2004 STANDARD CATALOG OF®

WORLD COINS

1901-Present

by Chester L. Krause • Clifford Mishler

Colin R. Bruce II
Senior Editor

Thomas Michael
Market Analyst

George Cuhaj
Technical Editor

Merna Dudley
Coordinating Editor

Deb McCue
Database Coordinator

Joel T. Edler
U.S. Market Analyst

Fred J. Borgmann
New Issues Editor

Randy Thern
Numismatic Cataloging Supervisor

Special Contributors
Albert Beck, Ray Hackett, Oen E. Nelson

UNCIRCULATED VALUATIONS

The uncirculated valuations represented in this edition are for typical quality specimens, for some of the more popularly collected series. Brilliant uncirculated (BU), or superior quality examples may easily command 10% to 50% premiums, or even greater where particularly popular or rare types or dates are concerned.

BULLION VALUE (BV) MARKET VALUATIONS

Valuations for all platinum, gold, palladium or silver coins of the more common, basically bullion types, or those possessing only modest numismatic premiums are presented in this edition based on market levels of $680 per ounce for platinum, $350 for gold, $245 for palladium and $4.60 per ounce for silver. Further information on using this catalog to evaluate platinum, gold, palladium or silver coins amid fluctuating precious metal market conditions is presented in the introduction.

2004 Standard Catalog of®

WORLD COINS

by Chester L. Krause • Clifford Mishler

Published in the United States by

kp krause publications
An F&W Publications Company

700 East State Street • Iola, WI 54990-0001
715-445-2214 • 888-457-2873
www.krause.com

Library of Congress Catalog Card Number: 79-940940
International Standard Book Number: 0-87349-593-4

Printed in the United States of America

TABLE OF CONTENTS

Title Page II
Copyright Page II
Table of Contents III
Introduction IV
Standard International Numeral Systems VI
Acknowledgments VIII
Country Index X
A Guide To International Numerics XVIII
Foreign Exchange XX
How To Use This Catalog XXII
Instant Identifier XXXII
Coin Denomination Index XXXVII
Hejira Date Conversion Chart XL
Mint Index XL
Silver Bullion Chart XLIII
Gold & Platinum Bullion Chart XLIV
Circle Chart XLV
Monograms XLVI
Eastern Mint Names XLIX

ADVERTISING INDEX

Ponterio and Associates, Inc. V
Pobjoy Mint VII
Stack's XI
I.A.P.N. (International Association of Professional Numismatists) XIII
N.Y.I.N.C. (New York International Numismatic Convention) XV
Numis-Phil (s) Pte Ltd. XVII
Northeast Numismatics, Inc. XIX
Mietens & Partner GMBH XXI
C.P.M.X. (Chicago Paper Money Expo) XXIII
Steinberg's XXV
Allan Davisson XXV
PomeXport XXV
William Rosenblum Rare Coins XXV
C.I.C.F. (Chicago International Coin Fair) XLVIII

INTRODUCTION

Welcome to the All New 31st Edition of the *Standard Catalog of World Coins*. What began in 1972 as a single-volume chronicle of world coinage from the mid-1800's to the first issues of the 1970's has grown into a century-specific, four-volume set that catalogs a wealth of numismatic history spanning over four centuries, from 1601 to the dawn of the 21st century. What you hold in your hands is the oldest sibling in that family of numismatic reference materials.

Through the years, research conducted by contributors and staff editors gradually expanded the parameters of the individual coin listings, introducing earlier eras and sometimes somewhat esoteric issues. As a result, the database from which annual editions of the Standard Catalog of World Coins developed had proliferated to include the first half of the 19th century, then the 18th and 17th centuries, on a selective basis as useful and reliable listings could be utilized.

Eventually supplementing the circulating coin listings were such specialized categories as Patterns, Piefors, Trial Strikes and Pretender issues, related Token coinage, NCLT's (non-circulating legal tender), and Collector and Presentation Sets - any "coins" individuals pursuing an interest in a given country might logically expect to encounter.

Annual editions of the Standard Catalog gradually developed growing pains, becoming heavy and unwieldy. In an effort to manage the swelling tome, lighter-weight paper was introduced, listings were condensed, photos were overlaid, and coverage of the more esoteric realms were selectively removed from edition to edition. By the mid-1990's, coverage was, for all intents and purposes, devoted exclusively to regular issue and commemorative coinages of the 19th and 20th centuries. A wealth of available, desirable information on world coinages had been placed on hold. The demand for the return of this excised data to the listings mounted as editions passed. Effective with the 24th edition of the Standard Catalog of World Coins, we resolved that the logical solution to the content vs. capacity dilemma was to dedicate individual volumes to the numismatic evolution of each century.

With the explosion of world commemorative programs and the steady accumulation of data, the resulting mass of the 20th Century Standard Catalog of World Coins earned the nickname "the telephone book" of world numismatics. The astounding 2,280-page 31st Edition maintains this reputation, representing a third of the nearly 7,000-page Standard Catalog database.

The volume before you embraces within the confines of the 20th and now 21st centuries comprehensive, detailed coverage that is complete with detailed treatments of the aforementioned specialized categories. But again, with the advent of a new century and the continuing march of new issues, the 20th century catalog is pressing its boundaries.

If your collecting interests pull you back to earlier eras, we refer you to the sister volumes, which explore coverage by century. The 19th Century (1801-1900), 18th Century (1701-1800) and 17th Century (1601-1700) editions provide similar comprehensive and detailed representation. These three volumes, plus the present 20th century volume, provide collectors and dealers with a comprehensive, nearly 7,000-page source - a veritable library of international numismatic history with the user-friendly convenience of century-specific data.

We are pleased to offer the numismatic enthusiast this living and breathing reference set, which authoritatively embraces exhaustive and definitive treatments of the diverse and sometimes challenging scopes of coverage spanning a rich, four-century run of world coinage. This resource presents a body of knowledge that will augment and stimulate your future interests. In the presentation of successor editions of each as the marketplace demands, the set becomes a dynamic, scholarly effort to the measure of what you, the user, contribute to make them something more than what they presently are. Toward that end, you are invited - make that encouraged - as were those who became users of the first Standard Catalog of World Coins 31 years ago, to suggest revisions and enhancements.

The present edition features thousands of changes and enhancements to previous listings. Tens of thousands of revised and updated valuations, as well as hundreds of fully illustrated listings of new regular-issue and commemorative coins released by world mints over the past couple of years represent only a fraction of the improvements offered in this edition. A further enhanced format has been employed for this 31st edition, which features an easier-to-use alphabetical organization, full composition details and denominations included with each type listing, a renewed emphasis on Political structure and more distinct separation by coinage types. The perceptive user of the Standard Catalog of World Coins will also appreciate myriad revisions and improvements of the descriptive text incorporated in the listings. These major rearrangements have been designed to make the catalog more useful to those of us who love the study of coins. Upon the introduction of this new format with the 30th edition, many readers contacted our office with suggestions for further style & presentation improvements, many of which were incorporated in the 31st edition.

Welcome to the complete, one-volume reference for 20th and 21st century world coins collecting — "basically a compilation of the digested knowledge," as stated in the introduction to the first edition, "which students of the numismatic science have contributed to the coin collecting hobby through the years," enhanced through the incorporation of original contributions that have substantially enriched the scope of awareness...humble still, but hopefully a worthy successor to the ideals embodied in the publication of the first Standard Catalog of World Coins in 1972.

Clifford Mishler

STANDARD INTERNATIONAL NUMERAL SYSTEMS

PREPARED ESPECIALLY FOR THE **STANDARD CATALOG OF WORLD COINS**

WESTERN	0	½	1	2	3	4	5	6	7	8	9	10	50	100	500	1000
ROMAN			I	II	III	IV	V	VI	VII	VIII	IX	X	L	C	D	M
ARABIC-TURKISH	٠	١/٢	١	٢	٣	٤	٥	٦	٧	٨	٩	١٠	٥٠	١٠٠	٥٠٠	١٠٠٠
MALAY-PERSIAN	٠	١/٢	١	٢	٣	۴	۵	۶	٧	٨	٩	١٠	۵٠	١٠٠	۵٠٠	١٠٠٠
EASTERN ARABIC	۰	۱/۲	۱	۲	۳	۴	۵	۶	۷	۸	۹	۱۰	۵۰	۱۰۰	۵۰۰	۱۰۰۰
HYDERABAD ARABIC	٠	١/٢	١	٢	٣	٤	٥	٦	٧	٨	٩	١٠	٥٠	١٠٠	٥٠٠	١٠٠٠
INDIAN (Sanskrit)	०	१/२	१	२	३	४	५	६	७	८	९	१०	५०	१००	५००	१०००
ASSAMESE	০	১/২	১	২	৩	৪	৫	৬	৭	৮	৯	১০	৫০	১০০	৫০০	১০০০
BENGALI	০	১/২	১	২	৩	৪	৫	৬	৭	৮	৯	১০	৫০	১০০	৫০০	১০০০
GUJARATI	૦	૧/૨	૧	૨	૩	૪	૫	૬	૭	૮	૯	૧૦	૫૦	૧૦૦	૫૦૦	૧૦૦૦
KUTCH	0	१/२	१	२	३	४	५	६	७	८	९	१०	५०	१००	५००	१०००
DEVAVNAGRI	०	१/२	१	२	३	४	५	६ or ६	७	८	९ or ९	१०	५०	१००	५००	१०००
NEPALESE	०	१/२	१ or १	२	३	४	५ or ५	६	७	८ or ८	९ or ९	१०	५०	१००	५००	१०००
TIBETAN	༠	༡/༢	༡	༢	༣	༤	༥	༦	༧	༨	༩	༡༠	༥༠	༡༠༠	༥༠༠	༡༠༠༠
MONGOLIAN	᠐	᠑/᠒	᠑	᠒	᠓	᠔	᠕	᠖	᠗	᠘	᠙	᠑᠐	᠕᠐	᠑᠐᠐	᠕᠐᠐	᠑᠐᠐᠐
BURMESE	၀	၁/၂	၁	၂	၃	၄	၅	၆	၇	၈	၉	၁၀	၅၀	၁၀၀	၅၀၀	၁၀၀၀
THAI-LAO	๐	๑/๒	๑	๒	๓	๔	๕	๖	๗	๘	๙	๑๐	๕๐	๑๐๐	๕๐๐	๑๐๐๐
JAVANESE	꧐		꧑	꧒	꧓	꧔	꧕	꧖	꧗	꧘	꧙	꧑꧐	꧕꧐	꧑꧐꧐	꧕꧐꧐	꧑꧐꧐꧐
ORDINARY CHINESE JAPANESE-KOREAN	零	半	一	二	三	四	五	六	七	八	九	十	十五	百	百五	千
OFFICIAL CHINESE			壹	貳	叁	肆	伍	陸	柒	捌	玖	拾	拾伍	佰	佰伍	仟
COMMERCIAL CHINESE			〡	〢	〣	〤	〥	〦	〧	〨	〩	十	〥十	〡百	〥百	〡千
KOREAN		반	일	이	삼	사	오	육	칠	팔	구	십	오십	백	오백	천
GEORGIAN			ა	ბ	გ	დ	ე	ვ	ზ	ჱ	თ	ი	ნ	რ	ფ	ჩ
			11 [illegible]	20 კ	30 ლ	40 მ	50 ნ	60 ჲ	70 ო	80 პ	90 ჟ	100 რ	200 ს, 300 ტ	400 ჳ	600 ქ, 700 ღ	800 ყ
ETHIOPIAN	◆		፩	፪	፫	፬	፭	፮	፯	፰	፱	፲	፶	፻	፭፻	፲፻
				20 ፳	30 ፴	40 ፵		60 ፷	70 ፸	80 ፹	90 ፺					
HEBREW			א	ב	ג	ד	ה	ו	ז	ח	ט	י	נ	ק	תק	
				20 כ	30 ל	40 מ		60 ס	70 ע	80 פ	90 צ		200 ר, 300 ש	400 ת	600 תר	700 תש, 800 תת
GREEK			Α	Β	Γ	Δ	Ε	ΣΤ	Ζ	Η	Θ	Ι	Ν	Ρ	Φ	Α
				20 Κ	30 Λ	40 Μ	60 Ξ	70 Ο	80 Π		200 Σ	300 Τ	400 Υ	600 Χ	700 Ψ	800 Ω

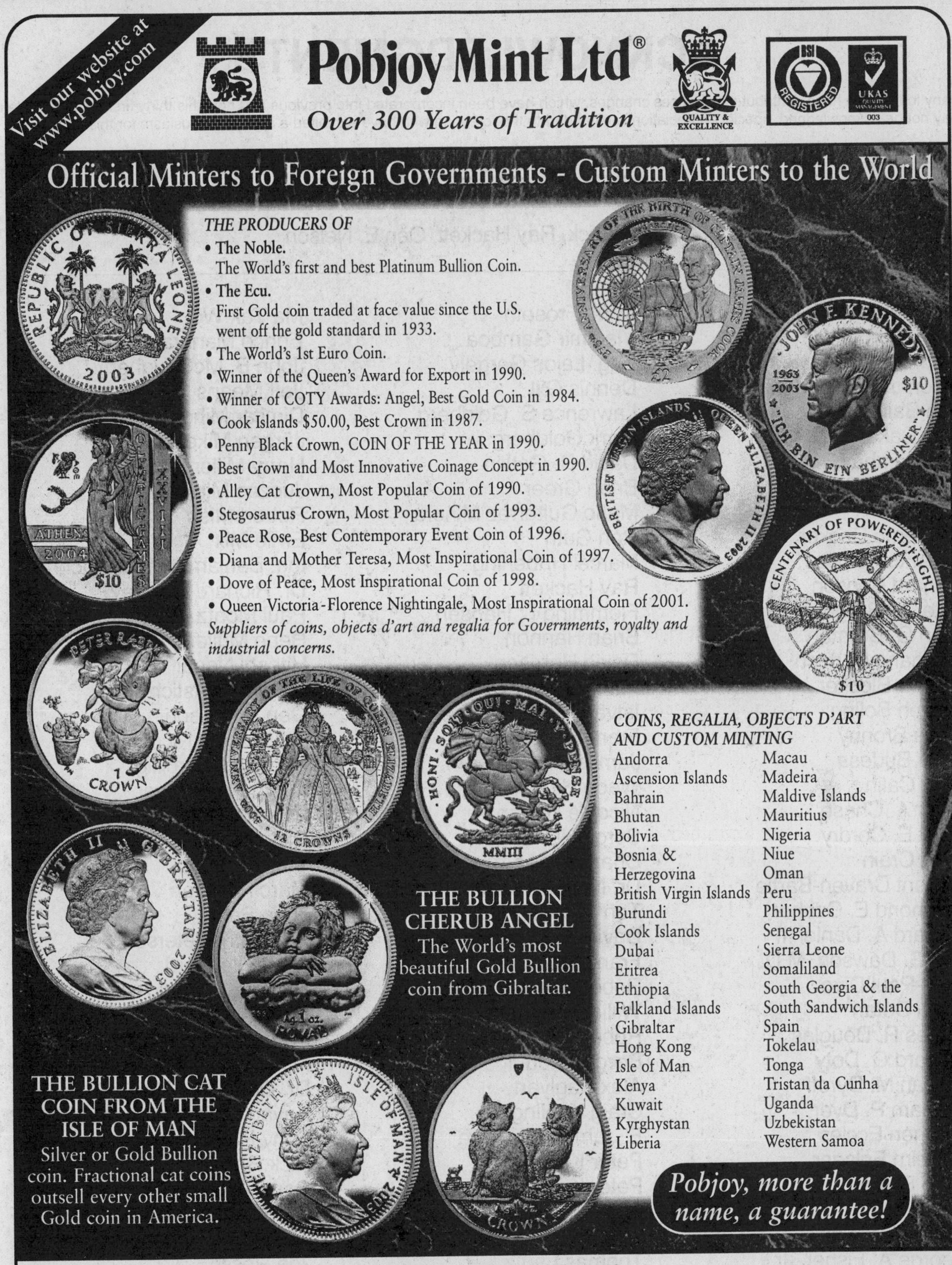
Visit our website at www.pobjoy.com
Pobjoy Mint Ltd®
Over 300 Years of Tradition
QUALITY & EXCELLENCE
BSI REGISTERED
UKAS QUALITY MANAGEMENT 003
Official Minters to Foreign Governments - Custom Minters to the World
THE PRODUCERS OF
• The Noble.
The World's first and best Platinum Bullion Coin.
• The Ecu.
First Gold coin traded at face value since the U.S. went off the gold standard in 1933.
• The World's 1st Euro Coin.
• Winner of the Queen's Award for Export in 1990.
• Winner of COTY Awards: Angel, Best Gold Coin in 1984.
• Cook Islands $50.00, Best Crown in 1987.
• Penny Black Crown, COIN OF THE YEAR in 1990.
• Best Crown and Most Innovative Coinage Concept in 1990.
• Alley Cat Crown, Most Popular Coin of 1990.
• Stegosaurus Crown, Most Popular Coin of 1993.
• Peace Rose, Best Contemporary Event Coin of 1996.
• Diana and Mother Teresa, Most Inspirational Coin of 1997.
• Dove of Peace, Most Inspirational Coin of 1998.
• Queen Victoria-Florence Nightingale, Most Inspirational Coin of 2001.
Suppliers of coins, objects d'art and regalia for Governments, royalty and industrial concerns.
COINS, REGALIA, OBJECTS D'ART AND CUSTOM MINTING
Andorra
Ascension Islands
Bahrain
Bhutan
Bolivia
Bosnia & Herzegovina
British Virgin Islands
Burundi
Cook Islands
Dubai
Eritrea
Ethiopia
Falkland Islands
Gibraltar
Hong Kong
Isle of Man
Kenya
Kuwait
Kyrghystan
Liberia
Macau
Madeira
Maldive Islands
Mauritius
Nigeria
Niue
Oman
Peru
Philippines
Senegal
Sierra Leone
Somaliland
South Georgia & the South Sandwich Islands
Spain
Tokelau
Tonga
Tristan da Cunha
Uganda
Uzbekistan
Western Samoa
THE BULLION CHERUB ANGEL
The World's most beautiful Gold Bullion coin from Gibraltar.
THE BULLION CAT COIN FROM THE ISLE OF MAN
Silver or Gold Bullion coin. Fractional cat coins outsell every other small Gold coin in America.
Pobjoy, more than a name, a guarantee!
Pobjoy Mint Ltd®
USA Branch: P.O. Box 109, Rosemount, MN 55068 USA TEL: Toll Free 1-877-4 POBJOY (1-877-476 2569) FAX: (651) 322 5527
Head Office: Millennia House, Kingswood Park, Bonsor Drive, Kingswood, Surrey, KT20 6AY, U.K.
TEL: (+44) 1737 818181 FAX: (+44) 1737 818199 Internet: www.pobjoy.com Email: mint@pobjoy.com

ACKNOWLEDGMENTS

Many individuals have contributed countless changes, which have been incorporated into previous and now this thirty first edition. While all may not be acknowledged, special appreciation is extended to the following who have exhibited a special enthusiasm for this edition.

SPECIAL CONTRIBUTORS

Albert Beck, Ray Hackett, Oen E. Nelson

Dr. Lawrence A. Adams
Esko Ahlroth
Stephen Album
Antonio Alessandrini
Don Bailey
Paul Baker
Yuri Barshay
Mitchell A. Battino
Albert Beck
Dr. Bernd Becker
Dr. Anton Belcev
Richard Benson
Peter N. Berger
Allen G. Berman
Wolfgang Bertsch
Sharon Blocker
Joseph Boling
Klaus Bronny
Chris Budesa
Doru Calin
Peter A. Chase
Scott E. Cordry
Jerry Crain
Vincent Craven-Bartle
Raymond E. Czahor
Howard A. Daniel III
Eric G. Dawson, M.D.
Jean-Paul Divo
Yossi Dotan
James R. Douglas
Richard G. Doty
Dr. Jan M. Dyroff
Graham P. Dyer
Stephen Eccles
Wilhelm Eglseer
Esko Ekman
Jack Erb
Michael Findlay
George A. Fisher, Jr.
Joe Flores
Luis H. Flores
Donald T. Fox
Arthur Friedberg
K. M. Froseth
Vladimir Gamboa
Eng. Lajos Gergely
Dennis Gill
Lawrence S. Goldberg
Mark Goldberg
David R. Gotkin
Brian Greer
Mario Guiterrez Minera
Ron Guth
Marcel Häberling
Ray Hackett
Flemming L. Hansen
Brian Hannon
David Harrison
Martin Rodney Hayter
Istvan Hegedus
Frans Hellendall
James H. Higby
Wade Hinderling
Nicolae Hridan
Serge Huard
Charles L. Huff
Dr. Norman Jacobs
Ton Jacobs
David Jen (deceased)
Francisco Jovel
Roberto Jovel
William M. Judd
Robert W. Julian
Børge R. Juul
Alex Kaglyan
Craig Keplinger
E. James Kindrake
Peter Kraneveld
Peter Krix
Russell Kruzell
Joseph E. Lang
Thomas Lautz
Nirat Lertchitvikul
Jim Long
Rudi Lotter
Alan Luedeking
Ma Tak Wo
Enrico Manara
John B. McCaugherty
Jeff Means
Dimitar Mihov
Jürgen Mikeska
Harry Miller
Juozas Minikevicius
Robert Mish
Ernie Mix
Ing. Benjamin M. Mizrachi R.
Dr. Richard Montrey
Paul Montz
René Müller
Hitoshi Nagai
Vladimir Nastich
Oen E. Nelson
N. Douglas Nicol
Andrew Oberbillig
Wayne N. Palmer
Gus A. Pappas
Dick Parker
Frank Passic
Marc Pelletier
Juan Pena
Kirsten F. Petersen
Jens Pilegaard
Richard Ponterio
Kent Ponterio
Michel Prier
Mircea Raicopol
Dr. Dennis G. Rainey
Kavan U. Ratnatunga
Tony Raymond
Nick Rhodes
Dana Roberts
Dr. K. A. Rodgers
William M. Rosenblum
Joe Ross
Clinton P. Rusaw
Arnaldo Russo
John Sacher
T.M.U. Sallay

Leon Saryan
Erwin Schaffer
Gerhard Schön
Dr. Wolfgang Schuster
Ladislav Sin
Evzen Sknouril
Jørgen Sømod
William F. Spengler
Tom Steinmetz
Benjamin Swagerty
Alim A. Sumana
M. Louis Teller
Tonin Thaci
Anthony Tumonis
Robert van Bebber
J. L. Van der Schueren
J. J. Van Grover
Erik J. Van Loon
Helen Wallace
R.W. Walter
Justin C. Wang
John Wells
Paul Welz
Stewart Westdal
J. Hugh Witherow
Joseph Zaffern
Christof Zellweger

AUCTION HOUSES AND DISTRIBUTORS

David Akers Numismatics
Bowers and Merena Galleries
Educational Coin Company
Heritage Numismatic Auctions
Hess-Divo Ltd.
Gerhard Hirsch
Thomas Høiland Møntauktion
Fritz Rudolf Künker
Leu Numismatik AG
Münzenhandlung Harald Möller, GmbH
Noble Numismatics, Pty. Ltd.
Omni Trading B. V.
Ponterio & Associates
Stack's
UBS, AG
World Wide Coins of California

SOCIETIES, INSTITUTIONS AND INTERNATIONAL MINTS

American Numismatic Association
American Numismatic Society
Austrian Mint
British Museum
British Royal Mint
Central Bank of The Russian Federation
Johns Hopkins University
Mint of Finland
Norwegian Mint
Numismatics International
Pobjoy Mint
Royal Dutch Mint
Singapore Mint
Smithsonian Institution
Vatican City Government Numismatic Office

PUBLICATIONS

The Statesman's Yearbook, 2001.
137th Edition
by Barry Turner, editor, The Statesman's Yearbook Office, The Macmillan Press Ltd., 25 Eccleston Place, London SW1W 9NF, United Kingdom
(Statistical and Historical Annual of the States of the World)

A special thanks to these members of the Krause Publications production team:

Sandra Morrison - Database Publishing Specialist
Sally Olson
Stacy Bloch
Mary Lou Marshall - Pre-Press Operations Manager
Kay Sanders
Ethel Thulien
Gordon Ullom

COUNTRY INDEX

A

Afghanistan 1
Aguascalientes 1408
Ajman 13
Albania 15
Alderney 23
Algeria 26
American Samoa 30
Andorra 31
Angola 42
Anguilla 45
Anhalt-Dessau 763
Anhwei Province 338
Annam 2172
Antigua & Barbuda 47
Antigua 46
Arenys De Mar 1904
Argentina 47
Armavir 1754
Armenia 55
Aruba 58
Ascension Island 60
Asturias And Leon 1904
Australia 61
Austria 101
Azerbaijan 125
Azores 125

B

Baden 764
Bahamas 126
Bahawalpur 993
Bahrain 141
Bangladesh 143
Barbados 144
Baroda 994
Bavaria 765
Belarus 149
Belgian Congo 152
Belgium 154
Belize 171
Benin 179
Bermuda 181
Bhaunagar 994
Bhutan 189
Biafra 197
Bohemia & Moravia 198
Bolivia 198
Bosnia-Herzegovina 201
Botswana 206
Brazil 209
Bremen 767
British Honduras 220
British North Borneo 222
British Virgin Islands 223
British West Africa 238
Brunei 242
Brunswick-Wolfenbuttel 767
Bulgaria 246
Bundi 994
Burundi 261

C

Cambay 995
Cambodia 262
Cameroon 266
Canada 268
Cape Verde 301
Catamarca 54
Cayman Islands 304
Cazalla De Sierra 1904
Ceara 220
Central African Republic 314
Central African States 315
Ceylon 316
Chad 319
Chechnya 1754
Chekiang Province 340
Chihli Province 341
Chihuahua 1408
Chile 320
China, Japanese Puppet States 405
China, People's Republic 411
China, Republic Of 395
China 328
Chinese Soviet Republic 407
Cis-sutlej States - Maler Kolta 996
Cis-sutlej States - Patiala 996
Cis-sutlej States 996
Colombia 470
Comoros 480
Congo Free State 481
Congo Republic 482
Congo, Democratic Republic 485
Cooch Behar 996
Cook Islands 491
Costa Rica 517
Crete 525
Croatia 525
Cuba 530
Culion Island 1617
Curacao 571
Cyprus 572
Czech Republic 578
Czechoslovakia 584

D

Dahomey 597
Danish West Indies 598
Danzig 1662
Darfur 1920
Datia 997
Denmark 599
Dewas 997
Djibouti 611
Dominica 612
Dominican Republic 614
Dungarpur 997
Durango 1409

E

East Africa 622
East Carribean States 625
East Hopei 405
Ecuador 629
Egypt 633
El Arahal 1904
El Salvador 666
Emirate Of Bukhara 2140
Equatorial African States 670
Equatorial Guinea 671
Eritrea 679
Estonia 681
Ethiopia 683
Euzkadi 1905

F

Faeroe Islands 688
Falkland Islands 688
Fengtien Province 343
Fiji 695
Finland 702
France 712
French Afars & Issas 745
French Equatorial Africa 746
French Indo-china 746
French Oceania 750
French Polynesia 750
French Somaliland 752
French West Africa 753
Fujairah 753
Fukien Province 344

G

Gabon 755
Georgia 761
German East Africa 762
German States 763
German-Democratic Republic 816
Germany - Federal Republic 794
Germany, Third Reich 790
Germany, Weimar Republic 783
Germany-Empire 779
Ghana 827
Ghent 170
Gibraltar 830
Great Britain 883
Greece 909
Greenland 918
Grenada 920
Guadeloupe 920
Guatemala 921
Guernsey 926
Guerrero 1410
Guinea 935
Guinea-Bissau 939
Guyana 941
Gwalior 997

H

Haiti 944
Hamburg 768

Heilungkiang Province 347
Hejaz & Nejd. 955
Hejaz 953
Hesse-darmstadt 769
Honan Province 347
Honduras 955
Hong Kong 958
Hsiang-o-hsi Soviet. 408
Hunan Province 349
Hunan Soviet 408
Hungary 963
Hupeh Province 354
Hupeh-Honan-Anwhei Soviet 408
Hyderabad 998

I

Ibi 1905
Iceland 988
India - Princely States. 992
India-British. 1018
India-Portugese 1016
India-Republic. 1027
Indonesia 1044
Indore 1001
Iran 1049
Iraq 1065
Ireland Republic 1070
Irian Barat. 1048
Isle Of Man 1074
Israel. 1146
Italian Somaliland. 1170
Italy. 1171
Ivory Coast 1187

J

Jaipur 1002
Jalisco. 1413
Jamaica 1188
Japan 1202
Jersey. 1212
Jodhpur. 1004
Jordan. 1220
Junagadh 1006

K

Kansu Province. 357
Katanga 1225
Kazakhstan. 1225
Keeling Cocos Islands 1228
Kelantan 1334
Kenya 1230
Khanate Of Khiva (Khwarezm) 2141
Kiangnan 358
Kiangsi Province. 361
Kiangsu-kiangsoo Province 363
Kiau Chau. 1232
Kiribati. 1232
Kirin Province 366
Kishangarh 1007
Korea 1235
Korea-North 1236
Korea-South 1252
Kutch 1008
Kuwait 1259
Kwangsi-Kwangsea 369
Kwangtung Province 369
Kweichow Province 371
Kyrgyzstan. 1262

L

L'ametlla Del Valles 1905
La Puebla De Cazalla 1905
La Rioja 54
Laos. 1262
Latvia 1268
Lebanon. 1272
Lesotho 1275
Liberia 1279
Libya 1308
Liechtenstein 1309
Lippe-Detmold 769
Lithuania 1311
Lora Del Rio. 1905
Lubeck 769
Lunavada. 1010
Luxembourg. 1315

M

Macao 1320
Macedonia. 1326
Madagascar. 1327
Madeira Islands 1329
Makrai 1011
Malawi 1330
Malay Peninsula 1334
Malaya & British Borneo 1333
Malaya. 1332
Malaysia. 1335
Maldive Islands 1340
Mali 1344
Malta 1345
Manchukuo 405
Manchurian Provinces 372
Maracaibo 2170
Marchena. 1905
Marshall Islands. 1353
Martinique 1381
Mauritania 1381
Mauritius 1382
Mecca 954
Mecklenburg-Schwerin 770
Mecklenburg-Strelitz 771
Meng Chiang 407
Menorca. 1906
Mewar 1011
Mexico, Estado De. 1413
Mexico 1386
Mexico-Revolutionary 1408
Min-che-kan Soviet 408
Moldova 1419
Monaco 1420
Mongolia 1425
Montenegro 1435
Montserrat 1436
Morelos 1414
Morocco 1436
Mozambique 1445
Muscat & Oman 1450
Mutawakkilite 1451
Myanmar. 1457

N

Nagorno-Karabakh 1459
Namibia. 1460
Nauru 1461
Nejd. 1463
Nepal. 1464
Netherlands Antilles 1497
Netherlands East Indies 1503
Netherlands. 1487
New Caledonia 1505
New Guinea 1509
New Hebrides 1509
New Zealand. 1511
Newfoundland 1507
Nicaragua 1523
Niger 1529
Nigeria. 1530
Niue. 1532
North Viet Nam 2174
Norway 1540
Nulles 1906

O

Oaxaca 1415
Oldenburg 771
Olot 1906
Oman 1550

P

P'ing Chiang County Soviet 409
Pakistan 1558
Palau. 1562
Palestine 1568
Palo Seco 1579
Panama. 1569
Papua New Guinea. 1580
Paraguay. 1584
Peru 1594
Philippines. 1607
Pitcairn Islands 1618
Poland 1619
Portugal. 1664
Provisional Govt. Of China 407
Prussia 771
Puebla. 1418

Q

Qatar & Dubai 1682
Qatar 1681
Quaiti State Of Hadhramaut 1683

R

Ras Al-khaimah. 1683
Ratlam. 1012
Reformed Govt. Of China 407
Reunion. 1685
Reuss-Obergreiz. 773

Rewa 1012
Rhodesia And Nyasaland 1686
Rhodesia 1687
Riau Archipelago 1048
Romania 1688
Ruanda-Urundi 153
Ruess 773
Russia 1700
Russian Caucasia 1754
Rwanda & Burundi 1756
Rwanda 1754

S

Saarland 1756
Saharawi Arab Democratic Republic 1757
Sailana 1013
Saint Helena & Ascension 1762
Saint Helena 1760
Saint Kitts & Nevis 1763
Saint Lucia 1764
Saint Pierre & Miquelon 1765
Saint Thomas & Prince Island 1766
Saint Vincent 1774
San Marino 1775
Santander, Palencia & Burgos 1906
Sarawak 1799
Saudi Arabia 1800
Saxe-Altenburg 773
Saxe-Coburg-Gotha 773
Saxe-Meiningen 774
Saxe-Weimar-Eisenach 775
Saxony 775
Schaumburg-Lippe 777
Schleswig-Holstein 777
Schwarzburg-Rudolstadt 777
Schwarzburg-Sondershausen 777
Segarra De Gaia 1907
Senegal 1803
Serbia 1804
Seychelles 1805
Shah Dynasty 1465
Shansi Province 373
Shantung Province 373
Sharjah 1813
Shensi Province 374
Shensi-North Soviet 409
Sierra Leone 1814
Sikang Province 374
Sinaloa 1419
Singapore 1824
Sinkiang Province 374
Slovakia 1836
Slovenia 1842
Socialist Republic 2175
Solomon Islands 1846
Somalia 1852
Somaliland 1860
South Africa 1860
South Arabia 1881
South Georgia And The South Sandwich Islands 1881
Southern Rhodesia 1882
Spain Civil War 1904
Spain 1885
Spitzbergen 1907
Sri Lanka 1908
State Of South Viet Nam 2174
Straits Settlements 1911
Sudan 1913
Suiyuan Province 386
Suriname 1920
Swaziland 1924
Sweden 1928
Switzerland 1937
Syria 1949
Szechuan Province 387
Szechuan-Shensi Soviet 409

T

Taiwan 402
Tajikistan 1953
Tannu Tuva 1953
Tanzania 1954
Tatarstan 1958
Thailand 1958
The Gambia 757
Thule-Kap York 919
Tibet 1980
Timor 1987
Togo 1988
Tokelau Islands 1990
Tonga 1992
Tonk 1013
Tonkin 2004
Transdniestra 2004
Travancore 1014
Trengganu 1334
Trinidad & Tobago 2005
Tristan Da Cunha 2011
Tunis 2013
Tunisia 2013
Tunisia 2020
Turkey 2020
Turkmenistan 2052
Turks & Caicos Islands 2054
Tuvalu 2071

U

Uganda 2074
Ukraine 2083
Umm Al Qaiwain 2095
United Arab Emirates 2095
United States 2099
Uruguay 2132
Uzbekistan 2139

V

Vanuatu 2142
Vatican City 2145
Venezuela 2165
Viet Nam 2172

W

Waldeck-pyrmont 778
Wan-Hsi-Pei-Soviet 411
West African States 2180
Western Samoa 2182
Wurttemberg 778

Y

Yemen Arab Republic 2190
Yemen Republic 2194
Yemen, Democratic Republic Of 2195
Yugoslavia 2196
Yunnan Province 392
Yunnan-Szechuan 394

Z

Zaire 2207
Zambia 2209
Zanzibar 2223
Zimbabwe 2223

NYINC

NEW YORK
INTERNATIONAL
NUMISMATIC
CONVENTION

January 15-16-17-18, 2004
(Early Birds - Thursday, January 15, 2PM-7PM - $100 Registration)
Friday, January 16 10AM-7PM

Saturday, January 17 10AM-7PM

Sunday, January 18 10AM-3PM
(Admission - $10 for a three-day pass. Present this ad for a $5 admission discount)

Waldorf Astoria Hotel
Park Avenue between 49th & 50th Sts., New York, NY
Hotel Reservations:
(212) 355-3000
Ask for our Special NYINC rates: $190, $219 or $229

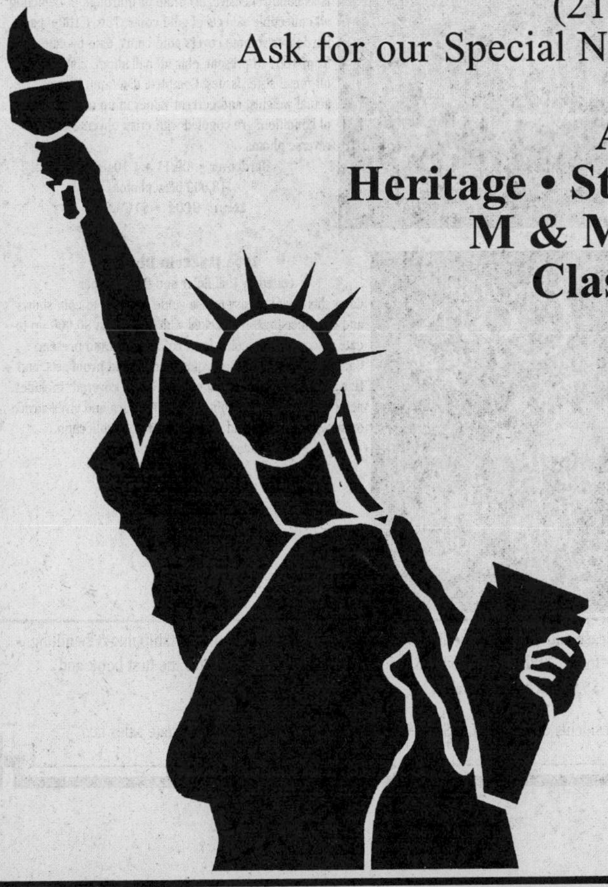

Auctions by:
Heritage • Stack's • Dmitry Markov • M & M Numismatics • Baldwin's • Classical Numismatic Group • Ponterio & Associates

Bourse Chairman:
Kevin Foley
P.O. Box 370650
Milwaukee, WI 53237
(414) 421-3484
Fax: (414) 423-0343
E-mail: kfoley2@wi.rr.com

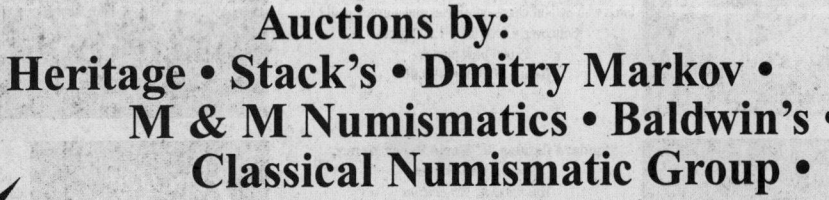

Visit our Web Site:
www.nyinc.info

Rely On The Experts When Pricing Your Collection

Standard Catalog of® World Coins 1601-1700
17th Century, 3rd Edition
by Chester L. Krause and Clifford Mishler,
Colin R. Bruce II, Senior Editor

Now in its 3rd edition, this classic reference has been updated and reformatted, providing far more detail than any previous volume. Every valuation from the second edition has been reviewed and adjusted to reflect market values in up to 5 grades of condition. Hundreds of new photographs have been added and vast improvements have been made to the existing images. With coinage types clearly identified, political structures outlined, and expanded coverage of German States and Central Asia, no collector can be without this edition.

Softcover • 8¼x10⅞ • 1,296 pages
18,500 b&w photos
Item# C403 • $65.00

Standard Catalog of® World Coins 1701-1800
3rd Edition
by Chester L. Krause and Clifford Mishler,
Colin R. Bruce II, Senior Editor

Based on 30 years of research, this third edition contains massive price revisions throughout. 18th Century coins are conveniently listed by country and denomination in up to five grades of preservation. Listings are presented in a new easy-to-use format with more descriptive information and the denomination appearing next to each Krause-Mishler number. More than 17,900 actual size photos of the obverse and reverse enable easy identification.

Softcover • 8¼x10⅞ • 1,272 pages
17,900+ b&w photos
Item# SE03 • $70.00

Standard Catalog of® World Coins 19th Century 1801-1900
3rd Edition
by Chester L. Krause and Clifford Mishler,
Colin R. Bruce II, Senior Editor

This prestigious guide is the only volume you need to identify and value 19th century world coins. Veteran coin experts have amassed coin denomination listings for every coin minted from 1801 to 1900 with tens of thousands of coins cataloged in up to four grades of condition. This third edition is heavily illustrated with new and improved photos and will appeal to all skill levels with helpful charts, glossaries and a user's guide.

Softcover • 8¼x10⅞ • 1,200 pages
25,000 b&w photos
Item# SCN03 • $50.00

Standard Catalog of® World Paper Money, Specialized Issues
Volume One, 9th Edition
edited by Neil Shafer and George S. Cuhaj

More than 52,000 updated prices for more than 17,500 notes are presented along with more than 10,000 obverse and reverse photos for easy identification. Helpful currency exchange and translation information provides additional insight into the world paper money collecting hobby. Contains listings for specialized issue notes in Central and South America, China, Europe and for worldwide guerilla, revolutionary, and siege issues.

Softcover • 8¼x10⅞ • 1,224 pages
10,000+ b&w photos
Item# PS09 • $65.00

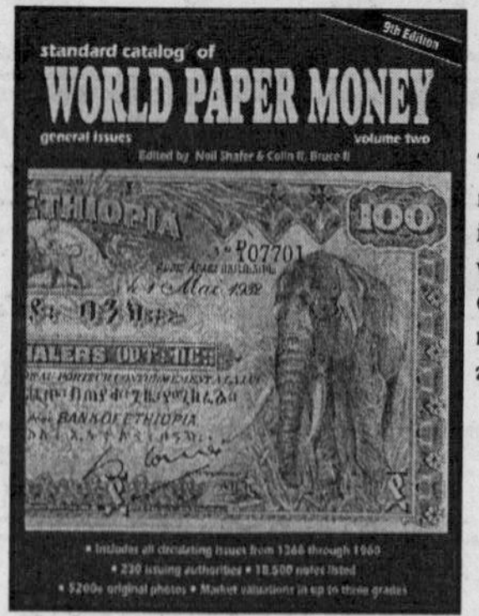

Standard Catalog of® World Paper Money, General Issues 1368-1960
Volume Two, 9th Edition
edited by Neil Shafer & Colin R. Bruce II

This is the world's most comprehensive world paper money price guide and reference. The new 9th Edition includes 19,000+ listings of paper money circulating worldwide from 1368 through 1960 in three grades of condition and well over 50,000 up-to-date prices that reflect recent market activity. Introductory chapters are updated.

Softcover • 8½x11 • 1,184 pages
5,200+ b&w photos
Item# PM09 • $65.00

Standard Catalog of® World Paper Money, Modern Issues 1961-Date
Volume Three, 9th Edition
edited by Neil Shafer & George S. Cuhaj

Stay on top of the most recent releases, discoveries, and prices of world paper money. Identify and price more than 11,500 legal tender notes issued and circulated by more than 380 note-issuing authorities. Notes are priced in three grades of condition. Learn more about the paper money collecting hobby with the detailed user's guide and other helpful resources.

Softcover • 8½x11 • 968 pages
7,500 b&w photos • 8-page color section
Item# WP09 • $45.00

Standard Catalog of® World Gold Coins
Fourth Edition
by Chester L. Krause, Clifford Mishler,
Colin R. Bruce II, Senior Editor

The 4th edition of this extraordinary volume is the most recent revision since 1993, and no other volume is as comprehensive, accurate or thorough in depicting all collectible aspects of gold coins. This 1,100+ page, hardcover volume covers gold coins, date-by-date, from 1601 to present, plus all palladium, platinum and off-metal sister issues. Complete date/mint listings, actual weights, and current values in up to four grades of condition, are coupled with crisp obverse and reverse photos.

Hardcover • 8½x11 • 1,104 pages
18,000 b&w photos
Item# GC04 • $100.00

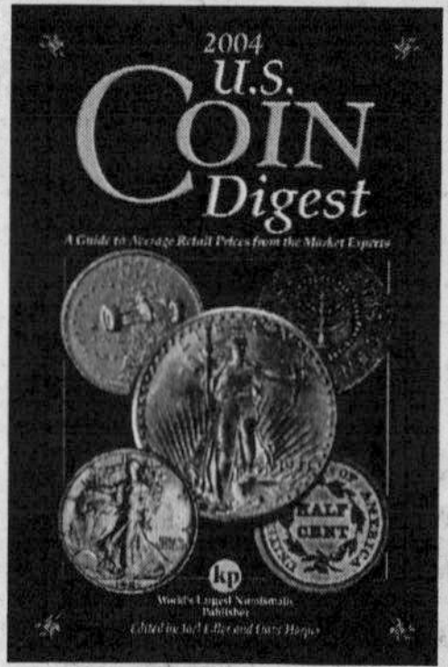

2004 U.S. Coin Digest
edited by Joel Edler and Dave Harper

Carry this updated easy-to-use guide with you to coin shows and club meetings. It's packed with more than 80,000 up-to-date prices for U.S. coins from colonial times to present. Commemoratives, bullion coinage, mint and proof sets, and Hawaiian and Puerto Rican coins are also covered. Includes news from the largest coin show in America and gives advice on how to organize and care for your coin collection.

Softcover W/Concealed Spiral
6x9 • 264 pages
1,100 b&w photos
Item# USCD2 • $11.99

To order call 800-258-0929 Offer NUB3

Krause Publications, Offer NUB3
P.O. Box 5009, Iola WI 54945-5009
www.krausebooks.com

Please add $4.00 for the first book and $2.25 each additional for shipping & handling to U.S. addresses. Non-U.S. addresses please add $20.95 for the first book and $5.95 each additional.

Residents of CA, IA, IL, KS, NJ, PA, SD, TN, WI please add appropriate sales tax.

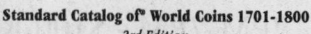

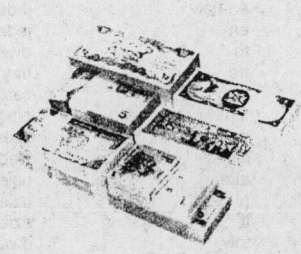

A GUIDE TO INTERNATIONAL NUMERICS

	ENGLISH	CZECH	DANISH	DUTCH	ESPERANTO	FRENCH
1/4	one-quarter	jeden-ctvrt	én kvart	een-kwart	unu-kvar'ono	un-quart
1/2	one-half	jeden-polovieni or pul	én halve	een-half	unu-du'one	un-demi
1	one	jeden	én	een	unu	un
2	two	dve	to	twee	du	deux
3	three	tri	trre	drie	tri	trois
4	four	ctyri	fire	vier	kvar	quatre
5	five	pet	fem	vijf	kvin	cinq
6	six	sest	seks	zes	ses	six
7	seven	sedm	syv	zeven	sep	sept
8	eight	osm	otte	acht	ok	huit
9	nine	devet	ni	negen	nau	neuf
10	ten	deset	ti	tien	dek	dix
12	twelve	dvanáct	tolv	twaalf	dek du	douze
15	fifteen	patnáct	femten	vijftien	dek kvin	quinze
20	twenty	dvacet	tyve	twintig	du'dek	vingt
24	twenty-four	dvacet-ctyri	fireog tyve	twintig-vier	du'dek kvar	vingt-quatre
25	twenty-five	dvacet-pet	fem og tyve	twintig-vijf	du'dek kvin	vingt-cinq
30	thirty	tricet	tredive	dertig	tri'dek	trente
40	forty	ctyricet	fyrre	veertig	kvar'dek	quarante
50	fifty	padesát	halytreds	vijftig	kvin'dek	cinquante
60	sixty	sedesát	tres	zestig	ses'dek	soixante
70	seventy	sedmdesát	halvfjerds	zeventig	sep'dek	soixante dix
80	eighty	osemdesát	firs	tachtig	ok'dek	quatre-vingt
90	ninety	devadesát	halvfjerds	negentig	nau'dek	quatre-vingt-dix
100	one hundred	jedno sto	et hundrede	een-honderd	unu-cento	un-cent
1000	thousand	tisíc	tusind	duizend	mil	mille

	GERMAN	HUNGARIAN	INDONESIAN	ITALIAN	NORWEGIAN	POLISH
1/4	ein viertel	egy-negyed	satu-suku	uno-guarto	en-fjeerdedel	jeden-c weirc
1/2	einhalb	egy-fél	satu-setengah	uno-mezzo	en-halv	jeden-polowa
1	ein	egy	satu	uno	en	jeden
2	zwei	kettö	dud	due	to	dwa
3	drei	három	tiga	tre	tre	trzy
4	vier	négy	empot	quattro	fire	cztery
5	fünf	öt	lima	cinque	fem	piec'
6	sechs	hat	enam	sei	seks	szes'c'
7	sieben	hét	tudjuh	sette	sju	siedem
8	acht	nyolc	delapan	otto	atte	osiem
9	neun	kilenc	sembilan	nove	ni	dziewiec'
10	zehn	tí z	sepuluh	dieci	ti	dziesiec'
12	zwölf	tizenketto	duabelas	dodici	tolv	dwanas' cie
15	fünfzehn	tizenöt	lima belas	quindici	femten	pietnas'cie
20	zwanzig	húsz	dua pulah	venti	tjue or tyve	dwadzies'cia
24	vierundzwanzig	húsz-négy	dua pulah-empot	venti-quattro	tjue-fire or tyve-fire	dwadzies'cia-cztery
25	fünfundzwanzig	húsz-öt	dua-pulah-lima	venti-cinque	tjue-fem or tyve-fem	dwadzies'cia-piec
30	dreissig	harminc	tigapulah	trenta	tredve	trydzies'ci
40	vierzig	negyven	empat pulah	quaranta	forti	czterdries'ci
50	fünfzig	otven	lima pulah	cinquanta	femti	piec'dziesiat
60	sechzig	hatvan	enam pulah	sessanta	seksti	szes'c'dziesiat
70	siebzig	hetven	tudjuh pulu	settanta	sytti	siedemdziesiat
80	achtzig	nyolvan	delapan puluh	ottonta	atti	osiemdziesiat
90	neunzig	kilencven	sembilan puluh	novanta	nitty	dziewiec'dziesiat
100	ein hundert	egy-száz	satu-seratus	uno-cento	en-hundre	jeden-sto
1000	tausend	ezer	seribu	mille	tusen	tysiac

	PORTUGUESE	ROMANIAN	SERBO-CROATIAN	SPANISH	SWEDEN	TURKISH
1/4	um-quarto	un-sfert	jedan-ceturtina	un-cuarto	en-fjärdedel	bir-ceyrek
1/2	un-meio	o-jumatate	jedan-polovina	un-medio	en-hälft	bir-yarim
1	um	un	jedan	uno	en	bir
2	dois	doi	dva	dos	tva	iki
3	trés	trei	tri	tres	tre	üc
4	quatro	patru	cetiri	cuatro	fyra	dört
5	cinco	cinci	pet	cinco	fem	bes
6	seis	sase	sest	seis	sex	alti
7	sete	sapte	sedam	siete	sju	yedi
8	oito	opt	osam	ocho	atta	sekiz
9	nove	noua	devet	nueve	io	dokuz
10	dez	zece	deset	diez	tio	on
12	doze	doisprezece	dvanaest	doce	tolv	on iki
15	quinze	cincisprezece	petnaest	quince	femton	on bes
20	vinte	douazeci	dvadset	veinte	tjugu	yirmi
24	vinte-quatro	douazeci-patru	dvadesel-citiri	veinticuatro	tjugu-fyra	yirmi-dört
25	vinte-cinco	douazeci-cinci	dvadeset-pet	veinticinco	tjugu-fem	yirmi-bes
30	trinta	treizeci	trideset	treinta	trettio	otuz
40	quarenta	patruzeci	cetrdeset	cuarenta	fyrtio	kirk
50	cinqüenta	cincizeci	padeset	cincuenta	femtio	elli
60	sessenta	saizeci	sezdeset	sesenta	sextio	altmis
70	setenta	saptezeci	sedamdeset	setenta	sjuttió	yetmis
80	oitenta	optzeci	osamdeset	ochenta	attio	seksen
90	noventa	novazeci	devedeset	noventa	nittio	doksan
100	un-cem	o-suta	jedan-sto	cien	en-hundra	bir-yüz
1000	mil	mie	hiljada	mil	tusen	bin

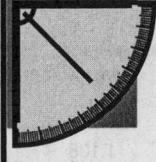

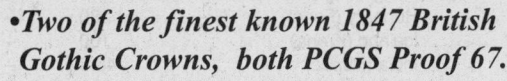

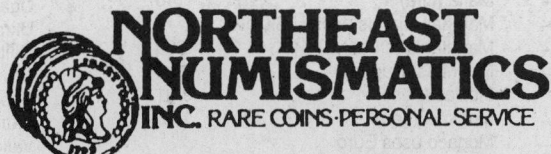

Foreign Exchange Table

The latest foreign exchange rates below apply to trade with banks in the country of origin. The left column shows the number of units per U.S. dollar at the official rate. The right column shows the number of units per dollar at the free market rate.

Country	Official #/$	Market #/$
Afghanistan (Afghan)	4,750	28,700
Albania (Lek)	143	–
Algeria (Dinar)	80	–
Andorra uses Euro		
Angola (Readjust Kwanza)	37.4	–
Anguilla uses E.C. Dollar	2.67	–
Antigua uses E.C. Dollar	2.67	–
Argentina (Peso)	2.77	–
Armenia (Dram)	575	–
Aruba (Florin)	1.79	–
Australia (Dollar)	1.89	–
Austria (Euro)	1.138	–
Azerbaijan (Manat)	4,775	–
Bahamas (Dollar)	1.00	–
Bahrain Is.(Dinar)	.377	–
Bangladesh (Taka)	57	–
Barbados (Dollar)	1.99	–
Belarus (Ruble)	1,725	–
Belgium (Euro)	1.138	–
Belize (Dollar)	1.97	–
Benin uses CFA Franc West	746	–
Bermuda (Dollar)	.99	–
Bhutan (Ngultrum)	49	–
Bolivia (Boliviano)	7.05	–
Bosnia-Herzegovina (Deutschmark)	2.22	–
Botswana (Pula)	6.65	–
British Virgin Islands uses U.S. Dollar	1.00	–
Brazil (Real)	2.28	–
Brunei (Dollar)	1.84	–
Bulgaria (Lev)	2.22	–
Burkina Faso uses CFA Fr.West	746	–
Burma (Kyat)	6.79	–
Burundi (Franc)	870	–
Cambodia (Riel)	3,835	–
Cameron uses CFA Franc Central	746	–
Canada (Dollar)	1.589	–
Cape Verde (Escudo)	120	–
Cayman Is.(Dollar)	0.82	–
Central African Rep.	746	–
CFA Franc Central	746	–
CFA Franc West	746	–
CFP Franc	136.5	–
Chad uses CFA Franc Central	746	–
Chile (Peso)	550	–
China, P.R. (Renminbi Yuan)	8.277	–
Colombia (Peso)	2,260	–
Comoros (Franc)	560	–
Congo uses CFA Franc Central	746	–
Congo-Dem.Rep. (Congolese Franc)	325	–
Cook Islands (Dollar)	1.73	–
Costa Rica (Colon)	350	–
Croatia (Kuna)	8.4	–
Cuba (Peso)	22.00	37.00
Cyprus (Pound)	.65	–
Czech Republic (Koruna)	35	–
Denmark (Danish Krone)	8.5	–
Djibouti (Franc)	170	–
Dominica uses E.C. Dollar	2.67	–
Dominican Republic (Peso)	17.4	–
East Caribbean (Dollar)	2.67	–
Ecuador uses U.S. Dollar		
Egypt (Pound)	4.61	–
El Salvador (Colon)	8.75	–
England (Sterling Pound)	.698	–
Equatorial Guinea uses CFA Franc Central	746	–
Eritrea (Nafka)	7.67	–
Estonia (Kroon)	17.8	–
Ethiopia (Birr)	8.4	–
Euro	1.138	–

Country	Official #/$	Market #/$
Falkland Is. (Pound)	.70	–
Faroe Islands (Krona)	8.45	–
Fiji Islands (Dollar)	2.25	–
Finland (Euro)	1.138	–
France (Euro)	1.138	–
French Polynesia uses CFP Franc	136.5	–
Gabon (CFA Franc)	746	–
Gambia (Dalasi)	18.4	–
Georgia (Lari)	1.97	–
Germany (Euro)	1.138	–
Ghana (Cedi)	7,750	–
Gibraltar (Pound)	.697	–
Greece (Euro)	1.138	–
Greenland uses Danish Krone		
Grenada uses E.C. Dollar	2.67	–
Guatemala (Quetzal)	7.89	–
Guernsey uses Sterling Pound	.698	–
Guinea Bissau (CFA Franc)	746	–
Guinea Conakry (Franc)	1,980	–
Guyana (Dollar)	180	–
Haiti (Gourde)	27	–
Honduras (Lempira)	16.2	–
Hong Kong (Dollar)	7.8	–
Hungary (Forint)	280	–
Iceland (Krona)	100	–
India (Rupee)	48.8	–
Indonesia (Rupiah)	9,500	–
Iran (Rial)	1,750	8,100
Iraq (Dinar)	.31	1,800
Ireland (Euro)	1.138	–
Isle of Man uses Sterling Pound	.698	–
Israel (New Sheqalim)	4.75	–
Italy (Euro)	1.138	–
Ivory Coast uses CFA Franc West	746	–
Jamaica (Dollar)	47.6	–
Japan (Yen)	130	–
Jersey uses Sterling Pound	.698	–
Jordan (Dinar)	.71	–
Kazakhstan (Tenge)	150	–
Kenya (Shilling)	78	–
Kiribati uses Australian Dollar		
Korea-PDR (Won)	2.20	170.0
Korea-Rep. (Won)	1,325	–
Kuwait (Dinar)	.307	–
Kyrgyzstan (Som)	48.3	–
Laos (Kip)	7,600	–
Latvia (Lat)	.63	–
Lebanon (Pound)	1,500	–
Lesotho (Maloti)	11.1	–
Liberia (Dollar) "JJ"	1.00	20.00
"Liberty"	–	40.00
Libya (Dinar)	1.32	
Liechtenstein uses Swiss Franc		
Lithuania (Litas)	3.93	–
Luxembourg (Euro)	1.138	–
Macao (Pataca)	8.03	–
Macedonia (New Denar)	70.5	–
Madagascar (Franc)	6,500	–
Malawi (Kwacha)	75	–
Malaysia (Ringgit)	3.8	–
Maldives (Rufiya)	11.77	–
Mali uses CFA Franc West	746	–
Malta (Lira)	.45	–
Marshall Islands uses U.S.Dollar		
Mauritania (Ouguiya)	280	–
Mauritius (Rupee)	30.4	–
Mexico (Peso)	9.01	–
Moldova (Leu)	13.5	–
Monaco uses Euro		
Mongolia (Tugrik)	1,100	–
Montenegro uses Yugo New Dinar		
Montserrat uses E.C. Dollar	2.67	–
Morocco (Dirham)	11.6	–
Mozambique (Metical)	23,100	–
Myanmar (Burma) (Kyat)	6.79	–
Namibia (Rand)	11.16	–

Country	Official #/$	Market #/$
Nauru uses Australian Dollar		
Nepal (Rupee)	77	–
Netherlands (Euro)	1.138	–
Netherlands Antilles (Gulden)	1.78	–
New Caledonia uses CFP Franc	136.5	–
New Zealand (Dollar)	2.283	–
Nicaragua (Cordoba Oro)	14.03	–
Niger uses CFA Franc West	746	–
Nigeria (Naira)	116	–
Northern Ireland uses Sterling Pound	.698	–
Norway (Krone)	8.7	–
Oman (Rial)	.385	–
Pakistan (Rupee)	60	–
Palau uses U.S.Dollar		
Panama (Balboa) uses U.S.Dollar		
Papua New Guinea (Kina)	3.72	–
Paraguay (Guarani)	4,900	–
Peru (Nuevo Sol)	3.45	–
Philippines (Peso)	51	–
Poland (Zloty)	4.08	–
Portugal (Euro)	1.138	–
Qatar (Riyal)	3.64	–
Romania (Leu)	33,000	–
Russia (New Ruble)	31.25	–
Rwanda (Franc)	450	–
St. Helena (Pound)	.697	–
St. Kitts uses E.C. Dollar	2.67	–
St. Lucia uses E.C. Dollar	2.67	–
St. Vincent uses E.C. Dollar	2.67	–
San Marino uses Euro		
Sao Tome e Principe (Dobra)	9,020	–
Saudi Arabia (Riyal)	3.75	–
Scotland uses Sterling Pound	.698	–
Senegal uses CFA Franc West	746	–
Seychelles (Rupee)	5.62	6.50
Sierra Leone (Leone)	2,025	2,500
Singapore (Dollar)	1.83	–
Slovakia (Sk.Koruna)	47.5	–
Slovenia (Tolar)	255	–
Solomon Is.(Dollar)	6.13	–
Somalia (Shilling)	2,600	–
Somaliland (Somali Shilling)	1,800	4,000
South Africa (Rand)	11.07	–
Spain (Euro)	1.138	–
Sri Lanka (Rupee)	96	–
Sudan (Dinar)	259	300
Surinam (Guilder)	2,180	–
Swaziland (Lilangeni)	11.2	–
Sweden (Krona)	10.25	–
Switzerland (Franc)	1.67	–
Syria (Pound)	52	–
Taiwan (NT Dollar)	35	–
Tajikistan (Ruble)	746	–
Tanzania (Shilling)	980	–
Thailand (Baht)	43.5	–
Togo uses CFA Franc West	746	–
Tonga (Pa'anga)	2.16	–
Transdniestra (New Ruble)	3,500,000	4,500,000
Trinidad & Tobago (Dollar)	6.12	–
Tunisia (Dinar)	1.49	–
Turkey (Lira)	1,310,000	–
Turkmenistan (Manat)	33.8	–
Turks & Caicos uses U.S. Dollar		
Tuvalu uses Australian Dollar		
Uganda (Shilling)	1,800	–
Ukraine (Hryvnia)	5.3	–
United Arab Emirates (Dirham)	3.673	–
Uruguay (Peso Uruguayo)	15.5	–
Uzbekistan (Som)	775	–
Vanuatu (Vatu)	145	–
Vatican City uses Euro		
Venezuela (Bolivar)	900	–
Vietnam (Dong)	15,200	–
Western Samoa (Tala)	3.45	–
Yemen (Rial)	174	–
Yugoslavia (Novih Dinar)	67	–
Zambia (Kwacha)	4,400	–
Zimbabwe (Dollar)	55.5	120

HOW TO USE THIS CATALOG

This catalog series is designed to serve the needs of both the novice and advanced collectors. It provides a comprehensive guide to over 400 years of world coinage. It is generally arranged so that persons with no more than a basic knowledge of world history and a casual acquaintance with coin collecting can consult it with confidence and ease. The following explanations summarize the general practices used in preparing this catalog's listings. However, because of specialized requirements, which may vary by country and era, these must not be considered ironclad. Where these standards have been set aside, appropriate notations of the variations are incorporated in that particular listing.

ARRANGEMENT

Countries are arranged alphabetically. Political changes within a country are arranged chronologically. In countries where Rulers are the single most significant political entity a chronological arrangement by Ruler has been employed. Distinctive sub-geographic regions are listed alphabetically following the countries main listings. A few exceptions to these rules may exist. Refer to the Country Index.

Diverse coinage types relating to fabrication methods, revaluations, denomination systems, non-circulating categories and such have been identified, separated and arranged in logical fashion. Chronological arrangement is employed for most circulating coinage, i.e., Hammered coinage will normally precede Milled coinage, monetary reforms will flow in order of their institution. Non-circulating types such as Essais, Piefort, Patterns, Trial Strikes, Mint and Proof sets will follow the main listings, as will Medallic coinage and Token coinage.

Within a coinage type coins will be listed by denomination, from smallest to largest. Numbered types within a denomination will be ordered by their first date of issue.

IDENTIFICATION

The most important step in the identification of a coin is the determination of the nation of origin. This is generally easily accomplished where English-speaking lands are concerned, however, use of the country index is sometimes required. The coins of Great Britain provide an interesting challenge. For hundreds of years the only indication of the country of origin was in the abbreviated Latin legends. In recent times there have been occasions when there has been no indication of origin. Only through the familiarity of the monarchical portraits, symbols and legends or indication of currency system are they identifiable.

The coins of many countries beyond the English-language realm, such as those of French, Italian or Spanish heritage, are also quite easy to identify through reference to their legends, which appear in the national languages based on Western alphabets. In many instances the name is spelled exactly the same in English as in the national language, such as France; while in other cases it varies only slightly, like Italia for Italy, Belgique or Belgie for Belgium, Brasil for Brazil and Danmark for Denmark.

This is not always the case, however, as in Norge for Norway, Espana for Spain, Sverige for Sweden and Helvetia for Switzerland. Some other examples include:

DEUTSCHES REICH - Germany 1873-1945

BUNDESREPUBLIC DEUTSCHLAND - Federal Republic of Germany.

DEUTSCHE DEMOKRATISCHE REPUBLIK - German Democratic Republic.

EMPIRE CHERIFIEN MAROC - Morocco.

ESTADOS UNIDOS MEXICANOS - United Mexican States (Mexico).

ETAT DU GRAND LIBAN - State of Great Lebanon (Lebanon).

Thus it can be seen there are instances in which a little schooling in the rudiments of foreign languages can be most helpful. In general, colonial possessions of countries using the Western alphabet are similarly identifiable as they often carry portraits of their current rulers, the familiar lettering, sometimes in combination with a companion designation in the local language.

Collectors have the greatest difficulty with coins that do not bear legends or dates in the Western systems. These include coins bearing Cyrillic lettering, attributable to Bulgaria, Russia, the Slavic states and Mongolia, the Greek script peculiar to Greece, Crete and the Ionian Islands; The Amharic characters of Ethiopia, or Hebrew in the case of Israel. Dragons and sunbursts along with the distinctive word characters attribute a coin to the Oriental countries of China, Japan, Korea, Tibet, Viet Nam and their component parts.

The most difficult coins to identify are those bearing only Persian or Arabic script and its derivatives, found on the issues of nations stretching in a wide swath across North Africa and East Asia, from Morocco to Indonesia, and the Indian subcontinent coinages which surely are more confusing in their vast array of Nagari, Sanskrit, Ahom, Assamese and other local dialects found on the local issues of the Indian Princely States. Although the task of identification on the more modern issues of these lands is often eased by the added presence of Western alphabet legends, a feature sometimes adopted as early as the late 19th Century, for the earlier pieces it is often necessary for the uninitiated to laboriously seek and find.

Except for the cruder issues, however, it will be found that certain characteristics and symbols featured in addition to the predominant legends are typi-

You're Invited to the...

10th ANNUAL CHICAGO PAPER MONEY EXPO

Featuring Stocks & Bonds '04

CPMX

Sponsored by
BANK NOTE REPORTER

Thursday, Friday, Saturday, Sunday
February 26 – 29, 2004

Holiday Inn – O'Hare
5440 North River Road, Rosemont, Illinois

The Chicago Paper Money Expo, featuring Stocks & Bonds '04, is sponsored by Krause Publications, the World's Largest Publisher of Hobby Related Publications, including **Bank Note Reporter & the Standard Catalog of United States Paper Money.** *For more info about this show and others, visit our Web site at www.collect.com*

* 100 Dealer Bourse Area
* Society Meetings
* Auction by Lyn F. Knight
* Educational Programs
* Complimentary Airport Shuttle

Show Hours

Thursday, February 26	2 pm - 6 pm
(Professional Preview - $50)	
Friday, February 27	10 am - 6 pm
Saturday, February 28	10 am - 6 pm
Sunday, February 29	10 am - 1 pm

(A three day pass valid Friday-Sunday is $5 Children 16 and under - Free)

Hotel Reservations

Please call the Holiday Inn O'Hare directly at (847) 671-6350 and ask for the special Chicago Paper Money Expo rate of $99 S/D.

Bourse Information:

Kevin Foley

P.O. Box 573, Milwaukee, WI 53201
(414) 421-3484 • FAX (414) 423-0343
E-Mail: kfoley2@wi.rr.com

cal on coins from a given country or group of countries. The toughra monogram, for instance, occurs on some of the coins of Afghanistan, Egypt, the Sudan, Pakistan, Turkey and other areas of the late Ottoman Empire. A predominant design feature on the coins of Nepal is the trident; while neighboring Tibet features a lotus blossom or lion on many of their issues.

To assist in identification of the more difficult coins, we have assembled the Instant Identifier and Monogram sections presented on the following pages. They are designed to provide a point of beginning for collectors by allowing them to compare unidentified coins with photographic details from typical issues.

We also suggest reference to the Index of Coin Denominations presented here and also the comprehensive Country Index, where the inscription will be found listed just as it appears on the coin for nations using the Western alphabet.

DATING

Coin dating is the final basic attribution consideration. Here, the problem can be more difficult because the reading of a coin date is subject not only to the vagaries of numeric styling, but to calendar variations caused by the observance of various religious eras or regal periods from country to country, or even within a country. Here again with the exception of the sphere from North Africa through the Orient, it will be found that most countries rely on Western date numerals and Christian (AD) era reckoning, although in a few instances, coin dating has been tied to the year of a reign or government. The Vatican, for example dates its coinage according to the year of reign of the current pope, in addition to the Christian-era date.

Countries in the Arabic sphere generally date their coins to the Muslim era (AH), which commenced on July 16, 622 AD (Julian calendar), when the prophet Mohammed fled from Mecca to Medina. As their calendar is reckoned by the lunar year of 354 days, which is about three percent (precisely 2.98%) shorter than the Christian year, a formula is required to convert AH dating to its Western equivalent. To convert an AH date to the approximate AD date, subtract three percent of the AH date (round to the closest whole number) from the AH date and add 622. A chart converting all AH years from 1010 (July 2, 1601) to 1421 (May 25, 2028) is presented as the Heijra Chart on page 35.

The Muslim calendar is not always based on the lunar year (AH), however, causing some confusion, particularly in Afghanistan and Iran, where a calendar based on the solar year (SH) was introduced around 1920. These dates can be converted to AD by simply adding 621. In 1976 the government of Iran implemented a new solar calendar based on the foundation of the Iranian monarchy in 559 BC. The first year observed on the new calendar was 2535 (MS), which commenced March 20, 1976. A reversion to the traditional SH dating standard occurred a few years later.

Several different eras of reckoning, including Christian and Muslim (AH), have been used to date coins of the Indian subcontinent. The two basic systems are the Vikrama Samvat (VS), which dates from Oct. 18, 58 BC, and the Saka era, the origin of which is reckoned from March 3, 78 AD. Dating according to both eras appears on various coins of the area.

Coins of Thailand (Siam) are found dated by three different eras. The most predominant is the Buddhist era (BE), which originated in 543 BC. Next is the Bangkok or Ratanakosindsok (RS) era, dating from 1781 AD; followed by the Chula-Sakarat (CS) era, dating from 638 AD. The latter era originated in Burma and is used on that country's coins.

Other calendars include that of the Ethiopian era (EE), which commenced seven years, eight months after AD dating; and that of the Jewish people, which commenced on Oct. 7, 3761 BC. Korea claims a legendary dating from 2333 BC, which is acknowledged in some of its coin dating. Some coin issues of the Indonesian area carry dates determined by the Javanese Aji Saka era (AS), a calendar of 354 days (100 Javanese years equal 97 Christian or Gregorian calendar years), which can be matched to AD dating by comparing it to AH dating.

The following table indicates the year dating for the various eras, which correspond to 2002 in Christian calendar reckoning, but it must be remembered that there are overlaps between the eras in some instances.

Christian era (AD)	-2003
Muslim era (AH)	-AH1424
Solar year (SH)	-SH1381
Monarchic Solar era (MS)	-MS2562
Vikrama Samvat (VS)	-VS2060
Saka era (SE)	-SE1925
Buddhist era (BE)	-BE2546
Bangkok era (RS)	-RS222
Chula-Sakarat era (CS)	-CS1365
Ethiopian era (EE)	-EE1997
Jewish era	-5763
Korean era	-4336
Javanese Aji Saka era (AS)	-AS1936
Fasli era (FE)	-FE1413

Coins of Asian origin - principally Japan, Korea, China, Turkestan and Tibet and some modern gold issues of Turkey - are generally dated to the year of the government, dynasty, reign or cyclic eras, with the dates indicated in Asian characters which usually read from right to left. In recent years, however, some dating has been according to the Christian calendar and in Western numerals. In Japan, Asian character dating was reversed to read from left to right in Showa year 23 (1948 AD).

More detailed guides to less prevalent coin dating systems, which are strictly local in nature, are presented with the appropriate listings.

Some coins carry dates according to both locally observed and Christian eras. This is particularly true in the Arabic world, where the Hejira date may be indicated in Arabic numerals and the Christian date in Western numerals, or both dates in either form.

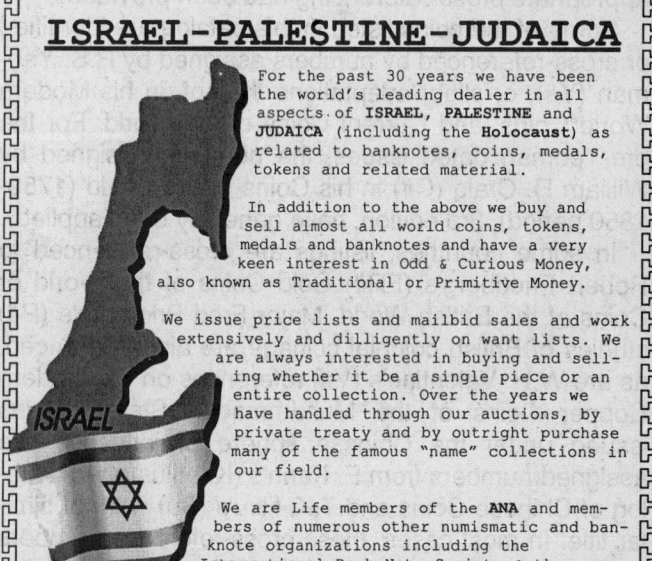

Sending Scanned Images by Email

Over the past 2 years or so, we have been receiving an ever-increasing flow of scanned images from sources worldwide. Unfortunately, many of these scans could not be used due to the type of scan, or simple incompatability with our systems. We appreciate the effort it takes to produce these images and accuracy they add to the catalog listings.

Here are a few simple instructions to follow when producing these scans. We encourage you to continue sending new images or upgrades to those currently illustrated and please do not hesitate to ask questions about this process.

— Scan all images within a resolution range of 200 dpi to 300 dpi
— Size setting should be at 100%
— Scan in true 4-color
— Save images as 'jpeg' or 'tiff' and name in such a way, which clearly identifies the country of origin of the note
— Please email with a request to confirm receipt of the attachment
— Please send images to thernr@krause.com

The date actually carried on a given coin is generally cataloged here in the first column (Date) to the right of the catalog number. If this date is by a non-Christian dating system, such as 'AH'(Muslim), the Christian equivalent date will appear in parentheses(), for example AH1336(1917). Dates listed alone in the date column which do not actually appear on a given coin, or dates which are known, but do not appear on the coin, are generally enclosed by parentheses with 'ND' at the left, for example ND(1926).

Timing differentials between some era of reckoning, particularly the 354-day Mohammedan and 365-day Christian years, cause situations whereby coins which carry dates for both eras exist bearing two year dates from one calendar combined with a single date from another.

Countermarked Coinage is presented with both 'Countermark Date' and 'Host Coin' date for each type. Actual date representation follows the rules outlined above.

NUMBERING SYSTEM

Some catalog numbers assigned in this volume are based on established references. This practice has been observed for two reasons: First, when world coins are listed chronologically they are basically self-cataloging; second, there was no need to confuse collectors with totally new numeric designations where appropriate systems already existed. As time progressed we found many of these established systems incomplete and inadequate and have now replaced many with new KM numbers. When numbers change appropriate cross-referencing has been provided.

Some of the coins listed in this catalog are identified or cross-referenced by numbers assigned by R.S. Yeoman (Y#), or slight adaptations thereof, in his Modern World Coins, and Current Coins of the World. For the pre-Yeoman dated issues, the numbers assigned by William D. Craig (C#) in his Coins of the World (1750-1850 period), 3rd edition, have generally been applied.

In some countries, listings are cross-referenced to Robert Friedberg's (FR#) Gold Coins of the World or Coins of the British World. Major Fred Pridmore's (P#) studies of British colonial coinage are also referenced, as are W.H. Valentine's (V#) references on the Modern Copper Coins of the Muhammadan States. Coins issued under the Chinese sphere of influence are assigned numbers from E. Kann's (K#) Illustrated Catalog of Chinese Coins and T.K. Hsu's (Su) work of similar title. In most cases, these cross-reference numbers are presented in the descriptive text for each type.

DENOMINATIONS

The second basic consideration to be met in the attribution of a coin is the determination of denomination. Since denominations are usually expressed in numeric, rather than word form on a coin, this is usually quite easily accomplished on coins from nations, which use Western numerals, except in those instances where issues are devoid of any mention of face value, and denomination must be attributed by size, metallic composition or weight. Coins listed in this volume are generally illustrated in actual size. Where size is critical to proper attribution, the coin's millimeter size is indicated.

The sphere of countries stretching from North Africa through the Orient, on which numeric symbols generally unfamiliar to Westerners are employed, often provide the collector with a much greater challenge. This is particularly true on nearly all pre-20th Century issues. On some of the more modern issues and increasingly so as the years progress, Western-style numerals usually presented in combination with the local numeric system are becoming more commonplace on these coins.

Determination of a coin's currency system can also be valuable in attributing the issue to its country of origin. A comprehensive alphabetical index of currency names, applicable to the countries as cataloged in this volume, with all individual nations of use for each, is presented in this section.

The included table of Standard International Numeral Systems presents charts of the basic numeric designations found on coins of non-Western origin. Although denomination numerals are generally prominently displayed on coins, it must be remembered that these are general representations of characters, which individual coin engravers may have rendered in widely varying styles. Where numeric or script denominations designation forms peculiar to a given coin or country apply, such as the script used on some Persian (Iranian) issues. They are so indicated or illustrated in conjunction with the appropriate listings.

MINTAGES

Quantities minted of each date are indicated where that information is available, generally stated in millions, and usually rounded off to the nearest 10,000 pieces. On quantities of a few thousand or less, actual mintages are generally indicated. For combined mintage figures the abbreviation "Inc. Above" means Included Above, while "Inc. Below" means Included Below. "Est." beside a mintage figure indicates the number given is an estimate or mintage limit.

MINT AND PRIVY MARKS

The presence of distinctive, but frequently inconspicuously placed, mintmarks indicates the mint of issue for many of the coins listed in this catalog. An appropriate designation in the date listings notes the presence, if any, of a mint mark on a particular coin type by incorporating the letter or letters of the mint mark adjoining the date, i.e., 1950D or 1927R.

The presence of mint and/or mintmaster's privy marks on a coin in non-letter form is indicated by incorporating the mint letter in lower case within parentheses adjoining the date; i.e. 1927(a). The corresponding mark is illustrated or identified in the introduction of the country.

In countries such as France and Mexico, where many mints may be producing like coinage in the same denomination during the same time period, divisions by mint have been employed. In these cases the mint mark may appear next to the individual date listings and/or the mint name or mint mark may be listed in the Note field of the type description.

Where listings incorporate mintmaster initials, they are always presented in capital letters separated from the date by one character space; i.e., 1850 MF. The different mintmark and mintmaster letters found on the coins of any country, state or city of issue are always shown at the beginning of listings.

METALS

Each numbered type listing will contain a description of the coins metallic content. The traditional coinage metals and their symbolic chemical abbreviations sometimes used in this catalog are:

Platinum - (PT)	Copper - (Cu)
Gold - (Au)	Brass -
Silver - (Ag)	Copper-nickel - (CN)
Billion -	Lead - (Pb)
Nickel - (Ni)	Steel -
Zinc - (Zn)	Tin - (Sn)
Bronze - (Ae)	Aluminum - (Al)

During the 18th and 19th centuries, most of the world's coins were struck of copper or bronze, silver and gold. Commencing in the early years of the 20th century, however, numerous new coinage metals, primarily non-precious metal alloys, were introduced. Gold has not been widely used for circulation coinages since World War I, although silver remained a popular coinage metal in most parts of the world until after World War II. With the disappearance of silver for circulation coinage, numerous additional compositions were introduced to coinage applications.

Most recent is the development of clad or plated planchets in order to maintain circulation life and extend the life of a set of production dies as used in the production of the copper-nickel clad copper 50 centesimos of Panama or in the latter case to reduce production costs of the planchets and yet provide a coin quite similar in appearance to its predecessor as in the case of the copper plated zinc core United States 1983 cent.

Modern commemorative coins have employed still more unusual methods such as bimetallic coins, color applications and precious metal or gem inlays.

OFF-METAL STRIKES

Off-metal strikes previously designated by "(OMS)" which also included the wide range of error coinage struck in other than their officially authorized compositions have been incorporated into Pattern listings along with special issues, which were struck for presentation or other reasons.

Collectors of Germanic coinage may be familiar with the term "Abschlag" which quickly identifies similar types of coinage.

PRECIOUS METAL WEIGHTS

Listings of weight, fineness and actual silver (ASW), gold (AGW), platinum or palladium (APW) content of most machine-struck silver, gold, platinum and palladium coins are provided in this edition. This information will be found incorporated in each separate type listing, along with other data related to the coin.

The ASW, AGW and APW figures were determined by multiplying the gross weight of a given coin by its known or tested fineness and converting the resulting gram or grain weight to troy ounces, rounded to the nearest ten-thousandth of an ounce. A silver coin with a 24.25-gram weight and .875 fineness for example, would have a fine weight of approximately 21.2188 grams, or a .6822 ASW, a factor that can be used to accurately determine the intrinsic value for multiple examples.

The ASW, AGW or APW figure can be multiplied by the spot price of each precious metal to determine the current intrinsic value of any coin accompanied by these designations.

Coin weights are indicated in grams (abbreviated "g") along with fineness where the information is of value in differentiating between types. These weights are based on 31.103 grams per troy (scientific) ounce, as opposed to the avoirdupois (commercial) standard of 28.35 grams. Actual coin weights are generally shown in hundredths or thousands of a gram; i.e., 0.500 SILVER 2.9200g.WEIGHTS AND FINENESSES

As the silver and gold bullion markets have advanced and declined sharply in recent years, the fineness and total precious metal content of coins has become especially significant where bullion coins - issues which trade on the basis of their intrinsic metallic content rather than numismatic value - are concerned. In many instances, such issues have become worth more in bullion form than their nominal collector values or denominations indicate.

Establishing the weight of a coin can also be valuable for determining its denomination. Actual weight is also necessary to ascertain the specific gravity of the coin's metallic content, an important factor in determining authenticity.

TROY WEIGHT STANDARDS

24 Grains = 1 Pennyweight
480 Grains = 1 Ounce
31.103 Grams = 1 Ounce

UNIFORM WEIGHTS

15.432 Grains = 1 Gram
0.0648 Gram = 1 Grain

AVOIRDUPOIS STANDARDS

27-11/32 Grains = 11 Dram
437-1/2 Grains = 1 Ounce
28.350 Grams = 1 Ounce

BULLION VALUE CHARTS

Universal silver, gold, and platinum bullion value charts are provided for use in combination with the ASW, AGW and APW factors to determine approximate intrinsic values of listed coins. By adding the component weights as shown in troy ounces on each chart, the approximate intrinsic value of any silver, gold or platinum coin's precious metal content can be determined.

Again referring to the examples presented in the above section, the intrinsic value of a silver coin with a .6822 ASW would be indicated as $4.43 + based on the application of the silver bullion chart. This result is obtained by moving across the top to the $6.50 column, then moving down to the line indicated .680 in the far left hand corner which reveals a bullion value of $4.420. To determine the value of the remaining .0022 of ASW, return up the same column to the .002 line, the closest factor available, where a $ .0130 value is indicted. The two factors total $4.433, which would be slightly less than actual value.

The silver bullion chart provides silver values in thousandths from .001 to .009 troy ounce, and in hundredths from .01 to 1.00 in 50¢ value increments from $3.00 to $10.50. If the market value of silver exceeds $10.50, doubling the increments presented will provide valuations in $1 steps from $6.00 to $21.00.

The gold/platinum bullion chart is similarly arranged in $10 increments from $350 to $490, and by doubling the increments presented, $20 steps from $700 to $980 can be determined.

Valuations for most of the silver, gold, platinum and palladium coins listed in this edition are based on assumed market values of $4.60 per troy ounce for silver, $350 for gold, $680 for platinum, and $245 for palladium. To arrive at accurate current market indications for these issues, increase or decrease the valuations appropriately based on any variations in these indicated levels.

HOMELAND TYPES

Homeland types are coins which colonial powers used in a colony, but do not bear that location's name. In some cases they were legal tender in the homeland, in others not. They are listed under the homeland and cross-referenced at the colony listing.

COUNTERMARKS/COUNTERSTAMPS

There is some confusion among collectors over the terms “countermark” and “counterstamp” when applied to a coin bearing an additional mark or change of design and/or denomination.

To clarify, a countermark might be considered similar to the “hall mark” applied to a piece of silverware, by which a silversmith assured the quality of the piece. In the same way, a countermark assures the quality of the coin on which it is placed, as, for example, when the royal crown of England was countermarked (punched into) on segmented Spanish reales, allowing them to circulate in commerce in the British West Indies. An additional countermark indicating the new denomination may also be encountered on these coins.

Coin Alignment

Medal Alignment

COIN vs MEDAL ALIGNMENT

Some coins are struck with obverse and reverse aligned at a rotation of 180 degrees from each other. When a coin is held for vertical viewing with the obverse design aligned upright and the index finger and thumb at the top and bottom, upon rotation from left to right for viewing the reverse, the latter will be upside down. Such alignment is called “coin rotation.” Other coins are struck with the obverse and reverse designs mated on an alignment of zero or 360 degrees. If such an example is held and rotated as described, the reverse will appear upright. This is the alignment, which is generally observed in the striking of medals, and for that reason coins produced in this manner are considered struck in “medal rotation”. In some instances, often through error, certain coin issues have been struck to both alignment standards, creating interesting collectible varieties, which will be found noted in some listings. In addition, some countries are now producing coins with other designated overse to reverse alignments which are considered standard for this type.

Countermarks are generally applied singularly and in most cases indiscriminately on either side of the "host" coin.

Counterstamped coins are more extensively altered. The counterstamping is done with a set of dies, rather than a hand punch. The coin being counterstamped is placed between the new dies and struck as if it were a blank planchet as found with the Manila 8 reales issue of the Philippines. A more unusual application where the counterstamp dies were smaller than the host coin in the revalidated 50 centimos and 1 colon of Costa Rica issued in 1923.

PHOTOGRAPHS

To assist the reader in coin identification, every effort has been made to present actual size photographs of every coinage type listed. Obverse and reverse are illustrated, except when a change in design is restricted to one side, and the coin has a diameter of 39mm or larger, in which case only the side required for identification of the type is generally illustrated. All coins up to 60mm are illustrated actual size, to the nearest 1/2mm up to 25mm, and to the nearest 1mm thereafter. Coins larger than 60mm diameter are illustrated in reduced size, with the actual size noted in the descriptive text block. Where slight change in size is important to coin type identification, actual millimeter measurements are stated.

TRADE COINS

From approximately 1750-1940, a number of nations, particularly European colonial powers and commercial traders, minted trade coins to facilitate commerce with the local populace of Africa, the Arab countries, the Indian subcontinental, Southeast Asia and the Far East. Such coins generally circulated at a value based on the weight and fineness of their silver or gold content, rather than their stated denomination. Examples include the sovereigns of Great Britain and the gold ducat issues of Austria, Hungary and the Netherlands. Trade coinage will sometimes be found listed at the end of the domestic issues.

VALUATIONS

Values quoted in this catalog represent the current market and are compiled from recommendations provided and verified through various source documents and specialized consultants. It should be stressed, however, that this book is intended to serve only as an aid for evaluating coins, actual market conditions are constantly changing and additional influences, such as particularly strong local demand for certain coin series, fluctuation of international exchange rates and worldwide collection patterns must also be considered. Publication of this catalog is not intended as a solicitation by the publisher, editors or contributors to buy or sell the coins listed at the prices indicated.

All valuations are stated in U.S. dollars, based on careful assessment of the varied international collector market. Valuations for coins priced below $100.00 are generally stated in full amounts - i.e. 37.50 or 95.00 - while valuations at or above that figure are rounded off in even dollars - i.e. $125.00 is expressed 125. A comma is added to indicate thousands of dollars in value.

For the convenience of overseas collectors and for U.S. collectors doing business with overseas dealers, the base exchange rate for the national currencies of approximately 180 countries are presented in the Foreign Exchange Table.

It should be noted that when particularly select uncirculated or proof-like examples of uncirculated coins become available they can be expected to command proportionately high premiums. Such examples in reference to choice Germanic Thalers are referred to as "erst schlage" or first strikes.

TOKEN COINAGE

At times local economic conditions have forced regular coinage from circulation or found mints unable to cope with the demand for coinage, giving rise to privately issued token coinage substitutes. British tokens of the late 1700s and early 1880s, and the German and French and French Colonial emergency emissions of the World War I era are examples of such tokens being freely accepted in monetary transactions over wide areas. Tokens were likewise introduced to satisfy specific restricted needs, such as the leper colony issues of Brazil, Colombia and the Philippines.

This catalog includes introductory or detailed listings with "Tn" prefixes of many token coinage issues, particularly those which enjoyed wide circulation and where the series was limited in diversity. More complex series, and those more restricted in scope of circulation are generally not listed, although a representative sample may be illustrated and a specialty reference provided.

MEDALLIC ISSUES

Medallic issues are segregated following the regular issue listings. Grouped there are coin-type issues, which can generally be identified as commemoratives produced to the country's established coinage standards but without the usual indicator of denomination. These pieces may or may not feature designs adapted from the country's regular issue or commemorative coinage, and may or may not have been issued in conjunction with related coinage issues.

RESTRIKES, COUNTERFEITS

Deceptive restrike and counterfeit (both contemporary and modern) examples exist of some coin issues. Where possible, the existence of restrikes is noted. Warnings are also incorporated in instances where particularly deceptive counterfeits are known to exist. Collectors who are uncertain about the authenticity of a coin held in their collection, or being offered for sale, should take the precaution of having it authenticated by the American Numismatic Association Authentication Bureau, 818 N. Cascade, Colorado Springs, CO 80903. Their reasonably priced certification tests are widely accepted by collectors and dealers alike.

NON-CIRCULATING LEGAL TENDER COINS

Coins of non-circulating legal tender (NCLT) origin are individually listed and integrated by denomination into the regular listings for each country. These coins fall outside the customary definitions of coin-of-the-realm issues, but where created and sold by, or under authorization of, agencies of sovereign governments expressly for collectors. These are primarily individual coins and sets of a commemorative nature, marketed at prices substantially in excess of face value, and usually do not have counterparts released for circulation.

EDGE VARIETIES

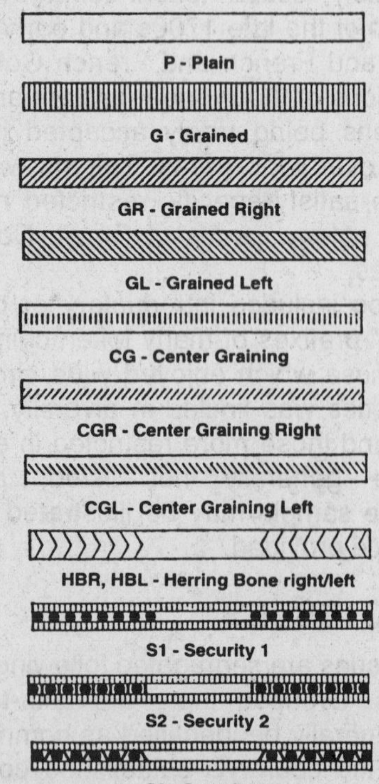

NEW ISSUES

All newly released coins that have been physically observed by our staff and those that have been confirmed by press time have been incorporated in this edition. Exceptions exist in some countries where current date coin production lags far behind and other countries whose fiscal year actually begins in the latter half of the current year.

Collectors and dealers alike are kept up to date with worldwide new issues having newly assigned catalog reference numbers in the monthly feature "World Coin Roundup" in World Coin News. A free sample copy will be sent upon request. Overseas requests should include 1 international postal reply coupon for surface mail or 2 international postal reply coupons for air mail dispatch: Write to World Coin News, 700 East State St., Iola, WI 54990 USA.

SETS

Listings in this catalog for specimen, proof and mint sets are for official, government-produced sets. In many instances privately packaged sets also exist.

Mint Sets/Fleur de Coin Sets: Specially prepared by worldwide mints to provide banks, collectors and government dignitaries with examples of current coinage. Usually subjected to rigorous inspection to insure that top quality specimens of selected business strikes are provided. One of the most popular mint set is that given out by the monarch of Great Britain each year on Maunday Thursday. This set contains four special coins in denominations of 1, 2, 3 and 4 pence, struck in silver and contained in a little pouch. They have been given away in a special ceremony for the poor for more than two centuries.

The Paris Mint introduced polyvinyl plastic cases packed within a cardboard box for homeland and colonial Fleur de Coin sets of the 1960s. British colonial sets were issued in velvet-lined metal cases similar to those used for proof sets. For its client nations, the Franklin Mint introduced a sealed composition of cardboard and specially molded hard clear plastic protective container inserted in a soft plastic wallet. Recent discovery that soft polyvinyl packaging has proved hazardous to coins has resulted in a change to the use of hard, inert plastics for virtually all mint sets.

Some of the highest quality mint sets ever produced were those struck by the Franklin Mint during 1972-74. In many cases matte finish dies were used to strike a polished proof planchet. Later on, from 1975, sets contained highly polished, glassy-looking coins (similar to those struck by the Bombay Mint) for collectors over a period of 12 years.

Specimen Sets: Forerunners of today's proof sets. In most cases the coins were specially struck, perhaps even double struck, to produce a very soft or matte finish on the effigies and fields, along with high, sharp, "wire" rims. The finish is rather dull to the naked eye.

The original purpose of these sets was to provide VIPs, monarchs and mintmasters around the world with samples of the highest quality workmanship of a particular mint. These were usually housed in elaborate velvet-lined leather and metal cases.

Proof-like Sets are relatively new to the field of numismatics. During the mid 1950s the Royal Canadian Mint furnished the hobby with specially selected early business strike coins that exhibited some qualities similar to proof coinage. However, the "proof-like" fields are generally flawed and the edges are rounded. These pieces are not double struck. These are commonly encountered in cardboard holders, later in soft plastic or pliofilm packaging. Of late, the Royal Canadian Mint packages such sets in rigid plastic cases.

Many worldwide officially issued proof sets would in reality fall into this category upon careful examination of the quality of the coin's finish.

Another term encountered in this category is "Special Select," used to describe the crowns of the Union of South Africa and 100-schilling coins produced for collectors in the late 1970s by the Austrian Mint.

Proof Sets: This is undoubtedly among the most misused terms in the hobby, not only by collectors and dealers, but also by many of the world mints.

A true proof set must be at least double-struck on specially prepared polished planchets and struck using dies (often themselves polished) of the highest quality.

Modern-day proof quality consists of frosted effigies surrounded by absolute mirror-like fields.

Listings for proof sets in this catalog are for officially issued proof sets so designated by the issuing authority, and may or may not possess what are considered modern proof quality standards.

It is necessary for collectors to acquire the knowledge to allow them to differentiate true proof sets from would-be proof sets and proof-like sets which may be encountered.

CONDITIONS/GRADING

Wherever possible, coin valuations are given in four or five grades of preservation. For modern commemoratives, which do not circulate, only uncirculated values are usually sufficient. Proof issues are indicated by the word "Proof" next to the date, with valuation proceeded by the word "value" following the mintage. For very recent circulating coins and coins of limited value, one, two or three grade values are presented.

There are almost no grading guides for world coins. What follows is an attempt to help bridge that gap until a detailed, illustrated guide becomes available.

In grading world coins, there are two elements to look for: 1) Overall wear, and 2) loss of design details, such as strands of hair, feathers on eagles, designs on coats of arms, etc.

The age, rarity or type of a coin should not be a consideration in grading.

Grade each coin by the weaker of the two sides. This method appears to give results most nearly consistent with conservative American Numismatic Association standards for U.S. coins. Split grades, i.e., F/VF for obverse and reverse, respectively, are normally no more than one grade apart. If the two sides are more than one grade apart, the series of coins probably wears differently on each side and should then be graded by the weaker side alone.

Grade by the amount of overall wear and loss of design detail evident on each side of the coin. On coins with a moderately small design element, which is prone to early wear, grade by that design alone. For example, the 5-ore (KM#554) of Sweden has a crown above the monogram on which the beads on the arches show wear most clearly. So, grade by the crown alone.

For **Brilliant Uncirculated** (BU) grades there will be no visible signs of wear or handling, even under a 30-power microscope. Full mint luster will be present. Ideally no bags marks will be evident.

For **Uncirculated** (Unc.) grades there will be no visible signs of wear or handling, even under a 30-power microscope. Bag marks may be present.

For **Almost Uncirculated** (AU), all detail will be visible. There will be wear only on the highest point of the coin. There will often be half or more of the original mint luster present.

On the **Extremely Fine** (XF or EF) coin, there will be about 95% of the original detail visible. Or, on a coin with a design with no inner detail to wear down, there will be a light wear over nearly all the coin. If a small design is used as the grading area, about 90% of the original detail will be visible. This latter rule stems from the logic that a smaller amount of detail needs to be present because a small area is being used to grade the whole coin.

The **Very Fine** (VF) coin will have about 75% of the original detail visible. Or, on a coin with no inner detail, there will be moderate wear over the entire coin. Corners of letters and numbers may be weak. A small grading area will have about 66% of the original detail.

For **Fine** (F), there will be about 50% of the original detail visible. Or, on a coin with no inner detail, there will be fairly heavy wear over all of the coin. Sides of letters will be weak. A typically uncleaned coin will often appear as dirty or dull. A small grading area will have just under 50% of the original detail.

On the **Very Good** (VG) coin, there will be about 25% of the original detail visible. There will be heavy wear on all of the coin.

The **Good** (G) coin's design will be clearly outlined but with substantial wear. Some of the larger detail may be visible. The rim may have a few weak spots of wear.

On the **About Good** (AG) coin, there will typically be only a silhouette of a large design. The rim will be worn down into the letters if any.

STANDARD INTERNATIONAL GRADING TERMINOLOGY AND ABBREVIATIONS

	PROOF	UNCIRCULATED	EXTREMELY FINE	VERY FINE	FINE	VERY GOOD	GOOD	POOR
U.S. and ENGLISH SPEAKING LANDS	PRF	UNC	EF or XF	VF	F	VG	G	PR
BRAZIL	—	(1)FDC or FC	(3) S	(5) MBC	(7) BC	(8) BC/R	(9) R	UT GeG
DENMARK	M	0	01	1+	1	1÷	2	3
FINLAND	00	0	01	1+	1	1?	2	3
FRANCE	FB Flan Bruni	FDC Fleur de Coin	SUP Superbe	TTB Très très beau	TB Très beau	B Beau	TBC Très Bien Conservée	BC Bien Conservée
GERMANY	PP Polierte Platte	STG Stempelglanz	VZ Vorzüglich	SS Sehr schön	S Schön	S.G.E. Sehr gut erhalten	G.E. Gut erhalten	Gering erhalten
ITALY	FS Fondo Specchio	FDC Fior di Conio	SPL Splendido	BB Bellissimo	MB Molto Bello	B Bello	M	—
JAPAN	—	未使用	極美品	美品	並品	—	—	—
NETHERLANDS	— Proef	FDC Fleur de Coin	Pr. Prachtig	Z.f. Zeer fraai	Fr. Fraai	Z.g. Zeer goed	G	—
NORWAY	M	0	01	1+	1	1÷	2	3
PORTUGAL	—	Soberba	Bela	MBC	BC	MREG	REG	MC
SPAIN	Prueba	SC	EBC	MBC	BC+	BC	RC	MC
SWEDEN	Polerad	0	01	1+	1	1?	2	—

Strong or weak strikes, partially weak strikes, damage, corrosion, attractive or unattractive toning, dipping or cleaning should be described along with the above grades. These factors affect the quality of the coin just as do wear and loss of detail, but are easier to describe.

In the case of countermarked/counterstamped coins, the condition of the host coin will have a bearing on the end valuation. The important factor in determining the grade is the condition, clarity and completeness of the countermark itself. This is in reference to countermarks/counterstamps having raised design while being struck in a depression.

Incuse countermarks cannot be graded for wear. They are graded by the clarity and completeness including the condition of the host coin which will also have more bearing on the final grade/valuation determined.

Sending Scanned Images by Email

Over the past 2 years or so, we have been receiving an ever-increasing flow of scanned images from sources worldwide. Unfortunately, many of these scans could not be used due to the type of scan, or simple incompatability with our systems. We appreciate the effort it takes to produce these images and accuracy they add to the catalog listings.

Here are a few simple instructions to follow when producing these scans. We encourage you to continue sending new images or upgrades to those currently illustrated and please do not hesitate to ask questions about this process.

— Scan all images within a resolution range of 200 dpi to 300 dpi
— Size setting should be at 100%
— Scan in true 4-color
— Save images as 'jpeg' or 'tiff' and name in such a way, which clearly identifies the country of origin of the note
— Please email with a request to confirm receipt of the attachment
— Please send images to thernr@krause.com

INSTANT IDENTIFIER

Aachen (German States)

Albania

Austria

Baden (German States)

Brandenburg Ansbach (German States)

Finland

Jever (German States)

Frankfurt (German States)

Furstenberg (German States)

Geneva (Swiss Cantons)

German Empire

Montenegro (Yugoslavia)

Nürnberg (German States)

Milan (Italian States)

Prussia (German States)

Russia (Czarist) Russian Poland

Schwarzburg-Rudolstadt (German States)

Schwarzburg-Sondershausen (German States)

Serbia (Yugoslavia)

Teutonic Order (German States)

Genoa (Italian States)

Syrian Arab Republic

United Arab Republic (Egypt, Syria)

Arab Republic of Egypt Libya

Yemen Arab Republic

Bulgaria

Burma (Myanmar)

Ethiopia

Finland

Norway

Gorizia (Italian States)

Hannover (German States)

Hesse-Darmstadt (German States)

Hohenlohe-Neuenstein-Oehringen (German States)

Iran (Persia)

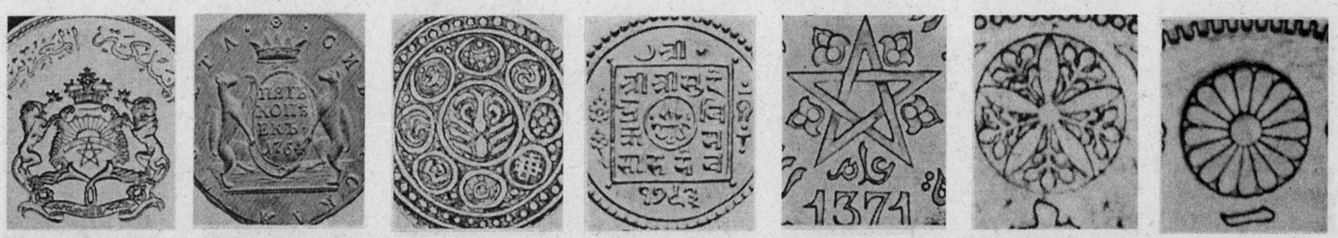

Morocco

Siberia

Tibet (China)

Nepal

Morocco (AH1371-1951AD)

Manchoukuo (Puppet State-China)

Japan

INSTANT IDENTIFIER

Hanau-Munzenberg (German States) | Nassau (German States) | Hesse-Cassel (German States) | Sri Lanka (Ceylon) | Tibet (China) | Utrecht (Netherlands) | Venice (Italian States)

Neuchatel (Swiss Cantons) | China (Empire-Provincial) | China (Empire-Provincial) | Japan | Japan | African States | Bretzenheim (German States)

Hall in Swabia (German States) | Greenland | German New Guinea (Papua New Guinea) | Lithuania | Mongolia | Sudan | Algeria

Lowenstein-Wertheim (German States) | Maldive Islands | Afghanistan | Ireland | Israel | Lebanon | Papal States (Italian States)

Regensburg (German States) | Sweden | North Korea | CCCP-Russia | CCCP-Russia | Yugoslavia | Taiwan (Rep. of China)

Mainz (German States) | Solms-Laubach (German States) | Ticino (Swiss Cantons) | Fugger (German States) | Naples & Sicily (Italian States) | Saxe-Saalfeld (German States) | Stolberg-Stolberg (German States)

INSTANT IDENTIFIER

French Colonial | French Colonial | French Colonial | Bangladesh | Isle of Man Sicily | Libya | Anhalt-Bernburg (German States)

Aargau (Swiss Cantons) | Augsburg (German States) | Basel (Swiss Cantons) | Bavaria (German States) | Brazil | Bremen (German States) | Luzern (Swiss Cantons)

Chur Pfalz (German States) | Fulda (German States) | Glarus (Swiss Cantons) | Grand Duchy of Warsaw (Poland) | Graubunden (Swiss Cantons) | Hamburg (German States) | Lucca (Italian States)

Hesse-Cassel (German States) | Hesse-Homburg (German States) | Hildesheim (German States) | Hohenzollern-Hechingen (German States) | Hungary | Julich-Berg (German States) | Gelderland (Netherlands)

Lippe-Detmold (German States) | Lübeck (German States) | Mecklenburg-Strelitz (German States) | Oldenburg (German States) | Passau (German States) | Portugal | Vaud (Swiss Cantons)

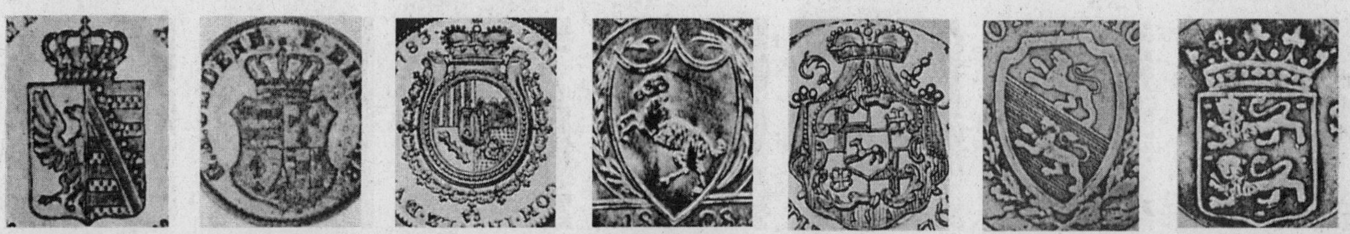

Anhalt (Joint Coinage) (German States) | Oldenburg (German States) | Schwarzenberg (German States) | Schaffhausen (Swiss Cantons) | Paderborn (German States) | Thurgau (Swiss Cantons) | Westfrisia (Netherlands)

INSTANT IDENTIFIER

Arenberg (German States)

Rhenish Confederation (German States)

Reuss-Greiz (German States)

Sardinia (Italian States)

Saxony (German States)

Schaumburg-Lippe (German States)

Schleswig-Holstein (German States)

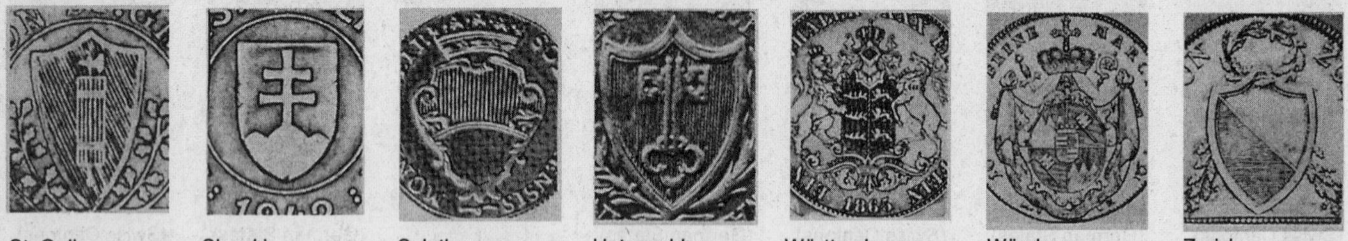

St. Gall (Swiss Cantons)

Slovakia

Solothurn (Swiss Cantons)

Unterwalden (Nidwalden) (Swiss Cantons)

Württemberg (German States)

Würzburg (German States)

Zurich (Swiss Cantons)

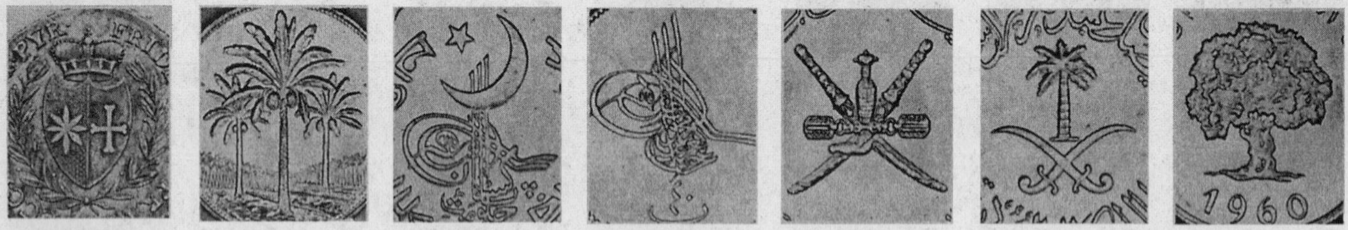

Waldeck-Pyrmont (German States)

Iraq

Pakistan

Turkey-Egypt Sudan, Algeria (Ottoman Empire)

Muscat & Oman, Oman

Saudi Arabia

Tunisia

Wismar (German States)

Order of Malta

Bamberg (German States)

Brunswick-Wolfenbüttel (German States)

Brunswick-Lüneburg (German States

Erfurt Mainz (German States)

Hannover (German States)

Albania

Israel

Eichstätt (German States)

Greece

Serbia

Switzerland

Thailand (Siam)

Japan (Dai Nippon)

South Korea

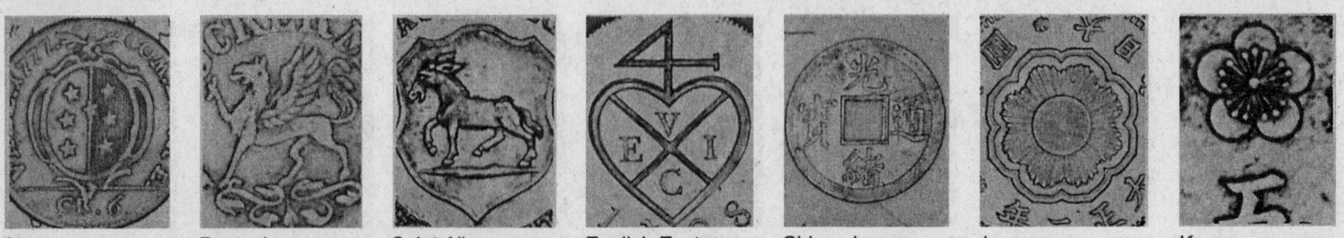

Sitten (Swiss Cantons)

Rostock (German States)

Saint Alban (German States)

English East India Co. (Sumatra)

China, Japan, Annam, Korea (All Holed 'cash' coins look quite similar.)

Japan

Korea

COIN DENOMINATION INDEX

ABBASI - Afghanistan
Iran
ADHIO - India - Independent Kingdoms
AFGHANI - Afghanistan
AGORAH - Israel
AGOROT - Israel
AMANI - Afghanistan
ANGEL - Isle Of Man
ANNA - India - Princely States
India-British
India-Republic
Muscat & Oman
Myanmar
Pakistan
ARGENTINO - Argentina
ARI - Albania
ARIARY - Madagascar
ASARFI - Nepal
ASARPHI - Nepal
ASHRAFI - India - Princely States
Iran
ASHRAPHI - Nepal
ATT - Laos
Thailand
AURAR - Iceland
AUSTRAL - Argentina
AVOS - Macao
Timor
AZADI - Iran
BAHT - Thailand
BAISA - Muscat & Oman
Oman
BALBOA - Panama
BAN - Moldova
Romania
BANI - Moldova
Romania
BANICA - Croatia
BESA - Italian Somaliland
BESE - Italian Somaliland
BIPKWELE - Equatorial Guinea
BIRR - Ethiopia
BOLIVAR - Venezuela
BOLIVIANO - Bolivia
BUQSHA - Yemen Arab Republic
BUTUT - Gambia, The
CASH - China
China, People'S Republic
China, Republic Of
India - Princely States
CASHES - China
CAURIS - Guinea
CEDI - Ghana
CEDIS - Ghana
CENT - Aruba
Australia
Bahamas
Barbados
Belize
Bermuda
Botswana
British Honduras
British North Borneo
British Virgin Islands
Canada
Cayman Islands
Ceylon
China
China, People'S Republic
China, Republic Of
Cook Islands
Curacao
Cyprus
Danish West Indies
Dominica
East Africa
East Carribean States
Eritrea
Ethiopia
Fiji
French Indo-China
Great Britain
Guyana
Hong Kong
Jamaica
Keeling Cocos Islands
Kenya
Kiau Chau
Kiribati
Laos
Liberia
Malay Peninsula
Malaya
Malaya & British Borneo
Malaysia
Malta
Mauritius
Namibia
Netherlands
Netherlands Antilles
Netherlands East Indies
New Zealand
Newfoundland
Panama
Rhodesia
Sarawak
Seychelles
Sierra Leone
Singapore
Solomon Islands
South Africa
Sri Lanka
Straits Settlements
Suriname
Swaziland
Trinidad & Tobago
Tuvalu
Uganda
United States
Zanzibar
Zimbabwe
CENTAI - Lithuania
CENTAS - Lithuania
CENTAVO - Angola
Argentina
Bolivia
Brazil
Cape Verde
Chile
Colombia
Costa Rica
Cuba
Dominican Republic
Ecuador
El Salvador
Guatemala
Guinea-Bissau
Honduras
India-Portugese
Mexico
Mexico-Revolutionary
Mozambique
Nicaragua
Paraguay
Peru
Philippines
Portugal
Saint Thomas & Prince Island
Timor
CENTESIMI - Italy
San Marino
Somalia
Vatican City
CENTESIMO - Chile
Italy
Panama
Sierra Leone
Somalia
Uruguay
CENTIM - Andorra
CENTIME - Algeria
Belgian Congo
Belgium
Cambodia
Cameroon
Comoros
Congo Free State
Congo, Democratic Republic
Djibouti
France
French Equatorial Africa
French Oceania
French Polynesia
French West Africa
Guadeloupe
Haiti
Luxembourg
Madagascar
Martinique
Monaco
Morocco
New Caledonia
Reunion
Senegal
Tunisia
CENTIMO - Angola
Costa Rica
Mozambique
Paraguay
Peru
Saint Thomas & Prince Island
Spain
Spain Civil War
Venezuela
CENTIMS - Andorra
CENTU - Lithuania
CH'IEN - China
CHERVONETZ - Russia
CHETRUM - Bhutan
CHHERTUM - Bhutan
CHIAO - China, Japanese Puppet States
China, Republic Of
CHIEN - China, Republic Of
CHON - Korea
Korea-North
CHUCKRAM - India - Princely States
COLON - Costa Rica
El Salvador
CONDOR - Ecuador
COPPERS - China
CORDOBA - Nicaragua
CORONA - Austria
CROWN - Australia
Bermuda
Biafra
Gibraltar
Great Britain
Ireland Republic
Isle Of Man
Malawi
New Zealand
Rhodesia And Nyasaland
Southern Rhodesia
Tristan Da Cunha
Turks & Caicos Islands
CROWNS - Isle Of Man
CRUZADO - Brazil
CRUZEIRO - Brazil
CRUZEIROS - Brazil
CRUZEIROS REAIS - Brazil
CRUZEIROS REAL - Brazil
DALASI - Gambia, The
DALER - Danish West Indies
DAM - Nepal
DECIMO - Colombia
Ecuador
DENAR - Macedonia
DENARI - Macedonia
DENI - Macedonia
DHABU - India - Independent Kingdoms
DHINGLO - India - Independent Kingdoms
DIME - United States
DINAR - Algeria
Bahrain
Fujairah, Al
Hejaz
Iran
Iraq
Jordan
Kuwait
Libya
Serbia
Sudan
Syria
Tunisia
Yemen, Democratic Republic Of
Yugoslavia
DINARA - Bosnia-Herzegovina
Serbia
Yugoslavia
DINER - Andorra
DINERO - Peru
DIRHAM - Ajman
Jordan
Libya
Morocco
Ras Al-Khaimah
United Arab Emirates
DIRHEM - Qatar
Qatar & Dubai
DOBRA - Saint Thomas & Prince Island
DOBRAS - Saint Thomas & Prince Island
DOKDA - India - Independent Kingdoms
India - Princely States
DOKDO - India - Independent Kingdoms
India - Princely States
DOLLAR - American Samoa
Anguilla
Antigua
Antigua & Barbuda
Australia
Bahamas
Barbados
Belize
Bermuda
British Virgin Islands
Brunei
Canada
Cayman Islands
China
China, People'S Republic
China, Republic Of
Cook Islands
Dominica
East Carribean States
Eritrea
Ethiopia
Fiji
Great Britain
Grenada
Guyana
Hong Kong
India-British
Jamaica
Kiribati
Liberia
Marshall Islands
Montserrat
Namibia
Nauru
New Zealand
Niue
Palau
Panama
Pitcairn Islands
Saint Kitts & Nevis
Saint Lucia
Saint Vincent
Sierra Leone
Singapore
Solomon Islands
Straits Settlements
Trinidad & Tobago
Turks & Caicos Islands
Tuvalu
United States
Zimbabwe
DOLYA - Russia
DONG - Viet Nam
DOUBLE - Guernsey
DRACHMA - Crete
Greece
DRACHMAI - Crete
Greece
DRACHMES - Greece
DRAM - Armenia
Nagorno-Karabakh
Tajikistan
DRAMS - Armenia
Nagorno-Karabakh
DUCAT - Austria
Croatia
Netherlands
Netherlands East Indies
DUKAT - Bosnia-Herzegovina
Czechoslovakia
Yugoslavia
DUKATA - Yugoslavia
DUKATU - Czechoslovakia
DUKATY - Czechoslovakia
ECU - Belgium
Bosnia-Herzegovina
Gibraltar
Isle Of Man
ECUS - Gibraltar
EKUELE - Equatorial Guinea
EMALANGENI - Swaziland
ESCUDO - Angola
Azores
Cape Verde
Chile
Guinea-Bissau
India-Portugese
Madeira Islands
Mozambique

Portugal
Saint Thomas & Prince Island
Timor
EURO - Austria
Belgium
Bosnia-Herzegovina
Finland
France
Germany - Federal Republic
Greece
Ireland Republic
Isle Of Man
Italy
Luxembourg
Monaco
Netherlands
Portugal
San Marino
Spain
Turkey
Vatican City
EYRIR - Iceland
FALUS - Uzbekistan
FANAM - India - Princely States
FARTHING - Great Britain
Ireland Republic
Jamaica
FEN - China
China, Japanese Puppet States
China, People'S Republic
China, Republic Of
FENIG - Poland
FENIGOW - Poland
FENINGA - Bosnia-Herzegovina
FIL - Bahrain
Fujairah, Al
Iraq
Jordan
Kuwait
South Arabia
United Arab Emirates
Yemen Arab Republic
Yemen, Democratic Republic Of
FILLER - Hungary
FLORIN - Aruba
Australia
East Africa
Fiji
Great Britain
Ireland Republic
Malawi
New Zealand
South Africa
FLORINI - Italy
FLORINO - Italy
FORINT - Hungary
FRANC - Algeria
Belgian Congo
Belgium
Benin
Burundi
Cambodia
Cameroon
Central African Republic
Central African States
Chad
Comoros
Congo Republic
Congo, Democratic Republic
Dahomey
Danish West Indies
Djibouti
Equatorial African States
Equatorial Guinea
France
French Afars & Issas
French Equatorial Africa
French Oceania
French Polynesia
French Somaliland
French West Africa
Gabon
Guadeloupe
Guinea
Ivory Coast
Katanga
Luxembourg
Madagascar
Mali
Martinique
Monaco
Morocco
New Caledonia
New Hebrides
Niger
Reunion
Rwanda
Rwanda & Burundi
Saint Pierre & Miquelon
Senegal
Switzerland
Togo
Tunisia
West African States
FRANCO - Equatorial Guinea
FRANCOS - Equatorial Guinea
FRANCS - Senegal
FRANG AR - Albania
FRANK - Liechtenstein
FRANKEN - Belgium
Liechtenstein
Saarland
FUANG - Thailand
FUN - Korea
GAUCHO - Uruguay
GERSH - Ethiopia
GHIRSH - Hejaz
Hejaz & Nejd
Saudi Arabia
Sudan
GOLDE - Sierra Leone
GOURDE - Haiti
GRAMO - Bolivia
GRAMS - Afghanistan
GROATS - Great Britain
GROSCHEN - Austria
GROSZ - Poland
GROSZE - Poland
GROSZY - Poland
GUARANI - Paraguay
GUILDER - Netherlands Antilles
Suriname
GUINEA - Saudi Arabia
GULDEN - Curacao
German States
Netherlands
Netherlands Antilles
Netherlands East Indies
Poland
Suriname
GUTSCHRIFTSMARKE - German States
HABIBI - Afghanistan
HALALA - Mutawakkilite
Saudi Arabia
HALER - Czechoslovakia
HALERE - Czechoslovakia
HALERU - Bohemia & Moravia
Czech Republic
Czechoslovakia
HALIEROV - Slovakia
HAO - Viet Nam
HARF - Mutawakkilite
HAU - Tonga
HELLER - Austria
German East Africa
Hungary
HRYVEN - Ukraine
HRYVNI - Ukraine
HRYVNIA - Ukraine
HWAN - Korea-South
IMADI RIYAL - Mutawakkilite
INTI - Peru
JIAO - China, People'S Republic
KABIR - Mutawakkilite
KARBOVANET - Ukraine
KARBOVANTSIV - Ukraine
KEPING - Malay Peninsula
KHUMSI - Quaiti State Of Hadhramaut
KILO - Tatarstan
KINA - Papua New Guinea
KIP - Laos
KOBO - Nigeria
KOPEEK - Transnistria
KOPEJEK - Tannu Tuva
KOPEK - Germany-Empire
Russia
Spitzbergen
KOPIYKA - Ukraine
KOPIYKY - Ukraine
KOPIYOK - Ukraine
KORI - India - Independent Kingdoms
India - Princely States
KORONA - Hungary
KORUN - Czech Republic
Czechoslovakia
Slovakia
KORUNA - Bohemia & Moravia
Czech Republic
Czechoslovakia
Slovakia
KOULA - Tonga
KRAN - Iran
KRONA - Iceland
Sweden
KRONE - Austria
Denmark
Greenland
Liechtenstein
Norway
KRONEN - Austria
Liechtenstein
KRONER - Denmark
Greenland
Norway
KRONOR - Sweden
KRONUR - Iceland
KROONI - Estonia
KRUGERRAND - South Africa
KUNA - Croatia
KURUS - Turkey
KWACHA - Malawi
Zambia
KWANZA - Angola
KYAT - Myanmar
KYATS - Myanmar
LAARI - Maldive Islands
LANG - Annam
LARI - Georgia
LARIAT - Maldive Islands
LARIN - Maldive Islands
LATI - Latvia
LATS - Latvia
LATU - Latvia
LEI - Moldova
Romania
LEK - Albania
LEKE - Albania
LEKU - Albania
LEMPIRA - Honduras
LEONE - Sierra Leone
LEPTA - Crete
Greece
LEPTON - Crete
LEU - Moldova
Romania
LEV - Bulgaria
LEVA - Bulgaria
LI - China
China, Japanese Puppet States
LIANG - China
LIBRA - Peru
LICENTE - Lesotho
LIKUTA - Congo, Democratic Republic
LILANGENI - Swaziland
LIP - Slovenia
LIPA - Croatia
Slovenia
LIPE - Croatia
Slovenia
LIRA - Italy
Malta
Mutawakkilite
San Marino
Syria
Turkey
Vatican City
LIRAH - Israel
LIRE - Italian Somaliland
Italy
San Marino
Vatican City
LIRI - Malta
LIROT - Israel
LISENTE - Lesotho
LITAI - Lithuania
LITAS - Lithuania
LITRES - Tatarstan
LITU - Lithuania
LIVRE - Lebanon
LIVRES - Lebanon
LOTI - Lesotho
LOWE - Bophuthatswana
LUHLANGA - Swaziland
LUMA - Armenia
LWEI - Angola
MACE - China
MAKUTA - Congo, Democratic Republic
Zaire
MALOTI - Lesotho
MANAT - Azerbaijan
Turkmenistan
MAREK - Poland
MARK - Estonia
German States
German-Democratic Republic
Germany - Federal Republic
Germany, Third Reich
Germany, Weimar Republic
Germany-Empire
Poland
MARKA - Bosnia-Herzegovina
Estonia
MARKKA - Finland
MARKKAA - Finland
MATONA - Ethiopia
MATONAS - Ethiopia
MAZUNAS - Morocco
MEI - China, Republic Of
METICA - Mozambique
METICAIS - Mozambique
METICAL - Mozambique
METICAS - Mozambique
MIL - Cyprus
Israel
Malta
Palestine
MILLIEME - Egypt
Libya
MILLIM - Sudan
Tunisia
MISCAL - China
MITQAL - Morocco
MOHAR - Nepal
MOHUR - India - Princely States
MOMME - Japan
MONGO - Mongolia
MU - Myanmar
MUZUNA - Morocco
NAIRA - Nigeria
NGULTRUM - Bhutan
NGWEE - Zambia
NKWE - Bophuthatswana
NOBLE - Isle Of Man
NON-DENOMINATED - French Equatorial Africa
Gabon
Germany-Empire
OCTORINO - Great Britain
ONZA - Chile
Mexico
ORE - Denmark
Faeroe Islands
Greenland
Iceland
Norway
Sweden
OUGUIYA - Mauritania
OUNCE - China, People'S Republic
South Africa
PA'ANGA - Tonga
PAHLAVI - Iran
PAI - India - Princely States
PAISA - Afghanistan
Bhutan
India - Princely States
India-Republic
Nepal
Pakistan
PAISE - Afghanistan
India-Republic
PARA - Hejaz
Montenegro
Serbia
Turkey
Yugoslavia
PARE - Montenegro
Serbia
PATACA - Macao
PAYALO - India - Independent Kingdoms
PE - Myanmar
PENCE - Ascension Island
Australia
Biafra
British West Africa
Falkland Islands
Fiji
Gambia, The
Ghana
Gibraltar
Great Britain
Guernsey
Guyana
Ireland Republic
Isle Of Man
Jersey
Malawi
New Guinea
New Zealand
Nigeria
Rhodesia
Rhodesia And Nyasaland
Saint Helena

Saint Helena & Ascension
South Africa
Southern Rhodesia
Tristan Da Cunha
Zambia
PENGO - Hungary
PENNIA - Finland
PENNY - Australia
British West Africa
Falkland Islands
Fiji
Gambia, The
Ghana
Gibraltar
Great Britain
Guernsey
Ireland Republic
Isle Of Man
Jamaica
Jersey
Malawi
New Guinea
New Zealand
Nigeria
Rhodesia And Nyasaland
Saint Helena & Ascension
South Africa
Southern Rhodesia
Zambia
PERPER - Montenegro
PERPERA - Montenegro
PESETA - Equatorial Guinea
Saharawi Arab Democratic Republic
Spain
Spain Civil War
PESEWA - Ghana
PESO - Argentina
Bolivia
Chile
Colombia
Cuba
Dominican Republic
El Salvador
Guatemala
Guinea-Bissau
Honduras
Mexico
Mexico-Revolutionary
Nicaragua
Paraguay
Philippines
Uruguay
PFENNIG - German East Africa
German States
German-Democratic Republic
Germany - Federal Republic
Germany, Third Reich
Germany, Weimar Republic
Germany-Empire
Poland
PFENNING - Germany-Empire
PHAN - Annam
PIASTRE - Cyprus
Egypt
Ethiopia
French Indo-China
Hejaz
Jordan
Lebanon
Libya
Nejd
Sudan
Syria
Tonkin
PICE - Bhutan
India - Princely States
India-British
India-Republic
PIE - India - Princely States
India-British
PISA - Philippines
PISO - Philippines
PITIS - Malay Peninsula
PLATINA - Isle Of Man
POISHA - Bangladesh
POLUSHKA - Russia
POND - South Africa
POUND - Alderney
Ascension Island
Australia
Biafra
Cyprus
Egypt
Falkland Islands
Gibraltar
Great Britain
Guernsey
Isle Of Man
Jersey
Malta
Rhodesia
Saint Helena
Saint Helena & Ascension
Saudi Arabia
South Africa
South Georgia And The South Sandwich Islands
Sudan
Syria
Tristan Da Cunha
PROTEA - South Africa
PRUTA - Israel
PRUTAH - Israel
PUL - Afghanistan
PULA - Botswana
PUNT - Ireland Republic
PYA - Myanmar
QAPIK - Azerbaijan
QINDAR AR - Albania
QINDAR ARI - Albania
QINDARKA - Albania
QIRSH - Egypt
Jordan
QUETZAL - Guatemala
QUINDAR LEKU - Albania
RAND - South Africa
RAPPEN - Switzerland
REAIS - Brazil
REAL - Brazil
El Salvador
Guatemala
REALES - Mexico
REICHSMARK - Germany, Third Reich
Germany, Weimar Republic
REICHSPFENNIG - Germany, Third Reich
Germany, Weimar Republic
REIS - Azores
Brazil
Portugal
RENTENPFENNIG - Germany, Weimar Republic
RIAL - Iran
Morocco
Muscat & Oman
Oman
Ras Al-Khaimah
Yemen Arab Republic
RIEL - Cambodia
RIELS - Cambodia
RIN - Japan
RINGGIT - Malaysia
RIYAL - Ajman
Fujairah, Al
Hejaz & Nejd
Iraq
Mutawakkilite
Qatar
Ras Al-Khaimah
Saudi Arabia
Sharjah
Umm Al Qaiwain
Yemen Arab Republic
Yemen Republic
RIYALS - Yemen Arab Republic
ROUBLE - Belarus
Russia
Russian Caucasia
Spitzbergen
Tajikistan
Uzbekistan
ROYAL - Gibraltar
RUBLEI - Transnistria
RUFIYAA - Maldive Islands
RUPEE - Afghanistan
Bhutan
Ceylon
Djibouti
India - Princely States
India-British
India-Republic
Keeling Cocos Islands
Mauritius
Nejd
Nepal
Pakistan
Seychelles
Sharjah
Sri Lanka
Tibet
RUPIA - India-Portugese
Indonesia
Italian Somaliland
RUPIAH - Indonesia
RUPIE - German East Africa
RUPIEN - German East Africa
S.M. - German States
SALUNG - Thailand
SANAR - Afghanistan
SANTIM - Morocco
SANTIMAT - Morocco
SANTIMI - Latvia
SANTIMS - Latvia
SANTIMU - Latvia
SAPEQUE - French Indo-China
SAR - China
SATANG - Thailand
SCELLINO - Somalia
SCHILLING - Austria
Malawi
SCUDI - Malta, Order Of
San Marino
SCUDO - Malta, Order Of
San Marino
SEN - Brunei
Cambodia
Indonesia
Japan
Malaysia
Netherlands East Indies
Thailand
SENE - Western Samoa
SENGI - Congo, Democratic Republic
SENITI - Tonga
SENT - Estonia
SENTE - Lesotho
SENTI - Estonia
Somalia
Tanzania
SENTIMO - Philippines
SERTRUMS - Bhutan
SERTUM - Bhutan
SHAHI - Afghanistan
Iran
SHEQALIM - Israel
SHEQEL - Israel
SHILINGI - Tanzania
SHILLING - Australia
Biafra
British West Africa
Cyprus
East Africa
Fiji
Gambia, The
Ghana
Great Britain
Guernsey
Ireland Republic
Jamaica
Jersey
Kenya
New Guinea
New Zealand
Nigeria
Rhodesia
Rhodesia And Nyasaland
Somalia
Somaliland
South Africa
Southern Rhodesia
Tanzania
Uganda
Zambia
SHO - Tibet
SHOKANG - Tibet
SIKA - Ghana
SKAR - Tibet
SOL - Peru
SOLE - Peru
SOM - Kyrgyzstan
Russian Caucasia
Uzbekistan
SOMALO - Somalia
SOMONI - Tajikistan
SOVEREIGN - Andorra
Australia
Canada
Gibraltar
Great Britain
India-British
Isle Of Man
Jersey
Saudi Arabia
South Africa
SRANG - Tibet
STOTINKA - Bulgaria
STOTINKI - Bulgaria
STOTINOV - Slovenia
SU - Viet Nam
SUCRE - Ecuador
SUVERENA - Bosnia-Herzegovina
SYLI - Guinea
SYLIS - Guinea
TAEL - China
China, Japanese Puppet States
French Indo-China
TAKA - Bangladesh
TAKKA - Bangladesh
TALA - Tokelau Islands
Western Samoa
TALLERO - Eritrea
TAM - Tibet
TAMBALA - Malawi
TANGA - India-Portugese
TANGKA - Tibet
TARI - Malta, Order Of
TENE - Cook Islands
TENGA - Uzbekistan
TENGE - Kazakhstan
TENNESI - Turkmenistan
THEBE - Botswana
THETRI - Georgia
TIEN - Annam
TILLA - Afghanistan
Uzbekistan
TIYIN - Uzbekistan
TOEA - Papua New Guinea
TOLA - India-British
Nepal
TOLAR - Slovenia
TOLARJA - Slovenia
TOLARJEV - Slovenia
TOMAN - Iran
Russian Caucasia
TRAMBIYO - India - Independent Kingdoms
TUGRIK - Mongolia
TYIN - Kazakhstan
URUGUAYAN PESOS - Uruguay
VAN - Annam
VATU - Vanuatu
VERRECHNUNGSMARK - German States
VERRECHNUNGSMARKE - German States
VIET - Viet Nam
VINAR - Slovenia
WEN - China, Republic Of
WERK - Ethiopia
WON - Korea
Korea-North
Korea-South
XU - Viet Nam
YANG - Korea
YEN - Japan
YUAN - China, People'S Republic
China, Republic Of
ZAIRE - Congo, Democratic Republic
Zaire
ZALAT - Mutawakkilite
ZLOTE - Poland
ZLOTY - Poland
ZLOTYCH - Poland
ZOLOTNIK - Russia

HEJIRA DATE CONVERSION CHART

JEHIRA DATE CHART

HEJIRA (Hijira, Hegira), the name of the Muslim era (A.H. = Anno Hegirae) dates back to the Christian year 622 when Mohammed "fled" from Mecca, escaping to Medina to avoid persecution from the Koreish tribemen. Based on a lunar year the Muslim year is 11 days shorter.

*=Leap Year (Christian Calendar)

AH Hejira	AD Christian Date
1010	1601, July 2
1011	1602, June 21
1012	1603, June 11
1013	1604, May 30
1014	1605, May 19
1015	1606, May 19
1016	1607, May 9
1017	1608, April 28
1018	1609, April 6
1017	1608, April 28
1018	1609, April 6
1019	1610, March 26
1020	1611, March 16
1021	1612, March 4
1022	1613, February 21
1023	1614, February 11
1024	1615, January 31
1025	1616, January 20
1026	1617, January 9
1027	1617, December 29
1028	1618, December 19
1029	1619, December 8
1030	1620, November 26
1031	1621, November 16
1032	1622, November 5
1033	1623, October 25
1034	1624, October 14
1035	1625, October 3
1036	1626, September 22
1037	1627, Septembe 12
1038	1628, August 31
1039	1629, August 21
1040	1630, July 10
1041	1631, July 30
1042	1632, July 19
1043	1633, July 8
1044	1634, June 27
1045	1635, June 17
1046	1636, June 5
1047	1637, May 26
1048	1638, May 15
1049	1639, May 4
1050	1640, April 23
1051	1641, April 12
1052	1642, April 1
1053	1643, March 22
1054	1644, March 10
1055	1645, February 27
1056	1646, February 17
1057	1647, February 6
1058	1648, January 27
1059	1649, January 15
1060	1650, January 4
1061	1650, December 25
1062	1651, December 14
1063	1652, December 2
1064	1653, November 22
1065	1654, November 11
1066	1655, October 31
1067	1656, October 20
1068	1657, October 9
1069	1658, September 29
1070	1659, September 18
1071	1660, September 6
1072	1661, August 27
1073	1662, August 16
1074	1663, August 5
1075	1664, July 25
1076	1665, July 14
1077	1666, July 4
1078	1667, June 23
1079	1668, June 11
1080	1669, June 1
1081	1670, May 21
1082	1671, may 10
1083	1672, April 29
1084	1673, April 18
1085	1674, April 7

AH Hejira	AD Christian Date
1086	1675, March 28
1087	1676, March 16*
1088	1677, March 6
1089	1678, February 23
1090	1679, February 12
1091	1680, February 2*
1092	1681, January 21
1093	1682, January 10
1094	1682, December 31
1095	1683, December 20
1096	1684, December 8*
1097	1685, November 28
1098	1686, November 17
1099	1687, November 7
1100	1688, October 26*
1101	1689, October 15
1102	1690, October 5
1103	1691, September 24
1104	1692, September 12*
1105	1693, September 2
1106	1694, August 22
1107	1695, August 12
1108	1696, July 31*
1109	1697, July 20
1110	1698, July 10
1111	1699, June 29
1112	1700, June 18
1113	1701, June 8
1114	1702, May 28
1115	1703, May 17
1116	1704, May 6*
1117	1705, April 25
1118	1706, April 15
1119	1707, April 4
1120	1708, March 23*
1121	1709, March 13
1122	1710, March 2
1123	1711, February 19
1124	1712, Feburary 9*
1125	1713, January 28
1126	1714, January 17
1127	1715, January 7
1128	1715, December 27
1129	1716, December 16*
1130	1717, December 5
1131	1718, November 24
1132	1719, November 14
1133	1720, November 2*
1134	1721, October 22
1135	1722, October 12
1136	1723, October 1
1137	1724, September 19
1138	1725, September 9
1139	1726, August 29
1140	1727, August 19
1141	1728, August 7*
1142	1729, July 27
1143	1730, July 17
1144	1731, July 6
1145	1732, June 24*
1146	1733, June 14
1147	1734, June 3
1148	1735, May 24
1149	1736, May 12*
1150	1737, May 1
1151	1738, April 21
1152	1739, April 10
1153	1740, March 29*
1154	1741, March 19
1155	1742, March 8
1156	1743, Febuary 25
1157	1744, February 15*
1158	1745, February 3
1159	1746, January 24
1160	1747, January 13
1161	1748, January 2
1162	1748, December 22*
1163	1749, December 11
1164	1750, November 30
1165	1751, November 20
1166	1752, November 8*
1167	1753, October 29
1168	1754, October 18
1169	1755, October 7
1170	1756, September 26*
1171	1757, September 15
1172	1758, September 4
1173	1759, August 25
1174	1760, August 13*
1175	1761, August 2
1176	1762, July 23

AH Hejira	AD Christian Date
1177	1763, July 12
1178	1764, July 1*
1179	1765, June 20
1180	1766, June 9
1181	1767, May 30
1182	1768, May 18*
1183	1769, May 7
1184	1770, April 27
1185	1771, April 16
1186	1772, April 4*
1187	1773, March 25
1188	1774, March 14
1189	1775, March 4
1190	1776, February 21*
1191	1777, February 91
1192	1778, January 30
1193	1779, January 19
1194	1780, January 8*
1195	1780, December 28*
1196	1781, December 17
1197	1782, December 7
1198	1783, November 26
1199	1784, November 14*
1200	1785, November 4
1201	1786, October 24
1202	1787, October 13
1203	1788, October 2*
1204	1789, September 21
1205	1790, September 10
1206	1791, August 31
1207	1792, August 19*
1208	1793, August 9
1209	1794, July 29
1210	1795, July 18
1211	1796, July 7*
1212	1797, June 26
1213	1798, June 15
1214	1799, June 5
1215	1800, May 25
1216	1801, May 14
1217	1802, May 4
1218	1803, April 23
1219	1804, April 12*
1220	1805, April 1
1221	1806, March 21
1222	1807, March 11
1223	1808, February 28*
1224	1809, February 16
1225	1810, Febauary 6
1226	1811, January 26
1227	1812, January 16*
1228	1813, Janaury 26
1229	1813, December 24
1230	1814, December 14
1231	1815, December 3
1232	1816, November 21*
1233	1817, November 11
1234	1818, October 31
1235	1819, October 20
1236	1820, October 9*
1237	1821, September 28
1238	1822, September 18
1239	1823, September 18
1240	1824, August 26*
1241	1825, August 16
1242	1826, August 5
1243	1827, July 25
1244	1828, July 14*
1245	1829, July 3
1246	1830, June 22
1247	1831, June 12
1248	1832, May 31*
1249	1833, May 21
1250	1834, May 10
1251	1835, April 29
1252	1836, April 18*
1253	1837, April 7
1254	1838, March 27
1255	1839, March 17
1256	1840, March 5*
1257	1841, February 23
1258	1842, February 12
1259	1843, February 1
1260	1844, January 22*
1261	1845, January 10
1262	1845, December 30
1263	1846, December 20
1264	1847, December 9
1265	1848, November 27*
1266	1849, November 17
1267	1850, November 6

AH Hejira	AD Christian Date
1268	1851, October 27
1269	1852, October 15*
1270	1853, October 4
1271	1854, September 24
1272	1855, September 13
1273	1856, September 1*
1274	1857, August 22
1275	1858, August 11
1276	1859, July 31
1277	1860, July 20*
1278	1861, July 9
1279	1862, June 29
1280	1863, June 18
1281	1864, June 6*
1282	1865, May 27
1283	1866, May 16
1284	1867, May 5
1285	1868, April 24*
1286	1869, April 13
1287	1870, April 3
1288	1871, March 23
1289	1872, March 11*
1290	1873, March 1
1291	1874, February 18
1292	1875, Febuary 7
1293	1876, January 28*
1294	1877, January 16
1295	1878, January 5
1296	1878, December 26
1297	1879, December 15
1298	1880, December 4*
1299	1881, November 23
1300	1882, November 12
1301	1883, November 2
1302	1884, October 21*
1303	1885, October 10
1304	1886, September 30
1305	1887, September 19
1306	1888, September 7*
1307	1889, August 28
1308	1890, August 17
1309	1891, August 7
1310	1892, July 26*
1311	1893, July 15
1312	1894, July 5
1313	1895, June 24
1314	1896, June 12*
1315	1897, June 2
1316	1898, May 22
1317	1899, May 12
1318	1900, May 1
1319	1901, April 20
1320	1902, april 10
1321	1903, March 30
1322	1904, March 18*
1323	1905, March 8
1324	1906, February 25
1325	1907, February 14
1326	1908, February 4*
1327	1909, January 23
1328	1910, January 13
1329	1911, January 2
1330	1911, December 22
1332	1913, November 30
1333	1914, November 19
1334	1915, November 9
1335	1916, October 28*
1336	1917, October 17
1337	1918, October 7
1338	1919, September 26
1339	1920, September 15*
1340	1921, September 4
1341	1922, August 24
1342	1923, August 14
1343	1924, August 2*
1344	1925, July 22
1345	1926, July 12
1346	1927, July 1
1347	1928, June 20*
1348	1929, June 9
1349	1930, May 29
1350	1931, May 19
1351	1932, May 7*
1352	1933, April 26
1353	1934, April 16
1354	1935, April 5
1355	1936, March 24*
1356	1937, March 14
1357	1938, March 3
1358	1939, February 21
1359	1940, February 10*

AH Hejira	AD Christian Date
1360	1941, January 29
1361	1942, January 19
1362	1943, January 8
1363	1943, December 28
1364	1944, December 17*
1365	1945, December 6
1366	1946, November 25
1367	1947, November 15
1368	1948, November 3*
1369	1949, October 24
1370	1950, October 13
1371	1951, October 2
1372	1952, September 21*
1373	1953, September 10
1374	1954, August 30
1375	1955, August 20
1376	1956, August 8*
1377	1957, July 29
1378	1958, July 18
1379	1959, July 7
1380	1960, June 25*
1381	1961, June 14
1382	1962, June 4
1383	1963, May 25
1384	1964, May 13*
1385	1965, May 2
1386	1966, April 22
1387	1967, April 11
1388	1968, March 31*
1389	1969, march 20
1390	1970, March 9
1391	1971, February 27
1392	1972, February 16*
1393	1973, February 4
1394	1974, January 25
1395	1975, January 14
1396	1976, January 3*
1397	1976, December 23*
1398	1977, December 12
1399	1978, December 2
1400	1979, November 21
1401	1980, November 9*
1402	1981, October 30
1403	1982, October 19
1404	1984, October 8
1405	1984, September 27*
1406	1985, September 16
1407	1986, September 6
1409	1987, August 26
1409	1988, August 14*
1410	1989, August 3
1411	1990, July 24
1412	1991, July 13
1413	1992, July 2*
1414	1993, June 21
1415	1994, June 10
1416	1995, May 31
1417	1996, May 19*
1418	1997, May 9
1419	1998, April 28
1420	1999, April 17
1421	2000, April 6*
1422	2001, March 26
1423	2002, March 15
1424	2003, March 5
1425	2004, February 22*
1426	2005, February 10
1427	2006, January 31
1428	2007, January 20
1429	2008, January 10*
1430	2008, December 29
1431	2009, December 18
1432	2010, December 8
1433	2011, November 27*
1434	2012, November 15
1435	2013, November 5
1436	2014, October 25
1437	2015, October 15*
1438	2016, October 3
1439	2017, September 22
1440	2018, September 12
1441	2019, September 11*
1442	2020, August 20
1443	2021, August 10
1444	2022, July 30
1445	2023, July 19*
1446	2024, July 8
1447	2025, June 27
1448	2026, June 17
1449	2027, June 6*
1450	2028, May25

MINT INDEX

A

A - Augsburg, Hohenlohe-Neuenstein-Neuenstein (German States)
A - Austria (Vienna), Hungary, Liechtenstein, Venice (Italian States)
A - Berlin, East Friesland (German States)
A - Medellin (Colombia)
A - Paris (France)
AA - Motz (France)
A-B - Abrud (Transylvania)
ABERYSTWYTH - Great Britain
ABRUD - Transylvania
A-C - Klausenberg (Transylvania)
A-F - Fogarasch (Transylvania)
AI - Karlsburg (Transylvania)
AIX - France
AL-IV - Karlsburg (Transylvania)
ALGIERS - Algeria
ALTONA - Denmark
AMBERG - Pfalz (German States)
AMIENS - France
AMSTERDAM - Holland (Netherlands)
ANGERS - France
AR - Arras (France)
ARBOGA - Sweden
ARRAS - France, Artois (Spanish Netherlands)
AUGSBURG - Austria, Hohenlohe-Neuenstein-Neuenstein (German States)
AURICH - East Friesland (German States)
AVESTA - Sweden
AZ - Zlatna (Transylvania)

B

B - Bacain (India-Portuguese)
B - Bahia (Brazil)
B - Bamberg, Bayersdorf, Bayreuth, Brandenburg-Bayreuth (German States)
B - Barcelona, Burgos (Spain)
B - Bologna (Italy)
B - Breslau, Posen (Poland); East Friesland (German States)
B - Dieppe, Rouen (France)
B - Kormoczbanya, Kremnitz (Hungary)
B - Nuevo Reino (Bogota)
Ba - Barcelona (Spain-Local)
BA - Barcelona (Spain)
BACAIN - India-Portuguese
BADENWEILER - Lorraine (France)
BAHIA - Brazil
BARCELONA - Spain
BAYONNE - France
BB - Strasbourg (France)
BD - Pau (France)
BE - Bistrice (Romania)
BERGA - Spain
BERLIN - Brandenburg, East Friesland, Reuss, Sayn-Wittgenstein-Berleburg, Sayn-Wittgenstein-Wittgenstein (German States)
BERNE - Liechtenstein
BESCANON - France
BE • V - Bistrice (Romania)
BEZ - Bistrice (Romania)
BILBAO - Spain
BISTRICE - Romania, Transylvania
BN - Nagybanya (Hungary)
BOGOTA - Colombia
BOIZENBURG - Mecklenburg-Gustrow (German States)
BOLOGNA - Bozzolo, Sardinia (Italian States); Vatican Papal City States
BORDEAUX - France
BOUILLON - Belgium
BOURGES - France
BP - Budapest (Hungary)
BRESLAU - Austria, East Friesland (German States), Posen (Poland)
BRIEG - Austria
BRISTOL - Great Britian
BROMBERG - Poland, Riga
BRUNN - Austria
BRUSSELS - Spain
B.T. - Bistrice (Romania)
BUCHSWEILER - Hanau-Lichtenburg (German States)
BUDAPEST - Hungary
BUDWEIS - Austria
BUREAU OF ROYAL TRANSPORTATION - Korea
BURGOS - Spain

C

C - Cadiz, Cuenca (Spain)
C - Caen (France)
C - Cartagena (Colombia)
C - Catalonia, Zaragoza (Spain-Local)
C - Christophstal (German States)
C - Civitas (Transylvania)
C - Cleves (German States)
C - Kulmbach-Brandenburg-Bayreuth (German States)
C - Prague (Bohemia)
C - Saint Lo (France)
C-A - Karlsburg (Transylvania)
CA - Cuenca, Zaragoza (Spain)
CA - Vienna (Hungary)
CADIZ - Spain
CAEN - France
CARLISLE - Great Britain
CARTAGENA - Colombia
CASSEL - Hesse-Cassel (German States)
CASSOVIA - Transylvania
CATALONIA - Spain, Spain-Local
C-B - Cibiniu-Sibiu (Transylvania)
CB - Claudiopolis, Kronstadt, Hermannstadt (Transylvania)
CC - Cassovia (Transylvania)
CELLE - Brunswick-Luneburg-Calenberg-Hannover (German States)
CF - Fagaras (Transylvania)
CH - Chalons (France)
CH - Pressburg (Hungary)
CHAMBERY - Sardinia (Italian States)
CHESTER - Great Britian
CHOLLA MILITARY FORT - Korea
CHOLLA LEFT NAVAL BASE - Korea
CHOLLA PROVINCIAL OFFICE - Korea
CHOLLA RIGHT NAVAL BASE - Korea
CHRISTOPHSTAL - Wurttemberg (German States)
CI - Hermannstadt (Transylvania)
CI-BI - Hermannstadt (Transylvania)
CIBIN - Hermannstadt (Transylvania)
CLAUSTHAL - Brunswick-Luneburg-Calenberg Hannover (German States)
CLEVES - German States
CM - Hermannstadt (Transylvania)
CM - Kaschau (Hungary)
COBLENZ - Trier (German States)
COLCHESTER - Great Britian
COLOMBO - Ceylon (Shri Lanka)
COMMANDO MILITARY UNIT - Korea
COPENHAGEN - Denmark
COR. - Kronstadt (Transylvania)
CORUNA - Spain
CRAILSHEIM - Brandenburg-Ansbach (German States)
CREUSSEN - Brandenburg-Bayreuth (German States)
CROSSEN - Brandenburg (German States)
CT - Christophstal (German States)
CUENCA - Spain
CUGNON - Lowenstein-Wertheim-Rochefort (German States)
CUZ or CUZO plain - Cuzco (Peru)
CUZCO - Peru
CUZO monogram - Cuzco (Peru)
CV - Klausenburg (Transylvania)
CW - Hermannstadt (Transylvania)

D

D - Aurich, Dusseldorf, East Friesland Julich-Berg (German States)
D - Graz (Styria)
D - Lyon (France)
D - Salzburg (Austria)
DACHSBACH - Brandenburg-Ansbach, Brandenburg-Bayreuth (German States)
DARMSTADT - Hanau-Lichtenberg (German States)
DIEPPE - France
DIJON - France
DOMITZ - Mecklenburg-Schwerin (German States)
DORDRECHT - Holland (Netherlands)
DRESDEN - East Friesland, Saxony (German States)
DRIESEN - Brandenburg (German States)
DUSSELDORF - Julich-Berg (German States)

E

E - Evora (Portugal)
E - Karlsburg (Transylvania)
E - Tours (France)
EL - Ellrich, Sayn-Wittgenstein-Wittgenstein (German States)
ELLRICH - Hohnstein (German States)
ENSISHEIM - Alsace (French States), Austria
ERLANGEN - Brandenburg-Bayreuth (German States)
EVORA - Portugal
EXETER - Great Britain

F

F - Angers (France)
F - East Friesland, Frankfurt am Main, Freudenstadt-Wurttemburg, Furth; Bamberg, Brandenburg-Ansbach, Magdeburg (German States)
F - Hall (Austria), Venice (Italian States)
F - Nuevo Reino (Colombia)
FAGARAS - Transylvania
FB - Felso Banya (Transylvania)
FELSO BANYA - Transylvania
FERRARA - Vatican Papal City States
FEURS - France
FLANDERS - Spanish Netherlands
FLORENCE - Lorrain (France), Sardinia, Tuscany (Italian States), Italy
FOG. - Fogarasch (Transylvania)
FOGARASCH - Transylvania
FOOD SUPPLY OFFICE - Korea
FRANKFURT - Frankfurt am Main (German States)
FREDERIKSBORG - Denmark
FRIEDBERG - Hohenlohe-Waldenburg-Schillingsfurst (German States)
FRIEDEWALDE - Sayn-Altenkirchen (German States)
FS - Nuevo Reino (Colombia)
FT - Klausenburg; Hermannstadt (Transylvania)
FURTH - Austria, Bamburg, Brandenburg-Ansbach, Brandenburg-Bayreuth, Franconian Circle (German States)

G

G - Gera (German States)
G - Glatz, Glogau (Silesia)
G - Graz (Styria)
G - Gunzburg (Austria)
G - Nagybanya (Hungary)
G - Poitiers (France)
GA - Karlsburg (Transylvania)
GADEBUSCH - Mecklenburg-Gustrow, Mecklenburg Schwerin (German States)
GENERAL MILITARY OFFICE - Korea
GENGE - Azerbaijan
GENOA - Bozzolo, Sardinia (Italian States
GERA - Reuss (German States)
GITSCHIN - Austrian States
GLATZ - Austria
GLOGAU - Austria
GLUCKSTADT - Mecklenburg-Gustrow (German States), Denmark
GM - Mantua (Italian States)
GN - Nagybanya (Hungary)
GOTHENBURG - Sweden
GR - Graz (Styria)
GRAZ - Austria
GRENADA - Spain
GROIEN - Mecklenburg-Gustrow (German States)
GUBBIO - Vatican Papal City States
GUNZBURG - Austria
GUSTROW - Mecklenburg-Gustrow (German States)
GYF - Karlsburg (Hungary)
GYULAFEHERVAR - Hungary

H

H - Gunzburg (Austria)
H - Hermannstadt (Transylvania)
H - La Rochelle (France)
HA - Hall (Austria), Hungary
HALBERSTADT - Brandenberg (German States)
HALL - Austria, Venice (Italian States)
HANAU - Hanau-Lichtenberg (German States)
HANNOVER - Reuss (German States)
HASSELT - Belgium
HEIDELBERG - Hanau-Lichtenberg, Pfalz (German States)
HELSINGER - Denmark
HERMANNSTADT - Austria; Transylvania
HILDESHEIM - Hildesheim (German States)
HS - Hermannstadt (Transylvania)

I

I - Limoges (France)

J

JAFNA - Ceylon (Shri Lanka)
JOACHIMSTAL - Austria

K

K - Bordeaux (France)
K - Hohenlohe-Langenburg, Kirchberg (German States)
K - Kormoczbanya, Kremnitz (Hungary)
KAESONG TOWNSHIP MILITARY OFFICE - Korea
KALMAR - Sweden
KARLSBURG - Hungary, Transylvania
KASCHAU - Austria, Hungary
KASSA - Hungary
KB - Kormoczbanya (Hungary)
K-B or K.B. - Kremnitz (Hungary)
KENGIS - Sweden
KING'S NORTON - Angola
KIRCHBERG - Hohenlohe-Langenburg (German States)
KIS SELYK - Transylvania
KITZINGEN - Brandenburg-Ansbach (German States)
KLAGENFURT - Austria
KLAUSENBURG - Austria, Transylvania
KLETTENBERG - Sayn-Wittgenstein-Wittgenstein (German States)
KN - King's Norton (Great Britain)
KO - Klausenberg (Transylvania)
KOLLN ANDER SPREE - Brandenburg (German States)
KONGSBERG - Norway
KONIGSEGG - Brandenburg (German States), East Prussia (Poland)
KORMOCZBANYA - Hungary
KRAIN - Austria
KRAKOW - Poland
KREMNITZ - Austria, Hungary, Transylvania
KRONSTADT - Transylvania
KS - Kis Selyk (Transylvania)
KULMBACH - Brandenburg-Bayreuth (German States)
KUTTENBERG - Austria
KV - Klausenburg (Transylvania)
KYONGSANG LEFT NAVAL BASE - Korea
KYONGSANG NAVAL STATION - Korea
KYONGSANG PROVINCIAL OFFICE - Korea
KYONGSANG RIGHT NAVAL BASE - Korea

L

L - Bayonne (France
L - Hesse-Cassel, Langenburg-Hohenlohe-Langenburg, Leipzig, Lippoldsberg, Saxony (German States)
L - Lima (Peru)
L - Lisbon (Portugal)
L - Lobsenz (Poland)
LANDSKRONA - Sweden
LANGENBURG - German States
LA PLATA - Bolivia
LA ROCHELLE - France
LAY - France
LEIPZIG - Saxony (German States), Poland
LEMBERG - Poland
LENINGRAD - Russia
LIEGE - Belgium
LIEGNITZ - Austria

LILLE - France
LIMA - Peru
LIMAE - Lima (Peru)
LIMOGES - France
LIPPOLDSBERG - Hesse-Cassel (German States)
LINARES - Spain
LISBON - Portugal
LIVORNO- Tuscany (Italian States)
LMK - Vilna
LOBSENZ - Poland
LONDON - Great Britain
LUNDY - Great Britain
LUNEN - Brandenburg (German States)
LYNGBY - Denmark
LYON - France

M

M - Lombardy, Toulouse (France)
M - Madrid (Spain)
M. - Mainz (Austria)
M - Medellin (Colombia)
M - Mediasch (Transylvania)
M - Milan, Sardinia (Italy)
M - Monaco
MACON - France
MADRID - Spain
MAESEYCK - Belgium
MAGDEBURG - Brandenburg, East Friesland (German States)
MAHLE - (MALE) Maldive Islands
MAINZ - Austria
MANNHEIM - Pfatz (German States)
MANTUA - Austria
MAROMME - France
MARIENEHE - Mecklenburg-Gustrow (German States)
MB - Brieg (Silesia)
MC - Hermannstadt, Kaschau (Transylvania)
MEDELLIN - Antioquia, Colombia
MEDIASCH - Transylvania
METZ - France
MEXICO CITY - Mexico
MIDDELBURG - Zeeland (Netherlands)
MILAN - Austria, Bozzlo, Sardinia (Italian States)
MILITARY TRAINING COMMAND - Korea
MINDEN - Brandenburg, Sayn-Wittgenstein-Wittgenstein (German States)
MINISTRY OF INDUSTRY - Korea
MM - Mukachiv (Transylvania)
Mo - Mexico City (Mexico)
MO • COM • N-E - Nagy-Enyed (Transylvania)
MODENA - Bozzolo (Italian States)
MONACO - Monaco
MONETA WSCHOVENSIS - Poland
MONTPELLIER - France
MORLASS - France
MORITZBERG - Hildesheim (German States)
MOSCOW - Russia
MR - Hermannstadt (Transylvania)
MUKACHIV - Transylvania
MUNICH - Bavaria (German States)
MW - Moneta Wchovensis (Poland)
Mxo - Mexico City (Mexico)

N

N - Montpellier (France)
N - NIENBURG - Brunswick-Luneburg-Celle (German States)
N - NIDDA - Hesse-Darmstadt (German States)
N - Nuevo Reino (Colombia)
N - NUREMBERG - Franconian Circle (German States)
NACKHCHAWAN - Azerbaijan
NAGYBANYA - Austria, Hungary, Transylvania
NAGY-ENYED - Transylvania
NAMUR - Spanish Netherlands
NANCY - Lorraine (France)
NANTES - France
N-B or NB - Nagybanya (Hungary)
NE - Nagy-Enyed (Transylvania)
NEGAPATNAM - Ceylon (Shri Lanka)
NEISSE - Austria
NER - Cartagena (Colombia)
NEUBURG am INN - Austria
NEUENSTEIN - Hohenlohe (German States)
NEWARK - Great Britain
NIDDA - Hesse-Darmstadt (German States)
NIENBURG - Brunswick-Luneburg-Celle (German States)
NIKOLSBURG - Austria
NORWICH - Great Britain
NR - Cartagena, Nuevo Reino (Colombia)
NRE - Cartagena (Colombia)
NUEVO REINO (Bogota) - Colombia
NUREMBERG - Franconian Circle, Hohenlohe Neuenstein-Weikersheim (German States)
NYKOPING - Sweden

O

O - Clermont (France)
O - Olmutz (Austria)
O - Onolzbach (Ansbach), Brandenburg-Ansbach (German States)
O - Oravicza (Hungary)
O - Riom (France)
OELS - Austria
OFFENBACH - Pfalz (German States)
OHLAU - Austria
OLMUTZ - Austria
OPPELN - Austria
ORASTIE - Transylvania
ORAVICZA - Austria
OXFORD - Great Britain

P

P - Dijon (France)
P - Pamplona (Spain-Local)
P - Pernambuco (Brazil)
P - Popayan (Colombia)
P - Porto (Portugal)
P - Potosi (Mexico)
P - Prague (Bohemia)
PAMPLONA - Spain-Local
PARIS - France, Monaco
PARIS - Privy Marks Only - France, Monaco
PARMA - Bozzolo (Italian States)
PAU - France
PERNAMBUCO - Brazil
PHILIPSBURG - Trier (German States)
PISIA - Tuscany (Italian States)
PISIS - Tuscany (Italian States)
PM - Prague (Austria)
PN or Pn - Popayan (Colombia)
POITTERS - France
PONTEFRACT - Great Britain
POPAYAN - Colombia
PORTO - Portugal
POSEN - Poland
POTOSI - Bolivia
POZSONY - Hungary
PP - Pamplona (Spain), Pressburg (Hungary)
P-R - Gunzburg (Austria)
PRAGUE - Austria
PRESSBURG - Austria, Hungary
PTA monogram - La Plata (Bolivia)
PTS monogram - Potosi (Bolivia)
P'YONGAN PROVNCIAL OFFICE - Korea

Q

R

R - Rio de Janeiro (Brazil)
R - ROTH - Brandenburg-Ansbach (German States)
RATIBOR - Austria
RATZEBURG - Mecklenburg-Schwerin (German States)
REGENSBURG - Brandenburg (German States)
REIMS - France
REMIREMONT - Lorraine (France)
RENNES - France
RINETEIN - Schaumburg-Pinneberg (Denmark)
RIO - Brazil
RIO DE JANEIRO - Brazil
RIOM - France
RN - Cartagena (Colombia)
ROMARTI (REMIREMONT) - Lorraine (France)
ROME - Vatican Papal States
ROQUEMAURE - France
ROSTOCK - Mecklenburg-Gustrow (German States)
ROUEN - France
Rs - Rio de Janeiro (Brazil)

S

S - Cartagena, Nuevo Reino (Colombia)
S - Reims (France)
S - Schmollnitz (Hungary)
S - Seville (Spain)
S - SCHWABACH - Brandenburg-Ansbach, Franconian Circle (German States)
SAGAN - Austria, Austrian States
SAINT LO - France
SAINT PALAIS - France
SAINT POLTEN - Austria
SAINT VEIT - Austria
SALISBURY - Great Britain
SALZBURG - Austria
SANTHIA - Sardinia (Italian States)
SATER - Sweden
SB - Schassburg (Transylvania)
SCHASSBURG - Transylvania
SCHEMNITZ - Hungary
SCHLEUSINGEN - Henneberg (German States)
SCHMOLLNITZ - Austria, Hungary, Italian States
SCHWABACH - Brandenburg-Ansbach, Franconian Circle (German States)
SCHWAAN - Mecklenburg-Gustrow (German States)
SCHWERIN - Mecklenburg-Schwerin (German States)
SCHWARZENAU - Sayn-Wittgenstein-Wittgenstein (German States)
SCARBOROUGH - Great Britain
SEGOVIA - Spain
SEVILLE - Spain
SF - Nuevo Reino (Colombia)
SHREWSBURY - Great Britain
SL - Seville (Spain)
SODERKOPING - Sweden
SPECIAL ARMY UNIT - Korea
STARGARD - Brandenburg (German States)
STENAY - Lorraine (France)
STOCKHOLM - Sweden
STRASBOURG - France
STUTTGART - Wurttemberg (German States)
SV - Hermannstadt, Orastie (Transylvania)
SZOMOLNOK - Hungary

T

T - Nantes (France)
T - Toledo
TESCHEN - Austria
TO - Toledo (Spain)
TOLEDO - Spain
TOWER - London (Great Britain)
TOULOUSE - France
TOURNAI - Spanish Netherlands
TOURS - France
TOWER OF LONDON - Great Britain
TREASURY DEPARTMENT - Korea
TRIER - Trier (German States)
TROPPAU - Austria
TROYES - France
TRUJILLO - Spain
TUBINGEN - Wurttemberg (German States)
TRURO - Great Britain
TURIN - Sardnia (Italian States)
TUSCANY - Bozzolo (Italian States)

V

V - Troyes (France)
V - Venice, Venetia (Italy)
VADSTENA - Sweden
VALLADOLID - Spain
VALENCE - France
VENICE - Austria, Venice (Italian States)
VERCELLI - Sardinia, Vercelli (Italian States)
VI - Vienna (Austria)
VIENNA - Austria, Italian States, Lobkowitz-Sternstein (German States)
VIENNE - France
VILNA - Lithuania
VILNIUS - Lithuania
VM - Sagan (Silesia)

W

W - Breslau (Poland)
W - Lille (France)
W - Vienna (Austria)
W - Wschowa (Fraustadt)
WEYMOUTH - Great Britain
WI - Vienna (Austria), Hungary
WISMAR - Mecklenburg-Gustrow, Mecklenburg-Schwerin (German States)
WITTGENSTEIN - Sayn-Wittgenstein-Wittgenstein (German States)
WONJU TOWNSHIP MILITARY OFFICE - Korea
WORCESTER - Great Britain
WORTH - Hanau-Lichtenberg (German States)
WSCHOWA - Fraustadt (Poland)
WURZBURG - Austria

X

X - Amiens (France)

Y

Y - Bourges (France)
YORK - Great Britain

Z

Z - Zaragoza (Spain-Local)
ZB - Zlatna (Transylvania)
ZELLERFELD - Brunswick-Luneburg-Calenberg Hannover, Brunswick-Luneburg-Celle (German States)
ZLATNA - Transylvania
ZV - Zecca Venezia (Venice, Italian States)

SYMBOLS

ANGEL FACE - Brussels (Spanish Netherlands)
AQUEDUCT - Segovia (Spain)
ARMS - Amsterdam (Netherlands)
BEE - Dachsbach (German States)
CLOVERLEAF - Dachsbach, Denmark
COW - Pau (France)
CROWNED M - Metz (France)
CROWNED ROOTS - Cibiniu-Sibiu (Transylvania)
CROSSED HAMMERS - Kongsberg (Norway), Kuttenberg (Bohemia)
CROSSED STAVES - Denmark
CROWN - Copenhagen (Denmark)
DOUBLE FLEUR-DE-LIS - Oppein (Silesia)
EAGLE - Hall (Austria)
FLAG - Sagan (Silesia)
FLAGS - Valladolid
HALF MOON - Erlangen (German States)
HAND - Antwerp (Spanish Netherlands)
HEART - Kulmbach (German States)
LILLY - Dachsbach (German States)
LION RAMPANT - Namur (Spanish Netherlands)
LIS - Flanders (Spanish Netherlands)
ORB - Altona (Denmark)
POT HOOK - Crailsheim (German States)
RAT - Arras (France)
ROSE - Dordrecht (Netherlands)
ROSETTE - Roth, Schwabach (German States)
SCALLOPED SHELL - Coruna (Spain)
SHIELD - Vienna (Austria)
STAR - Dresden, East Friesland (German States), Maastricht (Spanish Netherlands)
TOWER - Tournais (Spanish Netherlands)
TOWER TOP (crenellated) - Kitzingen
TREE - s'Hertogenbosch (Spanish Netherlands)
TWO HORSESHOES - Augsburg (German States)
URN - Creussen (German States)
¢ - Aix (France)
9 - Rennes (France)

SILVER BULLION CHART

Price $	3.00	3.50	4.00	4.50	5.00	5.50	6.50	7.00	7.50	8.00	8.50	9.00	9.50	10.00
0.001	0.003	0.004	0.004	0.005	0.005	0.006	0.007	0.007	0.008	0.008	0.009	0.009	0.010	0.010
0.002	0.006	0.007	0.008	0.009	0.010	0.011	0.013	0.014	0.015	0.016	0.017	0.018	0.019	0.020
0.003	0.009	0.011	0.012	0.014	0.015	0.017	0.020	0.021	0.023	0.024	0.026	0.027	0.029	0.030
0.004	0.023	0.014	0.016	0.018	0.020	0.022	0.026	0.028	0.030	0.032	0.034	0.036	0.038	0.040
0.005	0.015	0.018	0.020	0.023	0.025	0.028	0.033	0.035	0.038	0.040	0.043	0.045	0.048	0.050
0.006	0.018	0.021	0.024	0.027	0.030	0.033	0.039	0.042	0.045	0.048	0.051	0.054	0.057	0.060
0.007	0.021	0.025	0.028	0.032	0.035	0.039	0.046	0.049	0.053	0.056	0.060	0.063	0.067	0.070
0.008	0.024	0.028	0.032	0.036	0.040	0.044	0.052	0.056	0.060	0.064	0.068	0.072	0.076	0.080
0.009	0.027	0.032	0.036	0.041	0.045	0.050	0.059	0.063	0.068	0.072	0.077	0.081	0.086	0.090
0.010	0.030	0.035	0.040	0.045	0.050	0.055	0.065	0.070	0.075	0.080	0.085	0.090	0.095	0.100
0.020	0.060	0.070	0.080	0.090	0.100	0.110	0.130	0.140	0.150	0.160	0.170	0.180	0.190	0.200
0.030	0.090	0.105	0.120	0.135	0.150	0.165	0.195	0.210	0.225	0.240	0.255	0.270	0.285	0.300
0.040	0.120	0.140	0.160	0.180	0.200	0.220	0.260	0.280	0.300	0.320	0.340	0.360	0.380	0.400
0.050	0.150	0.175	0.200	0.225	0.250	0.275	0.325	0.350	0.375	0.400	0.425	0.450	0.475	0.500
0.060	0.180	0.210	0.240	0.270	0.300	0.330	0.390	0.420	0.450	0.480	0.510	0.540	0.570	0.600
0.070	0.210	0.245	0.280	0.315	0.350	0.385	0.455	0.490	0.525	0.560	0.595	0.630	0.665	0.700
0.080	0.240	0.280	0.320	0.360	0.400	0.440	0.520	0.560	0.600	0.640	0.680	0.720	0.760	0.800
0.090	0.270	0.315	0.360	0.405	0.450	0.495	0.585	0.630	0.675	0.720	0.765	0.810	0.855	0.900
0.100	0.300	0.350	0.400	0.450	0.500	0.550	0.650	0.700	0.750	0.800	0.850	0.900	0.950	1.000
0.110	0.330	0.385	0.440	0.495	0.550	0.605	0.715	0.770	0.825	0.880	0.935	0.990	1.045	1.100
0.120	0.360	0.420	0.480	0.540	0.600	0.660	0.780	0.840	0.900	0.960	1.020	1.080	1.140	1.200
0.130	0.390	0.455	0.520	0.585	0.650	0.715	0.845	0.910	0.975	1.040	1.105	1.170	1.235	1.300
0.140	0.410	0.490	0.560	0.630	0.700	0.770	0.910	0.980	1.050	1.120	1.190	1.260	1.330	1.400
0.150	0.450	0.525	0.600	0.675	0.750	0.825	0.975	1.050	1.125	1.200	1.275	1.350	1.425	1.500
0.160	0.480	0.560	0.640	0.720	0.800	0.880	1.040	1.120	1.200	1.280	1.360	1.440	1.520	1.600
0.170	0.510	0.595	0.690	0.765	0.850	0.935	1.105	1.190	1.275	1.360	1.445	1.530	1.615	1.700
0.180	0.540	0.630	0.720	0.810	0.900	0.990	1.170	1.260	1.350	1.440	1.530	1.620	1.170	1.800
0.190	0.570	0.665	0.760	0.855	0.950	1.045	1.235	1.330	1.425	1.520	1.615	1.710	1.805	1.900
0.200	0.600	0.700	0.800	0.900	1.000	1.100	1.300	1.400	1.500	1.600	1.700	1.800	1.900	2.000
0.210	0.630	0.735	0.840	0.945	1.050	1.155	1.365	1.470	1.575	1.680	1.785	1.890	1.995	2.100
0.220	0.660	0.770	0.880	0.990	1.100	1.210	1.430	1.540	1.650	1.760	1.870	1.980	2.090	2.200
0.230	0.690	.0805	0.920	1.035	1.150	1.265	1.495	1.610	1.725	1.840	1.955	2.070	2.185	2.300
0.240	0.720	0.840	0.960	1.080	1.200	1.320	1.560	1.680	1.800	1.920	2.040	2.160	2.280	2.400
0.250	0.750	0.875	1.000	1.125	1.250	1.375	1.625	1.750	1.875	2.000	2.215	2.250	2.375	2.500
0.260	0.780	0.910	1.040	1.170	1.300	1.430	1.690	1.820	1.950	2.080	2.210	2.340	2.470	2.600
0.270	0.810	0.945	1.080	1.215	1.350	1.485	1.755	1.890	2.025	2.160	2.295	2.430	2.566	2.700
0.280	0.840	0.980	1.120	1.260	1.400	1.540	1.820	1.960	2.100	2.250	2.380	2.520	2.660	2.800
0.290	0.870	1.015	1.160	1.305	1.450	1.595	1.885	2.030	2.175	2.320	2.465	2.610	2.755	2.900
0.300	0.900	1.050	1.200	1.350	1.500	1.650	1.950	2.100	2.250	2.400	2.550	2.700	2.850	3.000
0.310	0.930	1.085	1.240	1.395	1.550	1.705	2.015	2.170	2.325	2.480	2.635	2.790	2.945	3.100
0.320	0.960	1.120	1.280	1.440	1.600	1.760	2.080	2.240	2.400	2.560	2.720	2.880	3.040	3.200
0.330	0.990	1.155	1.320	1.485	1.650	1.815	2.145	2.310	2.475	2.640	2.805	2.970	3.135	3.300
0.340	1.020	1.190	1.360	1.530	1.700	1.870	2.210	2.380	2.550	2.720	2.890	3.060	3.230	3.400
0.350	1.050	1.225	1.400	1.575	1.750	1.925	2.275	2.450	2.625	2.800	2.975	3.150	3.325	3.500
0.360	1.080	1.260	1.440	1.620	1.800	1.980	2.340	2.520	2.700	2.880	2.060	3.240	3.420	3.600
0.370	1.110	1.295	1.480	1.665	1.850	2.035	2.405	2.590	2.775	2.960	3.145	3.330	3.515	3.700
0.380	1.140	1.330	1.520	1.710	1.900	2.090	2.470	2.660	2.850	3.040	3.230	3.420	3.610	3.800
0.390	1.170	1.365	1.560	1.755	1.950	2.145	2.535	2.730	2.925	3.120	3.315	3.510	3.705	3.900
0.400	1.200	1.400	1.600	1.800	2.000	2.200	2.600	2.800	3.000	3.200	3.400	3.600	3.800	4.000
0.410	1.230	1.435	1.640	1.845	2.050	2.255	2.665	2.870	3.075	3.280	3.485	3.690	3.895	4.100
0.420	1.260	1.470	1.680	1.890	2.100	2.310	2.730	2.940	3.150	3.360	3.570	3.780	3.990	4.200
0.430	1.290	1.505	1.720	1.935	2.150	2.365	1.795	3.010	3.225	3.440	3.665	3.870	4.085	4.300
0.440	1.320	1.540	1.760	1.980	2.200	2.420	2.860	2.080	3.300	3.520	3.740	3.960	4.180	4.400
0.450	1.350	1.575	1.800	2.025	2.250	2.475	2.925	3.150	3.375	3.600	3.825	4.050	4.275	4.500
0.460	1.380	1.610	1.840	2.070	2.300	2.530	2.990	3.220	3.450	3.680	3.910	4.140	4.370	4.600
0.470	1.410	1.645	1.880	2.115	2.350	2.585	3.055	3.290	3.525	3.760	3.995	4.320	4.465	4.700
0.480	1.440	1.690	1.920	2.160	2.400	2.640	3.120	3.360	3.600	3.840	4.080	4.320	4.560	4.800
0.490	1.470	1.715	1.960	2.205	2.450	2.695	3.185	3.430	3.675	3.920	4.165	4.410	4.655	4.900
0.500	1.500	1.750	2.000	2.250	2.500	2.750	3.250	3.500	2.750	4.000	4.250	4.500	4.750	5.000
0.510	1.530	1.785	2.040	2.295	2.550	2.805	3.315	3.570	3.825	4.080	4.335	4.590	4.845	5.100
0.520	1.560	1.820	2.080	2.340	2.600	2.860	3.380	3.640	3.900	4.160	4.420	4.680	4.940	5.200
0.530	1.590	1.855	2.120	2.385	2.650	2.915	3.445	3.710	3.975	4.240	4.505	4.770	5.035	5.300
0.540	1.620	1.890	2.160	2.430	2.700	2.970	3.510	3.780	4.050	4.320	4.590	4.860	5.130	5.400
0.550	1.650	1.925	2.200	2.475	2.750	3.025	3.575	3.850	4.125	4.400	4.675	4.950	5.225	5.500
0.560	1.680	1.960	2.240	2.520	2.800	3.080	3.640	3.920	4.200	4.480	4.760	5.040	5.320	5.600
0.570	1.710	1.995	2.280	2.565	2.850	3.135	3.705	3.990	4.275	4.560	4.845	5.130	5.145	5.700
0.580	1.740	2.030	2.320	2.610	2.900	3.190	3.770	4.060	4.350	4.640	4.930	5.220	5.510	5.800
0.590	1.770	2.065	2.360	2.655	2.950	3.245	3.835	4.130	4.425	4.720	5.015	5.310	5.605	5.900
0.600	1.800	2.100	2.400	2.700	3.000	3.300	3.900	4.200	4.500	4.800	5.100	5.400	5.700	6.000
0.610	1.830	2.135	2.440	2.745	3.050	3.355	3.965	4.270	4.575	4.880	5.185	5.490	5.795	6.100
0.620	1.860	2.170	2.480	2.970	3.100	3.410	4.030	4.340	4.650	4.960	5.270	5.580	5.890	6.200
0.630	1.890	2.205	2.520	2.835	3.150	3.465	4.095	4.410	4.725	5.040	5.355	5.670	5.985	6.300
0.640	1.920	2.240	2.560	2.880	3.200	3.520	4.160	4.480	4.800	5.120	5.440	5.760	6.080	6.400
0.650	1.950	2.275	2.600	2.925	3.250	3.575	4.225	4.550	4.875	5.200	5.525	5.850	6.175	6.500
0.660	1.980	2.310	2.640	2.970	3.300	3.630	4.290	4.620	4.950	5.280	5.610	5.940	6.270	6.600
0.670	2.010	2.345	2.680	3.015	3.350	3.685	4.335	4.690	5.025	5.360	5.695	6.030	6.363	6.700
0.680	2.040	2.380	2.720	3.060	3.400	3.740	4.420	4.760	5.100	5.440	5.780	6.120	6.460	6.800
0.690	2.070	2.415	2.760	3.105	3.450	2.795	4.485	4.830	5.175	5.520	5.865	6.210	6.555	6.900
0.700	2.100	2.450	2.800	3.150	3.500	3.850	4.550	4.900	5.250	5.600	5.950	6.300	6.650	7.000
0.710	2.130	2.485	2.840	3.195	3.550	3.905	4.615	4.970	5.325	5.680	6.035	6.390	6.745	7.100
0.720	2.160	2.520	2.880	3.240	3.600	3.960	4.680	5.040	5.400	5.760	6.120	6.480	6.840	7.200
0.730	2.910	2.555	2.920	3.285	2.650	4.015	4.745	5.110	5.475	5.840	6.205	6.570	6.935	7.300
0.740	2.220	2.590	2.960	3.350	3.700	4.070	4.810	5.180	5.550	5.920	6.290	6.660	7.030	7.400
0.750	2.250	2.625	3.000	3.375	2.750	4.125	4.875	5.250	5.625	6.000	6.375	6.750	7.125	7.500
0.760	2.280	2.660	3.040	3.420	3.800	4.180	4.940	5.320	5.700	6.080	6.460	6.840	7.220	7.600
0.770	2.310	2.695	3.080	3.465	3.850	4.235	5.005	5.390	5.775	6.160	6.545	6.930	7.315	7.700
0.780	2.340	2.730	3.120	3.510	3.900	4.290	5.070	5.460	5.850	6.240	6.630	7.020	7.410	7.800
0.790	2.370	2.765	3.160	3.555	3.950	4.345	5.135	5.530	5.935	6.320	6.715	7.110	7.505	7.900
0.800	2.400	2.800	3.200	3.600	4.000	4.400	5.200	5.600	6.000	6.400	6.800	7.200	7.600	8.000
0.810	2.430	2.835	3.240	3.645	4.050	4.455	5.265	5.670	6.075	6.480	6.885	7.290	7.695	8.100
0.820	2.460	2.870	3.280	3.690	4.100	4.510	5.330	5.740	6.150	6.560	6.970	7.380	7.790	8.200
0.830	2.490	2.905	3.320	3.735	4.150	4.565	5.395	5.810	6.225	6.640	7.055	7.470	7.885	8.300
0.840	2.520	2.940	3.360	3.780	4.200	4.620	5.460	5.880	6.300	6.720	7.140	7.560	7.890	8.400
0.850	2.550	2.975	3.400	3.825	4.250	4.675	5.525	5.950	6.375	6.800	7.225	7.650	8.075	8.500
0.860	2.580	3.010	3.440	3.870	4.300	4.730	5.590	6.020	6.450	6.880	7.310	7.740	8.170	8.600
0.870	2.610	3.045	3.480	3.915	4.350	4.875	5.655	6.090	6.525	6.960	7.395	7.830	8.265	8.700
0.880	2.640	3.080	3.520	3.960	4.400	4.840	5.720	6.160	6.600	7.040	7.480	7.920	8.360	8.800
0.890	2.670	3.115	3.560	4.005	4.450	4.895	5.785	6.230	6.675	7.120	7.565	8.010	8.445	8.900
0.900	2.700	3.150	3.600	4.050	4.500	4.950	5.850	6.300	6.750	7.200	7.650	8.100	8.550	9.000
0.910	2.730	3.185	3.640	4.095	4.550	5.005	5.915	6.370	6.825	7.280	7.735	8.190	8.645	9.100
0.920	2.760	3.220	3.680	4.140	4.600	5.060	5.980	6.440	6.900	7.360	7.820	8.280	8.740	9.200
0.930	2.790	3.255	3.270	4.185	4.650	5.115	6.045	6.510	6.975	7.440	7.905	8.370	8.835	9.300
0.940	2.820	3.290	3.760	4.230	4.700	5.170	6.110	6.580	7.050	7.520	7.990	8.460	8.930	9.400
0.950	2.850	3.325	3.800	4.275	4.750	5.225	6.175	6.650	7.125	7.600	8.075	8.550	9.025	9.500
0.960	2.880	3.360	3.840	4.320	4.800	5.280	6.240	6.720	7.200	7.680	8.160	8.640	9.120	9.600
0.970	2.910	3.395	3.880	4.365	4.850	5.335	6.305	6.790	7.275	7.760	8.245	8.730	9.215	9.700
0.980	2.940	3.430	3.290	4.410	4.900	5.390	6.370	6.860	7.350	7.840	8.330	8.820	9.310	9.800
0.990	2.970	3.465	3.960	4.455	4.950	5.445	6.435	6.930	7.425	7.920	8.415	8.910	9.405	9.900
1.000	3.000	3.500	4.000	4.500	5.000	5.500	6.500	7.000	7.500	8.000	8.500	9.000	9.500	10.000

GOLD & PLATINUM BULLION CHART

FRACTION OF ONE OUNCE

Oz.	$270.00	280.00	290.00	300.00	310.00	320.00	330.00	340.00	350.00	360.00	370.00	380.00	390.00	400.00	410.00
0.100	27.00	28.00	29.00	30.00	31.00	32.00	33.00	34.00	35.00	36.00	37.00	38.00	39.00	40.00	41.00
0.110	29.70	30.80	31.90	33.00	34.10	35.20	36.30	37.40	38.50	39.60	40.70	41.80	42.90	44.00	45.10
0.120	32.40	33.60	34.80	36.00	37.20	38.40	39.60	40.80	42.00	43.20	44.40	45.60	46.80	48.00	49.20
0.130	35.10	36.40	37.70	39.00	40.30	41.60	42.90	44.20	45.50	46.80	48.10	49.40	50.70	52.00	53.30
0.140	37.80	39.20	40.60	42.00	43.40	44.80	46.20	47.60	49.00	50.40	51.80	53.20	54.60	56.00	57.40
0.150	40.50	42.00	43.50	45.00	46.50	48.00	49.50	51.00	52.50	54.00	55.50	57.00	58.50	60.00	61.50
0.160	43.20	44.80	46.40	48.00	49.50	51.20	52.80	54.40	56.00	57.60	59.20	60.80	62.40	64.00	65.50
0.170	45.90	47.60	49.30	51.00	52.70	54.40	56.10	57.80	59.50	61.20	62.90	64.60	66.30	68.00	69.70
0.180	48.60	50.40	52.20	54.00	55.80	57.60	59.40	61.20	63.00	64.80	66.60	68.40	70.20	72.00	73.80
0.190	51.30	53.20	55.10	57.00	58.90	60.80	62.70	64.60	66.50	68.40	70.30	72.20	74.10	76.00	77.90
0.200	54.00	56.00	58.00	60.00	62.00	64.00	66.00	68.00	70.00	72.00	74.00	76.00	78.00	80.00	82.00
0.210	56.70	58.80	60.90	63.00	65.10	67.20	69.30	71.40	73.50	75.60	77.70	79.80	81.90	84.00	86.10
0.220	59.40	61.60	63.80	66.00	68.20	70.40	72.60	74.80	77.00	79.20	81.40	83.60	85.80	88.00	90.20
0.230	62.10	64.40	66.70	69.00	71.30	73.60	75.90	78.20	80.50	82.80	85.10	87.40	89.70	92.00	94.30
0.240	64.80	67.20	69.60	72.00	74.40	76.80	79.20	81.60	84.00	86.40	88.80	91.20	93.60	96.00	98.40
0.250	67.50	70.00	72.50	75.00	77.50	80.00	82.50	85.00	87.50	90.00	92.50	95.00	97.50	100.00	102.50
0.260	70.20	72.80	75.40	78.00	80.60	83.20	85.80	88.40	91.00	93.60	96.20	98.80	101.40	104.00	106.60
0.270	72.90	75.60	78.30	81.00	83.70	86.40	89.10	91.80	94.50	97.20	99.90	102.60	105.30	108.00	110.70
0.280	75.60	78.40	81.20	84.00	86.80	89.60	92.40	95.20	98.00	100.80	103.60	106.40	109.20	112.00	114.80
0.290	78.30	81.20	84.10	87.00	89.90	92.80	95.70	98.60	101.50	104.40	107.30	110.20	113.10	116.00	118.90
0.300	81.00	84.00	87.00	90.00	93.00	96.00	99.00	102.00	105.00	108.00	111.00	114.00	117.00	120.00	123.00
0.310	83.70	86.80	89.90	93.00	96.10	99.20	102.30	105.40	108.50	111.60	114.70	117.80	120.90	124.00	127.10
0.320	86.40	89.60	92.80	96.00	99.20	102.40	105.60	108.80	112.00	115.20	118.40	121.60	124.80	128.00	131.20
0.330	89.10	92.40	95.70	99.00	102.30	105.60	108.90	112.20	115.50	118.80	122.10	125.40	128.70	132.00	135.30
0.340	91.80	95.20	98.60	102.00	105.40	108.80	112.20	115.60	119.00	122.40	125.80	129.20	132.60	136.00	139.40
0.350	94.50	98.00	101.50	105.00	108.50	112.00	115.50	119.00	122.50	126.00	129.50	133.00	136.50	140.00	143.50
0.360	97.20	100.80	104.40	108.00	111.60	115.20	118.80	122.40	126.00	129.60	133.20	136.80	140.40	144.00	147.60
0.370	99.90	103.60	107.30	111.00	114.70	118.40	122.10	125.80	129.50	133.20	136.90	140.60	144.30	148.00	151.70
0.380	102.60	106.40	110.20	114.00	117.80	121.60	125.40	129.20	133.00	136.80	140.60	144.40	148.20	152.00	155.80
0.390	105.30	109.20	113.10	117.00	120.90	124.80	128.70	132.60	136.50	140.40	144.30	148.20	152.10	156.00	159.90
0.400	108.00	112.00	116.00	120.00	124.00	128.00	132.00	136.00	140.00	144.00	148.00	152.00	156.00	160.00	164.00
0.410	110.70	114.80	118.90	123.00	127.10	131.20	135.30	139.70	143.50	147.60	151.70	155.80	159.90	164.00	168.10
0.420	113.40	117.60	121.80	126.00	130.20	134.40	138.60	142.80	147.00	151.20	155.40	159.60	163.80	168.00	172.20
0.430	116.10	120.40	124.70	129.00	133.30	137.60	141.90	146.20	150.50	154.80	159.10	163.40	167.70	172.00	176.30
0.440	118.80	123.20	127.60	132.00	136.40	140.80	145.20	149.60	154.00	158.40	162.80	167.20	171.60	176.00	180.40
0.450	121.50	126.00	130.50	135.00	139.50	144.00	148.50	153.00	157.50	162.00	166.50	171.00	175.50	180.00	184.50
0.460	124.20	128.80	133.40	138.00	142.60	147.20	151.80	156.40	161.00	165.60	170.20	174.80	179.40	184.00	188.60
0.470	126.90	131.60	136.30	141.00	145.70	150.40	155.10	159.80	164.50	169.20	173.90	178.60	183.30	188.00	192.70
0.480	129.60	134.40	139.20	144.00	148.80	153.60	158.40	163.20	168.00	172.80	177.60	182.40	187.20	192.00	196.80
0.490	132.30	137.20	142.10	147.00	151.90	156.80	161.70	166.60	171.50	176.40	181.30	186.20	191.10	196.00	200.90
0.500	135.00	140.00	145.00	150.00	155.00	160.00	165.00	170.00	175.00	180.00	185.00	190.00	195.00	200.00	205.00
0.510	137.70	142.80	147.90	153.00	158.10	163.20	168.30	173.40	178.50	183.60	188.70	193.80	198.90	204.00	209.10
0.520	140.40	145.60	150.80	156.00	161.20	166.40	171.60	176.80	182.00	187.20	192.40	197.60	202.80	208.00	213.20
0.530	143.10	148.40	153.70	159.00	164.30	169.60	174.90	180.20	185.50	190.80	196.10	201.40	206.70	212.00	217.30
0.540	145.80	151.20	156.60	162.00	167.40	172.80	178.20	183.60	189.00	194.40	199.80	205.20	210.60	216.00	221.40
0.550	148.50	154.00	159.50	165.00	170.50	176.00	181.50	187.00	192.50	198.00	203.50	209.00	214.50	220.00	225.50
0.560	151.20	156.80	162.40	168.00	173.60	179.20	184.80	190.40	196.00	201.60	207.20	212.80	218.40	224.00	229.60
0.570	153.90	159.60	165.30	171.00	176.70	182.40	188.10	193.80	199.50	205.20	210.90	216.60	222.30	228.00	233.70
0.580	156.60	162.40	168.20	174.00	179.80	186.60	191.40	197.20	203.00	208.80	214.60	220.40	226.20	232.00	237.80
0.590	159.30	165.20	171.10	177.00	182.90	188.80	194.70	200.60	206.50	212.40	218.30	224.20	230.10	236.00	241.90
0.600	162.00	158.00	174.00	180.00	186.00	192.00	198.00	204.00	210.00	216.00	222.00	228.00	234.00	240.00	246.00
0.610	164.70	170.80	176.90	183.00	189.10	195.20	201.30	207.40	213.50	219.60	225.70	231.80	237.90	244.00	250.10
0.620	167.40	173.60	179.80	186.00	192.20	198.40	204.60	210.80	217.00	223.20	229.40	235.60	241.80	248.00	254.20
0.630	170.10	176.40	182.70	189.00	195.30	201.60	207.90	214.20	220.50	226.80	233.10	239.40	245.70	252.00	258.30
0.640	172.80	179.20	185.60	192.00	198.40	204.80	211.20	217.60	224.00	230.40	236.80	243.20	249.60	256.00	262.40
0.650	175.50	182.00	188.50	195.00	201.50	208.00	214.50	221.00	227.50	234.00	240.50	247.00	253.50	260.00	266.50
0.660	178.20	184.80	191.40	198.00	204.60	211.20	217.80	224.40	231.00	237.60	244.20	250.80	257.40	264.00	270.60
0.670	180.90	187.60	194.30	201.00	207.70	214.40	221.10	227.80	234.50	241.20	247.90	254.60	261.30	268.00	274.70
0.680	183.60	190.40	197.20	204.00	210.80	217.60	224.40	231.20	238.00	244.80	251.60	258.40	265.20	272.00	278.80
0.690	186.30	193.20	200.10	207.00	213.90	220.80	227.70	234.60	241.50	248.40	255.30	262.20	269.10	276.00	282.90
0.700	189.00	196.00	203.00	210.00	217.00	224.00	231.00	238.00	245.00	252.00	259.00	266.00	273.00	280.00	287.00
0.710	191.70	198.80	205.90	213.00	220.10	227.20	234.30	241.40	248.50	255.60	262.70	269.80	276.90	284.00	291.10
0.720	194.40	201.60	208.80	216.00	223.20	230.40	237.60	244.80	252.00	259.20	266.40	273.60	280.80	288.00	295.20
0.730	197.10	204.40	211.70	219.00	226.30	233.60	240.90	248.20	255.50	262.80	270.10	277.40	284.70	292.00	299.30
0.740	199.80	207.20	214.60	222.00	229.40	236.80	244.20	251.60	259.00	266.40	273.80	281.20	288.60	296.00	303.40
0.750	202.50	210.00	217.50	225.00	232.50	240.00	247.50	255.00	262.50	270.00	277.50	285.00	292.50	300.00	307.50
0.760	205.20	212.80	220.40	228.00	235.60	243.20	250.80	258.40	266.00	273.60	281.20	288.80	296.40	304.00	311.60
0.770	207.90	215.60	223.30	231.00	238.70	246.40	254.10	261.80	269.50	277.20	284.90	292.60	300.30	308.00	315.70
0.780	210.60	218.40	226.20	234.00	241.80	249.60	257.40	265.20	273.00	280.80	288.60	296.40	304.20	312.00	319.80
0.790	213.30	221.20	229.10	237.00	244.90	252.80	260.70	268.60	276.50	284.40	292.30	300.20	308.10	316.00	323.90
0.800	216.00	224.00	232.00	240.00	248.00	256.00	264.00	272.00	280.00	288.00	296.00	304.00	312.00	320.00	328.00
0.810	218.70	226.80	234.90	243.00	251.10	259.20	267.30	276.40	283.50	291.60	299.70	307.80	315.90	324.00	332.10
0.820	221.40	229.60	237.80	246.00	254.20	262.40	270.60	278.80	287.00	295.20	303.40	311.60	319.80	328.00	336.20
0.830	224.10	232.40	240.70	249.00	257.30	264.60	273.90	282.20	290.50	298.80	307.10	315.40	323.70	332.00	340.30
0.840	226.80	235.20	243.60	252.00	260.40	268.80	277.20	285.60	294.00	302.40	310.80	319.20	327.60	336.00	344.40
0.850	229.50	238.00	246.50	255.00	263.50	272.00	280.50	289.00	297.50	306.00	314.50	323.00	331.50	340.00	348.50
0.860	232.20	240.80	249.40	258.00	266.60	275.20	283.80	292.40	301.00	309.60	318.20	326.80	335.40	344.00	352.60
0.870	234.90	243.60	252.30	261.00	269.70	278.40	287.10	295.80	304.50	313.20	321.90	330.60	339.30	348.00	356.70
0.880	237.60	246.40	255.20	264.00	272.80	281.60	290.40	299.20	308.00	316.80	325.60	334.40	343.20	352.00	360.80
0.890	240.30	249.20	248.10	267.00	275.90	284.80	293.70	302.60	311.50	320.40	329.30	338.20	347.10	356.00	364.90
0.900	243.00	252.00	261.00	270.00	279.00	288.00	297.00	306.00	315.00	324.00	333.00	342.00	351.00	360.00	369.00
0.910	245.70	254.80	263.90	273.00	282.10	291.20	300.30	309.40	318.50	327.60	336.70	345.80	354.90	364.00	373.10
0.920	248.40	257.60	266.80	276.00	285.20	294.40	303.60	312.80	322.00	331.20	340.40	349.60	358.80	368.00	377.20
0.930	251.10	260.40	269.70	279.00	288.30	297.60	306.90	316.20	325.50	334.80	344.10	353.40	362.70	372.00	381.30
0.940	253.80	263.20	272.60	282.00	291.40	300.80	310.20	319.60	329.00	338.40	347.80	357.20	366.60	376.00	385.40
0.950	256.50	266.00	375.50	285.00	294.50	304.00	313.50	323.00	332.50	342.00	351.50	361.00	370.50	380.00	389.50
0.960	259.20	268.80	278.40	288.00	297.60	307.20	316.80	326.40	336.00	345.60	355.20	364.80	374.40	384.00	393.60
0.970	261.90	271.60	281.30	291.00	300.70	310.40	320.10	329.80	339.50	349.20	358.90	368.60	378.30	388.00	397.70
0.980	264.60	274.40	284.20	394.00	303.80	313.60	323.40	333.20	343.00	352.80	362.60	372.40	382.20	392.00	401.80
0.990	267.30	277.20	287.10	397.00	306.90	316.80	326.70	336.60	346.50	356.40	366.30	376.20	385.10	396.00	405.90
1.000	270.00	280.00	290.00	300.00	310.00	320.00	330.00	340.00	350.00	360.00	370.00	380.00	390.00	400.00	410.00

CHART OF COIN SIZES BY MILLIMETERS

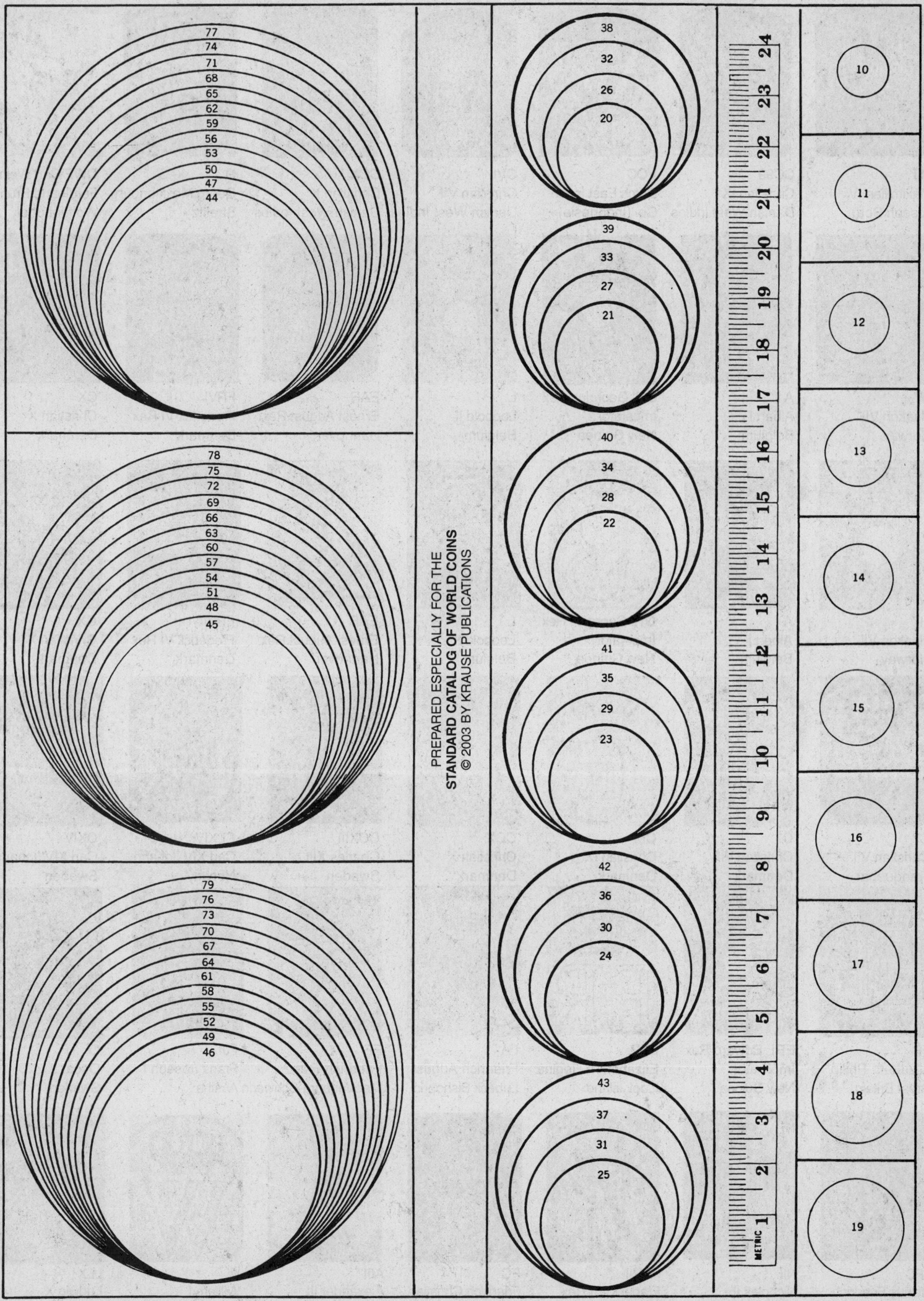

MONOGRAMS

MJ
Maximilian IV
Joseph Berg

CC99
Christian IX
Danish West Indies

VOC
Dutch East India
Co. (Indonesia)

CVII
Christian VII
Danish West Indies

CCX
Christian X
Danish West Indies

G
Georg Mexklenburg-
Strelitz

CWF Carl Welhelm
Ferdinand Brunswick-
Wolfenbuttel

H7
Haakon VII
Norway

A
Albert I
Belgium

GRI Georgius Rex
Imperator
New Guinea

L
Leopold II
Belgium

EAR
Ernest August Rex
Hannover

FRVI
Frederick VI Rex
Denmark

CX
Christian X
Denmark

H7
Haakon VII
Norway

A
Albert I
Belgium

GRI Georgius Rex
Imperator
New Guinea

L
Leopold II
Belgium

EAR
Ernest August Rex
Hannover

FRVI
Frederick VI Rex
Denmark

CX
Christian X
Denmark

C7
Christian VII
Tranquebar

C7
Christian VII
Denmark

CIX
Christian IX
Denmark

CCX
Christian X
Denmark

CCXIII
Charles XIII
Sweden

CLXIV
Carl XIV Johann
Norway

CXIV
Carl XIV Johann
Sweden

EP
Elizabeth-Philip
Great Britain

ERI Edward Rex
Imperator
New Guinea

EIIR
Elizabeth II Regina
Cook Island

FA
Friedrich August
Lubeck Bishopric

FF
Friedrich Franz
Mecklenburg-Schwerin

FJI
Franz Joseph I
Austria

O
Oscar I
Sweden

AFC
Alexius Friedrich
Great Britain
Anhalt-Bernburg

NII
Nicholas II
Russia

FRVII
Frederik VII Rex
Danish West Indies
Denmark

FC
Friedrich Christian
Brandenburg-
Bayreuth

AIII
Alexander III
Russia

W
William I
Netherlands

LLX
Ludwig X
Hesse-Darmstadt

MONOGRAMS

MJ
Maximilian IV Joseph
Berg

FI
Frederick IX & Ingrid
Denmark

F VI R
Fred. VI Denmark
Tranquebar

FVII
Frederick VII
Denmark

FF8
Frederick VIII
Denmark

F IX R
Frederick IX
Denmark

FVII
Ferdinand VII
Mexico

PI
Paul I
Russia

FVII
Ferdinand VII
Mexico

FW
Fredrich Wilhelm III
Prussia

GA IV
Gustav Adolf IV
Sweden

HI
Nicholas I
Russia

HC
Henri Christophe
Haiti

HVII
Haakon VII
Norway

HN Hieronymus
Napoleon
Westphalia

J
Joachim (Murat)
Berg

E(K)I II
Katherine II
Russia

L
Ludwig
Hesse-Darmstadt

L
Leopold
Belgium

LL III
Leopold III
Belgium

LL
Louis XVIII
Antwerp

C XIVJ
Carl XIV Johann
Norway

M Morelos
Revolutionary
Mexico

M 2 R
Margrethe II Regina
Denmark

NII
Nicholas II
Russia

NI
Nicholas I
Russia

NFP
Nicholas Friedrich
Peter Oldenburg

OII
Oscar II
Norway

E
Ernest I
Saxe-Coburg-Gotha

O V
Olav V
Norway

P I
Paul I
Russia

P III
Peter III
Russia

R
Rainier III
Monaco

WL
Wilhelm Landgraf
Hesse-Cassel

WR
William Rex
Hannover

PFA
Peter Friedrich
August Oldenburg

OII
Oscar II
Sweden

GR
Georgius Rex
Hannover

FRVI
Frederik VI Rex
Tranquebar

PF
Paul Friedrich
Mecklenburg-Schwerin

FII
Friedrich II
Wurttemberg

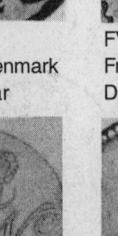

FER VII
Ferdinand VII
(Spain) Gerona

ILLUSTRATED GUIDE TO EASTERN MINT NAMES

PREPARED ESPECIALL FOR THE **STANDARD CATALOG OF WORLD COINS** © BY KRAUSE PUBLICATIONS

Compiled by Harry S. Scherzer.
Scrip typeset by Ketab Corporation

Eastern mint names are basically composed of the Arabic alphabet which in fact covers a number of languages — Arabic is Semitic; Persian is Indo-European; and Malayan is in the Malayo-Polynesian group. Differences are not just of dialect, they are of basic structure. However, Arabic itself is the rally important one, bearing a relationship to other Oriental languages not unlike that of Latin to the languages of Europe. Just as medieval European coins are inscribed in Latin, so are the majority of the coins of North African, Turkish, Persian, and Indian origin inscribed until very recent times in Arabic. A limited knowledge of Persian will also be necessary for unravelling the Persian poetic couplets found on Indian and Persian coins particulary during the seventeenth and eighteenth centuries A.D.

(Courtesy of Richard J. Plant)

ANKARA
Turkey
انقره

AL-'ARAISH
"Larache", Morocco
العرايش

AL-'ARAISHAN
"Larache", Morocco
العرايشة

ABUSHAHR
"Bushire", Iran
ابو شهر

ADRANAH
"Edirne", Turkey
ادرنة

AFGHANISTAN
افغانستان

AHMADABAD
Bombay, India-British
احمد اباد

AHMADNAGAR-FARRUKHABAD
Afghanistan
احمدنكر فرخ اباد

AHMADPUR
See "Bahawalpur", Afghanistan
احمد پور

AHMADSHAHI
See "Ashraf Al-Bilad" and "Qandar", Afghanistan
احمد شاهى

AJMAN
See "United Arab Emirates"
احمد شاهى

AKSU
China-Sinkiang
اقصو

ALGERIA
See "Al-Jaza 'Iriyat"
—

BI-ANGLAND
"In England" (Birmingham)
For Morocco
بانكلند

BI-ANGLAND
"In England" (London)
For Morocco
بانكلند

DAULAT ANJAZANCHIYAH
"The State of Anjazanchiyah"
See Comoros
دولة انجزنجية

ANWALA
"Aonla," Afghanistan
انوله

AL-ARABIYAT AS-SA'UDIYAT
"Saudi-Arabian", Saudi Arabia
العربية السعودية

ARDEBIL
Iran
اردبيل

ARKAT
"Arcot", India-French
اركات

ASHRAF AL-BILAD
"Most Noble of Cities"
See "Ahmadshahi", Afghanistan
اشرف البلاد

ASTARABAD
Iran
استراباد

ATCHEH
Indonesia
اجه

ATTOCK
Afghanistan
اتك

AZIMABAD
See "Patna", Bengal, India-British
عظيم اباد

ILLUSTRATED GUIDE TO EASTERN MINT NAMES

BACAIM (no legends)
See "India-Portuguese"
—

BADAKHSHAN
See Afghanistan
بد خشان

BAGCHIH-SERAI
See "Krim"
باغجه سراي

BAGHDAD
Iraq
بغداد

BAHAWALPUR
See "Ahmadpur" and
"Dar Es-Surur", Afghanistan
بها ولپور

BAHRAIN
See "El-Bahrain"
بحرين

EL-BAHRAIN
"Of the Two Seas", Bahrain
البحرين

BALKH
See "Umm Al-Bilad", Afghanistan
بلخ

BANARAS
"Awadh", Bengal, India-British
بنارس

BANDAR ABBAS
Iran
بندر عباس

BANJARMASIN
Indonesia
بنجرمسن

BARELI
Afghanistan
بريلي

BI BARIZ
"In Paris"
For Morocco
بباريز

BEHBEHAN
Iran
بهبهان

BERLIN
For Morocco
برلين

BHAKHAR
Afghanistan
بهكر

BOMBAY
See "Munbai", Bombay, India-British
—

BORUJERD
Iran
بروجرد

NEGRI BRUNEI
"State of Brunei", Brunei
نكري بروني

BRUSAH
"Bursa", Turkey
بروسة

BUKHARA
See Russian Turkestan
بخارا

BUSHIRE
See "Abushahr", Iran
—

CALCUTTA
See "Kalkatah", Bengal,
India-British
كلكته

COCHIN
See India-Dutch and
"V.O.C.", India-Dutch
—

COMOROS
See "Anjazanchiyah",
"The Largest of the Islands", Comoros
كموز

DACCA
See "Jahangirnager", Bengal,
India-British
—

DAMAO (no legends)
See India-Portuguese
—

DAR AL-AMAN
"Abode of Security" (honorific)
See "Multan"
دار الامان

DAR AL-ISLAM
See Bahawalpur, India
Princely States
دار الاسلام

DAR AL-MULK
"Abode of the King" (honorific)
See "Kabul"
دارالملك

DAR AL-NUSRAT
"Abode of the New (Town?)" (honorific)
See Herat"
دارالنصرت

DAR AL-KHILAFAT
"Abode of the Caliphate" (honorific)
See "Tehran" and "Yeman"
دار الخلافة

DAR AS-SALAM
"Abode of Peace" (honorific)
See "Ligkeh", Thailand
دار السلام

DAR AS-SULTANAT
"Abode of the sultanate" (honorific)
See "Herat" and "Kabul", Afghanistan
دارالسلطنة

DAR AS-SURUR
"Abode of Happiness" (honorific)
See "Bahawalpur", Afghanistan
دار السرور

DARBAND
Iran
دربند

ILLUSTRATED GUIDE TO EASTERN MINT NAMES

DARFUR
See "Al-Fasher", Sudan
الفشير

DEHLI
See "Shajahanabad", Afghanistan
دهلي

DELI
Indonesia
دلي

DERA
"Dera Ghazi Khan", Afghanistan
ديره

DERAJAT
"Dera Ishmael Khan", Afghanistan
ديره جات

DEZFUL
Iran
دزفول

DIU (no legends)
See India-Portuguese
—

DJIBOUTI
See "Jaibuti"
—

EDIRNE
See "Adranah", Turkey
—

EGYPT
See "Misr" and "Al-Misriyat"
—

ERAVAN
Iran
ايروان

FARRUKHABAD
Bengal, India-British
فرخ اباد

AL-FASHER
See "Darfur", Sudan
الفشير

FES
"Fez", Morocco
فاس

FERGANA
See "Khoqand",
Russian Turkestan
فرغانة

FILASTIN
"Palestine", Israel
فلسطين

AL-FUJAIRAH
See "United Arab Emirates"
الفجيره

GANJAH
Iran
كنجه

GERMAN EAST AFRICA
See "Sharakat Almaniyah", Tanzania
شراكة المانيا

GHAZNI
Afghanistan
غزني

GOA (no legends)
See India-Portuguese
—

HAIDARABAD SIND MINT
Afghanistan
حيدرآباد سند

HALEB
"Allepo", Syria
حلب

HAMADAN
Iran
ہمدان

AL-HARAR
Ethiopia-Eritrea
الهرر

AL-HEJAZ
Saudi Arabia-Hejaz
الحجاز

HERAT
See "Dar Al-Nushat" and
"Dar As-Sultanat", Afghanistan
هرات

HERAT
Iran
ہرات

ILI
China-Sinkiang
الي

IRAN
ايران

AL-IRAQ
"Iraque"
العراق

AL-IRAQIYAT
"Iraqi", Iraq
العراقية

ISFAHAN
Iran
اصفهان

ISLAMBUL (ISTABMUL)
Turkey
اسلامبول

ITALIAN SOMALILAND
See "Al-Somal Al-Italianiah",
Somalia
الصومال الايطليانية

JAHANGIRNAGAR
See "Dacca", Bengal, India-British
جهانكيرنكر

BI-JAIBUTI
"In Djibouti", Djibouti
بجيبوتي

JAVA
Indonesia
جاوا

JAZA'IR
Algeria-Algiers
جزاير

AL-JAZA'IRIYAT
Algeria-Algiers
الجزايرة

ILLUSTRATED GUIDE TO EASTERN MINT NAMES

JERING
"Jaring", Thailand
جريج

AL-JOMHURIYAT EL-IRAQIYAT
"The Iraqi Republic" Iraq
الجمهورية العرقية

AL-JOMHURIYAT EL-LUBNANIYAT
"The Lebanese Republic", Lebanon
الجمهورية البنانية

AL-JOMHURIYAT AL-MUTTAHIDAH AL-ARABIYAT
"United Arab Republic"
See "Egypt, Syria, Yemen"
الجمهورية المتحدة العربية

AL-JOMHURIYAT AS-SUDAN
"The Sudanese Republic", Sudan
لجمهورية السودان

AL-JOMHURIYAT AS-SURIYAT
"The Syrian Republic", Syria
الجمهورية السورية

AL-JOMHURIYAT AL-TUNISIAT
"The Tunisian Republic", Tunisia
الجمهورية التونسية

AL-JOMHURIYAT AL-TURKIYAH
"The Turkish Republic", Turkey
الجمهورية توركية

JORDON
See "Al-Urduniyat" and "Al-Mamlakat, etc.," Jordon
—

KABUL
See "Dar Al-Mulk" >AH1163 and "Dar As-Sultanat" >AH1164, Afghanistan
كابل

KAFFA
Krim, Russian Caucasia
كفه

KALKATAH
"Calcutta", Bengal, India-British
كلكته

KASHAN
Iran
كاشان

KASHMIR
Afghanistan
كشمير

KASHQUAR
China-Sinkiang
كشقر

KEDAH
See "Bilad Kedah" and "Bilad Al-Perlis Kedah", Malaysia
كداه

KELANTAN
See "Khalifat Al-Mu'Minin" and "Negri Kelantin", Malaysia
كلنتن

KEMASIN
Malaysia
كماسن

KERMAN
Iran
كرمان

KERMANSHAHAN
See "Kermanshah", Iran
كرمانشاهان

KHALIFAT AL-MU'MININ
"Commander of the Faithful" (honorific)
See "Kelantin" and "Trengganu"
خليفة المؤمنين

KHALIFAT AL-KARAM
"Noble Caliph" (honorific)
See "Patani"
خليفة الكرم

KHANABAD
Afghanistan
خان اباد

KHOQAND
See Russian Turkestan
خوقند

KHUI
See "Khoy", Iran
خوى

AL-KHURFAH
See "Yemen"
الخرفاه

KHUTAN
China-Sinkiang
خوتن

KHWAREZM
Russian Turkestan-Khiva
خوارزم

KOSOVAH
Turkey
قوصوه

KOTSHA
China-Sinkiang
كوتشر

AL-KUWAIT
Kuwait
الكويت

LADAKH
Afghanistan
لداخ

LAHEJ
See "Yemen"
لحج

LAHIJAN
See "Gilan", Iran
لاهيجان

LAHORE
Afghanistan
لاهور

LEBANON
See "Al-Lubnaniyat" and "Jomhuriyat, etc."
—

AL-LIBIYAT
"Libyan", Libya
الليبية

ILLUSTRATED GUIDE TO EASTERN MINT NAMES

LIBYA
See "Al-Libyat" and
"Mamlakat, etc."
ليبيا

NEGRI LIGKEH
"State of Ligeh (or Ligor)"
See "Dar As-Salam", Thialand
نكري لغكه

AL-LUBNANIYAT
"Lebanese", Lebanon
النلنية

MACHHLIPATAN
See "Mazulipatam", India-French
"Masulipatam", India-Madras
مجهلي بتن

MACHHLIPATAN-BANDAR
See "Machhlipatan", India-Madras
مچهلي پتن بندر

AL-MAGHRIBIYAT
"Moroccan", Morocco
المغربية

TANAH MALAYU
"Land of the Malays"
See "Sumatra", Indonesia and
"Malacca", Malaysia
تانه ملايو

PULU MALAYU
"Island of the Malays"
See "Sumatra", Indonesia
فولو ملايو

MALUKA
Indonesia
ملوكى

AL-MAMLAKAT AL-ARABIYAT
AL-SA'UDIYAT
"The Kingdom of Saudi Arabia"
المملكة
العربية السعودية

AL-MAMLAKAT AL-LIBIYAT
"The Kingdom of Libya"
المملكة الليبية

AL-MAMLAKAT AL-MAGHRIBIYAT
"The Kingdom of Morocco"
لمملكة المغربية

AL-MAMLAKAT AL-MUTAWAKELIYAT
AL-YEMENIAT
"The Mutawakkilite Kingdom of Yemen"
المملكة
المتوكلية اليمنية

AL-MAMLAKAT AL-MISRIYAT
"The Kingdom of Egypt"
المملكة المصرية

AL-MAMLAKAT AL-URDUNIYAT
AL-HASHEMIYAT
"The Hashemite Kingdom of Jordan"
المملكة
الاردنية الهاشمية

MANASTIR
Turkey
مناستر

MARAGHEH
Iran
مراغه

MARAKESH
"Marrakech", Morocco
مراكش

AL-MASCARA
Algeria-Algiers
المعسكر

MASH'HAD
Afghanistan
مشهد

MASH'HAD
Iran
مشهد

MASULIPATAM
See "Machhlipatan", India-Madras
—

MAZANDARAN
Iran
مازندران

MAZULIPATAM
See "Machhlipatan", India-French
—

MEDEA
Algeria-Algiers
مديه

MEKHA
"Mecca", Saudi-Arabia
مكة

MENANGKABAU
Indonesia
منفكابو

MIKNAS
"Meknes", Morocco
مكناس

MIKNASAH
"Meknes", Morocco
مكناسة

MISR
Egypt
مصر

AL-MISRIYAT
"Egptian", Egypt
المصرية

AL-MOHAMMEDIYAT ASH-SHERIFATE
"The Mohammedan Sherifate" or
"Empire Cherifien" (French), Morocco
المحمدية
الشريفة

MOMBASA
Kenya
ممباسه

MOROCCO
See "Al-Maghribyat" and
"Al-Mohammediyat Ash-Sherifate"
—

MOXOUDABAT
See "Murshidabad", India-French
—

MUBARAK
"Auspicious" (hnonorific)
See "Rikab"
مبارك

ILLUSTRATED GUIDE TO EASTERN MINT NAMES

AL-MAKALA "Mukalla" See "Yemen"	المكلا
MULTAN See "Dar Al-Aman", Afghanistan	ملتان
MUNBAI See "Bombay", India-British	منبي
MURADABAD Afghanistan	مراد اباد
MURSHIDABAD See "Moxoudabat", India-French	مرشد اباد
MURSHIDABAD Bengal, India-British	مرشد اباد
MUSCAT Oman	مسقط
NAJIBABAD Afghanistan	نجيب اباد
NAKAPATTANAM (Tamil legends) "Negapatnam", India-Dutch	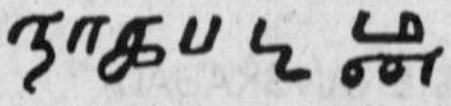
NAKHCHAWAN Iran	نخجوان
NEGAPATNAM See "Nakappattanam"	—
NEJD Saudi Arabia	نجد
NIHAWAND Iran	نهاوند
NUKHWI "Sheki", Iran	نخوى
NUKHWI See "Sheki", Russian Caucasia	نخوي
OMAN	عمان
OMDURMAN Sudan	ام درمان
PAHANG "Pahang Company", Malaysia	فاحغ
PAKISTAN	پاکستان
PALEMBANG Indonesia	فلمبغ
PALESTINE See "Filastin", Israel	—
PANA'HABAD "Shusha" See "Karabagh", Russian Caucasia	پناه باد
AL-PATANI See "Khalifat Al-Karam", "Khalifat Al-Mu'Minin" and "Bilad Al-Patani", Thailand	الفطاني
PATNA See "Azimabad", Bengal, India-British	پتنه
PULU PENANG "Prince of Wales Island", Malaysia	فولو فنيغ
NEGRI PERAQ "State of Perak", Malaysia	نكري فيرق
PULU PERCHA "Island of Sumatra", Indonesia	فولو فرج
PERLIS See "Kedah", Malaysia	—
PESHAWAR Afghanistan	پشاور
PHALICHERY See "Pondichery", India-French	پهلجري
PONDICHERY See "Phalichery", India-French	—
PONTIANAQ (no legends) Indonesia	—
PULICAT (no legends) See "India-Dutch"	—
QANDAHAR See "Ashraf Al-Bilad" and "Ahmadshahi", Afghanistan	قندهار
QATAR WA DUBAI "Qatar and Dubai", Qatar	قطرودبي
DAULAT QATAR "State of Qatar", Qatar	—
QAZWIN Iran	قزوين
QUAITI Yemen	قيطي
QUM Iran	قم

ILLUSTRATED GUIDE TO EASTERN MINT NAMES

QUSANTINAT
"Constantine", Algeria-Algiers
قسنطينة

QUSTINTINIYAH
"Constantinople", Turkey
قسطنطنية

RA'NASH
Iran
رعنش

RABAT
See "Rabat Al-Fath", Morocco
رشت

RABAT AL-FATH
"Rabat", Morocco
رباط الفتح

RAS AL-KHAIMASee
"United Arab Emirates"
راس الخيمه

RASHT
Iran
رشت

REHMAN
Thailand
رحمن

REZA'IYEH
See "Urumi", Iran
رظاعيه

RIKAB
See "Mubarak", Afghanistan
ركاب

RIKAB
Iran
ركاب

SA'UJBALAQ
Iran
ساوج بلاق

SAGAR
Bengal, India-British
ساكر

SAHRIND
Afghanistan
شهرند

AL-SAIWI
See "Bilad Al-Saiwi", "Sai", "Saiburi" and "Teluban", Thailand
السيوي

SAN'A
See "Yemen", Yemen Republic
سنة

SARAKHS
Iran
سرخس

SARHIND
See "Sahrind", Afghanistan
—

SARI
Iran
ساري

SARI POL
Afghanistan
سربل

SAUDI ARABIA
See "Al-Hejaz", "Nejd" and "Al-Arabiyat As-Sa'udiya", Saudi Arabia
—

NEGRI SELANGHUR
"State of Selangor", Malaysia
نكري سلاغور

SELANIK
"Salonika", Turkey
سلانيك

SHAJAHANABAD
See "Dehli", Afghanistan
شاجهان اباد

SHAMAKHI
Russian Caucasia
شماخ

SHAMAKHA
Russian Caucasia
شماخه

SHARAKAT ALMANIYAH
"German Company" or "German East Africa", Tanzania
شراكتة المانيا

ES-SHARJAH
See "United Arab Emirates"
الشارجة

SHIRAZ
Iran
شيراز

SHUSHTAR
Iran
شوشتر

NEGRI SIAK
"State of Siak", Indonesia
نكري سيك

SIMNAN
Iran
سمنان

SIND
Afghanistan
سند

AL-SOMAL AL-ITALIANIYAH
"Italian Somaliland", Somalia
لصومال الايطليانية

SULTANABAD
Iran
سلطاناباد

SUMENEP
Indonesia
سمنف

SURAT
See "Surate", India-French
سورت

SURAT
Bombay, India-British
سورت

AS-SURIYAT
"Syrian", Syria
السورية

AL-SUWAIR
"Essaouira Mogador", Morocco
السورية

AL-SUWAIRAH
"Essaouira Mogador", Morocco
الصوير

ILLUSTRATED GUIDE TO EASTERN MINT NAMES

SYRIA
See "Haleb", As-Suriyat", "Jomhuriyat, etc.", Syra
—

TABARISTAN
Iran
طبرستان

TABRIZ
Iran
تبريز

TANGIER
See "Tanjah", Morocco
—

TANJAH
"Tangier", Morocco
طنجة

TAQIDEMT
Algeria-Algiers
تاقدمت

TARABALUS GHARB
"Tripoli West", Libya
طرابلس غرب

TARIM
See "Yemen"
تريم

NEGRI TARUMON
"State of Tarumon", Indonesia
تاش قورغان

TASHQURGHAN
Afghanistan
تاش قورغان

TATTA
Afghanistan
تته

TEGNAPATAM (no legends)
"Fort St. David", Madras, India-British
—

TEHRAN
See "Dar Al-Khilafat", Iran
طهران

TELLICHERY
Bombay, India-British
تلچري

TETUAN
Morocco
تطوان

TIFLIS
See Russia, Georgia
تفليس

TRANQUEBAR (no legends)
See "India-Danish"
—

TRENGKANU
See "Khalifat Al-Mu'Minin", Malaysia
ترغكانو

TUNIS
Tunisia
تونس

TUNISIA
See "Tunis", "Al-Tunisiyat", "Jomhuriyat, etc."
—

AL-TUNISIYAT
"Tunisian," Tunisia
التونسية

TURKEY
See "Turkiyah", "Jomhuriyat, etc."
—

AL-TURKIYAH
"Turkish", Turkey
التوركية

TUTICORIN (degenerate Nagari legends)
See "India-Dutch"
—

TUYSERKAN
Iran
توی سرکان

TANAH UGI
"Land of the Bugis", Indonesia
تانه اغيسى

UMM AL-BILAD
"Mother of Cities"
See "Balkh", Afghanistan
ام البلاد

UMM AL-QAIWAIN
See "United Arab Emirates"
ام القوين

UNITED ARAB EMIRATES
—

UNITED ARAB REPUBLIC
See "Al-Jomhuriyat Al-Arabiyat Al-Muttahidah"
الامارات العربية
المتحدة

AL-URDUNIYAT
"Jordanian", Jordan
الاردنية

URUMCHI
China-Sinkiang
ارومجي

URUMI
See "Reza'iyeh", Iran
ارومى

USHI
China-Sinkiang
اوش

WAN
"Van", Turkey
وان

YARKHAND
China-Sinkiang
يارقند

YARKHISSARMARAN
"Yanghissar" China-Sinkiang
يارکسارمرن

YAZD
Iran
يزد

YEMEN
See "Sana", "Dar Al-Khilafat", Al-Yemeniyat", Mamlakat, etc."
—

AL-YEMENIYAT
"The Yemen"
اليمنية

ZANJAN
Iran
زنجان

ZANJIBARA
"Zanzibar", Tanzania
زنجباراه

AFGHANISTAN

The Islamic State of Afghanistan, which occupies a mountainous region of Southwest Asia, has an area of 251,825 sq. mi. (652,090 sq. km.) and a population of 25.59 million. Presently, about a fifth of the total population lives in exile as refugees, (mostly in Pakistan). Capital: Kabul. It is bordered by Iran, Pakistan, Turkmenistan, Uzbekistan, Tajikistan, and China's Sinkiang Province. Agriculture and herding are the principal industries; textile mills and cement factories add to the industrial sector. Cotton, wool, fruits, nuts, oil, sheepskin coats and hand-woven carpets are normally exported but foreign trade has been interrupted since 1979.

Because of its strategic position astride the ancient land route to India, Afghanistan (formerly known as Aryana and Khorasan) was invaded by Darius I, Alexander the Great, various Scythian tribes, the White Huns, the Arabs, the Turks, Genghis Khan, Tamerlane, the Mughals, the Persians, and in more recent times by Great Britain. It was a powerful empire under the Kushans, Hephthalites, Ghaznavids and Ghorids. The name Afghanistan, "Land of the Afghans," came into use in the eighteenth and nineteenth centuries to describe the realm of the Afghan kings. For a short period, this mountainous region was the easternmost frontier of the Iranian world, with strong cultural influences from the Turks and Mongols to the north and India to the south.

Previous to 1747, Afghan Kings ruled not only in Afghanistan, but also in India, of which Sher Shah Suri was one. Ahmad Shah Abdali, founder of the Durrani dynasty, established his rule at Qandahar in 1747. His clan was known as Saddozai. He conquered large territories in India and eastern Iran, which were lost by his grandson Shah Zaman. A new family, the Barakzai, drove the Durrani king out of Kabul, the capital, in 1819, but the Durranis were not eliminated completely until 1858. Further conflicts among the Barakzai prevented full unity until the reign of Abdur Rahman in 1880. In 1929, King Amanullah, grandson of Abdul Rahman, was driven out of the country by a commoner known as Baccha-i-Saqao, "Son of the Water-Carrier", who ruled as Habibullah for less than a year before he was defeated by Muhammad Nadir Shah, a relative of the Barakzai. The last king, Muhammad Zahir Shah, became a constitutional though still autocratic monarch in 1964. In 1973 a coup d'etat displaced him and created the Republic of Afghanistan. A subsequent military coup established the pro-Soviet Democratic Republic of Afghanistan in 1978. Mounting resistance in the countryside and violence within the government led to the Soviet invasion of late 1979 and the installation of Babrak Karmal as prime minister. A brutal civil war ensued, which continues to the present, even after Soviet forces withdrew in 1989 and Karmal's government was defeated. An unstable coalition of former *Mujahideen* (Freedom Fighters) factions attempted to govern for several years but have been gradually overcome by the Taliban, a Muslim fundamentalist force supported from Pakistan.

On September 11, 2001, a terrorist attack on the United States, supported by the Taliban, led to retaliatory strikes by the U.S. Military and subsequent dismantling of the Taliban regime. During a UN-sponsored conference on Afghanistan that was held in Bonn, Germany, in early November 2001, an agreement was reached for an Interim Authority, under the leadership of Hamid Karzai, to be instated in Afghanistan on December 22, 2001 and to hold power for the following four to six months. During that time a "loya jirga" (Grand Council) is scheduled to decide on the follow-on Transitional Authority.

Afghanistan's traditional coinage was much like that of its neighbors Iran and India. There were four major mints: Kabul, Qandahar, Balkh and Herat. The early Durranis also controlled mints in Iran and India. On gold and silver coins, the inscriptions in Persian (called *Dari* in Afghanistan) included the name of the mint city and, normally, of the ruler recognized there, but some issues are anonymous. The arrangement of the inscriptions, and frequently the name of the ruler, was different at each mint. Copper coins were controlled locally and usually did not name any ruler. For these reasons the coinage of each mint is treated separately. The relative values of gold, silver, and copper coins were not fixed but were determined in the marketplace.

In 1890 Abdur Rahman had a modern mint set up in Kabul using British minting machinery and the help of British advisors. The other mints were closed down, except for the issue of local coppers. The new system had 60 paisa equal one rupee; intermediate denominations also had special names. In 1901 the name Afghanistan appeared on coins for the first time. A decimal system, 100 puls to the afghani, was introduced in 1925. The gold amani, rated at 20 afghanis, was a bullion coin.

The national symbol on most coins of the kingdom is a stylized mosque, within which is seen the *mihrab*, a niche indicating the direction of Mecca, and the *minbar*, the pulpit, with a flight of steps leading up to it. Inscriptions in Pashtu were first used under the rebel Habibullah, but did not become standard until 1950.

Until 1919, coins were dated by the lunar Islamic Hejira calendar (AH), often with the king's regnal year as a second date. The solar Hejira (SH) calendar was introduced in 1919 (1337 AH, 1298 SH). The rebel Habibullah reinstated lunar Hejira dating (AH 1347-50), but the solar calendar was used thereafter. The solar Hejira year begins on the first day of spring, about March 21. Adding 621 to the SH year yields the AD year in which it begins.

RULERS

Names of rulers are shown in Perso-Arabic script in the style usually found on their coins; they are not always in a straight line.

BARAKZAI DYNASTY

Habibullah,

امان الله

AH1319-1337/1901-1919AD

Amanullah, AH1337,

حبيب الله
١٣٤٧(٥٣٨)

SH1298-1307/1919-1929AD

Habibullah (rebel, known as Baccha-i-Saqao),

حبيب الله

AH1347-1348/1929AD

Muhammed Nadir Shah, AH1348-1350,

محمد نادر شاه

SH1310-1312/1929-1933AD

Muhammad Zahir Shah,

محمد ظاهر شاه

SH1312-1352/1933-1973AD

Republic, SH1352-1358/1973-1979AD
Democratic Republic, SH1358-1373/1979-1994 AD
Islamic Republic, SH1373-1381/1994-2002AD

MINTNAMES

Coins were struck at numerous mints in Afghanistan and adjacent lands. These are listed below, together with their honorific titles, and shown in the style ordinarily found on the coins.

Afghanistan افغانستان

Ghazni غزني

Herat هرات

Kabul كابل

"Dar al-Mulk"
Abode of the King دار لملك

Qandahar

MINT MARKS

(k) – key Havana, Cuba

KINGDOM OF AFGHANISTAN

Habibullah
AH1319-1337/1901-1919AD
LOCAL COINAGE

KM# 956.1 PAISA **Composition:** Copper **Note:** Round or irregular flan. Struck at Herat.

Date	Good	VG	F	VF	XF
AH1322	2.50	4.00	7.50	12.50	—
AH1328	2.50	4.00	7.50	12.50	—
AH1329	2.50	4.00	7.50	12.50	—
AH1330	2.50	4.00	7.50	12.50	—
AH1331	2.50	4.00	7.50	12.50	—
AH1332	2.50	4.00	7.50	12.50	—
ND Date off flan	1.50	2.50	5.00	8.00	—

KM# 957 PAISA **Composition:** Copper **Note:** Struck over Iran, 50 Dinars, Y#4; Struck at Herat.

Date	Good	VG	F	VF	XF
AH1322	4.00	6.50	12.50	16.00	—
AH1328	3.00	5.00	10.00	12.50	—

KM# 956.2 PAISA **Composition:** Copper **Reverse:** In a rayed circle **Note:** Struck at Herat.

Date	Good	VG	F	VF	XF
AH1332	3.00	5.00	8.50	15.00	—

KM# 956.3 PAISA **Composition:** Copper **Obverse:** Scroll symbol **Note:** Struck at Herat.

Date	Good	VG	F	VF	XF
AH1325	3.00	5.00	8.50	15.00	—

KM# 960.4 PAISA **Composition:** Copper **Note:** Counterstamp on British East India Co., 1/4 Anna; Struck at Qandahar.

Date	Good	VG	F	VF	XF
AH1322	4.00	7.50	12.00	18.00	—
AH1330	4.00	7.50	12.00	18.00	—

KM# 960.2 PAISA **Composition:** Copper **Note:** Counterstamp on Iran 50 dinars, Y#4; Struck at Qandahar.

Date	Good	VG	F	VF	XF
AH1321	3.00	5.00	8.00	12.50	—
AH1322	3.00	5.00	8.00	12.50	—

KM# 960.1 PAISA **Composition:** Copper **Note:** Dump; Struck at Qandahar.

Date	Good	VG	F	VF	XF
AH1322	4.50	7.50	12.50	17.50	—

KM# 960.3 PAISA **Composition:** Copper **Note:** Counterstamp on Muscat and Oman, 1/4 Anna, KM#4; Struck at Qandahar.

Date	Good	VG	F	VF	XF
AH1322	3.75	6.50	10.00	15.00	—

KM# 960.5 PAISA Composition: Copper **Note:** Overstruck on Oman, 1/4 Anna, KM#3.1; Struck at Qandahar.

Date	Good	VG	F	VF	XF
AH1322	3.75	6.50	10.00	15.00	—

KM# 963 PAISA Composition: Copper **Note:** Struck over British East India Co., 1/4 Anna; Struck at Ghazni.

Date	Good	VG	F	VF	XF
AH1322	10.00	20.00	35.00	75.00	—

KM# 958.1 PAISA Composition: Copper **Obverse:** "Dar al-Nusrat" added above date **Note:** Struck at Herat.

Date	Good	VG	F	VF	XF
AH1331	2.50	4.00	7.50	12.50	—

KM# 958.2 PAISA Composition: Copper **Reverse:** Date below mosque **Note:** Struck at Herat.

Date	Good	VG	F	VF	XF
AH1331	3.50	5.00	8.50	15.00	—

KM# 964 PAISA Composition: Copper **Note:** Struck at Qandahar.

Date	Good	VG	F	VF	XF
AH1333	2.00	3.50	6.00	10.00	—
AH1334	2.00	3.50	6.00	10.00	—

KM# 973 PAISA Composition: Copper **Note:** Struck at Kabul.

Date	Good	VG	F	VF	XF
ND	—	—	—	—	—

KM# 959 2 PAISE Composition: Copper **Note:** Similar to Paisa, KM#965 but inscribed "Do Paisa" below mosque.

Date	Good	VG	F	VF	XF
AH1329	3.00	5.00	8.50	13.50	—

MILLED COINAGE

10 Dinar = 1 Paisa; 5 Paise = 1 Shahi; 2 Shahi = 1 Sanar; 2 Sanar = 1 Abbasi; 1-1/2 Abbasi = 1 Qiran; 2 Qiran = 1 Kabuli Rupee; 1 Tilla = 10 Rupees

KM# 848 PAISA Composition: Bronze Or Brass

Date	VG	F	VF	XF	Unc
AH1329	6.00	12.00	25.00	45.00	—
AH1329/17 on KM#828 obverse die	8.00	16.00	35.00	60.00	—

KM# 849 PAISA Composition: Bronze Or Brass **Size:** 21 mm.

Date	VG	F	VF	XF	Unc
AH1329	2.00	4.00	7.50	15.00	—
AH1331	2.00	4.00	7.50	15.00	—
AH1332	2.50	4.75	9.00	16.50	—
AH1334	3.00	6.00	11.50	20.00	—

KM# 854 PAISA Composition: Bronze Or Brass **Size:** 19 mm. **Note:** Thick flan, reduced size.

Date	VG	F	VF	XF	Unc
AH1336	3.00	6.00	12.00	25.00	—

KM# 855 PAISA Composition: Bronze Or Brass **Note:** Thin flan.

Date	VG	F	VF	XF	Unc
AH1336	6.50	10.00	20.00	35.00	—
AH1337	2.00	4.00	8.00	16.00	—

KM# 857 PAISA Composition: Bronze Or Brass **Size:** 20 mm. **Note:** Thin flan.

Date	VG	F	VF	XF	Unc
AH1337	6.50	10.00	20.00	35.00	—

KM# 858 PAISA Composition: Bronze Or Brass **Note:** Thin flan. Size varies: 19-20 millimeters.

Date	VG	F	VF	XF	Unc
AH1337 (1918)	3.00	6.00	10.00	20.00	—
SH1298 (1919)	4.50	8.00	15.00	32.50	—

Note: Three varieties are known dated AH1337

KM# 846 SANAR (10 Paisa) Weight: 1.5500 g. **Composition:** 0.5000 Silver .0249 oz. ASW

Date	VG	F	VF	XF	Unc
AH1325	10.00	20.00	35.00	60.00	—
AH1326	5.00	7.50	12.50	22.50	—
AH1328	5.00	7.50	12.50	22.50	—
AH1329	5.75	8.50	14.00	25.00	—

KM# 850 SANAR (10 Paisa) Weight: 1.5500 g. **Composition:** 0.5000 Silver .0249 oz. ASW **Note:** Coins dated AH1333 and 1337 are known in two varieties.

Date	VG	F	VF	XF	Unc
AH1329	4.00	7.00	12.00	22.00	—
AH1330	3.00	6.00	10.00	20.00	—
AH1331	3.00	6.00	10.00	20.00	—
AH1332	3.00	6.00	10.00	20.00	—
AH1333	3.00	5.00	9.00	16.00	—
AH1335	3.00	5.00	9.00	16.00	—
AH1337	3.00	6.00	10.00	20.00	—

KM# 863 3 SHAHI (15 Paisa) Composition: Copper **Obverse:** Without "Al-Ghazi" **Reverse:** Mosque in eight-pointed star **Note:** Size varies: 32-33 millimeters.

Date	VG	F	VF	XF	Unc
AH1337 (1918)	5.00	12.00	20.00	35.00	—

Note: Three varieties are known

KM# 869 3 SHAHI (15 Paisa) Composition: Copper **Obverse:** "Shamsi" left and below date

Date	VG	F	VF	XF	Unc
SH1298 (1919)	2.00	4.00	9.00	18.00	—

Note: Shamsi (Solar) is an additional word written on some of the coins dated SH1298, to show the change from a lunar to solar calendar

KM# 837 ABBASI (20 Paisa) Weight: 3.1100 g. **Composition:** 0.5000 Silver .0499 oz. ASW

Date	VG	F	VF	XF	Unc
AH1320	30.00	60.00	100	225	—

KM# 845 ABBASI (20 Paisa) Weight: 3.1100 g. **Composition:** 0.5000 Silver .0499 oz. ASW

Date	VG	F	VF	XF	Unc
AH1324	35.00	70.00	125	250	—
AH1328	35.00	70.00	125	250	—
AH1329	50.00	100	175	300	—

KM# 851 ABBASI (20 Paisa) Weight: 3.1100 g. **Composition:** 0.5000 Silver .0499 oz. ASW

Date	VG	F	VF	XF	Unc
AH1329	6.00	11.00	16.00	24.00	—
AH1330	6.00	11.00	16.00	24.00	—
AH1333	5.00	10.00	15.00	22.50	—
AH1334	5.00	10.00	15.00	22.50	—
AH1335	5.00	10.00	15.00	22.50	—
AH1337	5.00	10.00	15.00	22.50	—

KM# 831 1/2 RUPEE (Qiran) Weight: 4.6500 g. **Composition:** 0.5000 Silver .0747 oz. ASW **Obverse:** Toughra **Reverse:** Crossed cannons below mosque

Date	VG	F	VF	XF	Unc
AH1319	20.00	40.00	75.00	125	—

KM# 838 1/2 RUPEE (Qiran) Weight: 4.6500 g. **Composition:** 0.5000 Silver .0747 oz. ASW **Obverse:** Toughra divides date

Date	VG	F	VF	XF	Unc
AH1320	25.00	45.00	85.00	140	—
AH1325	20.00	40.00	75.00	125	—

KM# 841 1/2 RUPEE (Qiran) Weight: 4.6500 g. **Composition:** 0.5000 Silver .0747 oz. ASW **Obverse:** Date at upper right of toughra **Reverse:** Dated AH1320

Date	VG	F	VF	XF	Unc
AH1321	25.00	45.00	85.00	140	—
AH1323	30.00	55.00	100	170	—

KM# 844.1 (KM844) 1/2 RUPEE (Qiran) **Weight:** 4.6500 g. **Composition:** 0.5000 Silver .0747 oz. ASW **Obverse:** Inscription and date **Reverse:** Frozen date AH1320 split above mosque

Date	VG	F	VF	XF	Unc
AH1323	6.00	9.00	16.00	28.00	—
AH1323	6.00	9.00	16.00	28.00	—
AH1324	6.00	9.00	15.00	25.00	—
AH1324	6.00	9.00	15.00	25.00	—
AH1326	6.00	9.00	15.00	25.00	—
AH1326	6.00	9.00	15.00	25.00	—
AH1327/6	6.00	9.00	15.00	25.00	—
AH1327/6	6.00	9.00	15.00	25.00	—
AH1327	6.00	9.00	15.00	25.00	—
AH1327	6.00	9.00	15.00	25.00	—
AH1328	8.00	12.00	20.00	45.00	—
AH1328	8.00	12.00	20.00	45.00	—
AH1329	6.00	9.00	16.00	28.00	—
AH1329	6.00	9.00	16.00	28.00	—

KM# 844.2 1/2 RUPEE (Qiran) **Weight:** 4.6500 g. **Composition:** 0.5000 Silver .0747 oz. ASW **Obverse:** Inscription and date **Reverse:** Actual date at top

Date	VG	F	VF	XF	Unc
AH1326/3	25.00	45.00	75.00	135	—
Note: AH1326/0 for actual date on reverse					
AH1329	25.00	45.00	75.00	135	—

KM# 852 1/2 RUPEE (Qiran) **Weight:** 4.6000 g. **Composition:** 0.5000 Silver .0739 oz. ASW

Date	VG	F	VF	XF	Unc
AH1329	3.50	5.50	8.50	16.00	—
AH1333	3.50	5.50	8.50	16.00	—
AH1334	4.50	7.50	12.50	22.50	—
AH1335	4.50	7.50	12.50	22.50	—
AH1337	3.50	5.50	8.50	16.00	—

KM# 864 1/2 RUPEE (Qiran) **Weight:** 5.0000 g. **Composition:** Silver **Obv. Legend:** "Habibullah" **Reverse:** Star of Solomon

Date	VG	F	VF	XF	Unc
AH1335	—	300	500	—	—

KM# 865 1/2 RUPEE (Qiran) **Composition:** Silver **Obverse:** Uncircled inscription

Date	VG	F	VF	XF	Unc
AH1337 (1918)	4.00	9.00	15.00	25.00	—

Note: Five varieties are known

KM# 832 RUPEE **Weight:** 9.2000 g. **Composition:** 0.5000 Silver .0755 oz. ASW **Obverse:** Toughra of Habibullah in wreath, star above

Date	VG	F	VF	XF	Unc
AH1319	8.00	12.00	25.00	70.00	—

Note: Two varieties are known

KM# 833.1 RUPEE **Weight:** 9.2000 g. **Composition:** 0.5000 Silver .0755 oz. ASW **Obverse:** "Afghanistan" above small toughra, star at right **Reverse:** Large inverted pyramid dome

Date	VG	F	VF	XF	Unc
AH1319	4.00	5.50	10.00	25.00	—
AH1320	4.00	5.50	8.50	20.00	—
AH1325	7.00	15.00	25.00	50.00	—

KM# 833.2 RUPEE **Weight:** 9.2000 g. **Composition:** 0.5000 Silver .0755 oz. ASW **Obverse:** Without star

Date	VG	F	VF	XF	Unc
AH1319	4.00	5.50	10.00	25.00	—
AH1325	7.00	15.00	25.00	50.00	—

KM# 839 RUPEE **Weight:** 9.2000 g. **Composition:** 0.5000 Silver .0755 oz. ASW **Obverse:** "Afgahanistan" divided by a star above large toughra

Date	VG	F	VF	XF	Unc
AH1320	4.00	6.00	10.00	20.00	—

KM# 840.1 RUPEE **Weight:** 9.2000 g. **Composition:** 0.5000 Silver .0755 oz. ASW **Reverse:** Small dome mosque

Date	VG	F	VF	XF	Unc
AH1320	5.00	8.00	15.00	35.00	—

KM# 840.2 RUPEE **Weight:** 9.2000 g. **Composition:** 0.5000 Silver .0755 oz. ASW **Obverse:** Date in loop of toughra

Date	VG	F	VF	XF	Unc
AH1321	10.00	15.00	25.00	50.00	—

KM# 842.1 RUPEE **Weight:** 9.2000 g. **Composition:** 0.5000 Silver .0755 oz. ASW **Reverse:** "Afghanistan" above mosque, crossed swords and cannons

Date	VG	F	VF	XF	Unc
AH1321	4.00	7.00	10.50	22.00	—
Note: Two varieties exist for AH1321 date					
AH1322	4.00	7.00	10.50	22.00	—

KM# 842.2 RUPEE **Weight:** 9.2000 g. **Composition:** 0.5000 Silver .0755 oz. ASW **Reverse:** Crossed cannons

Date	VG	F	VF	XF	Unc
AH1322	4.00	5.00	9.00	20.00	—
AH1324	4.00	5.00	9.00	20.00	—

Date	VG	F	VF	XF	Unc
AH1325	5.00	8.00	12.00	25.00	—
AH1326	4.00	6.00	10.00	19.00	—
AH1327/6	6.00	8.00	15.00	30.00	—
AH1327	4.00	6.00	10.00	20.00	—
AH1328	6.00	8.00	15.00	30.00	—
Note: Two varieties exist for AH1328 date.					
AH1329	6.00	8.00	15.00	30.00	—

KM# 847.1 RUPEE **Weight:** 9.2000 g. **Composition:** 0.5000 Silver .0755 oz. ASW **Obverse:** Date divided 13 Arabic "j" 28 **Reverse:** Large dome mosque without "Afghanistan"

Date	VG	F	VF	XF	Unc
AH1328	7.00	15.00	25.00	50.00	—

KM# 847.2 RUPEE **Weight:** 9.2000 g. **Composition:** 0.5000 Silver .0755 oz. ASW **Obverse:** Date divided 132 Arabic "j" 8

Date	VG	F	VF	XF	Unc
AH1328	10.00	20.00	30.00	60.00	—

KM# 853 RUPEE **Weight:** 9.2000 g. **Composition:** 0.5000 Silver .0755 oz. ASW **Obverse:** Name and titles of Habibullah in sprays **Reverse:** Mosque within sunburst **Note:** Size varies: 25-26 millimeters. Two varieties exist for AH1330, 1331, and 1337 and three varieties exist for AH1333; thickness of obverse inscription and size of mosque dome on reverse vary

Date	VG	F	VF	XF	Unc
AH1329	4.00	6.00	10.00	20.00	—
AH1330	4.00	6.00	9.00	18.50	—
AH1331	4.00	6.00	9.00	18.50	—
AH1332	4.00	6.00	9.00	18.50	—
AH1333	4.00	6.00	9.00	18.50	—
AH1334	4.00	6.00	9.00	18.50	—
AH1335	4.00	6.00	9.00	18.50	—
AH1337	4.00	6.00	10.00	20.00	—

KM# 835 TILLA (10 Rupees) **Weight:** 4.6000 g. **Composition:** 0.9000 Gold .1331 oz. AGW **Obverse:** Star above toughra

Date	VG	F	VF	XF	Unc
AH1319	80.00	110	170	240	—

KM# 836.1 TILLA (10 Rupees) **Weight:** 4.6000 g. **Composition:** 0.9000 Gold .1331 oz. AGW **Obverse:** Legend divided by star above toughra **Obv. Legend:** "Afghanistan"

Date	VG	F	VF	XF	Unc
AH1319	90.00	120	180	250	—

KM# 836.2 TILLA (10 Rupees) **Weight:** 4.6000 g. **Composition:** 0.9000 Gold .1331 oz. AGW **Obverse:** Legend above toughra with star to right **Obv. Legend:** "Afghanistan"

Date	VG	F	VF	XF	Unc
AH1320	90.00	120	180	250	—

KM# A856 TILLA (10 Rupees) **Weight:** 4.6000 g. **Composition:** 0.9000 Gold .1331 oz. AGW **Obverse:** Date divided

Date	VG	F	VF	XF	Unc
AH1325	—	450	650	900	—

KM# 856 TILLA (10 Rupees) **Weight:** 4.6000 g. **Composition:** 0.9000 Gold .1331 oz. AGW **Obv. Legend:** Habibullah...

Date	VG	F	VF	XF	Unc
AH1335	170	200	260	330	—
AH1336	100	120	175	240	—
AH1337	110	130	180	220	—

KM# 879 2 TILLAS (20 Rupees) **Weight:** 9.2000 g. **Composition:** 0.9000 Gold .2661 oz. AGW **Size:** 22 mm.

Date	F	VF	XF	Unc
SH1298 (1919)	100	165	240	380

KM# 903 4 TILLAS (40 Rupees) **Weight:** 18.5300 g. **Composition:** 0.9000 Gold .1997 oz. AGW

Date	VG	F	VF	XF	Unc
AH1337 (1918) Rare	—	—	—	—	—

KM# 889 5 AMANI (50 Rupees) **Weight:** 23.0000 g. **Composition:** 0.9000 Gold .6656 oz. AGW **Obverse:** Persian "5" above toughra; "Al Ghazi" at right **Reverse:** Legend above mosque **Rev. Legend:** "Amaniya"

Date	VG	F	VF	XF	Unc
SH1299 (1920)	275	400	675	1,500	—

KM# 890 5 AMANI (50 Rupees) **Weight:** 23.0000 g. **Composition:** 0.9000 Gold .6656 oz. AGW **Obverse:** Star above toughta **Reverse:** Persian "5" above mosque

Date	VG	F	VF	XF	Unc
SH1299 (1920)	275	400	675	1,500	—

Amanullah
AH1337, SH1298-1307/1919-1929AD

LOCAL COINAGE

KM# 965 PAISA **Composition:** Copper **Obverse:** Denomination "Yek Paisa" **Note:** Crudely struck. Without mint name, believed to be struck at Kabul.

Date	Good	VG	F	VF	XF
SH1298 (1919)	4.50	7.50	12.50	20.00	—
SH1299 (1920)	4.50	7.50	12.50	20.00	—

KM# 966 PAISA **Composition:** Copper **Note:** Crudely struck; without mint name, believed to be struck at Kabul.

Date	Good	VG	F	VF	XF
SH1299 (1920)	6.00	10.00	16.50	24.00	—

KM# 967 SHAHI (5 Paise) **Composition:** Copper **Reverse:** Both denominations **Note:** Crudely struck; without mint name, believed to be struck at Kabul.

Date	Good	VG	F	VF	XF
SH1298 (1919)	6.00	10.00	16.50	24.00	—
SH1299 (1920)	7.50	12.50	20.00	30.00	—
SH1299 (1920)	6.00	10.00	16.50	24.00	—

KM# A846 10 PAISE **Composition:** Copper **Note:** Crudely struck; without mint name, believed to be struck at Kabul.

Date	Good	VG	F	VF	XF
SH1299 (1920)	7.50	12.50	20.00	30.00	—

MILLED COINAGE

10 Dinar = 1 Paisa; 5 Paise = 1 Shahi; 2 Shahi = 1 Sanar; 2 Sanar = 1 Abbasi; 1-1/2 Abbasi = 1 Qiran; 2 Qiran = 1 Kabuli Rupee; 1 Tilla = 10 Rupees

KM# 906 5 PUL **Weight:** 3.0000 g. **Composition:** Bronze Or Brass

Date	F	VF	XF	Unc
SH1304 (1925)	1.75	3.50	6.00	14.00
SH1305 (1926)	1.50	3.00	5.50	14.00

KM# 907 10 PUL **Weight:** 6.0000 g. **Composition:** Copper

Date	F	VF	XF	Unc
SH1304 (1925)	2.00	4.00	6.00	15.00
SH1305 (1926)	2.50	4.50	7.00	20.00
SH1306 (1927)	2.50	4.50	7.00	20.00

KM# 908 20 PUL **Weight:** 2.0000 g. **Composition:** Billon **Note:** Varieties exist.

Date	F	VF	XF	Unc
SH1304	50.00	75.00	100	170
SH134 Error	—	—	—	—
ND(ca.1926)	35.00	60.00	90.00	160

KM# 880 PAISA **Composition:** Bronze Or Brass

Date	VG	F	VF	XF	Unc
SH1299 (1920)	2.50	5.50	12.00	22.50	—
SH1300 (1921)	3.50	7.00	15.00	25.00	—
SH1301 (1922)	3.50	7.00	15.00	25.00	—
Note: 2 varieties are known dated SH1301					
SH1302 (1923)	2.50	5.50	12.00	22.50	—
SH1303 (1924)	2.50	5.50	12.00	22.50	—

KM# 909 1/2 AFGHANI (50 Pul) **Weight:** 5.0000 g. **Composition:** 0.5000 Silver .0803 oz. ASW **Obverse:** Date below toughra

Date	F	VF	XF	Unc
SH1304/7 (1925)	2.00	3.50	6.50	18.50
Note: Two varieties are known dated SH1304				
SH1305/8 (1926)	2.00	3.50	6.50	18.50
SH1306/9 (1927)	2.00	3.50	6.50	18.50

KM# 915 1/2 AFGHANI (50 Pul) **Weight:** 5.0000 g. **Composition:** 0.5000 Silver .0803 oz. ASW **Obverse:** Date below mosque

Date	F	VF	XF	Unc
SH1307/10 (1928)	3.00	6.00	12.00	35.00

KM# 910 AFGHANI (100 Pul) **Weight:** 10.0000 g. **Composition:** 0.9000 Silver .2893 oz. ASW **Obverse:** Date below toughra **Note:** Two varieties each are known for dates SH1305-06.

Date	F	VF	XF	Unc
SH1304/7 (1925)	3.00	6.00	12.00	28.00
Note: Three varieties are known for date SH1304				
SH1305/8 (1926)	3.00	6.00	12.00	28.00
SH1305/9 (1926)	3.00	6.00	12.00	28.00
SH1306/9 (1927)	3.00	6.00	12.00	28.00

KM# 859 SHAHI (5 Paise) **Composition:** Copper Or Brass **Note:** Thick flan.

Date	VG	F	VF	XF	Unc
AH1337	12.00	22.00	40.00	70.00	—

KM# 860 SHAHI (5 Paise) **Composition:** Copper Or Brass **Note:** Thin flan.

Date	VG	F	VF	XF	Unc
AH1337	10.00	20.00	35.00	55.00	—

KM# 861 SANAR (10 Paisa) **Composition:** Copper Or Brass **Note:** Thick flan.

Date	VG	F	VF	XF	Unc
AH1337	10.00	17.50	30.00	55.00	—

KM# 862 SANAR (10 Paisa) **Composition:** Copper Or Brass **Note:** Thin flan.

Date	VG	F	VF	XF	Unc
AH1337	9.00	14.00	20.00	35.00	—

KM# 872 3 SHAHI (15 Paisa) **Composition:** Copper **Obverse:** "Shamsi" **Reverse:** Mosque in seven-pointed star

Date	VG	F	VF	XF	Unc
SH1298 (1919)	2.00	4.00	9.00	18.00	—

KM# 881 3 SHAHI (15 Paisa) **Composition:** Copper **Obverse:** Without "Shamsi" **Note:** Four varieties for date SH1299 and three varieties for date SH1300 are known.

Date	VG	F	VF	XF	Unc
SH1298 (1919)	4.00	15.00	22.00	40.00	—
AH1299 (1920)	1.50	3.50	8.00	17.00	—
AH1300 (1921)	1.50	3.50	8.00	17.00	—

KM# 870 3 SHAHI (15 Paisa) **Composition:** Copper **Obverse:** "Al-Ghazi", without "Shamsi" by date **Reverse:** Mosque in eight-pointed star **Note:** Size varies: 32-33 millimeters.

Date	VG	F	VF	XF	Unc
SH1298 (1919)	3.00	5.00	10.00	20.00	—
SH1299 (1920)	3.00	5.00	10.00	20.00	—

Note: 2 varieties of SH1299 exist

KM# 871.1 3 SHAHI (15 Paisa) **Weight:** 11.5000 g. **Composition:** Copper **Obverse:** "Al-Ghazi, Shamsi" **Note:** Thick flan.

Date	VG	F	VF	XF	Unc
SH1298 (1919)	10.00	15.00	22.00	40.00	—

KM# 871.2 3 SHAHI (15 Paisa) **Weight:** 9.0000 g. **Composition:** Copper **Note:** Thin flan.

Date	VG	F	VF	XF	Unc
SH1298 (1919)	2.00	4.00	9.00	18.00	—

Note: Two reverse varieties with 10 or 11 circular stars exist

KM# 881a 3 SHAHI (15 Paisa) **Composition:** Brass **Note:** Previous KM#892.

Date	VG	F	VF	XF	Unc
SH1300 (1921)	4.00	8.00	15.00	30.00	—

KM# 893 3 SHAHI (15 Paisa) **Composition:** Copper **Reverse:** Mosque in seven-pointed star

Date	VG	F	VF	XF	Unc
SH1300 (1921)	1.50	3.50	8.00	17.00	—
SH1301 (1922)	1.50	3.50	8.00	17.00	—

Note: 2 varieties of SH1301 exist

Date	VG	F	VF	XF	Unc
SH130x (1923) (error)	—	—	—	—	—
SH1303 (1924)	1.50	3.50	8.00	17.00	—

KM# 891 3 SHAHI (15 Paisa) **Composition:** Brass **Obverse:** Eight stars around perimeter **Reverse:** Eight stars around perimeter

Date	VG	F	VF	XF	Unc
SH1300 (1921)	—	—	—	—	—

KM# 874 ABBASI (20 Paisa) **Composition:** Copper Or Billon

Date	VG	F	VF	XF	Unc
SH1298 (1919)	50.00	75.00	90.00	150	—

KM# 882 ABBASI (20 Paisa) **Composition:** Copper Or Billon **Size:** 25 mm.

Date	VG	F	VF	XF	Unc
SH1299 (1920)	15.00	30.00	50.00	75.00	—

KM# 883 ABBASI (20 Paisa) **Composition:** Copper Or Billon

Date	VG	F	VF	XF	Unc
SH1299 (1920)	2.00	6.00	15.00	30.00	—
SH1300 (1921)	2.00	6.00	15.00	30.00	—
SH1301 (1922)	2.00	6.00	15.00	30.00	—

Note: Two varieties for date SH1301 exist

Date	VG	F	VF	XF	Unc
SH1302 (1923)	2.00	6.00	15.00	30.00	—
SH2031 (1923) Error	7.00	15.00	30.00	50.00	—
SH1303 (1924)	2.00	6.00	15.00	30.00	—

KM# 866 1/2 RUPEE (Qiran) **Composition:** Silver **Obverse:** Legend within circle and wreath

Date	VG	F	VF	XF	Unc
AH1337 (1918)	150	300	500	725	—

KM# 875 1/2 RUPEE (Qiran) **Weight:** 4.7500 g. **Composition:** 0.5000 Silver .0763 oz. ASW **Obverse:** Star above inscription, "Shamsi"

Date	VG	F	VF	XF	Unc
SH1298 (1919)	3.00	6.00	10.00	20.00	—

Note: Two varieties are known

KM# 876 1/2 RUPEE (Qiran) **Weight:** 4.7500 g. **Composition:** 0.5000 Silver .0763 oz. ASW **Obverse:** "Al-Ghazi" above inscription, "Shamsi"

Date	VG	F	VF	XF	Unc
SH1298 (1919)	15.00	30.00	50.00	75.00	—

KM# 884 1/2 RUPEE (Qiran) **Weight:** 4.7500 g. **Composition:** 0.5000 Silver .0763 oz. ASW **Obverse:** Without "Shamsi"

Date	VG	F	VF	XF	Unc
SH1299 (1920)	3.00	4.00	7.00	15.00	—

Note: Two varieties are known dated 1299

Date	VG	F	VF	XF	Unc
SH1300 (1921)	3.00	4.00	7.00	15.00	—

KM# 894 1/2 RUPEE (Qiran) **Weight:** 4.7500 g. **Composition:** 0.5000 Silver .0763 oz. ASW

Date	VG	F	VF	XF	Unc
SH1300 (1921)	2.00	4.00	7.00	12.00	—
SH1301 (1922)	2.00	4.00	7.00	12.00	—
SH1302 (1923)	2.00	4.00	7.00	12.00	—
SH1303 (1924)	2.00	4.00	7.00	12.00	—

KM# 867 RUPEE **Weight:** 9.2000 g. **Composition:** 0.5000 Silver .0755 oz. ASW **Obverse:** Name and titles of Amanullah, star above inscription

Date	VG	F	VF	XF	Unc
AH1337 (1918)	6.00	10.00	18.00	30.00	—

Note: Seven varieties are known

KM# 877 RUPEE **Weight:** 9.0000 g. **Composition:** 0.9000 Silver .2604 oz. ASW **Obverse:** "Al-Ghazi" above inscription

Date	VG	F	VF	XF	Unc
SH1298 (1919)	4.50	6.50	10.00	18.50	—

Note: Four varieties are known for date SH1298

Date	VG	F	VF	XF	Unc
SH1299 (1920)	4.50	6.50	10.00	18.50	—

Note: Two varieties are known for date SH1299

KM# 885 RUPEE **Weight:** 9.2500 g. **Composition:** 0.9000 Silver .2676 oz. ASW **Obverse:** Toughra of Amanullah

Date	VG	F	VF	XF	Unc
SH1299 (1920)	4.00	5.00	8.00	16.50	—
SH1300 (1921)	4.00	5.00	8.00	16.50	—
SH1301 (1922)	4.00	5.00	8.00	16.50	—
SH1302/1 (1923)	4.00	5.00	8.00	16.50	—
SH1302 (1923)	4.00	5.00	8.00	16.50	—
SH1303 (1924)	4.00	5.00	8.00	16.50	—

KM# 878 2-1/2 RUPEES **Weight:** 22.9200 g. **Composition:** 0.9000 Silver .6632 oz. ASW **Note:** Two varieties each are known for dates SH 1298-1300.

Date	VG	F	VF	XF	Unc
SH1298 (1919)	12.50	16.50	20.00	45.00	—
SH1299 (1920)	8.50	12.50	17.50	40.00	—
SH1300 (1921)	8.50	12.50	17.50	40.00	—
SH1301 (1922)	8.50	12.50	15.00	35.00	—
SH1302 (1923)	8.50	12.50	15.00	35.00	—
SH1303 (1924)	8.50	12.50	15.00	35.00	—

KM# 834.1 5 RUPEES **Weight:** 45.6000 g. **Composition:** 0.9000 Silver 1.3194 oz. ASW **Reverse:** Similar to KM#826

Date	VG	F	VF	XF	Unc
AH1319	25.00	45.00	85.00	160	—

KM# 834.2 5 RUPEES **Weight:** 45.6000 g. **Composition:** 0.9000 Silver 1.3194 oz. ASW **Obverse:** Date at left of toughra

Date	VG	F	VF	XF	Unc
AH1319	25.00	45.00	85.00	160	—

KM# 843 5 RUPEES **Weight:** 45.6000 g. **Composition:** 0.9000 Silver 1.3194 oz. ASW **Note:** Most dates are recut dies. Two varieties are known for each date, AH1324 and 1327.

Date	VG	F	VF	XF	Unc
AH1322	20.00	25.00	45.00	90.00	—
AH1324	15.00	20.00	45.00	85.00	—
AH1326	15.00	20.00	45.00	85.00	—
AH1327/6	15.00	20.00	45.00	85.00	—
AH1328	22.50	30.00	55.00	110	—
AH1329	25.00	40.00	70.00	135	—

KM# 886 1/2 AMANI (5 Rupees) **Weight:** 2.3000 g. **Composition:** 0.9000 Gold .0665 oz. AGW

Date	VG	F	VF	XF	Unc
SH1299 (1920)	50.00	65.00	90.00	125	—

KM# 911 1/2 AMANI (5 Rupees) **Weight:** 3.0000 g. **Composition:** 0.9000 Gold .0868 oz. AGW

Date	F	VF	XF	Unc
SH1304/7 (1925)	55.00	85.00	110	150
SH1305/8 (1926)	55.00	85.00	110	150
SH1306/9 (1927)	55.00	85.00	110	150

KM# 868.1 TILLA (10 Rupees) **Weight:** 4.6000 g. **Composition:** 0.9000 Gold .1331 oz. AGW **Obv. Legend:** "Amanullah..." **Reverse:** Crossed swords below mosque

Date	VG	F	VF	XF	Unc
AH1337	100	125	160	225	—

KM# 868.2 TILLA (10 Rupees) **Weight:** 4.6000 g. **Composition:** 0.9000 Gold .1331 oz. AGW **Reverse:** 6-pointed star below mosque

Date	VG	F	VF	XF	Unc
AH1337	100	135	175	250	—

KM# 887 AMANI (10 Rupees) **Weight:** 4.6000 g. **Composition:** 0.9000 Gold .1331 oz. AGW

Date	VG	F	VF	XF	Unc
SH1299 (1920)	70.00	90.00	130	175	—

KM# 912 AMANI **Weight:** 6.0000 g. **Composition:** 0.9000 Gold .1736 oz. AGW

Date	F	VF	XF	Unc
SH1304/7 (1925)	75.00	95.00	125	180
SH1305/8 (1926)	75.00	95.00	150	220
SH1306/9 (1927)	75.00	95.00	125	180

KM# 888 2 AMANI (20 Rupees) **Weight:** 9.2000 g. **Composition:** 0.9000 Gold .2662 oz. AGW

Date	VG	F	VF	XF	Unc
SH1299 (1920)	100	125	185	265	300
SH1300 (1921)	100	125	185	265	300
SH1301 (1922)	100	125	185	265	300
SH1302 (1923)	100	125	185	265	300
SH1303 (1924)	100	125	185	265	300

KM# 914 2-1/2 AMANI **Weight:** 15.0000 g. **Composition:** 0.9000 Gold .4340 oz. AGW

Date	F	VF	XF	Unc
SH1306/9 (1927)	—	—	5,000	6,900

KM# 900 HABIBI (30 Rupees) **Weight:** 4.6000 g. **Composition:** 0.9000 Gold .1331 oz. AGW **Obverse:** Small star replaces "30 Rupees" in legend

Date	VG	F	VF	XF	Unc
AH1347	85.00	125	200	325	—

DECIMAL COINAGE

100 Pul = 1 Afghani; 20 Afghani = 1 Amani

KM# 905 2 PUL **Weight:** 2.0000 g. **Composition:** Bronze Or Brass

Date	F	VF	XF	Unc
SH1304 (1925)	3.00	5.00	9.00	15.00
SH1305 (1926)	3.00	5.00	9.00	15.00

KM# 913 2-1/2 AFGHANIS **Weight:** 25.0000 g. **Composition:** 0.9000 Silver .7234 oz. ASW **Note:** Two varieties are known for each date.

Date	F	VF	XF	Unc
SH1305/8 (1926)	15.00	25.00	50.00	125
SH1306/9 (1927)	15.00	20.00	40.00	80.00

Habibullah

Rebel known as Baccha - I - Saqao; AH1347-1348/1929AD

LOCAL COINAGE

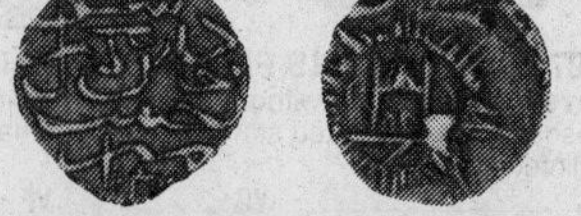

KM# 969 5 PAISE **Composition:** Brass **Note:** Struck at Herat.

Date	Good	VG	F	VF	XF
AH1347	5.00	8.50	15.00	22.50	—

KM# 970.1 10 PAISE **Composition:** Brass **Reverse:** Denomination "Dah" written above "Paisa" **Note:** Struck at Herat.

Date	Good	VG	F	VF	XF
AH1347	6.00	10.00	16.50	25.00	—

KM# 970.2 10 PAISE **Composition:** Brass **Reverse:** Denomination "Dah" written at right of "Paisa" **Note:** Struck at Herat.

Date	Good	VG	F	VF	XF
AH1347	7.50	12.50	20.00	30.00	—

KM# 972 20 PAISE **Composition:** Brass **Note:** Struck at Herat.

Date	Good	VG	F	VF	XF
AH1347	7.50	12.50	20.00	30.00	—

MILLED COINAGE

10 Dinar = 1 Paisa; 5 Paise = 1 Shahi; 2 Shahi = 1 Sanar; 2 Sanar = 1 Abbasi; 1-1/2 Abbasi = 1 Qiran; 2 Qiran = 1 Kabuli Rupee; 1 Tilla = 10 Rupees

KM# 901 10 PAISE **Composition:** Copper

Date	VG	F	VF	XF	Unc
AH1348	6.00	12.00	20.00	40.00	—

KM# 895 20 PAISE **Composition:** Bronze Or Brass

Date	VG	F	VF	XF	Unc
AH1347	3.00	5.00	7.50	17.50	—

KM# 896 1/2 RUPEE (Qiran) **Weight:** 4.7000 g. **Composition:** 0.5000 Silver .0755 oz. ASW

Date	VG	F	VF	XF	Unc
AH1347	4.00	7.00	12.00	20.00	—

KM# 902 1/2 RUPEE (Qiran) **Weight:** 4.7000 g. **Composition:** 0.5000 Silver .0755 oz. ASW

Date	VG	F	VF	XF	Unc
AH1348	12.00	20.00	32.00	50.00	—

KM# 897 RUPEE **Weight:** 9.1000 g. **Composition:** 0.9000 Silver .2633 oz. ASW **Obverse:** Name and titles of Amir Habibullah (The Usurper)

Date	VG	F	VF	XF	Unc
AH1347	4.00	8.00	15.00	25.00	—

KM# 898 RUPEE **Weight:** 9.1000 g. **Composition:** 0.9000 Silver .2633 oz. ASW **Obverse:** Title in circle

Date	VG	F	VF	XF	Unc
AH1347	25.00	35.00	55.00	90.00	—

KM# 899 HABIBI (30 Rupees) **Weight:** 4.6000 g. **Composition:** 0.9000 Gold .1331 oz. AGW

Date	VG	F	VF	XF	Unc
AH1347	85.00	125	200	325	—

Muhammed Nadir Shah
AH1348-1350, SH1310-1312/1929-1933AD

DECIMAL COINAGE

100 Pul = 1 Afghani; 20 Afghani = 1 Amani

KM# A922 PUL **Composition:** Bronze Or Brass

Date	F	VF	XF	Unc
AH1349 (1930)	0.75	1.25	1.75	2.50

KM# 922 PUL **Composition:** Bronze Or Brass **Obverse:** Toughra

Date	F	VF	XF	Unc
AH1349 (1930)	100	250	300	400

KM# 917 2 PUL **Weight:** 2.0000 g. **Composition:** Bronze Or Brass

Date	F	VF	XF	Unc
AH1348 (1929)	1.25	2.50	3.50	8.00
AH1349/8 (1930)	1.25	2.50	3.50	8.00

KM# 923 5 PUL **Weight:** 3.0000 g. **Composition:** Bronze Or Brass

Date	F	VF	XF	Unc
AH1349 (1930)	1.75	2.75	4.50	12.50
AH1350 (1931)	1.25	2.25	3.50	12.50

Note: Two varieties are known dated AH1350

KM# 929 5 PUL **Weight:** 3.0000 g. **Composition:** Bronze Or Brass

Date	F	VF	XF	Unc
SH1311 (1932)	2.50	5.50	9.00	20.00
SH1312 (1933)	2.50	5.50	9.00	20.00
SH1313 (1934)	2.50	5.50	9.00	20.00
SH1314 (1935)	2.50	5.50	9.00	20.00

KM# 918 10 PUL **Composition:** Copper Or Brass **Note:** Illustration shows an example struck off-center; prices are for properly struck specimens.

Date	F	VF	XF	Unc
AH1348 (1929)	2.00	3.50	5.00	15.00
AH1349 (1930) 2 varieties	2.25	4.00	5.50	15.00

KM# 930 10 PUL **Composition:** Bronze Or Brass

Date	F	VF	XF	Unc
SH1311 (1932)	1.50	2.50	4.00	15.00
SH1312 (1933)	1.50	2.50	4.00	15.00
SH1313 (1934)	1.50	2.50	4.00	15.00
SH1314 (1935)	1.50	2.50	4.00	15.00

KM# 919 20 PUL **Composition:** Copper Or Brass

Date	F	VF	XF	Unc
AH1348 (1929)	2.00	4.00	10.00	22.00
AH1349 (1930)	3.00	5.00	12.00	25.00

KM# 924 25 PUL **Composition:** Copper Or Brass

Date	F	VF	XF	Unc
AH1349	2.50	5.00	10.00	20.00

Note: Two varieties are known dated AH1349.

KM# 920 1/2 AFGHANI (50 Pul) **Weight:** 5.0000 g. **Composition:** 0.5000 Silver .0803 oz. ASW **Obverse:** Date below mosque **Note:** Previous KM#919.

Date	F	VF	XF	Unc
AH1348/1 (1929)	1.50	2.50	5.00	14.00
AH1349/2 (1930)	1.50	2.50	5.00	14.00
AH1350/3 (1931)	1.50	2.50	5.00	14.00

KM# 926 1/2 AFGHANI (50 Pul) **Weight:** 4.7500 g. **Composition:** 0.5000 Silver .0763 oz. ASW

Date	F	VF	XF	Unc
SH1310 (1931)	1.75	3.00	5.50	15.00
SH1311 (1932)	1.50	2.25	4.50	12.50

Note: Two die varieties exist

Date	F	VF	XF	Unc
SH1312 (1933)	1.75	3.00	5.50	15.00

Note: With and without diamond-shaped dot beneath the wreath on the obverse

KM# 921 AFGHANI (100 Pul) **Weight:** 9.9500 g. **Composition:** 0.9000 Silver .2879 oz. ASW

Date	F	VF	XF	Unc
AH1348 (1929)	3.00	5.00	9.00	16.50
AH1349 (1930)	3.00	5.00	9.00	16.50
AH1350 (1931)	3.00	5.00	9.00	16.50

KM# 927.1 AFGHANI (100 Pul) **Weight:** 10.0000 g. **Composition:** 0.9000 Silver .2893 oz. ASW

Date	F	VF	XF	Unc
SH1310 (1931)	40.00	55.00	70.00	100
SH1311 (1932)	110	160	180	260

KM# 927.2 AFGHANI (100 Pul) **Weight:** 10.0000 g. **Composition:** 0.9000 Silver .2893 oz. ASW **Note:** Thick flan.

Date	F	VF	XF	Unc
SH1310 (1931)	250	375	500	700

KM# 925 20 AFGHANIS **Weight:** 6.0000 g. **Composition:** 0.9000 Gold .1736 oz. AGW

Date	F	VF	XF	Unc
AH1348 (1929)	125	175	200	300
AH1349 (1930)	85.00	110	165	240
AH1350 (1931)	85.00	110	165	240

Muhammed Zahir Shah
SH1312-1352/1933-1973AD

DECIMAL COINAGE

100 Pul = 1 Afghani; 20 Afghani = 1 Amani

KM# 928 2 PUL **Weight:** 2.0000 g. **Composition:** Bronze Or Brass

Date	F	VF	XF	Unc
SH1311 (1932)	2.00	3.00	4.00	12.00
SH1312 (1933)	1.50	2.25	3.00	10.00
SH1313 (1934)	1.75	2.75	3.75	10.00
SH1314 (1935)	2.00	3.00	4.00	12.00

KM# 936 2 PUL **Composition:** Bronze

Date	F	VF	XF	Unc
SH1316 (1937)	0.15	0.20	0.35	1.00

KM# 937 3 PUL **Composition:** Bronze

Date	F	VF	XF	Unc
SH1316 (1937)	0.35	0.50	0.75	2.00

KM# 938 5 PUL **Composition:** Bronze

Date	F	VF	XF	Unc
SH1316 (1937)	0.35	0.50	0.75	2.00

KM# 939 10 PUL **Composition:** Copper-Nickel

Date	F	VF	XF	Unc
SH1316 (1937)	0.40	0.65	1.00	3.00

KM# 931 25 PUL **Composition:** Bronze Or Brass

Date	F	VF	XF	Unc
SH1312 (1933)	2.00	4.00	12.00	25.00
SH1313 (1934)	2.00	4.00	12.00	25.00
SH1314 (1935)	2.00	4.50	14.00	28.00
SH1316 (1937)	2.00	4.50	14.00	28.00

KM# 940 25 PUL **Composition:** Copper-Nickel

Date	F	VF	XF	Unc
SH1316 (1937)	0.60	0.75	1.50	3.50

KM# 941 25 PUL **Composition:** Bronze

Date	F	VF	XF	Unc
SH1330 (1951)	0.30	0.50	0.75	2.50
SH1331 (1952)	0.30	0.50	0.75	2.50
SH1332 (1953)	0.30	0.50	0.75	2.50
SH1333 (1954)	1.00	2.00	3.50	6.00

KM# 943 25 PUL **Composition:** Nickel Clad Steel **Edge:** Reeded

Date	F	VF	XF	Unc
SH1331 (1952)	1.00	2.00	3.50	7.00
SH1332 (1953)	1.50	3.00	5.00	9.00

KM# 944 25 PUL **Composition:** Nickel Clad Steel **Edge:** Plain

Date	F	VF	XF	Unc
SH1331 (1952)	0.35	0.65	1.00	3.00
SH1332 (1953)	0.35	0.65	1.00	3.00
SH1333 (1954)	0.35	0.65	1.00	3.00
SH1334/2 (1955)	1.50	3.00	5.00	9.00
SH1334 (1955)	0.35	0.65	1.00	3.00

KM# 945 25 PUL **Composition:** Aluminum **Note:** Struck on oversize 2 Afghani KM#949 planchets in 1970.

Date	F	VF	XF	Unc
SH1331 (1952)	0.50	1.00	3.00	10.00

KM# 932.1 1/2 AFGHANI (50 Pul) **Weight:** 4.7500 g. **Composition:** 0.5000 Silver .0763 oz. ASW **Obverse:** Smaller dotted circle

Date	F	VF	XF	Unc
SH1312 (1933)	1.75	3.00	6.00	16.00

KM# 932.2 1/2 AFGHANI (50 Pul) **Weight:** 4.7500 g. **Composition:** 0.5000 Silver .0763 oz. ASW **Obverse:** Larger dotted circle

Date	F	VF	XF	Unc
SH1313 (1934)	1.75	3.00	6.00	16.00
SH1314 (1935)	1.75	3.00	6.00	16.00
SH1315 (1936)	1.50	2.50	5.50	15.00
SH1316 (1937)	1.50	2.50	5.50	15.00

KM# 942.1 1/2 AFGHANI (50 Pul) **Composition:** Bronze **Obverse:** Denomination in numerals **Size:** 22.5 mm.

Date	F	VF	XF	Unc
SH1330 (1951)	0.50	1.00	2.00	4.00
SH133x (1951)	1.50	3.00	5.00	9.00

KM# 942.2 1/2 AFGHANI (50 Pul) **Composition:** Bronze **Size:** 24 mm.

Date	F	VF	XF	Unc
SH1330 (1951)	20.00	30.00	40.00	50.00

KM# 946 1/2 AFGHANI (50 Pul) **Composition:** Nickel Clad Steel

Date	F	VF	XF	Unc
SH1331 (1952)	0.20	0.35	0.65	2.00
SH1332 (1953)	0.20	0.35	0.65	2.00
SH1333 (1954)	1.00	2.00	3.50	6.00
SH1334/2 (1955)	0.40	0.65	1.00	2.50
SH1334 (1955)	0.20	0.35	0.65	2.00

KM# 947 1/2 AFGHANI (50 Pul) Composition: Nickel Clad Steel **Obverse:** Denomination in words

Date	F	VF	XF	Unc
SH1331 (1952)	0.50	1.00	2.00	4.00
SH133x (1953)	5.00	7.50	12.50	20.00

KM# 953 AFGHANI (100 Pul) Composition: Nickel Clad Steel

Date	F	VF	XF	Unc
SH1340 (1961)	0.20	0.35	0.60	1.25

KM# 949 2 AFGHANIS Composition: Aluminum **Note:** This issue was withdrawn and demonetized due to extensive counterfeiting.

Date	F	VF	XF	Unc
SH1337 (1958)	0.60	1.00	1.50	2.50

KM# 954.1 2 AFGHANIS Composition: Nickel Clad Steel **Note:** Coin type.

Date	F	VF	XF	Unc
SH1340 (1961)	0.25	0.45	0.85	2.00

KM# 954.2 2 AFGHANIS Composition: Nickel Clad Steel **Note:** Medallic die orientation.

Date	F	VF	XF	Unc
SH1340 (1961)	0.75	1.25	2.25	5.00

Note: Some evidence indicates that this variety was the first Republican issue struck in 1973

KM# 955 5 AFGHANIS Composition: Nickel Clad Steel **Note:** Mohammed Sahir Shah

Date	F	VF	XF	Unc
SH1340(1961) (1921)	0.35	0.75	1.50	3.00

KM# 950 5 AFGHANIS Composition: Aluminum **Note:** This issue was withdrawn and demonetized due to extensive counterfeiting.

Date	F	VF	XF	Unc
SH1337 (1958)	1.00	2.00	3.50	5.00

KM# 948 10 AFGHANIS Composition: Aluminum

Date	F	VF	XF	Unc
SH1336 (1957)	—	—	—	900

KM# 935 4 GRAMS Weight: 4.0000 g. **Composition:** 0.9000 Gold .1157 oz. AGW

Date	F	VF	XF	Unc
SH1315 (1936)	65.00	90.00	125	165
SH1317 (1938)	65.00	90.00	125	165

KM# 933 TILLA Weight: 6.0000 g. **Composition:** 0.9000 Gold .1736 oz. AGW

Date	F	VF	XF	Unc
SH1313 (1934)	125	150	185	275

KM# 934 8 GRAMS Weight: 8.0000 g. **Composition:** 0.9000 Gold .2314 oz. AGW

Date	F	VF	XF	Unc
SH1314 (1935)	95.00	120	160	250
SH1315 (1936)	95.00	120	160	250
SH1317 (1938)	95.00	120	160	250

KM# 952 8 GRAMS Weight: 8.0000 g. **Composition:** 0.9000 Gold .2314 oz. AGW

Date	Mintage	F	VF	XF	Unc
SH1339 (1960)	200	—	—	300	800

Note: Struck for royal presentation purposes. Specimens struck with the same dies (including the "8 grams", the "8" having been effaced after striking), but on thin planchets weighing 3.9-4.0 grams, exist, they are regarded as "mint sports". Market value $250.00 in Unc

REPUBLIC
SH1352-1357 / 1973-1978AD
STANDARD COINAGE

KM# 975 25 PUL Composition: Brass Clad Steel

Date	Mintage	F	VF	XF	Unc
SH1352(1973)	45,950,000	0.25	0.50	1.00	2.00

KM# 976 50 PUL Composition: Copper Clad Steel

Date	Mintage	F	VF	XF	Unc
SH1352(1973)	24,750,000	0.50	1.00	2.00	4.00

KM# 977 5 AFGHANIS Composition: Copper-Nickel Clad Steel

Date	Mintage	F	VF	XF	Unc
SH1352(1973)	34,750,000	1.75	3.50	5.00	10.00

KM# 978 250 AFGHANIS Weight: 28.5700 g. **Composition:** 0.9250 Silver .8496 oz. ASW **Series:** Conservation **Subject:** Snow Leopard

Date	Mintage	F	VF	XF	Unc
1978	4,370	—	—	—	30.00

KM# 979 250 AFGHANIS Weight: 28.2800 g. **Composition:** 0.9250 Silver .8410 oz. ASW **Series:** Conservation **Subject:** Snow Leopard

Date	Mintage	F	VF	XF	Unc
1978 Proof	4,387	Value: 38.00			

KM# 980 500 AFGHANIS Weight: 35.3000 g. **Composition:** 0.9250 Silver 1.0498 oz. ASW **Series:** Conservation **Subject:** Siberian Crane

Date	Mintage	F	VF	XF	Unc
1978	4,374	—	—	—	25.00

KM# 981 500 AFGHANIS Weight: 35.0000 g. **Composition:** 0.9250 Silver 1.0408 oz. ASW **Series:** Conservation **Subject:** Siberian Crane

Date	Mintage	F	VF	XF	Unc
1978 Proof	4,218	Value: 35.00			

KM# 982 10000 AFGHANIS Weight: 33.4370 g. **Composition:** 0.9000 Gold .9676 oz. AGW **Series:** Conservation **Subject:** Marco Polo Sheep

Date	Mintage	F	VF	XF	Unc
1978	694	—	—	—	550
1978 Proof	181	Value: 950			

DEMOCRATIC REPUBLIC

SH1358-1371 / 1979-1992AD

STANDARD COINAGE

KM# 990 25 PUL Composition: Aluminum-Bronze

Date	F	VF	XF	Unc
SH1357 (1978)	0.25	0.50	1.00	2.00

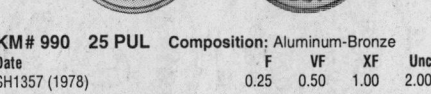

KM# 996 25 PUL Composition: Aluminum-Bronze

Date	F	VF	XF	Unc
SH1359 (1980)	0.20	0.35	0.70	1.50

KM# 992 50 PUL Weight: 3.0000 g. **Composition:** Aluminum-Bronze

Date	F	VF	XF	Unc
SH1357 (1978)	0.50	0.80	1.50	2.50

KM# 997 50 PUL Composition: Aluminum-Bronze

Date	F	VF	XF	Unc
SH1359 (1980)	0.25	0.50	1.00	2.00

KM# 993 AFGHANI Composition: Copper-Nickel

Date	F	VF	XF	Unc
SH1357 (1978)	0.60	1.00	2.00	4.00

KM# 998 AFGHANI Composition: Copper-Nickel

Date	F	VF	XF	Unc
SH1359 (1980)	0.50	0.80	1.50	2.50

KM# 994 2 AFGHANIS Composition: Copper-Nickel

Date	F	VF	XF	Unc
SH1357 (1978)	1.00	1.50	2.00	4.00
SH1358 (1979)	1.00	1.50	2.00	4.00

KM# 999 2 AFGHANIS Composition: Copper-Nickel **Obverse:** Similar to 1 Afghani, KM#998

Date	F	VF	XF	Unc
SH1359 (1980)	0.60	1.00	1.50	3.00

KM# 995 5 AFGHANIS Weight: 7.4000 g. **Composition:** Copper-Nickel

Date	F	VF	XF	Unc
SH1357 (1978)	1.00	2.00	4.00	6.50

KM# 1000 5 AFGHANIS Weight: 7.4000 g. **Composition:** Copper-Nickel

Date	F	VF	XF	Unc
SH1359 (1980)	1.00	1.50	2.00	4.00

KM# 1001 5 AFGHANIS Composition: Brass **Series:** F.A.O **Subject:** World Food Day

Date	F	VF	XF	Unc
SH1360 (1981)	0.25	0.50	1.00	1.75

KM# 1015 10 AFGHANIS Composition: Brass **Subject:** 70th Anniversary of Independence

Date	F	VF	XF	Unc
1989	—	—	—	3.50

KM# 1016 50 AFGHANIS Composition: Copper-Nickel **Subject:** 100 Years of the Automobile

Date	F	VF	XF	Unc
ND	—	—	—	14.00

KM# 1006 50 AFGHANIS Composition: Copper-Nickel **Series:** World Wildlife Fund **Subject:** Leopard

Date	Mintage	F	VF	XF	Unc
1987	28,000	—	—	—	15.00

KM# 1024 50 AFGHANIS Composition: Copper **Series:** Prehistoric Animals **Subject:** Deinotherium - Elephant

Date	F	VF	XF	Unc
1993	—	—	—	15.00

KM# 1032 50 AFGHANIS Composition: Copper **Series:** Prehistoric Animals **Subject:** Ankylosaurus

Date	Mintage	F	VF	XF	Unc
1995 Proof	100	Value: 65.00			

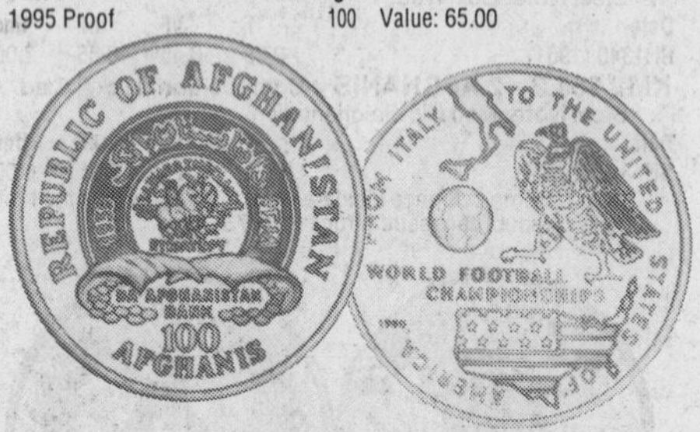

KM# 1014 100 AFGHANIS Composition: Copper-Nickel **Series:** World Soccer Championship **Subject:** Italy to U.S.A.

Date	Mintage	F	VF	XF	Unc
1990 Proof	10,000	Value: 14.00			

KM# 1017 250 AFGHANIS Weight: 20.3100 g. **Composition:** 0.9250 Silver .8716 oz. ASW **Series:** Conservation **Subject:** Snow Leopard

Date	F	VF	XF	Unc
1978 4 Known				500

KM# 1018 500 AFGHANIS **Weight:** 35.4400 g. **Composition:** 0.9250 Silver 1.0539 oz. ASW **Series:** Conservation **Subject:** Siberian Crane

Date	F	VF	XF	Unc
1978 4 known	—	—	—	500

KM# 1002 500 AFGHANIS **Weight:** 9.0600 g. **Composition:** 0.9000 Silver .2622 oz. ASW **Series:** F.A.O. **Subject:** World Food Day

Date	F	VF	XF	Unc
SH1360(1981) Proof	—	Value: 25.00		

KM# 1003 500 AFGHANIS **Weight:** 12.0000 g. **Composition:** 0.9990 Silver .3855 oz. ASW **Series:** 100th Anniversary of the Automobile

Date	Mintage	F	VF	XF	Unc
ND	2,000	—	—	—	40.00

KM# 1004 500 AFGHANIS **Weight:** 12.0000 g. **Composition:** 0.9990 Silver .3855 oz. ASW **Series:** 1988 Winter Olympics **Subject:** Skaters

Date	Mintage	F	VF	XF	Unc
ND	10,000	—	—	—	35.00

KM# 1005 500 AFGHANIS **Weight:** 12.0000 g. **Composition:** 0.9990 Silver .3855 oz. ASW **Series:** Wildlife Preservation **Subject:** Leopard

Date	Mintage	F	VF	XF	Unc
1986	5,000	—	—	—	35.00

KM# 1010 500 AFGHANIS **Weight:** 12.0000 g. **Composition:** 0.9990 Silver .3855 oz. ASW **Series:** 1988 Summer Olympics **Subject:** Volleyball **Note:** Struck at Havana.

Date	Mintage	F	VF	XF	Unc
1987 (k)	10,000	—	—	—	25.00

KM# 1007 500 AFGHANIS **Weight:** 12.0000 g. **Composition:** 0.9990 Silver .3855 oz. ASW **Subject:** European Soccer Championship - West Germany **Note:** Struck at Havana.

Date	F	VF	XF	Unc
1988 (k)	—	—	—	37.50

KM# 1009 500 AFGHANIS **Weight:** 16.0000 g. **Composition:** 0.9990 Silver .5145 oz. ASW **Series:** 1986 World Soccer Championship - Mexico

Date	Mintage	F	VF	XF	Unc
ND	5,000	—	—	—	32.00

KM# 1008.2 500 AFGHANIS **Weight:** 16.0000 g. **Composition:** 0.9990 Silver .5145 oz. ASW **Series:** 1992 Winter Olympics **Subject:** Bobsledding **Obverse:** Tall thin letters

Date	Mintage	F	VF	XF	Unc
1989 Proof	Inc. above	Value: 35.00			

KM# 1008.1 500 AFGHANIS **Weight:** 16.0000 g. **Composition:** 0.9990 Silver .5145 oz. ASW **Series:** 1992 Winter Olympics **Subject:** Bobsledding **Obverse:** Short thick letters

Date	Mintage	F	VF	XF	Unc
1989 Proof	Est. 10,000	Value: 30.00			

KM# 1011 500 AFGHANIS **Weight:** 16.0000 g. **Composition:** 0.9990 Silver .5145 oz. ASW **Series:** 1990 World Soccer Championship **Subject:** Italy

Date	Mintage	F	VF	XF	Unc
1989 Proof	10,000	Value: 30.00			

KM# 1012 500 AFGHANIS **Weight:** 16.0000 g. **Composition:** 0.9990 Silver .5145 oz. ASW **Series:** 1992 Summer Olympics **Subject:** Field Hockey

Date	Mintage	F	VF	XF	Unc
1989 Proof	10,000	Value: 30.00			

KM# 1013 500 AFGHANIS **Weight:** 12.0000 g. **Composition:** 0.9990 Silver .3855 oz. ASW **Series:** 1994 World Cup Soccer Games U.S.A.

Date	F	VF	XF	Unc
1991	—	—	—	30.00

KM# 1022 500 AFGHANIS **Weight:** 20.0000 g. **Composition:** 0.9990 Silver .6430 oz. ASW **Series:** 1994 World Cup Soccer Games - U.S.A.

Date	Mintage	F	VF	XF	Unc
1992 Proof	—	Value: 45.00			

KM# 1020 500 AFGHANIS **Weight:** 16.0000 g. **Composition:** 0.9990 Silver .5145 oz. ASW **Series:** Prehistoric Animals **Subject:** Deinotherium - Elephant

Date	Mintage	F	VF	XF	Unc
1993 Proof	—	Value: 42.50			

KM# 1021 500 AFGHANIS **Weight:** 16.0000 g. **Composition:** 0.9990 Silver .5145 oz. ASW **Series:** Prehistoric Animals **Subject:** Styracosaurus

Date	F	VF	XF	Unc
1994 Proof	—	Value: 45.00		

KM# 1035 500 AFGHANIS **Weight:** 16.0000 g. **Composition:** 0.9990 Silver .5145 oz. ASW **Series:** Prehistoric Animals **Subject:** Ankylosaurus

Date	F	VF	XF	Unc
1995 Proof	—	Value: 50.00		

KM# 1023 500 AFGHANIS **Weight:** 20.0000 g. **Composition:** 0.9990 Silver .6430 oz. ASW **Series:** 1996 Olympics **Subject:** Three runners and building

Date	Mintage	F	VF	XF	Unc
1995 Proof	15,000	Value: 22.50			

KM# 1019 10000 AFGHANIS **Weight:** 33.6600 g. **Composition:** 0.9000 Gold .9739 oz. AGW **Series:** Conservation **Subject:** Marco Polo Sheep

Date	F	VF	XF	Unc
1978 4 Known				2,000

ISLAMIC STATE

SH1373-1381 / 1994-2002AD

STANDARD COINAGE

KM# 1026 50 AFGHANIS **Composition:** Copper-Nickel **Series:** 50th Anniversary - United Nations **Obverse:** State emblem **Reverse:** Meditating figure with three doves

Date	F	VF	XF	Unc
1996 Proof	—	Value: 35.00		

KM# 1030 50 AFGHANIS **Composition:** Copper-Nickel **Series:** World Food Summit **Obverse:** State emblem **Reverse:** Gate of Zafar

Date	F	VF	XF	Unc
1996	—	—	—	8.50

KM# 1037 50 AFGHANIS **Composition:** Copper-Nickel **Series:** Sydney Olympics 2000 **Obverse:** National emblem **Reverse:** Equestrian event

Date	Mintage	F	VF	XF	Unc
1999	10,000	—	—	—	7.50

KM# 1031 500 AFGHANIS **Weight:** 28.4300 g. **Composition:** 0.9250 Silver .8455 oz. ASW **Series:** 50th Anniversary United Nations **Obverse:** State emblem **Reverse:** Meditating figure with three doves

Date	F	VF	XF	Unc
ND Proof	—	Value: 35.00		

KM# 1040 500 AFGHANIS **Weight:** 20.0000 g. **Composition:** 0.9990 Silver 0.6424 oz. ASW **Subject:** World Cup Soccer **Obverse:** National arms **Reverse:** Multi-color soccer players, flags and ball **Edge:** Reeded **Size:** 38 mm.

Date	F	VF	XF	Unc
1996 Proof	—	Value: 35.00		

KM# 1025 500 AFGHANIS **Weight:** 20.0000 g. **Composition:** 0.9990 Silver .6430 oz. ASW **Subject:** Multi-color Lynx

Date	F	VF	XF	Unc
1996 Proof	—	Value: 50.00		

KM# 1027 500 AFGHANIS **Weight:** 20.0000 g. **Composition:** 0.9990 Silver .6430 oz. ASW **Series:** XVI World Cup Soccer **Subject:** France **Obverse:** State emblem **Reverse:** Soccer player going for goal

Date	Mintage	F	VF	XF	Unc
1996	100	—	—	—	100
1996 Proof	—	Value: 45.00			

KM# 1028 500 AFGHANIS **Weight:** 20.1300 g. **Composition:** 0.9990 Silver .6465 oz. ASW **Series:** World Food Summit **Obverse:** State emblem **Reverse:** Zafar Gate, FAO logo, dates

Date	F	VF	XF	Unc
1996 Proof	—	Value: 45.00		

KM# 1029 500 AFGHANIS **Weight:** 14.9500 g. **Composition:** 0.9990 Silver .4802 oz. ASW **Series:** World of Adventure **Obverse:** State emblem **Reverse:** Multicolor enamel airplane and statue, cameo portrait

Date	F	VF	XF	Unc
1996 Proof	—	Value: 45.00		

KM# 1036 500 AFGHANIS **Weight:** 20.3100 g. **Composition:** 0.9990 Silver .6465 oz. ASW **Series:** Sydney Olympics 2000 **Obverse:** National emblem **Reverse:** Winged goddess bearing torch, Greek temples behind

Date	Mintage	F	VF	XF	Unc
1996 Proof	500	Value: 40.00			

KM# 1036a 500 AFGHANIS **Weight:** 15.0000 g. **Composition:** 0.9990 Silver .6465 oz. ASW **Series:** Sydney Olympics 2000 **Reverse:** Winged Goddess bearing torch, Greek temples behind

Date		F	VF	XF	Unc
1998 Proof	7,500	Value: 27.50			

KM# 1039 500 AFGHANIS **Weight:** 15.0000 g. **Composition:** 0.9990 Silver .4818 oz. ASW **Subject:** 16th World Cup - Soccer **Obverse:** National arms **Reverse:** Soccer player on ball background **Edge:** Plain

Date		F	VF	XF	Unc
1997 Proof	—	Value: 37.50			

KM# 1033 500 AFGHANIS **Weight:** 20.0000 g. **Composition:** 0.9990 Silver .4818 oz. ASW **Series:** Sydney Olympics 2000 **Obverse:** National emblem **Reverse:** Javelin thrower

Date	Mintage	F	VF	XF	Unc
1998 Proof	5,000	Value: 37.50			

KM# 1034 500 AFGHANIS **Weight:** 20.0000 g. **Composition:** 0.9990 Silver .6430 oz. ASW **Subject:** Fauna of Asia **Obverse:** National emblem **Reverse:** Marco Polo Sheep

Date	Mintage	F	VF	XF	Unc
1998	100	—	—	—	75.00

KM# 1038 500 AFGHANIS **Weight:** 20.0000 g. **Composition:** 0.9990 Silver .6430 oz. ASW **Series:** Sydney Olympics 2000 **Obverse:** National emblem **Reverse:** Equestrian event

Date	Mintage	F	VF	XF	Unc
1999 Proof	5,000	Value: 30.00			

PATTERNS

Including off metal strikes

KM#	Date	Mintage	Identification	Mkt Val
Pn1	1310	—	1/2 Afghani. Silver. 4.7500 g.	—
Pn2	1336	—	5 Afghanis. Silver. Legend with off-center circle, denomination. National emblem with wreath, date	350
Pn3	1336	—	10 Afghanis. Silver. Toughra with off-center circle, denomination. National emblem with wreath, date	350

PIEFORTS

KM#	Date	Mintage	Identification	Mkt Val
P1.1	1989	110	500 Afghanis. 0.9990 Silver. KM#1008.2	85.00
P1.2	1989	—	500 Afghanis. 0.9990 Silver. KM#1008.2, pine tree without needles	125
P1.3	1989	—	500 Afghanis. 0.9990 Silver. KM#1008.2, pine tree with sagging branches	85.00
P1.4	1989	—	500 Afghanis. 0.9990 Silver. KM#1008.2, pine tree with uplifted branches	85.00
p2	1996	—	500 Afghanis. Silver. KM#1029	65.00
P3	1998	—	500 Afghanis. KM#1033	120
P4	1999	—	500 Afghanis. KM#1038	80.00

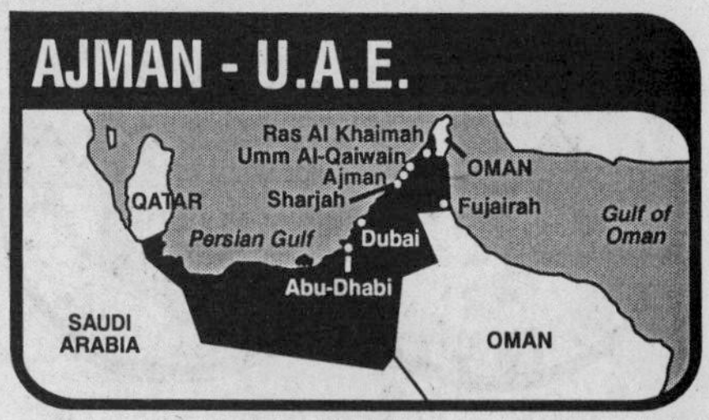

Ajman is the smallest and poorest of the emirates in the United Arab Emirates. It has an estimated area of 100sq. mi. (250 sq. km.) and a population of 6,000. Ajman's first act as an autonomous entity was entering into a treaty with Great Britain in 1820. On December 2, 1971 Ajman became one of the 6 original members of the United Arab Emirates.

TITLES

Ajman اجمان

RULERS

Abdul Aziz Bin Humaid al-Naimi, 1900-1908
Humaid Bin Abdul Aziz al-Naimi, 1908-1928
Rashid Bin Hamad al-Naimi, 1928-1981
Humaid Bin Rashid al-Naimi, 1981--

MONETARY SYSTEM

100 Dirhams = 1 Riyal

UNITED ARAB EMIRATE

NON-CIRCULATING LEGAL TENDER COINAGE

KM# 1.1 RIYAL **Weight:** 3.9500 g. **Composition:** 0.6400 Silver .0812 oz. ASW **Reverse:** Two dates

Date	Mintage	F	VF	XF	Unc	BU
AH1389 - 1969	20,000	—	—	—	7.50	—
AH1389 - 1969 Proof	1,200	Value: 15.00				

KM# 1.2 RIYAL **Weight:** 3.9500 g. **Composition:** 0.6400 Silver .0812 oz. ASW **Reverse:** Three dates

Date		F	VF	XF	Unc	BU
AH1390 - 1970		—	—	—	20.00	—

KM# 2.1 2 RIYALS **Weight:** 6.4500 g. **Composition:** 0.8350 Silver .1731 oz. ASW **Reverse:** Two dates

Date	Mintage	F	VF	XF	Unc	BU
AH1389-1969	20,000	—	—	—	15.00	—
AH1389-1969 Proof	1,200	Value: 25.00				

KM# 2.2 2 RIYALS **Weight:** 6.4500 g. **Composition:** 0.8350 Silver .1731 oz. ASW **Reverse:** Three dates

Date		F	VF	XF	Unc	BU
AH1390-1970		—	—	—	30.00	—

KM# 3.1 5 RIYALS **Weight:** 15.0000 g. **Composition:** 0.8350 Silver .4027 oz. ASW **Reverse:** Two dates

Date	Mintage	F	VF	XF	Unc	BU
AH1389-1969	10,000	—	—	—	22.50	—
AH1389-1969 Proof	1,200	Value: 40.00				

KM# 3.2 5 RIYALS **Weight:** 15.0000 g. **Composition:** 0.8350 Silver .4027 oz. ASW **Reverse:** Three dates

Date		F	VF	XF	Unc	BU
AH1390-1970		—	—	—	50.00	—
AH1390-1970 Proof	—	Value: 90.00				

KM# 12 5 RIYALS **Weight:** 15.0000 g. **Composition:** 0.9250 Silver .4460 oz. ASW **Subject:** Death of Gamal Abdel Nassar

Date	Mintage	F	VF	XF	Unc	BU
AH1390-1970 Proof	5,000	Value: 27.50				

KM# 17 5 RIYALS **Weight:** 15.0000 g. **Composition:** 0.9250 Silver .4460 oz. ASW **Reverse:** Dag Hammarskjold

Date	Mintage	F	VF	XF	Unc	BU
ND(1970) Proof	1,175	Value: 60.00				

KM# 18 5 RIYALS **Weight:** 15.0000 g. **Composition:** 0.9250 Silver .4460 oz. ASW **Reverse:** Mahatma Gandhi

Date	Mintage	F	VF	XF	Unc	BU
ND(1970) Proof	1,175	Value: 60.00				

KM# 19 5 RIYALS **Weight:** 15.0000 g. **Composition:** 0.9250 Silver .4460 oz. ASW **Reverse:** Martin Luther King

Date	Mintage	F	VF	XF	Unc	BU
ND(1970) Proof	1,175	Value: 60.00				

KM# 20 5 RIYALS **Weight:** 15.0000 g. **Composition:** 0.9250 Silver .4460 oz. ASW **Reverse:** George C. Marshall

Date	Mintage	F	VF	XF	Unc	BU
ND(1970) Proof	1,175	Value: 60.00				

KM# 21 5 RIYALS **Weight:** 15.0000 g. **Composition:** 0.9250 Silver .4460 oz. ASW **Reverse:** Bertrand A. Russell

Date	Mintage	F	VF	XF	Unc	BU
ND(1970) Proof	1,175	Value: 60.00				

KM# 22 5 RIYALS **Weight:** 15.0000 g. **Composition:** 0.9250 Silver .4460 oz. ASW **Reverse:** Albert Schweitzer

Date	Mintage	F	VF	XF	Unc	BU
ND(1970) Proof	1,175	Value: 60.00				

KM# 23 5 RIYALS **Weight:** 15.0000 g. **Composition:** 0.9250 Silver .4460 oz. ASW **Reverse:** Jan Palach

Date	Mintage	F	VF	XF	Unc	BU
ND(1970) Proof	1,175	Value: 60.00				

KM# 24 5 RIYALS **Weight:** 15.0000 g. **Composition:** 0.9250 Silver .4460 oz. ASW **Reverse:** Albert J. Luthuli

Date	Mintage	F	VF	XF	Unc	BU
ND(1970) Proof	1,175	Value: 60.00				

KM# 26 5 RIYALS **Weight:** 15.0000 g. **Composition:** 0.9250 Silver .4460 oz. ASW **Series:** F.A.O.

Date	Mintage	F	VF	XF	Unc	BU
AH1390-1970 Proof	2,000	Value: 70.00				

Note: This issue is not recognized by the FAO

KM# 27 5 RIYALS **Weight:** 15.0000 g. **Composition:** 0.9250 Silver .4460 oz. ASW **Subject:** Save Venice

Date	Mintage	F	VF	XF	Unc	BU
ND(1971) Proof	4,800	Value: 100				

KM# 5 7-1/2 RIYALS **Weight:** 23.0000 g. **Composition:** 0.9250 Silver .6840 oz. ASW **Subject:** Rashid bin Humaid al-Naimi **Reverse:** Bonefish

Date	Mintage	F	VF	XF	Unc	BU
AH1389-1970	4,350	—	—	—	55.00	—
AH1389-1970 Proof	650	Value: 85.00				

KM# 6 7-1/2 RIYALS **Weight:** 23.0000 g. **Composition:** 0.9250 Silver .6840 oz. ASW **Reverse:** Barbary Falcon

Date	Mintage	F	VF	XF	Unc	BU
AH1389-1970	4,350	—	—	—	55.00	—
AH1389-1970 Proof	650	Value: 85.00				

KM# 7 7-1/2 RIYALS **Weight:** 23.0000 g. **Composition:** 0.9250 Silver .6840 oz. ASW **Reverse:** Gazelle

Date	Mintage	F	VF	XF	Unc	BU
AH1389-1970	4,350	—	—	—	55.00	—
AH1389-1970 Proof	650	Value: 85.00				

KM# 13 7-1/2 RIYALS **Weight:** 23.0000 g. **Composition:** 0.8350 Silver .6175 oz. ASW **Subject:** Death of Gamal Abdel Nassar

Date	Mintage	F	VF	XF	Unc	BU
AH1390-1970 Proof	6,000	Value: 45.00				

KM# 9.1 10 RIYALS **Weight:** 30.0000 g. **Composition:** 0.9250 Silver .8923 oz. ASW **Reverse:** Vladimir Lenin

Date	F	VF	XF	Unc	BU
ND(1970) Proof	—	Value: 55.00			
ND(1970) Matte	—	—	—	—	—

KM# 9.2 10 RIYALS **Weight:** 30.0000 g. **Composition:** 0.9250 Silver .8923 oz. ASW **Obverse:** PROOF added

Date	Mintage	F	VF	XF	Unc	BU
ND(1970) Proof	3,200	Value: 45.00				

KM# 15 25 RIYALS **Weight:** 5.1750 g. **Composition:** 0.9000 Gold .1497 oz. AGW **Subject:** Death of Gamal Abdel Nassar

Date	Mintage	F	VF	XF	Unc	BU
AH1390 Proof	1,100	Value: 125				

Note: Some of these coins have a serial number on the obverse below the bust

KM# 28 25 RIYALS **Weight:** 5.1750 g. **Composition:** 0.9000 Gold .1497 oz. AGW **Reverse:** Dag Hammarskjold

Date	F	VF	XF	Unc	BU
ND(1970) Proof	—	Value: 135			

KM# 29 25 RIYALS **Weight:** 5.1750 g. **Composition:** 0.9000 Gold .1497 oz. AGW **Reverse:** Mahatma Gandi

Date	F	VF	XF	Unc	BU
ND(1970) Proof	—	Value: 135			

KM# 30 25 RIYALS **Weight:** 5.1750 g. **Composition:** 0.9000 Gold .1497 oz. AGW **Reverse:** Martin Luther King

Date	F	VF	XF	Unc	BU
ND(1970) Proof	—	Value: 135			

KM# 31 25 RIYALS **Weight:** 5.1750 g. **Composition:** 0.9000 Gold .1497 oz. AGW **Reverse:** George C. Marshall

Date	F	VF	XF	Unc	BU
ND(1970) Proof	—	Value: 135			

KM# 32 25 RIYALS **Weight:** 5.1750 g. **Composition:** 0.9000 Gold .1497 oz. AGW **Reverse:** Bertrand A. Russell

Date	F	VF	XF	Unc	BU
ND(1970) Proof	—	Value: 135			

KM# 33 25 RIYALS **Weight:** 5.1750 g. **Composition:** 0.9000 Gold .1497 oz. AGW **Reverse:** Albert Schweitzer

Date	F	VF	XF	Unc	BU
ND(1970) Proof	—	Value: 135			

KM# 34 25 RIYALS **Weight:** 5.1750 g. **Composition:** 0.9000 Gold .1497 oz. AGW **Reverse:** Jan Palach

Date	F	VF	XF	Unc	BU
ND(1970) Proof	—	Value: 135			

KM# 35 25 RIYALS **Weight:** 5.1750 g. **Composition:** 0.9000 Gold .1497 oz. AGW **Reverse:** Albert J. Luthuli

Date	F	VF	XF	Unc	BU
ND(1970) Proof	—	Value: 135			

KM# 36 25 RIYALS **Weight:** 5.1750 g. **Composition:** 0.9000 Gold .1497 oz. AGW **Rev. Legend:** Save Venice

Date	F	VF	XF	Unc	BU
ND(1971) Proof	—	Value: 150			

KM# 16 50 RIYALS **Weight:** 10.3500 g. **Composition:** 0.9000 Gold .2995 oz. AGW **Subject:** Death of Gamal Abdel Nassar **Obverse:** Arms **Reverse:** Gamal Abdel Nassar
Note: Similar to 7.5 Riyals, KM#13.

Date	Mintage	F	VF	XF	Unc	BU
AH1390 Proof	700	Value: 245				

Note: Some of these coins have a serial number below the bust on the obverse

KM# 39 50 RIYALS **Weight:** 10.3500 g. **Composition:** 0.9000 Gold .2995 oz. AGW **Subject:** Save Venice

Date	F	VF	XF	Unc	BU
ND(1971) Proof	—	Value: 265			

KM# 41 75 RIYALS **Weight:** 15.5300 g. **Composition:** 0.9000 Gold .4494 oz. AGW **Series:** F.A.O **Obverse:** Fish

Date	F	VF	XF	Unc	BU
AH1389-1969 Proof	—	Value: 385			

KM# 10 100 RIYALS **Weight:** 20.7000 g. **Composition:** 0.9000 Gold .5990 oz. AGW **Reverse:** Vladimir Lenin

Date	Mintage	F	VF	XF	Unc	BU
ND(1970) Proof	1,000	Value: 450				

KM# 40 100 RIYALS **Weight:** 20.7000 g. **Composition:** 0.9000 Gold .5990 oz. AGW **Subject:** Save Venice

Date	F	VF	XF	Unc	BU
ND(1971) Proof	—	Value: 465			

ESSAIS

With Assay or Proof

KM#	Date	Mintage	Identification	Mkt Val
E1	1969	1,250	Riyal. KM#1	15.00
E2	1969	1,250	2 Riyals. KM#2	20.00
E3	1969	1,250	5 Riyals. KM#3	30.00
E4	1970	100	Riyal.	35.00
E5	1970	100	2 Riyals.	40.00
E6	1970	100	5 Riyals.	75.00
E7	1970	—	5 Riyals. Aluminum. KM#12	40.00
E8	1970	—	7-1/2 Riyals. KM#5	90.00
E9	1970	—	7-1/2 Riyals. KM#6	90.00
E10	1970	—	7-1/2 Riyals. Aluminum. KM#13	55.00
E11	ND(1970)	800	10 Riyals.	75.00

PATTERNS

Including off metal strikes

KM#	Date	Mintage	Identification	Mkt Val
Pn1	1970	—	100 Dirhams. Copper-Nickel.	—

MINT SETS

KM#	Date	Mintage	Identification	Issue Price	Mkt Val
MS1	1969 (3)	—	KM#1.1-3.1	—	45.00
MS2	1970 (3)	4,350	KM#5-7	—	165

PROOF SETS

KM#	Date	Mintage	Identification	Issue Price	Mkt Val
PS1	1969 (3)	1,200	KM#1.1-3.1	11.22	80.00
PS10	1970 (3)	—	KM#12, 13, 15	—	200
PS11	1970 (3)	—	KM#9.1, 9.2, 10	—	550
PS2	1970 (8)	1,175	KM#17-24	—	485
PS3	1970 (8)	—	KM#28-35	—	1,100
PS4	1970 (4)	—	KM#12, 13, 15, 16	—	415
PS5	1970 (3)	100	KM#E4-6	—	190
PS6	1970 (3)	650	KM#5-7	19.50	260
PS7	1970 (3)	—	KM#E9, E7, 10	—	580
PS8	1970 (2)	800	KM#E7, 10	—	500
PS9	1970 (2)	5,000	KM#12, 13	9.50	75.00
PS12	1971 (4)	—	KM#27, 36, 39, 40	—	980

ALBANIA

The Republic of Albania, a Balkan republic bounded by Macedonia, Greece, Montenegro, and the Adriatic Sea, has an area of 11,100 sq. mi. (28,748 sq. km.) and a population of 3.49 million. Capital: Tirane. The country is predominantly agricultural, although recent progress has been made in the manufacturing and mining sectors. Petroleum, chrome, iron, copper, cotton textiles, tobacco and wood products are exported.

Since it had been part of the Greek and Roman empires little is known of the early history of Albania. After the disintegration of the Roman Empire Albania was overrun by Goths, Byzantines, Venetians and Turks. Skanderbeg, the national hero, resisted the Turks and established an independent Albania in 1443, but in 1468 the country again fell to the Turks and remained part of the Ottoman Empire for more than 400 years.

Independence was re-established by revolt in 1912, and the present borders established in 1913 by a conference of European powers, which, in 1914, placed Prince William of Wied on the throne; popular discontent forced his abdication within months. In 1920, following World War I occupancy by several nations, a republic was set up. Ahmed Zogu seized the presidency in 1925, and in 1928 he proclaimed himself king with the title of Zog I. King Zog fled when Italy occupied Albania in 1939 and enthroned King Victor Emanuel of Italy. Upon the surrender of Italy to the Allies in 1943, German troops occupied the country. They withdrew in 1944, and communist partisans seized power, naming Gen. Enver Hoxha provisional president. In 1946, following a victory by the communist front in the 1945 elections, a new constitution modeled on that of the USSR was adopted. In accordance with the constitution of Dec. 28, 1976, the official name of Albania was changed from the Peoples Republic of Albania to the Peoples Socialist Republic of Albania.

Albania's former Communists were routed in elections. March 1992, amid economic collapse and social unrest. Sali Berisha was elected as the first non-communist president since World War II. Rexhep Mejdani, elected president in 1997, succeeds him.

RULERS
Ahmed Bey Zogu - King Zog I, 1928-1939
Vittorio Emanuele III, 1939-1943

MINT MARKS
L – London
R – Rome
V – Vienna

MONETARY SYSTEM
100 Qindar Leku = 1 Lek
100 Qindar Ari = 1 Frang Ar = 5 Lek

KINGDOM

STANDARD COINAGE

KM# 1 5 QINDAR LEKU **Composition:** Bronze

Date	Mintage	F	VF	XF	Unc	BU
1926R	512,000	20.00	45.00	75.00	160	—

KM# 2 10 QINDAR LEKU **Composition:** Bronze

Date	Mintage	F	VF	XF	Unc	BU
1926R	511,000	14.00	30.00	65.00	140	—

KM# 14 QINDAR AR **Composition:** Bronze

Date	Mintage	F	VF	XF	Unc	BU
1935R	2,000,000	2.50	6.00	12.00	22.00	—

KM# 15 2 QINDAR ARI **Composition:** Bronze

Date	Mintage	F	VF	XF	Unc	BU
1935R	1,500,000	3.50	10.00	17.00	32.00	—

KM# 3 1/4 LEKU **Composition:** Nickel

Date	Mintage	F	VF	XF	Unc	BU
1926R	506,000	3.50	8.00	17.00	35.00	—
1927R	756,000	3.50	8.00	15.00	30.00	—

KM# 4 1/2 LEK **Composition:** Nickel

Date	Mintage	F	VF	XF	Unc	BU
1926R	1,002,000	3.00	6.00	14.00	25.00	—

KM# 13 1/2 LEK **Composition:** Nickel

Date	Mintage	F	VF	XF	Unc	BU
1930V	500,000	3.00	5.50	11.00	20.00	—
1931L Proof	—	—	—	—	—	—
1931L	500,000	3.00	5.50	11.00	20.00	—

KM# 5 LEK **Composition:** Nickel

Date	Mintage	F	VF	XF	Unc	BU
1926R	1,004,000	2.00	4.00	10.00	25.00	—
1927R	506,000	3.00	7.00	16.00	32.00	—
1930V	1,250,000	1.50	3.00	7.00	22.00	—
1931L	1,000,000	2.00	4.00	10.00	25.00	—
1931L Proof	—	—	—	—	—	—

KM# 6 FRANG AR **Weight:** 5.0000 g. **Composition:** 0.8350 Silver .1342 oz. ASW

Date	Mintage	F	VF	XF	Unc	BU
1927R	100,000	60.00	100	160	320	—
1928R	60,000	60.00	110	170	325	—

KM# 16 FRANG AR **Weight:** 5.0000 g. **Composition:** 0.8350 Silver .1342 oz. ASW

Date	Mintage	F	VF	XF	Unc	BU
1935R	700,000	5.00	10.00	22.00	60.00	—
1937R	600,000	5.00	12.00	27.50	70.00	—

KM# 18 FRANG AR **Weight:** 5.0000 g. **Composition:** 0.8350 Silver .1342 oz. ASW **Subject:** 25th Anniversary of Independence

Date	Mintage	F	VF	XF	Unc	BU
1937R	50,000	8.00	16.00	35.00	80.00	—

KM# 7 2 FRANGA ARI **Weight:** 10.0000 g. **Composition:** 0.8350 Silver .2684 oz. ASW

Date	Mintage	F	VF	XF	Unc	BU
1926R	50,000	50.00	115	230	335	—
1927R	50,000	60.00	140	250	365	—
1928R	60,000	50.00	115	230	335	—

KM# 17 2 FRANGA ARI **Weight:** 10.0000 g. **Composition:** 0.8350 Silver .2684 oz. ASW

Date	Mintage	F	VF	XF	Unc	BU
1935R	150,000	10.00	30.00	70.00	120	—

KM# 19 2 FRANGA ARI **Weight:** 10.0000 g. **Composition:** 0.8350 Silver .2684 oz. ASW **Subject:** 25th Anniversary of Independence

Date	Mintage	F	VF	XF	Unc	BU
1937R	25,000	13.00	28.00	55.00	110	—

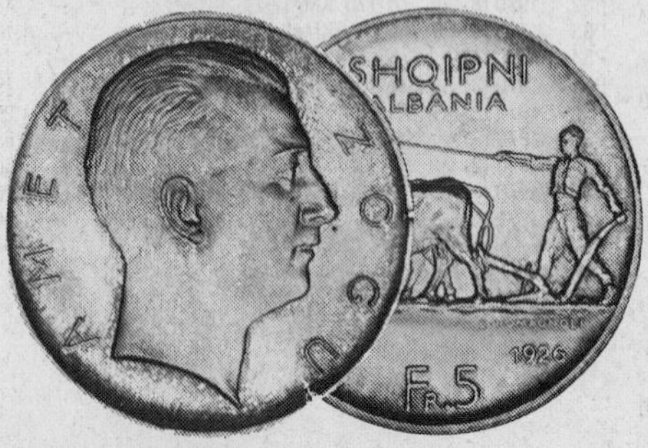

KM# 8.1 5 FRANGA ARI **Weight:** 25.0000 g. **Composition:** 0.9000 Silver .7234 oz. ASW

Date	F	VF	XF	Unc	BU
1926R	80.00	190	390	550	—
1927V	—	—	—	—	—

Note: Only exist as provas

KM# 8.2 5 FRANGA ARI **Weight:** 25.0000 g. **Composition:** 0.9000 Silver .7234 oz. ASW **Obverse:** Star below bust

Date	F	VF	XF	Unc	BU
1926R	120	290	470	650	—

KM# 9 10 FRANGA ARI **Weight:** 3.2258 g. **Composition:** 0.9000 Gold .933 oz. AGW

Date	Mintage	F	VF	XF	Unc	BU
1927R	6,000	100	140	210	300	—

KM# 10 20 FRANGA ARI **Weight:** 6.4516 g. **Composition:** 0.9000 Gold .1867 oz. AGW

Date	Mintage	F	VF	XF	Unc	BU
1926R	—	110	155	235	300	—
1927R	6,000	110	150	225	295	—

KM# 12 20 FRANGA ARI **Weight:** 6.4516 g. **Composition:** 0.9000 Gold .1867 oz. AGW **Subject:** George Kastrioti "Skanderbeg"

Date	Mintage	F	VF	XF	Unc	BU
1926R	5,900	120	160	275	385	—
1926 Fasces	100	—	—	3,500	5,500	—
Note: 90 pieces were reported melted						
1927V	5,053	—	140	240	310	—

KM# 20 20 FRANGA ARI **Weight:** 6.4516 g. **Composition:** 0.9000 Gold .1867 oz. AGW **Subject:** 25th Anniversary of Independence

Date	Mintage	F	VF	XF	Unc	BU
1937R	2,500	—	180	285	425	—

KM# 22 20 FRANGA ARI **Weight:** 6.4516 g. **Composition:** 0.9000 Gold .1867 oz. AGW **Subject:** Marriage of King Zog

Date	Mintage	F	VF	XF	Unc	BU
1938R	2,500	—	180	285	425	—

KM# 24 20 FRANGA ARI **Weight:** 6.4516 g. **Composition:** 0.9000 Gold .1867 oz. AGW **Subject:** 10th Anniversary - Reign of King Zog

Date	Mintage	F	VF	XF	Unc	BU
1938R	1,000	—	200	300	500	—

Note: Pieces struck in 1969 from new dies

KM# 25 50 FRANGA ARI **Weight:** 16.1290 g. **Composition:** 0.9000 Gold .4667 oz. AGW **Subject:** 10th Anniversary - Reign of King Zog

Date	Mintage	F	VF	XF	Unc	BU
1938R	600	—	500	800	1,450	—

Note: Pieces struck in 1969 from new dies

KM# 11.1 100 FRANGA ARI **Weight:** 32.2580 g. **Composition:** 0.9000 Gold .9335 oz. AGW

Date	Mintage	F	VF	XF	Unc	BU
1926R	6,614	—	550	750	1,150	—

Note: Mintage figures includes provas, Pr7-9

KM# 11.2 100 FRANGA ARI **Weight:** 32.2580 g. **Composition:** 0.9000 Gold .9335 oz. AGW **Obverse:** Star below bust

Date	F	VF	XF	Unc	BU
1926R	—	550	750	1,150	—

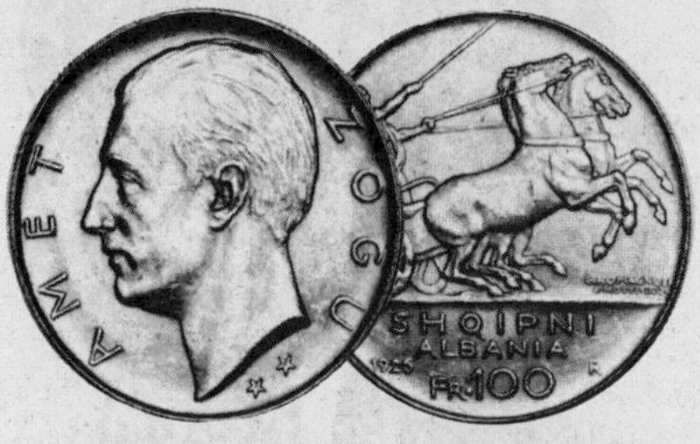

KM# 11.3 100 FRANGA ARI **Weight:** 32.2580 g. **Composition:** 0.9000 Gold .9335 oz. AGW **Obverse:** 2 stars below bust

Date	F	VF	XF	Unc	BU
1926R	—	550	750	1,150	—

KM# 11a.2 100 FRANGA ARI **Weight:** 32.2580 g. **Composition:** 0.9000 Gold .9335 oz. AGW **Obverse:** Star below bust

Date	F	VF	XF	Unc	BU
1927R	—	600	850	1,350	—

KM# 11a.3 100 FRANGA ARI **Weight:** 32.2580 g. **Composition:** 0.9000 Gold .9335 oz. AGW **Obverse:** 2 stars below bust

Date	F	VF	XF	Unc	BU
1927R	—	600	850	1,350	—

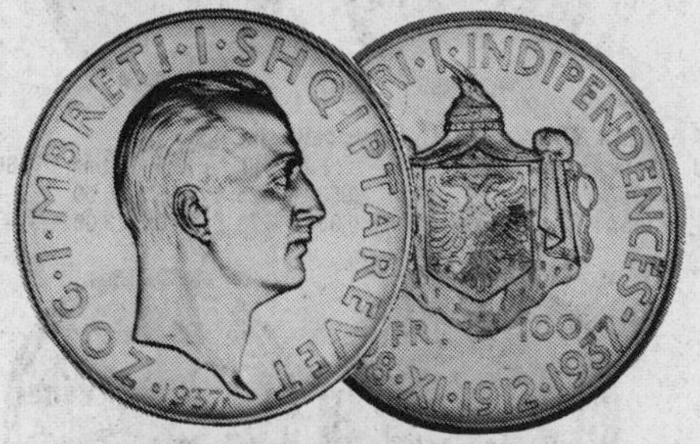

KM# 21 100 FRANGA ARI **Weight:** 32.2580 g. **Composition:** 0.9000 Gold .9335 oz. AGW **Subject:** 25th Anniversary of Independence

Date	Mintage	F	VF	XF	Unc	BU
1937R	500	—	750	1,150	1,650	—

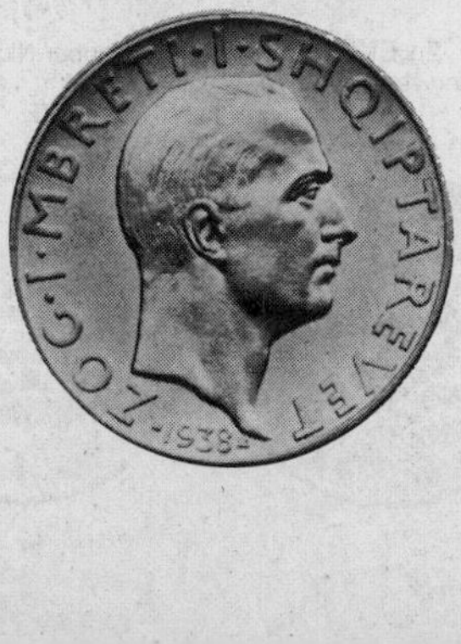

KM# 23 100 FRANGA ARI **Weight:** 32.2580 g. **Composition:** 0.9000 Gold .9335 oz. AGW **Subject:** Marriage of King Zog

Date	Mintage	F	VF	XF	Unc	BU
1938R	500	—	700	1,100	1,600	—

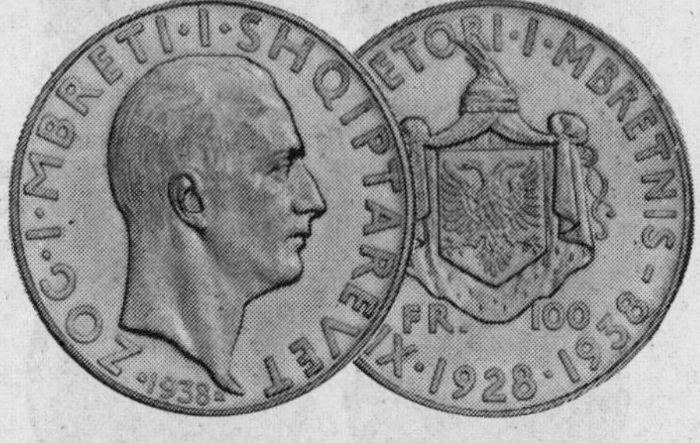

KM# 26 100 FRANGA ARI **Weight:** 32.2580 g. **Composition:** 0.9000 Gold .9335 oz. AGW **Subject:** 10th Anniversary - Reign of King Zog

Date	Mintage	F	VF	XF	Unc	BU
1938R	500	—	700	1,100	1,600	—

Note: Pieces restruck in 1969 from new dies

ITALIAN OCCUPATION WWII

STANDARD COINAGE

KM# 27 0.05 LEK **Composition:** Aluminum-Bronze

Date	Mintage	F	VF	XF	Unc	BU
1940R	1,400,000	3.00	6.00	14.00	25.00	—
1941R Rare	200,000	—	—	—	—	—

KM# 28 0.10 LEK **Composition:** Aluminum-Bronze

Date	Mintage	F	VF	XF	Unc	BU
1940R	550,000	4.00	8.00	18.00	30.00	—
1941R	250,000	18.00	47.00	85.00	145	—

KM# 29 0.20 LEK **Composition:** Stainless Steel

Date	Mintage	F	VF	XF	Unc	BU
1939R	900,000	1.00	4.00	8.00	14.00	—
Note: 1939 dated coins exist in 2 varieties, magnetic and non-magnetic						
1940R	700,000	1.00	2.00	4.00	12.00	—
1941R	1,400,000	1.00	2.00	4.00	12.00	—

KM# 30 0.50 LEK **Composition:** Stainless Steel

Date	Mintage	F	VF	XF	Unc	BU
1939R	100,000	1.50	4.00	8.00	20.00	—
Note: 1939 dated coins exist in 2 varieties, magnetic and on-magnetic						
1940R	500,000	1.50	3.00	6.00	16.00	—
1941R	—	1.50	3.00	7.00	18.00	—

KM# 31 LEK **Composition:** Stainless Steel **Note:** Coins dated after 1939 were not struck for circulation.

Date	Mintage	F	VF	XF	Unc	BU
1939R	2,100,000	1.50	2.50	5.00	15.00	—
Note: 1939 dated coins exist in 2 varieties, magnetic and on-magnetic						
1940R Rare	1,500,000	—	—	—	—	—
Note: The official mintage figure is large, but few examples are known						
1941R Rare	1,000,000	—	—	—	—	—
Note: The official mintage figure is large, but few examples are known						

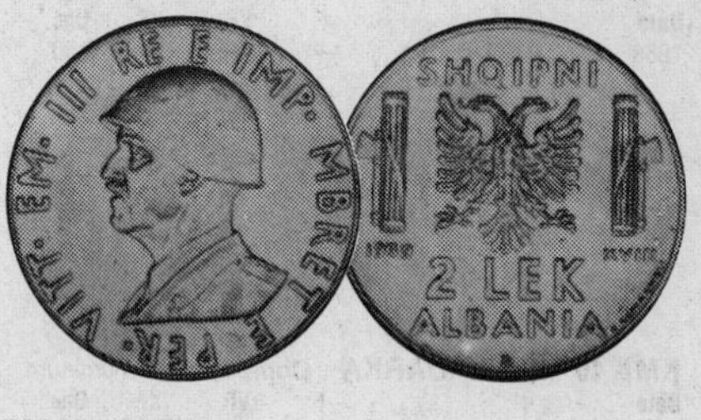

KM# 32 2 LEK **Composition:** Stainless Steel **Note:** Coins dated after 1939 were not struck for circuation.

Date	Mintage	F	VF	XF	Unc	BU
1939R	1,300,000	2.00	4.00	8.00	18.00	—
Note: 1939 dated coins exist in 2 varieties, magnetic and non-magnetic						
1940R Rare	—	—	—	—	—	—
1941R Rare	—	—	—	—	—	—

KM# 33 5 LEK **Weight:** 5.0000 g. **Composition:** 0.8350 Silver .1342 oz. ASW

Date	Mintage	F	VF	XF	Unc	BU
1939R	1,350,000	6.00	12.00	30.00	70.00	—

KM# 34 10 LEK **Weight:** 10.0000 g. **Composition:** 0.8350 Silver .2684 oz. ASW

Date	Mintage	F	VF	XF	Unc	BU
1939R	175,000	40.00	70.00	110	200	—

PEOPLES SOCIALIST REPUBLIC

STANDARD COINAGE

KM# 39 5 QINDARKA **Composition:** Aluminum

Date	F	VF	XF	Unc	BU
1964	0.10	0.25	0.50	1.25	—

KM# 44 5 QINDARKA **Composition:** Aluminum **Subject:** 25th Anniversary of Liberation

Date	F	VF	XF	Unc	BU
ND (1969)	0.10	0.20	0.30	0.85	—

KM# 71 5 QINDARKA **Composition:** Aluminum **Edge:** Plain

Date	F	VF	XF	Unc	BU
1988	—	—	—	0.50	—

KM# 40 10 QINDARKA **Composition:** Aluminum

Date	F	VF	XF	Unc	BU
1964	0.15	0.30	0.60	1.50	—

KM# 45 10 QINDARKA **Composition:** Aluminum **Subject:** 25th Anniversary of Liberation

Date	F	VF	XF	Unc	BU
ND (1969)	0.10	0.20	0.35	1.00	—

KM# 60 10 QINDARKA **Composition:** Aluminum

Date	F	VF	XF	Unc	BU
1988	—	—	—	0.60	—

KM# 41 20 QINDARKA **Composition:** Aluminum

Date	F	VF	XF	Unc	BU
1964	0.20	0.40	0.60	1.75	—

KM# 46 20 QINDARKA **Composition:** Aluminum **Subject:** 25th Anniversary of Liberation

Date	F	VF	XF	Unc	BU
ND (1969)	0.15	0.30	0.50	1.25	—

KM# 65 20 QINDARKA **Composition:** Aluminum

Date	F	VF	XF	Unc	BU
1988	—	—	—	0.75	—

KM# 42 50 QINDARKA **Composition:** Aluminum

Date	F	VF	XF	Unc	BU
1964	0.50	0.75	2.00	4.00	—

KM# 47 50 QINDARKA **Composition:** Aluminum **Subject:** 25th Anniversary of Liberation

Date	F	VF	XF	Unc	BU
ND (1969)	0.30	0.50	1.00	2.00	—

KM# 72 50 QINDARKA **Composition:** Aluminum **Edge:** Plain

Date	F	VF	XF	Unc	BU
1988	—	—	—	1.25	—

KM# 35 1/2 LEKU **Composition:** Zinc

Date	F	VF	XF	Unc	BU
1947	0.40	0.80	1.50	3.00	—
1957	0.25	0.50	1.00	2.00	—

KM# 36 LEK **Composition:** Zinc

Date	F	VF	XF	Unc	BU
1947	0.60	1.00	2.00	4.50	—
1957	0.35	0.75	1.50	3.00	—

KM# 43 LEK **Composition:** Aluminum

Date	F	VF	XF	Unc	BU
1964	0.50	1.00	2.00	4.00	—

KM# 48 LEK **Composition:** Aluminum **Subject:** 25th Anniversary of Liberation

Date	F	VF	XF	Unc	BU
ND (1969)	0.35	0.75	1.25	2.50	—

KM# 66 LEK **Composition:** Aluminum-Bronze

Date	F	VF	XF	Unc	BU
1988	—	—	—	1.75	—

KM# 74 LEK **Composition:** Aluminum

Date	F	VF	XF	Unc	BU
1988	—	—	—	1.50	—

KM# 75 LEK **Composition:** Bronze **Obverse:** Pelican **Reverse:** Denomination

Date	F	VF	XF	Unc	BU
1996	—	—	—	1.50	—

KM# 37 2 LEKE **Composition:** Zinc

Date	F	VF	XF	Unc	BU
1947	0.50	1.25	2.25	5.00	—
1957	0.35	0.75	1.50	3.00	—

KM# 67 2 LEKE **Composition:** Copper-Nickel **Subject:** 45th Anniversary - WWII

Date	F	VF	XF	Unc	BU
1989	—	—	—	3.50	—

KM# 73 2 LEKE **Composition:** Copper-Nickel

Date	F	VF	XF	Unc	BU
1989	—	—	—	3.25	—

KM# 38 5 LEKE **Composition:** Zinc

Date	F	VF	XF	Unc	BU
1947	1.00	1.75	3.50	7.00	—
1957	0.50	1.00	2.00	3.50	—

KM# 49.1 5 LEKE **Weight:** 16.6600 g. **Composition:** 0.9990 Silver .5165 oz. ASW **Subject:** 500th Anniversary - Liga Lissi Skanderbeg's Victory Over the Turks **Reverse:** Without date below arms, oval fineness countermark punched in

Date	Mintage	F	VF	XF	Unc	BU
ND (1969) Proof	8,540	Value: 20.00				

Note: Countermarks for 1968 and 1969 coins were hand positioned, then punched. The result is a variety of countermark positions, to the left and right of LEKE

KM# 49.2 5 LEKE **Weight:** 16.6600 g. **Composition:** 0.9990 Silver .5165 oz. ASW **Reverse:** Date below arms

Date	Mintage	F	VF	XF	Unc	BU
1969 Proof	1,500	Value: 25.00				

Note: Countermarks for 1968 and 1969 coins were hand positioned, then punched. The result is a variety of countermark positions, to the left and right of LEKE

KM# 49.3 5 LEKE **Weight:** 16.6600 g. **Composition:** 0.9990 Silver .5165 oz. ASW **Reverse:** Date below arms, oval fineness in relief

Date	Mintage	F	VF	XF	Unc	BU
1970 Proof	500	Value: 30.00				

Note: For the 1970 issue the fineness marking has been incorporated in the dies

KM# 57 5 LEKE **Composition:** Copper-Nickel **Subject:** Seaport of Durazzo

Date	F	VF	XF	Unc	BU
1987	—	—	—	10.00	—

KM# 57a 5 LEKE **Weight:** 50.0000 g. **Composition:** 0.9000 Gold 1.4470 oz. AGW **Subject:** Seaport of Durazzo

Date	Mintage	F	VF	XF	Unc	BU
1987 Proof	5	Value: 2,500				

KM# 61 5 LEKE **Composition:** Copper-Nickel **Subject:** 42nd Anniversary of First Railroad

Date	Mintage	F	VF	XF	Unc	BU
1988	20,000	—	—	—	15.00	—

KM# 76 5 LEKE **Composition:** Steel **Obverse:** Imperial eagle **Reverse:** Olive branch, denomination

Date	F	VF	XF	Unc	BU
1995	—	—	—	1.00	—

KM# 50.1 10 LEKE **Weight:** 33.3300 g. **Composition:** 0.9990 Silver 1.0354 oz. ASW **Subject:** 500th Anniversary - Death of Prince Skanderbeg **Reverse:** Oval finess countermark punched in, no date below

Date	Mintage	F	VF	XF	Unc	BU
ND Proof	8,540	Value: 35.00				

Note: Countermark for 1968 and 1969 coins were hand positioned, then punched. The result is a variety of countermark positions, to the left and right of LEKE

KM# 50.2 10 LEKE **Weight:** 33.3300 g. **Composition:** 0.9990 Silver 1.0354 oz. ASW **Reverse:** Date below arms

Date	Mintage	F	VF	XF	Unc	BU
1969 Proof	1,500	Value: 45.00				

Note: Countermark for 1968 and 1969 coins were hand positioned, then punched. The result is a variety of countermark positions, to the left and right of LEKE

KM# 50.3 10 LEKE **Weight:** 33.3300 g. **Composition:** 0.9990 Silver 1.0354 oz. ASW **Reverse:** Oval fineness is in relief, date below arms

Date	Mintage	F	VF	XF	Unc	BU
1970 Proof	500	Value: 50.00				

Note: For the 1970 issues the fineness marking has been incorporated in the dies

KM# 50.4 10 LEKE **Weight:** 33.3300 g. **Composition:** 0.9990 Silver 1.0354 oz. ASW **Reverse:** Hallmark countermark left of LEKE, oval fineness countermark in relief, date below arms

Date	Mintage	F	VF	XF	Unc	BU
1970 Proof	Inc. above	Value: 50.00				

Note: For the 1970 issues the fineness marking has been incorporated in the dies

KM# 68 10 LEKE **Weight:** 52.5000 g. **Composition:** 0.9250 Silver 1.5613 oz. ASW **Subject:** 1992 Summer Olympics - Equestrian **Reverse:** Horse and rider right, incuse design

Date	Mintage	F	VF	XF	Unc	BU
1991	980	—	—	—	200	—

KM# 69 10 LEKE **Weight:** 52.5000 g. **Composition:** 0.9250 Silver 1.5613 oz. ASW **Subject:** 1992 Summer Olympics - Equestrian **Reverse:** Horse and rider left, relief design

Date	Mintage	F	VF	XF	Unc	BU
1991	980	—	—	—	200	—

KM# 70 10 LEKE **Weight:** 28.4600 g. **Composition:** 0.9250 Silver .8464 oz. ASW **Subject:** 1992 Summer Olympics - Boxing

Date	Mintage	F	VF	XF	Unc	BU
1992 Proof	20,000	Value: 47.50				

KM# 77 10 LEKE **Composition:** Brass **Obverse:** Fortress **Reverse:** Denomination, sprig with berries

Date	F	VF	XF	Unc	BU
1996	—	—	—	1.25	—

KM# 51.1 20 LEKE **Weight:** 3.9500 g. **Composition:** 0.9000 Gold .1143 oz. AGW **Subject:** 500th Anniversary - Death of Prince Skanderbeg **Obverse:** Date on ribbon **Reverse:** Oval fineness countermark punched in

Date	Mintage	F	VF	XF	Unc	BU
1968	2,920	Value: 90.00				

Note: Countermark for 1968 and 1969 coins were hand positioned, then punched. The result is a variety of countermark positions, to the left and right of LEKE

KM# 51.2 20 LEKE **Weight:** 3.9500 g. **Composition:** 0.9000 Gold .1143 oz. AGW **Reverse:** Without fineness countermark (error)

Date	Mintage	F	VF	XF	Unc	BU
1968 Proof	Inc. above	Value: 90.00				

Note: Countermark for 1968 and 1969 coins were hand positioned, then punched. The result is a variety of countermark positions, to the left and right of LEKE

KM# 51.3 20 LEKE **Weight:** 3.9500 g. **Composition:** 0.9000 Gold .1143 oz. AGW **Reverse:** Cornucopia countermark at right of LEKE

Date	Mintage	F	VF	XF	Unc	BU
1968 Paris	24	—	—	—	400	—

Note: Countermarks for 1968 and 1969 coins were hand positioned, then punched. The result is a variety of countermark positions, to the left and right of LEKE

KM# 51.4 20 LEKE **Weight:** 3.9500 g. **Composition:** 0.9000 Gold .1143 oz. AGW **Reverse:** Date added below arms

Date	Mintage	F	VF	XF	Unc	BU
1969 Proof	650	Value: 125				

Note: Countermarks for 1968 and 1969 coins were hand positioned, then punched. The result is a variety of countermark positions, to the left and right of LEKE

KM# 51.5 20 LEKE **Weight:** 3.9500 g. **Composition:** 0.9000 Gold .1143 oz. AGW **Reverse:** Date below arms, oval fineness in relief

Date	Mintage	F	VF	XF	Unc	BU
1970 Proof	500	Value: 140				

Note: For the 1970 issues the fineness marking has been incorporated in the dies

KM# 51.6 20 LEKE **Weight:** 3.9500 g. **Composition:** 0.9000 Gold .1143 oz. AGW **Reverse:** Sunken countermark 1 AR left of LEKE and raised oval fineness countermark on right

Date	F	VF	XF	Unc	BU
1970 Proof	—	—	—	—	—

Note: For the 1970 issues the fineness marking has been incorporated in the dies

KM# 78 20 LEKE **Composition:** Brass **Obverse:** Ancient sailing vessel **Reverse:** Denomination

Date	F	VF	XF	Unc	BU
1996	—	—	—	1.50	—

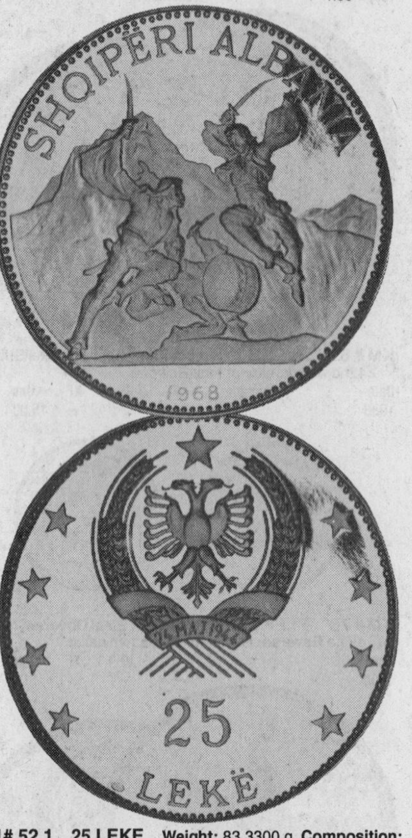

KM# 52.1 25 LEKE **Weight:** 83.3300 g. **Composition:** 0.9990 Silver 2.5887 oz. ASW **Obverse:** Dance with swords **Reverse:** Date below arms, oval fineness countermark

Date	Mintage	F	VF	XF	Unc	BU
1968 Proof	8,540	Value: 50.00				

Note: Countermarks for 1968 and 1969 coins were hand positioned, then punched; the result is a variety of countermark positions, to the left and the right of LEKE

KM# 52.2 25 LEKE **Weight:** 83.3300 g. **Composition:** 0.9990 Silver 2.5887 oz. ASW **Obverse:** Date below scene **Reverse:** Date below arms, oval fineness countermark

Date	F	VF	XF	Unc	BU
1969 Proof	—	Value: 60.00			

KM# 52.3 25 LEKE **Weight:** 83.3300 g. **Composition:** 0.9990 Silver 2.5887 oz. ASW **Obverse:** Without date **Reverse:** Oval fineness countermark in relief

Date	Mintage	F	VF	XF	Unc	BU
1970 Proof	500	Value: 80.00				

Note: For the 1970 issue the fineness amrking has been incorporated in the dies

KM# 53.1 50 LEKE **Weight:** 9.8700 g. **Composition:** 0.9000 Gold .2856 oz. AGW **Obverse:** Argirocastrum Ruins, date below **Reverse:** Oval fineness countermark

Date	Mintage	F	VF	XF	Unc	BU
1968 Proof	3,120	Value: 165				

KM# 53.2 50 LEKE **Weight:** 9.8700 g. **Composition:** 0.9000 Gold .2856 oz. AGW **Reverse:** Date below arms, oval fineness countermark

Date	Mintage	F	VF	XF	Unc	BU
1969 Proof	500	Value: 265				

KM# 53.3 50 LEKE **Weight:** 9.8700 g. **Composition:** 0.9000 Gold .2856 oz. AGW **Obverse:** Without date **Reverse:** Oval fineness countermark in relief

Date	Mintage	F	VF	XF	Unc	BU
1970 Proof	100	Value: 300				

Note: For the 1970 issue the fineness marking has been incorporated in the dies

KM# 58a 50 LEKE **Weight:** 155.5000 g. **Composition:** 0.9990 Gold 4.9950 oz. AGW **Subject:** Seaport of Durazzo

Date	Mintage	F	VF	XF	Unc	BU
1987 Proof	5	Value: 5,300				

KM# 58 50 LEKE **Weight:** 168.1500 g. **Composition:** 0.9250 Silver 5.0012 oz. ASW **Subject:** Seaport of Durazzo **Obverse:** Similar to 5 Leke, KM#57 **Note:** Illustration reduced. Actual size 65 millimeters.

Date	Mintage	F	VF	XF	Unc	BU
1987 Proof	Est. 15,000	Value: 120				

KM# 62 50 LEKE **Weight:** 168.1500 g. **Composition:** 0.9250 Silver 5.0012 oz. ASW **Subject:** 42nd Anniversary - First Railroad **Note:** Illustration reduced. Actual size 65 millimeters.

Date	Mintage	F	VF	XF	Unc	BU
1988 Proof	7,500	Value: 285				

KM# 79 50 LEKE **Composition:** Copper-Nickel **Obverse:** Ancient equestrian **Reverse:** Denomination, tied oak sprigs

Date	F	VF	XF	Unc	BU
1996	—	—	—	2.00	—

KM# 81 50 LEKE **Weight:** 7.5000 g. **Composition:** Copper Nickel **Subject:** Michaelangelo's "David" **Obverse:** Towered building. **Reverse:** Statue's head and denomination. **Edge:** Reeded. **Size:** 28 mm.

Date	Mintage	F	VF	XF	Unc	BU
2001	1,000	—	—	—	6.00	—

KM# 54.1 100 LEKE **Weight:** 19.7500 g. **Composition:** 0.9000 Gold .5715 oz. AGW **Obverse:** Peasant girl in national dress, date below **Reverse:** Oval fineness countermark

Date	Mintage	F	VF	XF	Unc	BU
1968 Proof	3,470	Value: 350				

Note: Countermarks for 1968 and 1969 coins were hand positioned, then punched. The result is a variety of countermark positions, to the left and the right of LEKE

KM# 54.2 100 LEKE **Weight:** 19.7500 g. **Composition:** 0.9000 Gold .5715 oz. AGW **Obverse:** Date below scene **Reverse:** Date below arms, oval fineness countermark

Date	Mintage	F	VF	XF	Unc	BU
1969 Proof	450	Value: 450				

Note: Countermarks for 1968 and 1969 coins were hand positioned, then punched. The result is a variety of countermark positions, to the left and the right of LEKE

KM# 54.3 100 LEKE **Weight:** 19.7500 g. **Composition:** 0.9000 Gold .5715 oz. AGW **Obverse:** Without date **Reverse:** Oval fineness countermark in relief

Date	Mintage	F	VF	XF	Unc	BU
1970 Proof	Inc. above	Value: 475				

KM# 59 100 LEKE **Weight:** 6.4500 g. **Composition:** 0.9000 Gold .1866 oz. AGW **Subject:** Seaport of Durazzo **Obverse:** Arms **Reverse:** Ship in harbor **Note:** Similar to 5 Leke, KM#57.

Date	Mintage	F	VF	XF	Unc	BU
1987 Proof	5,000	Value: 180				

KM# 63 100 LEKE **Weight:** 6.4500 g. **Composition:** 0.9000 Gold .1866 oz. AGW **Subject:** 42nd Anniversary - First Railroad **Obverse:** Train engine emerging from tunnel **Reverse:** Caboose leaving tunnel **Note:** Similar to 50 Leke, KM#62, but without hole in coin

Date	Mintage	F	VF	XF	Unc	BU
1988 Proof	2,000	Value: 280				

KM# 80 100 LEKE **Ring Composition:** Copper-Nickel**Center Weight:** 6.7000 g. **Center Composition:** Aluminum-Bronze **Obverse:** Allegorical figure, Teuta. **Reverse:** Denomination in wreath. **Edge:** Reeded **Size:** 24.7 mm.

Date	F	VF	XF	Unc	BU
2000	—	—	—	4.00	—

KM# 82 100 LEKE **Weight:** 15.7000 g. **Composition:** 0.9250 Silver 0.4669 oz. ASW **Subject:** Michaelangelo's "David" **Obverse:** Arch of Triumph. **Reverse:** Statue's upper half and denomination. **Edge:** Reeded. **Size:** 32.65 mm.

Date	Mintage	F	VF	XF	Unc	BU
2001	1,000	—	—	—	30.00	—

KM# 84 100 LEKE **Weight:** 15.0000 g. **Composition:** 0.9250 Silver 0.4461 oz. ASW **Subject:** Albanian-European Integration **Obverse:** Dove in flight. **Reverse:** European and Albanian maps. **Edge:** Reeded. **Size:** 32 mm.

Date	Mintage	F	VF	XF	Unc	BU
2001	1,000	—	—	—	25.00	—

KM# 55.1 200 LEKE **Weight:** 39.4900 g. **Composition:** 0.9000 Gold 1.1427 oz. AGW **Subject:** Buthrotum Ruins **Reverse:** Similar to 100 Leke, KM#54.1

Date	Mintage	F	VF	XF	Unc	BU
1968 Proof	2,170	Value: 600				

Note: Countermarks for 1968 and 1969 coins were hand positioned then punched. The result is a variety of countermark positions, to the left and right of LEKE

KM# 55.2 200 LEKE **Weight:** 39.4900 g. **Composition:** 0.9000 Gold 1.1427 oz. AGW **Reverse:** Date below arms, oval fineness countermark

Date	Mintage	F	VF	XF	Unc	BU
1969 Proof	200	Value: 775				

Note: Countermarks for 1968 and 1969 coins were hand positioned then punched. The result is a variety of countermark positions, to the left and right of LEKE

KM# 55.3 200 LEKE **Weight:** 39.4900 g. **Composition:** 0.9000 Gold 1.1427 oz. AGW **Obverse:** Without date **Reverse:** Oval fineness countermark in relief

Date	Mintage	F	VF	XF	Unc	BU
1970 Proof	Inc. above	Value: 800				

KM# 83 200 LEKE **Weight:** 7.6500 g. **Composition:** 0.9000 Gold 0.2214 oz. AGW **Subject:** Michaelangelo's "David" **Obverse:** City plaza **Reverse:** Statue of "David" and denomination **Edge:** Reeded **Size:** 25.45 mm.

Date	Mintage	F	VF	XF	Unc	BU
2001	500	—	—	—	175	—

KM# 85 200 LEKE **Weight:** 15.0000 g. **Composition:** 0.9250 Silver 0.4461 oz. ASW **Subject:** Albanian-European Integration **Obverse:** Dove in flight **Reverse:** Adult and infant hand **Edge:** Reeded **Size:** 32 mm.

Date	Mintage	F	VF	XF	Unc	BU
2001	1,000	—	—	—	35.00	—

KM# 56.1 500 LEKE **Weight:** 98.7400 g. **Composition:** 0.9000 Gold 2.8574 oz. AGW **Subject:** 500th Anniversary - Death of Prince Skanderbeg **Reverse:** Similar to 100 Leke, KM#54.1

Date	Mintage	F	VF	XF	Unc	BU
1968 Proof	1,520	Value: 1,350				

Note: Countermarks for 1968 and 1969 coins were hand positioned then punched. The result is a variety of countermark positions to the left and right of LEKE

KM# 56.2 500 LEKE **Weight:** 98.7400 g. **Composition:** 0.9000 Gold 2.8574 oz. AGW **Reverse:** Date below arms, oval fineness countermark

Date	Mintage	F	VF	XF	Unc	BU
1969 Proof	200	Value: 1,750				

Note: Countermarks for 1968 and 1969 coins were hand positioned then punched. The result is a variety of countermark positions to the left and right of LEKE

KM# 56.3 500 LEKE **Weight:** 98.7400 g. **Composition:** 0.9000 Gold 2.8574 oz. AGW **Obverse:** Without date **Reverse:** Oval fineness countermark in relief

Date	F	VF	XF	Unc	BU
1970 Proof	Inc. above	Value: 1,800			

KM# 64 7500 LEKE **Weight:** 483.7500 g. **Composition:** 0.9000 Gold 13.9992 oz. AGW **Subject:** 42nd Anniversary - First Railroad **Obverse:** Train engine emerging from tunnel **Reverse:** Caboose leaving tunnel **Note:** Similar to 50 Leke, KM#62.

Date	Mintage	F	VF	XF	Unc	BU
1988 Proof	50	Value: 8,000				

TRIAL STRIKE

KM#	Date	Mintage	Identification	Issue Price	Mkt Val
TS1	1969	—	500 Leke. Goldine-Brass. 56.3200 g. 55 mm. Blank with MET countermark. Like KM56.2.	—	175

PATTERNS

Including off-metal strikes

KM#	Date	Mintage	Identification	Mkt Val
Pn1	1927	—	Frang Ar. Silver. Plain edge.	500
	1927	—	Frang Ar. Silver. Plain edge.	500
Pn2	1927	—	5 Franga Ari. Copper.	—
	1927	—	5 Franga Ari. Copper.	—
Pn3	1928	—	2 Lek. Copper-Nickel.	—
	1928	—	2 Lek. Copper-Nickel.	—
Pn4	1968	—	10 Leke. 0.9990 Silver. 31.6000 g. Like 10 Leke, KM#50.. Blank except for MET in rectangle at 6 o'clock.. Reeded edge.	—

ESSAIS

KM#	Date	Mintage	Identification	Mkt Val
E1	1926	—	5 Qindar Leku. Bronze.	—
E2	1926	—	10 Qindar Ari. Bronze.	—
	1926	—	10 Qindar Ari. Bronze.	—
E3	1926	—	1/2 Lek. Nickel.	—
	1926	—	1/2 Lek. Nickel.	—
E4	1926	50	2 Franga Ari. Silver.	500
	1926	50	2 Franga Ari. Silver.	500
E6	1927	—	Frang Ar. Silver.	500
E8	1927	—	100 Franga Ari. Silver.	—
E5	1927	—	Lek. Nickel.	—
	1927	—	Lek. Nickel.	—
E8	1927	—	100 Franga Ari. Silver.	—
E6	1927	—	Frang Ar. Silver.	500
E7	1927	50	2 Franga Ari. Silver.	650
	1927	50	2 Franga Ari. Silver.	650
E10	1928	50	Frang Ar. Silver.	500
	1928	50	Frang Ar. Silver.	500
E11	1928	50	2 Franga Ari. Silver.	650
	1928	50	2 Franga Ari. Silver.	650
E9	1928	—	2 Lek. Nickel.	—
	1928	—	2 Lek. Nickel.	—
E12	1938	—	100 Franga Ari. Gold. Without signature.	—

KM#	Date	Mintage	Identification	Mkt Val
E13	1986	10	5 Leke. Copper-Nickel. 27.7900 g.	200

PIEFORTS

KM#	Date	Mintage	Identification	Mkt Val
P1	1988	250	50 Leke. 0.9250 Silver. KM#62 without tunnel hole.	500

PROVAS

Standard metals unless otherwise stated

KM#	Date	Mintage	Identification	Mkt Val
Pr1	1926R	50	5 Qindar Leku. Bronze. KM#1.	400
Pr2	1926R	50	10 Qindar Leku. Bronze. KM#2.	400

KM#	Date	Mintage	Identification	Mkt Val
Pr3	1926R	50	1/4 Leku. KM#3.	500
Pr4	1926	—	1/2 Lek. Nickel.	400
Pr5	1926R	—	1/2 Lek. Nickel. KM#4.	400
Pr6	1926R	50	Lek. KM#5.	500
Pr7	1926R	—	2 Franga Ari. Silver. KM#7.	500
Pr8	1926R	—	5 Franga Ari. KM#8. Modern copy of 5 Franga Ari exist in copper and bronze.	750
Pr9	1926R	—	5 Franga Ari. Copper. KM#8. Modern copy of 5 Franga Ari exist in copper and bronze.	450
Pr10	1926R	—	5 Franga Ari. KM#8. Modern copy of 5 Franga Ari exist in copper and bronze.	500
Pr11	1926R	—	5 Franga Ari. Copper. KM#8. Modern copy of 5 Franga Ari exist in copper and bronze.	450
Pr12	1926R	50	20 Franga Ari. KM#12.	650
Pr13	1926	—	20 Franga Ari. KM#12.	5,000
Pr14	1926R	—	100 Franga Ari. Gold. KM#11.1.	1,500
Pr15	1926R	—	100 Franga Ari. Star, KM#11.2.	1,600

KM#	Date	Mintage	Identification	Mkt Val
Pr16	1926R	—	100 Franga Ari. 2 stars, KM#11.3.	1,600
Pr17	1927R	—	1/4 Leku. Nickel. KM#3.	500
Pr18	1927R	—	Lek. Nickel. KM#5.	500

KM#	Date	Mintage	Identification	Mkt Val
Pr19	1927R	50	Frang Ar. KM#6.	300
Pr23	1927V	—	5 Franga Ari. Silver. Matte proof.	—

KM#	Date	Mintage	Identification	Mkt Val
PrA25	1927R	—	Frang Ar. Silver. similar to KM#9.	—
Pr20	1927V	—	Frang Ar. KM#6.	350

KM#	Date	Mintage	Identification	Mkt Val
Pr21	1927R	—	2 Franga Ari. KM#7.	300
Pr22	1927V	—	5 Franga Ari. Silver.	450
Pr24	1927	—	10 Franga Ari. Gold. KM#9.	700
Pr25	1927R	50	10 Franga Ari. KM#9.	700
Pr26	1927	—	20 Franga Ari. Gold. KM#10.	650
Pr27	1927V	—	20 Franga Ari. KM#12.	600
Pr28	1927R	50	20 Franga Ari. KM#10.	550
Pr29	1927R	—	100 Franga Ari. KM#11a.	1,500
Pr30	1927R	—	100 Franga Ari. Star, KM#11a.1.	1,600
Pr31	1927R	—	100 Franga Ari. 2 stars, KM#11a.2.	1,600

KM#	Date	Mintage	Identification	Mkt Val
PrA32	1927V	—	100 Franga Ari. Similar to 5 Franga Ari, KM#8.1.	1,260
Pr32	1928R	—	2 Lek. Copper-Nickel. KM#28.	200

KM#	Date	Mintage	Identification	Mkt Val
PrA34	1928R	—	2 Lek. Nickel. 9.7800 g. Portrait. Double eagle.	300
Pr34	1928R	—	Frang Ar. KM#6.	200
Pr35	1928R	—	2 Franga Ari. KM#7.	250

KM#	Date	Mintage	Identification	Mkt Val
PrA36	1928R	—	2 Franga Ari. Silver. 10.0400 g. Portrait. Double eagle.	350

KM#	Date	Mintage	Identification	Mkt Val
Pr36	1928R	50	100 Franga Ari. Gold. Bare head.	2,750

KM#	Date	Mintage	Identification	Mkt Val
Pr37	1928R	50	100 Franga Ari. Gold. Bare head, wreath.	2,750

KM#	Date	Mintage	Identification	Mkt Val

KM#	Date	Mintage	Identification	Mkt Val
Pr38	1928R	50	100 Franga Ari. Gold. Uniformed bust.	2,750
Pr33	1928R	—	2 Lek. Nickel. KM#28.	—

KM#	Date	Mintage	Identification	Mkt Val
Pr39	1929R	50	100 Franga Ari. Gold. Bare head, wreath.	2,750
Pr40	1935R	50	Qindar Ar. KM#14.	300
Pr41	1935R	50	2 Qindar Ari. KM#15.	300
Pr42	1935	50	Frang Ar. Silver.	400
Pr43	1935	50	2 Franga Ari. Silver.	500
Pr44	1935	—	5 Franga Ari. Silver. Pattern.	—
Pr48	1937R	—	10 Franga Ari. Gold.	—
Pr45	1937R	50	Frang Ar. KM#16.	450
Pr46	1937R	50	Frang Ar. Silver.	500
Pr47	1937R	50	2 Franga Ari. Silver.	525
Pr49	1937R	50	20 Franga Ari. Gold. KM#20.	550

KM#	Date	Mintage	Identification	Mkt Val
Pr50	1937R	50	100 Franga Ari. KM#21.	1,800
Pr51	1938R	50	20 Franga Ari. KM#22.	650
Pr52	1938R	50	20 Franga Ari. KM#24.	650
Pr53	1938R	50	50 Franga Ari.	1,750

KM#	Date	Mintage	Identification	Mkt Val
Pr54	1938R	50	100 Franga Ari. KM#26.	1,800
Pr55	1938R	50	100 Franga Ari. KM#23.	1,800
Pr56	1939	—	0.05 Lek. Proof.	400
Pr57	1939	—	0.10 Lek. Proof.	400
Pr58	1939	—	0.20 Lek. Proof	500
Pr59	1939	—	0.50 Lek. Proof.	500
Pr60	1939	—	Lek. Proof.	500
Pr61	1939	—	2 Lek. Proof.	525
Pr62	1939	—	5 Lek. Proof.	500
Pr63	1939	—	10 Lek. Silver. Proof.	625
Pr64	1947	—	10 Qindar Leku. Aluminum.	—
Pr65	1947	—	5 Qindar Leku. Tombac.	—
Pr66	1947	—	10 Qindar Leku. Aluminum.	—
Pr71	1947	—	50 Quindar Leku. Tombac.	—
Pr67	1947	—	10 Qindar Leku. Tombac.	—
Pr68	1947	—	20 Quindar Leku. Aluminum.	—
Pr69	1947	—	20 Quindar Leku. Tombac.	—
Pr70	1947	—	50 Quindar Leku. Aluminum.	—

MINT SETS

KM#	Date	Mintage	Identification	Issue Price	Mkt Val
MS1	1969 (5)	—	KM#44-48	5.00	25.00

PROOF SETS

KM#	Date	Mintage	Identification	Issue Price	Mkt Val
PS1	1968 (5)	1,520	KM#51, 53-56	470	2,550
PS2	1968 (8)	—	KM#49-56	—	2,650
PSA2	1968 (3)	8,540	KM#49, 50, 52	44.00	110
PS3	1969 (5)	—	KM#51, 53-56	470	3,385
PS4	1969 (8)	—	KM#49-56	—	3,520
PSA4	1969 (3)	1,500	KM#49, 50, 52	45.00	135
PS5	1970 (5)	—	KM#51.5, 53-56	516	3,515
PS6	1970 (3)	500	KM#49-50, 52	45.00	170
PS7	1991 (2)	980	KM#68-69	—	400

ALDERNEY

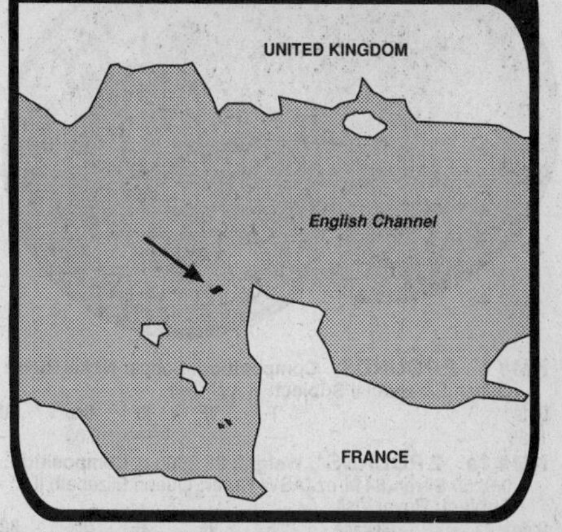

Alderney, the northernmost and third largest of the Channel Islands, separated from the coast of France by the dangerous 8-mile-wide tidal channel, has an area of 3 sq. mi. (8 km.) and a population of 1,686. It is a dependency of the British island of Guernsey, to the southwest. Capital: St. Anne. Principal industries are agriculture and raising cattle.

There is evidence of settlement in prehistoric times and Roman coins have been discovered on the island along with evidence of their buildings. Toward the close of the reign of Henry VIII, France began making plans to seize the Island of Sark. The English, realizing its strategic importance, began to build a defensive fort, which was abandoned some years later when Edward VI died. France constructed a large naval base at its northern tip, which incited the English into making Alderney the "Gibraltar of the Channel." Most of the Islanders were evacuated before the German occupation in 1940 but returned in 1945 when the Germans surrendered.

The Channel Islands have never been subject to the British Parliament and are self-governing units under the direct rule of the Crown acting through the Privy Council. Alderney is within the Bailiwick of Guernsey (q.v.). It is one of the nine Channel Islands, the only part of the Duchy of Normandy still belonging to the British Crown, and has been a British possession since the Norman Conquest of 1066. Legislation was only recently introduced for the issue of its own coinage, a right it now shares with Jersey and Guernsey. Alderney is a dependency of the British island of Guernsey, to the southwest.

RULERS
British

MONETARY SYSTEM
100 Pence = 1 Pound Sterling

DEPENDENCY

STANDARD COINAGE

KM# 4 POUND **Weight:** 9.5000 g. **Composition:** 0.9250 Silver .2826 oz. ASW **Ruler:** Queen Elizabeth II **Subject:** 40th Anniversary - Coronation

Date	Mintage	F	VF	XF	Unc	BU
1993 Proof	Est. 20,000	Value: 35.00				

KM# 12 POUND **Weight:** 9.5000 g. **Composition:** 0.9250 Silver .2826 oz. ASW **Ruler:** Queen Elizabeth II **Subject:** VE Day **Reverse:** VE Monogram and dove

Date	Mintage	F	VF	XF	Unc	BU
ND(1995) Proof	Est. 20,000	Value: 35.00				

KM# 12a POUND **Weight:** 15.8000 g. **Composition:** 0.9160 Gold .4653 oz. AGW **Ruler:** Queen Elizabeth II **Subject:** VE Day **Reverse:** VE Monogram and dove

Date	Mintage	F	VF	XF	Unc	BU
ND(1995) Proof	500	Value: 350				

KM# 1 2 POUNDS **Composition:** Copper-Nickel **Ruler:** Queen Elizabeth II **Subject:** Royal Visit

Date	F	VF	XF	Unc	BU
1989	—	—	—	10.00	—

KM# 1a 2 POUNDS **Weight:** 28.2800 g. **Composition:** 0.9250 Silver .8411 oz. ASW **Ruler:** Queen Elizabeth II **Subject:** Royal Visit

Date	Mintage	F	VF	XF	Unc	BU
1989 Proof	5,000	Value: 50.00				

KM# 1b 2 POUNDS **Weight:** 47.5400 g. **Composition:** 0.9170 Gold 1.4011 oz. AGW **Ruler:** Queen Elizabeth II **Subject:** Royal Visit

Date	Mintage	F	VF	XF	Unc	BU
1989 Proof	100	Value: 850				

KM# 2 2 POUNDS **Composition:** Copper-Nickel **Ruler:** Queen Elizabeth II **Subject:** Queen Mother's - 90th Birthday

Date	F	VF	XF	Unc	BU
1990	—	—	—	8.50	—

KM# 2b 2 POUNDS **Weight:** 47.5400 g. **Composition:** 0.9170 Gold 1.4011 oz. AGW **Ruler:** Queen Elizabeth II **Subject:** Queen Mother's - 90th Birthday

Date	Mintage	F	VF	XF	Unc	BU
1990 Proof	90	Value: 1,000				

KM# 2a 2 POUNDS **Weight:** 28.2800 g. **Composition:** 0.9250 Silver .8411 oz. ASW **Ruler:** Queen Elizabeth II **Subject:** Royal Visit

Date	Mintage	F	VF	XF	Unc	BU
1990 Proof	5,000	Value: 50.00				

KM# 3 2 POUNDS **Composition:** Copper-Nickel **Ruler:** Queen Elizabeth II **Subject:** 40th Anniversary - Queen's Reign

Date	F	VF	XF	Unc	BU
1992	—	—	—	8.50	—

KM# 3a 2 POUNDS **Weight:** 28.2800 g. **Composition:** 0.9250 Silver .8411 oz. ASW **Ruler:** Queen Elizabeth II **Subject:** 40th Anniversary - Queen's Reign

Date	Mintage	F	VF	XF	Unc	BU
1992 Proof	5,000	Value: 40.00				

KM# 3b 2 POUNDS **Weight:** 47.5400 g. **Composition:** 0.9170 Gold 1.4011 oz. AGW **Ruler:** Queen Elizabeth II **Subject:** 40th Anniversary - Queen's Reign

Date	Mintage	F	VF	XF	Unc	BU
1992 Proof	150	Value: 850				

KM# 5 2 POUNDS **Composition:** Copper-Nickel **Ruler:** Queen Elizabeth II **Subject:** 40th Anniversary - Coronation

Date	F	VF	XF	Unc	BU
1993	—	—	—	8.00	—

KM# 5a 2 POUNDS **Weight:** 28.2800 g. **Composition:** 0.9250 Silver .8411 oz. ASW **Ruler:** Queen Elizabeth II **Subject:** 40th Anniversary - Coronation

Date	Mintage	F	VF	XF	Unc	BU
1993 Proof	Est. 5,000	Value: 45.00				

KM# 7 2 POUNDS **Composition:** Copper-Nickel **Ruler:** Queen Elizabeth II **Subject:** Normandy Invasion **Reverse:** Normandy beach landing scene

Date	F	VF	XF	Unc	BU
1994	—	—	—	8.00	—

KM# 7a 2 POUNDS **Weight:** 28.2800 g. **Composition:** 0.9250 Silver .8411 oz. ASW **Ruler:** Queen Elizabeth II **Subject:** Normandy Invasion **Reverse:** Normandy beach landing scene

Date	Mintage	F	VF	XF	Unc	BU
1994 Proof	—	Value: 50.00				

KM# 13 2 POUNDS **Composition:** Copper-Nickel **Ruler:** Queen Elizabeth II **Subject:** Islander's Return **Reverse:** Steamship

Date	F	VF	XF	Unc	BU
ND(1995)	—	—	—	10.00	—

KM# 13a 2 POUNDS **Weight:** 28.2800 g. **Composition:** 0.9250 Silver .8411 oz. ASW **Ruler:** Queen Elizabeth II **Subject:** Islander's Return **Reverse:** Steamship

Date	Mintage	F	VF	XF	Unc	BU
ND(1995) Proof	10,000	Value: 50.00				

KM# 13b 2 POUNDS **Weight:** 47.5400 g. **Composition:** 0.9160 Gold 1.4011 oz. AGW **Ruler:** Queen Elizabeth II **Subject:** Islander's Return **Reverse:** Steamship

Date	Mintage	F	VF	XF	Unc	BU
ND(1995) Proof	250	Value: 850				

KM# 16 2 POUNDS **Composition:** Copper-Nickel **Ruler:** Queen Elizabeth II **Subject:** World Wildlife Fund **Obverse:** Queen's portrait **Reverse:** 2 Puffin birds

Date	F	VF	XF	Unc	BU
1997	—	—	—	10.00	—

KM# 16a 2 POUNDS **Weight:** 28.2800 g. **Composition:** 0.9250 Silver .8410 oz. ASW **Ruler:** Queen Elizabeth II **Subject:** World Wildlife Fund **Reverse:** 2 Puffin birds

Date	F	VF	XF	Unc	BU
1997 Proof	—	Value: 47.50			

KM# 17 2 POUNDS **Weight:** 28.2800 g. **Composition:** 0.9250 Silver .8410 oz. ASW **Ruler:** Queen Elizabeth II **Subject:** Queen's Golden Wedding Anniversary **Obverse:** Queen's portrait **Reverse:** Queen crowning Prince Charles

Date	F	VF	XF	Unc	BU
ND(1997)	—	—	—	8.50	—

KM# 18 2 POUNDS **Weight:** 28.2800 g. **Composition:** 0.9250 Silver .8410 oz. ASW **Ruler:** Queen Elizabeth II **Subject:** Total Eclipse of the Sun **Obverse:** Queen's portrait **Reverse:** 2 sea birds and church

Date	F	VF	XF	Unc	BU
1999	—	—	—	15.00	—

KM# 18a 2 POUNDS **Weight:** 28.2800 g. **Composition:** 0.9250 Silver .8410 oz. ASW **Ruler:** Queen Elizabeth II **Subject:** Total Eclipse of the Sun **Obverse:** Queen's portrait **Reverse:** 2 sea birds and church

Date	Mintage	F	VF	XF	Unc	BU
1999 Proof	Est. 10,000	Value: 47.50				

KM# 18b 2 POUNDS **Weight:** 47.5400 g. **Composition:** 0.9170 Gold 1.4011 oz. AGW **Ruler:** Queen Elizabeth II **Subject:** Total Eclipse of the Sun **Obverse:** Queen's portrait **Reverse:** 2 sea birds and church

Date	Mintage	F	VF	XF	Unc	BU
1999 Proof	Est. 100	Value: 1,300				

KM# 26 5 POUNDS **Weight:** 28.0300 g. **Composition:** 0.9250 Silver 0.8336 oz. ASW **Subject:** Millennium **Obverse:** Queen's portrait **Reverse:** Radiant light house and birds **Edge:** Reeded **Size:** 38.5 mm.

Date	Mintage	F	VF	XF	Unc	BU
ND(2000) Proof	20,000	Value: 45.00				

KM# 14 5 POUNDS **Composition:** Copper-Nickel **Ruler:** Queen Elizabeth II **Subject:** Queen Mother - Children

Date	F	VF	XF	Unc	BU
1995	—	—	—	15.00	—

KM# 14a 5 POUNDS **Weight:** 28.2800 g. **Composition:** 0.9250 Silver .8411 oz. ASW **Ruler:** Queen Elizabeth II **Subject:** Queen Morther - Children

Date	Mintage	F	VF	XF	Unc	BU
1995 Proof	10,000	Value: 50.00				

KM# 14b 5 POUNDS **Weight:** 47.5400 g. **Composition:** 0.9160 Gold 1.4011 oz. AGW **Ruler:** Queen Elizabeth II **Subject:** Queen Mother - Children

Date	Mintage	F	VF	XF	Unc	BU
1995 Proof	150	Value: 850				

KM# 15 5 POUNDS **Composition:** Copper-Nickel **Ruler:** Queen Elizabeth II **Subject:** Queen Elizabeth's 70th Birthday - Flowers

Date	F	VF	XF	Unc	BU
1996	—	—	—	16.00	—

KM# 15a 5 POUNDS **Weight:** 28.2800 g. **Composition:** 0.9250 Silver .8411 oz. ASW **Ruler:** Queen Elizabeth II **Subject:** Queen Elizabeth's 70th Birthday - Flowers

Date	Mintage	F	VF	XF	Unc	BU
1996 Proof	Est. 10,000	Value: 50.00				

KM# 15b 5 POUNDS **Weight:** 47.5400 g. **Composition:** 0.9170 Gold 1.4012 oz. AGW **Ruler:** Queen Elizabeth II **Subject:** Queen Elizabeth's 70th Birthday - Flowers

Date	Mintage	F	VF	XF	Unc	BU
1996 Proof	250	Value: 1,225				

KM# 19 5 POUNDS **Composition:** Copper-Nickel **Ruler:** Queen Elizabeth II **Subject:** Total Eclipse of the Sun **Obverse:** Portrait of Queen **Reverse:** Map of Alderney, pre, post and actual phases of eclipse

Date	F	VF	XF	Unc	BU
1999	—	—	—	18.00	—

KM# 19a 5 POUNDS **Weight:** 28.2800 g. **Composition:** 0.9250 Silver .8410 oz. ASW **Ruler:** Queen Elizabeth II

Date	Mintage	F	VF	XF	Unc	BU
1999 Proof	Est. 10,000	Value: 55.00				

KM# 20 5 POUNDS **Weight:** 28.2800 g. **Composition:** 0.9250 Silver 0.841 oz. ASW **Ruler:** Queen Elizabeth II **Subject:** Winston Churchill **Obverse:** Queen's portrait **Reverse:** Winston Churchill wearing hat **Edge:** Reeded **Note:** Struck at the British Royal Mint.

Date	F	VF	XF	Unc	BU
1999	—	—	—	—	—

KM# 20a 5 POUNDS **Weight:** 47.5400 g. **Composition:** 0.9166 Gold 1.4011 oz. AGW **Ruler:** Queen Elizabeth II **Subject:** Winston Churchill **Obverse:** Queen's portrait **Reverse:** Winston Churchill wearing hat **Edge:** Reeded **Note:** Struck at the British Royal Mint. Prev. KM#20.

Date	Mintage	F	VF	XF	Unc	BU
1999 Proof	125,000	Value: 865				

KM# 21 5 POUNDS **Weight:** 28.2800 g. **Composition:** Copper-Nickel **Ruler:** Queen Elizabeth II **Subject:** 60th Anniversary - Battle of Britain **Obverse:** Queen Elizabeth's head right **Reverse:** Two spitfires in flight, pilot at bottom center **Edge:** Reeded

Date	F	VF	XF	Unc	BU
2000	—	—	—	18.00	—

KM# 21a 5 POUNDS **Weight:** 28.2800 g. **Composition:** 0.9250 Silver .8410 oz. ASW **Ruler:** Queen Elizabeth II **Subject:** 60th Anniversary - Battle of Britain **Obverse:** Queen Elizabeth's head right **Reverse:** Two spitfires in flight, pilot at bottom center **Edge:** Reeded

Date	F	VF	XF	Unc	BU
2000 Proof	— Value: 55.00				

KM# 25 5 POUNDS **Weight:** 28.2800 g. **Composition:** 0.9250 Silver 0.841 oz. ASW **Ruler:** Queen Elizabeth II **Subject:** Queen's Golden Jubilee **Obverse:** Queen's portrait **Reverse:** Honor guard and trumpets **Edge:** Reeded **Size:** 38.6 mm.

Date	Mintage	F	VF	XF	Unc	BU
2002 Proof	15,000	Value: 50.00				

KM# 24 5 POUNDS **Weight:** 28.2800 g. **Composition:** 0.9250 Silver 0.841 oz. ASW **Ruler:** Queen Elizabeth II **Subject:** Queen Elizabeth II - 50 Years of Reign **Obverse:** Queen's head right **Reverse:** Sword hilt and denomination with royal arms background **Edge:** Reeded **Size:** 38.6 mm.

Date	Mintage	F	VF	XF	Unc	BU
2002 Proof	15,000	Value: 50.00				

KM# 27 5 POUNDS **Weight:** 28.2800 g. **Composition:** Copper Nickel **Ruler:** Queen Elizabeth II **Obverse:** Queen's portrait **Reverse:** Diana accepting flowers from girl **Edge:** Reeded **Size:** 38.6 mm.

Date	VG	F	VF	XF	Unc
2002	—	—	—	—	13.50

KM# 27a 5 POUNDS **Weight:** 28.2800 g. **Composition:** 0.9250 Silver 0.841 oz. ASW **Ruler:** Queen Elizabeth II **Subject:** Princess Diana **Obverse:** Queen's portrait **Reverse:** Diana accepting flowers from girl **Edge:** Reeded **Size:** 38.6 mm.

Date	Mintage	VG	F	VF	XF	Unc
2002 Proof	20,000	Value: 45.00				

KM# 27b 5 POUNDS **Weight:** 39.9400 g. **Composition:** 0.9167 Gold 1.1771 oz. AGW **Ruler:** Queen Elizabeth II **Subject:** Princess Diana **Obverse:** Queen's portrait **Reverse:** Diana accepting flowers from girl **Edge:** Reeded **Size:** 38.6 mm.

Date	Mintage	VG	F	VF	XF	Unc
2002 Proof	100	Value: 800				

KM# 29 5 POUNDS **Weight:** 28.2800 g. **Composition:** Copper-Nickel **Ruler:** Queen Elizabeth II **Subject:** The Duke of Wellington **Obverse:** Queen's portrait **Reverse:** Coat of arms, castle and portrait **Edge:** Reeded **Size:** 38.6 mm.

Date	F	VF	XF	Unc	BU
2002	—	—	—	12.50	—

KM# 29a 5 POUNDS **Weight:** 28.2800 g. **Composition:** 0.9250 Silver 0.841 oz. ASW **Ruler:** Queen Elizabeth II **Subject:** The Duke of Wellington **Obverse:** Queen's portrait **Reverse:** Multicolor coat of arms. Portrait and castle **Edge:** Reeded **Size:** 38.6 mm.

Date	Mintage	VG	F	VF	XF	Unc
2002 Proof	15,000	Value: 55.00				

KM# 29b 5 POUNDS **Weight:** 39.9400 g. **Composition:** 0.9166 Gold 1.177 oz. AGW **Ruler:** Queen Elizabeth II **Subject:** The Duke of Wellington **Obverse:** Queen's portrait **Reverse:** Coat of arms, castle and portrait **Edge:** Reeded **Size:** 38.6 mm.

Date	Mintage	VG	F	VF	XF	Unc
2002 Proof	200	Value: 775				

KM# 8 10 POUNDS **Weight:** 3.1300 g. **Composition:** 0.9990 Gold .1005 oz. AGW **Ruler:** Queen Elizabeth II **Subject:** Normandy Invasion **Reverse:** Paratroopers and Transport Plane

Date	Mintage	F	VF	XF	Unc	BU
1994 Proof	Est. 1,000	Value: 80.00				

KM# 6 25 POUNDS **Weight:** 8.5130 g. **Composition:** 0.9170 Gold .2507 oz. AGW **Ruler:** Queen Elizabeth II **Subject:** 40th Anniversary - Coronation **Reverse:** Royal Carriage

Date	Mintage	F	VF	XF	Unc	BU
1993 Proof	Est. 1,000	Value: 190				

KM# 9 25 POUNDS **Weight:** 7.8100 g. **Composition:** 0.9990 Gold .2509 oz. AGW **Ruler:** Queen Elizabeth II **Subject:** Normandy Invasion **Reverse:** Fighter Planes and Tank

Date	Mintage	F	VF	XF	Unc	BU
1994 Proof	Est. 1,000	Value: 190				

KM# 23 25 POUNDS **Weight:** 28.0000 g. **Composition:** Copper-Nickel **Ruler:** Queen Elizabeth II **Subject:** Golden Wedding Anniversary - Elizabeth and Philip **Obverse:** Queen Elizabeth's head right. **Reverse:** Queen Elizabeth crowning Charles as Prince of Wales, date (1947-1997) in legend

Date	F	VF	XF	Unc	BU
ND(1997)	—	—	—	18.00	—

KM# 23a 25 POUNDS **Weight:** 28.2800 g. **Composition:** 0.9250 Silver **Ruler:** Queen Elizabeth II **Subject:** Golden Wedding Anniversary - Elizabeth and Philip **Obverse:** Queen Elizabeth's head right **Reverse:** Queen Elizabeth crowning Charles as Prince of Wales, date (1947-1997) in legend

Date	F	VF	XF	Unc	BU
ND(1997) Proof	— Value: 19.50				

KM# 22 25 POUNDS **Weight:** 7.8100 g. **Composition:** 0.9160 Gold .2302 oz. AGW **Ruler:** Queen Elizabeth II **Subject:** 60th Anniversary - Battle of Britain **Obverse:** Queen Elizabeth's head right **Reverse:** Two spitfires in flight, pilot at bottom center **Edge:** Reeded

Date	F	VF	XF	Unc	BU
2000	— Value: 275				

KM# 28 25 POUNDS **Weight:** 7.9800 g. **Composition:** 0.9167 Gold 0.2352 oz. AGW **Ruler:** Queen Elizabeth II **Subject:** Princess Diana **Obverse:** Queen's portrait **Reverse:** Diana's cameo portrait above denomination **Edge:** Reeded **Size:** 22.05 mm.

Date	Mintage	VG	F	VF	XF	Unc
2002 Proof	2,500	Value: 290				

KM# 30 25 POUNDS **Weight:** 7.9800 g. **Composition:** 0.9166 Gold 0.2352 oz. AGW **Ruler:** Queen Elizabeth II **Subject:** The Duke of Wellington **Obverse:** Queen's portrait **Reverse:** Coat of arms, castle and portrait **Edge:** Reeded **Size:** 22 mm.

Date	Mintage	VG	F	VF	XF	Unc
2002 Proof	2,500	Value: 295				

KM# 10 50 POUNDS **Weight:** 15.6000 g. **Composition:** 0.9990 Gold .5014 oz. AGW **Ruler:** Queen Elizabeth II **Subject:** Normandy Invasion **Reverse:** British Gliders

Date	Mintage	F	VF	XF	Unc	BU
1994 In Proof sets only	Est. 1,000	Value: 400				

KM# 11 100 POUNDS **Weight:** 31.2100 g. **Composition:** 0.9990 Gold 1.0025 oz. AGW **Ruler:** Queen Elizabeth II **Subject:** Normandy Invasion **Reverse:** Normandy beach landing scene

Date		F	VF	XF	Unc	BU
1994 Proof	Est. 500	Value: 815				

PIEFORTS

KM#	Date	Mintage	Identification	Mkt Val
P1	1989	500	2 Pounds. 0.9250 Silver. KM#1a.	100
P2	1990	500	2 Pounds. 0.9250 Silver. KM#2a.	100
P3	1992	750	2 Pounds. 0.9250 Silver. KM#3a.	70.00
P4	1993	500	2 Pounds. 0.9250 Silver. KM#5a.	75.00
P5	1994	500	2 Pounds. 0.9250 Silver. KM#7a.	75.00
P6	ND(1995)	500	2 Pounds. 0.9250 Silver. KM#13a.	90.00
P7	1995	500	5 Pounds. 0.9250 Silver. KM#14a.	75.00
P8	1996	500	5 Pounds. 0.9250 Silver. KM#15a.	90.00

PROOF SETS

KM#	Date	Mintage	Identification	Issue Price	Mkt Val
PS1	1994 (5)	500	KM#7a, 8-11	—	1,550
PS2	1994 (4)	I.A.	KM#8-11	—	1,500
PS3	1994 (4)	500	KM#7a, 8-10	—	735
PS4	1994 (3)	I.A.	KM#8-10	—	675

ALGERIA

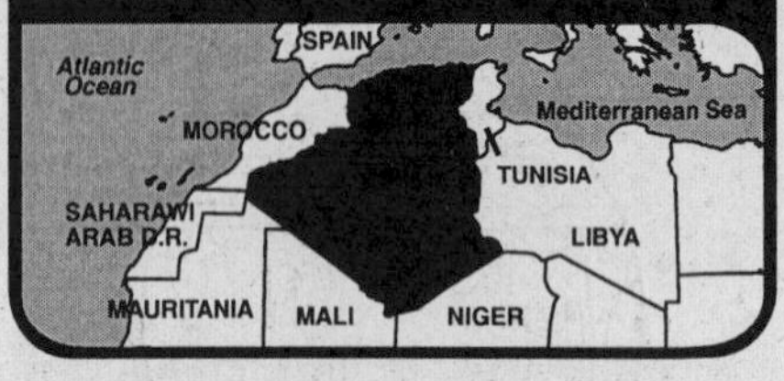

The Democratic and Popular Republic of Algeria, a North African country fronting on the Mediterranean Sea between Tunisia and Morocco, has an area of 919,595 sq. mi. (2,381,740 sq. km.) and a population of 31.6 million. Capital: Algiers (Alger). Most of the country's working population is engaged in agriculture although a recent industrial diversification, financed by oil revenues, is making steady progress. Wines, fruits, iron and zinc ores, phosphates, tobacco products, liquified natural gas, and petroleum are exported.

Algiers, the capital and chief seaport of Algeria, was the site of Phoenician and Roman settlements before the present Moslem city was founded about 950. Nominally part of the sultanate of Tilimsan, Algiers had a large measure of independence under the amirs of its own. In 1492 the Jews and Moors who had been expelled from Spain settled in Algiers and enjoyed an increasing influence until the imposition of Turkish control in 1518. For the following three centuries, Algiers was the headquarters of the notorious Barbary pirates as Turkish control became more and more nominal. The French took Algiers in 1830, and after a long and wearisome war completed the conquest of Algeria and annexed it to France, 1848. Following the armistice signed by France and Nazi Germany on June 22, 1940, Algeria fell under Vichy Government control until liberated by the Allied invasion forces under the command of Gen. D. D. Eisenhower on Nov. 8, 1942. The inability to obtain equal rights with Frenchmen led to an organized revolt, which began on Nov. 1, 1954 and lasted until a ceasefire was signed on July l, 1962. Independence was proclaimed on July 5, 1962, following a self-determination referendum, and the Republic was declared on September 25, 1962.

MINT MARKS

Paris – Privy marks only

MONETARY SYSTEMS

100 Centimes = 1 Franc

FRENCH OCCUPATION

COLONIAL COINAGE

KM# 91 20 FRANCS **Composition:** Copper-Nickel

Date	Mintage	F	VF	XF	Unc	BU
1949(a)	25,556,000	1.00	2.00	5.00	10.00	—
1956(a)	7,500,000	1.00	2.50	6.00	12.50	—

KM# 92 50 FRANCS **Composition:** Copper-Nickel

Date	Mintage	F	VF	XF	Unc	BU
1949(a)	18,000,000	1.50	3.00	9.00	18.00	—

KM# 93 100 FRANCS **Composition:** Copper-Nickel **Note:** During World War II homeland coins were struck at the Paris Mint and the French 2 Francs, Y#89 were struck at the Philadelphia Mint for use in French African Territories.

Date	Mintage	F	VF	XF	Unc	BU
1950(a)	22,189,000	1.50	3.00	10.00	20.00	—
1952(a)	12,000,000	2.00	4.00	12.00	25.00	—

TOKEN COINAGE

Alger

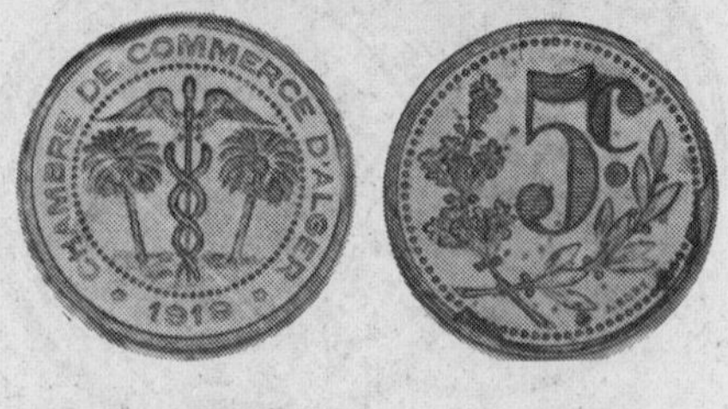

KM# TnA1 5 CENTIMES **Composition:** Aluminum **Issuer:** Alger Chamber of Commerce **Reverse:** With J. Bory

Date	F	VF	XF	Unc	BU
1916	5.00	10.00	18.00	35.00	—
1917	—	175	250	500	—

Note: The year 1917 is not a regular issue

Date	F	VF	XF	Unc	BU
1919	4.00	6.00	12.00	18.00	—
1921	5.00	10.00	18.00	35.00	—

KM# TnA2 5 CENTIMES **Composition:** Iron **Issuer:** Alger Chamber of Commerce

Date	F	VF	XF	Unc	BU
1916	30.00	50.00	100	200	—

KM# TnA3 5 CENTIMES **Composition:** Zinc **Issuer:** Alger Chamber of Commerce

Date	F	VF	XF	Unc	BU
1917	3.50	10.00	20.00	40.00	—
1919	—	35.00	70.00	150	—

Note: The year 1919 is not a regular issue

KM# TnA4 5 CENTIMES **Composition:** Brass **Issuer:** Alger Chamber of Commerce

Date	F	VF	XF	Unc	BU
1921	—	35.00	70.00	150	—

Note: Not a regular issue

KM# TnA5 10 CENTIMES **Composition:** Aluminum **Issuer:** Alger Chamber of Commerce

Date	F	VF	XF	Unc	BU
1916 Without J. Bory	6.00	10.00	20.00	45.00	—
1918 Without J. BOry	6.00	10.00	15.00	32.00	—
1919 With J. Bory	4.00	6.00	12.00	25.00	—
1921 With J. BOry	3.00	6.00	12.00	25.00	—
1921 Without J. Bory	6.00	10.00	20.00	45.00	—

KM# TnA6 10 CENTIMES **Composition:** Iron **Issuer:** Alger Chamber of Commerce **Reverse:** Without J. Bory

Date	F	VF	XF	Unc	BU
1916	10.00	22.00	50.00	100	—

KM# TnA7 10 CENTIMES **Composition:** Zinc **Issuer:** Alger Chamber of Commerce

Date	F	VF	XF	Unc	BU
1917	5.00	12.50	30.00	60.00	—
1918	—	40.00	80.00	160	—

Note: 1918 is not a regular issue

Date	F	VF	XF	Unc	BU
1919	—	40.00	80.00	160	—

Note: 1919 is not a regular issue

KM# TnA8 10 CENTIMES **Composition:** Brass **Issuer:** Alger Chamber of Commerce **Note:** Not a regular issue.

Date	F	VF	XF	Unc	BU
1919	—	50.00	110	225	—
1921	—	65.00	125	245	—

TOKEN COINAGE

Bone

KM# TnB1 5 CENTIMES **Composition:** Aluminum **Issuer:** Bone Chamber of Commerce

Date	F	VF	XF	Unc	BU
1915	6.00	10.00	15.00	30.00	—
ND(1915)	5.00	9.00	13.00	25.00	—

KM# TnB2 5 CENTIMES **Composition:** Brass **Issuer:** Bone Chamber of Commerce **Note:** Not a regular issue.

Date	F	VF	XF	Unc	BU
ND(1915)	—	30.00	60.00	120	—

KM# TnB3 10 CENTIMES **Composition:** Aluminum **Issuer:** Bone Chamber of Commerce

Date	F	VF	XF	Unc	BU
1915	4.00	10.00	22.00	40.00	—
ND(1915)	4.00	9.00	20.00	35.00	—

KM# TnB4 10 CENTIMES **Composition:** Brass **Issuer:** Bone Chamber of Commerce **Note:** Not a regular issue.

Date	F	VF	XF	Unc	BU
ND(1915)	—	32.50	65.00	130	—

KM# TnB5 50 CENTIMES **Composition:** Brass **Issuer:** Bone Chamber of Commerce

Date	F	VF	XF	Unc	BU
ND(1915)	15.00	30.00	50.00	75.00	—

KM# TnB6 50 CENTIMES **Composition:** Copper-Nickel **Issuer:** Bone Chamber of Commerce **Note:** Not a regular issue.

Date	F	VF	XF	Unc	BU
ND(1915)	—	40.00	90.00	200	—

KM# TnB7 FRANC **Composition:** Brass **Issuer:** Bone Chamber of Commerce

Date	F	VF	XF	Unc	BU
ND(1915)	20.00	35.00	60.00	100	—

KM# TnB8 FRANC **Composition:** Copper-Nickel **Issuer:** Bone Chamber of Commerce **Note:** Not a regular issue.

Date	F	VF	XF	Unc	BU
ND(1915)	—	60.00	120	225	—

KM# TnB9 FRANC **Composition:** Copper **Issuer:** Bone Chamber of Commerce **Note:** Not a regular issue.

Date	F	VF	XF	Unc	BU
ND(1915)	—	90.00	150	300	—

TOKEN COINAGE

Bougie

KM# TnC1 5 CENTIMES **Composition:** Aluminum **Issuer:** Bougie Chamber of Commerce

Date	F	VF	XF	Unc	BU
1915	3.50	8.00	20.00	40.00	—

KM# TnC2.1 10 CENTIMES **Composition:** Aluminum **Issuer:** Bougie Chamber of Commerce **Obverse:** Dots flank date

Date	F	VF	XF	Unc	BU
1915	3.50	10.00	25.00	50.00	—

KM# TnC2.2 10 CENTIMES **Composition:** Aluminum **Issuer:** Bougie Chamber of Commerce **Obverse:** Dot and triangle at right of date

Date	F	VF	XF	Unc	BU
1915	3.00	6.00	15.00	30.00	—

KM# TnC2a 10 CENTIMES **Composition:** Zinc **Issuer:** Bougie Chamber of Commerce

Date	F	VF	XF	Unc	BU
1915	30.00	50.00	120	250	—

TOKEN COINAGE

Constantine

KM# TnD1 5 CENTIMES **Composition:** Aluminum **Issuer:** Constantine Chamber of Commerce

Date	F	VF	XF	Unc	BU
1922	20.00	30.00	50.00	100	—

KM# TnD2 10 CENTIMES **Composition:** Aluminum **Issuer:** Constantine Chamber of Commerce

Date	F	VF	XF	Unc	BU
1922	15.00	25.00	45.00	90.00	—

TOKEN COINAGE

Oran

KM# TnE1 5 CENTIMES **Composition:** Aluminum **Issuer:** Oran Chamber of Commerce

Date	F	VF	XF	Unc	BU
1921	4.50	9.00	25.00	50.00	—

KM# TnE2 10 CENTIMES **Composition:** Aluminum **Issuer:** Oran Chamber of Commerce

Date	F	VF	XF	Unc	BU
1921	3.00	7.00	18.00	35.00	—

KM# TnE2a 10 CENTIMES **Composition:** Brass **Issuer:** Oran Chamber of Commerce

Date	F	VF	XF	Unc	BU
1921	—	75.00	150	300	—

KM# TnE3 25 CENTIMES **Composition:** Aluminum **Issuer:** Oran Chamber of Commerce **Obverse:** Similar to 10 Centimes, KM#TnE2 **Reverse:** Similar to 25 Centimes, KM#TnE4

Date	F	VF	XF	Unc	BU
1921	4.00	8.50	25.00	50.00	—

KM# TnE4 25 CENTIMES **Composition:** Aluminum **Issuer:** Oran Chamber of Commerce **Obverse:** Small crowned shield, chains

Date	F	VF	XF	Unc	BU
1921	5.00	10.00	30.00	60.00	—

KM# TnE5 25 CENTIMES **Composition:** Aluminum **Issuer:** Oran Chamber of Commerce **Note:** For further listings of private token issues refer to the catalogue of "French Emergency Tokens of 1914-1922" by Robert Lamb.

Date	F	VF	XF	Unc	BU
1922	5.00	10.00	30.00	60.00	—

REPUBLIC

STANDARD COINAGE

KM# 94 CENTIME **Composition:** Aluminum

Date	Mintage	F	VF	XF	Unc	BU
AH1383 (1964)	35,000,000	—	0.20	0.40	1.00	—

KM# 95 2 CENTIMES **Composition:** Aluminum

Date	Mintage	F	VF	XF	Unc	BU
AH1383 (1964)	50,000,000	—	0.20	0.40	1.00	—

KM# 96 5 CENTIMES **Composition:** Aluminum

Date	Mintage	F	VF	XF	Unc	BU
AH1383 (1964)	40,000,000	—	0.25	0.45	1.25	—

KM# 101 5 CENTIMES **Composition:** Aluminum **Series:** F.A.O. **Subject:** 1st Four Year Plan **Note:** Varieties exist.

Date	Mintage	F	VF	XF	Unc	BU
ND(1970)	10,000,000	—	0.15	0.30	0.75	—

KM# 106 5 CENTIMES **Composition:** Aluminum **Series:** F.A.O. **Subject:** 2nd Four Year Plan

Date	Mintage	F	VF	XF	Unc	BU
ND(1974)	10,000,000	—	0.15	0.30	0.75	—

KM# 113 5 CENTIMES **Composition:** Aluminum **Series:** F.A.O. **Subject:** 1st Five Year Plan

Date	F	VF	XF	Unc	BU
ND(1980)	2.00	5.00	12.00	25.00	—

KM# 116 5 CENTIMES **Composition:** Aluminum **Series:** F.A.O. **Subject:** 2nd Five Year Plan **Note:** Varieties exist in planchet thickness.

Date	F	VF	XF	Unc	BU
ND(1985)	—	0.10	0.25	0.70	—

KM# 97 10 CENTIMES **Composition:** Aluminum-Bronze

Date	F	VF	XF	Unc	BU
AH1383 (1964)	—	0.25	0.75	2.00	—

KM# 115 10 CENTIMES **Composition:** Aluminum **Note:** Varieties exist.

Date	F	VF	XF	Unc	BU
1984	0.15	0.25	0.75	3.00	—

KM# 98 20 CENTIMES **Composition:** Aluminum-Bronze

Date	F	VF	XF	Unc	BU
AH1383 (1964)	—	0.25	0.75	2.00	—

KM# 103 20 CENTIMES **Composition:** Brass **Series:** F.A.O. **Subject:** Agricultural Revolution

Date	Mintage	F	VF	XF	Unc	BU
1972	20,000,000	—	0.10	0.25	0.75	1.25

KM# 107.1 20 CENTIMES **Composition:** Aluminum-Bronze **Series:** F.A.O.

Date	Mintage	F	VF	XF	Unc	BU
1975	50,000,000	—	0.20	0.45	1.75	—

KM# 107.2 20 CENTIMES **Composition:** Aluminum-Bronze **Series:** F.A.O. **Obverse:** Small flower above 20

Date	F	VF	XF	Unc	BU
1975	—	0.15	0.30	1.50	—

KM# 118 20 CENTIMES **Composition:** Aluminum-Bronze **Series:** F.A.O.

Date	Mintage	F	VF	XF	Unc	BU
1987	60,000,000	0.50	1.00	2.00	8.00	—

KM# 99 50 CENTIMES **Composition:** Aluminum-Bronze

Date	F	VF	XF	Unc	BU
AH1383 (1964)	—	0.25	0.75	2.00	—

KM# 102 50 CENTIMES **Composition:** Copper-Nickel-Zinc

Date	Mintage	F	VF	XF	Unc	BU
AH1391 (1971)	10,000,000	0.25	0.50	1.50	6.00	—
AH1393 (1973)	—	0.25	0.50	1.50	6.00	—

KM# 109 50 CENTIMES **Composition:** Brass **Subject:** 30th Anniversary French-Algerian Clash

Date	Mintage	F	VF	XF	Unc	BU
ND(1975)	18,000,000	—	0.20	0.50	2.00	—

KM# 111 50 CENTIMES **Composition:** Aluminum-Bronze **Subject:** 1400th Anniversary of Mohammad's Flight

Date	F	VF	XF	Unc	BU
AH1400 (1980)	0.15	0.25	0.50	2.50	4.50
AH1401 (1981)	0.15	0.25	0.50	2.50	4.50

KM# 119 50 CENTIMES **Composition:** Aluminum-Bronze **Subject:** 25th Anniversary of Constitution

Date	F	VF	XF	Unc	BU
1988	0.15	0.25	0.75	3.00	6.00

KM# 127 1/4 DINAR **Composition:** Aluminum **Subject:** Fennec Fox

Date	F	VF	XF	Unc	BU
AH1413 (1992)	—	0.65	1.25	2.50	—
AH1413 (1992) Proof	—	Value: 12.00			
AH1418 (1998)	—	0.65	1.25	2.50	—

KM# 128 1/2 DINAR **Composition:** Steel **Subject:** Barbary Horse

Date	F	VF	XF	Unc	BU
AH1413 (1992)	—	0.65	1.25	2.50	—
AH1413 (1992) Proof	—	Value: 12.00			

KM# 100 DINAR **Composition:** Copper-Nickel

Date	Mintage	F	VF	XF	Unc	BU
AH1383 (1964)	15,000,000	0.25	0.50	1.00	4.00	—

KM# 104.1 DINAR **Composition:** Copper-Nickel **Series:** F.A.O.

Date	Mintage	F	VF	XF	Unc	BU
1972	20,000,000	0.25	0.50	1.00	2.50	3.50

KM# 104.2 DINAR **Composition:** Copper-Nickel **Obverse:** Legend touches inner circle

Date	F	VF	XF	Unc	BU
1972	0.20	0.45	0.85	2.00	3.00

KM# 112 DINAR **Composition:** Copper-Nickel **Subject:** 20th Anniversary of Independence

Date	F	VF	XF	Unc	BU
ND(1983)	0.35	0.75	1.50	4.50	6.50

KM# 117 DINAR **Composition:** Copper-Nickel **Subject:** 25th Anniversary of Independence - Monument

Date	F	VF	XF	Unc	BU
1987	0.35	0.75	1.50	4.00	6.00

KM# 120 DINAR **Weight:** 3.2200 g. **Composition:** 0.9200 Gold .0953 oz. AGW **Subject:** Historical Coin - 5 Aspers of Abd-el-Kader

Date	F	VF	XF	Unc	BU
AH1411 (1991)	—	—	—	125	145

KM# 129 DINAR **Composition:** Steel **Subject:** Prehistoric Buffalo

Date	F	VF	XF	Unc	BU
AH1413 (1992)	—	1.00	2.00	4.50	—
AH1413 (1992) Proof	—	Value: 15.00			
AH1417 (1997)	—	—	2.00	4.50	—

KM# 121 2 DINARS **Weight:** 6.4500 g. **Composition:** 0.9200 Gold .1908 oz. AGW **Subject:** Historical Coin - Dinar of 762 A.D. Rostomiden Dynasty

Date	F	VF	XF	Unc	BU
AH1411 (1991)	—	—	—	250	300

KM# 130 2 DINARS **Composition:** Steel **Subject:** Camel's Head

Date	F	VF	XF	Unc	BU
AH1413 (1992)	—	1.00	2.50	5.50	—
AH1413 (1992) Proof	—	Value: 18.00			
AH1417 (1996)	—	—	—	—	—
AH1417 (1997)	—	1.00	2.50	5.50	—

KM# 133 2 DINARS **Composition:** Gold **Subject:** Historical Coin - 2 Dinar of Abd Al-Qadir, AH1222-1300

Date	F	VF	XF	Unc	BU
AH1417 (1996)	—	—	—	265	325

KM# 105 5 DINARS **Weight:** 12.0000 g. **Composition:** 0.7500 Silver .2893 oz. ASW **Series:** F.A.O. **Subject:** 10th Anniversary **Note:** Privy mark owl.

Date	F	VF	XF	Unc	BU
ND(1972)(a)	—	5.00	10.00	16.50	—

KM# 105a.1 5 DINARS **Composition:** Nickel

Date	F	VF	XF	Unc	BU
ND(1972)(a)	—	4.00	8.00	14.50	—

KM# 105a.2 5 DINARS **Composition:** Nickel **Note:** Privy mark: dolphin.

Date	F	VF	XF	Unc	BU
ND(1974)(a)	—	4.00	8.00	14.50	—

KM# 108 5 DINARS **Composition:** Nickel **Subject:** 20th Anniversary of Revolution

Date	F	VF	XF	Unc	BU
ND(1974)(a)	—	3.50	7.00	12.50	—

KM# 114 5 DINARS **Composition:** Nickel **Subject:** 30th Anniversary of Revolution

Date	F	VF	XF	Unc	BU
ND(1984)	—	2.50	5.00	10.00	—

KM# 122 5 DINARS **Weight:** 16.1200 g. **Composition:** 0.9200 Gold .4768 oz. AGW **Subject:** Historical Coin - Denar of Numidian King Massinissa, 238-148 B.C.

Date	F	VF	XF	Unc	BU
AH1411 (1991)	—	—	—	550	625

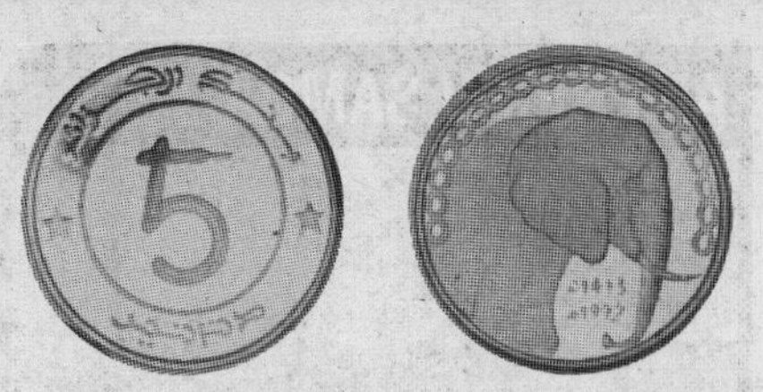

KM# 123 5 DINARS **Composition:** Steel **Obverse:** Denomination **Reverse:** Elephant

Date	F	VF	XF	Unc	BU
AH1413 (1992)	—	1.50	3.50	7.50	—
AH1413 (1992) Proof	—	Value: 20.00			
AH1414 (1993)	—	1.50	3.50	7.50	—
AH1418 (1997)	—	1.50	3.50	7.50	—
AH1417 (1997)	—	1.50	3.50	7.50	—
AH1418 (1998)	—	1.50	3.50	7.50	—
AH1419 (1998)	—	1.50	3.50	7.50	—

KM# 110 10 DINARS **Weight:** 11.3700 g. **Composition:** Aluminum-Bronze

Date	Mintage	F	VF	XF	Unc	BU
1979	25,001,000	—	2.00	4.50	8.50	—
1981(a)	40,000,000	—	2.00	4.50	8.50	—

KM# 110a 10 DINARS **Weight:** 14.6000 g. **Composition:** 0.9250 Silver .4342 oz. ASW

Date	Mintage	F	VF	XF	Unc	BU
1979	1,000	—	—	—	35.00	—

KM# 110b 10 DINARS **Weight:** 24.5000 g. **Composition:** 0.9000 Gold .7090 oz. AGW

Date	Mintage	F	VF	XF	Unc	BU
1979	100	—	—	—	1,250	—

KM# 124 10 DINARS **Ring Composition:** Steel **Center Composition:** Aluminum **Obverse:** Denomination **Reverse:** Falcon

Date	F	VF	XF	Unc	BU
AH1413 (1992)	—	2.00	6.00	12.00	—
AH1413 (1992) Proof	—	—	—	—	—
AH1414 (1993)	—	2.00	6.00	12.00	—
AH1418 (1997)	—	2.00	6.00	12.00	—

KM# 134 10 DINARS **Weight:** 14.6000 g. **Composition:** 0.8350 Silver 0.3919 oz. ASW **Subject:** Jugurtha, King of Numidia (154-104BC) **Obverse:** Denomination **Reverse:** Head of Jugurtha left **Edge:** Reeded **Size:** 31.5 mm.

Date	F	VF	XF	Unc	BU
AH1415 (1994)	—	—	—	75.00	—

KM# 135 10 DINARS **Weight:** 14.6000 g. **Composition:** 0.8350 Silver 0.3919 oz. ASW **Subject:** Abdelhamid Benbadis (1889-1940) **Obverse:** Denomination **Reverse:** 1/2 bust of Benbadis half left **Edge:** Reeded **Size:** 31.5 mm.

Date	F	VF	XF	Unc	BU
AH1415 (1994)	—	—	—	75.00	—

KM# 136 10 DINARS **Weight:** 14.6000 g. **Composition:** 0.8350 Silver 0.3919 oz. ASW **Subject:** Houari Boumediene (1922-1978) **Obverse:** Denomination **Reverse:** Bust of Boumediene half left **Edge:** Reeded **Size:** 31.5 mm.

Date	F	VF	XF	Unc	BU
AH1415 (1994)	—	—	—	75.00	—

KM# 125 20 DINARS **Ring Composition:** Steel **Center Composition:** Brass **Obverse:** Denomination **Reverse:** Lion

Date	F	VF	XF	Unc	BU
AH1413 (1992)	—	3.00	7.00	15.00	—
AH1413 (1992) Proof	—	—	—	—	—
AH1414 (1993)	—	3.00	7.00	15.00	—
AH1416 (1996)	—	3.00	7.00	15.00	—
AH1417 (1996)	—	3.00	7.00	15.00	—
AH1417 (1997)	—	3.00	7.00	15.00	—
AH1418 (1997)	—	3.00	7.00	15.00	—
AH1420 (1999)	—	3.00	7.00	15.00	—
AH1427 (2000)	—	3.00	7.00	15.00	—

KM# 126 50 DINARS **Ring Composition:** Brass **Center Composition:** Steel **Obverse:** Denomination **Reverse:** Gazelle

Date	F	VF	XF	Unc	BU
AH1413 (1992)	—	4.00	8.00	16.50	—
AH1413 (1992) Proof	—	Value: 35.00			
AH1414 (1993)	—	4.00	8.00	16.50	—
AH1416 (1996)	—	4.00	8.00	16.50	—
AH1417 (1996)	—	4.00	8.00	16.50	—
AH1414 (1996)	—	4.00	8.00	16.50	—
AH1418 (1998)	—	4.00	8.00	16.50	—
AH1419 (1999)	—	4.00	8.00	16.50	—

KM# 131 50 DINARS **Ring Composition:** Brass **Center Composition:** Steel **Subject:** 40th Anniversary - Revolution

Date	F	VF	XF	Unc	BU
ND(1994) (1994)	—	5.00	10.00	17.50	—
ND(1994) (1994) Proof	—	Value: 37.50			

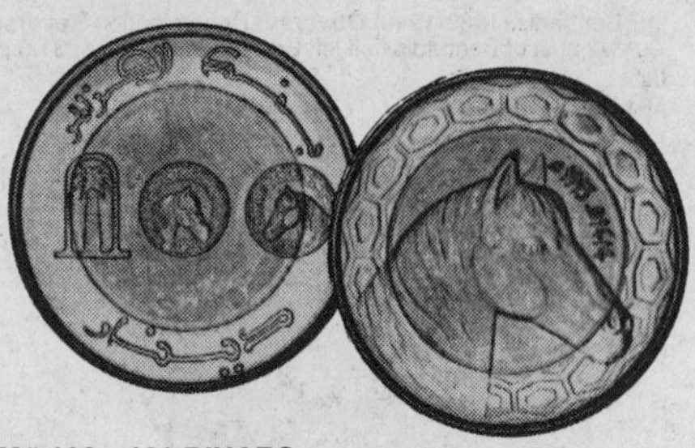

KM# 132 100 DINARS **Center Composition:** Aluminum-Bronze **Obverse:** Denomination stylized with reverse design **Reverse:** Horse head

Date	F	VF	XF	Unc	BU
AH1413 (1992)	—	6.50	12.50	22.50	—
AH1414 (1993)	—	6.50	12.50	22.50	—
AH1415 (1994)	—	6.50	12.50	22.50	—
AH1417 (1997)	—	6.50	12.50	22.50	—
AH1418 (1998)	—	6.50	12.50	22.50	—

ESSAIS

Standard metals unless otherwise noted

KM#	Date	Mintage	Identification	Issue Price	Mkt Val
E1	ND(1949)(a)	1,500	20 Francs. KM#91.	—	35.00
E2	ND(1949)(a)	1,500	50 Francs. KM#92.	—	45.00
E3	ND(1950)(a)	1,500	100 Francs. KM#93.	—	50.00

KM#	Date	Mintage	Identification	Issue Price	Mkt Val
E4	ND(1972)(a)	2,250	5 Dinars. KM#105.	—	25.00
E5	ND(1972)(a)	1,000	5 Dinars. KM#105a.	—	35.00

KM#	Date	Mintage	Identification	Issue Price	Mkt Val
E6	ND(1974)(a)	3,300	5 Dinars. KM#108.	—	20.00
E7	1981	2,670	10 Dinars. KM#110.	—	25.00

PIEFORTS WITH ESSAI

Double thickness - Standard metals unless otherwise noted

KM#	Date	Mintage	Identification	Issue Price	Mkt Val
PE1	1949(a)	104	20 Francs. KM#91.	—	100
PE2	1949(a)	104	50 Francs. KM#92.	—	110

KM#	Date	Mintage	Identification	Issue Price	Mkt Val
PE3	1950(a)	104	100 Francs. KM#93.	—	120

PROOF SETS

KM#	Date	Mintage	Identification	Issue Price	Mkt Val
PS1	AH1314 (1992) (8)	—	KM#123-130	—	160

AMERICAN SAMOA

The Territory of American Samoa, with a population of 41,000, consists of seven major islands with a total land area of 76 sq. mi. (199 sq. km.) which are located about 2300 miles south-southwest of Hawaii. American Samoa was settled by the Polynesians around 600 BC. The capital is Pago Pago.

Samoa's long isolation from the western world ended in 1722 when the Dutch explorer, Jacob Roggeveen, came upon the islands. However, it wasn't until 1831 that European influence had any real impact. In that year, John Williams of the London Missionary Society arrived with eight Tahitian missionaries.

By 1900 the Samoan islands were being claimed by both Germany and the United States. Germany annexed several islands, which now comprise Western Samoa; the U.S. took Tutuila to use Pago Pago Bay as a coaling station for naval ships.

As Japan began emerging as an international power in the mid-1930's, the U.S. Naval station on Tutuila began to acquire new strategic importance; and in 1940 the Samoan Islands became a training and staging area for the U.S. Marine Corps.

A. P. Lutali, Governor of American Samoa, signed a historic proclamation on May 23, 1988 that authorized the minting of the first numismatic issue for this unincorporated territory administered by the United States Department of the Interior.

MONETARY SYSTEM
100 Cents = 1 Dollar

U.S. TERRITORY

NON-CIRCULATING LEGAL TENDER COINAGE

KM# 1 DOLLAR **Composition:** Bronze **Subject:** America's Cup

Date	Mintage	F	VF	XF	Unc	BU
1988 Proof	2,000	Value: 16.00				

KM# 2 5 DOLLARS **Weight:** 31.1000 g. **Composition:** 0.9990 Silver 1.0000 oz. ASW **Subject:** America's Cup

Date	Mintage	F	VF	XF	Unc	BU
1988 Proof	1,000	Value: 45.00				

KM# 6.1 5 DOLLARS **Weight:** 31.1000 g. **Composition:** 0.9990 Silver 1.0000 oz. ASW **Subject:** Olympics **Note:** Coin die alignment.

Date	Mintage	F	VF	XF	Unc	BU
1988 Proof	1,000	Value: 60.00				

KM# 6.2 5 DOLLARS **Weight:** 31.1000 g. **Composition:** 0.9990 Silver 1.0000 oz. ASW **Note:** Medallic die alignment.

Date	F	VF	XF	Unc	BU
1988 Proof	—	Value: 165			

KM# 3 25 DOLLARS **Weight:** 155.5150 g. **Composition:** 0.9990 Silver 5.0000 oz. ASW **Subject:** America's Cup **Note:** Illustration reduced. Actual size: 63 millimeters.

Date	Mintage	F	VF	XF	Unc	BU
1988 Proof	100	Value: 220				

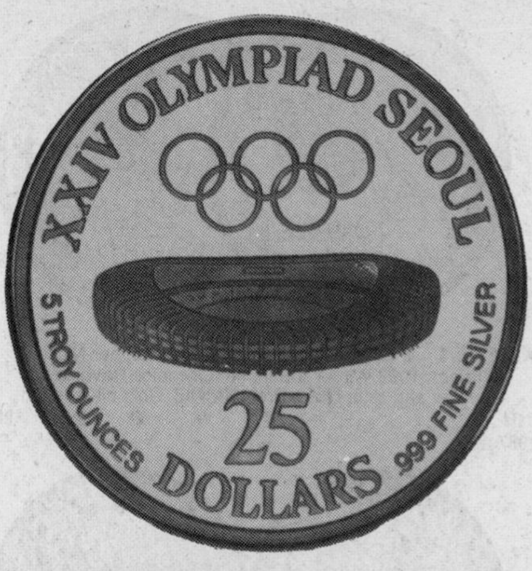

KM# 7 25 DOLLARS **Weight:** 155.5150 g. **Composition:** 0.9990 Silver 5.0000 oz. ASW **Subject:** Olympics **Obverse:** Gov. Lutali **Note:** Illustration reduced. Actual size: 63 millimeters.

Date	Mintage	F	VF	XF	Unc	BU
ND(1988) Proof	100	Value: 400				

KM# 9 25 DOLLARS **Weight:** 155.5150 g. **Composition:** 0.9990 Silver 5.0000 oz. ASW **Subject:** Olympics **Reverse:** Symbols **Note:** Illustration reduced. Actual size: 63 millimeters.

Date	Mintage	F	VF	XF	Unc	BU
1988 Proof	100	Value: 185				

KM# 10 25 DOLLARS **Weight:** 155.5150 g. **Composition:** 0.9990 Silver 5.0000 oz. ASW **Subject:** Olympics **Note:** Similar to KM#7 but denomination: TWENTY-FIVE.

Date	F	VF	XF	Unc	BU
1988 Proof	—	Value: 550			

KM# 4 50 DOLLARS (1/4 Ounce) **Weight:** 8.6397 g. **Composition:** 0.9000 Gold .2500 oz. AGW **Subject:** America's Cup

Date	Mintage	F	VF	XF	Unc	BU
1988 Proof	100	Value: 275				

KM# 5 100 DOLLARS (1 Ounce) **Weight:** 31.1000 g. **Composition:** 0.9990 Gold 1.0000 oz. AGW **Subject:** America's Cup **Obverse:** State seal **Reverse:** USA's yacht passing New Zealand's yacht

Date	Mintage	F	VF	XF	Unc	BU
1988 Proof	50	Value: 900				

KM# 8 100 DOLLARS (1 Ounce) **Weight:** 31.1000 g. **Composition:** 0.9990 Gold 1.0000 oz. AGW **Subject:** Olympics **Obverse:** State seal **Reverse:** Olympic rings and stadium above denomination

Date	Mintage	F	VF	XF	Unc	BU
1988 Proof	50	Value: 1,200				

KM# 11 100 DOLLARS (1 Ounce) **Weight:** 31.1000 g. **Composition:** 0.9990 Gold 1.0000 oz. AGW **Obverse:** Reverse of KM#5 **Reverse:** Reverse of KM#8 **Note:** Mule.

Date	Mintage	F	VF	XF	Unc	BU
1988 Proof	5	Value: 2,250				

PROOF SETS

KM#	Date	Mintage	Identification	Issue Price	Mkt Val
PS1	1988 (3)	—	KM#2-4	315	500

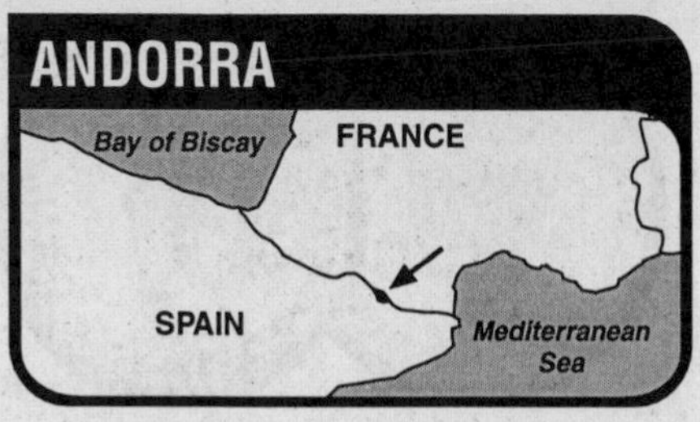

Principality of Andorra (Principat d'Andorra), situated on the southern slopes of the Pyrenees Mountains between France and Spain, has an area of 181 sq. mi. (453 sq. km.) and a population of 80,000. Capital: Andorra la Vella. Tourism is the chief source of income. Timber, cattle and derivatives, and furniture are exported.

According to tradition, the independence of Andorra derives from a charter Charlemagne granted the people of Andorra in 806 in recognition of their help in battling the Moors. An agreement between the Count of Foix (France) and the Bishop of Seo de Urgel (Spanish) in 1278 to recognize each other as Co-Princes of Andorra gave the state what has been its political form and territorial extent continuously to the present day. Over the years, the title on the French side passed to the Kings of Navarre, then to the Kings of France, and is now held by the President of France.

RULERS

Joan D.M. Bisbe D'Urgell I

MONETARY SYSTEM

100 Centims = 1 Diner
100 Pesetas = 1 Diner, 1983-85
125 Pesetas = 1 Diner, 1986-

NOTE: The Diners have been struck for collectors while French Francs and Spanish Pesetas are used in everyday commerce.

MINT MARKS

Crowned M = Madrid

PRINCIPALITY

DECIMAL COINAGE

KM# 171 CENTIM **Weight:** 1.2500 g. **Composition:** Aluminum **Subject:** F.A.O. **Obverse:** Denomination **Reverse:** Winged figure carrying wheat **Edge:** Plain

Date	F	VF	XF	Unc	BU
1999	—	—	—	1.50	—

KM# 178 CENTIM **Weight:** 1.2500 g. **Composition:** Aluminum **Subject:** Agnus Dei **Obverse:** National arms **Reverse:** Lamb of God **Edge:** Plain **Size:** 21.9 mm.

Date	F	VF	XF	Unc	BU
2002	—	—	—	1.00	—

KM# 176 CENTIM **Weight:** 1.2500 g. **Composition:** Aluminum **Subject:** Charlemagne **Obverse:** National arms **Reverse:** Crowned portrait **Edge:** Plain **Size:** 21.9 mm.

Date	F	VF	XF	Unc	BU
2002	—	—	—	1.00	—

KM# 177 CENTIM **Weight:** 1.2500 g. **Composition:** Aluminum **Subject:** Isard **Obverse:** National arms **Reverse:** Mountain goat **Edge:** Plain **Size:** 21.9 mm.

Date	F	VF	XF	Unc	BU
2002	—	—	—	1.00	—

KM# 179 2 CENTIMS **Composition:** Brass **Subject:** Grandalla **Obverse:** National arms **Reverse:** Edelweiss flower **Edge:** Plain

Date	F	VF	XF	Unc	BU
2002	—	—	—	1.50	—

KM# 180 5 CENTIMS **Composition:** Brass **Subject:** Esquirel **Obverse:** National arms **Reverse:** Squirrel on tree stump **Edge:** Plain

Date	F	VF	XF	Unc	BU
2002	—	—	—	2.00	—

KM# 181 5 CENTIMS **Composition:** Brass **Subject:** Gall Fer **Obverse:** National arms **Reverse:** Male turkey displaying plumage **Edge:** Plain

Date	F	VF	XF	Unc	BU
2002	—	—	—	2.00	—

KM# 164 10 CENTIMS **Weight:** 6.8100 g. **Composition:** Brass **Obverse:** National arms **Reverse:** Building and arms **Edge:** Plain

Date	F	VF	XF	Unc	BU
1997	—	—	—	4.00	—

KM# 182 10 CENTIMS **Composition:** Brass **Subject:** St. Joan de Caselles **Obverse:** National arms **Reverse:** Tower and building **Edge:** Plain

Date	F	VF	XF	Unc	BU
2002	—	—	—	3.00	—

KM# 33 25 CENTIMS **Composition:** Bronze **Obverse:** Joan D.M. Bisbe D'Urgell I

Date	Mintage	F	VF	XF	Unc	BU
1986	10,000	—	—	—	5.00	—

KM# 109 25 CENTIMS **Composition:** Copper-Nickel **Subject:** 50th Anniversary - F.A.O **Reverse:** People on globe adoring F.A.O. logo

Date	Mintage	F	VF	XF	Unc	BU
1995	50,000	—	—	—	7.00	—

KM# 134 50 CENTIMS **Weight:** 0.6221 g. **Composition:** 0.9990 Gold .0100 oz. AGW **Obverse:** Fleury cross **Reverse:** Portrait of Queen Isabella I **Note:** Similar to 20 Diners, KM#137.

Date	Mintage	F	VF	XF	Unc	BU
1997 Proof	Est. 50,000	Value: 30.00				

KM# 14 DINER **Composition:** Brass **Obverse:** Joan D.M. Bisbe D'Urgell I

Date	Mintage	F	VF	XF	Unc	BU
1983	28,000	—	—	—	8.00	—

KM# 15 DINER **Composition:** Cast Copper-Zinc

Date	Mintage	F	VF	XF	Unc	BU
1984	7,500	—	—	—	9.00	—

KM# 35 DINER **Composition:** Brass

Date	Mintage	F	VF	XF	Unc	BU
1986	10,000	—	—	—	8.00	—

KM# 49 DINER **Composition:** Copper-Nickel **Subject:** Pont de la Margineda

Date	Mintage	F	VF	XF	Unc	BU
1988	5,000	—	—	—	10.00	—

KM# 66 DINER **Weight:** 10.3000 g. **Composition:** 0.9990 Silver .3312 oz. ASW

Date	Mintage	F	VF	XF	Unc	BU
1990	6,000	—	—	—	25.00	—

KM# 127 DINER **Weight:** 10.0000 g. **Composition:** 0.5000 Silver .1607 oz. ASW **Subject:** Treaty of Rome **Obverse:** Crowned arms **Reverse:** Seated Europa placing laurel wreath on her head

Date	Mintage	F	VF	XF	Unc	BU
1997 Proof	30,000	Value: 20.00				

KM# 135 DINER **Weight:** 1.2441 g. **Composition:** 0.9990 Gold .0400 oz. AGW **Obverse:** Fleury cross **Reverse:** Portrait of Queen Isabella I **Note:** Similar to 20 Diners, KM#137.

Date	Mintage	F	VF	XF	Unc	BU
1997 Proof	Est. 10,000	Value: 50.00				

KM# 19 2 DINERS **Ring Composition:** Copper-Nickel **Center Composition:** Bronze **Subject:** Wildlife **Reverse:** Bear

Date	Mintage	F	VF	XF	Unc	BU
1984	5,000	—	—	—	27.50	—

KM# 20 2 DINERS **Ring Composition:** Copper-Nickel **Center Composition:** Bronze **Subject:** Wildlife **Reverse:** Red squirrel

Date	Mintage	F	VF	XF	Unc	BU
1984	5,000	—	—	—	27.50	—

KM# 21 2 DINERS **Ring Composition:** Copper-Nickel **Center Composition:** Bronze **Subject:** Wildlife **Reverse:** Ibex

Date	Mintage	F	VF	XF	Unc	BU
1984	5,000	—	—	—	27.50	—

KM# 27 2 DINERS **Ring Composition:** Copper-Nickel **Center Composition:** Bronze **Subject:** 1988 Winter Olympics **Reverse:** Skier

Date	Mintage	F	VF	XF	Unc	BU
1985	11,000	—	—	—	22.50	—

KM# 28 2 DINERS **Ring Composition:** Copper-Nickel **Subject:** 1988 Summer Olympics **Reverse:** High jumper

Date	Mintage	F	VF	XF	Unc	BU
1985	11,000	—	—	—	22.50	—

KM# 36 2 DINERS **Composition:** Brass **Obverse:** Joan D.M. Bisbe D'Urgell I

Date	Mintage	F	VF	XF	Unc	BU
1986	10,000	—	—	—	12.50	—

KM# 40 2 DINERS **Composition:** Copper-Nickel **Subject:** 1988 Summer Olympics **Reverse:** Tennis

Date	Mintage	F	VF	XF	Unc	BU
1987	20,000	—	—	—	14.50	—

KM# 46.2 2 DINERS **Composition:** Copper-Nickel **Subject:** 1992 Winter & Summer Olympics **Reverse:** Kayaker and skier **Note:** Medallic die rotation.

Date	F	VF	XF	Unc	BU
1987	—	—	—	13.50	—

KM# 46.1 2 DINERS **Composition:** Copper-Nickel **Subject:** 1992 Winter & Summer Olympics **Reverse:** Kayaker and skier **Note:** Prev. KM#46. Coin die rotation.

Date	F	VF	XF	Unc	BU
1987	—	—	—	13.50	—

KM# 50 2 DINERS **Composition:** Copper-Nickel **Obverse:** Church of Santa Coloma

Date	Mintage	F	VF	XF	Unc	BU
1988	5,000	—	—	—	15.00	—

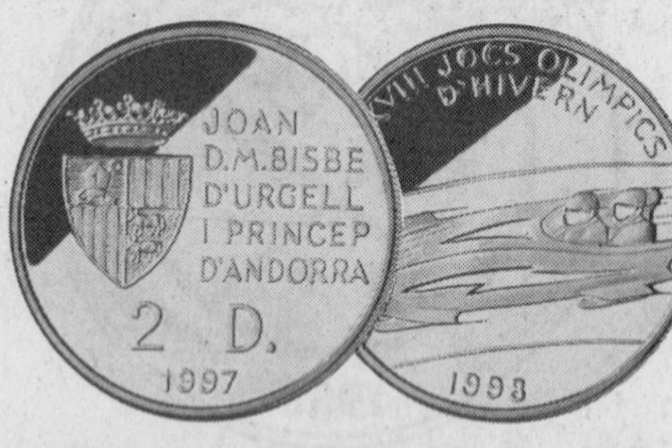

KM# 140 2 DINERS **Weight:** 20.0000 g. **Composition:** 0.9250 Silver .5948 oz. ASW **Subject:** 1988 Winter Olympics **Obverse:** Crowned arms, denomination **Reverse:** Bobsled

Date	Mintage	F	VF	XF	Unc	BU
1997 (1998) Proof	30,000	Value: 25.00				

KM# 16 5 DINERS **Composition:** Cast Copper **Obverse:** Joan D.M. Bisbe D'Urgell I

Date	Mintage	F	VF	XF	Unc	BU
1984	7,500	—	—	—	13.50	—

KM# 29 5 DINERS **Composition:** Cast Copper **Subject:** 2nd Congress of the Catalan Language

Date	Mintage	F	VF	XF	Unc	BU
1986	6,000	—	—	—	15.00	—

KM# 37 5 DINERS **Composition:** Bronze **Obverse:** Joan D.M. Bisbe D'Urgell I

Date	Mintage	F	VF	XF	Unc	BU
1986	10,000	—	—	—	17.50	—

KM# 51 5 DINERS **Composition:** Copper-Nickel **Obverse:** Church of St. Climent de Pal

Date	Mintage	F	VF	XF	Unc	BU
1988	5,000	—	—	—	17.50	—

KM# 80 5 DINERS **Weight:** 10.0000 g. **Composition:** 0.5000 Silver .1608 oz. ASW **Subject:** 1988 Winter Olympics **Reverse:** Cross-country skier

Date	Mintage	F	VF	XF	Unc	BU
1993 Proof	50,000	Value: 13.50				

KM# 102 5 DINERS **Weight:** 15.0000 g. **Composition:** 0.9250 Silver .4461 oz. ASW **Subject:** Andorran Circle of the Arts - 25th Anniversary

Date	Mintage	F	VF	XF	Unc	BU
1993 Proof	3,000	Value: 25.00				

KM# 111 5 DINERS **Weight:** 1.2500 g. **Composition:** 0.9990 Gold .0401 oz. AGW **Subject:** Wildlife **Obverse:** Crowned arms, denomination **Reverse:** Red squirrel

Date	Mintage	F	VF	XF	Unc	BU
1994 Proof	—	Value: 40.00				

KM# 112 5 DINERS **Weight:** 1.5552 g. **Composition:** 0.9990 Gold .0500 oz. AGW **Obverse:** Defiant eagle **Reverse:** Crowned denomination

Date	Mintage	F	VF	XF	Unc	BU
1995 Proof	—	Value: 50.00				

KM# 116 5 DINERS **Weight:** 15.0000 g. **Composition:** 0.9250 Silver .4461 oz. ASW **Subject:** XXIII Photographers Federation Congress

Date	Mintage	F	VF	XF	Unc	BU
1995 Proof	3,000	Value: 25.00				

KM# 117 5 DINERS **Weight:** 1.2441 g. **Composition:** 0.9990 Gold .0400 oz. AGW **Subject:** Wildlife **Reverse:** Chamois

Date	Mintage	F	VF	XF	Unc	BU
1996 Proof	Est. 100,000	Value: 40.00				

KM# 118 5 DINERS **Weight:** 1.2441 g. **Composition:** 0.9990 Gold .0400 oz. AGW **Subject:** Wildlife **Reverse:** Brown bear and cub

Date	Mintage	F	VF	XF	Unc	BU
1996 Proof	Est. 100,000	Value: 40.00				

KM# 141 5 DINERS **Weight:** 3.1103 g. **Composition:** 0.5850 Gold .0585 oz. AGW **Subject:** 1998 Winter Olympics **Obverse:** Crowned arms, denomination **Reverse:** Downhill skier

Date	Mintage	F	VF	XF	Unc	BU
1997 (1998) Proof	5,000	Value: 55.00				

KM# 155 5 DINERS **Ring Composition:** Brass **Center Weight:** 27.0000 g. **Center Composition:** Silver **Obverse:** World globe amid stars **Reverse:** World globe with sun, planets and stars **Note:** Silver center and brass ring are within a silver ring.

Date		F	VF	XF	Unc	BU
1999 Proof	—	Value: 30.00				

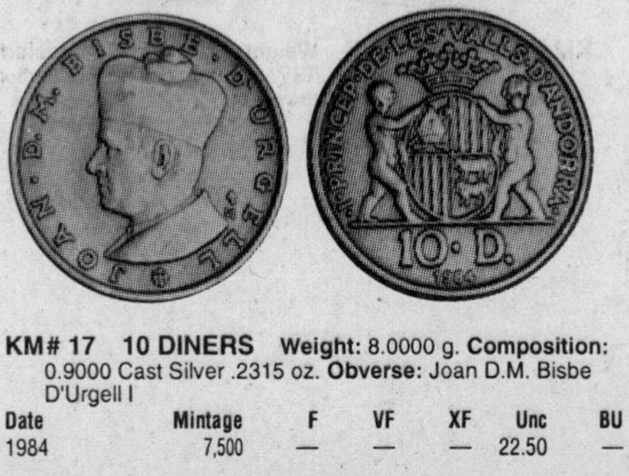

KM# 17 10 DINERS **Weight:** 8.0000 g. **Composition:** 0.9000 Cast Silver .2315 oz. **Obverse:** Joan D.M. Bisbe D'Urgell I

Date	Mintage	F	VF	XF	Unc	BU
1984	7,500	—	—	—	22.50	—

KM# 34 10 DINERS **Weight:** 8.0000 g. **Composition:** 0.9000 Cast Silver .2315 oz. **Subject:** 1988 World Cup Soccer Games

Date	Mintage	F	VF	XF	Unc	BU
1986 Prooflike	10,000	—	—	—	22.50	—

KM# 38 10 DINERS **Weight:** 8.0000 g. **Composition:** 0.9250 Silver .2379 oz. ASW **Obverse:** Joan D.M. Bisbe D'Urgell I

Date	Mintage	F	VF	XF	Unc	BU
1986	10,000	—	—	—	22.50	—

KM# 52 10 DINERS **Weight:** 8.0000 g. **Composition:** 0.9250 Silver .2379 oz. ASW **Obverse:** Church of St. Joan de Caselles

Date	Mintage	F	VF	XF	Unc	BU
1988	5,000	—	—	—	22.50	—

KM# 53 10 DINERS **Weight:** 12.0000 g. **Composition:** 0.9250 Silver .3569 oz. ASW **Subject:** 1990 World Cup Soccer Games

Date	Mintage	F	VF	XF	Unc	BU
1989 Proof	20,000	Value: 13.50				

KM# 55 10 DINERS **Weight:** 12.0000 g. **Composition:** 0.9250 Silver .3569 oz. ASW **Subject:** 1992 Winter Olympics **Reverse:** Downhill skier

Date	Mintage	F	VF	XF	Unc	BU
1989 Proof	15,000	Value: 17.50				

KM# 56 10 DINERS **Weight:** 12.0000 g. **Composition:** 0.9250 Silver .3569 oz. ASW **Subject:** 1992 Summer Olympics **Reverse:** Soccer

Date	Mintage	F	VF	XF	Unc	BU
1989 Proof	15,000	Value: 17.50				

KM# 60 10 DINERS **Weight:** 12.0000 g. **Composition:** 0.9250 Silver .3569 oz. ASW **Subject:** 1990 World Cup Soccer Games **Reverse:** Map of Italy and soccer ball

Date	Mintage	F	VF	XF	Unc	BU
1989 Proof	20,000	Value: 17.50				

KM# 71 10 DINERS **Weight:** 12.0000 g. **Composition:** 0.9250 Silver .3569 oz. ASW **Subject:** ECU Customs Union **Reverse:** Charlemagne

Date	Mintage	F	VF	XF	Unc	BU
ND(1992) Proof	15,000	Value: 40.00				

KM# 74 10 DINERS **Weight:** 31.1035 g. **Composition:** 0.9250 Silver .9250 oz. ASW **Subject:** Wildlife **Reverse:** Red squirrel

Date	Mintage	F	VF	XF	Unc	BU
1992 Proof	15,000	Value: 35.00				

KM# 75 10 DINERS **Weight:** 31.1035 g. **Composition:** 0.9250 Silver .9250 oz. ASW **Subject:** Wildlife **Reverse:** Chamois

Date	Mintage	F	VF	XF	Unc	BU
1992 Proof	15,000	Value: 30.00				

KM# 76 10 DINERS **Weight:** 31.1035 g. **Composition:** 0.9250 Silver .9250 oz. ASW **Subject:** Wildlife **Reverse:** Bears

Date	Mintage	F	VF	XF	Unc	BU
1992 Proof	15,000	Value: 35.00				

KM# 78 10 DINERS **Weight:** 31.1035 g. **Composition:** 0.9250 Silver .9250 oz. ASW **Subject:** Discovery of the New World **Reverse:** Stylized ship on globe

Date	Mintage	F	VF	XF	Unc	BU
1992 Proof	15,000	Value: 30.00				

KM# 84 10 DINERS **Weight:** 31.4700 g. **Composition:** 0.9250 Silver .9359 oz. ASW **Obverse:** Crowned arms above denomination and date **Reverse:** Stylized tree and birds

Date	Mintage	F	VF	XF	Unc	BU
1993 Proof	15,000	Value: 30.00				

KM# 85 10 DINERS **Weight:** 31.4700 g. **Composition:** 0.9250 Silver .9359 oz. ASW **Subject:** Space Exploration **Reverse:** Tethered space walker

Date	Mintage	F	VF	XF	Unc	BU
1993 Proof	15,000	Value: 32.50				

KM# 86 10 DINERS **Weight:** 31.4700 g. **Composition:** 0.9250 Silver .9359 oz. ASW **Subject:** 1994 World Cup Soccer **Reverse:** Player before world map

Date	Mintage	F	VF	XF	Unc	BU
1993 Proof	20,000	Value: 35.00				

KM# 87 10 DINERS **Weight:** 31.4700 g. **Composition:** 0.9250 Silver .9359 oz. ASW **Subject:** Pioneer Edward White

Date	Mintage	F	VF	XF	Unc	BU
1993 Proof	Est. 10,000	Value: 50.00				

KM# 89 10 DINERS **Weight:** 31.4700 g. **Composition:** 0.9250 Silver .9359 oz. ASW **Subject:** ECU Customs Union **Reverse:** St. George

Date	Mintage	F	VF	XF	Unc	BU
1993 Proof	25,000	Value: 30.00				

KM# 95 10 DINERS **Weight:** 31.4700 g. **Composition:** 0.9250 Silver .9359 oz. ASW **Subject:** 1996 Summer Olympic Games **Reverse:** Cyclists

Date	Mintage	F	VF	XF	Unc	BU
1994 Proof	50,000	Value: 27.50				

KM# 97 10 DINERS **Weight:** 31.4700 g. **Composition:** 0.9250 Silver .9359 oz. ASW **Subject:** Andorra U.N. Membership **Obverse:** Arms above "ECU"

Date	Mintage	F	VF	XF	Unc	BU
1994 Proof	25,000	Value: 37.50				

KM# 98 10 DINERS **Weight:** 31.4700 g. **Composition:** 0.9250 Silver .9359 oz. ASW **Subject:** Discovery of the New World

Date	Mintage	F	VF	XF	Unc	BU
1994 Proof	20,000	Value: 42.50				

KM# 99 10 DINERS **Weight:** 31.4700 g. **Composition:** 0.9250 Silver .9359 oz. ASW **Subject:** ECU Customs Union **Reverse:** Peter III of Catalonia and Aragon

Date	Mintage	F	VF	XF	Unc	BU
1994 Proof	25,000	Value: 40.00				

KM# 105 10 DINERS **Weight:** 31.4700 g. **Composition:** 0.9250 Silver .9359 oz. ASW **Subject:** ECU Customs Union **Reverse:** Ramon Berenguer III

Date	Mintage	F	VF	XF	Unc	BU
1995 Proof	30,000	Value: 42.50				

KM# 108 10 DINERS **Weight:** 31.6000 g. **Composition:** 0.9250 Silver .9308 oz. ASW **Subject:** Admission to the Council of Europe **Obverse:** Arms above "ECU"

Date	Mintage	F	VF	XF	Unc	BU
1995 Proof	35,000	Value: 37.50				

KM# 110 10 DINERS **Weight:** 31.1035 g. **Composition:** 0.9250 Silver .9250 oz. ASW **Subject:** 50th Anniversary - F.A.O. **Reverse:** Ceres holding grain

Date	Mintage	F	VF	XF	Unc	BU
1995 Proof	10,000	Value: 45.00				

KM# 113 10 DINERS **Weight:** 31.1035 g. **Composition:** 0.9250 Silver .9250 oz. ASW **Subject:** Wildlife **Reverse:** Wolf

Date	Mintage	F	VF	XF	Unc	BU
1995 Proof	20,000	Value: 50.00				

KM# 114 10 DINERS **Weight:** 31.1035 g. **Composition:** 0.9250 Silver .9250 oz. ASW **Subject:** Agnus Dei **Obverse:** Arms above "ECU"

Date	Mintage	F	VF	XF	Unc	BU
1995 Proof	Est. 35,000	Value: 35.00				

KM# 119 10 DINERS **Weight:** 31.4700 g. **Composition:** 0.9250 Silver .9359 oz. ASW **Obverse:** Arms above "ECU" **Reverse:** Frederic II on throne

Date	Mintage	F	VF	XF	Unc	BU
1996 Proof	Est. 30,000	Value: 35.00				

KM# A127 10 DINERS **Weight:** 31.4700 g. **Composition:** 0.9250 Copper .9359 oz. **Series:** Wildlife Protection **Subject:** Sea Otter **Obverse:** Crowned arms **Reverse:** Diving sea otter

Date	Mintage	F	VF	XF	Unc	BU
1996 Proof	15,000	Value: 42.50				

KM# 120 10 DINERS **Weight:** 31.4700 g. **Composition:** 0.9250 Silver .9359 oz. ASW **Reverse:** Sailing ship

Date	Mintage	F	VF	XF	Unc	BU
1996 Proof	Est. 20,000	Value: 40.00				

KM# 121 10 DINERS **Weight:** 31.4700 g. **Composition:** 0.9250 Silver .9359 oz. ASW **Obverse:** Arms above "ECU" **Reverse:** Pope crowning Charlemagne

Date	Mintage	F	VF	XF	Unc	BU
1996 Proof	Est. 30,000	Value: 32.50				

KM# 125 10 DINERS **Weight:** 31.4700 g. **Composition:** 0.9250 Silver .9359 oz. ASW **Subject:** 25th Anniversary - Msgr. Alanis, Co-prince and Bishop of Andorra **Obverse:** Crowned arms above "EURO" **Reverse:** Enthroned prince, date

Date	Mintage	F	VF	XF	Unc	BU
1996 Proof	30,000	Value: 32.50				

KM# 130 10 DINERS **Weight:** 31.4700 g. **Composition:** 0.9250 Silver .9359 oz. ASW **Subject:** Treaty of Rome **Obverse:** Crowned arms above "EURO" **Reverse:** Seated Europa with olive branch and "EURO" shield, dates

Date	Mintage	F	VF	XF	Unc	BU
1997 Proof	25,000	Value: 40.00				

KM#166 10 DINERS **Weight:** 31.5500 g. **Composition:** 0.9250 Silver .9383 oz. ASW **Subject:** Palau del Princep **Obverse:** Crowned arms **Reverse:** Crowned arms on house corner **Edge:** Reeded

Date	F	VF	XF	Unc	BU
1997 Proof	—	Value: 35.00			

KM#131 10 DINERS **Weight:** 31.4700 g. **Composition:** 0.9250 Silver .9359 oz. ASW **Subject:** Wildlife **Obverse:** Crowned arms **Reverse:** Vixen with kit

Date	Mintage	F	VF	XF	Unc	BU
1997 Proof	15,000	Value: 45.00				

KM#132 10 DINERS **Weight:** 31.4700 g. **Composition:** 0.9250 Silver .9359 oz. ASW **Obverse:** Crowned arms **Reverse:** Johan Sebastian Bach portrait

Date	Mintage	F	VF	XF	Unc	BU
1997 Proof	Est. 25,000	Value: 37.50				

KM#133 10 DINERS **Weight:** 31.4700 g. **Composition:** 0.9250 Silver .9359 oz. ASW **Obverse:** Crowned arms **Reverse:** Antonio Vivaldi portrait

Date	Mintage	F	VF	XF	Unc	BU
1997 Proof	Est. 25,000	Value: 37.50				

KM# 136 10 DINERS **Weight:** 3.1103 g. **Composition:** 0.9990 Gold .1000 oz. AGW **Obverse:** Fleury cross **Reverse:** Portrait of Isabella I **Note:** Similar to 20 Diners, KM#137

Date	Mintage	F	VF	XF	Unc	BU
1997 Proof	Est. 5,000	Value: 85.00				

KM#142 10 DINERS **Weight:** 31.4700 g. **Composition:** 0.9250 Silver .9359 oz. ASW **Subject:** 1998 World Cup Soccer **Obverse:** Crowned arms and denomination **Reverse:** Eiffel Tower and soccer ball

Date	Mintage	F	VF	XF	Unc	BU
1997 Proof	15,000	Value: 45.00				

KM#143 10 DINERS **Weight:** 31.4700 g. **Composition:** 0.9250 Silver .9359 oz. ASW **Subject:** Human Rights **Obverse:** Crowned arms **Reverse:** Allegorical figure of Justice

Date	Mintage	F	VF	XF	Unc	BU
1998 Proof	25,000	Value: 42.50				

KM#165 10 DINERS **Weight:** 31.1100 g. **Composition:** 0.9990 Silver 1 oz. ASW **Subject:** Year of the Tiger **Obverse:** Multicolored cartoon tiger and Chinese legend **Reverse:** Denomination in crowned wreath **Edge:** Reeded

Date	F	VF	XF	Unc	BU
1998 Proof	—	Value: 50.00			

KM#146 10 DINERS **Weight:** 31.4700 g. **Composition:** 0.9250 Silver .9359 oz. ASW **Obverse:** Crowned arms **Reverse:** Portraitof Claudio Monteverdi, dates

Date	Mintage	F	VF	XF	Unc	BU
1998 Proof	25,000	Value: 37.50				

KM#147 10 DINERS **Weight:** 31.4700 g. **Composition:** 0.9250 Silver .9359 oz. ASW **Subject:** George Friedrich Handel **Obverse:** Crowned arms **Reverse:** Portrait, dates

Date	Mintage	F	VF	XF	Unc	BU
1998 Proof	25,000	Value: 37.50				

KM#150 10 DINERS **Weight:** 31.4700 g. **Composition:** 0.9250 Silver .9359 oz. ASW **Subject:** Europa **Obverse:** Crowned arms **Reverse:** Seated Europa

Date	Mintage	F	VF	XF	Unc	BU
1998 Proof	25,000	Value: 40.00				

KM#151 10 DINERS **Weight:** 31.4700 g. **Composition:** 0.9250 Silver .9359 oz. ASW **Subject:** Europa **Obverse:** Crowned arms **Reverse:** Europa driving quadriga

Date	Mintage	F	VF	XF	Unc	BU
1998 Proof	25,000	Value: 40.00				

KM#153 10 DINERS **Weight:** 31.4700 g. **Composition:** 0.9250 Silver .9359 oz. ASW **Subject:** 50th Anniversary - European Council **Obverse:** Crowned arms **Reverse:** Statue of Democracy

Date	Mintage	F	VF	XF	Unc	BU
1999 Proof	15,000	Value: 42.50				

KM# 156 10 DINERS **Weight:** 31.4700 g. **Composition:** 0.9250 Silver .9359 oz. ASW **Subject:** Jubilee 2000 **Obverse:** National arms **Reverse:** Birth of Jesus **Edge:** Reeded **Size:** 38.6 mm.

Date	Mintage	F	VF	XF	Unc	BU
1999 Proof	15,000	Value: 40.00				

KM# 157 10 DINERS **Weight:** 31.4700 g. **Composition:** 0.9250 Silver .9359 oz. ASW **Subject:** Jubilee 2000 **Obverse:** National arms **Reverse:** Slaughter of the Innocents - Man with sword killing children

Date	Mintage	F	VF	XF	Unc	BU
1999 Proof	15,000	Value: 40.00				

KM# 154 10 DINERS **Weight:** 31.4700 g. **Composition:** 0.9250 Silver .9359 oz. ASW **Subject:** 50th Anniversary - European Council **Obverse:** Crowned arms **Reverse:** Statue of Human Rights

Date	Mintage	F	VF	XF	Unc	BU
1999 Proof	15,000	Value: 42.50				

KM# 158 10 DINERS **Weight:** 31.4700 g. **Composition:** 0.9250 Silver .9359 oz. ASW **Subject:** Jubilee 2000 **Obverse:** National arms **Reverse:** John the Baptist baptizing Jesus

Date	Mintage	F	VF	XF	Unc	BU
1999 Proof	15,000	Value: 40.00				

KM# 159 10 DINERS **Weight:** 31.4700 g. **Composition:** 0.9250 Silver .9359 oz. ASW **Subject:** Jubilee 2000 **Obverse:** National arms **Reverse:** Prodigal Son - Son kneeling before his father

Date	Mintage	F	VF	XF	Unc	BU
1999 Proof	15,000	Value: 40.00				

KM# 160 10 DINERS **Weight:** 31.4700 g. **Composition:** 0.9250 Silver .9359 oz. ASW **Subject:** Jubilee 2000 **Obverse:** National arms **Reverse:** Jesus' entry into Jerusalem

Date	Mintage	F	VF	XF	Unc	BU
1999 Proof	15,000	Value: 40.00				

KM# 161 10 DINERS **Weight:** 31.4700 g. **Composition:** 0.9250 Silver .9359 oz. ASW **Subject:** Jubilee 2000 **Obverse:** National arms **Reverse:** Last Supper scene

Date	Mintage	F	VF	XF	Unc	BU
1999 Proof	15,000	Value: 40.00				

KM# 162 10 DINERS **Weight:** 31.4700 g. **Composition:** 0.9250 Silver .9359 oz. ASW **Subject:** Jubilee 2000 **Obverse:** National arms **Reverse:** Jesus on the cross

Date	Mintage	F	VF	XF	Unc	BU
1999 Proof	15,000	Value: 40.00				

KM# 163 10 DINERS **Weight:** 31.4700 g. **Composition:** 0.9250 Silver .9359 oz. ASW **Subject:** Jubilee 2000 **Obverse:** National arms **Reverse:** Jesus standing in boat

Date	Mintage	F	VF	XF	Unc	BU
1999 Proof	15,000	Value: 40.00				

KM# 172 10 DINERS **Weight:** 31.4700 g. **Composition:** 0.9250 Silver 0.9359 oz. ASW **Subject:** Europa **Obverse:** National arms **Reverse:** Europa in chariot **Edge:** Reeded **Size:** 38.6 mm.

Date	Mintage	F	VF	XF	Unc	BU
2001 Proof	15,000	Value: 40.00				

KM# 173 10 DINERS **Weight:** 31.4700 g. **Composition:** 0.9250 Silver 0.9359 oz. ASW **Subject:** Concordia Europea **Obverse:** National arms **Reverse:** Two crowned women holding hands **Edge:** Reeded **Size:** 38.6 mm.

Date	Mintage	F	VF	XF	Unc	BU
2001 Proof	15,000	Value: 40.00				

KM# 175 10 DINERS **Weight:** 31.4700 g. **Composition:** 0.9250 Silver 0.9359 oz. ASW **Subject:** Olympics **Obverse:** National arms **Reverse:** Snowboarder **Edge:** Reeded **Size:** 38.6 mm.

Date	Mintage	F	VF	XF	Unc	BU
2002 Proof	15,000	Value: 40.00				

KM# 22 20 DINERS **Weight:** 16.0000 g. **Composition:** 0.8350 Silver .4296 oz. ASW **Subject:** Wildlife **Reverse:** Bear

Date	Mintage	F	VF	XF	Unc	BU
1984 Proof	5,000	Value: 35.00				

KM# 23 20 DINERS **Weight:** 16.0000 g. **Composition:** 0.8350 Silver .4296 oz. ASW **Subject:** Wildlife **Reverse:** Red squirrel

Date	Mintage	F	VF	XF	Unc	BU
1984 Proof	5,000	Value: 35.00				

KM# 24 20 DINERS **Weight:** 16.0000 g. **Composition:** 0.8350 Silver .4296 oz. ASW **Subject:** Wildlife **Obverse:** Similar to KM#23 **Reverse:** Ibex

Date	Mintage	F	VF	XF	Unc	BU
1984 Proof	5,000	Value: 35.00				

KM# 25 20 DINERS **Weight:** 16.0000 g. **Composition:** 0.9000 Silver .4630 oz. ASW **Subject:** 1984 Summer Olympics

Date	Mintage	F	VF	XF	Unc	BU
1984 Proof	10,000	Value: 35.00				

KM# 26 20 DINERS **Weight:** 16.0000 g. **Composition:** 0.9000 Silver .4630 oz. ASW **Subject:** Christmas

Date	Mintage	F	VF	XF	Unc	BU
1985 Proof	7,000	Value: 27.50				

KM# 39 20 DINERS **Weight:** 16.0000 g. **Composition:** 0.9000 Silver .4630 oz. ASW **Subject:** Olympic Tennis

Date	Mintage	F	VF	XF	Unc	BU
1987	10,000	—	—	—	50.00	—

KM# 43 20 DINERS **Weight:** 16.0000 g. **Composition:** 0.9000 Silver .4630 oz. ASW **Subject:** 1988 Summer Olympics **Reverse:** Stadium

Date	Mintage	F	VF	XF	Unc	BU
1988	12,000	—	—	—	50.00	—

KM# 47 20 DINERS **Weight:** 16.0000 g. **Composition:** 0.9250 Silver .4759 oz. ASW **Subject:** 1992 Winter Olympics **Reverse:** Pairs figure skating

Date	Mintage	F	VF	XF	Unc	BU
1988 Proof	15,000	Value: 35.00				

KM# 48 20 DINERS **Weight:** 16.0000 g. **Composition:** 0.9250 Silver .4759 oz. ASW **Subject:** 1992 Summer Olympics **Reverse:** Gymnast on rings

Date	Mintage	F	VF	XF	Unc	BU
1988 Proof	15,000	Value: 35.00				

KM# 54 20 DINERS **Weight:** 16.0000 g. **Composition:** 0.9250 Silver .4759 oz. ASW **Subject:** 1992 Summer Olympics **Reverse:** Wind surfer

Date	Mintage	F	VF	XF	Unc	BU
1989 Proof	15,000	Value: 35.00				

KM# 57 20 DINERS **Weight:** 16.0000 g. **Composition:** 0.9250 Silver .4759 oz. ASW **Subject:** 1992 Summer Olympics **Obverse:** Similar to KM#47 **Reverse:** Kayaker

Date	Mintage	F	VF	XF	Unc	BU
1989 Proof	15,000	Value: 35.00				

KM# 58 20 DINERS **Weight:** 16.0000 g. **Composition:** 0.9250 Silver .4759 oz. ASW **Subject:** 1992 Summer Olympics **Obverse:** Similar to KM#47 **Reverse:** Hurdler

Date	Mintage	F	VF	XF	Unc	BU
1990 Proof	15,000	Value: 35.00				

KM# 59 20 DINERS **Weight:** 16.0000 g. **Composition:** 0.9250 Silver .4759 oz. ASW **Subject:** 1992 Summer Olympics **Obverse:** Similar to KM#47 **Reverse:** Equestrian

Date	Mintage	F	VF	XF	Unc	BU
1990 Proof	15,000	Value: 35.00				

KM# 67 20 DINERS **Weight:** 21.0000 g. **Composition:** 0.9250 Silver .6246 oz. ASW **Subject:** European Small States Games **Reverse:** Equestrian

Date	Mintage	F	VF	XF	Unc	BU
1991 Proof	5,000	Value: 40.00				

KM# 72 20 DINERS **Weight:** 26.5000 g. **Composition:** 0.9250 Silver .7435 oz. ASW **Subject:** ECU Customs Union **Obverse:** Similar to 10 Diners, KM#71 **Reverse:** Charlemagne **Note:** With 1.5 g. 0.917 gold inlay, 0.0442 oz. AGW.

Date	Mintage	F	VF	XF	Unc	BU
ND(1992)	5,000	—	—	—	100	—

KM# 90 20 DINERS **Weight:** 26.5000 g. **Composition:** 0.9250 Silver .7435 oz. ASW **Subject:** ECU Customs Union **Reverse:** St. George **Note:** With 1.5 g. 0.917 gold inlay, 0.0442 oz. AGW.

Date	Mintage	F	VF	XF	Unc	BU
1993 Matte	5,000	—	—	—	110	—

KM# 100 20 DINERS **Weight:** 26.5000 g. **Composition:** 0.9250 Silver .7435 oz. ASW **Subject:** ECU Customs Union **Reverse:** Peter III of Catalonia and Aragon **Note:** With 1.5 g. 0.917 gold inlay, 0.0442 oz. AGW.

Date	Mintage	F	VF	XF	Unc	BU
1994	5,000	—	—	—	90.00	—

KM# 106 20 DINERS **Weight:** 25.0000 g. **Composition:** 0.9250 Silver .7435 oz. ASW **Subject:** ECU Customs Union **Reverse:** Ramon Berenger III **Note:** With 1.6 g. 0.917 gold inlay, 0.0442 oz. AGW.

Date	Mintage	F	VF	XF	Unc	BU
1995	6,000	—	—	—	85.00	—

KM# 122 20 DINERS **Weight:** 25.0000 g. **Composition:** 0.9250 Silver .7435 oz. ASW **Obverse:** Arms and "ECU" **Reverse:** Charlemagne being crowned **Note:** With 1.6 g. 0.917 gold inlay, 0.0442 oz. AGW.

Date	F	VF	XF	Unc	BU
1996	—	—	—	150	—

KM# 128 20 DINERS **Weight:** 25.0000 g. **Composition:** 0.9250 Silver .7435 oz. ASW **Subject:** Treaty at Rome **Obverse:** Crowned arms above "EURO" **Reverse:** Seated Europa with child holding "EURO" shield **Note:** With 1.6 g. 0.917 gold inlay, 0.0442 oz. AGW.

Date	Mintage	F	VF	XF	Unc	BU
1997	5,000	—	—	—	90.00	—

KM# 137 20 DINERS **Weight:** 6.2207 g. **Composition:** 0.9990 Gold .2000 oz. AGW **Obverse:** Fleury cross **Reverse:** Portrait of Isabella I

Date	Mintage	F	VF	XF	Unc	BU
1997 Proof	Est. 3,500	Value: 165				

KM# 144 20 DINERS **Weight:** 25.0000 g. **Composition:** 0.9250 Silver .7435 oz. ASW **Subject:** Human Rights **Obverse:** Crowned arms **Reverse:** Young family and broken chain **Note:** With 1.5 g. 0.917 gold inlay, 0.0442 oz. AGW.

Date	Mintage	F	VF	XF	Unc	BU
1998	5,000	—	—	—	80.00	—

KM# 148 20 DINERS **Weight:** 25.0000 g. **Composition:** 0.9250 Silver .7435 oz. ASW **Subject:** Olympics 2000 **Obverse:** Crowned arms **Reverse:** Javelin thrower **Note:** With 1.5 g. 0.917 gold inlay, 0.0442 oz. AGW.

Date	Mintage	F	VF	XF	Unc	BU
1998	5,000	—	—	—	75.00	—

KM# 149 20 DINERS **Weight:** 25.0000 g. **Composition:** 0.9250 Silver .7435 oz. ASW **Subject:** Olympics 2000 **Obverse:** Crowned arms **Reverse:** Discus thrower

Date	Mintage	F	VF	XF	Unc	BU
1998	5,000	—	—	—	75.00	—

KM# 167 20 DINERS **Weight:** 25.0000 g. **Composition:** 0.9250 Silver .7435 oz. ASW **Subject:** XXVII JOCS 2000 Olympics **Obverse:** Crowned arms, date and denomination **Reverse:** Hurdler on gold inlay **Edge:** Plain

Date	Mintage	F	VF	XF	Unc	BU
2000	6,000	—	—	—	75.00	—

KM# 168 20 DINERS **Weight:** 25.0000 g. **Composition:** 0.9250 Silver .7435 oz. ASW **Subject:** XXVII JOCS 2000 Olympics **Obverse:** Crowned arms, date and denomination **Reverse:** Runner on gold inlay **Edge:** Plain

Date	Mintage	F	VF	XF	Unc	BU
2000	6,000	—	—	—	75.00	—

KM# 169 20 DINERS **Weight:** 25.0000 g. **Composition:** 0.9250 Silver .7435 oz. ASW **Subject:** XXVII JOCS 2000 Olympics **Obverse:** Crowned arms, date and denomination **Reverse:** Long jumper on gold inlay **Edge:** Plain

Date	Mintage	F	VF	XF	Unc	BU
2000	6,000	—	—	—	75.00	—

KM# 170 20 DINERS **Weight:** 25.0000 g. **Composition:** 0.9250 Silver .7435 oz. ASW **Subject:** XXVII JOCS 2000 Olympics **Obverse:** Crowned arms, date and denomination **Reverse:** Pole vaulter on gold inlay **Edge:** Plain

Date	Mintage	F	VF	XF	Unc	BU
2000	6,000	—	—	—	75.00	—

KM# 18 25 DINERS Weight: 20.0000 g. **Composition:** 0.9000 Silver .5787 oz. ASW **Obverse:** Joan D.M. Bisbe D'Urgell I

Date	Mintage	F	VF	XF	Unc	BU
1984	4,450	—	—	—	45.00	—
1984 Proof	550	Value: 125				

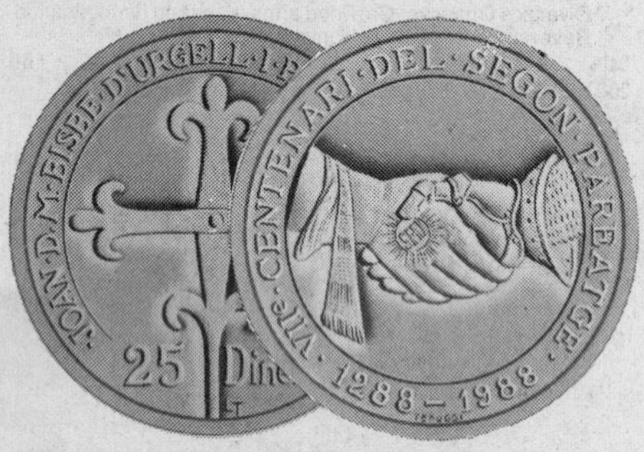

KM# 44.1 25 DINERS Weight: 20.0000 g. **Composition:** 0.9000 Silver .5787 oz. ASW **Subject:** 700th Anniversary - Andorra's Governing Charter **Note:** Medallic die rotation.

Date	Mintage	F	VF	XF	Unc	BU
ND(1988)	20,000	—	—	—	32.00	—

KM# 44.2 25 DINERS Weight: 20.0000 g. **Composition:** 0.9000 Silver .5787 oz. ASW **Subject:** 700th Anniversary - Andorra's Governing Charter **Note:** Medallic die rotation.

Date	Mintage	F	VF	XF	Unc	BU
ND(1988) Proof	10,000	Value: 40.00				

KM# 61 25 DINERS Weight: 20.0000 g. **Composition:** 0.9000 Silver .5787 oz. ASW **Subject:** Millenary of the Bishop of Sala

Date	F	VF	XF	Unc	BU
1989	—	—	—	50.00	—

KM# 65 25 DINERS Weight: 28.2800 g. **Composition:** 0.9250 Silver .8411 oz. ASW **Subject:** Red Cross

Date	Mintage	F	VF	XF	Unc	BU
1991 Proof	3,000	Value: 57.50				

KM# 69 25 DINERS Weight: 25.0000 g. **Composition:** 0.9250 Silver .7435 oz. ASW **Subject:** 20th Anniversary - Episcopal Co-prince **Note:** With 0.917 gold inlay, 0.0442 oz. AGW.

Date	Mintage	F	VF	XF	Unc	BU
1991	2,500	—	—	—	85.00	—

KM# 73 25 DINERS Weight: 7.7700 g. **Composition:** 0.5830 Gold .1456 oz. AGW **Subject:** ECU Customs Union **Reverse:** St. Ermengol

Date	Mintage	F	VF	XF	Unc	BU
1992 Proof	3,000	Value: 100				

KM# 81 25 DINERS Weight: 7.7700 g. **Composition:** 0.5830 Gold .1456 oz. AGW **Subject:** 1994 Winter Olympic Games **Reverse:** Downhill skier

Date	Mintage	F	VF	XF	Unc	BU
1993 Proof	6,000	Value: 115				

KM# 91 25 DINERS Weight: 7.7700 g. **Composition:** 0.5830 Gold .1456 oz. AGW **Subject:** ECU Customs Union **Reverse:** Bishop riding a horse

Date	Mintage	F	VF	XF	Unc	BU
1993 Proof	5,000	Value: 115				

KM# 92 25 DINERS Weight: 7.7700 g. **Composition:** 0.5830 Gold .1456 oz. AGW **Subject:** 1994 World Cup Soccer

Date	Mintage	F	VF	XF	Unc	BU
1993 Proof	5,000	Value: 115				

KM# 96 25 DINERS Weight: 7.7700 g. **Composition:** 0.5830 Gold .1456 oz. AGW **Subject:** 1994 Summer Olympic Games **Reverse:** Tennis

Date	Mintage	F	VF	XF	Unc	BU
1994 Proof	5,000	Value: 115				

KM# 101 25 DINERS Weight: 7.7700 g. **Composition:** 0.5830 Gold .1456 oz. AGW **Subject:** ECU Customs Union **Obverse:** Coat of arms **Reverse:** Bishop Pere D'Urg standing

Date	Mintage	F	VF	XF	Unc	BU
1994 Proof	5,000	Value: 115				

KM# 107 25 DINERS Weight: 7.7700 g. **Composition:** 0.5830 Gold .1456 oz. AGW **Subject:** ECU Customs Union **Obverse:** Coat of arms **Reverse:** Bishop Pere D'Urg seated

Date	Mintage	F	VF	XF	Unc	BU
1995 Proof	5,000	Value: 115				

KM# 123 25 DINERS Weight: 7.7700 g. **Composition:** 0.5830 Gold .1456 oz. AGW **Obverse:** Arms and "ECU" **Reverse:** Seated Europa

Date	Mintage	F	VF	XF	Unc	BU
1996 Proof	Est. 5,000	Value: 115				

KM# 129 25 DINERS Weight: 7.7700 g. **Composition:** 0.5830 Gold .1456 oz. AGW **Subject:** Treaty of Rome **Obverse:** Crowned arms **Reverse:** Europa on knee, holding large "EURO" shield

Date	Mintage	F	VF	XF	Unc	BU
1997 Proof	5,000	Value: 115				

KM# 139 25 DINERS Ring Weight: 3.1103 g. **Ring Composition:** 0.9995 Platinum .0999 oz. APW **Center Weight:** 3.1103 g. **Center Composition:** 0.9999 Gold .1000 oz. AGW **Obverse:** Fleury cross **Reverse:** Swan in water

Date	Mintage	F	VF	XF	Unc	BU
1997 Proof	10,000	Value: 235				

KM# 145 25 DINERS Weight: 7.7700 g. **Composition:** 0.5850 Gold .1461 oz. AGW **Subject:** Human Rights **Obverse:** Crowned arms **Reverse:** Seated woman with quill

A SPECIAL BONUS SUPPLEMENT FROM KRAUSE PUBLICATIONS

MAY/JUNE 2003

Mints of the World

NUMISMATIC NEWS • WORLD COIN NEWS • BANK NOTE REPORTER

Pride of AFRICA

Pobjoy Mint
Pobjoy International School of Minting Technology
Creative, Adventurous, Meticulous and Secure are words which are associated with the name of Pobjoy Mint, Europe's most consistently successful private mint. We are proud of our record of winning no less than eleven Coin of the Year Awards on behalf of five of our Governments and have recently qualified as a holder of the ISO 9001: 2000 standard of quality.
Pobjoy Mint leads where others follow and with the Peter Rabbit™ coin collection of 1993, it introduced a whole new concept of producing coins depicting the worlds favourite licensed characters. Over a period of ten years, coins have depicted such diverse images as Snoopy™, Pokémon™ and most recently Harry Potter™.
Ag 1 oz. CROWN
21ST CENTURY 1 CROWN
100th BIRTHDAY OF H.M. QUEEN ELIZABETH THE QUEEN MOTHER 1/5 CROWN
OF THE POSTAGE POST OFFICE MAURITIUS TWO PENCE 150TH ANNIVERSARY UNIFORM PENNY POST 5 POUNDS
2 CROWNS
.999 Ag 1 oz. ROYAL
BSI REGISTERED
UKAS QUALITY MANAGEMENT 003
Pobjoy Mint Ltd®
QUALITY & EXCELLENCE
CUSTOM MINTERS

A Family Affair
In addition to stunning images, produced to the highest standard, modern commemorative coins from Pobjoy Mint have featured new and unique production techniques, such as the first titanium coin, the first struck hologram, the first gold bullion bar coin, the first bejewelled coin. The list of unique developments grows each year and will continue to grow.
Having produced circulating or commemorative coinage for some twenty per cent of the World's Governments and Central Banks, the Pobjoy Mint has a pedigree to be admired and a reputation that is second to none. Not only does the Mint produce legal tender coins, but it produces high quality medallions for national and international organisations and offers a die making facility to other mints.
For further information concerning our services to Governments, Collectors and Commercial Organisations please contact Pobjoy Mint +44 1737 818181.
Pobjoy Mint Ltd, Kingswood Park, Bonsor Drive,
Kingswood, Surrey, KT20 6AY, U.K.
Tel: (+44) 1737 818181 Fax: (+44) 1737 818199
Internet: www.pobjoy.com Email: mint@pobjoy.com
TO THE WORLD
All legal tender coins made in England
HARRY POTTER
1 CROWN
1953 CORONATION 2003
GOD SAVE THE QUEEN
5 CROWNS
11th SEPT 2001
LEST WE FORGET
$100
CENTENARY OF THE TEDDY BEAR
$50
150th ANNIVERSARY
PENNY BLACK
POSTAGE
ONE PENNY
1 CROWN
PETER PAN
1 CROWN
YEAR OF THE GOAT
1 CROWN
XXVIII OLYMPIC GAMES
$10

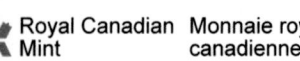

...VIATION
...TION

In the year of the Centenary of Flight...

The innovation of Australian Map coins has enchanted the collector world, with the 2002 Matthew Flinders Colour Coin Collection an overwhelming success. With the quality of the 2003 coins even better, demand for this new set is sure to be huge. This is especially so given the obvious international appeal of the Centenary of the First Flight by the Wright Brothers in 1903.

Order the 2003 Pioneers of Aviation Coin Collection now at the Official Issue Price!

Each Precious Metal Collection is...

- comprised of four pure silver (.999) 1 ounce $1 legal tender coins
- struck by The Perth Mint for the Commonwealth nation of Tuvalu
- housed in a timber case enriched with an impressive 'silver metallic' finish
- accompanied by an eight-page booklet with a numbered Certificate of Authenticity
- sensational value for such an innovative collection
- a lasting tribute to the pioneering feats of aviators

CELEBRATING THE 75TH ANNIVERSARY OF THE FIRST FLIGHT FROM USA TO AUSTRALIA

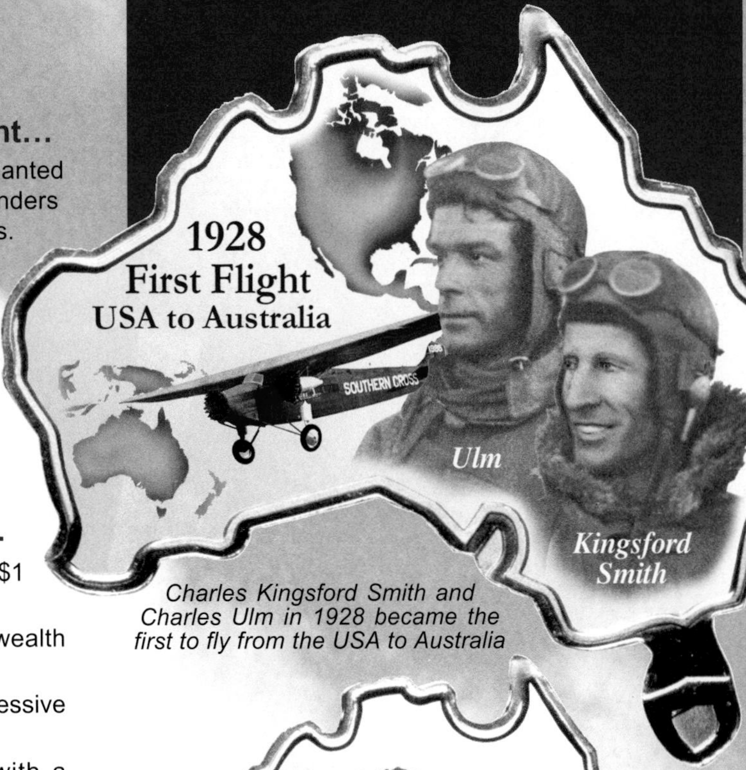

Charles Kingsford Smith and Charles Ulm in 1928 became the first to fly from the USA to Australia

Creating a world first, Bert Hinkler became the first to fly solo from Australia to Great Britain

Piloting the famous Southern Cross, Kingsford Smith took on treacherous conditions over the Tasman to become the first to fly from Australia to New Zealand

030404

Downie's Ltd
ESTABLISHED 1932

4533 MacArthur Blvd #888, Newport Beach CA 92660
Phone: (949) 838 0250 Fax: (949) 838 0013
Email: DowniesUSA@downies.com

ROYAL NORWEGIAN MINT

2000 Norway Souvenir Set

2002 Norway Souvenir Set

2002 Norway Proof set

2001 Norway Souvenir Set

2001 Nobel Commemorative Gold Coin

Internationally recognized for its restrictive issue policy, low mintages and unique designs, the Royal Norwegian Mint has minted coins for the Kingdom of Norway since 1686. Today, at 317 years old, RNM is one of the world's most reputable mints - proven by the fact that it has been the exclusive manufacturer of the gold medal for the Nobel Peace Prize since 1902. Norway is the most active collector's markets in the world, with an estimated 5% of the population actively collecting coins and medals. Norway is also not a member of the European Union, and is therefore one of a few remaining countries in Western Europe that has kept its own currency – the Krone.

The Mint annually issues currency and proof sets in limited editions that are sold to collectors all over the world. The souvenir coin set features English text and is a perfect gift for the novice collector, friend or family member – even if they're not of Norwegian heritage. On June 7 2005, Norway will celebrate the 100th anniversary of the dissolution of the union with Sweden, and its emergence as an independent nation. In a 1905 national referendum, 99.5% of voters backed the proposal to dissolve the union - only 184 people voted against – which led to Norway becoming its own monarchy under King Haakon VII. The Central Bank of Norway is marking this important occasion in Norwegian history with the issue of a three-year, six-coin commemorative program. The program will consist of three silver coins and three gold coins, to be issued in pairs starting in November 2003. Regrettably, the designs of the first pair of coins are currently embargoed and cannot be shown at this time.

However, interested collectors in North America can reserve their own personal copy of these items by contacting our sales representative, Royal Scandinavian Mint, by e-mail office@scandmint.com or phone 1-877-552-MINT (6468). To receive a catalog with products from the Royal Norwegian Mint, please visit our Internet site at www.dkm.no or contact Royal Scandinavian Mint using the contact information on the opposite page.

Royal Norwegian Mint PO Box 53 3602 Kongsberg Norway
Phone: +47 32 29 95 30 **Fax:** +47 32 29 95 50 **Email:** office@dkm.no

www.dkm.no

Krause Publications Coin Of The Year Program Nearly 20 Years Old

An awards program, the Coin of The Year, was launched in 1983 by WORLD COIN NEWS, a monthly periodical dedicated to collectors of world coins. The program is designed to enhance future design considerations, marketing techniques, aesthetic values and pride in workmanship in modern coinage. Each year a special worldwide blue-ribbon panel of experts selects the Coin of The Year and a winning coin in each of ten subsidiary classes:

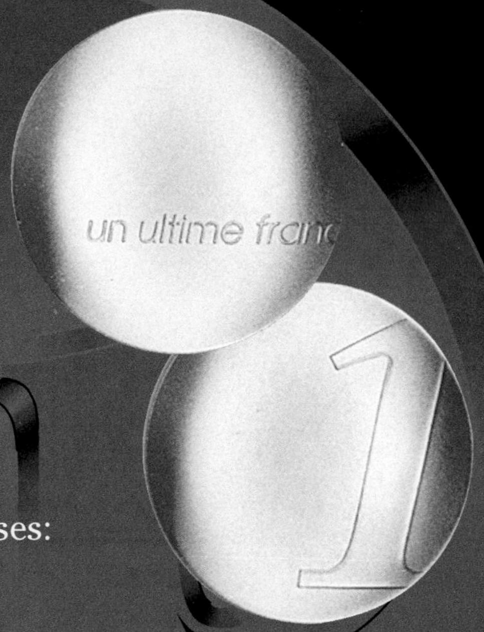

2003 Coin of the Year France 1-Franc Silver Coin

- **Most Artistic Coin**
- **Most Popular Coin**
- **Most Historically Significant Coin**
- **Best Gold Coin (This category includes coins struck of gold, platinum, palladium, or other exotic precious metals.)**
- **Best Silver Coin**
- **Best Crown**
- **Best Trade Coin**
- **Most Innovative Coinage Concept**
- **Most Inspirational Coin**
- **Best Contemporary Event Coin**

A distinguished panel of judges makes the selections. It consists of mint officials, engravers, officers of numismatic associations and coin dealer groups, world central bank and treasury officials, mass marketers of coins and independent experts from around the world, along with members of the Krause Publications' numismatic staff.

Date	Mintage	F	VF	XF	Unc	BU
1998 Proof	5,000	Value: 115				

KM# 174 25 DINERS **Weight:** 12.4414 g. **Composition:** 0.9990 Gold 0.3996 oz. AGW **Subject:** Christmas **Obverse:** National arms **Reverse:** Nativity scene **Edge:** Reeded **Size:** 26 mm.

Date	Mintage	F	VF	XF	Unc	BU
2001 Proof	3,000	Value: 225				

KM# 63 50 DINERS **Weight:** 15.5500 g. **Composition:** 0.9990 Gold .5000 oz. AGW **Note:** There is a similar 1988 half-ounce without the denomination.

Date	Mintage	F	VF	XF	Unc	BU
1989	3,000	—	—	—	225	—
1989 Proof	—	Value: 250				

KM# 62 50 DINERS **Weight:** 17.0250 g. **Composition:** 0.9170 Gold .5000 oz. AGW **Reverse:** Antoni Gaudi

Date	Mintage	F	VF	XF	Unc	BU
1990 Proof	3,000	Value: 300				

KM# 64 50 DINERS **Weight:** 15.5500 g. **Composition:** 0.9990 Gold .5000 oz. AGW **Subject:** Wildlife **Reverse:** Red squirrel

Date	Mintage	F	VF	XF	Unc	BU
1990 Proof	2,500	Value: 275				

KM# 68 50 DINERS **Weight:** 15.5500 g. **Composition:** 0.9990 Gold .5000 oz. AGW **Subject:** Wildlife **Reverse:** Chamois

Date	Mintage	F	VF	XF	Unc	BU
1991 Proof	Est. 2,500	Value: 275				

KM# 70 50 DINERS **Weight:** 13.3400 g. **Composition:** 0.5850 Gold .2509 oz. AGW **Subject:** 1992 Summer Olympic Games **Reverse:** Gymnast on rings

Date	Mintage	F	VF	XF	Unc	BU
1991 Proof	3,000	Value: 195				

KM# 93 50 DINERS **Weight:** 13.3400 g. **Composition:** 0.5850 Gold .2509 oz. AGW **Obverse:** Eagle

Date	F	VF	XF	Unc	BU
1992	—	—	—	195	—

KM# 77 50 DINERS **Weight:** 15.5520 g. **Composition:** 0.9999 Gold .4995 oz. AGW **Subject:** Wildlife **Reverse:** Bears

Date	Mintage	F	VF	XF	Unc	BU
1992 Proof	2,500	Value: 250				

KM# 82 50 DINERS **Weight:** 16.9650 g. **Composition:** 0.9160 Gold .4996 oz. AGW **Reverse:** Musician Pau Casals

Date	Mintage	F	VF	XF	Unc	BU
1993 Proof	5,000	Value: 250				

KM# 104 50 DINERS **Weight:** 155.5100 g. **Composition:** 0.9250 Silver 4.6253 oz. ASW **Subject:** 1st Anniversary - Andorran Constitution **Obverse:** Arms above "ECU" **Size:** 65 mm. **Note:** Illustration reduced.

Date	Mintage	F	VF	XF	Unc	BU
1994	5,000	—	—	—	185	—

KM# 115 50 DINERS **Weight:** 155.5100 g. **Composition:** 0.9250 Silver 4.5058 oz. ASW **Subject:** 1996 Olympic Games **Obverse:** Arms above date **Reverse:** Angel lighting Olympic flame **Size:** 65.8 mm. **Note:** Illustration reduced.

Date	Mintage	F	VF	XF	Unc	BU
1995	5,000	—	—	—	185	—

KM# 124 50 DINERS Weight: 155.5100 g. **Composition:** 0.9250 Silver 4.6253 oz. ASW **Subject:** Our Lady of Maritxell - Patroness of Andorra **Obverse:** Crowned arms in inner circle **Reverse:** Enthroned Madonna and child **Size:** 65 mm. **Note:** With insert of 2.5 g. 0.917 gold, 0.0737 AGW. Illustration reduced.

Date	Mintage	F	VF	XF	Unc	BU
1996	5,000	—	—	—	225	—

KM# 152 50 DINERS Weight: 15.5520 g. **Composition:** 0.9160 Gold .4583 oz. AGW **Subject:** 250th Anniversary - Synod Constitution **Obverse:** Clerical arms **Reverse:** Madonna and child

Date	Mintage	F	VF	XF	Unc	BU
1998 Proof	1,998	Value: 300				

KM# 41 100 DINERS Weight: 5.0000 g. **Composition:** 0.9990 Gold .1607 oz. AGW

Date	Mintage	F	VF	XF	Unc	BU
1987	2,000	—	—	—	150	—

KM# 42 100 DINERS Weight: 5.0000 g. **Composition:** 0.9990 Gold .1607 oz. AGW

Date	Mintage	F	VF	XF	Unc	BU
1988	2,000	—	—	—	225	—

KM# 79 100 DINERS Weight: 31.1035 g. **Composition:** 0.9990 Gold 1 oz. AGW **Note:** There is a similar 1988 one-ounce without the denomination.

Date	Mintage	F	VF	XF	Unc	BU
1989	3,000	—	—	—	450	—

KM# 94 100 DINERS Weight: 31.1035 g. **Composition:** 0.9990 Gold 1 oz. AGW **Obverse:** Eagle

Date	F	VF	XF	Unc	BU
1992	—	—	—	450	—

KM# 45 250 DINERS Weight: 12.0000 g. **Composition:** 0.9990 Gold .3858 oz. AGW **Subject:** 700th Anniversary - Andorra's Governing Charter

Date	Mintage	F	VF	XF	Unc	BU
ND(1988)	3,000	—	—	—	275	—

KM# 30 SOVEREIGN Weight: 8.0000 g. **Composition:** 0.9180 Gold .2361 oz. AGW **Note:** Latin legend.

Date	Mintage	F	VF	XF	Unc	BU
1982	1,500	—	—	—	165	—

KM# 31 SOVEREIGN Weight: 8.0000 g. **Composition:** 0.9180 Gold .2361 oz. AGW **Note:** Catalan legend.

Date	Mintage	F	VF	XF	Unc	BU
1982	1,500	—	—	—	165	—

KM# 32 SOVEREIGN Weight: 8.0000 g. **Composition:** 0.9180 Gold .2361 oz. AGW **Note:** Latin legends.

Date	Mintage	F	VF	XF	Unc	BU
1983	1,500	—	—	—	165	—

PATTERNS

KM#	Date	Mintage	Identification	Mkt Val
Pn1	1987	—	2 Diners. Nickel Plated Bronze. KM#46.	—

MINT SETS

KM#	Date	Mintage	Identification	Issue Price	Mkt Val
MS1	1986 (5)	—	KM#33, 35-38	31.00	67.50

ANGOLA

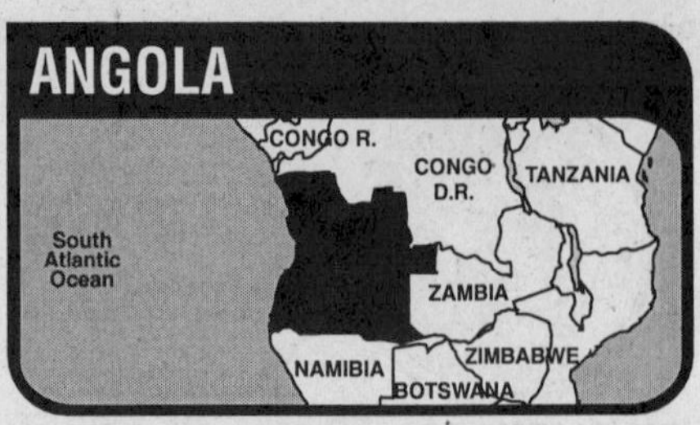

The Republic of Angola, a country on the west coast of southern Africa bounded by Congo Democratic Republic, Zambia, and Namibia (Southwest Africa), has an area of 481,351 sq. mi. (1,246,700 sq. km.) and a population of 12.78 million, predominantly Bantu in origin. Capital: Luanda. Most of the people are engaged in subsistence agriculture. However, important oil and mineral deposits make Angola potentially one of the richest countries in Africa. Iron and diamonds are exported.

The Portuguese navigator, Diogo Cao, discovered Angola in 1482 Angola. Portuguese settlers arrived in 1491, and established Angola as a major slaving center, which sent about 3 million slaves to the New World.

A revolt, characterized by guerrilla warfare, against Portuguese rule began in 1961 and continued until 1974, when a new regime in Portugal offered independence. The independence movement was actively supported by three groups; the National Front, based in Zaire, the Soviet-backed Popular Movement, and the moderate National Union. Independence was proclaimed on Nov. 11, 1975, and the Portuguese departed, leaving the Angolan people to work out their own political destiny. Within hours, each of the independence groups proclaimed itself Angola's sole ruler. A bloody intertribal civil war erupted in which the Communist Popular Movement, assisted by Soviet arms and Cuban mercenaries, was the eventual victor.

RULERS

Portuguese until 1975

MINT MARKS

KN - King's Norton

PORTUGUESE COLONY

DECIMAL COINAGE

Commencing 1910

100 Centavos = 20 Macutas = 1 Escudo

100 Centavos = 1 Escudo

KM# 60 CENTAVO Composition: Bronze

Date	Mintage	F	VF	XF	Unc	BU
1921	1,360,000	7.50	12.50	30.00	65.00	—

KM# 61 2 CENTAVOS Composition: Bronze

Date	Mintage	F	VF	XF	Unc	BU
1921	530,000	10.00	15.00	50.00	110	—

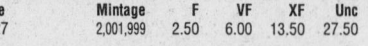

KM# 66 5 CENTAVOS (1 Macuta) Composition: Nickel-Bronze

Date	Mintage	F	VF	XF	Unc	BU
1927	2,001,999	2.50	6.00	13.50	27.50	—

KM# 62 5 CENTAVOS **Composition:** Bronze

Date	Mintage	F	VF	XF	Unc	BU
1921	720,000	5.00	18.00	45.00	80.00	—
1922	5,680,000	4.00	14.00	30.00	55.00	—
1923	5,840,000	4.00	14.00	30.00	55.00	—
1924	—	12.00	35.00	70.00	135	—

KM# 63 10 CENTAVOS (2 Macutas) **Composition:** Copper-Nickel

Date	Mintage	F	VF	XF	Unc	BU
1921	160,000	10.00	30.00	65.00	120	—
1922	340,000	7.50	15.00	45.00	85.00	—
1923	2,960,000	3.50	8.00	20.00	45.00	—

KM# 67 10 CENTAVOS (2 Macutas) **Composition:** Copper-Nickel

Date	Mintage	F	VF	XF	Unc	BU
1927	2,003,000	2.00	4.00	16.00	32.00	—
1928	1,000,000	2.00	4.00	16.00	32.00	—

KM# 70 10 CENTAVOS **Composition:** Bronze
Subject: 300th Anniversary - Revolution of 1648

Date	Mintage	F	VF	XF	Unc	BU
1948	10,000,000	0.50	1.00	3.50	7.50	—
1949	10,000,000	0.35	0.75	3.00	6.50	—

KM# 82 10 CENTAVOS **Composition:** Aluminum

Date	Mintage	F	VF	XF	Unc	BU
1974	4,000,000	—	—	—	17.50	—

Note: Not released for circulation, but relatively available

KM# 68 20 CENTAVOS (4 Macutas) **Composition:** Copper-Nickel

Date	Mintage	F	VF	XF	Unc	BU
1927	2,001,000	2.50	4.00	8.00	20.00	—
1928	500,000	3.50	6.00	13.50	27.50	—

KM# 64 20 CENTAVOS **Composition:** Copper-Nickel

Date	Mintage	F	VF	XF	Unc	BU
1921	2,115,000	4.00	9.00	22.00	40.00	—
1922	1,730,000	6.50	14.50	35.00	65.00	—

KM# 71 20 CENTAVOS **Composition:** Bronze
Subject: 300th Anniversary - Revolution of 1648

Date	Mintage	F	VF	XF	Unc	BU
1948	7,850,000	0.50	1.00	2.00	4.50	—
1949	2,150,000	4.00	7.50	12.50	22.50	—

KM# 78 20 CENTAVOS **Composition:** Bronze

Date	Mintage	F	VF	XF	Unc	BU
1962	3,000,000	—	0.25	0.65	1.75	—

KM# 65 50 CENTAVOS **Composition:** Nickel

Date	Mintage	F	VF	XF	Unc	BU
1922	6,000,000	3.00	10.00	20.00	40.00	—
1923 KN	6,000,000	—	—	225	375	—
1923	Inc. above	3.00	10.00	20.00	40.00	—

KM# 69 50 CENTAVOS **Composition:** Nickel-Bronze

Date	Mintage	F	VF	XF	Unc	BU
1927	1,608,000	5.00	18.00	35.00	70.00	—
1928/7	1,600,000	5.00	18.00	40.00	75.00	—
1928	Inc. above	3.50	12.50	30.00	65.00	—

KM# 72 50 CENTAVOS **Composition:** Nickel-Bronze
Subject: 300th Anniversary - Revolution of 1648

Date	Mintage	F	VF	XF	Unc	BU
1948	4,000,000	0.50	1.00	3.50	8.00	—
1950	4,000,000	0.50	1.00	3.50	8.00	—

KM# 75 50 CENTAVOS **Composition:** Bronze

Date	Mintage	F	VF	XF	Unc	BU
1953	5,000,000	—	0.25	0.65	2.50	—
1954	11,731,000	—	0.20	0.40	1.75	—
1955 Rare	1,126,000	1.00	3.00	10.00	40.00	—
1957	8,873,000	—	0.20	0.45	2.00	—
1958	17,520,000	—	0.15	0.35	1.50	—
1961	8,750,000	—	0.20	0.45	2.00	—

KM# 75a 50 CENTAVOS **Composition:** Copper-Nickel

Date	Mintage	F	VF	XF	Unc	BU
1974	150	—	—	125	250	—

Note: Not released for circulation

KM# 76 ESCUDO **Composition:** Bronze

Date	Mintage	F	VF	XF	Unc	BU
1953	2,001,000	—	1.50	6.00	15.00	—
1956	2,989,000	—	1.00	4.00	10.00	—
1963	5,000,000	—	1.00	2.00	7.00	—
1965	5,000,000	—	1.00	2.00	7.00	—
1972	10,000,000	—	0.75	1.50	4.50	—
1974	6,214,000	—	0.75	1.50	4.50	—

KM# 76a ESCUDO **Composition:** Copper-Nickel **Note:** Not released for circulation.

Date	F	VF	XF	Unc	BU
1972 Rare	—	—	—	—	—
1974 Rare	—	—	—	—	—

KM# 77 2-1/2 ESCUDOS **Composition:** Copper-Nickel

Date	Mintage	F	VF	XF	Unc	BU
1953	6,008,000	—	1.00	4.00	10.00	—
1956	9,992,000	—	0.35	2.00	4.00	—
1967	6,000,000	—	0.35	2.00	4.00	—
1968	5,000,000	—	0.35	2.00	4.00	—
1969	5,000,000	—	0.35	2.00	4.00	—
1974	19,999,000	—	0.25	1.00	3.00	—

KM# 81 5 ESCUDOS **Composition:** Copper-Nickel

Date	F	VF	XF	Unc	BU
1972	—	10.00	20.00	45.00	—
1974	—	—	100	200	—

Note: Not released for circulation

KM# 73 10 ESCUDOS **Weight:** 5.0000 g. **Composition:** 0.7200 Silver .1157 oz. ASW

Date	Mintage	F	VF	XF	Unc	BU
1952	2,023,000	—	2.50	5.00	10.00	—
1955	1,977,000	—	2.50	5.00	10.00	—

KM# 79 10 ESCUDOS **Composition:** Copper-Nickel

Date	Mintage	F	VF	XF	Unc	BU
1969	3,022,000	—	1.50	3.00	6.00	—
1970	978,000	—	2.00	4.00	7.00	—

KM# 74 20 ESCUDOS **Weight:** 10.0000 g. **Composition:** 0.7200 Silver .2315 oz. ASW

Date	Mintage	F	VF	XF	Unc	BU
1952	1,002,999	—	2.50	6.00	13.50	—
1955	997,000	—	2.50	5.00	10.00	—

KM# 80 20 ESCUDOS **Composition:** Nickel

Date	Mintage	F	VF	XF	Unc	BU
1971	1,572,000	—	0.75	2.00	4.00	—
1972	428,000	—	2.50	5.00	10.00	—

PEOPLES REPUBLIC

DECIMAL COINAGE

1975 - 1979

100 Lwei = 1 Kwanza

KM# 90 50 LWEI **Composition:** Copper-Nickel

Date	F	VF	XF	Unc	BU
ND(1975)	—	0.15	0.35	1.25	2.50
1979	—	0.10	0.30	1.00	1.50

KM# 83 KWANZA **Composition:** Copper-Nickel

Date	F	VF	XF	Unc	BU
ND(1975)	—	0.30	0.50	1.50	—
1978	—	0.25	0.40	1.50	—
1979	—	0.25	0.40	1.50	—

KM# 84 2 KWANZAS **Composition:** Copper-Nickel

Date	F	VF	XF	Unc	BU
ND(1975)	—	0.40	0.60	1.75	—

KM# 85 5 KWANZAS **Composition:** Copper-Nickel

Date	F	VF	XF	Unc	BU
ND(1975)	—	0.65	1.25	3.00	—

KM# 86.1 10 KWANZAS **Composition:** Copper-Nickel **Reverse:** Small date, dots near rim

Date	F	VF	XF	Unc	BU
ND(1975)	—	1.25	2.00	3.50	—
1978	—	1.50	2.50	4.50	—

KM# 86.2 10 KWANZAS **Composition:** Copper-Nickel **Reverse:** Large date, dots away from rim

Date	F	VF	XF	Unc	BU
1978	—	1.50	2.50	4.50	—

KM# 87 20 KWANZAS **Composition:** Copper-Nickel

Date	F	VF	XF	Unc	BU
1978	—	2.00	3.00	6.00	—

KM# 91 50 KWANZAS **Composition:** Copper **Obverse:** State emblem **Reverse:** Denomination

Date	F	VF	XF	Unc	BU
ND(1975)	—	2.50	4.50	9.00	—

KM# 92 100 KWANZAS **Composition:** Copper **Obverse:** State emblem **Reverse:** Denomination

Date	F	VF	XF	Unc	BU
ND(1975)	—	3.50	6.50	14.00	—

REFORM COINAGE

1999 -

KM# 95 10 CENTIMOS **Weight:** 1.5000 g. **Composition:** Copper Plated Steel **Obverse:** National arms, country name and date **Reverse:** Denomination **Edge:** Reeded **Size:** 15 mm.

Date	F	VF	XF	Unc	BU
1999	—	—	—	0.50	—

KM# 96 50 CENTIMOS **Weight:** 3.0000 g. **Composition:** Copper Plated Steel **Obverse:** National arms, country name and date **Reverse:** Denomination **Edge:** Reeded **Size:** 18 mm.

Date	F	VF	XF	Unc	BU
1999	—	—	—	1.00	—

KM# 97 KWANZA **Weight:** 4.5000 g. **Composition:** Copper-Nickel **Obverse:** National arms, country name and date **Reverse:** Denomination **Edge:** Reeded **Size:** 21 mm.

Date	F	VF	XF	Unc	BU
1999	—	—	—	1.50	—

KM# 98 2 KWANZAS **Weight:** 5.0000 g. **Composition:** Copper-Nickel **Obverse:** National arms, country name and date **Reverse:** Denomination **Edge:** Reeded **Size:** 22 mm.

Date	F	VF	XF	Unc	BU
1999	—	—	—	2.00	—

KM# 99 5 KWANZAS **Weight:** 7.0000 g. **Composition:** Copper-Nickel **Obverse:** National arms, country name and date **Reverse:** Denomination **Edge:** Reeded **Size:** 26 mm.

Date	F	VF	XF	Unc	BU
1999	—	—	—	3.50	—

KM# 93 10 KWANZAS **Weight:** 24.2250 g. **Composition:** Copper-Nickel **Subject:** Olympics **Obverse:** National arms **Reverse:** Olympic logo and allegory **Edge:** Reeded

Date	F	VF	XF	Unc	BU
1999 Proof	—	Value: 15.00			

KM# 100 10 KWANZAS **Weight:** 23.0500 g. **Composition:** Copper-Nickel **Subject:** Prince Henry the Navigator **Obverse:** Angolan arms **Reverse:** Prince Henry in armour half facing left **Edge:** Reeded

Date	F	VF	XF	Unc	BU
1999 Proof	—	Value: 15.00			

KM# 94 100 KWANZAS **Weight:** 25.0000 g. **Composition:** 0.9250 Silver .7435 oz. ASW **Subject:** Olympics **Obverse:** National arms **Reverse:** Olympic logo and allegory

Date	F	VF	XF	Unc	BU
1999 Proof	—	Value: 35.00			

PATTERNS

Including off metal strikes

KM#	Date	Mintage	Identification	Mkt Val
Pn7	1972	—	50 Escudos. Silver.	1,500

PROVAS

KM#	Date	Mintage	Identification	Issue Price	Mkt Val
Pr1	1921	—	Centavo. KM#60.	—	25.00
Pr2	1921	—	2 Centavos. KM#61.	—	25.00
Pr3	1921	—	5 Centavos. KM#62.	—	25.00
Pr4	1921	—	10 Centavos. KM#63.	—	35.00
Pr5	1921	—	20 Centavos. KM#64.	—	30.00
Pr6	1922	—	5 Centavos. KM#62.	—	25.00
Pr7	1922	—	10 Centavos. KM#63.	—	30.00
Pr8	1922	—	20 Centavos. KM#64.	—	30.00
Pr9	1923	—	5 Centavos. KM#62.	—	25.00
Pr10	1923	—	10 Centavos. KM#63.	—	30.00
Pr11	1923	—	20 Centavos. KM#64.	—	30.00
Pr12	1924	—	5 Centavos. KM#62.	—	100
Pr13	1927	—	5 Centavos. KM#66.	—	20.00
Pr14	1927	—	10 Centavos. KM#67.	—	20.00
Pr15	1927	—	20 Centavos. KM#68.	—	20.00
Pr16	1927	—	50 Centavos. KM#69.	—	20.00
Pr17	1928	—	10 Centavos. KM#67.	—	20.00
Pr18	1928	—	20 Centavos. KM#68.	—	20.00

KM#	Date	Mintage	Identification	Issue Price	Mkt Val
Pr19	1928	—	50 Centavos. KM#69.	—	20.00
Pr20	1948	—	10 Centavos. KM#70.	—	20.00
Pr21	1948	—	20 Centavos. KM#71.	—	20.00
Pr22	1948	—	50 Centavos. KM#72.	—	20.00
Pr23	1949	—	10 Centavos. KM#70.	—	20.00
Pr24	1949	—	20 Centavos. KM#71.	—	20.00
Pr25	1949	—	50 Centavos. KM#72.	—	20.00
Pr26	1950	—	50 Centavos. KM#72.	—	15.00
Pr27	1952	—	10 Escudos. KM#73.	—	30.00
Pr28	1952	—	20 Escudos. KM#74.	—	42.00
Pr29	1953	—	50 Centavos. KM#75.	—	15.00
Pr30	1953	—	Escudo. KM#76.	—	20.00
Pr31	1953	—	2-1/2 Escudos. KM#77.	—	30.00
Pr32	1954	—	50 Centavos. KM#75.	—	15.00
Pr33	1954	—	Escudo. KM#76.	—	20.00
Pr34	1954	—	2-1/2 Escudos. KM#77.	—	30.00
Pr35	1955	—	50 Centavos. KM#75.	—	15.00
Pr36	1955	—	Escudo. KM#76.	—	20.00
Pr37	1955	—	2-1/2 Escudos. KM#77.	—	30.00
Pr38	1955	—	10 Escudos. KM#73.	—	30.00
Pr39	1955	—	20 Escudos. KM#74.	—	42.00
Pr40	1956	—	50 Centavos. KM#75.	—	12.50
Pr41	1956	—	Escudo. KM#76.	—	12.50
Pr42	1956	—	2-1/2 Escudos. KM#77.	—	12.50
Pr43	1957	—	50 Centavos. KM#75.	—	12.50
Pr44	1957	—	Escudo. KM#76.	—	12.50
Pr45	1957	—	2-1/2 Escudos. KM#77.	—	12.50
Pr46	1958	—	50 Centavos. KM#75.	—	12.50
Pr47	1958	—	Escudo. KM#76.	—	12.50
Pr48	1958	—	2-1/2 Escudos. KM#77.	—	12.50
Pr49	1959	—	50 Centavos. KM#75.	—	12.50
Pr50	1959	—	Escudo. KM#76.	—	12.50
Pr51	1959	—	2-1/2 Escudos. KM#77.	—	12.50
Pr52	1960	—	50 Centavos. KM#75.	—	12.50
Pr53	1960	—	Escudo. KM#76.	—	12.50
Pr54	1960	—	2-1/2 Escudos. KM#77.	—	12.50
Pr55	1961	—	50 Centavos. KM#75.	—	12.50
Pr56	1961	—	Escudo. KM#76.	—	12.50
Pr57	1961	—	2-1/2 Escudos. KM#77.	—	12.50
Pr58	1962	—	20 Centavos. KM#78.	—	12.50
Pr59	1962	—	Escudo. KM#76.	—	12.50
Pr60	1962	—	2-1/2 Escudos. KM#77.	—	12.50
Pr61	1963	—	Escudo. KM#76.	—	12.50
Pr62	1963	—	2-1/2 Escudos. KM#77.	—	12.50
Pr63	1964	—	Escudo. KM#76.	—	12.50
Pr64	1964	—	2-1/2 Escudos. KM#77.	—	12.50
Pr65	1965	—	Escudo. KM#76.	—	12.50
Pr66	1965	—	2-1/2 Escudos. KM#77.	—	12.50
Pr67	1966	—	Escudo. KM#76.	—	12.50
Pr68	1966	—	2-1/2 Escudos. KM#77.	—	12.50
Pr69	1967	—	Escudo. KM#76.	—	12.50
Pr70	1967	—	2-1/2 Escudos. KM#77.	—	12.50
Pr71	1968	—	Escudo. KM#76.	—	12.50
Pr72	1968	—	2-1/2 Escudos. KM#77.	—	12.50
Pr73	1969	—	Escudo. KM#76.	—	12.50
Pr74	1969	—	2-1/2 Escudos. KM#77.	—	12.50
Pr75	1969	—	10 Escudos. KM#79.	—	12.50
Pr76	1970	—	Escudo. KM#76.	—	12.50
Pr77	1970	—	2-1/2 Escudos. KM#77.	—	12.50
Pr78	1970	—	10 Escudos. KM#79.	—	12.50
Pr79	1971	—	Escudo. KM#76.	—	12.50
Pr80	1971	—	2-1/2 Escudos. KM#77.	—	12.50
Pr81	1971	—	20 Escudos. KM#80.	—	12.50
Pr82	1972	—	Escudo. KM#76.	—	12.50
Pr83	1972	—	2-1/2 Escudos. KM#77.	—	12.50
Pr84	1972	—	5 Escudos. KM#81.	—	12.50
Pr85	1972	—	20 Escudos. KM#80.	—	12.50
Pr86	1974	—	Escudo. KM#76.	—	12.50

MINT SETS

KM#	Date	Mintage	Identification	Issue Price	Mkt Val
MS1	ND (1979) (6)	—	KM#83, 84, 85, 86.2, 87, 90	20.00	20.00

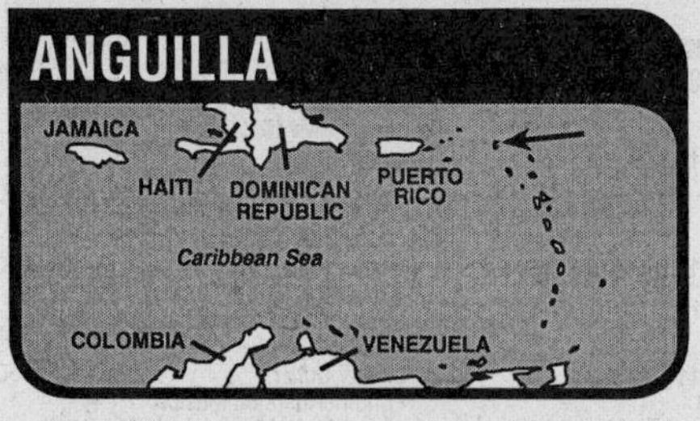

The British dependency of Anguilla, a self-governing British territory situated in the east Caribbean Sea about 60 miles (100 km.) northwest of St. Kitts, has an area of 35 sq. mi. (91 sq. km.) and an approximate population of 12,000. Capital: The Valley. In recent years, tourism has replaced the traditional fishing, stock raising and salt production as the main industry.

Anguilla was discovered by Columbus in 1493 and became a British colony in 1650. As the other British areas in the West Indies did, Anguilla officially adapted to sterling beginning in 1825. From 1950 to 1965, Anguilla was a member of the British Caribbean Territories (Eastern Group) Currency Board, whose coinage it used. In March 1967, Anguilla was joined politically with St. Christopher (St. Kitts), as it had been for much of its colonial history, and Nevis to form a British associated state.

On June 16, 1967, the Provisional Government of Anguilla unilaterally declared its independence and seceded from the Federation. Later, on July 11, 1967, a vote of confidence was taken and the results favored independence. Britain refused to accept the declaration (nor did any other country recognize it) and appointed a British administrator whom Anguilla accepted. However, in Feb. 1969 Anguilla ousted the British emissary, voted to sever all ties with Britain, and established the Republic of Anguilla. The following month Britain landed a force of paratroopers and policemen. This bloodless counteraction ended the self-proclaimed republic and resulted in the installation of a governing commissioner. The troops were withdrawn in Sept. 1969, and the Anguilla Act of July 1971 placed Anguilla directly under British control. A new constitution in 1976 established Anguilla as a self-governing British dependant territory. Britain retains power over defense, police and civil service, and foreign affairs. Since 1981, Anguilla has employed the coinage of the East Caribbean States.

NOTE: There is no evidence that the issues of the self-proclaimed Provisional Government ever actually circulated. The c/s series most likely served as souvenirs of the "revolution".

RULERS

British

BRITISH COLONY

DECIMAL COINAGE

KM# 15 1/2 DOLLAR **Weight:** 3.6100 g. **Composition:** 0.9990 Silver .1160 oz. ASW **Obverse:** St. Mary's Church

Date	Mintage	F	VF	XF	Unc	BU
ND Proof	4,200	Value: 20.00				
1969 Proof	—	Value: 20.00				
1970 Proof	Inc. above	Value: 20.00				

KM# 16 DOLLAR **Weight:** 7.1800 g. **Composition:** 0.9990 Silver .2308 oz. ASW **Obverse:** Map - Flora and Fauna

Date	Mintage	F	VF	XF	Unc	BU
ND Proof	4,450	Value: 25.00				
1969 Proof	—	Value: 25.00				
1970 Proof	Inc. above	Value: 25.00				

KM# 17 2 DOLLARS **Weight:** 14.1400 g. **Composition:** 0.9990 Silver .4546 oz. ASW **Obverse:** National flag and map

Date	Mintage	F	VF	XF	Unc	BU
ND Proof	4,150	Value: 30.00				
1969 Proof	—	Value: 30.00				
1970 Proof	Inc. above	Value: 30.00				

KM# 18.1 4 DOLLARS **Weight:** 28.4800 g. **Composition:** 0.9990 Silver .9156 oz. ASW **Obverse:** Ship - Atlantic Star

Date	Mintage	F	VF	XF	Unc	BU
ND Proof	5,100	Value: 60.00				
1969 Proof	—	Value: 60.00				
1970 Proof	Inc. above	Value: 60.00				

KM# 18.2 4 DOLLARS **Weight:** 28.4800 g. **Composition:** 0.9990 Silver .9156 oz. ASW **Reverse:** 2 hallmarks at 4 o'clock

Date	F	VF	XF	Unc	BU
1970 Proof	—	Value: 90.00			

KM# 20 5 DOLLARS **Weight:** 2.4600 g. **Composition:** 0.9000 Gold .0711 oz. AGW **Obverse:** Methodist Church of West End

Date	Mintage	F	VF	XF	Unc	BU
ND Proof	1,925	Value: 70.00				
1969 Proof	—	Value: 70.00				
1970 Proof	Inc. above	Value: 70.00				

KM# 21 10 DOLLARS **Weight:** 4.9300 g. **Composition:** 0.9000 Gold .1426 oz. AGW **Obverse:** Dolphin and sea creatures

Date	Mintage	F	VF	XF	Unc	BU
ND Proof	1,615	Value: 110				
1969 Proof	—	Value: 110				
1970 Proof	Inc. above	Value: 110				

KM# 22 20 DOLLARS **Weight:** 9.8700 g. **Composition:** 0.9000 Gold .2856 oz. AGW **Obverse:** Mermaids

Date	Mintage	F	VF	XF	Unc	BU
ND Proof	1,395	Value: 260				
1969 Proof	—	Value: 260				
1970 Proof	Inc. above	Value: 260				

KM# 23 100 DOLLARS **Weight:** 49.3700 g. **Composition:** 0.9000 Gold 1.4287 oz. AGW **Subject:** Demonstrating Population

Date	Mintage	F	VF	XF	Unc	BU
ND Proof	710	Value: 775				
1969 Proof	—	Value: 775				
1970 Proof	Inc. above	Value: 775				

PROVISIONAL GOVERNMENT COINAGE

Countermarked

KM#	Date	Mintage	Identification	Issue Price	Mkt Val
1	1951-1954	5,987	Liberty Dollar. Countermark on Mexico 5 Pesos, KM#467. 54,000 of the below pieces were remelted.	10.00	25.00
14	1921-1947	2	100 Liberty Dollars. Gold. Countermark on Mexico 50 Pesos, KM#481.	—	3,000
2	1947-1948	1,530	Liberty Dollar. Countermark on Mexico 5 Pesos, KM#465.	10.00	30.00
3	1923-1926	1,531	Liberty Dollar. Countermark on Peru Sol, KM#218.1.	10.00	30.00

KM#	Date	Mintage	Identification	Issue Price	Mkt Val
3a	AH1382	—	Liberty Dollar. Countermark on Yemen Riyal, Y#31.	10.00	45.00
4	AH1367-AH1381	494	Liberty Dollar. Countermark on Yemen Ahmadi Riyal, Y#17.	10.00	85.00
5	1907-1912	340	Liberty Dollar. Countermark on Philippines Peso, KM#172.	10.00	80.00

KM#	Date	Mintage	Identification	Issue Price	Mkt Val
6	1955-1956	250	100 Liberty Dollars. Countermark on Mexico 10 Pesos, KM#474.	10.00	80.00
7.1	1931-1947	91	100 Liberty Dollars. Countermark on Panama Balboa, KM#13.	10.00	115
7.2	1953	I.A.	Liberty Dollar. Countermark on Panama Balboa, KM#21.	—	115
8	1943-1944	21	Liberty Dollar. Countermark on Ecuador Cinco Sucres, KM#79.	—	175
9	1901-1905	15	Liberty Dollar. Countermark on Mexico Peso, KM#409.	—	220
10.1	1914	10	Liberty Dollar. Countermark on China Republic Yuan Shih Kai Dollar, KM#329.	—	250
10.2	1920-21	10	Liberty Dollar. Countermark on China Republic Yuan Shih Kai Dollar, KM#329.6.	—	250
11	1953	2	Liberty Dollar. Countermark on Mexico 5 Pesos, KM#468.	—	450
12	1901-1935	1	Liberty Dollar. Countermark on Great Britain Trade Coinage, Y-T5. The countermark was done in San Francisco, California, on various crown-sized coins.	—	500

TRIAL STRIKES

KM#	Date	Mintage	Identification	Mkt Val
TS1	ND (1969)	—	5 Dollars. Goldine-Brass. 1.5100 g. Design of KM-20.. Blank with MET countermark.. Reeded. edge. Uniface.	60.00
TS2	1969	—	100 Dollars. Goldine.	—
	1969	—	100 Dollars. Goldine.	—
TS3	ND (1969)	—	100 Dollars. Goldine-Brass. 29.2100 g. Design of KM-23. Blank with MET countermark. Reeded edge.	200

PROOF SETS

KM#	Date	Mintage	Identification	Issue Price	Mkt Val
PS1	1969 (8)	—	KM#15-18, 20-23	225	1,310
PS2	1969 (4)	—	KM#15-18	25.50	135
PS3	1969 (4)	—	KM#20-23	200	1,200
PS4	1970 (8)	—	KM#15-18, 20-23	225	1,310
PS5	1970 (4)	—	KM#15-18	25.50	135
PS6	1970 (4)	—	KM#20-23	200	1,200

ANTIGUA & BARBUDA

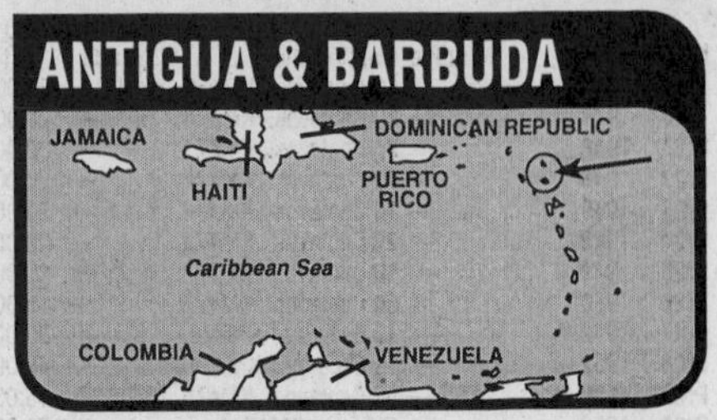

The Independent State of Antigua and Barbuda, located on the eastern edge of the Leeward Islands in the Caribbean Sea, has an area of 170 sq. mi. (440 sq. km.) and an estimated population of 68,000. Capital: St. John's. Prior to 1967, Antigua and its dependencies Barbuda and Redonda, comprised a presidency of the Leeward Islands. The mountainous island produces sugar, molasses, rum, cotton and fruit. Tourism is making an increasingly valuable contribution to the economy.

Antigua was discovered by Columbus in 1493, settled by British colonists from St. Kitts in 1632, occupied by the French in 1666, and ceded to Britain in 1667. It became an associated state with internal self-government on February 27, 1967. On November 1, 1981 it became independent as Antigua and Barbuda. As a constitutional monarchy, Elizabeth II is Queen of Antiqua and Barbuda and Head of State. Antigua & Barbuda is a member of the Commonwealth of Nations.

Spanish silver coinage and French colonial "Black Dogs" were used throughout the islands' early history; however, late in the seventeenth century the introduction of British tin farthings was attempted with complete lack of success. In 1822, British colonial Anchor Money was introduced.

From 1825 to 1955, Antigua was on the sterling standard and used British coins. Coins of the British Caribbean Territories (Eastern Group) and East Caribbean States circulated from 1955, and banknotes of East Caribbean Currency Authority are now used on the island. The early coinage was augmented by that of the East Caribbean States in 1981.

RULERS
British

ANTIGUA

BRITISH ADMINISTRATION

DECIMAL COINAGE

100 Cents = 1 Dollar

KM# 1 4 DOLLARS **Composition:** Copper-Nickel **Ruler:** Elizabeth II **Series:** F.A.O.

Date	Mintage	F	VF	XF	Unc	BU
1970	14,000	—	4.00	7.00	15.00	—
1970 Proof	2,000	Value: 30.00				

Note: For similar issues see Barbados, Dominica, Grenada, Montserrat, St. Kitts, St. Lucia and St. Vincent.

ANTIGUA & BARBUDA

BRITISH ADMINISTRATION

DECIMAL COINAGE

KM# 5 10 DOLLARS Composition: Copper-Nickel **Ruler:** Elizabeth II **Subject:** Royal Visit

Date	Mintage	F	VF	XF	Unc	BU
1985	100,000	—	—	—	9.00	—

KM# 5a 10 DOLLARS Weight: 28.2800 g. **Composition:** 0.9250 Silver .8409 oz. ASW **Ruler:** Elizabeth II

Date	Mintage	F	VF	XF	Unc	BU
1985 Proof	5,000	Value: 40.00				

KM# 5b 10 DOLLARS Weight: 47.5400 g. **Composition:** 0.9170 Gold 1.4013 oz. AGW **Ruler:** Elizabeth II

Date	Mintage	F	VF	XF	Unc	BU
1985 Proof	250	Value: 1,100				

KM# 2 30 DOLLARS Weight: 31.1000 g. **Composition:** 0.5000 Silver .5 oz. ASW **Ruler:** Elizabeth II **Subject:** George Washington - Yorktown, 1781

Date	Mintage	F	VF	XF	Unc	BU
1982 Proof	1,200	Value: 37.50				

KM# 3 30 DOLLARS Weight: 31.1000 g. **Composition:** 0.5000 Silver .5 oz. ASW **Ruler:** Elizabeth II **Subject:** George Washington - Inauguration, 1789 **Obverse:** Similar to KM#2

Date	Mintage	F	VF	XF	Unc	BU
1982 Proof	1,125	Value: 40.00				

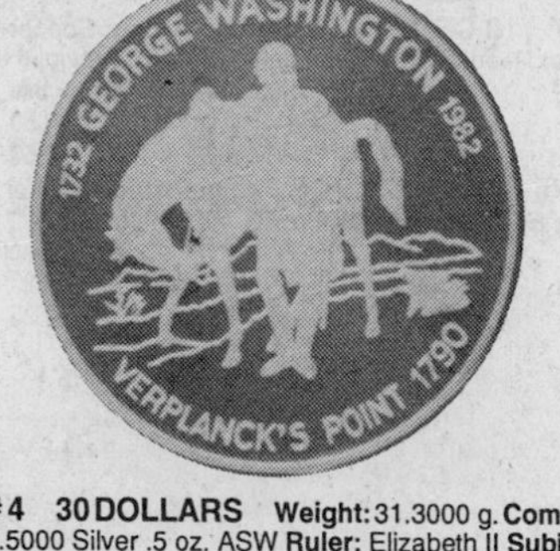

KM# 4 30 DOLLARS Weight: 31.3000 g. **Composition:** 0.5000 Silver .5 oz. ASW **Ruler:** Elizabeth II **Subject:** George Washington - Verplanck's Point, 1790 **Obverse:** Similar to KM#2

Date	Mintage	F	VF	XF	Unc	BU
1982 Proof	675	Value: 42.50				

KM# 6 100 DOLLARS Ruler: Elizabeth II **Subject:** Tropical Birds **Obverse:** Arms in circle, country name above, date below **Reverse:** Cattle Egret

Date	Mintage	F	VF	XF	Unc	BU
1988 Proof	10,000	Value: 110				

ARGENTINA

The Argentine Republic, located in southern South America, has an area of 1,073,518 sq. mi. (3,761,274 sq. km.) and an estimated population of 37.03 million. Capital: Buenos Aires. Its varied topography ranges from the subtropical lowlands of the north to the towering Andean Mountains in the west and the wind-swept Patagonian steppe in the south. The rolling, fertile pampas of central Argentina are ideal for agriculture and grazing, and support most of the republic's population. Meatpacking, flour milling, textiles, sugar refining and dairy products are the principal industries. Oil is found in Patagonia, but most mineral requirements must be imported.

Argentina was discovered in 1516 by the Spanish navigator Juan de Solis. A permanent Spanish colony was established at Buenos Aires in 1580, but the colony developed slowly. When Napoleon conquered Spain, the Argentines set up their own government on May 25, 1810. Independence was formally declared on July 9, 1816. A strong tendency toward local autonomy, fostered by difficult transportation, resulted in a federalized union with much authority left to the states or provinces, which resulted in the coinage of 1817-1867.

Internal conflict through the first half century of Argentine independence resulted in a provisional national coinage, chiefly of crown-sized silver. Provincial issues mainly of minor denominations supplemented this.

MINT MARKS

A = Korea
B = Great Britain
BA = Buenos Aires
CORDOBA, CORDOVA
C = France
PTS = Potosi monogram (Bolivia)
R, RA, RIOJA, RIOXA
SE = Santiago del Estero
T, TM = Tucuman
TIERRA DEL FUEGO

MONETARY SYSTEM

8 Reales = 8 Soles = 1/2 Escudo
16 Reales or Soles = 1 Escudo
10 Decimos = 1 Real
100 Centavos = 1 Peso
10 Pesos = 1 Argentino

(Commencing 1970)

100 Old Pesos = 1 New Peso

(Commencing June 1983)

10,000 New Pesos = 1 Peso Argentino
1,000 Pesos Argentino = 1 Austral

(Commencing 1985)

1,000 Pesos Argentinos = 1 Austral
100 Centavos = 1 Austral

(Commencing 1992)

10,000 Australs = 1 Peso

REPUBLIC

DECIMAL COINAGE

KM# 37 CENTAVO Composition: Bronze **Note:** Previous KM#12.

Date	Mintage	F	VF	XF	Unc	BU
1939	3,488,000	0.25	0.50	1.50	4.00	—
1940	3,140,000	0.15	0.35	1.00	2.00	—
1941	4,572,000	0.15	0.35	1.00	2.00	—
1942	496,000	0.30	0.75	1.50	7.50	—
1944	3,104,000	0.20	0.50	1.00	2.75	—
1973	1,294,000	0.10	0.25	0.55	1.50	—

KM# 37a CENTAVO **Composition:** Copper **Note:** Cruder diework. Previous KM#12a.

Date	Mintage	F	VF	XF	Unc	BU
1945	420,000	0.20	0.50	1.00	4.00	—
1946	4,450,000	0.15	0.35	0.50	2.00	—
1947	5,630,000	0.15	0.35	0.50	2.00	—
1948	4,420,000	0.15	0.35	0.50	2.00	—

KM# 38 2 CENTAVOS **Composition:** Bronze **Note:** Previous KM#13.

Date	Mintage	F	VF	XF	Unc	BU
1939	5,490,000	0.15	0.35	1.00	4.50	—
1940	4,625,000	0.15	0.35	1.00	5.00	—
1941	4,567,000	0.15	0.35	1.00	5.00	—
1942	2,082,000	0.15	0.35	1.00	5.50	—
1944	387,000	0.25	0.50	1.25	7.50	—
1945	4,585,000	0.15	0.35	1.00	5.00	—
1946	3,395,000	0.15	0.35	1.00	5.00	—
1947	4,395,000	0.15	0.35	1.00	5.00	—

KM# 38a 2 CENTAVOS **Composition:** Copper **Note:** Cruder diework. Previous KM#13a.

Date	Mintage	F	VF	XF	Unc	BU
1947	Inc. above	0.15	0.35	1.00	5.50	—
1948	3,645,000	0.15	0.35	1.00	5.50	—
1949	7,290,000	0.15	0.35	1.00	3.50	—
1950	903,000	0.25	0.65	1.25	6.50	—

KM# 34 5 CENTAVOS **Composition:** Copper-Nickel **Note:** Previous KM#9.

Date	Mintage	F	VF	XF	Unc	BU
1903	2,502,000	0.25	0.50	3.00	18.00	—
1904	2,518,000	0.25	0.50	3.00	18.00	—
1905	4,359,000	0.25	0.50	3.00	18.00	—
1906	3,939,000	0.25	0.50	3.00	18.00	—
1907	1,682,000	0.50	1.00	5.00	20.00	—
1908	1,693,000	0.50	1.00	5.00	20.00	—
1909	4,650,000	0.25	0.50	3.50	20.00	—
1910	1,469,000	0.75	2.00	6.00	24.00	—
1911	1,431,000	0.25	0.75	4.00	20.00	—
1912	2,377,000	0.25	0.75	4.00	20.00	—
1913	1,477,000	0.25	0.75	4.00	20.00	—
1914	1,097,000	0.50	1.00	5.00	22.00	—
1915	1,310,000	0.30	0.75	3.50	20.00	—
1916	1,310,000	0.30	0.75	3.50	18.00	—
1917	1,009,000	0.75	1.50	4.00	20.00	—
1918	2,287,000	0.25	0.50	3.00	15.00	—
1919	2,476,000	0.25	0.50	3.00	10.00	—
1920	5,235,000	0.25	0.50	3.00	10.00	—
1921	7,040,000	0.20	0.35	2.00	8.00	—
1922	9,427,000	0.20	0.35	2.00	10.00	—
1923	6,256,000	0.20	0.35	2.00	10.00	—
1924	6,355,000	0.20	0.35	2.00	10.00	—
1925	3,955,000	0.20	0.35	2.00	10.00	—
1926	3,560,000	0.20	0.35	2.00	10.00	—
1927	5,650,000	0.20	0.35	2.00	10.00	—
1928	6,380,000	0.20	0.35	2.00	10.00	—
1929	11,831,000	0.20	0.35	2.00	10.00	—
1930	7,110,000	0.20	0.35	2.00	10.00	—
1931	506,000	2.00	4.00	9.00	25.00	—
1933	5,537,000	0.10	0.25	1.00	4.00	—
1934	1,288,000	0.25	0.50	3.00	8.00	—
1935	3,052,000	0.10	0.25	1.00	4.00	—
1936	7,175,000	0.10	0.25	1.00	4.00	—
1937	7,063,000	0.10	0.25	1.00	4.00	—
1938	10,252,000	0.10	0.25	1.00	3.50	—
1939	7,171,000	0.10	0.25	1.00	4.00	—
1940	10,191,000	0.10	0.25	1.00	3.50	—
1941	951,000	0.50	1.00	3.00	12.00	—
1942	8,692,000	0.10	0.25	1.00	3.50	—

KM# 40 5 CENTAVOS **Composition:** Aluminum-Bronze **Note:** Previous KM#15.

Date	Mintage	F	VF	XF	Unc	BU
1942	2,130,000	0.25	0.50	1.50	5.00	—
1943	15,778,000	0.10	0.25	0.75	3.00	—
1944	21,081,000	0.10	0.25	0.75	3.00	—
1945	21,600,000	0.10	0.25	0.75	3.00	—
1946	20,460,000	0.10	0.25	0.75	3.00	—
1947	22,520,000	0.10	0.25	0.75	3.00	—
1948	42,790,000	0.10	0.25	0.50	2.00	—
1949	35,470,000	0.10	0.25	0.75	3.00	—
1950	13,500,000	0.10	0.25	0.75	3.00	—

KM# 43 5 CENTAVOS **Composition:** Copper-Nickel **Reverse:** Jose de San Martin bust facing right. **Edge:** Reeded. **Note:** Previous KM#18.

Date	Mintage	F	VF	XF	Unc	BU
1950	3,460,000	0.20	0.40	0.60	2.00	—

KM# 46 5 CENTAVOS **Composition:** Copper-Nickel **Reverse:** Jose de San Martin bust facing right **Edge:** Reeded **Note:** Previous KM#21.

Date	Mintage	F	VF	XF	Unc	BU
1951	34,994,000	—	0.20	0.30	0.50	—
1952	33,110,000	—	0.20	0.30	0.50	—
1953	20,129,000	—	0.20	0.30	0.50	—

KM# 46a 5 CENTAVOS **Composition:** Copper-Nickel Clad Steel **Reverse:** Jose de San Martin bust facing right **Edge:** Plain **Note:** Previous KM#21a.

Date	Mintage	F	VF	XF	Unc	BU
1953	56,300,000	—	0.15	0.20	0.35	—

KM# 50 5 CENTAVOS **Composition:** Copper-Nickel Clad Steel **Reverse:** Jose de San Martin bust facing right, smaller head **Edge:** Plain **Note:** Previous KM#25.

Date	Mintage	F	VF	XF	Unc	BU
1954	50,640,000	—	0.15	0.20	0.35	—
1955	42,200,000	—	0.15	0.20	0.35	—
1956	36,870,000	—	0.15	0.20	0.35	—

KM# 53 5 CENTAVOS **Composition:** Copper-Nickel Clad Steel **Reverse:** Smaller head **Edge:** Plain **Note:** Jose de San Martin. Previous KM#28.

Date	Mintage	F	VF	XF	Unc	BU
1957	26,930,000	—	0.15	0.20	0.35	—
1958	13,108,000	—	0.15	0.20	0.35	—
1959	14,971,000	—	0.15	0.20	0.35	—

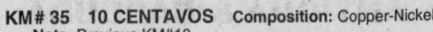

KM# 35 10 CENTAVOS **Composition:** Copper-Nickel **Note:** Previous KM#10.

Date	Mintage	F	VF	XF	Unc	BU
1905	3,785,000	0.50	1.00	3.50	20.00	—
1906	3,854,000	0.50	1.00	3.50	20.00	—
1907	2,355,000	0.50	1.00	4.50	22.00	—
1908	2,280,000	0.50	1.00	4.50	22.00	—
1909	3,738,000	0.50	1.00	3.50	20.00	—
1910	3,026,000	0.50	1.00	3.50	20.00	—
1911	2,142,000	0.75	2.00	5.00	24.00	—
1912	2,993,000	0.75	2.00	5.00	24.00	—
1913	1,828,000	1.00	2.50	5.50	25.00	—
1914	751,000	1.00	2.50	5.50	25.00	—
1915	2,607,000	0.50	1.00	3.50	20.00	—
1916	835,000	1.00	2.50	5.50	25.00	—
1918	3,897,000	0.50	1.00	3.50	20.00	—
1919	2,517,000	0.50	1.00	3.50	25.00	—
1920	7,509,000	0.25	0.75	2.50	20.00	—
1921	11,564,000	0.25	0.60	2.00	15.00	—
1922	6,542,000	0.20	0.50	2.00	20.00	—
1923	5,301,000	0.20	0.50	2.00	15.00	—
1924	3,489,000	0.20	0.50	1.75	10.00	—
1925	5,415,000	0.20	0.50	1.75	10.00	—
1926	5,055,000	0.15	0.35	1.50	9.00	—
1927	5,205,000	0.15	0.35	1.50	9.00	—
1928	8,255,000	0.15	0.35	1.50	9.00	—
1929	2,501,000	0.15	0.35	1.50	9.00	—
1930	14,586,000	0.15	0.35	1.00	6.00	—
1931	893,000	0.50	1.00	2.50	20.00	—
1933	5,394,000	0.15	0.35	1.50	8.00	—
1934	3,319,000	0.15	0.35	1.50	8.00	—
1935	1,018,000	0.30	0.75	2.00	15.00	—
1936	3,000,000	0.15	0.35	1.50	12.00	—
1937	11,766,000	0.15	0.35	1.00	4.00	—
1938	10,494,000	0.15	0.35	1.00	4.00	—
1939	5,585,000	0.15	0.35	1.00	5.00	—
1940	3,955,000	0.15	0.35	1.00	5.00	—
1941	4,101,000	0.15	0.35	1.00	5.00	—
1942	2,962,000	0.15	0.25	1.00	5.00	—

KM# 41 10 CENTAVOS **Composition:** Aluminum-Bronze **Note:** Previous KM#16.

Date	Mintage	F	VF	XF	Unc	BU
1942	15,541,000	0.15	0.25	1.00	4.00	—
1943	13,916,000	0.15	0.35	1.25	6.00	—
1944	16,411,000	0.15	0.25	1.00	4.00	—
1945	12,500,000	0.25	0.50	2.00	7.00	—
1946	15,790,000	0.15	0.25	1.00	4.00	—
1947	36,430,000	0.15	0.25	1.00	2.50	—
1948	54,685,000	0.15	0.25	1.00	2.50	—
1949	57,740,000	0.15	0.25	1.00	2.50	—
1950	42,825,000	0.15	0.25	1.00	2.50	—

KM# 44 10 CENTAVOS **Composition:** Copper-Nickel **Edge:** Reeded **Note:** Jose de San Martin. Previous KM#19.

Date	Mintage	F	VF	XF	Unc	BU
1950	17,505,000	0.20	0.40	0.60	1.75	—

KM# 47 10 CENTAVOS **Composition:** Copper-Nickel **Edge:** Reeded **Note:** Jose de San Martin. Previous KM#22.

Date	Mintage	F	VF	XF	Unc	BU
1951	98,521,000	—	0.20	0.30	0.50	—
1952	67,328,000	—	0.20	0.30	0.50	—

KM# 47a 10 CENTAVOS **Composition:** Nickel Clad Steel **Edge:** Plain **Note:** Previous KM#22a.

Date	Mintage	F	VF	XF	Unc	BU
1952	33,240,000	—	0.10	0.15	0.25	—
1953	106,685,000	—	0.10	0.15	0.25	—

KM# 51 10 CENTAVOS **Composition:** Nickel Clad Steel **Obverse:** Smaller head **Edge:** Plain **Note:** Previous KM#26.

Date	Mintage	F	VF	XF	Unc	BU
1954	117,200,000	—	0.10	0.15	0.25	—
1955	97,045,000	—	0.10	0.15	0.25	—
1956	122,630,000	—	0.10	0.15	0.25	—

KM# 54 10 CENTAVOS **Composition:** Nickel Clad Steel **Obverse:** Smaller head **Edge:** Plain **Note:** Previous KM#29.

Date	Mintage	F	VF	XF	Unc	BU
1957	52,810,000	—	0.10	0.15	0.25	—
1958	41,916,000	—	0.10	0.15	0.25	—
1959	29,183,000	—	0.10	0.15	0.25	—

KM# 36 20 CENTAVOS **Composition:** Copper-Nickel **Note:** Previous KM#11.

Date	Mintage	F	VF	XF	Unc	BU
1905	4,455,000	0.75	2.00	5.00	38.00	—
1906	4,331,000	0.75	2.00	5.00	38.00	—
1907	3,730,000	1.00	3.00	7.00	40.00	—
1908	719,000	2.25	5.00	10.00	45.00	—
1909	1,329,000	0.50	1.50	4.00	35.00	—
1910	1,845,000	0.50	1.50	4.00	35.00	—
1911	1,110,000	0.50	1.50	4.00	35.00	—
1912	2,402,000	0.50	1.50	4.00	35.00	—
1913	1,579,000	0.50	1.00	3.00	30.00	—
1914	527,000	2.25	5.00	12.00	50.00	—
1915	1,921,000	0.50	1.00	3.00	30.00	—
1916	985,000	0.50	1.25	4.00	35.00	—
1918	1,638,000	0.40	0.75	3.00	30.00	—
1919	2,280,000	0.40	0.75	3.00	30.00	—
1920	7,572,000	0.40	0.75	2.50	20.00	—
1921	5,286,000	0.25	0.60	2.50	30.00	—
1922	2,324,000	0.25	0.60	2.50	30.00	—
1923	4,416,000	0.25	0.60	2.50	30.00	—
1924	3,676,000	0.25	0.60	2.00	30.00	—
1925	3,799,000	0.25	0.60	2.00	30.00	—
1926	3,250,000	0.25	0.50	2.00	25.00	—
1927	2,880,000	0.25	0.50	2.00	25.00	—
1928	2,886,000	0.25	0.50	2.00	25.00	—
1929	8,361,000	0.25	0.50	1.25	12.00	—
1930	8,281,000	0.25	0.50	1.25	12.00	—
1931	315,000	2.25	5.00	10.00	35.00	—
1935	1,127,000	0.25	0.60	1.75	12.50	—
1936	855,000	0.50	1.25	2.50	15.00	—
1937	3,314,000	0.25	0.50	1.50	9.00	—
1938	6,449,000	0.25	0.50	1.25	9.00	—
1939	3,555,000	0.25	0.50	1.25	9.00	—
1940	4,465,000	0.25	0.50	1.25	9.00	—
1941	600,000	0.50	1.00	2.00	12.50	—
1942	4,844,000	0.25	0.50	1.25	9.00	—

KM# 42 20 CENTAVOS **Composition:** Aluminum-Bronze **Note:** Previous KM#17.

Date	Mintage	F	VF	XF	Unc	BU
1942	10,255,000	0.25	0.50	2.00	10.00	—
1943	13,775,000	0.15	0.35	1.50	7.00	—
1944	12,225,000	0.15	0.35	1.75	8.00	—
1945	13,340,000	0.15	0.35	1.50	7.00	—
1946	14,625,000	0.15	0.35	1.50	7.00	—
1947	23,165,000	0.15	0.25	1.25	6.00	—
1948	32,245,000	0.15	0.25	1.25	6.00	—
1949	67,115,000	0.15	0.25	1.25	6.00	—
1950	40,071,000	0.15	0.25	1.25	6.00	—

KM# 45 20 CENTAVOS **Composition:** Copper-Nickel **Reverse:** Jose de San Martín portrait right **Edge:** Reeded **Note:** Previous KM#20.

Date	Mintage	F	VF	XF	Unc	BU
1950	86,770,000	0.15	0.25	0.60	1.50	—

KM# 48 20 CENTAVOS **Composition:** Copper-Nickel **Reverse:** Jose de San Martin portrait right **Edge:** Reeded **Note:** Previous KM#23.

Date	Mintage	F	VF	XF	Unc	BU
1951	85,782,000	0.10	0.20	0.30	0.50	—
1952	69,796,000	0.10	0.20	0.30	0.50	—

KM# 48a 20 CENTAVOS **Composition:** Nickel Clad Steel **Reverse:** Jose de San Martín portrait right **Edge:** Plain **Note:** Previous KM#23a.

Date	Mintage	F	VF	XF	Unc	BU
1952	12,863,000	—	0.15	0.25	0.50	—
1953	36,893,000	—	0.15	0.40	1.00	—

KM# 52 20 CENTAVOS **Composition:** Nickel Clad Steel **Note:** Head size reduced slightly. Previous KM#27.

Date	Mintage	F	VF	XF	Unc	BU
1954	52,563,000	—	0.15	0.20	0.25	—
1955	46,952,000	—	0.15	0.20	0.25	—
1956	35,995,000	—	0.15	0.20	0.25	—

KM# 55 20 CENTAVOS **Composition:** Nickel Clad Steel **Note:** Previous KM#30.

Date	Mintage	F	VF	XF	Unc	BU
1957	89,365,000	—	0.15	0.20	0.25	—
1958	52,710,000	—	0.15	0.20	0.25	—
1959	56,585,000	—	0.15	0.20	0.25	—
1960	21,254,000	—	0.15	0.20	0.25	—
1961	2,083,000	—	0.25	0.50	1.50	—

KM# 39 50 CENTAVOS **Composition:** Nickel **Edge:** Reeded **Note:** Previous KM#14.

Date	Mintage	F	VF	XF	Unc	BU
1941	10,961	0.40	1.00	2.00	6.00	—

KM# 49 50 CENTAVOS **Composition:** Nickel Clad Steel **Reverse:** Jose de San Martín portrait right **Edge:** Plain **Note:** Previous KM#24.

Date	Mintage	F	VF	XF	Unc	BU
1952	29,736,000	0.10	0.20	0.35	1.25	—
1953	62,814,000	0.10	0.20	0.35	1.25	—
1954	132,224,000	0.10	0.20	0.35	1.00	—
1955	75,490,000	0.10	0.20	0.35	1.25	—
1956	19,120,000	0.10	0.20	0.50	2.00	—

KM# 56 50 CENTAVOS **Composition:** Nickel Clad Steel **Edge:** Plain **Note:** Previous KM#31.

Date	Mintage	F	VF	XF	Unc	BU
1957	18,139,000	0.10	0.20	0.45	1.25	—
1958	51,750,000	0.10	0.20	0.35	1.00	—
1959	13,997,000	0.10	0.20	0.45	1.25	—
1960	26,038,000	0.10	0.20	0.35	1.00	—
1961	11,106,000	0.10	0.20	0.45	1.25	—

KM# 57 PESO **Composition:** Nickel Clad Steel **Note:** Previous KM#32.

Date	Mintage	F	VF	XF	Unc	BU
1957	118,118,000	0.10	0.20	0.40	2.00	—
1958	118,151,000	0.10	0.20	0.40	2.00	—
1959	237,733,000	0.10	0.20	0.30	1.50	—
1960	75,048,000	0.10	0.30	0.50	2.50	—
1961	76,897,000	0.10	0.30	0.50	2.50	—
1962	30,006,000	0.10	0.30	0.50	3.00	—

KM# 58 PESO **Composition:** Nickel Clad Steel **Subject:** 150th Anniversary - Removal of Spanish Viceroy **Note:** Previous KM#33.

Date	Mintage	F	VF	XF	Unc	BU
ND(1960)	98,751,000	0.20	0.50	0.75	2.00	—

KM# 59 5 PESOS **Composition:** Nickel Clad Steel **Reverse:** Sailing ship - Presidente Sarmiento **Note:** Previous KM#34.

Date	Mintage	F	VF	XF	Unc	BU
1961	37,423,000	0.15	0.25	0.50	3.00	—
1962	42,362,000	0.15	0.25	0.50	3.00	—
1963	71,769,000	0.15	0.25	0.40	2.00	—
1964	12,302,000	0.20	0.35	0.60	3.50	—
1965	19,450,000	0.15	0.25	0.50	3.00	—
1966	17,259,000	0.15	0.25	0.50	3.00	—
1967	17,806,000	0.15	0.25	0.50	3.00	—
1968	12,634,000	0.20	0.35	0.60	3.50	—

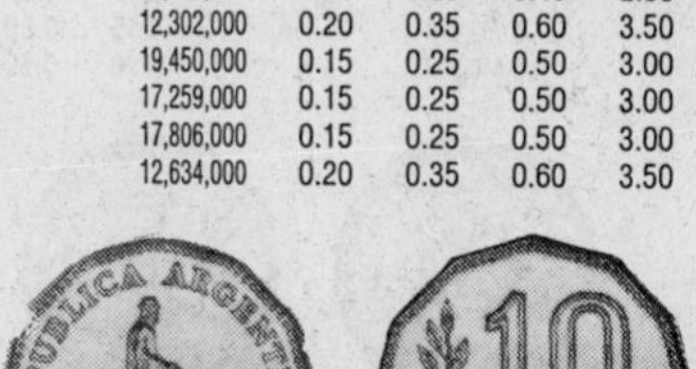

KM# 60 10 PESOS **Composition:** Nickel Clad Steel **Obverse:** Gaucho **Note:** Previous KM#35.

Date	Mintage	F	VF	XF	Unc	BU
1962	57,401,000	0.15	0.25	0.50	3.00	—
1963	136,792,000	0.15	0.20	0.35	2.00	—
1964	46,576,000	0.15	0.25	0.50	3.00	—
1965	40,640,000	0.15	0.25	0.50	3.00	—
1966	50,733,000	0.15	0.20	0.40	2.50	—

Date	Mintage	F	VF	XF	Unc	BU
1967	43,050,000	0.15	0.25	0.50	3.00	—
1968	36,588,000	0.15	0.25	0.50	3.00	—

KM# 62 10 PESOS **Composition:** Nickel Clad Steel **Subject:** 150th Anniversary - Declaration of Independence. **Note:** Previous KM#37.

Date	Mintage	F	VF	XF	Unc	BU
ND(1966)	29,336,000	0.15	0.25	0.50	3.00	—

KM# 61 25 PESOS **Composition:** Nickel Clad Steel **Subject:** 1st issue of National Coinage in 1813. **Note:** Previous KM#36.

Date	Mintage	F	VF	XF	Unc	BU
1964	20,485,000	0.15	0.25	0.50	3.00	—
1965	14,884,000	0.15	0.25	0.50	3.00	—
1966	16,426,000	0.15	0.25	0.50	3.00	—
1967	15,734,000	0.15	0.25	0.50	3.00	—
1968	4,446,000	0.15	0.25	0.75	3.50	—

KM# 63 25 PESOS **Composition:** Nickel Clad Steel **Subject:** 80th Anniversary - Death of D. Faustino Sarmiento. **Note:** Previous KM#38.

Date	Mintage	F	VF	XF	Unc	BU
1968	15,804,000	0.25	0.60	0.85	1.65	—

KM# 131 25 PESOS **Weight:** 26.9000 g. **Composition:** 0.9250 Silver 0.8 oz. ASW **Subject:** Ibero-America Series **Obverse:** Argentine arms within legend and circle of arms **Reverse:** Bronco busting scene **Edge:** Reeded **Size:** 40 mm.

Date	F	VF	XF	Unc	BU
2000 Proof				— Value: 60.00	

REFORM COINAGE

1970-1983; 100 Old Pesos = 1 New Peso

KM# 64 CENTAVO **Composition:** Aluminum **Note:** Previous KM#39.

Date	Mintage	F	VF	XF	Unc	BU
1970	47,801,000	—	—	0.10	0.30	—
1971	44,644,000	—	—	0.10	0.30	—
1972	92,430,000	—	—	0.10	0.30	—
1973	29,515,000	—	—	0.10	0.30	—
1974	5,162,000	—	—	0.15	0.35	—
1975	3,840,000	—	0.10	0.20	0.50	—

KM# 65 5 CENTAVOS **Composition:** Aluminum **Note:** Previous KM#40.

Date	Mintage	F	VF	XF	Unc	BU
1970	56,174,000	—	0.10	0.15	0.40	—
1971	3,798,000	0.10	0.20	0.35	0.65	—
1972	84,250,000	—	0.10	0.15	0.40	—
1973	113,912,000	—	0.10	0.15	0.40	—
1974	18,150,000	—	0.10	0.15	0.40	—
1975	6,940,000	0.10	0.20	0.35	0.65	—

KM# 66 10 CENTAVOS **Composition:** Brass **Note:** Previous KM#41.

Date	Mintage	F	VF	XF	Unc	BU
1970	52,903,000	—	0.10	0.15	0.35	—
1971	135,623,000	—	0.10	0.15	0.35	—
1973	19,930,000	—	0.10	0.15	0.35	—
1974	79,156,000	—	0.10	0.15	0.35	—
1975	31,270,000	—	0.10	0.15	0.35	—
1976	730,000	0.10	0.20	0.35	1.00	—

KM# 67 20 CENTAVOS **Composition:** Brass **Note:** Previous KM#42.

Date	Mintage	F	VF	XF	Unc	BU
1970	27,029,000	—	0.10	0.15	0.35	—
1971	32,211,000	—	0.10	0.15	0.35	—
1972	220,000	1.00	2.00	4.00	8.00	—
1973	9,676,000	—	0.10	0.15	0.35	—
1974	41,024,000	—	0.10	0.15	0.35	—
1975	26,540,000	—	0.10	0.15	0.35	—
1976	960,000	—	0.10	0.15	0.35	—

KM# 68 50 CENTAVOS **Composition:** Brass **Note:** Previous KM#43.

Date	Mintage	F	VF	XF	Unc	BU
1970	44,748,000	0.10	0.15	0.30	0.60	—
1971	34,947,000	0.10	0.15	0.30	0.60	—
1972	40,960,000	0.10	0.15	0.30	0.60	—
1973	69,472,000	0.10	0.15	0.30	0.60	—
1974	63,063,000	0.10	0.15	0.30	0.60	—
1975	64,859,000	0.10	0.15	0.30	0.60	—
1976	9,768,000	0.10	0.15	0.30	0.60	—

KM# 69 PESO **Composition:** Aluminum-Brass **Note:** Wide and narrow rim varieties exist. Previous KM#44.

Date	Mintage	F	VF	XF	Unc	BU
1974	77,292,000	—	0.10	0.25	0.75	—
1975	423,000,000	—	0.10	0.20	0.50	—
1976	100,075,000	—	0.10	0.20	0.50	—

KM# 71 5 PESOS **Composition:** Aluminum-Bronze **Note:** Previous KM#46.

Date	Mintage	F	VF	XF	Unc	BU
1976	118,353,000	—	0.10	0.20	0.65	—
1977	64,738,000	—	0.10	0.20	0.65	—

KM# 73 5 PESOS **Composition:** Aluminum-Bronze **Subject:** Admiral G. Brown Bicentennial **Note:** Previous KM#48.

Date	F	VF	XF	Unc	BU
1977	0.10	0.15	0.30	0.75	—

KM# 72 10 PESOS **Composition:** Aluminum-Bronze **Note:** Previous KM#47.

Date	Mintage	F	VF	XF	Unc	BU
1976	128,965,000	0.10	0.15	0.35	1.00	—
1977	113,400,000	0.10	0.15	0.35	1.00	—
1978	253,863,000	0.10	0.15	0.35	1.00	—

KM# 74 10 PESOS **Composition:** Aluminum-Bronze **Subject:** Admiral G. Brown Bicentennial **Note:** Previous KM#49.

Date	F	VF	XF	Unc	BU
1977	0.10	0.20	0.50	1.25	—

KM# 75 20 PESOS **Composition:** Aluminum-Bronze **Subject:** 1978 World Soccer Championship **Note:** Previous KM#50.

Date	Mintage	F	VF	XF	Unc	BU
1977	1,506,000	0.10	0.20	0.40	1.00	—
1978	2,000,000	0.10	0.20	0.40	1.00	—

KM# 76 50 PESOS **Composition:** Aluminum-Bronze **Subject:** 1978 World Soccer Championship **Note:** Previous KM#51.

Date	Mintage	F	VF	XF	Unc	BU
1977	1,506,000	0.10	0.20	0.40	1.00	—
1978	2,000,000	0.10	0.20	0.40	1.00	—

KM# 81 50 PESOS **Composition:** Aluminum-Bronze **Subject:** 200th Anniversary - Birth of Jose de San Martín **Note:** Previous KM#56.

Date	Mintage	F	VF	XF	Unc	BU
1978	40,601,000	0.20	0.50	1.00	2.00	—

KM# 83 50 PESOS **Composition:** Aluminum-Bronze **Reverse:** Jose de San Martín portrait right **Note:** Previous KM#58.

Date	Mintage	F	VF	XF	Unc	BU
1979	103,491,000	0.10	0.25	0.65	1.50	—
1980	—	0.10	0.25	0.65	1.50	—

KM# 83a 50 PESOS **Composition:** Brass Clad Steel **Reverse:** Jose de San Martín portrait right **Note:** Previous KM#58a.

Date	Mintage	F	VF	XF	Unc	BU
1980	94,730,000	0.10	0.25	0.65	1.25	—
1981	4,372,000	0.10	0.25	0.65	1.25	—

KM# 84 50 PESOS **Composition:** Aluminum-Bronze **Subject:** Conquest of Patagonia Centennial **Note:** Previous KM#59.

Date	F	VF	XF	Unc	BU
1979	0.10	0.25	0.65	1.50	—

KM# 77 100 PESOS **Composition:** Aluminum-Bronze **Subject:** 1978 World Soccer Championship **Note:** Previous KM#52.

Date	Mintage	F	VF	XF	Unc	BU
1977	1,506,000	0.15	0.30	0.75	1.50	—
1978	2,000,000	0.15	0.30	0.75	1.50	—

KM# 82 100 PESOS **Composition:** Aluminum-Bronze **Subject:** 200th Anniversary - Birth of Jose de San Martín **Note:** Previous KM#57.

Date	Mintage	F	VF	XF	Unc	BU
1978	113,826,000	—	0.50	1.00	2.00	—

KM# 85 100 PESOS **Composition:** Aluminum-Bronze **Reverse:** Jose de San Martín portrait right **Note:** Previous KM#60.

Date	Mintage	F	VF	XF	Unc	BU
1979	207,572,000	0.15	0.30	0.75	1.25	—
1980	154,260,000	0.15	0.30	0.75	1.25	—
1981	145,680,000	0.15	0.30	0.75	1.25	—

KM# 85a 100 PESOS **Composition:** Brass Clad Steel **Reverse:** Jose de San Martín portrait right **Note:** Previous KM#60a.

Date	F	VF	XF	Unc	BU
1980	0.15	0.30	0.75	1.50	—
1981	0.15	0.30	0.75	1.50	—

KM# 86 100 PESOS **Composition:** Aluminum-Bronze **Subject:** Conquest of Patagonia Centennial **Note:** Previous KM#61.

Date	F	VF	XF	Unc	BU
1979	0.15	0.30	0.75	1.50	—

KM# 78 1000 PESOS **Weight:** 10.0000 g. **Composition:** 0.9000 Silver .2893 oz. ASW **Subject:** 1978 World Soccer Championship **Note:** Previous KM#53.

Date	Mintage	F	VF	XF	Unc	BU
1977		—	—	3.00	6.00	—
1977 Proof	1,000	Value: 17.50				
1978		—	—	3.00	6.00	—
1978 Proof	1,750	Value: 17.50				

KM# 79 2000 PESOS **Weight:** 15.0000 g. **Composition:** 0.9000 Silver .4340 oz. ASW **Subject:** 1978 World Soccer Championship **Note:** Previous KM#54.

Date	Mintage	F	VF	XF	Unc	BU
1977		—	—	5.00	10.00	—
1977 Proof	1,000	Value: 22.50				
1978		—	—	5.00	9.50	—
1978 Proof	1,750	Value: 22.50				

KM# 80 3000 PESOS **Weight:** 25.0000 g. **Composition:** 0.9000 Silver .7234 oz. ASW **Subject:** 1978 World Soccer Championship **Note:** Previous KM#55.

Date	Mintage	F	VF	XF	Unc	BU
1977		—	—	8.00	15.50	—
1977 Proof	1,000	Value: 35.00				
1978		—	—	8.00	14.50	—
1978 Proof	1,750	Value: 35.00				

REFORM COINAGE

1983-1985; 10,000 Pesos = 1 Peso Argentino; 100 Centavos = 1 Peso Argentino

KM# 87 CENTAVO **Composition:** Aluminum **Note:** Previous KM#62.

Date	Mintage	F	VF	XF	Unc	BU
1983	19,959,000	—	—	—	0.20	—

KM# 88 5 CENTAVOS **Composition:** Aluminum **Note:** Previous KM#63.

Date	Mintage	F	VF	XF	Unc	BU
1983	59,870,000	—	—	—	0.25	—

KM# 89 10 CENTAVOS **Composition:** Aluminum **Note:** Previous KM#64.

Date	Mintage	F	VF	XF	Unc	BU
1983	307,513,000	—	—	—	0.25	—

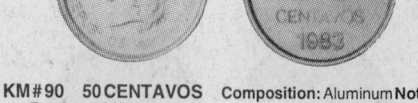

KM# 90 50 CENTAVOS **Composition:** Aluminum **Note:** Previous KM#65.

Date	Mintage	F	VF	XF	Unc	BU
1983	243,909,000	—	—	—	0.45	—

KM# 91 PESO **Composition:** Aluminum **Note:** National Congress. Previous KM#66.

Date	Mintage	F	VF	XF	Unc	BU
1984	785,791,000	—	—	—	0.50	—

KM# 92 5 PESOS **Composition:** Brass **Obverse:** Buenos Aires City Hall **Note:** Previous KM#67.

Date	Mintage	F	VF	XF	Unc	BU
1984	11,206,000	—	—	—	0.65	—
1985	14,168,000	—	—	—	0.65	—

KM# 93 10 PESOS **Composition:** Brass **Obverse:** Independence Hall at Tucuman **Note:** Previous KM#68.

Date	Mintage	F	VF	XF	Unc	BU
1984	16,528,000	—	—	—	0.85	—
1985	14,618,000	—	—	—	0.85	—

KM# 94 50 PESOS **Composition:** Aluminum-Bronze **Subject:** 50th Anniversary of Central Bank **Note:** Previous KM#69.

Date	Mintage	F	VF	XF	Unc	BU
1985	26,400,000	—	—	—	1.00	—

REFORM COINAGE

1985-1992; 1,000 Pesos Argentinos = 1 Austral; 100 Centavos = 1 Austral

KM# 95 1/2 CENTAVO **Composition:** Brass **Note:** Rufous Hornero Bird. Previous KM#70.

Date	Mintage	F	VF	XF	Unc	BU
1985	7,490,000	—	—	—	0.45	0.65

KM# 96.1 CENTAVO **Composition:** Brass **Obverse:** Common Rhea **Note:** Thick flan. Previous KM#71.1.

Date	Mintage	F	VF	XF	Unc	BU
1985	76,082,000	—	—	—	0.65	0.85

KM# 96.2 CENTAVO **Composition:** Brass **Obverse:** Common Rhea **Note:** Thin flan. Previous KM#71.2.

Date	Mintage	F	VF	XF	Unc	BU
1986	18,934,000	—	—	—	0.65	0.85
1987	87,315,000	—	—	—	0.65	0.85

KM# 97.1 5 CENTAVOS **Composition:** Brass **Obverse:** Pampas Cat **Note:** Thick flan. Previous KM#72.1.

Date	Mintage	F	VF	XF	Unc	BU
1985	36,924,000	—	—	—	1.50	2.00

KM# 97.2 5 CENTAVOS **Composition:** Brass **Obverse:** Pampas Cat **Note:** Thin flan. Previous KM#72.2.

Date	Mintage	F	VF	XF	Unc	BU
1986	66,414,000	—	—	—	1.45	1.85
1987	56,181,000	—	—	—	1.45	1.85
1988	23,895,000	—	—	—	1.45	1.85

KM# 98 10 CENTAVOS **Composition:** Brass **Note:** Previous KM#73.

Date	Mintage	F	VF	XF	Unc	BU
1985	23,268,000	—	—	—	0.65	0.85
1986	158,427,000	—	—	—	0.65	0.85
1987	184,330,000	—	—	—	0.65	0.85
1988	174,003,000	—	—	—	0.65	0.85

KM# 99 50 CENTAVOS **Composition:** Brass **Note:** Varieties exist. Previous KM#74.

Date	Mintage	F	VF	XF	Unc	BU
1985	13,884,000	—	—	—	1.50	2.00
1986	59,074,000	—	—	—	1.45	1.85
1987	64,525,000	—	—	—	1.45	1.85
1988	62,388,000	—	—	—	1.45	1.85

KM# 100 AUSTRAL **Composition:** Aluminum **Obverse:** Buenos Aires City Hall **Note:** Previous KM#75.

Date	F	VF	XF	Unc	BU
1989	—	—	—	0.15	—

KM# 101 5 AUSTRALES **Composition:** Aluminum **Obverse:** Independence Hall at Tucuman **Note:** Previous KM#76.

Date	F	VF	XF	Unc	BU
1989	—	—	—	0.25	—

KM# 102 10 AUSTRALES **Composition:** Aluminum **Obverse:** Casa del Acuerdo **Note:** Previous KM#77.

Date	F	VF	XF	Unc	BU
1989	—	—	—	0.35	—

KM# 103 100 AUSTRALES **Composition:** Aluminum **Note:** Previous KM#78.

Date	F	VF	XF	Unc	BU
1990	—	—	—	0.25	—
1991	—	—	—	0.25	—

KM# 104 500 AUSTRALES **Composition:** Aluminum **Note:** Previous KM#79.

Date	F	VF	XF	Unc	BU
1990	—	—	—	0.35	—
1991	—	—	—	0.35	—

KM# 105 1000 AUSTRALES **Composition:** Aluminum **Note:** Previous KM#80.

Date	F	VF	XF	Unc	BU
1990	—	—	—	0.60	—
1991	—	—	—	0.60	—

KM# 106 1000 AUSTRALES **Weight:** 27.0000 g. **Composition:** 0.9250 Silver .8029 oz. ASW **Subject:** Ibero - American Series **Note:** Previous KM#81.

Date	Mintage	F	VF	XF	Unc	BU
1991 Proof	70,000	Value: 45.00				

REFORM COINAGE

1992; 10,000 Australes = 1 Peso

KM# 108 CENTAVO **Composition:** Brass **Edge:** Plain **Note:** Octagonal. Previous KM#83.

Date	F	VF	XF	Unc	BU
1992	—	—	—	0.25	—

KM# 113 CENTAVO **Composition:** Brass **Edge:** Reeded

Date	F	VF	XF	Unc	BU
1992	—	—	—	0.25	—
1993	—	—	—	0.25	—

KM# 113a CENTAVO **Composition:** Bronze **Edge:** Reeded

Date	F	VF	XF	Unc	BU
1993	—	—	—	0.25	—
1997	—	—	—	0.25	—
1998	—	—	—	0.25	—
1999	—	—	—	0.25	—

KM# 109 5 CENTAVOS **Composition:** Brass **Obverse:** Radiant sunface **Note:** Previous KM#84.

Date	F	VF	XF	Unc	BU
1992	—	—	—	0.45	—
1993	—	—	—	0.45	—

KM# 109a.1 5 CENTAVOS **Composition:** Copper-Nickel **Obverse:** Radiant sunface. Fine, bold lettering **Note:** Previous KM#84a.1.

Date	F	VF	XF	Unc	BU
1993	—	—	—	0.45	—

KM# 109a.2 5 CENTAVOS **Composition:** Copper-Nickel **Obverse:** Radiant sunface. Bold lettering **Note:** Previous KM#84a.2.

Date	F	VF	XF	Unc	BU
1994	—	—	—	0.45	—

KM# 107 10 CENTAVOS **Composition:** Aluminum-Bronze **Edge:** Plain **Note:** Previous KM#82.

Date	Mintage	F	VF	XF	Unc	BU
1992	400,000,000	—	—	—	0.65	—
1993	—	—	—	—	0.65	—
1994	—	—	—	—	0.65	—

KM# 110.1 25 CENTAVOS **Composition:** Brass **Obverse:** Towered building, fine lettering **Note:** Previous KM#85.1.

Date	F	VF	XF	Unc	BU
1992	—	—	—	1.25	—

KM# 110.2 25 CENTAVOS **Composition:** Brass **Obverse:** Towered building, bold lettering **Note:** Previous KM#85.2.

Date	F	VF	XF	Unc	BU
1993	—	—	—	1.25	—

KM# 110a 25 CENTAVOS **Composition:** Copper-Nickel **Obverse:** Towered building, bold lettering **Note:** Previous KM#85a.

Date	F	VF	XF	Unc	BU
1993	—	—	—	1.25	—
1994	—	—	—	1.25	—
1995	—	—	—	1.25	—
1996	—	—	—	1.25	—

KM# 111.1 50 CENTAVOS **Composition:** Copper-Nickel **Obverse:** Tucuman Province Capital Building; fine lettering **Note:** Previous KM#86.1.

Date	F	VF	XF	Unc	BU
1992	—	—	—	1.75	—

KM# 111.2 50 CENTAVOS **Composition:** Copper-Nickel **Obverse:** Tucuman Province Capital Building; bold lettering. **Note:** Previous KM#86.2.

Date	F	VF	XF	Unc	BU
1993	—	—	—	1.75	—
1994	—	—	—	1.75	—
1995	—	—	—	1.75	—

KM# 119 50 CENTAVOS **Composition:** Copper-Aluminum **Subject:** 50th Anniversary - UNICEF **Obverse:** Girl with rag doll **Reverse:** UNICEF logo above denomination **Note:** Previous KM#94.

Date	F	VF	XF	Unc	BU
1996	—	—	—	2.00	—

KM# 121 50 CENTAVOS **Composition:** Copper-Aluminum **Subject:** 50th Anniversary - Women's Right to Vote **Obverse:** Eva Peron portrait **Reverse:** Denomination **Note:** Previous KM#96.

Date	Mintage	F	VF	XF	Unc	BU
1997	2,000	—	—	—	2.25	—

KM# 124 50 CENTAVOS **Composition:** Copper-Aluminum **Subject:** Mercosur **Obverse:** Southern Cross constellation **Reverse:** Denomination **Note:** Previous KM#99.

Date	F	VF	XF	Unc	BU
1998	—	—	—	2.25	—

KM# 112.1 PESO **Ring Composition:** Copper-Nickel **Center Composition:** Brass **Subject:** First Argentine Coin Design **Obverse:** Large legend **Reverse:** Large legend; pointed 9s **Note:** Previous KM#87.1.

Date	F	VF	XF	Unc	BU
1994A	—	—	—	4.50	—
1995A	—	—	—	4.50	—
1995B	—	—	—	4.50	—
1996A	—	—	—	4.50	—
1996A	—	—	—	4.50	—

KM# 112.2 PESO **Ring Composition:** Copper-Nickel **Center Composition:** Brass **Subject:** First Argentine Coin Design **Obverse:** Small legend **Reverse:** Small legend; rounded 9s **Note:** Previous KM#87.2.

Date	F	VF	XF	Unc	BU
1995C	—	—	—	4.50	—

KM# 126 PESO **Weight:** 25.0000 g. **Composition:** 0.9000 Silver .7234 oz. ASW **Subject:** 50th Anniversary - United Nations **Obverse:** Dove over national arms **Reverse:** UN logo, denomination, dates **Note:** Previous KM#101.

Date		F	VF	XF	Unc	BU
1995 Proof	100,000	Value: 35.00				

KM# 112.3 PESO **Ring Composition:** Copper-Nickel **Center Composition:** Brass **Subject:** First Argentine Coin Design **Obverse:** Small legend **Reverse:** 6 error, PROVINGIAS **Note:** Previous KM#87.3.

Date	F	VF	XF	Unc	BU
1995B	—	—	—	7.50	—

KM# 120 PESO **Ring Composition:** Copper-Nickel **Center Composition:** Brass **Subject:** 50th Anniversary - UNICEF **Obverse:** Girl with rag doll **Reverse:** UNICEF logo above denomination **Note:** Previous KM#95.

Date	Mintage	F	VF	XF	Unc	BU
1996	1,000,000	—	—	—	4.50	—

KM# 122 PESO **Ring Composition:** Copper-Nickel **Center Composition:** Brass **Subject:** 50th Anniversary - Women's Right to Vote **Obverse:** Eva Peron portrait **Reverse:** Denomination **Note:** Previous KM#97.

Date	Mintage	F	VF	XF	Unc	BU
1997	1,000,000	—	—	—	5.00	—

KM# 125 PESO **Ring Composition:** Copper-Nickel **Center Composition:** Brass **Subject:** Mercosur **Obverse:** Southern Cross constellation **Reverse:** Denomination **Note:** Previous KM#100.

Date	F	VF	XF	Unc	BU
1998	—	—	—	4.50	—

KM# 127 PESO **Weight:** 25.0000 g. **Composition:** 0.9000 Silver .7234 oz. ASW **Subject:** 100th Anniversary - Birth of Jorge Luis Borges **Obverse:** Profile portrait of Borges, dates **Reverse:** Labyrinth, sundial, denomination and date **Note:** Previous KM#102.

Date		F	VF	XF	Unc	BU
1999 Proof	5,000	Value: 37.50				

KM# 114 2 PESOS **Composition:** Nickel **Subject:** National Constitution Convention **Note:** Previous KM#89.

Date	Mintage	F	VF	XF	Unc	BU
ND(1994)	—	—	—	—	8.00	—
ND(1994) Proof	5,500	Value: 16.00				

KM# 114a 2 PESOS **Weight:** 12.4800 g. **Composition:** 0.9000 Silver .3612 oz. ASW **Subject:** National Constitution Convention **Note:** Previous KM#89a.

Date		F	VF	XF	Unc	BU
ND		—	—	—	12.50	—
ND Proof	1,500	Value: 25.00				

KM# 128 2 PESOS **Composition:** Copper-Nickel **Subject:** 100th Anniversary - Birth of Jorge Luis Borges **Obverse:** Profile head of Borges left **Reverse:** Labyrinth, sundial, denomination and date **Note:** Previous KM#103.

Date	F	VF	XF	Unc	BU
1999	—	—	—	8.00	—

KM# 115 5 PESOS **Composition:** Nickel **Subject:** National Constitution Convention **Note:** Previous KM#90.

Date	Mintage	F	VF	XF	Unc	BU
ND	—	—	—	—	15.00	—
ND Proof	5,500	Value: 25.00				

KM# 115a 5 PESOS **Weight:** 24.8000 g. **Composition:** 0.9000 Silver .7177 oz. ASW **Subject:** National Constitution Convention **Note:** Previous KM#90a.

Date		F	VF	XF	Unc	BU
ND(1994)		—	—	—	25.00	—
ND(1994) Proof	1,500	Value: 60.00				

KM# 116 25 PESOS **Weight:** 4.0320 g. **Composition:** 0.9000 Gold .1167 oz. AGW **Subject:** National Constitution Convention **Note:** Previous KM#91.

Date	Mintage	F	VF	XF	Unc	BU
ND(1994) Proof	1,500	Value: 115				

KM# 118 25 PESOS **Weight:** 27.0000 g. **Composition:** 0.9250 Silver .8030 oz. ASW **Subject:** Environmental Protection **Reverse:** Giant Armadillo **Note:** Previous KM#93.

Date	Mintage	F	VF	XF	Unc	BU
1997 Proof	—	Value: 45.00				

KM# 123 25 PESOS **Weight:** 27.0000 g. **Composition:** 0.9250 Silver .8030 oz. ASW **Subject:** Ibero-American Series - LaZamba **Obverse:** Argentine arms in center **Reverse:** Zamba dancers **Note:** Previous KM#98.

Date	Mintage	F	VF	XF	Unc	BU
1997 Proof	—	Value: 55.00				

KM# 117 50 PESOS **Weight:** 8.0640 g. **Composition:** 0.9000 Gold .2334 oz. AGW **Subject:** National Constitution Convention **Note:** Previous KM#92.

Date	Mintage	F	VF	XF	Unc	BU
ND Proof	1,500	Value: 225				

PATTERNS

Including off metal strikes

KM#	Date	Mintage	Identification	Mkt Val
Pn35	19xx	—	Centavo. Copper.	—
Pn36	19xx	—	2 Centavos. Copper.	—
Pn37	1925	—	2 Centavos. Copper.	—
Pn38	1925	—	2 Centavos. Bronze.	—
Pn39	1932	—	Argentino. Copper.	—
Pn40	1932	—	Argentino. Bronze.	—
Pn41	1933	—	Argentino. Bronze.	—
Pn42	1934	—	Argentino. Copper.	—
Pn43	1935	—	Centavo. Copper.	150
Pn44	1935	—	2 Centavos. Copper.	175
Pn46	1936	—	50 Centavos. Copper-Nickel.	175
Pn48	1936	—	Peso. Copper-Nickel.	250
Pn45	1936	—	50 Centavos. Bronze.	—
Pn47	1936	—	Peso. Bronze.	—
Pn49	1937	—	Centavo. Copper. Post horn mint mark.	—
Pn50	1938	—	Centavo. Copper.	175
Pn51	1938	—	2 Centavos. Copper.	195
Pn52	1940	—	50 Centavos. Bronze.	200
Pn53	1940	—	50 Centavos. Copper-Nickel. Head by Oudine.	—
Pn54	1940	—	50 Centavos. Nickel. Head by L. Bazor.	—
Pn55	1941	—	50 Centavos. Nickel.	—
Pn56	1943	—	Peso. Bronze.	—
Pn57	1943	—	Peso. Nickel.	—
Pn58	1943	—	Peso. Bronze. Condor.	—
Pn59	1945	—	Peso. Bronze.	—
Pn60	1945	—	Peso. Copper-Nickel.	—
Pn61	1946	—	Peso. Bronze.	—
Pn62	1946	—	Peso. Copper-Nickel.	200
Pn63	1971	—	50 Centavos. Silverish Aluminum. KM#43	75.00
Pn64	1975	—	Peso. Aluminum-Brass. KM#45	125
Pn65	1976	—	5 Pesos. Silverish Aluminum. KM#46	—
Pn66	1977	—	10 Pesos. Silverish Aluminum-Brass. KM#47	—

MINT SETS

KM#	Date	Mintage	Identification	Issue Price	Mkt Val
MS2	1970 (5)	—	KM#64-68	—	2.00
MS3	1977 (6)	—	KM#75-80	—	32.00
MS4	1977 (3)	—	KM#75-77	—	4.00
MS5	1978 (6)	—	KM#75-80	—	30.00
MS6	1983 (4)	—	KM#87-90	—	2.00

PROOF SETS

KM#	Date	Mintage	Identification	Issue Price	Mkt Val
PS1	1977 (3)	1,000	KM#78-80	—	75.00
PS2	1978 (3)	1,750	KM#78-80	153	75.00
PS5	ND(1994) (2)	1,000	KM#116, 117	375	345
PS3	ND(1994) (2)	5,500	KM#114, 115	—	40.00
PS4	ND(1994) (2)	1,000	KM#114a, 115a	79.50	85.00

CATAMARCA

A province located in northwest Argentina having an area of 38,540 sq. mi. and a population of 172,323. Capital: Catamarca. Agriculture and mining are the main industries.

PROVINCE

TOKEN COINAGE

Stabilization Currency Unit

KM# Tn1 100000 AUSTRALES **Weight:** 15.0000 g. **Composition:** 0.9000 Silver .4341 oz. ASW **Subject:** Fray Mamerto Esquiu

Date	Mintage	F	VF	XF	Unc	BU
1990	200,000	—	—	—	28.50	—

KM# Tn3 100000 AUSTRALES **Weight:** 14.8500 g. **Composition:** 0.9000 Silver .4297 oz. ASW **Subject:** 100th Anniversary - Coronation of Our Lady of the Valley

Date	F	VF	XF	Unc	BU
1991	—	—	—	28.50	—

KM# Tn2 4000000 AUSTRALES **Weight:** 20.0000 g. **Composition:** 0.7500 Gold .4823 oz. AGW **Subject:** Fray Mamerto Esquiu **Note:** Denomination determined upon release.

Date	Mintage	F	VF	XF	Unc	BU
1990	200	—	—	—	920	—

LA RIOJA

La Rioja (Rioxa), a city and province in northwest Argentina, was the source of rich mineral wealth. In this province the city of Chilecito was significant as the spot where gold and silver mines within the Famatina Mountains had been worked since colonial times. After independence was gained from Spain, Governor Nicolas Davila authorized a mint at Chilecito, which was established in 1820. The first attempts at coinage came in 1821 and were nothing more than poor imitations of the Potosi 2 real cobs of Ferdinand VII, crude in all respects because the mint had no machinery with which to make proper dies, punches for collars. No examples of these types are distinguishable today as they are in essence identical to all other contemporary cob copies of the period. However, some experts believe that the presence of the letter A on provisional cobs of this type can be considered a mint mark or assayer initial tying the coins to the Chilecito mint.

The next coins to emerge from Chilecito were cob types dated 1821, 1822, and 1823, bearing the legend RIOXA. All of these cob coins circulated in the area until the middle of 1824 when they were officially recalled. These rare types were well received in their day as they were made of good silver. They can be distinguished today by their crude and uneven strike quality as opposed to the well made, attractive look of modern fakes.

In 1824 the mint at Chilecito was transferred to the capital of La Rioja where minting continued from 1824 to 1860. Chilecito's mines at Famatina Mountain continued to produce gold and silver for the new mint and Famatina is featured as a central design on many coins of the period.

NOTE: Virtually all of the early pieces are false. All pieces dated between 1820 and 1824 should only be bought with certification of two or more authorities.

PROVINCE

TOKEN COINAGE

Stabilization Currency Unit

KM# Tn1 100000 AUSTRALES **Weight:** 15.0000 g. **Composition:** 0.9000 Silver .4341 oz. ASW **Subject:** 400th Anniversary - Foundation of La Rioja

Date	Mintage	VG	F	VF	XF	Unc
1991	200,000	—	—	—	—	28.50

KM# Tn2 4000000 AUSTRALES **Weight:** 20.0000 g. **Composition:** 0.7500 Gold .4823 oz. AGW **Subject:** 400th Anniversary - Foundation of La Rioja

Date	Mintage	VG	F	VF	XF	Unc
1991	1,000	—	—	—	900	—

ARMENIA

The Republic of Armenia, formerly Armenian S.S.R., is bordered to the north by Georgia, the east by Azerbaijan and the south and west by Turkey and Iran. It has an area of 11,506 sq. mi. (29,800 sq. km) and an estimated population of 3.66 million. Capital: Yerevan. Agriculture including cotton, vineyards and orchards, hydroelectricity, chemicals - primarily synthetic rubber and fertilizers, vast mineral deposits of copper, zinc and aluminum, and production of steel and paper are major industries.

Russia occupied Armenia in 1801 until the Russo-Turkish war of 1878. British intervention excluded either side from remaining although the Armenians remained more loyal to the Ottoman Turks, but in 1894 the Ottoman Turks sent in an expeditionary force of Kurds fearing a revolutionary movement. Large massacres were followed by retaliations, then amnesty was proclaimed which led right into WW I and once again occupation by Russian forces in 1916. After the Russian revolution the Georgians, Armenians and Azerbaijanis formed the short-lived Transcaucasian Federal Republic on Sept. 20, 1917, which broke up into three independent republics on May 26, 1918. Communism developed and in Sept. 1920 the Turks attacked the Armenian Republic; the Russians soon followed suit from Azerbaijan routing the Turks. On Nov. 29, 1920 Armenia was proclaimed a Soviet Socialist Republic. On March 12, 1922, Armenia, Georgia and Azerbaijan were combined to form the Transcaucasian Soviet Federated Socialist Republic, which on Dec. 30, 1922, became a part of U.S.S.R. On Dec. 5, 1936, the Transcaucasian federation was dissolved and Armenia became a constituent Republic of the U.S.S.R. A new constitution was adopted in April 1978. Elections took place on May 20, 1990. The Supreme Soviet adopted a declaration of sovereignty in Aug. 1991, voting to unite Armenia with Nagorno - Karabakh. This newly constituted "Republic of Armenia" became fully independent by popular vote in Sept. 1991. It became a member of the CIS in Dec. 1991.

Fighting between Christians in Armenia and Muslim forces of Azerbaijan escalated in 1992 and continued through early 1994. Each country claimed the Nagorno-Karabakh, an Armenian ethnic enclave, in Azerbaijan. A temporary cease-fire was announced in May 1994.

MONETARY SYSTEM
50 Luma = 1 Dram

MINTNAMES
Revan, (Erevan, now Yerevan)

REPUBLIC

STANDARD COINAGE

KM# 51 10 LUMA Composition: Aluminum

Date	F	VF	XF	Unc	BU
1994	—	—	—	0.25	—

KM# 52 20 LUMA Composition: Aluminum

Date	F	VF	XF	Unc	BU
1994	—	—	—	0.25	—

KM# 53 50 LUMA Composition: Aluminum

Date	F	VF	XF	Unc	BU
1994	—	—	—	0.45	—

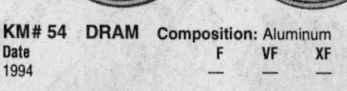

KM# 54 DRAM Composition: Aluminum

Date	F	VF	XF	Unc	BU
1994	—	—	—	0.65	—

KM# 55 3 DRAM Composition: Aluminum

Date	F	VF	XF	Unc	BU
1994	—	—	—	0.85	—

KM# 56 5 DRAM Composition: Aluminum

Date	F	VF	XF	Unc	BU
1994	—	—	—	1.20	—

KM# 81 5 DRAM Weight: 31.3700 g. **Composition:** 0.9990 Silver 1.0076 oz. ASW **Subject:** 5th Anniversary - National Currency **Obverse:** National arms **Reverse:** 6 banknote designs **Size:** 38 mm.

Date		F	VF	XF	Unc	BU
1998 Proof	Est. 500	Value: 70.00				

KM# 58 10 DRAM Composition: Aluminum

Date	F	VF	XF	Unc	BU
1994	—	—	—	2.00	—

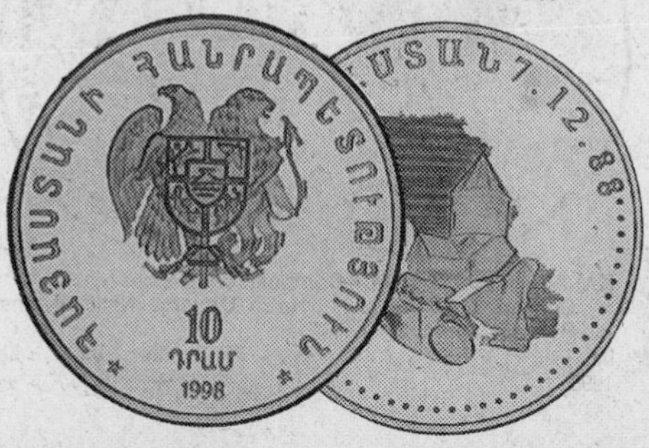

KM# 82 10 DRAM Weight: 31.4500 g. **Composition:** 0.9990 Silver 1.0130 oz. ASW **Subject:** 10th Anniversary - Earthquake **Obverse:** National arms **Reverse:** Map and building **Size:** 38 mm.

Date	F	VF	XF	Unc	BU
1998 Proof	—	Value: 70.00			

KM# 57 25 DRAM Weight: 31.1035 g. **Composition:** 0.9990 Silver 1.0000 oz. ASW **Subject:** 1918 Battle of Sardarapat **Obverse:** National arms **Reverse:** Symbolic design **Size:** 38 mm.

Date	Mintage	F	VF	XF	Unc	BU
1994 Proof	3,000	Value: 55.00				

KM# 59 25 DRAM Weight: 28.2800 g. **Composition:** 0.9250 Silver .8411 oz. ASW **Reverse:** Apricot **Size:** 38.61 mm.

Date		F	VF	XF	Unc	BU
1994 Proof	Est. 10,000	Value: 50.00				

KM# 60 25 DRAM Weight: 31.1035 g. **Composition:** 0.9990 Silver 1.0000 oz. ASW **Subject:** David of Sasun **Obverse:** National arms above denomination **Reverse:** Monument

Date	Mintage	F	VF	XF	Unc	BU
1994 Proof	5,000	Value: 45.00				

KM# 61 25 DRAM Weight: 31.1035 g. **Composition:** 0.9990 Silver 1.0000 oz. ASW **Subject:** Temple of Garni **Reverse:** Ancient building **Size:** 38 mm.

Date	Mintage	F	VF	XF	Unc	BU
1994 Proof	5,000	Value: 40.00				

KM# 62 25 DRAM Weight: 31.1035 g. **Composition:** 0.9990 Silver 1.0000 oz. ASW **Subject:** Jakharak

Date	F	VF	XF	Unc	BU
1994 Proof	—	Value: 42.50			

KM# 63 25 DRAM **Weight:** 31.1035 g. **Composition:** 0.9990 Silver 1.0000 oz. ASW **Subject:** Artsakh

Date	F	VF	XF	Unc	BU
1994 Proof	—	Value: 40.00			

KM# 72 100 DRAM **Weight:** 28.2800 g. **Composition:** 0.9250 Silver .8411 oz. ASW **Subject:** 50th Anniversary - United Nations **Obverse:** National arms **Reverse:** Seated Madonna and child

Date	Mintage	F	VF	XF	Unc	BU
1995 Proof	100,000	Value: 40.00				

KM# 64 100 DRAM **Weight:** 31.1035 g. **Composition:** 0.9990 Silver 1.0000 oz. ASW **Subject:** Chess Olympics

Date	Mintage	F	VF	XF	Unc	BU
1996 Proof	2,000	Value: 50.00				

KM# 69 100 DRAM **Composition:** Copper-Nickel **Subject:** XXXII CHess Olympiad **Obverse:** Eagle and lion support arms **Reverse:** Stylized stork and chessboard in inner circle

Date	F	VF	XF	Unc	BU
1996	—	—	—	7.00	—
1996 Proof	—	Value: 12.50			

KM# 70 100 DRAM **Weight:** 28.2800 g. **Composition:** 0.9250 Silver .8411 oz. ASW **Subject:** XXXII Chess Olympiad **Obverse:** Eagle and lion support arms **Reverse:** Stylized stork and chessboard

Date	Mintage	F	VF	XF	Unc	BU
1996 Proof	10,000	Value: 55.00				

KM# 71 100 DRAM **Composition:** Copper-Nickel **Subject:** WWF Conserving Nature 1997 **Obverse:** National emblem **Reverse:** Caucasian otter

Date	F	VF	XF	Unc	BU
1997	—	—	—	16.00	—

KM# 71a 100 DRAM **Weight:** 28.2800 g. **Composition:** 0.9250 Silver .8410 oz. ASW

Date	Mintage	F	VF	XF	Unc	BU
1997 Proof	15,000	Value: 50.00				

KM# 76 100 DRAM **Composition:** Copper-Nickel **Subject:** Charents **Obverse:** National emblem **Reverse:** Facial portrait

Date	F	VF	XF	Unc	BU
1997	—	—	—	4.00	—

KM# 77 100 DRAM **Weight:** 31.1500 g. **Composition:** 0.9990 Silver 1.0005 oz. ASW **Subject:** Marshal Bagramian **Obverse:** National arms **Reverse:** Uniformed portrait

Date	F	VF	XF	Unc	BU
1997 Proof	—	Value: 45.00			

KM# 78 100 DRAM **Composition:** Copper-Nickel **Subject:** WWF Conserving Nature **Obverse:** National arms **Reverse:** Armenian gull

Date	F	VF	XF	Unc	BU
1998	—	—	—	8.00	—

KM# 79 100 DRAM **Weight:** 28.2800 g. **Composition:** 0.9250 Silver .8410 oz. ASW **Subject:** XVII Olympic Winter Games **Obverse:** Arms **Reverse:** Downhill skiers

Date	F	VF	XF	Unc	BU
1998 Proof	—	Value: 40.00			

KM# 80 100 DRAM **Weight:** 28.2800 g. **Composition:** 0.9250 Silver .8410 oz. ASW **Subject:** XVII Olympic Winter Games **Obverse:** Arms **Reverse:** Soccer players, map of France

Date	F	VF	XF	Unc	BU
1998 Proof	—	Value: 50.00			

KM# 86 100 DRAM **Weight:** 31.0400 g. **Composition:** 0.9990 Silver 0.997 oz. ASW **Obverse:** National arms **Reverse:** Bust of General Garegen Nzhdeh facing at right **Edge:** Plain **Edge Lettering:** Serial number **Size:** 38 mm.

Date	Mintage	F	VF	XF	Unc	BU
2001 Proof	170	Value: 100				

KM# 86a 100 DRAM **Weight:** 31.0400 g. **Composition:** 0.9990 Gold Plated Silver 0.997 oz. ASW AGW **Obverse:** National arms **Obv. Inscription:** Bust of General Garegen Nzhdeh facing at right **Edge:** Plain **Edge Lettering:** Serial number **Size:** 38 mm.

Date	Mintage	F	VF	XF	Unc	BU
2001 Proof	30	Value: 125				

KM# 87 100 DRAM **Weight:** 31.0400 g. **Composition:** 0.9990 Silver 0.997 oz. ASW **Subject:** Armenian Membership in the Council of Europe **Obverse:** National arms **Reverse:** Spiral design with star circle **Edge:** Plain **Edge Lettering:** Serial number **Size:** 38 mm.

Date	Mintage	F	VF	XF	Unc	BU
2001 Proof	170	Value: 100				

KM# 87a 100 DRAM **Weight:** 31.0400 g. **Composition:** 0.9990 Gold Plated Silver 0.997 oz. ASW AGW **Subject:** Armenian Membership in the Council of Europe **Obverse:** National arms **Reverse:** Spiral design with star circle **Edge:** Plain **Edge Lettering:** Serial number **Size:** 38 mm.

Date	Mintage	F	VF	XF	Unc	BU
2001 Proof	30	Value: 125				

KM# 65 500 DRAM **Weight:** 155.5175 g. **Composition:** 0.9990 Silver 5.000 oz. ASW **Subject:** National Assembly Building **Edge:** 5TO .999 AG and serial number **Edge Lettering:** Plain

Date	Mintage	F	VF	XF	Unc	BU
1995 Proof	300	Value: 185				

KM# 73 500 DRAM **Weight:** 155.5175 g. **Composition:** 0.9990 Silver 5.000 oz. ASW **Subject:** Historical Armenian Coat of Arms - Lion **Obverse:** Similar to KM#74 **Edge:** WIth 5T0 .999 AG and serial number **Edge Lettering:** Plain

Date	Mintage	F	VF	XF	Unc	BU
1995 Proof	300	Value: 185				

KM# 66 500 DRAM **Weight:** 155.5175 g. **Composition:** 0.9990 Silver 5.000 oz. ASW **Subject:** Historical Armenian Coat of Arms Series **Obverse:** Similar to KM#74 **Reverse:** Crowned lion with staff, 11th century **Note:** Illustration reduced.

Date	Mintage	F	VF	XF	Unc	BU
1995 Proof	300	Value: 185				

KM# 67 500 DRAM **Weight:** 155.5175 g. **Composition:** 0.9990 Silver 5.000 oz. ASW **Subject:** Historical Armenian Coat of Arms Series **Obverse:** Similar to KM#74 **Reverse:** Double eagle of the Arsacid Dynasty (63-428AD) **Note:** Illustration reduced.

Date	Mintage	F	VF	XF	Unc	BU
1995 Proof	300	Value: 185				

KM# 74 500 DRAM **Weight:** 155.5175 g. **Composition:** 0.9990 Silver 5.000 oz. ASW **Subject:** Historical Armenian Coat of Arms - Double Eagle **Note:** Illustration reduced.

Date	Mintage	F	VF	XF	Unc	BU
1995 Proof	300	Value: 185				

KM# 68 1000 DRAM **Weight:** 31.1035 g. **Composition:** 0.9990 Silver 1.0000 oz. ASW **Subject:** Armenian Money - Vignette from 100 Rouble Note

Date	Mintage	F	VF	XF	Unc	BU
1994 Proof	5,000	Value: 47.50				

KM# 83 1000 DRAM **Weight:** 31.3100 g. **Composition:** 0.9990 Silver 1.0056 oz. ASW **Subject:** 300th Anniversary - Christian Armenia **Obverse:** National arms **Reverse:** Etchmiadzin church

Date		F	VF	XF	Unc	BU
1998 Proof	—	Value: 65.00				

KM# 84 1000 DRAM **Weight:** 31.3100 g. **Composition:** 0.9990 Silver 1.0056 oz. ASW **Subject:** 300th Anniversary - Christian Armenia **Obverse:** National arms **Reverse:** Ani church tower

Date		F	VF	XF	Unc	BU
1998 Proof	—	Value: 65.00				

KM# 85 1000 DRAM **Weight:** 31.3100 g. **Composition:** 0.9990 Silver 1.0056 oz. ASW **Subject:** 300th Anniversary - Christian Armenia **Obverse:** National arms **Reverse:** Haghpat carved stone cross

Date		F	VF	XF	Unc	BU
1998 Proof	—	Value: 65.00				

KM# 88 2000 DRAMS **Weight:** 28.5000 g. **Composition:** 0.9250 Silver 0.8476 oz. ASW **Subject:** Millennium **Obverse:** National arms **Reverse:** Mounted St. George left holding banner **Edge:** Plain **Shape:** Octagonal **Size:** 38.6 mm.

Date	Mintage	F	VF	XF	Unc	BU
2000 Proof	30,000	Value: 75.00				

KM# 89 5000 DRAMS **Weight:** 31.2600 g. **Composition:** 0.9990 Silver 1.004 oz. ASW **Subject:** Christian Armenia - Akhtamar **Obverse:** National arms **Reverse:** Church on an island **Edge:** Plain **Edge Lettering:** Serial number **Size:** 38 mm.

Date	Mintage	F	VF	XF	Unc	BU
1999 Proof	1,700	Value: 65.00				

KM# 90 10000 DRAMS Weight: 8.6400 g. **Composition:** 0.9000 Gold 0.25 oz. AGW **Subject:** Christian Armenia - Ani **Obverse:** National arms **Reverse:** Church tower **Edge:** Plain **Edge Lettering:** Serial number **Size:** 22 mm.

Date	Mintage	F	VF	XF	Unc	BU
1998 Proof	1,700	Value: 200				

KM# 91 10000 DRAMS Weight: 8.6400 g. **Composition:** 0.9000 Gold 0.25 oz. AGW **Subject:** Christian Armenia - Etchmiadzin **Obverse:** National arms **Reverse:** Multi-towered church **Edge:** Plain **Edge Lettering:** Serial number **Size:** 22 mm.

Date	Mintage	F	VF	XF	Unc	BU
1998 Proof	1,700	Value: 200				

KM# 75.1 25000 DRAM Weight: 4.3000 g. **Composition:** 0.9000 Gold .1244 oz. AGW **Obverse:** National arms **Reverse:** Portrait of goddess Anahit **Edge:** Reeded

Date		F	VF	XF	Unc	BU
1997 Proof	—	Value: 75.00				

KM# 75.2 25000 DRAM Weight: 4.3000 g. **Composition:** 0.9000 Gold .1244 oz. AGW **Edge:** Plain

Date		F	VF	XF	Unc	BU
1997 Proof	—	Value: 120				

KM# 92 50000 DRAMS Weight: 8.6400 g. **Composition:** 0.9000 Gold 0.25 oz. AGW **Subject:** Christian Armenia - Akhtamar **Obverse:** National arms **Reverse:** Church **Edge:** Plain **Edge Lettering:** Serial number **Size:** 22 mm.

Date	Mintage	F	VF	XF	Unc	BU
1999 Proof	1,700	Value: 200				

ARUBA

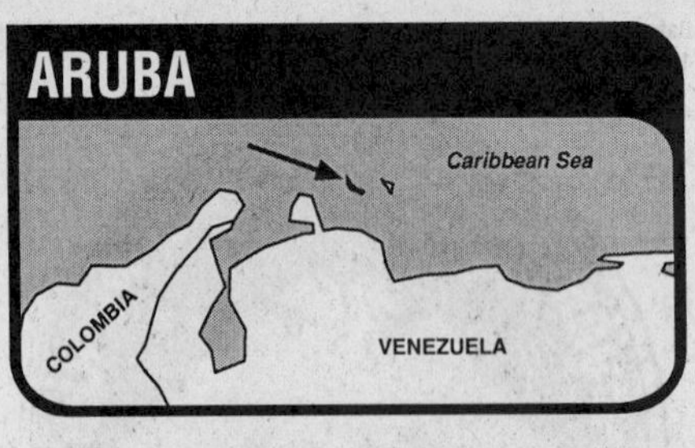

Aruba, formerly a part of the Netherlands Antilles, achieved on Jan. 1, 1986 a special status, "status aparte" as the third state under the Dutch crown, together with the Netherlands and the remaining five islands of the Netherlands Antilles. On Dec. 15, 1954 the Netherlands Antilles were given complete domestic autonomy and granted equality within the Kingdom of the Netherlands. The separate constitution put in place for Aruba in 1986 established it as an autonomous government within the Kingdom of the Netherlands. In 1990 Aruba opted to remain a part of the Kingdom without the promise of future independence.

The second largest island of the Netherlands Antilles, Aruba is situated near the Venezuelan coast. The island has an area of 74-1/2 sq. mi. (193 sq. km.) and a population of 65,974. Capital: Oranjestad, named after the Dutch royal family. Aruba was important in the processing and transportation of petroleum products in the first part of the twentieth century, but today the chief industry is tourism.

For earlier issues see Curacao and the Netherlands Antilles.

RULERS

Dutch

MINT MARKS

(u) Utrecht - Privy marks only
- Anvil, 1986-1988
- Bow and Arrow, 1989-1999
- Bow and Arrow w/star, 2000
- Winetendril with grapes, 2001-
- Winetendril with grapes plus star, 2002-
- Sails of a clipper, 2003-

MONETARY SYSTEM

100 Cents = 1 Florin

DUTCH STATE
"Status Aparte"
REGULAR COINAGE

KM# 1 5 CENTS Weight: 2.0000 g. **Composition:** Nickel Bonded Steel **Obverse:** Arms **Reverse:** Geometric design

Date	Mintage	F	VF	XF	Unc	BU
1986(u)	776,000	—	0.10	0.25	0.50	—
1987(u)	461,651	—	0.10	0.25	0.50	—
1988(u)	656,500	—	—	—	0.30	—
1989(u)	770,000	—	—	—	0.30	—
1990(u)	612,000	—	—	—	0.30	—
1991(u)	412,000	—	—	—	0.30	—
1995(u)	808,500	—	—	—	0.25	—
1996(u)	587,500	—	—	—	0.25	—
1997(u)	535,500	—	—	—	0.25	—
1998(u)	920,000	—	—	—	0.25	—
1999(u)	823,000	—	—	—	0.25	—
2001(u)	947,000	—	—	—	0.25	—
2002(u)	—	—	—	—	0.25	—
2003(u)	—	—	—	—	0.25	—

KM# 2 10 CENTS Weight: 3.0000 g. **Composition:** Nickel Bonded Steel **Obverse:** Arms **Reverse:** Geometric design

Date	Mintage	F	VF	XF	Unc	BU
1986(u)	856,200	—	0.20	0.40	0.75	—
1988(u)	986,500	—	—	0.10	0.35	—
1989(u)	610,000	—	—	0.10	0.35	—
1990(u)	762,000	—	—	0.10	0.35	—
1991(u)	512,000	—	—	0.10	0.35	—
1992(u)	610,500	—	—	0.10	0.35	—
1993(u)	1,009,100	—	—	—	0.30	—
1994(u)	409,100	—	—	—	0.30	—
1995(u)	918,500	—	—	—	0.30	—
1996(u)	457,500	—	—	—	0.30	—
1997(u)	423,500	—	—	—	0.30	—
1998(u)	954,000	—	—	—	0.30	—
1999(u)	1,004,000	—	—	—	0.30	—

Date	Mintage	F	VF	XF	Unc	BU
2001(u)	1,007,000	—	—	—	0.30	—
2002(u)	—	—	—	—	0.30	—
2003(u)	—	—	—	—	0.30	—

KM# 3 25 CENTS Weight: 3.5000 g. **Composition:** Nickel Bonded Steel **Obverse:** Arms **Reverse:** Geometric design

Date	Mintage	F	VF	XF	Unc	BU
1986(u)	856,200	—	0.20	0.40	0.75	—
1987(u)	331,651	—	0.20	0.40	0.75	—
1988(u)	116,500	—	—	—	0.45	—
1989(u)	360,000	—	—	—	0.45	—
1990(u)	512,000	—	—	—	0.45	—
1991(u)	612,000	—	—	—	0.45	—
1992(u)	460,500	—	—	—	0.45	—
1993(u)	609,100	—	—	—	0.45	—
1994(u)	109,100	—	—	—	0.45	—
1995(u)	608,500	—	—	—	0.45	—
1996(u)	287,500	—	—	—	0.45	—
1997(u)	467,500	—	—	—	0.45	—
1998(u)	641,000	—	—	—	0.45	—
1999(u)	332,000	—	—	—	0.45	—
2001(u)	717,000	—	—	—	0.45	—
2002(u)	—	—	—	—	0.45	—

KM# 4 50 CENTS Weight: 5.0000 g. **Composition:** Nickel Bonded Steel **Obverse:** Arms **Reverse:** Geometric design

Date	Mintage	F	VF	XF	Unc	BU
1986(u)	486,200	—	0.30	0.50	1.00	—
1987(u)	121,651	—	0.30	0.50	1.00	—
1988(u)	216,500	—	—	0.35	0.75	—
1989(u)	110,000	—	—	0.35	0.75	—
1990(u)	262,000	—	—	0.35	0.75	—
1991(u)	312,000	—	—	0.35	0.75	—
1992(u)	310,500	—	—	0.35	0.75	—
1993(u)	459,100	—	—	0.35	0.75	—
1994(u)	309,100	—	—	0.35	0.75	—
1995(u)	258,500	—	—	0.35	0.75	—
1996(u)	392,500	—	—	0.35	0.75	—
1997(u)	27,500	—	—	0.60	1.25	—
1998(u)	197,000	—	—	0.35	0.75	—
1999(u)	445,000	—	—	0.35	0.75	—
2001(u)	507,000	—	—	0.35	0.75	—
2002(u)	—	—	—	0.35	0.75	—
2003(u)	—	—	—	—	0.75	—

KM# 5 FLORIN **Composition:** 8.5000 Nickel Bonded Steel **Obverse:** Head of Queen Beatrix left **Reverse:** Arms

Date	Mintage	F	VF	XF	Unc	BU
1986(u)	586,200	—	0.60	1.00	2.00	—
1987(u)	271,651	—	0.60	1.00	2.00	—
1988(u)	566,500	—	—	0.65	1.25	—
1989(u)	410,000	—	—	0.65	1.25	—
1990(u)	412,000	—	—	0.65	1.25	—
1991(u)	162,000	—	—	0.65	1.25	—
1992(u)	510,500	—	—	0.65	1.25	—
1993(u)	409,100	—	—	0.65	1.25	—
1994(u)	109,100	—	—	0.65	1.25	—
1995(u)	208,500	—	—	0.65	1.25	—
1996(u)	132,500	—	—	0.65	1.25	—
1997(u)	415,500	—	—	0.65	1.25	—
1998(u)	300,000	—	—	0.65	1.25	—
1999(u)	430,000	—	—	0.65	1.25	—
2002(u)	—	—	—	0.65	1.25	—
2003(u)	—	—	—	0.70	1.35	—

KM# 6 2-1/2 FLORIN **Weight:** 10.3000 g. **Composition:** Nickel Bonded Steel **Obverse:** Head of Queen Beatrix left **Reverse:** Arms

Date	Mintage	F	VF	XF	Unc	BU
1986(u)	106,200	—	—	1.75	3.50	—
1987(u)	31,651	—	—	1.75	3.50	—
1988(u)	26,500	—	—	—	2.00	—
1989(u)	15,000	—	—	—	2.00	—
1990(u)	17,000	—	—	—	2.00	—
1991(u)	17,000	—	—	—	2.00	—
1992(u)	12,500	—	—	—	2.00	—
1993(u)	11,100	—	—	—	2.00	—
1994(u)	11,100	—	—	—	2.00	—
1995(u)	10,500	—	—	—	2.00	—
1996(u) In set only	7,500	—	—	—	3.50	—
1997(u) In set only	7,500	—	—	—	3.50	—
1998(u) In set only	8,000	—	—	—	3.50	—
1999(u) In set only	7,500	—	—	—	2.25	—
2001(u) In set only	7,000	—	—	—	2.25	—
2002(u) In set only	—	—	—	—	2.25	—
2003(u)	—	—	—	—	2.25	—

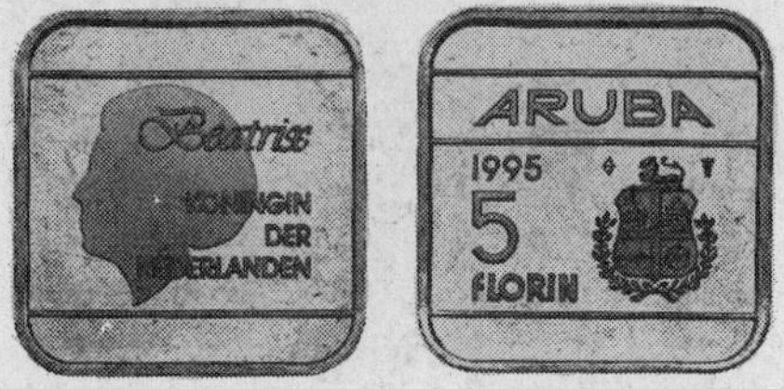

KM# 12 5 FLORIN **Weight:** 8.6400 g. **Composition:** Nickel Bonded Steel **Obverse:** Head of Queen Beatrix left **Reverse:** Arms

Date	Mintage	F	VF	XF	Unc	BU
1995(u)	200,500	—	—	—	6.00	—
1996(u)	357,500	—	—	—	6.00	—
1997(u)	27,500	—	—	—	7.50	—
1998(u)	162,000	—	—	—	6.00	—
1999(u)	86,200	—	—	—	6.00	—
2001(u) In set only	17,000	—	—	—	6.50	—
2002(u)	—	—	—	—	6.00	—
2003(u)	—	—	—	—	5.50	—

KM# 20 10 FLORIN **Weight:** 25.0000 g. **Composition:** 0.9250 Silver 0.7435 oz. ASW **Subject:** Green Sea Turtles **Obverse:** Head of Queen Beatrix left **Reverse:** Seven sea turtles **Edge:** Plain **Size:** 38 mm.

Date	F	VF	XF	Unc	BU
2001(u) Prooflike	—	—	—	—	—

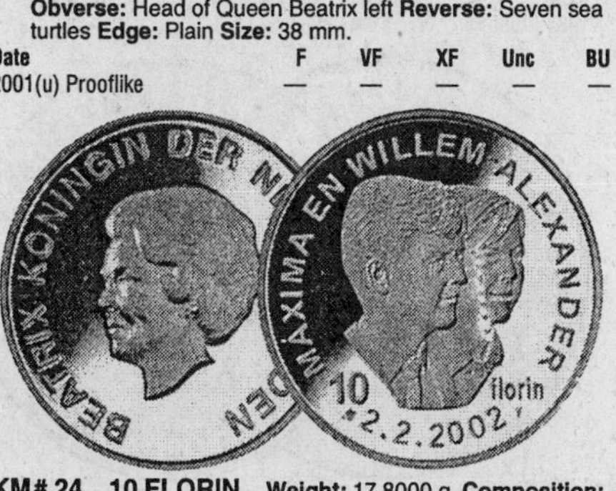

KM# 24 10 FLORIN **Weight:** 17.8000 g. **Composition:** 0.9250 Silver 0.5294 oz. ASW **Subject:** Crown Prince's Wedding **Obverse:** Head of Queen Beatrix left **Reverse:** Portraits of the prince and **Edge Lettering:** "God Zij Met ons" **Size:** 33 mm.

Date	F	VF	XF	Unc	BU
ND(2002)(u) Proof like	—	—	—	35.00	—

KM# 7 25 FLORIN **Weight:** 25.0000 g. **Composition:** 0.9250 Silver .7435 oz. ASW **Subject:** Independence **Obverse:** Queen Beatrix **Reverse:** Arms, treaty name and date

Date	Mintage	F	VF	XF	Unc	BU
1986(u)	5,000	—	—	—	30.00	—
1986(u) Proof	10,250	Value: 25.00				

KM# 8 25 FLORIN **Weight:** 25.0000 g. **Composition:** 0.9250 Silver .7435 oz. ASW **Subject:** Independence **Obverse:** Queen Beatrix **Reverse:** Triangular portion of flag, treaty name and date

Date	Mintage	F	VF	XF	Unc	BU
1991(u)	2,500	—	—	—	25.00	—
1991(u) Proof	4,600	Value: 40.00				

KM# 10 25 FLORIN **Weight:** 25.0000 g. **Composition:** 0.9250 Silver .7435 oz. ASW **Series:** 1992 Olympics **Subject:** Windsurfing **Obverse:** Head of Queen Beatrix left **Reverse:** Sailing ship

Date	Mintage	F	VF	XF	Unc	BU
1992(u)	2,000	—	—	—	37.50	—
1992(u) Proof	16,000	Value: 42.50				

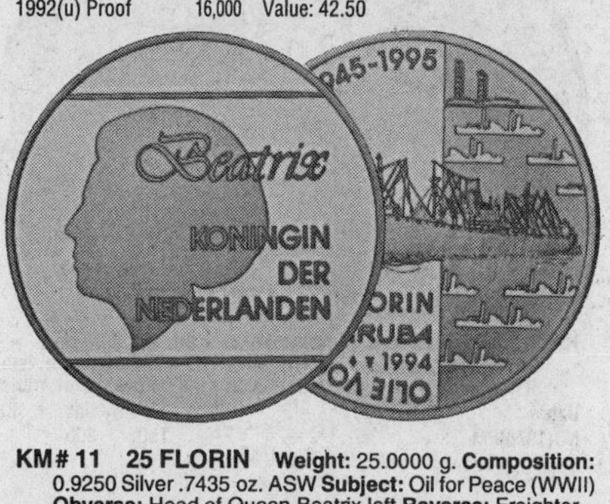

KM# 11 25 FLORIN **Weight:** 25.0000 g. **Composition:** 0.9250 Silver .7435 oz. ASW **Subject:** Oil for Peace (WWII) **Obverse:** Head of Queen Beatrix left **Reverse:** Freighter, tankers and refinery

Date	Mintage	F	VF	XF	Unc	BU
1994(u)	1,500	—	—	—	37.50	—
1994(u) Proof	4,000	Value: 40.00				

KM# 13 25 FLORIN **Weight:** 25.0000 g. **Composition:** 0.9250 Silver .7435 oz. ASW **Subject:** 100th Anniversary of the Olympics **Obverse:** Head of Queen Beatrix left **Reverse:** Cyclist and logo

Date	Mintage	F	VF	XF	Unc	BU
1995(u)	1,000	—	—	—	35.00	—
1995(u) Proof	2,100	Value: 42.50				

KM# 14 25 FLORIN **Weight:** 25.0000 g. **Composition:** 0.9250 Silver .7435 oz. ASW **Subject:** 100th Anniversary of the Olympics **Obverse:** Head of Queen Beatrix left **Reverse:** Cyclist, without logo

Date	Mintage	F	VF	XF	Unc	BU
1995(u) Proof	1,700	Value: 50.00				

KM# 15 25 FLORIN **Weight:** 25.0000 g. **Composition:** 0.9250 Silver .7435 oz. ASW **Obverse:** Head of Queen Beatrix left **Reverse:** Sea turtles with pre-Columbian design

Date	Mintage	F	VF	XF	Unc	BU
1995(u)	3,500	—	—	—	35.00	—
1995(u) Proof	2,000	Value: 45.00				

KM# 18 25 FLORIN **Weight:** 25.0000 g. **Composition:** 0.9250 Silver .7435 oz. ASW **Subject:** Tradition With Vision - Discovery 1499 **Obverse:** Portrait of Vespucci, sailing vessel, map **Reverse:** Spanish fan and aboriginal design, dates

Date	Mintage	F	VF	XF	Unc	BU
ND(1999)(u) Proof	1,850	Value: 45.00				

KM# 21 25 FLORIN **Weight:** 25.0000 g. **Composition:** 0.9250 Silver 0.7435 oz. ASW **Subject:** Olympics **Obverse:** Head of Queen Beatrix left **Reverse:** Catamaran sailboat **Edge:** Plain **Size:** 38 mm.

Date	Mintage	F	VF	XF	Unc	BU
2000(u) Proof	3,500	Value: 40.00				

KM# 22 25 FLORIN **Weight:** 25.0000 g. **Composition:** 0.9250 Silver 0.7435 oz. ASW **Subject:** 15th Anniversary of Autonomy **Obverse:** Head of Queen Beatrix left **Reverse:** National arms and inscription **Edge:** Plain **Size:** 38 mm.

Date	Mintage	F	VF	XF	Unc	BU
2001(u) Proof	3,000	Value: 40.00				

KM# 9 50 FLORIN **Weight:** 6.7200 g. **Composition:** 0.9000 Gold .1945 oz. AGW **Subject:** Independence

Date	Mintage	F	VF	XF	Unc	BU
1991(u) Proof	2,600	Value: 140				

KM# 16 50 FLORIN **Weight:** 25.0000 g. **Composition:** 0.9250 Silver .7435 oz. ASW **Subject:** 10th Anniversary of Autonomy **Obverse:** Head of Queen Beatrix left **Reverse:** Portions of national flag and anthem score **Note:** Similar to 100 Florin, KM#17

Date	Mintage	F	VF	XF	Unc	BU
1996(u)	500	—	—	—	47.50	—
1996(u) Proof	2,000	Value: 42.50				

KM# 17 100 FLORIN **Weight:** 6.7200 g. **Composition:** 0.9000 Gold .1945 oz. AGW **Subject:** 10th Anniversary of Autonomy **Obverse:** Head of Queen Beatrix left **Reverse:** Portions of national flag and anthem score

Date	Mintage	F	VF	XF	Unc	BU
1996(u) Proof	535	Value: 200				

KM# 19 100 FLORIN **Weight:** 6.7200 g. **Composition:** 0.9000 Gold .1945 oz. AGW **Subject:** Tradition With Vision - Discovery 1499 **Obverse:** Portrait of Vespucci, sailing vessel, map **Reverse:** Spanish fan and aboriginal design, dates **Note:** Similar to 25 Florin, KM#19.

Date	Mintage	F	VF	XF	Unc	BU
ND(1999)(u) Proof	1,100	Value: 175				

KM# 23 100 FLORIN **Weight:** 6.7200 g. **Composition:** Gold **Subject:** Independence **Obverse:** Arms, treaty name, dates **Reverse:** Head of Queen Beatrix left

Date	Mintage	F	VF	XF	Unc	BU
2001 Proof	—	Value: 180				

MINT SETS

KM#	Date	Mintage	Identification	Issue Price	Mkt Val
MS1	1986 (6)	36,200	KM#1-6, with medal	8.95	11.50
MS2	1987 (6)	21,650	KM#1-6, with medal	9.95	12.00
MS3	1988 (6)	16,500	KM#1-6, with medal	12.95	12.00
MS4	1989 (6)	10,000	KM#1-6, with medal	12.00	12.00
MS5	1990 (6)	12,000	KM#1-6, with medal	—	13.00
MS6	1991 (6)	12,000	KM#1-6, with medal	14.50	13.00
MS7	1992 (6)	10,500	KM#1-6, with medal	—	13.00
MS8	1993 (6)	9,100	KM#1-6, with medal	—	14.50
MS9	1994 (6)	9,100	KM#1-6, with medal	14.50	15.50
MS10	1995 (1)	1,000	KM#12	—	20.00
MS11	1995 (6)	8,500	KM#1-6, with medal	17.50	13.50
MS12	1995 (2)	2,500	KM#15, 5 Florin banknote, with medal	56.50	50.00
MS13	1996 (7)	7,500	KM#1-6, 12, with medal	17.50	14.50
MS14	1997 (7)	7,500	KM#1-6, 12, with medal	17.50	14.50
MS15	1998 (7)	8,000	KM#1-6, 12, with medal	17.50	14.50
MS16	1999 (7)	7,000	KM#1-6, 12, with medal	17.50	14.50
MS19	2001 (7)	7,000	KM#1-6, 12	13.25	15.00
MS20	2002 (7)	—	KM# 1-6, 12	15.00	16.50

PROOF SETS

KM#	Date	Mintage	Identification	Issue Price	Mkt Val
PS1	1999 (5)	—	KM#18-19, with Netherlands Antilles KM#45-47	580	615

ASCENSION ISLAND

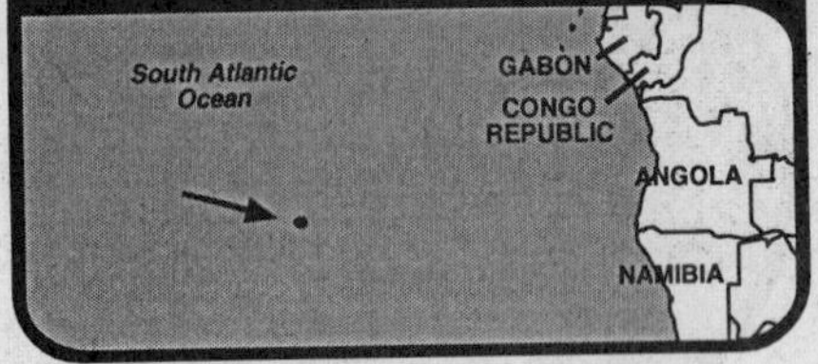

An island of volcanic origin, Ascension Island lies in the South Atlantic, 700 miles (1,100 km.) northwest of St. Helena. It has an area of 34 sq. mi. (88 sq. km.) on an island 9 miles (14 km.) long and 6 miles (10 km.) wide. Approximate population: 1,146. Although having little vegetation and scant rainfall, the island has a very healthy climate. The island is the nesting place for a large number of sea turtles and sooty terns. Phosphates and guano are the chief natural sources of income.

The island was discovered on Ascension Day, 1501, by Joao da Nova, a Portuguese navigator. It lay unoccupied until 1815, when occupied by the British. It was under Admiralty rule until 1922 when it was annexed as a dependency of St. Helena. During World War II an airfield was built that has been used as a fueling stop for Transatlantic flights to Southern Europe, North Africa and the Near-East.

RULERS
British

MINT MARKS
PM - Pobjoy Mint

BRITISH ADMINISTRATION

STANDARD COINAGE

KM# 1 25 PENCE (Crown) **Composition:** Copper-Nickel **Subject:** 25th Anniversary of Coronation

Date	F	VF	XF	Unc	BU
1978PM	—	—	—	7.50	—

KM# 1a 25 PENCE (Crown) **Weight:** 28.2800 g. **Composition:** 0.9250 Silver .8411 oz. ASW **Subject:** 25th Anniversary of Coronation

Date	Mintage	F	VF	XF	Unc	BU
1978PM	70,000	—	—	—	15.00	—
1978PM Proof	25,000	Value: 22.50				

KM# 2 25 PENCE (Crown) **Weight:** 28.2800 g. **Composition:** 0.9250 Silver .8411 oz. ASW **Obverse:** Isle of Man crown **Reverse:** Ascension KM#1 **Note:** Error; mule.

Date	Mintage	F	VF	XF	Unc	BU
ND(1978)PM	367	—	—	150	200	—

KM# 3 25 PENCE (Crown) **Composition:** Copper-Nickel **Subject:** Wedding of Prince Charles and Lady Diana

Date	Mintage	F	VF	XF	Unc	BU
1981PM	50,000	—	—	—	4.50	—

KM# 3a 25 PENCE (Crown) **Weight:** 28.2800 g. **Composition:** 0.5000 Silver .4546 oz. ASW **Subject:** Wedding of Prince Charles and Lady Diana

Date	Mintage	F	VF	XF	Unc	BU
1981	500	—	—	—	50.00	—

KM# 3b 25 PENCE (Crown) **Weight:** 28.2800 g. **Composition:** 0.9250 Silver .8411 oz. ASW **Subject:** Wedding of Prince Charles and Lady Diana

Date	Mintage	F	VF	XF	Unc	BU
1981 Proof	30,000	Value: 22.50				

KM# 4 25 PENCE (Crown) **Weight:** 28.2800 g. **Composition:** 0.9250 Silver .8411 oz. ASW **Series:** International Year of the Scout

Date	Mintage	F	VF	XF	Unc	BU
ND(1983)	10,000	—	—	—	30.00	—
ND(1983) Proof	10,000	Value: 42.50				

KM# 6 50 PENCE **Composition:** Copper-Nickel **Subject:** Royal visit of Prince Andrew

Date	Mintage	F	VF	XF	Unc	BU
1984	125,000	—	—	—	4.00	—

KM# 6a 50 PENCE **Weight:** 28.2800 g. **Composition:** 0.9250 Silver .8411 oz. ASW **Subject:** Royal visit of Prince Andrew

Date	Mintage	F	VF	XF	Unc	BU
1984 Proof	5,000	Value: 22.50				

KM# 7 50 PENCE **Composition:** Copper-Nickel **Reverse:** Queen Mother fishing

Date	F	VF	XF	Unc	BU
1995	—	—	—	4.00	—

KM# 7a 50 PENCE **Weight:** 28.2800 g. **Composition:** 0.9250 Silver .841 oz. ASW **Reverse:** Queen Mother fishing

Date		F	VF	XF	Unc	BU
1995 Proof	—	Value: 32.50				

KM# 7b 50 PENCE **Weight:** 47.5400 g. **Composition:** 0.9160 Gold 1.4001 oz. AGW **Reverse:** Queen Mother fishing

Date		F	VF	XF	Unc	BU
1995 Proof	150	Value: 600				

KM# 8 50 PENCE **Composition:** Copper-Nickel **Subject:** 70th birthday - Queen Elizabeth II

Date	F	VF	XF	Unc	BU
1996	—	—	—	6.00	—

KM# 8a 50 PENCE **Weight:** 28.2800 g. **Composition:** 0.9250 Silver .8411 oz. ASW **Subject:** 70th birthday - Queen Elizabeth II

Date	Mintage	F	VF	XF	Unc	BU
1996 Proof	5,000	Value: 50.00				

KM# 11 50 PENCE **Composition:** Copper-Nickel **Series:** Montreal Olympics **Subject:** Queen's portrait **Reverse:** Royal couple behind horse and rider jumping British arms

Date	F	VF	XF	Unc	BU
1997	—	—	—	8.00	—

KM# 9 50 PENCE **Composition:** Copper-Nickel **Subject:** World Wildlife Fund - conserving nature **Reverse:** Frigate birds

Date	F	VF	XF	Unc	BU
1998	—	—	—	9.00	—

KM# 10 50 PENCE **Composition:** Copper-Nickel **Subject:** World Wildlife Fund - conserving nature **Reverse:** Long-tailed birds

Date	F	VF	XF	Unc	BU
1998	—	—	—	9.00	—

KM# 12 50 PENCE **Weight:** 28.7600 g. **Composition:** Copper-Nickel **Subject:** 100th Birthday of the Queen Mother **Obverse:** Queen's bust right **Reverse:** Queen Mother's bust 3/4 facing half left **Edge:** Reeded **Size:** 38.5 mm.

Date	F	VF	XF	Unc	BU
ND(2000)	—	—	—	8.50	—

KM# 13 50 PENCE **Weight:** 28.6300 g. **Composition:** Copper-Nickel **Subject:** 75th Birthday of Queen Elizabeth **Obverse:** Queen's head right **Reverse:** Crowned monogram above flowers **Edge:** Reeded **Size:** 38.6 mm.

Date	F	VF	XF	Unc	BU
2001	—	—	—	8.00	—

KM# 14 50 PENCE **Weight:** 28.6300 g. **Composition:** Copper-Nickel **Subject:** Centennial - Queen Victoria's Death **Obverse:** Queen's bust right **Reverse:** Queen Victoria's 3/4 bust left **Edge:** Reeded **Size:** 38.6 mm.

Date	F	VF	XF	Unc	BU
2001	—	—	—	8.00	—

KM# 5 2 POUNDS **Weight:** 15.9800 g. **Composition:** 0.9170 Gold .4712 oz. AGW **Series:** International Year of the Scout **Reverse:** Boy Scout

Date	Mintage	F	VF	XF	Unc	BU
1983	2,000	—	—	—	450	—
1983 Proof	2,000	Value: 500				

PIEFORTS

KM#	Date	Mintage	Identification	Mkt Val
P1	1995	500	50 Pence. KM7a.	55.00

The Commonwealth of Australia, the smallest continent in the world, is located south of Indonesia between the Indian and Pacific oceans. It has an area of 2,967,893 sq. mi. (7,686,850 sq. km.) and an estimated population of 18.84 million. Capital: Canberra. Due to its early and sustained isolation, Australia is the habitat of such curious and unique fauna as the kangaroo, koala, platypus, wombat, echidna and frilled-necked lizard. The continent possesses extensive mineral deposits, the most important of which are iron ore, coal, gold, silver, nickel, uranium, lead and zinc. Raising livestock, mining and manufacturing are the principal industries. Chief exports are wool, meat, wheat, iron ore, coal and nonferrous metals.

The first Caucasians to see Australia probably were Portuguese and Spanish navigators of the late 16th century. In 1770, Captain James Cook explored the east coast and annexed it for Great Britain. New South Wales was founded as a penal colony, following the loss of British North America by Captain Arthur Phillip on January 26, 1788, a date now celebrated as Australia Day. Dates of creation of the six colonies that now comprise the states of the Australian Commonwealth are: New South Wales, 1823; Tasmania, 1825; Western Australia, 1838; South Australia, 1842; Victoria, 1851; Queensland, 1859. The British Parliament approved a constitution providing for the federation of the colonies in 1900. The Commonwealth of Australia came into being in 1901. Australia passed the Statute of Westminster Adoption Act on October 9, 1942, which officially established Australia's complete autonomy in external and internal affairs, thereby formalizing a situation that had existed for years. Australia is a member of the Commonwealth of Nations. Elizabeth II is Head of State as Queen of Australia.

Australia's currency system was changed from Pounds-Shillings-Pence to a decimal system of Dollars and Cents on Feb. 14, 1966.

RULERS

British until 1942

MINT MARKS

Abbr.	Mint	Mint Marks
A	Adelaide	-
(b)	Bombay	I below bust; dots before and after HALF PENNY, 1942-43
(b)	Bombay	I below bust dots before and after PENNY, 1942-43
B	Brisbane	-
(c)	Calcutta	I above date, 1916-18
(c)	Canberra	None, 1966 to date
C	Canberra	-
D	Denver	D above date 1/-& 2/-, below date on 3d
D	Denver	D below date on 6d
H	Heaton	H below date on silvere coins, 1914-15
H	Heaton	H above date on bronze coins
(L)	London	1910-1915 (no marks), 1966
M	Melbourne	M below date on silver coins, 1916-20
M	Melbourne	M above date on the ground on gold coins w/St. George
M	Melbourne	-
(m)	Melbourne	Dot below scroll on penny, 1919-20
(m)	Melbourne	Two dots; below lower scroll and above upper, 1919-20
(m)	Melbourne	None, 1921-1964, 1966
P	Perth	P above date on the ground on gold coins w/St. George
(p)	Perth	Dot between KG (designer's initials), 1940-41
(p)	Perth	Dot after PENNY, 1941-51, 1954-64
(p)	Perth	Dot after AUSTRALIA, 1952-53
(p)	Perth	Dot before SHILLING, 1946
(p)	Perth	None, 1922 penny, 1966
P	Perth	Nuggets, 1986
PL	London	PL after PENNY in 1951
PL	London	PL on bottom folds of ribbon, 1951 threepence

PL	London	PL above date on sixpence
PL		1951
S	San Francisco	S above or below date, 1942-44, mm exists w/ and w/o bulbous serifs
S	Sydney	S above date on the ground on gold coins w/St. George
S	Sydney	-
(sy)	Sydney	Dot above bottom scroll on penny 1920
(sy)	Sydney	None, 1919-1926

Mint designations are shown in ( ). Ex. 1978(m). Mint marks are shown after date. Ex. 1978M.

PRIVY MARKS

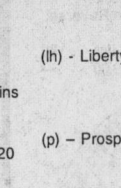

(ae) - American Eagle 

(aa) - Adelaide Assay 

(ba) - Basler Stab 

(bg) - Brandenburg Gate 

(d) – Ducat 

(dp) - Dump 

(e) – Emu 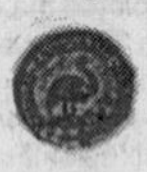

(ev) - Edward V

(f) – Fok 

(f1) - Rev. 1 Florin, KM#31 

(f3) - Rev. 1 Florin, KM#33 

(f7) - Rev. 1 Florin, KM#47 

(ge) - Golden Eagle 

(gv) - George V, small head 

(gV) - George V, large head

(h) – Hague 

(hd) - Holey Dollar 

(j) – Johanna 

(jw) - Japanese Royal Wedding 

(l) – Luk 

(lh) - Liberty Head 

(p) – Prospector 

(qv) - Queen Victoria 

(rv) - Royal Visit Florin, Rev. 1 Florin, KM#55 

(s) – Shu 

(sg) - Spade Guinea 

(sm) - Sydney Mint Sovereign 

(so) - Sydney Opera House 

(sp) - Star Pagoda 

(sq) – State Quarter

(sr) - Swan River/Rottnest Island Tercentenary 

(ta) - Team Australia (Commonwealth Games) 

(w) – Whales 

(ww) - 50 Years Beyond WWII 

MONETARY SYSTEM

Sterling Coinage (Until 1966)
12 Pence = 1 Shilling
2 Shillings = 1 Florin
5 Shillings = 1 Crown
20 Shillings = 1 Pound
1 Sovereign = 1 Pound

Decimal Coinage (Commencing 1966)
100 Cents = 1 Dollar

COMMONWEALTH OF AUSTRALIA

STERLING COINAGE

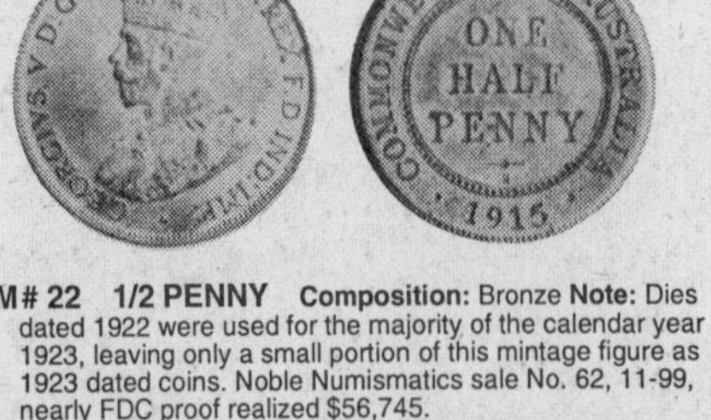

KM# 22 1/2 PENNY Composition: Bronze **Note:** Dies dated 1922 were used for the majority of the calendar year 1923, leaving only a small portion of this mintage figure as 1923 dated coins. Noble Numismatics sale No. 62, 11-99, nearly FDC proof realized $56,745.

Date		F	VF	XF	Unc	BU
1911(L)		0.35	1.75	17.50	90.00	—
1911(L) Proof	—	Value: 1,600				
1912H		0.35	3.00	21.50	140	—
1912H Proof	—	Value: 1,600				
1913(L) Wide date		1.00	5.00	23.50	145	—
1913(L) Narrow date		1.00	5.00	23.50	145	—
1914(L)		1.75	7.50	35.00	225	—
1914H		2.00	8.00	37.50	225	—
1915H		15.00	35.00	170	820	—
1916(c) I		0.30	1.50	11.50	90.00	—
1916(c) I Proof	—	Value: 1,600				
1916(c) I Without I		0.30	1.50	11.50	90.00	—
1917(c) I		0.30	1.75	11.50	90.00	—
1918(c) I		5.00	15.50	100	865	—
1919(sy)		0.20	1.25	11.50	90.00	—
1919(sy) Proof	—	Value: 1,600				
1920(sy)		1.00	2.25	22.00	135	—
1920(m) Proof	—	Value: 1,600				
1921(sy)		0.30	1.50	13.50	90.00	—
1922(sy)		0.50	1.50	13.50	90.00	—
1923(sy)		335	525	2,350	9,500	—
1923(sy) Proof; Rare		—	—	—	—	—
1924(m)		1.75	4.75	55.00	290	—
1924(m) Proof	—	Value: 1,600				
1925(m)		0.50	2.00	23.50	225	—
1925(m) Proof	—	Value: 2,750				
1926(m & sy)		0.20	1.00	15.00	125	—
1926(m) Proof	—	Value: 1,550				
1927(m)		0.20	0.65	15.00	100	—
1927(m) Proof	50	Value: 1,500				
1928(m)		1.00	2.75	21.50	285	—
1928(m) Proof	—	Value: 1,500				
1929(m)		0.20	0.65	15.00	140	—
1929(m) Proof	—	Value: 1,600				
1930(m)		2.00	3.75	50.00	245	—
1930(m) Proof	—	Value: 10,000				
1931(m)		2.00	3.75	27.50	245	—
1931(m) Proof	—	Value: 1,500				
1932(m)		0.20	0.65	8.50	80.00	—
1932(m) Proof	—	Value: 1,500				
1933(m)		0.20	0.65	7.00	60.00	—
1933(m) Proof	—	Value: 1,250				
1934(m)		0.20	0.65	7.00	60.00	—
1934(m) Proof	100	Value: 750				
1935(m)		0.20	0.65	4.00	40.00	—
1935(m) Proof	100	Value: 750				
1936(m)		0.20	0.65	4.00	40.00	—
1936(m) Proof	—	Value: 1,000				

KM# 30 1/2 PENNY Composition: Bronze **Obverse:** India 1/4 Anna, KM#511 **Reverse:** KM#22 **Note:** Mule.

Date	F	VF	XF	Unc	BU
1916(c) I	4,000	7,500	—	—	—

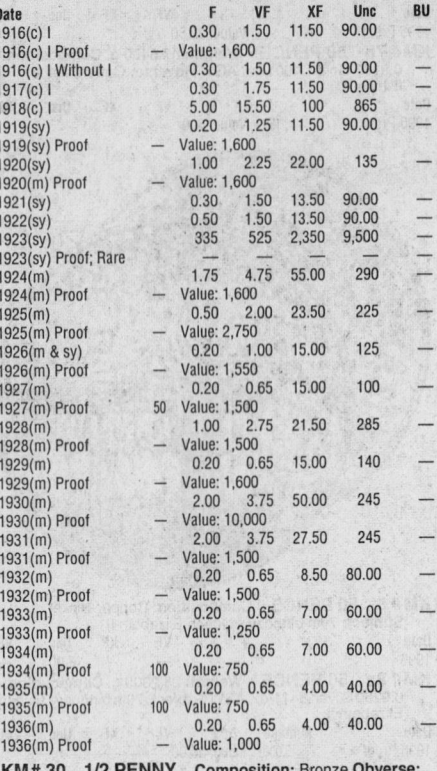

KM# 35 1/2 PENNY Composition: Bronze

Date	Mintage	F	VF	XF	Unc	BU
1938(m)	3,014,000	0.20	0.50	1.75	20.00	—
1938(m) Proof	250	Value: 650				
1939(m)	4,382,000	0.20	0.50	3.50	30.00	—
1939(m) Proof	—	Value: 1,400				

KM# 41 1/2 PENNY Composition: Bronze

Date	Mintage	F	VF	XF	Unc	BU
1939(m)	504,000	3.75	6.50	42.50	325	—
1939(m) Proof	100	Value: 1,500				
1940(m)	2,294,000	0.20	0.75	5.00	40.00	—
1940(m) Proof	—	Value: 900				
1941(m)	5,011,000	0.20	0.65	3.00	25.00	—
1941(m) Proof	—	Value: 1,000				
1941(p) Proof	—	Value: 1,000				
1942(m)	720,000	1.75	3.75	21.50	110	—
1942(m) Proof	—	Value: 900				
1942(p)	4,334,000	0.20	0.50	1.75	17.50	—
1942(p) Proof	—	Value: 1,000				
1942(b) I	6,000,000	0.15	0.25	1.75	20.00	—
1942(b) I Proof	—	Value: 800				
1943(m)	33,989,000	0.15	0.25	1.25	7.00	—
1943(p) Proof	—	Value: 1,000				
1943(b) I	6,000,000	0.20	0.35	2.75	12.50	—
1943(b) I Proof	—	Value: 800				
1944(m)	720,000	1.75	3.00	22.00	100	—
1944(m) Proof	—	Value: 1,200				
1945(p)	3,033,000	0.75	2.50	10.00	75.00	—
1945(p) Proof	—	Value: 850				
1945(p) Without dot	Inc. above	1.25	2.50	12.50	55.00	—
1946(p)	13,747,000	0.15	0.25	1.25	10.00	—
1946(p) Proof	—	Value: 850				
1947(p)	9,293,000	0.15	0.25	1.25	10.00	—
1947(p) Proof	—	Value: 850				
1948(m)	4,608,000	0.25	0.50	2.75	20.00	—

Date	Mintage	F	VF	XF	Unc	BU
1948(m) Proof	—	Value: 1,000				
1948(p)	25,553,000	0.15	0.25	1.25	7.00	—
1948(p) Proof	—	Value: 850				

KM# 42 1/2 PENNY **Composition:** Bronze **Obv. Legend:** IND: IMP: dropped

Date	Mintage	F	VF	XF	Unc	BU
1949(m) Proof	—	Value: 1,000				
1949(p)	22,310,000	0.15	0.25	2.00	10.00	—
1949(p) Proof	—	Value: 1,000				
1950(p)	12,014,000	0.15	0.50	3.50	12.50	—
1950(p) Proof	—	Value: 850				
1951(p) with dot	—	0.15	0.35	2.00	10.00	—
1951(p) with dot, Proof	—	Value: 850				
1951(p) Without dot	29,422,000	0.15	0.35	2.50	12.50	—
1951(p) Without dot; Proof	—	Value: 850				
1951PL	17,040,000	0.15	0.35	1.25	7.00	—

Note: 5.040 struck at the Birmingham Mint

Date	Mintage	F	VF	XF	Unc	BU
1951PL Proof	—	Value: 1,000				
1952(p)	1,832,000	0.50	2.25	7.00	25.00	—
1952(p) Proof	—	Value: 850				

KM# 49 1/2 PENNY **Composition:** Bronze

Date	Mintage	F	VF	XF	Unc	BU
1953(p)	23,967,000	0.15	0.25	0.50	5.00	—
1953(p) Proof	16	Value: 850				
1954(p)	21,963,000	0.15	0.25	0.50	6.00	—
1954(p) Proof	—	Value: 850				
1955(p) Without dot	9,343,000	0.15	0.25	0.50	6.00	—
1955(p) Without dot; Proof	301	Value: 600				

KM# 61 1/2 PENNY **Composition:** Bronze **Obv. Legend:** F:D: added

Date	Mintage	F	VF	XF	Unc	BU
1959(m)	10,166,000	0.10	0.15	0.25	1.50	2.50
1959(m) Proof	1,506	Value: 75.00				
1960(p)	17,812,000	0.10	0.15	0.25	1.00	1.50
1960(p) Proof	1,030	Value: 95.00				
1961(p)	20,183,000	0.10	0.15	0.25	1.00	1.50
1961(p) Proof	1,040	Value: 95.00				
1962(p)	10,259,000	0.10	0.15	0.25	2.00	2.50
1962(p) Proof	1,064	Value: 85.00				
1963(p)	16,410,000	0.10	0.15	0.25	1.00	1.50
1963(p) Proof	1,060	Value: 85.00				
1964(p)	18,230,000	0.10	0.15	0.25	1.00	1.50
1964(p) Proof; 1 known	—	Value: 3,000				

KM# 23 PENNY **Composition:** Bronze **Obverse:** Bust King George V left **Reverse:** Value in inner circle

Date		F	VF	XF	Unc	BU
1911(L)		0.75	3.00	17.50	90.00	—
1911(L) Proof	—	Value: 1,800				
1912H		0.75	3.00	21.50	150	—
1912H Proof	—	Value: 1,800				
1913(L)		1.25	7.50	27.50	200	—
1914(L)		3.00	8.50	60.00	425	—
1915(L)		2.25	15.50	75.00	600	—
1915H		1.75	8.50	55.00	500	—
1916(c) I		0.50	1.50	15.00	100	—
1916(c) I Proof	—	Value: 1,800				
1917(c) I		0.40	1.00	12.50	125	—
1918(c) I		3.75	15.50	70.00	550	—
1919(m) Without dots		0.50	2.25	21.50	180	—
1919(m) Dot below bottom scroll		1.00	3.75	35.00	180	—
1919(m) Dots below bottom scroll and above upper		10.00	27.50	110	—	—
1919(m) Proof	—	Value: 1,800				
1920(m & sy) Without dots		0.75	7.50	190	1,550	—
1920(m) Dot beow bottom scroll		2.00	7.50	42.50	315	—
1920(m) Proof	—	Value: 1,800				
1920(sy) Dot above bottom scroll		3.00	7.50	42.50	470	—
1920 Dots below bottom scroll and above upper		5.50	30.00	110	—	—
1921(m & sy)		0.25	3.00	27.50	225	—
1922(m & p)		0.25	2.50	27.50	225	—
1923(m)		0.25	2.50	23.50	225	—
1923(m) Proof	—	Value: 1,600				
1924(m & sy)		0.25	1.50	18.50	210	—
1924(m) Proof	—	Value: 1,500				
1925(m)		12.50	50.00	190	3,750	—
1925(m) Proof	—	Value: 10,500				
1926(m & sy)		1.00	3.75	35.00	315	—
1926(m) Proof	—	Value: 1,800				
1927(m)		0.30	2.25	20.00	110	—
1927(m) Proof	50	Value: 1,200				
1928(m)		0.30	3.50	21.50	260	—
1928(m) Proof	—	Value: 1,800				
1929(m)		0.30	2.50	22.00	320	—
1929(m) Proof	—	Value: 1,750				
1930(m)		4,250	7,200	20,000	40,000	—
1930(m) Proof; Rare		—	—	—	—	—

Note: Noble Numismatics sale No. 52, 7-97, nearly FDC proof realized $126,500. Noble Numismatics sale No. 62, 11-99, FDC proof realized $162,665.

Date		F	VF	XF	Unc	BU
1931(m)		1.75	1.50	35.00	600	—
1931(m) Proof	—	Value: 1,750				
1932(m)		0.30	2.50	35.00	150	—
1933/2(m)		3.00	15.00	50.00	350	—
1933(m)		0.25	1.50	13.50	70.00	—
1933(m) Proof Sets	—	Value: 1,400				
1934(m)		0.25	0.85	13.50	60.00	—
1934(m) Proof	100	Value: 900				
1935(m)		0.25	0.75	12.50	55.00	—
1935(m) Proof	100	Value: 900				
1936(m)		0.25	0.75	10.00	45.00	—
1936(m) Proof	—	Value: 1,000				

KM# 36 PENNY **Composition:** Bronze **Obverse:** Head of King George VI left **Reverse:** Kangaroo leaping left

Date	Mintage	F	VF	XF	Unc	BU
1938(m)	5,552,000	0.25	0.50	3.75	22.50	—
1938(m) Proof	250	Value: 750				
1939(m)	6,240,000	0.25	0.50	3.75	27.50	—
1939(m) Proof	—	Value: 1,250				
1940(m)	4,075,000	0.30	1.00	6.50	45.00	—
1940(p) K.G.	1,114,000	1.50	3.00	40.00	300	—
1941(m)	1,588,000	0.30	1.00	8.50	45.00	—
1941(p) K.G.	12,794,000	0.75	2.00	21.50	90.00	—
1941(p) Proof	—	Value: 1,600				
1941(p)	Inc. above	0.25	0.75	6.50	45.00	—
1941(p) K.G. high dot after Y	Inc. above	0.50	1.25	8.50	42.50	—
1942(p)	12,245,000	0.15	0.75	4.25	28.00	—
1942(p) Proof	—	Value: 1,200				
1942(b) I	9,000,000	0.15	0.50	3.50	22.50	—
1942(b) Without I	Inc. above	1.75	3.75	10.00	60.00	—
1942(b) Proof	—	Value: 1,200				
1943(m)	11,112,000	0.20	0.50	5.00	25.00	—
1943(p)	33,086,000	0.15	0.50	5.00	25.00	—
1943(p) Proof	—	Value: 1,000				
1943(b) I	9,000,000	0.20	0.50	4.25	20.00	—
1943(b) I Without I	Inc. above	1.75	3.75	10.00	55.00	—
1943(b) Proof	—	Value: 800				
1944(m)	2,112,000	0.50	3.75	21.50	100	—
1944(p)	27,830,000	0.15	0.50	3.50	25.00	—
1944(p) Proof	—	Value: 1,200				
1945(p)	15,173,000	0.20	0.75	4.75	32.00	—
1945(p) Proof	—	Value: 1,400				
1945(b) I Rare	6	—	—	—	—	—
1945(m)	—	—	—	—	15,000	—
1946(m)	240,000	5.50	15.50	42.50	470	—
1947(m)	6,864,000	0.15	0.40	2.25	12.50	—
1947(p)	4,490,000	0.50	1.25	6.50	45.00	—
1947(p) Proof	—	Value: 1,400				
1948(m)	26,616,000	0.15	0.40	2.25	12.50	—
1948(p)	1,534,000	0.75	3.00	35.00	200	—
1948(p) Proof	—	Value: 1,500				

KM# 43 PENNY **Composition:** Bronze **Obverse:** Head of King George VI left **Obv. Legend:** IND: IMP. dropped **Reverse:** Kangaroo leaping left

Date	Mintage	F	VF	XF	Unc	BU
1949(m)	27,065,000	0.15	0.25	2.00	10.00	—
1949(m) Proof	—	Value: 2,000				
1950(m)	36,359,000	0.15	0.25	2.00	14.50	—
1950(m) Proof	—	Value: 2,000				
1950(p)	21,488,000	0.20	1.00	6.50	35.00	—
1950(p) Proof	—	Value: 1,200				
1951(m)	21,240,000	0.15	0.20	1.00	9.00	—
1951(p)	12,888,000	0.20	0.40	4.00	22.50	—
1951(p) Proof	—	Value: 1,200				
1951PL	18,000,000	0.15	0.25	0.85	7.00	—
1951PL Proof	—	Value: 1,250				
1952(m)	12,408,000	0.15	0.30	1.00	7.00	—
1952(m) Proof	—	Value: 2,500				
1952(p)	45,514,000	0.15	0.30	1.00	6.50	—
1952(p) Proof	—	Value: 1,250				

KM# 50 PENNY **Composition:** Bronze **Obverse:** Bust of Queen Elizabeth II right **Reverse:** Kangaroo leaping left

Date	Mintage	F	VF	XF	Unc	BU
1953(m)	6,936,000	0.20	0.75	3.00	14.50	—
1953(m) Proof	—	Value: 800				
1953(p)	6,203,000	0.20	0.65	1.50	16.50	—
1953(p) Proof	16	Value: 1,400				

KM# 56 PENNY **Composition:** Bronze **Obverse:** Bust of Queen Elizabeth II right **Obv. Legend:** F:D: added **Reverse:** Kangaroo leaping left

Date	Mintage	F	VF	XF	Unc	BU
1955(m)	6,336,000	0.50	1.00	2.50	12.00	20.00
1955(m) Proof	1,200	Value: 100				
1955(p)	11,110,000	0.10	0.20	0.85	9.00	12.00
1955(p) Proof	301	Value: 900				
1956(m)	13,872,000	0.10	0.20	0.85	7.00	10.00
1956(m) Proof	1,500	Value: 75.00				
1956(p)	12,121,000	0.10	0.20	0.85	6.50	10.00
1956(p) Proof	417	Value: 750				
1957(p)	15,978,000	0.10	0.20	0.85	6.00	9.00
1957(p) Proof	1,112	Value: 150				
1958(m)	10,012,000	0.10	0.20	0.85	6.00	9.00
1958(m) Proof	1,506	Value: 75.00				
1958(p)	14,428,000	0.10	0.20	0.85	6.50	9.00
1958(p) Proof	1,028	Value: 125				
1959(m)	1,617,000	0.50	1.25	6.50	30.00	—
1959(m) Proof	1,506	Value: 75.00				
1959(p)	14,428,000	0.10	0.20	0.85	5.50	9.00
1959(p) Proof	1,030	Value: 125				
1960(p)	20,515,000	0.10	0.20	0.85	1.75	2.50
1960(p) Proof	1,030	Value: 100				
1961(p)	30,607,000	0.10	0.20	0.40	1.25	2.00

Date	Mintage	F	VF	XF	Unc	BU
1961(p) Proof	1,040	Value: 100				
1962(p)	34,851,000	0.10	0.20	0.40	1.25	2.00
1962(p) Proof	1,064	Value: 95.00				
1963(p)	10,258,000	0.10	0.20	0.40	1.25	2.00
1963(p) Proof	1,100	Value: 95.00				
1964(m)	49,130,000	0.10	0.20	0.50	1.25	1.50
1964(p)	54,590,000	0.10	0.20	0.50	1.25	1.50
1964(p) Proof; 1 known	—	Value: 4,000				

KM# 18 THREEPENCE **Weight:** 1.4100 g. **Composition:** 0.9250 Silver .0419 oz. ASW **Obverse:** Bust of King Edward VII right **Reverse:** Arms

Date	Mintage	F	VF	XF	Unc	BU
1910(L)	4,000,000	1.75	3.75	8.50	45.00	—
1910(L) Proof	—	Value: 700				

KM# 24 THREEPENCE **Weight:** 1.4100 g. **Composition:** 0.9250 Silver .0419 oz. ASW **Obverse:** George V left **Reverse:** Arms

Date	Mintage	F	VF	XF	Unc	BU
1911(L)	2,000,000	4.25	10.00	42.50	210	—
1911(L) Proof	—	Value: 2,000				
1911(L) Reeded edge; Proof	—	Value: 10,000				
1912(L)	2,400,000	5.50	50.00	170	1,000	—
1914(L)	1,600,000	8.50	27.50	100	580	—
1915(L)	800,000	12.50	55.00	180	900	—
1916M	1,913,000	5.00	11.50	55.00	385	—
1916M Proof	25	Value: 1,000				
1917M	3,808,000	1.75	5.50	18.50	135	—
1918M	3,119,000	1.75	5.50	21.50	125	—
1919M	3,201,000	2.50	8.50	27.50	145	—
1919M Proof	—	Value: 1,000				
1920M	4,196,000	6.50	15.00	55.00	380	—
1920M Proof	—	Value: 1,000				
1921M	7,378,000	1.75	4.25	17.50	95.00	—
1921(m)	Inc. above	7.50	13.50	85.00	450	—
1922/1(m)	5,531,000	2,125	4,750	9,500	17,500	—
1922(m)	Inc. above	1.75	7.50	21.50	165	—
1922(m) Proof	—	Value: 1,000				
1923(m)	815,000	11.50	30.00	125	765	—
1924(m & sy)	2,013,999	5.50	11.50	50.00	320	—
1924(m) Proof	—	Value: 900				
1925(m & sy) Proof	4,347,000	0.50	3.50	17.50	100	—
1925(m) Proof	—	Value: 900				
1926(m & sy)	6,158,000	0.50	2.00	16.50	90.00	—
1926(m) Proof	—	Value: 900				
1927(m)	6,720,000	0.50	2.00	13.50	80.00	—
1927(m) Proof	50	Value: 900				
1928(m)	5,000,000	0.50	2.00	16.50	85.00	—
1928(m) Proof	—	Value: 900				
1934/3(m)	1,616,000	20.00	38.50	150	700	—
1934(m)	Inc. above	0.50	2.00	15.00	80.00	—
1934(m) Proof	100	Value: 750				
1935(m)	2,800,000	0.50	2.00	18.50	110	—
1935(m) Proof	—	Value: 550				
1936(m)	3,600,000	0.30	1.25	7.00	40.00	—
1936(m) Proof	—	Value: 650				

KM# 37 THREEPENCE **Weight:** 1.4100 g. **Composition:** 0.9250 Silver .0419 oz. ASW **Obverse:** George VI **Reverse:** Three wheat stalks divide date

Date	Mintage	F	VF	XF	Unc	BU
1938(m)	4,560,000	0.30	1.25	6.50	12.50	—
1938(m) Proof	250	Value: 300				
1939(m)	3,856,000	0.30	1.50	7.00	25.00	—
1939(m) Proof	—	Value: 450				
1940(m)	3,840,000	0.30	1.50	7.00	37.50	—
1941(m)	7,584,000	0.30	1.00	3.75	20.00	—
1942(m)	528,000	8.50	25.00	115	650	—
1942D	16,000,000	BV	0.40	1.00	3.50	—
1942S	8,000,000	BV	0.65	1.25	4.50	—
1943(m)	24,912,000	BV	0.40	0.85	3.00	—
1943D	16,000,000	BV	0.40	1.00	3.50	—
1943S	8,000,000	BV	0.65	1.25	4.50	—
1944S	32,000,000	BV	0.40	0.85	3.50	—

KM# 37a THREEPENCE **Weight:** 1.4100 g. **Composition:** 0.5000 Silver .0226 oz. ASW

Date	Mintage	F	VF	XF	Unc	BU
1947(m)	4,176,000	0.85	2.00	7.00	25.00	—
1948(m)	26,208,000	—	BV	1.75	5.00	—

KM# 44 THREEPENCE **Weight:** 1.4100 g. **Composition:** 0.5000 Silver .0226 oz. ASW **Obverse:** George VI **Obv. Legend:** IND: IMP. dropped **Reverse:** Three wheat stalks divide date

Date	Mintage	F	VF	XF	Unc	BU
1949(m)	26,400,000	—	BV	1.75	5.50	—
1949(m) Proof	—	Value: 700				
1950(m)	35,456,000	—	BV	1.75	7.00	—
1951(m)	15,856,000	—	0.50	2.50	10.00	—
1951PL	40,000,000	—	BV	1.00	3.00	—
1951PL Proof	—	Value: 500				
1952(m)	21,560,000	—	BV	1.75	7.00	—

KM# 51 THREEPENCE **Weight:** 1.4100 g. **Composition:** 0.5000 Silver .0226 oz. ASW **Obverse:** Queen Elizabeth II right **Reverse:** Three wheat stalks divide date

Date	Mintage	F	VF	XF	Unc	BU
1953(m)	7,664,000	BV	1.75	4.75	22.50	—
1953(m) Proof	—	Value: 500				
1954(m)	2,672,000	0.85	2.50	5.50	35.00	—
1954(m) Proof	—	Value: 600				

KM# 57 THREEPENCE **Weight:** 1.4100 g. **Composition:** 0.5000 Silver .0226 oz. ASW **Obverse:** Queen Elizabeth Ii right **Obv. Legend:** F:D: added **Reverse:** Three wheat stalks divide date

Date	Mintage	F	VF	XF	Unc	BU
1955(m)	27,088,000	—	BV	1.25	4.00	—
1955(m) Proof	1,040	Value: 45.00				
1956(m)	14,088,000	—	BV	1.25	4.50	—
1956(m) Proof	1,500	Value: 40.00				
1957(m)	26,704,000	—	BV	0.85	2.50	—
1957(m) Proof	1,256	Value: 40.00				
1958(m)	11,248,000	—	BV	1.75	4.50	—
1958(m) Proof	1,506	Value: 40.00				
1959(m)	19,888,000	—	BV	0.85	2.25	—
1959(m) Proof	1,506	Value: 40.00				
1960(m)	19,600,000	—	BV	0.60	1.00	—
1960(m) Proof	1,509	Value: 35.00				
1961(m)	33,840,000	—	BV	0.60	1.00	—
1961(m) Proof	1,506	Value: 35.00				
1962(m)	15,968,000	—	BV	0.60	1.00	—
1962(m) Proof	2,016	Value: 35.00				
1963(m)	44,016,000	—	BV	0.50	1.00	—
1963(m) Proof	5,042	Value: 25.00				
1964(m)	20,320,000	—	BV	0.50	1.25	—

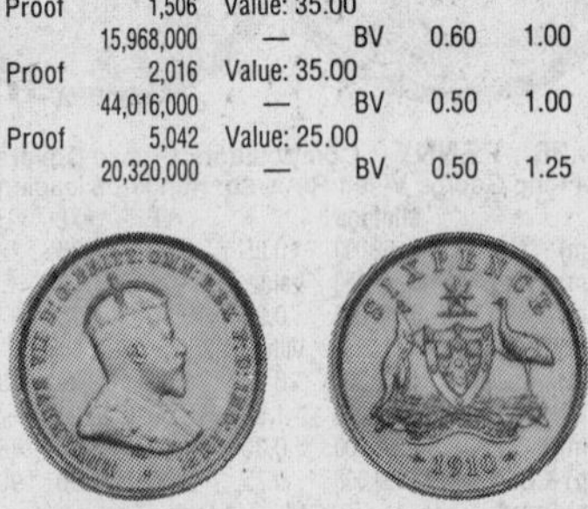

KM# 19 SIXPENCE **Weight:** 2.8200 g. **Composition:** 0.9250 Silver .0838 oz. ASW **Obverse:** Edward VII bust right **Reverse:** Arms

Date	Mintage	F	VF	XF	Unc	BU
1910(L)	3,046,000	5.00	12.50	35.00	150	—
1910(L) Proof	—	Value: 800				

KM# 25 SIXPENCE **Weight:** 2.8200 g. **Composition:** 0.9250 Silver .0838 oz. ASW **Obverse:** George V left **Reverse:** Arms

Date	Mintage	F	VF	XF	Unc	BU
1911(L)	1,000,000	7.00	21.50	125	540	—
1911(L) Proof	—	Value: 2,000				
1912(L)	1,600,000	13.50	50.00	150	850	—
1914(L)	1,800,000	5.50	12.50	70.00	400	—
1916M	1,769,000	7.50	21.50	120	600	—
1916M Proof	25	Value: 1,750				
1917M	1,632,000	7.50	20.00	100	470	—
1918M	915,000	20.00	65.00	235	1,125	—
1919M	1,521,000	7.50	19.50	65.00	350	—
1919M Proof	—	Value: 1,600				
1920M	1,476,000	8.50	25.00	120	600	—
1920M Proof	—	Value: 2,500				
1921(m) Proof	—	Value: 2,000				
1921(m & sy)	3,795,000	5.00	10.00	35.00	225	—
1922(sy)	1,488,000	13.50	38.50	200	850	—
1922(sy) Proof	—	Value: 2,500				
1923(m & sy)	1,458,000	8.50	21.50	120	585	—
1924(m) Proof	—	Value: 2,000				
1924(m & sy)	1,038,000	8.50	21.50	150	800	—
1925(m) Proof	—	Value: 900				
1925(m & sy)	3,266,000	0.75	8.50	42.50	180	—
1926(m) Proof	—	Value: 900				
1926(m & sy)	3,609,000	0.75	7.00	27.50	100	—
1927(m)	3,592,000	0.75	6.00	21.50	100	—
1927(m) Proof	50	Value: 900				
1928(m)	2,721,000	0.75	6.00	21.50	135	—
1928(m) Proof	—	Value: 900				
1934(m)	1,024,000	2.50	7.00	30.00	225	—
1934(m) Proof	100	Value: 700				
1935(m)	392,000	4.25	10.00	50.00	375	—
1935(m) Proof	—	Value: 1,000				
1936(m)	1,800,000	0.75	3.00	10.00	120	—
1936(m) Proof	—	Value: 900				

KM# 38 SIXPENCE **Weight:** 2.8200 g. **Composition:** 0.9250 Silver .0838 oz. ASW **Obverse:** George VI left **Reverse:** Arms

Date	Mintage	F	VF	XF	Unc	BU
1938(m)	2,864,000	0.65	2.00	7.00	35.00	—
1938(m) Proof	250	Value: 400				
1939(m)	1,600,000	0.65	2.50	13.50	175	—
1939(m) Proof	—	Value: 900				
1940(m)	1,600,000	0.65	2.50	10.00	70.00	—
1941(m)	2,912,000	0.65	2.00	5.50	30.00	—
1942(m)	8,968,000	BV	1.25	3.50	22.50	—
1942D	12,000,000	BV	0.75	2.00	10.00	—
1942S	4,000,000	BV	0.75	2.00	18.00	—
1943D	8,000,000	BV	0.75	2.00	8.50	—
1943S	4,000,000	BV	0.75	2.00	15.00	—
1944S	4,000,000	BV	1.00	2.50	12.00	—
1945(m)	10,096,000	BV	1.00	2.50	10.00	—

KM# 38a SIXPENCE **Weight:** 2.8200 g. **Composition:** 0.5000 Silver .0453 oz. ASW

Date	Mintage	F	VF	XF	Unc	BU
1946(m)	10,024,000	BV	0.85	3.50	20.00	—
1946(m) Proof	—	Value: 900				
1948(m)	1,584,000	BV	0.85	3.50	22.50	—

KM# 45 SIXPENCE **Weight:** 1.4100 g. **Composition:** 0.5000 Silver .0463 oz. ASW **Obverse:** George VI left **Obv. Legend:** IND: IMP. dropped **Reverse:** Arms

Date	Mintage	F	VF	XF	Unc	BU
1950(m)	10,272,000	BV	2.00	3.50	25.00	—
1950(m) Proof	—	Value: 1,500				
1951(m)	13,760,000	BV	1.50	2.75	16.50	—
1951PL	20,024,000	BV	0.50	1.75	7.00	—
1951PL Proof	—	Value: 650				
1952(m)	2,112,000	0.75	4.25	21.50	200	—

KM# 52 SIXPENCE **Weight:** 1.4100 g. **Composition:** 0.5000 Silver .0463 oz. ASW **Obverse:** Elizabeth II right **Reverse:** Arms

Date	Mintage	F	VF	XF	Unc	BU
1953(m)	1,152,000	0.75	3.50	10.00	90.00	—
1953(m) Proof	—	Value: 700				
1954(m)	7,672,000	BV	0.85	1.50	5.00	—
1954(m) Proof	—	Value: 750				

KM# 58 SIXPENCE Weight: 1.4100 g. Composition: 0.5000 Silver .0226 oz. ASW Obverse: Elizabeth II right Obv. Legend: F:D: added Reverse: Arms

Date	Mintage	F	VF	XF	Unc	BU
1955(m)	14,248,000	BV	0.75	1.75	8.00	—
1955(m) Proof	1,200	Value: 70.00				
1956(m)	7,904,000	BV	2.25	4.25	25.00	—
1956(m) Proof	1,500	Value: 55.00				
1957(m)	13,752,000	BV	0.50	0.85	3.50	—
1957(m) Proof	1,256	Value: 55.00				
1958(m)	17,944,000	BV	0.50	0.85	3.00	—
1958(m) Proof	1,506	Value: 50.00				
1959(m)	11,728,000	BV	0.50	1.00	5.00	—
1959(m) Proof	1,506	Value: 50.00				
1960(m)	18,592,000	BV	0.50	0.85	4.50	—
1960(m) Proof	1,509	Value: 45.00				
1961(m)	9,152,000	BV	0.50	0.85	2.75	—
1961(m) Proof	1,506	Value: 45.00				
1962(m)	44,816,000	BV	0.50	0.75	1.75	—
1962(m) Proof	2,016	Value: 45.00				
1963(m)	25,056,000	BV	0.50	0.75	1.75	—
1963(m) Proof	5,042	Value: 30.00				

KM# 20 SHILLING Weight: 5.6500 g. Composition: 0.9250 Silver .1680 oz. ASW Obverse: Bust King Edward VII right Reverse: Arms

Date	Mintage	F	VF	XF	Unc	BU
1910(L)	2,536,000	3.75	15.00	65.00	150	—
1910(L) Proof	—	Value: 900				

KM# 26 SHILLING Weight: 5.6500 g. Composition: 0.9250 Silver .1680 oz. ASW Obverse: George V left Reverse: Arms

Date	Mintage	F	VF	XF	Unc	BU
1911(L)	1,700,000	9.50	27.50	85.00	525	—
1911(L) Proof	—	Value: 5,000				
1912(L)	1,000,000	20.00	95.00	185	1,850	—
1913(L)	1,200,000	11.50	35.00	145	1,350	—
1914(L)	3,300,000	6.50	17.50	65.00	400	—
1915(L)	800,000	20.00	100	255	1,650	—
1915H	500,000	30.00	115	375	3,400	—
1916M	5,141,000	1.25	5.50	21.50	150	—
1916M Proof	25	Value: 1,750				
1917M	5,274,000	1.25	5.50	21.50	150	—
1918M	3,761,000	3.75	13.50	42.50	170	—
1919M Proof	—	Value: 20,000				
1920M	520,000	5.50	21.50	120	975	—
1920M Proof	—	Value: 6,000				
1921(sy) Star	1,641,000	15.50	75.00	265	2,250	—
1921(m) Star; Proof	—	Value: 7,500				
1922(m)	2,040,000	7.80	20.00	85.00	375	—
1922(m) Proof	—	Value: 2,700				
1924(m & sy)	674,000	15.50	45.00	220	1,000	—
1924(m) Proof	—	Value: 4,000				
1925/3(m & sy)	1,448,000	1.25	10.00	35.00	180	—
1925(m) Proof	—	Value: 1,500				
1926(m & sy)	2,352,000	1.25	10.00	42.50	160	—
1926(m) Proof	—	Value: 2,000				
1927(m)	1,146,000	3.75	10.00	30.00	155	—
1927(m) Proof	50	Value: 1,850				
1928(m)	664,000	10.00	22.50	135	850	—
1928(m) Proof	—	Value: 3,000				
1931(m)	1,000,000	3.75	10.00	42.50	190	—
1931(m) Proof	—	—	—	—	—	—
1933(m)	220,000	35.00	125	785	1,850	—
1933(m) Proof	—	Value: 10,000				
1934(m)	480,000	7.50	18.50	75.00	275	—
1934(m) Proof	100	Value: 900				
1935(m)	500,000	5.00	10.00	22.50	160	—
1935(m) Proof	—	Value: 1,000				
1936(m)	2,000,000	2.50	7.50	25.00	155	—
1936(m) Proof	—	Value: 1,250				

KM# 39 SHILLING Weight: 5.6500 g. Composition: 0.9250 Silver .1680 oz. ASW Obverse: George VI left Reverse: Ram left above value, date

Date	Mintage	F	VF	XF	Unc	BU
1938(m)	1,484,000	2.25	4.50	8.50	35.00	—
1938(m) Proof	250	Value: 500				
1939(m)	1,520,000	2.25	4.50	10.00	85.00	—
1939(m) Proof	—	Value: 2,000				
1940(m)	760,000	5.00	11.50	35.00	200	—
1941(m)	3,040,000	BV	3.75	6.75	30.00	—
1942(m)	1,380,000	BV	3.00	6.00	22.50	—
1942S	4,000,000	BV	1.25	3.00	12.00	—
1943(m)	2,720,000	2.25	5.00	13.50	65.00	—
1943S	16,000,000	BV	1.25	2.50	10.00	—
1944(m)	14,576,000	BV	2.50	6.00	27.50	—
1944S	8,000,000	BV	1.25	2.50	10.00	—

KM# 39a SHILLING Weight: 5.6500 g. Composition: 0.5000 Silver .0908 oz. ASW

Date	Mintage	F	VF	XF	Unc	BU
1946(m)	10,072,000	BV	2.50	4.50	18.00	—
1946(p)	1,316,000	4.50	11.50	27.50	95.00	—
1948(m)	4,131,999	BV	3.00	5.50	18.00	—

KM# 46 SHILLING Weight: 5.6500 g. Composition: 0.5000 Silver .0908 oz. ASW Obverse: George VI left Obv. Legend: IND: IMP. dropped Reverse: Ram left above value, date

Date	Mintage	F	VF	XF	Unc	BU
1950(m)	7,188,000	BV	2.50	4.25	14.00	—
1952(m)	19,644,000	BV	2.25	3.50	8.00	—

KM# 53 SHILLING Weight: 2.8200 g. Composition: 0.5000 Silver .0908 oz. ASW Obverse: Queen Elizabeth II right Reverse: Ram left above value, date

Date	Mintage	F	VF	XF	Unc	BU
1953(m)	12,204,000	BV	2.00	3.50	7.00	—
1953(m) Proof	—	Value: 700				
1954(m)	16,187,999	BV	2.00	3.50	8.00	—
1954(m) Proof	—	Value: 800				

KM# 59 SHILLING Weight: 2.8200 g. Composition: 0.5000 Silver .0908 oz. ASW Obverse: Queen Elizabeth II right Obv. Legend: F:D: added Reverse: Ram left above value, date

Date	Mintage	F	VF	XF	Unc	BU
1955(m)	7,492,000	BV	1.50	3.50	12.50	—
1955(m) Proof	1,200	Value: 80.00				
1956(m)	6,064,000	BV	0.85	2.50	16.00	—
1956(m) Proof	1,500	Value: 70.00				
1957(m)	12,668,000	BV	0.65	1.25	5.00	—
1957(m) Proof	1,256	Value: 75.00				
1958(m)	7,412,000	BV	0.65	1.25	5.00	—
1958(m) Proof	1,506	Value: 55.00				
1959(m)	10,876,000	BV	0.65	1.00	4.50	—
1959(m) Proof	1,506	Value: 55.00				
1960(m)	14,512,000	—	BV	0.85	3.00	—
1960(m) Proof	1,509	Value: 50.00				
1961(m)	31,864,000	—	BV	0.65	1.75	—
1961(m) Proof	1,506	Value: 50.00				
1962(m)	6,592,000	—	BV	0.65	1.75	—
1962(m) Proof	2,016	Value: 50.00				
1963(m)	10,072,000	—	BV	0.65	1.75	—
1963(m) Proof	5,042	Value: 35.00				

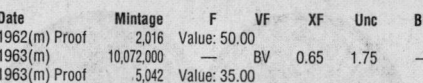

KM# 21 FLORIN Weight: 11.3100 g. Composition: 0.9250 Silver .3363 oz. ASW Obverse: Edward VII right Reverse: Arms

Date	Mintage	F	VF	XF	Unc	BU
1910(L)	1,259,000	25.00	115	275	700	—
1910(L) Proof	—	Value: 1,500				

KM# 27 FLORIN Weight: 11.3100 g. Composition: 0.9250 Silver .3363 oz. ASW Obverse: King George V left Reverse: Arms

Date	Mintage	F	VF	XF	Unc	BU
1911(L)	950,000	25.00	115	365	2,000	—
1911(L) Proof	—	Value: 7,000				
1912(L)	1,000,000	20.00	125	425	2,600	—
1913(L)	1,200,000	20.00	125	425	2,250	—
1914(L)	2,300,000	10.00	30.00	100	625	—
1914H	500,000	65.00	190	850	3,850	—
1914H Proof	—	Value: 9,500				
1915(L)	500,000	70.00	220	540	3,325	—
1915H	750,000	42.50	135	300	1,800	—
1916M	2,752,000	7.50	27.50	120	500	—
1916M Proof	25	Value: 2,250				
1917M	4,305,000	7.50	27.50	120	500	—
1918M	2,095,000	8.50	37.50	125	600	—
1919M	1,677,000	20.00	110	350	1,500	—
1920M Star; Proof	—	Value: 40,000				
1921(m)	1,247,000	20.00	120	385	1,575	—
1921(m) Proof	—	Value: 6,000				
1922(m)	2,057,999	15.50	100	240	1,400	—
1922(m) Proof	—	Value: 3,700				
1923(m)	1,038,000	11.50	75.00	190	1,000	—
1924(m) Proof	—	Value: 2,500				
1924(m & sy)	1,582,000	8.50	45.00	150	850	—
1925(m & sy)	2,960,000	7.50	25.00	100	460	—
1925(m) Proof	—	Value: 2,300				
1926(m & sy)	2,487,000	7.50	25.00	110	500	—
1926(m) Proof	—	Value: 3,000				
1927(m)	3,420,000	6.00	15.50	75.00	325	—
1927(m) Proof	50	Value: 1,850				
1928(m)	1,962,000	7.00	21.50	100	375	—
1928(m) Proof	—	Value: 2,000				
1931(m)	3,129,000	3.75	11.50	60.00	170	—
1931(m) Proof	—	Value: 1,850				
1932(m)	188,000	100	270	820	4,000	—
1933(m)	488,000	25.00	140	625	3,500	—
1934(m)	1,674,000	4.25	12.50	60.00	290	—
1934(m) Proof	100	Value: 1,250				
1935(m)	915,000	3.00	14.00	62.50	300	—
1935(m) Proof	—	Value: 1,250				
1936(m)	2,382,000	2.00	4.50	17.50	135	—
1936(m) Proof	—	Value: 1,350				

KM# 31 FLORIN Weight: 11.3100 g. Composition: 0.9250 Silver .3363 oz. ASW Subject: Opening of Parliament House, Canberra Obverse: King George V left

Date	Mintage	F	VF	XF	Unc	BU
1927(m)	2,000,000	1.75	5.50	10.00	45.00	—
1927(m) Proof	400	Value: 2,000				

KM# 33 FLORIN **Weight:** 11.3100 g. **Composition:** 0.9250 Silver .3363 oz. ASW **Subject:** Centennial of Victoria and Melbourne **Obverse:** King George V left **Reverse:** Horse with rider prancing left

Date	F	VF	XF	Unc	BU
ND(1934)	75.00	95.00	185	250	—

Note: 21,000 pieces were melted

Date	F	VF	XF	Unc	BU
ND(1934) Proof	—	Value: 6,500			

KM# 40 FLORIN **Weight:** 11.3100 g. **Composition:** 0.9250 Silver .3363 oz. ASW **Obverse:** King George VI left **Reverse:** Arms

Date	Mintage	F	VF	XF	Unc	BU
1938(m)	2,990,000	2.00	4.50	17.50	55.00	—
1938(m) Proof	—	Value: 800				
1939(m)	630,000	7.50	15.50	45.00	550	—
1939(m) Proof	—	Value: 2,500				
1940(m)	8,410,000	BV	3.75	8.50	30.00	—
1941(m)	7,614,000	BV	3.75	7.50	30.00	—
1942(m)	17,986,000	BV	3.50	5.00	20.00	—
1942S	6,000,000	BV	3.75	6.00	22.50	—
1943(m)	12,762,000	BV	3.00	4.25	20.00	—
1943S	11,000,000	BV	3.00	4.25	18.00	—
1944(m)	22,440,000	BV	3.00	4.25	22.50	—
1944S	11,000,000	BV	3.00	4.25	18.00	—
1945(m)	11,970,000	BV	3.75	7.50	35.00	—

KM# 40a FLORIN **Weight:** 11.3100 g. **Composition:** 0.5000 Silver .1818 oz. ASW

Date	Mintage	F	VF	XF	Unc	BU
1946(m)	22,154,000	BV	1.75	3.50	13.50	—
1946(m) Proof	—	Value: 600				
1947(m)	39,292,000	BV	1.75	3.50	13.50	—
1947(m) Proof	—	Value: 600				

KM# 47 FLORIN **Weight:** 11.3100 g. **Composition:** 0.5000 Silver .1818 oz. ASW **Subject:** 50th Year Jubilee **Obverse:** King George VI left **Reverse:** Crowned crossed scepter and sword divide Jubilee dates

Date	Mintage	F	VF	XF	Unc	BU
1951(m)	2,000,000	BV	2.00	3.50	10.00	—

KM# 47a FLORIN **Composition:** Copper-Nickel

Date	F	VF	XF	Unc	BU
1951(L) Proof	—	Value: 5,000			

KM# 48 FLORIN **Weight:** 11.3100 g. **Composition:** 0.5000 Silver .1818 oz. ASW **Obverse:** King George VI left **Obv. Legend:** IND: IMP. dropped **Reverse:** Arms

Date	Mintage	F	VF	XF	Unc	BU
1951(m)	10,068,000	2.00	5.00	10.00	30.00	—
1952(m)	10,044,000	2.00	5.50	11.00	32.00	—

KM# 54 FLORIN **Weight:** 11.3100 g. **Composition:** 0.5000 Silver .1818 oz. ASW **Obverse:** Elizabeth II bust right **Reverse:** Arms

Date	Mintage	F	VF	XF	Unc	BU
1953(m)	12,658,000	BV	2.00	5.00	11.00	—
1953(m) Proof	—	Value: 900				
1954(m)	15,366,000	BV	3.00	5.00	15.00	—
1954(m) Proof	—	Value: 1,000				

KM# 55 FLORIN **Weight:** 11.3100 g. **Composition:** 0.5000 Silver .1818 oz. ASW **Subject:** Royal Visit **Obverse:** Elizabeth II bust right **Reverse:** Lion and kangaroo facing right

Date	Mintage	F	VF	XF	Unc	BU
1954(m)	4,000,000	BV	2.00	3.50	12.00	—

KM# 60 FLORIN **Weight:** 11.3100 g. **Composition:** 0.5000 Silver .1818 oz. ASW **Obverse:** Elizabeth II bust right **Obv. Legend:** F:D: added **Reverse:** Arms

Date	Mintage	F	VF	XF	Unc	BU
1956(m)	8,090,000	2.00	3.50	10.00	35.00	—
1956(m) Proof	1,500	Value: 85.00				
1957(m)	9,278,000	BV	2.00	2.75	6.00	—
1957(m) Proof	1,256	Value: 55.00				
1958(m)	8,972,000	BV	2.00	2.75	6.00	—
1958(m) Proof	1,506	Value: 50.00				
1959(m)	3,500,000	BV	2.00	2.75	6.00	—
1959(m) Proof	1,506	Value: 45.00				
1960(m)	15,760,000	BV	1.25	2.35	4.00	—
1960(m) Proof	1,509	Value: 40.00				
1961(m)	9,452,000	BV	1.25	2.50	4.50	—
1961(m) Proof	1,506	Value: 40.00				
1962(m)	13,748,000	BV	1.25	2.35	4.00	—
1962(m) Proof	2,016	Value: 40.00				
1963(m)	12,002,000	BV	1.25	2.35	4.00	—
1963(m) Proof	5,042	Value: 30.00				

KM# 34 CROWN **Weight:** 28.2800 g. **Composition:** 0.9250 Silver .8411 oz. ASW **Obverse:** George VI left **Reverse:** Crown above date and value

Date	Mintage	F	VF	XF	Unc	BU
1937(m)	1,008,000	BV	7.50	15.00	50.00	—
1937(m) Proof	100	Value: 4,000				
1938(m)	102,000	20.00	35.00	85.00	320	—
1938(m) Proof	250	Value: 4,500				

TRADE COINAGE

KM# 12 1/2 SOVEREIGN **Weight:** 3.9940 g. **Composition:** 0.9170 Gold .1177 oz. AGW **Obverse:** Older veiled head of Queen Victoria left **Reverse:** Mint mark above date

Date	F	VF	XF	Unc	BU
1901M Proof	—	Value: 11,500			
1901P Proof	—	Value: 20,000			

KM# 14 1/2 SOVEREIGN **Weight:** 3.9940 g. **Composition:** 0.9170 Gold .1177 oz. AGW

Date	Mintage	F	VF	XF	Unc	BU
1902S	84,000	65.00	90.00	180	600	—
1902S Proof	—	Value: 7,500				
1903S	231,000	65.00	90.00	200	600	—
1904P	60,000	100	300	900	2,400	—
1906S	308,000	60.00	75.00	100	400	—
1906M	82,000	60.00	80.00	170	650	—
1907M	400,000	60.00	75.00	100	500	—
1908S	538,000	60.00	75.00	100	425	—
1908M	—	60.00	75.00	100	400	—
1908P	25,000	150	350	950	2,400	—
1909M	186,000	60.00	75.00	140	550	—
1909P	44,000	115	250	625	1,600	—
1910S	474,000	60.00	75.00	100	300	—
1915P	138,000	75.00	95.00	135	250	—
1916S	448,000	BV	50.00	65.00	95.00	—
1918P 200-250 pieces	—	250	450	650	1,200	—

KM# 28 1/2 SOVEREIGN **Weight:** 3.9940 g. **Composition:** 0.9170 Gold .1177 oz. AGW

Date	Mintage	F	VF	XF	Unc	BU
1911S	252,000	BV	55.00	75.00	95.00	—
1911S Matte Proof	—	—	—	—	11,500	—
1911P	130,000	75.00	95.00	135	270	—
1912S	278,000	BV	55.00	75.00	95.00	—
1914S	322,000	BV	55.00	75.00	95.00	—
1915S	892,000	BV	40.00	65.00	90.00	—
1915M	125,000	BV	55.00	75.00	110	—
1916S	448,000	BV	50.00	65.00	95.00	—
1918P Estimated 200-250 pieces minted	—	250	450	650	1,200	—

KM# 13 SOVEREIGN **Weight:** 7.9881 g. **Composition:** 0.9170 Gold .2354 oz. AGW **Obverse:** Older veiled head

Date	Mintage	F	VF	XF	Unc	BU
1901S	3,012,000	—	BV	85.00	130	—
1901S	3,012,000	—	BV	85.00	130	—
1901M	3,987,000	—	BV	85.00	130	—
1901M Proof	—	Value: 10,000				
1901P	2,889,000	—	BV	110	220	—
1901P Proof	—	Value: 12,500				

KM# 15 SOVEREIGN **Weight:** 7.9881 g. **Composition:** 0.9170 Gold .2354 oz. AGW

Date	Mintage	F	VF	XF	Unc	BU
1902S	2,813,000	—	—	BV	100	—
1902S Proof	—	Value: 12,500				
1902M	4,267,000	—	—	BV	100	—
1902P	4,289,000	—	—	BV	100	—
1902P Proof	—	Value: 12,500				
1903S	2,806,000	—	—	BV	100	—
1903M	3,521,000	—	—	BV	100	—
1903P	4,674,000	—	—	BV	100	—
1904S	2,986,000	—	—	BV	100	—
1904M	3,743,000	—	—	BV	100	—
1904M Proof	—	Value: 12,500				
1904P	4,506,000	—	—	BV	100	—
1905S	2,778,000	—	—	BV	100	—
1905M	3,633,000	—	—	BV	100	—
1905P	4,876,000	—	—	BV	100	—
1906S	2,792,000	—	—	BV	100	—
1906M	3,657,000	—	—	BV	100	—
1906P	4,829,000	—	—	BV	100	—
1907S	2,539,000	—	—	BV	100	—
1907M	3,332,000	—	—	BV	100	—
1907P	4,972,000	—	—	BV	100	—
1908S	2,017,000	—	—	BV	100	—
1908M	3,080,000	—	—	BV	100	—
1908P	4,875,000	—	—	BV	100	—
1909S	2,057,000	—	—	BV	100	—
1909M	3,029,000	—	—	BV	100	—
1909P	4,524,000	—	—	BV	100	—
1910S	2,135,000	—	—	BV	100	—
1910M	3,054,000	—	—	BV	100	—
1910M Proof	—	Value: 12,500				
1910P	4,690,000	—	—	BV	100	—

KM# 29 SOVEREIGN **Weight:** 7.9881 g. **Composition:** 0.9170 Gold .2354 oz. AGW

Date	Mintage	F	VF	XF	Unc	BU
1911S	2,519,000	—	—	BV	110	—
1911S Proof	—	Value: 12,500				
1911M	2,851,000	—	—	BV	110	—
1911M Proof	—	Value: 12,500				
1911P	4,373,000	—	—	BV	110	—
1912S	2,227,000	—	—	BV	110	—
1912M	2,467,000	—	—	BV	110	—
1912P	4,278,000	—	—	BV	110	—
1913S	2,249,000	—	—	BV	110	—
1913M	2,323,000	—	—	BV	110	—
1913P	4,635,000	—	—	BV	110	—
1914S	1,774,000	—	—	BV	110	—
1914S Proof	—	Value: 11,500				
1914M	2,012,000	—	—	BV	110	—
1914P	4,815,000	—	—	BV	110	—
1915S	1,346,000	—	—	BV	110	—
1915M	1,637,000	—	—	BV	110	—
1915P	4,373,000	—	—	BV	110	—
1916S	1,242,000	—	—	BV	110	—
1916M	1,277,000	—	—	BV	110	—
1916P	4,906,000	—	—	BV	110	—
1917S	1,666,000	—	—	BV	110	—
1917M	934,000	—	—	BV	110	—
1917P	4,110,000	—	—	BV	110	—
1918S	3,716,000	—	—	BV	110	—
1918M	4,969,000	—	—	BV	110	—
1918P	3,812,000	—	—	BV	110	—
1919S	1,835,000	—	—	BV	110	—
1919M	514,000	—	BV	90.00	145	—
1919P	2,995,000	—	—	BV	100	—
1920S	360,000	20,000	30,000	50,000	120,000	—
1920M	530,000	1,000	1,500	2,150	4,550	—
1920P	2,421,000	—	—	BV	120	—
1921S	839,000	8,500	1,250	1,850	4,250	—
1921M	240,000	1,500	3,500	5,750	9,500	—
1921P	2,314,000	—	—	BV	110	—
1922S	578,000	3,000	8,000	11,500	18,500	—
1922M	608,000	1,000	3,000	5,250	9,500	—
1922P	2,298,000	—	—	BV	125	—
1923S	416,000	1,200	3,250	5,500	9,500	—
1923M	510,000	—	BV	100	150	—
1923P	2,124,000	—	—	BV	120	—
1924S	394,000	150	600	1,000	1,800	—
1924M	278,000	—	BV	100	150	—
1924P	1,464,000	BV	135	185	285	—
1925S	5,632,000	—	—	BV	110	—
1925M	3,311,000	—	—	BV	110	—
1925P	1,837,000	BV	165	200	350	—
1926S	1,030,999	7,000	12,000	17,000	24,000	—
1926S Proof	—	Value: 27,000				
1926M	211,000	—	BV	100	140	—
1926P	1,131,000	200	500	1,000	2,850	—
1927M	310,000	—	—	—	—	—
1927P	1,383,000	BV	165	200	350	—
1928M	413,000	750	1,250	2,000	3,200	—
1928P	1,333,000	BV	145	185	285	—

KM# 32 SOVEREIGN **Weight:** 7.9881 g. **Composition:** 0.9170 Gold .2354 oz. AGW **Obverse:** Smaller head

Date	Mintage	F	VF	XF	Unc	BU
1929M	436,000	600	1,000	1,750	3,150	—
1929M Proof	—	Value: 10,000				
1929P	1,606,000	—	BV	100	135	—
1930M	77,000	90.00	120	185	250	—
1930M Proof	—	Value: 10,000				
1930P	1,915,000	—	BV	100	135	—
1931M	57,000	120	220	400	575	—
1931M Proof	—	Value: 10,000				
1931P	1,173,000	—	BV	100	135	—

KM# 16 2 POUNDS **Weight:** 15.9761 g. **Composition:** 0.9170 Gold .4707 oz. AGW **Note:** Gilt lead electrotypes exist.

Date	Mintage	F	VF	XF	Unc	BU
1902S Matte Proof	4	Value: 35,000				

KM# 17 5 POUNDS **Weight:** 39.9403 g. **Composition:** 0.9170 Gold 1.1771 oz. AGW **Note:** Gilt lead electrotypes exist.

Date	F	VF	XF	Unc	BU
1902S Proof; Rare	—	—	—	—	—
1902S Matte Proof; Rare	—	—	—	—	—

Note: Spink Australia Sale #30 11-89 nearly FDC realized $38,500

DECIMAL COINAGE

KM# 62 CENT **Composition:** Bronze **Reverse:** Ring-tailed opossum

Date	Mintage	F	VF	XF	Unc	BU
1966(c)	146,457,000	—	—	0.15	0.45	—
1966(c) Proof	18,000	Value: 2.50				
1966(m) Blunted whisker on right	238,990,000	—	0.15	0.25	1.25	—
1966(p) Blunted 2nd whisker from right	26,620,000	0.15	0.30	1.25	7.00	—
1967	110,055,000	—	0.15	0.25	1.75	—
1968	19,930,000	—	0.15	0.45	6.00	—
1969	87,680,000	—	—	0.15	0.50	—
1969 Proof	13,000	Value: 2.50				
1970	72,560,000	—	—	0.15	0.50	—
1970 Proof	15,000	Value: 2.50				
1971	102,455,000	—	—	0.15	0.45	—
1971 Proof	10,000	Value: 2.50				
1972	82,400,000	—	—	0.10	0.45	—
1972 Proof	10,000	Value: 2.50				
1973	140,710,000	—	—	0.10	0.25	—
1973 Proof	10,000	Value: 2.50				
1974	131,720,000	—	—	0.10	0.25	—
1974 Proof	11,000	Value: 2.50				
1975	134,775,000	—	—	—	0.25	—
1975 Proof	23,000	Value: 0.65				
1976	172,935,000	—	—	—	0.25	—
1976 Proof	21,000	Value: 1.50				
1977	153,430,000	—	—	—	0.25	—
1977 Proof	55,000	Value: 0.65				
1978	97,253,000	—	—	—	0.25	—
1978 Proof	39,000	Value: 0.65				
1979	130,339,000	—	—	—	0.25	—
1979 Proof	36,000	Value: 0.65				
1980	137,892,000	—	—	—	0.25	—
1980 Proof	68,000	Value: 0.65				
1981	223,900,000	—	—	—	0.25	—
1981 Proof	86,000	Value: 0.65				
1982	134,290,000	—	—	—	0.25	—
1982 Proof	100,000	Value: 0.65				
1983	205,625,000	—	—	—	0.25	—
1983 Proof	80,000	Value: 0.65				
1984	74,735,000	—	—	—	0.25	—
1984 Proof	61,000	Value: 0.65				

KM# 78 CENT **Composition:** Bronze

Date	Mintage	F	VF	XF	Unc	BU
1985	38,300,000	—	—	—	0.25	—
1985 Proof	75,000	Value: 0.45				
1986 In sets only	180,000	—	—	—	2.25	—
1986 Proof	67,000	Value: 0.45				
1987	127,000,000	—	—	—	0.25	—
1987 Proof	70,000	Value: 0.45				
1988	56,910,000	—	—	—	0.25	—
1988 Proof	106,000	Value: 0.45				
1989	—	—	—	—	0.25	—
1989 Proof	—	Value: 0.45				
1990	—	—	—	—	0.25	—
1990 Proof	—	Value: 0.45				
1991	—	—	—	—	0.25	—
1991 Proof	—	Value: 0.45				

KM# 78a CENT **Weight:** 3.0100 g. **Composition:** 0.9250 Silver .0895 oz. ASW

Date	Mintage	F	VF	XF	Unc	BU
1991 Proof	23,000	Value: 10.00				

Note: In Proof sets only

KM# 63 2 CENTS **Composition:** Bronze **Reverse:** Frilled Lizard

Date	Mintage	F	VF	XF	Unc	BU
1966(c)	145,226,000	—	—	0.10	0.45	—
1966(c) Proof	18,000	Value: 5.00				
1966(m) Blunted 3rd left claw	66,575,000	—	0.15	0.35	2.25	—
1966(p) Blunted 1st right claw	217,735,000	—	0.15	0.25	1.25	—
1967	73,250,000	—	0.15	0.30	3.50	—
1968	17,000,000	—	0.15	0.55	4.25	—
1969	12,940,000	—	0.15	0.30	2.25	—
1969 Proof	13,000	Value: 4.75				
1970	39,872,000	—	—	0.15	0.75	—
1970 Proof	15,000	Value: 4.75				
1971	60,735,000	—	—	0.15	0.75	—
1971 Proof	10,000	Value: 4.75				
1972	77,570,000	—	—	0.10	0.75	—
1972 Proof	10,000	Value: 4.25				
1973	94,058,000	—	—	0.10	0.75	—
1973 Proof	10,000	Value: 4.25				
1974	177,723,000	—	—	0.10	0.65	—
1974 Proof	11,000	Value: 4.25				
1975	100,045,000	—	—	0.10	0.75	—
1975 Proof	23,000	Value: 0.75				
1976	121,882,000	—	—	0.10	0.50	—
1976 Proof	21,000	Value: 2.25				
1977	102,000,000	—	—	0.10	0.50	—
1977 Proof	55,000	Value: 0.75				
1978	128,252,999	—	—	0.10	0.50	—
1978 Proof	39,000	Value: 0.75				
1979	69,705,000	—	—	0.10	0.50	—
1979 Proof	36,000	Value: 0.75				
1980	145,603,000	—	—	0.10	0.50	—
1980 Proof	68,000	Value: 0.75				
1981	219,176,000	—	—	0.10	0.50	—
1981 Proof	86,000	Value: 0.75				
1982	121,770,000	—	—	0.10	0.50	—
1982 Proof	100,000	Value: 0.75				
1983	177,227,000	—	—	0.10	0.50	—
1983 Proof	80,000	Value: 0.75				
1984	57,963,000	—	—	0.10	0.50	—
1984 Proof	61,000	Value: 0.75				

KM# 79 2 CENTS **Composition:** Bronze

Date	Mintage	F	VF	XF	Unc	BU
1985	34,500,000	—	—	0.10	0.25	—
1985 Proof	75,000	Value: 0.45				
1986 In sets only	180,000	—	—	—	0.75	—
1986 Proof	67,000	Value: 0.45				
1987 In sets only	200,000	—	—	—	0.75	—
1987 Proof	70,000	Value: 0.45				
1988	28,905,000	—	—	0.10	0.50	—
1988 Proof	106,000	Value: 0.45				
1989	—	—	—	0.10	0.50	—
1989 Proof	—	Value: 0.45				
1990	—	—	—	0.10	0.25	—
1990 Proof	—	Value: 0.45				
1991	—	—	—	0.10	0.25	—
1991 Proof	—	Value: 0.45				

KM# 79a 2 CENTS **Weight:** 6.0600 g. **Composition:** 0.9250 Silver .1802 oz. ASW

Date	Mintage	F	VF	XF	Unc	BU
1991 Proof	23,000	Value: 10.00				

Note: In Proof sets only

KM# 64 5 CENTS **Composition:** Copper-Nickel
Reverse: Short-beaked Spiny Anteater **Note:** For 1966 dated examples, the length of the whisker on top of the forward-most claw at left will indicate the mint: Canberra (less than .5mm) or London (greater than .6mm).

Date	Mintage	F	VF	XF	Unc	BU
1966(c)	45,427,000	—	0.15	0.25	1.25	—
1966(c) Proof	18,000	Value: 7.50				
1966(L)	30,000,000	—	0.15	0.25	1.25	—
1966(L) Proof	—	Value: 12.50				
1967	62,144,000	—	0.15	0.35	2.25	—
1968	67,336,000	—	0.15	0.40	3.00	—
1969	38,170,000	—	0.15	0.20	1.75	—
1969 Proof	13,000	Value: 10.00				
1970	46,058,000	—	—	0.15	2.25	—
1970 Proof	15,000	Value: 10.00				
1971	39,516,000	—	0.15	0.25	2.50	—
1971 Proof	10,000	Value: 10.00				
1972	8,256,000	0.15	0.30	1.00	7.50	—
1972 Proof	10,000	Value: 8.50				
1973	48,816,000	—	0.15	0.20	0.75	—
1973 Proof	10,000	Value: 8.50				
1974	64,248,000	—	0.15	0.20	0.75	—
1974 Proof	11,000	Value: 8.50				
1975	44,256,000	—	—	0.10	0.40	—
1975 Proof	23,000	Value: 1.75				
1976	113,180,000	—	—	0.10	0.25	—
1976 Proof	21,000	Value: 3.75				
1977	108,800,000	—	—	0.10	0.25	—
1977 Proof	55,000	Value: 1.75				
1978	25,210,000	—	—	0.10	0.25	—
1978 Proof	39,000	Value: 1.75				
1979	44,533,000	—	—	0.10	0.25	—
1979 Proof	36,000	Value: 1.75				
1980	115,042,000	—	—	0.10	0.25	—
1980 Proof	68,000	Value: 1.25				
1981	162,264,000	—	—	0.10	0.25	—
1981 Proof	86,000	Value: 1.25				
1982	139,468,000	—	—	0.10	0.25	—
1982 Proof	100,000	Value: 1.25				
1983	131,568,000	—	—	0.10	0.25	—
1983 Proof	80,000	Value: 1.75				
1984	35,436,000	—	—	0.10	0.25	—
1984 Proof	61,000	Value: 1.75				

KM# 80 5 CENTS **Composition:** Copper-Nickel

Date	Mintage	F	VF	XF	Unc	BU
1985 In Mint sets only	170,000	—	—	—	3.50	—
1985 Proof	75,000	Value: 2.50				
1986 In Mint sets only	180,000	—	—	—	0.75	—
1986 Proof	67,000	Value: 0.75				
1987	73,500,000	—	—	—	0.25	—
1987 Proof	70,000	Value: 0.75				
1988	65,424,000	—	—	—	0.25	—
1988 Proof	106,000	Value: 0.75				
1989	—	—	—	—	0.25	—
1989 Proof	—	Value: 0.75				
1990	1,446,000	—	—	—	0.25	—
1990 Proof	—	Value: 0.75				
1991	29,889,000	—	—	—	0.25	—
1991 Proof	—	Value: 0.75				
1992	3,000,000	—	—	—	0.25	—
1992 Proof	47,000	Value: 0.75				
1993	—	—	—	—	0.25	—
1993 Proof	—	Value: 0.75				
1994	—	—	—	—	0.25	—
1994 Proof	—	Value: 0.75				
1995	—	—	—	—	0.25	—
1995 Proof	—	Value: 0.75				
1996	—	—	—	—	0.25	—
1996 Proof	—	Value: 0.75				
1997	—	—	—	—	0.25	—
1997 Proof	—	Value: 0.75				
1998	—	—	—	—	0.25	—
1998 Proof	—	Value: 0.75				

KM# 80a 5 CENTS **Weight:** 3.2700 g. **Composition:** 0.9250 Silver .0972 oz. ASW

Date	Mintage	F	VF	XF	Unc	BU
1991 Proof	23,000	Value: 15.00				

Note: In Proof sets only

KM# 401 5 CENTS **Composition:** Copper-Nickel
Obverse: Queen's new portrait by Rank-Broadley

Date		F	VF	XF	Unc	BU
1999		—	—	—	0.20	—
1999 Proof	—	Value: 0.75				
2000		—	—	—	0.20	—
2000 Proof	—	Value: 0.75				
2001		—	—	—	0.20	—
2001 Proof	—	Value: 0.75				
2002		—	—	—	0.20	—
2002 Proof	—	Value: 0.75				

KM# 481 5 CENTS **Weight:** 5.5300 g. **Composition:** 0.9990 Silver .1776 oz. ASW **Series:** Masterpieces in Silver **Reverse:** Half penny reverse design of KM#41. **Edge:** Reeded. **Size:** 25 mm.

Date	Mintage	F	VF	XF	Unc	BU
1999 Proof	15,000	Value: 8.00				

KM# 65 10 CENTS **Composition:** Copper-Nickel
Reverse: Superb Lyre-bird **Note:** For 1966 dated examples, 11 spikes on the left Lyre-bird indicates a strike from Canberra, 12 spikes indicate a London strike.

Date	Mintage	F	VF	XF	Unc	BU
1966(c)	10,984,000	—	0.15	0.30	1.75	—
1966(c) Proof	18,000	Value: 8.00				
1966(L)	30,000,000	—	0.15	0.30	1.75	—
1966(L) Proof	—	Value: 12.00				
1967	51,032,000	—	0.15	0.55	6.00	—
1968	57,194,000	—	0.15	0.45	4.25	—
1969	22,146,000	—	0.15	0.25	2.25	—
1969 Proof	13,000	Value: 8.50				
1970	22,306,000	—	0.15	0.25	2.25	—
1970 Proof	15,000	Value: 8.50				
1971	20,726,000	—	0.10	0.25	3.00	—
1971 Proof	10,000	Value: 8.00				
1972	12,502,000	—	0.10	0.25	3.50	—
1972 Proof	10,000	Value: 7.00				
1973	27,320,000	—	0.10	0.15	1.25	—
1973 Proof	10,000	Value: 7.00				
1974	46,550,000	—	0.10	0.15	1.25	—
1974 Proof	11,000	Value: 7.00				
1975	50,900,000	—	0.10	0.15	0.65	—
1975 Proof	23,000	Value: 1.75				
1976	57,060,000	—	0.10	0.15	0.65	—
1976 Proof	21,000	Value: 3.75				
1977	10,940,000	—	0.10	0.15	0.75	—
1977 Proof	55,000	Value: 1.75				
1978	48,400,000	—	0.10	0.15	0.40	—
1978 Proof	39,000	Value: 1.75				
1979	36,950,000	—	0.10	0.15	0.40	—
1979 Proof	36,000	Value: 1.75				
1980	55,084,000	—	0.10	0.15	0.40	—
1980 Proof	68,000	Value: 1.50				
1981	116,060,000	—	0.10	0.15	0.25	—

Note: One 1981 coin was struck on a Sri Lanka 50 cents planchet, KM#135.1. It carries an approximate value of $600

Date	Mintage	F	VF	XF	Unc	BU
1981 Proof	86,000	Value: 1.50				
1982	61,492,000	—	0.10	0.15	0.25	—
1982 Proof	100,000	Value: 1.50				
1983	82,318,000	—	0.10	0.15	0.25	—
1983 Proof	80,000	Value: 1.75				
1984	25,728,000	—	0.10	0.15	0.25	—
1984 Proof	61,000	Value: 1.75				

KM# 81 10 CENTS **Composition:** Copper-Nickel

Date	Mintage	F	VF	XF	Unc	BU
1985	2,100,000	—	—	0.10	0.25	—
1985 Proof	75,000	Value: 1.00				
1986 In sets only	180,000	—	—	—	0.75	—
1986 Proof	67,000	Value: 1.00				
1987 In sets only	200,000	—	—	—	0.75	—
1987 Proof	70,000	Value: 1.00				
1988	35,095,000	—	—	—	0.25	—
1988 Proof	106,000	Value: 1.00				
1989	—	—	—	—	0.25	—
1989 Proof	—	Value: 1.00				
1990	5,452,000	—	—	—	0.25	—
1990 Proof	—	Value: 1.00				
1991	3,174,000	—	—	—	0.25	—
1991 Proof	—	Value: 1.00				
1992	5,589,000	—	—	—	0.25	—
1992 Proof	47,000	Value: 1.00				
1993	—	—	—	—	0.25	—
1993 Proof	—	Value: 1.00				
1994	—	—	—	—	0.25	—
1994 Proof	—	Value: 1.00				
1995	—	—	—	—	0.25	—
1995 Proof	—	Value: 1.00				
1996	—	—	—	—	0.25	—
1996 Proof	—	Value: 1.00				
1997	—	—	—	—	0.25	—
1997 Proof	—	Value: 2.00				
1998	—	—	—	—	0.25	—
1998 Proof	—	Value: 2.00				

KM# 81a 10 CENTS **Weight:** 6.5200 g. **Composition:** 0.9250 Silver .1939 oz. ASW

Date	Mintage	F	VF	XF	Unc	BU
1991 Proof	23,000	Value: 15.00				

Note: In Proof sets only

KM# 402 10 CENTS **Composition:** Copper-Nickel
Obverse: Queen's portrait by Rank-Broadley

Date		F	VF	XF	Unc	BU
1999		—	—	—	0.30	—
1999 Proof	—	Value: 1.00				
2000		—	—	—	0.30	—
2000 Proof	—	Value: 1.00				
2001		—	—	—	0.30	—
2001 Proof	—	Value: 1.00				
2002		—	—	—	0.30	—
2002 Proof	—	Value: 1.00				

KM# 482 10 CENTS **Weight:** 8.3600 g. **Composition:** 0.9990 Silver .2685 oz. ASW **Series:** Masterpieces in Silver **Obverse:** Queen's head right **Reverse:** Penny reverse design of KM#23 **Edge:** Reeded **Size:** 30 mm.

Date	Mintage	F	VF	XF	Unc	BU
1999 Proof	15,000	Value: 12.00				

KM# 66 20 CENTS **Composition:** Copper-Nickel
Reverse: Duckbill Platypus

Date	Mintage	F	VF	XF	Unc	BU
1966(c)	28,223,000	—	0.20	0.75	8.50	—

Note: For 1966 dated examples, strikes from Canberra show a gap between sea line and right face of platypus

Date	Mintage	F	VF	XF	Unc	BU
1966(c) Proof	18,000	Value: 10.00				

Note: For 1966 dated examples, strikes from Canberra show a gap between sea line and right face of platypus

Date	Mintage	F	VF	XF	Unc	BU
1966(L) Wave on base of 2	—	—	—	—	165	—
1966(L)	30,000,000	—	0.20	0.65	7.00	—
1966(L) Proof	—	Value: 12.50				
1967	83,848,000	—	0.20	1.15	12.50	—
1968	40,537,000	—	0.20	1.00	11.00	—
1969	16,501,999	—	0.20	1.00	11.00	—
1969 Proof	13,000	Value: 13.50				
1970	23,271,000	—	0.20	0.50	4.75	—
1970 Proof	15,000	Value: 11.50				
1971	8,947,000	—	0.15	0.65	11.00	—
1971 Proof	10,000	Value: 11.50				
1972	16,643,000	—	0.15	0.50	6.00	—

Date	Mintage	F	VF	XF	Unc	BU
1972 Proof	10,000	Value: 10.00				
1973	23,356,000	—	0.15	0.45	7.00	—
1973 Proof	10,000	Value: 10.00				
1974	33,548,000	—	0.15	0.45	6.50	—
1974 Proof	11,000	Value: 10.00				
1975	53,300,000	—	0.15	0.20	1.75	—
1975 Proof	23,000	Value: 2.25				
1976	59,774,000	—	0.15	0.20	0.75	—
1976 Proof	21,000	Value: 3.75				
1977	41,272,000	—	0.15	0.20	0.75	—
1977 Proof	55,000	Value: 1.75				
1978	38,781,000	—	0.15	0.20	0.75	—
1978 Proof	39,000	Value: 1.75				
1979	22,300,000	—	0.15	0.20	0.75	—
1979 Proof	36,000	Value: 1.75				
1980	77,673,000	—	0.15	0.20	0.50	—
1980 Proof	68,000	Value: 1.25				
1981	164,500,000	—	0.15	0.20	0.50	—

Note: Some 1981 dated coins were struck on a Hong Kong 2 Dollar planchet, KM#37. 6 pieces are reported. Each carries an approximate value of $800

Date	Mintage	F	VF	XF	Unc	BU
1981 Proof	86,000	Value: 1.25				
1982	76,600,000	—	0.15	0.20	0.50	—
1982 Proof	100,000	Value: 1.25				
1983	55,113,000	—	0.15	0.20	0.50	—
1983 Proof	80,000	Value: 1.75				
1984	27,820,000	—	0.15	0.20	0.50	—
1984 Proof	61,000	Value: 1.75				

KM# 82 20 CENTS Composition: Copper-Nickel

Date	Mintage	F	VF	XF	Unc	BU
1985	27,000,000	—	0.15	0.20	0.30	—
1985 Proof	75,000	Value: 1.75				
1986 In sets only	180,000	—	—	—	0.85	—
1986 Proof	67,000	Value: 2.50				
1987 In sets only	200,000	—	—	—	0.85	—
1987 Proof	70,000	Value: 1.25				
1988 In sets only	240,000	—	—	—	0.85	—
1988 Proof	106,000	Value: 1.25				
1989	—	—	—	—	0.50	—
1989 Proof	—	Value: 1.25				
1990	—	—	—	—	0.50	—
1990 Proof	—	Value: 1.25				
1991	—	—	—	—	0.50	—
1991 Proof	—	Value: 1.25				
1992	—	—	—	—	0.50	—
1992 Proof	47,000	Value: 1.25				
1993	—	—	—	—	0.50	—
1993 Proof	—	Value: 1.25				
1994	—	—	—	—	0.50	—
1994 Proof	—	Value: 1.25				
1995	—	—	—	—	0.50	—
1995 Proof	—	Value: 1.25				
1996	—	—	—	—	0.50	—
1996 Proof	—	Value: 1.25				
1997	—	—	—	—	0.50	—
1997 Proof	—	Value: 1.25				
1998	—	—	—	—	0.50	—
1998 Proof	—	Value: 1.25				

KM# 82a 20 CENTS Weight: 13.0900 g. **Composition:** 0.9250 Silver .3893 oz. ASW

Date	Mintage	F	VF	XF	Unc	BU
1991 Proof	23,000	Value: 20.00				

Note: In Proof sets only

KM# 295 20 CENTS Weight: 13.0900 g. **Composition:** 0.9250 Silver .3893 oz. ASW **Subject:** 50th Anniversary - United Nations

Date	F	VF	XF	Unc	BU
1995	—	—	—	1.25	—

KM# 410 20 CENTS Weight: 13.3600 g. **Composition:** 0.9990 Silver .4291 oz. ASW **Subject:** Masterpieces in Silver **Obverse:** Queen's portrait **Reverse:** 1927 florin design

Date	F	VF	XF	Unc	BU
1998 Proof	—	Value: 20.00			

KM# 403 20 CENTS Composition: Copper-Nickel **Obverse:** Queen's portrait by Rank-Broadley **Reverse:** Similar to KM#82

Date	F	VF	XF	Unc	BU
1999	—	—	—	0.50	—
1999 Proof	—	Value: 2.50			
2000	—	—	—	0.50	—
2000 Proof	—	Value: 2.50			
2001	—	—	—	0.50	—
2001 Proof	—	Value: 2.50			
2002	—	—	—	0.50	—
2002 Proof	—	Value: 2.50			

KM# 483 20 CENTS Weight: 2.9900 g. **Composition:** 0.9990 Silver .0960 oz. ASW **Series:** Masterpieces in Silver **Obverse:** Queen's head right **Reverse:** Threepence reverse design of KM#37 **Edge:** Reeded **Size:** 17.5 mm.

Date	Mintage	F	VF	XF	Unc	BU
1999 Proof	15,000	Value: 8.00				

KM# 496 20 CENTS Weight: 13.3600 g. **Composition:** 0.9990 Silver .4291 oz. ASW **Series:** Masterpieces in Silver - 2000 Set **Obverse:** Queen's head right **Reverse:** Edward VII bust right **Edge:** Reeded **Size:** 28.5 mm.

Date	Mintage	F	VF	XF	Unc	BU
2000 Proof	15,000	Value: 25.00				

KM# 497 20 CENTS Weight: 13.3600 g. **Composition:** 0.9990 Silver .4291 oz. ASW **Series:** Masterpieces in Silver - 2000 Set **Obverse:** Queen's head right **Reverse:** George V bust left **Edge:** Reeded **Size:** 28.5 mm.

Date	Mintage	F	VF	XF	Unc	BU
2000 Proof	15,000	Value: 25.00				

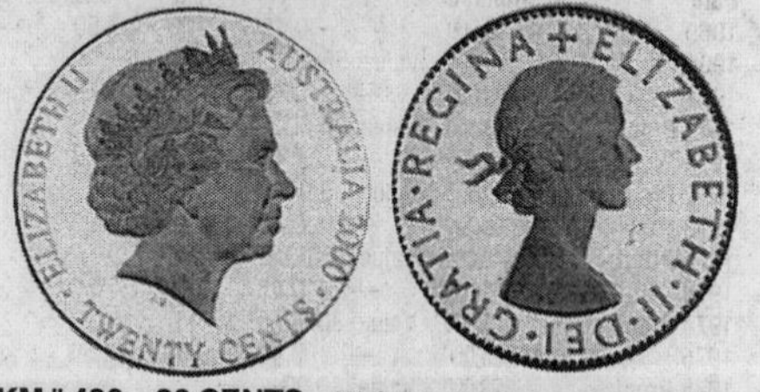

KM# 498 20 CENTS Weight: 13.3600 g. **Composition:** 0.9990 Silver .4291 oz. ASW **Series:** Masterpieces in Silver - 2000 Set **Obverse:** Queen's head right **Reverse:** Queen Elizabeth's first coin design **Edge:** Reeded **Size:** 28.5 mm.

Date	Mintage	F	VF	XF	Unc	BU
2000 Proof	15,000	Value: 25.00				

KM# 532 20 CENTS Weight: 11.3300 g. **Composition:** Copper-Nickel **Subject:** Centennial of Federation - Norfolk **Obverse:** Queen's head right **Reverse:** Plant on island map **Size:** 28.5 mm.

Date	F	VF	XF	Unc	BU
2001	—	—	—	1.75	—

KM# 550 20 CENTS Weight: 11.3000 g. **Composition:** Copper-Nickel **Series:** Centenary of Federation - New South Wales **Obverse:** Queen's head right **Reverse:** Flower on state map **Edge:** Reeded **Size:** 28.5 mm.

Date	F	VF	XF	Unc	BU
2001	—	—	—	1.75	—
2001 Proof	—	Value: 2.50			

KM# 552 (KM551) 20 CENTS Weight: 11.3000 g. **Composition:** Copper-Nickel **Series:** Centenary of Federation - Australian Capital Territory **Obverse:** Queen's head right **Reverse:** Parliament house, map, flowers **Edge:** Reeded **Size:** 28.5 mm.

Date	F	VF	XF	Unc	BU
2001	—	—	—	1.75	—
2001	—	—	—	1.75	—
2001 Proof	—	Value: 2.50			
2001 Proof	—	Value: 2.50			

KM# 554 20 CENTS Weight: 11.3000 g. **Composition:** Copper-Nickel **Series:** Centenary of Federation - Queensland **Obverse:** Queen's head right **Reverse:** Radiant design **Edge:** Reeded **Size:** 28.5 mm.

Date	F	VF	XF	Unc	BU
2001	—	—	—	1.75	—
2001 Proof	—	Value: 2.50			

KM# 556 20 CENTS Weight: 11.3000 g. **Composition:** Copper-Nickel **Series:** Centenary of Federation - Victoria **Obverse:** Queen's head right **Reverse:** Capital building **Edge:** Reeded **Size:** 28.5 mm.

Date	F	VF	XF	Unc	BU
2001	—	—	—	1.75	—
2001 Proof	—	Value: 2.50			

KM# 558 20 CENTS Weight: 11.3000 g. **Composition:** Copper-Nickel **Series:** Centenary of Federation - Northern Territory **Obverse:** Queen's head right **Reverse:** Two brolga cranes in ritual dance **Edge:** Reeded **Size:** 28.5 mm.

Date	F	VF	XF	Unc	BU
2001	—	—	—	1.75	—
2001 Proof	—	Value: 2.50			

KM# 560 20 CENTS Weight: 11.3000 g. **Composition:** Copper-Nickel **Series:** Centenary of Federation - South Australia **Obverse:** Queen's head right **Reverse:** Flower, landscape and stars **Edge:** Reeded **Size:** 28.5 mm.

Date	F	VF	XF	Unc	BU
2001	—	—	—	2.00	—
2001 Proof	—	Value: 2.50			

KM# 562 20 CENTS **Weight:** 11.3000 g. **Composition:** Copper-Nickel **Series:** Centenary of Federation - Western Australia **Obverse:** Queen's head right **Reverse:** Rabbit-eared Bandicoot (bilby), plant and map **Edge:** Reeded **Size:** 28.5 mm.

Date	Mintage	F	VF	XF	Unc	BU
2001		—	—	—	2.00	—
2001 Proof	—	Value: 2.50				

KM# 564 20 CENTS **Weight:** 11.3000 g. **Composition:** Copper-Nickel **Series:** Centenary of Federation - Tasmania **Obverse:** Queen's head right **Reverse:** Tasmanian Devil on map **Edge:** Reeded **Size:** 28.5 mm.

Date	Mintage	F	VF	XF	Unc	BU
2001		—	—	—	2.00	—
2001 Proof	—	Value: 2.50				

KM# 589 20 CENTS **Weight:** 11.3000 g. **Composition:** Copper Nickel **Subject:** Sir Donald Bradman **Obverse:** Bust of Queen Elizabeth II right **Reverse:** Cricket player batsman **Edge:** Reeded **Size:** 28.5 mm.

Date	Mintage	F	VF	XF	Unc	BU
2001	10,000,000				2.00	

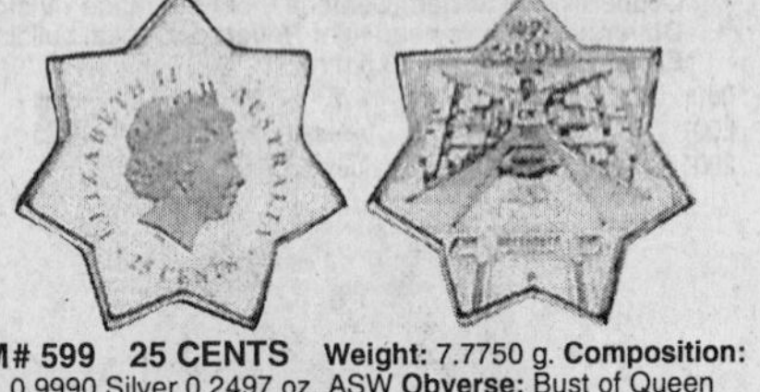

KM# 599 25 CENTS **Weight:** 7.7750 g. **Composition:** 0.9990 Silver 0.2497 oz. ASW **Obverse:** Bust of Queen Elizabeth II right **Reverse:** Parliament House. **Edge:** Plain **Shape:** Star **Size:** 24.5 mm. **Note:** "The Dump" portion of the "Holey Dollar" KM#598.

Date	Mintage	F	VF	XF	Unc	BU
2001 Prooflike	30,000	—	—	—	15.00	—

KM# 113 25 CENTS (The Dump) **Weight:** 7.7750 g. **Composition:** 0.9990 Silver .2500 oz. ASW **Reverse:** Aboriginal Culture

Date	Mintage	F	VF	XF	Unc	BU
1988 Proof	—	Value: 15.00				

KM# 132 25 CENTS (The Dump) **Weight:** 7.7750 g. **Composition:** 0.9990 Silver .2500 oz. ASW **Reverse:** Wandjina of Aboriginal Mythology

Date	Mintage	F	VF	XF	Unc	BU
1989 Proof	45,000	Value: 15.00				

KM# 155 25 CENTS (The Dump) **Weight:** 7.7750 g. **Composition:** 0.9990 Silver .2500 oz. ASW **Reverse:** 3 Mythological Creatures

Date	Mintage	F	VF	XF	Unc	BU
1990 Proof	30,000	Value: 15.00				

KM# 67 50 CENTS **Weight:** 13.2800 g. **Composition:** 0.8000 Silver .3416 oz. ASW

Date	Mintage	F	VF	XF	Unc	BU
1966	36,454,000	—	—	BV	5.50	—
1966 Proof	18,000	Value: 70.00				

KM# 68 50 CENTS **Composition:** Copper-Nickel

Date	Mintage	F	VF	XF	Unc	BU
1969	14,015,000	—	0.45	1.00	7.50	—
1969 Proof	13,000	Value: 55.00				
1971	21,056,000	—	0.45	1.75	7.75	—
1971 Proof	10,000	Value: 35.00				
1972	5,586,000	—	0.45	2.00	8.50	—
1972 Proof	10,000	Value: 35.00				
1973	4,009,000	—	0.45	2.25	15.00	—
1973 Proof	10,000	Value: 35.00				
1974	8,962,000	—	0.45	0.85	7.50	—
1974 Proof	11,000	Value: 30.00				
1975	19,025,000	—	0.40	0.50	2.50	—
1975 Proof	23,000	Value: 10.00				
1976	27,280,000	—	0.40	0.50	2.00	—
1976 Proof	21,000	Value: 20.00				
1978	25,765,000	—	0.40	0.50	0.85	—
1978 Proof	39,000	Value: 6.75				
1979	24,886,000	—	0.40	0.50	0.85	—
1979 Proof	36,000	Value: 7.75				
1980	38,681,000	—	0.40	0.50	0.85	—
1980 Proof	68,000	Value: 5.50				
1981	24,168,000	—	0.40	0.50	0.75	—
1981 Proof	86,000	Value: 5.50				
1983	48,923,000	—	—	0.40	0.75	—
1983 Proof	80,000	Value: 7.75				
1984	26,281,000	—	—	0.40	0.75	—
1984 Proof	61,000	Value: 7.75				

KM# 69 50 CENTS **Composition:** Copper-Nickel **Subject:** 200th Anniversary - Cook's Australian Voyage

Date	Mintage	F	VF	XF	Unc	BU
1970	17,100,000	—	0.40	1.25	3.50	—
1970 Proof	15,000	Value: 50.00				

KM# 70 50 CENTS **Composition:** Copper-Nickel **Subject:** Queen's Silver Jubilee

Date	Mintage	F	VF	XF	Unc	BU
1977	25,076,000	—	0.40	0.50	1.25	—
1977 Proof	55,000	Value: 6.75				

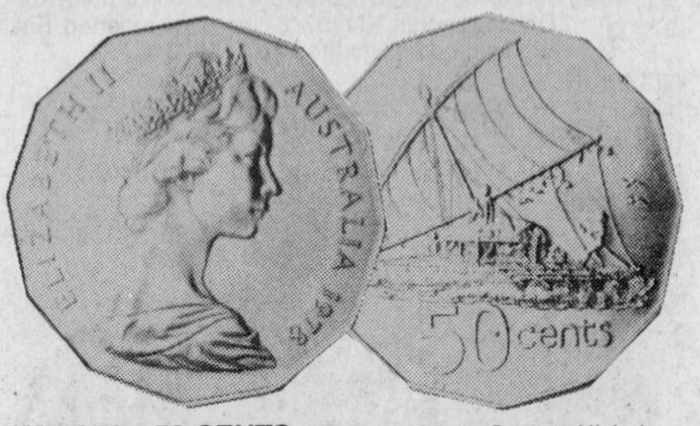

KM# A72 50 CENTS **Composition:** Copper-Nickel **Subject:** Mule **Obverse:** KM#70 **Reverse:** Fiji 50 Cent, KM#36

Date	F	VF	XF	Unc	BU
1978	—	—	—	—	—

KM# 72 50 CENTS **Composition:** Copper-Nickel **Subject:** Wedding of Prince Charles and Lady Diana

Date	Mintage	F	VF	XF	Unc	BU
1981	44,100,000	—	0.40	0.50	1.25	—

KM# 74 50 CENTS **Composition:** Copper-Nickel **Subject:** XII Commonwealth Games - Birsbane

Date	Mintage	F	VF	XF	Unc	BU
1982	23,287,000	—	0.40	0.50	1.25	—
1982 Proof	100,000	Value: 5.50				

KM# 83 50 CENTS **Composition:** Copper-Nickel

Date	Mintage	F	VF	XF	Unc	BU
1985	1,000,000	—	—	0.40	0.60	—
1985 Proof	75,000	Value: 3.50				
1986 In sets only	180,000	—	—	—	3.00	—
1986 Proof	67,000	Value: 3.50				
1987 In sets only	200,000	—	—	—	3.00	—
1987 Proof	70,000	Value: 3.50				
1989	—	—	—	—	2.25	—
1989 Proof	—	Value: 3.50				
1990	—	—	—	—	2.25	—
1990 Proof	—	Value: 3.50				
1992	—	—	—	—	2.25	—

Date	Mintage	F	VF	XF	Unc	BU
1992 Proof	47,000	Value: 3.50				
1993	—	—	—	—	2.25	—
1993 Proof	—	Value: 3.50				
1996	—	—	—	—	2.25	—
1996 Proof	—	Value: 3.50				
1997	—	—	—	—	2.25	—
1997 Proof	—	Value: 3.50				

KM# 99 50 CENTS Composition: Copper-Nickel **Subject:** Australian Bicentennial

Date	Mintage	F	VF	XF	Unc	BU
1988	2,793,000	—	—	—	2.25	—
1988 Proof	106,000	Value: 3.50				

KM# 99a 50 CENTS Weight: 18.0000 g. **Composition:** 0.9250 Silver .5353 oz. ASW

Date	Mintage	F	VF	XF	Unc	BU
1988 Proof	25,000	Value: 22.50				
1989 Proof	25,000	Value: 22.50				

KM# 127 50 CENTS Weight: 18.0000 g. **Composition:** 0.9250 Silver .5353 oz. ASW **Subject:** Cook Commemorative **Obverse:** Similar to KM#99 **Reverse:** Similar to KM#69

Date	Mintage	F	VF	XF	Unc	BU
1989 Proof	25,000	Value: 22.50				

KM# 128 50 CENTS Weight: 18.0000 g. **Composition:** 0.9250 Silver .5353 oz. ASW **Subject:** Queen's Silver Jubilee **Obverse:** Similar to KM#99 **Reverse:** Similar to KM#70

Date	Mintage	F	VF	XF	Unc	BU
1989 Proof	25,000	Value: 22.50				

KM# 129 50 CENTS Weight: 18.0000 g. **Composition:** 0.9250 Silver .5353 oz. ASW **Subject:** Wedding of Prince Charles and Lady Diana **Obverse:** Similar to KM#99 **Reverse:** Similar to KM#72

Date	Mintage	F	VF	XF	Unc	BU
1989 Proof	25,000	Value: 22.50				

KM# 130 50 CENTS Weight: 18.0000 g. **Composition:** 0.9250 Silver .5353 oz. ASW **Subject:** XII Commonwealth Games - Brisbane **Obverse:** Similar to KM#99 **Reverse:** Similar to KM#74

Date	Mintage	F	VF	XF	Unc	BU
1989 Proof	25,000	Value: 22.50				

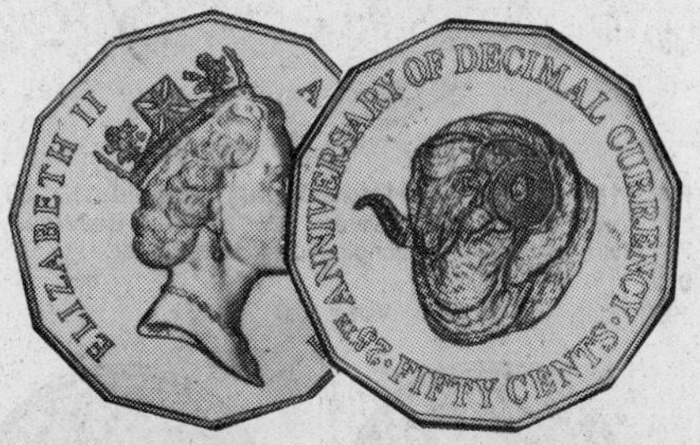

KM# 139 50 CENTS Composition: Copper-Nickel **Subject:** 25th Anniversary of Decimal Currency - Merino Ram

Date	Mintage	F	VF	XF	Unc	BU
1991	4,364,000	—	—	1.00	3.00	—
1991 Proof	—	Value: 11.50				

KM# 139a 50 CENTS Weight: 18.0000 g. **Composition:** 0.9250 Silver .5353 oz. ASW

Date	Mintage	F	VF	XF	Unc	BU
1991 Proof	23,000	Value: 18.00				

Note: In Proof sets only

KM# 257 50 CENTS Weight: 18.0000 g. **Composition:** 0.9250 Silver .5353 oz. ASW **Subject:** International Year of the Family

Date	F	VF	XF	Unc	BU
1994	—	—	1.00	3.00	—
1994 Proof	— Value: 11.50				

KM# 294 50 CENTS Weight: 18.0000 g. **Composition:** 0.9250 Silver .5353 oz. ASW **Subject:** Weary Dunlop

Date	F	VF	XF	Unc	BU
1995	—	—	0.85	2.75	—
1995 Proof	— Value: 11.50				

KM# 364 50 CENTS Weight: 18.0000 g. **Composition:** 0.9250 Silver .5353 oz. ASW **Subject:** George Bass and Matthew Flinders **Obverse:** Queen's portrait **Reverse:** Portraits of Bass and Flinders

Date	F	VF	XF	Unc	BU
1998	—	—	0.85	2.75	—
1998 Proof	— Value: 11.50				

KM# 411 50 CENTS Weight: 36.3100 g. **Composition:** 0.9990 Silver 1.1662 oz. ASW **Subject:** Masterpieces in Silver **Obverse:** Queen's portrait **Reverse:** 1937 crown design

Date	Mintage	F	VF	XF	Unc	BU
1998 Proof	15,000	Value: 25.00				

KM# 404 50 CENTS Composition: Copper-Nickel **Obverse:** Queen's portrait by Rank-Broadley **Reverse:** Similar to KM#83

Date	F	VF	XF	Unc	BU
1999	—	—	0.85	2.75	—
1999 Proof	— Value: 6.50				
2001	—	—	0.85	2.75	—

KM# 484 50 CENTS Weight: 3.2400 g. **Composition:** 0.9990 Silver .1041 oz. ASW **Series:** Masterpieces in Silver **Obverse:** Queen's head right **Reverse:** Sixpence reverse design of KM#25 **Edge:** Reeded **Size:** 19.4 mm.

Date	Mintage	F	VF	XF	Unc	BU
1999 Proof	15,000	Value: 10.00				

KM# 501 50 CENTS Weight: 16.8860 g. **Composition:** 0.9990 Silver .5424 oz. ASW **Subject:** Year of the Rabbit **Obverse:** Queen's head right **Reverse:** Rabbit **Edge:** Reeded **Size:** 32.1 mm.

Date	Mintage	F	VF	XF	Unc	BU
1999	—	—	—	—	15.00	—
1999 Proof	5,000	Value: 25.00				

KM# 437 50 CENTS Composition: Copper-Nickel **Subject:** Royal Visit **Obverse:** Queen's head right **Reverse:** Australian flag above Canberra Parliament House, British crown at right **Edge:** Plain 12-sided edge

Date	Mintage	F	VF	XF	Unc	BU
2000 Proof	5,000	Value: 2.50				

KM# 437a 50 CENTS Weight: 18.2400 g. **Composition:** 0.9990 Silver .5858 oz. ASW **Subject:** Royal Visit **Obverse:** Queen's head right **Reverse:** Australian flag above Canberra Parliament House, British crown at right

Date	Mintage	F	VF	XF	Unc	BU
2000 Proof	25,000	Value: 27.50				

KM# 488.1 (KM488) 50 CENTS Weight: 15.5500 g. **Composition:** Copper-Nickel **Subject:** Millennium **Obverse:** Queen's head right **Reverse:** Australian flag **Edge:** Plain, 12-sided **Size:** 31.5 mm.

Date	F	VF	XF	Unc	BU
2000	—	—	—	3.00	—
2000	—	—	—	3.00	—

KM# 488.2 (KM488.1) 50 CENTS Weight: 15.5500 g. **Composition:** Copper-Nickel **Subject:** Millennium **Obverse:** Queen's head right **Reverse:** Multicolor Australian flag **Edge:** Plain, 12-sided **Size:** 31.5 mm.

Date	F	VF	XF	Unc	BU
2000 Proof	— Value: 12.50				
2000 Proof	— Value: 12.50				

KM# 522 50 CENTS Weight: 16.8860 g. **Composition:** 0.9990 Silver .5424 oz. ASW **Series:** Dragons **Obverse:** Queen's head right **Reverse:** Dragon **Edge:** Reeded **Size:** 32.1 mm.

Date	F	VF	XF	Unc	BU
2000 Proof	— Value: 25.00				

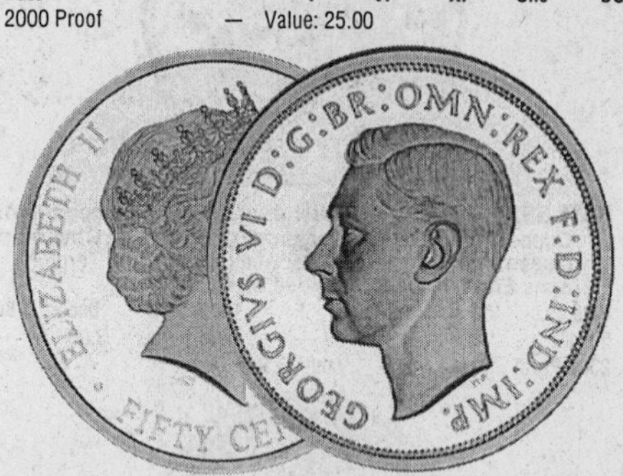

KM# 499 50 CENTS Weight: 36.3100 g. **Composition:** 0.9990 Silver 1.1662 oz. ASW **Series:** Masterpieces in Silver - 2000 Set **Obverse:** Queen's head right **Reverse:** George VI's head left **Edge:** Reeded **Size:** 38.7 mm.

Date	Mintage	F	VF	XF	Unc	BU
2000 Proof	15,000	Value: 30.00				

KM# 491.1 (KM491) 50 CENTS Composition: Copper-Nickel **Subject:** Centenary of Federation, 1901-2001 **Obverse:** Queen's head right **Reverse:** Commonwealth coat of arms **Edge:** Plain 12-sided **Size:** 31.5 mm.

Date	F	VF	XF	Unc	BU
2001	—	—	—	2.50	—

KM# 491.2a (KM491a) 50 CENTS Weight: 18.2400 g. **Composition:** 0.9990 Silver .5858 oz. ASW **Subject:** Centenary of Federation, 1901-2001 **Obverse:** Queen's head right **Reverse:** Commonwealth coat of arms **Edge:** Plain 12-sided **Size:** 31.5 mm.

Date	F	VF	XF	Unc	BU
2001 Proof	— Value: 27.50				

KM# 533 50 CENTS Weight: 15.6000 g. **Composition:** Copper-Nickel **Subject:** Centennial - Norfolk Island Federation **Obverse:** Queen's head right **Reverse:** Norfolk Island coat of arms **Edge:** Plain 12-sided **Size:** 31.4 mm.

Date	F	VF	XF	Unc	BU
2001	—	—	—	2.50	—

KM# 535 50 CENTS Weight: 16.8860 g. **Composition:** 0.9990 Silver .5424 oz. ASW **Subject:** Year of the Snake

Obverse: Bust of Queen Elizabeth II right **Reverse:** Snake with eggs **Edge:** Reeded **Size:** 32.1 mm.

Date	Mintage	F	VF	XF	Unc	BU
2001	500,000	—	—	—	15.00	—
2001P Proof	5,000	Value: 36.00				

KM# 551 50 CENTS **Weight:** 15.5500 g. **Composition:** Copper-Nickel **Series:** Centenary of Federation **Obverse:** Queen's head right **Reverse:** New South Wales state arms **Edge:** Reeded, 12-sided **Size:** 31.5 mm.

Date	F	VF	XF	Unc	BU
2001	—	—	—	3.00	—
2001 Proof	— Value: 6.50				

KM# 553 50 CENTS **Weight:** 15.5500 g. **Composition:** Copper-Nickel **Series:** Centenary of Federation **Obverse:** Queen's head right **Reverse:** Australian Capital Territory arms **Edge:** Reeded, 12-sided **Size:** 31.5 mm.

Date	F	VF	XF	Unc	BU
2001	—	—	—	3.00	—
2001 Proof	— Value: 6.50				

KM# 555 50 CENTS **Weight:** 15.5500 g. **Composition:** Copper-Nickel **Series:** Centenary of Federation **Obverse:** Queen's head right **Reverse:** Queensland state arms **Edge:** Reeded, 12-sided **Size:** 31.5 mm.

Date	F	VF	XF	Unc	BU
2001	—	—	—	3.00	—
2001 Proof	— Value: 6.50				

KM# 557 50 CENTS **Weight:** 15.5500 g. **Composition:** Copper-Nickel **Series:** Centenary of Federation **Obverse:** Queen's head right **Reverse:** Victoria state arms **Edge:** Reeded, 12-sided **Size:** 31.5 mm.

Date	F	VF	XF	Unc	BU
2001	—	—	—	3.00	—
2001 Proof	— Value: 6.50				

KM# 559 50 CENTS **Weight:** 15.5500 g. **Composition:** Copper-Nickel **Series:** Centenary of Federation **Obverse:** Queen's head right **Reverse:** Northern Territory state arms **Edge:** Reeded, 12-sided **Size:** 31.5 mm.

Date	F	VF	XF	Unc	BU
2001	—	—	—	3.00	—
2001 Proof	— Value: 6.50				

KM# 561 50 CENTS **Weight:** 15.5500 g. **Composition:** Copper-Nickel **Series:** Centenary of Federation **Obverse:** Queen's head right **Reverse:** South Australia state arms **Edge:** Reeded, 12-sided **Size:** 31.5 mm.

Date	F	VF	XF	Unc	BU
2001	—	—	—	3.00	—
2001 Proof	— Value: 6.50				

KM# 563 50 CENTS **Weight:** 15.5500 g. **Composition:** Copper-Nickel **Series:** Centenary of Federation **Obverse:** Queen's head right **Reverse:** Western Australia state arms **Edge:** Reeded, 12-sided **Size:** 31.5 mm.

Date	F	VF	XF	Unc	BU
2001	—	—	—	3.00	—
2001 Proof	— Value: 6.50				

KM# 565 50 CENTS **Weight:** 15.5500 g. **Composition:** Copper-Nickel **Series:** Centenary of Federation **Obverse:** Queen's head right **Reverse:** Tasmania state arms **Edge:** Reeded, 12-sided **Size:** 31.5 mm.

Date	F	VF	XF	Unc	BU
2001	—	—	—	3.00	—
2001 Proof	— Value: 6.50				

KM# 579 50 CENTS **Weight:** 15.5518 g. **Composition:** 0.9990 Silver 0.4995 oz. ASW **Subject:** Year of the Horse **Obverse:** Bust of Queen Elizabeth II right **Reverse:** Horse running left **Edge:** Reeded **Size:** 32.1 mm.

Date	Mintage	F	VF	XF	Unc	BU
2002P Proof	5,000	Value: 36.00				

KM# 602 50 CENTS **Weight:** 15.5500 g. **Composition:** Copper Nickel **Subject:** The Outback Region **Obverse:** Bust of Queen Elizabeth II right **Reverse:** Windmill **Edge:** Plain, 12-sided **Size:** 31.5 mm.

Date	F	VF	XF	Unc	BU
2002	—	—	—	3.00	—
2002 Proof	—	—	—	—	—

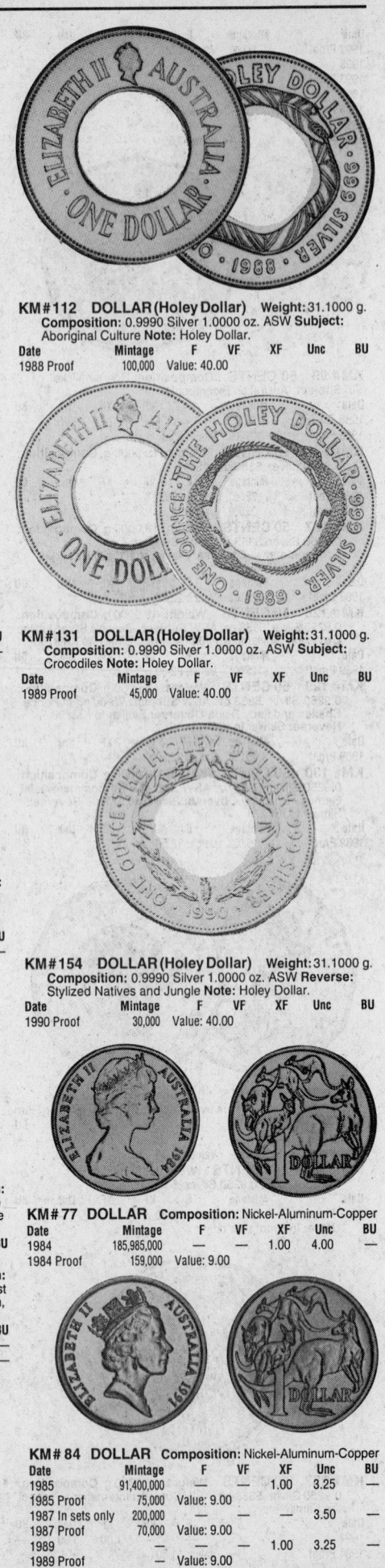

KM# 112 DOLLAR (Holey Dollar) **Weight:** 31.1000 g. **Composition:** 0.9990 Silver 1.0000 oz. ASW **Subject:** Aboriginal Culture **Note:** Holey Dollar.

Date	Mintage	F	VF	XF	Unc	BU
1988 Proof	100,000	Value: 40.00				

KM# 131 DOLLAR (Holey Dollar) **Weight:** 31.1000 g. **Composition:** 0.9990 Silver 1.0000 oz. ASW **Subject:** Crocodiles **Note:** Holey Dollar.

Date	Mintage	F	VF	XF	Unc	BU
1989 Proof	45,000	Value: 40.00				

KM# 154 DOLLAR (Holey Dollar) **Weight:** 31.1000 g. **Composition:** 0.9990 Silver 1.0000 oz. ASW **Reverse:** Stylized Natives and Jungle **Note:** Holey Dollar.

Date	Mintage	F	VF	XF	Unc	BU
1990 Proof	30,000	Value: 40.00				

KM# 77 DOLLAR **Composition:** Nickel-Aluminum-Copper

Date	Mintage	F	VF	XF	Unc	BU
1984	185,985,000	—	—	1.00	4.00	—
1984 Proof	159,000	Value: 9.00				

KM# 84 DOLLAR **Composition:** Nickel-Aluminum-Copper

Date	Mintage	F	VF	XF	Unc	BU
1985	91,400,000	—	—	1.00	3.25	—
1985 Proof	75,000	Value: 9.00				
1987 In sets only	200,000	—	—	—	3.50	—
1987 Proof	70,000	Value: 9.00				
1989	—	—	—	1.00	3.25	—
1989 Proof	—	Value: 9.00				
1990	—	—	—	1.00	3.25	—

Date	Mintage	F	VF	XF	Unc	BU
1990 Proof	—	Value: 9.00				
1991	—	—	—	1.00	3.25	—
1991 Proof	—	Value: 9.00				
1994	—	—	—	1.00	3.25	—
1994 Proof	—	Value: 9.00				
1995	—	—	—	1.00	3.25	—
1995 Proof	—	Value: 9.00				
1998	—	—	—	1.00	3.25	—
1998 Proof	—	Value: 9.00				

KM# 87 DOLLAR **Composition:** Nickel-Aluminum-Copper **Subject:** International Year of Peace

Date	Mintage	F	VF	XF	Unc	BU
1986	25,100,000	—	—	1.00	4.00	—
1986 Proof	67,000	Value: 20.00				

KM# 100 DOLLAR **Composition:** Aluminum-Bronze **Subject:** Aboriginal Art

Date	Mintage	F	VF	XF	Unc	BU
1988	1,564,000	—	—	—	4.00	—
1988 Proof	106,000	Value: 18.50				

KM# 100a DOLLAR **Weight:** 11.4900 g. **Composition:** 0.9250 Silver .3417 oz. ASW **Subject:** Masterpieces in Silver

Date	Mintage	F	VF	XF	Unc	BU
1988 Proof	25,000	Value: 35.00				
1990 Proof	25,000	Value: 35.00				

KM# 84a DOLLAR **Weight:** 11.4900 g. **Composition:** 0.9250 Silver .3417 oz. ASW **Subject:** Masterpieces in Silver

Date	Mintage	F	VF	XF	Unc	BU
1990 Proof	25,000	Value: 35.00				
1991 Proof	23,000	Value: 35.00				

Note: In Proof sets only

KM# 87a DOLLAR **Weight:** 11.4900 g. **Composition:** 0.9250 Silver .3417 oz. ASW **Subject:** Masterpieces in Silver

Date	Mintage	F	VF	XF	Unc	BU
1990 Proof	25,000	Value: 35.00				

KM# 164 DOLLAR **Weight:** 31.1000 g. **Composition:** 0.9990 Silver 1.0000 oz. ASW **Reverse:** Australian Kookaburra

Date	Mintage	F	VF	XF	Unc	BU
1992	300,000	—	—	—	12.00	—
1993	300,000	—	—	—	12.00	—

KM# 175 DOLLAR **Composition:** Nickel-Aluminum-Copper **Subject:** Olympics - Female Javelin Thrower **Edge:** Alternating reeded and plain sections

Date	Mintage	F	VF	XF	Unc	BU
1992	16,000	—	—	—	4.00	—
1992 Proof	47,000	Value: 20.00				

KM# 175a.1 DOLLAR **Weight:** 11.4900 g. **Composition:** 0.9250 Silver .3412 oz. ASW

Date	Mintage	F	VF	XF	Unc	BU
1992 Proof	12,500	Value: 85.00				

Note: In Proof sets only

KM# 175a.2 DOLLAR **Weight:** 11.4900 g. **Composition:** 0.9250 Silver .3412 oz. ASW **Edge:** Reeded

Date	Mintage	F	VF	XF	Unc	BU
1992 Proof	2,500	Value: 300				

KM# 209 DOLLAR **Weight:** 31.1000 g. **Composition:** 0.9990 Silver 1.0000 oz. ASW **Subject:** Australian Kookaburra

Date		F	VF	XF	Unc	BU
1992 Proof	—	Value: 40.00				
1992 (ae) Proof	750	Value: 185				
1993		—	—	—	12.50	—

KM# 211.1 DOLLAR **Weight:** 31.5700 g. **Composition:** 0.9990 Silver 1.0140 oz. ASW **Reverse:** Kangaroo **Edge:** Reeded

Date	Mintage	F	VF	XF	Unc	BU
1993C	73,000	—	—	—	20.00	—

KM# 211.2 DOLLAR **Weight:** 31.5700 g. **Composition:** 0.9990 Silver 1.0140 oz. ASW **Edge:** Reeded and plain sections

Date	Mintage	F	VF	XF	Unc	BU
1993C	5,000	—	—	—	50.00	—

KM# 212.1 DOLLAR **Weight:** 31.1035 g. **Composition:** 0.9990 Silver 1.0000 oz. ASW **Reverse:** Pair of Kookaburras

Date	Mintage	F	VF	XF	Unc	BU
1993 AE Proof	—	Value: 18.00				
1993 AE Proof	—	Value: 18.00				
1993 (ge) Proof	500	Value: 65.00				
1993 (so) Proof	13,000	Value: 45.00				
1994 Proof	2,500	Value: 25.00				
1994 (ta) Specimen	15,000	—	—	—	22.50	—

KM# 212.2 DOLLAR **Weight:** 31.1035 g. **Composition:** 0.9990 Silver 1.0000 oz. ASW **Reverse:** American Eagle privy mark above date

Date		F	VF	XF	Unc	BU
1993 AE Proof		—	—	—	—	—
1993 AE Proof	500	Value: 65.00				

KM# 208 DOLLAR **Composition:** Nickel-Aluminum-Copper **Note:** Visitors at mints and coin shows were allowed to strike a coin for a fee at the following C - Canberra, M - Hall of Manufacturers Pavilion Coin Show, Melbourne and S - Sydney International Coin Fair.

Date	Mintage	F	VF	XF	Unc	BU
1993	15,000,000	—	—	—	2.85	—
1993 Proof	—	Value: 16.50				
1993C	92,000	—	—	—	3.00	—
1993M	60,000	—	—	—	3.00	—
1993S Proof	88,000	—	—	—	3.00	—

KM# 208a.1 DOLLAR **Composition:** Silver **Edge:** Alternating reeded and plain sections

Date	Mintage	F	VF	XF	Unc	BU
1993 Proof	20,000	Value: 42.50				

KM# 208a.2 DOLLAR **Composition:** Silver **Edge:** Reeded

Date	Mintage	F	VF	XF	Unc	BU
1993 Proof	5,001	Value: 120				

KM# 258 DOLLAR **Composition:** Nickel-Aluminum-Copper **Subject:** 10th Anniversary - Introduction of Dollar Coin

Date	Mintage	F	VF	XF	Unc	BU
1994C	123,000	—	—	—	3.00	—
1994M	65,000	—	—	—	3.50	—
1994S	74,000	—	—	—	3.50	—

KM# 258a.1 DOLLAR **Weight:** 14.4900 g. **Composition:** 0.9250 Silver .3417 oz. ASW **Edge:** Reeded and plain sections

Date	Mintage	F	VF	XF	Unc	BU
1994 Proof	20,000	Value: 42.50				

KM# 258a.2 DOLLAR **Weight:** 14.4900 g. **Composition:** 0.9250 Silver .3417 oz. ASW **Edge:** Reeded

Date	Mintage	F	VF	XF	Unc	BU
1994 Proof	5,000	Value: 135				

KM# 260 DOLLAR **Weight:** 31.1035 g. **Composition:** 0.9990 Silver 1.0000 oz. ASW **Reverse:** Kookaburra on branch

Date	Mintage	F	VF	XF	Unc	BU
1994 Proof	2,500	Value: 45.00				
1995 Proof	300,000	Value: 12.50				

KM# 263.1 DOLLAR **Weight:** 31.6350 g. **Composition:** 0.9990 Silver 1.0161 oz. ASW **Obverse:** Queen Elizabeth portrait **Reverse:** Kangaroo leaping right **Edge:** Reeded

Date	Mintage	F	VF	XF	Unc	BU
1994C	45,000	—	—	—	20.00	—

KM# 263.2 DOLLAR **Weight:** 31.6350 g. **Composition:** 0.9990 Silver 1.0161 oz. ASW **Edge:** Reeded and plain sections

Date	Mintage	F	VF	XF	Unc	BU
1994C	2,500	—	—	—	120	—

KM# 289.1 DOLLAR **Weight:** 31.6350 g. **Composition:** 0.9990 Silver 1.0161 oz. ASW **Reverse:** Kookaburra in flight

Date	Mintage	F	VF	XF	Unc	BU
1995P Proof	4,900	Value: 20.00				
1996	300,000	—	—	—	18.00	—
1996 (bg)	5,000	—	—	—	40.00	—
1996 (ba)	2,500	—	—	—	42.00	—
1996 (sr)	5,000	—	—	—	40.00	—

KM# 269 DOLLAR **Composition:** Nickel-Aluminum-Copper **Subject:** A.B. Banjo Paterson - Waltzing Matilda

Date	Mintage	F	VF	XF	Unc	BU
1995B	74,000	—	—	—	5.00	—
1995C	156,000	—	—	—	4.50	—
1995M	74,000	—	—	—	5.00	—
1995S	83,000	—	—	—	5.00	—

KM# 269a.1 DOLLAR **Weight:** 14.4900 g. **Composition:** 0.9250 Silver .3417 oz. ASW **Edge:** Alternating reeded and plain sections

Date	Mintage	F	VF	XF	Unc	BU
1995 Proof	20,000	Value: 30.00				

KM# 269a.2 DOLLAR **Weight:** 14.4900 g. **Composition:** 0.9250 Silver .3417 oz. ASW **Edge:** Reeded

Date		F	VF	XF	Unc	BU
1995 Proof	Est. 2,500	Value: 50.00				

KM# 289.2 DOLLAR **Weight:** 31.1035 g. **Composition:** 0.9990 Silver 1.0000 oz. ASW **Edge:** Reeded and inscribed with date and serial

Date	Mintage	F	VF	XF	Unc	BU
1996	1,500	—	—	—	45.00	—

KM# 293.1 DOLLAR **Weight:** 31.6350 g. **Composition:** 0.9990 Silver 1.0161 oz. ASW **Reverse:** Kangaroo portrait **Edge:** Reeded

Date	Mintage	F	VF	XF	Unc	BU
1995C	73,000	—	—	—	20.00	—

KM# 293.2 DOLLAR **Weight:** 31.6350 g. **Composition:** 0.9990 Silver 1.0161 oz. ASW **Edge:** Reeded and plain sections

Date	Mintage	F	VF	XF	Unc	BU
1995C	2,500	—	—	—	110	—

KM# 297 DOLLAR **Weight:** 31.6350 g. **Composition:** 0.9990 Silver 1.0161 oz. ASW **Reverse:** Mother and Baby Kangaroo

Date	F	VF	XF	Unc	BU
1996	—	—	—	22.50	—

KM# 310 DOLLAR **Composition:** Nickel-Aluminum-Copper **Subject:** Sir Henry Parks

Date	Mintage	F	VF	XF	Unc	BU
1996	—	—	—	—	4.00	—
1996 Proof	—	—	—	—	—	—
1996A	—	—	—	—	4.50	—
1996B	—	—	—	—	4.50	—
1996C	25,000	—	—	—	5.50	—
1996M	—	—	—	—	4.50	—
1996S	64,000	—	—	—	4.50	—

KM# 310a DOLLAR **Weight:** 11.4900 g. **Composition:** 0.9250 Silver .3417 oz. ASW

Date	Mintage	F	VF	XF	Unc	BU
1996 Proof	20,000	Value: 17.50				

KM# 326 DOLLAR **Weight:** 31.1035 g. **Composition:** 0.9990 Silver 1.0000 oz. ASW **Subject:** 30th Anniversary - Decimal Coinage **Obverse:** Queen's portrait **Reverse:** Map and seven different coin designs

Date	F	VF	XF	Unc	BU
1996 Proof	—	Value: 60.00			

KM# 325 DOLLAR **Weight:** 31.5600 g. **Composition:** 0.9990 Silver 1.0136 oz. ASW **Obverse:** Queen's portrait **Reverse:** Kangaroo drinking water, reflection

Date	F	VF	XF	Unc	BU
1997C	—	—	—	22.50	—

KM# 327 DOLLAR **Composition:** Nickel-Aluminum-Copper **Subject:** Sir Charles Kingsford Smith **Obverse:** Queen's portrait **Reverse:** Pilot above airplane, dates

Date	F	VF	XF	Unc	BU
1997	—	—	—	4.00	—

KM# 355 DOLLAR **Composition:** Nickel-Aluminum-Copper **Subject:** Sir Charles Kingsford Smith **Obverse:** Queen's portrait **Reverse:** Portrait and airplane over map

Date	F	VF	XF	Unc	BU
1997A	—	—	—	3.00	—
1997B	—	—	—	3.00	—
1997C	—	—	—	3.00	—
1997M	—	—	—	3.00	—
1997S	—	—	—	3.00	—

KM# 355a DOLLAR **Weight:** 11.6600 g. **Composition:** 0.9990 Silver .3752 oz. ASW

Date	Mintage	F	VF	XF	Unc	BU
1997 Proof	20,000	Value: 17.50				

KM# 362 DOLLAR **Weight:** 31.1035 g. **Composition:** 0.9990 Silver 1.0000 oz. ASW **Subject:** Kookaburra **Obverse:** Queen's portrait **Reverse:** Bird on fence

Date	Mintage	F	VF	XF	Unc	BU
1997 Proof	2,000	Value: 30.00				
1998 (1997)	—	—	—	—	15.00	—

KM# 318 DOLLAR **Weight:** 31.1035 g. **Composition:** 0.9990 Silver 1.0000 oz. ASW **Reverse:** Kookaburra and Nestlings **Note:** With Utrecht Coat of Arms privy mark.

Date	Mintage	F	VF	XF	Unc	BU
1997	300,000	—	—	—	13.50	—

KM# 365 DOLLAR **Weight:** 32.0000 g. **Composition:** 0.9990 Silver 1.0278 oz. ASW **Obverse:** Queen's portrait **Reverse:** Kangaroo bounding left

Date	F	VF	XF	Unc	BU
1998C	—	—	—	20.00	—

KM# 366 DOLLAR **Composition:** Nickel-Aluminum-Copper **Subject:** Howard Florey **Obverse:** Queen's portrait **Reverse:** Portrait of Florey

Date	F	VF	XF	Unc	BU
1998A	—	—	—	4.25	—
1998B	—	—	—	4.25	—
1998C	—	—	—	4.25	—
1998M	—	—	—	4.25	—
1998S	—	—	—	4.25	—

KM# 366a DOLLAR **Weight:** 11.6600 g. **Composition:** 0.9990 Silver .3745 oz. ASW

Date	Mintage	F	VF	XF	Unc	BU
1998 Proof only	20,000	Value: 20.00				

KM# 412 DOLLAR **Weight:** 31.1035 g. **Composition:** 0.9990 Silver 1.0000 oz. ASW **Subject:** 10th Anniversary - New Parliament House **Obverse:** Queen's portrait **Reverse:** Parliament building

Date	Mintage	F	VF	XF	Unc	BU
1998 Proof	17,000	Value: 60.00				

KM# 398 DOLLAR **Weight:** 32.2500 g. **Composition:** 0.9990 Silver 1.0358 oz. ASW **Obverse:** Queen's portrait by Rank-Broadley **Reverse:** Pair of kangaroos

Date	F	VF	XF	Unc	BU
1999	—	—	—	20.00	—
1999 Proof	—	Value: 30.00			

KM# 399 DOLLAR **Weight:** 32.2500 g. **Composition:** 0.9990 Silver 1.0358 oz. ASW **Obverse:** Queen's portrait **Reverse:** Adult and chick kookaburras on branch

Date	F	VF	XF	Unc	BU
1999	—	—	—	14.00	—

KM# 400 DOLLAR **Composition:** Nickel-Aluminum-Copper **Subject:** The Last of the Anzaca **Obverse:** Queen's portrait **Reverse:** Anzac soldier wearing bush hat

Date	F	VF	XF	Unc	BU
1999A	—	—	—	4.25	—
1999C	—	—	—	4.25	—
1999M	—	—	—	4.25	—
1999S	—	—	—	4.25	—
1999B	—	—	—	4.25	—
2000	—	—	—	4.25	—

KM# 400a DOLLAR **Weight:** 11.6600 g. **Composition:** 0.9990 Silver .3745 oz. ASW **Subject:** The Last of the Anzacs **Obverse:** Queen's head right **Reverse:** Anzac soldier wearing bush hat **Edge:** Reeded and plain sections on edge

Date	Mintage	F	VF	XF	Unc	BU
1999 Proof	25,000	Value: 25.00				

KM# 405 DOLLAR **Composition:** Nickel-Aluminum-Copper **Subject:** International Year of Older People **Obverse:** Queen's portrait **Reverse:** IYPO logo **Size:** 25 mm.

Date	F	VF	XF	Unc	BU
1999	—	—	—	4.25	—
1999 Proof	—	Value: 14.00			

KM# 416 DOLLAR **Weight:** 31.7700 g. **Composition:** 0.9990 Silver 1.0204 oz. ASW **Obverse:** Queen's head right **Reverse:** Kookaburra on branch

Date	F	VF	XF	Unc	BU
1999	—	—	—	16.00	—
2000 (1999)	—	—	—	16.00	—

KM# 476 DOLLAR **Weight:** 31.1035 g. **Composition:** 0.9990 Silver 1.0000 oz. ASW **Subject:** Majestic Images **Obverse:** Queen's head right **Reverse:** Queen's 3 previous portraits **Edge:** Reeded

Date	Mintage	F	VF	XF	Unc	BU
1999 Proof	17,000	Value: 65.00				

KM# 502 DOLLAR **Weight:** 31.6350 g. **Composition:** 0.9990 Silver 1.0161 oz. ASW **Subject:** Year of the Rabbit **Obverse:** Queen's head right **Edge:** Reeded **Size:** 40.6 mm.

Date	Mintage	F	VF	XF	Unc	BU
1999	—	—	—	—	20.00	—
1999 Proof	2,500	Value: 45.00				

KM# 604 DOLLAR **Weight:** 31.1035 g. **Composition:** 0.9990 Silver 0.999 oz. ASW **Subject:** U.S. State Quarter - Delaware **Size:** 40.4 mm.

Date	Mintage	F	VF	XF	Unc	BU
1999	75,000	—	—	—	24.50	—

KM# 605 DOLLAR **Weight:** 31.1035 g. **Composition:** 0.9990 Silver 0.999 oz. ASW **Subject:** U.S. State Quarter - Pennsylvania **Size:** 40.4 mm.

Date	Mintage	F	VF	XF	Unc	BU
1999	75,000	—	—	—	24.50	—

KM# 606 DOLLAR **Weight:** 31.1035 g. **Composition:** 0.9990 Silver 0.999 oz. ASW **Subject:** U.S. State Quarter - New Jersey **Size:** 40.4 mm.

Date	Mintage	F	VF	XF	Unc	BU
1999	75,000	—	—	—	24.50	—

KM# 607 DOLLAR **Weight:** 31.1035 g. **Composition:** 0.9990 Silver 0.999 oz. ASW **Subject:** U.S. State Quarter - Georgia **Size:** 40.4 mm.

Date	Mintage	F	VF	XF	Unc	BU
1999	75,000	—	—	—	24.50	—

KM# 608 DOLLAR **Weight:** 31.1035 g. **Composition:** 0.9990 Silver 0.999 oz. ASW **Subject:** U.S. State Quarter - Connecticut **Size:** 40.4 mm.

Date	Mintage	F	VF	XF	Unc	BU
1999	75,000	—	—	—	24.50	—

KM# 485 DOLLAR **Weight:** 6.5700 g. **Composition:** 0.9990 Silver .2110 oz. ASW **Series:** Masterpieces in Silver **Obverse:** Queen's head right **Reverse:** Shilling reverse design of KM#39 **Edge:** Reeded **Size:** 23.6 mm.

Date	Mintage	F	VF	XF	Unc	BU
1999 Proof	15,000	Value: 18.00				

KM# 489 DOLLAR **Weight:** 9.0000 g. **Composition:** Nickel-Aluminum-Copper **Subject:** Kangaroos **Obverse:** Queen's head by Rank-Broadly right **Reverse:** Same as KM#84 **Edge:** Reeded and plain sections **Size:** 25 mm.

Date	F	VF	XF	Unc	BU
2000 Proof	—	Value: 10.00			
2000	—	—	—	4.00	—

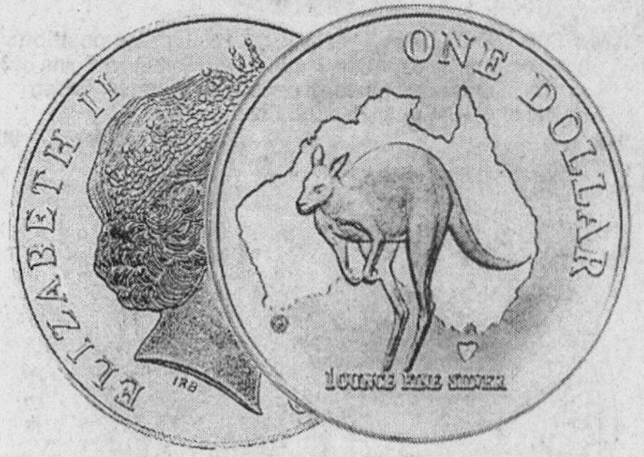

KM# 490 DOLLAR **Weight:** 31.1035 g. **Composition:** 0.9990 Silver 1. oz. ASW **Subject:** Kangaroo Bullion **Obverse:** Queen's portrait by Rank-Broadly right **Reverse:** Kangaroo with Australian map background **Edge:** Reeded **Size:** 40 mm.

Date	F	VF	XF	Unc	BU
2000 Proof	—	Value: 23.50			
2000	—	—	—	12.50	—

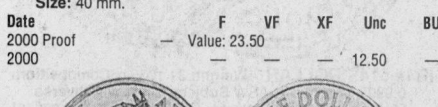

KM# 600 DOLLAR **Weight:** 9.0000 g. **Composition:** Aluminum-Bronze **Subject:** "The Outback" **Obverse:** Bust of Queen Elizabeth II right **Reverse:** Stylized Australian map **Edge:** Reeded and plain sections **Size:** 24.9 mm.

Date	F	VF	XF	Unc	BU
2000C	—	—	—	2.50	—
2002	—	—	—	—	—
2002 Proof	—	—	—	—	—

KM# 422 DOLLAR **Composition:** Nickel-Aluminum-Copper **Subject:** HMAS Sydney II **Obverse:** Queen's head right **Reverse:** Ship above denomination **Edge:** Reeded

Date	F	VF	XF	Unc	BU
2000	—	—	—	5.00	—
2000C	—	—	—	5.00	—
2000S	—	—	—	5.00	—

KM# 422a DOLLAR **Weight:** 11.6600 g. **Composition:** 0.9990 Silver .3754 oz. ASW **Obverse:** Queen's head right **Reverse:** HMAS Sydney II above denomination

Date	Mintage	F	VF	XF	Unc	BU
2000 Proof	20,000	Value: 30.00				

KM# 424 DOLLAR **Weight:** 31.1035 g. **Composition:** 0.9990 Silver 1.0000 oz. ASW **Obverse:** Queen's portrait **Reverse:** Dragon

Date	F	VF	XF	Unc	BU
2000	—	—	—	25.00	—

KM# 493 DOLLAR **Weight:** 9.0000 g. **Composition:** Nickel-Aluminum-Copper **Subject:** Victoria Cross **Obverse:** Queen's head right **Reverse:** The Victoria Cross **Edge:** Reeded and plain sections **Size:** 24.9 mm.

Date	F	VF	XF	Unc	BU
2000	—	—	—	4.50	—

KM# 509 DOLLAR **Weight:** 31.1035 g. **Composition:** 0.9990 Silver 1. oz. ASW **Subject:** Proclamation Coins of Australia **Obverse:** Queen's head right **Reverse:** British penny of 1797 **Edge:** Reeded **Size:** 40 mm.

Date	F	VF	XF	Unc	BU
2000 Proof	—	Value: 65.00			

KM# 514 DOLLAR **Weight:** 31.1035 g. **Composition:** 0.9990 Silver 1. oz. ASW **Subject:** Millenium **Obverse:** Queen's head right **Reverse:** Gold inlay earth and radiant sun as seen from the moon's surface **Edge:** Reeded **Size:** 40.4 mm.

Date	Mintage	F	VF	XF	Unc	BU
2000 Prooflike	30,000	—	—	—	35.00	—

KM# 529.1 DOLLAR **Weight:** 9.0000 g. **Composition:** Nickel-Aluminum-Copper **Subject:** Olymphilex Exhibition **Obverse:** Queen's head right **Reverse:** Denomination and Olympic logo **Edge:** Plain **Edge Lettering:** Incuse SYDNEY **Size:** 24.9 mm.

Date	F	VF	XF	Unc	BU
2000	—	—	—	4.00	—

KM# 529.2 DOLLAR **Weight:** 9.0000 g. **Composition:** Nickel-Aluminum-Copper **Obverse:** Queen's head right **Reverse:** Denomination and Olympic logo. **Edge:** Plain **Edge Lettering:** Incuse CANBERRA **Size:** 24.9 mm.

Date	F	VF	XF	Unc	BU
2000	—	—	—	4.50	—

KM# 611 DOLLAR **Weight:** 31.1035 g. **Composition:** 0.9990 Silver 0.999 oz. ASW **Subject:** U.S. State Quarter - Massachusetts **Size:** 40.4 mm.

Date	Mintage	F	VF	XF	Unc	BU
2000	75,000	—	—	—	24.50	—

KM# 612 DOLLAR **Weight:** 31.1035 g. **Composition:** 0.9990 Silver 0.999 oz. ASW **Subject:** U.S. State Quarter - Maryland **Size:** 40.4 mm.

Date	Mintage	F	VF	XF	Unc	BU
2000	75,000	—	—	—	24.50	—

KM# 613 DOLLAR **Weight:** 31.1035 g. **Composition:** 0.9990 Silver 0.999 oz. ASW **Subject:** U.S. State Quarter - South Carolina **Size:** 40.4 mm.

Date	Mintage	F	VF	XF	Unc	BU
2000	75,000	—	—	—	24.50	—

KM# 614 DOLLAR **Weight:** 31.1035 g. **Composition:** 0.9990 Silver 0.999 oz. ASW **Subject:** U.S. State Quarter - New Hampshire **Size:** 40.4 mm.

Date	Mintage	F	VF	XF	Unc	BU
2000	75,000	—	—	—	24.50	—

KM# 615 DOLLAR **Weight:** 31.1035 g. **Composition:** 0.9990 Silver 0.999 oz. ASW **Subject:** U.S. State Quarter - Virginia **Size:** 40.4 mm.

Date	Mintage	F	VF	XF	Unc	BU
2000	75,000	—	—	—	24.50	—

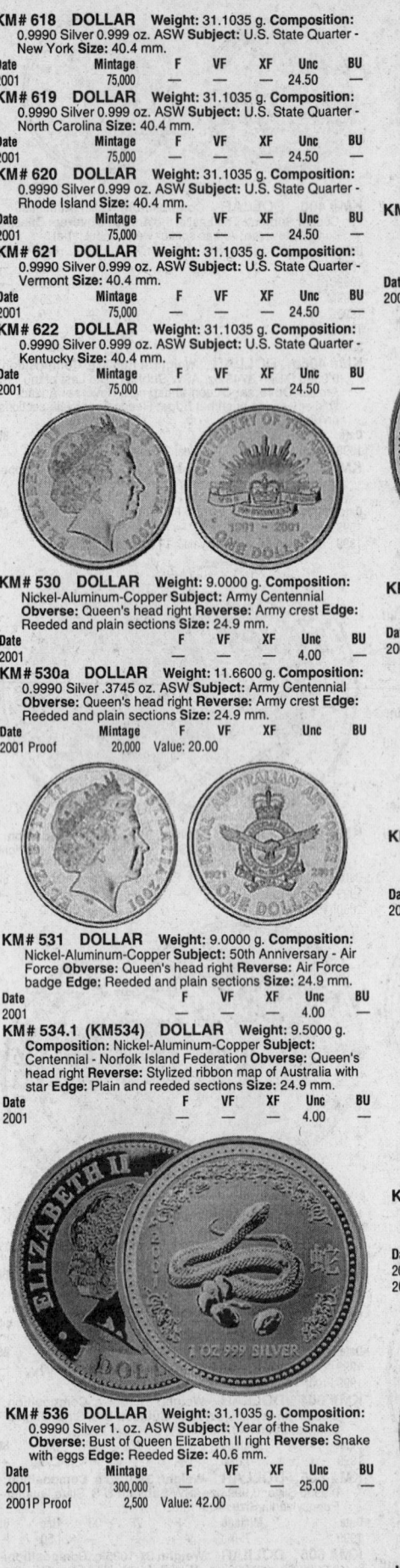

KM# 618 DOLLAR **Weight:** 31.1035 g. **Composition:** 0.9990 Silver 0.999 oz. ASW **Subject:** U.S. State Quarter - New York **Size:** 40.4 mm.

Date	Mintage	F	VF	XF	Unc	BU
2001	75,000	—	—	—	24.50	—

KM# 619 DOLLAR **Weight:** 31.1035 g. **Composition:** 0.9990 Silver 0.999 oz. ASW **Subject:** U.S. State Quarter - North Carolina **Size:** 40.4 mm.

Date	Mintage	F	VF	XF	Unc	BU
2001	75,000	—	—	—	24.50	—

KM# 620 DOLLAR **Weight:** 31.1035 g. **Composition:** 0.9990 Silver 0.999 oz. ASW **Subject:** U.S. State Quarter - Rhode Island **Size:** 40.4 mm.

Date	Mintage	F	VF	XF	Unc	BU
2001	75,000	—	—	—	24.50	—

KM# 621 DOLLAR **Weight:** 31.1035 g. **Composition:** 0.9990 Silver 0.999 oz. ASW **Subject:** U.S. State Quarter - Vermont **Size:** 40.4 mm.

Date	Mintage	F	VF	XF	Unc	BU
2001	75,000	—	—	—	24.50	—

KM# 622 DOLLAR **Weight:** 31.1035 g. **Composition:** 0.9990 Silver 0.999 oz. ASW **Subject:** U.S. State Quarter - Kentucky **Size:** 40.4 mm.

Date	Mintage	F	VF	XF	Unc	BU
2001	75,000	—	—	—	24.50	—

KM# 530 DOLLAR **Weight:** 9.0000 g. **Composition:** Nickel-Aluminum-Copper **Subject:** Army Centennial **Obverse:** Queen's head right **Reverse:** Army crest **Edge:** Reeded and plain sections **Size:** 24.9 mm.

Date	F	VF	XF	Unc	BU
2001	—	—	—	4.00	—

KM# 530a DOLLAR **Weight:** 11.6600 g. **Composition:** 0.9990 Silver .3745 oz. ASW **Subject:** Army Centennial **Obverse:** Queen's head right **Reverse:** Army crest **Edge:** Reeded and plain sections **Size:** 24.9 mm.

Date	Mintage	F	VF	XF	Unc	BU
2001 Proof	20,000	Value: 20.00				

KM# 531 DOLLAR **Weight:** 9.0000 g. **Composition:** Nickel-Aluminum-Copper **Subject:** 50th Anniversary - Air Force **Obverse:** Queen's head right **Reverse:** Air Force badge **Edge:** Reeded and plain sections **Size:** 24.9 mm.

Date	F	VF	XF	Unc	BU
2001	—	—	—	4.00	—

KM# 534.1 (KM534) DOLLAR **Weight:** 9.5000 g. **Composition:** Nickel-Aluminum-Copper **Subject:** Centennial - Norfolk Island Federation **Obverse:** Queen's head right **Reverse:** Stylized ribbon map of Australia with star **Edge:** Plain and reeded sections **Size:** 24.9 mm.

Date	F	VF	XF	Unc	BU
2001	—	—	—	4.00	—

KM# 536 DOLLAR **Weight:** 31.1035 g. **Composition:** 0.9990 Silver 1. oz. ASW **Subject:** Year of the Snake **Obverse:** Bust of Queen Elizabeth II right **Reverse:** Snake with eggs **Edge:** Reeded **Size:** 40.6 mm.

Date	Mintage	F	VF	XF	Unc	BU
2001	300,000	—	—	—	25.00	—
2001P Proof	2,500	Value: 42.00				

KM# 534.2 DOLLAR **Weight:** 9.5000 g. **Composition:** Nickel-Aluminum-Copper **Subject:** Centenary of Norfolk Island Federation **Obverse:** Queen's head right **Reverse:** Multi-color ribbon design of Australia with star **Edge:** Plain and reeded sections **Size:** 24.9 mm.

Date	F	VF	XF	Unc	BU
2001 Proof	—	Value: 13.50			

KM# 479 DOLLAR **Weight:** 31.9700 g. **Composition:** 0.9990 Silver 1.0268 oz. ASW **Obverse:** Queen's head right **Reverse:** Two Kookaburras back to back on branch

Date	F	VF	XF	Unc	BU
2001	—	—	—	17.50	—

KM# 588 DOLLAR **Weight:** 9.0000 g. **Composition:** Aluminum-Bronze **Subject:** Royal Australian Navy **Obverse:** Head of Queen Elizabeth II right **Reverse:** Navy emblem **Edge:** Reeded and plain sections **Size:** 25 mm.

Date	F	VF	XF	Unc	BU
2001	—	—	—	2.50	—

KM# 590 DOLLAR **Weight:** 31.1035 g. **Composition:** 0.9990 Silver 0.999 oz. ASW **Subject:** Silver Kangaroo Series **Obverse:** Bust of Queen Elizabeth II right **Reverse:** Aboriginal kangaroo design **Edge:** Reeded **Size:** 40 mm.

Date	F	VF	XF	Unc	BU
2001 Frosted	—	—	—	2.00	—
2001 Proof	—	Value: 25.00			

KM# 594 DOLLAR **Weight:** 31.1035 g. **Composition:** 0.9990 Silver 0.999 oz. ASW **Subject:** Millennium **Obverse:** Bust of Queen Elizabeth II right **Reverse:** Gold inset Sun on multicolor Earth above Egyptian obelisk **Edge:** Reeded **Size:** 40 mm.

Date	Mintage	F	VF	XF	Unc	BU
2001 Prooflike	30,000	—	—	—	35.00	—

KM# 598 DOLLAR **Weight:** 31.1000 g. **Composition:** 0.9990 Silver 0.9989 oz. ASW **Subject:** Centenary of Federation "Holey Dollar" **Obverse:** Legend around star shaped center hole **Reverse:** Seven coats of arms around star-shaped hole **Edge:** Reeded **Size:** 38.1 mm.

Date	Mintage	F	VF	XF	Unc	BU
ND(2001) Prooflike	30,000	—	—	—	40.00	—

KM# 580 DOLLAR **Weight:** 31.1035 g. **Composition:** 0.9990 Silver 0.999 oz. ASW **Subject:** Year of the Horse **Obverse:** Bust of Queen Elizabeth II right **Reverse:** Horse running left **Edge:** Reeded **Size:** 40.6 mm.

Date	Mintage	F	VF	XF	Unc	BU
2002P	—	—	—	—	15.00	—
2002P Proof	2,500	Value: 42.00				

KM# 625 DOLLAR **Weight:** 31.1035 g. **Composition:** 0.9990 Silver 0.999 oz. ASW **Subject:** U.S. State Quarter - Tennessee **Size:** 40.4 mm.

Date	Mintage	F	VF	XF	Unc	BU
2002	75,000	—	—	—	24.50	—

KM# 626 DOLLAR **Weight:** 31.1035 g. **Composition:** 0.9990 Silver 0.999 oz. ASW **Subject:** U.S. State Quarter - Ohio **Size:** 40.4 mm.

Date	Mintage	F	VF	XF	Unc	BU
2002	75,000	—	—	—	24.50	—

KM# 627 DOLLAR **Weight:** 31.1035 g. **Composition:** 0.9990 Silver 0.999 oz. ASW **Subject:** U.S. State Quarter - Louisiana **Size:** 40.4 mm.

Date	Mintage	F	VF	XF	Unc	BU
2002	75,000	—	—	—	24.50	—

KM# 628 DOLLAR **Weight:** 31.1035 g. **Composition:** 0.9990 Silver 0.999 oz. ASW **Subject:** U.S. State Quarter - Indiana **Size:** 40.4 mm.

Date	Mintage	F	VF	XF	Unc	BU
2002	75,000	—	—	—	24.50	—

KM# 629 DOLLAR **Weight:** 31.1035 g. **Composition:** 0.9990 Silver 0.999 oz. ASW **Subject:** U.S. State Quarter - Mississippi **Size:** 40.4 mm.

Date	Mintage	F	VF	XF	Unc	BU
2002	75,000	—	—	—	24.50	—

KM# 101 2 DOLLARS **Composition:** Aluminum-Bronze **Subject:** Aboriginal Man

Date	Mintage	F	VF	XF	Unc	BU
1988	59,679,000	—	—	—	4.25	—
1988 Proof	106,000	Value: 7.50				
1989	—	—	—	—	4.25	—
1989 Proof	—	Value: 7.50				
1990	339,000	—	—	—	4.25	—
1990 Proof	—	Value: 7.50				
1991	—	—	—	—	4.25	—
1991 Proof	—	Value: 7.50				
1992	—	—	—	—	4.25	—
1992 Proof	47,000	Value: 7.50				
1993	—	—	—	—	4.25	—
1993 Proof	—	Value: 7.50				
1994	—	—	—	—	4.25	—
1994 Proof	—	Value: 7.50				
1995	—	—	—	—	4.25	—
1995 Proof	—	Value: 7.50				
1996	—	—	—	—	4.25	—
1996 Proof	—	Value: 7.50				
1997	—	—	—	—	4.25	—
1997 Proof	—	Value: 7.50				
1998	—	—	—	—	4.25	—
1998 Proof	—	Value: 7.50				

KM# 101a 2 DOLLARS **Weight:** 8.4300 g. **Composition:** 0.9250 Silver .2507 oz. ASW

Date	Mintage	F	VF	XF	Unc	BU
1988 Proof	25,000	Value: 14.50				
1991 Proof	23,000	Value: 14.50				

Note: In Proof sets only

KM# 179 2 DOLLARS **Weight:** 62.2070 g. **Composition:** 0.9990 Silver 2.0000 oz. ASW **Subject:** Australian Kookaburra - On Stump **Obverse:** Head of Queen Elizabeth II right

Date	Mintage	F	VF	XF	Unc	BU
1992	—	—	—	—	25.00	—
1992 Proof	5,000	Value: 85.00				
1992 (gv) Proof	500	Value: 160				
1992 (hd) Specimen	1,000	—	—	—	125	—
1993 (dp) Specimen	1,000	—	—	—	125	—
1993 (w) Specimen	1,000	—	—	—	135	—
1993 (e) Specimen	1,000	—	—	—	115	—
1993 (ta) Specimen	1,000	—	—	—	115	—

KM# 227 2 DOLLARS **Weight:** 62.2070 g. **Composition:** 0.9990 Silver 2.0000 oz. ASW **Obverse:** Head of Queen Elizabeth II right **Reverse:** Kookaburra feeding nestling

Date	Mintage	F	VF	XF	Unc	BU
1992 Proof	—	Value: 85.00				
1992 (aa) Proof	500	Value: 375				
1993	—	—	—	—	25.00	—
1993 Proof	—	Value: 85.00				

KM# 230 2 DOLLARS **Weight:** 62.2070 g. **Composition:** 0.9990 Silver 2.0000 oz. ASW **Obverse:** Head of Queen Elizabeth II right **Reverse:** Pair of Kookaburras on branch

Date	Mintage	F	VF	XF	Unc	BU
1993	—	—	—	—	25.00	—
1993 Proof	—	Value: 85.00				
1993 (sm) Proof	750	Value: 200				
1993 (ae) Proof	500	Value: 300				
1994	—	—	—	—	25.00	—
1994 Proof	—	Value: 85.00				
1994 (gv) Specimen	1,000	—	—	—	275	—
1994 (ev) Proof	1,500	Value: 200				
1994 (gv) Specimen	1,500	—	—	—	180	—

KM# 261 2 DOLLARS **Weight:** 62.2070 g. **Composition:** 0.9990 Silver 2.0000 oz. ASW **Obverse:** Head of Queen Elizabeth II right **Reverse:** Kookaburra on branch

Date	Mintage	F	VF	XF	Unc	BU
1995	—	—	—	—	28.00	—
1995 (f1) Proof	1,500	Value: 120				
1995 (f3) Proof	1,500	Value: 135				
1995 (f7) Proof	1,500	Value: 100				
1995 (rv) Proof	1,500	Value: 90.00				

KM# 290 2 DOLLARS **Weight:** 62.2070 g. **Composition:** 0.9990 Silver 2.0000 oz. ASW **Reverse:** Kookaburra in flight

Date	Mintage	F	VF	XF	Unc	BU
1995P Proof	650	Value: 65.00				
1995P (ww) Proof	1,300	Value: 135				
1995 (ge) Proof	800	Value: 135				
Note: Privy marks on gold insert						
1996	—	—	—	—	22.50	—
1996 (h) Proof	1,500	Value: 70.00				
1996 (d) Proof	1,500	Value: 115				
Note: Privy marks on gold insert						
1996 (j) Proof	1,500	Value: 120				
Note: Privy marks on gold insert						
1996 (sg) Proof	1,500	Value: 130				
Note: Privy marks on gold insert						
1996 (sp) Proof	1,500	Value: 135				
Note: Privy marks on gold insert						

KM# 319 2 DOLLARS **Weight:** 62.2070 g. **Composition:** 0.9990 Silver 2.0000 oz. ASW **Obverse:** Head of Queen Elizabeth II right **Reverse:** Kookaburra and nestling; similar to 1 Dollar, KM#318

Date	F	VF	XF	Unc	BU
1997	—	—	—	25.00	—

KM# 363 2 DOLLARS **Weight:** 62.2070 g. **Composition:** 0.9990 Silver 2.0000 oz. ASW **Subject:** Kookaburra **Obverse:** Queen's portrait **Reverse:** Bird on fence

Date	Mintage	F	VF	XF	Unc	BU
1998 (1997)	—	—	—	—	25.00	—
1997 Proof	2,000	Value: 110				

KM# 406 2 DOLLARS **Composition:** Aluminum-Bronze **Obverse:** Queen's portrait by Rank-Broadley **Reverse:** Similar to KM#101

Date	F	VF	XF	Unc	BU
1999	—	—	—	4.50	—
1999 Proof	—	Value: 11.50			
2000	—	—	—	4.50	—
2000 Proof	—	Value: 11.50			
2001	—	—	—	4.50	—
2001 Proof	—	Value: 11.50			
2002	—	—	—	4.50	—
2002 Proof	—	Value: 11.50			

KM# 445 2 DOLLARS **Weight:** 62.7700 g. **Composition:** 0.9990 Silver 2.0000 oz. ASW **Obverse:** Queen's head right **Reverse:** 2 Kookaburras on branch **Edge:** Interrupted reeding on edge

Date	F	VF	XF	Unc	BU
1999	—	—	—	25.00	—

KM# 486 2 DOLLARS **Weight:** 13.3600 g. **Composition:** 0.9990 Silver .4291 oz. ASW **Series:** Masterpieces in Silver **Obverse:** Queen's head right. **Reverse:** Gold sovereign reverse design of KM#29. **Edge:** Reeded. **Size:** 28.5 mm.

Date	Mintage	F	VF	XF	Unc	BU
1999 Proof	15,000	Value: 22.00				

KM# 503 2 DOLLARS **Weight:** 62.7700 g. **Composition:** 0.9990 Silver 2.0161 oz. ASW **Subject:** Year of the Rabbit **Obverse:** Queen's head right **Reverse:** Rabbit **Edge:** Reeded and plain sections **Size:** 49.9 mm.

Date	Mintage	F	VF	XF	Unc	BU
1999	—	—	—	—	25.00	—
1999 Proof	2,500	Value: 95.00				

KM# 417.1 2 DOLLARS **Weight:** 62.8500 g. **Composition:** 0.9990 Silver 2.0187 oz. ASW **Obverse:** Queen's head right **Reverse:** Kookaburra on branch

Date	F	VF	XF	Unc	BU
1999	—	—	—	25.00	—
1999 Proof	—	—	—	—	—
2000(1999)	—	—	—	25.00	—

KM# 609 2 DOLLARS **Weight:** 62.2070 g. **Composition:** 0.9990 Silver 1.998 oz. ASW **Subject:** USA State Quarters - 1999 **Obverse:** Queen's head right. **Reverse:** Kookaburra on branch with five state quarter designs added below. **Edge:** Reeded and plain sections.

Date	Mintage	F	VF	XF	Unc	BU
1999	10,000	—	—	—	42.00	—

KM# 417.3 2 DOLLARS **Weight:** 62.8500 g. **Composition:** 0.9990 Silver 2.0187 oz. ASW **Subject:** USA State Quarters - 2000 **Obverse:** Queen's head right **Reverse:** Kookaburra on branch with five state quarter designs added below **Edge:** Reeded and plain sections **Note:** Rev. with 1933 Shilling obv. & rev. design copper inserts.

Date	Mintage	F	VF	XF	Unc	BU
1999	1,500	—	—	—	60.00	—

KM# 417.4 2 DOLLARS **Weight:** 62.8500 g. **Composition:** 0.9999 Silver 2.0205 oz. ASW **Subject:** USA State Quarters - 2000 **Obverse:** Queen's head right **Reverse:** Kookaburra on branch with five state quarter designs added below **Edge:** Reeded and plain sections **Note:** Reverse with 1930 Penny obverse and reverse design copper inserts

Date	F	VF	XF	Unc	BU
1999 Proof	—	Value: 95.00			

KM# 417.5 2 DOLLARS **Weight:** 62.8500 g. **Composition:** 0.9990 Silver 2.0187 oz. ASW **Subject:** USA State Quarters - 2000 **Obverse:** Queen's head right **Reverse:** Kookaburra on branch with five state quarter designs added below **Edge:** Reeded and plain sections **Note:** Reverse with 1932 Florin obverse and reverse design copper inserts.

Date	F	VF	XF	Unc	BU
1999 Proof	—	Value: 95.00			

KM# 616 2 DOLLARS **Weight:** 62.2070 g. **Composition:** 0.9990 Silver 1.998 oz. ASW **Subject:** USA State Quarters - 2000 **Obverse:** Queen's head right. **Reverse:** Kookaburra on branch with five state quarter designs added below. **Edge:** Reeded and plain sections. **Note:** Prev. KM#417.2.

Date	Mintage	F	VF	XF	Unc	BU
2000	10,000	—	—	—	42.00	—

KM# 523 2 DOLLARS **Weight:** 62.2070 g. **Composition:** 0.9990 Silver 2. oz. ASW **Series:** Dragons **Obverse:** Queen's head right **Reverse:** Dragon **Edge:** Segmented reeding **Size:** 50.3 mm.

Date	F	VF	XF	Unc	BU
2000 Proof	—	Value: 100			

KM# 500 2 DOLLARS **Weight:** 8.5500 g. **Composition:** 0.9990 Silver .2746 oz. ASW **Series:** Masterpieces in Silver - 2000 Set **Obverse:** Queen's head right **Reverse:** Queen Victoria's bust left **Edge:** Reeded **Size:** 20.5 mm.

Date	Mintage	F	VF	XF	Unc	BU
2000 Proof	15,000	Value: 27.50				

KM# 417.6 2 DOLLARS **Weight:** 62.8500 g. **Composition:** 0.9990 Silver 2.0187 oz. ASW **Subject:** USA State Quarters - 2000 **Obverse:** Queen's head right **Reverse:** Kookaburra on branch with five state quarter designs added below **Edge:** Reeded and plain sections

Date	F	VF	XF	Unc	BU
2000 (1999) (sq)	—	—	—	150	—

KM# 537 2 DOLLARS **Weight:** 62.2070 g. **Composition:** 0.9990 Silver 2. oz. ASW **Subject:** Year of the Snake **Obverse:** Queen's head right **Reverse:** Snake with eggs **Edge:** Segmented reeding **Size:** 50.3 mm.

Date	Mintage	F	VF	XF	Unc	BU
2001	—	—	—	—	35.00	—
2001P Proof	1,000	Value: 87.00				

KM# 581 2 DOLLARS **Weight:** 62.2070 g. **Composition:** 0.9990 Silver 1.998 oz. ASW **Subject:** Year of the Horse **Obverse:** Bust of Queen Elizabeth II right **Reverse:** Horse running left **Edge:** Reeded **Size:** 50 mm.

Date	Mintage	F	VF	XF	Unc	BU
2002P Proof	1,000	Value: 87.00				

KM# 102 5 DOLLARS **Composition:** Aluminum-Bronze **Subject:** Parliament House

Date	Mintage	F	VF	XF	Unc	BU
1988	—	—	—	—	—	5.00
1988 Proof	80,000	Value: 15.00				

KM# 102a 5 DOLLARS **Weight:** 35.7900 g. **Composition:** 0.9250 Silver 1.0645 oz. ASW

Date	Mintage	F	VF	XF	Unc	BU
1988 Proof	25,000	Value: 18.50				

KM# 117 5 DOLLARS **Weight:** 1.5710 g. **Composition:** 0.9990 Gold .0500 oz. AGW **Subject:** Red Kangaroo **Obverse:** Elizabeth II

Date	Mintage	F	VF	XF	Unc	BU
1989 Proof	2,200	Value: 30.00				
1990	—	—	—	—	BV+ 35%	—

KM# 122 5 DOLLARS **Weight:** 1.5710 g. **Composition:** 0.9990 Platinum .0500 oz. APW **Note:** Similar to 100 Dollars, KM#126.

Date	Mintage	F	VF	XF	Unc	BU
1989 Proof	2,400	Value: 38.00				
1990 Proof	—	Value: 38.00				

KM# 138 5 DOLLARS **Weight:** 31.1030 g. **Composition:** 0.9990 Silver 1.0000 oz. ASW **Reverse:** Australian Kookaburra **Note:** Special coin fair issues exist.

Date	Mintage	F	VF	XF	Unc	BU
1990 Proof	22,000	Value: 27.50				
1991	300,000	—	—	—	11.50	—
1991 Proof	—	Value: 27.50				

KM# 134 5 DOLLARS **Composition:** Aluminum-Bronze **Subject:** ANZAC Memorial

Date	F	VF	XF	Unc	BU
1990	—	—	—	5.50	—
1990 Proof	—	Value: 32.50			

KM# 140 5 DOLLARS **Weight:** 1.5710 g. **Composition:** 0.9990 Gold .0500 oz. AGW **Reverse:** Gray Kangaroo

Date	Mintage	F	VF	XF	Unc	BU
1990 Proof	7,000	Value: 28.00				
1991	200,000	—	—	—	BV+35%	—

KM# 145 5 DOLLARS **Weight:** 1.5710 g. **Composition:** 0.9990 Platinum .0500 oz. APW **Obverse:** Similar to 100 Dollars, KM#149. **Reverse:** Koala

Date	Mintage	F	VF	XF	Unc	BU
1990 Proof	2,500	Value: 38.00				
1991	20,000	—	—	—	BV+ 35%	—
1991 Proof	1,000	Value: 38.00				

KM# 189 5 DOLLARS **Weight:** 31.1030 g. **Composition:** 0.9990 Silver 1.0000 oz. ASW **Reverse:** Australian Kookaburra

Date	Mintage	F	VF	XF	Unc	BU
1990	300,000	—	—	—	15.00	—

KM# 165 5 DOLLARS **Weight:** 1.5710 g. **Composition:** 0.9990 Gold .0500 oz. AGW **Subject:** Common Wallaroo **Obverse:** Elizabeth II **Reverse:** Similar to 100 Dollars, KM#169 **Note:** 1992 (ae) previously listed here is now KM#389.

Date	Mintage	F	VF	XF	Unc	BU
1991 Proof	3,525	Value: 30.00				
1992	200,000	—	—	—	BV+ 35%	—

KM# 389 5 DOLLARS **Weight:** 1.5710 g. **Composition:** 0.9990 Gold .0500 oz. AGW **Obverse:** Queen's portrait **Reverse:** Nail-tailed Wallaby **Note:** Similar to 25 Dollars, KM#391.

Date	Mintage	F	VF	XF	Unc	BU
1992 (ae) Proof	500	Value: 50.00				

KM# 170 5 DOLLARS **Weight:** 1.5710 g. **Composition:** 0.9990 Platinum .0500 oz. APW **Subject:** Koala **Obverse:** Elizabeth II **Reverse:** Similar to 100 Dollars, KM#174

Date	Mintage	F	VF	XF	Unc	BU
1992	20,000	—	—	—	BV+ 35%	—

KM# 190 5 DOLLARS **Composition:** Aluminum-Bronze **Subject:** Australian Role in Space Industry

Date	Mintage	F	VF	XF	Unc	BU
1992	218,000	—	—	—	6.00	—
1992 Proof	25,000	Value: 20.00				

KM# 191 5 DOLLARS **Weight:** 1.5710 g. **Composition:** 0.9990 Platinum .0500 oz. APW **Obverse:** Similar to 100 Dollars, KM#195

Date	F	VF	XF	Unc	BU
1993	—	—	—	BV+ 35%	—

KM# 213 5 DOLLARS **Weight:** 35.7900 g. **Composition:** 0.9250 Silver 1.0645 oz. ASW **Subject:** Aboriginal Exploration

Date	Mintage	F	VF	XF	Unc	BU
1993 Proof	20,000	Value: 22.50				

KM# 214 5 DOLLARS **Weight:** 35.7900 g. **Composition:** 0.9250 Silver 1.0645 oz. ASW **Subject:** Abel Tasman

Date	Mintage	F	VF	XF	Unc	BU
1993 Proof	20,000	Value: 22.50				

KM# 215 5 DOLLARS **Weight:** 35.7900 g. **Composition:** 0.9250 Silver 1.0645 oz. ASW **Subject:** Captain James Cook

Date	Mintage	F	VF	XF	Unc	BU
1993 Proof	20,000	Value: 22.50				

KM# 216 5 DOLLARS **Weight:** 35.7900 g. **Composition:** 0.9250 Silver 1.0645 oz. ASW **Subject:** Matthew Flinders

Date	Mintage	F	VF	XF	Unc	BU
1993 Proof	20,000	Value: 22.50				

KM# 217 5 DOLLARS **Weight:** 35.7900 g. **Composition:** 0.9250 Silver 1.0645 oz. ASW **Subject:** W. Lawson, G. Blayland and W.C. Wentworth

Date	Mintage	F	VF	XF	Unc	BU
1993 Proof	20,000	Value: 22.50				

KM# 233 5 DOLLARS **Weight:** 1.5710 g. **Composition:** 0.9990 Gold .0500 oz. AGW **Obverse:** Elizabeth II **Reverse:** Whiptail Wallaby

Date	F	VF	XF	Unc	BU
1993 Proof	—	Value: 35.00			
1994	—	—	—	BV+ 35%	—

KM# 224 5 DOLLARS **Ring Composition:** Stainless Steel **Center Composition:** Aluminum-Bronze **Subject:** Women's Enfranchisement

Date	Mintage	F	VF	XF	Unc	BU
1994	250,000	—	—	—	11.00	—
1994 Proof	23,000	Value: 25.00				

KM# 224a 5 DOLLARS **Composition:** Aluminum-Bronze

Date	Mintage	F	VF	XF	Unc	BU
1994 Proof	2,500	Value: 35.00				

KM# 241 5 DOLLARS **Weight:** 1.5710 g. **Composition:** 0.9990 Gold .0500 oz. AGW **Reverse:** Red Kangaroo

Date	Mintage	F	VF	XF	Unc	BU
1994 Proof	—	Value: 35.00				
1995	200,000	—	—	—	BV+ 35%	—

KM# 249 5 DOLLARS **Weight:** 1.5710 g. **Composition:** 0.9990 Platinum .0500 oz. APW **Reverse:** Koala mother and baby

Date	Mintage	F	VF	XF	Unc	BU
1994	20,000	—	—	—	BV+35%	—

KM# 264 5 DOLLARS **Weight:** 31.1040 g. **Composition:** 0.9250 Silver 1.0870 oz. ASW **Subject:** Explorer - Ludwig Leichhardt **Obverse:** Queen Elizabeth II portrait

Date	Mintage	F	VF	XF	Unc	BU
1994 Proof	Est. 20,000	Value: 18.50				

KM# 265 5 DOLLARS **Weight:** 31.1040 g. **Composition:** 0.9250 Silver 1.0870 oz. ASW **Subject:** Explorer - Charles Sturt

Date	Mintage	F	VF	XF	Unc	BU
1994 Proof	Est. 20,000	Value: 18.50				

KM# 266 5 DOLLARS **Weight:** 31.1040 g. **Composition:** 0.9250 Silver 1.0870 oz. ASW **Subject:** Explorer - Sir John Forrest

Date	Mintage	F	VF	XF	Unc	BU
1994 Proof	Est. 20,000	Value: 18.50				

KM# 267 5 DOLLARS **Weight:** 31.1040 g. **Composition:** 0.9250 Silver 1.0870 oz. ASW **Subject:** Explorer - John McDouall Stuart

Date	Mintage	F	VF	XF	Unc	BU
1994 Proof	Est. 20,000	Value: 18.00				

KM# 268 5 DOLLARS **Weight:** 31.1040 g. **Composition:** 0.9250 Silver 1.0870 oz. ASW **Subject:** Explorer - Sir Douglas Mawson

Date	Mintage	F	VF	XF	Unc	BU
1994 Proof	Est. 20,000	Value: 18.00				

KM# 278 5 DOLLARS **Weight:** 1.5710 g. **Composition:** 0.9990 Platinum .0500 oz. APW **Reverse:** Koala in fork of tree

Date	Mintage	F	VF	XF	Unc	BU
1994 Proof	—	Value: 40.00				
1995	—	—	—	—BV+35%		—

KM# 272 5 DOLLARS **Weight:** 1.5710 g. **Composition:** 0.9990 Gold .0500 oz. AGW **Reverse:** Two kangaroos

Date	Mintage	F	VF	XF	Unc	BU
1995 Proof	300	Value: 35.00				
1996	200,000	—	—	—BV+35%		—

KM# 283 5 DOLLARS **Weight:** 1.5710 g. **Composition:** 0.9990 Platinum .0500 oz. APW **Reverse:** Baby koala on branch

Date	Mintage	F	VF	XF	Unc	BU
1995 Proof	200	Value: 40.00				
1996	20,000	—	—	—BV+35%		—

KM# 303 5 DOLLARS **Weight:** 35.7900 g. **Composition:** 0.9250 Silver 1.0645 oz. ASW **Subject:** The Gold Rush Era

Date	Mintage	F	VF	XF	Unc	BU
1995 Proof	20,000	Value: 17.50				

KM# 304 5 DOLLARS **Weight:** 35.7900 g. **Composition:** 0.9250 Silver 1.0645 oz. ASW **Subject:** Cobb and Co. 1853, Stagecoach

Date	Mintage	F	VF	XF	Unc	BU
1995 Proof	20,000	Value: 17.50				

KM# 305 5 DOLLARS **Weight:** 35.7900 g. **Composition:** 0.9250 Silver 1.0645 oz. ASW **Subject:** Elizabeth MacArthur, 1766-1850 - Sheep

Date	Mintage	F	VF	XF	Unc	BU
1995 Proof	20,000	Value: 17.50				

KM# 306 5 DOLLARS **Weight:** 35.7900 g. **Composition:** 0.9250 Silver 1.0645 oz. ASW **Subject:** Col. William Light, 1786-1839 - City Plan

Date	Mintage	F	VF	XF	Unc	BU
1995 Proof	20,000	Value: 17.50				

KM# 307 5 DOLLARS **Weight:** 35.7900 g. **Composition:** 0.9250 Silver 1.0645 oz. ASW **Subject:** Charles Todd, 1827-1910 - Telegraph Line

Date	Mintage	F	VF	XF	Unc	BU
1995 Proof	20,000	Value: 17.50				

KM# 311 5 DOLLARS **Ring Composition:** Stainless Steel **Center Composition:** Aluminum-Bronze **Subject:** Sir Donald Bradman - Cricket Player

Date	Mintage	F	VF	XF	Unc	BU
1996	500,000	—	—	—	11.00	—
1997	—	—	—	—	11.00	—

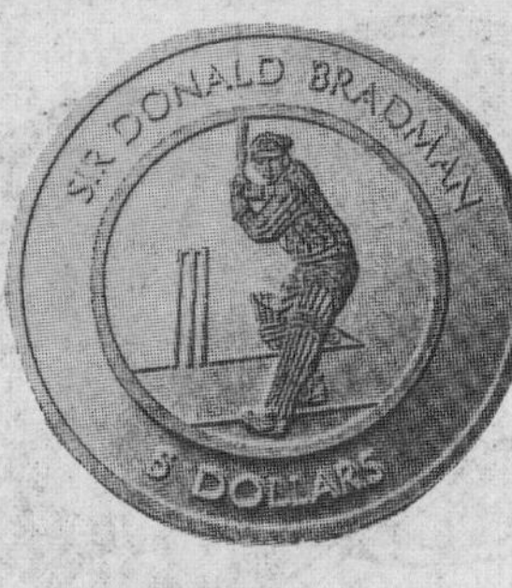

KM# 312 5 DOLLARS **Composition:** Aluminum-Bronze **Subject:** Sir Donald Bradman Full Length Cricket Player

Date	Mintage	F	VF	XF	Unc	BU
1996 Proof	23,000	Value: 40.00				

KM# 320 5 DOLLARS **Weight:** 1.5710 g. **Composition:** 0.9990 Gold .0500 oz. AGW **Obverse:** Queen's portrait **Reverse:** Kangaroo bounding right

Date	F	VF	XF	Unc	BU
1996P Proof	—	Value: 50.00			

Note: In proof sets only

KM# 328 5 DOLLARS **Weight:** 35.7900 g. **Composition:** 0.9250 Silver 1.0645 oz. ASW **Subject:** Stockman **Obverse:** Queen's portrait **Reverse:** Cowboy with whip

Date	Mintage	F	VF	XF	Unc	BU
1996 Proof	20,000	Value: 17.50				

KM# 329 5 DOLLARS **Weight:** 35.7900 g. **Composition:** 0.9250 Silver 1.0645 oz. ASW **Subject:** Horse Racing **Obverse:** Queen's portrait **Reverse:** Horse racing scene

Date	Mintage	F	VF	XF	Unc	BU
1996 Proof	20,000	Value: 17.50				

KM# 330 5 DOLLARS **Weight:** 35.7900 g. **Composition:** 0.9250 Silver 1.0645 oz. ASW **Subject:** Dame Nellie Melba **Obverse:** Queen's portrait **Reverse:** Melba's portrait

Date	Mintage	F	VF	XF	Unc	BU
1996 Proof	20,000	Value: 17.50				

KM# 331 5 DOLLARS **Weight:** 35.7900 g. **Composition:** 0.9250 Silver 1.0645 oz. ASW **Subject:** Tom Roberts **Obverse:** Queen's portrait **Reverse:** Painter and painting

Date	Mintage	F	VF	XF	Unc	BU
1996 Proof	20,000	Value: 17.50				

KM# 332 5 DOLLARS **Weight:** 35.7900 g. **Composition:** 0.9250 Silver 1.0645 oz. ASW **Subject:** Henry Lawson **Obverse:** Queen's portrait **Reverse:** Author's portrait and letter to friends

Date	Mintage	F	VF	XF	Unc	BU
1996 Proof	20,000	Value: 17.50				

KM# 566 5 DOLLARS **Weight:** 1.5552 g. **Composition:** 0.9990 Gold 0.05 oz. AGW **Subject:** Year of the Rat **Obverse:** Bust of Queen Elizabeth II right **Reverse:** Rat **Edge:** Reeded **Size:** 14.1 mm.

Date	Mintage	F	VF	XF	Unc	BU
1996P	100,000	—	—	—	27.00	—

KM# 567 5 DOLLARS **Weight:** 1.5552 g. **Composition:** 0.9990 Gold 0.05 oz. AGW **Subject:** Year of the Ox **Obverse:** Bust of Queen Elizabeth II right **Reverse:** Ox **Edge:** Reeded **Size:** 14.1 mm.

Date	Mintage	F	VF	XF	Unc	BU
1997P	100,000	—	—	—	27.00	—

KM# 544 5 DOLLARS **Weight:** 35.7900 g. **Composition:** 0.9250 Silver 1.0644 oz. ASW **Series:** Masterpieces of Transportation **Obverse:** Queen's head right **Reverse:** Camel pack train **Edge:** Reeded **Size:** 38.9 mm.

Date	Mintage	F	VF	XF	Unc	BU
1997 Proof	10,000	Value: 25.00				

KM# 545 5 DOLLARS **Weight:** 35.7900 g. **Composition:** 0.9250 Silver 1.0644 oz. ASW **Series:** Masterpieces of Transportation **Obverse:** Queen's head right **Reverse:** Riverboat **Edge:** Reeded **Size:** 38.9 mm.

Date	Mintage	F	VF	XF	Unc	BU
1997 Proof	10,000	Value: 25.00				

KM# 546 5 DOLLARS **Weight:** 35.7900 g. **Composition:** 0.9250 Silver 1.0644 oz. ASW **Series:** Masterpieces of Transportation **Obverse:** Queen's head right **Reverse:** Steam locomotive **Edge:** Reeded **Size:** 38.9 mm.

Date	Mintage	F	VF	XF	Unc	BU
1997 Proof	10,000	Value: 25.00				

KM# 547 5 DOLLARS **Weight:** 35.7900 g. **Composition:** 0.9250 Silver 1.0644 oz. ASW **Series:** Masterpieces of Transportation **Obverse:** Queen's head right **Reverse:** Ox drawn wagons **Edge:** Reeded **Size:** 38.9 mm.

Date	Mintage	F	VF	XF	Unc	BU
1997 Proof	10,000	Value: 25.00				

KM# 548 5 DOLLARS **Weight:** 35.7900 g. **Composition:** 0.9250 Silver 1.0644 oz. ASW **Series:** Masterpieces of Transportation **Obverse:** Queen's head right **Reverse:** Steam tractor **Edge:** Reeded **Size:** 38.9 mm.

Date	Mintage	F	VF	XF	Unc	BU
1997 Proof	10,000	Value: 25.00				

KM# 338 5 DOLLARS **Weight:** 1.5710 g. **Composition:** 0.9999 Gold .0500 oz. AGW **Subject:** Kangaroo **Obverse:** Queen's portrait **Reverse:** Kangaroo bounding right

Date	Mintage	F	VF	XF	Unc	BU
1997	200,000	—	—	—	BV+ 35%	—
1997 Proof	—	Value: 30.00				

KM# 344 5 DOLLARS **Weight:** 1.5710 g. **Composition:** 0.9995 Platinum .0500 oz. APW **Subject:** Koalas **Obverse:** Queen's portrait **Reverse:** Cuddling koalas

Date	Mintage	F	VF	XF	Unc	BU
1997	20,000	—	—	—	BV+ 35%	—
1997 Proof	—	Value: 40.00				

KM#356 5 DOLLARS **Composition:** Aluminum-Bronze **Subject:** Sydney 2000 **Obverse:** Queen's portrait **Reverse:** Runner

Date	F	VF	XF	Unc	BU
2000 (1997)	—	—	—	9.00	—

KM#360 5 DOLLARS **Composition:** Aluminum-Bronze **Series:** Sydney 2000 Olympics **Obverse:** Queen's portrait **Reverse:** Field hockey player

Date	F	VF	XF	Unc	BU
2000 (1997)	—	—	—	8.00	—

KM#369 5 DOLLARS **Composition:** Aluminum-Bronze **Series:** Sydney 2000 Olympics **Obverse:** Queen's portrait **Reverse:** Soccer player

Date	F	VF	XF	Unc	BU
2000 (1998)	—	—	—	9.00	—

KM#357 5 DOLLARS **Composition:** Aluminum-Bronze **Series:** Sydney 2000 Olympics **Obverse:** Queen's portrait **Reverse:** Gymnast

Date	F	VF	XF	Unc	BU
2000 (1997)	—	—	—	8.00	—

KM#361 5 DOLLARS **Composition:** Aluminum-Bronze **Series:** Sydney 2000 Olympics **Obverse:** Queen's portrait **Reverse:** Power lifter

Date	F	VF	XF	Unc	BU
2000 (1997)	—	—	—	8.00	—

KM#370 5 DOLLARS **Composition:** Aluminum-Bronze **Series:** Sydney 2000 Olympics **Obverse:** Queen's portrait **Reverse:** Triathalon swimmer

Date	F	VF	XF	Unc	BU
2000 (1998)	—	—	—	9.00	—

KM#358 5 DOLLARS **Composition:** Aluminum-Bronze **Series:** Sydney 2000 Olympics **Obverse:** Queen's portrait **Reverse:** Sailors

Date	F	VF	XF	Unc	BU
2000 (1997)	—	—	—	9.00	—

KM#386 5 DOLLARS **Composition:** Aluminum-Bronze **Subject:** 70th Anniversary - Royal Flying Doctor **Obverse:** Queen's portrait **Reverse:** Radio dispatcher and airplane

Date	Mintage	F	VF	XF	Unc	BU
1998 Proof	Est. 20,000	Value: 18.50				

KM# 371 5 DOLLARS **Weight:** 31.6350 g. **Composition:** 0.9990 Silver 1.0161 oz. ASW **Series:** Sydney 2000 Olympics **Obverse:** Queen's portrait **Reverse:** Australian map above multicolor logo

Date	Mintage	F	VF	XF	Unc	BU
2000 (1998) Proof	Est. 100,000	Value: 40.00				

KM#359 5 DOLLARS **Composition:** Aluminum-Bronze **Subject:** Sydney 2000 **Obverse:** Queen's portrait **Reverse:** Archer

Date	F	VF	XF	Unc	BU
2000 (1997)	—	—	—	9.00	—

KM#368 5 DOLLARS **Composition:** Aluminum-Bronze **Series:** Sydney 2000 Olympics **Obverse:** Queen's portrait **Reverse:** Cyclist

Date	F	VF	XF	Unc	BU
2000 (1998)	—	—	—	9.00	—

KM# 372 5 DOLLARS **Weight:** 31.6350 g. **Composition:** 0.9990 Silver 1.0161 oz. ASW **Series:** Sydney 2000 Olympics **Obverse:** Queen's portrait **Reverse:** Two Great White sharks

Date	Mintage	F	VF	XF	Unc	BU
2000 (1998) Proof	Est. 100,000	Value: 45.00				

KM# 374 5 DOLLARS **Ring Composition:** Stainless Steel **Center Composition:** Aluminum-Bronze **Subject:** 70 Years - Royal Flying Doctor Service **Obverse:** Queen's portrait **Reverse:** Insignia above bi-plane

Date	F	VF	XF	Unc	BU
1998	—	—	—	10.00	—

KM# 375 5 DOLLARS **Composition:** Aluminum-Bronze **Series:** Sydney 2000 Olympics **Obverse:** Queen's portrait **Reverse:** Two handball players

Date	F	VF	XF	Unc	BU
2000 (1998)	—	—	—	9.00	—

KM# 376 5 DOLLARS **Composition:** Aluminum-Bronze **Series:** Sydney 2000 Olympics **Obverse:** Queen's portrait **Reverse:** Two wrestlers

Date	F	VF	XF	Unc	BU
2000 (1998)	—	—	—	9.00	—

KM# 377 5 DOLLARS **Composition:** Aluminum-Bronze **Series:** Sydney 2000 Olympics **Obverse:** Queen's portrait **Reverse:** Canoeing

Date	F	VF	XF	Unc	BU
2000 (1998)	—	—	—	9.00	—

KM# 378 5 DOLLARS **Composition:** Aluminum-Bronze **Series:** Sydney 2000 Olympics **Obverse:** Queen's portrait **Reverse:** Softball player at bat

Date	F	VF	XF	Unc	BU
2000 (1998)	—	—	—	9.00	—

KM# 379 5 DOLLARS **Weight:** 31.6350 g. **Composition:** 0.9990 Silver 1.0161 oz. ASW **Series:** Sydney 2000 Olympics **Obverse:** Queen's portrait **Reverse:** Frill-necked lizard

Date	Mintage	F	VF	XF	Unc	BU
2000 (1998) Proof	Est. 100,000	Value: 50.00				

KM# 380 5 DOLLARS **Weight:** 31.6350 g. **Composition:** 0.9990 Silver 1.0161 oz. ASW **Series:** Sydney 2000 Olympics **Obverse:** Queen's portrait **Reverse:** 9 Australian faces of different races

Date	Mintage	F	VF	XF	Unc	BU
2000 (1998) Proof	Est. 100,000	Value: 40.00				

KM# 381 5 DOLLARS **Weight:** 31.6350 g. **Composition:** 0.9990 Silver 1.0161 oz. ASW **Series:** Sydney 2000 Olympics **Obverse:** Queen's portrait **Reverse:** Two dancing figures in dream circle, Olympic logo

Date	Mintage	F	VF	XF	Unc	BU
2000 (1998) Proof	Est. 100,000	Value: 40.00				

KM# 382 5 DOLLARS **Weight:** 31.6350 g. **Composition:** 0.9990 Silver 1.0161 oz. ASW **Series:** Sydney 2000 Olympics **Obverse:** Queen's portrait **Reverse:** Kangaroo in circle of grass trees above games logo

Date	Mintage	F	VF	XF	Unc	BU
2000 (1998) Proof	Est. 100,000	Value: 40.00				

KM# 568 5 DOLLARS **Weight:** 1.5552 g. **Composition:** 0.9990 Gold 0.05 oz. AGW **Subject:** Year of the Tiger **Obverse:** Bust of Queen Elizabeth II right **Reverse:** Tiger springing right **Edge:** Reeded **Size:** 14.1 mm.

Date	Mintage	F	VF	XF	Unc	BU
1998P	100,000	—	—	—	27.00	—

KM# 438 5 DOLLARS **Weight:** 31.6350 g. **Composition:** 0.9990 Silver 1.0161 oz. ASW **Series:** Sydney 2000 Olympics **Obverse:** Queen's head right **Reverse:** Two emus with eggs and chicks **Edge:** Reeded

Date	Mintage	F	VF	XF	Unc	BU
2000 (1999) Proof	100,000	Value: 40.00				

KM# 439 5 DOLLARS **Weight:** 31.6350 g. **Composition:** 0.9990 Silver 1.0161 oz. ASW **Series:** Sydney 2000 Olympics **Obverse:** Queen's head right **Reverse:** Koala in tree

Date	Mintage	F	VF	XF	Unc	BU
2000 (1999) Proof	100,000	Value: 40.00				

KM# 448 5 DOLLARS **Weight:** 1.5710 g. **Composition:** 0.9990 Gold .0505 oz. AGW **Obverse:** Queen's portrait right **Reverse:** Kangaroo facing left **Edge:** Reeded

Date	Mintage	F	VF	XF	Unc	BU
1999	200,000	—	—	—	30.00	—

KM# 456 5 DOLLARS **Weight:** 1.5710 g. **Composition:** 0.9990 Platinum .0500 oz. APW **Obverse:** Queen's head right **Reverse:** Koala on log

Date	Mintage	F	VF	XF	Unc	BU
1999	20,000	—	—	—	40.00	—

KM# 425 5 DOLLARS **Weight:** 1.5710 g. **Composition:** 0.9999 Gold .0500 oz. AGW **Subject:** Year of the Rabbit

Obverse: Queen's portrait **Reverse:** Rabbit **Note:** Similar to 100 Dollars, KM#428.

Date	F	VF	XF	Unc	BU
1999	—	—	—	35.00	—

KM# 407 5 DOLLARS **Composition:** Brass **Series:** Sydney 2000 Olympics **Obverse:** Queen's portrait **Reverse:** Two basketball players

Date	F	VF	XF	Unc	BU
2000 (1999)	—	—	—	8.00	—

KM# 408 5 DOLLARS **Composition:** Brass **Series:** Sydney 2000 Olympics **Obverse:** Queen's portrait **Reverse:** Tae Kwon Do competitor

Date	F	VF	XF	Unc	BU
2000 (1999)	—	—	—	8.00	—

KM# 409 5 DOLLARS **Composition:** Brass **Series:** Sydney 2000 Olympics **Obverse:** Queen's portrait **Reverse:** Tennis player

Date	F	VF	XF	Unc	BU
2000 (1999)	—	—	—	8.00	—

KM# 418 5 DOLLARS **Weight:** 20.0000 g. **Composition:** Brass **Series:** Sydney 2000 Olympics **Obverse:** Queen's head right **Reverse:** Shooter with shotgun

Date	F	VF	XF	Unc	BU
2000 (1999)	—	—	—	8.00	—

KM# 419 5 DOLLARS **Weight:** 20.0000 g. **Composition:** Brass **Series:** Sydney 2000 Olympics **Obverse:** Queen's head right **Reverse:** Table tennis player

Date	F	VF	XF	Unc	BU
2000 (1999)	—	—	—	8.00	—

KM# 420 5 DOLLARS **Weight:** 20.0000 g. **Composition:** Brass **Series:** Sydney 2000 Olympics **Obverse:** Queen's head right **Reverse:** Fencer in action

Date	F	VF	XF	Unc	BU
2000 (1999)	—	—	—	8.00	—

KM# 421 5 DOLLARS **Weight:** 20.0000 g. **Composition:** Brass **Series:** Sydney 2000 Olympics **Obverse:** Queen's head right **Reverse:** Badminton player

Date	F	VF	XF	Unc	BU
2000 (1999)	—	—	—	9.00	—

KM# 429 5 DOLLARS **Weight:** 20.0000 g. **Composition:** Brass **Series:** Sydney 2000 Olympics **Obverse:** Queen's head right **Reverse:** Pentathlon events portrayed by 5 participants

Date	F	VF	XF	Unc	BU
2000	—	—	—	9.00	—

KM# 430 5 DOLLARS **Weight:** 20.0000 g. **Composition:** Brass **Obverse:** Queen's head right **Reverse:** Judo match

Date	F	VF	XF	Unc	BU
2000	—	—	—	8.00	—

KM# 431 5 DOLLARS **Weight:** 20.0000 g. **Composition:** Brass **Series:** Sydney 2000 Olympics **Obverse:** Queen's head right **Reverse:** Rower

Date	F	VF	XF	Unc	BU
2000	—	—	—	9.00	—

KM# 432 5 DOLLARS **Weight:** 20.0000 g. **Composition:** Brass **Series:** Sydney 2000 Olympics **Obverse:** Queen's head right **Reverse:** Two men boxing

Date	F	VF	XF	Unc	BU
2000	—	—	—	9.00	—

KM# 433 5 DOLLARS **Weight:** 20.0000 g. **Composition:** Brass **Series:** Sydney 2000 Olympics **Obverse:** Queen's head right **Reverse:** Volleyball player

Date	F	VF	XF	Unc	BU
2000	—	—	—	9.00	—

KM# 434 5 DOLLARS **Weight:** 1.5710 g. **Composition:** 0.9999 Gold .0500 oz. AGW **Series:** Sydney 2000 Olympics **Obverse:** Queen's head right **Reverse:** Equestrian putting horse through jumps

Date	F	VF	XF	Unc	BU
2000	—	—	—	9.00	—

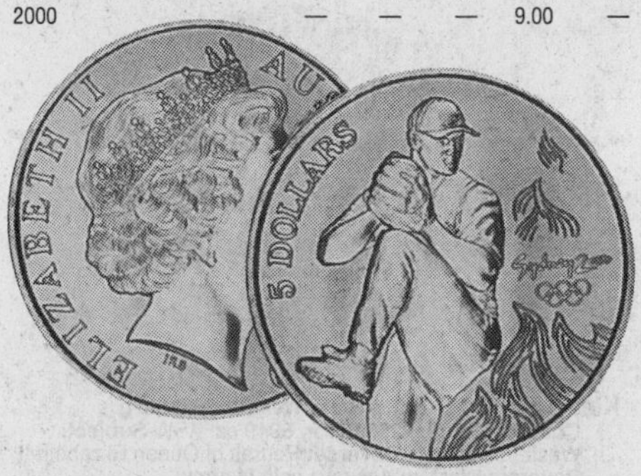

KM# 435 5 DOLLARS **Weight:** 1.5710 g. **Composition:** 0.9999 Gold .0500 oz. AGW **Series:** Sydney 2000 Olympics **Obverse:** Queen's head right **Reverse:** Pitcher winding up

Date	F	VF	XF	Unc	BU
2000	—	—	—	9.00	—

KM# 436 5 DOLLARS **Weight:** 20.0000 g. **Composition:** Brass **Series:** Sydney 2000 Olympics **Obverse:** Queen's head right **Reverse:** Swimmer

Date	F	VF	XF	Unc	BU
2000	—	—	—	9.00	—

KM# 601 5 DOLLARS **Ring Composition:** Stainless Steel**Center Weight:** 10.5200 g. **Center Composition:** Aluminum-Bronze **Subject:** Battle of Sunda Strait **Obverse:** Bust of Queen Elizabeth II right **Reverse:** Ships bell from the "USS Houston" **Edge:** Plain **Shape:** 24-sided **Size:** 27.8 mm. **Note:** Demagnetized.

Date	F	VF	XF	Unc	BU
2000	—	—	—	7.50	—

KM# 464 5 DOLLARS **Weight:** 1.5710 g. **Composition:** 0.9990 Gold .0505 oz. AGW **Obverse:** Queen's head right **Reverse:** Two kangaroos bounding left

Date	F	VF	XF	Unc	BU
2000	—	—	—	30.00	—

KM# 469 5 DOLLARS **Weight:** 1.5710 g. **Composition:** 0.9990 Platinum .0500 oz. APW **Obverse:** Queen's portrait **Reverse:** Seated koala

Date	F	VF	XF	Unc	BU
2000	—	—	—	40.00	—

KM# 478 5 DOLLARS **Ring Composition:** Stainless Steel**Center Weight:** 10.5200 g. **Center Composition:** Aluminum-Bronze **Subject:** Phar Lap **Obverse:** Queen's head right within ring **Reverse:** Jockey atop Phar Lap racing right **Edge:** Plain, 24-sided

Date	F	VF	XF	Unc	BU
2000	—	—	—	10.00	—

KM# 510 5 DOLLARS **Weight:** 28.0000 g. **Composition:** Aluminum-Bronze **Subject:** Phar Lap **Obverse:** Queen's head right **Reverse:** Phar Lap and jockey **Edge:** Reeded **Size:** 38.7 mm.

Date	Mintage	F	VF	XF	Unc	BU
2000 Proof	20,000	Value: 25.00				

KM# 515 5 DOLLARS **Weight:** 31.6350 g. **Composition:** 0.9990 Silver 1.0161 oz. ASW **Series:** Olympics - Sydney Harbor Bridge **Obverse:** Queen's head right **Reverse:** Sydney suspension bridge **Edge Lettering:** GAMES OF THE XXVII OLYMPIAD twice **Size:** 40.5 mm.

Date	Mintage	F	VF	XF	Unc	BU
2000 Prooflike	100,000	—	—	—	40.00	—

KM# 516 5 DOLLARS **Weight:** 31.6350 g. **Composition:** 0.9990 Silver 1.0161 oz. ASW **Series:** Olympics - Kookaburra **Obverse:** Queen's head right **Reverse:** Kookaburra with Waratah leaves **Size:** 40.5 mm.

Date	Mintage	F	VF	XF	Unc	BU
2000 Prooflike	100,000	—	—	—	40.00	—

KM# 517 5 DOLLARS **Composition:** Aluminum-Bronze **Subject:** Paralympics **Obverse:** Queen's head right **Reverse:** Wheelchair racer and multi-color logo **Edge:** Reeded **Size:** 38.6 mm.

Date	F	VF	XF	Unc	BU
2000	—	—	—	12.50	—

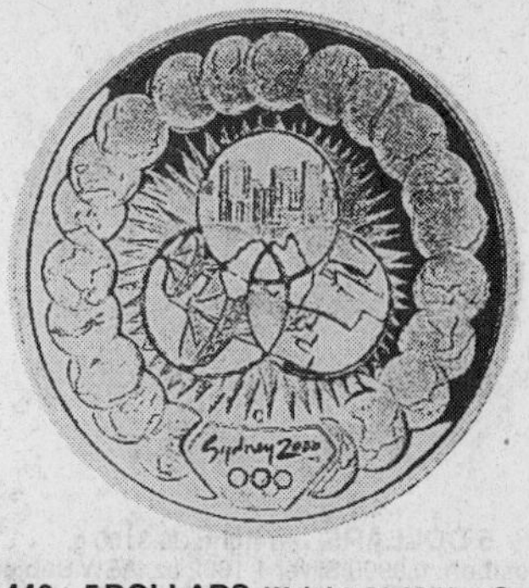

KM# 440 5 DOLLARS **Weight:** 31.6350 g. **Composition:** 0.9990 Silver 1.0161 oz. ASW **Series:** Sydney 2000 Olympics **Obverse:** Queen's head right **Reverse:** Three radiant circular views within circle of round maps

Date	Mintage	F	VF	XF	Unc	BU
2000 Proof	100,000	Value: 37.50				

KM# 441 5 DOLLARS **Weight:** 31.6350 g. **Composition:** 0.9990 Silver 1.0161 oz. ASW **Series:** Sydney 2000 Olympics **Obverse:** Queen's head right **Reverse:** 7 figures like spokes in a wheel

Date	Mintage	F	VF	XF	Unc	BU
2000 Proof	100,000	Value: 37.50				

KM# 569 5 DOLLARS **Weight:** 1.5552 g. **Composition:** 0.9990 Gold 0.05 oz. AGW **Subject:** Year of the Dragon **Obverse:** Bust of Queen Elizabeth II right **Reverse:** Dragon **Edge:** Reeded **Size:** 14.1 mm.

Date	Mintage	F	VF	XF	Unc	BU
2000P	100,000	—	—	—	27.00	—

KM# 538 5 DOLLARS **Weight:** 1.5710 g. **Composition:** 0.9990 Gold .0500 oz. AGW **Subject:** Year of the Snake **Obverse:** Queen's head right **Reverse:** Snake in tree **Edge:** Reeded **Size:** 14.1 mm.

Date	Mintage	F	VF	XF	Unc	BU
2001	—	—	—	—	45.00	—
2001P Proof	100,000	Value: 27.00				

KM# 591 5 DOLLARS **Weight:** 36.3100 g. **Composition:** 0.9990 Silver 1.1662 oz. ASW **Subject:** Centennial of Federation Series Finale **Obverse:** Bust of Queen Elizabeth II right **Reverse:** Multi-color dual hologram: map and rotunda **Edge:** Reeded **Size:** 38.74 mm.

Date	F	VF	XF	Unc	BU
2001 Proof	— Value: 30.00				

KM# 592 5 DOLLARS **Weight:** 36.3100 g. **Composition:** 0.9990 Silver 1.1662 oz. ASW **Subject:** Barton and Reid **Obverse:** Bust of Queen Elizabeth II right **Reverse:** Portraits of Dame Flora Reid and Lady Jean Barton **Edge:** Reeded **Size:** 38.74 mm.

Date	F	VF	XF	Unc	BU
2001 Proof	—	Value: 20.00			

KM# 582 5 DOLLARS **Weight:** 1.5552 g. **Composition:** 0.9990 Gold 0.05 oz. AGW **Subject:** Year of the Horse **Obverse:** Bust of Queen Elizabeth II right **Reverse:** Horse galloping towards us **Edge:** Reeded **Size:** 14.1 mm.

Date	Mintage	F	VF	XF	Unc	BU
2002P	100,000	—	—	—	27.00	—

KM# 75 10 DOLLARS **Weight:** 20.0000 g. **Composition:** 0.9250 Silver .5949 oz. ASW **Subject:** XII Commonwealth Games - Brisbane

Date	Mintage	F	VF	XF	Unc	BU
1982	126,000	—	—	—	7.00	—
1982 Proof	85,000	Value: 10.00				

KM# 85 10 DOLLARS **Weight:** 20.0000 g. **Composition:** 0.9250 Silver .5949 oz. ASW **Subject:** 150th Anniversary - State of Victoria

Date	Mintage	F	VF	XF	Unc	BU
1985	82,000	—	—	—	8.00	—
1985 Proof	56,000	Value: 16.00				

KM# 88 10 DOLLARS **Weight:** 20.0000 g. **Composition:** 0.9250 Silver .5949 oz. ASW **Subject:** 150th Anniversary - South Australia

Date	Mintage	F	VF	XF	Unc	BU
1986	78,000	—	—	—	8.00	—
1986 Proof	52,000	Value: 16.00				

KM# 93 10 DOLLARS **Weight:** 20.0000 g. **Composition:** 0.9250 Silver .5949 oz. ASW **Subject:** New South Wales

Date	Mintage	F	VF	XF	Unc	BU
1987	65,000	—	—	—	8.00	—
1987 Proof	50,000	Value: 16.00				

KM# 103 10 DOLLARS **Weight:** 20.0000 g. **Composition:** 0.9250 Silver .5949 oz. ASW **Subject:** Landing of Governor Philip

Date	F	VF	XF	Unc	BU
1988	—	—	—	10.00	—
1988 Proof	—	Value: 18.00			

KM# 114 10 DOLLARS **Weight:** 20.0000 g. **Composition:** 0.9250 Silver .5949 oz. ASW **Subject:** Queensland

Date	F	VF	XF	Unc	BU
1989	—	—	—	8.50	—
1989 Proof	—	Value: 16.50			

KM# 133 10 DOLLARS **Weight:** 20.0000 g. **Composition:** 0.9250 Silver .5949 oz. ASW **Obverse:** Portrait of Queen Elizabeth II **Reverse:** Kookaburras

Date	F	VF	XF	Unc	BU
1989 Proof	—	Value: 50.00			

KM# 136 10 DOLLARS **Weight:** 20.0000 g. **Composition:** 0.9250 Silver .5949 oz. ASW **Obverse:** Portrait of Queen Elizabeth II **Reverse:** Sulpher-crested cockatoo

Date	F	VF	XF	Unc	BU
1990 Proof	—	Value: 50.00			

KM# 137 10 DOLLARS **Weight:** 20.0000 g. **Composition:** 0.9250 Silver .5949 oz. ASW **Subject:** Western Australia **Obverse:** Portrait of Queen Elizabeth II **Reverse:** Western Australia coat of arms

Date	F	VF	XF	Unc	BU
1990	—	—	—	12.00	—
1990 Proof	—	Value: 22.50			

KM# 153 10 DOLLARS **Weight:** 20.0000 g. **Composition:** 0.9250 Silver .5949 oz. ASW **Subject:** Tasmania

Date	Mintage	F	VF	XF	Unc	BU
1991	5,691	—	—	—	12.00	—
1991 Proof	5,504	Value: 30.00				

KM# 156 10 DOLLARS **Weight:** 20.0000 g. **Composition:** 0.9250 Silver .5949 oz. ASW **Reverse:** Birds of Australia- Jabiru Stork

Date	Mintage	F	VF	XF	Unc	BU
1991 Proof	50,000	Value: 42.00				

KM# 161 10 DOLLARS **Weight:** 62.2140 g. **Composition:** 0.9990 Silver 2.0000 oz. ASW **Reverse:** Australian Kookaburra

Date	Mintage	F	VF	XF	Unc	BU
1991	—	—	—	—	15.00	—
1991 Proof	5,000	Value: 55.00				

KM# 180 10 DOLLARS **Weight:** 311.0670 g. **Composition:** 0.9990 Silver 10.0000 oz. ASW **Reverse:** Australian kookaburra sitting on branch; similar to 30 Dollars, KM#181

Date	Mintage	F	VF	XF	Unc	BU
1992	—	—	—	—	85.00	—
1992 Proof	2,500	Value: 325				

KM# 221 10 DOLLARS **Weight:** 20.0000 g. **Composition:** 0.9250 Silver .5949 oz. ASW **Reverse:** Palm cockatoo

Date	Mintage	F	VF	XF	Unc	BU
1993 Proof	Est. 35,000	Value: 45.00				

KM# 225 10 DOLLARS **Weight:** 20.7700 g. **Composition:** 0.9990 Silver .6678 oz. ASW **Series:** Olympic Gold Medalists - Edwin Flack 1896

Date	Mintage	F	VF	XF	Unc	BU
1994 Matte Proof	Est. 30,000	Value: 20.00				

KM# 317 10 DOLLARS **Weight:** 20.0000 g. **Composition:** 0.9250 Silver .5949 oz. ASW **Subject:** UNEP - Palm Cockatoo **Obverse:** Queen's portrait **Reverse:** Palm cockatoo with UNEP logo

Date	Mintage	F	VF	XF	Unc	BU
1993 Proof	Est. 55,000	Value: 40.00				

KM# 226 10 DOLLARS **Weight:** 20.7700 g. **Composition:** 0.9990 Silver .6678 oz. ASW **Series:** Olympic Gold Medalists - Sarah Durack 1912

Date	Mintage	F	VF	XF	Unc	BU
1994 Matte Proof	Est. 30,000	Value: 20.00				

KM# 188 10 DOLLARS **Weight:** 20.0000 g. **Composition:** 0.9250 Silver .5949 oz. ASW **Reverse:** Northern Territory state arms

Date	Mintage	F	VF	XF	Unc	BU
1992	23,000	—	—	—	10.00	—
1992 Proof	18,000	Value: 20.00				

KM# 296 10 DOLLARS **Weight:** 20.7700 g. **Composition:** 0.9990 Silver .6678 oz. ASW **Reverse:** Numbat

Date	Mintage	F	VF	XF	Unc	BU
1995 Proof	25,000	Value: 32.50				

KM# 301 10 DOLLARS **Weight:** 20.7700 g. **Composition:** 0.9990 Silver .6678 oz. ASW **Series:** Olympic Gold Medalists - Dawn Fraser **Obverse:** Queen's portrait **Reverse:** Half-length portrait

Date	Mintage	F	VF	XF	Unc	BU
1995 Matte Proof	Est. 30,000	Value: 25.00				

KM# 302 10 DOLLARS **Weight:** 20.7700 g. **Composition:** 0.9990 Silver .6678 oz. ASW **Series:** Olympic Gold Medalists - Murray Rose **Obverse:** Swimmer's portrait

Date	Mintage	F	VF	XF	Unc	BU
1995 Matte Proof	Est. 30,000	Value: 25.00				

KM# 270 10 DOLLARS **Weight:** 311.0670 g. **Composition:** 0.9990 Silver 10.0000 oz. ASW **Reverse:** Kookaburra on branch **Note:** Similar to 1 Dollar, KM#260.

Date	F	VF	XF	Unc	BU
1995	—	—	—	85.00	—
1995 Proof	—	Value: 300			

KM# 231 10 DOLLARS **Weight:** 311.0350 g. **Composition:** 0.9990 Silver 10.0000 oz. ASW **Subject:** The Australian Kookaburra **Obverse:** Queen's portrait **Reverse:** Pair of Kookaburras on branch **Note:** Illustration reduced. Actual size: 75 millimeters.

Date	Mintage	F	VF	XF	Unc	BU
1993 (ae) Proof	500	Value: 550				
1994	—	—	—	—	75.00	—
1994 Proof	—	Value: 200				

KM# 228 10 DOLLARS **Weight:** 311.0670 g. **Composition:** 0.9990 Silver 10.0000 oz. ASW **Reverse:** Kookaburra feeding nestling **Note:** Similar to 1 Dollar, KM#209.

Date	F	VF	XF	Unc	BU
1993	—	—	—	75.00	—
1993 Proof	—	Value: 200			

KM# 199 10 DOLLARS **Weight:** 20.0000 g. **Composition:** 0.9250 Silver .5949 oz. ASW **Reverse:** Emperor Penguin

Date	Mintage	F	VF	XF	Unc	BU
1992 Proof	Est. 35,000	Value: 45.00				

KM# 210 10 DOLLARS **Weight:** 20.0000 g. **Composition:** 0.9250 Silver .5949 oz. ASW **Reverse:** Australian Capital Territory state arms

Date	F	VF	XF	Unc	BU
1993	—	—	—	12.00	—
1993 Proof	—	Value: 20.00			

KM# 223 10 DOLLARS **Weight:** 20.0000 g. **Composition:** 0.9250 Silver .5949 oz. ASW **Reverse:** Wedge-tailed eagle

Date	Mintage	F	VF	XF	Unc	BU
1994 Proof	34,000	Value: 45.00				

KM# 291 10 DOLLARS **Weight:** 311.0670 g. **Composition:** 0.9990 Silver 10.0000 oz. ASW **Reverse:**

Kookaburra in flight **Note:** Illustration reduced. Actual size: 75.5 millimeters.

Date	Mintage	F	VF	XF	Unc	BU
1995P Proof	1,300	Value: 275				
1995 (ge) Proof	800	Value: 300				
Note: Privy mark on gold insert						
1996	—	—	—	—	75.00	—

KM# 314 10 DOLLARS **Weight:** 20.0000 g. **Composition:** 0.9250 Silver .5949 oz. ASW **Reverse:** Southern right whale with baby

Date	Mintage	F	VF	XF	Unc	BU
1996 Proof	24,000	Value: 40.00				

KM# 315 10 DOLLARS **Weight:** 20.7700 g. **Composition:** 0.9990 Silver .6678 oz. ASW **Series:** Australia's Greatest Olympics **Reverse:** Betty Cuthbert

Date	Mintage	F	VF	XF	Unc	BU
1996 Matte Unc	30,000	—	—	—	22.50	—

KM# 316 10 DOLLARS **Weight:** 20.7700 g. **Composition:** 0.9990 Silver .6678 oz. ASW **Series:** Australia's Greatest Olympics **Reverse:** Shirley Strickland

Date	Mintage	F	VF	XF	Unc	BU
1996 Matte Unc	30,000	—	—	—	22.50	—

KM# 353 10 DOLLARS **Weight:** 20.7700 g. **Composition:** 0.9990 Silver .6678 oz. ASW **Subject:** Sydney Opera House **Obverse:** Queen's portrait **Reverse:** Opera house and Sydney shoreline

Date	Mintage	F	VF	XF	Unc	BU
1997 Matte Proof	20,000	Value: 28.00				

KM# 354 10 DOLLARS **Weight:** 20.7700 g. **Composition:** 0.9990 Silver .6678 oz. ASW **Subject:** Sydney Harbour Bridge **Obverse:** Queen's portrait **Reverse:** Bridge over harbour

Date	Mintage	F	VF	XF	Unc	BU
1997 Matte Proof	20,000	Value: 28.00				

KM# 367.1 10 DOLLARS **Weight:** 20.0000 g. **Composition:** 0.9990 Silver .6678 oz. ASW **Subject:** Red-tailed Black Cockatoo **Obverse:** Queen's portrait **Reverse:** Cockatoo perched in dead tree

Date	Mintage	F	VF	XF	Unc	BU
1997 Proof	24,000	Value: 35.00				

KM# 367.2 10 DOLLARS **Weight:** 40.0000 g. **Composition:** 0.9250 Silver 1.1896 oz. ASW

Date	Mintage	F	VF	XF	Unc	BU
1997 Proof	14,000	Value: 50.00				

KM# 494 10 DOLLARS **Weight:** 311.0350 g. **Composition:** 0.9990 Silver 10.0000 oz. ASW **Subject:** Kookaburra Bullion **Obverse:** Queen's head right. **Reverse:** Kookaburra on fence. **Edge:** Reeded and plain sections. **Size:** 75 mm. **Note:** Illustration reduced.

Date	Mintage	F	VF	XF	Unc	BU
1997P Proof	—	Value: 325				

KM# 351 10 DOLLARS **Weight:** 311.0670 g. **Composition:** 0.9990 Silver 10.0000 oz. ASW **Subject:** Kookaburra and Nestling **Obverse:** Queen's portrait **Reverse:** Kookaburra looking right, nestling **Note:** Similar to 1 Dollar, KM#318.

Date	F	VF	XF	Unc	BU
1997	—	—	—	75.00	—

KM# 387 10 DOLLARS **Weight:** 20.7700 g. **Composition:** 0.9990 Silver .6671 oz. ASW **Subject:** Melbourne **Obverse:** Queen's portrait **Reverse:** Melbourne cricket grounds

Date	Mintage	F	VF	XF	Unc	BU
1998 Matte Proof	20,000	Value: 18.00				

KM# 388 10 DOLLARS **Weight:** 20.7700 g. **Composition:** 0.9990 Silver .6671 oz. ASW **Subject:** Melbourne **Obverse:** Queen's portrait **Reverse:** Street car

Date	Mintage	F	VF	XF	Unc	BU
1998 Matte Proof	20,000	Value: 18.00				

KM# 397 10 DOLLARS **Weight:** 20.0000 g. **Composition:** 0.9250 Silver .5948 oz. ASW **Subject:** Northern Hairy-Nosed Wombat **Obverse:** Queen's portrait **Reverse:** Wombat above denomination

Date	Mintage	F	VF	XF	Unc	BU
1998 Proof	24,000	Value: 32.50				

KM# 414 10 DOLLARS **Weight:** 20.7700 g. **Composition:** 0.9990 Silver .6671 oz. ASW **Subject:** The Snowy Mountain Scheme **Obverse:** Queen's portrait **Reverse:** Tunnel building scene

Date	F	VF	XF	Unc	BU
1999	—	—	—	18.00	—

KM# 415 10 DOLLARS **Weight:** 20.7700 g. **Composition:** 0.9990 Silver .6671 oz. ASW **Subject:** The Snowy Mountain Scheme **Obverse:** Queen's portrait **Reverse:** Dam building scene

Date	F	VF	XF	Unc	BU
1999	—	—	—	18.00	—

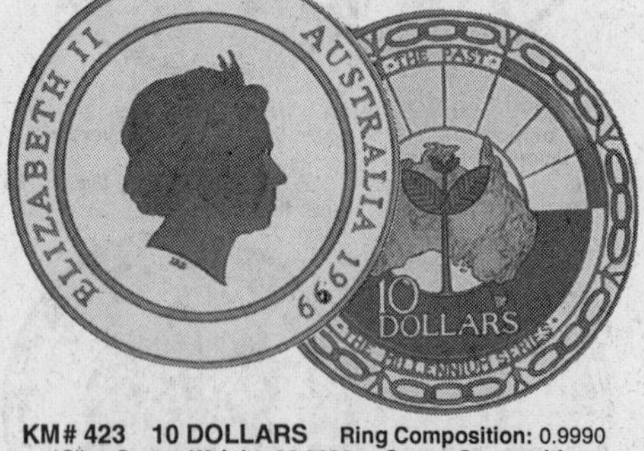

KM# 423 10 DOLLARS **Ring Composition:** 0.9990 Silver **Center Weight:** 33.5300 g. **Center Composition:** Copper **Subject:** Millennium Series, The Past **Obverse:** Queen's head right **Reverse:** Seedling on Australian map above denomination with rising sun background **Edge:** Reeded

Date	Mintage	F	VF	XF	Unc	BU
1999 Proof	20,000	Value: 40.00				

KM# 504 10 DOLLARS **Weight:** 312.3470 g. **Composition:** 0.9990 Silver 10.0321 oz. ASW **Subject:** Year of the Rabbit **Obverse:** Queen's head right **Reverse:** Rabbit **Edge:** Reeded and plain sections **Size:** 75.5 mm.

Date	Mintage	F	VF	XF	Unc	BU
1999	—	—	—	—	80.00	—
1999 Proof	2,500	Value: 350				

KM# 511 10 DOLLARS **Weight:** 36.0100 g. **Composition:** 0.9990 Silver 1.1566 oz. ASW **Series:** Millennium - The Present **Obverse:** Queen's head right **Reverse:** Australian map behind young tree **Edge:** Reeded **Size:** 38.7 mm.

Date	Mintage	F	VF	XF	Unc	BU
2000 Proof	20,000	Value: 40.00				

KM# 524 10 DOLLARS **Weight:** 311.0350 g. **Composition:** 0.9990 Silver 10.0000 oz. ASW **Series:** Dragons **Obverse:** Queen's head right **Reverse:** Dragon **Edge:** Segmented reeding **Size:** 75.5 mm.

Date		F	VF	XF	Unc	BU
2000 Proof	—	Value: 275				

KM# 518 10 DOLLARS **Weight:** 311.0350 g. **Composition:** 0.9990 Silver 10.0000 oz. ASW **Subject:** Paralympics **Obverse:** Queen's head right **Reverse:** Sydney Opera House and harbor bridge **Edge:** Lettering with logo **Edge Lettering:** GAMES OF THE XI PARALYMPIAD **Size:** 75 mm. **Note:** Illustration reduced.

Date	Mintage	F	VF	XF	Unc	BU
2000 Prooflike	3,000	—	—	—	300	—

KM# 446 10 DOLLARS **Weight:** 312.3470 g. **Composition:** 0.9990 Silver 10.0000 oz. ASW **Obverse:** Queen's head right **Reverse:** Two kookaburras on branch **Edge:** Interrupted reeding

Date		F	VF	XF	Unc	BU
2000		—	—	—	75.00	—

KM# 539 10 DOLLARS **Weight:** 311.0350 g. **Composition:** 0.9990 Silver 10.0000 oz. ASW **Subject:** Year of the Snake **Obverse:** Queen's head right **Reverse:** Snake with eggs **Edge:** Segmented reeding **Size:** 75.5 mm.

Date	Mintage	F	VF	XF	Unc	BU
2001		—	—	—	150	—
2001P Proof	250	Value: 275				

KM# 593 10 DOLLARS **Ring Composition:** Copper **Center Weight:** 33.1500 g. **Center Composition:** 0.9990 Gold Plated Silver 1.0647 oz. AGW **Subject:** "The Future" **Obverse:** Bust of Queen Elizabeth II right **Reverse:** Tree, map and denomination **Edge:** Reeded **Size:** 38.74 mm.

Date	Mintage	F	VF	XF	Unc	BU
2001	20,000	Value: 40.00				

KM# 596 10 DOLLARS **Weight:** 311.0350 g. **Composition:** 0.9990 Silver 9.99 oz. ASW **Subject:** Calendar Evolution **Obverse:** Bust of Queen Elizabeth II right **Reverse:** Multicolor solar system in center **Edge:** Segmented reeding **Size:** 75.5 mm. **Note:** Illustration reduced. Actual size: 75.5 millimeters.

Date	Mintage	F	VF	XF	Unc	BU
ND(2001) Proof	15,000	Value: 300				

KM# 583 10 DOLLARS **Weight:** 311.0350 g. **Composition:** 0.9990 Silver 9.99 oz. ASW **Subject:** Year of the Horse **Obverse:** Bust of Queen Elizabeth II right **Reverse:** Horse running left **Edge:** Segmented reeding **Size:** 75.5 mm.

Date	Mintage	F	VF	XF	Unc	BU
2002P Proof	500	Value: 275				

KM# 603 10 DOLLARS **Weight:** 311.0350 g. **Composition:** 0.9990 Silver 9.99 oz. ASW **Subject:** Kookaburra **Obverse:** Queen's portrait **Reverse:** Flying bird over map **Edge:** Reeded **Size:** 74.9 mm.

Date		F	VF	XF	Unc	BU
2002 Proof	—	Value: 150				

KM# 89 15 DOLLARS **Weight:** 3.1103 g. **Composition:** 0.9990 Gold .1000 oz. AGW **Obverse:** Elizabeth II **Reverse:** Little Hero

Date	Mintage	F	VF	XF	Unc	BU
1986P Proof	15,000	Value: 60.00				
1987	266,000	—	—	—	BV+12%	—
1988	104,000	—	—	—	BV+12%	—
1989	—	—	—	—	BV+12%	—

KM# 95 15 DOLLARS **Weight:** 3.1103 g. **Composition:** 0.9990 Gold .1000 oz. AGW **Reverse:** Golden Aussie

Date	Mintage	F	VF	XF	Unc	BU
1987P Proof	15,000	Value: 60.00				

KM# 104 15 DOLLARS **Weight:** 3.1103 g. **Composition:** 0.9990 Gold .1000 oz. AGW **Reverse:** Jubilee Nugget

Date	Mintage	F	VF	XF	Unc	BU
1988P Proof	Est. 10,000	Value: 60.00				

KM# 108 15 DOLLARS **Weight:** 3.1370 g. **Composition:** 0.9990 Platinum .1000 oz. APW **Note:** Similar to 100 Dollars, KM#111.

Date		F	VF	XF	Unc	BU
1988		—	—	—	BV+15%	—
1989 Proof	—	Value: 75.00				

KM# 123 15 DOLLARS **Weight:** 3.1370 g. **Composition:** 0.9990 Platinum .1000 oz. APW **Note:** Similar to 100 Dollars, KM#126.

Date	Mintage	F	VF	XF	Unc	BU
1989 Proof	2,400	Value: 75.00				
1990 Proof	—	Value: 75.00				

KM# 118 15 DOLLARS **Weight:** 3.1103 g. **Composition:** 0.9990 Gold .1000 oz. AGW **Reverse:** Red kangaroo

Date	Mintage	F	VF	XF	Unc	BU
1989 Proof	2,200	Value: 60.00				
1990	200,000	—	—	—	BV+12%	—

KM# 141 15 DOLLARS **Weight:** 3.1103 g. **Composition:** 0.9990 Gold .1000 oz. AGW **Reverse:** Gray kangaroo

Date	Mintage	F	VF	XF	Unc	BU
1990 Proof	7,000	Value: 55.00				
1991	150,000	—	—	—	BV+12%	—

KM# 146 15 DOLLARS **Weight:** 3.1370 g. **Composition:** 0.9990 Platinum .1000 oz. APW **Subject:** Koala **Obverse:** Similar to 100 Dollars, KM#149

Date	Mintage	F	VF	XF	Unc	BU
1990 Proof	2,500	Value: 75.00				
1991	20,000	—	—	—	BV+15%	—
1991 Proof	1,000	Value: 85.00				

KM# 166 15 DOLLARS **Weight:** 3.1103 g. **Composition:** 0.9990 Gold .1000 oz. AGW **Subject:** Common Wallaroo **Obverse:** Elizabeth II **Reverse:** Similar to 100 Dollars, KM#169

Date	Mintage	F	VF	XF	Unc	BU
1991 Proof	1,975	Value: 70.00				
1992	150,000	—	—	—	BV+12%	—

KM# 171 15 DOLLARS **Weight:** 3.1370 g. **Composition:** 0.9990 Platinum .1000 oz. APW **Subject:** Koala **Obverse:** Elizabeth II **Reverse:** Similar to 100 Dollars, KM#174

Date	Mintage	F	VF	XF	Unc	BU
1992	20,000	—	—	—	BV+ 15%	—

KM# 390 15 DOLLARS **Weight:** 3.1103 g. **Composition:** 0.9990 Gold .1000 oz. AGW **Obverse:** Queen's portrait **Reverse:** Nail-tailed wallaby **Note:** Similar to 25 Dollars, KM#391.

Date	Mintage	F	VF	XF	Unc	BU
1992 (ae) Proof	500	Value: 100				

KM# 192 15 DOLLARS **Weight:** 3.1370 g. **Composition:** 0.9990 Platinum .1000 oz. APW **Obverse:** Similar to 100 Dollars, KM#195

Date		F	VF	XF	Unc	BU
1993		—	—	—	BV+15%	—

KM# 234 15 DOLLARS **Weight:** 3.1103 g. **Composition:** 0.9990 Gold .1000 oz. AGW **Subject:** Whiptail Wallaby **Obverse:** Queen Elizabeth II **Reverse:** Whiptail wallaby

Date		F	VF	XF	Unc	BU
1993 Proof	—	Value: 75.00				
1994		—	—	—	BV+12%	—

KM# 242 15 DOLLARS **Weight:** 3.1103 g. **Composition:** 0.9990 Gold .1000 oz. AGW **Reverse:** Red Kangaroo

Date	Mintage	F	VF	XF	Unc	BU
1994 Proof	—	Value: 75.00				
1995	200,000	—	—	—	BV+12%	—

KM# 250 15 DOLLARS **Weight:** 3.1370 g. **Composition:** 0.9990 Platinum .1000 oz. APW **Reverse:** Koala mother and baby

Date	Mintage	F	VF	XF	Unc	BU
1994	20,000	—	—	—	BV+15%	—

KM# 279 15 DOLLARS Weight: 3.1370 g. **Composition:** 0.9990 Platinum .1000 oz. APW **Reverse:** Koala in fork of tree

Date	F	VF	XF	Unc	BU
1994 Proof	—	Value: 65.00			
1995	—	—	—	BV+15%	—

KM# 273 15 DOLLARS Weight: 3.1103 g. **Composition:** 0.9990 Gold .1000 oz. AGW **Reverse:** Two kangaroos

Date	Mintage	F	VF	XF	Unc	BU
1995 Proof	900	Value: 75.00				
1996	200,000	—	—	—	BV+12%	—

KM# 284 15 DOLLARS Weight: 3.1370 g. **Composition:** 0.9990 Platinum .1000 oz. APW **Reverse:** Baby koala on branch

Date	Mintage	F	VF	XF	Unc	BU
1995 Proof	800	Value: 80.00				
1996	20,000	—	—	—	BV+15%	—

KM# 298 15 DOLLARS Weight: 3.1103 g. **Composition:** 0.9990 Gold .1000 oz. AGW **Subject:** Year of the Rat

Date	F	VF	XF	Unc	BU
1996 Proof	—	Value: 60.00			

KM# 321 15 DOLLARS Weight: 3.1103 g. **Composition:** 0.9990 Gold .1000 oz. AGW **Obverse:** Queen's portrait **Reverse:** Kangaroo bounding right

Date	Mintage	F	VF	XF	Unc	BU
1996P Proof	400	Value: 200				

Note: In Proof sets only

KM# 339 15 DOLLARS Weight: 3.1103 g. **Composition:** 0.9990 Gold .1000 oz. AGW **Subject:** Kangaroo **Obverse:** Queen's portrait **Reverse:** Kangaroo bounding right

Date	Mintage	F	VF	XF	Unc	BU
1997	200,000	—	—	—	35.00	—
1997 Proof	—	Value: 50.00				

KM# 345 15 DOLLARS Weight: 3.1103 g. **Composition:** 0.9995 Platinum .1000 oz. APW **Subject:** Koalas **Obverse:** Queen's portrait **Reverse:** Cuddling koalas

Date	Mintage	F	VF	XF	Unc	BU
1997	20,000	—	—	—	BV+15%	—
1997 Proof	—	Value: 75.00				

KM# 335 15 DOLLARS Weight: 3.1103 g. **Composition:** 0.9990 Gold .1000 oz. AGW **Subject:** Year of the Ox **Obverse:** Queen's portrait **Reverse:** Bull ox looking right **Note:** Similar to 100 Dollars, KM#337.

Date	F	VF	XF	Unc	BU
1997	—	—	—	55.00	—
1997 Proof	—	Value: 65.00			

KM# 506 15 DOLLARS Weight: 3.1103 g. **Composition:** 0.9990 Gold 0.0999 oz. AGW **Subject:** Year of the Tiger **Obverse:** Bust of Queen Elizabeth II right **Reverse:** Tiger springing right **Edge:** Reeded **Size:** 16.1 mm.

Date	F	VF	XF	Unc	BU
1998P	—	—	—	85.00	—

KM# 426 15 DOLLARS Weight: 3.1130 g. **Composition:** 0.9999 Gold .1000 oz. AGW **Subject:** Year of the Rabbit **Obverse:** Queen's portrait **Reverse:** Rabbit **Note:** Similar to 100 Dollars, KM#428.

Date	F	VF	XF	Unc	BU
1999	—	—	—	55.00	—
1999 Proof	—	Value: 75.00			

KM# 449 15 DOLLARS Weight: 3.1330 g. **Composition:** 0.9990 Gold .1000 oz. AGW **Obverse:** Queen's head right **Reverse:** Kangaroo facing left **Edge:** Reeded

Date	Mintage	F	VF	XF	Unc	BU
1999	200,000	—	—	—	40.00	—

KM# 457 15 DOLLARS Weight: 3.1370 g. **Composition:** 0.9990 Platinum .1000 oz. APW **Obverse:** Queen's head right **Reverse:** Koala on log **Edge:** Reeded

Date	Mintage	F	VF	XF	Unc	BU
1999	20,000	—	—	—	BV+15%	—

KM# 465 15 DOLLARS Weight: 3.1330 g. **Composition:** 0.9990 Gold .1000 oz. AGW **Obverse:** Queen's head right **Reverse:** Two kangaroos bounding left **Edge:** Reeded

Date	F	VF	XF	Unc	BU
2000	—	—	—	40.00	—

KM# 470 15 DOLLARS Weight: 3.1370 g. **Composition:** 0.9990 Platinum .1000 oz. APW **Obverse:** Queen's head right **Reverse:** Seated koala **Edge:** Reeded

Date	F	VF	XF	Unc	BU
2000	—	—	—	BV+15%	—

KM# 526 15 DOLLARS Weight: 3.1103 g. **Composition:** 0.9990 Gold .1000 oz. AGW **Series:** Dragons **Obverse:** Queen's head right. **Reverse:** Dragon. **Edge:** Reeded. **Size:** 16.1 mm.

Date	F	VF	XF	Unc	BU
2000 Proof	—	Value: 65.00			

KM# 540 15 DOLLARS Weight: 3.1103 g. **Composition:** 0.9990 Gold .1000 oz. AGW **Subject:** Year of the Snake **Obverse:** Queen's head right **Reverse:** Snake in tree **Edge:** Reeded **Size:** 16.1 mm.

Date	Mintage	F	VF	XF	Unc	BU
2001	—	—	—	—	65.00	—
2001P Proof	7,000	Value: 85.00				

KM# 584 15 DOLLARS Weight: 3.1103 g. **Composition:** 0.9990 Gold 0.0999 oz. AGW **Subject:** Year of the Horse **Obverse:** Bust of Queen Elizabeth II right **Reverse:** Horse galloping towards half left **Edge:** Reeded **Size:** 16.1 mm.

Date	Mintage	F	VF	XF	Unc	BU
2002P Proof	7,000	Value: 85.00				

KM# 218 20 DOLLARS Weight: 33.6200 g. **Composition:** 0.9250 Silver 1.0000 oz. ASW **Series:** Olympics **Subject:** Track Winners

Date	Mintage	F	VF	XF	Unc	BU
1993 Proof	100,000	Value: 28.00				

KM# 219 20 DOLLARS Weight: 33.6200 g. **Composition:** 0.9250 Silver 1.0000 oz. ASW **Series:** Olympics **Subject:** Swimmers

Date	Mintage	F	VF	XF	Unc	BU
1993 Proof	100,000	Value: 28.00				

KM# 519 20 DOLLARS Ring Weight: 5.0077 g. **Ring Composition:** 0.9990 Silver .1610 oz. ASW **Center Weight:** 8.3979 g. **Center Composition:** 0.9990 Gold .6938 oz. AGW **Subject:** Millennium **Obverse:** Queen's head right **Reverse:** Earth view from space **Edge:** Reeded **Size:** 32 mm.

Date	F	VF	XF	Unc	BU
2000 Prooflike	—	—	—	200	—

KM# 623 20 DOLLARS Weight: 62.2070 g. **Composition:** 0.9990 Silver 1.998 oz. ASW **Subject:** USA State Quarters - 2001 **Obverse:** Queen's head right. **Reverse:** Kookaburra on branch with five state quarter designs added below. **Edge:** Reeded and plain sections.

Date	Mintage	F	VF	XF	Unc	BU
2001	10,000	—	—	—	42.00	—

KM# 595 20 DOLLARS Ring Weight: 9.4990 g. **Ring Composition:** 0.9999 Gold .3054 oz. AGW **Center Weight:** 4.5287 g. **Center Composition:** 0.9990 Silver 0.1455 oz. ASW **Subject:** Gregorian Millennium **Obverse:** Bust of Queen Elizabeth II right **Reverse:** Chronograph watch face with observatory in center and three depictions of the Earth's rotation **Edge:** Reeded **Size:** 32.1 mm. **Note:** 14.03 grams total weight.

Date	Mintage	F	VF	XF	Unc	BU
2001 Prooflike	7,500	—	—	—	200	—

KM# 597 20 DOLLARS Ring Weight: 10.7618 g. **Ring Composition:** 0.9990 Silver .3457 oz. ASW **Center Weight:** 8.8645 g. **Center Composition:** 0.9999 Gold 0.285 oz. AGW **Subject:** Centenary of Federation **Obverse:** Bust of Queen Elizabeth II right **Reverse:** National arms on a flowery background **Edge:** Reeded **Size:** 32.1 mm. **Note:** 19.63 grams total weight.

Date	Mintage	F	VF	XF	Unc	BU
ND(2001) Prooflike	7,500	—	—	—	200	—

KM# 630 20 DOLLARS Weight: 62.2070 g. **Composition:** 0.9990 Silver 1.998 oz. ASW **Subject:** USA State Quarters - 2002 **Obverse:** Queen's head right. **Reverse:** Kookaburra on branch with five state quarter designs added below. **Edge:** Reeded and plain sections.

Date	Mintage	F	VF	XF	Unc	BU
2002	10,000	—	—	—	42.00	—

KM# 90 25 DOLLARS Weight: 7.7508 g. **Composition:** 0.9990 Gold .2500 oz. AGW **Obverse:** Elizabeth II **Reverse:** Gold Eagle

Date	Mintage	F	VF	XF	Unc	BU
1986P Proof	15,000	Value: 125				
1987	233,000	—	—	—	BV+10%	—
1988	75,000	—	—	—	BV+10%	—
1989	—	—	—	—	BV+10%	—

KM# 96 25 DOLLARS **Weight:** 7.7508 g. **Composition:** 0.9990 Gold .2500 oz. AGW **Reverse:** Father's Day

Date	Mintage	F	VF	XF	Unc	BU
1987P Proof	15,000	Value: 125				

KM# 105 25 DOLLARS **Weight:** 7.7508 g. **Composition:** 0.9990 Gold .2500 oz. AGW **Reverse:** Ruby Well Nugget

Date	Mintage	F	VF	XF	Unc	BU
1988P Proof	Est. 10,000	Value: 125				

KM# 109 25 DOLLARS **Weight:** 7.8150 g. **Composition:** 0.9990 Platinum .2500 oz. APW **Note:** Similar to 100 Dollars, KM#111.

Date		F	VF	XF	Unc	BU
1988		—	—	—	BV+10%	—
1989 Proof	—	Value: 200				

KM# 124 25 DOLLARS **Weight:** 7.7508 g. **Composition:** 0.9990 Gold .2500 oz. AGW **Note:** Similar to 100 Dollars, KM#126.

Date	Mintage	F	VF	XF	Unc	BU
1989 Proof	2,400	Value: 185				
1990 Proof	—	Value: 185				

KM# 119 25 DOLLARS **Weight:** 7.7508 g. **Composition:** 0.9990 Gold .2500 oz. AGW **Reverse:** Red Kangaroo

Date	Mintage	F	VF	XF	Unc	BU
1989 Proof	2,200	Value: 145				
1990		—	—	—	BV+10%	—

KM# 142 25 DOLLARS **Weight:** 7.7508 g. **Composition:** 0.9990 Gold .2500 oz. AGW **Reverse:** Gray kangaroo

Date	Mintage	F	VF	XF	Unc	BU
1990 Proof	7,000	Value: 125				
1991	100,000	—	—	—	BV+10%	—

KM# 147 25 DOLLARS **Weight:** 7.8150 g. **Composition:** 0.9990 Platinum .2500 oz. APW **Obverse:** Similar to 100 Dollars, KM#149 **Reverse:** Koala

Date	Mintage	F	VF	XF	Unc	BU
1990 Proof	2,500	Value: 200				
1991	20,000	—	—	—	BV+10%	—
1991 Proof	1,000	Value: 210				

KM# 167 25 DOLLARS **Weight:** 7.7508 g. **Composition:** 0.9990 Gold .2500 oz. AGW **Subject:** Common Wallaroo **Obverse:** Elizabeth II **Reverse:** Similar to 100 Dollars, KM#169

Date	Mintage	F	VF	XF	Unc	BU
1991 Proof	1,991	Value: 140				
1992	100,000	—	—	—	BV+10%	—

KM# 172 25 DOLLARS **Weight:** 7.8150 g. **Composition:** 0.9990 Platinum .2500 oz. APW **Subject:** Koala **Obverse:** Elizabeth II **Reverse:** Similar to 100 Dollars, KM#174

Date	Mintage	F	VF	XF	Unc	BU
1992	20,000	—	—	—	BV+10%	—

KM# 200 25 DOLLARS **Weight:** 33.6300 g. **Composition:** 0.9250 Silver 1.0001 oz. ASW **Subject:** 40th Anniversary - Reign of Queen Elizabeth II - Queen Mother **Obverse:** Portrait of Queen Elizabeth II

Date		F	VF	XF	Unc	BU
1992 Proof	—	Value: 25.00				

KM# 201 25 DOLLARS **Weight:** 33.6300 g. **Composition:** 0.9250 Silver 1.0001 oz. ASW **Subject:** 40th Anniversary - Reign of Queen Elizabeth II - Princess Diana

Date		F	VF	XF	Unc	BU
1992 Proof	—	Value: 25.00				

KM# 202 25 DOLLARS **Weight:** 33.6300 g. **Composition:** 0.9250 Silver 1.0001 oz. ASW **Subject:** 40th Anniversary - Reign of Queen Elizabeth II - Princess Anne

Date		F	VF	XF	Unc	BU
1992 Proof	—	Value: 25.00				

KM# 203 25 DOLLARS **Weight:** 33.6300 g. **Composition:** 0.9250 Silver 1.0001 oz. ASW **Subject:** 40th Anniversary - Reign of Queen Elizabeth II - Prince Margaret

Date		F	VF	XF	Unc	BU
1992 Proof	—	Value: 25.00				

KM# 391 25 DOLLARS **Weight:** 7.7508 g. **Composition:** 0.9990 Gold .2500 oz. AGW **Obverse:** Queen's portrait **Reverse:** Nail-tailed wallaby

Date	Mintage	F	VF	XF	Unc	BU
1992 (ae) Proof	500	Value: 215				

KM# 193 25 DOLLARS **Weight:** 7.8150 g. **Composition:** 0.9990 Platinum .2500 oz. APW **Obverse:** Similar to 100 Dollars, KM#195

Date	Mintage	F	VF	XF	Unc	BU
1992 (ae) Proof	750	Value: 220				
1993		—	—	—	BV+10%	—

KM# 235 25 DOLLARS **Weight:** 7.7508 g. **Composition:** 0.9990 Gold .2500 oz. AGW **Obverse:** Queen Elizabeth II **Reverse:** Whiptail wallaby

Date	Mintage	F	VF	XF	Unc	BU
1993 (f) Proof	200	—	—	—	—	
1993 Proof	—	Value: 160				
1994	—	—	—	—	BV+10%	—

KM# 243 25 DOLLARS **Weight:** 7.7508 g. **Composition:** 0.9990 Gold .2500 oz. AGW **Reverse:** Red kangaroo

Date	Mintage	F	VF	XF	Unc	BU
1994 Proof	—	Value: 160				
1995	150,000	—	—	—	BV+10%	—

KM# 251 25 DOLLARS **Weight:** 7.8150 g. **Composition:** 0.9990 Platinum .2500 oz. APW **Subject:** Koala Mother and Baby **Obverse:** Queen Elizabeth II **Reverse:** Similar to 100 Dollars, KM#253

Date	Mintage	F	VF	XF	Unc	BU
1994	20,000	—	—	—	BV+10%	—

KM# 280 25 DOLLARS **Weight:** 7.8150 g. **Composition:** 0.9990 Platinum .2500 oz. APW **Reverse:** Koala in fork of tree

Date		F	VF	XF	Unc	BU
1994 Proof	—	Value: 225				
1995		—	—	—	BV+10%	—

KM# 274 25 DOLLARS **Weight:** 7.7508 g. **Composition:** 0.9990 Gold .2500 oz. AGW **Reverse:** Two kangaroos

Date	Mintage	F	VF	XF	Unc	BU
1995 Proof	650	Value: 160				
1996	150,000	—	—	—	BV+10%	—

KM# 285 25 DOLLARS Weight: 7.8150 g. **Composition:** 0.9990 Platinum .2500 oz. APW **Reverse:** Baby koala on branch

Date	Mintage	F	VF	XF	Unc	BU
1995 Proof	200	Value: 225				
1996	20,000	—	—	—	BV+10%	—

KM# 299 25 DOLLARS Weight: 7.7508 g. **Composition:** 0.9990 Gold .2500 oz. AGW **Subject:** Year of the Rat

Date	F	VF	XF	Unc	BU
1996 Proof	— Value: 125				

KM# 322 25 DOLLARS Weight: 7.7508 g. **Composition:** 0.9990 Gold .2500 oz. AGW **Obverse:** Queen's portrait **Reverse:** Kangaroo bounding right

Date	Mintage	F	VF	XF	Unc	BU
1996(p) Proof	400	Value: 350				

Note: In Proof sets only

KM# 340 25 DOLLARS Weight: 7.7508 g. **Composition:** 0.9990 Gold .2500 oz. AGW **Subject:** Kangaroo **Obverse:** Queen's portrait **Reverse:** Kangaroo bounding right

Date	Mintage	F	VF	XF	Unc	BU
1997	200,000	—	—	—	BV+10%	—
1997 Proof	—	Value: 120				

KM# 346 25 DOLLARS Weight: 7.7508 g. **Composition:** 0.9995 Platinum .2500 oz. APW **Subject:** Koalas **Obverse:** Queen's portrait **Reverse:** Cuddling koalas

Date	Mintage	F	VF	XF	Unc	BU
1997	20,000	—	—	—	BV+10%	—
1997 Proof	—	Value: 210				

KM# 336 25 DOLLARS Weight: 7.7508 g. **Composition:** 0.9990 Gold .2500 oz. AGW **Subject:** Year of the Ox **Obverse:** Queen's portrait **Reverse:** Bull ox looking right **Note:** Similar to 100 Dollars, KM#337.

Date	Mintage	F	VF	XF	Unc	BU
1997	—	—	—	—	125	—
1997 Proof	8,888	Value: 160				

KM# 507 25 DOLLARS Weight: 7.7759 g. **Composition:** 0.9990 Gold 0.2498 oz. AGW **Subject:** Year of the Tiger **Obverse:** Bust of Queen Elizabeth II right **Reverse:** Tiger springing right **Edge:** Reeded **Size:** 20.1 mm.

Date	F	VF	XF	Unc	BU
1998P Proof	— Value: 205				

KM# 427 25 DOLLARS Weight: 7.8070 g. **Composition:** 0.9999 Gold .2510 oz. AGW **Subject:** Year of the Rabbit **Obverse:** Queen's portrait **Reverse:** Rabbit **Edge:** Reeded **Note:** Similar to 100 Dollars, KM#428.

Date	F	VF	XF	Unc	BU
1999	—	—	—	125	—
1999 Proof	— Value: 200				

KM# 450 25 DOLLARS Weight: 7.8070 g. **Composition:** 0.9990,Gold .2500 oz. AGW **Obverse:** Queen's head right **Reverse:** Kangaroo facing left **Edge:** Reeded

Date	Mintage	F	VF	XF	Unc	BU
1999	150,000	—	—	—	BV+10%	—

KM# 458 25 DOLLARS Weight: 7.8150 g. **Composition:** 0.9990 Platinum .2500 oz. APW **Obverse:** Queen's head right **Reverse:** Koala on log **Edge:** Reeded

Date	Mintage	F	VF	XF	Unc	BU
1999	20,000	—	—	—	BV+10%	—

KM# 466 25 DOLLARS Weight: 7.8070 g. **Composition:** 0.9990 Gold .2500 oz. AGW **Obverse:** Queen's head right **Reverse:** Two kangaroos bounding left **Edge:** Reeded

Date	F	VF	XF	Unc	BU
2000	—	—	—	BV+10%	—

KM# 471 25 DOLLARS Weight: 7.8150 g. **Composition:** 0.9990 Platinum .2500 oz. APW **Obverse:** Queen's head right **Reverse:** Seated koala **Edge:** Reeded

Date	F	VF	XF	Unc	BU
2000	—	—	—	BV+10%	—

KM# 527 25 DOLLARS Weight: 7.7508 g. **Composition:** 0.9990 Gold .2500 oz. AGW **Series:** Dragons **Obverse:** Queen's head right **Reverse:** Dragon **Edge:** Reeded **Size:** 20.1 mm.

Date	F	VF	XF	Unc	BU
2000 Proof	— Value: 150				

KM# 541 25 DOLLARS Weight: 7.7508 g. **Composition:** 0.9990 Gold .2500 oz. AGW **Subject:** Year of the Snake **Obverse:** Queen's head right **Reverse:** Snake in tree **Edge:** Reeded **Size:** 20.1 mm.

Date	Mintage	F	VF	XF	Unc	BU
2001	—	—	—	—	125	—
2001P Proof	7,000	Value: 205				

KM# 585 25 DOLLARS Weight: 7.7759 g. **Composition:** 0.9990 Gold 0.2498 oz. AGW **Subject:** Year of the Horse **Obverse:** Bust of Queen Elizabeth II right **Reverse:** Horse galloping half left **Edge:** Reeded **Size:** 20.1 mm.

Date	Mintage	F	VF	XF	Unc	BU
2002P Proof	7,000	Value: 205				

KM# 181 30 DOLLARS Weight: 1100.1000 g. **Composition:** 0.9990 Silver 35.3376 oz. ASW **Obverse:** Head of Queen Elizabeth II right **Reverse:** Australian Kookaburra on stump **Note:** Illustration reduced. Actual size: 100 millimeters.

Date	Mintage	F	VF	XF	Unc	BU
1992	—	—	—	—	250	—
1992 Proof	1,000	Value: 600				
1993	—	—	—	—	250	—
1993 (jw) Proof	210	Value: 400				

KM# 229 30 DOLLARS Weight: 1000.2108 g. **Composition:** 0.9990 Silver 32.1575 oz. ASW **Reverse:** Kookaburra feeding nestling **Note:** Similar to 1 Dollar, KM#209.

Date	F	VF	XF	Unc	BU
1993	—	—	—	220	—
1993 Proof	— Value: 350				

KM# 232 30 DOLLARS Weight: 1000.2108 g. **Composition:** 0.9990 Silver 32.1575 oz. ASW **Reverse:** Pair of kookaburras on branch **Note:** Illustration reduced. Actual size: 100 millimeters.

Date	F	VF	XF	Unc	BU
1994	—	—	—	220	—
1994 Proof	— Value: 350				

KM# 292 30 DOLLARS Weight: 1000.2108 g. **Composition:** 0.9990 Silver 32.1575 oz. ASW **Reverse:** Kookaburra in flight **Note:** Illustration reduced. Actual size: 101 millimeters.

Date	Mintage	F	VF	XF	Unc	BU
1995 (lh) Proof	500	Value: 375				
1995P Proof	1,000	Value: 400				
1996	—	—	—	—	200	—

KM# 271 30 DOLLARS Weight: 1000.2108 g. **Composition:** 0.9990 Silver 32.1575 oz. ASW **Obverse:** Queen's portrait **Reverse:** Kookaburra on branch

Date	F	VF	XF	Unc	BU
1995	—	—	—	250	—
1995 Proof	— Value: 525				

KM# 495 30 DOLLARS Weight: 1100.1000 g. **Composition:** 0.9990 Silver 35.3376 oz. ASW **Subject:** Kookaburra Bullion **Obverse:** Queen's head right **Reverse:** Kookaburra on fence **Edge:** Reeded and plain sections with serial number **Size:** 100 mm. **Note:** Illustration reduced.

Date	F	VF	XF	Unc	BU
1997P Proof	— Value: 450				
1998P	—	—	—	280	—

KM# 447 30 DOLLARS Weight: 1002.5020 g. **Composition:** 0.9990 Silver 32.1989 oz. ASW **Obverse:** Queen's head right **Reverse:** Two kookaburras on branch **Edge:** Reeded

Date	F	VF	XF	Unc	BU
1999	—	—	—	250	—

KM# 505 30 DOLLARS Weight: 1002.5020 g. **Composition:** 0.9990 Silver 32.1989 oz. ASW **Subject:** Year of the Rabbit **Obverse:** Queen's head right **Reverse:** Rabbit **Edge:** Reeded and plain sections **Size:** 101 mm.

Date	Mintage	F	VF	XF	Unc	BU
1999	—	—	—	—	225	—
1999 Proof	2,500	Value: 500				

KM# 610 30 DOLLARS **Weight:** 1002.5020 g. **Composition:** 0.9990 Shell Casing Brass 32.1989 oz. **Subject:** USA State Quarters - 1999 **Obverse:** Queen's head right. **Reverse:** Kookaburra on branch with five state quarter designs added below. **Edge:** Reeded and plain sections.

Date	Mintage	F	VF	XF	Unc	BU
1999	1,000	—	—	—	385	—

KM# 617 30 DOLLARS **Weight:** 1002.5020 g. **Composition:** 0.9990 Silver 32.1989 oz. ASW **Subject:** USA State Quarters - 2000 **Obverse:** Queen's head right. **Reverse:** Kookaburra on branch with five state quarter designs added below. **Edge:** Reeded and plain sections.

Date	Mintage	F	VF	XF	Unc	BU
2000	1,000	—	—	—	385	—

KM# 525.1 (KM525) 30 DOLLARS **Weight:** 1002.5020 g. **Composition:** 0.9990 Silver 32.2312 oz. ASW **Series:** Dragons **Obverse:** Queen's head right **Reverse:** Dragon **Edge:** Segmented reeding **Size:** 101 mm.

Date		F	VF	XF	Unc	BU
2000 Proof	—	Value: 350				
2000 Proof	—	Value: 350				

KM# 525.2 30 DOLLARS **Composition:** 0.9990 Silver **Series:** Dragons **Obverse:** Queen's head right **Reverse:** Dragon with diamonds for eyes and multi-color ornamentation

Date	Mintage	F	VF	XF	Unc	BU
2000 Proof	5,000	Value: 400				

KM# 520 30 DOLLARS **Weight:** 1002.5020 g. **Composition:** 0.9990 Silver 32.2312 oz. ASW **Series:** Olympics **Obverse:** Queen's head right **Reverse:** Multi-color logo in center **Rev. Legend:** 1 KILO .999 SILVER **Edge Lettering:** GAMES OF THE XXVII OLYMPIAD **Size:** 100 mm. **Note:** Illustration reduced.

Date	Mintage	F	VF	XF	Unc	BU
2000 Proof	20,000	Value: 470				

KM# 542 30 DOLLARS **Weight:** 1002.5020 g. **Composition:** 0.9990 Silver 32.2312 oz. ASW **Subject:** Year of the Snake **Obverse:** Queen's head right **Reverse:** Snake with eggs **Edge:** Segmented reeding **Size:** 101 mm.

Date	Mintage	F	VF	XF	Unc	BU
2001	—	—	—	—	335	—
2001P Proof	250	Value: 482				

KM# 624 30 DOLLARS **Weight:** 1002.5020 g. **Composition:** 0.9990 Silver 32.1989 oz. ASW **Subject:** USA State Quarters - 2001 **Obverse:** Queen's head right. **Reverse:** Kookaburra on branch with five state quarter designs added below. **Edge:** Reeded and plain sections.

Date	Mintage	F	VF	XF	Unc	BU
2001	1,000	—	—	—	385	—

KM# 631 30 DOLLARS **Weight:** 1002.5020 g. **Composition:** 0.9990 Silver 32.1989 oz. ASW **Subject:** USA State Quarters - 2002 **Obverse:** Queen's head right. **Reverse:** Kookaburra on branch with five state quarter designs added below. **Edge:** Reeded and plain sections.

Date	Mintage	F	VF	XF	Unc	BU
2002	1,000	—	—	—	385	—

KM# 586 30 DOLLARS **Weight:** 1002.5020 g. **Composition:** 0.9990 Silver 32.1989 oz. ASW **Subject:** Year of the Horse **Obverse:** Bust of Queen Elizabeth II right **Reverse:** Horse running left **Edge:** Segmented reeding **Size:** 101 mm. **Note:** Illustration reduced. Actual size: 101 millimeters.

Date	Mintage	F	VF	XF	Unc	BU
2002P Proof	250	Value: 482				

KM# 313 40 DOLLARS **Weight:** 31.1850 g. **Composition:** 0.9995 Palladium 1.0021 oz. **Reverse:** The Australian emu

Date	Mintage	F	VF	XF	Unc	BU
1995	—	—	—	—	600	—
1995 Proof	Est. 2,500	Value: 650				

KM# 343 40 DOLLARS **Weight:** 31.1850 g. **Composition:** 0.9995 Palladium 1.0021 oz. **Obverse:** Queen's portrait **Reverse:** Emu and chicks

Date	Mintage	F	VF	XF	Unc	BU
1996 Proof	Est. 2,500	Value: 650				

KM# 91 50 DOLLARS **Weight:** 15.5017 g. **Composition:** 0.9990 Gold .5000 oz. AGW **Obverse:** Elizabeth II **Reverse:** Hand of Faith

Date	Mintage	F	VF	XF	Unc	BU
1986P Proof	15,000	Value: 250				
1987	188,000	—	—	—	BV+7%	—
1988	75,000	—	—	—	BV+7%	—
1989	100,000	—	—	—	BV+7%	—

KM# 97 50 DOLLARS **Weight:** 15.5017 g. **Composition:** 0.9990 Gold .5000 oz. AGW **Reverse:** Bobby Dazzler

Date	Mintage	F	VF	XF	Unc	BU
1987P Proof	15,000	Value: 250				

KM# 106 50 DOLLARS **Weight:** 15.5017 g. **Composition:** 0.9990 Gold .5000 oz. AGW **Reverse:** Welcome nugget

Date	Mintage	F	VF	XF	Unc	BU
1988P Proof	Est. 10,000	Value: 250				

KM# 110 50 DOLLARS **Weight:** 15.6050 g. **Composition:** 0.9990 Platinum .5000 oz. APW **Obverse:** Head of Queen Elizabeth II right **Reverse:** Koala bear facing

Date	Mintage	F	VF	XF	Unc	BU
1988	—	—	—	—	BV+7%	—
1988 Proof	12,000	Value: 335				
1989 Proof	—	Value: 320				

KM# 120 50 DOLLARS **Weight:** 15.5017 g. **Composition:** 0.9990 Gold .5000 oz. AGW **Obverse:** Head of Queen Elizabeth II right **Reverse:** Red kangaroo

Date	Mintage	F	VF	XF	Unc	BU
1989 Proof	2,200	Value: 275				
1990	—	—	—	—	BV+7%	—

KM# 125 50 DOLLARS **Weight:** 15.6050 g. **Composition:** 0.9990 Platinum .5000 oz. APW **Note:** Similar to 100 Dollars, KM#126.

Date	Mintage	F	VF	XF	Unc	BU
1989 Proof	2,400	Value: 365				
1990 Proof	8,000	Value: 335				

KM# 143 50 DOLLARS **Weight:** 15.5017 g. **Composition:** 0.9990 Gold .5000 oz. AGW **Reverse:** Gray kangaroo

Date	Mintage	F	VF	XF	Unc	BU
1990 Proof	5,000	Value: 250				
1991	100,000	—	—	—	BV+7%	—

KM# 148 50 DOLLARS **Weight:** 15.6050 g. **Composition:** 0.9990 Platinum .5000 oz. APW **Reverse:** Koala bear in tree

Date	Mintage	F	VF	XF	Unc	BU
1990 Proof	5,500	Value: 335				
1991	20,000	—	—	—	BV+7%	—
1991 Proof	2,000	Value: 365				

KM# 162 50 DOLLARS **Weight:** 311.0670 g. **Composition:** 0.9990 Silver 10.0000 oz. ASW **Subject:** Australian Kookaburra **Obverse:** Queen Elizabeth II above denomination **Reverse:** Kookaburra bird

Date	Mintage	F	VF	XF	Unc	BU
1991	—	—	—	—	60.00	—
1991 Proof	2,500	Value: 250				

KM# 168 50 DOLLARS **Weight:** 15.5017 g. **Composition:** 0.9990 Gold .5000 oz. AGW **Subject:** Common Wallaroo **Obverse:** Elizabeth II **Reverse:** Similar to 100 Dollars, KM#169

Date	Mintage	F	VF	XF	Unc	BU
1991 Proof	1,096	Value: 300				
1992	100,000	—	—	—	BV+7%	—

KM# 173 50 DOLLARS **Weight:** 15.6050 g. **Composition:** 0.9990 Platinum .5000 oz. APW **Subject:** Koala **Obverse:** Queen Elizabeth II **Reverse:** Similar to 100 Dollars, KM#174

Date	Mintage	F	VF	XF	Unc	BU
1992	20,000	—	—	—	BV+7%	—

KM# 392 50 DOLLARS **Weight:** 15.5017 g. **Composition:** 0.9990 Gold .5000 oz. AGW **Obverse:** Queen's portrait **Reverse:** Nail-tailed wallaby **Note:** Similar to 25 Dollars, KM#391.

Date	Mintage	F	VF	XF	Unc	BU
1992 (ae) Proof	500	Value: 500				

KM# 194 50 DOLLARS **Weight:** 15.6050 g. **Composition:** 0.9990 Platinum .5000 oz. APW **Obverse:** Similar to 100 Dollars, KM#195

Date	F	VF	XF	Unc	BU
1993	—	—	—	BV+7%	—

KM# 236 50 DOLLARS **Weight:** 15.5017 g. **Composition:** 0.9990 Gold .5000 oz. AGW **Obverse:** Queen Elizabeth II **Reverse:** Whiptail wallaby

Date	F	VF	XF	Unc	BU
1993 Proof	— Value: 325				
1994	—	—	—	BV+7%	—

KM# 244 50 DOLLARS **Weight:** 15.5017 g. **Composition:** 0.9990 Gold .5000 oz. AGW **Reverse:** Red kangaroo

Date	Mintage	F	VF	XF	Unc	BU
1994 Proof	—	Value: 325				
1995	30,000	—	—	—	BV+10%	—
1995 (f) Proof	10,000	Value: 225				

KM# 252 50 DOLLARS **Weight:** 15.6050 g. **Composition:** 0.9990 Platinum .5000 oz. APW **Reverse:** Koala mother and baby

Date	Mintage	F	VF	XF	Unc	BU
1994	5,000	—	—	—	BV+7%	—

KM# 281 50 DOLLARS **Weight:** 15.6050 g. **Composition:** 0.9990 Platinum .5000 oz. APW **Reverse:** Koala in fork of tree

Date	F	VF	XF	Unc	BU
1994 Proof	— Value: 375				
1995	—	—	—	BV+7%	—

KM# 275.1 50 DOLLARS **Weight:** 15.5017 g. **Composition:** 0.9990 Gold .5000 oz. AGW **Reverse:** Two kangaroos

Date	Mintage	F	VF	XF	Unc	BU
1995 Proof	300	Value: 325				
1996	100,000	—	—	—	BV+7%	—
1996 (s) Proof	13,000	Value: 225				
1996 (l) Proof	3,000	Value: 235				

Note: In Proof sets only

Date	Mintage	F	VF	XF	Unc	BU
1996 (f) Proof	13,000	Value: 225				

KM# 286 50 DOLLARS **Weight:** 15.6050 g. **Composition:** 0.9990 Platinum .5000 oz. APW **Reverse:** Baby koala on branch

Date	Mintage	F	VF	XF	Unc	BU
1995 (ww) Proof	300	Value: 425				

Note: In Proof sets only

Date	Mintage	F	VF	XF	Unc	BU
1995 Proof	450	Value: 375				
1996	5,000	—	—	—	BV+7%	—

KM# 275.2 50 DOLLARS **Weight:** 15.5017 g. **Composition:** 0.9990 Gold .5000 oz. AGW **Edge:** Reeded and inscribed with date and serial number

Date	Mintage	F	VF	XF	Unc	BU
1996 Proof	500	Value: 235				

KM# 341 50 DOLLARS **Weight:** 15.5017 g. **Composition:** 0.9990 Gold .5000 oz. AGW **Subject:** Kangaroo **Obverse:** Queen's portrait **Reverse:** Kangaroo bounding right

Date	Mintage	F	VF	XF	Unc	BU
1996 (p) Proof	400	Value: 600				

Note: In Proof sets only

Date	Mintage	F	VF	XF	Unc	BU
1997	100,000	—	—	—	165	—
1997 Proof	—	Value: 185				
1997 (f) Proof	13,000	Value: 225				
1997 (l) Proof	10,000	Value: 225				

Note: In Proof sets only

Date	Mintage	F	VF	XF	Unc	BU
1997 (s) Proof	13,000	Value: 225				

KM# 347 50 DOLLARS **Weight:** 15.5518 g. **Composition:** 0.9995 Platinum .5000 oz. APW **Subject:** Koalas **Obverse:** Queen's portrait **Reverse:** Cuddling koalas

Date	Mintage	F	VF	XF	Unc	BU
1997	5,000	—	—	—	BV+7%	—
1997 Proof	—	Value: 375				

KM# 451 50 DOLLARS **Weight:** 15.5940 g. **Composition:** 0.9990 Gold .5000 oz. AGW **Obverse:** Queen's head right **Reverse:** Kangaroo facing left **Edge:** Reeded

Date	Mintage	F	VF	XF	Unc	BU
1999	100,000	—	—	—	165	—

KM# 459 50 DOLLARS **Weight:** 15.6050 g. **Composition:** 0.9990 Platinum .5000 oz. APW **Obverse:** Queen's head right **Reverse:** Koala on log **Edge:** Reeded

Date	Mintage	F	VF	XF	Unc	BU
1999	5,000	—	—	—	375	—

KM# 467 50 DOLLARS **Weight:** 15.5940 g. **Composition:** 0.9990 Gold .5000 oz. AGW **Obverse:** Queen's head right **Reverse:** Two kangaroos bounding left **Edge:** Reeded

Date	F	VF	XF	Unc	BU
2000	—	—	—	165	—

KM# 472 50 DOLLARS **Weight:** 15.6050 g. **Composition:** 0.9990 Platinum .5000 oz. APW **Obverse:** Queen's head right **Reverse:** Seated koala **Edge:** Reeded

Date	F	VF	XF	Unc	BU
2000	—	—	—	375	—

KM# 92 100 DOLLARS **Weight:** 31.1035 g. **Composition:** 0.9990 Gold 1.0000 oz. AGW **Reverse:** Welcome Stranger

Date	Mintage	F	VF	XF	Unc	BU
1986P Proof	15,000	Value: 425				
1987	259,000	—	—	—	BV+4%	—
1988	116,000	—	—	—	BV+4%	—
1989	—	—	—	—	BV+4%	—

KM# 98 100 DOLLARS **Weight:** 31.1035 g. **Composition:** 0.9990 Gold 1.0000 oz. AGW **Reverse:** Poseidon

Date	Mintage	F	VF	XF	Unc	BU
1987P Proof	15,000	Value: 425				

KM# 107 100 DOLLARS **Weight:** 31.1035 g. **Composition:** 0.9990 Gold 1.0000 oz. AGW **Reverse:** Pride of Australia nugget

Date	Mintage	F	VF	XF	Unc	BU
1988P Proof	Est. 10,000	Value: 425				

KM# 111 100 DOLLARS **Weight:** 31.1850 g. **Composition:** 0.9990 Platinum 1.0000 oz. APW

Date	F	VF	XF	Unc	BU
1988	—	—	—	BV+4%	—
1989 Proof	— Value: 650				

KM# 121 100 DOLLARS **Weight:** 31.1035 g. **Composition:** 0.9990 Gold 1.0000 oz. AGW **Reverse:** Red kangaroo

Date	Mintage	F	VF	XF	Unc	BU
1989 Proof	2,200	Value: 525				
1990	—	—	—	—	BV+4%	—

KM# 126 100 DOLLARS **Weight:** 31.1850 g. **Composition:** 0.9990 Platinum 1.0000 oz. APW

Date	Mintage	F	VF	XF	Unc	BU
1989 Proof	2,400	Value: 650				
1990 Proof	—	Value: 650				

KM# 144 100 DOLLARS **Weight:** 31.1035 g. **Composition:** 0.9990 Gold 1.0000 oz. AGW **Reverse:** Gray kangaroo

Date	Mintage	F	VF	XF	Unc	BU
1990 Proof	8,000	Value: 425				
1991	250,000	—	—	—	BV+4%	—

KM# 149 100 DOLLARS **Weight:** 31.1850 g. **Composition:** 0.9990 Platinum 1.0000 oz. APW **Reverse:** Koala bear in tree

Date	Mintage	F	VF	XF	Unc	BU
1990 Proof	3,500	Value: 650				
1991	75,000	—	—	—	BV+4%	—
1991 Proof	1,000	Value: 650				

KM# 169 100 DOLLARS **Weight:** 31.1035 g. **Composition:** 0.9990 Gold 1.0000 oz. AGW **Reverse:** Common wallaroo

Date	Mintage	F	VF	XF	Unc	BU
1991 Proof	3,000	Value: 550				
1992	250,000	—	—	—	BV+4%	—

KM# 174 100 DOLLARS **Weight:** 31.1850 g. **Composition:** 0.9990 Platinum 1.0000 oz. APW **Obverse:** Queen Elizabeth II **Reverse:** Koala

Date	Mintage	F	VF	XF	Unc	BU
1992	75,000	—	—	—	BV+4%	—

KM# 393 100 DOLLARS **Weight:** 31.1035 g. **Composition:** 0.9990 Gold 1.0000 oz. AGW **Obverse:** Queen's portrait **Reverse:** Nail-tailed wallaby **Note:** Similar to 25 Dollars, KM#391.

Date	Mintage	F	VF	XF	Unc	BU
1992 Proof	784	Value: 475				
1993	—	—	—	—	BV+4%	—

KM# 195 100 DOLLARS **Weight:** 31.1850 g. **Composition:** 0.9990 Platinum 1.0000 oz. APW

Date	F	VF	XF	Unc	BU
1993	—	—	—	BV+4%	—

KM# 237 100 DOLLARS **Weight:** 31.1035 g. **Composition:** 0.9990 Gold 1.0000 oz. AGW **Obverse:** Queen Elizabeth II **Reverse:** Whiptail wallaby

Date	Mintage	F	VF	XF	Unc	BU
1993 Proof	—	Value: 600				
1993 (f) Proof	150	Value: 650				
1994	—	—	—	—	BV+4%	—

KM# 245 100 DOLLARS **Weight:** 31.1035 g. **Composition:** 0.9990 Gold 1.0000 oz. AGW **Reverse:** Red kangaroo

Date	Mintage	F	VF	XF	Unc	BU
1994 Proof	—	Value: 425				
1995	350,000	—	—	—	BV+4%	—

KM# 253 100 DOLLARS **Weight:** 31.1850 g. **Composition:** 0.9990 Platinum 1.0000 oz. APW **Reverse:** Koala mother and baby

Date	Mintage	F	VF	XF	Unc	BU
1994 Prooflike	100,000	—	—	—	BV+4%	—

KM# 282 100 DOLLARS **Weight:** 31.1850 g. **Composition:** 0.9990 Platinum 1.0000 oz. APW **Reverse:** Koala in fork of tree

Date	F	VF	XF	Unc	BU
1994 Proof	—	Value: 675			
1995	—	—	—	BV+4%	—

KM# 276 100 DOLLARS **Weight:** 31.1035 g. **Composition:** 0.9990 Gold 1.0000 oz. AGW **Reverse:** Two kangaroos

Date	Mintage	F	VF	XF	Unc	BU
1995 Proof	300	Value: 600				
1995 (ww) Proof	600	Value: 575				
1996	350,000	—	—	—	BV+4%	—

KM# 287 100 DOLLARS **Weight:** 31.1850 g. **Composition:** 0.9990 Platinum 1.0000 oz. APW **Reverse:** Baby koala on branch

Date	Mintage	F	VF	XF	Unc	BU
1995 Proof	200	Value: 675				
1996	100,000	—	—	—	BV+4%	—

KM# 308 100 DOLLARS **Weight:** 10.3678 g. **Composition:** 0.9160 Gold .3053 oz. AGW **Reverse:** The Waratah Flower

Date	Mintage	F	VF	XF	Unc	BU
1995	3,000	—	—	—	165	—

KM# 308a 100 DOLLARS **Weight:** 10.3678 g. **Composition:** 0.9999 Gold .3333 oz. AGW

Date	Mintage	F	VF	XF	Unc	BU
1995 Proof	2,500	Value: 275				

KM# 300 100 DOLLARS **Weight:** 31.1035 g. **Composition:** 0.9990 Gold 1.0000 oz. AGW **Subject:** Year of the Rat

Date	F	VF	XF	Unc	BU
1996 Proof	—	Value: 425			

KM# 333a 100 DOLLARS **Weight:** 10.3678 g. **Composition:** 0.9999 Gold .3333 oz. AGW

Date	F	VF	XF	Unc	BU
1996 Proof	—	Value: 275			

KM# 342 100 DOLLARS **Weight:** 31.1035 g. **Composition:** 0.9990 Gold 1.0000 oz. AGW **Subject:** Kangaroo **Obverse:** Queen's portrait **Reverse:** Kangaroo bounding right

Date	Mintage	F	VF	XF	Unc	BU
1996 (p) Proof	—	Value: 550				
Note: In Proof sets only						
1997	350,000	—	—	—	300	—
1997 Proof	—	Value: 350				

KM# 333 100 DOLLARS **Weight:** 10.3678 g. **Composition:** 0.9160 Gold .3053 oz. AGW **Subject:** Tasmanial Blue Gum Flower **Obverse:** Queen's portrait **Reverse:** Flowering plant with long, droopy leaves **Note:** Similar to 150 Dollars, KM#334.

Date	F	VF	XF	Unc	BU
1996	—	—	—	165	—

KM# 337 100 DOLLARS **Weight:** 31.1035 g. **Composition:** 0.9990 Gold 1.0000 oz. AGW **Subject:** Year of the Ox **Obverse:** Queen's portrait **Reverse:** Ox looking right

Date	Mintage	F	VF	XF	Unc	BU
1997	—	—	—	—	400	—
1997 Proof	8,888	Value: 525				

KM# 348 100 DOLLARS **Weight:** 31.1850 g. **Composition:** 0.9990 Platinum 1.0000 oz. APW **Subject:** Koalas **Obverse:** Queen's portrait **Reverse:** Cuddling koalas

Date	Mintage	F	VF	XF	Unc	BU
1997	100,000	—	—	—	BV+4%	—
1997 Proof	—	Value: 675				

KM# 384 100 DOLLARS **Weight:** 10.3678 g. **Composition:** 0.9167 Gold .3053 oz. AGW **Subject:** Mangles' Kangaroo Paw Flower **Obverse:** Queens' portrait **Reverse:** Flower

Date	Mintage	F	VF	XF	Unc	BU
1997	3,000	—	—	—	165	—

KM# 373 100 DOLLARS **Weight:** 10.0210 g. **Composition:** 0.9999 Gold .3222 oz. AGW **Series:** Sydney Olympics 2000 **Obverse:** Queen's portrait **Reverse:** Runner training in rain

Date	F	VF	XF	Unc	BU
2000 (1998) Proof	—	Value: 250			

KM# 383 100 DOLLARS **Weight:** 10.0210 g. **Composition:** 0.9999 Gold .3222 oz. AGW **Series:** Sydney Olympics 2000 **Obverse:** Queen's portrait **Reverse:** Multicolor games logo

Date	Mintage	F	VF	XF	Unc	BU
2000 (1998) Proof	Est. 30,000	Value: 250				

KM# 508 100 DOLLARS **Weight:** 31.1035 g. **Composition:** 0.9990 Gold 0.999 oz. AGW **Subject:** Year of the Tiger **Obverse:** Bust of Queen Elizabeth II right **Reverse:** Tiger springing right **Edge:** Reeded **Size:** 32.1 mm.

Date	F	VF	XF	Unc	BU
1998P	—	—	—	525	—

KM# 480 100 DOLLARS **Weight:** 10.3678 g. **Composition:** 0.9160 Gold .3056 oz. AGW **Subject:** Stuart's Desert Pea **Obverse:** Queen's head right **Reverse:** Plant with pods **Edge:** Reeded **Size:** 25 mm.

Date	Mintage	F	VF	XF	Unc	BU
1998	3,000	—	—	—	140	—

KM# 480a 100 DOLLARS **Weight:** 10.3678 g. **Composition:** 0.9990 Gold .3333 oz. AGW **Subject:** Stuart's Desert Pea **Obverse:** Queen's head right **Reverse:** Plant with pods **Edge:** Reeded **Size:** 25 mm.

Date	Mintage	F	VF	XF	Unc	BU
1998 Proof	2,500	Value: 190				

KM# 487 100 DOLLARS **Weight:** 10.3678 g. **Composition:** 0.9160 Gold .3056 oz. AGW **Obverse:** Queen's head right **Reverse:** Common Heath flowers **Edge:** Reeded **Size:** 25 mm.

Date	Mintage	F	VF	XF	Unc	BU
1999	3,000	—	—	—	140	—

KM# 487a 100 DOLLARS **Weight:** 10.3678 g. **Composition:** 0.9990 Gold .3333 oz. AGW **Obverse:** Queen's head right **Reverse:** Common Heath flowers **Edge:** Reeded **Size:** 25 mm.

Date	Mintage	F	VF	XF	Unc	BU
1999 Proof	2,500	Value: 190				

KM# 428 100 DOLLARS **Weight:** 31.1620 g. **Composition:** 0.9999 Gold 1.0529 oz. AGW **Subject:** Year of the Rabbit **Obverse:** Queen's portrait **Reverse:** Rabbit **Edge:** Reeded

Date	F	VF	XF	Unc	BU
1999	—	—	—	400	—
1999 Proof	—	Value: 600			

KM# 442 100 DOLLARS **Weight:** 10.0000 g. **Composition:** 0.9990 Gold .3215 oz. AGW **Series:** Sydney Olympics 2000 **Obverse:** Queen's head right **Reverse:** 3 athletic workout scenes **Edge:** Reeded

Date	Mintage	F	VF	XF	Unc	BU
2000 (1999) Proof	30,000	Value: 250				

KM# 443 100 DOLLARS **Weight:** 10.0000 g. **Composition:** 0.9990 Gold .3215 oz. AGW **Series:** Sydney Olympics 2000 **Obverse:** Queen's head right **Reverse:** Shot putter teaching seated children **Edge:** Reeded

Date	Mintage	F	VF	XF	Unc	BU
2000 (1999) Proof	30,000	Value: 250				

KM# 444 100 DOLLARS **Weight:** 10.0000 g. **Composition:** 0.9990 Gold .3215 oz. AGW **Series:** Sydney Olympics 2000 **Obverse:** Queen's head right **Reverse:** Sprinter being coached **Edge:** Reeded

Date	Mintage	F	VF	XF	Unc	BU
2000 (1999) Proof	30,000	Value: 250				

KM# 452 100 DOLLARS **Weight:** 31.1620 g. **Composition:** 0.9990 Gold 1.0000 oz. AGW **Obverse:** Queen's head right **Reverse:** Kangaroo facing left **Edge:** Reeded

Date	Mintage	F	VF	XF	Unc	BU
1999	350,000	—	—	—	400	—

KM# 460 100 DOLLARS **Weight:** 31.1850 g. **Composition:** 0.9990 Platinum 1.0000 oz. APW **Obverse:** Queen's head right **Reverse:** Koala on log **Edge:** Reeded

Date	Mintage	F	VF	XF	Unc	BU
1999	100,000	—	—	—	675	—

KM# 474 100 DOLLARS **Ring Weight:** 5.0119 g. **Ring Composition:** 0.9990 Silver .1611 oz. ASW **Center Weight:** 7.9881 g. **Center Composition:** 0.9170 Gold .2354 oz. AGW **Subject:** Perth Mint Centennial Sovereign **Obverse:** Queen's head right **Reverse:** St. George slaying the dragon **Edge:** Reeded

Date	Mintage	F	VF	XF	Unc	BU
ND(1999) Proof	7,500	Value: 500				

KM# 468 100 DOLLARS **Weight:** 31.1620 g. **Composition:** 0.9990 Gold 1.0000 oz. AGW **Obverse:** Queen's head right **Reverse:** Two kangaroos bounding left **Edge:** Reeded

Date	F	VF	XF	Unc	BU
2000	—	—	—	400	—

KM# 473 100 DOLLARS **Weight:** 31.1850 g. **Composition:** 0.9990 Platinum 1.0000 oz. APW **Obverse:** Queen's head right **Reverse:** Seated koala **Edge:** Reeded

Date	F	VF	XF	Unc	BU
2000	—	—	—	675	—

KM# 512 100 DOLLARS **Weight:** 10.3678 g. **Composition:** 0.9160 Gold .3056 oz. AGW **Subject:** Cooktown Orchid **Obverse:** Queen's head right **Reverse:** Orchid and denomination **Edge:** Reeded **Size:** 25 mm.

Date	Mintage	F	VF	XF	Unc	BU
2000	3,000	—	—	—	150	—

KM# 512a 100 DOLLARS **Weight:** 10.3678 g. **Composition:** 0.9990 Gold .3333 oz. AGW **Subject:** Cooktown Orchid **Obverse:** Queen's head right **Reverse:** Orchid and denomination **Edge:** Reeded **Size:** 25 mm.

Date	Mintage	F	VF	XF	Unc	BU
2000 Proof	2,500	Value: 200				

KM# 521 100 DOLLARS **Weight:** 10.0000 g. **Composition:** 0.9990 Gold .3215 oz. AGW **Series:** Olympics **Obverse:** Queen's head right **Reverse:** Multicolor torch flames **Edge:** Reeded **Size:** 25 mm.

Date	Mintage	F	VF	XF	Unc	BU
2000 Proof	20,000	Value: 385				

KM# 528 100 DOLLARS **Weight:** 31.1035 g. **Composition:** 0.9990 Gold 1. oz. AGW **Series:** Dragons **Obverse:** Queen's head right **Reverse:** Dragon **Edge:** Reeded **Size:** 32.1 mm.

Date	F	VF	XF	Unc	BU
2000 Proof	—	Value: 460			

KM# 543 100 DOLLARS **Weight:** 31.1035 g. **Composition:** 0.9990 Gold 1. oz. AGW **Subject:** Year of the Snake **Obverse:** Queen's head right **Reverse:** Snake in tree **Edge:** Reeded **Size:** 32.1 mm.

Date	Mintage	F	VF	XF	Unc	BU
2001	30,000	—	—	—	450	—
2001P Proof	—	Value: 525				

KM# 587 100 DOLLARS **Weight:** 31.1035 g. **Composition:** 0.9990 Gold 0.999 oz. AGW **Subject:** Year of the Horse **Obverse:** Bust of Queen Elizabeth II right **Reverse:** Horse running left **Edge:** Reeded **Size:** 32.1 mm.

Date	F	VF	XF	Unc	BU
2002P	—	—	—	525	—

KM# 163 150 DOLLARS **Weight:** 1000.1000 g. **Composition:** 0.9990 Silver 32.1575 oz. ASW **Subject:** Australian Kookaburra **Obverse:** Queen Elizabeth II above denomination **Reverse:** Kookaburra bird **Note:** Kilo

Date	Mintage	F	VF	XF	Unc	BU
1991	—	—	—	—	200	—
1991 Proof	1,000	Value: 600				

KM# 309 150 DOLLARS **Weight:** 15.5517 g. **Composition:** 0.9999 Gold .5000 oz. AGW **Reverse:** The Waratah Flower

Date	Mintage	F	VF	XF	Unc	BU
1995 Proof	1,500	Value: 400				

KM# 334 150 DOLLARS **Weight:** 15.5517 g. **Composition:** 0.9999 Gold .5000 oz. AGW **Subject:** Tasmanian Blue Gum Flower **Obverse:** Queen's portrait **Reverse:** Flowering plant with long, dropping leaves

Date	F	VF	XF	Unc	BU
1996 Proof	—	Value: 400			

KM# 413 150 DOLLARS **Weight:** 15.5517 g. **Composition:** 0.9999 Gold .5000 oz. AGW **Obverse:** Queen's portrait **Reverse:** Stuart's desert pea

Date	Mintage	F	VF	XF	Unc	BU
1998 Proof	1,500	Value: 400				

KM# 475 150 DOLLARS **Weight:** 15.5517 g. **Composition:** 0.9999 Gold .5000 oz. AGW **Subject:** Common Heath Flower **Obverse:** Queen's head right **Reverse:** Flowers **Edge:** Reeded

Date	Mintage	F	VF	XF	Unc	BU
1999 Proof	1,500	Value: 400				

KM# 513 150 DOLLARS **Weight:** 15.5518 g. **Composition:** 0.9990 Gold .5000 oz. AGW **Subject:** Cooktown Orchid **Obverse:** Queen's head right **Reverse:** Orchid and denomination **Edge:** Reeded **Size:** 30 mm.

Date	Mintage	F	VF	XF	Unc	BU
2000 Proof	1,500	Value: 500				

KM# 71 200 DOLLARS **Weight:** 10.0000 g. **Composition:** 0.9170 Gold .2948 oz. AGW **Reverse:** Koala

Date	Mintage	F	VF	XF	Unc	BU
1980	208,000	—	—	—	125	—
1980 Proof	50,000	Value: 130				
1983	88,000	—	—	—	125	—
1983 Proof	16,000	Value: 130				
1984	49,000	—	—	—	125	—
1984 Proof	13,000	Value: 130				

KM# 73 200 DOLLARS **Weight:** 10.0000 g. **Composition:** 0.9170 Gold .2948 oz. AGW **Subject:** Wedding of Prince Charles and Lady Diana

Date	Mintage	F	VF	XF	Unc	BU
1981	78,000	—	—	—	125	—

KM# 76 200 DOLLARS **Weight:** 10.0000 g. **Composition:** 0.9170 Gold .2948 oz. AGW **Subject:** XII Commonwealth Games - Brisbane

Date	Mintage	F	VF	XF	Unc	BU
1982	77,000	—	—	—	125	—
1982 Proof	30,000	Value: 125				

KM# 86 200 DOLLARS **Weight:** 10.0000 g. **Composition:** 0.9170 Gold .2948 oz. AGW **Reverse:** Koala in tree

Date	Mintage	F	VF	XF	Unc	BU
1985	29,000	—	—	—	125	—
1985 Proof	17,000	Value: 130				
1986	15,000	—	—	—	125	—
1986 Proof	17,000	Value: 130				

KM# 94 200 DOLLARS **Weight:** 10.0000 g. **Composition:** 0.9170 Gold .2948 oz. AGW **Subject:** Arthur Phillip

Date	Mintage	F	VF	XF	Unc	BU
1987	21,000	—	—	—	125	—
1987 Proof	20,000	Value: 130				

KM# 115 200 DOLLARS **Weight:** 10.0000 g. **Composition:** 0.9170 Gold .2948 oz. AGW **Subject:** Bicentennial of Australia

Date	Mintage	F	VF	XF	Unc	BU
1988	11,000	—	—	—	125	—
1988 Proof	20,000	Value: 130				

KM# 116 200 DOLLARS **Weight:** 10.0000 g. **Composition:** 0.9170 Gold .2948 oz. AGW **Subject:** Pride of Australia - Frilled-neck lizard **Obverse:** Similar to KM#115

Date	Mintage	F	VF	XF	Unc	BU
1989		—	—	—	125	—
1989 Proof	Est. 25,000	Value: 130				

KM# 135 200 DOLLARS **Weight:** 10.0000 g. **Composition:** 0.9170 Gold .2948 oz. AGW **Subject:** Pride of Australia - Platypus

Date	Mintage	F	VF	XF	Unc	BU
1990		—	—	—	125	—
1990 Proof	—	Value: 130				

KM# 160 200 DOLLARS **Weight:** 10.0000 g. **Composition:** 0.9170 Gold .2948 oz. AGW **Subject:** Pride of Australia - Emu

Date	Mintage	F	VF	XF	Unc	BU
1991		—	—	—	125	—
1991 Proof	—	Value: 130				

KM# 182 200 DOLLARS **Weight:** 62.2140 g. **Composition:** 0.9990 Gold 2.0000 oz. AGW **Obverse:** Portrait of Queen Elizabeth II **Reverse:** Red kangaroo

Date	F	VF	XF	Unc	BU
1992	—	—	—	BV+4%	—
1994 Prooflike	—	—	—	BV+4%	—
1995	—	—	—	BV+4%	—
1996	—	—	—	BV+4%	—
1997	—	—	—	BV+4%	—

KM# 185 200 DOLLARS **Weight:** 62.2140 g. **Composition:** 0.9995 Platinum 2.0000 oz. APW **Obverse:** Portrait of Queen Elizabeth II **Reverse:** Koala bear in tree

Date	F	VF	XF	Unc	BU
1992	—	—	—	BV+4%	—
1992 Proof	—	Value: 1,500			
1996	—	—	—	BV+4%	—

KM# 259 200 DOLLARS **Weight:** 10.0000 g. **Composition:** 0.9170 Gold .2948 oz. AGW **Subject:** Pride of Australia - Echidna

Date	F	VF	XF	Unc	BU
1992	—	—	—	125	—
1992 Proof	—	Value: 130			

KM# 394 200 DOLLARS **Weight:** 62.2140 g. **Composition:** 0.9990 Gold 2.0000 oz. AGW **Obverse:** Queen's portrait **Reverse:** Nail-tailed wallaby **Note:** Similar to 25 Dollars, KM#391.

Date	Mintage	F	VF	XF	Unc	BU
1992 Proof	152	Value: 1,000				

KM# 196 200 DOLLARS **Weight:** 62.2140 g. **Composition:** 0.9995 Platinum 2.0000 oz. APW **Obverse:** Similar to 100 Dollars, KM#195

Date	F	VF	XF	Unc	BU
1993	—	—	—	BV+4%	—
1994	—	—	—	BV+4%	—
1995	—	—	—	BV+4%	—
1997	—	—	—	BV+4%	—

KM# 220 200 DOLLARS **Weight:** 16.8200 g. **Composition:** 0.9170 Gold .4958 oz. AGW **Series:** Olympics **Reverse:** Gymnast in flight

Date	Mintage	F	VF	XF	Unc	BU
1993 Proof	60,000	Value: 200				

KM# 222 200 DOLLARS **Weight:** 10.0000 g. **Composition:** 0.9170 Gold .2948 oz. AGW **Reverse:** Squirrel glider possum

Date	Mintage	F	VF	XF	Unc	BU
1993	3,014	—	—	—	125	—
1993 Proof	5,000	Value: 130				

KM# 238 200 DOLLARS **Weight:** 62.2140 g. **Composition:** 0.9999 Gold 2.0000 oz. AGW **Obverse:** Queen Elizabeth I **Reverse:** Whiptail wallaby

Date	F	VF	XF	Unc	BU
1993 Proof	—	Value: 1,450			

KM# 254 200 DOLLARS **Weight:** 62.2140 g. **Composition:** 0.9995 Platinum 2.0000 oz. APW **Subject:** Koala Mother and Baby **Obverse:** Queen Elizabeth II **Reverse:** Similar to 100 Dollars, KM#253

Date	F	VF	XF	Unc	BU
1994 Proof	—	Value: 1,750			

KM# 262 200 DOLLARS **Weight:** 10.0000 g. **Composition:** 0.9170 Gold .2948 oz. AGW **Reverse:** Tasmanian devil

Date	Mintage	F	VF	XF	Unc	BU
1994 Proof	5,000	Value: 200				

KM# 246 200 DOLLARS **Weight:** 62.2140 g. **Composition:** 0.9999 Gold 2.0000 oz. AGW **Reverse:** Red kangaroo **Note:** Similar to 100 Dollars, KM#245.

Date	Mintage	F	VF	XF	Unc	BU
1994 Proof	325	Value: 1,500				

KM# 277 200 DOLLARS **Weight:** 62.2140 g. **Composition:** 0.9999 Gold 2.0000 oz. AGW **Reverse:** Two kangaroos

Date	Mintage	F	VF	XF	Unc	BU
1995 Proof	100	Value: 1,600				

KM# 288 200 DOLLARS **Weight:** 62.2140 g. **Composition:** 0.9995 Platinum 2.0000 oz. APW **Reverse:** Baby koala on branch

Date	Mintage	F	VF	XF	Unc	BU
1995 Proof	100	Value: 1,650				

KM# 385 200 DOLLARS **Weight:** 15.5517 g. **Composition:** 0.9999 Gold .5000 oz. AGW **Subject:** Mangles' Kangaroo Paw Flower **Obverse:** Queen's portrait **Reverse:** Flower **Note:** Similar to 100 Dollars, KM#384.

Date	F	VF	XF	Unc	BU
1997 Proof	—	Value: 400			

KM# 461 200 DOLLARS **Weight:** 62.3130 g. **Composition:** 0.9990 Platinum 2.0000 oz. APW **Obverse:** Queen's head right **Reverse:** Koala in tree **Edge:** Reeded

Date	F	VF	XF	Unc	BU
1999	—	—	—	1,500	—

KM# 204 250 DOLLARS **Weight:** 16.9500 g. **Composition:** 0.9170 Gold .4995 oz. AGW **Subject:** 40th Anniversary - Reign of Queen Elizabeth II - Queen Mother **Reverse:** Portrait of Queen Mother right in circle of crowns

Date	Mintage	F	VF	XF	Unc	BU
1992 Proof	Est. 5,000	Value: 275				

KM# 205 250 DOLLARS **Weight:** 16.9500 g. **Composition:** 0.9170 Gold .4995 oz. AGW **Subject:** 40th Anniversary - Reign of Queen Elizabeth II - Princess Diana **Reverse:** Portrait of Princess Diana right in circle of crowns

Date	Mintage	F	VF	XF	Unc	BU
1992 Proof	Est. 5,000	Value: 300				

KM# 206 250 DOLLARS **Weight:** 16.9500 g. **Composition:** 0.9170 Gold .4995 oz. AGW **Subject:** 40th Anniversary - Reign of Queen Elizabeth II - Princess Anne **Reverse:** Portrait of Princess Anne right in circle of crowns

Date	Mintage	F	VF	XF	Unc	BU
1992 Proof	Est. 5,000	Value: 275				

KM# 207 250 DOLLARS **Weight:** 16.9500 g. **Composition:** 0.9170 Gold .4995 oz. AGW **Subject:** 40th Anniversary - Reign of Queen Elizabeth II - Princess Margaret **Reverse:** Portrait of Princess Margaret left in circle of crowns

Date	Mintage	F	VF	XF	Unc	BU
1992 Proof	Est. 5,000	Value: 285				

KM# 157 500 DOLLARS **Weight:** 62.2140 g. **Composition:** 0.9990 Platinum 2.0000 oz. APW **Subject:** Koala **Obverse:** Queen Elizabeth II **Reverse:** Koala in tree

Date	Mintage	F	VF	XF	Unc	BU
1991	—	—	—	—	BV+4%	—
1991 Proof	250	Value: 1,650				

KM# 150 500 DOLLARS **Weight:** 62.2140 g. **Composition:** 0.9990 Gold 2.0000 oz. AGW **Reverse:** Red kangaroo **Note:** Similar to 100 Dollars, KM#121.

Date	Mintage	F	VF	XF	Unc	BU
1991	—	—	—	—	BV+4%	—
1991 Proof	491	Value: 1,450				

KM# 186 1000 DOLLARS **Weight:** 311.0670 g. **Composition:** 0.9995 Platinum 10.0000 oz. APW **Reverse:** Koala **Note:** Similar to 200 Dollars, KM#185.

Date	F	VF	XF	Unc	BU
1992	—	—	—	BV+4%	—
1992 Proof	—	Value: 7,750			
1996	—	—	—	BV+4%	—

KM# 395 1000 DOLLARS **Weight:** 311.0670 g. **Composition:** 0.9990 Gold 10.0000 oz. AGW **Obverse:** Queen's portrait **Reverse:** Nail-tailed wallaby **Note:** Similar to 25 Dollars, KM#391.

Date	Mintage	F	VF	XF	Unc	BU
1992 Proof	40	Value: 7,500				

KM# 197 1000 DOLLARS **Weight:** 311.0670 g. **Composition:** 0.9995 Platinum 10.0000 oz. APW **Obverse:** Similar to 100 Dollars, KM#195 **Note:** Illustration reduced. Actual size: 60.3 millimeters.

Date	F	VF	XF	Unc	BU
1993	—	—	—	BV+4%	—
1994	—	—	—	BV+4%	—
1995	—	—	—	BV+4%	—
1997	—	—	—	BV+4%	—

KM# 239 1000 DOLLARS **Weight:** 311.0670 g. **Composition:** 0.9999 Gold 10.0000 oz. AGW **Obverse:** Queen Elizabeth II **Reverse:** Red kangaroo

Date	F	VF	XF	Unc	BU
1993 Proof	—	Value: 7,000			

KM# 247 1000 DOLLARS **Weight:** 311.0670 g. **Composition:** 0.9999 Gold 10.0000 oz. AGW **Reverse:** Kangaroo in diamond shape

Date	F	VF	XF	Unc	BU
1994 Proof	—	Value: 7,000			

KM# 255 1000 DOLLARS **Weight:** 311.0670 g. **Composition:** 0.9995 Platinum 10.0000 oz. APW **Subject:** Koala Mother and Baby **Obverse:** Queen Elizabeth II **Reverse:** Similar to 100 Dollars, KM#253

Date	F	VF	XF	Unc	BU
1994	—	—	—	BV+4%	—

KM# 183 1000 DOLLARS **Weight:** 311.0670 g. **Composition:** 0.9999 Gold 10.0000 oz. AGW **Reverse:** Red kangaroo **Note:** Similar to 200 Dollars, KM#182.

Date	F	VF	XF	Unc	BU
1995	—	—	—	BV+3%	—
1996	—	—	—	BV+3%	—
1997	—	—	—	BV+3%	—

KM# 454 1000 DOLLARS **Weight:** 311.3170 g. **Composition:** 0.9990 Gold 10.0000 oz. AGW **Obverse:** Queen's head right **Reverse:** Red kangaroo bounding left **Edge:** Reeded

Date	F	VF	XF	Unc	BU
1999	—	—	—	6,500	—

KM# 462 1000 DOLLARS **Weight:** 311.6910 g. **Composition:** 0.9990 Platinum 10.0000 oz. APW **Obverse:** Queen's portrait right **Reverse:** Koala in tree **Edge:** Reeded

Date	F	VF	XF	Unc	BU
1999	—	—	—	BV+4%	—

KM# 158 2500 DOLLARS **Weight:** 311.0670 g. **Composition:** 0.9990 Platinum 10.0000 oz. APW **Subject:** Koala **Obverse:** Queen Elizabeth II **Reverse:** Koala in tree

Date	Mintage	F	VF	XF	Unc	BU
1991	—	—	—	—	BV+4%	—
1991 Proof	100	Value: 7,750				

KM# 151 2500 DOLLARS **Weight:** 311.0670 g. **Composition:** 0.9990 Gold 10.0000 oz. AGW **Reverse:** Red kangaroo **Note:** Similar to 100 Dollars, KM#121.

Date	Mintage	F	VF	XF	Unc	BU
1991	—	—	—	—	BV+3%	—
1991 Proof	124	Value: 7,000				

KM# 184 3000 DOLLARS **Weight:** 1000.1000 g. **Composition:** 0.9999 Gold 32.1575 oz. AGW **Reverse:** Red kangaroo **Note:** Similar to 200 Dollars, KM#182.

Date	F	VF	XF	Unc	BU
1992	—	—	—	BV+3%	—
1992 Proof	25 Value: 24,500				
1995	—	—	—	BV+4%	—
1996	—	—	—	BV+3%	—
1997	—	—	—	BV+3%	—

KM# 187 3000 DOLLARS **Weight:** 1000.1000 g. **Composition:** 0.9999 Platinum 32.1575 oz. APW **Reverse:** Koala **Note:** Similar to 200 Dollars, KM#185.

Date	F	VF	XF	Unc	BU
1992	—	—	—	BV+3.5%	—
1992 Proof	—	Value: 21,500			
1996	—	—	—	BV+3.5%	—

KM# 396 3000 DOLLARS **Weight:** 1000.1000 g. **Composition:** 0.9999 Platinum 32.1575 oz. APW **Obverse:** Queen's portrait **Reverse:** Nail-tailed wallaby **Note:** Similar to 25 Dollars, KM#391.

Date	Mintage	F	VF	XF	Unc
1992 Proof	25	Value: 20,000			

KM# 198 3000 DOLLARS **Weight:** 1000.1000 g. **Composition:** 0.9999 Platinum 32.1575 oz. APW **Obverse:** Similar to 100 Dollars, KM#195 **Note:** Illustration reduced. Actual size: 75.3 millimeters.

Date	F	VF	XF	Unc	BU
1993	—	—	—	BV+3.5%	—
1994	—	—	—	BV+3.5%	—
1995	—	—	—	BV+3.5%	—
1997	—	—	—	BV+3.5%	—

KM# 240 3000 DOLLARS **Weight:** 1000.1000 g. **Composition:** 0.9999 Gold 32.1575 oz. AGW **Obverse:** Queen Elizabeth II **Reverse:** Whiptail wallaby

Date	F	VF	XF	Unc	BU
1993 Proof	—	Value: 21,500			

KM# 248 3000 DOLLARS **Weight:** 1000.1000 g. **Composition:** 0.9999 Gold 32.1575 oz. AGW **Subject:** Kangaroo **Reverse:** Kangaroo in diamond shape

Date	F	VF	XF	Unc	BU
1994 Proof	—	Value: 21,500			

KM# 256 3000 DOLLARS **Weight:** 1000.1000 g. **Composition:** 0.9995 Platinum 32.1575 oz. APW **Subject:** Koala Mother and Baby **Obverse:** Queen Elizabeth II **Reverse:** Similar to 100 Dollars, KM#253

Date	F	VF	XF	Unc	BU
1994	—	—	—	BV+3.5%	—

KM# 455 3000 DOLLARS **Weight:** 1000.3500 g. **Composition:** 0.9990 Gold 32.1588 oz. AGW **Obverse:** Queen's head right **Reverse:** Red Kangaroo bounding left **Edge:** Reeded

Date	F	VF	XF	Unc	BU
1999	—	—	—	18,500	—

KM# 463 3000 DOLLARS **Weight:** 1001.0000 g. **Composition:** 0.9990 Platinum 32.1668 oz. APW **Obverse:** Queen's head right **Reverse:** Koala in tree **Edge:** Reeded

Date	F	VF	XF	Unc	BU
1999	—	—	—	BV+3.5%	—

KM# 159 10000 DOLLARS **Weight:** 1000.1000 g. **Composition:** 0.9990 Platinum 32.1575 oz. APW **Subject:** Koala **Obverse:** Queen Elizabeth II **Reverse:** Red kangaroo

Date	Mintage	F	VF	XF	Unc	BU
1991	—	—	—	—	BV+3.5%	—
1991 Proof	50	Value: 25,000				

KM# 152 10000 DOLLARS **Weight:** 1000.1000 g. **Composition:** 0.9990 Gold 32.1575 oz. AGW **Subject:** Koala **Reverse:** Red kangaroo **Note:** Similar to 100 Dollars, KM#121.

Date	Mintage	F	VF	XF	Unc	BU
1991	—	—	—	—	BV+3%	—
1991 Proof	95	Value: 21,500				

TOKEN COINAGE

P.O.W.

WWI Liverpool (NSW)

KM# Tn-B1 THREEPENCE **Composition:** Aluminum **Issuer:** WWI Liverpool (NSW) **Note:** Oval.

Date	F	VF	XF	Unc	BU
ND	—	400	750	1,500	—

KM# Tn-A1 THREEPENCE **Composition:** Aluminum **Issuer:** WWI Liverpool (NSW) **Note:** Square.

Date	F	VF	XF	Unc	BU
ND	—	100	150	250	—

TOKEN COINAGE

P.O.W.

WWII Internment Camp

KM# Tn1.1 PENNY **Composition:** Brass **Issuer:** WWII Internment Camp

Date	F	VF	XF	Unc	BU
ND	15.00	25.00	40.00	65.00	—

KM# Tn1.2 PENNY **Composition:** Brass **Issuer:** WWII Internment Camp **Note:** Center hole misplaced (error).

Date	F	VF	XF	Unc	BU
ND	25.00	35.00	50.00	—	—

KM# Tn1.1a PENNY **Composition:** Copper-Nickel **Issuer:** WWII Internment Camp **Note:** Spink Australia Sale Nov. 1981. Lot 666A $600.

Date	F	VF	XF	Unc	BU
ND	—	—	—	—	—

KM# Tn2.1 THREEPENCE **Composition:** Bronze **Issuer:** WWII Internment Camp **Obv. Legend:** INTERNMENT CAMPS

Date	F	VF	XF	Unc	BU
ND	25.00	40.00	60.00	110	—

KM# Tn2.2 THREEPENCE **Composition:** Bronze **Issuer:** WWII Internment Camp **Obv. Legend:** INTERNMENT CAMP

Date	F	VF	XF	Unc	BU
ND	—	—	—	—	—

Note: Reported, not confirmed

KM# Tn3 SHILLING **Composition:** Bronze **Issuer:** WWII Internment Camp

Date	F	VF	XF	Unc	BU
ND	30.00	50.00	70.00	120	—

KM# Tn5.1 5 SHILLING **Composition:** Bronze

Date	F	VF	XF	Unc	BU
ND	—	500	600	900	—

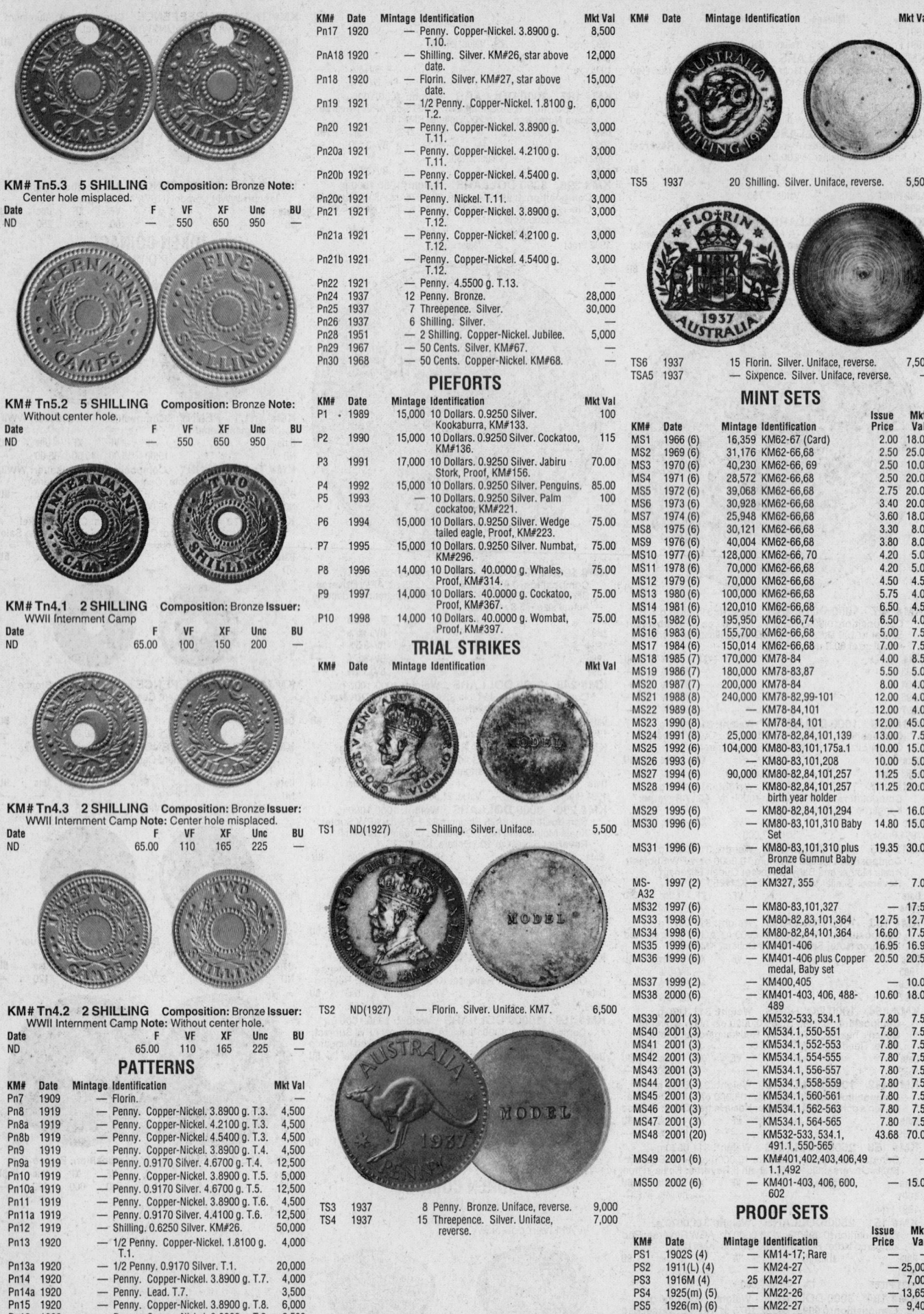

KM# Tn5.3 5 SHILLING Composition: Bronze Note: Center hole misplaced.

Date	F	VF	XF	Unc	BU
ND	—	550	650	950	—

KM# Tn5.2 5 SHILLING Composition: Bronze Note: Without center hole.

Date	F	VF	XF	Unc	BU
ND	—	550	650	950	—

KM# Tn4.1 2 SHILLING Composition: Bronze Issuer: WWII Internment Camp

Date	F	VF	XF	Unc	BU
ND	65.00	100	150	200	—

KM# Tn4.3 2 SHILLING Composition: Bronze Issuer: WWII Internment Camp Note: Center hole misplaced.

Date	F	VF	XF	Unc	BU
ND	65.00	110	165	225	—

KM# Tn4.2 2 SHILLING Composition: Bronze Issuer: WWII Internment Camp Note: Without center hole.

Date	F	VF	XF	Unc	BU
ND	65.00	110	165	225	—

PATTERNS

KM#	Date	Mintage	Identification	Mkt Val
Pn7	1909	—	Florin.	—
Pn8	1919	—	Penny. Copper-Nickel. 3.8900 g. T.3.	4,500
Pn8a	1919	—	Penny. Copper-Nickel. 4.2100 g. T.3.	4,500
Pn8b	1919	—	Penny. Copper-Nickel. 4.5400 g. T.3.	4,500
Pn9	1919	—	Penny. Copper-Nickel. 3.8900 g. T.4.	4,500
Pn9a	1919	—	Penny. 0.9170 Silver. 4.6700 g. T.4.	12,500
Pn10	1919	—	Penny. Copper-Nickel. 3.8900 g. T.5.	5,000
Pn10a	1919	—	Penny. 0.9170 Silver. 4.6700 g. T.5.	12,500
Pn11	1919	—	Penny. Copper-Nickel. 3.8900 g. T.6.	4,500
Pn11a	1919	—	Penny. 0.9170 Silver. 4.4100 g. T.6.	12,500
Pn12	1919	—	Shilling. 0.6250 Silver. KM#26.	50,000
Pn13	1920	—	1/2 Penny. Copper-Nickel. 1.8100 g. T.1.	4,000
Pn13a	1920	—	1/2 Penny. 0.9170 Silver. T.1.	20,000
Pn14	1920	—	Penny. Copper-Nickel. 3.8900 g. T.7.	4,000
Pn14a	1920	—	Penny. Lead. T.7.	3,500
Pn15	1920	—	Penny. Copper-Nickel. 3.8900 g. T.8.	6,000
Pn16	1920	—	Penny. Copper-Nickel. 3.8900 g. T.9.	6,500
Pn17	1920	—	Penny. Copper-Nickel. 3.8900 g. T.10.	8,500
PnA18	1920	—	Shilling. Silver. KM#26, star above date.	12,000
Pn18	1920	—	Florin. Silver. KM#27, star above date.	15,000
Pn19	1921	—	1/2 Penny. Copper-Nickel. 1.8100 g. T.2.	6,000
Pn20	1921	—	Penny. Copper-Nickel. 3.8900 g. T.11.	3,000
Pn20a	1921	—	Penny. Copper-Nickel. 4.2100 g. T.11.	3,000
Pn20b	1921	—	Penny. Copper-Nickel. 4.5400 g. T.11.	3,000
Pn20c	1921	—	Penny. Nickel. T.11.	3,000
Pn21	1921	—	Penny. Copper-Nickel. 3.8900 g. T.12.	3,000
Pn21a	1921	—	Penny. Copper-Nickel. 4.2100 g. T.12.	3,000
Pn21b	1921	—	Penny. Copper-Nickel. 4.5400 g. T.12.	3,000
Pn22	1921	—	Penny. 4.5500 g. T.13.	—
Pn24	1937	12	Penny. Bronze.	28,000
Pn25	1937	7	Threepence. Silver.	30,000
Pn26	1937	6	Shilling. Silver.	—
Pn28	1951	—	2 Shilling. Copper-Nickel. Jubilee.	5,000
Pn29	1967	—	50 Cents. Silver. KM#67.	—
Pn30	1968	—	50 Cents. Copper-Nickel. KM#68.	—

PIEFORTS

KM#	Date	Mintage	Identification	Mkt Val
P1	1989	15,000	10 Dollars. 0.9250 Silver. Kookaburra, KM#133.	100
P2	1990	15,000	10 Dollars. 0.9250 Silver. Cockatoo, KM#136.	115
P3	1991	17,000	10 Dollars. 0.9250 Silver. Jabiru Stork, Proof, KM#156.	70.00
P4	1992	15,000	10 Dollars. 0.9250 Silver. Penguins.	85.00
P5	1993	—	10 Dollars. 0.9250 Silver. Palm cockatoo, KM#221.	100
P6	1994	15,000	10 Dollars. 0.9250 Silver. Wedge tailed eagle, Proof, KM#223.	75.00
P7	1995	15,000	10 Dollars. 0.9250 Silver. Numbat, KM#296.	75.00
P8	1996	14,000	10 Dollars. 40.0000 g. Whales, Proof, KM#314.	75.00
P9	1997	14,000	10 Dollars. 40.0000 g. Cockatoo, Proof, KM#367.	75.00
P10	1998	14,000	10 Dollars. 40.0000 g. Wombat, Proof, KM#397.	75.00

TRIAL STRIKES

KM#	Date	Mintage	Identification	Mkt Val
TS1	ND(1927)	—	Shilling. Silver. Uniface.	5,500

KM#	Date	Mintage	Identification	Mkt Val
TS2	ND(1927)	—	Florin. Silver. Uniface. KM7.	6,500

KM#	Date	Mintage	Identification	Mkt Val
TS3	1937	8	Penny. Bronze. Uniface, reverse.	9,000
TS4	1937	15	Threepence. Silver. Uniface, reverse.	7,000

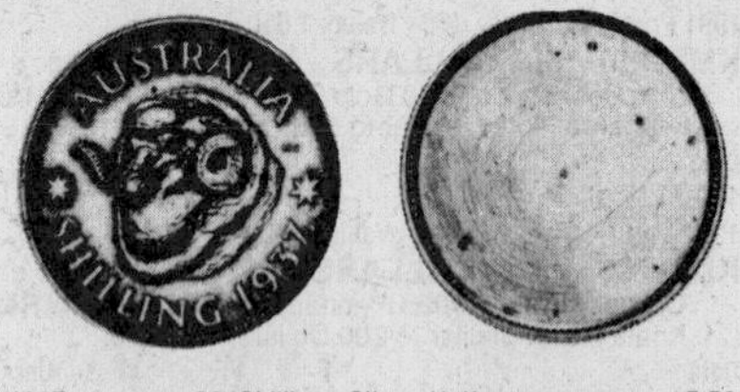

KM#	Date	Mintage	Identification	Mkt Val
TS5	1937	20	Shilling. Silver. Uniface, reverse.	5,500

KM#	Date	Mintage	Identification	Mkt Val
TS6	1937	15	Florin. Silver. Uniface, reverse.	7,500
TSA5	1937	—	Sixpence. Silver. Uniface, reverse.	—

MINT SETS

KM#	Date	Mintage	Identification	Issue Price	Mkt Val
MS1	1966 (6)	16,359	KM62-67 (Card)	2.00	18.00
MS2	1969 (6)	31,176	KM62-66,68	2.50	25.00
MS3	1970 (6)	40,230	KM62-66, 69	2.50	10.00
MS4	1971 (6)	28,572	KM62-66,68	2.50	20.00
MS5	1972 (6)	39,068	KM62-66,68	2.75	20.00
MS6	1973 (6)	30,928	KM62-66,68	3.40	20.00
MS7	1974 (6)	25,948	KM62-66,68	3.60	18.00
MS8	1975 (6)	30,121	KM62-66,68	3.30	8.00
MS9	1976 (6)	40,004	KM62-66,68	3.80	8.00
MS10	1977 (6)	128,000	KM62-66, 70	4.20	5.00
MS11	1978 (6)	70,000	KM62-66,68	4.20	5.00
MS12	1979 (6)	70,000	KM62-66,68	4.50	4.50
MS13	1980 (6)	100,000	KM62-66,68	5.75	4.00
MS14	1981 (6)	120,010	KM62-66,68	6.50	4.50
MS15	1982 (6)	195,950	KM62-66,74	6.50	4.00
MS16	1983 (6)	155,700	KM62-66,68	5.00	7.50
MS17	1984 (6)	150,014	KM62-66,68	7.00	7.50
MS18	1985 (7)	170,000	KM78-84	4.00	8.50
MS19	1986 (7)	180,000	KM78-83,87	5.50	5.00
MS20	1987 (7)	200,000	KM78-84	8.00	4.00
MS21	1988 (8)	240,000	KM78-82,99-101	12.00	4.00
MS22	1989 (8)	—	KM78-84,101	12.00	4.00
MS23	1990 (8)	—	KM78-84, 101	12.00	45.00
MS24	1991 (8)	25,000	KM78-82,84,101,139	13.00	7.50
MS25	1992 (6)	104,000	KM80-83,101,175a.1	10.00	15.00
MS26	1993 (6)	—	KM80-83,101,208	10.00	5.00
MS27	1994 (6)	90,000	KM80-82,84,101,257	11.25	5.00
MS28	1994 (6)	—	KM80-82,84,101,257 birth year holder	11.25	20.00
MS29	1995 (6)	—	KM80-82,84,101,294	—	16.00
MS30	1996 (6)	—	KM80-83,101,310 Baby Set	14.80	15.00
MS31	1996 (6)	—	KM80-83,101,310 plus Bronze Gumnut Baby medal	19.35	30.00
MS-A32	1997 (2)	—	KM327, 355	—	7.00
MS32	1997 (6)	—	KM80-83,101,327	—	17.50
MS33	1998 (6)	—	KM80-82,83,101,364	12.75	12.75
MS34	1998 (6)	—	KM80-82,84,101,364	16.60	17.50
MS35	1999 (6)	—	KM401-406	16.95	16.95
MS36	1999 (6)	—	KM401-406 plus Copper medal, Baby set	20.50	20.50
MS37	1999 (2)	—	KM400,405	—	10.00
MS38	2000 (6)	—	KM401-403, 406, 488-489	10.60	18.00
MS39	2001 (3)	—	KM532-533, 534.1	7.80	7.50
MS40	2001 (3)	—	KM534.1, 550-551	7.80	7.50
MS41	2001 (3)	—	KM534.1, 552-553	7.80	7.50
MS42	2001 (3)	—	KM534.1, 554-555	7.80	7.50
MS43	2001 (3)	—	KM534.1, 556-557	7.80	7.50
MS44	2001 (3)	—	KM534.1, 558-559	7.80	7.50
MS45	2001 (3)	—	KM534.1, 560-561	7.80	7.50
MS46	2001 (3)	—	KM534.1, 562-563	7.80	7.50
MS47	2001 (3)	—	KM534.1, 564-565	7.80	7.50
MS48	2001 (20)	—	KM532-533, 534.1, 491.1, 550-565	43.68	70.00
MS49	2001 (6)	—	KM#401,402,403,406,491.1,492	—	—
MS50	2002 (6)	—	KM401-403, 406, 600, 602	—	15.00

PROOF SETS

KM#	Date	Mintage	Identification	Issue Price	Mkt Val
PS1	1902S (4)	—	KM14-17; Rare	—	—
PS2	1911(L) (4)	—	KM24-27	—	25,000
PS3	1916M (4)	25	KM24-27	—	7,000
PS4	1925(m) (5)	—	KM22-26	—	13,650
PS5	1926(m) (6)	—	KM22-27	—	9,400
PS6	1927(m) (6)	50	KM22-27	—	7,150
PS7	1928(m) (6)	—	KM22-27	—	9,550

KM#	Date	Mintage	Identification	Issue Price	Mkt Val
PS8	1929(m) (2)	—	KM22-23	—	3,250
PSA9	1930(m) (2)	—	KM22-23	—	85.00
PS9	1931(m) (4)	—	KM22-27	—	7,000
PS10	1933(m) (2)	—	KM22-23	—	2,000
PS11	1934(m) (6)	100	KM22-27	—	7,500
PS12	1935(m) (6)	100	KM22-27	—	4,800
PS13	1936(m) (6)	—	KM22-27	—	6,350
PS14	1938(m) (6)	250	KM35-40	—	5,500
PS15	1953(p) (2)	—	KM49-50	—	3,500
PS16	1955(m) (4)	1,200	KM56-59	—	250
PS17	1955(p) (2)	301	KM49,56	—	2,000
PS18	1956(m) (5)	1,500	KM56-60	—	325
PS19	1957(m) (4)	1,256	KM57-60	—	225
PS20	1958(m) (5)	1,506	KM56-60	—	250
PS21	1959(m) (6)	1,506	KM56-61	—	325
PS22	1960(m) (4)	1,509	KM57-60	—	175
PS23	1960(p) (2)	1,030	KM56,61	—	225
PS24	1961(m) (4)	1,506	KM57-60	—	175
PS25	1961(p) (2)	1,040	KM56,61	—	225
PS26	1962(m) (4)	2,016	KM57-60	—	150
PS27	1962(p) (2)	1,064	KM56,61	—	200
PS28	1963(m) (4)	5,042	KM57-60	—	125
PS29	1963(p) (2)	1,064	KM56,61	—	225
PS30	1966 (6)	18,110	KM62-67	15.70	120
PS31	1969 (6)	12,696	KM62-66,68	11.25	110
PS32	1970 (6)	15,112	KM62-66,69	11.30	55.00
PS33	1971 (6)	10,066	KM62-66,68	11.30	50.00
PS34	1972 (6)	10,272	KM62-66,68	14.00	55.00
PS35	1973 (6)	10,090	KM62-66,68	15.50	70.00
PS36	1974 (6)	11,103	KM62-66,68	18.00	45.00
PS37	1975 (6)	23,021	KM62-66,68	17.00	15.00
PS38	1976 (6)	21,200	KM62-66,68	20.20	20.00
PS39	1977 (6)	55,000	KM62-66,70	20.20	12.00
PS40	1978 (6)	38,513	KM62-66,68	—	10.00
PS41	1979 (6)	36,000	KM62-66,68	—	10.00
PS42	1980 (6)	68,000	KM62-66,68	—	8.00
PS43	1981 (6)	86,008	KM62-66,68	48.00	8.00
PS44	1982 (6)	100,000	KM62-66,74	50.00	8.00
PS45	1983 (6)	80,000	KM62-66,68	39.00	10.00
PS46	1984 (6)	61,398	62-66,68	39.00	10.00
PS47	1985 (7)	74,809	KM78-84	27.50	20.00
PS49	1986P (4)	12,000	KM89-92	1,445	1,200
PS50	1986P (2)	3,000	KM89,90	305	310
PS48	1986 (7)	67,000	KM78-83,87	40.00	15.00
PS52	1987 (4)	12,000	KM95-98	1,440	1,000
PS53	1987 (2)	3,000	KM95, 96	305	350
PS51	1987 (7)	69,684	KM78-84	40.00	12.00
PS56	1988 (4)	25,000	KM99a-102a	85.00	130
PS57	1988	9,000	KM104-107	—	1,000
PS58	1988 (2)	1,000	KM104-105	—	200
PS59	1988 (2)	—	KM112-113	50.00	42.50
PS54	1988 (8)	101,000	KM78-82, 99-101	—	15.00
PS55	1988 (8)	5,000	KM78-82, 99-101, Coin Fair	—	80.00
PS62	1989 (5)	2,200	KM117-121	1,595	1,100
PS63	1989 (5)	2,400	KM122-126	1,995	1,300
PS64	1989 (5)	25,000	KM99a,127-130	—	130
PS65	1989 (2)	—	KM131-132	—	42.50
PS60	1989 (8)	2,500	KM78-84,101	—	15.00
PS61	1989 (8)	—	KM78-84, 101 Coin Fair	—	70.00
PS-A72	1990 (2)	—	KM154-155	—	42.50
PS68	1990 (5)	5,000	KM140-144	—	1,050
PS69	1990 (5)	2,500	KM145-149	—	1,300
PS70	1990 (3)	2,000	KM140-142	464	250
PS71	1990 (3)	1,000	KM138,144,149	1,900	1,200
PS76	1990 (3)	25,000	KM84a, 87a, 100a. Sydney Coin Fair.	135	110
PS66	1990 (8)	—	KM78-84,101	55.00	20.00
PS67	1990 (8)	—	KM78-84, 101 Coin Fair	—	80.00
PS73	1991 (8)	1,000	KM78-82,84,101a,139	—	70.00
PS74	1991 (5)	2,000	KM140-144	—	1,050
PS77	1991 (3)	1,000	KM140-142	—	250
PSA-74	1991 (8)	23,000	KM78a-82a,84a,101a,139a	—	140
PS72	1991 (8)	24,000	KM78-82,84,101,139	55.00	30.00
PS75	1991 (5)	1,000	PS145-149	—	1,050
PS-A79	1992 (4)	500	KM165-168	—	1,000
PS-A81	1992 (3)	264	KM389-391	251	350
PS-B81	1992 (5)	628	KM389-393	1,058	1,350
PS-C81	1992 (4)	500	KM389-392 plus medal	758	875
PS-D81	1992(ae) (3)	750	KM193, 209, 391	—	800
PS78	1992 (6)	47,000	KM80-83, 101, 175.1	40.00	25.00
PS79	1992 (4)	—	KM200-203, plus medal	120	120
PS80	1992 (4)	5,000	KM204-207 plus medal	1,520	1,520
PS-E81	1993 (4)	500	KM212, 230, 231 plus silver bar	—	300
PS82	1993 (5)	20,000	KM213-217	94.50	100
PS81	1993 (6)	—	KM80-83, 101, 208	—	20.00
PS84	1994 (5)	20,000	KM264-268	101	125
PS85	1994 (4)	20,000	KM182, 232 (2), 253	—	2,000
PS86	1994 (3)	25	KM241, 260, 278	303	350
PS83	1994 (6)	45,000	KM80-82, 84, 101, 257	—	20.00
PS-A89	1995 (3)	300	KM276, 286, 290	—	1,150
PS-A92	1995 (2)	800	KM290-291	—	395
PS87	1995 (5)	300	KM272-276	—	1,000
PS88	1995 (5)	200	KM283-287	—	1,300
PS89	1995 (4)	1,000	KM289-292	—	1,290
PS90	1995 (3)	300	KM289-291	—	390
PS91	1995 (2)	600	KM289-290	—	42.00
PSA87	1995 (6)	—	KM80-82, 84, 101, 294	—	35.00
PS-A95	1996 (3)	400	KM321-322, 341	1,500	1,350
PS-B95	1996 (6)	—	KM80-83, 101, 310	—	20.00
PS92	1996 (3)	3,000	KM275, (f), (l), (s) privy marks	—	800
PS93	1996 (6)	45,000	KM80-83, 101, 310. Baby set.	47.40	18.00
PS94	1996 (7)	—	KM80-83, 101, 310, plus silver gumnut baby medal	59.25	75.00
PS95	1997 (3)	3,888	KM335-337	914	925
PS96	1997 (3)	3,000	KM341 (f), (l), (s) privy marks	782	800
PS97	1998 (6)	—	KM80-82, 84, 101, 364	40.60	30.00
PS98	1998 (6)	—	KM80-82, 84, 101, 364. Baby set.	50.75	52.50
MS-B36	1999 (5)	500	KM501-505	—	1,050
MS-C36	1999 (3)	—	KM426-428	—	875
PS-A10	1999 (3)	1,000	KM501-503	—	170
PS100	1999 (6)	15,000	KM481-486	66.25	75.00
PS99	1999 (6)	—	KM401-406	—	35.00
PS101	2000 (6)	—	KM401-403, 406, 488.1, 489	34.35	40.00
PS102	2000 (5)	—	KM496-500 plus 20.5-gram silver ingot	—	135
PS103	2001 (3)	—	KM532-533, 534.2	21.00	22.50
PS104	2001 (3)	—	KM534.2, 550-551	21.00	22.50
PS105	2001 (3)	—	KM534.2, 552-553	21.00	22.50
PS106	2001 (3)	—	KM534.2, 554-555	21.00	22.50
PS107	2001 (3)	—	KM534.2, 556-557	21.00	22.50
PS108	2001 (3)	—	KM534.2, 558-559	21.00	22.50
PS109	2001 (3)	—	KM534.2, 560-561	21.00	22.50
PS110	2001 (3)	—	KM534.2, 562-563	21.00	22.50
PS111	2001 (3)	—	KM534.2, 564-565	21.00	22.50
PS112	2001 (20)	—	KM532-533, 534.2, 549.2, 550-565	120	200

AUSTRIA

The Republic of Austria, a parliamentary democracy located in mountainous central Europe, has an area of 32,374 sq. mi. (83,850 sq. km.) and a population of 8.08 million. Capital: Wien (Vienna). Austria is primarily an industrial country. Machinery, iron, steel, textiles, yarns and timber are exported.

The territories later to be known as Austria were overrun in pre-Roman times by various tribes, including the Celts. Upon the fall of the Roman Empire, the country became a margravate of Charlemagne's Empire. Premysl II of Otakar, King of Bohemia, gained possession in 1252, only to lose the territory to Rudolf of Habsburg in 1276. Thereafter, until World War I, the story of Austria was conducted by the ruling Habsburgs.

During the 17th century, Austrian coinage reflected the geo-political strife of three wars. From 1618-1648, the Thirty Years' War between northern Protestants and southern Catholics produced low quality, "kipperwhipper" strikes of 12, 24, 30, 60, 75 and 150 Kreuzer. Later, during the Austrian-Turkish War, 1660-1664, coinages used to maintain soldier's salaries also reported the steady division of Hungarian territories. Finally, between 1683 and 1699, during the second Austrian-Turkish conflict, new issues of 3, 6 and 15 Kreuzers were struck, being necessary to help defray mounting expenses of the war effort.

During World War I, the Austro-Hungarian Empire was one of the Central Powers with Germany, Bulgaria and Turkey. At the end of the war, the Empire was dismembered and Austria established as an independent republic. In March 1938, Austria was incorporated into Hitler's short-lived Greater German Reich. Allied forces of both East and West occupied Austria in April 1945, and subsequently divided it into 4 zones of military occupation. On May 15, 1955, the 4 powers formally recognized Austria as a sovereign independent democratic state.

NOTE: During the **GERMAN OCCUPATION** (1938-1945), the German Reichsmark coins and banknotes were circulated.

150 Schillings = 100 Reichsmark

RULERS

Franz Joseph I, 1848-1916
Karl I, 1916-1918

EMPIRE

REFORM COINAGE

100 Heller = 1 Corona

KM# 2800 HELLER **Composition:** Bronze **Ruler:** Franz Joseph

Date	Mintage	F	VF	XF	Unc	BU
1900	26,981,000	0.20	0.50	1.50	4.00	—
1901	52,096,000	0.20	0.35	0.50	2.00	—
1902	20,553,000	0.20	0.50	1.25	3.00	—
1903	13,779,000	0.20	0.35	0.50	2.50	—
1909	12,668,000	0.20	0.35	0.50	2.50	—
1910	21,900,000	0.20	0.35	0.50	2.50	—
1911	18,387,000	0.20	0.35	0.50	2.50	—
1912	27,053,000	0.20	0.35	0.50	2.50	—
1913	8,782,000	0.20	0.35	0.50	2.50	—
1914	9,906,000	0.20	0.35	0.50	2.50	—
1915	5,670,000	0.20	0.35	0.75	2.50	—
1916	12,484,000	0.35	0.75	1.50	4.00	—

KM# 2823 HELLER **Composition:** Bronze **Ruler:** Franz Joseph **Obverse:** Austrian shield on eagle's breast

Date	F	VF	XF	Unc	BU
1916	4.00	6.00	10.00	17.50	—

KM# 2801 2 HELLER **Composition:** Bronze **Ruler:** Franz Joseph

Date	Mintage	F	VF	XF	Unc	BU
1900	7,942,000	0.50	1.00	3.00	9.00	—
1901	12,157,000	2.00	3.00	6.00	25.00	—
1902	18,760,000	0.15	0.50	1.50	3.00	—
1903	26,983,000	0.50	1.50	3.00	8.00	—
1904	12,863,000	0.15	0.50	1.75	7.00	—
1905	6,679,000	0.75	2.75	5.50	15.00	—
1906	20,104,000	0.50	1.50	3.00	8.00	—
1907	23,804,000	0.15	0.25	0.75	3.00	—
1908	21,984,000	0.15	0.25	0.75	3.00	—
1909	25,975,000	0.15	0.25	0.75	3.00	—
1910	28,406,000	0.50	1.50	3.00	8.00	—
1911	50,007,000	0.15	0.25	0.50	2.00	—
1912	74,234,000	0.15	0.20	0.35	2.00	—
1913	27,432,000	0.35	0.75	2.25	6.00	—
1914	60,674,000	0.15	0.20	0.35	2.00	—
1915	7,870,000	0.15	0.20	0.35	2.00	—

KM# 2824 2 HELLER **Composition:** Iron **Ruler:** Karl I **Obverse:** Austrian shield on eagle's breast

Date	Mintage	F	VF	XF	Unc	BU
1916	61,909,000	0.50	1.00	2.00	7.50	—
1917	81,186,000	0.25	0.50	1.00	5.00	—
1918	66,352,999	0.25	0.50	1.00	4.00	—

KM# 2802 10 HELLER **Composition:** Nickel **Ruler:** Franz Joseph

Date	Mintage	F	VF	XF	Unc	BU
1907	8,662,000	0.25	0.50	1.00	4.00	—
1908	7,772,000	0.75	1.50	2.50	6.00	—
1909	20,462,000	0.15	0.25	0.75	2.50	—
1910	10,100,000	0.15	0.25	0.75	2.50	—
1911	3,634,000	1.00	2.00	3.50	8.00	—

KM# 2822 10 HELLER **Composition:** Copper-Nickel-Zinc **Ruler:** Franz Joseph

Date	Mintage	F	VF	XF	Unc	BU
1915	18,366,000	0.15	0.25	0.50	2.00	—
1916	27,487,000	0.15	0.25	0.50	2.00	—

KM# 2825 10 HELLER **Composition:** Copper-Nickel-Zinc **Ruler:** Franz Joseph **Obverse:** Austrian shield on eagle's breast

Date	Mintage	F	VF	XF	Unc	BU
1916	14,804,000	0.75	1.50	3.00	7.00	—

KM# 2803 20 HELLER **Composition:** Nickel **Ruler:** Franz Joseph

Date	Mintage	F	VF	XF	Unc	BU
1907	7,650,000	0.75	1.50	3.00	12.00	—
1908	7,469,000	0.75	1.25	2.50	9.00	—
1909	7,592,000	1.00	2.00	4.00	15.00	—
1911	19,560,000	0.25	0.35	1.00	5.00	—
1914	2,342,000	5.00	15.00	25.00	50.00	—

KM# 2826 20 HELLER **Composition:** Iron **Ruler:** Karl I **Obverse:** Austrian shield on eagle's breast

Date	Mintage	F	VF	XF	Unc	BU
1916	130,770,000	0.50	1.25	2.00	6.50	—
1917	127,420,000	0.50	1.25	2.00	5.50	—
1918	48,985,000	0.25	0.65	1.25	4.50	—

KM# 2804 CORONA **Weight:** 5.0000 g. **Composition:** 0.8350 Silver .1342 oz. ASW **Ruler:** Franz Joseph

Date	Mintage	F	VF	XF	Unc	BU
1901	10,387,000	1.75	2.75	5.00	10.00	—
1902	2,947,000	2.00	4.25	7.50	15.00	—
1903	2,198,000	2.00	4.25	8.00	25.00	—
1904	993,000	4.00	8.50	17.50	40.00	—
1905	505,000	10.00	25.00	45.00	85.00	—
1906	165,000	80.00	125	200	450	—
1907	244,000	30.00	60.00	100	300	—

KM# 2808 CORONA **Weight:** 5.0000 g. **Composition:** 0.8350 Silver .1342 oz. ASW **Ruler:** Franz Joseph **Subject:** 60th Anniversary of Reign

Date	Mintage	F	VF	XF	Unc	BU
ND(1908)	4,784,000	2.50	3.50	6.00	12.00	—

KM# 2820 CORONA **Weight:** 5.0000 g. **Composition:** 0.8350 Silver .1342 oz. ASW **Ruler:** Franz Joseph

Date	Mintage	F	VF	XF	Unc	BU
1912	8,457,000	1.50	2.00	3.00	8.00	—
1913	9,345,000	1.50	2.00	3.00	7.00	—
1914	37,897,000	1.50	2.00	3.00	6.00	—
1915	23,000,000	1.50	2.00	3.00	6.00	—
1916	12,415,000	1.50	2.00	3.00	6.00	—

KM# 2821 2 CORONA **Weight:** 10.0000 g. **Composition:** 0.8350 Silver .2684 oz. ASW **Ruler:** Franz Joseph

Date	Mintage	F	VF	XF	Unc	BU
1912	10,245,000	3.50	5.00	7.00	10.00	—
1913	7,256,000	3.50	5.00	7.00	10.00	—

KM# 2807 5 CORONA **Weight:** 24.0000 g. **Composition:** 0.9000 Silver .6945 oz. ASW **Ruler:** Franz Joseph

Date	Mintage	F	VF	XF	Unc	BU
1900	8,525,000	8.00	12.50	30.00	75.00	—
1907	1,539,000	10.00	15.00	35.00	100	—
1907 Proof	—	Value: 650				

KM# 2809 5 CORONA **Weight:** 24.0000 g. **Composition:** 0.9000 Silver .6945 oz. ASW **Ruler:** Franz Joseph **Subject:** 60th Anniversary of Reign

Date	Mintage	F	VF	XF	Unc	BU
ND(1908)	5,090,000	7.50	12.50	27.50	65.00	—
ND(1908) Proof	—	Value: 650				

KM# 2813 5 CORONA **Weight:** 24.0000 g. **Composition:** 0.9000 Silver .6945 oz. ASW **Ruler:** Franz Joseph **Obverse:** Large head without wreath, continuous legend

Date	Mintage	F	VF	XF	Unc	BU
1909	1,709,000	10.00	16.00	40.00	125	—

KM# 2814 5 CORONA **Weight:** 24.0000 g. **Composition:** 0.9000 Silver .6945 oz. ASW **Ruler:** Franz Joseph **Obverse:** Similar to KM#2809, with smaller head **Reverse:** Similar to KM#2813

Date	Mintage	F	VF	XF	Unc	BU
1909	1,776,000	10.00	15.00	35.00	90.00	—

KM# 2805 10 CORONA **Weight:** 3.3875 g. **Composition:** 0.9000 Gold .0980 oz. AGW **Ruler:** Franz Joseph **Obverse:** Laureate head of Franz Joseph I right **Reverse:** Eagle with value and date below

Date	Mintage	F	VF	XF	Unc	BU
1905	1,933,000	BV	50.00	60.00	85.00	—
1905	1,933,000	BV	50.00	60.00	85.00	—
1906	1,081,000	BV	50.00	60.00	85.00	—

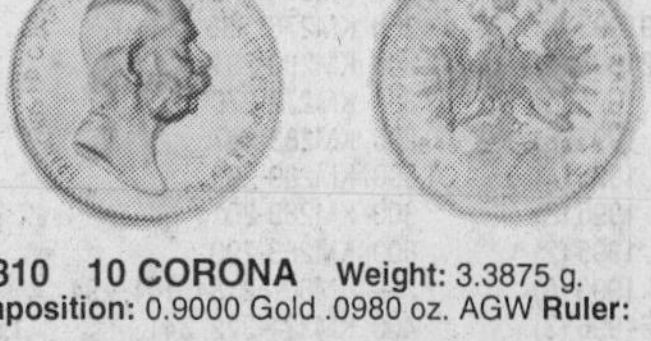

KM# 2810 10 CORONA **Weight:** 3.3875 g. **Composition:** 0.9000 Gold .0980 oz. AGW **Ruler:**

Franz Joseph **Subject:** 60th Anniversary of Reign **Obverse:** Small plain head of Franz Joseph I right **Reverse:** Eagle, value below, two dates above

Date	Mintage	F	VF	XF	Unc	BU
1908	654,000	BV	55.00	65.00	100	—

KM# 2815 10 CORONA Weight: 3.3875 g. **Composition:** 0.9000 Gold .0980 oz. AGW **Ruler:** Franz Joseph **Reverse:** Eagle, value and date below

Date	Mintage	F	VF	XF	Unc	BU
1909	2,320,000	BV	50.00	60.00	80.00	—

KM# 2816 10 CORONA Weight: 3.3875 g. **Composition:** 0.9000 Gold .0980 oz. AGW **Ruler:** Franz Joseph **Obverse:** Large head

Date	Mintage	F	VF	XF	Unc	BU
1909	192,000	55.00	60.00	75.00	90.00	—
1910	1,004,999	BV	50.00	60.00	80.00	—
1911	1,286,000	BV	50.00	60.00	80.00	—
1912 Restrike	—	—	—	—	BV+ 10%	—

KM# 2806 20 CORONA Weight: 6.7751 g. **Composition:** 0.9000 Gold .1960 oz. AGW **Ruler:** Franz Joseph

Date	Mintage	F	VF	XF	Unc	BU
1900	27,000	200	400	600	800	—
1901	49,000	150	225	325	400	—
1901	49,000	150	225	325	400	—
1902	441,000	BV	100	125	150	—
1903	323,000	BV	100	125	150	—
1904	494,000	BV	100	125	150	—
1905	146,000	100	120	150	170	—

KM# 2811 20 CORONA Weight: 6.7751 g. **Composition:** 0.9000 Gold .1960 oz. AGW **Ruler:** Franz Joseph **Subject:** 60th Anniversary of Reign **Reverse:** Two dates above eagle

Date	Mintage	F	VF	XF	Unc	BU
1908	188,000	100	125	150	200	—

KM# 2817 20 CORONA Weight: 6.7751 g. **Composition:** 0.9000 Gold .1960 oz. AGW **Ruler:** Franz Joseph

Date	Mintage	F	VF	XF	Unc	BU
1909	228,000	450	750	1,250	1,750	—

KM# 2818 20 CORONA Weight: 6.7751 g. **Composition:** 0.9000 Gold .1960 oz. AGW **Ruler:** Franz Joseph

Date	Mintage	F	VF	XF	Unc	BU
1909	102,000	575	850	1,250	1,750	—
1910	386,000	110	150	250	350	—
1911	59,000	120	175	275	375	—
1912	4,460	250	325	400	500	—
1913	28,000	350	500	750	1,000	—
1914	82,000	125	225	300	500	—
1915 Restrike	—	—	—	—	BV+ 5%	—
1916	72,000	2,500	3,500	5,500	7,500	—

KM# 2827 20 CORONA Weight: 6.7751 g. **Composition:** 0.9000 Gold .1960 oz. AGW **Ruler:** Franz Joseph **Reverse:** Austrian shield on eaegle

Date	F	VF	XF	Unc	BU
1916	450	550	900	1,200	—

KM# 2828 20 CORONA Weight: 6.7751 g. **Composition:** 0.9000 Gold .1960 oz. AGW **Ruler:** Franz Joseph **Obverse:** Head of Kaiser Karl I **Reverse:** Similar to KM#2818 **Note:** All but one specimen were remelted.

Date	F	VF	XF	Unc	BU
1918 Unique	—	—	—	—	—

KM# 2812 100 CORONA Weight: 33.8753 g. **Composition:** 0.9000 Gold .9803 oz. AGW **Ruler:** Franz Joseph **Subject:** 60th Anniversary of Reign

Date	Mintage	F	VF	XF	Unc	BU
1908	16,000	500	600	900	1,400	—
1908 Proof	—	Value: 1,850				

KM# 2819 100 CORONA Weight: 33.8753 g. **Composition:** 0.9000 Gold .9803 oz. AGW **Ruler:** Franz Joseph

Date	Mintage	F	VF	XF	Unc	BU
1909	3,203	500	650	950	1,500	—
1910	3,074	500	650	950	1,500	—
1911	11,165	500	650	950	1,500	—
1912	3,591	550	850	1,150	2,000	—
1913	2,696	500	800	1,200	1,700	—
1914	1,195	500	650	1,000	1,600	—
1915 Restrike	—	—	—	—	BV+ 2%	—
1915 Restrike, Proof	—	—	—	—	—	—

TRADE COINAGE

Uniform

KM# 2267 DUCAT Weight: 3.4909 g. **Composition:** 0.9860 Gold .1106 oz. AGW **Ruler:** Franz Joseph **Note:** 996,721 pieces were struck from 1920-1936.

Date	Mintage	F	VF	XF	Unc	BU
1901	349,000	60.00	100	125	175	—
1902	311,000	60.00	100	125	175	—
1903	380,000	60.00	100	125	175	—
1904	517,000	60.00	100	125	175	—
1905	392,000	60.00	125	150	200	—
1906	492,000	60.00	125	150	200	—
1907	554,000	60.00	125	175	250	—
1908	409,000	60.00	80.00	125	175	—
1909	366,000	60.00	80.00	100	150	—
1910	440,000	60.00	80.00	100	150	—
1911	591,000	60.00	80.00	100	125	—
1912	495,000	60.00	80.00	100	125	—
1913	320,000	60.00	80.00	100	125	—
1914	378,000	60.00	80.00	100	125	—
1915 Restrike	—	—	—	—	BV+ 10%	—
1915 Restrike, Proof	—	Value: 50.00				
1951 Error for 1915	—	75.00	125	150	225	—

KM# 2276 4 DUCAT Weight: 13.9636 g. **Composition:** 0.9860 Gold .4430 oz. AGW **Ruler:** Franz Joseph **Obverse:** Similar to 4 Ducat, KM#2272, but without mint

Date	Mintage	F	VF	XF	Unc	BU
1900	47,000	225	250	500	600	—
1901	47,000	225	250	500	600	—
1901	52,000	225	250	450	600	—
1902	69,000	225	250	400	600	—
1903	73,000	225	250	400	600	—
1904	80,000	225	250	400	600	—
1905	91,000	225	250	400	550	—
	123,000					
1907	104,000	225	250	300	500	—
1908	80,000	225	250	450	600	—
1909	84,000	225	250	375	500	—
1910	101,000	225	250	275	400	—
1911	142,000	225	250	275	350	—
1912	151,000	225	250	275	350	—
1913	119,000	225	250	275	350	—
1914	102,000	225	250	275	350	—
1915 (- 1936) Restrike	—	—	—	—	BV+ 8%	—

Note: 496,501 pieces were struck from 1920-1936

REPUBLIC

REFORM COINAGE

10,000 Kronen = 1 Schilling

KM# 2830 20 KRONEN Weight: 6.7751 g. **Composition:** 0.9000 Gold .1960 oz. AGW

Date	Mintage	F	VF	XF	Unc	BU
1923	6,988	650	1,400	1,850	2,500	—
1924	10,337	650	1,400	1,850	2,500	—

KM# 2831 100 KRONEN Weight: 33.8753 g. **Composition:** 0.9000 Gold .9802 oz. AGW

Date	Mintage	F	VF	XF	Unc	BU
1923	617	750	1,550	2,250	3,500	—
1923 Proof	—	Value: 4,000				
1924	2,851	750	1,550	2,250	3,500	—

KM# 2832 100 KRONEN Composition: Bronze

Date	Mintage	F	VF	XF	Unc	BU
1923	6,404,000	4.00	8.00	15.00	30.00	—
1924	43,014,000	0.25	0.50	1.50	4.50	—

KM# 2833 200 KRONEN Composition: Bronze

Date	Mintage	F	VF	XF	Unc	BU
1924	57,160,000	0.50	1.00	2.00	6.50	—

KM# 2834 1000 KRONEN Composition: Copper-Nickel

Date	Mintage	F	VF	XF	Unc	BU
1924	72,353,000	0.75	1.50	3.00	8.00	—

PRE WWII DECIMAL COINAGE

100 Groschen - 1 Schilling

KM# 2836 GROSCHEN Composition: Bronze

Date	Mintage	F	VF	XF	Unc	BU
1925	30,465,000	0.10	0.20	0.50	2.00	—
1926	15,487,000	0.10	0.30	0.75	2.00	—
1927	9,318,000	0.10	0.30	0.75	2.50	—
1928	17,189,000	0.10	0.30	0.75	2.50	—
1929	11,400,000	0.10	0.30	0.75	2.50	—
1930	8,893,000	0.10	0.30	0.75	2.50	—
1931	971,000	10.00	20.00	30.00	60.00	—
1932	3,040,000	1.00	2.50	5.00	7.50	—
1933	3,940,000	0.50	1.00	2.00	6.00	—
1934	4,232,000	0.15	0.50	1.00	4.00	—
1935	3,740,000	0.15	0.50	1.00	4.00	—
1936	6,020,000	0.50	1.00	3.00	9.00	—
1937	5,830,000	0.50	1.00	2.00	7.50	—
1938	1,650,000	2.00	3.00	6.00	15.00	—

KM# 2837 2 GROSCHEN Composition: Bronze

Date	Mintage	F	VF	XF	Unc	BU
1925	29,892,000	0.10	0.25	0.50	1.50	—
1926	17,700,000	0.10	0.30	0.75	2.00	—
1927	7,757,000	0.20	0.75	2.00	5.00	—
1928	19,478,000	0.10	0.30	0.75	2.00	—
1929	16,184,000	0.10	0.30	0.75	2.00	—
1930	5,709,000	0.20	0.60	1.50	4.00	—
1934	812,000	7.00	12.00	15.00	25.00	—
1935	3,148,000	0.20	0.60	1.50	4.00	—
1936	4,410,000	0.15	0.30	1.00	3.00	—
1937	3,790,000	0.20	0.40	1.25	3.50	—
1938	860,000	2.50	4.00	6.50	12.50	—

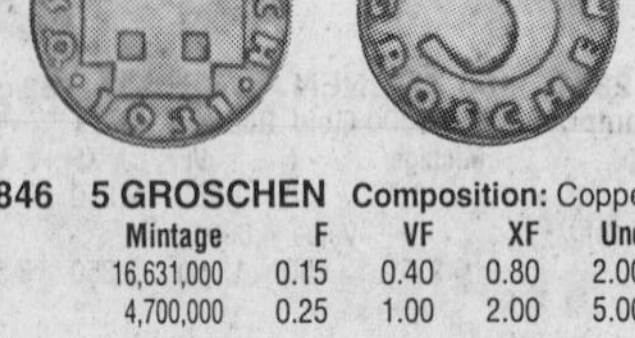

KM# 2846 5 GROSCHEN Composition: Copper-Nickel

Date	Mintage	F	VF	XF	Unc	BU
1931	16,631,000	0.15	0.40	0.80	2.00	—
1932	4,700,000	0.25	1.00	2.00	5.00	—

Date	Mintage	F	VF	XF	Unc	BU
1934	3,210,000	0.30	1.00	2.50	6.00	—
1936	1,240,000	2.00	4.00	7.50	15.00	—
1937	1,540,000	20.00	30.00	45.00	80.00	—
1938	870,000	125	175	250	425	—

KM# 2838 10 GROSCHEN Composition: Copper-Nickel

Date	Mintage	F	VF	XF	Unc	BU
1925	66,199,000	0.10	0.25	0.50	3.00	—
1928	11,468,000	0.50	1.00	4.00	12.00	—
1929	12,000,000	0.40	0.75	1.50	4.50	—

KM# 2850 50 GROSCHEN Composition: Copper-Nickel

Date	Mintage	F	VF	XF	Unc	BU
1934	8,225,000	20.00	35.00	50.00	90.00	—
1934 Proof	Inc. above	Value: 125				

KM# 2854 50 GROSCHEN Composition: Copper-Nickel

Date	Mintage	F	VF	XF	Unc	BU
1935	11,435,000	0.75	1.25	2.50	5.00	—
1935 Proof	Inc. above	Value: 80.00				
1936	1,000,000	30.00	40.00	60.00	115	—
1936 Proof	Inc. above	Value: 140				

KM# 2839 1/2 SCHILLING Weight: 3.0000 g. Composition: 0.6400 Silver .0617 oz. ASW

Date	Mintage	F	VF	XF	Unc	BU
1925	18,370,000	1.00	2.00	3.00	8.00	—
1926	12,943,000	2.00	4.00	6.00	12.00	—

KM# 2835 SCHILLING Weight: 7.0000 g. Composition: 0.8000 Silver .1800 oz. ASW Reverse: Coat of arms on spray of Edelweiss

Date	Mintage	F	VF	XF	Unc	BU
1924	11,086,000	1.50	2.50	4.50	10.00	—

KM# 2840 SCHILLING Weight: 6.0000 g. Composition: 0.6400 Silver .1235 oz. ASW

Date	Mintage	F	VF	XF	Unc	BU
1925	38,209,000	1.25	2.00	3.50	7.00	—
1926	20,157,000	1.25	2.00	4.00	8.00	—
1932	700,000	30.00	40.00	60.00	100	—

KM# 2851 SCHILLING Composition: Copper-Nickel

Date	Mintage	F	VF	XF	Unc	BU
1934	30,641,000	1.00	2.00	3.50	7.50	—
1934 Proof	—	Value: 150				
1935	11,987,000	3.00	6.00	12.50	30.00	—

KM# 2843 2 SCHILLING Weight: 12.0000 g. Composition: 0.6400 Silver .2469 oz. ASW Subject: Centennial - Death of Franz Schubert

Date	Mintage	F	VF	XF	Unc	BU
1928	6,900,000	3.50	4.50	8.00	16.00	—

KM# 2844 2 SCHILLING Weight: 12.0000 g. Composition: 0.6400 Silver .2469 oz. ASW Subject: 100th Anniversary - Birth of Dr. Theodor Billroth

Date	Mintage	F	VF	XF	Unc	BU
1929	2,000,000	5.00	8.00	16.00	32.50	—

KM# 2845 2 SCHILLING Weight: 12.0000 g. Composition: 0.6400 Silver .2469 oz. ASW Subject: 7th Centennial - Death of Walther von der Vogelweide

Date	Mintage	F	VF	XF	Unc	BU
1930	500,000	5.00	6.00	9.00	18.00	—
1930 Proof	Inc. above	Value: 125				

KM# 2847 2 SCHILLING Weight: 12.0000 g. Composition: 0.6400 Silver .2469 oz. ASW Subject: 175th Anniversary - Birth of Wolfgang Mozart

Date	Mintage	F	VF	XF	Unc	BU
1931	500,000	7.00	14.00	22.00	50.00	—
1931 Proof	Inc. above	Value: 300				

KM# 2848 2 SCHILLING **Weight:** 12.0000 g. **Composition:** 0.6400 Silver .2469 oz. ASW **Subject:** 200th Anniversary - Birth of Joseph Haydn

Date	Mintage	F	VF	XF	Unc	BU
1932	300,000	22.00	45.00	100	165	—
1932 Proof	Inc. above	Value: 500				

KM# 2849 2 SCHILLING **Weight:** 12.0000 g. **Composition:** 0.6400 Silver .2469 oz. ASW **Subject:** Death of Dr. Ignaz Seipel

Date	Mintage	F	VF	XF	Unc	BU
ND(1933)	400,000	8.00	16.00	30.00	50.00	—
ND(1933) Proof	Inc. above	Value: 400				

KM# 2852 2 SCHILLING **Weight:** 12.0000 g. **Composition:** 0.6400 Silver .2469 oz. ASW **Subject:** Death of Dr. Engelbert Dollfuss

Date	Mintage	F	VF	XF	Unc	BU
1934	1,500,000	7.00	12.00	20.00	32.50	—
1934 Proof	Inc. above	Value: 275				

KM# 2855 2 SCHILLING **Weight:** 12.0000 g. **Composition:** 0.6400 Silver .2469 oz. ASW **Subject:** 25th Anniversary - Death of Dr. Karl Lueger

Date	Mintage	F	VF	XF	Unc	BU
1935	500,000	8.00	16.00	25.00	45.00	—
1935 Proof	Inc. above	Value: 285				

KM# 2858 2 SCHILLING **Weight:** 12.0000 g. **Composition:** 0.6400 Silver .2469 oz. ASW **Subject:** Bicentennial - Death of Prince Eugen of Savoy

Date	Mintage	F	VF	XF	Unc	BU
1936	500,000	6.00	9.00	18.00	30.00	—
1936 Proof	Inc. above	Value: 225				

KM# 2859 2 SCHILLING **Weight:** 12.0000 g. **Composition:** 0.6400 Silver .2469 oz. ASW **Subject:** Bicentennial - Completeion of St. Charles Church

Date	Mintage	F	VF	XF	Unc	BU
1937	500,000	6.00	9.00	18.00	30.00	—
1937 Proof	Inc. above	Value: 185				

KM# 2853 5 SCHILLING **Weight:** 15.0000 g. **Composition:** 0.8350 Silver .4027 oz. ASW **Reverse:** Madonna of Mariazell

Date	Mintage	F	VF	XF	Unc	BU
1934	3,066,000	11.50	17.50	30.00	55.00	—
1934 Proof	—	Value: 200				
1935	5,377,000	11.50	17.50	30.00	55.00	—
1936	1,557,000	42.50	75.00	115	220	—

KM# 2841 25 SCHILLING **Weight:** 5.8810 g. **Composition:** 0.9000 Gold .1702 oz. AGW

Date	Mintage	F	VF	XF	Unc	BU
1926 Prooflike	276,000	—	—	—	125	—
1927 Prooflike	73,000	—	—	—	135	—
1928 Prooflike	134,000	—	—	—	125	—
1929 Prooflike	243,000	—	—	—	125	—
1930 Prooflike	130,000	—	—	—	135	—
1931 Prooflike	169,000	—	—	—	125	—
1933 Prooflike	4,944	—	—	—	1,850	—
1934 Prooflike	11,000	—	—	—	600	—

KM# 2856 25 SCHILLING **Weight:** 5.8810 g. **Composition:** 0.9000 Gold .1702 oz. AGW **Reverse:** St. Leopold

Date	Mintage	F	VF	XF	Unc	BU
1935 Prooflike	2,880	—	—	—	1,000	—
1936 Prooflike	7,260	—	—	—	850	—
1937 Prooflike	7,660	—	—	—	850	—
1938 Prooflike	1,360	—	—	—	25,000	—

KM# 2842 100 SCHILLING **Weight:** 23.5245 g. **Composition:** 0.9000 Gold .6806 oz. AGW

Date	Mintage	F	VF	XF	Unc	BU
1926 Prooflike	64,000	—	—	—	450	—
1927 Prooflike	69,000	—	—	—	450	—
1928 Prooflike	40,000	—	—	—	550	—
1929 Prooflike	75,000	—	—	—	450	—
1930 Prooflike	25,000	—	—	—	450	—
1931 Prooflike	102,000	—	—	—	450	—
1933 Prooflike	4,700	—	—	—	1,550	—
1934 Prooflike	9,383	—	—	—	600	—

KM# 2857 100 SCHILLING **Weight:** 23.5245 g. **Composition:** 0.9000 Gold .6806 oz. AGW **Reverse:** Madonna of Mariazell

Date	Mintage	F	VF	XF	Unc	BU
1935 Prooflike	951	—	—	—	5,500	—
1936 Prooflike	12,000	—	—	—	1,650	—
1937 Prooflike	2,900	—	—	—	2,250	—
1938 Prooflike	1,400	—	—	—	25,000	—

POST WWII DECIMAL COINAGE

100 Groschen - 1 Schilling

KM# 2873 GROSCHEN **Composition:** Zinc

Date	Mintage	F	VF	XF	Unc	BU
1947	23,758,000	0.15	0.25	0.75	2.50	—

KM# 2876 2 GROSCHEN **Composition:** Aluminum

Date	Mintage	F	VF	XF	Unc	BU
1950	21,600,000	—	0.15	0.60	4.00	—
1950 Proof	—	Value: 28.00				
1951	7,370,000	—	0.25	1.00	4.50	—
1951 Proof	—	Value: 300				
1952	37,851,000	—	0.15	0.50	2.50	—
1952 Proof	—	Value: 25.00				
1954	49,879,000	—	0.15	0.50	2.50	—
1954 Proof	—	Value: 50.00				
1957	23,211,000	—	0.15	0.50	3.00	—
1957 Proof	—	Value: 45.00				
1962	6,692,000	—	0.15	0.50	2.50	—
1962 Proof	—	Value: 28.00				
1964 Proof	173,000	Value: 6.50				
1965	11,865,000	—	0.10	0.30	1.50	—
1965 Proof	—	Value: 2.50				
1966	7,454,000	—	0.10	0.30	1.50	—
1966 Proof	—	Value: 7.50				
1967 Proof	13,000	Value: 100				
1968	176,000	—	0.10	0.30	1.50	—
1968 Proof	22,000	Value: 10.00				
1969 Proof	62,000	Value: 6.00				
1970 Proof	277,000	Value: 2.50				
1971 Proof	145,000	Value: 2.50				
1972	2,763,000	—	—	0.20	0.50	—
1972 Proof	132,000	Value: 1.00				
1973	5,883,000	—	—	0.20	0.50	—
1973 Proof	149,000	Value: 1.00				
1974	1,387,000	—	—	0.20	0.50	—
1974 Proof	93,000	Value: 1.00				
1975	1,096,000	—	—	0.20	0.50	—
1975 Proof	52,000	Value: 1.00				
1976	2,755,000	—	—	0.20	0.50	—
1976 Proof	45,000	Value: 1.00				
1977	1,837,000	—	—	0.20	0.50	—
1977 Proof	47,000	Value: 1.00				
1978	1,527,000	—	—	0.20	0.50	—
1978 Proof	44,000	Value: 1.00				
1979	2,434,000	—	—	0.20	0.50	—
1979 Proof	44,000	Value: 1.00				
1980	1,893,000	—	—	0.20	0.50	—
1980 Proof	48,000	Value: 10.00				
1981	950,000	—	—	0.20	0.50	—
1981 Proof	49,000	Value: 10.00				
1982	3,950,000	—	—	0.20	0.50	—
1982 Proof	50,000	Value: 3.00				
1983	2,665,000	—	—	0.20	0.50	—
1983 Proof	65,000	Value: 2.00				

Date	Mintage	F	VF	XF	Unc	BU
1984	500,000	—	—	0.20	0.50	—
1984 Proof	65,000	Value: 2.00				
1985	1,060,000	—	—	0.20	0.50	—
1985 Proof	45,000	Value: 5.00				
1986	1,800,000	—	—	0.20	0.50	—
1986 Proof	42,000	Value: 10.00				
1987	958,000	—	—	0.20	0.50	—
1987 Proof	42,000	Value: 6.00				
1988	1,061,000	—	—	0.20	0.50	—
1988 Proof	39,000	Value: 2.00				
1989	950,000	—	—	0.20	0.50	—
1989 Proof	38,000	Value: 2.00				
1990 Proof	35,000	Value: 22.00				
1991	2,600,000	—	—	0.20	0.50	—
1991 Proof	27,000	Value: 5.00				
1992 In sets only	25,000	—	—	—	20.00	—
1992 Proof	25,000	Value: 15.00				
1993 In sets only	35,000	—	—	—	20.00	—
1993 Proof	28,000	Value: 7.00				
1994 In sets only	25,000	—	—	—	25.00	—
1994 Proof	25,000	Value: 30.00				

KM# 2875 5 GROSCHEN Composition: Zinc

Date		F	VF	XF	Unc	BU
1948		—	0.20	0.75	12.00	—
1950		—	0.20	0.75	8.00	—
1950 Proof	—	Value: 200				
1951		—	0.20	0.75	12.00	—
1951 Proof	—	Value: 35.00				
1953		—	0.15	0.75	8.00	—
1955		—	0.15	0.75	12.00	—
1957		—	0.15	0.75	6.00	—
1957 Proof	—	Value: 50.00				
1961		—	0.20	0.75	8.00	—
1961 Proof	—	Value: 25.00				
1962		—	0.20	0.75	8.00	—
1963		—	0.15	0.75	8.00	—
1963 Proof	—	Value: 40.00				
1964		—	0.15	0.75	4.00	—
1964 Proof	—	Value: 2.50				
1965		—	0.10	0.50	3.00	—
1965 Proof	—	Value: 2.50				
1966		—	0.10	0.50	3.00	—
1966 Proof	—	Value: 8.00				
1967		—	0.10	0.50	3.00	—
1967 Proof	—	Value: 10.00				
1968		—	0.10	0.50	3.00	—
1968 Proof	16,000	Value: 8.00				
1969		—	0.10	0.50	3.00	—
1969 Proof	44,000	Value: 10.00				
1970		—	0.10	0.50	3.00	—
1970 Proof	Est. 179,000	Value: 2.50				
1971		—	—	—	—	—
1971 Proof	125,000	Value: 2.50				
1972		—	—	0.20	0.75	—
1972 Proof	116,000	Value: 1.00				
1973		—	—	0.20	0.75	—
1973 Proof	120,000	Value: 1.00				
1974		—	—	0.20	0.75	—
1974 Proof	87,000	Value: 1.00				
1975		—	—	0.20	0.75	—
1975 Proof	51,000	Value: 1.00				
1976		—	—	0.20	0.75	—
1976 Proof	45,000	Value: 1.00				
1977		—	—	0.20	0.75	—
1977 Proof	45,000	Value: 1.00				
1978		—	—	0.20	0.75	—
1978 Proof	44,000	Value: 1.00				
1979		—	—	0.20	0.75	—
1979 Proof	44,000	Value: 1.00				
1980		—	—	0.20	0.75	—
1980 Proof	48,000	Value: 8.00				
1981		—	—	0.20	0.75	—
1981 Proof	49,000	Value: 8.00				
1982		—	—	0.20	0.75	—
1982 Proof	50,000	Value: 2.50				
1983		—	—	0.20	0.75	—
1983 Proof	65,000	Value: 2.50				
1984		—	—	0.20	0.75	—
1984 Proof	65,000	Value: 2.50				
1985		—	—	0.20	0.75	—
1985 Proof	45,000	Value: 4.00				
1986		—	—	0.20	0.75	—
1986 Proof	42,000	Value: 7.00				
1987		—	—	0.20	0.75	—
1987 Proof	42,000	Value: 4.00				
1988		—	—	0.20	0.75	—
1988 Proof	39,000	Value: 3.00				
1989		—	—	0.20	0.75	—
1989 Proof	38,000	Value: 2.00				
1990		—	—	0.20	0.75	—
1990 Proof	35,000	Value: 6.00				
1991		—	—	0.20	0.75	—

Date		F	VF	XF	Unc	BU
1991 Proof	27,000	Value: 6.00				
1992		—	—	0.20	0.75	—
1992 Proof	25,000	Value: 10.00				
1993 In sets only		—	—	—	12.00	—
1993 Proof	28,000	Value: 7.00				
1994 In sets only		—	—	—	15.00	—
1994 Proof	25,000	Value: 20.00				

KM# 2874 10 GROSCHEN Composition: Zinc

Date	Mintage	F	VF	XF	Unc	BU
1947	6,845,000	0.75	2.00	4.00	22.00	—
1947 Proof	—	Value: 55.00				
1948	66,205,000	0.20	0.50	1.00	3.50	—
1948 Proof	—	Value: 65.00				
1949	51,202,000	0.20	0.50	1.00	3.50	—
1949 Proof	—	Value: 75.00				

KM# 2878 10 GROSCHEN Composition: Aluminum

Date	Mintage	F	VF	XF	Unc	BU
1951	9,573,000	—	0.20	0.75	8.00	—
1951 Proof	—	Value: 85.00				
1952	45,911,000	—	0.10	0.50	4.00	—
1952 Proof	—	Value: 50.00				
1953	39,002,000	—	0.10	0.50	4.00	—
1953 Proof	—	Value: 175				
1955	27,525,000	—	0.10	0.50	4.00	—
1955 Proof	—	Value: 28.00				
1957	33,509,000	—	0.10	0.50	4.00	—
1957 Proof	—	Value: 150				
1959	80,719,000	—	0.10	0.35	3.50	—
1959 Proof	—	Value: 45.00				
1961	11,183,000	—	0.20	0.75	8.00	—
1961 Proof	—	—	—	—	—	—
1962	24,635,000	—	0.10	0.35	3.50	—
1962 Proof	—	Value: 40.00				
1963	38,062,000	—	0.10	0.35	3.50	—
1963 Proof	—	Value: 45.00				
1964	34,928,000	—	0.10	0.20	2.00	—
1964 Proof	—	Value: 1.50				
1965	37,025,000	—	0.10	0.20	2.00	—
1965 Proof	—	Value: 1.50				
1966	24,991,000	—	0.10	0.20	2.00	—
1966 Proof	—	Value: 6.00				
1967	32,552,999	—	0.10	0.20	2.00	—
1967 Proof	—	Value: 12.00				
1968	42,412,000	—	0.10	0.20	2.00	—
1968 Proof	16,000	Value: 8.00				
1969	19,953,000	—	0.10	0.20	2.00	—
1969 Proof	27,000	Value: 5.00				
1970	36,998,000	—	—	0.10	0.45	—
1970 Proof	102,000	Value: 1.00				
1971	57,450,000	—	—	0.10	0.45	—
1971 Proof	82,000	Value: 1.00				
1972	75,661,000	—	—	0.10	0.45	—
1972 Proof	81,000	Value: 1.00				
1973	60,244,000	—	—	0.10	0.45	—
1973 Proof	97,000	Value: 0.75				
1974	55,924,000	—	—	0.10	0.45	—
1974 Proof	78,000	Value: 0.75				
1975	60,576,000	—	—	0.10	0.45	—
1975 Proof	49,000	Value: 0.75				
1976	39,367,000	—	—	0.10	0.45	—
1976 Proof	44,000	Value: 0.75				
1977	53,610,000	—	—	0.10	0.45	—
1977 Proof	44,000	Value: 0.75				
1978	57,857,000	—	—	0.10	0.45	—
1978 Proof	43,000	Value: 0.75				
1979	103,686,000	—	—	—	0.45	—
1979 Proof	44,000	Value: 0.75				
1980	79,848,000	—	—	—	0.45	—
1980 Proof	48,000	Value: 2.00				
1981	92,268,000	—	—	—	0.45	—
1981 Proof	49,000	Value: 2.00				
1982	99,950,000	—	—	—	0.45	—
1982 Proof	50,000	Value: 0.75				
1983	93,768,000	—	—	—	0.45	—
1983 Proof	65,000	Value: 0.75				
1984	86,603,000	—	—	—	0.45	—
1984 Proof	65,000	Value: 0.75				
1985	86,304,000	—	—	—	0.45	—
1985 Proof	45,000	Value: 0.75				
1986	108,910,000	—	—	—	0.45	—

Date	Mintage	F	VF	XF	Unc	BU
1986 Proof	42,000	Value: 1.50				
1987	114,058,000	—	—	—	0.45	—
1987 Proof	42,000	Value: 0.75				
1988	114,461,000	—	—	—	0.45	—
1988 Proof	39,000	Value: 0.75				
1989	127,784,000	—	—	—	0.45	—
1989 Proof	38,000	Value: 0.75				
1990	182,050,000	—	—	—	0.45	—
1990 Proof	35,000	Value: 1.50				
1991	140,000,000	—	—	—	0.45	—
1991 Proof	27,000	Value: 1.50				
1992	125,000,000	—	—	—	0.45	—
1992 Proof	25,000	Value: 1.50				
1993	120,000,000	—	—	—	0.45	—
1993 Proof	28,000	Value: 1.50				
1994	110,000,000	—	—	—	0.45	—
1994 Proof	25,000	Value: 2.00				
1995	110,000,000	—	—	—	0.45	—
1995 Proof	27,000	Value: 1.50				
1996	100,000,000	—	—	—	0.45	—
1996 Proof	25,000	Value: 2.50				
1997	—	—	—	—	0.45	—
1997 Proof	25,000	Value: 2.50				
1998	—	—	—	—	0.45	—
1998 Proof	25,000	Value: 3.00				
1999	—	—	—	—	0.45	—
1999 Proof	50,000	Value: 1.50				
2000	—	—	—	—	0.45	—
2000 Proof	—	Value: 1.50				
2001	—	—	—	—	0.45	—
2001 Proof	—	Value: 1.50				

KM# 2877 20 GROSCHEN Composition: Aluminum-Bronze

Date	Mintage	F	VF	XF	Unc	BU
1950	1,610,000	0.20	0.50	2.00	13.50	—
1950 Proof	—	Value: 40.00				
1951	7,781,000	0.10	0.25	0.75	2.75	—
1951 Proof	—	Value: 25.00				
1954	5,343,000	0.10	0.25	0.75	2.75	—
1954 Proof	—	Value: 275				

KM# 2870 50 GROSCHEN Composition: Aluminum

Date	Mintage	F	VF	XF	Unc	BU
1946	13,058,000	0.20	0.50	1.75	10.00	—
1946 Proof	—	Value: 75.00				
1947	26,990,000	0.15	0.35	1.25	6.50	—
1947 Proof	—	Value: 35.00				
1952	7,455,000	0.40	1.00	2.50	8.50	—
1952 Proof	—	Value: 55.00				
1955	16,919,000	0.20	0.40	1.25	4.50	—
1955 Proof	—	Value: 55.00				

KM# 2885 50 GROSCHEN Composition: Aluminum-Bronze

Date	Mintage	F	VF	XF	Unc	BU
1959	14,122,000	—	0.50	2.00	15.00	—
1959 Proof	—	Value: 25.00				
1960	22,404,000	—	0.20	1.50	12.00	—
1960 Proof	—	Value: 100				
1961	19,891,000	—	0.50	2.00	15.00	—
1961 Proof	—	Value: 75.00				
1962	10,008,000	—	0.40	1.75	15.00	—
1962 Proof	—	Value: 40.00				
1963	9,483,000	—	0.50	2.00	18.00	—
1963 Proof	—	Value: 40.00				
1964	5,331,000	—	0.15	0.75	3.00	—
1964 Proof	—	Value: 1.50				
1965	7,849,000	—	0.15	0.75	3.00	—
1965 Proof	—	Value: 1.50				
1966	7,322,000	—	0.15	0.75	3.00	—
1966 Proof	—	Value: 10.00				
1967	8,237,000	—	0.15	0.75	3.00	—

Date	Mintage	F	VF	XF	Unc	BU
1967 Proof	—	Value: 15.00				
1968	7,757,000	—	0.15	0.75	3.00	—
1968 Proof	15,000	Value: 10.00				
1969	7,070,000	—	0.15	0.75	3.00	—
1969 Proof	26,000	Value: 5.00				
1970	2,994,000	—	0.10	0.50	2.00	—
1970 Proof	129,000	Value: 3.00				
1971	14,217,000	—	—	0.25	1.50	—
1971 Proof	84,000	Value: 2.50				
1972	17,367,000	—	—	0.25	1.50	—
1972 Proof	80,000	Value: 2.00				
1973	17,902,000	—	—	0.25	1.50	—
1973 Proof	90,000	Value: 2.00				
1974	15,852,000	—	—	0.25	1.50	—
1974 Proof	76,000	Value: 2.00				
1975	7,726,000	—	—	0.15	1.00	—
1975 Proof	49,000	Value: 1.50				
1976	11,150,000	—	—	0.15	1.00	—
1976 Proof	44,000	Value: 1.50				
1977	7,258,000	—	—	0.15	1.00	—
1977 Proof	44,000	Value: 1.50				
1978	12,407,000	—	—	0.15	1.00	—
1978 Proof	43,000	Value: 1.50				
1979	16,351,000	—	—	0.15	1.00	—
1979 Proof	44,000	Value: 1.50				
1980	29,884,000	—	—	0.15	1.25	—
1980 Proof	48,000	Value: 3.50				
1981	12,993,000	—	—	0.15	1.25	—
1981 Proof	49,000	Value: 3.50				
1982	9,950,000	—	—	0.15	1.00	—
1982 Proof	50,000	Value: 1.50				
1983	15,182,000	—	—	0.15	1.00	—
1983 Proof	65,000	Value: 1.50				
1984	20,742,000	—	—	0.15	1.00	—
1984 Proof	65,000	Value: 2.00				
1985	15,654,000	—	—	0.15	1.00	—
1985 Proof	45,000	Value: 2.00				
1986	17,016,000	—	—	0.15	0.75	—
1986 Proof	42,000	Value: 2.00				
1987	7,258,000	—	—	0.15	0.75	—
1987 Proof	42,000	Value: 2.00				
1988	16,267,000	—	—	0.15	0.75	—
1988 Proof	39,000	Value: 2.00				
1989	17,352,000	—	—	0.15	0.75	—
1989 Proof	38,000	Value: 2.00				
1990	29,653,000	—	—	0.15	0.75	—
1990 Proof	35,000	Value: 2.00				
1991	44,990,000	—	—	0.15	0.75	—
1991 Proof	27,000	Value: 2.00				
1992	20,000,000	—	—	—	0.45	—
1992 Proof	25,000	Value: 2.00				
1993	15,000,000	—	—	—	0.45	—
1993 Proof	28,000	Value: 2.00				
1994	10,000,000	—	—	—	0.45	—
1994 Proof	25,000	Value: 2.50				
1995	20,000,000	—	—	—	0.45	—
1995 Proof	27,000	Value: 2.00				
1996	15,000,000	—	—	—	0.45	—
1996 Proof	25,000	Value: 2.50				
1997	—	—	—	—	0.45	—
1997 Proof	25,000	Value: 2.50				
1998	—	—	—	—	0.45	—
1998 Proof	25,000	Value: 3.00				
1999	—	—	—	—	0.45	—
1999 Proof	50,000	Value: 2.00				
2000	—	—	—	—	0.45	—
2000 Proof	—	Value: 2.00				
2001	—	—	—	—	0.45	—
2001 Proof	—	Value: 2.00				

KM# 2871 SCHILLING **Composition:** Aluminum

Date	Mintage	F	VF	XF	Unc	BU
1946	27,336,000	0.30	1.00	2.50	20.00	—
1946 Proof	—	Value: 500				
1947	35,838,000	0.20	0.50	1.50	6.00	—
1947 Proof	—	Value: 35.00				
1952	23,231,000	0.25	0.75	1.65	7.00	—
1952 Proof	—	Value: 50.00				
1957	28,649,000	0.25	0.75	1.65	7.00	—
1957 Proof	—	Value: 145				

KM# 2886 SCHILLING **Composition:** Aluminum-Bronze

Date	Mintage	F	VF	XF	Unc	BU
1959	46,726,000	—	0.25	0.75	12.00	—
1959 Proof	—	Value: 15.00				
1960	46,111,000	—	0.25	1.50	20.00	—
1960 Proof	—	Value: 200				
1961	51,115,000	—	0.25	1.50	15.00	—
1961 Proof	—	Value: 400				
1962	9,303,000	—	0.25	1.50	15.00	—
1962 Proof	—	Value: 65.00				
1963	20,863,000	—	0.25	1.50	20.00	—
1963 Proof	—	Value: 45.00				
1964	15,651,000	—	0.25	1.25	3.50	—
1964 Proof	—	Value: 2.00				
1965	21,290,000	—	0.25	0.75	3.50	—
1965 Proof	—	Value: 8.00				
1966	18,688,000	—	0.25	0.75	3.50	—
1966 Proof	—	Value: 8.00				
1967	22,214,000	—	0.25	0.75	3.50	—
1967 Proof	—	Value: 12.00				
1968	30,860,000	—	0.25	0.75	3.50	—
1968 Proof	17,000	Value: 8.00				
1969	10,285,000	—	0.25	0.75	3.50	—
1969 Proof	28,000	Value: 4.00				
1970	10,679,000	—	0.20	0.50	2.50	—
1970 Proof	100,000	Value: 1.75				
1971	27,974,000	—	0.20	0.50	2.50	—
1971 Proof	82,000	Value: 1.75				
1972	54,577,000	—	0.15	0.30	1.50	—
1972 Proof	78,000	Value: 1.25				
1973	41,332,000	—	0.15	0.30	1.50	—
1973 Proof	90,000	Value: 1.25				
1974	43,712,000	—	0.15	0.30	1.50	—
1974 Proof	77,000	Value: 1.25				
1975	13,989,000	—	0.15	0.30	1.50	—
1975 Proof	49,000	Value: 1.25				
1976	28,748,000	—	0.15	0.30	1.50	—
1976 Proof	44,000	Value: 1.25				
1977	19,584,000	—	0.15	0.30	1.50	—
1977 Proof	44,000	Value: 1.25				
1978	35,632,000	—	0.15	0.30	1.50	—
1978 Proof	43,000	Value: 1.25				
1979	64,802,000	—	0.15	0.30	1.50	—
1979 Proof	44,000	Value: 1.25				
1980	49,855,000	—	—	0.15	0.75	—
1980 Proof	48,000	Value: 2.50				
1981	37,502,000	—	—	0.15	0.75	—
1981 Proof	49,000	Value: 2.50				
1982	29,950,000	—	—	0.15	0.75	—
1982 Proof	50,000	Value: 1.50				
1983	38,186,000	—	—	0.15	0.75	—
1983 Proof	65,000	Value: 1.50				
1984	31,891,000	—	—	0.15	0.75	—
1984 Proof	65,000	Value: 1.50				
1985	49,150,000	—	—	0.15	0.75	—
1985 Proof	45,000	Value: 1.50				
1986	57,618,000	—	—	—	0.65	—
1986 Proof	42,000	Value: 1.50				
1987	44,158,000	—	—	—	0.65	—
1987 Proof	42,000	Value: 1.50				
1988	51,561,000	—	—	—	0.65	—
1988 Proof	39,000	Value: 1.50				
1989	62,821,000	—	—	—	0.65	—
1989 Proof	38,000	Value: 1.50				
1990	103,710,000	—	—	—	0.50	—
1990 Proof	35,000	Value: 1.50				
1991	117,700,000	—	—	—	0.50	—
1991 Proof	27,000	Value: 1.50				
1992	55,000,000	—	—	—	1.25	—
1992 Proof	25,000	Value: 2.00				
1993	60,000,000	—	—	—	1.25	—
1993 Proof	28,000	Value: 2.00				
1994	50,000,000	—	—	—	1.25	—
1994 Proof	25,000	Value: 3.00				
1995	70,000,000	—	—	—	1.25	—
1995 Proof	27,000	Value: 2.50				
1996	—	—	—	—	1.25	—
1996 Proof	25,000	Value: 3.50				
1997	—	—	—	—	1.25	—
1997 Proof	25,000	Value: 4.00				
1998	—	—	—	—	1.25	—
1998 Proof	25,000	Value: 4.50				
1999	—	—	—	—	1.25	—
1999 Proof	50,000	Value: 2.00				
2000	—	—	—	—	1.25	—
2000 Proof	—	Value: 2.00				
2001	—	—	—	—	1.25	—
2001 Proof	—	Value: 2.00				

KM# 2872 2 SCHILLING **Composition:** Aluminum

Date	Mintage	F	VF	XF	Unc	BU
1946	10,082,000	0.45	1.25	2.75	25.00	—
1946 Proof	—	Value: 700				
1947	20,140,000	0.45	1.25	2.50	20.00	—
1947 Proof	—	Value: 40.00				
1952	149,000	55.00	100	200	350	—
1952 Proof	—	Value: 900				

KM# 2879 5 SCHILLING **Composition:** Aluminum

Date	Mintage	F	VF	XF	Unc	BU
1952	29,873,000	1.00	2.00	5.00	12.50	—
1952 Proof	—	Value: 45.00				
1957	240,000	100	200	300	500	—
1957 Proof	—	Value: 700				

KM# 2889 5 SCHILLING **Weight:** 5.2000 g. **Composition:** 0.6400 Silver .1070 oz. ASW **Edge:** Reeded

Date	Mintage	F	VF	XF	Unc	BU
1960	12,618,000	—	BV	2.50	5.50	—
1960 Proof	1,000	Value: 65.00				
1961	17,902,000	—	BV	2.50	4.50	—
1961 Proof	—	Value: 25.00				
1962	6,771,000	—	BV	2.50	4.50	—
1962 Proof	—	Value: 50.00				
1963	1,811,000	BV	2.00	4.00	14.50	—
1963 Proof	—	Value: 120				
1964	4,030,000	—	BV	2.00	3.50	—
1964 Proof	—	Value: 3.50				
1965	3,030,000	—	BV	2.00	3.50	—
1965 Proof	—	Value: 3.50				
1966	4,481,000	—	BV	2.00	3.50	—
1966 Proof	—	Value: 8.00				
1967	1,900,000	BV	2.00	4.00	6.00	—
1967 Proof	—	Value: 15.00				
1968	4,792,000	—	BV	2.00	3.50	—
1968 Proof	20,000	Value: 8.00				

KM# 2889a 5 SCHILLING **Composition:** Copper-Nickel **Edge:** Plain

Date	Mintage	F	VF	XF	Unc	BU
1968	2,075,000	—	1.00	2.50	5.00	—
1969	41,222,000	—	0.75	1.50	4.00	—
1969 Proof	21,000	Value: 6.00				
1970	15,771,000	—	—	1.00	4.00	—
1970 Proof	92,000	Value: 2.00				
1971	14,408,000	—	—	1.00	4.00	—
1971 Proof	84,000	Value: 2.00				
1972	12,444,000	—	—	1.00	4.00	—
1972 Proof	75,000	Value: 2.00				
1973	8,259,000	—	—	1.00	4.00	—
1973 Proof	87,000	Value: 1.50				
1974	17,956,000	—	—	1.00	4.00	—
1974 Proof	76,000	Value: 1.50				
1975	6,849,000	—	—	0.75	4.00	—
1975 Proof	49,000	Value: 1.50				
1976	1,458,000	—	—	1.00	5.00	—
1976 Proof	44,000	Value: 4.00				
1977	6,423,000	—	—	0.65	2.00	—
1977 Proof	44,000	Value: 1.75				
1978	9,907,000	—	—	0.65	2.00	—
1978 Proof	43,000	Value: 1.75				
1979	11,607,000	—	—	0.65	2.00	—
1979 Proof	44,000	Value: 1.75				
1980	14,448,000	—	—	0.65	2.00	—
1980 Proof	48,000	Value: 3.50				
1981	13,837,000	—	—	0.65	2.00	—

Date	Mintage	F	VF	XF	Unc	BU
1981 Proof	49,000	Value: 3.50				
1982	4,950,000	—	—	0.65	1.50	—
1982 Proof	50,000	Value: 2.50				
1983	9,268,000	—	—	0.65	1.50	—
1983 Proof	65,000	Value: 2.50				
1984	13,763,000	—	—	0.65	1.50	—
1984 Proof	65,000	Value: 2.50				
1985	12,750,000	—	—	0.60	1.25	—
1985 Proof	45,000	Value: 3.00				
1986	16,559,999	—	—	0.60	1.25	—
1986 Proof	42,000	Value: 3.00				
1987	9,758,000	—	—	0.60	1.25	—
1987 Proof	42,000	Value: 3.00				
1988	10,161,000	—	—	0.60	1.25	—
1988 Proof	39,000	Value: 3.00				
1989	24,043,000	—	—	0.60	1.25	—
1989 Proof	38,000	Value: 3.00				
1990	36,512,000	—	—	0.60	1.25	—
1990 Proof	35,000	Value: 2.50				
1991	24,000,000	—	—	0.60	1.25	—
1991 Proof	27,000	Value: 2.50				
1992	20,000,000	—	—	—	1.25	—
1992 Proof	25,000	Value: 2.50				
1993	20,000,000	—	—	—	1.25	—
1993 Proof	28,000	Value: 2.50				
1994	10,000,000	—	—	—	1.25	—
1994 Proof	25,000	Value: 3.50				
1995	20,000,000	—	—	—	1.25	—
1995 Proof	27,000	Value: 2.50				
1996	—	—	—	—	1.25	—
1996 Proof	25,000	Value: 3.50				
1997	—	—	—	—	1.25	—
1997 Proof	25,000	Value: 4.00				
1998	—	—	—	—	1.25	—
1998 Proof	25,000	Value: 4.50				
1999	—	—	—	—	1.25	—
1999 Proof	50,000	Value: 2.50				
2000	—	—	—	—	1.25	—
2000 Proof	—	Value: 2.50				
2001	—	—	—	—	1.25	—
2001 Proof	—	Value: 2.50				

KM# 2882 10 SCHILLING Weight: 7.5000 g. **Composition:** 0.6400 Silver .1543 oz. ASW

Date	Mintage	F	VF	XF	Unc	BU
1957	15,636,000	BV	1.50	3.00	7.50	—
1957 Proof	—	Value: 80.00				
1958	27,280,000	BV	1.50	3.00	7.50	—
1958 Proof	—	Value: 700				
1959	3,923,000	BV	1.50	3.50	11.50	—
1959 Proof	—	Value: 40.00				
1964	195,000	7.00	10.00	25.00	45.00	—
1964 Proof	27,000	Value: 15.00				
1965	1,896,000	BV	1.50	3.50	11.50	—
1965 Proof	—	Value: 8.00				
1966	3,392,000	BV	1.50	3.50	9.00	—
1966 Proof	—	Value: 12.00				
1967	1,394,000	BV	1.50	3.50	11.50	—
1967 Proof	—	Value: 15.00				
1968	1,525,000	BV	1.50	3.50	10.00	—
1968 Proof	15,000	Value: 9.00				
1969	1,316,000	BV	1.50	3.50	11.50	—
1969 Proof	20,000	Value: 12.00				
1970	4,493,000	—	BV	2.50	6.50	—
1970 Proof	89,000	Value: 5.00				
1971	7,320,000	—	BV	2.50	5.50	—
1971 Proof	80,000	Value: 5.00				
1972	14,210,000	—	BV	2.50	4.50	—
1972 Proof	75,000	Value: 5.00				
1973	14,559,000	—	BV	2.50	4.50	—
1973 Proof	80,000	Value: 5.00				

KM# 2918 10 SCHILLING Composition: Copper-Nickel Plated Nickel

Date	Mintage	F	VF	XF	Unc	BU
1974	59,877,000	—	—	2.00	6.00	—
1974 Proof	75,000	Value: 4.00				
1975	16,869,000	—	—	2.00	6.00	—

Date	Mintage	F	VF	XF	Unc	BU
1975 Proof	49,000	Value: 3.00				
1976	13,459,000	—	—	2.00	6.00	—
1976 Proof	44,000	Value: 3.00				
1977	3,804,000	—	—	2.00	6.00	—
1977 Proof	44,000	Value: 3.00				
1978	6,813,000	—	—	2.00	6.00	—
1978 Proof	43,000	Value: 3.00				
1979	11,691,000	—	—	2.00	6.00	—
1979 Proof	44,000	Value: 2.50				
1980	10,884,000	—	—	2.00	6.00	—
1980 Proof	48,000	Value: 6.50				
1981	9,470,000	—	—	2.00	6.00	—
1981 Proof	49,000	Value: 6.50				
1982	3,470,000	—	—	2.00	5.00	—
1982 Proof	50,000	Value: 2.50				
1983	8,993,000	—	—	1.50	4.00	—
1983 Proof	65,000	Value: 2.50				
1984	7,936,000	—	—	1.50	4.00	—
1984 Proof	65,000	Value: 2.50				
1985	9,009,000	—	—	1.50	4.00	—
1985 Proof	45,000	Value: 2.50				
1986	8,768,000	—	—	1.50	4.00	—
1986 Proof	42,000	Value: 2.50				
1987	9,258,000	—	—	1.50	4.00	—
1987 Proof	42,000	Value: 2.50				
1988	9,011,000	—	—	1.50	4.00	—
1988 Proof	39,000	Value: 4.50				
1989	16,233,000	—	—	1.25	3.00	—
1989 Proof	38,000	Value: 2.50				
1990	27,150,000	—	—	1.25	3.00	—
1990 Proof	35,000	Value: 2.50				
1991	18,000,000	—	—	1.25	3.00	—
1991 Proof	27,000	Value: 2.50				
1992	11,000,000	—	—	—	2.00	—
1992 Proof	25,000	Value: 2.50				
1993	12,500,000	—	—	—	2.00	—
1993 Proof	28,000	Value: 2.50				
1994	15,000,000	—	—	—	2.00	—
1994 Proof	25,000	Value: 3.50				
1995	12,500,000	—	—	—	2.00	—
1995 Proof	27,000	Value: 2.50				
1996	10,000,000	—	—	—	2.00	—
1996 Proof	25,000	Value: 4.00				
1997	—	—	—	—	2.00	—
1997 Proof	25,000	Value: 4.50				
1998	—	—	—	—	2.00	—
1998 Proof	25,000	Value: 5.00				
1999	—	—	—	—	2.00	—
1999 Proof	50,000	Value: 2.50				
2000	—	—	—	—	2.00	—
2000 Proof	—	Value: 2.50				
2001	—	—	—	—	2.00	—
2001 Proof	—	Value: 2.50				

KM# 2946.1 20 SCHILLING Composition: Copper-Aluminum-Nickel **Edge:** Edge with incuse dots

Date	Mintage	F	VF	XF	Unc	BU
1980	9,850,000	—	—	2.50	3.50	—
1980 Proof	48,000	Value: 20.00				
1981	450,000	—	—	4.50	7.50	—
1981 Proof	49,000	Value: 22.50				
1991	140,000	—	—	2.25	5.00	—
1992	100,000	—	—	2.25	6.00	—
1992 Proof	25,000	Value: 10.00				

KM# 2946.2 20 SCHILLING Composition: Copper-Aluminum-Nickel **Edge:** Plain

Date	Mintage	F	VF	XF	Unc	BU
1993	180,000	—	—	2.25	5.00	—
1993 Proof	28,000	Value: 10.00				

KM# 2955.1 20 SCHILLING Composition: Copper-Aluminum-Nickel **Subject:** 250th Anniversary - Birth of Joseph Haydn **Edge:** Edge with incuse dots

Date	Mintage	F	VF	XF	Unc	BU
1982	3,100,000	—	—	2.25	3.50	—
1982 Proof	50,000	Value: 9.00				
1991	140,000	—	—	2.25	5.00	—
1992	100,000	—	—	2.25	6.00	—

KM# 2955.2 20 SCHILLING Composition: Copper-Aluminum-Nickel **Edge:** Plain

Date	Mintage	F	VF	XF	Unc	BU
1993	180,000	—	—	2.25	5.00	—

KM# 2960.1 20 SCHILLING Composition: Copper-Aluminum-Nickel **Reverse:** Hochosterwitz Castle **Edge:** Edge with incuse dots

Date	Mintage	F	VF	XF	Unc	BU
1983	1,002,000	—	—	2.25	3.50	—
1983 Proof	65,000	Value: 7.50				
1991	140,000	—	—	2.25	4.50	—
1992	100,000	—	—	2.25	5.00	—

KM# 2960.2 20 SCHILLING Composition: Copper-Aluminum-Nickel **Edge:** Plain

Date	Mintage	F	VF	XF	Unc	BU
1993	180,000	—	—	2.25	4.50	—

KM# 2965.1 20 SCHILLING Composition: Copper-Aluminum-Nickel **Reverse:** Grafenegg Palace **Edge:** Edge with incuse dots

Date	Mintage	F	VF	XF	Unc	BU
1984	1,203,000	—	—	2.25	3.50	—
1984 Proof	65,000	Value: 7.50				
1991	140,000	—	—	2.25	4.50	—
1992	100,000	—	—	2.25	5.00	—

KM# 2965.2 20 SCHILLING Composition: Copper-Aluminum-Nickel **Edge:** Plain

Date	Mintage	F	VF	XF	Unc	BU
1993	180,000	—	—	2.25	4.50	—

KM# 2970.1 20 SCHILLING Composition: Copper-Aluminum-Nickel **Subject:** 200th Anniversary - Diocese of Linz **Edge:** Edge with incuse dots

Date	Mintage	F	VF	XF	Unc	BU
1985	814,000	—	—	2.25	4.50	—
1985 Proof	45,000	Value: 11.50				
1991	140,000	—	—	2.25	4.50	—
1992	100,000	—	—	2.25	5.00	—

KM# 2970.2 20 SCHILLING Composition: Copper-Aluminum-Nickel **Edge:** Plain

Date	Mintage	F	VF	XF	Unc	BU
1993	180,000	—	—	2.25	4.50	—

KM# 2975.1 20 SCHILLING Composition: Copper-Aluminum-Nickel **Subject:** 800th Anniversary - Georgenberger Treaty **Edge:** Edge with incuse dots

Date	Mintage	F	VF	XF	Unc	BU
1986	801,000	—	—	2.25	4.50	—
1986 Proof	42,000	Value: 16.50				
1991	140,000	—	—	2.25	4.50	—
1992	100,000	—	—	2.25	5.00	—

KM# 2975.2 20 SCHILLING Composition: Copper-Aluminum-Nickel **Edge:** Plain

Date	Mintage	F	VF	XF	Unc	BU
1993	180,000	—	—	2.25	4.50	—

KM# 2980.1 20 SCHILLING Composition: Copper-Aluminum-Nickel **Subject:** 300th Anniversary - Birth of Salzburg's Archbishop Thun **Edge:** Edge with incuse dots

Date	Mintage	F	VF	XF	Unc	BU
1987	508,000	—	—	2.25	4.50	—
1987 Proof	42,000	Value: 11.50				
1991	140,000	—	—	2.25	4.50	—
1992	100,000	—	—	2.25	5.00	—

KM# 2980.2 20 SCHILLING Composition: Copper-Aluminum-Nickel **Edge:** Plain

Date	Mintage	F	VF	XF	Unc	BU
1993	180,000	—	—	2.25	4.50	—

KM# 2988.1 20 SCHILLING Composition: Copper-Aluminum-Nickel **Reverse:** Crowned eagle - Tyrol **Edge:** Edge with incuse dots

Date	Mintage	F	VF	XF	Unc	BU
1989	242,000	—	—	2.25	4.50	—
1989 Proof	38,000	Value: 8.00				
1991	140,000	—	—	2.25	4.50	—
1992	100,000	—	—	2.25	5.00	—

KM# 2993.1 20 SCHILLING Composition: Copper-Aluminum-Nickel **Reverse:** Martinsturm in Bregenz **Edge:** Edge with incuse dots

Date	Mintage	F	VF	XF	Unc	BU
1990	250,000	—	—	2.25	4.50	—
1990 Proof	35,000	Value: 10.00				
1991	—	—	—	—	—	—
1991	140,000	—	—	2.25	4.50	—
1992	100,000	—	—	2.25	6.50	—

KM# 2993.2 20 SCHILLING Composition: Copper-Aluminum-Nickel **Edge:** Plain

Date	Mintage	F	VF	XF	Unc	BU
1993	180,000	—	—	2.25	4.50	—

KM# 2995.1 20 SCHILLING Composition: Copper-Aluminum-Nickel **Subject:** 200th Anniversary - Birth of Franz Grillparzer **Edge:** Edge wit incuse dots

Date	Mintage	F	VF	XF	Unc	BU
1991	610,000	—	—	2.25	4.50	—
1991 Proof	27,000	Value: 10.00				
1992	100,000	—	—	2.25	5.00	—

KM# 2995.2 20 SCHILLING Composition: Copper-Aluminum-Nickel **Edge:** Plain

Date	Mintage	F	VF	XF	Unc	BU
1993	180,000	—	—	2.25	4.50	—

KM# 2988.2 20 SCHILLING Composition: Copper-Aluminum-Nickel **Edge:** Plain

Date	Mintage	F	VF	XF	Unc	BU
1993	180,000	—	—	2.25	4.50	—

KM# 3016 20 SCHILLING Composition: Copper-Aluminum-Nickel **Subject:** 800th Anniversary - Vienna Mint

Date	Mintage	F	VF	XF	Unc	BU
1994	2,000,000	—	—	—	4.50	—
1994 Proof	25,000	Value: 12.50				

KM# 3022 20 SCHILLING Composition: Copper-Aluminum-Nickel **Subject:** 1000th Anniversary - Krems

Date	Mintage	F	VF	XF	Unc	BU
1995	2,000,000	—	—	—	4.50	—
1995 Proof	27,000	Value: 10.00				

KM# 3033 20 SCHILLING Composition: Copper-Aluminum-Nickel **Reverse:** Anton Bruckner

Date	Mintage	F	VF	XF	Unc	BU
1996	—	—	—	—	4.50	—
1996 Proof	25,000	Value: 15.00				

KM# 3041 20 SCHILLING Composition: Copper-Aluminum-Nickel **Subject:** 850th Anniversary of St. Stephen's Cathedral **Obverse:** Denomination **Reverse:** Cathedral, dates

Date	Mintage	F	VF	XF	Unc	BU
1997	—	—	—	—	4.50	—
1997 Proof	25,000	Value: 16.50				

KM# 3048 20 SCHILLING Composition: Copper-Aluminum-Nickel **Subject:** 500th Anniversary of Michael Pacher's Death **Obverse:** Denomination **Reverse:** Pacher's altar at St. Wolfgang

Date	Mintage	F	VF	XF	Unc	BU
1998	—	—	—	—	5.00	—
1998 Proof	25,000	Value: 17.50				

KM# 3056 20 SCHILLING Composition: Copper-Aluminum-Nickel **Obverse:** Denomination **Reverse:** Hugo Von Hofmannsthal

Date	F	VF	XF	Unc	BU
1999	—	—	—	4.50	—
1999 Proof	—	Value: 12.50			

KM# 3064 20 SCHILLING Composition: Brass **Subject:** 150th Anniversary - First Austrian Postage Stamp **Obverse:** Denomination **Reverse:** Canceled stamp design **Edge:** Plain

Date	F	VF	XF	Unc	BU
2000	—	—	—	4.50	—
2000 Proof	—	Value: 12.50			

KM# 3075 20 SCHILLING Weight: 8.1300 g. **Composition:** Brass **Subject:** Johann Nepomuk Nestroy **Obverse:** Denomination **Reverse:** Bust of Nestroy half facing left **Edge:** Plain **Size:** 27.8 mm.

Date	Mintage	F	VF	XF	Unc	BU
2001	75,000	—	—	—	4.50	—

KM# 2880 25 SCHILLING Weight: 13.0000 g. **Composition:** 0.8000 Silver .3344 oz. ASW **Subject:** Reopening of the National Theater in Vienna

Date	Mintage	F	VF	XF	Unc	BU
1955		3.50	7.50	10.00	20.00	—
1955 Proof	Est. 5,000	Value: 100				

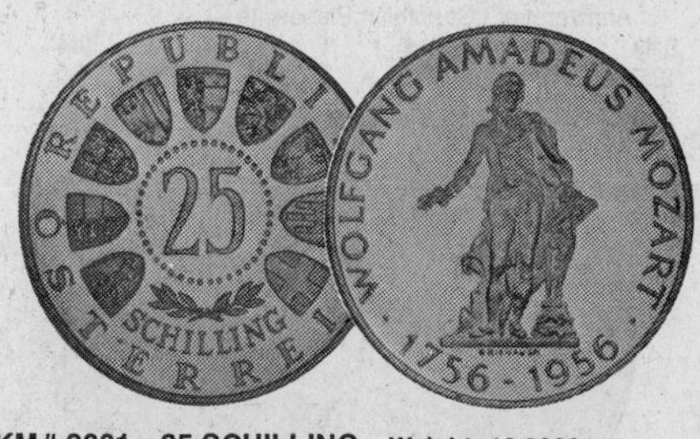

KM# 2881 25 SCHILLING Weight: 13.0000 g. **Composition:** 0.8000 Silver .3344 oz. ASW **Subject:** 200th Anniversary - Birth of Wolfgang Mozart

Date	Mintage	F	VF	XF	Unc	BU
1956		—	—	3.00	5.50	—
1956 Proof	Est. 1,500	Value: 350				

KM# 2883 25 SCHILLING **Weight:** 13.0000 g. **Composition:** 0.8000 Silver .3344 oz. ASW **Subject:** 8th Centennial - Mariazell Basilica

Date	Mintage	F	VF	XF	Unc	BU
1957	—	—	—	3.00	5.50	—
1957 Proof	Est. 1,500	Value: 300				

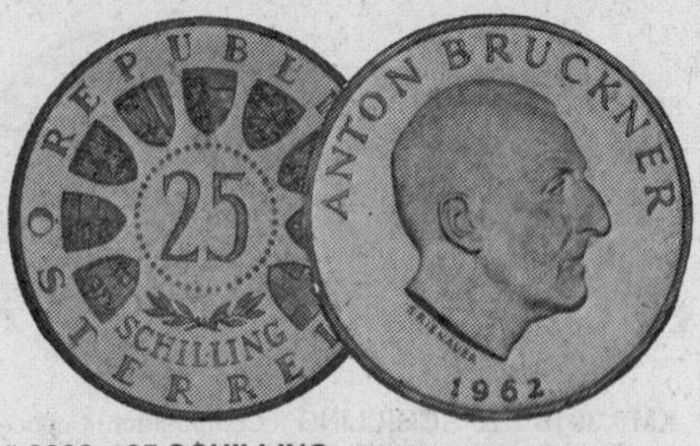

KM# 2892 25 SCHILLING **Weight:** 13.0000 g. **Composition:** 0.8000 Silver .3344 oz. ASW **Reverse:** Anton Bruckner

Date	Mintage	F	VF	XF	Unc	BU
1962	—	—	—	3.00	5.50	—
1962 Proof	Est. 3,000	Value: 150				

KM# 2899 25 SCHILLING **Weight:** 13.0000 g. **Composition:** 0.8000 Silver .3344 oz. ASW **Subject:** 130th Anniversary - Death of Ferdinand Raimund

Date	Mintage	F	VF	XF	Unc	BU
1966	1,388,000	—	—	3.50	6.00	—
1966 Proof	11,800	Value: 50.00				

KM# 2884 25 SCHILLING **Weight:** 13.0000 g. **Composition:** 0.8000 Silver .3344 oz. ASW **Subject:** 100th Anniversary - Birth of Auer von Welsbach

Date	Mintage	F	VF	XF	Unc	BU
1958	—	—	—	3.00	5.50	—
1958 Proof	Est. 500	Value: 1,500				

KM# 2893 25 SCHILLING **Weight:** 13.0000 g. **Composition:** 0.8000 Silver .3344 oz. ASW **Subject:** 300th Anniversary - Birth of Prince Eugen

Date	Mintage	F	VF	XF	Unc	BU
1963	1,994,000	—	—	3.00	5.50	—
1963 Proof	5,931	Value: 80.00				

KM# 2901 25 SCHILLING **Weight:** 13.0000 g. **Composition:** 0.8000 Silver .3344 oz. ASW **Subject:** 250th Anniversary - Birth of Maria Theresa

Date	Mintage	F	VF	XF	Unc	BU
1967	2,472,000	—	—	3.00	5.50	—
1967 Proof	28,000	Value: 25.00				

KM# 2887 25 SCHILLING **Weight:** 13.0000 g. **Composition:** 0.8000 Silver .3344 oz. ASW **Subject:** Centennial - Death of Archduke Johann

Date	Mintage	F	VF	XF	Unc	BU
1959	—	—	—	3.50	6.00	—
1959 Proof	Est. 1,000	Value: 300				

KM# 2895.1 25 SCHILLING **Weight:** 13.0000 g. **Composition:** 0.8000 Silver .3344 oz. ASW **Reverse:** Franz Grillparzer

Date	Mintage	F	VF	XF	Unc	BU
1964	1,664,000	—	—	3.50	6.00	—
1964 Proof	36,000	Value: 8.00				

KM# 2903 25 SCHILLING **Weight:** 13.0000 g. **Composition:** 0.8000 Silver .3344 oz. ASW **Subject:** 300th Anniversary - Birth of Von Hildebrandt

Date	Mintage	F	VF	XF	Unc	BU
1968	1,258,000	BV	2.50	4.00	8.50	—
1968 Proof	42,000	Value: 18.00				

KM# 2890 25 SCHILLING **Weight:** 13.0000 g. **Composition:** 0.8000 Silver .3344 oz. ASW **Subject:** 40th Anniversary - Carinthian Plebescite

Date	Mintage	F	VF	XF	Unc	BU
1960	—	—	—	3.50	6.00	—
1960 Proof	Est. 900	Value: 350				

KM# 2895.2 25 SCHILLING **Weight:** 13.0000 g. **Composition:** 0.8000 Silver .3344 oz. ASW **Obverse:** 9 shields (error)

Date	Mintage	F	VF	XF	Unc	BU
1964 Proof	3,660	Value: 300				

KM# 2905 25 SCHILLING **Weight:** 13.0000 g. **Composition:** 0.8000 Silver .3344 oz. ASW **Reverse:** Peter Rosegger

Date	Mintage	F	VF	XF	Unc	BU
1969	1,356,000	—	—	3.50	5.50	—
1969 Proof	44,000	Value: 18.00				

KM# 2891 25 SCHILLING **Weight:** 13.0000 g. **Composition:** 0.8000 Silver .3344 oz. ASW **Subject:** 40th Anniversary - Burgenland

Date	Mintage	F	VF	XF	Unc	BU
1961	—	—	—	3.50	6.00	—
1961 Proof	Est. 1,200	Value: 175				

KM# 2897 25 SCHILLING **Weight:** 13.0000 g. **Composition:** 0.8000 Silver .3344 oz. ASW **Subject:** 150th Anniversary - Vienna Technical High School

Date	Mintage	F	VF	XF	Unc	BU
1965	1,563,000	—	—	3.50	6.00	—
1965 Proof	37,000	Value: 15.00				

KM# 2907 25 SCHILLING **Weight:** 13.0000 g. **Composition:** 0.8000 Silver .3344 oz. ASW **Subject:** 100th Anniversary - Birth of Franz Lehar

Date	Mintage	F	VF	XF	Unc	BU
1970	1,661,000	—	—	3.00	5.00	—
1970 Proof	139,000	Value: 7.50				

KM# 2910 25 SCHILLING **Weight:** 13.0000 g. **Composition:** 0.8000 Silver .3344 oz. ASW **Subject:** 200th Anniversary - Vienna Bourse

Date	Mintage	F	VF	XF	Unc	BU
1971	1,804,000	—	—	3.00	4.50	—
1971 Proof	196,000	Value: 5.50				

KM# 2912 25 SCHILLING **Weight:** 13.0000 g. **Composition:** 0.8000 Silver .3344 oz. ASW **Subject:** 50th Anniversary - Death of Carl M. Ziehrer

Date	Mintage	F	VF	XF	Unc	BU
ND(1972)	1,955,000	—	—	3.00	4.50	—
ND(1972) Proof	145,000	Value: 5.50				

KM# 2915 25 SCHILLING **Weight:** 13.0000 g. **Composition:** 0.8000 Silver .3344 oz. ASW **Subject:** 100th Anniversary - Birth of Max Reinhardt

Date	Mintage	F	VF	XF	Unc	BU
ND(1973)	2,323,000	—	—	3.00	4.50	—
ND(1973) Proof	177,000	Value: 5.50				

KM# 2888 50 SCHILLING **Weight:** 20.0000 g. **Composition:** 0.9000 Silver .5787 oz. ASW **Subject:** 150th Anniversary - Liberation of Tyrol

Date	Mintage	F	VF	XF	Unc	BU
ND(1959)	—	5.00	6.00	9.00	—	
ND(1959) Proof	Est. 800	Value: 425				

KM# 2894 50 SCHILLING **Weight:** 20.0000 g. **Composition:** 0.9000 Silver .5787 oz. ASW **Subject:** 600th Anniversary - Union with Tirol

Date	Mintage	F	VF	XF	Unc	BU
ND(1963)	2,990,000	—	5.00	5.50	7.50	—
ND(1963) Proof	10,000	Value: 75.00				

KM# 2896 50 SCHILLING **Weight:** 20.0000 g. **Composition:** 0.9000 Silver .5787 oz. ASW **Series:** Winter Olympics **Reverse:** Innsbruck - Ski jump

Date	Mintage	F	VF	XF	Unc	BU
1964	2,832,000	—	5.00	5.50	8.00	—
1964 Proof	68,000	Value: 20.00				

KM# 2898 50 SCHILLING **Weight:** 20.0000 g. **Composition:** 0.9000 Silver .5787 oz. ASW **Subject:** 600th Anniversary - Vienna University

Date	Mintage	F	VF	XF	Unc	BU
ND(1965)	2,163,000	—	5.00	5.50	7.50	—
ND(1965) Proof	37,000	Value: 30.00				

KM# 2900 50 SCHILLING **Weight:** 20.0000 g. **Composition:** 0.9000 Silver .5787 oz. ASW **Subject:** 150th Anniversary - National Bank

Date	Mintage	F	VF	XF	Unc	BU
ND(1966)	1,782,000	—	5.00	5.50	7.50	—
ND(1966) Proof	17,000	Value: 60.00				

KM# 2902 50 SCHILLING **Weight:** 20.0000 g. **Composition:** 0.9000 Silver .5787 oz. ASW **Subject:** Centennial of the Blue Danube Waltz

Date	Mintage	F	VF	XF	Unc	BU
1967	2,974,000	—	5.00	5.50	7.50	—
1967 Proof	26,000	Value: 60.00				

KM# 2904.1 50 SCHILLING **Weight:** 20.0000 g. **Composition:** 0.9000 Silver .5787 oz. ASW **Subject:** 50th Anniversary - The Republic **Reverse:** Matte surface between pillars

Date	Mintage	F	VF	XF	Unc	BU
ND(1968)	1,660,000	—	5.00	5.50	7.50	—
ND(1968) Proof	40,000	Value: 22.50				

KM# 2904.2 50 SCHILLING **Weight:** 20.0000 g. **Composition:** 0.9000 Silver .5787 oz. ASW **Reverse:** Proof surface between pillars

Date		F	VF	XF	Unc	BU
1968 Proof	—	Value: 150				

KM# 2906 50 SCHILLING **Weight:** 20.0000 g. **Composition:** 0.9000 Silver .5787 oz. ASW **Subject:** 450th Anniversary - Death of Maximilian I

Date	Mintage	F	VF	XF	Unc	BU
1969	2,045,000	—	5.00	5.50	7.50	—
1969 Proof	55,000	Value: 22.50				

KM# 2908 50 SCHILLING **Weight:** 20.0000 g. **Composition:** 0.9000 Silver .5787 oz. ASW **Subject:** 300th Anniversary - Innsbruck University

Date	Mintage	F	VF	XF	Unc	BU
1970	2,087,000	—	5.00	5.50	7.50	—
1970 Prof	113,000	Value: 9.00				

KM# 2909 50 SCHILLING **Weight:** 20.0000 g. **Composition:** 0.9000 Silver .5787 oz. ASW **Subject:** 100th Anniversary - Birth of Dr. Karl Renner

Date	Mintage	F	VF	XF	Unc	BU
1970	2,214,000	—	5.00	5.50	6.50	—
1970 Proof	286,000	Value: 8.00				

KM# 2911 50 SCHILLING **Weight:** 20.0000 g. **Composition:** 0.9000 Silver .5787 oz. ASW **Subject:** 80th Anniversary - Birth of Julius Raab

Date	Mintage	F	VF	XF	Unc	BU
1971	2,317,000	—	5.00	5.50	6.50	—
1971 Proof	183,000	Value: 8.00				

KM# 2913 50 SCHILLING **Weight:** 20.0000 g. **Composition:** 0.9000 Silver .5787 oz. ASW **Subject:** 350th Anniversary - Salzburg University

Date	Mintage	F	VF	XF	Unc	BU
ND(1972)	2,863,000	—	5.00	5.50	6.50	—
ND(1972) Proof	136,000	Value: 8.00				

KM# 2914 50 SCHILLING **Weight:** 20.0000 g. **Composition:** 0.9000 Silver .5787 oz. ASW **Subject:** 100th Anniversary - Institute of Agriculture

Date	Mintage	F	VF	XF	Unc	BU
ND(1972)	1,891,000	—	5.00	5.50	6.50	—
ND(1972) Proof	109,000	Value: 8.00				

KM# 2916 50 SCHILLING **Weight:** 20.0000 g. **Composition:** 0.9000 Silver .5787 oz. ASW **Subject:** 500th Anniversary - Bummerl House

Date	Mintage	F	VF	XF	Unc	BU
1973	2,842,000	—	5.00	5.50	6.50	—
1973 Proof	158,000	Value: 8.00				

KM# 2917 50 SCHILLING **Weight:** 20.0000 g. **Composition:** 0.9000 Silver .5787 oz. ASW **Subject:** 100th Anniversary - Birth of Dr. Theodor Korner

Date	Mintage	F	VF	XF	Unc	BU
ND(1973)	2,868,000	—	5.00	5.50	6.50	—
ND(1973) Proof	132,000	Value: 8.00				

KM# 2919 50 SCHILLING **Weight:** 20.0000 g. **Composition:** 0.6400 Silver .4115 oz. ASW **Subject:** International Garden Exhibition

Date	Mintage	F	VF	XF	Unc	BU
1974	2,279,000	—	—	5.00	6.00	—
1974 Proof	221,000	Value: 7.00				

KM# 2920 50 SCHILLING **Weight:** 20.0000 g. **Composition:** 0.6400 Silver .4115 oz. ASW **Subject:** 125th Anniversary - Austrian Police Force

Date	Mintage	F	VF	XF	Unc	BU
ND(1974)	2,259,000	—	—	5.00	6.00	—
ND(1974) Proof	241,000	Value: 7.00				

KM# 2921 50 SCHILLING **Weight:** 20.0000 g. **Composition:** 0.6400 Silver .4115 oz. ASW **Subject:** 1200th Anniversary - Salzburg Cathedral

Date	Mintage	F	VF	XF	Unc	BU
1974	2,293,000	—	—	5.00	6.00	—
1974 Proof	207,000	Value: 7.00				

KM# 2922 50 SCHILLING **Weight:** 20.0000 g. **Composition:** 0.6400 Silver 04115 oz. ASW **Subject:** 50th Year Austrian Broadcasting

Date	Mintage	F	VF	XF	Unc	BU
1974	2,290,000	—	—	5.00	6.00	—
1974 Proof	210,000	Value: 7.00				

KM# 2937 50 SCHILLING **Weight:** 20.0000 g. **Composition:** 0.6400 Silver 04115 oz. ASW **Subject:** 150th Anniversary - Death of Franz Schubert

Date	Mintage	F	VF	XF	Unc	BU
1978	1,868,000	—	—	5.00	6.00	—
1978 Proof	132,000	Value: 7.00				

KM# 3038 50 SCHILLING **Ring Composition:** Aluminum-Bronze **Center Composition:** Copper-Nickel Clad Nickel **Subject:** Austrian Millenium **Obverse:** Circle of provincial arms around denomination **Reverse:** Arms below Heinrich I as knight on horse back

Date	Mintage	F	VF	XF	Unc	BU
ND(1996)	900,000	—	—	—	14.00	—
ND(1996) BU	100,000	—	—	—	25.00	—

KM# 3044 50 SCHILLING **Ring Composition:** Brass **Center Composition:** Copper-Nickel Plated Nickel **Subject:** 100th Anniversary - Wiener Secession **Obverse:** Circle of provincial arms **Reverse:** Vienna secession building portal

Date	Mintage	F	VF	XF	Unc	BU
ND(1997)	1,400,000	—	—	—	8.00	—
ND(1997) BU	100,000	—	—	—	11.50	—

KM# 3050 50 SCHILLING **Ring Composition:** Brass **Center Composition:** Copper-Nickel Plated Nickel **Subject:** Austrian Presidency of the European Union **Obverse:** Denomination **Reverse:** New Hofburg palace with logo

Date	Mintage	F	VF	XF	Unc	BU
1998	1,200,000	—	—	—	8.00	—
1998 BU	100,000	—	—	—	11.50	—

KM# 3053 50 SCHILLING **Ring Composition:** Brass **Center Composition:** Copper-Nickel Plated Nickel **Obverse:** Denomination in circle of shields **Reverse:** Konrad Lorenz with three Greylag geese

Date	Mintage	F	VF	XF	Unc	BU
1998	1,200,000	—	—	—	7.00	—
1998 Special Unc	100,000	—	—	—	9.00	—

KM# 3057 50 SCHILLING **Ring Composition:** Brass **Center Composition:** Copper-Nickel Plated Nickel **Subject:** Euro Currency **Obverse:** Denomination in circle of shields **Reverse:** Euro currency designs

Date	Mintage	F	VF	XF	Unc	BU
1999	1,200,000	—	—	—	7.00	—
1999 Special Unc	100,000	—	—	—	9.00	—

KM# 3061 50 SCHILLING Ring Composition: Brass **Center Composition:** Copper-Nickel Plated Nickel **Subject:** Centenary - Death of Johann Strauss **Obverse:** Circle of arms **Reverse:** Bust of Johann Strauss facing in right

Date	Mintage	F	VF	XF	Unc	BU
ND(1999)	600,000	—	—	—	7.00	—
ND(1999) Special Unc	100,000	—	—	—	9.00	—

KM# 3066 50 SCHILLING Ring Composition: Brass **Center Composition:** Copper-Nickel Plated Nickel **Obverse:** Circle of arms **Reverse:** Bust of Sigmund Freud facing in right **Edge:** Plain

Date	Mintage	F	VF	XF	Unc	BU
ND(2000)	600,000	—	—	—	7.00	—
ND(2000) Special Unc	100,000	—	—	—	9.00	—

KM# 3070 50 SCHILLING Ring Composition: Brass **Center Composition:** Copper-Nickel Plated Nickel **Obverse:** Circle of arms **Reverse:** Antique automobile and portrait of Ferdinand Porsche **Edge:** Plain **Note:** 100,000 of which are in blister-packs, with a value of $8.00 each.

Date	Mintage	F	VF	XF	Unc	BU
2000	700,000	—	—	—	6.50	—

KM# 3076 50 SCHILLING Ring Composition: BrassCenter **Weight:** 8.1100 g. **Center Composition:** Copper-Nickel Plated Nickel **Subject:** The Schilling Era **Obverse:** Denomination and shields **Reverse:** Four old coin designs **Edge:** Plain **Size:** 26.5 mm.

Date	Mintage	F	VF	XF	Unc	BU
2001	700,000	—	—	—	7.50	—

KM# 2926 100 SCHILLING Weight: 23.9300 g. **Composition:** 0.6400 Silver .4924 oz. ASW **Series:** Winter Olympics - Innsbruck **Reverse:** Emblem

Date	Mintage	F	VF	XF	Unc	BU
ND(1974)	2,826,000	—	—	—	9.00	—
ND(1974) Proof	374,000	Value: 10.00				

KM# 2927 100 SCHILLING Weight: 23.9300 g. **Composition:** 0.6400 Silver .4924 oz. ASW **Series:** Winter Olympics - Innsbruck **Reverse:** Buildings and Olympic Rings

Date	Mintage	F	VF	XF	Unc	BU
ND(1974)(h)	2,692,000	—	—	—	9.00	—
ND(1974)(v) Select	Inc. above	—	—	—	12.50	—
ND(1974)(h) Proof	223,000	Value: 10.00				
ND(1974)(v)	2,718,000	—	—	—	9.00	—
ND(1974)(h) Select	Inc. above	—	—	—	12.50	—
ND(1974)(v) Proof	232,000	Value: 10.00				

KM# 2928 100 SCHILLING Weight: 23.9300 g. **Composition:** 0.6400 Silver .4924 oz. ASW **Series:** Winter Olympics - Innsbruck **Reverse:** Skier

Date	Mintage	F	VF	XF	Unc	BU
ND(1974)(h)	2,636,000	—	—	—	9.00	—
ND(1974)(v) Select	Inc. above	—	—	—	12.50	—
ND(1974)(h) Proof	179,000	Value: 10.00				
ND(1974)(v)	2,641,000	—	—	—	9.00	—
ND(1974)(h) Select	Inc. above	—	—	—	12.50	—
ND(1974)(v) Proof	184,000	Value: 10.00				

KM# 2929 100 SCHILLING Weight: 23.9300 g. **Composition:** 0.6400 Silver .4924 oz. ASW **Series:** Winter Olympics - Innsbruck **Reverse:** Ski jump and symbols

Date	Mintage	F	VF	XF	Unc	BU
ND(1974)(h)	2,611,000	—	—	—	9.00	—
ND(1974)(h) Select	Inc. above	—	—	—	12.50	—
ND(1974)(h) Proof	179,000	Value: 10.00				
ND(1974)(v)	2,627,000	—	—	—	9.00	—
ND(1974)(v) Select	Inc. above	—	—	—	12.50	—
ND(1974)(v) Proof	188,000	Value: 10.00				

KM# 2923 100 SCHILLING Weight: 23.9300 g. **Composition:** 0.6400 Silver .4924 oz. ASW **Subject:** 150th Anniversary - Birth of Johann Strauss

Date	Mintage	F	VF	XF	Unc	BU
1975	2,646,000	—	—	—	9.00	—
1975 Select	Inc. above	—	—	—	12.00	—
1975 Proof	209,000	Value: 10.00				

KM# 2924 100 SCHILLING Weight: 23.9300 g. **Composition:** 0.6400 Silver .4924 oz. ASW **Subject:** 20th Anniversary - State Treaty

Date	Mintage	F	VF	XF	Unc	BU
1975	3,215,000	—	—	—	9.00	—
1975 Select	Inc. above	—	—	—	10.00	—
1975 Proof	225,000	Value: 10.00				

KM# 2925 100 SCHILLING Weight: 23.9300 g. **Composition:** 0.6400 Silver .4924 oz. ASW **Subject:** 50th Anniversary - Schilling

Date	Mintage	F	VF	XF	Unc	BU
1975	3,234,000	—	—	—	9.00	—
1975 Select	Inc. above	—	—	—	10.00	—
1975 Proof	201,000	Value: 10.00				

KM# 2930 100 SCHILLING Weight: 23.9300 g. **Composition:** 0.6400 Silver .4924 oz. ASW **Subject:** 200th Anniversary - Burgtheater

Date	Mintage	F	VF	XF	Unc	BU
ND(1976)	1,630,000	—	—	—	9.50	—
ND(1976) Select	Inc. above	—	—	—	11.50	—
ND(1976) Proof	220,000	Value: 11.50				

KM# 2931 100 SCHILLING Weight: 23.9300 g. **Composition:** 0.6400 Silver .4924 oz. ASW **Subject:** 1000th Anniversary - Carinthia

Date	Mintage	F	VF	XF	Unc	BU
ND(1976)	1,632,000	—	—	—	9.50	—
ND(1976) Select	Inc. above	—	—	—	11.50	—
ND(1976) Proof	168,000	Value: 11.50				

KM# 2932 100 SCHILLING **Weight:** 23.9300 g. **Composition:** 0.6400 Silver .4924 oz. ASW **Subject:** 175th Anniversary - Birth of Johann Nestroy

Date	Mintage	F	VF	XF	Unc	BU
1976	1,761,000	—	—	—	9.50	—
1976 Select	—	—	—	—	11.50	—
1976 Proof	139,000	Value: 11.50				

KM# 2938 100 SCHILLING **Weight:** 23.9300 g. **Composition:** 0.6400 Silver .4924 oz. ASW **Subject:** 700th Anniversary - Gmunden

Date	Mintage	F	VF	XF	Unc	BU
1978	1,870,000	—	—	—	9.50	—
1978 Select	Inc. above	—	—	—	11.50	—
1978 Proof	130,000	Value: 12.50				

KM# 2942 100 SCHILLING **Weight:** 23.9300 g. **Composition:** 0.6400 Silver .4924 oz. ASW **Subject:** 700th Anniversary - Cathedral of Wiener Neustadt

Date	Mintage	F	VF	XF	Unc	BU
1979	1,796,000	—	—	—	9.50	—
1979 Select	70,000	—	—	—	11.50	—
1979 Proof	134,000	Value: 12.50				

KM# 2934 100 SCHILLING **Weight:** 23.9300 g. **Composition:** 0.6400 Silver .4924 oz. ASW **Subject:** 1200th Anniversary - Kremsmunster Monastery

Date	Mintage	F	VF	XF	Unc	BU
ND(1977)	1,865,000	—	—	—	9.50	—
ND(1977) Select	Inc. above	—	—	—	11.50	—
ND(1977) Proof	135,000	Value: 12.50				

KM# 2939 100 SCHILLING **Weight:** 23.9300 g. **Composition:** 0.6400 Silver .4924 oz. ASW **Subject:** 700th Anniversary - Battle of Durnkrut and Jedenspeigen

Date	Mintage	F	VF	XF	Unc	BU
1978	1,677,000	—	—	—	9.50	—
1978 Select	Inc. above	—	—	—	11.50	—
1978 Proof	123,000	Value: 12.50				

KM# 2943 100 SCHILLING **Weight:** 23.9300 g. **Composition:** 0.6400 Silver .4924 oz. ASW **Subject:** 200th Anniversary - Inn District

Date	Mintage	F	VF	XF	Unc	BU
1979	1,795,000	—	—	—	9.50	—
1979 Select	75,000	—	—	—	11.50	—
1979 Proof	130,000	Value: 12.50				

KM# 2935 100 SCHILLING **Weight:** 23.9300 g. **Composition:** 0.6400 Silver .4924 oz. ASW **Subject:** 900th Anniversary - Hohensalzburg Fortress

Date	Mintage	F	VF	XF	Unc	BU
1977	1,878,000	—	—	—	9.50	—
1977 Select	Inc. above	—	—	—	11.50	—
1977 Proof	122,000	Value: 12.50				

KM# 2940 100 SCHILLING **Weight:** 23.9300 g. **Composition:** 0.6400 Silver .4924 oz. ASW **Subject:** 1100th Anniversary - Founding of Villach

Date	Mintage	F	VF	XF	Unc	BU
ND(1978)	1,569,000	—	—	—	9.50	—
ND(1978) Select	Inc. above	—	—	—	11.50	—
ND(1978) Proof	131,000	Value: 12.50				

KM# 2944 100 SCHILLING **Weight:** 23.9300 g. **Composition:** 0.6400 Silver .4924 oz. ASW **Reverse:** Vienna International Center

Date	Mintage	F	VF	XF	Unc	BU
1979	1,780,000	—	—	—	9.50	—
1979 Select	75,000	—	—	—	11.50	—
1979 Proof	145,000	Value: 12.50				

KM# 2936 100 SCHILLING **Weight:** 23.9300 g. **Composition:** 0.6400 Silver .4924 oz. ASW **Subject:** 500th Anniversary - Hall Mint

Date	Mintage	F	VF	XF	Unc	BU
1977	1,868,000	—	—	—	9.50	—
1977 Select	Inc. above	—	—	—	11.50	—
1977 Proof	132,000	Value: 16.50				

KM# 2941 100 SCHILLING **Weight:** 23.9300 g. **Composition:** 0.6400 Silver .4924 oz. ASW **Subject:** Opening of Arlberg Tunnel

Date	Mintage	F	VF	XF	Unc	BU
1978	1,764,000	—	—	—	9.50	—
1978 Select	80,000	—	—	—	11.50	—
1978 Proof	156,000	Value: 12.50				

KM# 2945 100 SCHILLING **Weight:** 23.9300 g. **Composition:** 0.6400 Silver .4924 oz. ASW **Reverse:** Festival and Congress Hall at Bregenz

Date	Mintage	F	VF	XF	Unc	BU
1979	1,498,000	—	—	—	9.50	—
1979 Select	75,000	—	—	—	11.50	—
1979 Proof	161,000	Value: 12.50				

KM# 2996 100 SCHILLING **Weight:** 18.0000 g. **Composition:** 0.9000 Silver .5209 oz. ASW **Reverse:** Mozart - Salsburg

Date	Mintage	F	VF	XF	Unc	BU
1991 Proof	99,000	Value: 32.50				

KM# 2998 100 SCHILLING **Weight:** 18.0000 g. **Composition:** 0.9000 Silver .5209 oz. ASW **Reverse:** Mozart's Vienna Years - Burgtheater

Date	Mintage	F	VF	XF	Unc	BU
1991 Proof	97,000	Value: 32.50				

KM# 3001 100 SCHILLING **Weight:** 18.0000 g. **Composition:** 0.9000 Silver .5209 oz. ASW **Reverse:** Rudolph I

Date	Mintage	F	VF	XF	Unc	BU
1991 Proof	75,000	Value: 135				

KM# 3003 100 SCHILLING **Weight:** 18.0000 g. **Composition:** 0.9000 Silver .5209 oz. ASW **Reverse:** Maximilian I

Date	Mintage	F	VF	XF	Unc	BU
1992 Proof	75,000	Value: 75.00				

KM# 3005 100 SCHILLING **Weight:** 20.0000 g. **Composition:** 0.9000 Silver .5788 oz. ASW **Reverse:** Otto Nicolai

Date	Mintage	F	VF	XF	Unc	BU
1992 Proof	68,000	Value: 35.00				

KM# 3007 100 SCHILLING **Weight:** 18.0000 g. **Composition:** 0.9000 Silver .5209 oz. ASW **Reverse:** Karl V

Date	Mintage	F	VF	XF	Unc	BU
1992 Proof	74,000	Value: 50.00				

KM# 3009 100 SCHILLING **Weight:** 18.0000 g. **Composition:** 0.9000 Silver .5209 oz. ASW **Reverse:** Kaiser Leopold I

Date	Mintage	F	VF	XF	Unc	BU
1993 Proof	73,000	Value: 35.00				

KM# 3019 100 SCHILLING **Weight:** 18.0000 g. **Composition:** 0.9000 Silver .5209 oz. ASW **Reverse:** Franz Joseph I

Date	Mintage	F	VF	XF	Unc	BU
1994 Proof	74,000	Value: 35.00				

KM# 3020 100 SCHILLING **Weight:** 18.0000 g. **Composition:** 0.9000 Silver .5209 oz. ASW **Subject:** 1848 Revolution **Reverse:** Archduke Johann

Date	Mintage	F	VF	XF	Unc	BU
1994 Proof	74,000	Value: 35.00				

KM# 3034 100 SCHILLING **Weight:** 18.0000 g. **Composition:** 0.9000 Silver .5209 oz. ASW **Reverse:** First Republic - Coin, Buildings and Symbols

Date	Mintage	F	VF	XF	Unc	BU
1995 Proof	68,000	Value: 35.00				

KM# 3036 100 SCHILLING **Weight:** 18.0000 g. **Composition:** 0.9000 Silver .5209 oz. ASW **Reverse:** Leopold III

Date	Mintage	F	VF	XF	Unc	BU
1996 Proof	69,000	Value: 35.00				

KM# 3046 100 SCHILLING **Weight:** 18.0000 g. **Composition:** 0.9000 Silver .5209 oz. ASW **Series:** Habsburg Tragedies **Obverse:** Standing portrait in uniform of Emperor Maximilian of Mexico **Reverse:** Miramar palace and the SMS Novard

Date	Mintage	F	VF	XF	Unc	BU
1997 Proof	65,000	Value: 40.00				

KM# 3051 100 SCHILLING **Weight:** 18.0000 g. **Composition:** 0.9000 Silver .5209 oz. ASW **Series:** Habsburg Tragedies **Obverse:** Standing portrait in uniform of Crown Prince Rudolf **Reverse:** Hearse with military honor guard

Date		F	VF	XF	Unc	BU
1998 Proof	Est. 50,000	Value: 40.00				

KM# 3059 100 SCHILLING **Weight:** 18.0000 g. **Composition:** 0.9000 Silver .5209 oz. ASW **Series:** Habsburg Tragedies **Obverse:** Archduke Franz Ferdinand and Sophie **Reverse:** The couple getting into the car

Date		F	VF	XF	Unc	BU
1999 Proof	Est. 50,000	Value: 40.00				

KM# 3063 100 SCHILLING **Ring Composition:** 0.9000 Silver**Center Weight:** 9.0000 g. **Center Composition:** Titanium .2604 oz. **Subject:** Communications **Obverse:** Computer chip design **Reverse:** World map at center in ring **Edge:** Plain

Date	Mintage	F	VF	XF	Unc	BU
2000 Proof	50,000	Value: 45.00				

KM# 3068 100 SCHILLING **Weight:** 18.0000 g. **Composition:** 0.9000 Silver .5209 oz. ASW **Obverse:** Celtic salt miner **Reverse:** Celtic coin design with mounted warrior **Edge:** Reeded **Size:** 34 mm.

Date	Mintage	F	VF	XF	Unc	BU
2000 Proof	50,000	Value: 40.00				

KM# 3069 100 SCHILLING **Weight:** 18.0000 g. **Composition:** 0.9000 Silver .5209 oz. ASW **Obverse:** Ancient Roman troops crossing pontoon bridge **Reverse:** Bust of Marcus Aurelius right **Edge:** Reeded

Date	Mintage	F	VF	XF	Unc	BU
2000 Proof	50,000	Value: 40.00				

KM# 3073 100 SCHILLING **Ring Weight:** 7.0000 g. **Ring Composition:** 0.9000 Silver .2604 oz. ASW **Center Weight:** 3.7500 g. **Center Composition:** Titanium **Subject:** Transportation **Obverse:** Automobile engine **Reverse:** Car, train, truck, and plane **Edge:** Plain **Size:** 34 mm.

Date	Mintage	F	VF	XF	Unc	BU
2001 Proof	50,000	Value: 40.00				

KM# 3077 100 SCHILLING **Weight:** 18.0000 g. **Composition:** 0.9000 Silver .5209 oz. ASW **Subject:** Charlemagne **Obverse:** Holy Roman Emperor's crown above denomination **Reverse:** Bust of Charlemagne facing half right holding sceptre **Edge:** Reeded **Size:** 34 mm.

Date	Mintage	F	VF	XF	Unc	BU
2001 Proof	50,000	Value: 40.00				

KM# 3079 100 SCHILLING **Weight:** 18.0000 g. **Composition:** 0.9000 Silver .5209 oz. ASW **Subject:** Duke Rudolf IV **Obverse:** University teaching scene **Reverse:** Bust of Duke Rudolf IV at right facing half left, St. Stephen's Cathedral at left **Edge:** Reeded **Size:** 34 mm.

Date	Mintage	F	VF	XF	Unc	BU
2001 Proof	50,000	Value: 40.00				

KM# 3004 200 SCHILLING **Weight:** 3.1100 g. **Composition:** 0.9999 Gold .1000 oz. AGW **Series:** Vienna Philharmonic Orchestra **Obverse:** Building **Reverse:** Instruments

Date	Mintage	F	VF	XF	Unc	BU
1991	83,000	—	—	—	BV+13%	—
1992	99,000	—	—	—	BV+13%	—
1993	10,000	—	—	—	BV+13%	—
1994	110,000	—	—	—	BV+13%	—
1995	151,000	—	—	—	BV+13%	—
1996	128,000	—	—	—	BV+13%	—
1997	12,000	—	—	—	BV+13%	—
1998	—	—	—	—	BV+13%	—
1999	—	—	—	—	BV+13%	—

KM# 3026 200 SCHILLING **Weight:** 33.6300 g. **Composition:** 0.9250 Silver 1.0000 oz. ASW **Series:** Olympics **Reverse:** Ribbon Dancer **Edge Lettering:** CITIUS ALTIUS FORTIUS

Date	Mintage	F	VF	XF	Unc	BU
1995 Proof	Est. 100,000	Value: 32.50				

KM# 3027 200 SCHILLING **Weight:** 33.6300 g. **Composition:** 0.9250 Silver 1.0000 oz. ASW **Series:** Olympics **Reverse:** Skier

Date	Mintage	F	VF	XF	Unc	BU
1995 Proof	Est. 100,000	Value: 32.50				

KM# 2947 500 SCHILLING **Weight:** 23.9600 g. **Composition:** 0.6400 Silver .4930 oz. ASW **Subject:** Millennium **Reverse:** City of Steyr

Date	Mintage	F	VF	XF	Unc	BU
1980	825,000	—	—	—	50.00	—
1980 Select	63,000	—	—	—	52.00	—
1980 Proof	111,000	Value: 58.00				

KM# 2948 500 SCHILLING **Weight:** 23.9600 g. **Composition:** 0.6400 Silver .4930 oz. ASW **Subject:** 25th Anniversary - State Treaty

Date	Mintage	F	VF	XF	Unc	BU
ND(1980)	787,000	—	—	—	50.00	—
ND(1980) Select	79,000	—	—	—	52.00	—
ND(1980) Proof	134,000	Value: 58.00				

KM# 2949 500 SCHILLING **Weight:** 23.9600 g. **Composition:** 0.6400 Silver .4930 oz. ASW **Subject:** Bicentennial - Death of Maria Theresa

Date	Mintage	F	VF	XF	Unc	BU
1980	841,600	—	—	—	50.00	—
1980 Select	86,400	—	—	—	50.00	—
1980 Proof	172,000	Value: 55.00				

KM# 2950 500 SCHILLING **Weight:** 23.9600 g. **Composition:** 0.6400 Silver .4930 oz. ASW **Subject:** Centennial - Austrian Red Cross

Date	Mintage	F	VF	XF	Unc	BU
ND(1980)	860,000	—	—	—	50.00	—
ND(1980) Select	90,000	—	—	—	50.00	—
ND(1980) Proof	200,000	Value: 55.00				

KM# 2951 500 SCHILLING **Weight:** 23.9600 g. **Composition:** 0.6400 Silver .4930 oz. ASW **Subject:** 800th Anniversary - Verdun Altar

Date	Mintage	F	VF	XF	Unc	BU
ND(1981)	865,000	—	—	—	50.00	—
ND(1981) Select	85,000	—	—	—	50.00	—
ND(1981) Proof	200,000	Value: 58.00				

KM# 2952 500 SCHILLING **Weight:** 23.9600 g. **Composition:** 0.6400 Silver .4930 oz. ASW **Subject:** 100th Anniversary - Birth of Anton Wildgans

Date	Mintage	F	VF	XF	Unc	BU
1981	911,000	—	—	—	50.00	—
1981 Select	72,000	—	—	—	50.00	—
1981 Proof	167,000	Value: 55.00				

KM# 2953 500 SCHILLING **Weight:** 23.9600 g. **Composition:** 0.6400 Silver .4930 oz. ASW **Subject:** 100th Anniversary - Birth of Otto Bauer

Date	Mintage	F	VF	XF	Unc	BU
ND(1981)	929,000	—	—	—	50.00	—
ND(1981) Select	65,000	—	—	—	50.00	—
ND(1981) Proof	156,000	Value: 55.00				

KM# 2954 500 SCHILLING **Weight:** 23.9600 g. **Composition:** 0.6400 Silver .4930 oz. ASW **Subject:** 200th Anniversary - Religious Tolerance

Date	Mintage	F	VF	XF	Unc	BU
ND(1981)	792,000	—	—	—	50.00	—
ND(1981) Select	60,000	—	—	—	50.00	—
ND(1981) Proof	148,000	Value: 55.00				

KM# 2959 500 SCHILLING **Weight:** 23.9600 g. **Composition:** 0.6400 Silver .4930 oz. ASW **Subject:** 80th Anniversary - Birth of Leopold Figl

Date	Mintage	F	VF	XF	Unc	BU
1982	344,400	—	—	—	50.00	—
1982 Select	39,600	—	—	—	50.00	—
1982 Proof	116,000	Value: 60.00				

KM# 2964 500 SCHILLING **Weight:** 23.9600 g. **Composition:** 0.9250 Silver .7125 oz. ASW **Subject:** Centennial - Parliament Building

Date	Mintage	F	VF	XF	Unc	BU
1983	463,000	—	—	—	50.00	—
1983 Proof	137,000	Value: 55.00				

KM# 2956 500 SCHILLING **Weight:** 23.9600 g. **Composition:** 0.6400 Silver .4930 oz. ASW **Subject:** 1500th Anniversary - Death of St. Severin

Date	Mintage	F	VF	XF	Unc	BU
ND(1982)	837,400	—	—	—	50.00	—
ND(1982) Select	42,600	—	—	—	50.00	—
ND(1982) Proof	120,000	Value: 55.00				

KM# 2961 500 SCHILLING **Weight:** 23.9600 g. **Composition:** 0.9250 Silver .7125 oz. ASW **Subject:** World Cup Horse Jumping Championship

Date	Mintage	F	VF	XF	Unc	BU
1983	368,000	—	—	—	50.00	—
1983 Proof	132,000	Value: 55.00				

KM# 2966 500 SCHILLING **Weight:** 23.9600 g. **Composition:** 0.9250 Silver .7125 oz. ASW **Subject:** 175th Anniversary - Tirolean Revolution

Date	Mintage	F	VF	XF	Unc	BU
ND(1984)	454,000	—	—	—	50.00	—
ND(1984) Proof	146,000	Value: 55.00				

KM# 2957 500 SCHILLING **Weight:** 23.9600 g. **Composition:** 0.6400 Silver .4930 oz. ASW **Subject:** 500 Years of Austrian Printing

Date	Mintage	F	VF	XF	Unc	BU
1982	589,800	—	—	—	50.00	—
1982 Select	42,200	—	—	—	50.00	—
1982 Proof	118,000	Value: 55.00				

KM# 2962 500 SCHILLING **Weight:** 23.9600 g. **Composition:** 0.9250 Silver .7125 oz. ASW **Subject:** Centennial - Vienna City Hall

Date	Mintage	F	VF	XF	Unc	BU
ND(1983)	466,000	—	—	—	50.00	—
ND(1973) Proof	134,000	Value: 55.00				

KM# 2967 500 SCHILLING **Weight:** 23.9600 g. **Composition:** 0.9250 Silver .7125 oz. ASW **Subject:** 100th Anniversary - Commercial Shipping on Lake Constance

Date	Mintage	F	VF	XF	Unc	BU
1984	458,000	—	—	—	50.00	—
1984 Proof	142,000	Value: 55.00				

KM# 2958 500 SCHILLING **Weight:** 23.9600 g. **Composition:** 0.6400 Silver .4930 oz. ASW **Subject:** 825 Years of the Mariazell Shrine

Date	Mintage	F	VF	XF	Unc	BU
1982	590,400	—	—	—	50.00	—
1982 Select	41,600	—	—	—	50.00	—
1982 Proof	118,000	Value: 55.00				

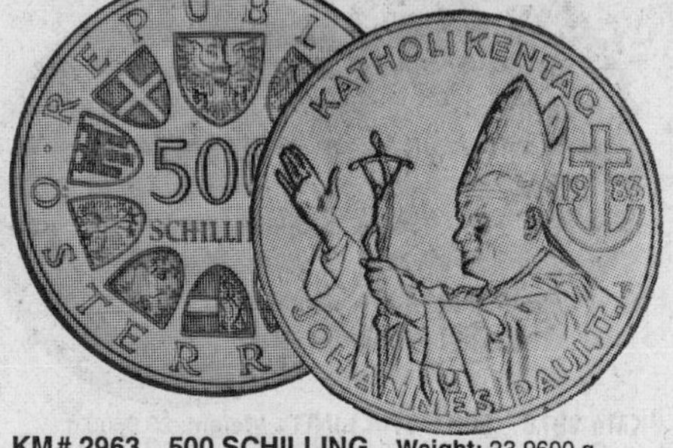

KM# 2963 500 SCHILLING **Weight:** 23.9600 g. **Composition:** 0.9250 Silver .7125 oz. ASW **Subject:** Catholic Day - Pope's Visit

Date	Mintage	F	VF	XF	Unc	BU
1983	600,000	—	—	—	50.00	—
1983 Select	60,000	—	—	—	50.00	—
1983 Proof	140,000	Value: 55.00				

KM# 2968 500 SCHILLING **Weight:** 23.9600 g. **Composition:** 0.9250 Silver .7125 oz. ASW **Subject:** 700th Anniversary - Stams Stift in Tirol

Date	Mintage	F	VF	XF	Unc	BU
1984	462,000	—	—	—	50.00	—
1984 Proof	138,000	Value: 55.00				

KM# 2969 500 SCHILLING **Weight:** 23.9600 g. **Composition:** 0.9250 Silver .7125 oz. ASW **Subject:** Centennial - Death of Fanny Elssler

Date	Mintage	F	VF	XF	Unc	BU
1984	465,000	—	—	—	50.00	—
1984 Proof	135,000	Value: 55.00				

KM# 2974 500 SCHILLING **Weight:** 23.9600 g. **Composition:** 0.9250 Silver .7125 oz. ASW **Subject:** 2000th Anniversary - Bregenz

Date	Mintage	F	VF	XF	Unc	BU
1985	388,000	—	—	—	50.00	—
1985 Proof	112,000	Value: 55.00				

KM# 2979 500 SCHILLING **Weight:** 23.9600 g. **Composition:** 0.9250 Silver .7125 oz. ASW **Subject:** European Conference on Security and Cooperation

Date	Mintage	F	VF	XF	Unc	BU
1986	202,000	—	—	—	50.00	—
1986 Proof	98,000	Value: 55.00				

KM# 2971 500 SCHILLING **Weight:** 23.9600 g. **Composition:** 0.9250 Silver .7125 oz. ASW **Subject:** 400th Anniversary - Graz University

Date	Mintage	F	VF	XF	Unc	BU
1985	481,000	—	—	—	50.00	—
1985 Proof	119,000	Value: 55.00				

KM# 2976 500 SCHILLING **Weight:** 23.9600 g. **Composition:** 0.9250 Silver .7125 oz. ASW **Subject:** 300th Anniversary - St. Florian's Abbey

Date	Mintage	F	VF	XF	Unc	BU
ND(1986)	303,000	—	—	—	50.00	—
ND(1986) Proof	97,000	Value: 55.00				

KM# 2981 500 SCHILLING **Weight:** 23.9600 g. **Composition:** 0.9250 Silver .7125 oz. ASW **Subject:** 150th Anniversary - Austrian Railroad

Date	Mintage	F	VF	XF	Unc	BU
ND(1987)	205,000	—	—	—	50.00	—
ND(1987) Proof	95,000	Value: 60.00				

KM# 2972 500 SCHILLING **Weight:** 23.9600 g. **Composition:** 0.9250 Silver .7125 oz. ASW **Subject:** 40 Years of Peace in Austria

Date	Mintage	F	VF	XF	Unc	BU
ND(1985)	384,000	—	—	—	50.00	—
ND(1985) Proof	116,000	Value: 55.00				

KM# 2977 500 SCHILLING **Weight:** 23.9600 g. **Composition:** 0.9250 Silver .7125 oz. ASW **Subject:** 500th Anniversary - First Thaler Coin Struck at Hall Mint

Date	Mintage	F	VF	XF	Unc	BU
ND(1986)	401,000	—	—	—	50.00	—
ND(1986) Proof	99,000	Value: 58.00				

KM# 2982 500 SCHILLING **Weight:** 23.9600 g. **Composition:** 0.9250 Silver .7125 oz. ASW **Subject:** 400th Anniversary - Birth of Salzburg's Archbishop von Raitenau

Date	Mintage	F	VF	XF	Unc	BU
ND(1987)	206,000	—	—	—	50.00	—
ND(1987) Proof	94,000	Value: 55.00				

KM# 2973 500 SCHILLING **Weight:** 23.9600 g. **Composition:** 0.9250 Silver .7125 oz. ASW **Subject:** 500th Anniversary - Canonization of Leopold III

Date	Mintage	F	VF	XF	Unc	BU
ND(1985)	388,000	—	—	—	50.00	—
ND(1985) Proof	112,000	Value: 55.00				

KM# 2978 500 SCHILLING **Weight:** 23.9600 g. **Composition:** 0.9250 Silver .7125 oz. ASW **Subject:** 250th Anniversary - Birth of Prince Eugene of Savoy

Date	Mintage	F	VF	XF	Unc	BU
1986	400,000	—	—	—	50.00	—
1986 Proof	100,000	Value: 55.00				

KM# 2983 500 SCHILLING **Weight:** 23.9600 g. **Composition:** 0.9250 Silver .7125 oz. ASW **Subject:** 800th Anniversary - Holy Cross Church

Date	Mintage	F	VF	XF	Unc	BU
1987	205,000	—	—	—	50.00	—
1987 Proof	95,000	Value: 55.00				

KM# 2984 500 SCHILLING **Weight:** 23.9600 g. **Composition:** 0.9250 Silver .7125 oz. ASW **Subject:** 850th Anniversary - St. Georgenberg Abbey

Date	Mintage	F	VF	XF	Unc	BU
ND(1988)	212,000	—	—	—	50.00	—
ND(1988) Proof	88,000	Value: 58.00				

KM# 2985 500 SCHILLING **Weight:** 23.9600 g. **Composition:** 0.9250 Silver .7125 oz. ASW **Subject:** Pope's Visit to Austria

Date	Mintage	F	VF	XF	Unc	BU
1988	211,000	—	—	—	50.00	—
1988 Proof	89,000	Value: 58.00				

KM# 2986 500 SCHILLING **Weight:** 23.9600 g. **Composition:** 0.9250 Silver .7125 oz. ASW **Subject:** 100th Anniversary - Victor Adler and Christian Socialist Party

Date	Mintage	F	VF	XF	Unc	BU
1988	213,000	—	—	—	50.00	—
1988 Proof	87,000	Value: 58.00				

KM# 2987 500 SCHILLING **Weight:** 23.9600 g. **Composition:** 0.9250 Silver .7125 oz. ASW **Obverse:** Gustav Klimt **Reverse:** Art Nouveau

Date	Mintage	F	VF	XF	Unc	BU
1989	237,000	—	—	—	50.00	—
1989 Proof	88,000	Value: 58.00				

KM# 2989 500 SCHILLING **Weight:** 7.7760 g. **Composition:** 0.9999 Gold .2505 oz. AGW **Series:** Vienna Philharmonic Orchestra **Obverse:** Similar to 2000 Schilling, KM#2990

Date	Mintage	F	VF	XF	Unc	BU
1989	68,000	—	—	—BV+10%		—
1990	41,000	—	—	—BV+10%		—
1991	37,000	—	—	—BV+10%		—
1992	44,000	—	—	—BV+10%		—
1992	44,000	—	—	—BV+10%		—
1994	30,000	—	—	—BV+10%		—
1995	157,000	—	—	—BV+10%		—
1996	138,000	—	—	—BV+10%		—
1997	25,000	—	—	—BV+10%		—
1998	—	—	—	—BV+10%		—
1999	—	—	—	—BV+10%		—

KM# 2991 500 SCHILLING **Weight:** 23.9600 g. **Composition:** 0.9250 Silver .7125 oz. ASW **Obverse:** Koloman Moser **Reverse:** Stained glass

Date	Mintage	F	VF	XF	Unc	BU
1989	228,000	—	—	—	50.00	—
1989 Proof	83,000	Value: 55.00				

KM# 2992 500 SCHILLING **Weight:** 23.9600 g. **Composition:** 0.9250 Silver .7125 oz. ASW **Obverse:** Egon Schiele **Reverse:** Expressionism

Date	Mintage	F	VF	XF	Unc	BU
1990	247,000	—	—	—	50.00	—
1990 Proof	81,000	Value: 55.00				

KM# 2994 500 SCHILLING **Weight:** 23.9600 g. **Composition:** 0.9250 Silver .7125 oz. ASW **Obverse:** Oskar Kokoschka **Reverse:** Expressionism

Date	Mintage	F	VF	XF	Unc	BU
1990	245,000	—	—	—	50.00	—
1990 Proof	81,000	Value: 55.00				

KM# 2997 500 SCHILLING **Weight:** 8.1130 g. **Composition:** 0.9860 Gold .2578 oz. AGW **Obverse:** Mozart **Reverse:** Don Giovanni

Date	Mintage	F	VF	XF	Unc	BU
1991 Proof	50,000	Value: 245				

KM# 3000 500 SCHILLING **Weight:** 24.0000 g. **Composition:** 0.9250 Silver .7125 oz. ASW **Obverse:** Herbert von Karajan **Reverse:** Salzburg Festspielhaus

Date	Mintage	F	VF	XF	Unc	BU
1991	240,000	—	—	—	47.50	—
1991 Proof	74,000	Value: 55.00				

KM# 3002 500 SCHILLING **Weight:** 24.0000 g. **Composition:** 0.9250 Silver .7125 oz. ASW **Obverse:** Karl Bohm

Date	Mintage	F	VF	XF	Unc	BU
1991	237,000	—	—	—	47.50	—
1991 Proof	71,000	Value: 55.00				

KM# 3006 500 SCHILLING **Weight:** 8.1130 g. **Composition:** 0.9860 Gold .2578 oz. AGW **Subject:** 150th Anniversary - Vienna Philharmonic

Date	Mintage	F	VF	XF	Unc	BU
1992 Proof	43,000	Value: 185				

KM# 3010 500 SCHILLING **Weight:** 24.0000 g. **Composition:** 0.9250 Silver .7125 oz. ASW **Obverse:** Gustav Mahler

Date	Mintage	F	VF	XF	Unc	BU
1992	256,000	—	—	—	47.50	—
1992 Proof	64,000	Value: 60.00				

KM# 3021 500 SCHILLING **Weight:** 24.0000 g. **Composition:** 0.9250 Silver .7125 oz. ASW **Obverse:** Richard Strauss

Date	Mintage	F	VF	XF	Unc	BU
1992	236,000	—	—	—	47.50	—
1992 Proof	63,000	Value: 60.00				

KM# 3011 500 SCHILLING Weight: 24.0000 g. **Composition:** 0.9250 Silver .7125 oz. ASW **Obverse:** Hallstatt and the Lakes Region

Date	Mintage	F	VF	XF	Unc	BU
1993	220,000	—	—	—	47.50	—
1993 Proof	60,000	Value: 60.00				

KM# 3012 500 SCHILLING Weight: 8.1130 g. **Composition:** 0.9860 Gold .2578 oz. AGW **Reverse:** Emperors Rudolf II, Ferdinand II and Archduke Leopold Wilhelm

Date	Mintage	F	VF	XF	Unc	BU
1993 Proof	50,000	Value: 650				

KM# 3014 500 SCHILLING Weight: 24.0000 g. **Composition:** 0.9250 Silver .7125 oz. ASW **Obverse:** Alpine Region

Date	Mintage	F	VF	XF	Unc	BU
1993	220,000	—	—	—	47.50	—
1993 Proof	60,000	Value: 60.00				

KM# 3015 500 SCHILLING Weight: 8.1130 g. **Composition:** 0.9860 Gold .2578 oz. AGW **Obverse:** Congress of Vienna

Date	Mintage	F	VF	XF	Unc	BU
1994 Proof	50,000	Value: 225				

KM# 3017 500 SCHILLING Weight: 24.0000 g. **Composition:** 0.9250 Silver .7125 oz. ASW **Obverse:** Pannonian Region **Reverse:** Dancers

Date	Mintage	F	VF	XF	Unc	BU
1994	190,000	—	—	—	47.50	—
1994 Proof	60,000	Value: 60.00				

KM# 3024 500 SCHILLING Weight: 24.0000 g. **Composition:** 0.9250 Silver .7125 oz. ASW **Obverse:** River Region **Reverse:** Folk Paraders

Date	Mintage	F	VF	XF	Unc	BU
1994	190,000	—	—	—	47.50	—
1994 Proof	60,000	Value: 60.00				

KM# 3025 500 SCHILLING Weight: 24.0000 g. **Composition:** 0.9250 Silver .7125 oz. ASW **Obverse:** Austrian Hill Country **Reverse:** Farm Couple

Date	Mintage	F	VF	XF	Unc	BU
1995	190,000	—	—	—	47.50	—
1995 Proof	60,000	Value: 60.00				

KM# 3029 500 SCHILLING Weight: 24.0000 g. **Composition:** 0.9250 Silver .7125 oz. ASW **Obverse:** Alpine Foothills **Reverse:** Lumberjack

Date	Mintage	F	VF	XF	Unc	BU
1995		—	—	—	47.50	—
1995 Proof	Est. 60,000	Value: 60.00				

KM# 3023 500 SCHILLING Ring Weight: 8.1130 g. **Ring Composition:** 0.9860 Gold .2578 oz. AGW **Center Weight:** 5.3330 g. **Center Composition:** 0.9000 Silver .1547 oz. ASW **Subject:** European Union - Austrian Membership **Note:** Stars in outer ring are completely punched through.

Date	Mintage	F	VF	XF	Unc	BU
1995 Proof	33,000	Value: 185				

KM# 3032 500 SCHILLING Weight: 8.1130 g. **Composition:** 0.9860 Gold .2578 oz. AGW **Reverse:** Heinrich II Jasomirgott

Date	Mintage	F	VF	XF	Unc	BU
1996 Proof	Est. 50,000	Value: 255				

KM# 3035 500 SCHILLING Weight: 24.0000 g. **Composition:** 0.9250 Silver .7125 oz. ASW **Obverse:** The Mill Region

Date	Mintage	F	VF	XF	Unc	BU
1996	190,000	—	—	—	47.50	—
1996 Proof	60,000	Value: 60.00				

KM# 3039 500 SCHILLING Weight: 24.0000 g. **Composition:** 0.9250 Silver .7125 oz. ASW **Series:** Town Series - Innsbruck Square **Obverse:** View of town square **Reverse:** Outdoor market scene

Date	Mintage	F	VF	XF	Unc	BU
1996	160,000	—	—	—	47.50	—
1996 BU	30,000	—	—	—	50.00	—
1996 Proof	60,000	Value: 60.00				

KM# 3040 500 SCHILLING Weight: 8.0400 g. **Composition:** 0.9950 Gold .2578 oz. AGW **Obverse:** People gathered at piano **Reverse:** Portrait, Franz Schubert dates, line of musical score

Date	Mintage	F	VF	XF	Unc	BU
1997 Proof	Est. 50,000	Value: 240				

KM# 3042 500 SCHILLING Weight: 24.0000 g. **Composition:** 0.9250 Silver .7125 oz. ASW **Series:** Town Series - Bruck an der Mur **Obverse:** Ornate pavilion on cobblestone street **Reverse:** Ironsmith at work

Date	Mintage	F	VF	XF	Unc	BU
1997	125,000	—	—	—	42.00	—
1997 Special Unc	25,000	—	—	—	50.00	—
1997 Proof	50,000	Value: 60.00				

KM# 3045 500 SCHILLING **Weight:** 24.0000 g. **Composition:** 0.9250 Silver .7125 oz. ASW **Obverse:** Stone pulpit of St. Stephen's cathedral **Reverse:** Stone mason at work

Date	Mintage	F	VF	XF	Unc	BU
1997	125,000	—	—	—	42.00	—
1997 Special Unc	25,000	—	—	—	50.00	—
1997 Proof	50,000	Value: 60.00				

KM# 3047 500 SCHILLING **Weight:** 8.0000 g. **Composition:** 0.9950 Gold .2559 oz. AGW **Obverse:** New York and Kyoto views **Reverse:** Vienna boys choir

Date	Mintage	F	VF	XF	Unc	BU
ND(1998) Proof	Est. 50,000	Value: 250				

KM# 3049 500 SCHILLING **Weight:** 22.2000 g. **Composition:** 0.9250 Silver .6602 oz. ASW **Obverse:** Interior view of Adimont Abbey Libary **Reverse:** Printers at work **Note:** Book printing.

Date	Mintage	F	VF	XF	Unc	BU
1998	125,000	—	—	—	42.00	—
1998 BU	25,000	—	—	—	50.00	—
1998 Proof	50,000	Value: 60.00				

KM# 3054 500 SCHILLING **Weight:** 22.2000 g. **Composition:** 0.9250 Silver .6602 oz. ASW **Obverse:** Gold chalice and church **Reverse:** Goldsmith at work **Note:** Gold smithing.

Date	Mintage	F	VF	XF	Unc	BU
1998	125,000	—	—	—	42.00	—
1998 Special Unc	25,000	—	—	—	50.00	—
1998 Proof	50,000	Value: 60.00				

KM# 3055 500 SCHILLING **Weight:** 8.0000 g. **Composition:** 0.9250 Gold .2559 oz. AGW **Obverse:** Waltzing couple and Strauss monument **Reverse:** Portrait of Johann Strauss and son, Johann

Date	Mintage	F	VF	XF	Unc	BU
1999 Proof	Est. 50,000	Value: 250				

KM# 3058 500 SCHILLING **Weight:** 24.0000 g. **Composition:** 0.9250 Silver .7137 oz. ASW **Obverse:** Rosenburg Castle, falcon on perch in castle jousting court **Reverse:** Jousting knights

Date	Mintage	F	VF	XF	Unc	BU
1999	—	—	—	—	42.00	—
1999 Special Unc	—	—	—	—	50.00	—
1999 Proof	Est. 50,000	Value: 60.00				

KM# 3060 500 SCHILLING **Weight:** 24.0000 g. **Composition:** 0.9250 Silver .7137 oz. ASW **Obverse:** Burg Lockenhaus **Reverse:** Two Templar knights on horseback

Date	Mintage	F	VF	XF	Unc	BU
1999	—	—	—	—	42.00	—
1999 Special Unc	—	—	—	—	50.00	—
1999 Proof	Est. 50,000	Value: 60.00				

KM# 3065 500 SCHILLING **Weight:** 10.0000 g. **Composition:** 0.9860 Gold .3170 oz. AGW **Subject:** 2000th Birthday of Jesus Christ **Obverse:** 3 wise men presenting gifts **Reverse:** Portrait of Jesus

Date	Mintage	F	VF	XF	Unc	BU
2000 Proof	Est. 50,000	Value: 250				

KM# 3067 500 SCHILLING **Weight:** 24.0000 g. **Composition:** 0.9250 Silver .7137 oz. ASW **Obverse:** Hochosterwitz Castle **Reverse:** Walter von der Vogelweide and royal couple **Edge:** Lettered **Size:** 37 mm.

Date	Mintage	F	VF	XF	Unc	BU
2000	95,000	—	—	—	42.00	—
2000 Special Unc	25,000	—	—	—	50.00	—
2000 Proof	505,000	Value: 55.00				

KM# 3071 500 SCHILLING **Weight:** 24.0000 g. **Composition:** 0.9250 Silver .7137 oz. ASW **Obverse:** Burg Hohenwerfen Castle **Reverse:** Medieval falcon training scene **Edge:** Lettered

Date	Mintage	F	VF	XF	Unc	BU
2000	95,000	—	—	—	42.00	—
2000 Special Unc	25,000	—	—	—	50.00	—
2000 Proof	50,000	Value: 55.00				

KM# 3074 500 SCHILLING **Weight:** 10.0000 g. **Composition:** 0.9860 Gold .3170 oz. AGW **Subject:** 2000 Years of Christianity - Bible **Obverse:** Bible and symbols of the saints: Matthew, Luke, Mark and John **Reverse:** St. Paul reading from a scroll to two listeners **Edge:** Reeded **Size:** 22 mm.

Date	Mintage	F	VF	XF	Unc	BU
2001	50,000	—	—	—	200	—

KM# 3078 500 SCHILLING **Weight:** 24.0000 g. **Composition:** 0.9250 Silver .7137 oz. ASW **Subject:** Kufstein Castle **Obverse:** Castle view above denomination **Reverse:** Emperor Maximilian being shown one of his new cannons **Edge:** Lettered **Size:** 37 mm.

Date	Mintage	F	VF	XF	Unc	BU
2001	120,000	—	—	—	45.00	—
2001 Proof	50,000	Value: 60.00				

KM# 3080 500 SCHILLING **Weight:** 24.0000 g. **Composition:** 0.9250 Silver .7137 oz. ASW **Subject:** Schattenburg Castle **Obverse:** Castle view **Reverse:** Two medieval armourers at work **Edge:** Lettered **Size:** 37 mm.

Date	Mintage	F	VF	XF	Unc	BU
2001	95,000	—	—	—	42.00	—
2001 Special Unc	25,000	—	—	—	50.00	—
2001 Proof	50,000	Value: 60.00				

KM# 2933 1000 SCHILLING **Weight:** 13.5000 g. **Composition:** 0.9000 Gold .3906 oz. AGW **Subject:** Babenberg Dynasty Millennium **Note:** Exists in shades of red to yellow gold.

Date	Mintage	F	VF	XF	Unc	BU
ND (1976)	1,800,000	—	—	—	175	—

KM# 2999 1000 SCHILLING **Weight:** 16.2250 g. **Composition:** 0.9860 Gold .5155 oz. AGW **Obverse:** Mozart **Reverse:** The Magic Flute Opera

Date	Mintage	F	VF	XF	Unc	BU
1991 Proof	30,000	Value: 475				

KM# 3008 1000 SCHILLING **Weight:** 16.2250 g. **Composition:** 0.9860 Gold .5155 oz. AGW **Reverse:** Johann Strauss - Violinist

Date	Mintage	F	VF	XF	Unc	BU
1992 Proof	42,000	Value: 300				

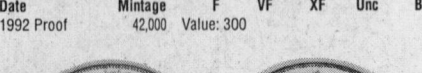

KM# 3013 1000 SCHILLING **Weight:** 16.2250 g. **Composition:** 0.9860 Gold .5155 oz. AGW **Reverse:** Maria Theresia

Date	Mintage	F	VF	XF	Unc	BU
1993 Proof	50,000	Value: 345				

KM# 3018 1000 SCHILLING **Weight:** 26.6660 g. **Composition:** 0.9860 Silver .7733 oz. ASW **Subject:** 800th Anniversary of the Vienna Mint

Date	Mintage	F	VF	XF	Unc	BU
ND (1994) Proof	48,000	Value: 300				

KM# 3031 1000 SCHILLING **Weight:** 15.5500 g. **Composition:** 0.9999 Gold .5000 oz. AGW **Series:** Vienna Philharmonic Orchestra

Date	Mintage	F	VF	XF	Unc	BU
1994	29,000	—	—	—	BV+8%	—
1995	95,000	—	—	—	BV+8%	—
1996	88,000	—	—	—	BV+8%	—
1997	34,000	—	—	—	BV+8%	—
1998	—	—	—	—	BV+8%	—
1999	—	—	—	—	BV+8%	—

KM# 3028 1000 SCHILLING **Weight:** 16.9700 g. **Composition:** 0.9170 Gold .5014 oz. AGW **Series:** Olympics **Reverse:** Zeus **Edge Lettering:** CITIUS ALTIUS FORTIUS

Date	Mintage	F	VF	XF	Unc	BU
1995 Proof	Est. 60,000	Value: 300				

KM# 3030 1000 SCHILLING **Weight:** 16.2250 g. **Composition:** 0.9860 Gold .5155 oz. AGW **Subject:** 50th Anniversary - Second Republic

Date	Mintage	F	VF	XF	Unc	BU
1995 Proof	49,000	Value: 345				

KM# 3037 1000 SCHILLING **Weight:** 16.2250 g. **Composition:** 0.9860 Gold .5155 oz. AGW **Subject:** Millennium of the Name Osterreich **Obverse:** Land grant **Reverse:** Otto III

Date	Mintage	F	VF	XF	Unc	BU
ND (1996) Proof	50,000	Value: 325				

KM# 3043 1000 SCHILLING **Weight:** 16.0000 g. **Composition:** 0.9950 Gold .5118 oz. AGW **Subject:** Habsburg Tragedies - Marie Antoinette **Obverse:** Marie holding flowers **Reverse:** Marie on trial

Date	Mintage	F	VF	XF	Unc	BU
1997 Proof	Est. 50,000	Value: 325				

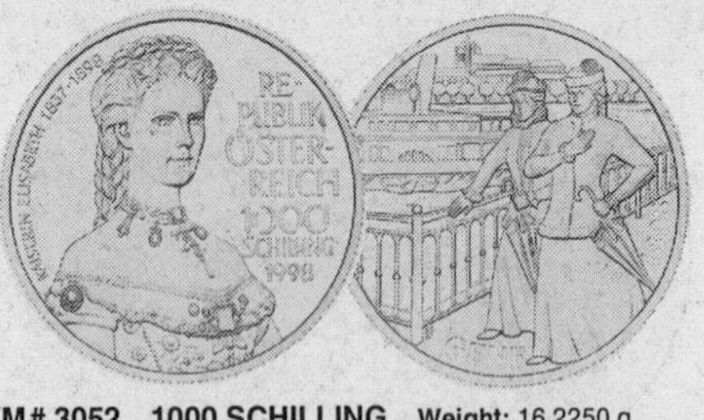

KM# 3052 1000 SCHILLING **Weight:** 16.2250 g. **Composition:** 0.9860 Gold .5155 oz. AGW **Obverse:** Empress Elizabeth bust right **Reverse:** Scene of Elizabeth's final moment

Date	Mintage	F	VF	XF	Unc	BU
1998 Proof	Est. 50,000	Value: 325				

KM# 3062 1000 SCHILLING **Weight:** 16.0000 g. **Composition:** 0.9950 Gold .5118 oz. AGW **Obverse:** Emperor Karl I bust facing **Reverse:** Interior view Habsburg crypt

Date	Mintage	F	VF	XF	Unc	BU
1999 Proof	Est. 50,000	Value: 325				

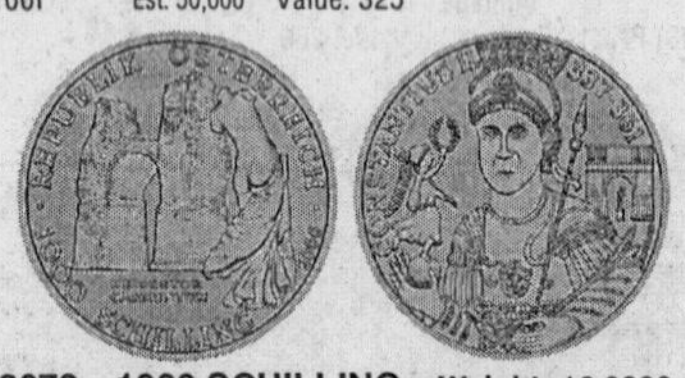

KM# 3072 1000 SCHILLING **Weight:** 16.0000 g. **Composition:** 0.9860 Gold .5027 oz. AGW **Obverse:** Heidentor ancient gate and statue **Reverse:** Constantius II portrait **Edge:** Reeded

Date	Mintage	F	VF	XF	Unc	BU
2000	30,000	—	—	—	325	—

KM# 3081 1000 SCHILLING **Weight:** 16.0000 g. **Composition:** 0.9860 Gold .5072 oz. AGW **Subject:** Austrian National Library **Obverse:** Archduke Maximilian as a student **Reverse:** Library interior view **Edge:** Reeded **Size:** 30 mm.

Date	Mintage	F	VF	XF	Unc	BU
2001	30,000	—	—	—	325	—

KM# 2990 2000 SCHILLING **Weight:** 31.1035 g. **Composition:** 0.9999 Gold 1.0002 oz. AGW **Series:** Vienna Philharmonic Orchestra

Date	Mintage	F	VF	XF	Unc	BU
1989	351,000	—	—	—	BV+4%	—
1990	484,000	—	—	—	BV+4%	—
1991	233,000	—	—	—	BV+4%	—
1992	537,000	—	—	—	BV+4%	—
1993	235,000	—	—	—	BV+4%	—
1994	218,000	—	—	—	BV+4%	—
1995	645,000	—	—	—	BV+4%	—
1996	377,000	—	—	—	BV+4%	—
1997	408,000	—	—	—	BV+4%	—

Date	Mintage	F	VF	XF	Unc	BU
1998	—	—	—	—	BV+4%	—
1999	—	—	—	—	BV+4%	—

EURO COINAGE

European Economic Community Issues

KM# 3082 EURO CENT **Weight:** 2.2700 g. **Composition:** Copper Plated Steel **Subject:** Euro Coinage **Obverse:** Flower **Reverse:** Denomination and globe **Edge:** Plain **Size:** 16.2 mm.

Date	F	VF	XF	Unc	BU
2002	—	—	—	0.35	—

KM# 3083 2 EURO CENTS **Weight:** 3.0300 g. **Composition:** Copper Plated Steel **Subject:** Euro Coinage **Obverse:** Flower in inner circle, stars in outer circle **Reverse:** Denomination and globe **Edge:** Grooved **Size:** 18.7 mm.

Date	F	VF	XF	Unc	BU
2002	—	—	—	0.50	—

KM# 3084 5 EURO CENTS **Weight:** 3.8600 g. **Composition:** Copper Plated Steel **Subject:** Euro Coinage **Obverse:** Flower in inner ring, stars in outer ring **Reverse:** Denomination and globe **Edge:** Plain **Size:** 21.2 mm.

Date	F	VF	XF	Unc	BU
2002	—	—	—	0.75	—

KM# 3085 10 EURO CENTS **Weight:** 4.0700 g. **Composition:** Brass **Subject:** Euro Coinage **Obverse:** Church steeples **Reverse:** Denomination and map **Edge:** Reeded **Size:** 19.7 mm.

Date	F	VF	XF	Unc	BU
2002	—	—	—	0.75	—

KM# 3086 20 EURO CENTS **Weight:** 5.7300 g. **Composition:** Brass **Subject:** Euro Coinage **Obverse:** Palace gate **Reverse:** Denomination and map **Edge:** Notched **Size:** 22.1 mm.

Date	F	VF	XF	Unc	BU
2002	—	—	—	1.00	—

KM# 3087 50 EURO CENTS **Weight:** 7.8100 g. **Composition:** Brass **Subject:** Euro Coinage **Obverse:** Building entrance **Reverse:** Denomination and map **Edge:** Reeded **Size:** 24.2 mm.

Date	F	VF	XF	Unc	BU
2002	—	—	—	1.25	—

KM# 3088 EURO **Ring Composition:** Brass**Center Weight:** 7.5000 g. **Center Composition:** Copper-Nickel **Subject:** Euro Coinage **Obverse:** Bust of Mozart right within inner circle, stars in outer circle **Reverse:** Denomination and map **Edge:** Reeded and plain sections **Size:** 23.2 mm.

Date	F	VF	XF	Unc	BU
2002	—	—	—	2.50	—

KM# 3089 2 EUROS **Ring Composition:** Copper-Nickel**Center Weight:** 8.5200 g. **Center Composition:** Brass **Subject:** Euro Coinage **Obverse:** Bust of Bertha von Suttner at right facing left in inner circle, stars in outer circle **Reverse:** Denomination and map **Edge:** Reeded **Size:** 25.7 mm.

Date	F	VF	XF	Unc	BU
2002	—	—	—	3.75	—

KM# 3091 5 EURO **Weight:** 8.0000 g. **Composition:** 0.8000 Silver 0.2058 oz. ASW **Subject:** Schoenbrunn Zoo **Obverse:** Circle of provincial arms around denomination **Reverse:** Building and animals **Edge:** Plain, nine-sided **Size:** 29 mm.

Date	Mintage	F	VF	XF	Unc	BU
ND(2002) Special Unc	100,000	—	—	—	9.00	—
ND(2002)	500,000	—	—	—	6.50	—

KM# 3092 10 EURO **Weight:** 3.1210 g. **Composition:** 0.9999 Gold 0.1003 oz. AGW **Subject:** Vienna Philharmonic **Obverse:** The Golden Hall organ **Reverse:** Musical instruments **Edge:** Segmented reeding **Size:** 16 mm.

Date	F	VF	XF	Unc	BU
2002	—	—	—	BV+13%	—

KM# 3096 10 EURO **Weight:** 16.0000 g. **Composition:** 0.9250 Silver 0.4758 oz. ASW **Subject:** Ambras Palace **Obverse:** Palace **Reverse:** Three strolling musicians **Edge:** Reeded **Size:** 32 mm.

Date	Mintage	F	VF	XF	Unc	BU
2002	130,000	—	—	—	15.00	—
2002 Special Unc	20,000	—	—	—	30.00	—
2002 Proof	50,000	Value: 40.00				

KM# 3099 10 EURO **Weight:** 16.0000 g. **Composition:** 0.9250 Silver 0.4758 oz. ASW **Subject:** Eggenberg Palace and Johannes kepler **Obverse:** Palace **Reverse:** Portrait **Edge:** Reeded **Size:** 32 mm.

Date	Mintage	F	VF	XF	Unc	BU
2002	20,000	—	—	—	20.00	—
2002 Proof	50,000	Value: 28.00				

KM# 3097 20 EURO **Weight:** 18.0000 g. **Composition:** 0.9000 Silver 0.5208 oz. ASW **Subject:** Ferdinand I - Renaissance **Obverse:** Hofburg Palace "Swiss Gate" with two guards **Reverse:** Ferdinand I and coat of arms **Edge:** Reeded **Size:** 34 mm.

Date	Mintage	F	VF	XF	Unc	BU
2002 Proof	50,000	Value: 37.50				

KM# 3098 20 EURO **Weight:** 18.0000 g. **Composition:** 0.9000 Silver 0.5208 oz. ASW **Subject:** Prince Eugen - Baroque Period **Obverse:** Baroque staircase with statues **Reverse:** Portrait **Edge:** Reeded **Size:** 34 mm.

Date	Mintage	F	VF	XF	Unc	BU
2002 Proof	50,000	Value: 40.00				

KM# 3093 25 EURO **Weight:** 7.7760 g. **Composition:** 0.9999 Gold 0.25 oz. AGW **Subject:** Vienna Philharmonic **Obverse:** The Golden Hall organ **Reverse:** Musical instruments **Edge:** Segmented reeding **Size:** 22 mm.

Date	F	VF	XF	Unc	BU
2002	—	—	—	BV+10%	—

KM# 3094 50 EURO **Weight:** 15.5520 g. **Composition:** 0.9999 Gold 0.5 oz. AGW **Subject:** Vienna Philharmonic **Obverse:** The Golden Hall organ **Reverse:** Musical instruments **Edge:** Segmented reeding **Size:** 28 mm.

Date	F	VF	XF	Unc	BU
2002	—	—	—	BV+8%	—

KM# 3095 100 EURO **Weight:** 31.1035 g. **Composition:** 0.9999 Gold 0.9999 oz. AGW **Subject:** Vienna Philharmonic **Obverse:** The Golden Hall organ **Reverse:** Musical instruments **Edge:** Segmented reeding **Size:** 37 mm.

Date	F	VF	XF	Unc	BU
2002	—	—	—	BV+4%	—

KM# 3100 100 EURO **Weight:** 16.0000 g. **Composition:** 0.9860 Gold 0.5072 oz. AGW **Subject:** Raphael Donner **Obverse:** Portrait in front of building **Reverse:** Providentia Fountain **Edge:** Reeded **Size:** 30 mm.

Date	Mintage	F	VF	XF	Unc	BU
2002	30,000	—	—	—	325	—

PATTERNS

Including off metal strikes

KM#	Date	Mintage	Identification	Mkt Val
Pn68	1908	—	100 Kronen. Without mm.	—
Pn69	1909	—	100 Kronen. Without mm.	—
Pn70	1910	—	2 Kronen. Silver. Similar to KM#2821.	2,350
Pn72	1913	—	2 Corona. Aluminum. KM#2821.	200
Pn73	ND	—	50 Heller. Iron.	235
Pn71	1913	—	Krone. Aluminum. KM#2820.	—
Pn74	1914	—	Heller. Copper. Privately produced by Karl Goetz in Munich, Germany.	150
Pn75	1914	—	Heller. Silver. Privately produced by Karl Goetz in Munich, Germany.	275
Pn78	1915	—	20 Heller. Iron. KM#2826.	450
Pn80	1915	—	Ducat. Aluminum. Plain edge.	100
Pn81	1915	—	Ducat. Copper. Reeded edge.	400
Pn76	1915	—	2 Heller. Bronze. KM#2801.	—
Pn77	1915	—	2 Heller. Iron. KM#2801.	—
Pn79	1915	—	1/2 Krone. Silver. 2.5200 g.	—
Pn83	1916	—	2 Heller. Iron.	—
Pn82	1916	—	Heller. Iron. KM#2823.	275

KM#	Date	Mintage	Identification	Mkt Val
Pn84	1916	—	10 Heller. Aluminum. KM#2825.	275
Pn85	1916	—	Krone. Aluminum. KM#2820.	145
Pn87	1917	—	10 Heller. Steel. Plain edge. 10 in square, thin planchet.	250
Pn86	1917	—	10 Heller. Steel. Plain edge. 10 in square, thick planchet.	—
Pn88	1917	—	10 Heller. Steel. Milled edge.	—
Pn89	1918	—	20 Heller. Aluminum. 20 in square.	—
Pn91	1918	—	5 Kronen. Brass.	—
Pn92	1918	—	20 Kronen. Copper.	—
Pn93	1918	—	20 Kronen. Gold.	—
Pn90	1918	—	20 Heller. Aluminum. KM#2826.	250
Pn94	ND	—	10 Schilling. Nickel.	180
Pn95	ND	—	20 Schilling. Nickel.	400
Pn96	1924	—	1/2 Schilling. KM#2839.	1,250
Pn97	1924	—	Schilling. Silver. KM#2835.	825
Pn98	1924	—	Schilling. Silver. KM#2835. KM#2835. Octagonal planchets, 1 pair.	700
Pn99	1924	—	20 Kronen. Copper. Reeded edge. KM#2830.	1,500
Pn100	1924	—	20 Kronen. Silver. Reeded edge. Uniface, KM#2830.	700
Pn101	1930	—	100 Schilling. Silver. Plain edge. KM#2842.	2,000
Pn103	1931	—	5 Groschen. Gold. KM#2846.	1,200
Pn104	1931	—	100 Schilling. Copper. KM#2842.	1,000
Pn102	1931	—	5 Groschen. Copper-Nickel.	—
Pn105	1934	—	50 Groschen. Copper-Nickel. Uniface.	—
Pn106	1934	—	50 Groschen. Copper-Nickel. Uniface.	—
Pn107	1934	—	Schilling. Copper-Nickel. Uniface.	1,750
Pn108	1934	—	Schilling. Copper-Nickel. Uniface.	1,750
Pn109	1934	—	2 Schilling. Zinc. KM#2852.	1,000
Pn110	1934	—	2 Schilling. Zinc. One side struck on octagonal planchet, KM#2852.	600
Pn111	1935	—	25 Schilling. Gold. J. Prinz.	—
Pn112	1935	—	100 Schilling. Gold. J. Prinz.	—
Pn113	1937	—	2 Schilling. Copper. KM#2859.	200
Pn114	1938	—	5 Groschen. Gold. KM#2846.	1,200
Pn115	1947	—	Schilling. Copper-Nickel. KM#2871.	500
Pn116	1959	—	Schilling. Similar to KM#2886.	850

TRIAL STRIKES

KM#	Date	Mintage	Identification	Mkt Val
TS1	1934	—	50 Groschen. Uniface.	—
TS2	1934	—	50 Groschen. Uniface.	—
TS3	ND(1973)	—	5 Schilling. Nickel.	275
TS4	ND(1973)	—	10 Schilling. Nickel.	200
TS5	ND(1973)	—	20 Schilling. Nickel.	350
TS6	ND(1984)	—	5 Groschen. Aluminum. Plain edge.	175

MINT SETS

KM#	Date	Mintage	Identification	Issue Price	Mkt Val
MS1	1992 (8)	25,000	KM#2875-2876, 2878, 2885-2886, 2889a, 2918, 2946.1	—	50.00
MS2	1993 (8)	35,000	KM#2875-2876, 2878, 2885-2886, 2889a, 2918, 2946.2	—	40.00
MS9	2000 (6)	—	KM#2878, 2885-2886, 2889a, 2918, 3064	—	22.50
MS3	1994 (8)	25,000	KM#2875-2876, 2878, 2885-2886, 2889a, 2918, 3016	—	70.00
MS4	1995 (6)	27,000	KM#2878, 2885-2886, 2889a, 2918, 3022	—	50.00
MS5	1996 (6)	25,000	KM#2878, 2885-2886, 2889a, 2918, 3033	—	35.00
MS6	1997 (6)	25,000	KM#2878, 2885-2886, 2889a, 2918, 3041	—	30.00
MS7	1998 (6)	—	KM#2878, 2885-2886, 2889a, 2918, 3048	—	22.50
MS8	1999 (6)	—	KM#2878, 2885-2886, 2889a, 2918, 3056	22.00	22.50
MS10	2001 (6)	75,000	KM#2878, 2885, 2886, 2889a, 2918, 3075	25.00	25.00

PROOF SETS

KM#	Date	Mintage	Identification	Issue Price	Mkt Val
PS1	1959 (2)	1,000	KM#2887-2888	—	725
PS2	1964 (9)	69,731	KM#2875-2876, 2878, 2882, 2885-2886, 2889, 2895.1, 2896	—	55.00
PS3	1964 (9)	2,700	KM#2875-2876, 2878, 2882, 2885-2886, 2889, 2895.2, 2896 (error set)	—	365
PS4	1964 (7)	—	KM#2875-2876, 2878, 2882, 2885-2886, 2889	—	22.50
PS5	1965 (7)	83,000	KM#2875-2876, 2878, 2882, 2885-2886, 2889	—	10.00
PS6	1965 (4)	38,000	KM#2882, 2889, 2897-2898	5.00	42.50
PS7	1966 (9)	1,765	KM#2875-2876, 2878, 2882, 2885-2886, 2889, 2899-2900	—	180
PS8	1966 (7)	—	KM#2875-2876, 2878, 2882, 2885-2886, 2889	—	60.00
PS10	1967 (7)	—	KM#2875-2876, 2878, 2882, 2885-2886, 2889	—	200
PS9	1967 (9)	1,163	KM#2875-2876, 2878, 2882, 2885-2886, 2889, 2901-2902	5.50	300
PS11	1968 (9)	15,200	KM#2875-2876, 2878, 2882, 2885-2886, 2889, 2903, 2904.1	5.75	110
PS12	1968 (7)	20,000	KM#2875-2876, 2878, 2882, 2885-2886, 2889	—	65.00
PS13	1969 (9)	20,000	KM#2875-2876, 2878, 2882, 2885-2886, 2889a, 2905-2906	7.50	90.00
PS14	1969 (7)	21,000	KM#2875-2876, 2878, 2882, 2885-2886, 2889a	—	50.00
PS15	1970 (9)	—	KM#2875-2876, 2878, 2882, 2885-2886, 2889a, 2907-2908	8.25	35.00
PS16	1970 (9)	—	KM#2875-2876, 2878, 2882, 2885-2886, 2889a, 2907, 2909	8.25	35.00
PS17	1970 (7)	92,000	KM#2875-2876, 2878, 2882, 2885-2886, 2889a	—	8.50
PS18	1970 (3)	—	KM#2907-2909	7.00	25.00
PS19	1971 (9)	—	KM#2875-2876, 2878, 2882, 2885-2886, 2889a, 2910-2911	8.25	28.00
PS20	1971 (7)	84,000	KM#2875-2876, 2878, 2882, 2885-2886, 2889a	—	8.50
PS21	1972 (9)	—	KM#2875-2876, 2878, 2882, 2885-2886, 2889a, 2912-2913	8.50	25.00
PS22	1972 (9)	—	KM#2875-2876, 2878, 2882, 2885-2886, 2889a, 2912, 2914	8.50	25.00
PS23	1972 (7)	75,000	KM#2875-2876, 2878, 2882, 2885-2886, 2889a	—	8.50
PS24	1972 (3)	—	KM#2912-2914	7.50	22.50
PS27	1972 (3)	—	KM#2912-2914	—	22.50
PS25	1973 (9)	—	KM#2875-2876, 2878, 2882, 2885-2886, 289a, 2915-2916	—	25.00
PS26	1973 (7)	87,000	KM#2875-2876, 2878, 2882, 2885-2886, 2889a	—	10.00
PS28	1974 (12)	—	KM#2875-2876, 2878, 2885-2886, 2889a, 2918-2922, 2926	29.70	55.00
PS29	1974 (8)	—	KM#2875-2876, 2878, 2885-2886, 2889a, 2918, 2921	—	20.00
PS30	1974 (7)	76,000	KM#2875-2876, 2878, 2885-2886, 2889a, 2918	—	8.50
PS31	1974 (5)	—	KM#2919-2922, 2926	27.00	42.00
PS32	1975 (10)	—	KM#2875-2876, 2878, 2885-2886, 289a, 2918, 2923-2925	30.00	45.00
PS34	1975 (3)	—	KM#2923-2925	27.00	35.00
PS33	1975 (7)	49,000	KM#2875-2876, 2878, 2885-2886, 2889a, 2918	—	8.50
PS37	1976-1977 (6)	—	KM#2930-2932, 2934-2936	27.00	85.00
PS35	1976 (7)	44,000	KM#2875-2876, 2878, 2885-2886, 2889a, 2918	3.00	9.50
PS36	1977 (7)	44,000	KM#2875-2876, 2878, 2885-2886, 2889a, 2918	3.15	8.50
PS38	1978 (7)	43,000	KM#2875-2876, 2878, 2885-2886, 2889a, 2918	—	9.50
PS39	1979 (7)	44,000	KM#2875-2876, 2878, 2885-2886, 2889a, 2918	—	9.50
PS40	1980 (8)	48,000	KM#2875-2876, 2878, 2885-2886, 2889a, 2918, 2946	—	28.00
PS42	1981 (8)	49,000	KM#2875-2876, 2878, 2885-2886, 2889a, 2918, 2946.1	—	28.00
PS43	1982 (8)	50,000	KM#2875-2876, 2878, 2885-2886, 2889a, 2918, 2955.1	—	14.00
PS44	1983 (8)	65,000	KM#2875-2876, 2878, 2885-2886, 2889a, 2918, 2960.1	—	12.50
PS45	1984 (8)	65,000	KM#2875-2876, 2878, 2885-2886, 2889a, 2918, 2965.1	—	12.50
PS46	1985 (8)	45,000	KM#2875-2876, 2878, 2885-2886, 2889a, 2918, 2970.1	—	20.00
PS47	1986 (8)	42,000	KM#2875-2876, 2878, 2885-2886, 2889a, 2918, 2975.1	—	30.00
PS48	1987 (8)	42,000	KM#2875-2876, 2878, 2885-2886, 2889a, 2918, 2980.1	—	22.00
PS49	1988 (7)	39,000	KM#2875-2876, 2878, 2885-2886, 2889a, 2918	—	12.50
PS50	1989 (8)	38,000	KM#2875-2876, 2878, 2885-2886, 2889a, 2918, 2988.1	—	17.50
PS51	1990 (8)	35,000	KM#2875-2876, 2878, 2885-2886, 2889a, 2918, 2993.1	—	42.50
PS52	1991 (8)	27,000	KM#2875-2876, 2878, 2885-2886, 2889a, 2918, 2995.1	—	22.00
PS53	1992 (8)	25,000	KM#2875-2876, 2878, 2885-2886, 2889a, 2918, 2946.1	—	45.00
PS54	1993 (8)	28,000	KM#2875-2876, 2878, 2885-2886, 2889a, 2918, 2946.2	—	35.00
PS55	1994 (8)	25,000	KM#2875-2876, 2878, 2885-2886, 2889a, 2918, 3016	—	75.00
PS56	1995 (6)	27,000	KM#2878, 2885, 2886, 2889a, 2918, 3022	—	37.50
PS57	1996 (6)	25,000	KM#2878, 2885, 2886, 2889a, 2918, 3033	—	45.00
PS58	1997	25,000	KM#2878, 2885, 2886, 2889a, 2918, 3041	—	50.00
PS59	1998 (6)	25,000	KM#2878, 2885, 2886, 2889a, 2918, 3048	—	60.00
PS60	1999 (6)	25,000	KM#2878, 2885, 2886, 2889a, 2918, 3056	—	27.50
PS61	2000 (6)	—	KM#2878, 2885, 2886, 2889a, 2918, 3064	—	27.50

AZERBAIJAN

The Republic of Azerbaijan (formerly Azerbaijan S.S.R.) includes the Nakhichevan Autonomous Republic. Situated in the eastern area of Transcaucasia, it is bordered in the west by Armenia, in the north by Georgia and Dagestan, to the east by the Caspian Sea and to the south by Iran. It has an area of 33,430 sq. mi. (86,600 sq. km.) and a population of 7.8 million. Capital: Baku. The area is rich in mineral deposits of aluminum, copper, iron, lead, salt and zinc, with oil as its leading industry. Agriculture and livestock follow in importance.

Ancient home of Scythian tribes and known under the Romans as Albania and to the Arabs as Arran, the country of Azerbaijan was formed at the time of its invasion by Seliuk Turks and grew into a prosperous state under Persian suzerainty. From the 16th century the country was a theatre of fighting and political rivalry between Turkey, Persia and later Russia. Baku was first annexed to Russia by Czar Peter I in 1723 and remained under Russian rule for 12 years. After the Russian retreat the whole of Azerbaijan north of the Aras River became a khanate under Persian control. Czar Alexander I, after an eight-year war with Persia, annexed it in 1813 to the Russian empire.

Until the Russian Revolution of 1905, there was no political life in Azerbaijan. A Mussavat (Equality) party was formed in 1911 by Mohammed Emin, Rasulzade, a former Social Democrat. After the Russian Revolution of March 1917, the party started a campaign for independence. Baku, however, the capital with its mixed population, constituted an alien enclave in the country While a national Azerbaijani government was established at Gandzha (Elizavetpol), a Communist controlled council assumed power at Baku with Stepan Shaumian, an Armenian, at its head. The Gandzha government joined first, on Sept. 20, 1917, a Transcaucasian federal republic, but on May 28, 1918, proclaimed the independence of Azerbaijan. On June 4, 1918, at Batum, a peace treaty was signed with Turkey. Turko-Azerbaijani forces started an offensive against Baku, occupied since Aug. 17, 1918 by 1,400 British troops coming by sea from Anzali, Persia. On Sept. 14 the British evacuated Baku, returning to Anzali, and three days later the Azerbaijan government, headed by Fath Khoysky, established itself at Baku.

After the collapse of the Ottoman Empire, the British returned to Baku, at first ignoring the Azerbaijan government. A general election with universal suffrage for the Azerbaijan constituent assembly took place on Dec. 7, 1918 and out of 120 members there were 84 Mussavat supporters. On Jan. 15, 1920, the Allied powers recognized Azerbaijan de facto, but on April 27 of the same year the Red army invaded the country, and a Soviet republic of Azerbaijan was proclaimed the next day. Later it became a member of the Transcaucasian Federation joining the U.S.S.R. on Dec. 30, 1922, it became a self-constituent republic in 1936.

The Azerbaijan Communist party held its first congress at Baku in Feb. 1920. From 1921 to 1925 its first secretary was a Russian, S.M. Kirov, who directed a mass deportation to Siberia of about 120,000 Azerbaijani "nationalist deviationists," among them the country's first two premiers.

In 1990 it adopted a declaration of republican sovereignty and in Aug. 1991 declared itself formally independent. This action was approved by a vote of referendum in Jan. 1992. It announced its intention of joining the CIS in Dec. 1991, but a parliamentary resolution of Oct. 1992 declined to confirm its involvement. On Sept. 20, 1993, Azerbaijan became a member of the CIS. Communist President Mutaibov was relieved of his office in May 1992. On June 7, in the first democratic election in the country's history, a National Council replaced Mutaibov with Abulfez Elchibey. Surat Huseynov led a military coup against Elchibey and seized power on June 30, 1993. Huseynov became prime minister with former communist Geidar Aliyev, president.

Fighting commenced between Muslim forces of Azerbaijan and Christian forces of Armenia in 1992 and continued through early 1994. Each faction claimed the Nagorno-Karabakh, an Armenian ethnic enclave, in Azerbaijan. A cease-fire was declared in May 1994.

MINTNAMES

Genge (Elisabethpol, Kirovabad)
Nackhchawan
Shamakhi
Shirvan

MONETARY SYSTEM

100 Qapik = 1 Manat

REPUBLIC

DECIMAL COINAGE

KM# 1 5 QAPIK Composition: Brass

Date	F	VF	XF	Unc	BU
1992	—	—	2.00	4.00	—

KM# 1a 5 QAPIK Composition: Aluminum

Date	F	VF	XF	Unc	BU
1993	—	—	—	1.00	—

KM# 2 10 QAPIK Composition: Copper Nickel **Obverse:** Denomination **Reverse:** Star with date

Date	F	VF	XF	Unc	BU
1992	—	—	1.00	2.00	—

KM# 2a 10 QAPIK Composition: Aluminum **Obverse:** Denomination **Reverse:** Star with date

Date	F	VF	XF	Unc	BU
1992	—	—	—	0.50	—

KM# 3 20 QAPIK Composition: Brass

Date	F	VF	XF	Unc	BU
1992	—	—	1.00	2.00	—
1993	—	—	1.00	2.00	—

KM# 3a 20 QAPIK Composition: Aluminum **Note:** Varieties in spelling of Respublikas exist.

Date	F	VF	XF	Unc	BU
1992	—	—	—	0.75	—
1993	—	—	—	0.75	—

Note: Two die varieties exist

KM# 4 50 QAPIK Composition: Copper-Nickel **Obverse:** Maiden tower ruins

Date	F	VF	XF	Unc	BU
1992	—	—	1.50	3.50	—
1994	—	—	1.50	3.50	—

KM# 4a 50 QAPIK Composition: Aluminum

Date	F	VF	XF	Unc	BU
1992	—	—	—	1.25	—
1993	—	—	—	0.75	—

KM# 5 50 MANAT Weight: 28.2800 g. **Composition:** 0.9250 Silver .8411 oz. ASW **Subject:** 500th Anniversary Mehemmed Fuzuli **Obverse:** Deer by man comforting fallen comrade **Reverse:** Portrait of Fuzuli

Date	Mintage	F	VF	XF	Unc	BU
1996 Proof	5,000	Value: 65.00				

KM# 6 100 MANAT Weight: 7.9800 g. **Composition:** 0.9167 Gold .2354 oz. AGW **Subject:** 500th Anniversary Mehemmed Fuzuli **Obverse:** Deer by man comforting fallen comrade **Reverse:** Portrait of Fuzuli

Date	Mintage	F	VF	XF	Unc	BU
1996 Proof	500	Value: 325				

AZORES

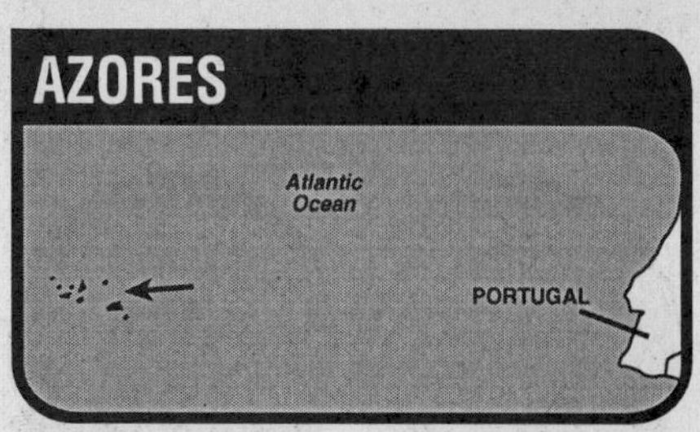

The Azores, an archipelago of nine islands of volcanic origin, are located in the Atlantic Ocean 740 miles (1,190 km.) west of Cape de Roca, Portugal. They are the westernmost region of Europe under the administration of Portugal and have an area of 902 sq. mi. (2,305 sq. km.) and a population of 236,000. Principal city: Ponta Delgada. The natives are mainly of Portuguese descent and earn their livelihood by fishing, wine making, basket weaving and the growing of fruit, grains and sugar cane. Pineapples are the chief item of export. The climate is particularly temperate, making the islands a favorite winter resort.

The Azores were discovered about 1427 by the Portuguese navigator Diogo de Sevill. Portugal secured the islands in the 15th century and established the first settlement on Santa Maria about 1439. From 1580 to 1640 the Azores were subject to Spain.

The Azores' first provincial coinage was ordered by law of August 19, 1750. Copper coins were struck for circulation in both the Azores and Madeira Islands. Keeping the same technical specifications but with different designs. In 1795 a second provincial coinage was introduced but the weight was reduced by 50 percent.

Angra on Terceira Island became the capital of the captaincy-general of the Azores in 1766 and it was here in 1826 that the constitutionalists set up a pro-Pedro government in opposition to King Miguel in Lisbon. The whole Portuguese fleet attacked Terceira and was repelled at Praia, after which Azoreans, Brazilians and British mercenaries defeated Miguel in Portugal. Maria de Gloria, Pedro's daughter, was proclaimed queen of Portugal on Terceira in 1828.

A U.S. naval base was established at Ponta Delgada in 1917.

After World War II, the islands acquired a renewed importance as a refueling stop for transatlantic air transport. The United States maintains defense bases in the Azores as part of the collective security program of NATO.

In 1976 the archipelago became the Autonomous Region of Azores.

RULERS

Portuguese

MONETARY SYSTEM

1000 Reis (Insulanos) = 1 Milreis

PORTUGUESE ADMINISTRATION

PROVINCIAL COINAGE

KM# 16 5 REIS Composition: Copper **Subject:** Carlos I

Date	Mintage	F	VF	XF	Unc	BU
1901	800,000	1.75	3.50	9.00	25.00	—

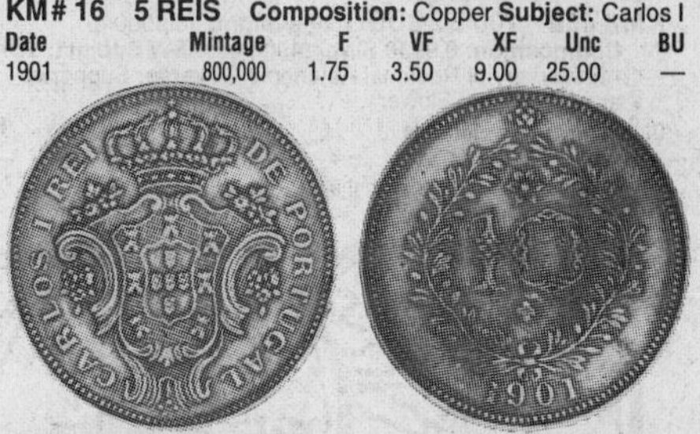

KM# 17 10 REIS Composition: Copper **Subject:** Carlos I

Date	Mintage	F	VF	XF	Unc	BU
1901	600,000	2.00	4.00	10.00	28.00	—

REPUBLIC

DECIMAL COINAGE

KM# 43 25 ESCUDOS Composition: Copper-Nickel **Subject:** Regional Autonomy **Obverse:** Shields above denomination, stars below **Reverse:** Supported arms

Date	Mintage	F	VF	XF	Unc	BU
1980	770,000	—	—	2.50	5.00	—

KM# 43a 25 ESCUDOS Weight: 11.0000 g. **Composition:** 0.9250 Silver .3272 oz. ASW **Subject:** Regional Autonomy **Obverse:** Shields above denomination, stars below **Reverse:** Supported arms

Date	Mintage	F	VF	XF	Unc	BU
1980 Proof	12,000	Value: 22.00				

KM# 44 100 ESCUDOS Composition: Copper-Nickel **Subject:** Regional Autonomy **Obverse:** Shields above denomination, stars below **Reverse:** Supported arms

Date	Mintage	F	VF	XF	Unc	BU
1980	270,000	—	—	4.50	10.00	—

KM# 44a 100 ESCUDOS Weight: 16.5000 g. **Composition:** 0.9250 Silver .4908 oz. ASW **Subject:** Regional Autonomy **Obverse:** Shields above denomination, stars below **Reverse:** Supported arms

Date	Mintage	F	VF	XF	Unc	BU
1980 Proof	12,000	Value: 42.50				

KM# 45 100 ESCUDOS Composition: Copper-Nickel **Subject:** 10th Anniversary of Regional Autonomy **Obverse:** Supported arms **Reverse:** Flower

Date	Mintage	F	VF	XF	Unc	BU
1986	750,000	—	—	—	6.50	—

KM# 45a 100 ESCUDOS Weight: 16.5000 g. **Composition:** 0.9250 Silver .4908 oz. ASW **Subject:** 10th Anniversary of Regional Autonomy **Obverse:** Supported arms **Reverse:** Flower

Date	Mintage	F	VF	XF	Unc	BU
1986	20,000	—	—	—	25.00	—
1986 Proof	10,000	Value: 35.00				

KM# 46 100 ESCUDOS Composition: Copper-Nickel **Subject:** 100th Anniversary - Death of Poet Antero de Quental **Obverse:** Offered hand with radiant sun behind, shield of arms below left **Reverse:** Bust of Antero de Quental facing

Date	Mintage	F	VF	XF	Unc	BU
1991	750,000	—	—	—	5.00	—

KM# 46a 100 ESCUDOS Weight: 18.5000 g. **Composition:** 0.9250 Silver .5503 oz. ASW **Subject:** 100th Anniversary - Death of Poet Antero de Quental **Obverse:** Offered hand with radiant sun behind, shield of arms below left **Reverse:** Bust of Antero de Quental facing **Size:** 36 mm.

Date	Mintage	F	VF	XF	Unc	BU
1991	20,000	—	—	—	30.00	—

KM# 46b 100 ESCUDOS Weight: 18.5000 g. **Composition:** 0.9250 Silver .5503 oz. ASW **Subject:** 100th Anniversary - Death of Poet Antero de Quental **Obverse:** Offered hand with radiant sun behind, shield of arms below left **Reverse:** Bust of Antero de Quental facing **Size:** 26 mm.

Date	Mintage	F	VF	XF	Unc	BU
1991 Proof	30,000	Value: 40.00				

KM# 47 100 ESCUDOS Composition: Copper-Nickel **Subject:** Centennial of Azorean Autonomy **Reverse:** Goshawk with wings spread below dates, 1895 above 1995

Date	Mintage	F	VF	XF	Unc	BU
ND(1995)	500,000	—	—	—	5.00	—

KM# 47a 100 ESCUDOS Weight: 18.5000 g. **Composition:** 0.9250 Silver .5502 oz. ASW **Subject:** Centennial of Azorean Autonomy **Reverse:** Goshawk with wings spread below dates, 1895 over 1995

Date	Mintage	F	VF	XF	Unc	BU
ND(1995)	5,000	—	—	—	35.00	—
ND(1995) Proof	10,000	Value: 50.00				

PATTERNS

Including off metal strikes

KM#	Date	Mintage	Identification	Mkt Val
Pn5	1901	—	5 Reis. Aluminum.	725
Pn6	1901	—	10 Reis. Aluminum.	725

PROVAS

KM#	Date	Mintage	Identification	Mkt Val
Pr1	1980	—	25 Escudos. Copper-Nickel. Incuse PROVA.	150

KM#	Date	Mintage	Identification	Mkt Val
Pr2	1980	—	100 Escudos. Copper-Nickel. Incuse PROVA.	175
Pr3	1986	—	100 Escudos. Copper-Nickel. Incuse PROVA.	175

PROOF SETS

KM#	Date	Mintage	Identification	Issue Price	Mkt Val
PS1	1980 (2)	12,000	KM43a-44a	40.00	70.00

BAHAMAS

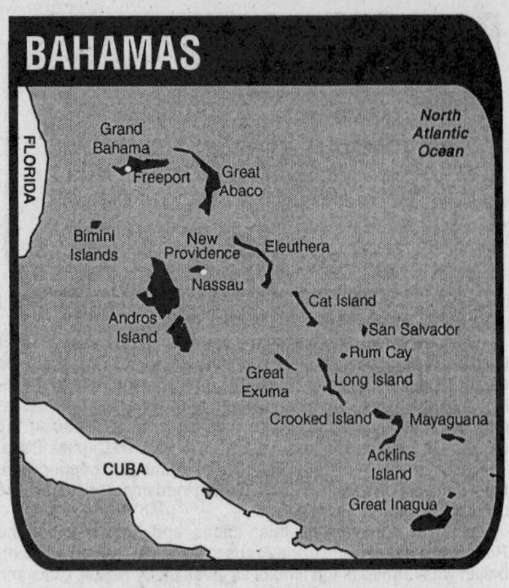

The Commonwealth of the Bahamas is an archipelago of about 3,000 islands, cays and rocks located in the Atlantic Ocean east of Florida and north of Cuba. The total land area of the 800 mile (1,287 km.) long chain of islands is 5,382 sq. mi. (13,935 sq. km.). They have a population of 302,000. Capital: Nassau. The Bahamas import most of their food and manufactured products and export cement, refined oil, pulpwood and lobsters. Tourism is the principal industry.

The Bahamas were discovered by Columbus October, 1492, upon his sighting of the island of San Salvador, but Spain made no attempt to settle them. British influence began in 1626 when Charles I granted them to the lord proprietors of Carolina, with settlements in 1629 at New Providence by colonists from the northern territory. Although the Bahamas were temporarily under Spanish control in 1641 and 1703, they continued under British proprietors until 1717, when, as the result of political and economic mismanagement, the civil and military governments were surrendered to the King and the islands designated a British Crown Colony. Full international agreement on British possession of the islands resulted from the Treaty of Versailles in 1783. The Bahamas obtained complete internal self-government under the constitution of Jan. 7, 1964. Full independence was achieved on July 10, 1973. The Bahamas is a member of the Caribbean community and the common market. Elizabeth II is Head of State, as Queen of the United Kingdom and is represented by a governor general.

The coinage of Great Britain was legal tender in the Bahamas from 1825 to the issuing of a definitive coinage in 1966.

RULERS

British

MINT MARKS

Through 1969 all decimal coinage of the Bahamas was executed at the Royal Mint in England. Since that time issues have been struck at both the Royal Mint and at the Franklin Mint (FM) in the U.S.A. While the mint mark of the latter appears on coins dated 1971 and subsequently, it is missing from the 1970 issues.

JP – John Pinches, London
None - Royal Mint
(t) - Tower of London
FM - Franklin Mint, U.S.A.

***NOTE:** From 1975-1985 the Franklin Mint produced coinage in up to 3 different qualities. Qualities of issue are designated in ( ) after each date and are defined as follows:

(M) MATTE - Normal circulation strike or a dull finish produced by sandblasting special uncirculated (polish finish) or proof quality dies.

(U) SPECIAL UNCIRCULATED - Polished or proof-like in appearance without any frosted features.

(P) PROOF - The highest quality obtainable having mirror-like fields and frosted features.

MONETARY SYSTEM

12 Pence = 1 Shilling

COMMONWEALTH

DECIMAL COINAGE

100 Cents = 1 Dollar

KM# 2 CENT Composition: Nickel-Brass **Reverse:** Starfish

Date	Mintage	F	VF	XF	Unc	BU
1966	7,312,000	—	—	0.10	0.50	—
1968	800,000	—	—	0.25	0.75	—
1969	4,036,000	—	—	0.10	0.50	—
1969 Proof	10,000	Value: 0.50				

KM# 15 CENT **Composition:** Bronze **Note:** Proof specimens of this date are struck in "special brass" which looks like a pale bronze.

Date	Mintage	F	VF	XF	Unc	BU
1970	125,000	—	0.10	0.25	0.50	1.00
1970 Proof	23,000	Value: 0.50				

KM# 16 CENT **Composition:** Brass

Date	Mintage	F	VF	XF	Unc	BU
1971FM	1,007,000	—	—	0.10	0.25	0.75
1971FM (P)	31,000	Value: 0.50				
1972FM	1,037,000	—	—	0.10	0.25	0.75
1972FM (P)	35,000	Value: 0.50				
1973	7,000,000	—	—	0.10	0.25	0.75
1973FM	1,040,000	—	—	0.10	0.25	0.75
1973FM (P)	35,000	Value: 0.50				

KM# 59 CENT **Composition:** Brass

Date	Mintage	F	VF	XF	Unc	BU
1974	11,000	—	—	0.20	0.40	1.00
1974FM	71,000	—	—	0.10	0.25	0.75
1974FM (P)	94,000	Value: 0.50				
1975FM (M)	60,000	—	—	0.10	0.25	0.75
1975FM (U)	3,845	—	—	0.10	0.50	1.00
1975FM (P)	29,000	Value: 0.50				
1976FM (M)	60,000	—	—	0.10	0.25	0.75
1976FM (U)	1,453	—	—	0.10	0.50	1.00
1976FM (P)	23,000	Value: 0.50				
1977	3,000,000	—	—	0.10	0.25	0.75
1977FM (M)	60,000	—	—	0.10	0.25	0.75
1977FM (U)	713	—	—	0.50	1.50	2.50
1977FM (P)	11,000	Value: 0.50				
1978FM (M)	60,000	—	—	0.10	0.25	0.75
1978FM (U)	767	—	—	0.50	1.50	2.50
1978FM (P)	6,931	Value: 0.75				
1979	—	—	—	0.10	0.25	0.75
1979FM (P)	2,053	Value: 1.00				
1980	4,000,000	—	—	0.10	0.25	0.75
1980FM (P)	2,084	Value: 1.00				
1981	5,000,000	—	—	0.10	0.25	0.75
1981FM (M)	—	—	—	0.10	0.25	0.75
1981FM (P)	1,980	Value: 1.00				
1982	5,000,000	—	—	0.10	0.25	0.75
1982FM (M)	—	—	—	0.10	0.25	0.75
1982FM (P)	1,217	Value: 1.00				
1983	8,000,000	—	—	0.10	0.25	0.75
1983FM (P)	1,020	Value: 1.00				
1984	—	—	—	0.10	0.25	0.75
1984FM (P)	7,500	Value: 0.75				
1985	12,000,000	—	—	0.10	0.25	0.75
1985FM (P)	7,500	Value: 0.50				

KM# 59a CENT **Composition:** Copper Plated Zinc

Date	Mintage	F	VF	XF	Unc	BU
1985	—	—	—	0.10	0.25	0.75
1987	12,000,000	—	—	0.10	0.25	0.75
1989	12,000,000	—	—	0.10	0.25	0.75
1989 Proof	—	Value: 1.00				
1990	—	—	—	0.10	0.25	0.75
1991	—	—	—	0.10	0.25	0.75
1992	—	—	—	0.10	0.25	0.75
1995	—	—	—	0.10	0.25	0.75
1997	—	—	—	0.10	0.25	0.75
1998	—	—	—	0.10	0.25	0.75
1999	—	—	—	0.10	0.25	0.75

KM# 3 5 CENTS **Composition:** Copper-Nickel **Reverse:** Pineapple **Note:** The obverse of this coin also comes muled with the reverse of a New Zealand 2-cent piece, KM#32. The undated 1967 error is listed as New Zealand KM#33.

Date	Mintage	F	VF	XF	Unc	BU
1966	2,571,000	—	—	0.10	0.25	—
1968	600,000	—	—	0.10	0.30	—
1969	2,026,000	—	—	0.10	0.25	—
1969 Proof	75,000	Value: 0.50				
1970	26,000	—	—	0.30	0.60	—
1970 Proof	23,000	Value: 0.75				

KM# 17 5 CENTS **Composition:** Copper-Nickel

Date	Mintage	F	VF	XF	Unc	BU
1971FM	13,000	—	—	0.15	0.40	—
1971FM (P)	31,000	Value: 0.50				
1972FM	11,000	—	—	0.15	0.40	—
1972FM (P)	35,000	Value: 0.50				
1973FM	21,000	—	—	0.15	0.40	—
1973FM (P)	35,000	Value: 0.50				

KM# 38 5 CENTS **Composition:** Copper-Nickel **Obv. Legend:** THE COMMONWEALTH OF THE BAHAMAS

Date	Mintage	F	VF	XF	Unc	BU
1973	1,000,000	—	—	0.10	0.65	—

KM# 60 5 CENTS **Composition:** Copper-Nickel

Date	Mintage	F	VF	XF	Unc	BU
1974FM	23,000	—	—	0.10	0.25	—
1974FM (P)	94,000	Value: 0.50				
1975	—	—	—	0.10	0.30	—
1975FM (M)	12,000	—	—	0.10	0.25	—
1975FM (U)	3,845	—	—	0.15	0.50	—
1975FM (P)	29,000	Value: 0.50				
1976FM (M)	12,000	—	—	0.10	0.25	—
1976FM (U)	1,453	—	—	0.15	0.75	—
1976FM (P)	23,000	Value: 0.50				
1977FM (M)	12,000	—	—	0.10	0.35	—
1977FM (U)	713	—	—	0.50	1.50	—
1977FM (P)	11,000	Value: 0.50				
1978FM (M)	12,000	—	—	0.10	0.35	—
1978FM (U)	767	—	—	0.50	1.50	—
1978FM (P)	6,931	Value: 0.50				
1979FM (P)	2,053	Value: 0.75				
1980FM (P)	2,084	Value: 0.75				
1981	—	—	—	0.10	0.25	—
1981FM (P)	1,980	Value: 0.75				
1982FM (P)	1,217	Value: 0.75				
1983	2,000,000	—	—	0.10	0.25	—
1983FM (P)	1,020	Value: 0.75				
1984	—	—	—	0.10	0.25	—
1984FM (P)	1,036	Value: 0.75				
1985FM (P)	7,500	Value: 0.75				
1987	4,000,000	—	—	0.10	0.25	—
1989	—	—	—	0.10	0.25	—
1989 (P)	—	Value: 0.75				
1991	—	—	—	0.10	0.25	—
1992	—	—	—	0.10	0.25	—
1998	—	—	—	0.10	0.25	—
1999	—	—	—	0.10	0.25	—
2000	—	—	—	—	—	—

KM# 4 10 CENTS **Composition:** Copper-Nickel **Reverse:** Bone Fish

Date	Mintage	F	VF	XF	Unc	BU
1966	2,198,000	—	—	0.10	0.30	—
1968	550,000	—	—	0.50	4.00	—
1969	2,026,000	—	—	0.10	0.30	—
1969 Proof	10,000	Value: 0.50				
1970	27,000	—	—	0.15	0.40	—
1970 Proof	23,000	Value: 0.50				

KM# 18 10 CENTS **Composition:** Copper-Nickel

Date	Mintage	F	VF	XF	Unc	BU
1971FM	13,000	—	—	0.15	0.50	—
1971FM (P)	31,000	Value: 0.50				
1972FM	11,000	—	—	0.15	0.50	—
1972FM (P)	35,000	Value: 0.50				
1973FM	15,000	—	—	0.15	0.50	—
1973FM (P)	35,000	Value: 0.50				

KM# 39 10 CENTS **Composition:** Copper-Nickel **Rev. Legend:** THE COMMONWEALTH OF THE BAHAMAS

Date	Mintage	F	VF	XF	Unc	BU
1973	1,000,000	—	—	0.15	0.85	—

KM# 61 10 CENTS **Composition:** Copper-Nickel

Date	Mintage	F	VF	XF	Unc	BU
1974FM	17,000	—	—	0.10	0.35	—
1974FM (P)	94,000	Value: 0.75				
1975	3,000,000	—	—	0.10	0.25	—
1975FM (M)	6,000	—	—	0.15	0.50	—
1975FM (U)	3,845	—	—	0.15	0.50	—
1975FM (P)	29,000	Value: 0.75				
1976FM (M)	6,000	—	—	0.15	0.50	—
1976FM (U)	1,453	—	—	0.25	1.00	—
1976FM (P)	23,000	Value: 0.75				
1977FM (M)	6,000	—	—	0.15	0.50	—
1977FM (U)	713	—	—	0.50	1.50	—
1977FM (P)	11,000	Value: 0.75				
1978FM (M)	6,000	—	—	0.15	0.50	—
1978FM (U)	767	—	—	0.50	1.50	—
1978FM (P)	6,931	Value: 1.00				
1979FM (P)	2,053	Value: 1.25				
1980	2,500,000	—	—	0.10	0.35	—
1980FM (P)	2,084	Value: 1.25				
1981FM (P)	1,980	Value: 1.25				
1982	2,000,000	—	—	0.10	0.35	—
1982FM (P)	1,217	Value: 1.25				
1983FM (P)	1,020	Value: 1.25				
1984FM (P)	1,036	Value: 1.25				
1985	2,000,000	—	—	0.10	0.35	—
1985FM (M)	—	—	—	0.15	0.50	—
1985FM (P)	7,500	Value: 1.00				
1987	3,000,000	—	—	0.15	0.50	—
1989	—	—	—	0.15	0.50	—
1989	—	Value: 1.00				
1991	—	—	—	0.15	0.50	—
1992	—	—	—	0.15	0.50	—
1998	—	—	—	0.15	0.50	—

KM# 5 15 CENTS **Composition:** Copper-Nickel **Reverse:** Hibiscus

Date	Mintage	F	VF	XF	Unc	BU
1966	930,000	—	—	0.20	0.75	—
1969	1,026,000	—	—	0.20	0.75	—
1969 Proof	10,000	Value: 1.00				
1970	28,000	—	—	0.25	0.75	—
1970 Proof	23,000	Value: 0.75				

KM# 19 15 CENTS **Composition:** Copper-Nickel

Date	Mintage	F	VF	XF	Unc	BU
1971FM	13,000	—	—	0.20	0.50	—
1971FM Proof	31,000	Value: 0.75				
1972FM	11,000	—	—	0.20	0.50	—
1972FM Proof	35,000	Value: 0.75				
1973FM	14,000	—	—	0.20	0.50	—
1973FM Proof	35,000	Value: 0.75				

KM# 62 15 CENTS **Composition:** Copper-Nickel

Date	Mintage	F	VF	XF	Unc	BU
1974FM	15,000	—	—	0.20	0.50	—
1974FM (P)	94,000	Value: 0.50				
1975FM (M)	3,500	—	—	0.25	1.00	—
1975FM (U)	3,845	—	—	0.25	1.00	—
1975FM (P)	29,000	Value: 0.50				
1976FM (M)	3,500	—	—	0.25	1.00	—
1976FM (U)	1,453	—	—	0.30	1.50	—
1976FM (P)	23,000	Value: 0.50				
1977FM (M)	3,500	—	—	0.25	1.00	—
1977FM (U)	713	—	—	0.50	2.00	—
1977FM (P)	11,000	Value: 0.50				
1978FM (M)	3,500	—	—	0.25	1.00	—
1978FM (U)	767	—	—	0.50	2.00	—
1978FM (P)	6,931	Value: 0.75				
1979FM (P)	2,053	Value: 1.00				
1980FM (P)	2,084	Value: 1.00				
1981FM (P)	1,980	Value: 1.00				
1982FM (P)	1,217	Value: 1.25				
1983FM (P)	1,020	Value: 1.25				
1984FM (P)	1,036	Value: 1.25				
1985FM (P)	7,500	Value: 0.75				
1989	—	—	—	0.20	0.50	—
1989 (P)	—	Value: 1.00				
1991	—	—	—	0.20	0.50	—
1992	—	—	—	0.20	0.50	—

KM# 6 25 CENTS **Composition:** Nickel **Reverse:** Bahaminian sloop

Date	Mintage	F	VF	XF	Unc	BU
1966	3,685,000	—	—	0.30	0.50	—
1969	1,026,000	—	—	0.30	0.50	—
1969	10,000	Value: 0.75				
1970	26,000	—	—	0.35	0.75	—
1970FM (P)	23,000	Value: 1.00				
1970FM (M)	—	—	—	—	—	—

KM# 20 25 CENTS **Composition:** Nickel

Date	Mintage	F	VF	XF	Unc	BU
1971FM	13,000	—	—	0.30	0.50	—
1971FM (P)	31,000	Value: 0.75				
1972FM	11,000	—	—	0.30	0.50	—
1972FM (M)	—	—	—	0.30	0.50	—

Date	Mintage	F	VF	XF	Unc	BU
1972FM (P)	35,000	Value: 0.75				
1973FM	12,000	—	—	0.30	0.50	—
1973FM (P)	35,000	Value: 0.75				

KM# 63.1 25 CENTS **Weight:** 6.9000 g. **Composition:** Nickel

Date	Mintage	F	VF	XF	Unc	BU
1974FM		—	—	0.30	0.50	—
1974FM (P)	94,000	Value: 0.75				
1975FM (M)		—	—	0.35	1.00	—
1975FM (U)		—	—	0.35	1.00	—
1975FM (P)	29,000	Value: 0.75				
1976FM (M)		—	—	0.35	1.00	—
1976FM (U)		—	—	0.35	1.25	—
1976FM (P)	23,000	Value: 0.75				
1977		—	—	0.30	0.50	—
1977FM (M)		—	—	0.35	1.00	—
1977FM (U)		—	—	0.50	3.00	—
1977FM (P)	11,000	Value: 0.75				
1978FM		—	—	0.35	1.00	—
1978FM (U)		—	—	0.50	3.00	—
1978FM (P)	6,931	Value: 1.00				
1979		—	—	0.30	0.50	—
1979FM (P)	2,053	Value: 1.25				
1980FM (P)	2,084	Value: 1.25				
1981		—	—	0.30	0.50	—
1981FM (P)	1,980	Value: 1.25				
1982FM (P)	1,217	Value: 1.50				
1983FM (P)	1,020	Value: 1.50				
1984FM (P)	1,036	Value: 1.50				
1985		—	—	0.30	0.50	—
1985FM (P)	7,500	Value: 1.00				
1987		—	—	0.30	0.50	—
1989		—	—	0.30	0.50	—
1989 (P)	—	Value: 1.25				
1991		—	—	0.30	0.50	—
1992		—	—	0.30	0.50	—
1997		—	—	0.30	0.50	—
1998		—	—	0.30	0.50	—

KM# 63.2 25 CENTS **Weight:** 5.7000 g. **Composition:** Nickel

Date	F	VF	XF	Unc	BU
1998	—	—	0.30	0.50	—
2000	—	—	0.30	0.50	—

KM# 7 50 CENTS **Weight:** 10.3700 g. **Composition:** 0.8000 Silver .2667 oz. ASW **Reverse:** Blue Marlin

Date	Mintage	F	VF	XF	Unc	BU
1966	701,000	—	BV	1.50	2.25	—
1969	26,000	—	BV	1.75	2.50	—
1969 Proof	10,000	Value: 3.00				
1970	25,000	—	BV	1.75	2.50	—
1970 Proof	23,000	Value: 3.00				

KM# 21 50 CENTS **Weight:** 10.3700 g. **Composition:** 0.8000 Silver .2667 oz. ASW

Date	Mintage	F	VF	XF	Unc	BU
1971FM	14,000	—	BV	1.75	2.50	—
1971FM (P)	31,000	Value: 3.00				
1972FM	12,000	—	BV	1.75	2.50	—
1972FM (P)	35,000	Value: 3.00				
1973FM	11,000	—	BV	1.75	2.50	—
1973FM (P)	35,000	Value: 3.00				

KM# 64 50 CENTS **Composition:** Copper-Nickel

Date	Mintage	F	VF	XF	Unc	BU
1974FM	12,000	—	—	0.60	2.00	—
1975FM (M)	1,200	—	—	1.00	8.00	—
1975FM (U)	3,828	—	—	0.65	4.00	—
1976FM (M)	1,200	—	—	0.75	5.00	—
1976FM (U)	1,453	—	—	0.65	4.00	—
1977FM (M)	1,200	—	—	0.75	5.00	—
1977FM (U)	713	—	—	1.25	10.00	—
1978FM (M)	1,200	—	—	1.00	8.00	—
1978FM (U)	767	—	—	1.25	10.00	—
1981FM (P)	1,980	Value: 3.00				
1982FM (P)	1,217	Value: 3.50				
1983FM (P)	1,020	Value: 3.50				
1984FM (P)	1,036	Value: 3.50				
1985FM (P)	7,500	Value: 2.50				
1989	—	—	—	0.75	2.00	—
1989 Proof	—	Value: 2.50				
1991	—	—	—	0.75	2.00	—
1992	—	—	—	0.75	2.00	—

KM# 64a 50 CENTS **Weight:** 10.3700 g. **Composition:** 0.8000 Silver .2667 oz. ASW

Date	Mintage	F	VF	XF	Unc	BU
1974FM (P)	94,000	Value: 4.00				
1975FM (P)	29,000	Value: 4.00				
1976FM (P)	23,000	Value: 4.00				
1977FM (P)	11,000	Value: 4.00				
1978FM (P)	6,931	Value: 6.00				
1979FM (P)	2,053	Value: 8.00				
1980FM (P)	2,084	Value: 8.00				

KM# 8 DOLLAR **Weight:** 18.1400 g. **Composition:** 0.8000 Silver .4666 oz. ASW **Reverse:** Conch shell

Date	Mintage	F	VF	XF	Unc	BU
1966	406,000	—	BV	3.00	5.00	—
1969	26,000	—	BV	3.00	5.00	—
1969 Proof	10,000	Value: 6.00				
1970	27,000	—	BV	3.00	5.00	—
1970 Proof	23,000	Value: 6.00				

KM# 22 DOLLAR **Weight:** 18.1400 g. **Composition:** 0.8000 Silver .4666 oz. ASW

Date	Mintage	F	VF	XF	Unc	BU
1971FM	15,000	—	BV	3.00	5.00	—
1971FM (P)	31,000	Value: 6.00				
1972FM	18,000	—	BV	3.00	5.00	—
1972FM (P)	35,000	Value: 6.00				
1973FM	10,000	—	BV	3.00	5.00	—
1973FM (P)	35,000	Value: 6.00				

KM# 65 DOLLAR **Composition:** Copper-Nickel **Size:** 34 mm.

Date	Mintage	F	VF	XF	Unc	BU
1974FM	12,000	—	—	1.25	3.50	—
1975FM (M)	600	—	—	7.50	25.00	—
1975FM (U)	3,845	—	—	1.50	6.00	—
1976FM (M)	600	—	—	7.50	25.00	—
1976FM (U)	1,453	—	—	1.75	8.00	—
1977FM (M)	600	—	—	7.50	25.00	—
1977FM (U)	713	—	—	5.00	25.00	—
1978FM (U)	1,367	—	—	2.00	10.00	—

KM# 65a DOLLAR **Weight:** 18.1400 g. **Composition:** 0.8000 Silver .4666 oz. ASW

Date	Mintage	F	VF	XF	Unc	BU
1974FM (P)	94,000	Value: 6.00				
1975FM (P)	29,000	Value: 8.00				
1976FM (P)	23,000	Value: 8.00				
1977FM (P)	11,000	Value: 8.00				
1978FM (P)	6,931	Value: 10.00				
1979FM (P)	2,053	Value: 15.00				
1980FM (P)	2,084	Value: 15.00				

KM# 65b DOLLAR **Composition:** Copper-Nickel **Size:** 32 mm.

Date	Mintage	F	VF	XF	Unc	BU
1981FM (P)	1,980	Value: 15.00				
1989		—	—	1.50	3.50	—
1989 (P)	Est. 2,000	Value: 15.00				
1991		—	—	1.50	3.50	—
1992		—	—	1.50	3.50	—

KM# 89 DOLLAR **Composition:** Copper-Nickel **Reverse:** Poinciana flower

Date	Mintage	F	VF	XF	Unc	BU
1982FM (P)	1,217	Value: 20.00				

KM# 93 DOLLAR **Composition:** Copper-Nickel **Subject:** 10th Anniversary of Independence **Reverse:** Allamanda flower

Date	Mintage	F	VF	XF	Unc	BU
1983FM (P)	1,020	Value: 20.00				

KM# 104 DOLLAR **Composition:** Copper-Nickel **Reverse:** Bougainvillea flower

Date	Mintage	F	VF	XF	Unc	BU
1984FM (P)	1,036	Value: 20.00				
1985FM (P)	7,500	Value: 10.00				

KM# 154 DOLLAR **Composition:** Copper-Nickel **Note:** Golf - Hole in One. Similar to 5 Dollars, KM#155.

Date	Mintage	F	VF	XF	Unc	BU
1994	20,000	—	—	—	15.00	—

KM# 186 DOLLAR **Weight:** 1.2442 g. **Composition:** 0.9999 Gold .0400 oz. AGW **Reverse:** Two flamingos **Note:** Similar to 5 Dollars, KM#188.

Date	Mintage	F	VF	XF	Unc	BU
1995 Proof	—	Value: 50.00				

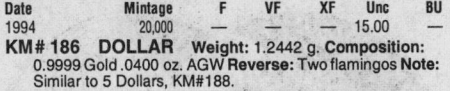

KM# 176 DOLLAR **Weight:** 31.1800 g. **Composition:** 0.9990 Silver 1.0015 oz. ASW **Subject:** Third Millennium - Year 2000

Date	Mintage	F	VF	XF	Unc	BU
1996 Proof	50,000	Value: 45.00				

KM# 9 2 DOLLARS **Weight:** 29.8000 g. **Composition:** 0.9250 Silver .8863 oz. ASW **Reverse:** National bird - two flamingos

Date	Mintage	F	VF	XF	Unc	BU
1966	104,000	—	BV	5.00	7.00	—
1969	26,000	—	BV	5.00	7.00	—
1969 Proof	10,000	Value: 8.00				
1970	32,000	—	BV	5.00	7.00	—
1970 Proof	23,000	Value: 9.00				

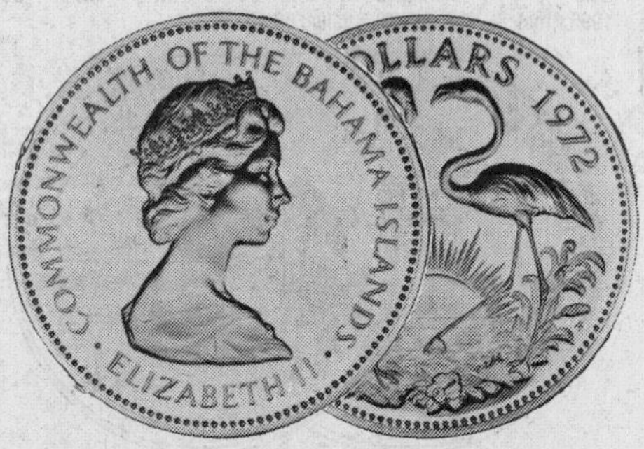

KM# 23 2 DOLLARS **Weight:** 29.8000 g. **Composition:** 0.9250 Silver .8863 oz. ASW

Date	Mintage	F	VF	XF	Unc	BU
1971FM	88,000	—	BV	5.00	8.00	—
1971FM (P)	60,000	Value: 10.00				
1972FM	65,000	—	BV	5.00	8.00	—
1972FM (P)	59,000	Value: 10.00				
1973FM	43,000	—	BV	5.00	8.00	—
1973FM (P)	50,000	Value: 10.00				

KM# 66 2 DOLLARS **Composition:** Copper-Nickel

Date	Mintage	F	VF	XF	Unc	BU
1974FM	37,000	—	—	2.25	5.00	—
1975FM (M)	300	—	—	9.00	25.00	—
1975FM (U)	8,810	—	—	2.25	5.00	—
1976FM (M)	300	—	—	9.00	25.00	—
1976FM (U)	4,381	—	—	2.50	8.00	—
1977FM (M)	300	—	—	9.00	25.00	—
1977FM (U)	946	—	—	3.00	20.00	—
1978FM (U)	1,067	—	—	3.00	15.00	—
1979FM (U)	300	—	—	7.50	25.00	—
1980FM (U)	—	—	—	—	—	—

KM# 66a 2 DOLLARS **Weight:** 29.8000 g. **Composition:** 0.9250 Silver .8863 oz. ASW

Date	Mintage	F	VF	XF	Unc	BU
1974FM (P)	129,000	Value: 9.00				
1975FM (P)	45,000	Value: 9.00				
1976FM (P)	35,000	Value: 9.00				
1977FM (P)	15,000	Value: 12.00				
1978FM (P)	11,000	Value: 17.50				
1979FM (P)	2,053	Value: 30.00				
1980FM (P)	2,084	Value: 30.00				

KM# 66b 2 DOLLARS **Composition:** Copper-Nickel

Date	Mintage	F	VF	XF	Unc	BU
1981FM (P)	1,980	Value: 30.00				
1989	—	—	—	2.25	6.00	—

KM# 90 2 DOLLARS **Composition:** Copper-Nickel **Reverse:** Bahama swallows

Date	Mintage	F	VF	XF	Unc	BU
1982FM (P)	1,217	Value: 30.00				

KM# 94 2 DOLLARS **Composition:** Copper-Nickel **Subject:** 10th Anniversary of Independence **Reverse:** Honeycreepers

Date	Mintage	F	VF	XF	Unc	BU
1983FM (P)	1,020	Value: 30.00				

KM# 105 2 DOLLARS **Composition:** Copper-Nickel **Reverse:** Flamingos in flight

Date	Mintage	F	VF	XF	Unc	BU
1984FM (P)	1,036	Value: 30.00				
1985FM (P)	7,500	Value: 15.00				

KM# 66c 2 DOLLARS **Weight:** 16.8500 g. **Composition:** 0.9250 Silver .5012 oz. ASW

Date	Mintage	F	VF	XF	Unc	BU
1989	Est. 4,000	Value: 40.00				
1991	—	—	—	—	100	—

KM# 158 2 DOLLARS **Weight:** 28.2800 g. **Composition:** 0.9250 Silver .8411 oz. ASW **Subject:** Royal Visit **Reverse:** Portraits and yacht

Date	Mintage	F	VF	XF	Unc	BU
1994 Proof	10,000	Value: 40.00				

KM# 164 2 DOLLARS **Weight:** 30.0800 g. **Composition:** 0.9990 Silver .9982 oz. ASW **Series:** Flora and Fauna **Reverse:** Hibiscus flower **Note:** "Applique"

Date	Mintage	F	VF	XF	Unc	BU
1995 Proof	25,000	Value: 45.00				

KM# 165 2 DOLLARS **Weight:** 31.4000 g. **Composition:** 0.9990 Silver 1.0085 oz. ASW **Series:** Flora and Fauna **Reverse:** Bahama Amazon Parrot **Note:** "Applique"

Date	Mintage	F	VF	XF	Unc	BU
1995 Proof	10,000	Value: 55.00				

KM# 166 2 DOLLARS **Weight:** 31.4000 g. **Composition:** 0.9990 Silver 1.0085 oz. ASW **Series:** Flora and Fauna **Reverse:** Caribbean Monk Seal **Note:** "Applique"

Date	Mintage	F	VF	XF	Unc	BU
1995 Proof	10,000	Value: 50.00				

KM# 183.1 2 DOLLARS **Weight:** 23.3300 g. **Composition:** 0.9250 Silver .6938 oz. ASW **Series:** Olympics **Subject:** Catamaran Sailing **Rev. Legend:** OLIMPIC GAMES...

Date	Mintage	F	VF	XF	Unc	BU
1995 Proof	30,000	Value: 40.00				

KM# 183.2 2 DOLLARS **Weight:** 23.3300 g. **Composition:** 0.9250 Silver .6938 oz. ASW **Series:** Olympics **Subject:** Catamaran Sailing **Rev. Legend:** OLYMPIC GAMES...

Date	F	VF	XF	Unc	BU
1995	—	—	—	150	—

KM# 187 2 DOLLARS **Weight:** 3.1103 g. **Composition:** 0.9999 Gold .1000 oz. AGW **Reverse:** Two flamingos **Note:** Similar to 5 Dollars, KM#188.

Date	F	VF	XF	Unc	BU
1995 Proof	—	Value: 100			

KM# 177 2 DOLLARS **Weight:** 3.1103 g. **Composition:** 0.9999 Gold .1000 oz. AGW **Subject:** Third Millennium - Year 2000 **Obverse:** Queen's portrait **Reverse:** Sea shell shaped map **Note:** Similar to 1 Dollar, KM#176.

Date	Mintage	F	VF	XF	Unc	BU
1996 Proof	10,000	Value: 80.00				

KM# 203 2 DOLLARS **Weight:** 23.3300 g. **Composition:** 0.9250 Silver .6938 oz. ASW **Subject:** Protect Our World **Obverse:** Queen's head right **Reverse:** Flamingo and map **Edge:** Reeded **Size:** 38.6 mm.

Date	F	VF	XF	Unc	BU
1996 Proof	—	Value: 50.00			

KM# 198 2 DOLLARS **Weight:** 28.2800 g. **Composition:** 0.9250 Silver .8410 oz. ASW **Subject:** WWF Conserving Nature **Obverse:** Queen's portrait **Reverse:** Spotfin Butterfly Fish and a Queen Angelfish

Date	Mintage	F	VF	XF	Unc	BU
1997 Proof	Est. 15,000	Value: 40.00				

KM# 206 2 DOLLARS **Weight:** 23.2300 g. **Composition:** 0.9250 Silver 0.6908 oz. ASW **Subject:** UNICEF **Obverse:** Bust of Queen Elizabeth II right. **Reverse:** Two boys and a dolphin. **Edge:** Reeded **Size:** 38.6 mm.

Date	Mintage	F	VF	XF	Unc	BU
1997 Proof	25,000	Value: 17.50				

KM# 204 2 DOLLARS **Weight:** 23.3200 g. **Composition:** 0.9250 Silver 0.6935 oz. ASW **Subject:** Queen Mother **Obverse:** Queen's portrait **Reverse:** Queen Mother's portrait circa 1908 **Edge:** Reeded **Size:** 38.5 mm.

Date	F	VF	XF	Unc	BU
1997 Proof	—	Value: 50.00			

KM# 10 5 DOLLARS **Weight:** 42.1200 g. **Composition:** 0.9250 Silver 1.2527 oz. ASW

Date	Mintage	F	VF	XF	Unc	BU
1966	100,000	—	BV	6.00	14.00	—
1969	36,000	—	BV	6.00	14.00	—
1969 Proof	10,000	Value: 15.00				
1970	43,000	—	BV	6.00	14.00	—
1970 Proof	23,000	Value: 15.00				

KM# 24 5 DOLLARS **Weight:** 42.1200 g. **Composition:** 0.9250 Silver 1.2527 oz. ASW

Date	Mintage	F	VF	XF	Unc	BU
1971FM	29,000	—	BV	6.00	10.00	—
1971FM (P)	31,000	Value: 11.00				

KM# 33 5 DOLLARS **Weight:** 42.1200 g. **Composition:** 0.9250 Silver 1.2527 oz. ASW **Obverse:** Similar to KM#24

Date	Mintage	F	VF	XF	Unc	BU
1972FM	32,000	—	BV	6.00	9.50	—
1972FM (P)	35,000	Value: 10.00				
1973FM	32,000	—	BV	6.00	9.50	—
1973FM (P)	35,000	Value: 10.00				

KM# 67 5 DOLLARS **Composition:** Copper-Nickel **Reverse:** National flag

Date	Mintage	F	VF	XF	Unc	BU
1974FM	32,000	—	—	—	8.00	—
1975FM (M)	200	—	—	—	40.00	—
1975FM (U)	7,058	—	—	—	9.00	—
1976FM (M)	200	—	—	—	40.00	—
1976FM (U)	2,591	—	—	—	15.00	—
1977FM (M)	200	—	—	—	40.00	—
1977FM (U)	801	—	—	—	25.00	—
1978FM (U)	1,244	—	—	—	15.00	—

KM# 67a 5 DOLLARS **Weight:** 42.1200 g. **Composition:** 0.9250 Silver 1.2527 oz. ASW

Date	Mintage	F	VF	XF	Unc	BU
1974FM (P)	94,000	Value: 12.00				
1975FM (P)	29,000	Value: 15.00				
1976FM (P)	23,000	Value: 15.00				
1977FM (P)	11,000	Value: 25.00				
1978FM (P)	6,931	Value: 30.00				
1979FM (P)	2,053	Value: 40.00				
1980FM (P)	2,084	Value: 40.00				

KM# 67b 5 DOLLARS **Weight:** 42.1200 g. **Composition:** 0.5000 Silver .6771 oz. ASW **Note:** Reduced diameter.

Date	Mintage	F	VF	XF	Unc	BU
1981FM (P)	1,980	Value: 40.00				

KM# 91 5 DOLLARS **Weight:** 42.1200 g. **Composition:** 0.5000 Silver .6771 oz. ASW **Note:** Columbus Memorial

Date	Mintage	F	VF	XF	Unc	BU
1982FM (P)	1,217	Value: 40.00				

KM# 95 5 DOLLARS **Weight:** 42.1200 g. **Composition:** 0.5000 Silver .6771 oz. ASW **Subject:** 10th Anniversary of Independence **Reverse:** Flamingo

Date	Mintage	F	VF	XF	Unc	BU
1983FM (P)	1,020	Value: 45.00				

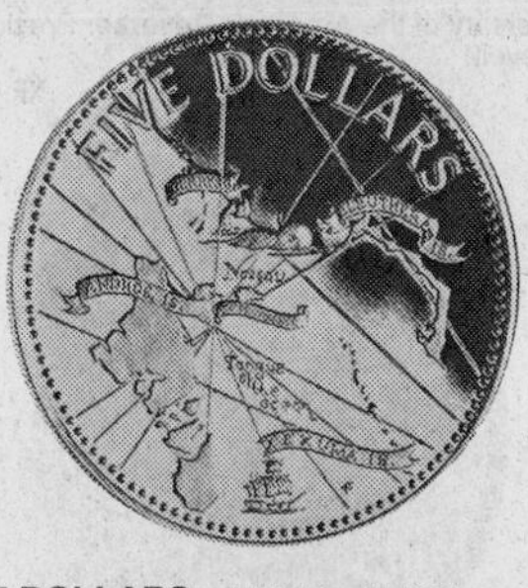

KM# 106 5 DOLLARS **Weight:** 42.1200 g. **Composition:** 0.5000 Silver .6771 oz. ASW **Note:** Historical map.

Date	Mintage	F	VF	XF	Unc	BU
1984FM (P)	1,036	Value: 45.00				

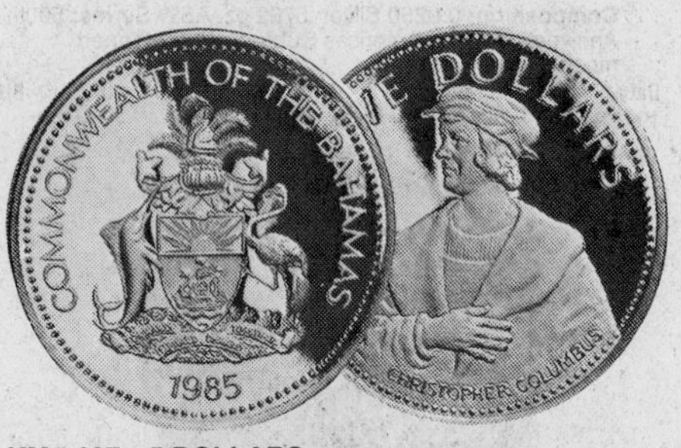

KM# 107 5 DOLLARS **Weight:** 42.1200 g. **Composition:** 0.5000 Silver .6771 oz. ASW **Reverse:** Half-length Christopher Columbus left

Date	Mintage	F	VF	XF	Unc	BU
1985FM (P)	7,847	Value: 30.00				

KM# 132 5 DOLLARS **Weight:** 19.4400 g. **Composition:** 0.9250 Silver .5782 oz. ASW **Reverse:** Standing Christopher Columbus in water holding sword, and flag before radiant sun

Date	Mintage	F	VF	XF	Unc	BU
1989 Proof	Est. 4,000	Value: 40.00				
1991	—	—	—	—	—	85.00
1991 Proof	7,000	Value: 50.00				
1992 Proof	Est. 25,000	Value: 30.00				

KM# 139 5 DOLLARS **Weight:** 19.4400 g. **Composition:** 0.9250 Silver .5782 oz. ASW **Series:** 500th Anniversary of the Americas **Reverse:** Columbus, along with Ferdinand and Isabella

Date	Mintage	F	VF	XF	Unc	BU
1991 Proof	Est. 25,000	Value: 27.50				

KM# 140 5 DOLLARS **Weight:** 19.4400 g. **Composition:** 0.9250 Silver .5782 oz. ASW **Series:** 500th Anniversary of the Americas **Subject:** Columbus sighting land

Date	Mintage	F	VF	XF	Unc	BU
1991 Proof	Est. 25,000	Value: 27.50				

KM# 141 5 DOLLARS **Weight:** 19.4400 g. **Composition:** 0.9250 Silver .5782 oz. ASW **Series:** 500th Anniversary of the Americas **Subject:** Columbus claiming the land

Date	Mintage	F	VF	XF	Unc	BU
1991 Proof	Est. 25,000	Value: 27.50				

KM# 142 5 DOLLARS **Weight:** 19.4400 g. **Composition:** 0.9250 Silver .5782 oz. ASW **Series:** 500th Anniversary of the Americas **Reverse:** Jacques Carter and map

Date	Mintage	F	VF	XF	Unc	BU
1991 Proof	Est. 25,000	Value: 27.50				

KM# 143 5 DOLLARS **Weight:** 19.4400 g. **Composition:** 0.9250 Silver .5782 oz. ASW **Series:** 500th Anniversary of the Americas **Reverse:** President Thomas Jefferson and Independence Hall

Date	Mintage	F	VF	XF	Unc	BU
1991 Proof	Est. 25,000	Value: 27.50				

KM# 144 5 DOLLARS **Weight:** 19.4400 g. **Composition:** 0.9250 Silver .5782 oz. ASW **Series:** 500th Anniversary of the Americas **Reverse:** Simon Bolivar and Jose San Martin

Date	Mintage	F	VF	XF	Unc	BU
1991 Proof	Est. 25,000	Value: 27.50				

KM# 146 5 DOLLARS Weight: 19.4400 g. **Composition:** 0.9250 Silver .5782 oz. ASW **Series:** 500th Anniversary of the Americas **Subject:** Electric light demonstration **Reverse:** Thomas Edison

Date	Mintage	F	VF	XF	Unc	BU
1991 Proof	Est. 25,000	Value: 30.00				

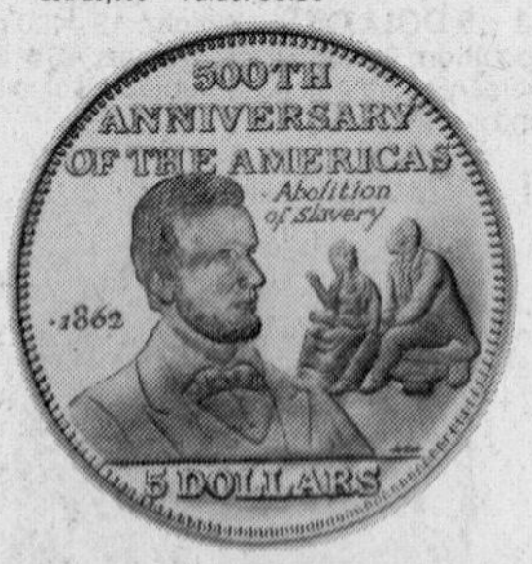

KM# 145 5 DOLLARS Weight: 19.4400 g. **Composition:** 0.9250 Silver .5782 oz. ASW **Series:** 500th Anniversary of the Americas **Subject:** Abolition of slavery **Reverse:** President Abraham Lincoln

Date	Mintage	F	VF	XF	Unc	BU
1991 Proof	Est. 25,000	Value: 30.00				

KM# 147 5 DOLLARS Weight: 19.4400 g. **Composition:** 0.9250 Silver .5782 oz. ASW **Series:** 500th Anniversary of the Americas **Subject:** Wright brothers' first airplane flight

Date	Mintage	F	VF	XF	Unc	BU
1991 Proof	Est. 25,000	Value: 30.00				

KM# 148 5 DOLLARS Weight: 19.4400 g. **Composition:** 0.9250 Silver .5782 oz. ASW **Series:** 500th Anniversary of the Americas **Reverse:** Henry Ford and automobiles

Date	Mintage	F	VF	XF	Unc	BU
1991 Proof	Est. 25,000	Value: 27.50				

KM# 149 5 DOLLARS Weight: 19.4400 g. **Composition:** 0.9250 Silver .5782 oz. ASW **Series:** 500th Anniversary of the Americas **Reverse:** President Teddy Roosevelt

Date	Mintage	F	VF	XF	Unc	BU
1991 Proof	Est. 25,000	Value: 27.50				

KM# 150 5 DOLLARS Weight: 19.4400 g. **Composition:** 0.9250 Silver .5782 oz. ASW **Series:** 500th Anniversary of the Americas **Subject:** First manned moonlanding

Date	Mintage	F	VF	XF	Unc	BU
1991 Proof	Est. 25,000	Value: 30.00				

KM# 138 5 DOLLARS Weight: 19.4400 g. **Composition:** 0.9250 Silver .5782 oz. ASW **Series:** Discovery of the New World **Obverse:** Coat of arms **Reverse:** Columbus' ships

Date	Mintage	F	VF	XF	Unc	BU
1992 Proof	Est. 25,000	Value: 30.00				

KM# 192 5 DOLLARS Weight: 1.5550 g. **Composition:** 0.5000 Gold .0250 oz. AGW **Obverse:** Queen's portrait **Reverse:** Facing pair of flamingos

Date	Mintage	F	VF	XF	Unc	BU
1992 Proof	Est. 750	Value: 70.00				

KM# 159 5 DOLLARS Weight: 23.3300 g. **Composition:** 0.9250 Silver .6939 oz. ASW **Reverse:** Pirate Captain Howell Davis

Date	Mintage	F	VF	XF	Unc	BU
1993 Proof	Est. 5,000	Value: 47.50				

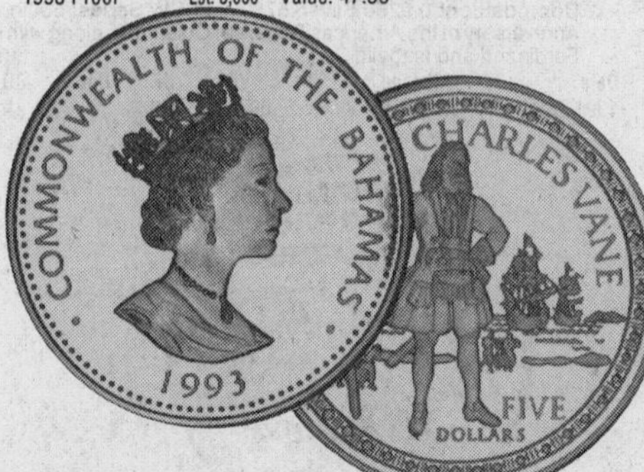

KM# 160 5 DOLLARS Weight: 23.3300 g. **Composition:** 0.9250 Silver .6939 oz. ASW **Reverse:** Pirate Captain Charles Vane

Date	Mintage	F	VF	XF	Unc	BU
1993 Proof	Est. 5,000	Value: 47.50				

KM# 161 5 DOLLARS Weight: 23.3300 g. **Composition:** 0.9250 Silver .6939 oz. ASW **Reverse:** Pirate Captain Edward Teach

Date	Mintage	F	VF	XF	Unc	BU
1993 Proof	Est. 5,000	Value: 47.50				

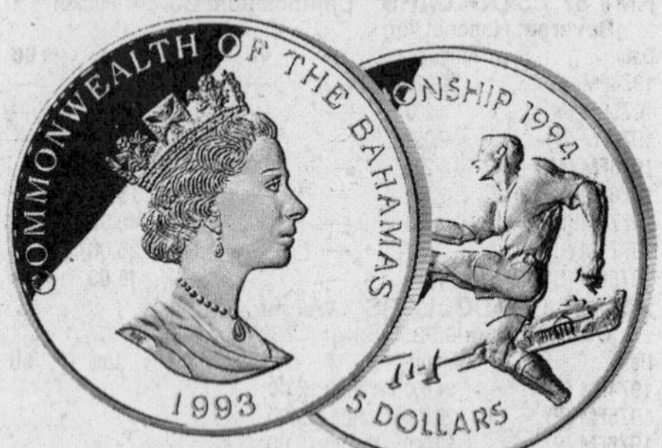

KM# 169 5 DOLLARS Weight: 23.3300 g. **Composition:** 0.9250 Silver .6939 oz. ASW **Subject:** World Soccer Championship

Date	Mintage	F	VF	XF	Unc	BU
1993 Proof	Est. 15,000	Value: 40.00				

KM# 170 5 DOLLARS Weight: 23.3300 g. **Composition:** 0.9250 Silver .6939 oz. ASW **Reverse:** Sailing boat

Date	Mintage	F	VF	XF	Unc	BU
1993 Proof	Est. 20,000	Value: 45.00				

KM# 155 5 DOLLARS Weight: 31.1035 g. **Composition:** 0.9990 Silver 1.0000 oz. ASW **Subject:** Golf - Hole in One **Obverse:** National arms, legend around, date below **Obv. Legend:** COMMONWEALTH OF THE BAHAMAS **Reverse:** Golf ball rolling towards cup

Date	Mintage	F	VF	XF	Unc	BU
1994 Proof	Est. 50,000	Value: 45.00				

KM# 201 5 DOLLARS Weight: 3.1103 g. **Composition:** 0.9990 Gold .1000 oz. AGW **Subject:** Golf - Hole in One **Obverse:** National arms, legend around, date below **Obv.**

Legend: COMMONWEALTH OF THE BAHAMAS **Reverse:** Golf ball rolling towards cup

Date	Mintage	F	VF	XF	Unc	BU
1994 Proof	250,000	Value: 125				

KM# 171 5 DOLLARS **Weight:** 3.1103 g. **Composition:** 0.9990 Gold .1000 oz. AGW **Reverse:** Space shuttle and satellite

Date	Mintage	F	VF	XF	Unc	BU
1994 Proof	Est. 10,000	Value: 50.00				

KM# 172 5 DOLLARS **Weight:** 3.1103 g. **Composition:** 0.9990 Gold .1000 oz. AGW **Reverse:** Two Whistling Ducks in flight

Date	Mintage	F	VF	XF	Unc	BU
1994 Proof	Est. 15,000	Value: 40.00				

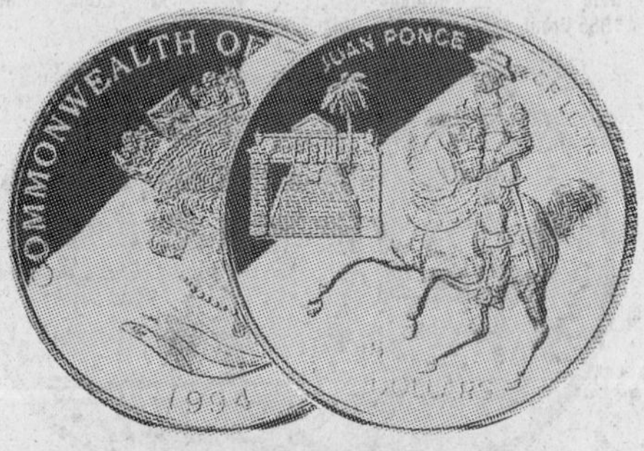

KM# 173 5 DOLLARS **Weight:** 31.4700 g. **Composition:** 0.9250 Silver .9359 oz. ASW **Reverse:** Ponce De Leon on horseback

Date	Mintage	F	VF	XF	Unc	BU
1994 Proof	Est. 10,000	Value: 45.00				

KM# 188 5 DOLLARS **Weight:** 6.2207 g. **Composition:** 0.9999 Gold .2000 oz. AGW **Obverse:** Queen's portrait **Reverse:** Two flamingos facing

Date	F	VF	XF	Unc	BU
1995 Proof	—	Value: 175			

KM# 178 5 DOLLARS **Weight:** 7.7758 g. **Composition:** 0.9999 Gold .2500 oz. AGW **Subject:** Third Millennium - Year 2000 **Obverse:** Queen's portrait **Reverse:** Sea shell-shaped world map

Date	Mintage	F	VF	XF	Unc	BU
1996 Proof	5,000	Value: 175				

KM# 11 10 DOLLARS **Weight:** 3.9943 g. **Composition:** 0.9170 Gold .1177 oz. AGW **Subject:** Adoption of New Constitution **Reverse:** Fortress

Date	Mintage	F	VF	XF	Unc	BU
1967	6,200	—	—	—	55.00	—
1967 Proof	850	Value: 95.00				

KM# 25 10 DOLLARS **Weight:** 3.9943 g. **Composition:** 0.9170 Gold .1177 oz. AGW

Date	Mintage	F	VF	XF	Unc	BU
1971	23,000	—	—	—	45.00	—
1971(t) Proof	1,250	Value: 70.00				

KM# 26 10 DOLLARS **Weight:** 3.9943 g. **Composition:** 0.9170 Gold .1177 oz. AGW **Reverse:** Hallmark and fineness stamped near bottom **Note:** Struck by the Gori and Zucchi Mint, Italy.

Date	F	VF	XF	Unc	BU
1971	—	—	—	45.00	—

KM# 34 10 DOLLARS **Weight:** 3.1950 g. **Composition:** 0.9170 Gold .0940 oz. AGW **Obverse:** Queen's portrait **Reverse:** Fortress

Date	Mintage	F	VF	XF	Unc	BU
1972	11,000	—	—	—	45.00	—
1972 Proof	1,250	Value: 70.00				

KM# 40.1 10 DOLLARS **Weight:** 1.4500 g. **Composition:** 0.7500 Gold .0349 oz. AGW **Subject:** Independence Day - July 10 **Obverse:** Tobacco Dove **Reverse:** Without fineness and date

Date	F	VF	XF	Unc	BU
1973	—	—	—	30.00	—
1973 Proof	—	Value: 32.00			

KM# 40.2 10 DOLLARS **Weight:** 1.4500 g. **Composition:** 0.7500 Gold .0349 oz. AGW **Obverse:** Tobacco Dove **Reverse:** Date without fineness

Date	F	VF	XF	Unc	BU
1973	—	—	25.00	32.00	—

KM# 41 10 DOLLARS **Weight:** 1.4500 g. **Composition:** 0.5850 Gold .0272 oz. AGW **Obverse:** Tobacco Dove **Reverse:** .585 fineness and date

Date	Mintage	F	VF	XF	Unc	BU
1973	9,960	—	—	—	32.00	—
1973 Proof	1,260	Value: 40.00				

KM# 42 10 DOLLARS **Weight:** 49.7500 g. **Composition:** 0.9250 Silver 1.4795 oz. ASW **Subject:** Independence Day - July 10 **Obverse:** Legend around queen's portrait

Date	Mintage	F	VF	XF	Unc	BU
1973FM	28,000	—	—	—	16.50	—
1973FM Proof	63,000	Value: 20.00				

KM# 68 10 DOLLARS **Composition:** Copper-Nickel **Subject:** 1st Anniversary of Independence **Obverse:** National arms, date below **Reverse:** National flag

Date	Mintage	F	VF	XF	Unc	BU
1974FM Proof	4,825	—	—	—	12.00	—

KM# 68a 10 DOLLARS **Weight:** 50.4200 g. **Composition:** 0.9250 Silver 1.4994 oz. ASW

Date	Mintage	F	VF	XF	Unc	BU
1974FM Proof	43,000	Value: 15.00				

KM# 76 10 DOLLARS **Composition:** Copper-Nickel **Subject:** Anniversary of Independence **Obverse:** National arms **Reverse:** Yellow Elder

Date	Mintage	F	VF	XF	Unc	BU
1975FM (M)	100	—	—	—	90.00	—
1975FM (U)	5,325	—	—	—	12.50	—
1976FM (M)	100	—	—	—	90.00	—
1976FM (U)	100	—	—	—	90.00	—
1977FM (M)	100	—	—	—	90.00	—
1977FM (U)	369	—	—	—	60.00	—

KM# 76a 10 DOLLARS **Weight:** 49.1000 g. **Composition:** 0.9250 Silver 1.4602 oz. ASW

Date	Mintage	F	VF	XF	Unc	BU
1975FM (P)	63,000	Value: 15.00				
1976FM (P)	10,000	Value: 18.50				
1977FM (P)	4,424	Value: 25.00				

KM# 78.1 10 DOLLARS **Weight:** 45.3600 g. **Composition:** 0.5000 Silver .7291 oz. ASW **Subject:** 5th Anniversary of Independence **Obverse:** National flag

Date	Mintage	F	VF	XF	Unc	BU
1978 Proof	50,000	Value: 25.00				

KM# 78.2 10 DOLLARS **Weight:** 45.3600 g. **Composition:** 0.5000 Silver .7291 oz. ASW **Reverse:** Tower mint mark after DOLLARS

Date	Mintage	F	VF	XF	Unc	BU
1978(t) Proof	—	Value: 25.00				

KM# 79 10 DOLLARS **Weight:** 45.3600 g. **Composition:** 0.5000 Silver .7291 oz. ASW **Subject:** 5th Anniversary of Independence **Obverse:** Arms

Date	Mintage	F	VF	XF	Unc	BU
1978 Proof	50,000	Value: 20.00				

KM# 84 10 DOLLARS **Weight:** 30.2800 g. **Composition:** 0.5000 Silver .4868 oz. ASW **Subject:** 10th Anniversary Caribbean Development Bank

Date	Mintage	F	VF	XF	Unc	BU
1980FM Proof	1,001	Value: 22.50				

KM# 85 10 DOLLARS **Weight:** 28.2800 g. **Composition:** 0.9250 Silver .8410 oz. ASW **Subject:** Wedding of Prince Charles and Lady Diana **Reverse:** Conjoined busts of royal couple left

Date	Mintage	F	VF	XF	Unc	BU
1981 Proof	39,000	Value: 30.00				

KM# 96 10 DOLLARS **Weight:** 30.2800 g. **Composition:** 0.5000 Silver .4867 oz. ASW **Subject:** 30th Anniversary - Coronation of Queen Elizabeth

Date	Mintage	F	VF	XF	Unc	BU
1983FM Proof	3,374	Value: 25.00				

KM# 97 10 DOLLARS **Weight:** 23.3300 g. **Composition:** 0.9250 Silver .6939 oz. ASW **Subject:** 10th Anniversary of Independence

Date	Mintage	F	VF	XF	Unc	BU
1983 Proof	800	Value: 37.50				

KM# 114 10 DOLLARS **Weight:** 23.3300 g. **Composition:** 0.9250 Silver .6939 oz. ASW **Subject:** Los Angeles Olympics **Obverse:** National arms **Reverse:** Sprinter

Date	Mintage	F	VF	XF	Unc	BU
1984 Proof	2,100	Value: 40.00				

KM# 127 10 DOLLARS **Weight:** 29.1700 g. **Composition:** 0.5000 Silver .4690 oz. ASW **Subject:** 10th Anniversary of Central Bank **Obverse:** National arms **Reverse:** Nummulite (Sand dollar)

Date	Mintage	F	VF	XF	Unc	BU
1984 Proof	1,001	Value: 50.00				

KM# 109 10 DOLLARS **Weight:** 28.2800 g. **Composition:** 0.9250 Silver .8411 oz. ASW **Subject:** Royal Visit

Date	Mintage	F	VF	XF	Unc	BU
1985 Proof	1,060	Value: 40.00				

KM# 109a 10 DOLLARS **Weight:** 47.5400 g. **Composition:** 0.9170 Gold 1.4013 oz. AGW **Subject:** Royal Visit

Date	Mintage	F	VF	XF	Unc	BU
1985 Proof	Est. 250	Value: 800				

KM# 113 10 DOLLARS **Weight:** 28.2800 g. **Composition:** 0.5000 Silver .4546 oz. ASW **Subject:** Commonwealth Games

Date	Mintage	F	VF	XF	Unc	BU
1986	899	—	—	—	32.00	—

KM# 113a 10 DOLLARS **Weight:** 28.2800 g. **Composition:** 0.9250 Silver .8411 oz. ASW

Date	Mintage	F	VF	XF	Unc	BU
1986 Proof	1,343	Value: 32.00				

KM# 120 10 DOLLARS **Weight:** 28.2800 g. **Composition:** 0.9250 Silver .8411 oz. ASW **Reverse:** Queen Isabella and Columbus

Date	Mintage	F	VF	XF	Unc	BU
1987 Proof	1,800	Value: 35.00				

KM# 123 10 DOLLARS **Weight:** 28.2800 g. **Composition:** 0.9250 Silver .8411 oz. ASW **Subject:** Columbus discovering America **Obverse:** Queen Elizabeth **Reverse:** Columbus sighting America

Date	Mintage	F	VF	XF	Unc	BU
1988 Proof	1,704	Value: 35.00				

KM# 128 10 DOLLARS **Weight:** 28.2800 g. **Composition:** 0.9250 Silver .8411 oz. ASW **Obverse:** Queen Elizabeth **Reverse:** Columbus with flag and sword

Date	Mintage	F	VF	XF	Unc	BU
1989 Proof	Est. 10,000	Value: 30.00				

KM# 133 10 DOLLARS **Weight:** 28.2800 g. **Composition:** 0.9250 Silver .8411 oz. ASW **Series:** Discovery of the New World **Obverse:** Queen Elizabeth **Reverse:** Columbus

Date	Mintage	F	VF	XF	Unc	BU
1990	550	—	—	—	125	—
1990 Proof	10,000	Value: 30.00				

KM# 196 10 DOLLARS **Weight:** 28.2800 g. **Composition:** 0.9250 Silver .8411 oz. ASW **Series:** Discovery of the New World **Obverse:** Queen's portrait **Reverse:** 5-man rowboat, Columbus' ships in background

Date	F	VF	XF	Unc	BU
1991 Proof	—	Value: 30.00			

KM# 193 10 DOLLARS **Weight:** 3.1450 g. **Composition:** 0.5000 Gold .0505 oz. AGW **Obverse:** Queen's portrait **Reverse:** Two flamingos facing

Date	Mintage	F	VF	XF	Unc	BU
1992 Proof	Est. 750	Value: 100				

KM# 197 10 DOLLARS **Weight:** 28.2800 g. **Composition:** 0.9250 Silver .8411 oz. ASW **Series:** Discovery of the New World **Obverse:** Queen's portrait **Reverse:** Nina, Pinta, Santa Maria ships

Date	F	VF	XF	Unc	BU
1992 Proof	—	Value: 30.00			

KM# 162 10 DOLLARS **Weight:** 136.0800 g. **Composition:** 0.9250 Silver 4.074 oz. ASW **Subject:** Expulsion of pirates **Obverse:** Queen's portrait, legend around, date below **Obv. Legend:** • COMMONWEALTH OF THE BAHAMAS • **Reverse:** Pirate ship **Rev. Legend:** • EXPULSIS PIRATIS • RESTITUTA COMMERCIA •

Date	Mintage	F	VF	XF	Unc	BU
1993 Proof	Est. 2,000	Value: 120				

KM# 156 10 DOLLARS **Weight:** 7.7759 g. **Composition:** 0.9990 Gold .2500 oz. AGW **Subject:** Golf - Hole in One **Obverse:** National arms **Reverse:** Golfer making hole in one. **Note:** Actual hole in coin.

Date	Mintage	F	VF	XF	Unc	BU
1994 Proof	2,500	Value: 250				

KM# 167 10 DOLLARS **Weight:** 155.5175 g. **Composition:** 0.9990 Silver 5.0000 oz. ASW **Obverse:** Multi-color National arms **Reverse:** Multicolor Bahama parrot

Date	Mintage	F	VF	XF	Unc	BU
1995 Proof	2,500	Value: 175				

KM# 168 10 DOLLARS **Weight:** 15.5518 g. **Composition:** 0.9990 Gold .5000 oz. AGW **Obverse:** Queen's portrait **Reverse:** Bahama Parrot

Date	Mintage	F	VF	XF	Unc	BU
1995 Proof	2,000	Value: 220				

KM# 174 10 DOLLARS **Weight:** 28.2800 g. **Composition:** 0.9250 Silver .8411 oz. ASW **Subject:** 25th Anniversary - Caribbean Development Bank **Obverse:** National arms

Date	Mintage	F	VF	XF	Unc	BU
1995 Proof	1,000	Value: 40.00				

KM# 189 10 DOLLARS **Weight:** 15.5517 g. **Composition:** 0.9999 Gold .5000 oz. AGW **Obverse:** Queen's portrait **Reverse:** Two flamingos facing

Date	F	VF	XF	Unc	BU
1995 Proof	—	Value: 300			

KM# 179 10 DOLLARS **Weight:** 15.5517 g. **Composition:** 0.9999 Gold .5000 oz. AGW **Subject:** Third Millennium - Year 2000 **Obverse:** Queen's portrait **Reverse:** Sea shell-shaped world map

Date	Mintage	F	VF	XF	Unc	BU
1996 Proof	5,000	Value: 300				

KM# 200 10 DOLLARS **Weight:** 31.1035 g. **Composition:** 0.9990 Silver 1.0000 oz. ASW **Subject:** 50th Anniversary of the University of the West Indies **Obverse:** National arms **Reverse:** University arms, dates

Date	Mintage	F	VF	XF	Unc	BU
1998 Proof	1,000	Value: 55.00				

KM# 12 20 DOLLARS **Weight:** 7.9880 g. **Composition:** 0.9170 Gold .2355 oz. AGW **Subject:** Adoption of New Constitution **Reverse:** Lighthouse

Date	Mintage	F	VF	XF	Unc	BU
1967	6,200	—	—	—	110	—
1967 Proof	850	Value: 150				

KM# 27 20 DOLLARS **Weight:** 7.9880 g. **Composition:** 0.9170 Gold .2355 oz. AGW

Date	Mintage	F	VF	XF	Unc	BU
1971	22,000	—	—	—	120	—
1971(t) Proof	1,250	Value: 140				

KM# 28 20 DOLLARS **Weight:** 7.9880 g. **Composition:** 0.9170 Gold .2355 oz. AGW **Reverse:** Hallmark and fineness stamped at bottom **Note:** Struck by the Gori and Zucchi Mint, Italy.

Date	F	VF	XF	Unc	BU
1971 Proof	—	—	—	110	—

KM# 35 20 DOLLARS **Weight:** 6.4800 g. **Composition:** 0.9170 Gold .1880 oz. AGW

Date	Mintage	F	VF	XF	Unc	BU
1972	10,000	—	—	—	100	—
1972 Proof	1,250	Value: 125				

KM# 43.1 20 DOLLARS **Weight:** 2.9000 g. **Composition:** 0.7500 Gold .0699 oz. AGW **Subject:** Independence Day - July 10 **Reverse:** Flamingos, without fineness and date

Date	F	VF	XF	Unc	BU
1973	—	—	—	35.00	—
1973 Proof	—	Value: 45.00			

KM# 43.2 20 DOLLARS **Weight:** 2.9000 g. **Composition:** 0.7500 Gold .0699 oz. AGW **Subject:** Independence Day - July 10 **Reverse:** Flamingos, without fineness, high date

Date	F	VF	XF	Unc	BU
1973	—	—	—	35.00	—
1973 Proof	—	Value: 45.00			

KM# 44 20 DOLLARS **Weight:** 2.9000 g. **Composition:** 0.5850 Gold .0545 oz. AGW **Reverse:** .585 fineness, low date

Date	Mintage	F	VF	XF	Unc	BU
1973	8,660	—	—	—	30.00	—
1973 Proof	1,260	Value: 40.00				

KM# 157 20 DOLLARS **Weight:** 15.5517 g. **Composition:** 0.9990 Gold .5000 oz. AGW **Obverse:** Arms **Reverse:** Golfer making hole in one **Note:** Actual hole in coin

Date	Mintage	F	VF	XF	Unc	BU
1994 Proof	2,500	Value: 350				

KM# 82 25 DOLLARS **Weight:** 37.3800 g. **Composition:** 0.9250 Silver 1.1117 oz. ASW **Subject:** 250th Anniversary of Parliament **Obverse:** Similar to 10 Dollars, KM#96

Date	Mintage	F	VF	XF	Unc	BU
1979 Proof	3,002	Value: 40.00				

KM# 110 25 DOLLARS **Weight:** 120.0000 g. **Composition:** 0.9250 Silver 3.5687 oz. ASW **Subject:** Columbus' Discovery of America **Obverse:** National arms

Date	Mintage	F	VF	XF	Unc	BU
1985 Proof	1,950	Value: 70.00				

KM# 115 25 DOLLARS **Weight:** 129.6000 g. **Composition:** 0.9250 Silver 3.8547 oz. ASW **Subject:** Bird Conservation **Obverse:** National arms **Reverse:** Flamingos

Date	Mintage	F	VF	XF	Unc	BU
1985 Proof	1,060	Value: 80.00				

KM# 118 25 DOLLARS **Weight:** 129.6000 g. **Composition:** 0.9250 Silver 3.8547 oz. ASW **Obverse:** Queen's portrait **Reverse:** Queen Isabella and Columbus

Date	Mintage	F	VF	XF	Unc	BU
1987 Proof	1,750	Value: 70.00				

KM# 124 25 DOLLARS **Weight:** 136.0000 g. **Composition:** 0.9250 Silver 4.0446 oz. ASW **Subject:** Columbus Discovering New World **Obverse:** Queen's portrait **Reverse:** Columbus on deck pointing towards land

Date	Mintage	F	VF	XF	Unc	BU
1988 Proof	954	Value: 110				

KM# 129 25 DOLLARS **Weight:** 136.0000 g. **Composition:** 0.9250 Silver 4.0446 oz. ASW **Obverse:** Queen Elizabeth **Reverse:** Christopher Columbus

Date	Mintage	F	VF	XF	Unc	BU
1989 Proof	1,572	Value: 70.00				

KM# 134 25 DOLLARS **Weight:** 136.0000 g. **Composition:** 0.9250 Silver 4.0446 oz. ASW **Series:** Discovery of the New World **Obverse:** Queen Elizabeth **Reverse:** Aborigine looking right

Date	Mintage	F	VF	XF	Unc	BU
1990 Proof	5,000	Value: 65.00				

KM# 153 25 DOLLARS **Weight:** 136.0000 g. **Composition:** 0.9250 Silver 4.0446 oz. ASW **Series:** Discovery of the New World **Obverse:** Queen Elizabeth **Reverse:** Facing half-bust of Columbus holding map, ship at left

Date	Mintage	F	VF	XF	Unc	BU
1991 Proof	Est. 500	Value: 175				

KM# 191 25 DOLLARS **Weight:** 136.0000 g. **Composition:** 0.9250 Silver 4.0446 oz. ASW **Series:** Discovery of the New World **Reverse:** Columbus meeting native Americans

Date	F	VF	XF	Unc	BU
1992 Proof	—	Value: 175			

KM# 194 25 DOLLARS **Weight:** 7.8300 g. **Composition:** 0.5000 Gold .1258 oz. AGW **Obverse:** Queen's portrait **Reverse:** Pair of flamingos

Date	Mintage	F	VF	XF	Unc	BU
1992 Proof	Est. 750	Value: 175				

KM# 202 25 DOLLARS **Weight:** 31.1035 g. **Composition:** 0.9999 Gold 1.0000 oz. AGW **Subject:** Golf - Hole in One **Obverse:** National arms **Reverse:** Golf ball rolling towards hole

Date	F	VF	XF	Unc	BU
1994 Proof	—	Value: 500			

KM# 190 25 DOLLARS **Weight:** 31.1035 g. **Composition:** 0.9999 Gold 1.0000 oz. AGW **Obverse:** Queen's portrait **Reverse:** Two flamingos

Date	F	VF	XF	Unc	BU
1995 Proof	—	Value: 475			

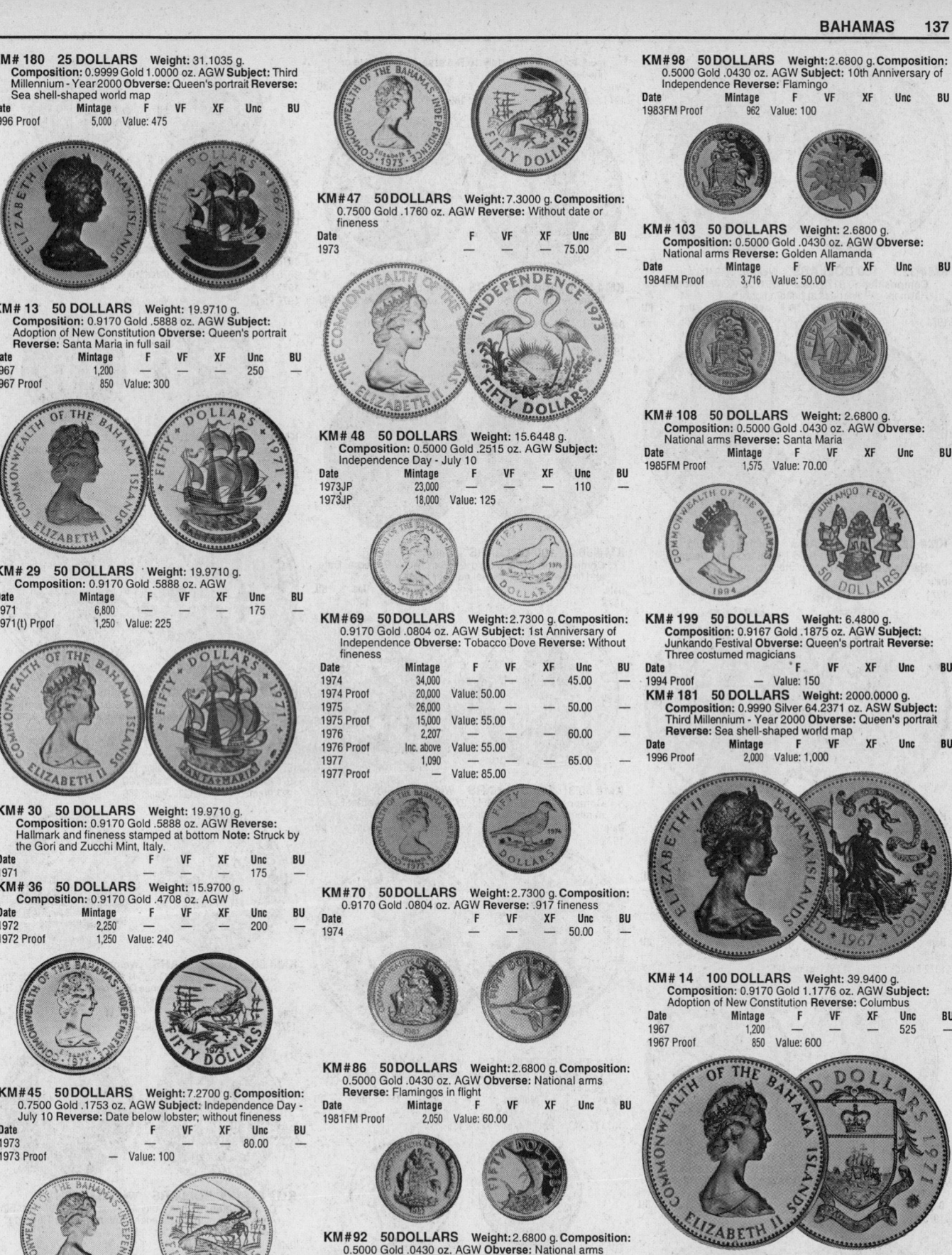

KM# 180 25 DOLLARS **Weight:** 31.1035 g. **Composition:** 0.9999 Gold 1.0000 oz. AGW **Subject:** Third Millennium - Year 2000 **Obverse:** Queen's portrait **Reverse:** Sea shell-shaped world map

Date	Mintage	F	VF	XF	Unc	BU
1996 Proof	5,000	Value: 475				

KM# 13 50 DOLLARS **Weight:** 19.9710 g. **Composition:** 0.9170 Gold .5888 oz. AGW **Subject:** Adoption of New Constitution **Obverse:** Queen's portrait **Reverse:** Santa Maria in full sail

Date	Mintage	F	VF	XF	Unc	BU
1967	1,200	—	—	—	250	—
1967 Proof	850	Value: 300				

KM# 29 50 DOLLARS **Weight:** 19.9710 g. **Composition:** 0.9170 Gold .5888 oz. AGW

Date	Mintage	F	VF	XF	Unc	BU
1971	6,800	—	—	—	175	—
1971(t) Proof	1,250	Value: 225				

KM# 30 50 DOLLARS **Weight:** 19.9710 g. **Composition:** 0.9170 Gold .5888 oz. AGW **Reverse:** Hallmark and fineness stamped at bottom **Note:** Struck by the Gori and Zucchi Mint, Italy.

Date	F	VF	XF	Unc	BU
1971	—	—	—	175	—

KM# 36 50 DOLLARS **Weight:** 15.9700 g. **Composition:** 0.9170 Gold .4708 oz. AGW

Date	Mintage	F	VF	XF	Unc	BU
1972	2,250	—	—	—	200	—
1972 Proof	1,250	Value: 240				

KM#45 50 DOLLARS **Weight:** 7.2700 g. **Composition:** 0.7500 Gold .1753 oz. AGW **Subject:** Independence Day - July 10 **Reverse:** Date below lobster; without fineness

Date	F	VF	XF	Unc	BU
1973	—	—	—	80.00	—
1973 Proof	—	Value: 100			

KM#46 50 DOLLARS **Weight:** 7.2700 g. **Composition:** 0.5850 Gold .1367 oz. AGW **Reverse:** .585 fineness to left, date to right

Date	Mintage	F	VF	XF	Unc	BU
1973	5,160	—	—	—	70.00	—
1973 Proof	1,260	Value: 85.00				

KM#47 50 DOLLARS **Weight:** 7.3000 g. **Composition:** 0.7500 Gold .1760 oz. AGW **Reverse:** Without date or fineness

Date	F	VF	XF	Unc	BU
1973	—	—	—	75.00	—

KM# 48 50 DOLLARS **Weight:** 15.6448 g. **Composition:** 0.5000 Gold .2515 oz. AGW **Subject:** Independence Day - July 10

Date	Mintage	F	VF	XF	Unc	BU
1973JP	23,000	—	—	—	110	—
1973JP	18,000	Value: 125				

KM#69 50 DOLLARS **Weight:** 2.7300 g. **Composition:** 0.9170 Gold .0804 oz. AGW **Subject:** 1st Anniversary of Independence **Obverse:** Tobacco Dove **Reverse:** Without fineness

Date	Mintage	F	VF	XF	Unc	BU
1974	34,000	—	—	—	45.00	—
1974 Proof	20,000	Value: 50.00				
1975	26,000	—	—	—	50.00	—
1975 Proof	15,000	Value: 55.00				
1976	2,207	—	—	—	60.00	—
1976 Proof	Inc. above	Value: 55.00				
1977	1,090	—	—	—	65.00	—
1977 Proof	—	Value: 85.00				

KM#70 50 DOLLARS **Weight:** 2.7300 g. **Composition:** 0.9170 Gold .0804 oz. AGW **Reverse:** .917 fineness

Date	F	VF	XF	Unc	BU
1974	—	—	—	50.00	—

KM#86 50 DOLLARS **Weight:** 2.6800 g. **Composition:** 0.5000 Gold .0430 oz. AGW **Obverse:** National arms **Reverse:** Flamingos in flight

Date	Mintage	F	VF	XF	Unc	BU
1981FM Proof	2,050	Value: 60.00				

KM#92 50 DOLLARS **Weight:** 2.6800 g. **Composition:** 0.5000 Gold .0430 oz. AGW **Obverse:** National arms **Reverse:** Marlin (Swordfish)

Date	Mintage	F	VF	XF	Unc	BU
1982FM Proof	841	Value: 125				

KM#98 50 DOLLARS **Weight:** 2.6800 g. **Composition:** 0.5000 Gold .0430 oz. AGW **Subject:** 10th Anniversary of Independence **Reverse:** Flamingo

Date	Mintage	F	VF	XF	Unc	BU
1983FM Proof	962	Value: 100				

KM# 103 50 DOLLARS **Weight:** 2.6800 g. **Composition:** 0.5000 Gold .0430 oz. AGW **Obverse:** National arms **Reverse:** Golden Allamanda

Date	Mintage	F	VF	XF	Unc	BU
1984FM Proof	3,716	Value: 50.00				

KM# 108 50 DOLLARS **Weight:** 2.6800 g. **Composition:** 0.5000 Gold .0430 oz. AGW **Obverse:** National arms **Reverse:** Santa Maria

Date	Mintage	F	VF	XF	Unc	BU
1985FM Proof	1,575	Value: 70.00				

KM# 199 50 DOLLARS **Weight:** 6.4800 g. **Composition:** 0.9167 Gold .1875 oz. AGW **Subject:** Junkando Festival **Obverse:** Queen's portrait **Reverse:** Three costumed magicians

Date	F	VF	XF	Unc	BU
1994 Proof	—	Value: 150			

KM# 181 50 DOLLARS **Weight:** 2000.0000 g. **Composition:** 0.9990 Silver 64.2371 oz. ASW **Subject:** Third Millennium - Year 2000 **Obverse:** Queen's portrait **Reverse:** Sea shell-shaped world map

Date	Mintage	F	VF	XF	Unc	BU
1996 Proof	2,000	Value: 1,000				

KM# 14 100 DOLLARS **Weight:** 39.9400 g. **Composition:** 0.9170 Gold 1.1776 oz. AGW **Subject:** Adoption of New Constitution **Reverse:** Columbus

Date	Mintage	F	VF	XF	Unc	BU
1967	1,200	—	—	—	525	—
1967 Proof	850	Value: 600				

KM# 31 100 DOLLARS **Weight:** 39.9400 g. **Composition:** 0.9170 Gold 1.1776 oz. AGW

Date	Mintage	F	VF	XF	Unc	BU
1971	6,800	—	—	—	450	—
1971(t) Proof	1,250	Value: 575				

KM# 32.1 100 DOLLARS **Weight:** 39.9400 g. **Composition:** 0.9170 Gold 1.1776 oz. AGW **Reverse:** Hallmark and fineness at bottom right

Date	F	VF	XF	Unc	BU
1971	—	—	—	465	—

KM# 32.2 100 DOLLARS **Weight:** 39.9400 g. **Composition:** 0.9170 Gold 1.1776 oz. AGW **Reverse:** Hallmark at bottom right, without fineness

Date	F	VF	XF	Unc	BU
1971	—	—	—	465	—

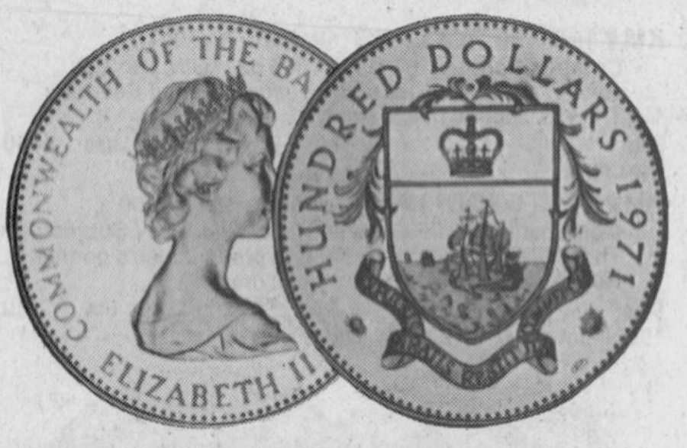

KM# 32.3 100 DOLLARS **Weight:** 39.9400 g. **Composition:** 0.9170 Gold 1.1776 oz. AGW **Reverse:** Fineness at bottom right without hallmark **Note:** Struck by the Gori and Zucchi Mint, Italy.

Date	F	VF	XF	Unc	BU
1971	—	—	—	465	—

KM# 37 100 DOLLARS **Weight:** 31.9500 g. **Composition:** 0.9170 Gold .9420 oz. AGW **Note:** The 1972 proof $100 is serially numbered on the edge.

Date	Mintage	F	VF	XF	Unc	BU
1972	2,250	—	—	—	400	—
1972 Proof	1,250	Value: 425				

KM# 49.1 100 DOLLARS **Weight:** 14.5400 g. **Composition:** 0.7500 Gold .3506 oz. AGW **Subject:** Independence Day - July 10 **Reverse:** Without fineness, date at bottom

Date	F	VF	XF	Unc	BU
1973	—	—	—	150	—

KM# 49.2 100 DOLLARS **Weight:** 14.5400 g. **Composition:** 0.7500 Gold .3506 oz. AGW **Subject:** Independence Day - July 10 **Reverse:** Without date or fineness

Date	F	VF	XF	Unc	BU
1973 Proof	—	Value: 160			

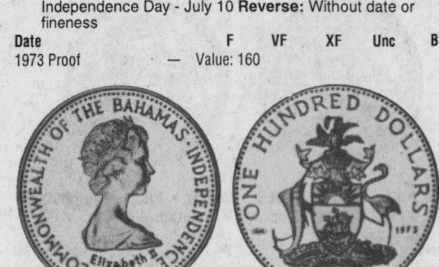

KM# 50.1 100 DOLLARS **Weight:** 14.5400 g. **Composition:** 0.5850 Gold .2735 oz. AGW **Reverse:** .585 fineness to left, date to right

Date	Mintage	F	VF	XF	Unc	BU
1973	4,660	—	—	—	125	—
1973 Proof	1,260	Value: 150				

Note: Serial number on reverse

KM# 50.2 100 DOLLARS **Weight:** 14.5400 g. **Composition:** 0.5850 Gold .2735 oz. AGW **Reverse:** Date and fineness at right, serial number at left

Date	F	VF	XF	Unc	BU
1973	—	—	—	140	—

KM# 50.3 100 DOLLARS **Weight:** 14.5400 g. **Composition:** 0.5850 Gold .2735 oz. AGW **Reverse:** Serial number at left, fineness below, date at right

Date	F	VF	XF	Unc	BU
1973	—	—	—	150	—

KM# 71 100 DOLLARS **Weight:** 18.0145 g. **Composition:** 0.5000 Gold .2896 oz. AGW **Subject:** 1st Anniversary of Independence

Date	Mintage	F	VF	XF	Unc	BU
1974	4,486	—	—	—	125	—
1974 Proof	4,153	Value: 135				

KM# 72 100 DOLLARS **Weight:** 5.4600 g. **Composition:** 0.9170 Gold .1609 oz. AGW **Reverse:** Broken waves behind flamingos' legs

Date	Mintage	F	VF	XF	Unc	BU
1974	29,000	—	—	—	70.00	—
1975	—	—	—	—	80.00	—

KM# 73 100 DOLLARS **Weight:** 5.4600 g. **Composition:** 0.9170 Gold .1609 oz. AGW **Reverse:** Unbroken waves behind flamingos' legs

Date	Mintage	F	VF	XF	Unc	BU
1974 Proof	17,000	Value: 75.00				
1975 Proof	—	Value: 85.00				
1976	—	—	—	—	90.00	—
1976 Proof	—	Value: 100				
1977	—	—	—	—	110	—
1977 Proof	—	Value: 120				

KM# 74 100 DOLLARS **Weight:** 5,4600 g. **Composition:** 0.9170 Gold .1609 oz. AGW **Reverse:** .917 fineness in oval

Date	F	VF	XF	Unc	BU
1974	—	—	—	75.00	—

KM# 77 100 DOLLARS **Weight:** 18.0145 g. **Composition:** 0.5000 Gold .2896 oz. AGW **Subject:** 2nd Anniversary of Independence **Reverse:** Bahama Amazon Parrot

Date	Mintage	F	VF	XF	Unc	BU
1975	3,694	—	—	—	120	—
1975 Proof	3,145	Value: 140				
1976 Proof	761	Value: 200				
1977 Proof	2,023	Value: 150				

KM# 80 100 DOLLARS **Weight:** 13.6000 g. **Composition:** 0.9630 Gold .4211 oz. AGW **Subject:** 5th Anniversary of Independence **Obverse:** Arms **Reverse:** Bust of H.R.H Prince Charles right

Date	Mintage	F	VF	XF	Unc	BU
1978 Proof	3,275	Value: 220				

KM# 81 100 DOLLARS **Weight:** 13.6000 g. **Composition:** 0.9630 Gold .4211 oz. AGW **Subject:** 5th Anniversary of Independence **Obverse:** Arms **Reverse:** Head of Sir Milo B. Butler half left

Date	Mintage	F	VF	XF	Unc	BU
1978 Proof	25,000	Value: 200				

KM# 87 100 DOLLARS **Weight:** 6.4800 g. **Composition:** 0.9000 Gold .1875 oz. AGW **Subject:**

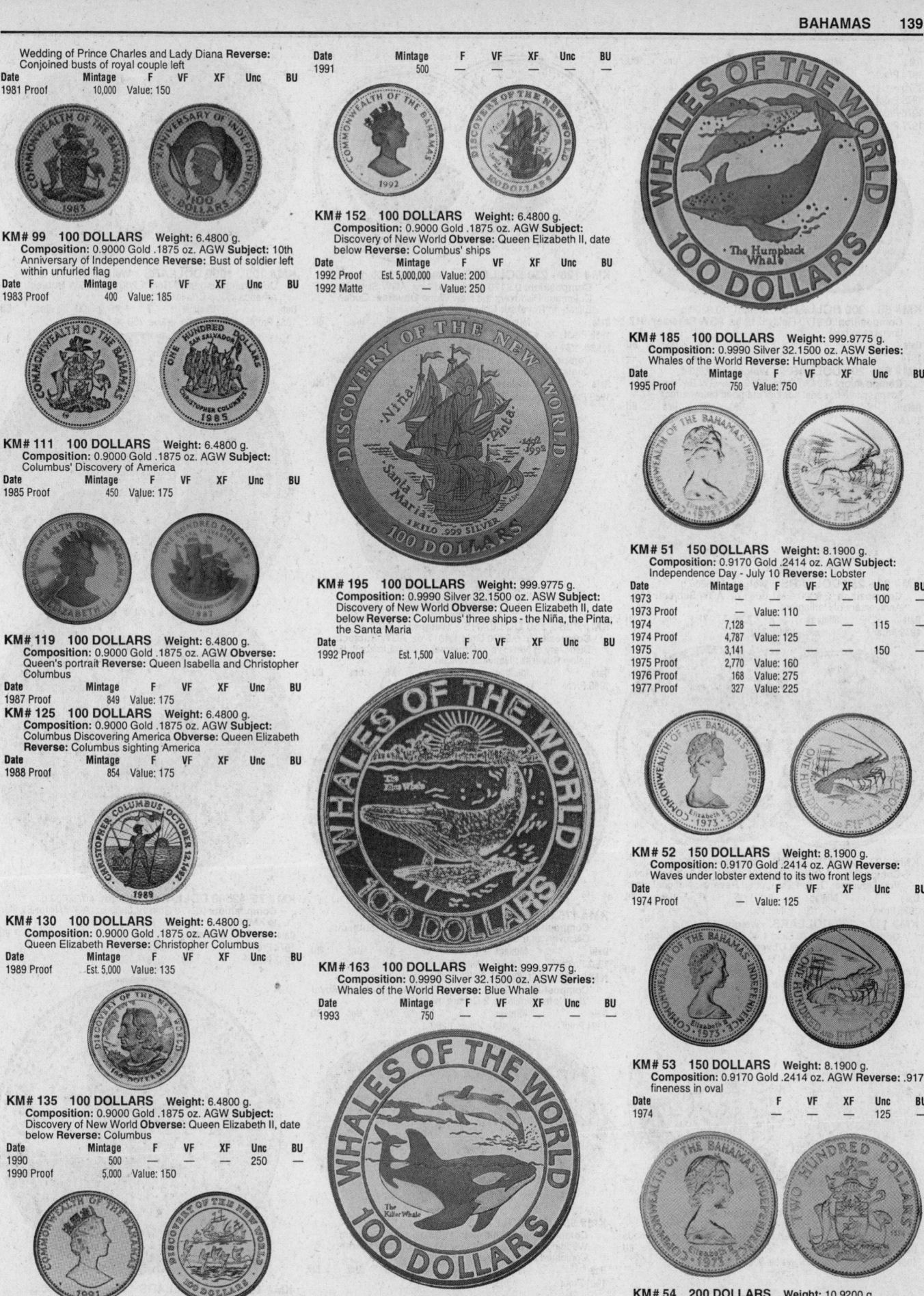

Wedding of Prince Charles and Lady Diana **Reverse:** Conjoined busts of royal couple left

Date	Mintage	F	VF	XF	Unc	BU
1981 Proof	10,000	Value: 150				

KM# 99 100 DOLLARS Weight: 6.4800 g. **Composition:** 0.9000 Gold .1875 oz. AGW **Subject:** 10th Anniversary of Independence **Reverse:** Bust of soldier left within unfurled flag

Date	Mintage	F	VF	XF	Unc	BU
1983 Proof	400	Value: 185				

KM# 111 100 DOLLARS Weight: 6.4800 g. **Composition:** 0.9000 Gold .1875 oz. AGW **Subject:** Columbus' Discovery of America

Date	Mintage	F	VF	XF	Unc	BU
1985 Proof	450	Value: 175				

KM# 119 100 DOLLARS Weight: 6.4800 g. **Composition:** 0.9000 Gold .1875 oz. AGW **Obverse:** Queen's portrait **Reverse:** Queen Isabella and Christopher Columbus

Date	Mintage	F	VF	XF	Unc	BU
1987 Proof	849	Value: 175				

KM# 125 100 DOLLARS Weight: 6.4800 g. **Composition:** 0.9000 Gold .1875 oz. AGW **Subject:** Columbus Discovering America **Obverse:** Queen Elizabeth **Reverse:** Columbus sighting America

Date	Mintage	F	VF	XF	Unc	BU
1988 Proof	854	Value: 175				

KM# 130 100 DOLLARS Weight: 6.4800 g. **Composition:** 0.9000 Gold .1875 oz. AGW **Obverse:** Queen Elizabeth **Reverse:** Christopher Columbus

Date	Mintage	F	VF	XF	Unc	BU
1989 Proof	Est. 5,000	Value: 135				

KM# 135 100 DOLLARS Weight: 6.4800 g. **Composition:** 0.9000 Gold .1875 oz. AGW **Subject:** Discovery of New World **Obverse:** Queen Elizabeth II, date below **Reverse:** Columbus

Date	Mintage	F	VF	XF	Unc	BU
1990	500	—	—	—	250	—
1990 Proof	5,000	Value: 150				

KM# 151 100 DOLLARS Weight: 6.4800 g. **Composition:** 0.9000 Gold .1875 oz. AGW **Subject:** Discovery of New World **Obverse:** Queen Elizabeth II, date below **Reverse:** 5-man rowboat

Date	Mintage	F	VF	XF	Unc	BU
1991	500	—	—	—	—	—

KM# 152 100 DOLLARS Weight: 6.4800 g. **Composition:** 0.9000 Gold .1875 oz. AGW **Subject:** Discovery of New World **Obverse:** Queen Elizabeth II, date below **Reverse:** Columbus' ships

Date	Mintage	F	VF	XF	Unc	BU
1992 Proof	Est. 5,000,000	Value: 200				
1992 Matte	—	Value: 250				

KM# 195 100 DOLLARS Weight: 999.9775 g. **Composition:** 0.9990 Silver 32.1500 oz. ASW **Subject:** Discovery of New World **Obverse:** Queen Elizabeth II, date below **Reverse:** Columbus' three ships - the Niña, the Pinta, the Santa Maria

Date	Mintage	F	VF	XF	Unc	BU
1992 Proof	Est. 1,500	Value: 700				

KM# 163 100 DOLLARS Weight: 999.9775 g. **Composition:** 0.9990 Silver 32.1500 oz. ASW **Series:** Whales of the World **Reverse:** Blue Whale

Date	Mintage	F	VF	XF	Unc	BU
1993	750	—	—	—	—	—

KM# 184 100 DOLLARS Weight: 999.9775 g. **Composition:** 0.9990 Silver 32.1500 oz. ASW **Series:** Whales of the World **Reverse:** Killer Whale

Date	Mintage	F	VF	XF	Unc	BU
1994 Proof	750	Value: 750				

KM# 185 100 DOLLARS Weight: 999.9775 g. **Composition:** 0.9990 Silver 32.1500 oz. ASW **Series:** Whales of the World **Reverse:** Humpback Whale

Date	Mintage	F	VF	XF	Unc	BU
1995 Proof	750	Value: 750				

KM# 51 150 DOLLARS Weight: 8.1900 g. **Composition:** 0.9170 Gold .2414 oz. AGW **Subject:** Independence Day - July 10 **Reverse:** Lobster

Date	Mintage	F	VF	XF	Unc	BU
1973	—	—	—	—	100	—
1973 Proof	—	Value: 110				
1974	7,128	—	—	—	115	—
1974 Proof	4,787	Value: 125				
1975	3,141	—	—	—	150	—
1975 Proof	2,770	Value: 160				
1976 Proof	168	Value: 275				
1977 Proof	327	Value: 225				

KM# 52 150 DOLLARS Weight: 8.1900 g. **Composition:** 0.9170 Gold .2414 oz. AGW **Reverse:** Waves under lobster extend to its two front legs

Date		F	VF	XF	Unc	BU
1974 Proof	—	Value: 125				

KM# 53 150 DOLLARS Weight: 8.1900 g. **Composition:** 0.9170 Gold .2414 oz. AGW **Reverse:** .917 fineness in oval

Date	F	VF	XF	Unc	BU
1974	—	—	—	125	—

KM# 54 200 DOLLARS Weight: 10.9200 g. **Composition:** 0.9170 Gold .3219 oz. AGW **Subject:** Independence Day - July 10

Date	Mintage	F	VF	XF	Unc	BU
1973	—	—	—	—	125	—
1973 Proof	—	Value: 135				
1974	5,528	—	—	—	135	—

Date	Mintage	F	VF	XF	Unc	BU
1974 Proof	3,587	Value: 140				
1975	1,545	—	—	—	150	—
1975 Proof	1,570	Value: 150				
1976 Proof	168	Value: 300				
1977 Proof	321	Value: 280				

KM# 56 200 DOLLARS **Weight:** 10.9200 g. **Composition:** 0.9170 Gold .3219 oz. AGW **Reverse:** .917 fineness in oval

Date	F	VF	XF	Unc	BU
1974	—	—	—	135	—

KM# 57 200 DOLLARS **Weight:** 10.9200 g. **Composition:** 0.9170 Gold .3219 oz. AGW **Reverse:** .916 fineness at left, serial number stamped below arms

Date	F	VF	XF	Unc	BU
1974	—	—	—	130	—

KM# 83 250 DOLLARS **Weight:** 10.5800 g. **Composition:** 0.9000 Gold .3061 oz. AGW **Subject:** 250 Anniversary of Parliament

Date	Mintage	F	VF	XF	Unc	BU
1979 Proof	1,835	Value: 240				

KM# 137 250 DOLLARS **Weight:** 47.5400 g. **Composition:** 0.9170 Gold 1.4017 oz. AGW **Subject:** Royal Visit **Obverse:** Queen Elizabeth II **Reverse:** National arms

Date	Mintage	F	VF	XF	Unc	BU
1985 Proof	100	Value: 800				

KM# 117 250 DOLLARS **Weight:** 47.5400 g. **Composition:** 0.9170 Gold 1.4017 oz. AGW **Subject:** Commonwealth Games **Obverse:** National arms **Note:** Similar to 10 Dollars, KM#113.

Date	Mintage	F	VF	XF	Unc	BU
1985 Proof	101	Value: 800				

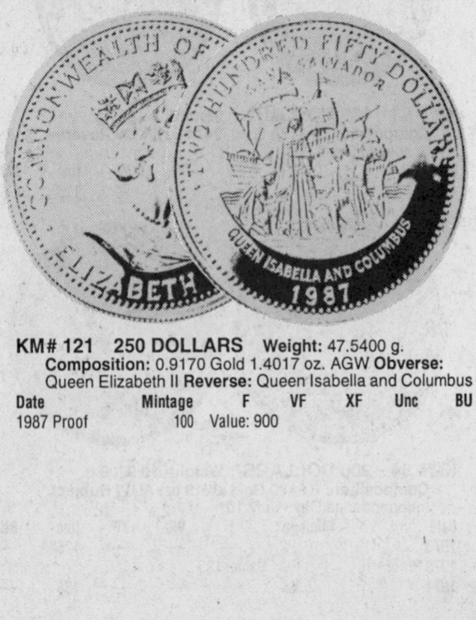

KM# 121 250 DOLLARS **Weight:** 47.5400 g. **Composition:** 0.9170 Gold 1.4017 oz. AGW **Obverse:** Queen Elizabeth II **Reverse:** Queen Isabella and Columbus

Date	Mintage	F	VF	XF	Unc	BU
1987 Proof	100	Value: 900				

KM# 126 250 DOLLARS **Weight:** 47.5400 g. **Composition:** 0.9170 Gold 1.4017 oz. AGW **Subject:** Columbus Discovers the New World **Obverse:** Queen Elizabeth **Reverse:** Columbus sighting land

Date	Mintage	F	VF	XF	Unc	BU
1988 Proof	53	Value: 1,000				

KM# 131 250 DOLLARS **Weight:** 47.5400 g. **Composition:** 0.9170 Gold 1.4017 oz. AGW **Obverse:** Queen Elizabeth **Reverse:** Christopher Columbus

Date	Mintage	F	VF	XF	Unc	BU
1989 Proof	Est. 250	Value: 900				

KM# 136 250 DOLLARS **Weight:** 47.5400 g. **Composition:** 0.9170 Gold 1.4017 oz. AGW **Subject:** Discovery of New World **Obverse:** Queen Elizabeth II, date below **Reverse:** Native American

Date	Mintage	F	VF	XF	Unc	BU
1990 Proof	500	Value: 850				

KM# 175 250 DOLLARS **Weight:** 47.5400 g. **Composition:** 0.9170 Gold 1.4017 oz. AGW **Subject:** Discovery of the New World

Date	Mintage	F	VF	XF	Unc	BU
1992 Proof	Est. 500	Value: 900				

KM# 182 250 DOLLARS **Weight:** 47.5400 g. **Composition:** 0.9170 Gold 1.4017 oz. AGW **Subject:** Royal Visit **Note:** Similar to 2 Dollars, KM#158.

Date	Mintage	F	VF	XF	Unc	BU
1994 Proof	100	Value: 1,200				

KM# 88 500 DOLLARS **Weight:** 25.9200 g. **Composition:** 0.9000 Gold .7500 oz. AGW **Subject:** Wedding of Prince Charles and Lady Diana **Reverse:** Conjoined busts of royal couple left

Date	Mintage	F	VF	XF	Unc	BU
1981 Proof	5,000	Value: 525				

KM# 100 1000 DOLLARS **Weight:** 41.4700 g. **Composition:** 0.9000 Gold 1.2001 oz. AGW **Subject:** America's Cup Challenge

Date	Mintage	F	VF	XF	Unc	BU
1983 Proof	300	Value: 750				

KM# 75 2500 DOLLARS **Weight:** 407.2600 g. **Composition:** 0.9170 Gold 12.0082 oz. AGW **Note:** Similar to KM#66, Two Dollars.

Date	Mintage	F	VF	XF	Unc	BU
1974 Proof	204	Value: 6,500				
1977 Proof	168	Value: 7,000				

KM# 101 2500 DOLLARS **Weight:** 407.2600 g. **Composition:** 0.9170 Gold 12.0082 oz. AGW **Subject:** 10th Anniversary of Independence

Date	Mintage	F	VF	XF	Unc	BU
1983 Proof	55	Value: 7,500				

KM# 112 2500 DOLLARS **Weight:** 407.2600 g. **Composition:** 0.9170 Gold 12.0082 oz. AGW **Subject:** Columbus' Discovery of America

Date	Mintage	F	VF	XF	Unc	BU
1985 Proof	37	Value: 7,500				

KM# 116 2500 DOLLARS **Weight:** 407.2600 g. **Composition:** 0.9170 Gold 12.0082 oz. AGW **Reverse:** Kneeling Columbus and Queen Isabella

Date	Mintage	F	VF	XF	Unc	BU
1987 Proof	20	Value: 9,000				

KM# 122 2500 DOLLARS **Weight:** 407.2600 g. **Composition:** 0.9170 Gold 12.0082 oz. AGW **Obverse:** Queen Elizabeth **Reverse:** Columbus sighting "New World"

Date	Mintage	F	VF	XF	Unc	BU
1988 Proof	32	Value: 9,000				

MINT SETS

KM#	Date	Mintage	Identification	Issue Price	Mkt Val
MS1	1966 (9)	75,050	KM#2-10	16.00	18.00
MS2	1966 (7)	500,000	KM#2-8	5.25	9.00
MS3	1967 (4)	1,200	KM#11-14	180	1,150
MS4	1969	26,221	KM#2-10	20.25	20.00
MS5	1970 (9)	25,135	KM#3-10, 15	20.25	20.00
MS6	1971 (9)	12,895	KM#16-24	20.25	20.00
MS7	1971 (4)	6,800	KM#25, 27, 29, 31	185	950
MS8	1972 (9)	10,128	KM#16-23, 33	22.75	19.00
MS9	1972 (4)	2,250	KM#34-37	185	700
MS10	1973 (9)	9,853	KM#16-23, 33	23.75	25.00
MS11	1973 (4)	4,660	KM#40, 43, 47, 49.1	—	310
MS12	1973 (2)	—	KM#40, 43	—	85.00
MS13	1974 (9)	11,004	KM#59-67	22.50	25.00
MS14	1974 (4)	5,528	KM#51, 54, 69, 72	—	450
MS15	1974 (2)	—	KM#68, 71	—	170
MS16	1975 (9)	3,845	KM#59-67	27.00	30.00
MS17	1975 (4)	1,545	KM#51, 54, 69, 72	—	500
MS18	1976 (9)	1,453	KM#59-67	27.00	35.00
MS19	1977 (9)	731	KM#59-67	27.00	75.00
MS20	1978 (9)	767	KM#59-67	27.00	75.00
MS21	1989 (7)	—	KM#59a, 60-64, 65b	—	30.00
MS22	1991 (7)	5,000	KM#59a, 60-64, 65b	—	30.00
MS23	1992 (7)	—	KM#59a, 60-64, 65b	24.00	30.00

PROOF SETS

KM#	Date	Mintage	Identification	Issue Price	Mkt Val
PS1	1967 (4)	850	KM#11-14	252	1,245
PS2	1969 (9)	10,381	KM#2-10	35.00	30.00
PS3	1970 (9)	22,827	KM#3-10, 15	35.00	30.00
PS5B	1971 (4)	—	KM#26, 28, 30, 32.1	—	800
PS4	1971 (9)	30,507	KM#16-24	35.00	30.00
PS5A	1971 (4)	1,250	KM#25, 27, 29, 31	298	1,100
PS6	1972 (9)	34,789	KM#16-23, 33	35.00	30.00
PS7	1972 (4)	1,250	KM#34-37	565	1,000
PS8	1973 (9)	34,815	KM#16-23, 33	35.00	30.00
PS9	1973 (4)	1,260	KM#41, 44, 46, 50	402	375
PS10	1974 (9)	93,776	KM#59-63, 64a-67a	45.00	30.00
PS11	1974 (4)	3,587	KM#51, 54, 69, 73	1,000	525
PS12	1975 (9)	29,095	KM#59-63, 64a-67a	59.00	35.00
PS13	1975 (4)	1,570	KM#51, 54, 69, 73	1,000	525
PS14	1976 (9)	22,570	KM#59-63, 64a-67a	59.00	35.00
PS15	1976 (4)	—	KM#51, 54, 69, 73	1,000	695
PS16	1977 (9)	10,812	KM#59-63, 64a-67a	59.00	45.00
PS17	1977 (4)	—	KM#51, 54, 69, 73	—	625
PS18	1978 (9)	6,931	KM#59-63, 64a-67a	59.00	55.00
PS19	1979 (9)	2,053	KM#59-63, 64a-67a	115	75.00
PS20	1979 (2)	—	KM#82-83	445	300
PS21	1980 (9)	2,084	KM#59-63, 64a-67a	145	75.00
PS22	1981 (9)	1,980	KM#59-64, 65b-67b	62.00	60.00
PS23	1982 (9)	—	KM#59-64, 89-91	67.00	75.00
PS24	1983 (9)	1,009	KM#59-64, 93-95	67.00	75.00
PS25	1984 (9)	7,500	KM#59-64, 104-106	72.00	60.00
PS26	1985 (9)	1,576	KM#59-64, 104, 105, 107	—	65.00
PS27	1989 (9)	2,000	KM#59a, 60-64, 65b, 66c, 132	106	100
PS28	1991 (12)	25,000	KM#139-150	425	400
PS29	1992 (3)	750	KM#192-194 + gold-plated silver ingot	—	400

BAHRAIN

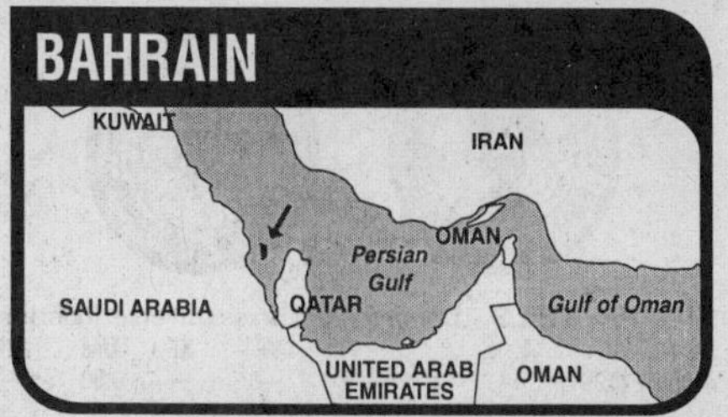

The State of Bahrain, a group of islands in the Persian Gulf off Saudi Arabia, has an area of 268 sq. mi. (622 sq. km.) and a population of 618,000. Capital: Manama. Prior to the depression of the 1930's, the economy was based on pearl fishing. Petroleum and aluminum industries and transit trade are the vital factors in the economy today.

The Portuguese occupied the islands in 1507 but were driven out in 1602 by Arab subjects of Persia. They in turn were ejected by Arabs of the Ataiba tribe from the Arabian mainland who have maintained possession up to the present time. The ruling sheikh of Bahrain entered into relations with Great Britain in 1805 and concluded a binding treaty of protection in 1861. In 1968 Great Britain decided to terminate treaty relations with the Persian Gulf sheikhdoms. Unable to agree on terms of union with the other sheikhdoms, Bahrain decided to seek independence as a separate entity and became fully independent on August 14, 1971.

Bahrain took part in the Arab oil embargo against the U.S. and other nations. The government bought controlling interest in the oil industry in 1975.

The coinage of the State of Bahrain was struck at the Royal Mint, London, England.

RULERS

Al Khalifa Dynasty
Isa Bin Ali, 1869-1932
Hamad Bin Isa, 1932-1942
Salman Bin Hamad, 1942-1961
Isa Bin Salman, 1961-1999
Hamed Bin Isa, 1999-

MINT MARKS

Bahrain بحرين

al-Bahrain = of the two seas البحرين

MONETARY SYSTEM

فلوس	فلس	فلسا
Falus, Fulus	Fals, Fils	Falsan

1000 Fils = 1 Dinar

ARAB STATE

STANDARD COINAGE

KM# 1 FILS **Composition:** Bronze

Date	Mintage	F	VF	XF	Unc	BU
AH1385 (1965)	1,500,000	—	0.10	0.20	0.40	—
AH1385 (1965) Proof	12,000	Value: 1.00				
AH1386 (1966)	1,500,000	—	0.10	0.20	0.40	—
AH1386 (1966) Proof	—	Value: 2.00				

KM# 1a FILS **Weight:** 1.5000 g. **Composition:** 0.9250 Silver .0446 oz. ASW

Date	Mintage	F	VF	XF	Unc	BU
AH1403 (1982) Proof	Est. 15,000	Value: 3.00				

KM# 2 5 FILS **Composition:** Bronze

Date	Mintage	F	VF	XF	Unc	BU
AH1385 (1965)	8,000,000	—	0.10	0.20	0.40	—
AH1385 (1965) Proof	12,000	Value: 1.00				

KM# 2a 5 FILS **Weight:** 2.0000 g. **Composition:** 0.9250 Silver .0595 oz. ASW

Date	Mintage	F	VF	XF	Unc	BU
AH1403 (1982) Proof	Est. 15,000	Value: 3.00				

KM# 16 5 FILS **Composition:** Brass **Obverse:** Palm tree

Date	F	VF	XF	Unc	BU
AH1412 (1991)	—	—	—	0.50	—

KM# 3 10 FILS **Composition:** Bronze

Date	Mintage	F	VF	XF	Unc	BU
AH1385 (1965)	8,500,000	—	0.10	0.25	0.50	—
AH1385 (1965) Proof	12,000	Value: 1.50				

KM# 3a 10 FILS **Weight:** 4.7500 g. **Composition:** 0.9250 Silver .1413 oz. ASW

Date	Mintage	F	VF	XF	Unc	BU
AH1403 (1982) Proof	Est. 15,000	Value: 4.00				

KM# 17 10 FILS **Composition:** Brass **Obverse:** Palm tree

Date	F	VF	XF	Unc	BU
AH1412 (1991)	—	—	—	0.75	—
AH1420 (2000)	—	—	—	0.75	—

KM# 4 25 FILS **Composition:** Copper Nickel

Date	Mintage	F	VF	XF	Unc	BU
AH1385 (1965)	11,250,000	—	0.20	0.35	0.75	—
AH1385 (1965) Proof	12,000	Value: 2.00				

KM# 4a 25 FILS **Weight:** 1.7500 g. **Composition:** 0.9250 Silver .0521 oz. ASW

Date	Mintage	F	VF	XF	Unc	BU
AH1403 (1982) Proof	Est. 15,000	Value: 4.00				

KM# 18 25 FILS **Composition:** Copper-Nickel **Obverse:** Ancient painting

Date	F	VF	XF	Unc	BU
AH1412 (1991)	—	—	—	1.25	—

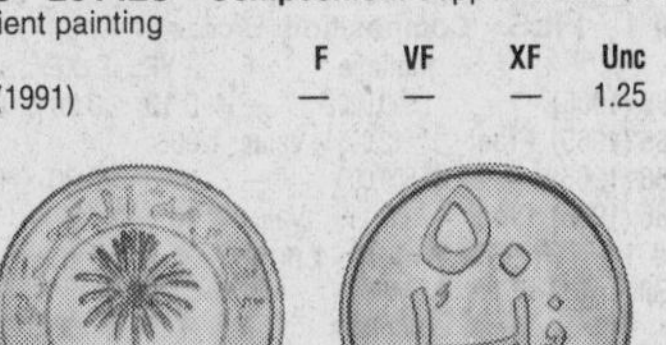

KM# 5 50 FILS **Composition:** Copper-Nickel

Date	Mintage	F	VF	XF	Unc	BU
AH1385 (1965)	6,909,000	—	0.25	0.55	1.25	—
AH1385 (1965) Proof	12,000	Value: 2.50				

KM# 5a 50 FILS **Weight:** 3.1000 g. **Composition:** 0.9250 Silver .0922 oz. ASW

Date	Mintage	F	VF	XF	Unc	BU
AH1403 (1982) Proof	Est. 15,000	Value: 5.00				

KM# 19 50 FILS **Composition:** Copper-Nickel **Obverse:** Stylized sail boats

Date	F	VF	XF	Unc	BU
AH1412 (1991)	—	—	—	1.50	—

KM# 6 100 FILS **Composition:** Copper-Nickel

Date	Mintage	F	VF	XF	Unc	BU
AH1385 (1965)	8,300,000	—	0.35	0.75	1.50	—
AH1385 (1965) Proof	12,000	Value: 3.50				

KM# 6a 100 FILS **Weight:** 6.5000 g. **Composition:** 0.9250 Silver .1933 oz. ASW

Date	Mintage	F	VF	XF	Unc	BU
AH1403 (1982) Proof	Est. 15,000	Value: 6.00				

KM# 20 100 FILS **Ring Composition:** Brass **Center Composition:** Copper-Nickel **Obverse:** Coat of arms

Date	F	VF	XF	Unc	BU
AH1412 (1992)	—	—	—	3.50	—
AH1415 (1994)	—	—	—	3.50	—
AH1417 (1996)	—	—	—	3.50	—

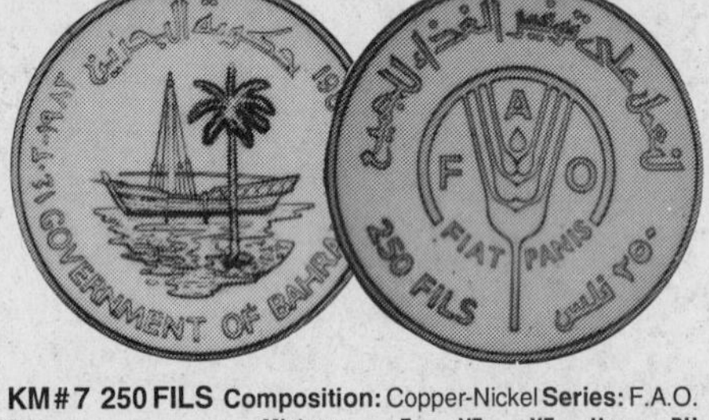

KM# 7 250 FILS **Composition:** Copper-Nickel **Series:** F.A.O.

Date	Mintage	F	VF	XF	Unc	BU
AH1389 (1969)	50,000	—	1.50	2.50	5.00	—
AH1389 (1969) Proof	—	Value: 8.00				
AH1403 (1982)	3,000	—	1.75	3.50	10.00	—

KM# 7a 250 FILS **Weight:** 15.0000 g. **Composition:** 0.9250 Silver .4461 oz. ASW

Date	Mintage	F	VF	XF	Unc	BU
AH1403 (1982) Proof	Est. 15,000	Value: 14.50				

KM# 8 500 FILS **Weight:** 18.3000 g. **Composition:** 0.8000 Silver .4707 oz. ASW **Reverse:** Opening of Isa Town

Date	Mintage	F	VF	XF	Unc	BU
AH1385 (1965) Proof	12,000	Value: 17.50				
AH1388 (1968)	50,000	—	2.50	5.50	12.50	—
AH1388 (1968) Proof	—	Value: 17.50				

KM# 8a 500 FILS **Weight:** 18.0600 g. **Composition:** 0.9250 Silver .5372 oz. ASW

Date	Mintage	F	VF	XF	Unc	BU
AH1403 (1982) Proof	Est. 15,000	Value: 35.00				

KM# 13 5 DINARS **Weight:** 19.4400 g. **Composition:** 0.9250 Silver .5782 oz. ASW **Reverse:** Gazelle **Edge Lettering:** World Wildlife Fund

Date	Mintage	F	VF	XF	Unc	BU
AH1406 (1985) Proof	Est. 25,000	Value: 35.00				

KM# 14 5 DINARS **Weight:** 19.4400 g. **Composition:** 0.9250 Silver .5782 oz. ASW **Reverse:** Save The Children

Date	Mintage	F	VF	XF	Unc	BU
AH1410 (1989) Proof	Est. 20,000	Value: 36.50				

KM# 21 5 DINARS **Weight:** 28.2300 g. **Composition:** 0.9250 Silver .8395 oz. ASW **Subject:** 50th Anniversary - United Nations **Obverse:** Portrait of Amir **Reverse:** UN building

Date	Mintage	F	VF	XF	Unc	BU
AH1416 (1995) Proof	—	Value: 37.50				

KM# 11 50 DINARS **Weight:** 15.9800 g. **Composition:** 0.9170 Gold .4712 oz. AGW **Subject:** 50th Anniversary of Bahrain Monetary Agency

Date	Mintage	F	VF	XF	Unc	BU
AH1398 (1977) Proof	5,000	Value: 300				

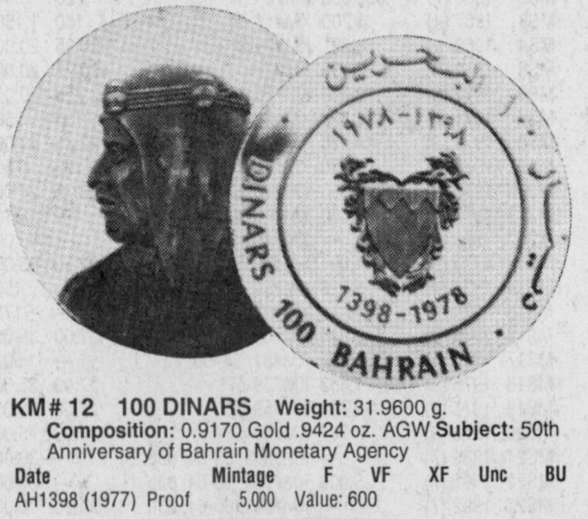

KM# 12 100 DINARS **Weight:** 31.9600 g. **Composition:** 0.9170 Gold .9424 oz. AGW **Subject:** 50th Anniversary of Bahrain Monetary Agency

Date	Mintage	F	VF	XF	Unc	BU
AH1398 (1977) Proof	5,000	Value: 600				

MINT SETS

KM#	Date	Mintage	Identification	Issue Price	Mkt Val
MS1	1992 (5)	—	KM#16-20	—	10.00

PROOF SETS

KM#	Date	Mintage	Identification	Issue Price	Mkt Val
PS2	1965 (7)	12,000	KM#1-6, 8	—	30.00
PS1	1965, 1968, 1969 (8)	20,000	KM#1-6 1965; KM7 1969; KM8 1968	32.00	35.00
PS3	1983 (7)	15,000	KM#1a-8a	99.00	75.00

BANGLADESH

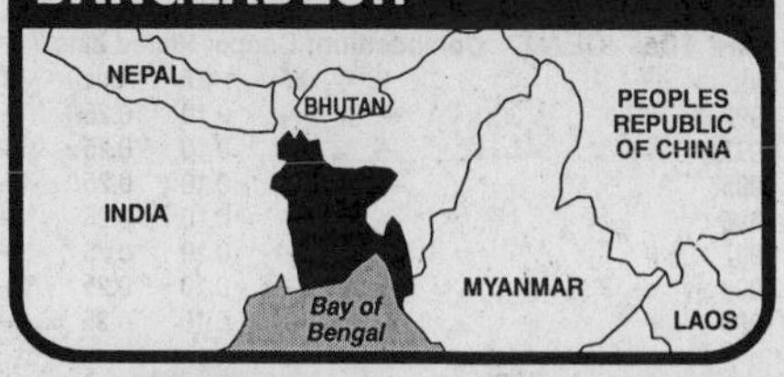

The Peoples Republic of Bangladesh (formerly East Pakistan), a parliamentary democracy located on the Bay of Bengal bordered by India and Burma, has an area of 55,598 sq. mi. (143,998 sq. km.) and a population of 128.1 million. Capital: Dhaka. The economy is predominantly agricultural. Jute products, jute and tea are exported.

British rule over the vast Indian sub-continent ended in 1947 when British India attained independence and was partitioned into the two successor states of India and Pakistan. Pakistan consisted of East and West Pakistan, two areas united by the Moslem religion but separated by culture and 1,000 miles of Indian territory. Restive under the de facto rule of the militant but fewer West Pakistanis, the East Pakistanis unsuccessfully demanded greater economic benefits and political reforms. The inability of the leaders of East and West Pakistan to resolve a political breakdown occasioned by the East Pakistan success in the general elections of 1970 precipitated massive civil disobedience in East Pakistan which West Pakistan sought to suppress militarily. East Pakistan seceded from Pakistan, March 26, 1971, and with the support of India declared an independent Peoples Republic of Bangladesh.

Bangladesh is a member of the Commonwealth of Nations. The president is the Head of State and the Government.

MONETARY SYSTEM
100 Poisha = 1 Taka

DATING
Christian era using Bengali numerals.

PEOPLES REPUBLIC

STANDARD COINAGE

KM# 5 POISHA **Composition:** Aluminum

Date	Mintage	F	VF	XF	Unc	BU
1974	300,000,000	—	—	0.10	0.15	—

KM# 1 5 POISHA **Composition:** Aluminum

Date	F	VF	XF	Unc	BU
1973	—	—	0.10	0.20	—
1974	—	—	0.10	0.20	—

KM# 6 5 POISHA **Composition:** Aluminum **Series:** F.A.O.

Date	Mintage	F	VF	XF	Unc	BU
1974	5,000,000	—	—	0.10	0.20	—
1975	3,000,000	—	—	0.10	0.20	—
1976	3,000,000	—	—	0.10	0.20	—
1977	—	—	—	0.10	0.20	—

KM# 10 5 POISHA **Composition:** Aluminum **Series:** F.A.O.

Date	Mintage	F	VF	XF	Unc	BU
1977	90,000,000	—	—	0.10	0.15	—
1978	52,432,000	—	—	0.10	0.25	—

Date	Mintage	F	VF	XF	Unc	BU
1979	120,096,000	—	—	0.10	0.15	—
1980	127,008,000	—	—	0.10	0.15	—
1981	72,992,000	—	—	0.10	0.15	—

KM# 2 10 POISHA **Composition:** Aluminum

Date	F	VF	XF	Unc	BU
1973	—	—	0.10	0.35	—
1974	—	—	0.10	0.35	—

KM# 7 10 POISHA **Composition:** Aluminum **Series:** F.A.O.

Date	Mintage	F	VF	XF	Unc	BU
1974	5,000,000	—	—	0.15	0.35	—
1975	4,000,000	—	—	0.15	0.35	—
1976	4,000,000	—	—	0.15	0.35	—
1977	4,000,000	—	—	0.15	0.35	—
1978	141,744,000	—	—	0.15	0.30	—
1979	—	—	—	0.15	0.40	—

KM# 11.1 10 POISHA **Composition:** Aluminum **Series:** F.A.O.

Date	Mintage	F	VF	XF	Unc	BU
1977	48,000,000	—	—	0.15	0.30	—
1978	77,518,000	—	—	0.15	0.30	—
1979	170,112,000	—	—	0.15	0.30	—
1980	200,000,000	—	—	0.15	0.30	—

KM# 11.2 10 POISHA **Composition:** Aluminum

Date	Mintage	F	VF	XF	Unc	BU
1981	—	—	—	0.25	0.50	—
1983	142,848,000	—	—	0.15	0.30	—
1984	57,152,000	—	—	0.15	0.30	—

KM# 3 25 POISHA **Composition:** Steel **Obverse:** Rohu

Date	F	VF	XF	Unc	BU
1973	—	—	0.25	0.75	—

KM# 8 25 POISHA **Composition:** Steel **Series:** F.A.O.

Date	Mintage	F	VF	XF	Unc	BU
1974	5,000,000	—	—	0.20	0.50	—
1975	6,000,000	—	—	0.20	0.50	—
1976	6,000,000	—	—	0.20	0.50	—
1977	51,300,000	—	—	0.15	0.35	—
1978	66,750,000	—	—	0.15	0.35	—
1979	—	—	—	0.15	0.35	—

KM# 12 25 POISHA **Composition:** Steel **Obverse:** Tiger head

Date	Mintage	F	VF	XF	Unc	BU
1977	45,300,000	—	—	0.15	0.40	—
1978	66,750,000	—	—	0.15	0.40	—
1979	56,704,000	—	—	0.15	0.40	—
1980	228,992,000	—	—	0.15	0.40	—
1981	45,072,000	—	—	0.15	0.40	—
1983	96,128,000	—	—	0.15	0.35	—
1984	203,872,000	—	—	0.15	0.35	—
1991	50,002,000	—	—	0.15	0.35	—

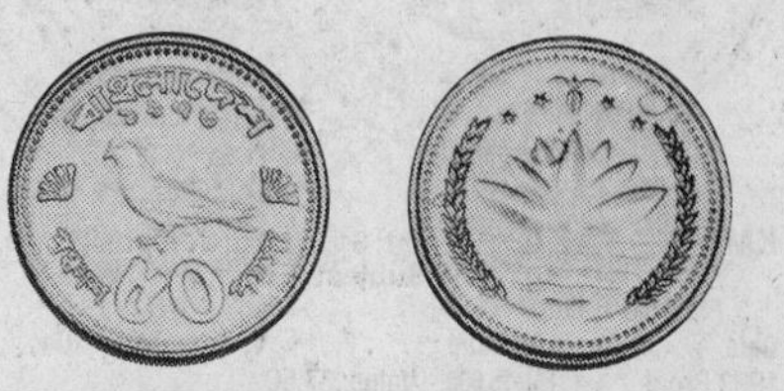

KM# 4 50 POISHA **Composition:** Steel

Date	Mintage	F	VF	XF	Unc	BU
1973	18,000,000	—	0.25	0.75	2.50	—

KM# 13 50 POISHA **Composition:** Steel **Series:** F.A.O.

Date	Mintage	F	VF	XF	Unc	BU
1977	12,700,000	—	—	0.20	0.75	—
1978	37,300,000	—	—	0.20	0.75	—
1979	2,208,000	—	—	0.20	0.75	—
1980	124,512,000	—	—	0.20	0.50	—
1981	36,680,000	—	—	0.20	0.75	—
1983	31,392,000	—	—	0.20	0.75	—
1984	168,608,000	—	—	0.20	0.50	—
1994	—	—	—	0.20	0.50	—

KM# 9.1 TAKA **Composition:** Copper-Nickel **Series:** F.A.O. **Obverse:** Stylized family **Reverse:** Shapla flower

Date	Mintage	F	VF	XF	Unc	BU
1975	4,000,000	—	0.15	0.45	1.00	—
1976	—	—	0.15	0.45	1.00	—
1977	—	—	0.15	0.45	1.00	—

KM# 9.2 TAKA **Composition:** Steel **Note:** Non-magnetic. Varieties exist.

Date	F	VF	XF	Unc	BU
1992	—	0.15	0.45	1.00	—
1993	—	0.15	0.45	1.00	—
1995	—	0.15	0.45	1.00	—

KM# 9.3 TAKA **Composition:** Copper-Nickel

Date	F	VF	XF	Unc	BU
1996	—	0.20	0.65	1.85	—
1997	—	0.20	0.65	1.85	—

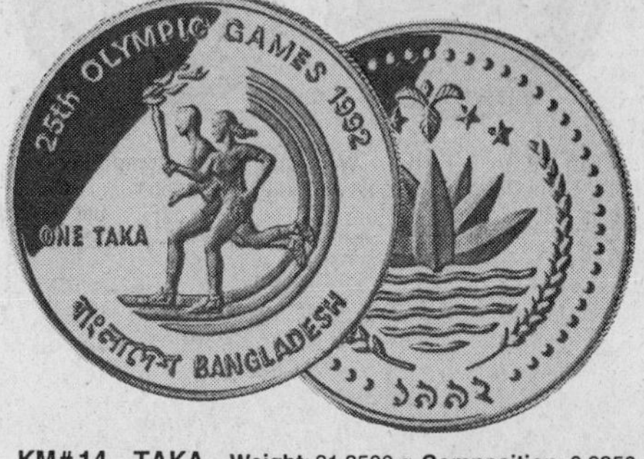

KM# 14 TAKA **Weight:** 31.3500 g. **Composition:** 0.9250 Silver .9323 oz. ASW **Reverse:** Olympics - Runners with Torch

Date	Mintage	F	VF	XF	Unc	BU
1992 Proof	Est. 40,000	Value: 32.50				

KM# 15 TAKA **Weight:** 31.3500 g. **Composition:** 0.9250 Silver .9323 oz. ASW **Subject:** Engangered Wildlife **Reverse:** Deer

Date	Mintage	F	VF	XF	Unc	BU
1993 Proof	Est. 15,000	Value: 37.50				

KM# 16 TAKA **Weight:** 31.3500 g. **Composition:** 0.9250 Silver .9323 oz. ASW **Subject:** World Cup Soccer, 1994

Date	Mintage	F	VF	XF	Unc	BU
1993 Proof	40,000	Value: 35.00				

KM# 17 TAKA **Weight:** 31.3500 g. **Composition:** 0.9250 Silver .9323 oz. ASW **Subject:** 20th Victory Day **Obverse:** Seven portraits **Reverse:** National memorial

Date	F	VF	XF	Unc	BU
1991 Proof	—	Value: 32.50			

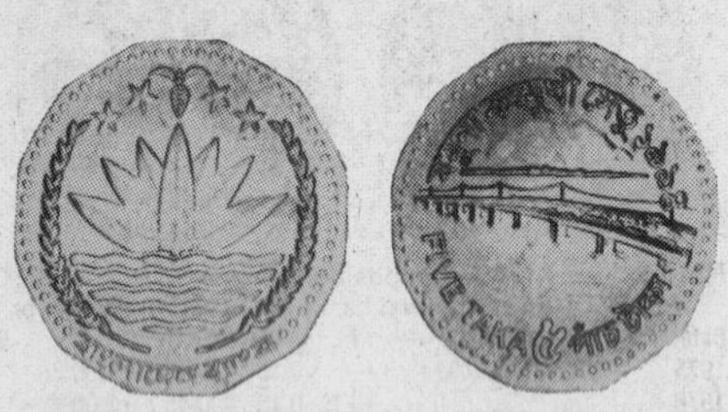

KM# 18.1 5 TAKA **Weight:** 7.8700 g. **Composition:** Steel **Obverse:** Shapla flower **Reverse:** Bridge

Date	F	VF	XF	Unc	BU
1994	—	—	—	1.75	—

KM# 18.2 5 TAKA **Weight:** 8.1700 g. **Composition:** Steel **Obverse:** Shapla flower, thicker design

Date	F	VF	XF	Unc	BU
1996	—	—	—	2.25	—

BARBADOS

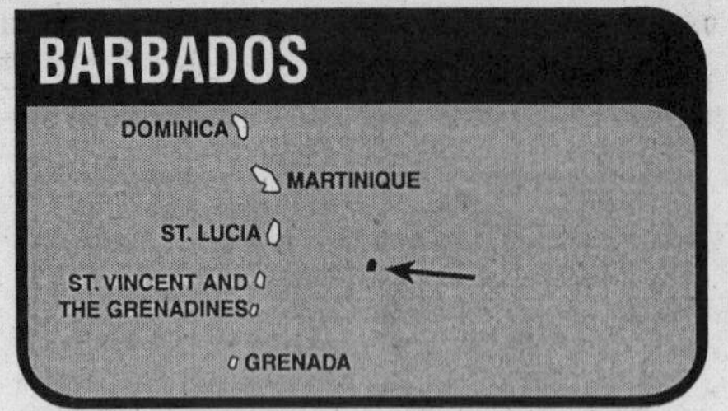

Barbados, an independent state within the British Commonwealth, is located in the Windward Islands of the West Indies east of St. Vincent. The coral island has an area of 166 sq. mi. (430 sq. km.) and a population of 269,000. Capital: Bridgetown. The economy is based on sugar and tourism. Sugar, petroleum products, molasses, and rum are exported.

Barbados was named by the Portuguese who achieved the first landing on the island in 1563. British sailors landed at the site of present-day Holetown in 1624. Barbados was under uninterrupted British control from the time of the first British settlement in 1627 until it obtained independence on Nov. 30, 1966. It is a member of the Commonwealth of Nations. Elizabeth II is Head of State as Queen of Barbados.

Unmarked side cut pieces of Spanish and Spanish Colonial 1, 2 and 8 reales were the principal coinage medium of 18th-century Barbados. The "Neptune" tokens issued by Sir Phillip Gibbs, a local plantation owner, circulated freely but were never established as legal coinage. The coinage and banknotes of the British Caribbean Territories (Eastern Group) were employed prior to 1973 when Barbados issued a decimal coinage.

RULERS

British, until 1966

MINT MARKS

FM - Franklin Mint, U.S.A.*
None - Royal Mint

*NOTE: From 1975-1985 the Franklin Mint produced coinage in up to 3 different qualities. Qualities of issue are designated in ( ) after each date and are defined as follows:

(M) MATTE - Normal circulation strike or a dull finish produced by sandblasting special uncirculated (polish finish) or proof quality dies.

(U) SPECIAL UNCIRCULATED - Polished or proof-like in appearance without any frosted features.

(P) PROOF - The highest quality obtainable having mirror-like fields and frosted features.

MONETARY SYSTEM

100 Cents = 1 Dollar

INDEPENDENT SOVEREIGN STATE
within the British Commonwealth

DECIMAL COINAGE

KM# 10 CENT **Composition:** Bronze

Date	Mintage	F	VF	XF	Unc	BU
1973	5,000,000	—	—	0.10	0.25	—
1973FM (M)	7,500	—	—	—	1.00	—
1973FM (P)	97,000	Value: 0.50				
1974FM (M)	8,708	—	—	—	1.00	—
1974FM (P)	36,000	Value: 0.50				
1975FM (M)	5,000	—	—	—	0.75	—
1975FM (U)	1,360	—	—	—	1.00	—
1975FM (P)	20,000	Value: 0.50				
1977FM (M)	2,102	—	—	—	0.75	—
1977FM (U)	468	—	—	—	3.00	—
1977FM (P)	5,014	Value: 0.50				
1978	4,807,000	—	—	0.10	0.25	—
1978FM (M)	2,000	—	—	—	1.00	—
1978FM (U)	2,517	—	—	—	1.50	—
1978FM (P)	4,436	Value: 1.00				
1979	5,606,000	—	—	0.10	0.25	—
1979FM (M)	1,500	—	—	—	1.00	—
1979FM (U)	523	—	—	—	2.50	—
1979FM (P)	4,126	Value: 1.00				
1980	14,400,000	—	—	0.10	0.25	—
1980FM (M)	1,500	—	—	—	1.00	—
1980FM (U)	649	—	—	—	2.00	—
1980FM (P)	2,111	Value: 1.50				
1981	10,160,000	—	—	0.10	0.25	—
1981FM (M)	1,500	—	—	—	1.00	—
1981FM (U)	327	—	—	—	2.00	—
1981FM (P)	943	Value: 1.50				
1982	5,040,000	—	—	0.10	0.25	—
1982FM (U)	1,500	—	—	—	1.25	—
1982FM (P)	843	Value: 1.50				
1983FM (M)	1,500	—	—	—	1.00	—
1983FM (U)	—	—	—	—	1.25	—
1983FM (P)	459	Value: 1.50				
1984	5,008,000	—	—	0.10	0.25	—
1984FM (M)	868	—	—	—	1.25	—
1984FM (P)	—	Value: 1.50				
1985	—	—	—	0.10	0.25	—
1986	—	—	—	0.10	0.25	—
1987	10,000,000	—	—	0.10	0.25	—
1988	12,136,000	—	—	0.10	0.25	—
1989	—	—	—	0.10	0.25	—
1990	—	—	—	0.10	0.25	—
1991	—	—	—	0.10	0.25	—

KM# 10a CENT **Composition:** Copper Plated Zinc

Date	F	VF	XF	Unc	BU
1992	—	—	0.10	0.25	—
1993	—	—	0.10	0.25	—
1995	—	—	0.10	0.25	—
1996	—	—	0.10	0.25	—
1997	—	—	0.10	0.25	—
1998	—	—	0.10	0.25	—
1999	—	—	0.10	0.25	—

KM# 19 CENT **Composition:** Copper Plated Zinc **Subject:** 10th Anniversary of Independence

Date	Mintage	F	VF	XF	Unc	BU
ND(1976)	6,406,000	—	—	0.10	0.20	—
ND(1976)FM (M)	5,000	—	—	—	0.50	—
ND(1976)FM (U)	996	—	—	—	1.00	—
ND(1976)FM (P)	12,000	Value: 0.50				

KM# 11 5 CENTS **Composition:** Brass **Reverse:** South Point Lighthouse

Date	Mintage	F	VF	XF	Unc	BU
1973FM (M)	7,500	—	—	—	1.25	—
1973	3,000,000	—	0.10	0.15	0.35	—
1973FM (P)	97,000	Value: 0.75				
1974FM (M)	8,708	—	—	—	1.25	—
1974FM (P)	36,000	Value: 0.75				
1975FM (M)	5,000	—	—	—	1.00	—
1975FM (U)	1,360	—	—	—	1.25	—
1975FM (P)	20,000	Value: 0.75				
1977FM (M)	2,100	—	—	—	2.00	—
1977FM (U)	468	—	—	—	3.00	—
1977FM (P)	5,014	Value: 0.75				
1978FM (M)	2,000	—	—	—	0.75	—
1978FM (U)	2,517	—	—	—	2.75	—
1978FM (P)	4,436	Value: 1.25				
1979	4,800,000	—	0.10	0.15	0.35	—
1979FM (M)	1,500	—	—	—	0.75	—
1979FM (U)	523	—	—	—	2.75	—
1979FM (P)	4,126	Value: 1.25				
1980FM (M)	1,500	—	—	—	1.00	—
1980FM (U)	649	—	—	—	2.25	—
1980FM (P)	2,111	Value: 1.75				
1981FM (M)	1,500	—	—	—	1.00	—
1981FM (U)	327	—	—	—	2.25	—
1981FM (P)	943	Value: 1.75				
1982	2,100,000	—	0.10	0.15	0.35	—
1982FM (U)	1,500	—	—	—	1.50	—
1982FM (P)	843	Value: 1.75				
1983FM (M)	1,500	—	—	—	1.50	—
1983FM (U)	—	—	—	—	1.50	—
1983FM (P)	459	Value: 1.75				
1984FM	1,737	—	—	—	1.50	—
1984FM (P)	—	Value: 2.00				
1985	—	—	—	—	0.25	—
1986	—	—	—	—	0.25	—
1988	4,200,000	—	—	—	0.25	—
1989	—	—	—	—	0.25	—
1991	—	—	—	—	0.25	—
1994	—	—	—	—	0.25	—
1996	—	—	—	—	0.25	—
1997	—	—	—	—	0.25	—
1998	—	—	—	—	0.25	—
1999	—	—	—	—	0.25	—

KM# 20 5 CENTS **Composition:** Brass **Subject:** 10th Anniversary of Independence

Date	Mintage	F	VF	XF	Unc	BU
ND(1976)FM (M)	5,000	—	—	—	1.00	—
ND(1976)FM (U)	12,000	—	—	—	1.00	—
ND(1976)FM (P)	—	Value: 0.75				

KM# 12 10 CENTS **Composition:** Copper-Nickel **Reverse:** Laughing Gull

Date	Mintage	F	VF	XF	Unc	BU
1973	4,000,000	—	0.10	0.15	0.50	—
1973FM (M)	5,000	—	—	—	1.50	—
1973FM (P)	97,000	Value: 1.00				
1974FM (M)	6,208	—	—	—	1.50	—
1974FM (P)	36,000	Value: 1.00				
1975FM (M)	2,500	—	—	—	1.00	—
1975FM (U)	1,360	—	—	—	1.50	—
1975FM (P)	20,000	Value: 1.00				
1977FM (M)	2,100	—	—	—	1.00	—
1977FM (U)	468	—	—	—	4.00	—
1977FM (P)	5,014	Value: 1.00				
1978FM (M)	2,000	—	—	—	1.00	—
1978FM (U)	2,517	—	—	—	3.00	—
1978FM (P)	4,436	Value: 1.50				
1979	2,500,000	—	0.10	0.20	0.60	—
1979FM (M)	1,500	—	—	—	2.50	—
1979FM (U)	523	—	—	—	3.00	—
1979FM (P)	4,126	Value: 1.50				
1980	3,500,000	—	0.10	0.15	0.50	—
1980FM (M)	1,500	—	—	—	1.00	—
1980FM (U)	649	—	—	—	2.50	—
1980FM (P)	2,111	Value: 2.00				
1981FM (M)	1,500	—	—	—	1.00	—
1981FM (U)	327	—	—	—	2.50	—
1981FM (P)	943	Value: 2.00				
1982FM (U)	1,500	—	—	—	1.75	—
1982FM (P)	843	Value: 2.00				
1983FM (M)	1,500	—	—	—	1.75	—
1983FM (U)	—	—	—	—	1.75	—
1983FM (P)	459	Value: 2.00				
1984	3,400,000	—	0.10	0.15	0.50	—
1984FM (P)	—	Value: 2.25				
1985	—	—	0.10	0.15	0.50	—
1986	—	—	0.10	0.15	0.50	—
1987	3,500,000	—	0.10	0.15	0.50	—
1988	—	—	0.10	0.15	0.50	—
1989	—	—	0.10	0.15	0.50	—
1990	—	—	0.10	0.15	0.50	—
1992	—	—	0.10	0.15	0.50	—
1995	—	—	0.10	0.15	0.50	—
1996	—	—	0.10	0.15	0.50	—
1998	—	—	0.10	0.15	0.50	—
2000	—	—	0.10	0.15	0.50	—
2001	—	—	0.10	0.15	0.50	—

KM# 21 10 CENTS **Composition:** Copper-Nickel **Subject:** 10th Anniversary of Independence

Date	Mintage	F	VF	XF	Unc	BU
ND(1976)FM (M)	2,500	—	—	—	0.75	—
ND(1976)FM (U)	996	—	—	—	1.75	—
ND(1976)FM (P)	12,000	Value: 1.50				

KM# 13 25 CENTS **Composition:** Copper-Nickel **Reverse:** Morgan Lewis Sugar Mill

Date	Mintage	F	VF	XF	Unc	BU
1973	6,000,000	—	0.15	0.30	0.60	—
1973FM (M)	4,300	—	—	—	1.75	—
1973FM (P)	97,000	Value: 1.25				
1974FM (M)	5,508	—	—	—	1.75	—
1974FM (P)	36,000	Value: 1.25				
1975FM (M)	1,800	—	—	—	1.25	—
1975FM (U)	1,360	—	—	—	1.75	—
1975FM (P)	20,000	Value: 1.25				
1977FM (M)	2,100	—	—	—	1.00	—
1977FM (U)	468	—	—	—	4.25	—
1977FM (P)	5,014	Value: 1.25				
1978	2,407,000	—	0.20	0.40	0.80	—
1978FM (M)	2,000	—	—	—	1.00	—
1978FM (U)	2,517	—	—	—	3.25	—
1978FM (P)	4,436	Value: 1.75				
1979	1,200,000	—	0.20	0.40	0.80	—
1979FM (M)	1,500	—	—	—	1.00	—
1979FM (U)	523	—	—	—	3.00	—
1979FM (P)	4,126,000	Value: 1.75				
1980	2,700,000	—	0.15	0.30	0.60	—
1980FM (M)	1,500	—	—	—	3.00	—
1980FM (U)	649	—	—	—	2.75	—
1980FM (P)	2,111	Value: 2.25				
1981	4,365,000	—	0.15	0.30	0.60	—
1981FM (M)	1,500	—	—	—	3.00	—
1981FM (U)	327	—	—	—	2.75	—
1981FM (P)	943	Value: 2.25				
1982FM (U)	1,500	—	—	—	2.00	—
1982FM (P)	843	Value: 2.25				
1983FM (M)	1,500	—	—	—	2.00	—
1983FM (U)	—	—	—	—	2.00	—
1983FM (P)	459	Value: 2.25				
1984FM	868	—	—	—	2.00	—
1984FM (P)	—	Value: 2.50				
1985	—	—	0.15	0.30	0.60	—
1986		—	0.15	0.30	0.60	—
1987	3,150,000	—	—	—	2.00	—
1988	—	—	0.15	0.30	0.60	—
1989	—	—	0.15	0.30	0.60	—
1990	—	—	0.15	0.30	0.60	—
1994	—	—	0.15	0.30	0.60	—
1996	—	—	0.15	0.30	0.60	—
1998	—	—	0.15	0.30	0.60	—
2000	—	—	0.15	0.30	0.60	—

KM# 22 25 CENTS **Composition:** Copper-Nickel **Subject:** 10th Anniversary of Independence

Date	Mintage	F	VF	XF	Unc	BU
ND(1976)FM (M)	1,800	—	—	—	1.25	—
ND(1976)FM (U)	996	—	—	—	2.00	—
ND(1976)FM (P)	12,000	Value: 1.50				

KM# 14.1 DOLLAR **Composition:** Copper-Nickel **Reverse:** Flying fish

Date	Mintage	F	VF	XF	Unc	BU
1973	3,955,000	—	0.60	0.75	1.00	—
1973FM (M)	3,000	—	—	—	2.00	—
1973FM (P)	97,000	Value: 1.50				
1974FM (M)	4,208	—	—	—	2.00	—
1974FM (P)	36,000	Value: 1.50				
1975FM (M)	500	—	—	—	3.50	—
1975FM (U)	1,360	—	—	—	2.00	—
1975FM (P)	20,000	Value: 1.50				
1977FM (M)	600	—	—	—	5.00	—
1977FM (U)	468	—	—	—	4.50	—
1977FM (P)	5,014	Value: 2.50				
1978FM (U)	1,017	—	—	—	3.50	—
1978FM (P)	4,436	Value: 2.50				
1979	2,000,000	—	0.75	1.25	1.75	—
1979FM (M)	600	—	—	—	3.00	—
1979FM (U)	523	—	—	—	3.50	—
1979FM (P)	4,126	Value: 2.50				
1980FM (M)	600	—	—	—	3.50	—
1980FM (U)	649	—	—	—	3.50	—
1980FM (P)	2,111	Value: 3.00				
1981FM (M)	600	—	—	—	3.00	—
1981FM (U)	327	—	—	—	3.50	—
1981FM (P)	943	Value: 3.50				
1982FM (U)	600	—	—	—	3.00	—
1982FM (P)	843	Value: 3.50				
1983FM (M)	600	—	—	—	3.00	—
1983FM (U)	—	—	—	—	3.00	—
1983FM (P)	459	Value: 4.00				
1984FM	469	—	—	—	3.50	—
1984FM (P)	—	Value: 4.50				
1985	—	—	—	—	1.00	—
1986	—	—	—	—	1.00	—

KM# 14.2 DOLLAR **Composition:** Copper-Nickel

Date	Mintage	F	VF	XF	Unc	BU
1988	3,145,000	—	—	—	2.25	—
1989	—	—	—	—	2.25	—
1994	—	—	—	—	2.25	—
1998	—	—	—	—	—	—

KM# 23 DOLLAR **Composition:** Copper-Nickel **Subject:** 10th Anniversary of Independence

Date	Mintage	F	VF	XF	Unc	BU
ND(1976)FM (M)	500	—	—	—	4.00	—
ND(1976)FM (U)	996	—	—	—	2.50	—
ND(1976)FM (P)	12,000	Value: 2.00				

KM# 57 DOLLAR **Weight:** 10.0000 g. **Composition:** 0.5000 Silver .1607 oz. ASW **Reverse:** Bust of Queen Mother

Date	Mintage	F	VF	XF	Unc	BU
1994 Proof	Est. 50,000	Value: 28.00				

KM# 65 DOLLAR **Weight:** 9.9400 g. **Composition:** 0.9250 Silver .2956 oz. ASW **Subject:** Queen Mother's 95th Birthday **Obverse:** National arms **Reverse:** Queen Mother's portrait

Date	Mintage	F	VF	XF	Unc	BU
1995 Proof	Est. 50,000	Value: 35.00				

KM# 15 2 DOLLARS **Composition:** Copper-Nickel **Reverse:** Staghorn coral

Date	Mintage	F	VF	XF	Unc	BU
1973FM (M)	3,000	—	—	—	4.00	—
1973FM (P)	97,000	Value: 4.50				
1974FM (M)	4,208	—	—	—	4.00	—
1974FM (P)	36,000	Value: 4.50				
1975FM (M)	500	—	—	—	5.00	—
1975FM (U)	1,360	—	—	—	4.00	—
1975FM (P)	20,000	Value: 4.50				
1977FM (M)	600	—	—	—	4.50	—
1977FM (U)	468	—	—	—	5.50	—
1977FM (P)	5,014	Value: 4.50				
1978FM (U)	1,017	—	—	—	5.00	—
1978FM (P)	4,436	Value: 4.50				
1979FM (M)	600	—	—	—	5.00	—
1979FM (U)	523	—	—	—	5.00	—
1979FM (P)	4,126	Value: 4.50				
1980FM (M)	600	—	—	—	5.00	—
1980FM (U)	649	—	—	—	5.00	—
1980FM (P)	2,111	Value: 4.50				
1981FM (M)	600	—	—	—	5.00	—
1981FM (U)	327	—	—	—	5.00	—
1981FM (P)	943	Value: 5.00				
1982FM (U)	600	—	—	—	5.00	—
1982FM (P)	843	Value: 5.00				
1983FM (U)	—	—	—	—	5.00	—
1983FM (P)	459	Value: 5.00				

Date	Mintage	F	VF	XF	Unc	BU
1984FM (U)	473	—	—	—	5.00	—
1984FM (P)	—	Value: 5.00				

KM# 24 2 DOLLARS **Composition:** Copper-Nickel **Subject:** 10th Anniversary of Independence

Date	Mintage	F	VF	XF	Unc	BU
ND(1976)FM (M)	500	—	—	—	5.00	—
ND(1976)FM (U)	996	—	—	—	5.00	—
ND(1976)FM (P)	12,000	Value: 4.00				

KM# A9 4 DOLLARS **Composition:** Copper-Nickel **Series:** F.A.O.

Date	Mintage	F	VF	XF	Unc	BU
1970	30,000	—	3.50	7.00	12.50	—
1970 Proof	2,000	Value: 22.50				

KM# 16 5 DOLLARS **Composition:** Copper-Nickel **Subject:** Shell Fountain in Bridgetown's Trafalgar Square **Obverse:** Similar to 2 Dollars, KM#15

Date	Mintage	F	VF	XF	Unc	BU
1974FM (M)	3,958	—	—	—	5.00	—
1975FM (M)	250	—	—	—	8.00	—
1975FM (U)	1,360	—	—	—	5.00	—
1977FM (M)	600	—	—	—	5.00	—
1977FM (U)	468	—	—	—	5.00	—
1978FM (U)	1,017	—	—	—	5.00	—
1979FM (M)	600	—	—	—	5.00	—
1979FM (U)	523	—	—	—	5.00	—
1980FM (M)	600	—	—	—	5.00	—
1980FM (U)	649	—	—	—	5.00	—
1981FM (M)	600	—	—	—	5.00	—
1981FM (U)	1,156	—	—	—	5.00	—
1982FM (U)	600	—	—	—	5.00	—
1982FM (P)	843	—	—	—	5.00	—
1983FM (M)	600	—	—	—	5.00	—
1983FM (U)	261	—	—	—	5.00	—
1984FM	470	—	—	—	5.00	—

KM# 16a 5 DOLLARS **Weight:** 31.1000 g. **Composition:** 0.8000 Silver .7999 oz. ASW

Date	Mintage	F	VF	XF	Unc	BU
1973FM (P)	97,000	Value: 7.00				
1973FM (M)	2,750	—	—	—	11.50	—
1974FM (P)	36,000	Value: 8.00				
1975FM (P)	20,000	Value: 9.00				
1977FM (P)	5,014	Value: 11.50				
1978FM (P)	4,436	Value: 11.50				
1979FM (P)	4,126	Value: 11.50				
1980FM (P)	2,111	Value: 14.50				
1981FM (P)	835	Value: 22.00				
1982FM (P)	658	Value: 22.00				
1983FM (P)	130	Value: 32.00				
1984FM (P)	—	Value: 32.00				

KM# 25 5 DOLLARS **Composition:** Copper-Nickel **Subject:** 10th Anniversary of Independence **Reverse:** Similar to KM#16

Date	Mintage	F	VF	XF	Unc	BU
ND(1976)FM (M)	250	—	—	—	25.00	—
ND(1976)FM (U)	996	—	—	—	12.50	—

KM# 25a 5 DOLLARS **Weight:** 31.1000 g. **Composition:** 0.8000 Silver .7999 oz. ASW

Date	Mintage	F	VF	XF	Unc	BU
ND(1976)FM (P)	12,000	Value: 15.00				

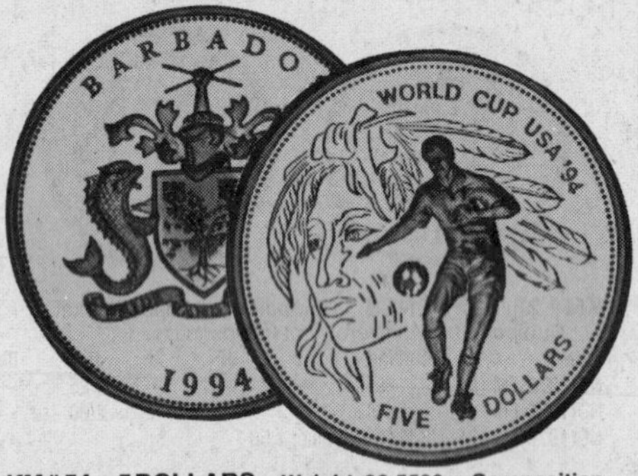

KM# 54 5 DOLLARS **Weight:** 28.5500 g. **Composition:** 0.9250 Silver .8492 oz. ASW **Reverse:** World Cup Soccer

Date	Mintage	F	VF	XF	Unc	BU
1994 Proof	Est. 10,000	Value: 37.50				

KM# 55 5 DOLLARS **Weight:** 28.2800 g. **Composition:** 0.9250 Silver .8411 oz. ASW **Subject:** UN Global SIDS Conference **Obverse:** Coat of arms **Reverse:** Stylized tropical island view

Date	Mintage	F	VF	XF	Unc	BU
1994 Proof	2,000	Value: 40.00				

KM# 58 5 DOLLARS **Weight:** 31.4700 g. **Composition:** 0.9250 Silver .9359 oz. ASW **Reverse:** Queen Mother's engagement portrait

Date	Mintage	F	VF	XF	Unc	BU
1994 Proof	Est. 20,000	Value: 50.00				

KM# 59 5 DOLLARS **Weight:** 28.2800 g. **Composition:** 0.9250 Silver .8411 oz. ASW **Reverse:** Pedro A. Campo

Date	Mintage	F	VF	XF	Unc	BU
1994 Proof	Est. 10,000	Value: 50.00				

KM# 62 5 DOLLARS **Composition:** Copper-Nickel **Subject:** 50th Anniversary - United Nations

Date	F	VF	XF	Unc	BU
1995	—	—	—	8.00	—

KM# 62a 5 DOLLARS **Weight:** 28.2800 g. **Composition:** 0.9250 Silver .8411 oz. ASW

Date	Mintage	F	VF	XF	Unc	BU
1995 Proof	Est. 105,000	Value: 32.50				

KM# 63 5 DOLLARS **Weight:** 28.2800 g. **Composition:** 0.9250 Silver .8411 oz. ASW **Reverse:** First European settlers, 1625

Date	Mintage	F	VF	XF	Unc	BU
1995 Proof	Est. 15,000	Value: 40.00				

KM# 68 5 DOLLARS **Weight:** 28.5000 g. **Composition:** 0.9250 Silver 0.8476 oz. ASW **Subject:** Queen's 70th Birthday **Obverse:** National arms **Reverse:** Royal couple **Edge:** Reeded **Size:** 38.5 mm.

Date	F	VF	XF	Unc	BU
1996 Proof	—	Value: 40.00			

KM# 67 5 DOLLARS **Weight:** 28.1000 g. **Composition:** 0.9250 Silver .8357 oz. ASW **Subject:** Eternal Flame **Obverse:** National arms **Reverse:** Denomination and eternal flame **Edge:** Reeded **Shape:** Octagonal **Size:** 38.6 mm.

Date	F	VF	XF	Unc	BU
1999-2000 Proof	—	Value: 60.00			

KM# 17 10 DOLLARS **Composition:** Copper-Nickel **Subject:** Neptune, God of the Sea **Obverse:** Similar to 2 Dollars, KM#15

Date	Mintage	F	VF	XF	Unc	BU
1974FM (M)	3,958	—	—	—	10.00	—
1975FM (M)	250	—	—	—	20.00	—
1975FM (U)	1,360	—	—	—	12.50	—
1977FM (M)	600	—	—	—	12.50	—
1977FM (U)	468	—	—	—	12.50	—

Date	Mintage	F	VF	XF	Unc	BU
1978FM (U)	1,017	—	—	—	12.50	—
1979FM (M)	600	—	—	—	12.50	—
1979FM (U)	523	—	—	—	12.50	—
1980FM (M)	600	—	—	—	12.50	—
1980FM (U)	649	—	—	—	12.50	—
1981FM (M)	600	—	—	—	12.50	—
1981FM (U)	1,156	—	—	—	12.50	—

KM# 17a 10 DOLLARS Weight: 37.9000 g. **Composition:** 0.9250 Silver 1.1271 oz. ASW

Date	Mintage	F	VF	XF	Unc	BU
1973FM (M)	2,750	—	—	—	15.00	—
1973FM (P)	97,000	Value: 11.50				
1974FM (P)	57,000	Value: 11.50				
1975FM (P)	29,000	Value: 11.50				
1977FM (P)	7,212	Value: 15.00				
1978FM (P)	7,079	Value: 15.00				
1979FM (P)	6,534	Value: 15.00				
1980FM (P)	3,618	Value: 17.50				
1981FM (P)	835	Value: 45.00				

KM# 26 10 DOLLARS Composition: Copper-Nickel **Subject:** 10th Anniversary of Independence **Reverse:** Similar to KM#17

Date	Mintage	F	VF	XF	Unc	BU
ND(1976)FM (M)	250	—	—	—	30.00	—
ND(1976)FM (U)	996	—	—	—	15.00	—

KM# 26a 10 DOLLARS Weight: 37.9000 g. **Composition:** 0.9250 Silver 1.1271 oz. ASW

Date	Mintage	F	VF	XF	Unc	BU
ND(1976)FM (P)	16,000	Value: 15.00				

KM# 34 10 DOLLARS Composition: Copper-Nickel **Subject:** 10th Anniversary of the Central Bank of Barbados **Obverse:** Similar to KM#26

Date	Mintage	F	VF	XF	Unc	BU
1982FM (U)	600	—	—	—	55.00	—

KM# 34a 10 DOLLARS Weight: 35.5200 g. **Composition:** 0.9250 Silver 1.0564 oz. ASW

Date	Mintage	F	VF	XF	Unc	BU
1982FM (P)	851	Value: 45.00				

KM# 36 10 DOLLARS Composition: Copper-Nickel **Subject:** Pelican

Date	Mintage	F	VF	XF	Unc	BU
1983FM (M)	600	—	—	—	60.00	—
1983FM (U)	141	—	—	—	100	—

KM# 36a 10 DOLLARS Weight: 35.5200 g. **Composition:** 0.9250 Silver 1.0564 oz. ASW

Date	Mintage	F	VF	XF	Unc	BU
1983FM (P)	679	Value: 115				

KM# 40 10 DOLLARS Weight: 35.5200 g. **Composition:** 0.9250 Silver 1.0564 oz. ASW **Subject:** Dolphins

Date	Mintage	F	VF	XF	Unc	BU
1984FM (M)	—	—	—	—	—	—
1984FM (P)	469	Value: 175				

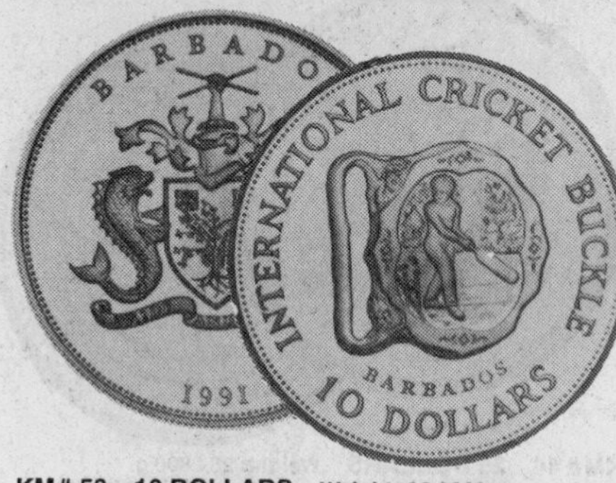

KM# 50 10 DOLLARS Weight: 28.2800 g. **Composition:** 0.9250 Silver .8411 oz. ASW **Subject:** International Cricket Belt Buckle

Date	Mintage	F	VF	XF	Unc	BU
1991 Proof	5,000	Value: 55.00				

KM# 52 10 DOLLARS Weight: 23.3300 g. **Composition:** 0.9250 Silver .6938 oz. ASW **Subject:** Discovery of America - Columbus and Native American - Ship and Scroll

Date	Mintage	F	VF	XF	Unc	BU
1991 Matte	750	Value: 65.00				
1991 Proof	Est. 25,000	Value: 35.00				

KM# 53 10 DOLLARS Weight: 23.3300 g. **Composition:** 0.9250 Silver .6938 oz. ASW **Subject:** Discovery of America - Columbus and Tribal Chief - Scroll

Date	Mintage	F	VF	XF	Unc	BU
1992 Matte	500	Value: 65.00				
1992 Proof	Est. 25,000	Value: 35.00				

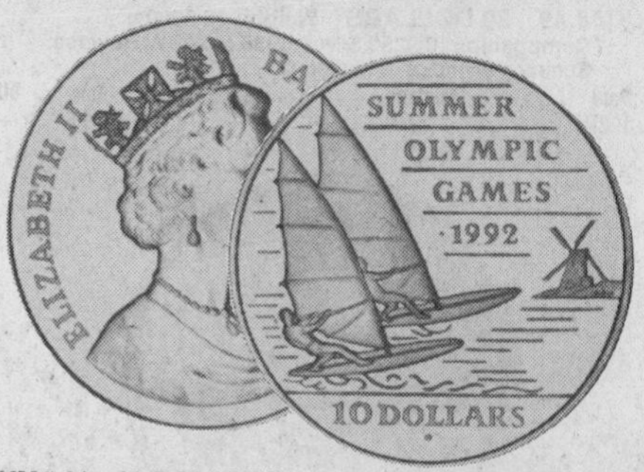

KM# 61 10 DOLLARS Weight: 23.3300 g. **Composition:** 0.9250 Silver .6938 oz. ASW **Subject:** 1992 Summer Olympics - Sailboards

Date	Mintage	F	VF	XF	Unc	BU
1992 Proof	10,000	Value: 50.00				

KM#60 10 DOLLARS Weight: 7.7800 g. **Composition:** 0.5830 Gold .1458 oz. AGW **Subject:** Queen Mother's Engagement Portrait

Date	Mintage	F	VF	XF	Unc	BU
1995 Proof	Est. 5,000	Value: 150				

KM# 66 10 DOLLARS Weight: 28.2800 g. **Composition:** 0.9250 Silver .8410 oz. ASW **Subject:** 50th Anniversary of the University of the West Indies **Obverse:** National arms **Reverse:** University arms, dates

Date	Mintage	F	VF	XF	Unc	BU
1998 Proof	1,000	Value: 55.00				

KM# 46 20 DOLLARS Weight: 23.3300 g. **Composition:** 0.9250 Silver .6938 oz. ASW **Subject:** Decade For Women

Date	Mintage	F	VF	XF	Unc	BU
1985 Proof	1,633	Value: 45.00				

KM# 49 20 DOLLARS **Weight:** 23.3300 g. **Composition:** 0.9250 Silver .6938 oz. ASW **Reverse:** Summer Olympics - Hurdler

Date	Mintage	F	VF	XF	Unc	BU
1988	15,000	—	—	—	28.00	—

KM# 27 25 DOLLARS **Weight:** 28.2800 g. **Composition:** 0.9250 Silver .8410 oz. ASW **Subject:** Coronation Jubilee **Obverse:** Portrait of Queen Elizabeth II

Date	Mintage	F	VF	XF	Unc	BU
1978FM (M)	300	—	—	—	90.00	—
1978FM (U)	69	—	—	—	250	—
1978FM (P)	8,728	Value: 16.00				

KM# 30 25 DOLLARS **Weight:** 30.2800 g. **Composition:** 0.5000 Silver .4868 oz. ASW **Subject:** 10th Anniversary of Caribbean Development Bank

Date	Mintage	F	VF	XF	Unc	BU
1980FM (P) Proof	2,345	Value: 25.00				

KM# 31 25 DOLLARS **Weight:** 30.2800 g. **Composition:** 0.5000 Silver .4868 oz. ASW **Subject:** Caribbean Festival of Arts **Obverse:** Similar to KM#30

Date	Mintage	F	VF	XF	Unc	BU
1981FM (P)	1,008	Value: 30.00				

KM# 37 25 DOLLARS **Weight:** 30.2800 g. **Composition:** 0.5000 Silver .4868 oz. ASW **Subject:** 30th Anniversary Coronation of Queen Elizabeth II

Date	Mintage	F	VF	XF	Unc	BU
1983FM (P)	2,951	Value: 22.50				

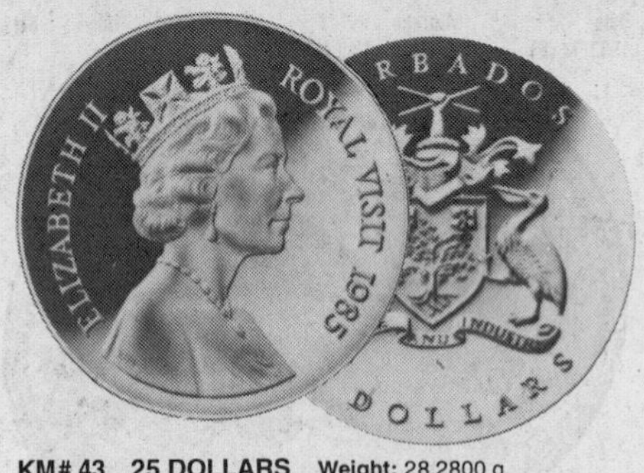

KM# 43 25 DOLLARS **Weight:** 28.2800 g. **Composition:** 0.9250 Silver .8410 oz. ASW **Subject:** Royal Visit

Date	F	VF	XF	Unc	BU
1985	—	—	—	32.50	—

KM# 43a 25 DOLLARS **Weight:** 47.5400 g. **Composition:** 0.9170 Gold 1.4013 oz. AGW **Subject:** Royal Visit

Date	Mintage	F	VF	XF	Unc	BU
1985	Est. 250	Value: 950				

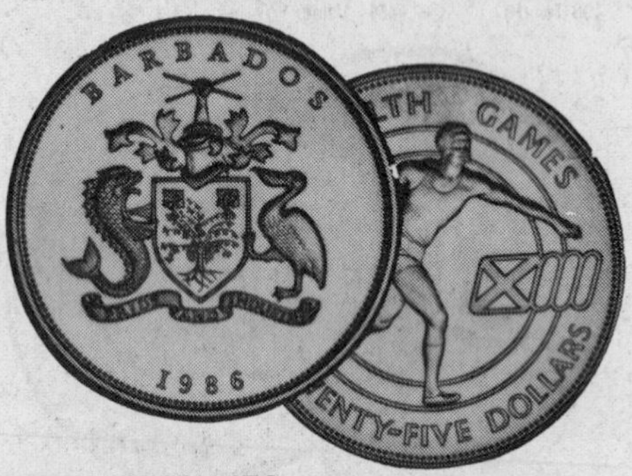

KM# 44 25 DOLLARS **Weight:** 28.2800 g. **Composition:** 0.5000 Silver .4546 oz. ASW **Subject:** Commonwealth Games

Date	F	VF	XF	Unc	BU
1986	—	—	—	25.00	—

KM# 44a 25 DOLLARS **Weight:** 28.2800 g. **Composition:** 0.9250 Silver .8410 oz. ASW

Date	Mintage	F	VF	XF	Unc	BU
1986	Est. 20,000	Value: 30.00				

KM# 32 50 DOLLARS **Weight:** 27.3500 g. **Composition:** 0.5000 Silver .4397 oz. ASW **Subject:** World Food Day - Black Belly Sheep

Date	Mintage	F	VF	XF	Unc	BU
1981FM (U)	6,012	—	—	—	30.00	—

KM# 42 50 DOLLARS **Weight:** 16.8500 g. **Composition:** 0.5000 Silver .2709 oz. ASW **Series:** F.A.O. **Reverse:** Four-wing flying fish

Date	Mintage	F	VF	XF	Unc	BU
1984	3,600	—	—	—	35.00	—

KM# 47 50 DOLLARS **Weight:** 33.6250 g. **Composition:** 0.9250 Silver 1.0000 oz. ASW **Subject:** 350th Anniversary of Parliament

Date	Mintage	F	VF	XF	Unc	BU
ND(1989) Proof	Est. 5,000	Value: 35.00				

KM# 51 50 DOLLARS **Weight:** 15.9800 g. **Composition:** 0.9170 Gold .4709 oz. AGW **Subject:** International Cricket Belt Buckle **Reverse:** Cricket player on belt buckle **Note:** Similar to 10 Dollars, KM#50.

Date	Mintage	F	VF	XF	Unc	BU
1991 Proof	500	Value: 530				

KM# 56 50 DOLLARS **Weight:** 15.9800 g. **Composition:** 0.9170 Gold .4709 oz. AGW **Subject:** UN Global SIDS Conference

Date	Mintage	F	VF	XF	Unc	BU
1994 Proof	100	Value: 550				

KM# 18 100 DOLLARS **Weight:** 6.2100 g. **Composition:** 0.5000 Gold .0998 oz. AGW **Subject:** 350th Anniversary - The English Ship - Olive Blossom

Date	Mintage	F	VF	XF	Unc	BU
ND(1975)FM (M)	50	—	—	—	250	—
ND(1975)FM (U)	16,000	—	—	—	50.00	—
ND(1975)FM (P)	23,000	Value: 65.00				

KM# 28 100 DOLLARS **Weight:** 4.0600 g. **Composition:** 0.9000 Gold .1174 oz. AGW **Subject:** Human Rights

Date	Mintage	F	VF	XF	Unc	BU
1978	1,114	—	—	—	125	—

KM# 28a 100 DOLLARS **Weight:** 5.0500 g. **Composition:** 0.9000 Gold .1461 oz. AGW

Date	Mintage	F	VF	XF	Unc	BU
1978 Proof	Inc. above	Value: 150				

KM# 38 100 DOLLARS **Weight:** 6.2100 g. **Composition:** 0.5000 Gold .0998 oz. AGW **Subject:** Neptune, God of the Sea

Date	Mintage	F	VF	XF	Unc	BU
1983FM (U)	3	—	—	—	—	—
1983FM (P)	484	Value: 220				

KM# 39 100 DOLLARS Weight: 6.2100 g. **Composition:** 0.5000 Gold .0998 oz. AGW **Subject:** Triton, Son of Neptune

Date	Mintage	F	VF	XF	Unc	BU
1984FM (P)	1,103	Value: 165				

KM# 41 100 DOLLARS Weight: 6.2100 g. **Composition:** 0.5000 Gold .0998 oz. AGW **Subject:** Amphitrite, Wife of Neptune

Date	Mintage	F	VF	XF	Unc	BU
1985FM (P)	1,276	Value: 160				

KM# 48 100 DOLLARS Weight: 15.9760 g. **Composition:** 0.9170 Gold .4709 oz. AGW **Subject:** 350th Anniversary of Parliament

Date		F	VF	XF	Unc	BU
ND(1989)FM	Est. 500	Value: 350				

KM# 33 150 DOLLARS Weight: 7.1300 g. **Composition:** 0.5000 Gold .1146 oz. AGW **Subject:** National Flower - Poinciana

Date	Mintage	F	VF	XF	Unc	BU
1981FM (U)	7	—	—	—	—	—
1981FM (P)	1,140	Value: 115				

KM# 29 200 DOLLARS Weight: 8.1200 g. **Composition:** 0.9000 Gold .2349 oz. AGW **Subject:** Year of the Child

Date	Mintage	F	VF	XF	Unc	BU
1979	1,121	—	—	—	225	—

KM# 29a 200 DOLLARS Weight: 10.1000 g. **Composition:** 0.9000 Gold .2922 oz. AGW

Date		F	VF	XF	Unc	BU
1979 Proof	Inc. above	Value: 275				

KM# 35 250 DOLLARS Weight: 6.6000 g. **Composition:** 0.9000 Gold .1910 oz. AGW **Subject:** 250th Anniversary of Birth of George Washington

Date	Mintage	F	VF	XF	Unc	BU
1982FM (P)	802	Value: 150				

KM# 45 250 DOLLARS Weight: 47.5400 g. **Composition:** 0.9170 Gold 1.4017 oz. AGW **Subject:** Commonwealth Games **Note:** Similar to 25 Dollars, KM#44.

Date	Mintage	F	VF	XF	Unc	BU
1986 Proof	150	Value: 1,000				

MINT SETS

KM#	Date	Mintage	Identification	Issue Price	Mkt Val
MS1	1973 (8)	2,500	KM#10-15, 16a, 17a	25.00	25.00
MS2	1974 (8)	3,708	KM#10-17	25.00	20.00
MS3	1975 (8)	1,360	KM#10-17	27.50	22.50
MS4	1976 (8)	996	KM#19-26	27.50	30.00
MS5	1977 (8)	468	KM#10-17	27.50	30.00
MS6	1978 (8)	517	KM#10-17	29.00	30.00
MS7	1979 (8)	523	KM#10-17	29.00	30.00
MS8	1980 (8)	649	KM#10-17	30.00	30.00
MS9	1981 (8)	327	KM#10-17	30.00	35.00
MS10	1982 (8)	—	KM#10-16, 34	35.00	45.00
MS11	1983 (8)	141	KM#10-16, 36	35.50	100
MS12	1989 (5)	—	KM#10-14.1	17.00	17.00

PROOF SETS

KM#	Date	Mintage	Identification	Issue Price	Mkt Val
PS1	1973 (8)	97,454	KM#109-15, 16a, 17a	37.50	30.00
PS2	1974 (8)	35,600	KM#10-15, 16a, 17a	50.00	30.00
PS3	1975 (8)	20,458	KM#10-15, 16a, 17a	55.00	30.00
PS4	1976 (8)	11,929	KM#19-24, 25a, 26a	55.00	40.00
PS5	1977 (8)	5,014	KM#10-15, 16a, 17a	55.00	35.00
PS6	1978 (8)	4,436	KM#10-15, 16a, 17a	58.00	37.50
PS7	1979 (8)	4,126	KM#10-15, 16a, 17a	60.00	37.50
PS8	1980 (8)	2,011	KM#10-15, 16a, 17a	117	45.00
PS9	1980 (2)	—	KM#16a, 17a	115	32.50
PS10	1981 (8)	—	KM#10-15, 16a, 17a	117	80.00
PS11	1982 (8)	—	KM#10-15, 16a, 34a	117	80.00
PS12	1983 (8)	—	KM#10-15, 16a, 36a	—	170
PS13	1984 (8)	—	KM#10-15, 16a, 40	132	200

BELARUS

Belarus (Byelorussia, Belorussia, or White Russia- formerly the Belorussian S.S.R.) is situated along the western Dvina and Dnieper Rivers, bounded in the west by Poland, to the north by Latvia and Lithuania, to the east by Russia and the south by the Ukraine. It has an area of 80,154 sq. mi. (207,600 sq. km.) and a population of 4.8 million. Capital: Minsk. Chief products: peat, salt, and agricultural products including flax, fodder and grasses for cattle breeding and dairy products.

There never existed an independent state of Byelorussia. Until the partitions of Poland at the end of the 18th century, the history of Byelorussia is identical with that of Lithuania.

When Russia incorporated the whole of Byelorussia into its territories in 1795, it claimed to be recovering old Russian lands and denied that the Byelorussians were a separate nation. Significant efforts for independence did not occur until 1918 and were met by external antagonism from German, Polish, and Russian influences.

Soviet and anti-Communist sympathies continued to reflect the political and social unrest of the U.S.S.R. for Byelorussia. Finally, on August 25, 1991, following an unsuccessful coup, the Supreme Soviet adopted a declaration of independence, and the "Republic of Belarus" was proclaimed in September. In December, it became a founder member of the CIS.

MONETARY SYSTEM
100 Kapeek = 1 Rouble

REPUBLIC

STANDARD COINAGE

KM# 6 ROUBLE **Composition:** Copper-Nickel **Subject:** United Nations 50th Anniversary **Obverse:** National emblem **Reverse:** Crane flying over map and UN logo

Date	F	VF	XF	Unc	BU
1996	—	—	—	10.00	—

KM# 6a ROUBLE Weight: 28.5100 g. **Composition:** 0.9250 Silver .8479 oz. ASW

Date	Mintage	F	VF	XF	Unc	BU
1996 Proof	20,000	Value: 35.00				

KM# 7 ROUBLE **Composition:** Copper-Nickel **Subject:** Olympics **Obverse:** National arms **Reverse:** Gymnast on the rings

Date	F	VF	XF	Unc	BU
1996 Prooflike	—	—	—	12.50	—

KM# 8 ROUBLE **Composition:** Copper-Nickel **Subject:** Olympics **Obverse:** National arms **Reverse:** Rhythmic gymnast

Date	F	VF	XF	Unc	BU
1996 Prooflike	—	—	—	12.50	—

KM# 31 ROUBLE **Weight:** 7.9800 g. **Composition:** 0.9167 Gold .2532 oz. AGW **Subject:** United Nations 50th Anniversary **Obverse:** National arms **Reverse:** Crane flying over map and U.N. logo

Date	Mintage	F	VF	XF	Unc	BU
1996 Proof	5,000	Value: 185				

KM# 9 ROUBLE **Weight:** 7.9800 g. **Composition:** 0.9167 Gold .2532 oz. AGW **Subject:** Third Anniversary of Independence **Obverse:** National arms **Reverse:** Monument

Date	F	VF	XF	Unc	BU
1997 Prooflike	—	—	—	12.50	—

KM# 34 ROUBLE **Composition:** Copper-Nickel **Subject:** Olympics **Obverse:** National arms **Reverse:** Biathlon skier with rifle

Date	Mintage	F	VF	XF	Unc	BU
1997 Prooflike	5,000	—	—	—	12.50	—

KM# 36 ROUBLE **Composition:** Copper-Nickel **Subject:** Olympics **Reverse:** Two hockey players

Date	Mintage	F	VF	XF	Unc	BU
1997 Prooflike	5,000	—	—	—	12.50	—

KM# 18 ROUBLE **Weight:** 7.9800 g. **Composition:** 0.9167 Gold .2532 oz. AGW **Subject:** Architecture of Belarus **Obverse:** National arms **Reverse:** Castle at Mir

Date	F	VF	XF	Unc	BU
1998 Proof	—	Value: 11.50			

KM# 19 ROUBLE **Weight:** 7.9800 g. **Composition:** 0.9167 Gold .2532 oz. AGW **Subject:** Cities of Belarus **Obverse:** National arms **Reverse:** Walled City of Polatsk with city arms

Date	F	VF	XF	Unc	BU
1998 Proof	—	Value: 11.50			

KM# 20 ROUBLE **Weight:** 7.9800 g. **Composition:** 0.9167 Gold .2532 oz. AGW **Subject:** 200th Anniversary - Birth of A. Mitskevich - Poet **Obverse:** National arms **Reverse:** Mitskevich portrait, dates

Date	F	VF	XF	Unc	BU
1998 Proof	—	Value: 11.50			

KM# 21 ROUBLE **Weight:** 7.9800 g. **Composition:** 0.9167 Gold .2532 oz. AGW **Subject:** Olympics **Obverse:** National arms and denomination **Reverse:** Hurdlers, Olympic crest

Date	F	VF	XF	Unc	BU
1998 Proof	—	Value: 11.50			

KM# 22 ROUBLE **Weight:** 7.9800 g. **Composition:** 0.9167 Gold .2532 oz. AGW **Subject:** Cities of Belarus **Obverse:** National arms **Reverse:** Minsk view with city arms

Date	F	VF	XF	Unc	BU
1999 Proof	—	Value: 11.50			

KM# 23 ROUBLE **Composition:** Copper-Nickel **Subject:** 100th Anniversary - Birth of Mikhas Lynkou **Obverse:** National arms **Reverse:** Head of Lynkou facing right

Date	F	VF	XF	Unc	BU
1999 Proof	—	Value: 11.50			

KM# 40 ROUBLE **Weight:** 14.5000 g. **Composition:** Copper-Nickel **Subject:** G.N. Glebats **Obverse:** National arms **Reverse:** Glebats portrait with two smaller portraits, dates **Edge:** Reeded

Date	F	VF	XF	Unc	BU
1999 Proof	—	Value: 11.50			

KM# 41 ROUBLE **Composition:** Copper-Nickel **Subject:** 2000 Years **Obverse:** National arms **Reverse:** Bethlehem view

Date	F	VF	XF	Unc	BU
1999 Proof	—	Value: 11.50			

KM# 24 10 ROUBLES **Weight:** 16.9600 g. **Composition:** 0.9250 Silver .5044 oz. ASW **Subject:** 200th Anniversary - Birth of A. Mitskevich **Obverse:** National arms **Reverse:** Portrait Mitskevich facing left, dates

Date	F	VF	XF	Unc	BU
1998 Proof	—	Value: 28.50			

KM# 25 10 ROUBLES **Weight:** 16.9600 g. **Composition:** 0.9250 Silver .5044 oz. ASW **Subject:** G.N. Glebats - Theatre Artist **Obverse:** National arms **Reverse:** Glebats portrait with two smaller portraits, dates

Date	F	VF	XF	Unc	BU
1999 Proof	—	Value: 27.50			

KM# 26 10 ROUBLES **Weight:** 16.9600 g. **Composition:** 0.9250 Silver .5044 oz. ASW **Subject:** 100th Anniversary - Birth of Mikhas Lynkou **Obverse:** National arms **Reverse:** Head of Lynkou facing right, dates

Date	F	VF	XF	Unc	BU
1999 Proof	—	Value: 27.50			

KM# 13 20 ROUBLES **Weight:** 33.8400 g. **Composition:** 0.9250 Silver 1.0064 oz. ASW **Subject:** Olympics **Obverse:** National arms and denomination **Reverse:** Olympic crest, gymnast on rings

Date	Mintage	F	VF	XF	Unc	BU
1996 Proof	1,000	Value: 50.00				

KM# 14 20 ROUBLES **Weight:** 33.8400 g. **Composition:** 0.9250 Silver 1.0064 oz. ASW **Subject:** Olympics **Obverse:** National arms **Reverse:** Ribbon dancer

Date	Mintage	F	VF	XF	Unc	BU
1996 Proof	1,000	Value: 50.00				

KM# 10 20 ROUBLES **Weight:** 34.7400 g. **Composition:** 0.9000 Silver 1.0052 oz. ASW **Subject:** Monument of Independence **Obverse:** National emblem

Date	Mintage	F	VF	XF	Unc	BU
1997 Proof	2,000	Value: 45.00				

KM# 11 20 ROUBLES **Weight:** 34.7400 g. **Composition:** 0.9000 Silver 1.0052 oz. ASW **Subject:** Russia-Belarus State Treaty **Obverse:** National emblem **Reverse:** 2 city views with respective national emblems

Date	F	VF	XF	Unc	BU
1997 Proof	—	Value: 45.00			

KM# 12 20 ROUBLES **Weight:** 31.4800 g. **Composition:** 0.9990 Silver 1.0110 oz. ASW **Subject:** 75th Anniversary - Banking System **Obverse:** National emblem **Reverse:** Bank building

Date	F	VF	XF	Unc	BU
1997 Proof	—	Value: 50.00			

KM# 15 20 ROUBLES **Weight:** 31.0300 g. **Composition:** 0.9250 Silver .9228 oz. ASW **Subject:** Olympics **Obverse:** National arms **Reverse:** Biathalon skier

Date	Mintage	F	VF	XF	Unc	BU
1997 Proof	Est. 1,000	Value: 35.00				

KM# 16 20 ROUBLES **Weight:** 31.1500 g. **Composition:** 0.9250 Silver .9264 oz. ASW **Subject:** Olympics **Obverse:** National arms **Reverse:** Two hockey players

Date	Mintage	F	VF	XF	Unc	BU
1997 Proof	Est. 1,000	Value: 35.00				

KM# 27 20 ROUBLES **Weight:** 33.5200 g. **Composition:** 0.9250 Silver .9969 oz. ASW **Subject:** Architecture of Belarus **Obverse:** National arms **Reverse:** Castle and Mir and seal

Date	F	VF	XF	Unc	BU
1998 Proof	—	Value: 35.00			

KM# 28 20 ROUBLES **Weight:** 33.5200 g. **Composition:** 0.9250 Silver .9969 oz. ASW **Subject:** Cities of Belarus **Obverse:** National arms **Reverse:** Polatsk with city arms above

Date	F	VF	XF	Unc	BU
1998 Proof	—	Value: 35.00			

KM# 29 20 ROUBLES **Weight:** 33.5200 g. **Composition:** 0.9250 Silver .9969 oz. ASW **Subject:** Olympics **Obverse:** National arms and denomination **Reverse:** Hurdlers, Olympic crest

Date	F	VF	XF	Unc	BU
1998 Proof	—	Value: 32.50			

KM# 17 20 ROUBLES **Weight:** 33.9000 g. **Composition:** 0.9250 Silver 1.0082 oz. ASW **Subject:** 80th Anniversary - Financial System **Obverse:** National arms **Reverse:** Anniversary logo

Date	F	VF	XF	Unc	BU
1999 Proof	—	Value: 30.00			

KM# 30 20 ROUBLES **Weight:** 33.5200 g. **Composition:** 0.9250 Silver .9969 oz. ASW **Subject:** Cities of Belarus **Obverse:** National arms **Reverse:** Minsk view with city arms

Date		F	VF	XF	Unc	BU
1999 Proof	—	Value: 35.00				

KM# 42 20 ROUBLES **Weight:** 33.8600 g. **Composition:** 0.9250 Silver 1.0070 oz. ASW **Subject:** 2000 Years of Christianity **Obverse:** National arms **Reverse:** Bethlehem view **Edge:** Reeded

Date		F	VF	XF	Unc	BU
1999 Proof	—	Value: 35.00				

KM# 43 20 ROUBLES **Weight:** 33.8600 g. **Composition:** 0.9250 Silver 1.0070 oz. ASW **Subject:** Jubilee 2000 **Obverse:** National arms **Reverse:** Three churches

Date		F	VF	XF	Unc	BU
1999 Proof	—	Value: 35.00				

KM# 32 50 ROUBLES **Weight:** 7.7800 g. **Composition:** 0.9990 Gold .2499 oz. AGW **Subject:** Olympics **Obverse:** National arms **Reverse:** Ribbon dancer

Date	Mintage	F	VF	XF	Unc	BU
1996 Proof	500	Value: 220				

KM# 33 50 ROUBLES **Weight:** 7.7800 g. **Composition:** 0.9990 Gold .2499 oz. AGW **Reverse:** Gymnast on rings

Date	Mintage	F	VF	XF	Unc	BU
1996 Proof	500	Value: 220				

KM# 35 50 ROUBLES **Weight:** 7.7800 g. **Composition:** 0.9990 Gold .2499 oz. AGW **Reverse:** Skier with rifle

Date	Mintage	F	VF	XF	Unc	BU
1997 Proof	500	Value: 220				

KM# 37 50 ROUBLES **Weight:** 7.7800 g. **Composition:** 0.9990 Gold .2499 oz. AGW **Reverse:** Two hockey players

Date	Mintage	F	VF	XF	Unc	BU
1997 Proof	500	Value: 220				

KM# 38 50 ROUBLES **Weight:** 7.7800 g. **Composition:** 0.9990 Gold .2499 oz. AGW **Reverse:** Two hurdlers

Date	Mintage	F	VF	XF	Unc	BU
1997 Proof	500	Value: 220				

BELGIAN CONGO

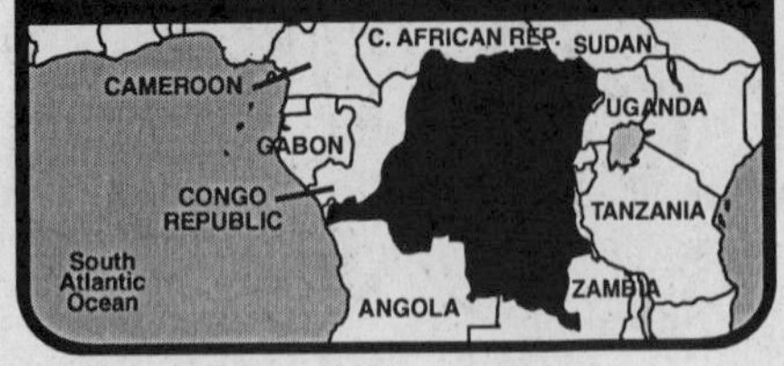

The Belgian Congo and Ruanda-Urundi were united administratively from 1925 to 1960. Ruanda-Urundi was made a U.N. Trust territory in 1946. Coins for these 2 areas were made jointly between 1952 and 1960. Ruanda-Urundi became the Republic of Rwanda on June 1, 1962.

MONETARY SYSTEM

100 Centimes = 1 Franc

PROVINCE

DECIMAL COINAGE

KM# 15 CENTIME **Composition:** Copper

Date	Mintage	F	VF	XF	Unc	BU
1910	2,000,000	1.00	2.00	3.00	9.00	—
1919	500,000	1.00	2.00	3.00	10.00	—

KM# 16 2 CENTIMES **Composition:** Copper

Date	Mintage	F	VF	XF	Unc	BU
1910	1,500,000	1.00	3.00	7.00	25.00	—
1919	500,000	1.50	3.50	10.00	30.00	—

KM# 12 5 CENTIMES **Composition:** Copper-Nickel

Date	Mintage	F	VF	XF	Unc	BU
1909	1,800,000	5.00	12.50	40.00	100	—

KM# 17 5 CENTIMES **Composition:** Copper-Nickel

Date	Mintage	F	VF	XF	Unc	BU
1910(H)	6,000,000	0.75	1.50	3.50	16.00	—
1911(H)	5,000,000	0.75	1.50	3.50	16.00	—
1917(H)	1,000,000	3.00	7.00	18.00	55.00	—
1917(H) Proof	—	Value: 175				
1919(H)	3,000,000	1.50	3.00	7.00	25.00	—
1919	6,850,000	0.50	1.00	2.50	16.00	—
1920	2,740,000	0.50	1.00	3.50	18.00	—
1921	17,260,000	0.25	0.75	1.50	10.00	—
1921(H)	3,000,000	1.00	2.00	6.00	20.00	—
1925	11,000,000	0.25	0.75	2.00	10.00	—
1926/5	5,770,000	2.25	4.50	—	—	—
1926	Inc. above	0.25	1.00	2.00	9.00	—
1927	2,000,000	0.50	1.00	2.50	10.00	—
1928/6	1,500,000	2.00	4.00	8.00	20.00	—
1928	Inc. above	0.75	1.25	3.00	10.00	—

KM# 13 10 CENTIMES Composition: Copper-Nickel

Date	Mintage	F	VF	XF	Unc	BU
1909	1,500,000	8.00	20.00	70.00	160	—

KM# 18 10 CENTIMES Composition: Copper-Nickel

Date	Mintage	F	VF	XF	Unc	BU
1910	5,000,000	0.50	1.00	3.00	15.00	—
1911	5,000,000	0.50	1.00	3.00	15.00	—
1917(H)	500,000	5.00	10.00	25.00	75.00	—
1919	3,430,000	0.50	1.00	3.50	16.50	—
1919(H)	1,500,000	0.75	1.25	4.00	18.00	—
1920	1,510,000	0.75	1.25	4.00	18.00	—
1921	13,540,000	0.25	0.75	2.00	10.00	—
1921(H)	3,000,000	0.75	1.50	3.50	16.50	—
1922	14,950,000	0.25	1.00	2.50	10.00	—
1924	3,600,000	0.50	1.50	3.00	15.00	—
1925/4	4,800,000	2.00	4.00	8.00	50.00	—
1925	Inc. above	0.25	1.00	3.00	15.00	—
1927	2,020,000	0.25	1.00	3.00	12.00	—
1928/7	5,600,000	1.00	3.00	8.00	40.00	—
1928	Inc. above	0.25	1.00	3.00	12.00	—

KM# 14 20 CENTIMES Composition: Copper-Nickel

Date	Mintage	F	VF	XF	Unc	BU
1909	300,000	10.00	25.00	65.00	180	—

KM# 19 20 CENTIMES Composition: Copper-Nickel

Date	Mintage	F	VF	XF	Unc	BU
1910	1,000,000	2.00	5.00	12.00	40.00	—
1911	1,250,000	1.50	4.00	10.00	35.00	—

KM# 22 50 CENTIMES Composition: Copper-Nickel **Reverse:** French legend **Rev. Legend:** CONGO BELGE

Date	Mintage	F	VF	XF	Unc	BU
1921	4,000,000	0.60	2.00	8.00	27.50	—
1922	6,000,000	0.60	2.00	8.00	27.50	—
1923	7,200,000	0.60	2.00	8.00	27.50	—
1924	1,096,000	0.75	3.00	10.00	32.50	—
1925	16,104,000	0.60	2.00	7.00	25.00	—
1926/5	16,000,000	1.00	4.00	12.00	45.00	—
1926	Inc. above	0.60	2.00	8.00	25.00	—
1927	10,000,000	0.60	2.00	8.00	27.50	—
1929/7	7,504,000	0.60	2.00	9.00	32.00	—
1929/8	Inc. above	1.00	4.00	15.00	90.00	—
1929	Inc. above	0.60	2.00	7.00	25.00	—

KM# 23 50 CENTIMES Composition: Copper-Nickel **Reverse:** Flemish legend **Rev. Legend:** BELGISCH CONGO

Date	Mintage	F	VF	XF	Unc	BU
1921	4,000,000	0.60	2.00	8.00	32.00	—
1922	5,592,000	0.60	2.00	7.00	27.50	—
1923	7,208,000	1.00	5.00	16.50	70.00	—
1923	Inc. above	0.60	2.00	7.00	25.00	—
1924	7,000,000	0.60	2.00	8.00	27.50	—
1925/4	10,600,000	1.50	7.00	20.00	90.00	—
1925	Inc. above	0.60	2.00	7.00	27.50	—
1926	25,200,000	0.60	2.00	7.00	25.00	—
1927	4,800,000	0.60	2.00	8.00	27.50	—
1928	7,484,000	0.60	2.00	7.00	25.00	—
1929/8	116,000	25.00	50.00	75.00	120	—
1929	Inc. above	20.00	40.00	70.00	100	—

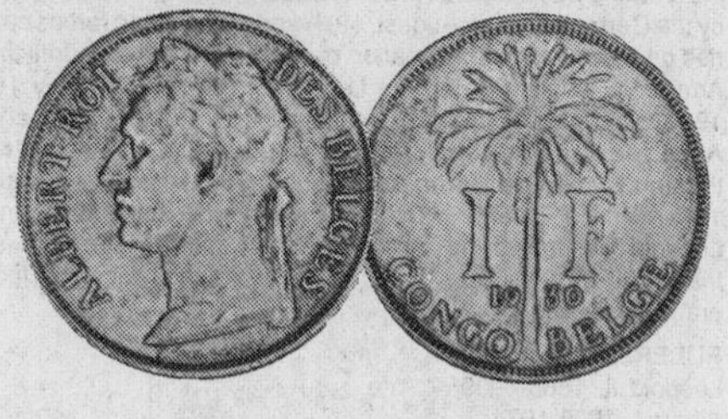

KM# 20 FRANC Composition: Copper-Nickel **Reverse:** French legend **Rev. Legend:** CONGO BELGE

Date	Mintage	F	VF	XF	Unc	BU
1920	4,000,000	0.85	2.75	10.00	37.50	—
1922	5,000,000	0.85	2.75	9.00	32.00	—
1923/2	5,000,000	2.00	7.00	16.00	45.00	—
1923	Inc. above	0.85	2.75	9.00	32.00	—
1924	6,030,000	0.85	2.75	9.00	35.00	—
1925	10,470,000	0.85	2.75	9.00	32.00	—
1926/5	12,500,000	2.00	7.00	16.50	50.00	—
1926	Inc. above	0.85	2.75	8.00	30.00	—
1927	15,250,000	0.85	2.75	8.00	30.00	—
1929	5,763,000	0.85	2.75	9.00	32.00	—
1930	5,000,000	0.85	2.75	10.00	40.00	—

KM# 21 FRANC Composition: Copper-Nickel **Reverse:** Flemish legend **Rev. Legend:** BELGISCH CONGO

Date	Mintage	F	VF	XF	Unc	BU
1920	475,000	2.00	5.00	16.50	50.00	—
1921	3,525,000	0.85	3.00	9.00	37.50	—
1922	5,000,000	0.85	3.00	9.00	37.50	—
1923/2	7,362,000	2.00	5.00	17.00	55.00	—
1923	Inc. above	0.85	2.75	9.00	32.00	—
1924	4,608,000	0.85	3.00	10.00	37.50	—
1925	9,530,000	0.85	2.75	9.00	32.00	—
1926/5	17,000,000	2.00	5.00	17.00	55.00	—
1926	Inc. above	0.85	2.75	9.00	32.00	—
1928	9,250,000	0.85	2.75	9.00	32.00	—
1929	4,250,000	0.85	3.00	10.00	37.50	—

KM# 26 FRANC Composition: Brass

Date	Mintage	F	VF	XF	Unc	BU
1944	25,000,000	0.50	1.00	3.00	7.50	12.50
1946	15,000,000	0.75	1.50	3.50	8.50	13.50
1949	15,000,000	0.75	1.50	3.00	8.00	13.50

KM# 25 2 FRANCS Composition: Brass

Date	Mintage	F	VF	XF	Unc	BU
1943	25,000,000	2.50	4.50	10.00	40.00	55.00

KM# 28 2 FRANCS Composition: Brass

Date	Mintage	F	VF	XF	Unc	BU
1946	13,000,000	1.00	2.00	3.50	15.00	—
1947	12,000,000	1.00	2.00	4.00	16.50	—

KM# 24 5 FRANCS Composition: Nickel-Bronze

Date	Mintage	F	VF	XF	Unc	BU
1936	2,600,000	5.00	10.00	20.00	95.00	—
1937	11,400,000	4.00	12.00	25.00	100	—

KM# 29 5 FRANCS Composition: Brass

Date	Mintage	F	VF	XF	Unc	BU
1947	10,000,000	3.00	7.00	15.00	50.00	—

KM# 27 50 FRANCS Weight: 17.5000 g. **Composition:** 0.5000 Silver .2814 oz. ASW

Date	Mintage	F	VF	XF	Unc	BU
1944	1,000,000	20.00	50.00	90.00	175	—

RUANDA-URUNDI

PROVINCE

DECIMAL COINAGE

KM# 2 50 CENTIMES **Composition:** Aluminum

Date	Mintage	F	VF	XF	Unc	BU
1954 DB	4,700,000	—	0.35	0.75	2.00	—
1955 DB	20,300,000	—	0.15	0.60	1.50	—

KM# 4 FRANC **Composition:** Aluminum

Date	Mintage	F	VF	XF	Unc	BU
1957	10,000,000	—	0.50	1.00	2.00	—
1958	20,000,000	—	0.50	1.00	2.00	—
1959	20,000,000	—	0.50	1.00	2.00	—
1960	20,000,000	—	0.50	1.00	2.00	—

KM# 1 5 FRANCS **Composition:** Brass

Date	Mintage	F	VF	XF	Unc	BU
1952	10,000,000	—	2.50	5.00	10.00	—

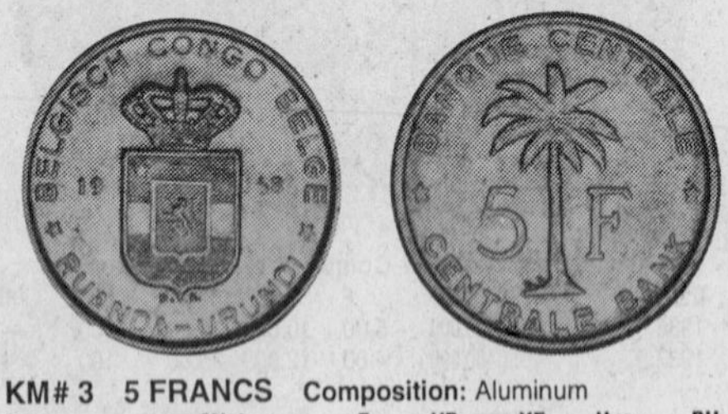

KM# 3 5 FRANCS **Composition:** Aluminum

Date	Mintage	F	VF	XF	Unc	BU
1956 DB	10,000,000	—	1.00	2.00	4.00	—
1958 DB	26,110,000	—	0.75	1.75	3.50	—
1959 DB	3,890,000	—	1.00	2.50	5.00	—

ESSAIS

KM#	Date	Mintage	Identification	Mkt Val

KM#	Date	Mintage	Identification	Mkt Val
E1	1952	—	5 Francs.	35.00
E2	1954	—	50 Centimes.	25.00
E3	1954	—	50 Centimes. Silver.	100

KM#	Date	Mintage	Identification	Mkt Val
E4	1956 DB	—	5 Francs.	30.00

KM#	Date	Mintage	Identification	Mkt Val
E5	1957	—	Franc.	20.00
E6	1960	—	Franc. Bronze.	90.00

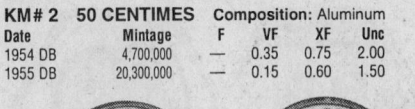

BELGIUM

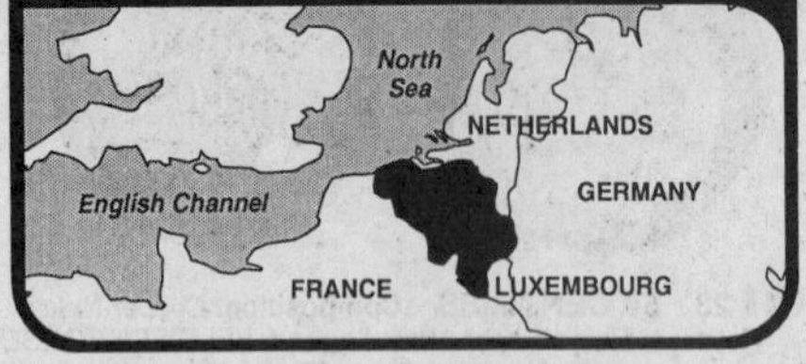

The Kingdom of Belgium, a constitutional monarchy in northwest Europe, has an area of 11,780 sq. mi. (30,519 sq. km.) and a population of 10.1 million, chiefly Dutch-speaking Flemish and French-speaking Walloons. Capital: Brussels. Agriculture, dairy farming, and the processing of raw materials for re-export are the principal industries. Beurs voor Diamant in Antwerp is the world's largest diamond trading center. Iron and steel, machinery motor vehicles, chemicals, textile yarns and fabrics comprise the principal exports.

At the Congress of Vienna in 1815 the area was reunited with the Netherlands, but in 1830 independence was gained and the constitutional monarchy of Belgium was established. A large part of the Duchy of Luxembourg was incorporated into Belgium and the first king was Leopold I of Saxe-Coburg-Gotha. It was invaded by the German Army in August, 1914 and the German forces carried on a devastating occupation of most of the territory until the Armistice. Belgium joined the League of Nations. On May 10, 1940 it was invaded again by the German army. The Belgian and Allied forces were quickly overwhelmed and were evacuated through Dunkirk. Allied troops reached Belgium again in Sept. 1944. Prince Charles, Count of Flanders, assumed King Leopold's responsibilities until liberation by the U.S. Army in Austria on May 8, 1945. As of January 1, 1989, Belgium became a federal kingdom.

RULERS

Leopold II, 1865-1909
Albert I, 1909-1934
Leopold III, 1934-1950
Baudouin I, 1951-1993
Albert II, 1993-

MINT MARKS

Angel head - Brussels

MINTMASTERS INITIALS & PRIVY MARKS

(b) - bird - Vogelier
Lamb head – Lambret

NOTE: Beginning in 1987, the letters "qp" appear on the coins - (quality proof)

MONETARY SYSTEM

100 Centimes = 1 Franc
1 Ecu - 1 Euro

LEGENDS

Belgian coins are usually inscribed either in Dutch, French or both. However some modern coins are being inscribed in Latin or German. The language used is best told by noting the spelling of the name of the country.

(Fr) French: BELGIQUE or BELGES
(Du) Dutch: BELGIE or BELGEN
(La) Latin: BELGICA
(Ge) German: BELGIEN

Many Belgian coins are collected by what is known as Position A and Position B edges. Some dates command a premium depending on the position which are as follows:

Position A: Coins with portrait side down having upright edge lettering.

Position B: Coins with portrait side up having upright edge lettering.

KINGDOM

DECIMAL COINAGE

KM# 33.1 CENTIME **Composition:** Copper **Obverse:** Legend in French **Obv. Legend:** DES BELGES

Date	Mintage	F	VF	XF	Unc	BU
1901/801 Near 1	3,743,000	0.50	1.50	3.50	15.00	—
1901/801 Far 1	Inc. above	0.50	1.50	3.50	15.00	—
1901	Inc. above	0.25	0.50	1.50	5.00	—
1902/802 Near 2	2,847,000	1.00	2.00	7.50	20.00	—
1902/802 Far 2	Inc. above	1.00	2.00	7.50	20.00	—
1902/801	Inc. above	1.00	2.00	7.50	25.00	—
1902/1	Inc. above	1.00	2.00	7.50	20.00	—
1902	Inc. above	0.20	0.50	1.50	5.00	—
1907	3,967,000	0.20	0.50	1.50	5.00	—

KM# 34.1 CENTIME **Composition:** Copper **Obverse:** Legend in Dutch **Obv. Legend:** DER BELGEN

Date	Mintage	F	VF	XF	Unc	BU
1901/899	Inc. above	0.75	2.25	4.50	10.00	—
1901	Inc. above	0.25	0.50	1.50	5.00	—
1902/1	2,482,000	1.25	3.50	9.00	15.00	—
1902	Inc. above	0.25	0.75	2.00	7.00	—
1907	3,966,000	0.25	0.75	1.50	5.00	—

KM# 33.2 CENTIME **Composition:** Copper **Note:** Thin flan.

Date	F	VF	XF	Unc	BU
1901	1.00	1.50	4.00	12.50	—
1902	1.00	1.50	6.00	15.00	—

KM# 34.2 CENTIME **Composition:** Copper **Note:** Thin flan.

Date	F	VF	XF	Unc	BU
1901	1.00	1.50	8.00	25.00	—
1902	1.00	1.50	8.00	25.00	—

KM# 33.3 CENTIME **Composition:** Copper **Reverse:** Additional stop in signature... BRAEMT.F.

Date	F	VF	XF	Unc	BU
1902	1.00	2.00	10.00	30.00	—

KM# 76 CENTIME **Composition:** Copper **Obverse:** Legend in French **Obv. Legend:** DES BELGES

Date	Mintage	F	VF	XF	Unc	BU
1912	2,540,000	0.20	0.50	2.50	7.00	—
1914	870,000	0.25	0.75	3.50	10.00	—

KM# 77 CENTIME **Composition:** Copper **Obverse:** Legend in Dutch **Obv. Legend:** DER BELGEN

Date	Mintage	F	VF	XF	Unc	BU
1912	2,542,000	0.20	0.50	1.50	5.00	—

KM# 35.1 2 CENTIMES **Composition:** Copper **Obverse:** Legend in French **Obv. Legend:** DES BELGES

Date	Mintage	F	VF	XF	Unc	BU
1902	2,490,000	0.15	0.50	4.00	12.00	—
1905	4,981,000	0.15	0.35	2.00	7.00	—
1909/5	4,983,000	0.75	1.50	8.00	25.00	—
1909	Inc. above	0.15	0.35	2.00	7.00	—

KM# 36 2 CENTIMES **Composition:** Copper **Obverse:** Legend in Dutch **Obv. Legend:** DER BELGEN

Date	Mintage	F	VF	XF	Unc	BU
1902	2,488,000	0.15	1.50	3.00	10.00	—
1905/2	4,986,000	1.50	3.00	15.00	40.00	—
1905	Inc. above	0.15	1.00	2.00	7.00	—
1909	565,000	0.50	2.00	12.00	25.00	—

KM# 35.2 2 CENTIMES **Composition:** Copper **Note:** Thin flan.

Date	F	VF	XF	Unc	BU
1902	3.00	5.00	35.00	100	—

KM# 65 2 CENTIMES **Composition:** Copper **Obverse:** Legend in Dutch **Obv. Legend:** DER BELGEN

Date	Mintage	F	VF	XF	Unc	BU
1910	1,248,000	0.25	0.50	3.00	7.00	—
1911 Large date	6,441,000	0.15	0.35	1.50	5.00	—
1911 Small date	Inc. above	0.15	0.35	1.50	5.00	—
1912	1,602,000	0.35	0.50	2.00	6.00	—
1919	4,998,000	0.15	0.35	0.75	3.00	—

KM# 64 2 CENTIMES Composition: Copper **Obverse:** Legend in French **Obv. Legend:** DES BELGES

Date	Mintage	F	VF	XF	Unc	BU
1911	645,000	1.50	3.00	14.00	40.00	—
1912/1	4,928,000	1.00	2.00	8.00	20.00	—
1912	Inc. above	0.15	0.50	2.00	5.00	—
1914	491,000	1.00	2.50	12.00	30.00	—
1919/4	5,000,000	0.75	1.00	5.00	10.00	—
1919	Inc. above	0.15	0.25	1.00	3.00	—

KM# 40.1 5 CENTIMES Composition: Copper-Nickel **Obverse:** Legend in French **Obv. Legend:** DES BELGES

Date	F	VF	XF	Unc	BU
1901	10.00	16.00	65.00	140	—

KM# 44 5 CENTIMES Composition: Copper-Nickel **Reverse:** Lion of different design

Date	Mintage	F	VF	XF	Unc	BU
1901	2,494,000	3.00	8.00	35.00	70.00	—

KM# 45 5 CENTIMES Composition: Copper-Nickel **Obverse:** Legend in Dutch **Obv. Legend:** DER BELGEN **Reverse:** Lion of different lower design

Date	Mintage	F	VF	XF	Unc	BU
1901	2,491,000	3.00	8.00	35.00	70.00	—

KM# 46 5 CENTIMES Composition: Copper-Nickel **Obverse:** Legend in French, small date **Obv. Legend:** BELGIQUE

Date	Mintage	F	VF	XF	Unc	BU
1901	202,000	15.00	30.00	75.00	150	—
1902/1	1,416,000	0.50	2.00	9.00	20.00	—
1902	Inc. above	0.25	1.50	6.00	14.00	—
1903	864,000	1.00	4.00	15.00	30.00	—

KM# 47 5 CENTIMES Composition: Copper-Nickel **Obverse:** Legend in Dutch, small date **Obv. Legend:** BELGIE

Date	Mintage	F	VF	XF	Unc	BU
1902/1	1,485,000	1.75	5.50	22.50	45.00	—
1902	Inc. above	0.15	1.50	7.00	20.00	—
1903	1,002,000	1.00	5.00	20.00	40.00	—

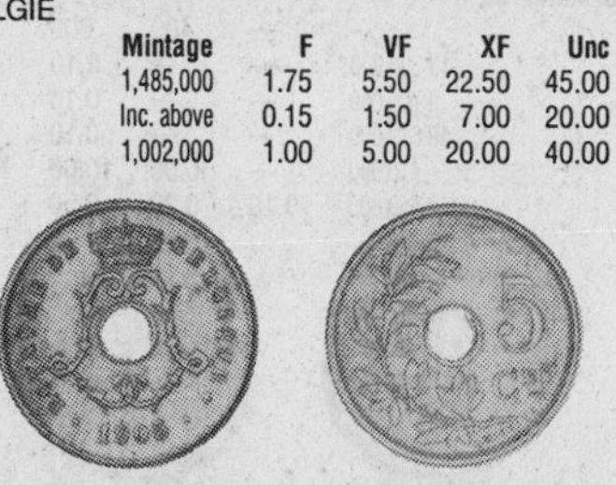

KM# 54 5 CENTIMES Composition: Copper-Nickel **Obverse:** Legend in French, large date **Obv. Legend:** BELGIQUE

Date	Mintage	F	VF	XF	Unc	BU
1904	5,814,000	0.15	0.35	2.00	7.00	—
1905/4	9,575,000	0.30	1.00	3.00	10.00	—
1905	Inc. above	0.15	0.35	2.00	7.00	—
1905 WICHAUX (error)	Inc. above	2.00	5.00	25.00	60.00	—
1905 A. MICHAUX	Inc. above	1.00	3.50	15.00	40.00	—
1906/5	8,463,000	0.30	1.50	3.00	10.00	—
1906	Inc. above	0.15	0.35	2.00	6.00	—
1907	993,000	1.00	3.00	12.00	30.00	—

KM# 55 5 CENTIMES Composition: Copper-Nickel **Obverse:** Legend in Dutch, large date **Obv. Legend:** BELGIE

Date	Mintage	F	VF	XF	Unc	BU
1904	5,812,000	0.15	0.35	2.00	7.00	—
1905/3	7,002,000	0.35	2.50	15.00	30.00	—
1905/4	Inc. above	0.30	1.50	10.00	25.00	—
1905	Inc. above	0.15	0.35	2.00	7.00	—
1905 Without cross	Inc. above	—	1.50	12.50	20.00	—
1906	11,016,000	0.15	0.35	2.00	7.00	—
1906 Without cross	Inc. above	2.00	5.00	15.00	35.00	—
1907	998,000	1.00	2.00	10.00	30.00	—

KM# 66 5 CENTIMES Composition: Copper-Nickel **Obverse:** Legend in French **Obv. Legend:** BELGIQUE **Reverse:** Plain field above 5

Date	Mintage	F	VF	XF	Unc	BU
1910	8,011,000	0.10	0.35	1.25	6.00	—
1913/0	5,005,000	0.20	0.75	2.25	10.00	—
1913	Inc. above	0.10	0.40	1.50	7.00	—
1914	1,004,000	1.00	3.00	8.00	20.00	—
1920/10	10,040,000	0.10	1.00	3.00	7.00	—
1920	Inc. above	0.10	0.35	1.25	4.00	—
1922/0	12,640,000	0.10	1.50	4.00	9.00	—
1922/1	Inc. above	0.10	1.50	3.50	9.00	—
1922	Inc. above	0.10	0.35	1.25	4.00	—
1923/13	9,000,000	0.10	0.75	2.50	8.00	—
1923	Inc. above	0.10	0.35	1.25	4.00	—
1925/13	15,860,000	0.10	0.50	2.00	8.00	—
1925	Inc. above	0.10	0.35	1.25	4.00	—
1926/5	7,000,000	0.10	1.00	2.50	8.00	—
1926	Inc. above	0.10	0.35	1.25	4.00	—
1927	2,000,000	0.10	1.00	2.50	9.00	—
1927 5 Cen	—	5.00	15.00	30.00	100	—
Note: Obverse of KM#66 paired with the reverse of KM#67						
1928	12,507,000	0.10	0.35	1.25	5.00	—
1932 Inc. KM93	—	5.00	15.00	50.00	150	—

KM# 67 5 CENTIMES Composition: Copper-Nickel **Obverse:** Legend in Dutch **Obv. Legend:** BELGIE **Reverse:** Plain field above 5

Date	Mintage	F	VF	XF	Unc	BU
1910	8,033,000	0.10	0.35	1.25	6.00	—
1914	6,040,000	0.10	0.35	1.25	4.00	—
1920/10	10,030,000	0.10	0.50	3.00	12.00	—
1920	Inc. above	0.10	0.35	1.25	4.00	—
1921/11	4,200,000	0.10	1.00	2.50	12.00	—
1921	Inc. above	0.10	1.00	2.00	9.00	—
1922/12	13,180,000	0.10	1.00	2.50	8.00	—
1922/0	Inc. above	0.10	1.00	3.00	9.00	—
1922	Inc. above	0.10	0.35	1.25	4.00	—
1923/13	3,530,000	0.10	1.00	3.00	14.00	—
1923	Inc. above	0.10	0.75	2.00	7.00	—
1924/11	5,260,000	0.10	1.00	2.50	9.00	—
1924/14	Inc. above	0.10	0.50	1.75	8.00	—
1924	Inc. above	0.10	0.35	1.25	4.00	—
1925/13	13,000,000	0.10	1.00	2.50	8.00	—
1925/15 High 2	Inc. above	0.10	1.00	2.00	9.00	—
1925/15 Level 2	Inc. above	0.10	1.00	2.00	9.00	—
1925/3	Inc. above	0.10	0.60	2.00	9.00	—
1925	Inc. above	0.10	0.35	1.25	4.00	—
1927	6,938,000	0.10	0.35	1.25	6.00	—
1928/3	6,252,000	0.10	0.75	2.50	9.00	—
1928	Inc. above	0.10	0.35	1.25	6.00	—
1930 Inc. KM94	—	5.00	15.00	50.00	150	—
1931 Inc. KM94	—	7.50	18.00	60.00	170	—

KM# 80 5 CENTIMES Composition: Zinc **Obverse:** Legend in French **Obv. Legend:** BELGIQUE-BELGIE **Note:** German Occupation WW I

Date	Mintage	F	VF	XF	Unc	BU
1915	10,199,000	0.15	2.00	4.00	15.00	—
1916	45,464,000	0.10	0.60	2.00	5.00	—

KM# 94 5 CENTIMES Composition: Nickel-Brass **Obverse:** Legend in Dutch **Obv. Legend:** BELGIE **Reverse:** Star added above 5

Date	Mintage	F	VF	XF	Unc	BU
1930	3,000,000	0.10	0.20	0.35	3.00	—
1931	7,430,000	0.10	0.20	0.35	3.00	—

KM# 93 5 CENTIMES Composition: Nickel-Brass **Obverse:** Legend in French **Obv. Legend:** BELGIQUE **Reverse:** Star added above 5

Date	Mintage	F	VF	XF	Unc	BU
1932	5,520,000	0.10	0.20	0.35	3.00	—

KM# 110.1 5 CENTIMES Composition: Nickel-Brass **Obverse:** Legend in French **Obv. Legend:** BELGIQUE-BELGIE

Date	Mintage	F	VF	XF	Unc	BU
1938	4,970,000	0.10	0.20	0.75	2.00	—
1939	—	—	—	—	—	—

Note: Struck at a later date

KM# 110.2 5 CENTIMES Composition: Nickel-Brass **Note:** Medal alignment.

Date	F	VF	XF	Unc	BU
1938	1.25	3.00	8.00	30.00	—

KM# 111 5 CENTIMES Composition: Nickel-Brass **Obverse:** Legend in Dutch **Obv. Legend:** BELGIE-BELGIQUE

Date	Mintage	F	VF	XF	Unc	BU
1939	3,000,000	0.10	0.20	0.75	2.00	—
1940	1,970,000	0.20	0.50	1.50	5.00	—

KM# 124 5 CENTIMES Composition: Zinc **Obverse:** Legend in Dutch **Obv. Legend:** BELGIE-BELGIQUE

Date	Mintage	F	VF	XF	Unc	BU
1941	4,000,000	0.15	0.75	2.50	8.00	—
1942	18,430,000	0.10	0.20	0.50	3.00	—

KM# 123 5 CENTIMES Composition: Zinc **Obverse:** Legend in French **Obv. Legend:** BELGIQUE-BELGIE **Note:** German Occupation WW II

Date	Mintage	F	VF	XF	Unc	BU
1941	10,000,000	0.10	0.20	1.00	4.00	—
1943	7,606,000	0.10	0.20	1.00	4.00	—

KM# 42 10 CENTIMES Composition: Copper-Nickel **Obverse:** Legend in French **Obv. Legend:** DES BELGES

Date	Mintage	F	VF	XF	Unc	BU
1901	551,000	30.00	50.00	150	275	—

KM# 43 10 CENTIMES Composition: Copper-Nickel **Obverse:** Legend in Dutch **Obv. Legend:** DER BELGEN

Date	Mintage	F	VF	XF	Unc	BU
1901	556,000	30.00	50.00	140	250	—

KM# 48 10 CENTIMES **Composition:** Copper-Nickel **Obverse:** Legend in French, small date **Obv. Legend:** BELGIQUE

Date	Mintage	F	VF	XF	Unc	BU
1901	582,000	6.00	15.00	40.00	130	—
1902/1	5,866,000	0.50	3.00	7.00	20.00	—
1902	Inc. above	0.15	1.00	3.00	9.00	—
1903	763,000	1.00	4.00	10.00	30.00	—

KM# 49 10 CENTIMES **Composition:** Copper-Nickel **Obverse:** Legend in Dutch, small date **Obv. Legend:** BELGIE

Date	Mintage	F	VF	XF	Unc	BU
1902	1,560,000	0.20	1.00	5.00	10.00	—
1903/2	—	0.50	1.25	7.00	18.00	—
1903	5,658,000	0.20	1.00	5.00	10.00	—

KM# 52 10 CENTIMES **Composition:** Copper-Nickel **Obverse:** Legend in French, large date **Obv. Legend:** BELGIQUE

Date	Mintage	F	VF	XF	Unc	BU
1903	Inc. above	2.00	7.00	17.00	40.00	—
1904	16,354,000	0.15	1.00	3.00	9.00	—
1905/4	14,392,000	0.25	1.00	5.00	15.00	—
1905	Inc. above	0.15	0.60	2.00	9.00	—
1906/5	1,483,000	0.50	1.50	5.00	18.00	—
1906	Inc. above	0.25	0.75	5.00	15.00	—

KM# 53 10 CENTIMES **Composition:** Copper-Nickel **Obverse:** Legend in Dutch, large date **Obv. Legend:** BELGIE

Date	Mintage	F	VF	XF	Unc	BU
1903	Inc. above	1.00	4.00	10.00	30.00	—
1904	16,834,000	0.20	0.50	2.00	9.00	—
1905/3	13,758,000	0.35	1.00	3.00	15.00	—
1905/4	Inc. above	0.30	1.00	3.00	10.00	—
1905	Inc. above	0.20	0.50	2.00	9.00	—
1906/5 Point above center of 6	2,017,000	0.50	1.25	4.00	15.00	—
1906/5 Point above right side of 6	Inc. above	0.50	1.25	4.00	15.00	—
1906	Inc. above	0.10	0.75	2.50	15.00	—

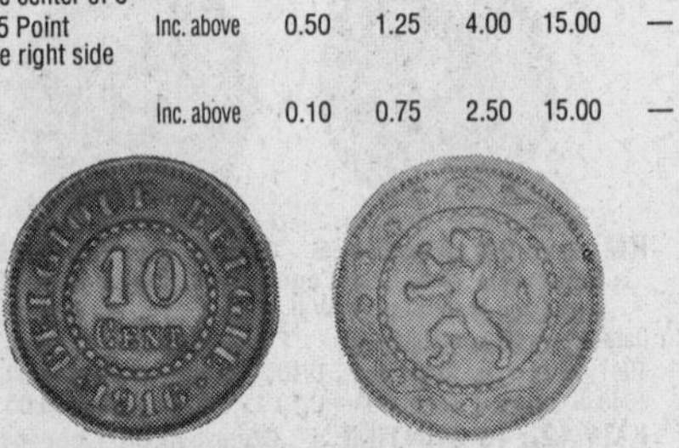

KM# 81 10 CENTIMES **Composition:** Zinc **Obverse:** Legend in French **Obv. Legend:** BELGIQUE-BELGIE **Note:** German Occupation. All of KM#81 have dots after the date. The 1916 is distinguished by a period after the date.

Date	Mintage	F	VF	XF	Unc	BU
1915	9,681,000	0.25	1.50	4.00	15.00	—
1916	37,382,000	0.15	0.75	3.00	12.00	—
1916.	Inc. above	10.00	17.50	70.00	150	—
1917	1,447,000	17.50	25.00	85.00	200	—

KM# 85.1 10 CENTIMES **Composition:** Copper-Nickel **Obverse:** Legend in French **Obv. Legend:** BELGIQUE

Date	Mintage	F	VF	XF	Unc	BU
1911	—	—	—	—	—	—
Note: Struck at a later date						
1920	6,520,000	0.15	0.40	1.50	5.50	—
1921	7,215,000	0.15	0.20	1.00	5.00	—
1923	20,625,000	0.10	0.20	1.00	5.00	—
1926/3	6,916,000	0.20	0.75	3.00	12.00	—
1926/5	Inc. above	0.20	0.75	3.00	12.00	—
1926	Inc. above	0.15	0.20	1.00	5.00	—
1927	8,125,000	0.15	0.20	1.00	5.00	—
1928/3	6,895,000	0.20	1.00	4.50	16.00	—
1928	Inc. above	0.15	0.20	1.00	5.00	—
1929	12,260,000	0.15	0.20	1.00	5.00	—

KM# 85.2 10 CENTIMES **Composition:** Copper-Nickel **Reverse:** Single line below ES of CES

Date	F	VF	XF	Unc	BU
1920	0.50	1.00	5.00	15.00	—
1921	1.50	4.00	12.00	45.00	—

KM# 86 10 CENTIMES **Composition:** Copper-Nickel **Obverse:** Legend in Dutch **Obv. Legend:** BELGIE **Reverse:** Plain field above 10

Date	Mintage	F	VF	XF	Unc	BU
1920	5,050,000	0.15	0.20	1.00	7.00	—
1921	7,580,000	0.15	0.20	1.00	5.00	—
1922	6,250,000	0.15	0.20	1.00	5.00	—
1924	5,825,000	0.15	0.20	1.00	8.00	—
1925/4	8,160,000	0.20	0.40	2.00	10.00	—
1925	Inc. above	0.10	0.20	1.00	5.00	—
1926/5	6,250,000	0.20	0.40	2.00	10.00	—
1926	Inc. above	0.15	0.20	1.00	5.00	—
1927	10,625,000	0.15	0.20	1.00	5.00	—
1928/5	6,750,000	0.20	0.40	2.00	10.00	—
1928	Inc. above	0.15	0.20	1.00	5.00	—
1929	4,668,000	0.15	0.20	1.00	5.00	—
1930	—	15.00	30.00	100	250	—

KM# 95.1 10 CENTIMES **Composition:** Nickel-Brass **Obverse:** Legend in French **Obv. Legend:** BELGIQUE **Reverse:** Star added above 10

Date	Mintage	F	VF	XF	Unc	BU
1930/20	2,000,000	50.00	75.00	200	375	—
1930	Inc. above	20.00	30.00	100	250	—
1931	6,270,000	1.00	5.00	15.00	40.00	—
1932	1,270,000	35.00	50.00	175	350	—
1932 A instead of signature	Inc. above	50.00	100	240	500	—

KM# 95.2 10 CENTIMES **Composition:** Nickel-Brass **Reverse:** Single line below ES of CES

Date	F	VF	XF	Unc	BU
1931	2.00	8.00	20.00	50.00	—
1932	45.00	90.00	200	500	—

KM# 96 10 CENTIMES **Composition:** Nickel-Brass **Obverse:** Legend in Dutch **Obv. Legend:** BELGIE **Reverse:** Star added above 10

Date	Mintage	F	VF	XF	Unc	BU
1930	1,581,000	0.30	0.75	3.00	10.00	—
1931	5,000,000	25.00	40.00	125	220	—

KM# 112 10 CENTIMES **Composition:** Nickel-Brass **Obverse:** Legend in French **Obv. Legend:** BELGIQUE-BELGIE

Date	Mintage	F	VF	XF	Unc	BU
1938	6,000,000	0.10	0.25	0.50	1.50	—
1939	7,000,000	0.50	1.00	3.00	12.00	—

KM# 113.1 10 CENTIMES **Composition:** Nickel-Brass **Obverse:** Legend in Dutch **Obv. Legend:** BELGIE-BELGIQUE

Date	Mintage	F	VF	XF	Unc	BU
1939	8,425,000	0.10	0.25	0.50	1.50	—

KM# 113.2 10 CENTIMES **Composition:** Nickel-Brass **Note:** Thin flan.

Date	F	VF	XF	Unc	BU
1939	1.25	3.00	10.00	35.00	—

KM# 126 10 CENTIMES **Composition:** Zinc **Obverse:** Legend in Dutch **Obv. Legend:** BELGIE-BELGIQUE **Note:**

Date	Mintage	F	VF	XF	Unc	BU
1941	7,000,000	0.15	0.25	1.50	6.00	—
1942	21,000,000	0.15	0.25	1.50	4.00	—
1943	22,000,000	0.15	0.25	1.50	4.00	—
1944	28,140,000	0.15	0.25	1.50	4.00	—
1945	8,000,000	0.15	0.50	2.00	6.00	—
1946	5,370,000	0.15	0.50	2.00	6.00	—

KM# 125 10 CENTIMES **Composition:** Zinc **Obverse:** Legend in French **Obv. Legend:** BELGIQUE-BELGIE **Note:** German Occupation WW II.

Date	F	VF	XF	Unc	BU
1941	0.15	0.25	1.50	4.00	—
1942	0.15	0.25	1.50	4.00	—
1943	0.15	0.25	1.50	4.00	—
1945	—	—	—	—	—
Note: Struck at a later date					
1946	—	—	—	—	—
Note: Not released for circulation					

KM# 146 20 CENTIMES **Composition:** Bronze **Obverse:** Legend in French **Obv. Legend:** BELGIQUE

Date	Mintage	F	VF	XF	Unc	BU
1953	14,150,000	—	0.10	0.20	0.50	—
1953 CENTIMES not touching rim	—	—	0.10	0.75	2.50	—
1954	—	—	400	600	800	—
1957	13,300,000	—	—	0.10	0.50	—
1958	8,700,000	—	—	0.10	0.50	—
1959	19,670,000	—	—	0.10	0.50	—
1962	410,000	—	6.00	10.00	12.50	—
1963	2,550,000	0.10	0.20	0.50	1.00	—

KM# 147.1 20 CENTIMES **Composition:** Bronze **Obverse:** Legend in Dutch **Obv. Legend:** BELGIE

Date	Mintage	F	VF	XF	Unc	BU
1954	50,130,000	—	—	0.10	0.50	—
1960	7,530,000	—	—	0.10	0.50	—

KM# 147.2 20 CENTIMES **Composition:** Bronze **Obverse:** CENTIMES touching rim

Date	F	VF	XF	Unc	BU
1954	—	0.15	0.75	2.50	—
1960	—	0.15	0.75	2.50	—

KM# 62 25 CENTIMES **Composition:** Copper-Nickel **Obverse:** Legend in French **Obv. Legend:** BELGIQUE

Date	Mintage	F	VF	XF	Unc	BU
1908	4,007,000	0.50	4.00	30.00	75.00	—
1909/8	1,998,000	4.00	30.00	110	200	—
1909	Inc. above	1.00	8.00	40.00	90.00	—

KM# 63 25 CENTIMES **Composition:** Copper-Nickel **Obverse:** Legend in Dutch **Obv. Legend:** BELGIE

Date	Mintage	F	VF	XF	Unc	BU
1908	4,011,000	0.50	4.00	30.00	75.00	—

KM# 69 25 CENTIMES **Composition:** Copper-Nickel **Obverse:** Legend in Dutch **Obv. Legend:** BELGIE

Date	Mintage	F	VF	XF	Unc	BU
1910	2,006,000	0.15	1.00	8.00	25.00	—
1911	—	—	—	—	—	—
Note: Struck at a later date						
1913	2,010,000	0.15	1.00	8.00	20.00	—
1921	11,173,000	0.15	0.25	2.00	6.00	—
1922/1	14,200,000	1.00	5.00	15.00	45.00	—
1922	Inc. above	0.15	0.25	2.00	6.00	—
1926/3	6,400,000	0.35	1.25	9.00	25.00	—
1926	Inc. above	0.10	0.40	2.00	6.00	—
1927/3	3,799,000	0.35	1.25	8.00	25.00	—
1927	Inc. above	0.10	0.25	2.00	8.00	—
1928	9,200,000	0.10	0.25	2.00	6.00	—
1929	8,980,000	0.10	0.25	2.00	6.00	—

KM# 68.1 25 CENTIMES **Composition:** Copper-Nickel **Obverse:** Legend in French **Obv. Legend:** BELGIQUE

Date	Mintage	F	VF	XF	Unc	BU
1913	2,011,000	0.15	0.75	6.00	20.00	—
1920	2,844,000	0.15	0.50	5.00	18.00	—
1921	7,464,000	0.10	0.25	2.00	6.00	—
1922	7,600,000	0.10	0.25	2.00	6.00	—
1923	11,356,000	0.15	0.25	2.00	6.00	—
1926/3	1,300,000	1.00	2.00	12.00	30.00	—
1926	Inc. above	0.50	1.00	7.00	25.00	—
1927/3	8,800,000	1.00	2.00	20.00	35.00	—
1927	Inc. above	0.10	0.25	2.00	6.00	—
1928	4,351,000	0.10	0.25	2.00	8.00	—
1929	9,600,000	0.10	0.25	2.00	6.00	—

KM# 68.2 25 CENTIMES **Composition:** Copper-Nickel **Reverse:** Single line below ES of CES

Date	F	VF	XF	Unc	BU
1920	0.50	1.00	8.00	25.00	—
1921	0.35	0.75	5.00	15.00	—

KM# 82 25 CENTIMES **Composition:** Zinc **Obverse:** Legend in French **Obv. Legend:** BELGIQUE-BELGIE **Note:** German Occupation WW I

Date	Mintage	F	VF	XF	Unc	BU
1915	8,080,000	0.50	2.00	9.00	25.00	—
1916	10,671,000	0.50	2.00	7.00	20.00	—
1917	3,555,000	2.00	4.00	18.00	50.00	—
1918	5,489,000	1.00	3.00	12.00	30.00	—

KM# 114.1 25 CENTIMES **Composition:** Nickel-Brass **Obverse:** Legend in French **Obv. Legend:** BELGIQUE-BELGIE

Date	Mintage	F	VF	XF	Unc	BU
1938	7,200,000	—	0.25	1.00	4.00	—
1939	7,732,000	—	0.25	1.00	4.00	—

KM# 114.2 25 CENTIMES **Composition:** Nickel-Brass **Note:** Medal alignment.

Date	F	VF	XF	Unc	BU
1939	1.75	3.00	10.00	30.00	—

KM# 115.1 25 CENTIMES **Composition:** Nickel-Brass **Obverse:** Legend in Dutch **Obv. Legend:** BELGIE-BELGIQUE

Date	Mintage	F	VF	XF	Unc	BU
1938	14,932,000	—	0.25	1.00	3.00	—

KM# 115.2 25 CENTIMES **Composition:** Nickel-Brass **Note:** Medal alignment.

Date	F	VF	XF	Unc	BU
1938	1.75	3.00	10.00	30.00	—

KM# 131 25 CENTIMES **Composition:** Zinc **Obverse:** Legend in French **Obv. Legend:** BELGIQUE-BELGIE **Note:** German Occupation WW II.

Date	F	VF	XF	Unc	BU
1941 Rare	—	—	—	—	—
1942	—	0.20	0.75	3.00	—
1943	—	0.20	0.75	3.00	—
1945	—	—	—	—	—
Note: Struck at a later date					
1946	—	0.20	0.75	3.00	—
1947	—	—	—	—	—
Note: Not released for circulation					

KM# 132 25 CENTIMES **Composition:** Zinc **Obverse:** Legend in Dutch **Obv. Legend:** BELGIE-BELGIQUE

Date	F	VF	XF	Unc	BU
1942	—	0.20	2.00	6.00	—
1943	—	0.20	0.75	3.00	—
1944	—	0.20	0.75	3.00	—
1945	—	0.50	2.50	8.00	—
1946	—	0.50	2.50	8.00	—
1947	—	—	—	—	—
Note: Not released for circulation					

KM# 153.1 25 CENTIMES **Composition:** Copper-Nickel **Obverse:** Legend in French **Obv. Legend:** BELGIQUE **Note:** Struck at Brussels Mint. Mint mark - Angel Head. Mintmaster Vogelier's privy mark - Bird.

Date	Mintage	F	VF	XF	Unc	BU
1964	21,770,000	—	—	0.10	0.15	—
1965	11,440,000	—	—	0.10	0.15	—
1966	19,990,000	—	—	0.10	0.15	—
1967	6,820,000	—	—	0.10	0.15	—
1968	25,250,000	—	—	0.10	0.15	—
1969	7,670,000	—	—	0.10	0.15	—
1970	27,000,000	—	—	0.10	0.15	—
1971	16,000,000	—	—	0.10	0.15	—
1972	20,000,000	—	—	0.10	0.15	—
1973	12,500,000	—	—	0.10	0.15	—
1974	20,000,000	—	—	0.10	0.15	—
1975	12,000,000	—	—	0.10	0.15	—

KM# 153.2 25 CENTIMES **Composition:** Copper-Nickel **Note:** Medal alignment. Struck at the Brussels Mint. Mint mark - Angel Head. Mintmaster Vogelier's privy mark - Bird.

Date	F	VF	XF	Unc	BU
1964	—	—	5.00	12.00	—
1965	—	—	10.00	25.00	—
1967	—	—	10.00	25.00	—
1970	—	—	5.00	12.00	—
1971	—	—	5.00	12.00	—
1974	—	—	10.00	25.00	—

KM# 154.1 25 CENTIMES **Composition:** Copper-Nickel **Obverse:** Legend in Dutch **Obv. Legend:** BELGIE **Note:** Struck at Brussels Mint. Mint mark - Angel Head. Mintmaster Vogelier's privy mark - Bird.

Date	Mintage	F	VF	XF	Unc	BU
1964	21,300,000	—	—	0.10	0.15	—
1965	7,900,000	—	—	0.10	0.15	—
1966	23,420,000	—	—	0.10	0.15	—
1967	7,720,000	—	—	0.10	0.15	—
1968	22,750,000	—	—	0.10	0.15	—
1969	25,190,000	—	—	0.10	0.15	—
1970	12,000,000	—	—	0.10	0.15	—
1971	16,000,000	—	—	0.10	0.15	—
1972	20,000,000	—	—	0.10	0.15	—
1973	12,500,000	—	—	0.10	0.15	—
1974	20,000,000	—	—	0.10	0.15	—
1975	12,000,000	—	—	0.10	0.15	—

KM# 154.2 25 CENTIMES **Composition:** Copper-Nickel **Note:** Medal alignment. Struck at Brussels Mint. Mint mark - Angel Head. Mintmaster Vogelier's privy mark - Bird.

Date	F	VF	XF	Unc	BU
1964	—	—	5.00	12.00	—
1965	—	—	5.00	15.00	—
1966	—	—	5.00	12.00	—
1967	—	—	6.00	15.00	—
1969	—	—	5.00	12.00	—
1971	—	—	6.00	15.00	—
1972	—	—	5.00	12.00	—

KM# 50 50 CENTIMES **Weight:** 2.5000 g. **Composition:** 0.8350 Silver .0671 oz. ASW **Obverse:** Legend in French **Obv. Legend:** DES BELGES

Date	Mintage	F	VF	XF	Unc	BU
1901	3,000,000	2.00	12.00	50.00	100	—

KM# 51 50 CENTIMES **Weight:** 2.5000 g. **Composition:** 0.8350 Silver .0671 oz. ASW **Obverse:** Legend in Dutch **Obv. Legend:** DER BELGEN

Date	Mintage	F	VF	XF	Unc	BU
1901	3,000,000	2.00	12.00	50.00	100	—

KM# 60.1 50 CENTIMES **Weight:** 2.5000 g. **Composition:** 0.8350 Silver .0671 oz. ASW **Obverse:** Legend in French **Obv. Legend:** DES BELGES

Date	Mintage	F	VF	XF	Unc	BU
1907	545,000	3.00	5.00	18.00	70.00	—
1909	2,503,000	1.00	2.50	10.00	30.00	—

KM# 60.2 50 CENTIMES **Weight:** 2.5000 g. **Composition:** 0.8350 Silver .0671 oz. ASW **Obverse:** Without period in signature

Date	F	VF	XF	Unc	BU
1907	4.00	10.00	25.00	100	—
1909	2.00	5.00	12.00	35.00	—

KM# 61.1 50 CENTIMES **Weight:** 2.5000 g. **Composition:** 0.8350 Silver .0671 oz. ASW **Obverse:** Legend in Dutch **Obv. Legend:** DER BELGEN

Date	Mintage	F	VF	XF	Unc	BU
1907	545,000	3.00	10.00	25.00	70.00	—
1909	2,510,000	1.00	2.50	9.00	30.00	—

KM# 61.2 50 CENTIMES **Weight:** 2.5000 g. **Composition:** 0.8350 Silver .0671 oz. ASW **Note:** Medal alignment

Date	F	VF	XF	Unc	BU
1909	12.50	15.00	40.00	125	—

KM# 61.3 50 CENTIMES **Weight:** 2.5000 g. **Composition:** 0.8350 Silver .0671 oz. ASW **Obverse:** Without periods in signature

Date	F	VF	XF	Unc	BU
1909	2.00	6.00	17.50	50.00	—

KM# 70 50 CENTIMES **Weight:** 2.5000 g. **Composition:** 0.8350 Silver .0671 oz. ASW **Obverse:** Legend in French **Obv. Legend:** DES BELGES

Date	Mintage	F	VF	XF	Unc	BU
1910	1,900,000	1.00	2.00	9.00	25.00	—
1911	2,063,000	1.00	3.00	10.00	30.00	—
1912	1,000,000	0.50	1.00	1.50	6.00	—
1914	240,000	2.50	5.00	20.00	65.00	—

KM# 71 50 CENTIMES **Weight:** 2.5000 g. **Composition:** 0.8350 Silver .0671 oz. ASW **Obverse:** Legend in Dutch **Obv. Legend:** DER BELGEN

Date	Mintage	F	VF	XF	Unc	BU
1910	1,900,000	1.00	3.00	10.00	35.00	—
1911	2,063,000	0.50	1.00	1.50	6.00	—
1912	1,000,000	0.50	1.00	1.50	6.00	—
1914	—	35.00	70.00	200	500	—

KM# 83 50 CENTIMES **Composition:** Zinc **Obverse:** Legend in Dutch **Obv. Legend:** BELGIE-BELGIQUE **Note:** German Occupation WW I

Date	Mintage	F	VF	XF	Unc	BU
1918	7,394,000	0.50	3.00	10.00	25.00	—

KM# 87 50 CENTIMES **Composition:** Nickel **Obverse:** Legend in French **Obv. Legend:** BELGIQUE

Date	Mintage	F	VF	XF	Unc	BU
1922	6,180,000	0.15	0.25	0.50	3.00	—
1923	8,820,000	0.15	0.25	0.50	3.00	—
1927	1,750,000	0.15	0.30	0.50	3.00	—
1928	3,000,000	0.15	0.35	1.00	4.00	—
1929	1,000,000	0.25	0.50	3.00	12.00	—
1930	1,000,000	0.25	0.50	3.00	10.00	—
1932/23	2,530,000	1.00	3.00	10.00	25.00	—
1932	Inc. above	0.15	0.50	1.00	4.00	—
1933	2,861,000	0.15	0.25	0.75	4.00	—

KM# 88 50 CENTIMES **Composition:** Nickel **Obverse:** Legend in Dutch **Obv. Legend:** BELGIE

Date	Mintage	F	VF	XF	Unc	BU
1922	—	—	—	—	—	—

Note: Struck at a later date

Date	Mintage	F	VF	XF	Unc	BU
1923	15,000,000	0.20	0.25	0.50	3.00	—
1928/3	10,000,000	0.25	0.50	3.00	15.00	—
1928	Inc. above	0.20	0.25	0.50	3.00	—
1930/20	2,252,000	0.50	2.00	3.50	16.00	—
1930	Inc. above	0.20	0.75	2.50	6.00	—
1932/22	—	0.25	0.50	3.00	15.00	—
1932	2,000,000	0.20	0.50	1.00	4.00	—
1933	1,189,000	1.00	2.00	4.00	16.50	—
1934	935,000	50.00	80.00	175	300	—

KM# 118 50 CENTIMES **Composition:** Nickel **Obverse:** Legend in French **Obv. Legend:** BELGIQUE-BELGIE **Note:** Striking interrupted by the war. Seems to have never been officially released into circulation.

Date	Mintage	F	VF	XF	Unc	BU
1939	15,500,000	200	400	800	1,200	—

KM# 144 50 CENTIMES **Composition:** Bronze **Obverse:** Legend in French **Obv. Legend:** BELGIQUE **Reverse:** Large head

Date	Mintage	F	VF	XF	Unc	BU
1952	3,520,000	—	0.10	0.25	1.00	—
1953	22,620,000	—	—	0.10	0.35	—

KM# 145 50 CENTIMES **Composition:** Bronze **Obverse:** Legend in Dutch **Obv. Legend:** BELGIE **Reverse:** Large head

Date	Mintage	F	VF	XF	Unc	BU
1952	5,830,000	—	0.10	0.25	1.00	—
1953	22,930,000	—	—	0.10	0.35	—
1954	15,730,000	—	—	0.10	0.35	—

KM# 148.1 50 CENTIMES **Composition:** Bronze **Obverse:** Legend in French **Obv. Legend:** BELGIQUE **Reverse:** Smaller head

Date	Mintage	F	VF	XF	Unc	BU
1955	29,160,000	—	—	0.10	0.25	—
1958	9,750,000	—	—	0.10	0.25	—
1959	17,350,000	—	—	0.10	0.20	—
1962	6,160,000	—	—	0.10	0.15	—
1964	5,860,000	—	—	0.10	0.15	—
1965	10,320,000	—	—	0.10	0.15	—
1966	11,040,000	—	—	0.10	0.15	—
1967	7,200,000	—	—	0.10	0.15	—
1968	2,000,000	—	—	0.10	0.20	—
1969	10,000,000	—	—	0.10	0.15	—
1970	16,000,000	—	—	0.10	0.15	—
1971	1,250,000	—	—	0.10	0.20	—
1972	3,000,000	—	—	0.10	0.15	—
1973	3,000,000	—	—	0.10	0.15	—
1974	5,000,000	—	—	0.10	0.15	—
1974 Wide rim	Inc. above	—	—	0.10	0.15	—
1975	7,000,000	—	—	0.10	0.15	—
1976	8,000,000	—	—	0.10	0.15	—
1977	13,000,000	—	—	0.10	0.15	—
1978	2,500,000	—	—	0.10	0.15	—
1979	20,000,000	—	—	0.10	0.15	—
1980	20,000,000	—	—	0.10	0.15	—
1981	2,000,000	—	—	0.10	0.15	—
1982	7,000,000	—	—	0.10	0.15	—
1983	14,100,000	—	—	0.10	0.15	—
1985	6,000,000	—	—	0.10	0.15	—
1987	9,000,000	—	—	0.10	0.15	—
1988	4,500,000	—	—	0.10	0.15	—
1989	60,000	—	—	—	0.50	—
1990	60,000	—	—	—	0.50	—
1991	60,000	—	—	—	0.50	—
1992	7,060,000	—	—	0.10	0.15	—
1993	—	—	—	0.10	0.15	—
1994	10,000,000	—	—	0.10	0.15	—
1995	60,000	—	—	—	0.50	—
1996	4,320,000	—	—	0.10	0.15	—
1997	95,060,000	—	—	—	0.10	—
1998	75,060,000	—	—	—	0.10	—
1999	60,000	—	—	—	0.50	—
2000	60,000	—	—	—	0.50	—

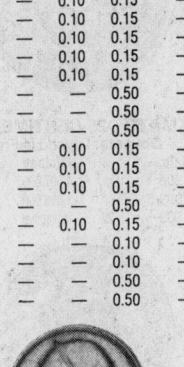

KM# 149.1 50 CENTIMES **Composition:** Bronze **Reverse:** Smaller head; legend in Dutch **Rev. Legend:** BELGIE

Date	Mintage	F	VF	XF	Unc	BU
1956	5,640,000	—	—	0.10	0.25	—
1957	13,800,000	—	—	0.10	0.25	—
1958	19,480,000	—	—	0.10	0.20	—
1962	4,150,000	—	—	0.10	0.15	—
1963	1,110,000	—	—	0.10	0.15	—
1964	10,340,000	—	—	0.10	0.15	—
1965	9,590,000	—	—	0.10	0.15	—
1966	6,930,000	—	—	0.10	0.15	—
1967	6,970,000	—	—	0.10	0.15	—
1968	2,000,000	—	—	0.10	0.20	—
1969	10,000,000	—	—	0.10	0.15	—
1970	12,000,000	—	—	0.10	0.15	—
1971	1,250,000	—	—	0.10	0.20	—
1972	7,000,000	—	—	0.10	0.15	—
1973	3,000,000	—	—	0.10	0.15	—
1974	5,000,000	—	—	0.10	0.15	—
1975	7,000,000	—	—	0.10	0.15	—
1976	8,000,000	—	—	0.10	0.15	—
1977	13,000,000	—	—	0.10	0.15	—
1978	2,500,000	—	—	0.10	0.15	—
1979	40,000,000	—	—	0.10	0.15	—
1980	20,000,000	—	—	0.10	0.15	—
1981	2,000,000	—	—	0.10	0.15	—
1982	7,000,000	—	—	0.10	0.15	—
1983	14,100,000	—	—	0.10	0.15	—
1985	6,000,000	—	—	0.10	0.15	—
1987	9,000,000	—	—	0.10	0.15	—
1988	9,000,000	—	—	0.10	0.15	—
1989	60,000	—	—	—	0.50	—
1990	60,000	—	—	—	0.50	—
1991	60,000	—	—	—	0.50	—
1992	7,060,000	—	—	0.10	0.15	—
1993	1,040,000	—	—	0.10	0.15	—
1994	10,000,000	—	—	0.10	0.15	—
1995	60,000	—	—	—	0.50	—
1996	60,000	—	—	—	0.50	—
1997	95,060,000	—	—	—	0.10	—
1998	75,060,000	—	—	—	0.10	—
1999	—	—	—	—	0.50	—
2000	—	—	—	—	0.50	—
2001	—	—	—	—	0.50	—

KM# 148.2 50 CENTIMES **Composition:** Bronze **Note:** Medal alignment.

Date	F	VF	XF	Unc	BU
1953	—	—	2.00	6.50	—
1959	—	—	2.00	5.00	—
1965	—	—	2.00	4.00	—
1966	—	—	2.00	4.00	—
1967	—	—	2.00	4.00	—
1969	—	—	2.00	4.00	—
1974	—	—	2.00	4.00	—
1976	—	—	2.00	4.00	—
1980	—	—	2.00	4.00	—

KM# 149.2 50 CENTIMES **Composition:** Bronze **Note:** Medal alignment.

Date	F	VF	XF	Unc	BU
1953	—	—	2.00	6.50	—
1958	—	—	2.00	6.50	—
1967	—	—	2.00	6.50	—
1969	—	—	2.00	6.50	—
1977	—	—	2.00	6.50	—
1979	—	—	2.00	6.50	—
1981	—	—	2.00	6.50	—

KM# 56.1 FRANC **Weight:** 5.0000 g. **Composition:** 0.8350 Silver .1342 oz. ASW **Obverse:** Legend in French **Obv. Legend:** DES BELGES

Date	Mintage	F	VF	XF	Unc	BU
1904	803,000	4.00	14.00	40.00	75.00	—
1909	2,250,000	2.00	10.00	30.00	45.00	—

KM# 56.2 FRANC **Weight:** 5.0000 g. **Composition:** 0.8350 Silver .1342 oz. ASW **Obverse:** Without period in signature

Date	F	VF	XF	Unc	BU
1904	7.00	25.00	60.00	90.00	—
1909	2.50	10.00	30.00	45.00	—

KM# 57.1 FRANC **Weight:** 5.0000 g. **Composition:** 0.8350 Silver .1342 oz. ASW **Obverse:** Legend in Dutch **Obv. Legend:** DER BELGEN

Date	Mintage	F	VF	XF	Unc	BU
1904	803,000	5.00	20.00	40.00	75.00	—
1909	2,250,000	2.00	10.00	30.00	45.00	—

KM# 57.2 FRANC **Weight:** 5.0000 g. **Composition:** 0.8350 Silver .1342 oz. ASW **Obverse:** Without period in signature

Date	F	VF	XF	Unc	BU
1904	10.00	60.00	110	200	—
1909	3.00	10.00	30.00	45.00	—

KM# 72.1 FRANC **Weight:** 5.0000 g. **Composition:** 0.8350 Silver .1342 oz. ASW **Obverse:** Legend in French **Obv. Legend:** DES BELGES

Date	Mintage	F	VF	XF	Unc	BU
1910	2,190,000	1.00	3.00	8.00	25.00	—
1911	2,810,000	0.75	1.50	5.00	12.00	—
1912	3,250,000	0.75	1.50	2.50	7.00	—
1913	3,000,000	0.75	1.50	2.50	7.00	—
1914	10,563,000	0.75	1.50	2.50	7.00	—
1917	8,540,000	350	700	1,500	2,000	—
1918	1,469,000	300	600	1,400	2,000	—

KM# 73.1 FRANC **Weight:** 5.0000 g. **Composition:** 0.8350 Silver .1342 oz. ASW **Obverse:** Legend in Dutch **Obv. Legend:** DER BELGEN

Date	Mintage	F	VF	XF	Unc	BU
1910	2,750,000	1.00	4.00	15.00	35.00	—
1911	2,250,000	0.75	1.50	5.00	10.00	—
1912	3,250,000	0.75	1.50	2.50	7.00	—
1913	3,000,000	0.75	1.50	2.50	7.00	—
1914	10,222,000	0.75	1.50	2.50	7.00	—
1918	—	300	600	1,400	2,000	—

KM# 72.2 FRANC **Weight:** 5.0000 g. **Composition:** 0.8350 Silver .1342 oz. ASW **Note:** Medal alignment.

Date	F	VF	XF	Unc	BU
1914	4.50	12.50	50.00	125	—

KM# 73.2 FRANC **Weight:** 5.0000 g. **Composition:** 0.8350 Silver .1342 oz. ASW **Note:** Medal alignment.

Date	F	VF	XF	Unc	BU
1914	4.50	12.50	50.00	125	—

KM# 89 FRANC **Composition:** Nickel **Obverse:** Legend in French **Obv. Legend:** BELGIQUE

Date	Mintage	F	VF	XF	Unc	BU
1922	14,000,000	0.15	0.25	1.00	3.00	—
1923	22,500,000	0.15	0.25	1.00	3.00	—
1928/3	5,000,000	0.25	1.50	5.00	12.00	—
1928/7	Inc. above	0.25	1.50	5.00	12.00	—
1928	Inc. above	0.15	0.25	1.00	4.00	—
1929	7,415,000	0.15	0.25	1.00	3.50	—
1930	5,365,000	0.15	0.25	1.00	3.50	—
1931	—	250	500	1,000	1,800	—
1933	1,998,000	0.25	1.50	5.00	12.00	—
1934/24	10,263,000	0.25	1.50	6.00	15.00	—
1934	Inc. above	0.15	0.25	1.00	3.00	—

KM# 90 FRANC **Composition:** Nickel **Obverse:** Legend in Dutch **Obv. Legend:** BELGIE

Date	Mintage	F	VF	XF	Unc	BU
1922	19,000,000	0.15	0.25	1.00	3.00	—
1923/2	17,500,000	0.20	1.50	4.00	12.00	—
1923	Inc. above	0.15	0.25	1.00	3.00	—
1928/3	4,975,000	0.20	2.00	5.00	12.00	—
1928/7	Inc. above	0.20	2.00	5.00	12.00	—
1928	Inc. above	0.15	0.50	2.00	7.00	—
1929	10,365,000	0.15	0.25	1.00	3.00	—
1933	786,000	200	400	900	2,000	—
1934/24	8,025,000	0.35	2.50	7.00	15.00	—
1934	Inc. above	0.15	0.50	1.00	3.00	—
1935/23	2,238,000	1.50	4.00	12.00	25.00	—
1935	Inc. above	0.25	0.75	2.00	6.00	—

KM# 119 FRANC **Composition:** Nickel **Obverse:** Legend in French **Obv. Legend:** BELGIQUE-BELGIE

Date	Mintage	F	VF	XF	Unc	BU
1939	46,865,000	0.15	0.25	0.50	1.50	—
1940	—	—	—	—	—	—

Note: Struck at a later date

KM# 120 FRANC **Composition:** Nickel **Obverse:** Legend in Dutch **Obv. Legend:** BELGIE-BELGIQUE

Date	Mintage	F	VF	XF	Unc	BU
1939	36,000,000	0.15	0.25	0.50	1.50	—
1940	10,865,000	0.20	0.40	0.75	2.50	—

KM# 127 FRANC **Composition:** Zinc **Obverse:** Legend in French **Obv. Legend:** BELGIQUE-BELGIE **Note:** German Occupation WW II.

Date	Mintage	F	VF	XF	Unc	BU
1941	16,000,000	0.20	0.75	1.50	6.00	—
1942	25,000,000	0.20	0.75	1.50	4.00	—
1943	28,000,000	0.20	0.75	1.50	4.00	—
1947	3,175,000	60.00	125	400	700	—

KM# 128 FRANC **Composition:** Zinc **Obverse:** Legend in Dutch **Obv. Legend:** BELGIE-BELGIQUE

Date	Mintage	F	VF	XF	Unc	BU
1942	42,000,000	0.20	0.75	1.50	4.00	—
1943	28,000,000	0.20	0.75	1.50	4.00	—
1944	24,190,000	0.20	0.75	1.50	4.00	—
1945	15,930,000	0.20	1.00	2.00	7.00	—
1946	36,000,000	0.20	0.75	1.50	4.00	—
1947	3,000,000	25.00	40.00	100	200	—

KM# 142.1 FRANC **Composition:** Copper-Nickel **Obverse:** Legend in French **Obv. Legend:** BELGIQUE

Date	Mintage	F	VF	XF	Unc	BU
1950	13,630,000	—	—	0.10	3.00	—
1951	51,025,000	—	—	0.10	2.00	—
1952	53,205,000	—	—	0.10	2.00	—
1954	4,980,000	—	0.10	0.25	3.00	—
1955	3,960,000	—	0.10	0.25	3.00	—
1956	10,000,000	—	—	0.10	1.00	—
1958	31,750,000	—	—	0.10	1.00	—
1959	9,000,000	—	—	0.10	1.00	—
1960	10,000,000	—	—	0.10	1.00	—
1961	5,030,000	—	—	0.10	1.00	—
1962	12,250,000	—	—	0.10	0.50	—
1963	18,700,000	—	—	0.10	0.50	—
1964	10,110,000	—	—	0.10	0.50	—
1965	10,185,000	—	—	0.10	0.50	—
1966	16,430,000	—	—	0.10	0.50	—
1967	32,945,000	—	—	0.10	0.30	—
1968	8,000,000	—	—	0.10	0.30	—
1969	21,950,000	—	—	0.10	0.30	—
1970	35,500,000	—	—	0.10	0.30	—
1971	10,000,000	—	—	0.10	0.30	—
1972	35,000,000	—	—	0.10	0.30	—
1973	42,500,000	—	—	0.10	0.30	—
1974	30,000,000	—	—	0.10	0.30	—
1975	80,000,000	—	—	0.10	0.30	—
1976	18,000,000	—	—	0.10	0.30	—
1977	68,500,000	—	—	0.10	0.30	—
1978	47,500,000	—	—	0.10	0.30	—
1979	25,000,000	—	—	0.10	0.30	—
1980	66,500,000	—	—	0.10	0.30	—
1981	2,000,000	0.10	0.20	0.50	0.75	—
1988	17,500,000	—	—	0.10	0.30	—

KM# 143.1 FRANC **Composition:** Copper-Nickel **Reverse:** Legend in Dutch **Rev. Legend:** BELGIE

Date	Mintage	F	VF	XF	Unc	BU
1950	10,000,000	—	—	0.10	3.00	—
1951	53,750,000	—	—	0.10	2.00	—
1952	49,145,000	—	—	0.10	2.00	—
1953	9,915,000	—	—	0.10	2.00	—
1954	4,940,000	—	0.10	0.25	3.00	—
1955	3,960,000	—	0.10	0.25	3.00	—
1956	10,040,000	—	—	0.10	1.00	—
1957	18,315,000	—	—	0.10	1.00	—
1958	17,365,000	—	—	0.10	1.00	—
1959	5,830,000	—	—	0.10	1.00	—
1960	5,555,000	—	—	0.10	1.00	—
1961	9,350,000	—	—	0.10	0.50	—
1962	10,720,000	—	—	0.10	0.50	—
1963	23,460,000	—	—	0.10	0.50	—
1964	7,430,000	—	—	0.10	0.50	—
1965	11,190,000	—	—	0.10	0.50	—
1966	20,990,000	—	—	0.10	0.50	—
1967	27,470,000	—	—	0.10	0.50	—
1968	8,170,000	—	—	0.10	0.30	—
1969	21,730,000	—	—	0.10	0.30	—
1970	35,730,000	—	—	0.10	0.30	—
1971	10,000,000	—	—	0.10	0.30	—
1972	35,000,000	—	—	0.10	0.30	—
1973	42,500,000	—	—	0.10	0.30	—
1974	30,000,000	—	—	0.10	0.30	—
1975	80,000,000	—	—	0.10	0.30	—
1976	18,000,000	—	—	0.10	0.30	—
1977	68,500,000	—	—	0.10	0.30	—
1978	47,500,000	—	—	0.10	0.30	—
1979	50,000,000	—	—	0.10	0.30	—
1980	66,500,000	—	—	0.10	0.30	—
1981	2,000,000	—	—	0.10	0.50	—
1988	17,500,000	—	—	0.10	0.30	—

KM# 142.2 FRANC **Composition:** Copper-Nickel **Note:** Medal alignment.

Date	F	VF	XF	Unc	BU
1952	—	3.00	9.00	20.00	—
1956	—	3.00	9.00	20.00	—
1958	—	3.00	9.00	20.00	—
1959	—	3.00	9.00	20.00	—
1963	—	3.00	9.00	20.00	—
1965	—	3.00	9.00	20.00	—
1966	—	3.00	9.00	25.00	—
1969	—	3.00	9.00	25.00	—
1970	—	3.00	9.00	25.00	—

Date	F	VF	XF	Unc	BU
1974	—	3.00	9.00	25.00	—
1975	—	3.00	9.00	25.00	—
1977	—	3.00	9.00	25.00	—
1978	—	3.00	9.00	25.00	—
1979	—	3.00	9.00	25.00	—
1988	—	3.00	9.00	25.00	—

KM# 143.2 FRANC Composition: Copper-Nickel **Note:** Medal alignment.

Date	F	VF	XF	Unc	BU
1951	—	3.00	9.00	20.00	—
1952	—	3.00	9.00	20.00	—
1956	—	3.00	9.00	20.00	—
1957	—	3.00	9.00	20.00	—
1958	—	3.00	9.00	20.00	—
1964	—	3.00	9.00	20.00	—
1970	—	3.00	9.00	20.00	—
1971	—	3.00	9.00	20.00	—
1973	—	3.00	9.00	20.00	—
1976	—	3.00	9.00	20.00	—
1977	—	3.00	9.00	20.00	—
1979	—	3.00	9.00	20.00	—
1981	—	3.00	9.00	20.00	—

KM# 171 FRANC Composition: Nickel Plated Iron **Obverse:** Dutch legend **Obv. Legend:** BOUDEWIJN I **Reverse:** Legend in Dutch **Rev. Legend:** BELGIE

Date	Mintage	F	VF	XF	Unc	BU
1989	200,060,000	—	—	—	0.35	—
1990	200,060,000	—	—	—	0.35	—
1991	200,060,000	—	—	—	0.35	—
1992	60,000	—	—	—	1.25	—
1993	15,060,000	—	—	—	0.35	—

KM# 170 FRANC Composition: Nickel Plated Iron **Obverse:** French legend **Obv. Legend:** BAUDOUIN I **Reverse:** Legend in French **Rev. Legend:** BELGIQUE

Date	Mintage	F	VF	XF	Unc	BU
1989	200,060,000	—	—	—	0.35	—
1990	200,060,000	—	—	—	0.35	—
1991	200,060,000	—	—	—	0.35	—
1992	60,000	—	—	—	1.25	—
1993	15,060,000	—	—	—	0.35	—

KM# 188 FRANC Composition: Nickel Plated Iron **Reverse:** Legend in Dutch **Rev. Legend:** BELGIE

Date	Mintage	F	VF	XF	Unc	BU
1994	75,060,000	—	—	—	0.30	—
1995	75,060,000	—	—	—	0.30	—
1996	75,060,000	—	—	—	0.30	—
1997	95,060,000	—	—	—	0.30	—
1998	75,060,000	—	—	—	0.30	—
1999	60,000	—	—	—	1.00	—
2000	60,000	—	—	—	1.00	—

KM# 187 FRANC Composition: Nickel Plated Iron **Obverse:** Albert II **Reverse:** Legend in French **Rev. Legend:** BELGIQUE **Note:** Struck at Brussels Mint. Mint mark - Angel Head. Unknown mintmaster's privy mark - scales.

Date	Mintage	F	VF	XF	Unc	BU
1994	75,060,000	—	—	—	0.30	—
1995	75,060,000	—	—	—	0.30	—
1996	75,060,000	—	—	—	0.30	—
1997	95,060,000	—	—	—	0.30	—
1998	75,060,000	—	—	—	0.30	—
1999	60,000	—	—	—	1.00	—
2000	60,000	—	—	—	1.00	—

KM# 58.1 2 FRANCS (2 Frank) Weight: 10.0000 g. **Composition:** 0.8350 Silver .2685 oz. ASW **Obverse:** Legend in French **Obv. Legend:** DES BELGES

Date	Mintage	F	VF	XF	Unc	BU
1904	400,000	6.00	10.00	45.00	90.00	—
1909	1,088,000	2.50	5.00	25.00	50.00	—

KM# 58.2 2 FRANCS (2 Frank) Weight: 10.0000 g. **Composition:** 0.8350 Silver .2685 oz. ASW **Obverse:** Without period in signature

Date	F	VF	XF	Unc	BU
1904	9.00	15.00	60.00	150	—
1909	10.00	20.00	75.00	200	—

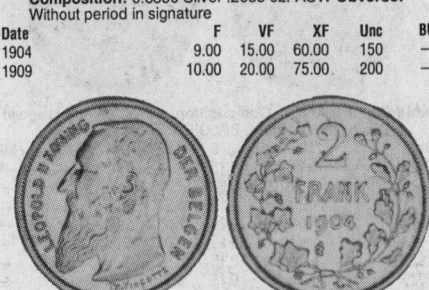

KM# 59.1 2 FRANCS (2 Frank) Weight: 10.0000 g. **Composition:** 0.8350 Silver .2685 oz. ASW **Obverse:** Legend in Dutch **Obv. Legend:** DER BELGEN

Date	Mintage	F	VF	XF	Unc	BU
1904	400,000	5.00	10.00	45.00	90.00	—
1909	1,088,000	2.50	4.00	25.00	50.00	—

KM# 59.2 2 FRANCS (2 Frank) Weight: 10.0000 g. **Composition:** 0.8350 Silver .2685 oz. ASW **Obverse:** Without period in signature

Date	F	VF	XF	Unc	BU
1904	12.50	30.00	75.00	200	—
1909	7.00	15.00	45.00	90.00	—

KM# 74 2 FRANCS (2 Frank) Weight: 10.0000 g. **Composition:** 0.8350 Silver .2685 oz. ASW **Obverse:** Legend in French **Obv. Legend:** DES BELGES

Date	Mintage	F	VF	XF	Unc	BU
1910	800,000	2.50	4.00	15.00	50.00	—
1911	1,000,000	2.00	3.00	10.00	30.00	—
1912	375,000	3.00	5.00	20.00	55.00	—

KM# 75 2 FRANCS (2 Frank) Weight: 10.0000 g. **Composition:** 0.8350 Silver .2685 oz. ASW **Obverse:** Legend in Dutch **Obv. Legend:** DER BELGEN

Date	Mintage	F	VF	XF	Unc	BU
1911	1,775,000	2.00	3.00	10.00	25.00	—
1912	375,000	2.50	4.00	20.00	50.00	—

KM# 91.1 2 FRANCS (2 Frank) Composition: Nickel **Obverse:** Legend in French **Obv. Legend:** BELGIQUE

Date	Mintage	F	VF	XF	Unc	BU
1923	7,500,000	0.50	1.50	8.00	15.00	—
1930/20	1,250,000	12.00	20.00	140	250	—
1930	Inc. above	10.00	17.00	100	200	—

KM# 92 2 FRANCS (2 Frank) Composition: Nickel **Obverse:** Legend in Dutch **Obv. Legend:** BELGIE

Date	Mintage	F	VF	XF	Unc	BU
1923	6,500,000	0.25	1.50	7.00	15.00	—
1924	1,000,000	5.00	15.00	65.00	125	—
1930/20	1,252,000	15.00	40.00	125	250	—
1930	Inc. above	8.00	15.00	100	200	—

KM# 91.2 2 FRANCS (2 Frank) Composition: Nickel **Note:** Medal alignment

Date	F	VF	XF	Unc	BU
1923	5.00	8.00	45.00	110	—

KM# 133 2 FRANCS (2 Frank) Composition: Zinc Coated Steel **Obverse:** Legend in French **Obv. Legend:** BELGIQUE-BELGIE **Note:** Allied Occupation issue. Made in U.S.A. on blanks for 1943 cents.

Date	Mintage	F	VF	XF	Unc	BU
1944	25,000,000	0.25	0.50	1.50	5.00	—

KM# 133a 2 FRANCS (2 Frank) Composition: Silver **Note:** Made in error in U.S.A. on blanks for Netherlands 25 cents.

Date	F	VF	XF	Unc	BU
1944	100	200	300	400	—

KM# 97.1 5 FRANCS - 5 FRANK (Un / Een Belga) Composition: Nickel **Obverse:** Legend in French **Obv. Legend:** DES BELGES **Reverse:** Value: UN BELGA **Note:** All dates exist in position A and B, values are the same.

Date	Mintage	F	VF	XF	Unc	BU
1930	1,600,000	1.50	6.00	12.00	25.00	—
1931	9,032,000	1.00	4.00	10.00	20.00	—
1932	3,600,000	1.50	7.00	14.00	30.00	—
1933	1,387,000	6.00	15.00	35.00	80.00	—
1934	1,000,000	30.00	75.00	160	300	—

KM# 98 5 FRANCS - 5 FRANK (Un / Een Belga) Composition: Nickel **Obverse:** Legend in Dutch **Obv. Legend:** DER BELGEN **Reverse:** Value: EEN BELGA **Note:** All dates exist in position A and B, values are the same.

Date	Mintage	F	VF	XF	Unc	BU
1930	5,086,000	2.00	8.00	16.00	30.00	—
1931	5,336,000	1.50	6.00	12.00	25.00	—
1932	3,683,000	1.50	7.00	14.00	30.00	—
1933	2,514,000	8.00	20.00	40.00	80.00	—

KM# 97.2 5 FRANCS - 5 FRANK (Un / Een Belga) Composition: Nickel **Note:** Medal alignment. Edge varieties exist.

Date	F	VF	XF	Unc	BU
1930	17.50	50.00	150	300	—

KM# 109.1 5 FRANCS - 5 FRANK (Un / Een Belga) Composition: Nickel **Reverse:** Legend in Dutch **Rev. Legend:** BELGIE **Note:** Both dates exist in position A and B, values are the same.

Date	Mintage	F	VF	XF	Unc	BU
1936	2,498,000	4.00	15.00	35.00	60.00	—
1937	—	—	—	—	—	—

KM# 108.1 5 FRANCS - 5 FRANK (Un / Een Belga) **Composition:** Nickel **Reverse:** Legend in French **Rev. Legend:** BELGIQUE **Note:** Both dates exist in position A and B, values are the same.

Date	Mintage	F	VF	XF	Unc	BU
1936	650,000	6.00	20.00	50.00	85.00	—
1937	1,848,000	6.00	17.50	40.00	70.00	—

KM# 108.2 5 FRANCS - 5 FRANK (Un / Een Belga) **Composition:** Nickel **Note:** Medal alignment.

Date	F	VF	XF	Unc	BU
1936	17.50	55.00	150	350	—

KM# 109.2 5 FRANCS - 5 FRANK (Un / Een Belga) **Composition:** Nickel **Note:** Medal alignment. Edge varieties exist.

Date	F	VF	XF	Unc	BU
1936	15.00	45.00	130	300	—

KM# 117.1 5 FRANCS - 5 FRANK (Un / Een Belga) **Composition:** Nickel **Obverse:** Legend in Dutch **Obv. Legend:** BELGIE-BELGIQUE **Note:** Milled edge, lettering with crown.

Date	Mintage	F	VF	XF	Unc	BU
1938 Position A	3,200,000	7.00	15.00	50.00	125	—
1938 Position B	Inc. above	7.00	15.00	50.00	125	—
1939 Position A	8,219,000	7.50	20.00	80.00	175	—
1939 Position B	Inc. above	7.50	20.00	80.00	175	—

KM# 117.2 5 FRANCS - 5 FRANK (Un / Een Belga) **Composition:** Nickel **Note:** Milled edge, lettering with star.

Date	F	VF	XF	Unc	BU
1938 Position B	6.00	20.00	70.00	160	—
1938 Position A	6.00	20.00	70.00	160	—
1939 Position A	0.15	0.50	1.25	4.00	—
1939 Position B	0.15	0.50	1.25	4.00	—

KM# 116.2 5 FRANCS - 5 FRANK (Un / Een Belga) **Composition:** Nickel **Note:** Milled edge, lettering with star.

Date	F	VF	XF	Unc	BU
1939 Position A	200	500	900	1,750	—
1939 Position B	200	500	900	1,750	—

KM# 116.1 5 FRANCS - 5 FRANK (Un / Een Belga) **Composition:** Nickel **Obverse:** Legend in French **Obv. Legend:** BELGIQUE-BELGIE **Note:** Milled edge, lettering with crown.

Date	Mintage	F	VF	XF	Unc	BU
1938 Position A	11,419,000	0.20	0.75	3.00	9.00	—
1938 Position B	Inc. above	0.30	1.00	4.00	10.00	—

KM# 116.3 5 FRANCS - 5 FRANK (Un / Een Belga) **Composition:** Nickel **Note:** Milled edge, without lettering (error).

Date	F	VF	XF	Unc	BU
1938	40.00	70.00	135	300	—

KM# 117.3 5 FRANCS - 5 FRANK (Un / Een Belga) **Composition:** Nickel **Note:** Milled edge, without lettering (error).

Date	F	VF	XF	Unc	BU
1939	30.00	60.00	175	350	—

KM# 129.1 5 FRANCS - 5 FRANK (Un / Een Belga) **Composition:** Zinc **Obverse:** Legend in French **Obv. Legend:** DES BELGES **Note:** German Occupation WW II.

Date	Mintage	F	VF	XF	Unc	BU
1941	15,200,000	0.35	0.75	2.50	10.00	—
1943	16,236,000	0.35	0.75	2.00	10.00	—
1944	1,868,000	0.75	3.00	18.00	50.00	—
1945	3,200,000	0.50	1.00	6.00	20.00	—
1946	4,452,000	1.00	4.50	15.00	40.00	—
1947	3,100,000	20.00	40.00	110	300	—

KM# 130 5 FRANCS - 5 FRANK (Un / Een Belga) **Composition:** Zinc **Obverse:** Legend in Dutch **Obv. Legend:** DER BELGEN

Date	Mintage	F	VF	XF	Unc	BU
1941	27,544,000	0.30	0.50	2.50	10.00	—
1945	3,200,000	15.00	30.00	75.00	200	—
1946 Rare	4,000,000	—	—	—	—	—
1947	36,000	75.00	150	375	900	—

KM# 129.2 5 FRANCS - 5 FRANK (Un / Een Belga) **Composition:** Zinc **Note:** Medal alignment.

Date	F	VF	XF	Unc	BU
1943	5.00	15.00	50.00	130	—

KM# 134.2 5 FRANCS - 5 FRANK (Un / Een Belga) **Composition:** Copper-Nickel **Note:** Medal alignment.

Date	F	VF	XF	Unc	BU
1949	—	4.00	10.00	30.00	—
1950	—	4.00	10.00	30.00	—
1958	—	4.00	10.00	30.00	—
1962	—	4.00	10.00	30.00	—
1963	—	4.00	10.00	30.00	—
1965	—	4.00	10.00	30.00	—
1966	—	4.00	10.00	30.00	—
1969	—	4.00	10.00	30.00	—
1975	—	4.00	10.00	30.00	—
1977	—	4.00	10.00	30.00	—

KM# 135.2 5 FRANCS - 5 FRANK (Un / Een Belga) **Composition:** Copper-Nickel **Note:** Medal alignment.

Date	F	VF	XF	Unc	BU
1950	—	4.00	10.00	30.00	—
1962	—	4.00	10.00	30.00	—
1963	—	4.00	10.00	30.00	—
1965	—	4.00	10.00	30.00	—
1966	—	4.00	10.00	30.00	—
1969	—	4.00	10.00	30.00	—
1974	—	4.00	10.00	30.00	—

KM# 134.1 5 FRANCS - 5 FRANK (Un / Een Belga) **Composition:** Copper-Nickel **Obverse:** Legend in French **Obv. Legend:** BELGIQUE

Date	Mintage	F	VF	XF	Unc	BU
1948	5,304,000	—	0.20	2.00	10.00	—
1949	38,752,000	—	—	0.20	4.00	—
1950	23,948,000	—	—	0.20	3.00	—
1958	9,088,000	—	—	0.20	2.00	—
1961	6,000,000	—	—	0.20	1.00	—
1962	6,576,000	—	—	0.20	1.00	—
1963	11,144,000	—	—	0.20	1.00	—
1964	3,520,000	—	—	0.20	1.50	—
1965	11,988,000	—	—	0.20	0.35	—
1966	6,772,000	—	—	0.20	0.40	—
1967	13,268,000	—	—	0.20	0.35	—
1968	5,192,000	—	—	0.20	0.40	—
1969	22,235,000	—	—	0.20	0.35	—
1969 Without engraver's name	Inc. above	1.00	2.50	9.00	20.00	—
1970	2,000,000	—	—	0.20	0.45	—

Date	Mintage	F	VF	XF	Unc	BU
1971	15,000,000	—	—	0.20	0.35	—
1972	17,500,000	—	—	0.20	0.35	—
1973	10,000,000	—	—	0.20	0.35	—
1974	25,000,000	—	—	0.20	0.35	—
1975	34,000,000	—	—	0.20	0.35	—
1975 Without engraver's name	—	1.00	2.00	6.00	10.00	—
1976	7,500,000	—	—	0.20	0.40	—
1977	22,500,000	—	—	0.20	0.35	—
1978	27,500,000	—	—	0.20	0.35	—
1979	5,000,000	—	—	0.20	0.40	—
1980	11,000,000	—	—	0.20	0.35	—
1981	2,000,000	—	—	0.20	0.40	—

KM# 135.1 5 FRANCS - 5 FRANK (Un / Een Belga) **Composition:** Copper-Nickel **Obverse:** Legend in Dutch **Obv. Legend:** BELGIE

Date	Mintage	F	VF	XF	Unc	BU
1948	4,800,000	—	0.20	2.00	10.00	—
1949	31,500,000	—	—	0.20	4.00	—
1950	34,728,000	—	—	0.20	3.00	—
1958	2,672,000	—	—	0.20	4.00	—
1960	5,896,000	—	—	0.20	2.00	—
1961	4,120,000	—	—	0.20	1.00	—
1962	7,624,000	—	—	0.20	1.00	—
1963	6,136,000	—	—	0.20	1.00	—
1964	8,128,000	—	—	0.20	0.40	—
1965	9,956,000	—	—	0.20	0.40	—
1966	7,136,000	—	—	0.20	0.40	—
1966 Without engraver's name	—	1.00	2.00	6.00	10.00	—
1967	16,132,000	—	—	0.20	0.35	—
1968	3,200,000	—	—	0.20	0.40	—
1969	21,500,000	—	—	0.20	0.35	—
1970	2,000,000	—	—	0.20	0.45	—
1971	15,000,000	—	—	0.20	0.35	—
1972	17,500,000	—	—	0.20	0.35	—
1972 Without engraver's name	Inc. above	1.00	2.50	9.00	20.00	—
1973	10,000,000	—	—	0.20	0.35	—
1974	25,000,000	—	—	0.20	0.35	—
1974 Without engraver's name	—	1.00	2.00	6.00	10.00	—
1975	34,000,000	—	—	0.20	0.35	—
1976	7,500,000	—	—	0.20	0.40	—
1977	22,500,000	—	—	0.20	0.35	—
1978	27,500,000	—	—	0.20	0.35	—
1979	10,000,000	—	—	0.20	0.35	—
1980	11,000,000	—	—	0.20	0.35	—
1981	2,000,000	—	—	0.20	0.40	—

KM# 163 5 FRANCS - 5 FRANK (Un / Een Belga) **Composition:** Brass Or Aluminum-Bronze **Reverse:** Legend in French **Rev. Legend:** BELGIQUE

Date	Mintage	F	VF	XF	Unc	BU
1986	208,400,000	—	—	0.35	0.65	—
1987	22,500,000	—	—	0.35	0.65	—
1988	26,500,000	—	—	0.35	0.65	—
1989	60,000	—	—	—	2.00	—
1990	60,000	—	—	—	2.00	—
1991	60,000	—	—	—	2.00	—
1992	5,060,000	—	—	0.35	0.65	—
1993	15,060,000	—	—	0.35	0.65	—

KM# 164 5 FRANCS - 5 FRANK (Un / Een Belga) **Composition:** Brass Or Aluminum-Bronze **Reverse:** Legend in Dutch **Rev. Legend:** BELGIE

Date	Mintage	F	VF	XF	Unc	BU
1986	208,400,000	—	—	0.35	0.65	—
1987	22,500,000	—	—	0.35	0.65	—
1988	26,500,000	—	—	0.35	0.65	—

Date	Mintage	F	VF	XF	Unc	BU
1989	60,000	—	—	—	2.00	—
1990	60,000	—	—	—	2.00	—
1991	60,000	—	—	—	2.00	—
1992	5,060,000	—	—	0.35	0.65	—
1993	15,060,000	—	—	0.35	0.65	—

KM# 189 5 FRANCS - 5 FRANK (Un / Een Belga) **Composition:** Aluminum-Bronze **Obverse:** Albert II **Reverse:** Legend in French **Rev. Legend:** BELGIQUE **Note:** Struck at Brussels Mint. Mint mark - Angel head. Unknown mintmaster's privy mark - Scales.

Date	Mintage	F	VF	XF	Unc	BU
1994	30,060,000	—	—	—	0.50	—
1995	60,000	—	—	—	5.00	—
1996	14,485,000	—	—	—	0.50	—
1997	60,000	—	—	—	5.00	—
1998	6,500,000	—	—	—	2.00	—

KM# 190 5 FRANCS - 5 FRANK (Un / Een Belga) **Composition:** Aluminum-Bronze **Reverse:** Legend in Dutch **Rev. Legend:** BELGIE **Note:** Struck at Brussels Mint. Mint mark - Angel head. Unknown mintmaster's privy mark - Scales.

Date	Mintage	F	VF	XF	Unc	BU
1994	30,060,000	—	—	—	0.50	—
1995	60,000	—	—	—	5.00	—
1996	3,133,000	—	—	—	2.00	—
1997	6,000	—	—	—	5.00	—
1998	6,500,000	—	—	—	1.00	—
1999	60,000	—	—	—	5.00	—
2000	60,000	—	—	—	5.00	—

KM# 99 10 FRANCS - 10 FRANK (Deux / Twee Belgas) **Composition:** Nickel **Subject:** Independence Cenntennial **Reverse:** Legend in French **Rev. Legend:** BELGIQUE **Note:** Exists in position A or B, values are the same.

Date	Mintage	F	VF	XF	Unc	BU
1930	2,699,000	25.00	70.00	130	200	—

KM# 100 10 FRANCS - 10 FRANK (Deux / Twee Belgas) **Composition:** Nickel **Reverse:** Legend in Dutch **Rev. Legend:** BELGIE **Note:** Exists in position A or B, values are the same.

Date	Mintage	F	VF	XF	Unc	BU
1930	3,000,000	30.00	75.00	140	250	—

KM# 155.2 10 FRANCS - 10 FRANK (Deux / Twee Belgas) **Composition:** Nickel **Note:** Medal alignment. Struck at Brussels Mint. Mint mark - Angel head. Mintmaster Vogelier's privy mark - Bird.

Date	F	VF	XF	Unc	BU
1969	—	6.00	12.00	35.00	—
1974	—	6.00	12.00	35.00	—
1977	—	6.00	12.00	35.00	—
1978	—	6.00	12.00	30.00	—

KM# 155.1 10 FRANCS - 10 FRANK (Deux / Twee Belgas) **Composition:** Nickel **Reverse:** Legend in French **Rev. Legend:** BELGIQUE **Note:** Struck at Brussels Mint. Mint mark - Angel head. Mintmaster Vogelier's privy mark - Bird.

Date	Mintage	F	VF	XF	Unc	BU
1969	22,235,000	—	—	0.40	0.70	—
1970	9,500,000	—	—	0.40	0.70	—
1971	15,000,000	—	—	0.40	0.70	—
1972	10,000,000	—	—	0.40	0.70	—
1973	10,000,000	—	—	0.40	0.70	—
1974	5,000,000	—	—	0.40	0.70	—
1975	5,000,000	—	—	0.40	0.70	—
1976	7,500,000	—	—	0.40	0.70	—
1977	7,000,000	—	—	0.40	0.70	—
1978	2,500,000	—	—	0.60	1.50	—
1979	5,000,000	—	—	0.60	1.50	—

KM# 156.1 10 FRANCS - 10 FRANK (Deux / Twee Belgas) **Composition:** Nickel **Reverse:** Legend in Dutch **Rev. Legend:** BELGIE **Note:** Struck at Brussels Mint. Mint mark - Angel head. Mintmaster Vogelier's privy mark - Bird.

Date	Mintage	F	VF	XF	Unc	BU
1969	21,500,000	—	—	0.40	0.70	—
1970	10,000,000	—	—	0.40	0.70	—
1971	15,000,000	—	—	0.40	0.70	—
1972	10,000,000	—	—	0.40	0.70	—
1973	10,000,000	—	—	0.40	0.70	—
1974	5,000,000	—	—	0.40	0.70	—
1975	5,000,000	—	—	0.40	0.70	—
1976	7,500,000	—	—	0.40	0.70	—
1977	7,000,000	—	—	0.40	0.70	—
1978	2,500,000	—	—	0.60	1.50	—
1979	10,000,000	—	—	0.60	1.50	—

KM# 156.2 10 FRANCS - 10 FRANK (Deux / Twee Belgas) **Composition:** Nickel **Note:** Medal alignment. Struck at Brussels Mint. Mint mark - Angel head. Mintmaster Vogelier's privy mark - Bird.

Date	F	VF	XF	Unc	BU
1971	—	6.00	12.00	35.00	—
1976	—	6.00	12.00	35.00	—

KM# 78 20 FRANCS (20 Frank) **Weight:** 6.4516 g. **Composition:** 0.9000 Gold .1867 oz. AGW **Obverse:** Legend in French **Obv. Legend:** DES BELGES

Date	Mintage	F	VF	XF	Unc	BU
1914 Position A	125,000	—	BV	75.00	110	—
1914 Position B	Inc. above	125	250	700	1,000	—

KM# 79 20 FRANCS (20 Frank) **Weight:** 6.4516 g. **Composition:** 0.9000 Gold .1867 oz. AGW **Obverse:** Legend in Dutch **Obv. Legend:** DER BELGEN

Date	Mintage	F	VF	XF	Unc	BU
1914 Position A	125,000	—	BV	75.00	110	—
1914 Position B	Inc. above	BV	80.00	90.00	130	—

KM# 101.1 20 FRANCS - 20 FRANK (Vier / Quatre Belgas) **Composition:** Nickel **Obverse:** Legend in French **Obv. Legend:** DES BELGES **Note:** All dates exist in position A and B, values are the same.

Date	Mintage	F	VF	XF	Unc	BU
1931	3,957,000	20.00	45.00	100	140	—
1932	5,472,000	15.00	40.00	90.00	130	—
1934	—	—	—	—	—	—

Note: Struck at a later date

KM# 102 20 FRANCS - 20 FRANK (Vier / Quatre Belgas) **Composition:** Nickel **Obverse:** Legend in Dutch **Obv. Legend:** DER BELGEN **Note:** All dates exist in position A and B, values are the same.

Date	Mintage	F	VF	XF	Unc	BU
1931	2,600,000	25.00	50.00	110	160	—
1932	6,950,000	15.00	40.00	90.00	130	—
1934	—	—	—	—	—	—

Note: Struck at a later date

KM# 101.2 20 FRANCS - 20 FRANK (Vier / Quatre Belgas) **Composition:** Nickel **Note:** Medal alignment. Edge varieties exist.

Date	F	VF	XF	Unc	BU
1932	65.00	175	400	600	—

KM# 103.1 20 FRANCS - 20 FRANK (Vier / Quatre Belgas) **Weight:** 11.0000 g. **Composition:** 0.6800 Silver .2405 oz. ASW **Obverse:** Legend in French **Obv. Legend:** DES BELGES

Date	Mintage	F	VF	XF	Unc	BU
1933 Position A	200,000	22.50	40.00	90.00	175	—
1933 Position B	Inc. above	25.00	45.00	100	200	—
1934 Position A	12,300,000	BV	2.00	4.00	8.00	—
1934 Position B	Inc. above	1.50	2.50	4.50	9.00	—

KM# 104.1 20 FRANCS - 20 FRANK (Vier / Quatre Belgas) **Weight:** 11.0000 g. **Composition:** 0.6800 Silver .2405 oz. ASW **Obverse:** Legend in Dutch **Obv. Legend:** DER BELGEN

Date	Mintage	F	VF	XF	Unc	BU
1933 Position B	Inc. above	16.00	32.50	65.00	125	—
1933 Position A	200,000	14.00	30.00	60.00	110	—
1934 Position A	12,300,000	BV	2.00	4.00	8.00	—
1934 Position B	Inc. above	1.50	2.50	4.50	9.00	—

KM# 103.2 20 FRANCS - 20 FRANK (Vier / Quatre Belgas) **Weight:** 11.0000 g. **Composition:** 0.6800 Silver .2405 oz. ASW **Note:** Medal alignment.

Date	F	VF	XF	Unc	BU
1934	35.00	80.00	190	400	—

KM# 104.2 20 FRANCS - 20 FRANK (Vier / Quatre Belgas) **Weight:** 11.0000 g. **Composition:** 0.6800 Silver .2405 oz. ASW **Note:** Medal alignment.

Date	F	VF	XF	Unc	BU
1934	30.00	70.00	170	350	—

KM# 105 20 FRANCS - 20 FRANK (Vier / Quatre Belgas) **Weight:** 11.0000 g. **Composition:** 0.6800 Silver .2405 oz. ASW **Note:** Both dates exist in position A and B, values are the same. Coins dated 1934 exist with and without umlauts above E in BELGIE.

Date	Mintage	F	VF	XF	Unc	BU
1934	1,250,000	2.00	4.00	8.00	15.00	—
1935	10,760,000	BV	2.50	5.00	7.00	—

KM# 140.2 20 FRANCS - 20 FRANK (Vier / Quatre Belgas) **Weight:** 8.0000 g. **Composition:** 0.8350 Silver .2148 oz. ASW **Note:** Medal alignment.

Date	F	VF	XF	Unc	BU
1949	15.00	35.00	75.00	125	—
1950	15.00	35.00	75.00	125	—

KM# 141.2 20 FRANCS - 20 FRANK (Vier / Quatre Belgas) **Weight:** 8.0000 g. **Composition:** 0.8350 Silver .2148 oz. ASW **Note:** Medal alignment.

Date	F	VF	XF	Unc	BU
1949	20.00	35.00	85.00	135	—
1951	15.00	40.00	95.00	150	—

KM# 140.1 20 FRANCS - 20 FRANK (Vier / Quatre Belgas) **Weight:** 8.0000 g. **Composition:** 0.8350 Silver .2148 oz. ASW **Obverse:** Legend in French **Obv. Legend:** BELGIQUE

Date	Mintage	F	VF	XF	Unc	BU
1949	4,600,000	BV	1.50	3.50	8.00	—
1950	12,957,000	BV	1.50	3.00	5.00	—
1951	—	—	—	—	—	—
1953	3,953,000	BV	2.00	4.00	12.00	—
1954	4,835,000	12.00	20.00	60.00	100	—
1955	1,730,000	150	250	650	900	—

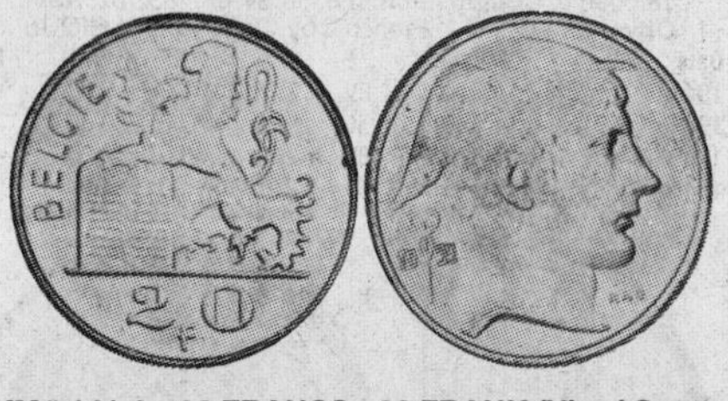

KM# 141.1 20 FRANCS - 20 FRANK (Vier / Quatre Belgas) **Weight:** 8.0000 g. **Composition:** 0.8350 Silver .2148 oz. ASW **Obverse:** Legend in Dutch **Obv. Legend:** BELGIE

Date	Mintage	F	VF	XF	Unc	BU
1949	5,545,000	BV	1.50	3.50	7.00	—
1950	—	150	400	600	1,000	—
1951	7,885,000	BV	1.50	3.00	5.00	—
1953	6,625,000	BV	1.50	3.00	8.00	—
1954	5,323,000	8.00	15.00	50.00	80.00	—
1955	3,760,000	15.00	50.00	125	200	—

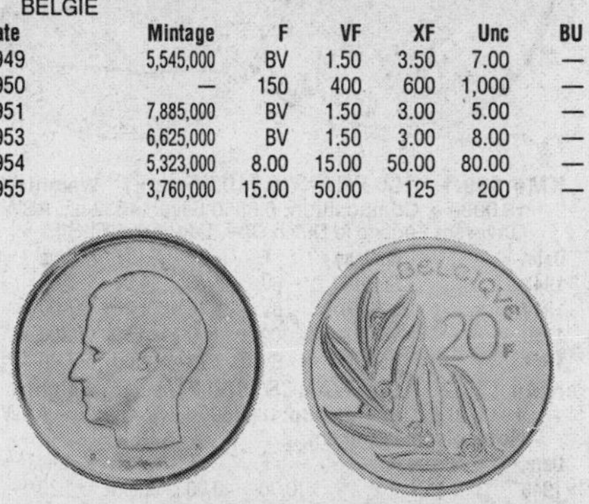

KM# 159 20 FRANCS - 20 FRANK (Vier / Quatre Belgas) **Composition:** Nickel-Bronze **Reverse:** Legend in French **Rev. Legend:** BELGIQUE

Date	Mintage	F	VF	XF	Unc	BU
1980	60,000,000	—	—	0.70	1.00	—
1981	60,000,000	—	—	0.70	1.00	—
1982	54,000,000	—	—	0.70	1.00	—
1989	60,000	—	—	—	3.50	—
1990	60,000	—	—	—	3.50	—
1991	60,000	—	—	—	3.50	—
1992	2,610,000	—	—	0.70	1.00	—
1993	7,540,000	—	—	0.70	1.00	—

KM# 160 20 FRANCS - 20 FRANK (Vier / Quatre Belgas) **Composition:** Nickel-Bronze **Reverse:** Legend in Dutch **Rev. Legend:** BELGIE

Date	Mintage	F	VF	XF	Unc	BU
1980	60,000,000	—	—	0.70	1.00	—
1981	60,000,000	—	—	0.70	1.00	—
1982	54,000,000	—	—	0.70	1.00	—
1989	60,000	—	—	—	3.50	—
1990	60,000	—	—	—	3.50	—
1991	60,000	—	—	—	3.50	—
1992	2,610,000	—	—	0.70	1.00	—
1993	7,540,000	—	—	0.70	1.00	—

KM# 191 20 FRANCS - 20 FRANK (Vier / Quatre Belgas) **Composition:** Nickel-Bronze **Obverse:** Albert II **Reverse:** Legend in French **Rev. Legend:** BELGIQUE **Note:** Struck at Brussels Mint. Mint mark - Angel head. Unknown mintmaster's privy mark - Scales.

Date	Mintage	F	VF	XF	Unc	BU
1994	12,560,000	—	—	0.70	1.00	—
1995	60,000	—	—	—	7.50	—
1996	60,000	—	—	—	7.50	—
1997	60,000	—	—	—	7.50	—
1998	3,000,000	—	—	—	3.75	—
1999	60,000	—	—	—	7.50	—
2000	60,000	—	—	—	7.50	—

KM# 192 20 FRANCS - 20 FRANK (Vier / Quatre Belgas) **Composition:** Nickel-Bronze **Reverse:** Legend in Dutch **Rev. Legend:** BELGIE **Note:** Struck at Brussels Mint. Mint mark - Angel head. Unknown mintmaster's privy mark - Scales.

Date	Mintage	F	VF	XF	Unc	BU
1994	12,560,000	—	—	0.70	1.00	—
1995	60,000	—	—	—	7.50	—
1996	11,352,000	—	—	—	7.50	—
1997	60,000	—	—	—	7.50	—
1998	300,000	—	—	—	3.75	—
1999	60,000	—	—	—	7.50	—
2000	60,000	—	—	—	7.50	—

KM# 106.1 50 FRANCS (50 Frank) **Weight:** 22.0000 g. **Composition:** 0.6800 Silver .4810 oz. ASW **Subject:** Brussels Exposition and Railway Centennial **Obv. Legend:** DE BELGIQUE **Reverse:** Legend in French **Rev. Legend:** DE FER BELGES **Note:** Exists in positions A and B, values are the same.

Date	Mintage	F	VF	XF	Unc	BU
1935	140,000	40.00	70.00	110	180	—

KM# 106.2 50 FRANCS (50 Frank) **Weight:** 22.0000 g. **Composition:** 0.6800 Silver .4810 oz. ASW **Note:** Medal alignment. Exists in positions A and B, values are the same.

Date	F	VF	XF	Unc	BU
1935	200	300	500	800	—

KM# 107.1 50 FRANCS (50 Frank) **Weight:** 22.0000 g. **Composition:** 0.6800 Silver .4810 oz. ASW **Obv. Legend:** BELGIE **Reverse:** Legend in Dutch **Rev. Legend:** DER BELGISCHE **Note:** Exists in positions A and B, values are the same.

Date	Mintage	F	VF	XF	Unc	BU
1935	140,000	50.00	100	150	225	—

KM# 107.2 50 FRANCS (50 Frank) **Weight:** 22.0000 g. **Composition:** 0.6800 Silver .4810 oz. ASW **Note:** Medal alignment. Exists in positions A and B, values are the same.

Date	F	VF	XF	Unc	BU
1935	300	600	900	1,500	—

KM# 122.2 50 FRANCS (50 Frank) **Weight:** 20.0000 g. **Composition:** 0.8350 Silver .5369 oz. ASW **Reverse:** Without cross on crown **Note:** Both dates exists in positions A and B, values are the same.

Date	F	VF	XF	Unc	BU
1939	6.00	15.00	20.00	40.00	—
1940	15.00	20.00	40.00	60.00	—

KM# 121.1 50 FRANCS (50 Frank) **Weight:** 20.0000 g. **Composition:** 0.8350 Silver .5369 oz. ASW **Reverse:** Legend in French **Rev. Legend:** BELGIQUE: BELGIE **Note:** Both dates exists in positions A and B, values are the same.

Date	Mintage	F	VF	XF	Unc	BU
1939	1,000,000	BV	8.00	12.00	18.00	—
1940	631,000	BV	10.00	18.00	27.50	—

KM# 121.2 50 FRANCS (50 Frank) **Weight:** 20.0000 g. **Composition:** 0.8350 Silver .5369 oz. ASW **Reverse:** Without cross on crown **Note:** Both dates exists in positions A and B, values are the same.

Date	F	VF	XF	Unc	BU
1939	5.00	10.00	15.00	25.00	—
1940	7.00	15.00	20.00	35.00	—

KM# 122.1 50 FRANCS (50 Frank) **Weight:** 20.0000 g. **Composition:** 0.8350 Silver .5369 oz. ASW **Reverse:** Legend in Dutch **Rev. Legend:** BELGIE: BELGIQUE **Note:** Both dates exists in positions A and B, values are the same.

Date	Mintage	F	VF	XF	Unc	BU
1939	1,000,000	BV	8.00	12.00	18.00	—
1940	631,000	BV	10.00	20.00	30.00	—

KM# 122.3 50 FRANCS (50 Frank) **Weight:** 20.0000 g. **Composition:** 0.8350 Silver .5369 oz. ASW **Reverse:** Triangle in third arms from left, cross on crown **Note:** Both dates exists in positions A and B, values are the same.

Date	F	VF	XF	Unc	BU
1940	15.00	25.00	35.00	70.00	—

KM# 122.4 50 FRANCS (50 Frank) **Weight:** 20.0000 g. **Composition:** 0.8350 Silver .5369 oz. ASW **Reverse:** Without cross on crown **Note:** Both dates exists in positions A and B, values are the same.

Date	F	VF	XF	Unc	BU
1940	30.00	60.00	100	180	—

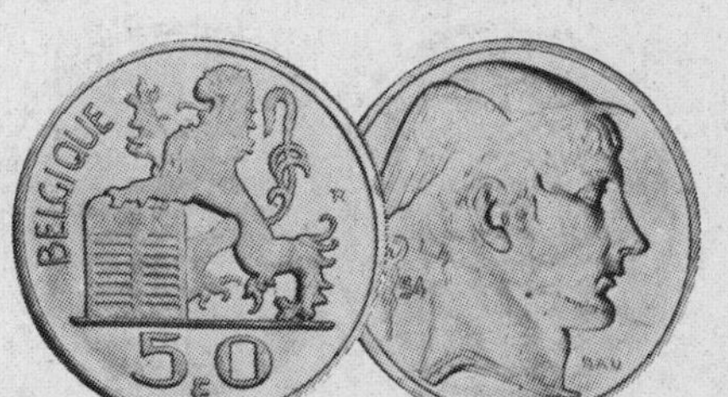

KM# 136.1 50 FRANCS (50 Frank) Weight: 12.5000 g. **Composition:** 0.8350 Silver .3356 oz. ASW **Obverse:** Legend in French **Obv. Legend:** BELGIQUE

Date	Mintage	F	VF	XF	Unc	BU
1948	2,000,000	BV	2.00	3.00	6.00	—

Note: Exists in position A and B, values are the same

Date	Mintage	F	VF	XF	Unc	BU
1949	4,354,000	BV	2.00	3.00	5.00	—
1950	—	200	400	800	1,750	—
1951	2,904,000	BV	2.00	3.00	5.00	—
1954	3,232,000	BV	7.50	15.00	30.00	—

KM# 137 50 FRANCS (50 Frank) Weight: 12.5000 g. **Composition:** 0.8350 Silver .3356 oz. ASW **Obverse:** Legend in Dutch **Obv. Legend:** BELGIE

Date	Mintage	F	VF	XF	Unc	BU
1948	3,000,000	BV	2.00	3.00	6.00	—
1950	4,110,000	BV	2.00	3.00	5.00	—
1951	1,698,000	BV	2.00	3.00	6.00	—
1954	2,978,000	BV	2.00	3.00	6.00	—

KM# 136.2 50 FRANCS (50 Frank) Weight: 12.5000 g. **Composition:** 0.8350 Silver .3356 oz. ASW **Note:** Medal alignment.

Date	F	VF	XF	Unc	BU
1949	10.00	30.00	90.00	175	—

KM# 150.1 50 FRANCS (50 Frank) Weight: 12.5000 g. **Composition:** 0.8350 Silver .3356 oz. ASW **Subject:** Brussels World Fair **Obverse:** Legend in French **Obv. Legend:** DES BELGES

Date	Mintage	F	VF	XF	Unc	BU
1958	476,000	BV	4.00	7.50	10.00	—

KM# 150.2 50 FRANCS (50 Frank) Weight: 12.5000 g. **Composition:** 0.8350 Silver .3356 oz. ASW **Note:** Medal alignment.

Date	F	VF	XF	Unc	BU
1958	18.00	45.00	100	180	—

KM# 151.1 50 FRANCS (50 Frank) Weight: 12.5000 g. **Composition:** 0.8350 Silver .3356 oz. ASW **Obverse:** Legend in Dutch **Obv. Legend:** DER BELGEN

Date	Mintage	F	VF	XF	Unc	BU
1958	382,000	BV	4.00	7.50	10.00	—

KM# 151.2 50 FRANCS (50 Frank) Weight: 12.5000 g. **Composition:** 0.8350 Silver .3356 oz. ASW **Note:** Medal alignment.

Date	F	VF	XF	Unc	BU
1958	15.00	35.00	75.00	125	—

KM# 152.1 50 FRANCS (50 Frank) Weight: 12.5000 g. **Composition:** 0.8350 Silver .3356 oz. ASW **Subject:** King Baudouin Marriage

Date	Mintage	F	VF	XF	Unc	BU
1960	500,000	BV	4.00	6.00	9.00	—

KM# 152.2 50 FRANCS (50 Frank) Weight: 12.5000 g. **Composition:** 0.8350 Silver .3356 oz. ASW **Note:** Medal alignment.

Date	F	VF	XF	Unc	BU
1960	12.50	30.00	60.00	120	—

KM# 168 50 FRANCS (50 Frank) Composition: Nickel **Reverse:** Legend in French **Rev. Legend:** BELGIQUE

Date	Mintage	F	VF	XF	Unc	BU
1987	30,000,000	—	—	2.00	4.00	—
1988	3,500,000	—	—	2.00	4.00	—
1989	15,060,000	—	—	2.00	4.00	—
1990	15,060,000	—	—	2.00	4.00	—
1991	3,500,000	—	—	2.00	4.00	—
1992	15,060,000	—	—	2.00	4.00	—
1993	15,060,000	—	—	2.00	4.00	—

KM# 169 50 FRANCS (50 Frank) Composition: Nickel **Reverse:** Legend in Dutch **Rev. Legend:** BELGIE

Date	Mintage	F	VF	XF	Unc	BU
1987	30,000,000	—	—	2.00	4.00	—
1988	3,500,000	—	—	2.00	4.00	—
1989	15,060,000	—	—	2.00	4.00	—
1990	15,060,000	—	—	2.00	4.00	—
1991	3,500,000	—	—	2.00	4.00	—
1992	15,060,000	—	—	2.00	4.00	—
1993	15,060,000	—	—	2.00	4.00	—

KM# 193 50 FRANCS (50 Frank) Composition: Nickel **Obverse:** Albert II **Reverse:** Legend in French **Rev. Legend:** BELGIQUE **Note:** Struck at Brussels Mint. Mint mark - Angel head. Unknown mintmaster's privy mark - Scales.

Date	Mintage	F	VF	XF	Unc	BU
1994	5,000,000	—	—	—	3.00	—
1995	60,000	—	—	—	10.00	—
1996	60,000	—	—	—	10.00	—
1997	60,000	—	—	—	10.00	—
1998	3,000,000	—	—	—	4.50	—
1999	60,000	—	—	—	10.00	—
2000	60,000	—	—	—	10.00	—

KM# 194 50 FRANCS (50 Frank) Composition: Nickel **Obverse:** Albert II **Reverse:** Legend in Dutch **Rev. Legend:** BELGIE **Note:** Struck at Brussels Mint. Mint mark - Angel head. Unknown mintmaster's privy mark - Scales.

Date	Mintage	F	VF	XF	Unc	BU
1994	5,000,000	—	—	—	4.50	—
1995	60,000	—	—	—	10.00	—
1996	60,000	—	—	—	10.00	—
1997	60,000	—	—	—	10.00	—
1998	3,000,000	—	—	—	4.50	—
1999	60,000	—	—	—	10.00	—
2000	60,000	—	—	—	10.00	—

KM# 213.1 50 FRANCS (50 Frank) Composition: Nickel **Subject:** European Soccer Championship **Obverse:** Head of Albert II left **Reverse:** Soccer ball, legend in French **Rev. Legend:** BELGIQUE **Edge:** Reeded

Date	Mintage	F	VF	XF	Unc	BU
2000	500,000	—	—	—	3.75	—

KM# 213.2 50 FRANCS (50 Frank) Composition: Nickel **Note:** Medal alignment.

Date	F	VF	XF	Unc	BU
2000	— Value: 15.00				

KM# 214.1 50 FRANCS (50 Frank) Composition: Nickel **Subject:** European Soccer Championship **Obverse:** Head of Albert II left **Reverse:** Soccer ball, legend in Dutch **Rev. Legend:** BELGIE **Edge:** Reeded

Date	Mintage	F	VF	XF	Unc	BU
2000	500,000	—	—	—	3.75	—

KM# 214.2 50 FRANCS (50 Frank) Composition: Nickel **Note:** Medal alignment.

Date	F	VF	XF	Unc	BU
2000	— Value: 15.00				

KM# 138.1 100 FRANCS (100 Frank) Weight: 18.0000 g. **Composition:** 0.8350 Silver .4832 oz. ASW **Obverse:** Legend in French **Obv. Legend:** BELGIQUE

Date	Mintage	F	VF	XF	Unc	BU
1948	1,000,000	BV	2.75	4.00	7.00	—
1949	106,000	12.50	25.00	40.00	60.00	—
1950	2,807,000	BV	2.75	4.00	7.00	—
1954	2,517,000	BV	2.75	4.00	7.00	—

KM# 139.1 100 FRANCS (100 Frank) Weight: 18.0000 g. **Composition:** 0.8350 Silver .4832 oz. ASW **Obverse:** Legend in Dutch **Obv. Legend:** BELGIE

Date	Mintage	F	VF	XF	Unc	BU
1948	1,000,000	BV	2.75	4.00	7.00	—
1949	2,271,000	BV	2.75	4.00	7.00	—
1950	—	300	500	850	1,200	—
1951	4,691,000	BV	2.75	4.00	7.00	—

KM# 138.2 100 FRANCS (100 Frank) Weight: 18.0000 g. **Composition:** 0.8350 Silver .4832 oz. ASW **Note:** Medal alignment.

Date	F	VF	XF	Unc	BU
1948	10.00	40.00	90.00	220	—
1950	10.00	40.00	90.00	200	—

KM# 139.2 100 FRANCS (100 Frank) Weight: 18.0000 g. **Composition:** 0.8350 Silver .4832 oz. ASW **Note:** Medal alignment.

Date	F	VF	XF	Unc	BU
1948	10.00	40.00	90.00	200	—
1949	7.50	30.00	75.00	160	—
1951	10.00	40.00	90.00	200	—

KM# 215 200 FRANCS (200 Frank) Composition: Silver **Subject:** The Universe **Obverse:** Legend in French **Obv. Legend:** BELGIQUE

Date	F	VF	XF	Unc	BU
2000	—	—	—	10.00	—
2000 (qp)	10,000	Value: 30.00			

KM# 216 200 FRANCS (200 Frank) Composition: Silver **Subject:** Nature **Obverse:** Legend in Dutch **Obv. Legend:** BELGIE

Date	F	VF	XF	Unc	BU
2000	—	—	—	10.00	—
2000 (qp)	10,000	Value: 30.00			

KM# 217 200 FRANCS (200 Frank) Composition: Silver **Subject:** The City **Obverse:** Legend in German **Obv. Legend:** BELGIEN

Date	F	VF	XF	Unc	BU
2000	—	—	—	10.00	—
2000 (qp)	—	—	—	30.00	—

KM# 157.1 250 FRANCS (250 Frank) Weight: 25.0000 g. **Composition:** 0.8350 Silver .6711 oz. ASW **Subject:** Silver Jubilee of King Baudouin **Obverse:** Legend in French **Obv. Legend:** ROI DES BELGES **Edge:** Reeded **Note:** Struck at Brussels Mint. Mint mark - Angel head. Mintmaster Vogelier's privy mark - Bird.

Date	Mintage	F	VF	XF	Unc	BU
1976 Large B, slant 5	1,000,000	—	BV	5.00	8.00	—
1976 Small B, upright 5	Inc. above	BV	8.00	10.00	15.00	—

KM# 157.2 250 FRANCS (250 Frank) Weight: 25.0000 g. **Composition:** 0.8350 Silver .6711 oz. ASW **Edge:** Stars **Note:** Struck at Brussels Mint. Mint mark - Angel head. Mintmaster Vogelier's privy mark - Bird.

Date	Mintage	F	VF	XF	Unc	BU
1976 Prooflike	100,000	—	—	—	15.00	—

KM# 158.1 250 FRANCS (250 Frank) Weight: 25.0000 g. **Composition:** 0.8350 Silver .6711 oz. ASW **Obverse:** Legend in Dutch **Obv. Legend:** KONING DER BELGEN **Edge:** Reeded **Note:** Struck at Brussels Mint. Mint mark - Angel head. Mintmaster Vogelier's privy mark - Bird.

Date	Mintage	F	VF	XF	Unc	BU
1976 Large B, slant 5	1,000,000	—	BV	5.00	8.00	—
1976 Small B, upright 5	Inc. above	BV	10.00	18.50	30.00	—

KM# 158.2 250 FRANCS (250 Frank) Weight: 25.0000 g. **Composition:** 0.8350 Silver .6711 oz. ASW **Edge:** Stars **Note:** Struck at Brussels Mint. Mint mark - Angel head. Mintmaster Vogelier's privy mark - Bird.

Date	Mintage	F	VF	XF	Unc	BU
1976 Prooflike	100,000	—	—	—	15.00	—

KM# 195 250 FRANCS (250 Frank) Weight: 18.7500 g. **Composition:** 0.9250 Silver .5571 oz. ASW **Subject:** BE-NE-LUX Treaty **Note:** Struck at Brussels Mint. Mint mark - Angel head. Unknown mintmaster's privy mark - Scales.

Date	Mintage	F	VF	XF	Unc	BU
1994	90,000	—	—	—	14.00	—
1994 Proof	1,800	Value: 45.00				

KM# 199 250 FRANCS (250 Frank) Weight: 18.7500 g. **Composition:** 0.9250 Silver .5571 oz. ASW **Subject:** Death of Queen Astrid **Note:** Struck at Brussels Mint. Mint mark - Angel head. Unknown mintmaster's privy mark - Scales.

Date	Mintage	F	VF	XF	Unc	BU
1995	177,000	—	—	—	14.00	—
1995 Proof	25,000	Value: 35.00				

KM# 202 250 FRANCS (250 Frank) Weight: 18.7500 g. **Composition:** 0.9250 Silver .5571 oz. ASW **Subject:** 20th Anniversary - King Baudouin Foundation **Obverse:** Royal couple and monogram **Reverse:** Denomination, stylized design and royal monogram

Date	Mintage	F	VF	XF	Unc	BU
ND(1996)	100,000	—	—	—	14.00	—
ND(1996) Proof	25,000	Value: 25.00				

KM# 207 250 FRANCS (250 Frank) Weight: 18.7500 g. **Composition:** 0.9250 Silver .5571 oz. ASW **Subject:** 60th Birthday - Queen Paola **Obverse:** Denomination **Reverse:** Portrait **Note:** Struck at Brussels Mint. Mint mark - Angel head. Unknown mintmaster's privy mark - Scales.

Date	Mintage	F	VF	XF	Unc	BU
1997	—	—	—	—	12.00	—
1997 Proof	25,000	Value: 25.00				

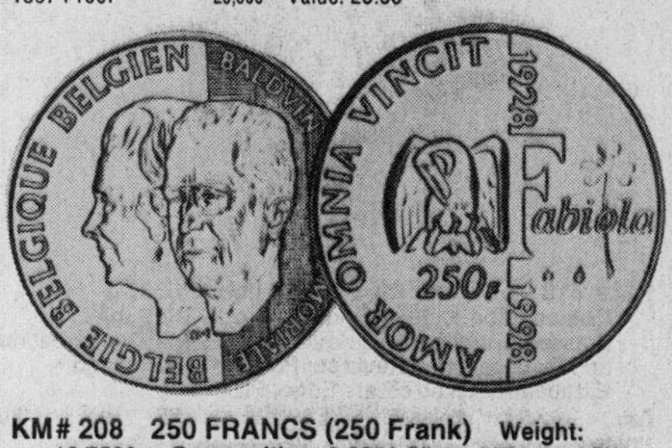

KM# 208 250 FRANCS (250 Frank) Weight: 18.7500 g. **Composition:** 0.9250 Silver .5571 oz. ASW **Subject:** King Boudewijn - Queen Fabiola **Obverse:** King and Queen's portraits **Reverse:** Pelican with nestlings

Date	F	VF	XF	Unc	BU
ND(1998)	—	—	—	12.00	—
ND(1998) Proof	25,000	Value: 25.00			

KM# 209 250 FRANCS (250 Frank) Weight: 18.7500 g. **Composition:** 0.9250 Silver .5571 oz. ASW **Subject:** 40th Wedding Anniversary - King Albert and Queen Paola **Obverse:** King and Queen's conjoining busts left **Reverse:** St. Gudule Cathedral and city hall **Edge:** Reeded

Date	F	VF	XF	Unc	BU
ND(1999)	—	—	—	12.00	—
ND(1999) Proof	25,000	Value: 25.00			

KM# 218 250 FRANCS (250 Frank) Weight: 18.7500 g. **Composition:** 0.9250 Silver .5571 oz. ASW **Subject:** Marriage of Prince Philip and Princess Mathilde **Reverse:** Two hands joined on a rose

Date	F	VF	XF	Unc	BU
1999	—	—	—	12.00	—
1999 Proof	25,000	Value: 25.00			

KM# 232 500 FRANCS Weight: 23.0000 g. **Composition:** 0.9250 Silver .6840 oz. ASW **Subject:** European Union **Obverse:** "E" emblem and map **Reverse:** Europa riding a bull; Roman numeral date **Edge:** Plain **Size:** 37 mm.

Date	F	VF	XF	Unc	BU
2001 Proof	—	Value: 35.00			

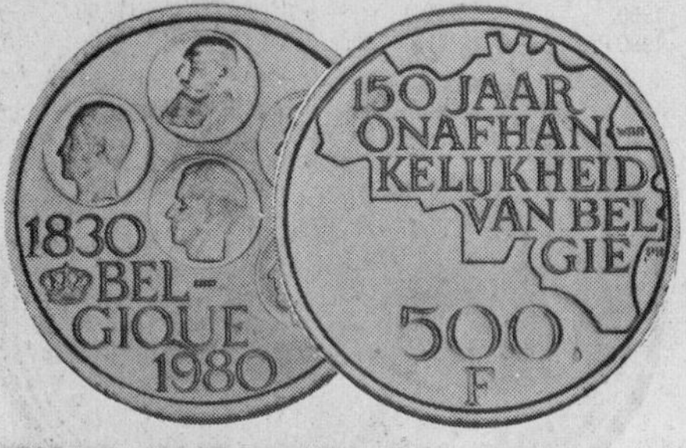

KM# 165 500 FRANCS (500 Frank) Weight: 25.0000 g. **Composition:** 0.5100 Silver .4099 oz. ASW **Obverse:** KM#161 **Reverse:** KM#162 **Note:** Mule. Struck at Brussels Mint. Mint mark - Angel head. Mintmaster Vogelier's privy mark - Bird.

Date	F	VF	XF	Unc	BU
1980	—	—	—	1,000	—

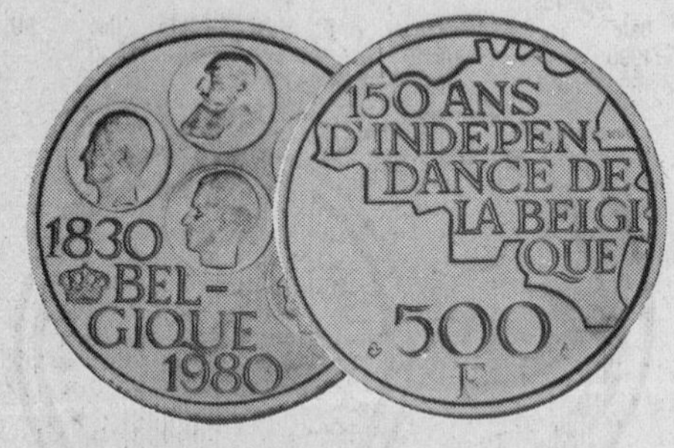

KM# 161 500 FRANCS (500 Frank) Composition: Silver Clad Copper-Nickel **Subject:** 150th Anniversary of Independence **Obverse:** French legend **Reverse:** French legend **Note:** Struck at Brussels Mint. Mint mark - Angel head. Mintmaster Vogelier's privy mark - Bird.

Date	Mintage	F	VF	XF	Unc	BU
1980	1,000,000	—	—	—	12.00	—

KM# 161a 500 FRANCS (500 Frank) Weight: 25.0000 g. **Composition:** 0.5100 Silver .4099 oz. ASW **Obverse:** French legend **Reverse:** French legend **Note:** Struck at Brussels Mint. Mint mark - Angel head. Mintmaster Vogelier's privy mark - Bird.

Date	Mintage	F	VF	XF	Unc	BU
1980 Proof	53,000	Value: 27.00				

KM# 162 500 FRANCS (500 Frank) Composition: Silver Clad Copper-Nickel **Obverse:** Dutch legend **Reverse:** Dutch legend **Note:** Struck at Brussels Mint. Mint mark - Angel head. Mintmaster Vogelier's privy mark - Bird.

Date	Mintage	F	VF	XF	Unc	BU
1980	1,000,000	—	—	—	12.00	—

KM# 162a 500 FRANCS (500 Frank) Weight: 25.0000 g. **Composition:** 0.5100 Silver .4099 oz. ASW

Reverse: Dutch legend **Note:** Struck at Brussels Mint. Mint mark - Angel Head. Mintmaster Vogelier's privy mark - Bird.

Date	Mintage	F	VF	XF	Unc	BU
1980 Proof	52,000	Value: 27.00				

KM# 178 500 FRANCS (500 Frank) **Weight:** 22.8500 g. **Composition:** 0.8330 Silver .6120 oz. ASW **Subject:** 60th Birthday of King Baudouin **Reverse:** Dutch legends

Date	Mintage	F	VF	XF	Unc	BU
1990	475,000	—	—	—	17.00	—
1990 Proof	10,000	Value: 35.00				

KM# 179 500 FRANCS (500 Frank) **Weight:** 22.8500 g. **Composition:** 0.8330 Silver .6120 oz. ASW **Subject:** 60th Birthday of King Baudouin **Reverse:** French legends

Date	Mintage	F	VF	XF	Unc	BU
1990	475,000	—	—	—	17.00	—
1990 Proof	10,000	Value: 35.00				

KM# 180 500 FRANCS (500 Frank) **Weight:** 22.8500 g. **Composition:** 0.8330 Silver .6120 oz. ASW **Subject:** 60th Birthday of King Baudouin **Reverse:** German legends

Date	Mintage	F	VF	XF	Unc	BU
1990	50,000	—	—	—	17.00	—
1990 Proof	10,000	Value: 35.00				

KM# 196 500 FRANCS (500 Frank) **Weight:** 22.8500 g. **Composition:** 0.8330 Silver .6120 oz. ASW **Subject:** 40th Year of Reign **Obverse:** Stylized design around **Reverse:** Crown above, denomination, year below, dutch legend

Date	Mintage	F	VF	XF	Unc	BU
1991	—	—	—	—	15.00	—
1991 Proof	10,000	Value: 25.00				

KM# 197 500 FRANCS (500 Frank) **Weight:** 22.8500 g. **Composition:** 0.8330 Silver .6120 oz. ASW **Subject:** 40th Year of Reign **Obverse:** Stylized design around **Reverse:** Crown above, denomination, year below, French legend

Date	Mintage	F	VF	XF	Unc	BU
1991	—	—	—	—	15.00	—
1991 Proof	10,000	Value: 25.00				

KM# 198 500 FRANCS (500 Frank) **Weight:** 22.8500 g. **Composition:** 0.8330 Silver .6120 oz. ASW **Subject:** 40th Year of Reign **Obverse:** Stylized design around **Reverse:** Crown above, denomination, year below, German legend

Date	Mintage	F	VF	XF	Unc	BU
1991	—	—	—	—	15.00	—
1991 Proof	10,000	Value: 25.00				

KM# 186 500 FRANCS (500 Frank) **Weight:** 22.8500 g. **Composition:** 0.8330 Silver .6120 oz. ASW **Subject:** Europalaia - Mexico Exposition **Note:** Struck at Brussels Mint. Mint mark - Angel head. Unknown mintmaster's privy mark - Scales.

Date	Mintage	F	VF	XF	Unc	BU
1993	52,000	—	—	—	15.00	—
1993 Proof	—	Value: 25.00				

KM# 212 500 FRANCS (500 Frank) **Weight:** 22.8500 g. **Composition:** 0.9250 Silver .6975 oz. ASW **Subject:** Brussels - European Culture Capital **Obverse:** Denomination and European map **Reverse:** Portraits of Albert and Elizabeth in ruffled collars **Edge:** Plain

Date	Mintage	F	VF	XF	Unc	BU
ND(1999)	—	—	—	—	20.00	—
ND(1999) (qp) Proof	30,000	Value: 35.00				

KM# 219 500 FRANCS (500 Frank) **Weight:** 22.8500 g. **Composition:** 0.9250 Silver .6975 oz. ASW **Subject:** Europe: Charles V **Obverse:** Map and denomination **Reverse:** Charles V of Spain and building **Edge:** Plain **Size:** 37 mm.

Date	Mintage	F	VF	XF	Unc	BU
ND(2000)	—	—	—	—	20.00	—
2000 Proof	40,000	Value: 35.00				

KM# 222 500 FRANCS (500 Frank) **Weight:** 22.8500 g. **Composition:** 0.9250 Silver .6795 oz. ASW **Subject:** Europe: Europa and the Bull **Obverse:** Map and denomination **Reverse:** Europa sitting on a bull **Edge:** Plain **Size:** 37 mm.

Date	Mintage	F	VF	XF	Unc	BU
2001 Proof	40,000	Value: 47.50				

KM# 210 5000 FRANCS **Weight:** 15.5500 g. **Composition:** 0.9990 Gold .4994 oz. AGW **Subject:** Brussels - European Culture Capital **Obverse:** Denomination and European map **Reverse:** Portraits of Albert and Elizabeth in ruffled collars **Edge:** Plain

Date	Mintage	F	VF	XF	Unc	BU
ND(1999) (qp) Proof	2,000	Value: 325				

KM# 220 5000 FRANCS **Weight:** 15.5500 g. **Composition:** 0.9990 Gold .4994 oz. AGW **Subject:** Europe: Charles V **Obverse:** Map and denomination **Reverse:** Charles V of Spain with building **Edge:** Plain **Size:** 29 mm.

Date	Mintage	F	VF	XF	Unc	BU
ND(2000) (qp) Proof	2,000	Value: 325				

KM# 223 5000 FRANCS **Weight:** 15.5500 g. **Composition:** 0.9990 Gold .4994 oz. AGW **Subject:** Europe: Europa and the Bull **Obverse:** Map and denomination **Reverse:** Europa sitting on a bull **Edge:** Plain **Size:** 29 mm.

Date	Mintage	F	VF	XF	Unc	BU
2001 Proof	2,000	Value: 325				

TRADE COINAGE

European Currency Units

KM# 166 5 ECU **Weight:** 22.8500 g. **Composition:** 0.8330 Silver .6120 oz. ASW **Subject:** 30th Anniversary - Treaties of Rome **Reverse:** Bust of Charles V right

Date	Mintage	F	VF	XF	Unc	BU
1987	985,000	—	—	—	10.00	—
1987 (qp)	15,000	Value: 50.00				
1988 (qp)	15,000	Value: 50.00				

KM# 183 5 ECU **Weight:** 22.8500 g. **Composition:** 0.8330 Silver .6120 oz. ASW **Reverse:** Charlemagne

Date	Mintage	F	VF	XF	Unc	BU
1991 (qp)	10,000	Value: 45.00				

KM# 185 5 ECU **Weight:** 22.8500 g. **Composition:** 0.9250 Silver .6796 oz. ASW **Subject:** Belgian Presidency of the E.C. **Obverse:** King Baudouin

Date	Mintage	F	VF	XF	Unc	BU
1993 (qp)	25,000	Value: 35.00				

KM# 200 5 ECU **Weight:** 22.8500 g. **Composition:** 0.9250 Silver .6796 oz. ASW **Subject:** 50th Anniversary - United Nations

Date	Mintage	F	VF	XF	Unc	BU
1995 (qp)	125,000	Value: 27.00				

KM# 203 5 ECU **Weight:** 22.8500 g. **Composition:** 0.9250 Silver .6796 oz. ASW **Subject:** 50th Anniversary - UNICEF **Obverse:** Royal couple **Reverse:** UNICEF logo

Date	Mintage	F	VF	XF	Unc	BU
1996 (qp)	Est. 40,000	Value: 28.00				

KM# 205 5 ECU Weight: 22.8500 g. **Composition:** 0.9250 Silver .6796 oz. ASW **Subject:** 40th Anniversary - Treaty of Rome **Obverse:** Portraits of Albert II and Baudouin **Reverse:** European Union map

Date	Mintage	F	VF	XF	Unc	BU
1997 (qp)	Est. 30,000	Value: 30.00				

KM# 221 5 ECU Weight: 22.8500 g. **Composition:** 0.9250 Silver .6796 oz. ASW **Subject:** 50th Anniversary - Human Rights Declaration

Date	Mintage	F	VF	XF	Unc	BU
1998 (qp)	30,000	Value: 27.00				

KM# 172 10 ECU Weight: 3.1100 g. **Composition:** 0.9990 Gold .1000 oz. AGW **Reverse:** Charles V bust right

Date	Mintage	F	VF	XF	Unc	BU
1989 (qp)	2,000	Value: 150				
1990 (qp)	5,000	Value: 100				

KM# 176 10 ECU Ring Composition: 0.8330 Silver **Center Weight:** 5.3000 g. **Center Composition:** 0.9000 Gold .1000 oz. AGW **Subject:** 60th Birthday of King Baudouin

Date	Mintage	F	VF	XF	Unc	BU
1990 (qp)	42,000	Value: 50.00				

KM# 181 10 ECU Ring Composition: 0.8330 Silver **Center Weight:** 5.3000 g. **Center Composition:** 0.9000 Gold .1000 oz. AGW **Subject:** 40th Year of Reign of King Baudouin

Date	Mintage	F	VF	XF	Unc	BU
1991 (qp)	16,000	Value: 80.00				

KM# 177 20 ECU Ring Composition: 0.8330 Silver **Center Weight:** 10.5000 g. **Center Composition:** 0.9000 Gold .2000 oz. AGW **Subject:** 60th Birthday of King Baudouin

Date	Mintage	F	VF	XF	Unc	BU
1990 (qp)	35,000	Value: 100				

KM# 182 20 ECU Ring Composition: 0.8330 Silver **Center Weight:** 10.5000 g. **Center Composition:** 0.9000 Gold .2000 oz. AGW **Subject:** 40th Year of Reign of King Baudouin

Date	Mintage	F	VF	XF	Unc	BU
1991 (qp)	13,000	Value: 160				

KM# 173 25 ECU Weight: 7.7750 g. **Composition:** 0.9990 Gold .2500 oz. AGW **Reverse:** Diocletian bust right

Date	Mintage	F	VF	XF	Unc	BU
1989	30,000	—	—	BV	90.00	—
1989 (qp)	2,000	Value: 200				
1990 (qp)	5,000	Value: 95.00				

KM# 167 50 ECU Weight: 17.2800 g. **Composition:** 0.9000 Gold .5000 oz. AGW **Subject:** 30th Anniversary - Treaties of Rome **Obverse:** Charles V bust right

Date	Mintage	F	VF	XF	Unc	BU
1987	1,502,000	—	—	BV	140	—
1987 (qp)	15,000	Value: 250				
1988 (qp)	15,000	Value: 250				

KM# 174 50 ECU Weight: 15.5550 g. **Composition:** 0.9990 Gold .5000 oz. AGW **Reverse:** Charlemagne seated on dais

Date	Mintage	F	VF	XF	Unc	BU
1989	60,000	—	—	BV	170	—
1989 (qp)	2,000	Value: 400				
1990 (qp)	5,000	Value: 200				

KM# 184 50 ECU Weight: 15.5550 g. **Composition:** 0.9990 Gold .5000 oz. AGW **Reverse:** Charlemagne bust right

Date	Mintage	F	VF	XF	Unc	BU
1991	—	—	—	—	—	—
1991 (qp)	4,000	Value: 300				

KM# 213 50 ECU Weight: 15.5550 g. **Composition:** 0.9990 Gold .5000 oz. AGW **Subject:** Belgian Presidency of the E.C.

Date	Mintage	F	VF	XF	Unc	BU
1993 (qp)	10,000	Value: 250				

KM# 201 50 ECU Weight: 15.5550 g. **Composition:** 0.9990 Gold .5000 oz. AGW **Subject:** 50th Anniversary - United Nations

Date	Mintage	F	VF	XF	Unc	BU
1995 (qp)	2,500	Value: 250				

KM# 204 50 ECU Weight: 15.5550 g. **Composition:** 0.9990 Gold .5000 oz. AGW **Subject:** 50th Anniversary - UNICEF **Obverse:** Conjoined busts of Royal couple left **Reverse:** UNICEF logo

Date	Mintage	F	VF	XF	Unc	BU
1996 (qp)	2,500	Value: 270				

KM# 206 50 ECU Weight: 15.5550 g. **Composition:** 0.9990 Gold .5000 oz. AGW **Subject:** 40th Anniversary - Treaty of Rome **Obverse:** Conjoined heads of Albert II and Baudouin **Reverse:** European Union map

Date	Mintage	F	VF	XF	Unc	BU
1997 (qp)	2,500	Value: 270				

KM# 211 50 ECU Weight: 15.5550 g. **Composition:** 0.9990 Gold .5000 oz. AGW **Subject:** 50th Anniversary - Human Rights Declaration

Date	Mintage	F	VF	XF	Unc	BU
1998 (qp)	2,500	Value: 270				

KM# 175 100 ECU Weight: 31.1030 g. **Composition:** 0.9990 Gold 1.0000 oz. AGW **Reverse:** Maria Theresa

Date	Mintage	F	VF	XF	Unc	BU
1989	50,000	—	—	BV	325	—
1989 (qp)	2,000	Value: 750				
1990 (qp)	5,000	Value: 400				

EURO COINAGE

European Economic Community Issues

KM# 224 EURO CENT Weight: 2.2700 g. **Composition:** Copper Plated Steel **Subject:** Euro Coinage **Obverse:** King's portrait **Reverse:** Denomination and globe **Edge:** Plain **Size:** 16.2 mm.

Date	F	VF	XF	Unc	BU
1999	—	—	—	0.35	—

KM# 225 2 EURO CENTS Weight: 3.0300 g. **Composition:** Copper Plated Steel **Subject:** Euro Coinage **Obverse:** King's portrait **Reverse:** Denomination and globe **Edge:** Grooved **Size:** 18.7 mm.

Date	F	VF	XF	Unc	BU
2000	—	—	—	0.50	—

KM# 226 5 EURO CENTS Weight: 3.8600 g. **Composition:** Copper Plated Steel **Subject:** Euro Coinage **Obverse:** King's portrait **Reverse:** Denomination and globe **Edge:** Plain **Size:** 21.2 mm.

Date	F	VF	XF	Unc	BU
1999	—	—	—	0.75	—

KM# 227 10 EURO CENTS Weight: 4.0700 g. **Composition:** Brass **Subject:** Euro Coinage **Obverse:** King's portrait **Reverse:** Denomination and map **Edge:** Reeded **Size:** 19.7 mm.

Date	F	VF	XF	Unc	BU
1999	—	—	—	0.75	—

KM# 228 20 EURO CENTS **Weight:** 5.7300 g. **Composition:** Brass **Subject:** Euro Coinage **Obverse:** King's portrait **Reverse:** Denomination and map **Edge:** Notched **Size:** 22.1 mm.

Date	F	VF	XF	Unc	BU
2000	—	—	—	1.00	—

KM# 229 50 EURO CENTS **Weight:** 7.8100 g. **Composition:** Brass **Subject:** Euro Coinage **Obverse:** King's portrait **Reverse:** Denomination and map **Edge:** Reeded **Size:** 24.2 mm.

Date	F	VF	XF	Unc	BU
1999	—	—	—	1.25	—

KM# 230 EURO **Ring Composition:** Brass**Center Weight:** 7.5000 g. **Center Composition:** Copper Nickel **Subject:** Euro Coinage **Obverse:** King's portrait **Reverse:** Denominaton and map **Edge:** Reeded and plain sections **Size:** 23.2 mm.

Date	F	VF	XF	Unc	BU
1999	—	—	—	2.50	—

KM# 231 2 EUROS **Ring Composition:** Copper Nickel**Center Weight:** 8.5200 g. **Center Composition:** Brass **Subject:** Euro Coinage **Obverse:** King's portrait **Reverse:** Denomination and map **Edge:** Reeded with 2's and stars **Size:** 25.7 mm.

Date	F	VF	XF	Unc	BU
2000	—	—	—	3.75	—

PATTERNS

Including off metal strikes

KM#	Date	Mintage	Identification	Mkt Val
Pn93	1901	—	5 Centimes. Brass Plated Nickel.	—
Pn94	1901	—	5 Centimes. Copper-Iron Alloy. KM#45	—
Pn95	1901	—	5 Centimes. Copper. Designer's initials as A.M.; KM#46	—
Pn96	1901	—	5 Centimes. Copper. Thin flan, KM#46	—
Pn97	1901	—	10 Centimes. Nickel. KM#48	—
Pn98	1901	—	10 Centimes. Copper-Nickel.	—
Pn100	1901	—	50 Centimes. Silver.	—
Pn101	1901	—	Franc. Silver.	—
Pn102	1901	—	Franc. Silver. Head left. Lion with constitution.	—
Pn103	1901	—	2 Francs. Silver.	—
Pn104	1901	—	2 Francs. Silver. Head left. Lion with constitution. Reeded edge.	—
Pn99	1901	—	50 Centimes. Copper. KM#50	250
Pn105	1902	—	5 Centimes. Nickel.	100
Pn107	19xx	—	Franc. Nickel-Brass.	400
Pn108	1902	—	Franc. Silver. Reeded edge. Small portrait, KM#56.1	350
Pn109	1902	—	Franc. Silver. Plain edge. Small portrait, KM#56.1	350
Pn106	1902	—	5 Centimes. Copper-Nickel. Without center hole; KM#47.	—
Pn112	1903	—	Franc. Silver.	—
Pn113	1903	—	Franc. Silver.	—
Pn114	1903	—	Franc. Silver.	—
Pn115	1903	—	Franc. Silver.	—
Pn116	1903	—	Franc. Silver.	—
Pn117	1903	—	Franc. Silver.	—
Pn118	1903	—	Franc. Silver.	—
Pn119	1903	—	Franc. Silver.	—
Pn110	1903	—	Franc. Silver. Reeded edge. Small portrait, KM#56.1	350
Pn111	1903	—	Franc. Silver. Plain edge. Small portrait, KM#56.1	350
Pn136	1904	—	50 Centimes. Silver. Plain edge. KM#60.1	—
Pn137	1904	—	50 Centimes. Silver. Reeded edge. KM#60.1	—
Pn138	1904	—	50 Centimes. Silver. Smaller designs, KM#60.1	—
Pn139	1904	—	Franc. Silver. Reeded edge. Thin flan, KM#56.1.	—
Pn140	1904	—	Franc. Silver. Plain edge. Thick flan, KM#56.1.	—
Pn141	1904	—	2 Francs. Silver. Plain edge. KM#58.1.	—
Pn142	1904	—	2 Francs. Silver. Reeded edge. Thin flan, KM#58.1.	—
Pn143	1904	—	2 Francs. Silver. Plain edge. Thick flan, KM#58.1.	—
Pn144	1904	—	2 Francs. Silver. Plain edge. KM#59.1.	—
Pn145	1904	—	2 Francs. Silver. Reeded edge. Thin flan, KM#59.1.	—
Pn146	1904	—	2 Francs. Silver. Plain edge. Thick flan, KM#59.1.	—
Pn147	1906	—	5 Centimes. Nickel-Brass. Restrike, KM#93.	—
Pn148	1907	—	Centime. Copper. Reeded edge. Thick flan, KM#34.1.	—
Pn149	1907	—	25 Centimes. Copper-Nickel.	—
Pn150	1909	—	Franc. Silver. Reeded edge. KM#73.1	—
Pn151	1910	—	5 Centimes. Gold. Not holed, KM#67	—
Pn152	1910	—	5 Centimes. Silver. Not holed, KM#67	—
Pn153	1910	—	5 Centimes. Bronze. Not holed, KM#67	—
Pn154	1910	—	5 Centimes. Aluminum. Not holed, KM#67	—
Pn155	1910	—	Franc. Silver. Reeded edge. KM#72.	—
Pn156	1910	—	Franc. Silver. Reeded edge. Thick planchet, KM#72.	—
Pn157	1910	—	Franc. Silver. Reeded edge. Thin planchet, KM#72.	—
Pn158	1910	—	Franc. Silver. Designer's name as Devreese, KM#72.	—
Pn159	1910	—	Franc. Silver. Plain edge. KM#73.1	—
Pn160	1910	—	2 Francs. Silver. Plain edge. KM#74.	—
Pn161	1911	—	Centime. Copper. Restrike.	—
Pn162	1911	—	10 Centimes. Copper. Not holed.	—
Pn163	1911	—	10 Centimes. Brass. Holed.	—
Pn164	1911	—	10 Centimes. Copper-Nickel. Not holed.	—
Pn165	1911	—	10 Centimes. Gold. KM#85.1.	—
Pn166	1911	—	10 Centimes. Silver. KM#85.1.	—
Pn167	1911	—	10 Centimes. Bronze. KM#85.1.	—
Pn168	1911	—	10 Centimes. Copper. KM#85.1.	—
Pn169	1911	—	10 Centimes. Aluminum. KM#85.1.	—
Pn170	1911	—	10 Centimes. Gold. KM#86	—
Pn171	1911	—	10 Centimes. Silver. KM#86.	—
Pn172	1911	—	10 Centimes. Bronze. KM#86.	—
Pn173	1911	—	10 Centimes. Copper. KM#86.	—
Pn174	1911	—	10 Centimes. Aluminum. KM#86.	—
Pn175	1911	—	Franc. Reeded edge. Designer's name as Devreese, KM#73.	—
Pn176	1911	—	Franc. Plain edge. Designer's name as Devreese, KM#73.	—
Pn181	1911	—	20 Francs. Brass Plated Copper.	—
Pn182	1911	—	20 Francs. Nickel.	—
Pn183	1911	—	20 Francs. Gold. Dutch legend.	—
Pn184	1911	—	20 Francs. Gold. French legend.	—
Pn185	1911	—	20 Francs. Pewter.	—
Pn186	1911	—	100 Francs. Aluminum-Nickel. Dutch legend.	—
Pn187	1911	—	100 Francs. Aluminum-Nickel. French legend.	—
Pn188	1911	—	100 Francs. Silver. Reeded edge.	—
Pn177	1911	—	2 Francs. Copper. KM#74.	350
Pn178	1911	—	2 Francs. Gold.	1,500
Pn179	1911	—	10 Francs. Gold. Dutch legend.	2,000
Pn180	1911	—	10 Francs. Gold. French legend.	2,000
Pn190	1912	—	10 Francs. Gold. Dutch legend.	2,000
Pn191	1912	—	10 Francs. Gold. French legend.	2,000
Pn193	1912	3	100 Francs. Gold. Dutch legend.	16,000
Pn194	1912	6	100 Francs. Gold. French legend.	12,500
Pn189	1912/1	—	Centime. Copper. Restrike, ESSAI.	—
Pn192	1912	—	10 Francs. Gold. Reeded edge.	—
Pn195	1914	—	2 Francs. Silver. Unadopted portrait. ESSAI/MONETAIRE/1914.	—
Pn196	ND(1915)	—	Centime. Zinc.	—
Pn197	1915	—	5 Centimes. Copper-Iron Bi-Metal. Reeded edge. KM#66.	—
Pn198	1915	—	10 Centimes. Copper-Iron Bi-Metal. KM#681.	—
Pn199	1915	—	25 Centimes. Pot Metal.	—
Pn200	1916	—	10 Centimes. Copper-Iron Bi-Metal. KM#81.	—
Pn201	1917	—	10 Centimes. Silver. Plain edge. KM#81.	—
Pn202	1918	—	25 Centimes. Silver. Plain edge. KM#82.	—
Pn203	ND(1918)	—	25 Centimes. Copper-Iron Bi-Metal. 2 branches around legend. ESSAI MONETAIRE. Legend around 25 CES.	—
Pn204	ND(1918)	—	25 Centimes. Zinc. Legend around 25 CENT.. Lion, ESSAI.	—
Pn205	ND(1918)	—	25 Centimes. Silver. 16 sided.	—
Pn206	1918	—	50 Centimes. Gold. KM#83.	—
Pn207	1918	—	50 Centimes. Silver. KM#83.	—
Pn208	1918	—	50 Centimes. Tan Bronze. KM#83.	—
Pn209	1918	—	50 Centimes. Red Bronze. KM#83.	—
Pn210	1918	—	50 Centimes. Aluminum. KM#83.	—
Pn211	1918	—	50 Centimes. Silver. Not holed.	—
Pn212	1918	—	50 Centimes. Nickel. Not holed.	—
Pn213	1918	—	50 Centimes. Copper-Nickel. Not holed.	—
Pn214	1920	—	5 Centimes. Nickel. Reeded edge. Not holed, KM#66.	—
PnA215	1920	—	20 Francs. Silver. Victory and Peace.	400
Pn216	1921	—	5 Centimes. Nickel. KM#69	—
Pn217	1922	—	5 Centimes. Nickel-Brass. Restrike, KM#94	—
Pn218	1922	—	50 Centimes. Bronze.	—
Pn219	1922	—	50 Centimes. Silver. Plain edge. KM#87	—
Pn220	1922	—	50 Centimes. Bronze. Plain edge. KM#87	—
Pn221	1922	—	50 Centimes. Aluminum. Plain edge. KM#87	—
Pn222	1922	—	50 Centimes. Nickel. Plain edge. KM#87	—
Pn223	1922	—	50 Centimes. Copper. Plain edge. KM#87	—
Pn224	1922	—	50 Centimes. Copper-Tin Alloy. Plain edge. KM#87	—
Pn225	1922	—	50 Centimes. Silver. Reeded edge. KM#87	—
Pn226	1922	—	50 Centimes. Bronze. Reeded edge. KM#87	—
Pn227	1922	—	50 Centimes. Aluminum. Reeded edge. KM#87	—
Pn228	1922	—	50 Centimes. Nickel. Reeded edge. KM#87	—
Pn229	1922	—	50 Centimes. Copper. Reeded edge. KM#87	—
Pn230	1922	—	50 Centimes. Copper-Tin Alloy. Reeded edge. KM#87	—
Pn231	1922	—	50 Centimes. Silver. Plain edge. KM#88	—
Pn232	1922	—	50 Centimes. Bronze. Plain edge. KM#88	—
Pn233	1922	—	50 Centimes. Aluminum. Plain edge. KM#88	—
Pn234	1922	—	50 Centimes. Copper. Plain edge. KM#88	—
Pn235	1922	—	50 Centimes. Copper-Tin Alloy. Plain edge. KM#88	—
Pn236	1922	—	50 Centimes. Silver. Reeded edge. KM#88	—
Pn237	1922	—	50 Centimes. Bronze. Reeded edge. KM#88	—
Pn238	1922	—	50 Centimes. Aluminum. Reeded edge. KM#88	—
Pn239	1922	—	50 Centimes. Copper. Reeded edge. KM#88	—
Pn240	1922	—	50 Centimes. Copper-Tin Alloy. Reeded edge. KM#88	—
Pn241	1922	—	Franc. Silver. Plain edge. KM#89	—
Pn242	1922	—	Franc. Bronze. Plain edge. KM#89	—
Pn243	1922	—	Franc. Aluminum. Plain edge. KM#89	—
Pn244	1922	—	Franc. Copper. Plain edge. KM#89	—
Pn245	1922	—	Franc. Copper-Tin Alloy. Plain edge. KM#89	—
Pn246	1922	—	Franc. Silver. Reeded edge. KM#89	—
Pn247	1922	—	Franc. Bronze. Reeded edge. KM#89	—
Pn248	1922	—	Franc. Aluminum. Reeded edge. KM#89	—
Pn249	1922	—	Franc. Copper. Reeded edge. KM#89	—
Pn250	1922	—	Franc. Copper-Tin Alloy. Reeded edge. KM#89	—
Pn251	1922	—	Franc. Silver. Plain edge. KM#90	—
Pn252	1922	—	Franc. Bronze. Plain edge. KM#90	—
Pn253	1922	—	Franc. Aluminum. Plain edge. KM#90	—
Pn254	1922	—	Franc. Nickel. Plain edge. Irregular flan, KM#90.	—
Pn255	1922	—	Franc. Copper. Plain edge. KM#90.	—
Pn256	1922	—	Franc. Copper-Tin Alloy. Plain edge. KM#90.	—
Pn257	1922	—	Franc. Silver. Reeded edge. KM#90.	—
Pn258	1922	—	Franc. Bronze. Reeded edge. KM#90.	—
Pn259	1922	—	Franc. Aluminum. Reeded edge. KM#90.	—
Pn260	1922	—	Franc. Copper. Reeded edge. KM#90.	—
Pn261	1922	—	Franc. Copper-Tin Alloy. Reeded edge. KM#90.	—
Pn262	1922	—	Franc. Nickel. KM#89. KM#90.	—

KM#	Date	Mintage	Identification	Mkt Val
Pn263	1923	—	2 Francs. Silver. ESSAI, KM#91.1.	—
Pn264	1923	—	2 Francs. Bronze. ESSAI, KM#91.1.	—
Pn265	1923	—	2 Francs. Aluminum. ESSAI, KM#91.1.	—
Pn266	1923	—	2 Francs. Copper-Tin Alloy. ESSAI, KM#91.1.	—
Pn267	1926	—	5 Francs. Red Bronze. ESSAI	—
Pn268	1926	—	5 Francs. Silver. Head left. Wreath with 5 FR within.	—
Pn269	1926	—	5 Francs. Bronze. Head left. Wreath with 5 FR within.	—
Pn270	1926	—	5 Francs. Nickel. Head left. Wreath with 5 FR within.	—
Pn271	1926	—	5 Francs. Copper-Tin Alloy. Head left. Wreath with 5 FR within.	—
Pn272	1926	—	5 Francs. Silver. Crown above 5 Francs.	—
Pn273	1926	—	5 Francs. Bronze. Crown above 5 Francs.	—
Pn274	1926	—	5 Francs. Nickel. Crown above 5 Francs.	—
Pn275	1926	—	5 Francs. Copper-Tin Alloy. Crown above 5 Francs.	—
Pn276	1926	—	5 Francs. Silver. Crown above oak wreath, 5 Francs within.	—
Pn277	1926	—	5 Francs. Bronze. Crown above oak wreath, 5 Francs within.	—
Pn278	1926	—	5 Francs. Copper-Tin Alloy. Crown above oak wreath, 5 Francs within.	—
Pn279	1926	—	5 Francs. Gold. Wreath, UN BELGA CINQ FRANCS.	—
Pn280	1926	—	5 Francs. Silver. Wreath, UN BELGA CINQ FRANCS.	—
Pn281	1926	—	5 Francs. Bronze. Wreath, UN BELGA CINQ FRANCS.	—
Pn282	1926	—	5 Francs. Nickel. Wreath, UN BELGA CINQ FRANCS.	—
Pn283	1926	—	5 Francs. Copper-Tin Alloy. Wreath, UN BELGA CINQ FRANCS.	—
Pn284	1926	—	5 Francs. Gold. Lion in shield, SF flanking.	—
Pn285	1926	—	5 Francs. Silver. Lion in shield, SF flanking.	—
Pn286	1926	—	5 Francs. Bronze. Lion in shield, SF flanking.	—
Pn287	1926	—	5 Francs. Nickel. Lion in shield, SF flanking.	—
Pn288	1926	—	5 Francs. Copper-Tin Alloy. Lion in shield, SF flanking.	—
Pn289	1927	—	5 Francs. Silver. Head by Bonnetain. 2 laurel branches, UN BELGA/OU/5 FRANCS/ESSAI.	—
Pn290	1927	—	5 Francs. Copper. Head by Bonnetain. 2 laurel branches, UN BELGA/OU/5 FRANCS/ESSAI.	—
Pn291	1927	—	5 Francs. Copper-Tin Alloy. Head by Bonnetain. 2 laurel branches, UN BELGA/OU/5 FRANCS/ESSAI.	—
Pn292	1927	—	5 Francs. Nickel.	—
Pn293	1929	—	5 Centimes. Not holed, KM#67.	—
Pn294	1929	—	10 Centimes. Nickel. Not holed, ESSAI, KM#85.1.	—
Pn295	1929	—	10 Centimes. Gold. KM#85.1.	—
Pn296	1929	—	10 Centimes. Silver. KM#85.1.	—
Pn297	1929	—	10 Centimes. Bronze. KM#85.1.	—
Pn298	1929	—	10 Centimes. Copper. KM#85.1.	—
Pn299	1929	—	10 Centimes. Aluminum. KM#85.1.	—
Pn300	1929	—	25 Centimes. Gold. ESSAI, KM#68.1.	—
Pn301	1929	—	25 Centimes. Silver. ESSAI, KM#68.1.	—
Pn302	1929	—	25 Centimes. Bronze. ESSAI, KM#68.1.	—
Pn303	1929	—	25 Centimes. Copper. ESSAI, KM#68.1.	—
Pn304	1929	—	25 Centimes. Aluminum. ESSAI, KM#68.1.	—
Pn305	1929	—	25 Centimes. Gold. ESSAI, KM#69.	—
Pn306	1929	—	25 Centimes. Silver. ESSAI, KM#69.	—
Pn307	1929	—	25 Centimes. Bronze. ESSAI, KM#69.	—
Pn308	1929	—	25 Centimes. Copper. ESSAI, KM#69.	—
Pn309	1929	—	25 Centimes. Aluminum. ESSAI, KM#69.	—
Pn310	1929	—	5 Francs. Nickel.	—
Pn311	1929	—	5 Francs. Bronze.	—
Pn312	1930	—	2 Francs. Copper. KM#92.	—
Pn313	1930	—	2 Francs. Matte Bronze. KM#92.	—
Pn315	1930	—	20 Francs. Silver.	—
Pn314	1930	—	10 Francs. Brass.	250
Pn317	1931	—	20 Francs. Bronze. French legend.	250
Pn318	1931	—	20 Francs. Bronze. Dutch legend.	250
Pn316	1931	—	Franc. Nickel.	—
Pn319	1932	—	5 Centimes. Copper-Nickel.	—
Pn320	1932	—	5 Centimes. Dupriez's design.	—
Pn321	1932	—	5 Centimes. Copper. Not holed, KM#93.	—
Pn322	1932	—	50 Centimes. Nickel. KM#87. KM#88. Reeded edge.	—
Pn323	1932	—	50 Centimes. Nickel. KM#87. KM#88. Plain edge.	—
Pn324	1933	—	5 Francs. Silver.	—
Pn325	1933	—	10 Francs. Nickel.	—
Pn326	1933	—	10 Francs. Nickel. DEUX BELGAS/OU/10 FRANCS.	—
Pn327	1933	—	50 Francs. Silver. 10/BELGAS/50/FRANCS within 2 oak branches. Plain edge.	—
Pn328	1933	—	50 Francs. Silver. Cross ornaments on edge.	—
Pn329	1933	—	50 Francs. Silver. Reeded edge.	—
Pn330	1933	—	50 Francs. Silver. Small head of Albert within pellet circle. Value within 2 laurel branches.	—
Pn331	1933	—	50 Francs. Silver. Bust by Bonnetain. Value within laurel branches.	—
Pn333	1933	—	100 Francs. By Devreese	—
Pn332	1933	—	100 Francs. Silver. Bust by Bonnetain. 20/BELGAS/100/ FRANCS wtihin 2 laurel branches.	—
Pn334	1933	—	100 Francs. L'UNION FAIT LA FORCE/100 FRS. By Devreese	—
Pn335	1933	—	100 Francs. Bronze. 20/BELGAS/100 FRANCS between 2 branches.	—
Pn336	1933	—	500 Francs. Bronze. 20/BELGAS/500/FRANCS between laurel and oak branches.	—
Pn337	1933	—	500 Francs. Nickel.	—
Pn338	1934	—	5 Francs. Bronze.	100
Pn339	1934	—	20 Francs. Bronze.	125
Pn346	1935	—	40 Francs. 0.6800 Silver. Lettered edge.	14,000
Pn363	1935	—	50 Francs. 0.6800 Silver. Plain edge.	600
Pn340	1935	—	Franc. Copper-Tin Alloy. Reeded edge.	—
Pn341	1935	—	Franc. Nickel. Reeded edge.	—
Pn342	1935	—	Franc. Silver. Allegory of Belgium kneeling left; BELGIQUE \ BELGIE at sides. Caducesus between IF and date. Plain edge.	—
Pn343	1935	—	Franc. Silver. Allegory of Belgium kneeling left. Plain edge.	—
Pn344	1935	—	Franc. Copper. Allegory of Belgium kneeling left. Plain edge.	—
Pn345	1935	—	Franc. Nickel. Allegory of Belgium kneeling left. Plain edge.	—
Pn347	1935	—	40 Francs. Silver. Plain edge. Restrike.	—
Pn348	1935	—	40 Francs. Copper-Tin Alloy. Lettered edge. Expo commemorative.	—
Pn349	1935	—	40 Francs. Gold. Reeded edge. Expo commemorative.	—
Pn350	1935	—	40 Francs. Silver. Reeded edge. Expo commemorative.	—
Pn351	1935	—	40 Francs. Bronze. Reeded edge. Expo commemorative.	—
Pn352	1935	—	40 Francs. Copper. Reeded edge. Expo commemorative.	—
Pn353	1935	—	40 Francs. Copper-Tin Alloy. Reeded edge. Expo commemorative.	—
Pn354	1935	—	40 Francs. Nickel. Reeded edge. Expo commemorative.	—
Pn355	1935	—	40 Francs. Aluminum. Reeded edge. Expo commemorative.	—
Pn356	1935	—	40 Francs. Gold. Expo commemorative, thin planchet	—
Pn357	1935	—	40 Francs. Silver. Expo commemorative, thin planchet	—
Pn358	1935	—	40 Francs. Bronze. Expo commemorative, thin planchet	—
Pn359	1935	—	40 Francs. Copper. Expo commemorative, thin planchet	—
Pn360	1935	—	40 Francs. Copper-Tin Alloy. Expo commemorative.	—
Pn361	1935	—	40 Francs. Nickel. Expo commemorative, thin planchet	—
Pn362	1935	—	40 Francs. Aluminum. Expo commemorative, thin planchet	—
Pn364	1935	—	50 Francs. Silver. Plain edge. KM#106.1.	—
Pn365	1935	—	50 Francs. Copper. Plain edge. KM#106.1.	—
Pn366	1935	—	50 Francs. Copper-Tin Alloy. Plain edge. KM#106.1.	—
Pn367	1935	—	50 Francs. Copper-Tin Alloy. Edge inscription. KM#106.1.	—
Pn368	1935	—	50 Francs. Gold. Reeded edge. KM#106.1.	—
Pn369	1935	—	50 Francs. Silver. Reeded edge. KM#106.1.	—
Pn370	1935	—	50 Francs. Bronze. Reeded edge. KM#106.1.	—
Pn371	1935	—	50 Francs. Copper. Reeded edge. KM#106.1.	—
Pn372	1935	—	50 Francs. Copper-Tin Alloy. Reeded edge. KM#106.1.	—
Pn373	1935	—	50 Francs. Aluminum. Reeded edge. KM#106.1.	—
Pn374	1935	—	50 Francs. Silver. Plain edge. KM#107.1.	—
Pn375	1935	—	50 Francs. Copper-Tin Alloy. Plain edge. KM#107.1.	—
Pn376	1935	—	50 Francs. Bronze. Edge inscription, KM#107.1.	—
Pn377	1935	—	50 Francs. Copper-Tin Alloy. Reeded edge. KM#107.1.	—
Pn378	1936	—	5 Francs. Nickel.	—
Pn379	1938	—	5 Centimes. Copper-Tin Alloy. KM#110.1	—
Pn380	1938	—	5 Centimes. Bronze. KM#110.1	—
Pn381	1938	—	5 Centimes. Tin. Not holed, KM#110.1	—
Pn382	1938	—	10 Centimes. Copper-Tin Alloy. Thin planchet, KM#112.	—
Pn383	1938	—	10 Centimes. Copper-Tin Alloy. Thick planchet, KM#112.	—
Pn384	1938	—	10 Centimes. Bronze. KM#112.	—
Pn385	1938	—	10 Centimes. Copper-Tin Alloy. Large letters, not holed.	—
Pn386	1938	—	25 Centimes. Nickel. Large shields.	—
Pn387	1938	—	25 Centimes. Copper-Tin Alloy. Not holed.	—
Pn388	1938	—	20 Francs. Silver.	—
Pn389	1938	—	20 Francs. Silver. Similar to KM#121.	—
Pn390	1938	—	20 Francs. Bronze. Similar to KM#121.	—
Pn391	1938	—	20 Francs. Copper. Similar to KM#121.	—
Pn392	1938	—	20 Francs. Copper-Tin Alloy. Similar to KM#121.	—
Pn393	1938	—	20 Francs. Nickel. Similar to KM#121.	—
Pn394	1938	—	20 Francs. Silver.	—
Pn395	1938	—	20 Francs. Copper-Tin Alloy.	—
Pn396	1938	—	20 Francs. Tin.	—
Pn397	1938	—	20 Francs. Silver. Thick planchet.	—
Pn398	1938	—	20 Francs. Copper-Tin Alloy. Thick planchet.	—
Pn399	1938	—	20 Francs. Tin. Thick planchet.	—
Pn400	1938	—	20 Francs. Silver. Small portrait.	—
Pn401	1938	—	20 Francs. Bronze. Small portrait.	—
Pn402	1938	—	20 Francs. Copper-Tin Alloy. Small portrait.	—
Pn403	1938	—	20 Francs. Tin. Small portrait.	—
Pn404	1938	—	50 Francs. Silver. Plain edge. KM#121.1.	—
Pn405	1938	—	50 Francs. Copper-Tin Alloy. Plain edge. KM#121.1.	—
Pn406	1938	—	50 Francs. Copper. Plain edge.	—
Pn407	1938	—	50 Francs. Copper. Plain edge. ESSAI	—
Pn408	1939	—	25 Centimes. Copper-Tin Alloy. Not holed, KM#114.1.	—
Pn409	1939	—	25 Centimes. Bronze. KM#114.1.	—
Pn410	1939	—	Franc. Nickel. KM#120.	—
Pn411	1939	—	Franc. Bronze. Reeded edge. KM#120.	—
Pn412	1939	—	Franc. Copper-Tin Alloy. Reeded edge. KM#120.	—
Pn413	1939	—	50 Francs. Copper-Tin Alloy. Lettered edge. KM#121.1.	—
Pn414	1939	—	50 Francs. Bronze. Lettered edge. KM#121.1.	—
Pn415	1940	—	Franc. Nickel. Restrike, KM#119.	—
Pn416	1940	—	5 Francs. Copper-Tin Alloy. Portrait by Rau, Leopold III ROI DE BELGES. 5/FRANCS/1940 between oak and laurel brnaches.	—
Pn417	1940	—	5 Francs. Copper-Tin Alloy. Portrait by Rau. Thick planchet.	—
Pn418	1940	—	5 Francs. Copper-Tin Alloy. Portrait by Rau. KM#108.1.	—
Pn419	1940	—	5 Francs. Copper-Tin Alloy. Portrait by Rau. KM#108.1. Thick planchet.	—
Pn420	1940	—	5 Francs. Copper-Tin Alloy. Leopold III.	—
Pn421	1940	—	5 Francs. Copper-Tin Alloy. Leopold III. Thick planchet.	—
Pn422	1940	—	5 Francs. Nickel. Leopold III. Reeded edge.	—
Pn423	1940	—	5 Francs. Nickel. Leopold III. Reeded edge. Thick planchet.	—
Pn424	1940	—	5 Francs. Silver. Leopold III. KM#108.1.	—
Pn425	1940	—	5 Francs. Silver. Leopold III. KM#108.1. Thick planchet.	—
Pn426	1940	—	5 Francs. Copper-Tin Alloy. Leopold III, ROI DES BELGES. KM#108.1. Thick planchet.	—
Pn427	1941	—	10 Centimes. Silver. Reeded edge. KM#130.	—
Pn428	1941	—	5 Francs. Silver. Reeded edge. KM#130.	—
Pn429	1944	—	2 Francs. Silver. KM#133.	—
Pn430	1948	—	100 Francs. Copper. ESSAI, KM#138.	—
Pn431	1948	—	100 Francs. Copper. ESSAI, KM#139.1.	—
Pn432	1949	—	5 Francs. Copper. KM#134.1.	—
Pn433	1949	—	5 Francs. Copper. KM#135.1.	—
Pn434	1949	—	50 Francs. Bronze.	—
Pn435	1949	—	100 Francs. Silver.	—
Pn436	1949	—	100 Francs. Silver.	—
Pn437	1949	—	1000 Francs. Bronze. Plain edge.	—
Pn438	1949	—	1000 Francs. Silver.	—
Pn440	ND	—	1000 Francs. Bronze.	—
Pn441	1949	—	1000 Francs. Bronze. Milled edge.	—
Pn439	1949	—	1000 Francs. Gold. ESSAI	10,920
Pn442	1951	—	20 Francs. Copper. ESSAI, KM#140.1	—

KM#	Date	Mintage	Identification	Mkt Val
Pn443	1951	—	20 Francs. Copper. ESSAI, KM#141.1	—
Pn444	1951	—	20 Francs. Copper. ESSAI, KM#136.1.	—
Pn445	1951	—	50 Francs. Copper. ESSAI, KM#137	—
Pn446	1952	—	Franc. Copper. KM#142.1	—
Pn447	1952	—	Franc. Copper. KM#143.1	—

PIEFORTS

KM#	Date	Mintage	Identification	Mkt Val
P6	1918	—	50 Centimes. Zinc. Plain edge. Not holed, KM#83.	—
P7	1920	—	25 Centimes. Nickel. Plain edge. KM#68.1.	—
P8	1926	—	5 Centimes. Copper. Plain edge. Not holed, KM#66.	—
P9	1935	—	Franc. Silver.	—
P10	1935	—	Franc. Copper.	—
P11	1935	—	Franc. Nickel.	—
P12	1989	—	100 Ecu. Gold. KM#175	1,000

TRIAL STRIKES

KM#	Date	Mintage	Identification	Mkt Val
TS5	1903	—	Franc. Pewter. Uniface. Rectangle planchet.	—
TS6	1904	—	Franc. Pewter. Uniface. Rectangle planchet.	—
TS7	ND(1904)	—	2 Francs. Lead. Uniface.	50.00
TS8	1910	—	2 Francs. Portrait, uniface.	—
TS9	1910	—	2 Francs. KM#74. Uniface.	—
TS10	1911	—	20 Francs. Gold. Error obverse.	—
TS11	1911	—	20 Francs. Aluminum. Error obverse.	—
TS12	1918	—	50 Centimes. Klippe.	—
TS13	1926	—	5 Francs. Nickel. Klippe.	—
TS14	1933	—	10 Francs. Silver. Legend within 2 branches.	—
TS15	1933	—	50 Francs. Silver. Irregular flan.	—
TS16	1949	—	1000 Francs. Red Copper. Klippe.	—
TS17	1949	—	1000 Francs. Yellow Copper. Klippe.	—
TS20	1949	—	1000 Francs. Silver. Klippe.	—
TS18	1949	—	1000 Francs. Red Copper. Klippe.	—
TS19	1949	—	1000 Francs. Yellow Copper. Klippe.	—

"FDC" SETS

This fleur-de-coin set was issued with New Caledonia and French Polynesia 1967 sets.

KM#	Date	Mintage	Identification	Issue Price	Mkt Val
SS1	1970 (5)	5,000	KM#135.1, 143.1, 149.1, 154.1, 156.1 DU	0.60	130
SS2	1970 (5)	5,000	KM#134.1, 142.1, 148.1, 153.1, 155.1 FR	0.60	130
SS3	1971 (5)	10,000	KM#135.1, 143.1, 149.1, 154.1, 156.1 DU	0.63	55.00
SS4	1971 (5)	10,000	KM#134.1, 142.1, 148.1, 153.1, 155.1 FR	0.63	55.00
SS5	1972 (5)	10,000	KM#135.1, 143.1, 149.1, 154.1, 156.1 DU	0.70	80.00
SS6	1972 (5)	10,000	KM#134.1, 142.1, 148.1, 153.1, 155.1 FR	0.70	80.00
SS7	1973 (5)	16,778	KM#135.1, 143.1, 149.1, 154.1, 156.1 DU	0.80	30.00
SS8	1973 (5)	15,000	KM#134.1, 142.1, 148.1, 153.1, 155.1 FR	0.80	30.00
SS10	1974 (5)	19,000	KM#134.1, 142.1, 148.1, 153.1, 155.1 FR	1.10	22.00
SS9	1974 (5)	20,608	KM#135.1, 143.1, 149,.1 154.1, 156.1 DU	1.10	22.00
SS11	1975 (10)	45,752	KM#135.1, 143.1, 149.1, 154.1, 156.1 DU, 134.1, 142.1, 148.1, 153.1, 155.1 FR	2.50	8.00
SS12	1976 (10)	15,000	KM#135, 143, 149, 156, 158.1 DU, 134, 142, 148, 155, 157.1 FR	20.75	60.00
SS13	1977 (8)	45,938	KM#135, 143, 149, 156 DU, 134, 142, 148, 155 FR	2.65	5.00
SS14	1978 (8)	46,237	KM#135, 143, 149, 156 DU, 134, 142, 148, 155 FR	4.00	6.00
SS15	1979 (8)	49,997	KM#135, 143, 149, 156 DU, 134, 142, 148, 155 FR	4.00	5.00
SS16	1980 (8)	60,000	KM#135, 143, 149, 160 DU, 134, 142, 148, 159 FR	4.00	5.00
SS17	1981 (8)	54,331	KM#135, 143, 149, 160 DU, 134, 142, 148, 159 FR	3.25	5.00

MINT SETS

KM#	Date	Mintage	Identification	Issue Price	Mkt Val
MS1	1989 (10)	60,000	KM#149, 160, 164, 169, 171 DU; 148, 159, 163, 168, 170 FR	11.00	25.00
MS2	1990 (10)	60,000	KM#149, 160, 164, 169, 171 DU; 148, 159, 163, 168, 170 FR	13.00	18.00
MS3	1991 (10)	60,000	KM#149, 160, 164, 169, 171 DU; 148, 159, 163, 168, 170 FR	13.00	10.00
MS4	1991 (3)	—	KM#196-198	—	30.00
MS5	1992 (10)	60,000	KM#149, 160, 164, 169, 171 DU; 148, 159,	15.00	10.00
MS6	1993 (10)	40,000	KM#149, 160, 164, 169, 171 DU; 148, 159, 163, 168, 170 FR	15.00	10.00
MS7	1994 (10)	60,000	KM#148.1, 149.1, 187-194, medal	15.00	12.00
MS8	1995 (10)	60,000	KM#148.1, 149.1, 187-194, medal	15.00	16.00
MS9	1996 (10)	60,000	KM#148.1, 149.1, 187-194, medal	15.00	12.00
MS10	1997 (10)	60,000	KM#148.1, 149.1, 187-194, medal	—	14.00
MS11	1998 (10)	60,000	KM#148.1, 149.1, 187-194	15.00	12.00
MS12	1999 (10)	60,000	KM#148.1, 149.1, 187-194	15.00	12.00
MS13	2000 (10)	60,000	KM#148.1, 149.1, 187-194	15.00	12.00

PROOF SETS

KM#	Date	Mintage	Identification	Issue Price	Mkt Val
PS1	1987 (2)	15,000	KM#166-167	395	300
PS2	1988 (2)	15,000	KM#166-167	395	300
PS3	1989 (4)	2,000	KM#172-175	1,300	1,500
PS4	1990 (4)	5,000	KM#172-175	1,300	900
PS5	1990 (3)	10,000	KM#178-180	100	110
PS6	1991 (3)	10,000	KM#196-198	100	80.00
PS7	2000 (3)	10,000	KM#215-217	75.00	80.00

GHENT

GERMAN OCCUPATION WWI

TOKEN COINAGE

KM# Tn1a 50 CENTIMES Composition: Iron **Reverse:** Thick "50"

Date	Mintage	F	VF	XF	Unc	BU
1915		3.00	6.00	12.00	35.00	—

KM# Tn1 50 CENTIMES Composition: Iron **Obverse:** Brass and iron **Reverse:** Copper plated **Note:** Similar to KM#Tn1a, thin "50".

Date	Mintage	F	VF	XF	Unc	BU
1915	512,000	3.00	6.00	12.00	35.00	—

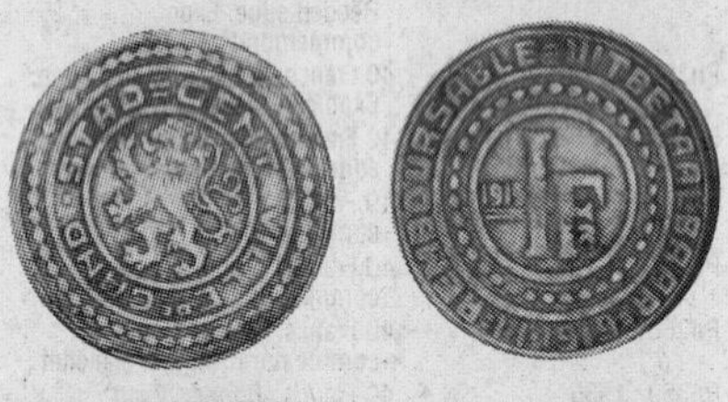

KM# Tn2 FRANKEN Composition: Iron **Obverse:** Brass **Reverse:** Copper plated

Date	Mintage	F	VF	XF	Unc	BU
1915	370,000	5.00	8.00	15.00	40.00	—

KM# Tn2a FRANKEN Composition: Iron **Reverse:** 11. 1919 instead of 1.1. 1919

Date	Mintage	F	VF	XF	Unc	BU
1915		3.75	7.50	15.00	40.00	—

KM# Tn3 FRANKEN Composition: Gilt Copper **Obverse:** Lion in circle, STAD GENT VILLE DE GAND around **Reverse:** 1915 1 FR in circle, UIT BETAALBAAR 1 JANUARI 1918 REMBOURSABLE 1 JANVIER 1920 along sides of square **Shape:** Square **Note:** This token was struck in 1920 for the benefit of charity.

Date	Mintage	F	VF	XF	Unc	BU
1915		30.00	60.00	120	250	—

KM# Tn4 2 FRANKEN Composition: Iron **Obverse:** Brass and iron **Reverse:** Copper plated

Date	Mintage	F	VF	XF	Unc	BU
1915	314,000	5.00	10.00	20.00	50.00	—

KM# Tn5 2 FRANKEN Composition: Gilt Copper **Obverse:** Arms in circle, STAD GENT FIDES ET AMOR around **Reverse:** 1928 2 FRANK in circle, UIT BETAAL BAAR JANUARI 1922 PAX ET LABOR around **Note:** This token was struck in 1920 for the benefit of charity.

Date	Mintage	F	VF	XF	Unc	BU
1918		25.00	50.00	100	200	—

KM# Tn6 5 FRANKEN Composition: Iron **Obverse:** Brass plated **Reverse:** Brass plated

Date	Mintage	F	VF	XF	Unc	BU
1917	108,000	17.50	30.00	45.00	100	—

KM# Tn7 5 FRANKEN Composition: Iron

Date	Mintage	F	VF	XF	Unc	BU
1918	339,000	12.50	22.50	35.00	80.00	—

BELIZE

Belize, formerly British Honduras, but now an independent member of the Commonwealth of Nations, is situated in Central America south of Mexico and east and north of Guatemala, with an area of 8,867 sq. mi. (22,960 sq. km.) and a population of *242,000. Capital: Belmopan. Tourism now augments Belize's economy, in addition to sugar, citrus fruits, chicle and hardwoods, which are exported.

In Dec. 1975, the U.N. General Assembly adopted a resolution supporting the right of the people of Belize to self-determination, and asking Britain and Guatemala to renew their negotiations on the future of Belize. Independence was obtained on Sept. 21, 1981. Belize is a member of the Caribbean community and the common market. Elizabeth II is Head of State as Queen of the United Kingdom.

RULERS

British, until 1981

MINT MARKS

H - Birmingham Mint

No mm - Royal Mint

MONETARY SYSTEM

commencing 1864

100 Cents = 1 Dollar

***NOTE:** From 1975-1985 the Franklin Mint produced coinage in up to 3 different qualities. Qualities of issue are designated in ( ) after each date and are defined as follows:

(M) MATTE - Normal circulation strike or a dull finish produced by sandblasting special uncirculated (polish finish) or proof quality dies.

(U) SPECIAL UNCIRCULATED - Polished or proof-like in appearance without any frosted features.

(P) PROOF - The highest quality obtainable having mirror-like fields and frosted features.

BRITISH COLONIAL & CONSTITUTIONAL

DECIMAL COINAGE

KM# 33 CENT Composition: Bronze **Obverse:** Bust of Queen Elizabeth right **Reverse:** Denomination within circle **Edge:** Scalloped

Date	Mintage	F	VF	XF	Unc	BU
1973	400,000	—	—	0.10	0.25	—
1974	2,000,000	—	—	0.10	0.20	—
1975	Inc. above	—	—	0.10	0.15	—
1976	3,000,000	—	—	0.10	0.15	—

KM#33a CENT Composition: Aluminum **Obverse:** Bust of Queen Elizabeth right **Reverse:** Denomination within circle **Edge:** Scalloped

Date	Mintage	F	VF	XF	Unc	BU
1976	2,049,999	—	—	0.10	0.25	—
1979	2,505,000	—	—	0.10	0.25	—
1980	1,505,000	—	—	0.10	0.25	—
1982	—	—	—	0.10	0.25	—
1983	—	—	—	0.10	0.25	—
1986	—	—	—	0.10	0.25	—
1987	—	—	—	0.10	0.25	—
1989	—	—	—	0.10	0.25	—
1991	—	—	—	0.10	0.25	—
1996	—	—	—	0.10	0.25	—

KM# 38 CENT Composition: Bronze **Reverse:** Swallow-tailed kite

Date	Mintage	F	VF	XF	Unc	BU
1974FM (M)	225,000	—	—	0.40	0.75	—
1974FM (P)	21,000	Value: 1.25				

KM#38a CENT Weight: 3.0200 g. **Composition:** 0.9250 Silver .0898 oz. ASW **Reverse:** Swallow-tailed kite

Date	Mintage	F	VF	XF	Unc	BU
1974FM (P)	31,000	Value: 2.50				

KM# 46 CENT Composition: Bronze **Reverse:** Swallow-tailed kite **Edge:** Scalloped

Date	Mintage	F	VF	XF	Unc	BU
1975FM (M)	118,000	—	—	0.10	0.75	—
1975FM (U)	1,095	—	—	0.20	1.00	—
1975FM (P)	8,794	Value: 1.00				
1976FM (M)	126,000	—	—	0.10	0.75	—
1976FM (U)	759	—	—	0.20	1.00	—
1976FM (P)	4,893	Value: 1.00				

KM# 46a CENT Weight: 3.0200 g. **Composition:** 0.9250 Silver .0898 oz. ASW **Reverse:** Swallow-tailed kite **Edge:** Scalloped

Date	Mintage	F	VF	XF	Unc	BU
1975FM (P)	13,000	Value: 2.00				
1976FM (P)	5,897	Value: 2.00				
1977FM (P)	3,197	Value: 2.00				
1978FM (P)	3,342	Value: 2.00				
1979FM (P)	2,445	Value: 2.00				
1980FM (P)	1,826	Value: 2.00				
1981FM (P)	615	Value: 2.50				

KM# 46b CENT Composition: Aluminum **Reverse:** Swallow-tailed kite **Edge:** Scalloped

Date	Mintage	F	VF	XF	Unc	BU
1977FM (U)	126,000	—	—	0.10	0.30	—
1977FM (P)	2,107	Value: 1.00				
1978FM (U)	125,000	—	—	0.10	0.30	—
1978FM (P)	1,671	Value: 1.00				
1979FM (U)	808	—	—	0.15	0.75	—
1979FM (P)	1,287	Value: 1.00				
1980FM (U)	761	—	—	0.15	0.75	—
1980FM (P)	920	Value: 1.00				
1981FM (U)	297	—	—	0.15	0.75	—
1981FM (P)	643	Value: 1.00				

KM# 83 CENT Composition: Aluminum **Reverse:** Swallow-tailed kite **Edge:** Scalloped

Date		F	VF	XF	Unc	BU
1982FM (U)		—	0.15	0.25	1.50	—
1982FM (P)	—	Value: 2.00				
1983FM (U)		—	0.15	0.25	1.50	—
1983FM (P)	—	Value: 2.00				

KM#83a CENT Weight: 3.0200 g. **Composition:** 0.9250 Silver .0898 oz. ASW **Reverse:** Swallow-tailed kite **Edge:** Scalloped

Date	Mintage	F	VF	XF	Unc	BU
1982FM (P)	381	Value: 6.50				
1983FM (P)	336	Value: 6.50				

KM# 90 CENT Composition: Aluminum **Reverse:** Swallow-tailed kite **Edge:** Scalloped

Date		F	VF	XF	Unc	BU
1984FM (U)		—	0.15	0.25	1.50	—
1984FM (P)	—	Value: 2.00				

KM#90a CENT Weight: 3.0200 g. **Composition:** 0.9250 Silver .0898 oz. ASW **Reverse:** Swallow-tailed kite **Edge:** Scalloped

Date	Mintage	F	VF	XF	Unc	BU
1984FM (P)	—	Value: 6.50				
1985 Proof	212	Value: 7.50				

KM# 114 CENT Composition: Aluminum **Obverse:** New portrait of Queen Elizabeth II

Date	F	VF	XF	Unc	BU
1992	—	—	0.10	0.15	—
1994	—	—	0.10	0.15	—
1996	—	—	0.10	0.15	—
1998	—	—	—	—	—

KM# 34 5 CENTS Composition: Nickel-Brass **Obverse:** Bust of Queen Elizabeth II right **Reverse:** Denomination within circle

Date	Mintage	F	VF	XF	Unc	BU
1973	210,000	—	—	0.50	1.00	—
1974	210,000	—	—	0.50	1.00	—
1975	420,000	—	—	0.15	0.40	—
1976	570,000	—	—	0.15	0.40	—
1979	—	—	—	0.15	0.40	—

KM# 39 5 CENTS Composition: Nickel-Brass **Reverse:** Fork-tailed flycatcher

Date	Mintage	F	VF	XF	Unc	BU
1974FM (M)	50,000	—	—	0.25	1.25	—
1974FM (P)	21,000	Value: 1.50				

KM# 39a 5 CENTS Weight: 4.3500 g. **Composition:** 0.9250 Silver .1293 oz. ASW **Reverse:** Fork-tailed flycatcher

Date	Mintage	F	VF	XF	Unc	BU
1974FM (P)	31,000	Value: 3.00				

KM# 47 5 CENTS Composition: Nickel-Brass **Reverse:** Fork-tailed flycatcher

Date	Mintage	F	VF	XF	Unc	BU
1975FM (M)	24,000	—	—	0.25	1.50	—
1975FM (U)	1,095	—	—	0.25	1.50	—
1975FM (P)	8,794	Value: 1.25				
1976FM (M)	25,000	—	—	0.25	1.50	—
1976FM (U)	759	—	—	0.25	1.50	—
1976FM (P)	4,893	Value: 1.25				

KM# 47a 5 CENTS Weight: 4.3500 g. **Composition:** 0.9250 Silver .1293 oz. ASW **Reverse:** Fork-tailed flycatcher

Date	Mintage	F	VF	XF	Unc	BU
1975FM (P)	13,000	Value: 2.50				
1976FM (P)	5,897	Value: 2.50				
1977FM (P)	3,197	Value: 2.50				
1978FM (P)	3,342	Value: 2.50				
1979FM (P)	2,445	Value: 2.50				
1980FM (P)	1,826	Value: 2.50				
1981FM (P)	615	Value: 3.00				

KM# 34a 5 CENTS Composition: Aluminum **Obverse:** Bust of Queen Elizabeth II right **Reverse:** Denomination within circle

Date	Mintage	F	VF	XF	Unc	BU
1976	1,000,000	—	—	0.10	0.25	—
1979	960,000	—	—	0.10	0.25	—
1980	1,040,000	—	—	0.10	0.25	—
1986	—	—	—	0.10	0.25	—
1987	—	—	—	0.10	0.25	—
1989	—	—	—	0.10	0.25	—
1991	—	—	—	0.10	0.25	—
1992	—	—	—	0.10	0.25	—
1993	—	—	—	0.10	0.25	—
1994	—	—	—	0.10	0.25	—

KM# 47b 5 CENTS Composition: Aluminum **Reverse:** Fork-tailed flycatcher

Date	Mintage	F	VF	XF	Unc	BU
1977FM (U)	26,000	—	—	0.10	0.50	—
1977FM (P)	2,107	Value: 1.50				
1978FM (U)	25,000	—	—	0.10	0.50	—
1978FM (P)	1,671	Value: 1.50				
1979FM (U)	808	—	—	0.15	0.75	—
1979FM (P)	1,287	—	—	0.25	1.75	—
1980FM (U)	761	—	—	0.15	0.75	—
1980FM (P)	920	Value: 1.75				
1981FM (U)	297	—	—	0.15	0.75	—
1981FM (P)	643	Value: 1.75				

KM# 64 5 CENTS Composition: Aluminum **Series:** World Food Day **Obverse:** Bust of Queen Elizabeth right **Reverse:** Denomination

Date	F	VF	XF	Unc	BU
1981	—	—	0.10	0.35	—

KM# 84a 5 CENTS Weight: 4.3500 g. **Composition:** 0.9250 Silver .1293 oz. ASW **Reverse:** Fork-tailed flycatcher

Date	Mintage	F	VF	XF	Unc	BU
1982FM (P)	381	Value: 12.00				
1983FM (P)	479	Value: 12.00				

KM# 84 5 CENTS Composition: Aluminum **Reverse:** Fork-tailed flycatcher

Date	F	VF	XF	Unc	BU
1982FM (U)	—	0.15	0.35	1.50	—
1982FM (P)	— Value: 2.50				
1983FM (U)	—	0.15	0.35	1.50	—
1983FM (P)	— Value: 2.50				

KM# 91 5 CENTS Composition: Aluminum

Date	F	VF	XF	Unc	BU
1984FM (U)	—	0.25	0.50	2.00	—
1984FM (P)	— Value: 2.50				

KM# 91a 5 CENTS Weight: 4.3500 g. **Composition:** 0.9250 Silver .1293 oz. ASW

Date	Mintage	F	VF	XF	Unc	BU
1984FM (P)	—	Value: 12.00				
1985 Proof	212	Value: 13.50				

KM# 115 5 CENTS Composition: Aluminum

Date	F	VF	XF	Unc	BU
1992	—	—	0.10	0.20	—
1993	—	—	0.10	0.20	—

KM# 35 10 CENTS Composition: Copper-Nickel **Obverse:** Bust of Queen Elizabeth right **Reverse:** Denomination within circle

Date	Mintage	F	VF	XF	Unc	BU
1974	100,000	—	0.15	0.35	0.60	—
1975	200,000	—	0.10	0.25	0.50	—
1976	700,000	—	0.10	0.20	0.45	—
1979	800,000	—	0.10	0.20	0.40	—
1980	—	—	0.10	0.20	0.40	—
1981	—	—	0.10	0.20	0.40	—
1992	—	—	0.10	0.20	0.40	—

KM# 40 10 CENTS Composition: Copper-Nickel **Reverse:** Long-tailed hermit

Date	Mintage	F	VF	XF	Unc	BU
1974FM (M)	27,000	—	—	0.50	2.00	—
1974FM (P)	21,000	Value: 1.75				

KM# 40a 10 CENTS Weight: 2.7900 g. **Composition:** 0.9250 Silver .0829 oz. ASW **Reverse:** Long-tailed hermit

Date	Mintage	F	VF	XF	Unc	BU
1974FM (P)	31,000	Value: 3.50				

KM# 48 10 CENTS Composition: Copper-Nickel **Reverse:** Long-tailed hermit

Date	Mintage	F	VF	XF	Unc	BU
1975FM (M)	12,000	—	—	0.25	1.50	—
1975FM (U)	1,095	—	—	0.30	2.00	—
1975FM (P)	8,794	Value: 1.50				
1976FM (M)	13,000	—	—	0.25	1.50	—
1976FM (U)	759	—	—	0.35	2.50	—
1976FM (P)	4,893	Value: 1.50				
1977FM (U)	14,000	—	—	0.25	1.50	—
1977FM (P)	2,107	Value: 2.00				
1978FM (U)	13,000	—	—	0.25	1.50	—
1978FM (P)	1,671	Value: 2.00				
1979FM (U)	808	—	—	0.25	1.50	—
1979FM (P)	1,287	Value: 2.50				
1980FM (U)	761	—	—	0.25	1.50	—
1980FM (P)	920	Value: 2.50				
1981FM (U)	297	—	—	0.25	1.50	—
1981FM (P)	643	Value: 2.50				

KM# 48a 10 CENTS Weight: 2.7900 g. **Composition:** 0.9250 Silver .0829 oz. ASW **Reverse:** Long-tailed hermit

Date	Mintage	F	VF	XF	Unc	BU
1975FM (P)	13,000	Value: 3.00				
1976FM (P)	5,897	Value: 3.00				
1977FM (P)	3,197	Value: 3.00				
1978FM (P)	3,342	Value: 3.00				
1979FM (P)	2,445	Value: 3.00				
1980FM (P)	1,826	Value: 3.00				
1981FM (P)	615	Value: 4.00				

KM# 85 10 CENTS Composition: Copper-Nickel **Reverse:** Long-tailed hermit

Date	F	VF	XF	Unc	BU
1982FM (U)	—	0.25	0.50	2.50	—
1982FM (P)	— Value: 3.50				
1983FM (U)	—	0.25	0.50	2.50	—
1983FM (P)	— Value: 3.50				

KM# 85a 10 CENTS Weight: 2.7900 g. **Composition:** 0.9250 Silver .0829 oz. ASW **Reverse:** Long-tailed hermit

Date	Mintage	F	VF	XF	Unc	BU
1982FM (P)	381	Value: 13.50				
1983FM (P)	312	Value: 13.50				

KM# 92 10 CENTS Composition: Copper-Nickel **Reverse:** Long-tailed hermit

Date	F	VF	XF	Unc	BU
1984FM (U)	—	0.25	0.50	2.50	—
1984FM (P)	— Value: 3.50				

KM# 92a 10 CENTS Weight: 2.7900 g. **Composition:** 0.9250 Silver .0829 oz. ASW **Reverse:** Long-tailed hermit

Date	Mintage	F	VF	XF	Unc	BU
1984FM (P)	—	Value: 13.50				
1985 Proof	212	Value: 15.50				

KM# 116 10 CENTS Composition: Copper-Nickel **Obverse:** New portrait of Queen Elizabeth II

Date	F	VF	XF	Unc	BU
1992	—	—	0.15	0.40	—

KM# 36 25 CENTS Composition: Copper-Nickel **Obverse:** Bust of Queen Elizabeth right **Reverse:** Denomination within circle

Date	Mintage	F	VF	XF	Unc	BU
1974	100,000	—	0.35	0.65	1.25	—
1975	200,000	—	0.20	0.35	0.75	—
1976	790,000	—	0.20	0.35	0.75	—
1979	500,000	—	0.20	0.35	0.75	—
1980	—	—	0.20	0.35	0.75	—
1981	—	—	0.20	0.35	0.75	—
1986	—	—	0.20	0.35	0.75	—
1987	—	—	0.20	0.35	0.75	—
1988	—	—	0.20	0.35	0.75	—
1989	—	—	0.20	0.35	0.75	—
1991	—	—	0.20	0.35	0.75	—
1992	—	—	0.20	0.35	0.75	—
1993	—	—	0.20	0.35	0.75	—
1994	—	—	0.20	0.35	0.75	—

KM# 41 25 CENTS Composition: Copper-Nickel **Reverse:** Blue-crowned motmot

Date	Mintage	F	VF	XF	Unc	BU
1974FM (M)	13,000	—	—	1.00	3.50	—
1974FM (P)	21,000	Value: 2.50				

KM# 41a 25 CENTS Weight: 6.6000 g. **Composition:** 0.9250 Silver .1962 oz. ASW **Reverse:** Blue-crowned motmot

Date	Mintage	F	VF	XF	Unc	BU
1974FM (P)	31,000	Value: 5.00				

KM# 49 25 CENTS Composition: Copper-Nickel **Reverse:** Blue-crowned motmot

Date	Mintage	F	VF	XF	Unc	BU
1975FM (M)	4,716	—	—	0.40	3.00	—
1975FM (U)	1,095	—	—	0.40	3.00	—
1975FM (P)	8,794	Value: 2.50				
1976FM (M)	5,000	—	—	0.50	4.00	—
1976FM (U)	759	—	—	0.45	3.50	—
1976FM (P)	4,893	Value: 2.50				
1977FM (U)	5,520	—	—	0.30	2.00	—
1977FM (P)	2,107	Value: 2.75				
1978FM (U)	5,458	—	—	0.30	2.00	—
1978FM (P)	1,671	Value: 2.75				
1979FM (U)	808	—	—	0.40	3.00	—
1979FM (P)	1,287	Value: 3.00				
1980FM (U)	761	—	—	0.40	3.00	—
1980FM (P)	920	Value: 3.00				
1981FM (U)	297	—	—	0.40	3.00	—
1981FM (P)	643	Value: 3.00				

KM# 49a 25 CENTS Weight: 6.6000 g. **Composition:** 0.9250 Silver .1962 oz. ASW **Reverse:** Blue-crowned motmot

Date	Mintage	F	VF	XF	Unc	BU
1975FM (P)	13,000	Value: 3.50				
1976FM (P)	5,897	Value: 3.50				
1977FM (P)	3,197	Value: 3.50				
1978FM (P)	3,342	Value: 3.50				
1979FM (P)	2,445	Value: 3.50				
1980FM (P)	1,826	Value: 3.50				
1981FM (P)	615	Value: 5.00				

KM# 86 25 CENTS Composition: Copper-Nickel **Reverse:** Blue-crowned motmot

Date	F	VF	XF	Unc	BU
1982FM (U)	—	0.50	1.00	4.00	—
1982FM (P)	—	Value: 5.00			
1983FM (U)	—	0.50	1.00	4.00	—
1983FM (P)	—	Value: 5.00			

KM# 86a 25 CENTS Weight: 6.6000 g. **Composition:** 0.9250 Silver .1962 oz. ASW **Reverse:** Blue-crowned motmot

Date	Mintage	F	VF	XF	Unc	BU
1982FM (P)	381	Value: 18.50				
1983FM (P)	314	Value: 18.50				

KM# 93 25 CENTS Composition: Copper-Nickel **Reverse:** Blue-crowned motmot

Date	F	VF	XF	Unc	BU
1984FM (U)	—	0.50	1.00	4.00	—
1984FM (P)	—	Value: 5.00			

KM# 93a 25 CENTS Weight: 6.6000 g. **Composition:** 0.9250 Silver .1962 oz. ASW **Reverse:** Blue-crowned motmot

Date	Mintage	F	VF	XF	Unc	BU
1984FM (P)	—	Value: 18.50				
1985 Proof	212	Value: 22.50				

KM# 77 25 CENTS Composition: Copper-Nickel **Subject:** World Forestry Congress **Obverse:** Bust of Queen Elizabeth right **Reverse:** Denomination

Date	F	VF	XF	Unc	BU
1985	—	0.25	0.40	0.85	—

KM# 117 25 CENTS Composition: Copper-Nickel **Obverse:** New portrait of Queen Elizabeth II

Date	F	VF	XF	Unc	BU
1991	—	0.20	0.35	0.75	—
1992	—	0.20	0.35	0.75	—
1993	—	0.20	0.35	0.75	—

KM# 37 50 CENTS Composition: Copper-Nickel **Obverse:** Bust of Queen Elizabeth right **Reverse:** Denomination within circle

Date	Mintage	F	VF	XF	Unc	BU
1974	123,000	—	0.50	1.50	3.00	—
1975	Inc. above	—	0.40	0.75	2.00	—
1976	312,000	—	0.40	0.75	2.00	—
1979	125,000	—	0.50	1.50	3.00	—
1980	—	—	0.40	0.75	1.75	—
1989	—	—	0.40	0.75	1.75	—
1991	—	—	0.40	0.75	1.75	—
1992	—	—	0.40	0.75	1.75	—
1993	—	—	0.40	0.75	1.75	—

KM# 42 50 CENTS Composition: Copper-Nickel **Reverse:** Frigate bird

Date	Mintage	F	VF	XF	Unc	BU
1974FM (M)	8,806	—	—	0.40	4.00	—
1974FM (P)	21,000	Value: 3.50				

KM# 42a 50 CENTS Weight: 9.9400 g. **Composition:** 0.9250 Silver .3197 oz. ASW **Reverse:** Frigate bird

Date	Mintage	F	VF	XF	Unc	BU
1974FM (P)	31,000	Value: 7.50				

KM# 50 50 CENTS Composition: Copper-Nickel **Reverse:** Frigate bird

Date	Mintage	F	VF	XF	Unc	BU
1975FM (M)	2,358	—	—	0.65	6.00	—
1975FM (U)	1,095	—	—	0.45	4.50	—
1975FM (P)	8,794	Value: 4.00				
1976FM (M)	3,259	—	—	0.55	5.00	—
1976FM (U)	759	—	—	0.55	5.00	—
1976FM (P)	4,893	Value: 4.00				
1977FM (U)	3,540	—	—	0.45	4.00	—
1977FM (P)	2,107	Value: 4.00				
1978FM (U)	2,958	—	—	0.45	4.00	—
1978FM (P)	1,671	Value: 4.00				
1979FM (U)	808	—	—	0.55	5.00	—
1979FM (P)	1,287	Value: 4.00				
1980FM (U)	761	—	—	0.55	5.00	—
1980FM (P)	920	Value: 5.00				
1981FM (U)	297	—	—	0.55	5.00	—
1981FM (P)	643	Value: 5.00				

KM# 50a 50 CENTS Weight: 9.9400 g. **Composition:** 0.9250 Silver .3197 oz. ASW **Reverse:** Frigate bird

Date	Mintage	F	VF	XF	Unc	BU
1975FM (P)	13,000	Value: 6.50				
1976FM (P)	5,897	Value: 6.50				
1977FM (P)	3,197	Value: 6.50				
1978FM (P)	3,342	Value: 6.50				
1979FM (P)	2,445	Value: 6.50				
1980FM (P)	1,826	Value: 6.50				
1981FM (P)	615	Value: 8.50				

KM# 87 50 CENTS Composition: Copper-Nickel **Reverse:** Frigate bird

Date	F	VF	XF	Unc	BU
1982FM (U)	—	0.75	1.50	6.50	—
1982FM (P)	—	Value: 7.50			
1983FM (U)	—	0.75	1.50	6.50	—
1983FM (P)	—	Value: 7.50			

KM# 87a 50 CENTS Weight: 9.9400 g. **Composition:** 0.9250 Silver .3197 oz. ASW **Reverse:** Frigate bird

Date	Mintage	F	VF	XF	Unc	BU
1982FM (P)	381	Value: 27.50				
1983FM (P)	312	Value: 27.50				

KM# 94 50 CENTS Composition: Copper-Nickel **Reverse:** Frigate bird

Date	F	VF	XF	Unc	BU
1984FM (U)	—	0.75	1.50	6.50	—
1984FM (P)	—	Value: 7.50			

KM# 94a 50 CENTS Weight: 9.9400 g. **Composition:** 0.9250 Silver .3197 oz. ASW **Reverse:** Frigate bird

Date	Mintage	F	VF	XF	Unc	BU
1984FM (P)	—	Value: 27.50				
1985 Proof	212	Value: 32.50				

KM# 118 50 CENTS Composition: Copper-Nickel **Obverse:** New portrait of Queen Elizabeth II

Date	F	VF	XF	Unc	BU
1992	—	0.40	0.75	1.75	—
1993	—	0.40	0.75	1.75	—

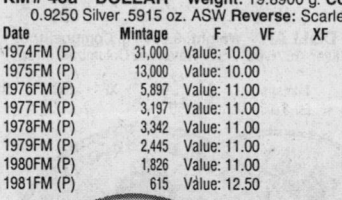

KM# 43 DOLLAR Composition: Copper-Nickel **Reverse:** Scarlet macaw

Date	Mintage	F	VF	XF	Unc	BU
1974FM (M)	6,656	—	—	1.00	8.00	—
1974FM (P)	21,000	Value: 5.00				
1975FM (M)	1,182	—	—	1.50	10.00	—
1975FM (U)	1,095	—	—	0.75	8.00	—
1975FM (P)	8,794	Value: 5.00				
1976FM (M)	1,250	—	—	1.50	10.00	—
1976FM (U)	759	—	—	1.25	9.00	—
1976FM (P)	4,893	Value: 5.00				
1977FM (U)	1,770	—	—	1.00	8.00	—
1977FM (P)	2,107	Value: 6.00				
1978FM (U)	1,708	—	—	1.00	8.00	—
1978FM (P)	1,671	Value: 6.00				
1979FM (U)	808	—	—	1.25	9.00	—
1979FM (P)	1,287	Value: 6.00				
1980FM (U)	761	—	—	1.25	9.00	—
1980FM (P)	920	Value: 6.00				
1981FM (U)	297	—	—	1.50	10.00	—
1981FM (P)	643	Value: 8.50				

KM# 43a DOLLAR Weight: 19.8900 g. **Composition:** 0.9250 Silver .5915 oz. ASW **Reverse:** Scarlet macaw

Date	Mintage	F	VF	XF	Unc	BU
1974FM (P)	31,000	Value: 10.00				
1975FM (P)	13,000	Value: 10.00				
1976FM (P)	5,897	Value: 11.00				
1977FM (P)	3,197	Value: 11.00				
1978FM (P)	3,342	Value: 11.00				
1979FM (P)	2,445	Value: 11.00				
1980FM (P)	1,826	Value: 11.00				
1981FM (P)	615	Value: 12.50				

KM# 88 DOLLAR Composition: Copper-Nickel **Reverse:** Scarlet macaw

Date	F	VF	XF	Unc	BU
1982FM (U)	—	1.50	3.00	10.00	—
1982FM (P)	—	Value: 8.50			
1983FM (U)	—	1.50	3.00	10.00	—
1983FM (P)	—	Value: 8.50			

KM# 88a DOLLAR Weight: 19.8900 g. **Composition:** 0.9250 Silver .5915 oz. ASW **Reverse:** Scarlet macaw

Date	Mintage	F	VF	XF	Unc	BU
1982FM (P)	381	Value: 37.50				
1983FM (P)	1,589	Value: 37.50				

KM# 95 DOLLAR **Composition:** Copper-Nickel
Reverse: Scarlet macaw

Date	F	VF	XF	Unc	BU
1984FM (U)	—	1.50	3.00	8.00	—
1984FM (P)	— Value: 8.50				

KM# 95a DOLLAR **Weight:** 19.8900 g. **Composition:** 0.9250 Silver .5915 oz. ASW **Reverse:** Scarlet macaw

Date	Mintage	F	VF	XF	Unc	BU
1984FM (P)	—	Value: 37.50				
1985 Proof	212	Value: 45.00				

KM# 99 DOLLAR **Composition:** Nickel-Brass **Reverse:** Columbus' three ships

Date	F	VF	XF	Unc	BU
1990	—	—	—	2.25	—
1991	—	—	—	2.25	—
1992	—	—	—	2.25	—

KM# 99a DOLLAR **Weight:** 9.0000 g. **Composition:** 0.9250 Silver .2676 oz. ASW **Reverse:** Columbus' three ships

Date	Mintage	F	VF	XF	Unc	BU
1990 Proof	Est. 5,000	Value: 32.50				

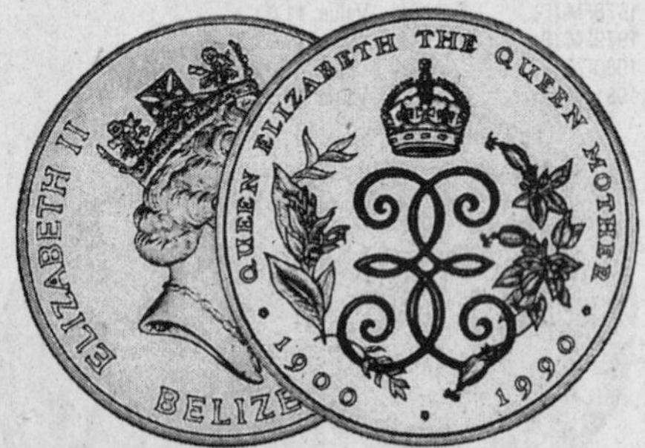

KM# 100 2 DOLLARS **Composition:** Copper-Nickel
Subject: Queen Mother's 90th Birthday

Date	F	VF	XF	Unc	BU
ND(1990)	—	—	—	6.00	—

KM# 100a 2 DOLLARS **Weight:** 28.2800 g. **Composition:** 0.9250 Silver .8411 oz. ASW **Subject:** Queen Mother's 90th Birthday

Date	Mintage	F	VF	XF	Unc	BU
ND(1990) Proof	Est. 10,000	Value: 45.00				

KM# 119 2 DOLLARS **Weight:** 28.2800 g. **Composition:** 0.9250 Silver .8411 oz. ASW **Subject:** 40th Anniversary - Coronation of Queen Elizabeth II

Date	Mintage	F	VF	XF	Unc	BU
ND(1993) Proof	Est. 10,000	Value: 45.00				

KM# 131 2 DOLLARS **Composition:** Copper-Nickel **Subject:** Battle of St. George's Caye **Obverse:** National arms **Reverse:** Oar-powered landing craft shorebound

Date	F	VF	XF	Unc	BU
ND(1998)	—	—	—	5.00	—

KM# 132 2 DOLLARS **Weight:** 28.2800 g. **Composition:** 0.9250 Silver .8410 oz. ASW **Subject:** Heritage Protection **Obverse:** National arms **Reverse:** Large building, people, jaguar and arms **Edge:** Reeded **Size:** 38.6 mm.

Date	Mintage	F	VF	XF	Unc	BU
1998 Proof	5,000	Value: 55.00				

KM# 44 5 DOLLARS **Composition:** Copper-Nickel
Reverse: Keel-billed toucan

Date	Mintage	F	VF	XF	Unc	BU
1974FM (M)	4,936	—	—	2.75	5.00	—
1974FM (P)	21,000	Value: 6.50				
1975FM (M)	237	—	—	5.00	22.50	—
1975FM (U)	1,095	—	—	2.75	5.00	—
1975FM (P)	8,794	Value: 6.50				
1976FM (M)	250	—	—	5.00	20.00	—
1976FM (U)	759	—	—	2.75	5.00	—
1976FM (P)	4,893	Value: 6.50				
1977FM (U)	720	—	—	2.75	6.50	—
1977FM (P)	2,107	Value: 7.50				
1978FM (U)	708	—	—	2.75	6.50	—
1978FM (P)	1,671	Value: 7.50				
1979FM (U)	808	—	—	2.75	5.00	—
1979FM (P)	1,287	Value: 7.50				
1980FM (U)	761	—	—	2.75	5.00	—
1980FM (P)	920	Value: 7.50				
1981FM (U)	297	—	—	2.75	6.50	—
1981FM (P)	643	Value: 8.50				

KM# 44a 5 DOLLARS **Weight:** 26.4000 g. **Composition:** 0.9250 Silver .7851 oz. ASW **Reverse:** Keel-billed toucan

Date	Mintage	F	VF	XF	Unc	BU
1974FM (P)	31,000	Value: 8.50				
1975FM (P)	13,000	Value: 9.00				
1976FM (P)	5,897	Value: 11.50				
1977FM (P)	3,197	Value: 11.50				
1978FM (P)	3,342	Value: 11.50				
1979FM (P)	2,445	Value: 11.50				
1980FM (P)	1,826	Value: 11.50				
1981FM (P)	615	Value: 16.00				

KM# 89 5 DOLLARS **Composition:** Copper-Nickel
Reverse: Keel-billed toucan

Date	F	VF	XF	Unc	BU
1982FM (U)	—	2.00	4.00	12.00	—
1982FM (P)	— Value: 15.00				
1983FM (U)	—	2.00	4.00	12.00	—
1983FM (P)	— Value: 15.00				

KM# 89a 5 DOLLARS **Weight:** 26.4000 g. **Composition:** 0.9250 Silver .7851 oz. ASW **Reverse:** Keel-billed toucan

Date	Mintage	F	VF	XF	Unc	BU
1982FM (P)	381	Value: 50.00				
1983FM (P)	311	Value: 50.00				

KM# 96 5 DOLLARS **Composition:** Copper-Nickel
Reverse: Keel-billed toucan

Date	F	VF	XF	Unc	BU
1984FM (U)	—	2.00	4.00	12.00	—
1984FM (P)	— Value: 15.00				

KM# 96a 5 DOLLARS **Weight:** 26.4000 g. **Composition:** 0.9250 Silver .7851 oz. ASW **Reverse:** Keel-billed toucan

Date	Mintage	F	VF	XF	Unc	BU
1984FM (P)	—	Value: 50.00				
1985 Proof	212	Value: 60.00				

KM# 107 5 DOLLARS **Weight:** 28.2800 g. **Composition:** 0.9250 Silver .8411 oz. ASW **Subject:** 50th anniversary - Battle of El Alamein - Field Marshall Rommel **Obverse:** Portrait of Queen Elizabeth II **Reverse:** Similar to 50 Dollars, KM#111

Date	Mintage	F	VF	XF	Unc	BU
1992 Proof	Est. 5,000	Value: 45.00				

KM# 108 5 DOLLARS **Weight:** 28.2800 g. **Composition:** 0.9250 Silver .8411 oz. ASW **Subject:** 50th anniversary - Battle of El Alamein - Lt. Gen. Montgomery **Obverse:** Portrait of Queen Elizabeth II **Reverse:** Similar to 250 Dollars, KM#113

Date	Mintage	F	VF	XF	Unc	BU
1992 Proof	Est. 5,000	Value: 45.00				

KM# 126 5 DOLLARS **Weight:** 28.2800 g. **Composition:** 0.9250 Silver .8411 oz. ASW **Subject:** Queen Mother - Balmoral Castle

Date	Mintage	F	VF	XF	Unc	BU
1995 Proof	Est. 40,000	Value: 35.00				

KM# 133 5 DOLLARS **Weight:** 28.5000 g. **Composition:** 0.9250 Silver 0.8476 oz. ASW **Subject:** Queen Elizabeth II's Golden Wedding Anniversary **Obverse:** National arms **Reverse:** Royal couple below gold inset shield **Edge:** Reeded **Size:** 38.5 mm.

Date		F	VF	XF	Unc	BU
1997 Proof	—	Value: 45.00				

KM# 45 10 DOLLARS **Composition:** Copper-Nickel **Reverse:** Great curassow

Date	Mintage	F	VF	XF	Unc	BU
1974FM (M)	4,726	—	—	3.50	7.50	—
1974FM (P)	21,000	Value: 8.00				
1975FM (M)	117	—	—	12.50	45.00	—
1975FM (U)	1,095	—	—	3.50	10.00	—
1975FM (P)	8,794	Value: 9.00				
1976FM (M)	125	—	—	10.00	35.00	—
1976FM (U)	759	—	—	3.50	10.00	—
1976FM (P)	4,893	Value: 10.00				
1977FM (U)	645	—	—	4.00	12.00	—
1977FM (P)	2,107	Value: 12.50				
1978FM (U)	583	—	—	5.00	12.00	—
1978FM (P)	1,671	Value: 12.50				

KM# 45a 10 DOLLARS **Weight:** 29.8000 g. **Composition:** 0.9250 Silver .8863 oz. ASW **Reverse:** Great curassow

Date	Mintage	F	VF	XF	Unc	BU
1974FM (P)	31,000	Value: 10.00				
1975FM (P)	13,000	Value: 11.50				
1976FM (P)	5,897	Value: 12.50				
1977FM (P)	3,197	Value: 14.00				
1978FM (P)	3,342	Value: 14.00				

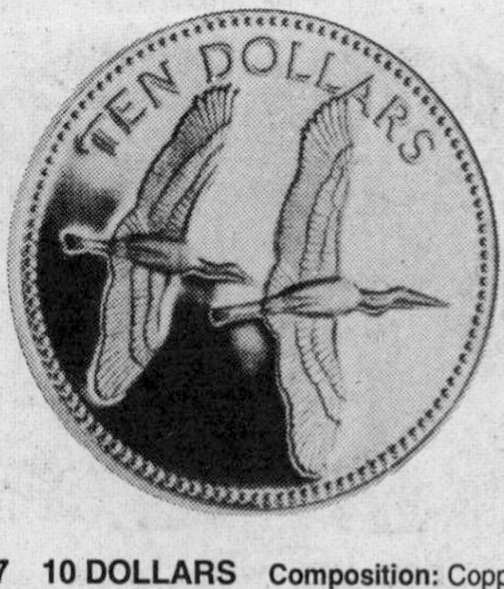

KM# 57 10 DOLLARS **Composition:** Copper-Nickel **Obverse:** Similar to Dollar, KM#43 **Reverse:** Flying jabirus

Date	Mintage	F	VF	XF	Unc	BU
1979FM (U)	808	—	—	5.00	20.00	—
1979FM (P)	1,287	Value: 25.00				

KM# 57a 10 DOLLARS **Weight:** 29.8000 g. **Composition:** 0.9250 Silver .8863 oz. ASW **Obverse:** Similar to Dollar, KM#43 **Reverse:** Flying jabirus

Date	Mintage	F	VF	XF	Unc	BU
1979FM (P)	2,445	Value: 40.00				

KM# 60 10 DOLLARS **Composition:** Copper-Nickel **Reverse:** Scarlet ibis

Date	Mintage	F	VF	XF	Unc	BU
1980FM (U)	761	—	—	5.00	25.00	—
1980FM (P)	920	Value: 28.00				

KM# 60a 10 DOLLARS **Weight:** 25.5000 g. **Composition:** 0.9250 Silver .7583 oz. ASW **Reverse:** Scarlet ibis

Date	Mintage	F	VF	XF	Unc	BU
1980FM (P)	1,826	Value: 50.00				

KM# 65 10 DOLLARS **Composition:** Copper-Nickel **Obverse:** Similar to Dollar, KM#43 **Reverse:** Roseate spoonbill

Date	Mintage	F	VF	XF	Unc	BU
1981FM (U)	297	—	7.50	15.00	40.00	—
1981FM (P)	643	Value: 50.00				

KM# 65a 10 DOLLARS **Weight:** 25.5000 g. **Composition:** 0.9250 Silver .7583 oz. ASW **Obverse:** Similar to Dollar, KM#43 **Reverse:** Roseate spoonbill

Date	Mintage	F	VF	XF	Unc	BU
1981FM (P)	615	Value: 75.00				

KM# 69 10 DOLLARS **Composition:** Copper-Nickel **Obverse:** Similar to Dollar, KM#80 **Reverse:** Yellow-crowned Amazon parrot

Date		F	VF	XF	Unc	BU
1982FM (U)		—	10.00	20.00	45.00	—
1982FM (P)	—	Value: 65.00				

KM# 69a 10 DOLLARS **Weight:** 25.5000 g. **Composition:** 0.9250 Silver .7583 oz. ASW **Obverse:** Similar to Dollar, KM#80 **Reverse:** Yellow-crowned Amazon parrot

Date	Mintage	F	VF	XF	Unc	BU
1982FM (P)	381	Value: 120				

KM# 80 10 DOLLARS **Composition:** Copper-Nickel **Obverse:** KM#69 **Reverse:** KM#45 **Note:** Mule.

Date	F	VF	XF	Unc	BU
1982FM (U)	—	—	—	25.00	—

KM# 71 10 DOLLARS **Composition:** Copper-Nickel **Reverse:** Ringed kingfisher

Date		F	VF	XF	Unc	BU
1983FM (U)		—	10.00	20.00	50.00	—
1983FM (P)	—	Value: 65.00				

KM# 71a 10 DOLLARS **Weight:** 25.5000 g. **Composition:** 0.9250 Silver .7583 oz. ASW **Reverse:** Ringed kingfisher

Date	Mintage	F	VF	XF	Unc	BU
1983FM (P)	334	Value: 135				

KM# 75 10 DOLLARS **Composition:** Copper-Nickel **Reverse:** Laughing falcon

Date		F	VF	XF	Unc	BU
1984FM (U)		—	—	—	50.00	—
1984FM (P)	—	Value: 60.00				

KM# 75a 10 DOLLARS **Weight:** 25.5000 g. **Composition:** 0.9250 Silver .7583 oz. ASW **Reverse:** Laughing falcon

Date	Mintage	F	VF	XF	Unc	BU
1984FM (P)	—	Value: 115				
1985 Proof	212	Value: 135				

KM# 102 10 DOLLARS **Composition:** Copper-Nickel **Subject:** 10th Anniversary of Independence

Date	Mintage	F	VF	XF	Unc	BU
ND(1991)	1,000,000	—	—	—	8.50	—

KM# 102a 10 DOLLARS **Weight:** 28.2800 g. **Composition:** 0.9250 Silver .8411 oz. ASW **Subject:** 10th Anniversary of Independence

Date	Mintage	F	VF	XF	Unc	BU
ND(1991) Proof	Est. 1,000	Value: 37.50				

KM# 104 10 DOLLARS **Weight:** 28.2800 g. **Composition:** 0.9250 Silver .8411 oz. ASW **Subject:** 10th Anniversary of Central Bank **Reverse:** Jabiru stork

Date	Mintage	F	VF	XF	Unc	BU
1992 Proof	Est. 1,000	Value: 40.00				

KM# 109 10 DOLLARS **Weight:** 155.6000 g. **Composition:** 0.9990 Silver 5.0032 oz. ASW **Subject:** 50th Anniversary - Battle of El Alamein - Lt. Gen. Montgomery **Obverse:** Portrait of Queen Elizabeth II **Reverse:** Similar to 250 Dollars, KM#113

Date	Mintage	F	VF	XF	Unc	BU
1992 Proof	Est. 2,500	Value: 150				

KM# 121 10 DOLLARS **Weight:** 28.2800 g. **Composition:** 0.9250 Silver .8411 oz. ASW **Subject:** Royal visit **Obverse:** Queen's portrait **Reverse:** Cameo portraits above flowers

Date	F	VF	XF	Unc	BU
1994 Proof	—	Value: 42.50			

KM# 123 10 DOLLARS **Weight:** 28.2800 g. **Composition:** 0.9250 Silver .8411 oz. ASW **Subject:** World Cup Soccer

Date	Mintage	F	VF	XF	Unc	BU
1994 Proof	Est. 10,000	Value: 45.00				

KM# 124 10 DOLLARS **Weight:** 28.2800 g. **Composition:** 0.9250 Silver .8411 oz. ASW **Reverse:** Carrack sailing ship

Date	Mintage	F	VF	XF	Unc	BU
1995 Proof	Est. 15,000	Value: 40.00				

KM# 125 10 DOLLARS **Weight:** 28.2800 g. **Composition:** 0.9250 Silver .8411 oz. ASW **Series:** Endangered wildlife **Reverse:** Howler monkey on branch

Date	Mintage	F	VF	XF	Unc	BU
1995 Proof	Est. 10,000	Value: 45.00				

KM# 127 10 DOLLARS **Weight:** 28.2800 g. **Composition:** 0.9250 Silver .8411 oz. ASW **Series:** Olympic Games 1996 **Obverse:** Wreathed arms **Reverse:** Female softball player

Date	Mintage	F	VF	XF	Unc	BU
1996 Proof	Est. 10,000	Value: 45.00				

KM# 128 10 DOLLARS **Weight:** 28.2800 g. **Composition:** 0.9250 Silver .8411 oz. ASW **Subject:** Battle of St. George's Caye **Obverse:** National arms **Reverse:** Oar-powered gunboats

Date	F	VF	XF	Unc	BU
ND(1998) Proof	—	Value: 55.00			

KM# 130 10 DOLLARS **Weight:** 28.2800 g. **Composition:** 0.9250 Silver .8411 oz. ASW **Subject:** 50th Anniversary - University of the West Indies **Obverse:** National arms **Reverse:** University arms

Date	Mintage	F	VF	XF	Unc	BU
ND(1999) Proof	1,000	Value: 55.00				

KM# 79 20 DOLLARS **Weight:** 23.3300 g. **Composition:** 0.9250 Silver .6938 oz. ASW **Series:** Los Angeles Olympics **Obverse:** National arms **Reverse:** Bicyclist

Date	Mintage	F	VF	XF	Unc	BU
1984 Proof	1,050	Value: 45.00				

KM# 82 20 DOLLARS **Weight:** 23.3300 g. **Composition:** 0.9250 Silver .6938 oz. ASW **Series:** Decade for Women **Obverse:** National arms

Date	Mintage	F	VF	XF	Unc	BU
1985 Proof	Est. 20,000	Value: 27.50				

KM# 54 25 DOLLARS **Weight:** 27.8100 g. **Composition:** 0.9250 Silver .8270 oz. ASW **Subject:** 25th Anniversary of Coronation **Obverse:** Queen Elizabeth II

Date	Mintage	F	VF	XF	Unc	BU
1978FM (U)	352	—	—	22.00	50.00	—
1978FM (P)	8,438	Value: 16.50				

KM# 61 25 DOLLARS **Weight:** 30.2800 g. **Composition:** 0.5000 Silver .4686 oz. ASW **Subject:** 10th Anniversary - Caribbean Development Bank

Date	Mintage	F	VF	XF	Unc	BU
1980FM (P)	2,647	Value: 25.00				

KM# 72 25 DOLLARS **Weight:** 30.2800 g. **Composition:** 0.5000 Silver .4686 oz. ASW **Subject:** 30th Anniversary of Coronation

Date	Mintage	F	VF	XF	Unc	BU
1983FM (P)	2,944	Value: 20.00				

KM# 78 25 DOLLARS **Weight:** 28.2800 g. **Composition:** 0.9250 Silver .8411 oz. ASW **Subject:** Royal visit

Date	Mintage	F	VF	XF	Unc	BU
1985 Proof	Est. 5,000	Value: 22.50				

KM# 97 25 DOLLARS **Weight:** 28.2800 g. **Composition:** 0.9250 Silver .8411 oz. ASW **Subject:** 500th Anniversary - Columbus Discovery of New World

Date	Mintage	F	VF	XF	Unc	BU
1989 Proof	Est. 5,000	Value: 35.00				

KM# 106 25 DOLLARS **Weight:** 28.2800 g. **Composition:** 0.9250 Silver .8411 oz. ASW **Series:** 25th Olympic Games **Reverse:** Hurdlers

Date	Mintage	F	VF	XF	Unc	BU
1992 Proof	30,000	Value: 27.50				

KM# 110 25 DOLLARS **Weight:** 3.1300 g. **Composition:** 0.9990 Gold .1 oz. AGW **Subject:** 50th Anniversary - Battle of El Alamein **Obverse:** Portrait of Queen Elizabeth II **Reverse:** 4 tanks

Date	Mintage	F	VF	XF	Unc	BU
1992 Proof	Est. 500	Value: 100				

KM#66 50 DOLLARS **Weight:** 1.5000 g. **Composition:** 0.5000 Gold .0241 oz. AGW **Reverse:** White-necked Jacobin hummingbird

Date	Mintage	F	VF	XF	Unc	BU
1981FM (U)	200	—	—	—	65.00	—
1981FM (P)	2,873	Value: 50.00				

KM# 81 50 DOLLARS **Weight:** 129.6000 g. **Composition:** 0.9250 Silver 3.8547 oz. ASW **Subject:** Bird conservation **Obverse:** Similar to 25 Dollars, KM#72 **Reverse:** Red-footed booby

Date	Mintage	F	VF	XF	Unc	BU
1985 Proof	Est. 10,000	Value: 80.00				

KM# 111 50 DOLLARS **Weight:** 7.8100 g. **Composition:** 0.9990 Gold .2511 oz. AGW **Subject:** 50th Anniversary - Battle of El Alamein **Obverse:** Portrait of Queen Elizabeth II **Reverse:** Field Marshall Rommel

Date	Mintage	F	VF	XF	Unc	BU
1992 Proof	Est. 500	Value: 250				

KM# 51 100 DOLLARS **Weight:** 6.2100 g. **Composition:** 0.5000 Gold .0998 oz. AGW **Subject:** 30th Anniversary of United Nations

Date	Mintage	F	VF	XF	Unc	BU
1975FM (M)	100	—	—	—	200	—
1975FM (U)	2,028	—	—	—	60.00	—
1975FM (P)	8,126	Value: 55.00				

KM# 52 100 DOLLARS **Weight:** 6.2100 g. **Composition:** 0.5000 Gold .0998 oz. AGW **Reverse:** Ancient Mayan symbols

Date	Mintage	F	VF	XF	Unc	BU
1976FM (M)	216	—	—	—	175	—
1976FM (P)	11,000	Value: 55.00				

KM# 53 100 DOLLARS **Weight:** 6.2100 g. **Composition:** 0.5000 Gold .0998 oz. AGW **Reverse:** Kinich Ahau, Mayan sun god

Date	Mintage	F	VF	XF	Unc	BU
1977FM (M)	200	—	—	—	135	—
1977FM (U)	51	—	—	—	350	—
1977FM (P)	7,859	Value: 55.00				

KM# 55 100 DOLLARS **Weight:** 6.2100 g. **Composition:** 0.5000 Gold .0998 oz. AGW **Reverse:** Itzamna Mayan god

Date	Mintage	F	VF	XF	Unc	BU
1978FM (U)	351	—	—	—	150	—
1978FM (P)	7,178	Value: 55.00				

KM# 58 100 DOLLARS **Weight:** 6.2100 g. **Composition:** 0.5000 Gold .0998 oz. AGW **Reverse:** Queen angelfish

Date	Mintage	F	VF	XF	Unc	BU
1979FM (U)	400	—	—	—	125	—
1979FM (P)	4,465	Value: 80.00				

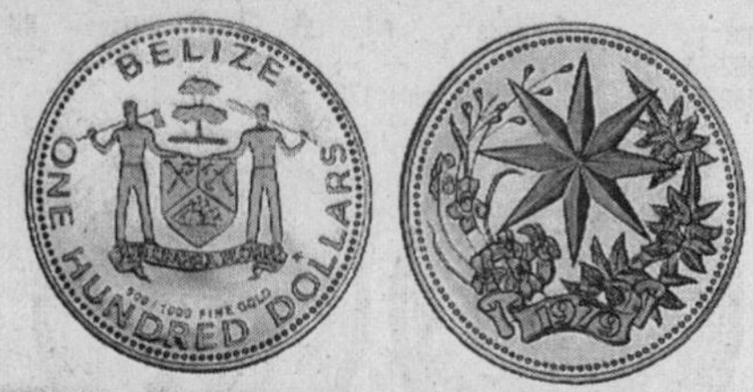

KM# 59 100 DOLLARS **Weight:** 6.4700 g. **Composition:** 0.5000 Gold .1040 oz. AGW **Reverse:** Star of Bethlehem

Date	F	VF	XF	Unc	BU
1979FM (U)	—	—	—	120	—
1979FM (P)	—	Value: 70.00			

KM# 62 100 DOLLARS **Weight:** 6.2100 g. **Composition:** 0.5000 Gold .0998 oz. AGW **Reverse:** Moorish idol reef fish

Date	Mintage	F	VF	XF	Unc	BU
1980FM (U)	400	—	—	—	150	—
1980FM (P)	3,993	Value: 90.00				

KM# 63 100 DOLLARS **Weight:** 6.2100 g. **Composition:** 0.5000 Gold .0998 oz. AGW **Reverse:** Orchids

Date	Mintage	F	VF	XF	Unc	BU
1980FM (U)	250	—	—	—	140	—
1980FM (P)	2,454	Value: 85.00				

KM# 67 100 DOLLARS **Weight:** 6.2100 g. **Composition:** 0.5000 Gold .0998 oz. AGW **Reverse:** Yellow swallowtail butterfly

Date	Mintage	F	VF	XF	Unc	BU
1981FM (U)	200	—	—	—	180	—
1981FM (P)	1,658	Value: 200				

KM# 68 100 DOLLARS **Weight:** 6.2100 g. **Composition:** 0.5000 Gold .0998 oz. AGW **Subject:** National independence

Date	Mintage	F	VF	XF	Unc	BU
1981FM (U)	50	—	—	—	325	—
1981FM (P)	1,401	Value: 125				

KM# 70 100 DOLLARS **Weight:** 6.2100 g. **Composition:** 0.5000 Gold .0998 oz. AGW **Reverse:** Kinkajou

Date	Mintage	F	VF	XF	Unc	BU
1982FM (U)	10	—	—	—	450	—
1982FM (P)	586	Value: 175				

KM# 73 100 DOLLARS **Weight:** 6.2100 g. **Composition:** 0.5000 Gold .0998 oz. AGW **Reverse:** Margay jungle cat

Date	Mintage	F	VF	XF	Unc	BU
1983FM (U)	20	—	—	—	400	—
1983FM (P)	494	Value: 200				

KM# 74 100 DOLLARS **Weight:** 6.2100 g. **Composition:** 0.5000 Gold .0998 oz. AGW **Reverse:** White-tailed deer

Date	Mintage	F	VF	XF	Unc	BU
1984FM (P)	965	Value: 150				

KM# 76 100 DOLLARS **Weight:** 6.2100 g. **Composition:** 0.5000 Gold .0998 oz. AGW **Reverse:** Ocelot

Date	Mintage	F	VF	XF	Unc	BU
1985FM (P) Proof	899	Value: 220				

KM# 103 100 DOLLARS **Weight:** 15.9760 g. **Composition:** 0.9170 Gold .4708 oz. AGW **Subject:** 10th Anniversary of Independence **Note:** Similar to 10 Dollars, KM#102.

Date	Mintage	F	VF	XF	Unc	BU
1991 Proof	Est. 500	Value: 550				

KM# 112 100 DOLLARS **Weight:** 15.6000 g. **Composition:** 0.9990 Gold .5016 oz. AGW **Subject:** 50th Anniversary - Battle of El Alamein **Obverse:** Portrait of Queen Elizabeth II **Reverse:** Infantry advancing

Date	Mintage	F	VF	XF	Unc	BU
1992 Proof	Est. 500	Value: 500				

KM# 129 100 DOLLARS **Weight:** 15.9700 g. **Composition:** 0.9170 Gold .4707 oz. AGW **Subject:** Battle of St. George's Caye **Note:** Similar to KM#128.

Date		F	VF	XF	Unc	BU
ND(1998) Proof	—	Value: 675				

KM# 56 250 DOLLARS **Weight:** 8.8100 g. **Composition:** 0.9000 Gold .2549 oz. AGW **Reverse:** Jaguar

Date	Mintage	F	VF	XF	Unc	BU
1978FM (U)	—	—	—	—	225	—
1978FM (P)	Est. 3,399	Value: 235				

Note: 1,712 pieces were used in first-day covers

KM# 98 250 DOLLARS **Weight:** 15.9800 g. **Composition:** 0.9170 Gold .4708 oz. AGW **Subject:** 500th Anniversary of Columbus discovery of America

Date	Mintage	F	VF	XF	Unc	BU
1989 Proof	Est. 500	Value: 375				

KM# 105 250 DOLLARS **Weight:** 15.9800 g. **Composition:** 0.9170 Gold .4708 oz. AGW **Subject:** 10th Anniversary of Central Bank **Reverse:** Jabiru stork **Note:** Similar to KM#104.

Date	Mintage	F	VF	XF	Unc	BU
1992	Est. 500	Value: 375				

KM# 113 250 DOLLARS **Weight:** 31.2100 g. **Composition:** 0.9990 Gold 1.0035 oz. AGW **Subject:** 50th Anniversary - Battle of El Alamein **Obverse:** Portrait of Queen Elizabeth II **Reverse:** Lt. Gen. Montgomery

Date	Mintage	F	VF	XF	Unc	BU
1992 Proof	Est. 500	Value: 750				

KM# 101 500 DOLLARS **Weight:** 47.5400 g. **Composition:** 0.9170 Gold 1.4018 oz. AGW **Subject:** Royal visit **Note:** Similar to KM#78.

Date	Mintage	F	VF	XF	Unc	BU
1985 Proof	Est. 250	Value: 1,000				

KM# 120 500 DOLLARS **Weight:** 47.5400 g. **Composition:** 0.9170 Gold 1.4018 oz. AGW **Subject:** 40th Anniversary - Coronation of Queen Elizabeth II

Date	Mintage	F	VF	XF	Unc	BU
1993 Proof	Est. 100	Value: 1,150				

KM# 122 500 DOLLARS **Weight:** 47.5400 g. **Composition:** 0.9170 Gold 1.4018 oz. AGW **Subject:** Royal visit **Reverse:** Cameo portraits

Date		F	VF	XF	Unc	BU
1994 Proof	—	Value: 1,150				

PIEFORTS

KM#	Date	Mintage	Identification	Mkt Val
P1	1990	1,000	Dollar. 0.9250 Silver. KM99a.	60.00

MINT SETS

KM#	Date	Mintage	Identification	Issue Price	Mkt Val
MS1	1974 (8)	4,506	KM38-45	20.00	20.00
MS2	1975 (8)	1,095	KM43-50	27.50	30.00
MS4	1977 (8)	—	KM43-45, 46b -47b, 48-50	27.50	30.00
MS3	1976 (8)	759	KM43-50	27.50	32.00
MS5	1978 (8)	458	KM43-45, 46b-47b, 48-50	28.50	32.00
MS6	1979 (8)	808	KM43-44, 46b-47b, 48-50, 57	28.50	32.00
MS7	1980 (8)	761	KM43-44, 46b-47b, 48-50, 60	29.50	40.00
MS8	1981 (8)	297	KM43-44, 46b-47b, 48-50, 65	29.50	60.00
MS9	1982 (8)	—	KM69, 83-89	29.50	60.00
MS10	1983 (8)	—	KM71, 83-89	29.50	65.00
MS11	1984 (8)	—	KM75, 90-96	—	75.00
MS12	1992 (6)	—	KM33a, 34a, 35-37, 99	24.00	24.00

PROOF SETS

KM#	Date	Mintage	Identification	Issue Price	Mkt Val
PS2	1974 (8)	31,368	KM38a-45a	100	40.00
PS1	1974 (8)	21,470	KM38-45	35.00	18.00
PS4	1975 (8)	13,275	KM43a-50a	110	40.00
PS3	1975 (8)	8,794	KM43-50	37.50	22.00
PS6	1976 (8)	5,897	KM43a-50a	110	45.00
PS5	1976 (8)	4,893	KM43-50	37.50	25.00
PS8	1977 (8)	3,197	KM43a-50a	110	47.50
PS7	1977 (8)	2,107	KM43-45, 46b-47b, 48-50	37.50	30.00
PS10	1978 (8)	3,342	KM43a-50a	110	47.50
PS9	1978 (8)	1,671	KM43-45, 46b, 47b, 48-50	39.50	30.00
PS11	1979 (8)	1,287	KM43-44, 46b-47b, 48-50, 57	41.50	35.00
PS12	1979 (8)	2,445	KM43a-44a, 46a-50a, 57a	112	70.00
PS14	1980 (8)	1,826	KM43a-44a, 46a-50a, 60a	222	80.00
PS13	1980 (8)	920	KM43-44, 46b-47b, 48-50, 60	41.50	40.00
PS15	1981 (8)	643	KM43-44, 46b-47b, 48-50, 65	41.50	60.00
PS16	1981 (8)	615	KM43a-44a, 46a-50a, 65a	—	115
PS18	1982 (8)	381	KM69a, 83a-89a	222	285
PS17	1982 (8)	—	KM69, 83-89	49.50	75.00
PS20	1983 (8)	241	KM71a, 83a-89a	197	300
PS19	1983 (8)	306	KM71, 83-89	37.00	70.00
PS21	1984 (8)	—	KM75, 90-96	37.00	65.00
PS22	1984 (8)	397	KM75a, 90a-96a	197	280
PS23	1985 (8)	212	KM75a, 90a-96a	—	325
PS24	1992 (4)	500	KM110-113	1,600	1,600
PS25	1992 (2)	—	KM107-108	100	100

BENIN (Dahomey)

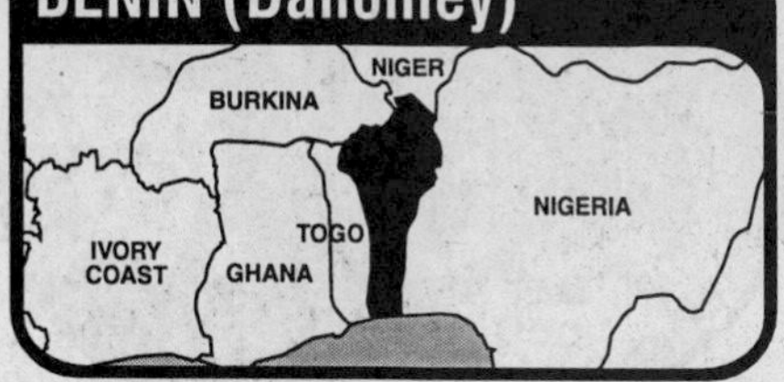

The Republic of Benin (formerly the Republic of Dahomey), located on the south side of the African bulge between Togo and Nigeria, has an area of 43,500 sq. mi. (112,620 sq. km.) and a population of 5.5 million. Capital: Porto-Novo. The principal industry of Benin, one of the poorest countries of West Africa, is the processing of palm oil products. Palm kernel oil, peanuts, cotton, and coffee are exported.

PEOPLES REPUBLIC

STANDARD COINAGE

KM# 10 200 FRANCS Composition: Copper **Reverse:** Sailing ship - Preussen

Date	Mintage	F	VF	XF	Unc	BU
1993	—	—	—	—	7.50	—
1993 Proof	100	Value: 55.00				

KM# 8 200 FRANCS Composition: Copper-Nickel **Series:** Prehistoric Animals **Reverse:** Dinosaurs - Acanthopholis

Date		F	VF	XF	Unc	BU
1994		—	—	—	20.00	—

KM# 15 200 FRANCS Composition: Copper **Series:** Prehistoric Animals **Reverse:** Dinosaurs - Tyrannosaurus Rex

Date	Mintage	F	VF	XF	Unc	BU
1994	—	—	—	—	15.00	—
1994 Proof	100	Value: 55.00				

KM# 16 200 FRANCS Composition: Copper-Nickel **Subject:** United Nations - 50 Years **Reverse:** Family in boat

Date	F	VF	XF	Unc	BU
ND(1995)	—	—	—	8.50	—

KM# 17 200 FRANCS Composition: Nickel-Bonded Steel And Enamel **Reverse:** WWI Austrian Hansa - Brandenburg D. I

Date	Mintage	F	VF	XF	Unc	BU
1995	25,000	—	—	—	30.00	—

KM# 23 200 FRANCS Composition: Copper **Series:** Prehistoric Animals **Obverse:** National arms **Reverse:** Iguanodon

Date	Mintage	F	VF	XF	Unc	BU
1995 Proof	100	Value: 65.00				

KM# 25 200 FRANCS Composition: Copper-Nickel **Series:** Sydney 2000 **Obverse:** National arms **Reverse:** Classic sculpture and racing scullcraft

Date	Mintage	F	VF	XF	Unc	BU
1999	10,000	—	—	—	7.50	—

KM# 3 500 FRANCS Weight: 12.0000 g. **Composition:** 0.9990 Silver .3858 oz. ASW **Subject:** 1992 World Cup Soccer **Reverse:** Soccer goalie

Date		F	VF	XF	Unc	BU
1992		—	—	—	45.00	—

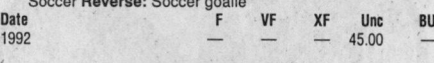

KM# 14 500 FRANCS Weight: 8.2500 g. **Composition:** 0.9990 Silver .2650 oz. ASW **Reverse:** Soccer - Eifel Tower, flag and ball **Edge Lettering:** 1995 World Cup Soccer

Date	Mintage	F	VF	XF	Unc	BU
1995 Proof	30,000	Value: 22.50				

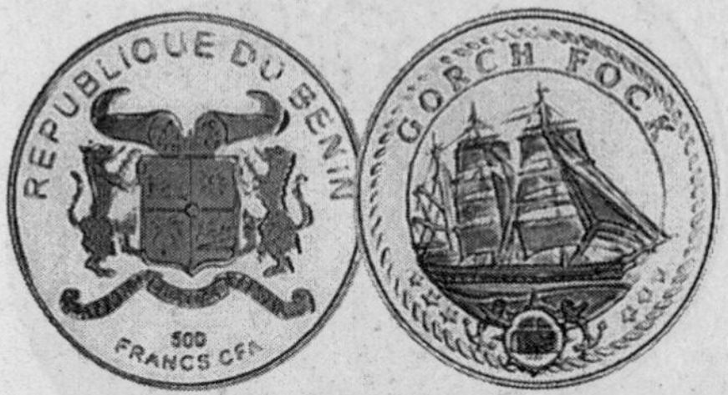

KM# 31 500 FRANCS Weight: 8.2500 g. **Composition:** 0.9990 Silver .2650 oz. ASW **Obverse:** National arms **Reverse:** Sailing ship, Gorch Fock **Edge:** Plain **Size:** 30.1 mm.

Date	Mintage	F	VF	XF	Unc	BU
1996 Proof	10,000	Value: 22.50				

KM# 2 1000 FRANCS Weight: 19.9100 g. **Composition:** 0.9990 Silver .6402 oz. ASW **Reverse:** National map in radiant sun.

Date	Mintage	F	VF	XF	Unc	BU
ND(1992) Proof	1,000	Value: 37.50				

KM# 4 1000 FRANCS Weight: 20.0000 g. **Composition:** 0.9990 Silver .6430 oz. ASW **Series:** Olympics **Reverse:** Gymnast

Date	Mintage	F	VF	XF	Unc	BU
1992 Proof	Est. 5,000	Value: 28.00				

KM# 5 1000 FRANCS Weight: 20.0000 g. **Composition:** 0.9990 Silver .6430 oz. ASW **Subject:** 1992 World Cup Soccer **Reverse:** Player kicking ball

Date	Mintage	F	VF	XF	Unc	BU
1992 Proof	Est. 10,000	Value: 35.00				

KM# 1 1000 FRANCS **Weight:** 19.9100 g. **Composition:** 0.9990 Silver .6402 oz. ASW **Note:** Five hands holding jar

Date	Mintage	F	VF	XF	Unc	BU
ND(1992) Proof	1,000	Value: 38.00				

KM# 6 1000 FRANCS **Weight:** 20.0000 g. **Composition:** 0.9990 Silver .6430 oz. ASW **Subject:** Protection of Nature **Reverse:** Elephant

Date	F	VF	XF	Unc	BU
1993 Proof	—	Value: 60.00			

KM# 7 1000 FRANCS **Weight:** 20.0000 g. **Composition:** 0.9990 Silver .6430 oz. ASW **Reverse:** Sailing ship - Preussen

Date	Mintage	F	VF	XF	Unc	BU
1993	100	—	—	—	125	—
1993 Proof	—	Value: 32.50				

KM# 27 1000 FRANCS **Weight:** 20.0000 g. **Composition:** 0.9990 Silver .6430 oz. ASW **Series:** Protection of Nature **Reverse:** Elephant

Date	F	VF	XF	Unc	BU
1993 Proof	—	Value: 35.00			

KM# 9 1000 FRANCS **Weight:** 15.8600 g. **Composition:** 0.9940 Silver .5095 oz. ASW **Series:** Dinosaurs **Reverse:** Tyrannosaurus Rex

Date	F	VF	XF	Unc	BU
1994 Proof	—	Value: 50.00			

KM# 12 1000 FRANCS **Weight:** 20.0000 g. **Composition:** 0.9990 Silver .6424 oz. ASW **Series:** 1996 Olympics **Reverse:** Three runners

Date	Mintage	F	VF	XF	Unc	BU
1995 Proof	15,000	Value: 28.00				

KM# 13 1000 FRANCS **Weight:** 20.0000 g. **Composition:** 0.9990 Silver .6424 oz. ASW **Subject:** 32 Years of Independence

Date	Mintage	F	VF	XF	Unc	BU
1995 Proof	2,000	Value: 35.00				

KM# 18 1000 FRANCS **Weight:** 20.0000 g. **Composition:** 0.9990 Silver .6424 oz. ASW **Reverse:** WWI Austrian Hansa - Brandenburg D. I

Date	Mintage	F	VF	XF	Unc	BU
1995 Proof	15,000	Value: 45.00				

KM# 28 1000 FRANCS **Weight:** 20.0000 g. **Composition:** 0.9990 Silver .6424 oz. ASW **Series:** Prehistoric Animals **Reverse:** Iguanodon **Edge:** Plain

Date	F	VF	XF	Unc	BU
1995 Proof	—	Value: 35.00			

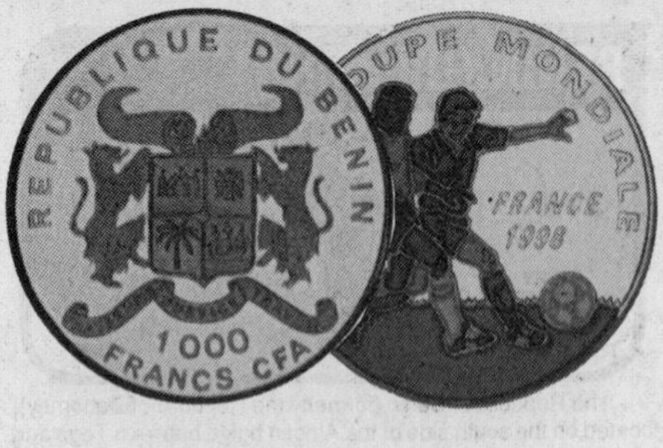

KM# 20 1000 FRANCS **Weight:** 15.0000 g. **Composition:** 0.9990 Silver .4817 oz. ASW **Subject:** 1996 World Cup Soccer **Obverse:** National arms **Reverse:** Two multi-colored soccer players

Date	F	VF	XF	Unc	BU
1996 Proof	—	Value: 45.00			

KM# 19 1000 FRANCS **Weight:** 20.0000 g. **Composition:** 0.9990 Silver .6424 oz. ASW **Note:** Multi-colored panther.

Date	F	VF	XF	Unc	BU
1996 Proof	—	Value: 60.00			

KM# 21 1000 FRANCS **Weight:** 15.0000 g. **Composition:** 0.9990 Silver .4817 oz. ASW **Series:** 2000 Summer Olympics **Obverse:** National arms **Reverse:** Multi-colored shot-putter and Olympic torch

Date	Mintage	F	VF	XF	Unc	BU
1997	100	—	—	—	110	—
1997 Proof	—	Value: 40.00				

KM# 24 1000 FRANCS **Weight:** 20.0000 g. **Composition:** 0.9990 Silver .6430 oz. ASW **Series:** 2000 Summer Olympics **Obverse:** National arms **Reverse:** Two runners and statue

Date	Mintage	F	VF	XF	Unc	BU
1997	—	—	—	—	75.00	—
1997 Proof	7,500	Value: 32.50				

KM# 39 1000 FRANCS **Weight:** 14.9600 g. **Composition:** 0.9990 Silver 0.4805 oz. ASW **Subject:** Gutenberg **Obverse:** National arms **Reverse:** Portrait and printing press **Edge:** Plain **Size:** 34.9 mm.

Date	F	VF	XF	Unc	BU
1999 Proof	—	Value: 30.00			

KM# 26 1000 FRANCS **Weight:** 20.1300 g. **Composition:** 0.9990 Silver .6465 oz. ASW **Series:** 2000 Summer Olympics **Obverse:** National arms **Reverse:** Classic statue and racing scullcraft

Date	Mintage	F	VF	XF	Unc	BU
1999 Proof	5,000	Value: 35.00				

KM# 37 1000 FRANCS **Weight:** 14.9500 g. **Composition:** 0.9990 Silver .4802 oz. ASW **Subject:** Leif Ericksson **Obverse:** National arms **Reverse:** Head of Eriksson at left, Viking ship at right **Edge:** Plain **Size:** 35 mm.

Date	F	VF	XF	Unc	BU
2001 Proof	—	Value: 28.00			

KM# 38 1000 FRANCS **Weight:** 20.0000 g. **Composition:** 0.9990 Silver 0.6424 oz. ASW **Subject:** Endangered Species **Obverse:** National arms **Reverse:** Two zebras grazing **Edge:** Reeded **Size:** 37.9 mm.

Date	F	VF	XF	Unc	BU
2001 Proof	—	Value: 40.00			

KM# 11 6000 FRANCS **Weight:** 20.1300 g. **Composition:** 0.9990 Silver .6465 oz. ASW **Series:** Protection of Nature **Reverse:** Elephant

Date	F	VF	XF	Unc	BU
1993 Proof	—	Value: 60.00			

KM# 22 6000 FRANCS **Weight:** 28.3400 g. **Composition:** 0.9250 Silver .8248 oz. ASW **Subject:** 50th Anniversary U.N. **Obverse:** National arms **Reverse:** Family in boat

Date	F	VF	XF	Unc	BU
ND(1995) Proof	—	Value: 42.50			

KM# 34 15000 FRANCS **Weight:** 500.0000 g. **Composition:** 0.9990 Silver 16.0593 oz. ASW **Subject:** Wildlife Protection **Obverse:** National arms **Reverse:** Multi-colored crocodile **Edge:** Reeded **Size:** 84.8 mm. **Note:** Illustration reduced.

Date	F	VF	XF	Unc	BU
1996 Proof	—	Value: 450			

KM# 36 20000 FRANCS **Weight:** 846.0152 g. **Composition:** 0.9990 Silver 27.2 oz. ASW **Subject:** African Fauna **Obverse:** National arms **Reverse:** Multi-colored zebra **Edge:** Plain **Size:** 90.4 mm. **Note:** Illustration reduced.

Date	F	VF	XF	Unc	BU
1997 Proof	—	Value: 700			

KM# 29 30000 FRANCS **Weight:** 15.5500 g. **Composition:** 0.9990 Gold .4494 oz. AGW **Obverse:** National arms **Reverse:** Map in radiant sun **Edge:** Reeded

Date	Mintage	F	VF	XF	Unc	BU
ND(1992) Proof	Est. 100	Value: 450				

KM# 30 100000 FRANCS **Weight:** 31.1035 g. **Composition:** 0.9990 Gold 1.0000 oz. AGW **Obverse:** National arms **Reverse:** President **Edge:** Reeded

Date	Mintage	F	VF	XF	Unc	BU
1992 Rare	Est. 10	Value: 950				

PIEFORTS

KM#	Date	Mintage	Identification	Mkt Val
P1	1997	—	1000 Francs. KM#21	135
P2	1997	—	1000 Francs. KM#24.	125
P3	1999	—	1000 Francs. KM#26.	85.00

BERMUDA

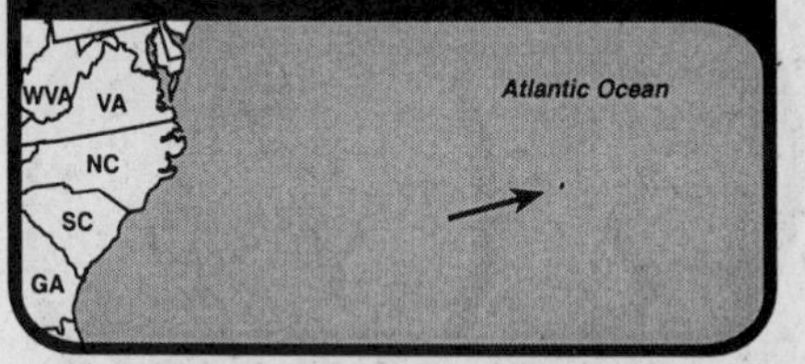

The Parliamentary British Colony of Bermuda, situated in the western Atlantic Ocean 660 miles (1,062 km.) east of North Carolina, has an area of 20.6 sq. mi. (53 sq. km.) and a population of 61,600. Capital: Hamilton. Concentrated essences, beauty preparations, and cut flowers are exported. Most Bermudians derive their livelihood from tourism. The British monarch is the head of state and is represented by a governor.

Bermuda was discovered by Juan de Bermudez, a Spanish navigator, in about 1503. British influence dates from 1609 when a group of Virginia-bound British colonists under the command of Sir George Somers was shipwrecked on the islands for 10 months. The islands were settled in 1612 by 60 British colonists from the Virginia Colony and became a crown colony in 1684. The earliest coins issued for the island were the "Hogge Money" series of 2, 3, 6 and 12 pence, the name derived from the pig in the obverse design, a recognition of the quantity of such animals then found there. The next issue for Bermuda was the Birmingham coppers of 1793; all locally circulating coinage was demonetized in 1842, when the currency of the United Kingdom became standard. Internal autonomy was obtained by the constitution of June 8, 1968.

In February, 1970, Bermuda converted from its former currency, which was sterling, to a decimal currency, the dollar unit which is equal to one U.S. dollar. On July 31, 1972, Bermuda severed its monetary link with the British pound sterling and pegged its dollar to be the same gold value as the U.S. dollar.

RULERS

British

MINT MARKS

CHI - Valcambi, Switzerland

FM - Franklin Mint, U.S.A.*

***NOTE**: From 1975-1985 the Franklin Mint produced coinage in up to 3 different qualities. Qualities of issue are designated in ( ) after each date and are defined as follows:

(M) MATTE - Normal circulation strike or a dull finish produced by sandblasting special uncirculated (polish finish) or proof quality dies.

(U) SPECIAL UNCIRCUALTED - Polished or proof-like in appearance without any frosted features.

(P) PROOF - The highest quality obtainable having mirror-like fields and frosted features.

MONETARY SYSTEM

12 Pence = 1 Shilling

20 Shillings = 1 Pound

BRITISH ADMINISTRATION

POUND STERLING COINAGE

KM# 13 CROWN **Weight:** 28.2800 g. **Composition:** 0.9250 Silver .8411 oz. ASW **Subject:** 350th Anniversary - Colony Founding

Date	Mintage	F	VF	XF	Unc	BU
1959	100,000	BV	5.00	7.00	12.50	—
1959 Matte proof	—	Value: 1,000				

Note: Mintage: 6-10

KM# 14 CROWN Weight: 22.6200 g. **Composition:** 0.5000 Silver .3636 oz. ASW

Date	Mintage	F	VF	XF	Unc	BU
1964	470,000	—	—	BV	5.00	—
1964 Proof	30,000	Value: 7.50				

DECIMAL COINAGE

100 Cents = 1 Dollar

KM# 15 CENT Composition: Bronze **Reverse:** Wild boar

Date	Mintage	F	VF	XF	Unc	BU
1970	5,500,000	—	—	0.10	0.20	—
1970 Proof	11,000	Value: 0.50				
1971	4,256,000	—	—	0.10	0.20	—
1973	2,144,000	—	—	0.10	0.20	—
1974	856,000	—	—	0.10	0.25	—
1975	1,000,000	—	—	0.10	0.20	—
1976	1,000,000	—	—	0.10	0.20	—
1977	2,000,000	—	—	0.10	0.20	—
1978	3,160,000	—	—	0.10	0.20	—
1980	3,520,000	—	—	0.10	0.20	—
1981	3,200,000	—	—	0.10	0.20	—
1982	320,000	—	—	0.10	0.20	—
1983	800,000	—	—	0.10	0.20	—
1983 Proof	10,000	Value: 1.00				
1984	800,000	—	—	0.10	0.20	—
1985	—	—	—	0.10	0.20	—

KM# 44 CENT Composition: Bronze **Reverse:** Wild boar

Date	Mintage	F	VF	XF	Unc	BU
1986	960,000	—	—	0.10	0.20	—
1986 Proof	Inc. above	Value: 2.00				
1987	—	—	—	0.10	0.20	—
1988	—	—	—	0.10	0.20	—
1990	—	—	—	0.10	0.20	—
1991	—	—	—	0.10	0.20	—

KM# 44a CENT Composition: Steel **Reverse:** Wild boar **Note:** Copper coated.

Date	F	VF	XF	Unc	BU
1988	—	—	—	2.50	—

KM# 44b CENT Composition: Copper Plated Zinc **Reverse:** Wild boar

Date	F	VF	XF	Unc	BU
1991	—	—	0.10	0.20	—
1993	—	—	0.10	0.20	—
1994	—	—	0.10	0.20	—
1995	—	—	0.10	0.20	—
1996	—	—	0.10	0.20	—
1997	—	—	0.10	0.20	—

KM# 44c CENT Weight: 3.7000 g. **Composition:** 0.9250 Silver .11 oz. ASW **Reverse:** Wild boar **Note:** In sets only.

Date	Mintage	F	VF	XF	Unc	BU
1995	2,000	—	—	—	4.00	—

KM# 44d CENT Weight: 6.2000 g. **Composition:** 0.9170 Gold .1827 oz. AGW **Reverse:** Wild boar **Note:** In sets only.

Date	Mintage	F	VF	XF	Unc	BU
1995	500	—	—	—	135	—

KM# 107 CENT Composition: Copper Plated Zinc **Obverse:** Queen's portrait **Obv. Designer:** Rank-Broadley **Reverse:** Wild boar

Date	Mintage	F	VF	XF	Unc	BU
1999		—	—	—	0.50	—
1999 Proof	2,500	Value: 2.50				
2000		—	—	—	0.50	—
2000 Proof	—	Value: 2.50				

KM# 16 5 CENTS Composition: Copper-Nickel **Reverse:** Queen angel fish

Date	Mintage	F	VF	XF	Unc	BU
1970	2,190,000	—	0.10	0.15	0.35	—
1970 Proof	11,000	Value: 0.50				
1974	310,000	—	0.10	0.15	0.35	—
1975	500,000	—	0.10	0.15	0.35	—
1977	500,000	—	0.10	0.15	0.35	—
1979	500,000	—	0.10	0.15	0.35	—
1980	1,100,000	—	0.10	0.15	0.35	—
1981	900,000	—	0.10	0.15	0.35	—
1982	200,000	—	0.10	0.15	0.35	—
1983	800,000	—	0.10	0.15	0.35	—
1983 Proof	10,000	Value: 1.50				
1984	500,000	—	0.10	0.15	0.35	—
1985	—	—	0.10	0.15	0.35	—

KM# 45 5 CENTS Composition: Copper-Nickel **Reverse:** Queen angel fish

Date	Mintage	F	VF	XF	Unc	BU
1986	700,000	—	0.10	0.15	0.35	—
1986 Proof	Inc. above	Value: 2.50				
1987	—	—	0.10	0.15	0.35	—
1988	—	—	0.10	0.15	0.35	—
1990	—	—	0.10	0.15	0.35	—
1993	—	—	0.10	0.15	0.35	—
1994	—	—	0.10	0.15	0.35	—
1995	—	—	0.10	0.15	0.35	—
1996	—	—	—	—	—	—
1997	—	—	0.10	0.15	0.35	—

KM# 45a 5 CENTS Weight: 5.7000 g. **Composition:** 0.9250 Silver .1695 oz. ASW **Reverse:** Queen angel fish **Note:** In sets only.

Date	Mintage	F	VF	XF	Unc	BU
1995	2,000	—	—	—	8.00	—

KM# 45b 5 CENTS Weight: 5.7000 g. **Composition:** 0.9170 Gold .2859 oz. AGW **Reverse:** Queen angel fish **Note:** In sets only.

Date	Mintage	F	VF	XF	Unc	BU
1995	500	—	—	—	200	—

KM# 108 5 CENTS Composition: Copper-Nickel **Obverse:** Queen's portrait **Obv. Designer:** Rank-Broadley **Reverse:** Queen angel fish

Date	Mintage	F	VF	XF	Unc	BU
1999		—	—	—	0.75	—
1999 Proof	2,500	Value: 3.50				
2000		—	—	—	0.75	—
2000 Proof	—	Value: 3.50				

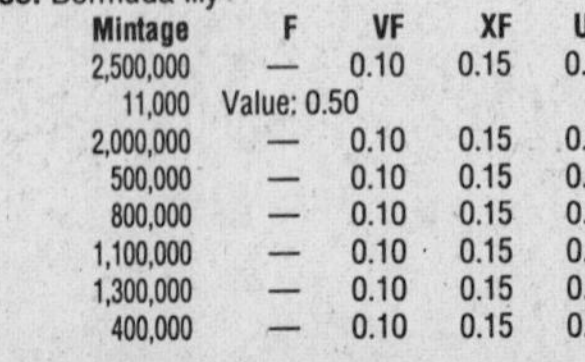

KM# 17 10 CENTS Composition: Copper-Nickel **Reverse:** Bermuda lily

Date	Mintage	F	VF	XF	Unc	BU
1970	2,500,000	—	0.10	0.15	0.35	—
1970 Proof	11,000	Value: 0.50				
1971	2,000,000	—	0.10	0.15	0.35	—
1978	500,000	—	0.10	0.15	0.40	—
1979	800,000	—	0.10	0.15	0.40	—
1980	1,100,000	—	0.10	0.15	0.35	—
1981	1,300,000	—	0.10	0.15	0.35	—
1982	400,000	—	0.10	0.15	0.40	—
1983	1,000,000	—	0.10	0.15	0.35	—
1983 Proof	10,000	Value: 2.00				
1984	500,000	—	0.10	0.15	0.40	—
1985	—	—	0.10	0.15	0.40	—

KM# 46 10 CENTS Composition: Copper-Nickel **Reverse:** Bermuda lily

Date	Mintage	F	VF	XF	Unc	BU
1986	350,000	—	0.10	0.15	0.40	—
1986 Proof	Inc. above	Value: 3.50				
1987	—	—	0.10	0.15	0.40	—
1988	—	—	0.10	0.15	0.40	—
1990	—	—	0.10	0.15	0.40	—
1993	—	—	0.10	0.15	0.40	—
1994	—	—	0.10	0.15	0.40	—
1995	—	—	0.10	0.15	0.40	—
1996	—	—	0.10	0.15	0.40	—
1997	—	—	0.10	0.15	0.40	—

KM# 46a 10 CENTS Weight: 2.8000 g. **Composition:** 0.9250 Silver .0833 oz. ASW **Reverse:** Bermuda lily **Note:** In sets only.

Date	Mintage	F	VF	XF	Unc	BU
1995	2,000	—	—	—	10.00	—

KM# 46b 10 CENTS Weight: 4.7500 g. **Composition:** 0.9170 Gold .14 oz. AGW **Reverse:** Bermuda lily **Note:** In sets only.

Date	Mintage	F	VF	XF	Unc	BU
1995	500	—	—	—	135	—

KM# 109 10 CENTS Composition: Copper-Nickel **Obverse:** Queen's portrait **Obv. Designer:** Rank-Broadley **Reverse:** Bermuda lily

Date	Mintage	F	VF	XF	Unc	BU
1999		—	—	—	0.85	—
1999 Proof	2,500	Value: 6.00				
2000		—	—	—	0.85	—
2000 Proof	—	Value: 6.00				

KM# 18 25 CENTS Composition: Copper-Nickel **Reverse:** Yellow-billed tropical bird

Date	Mintage	F	VF	XF	Unc	BU
1970	1,500,000	—	0.30	0.50	1.25	—
1970 Proof	11,000	Value: 2.00				
1973	1,000,000	—	0.30	0.50	1.25	—
1979	570,000	—	0.30	0.50	1.25	—
1980	1,120,000	—	0.30	0.50	1.25	—
1981	2,200,000	—	0.30	0.50	1.25	—
1982	160,000	—	0.30	0.50	1.50	—
1983	600,000	—	0.30	0.50	1.25	—
1983 Proof	10,000	Value: 2.50				
1984	400,000	—	0.30	0.50	1.25	—
1985	—	—	0.30	0.50	1.25	—

KM# 32 25 CENTS Composition: Copper-Nickel **Subject:** 375th Anniversary of Bermuda **Obverse:** Similar to KM#18 **Reverse:** Arms of the Bermudas

Date	F	VF	XF	Unc	BU
1984	—	—	1.50	4.50	—

KM# 32a 25 CENTS Weight: 5.9600 g. **Composition:** 0.9250 Silver .1772 oz. ASW **Subject:** 375th Anniversary of Bermuda **Obverse:** Similar to KM#18 **Reverse:** Arms of the Bermudas

Date	Mintage	F	VF	XF	Unc	BU
1984 Proof	1,750	Value: 18.50				

KM# 33 25 CENTS **Composition:** Copper-Nickel **Subject:** 375th Anniversary of Bermuda **Obverse:** Similar to KM#18 **Reverse:** City of Hamilton

Date	F	VF	XF	Unc	BU
1984	—	—	1.00	4.50	—

KM# 33a 25 CENTS **Weight:** 5.9600 g. **Composition:** 0.9250 Silver .1772 oz. ASW **Subject:** 375th Anniversary of Bermuda **Obverse:** Similar to KM#18 **Reverse:** City of Hamilton

Date	Mintage	F	VF	XF	Unc	BU
1984 Proof	1,750	Value: 18.50				

KM# 34 25 CENTS **Composition:** Copper-Nickel **Subject:** 375th Anniversary of Bermuda **Obverse:** Similar to KM#18 **Reverse:** Town of St. George

Date	F	VF	XF	Unc	BU
1984	—	—	1.50	4.50	—

KM# 34a 25 CENTS **Weight:** 5.9600 g. **Composition:** 0.9250 Silver .1772 oz. ASW **Subject:** 375th Anniversary of Bermuda **Obverse:** Similar to KM#18 **Reverse:** Town of St. George

Date	Mintage	F	VF	XF	Unc	BU
1984 Proof	1,750	Value: 18.50				

KM# 35 25 CENTS **Composition:** Copper-Nickel **Subject:** 375th Anniversary of Bermuda **Obverse:** Similar to KM#18 **Reverse:** Warwick Parish

Date	F	VF	XF	Unc	BU
1984	—	—	1.50	4.50	—

KM# 35a 25 CENTS **Weight:** 5.9600 g. **Composition:** 0.9250 Silver .1772 oz. ASW **Subject:** 375th Anniversary of Bermuda **Obverse:** Similar to KM#18 **Reverse:** Warwick Parish

Date	Mintage	F	VF	XF	Unc	BU
1984 Proof	1,750	Value: 18.50				

KM# 36 25 CENTS **Composition:** Copper-Nickel **Subject:** 375th Anniversary of Bermuda **Obverse:** Similar to KM#18 **Reverse:** Smith's Parish

Date	F	VF	XF	Unc	BU
1984	—	—	1.50	4.50	—

KM# 36a 25 CENTS **Weight:** 5.9600 g. **Composition:** 0.9250 Silver .1772 oz. ASW **Subject:** 375th Anniversary of Bermuda **Obverse:** Similar to KM#18 **Reverse:** Smith's Parish

Date	Mintage	F	VF	XF	Unc	BU
1984 Proof	1,750	Value: 18.50				

KM# 37 25 CENTS **Composition:** Copper-Nickel **Subject:** 375th Anniversary of Bermuda **Obverse:** Similar to KM#18 **Reverse:** Devonshire Parish

Date	F	VF	XF	Unc	BU
1984	—	—	1.50	4.50	—

KM# 37a 25 CENTS **Weight:** 5.9600 g. **Composition:** 0.9250 Silver .1772 oz. ASW **Subject:** 375th Anniversary of Bermuda **Obverse:** Similar to KM#18 **Reverse:** Devonshire Parish

Date	Mintage	F	VF	XF	Unc	BU
1984 Proof	1,750	Value: 18.50				

KM# 38 25 CENTS **Composition:** Copper-Nickel **Subject:** 375th Anniversary of Bermuda **Obverse:** Similar to KM#18 **Reverse:** Sandy's Parish

Date	F	VF	XF	Unc	BU
1984	—	—	1.50	4.50	—

KM# 38a 25 CENTS **Weight:** 5.9600 g. **Composition:** 0.9250 Silver .1772 oz. ASW **Subject:** 375th Anniversary of Bermuda **Obverse:** Similar to KM#18 **Reverse:** Sandy's Parish

Date	Mintage	F	VF	XF	Unc	BU
1984 Proof	1,750	Value: 18.50				

KM# 39 25 CENTS **Composition:** Copper-Nickel **Subject:** 375th Anniversary of Bermuda **Obverse:** Similar to KM#18 **Reverse:** Hamilton Parish

Date	F	VF	XF	Unc	BU
1984	—	—	1.50	4.50	—

KM# 39a 25 CENTS **Weight:** 5.9600 g. **Composition:** 0.9250 Silver .1772 oz. ASW **Subject:** 375th Anniversary of Bermuda **Obverse:** Similar to KM#18 **Reverse:** Hamilton Parish

Date	Mintage	F	VF	XF	Unc	BU
1984 Proof	1,750	Value: 18.50				

KM# 40 25 CENTS **Composition:** Copper-Nickel **Subject:** 375th Anniversary of Bermuda **Obverse:** Similar to KM#18 **Reverse:** Southampton Parish

Date	F	VF	XF	Unc	BU
1984	—	—	1.50	4.50	—

KM# 40a 25 CENTS **Weight:** 5.9600 g. **Composition:** 0.9250 Silver .1772 oz. ASW **Subject:** 375th Anniversary of Bermuda **Obverse:** Similar to KM#18 **Reverse:** Southampton Parish

Date	Mintage	F	VF	XF	Unc	BU
1984 Proof	1,750	Value: 18.50				

KM# 41 25 CENTS **Composition:** Copper-Nickel **Subject:** 375th Anniversary of Bermuda **Obverse:** Similar to KM#18 **Reverse:** Pembroke Parish

Date	F	VF	XF	Unc	BU
1984	—	—	1.50	4.50	—

KM# 41a 25 CENTS **Weight:** 5.9600 g. **Composition:** 0.9250 Silver .1772 oz. ASW **Subject:** 375th Anniversary of Bermuda **Obverse:** Similar to KM#18 **Reverse:** Pembroke Parish

Date	Mintage	F	VF	XF	Unc	BU
1984 Proof	1,750	Value: 18.50				

KM# 42 25 CENTS **Composition:** Copper-Nickel **Subject:** 375th Anniversary of Bermuda **Obverse:** Similar to KM#18 **Reverse:** Paget Parish

Date	F	VF	XF	Unc	BU
1984	—	—	1.50	4.50	—

KM# 42a 25 CENTS **Weight:** 5.9600 g. **Composition:** 0.9250 Silver .1772 oz. ASW **Subject:** 375th Anniversary of Bermuda **Obverse:** Similar to KM#18 **Reverse:** Paget Parish

Date	Mintage	F	VF	XF	Unc	BU
1984 Proof	1,750	Value: 18.50				

KM# 47 25 CENTS **Composition:** Copper-Nickel **Subject:** Yellow-billed tropical bird **Obverse:** Similar to KM#18 **Reverse:** Paget Parish

Date	Mintage	F	VF	XF	Unc	BU
1986	560,000	—	0.30	0.40	0.75	—
1986 Proof	Inc. above	Value: 6.00				
1987	—	—	0.30	0.40	0.75	—
1988	—	—	0.30	0.40	0.75	—
1993	—	—	0.30	0.40	0.75	—
1994	—	—	0.30	0.40	0.75	—
1995	—	—	0.30	0.40	0.75	—
1996	—	—	0.30	0.40	0.75	—
1997	—	—	0.30	0.40	0.75	—
1998	—	—	—	—	—	—

KM# 47a 25 CENTS **Weight:** 7.0000 g. **Composition:** 0.9250 Silver .2082 oz. ASW **Subject:** Yellow-billed tropical bird **Obverse:** Similar to KM#18 **Note:** In sets only.

Date	Mintage	F	VF	XF	Unc	BU
1995	2,000	—	—	—	18.00	—

KM# 47b 25 CENTS **Weight:** 11.7000 g. **Composition:** 0.9170 Gold .3448 oz. AGW **Subject:** Yellow-billed tropical bird **Obverse:** Similar to KM#18 **Note:** In sets only.

Date	Mintage	F	VF	XF	Unc	BU
1995	500	—	—	—	225	—

KM# 110 25 CENTS **Composition:** Copper-Nickel **Obverse:** Queen's portrait **Obv. Designer:** Rank-Broadley **Reverse:** Yellow-billed tropical bird

Date	Mintage	F	VF	XF	Unc	BU
1999	—	—	—	—	1.50	—
1999 Proof	2,500	Value: 12.00				
2000	—	—	—	—	1.50	—
2000 Proof	—	Value: 9.00				

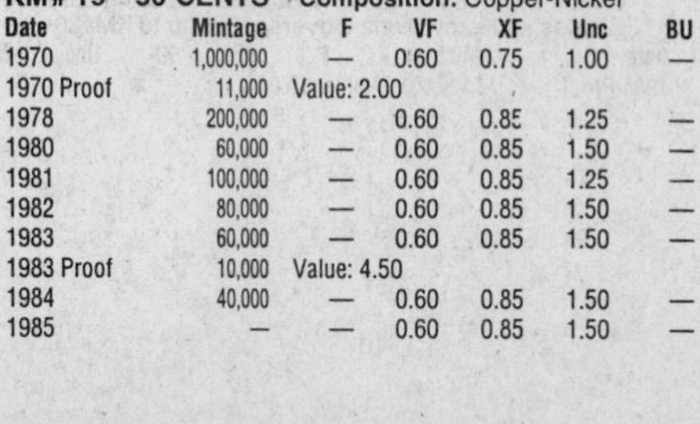

KM# 19 50 CENTS **Composition:** Copper-Nickel

Date	Mintage	F	VF	XF	Unc	BU
1970	1,000,000	—	0.60	0.75	1.00	—
1970 Proof	11,000	Value: 2.00				
1978	200,000	—	0.60	0.85	1.25	—
1980	60,000	—	0.60	0.85	1.50	—
1981	100,000	—	0.60	0.85	1.25	—
1982	80,000	—	0.60	0.85	1.50	—
1983	60,000	—	0.60	0.85	1.50	—
1983 Proof	10,000	Value: 4.50				
1984	40,000	—	0.60	0.85	1.50	—
1985	—	—	0.60	0.85	1.50	—

KM# 48 50 CENTS **Composition:** Copper-Nickel

Date	Mintage	F	VF	XF	Unc	BU
1986	60,000	—	0.60	0.85	1.50	—
1986 Proof	Inc. above	Value: 7.50				
1988	—	—	0.60	0.85	1.50	—

KM# 20 DOLLAR **Weight:** 28.2800 g. **Composition:** 0.8000 Silver .7273 oz. ASW

Date	Mintage	F	VF	XF	Unc	BU
1970 Proof	11,000	Value: 15.00				

KM# 22 DOLLAR **Weight:** 28.2800 g. **Composition:** 0.5000 Silver .4546 oz. ASW **Subject:** Silver wedding anniversary

Date	Mintage	F	VF	XF	Unc	BU
1972	75,000	—	—	—	7.50	—

KM# 22a DOLLAR **Weight:** 28.2800 g. **Composition:** 0.9250 Silver .8411 oz. ASW **Subject:** Silver wedding anniversary

Date	Mintage	F	VF	XF	Unc	BU
1972 Proof	15,000	Value: 12.00				

KM# 28 DOLLAR **Composition:** Copper-Nickel **Subject:** Wedding of Prince Charles and Lady Diana **Obverse:** Similar to KM#20

Date	Mintage	F	VF	XF	Unc	BU
1981	65,000	—	—	—	7.00	—

KM# 28a DOLLAR **Weight:** 28.2800 g. **Composition:** 0.9250 Silver .8411 oz. ASW **Subject:** Wedding of Prince Charles and Lady Diana **Obverse:** Similar to KM#20

Date	Mintage	F	VF	XF	Unc	BU
1981 Proof	17,000	Value: 15.00				

KM# 30 DOLLAR **Composition:** Nickel-Brass **Subject:** Cahow over Bermuda **Obverse:** Similar to KM#20

Date	Mintage	F	VF	XF	Unc	BU
1983	250,000	—	—	—	4.00	—
1983 Proof	10,000	Value: 7.00				

KM# 43 DOLLAR **Composition:** Copper-Nickel **Subject:** Cruise ship tourism

Date	Mintage	F	VF	XF	Unc	BU
1985	11,000	—	—	—	5.00	—

KM# 43a DOLLAR **Weight:** 28.2800 g. **Composition:** 0.9250 Silver .8411 oz. ASW **Subject:** Cruise ship tourism

Date	Mintage	F	VF	XF	Unc	BU
1985	2,500	—	—	—	25.00	—
1985 Proof	4,000	Value: 25.00				

KM# 49 DOLLAR **Composition:** Copper-Nickel **Series:** World Wildlife Fund **Reverse:** Sea turtle

Date	F	VF	XF	Unc	BU
1986	—	—	—	12.00	—

KM# 49a DOLLAR **Weight:** 28.2800 g. **Composition:** 0.9250 Silver .8411 oz. ASW **Series:** World Wildlife Fund **Reverse:** Sea turtle

Date	Mintage	F	VF	XF	Unc	BU
1986	—	—	—	—	17.50	—
1986 Proof	Est. 25,000	Value: 22.50				

KM# 50 DOLLAR **Composition:** Nickel-Brass **Obverse:** Similar to KM#43 **Reverse:** Cahow over Bermuda

Date	F	VF	XF	Unc	BU
1986 Proof	—	Value: 12.50			

KM# 52 DOLLAR **Composition:** Copper-Nickel **Subject:** 50th anniversary of commercial aviation **Reverse:** Amphibious plane

Date	F	VF	XF	Unc	BU
1987	—	—	—	7.00	—

KM# 52a DOLLAR **Weight:** 28.2800 g. **Composition:** 0.6250 Silver .8411 oz. ASW **Subject:** 50th anniversary of commercial aviation **Reverse:** Amphibious plane

Date	Mintage	F	VF	XF	Unc	BU
1987	4,000	—	—	—	20.00	—
1987 Proof	5,000	Value: 25.00				

KM# 56a DOLLAR **Weight:** 9.2000 g. **Composition:** 0.9250 Silver .2736 oz. ASW

Date	Mintage	F	VF	XF	Unc	BU
1988 Proof	Est. 3,000	Value: 25.00				
1995	—	—	—	—	40.00	—

Note: In sets only.

KM# 56 DOLLAR **Composition:** Nickel-Brass **Note:** Circulation type.

Date	Mintage	F	VF	XF	Unc	BU
1988	—	—	—	—	3.00	—
1993	15,000	—	—	—	5.00	—

Note: In sets only.

Date	Mintage	F	VF	XF	Unc	BU
1996	—	—	—	—	3.00	—
1997	—	—	—	—	3.00	—

KM# 55 DOLLAR **Composition:** Copper-Nickel **Subject:** Railroad

Date	F	VF	XF	Unc	BU
1988	—	—	—	7.00	—

KM# 55a DOLLAR **Weight:** 28.2800 g. **Composition:** 0.9250 Silver .8411 oz. ASW **Subject:** Railroad

Date	F	VF	XF	Unc	BU
1988	—	—	—	20.00	—
1988 Proof	—	Value: 30.00			

KM# 56b DOLLAR **Weight:** 15.5000 g. **Composition:** 0.9170 Gold .4568 oz. AGW

Date	Mintage	F	VF	XF	Unc	BU
1995	500	—	—	—	450	—

Note: In sets only.

KM# 61 DOLLAR **Composition:** Copper-Nickel **Subject:** Monarch Conservation Project

Date	F	VF	XF	Unc	BU
1989	—	—	—	9.00	—

KM# 61a DOLLAR **Weight:** 28.2800 g. **Composition:** 0.9250 Silver .8411 oz. ASW **Subject:** Monarch Conservation Project

Date	Mintage	F	VF	XF	Unc	BU
1989	—	—	—	—	25.00	—
1989 Proof	Est. 5,000	Value: 37.50				

KM# 67 DOLLAR **Composition:** Copper-Nickel **Subject:** Queen Mother's 90th birthday

Date	F	VF	XF	Unc	BU
1990	—	—	—	5.00	—

KM# 67a DOLLAR **Weight:** 28.2800 g. **Composition:** 0.9250 Silver .8411 oz. ASW **Subject:** Queen Mother's 90th birthday

Date	Mintage	F	VF	XF	Unc	BU
1990 Proof	1,473	Value: 50.00				

KM# 78 DOLLAR **Composition:** Bronze **Series:** Olympics **Obverse:** Portrait of Queen Elizabeth **Reverse:** Rings, similar to 5 Dollars, KM#79

Date	Mintage	F	VF	XF	Unc	BU
1992 Proof	Est. 250	Value: 35.00				

KM# 85 DOLLAR **Weight:** 31.4700 g. **Composition:** 0.9250 Silver .9359 oz. ASW **Series:** 1992 Olympics **Reverse:** Sailboats

Date	Mintage	F	VF	XF	Unc	BU
ND(1993) Proof	Est. 25,000	Value: 50.00				

KM# 91 DOLLAR **Composition:** Copper-Nickel **Subject:** International Senior Games

Date	Mintage	F	VF	XF	Unc	BU
1996	1,000	—	—	—	25.00	—

KM# 94 DOLLAR **Composition:** Copper-Nickel **Subject:** Queen Elizabeth II's 70th birthday **Obverse:** Queen's portrait **Reverse:** Horse-drawn carriage

Date	F	VF	XF	Unc	BU
ND(1996)	—	—	—	12.00	—

KM# 105 DOLLAR **Weight:** 28.2800 g. **Composition:** 0.9250 Silver .8416 oz. ASW **Series:** Olympic Games **Obverse:** Queen's portrait **Reverse:** Horse jumping

Date	F	VF	XF	Unc	BU
1996 Proof	—	Value: 50.00			

KM# 95 DOLLAR **Composition:** Copper-Nickel **Subject:** Wreck of the Sea Venture **Obverse:** Queen's portrait **Reverse:** Shipwreck from Bermudan arms **Shape:** Triangular

Date	F	VF	XF	Unc	BU
1997	—	—	—	12.00	—

KM# 119 DOLLAR **Weight:** 28.2800 g. **Composition:** 0.9250 Silver .8410 oz. ASW **Subject:** World Wildlife Fund - Conserving Nature **Obverse:** Queen's head right. **Reverse:** Bermuda Rock Skink (Eumeces longirostris) on rock. **Edge:** Reeded. **Size:** 39 mm.

Date	F	VF	XF	Unc	BU
1997 Proof	—	Value: 37.50			

KM# 104 DOLLAR **Composition:** Copper-Nickel **Obverse:** Queen's portrait **Reverse:** Ship and map **Shape:** Triangular

Date	F	VF	XF	Unc	BU
1998	—	—	—	12.00	—

KM# 111 DOLLAR **Composition:** Nickel-Brass **Obverse:** Queen's portrait **Obv. Designer:** Rank-Broadley **Reverse:** Sailboat

Date	Mintage	F	VF	XF	Unc	BU
1999	—	—	—	—	3.00	—
1999 Proof	2,500	Value: 25.00				
2000	—	—	—	—	3.00	—
2000 Proof	—	Value: 25.00				

KM# 117 DOLLAR **Weight:** 28.2800 g. **Composition:** Copper-Nickel **Subject:** Tall Ships **Obverse:** Queen's head right **Reverse:** Three-masted sailing ship **Edge:** Reeded **Size:** 38.6 mm.

Date	Mintage	F	VF	XF	Unc	BU
2000	10,000	—	—	—	15.00	—

KM# 117a DOLLAR **Weight:** 28.2800 g. **Composition:** 0.9250 Silver .8410 oz. ASW **Subject:** Tall Ships **Obverse:** Queen's head right **Reverse:** Three-masted sailing ship **Edge:** Reeded **Size:** 38.6 mm.

Date	Mintage	F	VF	XF	Unc	BU
2000 Proof	1,500	Value: 300				

KM# 64 2 DOLLARS **Weight:** 28.2800 g. **Composition:** 0.9250 Silver .8411 oz. ASW **Reverse:** Cicada insects

Date	Mintage	F	VF	XF	Unc	BU
1990 Proof	2,500	Value: 30.00				

KM# 65 2 DOLLARS **Weight:** 28.2800 g. **Composition:** 0.9250 Silver .8411 oz. ASW **Subject:** Wildlife **Reverse:** Tree frog

Date	Mintage	F	VF	XF	Unc	BU
1990 Proof	2,500	Value: 35.00				

KM# 68 2 DOLLARS **Weight:** 28.2800 g. **Composition:** 0.9250 Silver .8411 oz. ASW **Reverse:** Yellow-crowned night heron

Date	Mintage	F	VF	XF	Unc	BU
1991 Proof	Est. 2,500	Value: 27.50				

KM# 69 2 DOLLARS **Weight:** 28.2800 g. **Composition:** 0.9250 Silver .8411 oz. ASW **Reverse:** Spiny lobster

Date	Mintage	F	VF	XF	Unc	BU
1991 Proof	Est. 2,500	Value: 27.50				

KM#71 2 DOLLARS **Weight:** 28.2800 g. **Composition:** 0.9250 Silver .8411 oz. ASW **Reverse:** Bluebird feeding nestling

Date	Mintage	F	VF	XF	Unc	BU
1992 Proof	Est. 2,500	Value: 32.50				

KM#72 2 DOLLARS **Weight:** 28.2800 g. **Composition:** 0.9250 Silver .8411 oz. ASW **Reverse:** Cedar tree

Date	Mintage	F	VF	XF	Unc	BU
1992 Proof	Est. 2,500	Value: 30.00				

KM#81 2 DOLLARS **Weight:** 23.0000 g. **Composition:** 0.9250 Silver .684 oz. ASW **Subject:** 200 years of Bermudan coinage

Date	Mintage	F	VF	XF	Unc	BU
1993 Proof	5,000	Value: 35.00				

KM#83 2 DOLLARS **Weight:** 28.2800 g. **Composition:** 0.9250 Silver .8411 oz. ASW **Reverse:** Humpback whale

Date	Mintage	F	VF	XF	Unc	BU
1993 Proof	Est. 2,500	Value: 45.00				

KM#84 2 DOLLARS **Weight:** 28.2800 g. **Composition:** 0.9250 Silver .8411 oz. ASW **Reverse:** Bermuda longtail bird

Date	Mintage	F	VF	XF	Unc	BU
1993 Proof	Est. 2,500	Value: 40.00				

KM#89 2 DOLLARS **Weight:** 28.2800 g. **Composition:** 0.9250 Silver .8411 oz. ASW **Subject:** City of Hamilton's 200th anniversary **Reverse:** Ship at dock

Date	Mintage	F	VF	XF	Unc	BU
1993 Proof	250	Value: 70.00				

KM#86 2 DOLLARS **Weight:** 27.2800 g. **Composition:** 0.9250 Silver .8411 oz. ASW **Subject:** Royal visit **Reverse:** Map

Date		F	VF	XF	Unc	BU
1994 Proof	—	Value: 40.00				

KM#87 2 DOLLARS **Weight:** 28.2800 g. **Composition:** 0.9250 Silver .8411 oz. ASW **Reverse:** Long-snout seahorse

Date	Mintage	F	VF	XF	Unc	BU
1994 Proof	Est. 2,500	Value: 45.00				

KM#88 2 DOLLARS **Weight:** 28.2800 g. **Composition:** 0.9250 Silver .8411 oz. ASW **Reverse:** Lightbourn's fusinus (seashell)

Date	Mintage	F	VF	XF	Unc	BU
1994 Proof	Est. 2,500	Value: 45.00				

KM# 121 2 DOLLARS **Weight:** 28.1300 g. **Composition:** 0.9250 Silver 0.8366 oz. ASW **Subject:** Queen's golden wedding anniversary **Obverse:** Queen's portrait **Reverse:** Royal couple descending stairs with gold insert shield at right **Edge:** Reeded **Size:** 38.5 mm.

Date		F	VF	XF	Unc	BU
ND Proof	—	Value: 45.00				

KM# 116 2 DOLLARS **Weight:** 28.2800 g. **Composition:** Copper-Nickel **Subject:** Millennium **Obverse:** Queen's head right **Reverse:** Radiant sun with sailing ship dividing dates 1999-2000 above map **Edge:** Scalloped **Size:** 38.6 mm.

Date	F	VF	XF	Unc	BU
1999-2000	—	—	—	25.00	—

KM# 116a 2 DOLLARS **Weight:** 28.2800 g. **Composition:** 0.9250 Silver .8410 oz. ASW **Subject:** Millennium **Obverse:** Queen's head right **Reverse:** Radiant sun behind sailing ship dividing dates 1999-2000 above map **Edge:** Scalloped **Size:** 38.6 mm.

Date		F	VF	XF	Unc	BU
1999-2000 Proof	—	Value: 65.00				

KM#92 3 DOLLARS **Weight:** 20.0000 g. **Composition:** 0.9250 Silver .5948 oz. ASW **Subject:** Bermuda Triangle **Obverse:** Queen's portrait **Reverse:** Map, compass, capsizing ship **Note:** Similar to 60 Dollars, KM#93.

Date	Mintage	F	VF	XF	Unc	BU
1996 Proof	5,000	Value: 65.00				

KM#99 3 DOLLARS **Weight:** 20.2500 g. **Composition:** 0.9250 Silver .6022 oz. ASW **Subject:** Wreck of the Sea Venture **Obverse:** Queen's portrait **Reverse:** Ship wreck scene

Date	Mintage	F	VF	XF	Unc	BU
1997 Proof	Est. 6,500	Value: 50.00				

KM# 106 3 DOLLARS **Weight:** 20.0000 g. **Composition:** 0.9250 Silver .5948 oz. ASW **Obverse:** Queen's portrait **Reverse:** Sailing ship, map **Shape:** Triangular

Date	Mintage	F	VF	XF	Unc	BU
1998 Proof	Est. 6,500	Value: 50.00				

KM# 31 5 DOLLARS **Composition:** Nickel-Brass

Date	Mintage	F	VF	XF	Unc	BU
1983	100,000	—	—	—	6.00	—
1983 Proof	10,000	Value: 10.00				

KM# 51 5 DOLLARS **Composition:** Brass **Obverse:** Similar to Dollar, KM#43 **Reverse:** Onion superimposed over Bermuda map

Date		F	VF	XF	Unc	BU
1986 Proof	—	Value: 12.50				

KM# 54 5 DOLLARS **Weight:** 155.5150 g. **Composition:** 0.9990 Silver 5 oz. ASW **Subject:** Sea Venture wreck **Obverse:** Similar to Dollar, KM#43 **Reverse:** Sailing ship **Size:** 65 mm. **Note:** Illustration reduced.

Date	Mintage	F	VF	XF	Unc	BU
1987 Proof	Est. 20,000	Value: 75.00				

KM# 62 5 DOLLARS **Weight:** 155.5150 g. **Composition:** 0.9990 Silver 5 oz. ASW **Subject:** San Antonio **Obverse:** Portrait of Queen Elizabeth **Reverse:** Sailing ship **Size:** 65 mm. **Note:** Illustration reduced.

Date	Mintage	F	VF	XF	Unc	BU
1988 Proof	1,500	Value: 135				

KM# 79 5 DOLLARS **Weight:** 155.5150 g. **Composition:** 0.9990 Silver 5 oz. ASW **Series:** Olympics **Obverse:** Portrait of Queen Elizabeth **Reverse:** Rings **Size:** 65 mm. **Note:** Illustration reduced.

Date	Mintage	F	VF	XF	Unc	BU
1992 Proof	Est. 1,250	Value: 135				

KM# 90 5 DOLLARS **Weight:** 56.5600 g. **Composition:** 0.9250 Silver 1.6822 oz. ASW **Subject:** 375th anniversary of Bermudan Parliament

Date	Mintage	F	VF	XF	Unc	BU
1995 Proof	375	Value: 130				

KM# 120 5 DOLLARS **Weight:** 28.2800 g. **Composition:** 0.9250 Silver .8410 oz. ASW **Subject:** Gombey Dancers **Obverse:** Queen's head right **Reverse:** Multi-color costumed dancers **Edge:** Reeded **Size:** 38.6 mm.

Date	Mintage	F	VF	XF	Unc	BU
2001 Proof	3,500	Value: 65.00				

KM# 96 9 DOLLARS **Weight:** 155.5175 g. **Composition:** 0.9990 Silver 5 oz. ASW **Subject:** Bermuda Triangle **Obverse:** Queen's portrait **Reverse:** Map, compass, capsizing ship **Note:** Similar to 60 Dollars, KM#93.

Date	Mintage	F	VF	XF	Unc	BU
1996 Proof	Est. 1,000	Value: 200				

KM# 100 9 DOLLARS **Weight:** 155.5175 g. **Composition:** 0.9990 Silver 5 oz. ASW **Subject:** Wreck of the Sea Venture **Obverse:** Queen's portrait **Reverse:** Ship wreck scene **Note:** Similar to 60 Dollars, KM#102.

Date	Mintage	F	VF	XF	Unc	BU
1997 Proof	Est. 1,000	Value: 200				

KM# 112 9 DOLLARS **Weight:** 155.5200 g. **Composition:** 0.9990 Silver 4.9951 oz. ASW **Subject:** Bermuda Triangle **Obverse:** Queen's portrait **Reverse:** Map and ship, The Deliverance

Date	Mintage	F	VF	XF	Unc	BU
1998 Proof	Est. 1,000	Value: 200				

KM# 57 10 DOLLARS **Weight:** 3.1340 g. **Composition:** 0.9990 Gold .1007 oz. AGW **Subject:** Hogge money **Reverse:** Wild pig

Date	Mintage	F	VF	XF	Unc	BU
1989 Proof	500	Value: 100				

KM# 74 10 DOLLARS **Weight:** 3.1340 g. **Composition:** 0.9990 Gold .1007 oz. AGW **Subject:** Hogge money **Reverse:** Ship

Date	Mintage	F	VF	XF	Unc	BU
1990 Proof	500	Value: 100				

KM# 66 10 DOLLARS **Weight:** 3.1340 g. **Composition:** 0.9990 Gold .1007 oz. AGW **Subject:** Wildlife **Reverse:** Tree frog **Note:** Similar to 2 Dollars, KM#65.

Date	Mintage	F	VF	XF	Unc	BU
1990	1,000	—	—	—	75.00	—

KM# 70 10 DOLLARS **Weight:** 3.1340 g. **Composition:** 0.9990 Gold .1007 oz. AGW **Obverse:** Queen Elizabeth II **Reverse:** Yellow-crowned night heron

Date	Mintage	F	VF	XF	Unc	BU
1991 Proof	Est. 2,500	Value: 70.00				

KM# 73 10 DOLLARS **Weight:** 3.1340 g. **Composition:** 0.9990 Gold .1007 oz. AGW **Reverse:** Bluebird feeding nestling **Note:** Similar to KM#71.

Date	Mintage	F	VF	XF	Unc	BU
1992 Proof	Est. 2,500	Value: 70.00				

KM# 118 15 DOLLARS **Weight:** 15.9700 g. **Composition:** 0.9990 Gold .5129 oz. AGW **Subject:** Tall Ships **Obverse:** Queen's head right **Reverse:** Three-masted sailing ship **Edge:** Reeded **Size:** 28.4 mm.

Date	Mintage	F	VF	XF	Unc	BU
2000 Proof	1,500	Value: 375				

KM# 21 20 DOLLARS **Weight:** 7.9881 g. **Composition:** 0.9170 Gold .2355 oz. AGW **Reverse:** Cahow in flight

Date	Mintage	F	VF	XF	Unc	BU
1970 Proof	1,000	Value: 220				

KM# 23 25 DOLLARS **Composition:** Copper-Nickel **Subject:** Royal visit

Date	Mintage	F	VF	XF	Unc	BU
1975FM (M)	1,193	—	—	—	45.00	—
1975FM (U)	100	—	—	—	60.00	—

KM# 23a 25 DOLLARS **Weight:** 48.7000 g. **Composition:** 0.9250 Silver 1.4483 oz. ASW **Subject:** Royal visit

Date	Mintage	F	VF	XF	Unc	BU
1975FM (P) Proof	15,000	Value: 25.00				

KM# 25 25 DOLLARS **Weight:** 54.7500 g. **Composition:** 0.9250 Silver 1.6283 oz. ASW **Subject:** Queen's silver jubilee

Date	Mintage	F	VF	XF	Unc	BU
1977Chi		—	—	—	35.00	—
1977Chi Proof	11,000	Value: 40.00				
1977		—	—	—	250	—

Note: Struck at the Royal Canadian Mint

Date	Mintage	F	VF	XF	Unc	BU
1977 Proof	Est. 550	Value: 270				

Note: Struck at the Royal Canadian Mint

KM# 53 25 DOLLARS **Weight:** 31.1000 g. **Composition:** 0.9990 Palladium 1 oz. **Subject:** Sea Venture **Reverse:** Ship

Date	Mintage	F	VF	XF	Unc	BU
1987 Proof	Est. 20,000	Value: 1,000				

KM# 63 25 DOLLARS **Weight:** 31.1000 g. **Composition:** 0.9990 Palladium 1 oz. **Subject:** Ship wreck of San Antonio **Obverse:** Portrait of Queen Elizabeth

Date	Mintage	F	VF	XF	Unc	BU
1988 Proof	2,000	Value: 1,100				

KM#58 25 DOLLARS **Weight:** 7.8140 g. **Composition:** 0.9990 Gold .2512 oz. AGW **Subject:** Hogge money **Reverse:** Ship

Date	Mintage	F	VF	XF	Unc	BU
1989 Proof	500	Value: 220				

KM#75 25 DOLLARS **Weight:** 7.8140 g. **Composition:** 0.9990 Gold .2512 oz. AGW **Subject:** Hogge money **Reverse:** Wild pig

Date	Mintage	F	VF	XF	Unc	BU
1990 Proof	500	Value: 220				

KM# 97 30 DOLLARS **Weight:** 15.5518 g. **Composition:** 0.9990 Gold .5 oz. AGW **Subject:** Bermuda Triangle **Obverse:** Queen's portrait **Reverse:** Map, compass, capsizing ship **Note:** Similar to 60 Dollars, KM#93.

Date	Mintage	F	VF	XF	Unc	BU
1996 Proof	Est. 1,500	Value: 450				

KM# 101 30 DOLLARS **Weight:** 15.5518 g. **Composition:** 0.9990 Gold .5 oz. AGW **Subject:** Wreck of the Sea Venture **Obverse:** Queen's portrait **Reverse:** Ship wreck scene **Note:** Similar to 60 Dollars, KM#102.

Date	Mintage	F	VF	XF	Unc	BU
1997 Proof	Est. 1,500	Value: 450				

KM# 113 30 DOLLARS **Weight:** 15.5500 g. **Composition:** 0.9990 Gold .4994 oz. AGW **Obverse:** Queen's portrait **Reverse:** Map, ship, The Deliverance **Note:** Similar to 60 Dollars, KM#112.

Date	Mintage	F	VF	XF	Unc	BU
1998 Proof	Est. 1,500	Value: 450				

KM#26 50 DOLLARS **Weight:** 4.0500 g. **Composition:** 0.9000 Gold .1172 oz. AGW **Subject:** Queen's silver jubilee

Date	Mintage	F	VF	XF	Unc	BU
1977Chi	—	—	—	—	75.00	—
1977Chi Proof	4,070	Value: 85.00				
1977	—	—	—	—	250	—

Note: Struck at the Royal Canadian Mint

Date	Mintage	F	VF	XF	Unc	BU
1977 Proof	Est. 580	Value: 250				

Note: Struck at the Royal Canadian Mint

KM# 59 50 DOLLARS **Weight:** 15.6080 g. **Composition:** 0.9990 Gold .5018 oz. AGW **Subject:** Hogge money **Reverse:** Wild pig

Date	Mintage	F	VF	XF	Unc	BU
1989 Proof	500	Value: 250				

KM# 76 50 DOLLARS **Weight:** 15.6080 g. **Composition:** 0.9990 Gold .5018 oz. AGW **Subject:** Hogge money **Reverse:** Ship

Date	Mintage	F	VF	XF	Unc	BU
1990 Proof	500	Value: 250				

KM# 93 60 DOLLARS **Weight:** 31.4890 g. **Composition:** 0.9990 Gold 1.0124 oz. AGW **Subject:** Bermuda Triangle **Obverse:** Queen's portrait **Reverse:** Map, compass, capsizing ship

Date	Mintage	F	VF	XF	Unc	BU
1996 Proof	1,500	Value: 800				

KM# 102 60 DOLLARS **Weight:** 31.4890 g. **Composition:** 0.9990 Gold 1.0124 oz. AGW **Subject:** Wreck of the Sea Venture **Obverse:** Queen's portrait **Reverse:** Ship wreck scene

Date	Mintage	F	VF	XF	Unc	BU
1997 Proof	Est. 1,500	Value: 800				

KM# 114 60 DOLLARS **Weight:** 31.4800 g. **Composition:** 0.9990 Gold 1.0111 oz. AGW **Obverse:** Queen's portrait **Reverse:** Map, ship, The Deliverance **Shape:** Triangular

Date	Mintage	F	VF	XF	Unc	BU
1998 Proof	Est. 1,500	Value: 800				

KM# 24 100 DOLLARS **Weight:** 7.0300 g. **Composition:** 0.9000 Gold .2034 oz. AGW **Subject:** Royal visit

Date	Mintage	F	VF	XF	Unc	BU
1975FM (M)	25	—	—	—	350	—
1975FM (M)	19,000	—	—	—	95.00	—
1975FM (M) Proof	27,000	Value: 100				

KM# 27 100 DOLLARS **Weight:** 8.1000 g. **Composition:** 0.9000 Gold .2344 oz. AGW **Subject:** Queen's silver jubilee

Date	Mintage	F	VF	XF	Unc	BU
1977Chi	—	—	—	—	120	—
1977Chi Proof	5,613	Value: 135				
1977	—	—	—	—	200	—

Note: Struck at the Royal Canadian Mint

Date	Mintage	F	VF	XF	Unc	BU
1977 Proof	Est. 1,887	Value: 240				

Note: Struck at the Royal Canadian Mint

KM# 60 100 DOLLARS **Weight:** 31.2100 g. **Composition:** 0.9990 Gold 1.0035 oz. AGW **Subject:** Hogge money **Reverse:** Ship

Date	Mintage	F	VF	XF	Unc	BU
1989 Proof	500	Value: 500				

KM# 77 100 DOLLARS **Weight:** 31.2100 g. **Composition:** 0.9990 Gold 1.0035 oz. AGW **Subject:** Hogge money **Reverse:** Wild pig

Date	Mintage	F	VF	XF	Unc	BU
1990 Proof	500	Value: 500				

KM# 80 100 DOLLARS **Weight:** 47.5400 g. **Composition:** 0.9170 Gold 1.4017 oz. AGW **Series:** Olympics **Subject:** Portrait of Queen Elizabeth II **Reverse:** Rings, similar to 5 Dollars, KM#79

Date	Mintage	F	VF	XF	Unc	BU
1992 Proof	Est. 250	Value: 800				

KM# 98 180 DOLLARS **Weight:** 155.5175 g. **Composition:** 0.9990 Gold 5 oz. AGW **Subject:** Bermuda Triangle **Obverse:** Queen's portrait **Reverse:** Map, compass, capsizing ship **Note:** Similar to 60 Dollars, KM#93.

Date	Mintage	F	VF	XF	Unc	BU
1996 Proof	Est. 1,500	Value: 3,000				

KM# 103 180 DOLLARS **Weight:** 155.5175 g. **Composition:** 0.9990 Gold 5 oz. AGW **Subject:** Wreck of the Sea Venture **Obverse:** Queen's portrait **Reverse:** Ship wreck scene **Note:** Similar to 60 Dollars, KM#102.

Date	Mintage	F	VF	XF	Unc	BU
1997 Proof	Est. 99	Value: 4,000				

KM# 115 180 DOLLARS **Weight:** 155.5200 g. **Composition:** 0.9990 Gold 4.9951 oz. AGW **Obverse:** Queen's portrait **Reverse:** Map, ship, The Deliverance **Note:** Similar to 60 Dollars, KM#114.

Date	Mintage	F	VF	XF	Unc	BU
1998 Proof	Est. 99	Value: 4,000				

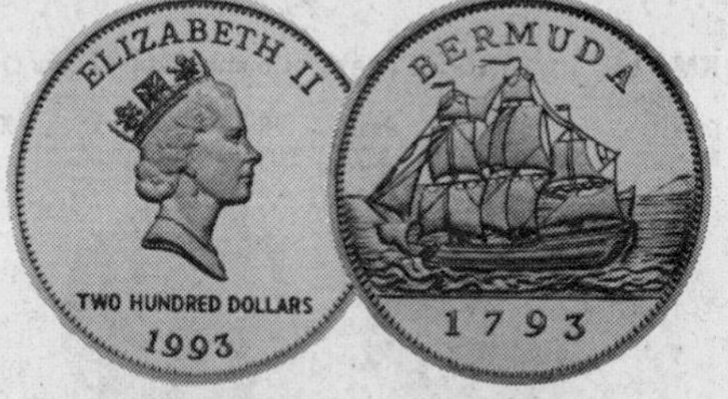

KM# 82 200 DOLLARS **Weight:** 28.5000 g. **Composition:** 0.9990 Gold .9154 oz. AGW **Subject:** 200 years - Bermudan coinage

Date	Mintage	F	VF	XF	Unc	BU
1993 Proof	200	Value: 550				

KM# 29 250 DOLLARS **Weight:** 15.9760 g. **Composition:** 0.9170 Gold .471 oz. AGW **Subject:** Wedding of Prince Charles and Lady Diana **Obverse:** Similar to 20 Dollars, KM#21

Date	Mintage	F	VF	XF	Unc	BU
1981	217	—	—	—	550	—
1981 Proof	790	Value: 400				

PIEFORTS

KM#	Date	Mintage	Identification	Issue Price	Mkt Val
P1	1981	690	250 Dollars. 31.9520 g. KM29.	920	750
P2	1988	500	Dollar. 0.9250 Silver. 16.8000 g. KM56a.	35.00	175

MINT SETS

KM#	Date	Mintage	Identification	Issue Price	Mkt Val
MS1	1970 (5)	90,000	KM15-19	3.25	4.00
MS2	1977Chi (3)	—	KM25-27	175	235
MS3	1977Chi (2)	—	KM26-27	150	200
MSA2	1977 (3)	—	KM25-27	—	685
MS4	1984 (11)	3,350	KM32-42	24.95	27.50
MS5	1993 (5)	15,000	KM44b, 45-47, 56	—	10.00
MS6	1995 (5)	2,000	KM44c, 45a-47a, 56a	100	80.00
MS7	1999 (5)	5,000	KM107-111	15.00	20.00

PROOF SETS

KM#	Date	Mintage	Identification	Issue Price	Mkt Val
PS1	1970 (6)	10,000	KM15-20	24.00	20.00
PS2	1970 (7)	1,000	KM15-21	216	280
PS3	1977Chi (3)	—	KM25-27	245	325
PS4	1977Chi (2)	—	KM26-27	210	275
PSA2	1977 (3)	—	KM25-27	—	760
PS5	1981 (3)	500	KM28a, 29, (P1), numbered set	1,500	1,050
PS6	1983 (7)	6,474	KM15-19, 30, 31	30.00	30.00
PS7	1984 (11)	1,750	KM32a-42a	250	200
PS8	1986 (7)	—	KM44-48, 50-51	50.00	50.00
PS14	1995 (5)	500	KM44d, 45b-47b, 56b	1,100	1,200
PS10	1989 (4)	500	KM57-60	1,495	1,250
PS11	1990 (4)	500	KM74-77	—	1,250
PS12	1992 (3)	250	KM78-80	1,075	1,250
PS13	1992 (2)	500	KM71-72	75.00	100
PS15	1996 (2)	1,000	KM96-97	—	700
PS16	1999 (5)	2,500	KM107-111	50.00	50.00

BHUTAN

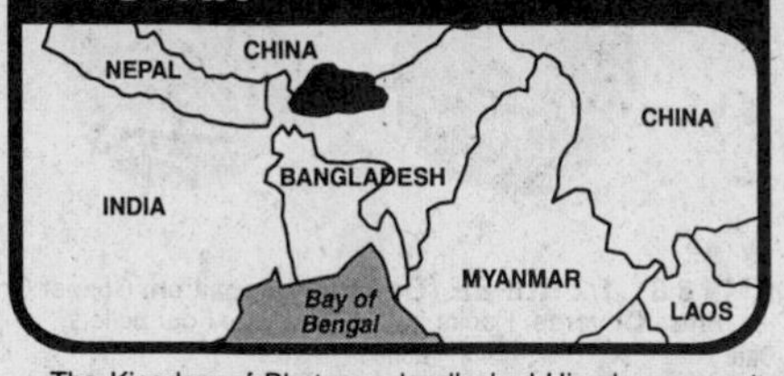

The Kingdom of Bhutan, a landlocked Himalayan country bordered by Tibet and India, has an area of 18,150 sq. mi. (47,000 sq. km.) and a population of *2.03 million. Capital: Thimphu. Virtually the entire population is engaged in agricultural and pastoral activities. Rice, wheat, barley, and yak butter are produced in sufficient quantity to make the country self-sufficient in food. The economy of Bhutan is primitive and many transactions are conducted on a barter basis.

Bhutan's early history is obscure, but is thought to have resembled that of rural medieval Europe. The country was conquered by Tibet in the 9th century, and a dual temporal and spiritual rule developed which operated until the mid-19th century, when the southern part of the country was occupied by the British and annexed to British India. Bhutan was established as a hereditary monarchy in 1907, and in 1910 agreed to British control of its external affairs. In 1949, India and Bhutan concluded a treaty whereby India assumed Britain's role in subsidizing Bhutan and guiding its foreign affairs. In 1971 Bhutan became a full member of the United Nations.

RULERS
Ugyen Wangchuck, 1907-1926
Jigme Wangchuck, 1926-1952
Jigme Dorji Wangchuck, 1952-1972
Jigme Singye Wangchuck, 1972-

KINGDOM
under British Adminstration

HAMMERED 'DUMP' COINAGE
Period III, 1835-1910AD

'Sa'

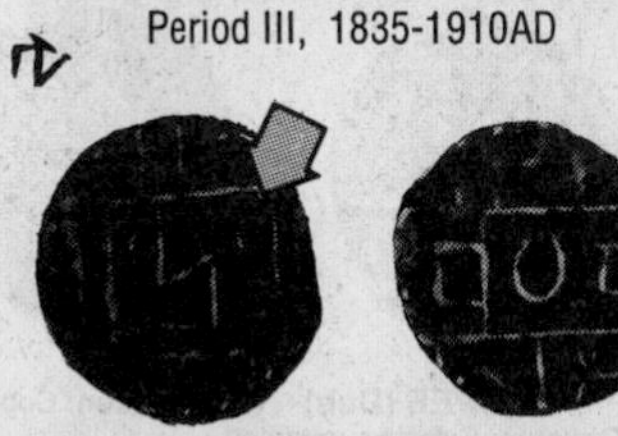

KM# A7 1/2 RUPEE (Deb) **Composition:** Copper Or Brass **Obverse:** Small "Sa" at upper right

Date	Good	VG	F	VF	XF
ND	1.00	2.25	4.50	7.50	—

'Sa'

KM# 7.1 1/2 RUPEE (Deb) **Composition:** Copper Or Brass **Obverse:** "Sa" at lower left

Date	Good	VG	F	VF	XF
ND	1.00	1.50	3.00	6.00	—

KM# 7.1a 1/2 RUPEE (Deb) **Weight:** 1.8500 g. **Composition:** Copper Or Brass **Obverse:** "Sa" at lower left **Note:** Small flan.

Date	Good	VG	F	VF	XF
ND	1.00	1.50	3.00	6.00	—

KM# 7.2 1/2 RUPEE (Deb) **Composition:** Copper Or Brass **Obverse:** Dots added

Date	Good	VG	F	VF	XF
ND	1.00	1.50	3.00	6.00	—

KM# 7.3 1/2 RUPEE (Deb) **Composition:** Copper Or Brass **Obverse:** "Sa" at upper right

Date	Good	VG	F	VF	XF
ND	1.00	1.50	3.00	6.00	—

KM# 7.4 1/2 RUPEE (Deb) **Composition:** Copper Or Brass **Obverse:** Large "Sa" below 5 pellets

Date	Good	VG	F	VF	XF
ND	1.00	1.50	3.00	6.00	—

KM# 7.5 1/2 RUPEE (Deb) **Composition:** Copper Or Brass **Obverse:** Large "Sa" below swastika

Date	Good	VG	F	VF	XF
ND	1.00	1.50	3.00	6.00	—

KM# 7.6 1/2 RUPEE (Deb) **Composition:** Copper Or Brass **Reverse:** Branch

Date	Good	VG	F	VF	XF
ND	1.00	1.50	3.00	6.00	—

KM# A8.1 1/2 RUPEE (Deb) **Composition:** Copper Or Brass **Obv. Legend:** Retrograde **Rev. Legend:** Retrograde

Date	Good	VG	F	VF	XF
ND	1.00	2.00	3.50	7.00	—

KM# A8.2 1/2 RUPEE (Deb) **Composition:** Copper Or Brass **Reverse:** Dots added

Date	Good	VG	F	VF	XF
ND	1.00	1.50	3.00	6.00	—

KM# A8.3 1/2 RUPEE (Deb) **Composition:** Copper Or Brass **Reverse:** Four pellets

Date	Good	VG	F	VF	XF
ND	1.00	1.50	3.00	6.00	—

KM# A8.4 1/2 RUPEE (Deb) **Composition:** Copper Or Brass **Obverse:** Two dots above crescent

Date	Good	VG	F	VF	XF
ND	1.00	1.50	3.00	6.00	—

KM# 8.1 1/2 RUPEE (Deb) **Composition:** Copper Or Brass **Obverse:** X above crescent

Date	Good	VG	F	VF	XF
ND	1.00	1.50	3.00	6.00	—

KM# 8.2 1/2 RUPEE (Deb) **Composition:** Copper Or Brass **Obverse:** One or two dots in center inscription

Date	Good	VG	F	VF	XF
ND	0.50	1.00	2.00	4.00	—

KM# 8.3 1/2 RUPEE (Deb) **Composition:** Copper Or Brass **Obverse:** Crescent above "*" at left

Date	Good	VG	F	VF	XF
ND	1.00	2.00	3.50	7.00	—

KM# 8.4 1/2 RUPEE (Deb) **Composition:** Copper Or Brass **Obverse:** "*" above crescent

Date	Good	VG	F	VF	XF
ND	1.00	2.00	3.50	7.00	—

KM# 8.6 1/2 RUPEE (Deb) **Composition:** Copper Or Brass **Obverse:** Low "*" at left

Date	Good	VG	F	VF	XF
ND	1.00	2.00	3.50	7.00	—

KM# 8.7 1/2 RUPEE (Deb) **Composition:** Copper Or Brass **Obverse:** Three pellets at left, low "*" at right

Date	Good	VG	F	VF	XF
ND	1.00	2.00	3.50	7.00	—

KM# 8.8 1/2 RUPEE (Deb) **Composition:** Copper Or Brass **Obverse:** Hooks added **Reverse:** Four pellets

Date	Good	VG	F	VF	XF
ND	1.00	2.00	3.50	7.00	—

KM# 8.9 1/2 RUPEE (Deb) **Composition:** Copper Or Brass **Obverse:** Two rows of pellets, high "*" at right

Date	Good	VG	F	VF	XF
ND	1.00	2.00	3.50	7.00	—

KM# 9.1 1/2 RUPEE (Deb) **Composition:** Copper Or Brass **Obverse:** Swastika

Date	Good	VG	F	VF	XF
ND	2.00	3.00	5.00	9.00	—

KM# 9.2 1/2 RUPEE (Deb) **Composition:** Copper Or Brass **Obverse:** Swastika reversed

Date	Good	VG	F	VF	XF
ND	2.00	3.00	5.00	9.00	—

KM# 10 1/2 RUPEE (Deb) **Composition:** Copper Or Brass

Date	Good	VG	F	VF	XF
ND	3.00	5.00	8.00	12.00	—

KM# 11 1/2 RUPEE (Deb) **Composition:** Copper Or Brass

Date	Good	VG	F	VF	XF
ND	3.00	5.00	8.00	12.00	—

KM# 11a 1/2 RUPEE (Deb) **Composition:** Copper Or Brass

Date	Good	VG	F	VF	XF
ND	3.00	5.00	8.00	12.00	—

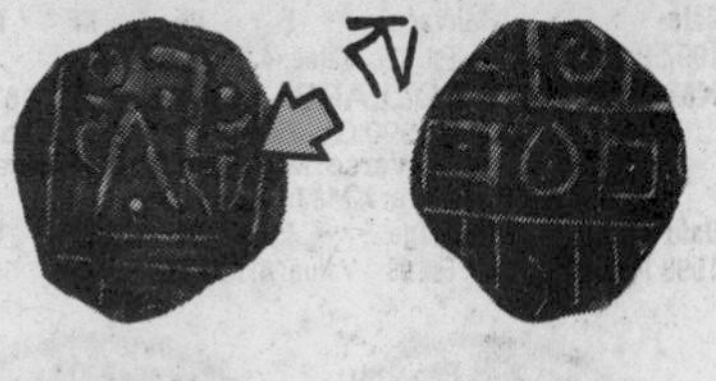

KM# 11b 1/2 RUPEE (Deb) **Composition:** Copper Or Brass

Date	Good	VG	F	VF	XF
ND	3.00	5.00	8.00	12.00	—

KM# 12 1/2 RUPEE (Deb) **Composition:** Copper Or Brass **Obverse:** Rosette **Reverse:** Swastika

Date	Good	VG	F	VF	XF
ND	3.00	5.00	8.00	12.00	—

KM# 13 1/2 RUPEE (Deb) **Composition:** Copper Or Brass **Obverse:** Rosette **Reverse:** Two fish

Date	Good	VG	F	VF	XF
ND	3.00	5.00	8.00	12.00	—

KM# 14 1/2 RUPEE (Deb) **Composition:** Copper Or Brass **Reverse:** Two fish **Note:** Varieties exist.

Date	Good	VG	F	VF	XF
ND	2.00	3.00	5.00	9.00	—

KM# 15 1/2 RUPEE (Deb) **Composition:** Copper Or Brass **Obverse:** Knot **Reverse:** Conch shell

Date	Good	VG	F	VF	XF
ND	1.50	2.50	4.00	8.00	—

HAMMERED 'DUMP' COINAGE

Period IV, 1910-1927

KM# 16 1/2 RUPEE (Deb) **Composition:** Copper

Date	Good	VG	F	VF	XF
ND	2.00	3.50	7.50	12.00	—

KM# 17 1/2 RUPEE (Deb) **Composition:** Silver

Date	Good	VG	F	VF	XF
ND	10.00	15.00	25.00	35.00	—

KM# 17a 1/2 RUPEE (Deb) **Composition:** Copper
Note: Obverse is similar to KM#17, but symbols on reverse are arranged differently.

Date	Good	VG	F	VF	XF
ND	2.00	3.50	5.00	9.00	—

KM# 18 1/2 RUPEE (Deb) **Composition:** Silver

Date	Good	VG	F	VF	XF
ND	10.00	15.00	25.00	35.00	—

KM# 18a 1/2 RUPEE (Deb) **Composition:** Copper
Note: Obverse is similar to KM#18, but symbols on reverse are arranged differently.

Date	Good	VG	F	VF	XF
ND	2.00	3.50	5.00	9.00	—

KM# 18b 1/2 RUPEE (Deb) **Composition:** Brass **Note:** Different reverse than KM18, this was heretofore an unpublished variety.

Date	Good	VG	F	VF	XF
ND	2.00	3.50	5.00	9.00	—

KM# 19 1/2 RUPEE (Deb) **Composition:** Silver

Date	Good	VG	F	VF	XF
ND	10.00	15.00	25.00	35.00	—

KM# 19a 1/2 RUPEE (Deb) **Composition:** Copper
Note: Obverse is similar to KM#19, but symbols on reverse are arranged differently.

Date	Good	VG	F	VF	XF
ND	2.00	3.50	5.00	9.00	—

KM# 20 1/2 RUPEE (Deb) **Composition:** Silver

Date	Good	VG	F	VF	XF
ND	10.00	15.00	25.00	35.00	—

KM# 20a 1/2 RUPEE (Deb) **Composition:** Copper
Note: Obverse is similar to KM#20, but symbols on reverse are arranged differently.

Date	Good	VG	F	VF	XF
ND	3.00	4.50	6.00	10.00	—

KM# 21 1/2 RUPEE (Deb) **Composition:** Copper

Date	Good	VG	F	VF	XF
ND	1.50	2.50	3.50	6.00	—

KM# 22 1/2 RUPEE (Deb) **Composition:** Copper
Obverse: Interlacing opposite of KM#21 **Reverse:** Interlacing opposite of KM#21 **Note:** Varieties exist.

Date	Good	VG	F	VF	XF
ND	1.50	2.50	3.50	6.00	—

GENERAL COINAGE

KM# 23.1 PICE **Weight:** 7.0000 g. **Composition:** Bronze **Size:** 26.5 mm. **Note:** Similar to KM#23.2.

Date	F	VF	XF	Unc	BU
1928	22.50	40.00	65.00	100	—

KM# 23.2 PICE **Weight:** 4.9000 g. **Composition:** Bronze **Size:** 25.1 mm. **Note:** Actually struck in 1931.

Date	Mintage	F	VF	XF	Unc	BU
1928	10,000	20.00	35.00	60.00	90.00	—
1928 Proof	—	Value: 100				

KM# A27 PICE **Weight:** 3.3000 g. **Composition:** Bronze

Date	F	VF	XF	Unc	BU
ND	—	—	—	—	—

KM# 27 PICE **Weight:** 2.9000 g. **Composition:** Bronze
Note: Actually struck in 1951 and 1955. Later strikes of 1955 dates differ in detail because of recut dies.

Date	F	VF	XF	Unc	BU
ND	0.75	1.00	1.50	2.25	—

KM# 26 1/2 RUPEE **Composition:** Nickel **Obverse:** Normal legend **Note:** Weight varies: 5.78-5.90 grams.

Date	Mintage	F	VF	XF	Unc	BU
ND(1928)	20,000	2.00	3.00	4.50	7.00	—
Note: Actually struck in 1951						
ND(1950)	202,000	1.50	2.50	3.00	4.50	—
Note: Actually struck in 1955						

KM# 24 1/2 RUPEE **Composition:** Silver **Note:** Weight varies: 5.83-5.85 grams.

Date	Mintage	F	VF	XF	Unc	BU
ND(1928)	50,000	10.00	15.00	22.50	35.00	—
Note: Actually struck in 1929						
ND(1928) Proof	—	Value: 100				

KM# 25 1/2 RUPEE **Composition:** Silver **Obverse:** Legend modified

Date	F	VF	XF	Unc	BU
ND(1928)	10.00	15.00	22.50	35.00	—
Note: Actually struck in 1930					

KM# 28 1/2 RUPEE **Weight:** 5.0800 g. **Composition:** Nickel **Obverse:** Legend normal

Date	Mintage	F	VF	XF	Unc	BU
ND(1950)	10,000,000	0.75	1.00	1.50	2.25	—
Note: Actually struck in 1967-1968						

DECIMAL COINAGE

KM# 29 25 NAYA PAISA **Composition:** Copper-Nickel **Subject:** 40th anniversary - accession of Jigme Wangchuk

Date	Mintage	F	VF	XF	Unc	BU
1966	10,000	—	0.25	0.50	1.00	2.00
1966 Proof	6,000	Value: 1.50				

KM# 30 50 NAYA PAISA **Composition:** Copper-Nickel **Subject:** 40th anniversary - accession of Jigme Wangchuk

Date	Mintage	F	VF	XF	Unc	BU
1966	10,000	—	0.35	0.75	1.50	3.00
1966 Proof	6,000	Value: 2.50				

KM# 31 RUPEE **Composition:** Copper-Nickel **Subject:** 40th anniversary - accession of Jigme Wangchuk

Date	Mintage	F	VF	XF	Unc	BU
1966	10,000	—	0.50	1.00	2.00	4.00
1966 Proof	6,000	Value: 3.50				

KM# 32 3 RUPEE **Composition:** Copper-Nickel **Subject:** 40th anniversary - accession of Jigme Wangchuk

Date	Mintage	F	VF	XF	Unc	BU
1966	5,826	—	—	—	6.00	9.00
1966 Proof	6,000	Value: 7.50				

KM# 32a 3 RUPEE **Weight:** 28.2800 g. **Composition:** 0.9250 Silver .8411 oz. ASW **Subject:** 40th anniversary - accession of Jigme Wangchuk

Date	Mintage	F	VF	XF	Unc	BU
1966	—	—	—	—	375	—
1966 Proof	2,000	Value: 25.00				
1966 Matte proof	—	Value: 375				

KM# 33 SERTUM **Weight:** 7.9800 g. **Composition:** 0.9170 Gold .2352 oz. AGW **Subject:** 40th anniversary - accession of Jigme Wangchuk

Date	Mintage	F	VF	XF	Unc	BU
1966	2,300	—	—	—	125	—
1966 Proof	598	Value: 165				

KM# 33a SERTUM **Weight:** 9.8400 g. **Composition:** 0.9500 Platinum .3005 oz. APW **Subject:** 40th anniversary - accession of Jigme Wangchuk

Date	Mintage	F	VF	XF	Unc	BU
1966 Proof	72	Value: 300				

KM# 36 SERTUM **Weight:** 7.9800 g. **Composition:** 0.9170 Gold .2352 oz. AGW

Date	Mintage	F	VF	XF	Unc	BU
1970	3,111	—	—	—	125	—

KM# 34 2 SERTUMS **Weight:** 15.9800 g. **Composition:** 0.9170 Gold .4711 oz. AGW **Subject:** 40th anniversary - accession of Jigme Wangchuk

Date	Mintage	F	VF	XF	Unc	BU
1966	800	—	—	—	225	—
1966 Proof	598	Value: 300				

KM# 34a 2 SERTUMS **Weight:** 19.6700 g. **Composition:** 0.9500 Platinum .6008 oz. APW **Subject:** 40th anniversary - accession of Jigme Wangchuk

Date	Mintage	F	VF	XF	Unc	BU
1966 Proof	72	Value: 420				

KM# 35 5 SERTUMS **Weight:** 39.9400 g. **Composition:** 0.9170 Gold 1.1776 oz. AGW **Subject:** 40th anniversary - accession of Jigme Wangchuk

Date	Mintage	F	VF	XF	Unc	BU
1966	800	—	—	—	500	—
1966 Proof	598	Value: 700				

KM# 35a 5 SERTUMS **Weight:** 49.1800 g. **Composition:** 0.9500 Platinum 1.5022 oz. APW **Subject:** 40th anniversary - accession of Jigme Wangchuk

Date	Mintage	F	VF	XF	Unc	BU
1966 Proof	72	Value: 950				

REFORM COINAGE

Commencing 1974; 100 Chetrums (Paisa) = 1 Ngultrum (Rupee); 100 Ngultrums = 1 Sertum

KM# 37 5 CHETRUMS **Composition:** Aluminum

Date	Mintage	F	VF	XF	Unc	BU
1974	—	—	0.10	0.20	0.50	0.75
1974 Proof	1,000	Value: 1.25				
1975	—	—	0.10	0.15	0.20	0.50
1975 Proof	—	Value: 1.25				

KM# 45 5 CHHERTUM **Composition:** Bronze

Date	F	VF	XF	Unc	BU
1979	—	0.10	0.20	0.50	0.75
1979 Proof	—	Value: 1.00			

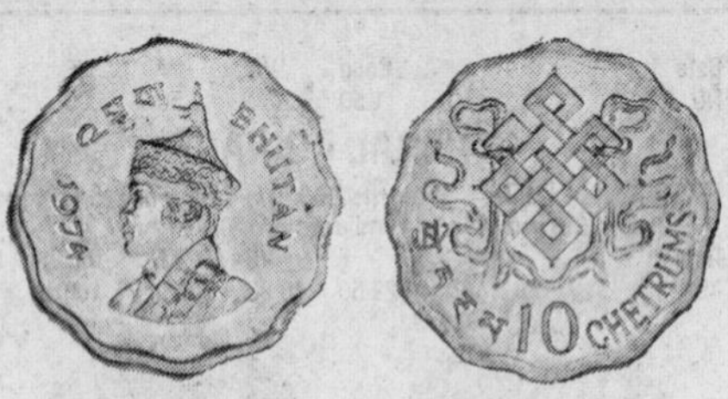

KM# 38 10 CHETRUMS **Composition:** Aluminum

Date	Mintage	F	VF	XF	Unc	BU
1974	—	—	0.15	0.25	0.50	1.00
1974 Proof	1,000	Value: 1.50				

KM# 43 10 CHETRUMS **Composition:** Aluminum **Series:** F.A.O. and International Women's Year

Date	Mintage	F	VF	XF	Unc	BU
1975	4,000,000	—	0.15	0.25	0.65	1.25
1975 Proof	—	Value: 2.50				

KM# 46 10 CHHERTUM **Composition:** Bronze

Date	F	VF	XF	Unc	BU
1979	—	0.15	0.30	1.00	1.50
1979 Proof	—	Value: 2.00			

KM# 39 20 CHETRUMS **Composition:** Aluminum-Bronze **Series:** F.A.O.

Date	Mintage	F	VF	XF	Unc	BU
1974	1,194,000	—	0.15	0.25	0.50	0.75
1974 Prooflike	—	—	—	—	1.50	—

Note: In mint sets only

Date	Mintage	F	VF	XF	Unc	BU
1974 Proof	1,000	Value: 2.00				

KM# 40.1 25 CHETRUMS **Composition:** Copper-Nickel **Reverse:** Type I

Date	Mintage	F	VF	XF	Unc	BU
1974	—	—	0.10	0.20	0.75	1.25
1974 Proof	1,000	Value: 3.00				

KM# 40.2 25 CHETRUMS **Composition:** Copper-Nickel **Reverse:** Type II

Date	F	VF	XF	Unc	BU
1974	—	0.10	0.20	0.75	1.25
1975	—	0.10	0.20	0.75	1.25
1975 Proof	—	Value: 3.00			

KM# 47 25 CHHERTUM **Composition:** Copper-Nickel

Date	F	VF	XF	Unc	BU
1979	—	0.25	0.50	1.25	1.75
1979 Proof	—	Value: 4.00			

KM# 47a 25 CHHERTUM **Composition:** Steel **Note:** Aluminum-bronze clad.

Date	F	VF	XF	Unc	BU
1979	—	—	—	2.50	3.00

KM# 48 50 CHHERTUM **Composition:** Copper-Nickel

Date	F	VF	XF	Unc	BU
1979	—	0.25	0.65	1.50	2.00
1979 Proof	—	Value: 5.00			

KM# 41 NGULTRUM **Composition:** Copper-Nickel

Date	Mintage	F	VF	XF	Unc	BU
1974	—	—	0.20	0.50	1.25	1.75
1974 Proof	1,000	Value: 5.00				
1975	—	—	0.20	0.50	1.25	1.75
1975 Proof	—	Value: 5.00				

KM# 49 NGULTRUM **Composition:** Copper-Nickel

Date	F	VF	XF	Unc	BU
1979	—	0.30	0.75	2.00	2.75
1979 Proof	—	Value: 5.50			

KM# 49a NGULTRUM **Composition:** Copper-Nickel Clad Steel

Date	F	VF	XF	Unc	BU
1979	—	—	—	3.00	3.50

KM# 50 3 NGULTRUMS **Composition:** Copper-Nickel

Date	F	VF	XF	Unc	BU
1979	—	1.25	2.50	5.50	—
1979 Proof	—	Value: 8.50			

KM# 50a 3 NGULTRUMS **Weight:** 28.2800 g. **Composition:** 0.9250 Silver .8411 oz. ASW

Date	F	VF	XF	Unc	BU
1979 Proof	Est. 10,000	Value: 32.50			

KM# 42 15 NGULTRUMS **Weight:** 22.3000 g. **Composition:** 0.5000 Silver .3584 oz. ASW **Series:** F.A.O.

Date	Mintage	F	VF	XF	Unc	BU
1974	30,000	—	—	—	8.00	—
1974 Prooflike	—	—	—	—	10.00	—

Note: In mint sets only

Date	Mintage	
1974 Proof	1,000	Value: 42.50

KM# 44 30 NGULTRUMS **Weight:** 25.0000 g. **Composition:** 0.5000 Silver .4018 oz. ASW **Series:** F.A.O. and International Women's Year

Date	Mintage	F	VF	XF	Unc	BU
1975	14,000	—	—	—	10.00	—
1975 Proof	—	Value: 20.00				

KM# 54 50 NGULTRUMS **Weight:** 28.2800 g. **Composition:** 0.9250 Silver .8411 oz. ASW **Series:** World Food Day

Date	Mintage	F	VF	XF	Unc	BU
1981	15,000	—	—	—	32.50	—
1981 Proof	5,000	Value: 45.00				

KM# 83 50 NGULTRUMS **Composition:** Copper-Nickel **Subject:** 50 years - United Nations

Date	F	VF	XF	Unc	BU
1995	—	—	—	8.00	—

KM# 58 100 NGULTRUMS **Weight:** 23.3300 g. **Composition:** 0.9250 Silver .6938 oz. ASW **Series:** Decade for Women

Date	Mintage	F	VF	XF	Unc	BU
1984 Proof	1,050	Value: 28.00				

KM# 84 100 NGULTRUMS **Composition:** Copper-Nickel **Subject:** St. Paul's Walden Bury Palace

Date	F	VF	XF	Unc	BU
1995	—	—	—	12.50	—

KM# 103 100 NGULTRUMS **Weight:** 20.0000 g. **Composition:** 0.9250 Silver .5948 oz. ASW **Subject:** Olympic Games 2000 **Obverse:** National arms **Reverse:** Archer at left sighting in on target at right **Edge:** Reeded **Size:** 34 mm.

Date	F	VF	XF	Unc	BU
1998 Proof	—	Value: 17.50			

KM# 57 200 NGULTRUMS **Weight:** 28.2800 g. **Composition:** 0.9250 Silver .8411 oz. ASW **Series:** International Year of Disabled Persons

Date	Mintage	F	VF	XF	Unc	BU
1981	10,000	—	—	—	40.00	—
1981 Proof	10,000	Value: 45.00				

KM# 55 200 NGULTRUMS **Weight:** 28.2800 g. **Composition:** 0.9250 Silver .8411 oz. ASW **Subject:** 75th anniversary of monarchy

Date	Mintage	F	VF	XF	Unc	BU
1982(1983)	10,000	—	—	—	30.00	—
1982(1983) Proof	5,000	Value: 40.00				

KM# 86 200 NGULTRUMS **Weight:** 10.0000 g. **Composition:** 0.5000 Silver .1607 oz. ASW **Series:** Olympics **Reverse:** Two basketball players

Date	F	VF	XF	Unc	BU
1996	—	—	—	20.00	—

KM# 87 200 NGULTRUMS **Weight:** 10.0000 g. **Composition:** 0.5000 Silver .1607 oz. ASW **Series:** Olympics **Reverse:** Skiing scene

Date	F	VF	XF	Unc	BU
1996	—	—	—	15.00	—

KM# 61 300 NGULTRUMS **Weight:** 28.2800 g. **Composition:** 0.9250 Silver .8411 oz. ASW **Subject:** World Championship Soccer

Date	Mintage	F	VF	XF	Unc	BU
1990 Proof	20,000	Value: 35.00				

KM# 65 300 NGULTRUMS **Weight:** 31.4700 g. **Composition:** 0.9250 Silver .9359 oz. ASW **Series:** Endangered wildlife **Reverse:** Snow leopard

Date	Mintage	F	VF	XF	Unc	BU
1991 Proof	Est. 25,000	Value: 35.00				

KM# 63 300 NGULTRUMS **Weight:** 28.2800 g. **Composition:** 0.9250 Silver .8411 oz. ASW **Reverse:** Solar system scene

Date		F	VF	XF	Unc	BU
1992 Proof	—	Value: 32.50				

KM# 72 300 NGULTRUMS **Weight:** 31.4700 g. **Composition:** 0.9250 Silver .9359 oz. ASW **Subject:** World Cup soccer **Reverse:** Two soccer players, radiant sunset behind

Date	Mintage	F	VF	XF	Unc	BU
1992 Proof	20,000	Value: 27.50				

KM# 74 300 NGULTRUMS **Weight:** 31.4700 g. **Composition:** 0.9250 Silver .9359 oz. ASW **Series:** 1994 Olympic Games **Reverse:** Figure speed skating

Date	Mintage	F	VF	XF	Unc	BU
1992 Proof	40,000	Value: 22.50				

KM# 75 300 NGULTRUMS **Weight:** 31.4700 g. **Composition:** 0.9250 Silver .9359 oz. ASW **Series:** Endangered wildlife **Reverse:** Golden langur monkey

Date		F	VF	XF	Unc	BU
1992 Proof	—	Value: 32.50				

KM# 76 300 NGULTRUMS **Weight:** 31.4700 g. **Composition:** 0.9250 Silver .9359 oz. ASW **Series:** 1992 Olympic Games **Reverse:** Archery scene

Date	Mintage	F	VF	XF	Unc	BU
1992 Proof	20,000	Value: 18.50				

KM# 77 300 NGULTRUMS **Weight:** 31.4700 g. **Composition:** 0.9250 Silver .9359 oz. ASW **Series:** 1992 Olympic Games **Reverse:** Boxer

Date	Mintage	F	VF	XF	Unc	BU
1992 Proof	20,000	Value: 20.00				

KM# 66 300 NGULTRUMS **Weight:** 31.4700 g. **Composition:** 0.9250 Silver .9359 oz. ASW **Subject:** 40th anniversary - coronation of Queen Elizabeth II

Date	Mintage	F	VF	XF	Unc	BU
1993 Proof	Est. 10,000	Value: 32.50				

KM# 67 300 NGULTRUMS **Weight:** 31.4700 g. **Composition:** 0.9250 Silver .9359 oz. ASW **Series:** Endangered Wildlife **Reverse:** Takin

Date	Mintage	F	VF	XF	Unc	BU
1993 Proof	Est. 10,000	Value: 35.00				

KM# 68 300 NGULTRUMS **Weight:** 31.4700 g. **Composition:** 0.9250 Silver .9359 oz. ASW **Subject:** Protect our world **Reverse:** Elephant, rhino, tree, and tiger

Date	Mintage	F	VF	XF	Unc	BU
1993 Proof	Est. 10,000	Value: 50.00				

KM# 78 300 NGULTRUMS **Weight:** 31.3200 g. **Composition:** 0.9250 Silver .9314 oz. ASW **Subject:** World Championship Soccer **Reverse:** Ball in flight

Date	Mintage	F	VF	XF	Unc	BU
1993 Proof	30,000	Value: 40.00				

KM# 79 300 NGULTRUMS **Weight:** 31.3200 g. **Composition:** 0.9250 Silver .9314 oz. ASW **Series:** Olympic Games **Reverse:** Soccer

Date	Mintage	F	VF	XF	Unc	BU
1993 Proof	30,000	Value: 25.00				

KM# 89 300 NGULTRUMS **Weight:** 31.3200 g. **Composition:** 0.9250 Silver .9314 oz. ASW **Subject:** Maurice Ravel **Obverse:** National emblem **Reverse:** Portrait, musician, dancer, and dates

Date		F	VF	XF	Unc	BU
1993 Proof	—	Value: 42.50				

KM# 69 300 NGULTRUMS **Weight:** 31.3200 g. **Composition:** 0.9250 Silver .9314 oz. ASW **Subject:** Protect Our World **Reverse:** Rain forest

Date	Mintage	F	VF	XF	Unc	BU
1994 Proof	Est. 10,000	Value: 45.00				

KM# 80 300 NGULTRUMS **Weight:** 28.2800 g. **Composition:** 0.9250 Silver .8411 oz. ASW **Subject:** 50th anniversary - United Nations

Date	Mintage	F	VF	XF	Unc	BU
1995 Proof	Est. 100,000	Value: 32.50				

KM# 92 300 NGULTRUMS **Weight:** 31.5000 g. **Composition:** 0.9250 Silver .9368 oz. ASW **Subject:** Chinese lunar year **Obverse:** National emblem **Reverse:** Stylized dog

Date	F	VF	XF	Unc	BU
1996 Proof	—	Value: 28.50			

KM# 73 300 NGULTRUMS **Weight:** 31.3200 g. **Composition:** 0.9250 Silver .9314 oz. ASW **Series:** 1996 Olympic Games **Reverse:** Basketball

Date	Mintage	F	VF	XF	Unc	BU
1994 Proof	30,000	Value: 25.00				

KM# 90 300 NGULTRUMS **Weight:** 31.5000 g. **Composition:** 0.9250 Silver .9368 oz. ASW **Subject:** Chinese lunar year **Obverse:** National emblem **Reverse:** Seated monkey

Date	F	VF	XF	Unc	BU
1996 Proof	—	Value: 28.50			

KM# 93 300 NGULTRUMS **Weight:** 31.5000 g. **Composition:** 0.9250 Silver .9368 oz. ASW **Subject:** Chinese lunar year **Obverse:** National emblem **Reverse:** Stylized pig

Date	F	VF	XF	Unc	BU
1996 Proof	—	Value: 28.50			

KM# 88 300 NGULTRUMS **Weight:** 31.4500 g. **Composition:** 0.9250 Silver .9353 oz. ASW **Series:** Endangered wildlife **Reverse:** Kalij pheasant

Date	F	VF	XF	Unc	BU
1994 Proof	—	Value: 37.50			

KM# 98 300 NGULTRUMS **Weight:** 31.5000 g. **Composition:** 0.9250 Silver .9368 oz. ASW **Subject:** Chinese lunar year **Obverse:** National emblem **Reverse:** Stylized dragon

Date	F	VF	XF	Unc	BU
1996 Proof	—	Value: 30.00			

KM# 94 300 NGULTRUMS **Weight:** 31.5000 g. **Composition:** 0.9250 Silver .9368 oz. ASW **Subject:** Chinese lunar year **Obverse:** National emblem **Reverse:** Stylized rat

Date	F	VF	XF	Unc	BU
1996 Proof	—	Value: 30.00			

KM# 81 300 NGULTRUMS **Weight:** 31.4500 g. **Composition:** 0.9250 Silver .9353 oz. ASW **Subject:** Joao Cabral **Obverse:** National emblem **Reverse:** Two explorers

Date	Mintage	F	VF	XF	Unc	BU
1994 Proof	Est. 10,000	Value: 32.50				

KM# 91 300 NGULTRUMS **Weight:** 31.5000 g. **Composition:** 0.9250 Silver .9368 oz. ASW **Subject:** Chinese lunar year **Obverse:** National emblem **Reverse:** Stylized rooster

Date	F	VF	XF	Unc	BU
1996 Proof	—	Value: 28.50			

KM# 95 300 NGULTRUMS **Weight:** 31.5000 g. **Composition:** 0.9250 Silver .9368 oz. ASW **Subject:** Chinese lunar year **Obverse:** National emblem **Reverse:** Stylized ox

Date	F	VF	XF	Unc	BU
1996 Proof	—	Value: 28.50			

KM# 96 300 NGULTRUMS **Weight:** 31.5000 g. **Composition:** 0.9250 Silver .9368 oz. ASW **Subject:** Chinese lunar year **Obverse:** National emblem **Reverse:** Stylized tiger

Date		F	VF	XF	Unc	BU
1996 Proof	—	Value: 30.00				

KM# 97 300 NGULTRUMS **Weight:** 31.5000 g. **Composition:** 0.9250 Silver .9368 oz. ASW **Subject:** Chinese lunar year **Obverse:** National emblem **Reverse:** Stylized rabbit

Date		F	VF	XF	Unc	BU
1996 Proof	—	Value: 28.50				

KM# 99 300 NGULTRUMS **Weight:** 31.5000 g. **Composition:** 0.9250 Silver .9368 oz. ASW **Subject:** Chinese lunar year **Obverse:** National emblem **Reverse:** Stylized snake

Date		F	VF	XF	Unc	BU
1996 Proof	—	Value: 30.00				

KM# 100 300 NGULTRUMS **Weight:** 31.5000 g. **Composition:** 0.9250 Silver .9368 oz. ASW **Subject:** Chinese lunar year **Obverse:** National emblem **Reverse:** Stylized horse

Date		F	VF	XF	Unc	BU
1996 Proof	—	Value: 28.50				

KM# 101 300 NGULTRUMS **Weight:** 31.5000 g. **Composition:** 0.9250 Silver .9368 oz. ASW **Subject:** Chinese lunar year **Obverse:** National emblem **Reverse:** Stylized ram

Date		F	VF	XF	Unc	BU
1996 Proof	—	Value: 28.50				

KM# 102 300 NGULTRUMS **Weight:** 1.2441 g. **Composition:** 0.9990 Gold .04 oz. AGW **Obverse:** National emblem **Reverse:** Mask

Date		F	VF	XF	Unc	BU
1997 Proof	—	Value: 45.00				

KM# 51 SERTUM **Weight:** 7.9800 g. **Composition:** 0.9170 Gold .2352 oz. AGW **Obverse:** Similar to 5 Sertums, KM#35 **Reverse:** Two dragons around inner circle

Date	Mintage	F	VF	XF	Unc	BU
1979	1,000	—	—	—	125	—
1979 Proof	1,000	Value: 160				

KM# 51a SERTUM **Weight:** 9.8500 g. **Composition:** 0.9500 Platinum .3008 oz. APW **Obverse:** Similar to 5 Sertums, KM#35 **Reverse:** Two dragons around inner circle

Date		F	VF	XF	Unc	BU
1979 Proof	—	Value: 300				

KM# 56 SERTUM **Weight:** 7.9900 g. **Composition:** 0.9170 Gold .2356 oz. AGW **Subject:** 75th anniversary of monarchy

Date	Mintage	F	VF	XF	Unc	BU
1982(1983)	1,000	—	—	—	135	—
1982(1983) Proof	1,000	Value: 165				

KM# 85 SERTUM **Weight:** 1.2442 g. **Composition:** 0.9999 Gold .04 oz. AGW **Subject:** 40th anniversary - Queen Elizabeth II's coronation

Date	F	VF	XF	Unc	BU
1995	—	—	—	50.00	—

KM# 52 2 SERTUMS **Weight:** 15.9800 g. **Composition:** 0.9170 Gold .4711 oz. AGW **Obverse:** Similar to 5 Sertums, KM#35 **Reverse:** Two dragons around inner circle

Date	Mintage	F	VF	XF	Unc	BU
1979	1,000	—	—	—	225	—
1979 Proof	1,000	Value: 285				

KM# 52a 2 SERTUMS **Weight:** 19.7000 g. **Composition:** 0.9500 Platinum .6017 oz. APW **Obverse:** Similar to 5 Sertums, KM#35 **Reverse:** Two dragons around inner circle

Date		F	VF	XF	Unc	BU
1979 Proof	—	Value: 420				

KM# 60 2 SERTUMS **Weight:** 15.9800 g. **Composition:** 0.9170 Gold .4711 oz. AGW **Series:** International Year of Disabled Persons

Date	F	VF	XF	Unc	BU
1981	—	—	—	700	—
1981 Proof	— Value: 900				

KM# 53 5 SERTUMS **Weight:** 39.9400 g. **Composition:** 0.9170 Gold 1.1776 oz. AGW **Obverse:** Similar to 5 Sertums, KM#35 **Reverse:** Two dragons around inner circle

Date	Mintage	F	VF	XF	Unc	BU
1979	1,000	—	—	—	500	—
1979 Proof	1,000	Value: 675				

KM# 53a 5 SERTUMS **Weight:** 49.2000 g. **Composition:** 0.9500 Platinum 1.5022 oz. APW **Obverse:** Similar to 5 Sertums, KM#35 **Reverse:** Two dragons around inner circle

Date		F	VF	XF	Unc	BU
1979 Proof	—	Value: 950				

KM# 64 5 SERTRUMS **Weight:** 7.7760 g. **Composition:** 0.5833 Gold .1458 oz. AGW **Series:** Endangered wildlife **Reverse:** Black-necked crane

Date	Mintage	F	VF	XF	Unc	BU
1992 Proof	2,000	Value: 85.00				

KM# 70 5 SERTRUMS **Weight:** 7.7760 g. **Composition:** 0.5833 Gold .1458 oz. AGW **Series:** 1992 Olympics **Reverse:** Archer

Date	Mintage	F	VF	XF	Unc	BU
1993 Proof	Est. 3,000	Value: 125				

KM# 71 5 SERTRUMS **Weight:** 7.7760 g. **Composition:** 0.5833 Gold .1458 oz. AGW **Subject:** World Cup '94 soccer

Date	Mintage	F	VF	XF	Unc	BU
1993 Proof	Est. 2,000	Value: 125				

KM# 82 5 SERTRUMS **Weight:** 7.7760 g. **Composition:** 0.5833 Gold .1458 oz. AGW **Series:** Olympics **Subject:** Tae kwon do **Obverse:** National emblem **Reverse:** Karate practitioner

Date	Mintage	F	VF	XF	Unc	BU
1994 Proof	Est. 3,000	Value: 125				

PIEFORTS

KM#	Date	Mintage	Identification	Mkt Val
P1	1981	—	2 Sertums. KM60.	1,450
P2	1981	—	200 Ngultrums. KM57.	300

MINT SETS

KM#	Date	Mintage	Identification	Issue Price	Mkt Val
MS1	1966 (3)	300	KM33-35	175	850
MS3	1974 (4)	—	KM37-38, 40-41	6.00	3.00
MS2	1974 (2)	—	KM39, 42	4.00	11.50
MS4	1979 (3)	1,000	KM51-53	1,575	850

PROOF SETS

KM#	Date	Mintage	Identification	Issue Price	Mkt Val
PS1	1966 (4)	6,000	KM29-32	11.50	15.00
PS2	1966 (3)	598	KM33-35	300	1,175
PS3	1966 (3)	72	KM33a-35a	685	1,675
PS4	1974 (6)	1,000	KM37-42	18.00	65.00
PS5	1975 (5)	—	KM37, 40-41, 43-44; rare	—	—
PS6	1979 (5)	20,000	KM45-49	30.00	15.00
PS7	1979 (3)	1,000	KM51-53	2,100	1,125
PS8	1979 (3)	—	KM51a-53a	2,400	1,675

BIAFRA

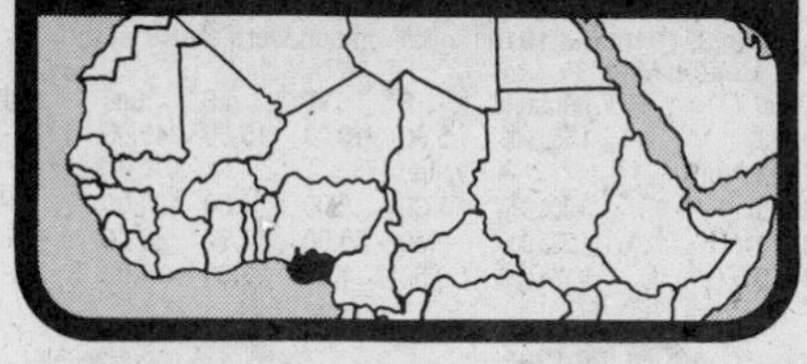

On May 30, 1967, the Eastern Region of the Republic of Nigeria, an area occupied principally by the proud and resourceful Ibo tribe, seceded from Nigeria and proclaimed itself the independent Republic of Biafra with Odumegwu Ojukwu as Chief of State. Civil war erupted and raged for 31 months. Casualties, including civilian, were about two million, the majority succumbing to malnutrition and disease. Biafra surrendered to the federal government on January 15, 1970.

MONETARY SYSTEM
12 Pence = 1 Shilling
20 Shillings = 1 Pound

INDEPENDANT REPUBLIC OF BIAFRA

STANDARD COINAGE

KM# 1 3 PENCE **Composition:** Aluminum

Date	F	VF	XF	Unc	BU
1969	—	15.00	20.00	30.00	—

KM# 12 6 PENCE **Composition:** Aluminum **Obverse:** Value: 6 PENCE

Date	F	VF	XF	Unc	BU
1969 2 pieces known	—	—	—	—	—

KM# 2 SHILLING **Composition:** Aluminum

Date	F	VF	XF	Unc	BU
1969	—	10.00	15.00	22.50	—

KM# 3 SHILLING **Composition:** Aluminum **Obverse:** Value: ONE SHILLING

Date	F	VF	XF	Unc	BU
1969	—	—	250	350	—

KM# 4 2-1/2 SHILLING **Composition:** Aluminum

Date	F	VF	XF	Unc	BU
1969	—	11.50	17.50	30.00	—

KM# 5 CROWN **Composition:** Silver **Subject:** Independence and Liberty

Date	F	VF	XF	Unc	BU
1969 Rare	—	—	—	—	—

KM# 6 POUND **Weight:** 19.7600 g. **Composition:** 0.7500 Silver .4765 oz. ASW

Date	F	VF	XF	Unc	BU
1969	—	—	75.00	95.00	—

KM# 7 POUND **Weight:** 3.9940 g. **Composition:** 0.9170 Gold .1177 oz. AGW **Subject:** 2nd Anniversary of Independence **Obverse:** Similar to 25 Pounds, KM#11

Date	Mintage	F	VF	XF	Unc	BU
1969 Proof	3,000	Value: 65.00				

KM# 8 2 POUNDS **Weight:** 7.9881 g. **Composition:** 0.9170 Gold .2354 oz. AGW **Subject:** 2nd Anniversary of Independence **Obverse:** Similar to 25 Pounds, KM#11

Date	Mintage	F	VF	XF	Unc	BU
1969 Proof	3,000	Value: 130				

KM# 9 5 POUNDS **Weight:** 15.9761 g. **Composition:** 0.9170 Gold .4710 oz. AGW **Subject:** 2nd Anniversary of Independence **Obverse:** Similar to 25 Pounds, KM#11

Date	Mintage	F	VF	XF	Unc	BU
1969 Proof	3,000	Value: 260				

KM#10 10 POUNDS **Weight:** 39.9403 g. **Composition:** 0.9170 Gold 1.1776 oz. AGW **Subject:** 2nd Anniversary of Independence **Obverse:** Similar to 25 Pounds, KM#11

Date	Mintage	F	VF	XF	Unc	BU
1969 Proof	3,000	Value: 625				

KM#11 25 POUNDS **Weight:** 79.8805 g. **Composition:** 0.9170 Gold 2.3553 oz. AGW **Subject:** 2nd Anniversary of Independence

Date	Mintage	F	VF	XF	Unc	BU
1969 Proof	3,000	Value: 1,275				

PROOF SETS

KM#	Date	Mintage	Identification	Issue Price	Mkt Val
PS1	1969 (5)	3,000	KM7-11	464	2,350

BOHEMIA & MORAVIA

Bohemia, a western province in the Czech Republic, was combined with the majority of Moravia in central Czechoslovakia (excluding parts of north and south Moravia which were joined with Silesia in 1938) to form the German protectorate in March, 1939, after the German invasion. Toward the end of war in 1945 the protectorate was dissolved and Bohemia and Moravia once again became part of Czechoslovakia.

MONETARY SYSTEM
100 Haleru = 1 Koruna

GERMAN PROTECTORATE

STANDARD COINAGE

KM# 1 10 HALERU Composition: Zinc

Date	Mintage	F	VF	XF	Unc	BU
1940	82,114,000	0.25	0.50	1.00	6.00	—
1941	Inc. above	0.25	0.50	1.00	7.50	—
1942	Inc. above	0.25	0.50	1.00	7.50	—
1943	Inc. above	0.50	0.75	1.50	10.00	—
1944	Inc. above	0.75	1.50	2.50	12.00	—

KM# 2 20 HALERU Composition: Zinc

Date	Mintage	F	VF	XF	Unc	BU
1940	106,526,000	0.25	0.50	1.00	7.50	—
1941	Inc. above	0.25	0.50	1.00	7.50	—
1942	Inc. above	0.25	0.50	1.00	7.50	—
1943	Inc. above	0.50	0.75	1.50	10.00	—
1944	Inc. above	0.50	1.00	1.75	12.00	—

KM# 3 50 HALERU Composition: Zinc

Date	Mintage	F	VF	XF	Unc	BU
1940	53,270,000	0.35	0.75	1.25	10.00	—
1941	Inc. above	0.35	0.75	1.25	10.00	—
1942	Inc. above	0.35	0.75	1.25	10.00	—
1943	Inc. above	0.75	1.50	3.00	15.00	—
1944	Inc. above	0.35	0.75	1.25	10.00	—

KM# 4 KORUNA Composition: Zinc

Date	Mintage	F	VF	XF	Unc	BU
1941	102,817,000	0.50	0.75	1.50	12.50	—
1942	Inc. above	0.50	0.75	1.50	12.50	—
1943	Inc. above	0.50	0.75	1.50	12.50	—
1944	Inc. above	0.50	0.75	1.50	12.50	—

BOLIVIA

The Republic of Bolivia, a landlocked country in west central South America, has an area of 424,165 sq. mi. (1,098,580 sq. km.) and a population of *8.33 million. Its capitals are: La Paz (administrative) and Sucre (constitutional). Principal exports are tin, zinc, antimony, tungsten, petroleum, natural gas, cotton and coffee.

Much of present-day Bolivia was first dominated by the Tiahuanaco Culture ca.400 BC. It had in turn been incorporated into the Inca Empire by 1440AD prior to the arrival of the Spanish, in 1535, who reduced the Indian population to virtual slavery. When Joseph Napoleon was placed upon the throne of occupied Spain in 1809, a fervor of revolutionary activity quickened throughout Alto Peru - culminating in the 1809 Proclamation of Liberty. Sixteen bloody years of struggle ensued before the republic, named for the famed liberator Simon Bolivar, was established on August 6, 1825. Since then Bolivia has survived more than 16 constitutions, 78 Presidents, 3 military juntas and over 160 revolutions.

MINT MARKS
A - Paris
(a) - Paris, privy marks only
CHI - Valcambia
H - Heaton
KN - Kings' Norton

MONETARY SYSTEM
100 Centavos = 1 Boliviano

REPUBLIC

REFORM COINAGE

1870 - 1951

The low quality of steel used for production of dies from the beginning of Republican coinage thru the late 1890s resulted in most series having multiple dies with differences in spacing, dots and even style of letters and numbers. Only major differences or errors will be listed.

KM# 173.1 5 CENTAVOS Composition: Copper-Nickel **Note:** Coins dated 1893, 1918 and 1919 medal rotation were struck at the Heaton Mint.

Date	Mintage	F	VF	XF	Unc	BU
1893	2,500,000	3.50	6.00	12.00	35.00	—
1893 Proof	—	Value: 100				
1899	2,000,000	1.00	1.75	5.00	25.00	—
1909	4,000,000	0.50	1.00	4.00	20.00	—
1918	530,000	4.00	6.00	20.00	50.00	—
1919	4,370,000	3.00	5.00	12.00	32.00	—

KM# 173.3 5 CENTAVOS Composition: Copper-Nickel **Reverse:** Cornucopia and torch flank date

Date	Mintage	F	VF	XF	Unc	BU
1897(a)	1,500,000	0.50	1.25	5.00	25.00	—
1902	2,000,000	0.50	1.25	5.00	25.00	—
1907(a)	2,000,000	1.75	3.75	7.50	30.00	—
1908	3,000,000	0.50	1.00	5.00	35.00	—
1909	—	2.00	4.00	9.00	40.00	—

KM# 178 5 CENTAVOS Composition: Copper-Nickel

Date	Mintage	F	VF	XF	Unc	BU
1935	5,000,000	0.50	1.00	3.00	9.00	—

KM# 174.1 10 CENTAVOS Composition: Copper-Nickel **Reverse:** Without privy marks **Note:** Coins dated 1893, 1918 and 1919 medal rotation were struck at the Heaton Mint.

Date	Mintage	F	VF	XF	Unc	BU
1893	1,250,000	5.00	10.00	15.00	45.00	—
1893 Proof	—	Value: 175				
1899	3,000,000	1.00	2.00	4.00	28.00	—
1918	1,335,000	2.50	5.00	7.50	30.00	—
1919	6,165,000	0.50	1.00	3.00	25.00	—

KM# 174.3 10 CENTAVOS Composition: Copper-Nickel **Reverse:** Cornucopia and torch flank date

Date	Mintage	F	VF	XF	Unc	BU
1901	—	17.50	27.50	45.00	75.00	—
1902	8,500,000	0.50	1.00	4.00	25.00	—
1907/2	4,000,000	1.25	2.50	7.00	30.00	—
1907	Inc. above	0.50	1.00	4.00	25.00	—
1908	6,000,000	0.50	1.00	4.00	25.00	—
1909	8,000,000	0.50	1.00	4.00	25.00	—

KM# 179.1 10 CENTAVOS Composition: Copper-Nickel **Reverse:** Wide O in value

Date	Mintage	F	VF	XF	Unc	BU
1935	10,000,000	0.50	1.00	2.50	10.00	—
1936	10,000,000	0.50	1.00	2.50	10.00	—

KM# 179.2 10 CENTAVOS Composition: Copper-Nickel **Reverse:** Narrow O in value

Date	F	VF	XF	Unc	BU
1939	0.50	1.00	2.50	10.00	—

KM# 179a 10 CENTAVOS Composition: Zinc

Date	Mintage	F	VF	XF	Unc	BU
1942 (p)	10,000,000	0.50	1.00	2.50	10.00	—

KM# 180 10 CENTAVOS Composition: Copper-Nickel

Date	Mintage	F	VF	XF	Unc	BU
1937	20,000,000	0.50	1.00	2.50	10.00	—

KM# 159.2 20 CENTAVOS Weight: 4.6000 g. **Composition:** 0.9000 Silver .1331 oz. ASW **Note:** Reduced size dates and lettering, bar below CENTS. The small bar

usually found below "S" in "9DS" is missing in the 1886-1888 and 1902 dates, Mint mark in monogram.

Date	Mintage	VG	F	VF	XF	Unc
1901PTS MM	40,000	2.50	5.00	13.50	20.00	50.00
1901PTS MM/.WM	—	2.50	5.00	16.50	35.00	75.00
1902PTS MM	—	6.50	10.00	20.00	50.00	100
1903PTS MM	10,000	10.00	15.00	30.00	75.00	125
1904PTS MM	—	7.00	12.00	20.00	75.00	125
1907PTS MM	—	45.00	90.00	150	300	500

KM# 176 20 CENTAVOS Weight: 4.0000 g. **Composition:** 0.8330 Silver .1071 oz. ASW

Date	Mintage	F	VF	XF	Unc	BU
1909H	1,500,000	2.50	5.00	15.00	30.00	—
1909H Proof	—	Value: 500				

KM# 183 20 CENTAVOS Composition: Zinc **Note:** Medal rotation strike.

Date	Mintage	F	VF	XF	Unc	BU
1942 (p)	10,000,000	1.00	2.00	6.00	20.00	—

KM# 175.1 50 CENTAVOS (1/2 Boliviano) Weight: 11.5000 g. **Composition:** 0.9000 Silver .3328 oz. ASW **Note:** Mint mark in monogram.

Date	Mintage	VG	F	VF	XF	Unc
1901/0PTS MM	—	BV	7.00	18.50	37.50	60.00
1901PTS MM	Inc. above	BV	3.50	8.00	16.50	45.00
1902PTS MM	1,530,000	BV	3.50	8.00	16.50	45.00
1903/2PTS MM	690,000	BV	5.00	16.00	37.50	60.00
1903PTS MM	Inc. above	BV	3.50	8.00	16.50	45.00
1904PTS MM	1,290,000	BV	3.50	8.00	16.50	45.00
1905PTS MM	1,690,000	BV	3.50	8.00	16.50	45.00
1905PTS AB	Inc. above	BV	3.50	8.00	16.50	45.00
1906PTS MM	630,000	BV	4.50	10.00	21.50	55.00
1906PTS AB	5,500,000	BV	3.50	8.00	16.50	45.00
1907PTS MM	50,000	BV	4.50	10.00	21.50	55.00
1908PTS MM	—	BV	3.50	8.00	16.50	45.00
1908PTS MM Inverted 8	—	BV	10.00	25.00	50.00	75.00

KM# 177 50 CENTAVOS (1/2 Boliviano) Weight: 10.0000 g. **Composition:** 0.8330 Silver .2678 oz. ASW

Date	Mintage	VG	F	VF	XF	Unc
1909H	1,400,000	BV	5.00	10.00	25.00	40.00
1909H	—	Value: 500				

KM# 181 50 CENTAVOS (1/2 Boliviano) Composition: Copper Nickel **Note:** Most melted upon receipt in Bolivia. Medal rotation strike.

Date	Mintage	F	VF	XF	Unc	BU
1937	8,000,000	10.00	25.00	45.00	75.00	—

KM# 182 50 CENTAVOS (1/2 Boliviano) Composition: Copper Nickel **Note:** Medal rotation strike.

Date	F	VF	XF	Unc	BU
1939	0.25	0.50	1.00	5.00	—

KM# 182a.1 50 CENTAVOS (1/2 Boliviano) Composition: Bronze **Note:** Medal rotation strike.

Date	Mintage	F	VF	XF	Unc	BU
1942 (p)	10,000,000	0.35	0.60	1.25	5.00	—

KM# 182a.2 50 CENTAVOS (1/2 Boliviano) Composition: Bronze **Note:** Restrike - poor detail. Medal rotation strike.

Date	Mintage	F	VF	XF	Unc	BU
1942	5,310,000	0.25	0.50	1.00	4.00	—

KM# 184 BOLIVIANO Composition: Bronze **Note:** Medal rotation strike. Mint mark in monogram.

Date	Mintage	F	VF	XF	Unc	BU
1951PTS	10,000,000	0.10	0.20	0.50	2.00	—
1951PTS Proof	10	Value: 200				
1951PTS H	15,000,000	0.10	0.20	0.40	1.75	—
1951PTS KN	15,000,000	0.25	0.50	1.00	3.00	—

KM# 185 5 BOLIVIANOS Composition: Bronze **Note:** Medal rotation strike.

Date	Mintage	F	VF	XF	Unc	BU
1951	7,000,000	0.25	0.50	1.00	3.50	—
1951 Proof	—	Value: 150				
1951 H	15,000,000	0.25	0.50	1.00	3.50	—
1951 KN	15,000,000	0.60	0.90	1.50	4.00	—

KM# 186 10 BOLIVIANOS (1 Bolivar) Composition: Bronze **Note:** Medal rotation strike.

Date	Mintage	F	VF	XF	Unc	BU
1951	40,000,000	0.60	1.00	1.75	3.50	—
1951 Proof	—	—	—	—	—	—

REFORM COINAGE

1965-1979; 100 Centavos = 1 Peso Boliviano

KM# 187 5 CENTAVOS Composition: Copper Clad Steel

Date	Mintage	F	VF	XF	Unc	BU
1965	10,000,000	0.20	0.30	0.65	1.50	—
1970	100,000	0.20	0.30	0.65	2.00	—

KM# 188 10 CENTAVOS Composition: Copper Clad Steel

Date	Mintage	F	VF	XF	Unc	BU
1965	10,000,000	0.10	0.25	0.50	1.50	—
1967	—	0.10	0.20	0.40	1.00	—
1969	5,700,000	0.10	0.20	0.40	1.00	—
1971	200,000	0.15	0.25	0.50	1.00	—
1972	100,000	0.20	0.40	0.80	1.50	—
1973	6,000,000	0.10	0.20	0.40	1.00	—

KM# 189 20 CENTAVOS Composition: Nickel Clad Steel

Date	Mintage	F	VF	XF	Unc	BU
1965	5,000,000	0.20	0.40	0.70	2.00	—
1967	—	0.20	0.40	0.65	1.75	—
1970	400,000	0.20	0.40	0.80	2.50	—
1971	400,000	0.20	0.40	0.80	2.50	—
1973	5,000,000	0.20	0.40	0.60	1.50	—

KM# 193 25 CENTAVOS Composition: Nickel Clad Steel

Date	Mintage	F	VF	XF	Unc	BU
1971	—	0.15	0.30	0.60	1.00	—
1972	9,998,000	0.15	0.30	0.60	1.00	—

KM# 190 50 CENTAVOS Composition: Nickel Clad Steel

Date	Mintage	F	VF	XF	Unc	BU
1965	10,000,000	—	0.25	0.65	1.75	—
1967	—	—	0.25	0.65	1.25	—
1972	—	—	0.25	0.65	1.25	—
1973	5,000,000	—	0.25	0.65	1.25	—
1974	15,000,000	—	0.25	0.65	1.25	—

Date	Mintage	F	VF	XF	Unc	BU
1978	5,000,000	—	0.25	0.65	1.25	—
1980	3,600,000	—	0.25	0.65	1.25	—

KM# 192 PESO BOLIVIANOS **Composition:** Nickel Clad Steel **Series:** F.A.O.

Date	Mintage	F	VF	XF	Unc	BU
1968	10,000,000	0.20	0.35	0.80	1.75	—
1969	—	0.20	0.35	0.80	1.75	—
1970	10,000,000	0.15	0.25	0.80	1.75	—
1972	—	0.20	0.35	0.80	1.75	—
1973	5,000,000	0.15	0.25	0.80	1.75	—
1974 small date	15,000,000	0.15	0.25	0.80	1.75	—
1978	10,000,000	0.15	0.25	0.80	1.75	—
1980 large date	2,993,000	0.15	0.25	0.80	1.75	—

KM# 191 PESO BOLIVIANOS **Composition:** Nickel Clad Steel **Series:** F.A.O.

Date	Mintage	F	VF	XF	Unc	BU
ND(1968)	40,000	—	2.50	3.50	6.50	—

KM# 197 5 PESOS BOLIVIANOS **Composition:** Nickel Clad Steel

Date	Mintage	F	VF	XF	Unc	BU
1976	20,000,000	0.65	1.25	2.50	5.00	—
1978	10,000,000	0.65	1.25	2.50	5.00	—
1980	5,231,000	0.65	1.25	2.50	5.00	—

KM# 194 100 PESOS BOLIVIANOS **Weight:** 10.0000 g. **Composition:** 0.9330 Silver .3000 oz. ASW **Subject:** 150th Anniversary of Independence

Date	Mintage	F	VF	XF	Unc	BU
ND(1975)	160,000	BV	3.50	5.00	8.50	—

KM# 198 200 PESOS BOLIVIANOS **Weight:** 23.3300 g. **Composition:** 0.9250 Silver .6938 oz. ASW **Subject:** International Year of the Child

Date	Mintage	F	VF	XF	Unc	BU
1979	15,000	Value: 16.50				

KM# 195 250 PESOS BOLIVIANOS **Weight:** 15.0000 g. **Composition:** 0.9330 Silver .4500 oz. ASW **Subject:** 150th Anniversary of Independence

Date	Mintage	F	VF	XF	Unc	BU
ND(1975)	140,000	BV	4.00	6.00	12.50	—

KM# 196 500 PESOS BOLIVIANOS **Weight:** 22.0000 g. **Composition:** 0.9330 Silver .6600 oz. ASW **Subject:** 150th Anniversary of Independence

Date	Mintage	F	VF	XF	Unc	BU
ND(1975)	100,000	BV	6.00	12.00	20.00	—

KM# 199 4000 PESOS BOLIVIANOS **Weight:** 17.1700 g. **Composition:** 0.9000 Gold .4968 oz. AGW **Subject:** International Year of the Child

Date	Mintage	F	VF	XF	Unc	BU
1979 Proof	6,315	Value: 200				

MONETARY REFORM COINAGE

1,000,000 Peso Bolivianos = 1 Boliviano; 100 Centavos = 1 Boliviano

KM# 200 2 CENTAVOS **Composition:** Stainless Steel

Date	Mintage	F	VF	XF	Unc	BU
1987	20,000,000	—	—	—	0.35	—

KM# 201 5 CENTAVOS **Composition:** Stainless Steel

Date	Mintage	F	VF	XF	Unc	BU
1987	20,000,000	—	—	—	0.50	—

KM# 202 10 CENTAVOS **Composition:** Stainless Steel

Date	Mintage	F	VF	XF	Unc	BU
1987	20,000,000	—	—	—	0.65	—
1991	23,000,000	—	—	—	0.50	—
1995	14,000,000	—	—	—	0.50	—
1997	33,000,000	—	—	—	0.50	—

KM# 202a 10 CENTAVOS **Composition:** Copper Clad Steel

Date	F	VF	XF	Unc	BU
1997	—	—	—	0.50	—

KM# 203 20 CENTAVOS **Composition:** Stainless Steel

Date	Mintage	F	VF	XF	Unc	BU
1987	20,000,000	—	—	—	0.75	—
1991	20,000,000	—	—	—	0.65	—
1995	14,000,000	—	—	—	0.65	—
1997	19,000,000	—	—	—	0.65	—

KM# 204 50 CENTAVOS **Composition:** Stainless Steel

Date	Mintage	F	VF	XF	Unc	BU
1987	15,000,000	—	—	—	1.00	—
1991	20,000,000	—	—	—	0.75	—
1995	14,000,000	—	—	—	0.75	—
1997	15,000,000	—	—	—	0.75	—

KM# 205 BOLIVIANO **Composition:** Stainless Steel

Date	Mintage	F	VF	XF	Unc	BU
1987	10,000,000	—	—	—	1.75	—
1991	20,000,000	—	—	—	1.00	—
1995	9,000,000	—	—	—	1.00	—
1997	17,000,000	—	—	—	1.00	—

KM# 210 BOLIVIANO **Weight:** 27.0000 g. **Composition:** 0.9250 Silver .8030 oz. ASW **Subject:** 70th Anniversary - Bolivian Central Bank **Obverse:** National arms **Reverse:** Denomination above bank emblem

Date	Mintage	F	VF	XF	Unc	BU
1998 Proof	1,000	Value: 65.00				

KM# 206.1 2 BOLIVIANOS **Composition:** Stainless Steel

Date	Mintage	F	VF	XF	Unc	BU
1991	18,000,000	—	—	—	2.00	—

KM# 206.2 2 BOLIVIANOS Composition: Stainless Steel **Size:** 29 mm. **Note:** Increased size.

Date	Mintage	F	VF	XF	Unc	BU
1995	11,000,000	—	—	—	2.00	—
1997	—	—	—	—	2.00	—

KM# 207 10 BOLIVIANOS Weight: 27.0000 g. **Composition:** 0.9250 Silver .8029 oz. ASW **Series:** Ibero - American

Date	Mintage	F	VF	XF	Unc	BU
1991 Proof	Est. 50,000	Value: 60.00				

KM# 209 10 BOLIVIANOS Weight: 27.1300 g. **Composition:** 0.9250 Silver .8068 oz. ASW **Series:** Ibero - American **Obverse:** Bolivian arms **Reverse:** Folk dancer

Date	Mintage	F	VF	XF	Unc	BU
1997 Proof	33,000	Value: 60.00				

KM# 211 50 BOLIVIANOS Weight: 27.0000 g. **Composition:** 0.9250 Silver .8030 oz. ASW **Subject:** 450th Anniversary of La Paz **Obverse:** National arms **Reverse:** City arms above church building

Date	Mintage	F	VF	XF	Unc	BU
1998 Proof	2,000	Value: 65.00				

REFORM COINAGE

1987-; 100 Centavos = 1 Boliviana

KM# 212 5 BOLIVIANOS Center Weight: 5.0000 g. **Center Composition:** Brass Clad Steel **Obverse:** National arms **Reverse:** Denomination within inner ring **Edge:** Reeded **Size:** 23 mm.

Date	F	VF	XF	Unc	BU
2001 Proof	—	Value: 3.50			

PATTERNS

Including off metal strikes

KM#	Date	Mintage	Identification	Mkt Val
Pn54	1902 MM	—	20 Centavos. Brass. Struck at La Paz.	75.00
Pn55	1902 MM	—	20 Centavos. Brass. Struck at La Paz. 1/2 Medio Boliviano/20 Centavos error.	75.00

KM#	Date	Mintage	Identification	Mkt Val
Pn56	1902 MM	—	50 Centavos. Brass.	100
Pn57	1942	—	50 Centavos. Silver. Struck at La Paz. KM#182a.1.	200
Pn58	1952	—	35 Gramos. Brass. Struck at La Paz. KM MB4.	—

PIEFORTS

KM#	Date	Mintage	Identification	Issue Price	Mkt Val
P9	1979	90	200 Pesos. KM#198.	—	200
P10	1979	47	4000 Pesos. KM#199.	—	1,000

TRIAL STRIKES

KM#	Date	Mintage	Identification	Issue Price	Mkt Val
Ts1	ND(1909)	—	20 Centavos. Silver. 23.2 mm. Uniface.	—	—

The Republic of Bosnia-Herzegovina borders Croatia to the north and west, Serbia to the east and Montenegro in the southeast with only 12.4 mi. of coastline. The total land area is 19,735 sq. mi. (51,129 sq. km.). They have a population of *4.34 million. Capital: Sarajevo. Electricity, mining and agriculture are leading industries.

After the defeat of Germany in WWII, during which Bosnia was under the control of Pavelic of Croatia, a new Socialist Republic was formed under Marshall Tito having six constituent republics, all subservient, quite similar to the constitution of the U.S.S.R. Military and civil loyalty was with Tito, not with Moscow. In Jan. 1990, the Yugoslav Government announced a rewriting of the Constitution, abolishing the Communist Party's monopoly of power. Opposition parties were legalized in July 1990. On Oct. 15, 1991 the National Assembly adopted a "Memorandum on Sovereignty", the envisaged Bosnian autonomy within a Yugoslav federation. In March 1992, an agreement was reached under EC auspices by Moslems, Serbs and Croats to set up 3 autonomous ethnic communities under a central Bosnian authority. Independence was declared on April 5, 1992. The 2 Serbian members of government resigned and fighting broke out between all 3 ethnic communities. The Dayton (Ohio) Peace Accord was signed in 1995, which recognized the Federation of Bosnia-Herzegovina and the Srpska (Serbian) Republic. Both governments maintain separate military forces, school systems, etc. The United Nations is currently providing humanitarian aid while a recent peace treaty allowed NATO "Peace Keeping" forces to be deployed in Dec. 1995 replacing the United Nations troops previously acting in a similar role.

MINT MARKS

PM - Pobjoy Mint

MONETARY SYSTEM

1 Dinara = 100 Para, 1992-1998
1 Convertible Marka = 100 Convertible Feniga = 1 Deutschemark 1998-

NOTE: German Marks and Yugoslavian Dinara circulate freely.

REPUBLIC

STANDARD COINAGE

KM# 115 10 FENINGA Composition: Copper-Plated-Steel **Obverse:** Denomination on map **Reverse:** Triangle and stars

Date	F	VF	XF	Unc	BU
1998	—	—	—	0.50	—
2000	—	—	—	0.50	—

KM# 116 20 FENINGA Composition: Copper-Plated-Steel **Obverse:** Denomination on map **Reverse:** Triangle and stars

Date	F	VF	XF	Unc	BU
1998	—	—	—	1.00	—
2000	—	—	—	1.00	—

KM# 117 50 FENINGA Composition: Copper-Plated-Steel **Obverse:** Denomination on map **Reverse:** Triangle and stars

Date	F	VF	XF	Unc	BU
1998	—	—	—	2.25	—
2000	—	—	—	2.25	—

KM# 118 KONVERTIBLE MARKA **Weight:** 4.9000 g. **Composition:** Nickel Plated Steel **Obverse:** Denomination **Reverse:** Coat of arms above date **Edge:** Reeded and plain sections **Size:** 23.23 mm.

Date	F	VF	XF	Unc	BU
2000	—	—	—	5.50	—

KM# 119 2 KONVERTIBLE MARKA **Ring Composition:** Nickel-Brass**Center Weight:** 6.9000 g. **Center Composition:** Copper-Nickel **Obverse:** Denomination **Reverse:** Dove of peace **Edge:** Reeded and plain sections **Size:** 25.75 mm.

Date	F	VF	XF	Unc	BU
2000	—	—	—	11.50	—

DINARA COINAGE

KM# 1 500 DINARA **Composition:** Copper-Nickel **Series:** Preserve Planet Earth **Subject:** Brontosaurus

Date	F	VF	XF	Unc	BU
1993 Proof	—	Value: 8.50			

KM# 4 500 DINARA **Composition:** Copper-Nickel **Series:** Preserve Planet Earth **Subject:** Tyrannosaurus Rex

Date	F	VF	XF	Unc	BU
1993 Proof	—	Value: 10.00			

KM# 23 500 DINARA **Composition:** Copper-Nickel **Series:** Preserve Planet Earth **Subject:** Gray Wolf

Date	F	VF	XF	Unc	BU
1994 Proof	—	—	—	9.00	—

KM# 24 500 DINARA **Composition:** Copper-Nickel **Series:** Preserve Planet Earth **Subject:** Black Bears

Date	F	VF	XF	Unc	BU
1994 Proof	—	—	—	9.00	—

KM# 25 500 DINARA **Composition:** Copper-Nickel **Series:** Preserve Planet Earth **Subject:** River Kingfisher

Date	F	VF	XF	Unc	BU
1994	—	—	—	9.00	—

KM# 20 500 DINARA **Composition:** Copper-Nickel **Series:** Preserve Planet Earth **Subject:** Eohippus **Note:** Similar to 10,000 Dinara, KM#22.

Date	F	VF	XF	Unc	BU
1994 Proof	—	—	—	9.00	—

KM# 39 500 DINARA **Composition:** Copper-Nickel **Series:** Preserve Planet Earth **Subject:** Przewalskii Horses **Note:** Similar to 750 Dinara, KM#40.

Date	F	VF	XF	Unc	BU
1995	—	—	—	9.00	—

KM# 42 500 DINARA **Composition:** Copper-Nickel **Series:** Preserve Planet Earth **Subject:** Hedgehogs **Note:** Similar to 750 Dinara, KM#40.

Date	F	VF	XF	Unc	BU
1995	—	—	—	10.00	—

KM# 64 500 DINARA **Composition:** Copper-Nickel **Series:** European Youth Olympics **Subject:** Flame **Note:** Similar to 750 Dinara, KM#66.

Date	F	VF	XF	Unc	BU
1995	—	—	—	8.50	—

KM# 65 500 DINARA **Composition:** Copper-Nickel **Series:** European Youth Olympics **Subject:** Rings **Note:** Similar to 750 Dinara, KM#67.

Date	F	VF	XF	Unc	BU
1995	—	—	—	8.50	—

KM# 76 500 DINARA **Composition:** Copper-Nickel **Series:** Preserve Planet Earth **Subject:** Hoopoe Birds **Note:** Similar to 750 Dinara, KM#77.

Date	F	VF	XF	Unc	BU
1996	—	—	—	8.50	—

KM# 52 500 DINARA **Composition:** Copper-Nickel **Series:** Olympics **Subject:** Long Jump **Note:** Similar to 750 Dinara, KM#56.

Date	F	VF	XF	Unc	BU
1996	—	—	—	8.50	—

KM# 53 500 DINARA **Composition:** Copper-Nickel **Series:** Olympics **Subject:** Sprinter **Note:** Similar to 750 Dinara, KM#57.

Date	F	VF	XF	Unc	BU
1996	—	—	—	8.50	—

KM# 54 500 DINARA **Composition:** Copper-Nickel **Series:** Olympics **Subject:** Wrestlers **Note:** Similar to 750 Dinara, KM#58.

Date	F	VF	XF	Unc	BU
1996	—	—	—	8.50	—

KM# 55 500 DINARA **Composition:** Copper-Nickel **Series:** Olympics **Subject:** Fencers **Note:** Similar to 750 Dinara, KM#59.

Date	F	VF	XF	Unc	BU
1996	—	—	—	8.50	—

KM# 79 500 DINARA **Composition:** Copper-Nickel **Series:** Preserve Planet Earth **Subject:** Goosander Birds **Note:** Similar to 750 Dinars, KM#80.

Date	F	VF	XF	Unc	BU
1996	—	—	—	8.50	—

KM# 95 500 DINARA **Composition:** Copper-Nickel **Subject:** Jurassic Park **Obverse:** Arms above bridge **Reverse:** Tyrannosaurus Rex, Jurassic Park logo **Note:** Similar to 750 Dinara, KM#96.

Date	F	VF	XF	Unc	BU
1997	—	—	—	10.00	—

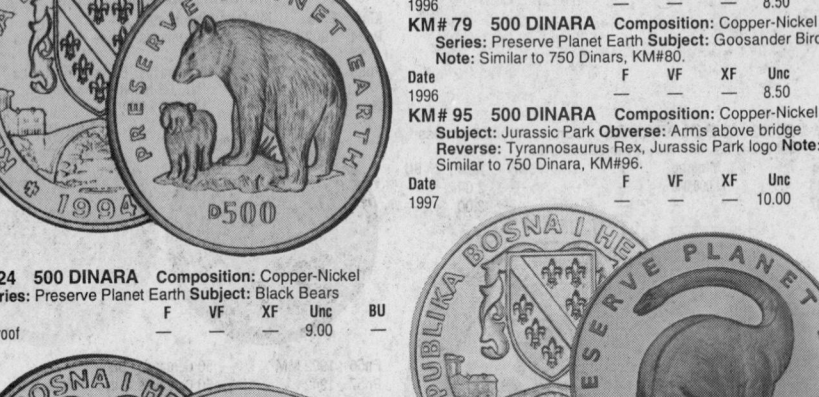

KM# 2 750 DINARA **Weight:** 28.2800 g. **Composition:** 0.9250 Silver .8411 oz. ASW **Series:** Preserve Planet Earth **Subject:** Brontosaurus

Date	Mintage	F	VF	XF	Unc	BU
1993 Proof	Est. 30,000	Value: 37.50				

KM# 5 750 DINARA **Weight:** 28.2800 g. **Composition:** 0.9250 Silver .8411 oz. ASW **Series:** Preserve Planet Earth **Subject:** Tyrannosaurus Rex

Date	Mintage	F	VF	XF	Unc	BU
1993 Proof	Est. 30,000	Value: 37.50				

KM# 7 750 DINARA **Weight:** 28.2800 g. **Composition:** 0.9250 Silver .8411 oz. ASW **Series:** Olympics **Subject:** Bobsledding

Date	Mintage	F	VF	XF	Unc	BU
1993 Proof	Est. 30,000	Value: 45.00				

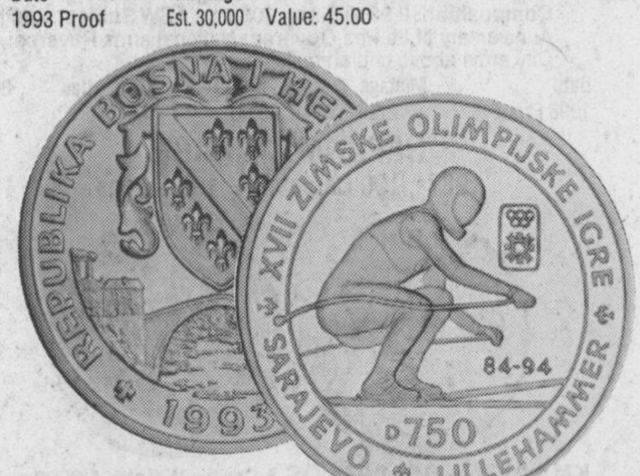

KM# 9 750 DINARA **Weight:** 28.2800 g. **Composition:** 0.9250 Silver .8411 oz. ASW **Series:** Olympics **Subject:** Downhill Skiing

Date	Mintage	F	VF	XF	Unc	BU
1993 Proof	Est. 30,000	Value: 45.00				

KM# 11 750 DINARA **Weight:** 28.2800 g. **Composition:** 0.9250 Silver .8411 oz. ASW **Series:** Olympics **Subject:** Cross Country Skiing

Date	Mintage	F	VF	XF	Unc	BU
1993 Proof	Est. 30,000	Value: 45.00				

KM# 13 750 DINARA **Weight:** 28.2800 g. **Composition:** 0.9250 Silver .8411 oz. ASW **Series:** Olympics **Subject:** Pairs Figure Skating

Date	Mintage	F	VF	XF	Unc	BU
1993 Proof	Est. 30,000	Value: 45.00				

KM# 26 750 DINARA **Weight:** 28.2800 g. **Composition:** 0.9250 Silver .8411 oz. ASW **Series:** Preserve Planet Earth **Subject:** Wolf

Date	Mintage	F	VF	XF	Unc	BU
1994 Proof	Est. 30,000	Value: 37.50				

KM# 27 750 DINARA **Weight:** 28.2800 g. **Composition:** 0.9250 Silver .8411 oz. ASW **Series:** Preserve Planet Earth **Subject:** Black Bears

Date	Mintage	F	VF	XF	Unc	BU
1994 Proof	Est. 30,000	Value: 32.50				

KM# 28 750 DINARA **Weight:** 28.2800 g. **Composition:** 0.9250 Silver .8411 oz. ASW **Series:** Preserve Planet Earth **Subject:** River Kingfisher

Date	Mintage	F	VF	XF	Unc	BU
1994 Proof	Est. 30,000	Value: 32.50				

KM# 21 750 DINARA **Weight:** 28.2800 g. **Composition:** 0.9250 Silver .8411 oz. ASW **Series:** Preserve Planet Earth **Subject:** Eohippu **Note:** Similar to 10,000 Dinara, KM#22.

Date	Mintage	F	VF	XF	Unc	BU
1994 Proof	Est. 30,000	Value: 32.50				

KM# 40 750 DINARA **Weight:** 28.2800 g. **Composition:** 0.9250 Silver .8411 oz. ASW **Series:** Preserve Planet Earth **Subject:** Przewalskii Horses

Date	Mintage	F	VF	XF	Unc	BU
1995 Proof	Est. 30,000	Value: 32.50				

KM# 43 750 DINARA **Weight:** 28.2800 g. **Composition:** 0.9250 Silver .8411 oz. ASW **Series:** Preserve Planet Earth **Subject:** Hedgehogs

Date	Mintage	F	VF	XF	Unc	BU
1995 Proof	Est. 30,000	Value: 35.00				

KM# 66 750 DINARA **Weight:** 28.2800 g. **Composition:** 0.9250 Silver .8411 oz. ASW **Series:** European Youth Olympics **Subject:** Flame

Date	Mintage	F	VF	XF	Unc	BU
1995 Proof	Est. 30,000	Value: 37.50				

KM# 67 750 DINARA **Weight:** 28.2800 g. **Composition:** 0.9250 Silver .8411 oz. ASW **Series:** European Youth Olympics **Subject:** Rings

Date	Mintage	F	VF	XF	Unc	BU
1995 Proof	Est. 30,000	Value: 37.50				

KM# 56 750 DINARA **Weight:** 28.2800 g. **Composition:** 0.9250 Silver .8411 oz. ASW **Series:** Olympics **Subject:** Long Jump

Date	Mintage	F	VF	XF	Unc	BU
1996 Proof	Est. 30,000	Value: 35.00				

KM# 57 750 DINARA **Weight:** 28.2800 g. **Composition:** 0.9250 Silver .8411 oz. ASW **Series:** Olympics **Subject:** Sprinter

Date	Mintage	F	VF	XF	Unc	BU
1996 Proof	Est. 30,000	Value: 35.00				

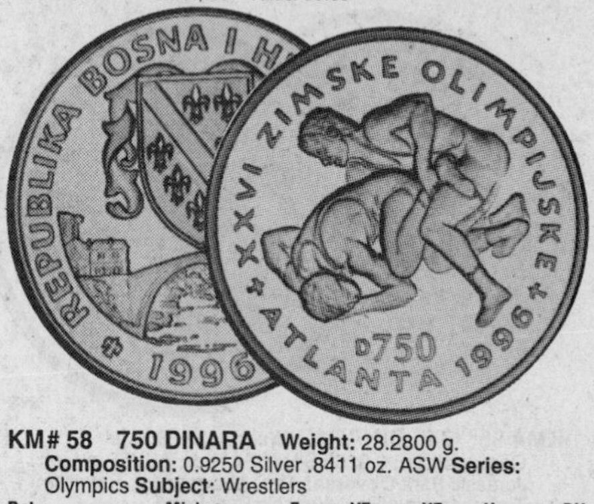

KM# 58 750 DINARA **Weight:** 28.2800 g. **Composition:** 0.9250 Silver .8411 oz. ASW **Series:** Olympics **Subject:** Wrestlers

Date	Mintage	F	VF	XF	Unc	BU
1996 Proof	Est. 30,000	Value: 35.00				

KM# 59 750 DINARA **Weight:** 28.2800 g. **Composition:** 0.9250 Silver .8411 oz. ASW **Series:** Olympics **Subject:** Fencers

Date	Mintage	F	VF	XF	Unc	BU
1996 Proof	Est. 30,000	Value: 35.00				

KM# 77 750 DINARA **Weight:** 28.2800 g. **Composition:** 0.9250 Silver .8411 oz. ASW **Series:** Preserve Planet Earth **Subject:** Hoopoe Birds

Date	Mintage	F	VF	XF	Unc	BU
1996 Proof	Est. 30,000	Value: 32.50				

KM# 80 750 DINARA **Weight:** 28.2800 g. **Composition:** 0.9250 Silver .8411 oz. ASW **Series:** Preserve Planet Earth **Subject:** Goosander Birds

Date	Mintage	F	VF	XF	Unc	BU
1996 Proof	Est. 30,000	Value: 32.50				

KM# 96 750 DINARA **Weight:** 28.2800 g. **Composition:** 0.9250 Silver .8411 oz. ASW **Subject:** Jurassic Park **Obverse:** Arms above bridge **Reverse:** Tyrannosaurus Rex, Jurassic Park logo

Date	Mintage	F	VF	XF	Unc	BU
1997 Proof	Est. 10,000	Value: 48.00				

KM# 3 10000 DINARA **Weight:** 6.2200 g. **Composition:** 0.9990 Gold .1998 oz. AGW **Series:** Preserve Planet Earth **Subject:** Brontosaurus

Date	Mintage	F	VF	XF	Unc	BU
1993 Proof	Est. 5,000	Value: 170				

KM# 6 10000 DINARA **Weight:** 6.2200 g. **Composition:** 0.9990 Gold .1998 oz. AGW **Series:** Preserve Planet Earth **Subject:** Tyrannosaurus Rex

Date	Mintage	F	VF	XF	Unc	BU
1993 Proof	Est. 5,000	Value: 170				

KM# 12 10000 DINARA **Weight:** 6.2200 g. **Composition:** 0.9990 Gold .1998 oz. AGW **Series:** Olympics **Subject:** Cross Country Skiing **Obverse:** Similar to KM#6 **Reverse:** Cross country skier **Note:** Similar to 750 Dinara, KM#11.

Date	Mintage	F	VF	XF	Unc	BU
1993 Proof	Est. 5,000	Value: 175				

KM# 14 10000 DINARA **Weight:** 6.2200 g. **Composition:** 0.9990 Gold .1998 oz. AGW **Series:** Olympics **Subject:** Pairs Figure Skating **Obverse:** Similar to KM#6 **Reverse:** Pair skating **Note:** Similar to 750 Dinara, KM#13.

Date	Mintage	F	VF	XF	Unc	BU
1993 Proof	Est. 5,000	Value: 175				

KM# 8 10000 DINARA **Weight:** 6.2200 g. **Composition:** 0.9990 Gold .1998 oz. AGW **Series:** Olympics **Subject:** Bobsledding **Obverse:** Similar to KM#6 **Reverse:** Two bobsledders starting race **Note:** Similar to 750 Dinara, KM#7.

Date	Mintage	F	VF	XF	Unc	BU
1993 Proof	Est. 5,000	Value: 175				

KM# 10 10000 DINARA **Weight:** 6.2200 g. **Composition:** 0.9990 Gold .1998 oz. AGW **Series:** Olympics **Subject:** Downhill Skiing **Obverse:** Similar to KM#6 **Reverse:** Downhill skier **Note:** Similar to 750 Dinara, KM#9.

Date	Mintage	F	VF	XF	Unc	BU
1993	Est. 5,000	Value: 175				

KM# 29 10000 DINARA **Weight:** 6.2200 g. **Composition:** 0.9990 Gold .1998 oz. AGW **Series:** Preserve Planet Earth **Subject:** Wolf **Reverse:** Wolf walking right **Note:** Similar to 750 Dinara, KM#26.

Date	Mintage	F	VF	XF	Unc	BU
1994 Proof	5,000	Value: 170				

KM# 30 10000 DINARA **Weight:** 6.2200 g. **Composition:** 0.9990 Gold .1998 oz. AGW **Series:** Preserve Planet Earth **Subject:** Black Bears **Reverse:** Black bear and cub walking right **Note:** Similar to 750 Dinara, KM#27.

Date	Mintage	F	VF	XF	Unc	BU
1994 Proof	5,000	Value: 170				

KM# 31 10000 DINARA **Weight:** 6.2200 g. **Composition:** 0.9990 Gold .1998 oz. AGW **Series:** Preserve Planet Earth **Subject:** Kingfisher **Reverse:** Kingfisher left with fish in bill **Note:** Similar to 750 Dinara, KM#28.

Date	Mintage	F	VF	XF	Unc	BU
1994 Proof	5,000	Value: 170				

KM# 22 10000 DINARA **Weight:** 6.2200 g. **Composition:** 0.9990 Gold .1998 oz. AGW **Series:** Preserve Planet Earth **Subject:** Eohippu

Date	Mintage	F	VF	XF	Unc	BU
1994 Proof	Est. 5,000	Value: 170				

KM# 41 10000 DINARA **Weight:** 6.2200 g. **Composition:** 0.9990 Gold .1998 oz. AGW **Series:** Preserve Planet Earth **Subject:** Przewalskii Horses **Note:** Similar to 750 Dinara, KM#40.

Date	Mintage	F	VF	XF	Unc	BU
1995 Proof	Est. 5,000	Value: 170				

KM# 44 10000 DINARA **Weight:** 6.2200 g. **Composition:** 0.9990 Gold .1998 oz. AGW **Series:** Preserve Planet Earth **Subject:** Hedgehogs **Note:** Similar to 750 Dinara, KM#43.

Date	Mintage	F	VF	XF	Unc	BU
1995 Proof	Est. 5,000	Value: 170				

KM# 60 10000 DINARA **Weight:** 6.2200 g. **Composition:** 0.9990 Gold .1998 oz. AGW **Series:** Olympics **Subject:** Long Jump **Obverse:** Coat of arms above bridge **Reverse:** Jumper **Note:** Similar to 750 Dinara, KM#56.

Date	Mintage	F	VF	XF	Unc	BU
1996 Proof	Est. 5,000	Value: 190				

KM# 61 10000 DINARA **Weight:** 6.2200 g. **Composition:** 0.9990 Gold .1998 oz. AGW **Series:** Olympics **Subject:** Sprinter **Obverse:** Coat of arms **Reverse:** Sprinter **Note:** Similar to 750 Dinara, KM#57.

Date	Mintage	F	VF	XF	Unc	BU
1996 Proof	Est. 5,000	Value: 190				

KM# 78 10000 DINARA **Weight:** 6.2200 g. **Composition:** 0.9990 Gold .1998 oz. AGW **Series:** Preserve Planet Earth **Subject:** Hoopoe Birds **Note:** Similar to 750 Dinara, KM#77.

Date	Mintage	F	VF	XF	Unc	BU
1996 Proof	Est. 5,000	Value: 175				

KM# 62 10000 DINARA **Weight:** 6.2200 g. **Composition:** 0.9990 Gold .1998 oz. AGW **Series:** Olympics **Subject:** Wrestlers **Obverse:** Coat of arms **Reverse:** Wrestlers **Note:** Similar to 750 Dinara, KM#58.

Date	Mintage	F	VF	XF	Unc	BU
1996 Proof	Est. 5,000	Value: 190				

KM# 63 10000 DINARA **Weight:** 6.2200 g. **Composition:** 0.9990 Gold .1998 oz. AGW **Series:** Olympics **Subject:** Fencers **Obverse:** Coat of arms **Reverse:** Fencers **Note:** Similar to 750 Dinara, KM#59.

Date	Mintage	F	VF	XF	Unc	BU
1996 Proof	Est. 5,000	Value: 190				

KM# 81 10000 DINARA **Weight:** 6.2200 g. **Composition:** 0.9990 Gold .1998 oz. AGW **Series:** Preserve Planet Earth **Subject:** Goosander Birds **Note:** Similar to 750 Dinara, KM#80.

Date	Mintage	F	VF	XF	Unc	BU
1996 Proof	Est. 5,000	Value: 175				

KM# 97 10000 DINARA **Weight:** 6.2200 g. **Composition:** 0.9990 Gold .1998 oz. AGW **Subject:** Jurassic Park **Note:** Similar to 750 Dinara, KM#96.

Date	Mintage	F	VF	XF	Unc	BU
1997 Proof	Est. 2,500	Value: 175				

MARKA / MARAKA COINAGE

KM# 111 5 MARKA **Composition:** Copper-Nickel **Subject:** Summer Olympics 2000 **Obverse:** Arms above bridge **Reverse:** Javelin thrower

Date	F	VF	XF	Unc	BU
1998	—	—	—	8.50	—

KM# 98 5 MARKA **Composition:** Copper-Nickel **Subject:** Princess Diana **Obverse:** Arms above bridge **Reverse:** Portrait and map **Note:** Similar to 10 Marka, KM#99.

Date	F	VF	XF	Unc	BU
1998	—	—	—	8.50	—

KM# 99 10 MARKA **Weight:** 28.2800 g. **Composition:** 0.9250 Silver .8410 oz. ASW **Subject:** Princess Diana **Obverse:** Arms above bridge **Reverse:** Portrait and map

Date	Mintage	F	VF	XF	Unc	BU
1998 Proof	Est. 10,000	Value: 50.00				

KM# 112 10 MARKA **Weight:** 28.2800 g. **Composition:** 0.9250 Silver .8410 oz. ASW **Subject:** Summer Olympics 2000 **Obverse:** Arms above bridge **Reverse:** Javelin thrower

Date	Mintage	F	VF	XF	Unc	BU
1998 Proof	Est. 10,000	Value: 50.00				

KM# 100 20 MARKA **Weight:** 1.2441 g. **Composition:** 0.9999 Gold .0400 oz. AGW **Subject:** Princess Diana **Obverse:** Arms above bridge **Reverse:** Portrait and map **Note:** Similar to 10 Marka, KM#99.

Date	Mintage	F	VF	XF	Unc	BU
1998 Proof	Est. 10,000	Value: 50.00				

KM# 101 50 MARKA **Weight:** 3.1103 g. **Composition:** 0.9999 Gold .1000 oz. AGW **Subject:** Princess Diana **Obverse:** Arms above bridge **Reverse:** Portrait and map **Note:** Similar to 10 Marka, KM#99.

Date	Mintage	F	VF	XF	Unc	BU
1998 Proof	Est. 7,500	Value: 100				

KM# 113 100 MARKA **Weight:** 6.2206 g. **Composition:** 0.9999 Gold .2000 oz. AGW **Subject:** Summer Olympics 2000 **Obverse:** Arms above bridge **Reverse:** Javelin thrower **Note:** Similar to 10 Marka, KM#112.

Date	Mintage	F	VF	XF	Unc	BU
1998 Proof	Est. 5,000	Value: 185				

KM# 102 100 MARKA Weight: 6.2206 g. **Composition:** 0.9999 Gold .2000 oz. AGW **Subject:** Princess Diana **Obverse:** Arms above bridge **Reverse:** Portrait and map **Note:** Similar to 10 Marka, KM#99.

Date	Mintage	F	VF	XF	Unc	BU
1998 Proof	Est. 5,000	Value: 185				

KM# 103 250 MARKA Weight: 15.5517 g. **Composition:** 0.9999 Gold .5000 oz. AGW **Subject:** Princess Diana **Obverse:** Arms above bridge **Reverse:** Portrait and map **Note:** Similar to 10 Marka, KM#99.

Date	Mintage	F	VF	XF	Unc	BU
1998 Proof	Est. 3,000	Value: 365				

TRADE COINAGE

KM# 15 1/25 DUKAT Weight: 1.2440 g. **Composition:** 0.9999 Gold .0400 oz. AGW **Subject:** Hajj - Kaaba in Mecca **Note:** Similar to 1 Dukat, KM#19.

Date	Mintage	F	VF	XF	Unc	BU
1993 Proof	Est. 25,000	Value: 40.00				

KM# 16 1/10 DUKAT Weight: 3.1103 g. **Composition:** 0.9999 Gold .1000 oz. AGW **Subject:** Hajj - Kaaba in Mecca **Note:** Similar to 1 Dukat, KM#19.

Date	Mintage	F	VF	XF	Unc	BU
1993 Proof	Est. 20,000	Value: 80.00				

KM# 17 1/5 DUKAT Weight: 6.2200 g. **Composition:** 0.9999 Gold .2000 oz. AGW **Subject:** Hajj - Kaaba in Mecca **Note:** Similar to 1 Dukat, KM#19.

Date	Mintage	F	VF	XF	Unc	BU
1993 Proof	Est. 5,000	Value: 160				

KM# 18 1/10 DUKAT Weight: 15.5510 g. **Composition:** 0.9999 Gold .5000 oz. AGW **Subject:** Hajj - Kaaba in Mecca **Note:** Similar to 1 Dukat, KM#19.

Date	Mintage	F	VF	XF	Unc	BU
1993 Proof	Est. 5,000	Value: 320				

KM# 19 DUKAT Weight: 31.1030 g. **Composition:** 0.9999 Gold 1.0000 oz. AGW **Subject:** Hajj - Kaaba in Mecca

Date	Mintage	F	VF	XF	Unc	BU
1993 Proof	Est. 5,000	Value: 600				
1994 Proof	—	Value: 600				

KM# 32 1/25 SUVERENA Weight: 1.2441 g. **Composition:** 0.9999 Gold .0400 oz. AGW **Subject:** Lipizzaner Stallion **Note:** Similar to 1 Suverena, KM#37a.

Date		F	VF	XF	Unc	BU
1994 Proof	—	Value: 50.00				

KM# 45 1/25 SUVERENA Weight: 1.2441 g. **Composition:** 0.9999 Gold .0400 oz. AGW **Subject:** English Hack **Note:** Similar to 1 Suverena, KM#51.

Date	Mintage	F	VF	XF	Unc	BU
1995 Proof	Est. 15,000	Value: 50.00				

KM# 70 1/25 SUVERENA Weight: 1.2441 g. **Composition:** 0.9999 Gold .0400 oz. AGW **Subject:** Hanoverian Stallion **Note:** Similar to 1 Suverena, KM#76.

Date	Mintage	F	VF	XF	Unc	BU
1996 Proof	Est. 15,000	Value: 50.00				

KM# 89 1/25 SUVERENA Weight: 1.2441 g. **Composition:** 0.9999 Gold .0400 oz. AGW **Subject:** The Arab **Note:** Similar to 1 Suverena, KM#95.

Date	Mintage	F	VF	XF	Unc	BU
1997 Proof	Est. 15,000	Value: 50.00				

KM# 104 1/25 SUVERENA Weight: 1.2441 g. **Composition:** 0.9999 Gold .0400 oz. AGW **Subject:** Chinese Horse **Obverse:** Arms above bridge **Reverse:** Horse **Note:** Similar to 1 Suverena, KM#108.

Date	Mintage	F	VF	XF	Unc	BU
1998 Proof	Est. 15,000	Value: 50.00				

KM# 33 1/10 SUVERENA Weight: 3.1103 g. **Composition:** 0.9999 Gold .1000 oz. AGW **Subject:** Lipizzaner Stallion **Note:** Similar to 1 Suverena, KM#37a.

Date		F	VF	XF	Unc	BU
1994 Proof	—	Value: 100				

KM# 46 1/10 SUVERENA Weight: 3.1103 g. **Composition:** 0.9999 Gold .1000 oz. AGW **Subject:** English Hack **Note:** Similar to 1 Suverena, KM#51.

Date	Mintage	F	VF	XF	Unc	BU
1995 Proof	Est. 10,000	Value: 100				

KM# 71 1/10 SUVERENA Weight: 3.1103 g. **Composition:** 0.9999 Gold .1000 oz. AGW **Subject:** Hanoverian Stallion **Note:** Similar to 1 Suverena, KM#76.

Date	Mintage	F	VF	XF	Unc	BU
1996 Proof	Est. 10,000	Value: 100				

KM# 90 1/10 SUVERENA Weight: 3.1103 g. **Composition:** 0.9999 Gold .1000 oz. AGW **Subject:** The Arab **Note:** Similar to 1 Suverena, KM#95.

Date	Mintage	F	VF	XF	Unc	BU
1997 Proof	Est. 10,000	Value: 100				

KM# 105 1/10 SUVERENA Weight: 3.1103 g. **Composition:** 0.9999 Gold .1000 oz. AGW **Subject:** Chinese Horse **Obverse:** Arms above bridge **Reverse:** Horse **Note:** Similar to 1 Suverena, KM#108.

Date	Mintage	F	VF	XF	Unc	BU
1998 Proof	Est. 10,000	Value: 100				

KM# 34 1/5 SUVERENA Weight: 6.2207 g. **Composition:** 0.9999 Gold .2000 oz. AGW **Subject:** Lipizzaner Stallion **Note:** Similar to 1 Suverena, KM#37a.

Date		F	VF	XF	Unc	BU
1994 Proof	—	Value: 180				

KM# 47 1/5 SUVERENA Weight: 6.2207 g. **Composition:** 0.9999 Gold .2000 oz. AGW **Subject:** English Hack **Note:** Similar to 1 Suverena, KM#51.

Date	Mintage	F	VF	XF	Unc	BU
1995 Proof	Est. 5,000	Value: 180				

KM# 72 1/5 SUVERENA Weight: 6.2207 g. **Composition:** 0.9999 Gold .2000 oz. AGW **Subject:** Hanoverian Stallion **Note:** Similar to 1 Suverena, KM#76.

Date	Mintage	F	VF	XF	Unc	BU
1996 Proof	Est. 5,000	Value: 180				

KM# 91 1/5 SUVERENA Weight: 6.2207 g. **Composition:** 0.9999 Gold .2000 oz. AGW **Subject:** The Arab **Note:** Similar to 1 Suverena, KM#95.

Date	Mintage	F	VF	XF	Unc	BU
1997 Proof	Est. 5,000	Value: 180				

KM# 106 1/5 SUVERENA Weight: 6.2207 g. **Composition:** 0.9999 Gold .2000 oz. AGW **Subject:** Chinese Horse **Obverse:** Arms above bridge **Reverse:** Horse **Note:** Similar to 1 Suverena, KM#108.

Date	Mintage	F	VF	XF	Unc	BU
1998 Proof	Est. 5,000	Value: 175				

KM# 35 1/2 SUVERENA Weight: 15.5517 g. **Composition:** 0.9999 Gold .5000 oz. AGW **Subject:** Lipizzaner Stallion **Note:** Similar to 1 Suverena, KM#37a.

Date		F	VF	XF	Unc	BU
1994 Proof	—	Value: 365				

KM# 48 1/2 SUVERENA Weight: 15.5517 g. **Composition:** 0.9999 Gold .5000 oz. AGW **Subject:** English Hack **Note:** Similar to 1 Suverena, KM#51.

Date	Mintage	F	VF	XF	Unc	BU
1995 Proof	Est. 2,500	Value: 365				

KM# 73 1/2 SUVERENA Weight: 15.5517 g. **Composition:** 0.9999 Gold .5000 oz. AGW **Subject:** Hanoverian Stallion **Note:** Similar to 1 Suverena, KM#76.

Date	Mintage	F	VF	XF	Unc	BU
1996 Proof	Est. 2,500	Value: 365				

KM# 92 1/2 SUVERENA Weight: 15.5517 g. **Composition:** 0.9999 Gold .5000 oz. AGW **Subject:** The Arab **Note:** Similar to 1 Suverena, KM#95.

Date	Mintage	F	VF	XF	Unc	BU
1997 Proof	Est. 2,500	Value: 365				

KM# 107 1/2 SUVERENA Weight: 15.5517 g. **Composition:** 0.9999 Gold .5000 oz. AGW **Subject:** Chinese Horse **Obverse:** Arms above bridge **Reverse:** Horse **Note:** Similar to 1 Suverena, KM#108.

Date	Mintage	F	VF	XF	Unc	BU
1998 Proof	Est. 2,500	Value: 365				

KM# 37 SUVERENA Weight: 31.1035 g. **Composition:** 0.9999 Silver 1.0000 oz. ASW **Note:** Similar to KM#37a.

Date		F	VF	XF	Unc	BU
1994 Proof	—	Value: 50.00				

KM# 37a SUVERENA Weight: 31.1035 g. **Composition:** 0.9999 Gold 1.0000 oz. AGW

Date		F	VF	XF	Unc	BU
1994 Proof	—	Value: 700				

KM# 36 SUVERENA Composition: Copper-Nickel **Subject:** Lipizzaner Stallion **Obverse:** Arms **Reverse:** Lipizzaner Stallion rearing **Note:** Similar to KM#37a.

Date	F	VF	XF	Unc	BU
1994	—	—	—	8.50	—

KM# 49 SUVERENA Composition: Copper-Nickel **Subject:** English Hack **Note:** Similar to 1 Suverena, KM#51.

Date	F	VF	XF	Unc	BU
1995	—	—	—	9.00	—

KM# 50 SUVERENA Weight: 31.1035 g. **Composition:** 0.9999 Silver 1.0000 oz. ASW

Date	Mintage	F	VF	XF	Unc	BU
1995 Proof	Est. 30,000	Value: 50.00				

KM# 51 SUVERENA Weight: 31.1035 g. **Composition:** 0.9999 Gold 1.0000 oz. AGW

Date	Mintage	F	VF	XF	Unc	BU
1995 Proof	Est. 850	Value: 700				

KM# A76 SUVERENA Weight: 31.1035 g. **Composition:** 0.9999 Gold 1.0000 oz. AGW **Subject:** Hanoverian Stallion

Date	Mintage	F	VF	XF	Unc	BU
1996 Proof	850	Value: 700				

KM# 75 SUVERENA Weight: 31.1035 g. **Composition:** 0.9999 Silver 1.0000 oz. ASW **Note:** Similar to 1 Suverena, KM#76.

Date	Mintage	F	VF	XF	Unc	BU
1996 Proof	Est. 30,000	Value: 50.00				

KM# 74 SUVERENA Composition: Copper-Nickel **Subject:** Hanoverian Stallion **Note:** Similar to KM#76.

Date	F	VF	XF	Unc	BU
1996	—	—	—	8.50	—

KM# 93 SUVERENA Composition: Copper-Nickel **Subject:** The Arab **Obverse:** National arms over bridge **Reverse:** Arabian horse

Date	F	VF	XF	Unc	BU
1997	—	—	—	12.00	—

KM# 93a SUVERENA Weight: 31.1035 g. **Composition:** 0.9999 Silver 1.0000 oz. ASW

Date	Mintage	F	VF	XF	Unc	BU
1997 Proof	Est. 30,000	Value: 50.00				

KM# 93b SUVERENA Weight: 31.1035 g. **Composition:** 0.9999 Gold 1.0000 oz. AGW

Date	Mintage	F	VF	XF	Unc	BU
1997 Proof	850	Value: 700				

KM# 108 SUVERENA Composition: Copper-Nickel **Subject:** Chinese Horse **Obverse:** Arms over bridge **Reverse:** Horse

Date	F	VF	XF	Unc	BU
1998	—	—	—	10.00	—

KM# 108a SUVERENA Weight: 31.1035 g. **Composition:** 0.9999 Silver 1.0000 oz. ASW

Date	Mintage	F	VF	XF	Unc	BU
1998 Proof	Est. 30,000	Value: 50.00				

KM# 109 SUVERENA Weight: 31.1035 g. **Composition:** 0.9999 Gold 1.0000 oz. AGW **Note:** Similar to KM#108.

Date		F	VF	XF	Unc	BU
1998 Proof	—	Value: 700				

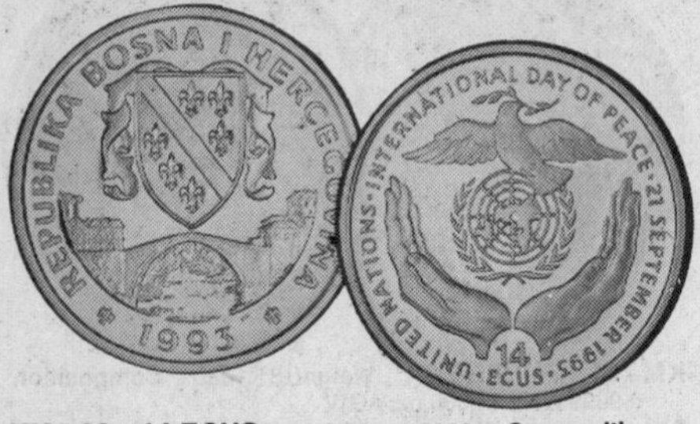

KM# 82 14 ECUS **Weight:** 10.0000 g. **Composition:** 0.9250 Silver .8921 oz. ASW **Subject:** International Day of Peace

Date	Mintage	F	VF	XF	Unc	BU
1993 Proof	Est. 20,000	Value: 45.00				

KM# 83 14 ECUS **Weight:** 10.0000 g. **Composition:** 0.9250 Silver .8921 oz. ASW **Subject:** Peace - Teddy Bear

Date	Mintage	F	VF	XF	Unc	BU
1994 Proof	20,000	Value: 50.00				

KM# 84 14 ECUS **Weight:** 10.1000 g. **Composition:** 0.9250 Silver .3004 oz. ASW **Subject:** Peace - Allegorical Europa

Date	Mintage	F	VF	XF	Unc	BU
1995 Proof	Est. 20,000	Value: 27.50				

KM# 85 14 ECUS + 2 **Weight:** 9.9700 g. **Composition:** 0.9990 Silver .3205 oz. ASW **Subject:** War Relief Funding - Sarajevo Mosque

Date	Mintage	F	VF	XF	Unc	BU
1993 Proof	20,000	Value: 30.00				

KM#86 21 ECUS + 3 **Weight:** 15.5600 g. **Composition:** 0.9990 Silver .5002 oz. ASW **Subject:** War Relief Funding - Sarajevo Mosque

Date	Mintage	F	VF	XF	Unc	BU
1993 Proof	Est. 15,000	Value: 60.00				

KM#87 70 ECUS + 10 **Weight:** 6.2200 g. **Composition:** 0.9990 Gold .2000 oz. AGW **Subject:** War Relief Funding - Sarajevo Mosque **Obverse:** Coat of arms above bridge **Reverse:** Dove **Mintage**of peace above Sarajevo Mosque

Date	Mintage	F	VF	XF	Unc	BU
1993 Proof	Est. 5,000	Value: 165				

KM# 88 14 EURO **Weight:** 10.0000 g. **Composition:** 0.9250 Silver .2974 oz. ASW **Subject:** Peace **Obverse:** Arms over bridge **Reverse:** Rose and the word PEACE in many languages

Date	Mintage	F	VF	XF	Unc	BU
1996 Proof	Est. 20,000	Value: 35.00				

KM# 110 14 EURO **Weight:** 10.0000 g. **Composition:** 0.9250 Silver .2974 oz. ASW **Subject:** Peace II **Obverse:** Arms over bridge **Reverse:** Dove in flight

Date	Mintage	F	VF	XF	Unc	BU
1998 Proof	Est. 20,000	Value: 40.00				

KM# 114 14 EURO **Weight:** 10.0000 g. **Composition:** 0.9250 Silver .2974 oz. ASW **Subject:** The Tree of Stability **Obverse:** National arms above bridge **Reverse:** Woman planting oak tree

Date	Mintage	F	VF	XF	Unc	BU
1999 Proof	Est. 20,000	Value: 40.00				

MINT SETS

KM#	Date	Mintage	Identification	Issue Price	Mkt Val
MS1	2000 (5)	—	KM#115, 116, 117, 118, 119	20.00	22.00

PROOF SETS

KM#	Date	Mintage	Identification	Issue Price	Mkt Val
PS1	1996 (5)	500	KM#70-73, 76	—	1,400

BOTSWANA

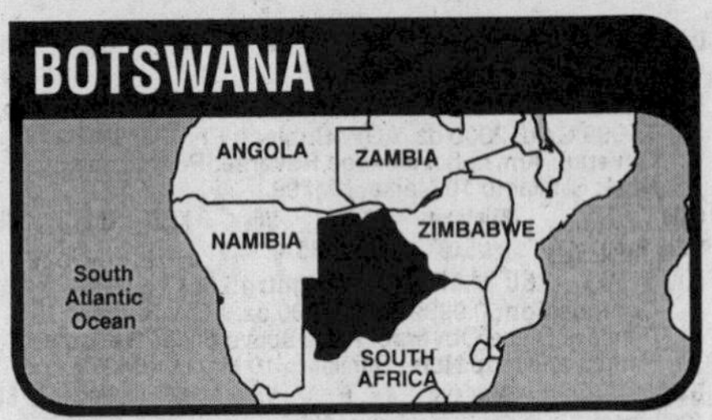

The Republic of Botswana (formerly Bechuanaland), located in south central Africa between Namibia and Zimbabwe, has an area of 224,607 sq. mi. (600,370 sq. km.) and a population of *1.62 million. Capital: Gaborone. Botswana is a member of a Customs Union with South Africa, Lesotho, and Swaziland. The economy is primarily pastoral with a rapidly developing mining industry, of which diamonds, copper and nickel are the chief elements. Meat products and diamonds comprise 85 percent of the exports.

Little is known of the origin of the peoples of Botswana. The early inhabitants, the Bushmen, did not develop a recorded history and are now dying out. The ancestors of the present Botswana residents probably arrived about 1600AD in Bantu migrations from the north and east. Bechuanaland was first united early in the 19th century under Chief Khama III to more effectively resist incursions by the Boer trekkers from Transvaal and by the neighboring Matabeles. As the Boer threat intensified, appeals for protection were made to the British Government, which proclaimed the whole of Bechuanaland a British protectorate in 1885. In 1895, the southern part of the protectorate was annexed to Cape Province. The northern part, known as the Bechuanaland Protectorate, remained under British administration until it became the independent Republic of Botswana on Sept. 30, 1966. Botswana is a member of the Commonwealth of Nations. The president is Chief of State and Head of government.

MINT MARKS

B - Berne

MONETARY SYSTEM

100 Cents = 1 Thebe

REPUBLIC

STANDARD COINAGE

KM# 1 50 CENTS **Weight:** 10.0000 g. **Composition:** 0.8000 Silver .2572 oz. ASW **Subject:** Independence Commemorative

Date	Mintage	F	VF	XF	Unc	BU
ND(1966)B	40,000	—	2.50	3.50	5.00	—
ND(1966)B Proof	10,000	Value: 7.50				

KM# 2 10 THEBE **Weight:** 11.2900 g. **Composition:** 0.9000 Gold .3270 oz. AGW **Subject:** Independence Commemorative

Date	Mintage	F	VF	XF	Unc	BU
ND(1966)B	5,100	—	—	—	160	—

REFORM COINAGE

100 Thebe = 1 Pula

KM# 3 THEBE **Composition:** Aluminum **Reverse:** Turako

Date	Mintage	F	VF	XF	Unc	BU
1976	15,000,000	—	0.10	0.15	0.25	—
1976 Proof	26,000	Value: 0.75				
1981 Proof	10,000	Value: 1.00				
1983	5,000,000	—	0.10	0.20	0.35	—
1984	5,000,000	—	0.10	0.20	0.35	—

Date	Mintage	F	VF	XF	Unc	BU
1985	—	—	0.10	0.20	0.35	—
1987	—	—	0.10	0.20	0.30	—
1988	—	—	0.10	0.20	0.30	—
1989	—	—	0.10	0.20	0.30	—
1991	—	—	0.10	0.20	0.30	—

KM# 14 2 THEBE Composition: Bronze **Subject:** World Food Day **Reverse:** Millet

Date	Mintage	F	VF	XF	Unc	BU
1981	9,990,000	—	0.15	0.25	0.50	—
1981 Proof	10,000	Value: 1.00				
1985	—	—	0.15	0.25	0.50	—

KM# 4 5 THEBE Composition: Bronze **Reverse:** Toko **Edge:** Reeded

Date	Mintage	F	VF	XF	Unc	BU
1976	3,000,000	—	0.15	0.25	0.50	—
1976 Proof	26,000	Value: 1.00				
1977	250,000	—	0.15	0.25	0.50	—
1979	200,000	—	0.15	0.25	0.50	—
1980	1,000,000	—	0.15	0.25	0.50	—
1981	4,990,000	—	0.15	0.25	0.50	—
1981 Proof	10,000	Value: 1.25				
1984	2,000,000	—	0.15	0.25	0.50	—
1985	—	—	0.15	0.25	0.50	—
1988	—	—	0.15	0.25	0.50	—
1989	—	—	0.15	0.25	0.50	—

KM# 4a.1 5 THEBE Composition: Bronze Clad Steel **Edge:** Plain

Date	F	VF	XF	Unc	BU
1991	—	0.15	0.25	0.50	—

KM# 4a.2 5 THEBE Composition: Bronze Clad Steel **Edge:** Reeded **Note:** Modified design.

Date	F	VF	XF	Unc	BU
1996	—	0.15	0.25	0.50	—

KM# 26 5 THEBE Composition: Bronze Clad Steel **Obverse:** National arms **Reverse:** Toko bird

Date	F	VF	XF	Unc	BU
1998	—	0.15	0.25	0.50	—

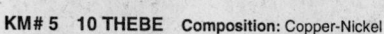

KM# 5 10 THEBE Composition: Copper-Nickel **Reverse:** South African Oryx

Date	Mintage	F	VF	XF	Unc	BU
1976	1,500,000	—	0.25	0.40	0.75	—
1976 Proof	26,000	Value: 1.50				
1977	500,000	—	0.25	0.40	0.75	—
1979	750,000	—	0.25	0.40	0.75	—
1980	—	—	0.25	0.40	0.75	—
1981	2,590,000	—	0.25	0.40	0.75	—
1981 Proof	10,000	Value: 1.75				
1984	4,000,000	—	0.20	0.30	0.60	—
1985	—	—	0.20	0.30	0.60	—
1989	—	—	0.20	0.30	0.60	—

KM# 5a 10 THEBE Composition: Nickel Clad Steel

Date	F	VF	XF	Unc	BU
1991	—	0.20	0.30	0.65	—

KM# 27 10 THEBE Composition: Nickel Clad Steel **Obverse:** National arms **Reverse:** South African Oryx

Date	F	VF	XF	Unc	BU
1998	—	0.20	0.30	0.65	—

KM# 6 25 THEBE Composition: Copper-Nickel **Reverse:** Zebu

Date	Mintage	F	VF	XF	Unc	BU
1976	1,500,000	—	0.25	0.55	1.50	—
1976 Proof	26,000	Value: 2.00				
1977	265,000	—	0.25	0.60	1.75	—
1980	—	—	0.25	0.60	1.35	—
1981	740,000	—	0.25	0.60	1.35	—
1981 Proof	10,000	Value: 2.50				
1982	400,000	—	0.25	0.60	1.75	—
1984	2,000,000	—	0.25	0.55	1.35	—
1985	—	—	0.30	0.60	1.35	—
1989	—	—	0.30	0.60	1.35	—

KM# 6a 25 THEBE Composition: Nickel Clad Steel

Date	F	VF	XF	Unc	BU
1991	—	0.30	0.60	1.35	—

KM# 28 25 THEBE Composition: Nickel Clad Steel **Obverse:** National arms **Reverse:** Zebu bull

Date	F	VF	XF	Unc	BU
1998	—	0.30	0.60	1.35	—

KM# 7 50 THEBE Composition: Copper-Nickel **Reverse:** African Fish Eagle

Date	Mintage	F	VF	XF	Unc	BU
1976	266,000	—	0.65	1.35	2.25	—
1976 Proof	26,000	Value: 3.00				
1977	250,000	—	0.65	1.35	2.25	—
1980	—	—	0.65	1.35	2.25	—
1981 Proof	10,000	Value: 3.50				
1984	2,000,000	—	0.65	1.35	2.25	—
1985	—	—	0.65	1.35	2.25	—

KM# 7a 50 THEBE Composition: Nickel Clad Steel

Date	F	VF	XF	Unc	BU
1991	—	0.65	1.35	2.25	—

KM# 29 50 THEBE Composition: Nickel Clad Steel **Obverse:** National arms **Reverse:** African Fish Eagle

Date	F	VF	XF	Unc	BU
1998	—	0.50	1.00	2.00	—

KM# 8 PULA Composition: Copper-Nickel **Reverse:** Zebra

Date	Mintage	F	VF	XF	Unc	BU
1976	166,000	—	1.50	2.50	5.00	—
1976 Proof	26,000	Value: 6.00				
1977	500,000	—	1.50	2.50	4.50	—
1981	—	—	1.50	2.50	4.50	—
1981 Proof	10,000	Value: 6.50				
1985	—	—	1.50	2.50	4.50	—
1987	—	—	1.50	2.50	4.50	—

KM# 24 PULA Composition: Nickel-Brass **Reverse:** Zebra

Date	F	VF	XF	Unc	BU
1991	—	1.00	1.75	3.50	—

KM# 17 2 PULA Weight: 28.2800 g. **Composition:** 0.5000 Silver .4546 oz. ASW **Subject:** Commonwealth Games

Date	F	VF	XF	Unc	BU
1986	—	—	—	12.50	—

KM# 17a 2 PULA Weight: 28.2800 g. **Composition:** 0.9250 Silver .8411 oz. ASW

Date	Mintage	F	VF	XF	Unc	BU
1986 Proof	Est. 20,000	Value: 25.00				

KM# 18 2 PULA Weight: 28.2800 g. **Composition:** 0.9250 Silver .8411 oz. ASW **Subject:** Wildlife **Reverse:** Slaty Egret

Date	Mintage	F	VF	XF	Unc	BU
1986 Proof	Est. 25,000	Value: 24.00				

KM# 22 2 PULA Weight: 28.2800 g. **Composition:** 0.9250 Silver .8411 oz. ASW **Subject:** Save The Children Fund **Obverse:** Coat of arms **Reverse:** Child milking goat

Date	Mintage	F	VF	XF	Unc	BU
1989 Proof	Est. 20,000	Value: 30.00				

KM# 25 2 PULA **Composition:** Nickel-Brass **Subject:** Wildlife **Reverse:** Rhinoceros

Date	F	VF	XF	Unc	BU
1994	—	1.75	2.75	5.50	—

KM# 19 5 PULA **Weight:** 15.9800 g. **Composition:** 0.9170 Gold .4711 oz. AGW **Subject:** Wildlife **Reverse:** Red Lechwes

Date	Mintage	F	VF	XF	Unc	BU
1986 Proof	Est. 5,000	Value: 300				

KM# 12 10 PULA **Weight:** 35.0000 g. **Composition:** 0.5000 Silver .5627 oz. ASW **Subject:** Wildlife **Obverse:** Similar to 5 Pula, KM#21 **Reverse:** Klipspringer

Date	Mintage	F	VF	XF	Unc	BU
1978	4,088	—	—	—	25.00	—

KM# 12a 10 PULA **Weight:** 35.0000 g. **Composition:** 0.9250 Silver 1.0408 oz. ASW

Date	Mintage	F	VF	XF	Unc	BU
1978 Proof	3,989	Value: 35.00				

KM# 9 5 PULA **Weight:** 28.2800 g. **Composition:** 0.5000 Silver .4546 oz. ASW **Subject:** 10th Anniversary of Independence

Date	Mintage	F	VF	XF	Unc	BU
ND(1976)	31,000	—	—	—	15.00	—

KM# 9a 5 PULA **Weight:** 28.2800 g. **Composition:** 0.9250 Silver .8411 oz. ASW

Date	Mintage	F	VF	XF	Unc	BU
ND(1976) Proof	22,000	Value: 22.50				

KM# 20 5 PULA **Composition:** Copper-Nickel **Subject:** Pope's Visit

Date	F	VF	XF	Unc	BU
1988	—	—	—	8.50	—

KM# 20a 5 PULA **Weight:** 28.2800 g. **Composition:** 0.9250 Silver .8411 oz. ASW

Date	Mintage	F	VF	XF	Unc	BU
1988 Proof	Est. 5,000	Value: 45.00				

KM# 10 150 PULA **Weight:** 15.9800 g. **Composition:** 0.9170 Gold .4711 oz. AGW **Subject:** 10th Anniversary of Independence

Date	Mintage	F	VF	XF	Unc	BU
ND(1976)	2,520	—	—	—	225	—
ND(1976) Proof	2,000	Value: 265				

KM# 11 5 PULA **Weight:** 28.5000 g. **Composition:** 0.5000 Silver .4582 oz. ASW **Subject:** Wildlife **Obverse:** Similar to KM#15 **Reverse:** Gemsbok

Date	Mintage	F	VF	XF	Unc	BU
1978	4,026	—	—	—	22.50	—

KM# 11a 5 PULA **Weight:** 28.5000 g. **Composition:** 0.9250 Silver .8477 oz. ASW

Date	Mintage	F	VF	XF	Unc	BU
1978 Proof	4,172	Value: 30.00				

KM# 21 5 PULA **Weight:** 28.2800 g. **Composition:** 0.9250 Silver .8411 oz. ASW **Subject:** 1988 Summer Olympics **Reverse:** Runners

Date	Mintage	F	VF	XF	Unc	BU
1988 Proof	25,000	Value: 25.00				

Note: A copper-nickel strike variety of this coin does not exist

KM# 13 150 PULA **Weight:** 33.4370 g. **Composition:** 0.9000 Gold .9676 oz. AGW **Subject:** Wildlife **Reverse:** Brown Hyaena

Date	Mintage	F	VF	XF	Unc	BU
1978	664	—	—	—	525	—
1978 Proof	219	Value: 950				

KM# 15 5 PULA **Weight:** 28.5000 g. **Composition:** 0.9250 Silver .8477 oz. ASW **Subject:** International Year of Disabled Persons

Date	Mintage	F	VF	XF	Unc	BU
1981	13,000	—	—	—	22.50	—
1981 Proof	11,000	Value: 32.50				

KM# 23 5 PULA **Weight:** 10.0000 g. **Composition:** 0.9170 Gold .2948 oz. AGW **Subject:** Save the Children Fund

Date	Mintage	F	VF	XF	Unc	BU
1989 Proof	Est. 3,000	Value: 350				

KM# 16 150 PULA **Weight:** 15.9800 g. **Composition:** 0.9170 Gold .4711 oz. AGW **Subject:** International Year of Disabled Persons

Date	Mintage	F	VF	XF	Unc	BU
1981	4,158	—	—	—	225	—
1981 Proof	4,155	Value: 265				

KM# 30 5 PULA **Ring Composition:** Brass**Center Weight:** 6.2000 g. **Center Composition:** Copper-Nickel **Obverse:** National arms. **Reverse:** Caterpillar on plant. **Edge:** Reeded. **Size:** 23.4 mm.

Date	F	VF	XF	Unc	BU
2000	—	—	—	4.50	—

PIEFORTS

KM#	Date	Mintage	Identification	Issue Price	Mkt Val
P1	1981	1,000	5 Pula. KM#15.	—	65.00
P2	1981	510	150 Pula. KM#16.	—	1,150

MINT SETS

KM#	Date	Mintage	Identification	Issue Price	Mkt Val
MS1	1978 (2)	—	KM#11, 12	—	50.00

PROOF SETS

KM#	Date	Mintage	Identification	Issue Price	Mkt Val
PS1	1976 (6)	20,000	KM#3-8	18.00	14.50
PS2	1978 (2)	—	KM#11a, 12a	—	65.00
PS3	1981 (7)	10,000	KM#3-8, 14	33.00	17.50

The Federative Republic of Brazil, which comprises half the continent of South America and is the only Latin American country deriving its culture and language from Portugal, has an area of 3,286,488 sq. mi. (8,511,965 sq. km.) and a population of *169.2 million. Capital: Brasilia. The economy of Brazil is as varied and complex as any in the developing world. Agriculture is a mainstay of the economy, while only 4 percent of the area is under cultivation. Known mineral resources are almost unlimited in variety and size of reserves. A large, relatively sophisticated industry ranges from basic steel and chemical production to finished consumer goods. Coffee, cotton, iron ore and cocoa are the chief exports.

Brazil was discovered and claimed for Portugal by Admiral Pedro Alvares Cabral in 1500. Portugal established a settlement in 1532 and proclaimed the area a royal colony in 1549. During the Napoleonic Wars, Dom Joao VI established the seat of Portuguese government in Rio de Janeiro. When he returned to Portugal, his son Dom Pedro I declared Brazil's independence on Sept. 7, 1822, and became emperor of Brazil. The Empire of Brazil was maintained until 1889 when the federal republic was established. The Federative Republic was established in 1946 by terms of a constitution drawn up by a constituent assembly. Following a coup in 1964 the armed forces retained overall control under a dictatorship until civilian government was restored on March 15, 1985. The current constitution was adopted in 1988.

MINT MARKS

(a) - Paris, privy marks only
A - Berlin 1913
B - Bahia

MONETARY SYSTEM

(1833-1942)
1000 Reis = 1 Milreis
(1942-1967)
100 Centavos = 1 Cruzeiro

REPUBLIC

DECIMAL COINAGE

1889-1942

KM# 490 20 REIS **Composition:** Bronze

Date	Mintage	F	VF	XF	Unc	BU
1901	713,000	1.00	4.50	9.50	20.00	—
1904	850,000	1.00	4.50	9.50	20.00	—
1905	1,075,000	3.50	7.00	14.50	48.00	—
1906	215,000	2.00	5.00	12.00	30.00	—
1908	4,558,000	1.00	4.50	9.50	20.00	—
1909	1,215,000	5.00	10.00	22.00	95.00	—
1910	828,000	1.00	4.50	9.50	20.00	—
1911	1,545,000	1.00	4.50	9.50	20.00	—
1912	480,000	1.00	4.50	9.50	25.00	—

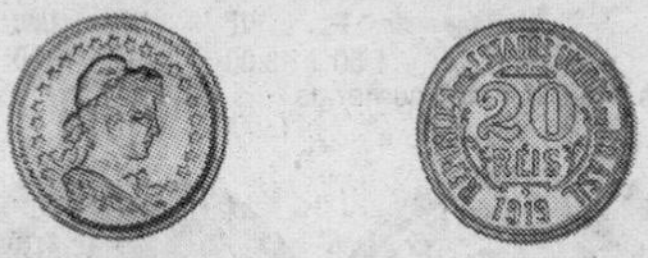

KM# 516 20 REIS **Composition:** Copper-Nickel

Date	Mintage	F	VF	XF	Unc	BU
1918	373,000	0.25	0.50	2.00	4.50	—
1919	2,870,000	0.25	0.50	1.00	3.50	—
1920	825,000	0.25	0.50	1.25	4.50	—
1921	1,020,000	0.25	0.50	1.25	4.50	—
1927	53,000	5.00	10.00	30.00	80.00	—
1935	100	200	450	900	1,500	—

KM# 491 40 REIS **Composition:** Bronze **Reverse:** FC above star

Date	Mintage	F	VF	XF	Unc	BU
1901	525,000	0.75	2.00	3.00	14.50	—
1907	218,000	0.75	2.00	3.00	14.50	—
1908	4,639,000	0.75	2.00	3.00	14.50	—
1909	4,226,000	0.75	2.00	3.50	16.50	—
1910	848,000	0.75	2.00	4.00	18.50	—
1911	1,660,000	0.75	2.00	4.00	18.50	—
1912	819,000	1.00	2.50	4.50	21.50	—

KM# 517 50 REIS **Composition:** Copper-Nickel

Date	Mintage	F	VF	XF	Unc	BU
1918	558,000	0.15	0.35	0.75	5.50	—
1919	558,000	0.15	0.35	0.75	5.50	—
1920	72,000	0.40	1.00	3.50	15.00	—
1921	682,000	0.15	0.35	0.75	5.50	—
1922	176,000	0.40	1.00	3.50	15.00	—
1925	128,000	0.40	1.50	4.00	18.50	—
1926	194,000	0.40	1.50	4.00	18.50	—
1931	20,000	2.00	10.00	40.00	80.00	—
1935	100	125	300	800	1,500	—

KM# 503 100 REIS **Composition:** Copper-Nickel

Date	Mintage	F	VF	XF	Unc	BU
1901	15,775,000	0.40	1.50	3.25	18.50	—

Note: Date in romal numerals

KM# 518 100 REIS **Composition:** Copper-Nickel

Date	Mintage	F	VF	XF	Unc	BU
1918	600,000	0.40	1.50	3.25	16.50	—
1919	1,219,000	0.40	1.50	3.25	16.50	—
1920	1,251,000	0.40	1.50	3.25	16.50	—
1921	853,000	0.40	1.50	3.25	16.50	—
1922	347,000	0.40	1.50	4.75	18.50	—
1923	956,000	0.40	1.50	4.75	18.50	—
1924	1,478,000	1.00	2.50	8.50	23.50	—
1925	2,502,000	0.30	1.25	2.75	16.50	—
1926	1,807,000	0.50	1.50	4.75	18.50	—
1927	1,451,000	0.30	1.25	2.75	16.50	—
1928	1,514,000	0.30	1.25	2.75	16.50	—
1929	2,503,000	0.30	1.25	2.75	16.50	—
1930	2,398,000	0.30	1.25	2.75	16.50	—
1931	2,500,000	0.25	1.00	2.25	16.50	—
1932	948,000	0.25	1.00	2.25	16.50	—
1933	1,314,000	0.25	1.00	2.25	16.50	—
1934	3,614,000	0.25	1.00	2.25	16.50	—
1935	3,442,000	0.25	1.00	2.25	16.50	—

KM# 527 100 REIS **Composition:** Copper-Nickel **Subject:** 400th Anniversary of Colonization **Obverse:** Cazique Tibirica

Date	Mintage	F	VF	XF	Unc	BU
1932	1,012,000	0.50	1.00	2.25	6.50	—

KM# 536 100 REIS **Composition:** Copper-Nickel **Reverse:** Admiral Marques Tamandare

Date	Mintage	F	VF	XF	Unc	BU
1936	3,928,000	0.20	0.50	1.50	3.00	—
1937	7,905,000	0.10	0.35	1.00	2.50	—
1938	8,618,000	0.10	0.35	1.00	2.50	—

KM# 544 100 REIS **Composition:** Copper-Nickel **Reverse:** Dr. Getulio Vargas **Edge:** Fluted

Date	Mintage	F	VF	XF	Unc	BU
1938	8,106,000	0.10	0.20	0.50	1.50	—
1940	8,797,000	0.10	0.20	0.50	1.50	—
1942	1,285,000	0.10	0.20	0.50	1.50	—

Note: The 1942 issue has a deeper yellow cast due to higher copper content

KM# 504 200 REIS **Composition:** Copper-Nickel

Date	Mintage	F	VF	XF	Unc	BU
1901	12,625,000	0.35	1.00	2.00	12.50	—

Note: Date in romal numerals

KM# 519 200 REIS **Composition:** Copper-Nickel

Date	Mintage	F	VF	XF	Unc	BU
1918	625,000	0.35	1.00	2.00	14.00	—
1919	882,000	0.35	1.00	2.00	14.00	—
1920	1,657,000	0.35	1.00	2.00	14.00	—
1921	1,135,000	0.35	1.00	2.00	14.00	—
1922	678,000	0.35	1.00	2.00	14.00	—
1923	1,655,000	0.35	1.00	2.00	14.00	—
1924	1,750,000	0.35	1.00	2.00	14.00	—
1925	2,081,999	0.35	1.00	2.00	14.00	—
1926	324,000	1.00	3.00	8.00	21.50	—
1927	1,806,000	0.35	1.00	2.00	14.00	—
1928	782,000	0.35	1.00	2.00	14.00	—
1929	2,440,000	0.25	1.00	2.00	14.00	—
1930	1,697,000	0.25	1.00	2.00	14.00	—
1931	1,830,000	0.25	1.00	2.00	14.00	—
1932	761,000	0.25	1.00	2.00	14.00	—
1933	173,000	0.35	1.00	2.00	14.00	—
1934	612,000	0.25	1.00	2.00	14.00	—
1935	1,329,000	0.25	1.00	2.00	14.00	—

KM# 528 200 REIS **Composition:** Copper-Nickel
Subject: 400th Anniversary of Colonization **Reverse:** Ship

Date	Mintage	F	VF	XF	Unc	BU
ND(1932)	596,000	0.75	1.75	3.50	15.00	—

KM# 537 200 REIS **Composition:** Copper-Nickel
Obverse: Train **Reverse:** Viscount de Maua

Date	Mintage	F	VF	XF	Unc	BU
1936	2,256,000	0.30	0.75	2.00	8.50	—
1937	6,506,000	0.30	0.75	2.00	8.50	—
1938	5,787,000	0.30	0.75	2.00	8.50	—

KM# 545 200 REIS **Composition:** Copper-Nickel
Reverse: Dr. Getulio Vargas **Edge:** Fluted

Date	Mintage	F	VF	XF	Unc	BU
1938	7,666,000	0.20	0.50	0.85	2.75	—
1940	10,161,000	0.15	0.40	0.60	2.25	—
1942	1,966,000	0.15	0.40	0.60	2.25	—

Note: The 1942 issue has a yellow cast due to higher copper content

KM# 538 300 REIS **Composition:** Copper-Nickel
Obverse: Harp **Reverse:** Antonio Carlos Gomes

Date	Mintage	F	VF	XF	Unc	BU
1936	3,029,000	0.30	1.25	4.00	11.50	—
1937	4,507,000	0.30	1.25	4.00	11.50	—
1938	3,753,000	0.30	1.25	4.00	11.50	—

KM# 546 300 REIS **Composition:** Copper-Nickel
Reverse: Dr. Getulio Vargas **Edge:** Fluted

Date	Mintage	F	VF	XF	Unc	BU
1938	12,080,000	0.20	0.35	0.50	2.25	—
1940	8,124,000	0.20	0.35	0.50	2.25	—
1942	2,020,000	0.25	0.40	0.75	3.25	—

Note: The 1942 issue has a yellow cast due to higher copper content

KM# 505 400 REIS **Composition:** Copper-Nickel

Date	Mintage	F	VF	XF	Unc	BU
1901	5,531,000	1.50	3.00	6.00	26.00	—

Note: Date in romal numerals

KM# 515 400 REIS **Composition:** Copper-Nickel

Date	Mintage	F	VF	XF	Unc	BU
1914	646,000	15.00	35.00	75.00	150	—

Note: This is considered a pattern by many authorities

KM# 520 400 REIS **Composition:** Copper-Nickel

Date	Mintage	F	VF	XF	Unc	BU
1918	491,000	0.75	2.00	5.50	17.00	—
1919	891,000	0.75	2.00	5.50	17.00	—
1920	1,521,000	0.75	2.00	5.50	17.00	—
1921	871,000	0.50	1.75	5.50	17.00	—
1922	1,275,000	0.50	1.75	5.50	17.00	—
1923	764,000	0.50	1.75	5.50	17.00	—
1925	2,048,000	0.50	1.75	5.50	17.00	—
1926	1,034,000	0.50	1.75	5.50	17.00	—
1927	738,000	0.50	1.75	5.50	17.00	—
1929	869,000	0.50	1.75	5.50	17.00	—
1930	1,030,999	0.50	1.75	5.50	17.00	—
1931	1,431,000	0.50	1.75	5.50	17.00	—
1932	588,000	0.50	1.75	5.50	17.00	—
1935	225,000	0.50	1.75	5.50	17.00	—

KM# 529 400 REIS **Composition:** Copper-Nickel
Subject: 400th Anniversary of Colonization

Date	Mintage	F	VF	XF	Unc	BU
ND(1932)	416,000	1.00	2.75	4.75	11.50	—

KM# 539 400 REIS **Composition:** Copper-Nickel
Obverse: Oil lamp **Reverse:** Oswaldo Cruz

Date	Mintage	F	VF	XF	Unc	BU
1936	2,079,000	0.50	1.00	2.75	8.50	—
1937	3,111,000	0.50	1.00	2.75	8.50	—
1938	2,681,000	0.50	1.00	2.75	8.50	—

KM# 547 400 REIS **Composition:** Copper-Nickel
Reverse: Dr. Getulio Vargas **Edge:** Fluted

Date	Mintage	F	VF	XF	Unc	BU
1938	10,620,000	0.25	0.50	1.00	2.25	—
1940	7,312,000	0.25	0.50	1.00	2.25	—
1942	1,496,000	0.25	0.50	1.50	3.25	—

Note: The 1942 issue has a yellow cast due to higher copper content

KM# 506 500 REIS **Weight:** 5.0000 g. **Composition:** 0.9000 Silver .1446 oz. ASW

Date	F	VF	XF	Unc	BU
1906	BV	2.75	4.75	14.00	—
1907	BV	2.75	4.75	14.00	—
1908	BV	2.75	4.75	14.00	—
1911	20.00	35.00	70.00	150	—
1912	20.00	40.00	80.00	200	—

KM# 509 500 REIS **Weight:** 5.0000 g. **Composition:** 0.9000 Silver .1446 oz. ASW

Date	F	VF	XF	Unc	BU
1912	3.00	7.00	14.00	38.00	—

KM# 512 500 REIS **Weight:** 5.0000 g. **Composition:** 0.9000 Silver .1446 oz. ASW

Date	F	VF	XF	Unc	BU
1913 A	1.25	2.50	4.50	15.00	—

KM# 521.1 500 REIS **Composition:** Aluminum-Bronze
Subject: Independence Centennial

Date	Mintage	F	VF	XF	Unc	BU
ND(1922)	13,744,000	0.25	0.60	1.25	4.75	—

KM# 521.2 500 REIS **Composition:** Aluminum-Bronze
Note: Error: BBASIL instead of BRASIL.

Date	F	VF	XF	Unc	BU
ND(1922)	17.50	35.00	55.00	120	—

KM# 524 500 REIS **Composition:** Aluminum-Bronze

Date	Mintage	F	VF	XF	Unc	BU
1924	7,400,000	0.30	0.75	1.50	7.00	—
1927	2,725,000	0.30	0.75	1.50	7.00	—
1928	9,432,000	0.30	0.75	1.50	7.00	—
1930	146,000	1.00	2.00	3.75	9.00	—

KM# 530 500 REIS Composition: Aluminum-Bronze **Subject:** 400th Anniversary of Colonization

Date	Mintage	F	VF	XF	Unc	BU
ND(1932)	34,000	1.50	4.00	11.50	18.50	—

KM# 533 500 REIS Weight: 4.0000 g. **Composition:** Aluminum-Bronze **Reverse:** Diogo Feijo; CB on truncation

Date	Mintage	F	VF	XF	Unc	BU
1935	14,000	2.00	9.00	20.00	40.00	—

KM# 540 500 REIS Weight: 5.0000 g. **Composition:** Aluminum-Bronze **Reverse:** Diogo Feijo

Date	Mintage	F	VF	XF	Unc	BU
1936	1,326,000	0.60	1.25	4.75	9.00	—
1937	Inc. above	0.60	1.25	4.75	9.00	—
1938	—	0.60	1.25	4.75	9.00	—

KM# 549 500 REIS Weight: 5.0000 g. **Composition:** Aluminum-Bronze **Reverse:** Joaquim Machado de Assis

Date	Mintage	F	VF	XF	Unc	BU
1939	5,928,000	0.50	1.00	3.00	8.00	—

KM# 507 1000 REIS Weight: 10.0000 g. **Composition:** 0.9000 Silver .2894 oz. ASW **Edge:** Reeded

Date	F	VF	XF	Unc	BU
1906	BV	4.75	8.50	23.50	—
1907	BV	4.75	8.50	23.50	—
1908	BV	4.75	8.50	23.50	—
1909	BV	4.75	8.50	23.50	—
1910	BV	4.75	8.50	23.50	—
1911	BV	4.75	8.50	23.50	—
1912	BV	4.75	8.50	23.50	—

KM# 510 1000 REIS Weight: 10.0000 g. **Composition:** 0.9000 Silver .2894 oz. ASW

Date	Mintage	F	VF	XF	Unc	BU
1912	Inc. above	3.75	5.50	10.00	32.50	—
1913	2,525,000	3.75	5.50	10.00	32.50	—

KM# 513 1000 REIS Weight: 10.0000 g. **Composition:** 0.9000 Silver .2894 oz. ASW

Date	F	VF	XF	Unc	BU
1913 A	BV	3.25	6.00	17.50	—

KM# 522.1 1000 REIS Composition: Aluminum-Bronze **Subject:** Independence Centennial

Date	Mintage	F	VF	XF	Unc	BU
ND(1922)	16,698,000	0.40	0.60	2.00	5.50	—

KM# 522.2 1000 REIS Composition: Aluminum-Bronze **Note:** Error: BBASIL instead of BRASIL.

Date	F	VF	XF	Unc	BU
ND(1922)	2.50	5.00	10.00	18.00	—

KM# 525 1000 REIS Composition: Aluminum-Bronze **Obverse:** Monogram left of knot

Date	Mintage	F	VF	XF	Unc	BU
1924	9,354,000	0.50	1.00	2.25	7.50	—
1925	6,205,000	0.50	1.00	2.25	7.50	—
1927	35,817,000	0.50	1.00	2.25	7.50	—
1928	1,899,000	0.50	1.00	2.25	7.50	—
1929	83,000	3.50	14.00	45.00	100	—
1930	45,000	3.50	14.00	45.00	100	—
1931	200,000	1.00	4.50	8.00	14.00	—

KM# 531 1000 REIS Composition: Aluminum-Bronze **Subject:** 400th Anniversary of Colonization **Obverse:** Martim Affonso da Sousa

Date	Mintage	F	VF	XF	Unc	BU
ND(1932)	56,000	2.00	4.00	7.50	15.00	—

KM# 534 1000 REIS Composition: Aluminum-Bronze **Reverse:** Jose de Anchieta; CB under chin

Date	Mintage	F	VF	XF	Unc	BU
1935	138,000	1.00	2.00	4.00	9.00	—

KM# 541 1000 REIS Composition: Aluminum-Bronze **Reverse:** Jose de Anchieta, LGCB under chin **Note:** Size reduced.

Date	Mintage	F	VF	XF	Unc	BU
1936	926,000	0.50	1.00	2.50	7.00	—
1937	Inc. above	0.50	1.00	2.50	7.00	—
1938 LGCB under chin	—	0.50	1.00	2.50	7.00	—
1938 CB under chin	—	0.50	1.00	2.50	7.00	—

KM# 550 1000 REIS Composition: Aluminum-Bronze **Reverse:** Tobias Barreto de Menezes; BR monogram right of bust

Date	Mintage	F	VF	XF	Unc	BU
1939	9,586,000	0.25	0.75	2.00	6.50	—

KM# 508 2000 REIS Weight: 20.0000 g. **Composition:** 0.9000 Silver .5787 oz. ASW

Date	Mintage	F	VF	XF	Unc	BU
1906	256,000	4.75	9.00	16.50	55.00	—
1907	2,863,000	BV	6.00	11.50	45.00	—
1908	1,707,000	BV	6.00	11.50	45.00	—
1910	585,000	4.75	9.00	16.50	55.00	—
1911	1,929,000	BV	6.00	11.50	45.00	—
1912	741,000	4.75	9.00	16.50	55.00	—

KM# 511 2000 REIS Weight: 20.0000 g. **Composition:** 0.9000 Silver .5787 oz. ASW **Reverse:** Arms break behind

Date	Mintage	F	VF	XF	Unc	BU
1912	Inc. above	6.00	11.50	23.50	58.00	—
1913	395,000	6.00	11.50	23.50	62.00	—

KM# 514 2000 REIS **Weight:** 20.0000 g. **Composition:** 0.9000 Silver .5787 oz. ASW **Reverse:** Continuous legend

Date	F	VF	XF	Unc	BU
1913 A	4.75	9.00	14.50	42.50	—

KM# 523 2000 REIS **Weight:** 7.9000 g. **Composition:** 0.9000 Silver .2285 oz. ASW **Subject:** Independence Centennial

Date	Mintage	F	VF	XF	Unc	BU
ND(1922)	1,560,000	BV	2.75	3.75	8.50	—

KM# 523a 2000 REIS **Weight:** 7.9000 g. **Composition:** 0.5000 Silver .1269 oz. ASW

Date	F	VF	XF	Unc	BU
ND(1922)	BV	2.75	3.75	8.50	—

Note: Struck in both .900 and .500 fine silver, but can only be distinguished by analysis (and color), on worn specimens

KM# 526 2000 REIS **Weight:** 7.9000 g. **Composition:** 0.5000 Silver .1269 oz. ASW

Date	Mintage	F	VF	XF	Unc	BU
1924	9,147,000	BV	1.50	3.75	12.00	—
1925	723,000	BV	1.50	3.75	12.00	—
1926	1,787,000	BV	1.50	3.75	12.00	—
1927	1,008,999	BV	2.50	4.75	14.00	—
1928	1,250,000	BV	1.50	3.75	12.00	—
1929	1,744,000	BV	1.50	3.75	12.00	—
1930	1,240,000	BV	1.50	3.75	12.00	—
1931	546,000	BV	1.50	3.75	12.00	—
1934	938,000	BV	1.50	3.75	12.00	—

KM# 532 2000 REIS **Weight:** 7.9000 g. **Composition:** 0.5000 Silver .1269 oz. ASW **Subject:** 400th Anniversary of Colonization **Obverse:** John III

Date	Mintage	F	VF	XF	Unc	BU
ND(1922)	695,000	2.00	2.50	4.75	14.00	—

KM# 535 2000 REIS **Weight:** 7.9000 g. **Composition:** 0.5000 Silver .1269 oz. ASW **Reverse:** Duke of Caxias; CB below chin

Date	Mintage	F	VF	XF	Unc	BU
1935	2,131,000	BV	1.50	3.75	12.50	—

KM# 542 2000 REIS **Composition:** Aluminum-Bronze **Reverse:** Duke of Caxias **Edge:** Reeded

Date	Mintage	F	VF	XF	Unc	BU
1936	665,000	0.50	1.00	2.00	5.50	—
1937	Inc. above	0.50	1.00	2.00	5.50	—
1938	—	2.50	4.75	11.50	28.00	—

KM# 548 2000 REIS **Composition:** Aluminum-Bronze **Edge:** Plain **Note:** Polygonal planchet.

Date	F	VF	XF	Unc	BU
1937	25.00	50.00	125	300	—
1938	0.75	1.50	3.25	7.50	—

KM# 551 2000 REIS **Composition:** Aluminum-Bronze **Reverse:** Floriano Peixoto

Date	Mintage	F	VF	XF	Unc	BU
1939	5,048,000	0.50	1.00	2.00	5.50	—

KM# 543 5000 REIS **Weight:** 10.0000 g. **Composition:** 0.6000 Silver .1929 oz. ASW **Reverse:** Alberto Santos Dumont

Date	Mintage	F	VF	XF	Unc	BU
1936	1,986,000	BV	2.00	3.50	8.50	—
1937	414,000	BV	2.00	3.50	8.50	—
1938	994,000	BV	2.00	3.50	8.50	—

KM# 496 10000 REIS **Weight:** 8.9645 g. **Composition:** 0.9170 Gold .2643 oz. AGW

Date	Mintage	F	VF	XF	Unc	BU
1898	216	250	500	1,500	2,000	—
1901	111	150	250	700	1,150	—
1902 Unique	—	—	—	—	—	—
1903	391	150	250	700	1,150	—
1904	541	150	250	700	1,150	—
1906	572	150	250	700	1,150	—
1907	878	150	250	600	1,100	—
1908	689	150	250	600	1,100	—
1909	1,069	150	250	600	1,100	—
1911	137	175	350	800	1,350	—
1914	969	250	500	1,500	2,400	—
1915	4,314	250	500	1,400	2,000	—
1916	4,720	150	250	700	1,150	—
1919	526	150	250	700	1,150	—
1921	2,435	150	250	600	1,000	—
1922 Rare	6	—	—	—	—	—

KM# 497 20000 REIS **Weight:** 17.9290 g. **Composition:** 0.9170 Gold .5286 oz. AGW

Date	Mintage	F	VF	XF	Unc	BU
1894	4,267	BV	300	550	1,100	—
1901	784	BV	350	700	1,350	—
1902	884	BV	350	700	1,350	—
1903	675	BV	350	700	1,350	—
1904	444	BV	350	700	1,350	—
1906	396	BV	500	900	1,600	—
1907	3,310	BV	300	550	1,100	—
1908	6,001,000	BV	300	550	1,100	—
1909	4,427	BV	300	550	1,100	—
1910	5,119	BV	300	550	1,100	—
1911	8,467	BV	300	550	1,100	—
1912	4,878	BV	300	550	1,100	—
1913	5,182	BV	300	600	1,200	—
1914	1,980	BV	350	700	1,400	—
1917	2,269	BV	400	800	1,550	—
1918	1,216	BV	400	800	1,550	—
1921	5,924	BV	300	600	1,200	—
1922	2,681	BV	400	800	1,550	—

REFORM COINAGE

100 Centavos = 1 Cruzeiro; 1942-1967

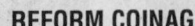

KM# 555 10 CENTAVOS **Composition:** Copper-Nickel **Obverse:** Getulio Vargas **Note:** KM#555 has a very light yellowish appearance while KM#555a is a deeper yellow.

Date	Mintage	F	VF	XF	Unc	BU
1942	3,826,000	—	0.35	0.50	1.00	—
1943	13,565,000	—	0.25	0.35	0.75	—

KM# 555a 10 CENTAVOS **Composition:** Aluminum-Bronze **Note:** KM#555 has a very light yellowish appearance while KM#555a is a deeper yellow.

Date	Mintage	F	VF	XF	Unc	BU
1943	Inc. above	—	0.25	0.35	0.75	—
1944	12,617,000	—	0.25	0.60	1.00	—
1945	24,674,000	—	0.25	0.60	1.00	—
1946	35,159,000	—	0.25	0.60	1.00	—
1947	20,664,000	—	0.25	0.35	0.75	—

KM# 561 10 CENTAVOS **Composition:** Aluminum-Bronze **Obverse:** Jose Bonifacio de Andrada e Silva

Date	Mintage	F	VF	XF	Unc	BU
1947	Inc. above	—	0.15	0.20	0.35	—
1948	45,041,000	—	0.15	0.20	0.35	—
1949	21,763,000	—	0.15	0.20	0.35	—
1950	16,329,999	—	0.15	0.20	0.35	—
1951	15,561,000	—	0.10	0.15	0.35	—
1952	10,966,000	—	0.10	0.20	0.50	—
1953	25,883,000	—	0.10	0.15	0.35	—
1954	17,031,000	—	0.10	0.15	0.35	—
1955	25,172,000	—	0.10	0.15	0.35	—

KM# 564 10 CENTAVOS **Composition:** Aluminum **Obverse:** National Arms

Date	Mintage	F	VF	XF	Unc	BU
1956	741,000	—	0.10	0.15	0.50	—
1957	25,311,000	—	0.10	0.15	0.25	—
1958	5,813,000	—	0.10	0.15	0.25	—
1959	2,611,000	—	0.10	0.15	0.25	—
1960	624,000	—	0.10	0.15	0.50	—
1961	951,000	—	0.10	0.15	0.50	—

KM# 556 20 CENTAVOS **Composition:** Copper-Nickel **Obverse:** Getulio Vargas **Note:** KM#556 has a very light yellowish appearance while KM#556a is a deeper yellow.

Date	Mintage	F	VF	XF	Unc	BU
1942	3,007,000	—	0.25	0.50	1.00	—
1943	13,392,000	—	0.15	0.40	0.75	—

KM# 556a 20 CENTAVOS **Composition:** Aluminum-Bronze **Note:** KM#556 has a very light yellowish appearance while KM#556a is a deeper yellow.

Date	Mintage	F	VF	XF	Unc	BU
1943	Inc. above	—	0.15	0.35	0.75	—
1944	12,673,000	—	0.15	0.35	0.75	—

Note: Coins dated 1944 exist with and without designer's initials and straight or curved-back 9 in date

Date	Mintage	F	VF	XF	Unc	BU
1945	61,632,000	—	0.15	0.35	0.60	—
1946	31,526,000	—	0.15	0.35	0.60	—
1947	36,422,000	—	0.15	0.35	0.75	—
1948	39,671,000	—	0.15	0.35	0.75	—

KM# 562 20 CENTAVOS Composition: Aluminum-Bronze **Obverse:** Ruy Barbosa

Date	Mintage	F	VF	XF	Unc	BU
1948	Inc. above	—	0.15	0.25	0.50	—
1949	24,805,000	—	0.15	0.25	0.50	—
1950	15,145,000	—	0.15	0.25	0.50	—
1951	14,964,000	—	0.15	0.25	0.50	—
1952	10,942,000	—	0.15	0.25	0.50	—
1953	25,585,000	—	0.15	0.25	0.50	—
1954	16,477,000	—	0.15	0.25	0.50	—
1955	25,122,000	—	0.15	0.25	0.50	—
1956	6,716,000	—	0.15	0.25	0.50	—

KM# 565 20 CENTAVOS Composition: Aluminum **Obverse:** National Arms **Note:** Varieties exist in the thickness of the planchet for year 1956.

Date	Mintage	F	VF	XF	Unc	BU
1956	Inc. above	—	0.10	0.25	0.50	—
1957	27,110,000	—	0.10	0.20	0.40	—
1958	8,552,000	—	0.10	0.20	0.40	—
1959	4,810,000	—	0.10	0.20	0.40	—
1960	510,000	—	0.10	0.25	0.50	—
1961	2,332,000	—	0.10	0.20	0.40	—

KM# 557 50 CENTAVOS Composition: Copper-Nickel **Obverse:** Getulio Vargas **Note:** KM#557 has a very light yellowish appearance while KM#557a is a deeper yellow.

Date	Mintage	F	VF	XF	Unc	BU
1942	2,358,000	—	0.40	0.75	1.50	—
1943	13,392,000	—	0.35	0.50	1.00	—

KM# 557a 50 CENTAVOS Composition: Aluminum-Bronze **Note:** KM#557 has a very light yellowish appearance while KM#557a is a deeper yellow.

Date	Mintage	F	VF	XF	Unc	BU
1943	Inc. above	—	0.30	0.50	1.00	—
1944	12,102,000	—	0.30	0.50	1.00	—
1945	73,222,000	—	0.30	0.50	1.00	—
1946	13,941,000	—	0.30	0.50	1.00	—
1947	23,588,000	—	0.20	0.50	1.00	—

KM# 563 50 CENTAVOS Composition: Aluminum-Bronze **Obverse:** General Eurico Gaspar Dutra

Date	Mintage	F	VF	XF	Unc	BU
1948	32,023,000	—	0.15	0.25	0.50	—
1949	11,392,000	—	0.15	0.25	0.50	—
1950	7,804,000	—	0.15	0.35	0.75	—
1951	7,523,000	—	0.15	0.35	0.75	—
1952	6,863,000	—	0.15	0.35	0.75	—
1953	17,372,000	—	0.15	0.25	0.50	—
1954	11,353,000	—	0.15	0.25	0.50	—
1955	27,150,000	—	0.15	0.25	0.50	—
1956	32,130,000	—	0.15	0.25	0.50	—

KM# 566 50 CENTAVOS Composition: Aluminum-Bronze **Obverse:** National arms

Date	F	VF	XF	Unc	BU
1956	—	0.15	0.25	0.50	—

KM# 569 50 CENTAVOS Composition: Aluminum **Obverse:** National Arms

Date	Mintage	F	VF	XF	Unc	BU
1957	49,350,000	—	0.10	0.20	0.35	—
1958	59,815,000	—	0.10	0.20	0.35	—
1959	32,891,000	—	0.10	0.20	0.35	—
1960	15,997,000	—	0.10	0.20	0.35	—
1961	18,456,000	—	0.10	0.20	0.35	—

KM# 558 CRUZEIRO Composition: Aluminum-Bronze **Obverse:** Topographical map

Date	Mintage	F	VF	XF	Unc	BU
1942	381,000	—	0.50	1.00	3.50	—
1943	2,728,000	—	0.25	0.50	1.00	—
1944	3,820,000	—	0.25	0.50	1.00	—
1945	32,543,999	—	0.25	0.50	0.75	—
1946	49,794,000	—	0.25	0.50	1.00	—
1947	15,391,000	—	0.25	0.50	1.00	—
1949	7,889,000	—	0.25	0.50	1.00	—
1950	5,163,000	—	0.25	0.50	1.00	—
1951	3,757,000	—	0.25	0.50	1.00	—
1952	1,769,000	—	0.50	1.00	3.50	—
1953	5,195,000	—	0.25	0.50	1.00	—
1954	1,145,000	—	0.25	0.50	1.50	—
1955	1,758,000	—	0.25	0.50	1.00	—
1956	668,000	—	6.00	12.00	20.00	—

KM# 567 CRUZEIRO Composition: Aluminum-Bronze **Obverse:** National Arms

Date	F	VF	XF	Unc	BU
1956	—	0.20	0.35	0.65	—

KM# 570 CRUZEIRO Composition: Aluminum **Obverse:** National Arms

Date	Mintage	F	VF	XF	Unc	BU
1957	11,849,000	—	0.20	0.75	2.50	—
1958	15,443,000	—	0.20	1.00	3.00	—
1959	25,010,000	—	0.20	0.75	2.50	—
1960	35,267,000	—	0.20	0.75	2.50	—
1961	22,181,000	—	0.20	1.00	3.00	—

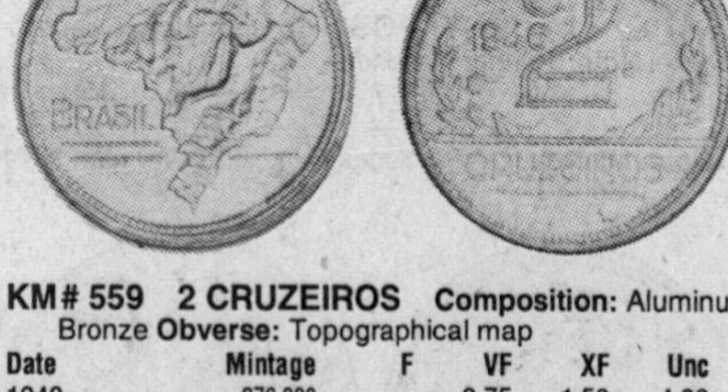

KM# 559 2 CRUZEIROS Composition: Aluminum-Bronze **Obverse:** Topographical map

Date	Mintage	F	VF	XF	Unc	BU
1942	276,000	—	0.75	1.50	4.00	—
1943	1,929,000	—	0.25	0.50	1.00	—
1944	3,820,000	—	0.25	0.50	1.00	—
1945	32,543,999	—	0.20	0.40	1.00	—
1946	33,650,000	—	0.20	0.40	1.00	—
1947	9,908,000	—	0.20	0.40	1.00	—
1949	11,252,000	—	0.20	0.40	1.00	—
1950	7,754,000	—	0.25	0.50	1.00	—
1951	390,000	—	0.40	1.00	3.00	—
1952	1,456,000	—	1.00	2.00	5.00	—
1953	3,582,000	—	0.20	0.40	1.00	—

Date	Mintage	F	VF	XF	Unc	BU
1954	1,197,000	—	0.25	1.00	2.00	—
1955	1,838,000	—	0.20	0.50	1.00	—
1956	—	—	2.00	4.00	10.00	—

KM# 568 2 CRUZEIROS Composition: Aluminum-Bronze **Obverse:** National Arms

Date	F	VF	XF	Unc	BU
1956	—	0.20	0.40	1.50	—

KM# 571 2 CRUZEIROS Composition: Aluminum **Obverse:** National Arms

Date	Mintage	F	VF	XF	Unc	BU
1957	194,000	—	0.20	0.30	1.25	—
1958	13,687,000	—	0.15	0.25	1.00	—
1959	20,894,000	—	0.15	0.25	1.00	—
1960	19,624,000	—	0.15	0.25	1.00	—
1961	24,924,000	—	0.15	0.25	1.00	—

KM# 560 5 CRUZEIROS Composition: Aluminum-Bronze **Obverse:** Topographical map

Date	Mintage	F	VF	XF	Unc	BU
1942	115,000	—	1.00	3.00	8.00	—
1943	222,000	—	0.75	2.00	6.50	—

KM# 572 10 CRUZEIROS Composition: Aluminum

Date	Mintage	F	VF	XF	Unc	BU
1965	19,656,000	—	0.10	0.20	0.50	—

KM# 573 20 CRUZEIROS Composition: Aluminum

Date	Mintage	F	VF	XF	Unc	BU
1965	25,930,000	—	0.15	0.25	0.75	—

KM# 574 50 CRUZEIROS Composition: Copper-Nickel

Date	Mintage	F	VF	XF	Unc	BU
1965	18,001,000	—	0.15	0.35	1.00	—

REFORM COINAGE

1000 Old Cruzeiros = 1 Cruzeiro Novo (New); 100 Centavos = 1 (New) Cruzeiro; 1967-1985

KM# 575.1 CENTAVO **Composition:** Stainless Steel

Date	Mintage	F	VF	XF	Unc	BU
1967	57,499,000	—	—	—	0.15	—

KM# 575.2 CENTAVO **Composition:** Stainless Steel **Note:** Thinner planchet.

Date	Mintage	F	VF	XF	Unc	BU
1969	243,855,000	—	—	—	0.15	—
1975	—	—	—	0.15	0.30	—
1976	—	—	—	0.15	0.30	—

KM# 585 CENTAVO **Composition:** Stainless Steel **Series:** F.A.O. **Subject:** Sugar Cane

Date	Mintage	F	VF	XF	Unc	BU
1975	31,700,000	—	—	0.15	0.30	—
1976	18,355,000	—	—	—	0.20	—
1977	100,000	—	—	—	0.20	—
1978	50,000	—	—	0.15	0.30	—

KM# 589 CENTAVO **Composition:** Stainless Steel **Series:** F.A.O **Subject:** Soja

Date	Mintage	F	VF	XF	Unc	BU
1979	100,000	—	0.15	0.35	1.00	—
1980	60,000	—	0.15	0.35	1.00	—
1981	100,000	—	0.15	0.35	1.00	—
1982	100,000	—	0.15	0.35	1.00	—
1983	—	—	0.15	0.35	1.00	—
1984	—	—	0.15	0.35	1.00	—

KM# 576.1 2 CENTAVOS **Composition:** Stainless Steel

Date	Mintage	F	VF	XF	Unc	BU
1967	65,226,000	—	—	—	0.25	—

KM# 576.2 2 CENTAVOS **Composition:** Stainless Steel **Note:** Thinner planchet.

Date	F	VF	XF	Unc	BU
1969	—	—	—	0.50	—

Note: Mintage figure includes coins struck through 1974 dated 1969

Date	F	VF	XF	Unc	BU
1975	—	—	0.25	0.75	—
1976	—	—	0.25	0.75	—

KM# 586 2 CENTAVOS **Composition:** Stainless Steel **Series:** F.A.O. **Subject:** Soja

Date	Mintage	F	VF	XF	Unc	BU
1975	31,400,000	—	—	—	0.25	—
1976	18,754,000	—	—	—	0.25	—
1977	100,000	—	—	—	0.25	—
1978	50,000	—	—	0.20	0.50	—

KM# 577.1 5 CENTAVOS **Composition:** Stainless Steel

Date	Mintage	F	VF	XF	Unc	BU
1967	69,304,000	—	—	0.20	0.50	—

KM# 577.2 5 CENTAVOS **Composition:** Stainless Steel **Note:** Thinner planchet.

Date	F	VF	XF	Unc	BU
1969	—	—	0.20	0.50	—

Note: Mintage figure includes coins struck through 1974 dated 1969

Date	F	VF	XF	Unc	BU
1975	—	—	0.20	0.50	—
1976	—	—	0.20	0.50	—

KM# 587.1 5 CENTAVOS **Composition:** Stainless Steel **Series:** F.A.O. **Subject:** Zebu **Reverse:** Plain 5

Date	Mintage	F	VF	XF	Unc	BU
1975	44,500,000	—	—	0.20	0.50	—
1976	134,267,000	—	—	0.20	0.50	—
1977	85,360	—	—	0.20	0.50	—
1978	34,090,000	—	—	0.20	0.65	—

KM# 587.2 5 CENTAVOS **Composition:** Stainless Steel **Reverse:** 5 over wavy lines

Date	F	VF	XF	Unc	BU
1975	—	—	0.20	0.50	—
1976	—	—	0.20	0.50	—
1977	—	—	0.20	0.50	—
1978	—	—	0.20	0.65	—

KM# 578.1 10 CENTAVOS **Composition:** Copper-Nickel

Date	Mintage	F	VF	XF	Unc	BU
1967	22,420,000	—	—	0.20	0.50	—

KM# 578.1a 10 CENTAVOS **Composition:** Stainless Steel

Date	Mintage	F	VF	XF	Unc	BU
1974	114,598,000	—	—	0.20	0.40	—
1975	—	—	—	0.20	0.40	—
1976	—	—	—	0.20	0.40	—
1977	225,213,000	—	—	0.20	0.40	—
1978	225,000,000	—	—	0.20	0.40	—
1979	100,000	—	—	0.20	0.40	—

KM# 578.2 10 CENTAVOS **Composition:** Copper-Nickel **Note:** Thinner planchet.

Date	F	VF	XF	Unc	BU
1970	—	—	0.20	0.40	—

Note: Mintage figure includes coins struck through 1974 dated 1970

KM# 579.1 20 CENTAVOS **Composition:** Copper-Nickel

Date	Mintage	F	VF	XF	Unc	BU
1967	123,610,000	—	—	0.20	0.50	—
1970	—	—	—	0.20	0.50	—

KM# 579.1a 20 CENTAVOS **Composition:** Stainless Steel

Date	Mintage	F	VF	XF	Unc	BU
1975	102,367,000	—	—	0.20	0.50	—
1976	—	—	—	0.20	0.50	—
1977	240,001,000	—	—	0.20	0.50	—
1978	255,000,000	—	—	0.20	0.50	—
1979	116,000	—	—	0.20	0.50	—

KM# 579.2 20 CENTAVOS **Composition:** Copper-Nickel **Note:** Thinner planchet.

Date	F	VF	XF	Unc	BU
1970	—	—	0.20	0.60	—

Note: Mintage figure includes coins struck through 1974 dated 1970

KM# 580 50 CENTAVOS **Composition:** Nickel

Date	Mintage	F	VF	XF	Unc	BU
1967	12,987,000	—	0.25	0.50	1.25	—

KM# 580a 50 CENTAVOS **Composition:** Copper-Nickel **Edge:** Reeded.

Date	Mintage	F	VF	XF	Unc	BU
1970	503,895,000	—	0.20	0.35	1.00	—
1975	—	—	0.20	0.35	1.00	—

KM# 580b 50 CENTAVOS **Composition:** Stainless Steel **Edge:** Plain.

Date	Mintage	F	VF	XF	Unc	BU
1975	79,062,000	—	0.20	0.35	1.00	—
1976	—	—	0.20	0.35	1.00	—
1977	160,019,000	—	0.20	0.35	1.00	—
1978	200,000,000	—	0.20	0.35	1.00	—
1979	104,000	—	0.20	0.35	1.00	—

KM# 581 CRUZEIRO **Composition:** Nickel

Date	F	VF	XF	Unc	BU
1970	—	0.25	0.50	1.00	—

Note: Mintage figure includes coins struck through 1972 dated 1970

1970 Proof 18,000 Value: 3.00

KM# 581a CRUZEIRO **Composition:** Copper-Nickel

Date	Mintage	F	VF	XF	Unc	BU
1975	21,613,000	—	0.20	0.45	1.00	—
1976	—	—	0.20	0.45	1.00	—
1977	98,000	—	0.20	0.45	1.00	—
1978	77,000	—	0.20	0.45	1.00	—

KM# 582 CRUZEIRO **Composition:** Nickel **Subject:** 150th Anniversary of Independence

Date	Mintage	F	VF	XF	Unc	BU
1972 Lettered edge	5,600,000	—	0.35	0.85	1.65	—
1972 Plain edge	Inc. above	—	0.35	0.85	1.65	—

Note: Coins with plain edge are believed by some to be errors

1972 Lettered edge; Proof — Value: 3.00

1972 Plain edge; Proof — Value: 3.00

Note: Coins with plain edge are believed by some to be errors

KM# 590 CRUZEIRO **Composition:** Stainless Steel **Obverse:** Sugar cane **Reverse:** Value, date

Date	Mintage	F	VF	XF	Unc	BU
1979	596,000	—	0.15	0.25	0.65	—
1980	690,497,000	—	0.15	0.25	0.65	—
1981	560,000,000	—	0.15	0.25	0.65	—
1982	300,000,000	—	0.15	0.25	0.65	—
1983	100,000	—	0.15	0.25	0.65	—
1984	62,100,000	—	0.15	0.25	0.65	—

KM# 598 CRUZEIRO **Composition:** Stainless Steel **Series:** F.A.O. **Obverse:** Sugar cane **Reverse:** Value, date

Date	Mintage	F	VF	XF	Unc	BU
1985	10,000,000	—	—	0.20	0.50	—

KM# 591 5 CRUZEIROS Composition: Stainless Steel **Obverse:** Coffee plant **Reverse:** Value, date

Date	Mintage	F	VF	XF	Unc	BU
1980	288,200,000	—	0.20	0.35	0.75	—
1981	82,000,000	—	0.20	0.35	0.75	—
1982	108,000,000	—	0.20	0.35	0.75	—
1983	113,400,000	—	0.20	0.35	0.75	—
1984	243,000,000	—	0.20	0.35	0.75	—

KM# 599 5 CRUZEIROS Composition: Stainless Steel **Series:** F.A.O. **Obverse:** Coffee plant **Reverse:** Value, date

Date	Mintage	F	VF	XF	Unc	BU
1985	10,000,000	—	0.20	0.40	0.85	—

KM# 588 10 CRUZEIROS Weight: 11.3000 g. **Composition:** 0.8000 Silver .2906 oz. ASW **Subject:** 10th Anniversary of Central Bank **Obverse:** Bust of Humberto de Alencar Castelo Branco left

Date	Mintage	F	VF	XF	Unc	BU
1975	20,000	—	—	—	55.00	—

KM# 592.1 10 CRUZEIROS Composition: Stainless Steel **Obverse:** Map of Brazil **Reverse:** Value, date

Date	Mintage	F	VF	XF	Unc	BU
1980	100,010,000	—	—	0.50	0.75	—
1981	200,000,000	—	—	0.50	0.75	—
1982	331,000,000	—	—	0.50	0.75	—
1983	390,000,000	—	—	0.50	0.75	—
1984	390,000,000	—	—	0.50	0.75	—

KM# 592.2 10 CRUZEIROS Composition: Stainless Steel **Obverse:** Map of Brazil **Reverse:** Value, date **Note:** Reduced weight.

Date	Mintage	F	VF	XF	Unc	BU
1985	201,000,000	—	—	0.50	0.75	—
1986	—	—	—	0.50	0.75	—

KM# 583 20 CRUZEIROS Weight: 18.0000 g. **Composition:** 0.9000 Silver .5208 oz. ASW **Subject:** 150th Anniversary of Independence

Date	Mintage	F	VF	XF	Unc	BU
1972 A	250,000	—	BV	6.00	10.00	—

KM# 593.1 20 CRUZEIROS Composition: Stainless Steel **Subject:** Francis of Assisi Church

Date	Mintage	F	VF	XF	Unc	BU
1981	88,297,000	—	—	0.25	0.85	—
1982	158,200,000	—	—	0.20	0.65	—
1983	312,000,000	—	—	0.20	0.65	—
1984	226,000,000	—	—	0.20	0.65	—

KM# 593.2 20 CRUZEIROS Composition: Stainless Steel **Note:** Reduced weight.

Date	Mintage	F	VF	XF	Unc	BU
1985	205,000,000	—	—	0.20	0.65	—
1986	—	—	—	0.20	0.65	—

KM# 594.1 50 CRUZEIROS Composition: Stainless Steel

Date	Mintage	F	VF	XF	Unc	BU
1981	57,000,000	—	—	0.35	1.00	—
1982	134,000,000	—	—	0.20	0.65	—
1983	181,800,000	—	—	0.20	0.65	—
1984	292,418,000	—	—	0.20	0.65	—

KM# 594.2 50 CRUZEIROS Composition: Stainless Steel **Note:** Reduced weight.

Date	Mintage	F	VF	XF	Unc	BU
1985	180,000,000	—	—	0.20	0.65	—
1986	—	—	—	0.20	0.65	—

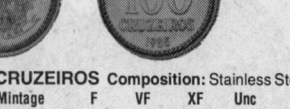

KM# 595 100 CRUZEIROS Composition: Stainless Steel

Date	Mintage	F	VF	XF	Unc	BU
1985	162,000,000	—	—	0.20	0.40	—
1986	—	—	—	—	0.35	—

KM# 596 200 CRUZEIROS Composition: Stainless Steel

Date	Mintage	F	VF	XF	Unc	BU
1985	55,000,000	—	—	0.25	0.50	—
1986	—	—	—	—	0.40	—

KM# 584 300 CRUZEIROS Weight: 16.6500 g. **Composition:** 0.9200 Gold .4925 oz. AGW **Subject:** 150th Anniversary of Independence

Date	Mintage	F	VF	XF	Unc	BU
1972 A	30,000	—	—	—	300	—

KM# 597 500 CRUZEIROS Composition: Stainless Steel

Date	Mintage	F	VF	XF	Unc	BU
1985	74,000,000	—	—	0.35	1.00	—
1986	—	—	—	—	0.65	—

REFORM COINAGE

1000 Cruzeiros Novos = 1 Cruzado; 100 Centavos = 1 Cruzado; 1986-1989

KM# 600 CENTAVO Composition: Stainless Steel

Date	Mintage	F	VF	XF	Unc	BU
1986	100,000,000	—	—	—	0.15	—
1987	1,000,000	—	—	—	0.20	—
1988	1,000,000	—	—	—	0.20	—

KM# 601 5 CENTAVOS Composition: Stainless Steel

Date	Mintage	F	VF	XF	Unc	BU
1986	99,282,000	—	—	—	0.15	—
1987	1,000,000	—	—	—	0.20	—
1988	1,000,000	—	—	—	0.20	—

KM# 602 10 CENTAVOS Composition: Stainless Steel

Date	Mintage	F	VF	XF	Unc	BU
1986	200,000,000	—	—	—	0.15	—
1987	245,628,000	—	—	—	0.15	—
1988	21,293,000	—	—	—	0.20	—

KM# 603 20 CENTAVOS Composition: Stainless Steel

Date	Mintage	F	VF	XF	Unc	BU
1986	140,000,000	—	—	—	0.20	—
1987	157,500,000	—	—	—	0.20	—
1988	16,000,000	—	—	—	0.25	—

KM# 604 50 CENTAVOS Composition: Stainless Steel

Date	Mintage	F	VF	XF	Unc	BU
1986	200,000,000	—	—	—	0.35	—
1987	201,884,000	—	—	—	0.35	—
1988	131,255,000	—	—	—	0.35	—

KM# 605 CRUZADO Composition: Stainless Steel

Date	Mintage	F	VF	XF	Unc	BU
1986	—	—	—	—	1.00	—
1987	383,087,000	—	—	—	0.45	—
1988	321,216,000	—	—	—	0.45	—

KM# 606 5 CRUZADOS **Composition:** Stainless Steel

Date	Mintage	F	VF	XF	Unc	BU
1986	—	—	—	—	1.50	—
1987	141,000,000	—	—	—	0.65	—
1988	291,906,000	—	—	—	0.65	—

KM# 607 10 CRUZADOS **Composition:** Stainless Steel

Date	Mintage	F	VF	XF	Unc	BU
1987	131,500,000	—	—	—	1.75	—
1988	457,977,000	—	—	—	0.85	—

KM# 608 100 CRUZADOS **Composition:** Stainless Steel **Subject:** Abolition of Slavery Centennial - Male

Date	Mintage	F	VF	XF	Unc	BU
ND	200,000	—	—	1.00	3.00	—

KM# 609 100 CRUZADOS **Composition:** Stainless Steel **Subject:** Abolition of Slavery Centennial - Female

Date	Mintage	F	VF	XF	Unc	BU
ND	200,000	—	—	1.00	3.00	—

KM# 610 100 CRUZADOS **Composition:** Stainless Steel **Subject:** Abolition of Slavery Centennial - Child

Date	Mintage	F	VF	XF	Unc	BU
ND	200,000	—	—	1.00	3.00	—

REFORM COINAGE

1000 Old Cruzados = 1 Novo Cruzado; 1989-1990

KM# 611 CENTAVO **Composition:** Stainless Steel

Date	F	VF	XF	Unc	BU
1989	—	—	—	0.35	—
1990	—	—	—	0.35	—

KM# 612 5 CENTAVOS **Composition:** Stainless Steel

Date	F	VF	XF	Unc	BU
1989	—	—	—	0.45	—
1990	—	—	—	0.45	—
1991	—	—	—	0.45	—
1992	—	—	—	0.45	—

KM# 613 10 CENTAVOS **Composition:** Stainless Steel

Date	F	VF	XF	Unc	BU
1989	—	—	—	0.60	—
1990	—	—	—	0.60	—
1991	—	—	—	0.60	—
1992	—	—	—	0.60	—
1993	—	—	—	0.60	—

KM# 614 50 CENTAVOS **Composition:** Stainless Steel

Date	F	VF	XF	Unc	BU
1989	—	—	—	1.25	—
1990	—	—	—	1.25	—
1991	—	—	—	1.25	—
1992	—	—	—	1.25	—

KM# 615 NOVO CRUZADO **Composition:** Stainless Steel **Subject:** Centennial of the Republic

Date	F	VF	XF	Unc	BU
ND(1989)	—	—	—	2.00	—

KM# 616 200 NOVOS CRUZADOS **Weight:** 13.4700 g. **Composition:** 0.9990 Silver .4331 oz. ASW **Subject:** Centennial of the Republic

Date	Mintage	F	VF	XF	Unc	BU
ND (1989) Proof	30,000	Value: 35.00				
ND(1989) Proof	30,000	Value: 35.00				

REFORM COINAGE

100 Centavos = 1 Cruzeiro; 1 Novo Cruzado = 1 Cruzeiro; 1990-1993

KM# 617 CRUZEIRO **Composition:** Stainless Steel

Date	F	VF	XF	Unc	BU
1990	—	—	—	0.35	—

KM# 618.1 5 CRUZEIROS **Composition:** Stainless Steel

Date	F	VF	XF	Unc	BU
1990	—	—	—	0.45	—

KM# 618.2 5 CRUZEIROS **Composition:** Stainless Steel **Note:** Thinner planchet.

Date	F	VF	XF	Unc	BU
1991	—	—	—	0.45	—
1992	—	—	—	0.45	—

KM# 619.1 10 CRUZEIROS **Composition:** Stainless Steel

Date	F	VF	XF	Unc	BU
1990	—	—	—	0.50	—

KM# 619.2 10 CRUZEIROS **Composition:** Stainless Steel **Note:** Thinner planchet.

Date	F	VF	XF	Unc	BU
1991	—	—	—	0.50	—
1992	—	—	—	0.50	—

KM# 620.1 50 CRUZEIROS **Composition:** Stainless Steel

Date	F	VF	XF	Unc	BU
1990	—	—	—	0.65	—

KM# 620.2 50 CRUZEIROS **Composition:** Stainless Steel **Note:** Thinner planchet.

Date	F	VF	XF	Unc	BU
1991	—	—	—	0.60	—
1992	—	—	—	0.60	—

KM# 623 100 CRUZEIROS **Composition:** Stainless Steel **Reverse:** Manatee

Date	F	VF	XF	Unc	BU
1992	—	—	—	0.65	—
1993	—	—	—	0.65	—

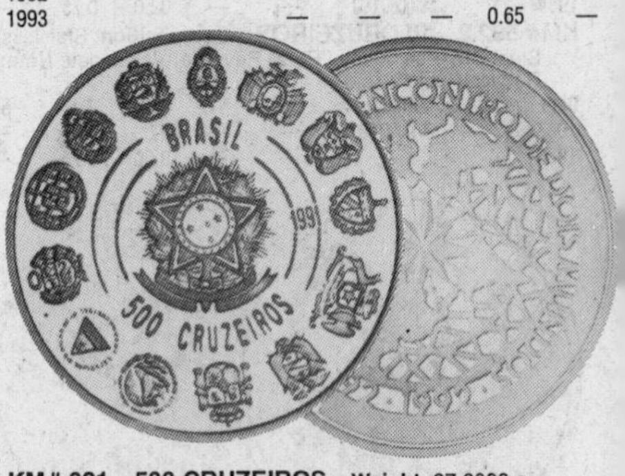

KM# 621 500 CRUZEIROS **Weight:** 27.0000 g. **Composition:** 0.9250 Silver .8029 oz. ASW **Reverse:** Ibero - American Series

Date	Mintage	F	VF	XF	Unc	BU
1991 Proof	70,000	Value: 55.00				

KM# 624 500 CRUZEIROS **Composition:** Stainless Steel **Reverse:** Loggerhead Sea Turtle

Date	F	VF	XF	Unc	BU
1992	—	—	—	0.75	—
1993	—	—	—	0.75	—

KM# 626 1000 CRUZEIROS **Composition:** Stainless Steel **Reverse:** Fish - Acara

Date	F	VF	XF	Unc	BU
1992	—	—	—	1.00	—
1993	—	—	—	1.00	—

KM# 622 2000 CRUZEIROS **Weight:** 28.2000 g. **Composition:** 0.9250 Silver .7977 oz. ASW **Subject:** U.N. Conference on Environment and Development **Obverse:** Hummingbird and flower

Date	Mintage	F	VF	XF	Unc	BU
1992 Proof	50,000	Value: 50.00				

KM# 625 5000 CRUZEIROS **Composition:** Stainless Steel **Subject:** 200th Anniversary of Tiradentes' Death **Reverse:** Bust left

Date	F	VF	XF	Unc	BU
ND	—	—	—	2.50	—

REFORM COINAGE

1000 Cruzeiros = 1 Cruzeiro Real; 1993 - June 30, 1994

KM# 627 5 CRUZEIROS REAIS **Composition:** Stainless Steel **Reverse:** Macaw Parrots - Arara

Date	F	VF	XF	Unc	BU
1993	—	—	—	0.75	—
1994	—	—	—	0.75	—

KM# 628 10 CRUZEIROS REAL **Composition:** Stainless Steel **Reverse:** Anteater - Tamandua

Date	F	VF	XF	Unc	BU
1993	—	—	—	1.00	—
1994	—	—	—	1.00	—

KM# 629 50 CRUZEIROS REAIS **Composition:** Stainless Steel **Reverse:** Mother jaguar and cub

Date	F	VF	XF	Unc	BU
1993	—	—	—	1.00	—
1994	—	—	—	1.00	—

KM# 630 100 CRUZEIROS REAIS **Composition:** Stainless Steel **Reverse:** Maned wolf

Date	F	VF	XF	Unc	BU
1993	—	—	—	1.50	—
1994	—	—	—	1.50	—

REFORM COINAGE

2750 Cruzeiros Reals = 1 Real; 100 Centavos = 1 Real; July 1, 1994 --

KM# 631 CENTAVO **Composition:** Stainless Steel

Date	F	VF	XF	Unc	BU
1994	—	—	—	0.35	—
1995	—	—	—	0.35	—
1996	—	—	—	0.35	—
1997	—	—	—	0.35	—

KM# 647 CENTAVO **Composition:** Copper Plated Steel **Subject:** Cabra; **Obverse:** Cabral's portrait **Reverse:** Denomination

Date	F	VF	XF	Unc	BU
1998	—	—	—	0.35	—
1999	—	—	—	0.10	—
2000	—	—	—	0.10	—

KM# 632 5 CENTAVOS **Composition:** Stainless Steel

Date	F	VF	XF	Unc	BU
1994	—	—	—	0.45	—
1995	—	—	—	0.45	—
1996	—	—	—	0.45	—
1997	—	—	—	0.45	—

KM# 648 5 CENTAVOS **Composition:** Copper Plated Steel **Subject:** Tiradentes **Obverse:** Tiradente's portrait **Reverse:** Denomination

Date	F	VF	XF	Unc	BU
1998	—	—	—	0.45	—
1999	—	—	—	0.45	—
2000	—	—	—	0.45	—

KM# 633 10 CENTAVOS **Composition:** Stainless Steel

Date	F	VF	XF	Unc	BU
1994	—	—	—	0.60	—
1995	—	—	—	0.60	—
1996	—	—	—	0.60	—
1997	—	—	—	0.60	—

KM# 641 10 CENTAVOS **Composition:** Stainless Steel **Series:** F.A.O. **Subject:** Seedling in Hand

Date	Mintage	F	VF	XF	Unc	BU
1995	10,000,000	—	—	—	0.65	—

KM# 649.1 10 CENTAVOS **Composition:** Brass Plated Steel **Subject:** Pedro I **Obverse:** Bust of Pedro, horseman with sword in left hand **Reverse:** Denomination **Note:** Majority of mintage recalled and melted.

Date	F	VF	XF	Unc	BU
1997	—	—	—	—	—
1998	—	—	—	—	—

KM# 649.2 10 CENTAVOS **Composition:** Brass Plated Steel **Obverse:** Bust of Pedro, horseman with sword in right hand

Date	F	VF	XF	Unc	BU
1998	—	—	—	0.60	—
1999	—	—	—	0.60	—
2000	—	—	—	0.60	—

KM# 634 25 CENTAVOS **Composition:** Stainless Steel

Date	F	VF	XF	Unc	BU
1994	—	—	—	0.75	—
1995	—	—	—	0.75	—

KM# 642 25 CENTAVOS **Composition:** Stainless Steel **Series:** F.A.O. **Obverse:** Farmer working **Reverse:** Denomination

Date	Mintage	F	VF	XF	Unc	BU
1995	10,000,000	—	—	—	0.80	—

KM# 650 25 CENTAVOS **Composition:** Brass Plated Steel **Subject:** Deodoro **Obverse:** Deodoro's portrait and national emblem **Reverse:** Denomination

Date	F	VF	XF	Unc	BU
1998	—	—	—	0.75	—
1999	—	—	—	0.75	—
2000	—	—	—	0.75	—

KM# 635 50 CENTAVOS **Composition:** Stainless Steel

Date	F	VF	XF	Unc	BU
1994	—	—	—	1.25	—
1995	—	—	—	1.25	—

KM# 651 50 CENTAVOS **Composition:** Copper-Nickel **Subject:** Rio Branco **Obverse:** Rio Branco's portrait **Reverse:** Denomination

Date	F	VF	XF	Unc	BU
1998	—	—	—	1.25	—
1999	—	—	—	1.25	—
2000	—	—	—	1.25	—

KM# 636 REAL **Composition:** Stainless Steel

Date	F	VF	XF	Unc	BU
1994	—	—	—	2.50	—
1997	—	—	—	2.50	—

KM# 652 REAL **Ring Composition:** Brass **Center Composition:** Copper-Nickel **Obverse:** Allegorical portrait **Reverse:** Denomination

Date	F	VF	XF	Unc	BU
1998	—	—	—	2.65	—
1999	—	—	—	2.65	—
2000	—	—	—	2.65	—

KM# 653 REAL **Center Composition:** Copper-Nickel **Subject:** Universal Declaration of Human Rights **Obverse:** Globe **Reverse:** Denomination

Date	F	VF	XF	Unc	BU
1998	—	—	—	2.75	—

KM# 652a REAL **Weight:** 7.0000 g. **Composition:** Bi-Metallic **Obverse:** Allegorical portrait **Reverse:** Denomination **Edge:** Reeded and plain sections **Size:** 26.9 mm.

Date	F	VF	XF	Unc	BU
2002	—	—	—	3.00	—

KM# 656 REAL **Weight:** 7.0000 g. **Composition:** Bi-Metallic **Subject:** Centennial of Juscelino Kubitschek **Obverse:** Portrait **Reverse:** Denomination **Edge:** Reeded and plain sections **Size:** 26.9 mm.

Date	F	VF	XF	Unc	BU
2002	—	—	—	3.00	—

KM# 637 2 REAIS **Weight:** 27.0000 g. **Composition:** 0.9250 Silver .8029 oz. ASW **Subject:** 300th Anniversary - First Brazilian Mint

Date	Mintage	F	VF	XF	Unc	BU
1994 Proof	10,000	Value: 65.00				

KM# 643 2 REAIS **Weight:** 27.0000 g. **Composition:** 0.9250 Silver .8029 oz. ASW **Subject:** Ayrton Senna - Race Driver

Date	Mintage	F	VF	XF	Unc	BU
1995 Proof	10,000	Value: 75.00				

KM# 640 3 REAIS **Weight:** 11.5000 g. **Composition:** 0.9250 Silver .3420 oz. ASW **Subject:** 30th Anniversary - Central Bank

Date	Mintage	F	VF	XF	Unc	BU
ND Proof	Est. 10,000	Value: 40.00				

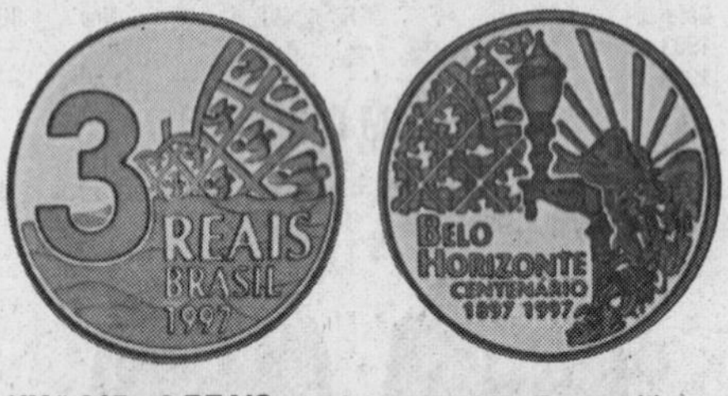

KM# 645 3 REAIS **Weight:** 11.5000 g. **Composition:** 0.9250 Silver .3420 oz. ASW **Subject:** Centennial of Belo Horizonte **Obverse:** Denomination **Reverse:** Collage, name, dates

Date	Mintage	F	VF	XF	Unc	BU
1997 Proof	Est. 20,000	Value: 40.00				

KM# 638 4 REAIS **Weight:** 27.0000 g. **Composition:** 0.9250 Silver .8030 oz. ASW **Subject:** World Cup Soccer

Date	Mintage	F	VF	XF	Unc	BU
1994 Proof	Est. 10,000	Value: 75.00				

KM# 654 5 REAIS **Weight:** 28.0000 g. **Composition:** 0.9990 Silver .8993 oz. ASW **Subject:** 500 Years - Discovery of Brazil **Obverse:** Partial compass face and feathers **Reverse:** Indian at left, ship at right, partial compass face and feathers at lower right **Edge:** Reeded **Size:** 40 mm.

Date	F	VF	XF	Unc	BU
ND(2000) Proof	—	Value: 65.00			

KM# 639 20 REAIS **Weight:** 8.0000 g. **Composition:** 0.9000 Gold .2315 oz. AGW **Subject:** World CUp Soccer **Obverse:** Hand held trophy **Reverse:** Denomination in net; similar to 4 Reais, KM#638

Date	Mintage	F	VF	XF	Unc	BU
1994 Proof	Est. 2,000	Value: 245				

KM# 644 20 REAIS **Weight:** 8.0000 g. **Composition:** 0.9000 Gold .2315 oz. AGW **Subject:** Ayrton Senna - Race Driver

Date	Mintage	F	VF	XF	Unc	BU
1995 Proof	5,000	Value: 245				

KM# 655 20 REAIS **Weight:** 8.0000 g. **Composition:** 0.9000 Gold .2315 oz. AGW **Subject:** 500 Years - Discovery of Brazil **Obverse:** Partial compass face and feathers at right, anniversary dates at left **Reverse:** Ornamented map **Edge:** Reeded **Size:** 22 mm.

Date	F	VF	XF	Unc	BU
ND(2000) Proof	—	Value: 245			

LEPROSARIUM COINAGE

KM# L1 100 REIS **Composition:** Brass **Issuer:** Colonia Santa Teresa

Date	F	VF	XF	Unc	BU
ND(ca.1940) Rare	150	200	300	400	—

KM# L2 200 REIS **Composition:** Brass **Issuer:** Colonia Santa Teresa

Date	F	VF	XF	Unc	BU
ND(ca.1940)	175	250	350	450	—

KM# L3 300 REIS **Composition:** Brass **Issuer:** Colonia Santa Teresa

Date	F	VF	XF	Unc	BU
ND(ca.1940) Rare	200	300	400	500	—

KM# L4 500 REIS **Composition:** Brass **Issuer:** Colonia Santa Teresa

Date	F	VF	XF	Unc	BU
ND(ca.1940) Rare	250	350	450	550	—

KM# L5 1000 REIS **Composition:** Brass **Issuer:** Colonia Santa Teresa

Date	F	VF	XF	Unc	BU
ND(ca.1940) Rare	300	400	500	600	—

KM# L6 1.00 REIS **Composition:** Brass **Issuer:** Santa Casa de Misericordia

Date	F	VF	XF	Unc	BU
ND(ca.1920) Rare	—	—	—	—	—

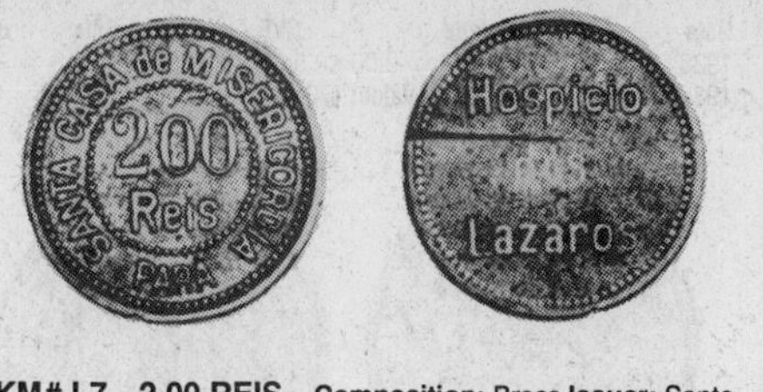

KM# L7 2.00 REIS Composition: Brass Issuer: Santa Casa de Misericordia

Date	F	VF	XF	Unc	BU
ND(ca.1920)	—	250	450	—	—

KM# L8 5.00 REIS Composition: Brass Issuer: Santa Casa de Misericordia

Date	F	VF	XF	Unc	BU
ND(ca.1920) Rare	—	—	—	—	—

KM# L9 1.000 REIS Composition: Brass Issuer: Santa Casa de Misericordia

Date	F	VF	XF	Unc	BU
ND(ca.1920) Rare	—	—	—	—	—

KM# L10 5.000 REIS Composition: Brass Issuer: Santa Casa de Misericordia

Date	F	VF	XF	Unc	BU
ND(ca.1920) Rare	—	—	—	—	—

PATTERNS

Including off metal strikes

KM#	Date	Mintage	Identification	Mkt Val
Pn179	1901	—	100 Reis. Nickel-Silver.	185
Pn180	1901	—	100 Reis. Nickel. Birmingham Mint	185
Pn181	1901	—	100 Reis. Nickel. Hamburg Mint	185
Pn182	1901	—	100 Reis. Silver.	285
Pn183	1901	—	100 Reis. Gold.	1,150
Pn184	1901	—	200 Reis. Nickel-Silver.	235
Pn185	1901	—	200 Reis. Nickel. Birmingham Mint	235
Pn186	1901	—	200 Reis. Nickel. Hamburg Mint	235
Pn187	1901	—	200 Reis. Silver.	285
Pn188	1901	—	200 Reis. Gold.	1,900
Pn189	1901	—	400 Reis. Nickel-Silver.	235
Pn190	1901	—	400 Reis. Nickel. Birmingham Mint	235
Pn192	1901	—	400 Reis. Silver.	575
Pn193	1901	—	400 Reis. Gold.	2,850
Pn191	1901	—	400 Reis. Nickel. Hamburg Mint	235
Pn194	1902	—	100 Reis. Nickel. MCMI. 1902.	375
Pn195	1907	—	100 Reis. Silver.	375
Pn196	1907	—	200 Reis. Silver.	575
Pn197	1907	—	500 Reis. Silver.	375
Pn198	1907	—	1000 Reis. Silver.	375
Pn199	1907	—	2000 Reis. Silver.	375
Pn200	1908	—	50 Reis. Silver.	375
Pn201	1908	—	500 Reis. Silver.	375
Pn202	1908	—	1000 Reis. Silver.	375
Pn203	1908	—	2000 Reis. Silver.	375
Pn204	1910	—	40 Reis. Silver.	375
Pn205	1910	—	1000 Reis. Silver.	375
Pn206	1910	—	2000 Reis. Silver.	425
Pn207	1912	—	2000 Reis. Copper.	325
Pn208	1913	—	1000 Reis. Copper.	325
Pn209	1914	—	50 Reis. Silver.	325
Pn210	1914	—	400 Reis. Nickel.	325
Pn211	1914	—	2000 Reis. Silver.	750
Pn212	1916	—	20 Reis. Silver.	285
Pn213	1916	—	200 Reis. Nickel.	285
Pn214	1916	—	200 Reis. Silver.	475
Pn215	1916	—	2000 Reis. Silver.	750
Pn216	1917	—	50 Reis. Nickel.	325
Pn217	1917	—	100 Reis. Nickel.	325
Pn218	1917	—	200 Reis. Nickel.	325
Pn219	1917	—	400 Reis. Nickel.	325
Pn220	1917	—	500 Reis. Nickel.	375
Pn221	1917	—	1000 Reis. Nickel.	325
Pn222	1917	—	2000 Reis. Nickel.	325
Pn223	1918	—	20 Reis. Nickel.	235
Pn224	1918	—	20 Reis. Nickel. Large planchet.	185
Pn225	1918	—	20 Reis. Silver.	325
Pn226	1918	—	2000 Reis. Nickel. Center hole.	285
Pn227	1921	—	1000 Reis.	185
Pn228	1921	—	2000 Reis.	375
Pn229	1921	—	10000 Reis. Gold.	950
Pn230	1921	—	20000 Reis. Gold.	950
Pn231	1922	—	50 Reis. Copper-Nickel.	285
Pn232	1922	—	50 Reis. Nickel-Silver.	185
Pn233	1922	—	500 Reis. Aluminum-Bronze.	185
Pn234	1922	—	500 Reis. Silver. Large planchet.	285
Pn235	1922	—	1000 Reis. Aluminum-Bronze.	185
Pn236	1922	—	2000 Reis. Silver.	285
Pn237	1922	—	2000 Reis. Silver.	265
Pn238	ND	—	2000 Reis. Silver.	265
Pn239	1922	—	2000 Reis. Silver.	265
Pn240	1922	—	2000 Reis. 0.6500 Silver.	265
Pn241	1922	—	2000 Reis. 0.8350 Silver.	265
Pn242	1922	—	2000 Reis. 0.9000 Silver.	265
Pn243	1923	—	1000 Reis. Silver.	375
Pn244	1923	—	2000 Reis. Silver.	265
Pn245	1923	—	2000 Reis. Silver.	265
Pn246	1923	—	2000 Reis. Silver.	265
Pn247	1923	—	2000 Reis. Silver.	265
Pn248	1923	—	2000 Reis. Silver.	265
Pn249	1923	—	2000 Reis. Silver.	265

KM#	Date	Mintage	Identification	Mkt Val
Pn250	1924	—	100 Reis. Nickel.	185
Pn251	1924	—	400 Reis. Nickel.	185
Pn252	1924	—	500 Reis. Nickel.	185
Pn253	1924	—	500 Reis. Silver.	185
Pn254	1924	—	1000 Reis. Silver.	185
Pn255	1924	—	1000 Reis. Silver.	185
Pn256	1924	—	1000 Reis. Silver.	90.00
Pn257	1924	—	1000 Reis. Silver.	90.00
Pn258	1927	—	Cruzeiro. Copper.	185
Pn259	1927	—	Cruzeiro. Silver.	235
Pn260	1927	—	Cruzeiro. Gold.	235
Pn261	1927	—	2 Cruzeiros. Gold.	235
Pn262	1928	—	Cruzeiro. Nickel.	235
Pn263	1928	—	2 Cruzeiros. Nickel.	235
Pn265	1928	—	5 Cruzeiros. Nickel.	235
Pn264	1928	—	4 Cruzeiros. Nickel.	235
Pn266	1928	—	10 Cruzeiros. Nickel.	375
Pn267	1931	—	10 Reis. Silver.	185
Pn268	1932	—	100 Reis. Nickel-Silver. St. Vincent.	185
Pn269	1932	—	100 Reis. Silver. St. Vincent.	375
Pn270	1932	—	200 Reis. Nickel-Silver.	235
Pn271	1932	—	200 Reis. Copper-Nickel. St. Vincent.	235
Pn272	1932	—	200 Reis. Silver. St. Vincent.	235
Pn273	1932	—	400 Reis. Nickel-Silver.	265
Pn274	1932	—	400 Reis. Silver. St. Vincent.	265
Pn275	1932	—	500 Reis. Copper. Large planchet.	265
Pn276	1932	—	1000 Reis. Copper. St. Vincent.	285
Pn277	1932	—	1000 Reis. Aluminum-Bronze. Arms.	285
Pn278	1932	—	1000 Reis. Silver.	285
Pn279	1932	—	1000 Reis. Silver. Large planchet.	375
Pn280	1932	—	2000 Reis. Silver. St. Vincent.	265
Pn281	1935	—	200 Reis. Nickel. Large planchet.	185
Pn282	1935	—	400 Reis. Silver.	185
Pn283	1935	—	500 Reis. Nickel. 3.8500 g.	375
Pn284	1935	—	500 Reis. Nickel-Silver. 6.0000 g.	375
Pn285	1935	—	1000 Reis. Copper.	185
Pn286	1935	—	1000 Reis. Nickel.	185
Pn287	1935	—	1000 Reis. Nickel-Silver.	375
Pn288	1935	—	1000 Reis. Silver.	375
Pn289	1935	—	2000 Reis. Zinc.	285
Pn290	1935	—	2000 Reis. Bronze.	265
Pn291	1935	—	2000 Reis. Copper.	265
Pn292	1935	—	2000 Reis. Nickel-Silver.	375
Pn293	1935	—	2000 Reis. Silver.	325
Pn294	1936	—	100 Reis. Nickel-Silver.	185
Pn295	1936	—	100 Reis. Silver.	325
Pn296	1936	—	200 Reis. Nickel-Silver.	90.00
Pn297	1936	—	200 Reis. Silver.	90.00
Pn298	1936	—	300 Reis. Nickel-Silver.	90.00
Pn299	1936	—	400 Reis. Nickel-Silver.	90.00
Pn300	1936	—	400 Reis. Silver.	90.00
Pn301	1936	—	500 Reis. Nickel-Silver.	90.00
Pn302	1936	—	500 Reis. Silver.	90.00
Pn303	1936	—	1000 Reis. Nickel-Silver.	90.00
Pn304	1936	—	1000 Reis. Silver.	90.00
Pn305	1936	—	2000 Reis. Nickel-Silver.	90.00
Pn306	1936	—	5000 Reis. Zinc.	90.00
Pn307	1936	—	5000 Reis. Nickel-Silver.	90.00
Pn308	1936	—	5000 Reis. Silver.	90.00
Pn309	1937	—	100 Reis. Nickel.	90.00
Pn310	1937	—	300 Reis. Nickel-Silver.	90.00
Pn311	1937	—	300 Reis. Nickel.	90.00
Pn312	1938	—	200 Reis. Nickel.	90.00
Pn313	1938	—	2000 Reis. Copper.	90.00
Pn314	1939	—	500 Reis. Nickel.	90.00
Pn315	1939	—	1000 Reis.	90.00
Pn316	1939	—	2000 Reis. Aluminum-Bronze.	90.00
Pn317	1939	—	2000 Reis. Aluminum-Bronze. Peixoto.	90.00
Pn318	1940	—	10 Centavos. Silver.	90.00
Pn319	1940	—	100 Reis. Copper-Nickel.	90.00
Pn320	1940	—	100 Reis. Nickel.	90.00
Pn321	1940	—	200 Reis. Copper-Nickel.	90.00
Pn322	1940	—	200 Reis. Nickel.	90.00
Pn323	1940	—	300 Reis. Copper-Nickel.	90.00
Pn324	1940	—	300 Reis. Nickel.	90.00
Pn325	1940	—	400 Reis. Copper-Nickel.	90.00
Pn326	1940	—	400 Reis. Nickel.	90.00
Pn327	1941	—	10 Centavos. Nickel.	90.00
Pn328	1941	—	10 Centavos. Nickel-Silver.	90.00
Pn329	1941	—	50 Centavos. Brass.	90.00
Pn330	1941	—	50 Centavos. Nickel.	90.00
Pn331	1941	—	50 Centavos. Nickel-Silver.	90.00
Pn332	1941	—	50 Centavos. Nickel-Silver.	90.00
Pn333	1941	—	50 Centavos. Silver.	90.00
Pn334	1941	—	50 Centavos. Silver.	90.00
Pn335	1941	—	Cruzeiro. Nickel-Silver.	90.00
Pn336	1941	—	2 Cruzeiros. Nickel.	90.00
Pn337	1941	—	2 Cruzeiros. Nickel-Silver.	45.00
Pn338	1941	—	2 Cruzeiros. Silver.	65.00
Pn339	1942	—	100 Reis. Nickel.	45.00
Pn340	1942	—	200 Reis. Nickel.	45.00
Pn341	1942	—	300 Reis. Nickel.	45.00
Pn342	1942	—	400 Reis. Nickel.	45.00
Pn343	1942	—	2 Cruzeiros. Nickel.	45.00
Pn344	1942	—	2 Cruzeiros. Nickel-Silver.	45.00
Pn345	1943	—	10 Centavos. Nickel-Silver.	45.00
Pn346	1943	—	20 Centavos. Nickel-Silver.	45.00
Pn347	1943	—	20 Centavos. Silver.	45.00
Pn348	1943	—	50 Centavos. Nickel-Silver.	45.00

KM#	Date	Mintage	Identification	Mkt Val
Pn349	1943	—	Cruzeiro. Silver.	45.00
Pn350	1945	—	10 Centavos. Nickel-Silver.	45.00
Pn351	1945	—	10 Centavos. Silver.	45.00
Pn352	1945	—	50 Centavos. Nickel-Silver.	45.00
Pn353	1945	—	50 Centavos. Silver.	45.00
Pn354	1945	—	Cruzeiro. Nickel.	45.00
Pn355	1945	—	Cruzeiro. Nickel-Silver.	45.00
Pn356	1947	—	20 Centavos. Aluminum-Bronze.	150
Pn357	1947	—	50 Centavos. Aluminum-Bronze.	150
Pn358	1947	—	2 Cruzeiros. Aluminum-Bronze.	90.00
Pn360	1950	—	Cruzeiro. Silver.	55.00
Pn361	1950	—	Cruzeiro. Gold.	—
Pn362	1955	—	50 Centavos. Aluminum.	45.00
Pn363	1956	—	10 Centavos. Aluminum. Arms.	45.00
Pn364	1956	—	10 Centavos. Aluminum-Bronze. Arms.	45.00
Pn365	1956	—	10 Centavos. Aluminum-Bronze. Bonifacio.	45.00
Pn366	1956	—	20 Centavos. Aluminum-Bronze.	45.00
Pn367	1956	—	50 Centavos. Aluminum.	45.00
Pn368	1956	—	Cruzeiro. Aluminum.	45.00
Pn369	1961	—	2 Cruzeiros. Aluminum-Bronze.	90.00
Pn370	1962	—	5 Cruzeiros.	90.00
Pn371	1963	—	5 Cruzeiros. Aluminum. Map.	90.00
Pn372	1963	—	5 Cruzeiros. Aluminum. Arms.	90.00
Pn373	1963	—	5 Cruzeiros. Aluminum-Bronze. Arms.	90.00
Pn374	1964	—	5 Cruzeiros. Aluminum.	90.00
Pn375	1964	—	10 Cruzeiros. Aluminum.	90.00
Pn376	1964	—	20 Cruzeiros. Aluminum.	90.00
Pn377	1964	—	50 Cruzeiros. Nickel.	90.00
Pn378	1964	—	100 Cruzeiros. Nickel.	90.00
Pn379	1964	—	200 Cruzeiros. Nickel.	90.00
Pn380	1965	—	5 Cruzeiros. Aluminum. Map.	90.00
Pn381	1965	—	5 Cruzeiros. Aluminum. Arms.	90.00
Pn382	1966	—	Centavo. Stainless Steel.	90.00
Pn383	1966	—	2 Centavos. Stainless Steel.	90.00
Pn384	1966	—	5 Centavos. Stainless Steel.	90.00
Pn385	1966	—	5 Centavos. Nickel.	90.00
Pn386	1966	—	10 Centavos. Copper-Nickel.	90.00
Pn387	1966	—	20 Centavos. Copper-Nickel.	90.00
Pn388	1967	—	10 Centavos. Stainless Steel.	90.00
Pn389	1972	—	20 Cruzeiros. 0.9000 Silver. KM#583.	90.00

PROVAS

KM#	Date	Mintage	Identification	Mkt Val
Pr1	1967	—	Cruzeiro. Nickel. PROVA.	45.00
Pr2	1967	—	Cruzeiro. Nickel. PROVA.	45.00
Pr3	1970	—	20 Centavos. Stainless Steel. KM#579.1.	45.00
Pr4	1970	—	50 Centavos. Stainless Steel.	45.00
Pr5	1972	—	Cruzeiro. Nickel. Y#94.	150
Pr6	1972	—	20 Cruzeiros. Silver. KM#583.	45.00
Pr7	1972	—	300 Cruzeiros. Brass. KM#584.	115
Pr8	1972	—	300 Cruzeiros. Gold. KM#584.	325
Pr9	1974	—	10 Centavos. Stainless Steel. KM#578.1a.	45.00
Pr10	1974	—	Cruzeiro. Nickel. KM#581.	45.00
Pr11	1975	—	Centavo. Stainless Steel. KM#585.	45.00
Pr12	1975	—	2 Centavos. Stainless Steel. KM#586.	45.00
Pr13	1975	—	5 Centavos. Stainless Steel. KM#587.1.	45.00
Pr14	1975	—	10 Centavos. Stainless Steel. KM#578.1a.	45.00
Pr15	1975	—	50 Centavos. Stainless Steel. KM#580b.	45.00
Pr16	1975	—	10 Cruzeiros. Silver. KM#588.	70.00
Pr17	1976	—	Centavo. Silver. KM#585.	70.00
Pr18	1976	—	2 Centavos. Stainless Steel. KM#586.	28.00
Pr19	1976	—	5 Centavos. Stainless Steel. KM#587.1.	45.00
Pr20	1980	5,000	Centavo. Steel. KM#589.	28.00
Pr21	1980	5,000	10 Centavos. Steel.	28.00
Pr23	1980	5,000	Cruzeiro. Steel. KM#590.	28.00
Pr22	1980	5,000	50 Centavos. Steel.	28.00
Pr24	1980	5,000	5 Cruzeiros. Steel. KM#591.	28.00
Pr25	1980	5,000	10 Cruzeiros. Steel. KM#592.	28.00
PrA26	1988	—	100 Cruzados. Stainless Steel. KM#608.	45.00
PrB26	1988	—	100 Cruzados. Stainless Steel. KM#609.	45.00
PrC26	1988	—	100 Cruzados. Stainless Steel. KM#610.	45.00
Pr26	1989	—	Centavo. Steel. KM#611.	38.00
Pr27	1989	—	5 Centavos. Steel. KM#612.	38.00
Pr28	1989	—	10 Centavos. Steel. KM#613.	42.00
Pr29	1989	—	50 Centavos. Steel. KM#614.	45.00
Pr30	ND	—	200 Novos Cruzados. 0.9990 Silver. KM#616.	90.00
Pr31	1990	—	Cruzeiro. Steel. KM#617.	38.00
Pr32	1990	—	5 Cruzeiros. Steel. KM#618.	38.00
Pr33	1990	—	10 Cruzeiros. Steel. KM#619.	42.00
Pr34	1990	—	50 Cruzeiros. Steel. KM#620.	45.00
Pr35	1991	—	500 Cruzeiros. 0.9250 Silver. KM#621.	90.00
Pr36	1992	—	2000 Cruzeiros. Silver. KM#622.	140
Pr37	ND	—	5000 Cruzeiros. Steel. KM#625.	80.00
Pr38	1994	—	4 Reais. 0.9250 Silver. KM#638.	155

TRIAL STRIKES

KM#	Date	Mintage	Identification	Mkt Val
TS4	1948	—	1000 Cruzeiros. Uniface.	750

CEARA

Ceara is a state in northeastern Brazil. Due to coin shortages a law was passed October 3, 1833 that copper coins would be countermarked and pass for 1/2 of their face value. In November of 1834 legislation was passed to stop the star countermarks.

Coins of 10, 20, 40, and 80 Reis were countermarked CEARA in a 5-pointed star to indicate a 50 percent reduction in value (to 5, 10, 20, and 40 Reis).

NOTE: Values given are for most common host coins.

REPUBLIC

REFORM COINAGE

KM# 510 1000 REIS **Weight:** 10.0000 g. **Composition:** 0.9000 Silver .2894 oz. ASW

Date	Mintage	F	VF	XF	Unc	BU
1912	Inc. above	3.75	5.50	10.00	32.50	—
1913	2,525	3.75	5.50	10.00	32.50	—

REFORM COINAGE

1000 Cruzeiros Novos = 1 Cruzado; 100 Centavos = 1 Cruzado

KM# 588 10 CRUZEIROS **Weight:** 11.3000 g. **Composition:** 0.8000 Silver .2906 oz. ASW **Subject:** 10th Anniversary of Central Bank **Obverse:** Humberto de Alencar Castelo Branco

Date	Mintage	F	VF	XF	Unc	BU
1975	20,000	—	—	—	55.00	—

BRITISH HONDURAS

This area, site of the ancient Mayan civilization, was sighted by Columbus in 1502, and settled by shipwrecked English seamen in 1638. British buccaneers settled the former capital of Belize in the 17th century. Britain claimed administrative right over the area after the emancipation of Central America from Spain. In 1825, Imperial coins were introduced into the colony and were rated against the Spanish dollar and Honduran currency. It was declared a colony subordinate to Jamaica in 1862 and was established as the separate Crown Colony of British Honduras in 1884. In May, 1885 an order in Council authorized coins for the colony, with the first shipment arriving in July. While the Guatemalan peso was originally the standard of value, in 1894 the colony changed to the gold standard, based on the U.S. gold dollar. The anti-British Peoples United Party, which attained power in 1954, won a constitution, effective in 1964 which established self-government under a British appointed governor. British Honduras became Belize on June 1, 1973, following the passage of a surprise bill by the Peoples United Party, but the constitutional relationship with Britain remained unchanged.

MONETARY SYSTEM
commencing 1864
100 Cents = 1 Dollar

BRITISH COLONY

DECIMAL COINAGE

KM# 11 CENT **Composition:** Bronze

Date	Mintage	F	VF	XF	Unc	BU
1904	50,000	6.00	15.00	50.00	90.00	—
1904 Proof	—	Value: 200				
1904 Matte Proof	—	Value: 1,550				
1906	50,000	12.00	27.50	65.00	225	—
1906 Matte Proof	—	Value: 1,050				
1909	25,000	35.00	80.00	150	300	—

KM# 15 CENT **Composition:** Bronze

Date	Mintage	F	VF	XF	Unc	BU
1911	50,000	60.00	100	200	500	—
1912H	50,000	85.00	160	250	600	—
1913	25,000	100	200	300	700	—

KM# 19 CENT **Composition:** Bronze

Date	Mintage	F	VF	XF	Unc	BU
1914	175,000	3.00	7.50	25.00	120	—
1916H	125,000	3.50	8.50	27.50	125	—
1918	40,000	7.00	15.00	40.00	150	—
1919	50,000	7.00	15.00	40.00	150	—
1924	50,000	7.00	15.00	40.00	125	—
1924 Proof	—	Value: 250				
1926	50,000	5.00	12.00	35.00	125	—
1926 Proof	—	Value: 225				
1936	40,000	2.00	5.00	20.00	65.00	—
1936 Proof	50	Value: 170				

KM# 21 CENT **Composition:** Bronze

Date	Mintage	F	VF	XF	Unc	BU
1937	80,000	0.75	4.00	12.00	75.00	—
1937 Proof	—	Value: 170				
1939	50,000	2.00	7.00	20.00	150	—
1939 Proof	—	Value: 100				
1942	50,000	2.00	7.00	20.00	150	—
1942 Proof	—	Value: 125				
1943	100,000	1.00	5.00	15.00	125	—
1943 Proof	—	Value: 150				
1944	100,000	2.00	7.00	20.00	150	—
1944 Proof	—	Value: 200				
1945	130,000	0.75	2.00	7.50	50.00	—
1945 Proof	—	Value: 120				
1947	100,000	0.75	2.50	10.00	70.00	—
1947 Proof	—	Value: 150				

KM# 24 CENT **Composition:** Bronze **Obv. Legend:** Without EMPEROR OF INDIA

Date	Mintage	F	VF	XF	Unc	BU
1949	100,000	0.60	1.50	4.00	16.50	—
1949 Proof	—	Value: 135				
1950	100,000	0.40	1.00	2.50	6.50	—
1950 Proof	—	Value: 135				
1951	100,000	0.60	1.50	4.00	16.50	—
1951 Proof	—	Value: 135				

KM# 27 CENT **Composition:** Bronze

Date	Mintage	F	VF	XF	Unc	BU
1954	200,000	0.50	0.75	1.00	5.00	—
1954 Proof	—	Value: 150				

KM# 30 CENT **Composition:** Bronze

Date	Mintage	F	VF	XF	Unc	BU
1956	200,000	0.10	0.25	0.50	3.50	—
1956 Proof	—	Value: 80.00				
1958	400,000	1.00	2.00	9.00	80.00	—
1958 Proof	—	Value: 80.00				
1959	200,000	1.00	2.50	10.00	100	—
1959 Proof	—	Value: 100				
1961	800,000	—	0.15	0.25	0.50	—
1961 Proof	—	Value: 80.00				
1964	300,000	—	0.10	0.30	0.90	—
1965	400,000	—	—	0.10	0.50	—
1966	100,000	—	—	0.10	0.50	—
1967	400,000	—	—	0.10	0.50	—
1968	200,000	—	—	0.10	0.50	—
1969	520,000	—	—	0.10	0.40	—
1970	120,000	—	—	0.10	0.40	—
1971	800,000	—	—	0.10	0.40	—
1972	800,000	—	—	0.10	0.40	—
1973	400,000	—	—	0.10	0.40	—

KM# 14 5 CENTS Composition: Copper-Nickel

Date	Mintage	F	VF	XF	Unc	BU
1907	10,000	25.00	50.00	100	250	—
1909	10,000	25.00	50.00	100	250	—

KM# 16 5 CENTS Composition: Copper-Nickel

Date	Mintage	F	VF	XF	Unc	BU
1911	10,000	25.00	50.00	100	250	—
1912H	20,000	10.00	25.00	55.00	175	—
1912H Proof	—	Value: 550				
1916H	20,000	10.00	25.00	55.00	175	—
1918	20,000	10.00	25.00	55.00	175	—
1919	20,000	8.00	20.00	50.00	160	—
1936	60,000	2.50	5.00	20.00	75.00	—
1936 Proof	50	Value: 450				

KM# 22 5 CENTS Composition: Copper-Nickel

Date	Mintage	F	VF	XF	Unc	BU
1939	20,000	3.00	6.00	25.00	75.00	—
1939 Proof	—	Value: 275				

KM# 22a 5 CENTS Composition: Nickel-Brass

Date	Mintage	F	VF	XF	Unc	BU
1942	30,000	5.00	15.00	65.00	200	—
1942 Proof	—	Value: 300				
1943	40,000	2.00	12.00	60.00	190	—
1944	50,000	1.50	10.00	50.00	175	—
1944 Proof	—	Value: 275				
1945	65,000	1.00	5.00	15.00	75.00	—
1945 Proof	—	Value: 150				
1947	40,000	1.50	5.00	15.00	85.00	—
1947 Proof	—	Value: 185				

KM# 25 5 CENTS Composition: Nickel-Brass **Obv. Legend:** Without EMPEROR OF INDIA

Date	Mintage	F	VF	XF	Unc	BU
1949	40,000	1.50	3.00	10.00	50.00	—
1949 Proof	—	Value: 150				
1950	225,000	0.40	1.00	4.00	30.00	—
1950 Proof	—	Value: 200				
1952	100,000	0.50	2.00	6.00	35.00	—
1952 Proof	—	Value: 250				

KM# 31 5 CENTS Composition: Nickel-Brass

Date	Mintage	F	VF	XF	Unc	BU
1956	100,000	0.20	0.50	3.00	75.00	—
1956 Proof	—	Value: 125				
1957	100,000	0.30	0.75	1.50	10.00	—
1957 Proof	—	Value: 175				
1958	200,000	0.30	1.00	7.50	90.00	—
1958 Proof	—	Value: 125				
1959	100,000	0.40	2.00	10.00	100	—
1959 Proof	—	Value: 185				
1961	100,000	0.30	0.75	2.50	35.00	—
1961 Proof	—	Value: 120				

Date	Mintage	F	VF	XF	Unc	BU
1962	200,000	0.15	0.35	0.65	2.00	—
1962 Proof	—	Value: 115				
1963	100,000	0.10	0.20	0.50	1.50	—
1963 Proof	—	Value: 175				
1964	100,000	0.10	0.15	0.35	1.00	—
1965	150,000	—	0.10	0.25	0.75	—
1966	150,000	—	0.10	0.20	0.60	—
1968	200,000	—	0.10	0.15	0.50	—
1969	540,000	—	0.10	0.15	0.50	—
1970	240,000	—	0.10	0.15	0.50	—
1971	450,000	—	0.10	0.15	0.50	—
1972	200,000	—	0.10	0.15	0.50	—
1973	210,000	—	0.10	0.15	0.75	—

KM# 20 10 CENTS Weight: 2.3240 g. **Composition:** 0.9250 Silver .0691 oz. ASW

Date	Mintage	F	VF	XF	Unc	BU
1918	10,000	15.00	25.00	100	350	—
1919	10,000	15.00	25.00	100	350	—
1936	30,000	6.00	12.00	25.00	100	—
1936 Proof	50	Value: 325				

KM# 23 10 CENTS Weight: 2.3240 g. **Composition:** 0.9250 Silver .0691 oz. ASW

Date	Mintage	F	VF	XF	Unc	BU
1939	20,000	3.00	7.00	20.00	60.00	—
1939 Proof	—	Value: 300				
1942	10,000	10.00	20.00	60.00	250	—
1943	20,000	3.00	6.00	45.00	250	—
1944	30,000	2.50	5.00	35.00	150	—
1944 Proof	—	Value: 250				
1946	10,000	5.00	12.00	45.00	200	—
1946 Proof	—	Value: 450				

KM# 32 10 CENTS Composition: Copper-Nickel

Date	Mintage	F	VF	XF	Unc	BU
1956	100,000	0.40	1.00	2.00	7.50	—
1956 Proof	—	Value: 200				
1959	100,000	0.60	1.50	2.00	37.50	—
1959 Proof	—	Value: 135				
1961	50,000	0.30	0.75	1.25	3.00	—
1961 Proof	—	Value: 135				
1963	50,000	0.20	0.50	0.75	2.00	—
1963 Proof	—	Value: 135				
1964	60,000	0.15	0.25	0.50	1.00	—
1965/6	200,000	5.00	10.00	20.00	40.00	—
1965	Inc. above	—	0.10	0.15	0.50	—
1970	—	—	0.10	0.15	0.75	—

KM# 9 25 CENTS Weight: 5.8100 g. **Composition:** 0.9250 Silver .1728 oz. ASW

Date	Mintage	F	VF	XF	Unc	BU
1901	20,000	20.00	35.00	125	400	—
1901 Proof	30	Value: 650				

KM# 12 25 CENTS Weight: 5.8100 g. **Composition:** 0.9250 Silver .1728 oz. ASW

Date	Mintage	F	VF	XF	Unc	BU
1906	30,000	15.00	30.00	110	375	—
1907	60,000	10.00	25.00	95.00	325	—

KM# 17 25 CENTS Weight: 5.8100 g. **Composition:** 0.9250 Silver .1728 oz. ASW

Date	Mintage	F	VF	XF	Unc	BU
1911	14,000	25.00	60.00	150	400	—
1919	40,000	8.00	17.50	75.00	250	—

KM# 26 25 CENTS Composition: Copper-Nickel

Date	Mintage	F	VF	XF	Unc	BU
1952	75,000	2.00	5.00	50.00	200	—
1952 Proof	—	Value: 250				

KM# 29 25 CENTS Composition: Copper-Nickel

Date	Mintage	F	VF	XF	Unc	BU
1955	75,000	0.40	1.00	3.50	15.00	—
1955 Proof	—	Value: 150				
1960	75,000	0.40	1.00	5.00	100	—
1960 Proof	—	Value: 250				
1962	50,000	0.30	0.50	1.00	2.50	—
1962 Proof	—	Value: 150				
1963	50,000	0.30	0.50	2.00	7.50	—
1963 Proof	—	Value: 150				
1964	100,000	0.30	0.50	0.75	1.50	—
1965	75,000	—	0.50	1.00	2.00	—
1966	75,000	0.40	1.00	2.00	8.00	—
1968	125,000	0.25	0.50	1.00	2.00	—
1970	—	0.20	0.35	0.75	1.50	—
1971	150,000	0.20	0.30	0.50	1.50	—
1972	200,000	0.20	0.30	0.50	1.50	—
1973	100,000	0.20	0.30	0.60	1.75	—

KM# 10 50 CENTS Weight: 11.6200 g. **Composition:** 0.9250 Silver .3456 oz. ASW

Date	Mintage	F	VF	XF	Unc	BU
1895	36,000	15.00	40.00	120	400	—
1901	10,000	35.00	80.00	350	1,000	—
1901 Prof	30	Value: 1,000				

KM# 13 50 CENTS Weight: 11.6200 g. **Composition:** 0.9250 Silver .3456 oz. ASW

Date	Mintage	F	VF	XF	Unc	BU
1906	15,000	20.00	60.00	225	600	—
1907	19,000	18.00	55.00	170	500	—

KM# 18 50 CENTS **Weight:** 11.6200 g. **Composition:** 0.9250 Silver .3456 oz. ASW

Date	Mintage	F	VF	XF	Unc	BU
1911	12,000	30.00	75.00	250	850	—
1919	40,000	20.00	40.00	150	400	—
1919 Proof	—	Value: 1,250				

KM# 28 50 CENTS **Composition:** Copper-Nickel

Date	Mintage	F	VF	XF	Unc	BU
1954	75,000	0.30	0.50	1.00	4.00	—
1954 Proof	—	Value: 175				
1962	50,000	0.30	0.50	1.50	5.00	—
1962 Proof	—	Value: 200				
1964	50,000	0.30	0.50	1.50	3.50	—
1965	25,000	1.00	3.00	5.00	22.50	—
1966	25,000	0.75	2.00	4.00	15.00	—
1971	30,000	0.30	0.50	1.50	3.50	—

PROOF SETS

KM#	Date	Mintage	Identification	Issue Price	Mkt Val
PS2	1901 (2)	30	KM#9, 10	—	2,500
PS3	1936 (3)	50	KM#16, 19, 20	—	1,000
PS4	1939 (3)	—	KM#21-23	—	675
PS5	1949 (2)	—	KM#24, 25	—	300
PS6	1950 (2)	—	KM#24, 25	—	350
PS7	1954 (2)	—	KM#27, 28	—	300
PS8	1956 (3)	—	KM#30-32	—	400
PS9	1958 (2)	—	KM#30, 31	—	200

BRITISH NORTH BORNEO

British North Borneo (now known as *Sabah*), a former British protectorate and crown colony, occupies the northem tip of the island of Borneo. The island of Labuan, which lies 6 miles off the northwest coast of the island of Borneo, was attached to Singapore settlement in 1907. It became an independent settlement of the Straits Colony in 1912 and was incorporated with British North Borneo in 1946. In 1963 it became part of Malaysia.

RULERS
British

MINT MARKS
H - Heaton, Birmingham

MONETARY SYSTEM
100 Cents = 1 Straits Dollar

BRITISH PROTECTORATE

STANDARD COINAGE

KM# 1 1/2 CENT **Composition:** Bronze

Date	Mintage	F	VF	XF	Unc	BU
1907H	1,000,000	15.00	30.00	45.00	130	—

KM# 3 CENT **Composition:** Copper-Nickel

Date	Mintage	F	VF	XF	Unc	BU
1904H	2,000,000	2.00	3.50	8.50	22.50	—
1921H	1,000,000	2.00	3.50	12.50	27.50	—
1935H	1,000,000	1.25	2.50	6.50	22.50	—
1938H	1,000,000	1.25	2.50	6.50	22.50	—
1941H	1,000,000	1.25	2.50	6.50	22.50	—

KM# 2 CENT **Composition:** Bronze

Date	Mintage	F	VF	XF	Unc	BU
1907H	1,000,000	20.00	50.00	75.00	140	—
1907H Proof	—	Value: 400				

KM# 4 2-1/2 CENT **Composition:** Copper-Nickel

Date	Mintage	F	VF	XF	Unc	BU
1903H	2,000,000	2.50	5.00	20.00	50.00	—
1903H Proof	—	Value: 300				
1920H	280,000	5.00	15.00	35.00	80.00	—

KM# 5 5 CENTS **Composition:** Copper-Nickel

Date	Mintage	F	VF	XF	Unc	BU
1903H	1,000,000	2.50	5.00	15.00	42.50	—
1920H	100,000	5.00	10.00	32.00	65.00	—
1921H	500,000	2.50	5.00	15.00	45.00	—
1927H	150,000	3.00	5.00	15.00	45.00	—
1928H	150,000	2.00	4.00	12.00	40.00	—
1938H	500,000	1.50	3.00	7.50	22.50	—
1940H	500,000	1.50	3.00	7.50	22.50	—
1941H	1,000,000	1.50	3.00	7.50	22.50	—

KM# 6 25 CENTS **Weight:** 2.8300 g. **Composition:** 0.5000 Silver .0454 oz. ASW

Date	Mintage	F	VF	XF	Unc	BU
1929H	400,000	7.00	15.00	35.00	80.00	—
1929H Proof	—	Value: 175				

BRITISH VIRGIN ISLANDS

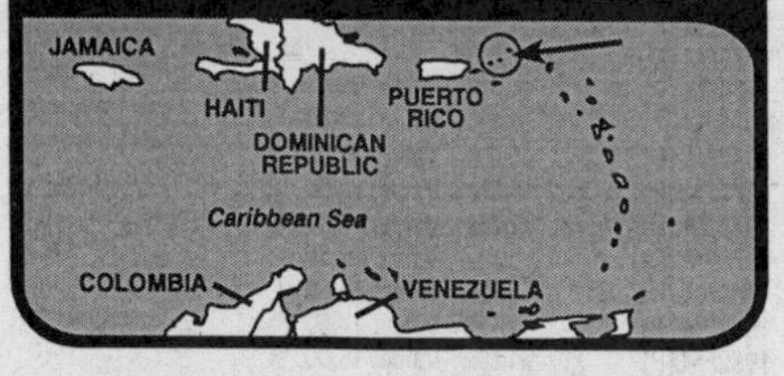

The Colony of the Virgin Islands, a British colony situated in the Caribbean Sea northeast of Puerto Rico and west of the Leeward Islands, has an area of 59 sq. mi. (155 sq. km.) and a population of 13,000. Capital: Road Town. The principal islands of the 36-island group are Tortola, Virgin Gorda, Anegada, and Jost Van Dyke. The chief industries are fishing and stock raising. Fish, livestock and bananas are exported.

The Virgin Islands were discovered by Columbus in 1493, and named by him, Las Virgienes, in honor of St. Ursula and her companions. The British Virgin Islands were formerly part of the administration of the Leeward Islands but received a separate administration as a Crown Colony in 1950. A new constitution promulgated in 1967 provided for a ministerial form of government headed by the Governor.

The Government of the British Virgin Islands issued the first official coinage in its history on June 30, 1973, in honor of 300 years of constitutional government in the islands. U.S. coins and currency continue to be the primary medium of exchange, though the coinage of the British Virgin Islands is legal tender.

***NOTE**: From 1975-1985 the Franklin Mint produced coinage in up to 3 different qualities. Qualities of issue are designated in ( ) after each date and are defined as follows:

(M) MATTE - Normal circulation strike or a dull finish produced by sandblasting special uncirculated (polish finish) or proof quality dies.

(U) SPECIAL UNCIRCULATED - Polished or proof-like in appearance without any frosted features.

(P) PROOF - The highest quality obtainable having mirror-like fields and frosted features.

BRITISH COLONY

STANDARD COINAGE

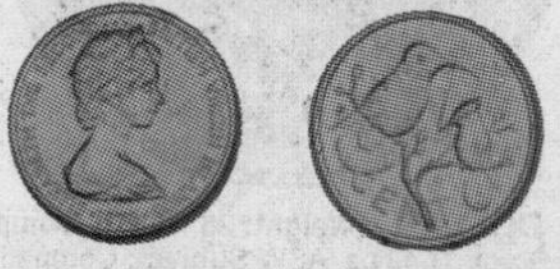

KM# 1 CENT Composition: Bronze **Reverse:** Green-throated Carib and Antillean Crested Hummingbird

Date	Mintage	F	VF	XF	Unc	BU
1973FM	53,000	—	—	0.10	0.50	—
1973FM (P)	181,000	Value: 1.00				
1974FM	22,000	—	—	0.10	0.50	—
1974FM (P)	94,000	Value: 1.00				
1975FM (M)	6,000	—	—	0.10	0.75	—
1975FM (U)	2,351	—	—	0.10	0.50	—
1975FM (P)	32,000	Value: 1.00				
1976FM (M)	12,000	—	—	0.10	0.50	—
1976FM (U)	996	—	—	0.10	0.50	—
1976FM (P)	15,000	Value: 1.00				
1977FM (M)	500	—	—	0.25	2.00	—
1977FM (U)	782	—	—	0.10	0.50	—
1977FM (P)	7,218	Value: 1.00				
1978FM (U)	1,443	—	—	0.10	0.50	—
1978FM (P)	7,059	Value: 1.00				
1979FM (U)	680	—	—	0.10	0.50	—
1979FM (P)	5,304	Value: 1.00				
1980FM (U)	1,007	—	—	0.10	0.50	—
1980FM (P)	3,421	Value: 1.00				
1981FM (U)	472	—	—	0.10	0.50	—
1981FM (P)	1,124	Value: 1.50				
1982FM (U)	—	—	—	0.10	0.50	—
1982FM (P)	—	Value: 1.50				
1983FM (U)	—	—	—	0.10	0.50	—
1983FM (P)	—	Value: 1.50				
1984FM (P)	—	Value: 1.50				

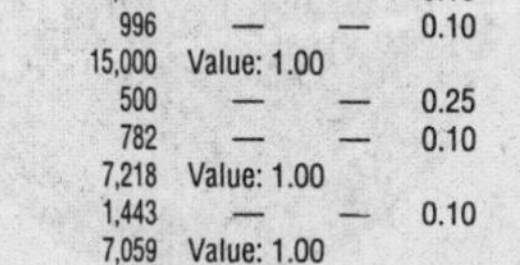

KM# 9 CENT Weight: 1.7500 g. **Composition:** 0.9250 Silver .0520 oz. ASW **Subject:** Queen's Silver Jubilee

Date	Mintage	F	VF	XF	Unc	BU
1977FM (P)	17,000	Value: 2.50				

KM# 16 CENT Weight: 1.7500 g. **Composition:** 0.9250 Silver .0520 oz. ASW **Subject:** Coronation Jubilee **Note:** Similar to KM#1.

Date	Mintage	F	VF	XF	Unc	BU
1978FM (P)	6,196	Value: 3.50				

KM# 42 CENT Composition: Bronze **Reverse:** Hawksbill Turtle

Date		F	VF	XF	Unc	BU
1985FM (P)	—	Value: 2.50				

KM# 42a CENT Weight: 1.7500 g. **Composition:** 0.9250 Silver .0520 oz. ASW

Date	Mintage	F	VF	XF	Unc	BU
1985FM (P)	1,474	Value: 5.00				

KM# 2 5 CENTS Composition: Copper-Nickel **Reverse:** Zenaida Dove

Date	Mintage	F	VF	XF	Unc	BU
1973FM	26,000	—	—	0.15	0.75	—
1973FM (P)	181,000	Value: 1.25				
1974FM	18,000	—	—	0.15	0.75	—
1974FM (P)	94,000	Value: 1.25				
1975FM (M)	3,800	—	—	0.20	1.00	—
1975FM (U)	2,351	—	—	0.15	0.75	—
1975FM (P)	32,000	Value: 1.25				
1976FM (M)	4,800	—	—	0.20	1.00	—
1976FM (U)	996	—	—	0.15	0.75	—
1976FM (P)	15,000	Value: 1.25				
1977FM (M)	500	—	—	0.35	3.50	—
1977FM (U)	782	—	—	0.15	0.75	—
1977FM (P)	7,218	Value: 1.25				
1978FM (U)	1,443	—	—	0.15	0.75	—
1978FM (P)	7,059	Value: 1.25				
1979FM (U)	680	—	—	0.15	0.75	—
1979FM (P)	5,304	Value: 1.25				
1980FM (U)	1,007	—	—	0.15	0.75	—
1980FM (P)	3,421	Value: 1.25				
1981FM (U)	472	—	—	0.15	0.75	—
1981FM (P)	1,124	Value: 1.25				
1982FM (U)	—	—	—	0.15	0.75	—
1982FM (P)	—	Value: 1.25				
1983FM (U)	—	—	—	0.15	0.75	—
1983FM (P)	—	Value: 1.25				
1984FM (P)	—	Value: 1.25				

KM# 10 5 CENTS Weight: 3.5500 g. **Composition:** 0.9250 Silver .1055 oz. ASW **Subject:** Queen's Silver Jubilee

Date	Mintage	F	VF	XF	Unc	BU
1977FM (P)	17,000	Value: 3.00				

KM# 17 5 CENTS Weight: 3.5500 g. **Composition:** 0.9250 Silver .1055 oz. ASW **Subject:** Coronation Jubilee

Date	Mintage	F	VF	XF	Unc	BU
ND(1978)FM (P)	6,196	Value: 4.50				

KM# 43 5 CENTS Composition: Copper-Nickel **Reverse:** Bonito Fish

Date		F	VF	XF	Unc	BU
1985FM (P)	—	Value: 2.00				

KM# 43a 5 CENTS Weight: 3.5550 g. **Composition:** 0.9250 Silver .1055 oz. ASW

Date	Mintage	F	VF	XF	Unc	BU
1985FM (P)	1,471	Value: 5.50				

KM# 3 10 CENTS Composition: Copper-Nickel **Reverse:** Ringed Kingfisher

Date	Mintage	F	VF	XF	Unc	BU
1973FM (U)	23,000	—	—	0.20	1.00	—
1973FM (P)	181,000	Value: 1.50				
1974FM (U)	13,000	—	—	0.20	1.00	—
1974FM (P)	94,000	Value: 1.50				
1975FM (M)	2,000	—	—	0.20	1.25	—
1975FM (U)	2,351	—	—	0.20	1.00	—
1975FM (P)	32,000	Value: 1.50				
1976FM (M)	3,000	—	—	0.20	1.00	—
1976FM (U)	996	—	—	0.20	1.00	—
1976FM (P)	15,000	Value: 1.50				
1977FM (M)	500	—	—	0.45	4.00	—
1977FM (U)	782	—	—	0.20	1.00	—
1977FM (P)	7,218	Value: 1.50				
1978FM (U)	1,443	—	—	0.20	1.00	—
1978FM (P)	7,059	Value: 1.50				
1979FM (U)	680	—	—	0.20	1.00	—
1979FM (P)	5,304	Value: 1.50				
1980FM (U)	1,007	—	—	0.20	1.00	—
1980FM (P)	3,421	Value: 1.50				
1981FM (U)	472	—	—	0.20	1.00	—
1981FM (P)	1,124	Value: 1.50				
1982FM (U)	—	—	—	0.20	1.00	—
1982FM (P)	—	Value: 1.50				
1983FM (U)	—	—	—	0.20	1.00	—
1983FM (P)	—	Value: 1.50				
1984FM (P)	—	Value: 1.50				

KM# 11 10 CENTS Weight: 6.4000 g. **Composition:** 0.9250 Silver .1903 oz. ASW **Subject:** Queen's Silver Jubilee

Date	Mintage	F	VF	XF	Unc	BU
1977FM (P)	17,000	Value: 5.00				

KM# 18 10 CENTS Weight: 6.4000 g. **Composition:** 0.9250 Silver .1903 oz. ASW **Subject:** Coronation Jubilee

Date	Mintage	F	VF	XF	Unc	BU
ND(1978)FM (P)	6,196	Value: 6.50				

KM# 44 10 CENTS Composition: Copper-Nickel **Reverse:** Great Barracuda

Date		F	VF	XF	Unc	BU
1985FM (P)	—	Value: 4.00				

KM# 44a 10 CENTS Weight: 6.4000 g. **Composition:** 0.9250 Silver .1903 oz. ASW

Date	Mintage	F	VF	XF	Unc	BU
1985FM (P)	1,474	Value: 7.50				

KM# 4 25 CENTS **Composition:** Silver **Reverse:** Mangrove Cuckoo

Date	Mintage	F	VF	XF	Unc	BU
1973FM	21,000	—	—	0.30	1.50	—
1973FM (P)	181,000	Value: 1.75				
1974FM	12,000	—	—	0.30	1.50	—
1974FM (P)	94,000	Value: 1.75				
1975FM (M)	1,000	—	—	0.35	3.00	—
1975FM (U)	2,351	—	—	0.30	1.50	—
1975FM (P)	32,000	Value: 1.75				
1976FM (M)	2,000	—	—	0.30	2.00	—
1976FM (U)	996	—	—	0.30	1.50	—
1976FM (P)	15,000	Value: 1.75				
1977FM (M)	500	—	—	0.50	5.00	—
1977FM (U)	782	—	—	0.30	1.50	—
1977FM (P)	7,218	Value: 1.75				
1978FM (U)	1,443	—	—	0.30	1.50	—
1978FM (P)	7,059	Value: 1.75				
1979FM (U)	680	—	—	0.30	1.50	—
1979FM (P)	5,304	Value: 1.75				
1980FM (U)	1,007	—	—	0.30	1.50	—
1980FM (P)	3,421	Value: 1.75				
1981FM (U)	472	—	—	0.30	1.50	—
1981FM (P)	1,124	Value: 1.75				
1982FM (U)	—	—	—	0.30	1.50	—
1982FM (P)	—	Value: 1.75				
1983FM (U)	—	—	—	0.30	1.50	—
1983FM (P)	—	Value: 1.75				
1984FM (P)	—	Value: 1.75				

KM# 12 25 CENTS **Weight:** 8.8100 g. **Composition:** 0.9250 Silver .2620 oz. ASW **Subject:** Queen's Silver Jubilee

Date	Mintage	F	VF	XF	Unc	BU
1977FM (P)	17,000	Value: 7.00				

KM# 19 25 CENTS **Weight:** 8.8100 g. **Composition:** 0.9250 Silver .2620 oz. ASW **Subject:** Coronation Jubilee

Date	Mintage	F	VF	XF	Unc	BU
ND(1978)FM (P)	6,196	Value: 8.50				

KM# 45 25 CENTS **Composition:** Copper-Nickel **Reverse:** Blue Marlin

Date		F	VF	XF	Unc	BU
1985FM (P)	—	Value: 5.00				

KM# 45a 25 CENTS **Weight:** 8.8100 g. **Composition:** 0.9250 Silver .2620 oz. ASW

Date	Mintage	F	VF	XF	Unc	BU
1985FM (P)	1,480	Value: 12.50				

KM# 5 50 CENTS **Composition:** Copper-Nickel **Reverse:** Brown Pelican

Date	Mintage	F	VF	XF	Unc	BU
1973FM	20,000	—	—	0.75	2.50	—
1973FM (P)	181,000	Value: 2.50				
1974FM	12,000	—	—	0.75	2.00	—
1974FM (P)	94,000	Value: 2.50				
1975FM (M)	1,000	—	—	1.00	5.00	—
1975FM (U)	2,351	—	—	0.75	2.50	—
1975FM (P)	32,000	Value: 2.50				
1976FM (M)	2,000	—	—	0.75	3.00	—
1976FM (U)	996	—	—	0.75	2.50	—
1976FM (P)	15,000	Value: 2.50				
1977FM (M)	600	—	—	1.00	6.00	—
1977FM (U)	782	—	—	0.75	2.50	—
1977FM (P)	7,218	Value: 2.50				
1978FM (U)	1,543	—	—	0.75	2.50	—
1978FM (P)	7,059	Value: 2.50				
1979FM (U)	680	—	—	0.75	2.50	—
1979FM (P)	5,304	Value: 2.50				
1980FM (U)	1,007	—	—	0.75	2.50	—
1980FM (P)	3,421	Value: 2.50				
1981FM (U)	472	—	—	0.75	2.50	—
1981FM (P)	1,124	Value: 2.50				
1982FM (U)	—	—	—	0.75	2.50	—
1982FM (P)	—	Value: 2.50				
1983FM (U)	—	—	—	0.75	2.50	—
1983FM (P)	—	Value: 2.50				
1984FM (P)	—	Value: 2.50				

KM# 13 50 CENTS **Weight:** 16.7200 g. **Composition:** 0.9250 Silver .4972 oz. ASW **Subject:** Queen's Silver Jubilee

Date	Mintage	F	VF	XF	Unc	BU
1977FM (P)	17,000	Value: 10.00				

KM# 20 50 CENTS **Weight:** 16.7200 g. **Composition:** 0.9250 Silver .4972 oz. ASW **Subject:** Coronation Jubilee

Date	Mintage	F	VF	XF	Unc	BU
ND(1978)FM (P)	6,196	Value: 11.50				

KM# 46 50 CENTS **Composition:** Copper-Nickel **Reverse:** Dolphin

Date		F	VF	XF	Unc	BU
1985FM (P)	—	Value: 7.50				

KM# 46a 50 CENTS **Weight:** 16.7200 g. **Composition:** 0.9250 Silver .4972 oz. ASW

Date	Mintage	F	VF	XF	Unc	BU
1985FM (P)	1,406	Value: 24.00				

KM# 6 DOLLAR **Composition:** Copper-Nickel **Reverse:** Magnificent Frigate

Date	Mintage	F	VF	XF	Unc	BU
1974FM (M)	12,000	—	—	2.50	6.50	—
1974FM (U)	—	—	—	—	—	—
1975FM (M)	800	—	—	2.50	8.00	—
1975FM (U)	2,351	—	—	2.50	6.50	—
1976FM (M)	1,800	—	—	2.50	6.50	—
1976FM (U)	996	—	—	2.50	8.00	—
1977FM (M)	800	—	—	2.50	8.00	—
1977FM (U)	782	—	—	2.50	8.00	—
1978FM (U)	1,743	—	—	2.50	6.50	—
1979FM (U)	680	—	—	2.50	8.00	—
1980FM (U)	1,007	—	—	2.50	6.50	—
1981FM (U)	472	—	—	2.50	8.00	—
1982FM (U)	—	—	—	2.50	8.00	—
1983FM (U)	—	—	—	2.50	8.00	—

KM# 6a DOLLAR **Weight:** 25.7000 g. **Composition:** 0.9250 Silver .7643 oz. ASW

Date	Mintage	F	VF	XF	Unc	BU
1973FM (P)	181,000	Value: 8.50				
1973FM (M)	20,000	—	—	8.00	11.00	—
1974FM (P)	94,000	Value: 9.00				
1975FM (P)	32,000	Value: 11.00				
1976FM (P)	15,000	Value: 11.00				
1977FM (P)	7,218	Value: 12.00				
1978FM (P)	7,059	Value: 12.00				
1979FM (P)	5,304	Value: 12.50				
1980FM (P)	3,421	Value: 13.50				
1981FM (P)	1,124	Value: 14.50				
1982FM (P)	1,865	Value: 15.00				
1983FM (P)	478	Value: 22.00				
1984FM (P)	—	Value: 15.00				

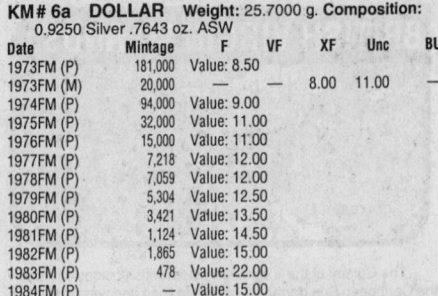

KM# 14 DOLLAR **Weight:** 25.7000 g. **Composition:** 0.9250 Silver .7643 oz. ASW **Subject:** Queen's Silver Jubilee

Date	Mintage	F	VF	XF	Unc	BU
1977FM (P)	17,000	Value: 15.00				

KM# 21 DOLLAR **Weight:** 25.7000 g. **Composition:** 0.9250 Silver .7643 oz. ASW **Subject:** Coronation Jubilee

Date	Mintage	F	VF	XF	Unc	BU
ND(1978)FM (P)	6,196	Value: 17.50				

KM# 47 DOLLAR **Composition:** Copper-Nickel **Reverse:** Butterfly Fish

Date		F	VF	XF	Unc	BU
1985FM (P)	—	Value: 30.00				

KM# 47a DOLLAR **Weight:** 24.7400 g. **Composition:** 0.9250 Silver .7358 oz. ASW

Date	Mintage	F	VF	XF	Unc	BU
1985FM (P)	1,372	Value: 40.00				

KM# 169 DOLLAR **Composition:** Copper-Nickel **Subject:** 500th Anniversary - Columbus' First Voyage to America **Obverse:** Queen's portrait **Reverse:** VIGILATE on banner below shield with woman and twelve lamps

Date		F	VF	XF	Unc	BU
ND(1992)	—	Value: 25.00				

KM# 172 DOLLAR Composition: Copper-Nickel **Subject:** Queen Mother's 100th Birthday **Obverse:** Queen's head right **Reverse:** Queen Mother facing **Edge:** Reeded **Size:** 38.6 mm.

Date	Mintage	F	VF	XF	Unc	BU
2000	100,000	—	—	—	7.50	—

KM# 175 DOLLAR Composition: Copper-Nickel **Subject:** 1st Anniversary - Earl and Countess of Wessex **Obverse:** Queen's head right **Reverse:** Half figures of Earl and Countess of Wessex facing, date below **Edge:** Reeded

Date	F	VF	XF	Unc	BU
2000	—	—	—	7.50	—

KM# 196 DOLLAR Weight: 28.2800 g. **Composition:** Copper-Nickel **Subject:** Queen's Golden Jubilee **Obverse:** Bust of Queen Elizabeth II right **Reverse:** Carnival dancers **Edge:** Reeded **Size:** 38.6 mm.

Date	F	VF	XF	Unc	BU
2002	—	—	—	10.00	—

KM# 180 DOLLAR Weight: 28.2800 g. **Composition:** Copper-Nickel **Subject:** Sir Francis Drake **Obverse:** Bust of Queen Elizabeth II right **Reverse:** Ship, portrait and map **Edge:** Reeded **Size:** 25.7 mm.

Date	F	VF	XF	Unc	BU
2002	—	—	—	10.00	—

KM# 183 DOLLAR Weight: 28.2800 g. **Composition:** Copper-Nickel **Subject:** Sir Walter Raleigh **Obverse:** Bust of Queen Elizabeth II right **Reverse:** Ship, portrait and map **Edge:** Reeded **Size:** 38.6 mm.

Date	F	VF	XF	Unc	BU
2002	—	—	—	10.00	—

KM# 187 DOLLAR Weight: 28.2800 g. **Composition:** Copper-Nickel **Subject:** Queen's Golden Jubilee **Obverse:** Bust of Queen Elizabeth II right **Reverse:** Queen on horse **Edge:** Reeded **Size:** 38.6 mm.

Date	F	VF	XF	Unc	BU
2002	—	—	—	10.00	—

KM# 190 DOLLAR Weight: 28.2800 g. **Composition:** Copper-Nickel **Subject:** Queen's Golden Jubilee **Obverse:** Bust of Queen Elizabeth II right **Reverse:** Queen on throne **Edge:** Reeded **Size:** 38.6 mm.

Date	F	VF	XF	Unc	BU
2002	—	—	—	10.00	—

KM# 193 DOLLAR Weight: 28.2800 g. **Composition:** Copper-Nickel **Subject:** Queen's Golden Jubilee **Obverse:** Bust of Queen Elizabeth II right **Reverse:** Queen with President Ronald Reagan and Mrs. Nancy Reagan **Edge:** Reeded **Size:** 38.6 mm.

Date	F	VF	XF	Unc	BU
2002	—	—	—	10.00	—

KM# 199 DOLLAR Weight: 28.2800 g. **Composition:** Copper-Nickel **Subject:** Teddy Bear Centennial **Obverse:** Bust of Queen Elizabeth II right **Reverse:** Teddy bear **Edge:** Reeded **Size:** 38.6 mm.

Date	F	VF	XF	Unc	BU
2002	—	—	—	10.00	—

KM# 204 DOLLAR Weight: 28.2800 g. **Composition:** Copper-Nickel **Subject:** Princess Diana **Obverse:** Bust of Queen Elizabeth II right **Reverse:** Diana's portrait **Edge:** Reeded **Size:** 38.6 mm.

Date	F	VF	XF	Unc	BU
2002	—	—	—	10.00	—

KM# 207 DOLLAR Weight: 28.2800 g. **Composition:** Copper-Nickel **Subject:** September 11, 2001 **Obverse:** Bust of Queen Elizabeth II right. **Reverse:** World Trade Center twin towers. **Edge:** Reeded. **Size:** 38.6 mm.

Date	F	VF	XF	Unc	BU
2002	—	—	—	14.00	—

KM# 210 DOLLAR Weight: 28.2800 g. **Composition:** Copper-Nickel **Subject:** September 11, 2001 **Obverse:** Bust of Queen Elizabeth II right **Reverse:** Statue of Liberty **Edge:** Reeded **Size:** 38.6 mm.

Date	F	VF	XF	Unc	BU
2002	—	—	—	14.00	—

KM# 213 DOLLAR Weight: 28.2800 g. **Composition:** Copper-Nickel **Subject:** Queen Mother **Obverse:** Queen's portrait **Reverse:** Queen Mother and a young Prince Charles **Edge:** Reeded **Size:** 38.6 mm.

Date	F	VF	XF	Unc	BU
2002	—	—	—	10.00	—

KM# 216 DOLLAR Weight: 28.2800 g. **Composition:** Copper-Nickel **Subject:** Queen Mother **Obverse:** Queen's portrait **Reverse:** Queen Mother with four grandchildren **Edge:** Reeded **Size:** 38.6 mm.

Date	F	VF	XF	Unc	BU
2002	—	—	—	10.00	—

KM# 219 DOLLAR Weight: 28.2800 g. **Composition:** Copper-Nickel **Subject:** Queen Mother Series **Obverse:** Queen's portrait **Reverse:** Queen Mother with uniformed Prince Charles **Edge:** Reeded **Size:** 38.6 mm.

Date	F	VF	XF	Unc	BU
2002	—	—	—	10.00	—

KM# 222 DOLLAR Weight: 28.2800 g. **Composition:** Copper-Nickel **Subject:** Queen Mother Series **Obverse:** Queen's portrait **Reverse:** Queen Mother's coffin **Edge:** Reeded **Size:** 38.6 mm.

Date	F	VF	XF	Unc	BU
2002	—	—	—	10.00	—

KM# 24 5 DOLLARS Composition: Copper-Nickel **Reverse:** Snowy Egret

Date	Mintage	F	VF	XF	Unc	BU
1979FM (U)	680	—	—	—	45.00	—

KM# 24a 5 DOLLARS Weight: 40.5000 g. **Composition:** 0.9250 Silver 1.2044 oz. ASW

Date	Mintage	F	VF	XF	Unc	BU
1979FM (P)	5,304	Value: 30.00				

KM# 26 5 DOLLARS Composition: Copper-Nickel **Reverse:** Great Blue Heron

Date	Mintage	F	VF	XF	Unc	BU
1980FM (U)	1,007	—	—	—	42.50	—

KM# 26a 5 DOLLARS Weight: 40.5000 g. **Composition:** 0.9250 Silver 1.2044 oz. ASW

Date	Mintage	F	VF	XF	Unc	BU
1980FM (P)	3,421	Value: 32.50				

KM# 30 5 DOLLARS Composition: Copper-Nickel **Subject:** Royal Tern **Obverse:** Similar to 50 Cents, KM#13

Date	Mintage	F	VF	XF	Unc	BU
1981FM (U)	472	—	—	—	45.00	—

KM# 30a 5 DOLLARS Weight: 40.5000 g. **Composition:** 0.9250 Silver 1.2044 oz. ASW

Date	Mintage	F	VF	XF	Unc	BU
1981FM (P)	1,124	Value: 35.00				

KM# 33 5 DOLLARS Composition: Copper-Nickel **Reverse:** White-tailed tropic birds

Date	F	VF	XF	Unc	BU
1982FM (U)	—	—	—	35.00	—

KM# 33a 5 DOLLARS Weight: 40.5000 g. **Composition:** 0.9250 Silver 1.2044 oz. ASW

Date	Mintage	F	VF	XF	Unc	BU
1982FM (P)	1,865	Value: 35.00				

KM# 35 5 DOLLARS Composition: Copper-Nickel **Subject:** Yellow Warblers **Obverse:** Similar to 50 Cents, KM#13

Date	F	VF	XF	Unc	BU
1983FM (U)	—	—	—	40.00	—

KM# 35a 5 DOLLARS Weight: 40.5000 g. **Composition:** 0.9250 Silver 1.2044 oz. ASW

Date	Mintage	F	VF	XF	Unc	BU
1983FM (P)	478	Value: 50.00				
1984FM (P)	—	Value: 50.00				

KM# 36 10 DOLLARS Weight: 30.2800 g. **Composition:** 0.5000 Silver .4868 oz. ASW **Subject:** 30th Anniversary - Coronation of Queen Elizabeth II

Date	Mintage	F	VF	XF	Unc	BU
1983FM (P)	2,957	Value: 17.50				

KM# 157 10 DOLLARS Composition: Copper-Nickel **Subject:** Discovery of America - Columbus Landing

Date	F	VF	XF	Unc	BU
ND(1992)FM (P)	—	Value: 12.50			

KM# 181 10 DOLLARS Weight: 28.2800 g. **Composition:** 0.9250 Silver 0.841 oz. ASW **Subject:** Sir Francis Drake **Obverse:** Bust of Queen Elizabeth II right. **Reverse:** Ship, portrait and map. **Edge:** Reeded. **Size:** 38.6 mm.

Date	F	VF	XF	Unc	BU
2002	—	—	—	47.50	—

KM# 197 10 DOLLARS Weight: 28.2800 g. **Composition:** 0.9250 Gold Clad Silver 0.841 oz. **Subject:** Queen's Golden Jubilee **Obverse:** Bust of Queen Elizabeth II right **Reverse:** Carnival dancers **Edge:** Reeded **Size:** 38.6 mm.

Date	Mintage	F	VF	XF	Unc	BU
2002 Proof	10,000	Value: 47.50				

KM# 173.1 (KM173) 10 DOLLARS Weight: 28.2800 g. **Composition:** 0.9250 Silver .8410 oz. ASW **Obverse:** Queen's head right **Reverse:** 1/2 bust Queen Mother facing **Edge:** Reeded **Size:** 38.6 mm.

Date	Mintage	F	VF	XF	Unc	BU
2000 Proof	10,000	Value: 47.50				

KM# 173.2 (KM173.1) 10 DOLLARS Weight: 28.2800 g. **Composition:** 0.9250 Silver 0.841 oz. ASW **Subject:** Queen Mother **Obverse:** Queen's portrait. **Reverse:** Queen Mother's portrait with a tiny sapphire mounted on her broach. **Edge:** Reeded. **Size:** 38.6 mm.

Date	Mintage
2000 Proof	1,000 Value: 50.00

KM# 184 10 DOLLARS Weight: 28.2800 g. **Composition:** 0.9250 Silver 0.841 oz. ASW **Subject:** Sir Walter Raleigh **Obverse:** Bust of Queen Elizabeth II right **Reverse:** Ship, portrait and map **Edge:** Reeded **Size:** 38.6 mm.

Date	F	VF	XF	Unc	BU
2002	—	—	—	47.50	—

KM# 200 10 DOLLARS Weight: 28.2800 g. **Composition:** 0.9250 Silver 0.841 oz. ASW **Subject:** Teddy Bear Centennial **Obverse:** Bust of Queen Elizabeth II right **Reverse:** Teddy bear **Edge:** Reeded **Size:** 38.6 mm.

Date	Mintage	F	VF	XF	Unc	BU
2002 Proof	10,000	Value: 47.50				

KM# 176 10 DOLLARS Weight: 28.2800 g. **Composition:** 0.9250 Silver .8410 oz. ASW **Subject:** 1st Anniversary - Earl and Countess of Wessex **Obverse:** Queen's head right **Reverse:** Half figures of Earl and Countess of Wessex facing, date below **Edge:** Reeded

Date	Mintage	F	VF	XF	Unc	BU
2000 Proof	10,000	Value: 47.50				

KM# 191 10 DOLLARS Weight: 28.2800 g. **Composition:** 0.9250 Gold Clad Silver 0.841 oz. **Subject:** Queen's Golden Jubilee **Obverse:** Bust of Queen Elizabeth II right **Reverse:** 3/4-length Queen seated on throne **Edge:** Reeded **Size:** 38.6 mm.

Date	Mintage	F	VF	XF	Unc	BU
2002 Proof	10,000	Value: 47.50				

KM# 205 10 DOLLARS Weight: 28.2800 g. **Composition:** 0.9250 Silver 0.841 oz. ASW **Subject:** Princess Diana **Obverse:** Bust of Queen Elizabeth II right **Reverse:** Diana's portrait **Edge:** Reeded **Size:** 38.6 mm.

Date	Mintage	F	VF	XF	Unc	BU
2002 Proof	10,000	Value: 47.50				

KM# 188 10 DOLLARS Weight: 28.2800 g. **Composition:** 0.9250 Gold Clad Silver 0.841 oz. **Subject:** Queen's Golden Jubilee **Obverse:** Bust of Queen Elizabeth II right **Reverse:** Queen on horse trotting left **Edge:** Reeded **Size:** 38.6 mm.

Date	F	VF	XF	Unc	BU
2002 Proof	10,000	Value: 47.50			

KM# 194 10 DOLLARS Weight: 28.2800 g. **Composition:** 0.9250 Gold Clad Silver 0.841 oz. **Subject:** Queen's Golden Jubilee **Obverse:** Bust of Queen Elizabeth II right **Reverse:** Queen with President Ronald Reagan and Mrs. Nancy Reagan **Edge:** Reeded **Size:** 38.6 mm.

Date	Mintage	F	VF	XF	Unc	BU
2002 Proof	10,000	Value: 47.50				

KM# 208.1 10 DOLLARS Weight: 28.2800 g. **Composition:** 0.9250 Silver 0.841 oz. ASW **Subject:** September 11, 2001 **Obverse:** Bust of Queen Elizabeth II right **Reverse:** World Trade Center twin towers **Edge:** Reeded **Size:** 38.6 mm.

Date	Mintage	F	VF	XF	Unc	BU
2002 Proof	10,000	Value: 49.00				

KM# 208.2 10 DOLLARS Weight: 28.2800 g. **Composition:** 0.9250 Silver 0.841 oz. ASW **Subject:** September 11, 2001 **Obverse:** Bust of Queen Elizabeth II right **Reverse:** Holographic multicolor World Trade Center twin towers **Edge:** Reeded **Size:** 38.6 mm.

Date	Mintage	F	VF	XF	Unc	BU
2002 Proof	10,000	Value: 55.00				

KM# 211 10 DOLLARS **Weight:** 28.2800 g. **Composition:** 0.9250 Silver 0.841 oz. ASW **Subject:** September 11, 2001 **Obverse:** Bust of Queen Elizabeth II right **Reverse:** Statue of Liberty **Edge:** Reeded **Size:** 38.6 mm.

Date	Mintage	F	VF	XF	Unc	BU
2002 Proof	10,000	Value: 49.00				

KM# 214 10 DOLLARS **Subject:** Queen Mother **Obverse:** Queen's portrait **Reverse:** Queen Mother with young Prince Charles **Edge:** Reeded **Size:** 38.6 mm.

Date	Mintage	F	VF	XF	Unc	BU
2002 Proof	10,000	Value: 47.50				

KM# 217 10 DOLLARS **Weight:** 28.2800 g. **Composition:** 0.9250 Silver 0.841 oz. ASW **Subject:** Queen Mother Series **Obverse:** Queen's portrait **Reverse:** Queen Mother with four grandchildren **Edge:** Reeded **Size:** 38.6 mm.

Date	Mintage	F	VF	XF	Unc	BU
2002 Proof	10,000	Value: 47.50				

KM# 220 10 DOLLARS **Weight:** 28.2800 g. **Composition:** 0.9250 Silver 0.841 oz. ASW **Subject:** Queen Mother Series **Obverse:** Queen's portrait **Reverse:** Queen Mother with uniformed Prince Charles **Edge:** Reeded **Size:** 38.6 mm.

Date	Mintage	F	VF	XF	Unc	BU
2002 Proof	10,000	Value: 47.50				

KM# 223 10 DOLLARS **Weight:** 28.2800 g. **Composition:** 0.9250 Silver 0.841 oz. ASW **Subject:** Queen Mother Series **Obverse:** Queen's portrait **Reverse:** Queen Mother's coffin **Edge:** Reeded **Size:** 38.6 mm.

Date	Mintage	F	VF	XF	Unc	BU
2002 Proof	10,000	Value: 47.50				

KM# 48 20 DOLLARS **Weight:** 19.0900 g. **Composition:** 0.9250 Silver .5678 oz. ASW **Reverse:** Crossed cannons

Date	F	VF	XF	Unc	BU
1985FM (P)	—	Value: 16.50			

KM# 49 20 DOLLARS **Weight:** 19.0900 g. **Composition:** 0.9250 Silver .5678 oz. ASW **Obverse:** Similar to KM#48 **Reverse:** Porcelain cup

Date	F	VF	XF	Unc	BU
1985FM (P)	—	Value: 16.50			

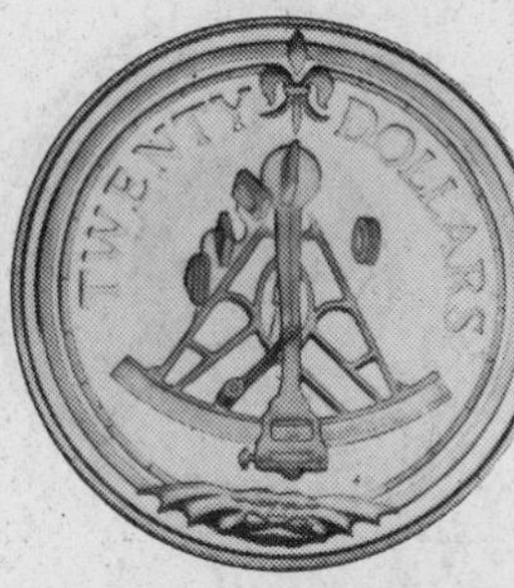

KM# 50 20 DOLLARS **Weight:** 19.0900 g. **Composition:** 0.9250 Silver .5678 oz. ASW **Obverse:** Similar to KM#48 **Reverse:** Sextant

Date	F	VF	XF	Unc	BU
1985FM (P)	—	Value: 16.50			

KM# 51 20 DOLLARS **Weight:** 19.0900 g. **Composition:** 0.9250 Silver .5678 oz. ASW **Obverse:** Similar to KM#48 **Reverse:** Emerald and gold ring

Date	F	VF	XF	Unc	BU
1985FM (P)	—	Value: 16.50			

KM# 52 20 DOLLARS **Weight:** 19.0900 g. **Composition:** 0.9250 Silver .5678 oz. ASW **Obverse:** Similar to KM#48 **Reverse:** Gold doubloon of 1702

Date	F	VF	XF	Unc	BU
1985FM (P)	—	Value: 16.50			

KM# 53 20 DOLLARS **Weight:** 19.0900 g. **Composition:** 0.9250 Silver .5678 oz. ASW **Obverse:** Similar to KM#48 **Reverse:** Anchor

Date	F	VF	XF	Unc	BU
1985FM (P)	—	Value: 16.50			

KM# 54 20 DOLLARS **Weight:** 19.0900 g. **Composition:** 0.9250 Silver .5678 oz. ASW **Obverse:** Similar to KM#48 **Reverse:** Brass nocturnal

Date	F	VF	XF	Unc	BU
1985FM (P)	—	Value: 16.50			

KM# 55 20 DOLLARS **Weight:** 19.0900 g. **Composition:** 0.9250 Silver .5678 oz. ASW **Obverse:** Similar to KM#48 **Reverse:** Sword guillon

Date	F	VF	XF	Unc	BU
1985FM (P)	—	Value: 16.50			

KM# 56 20 DOLLARS **Weight:** 19.0900 g. **Composition:** 0.9250 Silver .5678 oz. ASW **Obverse:** Similar to KM#48 **Reverse:** Gold bar

Date	F	VF	XF	Unc	BU
1985FM (P)	—	Value: 16.50			

KM# 57 20 DOLLARS **Weight:** 19.0900 g. **Composition:** 0.9250 Silver .5678 oz. ASW **Subject:** Gold Escudo **Obverse:** Similar to KM#48 **Reverse:** Obverse and reverse of gold escudo of 1733

Date	F	VF	XF	Unc	BU
1985FM (P)	—	Value: 16.50			

KM# 58 20 DOLLARS **Weight:** 19.0900 g. **Composition:** 0.9250 Silver .5678 oz. ASW **Obverse:** Similar to KM#48 **Reverse:** Ivory sundial

Date	F	VF	XF	Unc	BU
1985FM (P)	—	Value: 16.50			

KM# 59 20 DOLLARS **Weight:** 19.0900 g. **Composition:** 0.9250 Silver .5678 oz. ASW **Obverse:** Similar to KM#48 **Reverse:** Gold monstrance

Date	F	VF	XF	Unc	BU
1985FM (P)	—	Value: 16.50			

KM# 60 20 DOLLARS **Weight:** 19.0900 g. **Composition:** 0.9250 Silver .5678 oz. ASW **Obverse:** Similar to KM#48 **Reverse:** Teapot

Date	F	VF	XF	Unc	BU
1985FM (P)	—	Value: 16.50			

KM# 61 20 DOLLARS **Weight:** 19.0900 g. **Composition:** 0.9250 Silver .5678 oz. ASW **Obverse:** Similar to KM#48 **Reverse:** Brass religious medallion

Date	F	VF	XF	Unc	BU
1985FM (P)	—	Value: 16.50			

KM# 62 20 DOLLARS **Weight:** 19.0900 g. **Composition:** 0.9250 Silver .5678 oz. ASW **Obverse:** Similar to KM#48 **Reverse:** Astrolable

Date	F	VF	XF	Unc	BU
1985FM (P)	—	Value: 16.50			

KM# 64 20 DOLLARS **Weight:** 19.0900 g. **Composition:** 0.9250 Silver .5678 oz. ASW **Obverse:** Similar to KM#48 **Reverse:** Porcelain bottle

Date	F	VF	XF	Unc	BU
1985FM (P)	—	Value: 16.50			

KM# 65 20 DOLLARS **Weight:** 19.0900 g. **Composition:** 0.9250 Silver .5678 oz. ASW **Obverse:** Similar to KM#48 **Reverse:** Ship and Dutch cannons

Date	F	VF	XF	Unc	BU
1985FM (P)	—	Value: 16.50			

KM# 67 20 DOLLARS **Weight:** 19.0900 g. **Composition:** 0.9250 Silver .5678 oz. ASW **Obverse:** Similar to KM#48 **Reverse:** Ship's stern lantern

Date	F	VF	XF	Unc	BU
1985FM (P)	—	Value: 16.50			

KM# 68 20 DOLLARS **Weight:** 19.0900 g. **Composition:** 0.9250 Silver .5678 oz. ASW **Obverse:** Similar to KM#48 **Reverse:** Brass dividers

Date	F	VF	XF	Unc	BU
1985FM (P)	—	Value: 16.50			

KM# 69 20 DOLLARS **Weight:** 19.0900 g. **Composition:** 0.9250 Silver .5678 oz. ASW **Obverse:** Similar to KM#48 **Reverse:** Gold cross

Date	F	VF	XF	Unc	BU
1985FM (P)	—	Value: 16.50			

KM# 70 20 DOLLARS **Weight:** 19.0900 g. **Composition:** 0.9250 Silver .5678 oz. ASW **Obverse:** Similar to KM#48 **Reverse:** Perfume bottle

Date	F	VF	XF	Unc	BU
1985FM (P)	—	Value: 16.50			

KM# 71 20 DOLLARS **Weight:** 19.0900 g. **Composition:** 0.9250 Silver .5678 oz. ASW **Obverse:** Similar to KM#48 **Reverse:** Pocket watch

Date	F	VF	XF	Unc	BU
1985FM (P)	—	Value: 16.50			

KM# 72 20 DOLLARS **Weight:** 19.0900 g. **Composition:** 0.9250 Silver .5678 oz. ASW **Obverse:** Similar to KM#48 **Reverse:** Gold bracelet and button

Date	F	VF	XF	Unc	BU
1985FM (P)	—	Value: 16.50			

KM# 63.1 20 DOLLARS **Weight:** 19.0900 g. **Composition:** 0.9250 Silver .5678 oz. ASW **Obverse:** Similar to KM#48 **Reverse:** Bells **Note:** FM mint mark at right.

Date	F	VF	XF	Unc	BU
1985FM (P)	—	Value: 16.50			

KM# 63.2 20 DOLLARS **Weight:** 19.0900 g. **Composition:** 0.9250 Silver .5678 oz. ASW **Note:** FM mint mark in center.

Date	F	VF	XF	Unc	BU
1985FM (P)	—	Value: 16.50			

KM# 66 20 DOLLARS **Weight:** 19.0900 g. **Composition:** 0.9250 Silver .5678 oz. ASW **Obverse:** Similar to KM#48 **Note:** Spanish Colonial 8 Reales, Cob coin.

Date	F	VF	XF	Unc	BU
1985FM (P)	—	Value: 16.50			

KM# 201 20 DOLLARS **Weight:** 1.2441 g. **Composition:** 0.9999 Gold 0.04 oz. AGW **Subject:** Teddy Bear Centennial **Obverse:** Bust of Queen Elizabeth II right **Reverse:** Teddy bear **Edge:** Reeded **Size:** 13.92 mm.

Date	Mintage	F	VF	XF	Unc	BU
2002 Proof	10,000	Value: 49.50				

KM# 22 25 DOLLARS **Weight:** 28.1000 g. **Composition:** 0.9250 Silver .8356 oz. ASW **Subject:** Coronation Jubilee **Obverse:** Portrait of Queen

Date	Mintage	F	VF	XF	Unc	BU
1978FM (P)	8,438	Value: 25.00				

KM# 27 25 DOLLARS **Weight:** 1.5000 g. **Composition:** 0.5000 Gold .0241 oz. AGW **Reverse:** Diving Osprey

Date	Mintage	F	VF	XF	Unc	BU
1980FM (P)	11,000	Value: 50.00				

KM# 31.1 25 DOLLARS **Weight:** 1.5000 g. **Composition:** 0.5000 Gold .0241 oz. AGW **Reverse:** Caribbean Sparrow Hawk

Date	Mintage	F	VF	XF	Unc	BU
1981FM (P)	2,513	Value: 60.00				

KM# 31.2 25 DOLLARS **Weight:** 1.5000 g. **Composition:** 0.5000 Gold .0241 oz. AGW **Obverse:** Error. Without FM mint mark

Date	F	VF	XF	Unc	BU
1981 (P)	—	Value: 70.00			

KM# 41 25 DOLLARS **Weight:** 1.5000 g. **Composition:** 0.5000 Gold .0241 oz. AGW **Reverse:** Hawk

Date	Mintage	F	VF	XF	Unc	BU
1982FM (P)	3,819	Value: 52.20				

KM# 37 25 DOLLARS **Weight:** 1.5000 g. **Composition:** 0.5000 Gold .0241 oz. AGW **Reverse:** Merlin Hawk

Date	Mintage	F	VF	XF	Unc	BU
1983FM (P)	5,949	Value: 50.00				

KM# 40 25 DOLLARS **Weight:** 1.5000 g. **Composition:** 0.5000 Gold .0241 oz. AGW **Reverse:** Peregrine Falcon

Date	Mintage	F	VF	XF	Unc	BU
1984FM (P)	97	Value: 115				

KM# 73 25 DOLLARS **Weight:** 1.5000 g. **Composition:** 0.5000 Gold .0241 oz. AGW **Reverse:** Marsh Hawk

Date	Mintage	F	VF	XF	Unc	BU
1985FM (P)	1,294	Value: 80.00				

KM# 90 25 DOLLARS **Weight:** 20.0900 g. **Composition:** 0.9250 Silver .5977 oz. ASW **Series:** Sunken Ship Treasures **Reverse:** Ornamental lock plate

Date	F	VF	XF	Unc	BU
1988FM (P)	—	Value: 26.00			

KM# 91 25 DOLLARS **Weight:** 20.0900 g. **Composition:** 0.9250 Silver .5977 oz. ASW **Series:** Sunken Ship Treasures **Reverse:** Royal Coat of Arms on bottle

Date	F	VF	XF	Unc	BU
1988FM (P)	—	Value: 26.00			

KM# 92 25 DOLLARS **Weight:** 20.0900 g. **Composition:** 0.9250 Silver .5977 oz. ASW **Series:** Sunken Ship Treasures **Reverse:** Finger ring

Date	F	VF	XF	Unc	BU
1988FM (P)	—	Value: 26.00			

KM# 93 25 DOLLARS **Weight:** 20.0900 g. **Composition:** 0.9250 Silver .5977 oz. ASW **Series:** Sunken Ship Treasures **Reverse:** Hour glass

Date	F	VF	XF	Unc	BU
1988FM (P)	—	Value: 26.00			

KM# 94 25 DOLLARS **Weight:** 20.0900 g. **Composition:** 0.9250 Silver .5977 oz. ASW **Series:** Sunken Ship Treasures **Reverse:** Dagger and scabbard

Date	F	VF	XF	Unc	BU
1988FM (P)	—	Value: 26.00			

KM# 95 25 DOLLARS **Weight:** 20.0900 g. **Composition:** 0.9250 Silver .5977 oz. ASW **Series:** Sunken Ship Treasures **Reverse:** Jewel-encrusted cross

Date	F	VF	XF	Unc	BU
1988FM (P)	—	Value: 26.00			

KM# 96 25 DOLLARS **Weight:** 20.0900 g. **Composition:** 0.9250 Silver .5977 oz. ASW **Series:** Sunken Ship Treasures **Reverse:** Crossed keys

Date	F	VF	XF	Unc	BU
1988FM (P)	—	Value: 26.00			

KM# 97 25 DOLLARS **Weight:** 20.0900 g. **Composition:** 0.9250 Silver .5977 oz. ASW **Series:** Sunken Ship Treasures **Reverse:** Belt buckle

Date	F	VF	XF	Unc	BU
1988FM (P)	—	Value: 26.00			

KM# 98 25 DOLLARS **Weight:** 20.0900 g. **Composition:** 0.9250 Silver .5977 oz. ASW **Series:** Sunken Ship Treasures **Reverse:** American bottle

Date	F	VF	XF	Unc	BU
1988FM (P)	—	Value: 26.00			

KM# 99 25 DOLLARS **Weight:** 20.0900 g. **Composition:** 0.9250 Silver .5977 oz. ASW **Series:** Sunken Ship Treasures **Reverse:** Religious medallion

Date	F	VF	XF	Unc	BU
1988FM (P)	—	Value: 26.00			

KM# 100 25 DOLLARS **Weight:** 20.0900 g. **Composition:** 0.9250 Silver .5977 oz. ASW **Series:** Sunken Ship Treasures **Reverse:** Baby figurines

Date	F	VF	XF	Unc	BU
1988FM (P)	—	Value: 26.00			

KM# 101 25 DOLLARS **Weight:** 20.0900 g. **Composition:** 0.9250 Silver .5977 oz. ASW **Series:** Sunken Ship Treasures **Reverse:** Insignia of the Royal French Marines

Date	F	VF	XF	Unc	BU
1988FM (P)	—	Value: 26.00			

KM# 102 25 DOLLARS **Weight:** 20.0900 g. **Composition:** 0.9250 Silver .5977 oz. ASW **Series:** Sunken Ship Treasures **Reverse:** Engraved printing block

Date	F	VF	XF	Unc	BU
1988FM (P)	—	Value: 26.00			

KM# 103 25 DOLLARS **Weight:** 20.0900 g. **Composition:** 0.9250 Silver .5977 oz. ASW **Series:** Sunken Ship Treasures **Reverse:** Antique clock

Date	F	VF	XF	Unc	BU
1988FM (P)	—	Value: 26.00			

KM# 132 25 DOLLARS **Weight:** 20.0900 g. **Composition:** 0.9250 Silver .5977 oz. ASW **Reverse:** Flintlock pistol

Date	F	VF	XF	Unc	BU
1988FM (P)	—	Value: 26.00			

KM# 133 25 DOLLARS **Weight:** 20.0900 g. **Composition:** 0.9250 Silver .5977 oz. ASW **Reverse:** Stylized fish statue

Date	F	VF	XF	Unc	BU
1988FM (P)	—	Value: 26.00			

KM# 134 25 DOLLARS **Weight:** 20.0900 g. **Composition:** 0.9250 Silver .5977 oz. ASW **Reverse:** Mortar and pestle

Date	F	VF	XF	Unc	BU
1988FM (P)	—	Value: 26.00			

KM# 135 25 DOLLARS **Weight:** 20.0900 g. **Composition:** 0.9250 Silver .5977 oz. ASW **Reverse:** Open-mouthed dragon head sculpture

Date	F	VF	XF	Unc	BU
1988FM (P)	—	Value: 26.00			

KM# 136 25 DOLLARS **Weight:** 20.0900 g. **Composition:** 0.9250 Silver .5977 oz. ASW **Reverse:** Military mortar

Date	F	VF	XF	Unc	BU
1988FM (P)	—	Value: 26.00			

KM# 137 25 DOLLARS **Weight:** 20.0900 g. **Composition:** 0.9250 Silver .5977 oz. ASW **Reverse:** Seated figure sculpture

Date	F	VF	XF	Unc	BU
1988FM (P)	—	Value: 26.00			

KM# 138 25 DOLLARS **Weight:** 20.0900 g. **Composition:** 0.9250 Silver .5977 oz. ASW **Subject:** Lion Sculpture **Reverse:** Lion sculpture

Date	F	VF	XF	Unc	BU
1988FM (P)	—	Value: 26.00			

KM# 139 25 DOLLARS **Weight:** 20.0900 g. **Composition:** 0.9250 Silver .5977 oz. ASW **Reverse:** Violin

Date	F	VF	XF	Unc	BU
1988FM (P)	—	Value: 26.00			

KM# 140 25 DOLLARS **Weight:** 20.0900 g. **Composition:** 0.9250 Silver .5977 oz. ASW **Reverse:** Chalice

Date	F	VF	XF	Unc	BU
1988FM (P)	—	Value: 26.00			

KM# 141 25 DOLLARS **Weight:** 20.0900 g. **Composition:** 0.9250 Silver .5977 oz. ASW **Reverse:** Pitcher

Date	F	VF	XF	Unc	BU
1988FM (P)	—	Value: 26.00			

KM# 142 25 DOLLARS **Weight:** 20.0900 g. **Composition:** 0.9250 Silver .5977 oz. ASW **Reverse:** Cannon

Date	F	VF	XF	Unc	BU
1988FM (P)	—	Value: 26.00			

KM# 104 25 DOLLARS **Weight:** 21.5400 g. **Composition:** 0.9250 Silver .6406 oz. ASW **Series:** Discovery of America **Reverse:** Columbus planning voyage

Date	F	VF	XF	Unc	BU
ND(1992)FM (P)	—	Value: 32.00			

KM# 105 25 DOLLARS **Weight:** 21.5400 g. **Composition:** 0.9250 Silver .6406 oz. ASW **Series:** Discovery of America **Reverse:** Columbus lecturing

Date	F	VF	XF	Unc	BU
ND(1992)FM (P)	—	Value: 32.00			

KM# 106 25 DOLLARS **Weight:** 21.5400 g. **Composition:** 0.9250 Silver .6406 oz. ASW **Series:** Discovery of America **Reverse:** Queen Isabella offering jewels

Date	F	VF	XF	Unc	BU
ND(1992)FM (P)	—	Value: 32.00			

KM# 107 25 DOLLARS **Weight:** 21.5400 g. **Composition:** 0.9250 Silver .6406 oz. ASW **Series:** Discovery of America **Reverse:** Columbus aboard ship

Date	F	VF	XF	Unc	BU
ND(1992)FM (P)	—	Value: 32.00			

KM# 108 25 DOLLARS **Weight:** 21.5400 g. **Composition:** 0.9250 Silver .6406 oz. ASW **Series:** Discovery of America **Reverse:** Columbus on horseback

Date	F	VF	XF	Unc	BU
ND(1992)FM (P)	—	Value: 32.00			

KM# 112 25 DOLLARS **Weight:** 21.5400 g. **Composition:** 0.9250 Silver .6406 oz. ASW **Series:** Discovery of America **Reverse:** Shipwreck

Date	F	VF	XF	Unc	BU
ND(1992)FM (P)	—	Value: 32.00			

KM# 116 25 DOLLARS **Weight:** 21.5400 g. **Composition:** 0.9250 Silver .6406 oz. ASW **Series:** Discovery of America **Reverse:** Spanish figures

Date	F	VF	XF	Unc	BU
ND(1992)FM (P)	—	Value: 32.00			

KM# 109 25 DOLLARS **Weight:** 21.5400 g. **Composition:** 0.9250 Silver .6406 oz. ASW **Series:** Discovery of America **Reverse:** Ship under full sail

Date	F	VF	XF	Unc	BU
ND(1992)FM	—	Value: 32.00			

KM# 113 25 DOLLARS **Weight:** 21.5400 g. **Composition:** 0.9250 Silver .6406 oz. ASW **Series:** Discovery of America **Reverse:** Royal banquet

Date	F	VF	XF	Unc	BU
ND(1992)FM (P)	—	Value: 32.00			

KM# 117 25 DOLLARS **Weight:** 21.5400 g. **Composition:** 0.9250 Silver .6406 oz. ASW **Series:** Discovery of America **Reverse:** Columbus with shore party

Date	F	VF	XF	Unc	BU
ND(1992)FM (P)	—	Value: 32.00			

KM# 110 25 DOLLARS **Weight:** 21.5400 g. **Composition:** 0.9250 Silver .6406 oz. ASW **Series:** Discovery of America **Reverse:** Ship at anchor

Date	F	VF	XF	Unc	BU
ND(1992)FM (P)	—	Value: 32.00			

KM# 114 25 DOLLARS **Weight:** 21.5400 g. **Composition:** 0.9250 Silver .6406 oz. ASW **Series:** Discovery of America **Reverse:** Columbus predicting lunar eclipse to natives

Date	F	VF	XF	Unc	BU
ND(1992)FM (P)	—	Value: 32.00			

KM# 118 25 DOLLARS **Weight:** 21.5400 g. **Composition:** 0.9250 Silver .6406 oz. ASW **Series:** Discovery of America **Reverse:** Columbus on death bed

Date	F	VF	XF	Unc	BU
ND(1992)FM (P)	—	Value: 32.00			

KM# 111 25 DOLLARS **Weight:** 21.5400 g. **Composition:** 0.9250 Silver .6406 oz. ASW **Series:** Discovery of America **Reverse:** Natives offering gifts

Date	F	VF	XF	Unc	BU
ND(1992)FM (P)	—	Value: 32.00			

KM# 115 25 DOLLARS **Weight:** 21.5400 g. **Composition:** 0.9250 Silver .6406 oz. ASW **Series:** Discovery of America **Reverse:** Columbus on shore

Date	F	VF	XF	Unc	BU
ND(1992)FM (P)	—	Value: 32.00			

KM# 122 25 DOLLARS **Weight:** 21.5400 g. **Composition:** 0.9250 Silver .6406 oz. ASW **Series:** Discovery of America **Reverse:** Columbus bowing before King Ferdinand

Date	F	VF	XF	Unc	BU
ND(1992)FM (P)	—	Value: 32.00			

KM# 123 25 DOLLARS **Weight:** 21.5400 g. **Composition:** 0.9250 Silver .6406 oz. ASW **Series:** Discovery of America **Reverse:** Columbus before Queen Isabella

Date	F	VF	XF	Unc	BU
ND(1992)FM (P)	—	Value: 32.00			

KM# 127 25 DOLLARS **Weight:** 21.5400 g. **Composition:** 0.9250 Silver .6406 oz. ASW **Series:** Discovery of America **Reverse:** Columbus navigating by stars

Date	F	VF	XF	Unc	BU
ND(1992)FM (P)	—	Value: 32.00			

KM# 131 25 DOLLARS **Weight:** 21.5400 g. **Composition:** 0.9250 Silver .6406 oz. ASW **Series:** Discovery of America **Reverse:** Columbus as prisoner

Date	F	VF	XF	Unc	BU
ND(1992)FM (P)	—	Value: 32.00			

KM# 124 25 DOLLARS **Weight:** 21.5400 g. **Composition:** 0.9250 Silver .6406 oz. ASW **Series:** Discovery of America **Reverse:** Columbus before King Ferdinand and Queen Isabella

Date	F	VF	XF	Unc	BU
ND(1992)FM (P)	—	Value: 32.00			

KM# 128 25 DOLLARS **Weight:** 21.5400 g. **Composition:** 0.9250 Silver .6406 oz. ASW **Series:** Discovery of America **Reverse:** Sighting land

Date	F	VF	XF	Unc	BU
ND(1992)FM (P)	—	Value: 32.00			

KM# 186 25 DOLLARS **Weight:** 20.0900 g. **Composition:** 0.9250 Silver 0.5975 oz. ASW **Obverse:** Bust of Queen Elizabeth II right, 1988 type of KM#90-103 **Reverse:** Type of KM#122 originally minted in 1992 **Edge:** Reeded **Size:** 40 mm.

Date	F	VF	XF	Unc	BU
1988	—	—	—	800	—

KM# 125 25 DOLLARS **Weight:** 21.5400 g. **Composition:** 0.9250 Silver .6406 oz. ASW **Series:** Discovery of America **Reverse:** Columbus getting provisions for his ships

Date	F	VF	XF	Unc	BU
ND(1992)FM (P)	—	Value: 32.00			

KM# 129 25 DOLLARS **Weight:** 21.5400 g. **Composition:** 0.9250 Silver .6406 oz. ASW **Series:** Discovery of America **Reverse:** Columbus claiming the newly discovered land

Date	F	VF	XF	Unc	BU
ND(1992)FM (P)	—	Value: 32.00			

KM# 143 25 DOLLARS **Weight:** 20.0900 g. **Composition:** 0.9250 Silver .5977 oz. ASW **Series:** Endangered Wildlife **Reverse:** African elephants

Date	F	VF	XF	Unc	BU
1993FM (P)	—	Value: 40.00			

KM# 126 25 DOLLARS **Weight:** 21.5400 g. **Composition:** 0.9250 Silver .6406 oz. ASW **Series:** Discovery of America **Reverse:** Four sailing ships

Date	F	VF	XF	Unc	BU
ND(1992)FM (P)	—	Value: 32.00			

KM# 130 25 DOLLARS **Weight:** 21.5400 g. **Composition:** 0.9250 Silver .6406 oz. ASW **Series:** Discovery of America **Reverse:** Columbus seated on shore with shipwreck offshore

Date	F	VF	XF	Unc	BU
ND(1992)FM (P)	—	Value: 32.00			

KM# 144 25 DOLLARS **Weight:** 20.0900 g. **Composition:** 0.9250 Silver .5977 oz. ASW **Series:** Endangered Wildlife **Reverse:** Mountain gorilla

Date	F	VF	XF	Unc	BU
1993FM (P)	—	Value: 45.00			

KM# 145 25 DOLLARS **Weight:** 20.0900 g. **Composition:** 0.9250 Silver .5977 oz. ASW **Series:** Endangered Wildlife **Reverse:** Cape mountain zebra

Date		F	VF	XF	Unc	BU
1993FM (P)	—	Value: 35.00				

KM# 146 25 DOLLARS **Weight:** 20.0900 g. **Composition:** 0.9250 Silver .5977 oz. ASW **Series:** Endangered Wildlife **Reverse:** Polar bear

Date		F	VF	XF	Unc	BU
1993FM (P)	—	Value: 35.00				

KM# 147 25 DOLLARS **Weight:** 20.0900 g. **Composition:** 0.9250 Silver .5977 oz. ASW **Series:** Endangered Wildlife **Reverse:** Bald Eagle

Date		F	VF	XF	Unc	BU
1993FM (P)	—	Value: 32.50				

KM# 148 25 DOLLARS **Weight:** 20.0900 g. **Composition:** 0.9250 Silver .5977 oz. ASW **Series:** Endangered Wildlife **Reverse:** Snow Leopard

Date		F	VF	XF	Unc	BU
1993FM (P)	—	Value: 35.00				

KM# 149 25 DOLLARS **Weight:** 20.0900 g. **Composition:** 0.9250 Silver .5977 oz. ASW **Series:** Endangered Wildlife **Reverse:** Javan Rhinoceros

Date		F	VF	XF	Unc	BU
1993FM (P)	—	Value: 37.50				

KM# 150 25 DOLLARS **Weight:** 20.0900 g. **Composition:** 0.9250 Silver .5977 oz. ASW **Series:** Endangered Wildlife **Reverse:** Asian Lion

Date		F	VF	XF	Unc	BU
1993FM (P)	—	Value: 40.00				

KM# 151 25 DOLLARS **Weight:** 20.0900 g. **Composition:** 0.9250 Silver .5977 oz. ASW **Series:** Endangered Wildlife **Reverse:** Giant Panda

Date		F	VF	XF	Unc	BU
1993FM (P)	—	Value: 37.50				

KM# 152 25 DOLLARS **Weight:** 20.0900 g. **Composition:** 0.9250 Silver .5977 oz. ASW **Series:** Endangered Wildlife **Reverse:** Golden Lion Tamarin

Date		F	VF	XF	Unc	BU
1993FM (P)	—	Value: 35.00				

KM# 153 25 DOLLARS **Weight:** 20.0900 g. **Composition:** 0.9250 Silver .5977 oz. ASW **Series:** Endangered Wildlife **Reverse:** Pere David's deer

Date		F	VF	XF	Unc	BU
1993FM (P)	—	Value: 30.00				

KM# 154 25 DOLLARS **Weight:** 20.0900 g. **Composition:** 0.9250 Silver .5977 oz. ASW **Series:** Endangered Wildlife **Reverse:** Spectacled bear

Date		F	VF	XF	Unc	BU
1993FM (P)	—	Value: 40.00				

KM# 155 25 DOLLARS **Weight:** 20.0900 g. **Composition:** 0.9250 Silver .5977 oz. ASW **Series:** Endangered Wildlife **Obverse:** Queen's head right **Reverse:** Parrot on tree branch **Edge:** Reeded **Size:** 40 mm.

Date		F	VF	XF	Unc	BU
1993FM (P)	—	Value: 45.00				

KM# 158 25 DOLLARS **Weight:** 21.5900 g. **Composition:** 0.9250 Silver .6420 oz. ASW **Series:** Endangered Wildlife **Obverse:** Queen's portrait **Reverse:** Pair of black-footed ferrets, one standing

Date		F	VF	XF	Unc	BU
1993FM Proof	—	Value: 40.00				

KM# 159 25 DOLLARS Weight: 21.5900 g. **Composition:** 0.9250 Silver .6420 oz. ASW **Series:** Endangered Wildlife **Obverse:** Queen's portrait **Reverse:** Large rock lizard

Date	F	VF	XF	Unc	BU
1993FM Proof	—	Value: 40.00			

KM# 160 25 DOLLARS Weight: 21.5900 g. **Composition:** 0.9250 Silver .6420 oz. ASW **Series:** Endangered Wildlife **Obverse:** Queen's portrait **Reverse:** Two Parma wallabies, one with offspring

Date	F	VF	XF	Unc	BU
1993FM Proof	—	Value: 35.00			

KM# 161 25 DOLLARS Weight: 21.5900 g. **Composition:** 0.9250 Silver .6420 oz. ASW **Series:** Endangered Wildlife **Obverse:** Queen's portrait **Reverse:** Pair of leatherback sea turtles and Portuguese Man-o-War jelly fish

Date	F	VF	XF	Unc	BU
1993FM Proof	—	Value: 40.00			

KM# 170 25 DOLLARS Weight: 21.3500 g. **Composition:** 0.9250 Silver .6349 oz. ASW **Series:** Endangered Wildlife **Obverse:** Queen's portrait **Reverse:** Cheetah running left

Date	F	VF	XF	Unc	BU
1993FM (P)	—	Value: 35.00			

KM# 171 25 DOLLARS Weight: 21.3500 g. **Composition:** 0.9250 Silver .6349 oz. ASW **Series:** Endangered Wildlife **Obverse:** Queen's portrait **Reverse:** Bison in forest

Date	F	VF	XF	Unc	BU
1993FM (P)	—	Value: 30.00			

KM# 178 25 DOLLARS Weight: 21.6000 g. **Composition:** 0.9250 Silver .6424 oz. ASW **Series:** Endangered Wildlife **Obverse:** Queen's head right **Reverse:** Three flamingos and four nests **Edge:** Reeded **Size:** 40 mm.

Date	F	VF	XF	Unc	BU
1993 Proof	—	Value: 40.00			

KM# 179 25 DOLLARS Weight: 20.9000 g. **Composition:** 0.9250 Silver .5977 oz. ASW **Subject:** Endangered Wildlife **Obverse:** Queen's head right **Reverse:** Front half of tiger stalking left **Edge:** Reeded **Size:** 40 mm.

Date	F	VF	XF	Unc	BU
1993FM (P)	—	Value: 35.00			

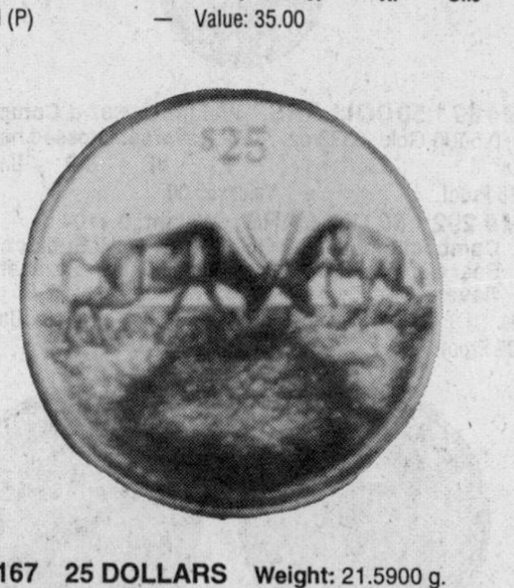

KM# 167 25 DOLLARS Weight: 21.5900 g. **Composition:** 0.9250 Silver .6420 oz. ASW **Series:** Endangered Wildlife **Obverse:** Queen's portrait **Reverse:** Pair of sparring antelope

Date	F	VF	XF	Unc	BU
1997	—	—	—	30.00	—

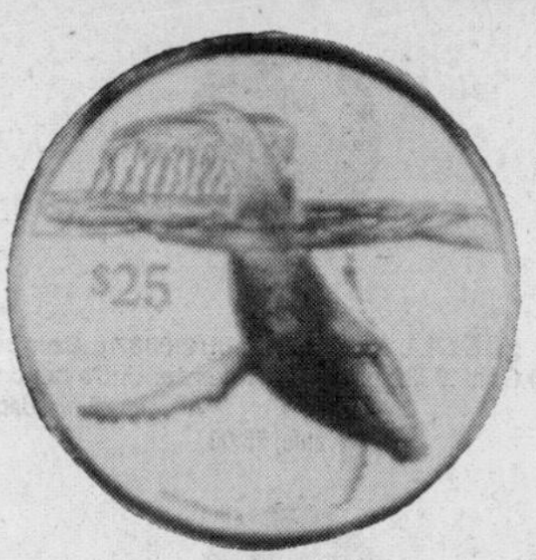

KM# 168 25 DOLLARS Weight: 21.5900 g. **Composition:** 0.9250 Silver .6420 oz. ASW **Series:** Endangered Wildlife **Obverse:** Queen's portrait **Reverse:** Diving humpback whale

Date	F	VF	XF	Unc	BU
1997	—	—	—	37.50	—

KM# 165 25 DOLLARS Weight: 21.5900 g. **Composition:** 0.9250 Silver .6420 oz. ASW **Series:** Endangered Wildlife **Obverse:** Queen's portrait **Reverse:** Two seals frolicking

Date	F	VF	XF	Unc	BU
1997	—	—	—	40.00	—

KM# 166 25 DOLLARS Weight: 21.5900 g. **Composition:** 0.9250 Silver .6420 oz. ASW **Series:** Endangered Wildlife **Obverse:** Queen's portrait **Reverse:** Sea otter holding a sea urchin

Date	F	VF	XF	Unc	BU
1997	—	—	—	40.00	—

KM# 28 50 DOLLARS Weight: 2.6800 g. **Composition:** 0.5000 Gold .0430 oz. AGW **Reverse:** Golden Dove of Christmas

Date	Mintage	F	VF	XF	Unc	BU
1980 Proof	6,379	Value: 65.00				

KM# 75 50 DOLLARS Weight: 2.0687 g. **Composition:** 0.5000 Gold .0332 oz. AGW **Reverse:** Flute player

Date	F	VF	XF	Unc	BU
1988 Proof	—	Value: 55.00			

KM#76 50 DOLLARS **Weight:** 2.0687 g. **Composition:** 0.5000 Gold .0332 oz. AGW **Reverse:** Bird's-head staff

Date		F	VF	XF	Unc	BU
1988 Proof	—	Value: 55.00				

KM#77 50 DOLLARS **Weight:** 2.0687 g. **Composition:** 0.5000 Gold .0332 oz. AGW **Reverse:** Double-spouted vessel

Date		F	VF	XF	Unc	BU
1988 Proof	—	Value: 55.00				

KM#78 50 DOLLARS **Weight:** 2.0687 g. **Composition:** 0.5000 Gold .0332 oz. AGW **Reverse:** Deer-top bell

Date		F	VF	XF	Unc	BU
1988 Proof	—	Value: 55.00				

KM#79 50 DOLLARS **Weight:** 2.0687 g. **Composition:** 0.5000 Gold .0332 oz. AGW **Reverse:** Two-headed animal

Date		F	VF	XF	Unc	BU
1988 Proof	—	Value: 55.00				

KM#80 50 DOLLARS **Weight:** 2.0687 g. **Composition:** 0.5000 Gold .0332 oz. AGW **Reverse:** Turtle

Date		F	VF	XF	Unc	BU
1988 Proof	—	Value: 55.00				

KM#81 50 DOLLARS **Weight:** 2.0687 g. **Composition:** 0.5000 Gold .0332 oz. AGW **Reverse:** Frog

Date		F	VF	XF	Unc	BU
1988 Proof	—	Value: 55.00				

KM#82 50 DOLLARS **Weight:** 2.0687 g. **Composition:** 0.5000 Gold .0332 oz. AGW **Reverse:** Mixtec mask

Date		F	VF	XF	Unc	BU
1988 Proof	—	Value: 55.00				

KM#83 50 DOLLARS **Weight:** 2.0687 g. **Composition:** 0.5000 Gold .0332 oz. AGW **Reverse:** Chimu gold beaker

Date		F	VF	XF	Unc	BU
1988 Proof	—	Value: 55.00				

KM#84 50 DOLLARS **Weight:** 2.0687 g. **Composition:** 0.5000 Gold .0332 oz. AGW **Reverse:** Bird vessel

Date		F	VF	XF	Unc	BU
1988 Proof	—	Value: 55.00				

KM#85 50 DOLLARS **Weight:** 2.0687 g. **Composition:** 0.5000 Gold .0332 oz. AGW **Reverse:** Ceremonial headdress

Date		F	VF	XF	Unc	BU
1988 Proof	—	Value: 55.00				

KM#86 50 DOLLARS **Weight:** 2.0687 g. **Composition:** 0.5000 Gold .0332 oz. AGW **Reverse:** Sacrifical knife

Date		F	VF	XF	Unc	BU
1988 Proof	—	Value: 55.00				

KM#87 50 DOLLARS **Weight:** 2.0687 g. **Composition:** 0.5000 Gold .0332 oz. AGW **Reverse:** Ceremonial dancer

Date		F	VF	XF	Unc	BU
1988 Proof	—	Value: 55.00				

KM#88 50 DOLLARS **Weight:** 2.0687 g. **Composition:** 0.5000 Gold .0332 oz. AGW **Reverse:** Spanish Colonial gold coin

Date		F	VF	XF	Unc	BU
1988 Proof	—	Value: 55.00				

KM#89 50 DOLLARS **Weight:** 2.0687 g. **Composition:** 0.5000 Gold .0332 oz. AGW **Reverse:** Crossed hands

Date		F	VF	XF	Unc	BU
1988 Proof	—	Value: 55.00				

KM# 202 50 DOLLARS **Weight:** 3.1104 g. **Composition:** 0.9999 Gold 0.1 oz. AGW **Subject:** Teddy Bear Centennial **Obverse:** Bust of Queen Elizabeth II right **Reverse:** Teddy bear **Edge:** Reeded **Size:** 17.95 mm.

Date	Mintage	F	VF	XF	Unc	BU
2002 Proof	7,000	Value: 70.00				

KM#7 100 DOLLARS **Weight:** 7.1000 g. **Composition:** 0.9000 Gold .2054 oz. AGW **Reverse:** Royal Tern

Date	Mintage	F	VF	XF	Unc	BU
1975FM (M) Rare	—	—	—	—	—	—
1975FM (U)	—	—	—	—	110	—
1975FM (P)	Est. 23,000	Value: 135				

Note: Includes 8,754 in First Day Covers

KM#8 100 DOLLARS **Weight:** 7.1000 g. **Composition:** 0.9000 Gold .2054 oz. AGW **Subject:** 50th Birthday of Queen Elizabeth II

Date	Mintage	F	VF	XF	Unc	BU
1976FM (M) Rare	10	—	—	—	—	—
1976FM (U)	1,752	—	—	—	125	—
1976FM (P)	12,000	Value: 150				

KM#15 100 DOLLARS **Weight:** 7.1000 g. **Composition:** 0.9000 Gold .2054 oz. AGW **Subject:** Queen's Silver Jubilee

Date	Mintage	F	VF	XF	Unc	BU
1977FM (U) Rare	10	—	—	—	—	—
1977FM (P)	6,715	Value: 150				

KM#23 100 DOLLARS **Weight:** 7.1000 g. **Composition:** 0.9000 Gold .2054 oz. AGW **Subject:** Coronation Jubilee

Date	Mintage	F	VF	XF	Unc	BU
1978FM (P)	5,772	Value: 160				

KM# 25 100 DOLLARS **Weight:** 7.1000 g. **Composition:** 0.9000 Gold .2054 oz. AGW **Reverse:** Bust of Sir Francis Drake with ruffed collar right

Date	Mintage	F	VF	XF	Unc	BU
1979FM (P)	3,216	Value: 175				

KM# 29 100 DOLLARS **Weight:** 7.1000 g. **Composition:** 0.9000 Gold .2054 oz. AGW **Subject:** 400th Anniversary of Drake's Voyage

Date	Mintage	F	VF	XF	Unc	BU
1980 Proof	5,412	Value: 125				

KM# 32 100 DOLLARS **Weight:** 7.1000 g. **Composition:** 0.9000 Gold .2054 oz. AGW **Subject:** Knighting of Sir Francis Drake

Date	Mintage	F	VF	XF	Unc	BU
1981FM (P)	1,321	Value: 180				

KM# 34 100 DOLLARS **Weight:** 7.1000 g. **Composition:** 0.9000 Gold .2054 oz. AGW **Subject:** 30th Anniversary - Reign of Queen Elizabeth II

Date	Mintage	F	VF	XF	Unc	BU
1982FM (P)	620	Value: 250				

KM# 38 100 DOLLARS **Weight:** 7.1000 g. **Composition:** 0.9000 Gold .2054 oz. AGW **Subject:** 30th Anniversary - Coronation of Queen Elizabeth II

Date	Mintage	F	VF	XF	Unc	BU
1983FM (P)	624	Value: 250				

KM# 39 100 DOLLARS **Weight:** 7.1000 g. **Composition:** 0.9000 Gold .2054 oz. AGW **Subject:** Flora - Ginger Thomas

Date	Mintage	F	VF	XF	Unc	BU
1984FM (P)	25	Value: 475				

KM# 74 100 DOLLARS **Weight:** 7.1000 g. **Composition:** 0.9000 Gold .2054 oz. AGW **Subject:** Sir Francis Drake's West Indian Voyage

Date	Mintage	F	VF	XF	Unc	BU
1985FM (P)	772	Value: 200				

KM# 119 100 DOLLARS **Weight:** 4.1180 g. **Composition:** 0.5000 Gold .0662 oz. AGW **Subject:** Discovery of America - King Ferdinand of Spain

Date	Mintage	F	VF	XF	Unc	BU
ND(1991)FM (P)	—	Value: 110				

KM# 162 100 DOLLARS **Weight:** 4.1180 g. **Composition:** 0.5000 Gold .0662 oz. AGW **Subject:** The Pinta **Obverse:** Queen's portrait **Reverse:** Ship sailing right

Date	Mintage	F	VF	XF	Unc	BU
ND(1994) Proof	—	Value: 125				

KM# 174.1 (KM174) 100 DOLLARS **Weight:** 6.2200 g. **Composition:** 0.9990 Gold .2000 oz. AGW **Subject:** Queen Mother's 100th Birthday **Obverse:** Queen's head right **Reverse:** 1/2 bust of Queen Mother facing **Edge:** Reeded

Date	Mintage	F	VF	XF	Unc	BU
2000 Proof	5,000	Value: 175				

KM# 174.2 (KM174.1) 100 DOLLARS **Weight:** 6.2200 g. **Composition:** 0.9999 Gold 0.2 oz. AGW **Subject:** Queen Mother **Obverse:** Queen's portrait **Reverse:** Queen Mother's portrait with a tiny black sapphire mounted on her broach **Edge:** Reeded **Size:** 22 mm.

Date	Mintage					
2000 Proof	1,000	Value: 180				

KM# 189 100 DOLLARS **Weight:** 6.2208 g. **Composition:** 0.9999 Gold 0.2 oz. AGW **Subject:** Queen's Golden Jubilee **Obverse:** Bust of Queen Elizabeth II right **Reverse:** Queen on horse **Edge:** Reeded **Size:** 22 mm.

Date	Mintage	F	VF	XF	Unc	BU
2002 Proof	2,002	Value: 175				

KM# 182 100 DOLLARS **Weight:** 6.2200 g. **Composition:** 0.9990 Gold 0.1998 oz. AGW **Subject:** Sir Francis Drake **Obverse:** Bust of Queen Elizabeth II right **Reverse:** Ship, portrait and map **Edge:** Reeded **Size:** 22 mm.

Date	Mintage	F	VF	XF	Unc	BU
2002 Proof	5,000	Value: 175				

KM# 185 100 DOLLARS **Weight:** 6.2200 g. **Composition:** 0.9990 Gold 0.1998 oz. AGW **Subject:** Sir Walter Raleigh **Obverse:** Bust of Queen Elizabeth II right **Reverse:** Ship, portrait and map **Edge:** Reeded **Size:** 22 mm.

Date	Mintage	F	VF	XF	Unc	BU
2002 Proof	5,000	Value: 175				

KM# 192 100 DOLLARS **Weight:** 6.2208 g. **Composition:** 0.9999 Gold 0.2 oz. AGW **Subject:** Queen's Golden Jubilee **Obverse:** Bust of Queen Elizabeth II right **Reverse:** Queen on throne **Edge:** Reeded **Size:** 22 mm.

Date	Mintage	F	VF	XF	Unc	BU
2002 Proof	2,002	Value: 175				

KM# 195 100 DOLLARS **Weight:** 6.2208 g. **Composition:** 0.9999 Gold 0.2 oz. AGW **Subject:** Queen's Golden Jubilee **Obverse:** Bust of Queen Elizabeth II right **Reverse:** Queen with President Ronald Reagan and Mrs. Nancy Reagan **Edge:** Reeded **Size:** 22 mm.

Date	Mintage	F	VF	XF	Unc	BU
2002 Proof	2,002	Value: 175				

KM# 198 100 DOLLARS **Weight:** 6.2208 g. **Composition:** 0.9999 Gold 0.2 oz. AGW **Subject:** Queen's Golden Jubilee **Obverse:** Bust of Queen Elizabeth II right **Reverse:** Carnival dancers **Edge:** Reeded **Size:** 22 mm.

Date	Mintage	F	VF	XF	Unc	BU
2002 Proof	2,002	Value: 175				

KM# 203 100 DOLLARS **Weight:** 6.2200 g. **Composition:** 0.9999 Gold 0.2 oz. AGW **Subject:** Teddy Bear Centennial **Obverse:** Bust of Queen Elizabeth II right **Reverse:** Teddy bear **Edge:** Reeded **Size:** 22 mm.

Date	Mintage	F	VF	XF	Unc	BU
2002 Proof	5,000	Value: 175				

KM# 206 100 DOLLARS **Weight:** 6.2200 g. **Composition:** 0.9999 Gold 0.2 oz. AGW **Subject:** Princess Diana **Obverse:** Bust of Queen Elizabeth II right **Reverse:** Diana's portrait **Edge:** Reeded **Size:** 22 mm.

Date	Mintage	F	VF	XF	Unc	BU
2002 Proof	5,000	Value: 175				

KM# 209.1 100 DOLLARS **Weight:** 6.2200 g. **Composition:** 0.9999 Gold 0.2 oz. AGW **Subject:** September 11, 2001 **Obverse:** Bust of Queen Elizabeth II right **Reverse:** World Trade Center twin towers **Edge:** Reeded **Size:** 22 mm.

Date	Mintage	F	VF	XF	Unc	BU
2002 Proof	5,000	Value: 175				

KM# 209.2 100 DOLLARS **Weight:** 6.2200 g. **Composition:** 0.9999 Gold 0.2 oz. AGW **Subject:** September 11, 2001 **Obverse:** Bust of Queen Elizabeth II right **Reverse:** Holographic multi-colored World Trade Center twin towers **Edge:** Reeded **Size:** 22 mm.

Date	Mintage	F	VF	XF	Unc	BU
2002 Proof	5,000	Value: 185				

KM# 212 100 DOLLARS **Weight:** 6.2200 g. **Composition:** 0.9999 Gold 0.2 oz. AGW **Subject:** September 11, 2001 **Obverse:** Bust of Queen Elizabeth II right **Reverse:** Statue of Liberty **Edge:** Reeded **Size:** 22 mm.

Date	Mintage	F	VF	XF	Unc	BU
2002 Proof	5,000	Value: 175				

KM# 215 100 DOLLARS **Weight:** 6.2200 g. **Composition:** 0.9999 Gold 0.2 oz. AGW **Subject:** Queen Mother Series **Obverse:** Queen's portrait **Reverse:** Queen Mother with young Prince Charles **Edge:** Reeded **Size:** 22 mm.

Date	Mintage	F	VF	XF	Unc	BU
2002 Proof	5,000	Value: 175				

KM# 218 100 DOLLARS **Weight:** 6.2200 g. **Composition:** 0.9999 Gold 0.2 oz. AGW **Subject:** Queen Mother Series **Obverse:** Queen's portrait **Reverse:** Queen Mother with four grandchildren **Edge:** Reeded **Size:** 22 mm.

Date	Mintage	F	VF	XF	Unc	BU
2002 Proof	5,000	Value: 175				

KM# 221 100 DOLLARS **Weight:** 6.2200 g. **Composition:** 0.9999 Gold 0.2 oz. AGW **Subject:** Queen Mother Series **Obverse:** Queen's portrait **Reverse:** Queen Mother with uniformed Prince Charles **Edge:** Reeded **Size:** 22 mm.

Date	Mintage	F	VF	XF	Unc	BU
2002 Proof	5,000	Value: 175				

KM# 224 100 DOLLARS **Weight:** 6.2200 g. **Composition:** 0.9999 Gold 0.2 oz. AGW **Subject:** Queen Mother Series **Obverse:** Queen's portrait **Reverse:** Queen Mother's coffin **Edge:** Reeded **Size:** 22 mm.

Date	Mintage	F	VF	XF	Unc	BU
2002 Proof	5,000	Value: 175				

KM# 120 250 DOLLARS **Weight:** 8.0494 g. **Composition:** 0.5000 Gold .1294 oz. AGW **Subject:** Discovery of America - Queen Isabella of Spain

Date	F	VF	XF	Unc	BU
ND(1991)FM (P)	—	Value: 265			

KM# 163 250 DOLLARS **Weight:** 8.0494 g. **Composition:** 0.5000 Gold .1294 oz. AGW **Subject:** The Nina **Obverse:** Queen's portrait **Reverse:** Ship sailing left

Date	F	VF	XF	Unc	BU
ND(1994) Proof	—	Value: 285			

KM# 121 500 DOLLARS **Weight:** 19.8126 g. **Composition:** 0.5000 Gold .3185 oz. AGW **Subject:** Discovery of America - Christopher Columbus

Date	F	VF	XF	Unc	BU
ND(1991)FM (P)	—	Value: 550			

KM# 164 500 DOLLARS **Weight:** 19.8126 g. **Composition:** 0.5000 Gold .3185 oz. AGW **Subject:** The Santa Maria **Obverse:** Queen's portrait **Reverse:** Ship sailing left, no gulls

Date	F	VF	XF	Unc	BU
ND(1994) Proof	—	Value: 575			

KM# 156 1000 DOLLARS **Weight:** 14.8000 g. **Composition:** 0.9990 Platinum .4758 oz. APW **Subject:** Discovery of America - Three Ships Sailing

Date	F	VF	XF	Unc	BU
ND(1992) Proof	—	Value: 1,150			

MINT SETS

KM#	Date	Mintage	Identification	Issue Price	Mkt Val
MS1	1973 (6)	18,402	KM#1-5, 6a	11.50	8.00
MS2	1974 (6)	9,474	KM#1-6	10.00	8.00
MS3	1975 (6)	2,351	KM#1-6	12.50	10.00
MS4	1976 (6)	996	KM#1-6	13.50	12.00
MS5	1977 (6)	782	KM#1-6	12.50	12.00
MS6	1978 (6)	943	KM#1-6	13.00	12.00
MS7	1979 (7)	680	KM#1-6, 24	20.00	25.00
MS8	1980 (7)	1,007	KM#1-6, 26	21.00	25.00
MS9	1981 (9)	472	KM#1-6, 30	20.00	30.00
MS10	1982 (7)	—	KM#1-6, 33	28.50	35.00
MS11	1983 (7)	203	KM#1-6, 35	22.00	50.00

PROOF SETS

KM#	Date	Mintage	Identification	Issue Price	Mkt Val
PS1	1973 (6)	146,581	KM#1-5, 6a. Includes 34,418 proofs in First Day Covers	15.00	15.00
PS2	1974 (6)	93,555	KM#1-5, 6a	20.00	16.50
PS3	1975 (6)	32,244	KM#1-5, 6a	25.00	18.50
PS4	1976 (6)	15,003	KM#1-5, 6a	25.00	18.50
PS5	1977 (6)	7,218	KM#1-5, 6a	26.00	20.00
PS6	1977 (6)	17,366	KM#9-14	60.00	40.00
PS7	1978 (6)	7,059	KM#1-5, 6a	25.00	20.00
PS8	1978 (6)	6,196	KM#16-21	—	40.00
PS9	1979 (7)	5,304	KM#1-5, 6a, 24a	39.50	37.50
PS10	1980 (7)	3,421	KM#105, 6a, 26a	97.00	47.50
PS11	1981 (7)	1,124	KM#1-5, 6a, 30a	97.00	60.00
PS12	1982 (7)	—	KM#1-5, 6a, 33a	97.00	60.00
PS13	1983 (7)	478	KM#1-5, 6a, 35a	77.00	65.00
PS14	1984 (7)	5,000	KM#1-5, 6a, 35a	77.00	60.00
PS15	1985 (6)	—	KM#42-47	20.50	45.00
PS16	1985 (6)	—	KM#42a-47a	76.00	95.00
PS17	ND (1991) (3)	—	KM#119-121	975	950
PS18	ND (1994) (3)	—	KM#162-164	975	985

BRITISH WEST AFRICA

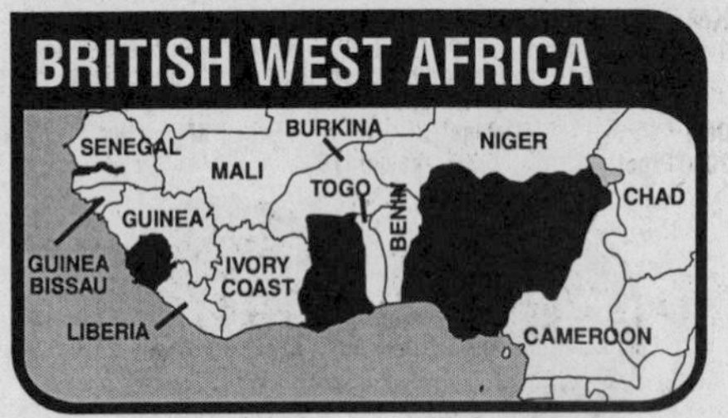

British West Africa was an administrative grouping of the four former British West African colonies of Gambia, Sierra Leone, Nigeria and Gold Coast (now Ghana). All are now independent republics and members of the British Commonwealth of Nations. See separate entries for individual statistics and history.

The Bank of British West Africa became the banker to the Colonial Government in 1894 and held this status until 1912. As such they were responsible for maintaining a proper supply of silver coinage for the colonies.

Through the subsidiary efforts of the Governor of Lagos, Nigeria a specific British West African coinage was put into use between 1907 and 1911. These coins bear the inscription, NIGERIA-BRITISH WEST AFRICA.

The four colonies were supplied with a common coinage and banknotes by the West African Currency Board from 1912 through 1958. This coinage bore the inscription BRITISH WEST AFRICA. The coinage, which includes three denominations of 1936 bearing the name of Edward VIII, is obsolete.

For later coinage see Gambia, Ghana, Sierra Leone and Nigeria.

RULERS

British, until 1958

MINT MARKS

G-J.R. Gaunt & Sons, Birmingham
H - Heaton Mint, Birmingham
K, KN - King's Norton, Birmingham
SA - Pretoria, South Africa
No mm - Royal Mint, London

MONETARY SYSTEM

12 Pence = 1 Shilling
20 Shillings = 1 Pound

BRITISH COLONIES

POUND COINAGE

KM# 1 1/10 PENNY Composition: Aluminum

Date	Mintage	F	VF	XF	Unc	BU
1907	1,254,000	2.00	4.00	10.00	20.00	35.00
1908	8,363,000	1.00	3.00	6.00	15.00	25.00
1908 Proof	—	Value: 300				

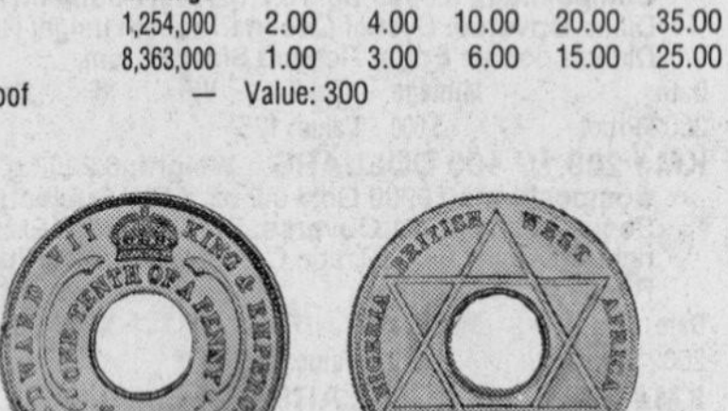

KM# 3 1/10 PENNY Composition: Copper-Nickel

Date	Mintage	F	VF	XF	Unc	BU
1908	9,600,000	0.30	0.50	1.00	2.00	3.50
1909	4,800,000	0.40	0.75	1.50	5.00	9.00
1910	7,200,000	0.50	1.00	2.00	7.50	12.50

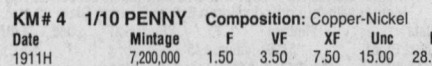

KM# 4 1/10 PENNY Composition: Copper-Nickel

Date	Mintage	F	VF	XF	Unc	BU
1911H	7,200,000	1.50	3.50	7.50	15.00	28.00

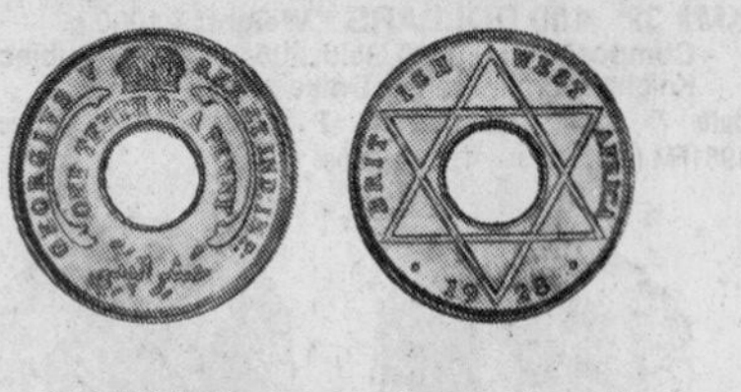

KM# 7 1/10 PENNY Composition: Copper-Nickel
Reverse: Legend without NIGERIA

Date	Mintage	F	VF	XF	Unc	BU
1912H	10,800,000	0.30	0.75	1.50	3.50	7.00
1913	4,632,000	1.00	2.00	3.50	6.50	11.50
1913H	1,080,000	0.30	0.75	1.50	3.50	7.00
1914	1,200,000	3.00	5.00	10.00	22.50	40.00
1914H	20,088,000	0.50	1.25	2.00	5.00	9.00
1915H	10,032,000	0.30	0.75	1.50	5.00	9.00
1916H	480,000	25.00	50.00	75.00	150	—
1917H	9,384,000	2.00	3.00	5.00	15.00	25.00
1919H	912,000	1.25	2.00	4.00	7.50	13.50
1919KN	480,000	10.00	25.00	50.00	75.00	—
1920H	1,560,000	2.00	3.00	5.00	10.00	18.00
1920KN	12,996,000	0.40	1.00	3.00	5.00	9.00
1920KN Proof	—	Value: 125				
1922KN	7,265,000	1.00	1.75	4.50	12.00	20.00
1923KN	12,000,000	0.30	0.75	1.50	5.00	9.00
1925	2,400,000	5.00	10.00	20.00	40.00	70.00
1925H	12,000,000	2.00	3.00	5.00	12.00	20.00
1925KN	12,000,000	0.75	1.50	3.00	8.00	15.00
1926	12,000,000	0.75	1.50	2.50	6.00	10.00
1927	3,984,000	0.20	0.50	1.50	3.00	6.00
1927 Proof	—	Value: 150				
1928	11,760,000	0.20	0.50	1.50	3.00	6.00
1928 Proof	—	Value: 150				
1928H	2,964,000	0.20	0.50	1.50	3.00	6.00
1928KN	3,151,000	2.00	3.00	6.00	15.00	25.00
1930	9,600,000	2.00	3.00	6.00	15.00	25.00
1930 Proof	—	Value: 150				
1931	9,840,000	0.20	0.50	1.00	3.00	6.00
1931 Proof	—	Value: 150				
1932	3,600,000	0.20	0.50	1.50	5.00	9.00
1932 Proof	—	Value: 150				
1933	7,200,000	0.20	0.50	1.50	3.50	7.00
1933 Proof	—	Value: 150				
1934	4,800,000	0.75	1.50	3.00	6.00	10.00
1934 Proof	—	Value: 150				
1935	13,200,000	0.75	1.50	3.00	7.50	12.50
1935 Proof	—	Value: 150				
1936	9,720,000	0.20	0.50	1.00	3.00	6.00
1936 Proof	—	Value: 150				

KM# 14 1/10 PENNY Composition: Copper-Nickel

Date	Mintage	F	VF	XF	Unc	BU
1936	5,880,000	0.25	0.50	1.00	2.50	4.50
1936 Proof	—	Value: 200				
1936H	1,404,000	50.00	75.00	125	250	—
1936H Proof	—	Value: 300				
1936KN	3,000,000	1.00	2.00	3.50	9.00	15.00
1936KN Proof	—	Value: 200				

KM# 20 1/10 PENNY Composition: Copper-Nickel

Date	Mintage	F	VF	XF	Unc	BU
1938	12,000,000	0.10	0.25	0.50	1.50	2.50
1938 Proof	—	Value: 125				
1938H	1,596,000	5.00	8.00	12.00	22.50	40.00
1938H Proof	—	Value: 100				
1939	9,840,000	0.25	0.50	1.00	3.50	6.00
1939 Proof	—	Value: 200				
1940	13,920,000	0.25	0.50	1.00	2.00	3.50
1940 Proof	—	Value: 125				
1941	16,560,000	1.00	2.00	4.00	8.00	14.00
1941 Proof	—	Value: 125				
1942	12,360,000	1.00	2.50	4.50	10.00	18.00
1942 Proof	—	Value: 125				
1943	22,560,000	1.00	2.50	5.00	10.00	18.00
1944	10,440,000	1.00	2.50	5.00	10.00	18.00
1944 Proof	—	Value: 150				
1945	25,706,000	0.50	1.00	1.75	6.00	10.00
1945 Proof	—	Value: 125				
1946	2,803,000	1.00	2.00	4.00	9.00	15.00
1946 Proof	—	Value: 125				

Date	Mintage	F	VF	XF	Unc	BU
1946H	5,004,000	1.00	2.00	4.00	9.00	15.00
1946KN	1,152,000	0.25	0.50	1.00	3.00	5.50
1946KN Proof	—	Value: 125				
1947	4,202,000	0.50	1.00	2.00	5.00	9.00
1947 Proof	—	Value: 125				
1947KN	3,900,000	200	300	500	600	—

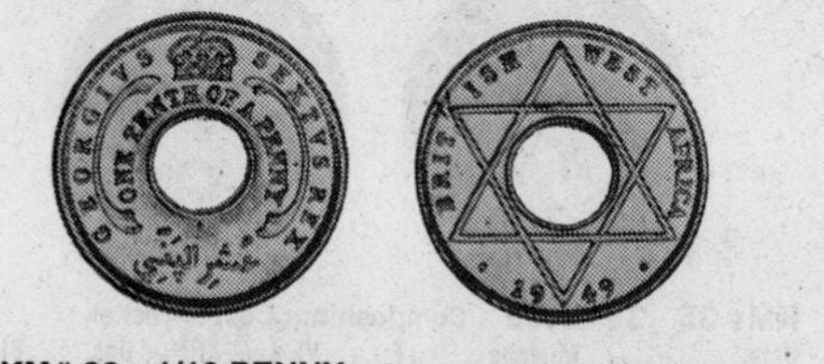

KM# 26 1/10 PENNY **Composition:** Copper-Nickel **Obverse:** Legend without IND: IMP:

Date	Mintage	F	VF	XF	Unc	BU
1949H	3,700,000	1.00	2.00	3.00	6.00	10.00
1949KN	3,036,000	1.00	2.00	3.00	5.00	9.00
1950KN	13,200,000	0.25	0.50	1.00	2.50	4.50
1950KN Proof	—	Value: 150				

KM# 26a 1/10 PENNY **Composition:** Bronze

Date	Mintage	F	VF	XF	Unc	BU
1952	15,060,000	0.50	1.00	2.00	6.00	10.00
1952 Proof	—	Value: 150				

KM# 32 1/10 PENNY **Composition:** Bronze

Date	Mintage	F	VF	XF	Unc	BU
1954	4,800,000	0.50	1.00	2.00	4.00	8.00
1954 Proof	—	Value: 150				
1956	2,400,000	100	200	400	700	—
1956 Proof	—	Value: 750				
1957	7,200,000	60.00	120	220	325	—
1957 Proof	—	Value: 600				

KM# 5 1/2 PENNY **Composition:** Copper-Nickel

Date	Mintage	F	VF	XF	Unc	BU
1911H	3,360,000	4.00	12.00	25.00	40.00	75.00

KM# 8 1/2 PENNY **Composition:** Copper-Nickel **Reverse:** Legend without NIGERIA

Date	Mintage	F	VF	XF	Unc	BU
1912H	3,120,000	2.00	5.00	7.00	20.00	35.00
1913	1,382,000	150	250	300	500	—
1913H	216,000	5.00	10.00	17.50	30.00	55.00
1914	240,000	10.00	20.00	35.00	60.00	110
1914H	586,000	20.00	30.00	50.00	75.00	135
1914K	3,360,000	3.00	6.00	17.50	30.00	55.00
1914K Proof	—	Value: 225				

Note: Issued with East Africa KM#11 in a double (4 pc.) specimen set

Date	Mintage	F	VF	XF	Unc	BU
1915K	3,577,000	1.00	2.00	4.00	15.00	25.00
1916H	4,046,000	1.00	3.00	5.00	15.00	25.00
1917H	214,000	6.00	12.00	28.00	50.00	90.00
1918H	490,000	2.50	5.00	10.00	30.00	55.00
1919H	4,950,000	1.25	2.50	6.00	20.00	35.00
1919KN	3,861,000	1.25	2.50	7.50	25.00	45.00
1920H	26,285,000	1.50	3.00	7.50	15.00	25.00
1920KN	13,844,000	0.50	3.00	8.50	16.50	30.00
1922KN	5,817,000	300	500	750	1,200	—
1927	528,000	20.00	30.00	65.00	135	250
1927 Proof	—	Value: 225				
1929	336,000	6.00	22.00	47.50	95.00	165
1929 Proof	—	Value: 225				
1931	96,000	500	800	1,200	1,500	—
1931 Proof	—	Value: 225				
1932	960,000	2.50	15.00	35.00	55.00	100
1932 Proof	—	Value: 225				

Date	Mintage	F	VF	XF	Unc	BU
1933	2,122,000	12.00	23.50	55.00	110	200
1933 Proof	—	Value: 225				
1934	1,694,000	2.50	15.00	35.00	75.00	135
1934 Proof	—	Value: 225				
1935	3,271,000	1.00	3.00	18.00	35.00	60.00
1935 Proof	—	Value: 225				
1936	5,400,000	2.50	5.00	18.00	32.00	55.00
1936	—	Value: 225				

KM# 15 1/2 PENNY **Composition:** Copper-Nickel

Date	Mintage	F	VF	XF	Unc	BU
1936	14,760,000	0.25	0.50	1.00	2.50	4.50
1936 Proof	—	Value: 200				
1936H	2,400,000	1.00	2.00	5.00	12.50	20.00
1936H Proof	—	Value: 200				
1936KN	2,298,000	0.65	1.25	2.25	4.00	7.00
1936KN Proof	—	Value: 200				

KM# 18 1/2 PENNY **Composition:** Copper-Nickel

Date	Mintage	F	VF	XF	Unc	BU
1937H	4,800,000	0.40	0.85	1.50	4.00	7.00
1937H Proof	—	Value: 125				
1937KN	5,577,000	0.40	0.85	3.00	5.00	9.00
1940KN	2,410,000	2.00	4.00	6.00	15.00	25.00
1940KN Proof	—	Value: 125				
1941H	2,400,000	0.40	2.00	4.00	12.00	20.00
1942	4,800,000	0.40	0.85	2.00	8.50	15.00
1943	3,360,000	0.50	1.00	5.00	10.00	18.00
1944	3,600,000	1.00	3.00	7.00	20.00	35.00
1944 Proof	—	Value: 125				
1946	3,600,000	0.25	1.00	3.00	7.00	12.50
1946 Proof	—	Value: 125				
1947H	15,218,000	0.35	0.75	1.25	5.00	9.00
1947KN	12,000,000	0.40	0.85	2.00	6.00	10.00

KM# 27 1/2 PENNY **Composition:** Copper-Nickel **Obverse:** Legend without IND: IMP:

Date	Mintage	F	VF	XF	Unc	BU
1949H	5,909,000	1.50	3.50	8.00	22.00	40.00
1949KN	3,413,000	1.50	3.50	8.00	25.00	45.00
1951	3,468,000	1.50	3.50	9.00	25.00	45.00
1951 Proof	—	Value: 250				

KM# 27a 1/2 PENNY **Composition:** Bronze

Date	Mintage	F	VF	XF	Unc	BU
1952	11,332,000	0.25	0.50	1.50	5.50	9.50
1952 Proof	—	Value: 150				
1952H	27,603,000	0.20	0.35	0.75	2.00	3.50
1952KN	4,800,000	0.50	2.00	5.00	10.00	18.00

KM# 2 PENNY **Composition:** Copper-Nickel

Date	Mintage	F	VF	XF	Unc	BU
1907	863,000	2.00	5.00	9.00	20.00	35.00
1908	3,217,000	2.00	4.00	8.00	17.50	30.00
1909	960,000	3.50	9.00	18.00	45.00	80.00
1910	2,520,000	2.75	7.00	12.00	25.00	45.00

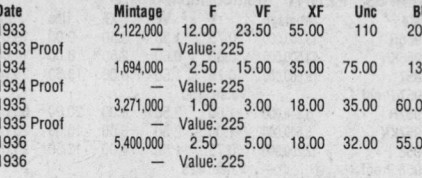

KM# 6 PENNY **Composition:** Copper-Nickel

Date	Mintage	F	VF	XF	Unc	BU
1911H	1,920,000	15.00	40.00	80.00	150	—

KM# 9 PENNY **Composition:** Copper-Nickel **Reverse:** Legend without NIGERIA

Date	Mintage	F	VF	XF	Unc	BU
1912H	1,560,000	1.50	3.00	7.50	22.50	40.00
1913	1,680,000	7.50	15.00	30.00	75.00	135
1913H	144,000	5.00	10.00	17.50	35.00	60.00
1914	3,000,000	2.50	5.00	10.00	22.50	40.00
1914H	72,000	35.00	50.00	100	200	—
1915H	3,295,000	1.25	2.00	5.00	15.00	25.00
1916H	3,461,000	1.25	2.00	7.00	20.00	35.00
1917H	444,000	5.00	7.00	18.00	45.00	80.00
1918H	994,000	7.50	15.00	35.00	75.00	135
1919H	21,864,000	1.25	2.50	5.00	15.00	25.00
1919KN	264,000	7.50	15.00	25.00	50.00	90.00
1920H	37,870,000	1.00	1.75	3.50	12.50	22.50
1920KN	20,685,000	1.00	2.00	5.00	17.50	30.00
1922KN	3,971,000	400	750	1,000	1,500	—
1926	8,039,999	2.00	4.00	10.00	30.00	55.00
1927	792,000	25.00	45.00	85.00	200	—
1927 Proof	—	Value: 225				
1928	6,672,000	2.00	4.00	10.00	25.00	45.00
1928 Proof	—	Value: 225				
1929	636,000	20.00	35.00	50.00	100	—
1929 Proof	—	Value: 225				
1933	2,806,000	2.00	14.00	32.50	65.00	120
1933 Proof	—	Value: 225				
1934	2,640,000	3.50	15.00	35.00	75.00	135
1934 Proof	—	Value: 225				
1935	8,551,000	1.25	12.50	27.50	45.00	80.00
1935 Proof	—	Value: 225				
1936	7,368,000	1.25	3.50	10.00	25.00	45.00
1936 Proof	—	Value: 225				

KM# 16 PENNY **Composition:** Copper-Nickel

Date	Mintage	F	VF	XF	Unc	BU
1936	7,992,000	0.50	1.00	3.50	7.00	12.50
1936 Proof	—	Value: 250				
1936H	12,600,000	0.35	0.75	1.00	2.25	4.00
1936H Proof	—	Value: 250				
1936KN	12,512,000	0.35	0.75	1.00	2.25	4.00
1936KN Proof	—	Value: 250				

KM# 17 PENNY **Composition:** Copper-Nickel **Obverse:** East Africa, KM#24 **Reverse:** KM#16 **Note:** Mule.

Date	F	VF	XF	Unc	BU
1936H	125	150	225	350	—

KM# 19 PENNY **Composition:** Copper-Nickel

Date	Mintage	F	VF	XF	Unc	BU
1937H	11,999,000	0.50	0.75	1.25	2.00	3.50
1937H Proof	—	Value: 200				
1937KN	11,999,000	0.50	0.75	1.25	2.00	3.50
1937KN Proof	—	Value: 200				
1940	3,840,000	0.50	0.75	1.25	2.00	3.50
1940 Proof	—	—	—	—	—	—
1940H	2,400,000	0.50	0.75	3.00	8.00	14.00
1940KN	2,400,000	0.75	1.50	4.50	10.00	18.00
1941	6,960,000	0.35	0.75	1.25	3.50	6.00
1941 Proof	—	—	—	—	—	—
1942	18,840,000	0.30	0.60	1.00	3.00	5.00
1943	28,920,000	0.30	0.60	1.00	3.00	5.00
1943H	7,140,000	2.00	5.00	10.00	20.00	35.00
1944	19,440,000	0.30	0.60	1.00	4.00	7.00
1945	6,072,000	0.45	0.90	1.75	5.00	9.00
1945 Proof	—	Value: 150				
1945H	9,000,000	1.00	2.00	4.50	10.00	18.00
1945KN	9,557,000	0.75	1.50	3.00	7.00	12.00
1946H	10,446,000	0.85	1.75	3.75	8.00	14.00
1946KN	11,976,000	0.30	0.60	1.00	5.00	9.00
1946SA	1,020,000	250	500	750	1,150	—
1947H	12,443,000	0.30	0.60	1.00	5.00	9.00
1947KN	9,829,000	0.30	0.60	1.00	5.00	9.00
1947SA	58,980,000	0.30	0.60	1.00	4.50	7.50

KM# 25 PENNY **Composition:** Copper-Nickel **Obverse:** KM#16 **Reverse:** KM#19 **Note:** Mule.

Date	F	VF	XF	Unc	BU
1945H	2,000	3,000	4,000	6,000	—

KM# 30 PENNY **Composition:** Copper-Nickel **Obverse:** Legend without IND: IMPL

Date	Mintage	F	VF	XF	Unc	BU
1951	1,258,000	7.50	12.50	27.50	45.00	80.00
1951 Proof	—	Value: 250				
1951KN	2,692,000	6.00	10.00	20.00	35.00	60.00

KM# 30a PENNY **Composition:** Bronze

Date	Mintage	F	VF	XF	Unc	BU
1952	10,542,000	0.75	1.50	3.00	8.50	15.00
1952 Proof	—	Value: 175				
1952H	30,794,000	0.20	0.40	0.60	3.00	5.00
1952KN	45,398,000	0.20	0.40	0.60	3.00	5.00
1952KN Proof	—	Value: 175				

KM# 33 PENNY **Composition:** Bronze

Date	Mintage	F	VF	XF	Unc	BU
1956H	13,503,000	0.75	1.50	3.50	9.00	16.00
1956KN	13,500,000	0.30	0.60	2.50	8.00	14.00
1957	9,000,000	0.75	1.50	6.00	13.50	25.00
1957 Proof	—	Value: 150				
1957H	5,340,000	1.00	2.50	8.00	20.00	35.00
1957KN	5,600,000	1.00	2.50	6.00	16.00	28.00
1958	12,200,000	0.75	1.50	4.00	13.50	25.00
1958 Proof	—	Value: 125				
1958KN	Inc. above	0.75	1.50	3.00	10.00	18.00

KM# 34 PENNY **Composition:** Bronze **Obverse:** KM#30 **Reverse:** KM#33 **Note:** Mule.

Date	F	VF	XF	Unc	BU
1956H	50.00	85.00	150	250	—

KM# 10 3 PENCE **Weight:** 1.1438 g. **Composition:** 0.9250 Silver .0420 oz. ASW

Date	Mintage	F	VF	XF	Unc	BU
1913	240,000	3.50	7.50	25.00	75.00	—
1913 Proof	—	Value: 250				
1913H	496,000	2.00	4.00	12.50	30.00	65.00
1914H	1,560,000	1.00	2.00	7.50	25.00	45.00
1915H	270,000	18.00	25.00	50.00	100	—
1916H	820,000	10.00	15.00	30.00	65.00	—
1917H	3,600,000	1.50	2.50	7.50	25.00	45.00
1918H	1,722,000	1.75	3.50	8.00	20.00	35.00
1919H	19,826,000	1.00	2.00	6.00	15.00	25.00
1919H Proof	—	Value: 200				

KM# 10a 3 PENCE **Weight:** 1.1438 g. **Composition:** 0.5000 Silver .0227 oz. ASW

Date	Mintage	F	VF	XF	Unc	BU
1920H	3,616,000	25.00	50.00	80.00	175	—

KM# 10b 3 PENCE **Composition:** Tin-Brass

Date	Mintage	F	VF	XF	Unc	BU
1920KN Unique	—	—	—	—	—	—

Note: Mint mark on obverse below bust

Date	Mintage	F	VF	XF	Unc	BU
1920KN	19,000,000	1.00	5.00	12.50	25.00	45.00
1920KN Proof	—	Value: 75.00				
1925	8,800,000	1.50	5.00	20.00	40.00	70.00
1926	1,600,000	10.00	25.00	50.00	85.00	—
1927	800,000	20.00	40.00	100	200	—
1928	1,760,000	10.00	35.00	70.00	125	—
1928 Proof	—	Value: 175				
1933	2,800,000	2.00	4.50	18.00	40.00	70.00
1933 Proof	—	Value: 200				
1934	6,400,000	1.00	12.50	20.00	35.00	60.00
1934 Proof	—	Value: 200				
1935	11,560,000	1.00	12.50	20.00	35.00	60.00
1935 Proof	—	Value: 200				
1936	17,160,000	1.00	3.50	15.00	28.00	50.00
1936 Proof	—	Value: 200				
1936H	1,000,000	15.00	25.00	45.00	85.00	—
1936H Proof	—	Value: 200				
1936KN	2,037,999	10.00	15.00	30.00	65.00	110

KM# 21 3 PENCE **Composition:** Copper-Nickel

Date	Mintage	F	VF	XF	Unc	BU
1938H	7,000,000	0.30	0.60	2.50	7.50	12.50
1938H Proof	—	Value: 200				
1938KN	9,056,000	0.35	0.75	2.50	8.00	14.00
1938KN Proof	—	Value: 250				
1939H	16,500,000	0.30	0.60	2.00	5.00	9.00
1939H Proof	—	Value: 300				
1939KN	15,500,000	0.30	0.60	2.00	8.00	14.00
1939KN Proof	—	Value: 200				
1940H	3,862,000	0.50	1.00	2.50	7.50	13.50
1940KN	10,000,000	0.30	0.60	2.00	5.00	9.00
1941H	5,032,000	0.40	0.85	3.50	9.00	16.00
1943H	5,106,000	0.40	0.85	6.00	15.00	25.00
1943KN	9,502,000	0.40	0.85	3.50	9.00	16.00
1944KN	2,536,000	0.40	0.85	6.50	15.00	25.00
1945H	998,000	3.00	5.00	10.00	20.00	35.00
1945KN	3,000,000	0.40	0.85	5.00	12.50	22.00
1946KN	7,488,000	0.40	0.85	3.50	9.00	16.00
1947H	10,000,000	0.35	0.75	3.50	8.00	14.00
1947KN	11,248,000	0.40	0.85	3.50	8.00	14.00

KM# 35 3 PENCE **Composition:** Copper-Nickel

Date	Mintage	F	VF	XF	Unc	BU
1957H	800,000	30.00	50.00	125	300	—

KM# 11 6 PENCE **Weight:** 2.8276 g. **Composition:** 0.9250 Silver .0841 oz. ASW

Date	Mintage	F	VF	XF	Unc	BU
1913	560,000	3.00	5.00	12.00	35.00	60.00
1913 Proof	—	Value: 350				
1913H	400,000	3.00	5.00	15.00	37.50	65.00
1914H	952,000	2.75	5.00	17.50	40.00	70.00
1916H	400,000	5.00	10.00	30.00	60.00	—
1917H	2,400,000	3.00	5.00	16.50	37.50	65.00
1918H	1,160,000	2.00	5.00	16.50	37.50	65.00
1919H	8,676,000	2.00	3.50	11.50	22.00	40.00
1919H Proof	—	Value: 200				

KM# 11a 6 PENCE **Weight:** 2.8276 g. **Composition:** 0.5000 Silver .0454 oz. ASW

Date	Mintage	F	VF	XF	Unc	BU
1920H	2,948,000	12.50	30.00	50.00	175	—
1920H Proof	—	Value: 275				

KM# 11b 6 PENCE **Composition:** Tin-Brass

Date	Mintage	F	VF	XF	Unc	BU
1920KN	12,000,000	1.00	5.00	20.00	37.50	65.00
1920KN Proof	—	Value: 125				
1923H	2,000,000	5.00	12.50	50.00	95.00	—
1924	1,000,000	15.00	30.00	80.00	150	—
1924H	1,000,000	15.00	30.00	80.00	150	—
1924KN	1,000,000	15.00	30.00	80.00	150	—
1925	2,800,000	3.50	7.00	30.00	60.00	100
1928	400,000	25.00	50.00	150	250	—
1928 Proof	—	Value: 200				
1933	1,000,000	20.00	40.00	100	175	—
1933 Proof	—	Value: 225				
1935	4,000,000	5.00	12.50	25.00	50.00	90.00
1935 Proof	—	Value: 225				
1936	10,400,000	7.50	15.00	25.00	50.00	90.00
1936 Proof	—	Value: 225				
1936H	480,000	25.00	50.00	125	200	—
1936H Proof	—	Value: 225				
1936KN	2,696,000	15.00	25.00	35.00	70.00	125
1936KN Proof	—	Value: 225				

KM# 22 6 PENCE **Composition:** Nickel-Brass

Date	Mintage	F	VF	XF	Unc	BU
1938	12,114,000	0.50	1.00	2.00	8.00	14.00
1938 Proof	—	Value: 200				
1940	17,829,000	0.75	1.50	3.00	10.00	18.00
1940 Proof	—	Value: 200				
1942	1,600,000	2.50	4.00	10.00	20.00	35.00
1943	10,586,000	0.75	1.75	5.00	11.00	20.00
1944	1,814,000	2.00	3.00	15.00	30.00	55.00
1945	4,000,000	1.00	2.00	12.50	25.00	45.00
1945 Proof	—	Value: 200				
1946	4,000,000	2.50	5.00	25.00	50.00	90.00
1946 Proof	—	Value: 225				
1947	6,120,000	0.50	1.50	5.00	15.00	25.00
1947 Proof	—	Value: 175				

KM# 31 6 PENCE **Composition:** Nickel-Brass **Obverse:** Legend without IND: IMP:

Date	Mintage	F	VF	XF	Unc	BU
1952	2,544,000	—	—	—	250	—
1952 Proof	—	Value: 300				

Note: This type was never released into circulation and the majority of the mintage was melted down at Riverside Metal Company in New Jersey; Approximately 167 pieces avoided the furnace and found their way into the numismtic market

KM# 12 SHILLING **Weight:** 5.6552 g. **Composition:** 0.9250 Silver .1682 oz. ASW

Date	Mintage	F	VF	XF	Unc	BU
1913	8,800,000	2.75	4.00	12.50	22.50	45.00
1913 Proof	—	Value: 400				
1913H	3,540,000	10.00	20.00	40.00	100	—
1914	3,000,000	2.75	4.00	15.00	35.00	65.00
1914H	11,292,000	2.75	4.00	12.50	30.00	55.00
1915H	254,000	20.00	40.00	80.00	150	—
1916H	11,838,000	2.75	4.00	15.00	35.00	65.00
1917H	15,018,000	2.75	4.00	15.00	35.00	65.00
1918H	9,486,000	2.75	5.50	17.50	40.00	70.00
1918H Proof	—	Value: 200				
1919	2,000,000	10.00	15.00	30.00	55.00	95.00
1919H	992,000	15.00	30.00	65.00	100	—
1919H Proof	—	Value: 200				
1920	828,000	22.50	40.00	85.00	150	—

KM# 12a SHILLING **Composition:** Tin-Brass

Date	Mintage	F	VF	XF	Unc	BU
1920KN Unique	—	—	—	—	—	—

Note: Mint mark on obverse below bust

Date	Mintage	F	VF	XF	Unc	BU
1920G	16,000	1,000	2,000	2,500	3,000	—
1920KN	38,800,000	1.50	5.00	12.50	32.50	55.00
1920KN Proof	—	Value: 200				
1922KN	32,324,000	2.00	6.50	35.00	70.00	—
1923H	24,384,000	4.00	7.50	25.00	45.00	80.00
1923KN	5,000,000	8.00	15.00	50.00	90.00	—
1924	17,000,000	2.00	6.50	30.00	60.00	110
1924H	9,567,000	10.00	20.00	65.00	125	—
1924KN	7,000,000	7.50	15.00	40.00	80.00	—
1925	19,800,000	4.00	8.00	18.00	45.00	80.00
1926	19,952,000	2.00	5.00	10.00	40.00	70.00
1927	22,248,000	1.50	4.00	8.50	35.00	60.00
1927 Proof	—	Value: 250				
1928	10,000,000	20.00	35.00	75.00	225	—
1928 Proof	—	Value: 300				
1936	70,200,000	3.00	6.50	11.00	32.50	55.00
1936 Proof	—	Value: 225				
1936H	10,920,000	12.50	22.50	35.00	75.00	—
1936KN	14,962,000	2.00	5.00	15.00	42.50	75.00
1936KN Proof	—	Value: 200				

KM# 23 SHILLING **Composition:** Nickel-Brass

Date	Mintage	F	VF	XF	Unc	BU
1938	57,806,000	0.50	1.25	4.50	12.00	20.00
1938 Proof	—	Value: 200				
1939	55,472,000	0.50	1.25	6.50	18.00	30.00
1939 Proof	—	Value: 200				
1940	40,311,000	0.50	1.25	5.50	15.00	25.00
1940 Proof	—	Value: 200				
1942	42,000,000	0.50	1.25	6.50	18.00	30.00
1943	133,600,000	0.50	1.25	5.50	15.00	25.00
1945	8,010,000	1.00	1.50	12.00	25.00	42.00
1945 Proof	—	Value: 200				
1945H	12,864,000	2.00	3.50	15.00	35.00	60.00
1945KN	11,120,000	1.00	2.00	12.00	25.00	42.00
1946	37,350,000	1.00	2.00	15.00	35.00	60.00
1946 Proof	—	Value: 200				
1946H	—	750	1,000	2,000	4,000	—
1947	99,200,000	0.50	1.00	4.50	12.00	20.00
1947 Proof	—	Value: 200				
1947H	10,000,000	1.50	3.00	15.00	30.00	50.00
1947KN	10,384,000	0.50	1.00	6.50	16.50	28.00

KM# 28 SHILLING **Composition:** Tin-Brass **Obverse:** Legend without IND: IMP:

Date	Mintage	F	VF	XF	Unc	BU
1949	70,000,000	0.50	2.50	12.00	25.00	42.00
1949 Proof	—	Value: 175				
1949H	10,000,000	1.25	4.00	12.50	27.50	47.50
1949KN	10,016,000	1.25	4.00	12.50	27.50	47.50
1949KN Proof	—	Value: 200				
1951	35,346,000	1.25	5.00	15.00	30.00	50.00
1951 Proof	—	Value: 175				
1951H	10,000,000	1.25	5.00	15.00	30.00	50.00
1951KN	16,832,000	1.25	5.00	15.00	30.00	50.00
1952	98,654,000	0.50	1.00	3.00	9.00	15.00
1952 Proof	—	Value: 200				
1952H	44,096,000	0.50	1.00	2.00	7.50	12.50
1952KN	41,653,000	0.50	1.00	2.00	6.00	10.00
1952KN Proof	—	Value: 175				

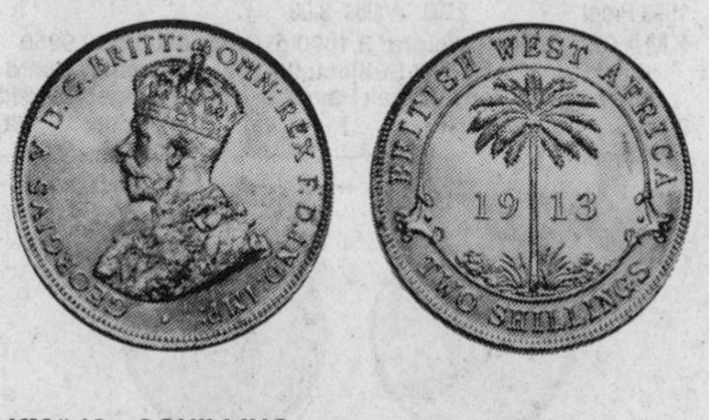

KM# 13 2 SHILLING **Weight:** 11.3104 g. **Composition:** 0.9250 Silver .3364 oz. ASW

Date	Mintage	F	VF	XF	Unc	BU
1913	2,100,000	5.00	8.00	16.50	45.00	80.00
1913 Proof	—	Value: 500				
1913H	1,176,000	6.00	15.00	27.50	55.00	95.00
1914	330,000	15.00	50.00	125	200	—
1914H	637,000	10.00	25.00	35.00	75.00	135
1915H	66,000	25.00	60.00	100	175	—
1916H	9,824,000	5.00	15.00	30.00	60.00	110
1917H	1,059,000	15.00	40.00	85.00	150	—
1917H Proof	—	Value: 300				
1918H	7,294,000	5.00	12.00	27.50	55.00	95.00
1919	2,000,000	6.00	20.00	40.00	85.00	150
1919H	10,866,000	4.50	10.00	32.00	65.00	115
1919H Proof	—	Value: 200				
1920	683,000	30.00	60.00	175	250	—

KM# 13a 2 SHILLING **Weight:** 11.3104 g. **Composition:** 0.5000 Silver .1818 oz. ASW

Date	Mintage	F	VF	XF	Unc	BU
1920H	1,926,000	30.00	55.00	100	275	—

KM# 13b 2 SHILLING **Composition:** Tin-Brass

Date	Mintage	F	VF	XF	Unc	BU
1920KN	15,856,000	2.50	5.00	15.00	40.00	70.00
1920KN Proof	—	Value: 250				
1922	10,000,000	3.00	9.00	17.50	55.00	95.00
1922KN	5,500,000	6.00	15.00	30.00	75.00	135
1922KN Proof	—	Value: 250				
1923H	12,696,000	4.00	12.00	22.50	65.00	115
1924	1,500,000	8.00	20.00	40.00	90.00	160
1925	3,700,000	4.00	12.00	25.00	70.00	125
1926	11,500,000	4.50	15.00	45.00	80.00	140
1927	11,100,000	6.00	20.00	60.00	100	185
1927 Proof	—	Value: 250				
1928	7,900,000	1,500	2,000	3,000	5,000	—
1928 Proof	—	Value: 3,000				
1936	32,939,999	5.00	12.00	35.00	60.00	100
1936 Proof	—	Value: 250				
1936H	8,703,000	6.00	18.00	45.00	75.00	130
1936KN	8,794,000	6.00	18.00	45.00	75.00	130

KM# 24 2 SHILLING **Composition:** Nickel-Brass

Date	Mintage	F	VF	XF	Unc	BU
1938H	32,000,000	1.00	2.00	3.50	15.00	28.00
1938KN	27,852,000	1.00	2.00	3.50	15.00	28.00

Note: Grained edge variety exists

Date	Mintage	F	VF	XF	Unc	BU
1939H	5,750,000	2.00	5.00	15.00	35.00	65.00
1939KN	6,250,000	1.00	4.00	12.00	30.00	55.00
1939KN Proof	—	Value: 200				
1942KN	10,000,000	1.25	4.50	14.00	30.00	55.00
1946H	10,500,000	1.25	4.00	12.00	27.50	50.00
1946KN	4,800,000	1.25	7.00	22.00	42.50	80.00
1947H	5,055,000	1.00	6.00	20.00	40.00	75.00
1947KN	4,200,000	1.25	7.00	22.00	42.50	80.00

KM# 29 2 SHILLING **Composition:** Nickel-Brass **Obverse:** Legend without IND: IMP:

Date	Mintage	F	VF	XF	Unc	BU
1949H	7,500,000	1.25	7.00	22.00	40.00	75.00
1949KN	7,576,000	1.25	6.00	20.00	35.00	65.00
1951H	6,566,000	1.25	7.00	22.00	40.00	75.00
1951H Proof	—	Value: 250				
1952H	4,410,000	2.00	8.00	22.50	42.00	80.00
1952KN	1,236,000	8.00	20.00	50.00	75.00	145

PATTERNS

Including off metal strikes

KM#	Date	Mintage	Identification	Mkt Val
Pn1	1906	4	1/10 Penny. Aluminum.	3,000
Pn2	1906	—	Penny. Copper-Nickel. Two varieties known, tick and thin flan.	3,000
Pn3	1920G	—	Shilling. Silver. 6.2700 g.	1,500
PnA4	1920	—	Penny. Brass. #KM9.	1,800
Pn4	1920KN	—	2 Shilling. Silver. Uniface.	250
Pn5	1925	—	Shilling. Nickel-Brass. Bare headed. ROYAL MINT 1925 edge.	2,000
Pn6	1936H	—	Shilling. Nickel-Brass. Security edge. Raised word SPECIMEN in field above date.	500
Pn7	1936KN	—	Shilling. Nickel-Brass. Fine reeded edge. Word SPECIMEN in field above date.	400
Pn8	1936KN	—	Shilling. Nickel-Brass. Security edge. Raised word SPECIMEN in field above date.	500
Pn9	1936KN	—	Shilling. Nickel-Brass. Coarser reeded edge. Without word SPECIMEN.	1,500
PnA10	1937H	—	Penny. Bronze. KM#19.	1,000
Pn10	1938KN	—	2 Shilling. Nickel-Brass. Security edge. Raised word SPECIMEN in field.	800
Pn11	1952KN	—	2 Shilling. Nickel-Brass. Raised word SPECIMEN in field below date.	400
Pn12	ND	—	Shilling. Nickel-Brass. KM#13b. Raided word MODEL.	1,000

TRIAL STRIKES

KM#	Date	Mintage	Identification	Mkt Val
TS1	1952	—	Shilling. Steel. Raised word TRIAL vertical in field on both sides.	100
TS2	1952	—	Shilling. Nickel. Raised word TRIAL vertical in field on both sides.	100
TS3	1952	—	Shilling. Steel. Raised word TRIAL vertical. Raised word TRIAL horizontal.	125
TS4	1952	—	Shilling. Nickel. Raised word TRIAL vertical. Raised word TRIAL horizontal.	85.00

SPECIMEN SETS (SS)

KM#	Date	Mintage	Identification	Issue Price	Mkt Val
SS1	1913 (8)	14	KM10-13	—	1,250
SS2	1913 (4)	200	KM10-13	—	550
SS3	1919H (8)	2	KM10-13	—	1,500
SS4	1920KN (8)	36	KM10b-11b, 12a, 13b	—	1,150
SSA5	1920KN (4)	4	KM10b-11b, 12a, 13b	—	—
SS5	1928 (4)	—	KM10b-11b, 12a, 13b	—	1,000
SS6	1936H (3)	—	KM14-16	—	450
SS7	1952 (4)	—	KM26a-27a, 30a, 31	—	750

BRUNEI

Negara Brunei Darussalam (State of Brunei), an independent sultanate on the northwest coast of the island of Borneo, has an area of 2,226 sq. mi. (5,765 sq. km.) and a population of *326,000. Capital: Bandar Seri Begawan. Crude oil and rubber are exported.

Magellan was the first European to visit Brunei in 1521. It was a powerful state, ruling over northern Borneo and adjacent islands from the 16th to the 19th century. Brunei became a British protectorate in 1888 and a British dependency in 1905. The Constitution of 1959 restored control over internal affairs to the sultan, while delegating responsibility for defense and foreign affairs to Britain. On January 1, 1984 it became independent and is a member of the Commonwealth of Nations.

TITLES

Negri Brunei نكري بروني

RULERS

Sultan Hashim Jalal, 1885-1906
British 1906-1950
Sultan Sir Omar Ali Saifuddin III, 1950-1967
Sultan Hassanal Bolkiah I, 1967-

MONETARY SYSTEM

100 Sen = 1 Dollar

SULTANATE

DECIMAL COINAGE

100 Sen = 1 Dollar (Ringgit)

KM# 4 SEN Composition: Bronze

Date	Mintage	F	VF	XF	Unc	BU
1967	1,000,000	—	0.15	0.35	0.75	—

KM# 9 SEN Composition: Bronze

Date	Mintage	F	VF	XF	Unc	BU
1968	60,000	—	0.25	0.50	1.75	—
1970	140,000	—	0.10	0.20	0.50	—
1970 Proof	4,000	Value: 4.00				
1971	400,000	—	0.10	0.15	0.40	—
1973	120,000	—	0.20	0.40	1.50	—
1974	640,000	—	—	0.10	0.30	—
1976	140,000	—	—	0.10	0.30	—
1977	140,000	—	—	0.10	0.30	—

KM# 15 SEN Composition: Bronze **Obverse:** Legend without numeral 'I' in title

Date	Mintage	F	VF	XF	Unc	BU
1977	280,000	—	—	0.10	0.20	—
1978	269,000	—	—	0.10	0.15	—
1979	250,000	—	0.10	0.20	0.50	—
1979 Proof	10,000	Value: 2.00				
1980	260,000	—	—	0.10	0.15	—
1981	540,000	—	—	0.10	0.15	—
1982	100,000	—	—	0.30	1.50	—
1983	500,000	—	—	0.10	0.15	—
1984	400,000	—	—	0.10	0.15	—
1984 Proof	3,000	Value: 2.00				
1985	200,000	—	—	0.10	0.15	—
1985 Proof	—	Value: 2.00				
1986	101,000	—	—	—	0.15	—
1986 Proof	7,000	Value: 2.00				

KM# 15a SEN Composition: Copper Clad Steel

Date	Mintage	F	VF	XF	Unc	BU
1986	102,000	—	—	—	0.30	—
1987	390,000	—	—	—	0.30	—
1988	500,000	—	—	—	0.30	—
1989	601,000	—	—	—	0.30	—
1990	680,000	—	—	—	0.30	—
1991	680,000	—	—	—	0.30	—
1992	887,000	—	—	—	0.30	—
1993	948,000	—	—	—	0.30	—

KM# 15b SEN Weight: 2.9200 g. **Composition:** 0.9250 Silver .0869 oz. ASW

Date	Mintage	F	VF	XF	Unc	BU
1987 Proof	2,000	Value: 3.00				
1988 Proof	2,000	Value: 3.00				
1989 Proof	2,000	Value: 3.00				
1990 Proof	2,000	Value: 3.00				
1991 Proof	2,000	Value: 3.00				
1992 Proof	2,000	Value: 3.00				
1993 Proof	2,000	Value: 3.00				

KM# 42 SEN Weight: 3.1000 g. **Composition:** 0.9250 Silver .0922 oz. ASW **Subject:** 25 Years - Currency Board **Obverse:** Sultan's portrait **Reverse:** Mosque **Edge:** Reeded

Date	Mintage	F	VF	XF	Unc	BU
1992 Proof	—	—	—	—	—	—
1992	2,000	—	—	—	5.00	—

KM# 34 SEN Composition: Copper Clad Steel

Date	Mintage	F	VF	XF	Unc	BU
1993	948,000	—	—	—	0.50	—
1994	—	—	—	—	0.50	—
1995	—	—	—	—	0.50	—
1996	—	—	—	—	0.50	—

KM# 54 SEN Composition: Copper Clad Steel **Subject:** 10 Years of Independence **Obverse:** Sultan's portrait **Reverse:** National arms

Date	Mintage	F	VF	XF	Unc	BU
ND(1994)		—	—	—	1.00	—

KM# 54a SEN Weight: 3.1000 g. **Composition:** 0.9250 Silver .0922 oz. ASW **Subject:** 10 Years of Independence **Obverse:** Sultan's portrait **Reverse:** National arms

Date	Mintage	F	VF	XF	Unc	BU
ND(1994) Proof	1,980	Value: 7.00				

KM# 5 5 SEN Composition: Copper-Nickel

Date	Mintage	F	VF	XF	Unc	BU
1967	1,160,000	—	0.20	0.40	1.00	—

KM# 10 5 SEN Composition: Copper-Nickel

Date	Mintage	F	VF	XF	Unc	BU
1968	320,000	—	0.10	0.35	0.80	—
1970	760,000	—	0.10	0.30	0.60	—
1970 Proof	4,000	Value: 4.00				
1971	320,000	—	0.10	0.20	0.70	—
1973	128,000	—	0.20	0.50	2.00	—
1974	576,000	—	0.10	0.15	0.40	—
1976	384,000	—	0.10	0.15	0.45	—
1977	384,000	—	0.10	0.15	0.45	—

KM# 16 5 SEN Composition: Copper-Nickel **Obverse:** Legend without numeral 'I' in title

Date	Mintage	F	VF	XF	Unc	BU
1977	920,000	—	—	0.10	0.30	—
1978	640,000	—	—	0.10	0.30	—
1979	650,000	—	0.10	0.20	0.50	—
1979 Proof	10,000	Value: 3.00				
1980	640,000	—	—	0.10	0.30	—
1981	960,000	—	—	0.10	0.30	—
1982	240,000	—	—	0.50	2.00	—
1983	1,280,000	—	—	0.10	0.30	—
1984	800,000	—	—	0.10	0.30	—
1984 Proof	3,000	Value: 3.00				
1985	800,000	—	—	0.10	0.30	—
1985 Proof	—	Value: 3.00				
1986	189,000	—	—	—	0.30	—
1986 Proof	7,000	Value: 3.00				
1987	960,000	—	—	—	0.30	—
1988	820,000	—	—	—	0.30	—
1989	1,504,000	—	—	—	0.30	—
1990	1,340,000	—	—	—	0.30	—
1991	1,340,000	—	—	—	0.30	—
1992	1,900,000	—	—	—	0.30	—
1993	1,951,000	—	—	—	0.30	—

KM# 16a 5 SEN Weight: 1.6500 g. **Composition:** 0.9250 Silver .0490 oz. ASW

Date	Mintage	F	VF	XF	Unc	BU
1987 Proof	2,000	Value: 3.00				
1988 Proof	2,000	Value: 3.00				
1989 Proof	2,000	Value: 3.00				
1990 Proof	2,000	Value: 3.00				
1991 Proof	2,000	Value: 3.00				
1992 Proof	2,000	Value: 3.00				
1993 Proof	2,000	Value: 3.00				

KM# 43 5 SEN Weight: 1.9000 g. **Composition:** 0.9250 Silver .0565 oz. ASW **Subject:** 25 Years - Currency Board **Obverse:** Sultan's portrait **Reverse:** Mosque **Edge:** Reeded

Date	Mintage	F	VF	XF	Unc	BU
1992 Proof	2,000	Value: 7.00				

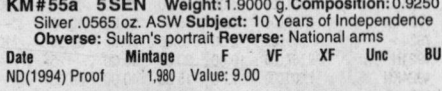

KM# 35 5 SEN Composition: Copper-Nickel

Date	Mintage	F	VF	XF	Unc	BU
1993	1,951,000	—	—	—	0.50	—
1994	—	—	—	—	0.50	—
1996	—	—	—	—	0.50	—

KM# 55 5 SEN Composition: Copper-Nickel .0565 oz. **Subject:** 10 Years of Independence **Obverse:** Sultan's portrait **Reverse:** National arms

Date	Mintage	F	VF	XF	Unc	BU
ND(1994)	3,000	—	—	—	1.50	—

KM# 55a 5 SEN Weight: 1.9000 g. **Composition:** 0.9250 Silver .0565 oz. ASW **Subject:** 10 Years of Independence **Obverse:** Sultan's portrait **Reverse:** National arms

Date	Mintage	F	VF	XF	Unc	BU
ND(1994) Proof	1,980	Value: 9.00				

KM# 6 10 SEN Composition: Copper-Nickel

Date	Mintage	F	VF	XF	Unc	BU
1967	3,510,000	—	0.15	0.35	0.75	—

KM# 11 10 SEN Composition: Copper-Nickel

Date	Mintage	F	VF	XF	Unc	BU
1968	580,000	—	0.10	0.25	0.60	—
1970	1,360,000	—	0.10	0.20	0.50	—
1970 Proof	4,000	Value: 4.00				
1971	420,000	—	0.10	0.20	0.50	—
1973	300,000	—	0.10	0.25	0.60	—
1974	1,410,000	—	0.10	0.20	0.50	—
1976	920,000	—	0.10	0.20	0.50	—
1977	920,000	—	—	0.15	0.40	—

KM# 17 10 SEN Composition: Copper-Nickel **Obverse:** Legend without numeral 'I' in title

Date	Mintage	F	VF	XF	Unc	BU
1977	1,800,000	—	0.10	0.15	0.40	—
1978	1,080,000	—	—	0.10	0.30	—
1979	2,050,000	—	—	0.10	0.30	—
1979 Proof	10,000	Value: 4.00				
1980	2,840,000	—	—	0.10	0.25	—
1981	976,000	—	—	0.10	0.25	—
1983	1,080,000	—	—	0.10	0.25	—
1984	1,400,000	—	—	0.10	0.25	—
1984 Proof	3,000	Value: 4.25				
1985	1,540,000	—	—	0.10	0.25	—
1985 Proof	—	Value: 4.25				

Date	Mintage	F	VF	XF	Unc	BU
1986	2,181,000	—	—	—	0.25	—
1986 Proof	7,000	Value: 4.25				
1987	2,560,000	—	—	—	0.25	—
1988	960,000	—	—	—	0.25	—
1989	1,000,000	—	—	—	0.25	—
1990	1,800,000	—	—	—	0.25	—
1991	1,800,000	—	—	—	0.25	—
1992	3,839,000	—	—	—	0.25	—
1993	3,973,000	—	—	—	0.25	—

KM# 17a 10 SEN Weight: 3.3500 g. **Composition:** 0.9250 Silver .0996 oz. ASW **Obverse:** Legend without numeral 'I' in title

Date	Mintage	F	VF	XF	Unc	BU
1987 Proof	2,000	Value: 6.00				
1988 Proof	2,000	Value: 6.00				
1989 Proof	2,000	Value: 6.00				
1990 Proof	2,000	Value: 6.00				
1991 Proof	2,000	Value: 6.00				
1992 Proof	2,000	Value: 6.00				
1993 Proof	2,000	Value: 6.00				

KM# 44 10 SEN Weight: 3.5000 g. **Composition:** 0.9250 Silver .1041 oz. ASW **Obverse:** Sultan's portrait **Reverse:** Mosque **Edge:** Reeded

Date	Mintage	F	VF	XF	Unc	BU
1992 Proof	2,000	Value: 10.00				

KM# 36 10 SEN Composition: Copper-Nickel

Date	Mintage	F	VF	XF	Unc	BU
1993	3,973,000	—	—	—	0.75	—
1994	—	—	—	—	0.75	—
1996	—	—	—	—	0.75	—

KM# 56 10 SEN Composition: Copper-Nickel **Subject:** 10 Years of Independence **Obverse:** Sultan's portrait **Reverse:** National arms

Date	Mintage	F	VF	XF	Unc	BU
ND(1994)	3,000	—	—	—	2.00	—

KM# 56a 10 SEN Weight: 3.5000 g. **Composition:** 0.9250 Silver .1041 oz. ASW **Subject:** 10 Years of Independence **Obverse:** Sultan's portrait **Reverse:** National arms

Date	Mintage	F	VF	XF	Unc	BU
ND(1994) Proof	1,980	Value: 12.00				

KM# 7 20 SEN Composition: Copper-Lead Alloy

Date	Mintage	F	VF	XF	Unc	BU
1967	2,130,000	—	0.35	1.00	2.00	—

KM# 12 20 SEN Composition: Copper-Nickel

Date	Mintage	F	VF	XF	Unc	BU
1968	510,000	—	0.20	0.50	1.00	—
1970	850,000	—	0.15	0.35	0.85	—
1970 Proof	4,000	Value: 4.00				
1971	450,000	—	0.20	0.50	1.00	—
1973	450,000	—	0.20	0.50	1.00	—
1974	700,000	—	0.15	0.35	0.85	—
1976	640,000	—	0.15	0.35	0.85	—
1977	640,000	—	0.15	0.35	0.85	—

KM# 18 20 SEN Composition: Copper-Nickel **Obverse:** Legend without numeral 'I' in title

Date	Mintage	F	VF	XF	Unc	BU
1977	1,200,000	—	0.10	0.25	0.75	—
1978	720,000	—	0.15	0.40	1.00	—
1979	1,060,000	—	0.20	0.50	1.25	—
1979 Proof	10,000	Value: 4.50				
1980	1,540,000	—	0.10	0.20	0.50	—
1981	2,140,000	—	0.10	0.20	0.50	—
1982	120,000	—	1.50	4.50	9.00	—
1983	1,350,000	—	0.10	0.15	0.40	—
1984	750,000	—	0.10	0.15	0.40	—
1984 Proof	3,000	Value: 4.75				
1985	1,000,000	—	0.10	0.15	0.40	—
1985 Proof	—	Value: 4.75				
1986	2,639,000	—	—	—	0.40	—
1986 Proof	7,000	Value: 4.75				
1987	2,400,000	—	—	—	0.40	—
1988	560,000	—	—	—	0.40	—
1989	500,000	—	—	—	0.40	—
1990	720,000	—	—	—	0.40	—
1991	725,000	—	—	—	0.40	—
1992	2,432,000	—	—	—	0.40	—
1993	2,521,000	—	—	—	0.40	—

KM# 18a 20 SEN Weight: 6.5100 g. **Composition:** 0.9250 Silver .1936 oz. ASW **Obverse:** Legend without numeral 'I' in title

Date	Mintage	F	VF	XF	Unc	BU
1987 Proof	2,000	Value: 10.00				
1988 Proof	2,000	Value: 10.00				
1989 Proof	2,000	Value: 10.00				
1990 Proof	2,000	Value: 10.00				
1991 Proof	2,000	Value: 10.00				
1992 Proof	2,000	Value: 10.00				
1993 Proof	2,000	Value: 10.00				

KM# 45 20 SEN Weight: 6.7000 g. **Composition:** 0.9250 Silver .1993 oz. ASW **Subject:** 25 Years - Currency Board **Obverse:** Sultan's portrait **Reverse:** Mosque **Edge:** Reeded

Date	Mintage	F	VF	XF	Unc	BU
1992 Proof	2,000	Value: 12.00				

KM# 37 20 SEN Composition: Copper-Nickel

Date	Mintage	F	VF	XF	Unc	BU
1993	—	—	—	—	1.25	—
1994	—	—	—	—	1.25	—
1996	—	—	—	—	1.25	—

KM# 57 20 SEN Composition: Copper-Nickel **Subject:** 10 Years of Independence **Obverse:** Sultan's portrait **Reverse:** National arms

Date	Mintage	F	VF	XF	Unc	BU
ND(1994)	3,000	—	—	—	2.50	—

KM# 57a 20 SEN Weight: 6.7000 g. **Composition:** 0.9250 Silver .1993 oz. ASW **Subject:** 10 Years of Independence **Obverse:** Sultan's portrait **Reverse:** National arms

Date	Mintage	F	VF	XF	Unc	BU
ND(1994) Proof	1,980	Value: 15.00				

KM# 8 50 SEN Composition: Copper-Nickel

Date	Mintage	F	VF	XF	Unc	BU
1967	788,000	—	0.75	1.75	3.50	—

KM# 13 50 SEN Composition: Copper-Nickel

Date	Mintage	F	VF	XF	Unc	BU
1968	212,000	—	0.30	1.00	1.75	—
1970	300,000	—	0.30	1.00	1.75	—
1970 Proof	4,000	Value: 6.50				
1971	320,000	—	0.30	1.00	1.75	—
1973	140,000	—	0.50	2.50	4.00	—
1974	244,000	—	0.30	1.00	1.75	—
1976	240,000	—	0.30	1.00	1.75	—
1977	240,000	—	0.30	1.00	1.75	—

KM# 19 50 SEN Composition: Copper-Nickel **Obverse:** Legend without numeral 'I' in title

Date	Mintage	F	VF	XF	Unc	BU
1977	499,000	—	0.30	0.85	1.65	—
1978	264,000	—	0.30	0.85	1.65	—
1979	730,000	—	0.30	0.85	1.65	—
1979 Proof	10,000	Value: 6.50				
1980	536,000	—	0.30	0.45	0.85	—
1981	960,000	—	0.30	0.40	0.75	—
1982	136,000	—	1.00	3.00	7.00	—
1983	408,000	—	0.30	0.40	0.75	—
1984	320,000	—	0.30	0.40	0.75	—
1984 Proof	3,000	Value: 6.75				
1985	450,000	—	0.30	0.40	0.75	—
1985 Proof	—	—	—	—	—	—
1986	1,067,000	—	—	—	0.75	—
1986 Proof	7,000	Value: 6.75				
1987	1,120,000	—	—	—	0.75	—
1988	250,000	—	—	—	0.75	—
1989	500,000	—	—	—	0.75	—
1990	472,000	—	—	—	0.75	—
1991	508,000	—	—	—	0.75	—
1992	1,072,000	—	—	—	0.75	—
1993	1,102,000	—	—	—	0.75	—

KM# 19a 50 SEN Weight: 10.8200 g. **Composition:** 0.9250 Silver .3218 oz. ASW **Obverse:** Legend without numeral 'I' in title

Date	Mintage	F	VF	XF	Unc	BU
1987 Proof	2,000	Value: 15.00				
1988 Proof	2,000	Value: 15.00				
1989 Proof	2,000	Value: 15.00				
1990 Proof	2,000	Value: 15.00				
1991 Proof	2,000	Value: 15.00				
1992 Proof	2,000	Value: 15.00				
1993 Proof	2,000	Value: 15.00				

KM# 46 50 SEN Weight: 11.1000 g. **Composition:** 0.9250 Silver .3301 oz. ASW **Subject:** 25 Years - Currency Board **Obverse:** Sultan's portrait **Reverse:** Mosque

Date	Mintage	F	VF	XF	Unc	BU
1992 Proof	2,000	Value: 20.00				

KM# 38 50 SEN Composition: Copper-Nickel

Date	Mintage	F	VF	XF	Unc	BU
1993	—	—	—	—	2.25	—
1994	—	—	—	—	2.25	—

KM# 58 50 SEN Composition: Copper-Nickel **Subject:** 10 Years of Independence **Obverse:** Sultan's portrait **Reverse:** National arms

Date	Mintage	F	VF	XF	Unc	BU
ND(1994)	3,000	—	—	—	4.50	—

KM# 58a 50 SEN Weight: 11.1000 g. **Composition:** 0.9250 Silver .3301 oz. ASW **Subject:** 10 Years of Independence **Obverse:** Sultan's portrait **Reverse:** National arms

Date	Mintage	F	VF	XF	Unc	BU
ND(1994) Proof	1,980	Value: 20.00				

KM# 64 50 SEN Composition: Copper-Nickel **Subject:** Sultan's 50th Birthday **Obverse:** Sultan's portrait **Reverse:** Waterfront building

Date	Mintage	F	VF	XF	Unc	BU
ND(1996) Proof	500	Value: 25.00				

KM# 14 DOLLAR **Composition:** Copper-Nickel

Date	Mintage	F	VF	XF	Unc	BU
1970 Proof	5,000	Value: 32.50				

KM# 20 DOLLAR **Composition:** Copper-Nickel
Obverse: Legend without numeral 'I' in title

Date	Mintage	F	VF	XF	Unc	BU
1979 Proof	10,000	Value: 20.00				
1984	5,000	—	—	—	10.00	—
1984 Proof	3,000	Value: 22.00				
1985	15,000	—	—	—	8.00	—
1985 Proof	10,000	Value: 20.00				
1986	10,000	—	—	—	8.00	—
1986 Proof	7,000	Value: 22.00				
1987	2,000	—	—	—	10.00	—
1988	2,000	—	—	—	10.00	—
1989	2,000	—	—	—	10.00	—
1990	3,000	—	—	—	10.00	—
1991	3,000	—	—	—	10.00	—
1992	—	—	—	—	10.00	—
1993	—	—	—	—	10.00	—

KM# 20a DOLLAR **Weight:** 18.0500 g. **Composition:** 0.9250 Silver .5368 oz. ASW **Obverse:** Legend without numeral 'I' in title

Date	Mintage	F	VF	XF	Unc	BU
1987 Proof	2,000	Value: 40.00				
1988 Proof	2,000	Value: 40.00				
1989 Proof	2,000	Value: 40.00				
1990 Proof	2,000	Value: 40.00				
1991 Proof	2,000	Value: 40.00				
1992 Proof	2,000	Value: 40.00				
1993 Proof	2,000	Value: 40.00				

KM# 47 DOLLAR **Weight:** 18.2000 g. **Composition:** 0.9250 Silver .5413 oz. ASW **Subject:** 25th Anniversary of Brunei Currency Board **Obverse:** Sultan Hassanal Bolkiah **Reverse:** Mosque

Date	Mintage	F	VF	XF	Unc	BU
1992 Proof	2,000	Value: 40.00				

KM# 47a DOLLAR **Composition:** 0.9170 Gold **Subject:** 25th Anniversary of Brunei Currency Board **Obverse:** Sultan Hassanal Bolkian **Reverse:** Mosque

Date	Mintage	F	VF	XF	Unc	BU
1992 Proof	1,000	Value: 300				

KM# 59 DOLLAR **Composition:** Copper-Nickel **Subject:** 10 Years of Independence **Obverse:** Sultan's portrait **Reverse:** National arms

Date	Mintage	F	VF	XF	Unc	BU
ND(1994)	3,000	—	—	—	8.00	—

KM# 59a DOLLAR **Weight:** 18.2000 g. **Composition:** 0.9250 Silver .5413 oz. ASW **Subject:** 10 Years of Independence **Obverse:** Sultan's portrait **Reverse:** National arms

Date	Mintage	F	VF	XF	Unc	BU
ND(1994) Proof	1,980	—	—	—	—	—

KM# 71 2 DOLLARS **Weight:** 9.3000 g. **Composition:** Copper-Nickel **Subject:** 20th SEA Games **Obverse:** Sultan's multi-colored portrait **Reverse:** Multicolor logo above stadium **Edge:** Reeded

Date	Mintage	F	VF	XF	Unc	BU
1999 Proof	1,350	Value: 25.00				

KM# 74 2 DOLLARS **Weight:** 9.8000 g. **Composition:** Copper-Nickel **Subject:** APEC **Obverse:** Multicolor bust of Sultan Haji Hassanal Bolkiah half facing **Reverse:** Multicolor flower and APEC initials above date below world map **Rev. Legend:** ASIA PACIFIC ECONOMIC COOPERATION NEGARA BRUNEI DARUSSALAM **Edge:** Reeded **Size:** 27.3 mm.

Date	Mintage	F	VF	XF	Unc	BU
2000	3,000	—	—	—	45.00	—

KM# 68 3 DOLLARS **Weight:** 10.0000 g. **Composition:** Copper-Nickel **Subject:** 30 Years ASEAN **Obverse:** Sultan's portrait **Reverse:** Map and sailboat **Edge:** Reeded

Date	Mintage	F	VF	XF	Unc	BU
1997 Proof	1,250	Value: 35.00				

KM# 23 5 DOLLARS **Composition:** Copper-Nickel **Subject:** Year of Hejira 1400 **Obverse:** Legend without numeral 'I' in title

Date	Mintage	F	VF	XF	Unc	BU
AH1400 (1979)	10,000	—	3.50	12.50	22.50	—

KM# 48 5 DOLLARS **Composition:** 0.9170 Gold **Subject:** 25th Anniversary of Brunei Currency Board **Obverse:** Sultan Hassanal Bolkiah **Reverse:** Mosque

Date	Mintage	F	VF	XF	Unc	BU
1992 Proof	1,000	Value: 350				

KM# 60 5 DOLLARS **Composition:** Copper-Nickel **Subject:** 10 Years of Independence **Obverse:** Sultan's portrait **Reverse:** National arms

Date	Mintage	F	VF	XF	Unc	BU
ND(1994)	3,000	—	—	—	16.00	—

KM# 60a 5 DOLLARS **Weight:** 28.2800 g. **Composition:** 0.9250 Silver .8410 oz. ASW **Subject:** 10 Years of Independence **Obverse:** Sultan's portrait **Reverse:** National arms

Date	Mintage	F	VF	XF	Unc	BU
ND(1994) Proof	1,980	Value: 35.00				

KM# 21 10 DOLLARS **Weight:** 28.2800 g. **Composition:** 0.9250 Silver .8411 oz. ASW **Subject:** 10th Anniversary of Brunei Currency Board **Obverse:** Legend without numeral 'I' in title

Date	Mintage	F	VF	XF	Unc	BU
1977 Proof	10,000	Value: 55.00				

KM# 26 10 DOLLARS **Composition:** Copper-Nickel **Subject:** Independence Day

Date	Mintage	F	VF	XF	Unc	BU
1984	15,000	—	—	—	22.50	—
1984 Proof	5,000	Value: 47.50				

KM# 49 10 DOLLARS **Composition:** 0.9170 Gold **Subject:** 25th Anniversary of Brunei Currency Board **Obverse:** Sultan Hassanal Bolkiah **Reverse:** Mosque

Date	Mintage	F	VF	XF	Unc	BU
1992 Proof	1,000	Value: 400				

KM# 61 10 DOLLARS **Composition:** Copper-Nickel **Subject:** 10 Years of Independence **Obverse:** Sultan's portrait **Reverse:** National arms

Date	Mintage	F	VF	XF	Unc	BU
ND	3,000	—	—	—	18.00	—

KM# 61a 10 DOLLARS **Weight:** 30.7000 g. **Composition:** 0.9250 Silver .9130 oz. ASW **Subject:** 10 Years of Independence **Obverse:** Sultan's portrait **Reverse:** National arms

Date	Mintage	F	VF	XF	Unc	BU
ND(1994) Proof	2,500	Value: 55.00				
ND(1994)	3,000	—	—	—	30.00	—

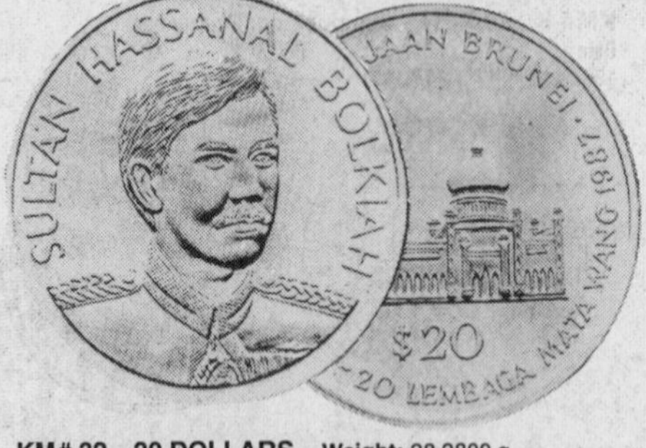

KM# 32 20 DOLLARS **Weight:** 28.2800 g. **Composition:** 0.9250 Silver .8411 oz. ASW **Subject:** 20th Anniversary of Brunei Currency Board

Date	Mintage	F	VF	XF	Unc	BU
1987 Proof	3,000	Value: 70.00				

KM# 29 20 DOLLARS **Weight:** 28.2800 g. **Composition:** 0.9250 Silver .8411 oz. ASW **Subject:** 20th Anniversary of Coronation

Date	Mintage	F	VF	XF	Unc	BU
ND(1988)	5,000	—	—	—	30.00	—
ND(1988) Proof	1,000	Value: 85.00				

KM# 72 20 DOLLARS **Weight:** 62.2000 g. **Composition:** 0.9990 Silver 2.0000 oz. ASW **Subject:** 20th SEA Games **Obverse:** Sultan's multi-colored portrait **Reverse:** Multicolor logo above stadium **Edge:** Reeded

Date	Mintage	F	VF	XF	Unc	BU
1999 Proof	850	Value: 100				

KM# 50 25 DOLLARS **Weight:** 31.1000 g. **Composition:** 0.9250 Silver .9249 oz. ASW **Subject:** 25th Anniversary of Brunei Currency Board **Obverse:** Sultan Hassanal Bolkiah **Reverse:** Mosque **Size:** 38.7 mm.

Date	Mintage	F	VF	XF	Unc	BU
1992 Proof	2,000	Value: 75.00				

KM# 39 25 DOLLARS **Composition:** Copper-Nickel **Subject:** 25th Anniversary of Accession

Date	Mintage	F	VF	XF	Unc	BU
ND(1992) Proof	7,500	Value: 35.00				

KM# 39a 25 DOLLARS **Composition:** 0.9170 Gold **Subject:** 25th Anniversary of Accession

Date	Mintage	F	VF	XF	Unc	BU
ND(1992) Proof	—	Value: 550				

KM# 70 30 DOLLARS **Weight:** 31.1000 g. **Composition:** 0.9170 Gold .9169 oz. AGW **Subject:** 30 Years - ASEAN **Obverse:** Sultan Hassanal Bolkiah **Reverse:** ASEAN logo

Date	Mintage	F	VF	XF	Unc	BU
1997 Proof	800	Value: 575				

KM# 69 30 DOLLARS **Weight:** 62.2070 g. **Composition:** 0.9990 Silver 2.0000 oz. ASW **Subject:** 30 Years - ASEAN **Obverse:** Sultan Hassanal Bolkiah **Reverse:** Seven multi-colored flags

Date	Mintage	F	VF	XF	Unc	BU
1997 Proof	1,000	Value: 135				

KM# 67 50 DOLLARS **Weight:** 31.1035 g. **Composition:** 0.9170 Gold 1.0000 oz. AGW **Subject:** 50th Birthday - Sultan Hassanal Bolkian **Obverse:** Sultan Hassanal Bolkiah **Reverse:** Mosque

Date	Mintage	F	VF	XF	Unc	BU
ND(1996) Proof	500	Value: 650				

KM# 24 50 DOLLARS **Weight:** 28.2800 g. **Composition:** 0.9250 Silver .8411 oz. ASW **Subject:** Year of Hejira 1400 **Obverse:** Legend without numeral 'I' in title

Date	Mintage	F	VF	XF	Unc	BU
AH1400 (1979) Proof	3,000	Value: 145				

KM# 40 50 DOLLARS **Weight:** 30.7000 g. **Composition:** 0.9250 Silver .9130 oz. ASW **Subject:** 25th Anniversary of Accession **Reverse:** Royal procession **Edge:** Reeded **Size:** 42 mm.

Date	Mintage	F	VF	XF	Unc	BU
ND(1992) Proof	3,500	Value: 50.00				

KM# 40a 50 DOLLARS **Composition:** 0.9170 Gold **Subject:** 25th Anniversary of Accession **Obverse:** Sultan Hassanal Bolkiah **Reverse:** Royal procession

Date	F	VF	XF	Unc	BU
ND(1992)	—	—	—	—	—

KM# 51 50 DOLLARS **Composition:** 0.9170 Gold **Subject:** 25th Anniversary of Brunei Currency Board **Obverse:** Sultan Hassanal Bolkiah **Reverse:** Mosque

Date	Mintage	F	VF	XF	Unc	BU
1992 Proof	1,000	Value: 450				

KM# 65 50 DOLLARS **Weight:** 62.2070 g. **Composition:** 0.9990 Silver 2.0000 oz. ASW **Subject:** 50th Birthday - Sultan Hassanal Bolkiah **Obverse:** Sultan Hassanal Bolkiah's multi-colored portrait **Reverse:** Buildings on waterfront

Date	Mintage	F	VF	XF	Unc	BU
ND Proof	500	Value: 175				

KM# 66 50 DOLLARS **Weight:** 62.2070 g. **Composition:** 0.9990 Silver 2.0000 oz. ASW **Subject:** 50th Birthday - Sultan Hassanal Bolkiah **Obverse:** Sultan Bolkian arms **Reverse:** Building

Date	Mintage	F	VF	XF	Unc	BU
ND(1996) Proof	500	Value: 225				

KM# 27 100 DOLLARS **Weight:** 28.2800 g. **Composition:** 0.9250 Silver .8411 oz. ASW **Subject:** Independence Day

Date	Mintage	F	VF	XF	Unc	BU
1984	5,000	—	—	—	140	—
1984 Proof	2,000	Value: 185				

KM# 33 100 DOLLARS **Weight:** 13.5000 g. **Composition:** 0.9170 Gold .3976 oz. AGW **Subject:** 20th Anniversary of Brunei Currency Board

Date	Mintage	F	VF	XF	Unc	BU
1987 Proof	1,000	Value: 450				

KM# 30 100 DOLLARS **Weight:** 31.1000 g. **Composition:** 0.9250 Silver .9250 oz. ASW **Subject:** 20th Anniversary of Coronation

Date	Mintage	F	VF	XF	Unc	BU
ND(1988) Proof	2,000	Value: 175				

KM# 52 100 DOLLARS **Composition:** 917.0000 Gold **Subject:** 25th Anniversary of Brunei Currency Board **Obverse:** Sultan Hassanal Bolkiah **Reverse:** Mosque

Date	Mintage	F	VF	XF	Unc	BU
1992 Proof	1,000	Value: 550				

KM# 62 100 DOLLARS **Composition:** 917.0000 White Gold **Subject:** 10th Years of Independence **Obverse:** Sultan Hassanal Bolkiah **Reverse:** National arms

Date	Mintage	F	VF	XF	Unc	BU
ND(1994)	1,980	—	—	—	475	—
ND(1994) Proof	1,500	Value: 525				

KM# 73 200 DOLLARS **Weight:** 31.1000 g. **Composition:** 0.9170 Gold .9169 oz. AGW **Subject:** 20th SEA Games **Obverse:** Sultan Hassanal Bolkiah **Reverse:** Multi-colored logo above stadium

Date	Mintage	F	VF	XF	Unc	BU
1999 Proof	450	Value: 650				

KM# 53 250 DOLLARS **Composition:** 0.9170 Gold **Subject:** 25th Anniversary of Brunei Currency Board **Obverse:** Sultan Hassanal Bolkiah **Reverse:** Mosque

Date	Mintage	F	VF	XF	Unc	BU
1992 Proof	1,000	Value: 700				

KM# 41 500 DOLLARS **Weight:** 50.0000 g. **Composition:** 0.9170 Gold 1.4727 oz. AGW **Subject:** 25th Anniversary of Accession **Obverse:** Sultan's portrait **Reverse:** Other portrait

Date	Mintage	F	VF	XF	Unc	BU
MS(1992) Proof	1,500	Value: 1,350				

KM# 25 750 DOLLARS **Weight:** 15.9800 g. **Composition:** 0.9170 Gold .4711 oz. AGW **Subject:** Year of Hejira 1400

Date	Mintage	F	VF	XF	Unc	BU
AH1400 (1979) Proof	1,000	Value: 650				

KM# 22 1000 DOLLARS **Weight:** 50.0000 g. **Composition:** 0.9170 Gold 1.4742 oz. AGW **Subject:** 10th Anniversary of Sultan's Coronation

Date	Mintage	F	VF	XF	Unc	BU
ND(1978) Proof	1,000	Value: 1,450				

KM# 28 1000 DOLLARS **Weight:** 50.0000 g. **Composition:** 0.9170 Gold 1.4742 oz. AGW **Subject:** Independence Day **Obverse:** Bust of Sultan Bolkiah half right **Reverse:** Off shore oil rig

Date	Mintage	F	VF	XF	Unc	BU
1984	4,000	—	—	—	1,000	—
1984 Proof	1,000	Value: 1,150				

KM# 31 1000 DOLLARS **Weight:** 50.0000 g. **Composition:** 0.9170 Gold 1.4742 oz. AGW **Subject:** 20th Anniversary of Coronation

Date	Mintage	F	VF	XF	Unc	BU
ND(1988) Proof	1,000	Value: 1,100				

KM# 63 1000 DOLLARS **Composition:** 0.9990 Gold **Subject:** 10 Years of Independence **Obverse:** Sultan Hassanal Bolkiah **Reverse:** National arms

Date	Mintage	F	VF	XF	Unc	BU
ND(1994)	980	—	—	—	1,275	—
ND(1994) Proof	1,000	Value: 1,325				

PROOF SETS

KM#	Date	Mintage	Identification	Issue Price	Mkt Val
PS16	1996 (4)	500	KM64-67	—	1,075
PSA1	1970 (5)	—	KM9-13	—	22.50
PS1	1979 (6)	10,000	KM15-20	30.00	60.00
PS2	1984 (6)	3,000	MS15-20	—	65.00
PS3	1984 (3)	500	KM26-28	—	1,450
PS4	1985 (6)	10,000	KM15-20	30.00	60.00
PS5	1986 (6)	5,000	KM15-20	30.00	65.00
PS6	1987 (6)	2,000	KM15b, 16a-20a	52.00	80.00
PS7	1988 (6)	2,000	KM15b, 16a-20a	—	80.00
PS8	1989 (6)	2,000	KM15b, 16a-20a	—	75.00
PS9	1990 (6)	2,000	KM15b, 16a-20a	—	75.00
PS10	1991 (6)	2,000	KM15b, 16a-20a	—	75.00
PS11	1992 (6)	2,000	KM15b, 16a-20a	—	75.00
PS12	1992 (7)	2,000	KM42-47, 50	—	170
PS13	1992 (7)	1,000	KM47a, 48-53	—	2,825
PS14	1993 (6)	2,000	KM15b, 16a-20a	—	75.00
PS15	1994 (8)	—	KM54a-61a	—	185
PS17	1997 (3)	500	KM68-70	—	740
PS18	1999 (3)	350	KM71-73	—	765

SPECIMEN SETS (SS)

KM#	Date	Mintage	Identification	Issue Price	Mkt Val
MS2	1984 (6)	5,000	KM15-20	—	15.00
MS3	1984 (3)	500	KM26-28	—	1,250
MS4	1985 (6)	15,000	KM15-20	10.00	22.50
MS5	1986 (6)	10,000	KM15-20	10.00	22.50
MS6	1987 (6)	3,000	KM15a, 16-20	15.60	22.50
MS7	1988 (6)	2,000	KM15a, 16-20	15.60	22.50
MS8	1989 (6)	2,000	KM15a, 16-20	—	22.50
MS9	1990 (6)	3,000	KM15a, 16-20	—	22.50
MS10	1991 (6)	3,000	KM15a, 16-20	—	22.50
MS11	1994 (8)	—	KM54-61	—	50.00

BULGARIA

The Republic of Bulgaria, formerly the Peoples Republic of Bulgaria, a Balkan country on the Black Sea in southeastern Europe, has an area of 42,855 sq. mi. (110,910 sq. km.) and a population of *8.31 million. Capital: Sofia. Agriculture remains a key component of the economy but industrialization, particularly heavy industry, has been emphasized since the late 1940s. Machinery, tobacco and cigarettes, wines and spirits, clothing and metals are the chief exports.

The area now occupied by Bulgaria was conquered by the Bulgars, an Asiatic tribe, in the 7th century. Bulgarian kingdoms continued to exist on the Bulgarian peninsula until it came under Turkish rule in 1395. In 1878, after nearly 500 years of Turkish rule, Bulgaria was made a principality under Turkish suzerainty. Union seven years later with Eastern Rumelia created a Balkan state with borders approximating those of present-day Bulgaria. A Bulgarian kingdom, fully independent of Turkey, was proclaimed Sept. 22, 1908. During WWI Bulgaria had been aligned with Germany. After the Armistice certain land concessions were given to Greece and Romania. In 1934 King Boris III suspended all political parties and established a dictatorial monarchy. In 1938 the military began rearming through the aide of the Anglo-French loan. As WW II developed, Bulgaria again supported the Germans but protected their Jewish community. Boris died mysteriously in 1943 and Simeon II became King at the age of six. The country was then ruled by a pro-Nazi regency until it was liberated by Soviet forces in 1944.

The monarchy was abolished and Simeon was ousted by plebiscite in 1946 and Bulgaria became a Peoples Republic on the Soviet pattern. After democratic reforms in 1989 the name was changed to the Republic of Bulgaria.

Coinage of the Peoples Republic features a number of politically oriented commemoratives.

RULERS

Ferdinand I, as Prince, 1887-1908
As King, 1908-1918
Boris III, 1918-1943

MINT MARKS

A - Berlin
(a) Cornucopia & torch - Paris
BP - Budapest
H - Heaton Mint, Birmingham
KB - Kormoczbanya
(p) Poissy - Thunderbolt

MONETARY SYSTEM

100 Stotinki = 1 Lev

TURKISH PRINCIPALITY

STANDARD COINAGE

KM# 22.1 STOTINKA **Composition:** Bronze **Ruler:** Ferdinand I as Prince **Reverse:** Privy marks and design name below denomination

Date	Mintage	F	VF	XF	Unc	BU
1901	20,000,000	1.00	2.00	6.00	12.50	—

KM# 22.2 STOTINKA **Composition:** Bronze **Ruler:** Ferdinand I as Prince **Reverse:** Without privy marks and designer name

Date	Mintage	F	VF	XF	Unc	BU
1912	20,000,000	0.50	1.00	2.50	5.00	—

KM# 23.1 2 STOTINKI **Composition:** Bronze **Ruler:** Ferdinand I **Reverse:** Privy marks and designer name below denomination

Date	Mintage	F	VF	XF	Unc	BU
1901(a)	40,000,000	1.00	2.00	5.00	10.00	—

KM# 23.2 2 STOTINKI **Composition:** Bronze **Reverse:** Without privy marks and designer name

Date	Mintage	F	VF	XF	Unc	BU
1912	40,000,000	0.50	1.00	2.00	4.00	—

KM# 24 5 STOTINKI **Composition:** Copper-Nickel

Date	Mintage	F	VF	XF	Unc	BU
1906	14,000,000	0.20	0.60	2.00	5.00	—
1912	14,000,000	0.20	0.40	1.00	2.50	—
1913	20,000,000	0.20	0.40	1.00	2.50	—
1913 Proof	—	—	—	—	—	—

KM# 24a 5 STOTINKI **Composition:** Zinc

Date	Mintage	F	VF	XF	Unc	BU
1917	53,200,000	0.60	1.00	2.50	6.00	—

KM# 25 10 STOTINKI **Composition:** Copper-Nickel

Date	Mintage	F	VF	XF	Unc	BU
1906	13,000,000	0.50	1.00	2.50	6.00	—
1912	13,000,000	0.20	0.40	1.00	2.50	—
1912 Proof	—	—	—	—	—	—
1913	20,000,000	0.20	0.40	1.00	2.50	—

KM# 25a 10 STOTINKI **Composition:** Zinc

Date	Mintage	F	VF	XF	Unc	BU
1917	59,100,000	0.40	1.00	2.00	5.00	—
1917 Proof	—	Value: 125				

KM# 26 20 STOTINKI **Composition:** Copper-Nickel

Date	Mintage	F	VF	XF	Unc	BU
1906	10,000,000	0.50	1.50	3.50	10.00	—
1912	10,000,000	0.20	0.50	1.25	5.00	—
1913	5,000,000	0.20	0.50	1.50	5.50	—
1913	—	—	—	—	—	—

KM# 26a 20 STOTINKI **Composition:** Zinc

Date	Mintage	F	VF	XF	Unc	BU
1917	40,000,000	0.50	1.75	4.00	8.50	—
1917 Proof	—	Value: 125				

KINGDOM

STANDARD COINAGE

KM# 27 50 STOTINKI **Weight:** 2.5000 g. **Composition:** 0.8350 Silver .0671 oz. ASW

Date	Mintage	F	VF	XF	Unc	BU
1910	400,000	1.75	3.50	6.00	14.00	—

KM# 30 50 STOTINKI **Weight:** 2.5000 g. **Composition:** 0.8350 Silver .0671 oz. ASW

Date	Mintage	F	VF	XF	Unc	BU
1912	2,000,000	1.00	2.00	4.50	10.00	—
1913	3,000,000	1.00	2.00	3.50	8.00	—
1916	4,562,000	50.00	100	175	275	—

KM# 46 50 STOTINKI **Composition:** Aluminum-Bronze

Date	Mintage	F	VF	XF	Unc	BU
1937	60,200,000	0.25	0.50	1.00	2.50	—

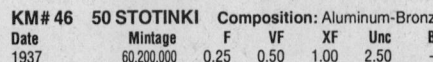

KM# 28 LEV **Weight:** 5.0000 g. **Composition:** 0.8350 Silver .1342 oz. ASW

Date	Mintage	F	VF	XF	Unc	BU
1910	3,000,000	2.00	4.00	7.00	16.00	—

KM# 31 LEV **Weight:** 5.0000 g. **Composition:** 0.8350 Silver .1342 oz. ASW

Date	Mintage	F	VF	XF	Unc	BU
1912	2,000,000	2.00	3.00	5.50	12.50	—
1913	3,500,000	2.00	3.00	5.00	10.00	—
1916	4,569,000	100	200	350	600	—

KM# 35 LEV **Composition:** Aluminum

Date	Mintage	F	VF	XF	Unc	BU
1923	40,000,000	2.50	5.00	12.00	35.00	—

KM# 37 LEV **Composition:** Copper-Nickel

Date	Mintage	F	VF	XF	Unc	BU
1925	35,000,000	0.20	0.50	1.00	2.50	—
1925(p)	34,982,000	0.25	0.60	1.25	3.00	—

Note: The Poissy issue bears the thunderbolt mint mark

KM# 37a LEV **Composition:** Iron

Date	Mintage	F	VF	XF	Unc	BU
1941	10,000,000	3.00	6.00	15.00	40.00	—

KM# 29 2 LEVA **Weight:** 10.0000 g. **Composition:** 0.8350 Silver .2685 oz. ASW

Date	Mintage	F	VF	XF	Unc	BU
1910	400,000	4.50	7.50	16.00	45.00	—

KM# 32 2 LEVA **Weight:** 10.0000 g. **Composition:** 0.8350 Silver .2685 oz. ASW

Date	Mintage	F	VF	XF	Unc	BU
1912	1,000,000	4.00	6.00	12.00	20.00	—
1913	500,000	4.00	6.00	12.00	20.00	—
1916	2,286,000	200	400	700	1,150	—

KM# 36 2 LEVA **Composition:** Aluminum

Date	Mintage	F	VF	XF	Unc	BU
1923	20,000,000	3.00	6.00	15.00	50.00	—

KM# 38 2 LEVA **Composition:** Copper-Nickel

Date	Mintage	F	VF	XF	Unc	BU
1925	20,000,000	0.40	0.80	1.75	4.00	—
1925(p)	20,000,000	0.50	1.00	2.00	4.50	—

Note: The Poissy issue bears the thunderbolt privy mark

KM# 38a 2 LEVA **Composition:** Iron

Date	Mintage	F	VF	XF	Unc	BU
1941	15,000,000	0.75	1.50	3.50	10.00	—

KM# 49 2 LEVA **Composition:** Iron

Date	Mintage	F	VF	XF	Unc	BU
1943	35,000,000	0.75	1.50	4.50	15.00	—

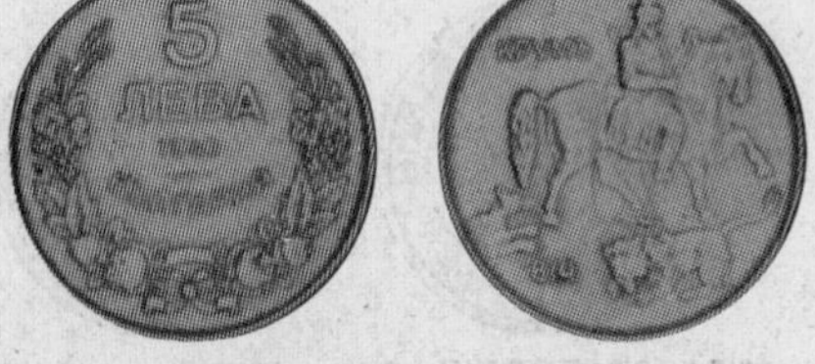

KM# 39 5 LEVA **Composition:** Copper-Nickel

Date	Mintage	F	VF	XF	Unc	BU
1930	20,001,000	0.60	1.25	2.75	7.00	—

KM# 39a 5 LEVA **Composition:** Iron

Date	Mintage	F	VF	XF	Unc	BU
1941	15,000,000	1.00	3.00	6.00	20.00	—

KM# 39b 5 LEVA **Composition:** Nickel Clad Steel

Date	Mintage	F	VF	XF	Unc	BU
1943	36,000,000	0.50	1.00	2.00	5.50	—

KM# 40 10 LEVA **Composition:** Copper-Nickel

Date	Mintage	F	VF	XF	Unc	BU
1930	15,001,000	0.75	1.50	3.50	9.00	—

KM# 40a 10 LEVA **Composition:** Iron

Date	Mintage	F	VF	XF	Unc	BU
1941	2,200,000	6.00	12.00	25.00	65.00	—

KM# 40b 10 LEVA **Composition:** Nickel Clad Steel

Date	Mintage	F	VF	XF	Unc	BU
1943	25,000,000	0.60	1.25	3.00	7.50	—

KM# 33 20 LEVA **Weight:** 6.4516 g. **Composition:** 0.9000 Gold .1867 oz. AGW **Subject:** Declaration of Independence

Date	Mintage	F	VF	XF	Unc	BU
1912	75,000	100	175	275	450	—
1912 Proof	—	Value: 2,000				

KM# 41 20 LEVA **Weight:** 4.0000 g. **Composition:** 0.5000 Silver .0643 oz. ASW

Date	Mintage	F	VF	XF	Unc	BU
1930BP	10,016,000	1.00	2.00	3.50	8.50	—

KM# 47 20 LEVA **Composition:** Copper-Nickel

Date	Mintage	F	VF	XF	Unc	BU
1940A	6,650,000	0.50	1.00	2.00	5.00	—

KM# 42 50 LEVA **Weight:** 10.0000 g. **Composition:** 0.5000 Silver .1607 oz. ASW

Date	Mintage	F	VF	XF	Unc	BU
1930BP	9,028,000	2.50	4.50	8.50	20.00	—

KM# 44 50 LEVA **Weight:** 10.0000 g. **Composition:** 0.5000 Silver .1607 oz. ASW

Date	Mintage	F	VF	XF	Unc	BU
1934	3,001,000	2.00	4.00	7.00	16.00	—
1934 Proof	—	—	—	—	—	—

KM# 48 50 LEVA **Composition:** Copper-Nickel

Date	Mintage	F	VF	XF	Unc	BU
1940A	12,340,000	0.75	1.50	3.00	7.50	—

KM# 48a 50 LEVA **Composition:** Nickel Clad Steel

Date	Mintage	F	VF	XF	Unc	BU
1943A	15,000,000	1.00	2.00	4.00	9.00	—

KM# 34 100 LEVA **Weight:** 32.2580 g. **Composition:** 0.9000 Gold .9334 oz. AGW **Subject:** Declaration of Independence

Date	Mintage	F	VF	XF	Unc	BU
1912	5,000	600	900	1,850	3,000	—
1912 Proof	—	Value: 3,500				

KM# 43 100 LEVA **Weight:** 20.0000 g. **Composition:** 0.5000 Silver .3215 oz. ASW

Date	Mintage	F	VF	XF	Unc	BU
1930BP	1,556,000	BV	6.00	12.00	30.00	—

KM# 45 100 LEVA **Weight:** 20.0000 g. **Composition:** 0.5000 Silver .3215 oz. ASW

Date	Mintage	F	VF	XF	Unc	BU
1934	2,506,000	BV	4.50	7.50	13.50	—
1934 Proof	—	—	—	—	—	—
1937	2,207,000	BV	4.50	7.50	13.50	—

PEOPLES REPUBLIC

STANDARD COINAGE

KM# 50 STOTINKA **Composition:** Brass

Date	F	VF	XF	Unc	BU
1951	—	—	0.10	0.25	—

KM# 59 STOTINKA **Composition:** Brass **Obverse:** Date 9 / IX / 1944 on ribbon

Date	F	VF	XF	Unc	BU
1962	—	—	0.10	0.25	—
1970	—	0.20	0.50	2.00	—

KM#84 STOTINKA **Composition:** Brass **Obverse:** Two dates on ribbon, '681-1944' **Note:** Edge varieties exist.

Date	Mintage	F	VF	XF	Unc	BU
1974	—	—	—	0.10	0.15	—
1979 Proof	2,000	Value: 1.50				
1980 Proof	2,000	Value: 1.50				
1981	137	—	—	—	2.00	—
1988	—	—	—	0.10	0.15	—
1989	—	—	—	0.10	0.15	—
1990	—	—	—	0.10	0.15	—

KM# 111 STOTINKA **Composition:** Brass **Subject:** 1300th Anniversary of Bulgaria

Date	F	VF	XF	Unc	BU
1981	—	0.10	0.20	0.50	—
1981 Proof	—	Value: 2.00			

KM# 60 2 STOTINKI **Composition:** Brass **Obverse:** Date 9 • IX • 1944 on ribbon

Date	F	VF	XF	Unc	BU
1962	—	—	0.10	0.25	—

KM# 85 2 STOTINKI **Composition:** Brass **Obverse:** Two dates on ribbon, '681-1944'

Date	Mintage	F	VF	XF	Unc	BU
1974	—	—	—	0.10	0.25	—
1979 Proof	2,000	Value: 2.00				
1980 Proof	2,000	Value: 2.00				
1981 Rare	20	—	—	—	—	—
1988	—	—	—	0.10	0.25	—
1989	—	—	—	0.10	0.25	—
1990	—	—	—	0.10	0.25	—

KM# 112 2 STOTINKI **Composition:** Brass **Subject:** 1300th Anniversary of Bulgaria

Date	F	VF	XF	Unc	BU
1981	—	0.10	0.20	0.60	—
1981 Proof	—	Value: 2.50			

KM# 51 3 STOTINKI **Composition:** Brass

Date	F	VF	XF	Unc	BU
1951	—	0.10	0.25	0.75	—

KM# 52 5 STOTINKI **Composition:** Brass

Date	F	VF	XF	Unc	BU
1951	0.10	0.15	0.25	0.75	—

KM# 61 5 STOTINKI **Composition:** Brass **Obverse:** Date 9 • IX • 1944 on ribbon

Date	F	VF	XF	Unc	BU
1962	—	0.10	0.20	0.50	—

KM# 86 5 STOTINKI **Composition:** Brass **Obverse:** Two dates on ribbon '681-1944'

Date	Mintage	F	VF	XF	Unc	BU
1974	—	—	0.10	0.15	0.25	—
1979 Proof	2,000	Value: 2.00				
1980 Proof	2,000	Value: 2.00				
1988	—	—	—	0.15	0.25	—
1989	—	—	—	0.15	0.25	—
1990	—	—	—	0.15	0.25	—

KM# 113 5 STOTINKI **Composition:** Brass **Subject:** 1300th Anniversary of Bulgaria

Date	F	VF	XF	Unc	BU
1981	—	0.10	0.25	0.75	—
1981 Proof	—	Value: 2.50			

KM# 53 10 STOTINKI **Composition:** Copper-Nickel

Date	F	VF	XF	Unc	BU
1951	—	0.10	0.20	0.40	—

KM# 62 10 STOTINKI **Composition:** Nickel-Brass **Obverse:** Date 9 • IX • 1944 on ribbon

Date	F	VF	XF	Unc	BU
1962	—	0.10	0.20	0.40	—

KM# 87 10 STOTINKI **Composition:** Nickel-Brass **Obverse:** Two dates on arms, '681-1944'

Date	Mintage	F	VF	XF	Unc	BU
1974	—	—	0.10	0.15	0.25	—
1979 Proof	2,000	Value: 3.50				
1980 Proof	2,000	Value: 3.50				
1988	—	—	—	0.15	0.25	—
1989	—	—	—	0.15	0.25	—
1990	—	—	—	0.15	0.25	—

KM# 114 10 STOTINKI **Composition:** Copper-Nickel **Subject:** 1300th Anniversary of Bulgaria

Date	F	VF	XF	Unc	BU
1981	—	0.20	0.50	1.50	—
1981 Proof	—	Value: 3.50			

KM# 55 20 STOTINKI **Composition:** Copper-Nickel

Date	F	VF	XF	Unc	BU
1952	1.00	2.50	7.50	20.00	—
1954	0.10	0.25	0.75	1.50	—

KM# 63 20 STOTINKI **Composition:** Nickel-Brass **Obverse:** Date 9 • IX • 1944 on ribbon

Date	F	VF	XF	Unc	BU
1962	0.10	0.20	0.30	0.75	—

KM# 88 20 STOTINKI **Composition:** Nickel-Brass **Obverse:** Two dates on ribbon, '681-1944'

Date	Mintage	F	VF	XF	Unc	BU
1974	—	0.10	0.20	0.30	0.60	—
1979 Proof	2,000	Value: 3.50				
1980 Proof	2,000	Value: 3.50				
1988	—	—	—	0.30	0.60	—
1989	—	—	—	0.30	0.60	—
1990	—	—	—	0.30	0.60	—

KM# 115 20 STOTINKI **Composition:** Copper-Nickel **Subject:** 1300th Anniversary of Bulgaria

Date	F	VF	XF	Unc	BU
1981	—	0.25	0.65	2.00	—
1981 Proof	—	Value: 4.00			

KM# 54 25 STOTINKI **Composition:** Copper-Nickel

Date	F	VF	XF	Unc	BU
1951	0.10	0.20	0.50	1.00	—

KM# 56 50 STOTINKI **Composition:** Copper-Nickel

Date	F	VF	XF	Unc	BU
1959	0.10	0.20	0.40	0.80	—

KM# 64 50 STOTINKI **Composition:** Nickel-Brass **Obverse:** Date 9 • IX • 1944 on ribbon

Date	F	VF	XF	Unc	BU
1962	0.10	0.40	0.65	1.00	—

KM# 89 50 STOTINKI **Composition:** Nickel-Brass **Obverse:** Two dates on ribbon, '681-1944'

Date	Mintage	F	VF	XF	Unc	BU
1974	—	0.10	0.40	0.65	1.50	—
1979 Proof	2,000	Value: 4.00				
1980 Proof	2,000	Value: 4.00				
1988	—	—	—	0.50	1.00	—
1989	—	—	—	0.50	1.00	—
1990	—	—	—	0.50	1.00	—

KM# 98 50 STOTINKI Composition: Copper-Nickel **Subject:** University Games at Sofia

Date	Mintage	F	VF	XF	Unc	BU
1977	2,000,000	0.20	0.40	0.75	1.50	—

KM# 116 50 STOTINKI Composition: Copper-Nickel **Subject:** 1300th Anniversary of Bulgaria

Date	F	VF	XF	Unc	BU
1981	—	0.30	0.60	1.80	—
1981 Proof	—	Value: 4.00			

KM# 57 LEV Composition: Copper-Nickel **Obverse:** Date 9 • IX • 1944 on ribbon

Date	F	VF	XF	Unc	BU
1960	0.10	0.25	0.60	1.00	—

KM# 58 LEV Composition: Nickel-Brass

Date	F	VF	XF	Unc	BU
1962	—	0.50	1.00	1.50	—

KM# 74 LEV Composition: Nickel-Brass **Subject:** 25th Anniversary of Socialist Revolution

Date	Mintage	F	VF	XF	Unc	BU
1969	2,410,196	0.35	0.60	1.25	2.50	—

KM# 76 LEV Composition: Nickel-Brass **Subject:** 90th Anniversary Liberation From Turks

Date	Mintage	F	VF	XF	Unc	BU
1969	1,290,373	0.35	0.65	1.50	2.75	—

KM# 90 LEV Composition: Nickel-Brass **Obverse:** Two dates '681-1944' on ribbon

Date	Mintage	F	VF	XF	Unc	BU
1974	—	—	0.50	1.00	2.00	—
1979 Proof	2,000	Value: 6.00				
1980 Proof	2,000	Value: 6.00				
1988	—	—	—	0.75	2.00	—
1989	—	—	—	0.75	2.00	—
1990	—	—	—	0.75	2.00	—

KM# 94 LEV Composition: Bronze **Subject:** 100th Anniversary of the "April Uprising" against the Turks

Date	Mintage	F	VF	XF	Unc	BU
1976	300,000	0.35	0.60	1.25	2.50	—
1976 Proof	—	Value: 4.00				

KM# 107 LEV Composition: Copper-Nickel **Subject:** World Cup Soccer Games in Spain

Date	Mintage	F	VF	XF	Unc	BU
1980	220,000	—	0.60	1.25	2.50	—
1980 Proof	30,000	Value: 3.50				

KM# 117 LEV Composition: Copper-Nickel **Subject:** 1300th Anniversary of Bulgaria

Date	F	VF	XF	Unc	BU
1981	—	0.50	1.00	2.00	—
1981 Proof	—	—	—	—	—

KM# 118 LEV Composition: Copper-Nickel **Subject:** International Hunting Exposition

Date	Mintage	F	VF	XF	Unc	BU
1981	250,000	—	0.60	1.25	2.50	—
1981 Proof	50,000	Value: 3.50				

KM# 119 LEV Composition: Copper-Nickel **Subject:** Russo-Bulgarian Friendship **Note:** The same reverse die was used for both Bulgaria 1 Lev, KM#19 and Russia 1 Rouble, KM#189.

Date	Mintage	F	VF	XF	Unc	BU
1981	220,800	—	0.60	1.25	2.50	—
1981 Proof	50,000	Value: 3.50				

KM#175 LEV Composition: Copper-Nickel **Series:** 1980 Winter Olympics **Reverse:** Hockey player

Date	Mintage	F	VF	XF	Unc	BU
1987	—	—	—	—	2.50	—
1987 Proof	300,000	Value: 3.50				

KM# 176 LEV Composition: Copper-Nickel **Series:** Summer Olympics **Reverse:** Sprinters

Date	Mintage	F	VF	XF	Unc	BU
1988	—	—	—	—	2.50	—
1988 Proof	300,000	Value: 3.50				

KM# 65 2 LEVA Weight: 8.8889 g. **Composition:** 0.9000 Silver .2572 oz. ASW **Subject:** 1100th Anniversary - Slovanic Alphabet

Date	Mintage	F	VF	XF	Unc	BU
ND(1963) Proof	10,000	Value: 7.50				

KM# 69 2 LEVA Weight: 8.8889 g. **Composition:** 0.9000 Silver .2572 oz. ASW **Subject:** 20th Anniversary Peoples Republic

Date	Mintage	F	VF	XF	Unc	BU
ND(1964) Proof	20,000	Value: 7.50				

KM# 73 2 LEVA Composition: Copper-Nickel **Subject:** 1050th Anniversary - Death of Ochridsky

Date	Mintage	F	VF	XF	Unc	BU
ND(1966)	506,000	—	1.00	2.00	4.00	—

KM# 75 2 LEVA Composition: Copper-Nickel **Subject:** 25th Anniversary of Socialist Revolution

Date	Mintage	F	VF	XF	Unc	BU
1969	1,082,210	—	0.75	1.75	3.50	—

KM# 77 2 LEVA **Composition:** Copper-Nickel **Subject:** 90th Anniversary - Liberation from Turks

Date	Mintage	F	VF	XF	Unc	BU
1969	756,759	—	0.75	1.75	3.50	—

KM# 80 2 LEVA **Composition:** Nickel-Brass **Subject:** 150th Anniversary - Birth of Dobri Chintulov

Date	Mintage	F	VF	XF	Unc	BU
1972	100,000	—	1.25	2.50	4.50	—

KM# 95.1 2 LEVA **Composition:** Copper-Nickel **Subject:** 100th Anniversary of the "April Uprising" against the Turks

Date	Mintage	F	VF	XF	Unc	BU
1976	224,800	—	0.75	1.50	3.00	—
1976 Proof	—	Value: 5.00				

KM# 95.2 2 LEVA **Composition:** Copper-Nickel **Edge:** Lettered

Date	Mintage	F	VF	XF	Unc	BU
1976	138	—	—	—	—	—

KM#108 2 LEVA **Composition:** Copper-Nickel **Subject:** World Cup Soccer Games in Spain

Date	Mintage	F	VF	XF	Unc	BU
1980	220,000	—	0.60	1.20	2.50	—
1980 Proof	30,000	Value: 4.50				

KM#110 2 LEVA **Composition:** Copper-Nickel **Subject:** 100th Anniversary - Birth of Yordan Yovkov

Date	Mintage	F	VF	XF	Unc	BU
1980	200,000	—	1.00	2.50	4.50	—

KM#120 2 LEVA **Composition:** Copper-Nickel **Subject:** International Hunting Exposition

Date	Mintage	F	VF	XF	Unc	BU
1981	250,000	—	0.75	1.50	3.00	—
1981 Proof	50,000	Value: 5.00				

KM#121 2 LEVA **Composition:** Copper-Nickel **Subject:** 1300th Anniversary of Nationhood **Reverse:** Equestrian figure

Date	F	VF	XF	Unc	BU
1981	—	—	—	2.50	—
1981 Proof	—	Value: 4.00			

KM#122 2 LEVA **Composition:** Copper-Nickel **Subject:** 1300th Anniversary of Nationhood **Reverse:** Mother and child

Date	F	VF	XF	Unc	BU
1981 Proof	—	Value: 4.00			

KM#123 2 LEVA **Composition:** Copper-Nickel **Subject:** 1300th Anniversary of Nationhood **Reverse:** Dimitrov

Date	F	VF	XF	Unc	BU
1981	—	—	—	3.50	—
1981 Proof	—	Value: 5.00			

KM#124 2 LEVA **Composition:** Copper-Nickel **Subject:** 1300th Anniversary of Nationhood **Reverse:** King and saint

Date	F	VF	XF	Unc	BU
1981	—	—	—	2.50	—
1981 Proof	—	Value: 4.00			

KM#125 2 LEVA **Composition:** Copper-Nickel **Subject:** 1300th Anniversary of Nationhood **Reverse:** Soldier

Date	F	VF	XF	Unc	BU
1981	—	—	—	2.50	—
1981 Proof	—	Value: 4.00			

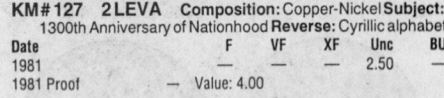

KM#126 2 LEVA **Composition:** Copper-Nickel **Subject:** 1300th Anniversary of Nationhood **Reverse:** Clandestine meeting

Date	F	VF	XF	Unc	BU
1981 Proof	—	Value: 4.00			

KM#127 2 LEVA **Composition:** Copper-Nickel **Subject:** 1300th Anniversary of Nationhood **Reverse:** Cyrillic alphabet

Date	F	VF	XF	Unc	BU
1981	—	—	—	2.50	—
1981 Proof	—	Value: 4.00			

KM#128 2 LEVA **Composition:** Copper-Nickel **Subject:** 1300th Anniversary of Nationhood **Reverse:** Rila Monastary

Date	F	VF	XF	Unc	BU
1981	—	—	—	2.50	—
1981 Proof	—	Value: 4.00			

KM#129 2 LEVA **Composition:** Copper-Nickel **Subject:** 1300th Anniversary of Nationhood **Reverse:** Russky monument

Date	F	VF	XF	Unc	BU
1981 Proof	—	Value: 4.50			

KM#130 2 LEVA Composition: Copper-Nickel **Subject:** 1300th Anniversary of Nationhood **Reverse:** Bojana church

Date	Mintage	F	VF	XF	Unc	BU
1981 Proof	300,000	Value: 4.50				

KM#161 2 LEVA Composition: Copper-Nickel **Subject:** 1300th Anniversary of Nationhood - Oboriste Assembly

Date	Mintage	F	VF	XF	Unc	BU
1981 Proof	300,000	Value: 4.50				

KM#162 2 LEVA Composition: Copper-Nickel **Subject:** 1300th Anniversary of Nationhood - Uprising of Assen and Peter

Date	Mintage	F	VF	XF	Unc	BU
1981 Proof	300,000	Value: 4.50				

KM#163 2 LEVA Composition: Copper-Nickel **Subject:** 1300th Anniversary of Nationhood - 100th Anniversary of Serbo-Bulgarian War

Date	F	VF	XF	Unc	BU
1981 Proof	—	Value: 4.50			

KM#155 2 LEVA Composition: Copper-Nickel **Subject:** Soccer

Date	Mintage	F	VF	XF	Unc	BU
1986 Proof	100,000	Value: 4.00				

KM#158 2 LEVA Composition: Copper-Nickel **Subject:** World Championship of Rhythmic Gymnastics

Date	Mintage	F	VF	XF	Unc	BU
1987 Proof	300,000	Value: 3.50				

KM#159 2 LEVA Composition: Copper-Nickel **Series:** Winter Olympics **Reverse:** Skier

Date	Mintage	F	VF	XF	Unc	BU
1987	300,000	Value: 5.00				

KM#165 2 LEVA Composition: Copper-Nickel **Subject:** 100th Anniversary of Sophia University

Date	F	VF	XF	Unc	BU
1988 Proof	—	Value: 4.00			

KM#166 2 LEVA Composition: Copper-Nickel **Subject:** Soviet-Bulgarian Space Flight

Date	Mintage	F	VF	XF	Unc	BU
1988 Proof	300,000	Value: 3.00				

KM#177 2 LEVA Composition: Copper-Nickel **Series:** Summer Olympics **Reverse:** High jumper

Date	Mintage	F	VF	XF	Unc	BU
1988 Proof	300,000	Value: 3.50				

KM#178 2 LEVA Composition: Copper-Nickel **Subject:** Sports **Reverse:** Rowers

Date	Mintage	F	VF	XF	Unc	BU
1989 Proof	300,000	Value: 3.00				

KM# 66 5 LEVA Weight: 16.6667 g. **Composition:** 0.9000 Silver .4823 oz. ASW **Subject:** 1100th Anniversary Slavic Alphabet

Date	Mintage	F	VF	XF	Unc	BU
ND(1963) Proof	5,000	Value: 13.50				

KM# 70 5 LEVA Weight: 16.6667 g. **Composition:** 0.9000 Silver .4823 oz. ASW **Subject:** 20th Anniversary Peoples Republic

Date	Mintage	F	VF	XF	Unc	BU
ND(1964) Proof	10,000	Value: 13.50				

KM# 78 5 LEVA Weight: 20.5000 g. **Composition:** 0.9000 Silver .5932 oz. ASW **Subject:** 120th Anniversary - Birth of Ivan Vazov

Date	Mintage	F	VF	XF	Unc	BU
1970	370,000	—	—	4.50	6.50	—
1970 Proof	109,700	Value: 7.50				

KM# 79 5 LEVA Weight: 20.5000 g. **Composition:** 0.9000 Silver .5932 oz. ASW **Subject:** 150th Anniversary - Birth of Georgi S. Rakovski

Date	Mintage	F	VF	XF	Unc	BU
1971 Prooflike	300,000	—	—	—	7.50	—

KM# 81 5 LEVA Weight: 20.5000 g. **Composition:** 0.9000 Silver .5932 oz. ASW **Subject:** 250th Anniversary - Birth of Paisii Hilendarski

Date	Mintage	F	VF	XF	Unc	BU
1972 Proof	200,000	Value: 7.50				

KM# 82 5 LEVA **Weight:** 20.5000 g. **Composition:** 0.9000 Silver .5932 oz. ASW **Subject:** Centennial - Death of Vasil Levski

Date	Mintage	F	VF	XF	Unc	BU
1973 Proof	200,000	Value: 7.50				

KM# 83 5 LEVA **Weight:** 20.5000 g. **Composition:** 0.9000 Silver .5932 oz. ASW **Subject:** 50th Anniversary - Anti-fascist Uprising

Date	Mintage	F	VF	XF	Unc	BU
1973 Proof	200,000	Value: 7.50				

KM# 91 5 LEVA **Weight:** 20.5000 g. **Composition:** 0.9000 Silver .5932 oz. ASW **Subject:** 50th Anniversary - Death of Alexander Stamboliiski

Date	Mintage	F	VF	XF	Unc	BU
1974 Proof	200,000	Value: 7.50				

KM# 92 5 LEVA **Weight:** 20.5000 g. **Composition:** 0.9000 Silver .5932 oz. ASW **Subject:** 30th Anniversary - Liberation from Fascism

Date	Mintage	F	VF	XF	Unc	BU
1974 Proof	200,000	Value: 8.00				

KM# 96 5 LEVA **Weight:** 20.5000 g. **Composition:** 0.9000 Silver .5932 oz. ASW **Subject:** Centennial - Death of Khristo Botev

Date	Mintage	F	VF	XF	Unc	BU
1976 Proof	196,660	Value: 7.50				

KM# 97 5 LEVA **Weight:** 20.5000 g. **Composition:** 0.5000 Silver .3295 oz. ASW **Subject:** 100th Anniversary of the "April Uprising" against the Turks

Date	Mintage	F	VF	XF	Unc	BU
1976 Proof	200,000	Value: 8.00				

KM# 99 5 LEVA **Weight:** 20.5000 g. **Composition:** 0.5000 Silver .3295 oz. ASW **Subject:** 150th Anniversary - Birth of Petko Slaveykov

Date	Mintage	F	VF	XF	Unc	BU
1977 Proof	200,000	Value: 8.00				

KM# 100 5 LEVA **Weight:** 20.5000 g. **Composition:** 0.5000 Silver .3295 oz. ASW **Subject:** 100th Anniversary - Birth of Peio Javoroff

Date	Mintage	F	VF	XF	Unc	BU
1978 Proof	200,000	Value: 8.00				

KM# 101 5 LEVA **Weight:** 20.5000 g. **Composition:** 0.5000 Silver .3295 oz. ASW **Subject:** 100th Anniversary - National Library

Date	Mintage	F	VF	XF	Unc	BU
ND(1978) Proof	200,000	Value: 8.00				

KM# 103 5 LEVA **Weight:** 20.5000 g. **Composition:** 0.5000 Silver .3295 oz. ASW **Subject:** 100th Anniversary - Communication Systems

Date	Mintage	F	VF	XF	Unc	BU
1979	35,000	—	—	—	8.50	—
1979 Proof	15,000	Value: 12.50				

KM# 109 5 LEVA **Composition:** Copper-Nickel **Subject:** World Cup Soccer Games in Spain

Date	Mintage	F	VF	XF	Unc	BU
1980	220,000	—	—	—	3.50	—
1980 Proof	30,000	Value: 6.00				

KM# 131 5 LEVA **Composition:** Copper-Nickel **Subject:** International Hunting Exposition

Date	Mintage	F	VF	XF	Unc	BU
1981	250,000	—	—	—	4.50	—
1981 Proof	50,000	Value: 7.00				

KM# 132 5 LEVA **Composition:** Copper-Nickel **Subject:** 1300th Anniversary of Nationhood - Friendship with Hungary

Date	Mintage	F	VF	XF	Unc	BU
1981	—	—	—	—	3.50	—
1981 Proof	47,000	Value: 7.00				

KM# 140 5 LEVA Composition: Copper-Nickel **Subject:** 100th Anniversary - Birth of Vladimir Dimitrov

Date	Mintage	F	VF	XF	Unc	BU
1982 Proof	283,050	Value: 5.00				

KM# 141 5 LEVA Composition: Copper-Nickel **Subject:** 40th Anniversary - Birth of Lyudmila Zhivkova

Date	Mintage	F	VF	XF	Unc	BU
1982 Proof	20,000	Value: 5.00				

KM# 142 5 LEVA Composition: Copper-Nickel **Subject:** 2nd International Children's Assembly

Date	Mintage	F	VF	XF	Unc	BU
1982 Proof	200,000	Value: 4.00				

KM# 151 5 LEVA Composition: Copper-Nickel **Subject:** 3rd International Children's Assembly

Date	Mintage	F	VF	XF	Unc	BU
1985 Proof	100,000	Value: 4.00				

KM# 152 5 LEVA Composition: Copper-Nickel **Subject:** 90th Anniversary of Tourism Movement - Konstantinov

Date	Mintage	F	VF	XF	Unc	BU
1985 Proof	100,000	Value: 4.50				

KM# 153 5 LEVA Composition: Copper-Nickel **Subject:** 4th Anniversary of UNESCO

Date	Mintage	F	VF	XF	Unc	BU
1985 Proof	100,000	Value: 4.50				

KM# 154 5 LEVA Composition: Copper-Nickel **Subject:** Young Inventors' Exposition

Date	Mintage	F	VF	XF	Unc	BU
1985 Proof	100,000	Value: 4.50				

KM# 167.1 5 LEVA Composition: Copper-Nickel **Subject:** Chiprovo Uprising **Edge:** Plain

Date	Mintage	F	VF	XF	Unc	BU
1988 Proof	100,000	Value: 4.50				

KM# 167.2 5 LEVA Composition: Copper-Nickel **Edge:** Reeded

Date		F	VF	XF	Unc	BU
1988 Proof	—	Value: 5.00				

KM# 168 5 LEVA Composition: Copper-Nickel **Subject:** 20th Anniversary - Dimitar and Karadzha

Date	Mintage	F	VF	XF	Unc	BU
1988 Proof	100,000	Value: 4.00				

KM# 170 5 LEVA Composition: Copper-Nickel **Subject:** Childrens' Assembly

Date	Mintage	F	VF	XF	Unc	BU
1988 Proof	100,000	Value: 4.00				

KM# 169 5 LEVA Composition: Copper-Nickel **Note:** Kremikovski

Date	Mintage	F	VF	XF	Unc	BU
1988 Proof	148,000	Value: 4.00				

KM# 179 5 LEVA Composition: Copper-Nickel **Subject:** 200th Birthday of Aprilov

Date	Mintage	F	VF	XF	Unc	BU
1989 Proof	100,000	Value: 4.00				

KM# 180 5 LEVA Composition: Copper-Nickel **Subject:** 250th Anniversary - Birth of Vrachanski

Date	Mintage	F	VF	XF	Unc	BU
1989 Proof	100,000	Value: 4.00				

KM# 67 10 LEVA Weight: 8.4444 g. **Composition:** 0.9000 Gold .2443 oz. AGW **Subject:** 1100th Anniversary - Slavic Alphabet

Date	Mintage	F	VF	XF	Unc	BU
ND(1963) Proof	7,000	Value: 165				

KM# 71 10 LEVA Weight: 8.4444 g. **Composition:** 0.9000 Gold .2443 oz. AGW **Subject:** 20th Anniversary - Peoples Republic **Reverse:** Head of Georgi Dmitrov left

Date	Mintage	F	VF	XF	Unc	BU
ND(1964) Proof	10,000	Value: 125				

KM# 93.1 10 LEVA **Weight:** 29.9500 g. **Composition:** 0.9000 Silver .8666 oz. ASW **Subject:** 10th Olympic Congress **Edge:** Inscription in Latin

Date	Mintage	F	VF	XF	Unc	BU
1975 Proof	50,000	Value: 16.50				

KM# 93.2 10 LEVA **Weight:** 29.9500 g. **Composition:** 0.9000 Silver .8666 oz. ASW **Edge:** Inscription in Cyrillic

Date	Mintage	F	VF	XF	Unc	BU
1975 Proof	50,000	Value: 16.50				

KM# 102 10 LEVA **Weight:** 29.8500 g. **Composition:** 0.5000 Silver .4798 oz. ASW **Subject:** 100th Anniversary - Liberation from Turks

Date	Mintage	F	VF	XF	Unc	BU
ND(1978) Proof	200,000	Value: 12.50				

KM# 104 10 LEVA **Weight:** 23.3280 g. **Composition:** 0.9250 Silver .6938 oz. ASW **Series:** International Year of the Child

Date	Mintage	F	VF	XF	Unc	BU
1979 Proof	16,906	Value: 22.50				

KM# 105 10 LEVA **Weight:** 14.0000 g. **Composition:** 0.5000 Silver .2251 oz. ASW **Subject:** Bulgarian-Soviet Cosmonaut Flight

Date	Mintage	F	VF	XF	Unc	BU
1979 Proof	35,000	Value: 20.00				

KM# 105a 10 LEVA **Weight:** 23.8500 g. **Composition:** 0.9000 Silver .6901 oz. ASW

Date	Mintage	F	VF	XF	Unc	BU
1979 Proof	15,000	Value: 27.50				

KM# 143 10 LEVA **Weight:** 18.8800 g. **Composition:** 0.5000 Silver .3035 oz. ASW **Subject:** Soccer Games **Reverse:** Ball and net

Date	Mintage	F	VF	XF	Unc	BU
1982 Proof	7,800	Value: 22.50				

KM# 144 10 LEVA **Weight:** 18.8800 g. **Composition:** 0.5000 Silver .3035 oz. ASW **Subject:** Soccer Games **Reverse:** Players

Date	Mintage	F	VF	XF	Unc	BU
1982 Proof	7,200	Value: 21.50				

KM# 146 10 LEVA **Weight:** 23.3300 g. **Composition:** 0.9250 Silver .6939 oz. ASW **Series:** Winter Olypics **Reverse:** Skier

Date	Mintage	F	VF	XF	Unc	BU
1984 Proof	8,464	Value: 14.50				

KM# 149 10 LEVA **Weight:** 23.3300 g. **Composition:** 0.9250 Silver .6939 oz. ASW **Subject:** International Decade for Women

Date	Mintage	F	VF	XF	Unc	BU
1984 Proof	5,572	Value: 32.50				

KM# 157 10 LEVA **Weight:** 18.7500 g. **Composition:** 0.6400 Silver .3858 oz. ASW **Reverse:** Cosmonauts

Date	Mintage	F	VF	XF	Unc	BU
1985 Proof	7,501	Value: 30.00				

KM# 184 10 LEVA **Weight:** 18.7500 g. **Composition:** 0.6400 Silver .3858 oz. ASW **Series:** 1988 Winter Olympics **Reverse:** Hockey player

Date	Mintage	F	VF	XF	Unc	BU
1987 Proof	15,000	Value: 20.00				

KM# 185 10 LEVA **Weight:** 18.7500 g. **Composition:** 0.6400 Silver .3858 oz. ASW **Series:** Summer Olympics **Reverse:** Sprinters

Date	Mintage	F	VF	XF	Unc	BU
1988 Proof	22,650	Value: 15.00				

KM# 244 10 LEVA **Weight:** 10.3500 g. **Composition:** 0.8000 Silver .2662 oz. ASW **Subject:** The Year 2000 **Obverse:** National arms above date with pierced zeros **Reverse:** Bell above date with pierced zeros **Edge:** Plain **Size:** 33.9 mm.

Date		F	VF	XF	Unc	BU
2000 Proof	—	Value: 50.00				

KM# 68 20 LEVA **Weight:** 16.8889 g. **Composition:** 0.9000 Gold .4887 oz. AGW **Subject:** 100th Anniversary - Slavic Alphabet

Date	Mintage	F	VF	XF	Unc	BU
ND(1963) Proof	3,000	Value: 325				

KM# 72 20 LEVA **Weight:** 16.8889 g. **Composition:** 0.9000 Gold .4887 oz. AGW **Subject:** 20th Anniversary - Peoples Republic **Reverse:** Head of Georgi Dmitrov left

Date	Mintage	F	VF	XF	Unc	BU
ND(1964) Proof	5,000	Value: 250				

KM# 106 20 LEVA **Weight:** 21.8000 g. **Composition:** 0.5000 Silver .3505 oz. ASW **Subject:** Centennial of Sophia as Capital

Date	Mintage	F	VF	XF	Unc	BU
1979	35,000	—	—	—	20.00	—

KM# 106a 20 LEVA **Weight:** 32.0000 g. **Composition:** 0.9000 Silver .9260 oz. ASW

Date	Mintage	F	VF	XF	Unc	BU
1979 Proof	15,000	Value: 32.50				

KM# 133.1 20 LEVA **Weight:** 14.0000 g. **Composition:** 0.5000 Silver .2250 oz. ASW **Subject:** 40th Anniversary - Birth of Lyudmila Zhivkova **Obverse:** Denomination with date to left **Reverse:** Head of Lyudmila Zhivkova left

Date	Mintage	F	VF	XF	Unc	BU
1982 Proof	10,000	Value: 20.00				

KM# 133.2 20 LEVA **Obverse:** Denomination between emblems of Children's Assembly and Year of the Child **Reverse:** Head of Lyudmila Zhivkova left

Date		F	VF	XF	Unc	BU
1982 Proof	—	Value: 150				

KM# 164 20 LEVA **Weight:** 11.2200 g. **Composition:** 0.5000 Silver .1804 oz. ASW **Note:** Vasil Levsky

Date	Mintage	F	VF	XF	Unc	BU
1987 Proof	100,000	Value: 12.50				

KM# 173 20 LEVA **Weight:** 11.5500 g. **Composition:** 0.5000 Silver .1855 oz. ASW **Subject:** 100th Anniversary of Sophia University

Date	Mintage	F	VF	XF	Unc	BU
1988 Proof	100,000	Value: 12.50				

KM# 174 20 LEVA **Weight:** 11.1900 g. **Composition:** 0.5000 Silver .1803 oz. ASW **Subject:** Soviet-Bulgarian Space Flight

Date	Mintage	F	VF	XF	Unc	BU
1988 Proof	100,000	Value: 12.50				

KM# 171 20 LEVA **Weight:** 11.3900 g. **Composition:** 0.5000 Silver .1830 oz. ASW **Subject:** Bulgarian Railways

Date	Mintage	F	VF	XF	Unc	BU
1988 Proof	93,000	Value: 11.50				

KM# 172 20 LEVA **Weight:** 11.2200 g. **Composition:** 0.5000 Silver .1804 oz. ASW **Subject:** 110th Anniversary of Liberation

Date	Mintage	F	VF	XF	Unc	BU
1988 Proof	100,000	Value: 11.50				

KM# 181 20 LEVA **Composition:** Copper-Nickel-Zinc

Date		F	VF	XF	Unc	BU
1989 Proof	—	Value: 8.00				

KM# 183 20 LEVA **Weight:** 12.1300 g. **Composition:** 0.5000 Silver .2138 oz. ASW **Subject:** Academy of Science

Date	Mintage	F	VF	XF	Unc	BU
1989 Proof	58,000	Value: 12.50				

KM# 134 25 LEVA **Weight:** 14.0000 g. **Composition:** 0.5000 Silver .2250 oz. ASW **Subject:** 1300th Anniversary of Nationhood

Date	Mintage	F	VF	XF	Unc	BU
1981 Proof	Est. 100,000	Value: 22.50				

KM# 145 25 LEVA **Weight:** 14.0000 g. **Composition:** 0.5000 Silver .2250 oz. ASW **Subject:** 100th Anniversary - Birth of George Dimitrov

Date	Mintage	F	VF	XF	Unc	BU
1982 Proof	15,000	Value: 12.50				

KM# 148 25 LEVA **Weight:** 14.0000 g. **Composition:** 0.5000 Silver .2250 oz. ASW **Subject:** 40th Anniversary of Peoples Republic

Date	Mintage	F	VF	XF	Unc	BU
ND(1984) Proof	91,000	Value: 11.50				

KM# 156.1 25 LEVA **Weight:** 23.3300 g. **Composition:** 0.9250 Silver .6939 oz. ASW **Subject:** Soccer

Date	Mintage	F	VF	XF	Unc	BU
1986 Proof	12,902	Value: 25.00				

KM# 156.2 25 LEVA **Weight:** 23.3300 g. **Composition:** 0.9250 Silver .6939 oz. ASW **Reverse:** Without date in field above eagle's head

Date	Mintage	F	VF	XF	Unc	BU
1986 Proof	Inc. above	Value: 30.00				

KM# 194 25 LEVA **Weight:** 23.3300 g. **Composition:** 0.9250 Silver .6939 oz. ASW **Subject:** Soccer **Reverse:** Player

Date	Mintage	F	VF	XF	Unc	BU
1986 Proof	12,250	Value: 20.00				

KM# 160 25 LEVA **Weight:** 23.3300 g. **Composition:** 0.9250 Silver .6939 oz. ASW **Series:** Winter Olympics **Reverse:** Skier

Date	Mintage	F	VF	XF	Unc	BU
1987 Proof	15,000	Value: 20.00				

KM# 190 25 LEVA **Weight:** 23.3800 g. **Composition:** 0.9250 Silver .6954 oz. ASW **Series:** 1992 Winter Olympics **Obverse:** Similar to KM#189 **Reverse:** Figure skating pairs competition

Date	Mintage	F	VF	XF	Unc	BU
1989 Proof	48,449	Value: 16.50				

KM# 195 25 LEVA **Weight:** 23.3800 g. **Composition:** 0.9250 Silver .6954 oz. ASW **Series:** Winter Olympics **Reverse:** Cross-country skiers

Date	Mintage	F	VF	XF	Unc	BU
1990 Proof	46,400	Value: 15.00				

KM# 186 25 LEVA **Weight:** 23.3300 g. **Composition:** 0.9250 Silver .6939 oz. ASW **Series:** Summer Olympics **Subject:** High Jump

Date	Mintage	F	VF	XF	Unc	BU
1988 Proof	20,000	Value: 21.50				

KM# 193 25 LEVA **Weight:** 23.3800 g. **Composition:** 0.9250 Silver .6954 oz. ASW **Subject:** Wildlife **Reverse:** Mother bear and cubs

Date	Mintage	F	VF	XF	Unc	BU
1989 Proof	15,000	Value: 32.50				

KM# 196 25 LEVA **Weight:** 23.3800 g. **Composition:** 0.9250 Silver .6954 oz. ASW **Series:** Summer Olympics **Reverse:** Runners

Date	Mintage	F	VF	XF	Unc	BU
1990 Proof	50,235	Value: 15.00				

KM# 187 25 LEVA **Weight:** 23.3300 g. **Composition:** 0.9250 Silver .6939 oz. ASW **Subject:** Soccer **Reverse:** Two players

Date	Mintage	F	VF	XF	Unc	BU
1989 Proof	17,600	Value: 25.00				

KM# 191 25 LEVA **Weight:** 23.3800 g. **Composition:** 0.9250 Silver .6954 oz. ASW **Subject:** Soccer **Reverse:** Globe, net, and shoe

Date	Mintage	F	VF	XF	Unc	BU
1990 Proof	15,600	Value: 22.50				

KM# 197 25 LEVA **Weight:** 23.3800 g. **Composition:** 0.9250 Silver .6954 oz. ASW **Subject:** Wildlife **Reverse:** Two lynx

Date	Mintage	F	VF	XF	Unc	BU
1990 Proof	14,840	Value: 32.50				

KM# 189 25 LEVA **Weight:** 23.3800 g. **Composition:** 0.9250 Silver .6954 oz. ASW **Series:** 1992 Summer Olympics **Reverse:** Two rowers

Date	Mintage	F	VF	XF	Unc	BU
1989 Proof	57,560	Value: 15.00				

KM# 192 25 LEVA **Weight:** 23.3800 g. **Composition:** 0.9250 Silver .6954 oz. ASW **Subject:** Soccer **Obverse:** Similar to KM#193 **Reverse:** Ball design

Date	Mintage	F	VF	XF	Unc	BU
1990 Proof	14,900	Value: 24.00				

KM# 135 50 LEVA **Weight:** 20.5000 g. **Composition:** 0.9000 Silver .5932 oz. ASW **Subject:** 1300th Anniversary of Nationhood **Obverse:** Dates above denomination **Reverse:** Equestrian figure

Date	Mintage	F	VF	XF	Unc	BU
1981 Proof	Est. 10,000	Value: 22.50				

KM# 136 50 LEVA **Weight:** 20.5000 g. **Composition:** 0.9000 Silver .5932 oz. ASW **Subject:** 1300th Anniversary of Nationhood **Obverse:** Head of Georgi Dmitrov left

Date	Mintage	F	VF	XF	Unc	BU
1981 Proof	1,000	Value: 25.00				

KM# 137 50 LEVA **Weight:** 20.5000 g. **Composition:** 0.9000 Silver .5932 oz. ASW **Subject:** 1300th Anniversary of Nationhood **Reverse:** Mother and child in front of radiant sun

Date	Mintage	F	VF	XF	Unc	BU
1981 Proof	1,000	Value: 30.00				

KM# 138 50 LEVA **Weight:** 20.5000 g. **Composition:** 0.9000 Silver .5932 oz. ASW **Subject:** 1300th Anniversary of Nationhood

Date	Mintage	F	VF	XF	Unc	BU
1981 Proof	Est. 10,000	Value: 23.50				

KM# 182 50 LEVA **Composition:** Copper-Nickel-Zinc

Date	F	VF	XF	Unc	BU
1989 Proof	—	Value: 12.00			

KM# 150 100 LEVA **Weight:** 8.4444 g. **Composition:** 0.9000 Gold .2443 oz. AGW **Subject:** International Womens Decade **Note:** .076 Silver, .024 Copper

Date	Mintage	F	VF	XF	Unc	BU
1984 Proof	500	Value: 260				

KM# 150a 100 LEVA **Weight:** 8.4444 g. **Composition:** 0.9000 Gold .2443 oz. AGW **Note:** .100 Copper

Date	Mintage	F	VF	XF	Unc	BU
1984	2,032	Value: 225				

KM# 139 1000 LEVA **Weight:** 16.8800 g. **Composition:** 0.9000 Gold .4885 oz. AGW **Subject:** 1300th Anniversary of Nationhood **Reverse:** Mother and child in front of radiant sun

Date	Mintage	F	VF	XF	Unc	BU
1981 Proof	2,000	Value: 385				

REPUBLIC

STANDARD COINAGE

KM# 199 10 STOTINKI **Composition:** Nickel-Brass **Note:** Ancient lion sculpture.

Date	F	VF	XF	Unc	BU
1992	—	—	—	0.25	—

KM# 200 20 STOTINKI **Composition:** Nickel-Brass **Note:** Ancient lion sculpture.

Date	F	VF	XF	Unc	BU
1992	—	—	—	0.35	—

KM# 201 50 STOTINKI **Composition:** Nickel-Brass **Note:** Ancient lion sculpture.

Date	F	VF	XF	Unc	BU
1992	—	—	—	0.50	—

KM# 202 LEV **Composition:** Nickel-Brass **Note:** Madara horseman

Date	F	VF	XF	Unc	BU
1992	—	—	—	0.75	—

KM# 254 LEV **Weight:** 7.0300 g. **Composition:** Bi-Metallic **Subject:** St. Rilski **Obverse:** Standing Saint **Reverse:** Denomination **Edge:** Reeded and plain sections **Size:** 24.3 mm.

Date	F	VF	XF	Unc	BU
2002	—	—	—	3.00	—

KM# 203 2 LEVA **Composition:** Nickel-Brass **Note:** Madara horseman

Date	F	VF	XF	Unc	BU
1992	—	—	—	1.25	—

KM# 204 5 LEVA **Composition:** Nickel-Brass **Note:** Madara horseman

Date	F	VF	XF	Unc	BU
1992	—	—	—	1.75	—

KM# 205 10 LEVA **Composition:** Copper-Nickel **Note:** Madara horseman

Date	F	VF	XF	Unc	BU
1992	—	—	—	2.50	—

KM# 224 10 LEVA **Composition:** Brass **Note:** Reduced size and metal change.

Date	F	VF	XF	Unc	BU
1997	—	—	—	1.25	—

KM# 248 10 LEVA **Weight:** 23.3300 g. **Composition:** 0.9250 Silver 0.6938 oz. ASW **Subject:** Todor Burmow **Obverse:** National arms **Reverse:** Portrait **Edge:** Plain **Size:** 38.5 mm.

Date	F	VF	XF	Unc	BU
1999 Proof	—	Value: 35.00			

KM# 249 10 LEVA **Weight:** 23.3300 g. **Composition:** 0.9250 Silver 0.6938 oz. ASW **Subject:** Euro Integration **Obverse:** National arms **Reverse:** Bulgarian National Bank building **Edge:** Plain **Size:** 38.5 mm.

Date	F	VF	XF	Unc	BU
1999 Proof	—	Value: 35.00			

KM# 250 10 LEVA **Weight:** 23.3300 g. **Composition:** 0.9250 Silver 0.6938 oz. ASW **Subject:** Summer Olympic Games **Obverse:** National arms **Reverse:** High Jumper **Edge:** Plain **Size:** 38.5 mm.

Date	F	VF	XF	Unc	BU
1999 Proof	—	Value: 35.00			

KM# 251 10 LEVA **Weight:** 23.3300 g. **Composition:** 0.9250 Silver 0.6938 oz. ASW **Subject:** Summer Olympics **Obverse:** National arms **Reverse:** Weight Lifter **Edge:** Plain **Size:** 38.5 mm.

Date	F	VF	XF	Unc	BU
2000 Proof	—	Value: 35.00			

KM# 252 10 LEVA **Weight:** 23.3300 g. **Composition:** 0.9250 Silver 0.6938 oz. ASW **Subject:** Christianity **Obverse:** National arms **Reverse:** Church Patriarch **Edge:** Plain **Size:** 38.5 mm.

Date	F	VF	XF	Unc	BU
2000 Proof	—	Value: 40.00			

KM# 253 10 LEVA **Weight:** 23.3300 g. **Composition:** 0.9250 Silver 0.6938 oz. ASW **Subject:** Bulgarian Association with the European Union **Obverse:** National Bank arms **Reverse:** Bulgarian coin design of the Middle Ages **Edge:** Plain **Size:** 38.5 mm.

Date	Mintage	F	VF	XF	Unc	BU
2000 Proof	20,000	Value: 40.00				

KM# 247 10 LEVA Weight: 23.3300 g. **Composition:** 0.9250 Silver 0.6938 oz. ASW **Subject:** Olympics **Obverse:** National arms **Reverse:** Ski jumper **Edge:** Plain with serial number **Size:** 38.5 mm.

Date	Mintage	F	VF	XF	Unc	BU
2001 Proof	25,000	Value: 40.00				

KM# 228 20 LEVA Composition: Brass **Obverse:** Madara horseman **Reverse:** Denomination

Date	F	VF	XF	Unc	BU
1997	—	—	—	1.50	—

KM# 198 50 LEVA Weight: 10.0700 g. **Composition:** 0.9250 Silver .2995 oz. ASW **Series:** Olympics **Reverse:** Downhill skier

Date	Mintage	F	VF	XF	Unc	BU
1992 Proof	52,390	Value: 11.50				

KM# 213 50 LEVA Composition: Copper-Nickel **Subject:** Centennial of Olympics in Bulgaria **Reverse:** Gymnasts

Date	Mintage	F	VF	XF	Unc	BU
1994 Proof	19,210	Value: 5.00				

KM# 225 50 LEVA Composition: Brass **Obverse:** Madara horseman **Reverse:** Denomination

Date	F	VF	XF	Unc	BU
1997	—	—	—	1.75	—

KM# 212 100 LEVA Weight: 23.2300 g. **Composition:** 0.9250 Silver .6908 oz. ASW **Reverse:** Old Ship Radetsky

Date	Mintage	F	VF	XF	Unc	BU
1992 Proof	28,765	Value: 25.00				

KM# 226 100 LEVA Weight: 23.2300 g. **Composition:** 0.9250 Silver .6908 oz. ASW **Obverse:** Denomination **Reverse:** Eagle descending on prey

Date	Mintage	F	VF	XF	Unc	BU
1992 Proof	27,651	Value: 30.00				

KM# 209 100 LEVA Weight: 23.3300 g. **Composition:** 0.9250 Silver .6939 oz. ASW **Series:** 1994 Olympics **Reverse:** Bobsled

Date	Mintage	F	VF	XF	Unc	BU
1993 Proof	33,690	Value: 22.50				

KM# 210 100 LEVA Weight: 23.3300 g. **Composition:** 0.9250 Silver .6939 oz. ASW **Subject:** 1994 World Cup Soccer

Date	Mintage	F	VF	XF	Unc	BU
1993 Proof	27,840	Value: 28.50				

KM# 227 100 LEVA Weight: 23.3300 g. **Composition:** 0.9250 Silver .6939 oz. ASW **Obverse:** Denomination **Reverse:** Ibex

Date	Mintage	F	VF	XF	Unc	BU
1993 Proof	20,000	Value: 30.00				

KM# 231 100 LEVA Weight: 23.3300 g. **Composition:** 0.9250 Silver .6939 oz. ASW **Obverse:** Denomination **Reverse:** Parliament building

Date	Mintage	F	VF	XF	Unc	BU
1993 Proof	15,000	Value: 30.00				

KM# 206 500 LEVA Weight: 33.6250 g. **Composition:** 0.9250 Silver 1.0000 oz. ASW **Subject:** European Community - St. Theodor Stratilat **Obverse:** ECU monogram and date in circle of stars

Date	Mintage	F	VF	XF	Unc	BU
1993 Proof	51,031	Value: 28.50				

KM# 211 500 LEVA Weight: 23.0000 g. **Composition:** 0.9250 Silver .6840 oz. ASW **Subject:** World Cup Soccer

Date	Mintage	F	VF	XF	Unc	BU
1994 Proof	24,351	Value: 32.50				

KM# 219 500 LEVA Weight: 10.0000 g. **Composition:** 0.9250 Silver .2974 oz. ASW **Subject:** Soccer **Obverse:** Denomination **Reverse:** Two soccer players

Date	Mintage	F	VF	XF	Unc	BU
1996 Proof	60,000	Value: 25.00				

KM# 229 500 LEVA Composition: Copper-Nickel-Zinc **Subject:** NATO **Obverse:** Denomination **Reverse:** City arms and NATO flag

Date	Mintage	F	VF	XF	Unc	BU
1997	30,000	—	—	—	5.00	—

KM# 223 500 LEVA Weight: 10.0000 g. **Composition:** 0.9250 Silver 0.2974 oz. ASW **Subject:** National Art Academy **Obverse:** Denomination within a wreath **Reverse:** Academy on paint palette **Edge:** Plain **Size:** 30 mm.

Date	F	VF	XF	Unc	BU
1996 Proof	—	Value: 50.00			

KM# 214 1000 LEVA **Weight:** 23.3300 g. **Composition:** 0.9250 Silver .6939 oz. ASW **Series:** 50 Years - F.A.O. **Reverse:** Wheat and globe

Date	Mintage	F	VF	XF	Unc	BU
1995 Proof	12,000	Value: 32.50				

KM# 220 1000 LEVA **Weight:** 23.3300 g. **Composition:** 0.9250 Silver .6939 oz. ASW **Obverse:** Denomination **Reverse:** Sailing Ship Kaliakra

Date	Mintage	F	VF	XF	Unc	BU
1996 Proof	23,052	Value: 35.00				

KM# 233 1000 LEVA **Weight:** 23.3300 g. **Composition:** 0.9250 Silver .6938 oz. ASW **Subject:** World Cup Soccer - France 1998 **Obverse:** Denomination **Reverse:** Three soccer players

Date	Mintage	F	VF	XF	Unc	BU
1997 Proof	22,606	Value: 35.00				

KM# 215 1000 LEVA **Weight:** 23.3300 g. **Composition:** 0.9250 Silver .6939 oz. ASW **Subject:** 100 Years of Olympic Games **Reverse:** Equestrian

Date	Mintage	F	VF	XF	Unc	BU
1995 Proof	28,713	Value: 30.00				

KM# 221 1000 LEVA **Weight:** 23.3300 g. **Composition:** 0.9250 Silver .6939 oz. ASW **Series:** Olympics **Obverse:** Denomination **Reverse:** Speed skater

Date	Mintage	F	VF	XF	Unc	BU
1996 Proof	22,602	Value: 30.00				

KM# 239 1000 LEVA **Composition:** Copper-Nickel-Zinc **Subject:** Bulgarian Telegraphic Agency Centennial **Obverse:** Crowned arms **Reverse:** World map and logo

Date	Mintage	F	VF	XF	Unc	BU
1998 Proof	—	Value: 5.50				

KM# 207 5000 LEVA **Weight:** 8.6400 g. **Composition:** 0.9000 Gold .2500 oz. AGW **Subject:** European Community - Slavonic Alphabet

Date	Mintage	F	VF	XF	Unc	BU
1993 Proof	Est. 2,500	Value: 200				

KM# 216 1000 LEVA **Weight:** 23.3300 g. **Composition:** 0.9250 Silver .6939 oz. ASW **Subject:** 110 Years - Union of Eastern Rumelia with the Bulgarian principality

Date	Mintage	F	VF	XF	Unc	BU
1995 Proof	15,000	Value: 32.50				

KM# 222 1000 LEVA **Weight:** 33.6250 g. **Composition:** 0.9250 Silver 1.0000 oz. ASW **Subject:** St. Ivan of Rila **Obverse:** ECU monogram **Reverse:** Standing saint, church, and denomination

Date	Mintage	F	VF	XF	Unc	BU
1996 Proof	42,445	Value: 32.50				

KM# 243 5000 LEVA **Weight:** 10.0000 g. **Composition:** 0.9250 Silver .2974 oz. ASW **Obverse:** National arms **Reverse:** Building above "EURO"

Date	F	VF	XF	Unc	BU
1998 Proof	—	Value: 18.50			

KM# 217 1000 LEVA **Weight:** 33.6250 g. **Composition:** 0.9250 Silver 1.0000 oz. ASW **Subject:** Rozhen Peak Astronomical Observatory

Date	Mintage	F	VF	XF	Unc	BU
1995 Proof	32,796	Value: 32.50				

KM# 232 1000 LEVA **Weight:** 23.3300 g. **Composition:** 0.9250 Silver .6938 oz. ASW **Subject:** UNICEF **Obverse:** Denomination **Reverse:** Singing child, UNICEF logo

Date	Mintage	F	VF	XF	Unc	BU
1997 Proof	6,001	Value: 30.00				

KM# 208 10000 LEVA **Weight:** 15.5670 g. **Composition:** 0.9990 Platinum .4999 oz. APW **Subject:** European Community - Desislava **Obverse:** Similar to 5000 Leva, KM#207

Date	Mintage	F	VF	XF	Unc	BU
1993 Proof	Est. 2,500	Value: 450				

KM# 218 10000 LEVA **Weight:** 8.6400 g. **Composition:** 0.9000 Gold .2500 oz. AGW **Reverse:** St. Alexander Nevski Cathedral

Date	Mintage	F	VF	XF	Unc	BU
1994 Proof	30,000	Value: 200				

KM# 234 10000 LEVA **Weight:** 23.3300 g. **Composition:** 0.9250 Silver .6938 oz. ASW **Subject:** 120th Anniversary of Liberation **Obverse:** National arms **Reverse:** Decorated soldier wtih flag

Date	Mintage	F	VF	XF	Unc	BU
1998 Proof	15,000	Value: 40.00				

KM# 235 10000 LEVA **Weight:** 23.3300 g. **Composition:** 0.9250 Silver .6938 oz. ASW **Subject:** United Europe **Obverse:** Rider of Madara over dead lion **Reverse:** Ancient cup and map

Date	Mintage	F	VF	XF	Unc	BU
1998 Proof	18,152	Value: 40.00				

KM# 236 20000 LEVA **Weight:** 1.5552 g. **Composition:** 0.9990 Gold .0500 oz. AGW **Subject:** Czar Ivan Alexander **Obverse:** Stylized lion **Reverse:** Four human figure sculptures

Date	F	VF	XF	Unc	BU
1998 Proof	—	Value: 75.00			

REFORM COINAGE

KM# 237 STOTINKA **Composition:** Brass **Obverse:** Madara horseman **Reverse:** Denomination

Date	F	VF	XF	Unc	BU
1999	—	—	—	0.25	—
2000	—	—	—	0.25	—

KM# 238 2 STOTINKI **Composition:** Brass **Obverse:** Madara horseman **Reverse:** Denomination

Date	F	VF	XF	Unc	BU
1999	—	—	—	0.35	—
2000	—	—	—	0.35	—

KM# A239 5 STOTINKI **Composition:** Brass **Obverse:** Madara horseman **Reverse:** Denomination

Date	F	VF	XF	Unc	BU
1999	—	—	—	0.50	—
2000	—	—	—	0.50	—

KM# 240 10 STOTINKI **Composition:** Copper-Nickel **Obverse:** Madara horseman **Reverse:** Denomination

Date	F	VF	XF	Unc	BU
1999	—	—	—	0.65	—

KM# 241 20 STOTINKI **Composition:** Copper-Nickel **Obverse:** Madara horseman **Reverse:** Denomination

Date	F	VF	XF	Unc	BU
1999	—	—	—	0.85	—

KM# 242 50 STOTINKI **Composition:** Copper-Nickel **Obverse:** Madara horseman **Reverse:** Denomination

Date	F	VF	XF	Unc	BU
1999	—	—	—	1.25	—

KM# 245 10 LEVA **Weight:** 23.3500 g. **Composition:** 0.9250 Silver 0.6944 oz. ASW **Obverse:** National arms **Reverse:** Mediterranean Monk Seal **Edge:** Plain **Size:** 38.5 mm.

Date	F	VF	XF	Unc	BU
1999 Proof	—	—	—	30.00	—

KM# 246 10 LEVA **Weight:** 23.6000 g. **Composition:** 0.9250 Silver 0.7019 oz. ASW **Subject:** Higher Education **Obverse:** National arms **Reverse:** Graduate before building **Edge:** Plain **Size:** 38.5 mm.

Date	F	VF	XF	Unc	BU
2001 Proof	—	Value: 40.00			

ESSAIS

KM#	Date	Mintage	Identification	Mkt Val
E5	1925(a)	—	2 Leva. Copper-Nickel.	150

PIEFORTS

KM#	Date	Mintage	Identification	Mkt Val
P3	1979	2,000	10 Leva. KM#104	75.00

TRIAL STRIKES

KM#	Date	Mintage	Identification	Mkt Val
TS1	1901	—	2 Stotinki. Bronze. Uniface.	—
TS2	1901	—	2 Stotinki. Bronze. Uniface.	—

PATTERNS

Including off metal strikes

KM#	Date	Mintage	Identification	Mkt Val
PnA6	1923H	—	Lev. Aluminum. Similar to KM#35	—
Pn6	1923H	—	Lev. Aluminum-Bronze.	—
PnA8	1923H	—	2 Leva. Aluminum. Similar to KM#36.	—
Pn8	1923H	—	2 Leva. Aluminum-Bronze.	—
Pn7	1923H	—	2 Leva. Aluminum.	275
Pn9	1928	2	5 Leva.	—
Pn10	1930	2	5 Leva.	—
Pn11	1930	2	10 Leva.	—
Pn12	1950	—	5 Leva.	—
Pn13	1984	1,500	10 Leva. Copper-Nickel. Reeded edge. PROBA I; KM#146.	35.00
Pn14	1984	250	10 Leva. 0.6400 Silver. Plain edge. PROBA II; KM#146a.	100
Pn15	1984	50	10 Leva. 0.9250 Silver. Lettered edge. SPECIMEN; KM#146a.	200
Pn16	1984	2,000	10 Leva. Copper-Nickel. Reeded edge. PROBA I; KM#147	55.00
Pn17	1984	300	10 Leva. 0.6400 Silver. Plain edge. PROBA II; KM#147a	150
Pn18	1984	50	10 Leva. 0.9250 Silver. Lettered edge. SPECIMEN; KM#147a	265

MINT SETS

KM#	Date	Mintage	Identification	Issue Price	Mkt Val
MS1	1981 (3)	—	KM#118, 120, 131	—	20.00

PROOF SETS

KM#	Date	Mintage	Identification	Issue Price	Mkt Val
PS1	1912 (2)	—	KM#33-34	—	5,500
PS2	1962/66 (9)	—	KM#58-64 (1962), 73 (1966)	—	—
PS3	1963 (2)	5,000	KM#65-66	—	27.50
PS5	1963/73 (8)	—	KM#65-66, 69-70, 78-79, 80-81 mixed date set, REPUBLIQUE DE BULGARIE	—	155
PS4	1964 (2)	10,000	KM#69-70	—	27.50
PS6	1979 (7)	2,000	KM#84-90	—	22.50
PS7	1980 (7)	2,000	KM#84-90	—	22.50

BURUNDI

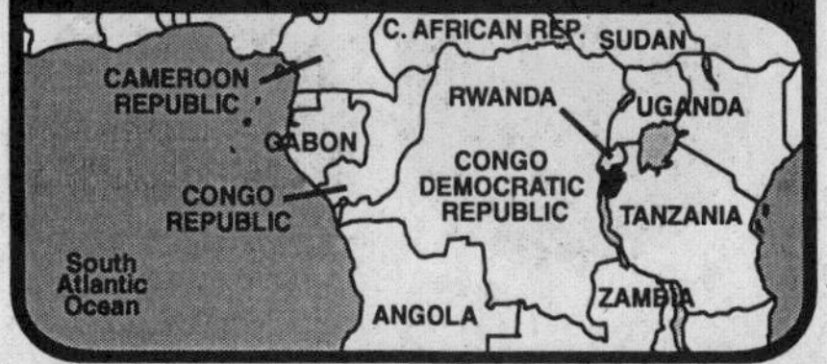

The Republic of Burundi, a landlocked country in central Africa, was a kingdom with a feudalistic society, caste system and Mwami (king) for more than 400 years before independence. It has an area of 10,740 sq. mi. (27,830 sq. km.) and a population of 6.3 million. Capital: Bujumbura. Plagued by poor soil, irregular rainfall and a single-crop economy, coffee, Burundi is barely able to feed itself. Coffee and tea are exported.

Although the area was visited by European explorers and missionaries in the latter half of the 19th century, it wasn't until the 1890s that it, together with Rwanda, fell under European domination as part of German East Africa. Following World War I, the territory was mandated to Belgium by the League of Nations and administered with the Belgian Congo. After World War II it became a U.N. Trust Territory. Limited self-government was established by U.N.-supervised elections in 1961. Burundi gained independence as a kingdom under Mwami Mwambutsa IV on July 1, 1962. The republic was established by military coup in 1966.

NOTE: For earlier coinage see Belgian Congo, and Rwanda and Burundi. For previously listed coinage dated 1966, coins of Mwambutsa IV and Ntare V, refer to *UNUSUAL WORLD COINS*, 3rd edition, Krause Publications, 1992.

RULERS
Mwambutsa IV, 1962-1966
Ntare V, 1966

MINT MARKS
PM - Pobjoy Mint
(b) - Privy Marks, Brussels

MONETARY SYSTEM
100 Centimes = 1 Franc

KINGDOM

STANDARD COINAGE

KM# 6 FRANC **Composition:** Brass

Date	Mintage	F	VF	XF	Unc	BU
1965	10,000,000	—	0.75	1.50	3.00	—

KM# 1 5 FRANCS **Composition:** Copper Nickel **Subject:** Burundi Independence

Date	F	VF	XF	Unc	BU
1962	—	—	—	—	—
1962 Proof	—	—	—	—	—

KM# 1a 5 FRANCS **Weight:** 24.1100 g. **Composition:** 0.9000 Silver .6976 oz. ASW **Subject:** Burundi Independence

Date	F	VF	XF	Unc	BU
1962 Proof	—	—	—	—	—

KM# 2 10 FRANCS **Weight:** 3.2000 g. **Composition:** 0.9000 Gold .0926 oz. AGW **Subject:** Burundi Independence

Date	Mintage	F	VF	XF	Unc	BU
1962 Proof	7,500	Value: 65.00				

KM# 7 10 FRANCS **Weight:** 3.0000 g. **Composition:** 0.9000 Gold .0868 oz. AGW **Subject:** 50th Anniversary - Reign of Mwambutsa IV

Date	Mintage	F	VF	XF	Unc	BU
ND(1965)	—	—	—	—	50.00	—
ND(1965) Proof	5,000	Value: 65.00				

KM# 3 25 FRANCS **Weight:** 8.0000 g. **Composition:** 0.9000 Gold .2315 oz. AGW **Subject:** Burundi Independence

Date	Mintage	F	VF	XF	Unc	BU
1962 Proof	15,000	Value: 125				

KM# 8 25 FRANCS **Weight:** 7.5000 g. **Composition:** 0.9000 Gold .217 oz. AGW **Subject:** 50th Anniversary - Reign of Mwambutsa IV

Date	Mintage	F	VF	XF	Unc	BU
ND(1965)	—	—	—	—	120	—
ND(1965) Proof	5,000	Value: 135				

KM# 4 50 FRANCS **Weight:** 16.0000 g. **Composition:** 0.9000 Gold .4630 oz. AGW **Subject:** Burundi Independence

Date	Mintage	F	VF	XF	Unc	BU
1962 Proof	3,500	Value: 320				

KM# 9 50 FRANCS **Weight:** 15.0000 g. **Composition:** 0.9000 Gold .4340 oz. AGW **Subject:** 50th Anniversary - Reign of Mwambutsa IV

Date	Mintage	F	VF	XF	Unc	BU
ND(1965)	—	—	—	—	215	—
ND(1965) Proof	5,000	Value: 285				

KM# 5 100 FRANCS **Weight:** 32.0000 g. **Composition:** 0.9000 Gold .9260 oz. AGW **Subject:** Burundi Independence

Date	Mintage	F	VF	XF	Unc	BU
1962 Proof	2,500	Value: 580				

KM# 10 100 FRANCS **Weight:** 30.0000 g. **Composition:** 0.9000 Gold .8681 oz. AGW **Subject:** 50th Anniversary - Reign of Mwambutsa IV

Date	Mintage	F	VF	XF	Unc	BU
ND(1965)	—	—	—	—	450	—
ND(1965) Proof	5,000	Value: 520				

REPUBLIC
1966-

STANDARD COINAGE

KM# 18 FRANC **Composition:** Aluminum

Date	Mintage	F	VF	XF	Unc	BU
1970	10,000,000	2.00	4.50	7.50	17.50	—

KM# 19 FRANC **Composition:** Aluminum

Date	Mintage	F	VF	XF	Unc	BU
1976	5,000,000	—	0.30	0.75	1.75	—
1980	—	—	0.20	0.65	1.75	—
1990PM	—	—	0.15	0.50	1.50	—
1993PM	—	—	0.15	0.50	1.50	—

KM# 16 5 FRANCS **Composition:** Aluminum

Date	Mintage	F	VF	XF	Unc	BU
1968(b)	2,000,000	—	0.25	0.85	2.00	—
1969(b)	2,000,000	—	0.25	0.85	2.00	—
1971(b)	2,000,000	—	0.25	0.85	2.00	—

KM# 20 5 FRANCS **Composition:** Aluminum

Date	Mintage	F	VF	XF	Unc	BU
1976	2,000,000	—	0.25	0.65	1.75	—
1980	—	—	0.25	0.65	1.75	—

KM# 11 10 FRANCS **Weight:** 3.2000 g. **Composition:** 0.9000 Gold .0926 oz. AGW **Subject:** First Anniversary of Republic

Date	F	VF	XF	Unc	BU
1967 Proof	—	Value: 85.00			

KM# 17 10 FRANCS **Composition:** Copper Nickel **Series:** F.A.O. **Subject:** First Anniversary of Republic

Date	Mintage	F	VF	XF	Unc	BU
1968	2,000,000	—	0.75	1.50	3.50	—
1971	2,000,000	—	0.75	1.50	3.50	—

KM# 12 20 FRANCS **Weight:** 6.4000 g. **Composition:** 0.9000 Gold .1852 oz. AGW **Subject:** First Anniversary of Republic

Date	F	VF	XF	Unc	BU
ND(1967) Proof	—	Value: 115			

KM# 13 25 FRANCS **Weight:** 8.0000 g. **Composition:** 0.9000 Gold .2315 oz. AGW **Subject:** First Anniversary of Republic

Date	F	VF	XF	Unc	BU
ND(1967) Proof	—	Value: 135			

KM# 14 50 FRANCS **Weight:** 16.0000 g. **Composition:** 0.9000 Gold .4630 oz. AGW **Subject:** First Anniversary of Republic

Date	F	VF	XF	Unc	BU
ND(1967) Proof	—	Value: 285			

KM# 15 100 FRANCS **Weight:** 32.0000 g. **Composition:** 0.9000 Gold .9261 oz. AGW **Subject:** First Anniversary of Republic

Date	F	VF	XF	Unc	BU
ND(1967) Proof	—	Value: 585			

PROOF SETS

KM#	Date	Mintage	Identification	Issue Price	Mkt Val
PS1	1962 (4)	2,500	KM2-5	—	1,100
PS2	1965 (4)	5,000	KM7-10	—	1,100
PS3	1967 (5)	—	KM11-15	—	1,200

CAMBODIA

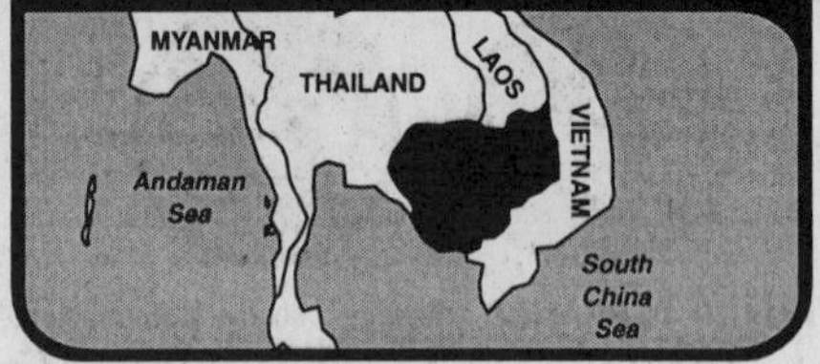

The State of Cambodia, formerly Democratic Kampuchea and the Khmer Republic, a land of paddy fields and forest-clad hills located on the Indo-Chinese peninsula, fronting on the Gulf of Thailand, has an area of 70,238 sq. mi. (181,040 sq. km.) and a population of *11.21 million. Capital: Phnom Penh. Agriculture is the basis of the economy, with rice the chief crop. Native industries include cattle breeding, weaving and rice milling. Rubber, cattle, corn, and timber are exported.

The region was the nucleus of the Khmer empire which flourished from the 5th to the 12th century and attained an excellence in art and architecture still evident in the magnificent ruins at Angkor. The Khmer empire once ruled over much of Southeast Asia, but began to decline in the 13th century as the Thai and Vietnamese invaded the region and attached its territories. At the request of the Cambodian king, a French protectorate attached to Cochin-China was established over the country in 1863, saving it from dissolution, and in 1885, Cambodia was included in the French Union of Indo-China.

France established a constitutional monarchy for Cambodia within the French Union in 1949. The 1954 Geneva Convention resulted in full independence for the Kingdom of Cambodia. King Sihanouk abdicated to his father and won the office of Prime Minister.

Prince Sihanouk was toppled by a bloodless coup led by Lon Nol in March of 1970. Sihanouk moved to Peking to head a government-in-exile. On Oct. 9, 1970, Cambodia became the Khmer Republic, and Lon Nol its President. The government of Lon Nol was in turn toppled, April 17, 1975, by the Khmer Rouge insurgents who took control of the government and renamed the country Democratic Kampuchea.

The Khmer Rouge completely eliminated the economy and created a state without money, exchange or barter while exterminating about 2 million Cambodians. These atrocities were finally halted at the beginning of 1979 when the Vietnamese regulars and Cambodian rebels launched an offensive that drove the Khmer Rouge out of Phnom Penh and the country acquired another new title - The Peoples Republic of Kampuchea.

In 1993 Prince Norodom Sihanouk returned to Kampuchea to lead the Supreme National Council.

RULERS

Kings of Cambodia

Norodom I, 1835-1904
Sisowath, 1904-1927
Sisowath Monivong, 1927-1941
Norodom Sihanouk, 1941-1955
Norodom Suramarit, 1955-1960
Heng Samrin, 1979-1985
Hun Sen, 1985-1991
Norodom Sihanouk, 1991-1993
Chairman, Supreme National Council
King, 1993-

MINT MARKS

(a) - Paris, privy marks only
(k) - Key, Havana, Cuba

MONETARY SYSTEM

(Commencing 1860)
100 Centimes = 1 Franc

KINGDOM

TOKEN COINAGE

KM# Tn1 10 CENTIMES **Composition:** Brass **Issuer:** Panom Penh Royal Palace **Obv. Legend:** SOMDACH PREA NORODOM... **Size:** 26 mm.

Date	F	VF	XF	Unc	BU
ND(1875-1904)	—	125	—	175	—

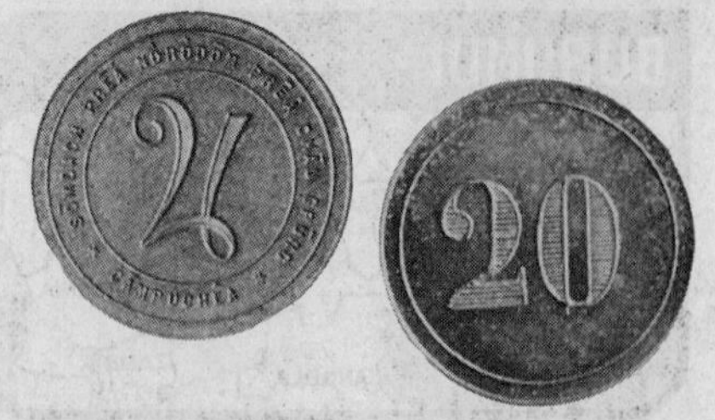

KM# Tn3 15 CENTIMES **Composition:** Brass **Issuer:** Panom Penh Royal Palace **Obv. Legend:** SOMDACH PREA NORODOM... **Size:** 26 mm.

Date	F	VF	XF	Unc	BU
ND(1875-1904)	—	175	—	225	—
ND(1875-1904)	—	175	—	225	—

KM# Tn4 25 CENTIMES **Composition:** Brass **Issuer:** Panom Penh Royal Palace **Obv. Legend:** SOMDACH PREA NORODOM... **Size:** 26 mm.

Date	F	VF	XF	Unc	BU
ND(1875-1904)	—	200	—	250	—

INDEPENDENT KINGDOM

DECIMAL COINAGE

KM# 51 10 CENTIMES **Composition:** Aluminum

Date	Mintage	F	VF	XF	Unc	BU
1953(a)	4,000,000	0.25	0.45	0.85	2.00	3.00

KM# 52 20 CENTIMES **Composition:** Aluminum

Date	Mintage	F	VF	XF	Unc	BU
1953(a)	3,000,000	0.25	0.65	1.50	3.00	4.50

KM# 55 20 CENTIMES **Composition:** Aluminum

Date	Mintage	F	VF	XF	Unc	BU
1959(a)	1,004,000	0.15	0.25	0.60	1.00	1.50

KM# 53 50 CENTIMES **Composition:** Aluminum

Date	Mintage	F	VF	XF	Unc	BU
1953(a)	3,170,000	0.45	0.85	2.00	4.00	6.00

KM# 54 5 SEN **Composition:** Aluminum

Date	Mintage	F	VF	XF	Unc	BU
1959(a)	1,000,000	0.10	0.20	0.35	0.65	1.00

KM# 56 50 SEN **Composition:** Aluminum

Date	Mintage	F	VF	XF	Unc	BU
1959(a)	3,399,000	0.20	0.35	0.75	1.50	2.50

KHMER REPUBLIC
1970 - 1975
DECIMAL COINAGE

KM# 59 RIEL **Composition:** Copper-Nickel **Series:** F.A.O.

Date	Mintage	F	VF	XF	Unc	BU
1970	5,000,000	—	—	7.50	16.50	22.50

Note: According to the Royal Mint of Great Britain, this coin was minted at the Llantrissant Branch Mint in 1972 but dated 1969. According to the FAO, the coin was to have been dated 1971, but was "not minted" due to the fall of the Cambodian government in 1970. However, this coin was released in limited numbers in 1983. The photograph of the coin, supplied by the FAO, is dated 1970. This type is currently available from many sources in the numismatic market

KM# 60 5000 RIELS **Weight:** 19.0100 g. **Composition:** 0.9250 Silver .5654 oz. ASW **Obverse:** Temple of Angkor Wat

Date	Mintage	F	VF	XF	Unc	BU
1974	500	—	—	—	65.00	—
1974 Proof	800	Value: 65.00				

KM# 61 5000 RIELS **Weight:** 19.0100 g. **Composition:** 0.9250 Silver .5654 oz. ASW **Obverse:** Cambodian dancers **Reverse:** Similar to KM#60.

Date	Mintage	F	VF	XF	Unc	BU
1974	500	—	—	—	85.00	—
1974 Proof	800	Value: 85.00				

KM# 62 10000 RIELS **Weight:** 38.0300 g. **Composition:** 0.9250 Silver 1.1310 oz. ASW **Obverse:** Bust of President Lon Nol left **Reverse:** Similar to 5,000 Riels, KM#60

Date	Mintage	F	VF	XF	Unc	BU
1974	500	—	—	—	110	—
1974 Proof	800	Value: 110				

KM# 63 10000 RIELS **Weight:** 38.0300 g. **Composition:** 0.9250 Silver 1.1310 oz. ASW **Obverse:** Celestial dancer **Reverse:** Similar to 5,000 Riels, KM#60

Date	Mintage	F	VF	XF	Unc	BU
1974	500	—	—	—	140	—
1974 Proof	800	Value: 140				

KM# 64 50000 RIELS **Weight:** 6.7100 g. **Composition:** 0.9000 Gold .1941 oz. AGW **Obverse:** Cambodian dancers

Date	Mintage	F	VF	XF	Unc	BU
1974	3,250	—	—	—	135	—
1974 Proof	2,300	Value: 190				

KM# 65 50000 RIELS **Weight:** 6.7100 g. **Composition:** 0.9000 Gold .1941 oz. AGW **Obverse:** Celestial dancer

Date	Mintage	F	VF	XF	Unc	BU
1974	450	—	—	—	245	—
1974 Proof	300	Value: 350				

KM# 66 100000 RIELS **Weight:** 19.1700 g. **Composition:** 0.9000 Gold .5547 oz. AGW **Obverse:** Bust of Presdient Lon Nol left **Reverse:** Similar to 50,000 Riels, KM#65

Date	Mintage	F	VF	XF	Unc	BU
1974	250	—	—	—	425	—
1974 Proof	100	Value: 685				

PEOPLE'S REPUBLIC OF KAMPUCHEA
1979 - 1990
DECIMAL COINAGE

KM# 69 5 SEN **Composition:** Aluminum

Date	F	VF	XF	Unc	BU
1979	—	0.60	1.25	3.00	—

KM# 71 4 RIELS **Composition:** Copper-Nickel **Subject:** Cambodian Transportation **Reverse:** Old sailing ship

Date	Mintage	F	VF	XF	Unc	BU
1988(k)	1,500	—	—	—	12.50	—

KM# 75 4 RIELS **Composition:** Copper **Subject:** 700th Anniversary of Swiss Unity

Date	Mintage	F	VF	XF	Unc	BU
ND(1988)	15,000	—	—	—	10.00	—

KM# 91 4 RIELS **Composition:** Copper **Reverse:** Angkot Wat Temples

Date	F	VF	XF	Unc	BU
ND(1988)	—	—	—	7.50	—

KM# 74 4 RIELS **Composition:** Copper-Nickel **Subject:** World Championship Soccer - Italy

Date	Mintage	F	VF	XF	Unc	BU
1989	2,000	—	—	—	7.00	—

KM# 90 4 RIELS **Composition:** Copper **Reverse:** Angkor Wat Temples

Date	F	VF	XF	Unc	BU
1989	—	—	—	8.50	—

KM# 70 20 RIELS **Weight:** 12.0600 g. **Composition:** 0.9990 Silver .3855 oz. ASW **Subject:** Cambodian Transportation **Reverse:** Old sailing ship

Date	Mintage	F	VF	XF	Unc	BU
1988(k)	3,000	—	—	—	30.00	—

KM# 72 20 RIELS **Weight:** 12.0600 g. **Composition:** 0.9990 Silver .3855 oz. ASW **Subject:** World Championship Soccer - Mexico

Date	Mintage	F	VF	XF	Unc	BU
1988	5,000	—	—	—	30.00	—

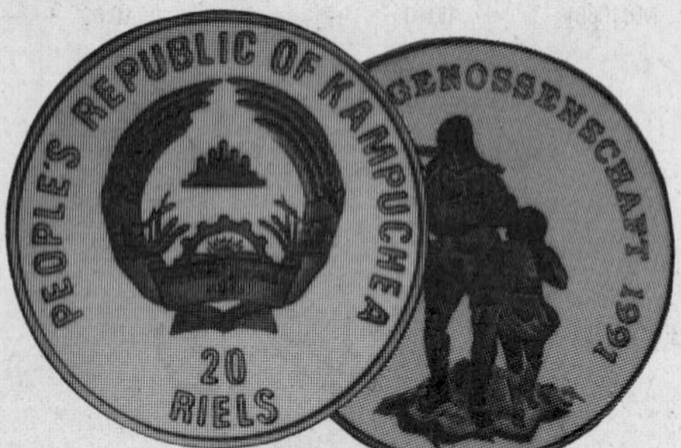

KM# 73 20 RIELS **Weight:** 16.0000 g. **Composition:** 0.9990 Silver .5145 oz. ASW **Subject:** 700th Anniversary of Swiss Unity - 1991

Date	Mintage	F	VF	XF	Unc	BU
ND Proof	2,000	Value: 45.00				

KM# 78 20 RIELS **Weight:** 12.0000 g. **Composition:** 0.9990 Silver .3855 oz. ASW **Subject:** European Soccer Championship - Germany

Date	Mintage	F	VF	XF	Unc	BU
1988(k)	5,000	—	—	—	40.00	—

KM# 76 20 RIELS **Weight:** 16.0000 g. **Composition:** 0.9990 Silver .5145 oz. ASW **Reverse:** Angkor Wat Temples

Date	Mintage	F	VF	XF	Unc	BU
1989 Proof	2,000	Value: 40.00				

KM# 79 20 RIELS **Weight:** 16.0000 g. **Composition:** 0.9990 Silver .5145 oz. ASW **Subject:** World Championship Soccer - Italy

Date	Mintage	F	VF	XF	Unc	BU
1989 Proof	10,000	Value: 28.00				

KM# 80 20 RIELS **Weight:** 16.0000 g. **Composition:** 0.9990 Silver .5145 oz. ASW **Subject:** Summer Olympics **Reverse:** Fencers

Date	Mintage	F	VF	XF	Unc	BU
1989 Proof	10,000	Value: 32.50				

KM# 81 20 RIELS **Weight:** 16.0000 g. **Composition:** 0.9990 Silver .5145 oz. ASW **Subject:** Winter Olympics **Reverse:** Skier

Date	Mintage	F	VF	XF	Unc	BU
1989 Proof	5,000	Value: 35.00				

KM# 77 40 RIELS **Weight:** 3.1500 g. **Composition:** 0.9990 Gold .1012 oz. AGW **Obverse:** Similar to KM#82. **Reverse:** Angkor Wat Temples

Date	Mintage	F	VF	XF	Unc	BU
1989	500	—	—	—	120	—

KM# 82 40 RIELS **Weight:** 3.1500 g. **Composition:** 0.9990 Gold .1012 oz. AGW **Reverse:** Folklore and dance

Date	Mintage	F	VF	XF	Unc	BU
1990	500	Value: 150				

STATE OF CAMBODIA

1990 - 1993

DECIMAL COINAGE

KM# 83 4 RIELS **Composition:** Nickel Plated Steel **Subject:** Olympics **Reverse:** Tennis

Date	Mintage	F	VF	XF	Unc	BU
1991	5,000	—	—	—	13.50	—

KM# 86 4 RIELS **Composition:** Copper-Nickel **Series:** Prehistoric Animals **Reverse:** Cryptocleidus

Date	F	VF	XF	Unc	BU
1993	—	—	—	25.00	—

KM# 89 4 RIELS **Composition:** Copper-Nickel **Series:** Prehistoric Animals **Reverse:** Anatosaurus

Date	F	VF	XF	Unc	BU
1994	—	—	—	25.00	—

KM# 84 20 RIELS **Weight:** 11.9600 g. **Composition:** 0.9990 Silver .3845 oz. ASW **Subject:** World Cup Soccer - 1994 **Reverse:** Player kicking ball

Date	Mintage	F	VF	XF	Unc	BU
1991	30,000	—	—	—	30.00	—

KM# 88 20 RIELS Weight: 11.9600 g. **Composition:** 0.9990 Silver .3845 oz. ASW **Subject:** World Cup Soccer - 1994 **Reverse:** 2 players kicking ball

Date	F	VF	XF	Unc	BU
1992 Proof	—	Value: 42.50			

KM# 87 20 RIELS Weight: 16.0600 g. **Composition:** 0.9990 Silver .5145 oz. ASW **Series:** Prehistoric Animals **Obverse:** Similar to KM#84. **Reverse:** Indricotherium

Date	F	VF	XF	Unc	BU
1993	—	Value: 40.00			

KM# 85 20 RIELS Weight: 19.9500 g. **Composition:** 0.9990 Silver .6408 oz. ASW **Subject:** Protection of Nature **Obverse:** Similar to KM#84 **Reverse:** Asian elephants

Date	F	VF	XF	Unc	BU
1993 Proof	—	Value: 50.00			

KM# 96 20 RIELS Weight: 16.1000 g. **Composition:** 0.9990 Silver .5171 oz. ASW **Series:** Prehistoric Animals **Obverse:** National flag **Reverse:** Nothosaurus at water's edge **Edge:** Plain

Date	F	VF	XF	Unc	BU
1994 Proof	—	Value: 50.00			

KINGDOM OF CAMBODIA

1993 -

DECIMAL COINAGE

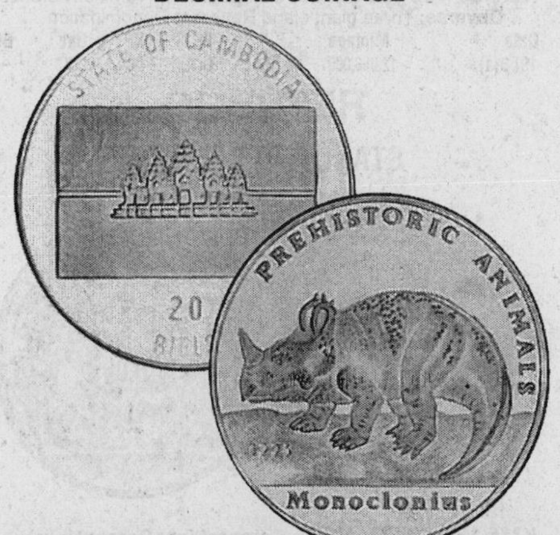

KM# 97 20 RIELS Weight: 16.1000 g. **Composition:** 0.9990 Silver 0.5171 oz. ASW **Subject:** Prehistoric Animals **Obverse:** National flag **Reverse:** Monoclonius **Edge:** Plain **Size:** 37.9 mm.

Date	F	VF	XF	Unc	BU
BE2539-1995 Proof	—	Value: 50.00			

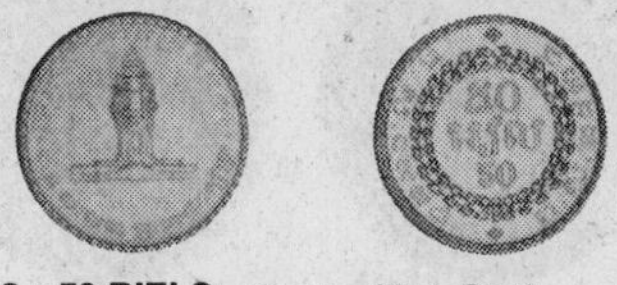

KM# 92 50 RIELS Composition: Steel

Date	F	VF	XF	Unc	BU
BE2538-1994	—	—	—	0.25	0.45

KM# 93 100 RIELS Composition: Steel **Obverse:** 3 towered building

Date	F	VF	XF	Unc	BU
BE2538-1994	—	—	—	0.50	0.85

KM# 94 200 RIELS Composition: Steel **Obverse:** 2 Ceremonial bowls

Date	F	VF	XF	Unc	BU
BE2538-1994	—	—	—	1.00	1.50

KM# 95 500 RIELS Ring Composition: Brass **Center Composition:** Steel **Obverse:** Royal emblem

Date	F	VF	XF	Unc	BU
BE2538-1994	—	—	—	4.00	6.00

KM# 98 500 RIELS Weight: 19.9200 g. **Composition:** Brass **Subject:** Angkor Wat **Obverse:** Arm-less statue of Jayavarman VII **Reverse:** View of Angkor Wat in center **Edge:** Reeded **Size:** 38.7 mm.

Date	Mintage	F	VF	XF	Unc	BU
2001	28,000	—	—	—	7.50	—

KM# 99 3000 RIELS Weight: 1.2441 g. **Composition:** 0.9999 Gold 0.04 oz. AGW **Subject:** Angkor Wat **Obverse:** Arm-less statue of Jayavarman VII **Reverse:** View of Angkor Wat in center **Edge:** Reeded **Size:** 13.92 mm.

Date	Mintage	F	VF	XF	Unc	BU
2001	28,000	—	—	—	45.00	—

KM# 100 3000 RIELS Weight: 20.0000 g. **Composition:** 0.9250 Silver 0.5948 oz. ASW **Subject:** Buddha **Obverse:** Arm-less statue of Jayavarman VII **Reverse:** Radiant Buddha next to a carved Buddha face **Edge:** Reeded **Size:** 38.7 mm.

Date	Mintage	F	VF	XF	Unc	BU
2001 Proof	10,000	Value: 45.00				

KM# 101 3000 RIELS Weight: 20.0000 g. **Composition:** 0.9250 Silver 0.5948 oz. ASW **Subject:** Apsara Dance **Obverse:** Armless statue of Jayavarman VII **Reverse:** Dancer next to multi-colored wall **Edge:** Reeded **Size:** 38.7 mm.

Date	Mintage	F	VF	XF	Unc	BU
2001 Proof	10,000	Value: 50.00				

KM# 102 10000 RIELS Weight: 31.1035 g. **Composition:** 0.9990 Silver .9990 oz. ASW**Center Weight:** 3.5000 g. **Center Composition:** 0.9999 Gold 0.1125 oz. AGW **Subject:** Angkor Wat **Obverse:** Armless statue of Jayavarman **Reverse:** Multicolor holographic view of Angkor Wat in center **Edge:** Reeded **Size:** 40.7 mm.

Date	Mintage	F	VF	XF	Unc	BU
2001 Proof	3,000	Value: 85.00				

ESSAIS

KM#	Date	Mintage	Identification	Issue Price	Mkt Val
E9	1953	1,200	10 Centimes.	—	20.00
E10	1953	1,200	20 Centimes.	—	22.00
E11	1953	1,200	50 Centimes.	—	25.00

PATTERNS

Including off metal strikes

KM#	Date	Mintage	Identification	Mkt Val
Pn15	1902	—	4 Francs. Silver. Palace at Phnom-Penh	250

PIEFORTS WITH ESSAI

Double thickness

Standard metals unless otherwise noted.

KM#	Date	Mintage	Identification	Issue Price	Mkt Val
PE9	1953	104	10 Centimes.	—	50.00
PE10	1953	104	20 Centimes.	—	65.00
PE11	1953	104	50 Centimes.	—	80.00

PIEFORTS

KM#	Date	Mintage	Identification	Mkt Val
P12	1989	110	20 Riels. 0.9990 Silver. KM80.	125
P13	1989	110	20 Riels. 0.9990 Silver. KM76.	125

MINT SETS

KM#	Date	Mintage	Identification	Issue Price	Mkt Val
MS1	1953 (3)	—	KM51,-53	—	10.00
MS2	1974 (7)	250	KM60-66	—	1,175
MS3	1974 (4)	500	KM60-63	—	365
MS4	BE2538 (1994) (4)	—	KM92-95 with 7 laminated banknotes	0.38	9.50

PROOF SETS

KM#	Date	Mintage	Identification	Issue Price	Mkt Val
PS1	1974 (7)	100	KM60-66	—	1,600
PS2	1974 (4)	800	KM60-63	—	365

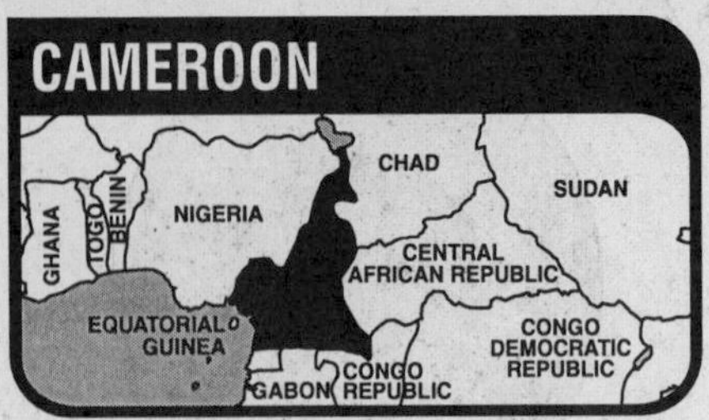

The Republic of Cameroon, located in west-central Africa on the Gulf of Guinea, has an area of 183,569 sq. mi. (475,445 sq. km.) and a population of *15.13 million. Capital: Yaounde. About 90 percent of the labor force is employed on the land; cash crops account for 80 percent of the country's export revenue. Cocoa, coffee, aluminum, cotton, rubber, and timber are exported.

European contact with what is now the United Republic of Cameroon began in the 16th century with the voyage of Portuguese navigator Fernando Po. The following three centuries saw continuous activity by Spanish, Dutch, and British traders and missionaries. The land was spared colonial rule until 1884, when treaties with tribal chiefs brought German domination. In 1919, the League of Nations divided the Cameroons between Great Britain and France, with the larger eastern area going to France. The French and British mandates were converted into United Nations trusteeships in 1946. French Cameroon became the independent Cameroon Republic on Jan. 1, 1960. The federation of East (French) and West (British) Cameroon was established in 1961 when the southern part of British Cameroon voted for reunification with the Cameroon Republic, and the northern part for union with Nigeria Cameroon joined the Commonwealth of Nations in November 1995.

Coins of French Equatorial Africa and of the monetary unions identified as the Equatorial African States and Central African States are also current in Cameroon.

MINT MARKS
(a) - Paris, privy marks only
SA - Pretoria, 1943

MONETARY SYSTEM
100 Centimes = 1 Franc

FRENCH MANDATE

STANDARD COINAGE

KM# 1 50 CENTIMES **Composition:** Aluminum-Bronze

Date	Mintage	F	VF	XF	Unc	BU
1924(a)	4,000,000	1.50	3.50	22.00	90.00	—
1925(a)	2,500,000	2.00	5.00	25.00	100	—
1926(a)	7,800,000	1.00	2.00	15.00	70.00	—

KM# 4 50 CENTIMES **Composition:** Bronze

Date	Mintage	F	VF	XF	Unc	BU
1943SA	4,000,000	2.00	3.50	7.00	18.00	—

KM# 6 50 CENTIMES **Composition:** Bronze **Obverse:** LIBRE added to legend

Date	Mintage	F	VF	XF	Unc	BU
1943SA	4,000,000	2.50	5.50	12.00	25.00	—

KM# 2 FRANC **Composition:** Aluminum-Bronze

Date	Mintage	F	VF	XF	Unc	BU
1924(a)	3,000,000	2.00	4.00	20.00	90.00	—
1925(a)	1,722,000	3.00	6.00	30.00	125	—
1926(a)	11,928,000	1.00	2.00	12.00	60.00	—

KM# 5 FRANC **Composition:** Bronze

Date	Mintage	F	VF	XF	Unc	BU
1943SA	3,000,000	2.50	4.50	17.50	40.00	—

KM# 7 FRANC **Composition:** Bronze **Obverse:** LIBRE added to legend

Date	Mintage	F	VF	XF	Unc	BU
1943SA	3,000,000	3.50	6.50	20.00	45.00	—

KM# 8 FRANC **Composition:** Aluminum

Date	Mintage	F	VF	XF	Unc	BU
1948(a)	8,000,000	0.15	0.35	0.85	1.75	—

KM# 3 2 FRANCS **Composition:** Aluminum-Bronze

Date	Mintage	F	VF	XF	Unc	BU
1924(a)	500,000	5.00	15.00	65.00	185	—
1925(a)	100,000	8.00	25.00	100	275	—

KM# 9 2 FRANCS **Composition:** Aluminum

Date	Mintage	F	VF	XF	Unc	BU
1948(a)	5,000,000	0.65	1.25	2.00	5.00	—

FRENCH EQUATORIAL AFRICA - CAMEROON

STANDARD COINAGE

KM# 24 5 FRANCS **Composition:** Aluminum-Bronze **Obverse:** Three giant eland **Reverse:** Denomination

Date	Mintage	F	VF	XF	Unc	BU
1958(a)	30,000,000	0.25	0.50	1.00	3.00	—

KM# 25 10 FRANCS **Composition:** Aluminum-Bronze **Obverse:** Three giant eland **Reverse:** Denomination

Date	Mintage	F	VF	XF	Unc	BU
1958(a)	25,000,000	0.25	0.50	1.50	4.00	—

KM# 26 25 FRANCS **Composition:** Aluminum-Bronze **Obverse:** Three giant eland **Reverse:** Denomination

Date	Mintage	F	VF	XF	Unc	BU
1958(a)	12,000,000	0.50	1.00	2.00	6.00	—

REPUBLIC

STANDARD COINAGE

KM# 13 50 FRANCS **Composition:** Copper-Nickel **Subject:** Independence Commemorative **Obverse:** Three Giant Eland **Reverse:** Denomination

Date	Mintage	F	VF	XF	Unc	BU
1960(a)	1,154,000	2.00	3.50	5.50	10.00	—

KM# 14 100 FRANCS **Composition:** Nickel **Obverse:** Three Giant Eland **Reverse:** Denomination **Note:** KM#14 was issued double thick and should not be considered a piefort.

Date	Mintage	F	VF	XF	Unc	BU
1966(a)	9,950,000	1.00	2.00	4.50	10.00	—
1967(a)	10,000,000	1.00	2.00	4.50	10.00	—
1968(a)	11,000,000	1.00	2.00	4.50	10.00	—

KM# 15 100 FRANCS **Composition:** Nickel **Obverse:** Three Giant Eland **Reverse:** Denomination **Note:** Refer also to Equatorial African States and Central African States.

Date	Mintage	F	VF	XF	Unc	BU
1971(a)	15,000,000	2.00	3.00	6.00	12.50	—
1972(a)	20,000,000	2.00	3.00	6.00	12.50	—

KM# 16 100 FRANCS **Composition:** Nickel **Obverse:** KM#17 **Reverse:** KM#15

Date	F	VF	XF	Unc	BU
1972(a)	6.50	12.50	22.50	45.00	—

KM# 17 100 FRANCS **Composition:** Nickel **Obverse:** Three Giant Eland **Reverse:** Denomination

Date	F	VF	XF	Unc	BU
1975(a)	1.00	2.00	3.00	5.50	—
1980(a)	1.00	2.00	3.00	5.50	—
1982(a)	0.75	1.50	2.50	4.50	—
1983(a)	0.75	1.50	2.50	4.50	—
1984(a)	0.75	1.50	2.50	4.50	—
1986(a)	0.75	1.50	2.50	4.50	—

KM# 23 500 FRANCS **Composition:** Copper-Nickel

Date	F	VF	XF	Unc	BU
1985(a)	2.00	3.50	5.50	10.00	—
1986(a)	2.00	3.50	5.50	10.00	—
1988(a)	2.00	3.50	5.50	10.00	—

KM# 18 1000 FRANCS **Weight:** 3.5000 g. **Composition:** 0.9000 Gold .1012 oz. AGW **Subject:** 10th Anniversary of Independence

Date	Mintage	F	VF	XF	Unc	BU
1970 Proof	4,000	Value: 75.00				

KM# 19 3000 FRANCS **Weight:** 10.5000 g. **Composition:** 0.9000 Gold .3038 oz. AGW **Subject:** 10th Anniversary of Independence

Date	Mintage	F	VF	XF	Unc	BU
1970 Proof	4,000	Value: 185				

Note: With or without cornucopia mint mark on reverse

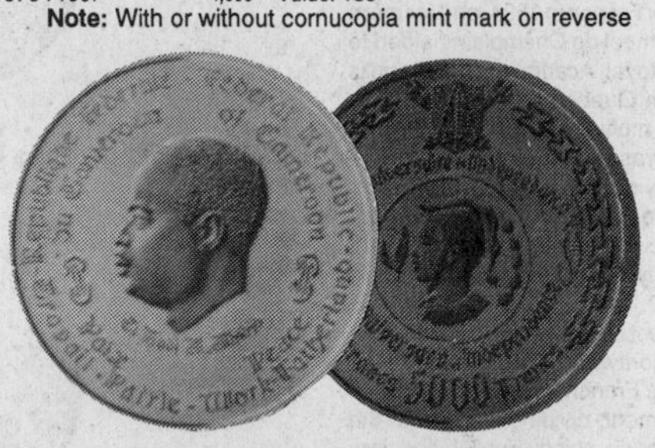

KM# 20 5000 FRANCS **Weight:** 17.5000 g. **Composition:** 0.9000 Gold .5064 oz. AGW **Subject:** 10th Anniversary of Independence

Date	Mintage	F	VF	XF	Unc	BU
1970 Proof	4,000	Value: 300				

KM# 21 10000 FRANCS **Weight:** 35.0000 g. **Composition:** 0.9000 Gold 1.0128 oz. AGW **Subject:** 10th Anniversary of Independence

Date	Mintage	F	VF	XF	Unc	BU
1970 Proof	4,000	Value: 650				

KM# 22 20000 FRANCS **Weight:** 70.0000 g. **Composition:** 0.9000 Gold 2.0257 oz. AGW **Subject:** 10th Anniversary of Independence **Obverse:** Similar to 10,000 Francs, KM#21

Date	Mintage	F	VF	XF	Unc	BU
1970 Proof	4,000	Value: 1,150				

TOKEN COINAGE

KM# TN3 50 CENTIMES **Composition:** Brass **Issuer:** Societe Nationale **Obverse:** SOCIETE NATIONALE DU CAMEROUN in legend **Reverse:** 50c

Date	VG	F	VF	XF	Unc
ND	40.00	100	175	320	—

KM# Tn4 FRANC **Composition:** Brass **Reverse:** 50c
Note: Similar to KM#TN3.

Date	VG	F	VF	XF	Unc
ND	50.00	120	220	375	—

ESSAIS

Standard metals unless otherwise noted

KM#	Date	Mintage	Identification	Issue Price	Mkt Val
E1	1924(a)	—	50 Centimes. KM1	—	85.00
E2	1924(a)	—	Franc. KM2	—	100

KM#	Date	Mintage	Identification	Issue Price	Mkt Val
E3	1924(a)	—	2 Francs. KM3	—	125
E4	1943	—	1/2 Franc.	—	600
E5	1948(a)	2,000	Franc. Copper-Nickel. KM8	—	30.00
E6	1948(a)	2,000	2 Francs. Copper-Nickel. KM9	—	35.00
E7	1958(a)	2,030	5 Francs. KM24	—	15.00
E8	1958(a)	2,030	10 Francs. KM25	—	17.50
E9	1958(a)	2,030	25 Francs. KM26	—	20.00
E10	1960(a)	1,500	50 Francs. KM13	—	27.50
E11	1966(a)	1,200	100 Francs. KM14	—	22.50
E12	1970(a)	—	1000 Francs. Bronze. KM18	—	95.00
E13	1971(a)	1,550	100 Francs. KM15	—	22.50
E14	1971	6	100 Francs. Gold. KM15	—	1,250
E15	1972(a)	1,550	100 Francs. KM16	—	30.00
E16	1975(a)	1,700	100 Francs. KM17	—	22.50
E17	1985(a)	—	500 Francs. KM23	—	35.00

PIEFORTS WITH ESSAI

Double thickness - Standard metals unless otherwise noted

KM#	Date	Mintage	Identification	Issue Price	Mkt Val
PE1	1948(a)	104	Franc. KM8	—	60.00
PE2	1948(a)	104	2 Francs. KM9	—	75.00
PE3	1948(a)	—	2 Francs. KM9, double piefort	—	250
PE4	1948(a)	—	2 Francs. Copper-Nickel. KM9	—	250

PROOF SETS

KM#	Date	Mintage	Identification	Issue Price	Mkt Val
PS1	1970 (5)	4,000	KM18-22	—	2,350

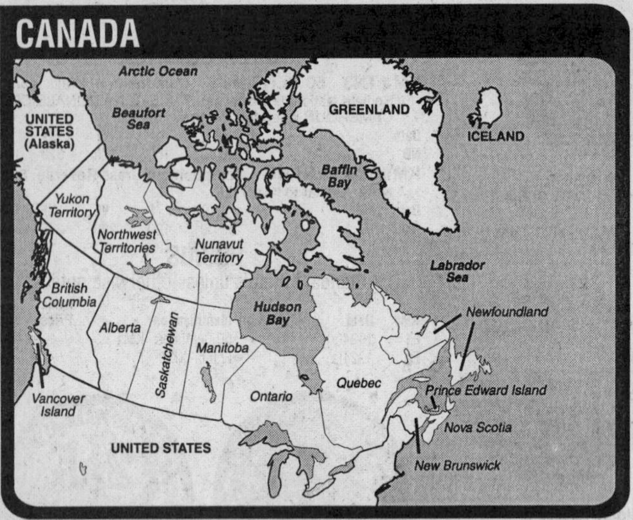

Canada is located to the north of the United States, and spans the full breadth of the northern portion of North America from Atlantic to Pacific oceans, except for the State of Alaska. It has a total area of 3,850,000 sq. mi. (9,971,550 sq. km.) and a population of 30.29 million. Capital: Ottawa.

Jacques Cartier, a French explorer, took possession of Canada for France in 1534, and for more than a century the history of Canada was that of a French colony. Samuel de Champlain helped to establish the first permanent colony in North America, in 1604 at Port Royal, Acadia – now Annapolis Royal, Nova Scotia. Four years later he founded the settlement in Quebec.

The British settled along the coast to the south while the French, motivated by a grand design, pushed into the interior. France's plan for a great American empire was to occupy the Mississippi heartland of the country, and from there to press in upon the narrow strip of English coastal settlements from the west. Inevitably, armed conflict erupted between the French and the British; consequently, Britain acquired Hudson Bay, Newfoundland and Nova Scotia from the French in 1713. British control of the rest of New France was secured in 1763, largely because of James Wolfe's great victory over Montcalm near Quebec in 1759.

During the American Revolution, Canada became a refuge for great numbers of American Royalists, most of whom settled in Ontario, thereby creating an English majority west of the Ottawa River. The ethnic imbalance contravened the effectiveness of the prevailing French type of government, and in 1791 the Constitutional act was passed by the British parliament, dividing Canada at the Ottawa River into two parts, each with its own government: Upper Canada, chiefly English and consisting of the southern section of what is now Ontario; and Lower Canada, chiefly French and consisting principally of the southern section of Quebec. Subsequent revolt by dissidents in both sections caused the British government to pass the Union Act, July 23, 1840, which united Lower and Upper Canada (as Canada East and Canada West) to form the Province of Canada, with one council and one assembly in which the two sections had equal numbers.

The union of the two provinces did not encourage political stability; the equal strength of the French and British made the task of government all but impossible. A further change was made with the passage of the British North American Act, which took effect on July 1, 1867, and established Canada as the first federal union in the British Empire. Four provinces entered the union at first: Upper Canada as Ontario, Lower Canada as Quebec, Nova Scotia and New Brunswick. The Hudson Bay Company's territories were acquired in 1869 out of which were formed the provinces of Manitoba, Saskatchewan and Alberta. British Columbia joined in 1871 and Prince Edward Island in 1873. Canada took over the Arctic Archipelago in 1895. In 1949 Newfoundland came into the confederation.

In the early years, Canada's coins were struck in England at the Royal Mint in London or at the Heaton Mint in Birmingham. Issues struck at the Royal Mint do not bear a mint mark, but those produced by Heaton carry an "H". All Canadian coins have been struck since January 2, 1908, at the Royal Canadian Mints at Ottawa and recently at Winnipeg except for some 1968 pure nickel dimes struck at the U.S. Mint in Philadelphia, and do not bear mint marks. Ottawa's mint mark (C) does not appear on some 20th Century Newfoundland issues, however, as it does on English type sovereigns struck there from 1908 through 1918.

Canada is a member of the Commonwealth of Nations. Elizabeth II is Head of State as Queen of Canada.

RULERS:
British 1763-

MONETARY SYSTEM
1 Dollar = 100 Cents

CONFEDERATION

CIRCULATION COINAGE

CENT Weight: 3.2400 g. **Composition:** Bronze

KM	Date	Mintage	VG-8	F-12	VF-20	XF-40	MS-60	MS-63	Proof
7	1901	4,100,000	1.50	2.50	3.00	5.00	22.00	70.00	—

CENT Weight: 3.2400 g. **Composition:** Bronze

KM	Date	Mintage	VG-8	F-12	VF-20	XF-40	MS-60	MS-63	Proof
8	1902	3,000,000	1.25	1.50	2.00	5.00	13.00	45.00	—
	1903	4,000,000	1.25	1.50	2.00	4.00	18.00	50.00	—
	1904	2,500,000	1.50	2.00	3.25	5.00	25.00	75.00	—
	1905	2,000,000	2.50	4.00	5.00	7.00	30.00	85.00	—
	1906	4,100,000	1.25	1.50	2.00	4.00	22.00	125	—
	1907	2,400,000	1.25	2.00	3.00	5.00	25.00	90.00	—
	1907H	800,000	8.00	11.00	16.00	30.00	80.00	350	—
	1908	2,401,506	1.25	2.00	3.00	5.00	22.00	80.00	150
	1909	3,973,339	1.25	1.50	2.00	4.00	18.00	65.00	—
	1910	5,146,487	1.25	1.50	2.00	3.00	13.00	65.00	—

CENT Weight: 3.2400 g. **Composition:** Bronze

KM	Date	Mintage	VG-8	F-12	VF-20	XF-40	MS-60	MS-63	Proof
15	1911	4,663,486	0.80	1.30	1.75	3.50	15.00	50.00	250

CENT Weight: 3.2400 g. **Composition:** Bronze

KM	Date	Mintage	VG-8	F-12	VF-20	XF-40	MS-60	MS-63	Proof
21	1912	5,107,642	0.75	1.00	1.50	2.50	15.00	50.00	—
	1913	5,735,405	0.75	1.00	1.50	2.50	15.00	75.00	—
	1914	3,405,958	0.75	1.00	1.50	2.50	25.00	90.00	—
	1915	4,932,134	0.75	1.00	1.50	2.50	18.00	65.00	—
	1916	11,022,367	0.50	0.65	0.90	2.00	12.00	45.00	—
	1917	11,899,254	0.50	0.65	0.90	1.50	8.00	40.00	—
	1918	12,970,798	0.50	0.65	0.90	1.50	8.00	40.00	—
	1919	11,279,634	0.50	0.65	0.90	1.50	8.00	40.00	—
	1920	6,762,247	0.60	0.75	1.00	2.00	10.00	50.00	—

CENT Weight: 3.2400 g. **Composition:** Bronze

KM	Date	Mintage	VG-8	F-12	VF-20	XF-40	MS-60	MS-63	Proof
28	1920	15,483,923	0.25	0.50	1.00	2.00	7.00	30.00	—
	1921	7,601,627	0.50	0.75	1.75	3.00	18.00	90.00	—
	1922	1,243,635	8.75	10.00	14.50	22.00	130	600	—
	1923	1,019,002	14.25	16.25	23.00	34.00	200	1,200	—
	1924	1,593,195	3.00	4.00	5.00	10.00	70.00	350	—
	1925	1,000,622	10.00	12.00	18.75	28.00	130	500	—
	1926	2,143,372	2.25	3.00	4.50	8.75	65.00	250	—
	1927	3,553,928	0.90	1.25	2.25	4.00	30.00	110	—
	1928	9,144,860	0.15	0.30	0.65	1.50	10.00	50.00	—
	1929	12,159,840	0.15	0.30	0.65	1.50	10.00	50.00	—
	1930	2,538,613	1.35	1.80	3.00	5.00	30.00	110	—
	1931	3,842,776	0.65	1.00	1.75	3.50	25.00	100	—
	1932	21,316,190	0.15	0.20	0.50	1.50	9.00	40.00	—
	1933	12,079,310	0.15	0.20	0.50	1.50	9.00	40.00	—
	1934	7,042,358	0.20	0.30	0.75	1.50	9.00	40.00	—
	1935	7,526,400	0.20	0.30	0.75	1.50	9.00	35.00	—
	1936	8,768,769	0.15	0.20	0.75	1.50	9.00	30.00	—
	1936 dot below date; Rare	678,823	—	—	—	—	—	—	—

Note: Only one possible business strike is known to exist. No other examples (or possible business strikes) have ever surfaced.

KM	Date	Mintage	VG-8	F-12	VF-20	XF-40	MS-60	MS-63	Proof
	1936 dot below date, specimen, 3 known	—	—	—	—	—	—	—	—

Note: At the David Akers auction of the John Jay Pittman collection (Part 1, 10-97), a gem specimen realized $121,000. At the David Akers auction of the John Jay Pittman collection (Part 3, 10-99), a near choice specimen realized $115,000.

CENT **Weight:** 3.2400 g. **Composition:** Bronze

KM	Date	Mintage	VG-8	F-12	VF-20	XF-40	MS-60	MS-63	Proof
32	1937	10,040,231	0.60	0.90	1.50	2.00	3.00	9.00	—
	1938	18,365,608	0.50	0.75	1.00	1.25	2.00	6.50	—
	1939	21,600,319	0.20	0.35	0.50	0.75	1.75	5.00	—
	1940	85,740,532	0.10	0.15	0.25	0.50	1.50	5.50	—
	1941	56,336,011	0.10	0.15	0.25	0.50	4.00	50.00	—
	1942	76,113,708	0.10	0.15	0.25	0.50	4.00	40.00	—
	1943	89,111,969	0.10	0.15	0.25	0.50	1.50	25.00	—
	1944	44,131,216	0.20	0.25	0.30	0.60	5.50	70.00	—
	1945	77,268,591	0.10	0.15	0.20	0.30	1.00	14.00	—
	1946	56,662,071	0.10	0.15	0.20	0.30	1.00	5.00	—
	1947	31,093,901	0.10	0.15	0.20	0.30	1.00	6.00	—
	1947 maple leaf	47,855,448	0.10	0.15	0.20	0.30	1.00	5.00	—

CENT **Weight:** 3.2400 g. **Composition:** Bronze **Obverse:** Modified legend

KM	Date	Mintage	VG-8	F-12	VF-20	XF-40	MS-60	MS-63	Proof
41	1948	25,767,779	—	0.10	0.25	0.60	2.25	20.00	—
	1949	33,128,933	—	0.10	0.15	0.25	1.25	6.00	—
	1950	60,444,992	—	0.10	0.15	0.25	0.85	6.00	—
	1951	80,430,379	—	0.10	0.15	0.20	0.85	8.00	—
	1952	67,631,736	—	0.10	0.15	0.20	0.85	4.00	—

CENT **Weight:** 3.2400 g. **Composition:** Bronze **Obverse:** Elizabeth II effigy **Obv. Designer:** Gillick

KM	Date	Mintage	VG-8	F-12	VF-20	XF-40	MS-60	MS-63	Proof
49	1953 without strap	67,806,016	0.15	0.20	0.25	0.30	0.65	1.50	—
	1953 with strap	Inc. above	0.50	1.00	1.50	2.50	10.00	35.00	—
	1954 with strap	22,181,760	0.10	0.15	0.30	0.40	1.00	4.00	—
	1954 without strap, proof-like only	Inc. above	—	—	—	—	150	300	—
	1955 with strap	56,403,193	—	0.10	0.15	0.20	0.35	1.00	—
	1955 without strap	Inc. above	70.00	100	125	225	400	1,000	—
	1956	78,658,535	—	—	—	0.10	0.50	0.90	—
	1957	100,601,792	—	—	—	0.10	0.25	0.50	—
	1958	59,385,679	—	—	—	0.10	0.25	0.50	—
	1959	83,615,343	—	—	—	0.10	0.25	0.30	—
	1960	75,772,775	—	—	—	0.10	0.25	0.30	—
	1961	139,598,404	—	—	—	—	0.15	0.20	—
	1962	227,244,069	—	—	—	—	0.10	0.20	—
	1963	279,076,334	—	—	—	—	0.10	0.20	—
	1964	484,655,322	—	—	—	—	0.10	0.20	—

CENT **Weight:** 3.2400 g. **Composition:** Bronze **Obverse:** Elizabeth II effigy **Obv. Designer:** Machin

KM	Date	Mintage	VG-8	F-12	VF-20	XF-40	MS-60	MS-63	Proof
59.1	1965 sm. beads, pointed 5	304,441,082	—	—	—	0.45	1.00	4.00	—
	1965 sm. beads, blunt 5	Inc. above	—	—	—	—	0.20	0.30	—
	1965 lg. beads, pointed 5	Inc. above	—	—	3.00	5.00	12.00	30.00	—
	1965 lg. beads, blunt 5	Inc. above	—	—	—	0.10	0.15	0.30	—
	1966	184,151,087	—	—	—	—	0.10	0.20	—
	1968	329,695,772	—	—	—	—	0.10	0.20	—
	1969	335,240,929	—	—	—	—	0.10	0.20	—
	1970	311,145,010	—	—	—	—	0.10	0.20	—
	1971	298,228,936	—	—	—	—	0.10	0.20	—
	1972	451,304,591	—	—	—	—	0.10	0.20	—
	1973	457,059,852	—	—	—	—	0.10	0.20	—
	1974	692,058,489	—	—	—	—	0.10	0.20	—
	1975	642,318,000	—	—	—	—	0.10	0.20	—
	1976	701,122,890	—	—	—	—	0.10	0.20	—
	1977	453,762,670	—	—	—	—	0.10	0.20	—
	1978	911,170,647	—	—	—	—	0.10	0.20	—

CENT **Weight:** 3.2400 g. **Composition:** Bronze **Obverse:** Elizabeth II effigy. Smaller bust **Obv. Designer:** Machin

KM	Date	Mintage	VG-8	F-12	VF-20	XF-40	MS-60	MS-63	Proof
59.2	1979	754,394,064	—	—	—	—	0.10	0.20	—

CENT **Weight:** 2.8000 g. **Composition:** Bronze **Obverse:** Elizabeth II effigy **Obv. Designer:** Machin **Note:** Reduced weight.

KM	Date	Mintage	VG-8	F-12	VF-20	XF-40	MS-60	MS-63	Proof
127	1980	912,052,318	—	—	—	—	0.10	0.15	—
	1981	1,209,468,500	—	—	—	—	0.10	0.15	—
	1981 Proof	199,000	—	—	—	—	—	—	1.50

CENT **Weight:** 2.5000 g. **Composition:** Bronze **Obverse:** Elizabeth II effigy **Obv. Designer:** Machin **Edge:** Multisided. **Note:** Reduced weight.

KM	Date	Mintage	VG-8	F-12	VF-20	XF-40	MS-60	MS-63	Proof
132	1982	911,001,000	—	—	—	—	0.10	0.15	—
	1982 Proof	180,908	—	—	—	—	—	—	1.50
	1983	975,510,000	—	—	—	—	0.10	0.15	—
	1983 Proof	168,000	—	—	—	—	—	—	1.50
	1984	838,225,000	—	—	—	—	0.10	0.15	—
	1984 Proof	161,602	—	—	—	—	—	—	1.50
	1985 pointed 5	771,772,500	—	—	—	5.00	10.00	18.50	—
	1985 blunt 5	Inc. above	—	—	—	—	0.10	0.15	—
	1985 blunt 5, proof	157,037	—	—	—	—	—	—	1.50
	1986	740,335,000	—	—	—	—	0.10	0.15	—
	1986 Proof	175,745	—	—	—	—	—	—	1.50
	1987	774,549,000	—	—	—	—	0.10	0.15	—
	1987 Proof	179,004	—	—	—	—	—	—	1.50
	1988	482,676,752	—	—	—	—	0.10	0.15	—
	1988 Proof	175,259	—	—	—	—	—	—	1.50
	1989	1,077,347,200	—	—	—	—	0.10	0.15	—
	1989 Proof	170,928	—	—	—	—	—	—	1.50

CENT **Weight:** 2.5000 g. **Composition:** Bronze **Obverse:** Elizabeth II effigy **Obv. Designer:** dePedery-Hunt

KM	Date	Mintage	VG-8	F-12	VF-20	XF-40	MS-60	MS-63	Proof
181	1990	218,035,000	—	—	—	—	0.10	0.15	—
	1990 Proof	140,649	—	—	—	—	—	—	2.50
	1991	831,001,000	—	—	—	—	0.10	0.15	—
	1991 Proof	131,888	—	—	—	—	—	—	3.50
	1993	752,034,000	—	—	—	—	0.10	0.15	—
	1993 Proof	145,065	—	—	—	—	—	—	2.00
	1994	639,516,000	—	—	—	—	0.10	0.15	—
	1994 Proof	146,424	—	—	—	—	—	—	2.50
	1995	624,983,000	—	—	—	—	0.10	0.15	—
	1996	445,746,000	—	—	—	—	0.10	0.15	—
	1996 Proof	—	—	—	—	—	—	—	2.50

CENT **Composition:** Copper Plated Zinc

KM	Date	Mintage	VG-8	F-12	VF-20	XF-40	MS-60	MS-63	Proof
181a	1996	445,746,000	—	—	—	—	0.10	0.15	2.50
	1996 Proof	—	—	—	—	—	—	—	—

CENT **Composition:** Bronze-Plated Zinc **Edge:** Round and plain.

KM	Date	Mintage	VG-8	F-12	VF-20	XF-40	MS-60	MS-63	Proof
289	1997	506,928,000	—	—	—	—	0.10	0.15	—
	1997 Proof	—	—	—	—	—	—	—	2.75
	1998	—	—	—	—	—	0.10	0.15	—
	1998 Proof	—	—	—	—	—	—	—	3.00
	1998W	—	—	—	—	—	—	1.75	—
	1999P	—	—	—	—	—	—	6.00	—
	Note: Plated, from test token set								
	1999	—	—	—	—	—	0.10	0.15	—
	1999 Proof	—	—	—	—	—	—	—	4.00
	1999W	—	—	—	—	—	—	—	—
	2000	—	—	—	—	—	0.10	0.15	—
	2000W	—	—	—	—	—	—	1.75	—
	2000 Proof	—	—	—	—	—	—	—	4.00
	2001	—	—	—	—	—	—	0.10	—
	2001 Proof	—	—	—	—	—	—	—	4.00

CENT **Composition:** Bronze

KM	Date	Mintage	VG-8	F-12	VF-20	XF-40	MS-60	MS-63	Proof
289a	1998 In Specimen sets only	—	—	—	—	—	—	0.75	—

5 CENTS **Weight:** 1.1620 g. **Composition:** 0.9250 Silver 0.0346 oz. ASW

KM	Date	Mintage	VG-8	F-12	VF-20	XF-40	MS-60	MS-63	Proof
2	1901	2,000,000	2.75	4.00	8.00	18.00	100	325	—

5 CENTS **Weight:** 1.1620 g. **Composition:** 0.9250 Silver 0.0346 oz. ASW

KM	Date	Mintage	VG-8	F-12	VF-20	XF-40	MS-60	MS-63	Proof
9	1902	2,120,000	1.50	2.00	3.25	7.00	30.00	50.00	—
	1902 lg. broad H	2,200,000	1.50	2.00	3.25	7.00	30.00	50.00	—
	1902 sm. narrow H	Inc. above	5.00	9.00	20.00	35.00	80.00	150	—

5 CENTS **Weight:** 1.1620 g. **Composition:** 0.9250 Silver 0.0346 oz. ASW

KM	Date	Mintage	VG-8	F-12	VF-20	XF-40	MS-60	MS-63	Proof
13	1903 22 leaves	1,000,000	4.00	7.00	14.00	30.00	120	280	—
	1903H 21 leaves	2,640,000	1.75	3.00	7.00	13.00	90.00	200	—
	1904	2,400,000	1.75	3.00	7.00	18.00	140	400	—
	1905	2,600,000	1.75	3.00	6.00	12.00	85.00	200	—
	1906	3,100,000	1.50	2.00	4.00	8.00	65.00	175	—
	1907	5,200,000	1.50	2.00	4.00	7.00	45.00	125	—
	1908	1,220,524	4.00	6.50	12.00	25.00	85.00	150	—
	1909 round leaves	1,983,725	2.00	3.75	7.00	15.00	125	350	—
	1909 pointed leaves	Inc. above	8.00	12.00	25.00	50.00	300	1,000	—
	1910 pointed leaves	3,850,325	1.50	1.75	3.25	7.00	45.00	75.00	—
	1910 round leaves	Inc. above	10.00	14.00	28.00	70.00	320	1,100	—

5 CENTS Weight: 1.1620 g. **Composition:** 0.9250 Silver 0.0346 oz. ASW

KM	Date	Mintage	VG-8	F-12	VF-20	XF-40	MS-60	MS-63	Proof
16	1911	3,692,350	1.25	2.00	4.00	8.00	50.00	85.00	—

5 CENTS Weight: 1.1620 g. **Composition:** 0.9250 Silver 0.0346 oz. ASW

KM	Date	Mintage	VG-8	F-12	VF-20	XF-40	MS-60	MS-63	Proof
22	1912	5,863,170	1.25	2.00	3.00	6.00	45.00	125	—
	1913	5,488,048	1.25	1.75	2.50	5.00	20.00	40.00	—
	1914	4,202,179	1.25	2.00	3.00	6.00	45.00	110	—
	1915	1,172,258	5.50	10.50	20.00	40.00	175	400	—
	1916	2,481,675	1.75	3.00	5.00	11.00	75.00	175	—
	1917	5,521,373	1.25	1.75	2.00	4.00	25.00	60.00	—
	1918	6,052,298	1.25	1.75	2.00	4.00	25.00	50.00	—
	1919	7,835,400	1.25	1.75	2.00	4.00	25.00	50.00	—

5 CENTS Weight: 1.1664 g. **Composition:** 0.8000 Silver .0300 oz. ASW

KM	Date	Mintage	VG-8	F-12	VF-20	XF-40	MS-60	MS-63	Proof
22a	1920	10,649,851	1.25	1.75	2.00	4.00	20.00	35.00	—
	1921	2,582,495	1,600	2,000	2,700	3,500	6,000	13,500	—

Note: Approximately 460 known; balance remelted. Stack's A.G. Carter Jr. Sale (12-89) choice BU, finest known, realized $57,200.

5 CENTS **Composition:** Nickel

KM	Date	Mintage	VG-8	F-12	VF-20	XF-40	MS-60	MS-63	Proof
29	1922	4,794,119	0.25	0.75	1.75	7.00	35.00	75.00	—
	1923	2,502,279	0.40	1.25	3.50	12.00	75.00	200	—
	1924	3,105,839	0.30	0.70	2.50	7.00	60.00	150	—
	1925	201,921	30.00	40.00	75.00	155	800	2,500	—
	1926 near 6	938,162	1.50	4.00	12.00	40.00	300	1,200	—
	1926 far 6	Inc. above	60.00	85.00	150	275	1,000	3,000	—
	1927	5,285,627	0.25	0.65	1.75	6.50	45.00	110	—
	1928	4,577,712	0.25	0.65	1.75	6.50	40.00	90.00	—
	1929	5,611,911	0.25	0.65	1.75	6.50	45.00	130	—
	1930	3,704,673	0.25	0.65	1.75	6.50	70.00	150	—
	1931	5,100,830	0.25	0.65	2.00	10.25	75.00	325	—
	1932	3,198,566	0.25	0.65	2.25	10.50	75.00	200	—
	1933	2,597,867	0.40	1.00	4.00	13.00	150	500	—
	1934	3,827,304	0.25	0.65	3.00	10.75	80.00	275	—
	1935	3,900,000	0.25	0.65	1.75	6.50	70.00	180	—
	1936	4,400,450	0.25	0.65	1.75	6.50	40.00	85.00	—

5 CENTS **Composition:** Nickel

KM	Date	Mintage	VG-8	F-12	VF-20	XF-40	MS-60	MS-63	Proof
33	1937 dot	4,593,263	0.20	0.30	1.25	2.50	9.00	22.00	—
	1938	3,898,974	0.20	1.00	2.00	7.00	50.00	100	—
	1939	5,661,123	0.20	0.30	1.25	3.00	30.00	55.00	—
	1940	13,920,197	0.15	0.20	0.75	2.25	12.00	35.00	—
	1941	8,681,785	0.10	0.20	0.75	2.25	15.00	42.00	—
	1942 round	6,847,544	0.20	0.25	0.75	1.75	12.00	35.00	—

5 CENTS **Composition:** Tombac

KM	Date	Mintage	VG-8	F-12	VF-20	XF-40	MS-60	MS-63	Proof
39	1942 - 12 sided	3,396,234	0.40	0.65	1.25	1.75	3.00	9.00	—

5 CENTS **Composition:** Nickel

KM	Date	Mintage	VG-8	F-12	VF-20	XF-40	MS-60	MS-63	Proof
39a	1946	6,952,684	0.15	0.25	0.50	2.00	8.00	18.00	—
	1947	7,603,724	0.15	0.25	0.50	1.25	6.50	12.50	—
	1947 dot	Inc. above	12.00	15.00	22.00	50.00	150	250	—
	1947 maple leaf	9,595,124	0.15	0.25	0.50	1.25	6.00	12.00	—

5 CENTS **Composition:** Nickel **Obverse:** Modified legend

KM	Date	Mintage	VG-8	F-12	VF-20	XF-40	MS-60	MS-63	Proof
42	1948	1,810,789	0.40	0.50	1.00	3.00	12.00	20.00	—
	1949	13,037,090	0.15	0.20	0.35	0.75	4.00	7.00	—
	1950	11,970,521	0.15	0.20	0.35	0.75	4.00	7.00	—

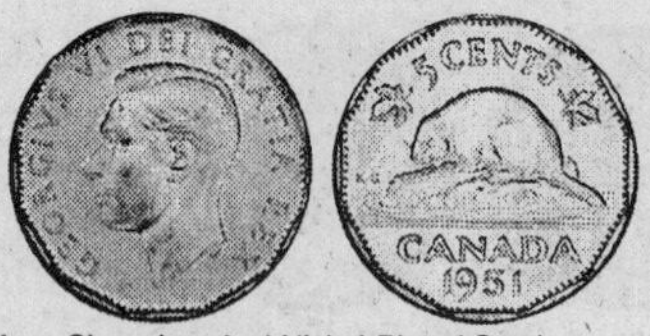

5 CENTS **Composition:** Chromium And Nickel-Plated Steel

KM	Date	Mintage	VG-8	F-12	VF-20	XF-40	MS-60	MS-63	Proof
42a	1951 Low relief	4,313,410	0.15	0.25	0.50	0.85	2.50	4.50	—
	Note: "A" in GRATIA points between denticles								
	1951 High relief	Inc. above	400	525	700	950	1,400	1,850	—
	Note: "A" in GRATIA points to a denticle								
	1952	10,891,148	0.15	0.25	0.50	0.85	3.00	5.00	—

5 CENTS **Composition:** Chromium And Nickel-Plated Steel **Obverse:** Elizabeth II effigy **Obv. Designer:** Gillick **Shape:** 12-sided

KM	Date	Mintage	VG-8	F-12	VF-20	XF-40	MS-60	MS-63	Proof
50	1953 without strap	16,635,552	0.15	0.25	0.40	1.00	3.00	4.50	—
	1953 without strap, near leaf	Inc. above	75.00	125	200	350	800	1,500	—
	1953 with strap, far leaf	Inc. above	75.00	100	150	250	600	1,500	—
	1953 with strap	Inc. above	0.15	0.25	0.45	1.00	3.50	7.00	—
	1954	6,998,662	0.15	0.25	0.50	1.00	4.00	8.00	—

5 CENTS **Composition:** Nickel

KM	Date	Mintage	VG-8	F-12	VF-20	XF-40	MS-60	MS-63	Proof
50a	1955	5,355,028	0.15	0.25	0.40	0.75	2.50	4.50	—
	1956	9,399,854	—	0.20	0.30	0.45	1.50	3.00	—
	1957	7,387,703	—	—	0.25	0.30	1.25	3.00	—
	1958	7,607,521	—	—	0.25	0.30	1.25	3.00	—
	1959	11,552,523	—	—	—	0.20	0.40	1.00	—
	1960	37,157,433	—	—	—	0.15	0.35	0.70	—
	1961	47,889,051	—	—	—	—	0.20	0.40	—
	1962	46,307,305	—	—	—	—	0.20	0.40	—

5 CENTS **Composition:** Nickel **Shape:** Round

KM	Date	Mintage	VG-8	F-12	VF-20	XF-40	MS-60	MS-63	Proof
57	1963	43,970,320	—	—	—	—	0.20	0.35	—
	1964	78,075,068	—	—	—	—	0.20	0.35	—
	1964 extra water line	—	8.00	10.00	12.00	15.00	25.00	40.00	—

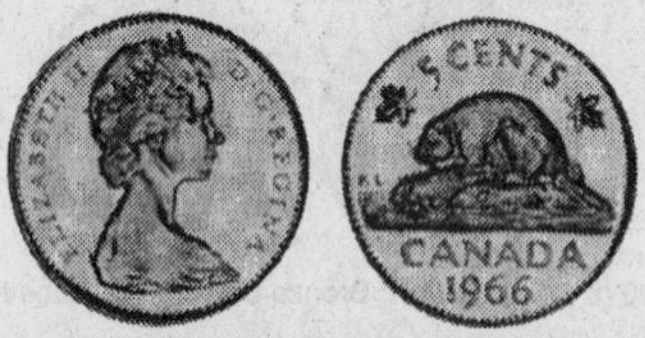

5 CENTS **Composition:** Nickel **Obverse:** Elizabeth II effigy **Obv. Designer:** Machin

KM	Date	Mintage	VG-8	F-12	VF-20	XF-40	MS-60	MS-63	Proof
60.1	1965	84,876,018	—	—	—	—	0.20	0.30	—
	1966	27,976,648	—	—	—	—	0.20	0.30	—
	1968	101,930,379	—	—	—	—	0.20	0.30	—
	1969	27,830,229	—	—	—	—	0.20	0.30	—
	1970	5,726,010	—	—	—	0.20	0.35	0.75	—
	1971	27,312,609	—	—	—	—	0.20	0.30	—
	1972	62,417,387	—	—	—	—	0.20	0.30	—
	1973	53,507,435	—	—	—	—	0.20	0.30	—
	1974	94,704,645	—	—	—	—	0.20	0.30	—
	1975	138,882,000	—	—	—	—	0.20	0.30	—
	1976	55,140,213	—	—	—	—	0.20	0.30	—
	1977	89,120,791	—	—	—	—	0.20	0.30	—
	1978	137,079,273	—	—	—	—	0.20	0.30	—

5 CENTS **Composition:** Nickel **Obverse:** Smaller bust

KM	Date	Mintage	VG-8	F-12	VF-20	XF-40	MS-60	MS-63	Proof
60.2	1979	186,295,825	—	—	—	—	0.20	0.30	—
	1980	134,878,000	—	—	—	—	0.20	0.30	—
	1981	99,107,900	—	—	—	—	0.20	0.30	—
	1981 Proof	199,000	—	—	—	—	—	—	1.50
	1982	—	—	—	—	—	—	—	—
	1982 Proof	—	—	—	—	—	—	—	—

5 CENTS **Composition:** Copper-Nickel

KM	Date	Mintage	VG-8	F-12	VF-20	XF-40	MS-60	MS-63	Proof
60.2a	1982	64,924,400	—	—	—	—	0.20	0.30	—
	1982 Proof	180,908	—	—	—	—	—	—	1.50
	1983	72,596,000	—	—	—	—	0.20	0.30	—
	1983 Proof	168,000	—	—	—	—	—	—	1.50
	1984	84,088,000	—	—	—	—	0.20	0.30	—
	1984 Proof	161,602	—	—	—	—	—	—	1.50
	1985	126,618,000	—	—	—	—	0.20	0.30	—
	1985 Proof	157,037	—	—	—	—	—	—	1.50
	1986	156,104,000	—	—	—	—	0.20	0.30	—
	1986 Proof	175,745	—	—	—	—	—	—	1.50
	1987	106,299,000	—	—	—	—	0.10	0.20	—
	1987 Proof	179,004	—	—	—	—	—	—	1.50

KM	Date	Mintage	VG-8	F-12	VF-20	XF-40	MS-60	MS-63	Proof
	1988	75,025,000	—	—	—	—	0.10	0.20	—
	1988 Proof	175,259	—	—	—	—	—	—	1.50
	1989	141,570,538	—	—	—	—	0.10	0.20	—
	1989 Proof	170,928	—	—	—	—	—	—	1.50

5 CENTS **Composition:** Copper-Nickel **Obverse:** Elizabeth II effigy **Obv. Designer:** dePedery-Hunt

KM	Date	Mintage	VG-8	F-12	VF-20	XF-40	MS-60	MS-63	Proof
182	1990	42,537,000	—	—	—	—	0.10	0.20	—
	1990 Proof	140,649	—	—	—	—	—	—	2.50
	1991	10,931,000	—	—	—	—	0.20	0.55	—
	1991 Proof	131,888	—	—	—	—	—	—	7.00
	1993	86,877,000	—	—	—	—	0.10	0.20	—
	1993 Proof	143,065	—	—	—	—	—	—	2.50
	1994	99,352,000	—	—	—	—	0.10	0.20	—
	1994 Proof	146,424	—	—	—	—	—	—	3.00
	1995	78,528,000	—	—	—	—	0.10	0.20	—
	1995 Proof	50,000	—	—	—	—	—	—	2.50
	1996 far 6	36,686,000	—	—	—	—	0.75	1.50	—
	1996 near 6	Inc. above	—	—	—	—	0.10	0.20	—
	1996 Proof	—	—	—	—	—	—	—	6.00
	1997 Proof	—	—	—	—	—	—	—	5.00
	1997	27,354,000	—	—	—	—	0.10	0.20	—
	1998	156,873,000	—	—	—	—	0.10	0.20	—
	1998 Proof	—	—	—	—	—	—	—	5.00
	1998W	—	—	—	—	—	—	1.50	—
	1999	124,861,000	—	—	—	—	0.10	0.20	—
	1999 Proof	—	—	—	—	—	—	—	5.00
	1999W	—	—	—	—	—	—	—	—
	2000 Proof	—	—	—	—	—	—	—	5.00
	2000	108,514,000	—	—	—	—	0.10	0.20	—
	2000W	—	—	—	—	—	—	1.50	—
	2001 Proof	—	—	—	—	—	—	—	5.00
	2001	20,036,000	—	—	—	—	0.10	0.20	—
	2002	—	—	—	—	—	0.10	—	—

5 CENTS **Weight:** 3.9000 g. **Composition:** Nickel Plated Steel **Obverse:** Queen's head right. **Reverse:** Beaver. **Edge:** Reeded. **Size:** 21.2 mm.

KM	Date	Mintage	VG-8	F-12	VF-20	XF-40	MS-60	MS-63	Proof
182b	1999 P	Est. 20,000	—	—	—	—	—	15.00	—
	2000 P	Est. 2,300,000	—	—	—	—	1.50	2.25	—
	2001 P	136,650	—	—	—	—	0.20	0.35	—
	2002 P	—	—	—	—	—	—	0.10	—

5 CENTS **Weight:** 5.3500 g. **Composition:** 0.9250 Silver 0.1591 oz. ASW

KM	Date	Mintage	VG-8	F-12	VF-20	XF-40	MS-60	MS-63	Proof
182a	1999	—	—	—	—	—	—	—	5.00
	2000	—	—	—	—	—	—	—	5.00
	2001	—	—	—	—	—	—	—	5.00
	2002 Proof	—	—	—	—	—	—	—	5.00

10 CENTS **Weight:** 2.3240 g. **Composition:** 0.9250 Silver 0.0691 oz. ASW **Obverse:** Victoria bust left

KM	Date	Mintage	VG-8	F-12	VF-20	XF-40	MS-60	MS-63	Proof
3	1901	1,200,000	6.75	10.50	25.00	60.00	150	390	—

10 CENTS **Weight:** 2.3240 g. **Composition:** 0.9250 Silver 0.0691 oz. ASW **Obverse:** Edward VII bust right

KM	Date	Mintage	VG-8	F-12	VF-20	XF-40	MS-60	MS-63	Proof
10	1902	720,000	3.50	9.00	20.00	50.00	250	650	—
	1902H	1,100,000	2.75	5.00	12.50	28.00	75.00	200	—
	1903	500,000	8.00	20.00	50.00	150	800	1,900	—
	1903H	1,320,000	4.50	7.00	20.00	42.00	200	450	—
	1904	1,000,000	4.50	9.00	30.00	65.00	250	450	—
	1905	1,000,000	4.00	10.00	30.00	80.00	350	800	—
	1906	1,700,000	2.75	7.50	15.00	40.00	200	400	—
	1907	2,620,000	2.75	7.50	15.00	30.00	180	350	—
	1908	776,666	5.00	10.00	27.00	65.00	180	250	—
	1909 Victorian leaves, similar to 1902-1908 coinage	1,697,200	3.50	9.00	25.00	60.00	285	800	—
	1909 broad leaves, similar to 1910-1912 coinage	Inc. above	6.00	12.00	30.00	70.00	375	1,000	—
	1910	4,468,331	2.75	5.00	12.50	28.00	100	250	—

10 CENTS **Weight:** 2.3240 g. **Composition:** 0.9250 Silver 0.0691 oz. ASW

KM	Date	Mintage	VG-8	F-12	VF-20	XF-40	MS-60	MS-63	Proof
17	1911	2,737,584	3.00	7.00	12.00	30.00	80.00	180	—

10 CENTS **Weight:** 2.3240 g. **Composition:** 0.9250 Silver 0.0691 oz. ASW

KM	Date	Mintage	VG-8	F-12	VF-20	XF-40	MS-60	MS-63	Proof
23	1912	3,235,557	1.75	2.50	6.00	22.00	150	400	—
	1913 sm. leaves	3,613,937	1.50	2.25	5.00	17.50	80.00	250	—
	1913 lg. leaves	Inc. above	70.00	125	250	650	4,000	10,000	—
	1914	2,549,811	1.50	2.50	5.50	18.50	80.00	350	—
	1915	688,057	4.00	10.00	22.00	70.00	225	550	—
	1916	4,218,114	1.25	1.50	4.00	11.00	60.00	200	—
	1917	5,011,988	1.00	1.50	3.00	8.75	40.00	70.00	—
	1918	5,133,602	1.00	1.50	3.00	6.00	35.00	65.00	—
	1919	7,877,722	1.00	1.50	3.00	6.00	35.00	65.00	—

10 CENTS **Weight:** 2.3328 g. **Composition:** 0.8000 Silver 0.0600 oz. ASW

KM	Date	Mintage	VG-8	F-12	VF-20	XF-40	MS-60	MS-63	Proof
23a	1920	6,305,345	1.00	1.50	3.00	8.00	40.00	75.00	—
	1921	2,469,562	1.25	2.00	4.00	12.50	50.00	150	—
	1928	2,458,602	1.00	1.75	4.00	8.00	40.00	100	—
	1929	3,253,888	1.00	2.25	3.50	8.00	40.00	90.00	—
	1930	1,831,043	1.00	2.50	4.50	9.00	40.00	90.00	—
	1931	2,067,421	1.00	1.75	4.00	8.00	40.00	90.00	—
	1932	1,154,317	1.50	2.50	6.00	15.00	60.00	120	—
	1933	672,368	2.00	3.00	8.00	25.00	100	275	—
	1934	409,067	3.00	6.00	16.00	40.00	200	400	—
	1935	384,056	3.50	6.00	15.00	40.00	200	400	—
	1936	2,460,871	0.60	1.25	3.00	6.00	30.00	65.00	—
	1936 dot on rev. Specimen, 4 known	—	—	—	—	—	—	—	—

Note: At the David Akers sale of the John Jay Pittman collection, Part 1, 10-97, a gem specimen realized $120,000.

10 CENTS **Weight:** 2.3328 g. **Composition:** 0.8000 Silver 0.0600 oz. ASW

KM	Date	Mintage	VG-8	F-12	VF-20	XF-40	MS-60	MS-63	Proof
34	1937	2,500,095	0.50	1.00	2.25	3.75	8.00	12.00	—
	1938	4,197,323	1.00	2.00	3.25	6.50	40.00	55.00	—
	1939	5,501,748	0.70	1.50	2.50	5.00	30.00	40.00	—
	1940	16,526,470	BV	0.50	1.50	3.00	10.00	20.00	—
	1941	8,716,386	BV	1.50	2.50	6.00	25.00	60.00	—
	1942	10,214,011	BV	0.50	1.25	4.00	20.00	30.00	—
	1943	21,143,229	BV	0.50	1.25	4.00	11.00	20.00	—
	1944	9,383,582	BV	0.50	1.50	4.50	15.00	25.00	—
	1945	10,979,570	BV	0.50	1.25	4.00	11.00	15.00	—
	1946	6,300,066	BV	1.00	2.00	4.50	20.00	30.00	—
	1947	4,431,926	BV	1.25	2.50	6.00	20.00	30.00	—
	1947 maple leaf	9,638,793	BV	0.50	1.50	3.00	7.00	10.00	—

10 CENTS **Weight:** 2.3328 g. **Composition:** 0.8000 Silver 0.0600 oz. ASW **Obverse:** Modified legend

KM	Date	Mintage	VG-8	F-12	VF-20	XF-40	MS-60	MS-63	Proof
43	1948	422,741	2.00	3.50	7.50	13.00	30.00	45.00	—
	1949	11,336,172	—	BV	0.85	2.00	6.00	10.00	—
	1950	17,823,075	—	BV	0.65	1.50	5.00	7.00	—
	1951	15,079,265	—	BV	0.50	1.50	4.00	7.00	—
	1951 Doubled die	—	—	1.50	2.50	7.00	22.00	—	—
	1952	10,474,455	—	BV	0.50	1.50	3.00	5.00	—

10 CENTS **Weight:** 2.3328 g. **Composition:** 0.8000 Silver 0.0600 oz. ASW **Obverse:** Elizabeth II effigy **Obv. Designer:** Gllick

KM	Date	Mintage	VG-8	F-12	VF-20	XF-40	MS-60	MS-63	Proof
51	1953 without straps	17,706,395	—	—	BV	1.25	2.00	4.00	—
	1953 with straps	Inc. above	—	—	BV	1.25	3.00	5.00	—
	1954	4,493,150	—	BV	1.00	2.25	5.00	8.00	—
	1955	12,237,294	—	—	BV	0.75	2.00	4.00	—
	1956	16,732,844	—	—	BV	0.75	2.00	3.50	—
	1956 dot below date	Inc. above	—	1.50	2.00	3.00	8.00	15.00	—
	1957	16,110,229	—	—	—	0.70	1.00	1.50	—
	1958	10,621,236	—	—	—	0.70	1.00	1.50	—
	1959	19,691,433	—	—	—	0.70	0.75	1.25	—
	1960	45,446,835	—	—	—	BV	0.50	1.00	—
	1961	26,850,859	—	—	—	BV	0.50	1.00	—
	1962	41,864,335	—	—	—	BV	0.50	1.00	—
	1963	41,916,208	—	—	—	BV	0.50	1.00	—
	1964	49,518,549	—	—	—	BV	0.50	1.00	—

10 CENTS **Weight:** 2.3328 g. **Composition:** 0.8000 Silver 0.0600 oz. ASW **Obverse:** Elizabeth II effigy **Obv. Designer:** Machin

KM	Date	Mintage	VG-8	F-12	VF-20	XF-40	MS-60	MS-63	Proof
61	1965	56,965,392	—	—	—	BV	0.50	0.75	—
	1966	34,567,898	—	—	—	BV	0.50	0.75	—

10 CENTS **Weight:** 2.3328 g. **Composition:** 0.8000 Silver 0.0600 oz. ASW

KM	Date	Mintage	VG-8	F-12	VF-20	XF-40	MS-60	MS-63	Proof
72	1968 Ottawa reeding	70,460,000	—	—	—	BV	0.50	0.75	—

10 CENTS **Composition:** Nickel

KM	Date	Mintage	VG-8	F-12	VF-20	XF-40	MS-60	MS-63	Proof
72a	1968 Ottawa reeding	87,412,930	—	—	—	0.15	0.25	0.35	—

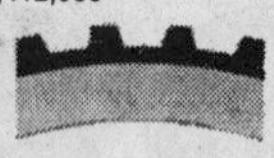

10 CENTS **Composition:** Nickel

KM	Date	Mintage	VG-8	F-12	VF-20	XF-40	MS-60	MS-63	Proof
73	1968 Philadelphia reeding	85,170,000	—	—	—	0.15	0.25	0.35	—
	1969 lg. date, lg. ship, 10-20 known	—	—	4,750	6,600	10,000	14,150	—	—

10 CENTS **Composition:** Nickel **Reverse:** Redesigned smaller ship

KM	Date	Mintage	VG-8	F-12	VF-20	XF-40	MS-60	MS-63	Proof
77.1	1969	55,833,929	—	—	—	0.15	0.25	0.35	—
	1970	5,249,296	—	—	—	0.25	0.45	0.95	—
	1971	41,016,968	—	—	—	0.15	0.25	0.35	—
	1972	60,169,387	—	—	—	0.15	0.25	0.35	—
	1973	167,715,435	—	—	—	0.15	0.25	0.35	—
	1974	201,566,565	—	—	—	0.15	0.25	0.35	—
	1975	207,680,000	—	—	—	0.15	0.25	0.35	—
	1976	95,018,533	—	—	—	0.15	0.25	0.35	—
	1977	128,452,206	—	—	—	0.15	0.25	0.35	—
	1978	170,366,431	—	—	—	0.15	0.25	0.35	—

10 CENTS **Composition:** Nickel **Obverse:** Smaller bust

KM	Date	Mintage	VG-8	F-12	VF-20	XF-40	MS-60	MS-63	Proof
77.2	1979	237,321,321	—	—	—	0.15	0.25	0.35	—
	1980	170,111,533	—	—	—	0.15	0.25	0.35	—
	1981	123,912,900	—	—	—	0.15	0.25	0.35	—
	1981 Proof	199,000	—	—	—	—	—	—	1.50
	1982	93,475,000	—	—	—	0.15	0.25	0.35	—
	1982 Proof	180,908	—	—	—	—	—	—	1.50
	1983	111,065,000	—	—	—	0.15	0.25	0.35	—
	1983 Proof	168,000	—	—	—	—	—	—	1.50
	1984	121,690,000	—	—	—	0.15	0.25	0.35	—
	1984 Proof	161,602	—	—	—	—	—	—	1.50
	1985	143,025,000	—	—	—	0.15	0.25	0.35	—
	1985 Proof	157,037	—	—	—	—	—	—	1.50
	1986	168,620,000	—	—	—	0.15	0.25	0.35	—
	1986 Proof	175,745	—	—	—	—	—	—	1.50
	1987	147,309,000	—	—	—	0.15	0.25	0.35	—
	1987 Proof	179,004	—	—	—	—	—	—	1.50
	1988	162,998,558	—	—	—	0.15	0.25	0.35	—
	1988 Proof	175,259	—	—	—	—	—	—	1.50
	1989	199,104,414	—	—	—	0.15	0.25	0.35	—
	1989 Proof	170,528	—	—	—	—	—	—	1.50

10 CENTS **Composition:** Nickel **Obverse:** Elizabeth II effigy **Obv. Designer:** dePedery-Hunt

KM	Date	Mintage	VG-8	F-12	VF-20	XF-40	MS-60	MS-63	Proof
183	1990	65,023,000	—	—	—	0.15	0.25	0.35	—
	1990 Proof	140,649	—	—	—	—	—	—	2.50
	1991	50,397,000	—	—	—	0.15	0.25	0.35	—
	1991 Proof	131,888	—	—	—	—	—	—	4.00
	1993	135,569,000	—	—	—	0.15	0.25	0.35	—
	1993 Proof	143,065	—	—	—	—	—	—	2.00
	1994	145,800,000	—	—	—	0.15	0.25	0.35	—
	1994 Proof	146,424	—	—	—	—	—	—	2.50
	1995	123,875,000	—	—	—	0.15	0.25	0.35	—
	1995 Proof	50,000	—	—	—	—	—	—	2.50
	1996 Proof	—	—	—	—	—	—	—	—
	1996	51,814,000	—	—	—	—	—	—	—
	1997	203,514,000	—	—	—	—	—	—	—
	1997 Proof	—	—	—	—	—	—	—	—
	1998 Proof	—	—	—	—	—	—	—	—
	1998	203,514,000	—	—	—	0.15	0.25	0.35	—
	1998W	—	—	—	—	—	—	1.50	—
	1999	258,462,000	—	—	—	0.15	0.25	0.35	—
	1999 Proof	—	—	—	—	—	—	—	—
	2000 Proof	—	—	—	—	—	—	—	—
	2000	159,125,000	—	—	—	0.15	0.25	0.35	—
	2000W	—	—	—	—	—	—	1.50	—
	2002	—	—	—	—	—	—	0.20	—

10 CENTS **Weight:** 2.4000 g. **Composition:** 0.9250 Silver 0.0713 oz. ASW

KM	Date	Mintage	VG-8	F-12	VF-20	XF-40	MS-60	MS-63	Proof
183a	1998 Proof	—	—	—	—	—	—	—	4.00
	19980 Proof	—	—	—	—	—	—	—	4.00
	1999 Proof	—	—	—	—	—	—	—	5.00
	2000 Proof	—	—	—	—	—	—	—	5.00
	2001 Proof	—	—	—	—	—	—	—	5.00
	2002 Proof	—	—	—	—	—	—	—	5.00

10 CENTS **Composition:** Nickel Plated Steel **Obverse:** Queen's head right **Reverse:** Sailboat **Edge:** Reeded **Size:** 18 mm.

KM	Date	Mintage	VG-8	F-12	VF-20	XF-40	MS-60	MS-63	Proof
183b	1999 P	Est. 20,000	—	—	—	—	—	15.00	—
	2000 P	Est. 200	—	—	—	—	400	600	—
	2001 P	266,000	—	—	—	—	0.30	0.65	—
	2002 P	—	—	—	—	—	—	0.20	—

25 CENTS **Weight:** 5.8100 g. **Composition:** 0.9250 Silver 0.1728 oz. ASW

KM	Date	Mintage	VG-8	F-12	VF-20	XF-40	MS-60	MS-63	Proof
5	1901	640,000	6.00	9.75	27.00	80.00	350	975	—

25 CENTS **Weight:** 5.8100 g. **Composition:** 0.9250 Silver 0.1728 oz. ASW

KM	Date	Mintage	VG-8	F-12	VF-20	XF-40	MS-60	MS-63	Proof
11	1902	464,000	7.00	12.00	35.00	110	500	1,450	—
	1902H	800,000	4.00	7.25	32.00	60.00	200	400	—
	1903	846,150	5.00	12.00	35.00	110	400	1,450	—
	1904	400,000	10.00	28.00	80.00	250	1,250	4,000	—
	1905	800,000	5.50	15.00	65.00	160	1,350	4,000	—
	1906 large crown	1,237,843	5.00	7.25	27.00	70.00	350	1,200	—
	1906 small crown; Rare	Inc. above	—	—	—	—	—	—	—
	1907	2,088,000	4.00	7.25	27.00	70.00	325	1,000	—
	1908	495,016	6.00	12.00	45.00	125	300	700	—
	1909	1,335,929	5.00	9.00	40.00	150	485	1,450	—

25 CENTS **Weight:** 5.8319 g. **Composition:** 0.9250 Silver 0.1734 oz. ASW

KM	Date	Mintage	VG-8	F-12	VF-20	XF-40	MS-60	MS-63	Proof
11a	1910	3,577,569	3.00	7.25	26.00	60.00	200	500	—

25 CENTS **Weight:** 5.8319 g. **Composition:** 0.9250 Silver 0.1734 oz. ASW

KM	Date	Mintage	VG-8	F-12	VF-20	XF-40	MS-60	MS-63	Proof
18	1911	1,721,341	4.00	12.00	25.00	60.00	200	350	—

25 CENTS **Weight:** 5.8319 g. **Composition:** 0.9250 Silver 0.1734 oz. ASW

KM	Date	Mintage	VG-8	F-12	VF-20	XF-40	MS-60	MS-63	Proof
24	1912	2,544,199	2.25	3.50	10.00	30.00	250	1,000	—
	1913	2,213,595	2.25	3.50	10.00	30.00	200	850	—
	1914	1,215,397	2.50	4.00	15.00	40.00	400	1,500	—
	1915	242,382	6.00	22.00	95.00	300	1,750	5,000	—
	1916	1,462,566	1.75	3.25	10.00	25.00	150	500	—
	1917	3,365,644	1.75	3.00	7.00	15.00	100	175	—
	1918	4,175,649	1.75	3.00	6.00	15.00	75.00	150	—
	1919	5,852,262	1.75	3.00	6.00	15.00	75.00	150	—

25 CENTS **Weight:** 5.8319 g. **Composition:** 0.8000 Silver 0.1500 oz. ASW

KM	Date	Mintage	VG-8	F-12	VF-20	XF-40	MS-60	MS-63	Proof
24a	1920	1,975,278	1.75	3.00	8.00	22.00	125	375	—
	1921	597,337	7.00	16.00	55.00	175	825	2,250	—
	1927	468,096	15.00	28.00	65.00	175	550	1,200	—
	1928	2,114,178	1.75	3.00	8.00	22.00	110	275	—
	1929	2,690,562	1.75	2.75	8.00	22.00	110	275	—
	1930	968,748	1.75	3.50	10.00	25.00	175	450	—
	1931	537,815	1.75	3.50	12.00	27.50	175	450	—
	1932	537,994	2.50	4.00	13.00	30.00	175	450	—
	1933	421,282	3.00	4.50	15.00	30.00	150	250	—
	1934	384,350	3.50	6.00	22.00	45.00	175	450	—
	1935	537,772	3.50	5.00	17.50	42.00	125	275	—
	1936	972,094	1.75	3.50	8.00	15.00	70.00	150	—
	1936 dot	153,322	20.00	50.00	120	225	600	1,400	—

Note: David Akers John Jay Pittman sale Part Three, 10-99, nearly Choice Unc. realized $6,900; considered a possible specimen example

25 CENTS **Weight:** 5.8319 g. **Composition:** 0.8000 Silver 0.1500 oz. ASW

KM	Date	Mintage	VG-8	F-12	VF-20	XF-40	MS-60	MS-63	Proof
35	1937	2,690,176	1.00	1.50	2.25	3.50	10.00	25.00	—
	1938	3,149,245	1.00	1.50	3.25	5.00	40.00	85.00	—
	1939	3,532,495	1.00	1.50	2.25	4.50	35.00	75.00	—
	1940	9,583,650	BV	1.00	1.50	2.50	10.00	20.00	—
	1941	6,654,672	BV	1.00	1.50	2.50	10.00	20.00	—
	1942	6,935,871	BV	1.00	1.50	2.50	10.00	20.00	—
	1943	13,559,575	BV	1.00	1.50	2.50	10.00	20.00	—
	1944	7,216,237	BV	1.00	1.50	2.50	15.00	25.00	—
	1945	5,296,495	BV	1.00	1.50	2.00	10.00	20.00	—
	1946	2,210,810	BV	1.50	3.00	5.00	30.00	45.00	—
	1947	1,524,554	BV	1.50	4.00	8.00	30.00	55.00	—
	1947 dot after 7	Inc. above	25.00	30.00	50.00	85.00	175	375	—
	1947 maple leaf	4,393,938	BV	1.00	2.00	3.00	10.00	20.00	—

25 CENTS **Weight:** 5.8319 g. **Composition:** 0.8000 Silver 0.1500 oz. ASW **Obverse:** Modified legend

KM	Date	Mintage	VG-8	F-12	VF-20	XF-40	MS-60	MS-63	Proof
44	1948	2,564,424	BV	1.50	3.00	5.00	35.00	70.00	—
	1949	7,988,830	—	BV	1.25	2.00	5.00	11.00	—
	1950	9,673,335	—	BV	1.25	1.50	4.00	9.00	—
	1951	8,290,719	—	BV	1.25	1.50	3.00	8.00	—
	1952	8,859,642	—	BV	1.25	1.50	3.00	7.00	—

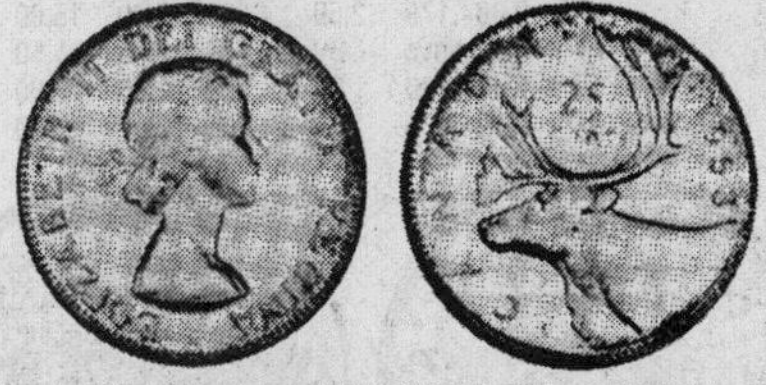

25 CENTS **Weight:** 5.8319 g. **Composition:** 0.8000 Silver 0.1500 oz. ASW **Obverse:** Elizabeth II effigy **Obv. Designer:** Gillick

KM	Date	Mintage	VG-8	F-12	VF-20	XF-40	MS-60	MS-63	Proof
52	1953 without strap	10,546,769	—	BV	1.25	1.50	3.00	7.00	—
	1953 with strap	Inc. above	—	BV	1.25	1.50	4.00	12.00	—
	1954	2,318,891	BV	1.25	2.00	4.00	15.00	25.00	—
	1955	9,552,505	—	—	BV	1.25	2.50	5.00	—
	1956	11,269,353	—	—	BV	1.25	2.00	4.00	—
	1957	12,770,190	—	—	BV	1.00	1.50	3.00	—
	1958	9,336,910	—	—	BV	1.00	1.50	3.00	—
	1959	13,503,461	—	—	—	BV	1.25	2.25	—
	1960	22,835,327	—	—	—	BV	1.00	1.50	—
	1961	18,164,368	—	—	—	BV	1.00	1.50	—
	1962	29,559,266	—	—	—	BV	1.00	1.25	—
	1963	21,180,652	—	—	—	BV	1.00	1.25	—
	1964	36,479,343	—	—	—	BV	1.00	1.25	—

25 CENTS **Weight:** 5.8319 g. **Composition:** 0.8000 Silver 0.1500 oz. ASW **Obverse:** Elizabeth II effigy **Obv. Designer:** Machin

KM	Date	Mintage	VG-8	F-12	VF-20	XF-40	MS-60	MS-63	Proof
62	1965	44,708,869	—	—	—	BV	1.00	1.25	—
	1966	25,626,315	—	—	—	BV	1.00	1.25	—

25 CENTS **Weight:** 5.8319 g. **Composition:** 0.5000 Silver 0.0937 oz. ASW **Obverse:** Elizabeth II effigy **Obv. Designer:** Machin

KM	Date	Mintage	VG-8	F-12	VF-20	XF-40	MS-60	MS-63	Proof
62a	1968	71,464,000	—	—	—	BV	0.75	1.25	—

25 CENTS **Composition:** Nickel **Obverse:** Elizabeth II effigy **Obv. Designer:** Machin

KM	Date	Mintage	VG-8	F-12	VF-20	XF-40	MS-60	MS-63	Proof
62b	1968	88,686,931	—	—	—	0.30	0.50	0.75	—
	1969	133,037,929	—	—	—	0.30	0.50	0.75	—
	1970	10,302,010	—	—	—	0.30	1.25	2.25	—
	1971	48,170,428	—	—	—	0.30	0.50	0.75	—
	1972	43,743,387	—	—	—	0.30	0.50	0.75	—
	1974	192,360,598	—	—	—	0.30	0.50	0.75	—
	1975	141,148,000	—	—	—	0.30	0.50	0.75	—
	1976	86,898,261	—	—	—	0.30	0.50	0.75	—
	1977	99,634,555	—	—	—	0.30	0.50	0.75	—
	1978	176,475,408	—	—	—	0.30	0.50	0.75	—

25 CENTS **Composition:** Nickel **Obverse:** Elizabeth II effigy, smaller bust **Obv. Designer:** Machin

KM	Date	Mintage	VG-8	F-12	VF-20	XF-40	MS-60	MS-63	Proof
74	1979	131,042,905	—	—	—	0.30	0.50	0.75	—
	1980	76,178,000	—	—	—	0.30	0.50	0.75	—
	1981	131,580,272	—	—	—	0.30	0.50	0.75	—
	1981 Proof	199,000	—	—	—	—	—	—	2.00
	1982	171,926,000	—	—	—	0.30	0.50	0.75	—
	1982 Proof	180,908	—	—	—	—	—	—	2.00
	1983	13,162,000	—	—	—	0.30	0.75	1.50	—
	1983 Proof	168,000	—	—	—	—	—	—	3.00
	1984	121,668,000	—	—	—	0.30	0.50	0.75	—
	1984 Proof	161,602	—	—	—	—	—	—	2.00
	1985	158,734,000	—	—	—	0.30	0.50	0.75	—
	1985 Proof	157,037	—	—	—	—	—	—	2.00
	1986	132,220,000	—	—	—	0.30	0.50	0.75	—
	1986 Proof	175,745	—	—	—	—	—	—	2.00
	1987	53,408,000	—	—	—	0.30	0.65	1.25	—
	1987 Proof	179,004	—	—	—	—	—	—	2.00
	1988	80,368,473	—	—	—	0.30	0.50	1.00	—
	1988 Proof	175,259	—	—	—	—	—	—	2.00
	1989	119,796,307	—	—	—	0.30	0.50	0.75	—
	1989 Proof	170,928	—	—	—	—	—	—	2.00

25 CENTS **Composition:** Nickel **Obverse:** Elizabeth II effigy **Obv. Designer:** dePedery-Hunt

KM	Date	Mintage	VG-8	F-12	VF-20	XF-40	MS-60	MS-63	Proof
184	1990	31,258,000	—	—	—	0.30	0.50	1.00	—
	1990 Proof	140,649	—	—	—	—	—	—	2.50
	1991	459,000	—	—	2.00	4.00	8.00	12.00	—
	1991 Proof	131,888	—	—	—	—	—	—	20.00
	1993	73,758,000	—	—	—	0.30	0.50	0.75	—
	1993 Proof	143,065	—	—	—	—	—	—	2.00
	1994	77,670,000	—	—	—	0.30	0.50	0.75	—
	1994 Proof	146,424	—	—	—	—	—	—	3.00
	1995	89,210,000	—	—	—	0.30	0.50	0.75	—
	1995 Proof	50,000	—	—	—	—	—	—	3.00
	1996 Proof	—	—	—	—	—	—	—	6.00
	1996	28,106,000	—	—	—	—	—	1.50	—
	1997	—	—	—	—	—	—	1.50	—
	1997 Proof	—	—	—	—	—	—	—	6.00
	1998W	—	—	—	—	—	—	5.00	—
	1999	—	—	—	—	—	—	1.50	—
	1999 Proof	—	—	—	—	—	—	—	6.00
	2000 Proof	—	—	—	—	—	—	—	6.00
	2000	—	—	—	—	—	—	1.50	—
	2000W	—	—	—	—	—	—	5.00	—
	2001 Proof	—	—	—	—	—	—	—	6.00
	2001	8,409,000	—	—	—	—	—	1.75	—
	2002	—	—	—	—	—	—	0.50	—

25 CENTS **Weight:** 5.9000 g. **Composition:** 0.9250 Silver 0.1754 oz. ASW

KM	Date	Mintage	VG-8	F-12	VF-20	XF-40	MS-60	MS-63	Proof
184a	1996 Proof	—	—	—	—	—	—	—	6.50
	1997 Proof	—	—	—	—	—	—	—	6.50
	1998 Proof	—	—	—	—	—	—	—	5.50
	1998O Proof	—	—	—	—	—	—	—	5.50
	1999 Proof	—	—	—	—	—	—	—	5.50
	2001 Proof	—	—	—	—	—	—	—	6.50
	2002 Proof	—	—	—	—	—	—	—	10.00

25 CENTS **Composition:** Nickel Plated Steel **Note:** No 2000 dated coins of this type were minted.

KM	Date	Mintage	VG-8	F-12	VF-20	XF-40	MS-60	MS-63	Proof
184b	1999 P	Est. 20,000	—	—	—	—	—	20.00	—

KM	Date	Mintage	VG-8	F-12	VF-20	XF-40	MS-60	MS-63	Proof
	2000 P 3-5 Known	—	—	—	—	—	—	2,000	—
	2001 P	52,153,000	—	—	—	—	0.60	1.00	—
	2002 P	—	—	—	—	—	—	0.50	—

50 CENTS

Weight: 11.6200 g. **Composition:** 0.9250 Silver .3456 oz. ASW

KM	Date	Mintage	VG-8	F-12	VF-20	XF-40	MS-60	MS-63	Proof
6	1901	80,000	42.00	70.00	165	400	4,200	10,500	—

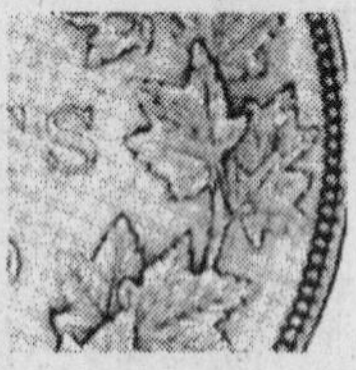

50 CENTS

Weight: 11.6200 g. **Composition:** 0.9250 Silver .3456 oz. ASW

KM	Date	Mintage	VG-8	F-12	VF-20	XF-40	MS-60	MS-63	Proof
12	1902	120,000	11.00	22.50	85.00	200	1,100	3,000	—
	1903H	140,000	16.00	35.00	100	225	1,100	3,000	—
	1904	60,000	85.00	150	285	625	2,650	7,000	—
	1905	40,000	100	200	425	1,000	4,000	10,000	—
	1906	350,000	10.00	25.00	70.00	190	1,000	3,000	—
	1907	300,000	8.00	25.00	70.00	200	1,000	3,500	—
	1908	128,119	14.75	45.00	125	275	800	1,650	—
	1909	302,118	13.00	40.00	150	350	2,000	6,000	—
	1910 Victorian leaves	649,521	8.00	25.00	75.00	225	1,100	3,500	—

50 CENTS

Weight: 11.6638 g. **Composition:** 0.9250 Silver .3461 oz. ASW

KM	Date	Mintage	VG-8	F-12	VF-20	XF-40	MS-60	MS-63	Proof
12a	1910 Edwardian leaves	Inc. above	8.00	22.00	65.00	200	1,000	3,150	—

50 CENTS

Weight: 11.6638 g. **Composition:** 0.9250 Silver .3461 oz. ASW

KM	Date	Mintage	VG-8	F-12	VF-20	XF-40	MS-60	MS-63	Proof
19	1911	209,972	6.00	55.00	200	425	1,100	2,900	—

50 CENTS

Weight: 11.6638 g. **Composition:** 0.9250 Silver .3461 oz. ASW **Obverse:** Modified legend

KM	Date	Mintage	VG-8	F-12	VF-20	XF-40	MS-60	MS-63	Proof
25	1912	285,867	4.00	16.00	65.00	175	850	2,200	—
	1913	265,889	4.00	16.00	85.00	200	1,100	4,000	—
	1914	160,128	8.00	40.00	120	375	2,000	6,000	—
	1916	459,070	3.00	9.00	35.00	95.00	550	1,800	—
	1917	752,213	3.00	7.00	25.00	70.00	350	950	—
	1918	754,989	3.00	6.00	20.00	60.00	300	800	—
	1919	1,113,429	3.00	6.00	20.00	60.00	300	1,100	—

50 CENTS

Weight: 11.6638 g. **Composition:** 0.8000 Silver .3000 oz. ASW

KM	Date	Mintage	VG-8	F-12	VF-20	XF-40	MS-60	MS-63	Proof
25a	1920	584,691	3.00	7.00	25.00	90.00	400	950	—
	1921 75 to 100 known	—	12,000	17,000	20,750	21,000	35,000	45,000	—

Note: David Akers John Jay Pittman sale, Part Three, 10-99, Gem Unc. realized $63,250

KM	Date	Mintage	VG-8	F-12	VF-20	XF-40	MS-60	MS-63	Proof
	1929	228,328	3.00	7.00	25.00	75.00	375	900	—
	1931	57,581	6.00	18.00	60.00	175	725	1,700	—
	1932	19,213	90.00	125	300	600	2,800	7,000	—
	1934	39,539	10.00	20.00	60.00	175	500	1,150	—
	1936	38,550	10.00	18.00	50.00	135	400	900	—

50 CENTS

Weight: 11.6638 g. **Composition:** 0.8000 Silver .3000 oz. ASW

KM	Date	Mintage	VG-8	F-12	VF-20	XF-40	MS-60	MS-63	Proof
36	1937	192,016	2.00	3.00	4.50	7.00	20.00	50.00	—
	1938	192,018	3.00	4.00	8.00	22.00	90.00	275	—
	1939	287,976	2.50	3.50	5.50	13.00	60.00	170	—
	1940	1,996,566	BV	1.75	2.50	4.00	18.00	60.00	—
	1941	1,714,874	BV	1.75	2.50	4.00	18.00	60.00	—
	1942	1,974,164	BV	1.75	2.50	4.00	18.00	60.00	—
	1943	3,109,583	BV	1.75	2.50	4.00	18.00	60.00	—
	1944	2,460,205	BV	1.75	2.50	4.00	18.00	60.00	—
	1945	1,959,528	BV	1.75	2.50	4.00	18.00	60.00	—
	1946	950,235	BV	2.00	3.50	7.00	40.00	110	—
	1946 hoof in 6	Inc. above	10.00	20.00	35.00	100	900	2,000	—
	1947 straight 7	424,885	BV	2.50	3.50	9.00	50.00	160	—
	1947 curved 7	Inc. above	BV	2.50	3.50	9.00	50.00	160	—
	1947 maple leaf, straight 7	38,433	14.00	18.00	25.00	50.00	125	230	—
	1947 maple leaf, curved 7	Inc. above	900	1,150	1,400	1,900	3,000	6,000	—

50 CENTS

Weight: 11.6638 g. **Composition:** 0.8000 Silver .3000 oz. ASW **Obverse:** Modified legend

KM	Date	Mintage	VG-8	F-12	VF-20	XF-40	MS-60	MS-63	Proof
45	1948	37,784	35.00	42.00	50.00	75.00	110	175	—
	1949	858,991	BV	2.00	3.50	7.00	25.00	100	—
	1949 hoof over 9	Inc. above	5.00	10.00	18.00	45.00	225	550	—
	1950 no lines	2,384,179	2.50	4.00	7.00	15.00	110	175	—
	1950 lines in 0	Inc. above	BV	1.75	2.75	3.50	8.00	20.00	—
	1951	2,421,730	BV	1.50	2.50	3.00	6.00	17.00	—
	1952	2,596,465	BV	1.50	2.50	3.00	6.00	11.00	—

50 CENTS

Weight: 11.6638 g. **Composition:** 0.8000 Silver .3000 oz. ASW **Obverse:** Elizabeth II Effigy **Obv. Designer:** Gillick

KM	Date	Mintage	VG-8	F-12	VF-20	XF-40	MS-60	MS-63	Proof
53	1953 small date	1,630,429	—	BV	2.00	2.50	4.50	10.00	—
	1953 lg. date, straps	Inc. above	—	BV	2.50	3.00	10.00	22.00	—
	1953 lg. date without straps	Inc. above	BV	2.00	3.50	9.00	50.00	90.00	—
	1954	506,305	BV	2.00	3.50	7.00	18.00	30.00	—
	1955	753,511	—	BV	2.50	3.50	10.00	20.00	—
	1956	1,379,499	—	BV	2.00	2.50	4.50	9.00	—
	1957	2,171,689	—	BV	—	1.75	3.50	6.00	—
	1958	2,957,266	—	BV	—	1.75	3.00	5.50	—

50 CENTS **Weight:** 11.6638 g. **Composition:** 0.8000 Silver .3000 oz. ASW **Reverse:** New shield

KM	Date	Mintage	VG-8	F-12	VF-20	XF-40	MS-60	MS-63	Proof
56	1959 horizontal shading	3,095,535	—	—	BV	1.75	2.50	4.50	—
	1960	3,488,897	—	—	—	BV	2.25	3.25	—
	1961	3,584,417	—	—	—	BV	2.00	3.00	—
	1962	5,208,030	—	—	—	BV	1.75	3.00	—
	1963	8,348,871	—	—	—	BV	1.75	3.00	—
	1964	9,377,676	—	—	—	BV	1.75	3.00	—

50 CENTS **Weight:** 11.6638 g. **Composition:** 0.8000 Silver .3000 oz. ASW **Obverse:** Elizabeth II effigy **Obv. Designer:** Machin

KM	Date	Mintage	VG-8	F-12	VF-20	XF-40	MS-60	MS-63	Proof
63	1965	12,629,974	—	—	—	BV	1.75	3.00	—
	1966	7,920,496	—	—	—	BV	1.75	3.00	—

50 CENTS **Composition:** Nickel

KM	Date	Mintage	VG-8	F-12	VF-20	XF-40	MS-60	MS-63	Proof
75.1	1968	3,966,932	—	—	—	0.50	0.65	1.00	—
	1969	7,113,929	—	—	—	0.50	0.65	1.00	—
	1970	2,429,526	—	—	—	0.50	0.65	1.00	—
	1971	2,166,444	—	—	—	0.50	0.65	1.00	—
	1972	2,515,632	—	—	—	0.50	0.65	1.00	—
	1973	2,546,096	—	—	—	0.50	0.65	1.00	—
	1974	3,436,650	—	—	—	0.50	0.65	1.00	—
	1975	3,710,000	—	—	—	0.50	0.65	1.00	—
	1976	2,940,719	—	—	—	0.50	0.65	1.00	—

50 CENTS **Composition:** Nickel **Obverse:** Smaller bust

KM	Date	Mintage	VG-8	F-12	VF-20	XF-40	MS-60	MS-63	Proof
75.2	1977	709,839	—	—	0.50	0.75	1.35	2.00	—

50 CENTS **Composition:** Nickel **Reverse:** Redesigned arms

KM	Date	Mintage	VG-8	F-12	VF-20	XF-40	MS-60	MS-63	Proof
75.3	1978 square jewels	3,341,892	—	—	—	0.50	0.65	1.00	—
	1978 round jewels	Inc. above	—	—	0.50	2.50	3.00	4.00	—
	1979	3,425,000	—	—	—	0.50	0.65	1.00	—
	1980	1,574,000	—	—	—	0.50	0.65	1.00	—
	1981	2,690,272	—	—	—	0.50	0.65	1.00	—
	1981 Proof	199,000	—	—	—	—	—	—	3.00
	1982 small beads	2,236,674	—	—	—	20.00	40.00	60.00	—
	1982 small beads; Proof	180,908	—	—	—	—	—	—	3.00
	1982 large beads	Inc. above	—	—	—	0.50	0.65	1.00	—
	1983	1,177,000	—	—	—	0.50	0.65	1.00	—
	1983 Proof	168,000	—	—	—	—	—	—	3.00
	1984	1,502,989	—	—	—	0.50	0.65	1.00	—
	1984 Proof	161,602	—	—	—	—	—	—	3.00
	1985	2,188,374	—	—	—	0.50	0.65	1.00	—
	1985 Proof	157,037	—	—	—	—	—	—	3.00
	1986	781,400	—	—	—	0.50	1.00	1.25	—
	1986 Proof	175,745	—	—	—	—	—	—	3.00
	1987	373,000	—	—	—	0.50	1.00	1.50	—
	1987 Proof	179,004	—	—	—	—	—	—	3.50
	1988	220,000	—	—	—	0.50	1.00	1.50	—
	1988 Proof	175,259	—	—	—	—	—	—	3.00
	1989	266,419	—	—	—	0.50	1.00	1.50	—
	1989 Proof	170,928	—	—	—	—	—	—	3.00

50 CENTS **Composition:** Nickel **Obverse:** Elizabeth II effigy **Obv. Designer:** dePedery-Hunt

KM	Date	Mintage	VG-8	F-12	VF-20	XF-40	MS-60	MS-63	Proof
185	1990	207,000	—	—	—	0.50	1.00	1.50	—
	1990 Proof	140,649	—	—	—	—	—	—	5.00
	1991	490,000	—	—	—	0.50	0.85	1.00	—
	1991 Proof	131,888	—	—	—	—	—	—	7.00
	1993	393,000	—	—	—	0.50	0.85	1.00	—
	1993 Proof	143,065	—	—	—	—	—	—	3.00
	1994	987,000	—	—	—	0.50	0.75	1.00	—
	1994 Proof	146,424	—	—	—	—	—	—	4.00
	1995	626,000	—	—	—	0.50	0.75	1.00	—
	1995 Proof	50,000	—	—	—	—	—	—	4.00
	1996	458,000	—	—	—	0.50	0.65	1.00	—
	1996 Proof	—	—	—	—	—	—	—	—

50 CENTS **Weight:** 11.6380 g. **Composition:** 0.9250 Silver .3461 oz. ASW

KM	Date	Mintage	VG-8	F-12	VF-20	XF-40	MS-60	MS-63	Proof
185a	1996 Proof	—	—	—	—	—	—	—	9.00

50 CENTS **Composition:** Nickel **Reverse:** Redesigned arms

KM	Date	Mintage	VG-8	F-12	VF-20	XF-40	MS-60	MS-63	Proof
290	1997 Proof	—	—	—	—	—	—	—	—
	1997	387,000	—	—	—	0.50	0.65	1.00	—
	1998	308,000	—	—	—	0.50	0.65	1.00	—
	1998 Proof	—	—	—	—	—	—	—	—
	1998W	—	—	—	—	—	—	2.00	—
	1999	496,000	—	—	—	0.50	0.65	1.00	—
	1999 Proof	—	—	—	—	—	—	—	—
	2000 Proof	—	—	—	—	—	—	—	—
	2000	559,000	—	—	—	0.50	0.65	1.00	—
	2000W	—	—	—	—	—	—	1.50	—

50 CENTS **Weight:** 11.6380 g. **Composition:** 0.9250 Silver .3461 oz. ASW

KM	Date	Mintage	VG-8	F-12	VF-20	XF-40	MS-60	MS-63	Proof
290a	1997 Proof	—	—	—	—	—	—	—	10.00
	1998 Proof	—	—	—	—	—	—	—	10.00
	1999 Proof	—	—	—	—	—	—	—	10.00
	2000 Proof	—	—	—	—	—	—	—	10.00
	2001 Proof	—	—	—	—	—	—	—	10.00
	2002 Proof	—	—	—	—	—	—	—	10.00

50 CENTS **Composition:** Nickel Plated Steel **Reverse:** Redesigned arms

KM	Date	Mintage	VG-8	F-12	VF-20	XF-40	MS-60	MS-63	Proof
290b	1999	Est. 20,000	—	—	—	—	—	15.00	—
	2000P	Est. 50	—	—	—	—	1,500	2,000	—
	Note: Available only in RCM presentation coin clocks								
	2001	—	—	—	—	—	1.25	2.50	—
	2002	—	—	—	—	—	1.25	2.50	—
	2002P	—	—	—	—	—	—	1.00	—

50 CENTS **Weight:** 6.8300 g. **Composition:** Nickel Plated Steel **Subject:** Queen's Golden Jubilee **Obverse:** Bust of Queen Elizabeth II right and monogram. **Reverse:** Canadian arms. **Edge:** Reeded. **Size:** 27 mm.

KM	Date	Mintage	VG-8	F-12	VF-20	XF-40	MS-60	MS-63	Proof
444	ND(2002)	—	—	—	—	—	1.00	—	—

DOLLAR **Weight:** 23.3276 g. **Composition:** 0.8000 Silver 0.6000 oz. ASW **Reverse:** Voyageur

KM	Date	Mintage	F-12	VF-20	XF-40	AU-50	MS-60	MS-63	Proof
31	1936	339,600	8.50	12.50	16.50	21.50	35.00	72.00	5,000

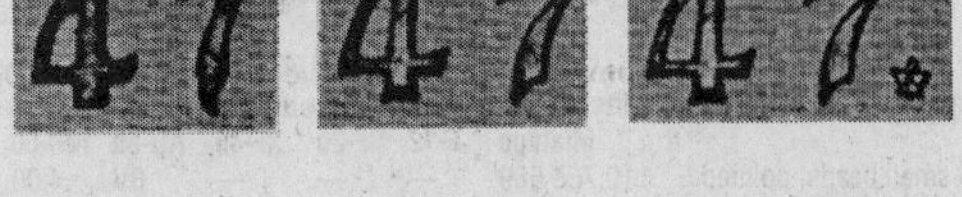

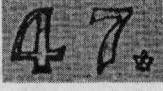

DOLLAR **Weight:** 23.3276 g. **Composition:** 0.8000 Silver 0.6000 oz. ASW **Reverse:** Voyageur

KM	Date	Mintage	F-12	VF-20	XF-40	AU-50	MS-60	MS-63	Proof
37	1937	207,406	9.00	9.50	11.00	13.00	25.00	65.00	—
	1937 Mirror Proof	1,295	—	—	—	—	—	—	650
	1937 Matte Proof	Inc. above	—	—	—	—	—	—	250
	1938	90,304	23.50	32.00	40.00	50.00	65.00	175	6,000
	1945	38,391	65.00	90.00	110	125	175	450	2,000
	1946	93,055	12.50	22.50	31.00	37.50	65.00	225	1,800
	1947 pointed 7		55.00	70.00	85.00	110	275	900	3,500
	1947 blunt 7	65,595	35.00	50.00	70.00	90.00	110	225	4,500
	1947 maple leaf	21,135	100	130	150	160	225	450	1,800

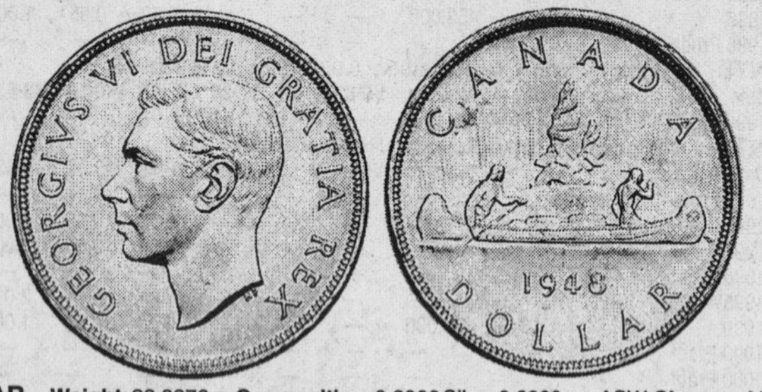

DOLLAR **Weight:** 23.3276 g. **Composition:** 0.8000 Silver 0.6000 oz. ASW **Obverse:** Modified left legend **Reverse:** Voyageur

KM	Date	Mintage	F-12	VF-20	XF-40	AU-50	MS-60	MS-63	Proof
46	1948	18,780	300	350	400	500	600	900	3,000
	1950 with 3 water lines	261,002	5.00	7.00	9.00	12.00	15.00	28.00	800
	1950 with 4 water lines, 1 known, Matte Proof	—	—	—	—	—	—	—	—
	1950 arnprior with 2-1/2 water lines	Inc. above	6.50	8.50	12.50	16.00	25.00	75.00	1,500
	1951 with 3 water lines	416,395	4.00	5.00	6.50	7.50	9.00	22.50	650
	1951 arnprior with 1-1/2 water lines	Inc. above	15.00	30.00	45.00	60.00	100	250	2,000
	1952 with 3 water lines	406,148	4.00	5.00	6.50	7.50	10.00	22.50	1,000
	1952 short water lines, arnprior type	Inc. above	8.00	12.00	15.00	18.00	25.00	60.00	1,250
	1952 without water lines	Inc. above	5.00	6.00	8.00	10.00	16.50	30.00	—

DOLLAR **Weight:** 23.3276 g. **Composition:** 0.8000 Silver 0.6000 oz. ASW **Obverse:** Elizabeth II effigy **Obv. Designer:** Gillick **Reverse:** Voyageur **Note:** All genuine circulation strike 1955 Arnprior dollars have a die break running along the top of TI in the word GRATIA on the obverse.

KM	Date	Mintage	F-12	VF-20	XF-40	AU-50	MS-60	MS-63	Proof
54	1953 without strap, wire rim	1,074,578	BV	3.90	4.50	5.00	7.00	13.00	400
	1953 with strap, flat rim	Inc. above	BV	3.90	4.50	5.00	7.00	13.00	—
	1954	246,606	4.00	6.00	8.00	10.00	16.50	31.50	—
	1955 with 3 water lines	268,105	4.50	6.00	8.00	10.00	15.00	25.00	—
	1955 arnprior with 1-1/2 water lines* and die break	Inc. above	40.00	45.00	55.00	65.00	75.00	140	—
	1956	209,092	7.00	9.00	12.50	15.50	19.00	30.00	—
	1957 with 3 water lines	496,389	—	BV	4.75	5.50	7.50	11.00	—
	1957 with 1 water line	Inc. above	4.50	5.50	7.50	8.50	10.00	20.00	—
	1959	1,443,502	—	—	—	BV	5.00	6.50	—
	1960	1,420,486	—	—	—	BV	5.00	6.50	—
	1961	1,262,231	—	—	—	BV	5.00	6.50	—
	1962	1,884,789	—	—	—	BV	5.00	6.50	—
	1963	4,179,981	—	—	—	BV	5.00	6.50	—

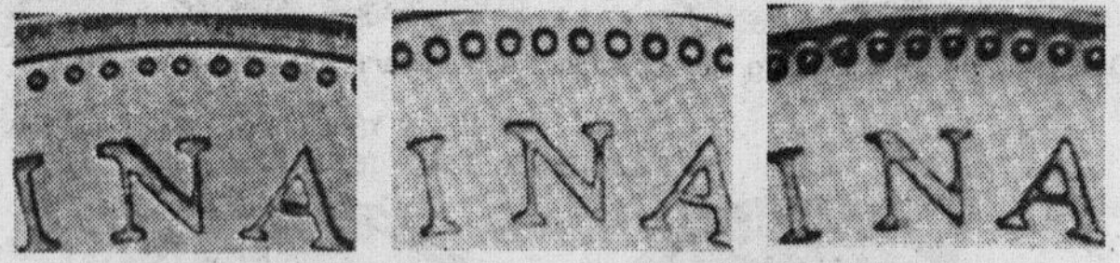

DOLLAR **Weight:** 23.3276 g. **Composition:** 0.8000 Silver 0.6000 oz. ASW **Obverse:** Elizabeth II effigy **Obv. Designer:** Machin **Reverse:** Voyageur

KM	Date	Mintage	F-12	VF-20	XF-40	AU-50	MS-60	MS-63	Proof
64.1	1965 small beads, pointed 5	10,768,569	—	—	—	BV	4.00	6.00	—
	1965 small beads, blunt 5	Inc. above	—	—	—	BV	4.00	6.00	—
	1965 large beads, blunt 5	Inc. above	—	—	—	BV	4.00	6.00	—
	1965 large beads, pointed 5	Inc. above	—	—	—	BV	4.75	8.00	—
	1965 medium beads, pointed 5	Inc. above	BV	5.00	7.00	9.00	12.00	25.00	—
	1966 large beads	9,912,178	—	—	—	BV	4.00	6.00	—
	1966 small beads	485	—	—	750	1,000	1,350	1,550	—

DOLLAR **Composition:** Nickel **Obverse:** Large bust **Reverse:** Voyageur **Size:** 32 mm.

KM	Date	Mintage	MS-63	P/L	Proof
76.1	1968	5,579,714	1.25	—	—
	1968	1,408,143	—	1.75	—
	1968 Small island	—	5.00	—	—
	1968 No island	—	—	4.00	—
	1968 Doubled die	—	—	25.00	—
	Note: Exhibits extra water lines				
	1969	4,809,313	1.25	—	—
	1969	594,258	—	2.00	—
	1972	2,676,041	1.50	—	—
	1972	405,865	—	2.50	—

DOLLAR **Weight:** 23.3276 g. **Composition:** 0.5000 Silver 0.3750 oz. ASW **Obverse:** Smaller bust **Reverse:** Voyageur **Size:** 36 mm.

KM	Date	Mintage	MS-63	P/L	Proof
64.2a	1972 Proof	341,598	—	—	5.00

Note: Specimen $5.50.

DOLLAR **Composition:** Nickel **Reverse:** Voyageur **Size:** 32 mm. **Note:** Only known in prooflike sets with 1976 obverse slightly modified.

KM	Date	Mintage	MS-63	P/L	Proof
76.3	1975 mule w/1976 obv.	Inc. above	—	3.00	—

DOLLAR **Composition:** Nickel **Obverse:** Smaller bust **Reverse:** Voyageur **Size:** 32 mm.

KM	Date	Mintage	MS-63	P/L	Proof
76.2	1975	3,256,000	1.50	—	—
	1975	322,325	—	2.50	—
	1976	2,498,204	1.50	—	—
	1976	274,106	—	2.50	—

DOLLAR **Composition:** Nickel **Reverse:** Voyageur modified **Size:** 32 mm.

KM	Date	Mintage	MS-63	P/L	Proof
117	1977	1,393,745	2.25	—	—

DOLLAR **Composition:** Nickel **Reverse:** Voyageur **Size:** 32 mm. **Note:** Modified design.

KM	Date	Mintage	MS-63	P/L	Proof
120.1	1978	2,948,488	1.50	—	—
	1979	2,954,842	1.50	—	—
	1980	3,291,221	1.50	—	—
	1981	2,778,900	1.50	—	—
	1981 Proof	—	—	—	—
	1982	1,098,500	1.50	2.50	—
	1982 Proof	180,908	—	—	5.25
	1983	2,267,525	1.50	4.00	—
	1983 Proof	166,779	—	—	5.25
	1984	1,223,486	1.50	—	—
	1984 Proof	161,602	—	—	6.00
	1985	3,104,092	1.50	3.50	—
	1985 Proof	153,950	—	—	7.00
	1986	3,089,225	2.00	4.00	—
	1986 Proof	176,224	—	—	7.50
	1987	287,330	3.50	5.00	—
	1987 Proof	175,686	—	—	7.50

DOLLAR **Composition:** Nickel **Reverse:** Voyageur **Size:** 32 mm. **Note:** Modified design.

KM	Date	Mintage	MS-63	P/L	Spec.
120.2	1985 mule w/New Zealand 50 cent, KM-37 obverse	—	1,200	—	—

DOLLAR **Composition:** Aureate-Bronze Plated Nickel **Obverse:** Elizabeth II effigy **Obv. Designer:** Machin **Reverse:** Loon

KM	Date	Mintage	MS-63	P/L	Proof
157	1987	205,405,000	2.25	—	—
	1987 Proof	178,120	—	—	8.00
	1988	138,893,539	2.25	4.00	—
	1988 Proof	175,259	—	—	6.75
	1989	184,773,902	3.00	4.00	—
	1989 Proof	170,928	—	—	6.75

DOLLAR **Composition:** Nickel **Obverse:** Elizabeth II effigy **Obv. Designer:** dePedery-Hunt **Reverse:** Loon

KM	Date	Mintage	MS-63	P/L	Proof
186	1990	68,402,000	1.75	4.00	—
	1990 Proof	140,649	—	—	7.00
	1991	23,156,000	1.75	6.50	—
	1991 Proof	—	—	—	13.00
	1993	33,662,000	2.00	3.00	—
	1993 Proof	—	—	—	6.00
	1994	36,237,000	2.00	3.50	—
	1994 Proof	—	—	—	7.00
	1995	41,813,000	3.00	4.50	—
	1995 Proof	—	—	—	7.00
	1996	17,101,000	2.00	6.00	—
	1996 Proof	—	—	—	7.50
	1997	—	5.00	6.00	—
	1997 Proof	—	—	—	8.00
	1998	—	3.50	6.00	—
	1998 Proof	—	—	—	10.00
	1998W	—	—	4.50	—
	1999	—	5.00	6.00	—
	1999 Proof	—	—	—	8.00
	2000	—	5.00	6.00	—
	2000 Proof	—	—	—	8.00
	2001	—	5.00	6.00	—
	2001 Proof	—	—	—	8.00
	2002	—	—	12.00	—
	2002 Proof	—	—	12.00	—

DOLLAR **Composition:** Gold Plated **Subject:** Olympic Win

KM	Date	Mintage	MS-63	P/L	Proof
186a	2002 Proof	—	—	—	30.00

2 DOLLARS **Ring Composition:** Nickel **Center Composition:** Aluminum-Bronze **Reverse:** Polar bear **Size:** 28 mm. **Note:** The Type III design has two lines outlining the star.

KM	Date	Mintage	MS-63	P/L	Proof
270	1996	375,483,000	3.25	5.00	10.00
	1997	16,942,000	3.25	—	—
	1998	4,926,000	3.25	—	—
	1998W	—	—	4.00	—
	1999	—	3.25	—	—
	2000	—	3.25	—	—
	2000W	—	—	—	—
	2001	11,910,000	3.25	—	—

2 DOLLARS **Ring Composition:** Silver 0.7434 oz. ASW **Center Weight:** 25.0000 g. **Center Composition:** 0.9250 Gold Plated Silver **Reverse:** Polar bear

KM	Date	Mintage	MS-63	P/L	Proof
270b	1996 Proof	10,000	—	—	50.00
	1998 Proof	—	—	—	—

2 DOLLARS **Ring Composition:** 0.9250 Silver 0.2626 oz. ASW **Center Weight:** 8.8300 g. **Center Composition:** 0.9250 Gold Plated Silver **Reverse:** Polar bear

KM	Date	Mintage	MS-63	P/L	Proof
270c	1997 Proof	—	—	—	10.00
	19980 Proof	—	—	—	12.00
	1999 Proof	—	—	—	12.00
	2000 Proof	—	—	—	12.00
	2001 Proof	—	—	—	12.00

5 DOLLARS **Weight:** 8.3592 g. **Composition:** 0.9000 Gold 0.2419 oz. AGW

KM	Date	Mintage	F-12	VF-20	XF-40	AU-50	MS-60	MS-63
26	1912	165,680	110	125	150	175	225	550
	1913	98,832	110	125	150	175	225	550
	1914	31,122	150	250	300	400	625	1,750

10 DOLLARS **Weight:** 16.7185 g. **Composition:** 0.9000 Gold 0.4838 oz. AGW

KM	Date	Mintage	F-12	VF-20	XF-40	AU-50	MS-60	MS-63
27	1912	74,759	225	275	325	375	500	2,000
	1913	149,232	225	275	325	375	525	2,650
	1914	140,068	225	275	350	400	575	2,750

SOVEREIGN **Weight:** 7.9881 g. **Composition:** 0.9170 Gold .2354 oz. AGW **Reverse:** Mint mark below horse's rear hooves

KM	Date	Mintage	VG-8	F-12	VF-20	XF-40	MS-60	MS-63	Proof
14	1908C	636	—	1,000	1,750	2,000	2,700	3,000	—
	1909C	16,273	—	110	170	200	475	1,600	—
	1910C	28,012	—	100	150	180	475	2,000	—

SOVEREIGN **Weight:** 7.9881 g. **Composition:** 0.9170 Gold 0.2354 oz. AGW

KM	Date	Mintage	VG-8	F-12	VF-20	XF-40	MS-60	MS-63	Proof
20	1911C	256,946	—	—	—	BV	90.00	150	—
	1913C	3,715	—	350	450	550	1,000	2,000	—
	1914C	14,871	—	150	200	275	325	600	—
	1916C about 20 known	—	—	8,000	12,500	11,000	16,000	25,000	—
	Note: Stacks' A.G. Carter Jr. Sale 12-89 Gem BU realized $82,500.								
	1917C	58,845	—	—	BV	85.00	100	300	—
	1918C	106,514	—	—	BV	85.00	110	450	—
	1919C	135,889	—	—	BV	85.00	100	350	—

COMMEMORATIVE COINAGE

CENT **Composition:** Bronze **Subject:** Confederation Centennial

KM	Date	Mintage	VG-8	F-12	VF-20	XF-40	MS-60	MS-63	Proof
65	ND(1967)	345,140,645	—	—	—	—	0.10	0.25	1.00

CENT **Composition:** Bronze **Subject:** Confederation 125

KM	Date	Mintage	VG-8	F-12	VF-20	XF-40	MS-60	MS-63	Proof
204	ND(1992)	673,512,000	—	—	—	—	0.10	0.15	—
	ND(1992) Proof	147,061	—	—	—	—	—	—	2.50

CENT **Weight:** 5.6700 g. **Composition:** 0.9250 Copper-Plated Silver 0.1677 oz. **Subject:** 90th Anniversary Royal Canadian Mint - 1908-1998

KM	Date	Mintage	VG-8	F-12	VF-20	XF-40	MS-60	MS-63	Proof
309	ND(1998)	25,000	—	—	—	—	—	16.00	—
	Note: Antique finish								
	ND(1998) Proof	—	—	—	—	—	—	—	—

CENT **Weight:** 5.6700 g. **Composition:** 0.9250 Silver .1677 oz. ASW **Subject:** 90th Anniversary Royal Canadian Mint - 1908-1998 **Obverse:** With "Canada" added to bust

KM	Date	Mintage	VG-8	F-12	VF-20	XF-40	MS-60	MS-63	Proof
332	• ND(2000) Proof	25,000	—	—	—	—	—	—	16.00
	Note: Mirror finish								

3 CENTS **Weight:** 31.1035 g. **Composition:** 0.9250 Silver .1600 oz. ASW **Subject:** 1st Canadian Postage Stamp **Obverse:** Queen's head right. **Reverse:** Partial stamp design. **Edge:** Plain. **Size:** 21.1 mm.

KM	Date	Mintage	MS-63	Proof
410	2001 Proof	90,000	—	25.00

5 CENTS **Composition:** Tombac **Subject:** Victory

KM	Date	Mintage	VG-8	F-12	VF-20	XF-40	MS-60	MS-63	Proof
40	1943	24,760,256	0.20	0.30	0.40	0.85	2.00	6.00	—
	1944 1 known	8,000	—	—	—	—	—	—	—

5 CENTS **Composition:** Chrome Plated Steel

KM	Date	Mintage	VG-8	F-12	VF-20	XF-40	MS-60	MS-63	Proof
40a	1944	11,532,784	0.15	0.25	0.45	1.00	2.00	4.00	—
	1945	18,893,216	0.15	0.25	0.45	1.00	2.00	4.00	—

5 CENTS **Composition:** Nickel **Subject:** Nickel Bicentennial

KM	Date	Mintage	VG-8	F-12	VF-20	XF-40	MS-60	MS-63	Proof
48	ND(1951)	9,028,507	0.15	0.20	0.25	0.50	1.75	3.50	—

5 CENTS **Composition:** Copper Nickel **Subject:** Confederation Centennial

KM	Date	Mintage	VG-8	F-12	VF-20	XF-40	MS-60	MS-63	Proof
66	ND(1967)	36,876,574	—	—	—	—	0.25	0.40	1.00

5 CENTS **Composition:** Copper-Nickel **Subject:** Confederation 125

KM	Date	Mintage	VG-8	F-12	VF-20	XF-40	MS-60	MS-63	Proof
205	ND(1992)	53,732,000	—	—	—	—	0.10	0.20	—
	ND(1992) Proof	147,061	—	—	—	—	—	—	4.00

5 CENTS **Weight:** 1.1670 g. **Composition:** 0.9250 Silver .0347 oz. ASW **Subject:** 90th Anniversary Royal Canadian Mint

KM	Date	Mintage	VG-8	F-12	VF-20	XF-40	MS-60	MS-63	Proof
310	ND(1998)	25,000	—	—	—	—	—	12.00	—
	ND(1998) Proof	25,000	—	—	—	—	—	—	12.00

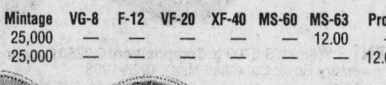

5 CENTS **Composition:** 0.9250 Silver **Subject:** First French-Canadian Regiment **Obverse:** Queen's portrait **Reverse:** Regimental drums, sash and baton **Edge:** Plain **Size:** 21.2 mm.

KM	Date	Mintage	VG-8	F-12	VF-20	XF-40	MS-60	MS-63	Proof
400	2000 Proof	—	—	—	—	—	—	—	11.50

5 CENTS **Weight:** 5.3500 g. **Composition:** 0.9250 Silver .1591 oz. ASW **Subject:** Royal Military College **Obverse:** Queen's head right **Reverse:** Marching cadets and arch **Edge:** Plain **Size:** 21.2 mm.

KM	Date	Mintage	VG-8	F-12	VF-20	XF-40	MS-60	MS-63	Proof
413	2001 Proof	—	—	—	—	—	—	—	11.50

10 CENTS **Weight:** 2.3328 g. **Composition:** 0.8000 Silver 0.0600 oz. ASW **Subject:** Confederation Centennial

KM	Date	Mintage	VG-8	F-12	VF-20	XF-40	MS-60	MS-63	Proof
67	ND(1967)	62,998,215	—	—	—	BV	0.50	1.00	2.00

10 CENTS **Weight:** 2.3328 g. **Composition:** 0.5000 Silver 0.0372 oz. ASW **Subject:** Confederation Centennial

KM	Date	Mintage	VG-8	F-12	VF-20	XF-40	MS-60	MS-63	Proof
67a	ND(1967)	Inc. above	—	—	—	BV	0.50	1.00	—

10 CENTS **Composition:** Nickel **Subject:** Confederation 125

KM	Date	Mintage	VG-8	F-12	VF-20	XF-40	MS-60	MS-63	Proof
206	ND(1992)	174,476,000	—	—	—	—	0.25	0.35	—
	ND(1992) Proof	147,061	—	—	—	—	—	—	3.00

10 CENTS **Weight:** 2.4000 g. **Composition:** 0.9250 Silver .0714 oz. ASW **Subject:** John Cabot

KM	Date	Mintage	VG-8	F-12	VF-20	XF-40	MS-60	MS-63	Proof
299	ND(1997) Proof	49,848	—	—	—	—	—	—	17.50

10 CENTS **Weight:** 2.3200 g. **Composition:** 0.9250 Silver .0690 oz. ASW **Subject:** 90th Anniversary Royal Canadian Mint

KM	Date	Mintage	VG-8	F-12	VF-20	XF-40	MS-60	MS-63	Proof
311	ND(1998) Matte	25,000	—	—	—	—	—	—	10.00
	ND(1998) Proof	25,000	—	—	—	—	—	—	10.00

10 CENTS **Weight:** 2.4000 g. **Composition:** 0.9250 Silver .0714 oz. ASW **Subject:** First Canadian Credit Union **Obverse:** Queen's head right. **Reverse:** Alphonse Desjardins' house, (founder of the first credit union in Canada). **Edge:** Reeded. **Size:** 18 mm.

KM	Date	Mintage	VG-8	F-12	VF-20	XF-40	MS-60	MS-63	Proof
409	ND(2000) Proof	66,336	—	—	—	—	—	—	11.00

10 CENTS **Weight:** 1.7700 g. **Composition:** Nickel Plated Steel **Subject:** Year of the Volunteer **Obverse:** Queen's head right. **Reverse:** Three portraits and radiant sun. **Edge:** Reeded. **Size:** 18 mm.

KM	Date	Mintage	VG-8	F-12	VF-20	XF-40	MS-60	MS-63	Proof
412	2001P Proof	—	—	—	—	—	—	—	—

10 CENTS **Weight:** 2.4000 g. **Composition:** 0.9250 Silver .0714 oz. ASW **Subject:** Year of the Volunteer **Obverse:** Queen's head right. **Reverse:** 3 conjoined busts above banner, radiant sun below. **Edge:** Reeded. **Size:** 18 mm.

KM	Date	Mintage	MS-63	Proof
412a	2001P Proof	50,000	—	12.50

25 CENTS **Weight:** 5.8319 g. **Composition:** 0.8000 Silver 0.1500 oz. ASW **Subject:** Confederation Centennial

KM	Date	Mintage	VG-8	F-12	VF-20	XF-40	MS-60	MS-63	Proof
68	ND(1967)	48,855,500	—	—	—	BV	1.00	1.75	—

25 CENTS **Weight:** 5.8319 g. **Composition:** 0.5000 Silver 0.0937 oz. ASW **Subject:** Confederation Centennial

KM	Date	Mintage	VG-8	F-12	VF-20	XF-40	MS-60	MS-63	Proof
68a	ND(1967)	Inc. above	—	—	—	BV	1.00	1.75	—

25 CENTS **Composition:** Nickel **Subject:** RCMP Centennial **Note:** 120 beads.

KM	Date	Mintage	VG-8	F-12	VF-20	XF-40	MS-60	MS-63	Proof
81.1	ND(1973)	134,958,587	—	—	—	0.30	0.50	0.80	—

25 CENTS **Composition:** Nickel **Subject:** RCMP Centennial **Note:** 132 beads.

KM	Date	Mintage	VG-8	F-12	VF-20	XF-40	MS-60	MS-63	Proof
81.2	ND(1973)	Inc. above	30.00	50.00	60.00	70.00	85.00	110	—

25 CENTS **Composition:** Nickel **Subject:** Confederation 125

KM	Date	Mintage	VG-8	F-12	VF-20	XF-40	MS-60	MS-63	Proof
207	ND(1992)	442,986	—	—	—	—	—	12.50	—
	ND(1992) Proof	147,061	—	—	—	—	—	—	20.00

25 CENTS **Composition:** Nickel **Series:** 125th Anniversary of Confederation **Subject:** New Brunswick

KM	Date	Mintage	VG-8	F-12	VF-20	XF-40	MS-60	MS-63	Proof
203	ND(1992)	12,174,000	—	—	—	—	0.35	0.75	—

25 CENTS **Weight:** 5.8319 g. **Composition:** 0.9250 Silver 0.1734 oz. ASW **Series:** 125th Anniversary of Confederation **Subject:** New Brunswick

KM	Date	Mintage	VG-8	F-12	VF-20	XF-40	MS-60	MS-63	Proof
203a	ND(1992) Proof	149,579	—	—	—	—	—	—	7.50

25 CENTS **Composition:** Nickel **Series:** 125th Anniversary of Confederation **Subject:** North West Territories

KM	Date	Mintage	VG-8	F-12	VF-20	XF-40	MS-60	MS-63	Proof
212	ND(1992)	12,582,000	—	—	—	—	0.35	0.75	—

25 CENTS **Weight:** 5.8319 g. **Composition:** 0.9250 Silver 0.1734 oz. ASW **Series:** 125th Anniversary of Confederation **Subject:** North West Territories

KM	Date	Mintage	VG-8	F-12	VF-20	XF-40	MS-60	MS-63	Proof
212a	ND(1992) Proof	149,579	—	—	—	—	—	—	7.50

25 CENTS **Composition:** Nickel **Series:** 125th Anniversary of Confederation **Subject:** Newfoundland

KM	Date	Mintage	VG-8	F-12	VF-20	XF-40	MS-60	MS-63	Proof
213	ND(1992)	11,405,000	—	—	—	—	0.35	0.75	—

25 CENTS **Weight:** 5.8319 g. **Composition:** 0.9250 Silver 0.1734 oz. ASW **Series:** 125th Anniversary of Confederation **Subject:** Newfoundland

KM	Date	Mintage	VG-8	F-12	VF-20	XF-40	MS-60	MS-63	Proof
213a	ND(1992) Proof	149,579	—	—	—	—	—	—	7.50

25 CENTS **Composition:** Nickel **Series:** 125th Anniversary of Confederation **Subject:** Manitoba

KM	Date	Mintage	VG-8	F-12	VF-20	XF-40	MS-60	MS-63	Proof
214	ND(1992)	11,349,000	—	—	—	—	0.35	0.75	—

25 CENTS **Weight:** 5.8319 g. **Composition:** 0.9250 Silver 0.1734 oz. ASW **Series:** 125th Anniversary of Confederation **Subject:** Manitoba

KM	Date	Mintage	VG-8	F-12	VF-20	XF-40	MS-60	MS-63	Proof
214a	ND(1992) Proof	149,579	—	—	—	—	—	—	7.50

25 CENTS **Composition:** Nickel **Series:** 125th Anniversary of Confederation **Subject:** Yukon

KM	Date	Mintage	VG-8	F-12	VF-20	XF-40	MS-60	MS-63	Proof
220	ND(1992)	10,388,000	—	—	—	—	0.35	0.75	—

25 CENTS **Weight:** 5.8319 g. **Composition:** 0.9250 Silver 0.1734 oz. ASW **Series:** 125th Anniversary of Confederation **Subject:** Yukon

KM	Date	Mintage	VG-8	F-12	VF-20	XF-40	MS-60	MS-63	Proof
220a	ND(1992) Proof	149,579	—	—	—	—	—	—	7.50

25 CENTS **Composition:** Nickel **Series:** 125th Anniversary of Confederation **Subject:** Alberta

KM	Date	Mintage	VG-8	F-12	VF-20	XF-40	MS-60	MS-63	Proof
221	ND(1992)	12,133,000	—	—	—	—	0.35	0.75	—

25 CENTS **Weight:** 5.8319 g. **Composition:** 0.9250 Silver 0.1734 oz. ASW **Series:** 125th Anniversary of Confederation **Subject:** Alberta

KM	Date	Mintage	VG-8	F-12	VF-20	XF-40	MS-60	MS-63	Proof
221a	ND(1992) Proof	—	—	—	—	—	—	—	7.50

25 CENTS **Composition:** Nickel **Series:** 125th Anniversary of Confederation **Subject:** Prince Edward Island

KM	Date	Mintage	VG-8	F-12	VF-20	XF-40	MS-60	MS-63	Proof
222	ND(1992)	13,001,000	—	—	—	—	0.35	0.75	—

25 CENTS **Weight:** 5.8319 g. **Composition:** 0.9250 Silver 0.1734 oz. ASW **Series:** 125th Anniversary of Confederation **Subject:** Prince Edward Island

KM	Date	Mintage	VG-8	F-12	VF-20	XF-40	MS-60	MS-63	Proof
222a	ND(1992) Proof	149,579	—	—	—	—	—	—	7.50

25 CENTS **Composition:** Nickel **Series:** 125th Anniversary of Confederation **Subject:** Ontario

KM	Date	Mintage	VG-8	F-12	VF-20	XF-40	MS-60	MS-63	Proof
223	ND(1992)	14,263,000	—	—	—	—	0.35	0.75	—

25 CENTS **Weight:** 5.8319 g. **Composition:** 0.9250 Silver 0.1734 oz. ASW **Series:** 125th Anniversary of Confederation **Subject:** Ontario

KM	Date	Mintage	VG-8	F-12	VF-20	XF-40	MS-60	MS-63	Proof
223a	ND(1992) Proof	149,579	—	—	—	—	—	—	7.50

25 CENTS **Composition:** Nickel **Series:** 125th Anniversary of Confederation **Subject:** Nova Scotia

KM	Date	Mintage	VG-8	F-12	VF-20	XF-40	MS-60	MS-63	Proof
231	ND(1992)	13,600,000	—	—	—	—	0.35	0.75	—

25 CENTS **Weight:** 5.8319 g. **Composition:** 0.9250 Silver 0.1734 oz. ASW **Series:** 125th Anniversary of Confederation **Subject:** Nova Scotia

KM	Date	Mintage	VG-8	F-12	VF-20	XF-40	MS-60	MS-63	Proof
231a	ND(1992) Proof	149,579	—	—	—	—	—	—	7.50

25 CENTS **Composition:** Nickel **Series:** 125th Anniversary of Confederation **Subject:** British Columbia

KM	Date	Mintage	VG-8	F-12	VF-20	XF-40	MS-60	MS-63	Proof
232	ND(1992)	14,001,000	—	—	—	—	0.35	0.75	—

25 CENTS **Weight:** 5.8319 g. **Composition:** 0.9250 Silver 0.1734 oz. ASW **Series:** 125th Anniversary of Confederation **Subject:** British Columbia

KM	Date	Mintage	VG-8	F-12	VF-20	XF-40	MS-60	MS-63	Proof
232a	ND(1992) Proof	149,579	—	—	—	—	—	—	7.50

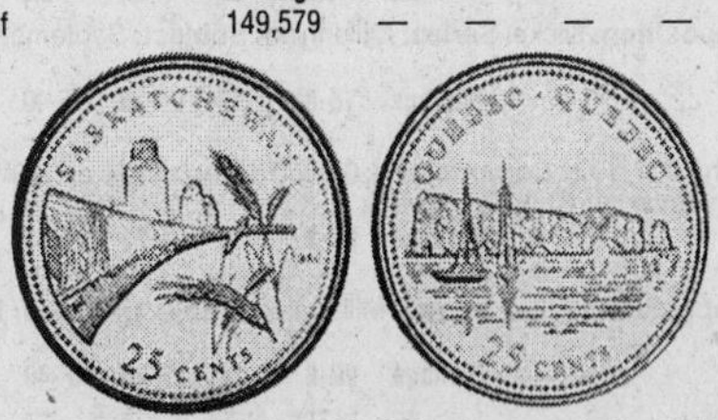

25 CENTS **Composition:** Nickel **Series:** 125th Anniversary of Confederation **Subject:** Saskatchewan

KM	Date	Mintage	VG-8	F-12	VF-20	XF-40	MS-60	MS-63	Proof
233	ND(1992)	14,165,000	—	—	—	—	0.35	0.75	—

25 CENTS **Weight:** 5.8319 g. **Composition:** 0.9250 Silver 0.1734 oz. ASW **Series:** 125th Anniversary of Confederation **Subject:** Saskatchewan

KM	Date	Mintage	VG-8	F-12	VF-20	XF-40	MS-60	MS-63	Proof
233a	ND(1992) Proof	149,579	—	—	—	—	—	—	7.50

25 CENTS **Composition:** Nickel **Series:** 125th Anniversary of Confederation **Subject:** Quebec

KM	Date	Mintage	VG-8	F-12	VF-20	XF-40	MS-60	MS-63	Proof
234	ND(1992)	13,607,000	—	—	—	—	0.35	0.75	—

25 CENTS **Weight:** 5.8319 g. **Composition:** 0.9250 Silver 0.1734 oz. ASW **Series:** 125th Anniversary of Confederation **Subject:** Quebec

KM	Date	Mintage	VG-8	F-12	VF-20	XF-40	MS-60	MS-63	Proof
234a	ND(1992) Proof	149,579	—	—	—	—	—	—	7.50

25 CENTS **Subject:** 90th Anniversary Royal Canadian Mint

KM	Date	Mintage	VG-8	F-12	VF-20	XF-40	MS-60	MS-63	Proof
312	ND(1998) Matte	25,000	—	—	—	—	—	—	15.00

25 CENTS **Composition:** Nickel **Series:** Millennium **Subject:** January **Reverse:** Totem pole, portraits

KM	Date	Mintage	VG-8	F-12	VF-20	XF-40	MS-60	MS-63	Proof
342	1999	—	—	—	—	—	0.50	0.70	—

25 CENTS **Weight:** 5.8319 g. **Composition:** 0.9250 Silver 0.1734 oz. ASW **Series:** Millennium **Subject:** January **Reverse:** Totem pole, portraits

KM	Date	Mintage	VG-8	F-12	VF-20	XF-40	MS-60	MS-63	Proof
342a	1999 Proof	—	—	—	—	—	—	—	8.00

25 CENTS **Composition:** Nickel **Series:** Millennium **Subject:** February **Reverse:** Native petroglyphs

KM	Date	Mintage	VG-8	F-12	VF-20	XF-40	MS-60	MS-63	Proof
343	1999	—	—	—	—	—	0.50	0.70	—

25 CENTS **Weight:** 5.8319 g. **Composition:** 0.9250 Silver 0.1734 oz. ASW **Series:** Millennium **Subject:** February **Reverse:** Native petroglyphs

KM	Date	Mintage	VG-8	F-12	VF-20	XF-40	MS-60	MS-63	Proof
343a	1999 Proof	—	—	—	—	—	—	—	8.00

25 CENTS **Composition:** Nickel **Series:** Millennium **Subject:** March **Reverse:** Lumberjack

KM	Date	Mintage	VG-8	F-12	VF-20	XF-40	MS-60	MS-63	Proof
344	1999	—	—	—	—	—	0.50	0.70	—

25 CENTS **Weight:** 5.8319 g. **Composition:** 0.9250 Silver 0.1734 oz. ASW **Series:** Millennium **Subject:** March **Reverse:** Lumberjack

KM	Date	Mintage	VG-8	F-12	VF-20	XF-40	MS-60	MS-63	Proof
344a	1999 Proof	—	—	—	—	—	—	—	8.00

25 CENTS **Composition:** Nickel **Series:** Millennium **Subject:** April **Reverse:** Owl, polar bear

KM	Date	Mintage	VG-8	F-12	VF-20	XF-40	MS-60	MS-63	Proof
345	1999	—	—	—	—	—	0.50	0.70	—

25 CENTS **Weight:** 5.8319 g. **Composition:** 0.9250 Silver 0.1734 oz. ASW **Series:** Millennium **Subject:** April **Reverse:** Owl, polar bear

KM	Date	Mintage	VG-8	F-12	VF-20	XF-40	MS-60	MS-63	Proof
345a	1999 Proof	—	—	—	—	—	—	—	8.00

25 CENTS **Composition:** Nickel **Series:** Millennium **Subject:** May **Reverse:** Voyageurs in canoe

KM	Date	Mintage	VG-8	F-12	VF-20	XF-40	MS-60	MS-63	Proof
346	1999	—	—	—	—	—	0.50	0.70	—

25 CENTS **Weight:** 5.8319 g. **Composition:** 0.9250 Silver 0.1734 oz. ASW **Series:** Millennium **Subject:** May **Reverse:** Voyageurs in canoe

KM	Date	Mintage	VG-8	F-12	VF-20	XF-40	MS-60	MS-63	Proof
346a	1999 Proof	—	—	—	—	—	—	—	8.00

25 CENTS **Composition:** Nickel **Series:** Millennium **Subject:** June **Reverse:** 19th-century locomotive

KM	Date	Mintage	VG-8	F-12	VF-20	XF-40	MS-60	MS-63	Proof
347	1999	—	—	—	—	—	0.50	0.70	—

25 CENTS **Weight:** 5.8319 g. **Composition:** 0.9250 Silver 0.1734 oz. ASW **Series:** Millennium **Subject:** June **Reverse:** 19th-century locomotive

KM	Date	Mintage	VG-8	F-12	VF-20	XF-40	MS-60	MS-63	Proof
347a	1999 Proof	—	—	—	—	—	—	—	8.00

25 CENTS **Composition:** Nickel **Series:** Millennium **Subject:** July **Reverse:** 6 stylized portraits

KM	Date	Mintage	VG-8	F-12	VF-20	XF-40	MS-60	MS-63	Proof
348	1999	—	—	—	—	—	0.50	0.70	—

25 CENTS **Weight:** 5.8319 g. **Composition:** 0.9250 Silver 0.1734 oz. ASW **Series:** Millennium **Subject:** July **Reverse:** 6 stylized portraits

KM	Date	Mintage	VG-8	F-12	VF-20	XF-40	MS-60	MS-63	Proof
348a	1999 Proof	—	—	—	—	—	—	—	8.00

25 CENTS **Composition:** Nickel **Series:** Millennium **Subject:** August **Reverse:** Hay harvesting

KM	Date	Mintage	VG-8	F-12	VF-20	XF-40	MS-60	MS-63	Proof
349	1999	—	—	—	—	—	0.50	0.70	—

25 CENTS **Weight:** 5.8319 g. **Composition:** 0.9250 Silver 0.1734 oz. ASW **Series:** Millennium **Subject:** August **Reverse:** Hay harvesting

KM	Date	Mintage	VG-8	F-12	VF-20	XF-40	MS-60	MS-63	Proof
349a	1999 Proof	—	—	—	—	—	—	—	8.00

25 CENTS **Composition:** Nickel **Series:** Millennium **Subject:** September **Reverse:** Childlike artwork

KM	Date	Mintage	VG-8	F-12	VF-20	XF-40	MS-60	MS-63	Proof
350	1999	—	—	—	—	—	0.50	0.70	—

25 CENTS **Weight:** 5.8319 g. **Composition:** 0.9250 Silver 0.1734 oz. ASW **Series:** Millennium **Subject:** September **Reverse:** Childlike artwork

KM	Date	Mintage	VG-8	F-12	VF-20	XF-40	MS-60	MS-63	Proof
350a	1999 Proof	—	—	—	—	—	—	—	8.00

25 CENTS **Composition:** Nickel **Series:** Millennium **Subject:** October **Reverse:** Aboriginal artwork

KM	Date	Mintage	VG-8	F-12	VF-20	XF-40	MS-60	MS-63	Proof
351	1999	—	—	—	—	—	0.50	0.70	—

25 CENTS **Weight:** 5.8319 g. **Composition:** 0.9250 Silver 0.1734 oz. ASW **Series:** Millennium **Subject:** October **Reverse:** Aboriginal artwork

KM	Date	Mintage	VG-8	F-12	VF-20	XF-40	MS-60	MS-63	Proof
351a	1999 Proof	—	—	—	—	—	—	—	8.00

25 CENTS **Composition:** Nickel **Series:** Millennium **Subject:** November **Reverse:** Bush plane with landing skis

KM	Date	Mintage	VG-8	F-12	VF-20	XF-40	MS-60	MS-63	Proof
352	1999	—	—	—	—	—	0.50	0.70	—

25 CENTS **Weight:** 5.8319 g. **Composition:** 0.9250 Silver 0.1734 oz. ASW **Series:** Millennium **Subject:** November **Reverse:** Bush plane with landing skis

KM	Date	Mintage	VG-8	F-12	VF-20	XF-40	MS-60	MS-63	Proof
352a	1999 Proof	—	—	—	—	—	—	—	8.00

25 CENTS **Composition:** Nickel **Series:** Millennium **Subject:** December **Reverse:** Eclectic geometric design

KM	Date	Mintage	VG-8	F-12	VF-20	XF-40	MS-60	MS-63	Proof

25 CENTS **Weight:** 5.8319 g. **Composition:** 0.9250 Silver 0.1734 oz. ASW **Series:** Millennium **Subject:** December **Reverse:** Eclectic geometric design

KM	Date	Mintage	VG-8	F-12	VF-20	XF-40	MS-60	MS-63	Proof
353a	1999 Proof	—	—	—	—	—	—	—	8.00

25 CENTS **Composition:** Nickel **Subject:** Health **Reverse:** Ribbon and caduceus

KM	Date	Mintage	VG-8	F-12	VF-20	XF-40	MS-60	MS-63	Proof
373	2000	—	—	—	—	—	0.50	0.70	—

25 CENTS **Composition:** 0.9250 Silver **Subject:** Health **Reverse:** Ribbon and caduceus

KM	Date	Mintage	VG-8	F-12	VF-20	XF-40	MS-60	MS-63	Proof

25 CENTS **Composition:** Nickel **Subject:** Freedom **Reverse:** 2 children and rising sun

KM	Date	Mintage	VG-8	F-12	VF-20	XF-40	MS-60	MS-63	Proof
374	2000	—	—	—	—	—	0.50	0.70	—

25 CENTS **Composition:** 0.9250 Silver **Subject:** Freedom **Reverse:** 2 children and rising sun

KM	Date	Mintage	VG-8	F-12	VF-20	XF-40	MS-60	MS-63	Proof
374a	2000 Proof	—	—	—	—	—	—	—	8.00

25 CENTS **Composition:** 0.9250 Silver **Subject:** Family **Reverse:** Circular native carvings

KM	Date	Mintage	VG-8	F-12	VF-20	XF-40	MS-60	MS-63	Proof
375a	2000 Proof	—	—	—	—	—	—	—	8.00

25 CENTS **Composition:** Nickel **Subject:** Family **Reverse:** Circular native carvings

KM	Date	Mintage	VG-8	F-12	VF-20	XF-40	MS-60	MS-63	Proof
375	2000	—	—	—	—	—	0.50	0.70	—

25 CENTS **Composition:** Nickel **Subject:** Community **Reverse:** Map on globe

KM	Date	Mintage	VG-8	F-12	VF-20	XF-40	MS-60	MS-63	Proof
376	2000	—	—	—	—	—	0.50	0.70	—

25 CENTS **Composition:** 0.9250 Silver **Subject;** Community **Reverse:** Map on globe

KM	Date	Mintage	VG-8	F-12	VF-20	XF-40	MS-60	MS-63	Proof
376a	2000 Proof	—	—	—	—	—	—	—	8.00

25 CENTS **Composition:** Nickel **Subject:** Harmony **Reverse:** Maple leaf

KM	Date	Mintage	VG-8	F-12	VF-20	XF-40	MS-60	MS-63	Proof
377	2000	—	—	—	—	—	0.50	0.70	—

25 CENTS **Composition:** 0.9250 Silver **Subject:** Harmony **Reverse:** Maple leaf

KM	Date	Mintage	VG-8	F-12	VF-20	XF-40	MS-60	MS-63	Proof
377a	2000 Proof	—	—	—	—	—	—	—	8.00

25 CENTS **Composition:** Nickel **Subject:** Wisdom **Reverse:** Man with young child

KM	Date	Mintage	VG-8	F-12	VF-20	XF-40	MS-60	MS-63	Proof
378	2000	—	—	—	—	—	0.50	0.70	—

25 CENTS **Composition:** 0.9250 Silver **Subject:** Wisdom **Reverse:** Man with young child

KM	Date	Mintage	VG-8	F-12	VF-20	XF-40	MS-60	MS-63	Proof
378a	2000 Proof	—	—	—	—	—	—	—	8.00

25 CENTS **Composition:** Nickel **Subject:** Creativity **Reverse:** Canoe full of children

KM	Date	Mintage	VG-8	F-12	VF-20	XF-40	MS-60	MS-63	Proof
379	2000	—	—	—	—	—	0.50	0.70	—

25 CENTS **Composition:** 0.9250 Silver **Subject:** Creativity **Reverse:** Canoe full of children

KM	Date	Mintage	VG-8	F-12	VF-20	XF-40	MS-60	MS-63	Proof
379a	2000 Proof	—	—	—	—	—	—	—	8.00

25 CENTS **Composition:** Nickel **Subject:** Ingenuity **Reverse:** Crescent-shaped city views

KM	Date	Mintage	VG-8	F-12	VF-20	XF-40	MS-60	MS-63	Proof
380	2000	—	—	—	—	—	0.50	0.70	—

25 CENTS **Composition:** 0.9250 Silver **Subject:** Ingenuity **Reverse:** Crescent-shaped city view

KM	Date	Mintage	VG-8	F-12	VF-20	XF-40	MS-60	MS-63	Proof
380a	2000 Proof	—	—	—	—	—	—	—	8.00

25 CENTS **Composition:** Nickel **Subject:** Achievement **Reverse:** Rocket above jagged design

KM	Date	Mintage	VG-8	F-12	VF-20	XF-40	MS-60	MS-63	Proof
381	2000	—	—	—	—	—	0.50	0.70	—

25 CENTS **Composition:** 0.9250 Silver **Subject:** Achievement **Reverse:** Rocket above jagged design

KM	Date	Mintage	VG-8	F-12	VF-20	XF-40	MS-60	MS-63	Proof
381a	2000 Proof	—	—	—	—	—	—	—	8.00

25 CENTS **Composition:** Nickel **Subject:** Natural legacy **Reverse:** Environmental elements

KM	Date	Mintage	VG-8	F-12	VF-20	XF-40	MS-60	MS-63	Proof
382	2000	—	—	—	—	—	0.50	0.70	—

25 CENTS **Composition:** 0.9250 Silver **Subject:** Natural legacy **Reverse:** Environmental elements

KM	Date	Mintage	VG-8	F-12	VF-20	XF-40	MS-60	MS-63	Proof
382a	2000 Proof	—	—	—	—	—	—	—	8.00

25 CENTS **Composition:** Nickel **Subject:** Celebration **Reverse:** Fireworks, children behind flag

KM	Date	Mintage	VG-8	F-12	VF-20	XF-40	MS-60	MS-63	Proof
383	2000	—	—	—	—	—	0.50	0.70	—

25 CENTS **Composition:** 0.9250 Silver **Subject:** Celebration **Reverse:** Fireworks, children behind flag

KM	Date	Mintage	VG-8	F-12	VF-20	XF-40	MS-60	MS-63	Proof
383a	2000 Proof	—	—	—	—	—	—	—	8.00

25 CENTS **Composition:** Nickel **Subject:** Pride **Reverse:** 2 with three small maple leaves on large maple leaf

KM	Date	Mintage	VG-8	F-12	VF-20	XF-40	MS-60	MS-63	Proof
384.2	2000	—	—	—	—	—	0.50	0.70	—

25 CENTS **Composition:** 0.9250 Silver **Subject:** Pride **Reverse:** 2 with 3 small maple leaves on large maple leaf

KM	Date	Mintage	VG-8	F-12	VF-20	XF-40	MS-60	MS-63	Proof
384.2a	2000 Proof	—	—	—	—	—	—	—	8.00

25 CENTS **Composition:** Nickel **Subject:** Pride **Obverse:** Queen's portrait **Reverse:** Red with 3 small maple leaves on large maple leaf **Edge:** Reeded **Size:** 23.9 mm. **Note:** Colorized version.

KM	Date	Mintage	VG-8	F-12	VF-20	XF-40	MS-60	MS-63	Proof
384.1	2000	—	—	—	—	—	—	6.50	

25 CENTS **Weight:** 5.0600 g. **Composition:** Nickel Plated Steel **Subject:** Spirit of Canada **Obverse:** Queen's head right. **Reverse:** Maple leaf at center, children holding hands below. **Edge:** Reeded. **Size:** 23.9 mm.

KM	Date	Mintage	VG-8	F-12	VF-20	XF-40	MS-60	MS-63	Proof
419	2001	—	—	—	—	—	—	—	—

50 CENTS **Weight:** 11.6638 g. **Composition:** 0.8000 Silver .3000 oz. ASW **Subject:** Confederation centennial

KM	Date	Mintage	VG-8	F-12	VF-20	XF-40	MS-60	MS-63	Proof
69	ND(1967)	4,211,392	—	—	—	2.50	3.00	5.00	—

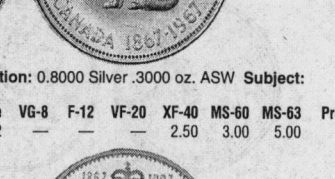

50 CENTS **Composition:** Nickel **Subject:** Confederation 125

KM	Date	Mintage	VG-8	F-12	VF-20	XF-40	MS-60	MS-63	Proof
208	ND(1992)	445,000	—	—	—	0.50	0.75	1.00	—
	ND(1992) Proof	147,061	—	—	—	—	—	—	5.00

50 CENTS **Weight:** 11.6638 g. **Composition:** 0.9250 Silver .3461 oz. ASW **Subject:** Atlantic puffin

KM	Date	Mintage	VG-8	F-12	VF-20	XF-40	MS-60	MS-63	Proof
261	1995 Proof	—	—	—	—	—	—	—	15.00

50 CENTS **Weight:** 11.6638 g. **Composition:** 0.9250 Silver .3461 oz. ASW **Subject:** Whooping crane

KM	Date	Mintage	VG-8	F-12	VF-20	XF-40	MS-60	MS-63	Proof
262	1995 Proof	—	—	—	—	—	—	—	15.00

50 CENTS **Weight:** 11.6638 g. **Composition:** 0.9250 Silver .3461 oz. ASW **Subject:** Gray jays

KM	Date	Mintage	VG-8	F-12	VF-20	XF-40	MS-60	MS-63	Proof
263	1995 Proof	—	—	—	—	—	—	—	20.00

50 CENTS **Weight:** 11.6638 g. **Composition:** 0.9250 Silver .3461 oz. ASW **Subject:** White-tailed ptarmigans

KM	Date	Mintage	VG-8	F-12	VF-20	XF-40	MS-60	MS-63	Proof
264	1995 Proof	—	—	—	—	—	—	—	20.00

50 CENTS **Weight:** 11.6638 g. **Composition:** 0.9250 Silver .3461 oz. ASW **Subject:** Moose calf

KM	Date	Mintage	VG-8	F-12	VF-20	XF-40	MS-60	MS-63	Proof
283	1996 Proof	—	—	—	—	—	—	—	14.00

50 CENTS **Weight:** 11.6638 g. **Composition:** 0.9250 Silver .3461 oz. ASW **Subject:** Wood ducklings

KM	Date	Mintage	VG-8	F-12	VF-20	XF-40	MS-60	MS-63	Proof
284	1996 Proof	—	—	—	—	—	—	—	14.00

50 CENTS **Weight:** 11.6638 g. **Composition:** 0.9250 Silver .3461 oz. ASW **Subject:** Cougar kittens

KM	Date	Mintage	VG-8	F-12	VF-20	XF-40	MS-60	MS-63	Proof
285	1996 Proof	—	—	—	—	—	—	—	14.00

50 CENTS **Weight:** 11.6638 g. **Composition:** 0.9250 Silver .3461 oz. ASW **Subject:** Black bear cubs

KM	Date	Mintage	VG-8	F-12	VF-20	XF-40	MS-60	MS-63	Proof
286	1996 Proof	—	—	—	—	—	—	—	14.00

50 CENTS **Weight:** 11.6638 g. **Composition:** 0.9250 Silver .3461 oz. ASW **Subject:** Duck tolling retriever

KM	Date	Mintage	VG-8	F-12	VF-20	XF-40	MS-60	MS-63	Proof
292	1997 Proof	—	—	—	—	—	—	—	14.00

50 CENTS **Weight:** 11.6638 g. **Composition:** 0.9250 Silver .3461 oz. ASW **Subject:** Labrador retriever

KM	Date	Mintage	VG-8	F-12	VF-20	XF-40	MS-60	MS-63	Proof
293	1997 Proof	—	—	—	—	—	—	—	14.00

50 CENTS **Weight:** 11.6638 g. **Composition:** 0.9250 Silver .3461 oz. ASW **Subject:** Newfoundland

KM	Date	Mintage	VG-8	F-12	VF-20	XF-40	MS-60	MS-63	Proof
294	1997 Proof	—	—	—	—	—	—	—	14.00

50 CENTS **Weight:** 11.6638 g. **Composition:** 0.9250 Silver .3461 oz. ASW **Subject:** Eskimo dog

KM	Date	Mintage	VG-8	F-12	VF-20	XF-40	MS-60	MS-63	Proof
295	1997 Proof	—	—	—	—	—	—	—	14.00

50 CENTS **Weight:** 11.6638 g. **Composition:** 0.9250 Silver .3461 oz. ASW **Subject:** 90th Anniversary Royal Canadian Mint

KM	Date	Mintage	VG-8	F-12	VF-20	XF-40	MS-60	MS-63	Proof
313	ND(1998) Matte	25,000	—	—	—	—	—	—	15.00
	ND(1998) Proof	25,000	—	—	—	—	—	—	15.00

50 CENTS **Weight:** 11.6638 g. **Composition:** 0.9250 Silver .3461 oz. ASW **Subject:** 110 years Canadian speed and figure skating

KM	Date	Mintage	VG-8	F-12	VF-20	XF-40	MS-60	MS-63	Proof
314	ND(1998) Proof	—	—	—	—	—	—	—	12.00

50 CENTS **Weight:** 11.6638 g. **Composition:** 0.9250 Silver .3461 oz. ASW **Subject:** 100 years Canadian ski racing

KM	Date	Mintage	VG-8	F-12	VF-20	XF-40	MS-60	MS-63	Proof
315	ND(1998) Proof	—	—	—	—	—	—	—	12.00

50 CENTS **Weight:** 11.6638 g. **Composition:** 0.9250 Silver .3461 oz. ASW **Subject:** Killer whales

KM	Date	Mintage	VG-8	F-12	VF-20	XF-40	MS-60	MS-63	Proof
318	1998 Proof	—	—	—	—	—	—	—	12.00

50 CENTS **Weight:** 11.6638 g. **Composition:** 0.9250 Silver .3461 oz. ASW **Subject:** Humpback whale

KM	Date	Mintage	VG-8	F-12	VF-20	XF-40	MS-60	MS-63	Proof
319	1998 Proof	—	—	—	—	—	—	—	12.00

50 CENTS **Weight:** 11.6638 g. **Composition:** 0.9250 Silver .3461 oz. ASW **Subject:** Beluga whale

KM	Date	Mintage	VG-8	F-12	VF-20	XF-40	MS-60	MS-63	Proof
320	1998 Proof	—	—	—	—	—	—	—	12.00

50 CENTS **Weight:** 11.6638 g. **Composition:** 0.9250 Silver .3461 oz. ASW **Subject:** Blue whale

KM	Date	Mintage	VG-8	F-12	VF-20	XF-40	MS-60	MS-63	Proof
321	1998 Proof	—	—	—	—	—	—	—	12.00

50 CENTS **Weight:** 11.6638 g. **Composition:** 0.9250 Silver .3461 oz. ASW **Subject:** 110 years Canadian soccer

KM	Date	Mintage	VG-8	F-12	VF-20	XF-40	MS-60	MS-63	Proof
327	ND(1998) Proof	—	—	—	—	—	—	—	12.00

50 CENTS **Weight:** 11.6638 g. **Composition:** 0.9250 Silver .3461 oz. ASW **Subject:** 20 years Canadian auto racing

KM	Date	Mintage	VG-8	F-12	VF-20	XF-40	MS-60	MS-63	Proof
328	ND(1998) Proof	—	—	—	—	—	—	—	12.00

50 CENTS **Weight:** 11.6638 g. **Composition:** 0.9250 Silver .3461 oz. ASW **Subject:** 1904 Canadian open

KM	Date	Mintage	VG-8	F-12	VF-20	XF-40	MS-60	MS-63	Proof
333	ND(1999) Proof	—	—	—	—	—	—	—	13.50

50 CENTS **Weight:** 11.6638 g. **Composition:** 0.9250 Silver .3461 oz. ASW **Subject:** First U.S.-Canadian yacht race

KM	Date	Mintage	VG-8	F-12	VF-20	XF-40	MS-60	MS-63	Proof
334	ND(1999) Proof	—	—	—	—	—	—	—	12.00

50 CENTS **Weight:** 11.6638 g. **Composition:** 0.9250 Silver .3461 oz. ASW **Series:** Canadian cats **Subject:** Cymric

KM	Date	Mintage	VG-8	F-12	VF-20	XF-40	MS-60	MS-63	Proof
335	1999 Proof	—	—	—	—	—	—	—	14.00

50 CENTS **Weight:** 11.6638 g. **Composition:** 0.9250 Silver .3461 oz. ASW **Series:** Canadian cats **Subject:** Tonkinese

KM	Date	Mintage	VG-8	F-12	VF-20	XF-40	MS-60	MS-63	Proof
336	1999 Proof	—	—	—	—	—	—	—	14.00

50 CENTS **Weight:** 11.6638 g. **Composition:** 0.9250 Silver .3461 oz. ASW **Series:** Canadian cats **Subject:** Cougar

KM	Date	Mintage	VG-8	F-12	VF-20	XF-40	MS-60	MS-63	Proof
337	1999 Proof	—	—	—	—	—	—	—	12.00

50 CENTS **Weight:** 11.6638 g. **Composition:** 0.9250 Silver .3461 oz. ASW **Series:** Canadian cats **Subject:** Lynx

KM	Date	Mintage	VG-8	F-12	VF-20	XF-40	MS-60	MS-63	Proof
338	1999 Proof	—	—	—	—	—	—	—	12.00

50 CENTS **Weight:** 9.3600 g. **Composition:** 0.9250 Silver 0.2784 oz. ASW **Subject:** Basketball **Obverse:** Queen's portrait **Reverse:** Basketball players **Edge:** Reeded **Size:** 27.1 mm.

KM	Date	Mintage	VG-8	F-12	VF-20	XF-40	MS-60	MS-63	Proof
371	ND(1999) Proof	—	—	—	—	—	—	—	12.00

50 CENTS **Weight:** 9.3600 g. **Composition:** 0.9250 Silver 0.2784 oz. ASW **Subject:** Football **Obverse:** Queen's portrait **Reverse:** Football players **Edge:** Reeded **Size:** 27.1 mm.

KM	Date	Mintage	VG-8	F-12	VF-20	XF-40	MS-60	MS-63	Proof
372	ND(1999) Proof	—	—	—	—	—	—	—	12.00

50 CENTS **Composition:** 0.9250 Silver **Subject:** Ice hockey **Reverse:** 4 hockey players

KM	Date	Mintage	VG-8	F-12	VF-20	XF-40	MS-60	MS-63	Proof
385	ND(2000) Proof	—	—	—	—	—	—	—	12.00

50 CENTS **Composition:** 0.9250 Silver **Subject:** Curling **Reverse:** Motion study of a curler

KM	Date	Mintage	VG-8	F-12	VF-20	XF-40	MS-60	MS-63	Proof
386	ND(2000) Proof	—	—	—	—	—	—	—	12.00

50 CENTS **Composition:** 0.9250 Silver **Subject:** Great horned owl

KM	Date	Mintage	VG-8	F-12	VF-20	XF-40	MS-60	MS-63	Proof
389	2000 Proof	—	—	—	—	—	—	—	12.00

50 CENTS **Composition:** 0.9250 Silver **Subject:** Red-tail hawk

KM	Date	Mintage	VG-8	F-12	VF-20	XF-40	MS-60	MS-63	Proof
390	2000 Proof	—	—	—	—	—	—	—	12.00

50 CENTS **Composition:** 0.9250 Silver **Subject:** Osprey

KM	Date	Mintage	VG-8	F-12	VF-20	XF-40	MS-60	MS-63	Proof
391	2000 Proof	—	—	—	—	—	—	—	12.00

50 CENTS **Composition:** 0.9250 Silver **Subject:** Bald eagle

KM	Date	Mintage	VG-8	F-12	VF-20	XF-40	MS-60	MS-63	Proof
392	2000 Proof	—	—	—	—	—	—	—	12.00

50 CENTS **Composition:** 0.9250 Silver **Subject:** Steeplechase

KM	Date	Mintage	VG-8	F-12	VF-20	XF-40	MS-60	MS-63	Proof
393	2000 Proof	—	—	—	—	—	—	—	12.00

50 CENTS **Composition:** 0.9250 Silver **Subject:** Bowling

KM	Date	Mintage	VG-8	F-12	VF-20	XF-40	MS-60	MS-63	Proof
394	2000 Proof	—	—	—	—	—	—	—	12.00

50 CENTS **Weight:** 9.3000 g. **Composition:** 0.9250 Silver .2766 oz. ASW **Series:** Festivals - Quebec **Obverse:** Queen's head right. **Reverse:** Snowman and Chateau Frontenac. **Edge:** Reeded. **Size:** 27.13 mm.

KM	Date	Mintage	VG-8	F-12	VF-20	XF-40	MS-60	MS-63	Proof
420	2001 Proof	—	—	—	—	—	—	—	15.00

50 CENTS **Weight:** 9.3000 g. **Composition:** 0.9250 Silver .2766 oz. ASW **Series:** Festivals - Nunavut **Obverse:** Queen's head right. **Reverse:** Dancer, dog sled and snowmobiles. **Edge:** Reeded. **Size:** 27.13 mm.

KM	Date	Mintage	VG-8	F-12	VF-20	XF-40	MS-60	MS-63	Proof
421	2001 Proof	—	—	—	—	—	—	—	15.00

50 CENTS **Weight:** 9.3000 g. **Composition:** 0.9250 Silver .2766 oz. ASW **Series:** Festivals - Newfoundland **Obverse:** Queen's head right. **Reverse:** Sailor and musical people. **Edge:** Reeded. **Size:** 27.13 mm.

KM	Date	Mintage	VG-8	F-12	VF-20	XF-40	MS-60	MS-63	Proof
422	2001 Proof	—	—	—	—	—	—	—	15.00

50 CENTS **Weight:** 9.3000 g. **Composition:** 0.9250 Silver .2766 oz. ASW **Series:** Festivals - Prince Edward Island **Obverse:** Queen's head right. **Reverse:** Family, juggler and building. **Edge:** Reeded. **Size:** 27.13 mm.

KM	Date	Mintage	VG-8	F-12	VF-20	XF-40	MS-60	MS-63	Proof
423	2001 Proof	—	—	—	—	—	—	—	15.00

50 CENTS **Weight:** 9.3000 g. **Composition:** 0.9250 Silver .2766 oz. ASW **Series:** Folklore - The Sled **Obverse:** Queen's head right. **Reverse:** Family scene. **Edge:** Reeded. **Size:** 27.13 mm.

KM	Date	Mintage	VG-8	F-12	VF-20	XF-40	MS-60	MS-63	Proof
424	2001 Proof	—	—	—	—	—	—	—	17.00

50 CENTS **Weight:** 9.3000 g. **Composition:** 0.9250 Silver .2766 oz. ASW **Series:** Folklore - The Maiden's Cave **Obverse:** Queen's head right. **Reverse:** Woman shouting. **Edge:** Reeded. **Size:** 27.13 mm.

KM	Date	Mintage	VG-8	F-12	VF-20	XF-40	MS-60	MS-63	Proof
425	2001 Proof	—	—	—	—	—	—	—	17.00

50 CENTS **Weight:** 9.3000 g. **Composition:** 0.9250 Silver .2766 oz. ASW **Series:** Folklore - The Small Jumpers **Obverse:** Queen's head right. **Reverse:** Jumping children on seashore. **Edge:** Reeded. **Size:** 27.13 mm.

KM	Date	Mintage	VG-8	F-12	VF-20	XF-40	MS-60	MS-63	Proof
426	2001 Proof	—	—	—	—	—	—	—	17.00

DOLLAR **Weight:** 23.3276 g. **Composition:** 0.8000 Silver 0.6000 oz. ASW **Subject:** Silver Jubilee

KM	Date	Mintage	F-12	VF-20	XF-40	AU-50	MS-60	MS-63	Proof
30	1935	428,707	11.50	17.50	28.00	32.00	36.50	60.00	4,500

DOLLAR **Weight:** 23.3276 g. **Composition:** 0.8000 Silver 0.6000 oz. ASW **Subject:** Royal Visit

KM	Date	Mintage	F-12	VF-20	XF-40	AU-50	MS-60	MS-63	Proof
38	1939	1,363,816	5.00	6.00	7.00	8.50	11.50	20.00	—
	1939 Matte specimen	—	—	—	—	—	—	—	475

DOLLAR **Weight:** 23.3276 g. **Composition:** 0.8000 Silver 0.6000 oz. ASW **Subject:** Newfoundland

KM	Date	Mintage	F-12	VF-20	XF-40	AU-50	MS-60	MS-63	Proof
47	1949	672,218	9.00	11.00	16.50	21.50	25.00	30.00	—
	1949 Specimen proof	—	—	—	—	—	—	—	1,200

DOLLAR **Weight:** 23.3276 g. **Composition:** 0.8000 Silver 0.6000 oz. ASW **Subject:** British Columbia

KM	Date	Mintage	F-12	VF-20	XF-40	AU-50	MS-60	MS-63	Proof
55	ND(1958)	3,039,630	BV	3.50	4.50	5.00	6.50	10.00	—

DOLLAR **Weight:** 23.3276 g. **Composition:** 0.8000 Silver 0.6000 oz. ASW **Subject:** Charlottetown

KM	Date	Mintage	F-12	VF-20	XF-40	AU-50	MS-60	MS-63	Proof
58	ND(1964)	7,296,832	—	—	—	BV	4.00	5.00	—
	ND(1964) Specimen proof	Inc. above	—	—	—	—	—	—	250

DOLLAR **Weight:** 23.3276 g. **Composition:** 0.8000 Silver 0.6000 oz. ASW **Subject:** Confederation Centennial **Reverse:** Goose

KM	Date	Mintage	MS-63	P/L	Proof
70	ND(1967)	6,767,496	6.00	7.00	10.00

DOLLAR **Composition:** Nickel **Subject:** Manitoba **Size:** 32 mm.

KM	Date	Mintage	MS-63	P/L	Proof
78	1970	4,140,058	2.00	—	—
	1970	645,869	—	2.50	—

DOLLAR **Composition:** Nickel **Subject:** British Columbia **Size:** 32 mm.

KM	Date	Mintage	MS-63	P/L	Proof
79	1971	4,260,781	2.00	—	—
	1971	468,729	—	2.25	—

DOLLAR **Weight:** 23.3276 g. **Composition:** 0.5000 Silver 0.3750 oz. ASW **Subject:** British Columbia **Size:** 36 mm.

KM	Date	Mintage	MS-63	P/L	Spec.
80	1971	585,674	—	—	5.50

DOLLAR **Weight:** 23.3276 g. **Composition:** 0.5000 Silver 0.3750 oz. ASW **Subject:** Mountie **Size:** 36 mm.

KM	Date	Mintage	MS-63	P/L	Spec.
83	1973	1,031,271	—	—	5.50

DOLLAR **Note:** Mountie Dollar in blue case with R.C.M.P. crest.

KM	Date	Mintage	MS-63	P/L	Spec.
83v	1973	Inc. above	—	—	15.00

DOLLAR **Composition:** Nickel **Subject:** Prince Edward Island **Size:** 32 mm.

KM	Date	Mintage	MS-63	P/L	Proof
82	1973	3,196,452	2.00	—	—
	1973 (c)	466,881	—	2.50	—

DOLLAR **Composition:** Nickel **Subject:** Winnipeg Centennial **Size:** 32 mm.

KM	Date	Mintage	MS-63	P/L	Proof
88	1974	2,799,363	2.00	—	—
	1974 (c)	363,786	—	2.50	—

DOLLAR **Composition:** 0.5000 Silver **Subject:** Winnipeg Centennial **Size:** 36 mm.

KM	Date	Mintage	MS-63	P/L	Spec.
88a	1974	728,947	—	—	5.50

DOLLAR **Weight:** 23.3276 g. **Composition:** 0.5000 Silver 0.3750 oz. ASW **Subject:** Calgary **Size:** 36 mm.

KM	Date	Mintage	MS-63	P/L	Spec.
97	1975	930,956	—	—	5.50

DOLLAR **Weight:** 23.3276 g. **Composition:** 0.5000 Silver 0.3750 oz. ASW **Subject:** Parliament Library **Size:** 36 mm.

KM	Date	Mintage	MS-63	P/L	Spec.
106	1976	578,708	—	—	6.00
	1976 blue case VIP	Inc. above	—	—	15.00

DOLLAR **Weight:** 23.3276 g. **Composition:** 0.5000 Silver 0.3750 oz. ASW **Subject:** Silver Jubilee **Size:** 36 mm.

KM	Date	Mintage	MS-63	P/L	Spec.
118	1977	744,848	—	—	5.00
	1977 red case VIP	Inc. above	—	—	25.00

DOLLAR **Weight:** 23.3276 g. **Composition:** 0.5000 Silver 0.3750 oz. ASW **Subject:** XI Commonwealth Games **Size:** 36 mm.

KM	Date	Mintage	MS-63	P/L	Spec.
121	1978	709,602	—	—	5.00

DOLLAR **Weight:** 23.3276 g. **Composition:** 0.5000 Silver 0.3750 oz. ASW **Subject:** Griffon **Size:** 36 mm.

KM	Date	Mintage	MS-63	P/L	Spec.
124	1979	826,695	—	—	8.00

DOLLAR **Weight:** 23.3276 g. **Composition:** 0.5000 Silver 0.3750 oz. ASW **Subject:** Arctic Territories **Size:** 36 mm.

KM	Date	Mintage	MS-63	P/L	Spec.
128	1980	539,617	—	—	17.50

DOLLAR **Weight:** 23.3276 g. **Composition:** 0.5000 Silver 0.3750 oz. ASW **Subject:** Transcontinental Railroad **Size:** 36 mm.

KM	Date	Mintage	MS-63	P/L	Proof
130	1981	699,494	7.50	—	13.50
	1981 Proof	—	—	—	—

DOLLAR **Weight:** 23.3276 g. **Composition:** 0.5000 Silver 0.3750 oz. ASW **Subject:** Regina **Size:** 36 mm.

KM	Date	Mintage	MS-63	P/L	Proof
133	1982	144,930	7.50	—	—
	1982 Proof	758,958	—	—	5.00

DOLLAR **Composition:** Nickel **Subject:** Constitution **Size:** 32 mm.

KM	Date	Mintage	MS-63	P/L	Proof
134	1982	9,709,422	3.00	6.00	—

DOLLAR **Weight:** 23.3276 g. **Composition:** 0.5000 Silver 0.3750 oz. ASW **Subject:** Edmonton University Games **Size:** 36 mm.

KM	Date	Mintage	MS-63	P/L	Proof
138	1983	159,450	5.00	—	—
	1983 Proof	506,847	—	—	6.00

DOLLAR **Weight:** 23.3276 g. **Composition:** 0.5000 Silver 0.3750 oz. ASW **Subject:** Toronto Sesquicentennial **Size:** 36 mm.

KM	Date	Mintage	MS-63	P/L	Proof
140	1984	133,610	7.50	—	—
	1984 Proof	732,542	—	—	5.00

DOLLAR **Composition:** Nickel **Subject:** Jacques Cartier **Size:** 32 mm.

KM	Date	Mintage	MS-63	P/L	Proof
141	1984	7,009,323	2.25	—	—
	1984 Proof	87,760	—	—	6.00

DOLLAR **Weight:** 23.3276 g. **Composition:** 0.5000 Silver 0.3750 oz. ASW **Subject:** National Parks/Moose **Size:** 36 mm.

KM	Date	Mintage	MS-63	P/L	Proof
143	1985	163,314	7.50	—	—
	1985 Proof	733,354	—	—	6.00

DOLLAR **Weight:** 23.3276 g. **Composition:** 0.5000 Silver 0.3750 oz. ASW **Subject:** Vancouver **Size:** 36 mm.

KM	Date	Mintage	MS-63	P/L	Proof
149	1986	125,949	7.50	—	—
	1986 Proof	680,004	—	—	7.00

DOLLAR **Weight:** 23.3276 g. **Composition:** 0.5000 Silver 0.3750 oz. ASW **Subject:** John Davis **Size:** 36 mm.

KM	Date	Mintage	MS-63	P/L	Proof
154	1987	118,722	7.50	—	—
	1987 Proof	602,374	—	—	9.00

DOLLAR **Weight:** 23.3276 g. **Composition:** 0.5000 Silver 0.3750 oz. ASW **Subject:** Ironworks **Size:** 36 mm.

KM	Date	Mintage	MS-63	P/L	Proof
161	1988	106,872	7.50	—	—
	1988 Proof	255,013	—	—	15.00

DOLLAR **Weight:** 23.3276 g. **Composition:** 0.5000 Silver 0.3750 oz. ASW **Subject:** MacKenzie River **Size:** 36 mm.

KM	Date	Mintage	MS-63	P/L	Proof
168	1989	99,774	7.50	—	—
	1989 Proof	244,062	—	—	15.00

DOLLAR **Weight:** 23.3276 g. **Composition:** 0.5000 Silver 0.3750 oz. ASW **Subject:** Henry Kelsey **Size:** 36 mm.

KM	Date	Mintage	MS-63	P/L	Proof
170	1990	99,455	7.50	—	—
	1990 Proof	254,959	—	—	12.50

DOLLAR **Weight:** 23.3276 g. **Composition:** 0.5000 Silver 0.3750 oz. ASW **Subject:** S.S. Frontenac **Size:** 36 mm.

KM	Date	Mintage	MS-63	P/L	Proof
179	1991	73,843	7.50	—	—
	1991 Proof	195,424	—	—	18.00

DOLLAR **Weight:** 25.1750 g. **Composition:** 0.9250 Silver 0.7487 oz. ASW **Subject:** Stagecoach service **Size:** 36 mm.

KM	Date	Mintage	MS-63	P/L	Proof
210	1992	78,160	7.50	—	—
	1992 Proof	187,612	—	—	12.50

DOLLAR **Composition:** Aureate **Subject:** Lcon **Size:** 32 mm.

KM	Date	Mintage	MS-63	P/L	Proof
209	ND(1992)	4,242,·85	2.00	4.00	8.00
	ND(1992) Proof	—	—	—	—

DOLLAR **Composition:** Aureate **Subject:** Parliament **Size:** 26 mm.

KM	Date	Mintage	MS-63	P/L	Proof
218	ND(1992)	23,915,000	2.25	5.00	—
	ND(1992) Proof	24,227	—	—	9.00

DOLLAR **Weight:** 25.1750 g. **Composition:** 0.9250 Silver 0.7487 oz. ASW **Subject:** Stanley Cup hockey **Size:** 36 mm.

KM	Date	Mintage	MS-63	P/L	Proof
235	1993	88,150	7.50	—	—
	1993 Proof	294,314	—	—	12.50

DOLLAR **Weight:** 25.1750 g. **Composition:** 0.9250 Silver 0.7487 oz. ASW **Subject:** Last RCMP sled-dog patrol **Size:** 36 mm.

KM	Date	Mintage	MS-63	P/L	Proof
251	1994	61,561	8.50	—	—
	1994 Proof	170,374	—	—	24.50

DOLLAR **Composition:** Aureate **Subject:** War Memorial **Size:** 26 mm.

KM	Date	Mintage	MS-63	P/L	Proof
248	1994	15,000,000	2.25	—	—
	1994 Proof	54,524	—	—	10.00

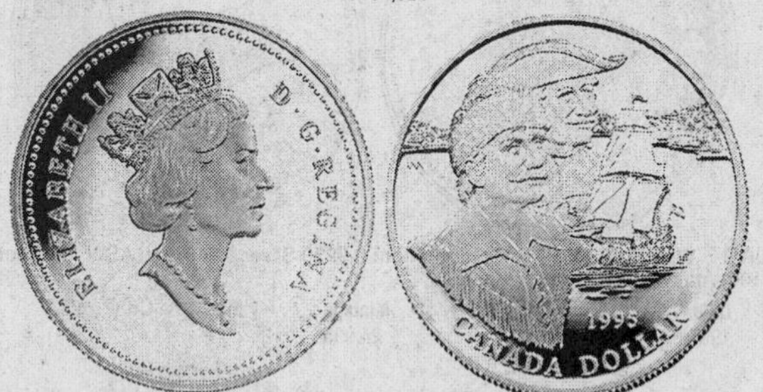

DOLLAR **Weight:** 25.1750 g. **Composition:** 0.9250 Silver 0.7487 oz. ASW **Subject:** Hudson Bay Co. **Size:** 36 mm.

KM	Date	Mintage	MS-63	P/L	Proof
259	1995	61,819	8.50	—	—
	1995 Proof	166,259	—	—	17.00

DOLLAR **Composition:** Aureate **Subject:** Peacekeeping Monument in Ottawa **Size:** 26 mm.
Note: Mintage included with KM#186.

KM	Date	Mintage	MS-63	P/L	Proof
258	1995	—	2.25	—	—
	1995 Proof	43,293	—	—	10.00

DOLLAR **Weight:** 25.1750 g. **Composition:** 0.9250 Silver 0.7487 oz. ASW **Subject:** McIntosh Apple **Size:** 36 mm.

KM	Date	Mintage	MS-63	P/L	Proof
274	1996	58,834	8.50	—	—
	1996 Proof	133,779	—	—	17.00

DOLLAR **Weight:** 25.1750 g. **Composition:** 0.9250 Silver 0.7487 oz. ASW **Subject:** 25th Anniversary Hockey Victory **Size:** 36 mm.

KM	Date	Mintage	MS-63	P/L	Proof
282	ND(1997)	155,252	8.50	—	—
	ND(1997) Proof	184,965	—	—	24.00

DOLLAR **Composition:** Aureate **Subject:** Loon Dollar 10th Anniversary **Size:** 26 mm.

KM	Date	Mintage	MS-63	P/L	Proof
291	1997	—	—	20.00	—

DOLLAR **Weight:** 25.1750 g. **Composition:** 0.9250 Silver 0.7487 oz. ASW **Subject:** Loon Dollar 10th Anniversary **Size:** 36 mm.

KM	Date	Mintage	MS-63	P/L	Proof
296	1997 Proof	24,995	—	—	65.00

DOLLAR **Weight:** 25.1750 g. **Composition:** 0.9250 Silver 0.7487 oz. ASW **Subject:** 120th Anniversary Royal Canadian Mounted Police **Size:** 36 mm. **Note:** Individually cased prooflikes, proofs or specimens are from broken-up prooflike or specimen sets.

KM	Date	Mintage	MS-63	P/L	Proof
306	1998	79,777	—	10.00	—
	1998 Proof	120,172	—	—	18.00

DOLLAR **Weight:** 25.1750 g. **Composition:** 0.9250 Silver 0.7487 oz. ASW **Subject:** International Year of Old Persons **Size:** 36 mm.

KM	Date	Mintage	MS-63	P/L	Proof
355	1999 Proof	24,976	—	—	32.50

DOLLAR **Weight:** 25.1750 g. **Composition:** 0.9250 Silver 0.7487 oz. ASW **Subject:** Discovery of Queen Charlotte Isle **Size:** 36 mm.

KM	Date	Mintage	MS-63	P/L	Proof
356	ND(1999)	67,655	—	10.00	—
	ND(1999) Proof	126,435	—	—	22.50

DOLLAR **Weight:** 25.1750 g. **Composition:** 0.9250 Silver 0.7487 oz. ASW **Subject:** Voyage of Discovery **Obverse:** Queen's portrait **Reverse:** Human and space shuttle **Size:** 36 mm.

KM	Date	Mintage	MS-63	P/L	Proof
401	2000	60,100	—	10.00	—
	2000 Proof	114,130	—	—	22.50

DOLLAR **Weight:** 25.1750 g. **Composition:** 0.9250 Silver 0.7487 oz. ASW **Subject:** Queen's Royal Jubilee **Obverse:** Queen's portrait with anniversary date **Reverse:** Queen in her coach and a view of the coach **Edge:** Reeded **Size:** 36 mm.

KM	Date	Mintage	MS-63	P/L	Proof
443	ND(2000) Proof	125,000	—	—	20.00
	2002	—	—	12.00	—
	2002 Proof	—	—	—	21.50

DOLLAR **Weight:** 25.1750 g. **Composition:** 0.9250 Silver 0.7487 oz. ASW **Subject:** National Ballet **Obverse:** Queen's head right. **Reverse:** Ballet dancers. **Edge:** Reeded. **Size:** 36 mm.

KM	Date	Mintage	MS-63	P/L	Proof
414	2001	65,000	—	12.00	—
	2001 Proof	225,000	—	—	21.50

DOLLAR **Weight:** 25.1750 g. **Composition:** 0.9250 Silver 0.7487 oz. ASW **Obverse:** Bust of Queen Elizabeth II right. **Reverse:** Recycled 1911 pattern dollar design: denomination, country name and dates in crowned wreath. **Edge:** Reeded. **Size:** 36 mm.

KM	Date	Mintage	MS-63	P/L	Proof
434	ND(2001) Proof	25,000	—	—	45.00

2 DOLLARS **Ring Weight:** 5.0958 g. **Ring Composition:** Silver 0.1638 oz. ASW **Center Weight:** 5.7456 g. **Center Composition:** Gold 0.1847 oz. AGW **Reverse:** Polar bear **Size:** 32 mm.

KM	Date	Mintage	MS-63	P/L	Proof
270a	1996 Proof	5,000	—	—	175

2 DOLLARS **Ring Composition:** Nickel **Center Composition:** Aluminum-Bronze **Subject:** Nunavut

KM	Date	Mintage	MS-63	P/L	Proof
357	1999	—	3.50	—	—

2 DOLLARS **Ring Weight:** 5.8600 g. **Ring Composition:** 0.9250 Silver .1743 oz. ASW **Center Weight:** 2.9600 g. **Center Composition:** 0.9250 Gold Plated Silver .0880 oz. ASW AGW **Subject:** Nunavut **Obverse:** Queen's head right. **Reverse:** Drum dancer. **Edge:** Interrupted reeding. **Size:** 28 mm.

KM	Date	Mintage	MS-63	P/L	Proof
357a	1999 Proof	—	—	—	14.00

2 DOLLARS **Ring Weight:** 6.3140 g. **Ring Composition:** 0.1708 White Gold .0347 oz. AGW **Center Weight:** 5.0900 g. **Center Composition:** 0.9167 Gold .15 oz. AGW **Subject:** Nunavut **Obverse:** Queen's head right. **Reverse:** Drum dancer.

KM	Date	Mintage	MS-63	P/L	Proof
357b	1999 Proof	10,000	—	—	175

2 DOLLARS **Ring Composition:** NickelCenter **Weight:** 5.9000 g. **Center Composition:** Aluminum-Bronze **Subject:** Knowledge **Reverse:** Polar bear and 2 cubs **Edge:** Reeded and plain sections. **Size:** 28 mm.

KM	Date	Mintage	MS-63	P/L	Proof
399	2000	—	3.50	5.00	—

2 DOLLARS **Ring Composition:** 0.1708 Gold **Center Composition:** 0.9167 Gold **Subject:** Knowledge **Reverse:** Polar bear and two cubs right.

KM	Date	Mintage	MS-63	P/L	Proof
399b	2000 Proof	—	—	—	175

2 DOLLARS **Ring Composition:** 0.9250 Silver **Center Composition:** 0.9250 Gold Plated Silver **Subject:** Knowledge **Reverse:** Polar bear and 2 cubs **Note:** Gold plated.

KM	Date	Mintage	MS-63	P/L	Proof
399a	2000 Proof	40,000	—	—	12.00

5 DOLLARS **Weight:** 24.3000 g. **Composition:** 0.9250 Silver 0.7227 oz. ASW **Subject:** 1976 Montreal Olympics **Reverse:** Sailboat "Kingston" **Size:** 38 mm. **Note:** Series I.

KM	Date	Mintage	MS-63	Proof
84	1973	—	5.00	—
	1973 Proof	165,203	—	6.25

5 DOLLARS **Composition:** 0.9250 Silver 0.7227 oz. ASW **Subject:** 1976 Montreal Olympics **Reverse:** North American map **Note:** Series I.

KM	Date	Mintage	MS-63	Proof
85	1973	—	5.00	—
	1973 Proof	165,203	—	6.25

5 DOLLARS **Weight:** 24.3000 g. **Composition:** 0.9250 Silver 0.7227 oz. ASW **Subject:** 1976 Montreal Olympics **Reverse:** Olympic rings **Size:** 38 mm. **Note:** Series II.

KM	Date	Mintage	MS-63	Proof
89	1974	—	5.00	—
	1974 Proof	97,431	—	6.25

5 DOLLARS **Weight:** 24.3000 g. **Composition:** 0.9250 Silver 0.7227 oz. ASW **Subject:** 1976 Montreal Olympics **Reverse:** Athlete with torch **Size:** 38 mm. **Note:** Series II.

KM	Date	Mintage	MS-63	Proof
90	1974	—	5.00	—
	1974 Proof	97,431	—	6.25

5 DOLLARS **Weight:** 24.3000 g. **Composition:** 0.9250 Silver 0.7227 oz. ASW **Subject:** 1976 Montreal Olympics **Reverse:** Rowing **Size:** 38 mm. **Note:** Series III.

KM	Date	Mintage	MS-63	Proof
91	1974	—	5.00	—
	1974 Proof	104,684	—	6.25

5 DOLLARS **Weight:** 24.3000 g. **Composition:** 0.9250 Silver 0.7227 oz. ASW **Subject:** 1976 Montreal Olympics **Reverse:** Canoeing **Size:** 38 mm. **Note:** Series III.

KM	Date	Mintage	MS-63	Proof
92	1974	—	5.00	—
	1974 Proof	104,684	—	6.25

5 DOLLARS **Weight:** 24.3000 g. **Composition:** 0.9250 Silver 0.7227 oz. ASW **Subject:** 1976 Montreal Olympics **Reverse:** Marathon **Size:** 38 mm. **Note:** Series IV.

KM	Date	Mintage	MS-63	Proof
98	1975	—	5.00	—
	1975 Proof	89,155	—	6.25

5 DOLLARS **Weight:** 24.3000 g. **Composition:** 0.9250 Silver 0.7227 oz. ASW **Subject:** 1976 Montreal Olympics **Reverse:** Women's javelin **Size:** 38 mm. **Note:** Series IV.

KM	Date	Mintage	MS-63	Proof
99	1975	—	5.00	—
	1975 Proof	89,155	—	6.25

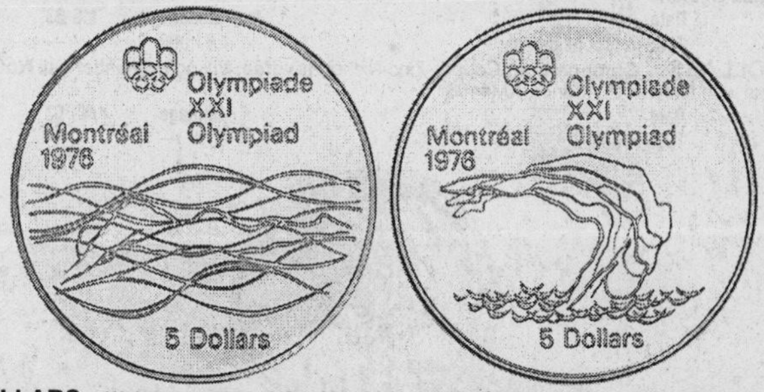

5 DOLLARS **Weight:** 24.3000 g. **Composition:** 0.9250 Silver 0.7227 oz. ASW **Subject:** 1976 Montreal Olympics **Reverse:** Swimmer **Size:** 38 mm. **Note:** Series V.

KM	Date	Mintage	MS-63	Proof
100	1975	—	5.00	—
	1975 Proof	89,155	—	6.25

5 DOLLARS **Weight:** 24.3000 g. **Composition:** 0.9250 Silver 0.7227 oz. ASW **Subject:** 1976 Montreal Olympics **Reverse:** Diver **Size:** 38 mm. **Note:** Series V.

KM	Date	Mintage	MS-63	Proof
101	1975	—	5.00	—
	1975 Proof	89,155	—	6.25

5 DOLLARS **Weight:** 24.3000 g. **Composition:** 0.9250 Silver 0.7227 oz. ASW **Subject:** 1976 Montreal Olympics **Reverse:** Fencing **Size:** 38 mm. **Note:** Series VI.

KM	Date	Mintage	MS-63	Proof
107	1976	—	5.00	—
	1976 Proof	82,302	—	6.50

5 DOLLARS **Weight:** 24.3000 g. **Composition:** 0.9250 Silver 0.7227 oz. ASW **Subject:** 1976 Montreal Olympics **Obv. Legend:** Boxing **Size:** 38 mm. **Note:** Series VI.

KM	Date	Mintage	MS-63	Proof
108	1976	—	5.00	—
	1976 Proof	82,302	—	6.50

5 DOLLARS **Weight:** 24.3000 g. **Composition:** 0.9250 Silver 0.7227 oz. ASW **Subject:** 1976 Montreal Olympics **Reverse:** Olympic village **Size:** 38 mm. **Note:** Series VII.

KM	Date	Mintage	MS-63	Proof
109	1976	—	5.00	—
	1976 Proof	76,908	—	6.50

5 DOLLARS **Weight:** 24.3000 g. **Composition:** 0.92:0 Silver 0.7227 oz. ASW **Subject:** 1976 Montreal Olympics **Reverse:** Olympic flame **Size:** 38 mm. **Note:** Series VII.

KM	Date	Mintage	MS-63	Proof
110	1976	—	5.00	—
	1976 Proof	79,102	—	6.50

5 DOLLARS **Weight:** 31.3900 g. **Composition:** 0.9999 Silver 1.0091 oz. ASW **Subject:** Dr. Norman Bethune

KM	Date	Mintage	MS-63	Proof
316	1998 in proof sets only	61,000	—	35.00

5 DOLLARS **Composition:** Copper-Zinc-Nickel **Reverse:** Viking ship under sail **Note:** Sold in sets with Norway 20 kroner, KM#465.

KM	Date	Mintage	MS-63	Proof
398	1999 Proof	—	—	16.50

5 DOLLARS **Weight:** 16.8600 g. **Composition:** 0.9250 Silver 0.5014 oz. ASW **Subject:** Guglielmo Marconi **Obverse:** Bust of Queen Elizabeth II right. **Reverse:** Gold-plated cameo portrait of Marconi. **Edge:** Reeded. **Size:** 28.4 mm. **Note:** Only issued in two coin set with British 2 pounds KM#1014a.

KM	Date	Mintage	F-12	VF-20	XF-40	AU-50	MS-60	MS-63
435	ND(2001) Proof	30,000	—	—	—	—	—	—

10 DOLLARS **Weight:** 48.6000 g. **Composition:** 0.9250 Silver 1.4454 oz. ASW **Subject:** 1976 Montreal Olympics **Reverse:** Montreal skyline **Size:** 87 mm. **Note:** Series I.

KM	Date	Mintage	MS-63	Proof
87	1973	—	10.00	—
	1973 Proof	165,203	—	11.50

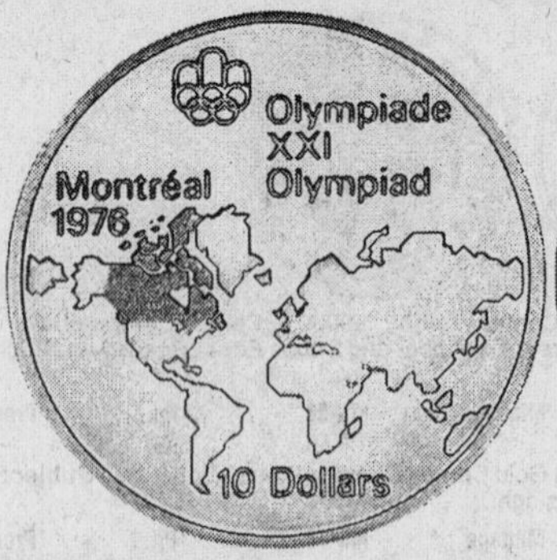

10 DOLLARS **Weight:** 48.6000 g. **Composition:** 0.9250 Silver 1.4454 oz. ASW **Subject:** 1976 Montreal Olympics **Reverse:** World map **Size:** 45 mm. **Note:** Series I.

KM	Date	Mintage	MS-63	Proof
86.1	1973	103,426	10.00	—
	1973 Proof	165,203	—	11.50

10 DOLLARS **Weight:** 48.6000 g. **Composition:** 0.9250 Silver 1.4454 oz. ASW **Subject:** 1976 Montreal Olympics **Reverse:** World map **Size:** 45 mm. **Note:** Series I.

KM	Date	Mintage	MS-63	Proof
86.2	1974 Error: mule	320	275	—

10 DOLLARS **Weight:** 48.6000 g. **Composition:** 0.9250 Silver 1.4454 oz. ASW **Subject:** 1976 Montreal Olympics **Reverse:** Head of Zeus **Size:** 45 mm. **Note:** Series II.

KM	Date	Mintage	MS-63	Proof
93	1974	—	10.00	—
	1974 Proof	104,684	—	11.50

10 DOLLARS **Weight:** 48.6000 g. **Composition:** 0.9250 Silver 1.4454 oz. ASW **Subject:** 1976 Montreal Olympics **Reverse:** Temple of Zeus **Size:** 45 mm. **Note:** Series II.

KM	Date	Mintage	MS-63	Proof
94	1974	—	10.00	—
	1974 Proof	104,684	—	11.50

10 DOLLARS **Weight:** 48.6000 g. **Composition:** 0.9250 Silver 1.4454 oz. ASW **Subject:** 1976 Montreal Olympics **Reverse:** Cycling **Size:** 45 mm. **Note:** Series III.

KM	Date	Mintage	MS-63	Proof
95	1974	—	10.00	—
	1974 Proof	97,431	—	11.50

10 DOLLARS **Weight:** 48.6000 g. **Composition:** 0.9250 Silver 1.4454 oz. ASW **Subject:** 1976 Montreal Olympics **Reverse:** Lacrosse **Size:** 45 mm. **Note:** Series III.

KM	Date	Mintage	MS-63	Proof
96	1974	—	10.00	—
	1974 Proof	97,431	—	11.50

10 DOLLARS **Weight:** 48.6000 g. **Composition:** 0.9250 Silver 1.4454 oz. ASW **Subject:** 1976 Montreal Olympics **Reverse:** Men's hurdles **Size:** 45 mm. **Note:** Series IV.

KM	Date	Mintage	MS-63	Proof
102	1975	—	10.00	—
	1975 Proof	82,302	—	11.50

10 DOLLARS **Weight:** 48.6000 g. **Composition:** 0.9250 Silver 1.4454 oz. ASW **Subject:** 1976 Montreal Olympics **Reverse:** Women's shot put **Size:** 45 mm. **Note:** Series IV.

KM	Date	Mintage	MS-63	Proof
103	1975	—	10.00	—
	1975 Proof	82,302	—	11.50

10 DOLLARS **Weight:** 48.6000 g. **Composition:** 0.9250 Silver 1.4454 oz. ASW **Subject:** 1976 Montreal Olympics **Reverse:** Sailing **Size:** 45 mm. **Note:** Series V.

KM	Date	Mintage	MS-63	Proof
104	1975	—	10.00	—
	1975 Proof	89,155	—	11.50

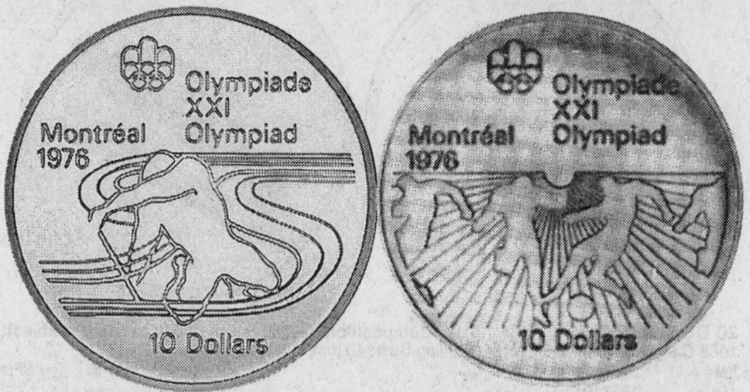

10 DOLLARS **Weight:** 48.6000 g. **Composition:** 0.9250 Silver 1.4454 oz. ASW **Subject:** 1976 Montreal Olympics **Reverse:** Canoeing **Size**. 45 mm. **Note:** Series V.

KM	Date	Mintage	MS-63	Proof
105	1975	—	10.00	—
	1975 Proof	89,155	—	11.50

10 DOLLARS **Weight:** 48.6000 g. **Composition:** 0.9250 Silver 1.4454 oz. ASW **Subject:** 1976 Montreal Olympics **Reverse:** Football **Size:** 45 mm. **Note:** Series VI.

KM	Date	Mintage	MS-63	Proof
111	1976	—	10.00	—
	1976 Proof	76,908	—	12.00

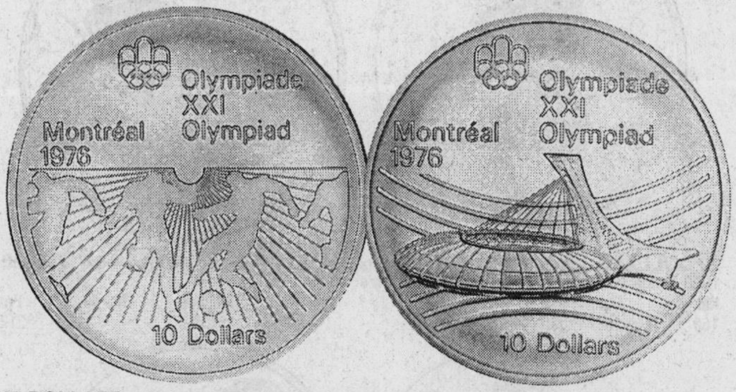

10 DOLLARS **Weight:** 48.6000 g. **Composition:** 0.9250 Silver 1.4454 oz. ASW **Subject:** 1976 Montreal Olympics **Reverse:** Field hockey **Size:** 45 mm. **Note:** Series VI.

KM	Date	Mintage	MS-63	Proof
112	1976	—	10.00	—
	1976 Proof	76,908	—	12.00

10 DOLLARS **Weight:** 48.6000 g. **Composition:** 0.9250 Silver 1.4454 oz. ASW **Subject:** 1976 Montreal Olympics **Reverse:** Olympic Stadium **Size:** 45 mm. **Note:** Series VII.

KM	Date	Mintage	MS-63	Proof
113	1976	—	10.00	—
	1976 Proof	79,102	—	12.00

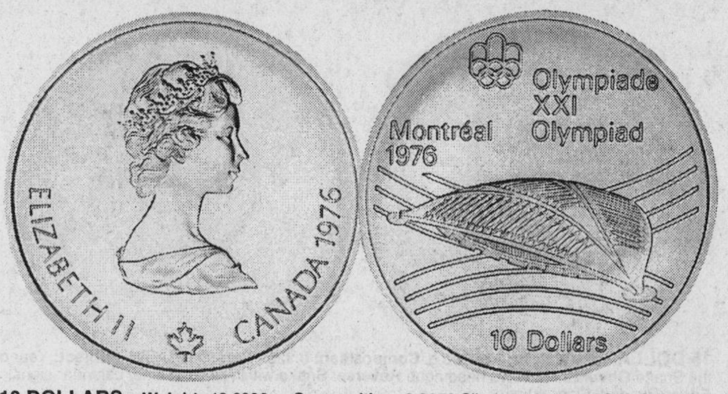

10 DOLLARS **Weight:** 48.6000 g. **Composition:** 0.9250 Silver 1.4454 oz. ASW **Subject:** 1976 Montreal Olympics **Reverse:** Olympic Velodrome **Size:** 45 mm. **Note:** Series VII.

KM	Date	Mintage	MS-63	Proof
114	1976	—	10.00	—
	1976 Proof	79,102	—	12.00

15 DOLLARS **Weight:** 33.6300 g. **Composition:** 0.9250 Silver 1.0000 oz. ASW **Subject:** 1992 Olympics **Reverse:** Coaching track **Size:** 39 mm.

KM	Date	Mintage	MS-63	Proof
215	1992 Proof	275,000	—	28.00

15 DOLLARS **Weight:** 33.6300 g. **Composition:** 0.9250 Silver 1.0000 oz. ASW **Subject:** 1992 Olympics **Reverse:** High jump, rings, speed skating

KM	Date	Mintage	MS-63	Proof
216	1992 Proof	275,000	—	28.00

15 DOLLARS **Ring Weight:** 33.6300 g. **Ring Composition:** 0.9250 Silver 1.0000 oz. ASW **Center Weight:** 0.3700 g. **Center Composition:** 0.9999 Gold 0.0118 oz. AGW **Subject:** Year of the Tiger **Size:** 32 mm.

KM	Date	Mintage	MS-63	Proof
304	1998 Proof	68,888	—	250

15 DOLLARS **Ring Weight:** 33.6300 g. **Ring Composition:** 0.9250 Silver 1.0000 oz. ASW **Center Weight:** 0.3700 g. **Center Composition:** 0.9999 Gold 0.0118 oz. AGW **Subject:** Year of the Rabbitt

KM	Date	Mintage	MS-63	Proof
331	1999 Proof	—	—	40.00

15 DOLLARS **Ring Weight:** 33.6300 g. **Ring Composition:** 0.9250 Silver 1 oz. ASW **Center Weight:** 0.3700 g. **Center Composition:** 0.9999 Gold 0.0118 oz. AGW **Subject:** Year of the Dragon

KM	Date	Mintage	MS-63	Proof
387	2000 Proof	—	—	55.00

15 DOLLARS **Weight:** 33.6300 g. **Composition:** 0.9250 Silver 1 oz. ASW **Subject:** Year of the Snake **Obverse:** Queen's head right. **Reverse:** Snake within circle of lunar calendar signs. **Edge:** Reeded. **Size:** 40 mm.

KM	Date	Mintage	MS-63	Proof
415	2001 Proof	—	—	50.00

20 DOLLARS **Weight:** 18.2733 g. **Composition:** 0.9000 Gold 0.5288 oz. AGW **Subject:** Centennial

KM	Date	Mintage	MS-63	Proof
71	1967 Proof	337,688	—	185

20 DOLLARS **Weight:** 33.6300 g. **Composition:** 0.9250 Silver 1.0000 oz. ASW **Subject:** 1988 Calgary Olympics **Reverse:** Downhill skier **Edge:** Lettered **Size:** 40 mm.

KM	Date	Mintage	MS-63	Proof
145	1985 Proof	406,360	—	21.50
	1985 Plain edge; Proof	Inc. above	—	175

20 DOLLARS **Weight:** 33.6300 g. **Composition:** 0.9250 Silver 1.0000 oz. ASW **Subject:** 1988 Calgary Olympics **Reverse:** Speed skater **Edge:** Lettered **Size:** 40 mm.

KM	Date	Mintage	MS-63	Proof
146	1985 Proof	354,222	—	21.50
	1985 Plain edge; Proof	Inc. above	—	175

20 DOLLARS **Weight:** 33.6300 g. **Composition:** 0.9250 Silver 1.0000 oz. ASW **Subject:** 1988 Calgary Olympics **Reverse:** Biathlon **Edge:** Lettered **Size:** 40 mm.

KM	Date	Mintage	MS-63	Proof
147	1986 Proof	308,086	—	21.50
	1986 Plain edge; Proof	Inc. above	—	175

20 DOLLARS **Weight:** 33.6300 g. **Composition:** 0.9250 Silver 1.0000 oz. ASW **Subject:** 1988 Calgary Olympics **Reverse:** Hockey **Edge:** Lettered **Size:** 40 mm.

KM	Date	Mintage	MS-63	Proof
148	1986 Proof	396,602	—	21.50
	1986 Plain edge; Proof	Inc. above	—	175

20 DOLLARS **Weight:** 33.6300 g. **Composition:** 0.9250 Silver 1.0000 oz. ASW **Subject:** 1988 Calgary Olympics **Reverse:** Cross-country skier **Size:** 40 mm.

KM	Date	Mintage	MS-63	Proof
150	1986 Proof	303,199	—	21.50

20 DOLLARS **Weight:** 33.6300 g. **Composition:** 0.9250 Silver 1.0000 oz. ASW **Subject:** 1988 Calgary Olympics **Reverse:** Free-style skier **Edge:** Lettered **Size:** 40 mm.

KM	Date	Mintage	MS-63	Proof
151	1986 Proof	294,322	—	21.50
	1986 Plain edge; Proof	Inc. above	—	175

20 DOLLARS **Weight:** 34.1070 g. **Composition:** 0.9250 Silver 1.0000 oz. ASW **Subject:** 1988 Calgary Olympics **Reverse:** Figure skater **Size:** 40 mm.

KM	Date	Mintage	MS-63	Proof
155	1987 Proof	334,875	—	21.50

20 DOLLARS **Weight:** 34.1070 g. **Composition:** 0.9250 Silver 1.0000 oz. ASW **Subject:** 1988 Calgary Olympics **Reverse:** Curling **Size:** 40 mm.

KM	Date	Mintage	MS-63	Proof
156	1987 Proof	286,457	—	21.50

20 DOLLARS **Weight:** 34.1070 g. **Composition:** 0.9250 Silver 1.0000 oz. ASW **Subject:** 1988 Calgary Olympics **Reverse:** Ski jumper **Size:** 40 mm.

KM	Date	Mintage	MS-63	Proof
159	1987 Proof	290,954	—	21.50

20 DOLLARS **Weight:** 34.1070 g. **Composition:** 0.9250 Silver 1.0000 oz. ASW **Subject:** 1988 Calgary Olympics **Reverse:** Bobsled **Size:** 40 mm.

KM	Date	Mintage	MS-63	Proof
160	1987 Proof	274,326	—	21.50

20 DOLLARS **Weight:** 31.1030 g. **Composition:** 0.9250 Silver 0.9743 oz. ASW **Subject:** Aviation **Reverse:** Lancaster/Fauquier **Size:** 38 mm.

KM	Date	Mintage	MS-63	Proof
172	1990 Proof	43,596	—	100

20 DOLLARS **Weight:** 31.1030 g. **Composition:** 0.9250 Silver 0.9743 oz. ASW **Subject:** Aviation **Reverse:** Anson and Harvard **Size:** 38 mm.

KM	Date	Mintage	MS-63	Proof
173	1990 Proof	41,844	—	35.00

20 DOLLARS **Weight:** 31.1030 g. **Composition:** 0.9250 Silver 0.9743 oz. ASW **Subject:** Aviation **Reverse:** Silver Dart **Size:** 38 mm.

KM	Date	Mintage	MS-63	Proof
196	1991 Proof	28,791	—	30.00

20 DOLLARS **Weight:** 31.1030 g. **Composition:** 0.9[illegible] Silver 0.9742 oz. ASW **Subject:** Aviation **Reverse:** de Haviland Beaver **Size:** 38 mm.

KM	Date	Mintage	MS-63	Proof
197	1991 Proof	29,399	—	30.00

20 DOLLARS **Weight:** 31.1030 g. **Composition:** 0.9250 Silver 0.9743 oz. ASW **Subject:** Aviation **Reverse:** Curtiss JN-4 Canuck ("Jenny") **Size:** 38 mm.

KM	Date	Mintage	MS-63	Proof
224	1992 Proof	33,105	—	30.00

20 DOLLARS **Weight:** 31.1030 g. **Composition:** 0.9250 Silver 0.9743 oz. ASW **Subject:** Aviation **Reverse:** de Havil[illegible]oth **Size:** 38 mm.

KM	Date	Mintage	MS-63	Proof
225	1992 Proof	32,537	—	30.00

20 DOLLARS **Weight:** 31.1030 g. **Composition:** 0.9250 Silver 0.0257 oz. ASW **Subject:** Aviation **Reverse:** Fairchild 71C float plane **Size:** 38 mm.

KM	Date	Mintage	MS-63	Proof
236	1993 Proof	32,199	—	30.00

20 DOLLARS **Weight:** 31.1030 g. **Composition:** 0.9250 Silver 0.9743 oz. ASW **Subject:** Aviation **Reverse:** Lockheed 14 **Size:** 38 mm.

KM	Date	Mintage	MS-63	Proof
237	1993 Proof	32,550	—	30.00

20 DOLLARS **Weight:** 31.1030 g. **Composition:** 0.9250 Silver 0.9743 oz. ASW **Subject:** Aviation **Reverse:** Curtiss HS-2L seaplane **Size:** 38 mm.

KM	Date	Mintage	MS-63	Proof
246	1994 Proof	31,242	—	30.00

20 DOLLARS **Weight:** 31.1030 g. **Composition:** 0.9250 Silver 0.9743 oz. ASW **Subject:** Aviation **Reverse:** Vickers Vedette **Size:** 38 mm.

KM	Date	Mintage	MS-63	Proof
247	1994 Proof	30,880	—	30.00

20 DOLLARS **Weight:** 31.1030 g. **Composition:** 0.9250 Silver 0.9743 oz. ASW **Subject:** Aviation **Reverse:** C-FEA1 Fleet Cannuck **Size:** 38 mm.

KM	Date	Mintage	MS-63	Proof
271	1995 Proof	17,438	—	30.00

20 DOLLARS **Weight:** 31.1030 g. **Composition:** 0.9250 Silver 0.9743 oz. ASW **Subject:** Aviation **Reverse:** DHC-1 Chipmunk **Size:** 38 mm.

KM	Date	Mintage	MS-63	Proof
272	1995 Proof	17,722	—	30.00

20 DOLLARS **Weight:** 31.1030 g. **Composition:** 0.9250 Silver 0.9743 oz. ASW **Subject:** Aviation **Reverse:** CF-100 Cannuck **Size:** 38 mm.

KM	Date	Mintage	MS-63	Proof
276	1996 Proof	18,508	—	30.00

20 DOLLARS **Weight:** 31.1030 g. **Composition:** 0.9250 Silver 0.9743 oz. ASW **Subject:** Aviation **Obv. Legend:** CF-105 Arrow **Size:** 38 mm.

KM	Date	Mintage	MS-63	Proof
277	1996 Proof	27,163	—	50.00

20 DOLLARS **Weight:** 31.1030 g. **Composition:** 0.9250 Silver 0.9743 oz. ASW **Subject:** Aviation **Reverse:** Canadair F-86 Sabre **Size:** 38 mm.

KM	Date	Mintage	MS-63	Proof
297	1997 Proof	14,389	—	30.00

20 DOLLARS **Weight:** 31.1030 g. **Composition:** 0.9250 Silver 0.9743 oz. ASW **Subject:** Aviation **Reverse:** Canadair CT-114 Tutor **Size:** 38 mm.

KM	Date	Mintage	MS-63	Proof
298	1997 Proof	15,669	—	3[illegible].00

20 DOLLARS **Weight:** 31.1030 g. **Composition:** 0.9250 Silver 0.9743 oz. ASW **Subject:** Aviation **Reverse:** CP-107 Argus **Size:** 38 mm.

KM	Date	Mintage	MS-63	Proof
329	1998 Proof	50,000,000	—	37[illegible]50

20 DOLLARS **Weight:** 31.10[illegible]0 g. **Composition:** 0.9250 Silver 0.9743 oz. ASW **Subject:** Aviation **Reverse:** CP-215 Water[illegible]mber **Size:** 38 mm.

KM	Date	Mintage	MS-63	Proof
330	1998 Proof	50,000,000	—	37.50

20 DOLLARS **Weight:** 31.10[illegible]0 g. **Composition:** 0.9250 Silver 0.9743 oz. ASW **Subject:** Aviation **Reverse:** DHC-6 Twin O[illegible]ter **Size:** 38 mm.

KM	Date	Mintage	MS-63	Proof
339	1999 Proof	50,000,000	—	37.50

20 DOLLARS **Weight:** 3[illegible].1030 g. **Composition:** 0.9250 Silver 0.9743 oz. ASW **Subject:** Aviation **Reverse:** DHC-8 Da[illegible]h 8 **Size:** 38 mm.

KM	Date	Mintage	MS-63	Proof
340	1999 Proof	50,000,000	—	37.50

20 DOLLARS **Compos**[illegible]**ion:** 0.9250 Silver **Subject:** First Canadian locomotive **Reverse:** Locomotive below multicolor[illegible]d cameo **Size:** 38 mm.

KM	Date	Mintage	MS-63	Proof
395	2000 Proof	—	—	40.00

20 DOLLARS **Compos**[illegible]**tion:** 0.9250 Silver **Subject:** First Canadian self-propelled car **Reverse:** Car below multico[illegible]ored cameo **Size:** 38 mm.

KM	Date	Mintage	MS-63	Proof
396	2000 Proof	—	—	40.00

20 DOLLARS **Compo**[illegible]**ition:** 0.9250 Silver **Subject:** Bluenose sailboat **Reverse:** Boat below multicolored cameo **Size:** 3[illegible] mm.

KM	Date	Mintage	MS-63	Proof
397	2000 Proof	—	—	125

20 DOLLARS **Wei**[illegible]**ht:** 31.1035 g. **Composition:** 0.9250 Silver .9250 oz. ASW **Subject:** First Canadian Steel Boiler S[illegible]eam Locomotive **Obverse:** Queen's head right. **Reverse:** Locomotive and cameo hologram. **Edg**[illegible]: Reeded and plain sections. **Size:** 38 mm.

KM	Date	Mintage	MS-63	Proof
411	2001 Proof	15,000	—	40.00

20 DOLLARS **W**[illegible]**eight:** 31.1030 g. **Composition:** 0.9250 Silver .9250 oz. ASW **Series:** Transportation - T[illegible]e Marco Polo **Obverse:** Queen's head right. **Reverse:** Sailship with hologram cameo. **Edge:** Re[illegible]ded and plain sections. **Size:** 38 mm.

KM	Date	Mintage	MS-63	Proof
427	2001 [illegible]roof	15,000	—	40.00

20 DOLLARS **Weight:** 31.1030 g. **Composition:** 0.9250 Silver .9250 oz. ASW **Series:** Transportation - R[illegible]ussell Touring Car **Obverse:** Queen's head right. **Reverse:** Russell touring car with hologram ca[illegible]eo. **Edge:** Reeded and plain sections. **Size:** 38 mm.

KM	Date	Mintage	MS-63	Proof
428	200[illegible] Proof	15,000	—	40.00

100 DOLLARS **Weight:** 13.3375 g. **Composition:** 0.5830 Gold 0.2500 oz. AGW **Subject:** 1976 Montreal Olympics **Obverse:** Beaded borders **Size:** 27 mm.

KM	Date	Mintage	MS-63	Proof
115	1976	650,000	85.00	—

100 DOLLAR[illegible] **Weight:** 16.9[illegible] g. **Composition:** 0.9170 Gold 0.5000 oz. AGW **Subject:** 1976 Montre[illegible]lympics **Obvers**[illegible]lain borders **Size:** 25 mm.

KM	Date	Mintage	MS-63	Proof
116	[illegible]76 Proof	337,342	—	180

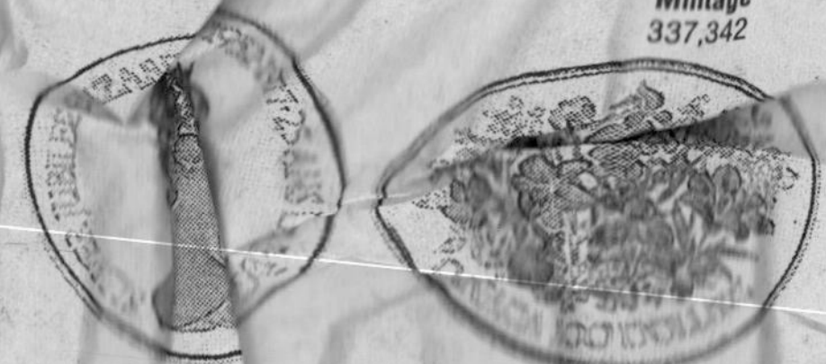

100 DOLLARS **Weight:** 16.9[illegible] **Composition:** 0.9170 Gold 0.5000 oz. AGW **Subject:** Queen's silver jubilee

KM	Date	Mintage	MS-63	Proof
119	[illegible]977) Proof	180,396	—	195

100 DOLLARS **We**[illegible]**.9655 g. Composition:** 0.9170 Gold 0.5000 oz. AGW **Subject:** Canadian unification

KM	Date	Mintage	MS-63	Proof
122	1978 Proof	200,000	—	180

100 DOLLARS **Weight:** 16.9655 g. **Composition:** 0.9170 Gold 0.5000 oz. AGW **Subject:** International Year of the Child

KM	Date	Mintage	MS-63	Proof
126	1979 Proof	250,000	—	180

100 DOLLARS **Weight:** 16.9655 g. **Composition:** 0.9170 Gold 0.5000 oz. AGW **Subject:** Arctic Territories

KM	Date	Mintage	MS-63	Proof
129	1980 Proof	300,000	—	190

100 DOLLARS **Weight:** 16.9655 g. **Composition:** 0.9170 Gold 0.5000 oz. AGW **Subject:** National anthem

KM	Date	Mintage	MS-63	Proof
131	1981 Proof	102,000	—	180

100 DOLLARS **Weight:** 16.9655 g. **Composition:** 0.9170 Gold 0.5000 oz. AGW **Subject:** New Constitution

KM	Date	Mintage	MS-63	Proof
137	1982 Proof	121,708	—	180

100 DOLLARS **Weight:** 16.9655 g. **Composition:** 0.9170 Gold 0.5000 oz. AGW **Subject:** 400th Anniversary of St. John's, Newfoundland

KM	Date	Mintage	MS-63	Proof
139	ND(1983) Proof	83,128	—	190

100 DOLLARS **Weight:** 16.9655 g. **Composition:** 0.9170 Gold 0.5000 oz. AGW **Subject:** Jacques Cartier

KM	Date	Mintage	MS-63	Proof
142	ND(1984) Proof	67,662	—	185

100 DOLLARS **Weight:** 16.9655 g. **Composition:** 0.9170 Gold 0.5000 oz. AGW **Subject:** National Parks **Reverse:** Big-horn sheep

KM	Date	Mintage	MS-63	Proof
144	ND(1985) Proof	61,332	—	190

100 DOLLARS **Weight:** 16.9655 g. **Composition:** 0.9170 Gold 0.5000 oz. AGW **Subject:** Peace

KM	Date	Mintage	MS-63	Proof
152	1986 Proof	76,409	—	180

100 DOLLARS **Weight:** 13.3375 g. **Composition:** 0.5830 Gold 0.2500 oz. AGW **Subject:** 1988 Calgary Olympics **Reverse:** Torch and logo

KM	Date	Mintage	MS-63	Proof
158	1987 lettered edge; Proof	142,750	—	90.00
	1987 plain edge; Proof	Inc. above	—	350

100 DOLLARS **Weight:** 13.3375 g. **Composition:** 0.5830 Gold 0.2500 oz. AGW **Subject:** Whales

KM	Date	Mintage	MS-63	Proof
162	1988 Proof	52,594	—	95.00

100 DOLLARS **Weight:** 13.3375 g. **Composition:** 0.5830 Gold 0.2500 oz. AGW **Subject:** Sainte-Marie

KM	Date	Mintage	MS-63	Proof
169	ND(1989) Proof	59,657	—	95.00

100 DOLLARS **Weight:** 13.3375 g. **Composition:** 0.5830 Gold 0.2500 oz. AGW **Subject:** International Literacy Year

KM	Date	Mintage	MS-63	Proof
171	1990 Proof	49,940	—	95.00

100 DOLLARS **Weight:** 13.3375 g. **Composition:** 0.5830 Gold 0.2500 oz. AGW **Subject:** S.S. Empress of India

KM	Date	Mintage	MS-63	Proof
180	1991 Proof	33,966	—	95.00

100 DOLLARS **Weight:** 13.3375 g. **Composition:** 0.5830 Gold 0.2500 oz. AGW **Subject:** Montreal

KM	Date	Mintage	MS-63	Proof
211	1992 Proof	28,162	—	95.00

100 DOLLARS **Weight:** 13.3375 g. **Composition:** 0.5830 Gold 0.2500 oz. AGW **Subject:** Antique Automobiles

KM	Date	Mintage	MS-63	Proof
245	1993 Proof	25,971	—	100

100 DOLLARS **Weight:** 13.3375 g. **Composition:** 0.5830 Gold 0.2500 oz. AGW **Subject:** World War II Home Front

KM	Date	Mintage	MS-63	Proof
249	1994 Proof	16,201	—	125

100 DOLLARS **Weight:** 13.3375 g. **Composition:** 0.5830 Gold 0.2500 oz. AGW **Subject:** Louisbourg

KM	Date	Mintage	MS-63	Proof
260	1995 Proof	16,916	—	125

100 DOLLARS **Weight:** 13.3375 g. **Composition:** 0.5830 Gold 0.2500 oz. AGW **Subject:** Klondike Gold Rush Centennial

KM	Date	Mintage	MS-63	Proof
273	ND(1996) Proof	17,973	—	135

100 DOLLARS **Weight:** 13.3375 g. **Composition:** 0.5830 Gold 0.2500 oz. AGW **Subject:** Alexander Graham Bell

KM	Date	Mintage	MS-63	Proof
287	1997 Proof	14,775	—	155

100 DOLLARS **Weight:** 13.3375 g. **Composition:** 0.5830 Gold 0.2500 oz. AGW **Subject:** Discovery of Insulin

KM	Date	Mintage	MS-63	Proof
307	1998 Proof	11,220	—	155

100 DOLLARS **Weight:** 13.3375 g. **Composition:** 0.5830 Gold 0.2500 oz. AGW **Subject:** 50th Anniversary Newfoundland Unity With Canada

KM	Date	Mintage	MS-63	Proof
341	1999 Proof	10,242	—	170

100 DOLLARS **Weight:** 13.3375 g. **Composition:** 0.5830 Gold 0.2500 oz. AGW **Subject:** McClure's Arctic expedition **Obverse:** Queen's portrait **Reverse:** Six men pulling supply sled to an icebound ship **Edge:** Reeded **Size:** 27 mm.

KM	Date	Mintage	MS-63	Proof
402	2000 Proof	9,767	—	185

100 DOLLARS **Weight:** 13.3375 g. **Composition:** 0.5830 Gold 0.2500 oz. AGW **Subject:** Library of Parliament **Obverse:** Queen's head right. **Reverse:** Statue in domed building. **Edge:** Reeded. **Size:** 27 mm.

KM	Date	Mintage	MS-63	Proof
416	2001 Proof	10,000	—	185

150 DOLLARS **Weight:** 13.6100 g. **Composition:** 0.7500 Gold .3282 oz. AGW **Subject:** Year of the Dragon

KM	Date	Mintage	MS-63	Proof
388	2000 Proof	8,851	—	475

150 DOLLARS **Weight:** 13.6100 g. **Composition:** 0.7500 Gold .3282 oz. AGW **Subject:** Year of the Snake **Obverse:** Queen's head right. **Reverse:** Multicolor snake hologram. **Edge:** Reeded. **Size:** 28 mm.

KM	Date	Mintage	MS-63	Proof
417	2001 Proof	6,888	—	265

175 DOLLARS **Weight:** 16.9700 g. **Composition:** 0.9170 Gold 0.5000 oz. AGW **Subject:** 1992 Olympics **Reverse:** Passing the torch

KM	Date	Mintage	MS-63	Proof
217	1992 Proof	22,092	—	210

200 DOLLARS **Weight:** 17.1060 g. **Composition:** 0.9170 Gold 0.5042 oz. AGW **Subject:** Canadian flag silver jubilee **Size:** 29 mm.

KM	Date	Mintage	MS-63	Proof
178	1990 Proof	20,980	—	185

200 DOLLARS **Weight:** 17.1060 g. **Composition:** 0.9170 Gold 0.5042 oz. AGW **Subject:** Hockey **Size:** 29 mm.

KM	Date	Mintage	MS-63	Proof
202	1991 Proof	10,215	—	200

200 DOLLARS **Weight:** 17.1060 g. **Composition:** 0.9170 Gold 0.5042 oz. AGW **Subject:** Niagara Falls **Size:** 29 mm.

KM	Date	Mintage	MS-63	Proof
230	1992 Proof	9,465	—	250

200 DOLLARS **Weight:** 17.1350 g. **Composition:** 0.9170 Gold 0.5500 oz. AGW **Subject:** Mounted police **Size:** 29 mm.

KM	Date	Mintage	MS-63	Proof
244	1993 Proof	10,807	—	190

200 DOLLARS **Weight:** 17.1350 g. **Composition:** 0.9170 Gold 0.5500 oz. AGW **Subject:** Novel: Anne of Green Gables **Size:** 29 mm.

KM	Date	Mintage	MS-63	Proof
250	1994 Proof	10,655	—	210

200 DOLLARS **Weight:** 17.1350 g. **Composition:** 0.9170 Gold 0.5500 oz. AGW **Subject:** Maple-syrup production **Size:** 29 mm.

KM	Date	Mintage	MS-63	Proof
265	1995 Proof	6,579	—	225

200 DOLLARS **Weight:** 17.1350 g. **Composition:** 0.9170 Gold 0.5500 oz. AGW **Subject:** Transcontinental Canadian Railway **Size:** 29 mm.

KM	Date	Mintage	MS-63	Proof
275	1996 Proof	8,047	—	265

200 DOLLARS **Weight:** 17.1350 g. **Composition:** 0.9170 Gold 0.5500 oz. AGW **Subject:** Haida mask **Size:** 29 mm.

KM	Date	Mintage	MS-63	Proof
288	1997 Proof	11,610	—	300

200 DOLLARS **Weight:** 17.1350 g. **Composition:** 0.9170 Gold 0.5500 oz. AGW **Subject:** Legendary white buffalo **Size:** 29 mm.

KM	Date	Mintage	MS-63	Proof
317	1998 Proof	7,149	—	275

200 DOLLARS **Weight:** 17.1350 g. **Composition:** 0.9170 Gold 0.5500 oz. AGW **Subject:** Mikmaq butterfly **Size:** 29 mm.

KM	Date	Mintage	MS-63	Proof
358	1999 Proof	6,510	—	280

200 DOLLARS **Weight:** 17.1350 g. **Composition:** 0.9170 Gold 0.5500 oz. AGW **Subject:** Motherhood **Reverse:** Inuit mother with infant **Edge:** Reeded **Size:** 29 mm.

KM	Date	Mintage	MS-63	Proof
403	2000 Proof	6,284	—	280

200 DOLLARS **Weight:** 17.1350 g. **Composition:** 0.9170 Gold 0.5500 oz. AGW **Subject:** Cornelius David Krieghoff **Obverse:** Queen's head right. **Reverse:** Farm homestead circa 1856. **Edge:** Reeded. **Size:** 29 mm.

KM	Date	Mintage	MS-63	Proof
418	2001 Proof	10,000	—	275

350 DOLLARS **Weight:** 38.0500 g. **Composition:** 0.9999 Gold 1.2233 oz. AGW **Subject:** Flowers of Canada's Coat of Arms

KM	Date	Mintage	MS-63	Proof
308	1998 Proof	664	—	800

350 DOLLARS **Weight:** 38.0500 g. **Composition:** 0.9999 Gold 1.2233 oz. AGW **Subject:** Lady's slipper

KM	Date	Mintage	MS-63	Proof
370	1999 Proof	1,990	—	665

350 DOLLARS **Weight:** 38.0500 g. **Composition:** 0.9999 Gold 1.2233 oz. AGW **Subject:** Pacific Dogwood **Obverse:** Queen's portrait **Reverse:** Three flowers **Edge:** Reeded **Size:** 34 mm.

KM	Date	Mintage	MS-63	Proof
404	2000 Proof	1,506	—	665

350 DOLLARS **Weight:** 38.0500 g. **Composition:** 0.9999 Gold 1.2233 oz. AGW **Subject:** The Mayflower Flower **Obverse:** Queen's head right. **Reverse:** Two flowers. **Edge:** Reeded. **Size:** 34 mm.

KM	Date	Mintage	MS-63	Proof
433	2001 Proof	—	—	676

SILVER BULLION COINAGE

5 DOLLARS **Weight:** 31.1000 g. **Composition:** 0.9999 Silver 1.0000 oz. ASW **Obverse:** Elizabeth II effigy **Obv. Designer:** Machin **Reverse:** Maple leaf

KM	Date	Mintage	MS-63	Proof
163	1988	1,155,931	8.00	—
	1989	3,288,235	7.25	—
	1989 Proof	43,965	—	28.50

5 DOLLARS **Weight:** 31.1000 g. **Composition:** 0.9999 Silver 1.0000 oz. ASW **Obverse:** New Elizabeth II effigy **Obv. Designer:** de Pedery-Hunt **Reverse:** Maple leaf

KM	Date	Mintage	MS-63	Proof
187	1990	1,708,800	8.00	—
	1991	644,300	10.00	—
	1992	343,800	9.50	—
	1993	889,946	7.50	—
	1994	1,133,900	7.75	—
	1995	326,244	8.50	—
	1996	250,445	30.00	—
	1997	100,970	12.00	—
	1998 Tiger privy mark	25,000	13.50	—
	1998 Proof; 20 Years ANS privy mark	—	—	35.00
	1998 Titanic privy mark	26,000	100	—
	1998 R.C.M.P. privy mark	25,000	15.00	—
	1998 90th Anniversary R.C.M. privy mark	13,025	16.50	—
	1999 Rabbit privy mark	25,000	13.50	—

KM	Date	Mintage	MS-63	Proof
	1999 "Y2K" privy mark	9,999	18.00	—
	2000 Expo Hanover privy mark	—	18.50	—
	2001 Snake privy mark	25,000	13.50	—

5 DOLLARS **Weight:** 31.1000 g. **Composition:** 0.9999 Silver 1 oz. ASW **Reverse:** Maple leaf with fireworks privy mark

KM	Date	Mintage	MS-63	Proof
363	1999/2000	298,775	9.50	—

5 DOLLARS **Weight:** 31.1035 g. **Composition:** 0.9999 Silver 0.9999 oz. ASW **Subject:** Maple Leaves **Obverse:** Queen's portrait. **Reverse:** Three maple leaves in multicolor. **Edge:** Reeded. **Size:** 38 mm.

KM	Date	Mintage	MS-63	Proof
436	2001	50,000	22.50	—

5 DOLLARS **Weight:** 31.1035 g. **Composition:** 0.9999 Silver 0.9999 oz. ASW **Subject:** Multicolor Holographic Maple Leaf **Obverse:** Queen's portrait. **Reverse:** Radiant maple leaf hologram ith date privy mark. **Edge:** Reeded. **Size:** 38 mm.

KM	Date	Mintage	MS-63	Proof
437	2001	30,000	25.50	—

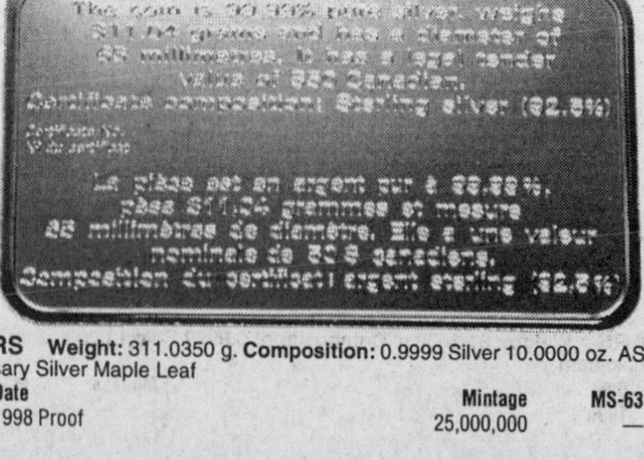

50 DOLLARS **Weight:** 311.0350 g. **Composition:** 0.9999 Silver 10.0000 oz. ASW **Subject:** 10th Anniversary Silver Maple Leaf

KM	Date	Mintage	MS-63	Proof
326	1998 Proof	25,000,000	—	125

GOLD BULLION COINAGE

DOLLAR **Weight:** 1.5551 g. **Composition:** 0.9999 Gold 0.05 oz. AGW

KM	Date	Mintage	MS-63	Proof
238	1993	37,080	BV+37%	—
	1994	78,860	BV+37%	—
	1995	85,920	BV+37%	—
	1996	56,520	BV+37%	—
	1997	59,720	BV+37%	—
	1998	44,260	BV+37%	—
	1999 Maple leaf with oval "20 Years ANS" privy mark	—	BV+46%	—

DOLLAR **Weight:** 1.5551 g. **Composition:** 0.9999 Gold 0.05 oz. AGW **Reverse:** Maple leaf hologram

KM	Date	Mintage	MS-63	Proof
365	1999	—	—	—

DOLLAR **Weight:** 1.5810 g. **Composition:** 0.9990 Gold 0.0508 oz. AGW **Subject:** Holographic Maple Leaves **Obverse:** Bust of Queen Elizabeth II right. **Reverse:** Three maple leaves multicolor hologram. **Edge:** Reeded. **Size:** 14.1 mm.

KM	Date	Mintage	MS-63	Proof
438	2001 in sets only	600	BV+37%	—

2 DOLLARS **Weight:** 2.0735 g. **Composition:** 0.9999 Gold 0.0666 oz. AGW **Reverse:** Maple leaf

KM	Date	Mintage	MS-63	Proof
256	1994	5,493	55.00	—

5 DOLLARS **Weight:** 3.1200 g. **Composition:** 0.9999 Gold .1000 oz. AGW **Obverse:** Elizabeth II effigy **Obv. Designer:** Machin **Reverse:** Maple leaf

KM	Date	Mintage	MS-63	Proof
135	1982	246,000	BV+14%	—
	1983	304,000	BV+14%	—
	1984	262,000	BV+14%	—
	1985	398,000	BV+14%	—
	1986	529,516	BV+14%	—
	1987	459,000	BV+14%	—
	1988	506,500	BV+14%	—
	1989	539,000	BV+14%	—
	1989 Proof	16,992	—	50.00

5 DOLLARS **Weight:** 3.1200 g. **Composition:** 0.9999 Gold 0.1000 oz. AGW **Obverse:** Elizabeth II effigy **Obv. Designer:** dePedery-Hunt **Reverse:** Maple leaf

KM	Date	Mintage	MS-63	Proof
188	1990	476,000	BV+14%	—
	1991	322,000	BV+14%	—
	1992	384,000	BV+14%	—
	1993	248,630	BV+14%	—
	1994	313,150	BV+14%	—
	1995	294,890	BV+14%	—
	1996	179,220	BV+14%	—
	1997	188,540	BV+14%	—
	1998	301,940	BV+14%	—
	1999 Maple leaf with oval "20 Years ANS" privy mark	—	BV+19%	—

5 DOLLARS **Weight:** 3.1200 g. **Composition:** 0.9999 Gold 0.1000 oz. AGW **Reverse:** Maple leaf hologram

KM	Date	Mintage	MS-63	Proof
366	1999	—	—	—

5 DOLLARS **Weight:** 3.1310 g. **Composition:** 0.9999 Gold 0.1007 oz. AGW **Subject:** Holographic Maple Leaves **Obverse:** Queen's portrait. **Reverse:** Three maple leaves multicolor hologram. **Edge:** Reeded. **Size:** 16 mm.

KM	Date	Mintage	MS-63	Proof
439	2001 in sets only	600	—	—

10 DOLLARS **Weight:** 7.7850 g. **Composition:** 0.9999 Gold 0.2500 oz. AGW **Obverse:** Elizabeth II effigy **Obv. Designer:** Machin **Reverse:** Maple leaf

KM	Date	Mintage	MS-63	Proof
136	1982	184,000	BV+10%	—
	1983	308,800	BV+10%	—
	1984	242,400	BV+10%	—
	1985	620,000	BV+10%	—
	1986	915,200	BV+10%	—
	1987	376,000	BV+10%	—
	1988	436,000	BV+10%	—
	1989	328,800	BV+10%	—
	1989 Proof	6,998	—	125

10 DOLLARS **Weight:** 7.7850 g. **Composition:** 0.9999 Gold 0.2500 oz. AGW **Obverse:** Elizabeth II effigy **Obv. Designer:** dePedery-Hunt **Reverse:** Maple leaf

KM	Date	Mintage	MS-63	Proof
189	1990	253,600	BV+10%	—
	1991	166,400	BV+10%	—
	1992	179,600	BV+10%	—
	1993	158,452	BV+10%	—
	1994	148,792	BV+10%	—
	1995	127,596	BV+10%	—
	1996	89,148	BV+10%	—
	1997	98,104	BV+10%	—
	1998	85,472	BV+10%	—
	1999 Maple leaf with oval "20 Years ANS" privy mark	—	BV+15%	—

10 DOLLARS **Weight:** 7.7850 g. **Composition:** 0.9999 Gold 0.2500 oz. AGW **Reverse:** Maple leaf hologram

KM	Date	Mintage	MS-63	Proof
367	1999	—	—	—

10 DOLLARS **Weight:** 7.7970 g. **Composition:** 0.9999 Gold 0.2507 oz. AGW **Subject:** Holographic Maples Leaves **Obverse:** Queen's portrait. **Reverse:** Three maple leaves multicolor hologram. **Edge:** Reeded. **Size:** 20 mm.

KM	Date	Mintage	MS-63	Proof
440	2001	15,000	196	—

20 DOLLARS **Weight:** 15.5515 g. **Composition:** 0.9999 Gold 0.5000 oz. AGW **Obverse:** Elizabeth II effigy **Obv. Designer:** Machin **Size:** 32 mm.

KM	Date	Mintage	MS-63	Proof
153	1986	529,200	BV+7%	—
	1987	332,800	BV+7%	—
	1988	538,400	BV+7%	—
	1989	259,200	BV+7%	—
	1989 Proof	6,998	—	225

20 DOLLARS **Weight:** 15.5515 g. **Composition:** 0.9999 Gold 0.5000 oz. AGW **Obverse:** Elizabeth II effigy **Obv. Designer:** dePedery-Hunt **Reverse:** Maple leaf

KM	Date	Mintage	MS-63	Proof
190	1990	174,400	BV+7%	—
	1991	96,200	BV+7%	—
	1992	108,000	BV+7%	—
	1993	99,492	BV+7%	—
	1994	104,766	BV+7%	—
	1995	103,162	BV+7%	—
	1996	66,246	BV+7%	—
	1997	63,354	BV+7%	—
	1998	65,366	BV+7%	—
	1999 Maple leaf with oval "20 Years ANS" privy mark	—	BV+12%	—

20 DOLLARS **Weight:** 15.5515 g. **Composition:** 0.9999 Gold 0.5000 oz. AGW **Reverse:** Maple leaf hologram

KM	Date	Mintage	MS-63	Proof
368	1999	—	—	—

20 DOLLARS **Weight:** 15.5840 g. **Composition:** 0.9999 Gold 0.501 oz. AGW **Subject:** Holographic Maples Leaves **Obverse:** Queen's portrait. **Reverse:** Three maple leaves multicolor hologram. **Edge:** Reeded. **Size:** 25 mm.

KM	Date	Mintage	MS-63	Proof
441	2001 in set only	600	465	—

50 DOLLARS **Weight:** 31.1030 g. **Composition:** 0.9990 Gold 1.0000 oz. AGW **Reverse:** Maple leaf flanked by .9999

KM	Date	Mintage	MS-63	Proof
125.1	1979	1,000,000	BV+4%	—
	1980	1,251,500	BV+4%	—
	1981	863,000	BV+4%	—
	1982	883,000	BV+4%	—

50 DOLLARS **Weight:** 31.1030 g. **Composition:** 0.9999 Gold 1.0000 oz. AGW **Reverse:** Maple leaf flanked by .9999

KM	Date	Mintage	MS-63	Proof
125.2	1983	843,000	BV+4%	—
	1984	1,067,500	BV+4%	—
	1985	1,908,000	BV+4%	—
	1986	779,115	BV+4%	—
	1987	978,000	BV+4%	—
	1988	826,500	BV+4%	—
	1989	856,000	BV+4%	—
	1989 Proof	17,781	—	375

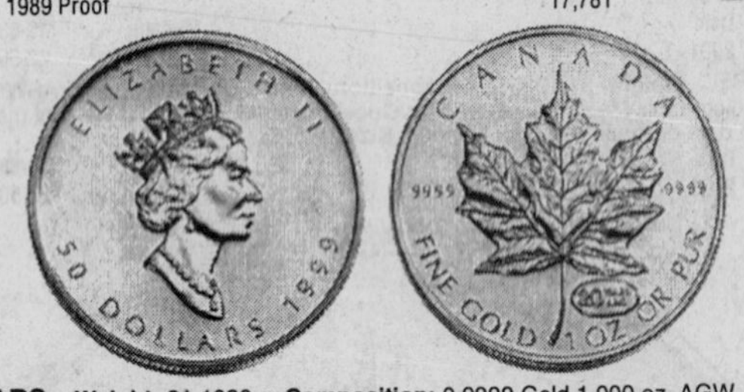

50 DOLLARS **Weight:** 31.1030 g. **Composition:** 0.9999 Gold 1.000 oz. AGW **Obverse:** Elizabeth II effigy **Obv. Designer:** dePedery-Hunt **Reverse:** Maple leaf flanked by .9999

KM	Date	Mintage	MS-63	Proof
191	1990	815,000	BV+4%	—
	1991	290,000	BV+4%	—
	1992	368,900	BV+4%	—
	1993	321,413	BV+4%	—
	1994	180,357	BV+4%	—
	1995	208,729	BV+4%	—
	1996	143,682	BV+4%	—
	1997	478,211	BV+4%	—
	1998	593,704	BV+4%	—
	1999 Maple leaf with oval "20 Years ANS" privy mark	—	BV+7%	—

50 DOLLARS **Weight:** 31.1030 g. **Composition:** 0.9999 Gold 1 oz. AGW **Reverse:** Mountie

KM	Date	Mintage	MS-63	Proof
305	1997	12,913	350	—

50 DOLLARS **Weight:** 31.1030 g. **Composition:** 0.9999 Gold 1.0000 oz. AGW **Reverse:** Maple leaf hologram

KM	Date	Mintage	MS-63	Proof
369	1999	—	—	—

50 DOLLARS **Weight:** 31.1030 g. **Composition:** 0.9999 Gold 1.0000 oz. AGW **Reverse:** Maple leaf with fireworks privy mark

KM	Date	Mintage	MS-63	Proof
364	1999/2000	—	—	—

50 DOLLARS **Weight:** 31.1500 g. **Composition:** 0.9999 Gold 1.0014 oz. AGW **Subject:** Holographic Maples Leaves **Obverse:** Queen's portrait. **Reverse:** Three maple leaves multicolor hologram. **Edge:** Reeded. **Size:** 30 mm.

KM	Date	Mintage	MS-63	Proof
442	2001 in set only	600	1,163	—

PLATINUM BULLION COINAGE

DOLLAR **Weight:** 1.5552 g. **Composition:** 0.9995 Platinum 0.0500 oz. APW **Reverse:** Maple leaf

KM	Date	Mintage	MS-63	Proof
239	1993	2,120	BV+35%	—
	1994	4,260	BV+35%	—
	1995	460	100	—
	1996	1,640	BV+35%	—
	1997	1,340	BV+35%	—
	1998	2,000	BV+35%	—
	1999	2,000	BV+35%	—

2 DOLLARS **Weight:** 2.0735 g. **Composition:** 0.9995 Platinum 0.0666 oz. APW **Reverse:** Maple leaf

KM	Date	Mintage	MS-63	Proof
257	1994	1,470	250	—

5 DOLLARS **Weight:** 3.1203 g. **Composition:** 0.9995 Platinum 0.1000 oz. APW **Obverse:** Elizabeth II effigy **Obv. Designer:** Machin

KM	Date	Mintage	MS-63	Proof
164	1988	74,000	BV+18%	—
	1989	18,000	BV+18%	—
	1989 Proof	11,999	—	75.00

5 DOLLARS **Weight:** 3.1203 g. **Composition:** 0.9995 Platinum 0.1000 oz. APW **Obverse:** Elizabeth II effigy **Obv. Designer:** dePedery-Hunt

KM	Date	Mintage	MS-63	Proof
192	1990	9,000	BV+18%	—
	1991	13,000	BV+18%	—
	1992	16,000	BV+18%	—
	1993	14,020	BV+18%	—
	1994	19,190	BV+18%	—
	1995	8,940	BV+18%	—
	1996	8,820	BV+18%	—
	1997	7,050	BV+18%	—
	1998	5,710	BV+18%	—
	1999	2,000	BV+18%	—

10 DOLLARS **Weight:** 7.7857 g. **Composition:** 0.9995 Platinum 0.2500 oz. APW **Obverse:** Elizabeth II effigy **Obv. Designer:** Machin **Reverse:** Maple leaf

KM	Date	Mintage	MS-63	Proof
165	1988	93,600	BV+13%	—
	1989	3,200	BV+13%	—
	1989 Proof	1,999	—	175

10 DOLLARS **Weight:** 7.7857 g. **Composition:** 0.9995 Platinum 0.2500 oz. APW **Obverse:** Elizabeth II effigy **Obv. Designer:** dePedery-Hunt **Reverse:** Maple leaf

KM	Date	Mintage	MS-63	Proof
193	1990	1,600	BV+13%	—
	1991	7,200	BV+13%	—
	1992	11,600	BV+13%	—
	1993	8,048	BV+13%	—
	1994	9,456	BV+13%	—
	1995	6,524	BV+13%	—
	1996	6,160	BV+13%	—
	1997	4,552	BV+13%	—
	1998	3,816	BV+13%	—
	1999	2,000	BV+13%	—

20 DOLLARS **Weight:** 15.5519 g. **Composition:** 0.9995 Platinum 0.5000 oz. APW **Obverse:** Elizabeth II effigy **Obv. Designer:** Machin **Reverse:** Maple leaf

KM	Date	Mintage	MS-63	Proof
166	1988	23,600	BV+9%	—
	1989	4,800	BV+9%	—
	1989 Proof	1,999	—	400

20 DOLLARS **Weight:** 15.5519 g. **Composition:** 0.9995 Platinum 0.5000 oz. APW **Obverse:** Elizabeth II effigy **Obv. Designer:** dePedery-Hunt **Reverse:** Maple leaf

KM	Date	Mintage	MS-63	Proof
194	1990	2,600	BV+9%	—
	1991	5,600	BV+9%	—
	1992	12,800	BV+9%	—
	1993	6,022	BV+9%	—
	1994	6,710	BV+9%	—
	1995	6,308	BV+9%	—
	1996	5,490	BV+9%	—
	1997	3,990	BV+9%	—
	1998	5,486	BV+9%	—
	1999	500	BV+15%	—

30 DOLLARS **Weight:** 3.1100 g. **Composition:** 0.9990 Platinum 0.1000 oz. APW **Reverse:** Polar bear swimming

KM	Date	Mintage	MS-63	Proof
174	1990 Proof	2,629	—	85.00

30 DOLLARS **Weight:** 3.1100 g. **Composition:** 0.9990 Platinum 0.1000 oz. APW **Reverse:** Snowy owl

KM	Date	Mintage	MS-63	Proof
198	1991 Proof	3,500	—	85.00

30 DOLLARS **Weight:** 3.1100 g. **Composition:** 0.9990 Platinum 0.1000 oz. APW **Reverse:** Cougar head and shoulders

KM	Date	Mintage	MS-63	Proof
226	1992 Proof	3,500	—	85.00

30 DOLLARS **Weight:** 3.1100 g. **Composition:** 0.9990 Platinum 0.1000 oz. APW **Reverse:** Arctic fox

KM	Date	Mintage	MS-63	Proof
240	1993 Proof	3,500	—	100

30 DOLLARS **Weight:** 3.1100 g. **Composition:** 0.9990 Platinum 0.1000 oz. APW **Reverse:** Sea otter **Note:** 1,500 sets only.

KM	Date	Mintage	MS-63	Proof
252	1994 Proof	1,500	—	110

30 DOLLARS **Weight:** 3.1100 g. **Composition:** 0.9990 Platinum 0.1000 oz. APW **Reverse:** Canadian lynx

KM	Date	Mintage	MS-63	Proof
266	1995 Proof	620	—	100

30 DOLLARS **Weight:** 3.1100 g. **Composition:** 0.9990 Platinum 0.1000 oz. APW **Reverse:** Falcon portrait

KM	Date	Mintage	MS-63	Proof
278	1996 Proof	489	—	100

30 DOLLARS **Weight:** 3.1320 g. **Composition:** 0.9995 Platinum 0.1006 oz. APW **Reverse:** Bison head

KM	Date	Mintage	MS-63	Proof
300	1997 Proof	5,000	—	100

30 DOLLARS **Weight:** 3.1100 g. **Composition:** 0.9990 Platinum 0.1 oz. APW **Reverse:** Grey wolf

KM	Date	Mintage	MS-63	Proof
322	ND(1998) Proof	2,000	—	100

30 DOLLARS **Weight:** 3.1320 g. **Composition:** 0.9995 Platinum 0.1006 oz. APW **Reverse:** Musk ox

KM	Date	Mintage	MS-63	Proof
359	1999 Proof	1,500	—	100

30 DOLLARS **Weight:** 3.1320 g. **Composition:** 0.9995 Platinum .1006 oz. APW **Obverse:** Queen's portrait **Reverse:** Pronghorn antelope head **Edge:** Reeded **Size:** 16 mm.

KM	Date	Mintage	MS-63	Proof
405	2000 Proof	600	—	100

30 DOLLARS **Weight:** 3.1320 g. **Composition:** 0.9995 Platinum .1006 oz. APW **Subject:** Platinum Collector Bullion **Obverse:** Queen's head right. **Reverse:** Harlequin duck's head. **Edge:** Reeded. **Size:** 16 mm.

KM	Date	Mintage	MS-63	Proof
429	2001 Proof	—	—	100

50 DOLLARS **Weight:** 31.1030 g. **Composition:** 0.9995 Platinum 1.0000 oz. APW **Obverse:** Elizabeth II effigy **Obv. Designer:** Machin **Reverse:** Maple leaf

KM	Date	Mintage	MS-63	Proof
167	1988	37,500	BV+4%	—
	1989	10,000	BV+4%	—
	1989 Proof	5,965	—	BV+15%

50 DOLLARS **Weight:** 31.1030 g. **Composition:** 0.9995 Platinum 1.0000 oz. APW **Obverse:** Elizabeth II effigy **Obv. Designer:** dePedery-Hunt **Reverse:** Maple leaf

KM	Date	Mintage	MS-63	Proof
195	1990	15,100	BV+4%	—
	1991	31,900	BV+4%	—
	1992	40,500	BV+4%	—
	1993	17,666	BV+4%	—
	1994	36,245	BV+4%	—
	1995	25,829	BV+4%	—
	1996	62,273	BV+4%	—
	1997	25,480	BV+4%	—
	1998	10,403	BV+4%	—
	1999	1,300	BV+10%	—

75 DOLLARS **Weight:** 7.7760 g. **Composition:** 0.9990 Platinum 0.2500 oz. APW **Reverse:** Polar bear resting

KM	Date	Mintage	MS-63	Proof
175	1990 Proof	2,629	—	200

75 DOLLARS **Weight:** 7.7760 g. **Composition:** 0.9990 Platinum 0.2500 oz. APW **Reverse:** Snowy owls perched on branch

KM	Date	Mintage	MS-63	Proof
199	1991 Proof	3,500	—	200

75 DOLLARS **Weight:** 7.7760 g. **Composition:** 0.9990 Platinum 0.2500 oz. APW **Reverse:** Cougar prowling

KM	Date	Mintage	MS-63	Proof
227	1992 Proof	3,500	—	225

75 DOLLARS **Weight:** 7.7760 g. **Composition:** 0.9990 Platinum 0.2500 oz. APW **Reverse:** Two Arctic foxes

KM	Date	Mintage	MS-63	Proof
241	1993 Proof	3,500	—	225

75 DOLLARS **Weight:** 7.7760 g. **Composition:** 0.9990 Platinum 0.2500 oz. APW **Reverse:** Sea otter eating urchin

KM	Date	Mintage	MS-63	Proof
253	1994 Proof	1,500	—	250

75 DOLLARS **Weight:** 7.7760 g. **Composition:** 0.9990 Platinum 0.2500 oz. APW **Reverse:** Two lynx kittens

KM	Date	Mintage	MS-63	Proof
267	1995 Proof	1,500	—	225

75 DOLLARS **Weight:** 7.7760 g. **Composition:** 0.9990 Platinum 0.2500 oz. APW **Reverse:** Peregrine falcon, diving falcon

KM	Date	Mintage	MS-63	Proof
279	1996 Proof	1,500	—	225

75 DOLLARS **Weight:** 7.7760 g. **Composition:** 0.9990 Platinum 0.2500 oz. APW **Reverse:** Two bison calves

KM	Date	Mintage	MS-63	Proof
301	1997 Proof	1,500	—	225

75 DOLLARS **Weight:** 7.7760 g. **Composition:** 0.9990 Platinum 0.2500 oz. APW **Reverse:** Gray wolf

KM	Date	Mintage	MS-63	Proof
323	1998 Proof	1,000	—	225

75 DOLLARS **Weight:** 7.7760 g. **Composition:** 0.9990 Platinum 0.2500 oz. APW **Reverse:** Musk ox

KM	Date	Mintage	MS-63	Proof
360	1999 Proof	500	—	250

75 DOLLARS **Weight:** 7.7760 g. **Composition:** 0.9990 Platinum .25 oz. APW **Obverse:** Queen's portrait **Reverse:** Standing pronghorn antelope **Edge:** Reeded **Size:** 20 mm.

KM	Date	Mintage	MS-63	Proof
406	2000 Proof	600	—	250

75 DOLLARS **Weight:** 7.8000 g. **Composition:** 0.9995 Platinum .2506 oz. APW **Subject:** Platinum Collector Bullion **Obverse:** Queen's head right. **Reverse:** Harlequin duck in flight. **Edge:** Reeded. **Size:** 20 mm.

KM	Date	Mintage	MS-63	Proof
430	2001 Proof	—	—	250

150 DOLLARS **Weight:** 15.5520 g. **Composition:** 0.9990 Platinum 0.5000 oz. APW **Reverse:** Polar bear walking

KM	Date	Mintage	MS-63	Proof
176	1990 Proof	2,629	—	400

150 DOLLARS **Weight:** 15.5520 g. **Composition:** 0.9990 Platinum 0.5000 oz. APW **Reverse:** Snowy owl flying

KM	Date	Mintage	MS-63	Proof
200	1991 Proof	3,500	—	400

150 DOLLARS **Weight:** 15.5520 g. **Composition:** 0.9990 Platinum 0.5000 oz. APW **Reverse:** Cougar mother and cub

KM	Date	Mintage	MS-63	Proof
228	1992 Proof	3,500	—	425

150 DOLLARS **Weight:** 15.5520 g. **Composition:** 0.9990 Platinum 0.5000 oz. APW **Reverse:** Arctic fox by lake

KM	Date	Mintage	MS-63	Proof
242	1993 Proof	3,500	—	425

150 DOLLARS **Weight:** 15.5520 g. **Composition:** 0.9990 Platinum 0.5000 oz. APW **Reverse:** Sea otter mother carrying pup

KM	Date	Mintage	MS-63	Proof
254	1994 Proof	—	—	450

150 DOLLARS **Weight:** 15.5520 g. **Composition:** 0.9990 Platinum 0.5000 oz. APW **Reverse:** Prowling lynx

KM	Date	Mintage	MS-63	Proof
268	1995 Proof	226	—	425

150 DOLLARS **Weight:** 15.5520 g. **Composition:** 0.9990 Platinum 0.5000 oz. APW **Reverse:** Peregrine falcon on branch

KM	Date	Mintage	MS-63	Proof
280	1996 Proof	100	—	425

150 DOLLARS **Weight:** 15.5520 g. **Composition:** 0.9990 Platinum 0.5000 oz. APW **Reverse:** Bison bull

KM	Date	Mintage	MS-63	Proof
302	1997 Proof	4,000	—	425

150 DOLLARS **Weight:** 15.5520 g. **Composition:** 0.9990 Platinum 0.5000 oz. APW **Reverse:** Two gray wolf cubs

KM	Date	Mintage	MS-63	Proof
324	1998 Proof	2,000	—	425

150 DOLLARS **Weight:** 15.5520 g. **Composition:** 0.9990 Platinum 0.5000 oz. APW **Reverse:** Musk ox

KM	Date	Mintage	MS-63	Proof
361	1999 Proof	500	—	450

150 DOLLARS **Weight:** 15.5520 g. **Composition:** 0.9990 Platinum .5 oz. APW **Obverse:** Queen's portrait **Reverse:** Two pronghorn antelope **Edge:** Reeded **Size:** 25 mm.

KM	Date	Mintage	MS-63	Proof
407	2000 Proof	600	—	450

150 DOLLARS **Weight:** 15.5900 g. **Composition:** 0.9995 Platinum .5010 oz. APW **Subject:** Platinum Collector Bullion **Obverse:** Queen's head right. **Reverse:** Two harlequin ducks. **Edge:** Reeded. **Size:** 25 mm.

KM	Date	Mintage	MS-63	Proof
431	2001 Proof	—	—	450

300 DOLLARS **Weight:** 31.1035 g. **Composition:** 0.9990 Platinum 1.0000 oz. APW **Reverse:** Polar bear mother and cub

KM	Date	Mintage	MS-63	Proof
177	1990 Proof	2,629	—	800

300 DOLLARS **Weight:** 31.1035 g. **Composition:** 0.9990 Platinum 1.0000 oz. APW **Reverse:** Snowy owl with chicks

KM	Date	Mintage	MS-63	Proof
201	1991 Proof	3,500	—	800

300 DOLLARS **Weight:** 31.1035 g. **Composition:** 0.9990 Platinum 1.0000 oz. APW **Reverse:** Cougar resting in tree

KM	Date	Mintage	MS-63	Proof
229	1992 Proof	3,500	—	800

300 DOLLARS **Weight:** 31.1035 g. **Composition:** 0.9990 Platinum 1.0000 oz. APW **Reverse:** Mother fox and three kits

KM	Date	Mintage	MS-63	Proof
243	1993 Proof	3,500	—	800

300 DOLLARS **Weight:** 31.1035 g. **Composition:** 0.9990 Platinum 1.0000 oz. APW **Reverse:** Two otters swimming

KM	Date	Mintage	MS-63	Proof
255	1994 Proof	—	—	900

300 DOLLARS **Weight:** 31.1035 g. **Composition:** 0.9990 Platinum 1.0000 oz. APW **Reverse:** Female lynx and three kittens

KM	Date	Mintage	MS-63	Proof
269	1995 Proof	1,500	—	800

300 DOLLARS **Weight:** 31.1035 g. **Composition:** 0.9990 Platinum 1.0000 oz. APW **Reverse:** Peregrine falcon feeding nestlings

KM	Date	Mintage	MS-63	Proof
281	1996 Proof	1,500	—	800

300 DOLLARS **Weight:** 31.1035 g. **Composition:** 0.9990 Platinum 1.0000 oz. APW **Reverse:** Bison family

KM	Date	Mintage	MS-63	Proof
303	1997 Proof	1,500	—	800

300 DOLLARS **Weight:** 31.1035 g. **Composition:** 0.9990 Platinum 1.0000 oz. APW **Reverse:** Gray wolf and two cubs

KM	Date	Mintage	MS-63	Proof
325	1998 Proof	—	—	850

300 DOLLARS **Weight:** 31.1035 g. **Composition:** 0.9990 Platinum 1.0000 oz. APW **Reverse:** Musk ox

KM	Date	Mintage	MS-63	Proof
362	1999 Proof	500	—	900

300 DOLLARS **Weight:** 31.1035 g. **Composition:** 0.9990 Platinum 1.0000 oz. APW **Obverse:** Queen's portrait **Reverse:** Four pronghorn antelope **Edge:** Reeded **Size:** 30 mm.

KM	Date	Mintage	MS-63	Proof
408	2000 Proof	600	—	900

300 DOLLARS **Weight:** 31.1600 g. **Composition:** 0.9995 Platinum 1.0013 oz. APW **Subject:** Platinum Collector Bullion **Obverse:** Queen's head right. **Reverse:** Two standing harlequin ducks. **Edge:** Reeded. **Size:** 30 mm.

KM	Date	Mintage	MS-63	Proof
432	2001 Proof	—	—	900

CUSTOM PROOF-LIKE SETS (CPL)

KM	Date	Mintage	Identification	Issue Price	Mkt Val
CPL1	1971	33,517	KM59.1 (2 pcs.), 60.1, 62b-75.1, 77.1 ,79	6.50	5.00
CPL2	1971	38,198	KM59.1 (2 pcs.), 60.1, 62b, 75.1-77.1	6.50	5.00
CPL3	1973	35,676	KM59.1 (2 pcs.), 60.1, 75.1, 77.1, 81.1 obv. 120 beads, 82	6.50	5.00
CPL4	1973	I.A.	KM59.1 (2 pcs.), 60.1, 75.1, 77.1, 81.1 obv. 132 beads, 82	6.50	140
CPL5	1974	44,296	KM59.1 (2 pcs.), 60.1, 62b-75.1, 88	8.00	5.00
CPL6	1975	36,851	KM59.1 (2 pcs.), 60.1, 62b-75.1, 76.2, 77.1	8.00	5.00
CPL7	1976	28,162	KM59.1 (2 pcs.), 60.1, 62b-75.1, 76.2, 77.1	8.00	5.50
CPL8	1977	44,198	KM59.1 (2 pcs.), 60.1, 62b-75.2, 77.1, 117	8.15	5.50
CPL9	1978	41,000	KM59.1 (2 pcs.), 60.1, 62b-75.3, 77.1, 120.1	—	5.50
CPL10	1979	31,174	KM59.2 (2 pcs.), 60.2, 74, 75.3, 77.2, 120.1	10.75	5.50
CPL11	1980	41,447	KM60.2, 74, 75.3, 77.2, 120.1, 127 (2 pcs.)	10.75	6.00

MINT SETS

KM	Date	Mintage	Identification	Issue Price	Mkt Val
MS1	1973	I.A.	KM84-85, 86.1, 87; Olympic Commemoratives, Series I	45.00	30.00
MS2	1974	I.A.	KM89-90, 93-94; Olympic Commemoratives, Series II	48.00	30.00
MS3	1974	I.A.	KM91-92, 95-96; Olympic Commemorative, Series III	48.00	30.00
MS4	1975	I.A.	KM98-99, 102-103; Olympic Commemoratives, Series IV	48.00	30.00
MS5	1975	I.A.	KM100-101, 104-105; Olympic Commemoratives, Series V	60.00	30.00
MS6	1976	I.A.	KM107-108, 111-112; Olympic Commemoratives, Series VI	60.00	30.00
MS7	1976	I.A.	KM109-110, 113-114; Olympic Commemoratives, Series VII	60.00	30.00
MS8	2001	600	KM438-442	1,996	—

OLYMPIC COMMEMORATIVES (OCP)

KM	Date	Mintage	Identification	Issue Price	Mkt Val
OCP1	1973	I.A.	KM84-87, Series I	78.50	37.50
OCP2	1974	I.A.	KM89-90, 93-94, Series II	88.50	37.50
OCP3	1974	I.A.	KM91-92, 95-96, Series III	88.50	37.50
OCP4	1975	I.A.	KM98-99, 102-103, Series IV	88.50	37.50
OCP5	1975	I.A.	KM100-101, 104-105, Series V	88.50	37.50
OCP6	1976	I.A.	KM107-108, 111-112, Series VI	88.50	38.50
OCP7	1976	I.A.	KM109-110, 113-114, Series VII	88.50	38.50

PROOF SETS

KM	Date	Mintage	Identification	Issue Price	Mkt Val
PS1	1981	199,000	KM60.2, 74, 75.3, 77.2, 120.1, 127, 130	36.00	17.50
PS2	1982	180,908	KM60.2a, 74, 75.3, 77.2, 120.1, 132-133	36.00	11.00
PS3	1983	166,779	KM60.2a, 74, 75.3, 77.2, 120.1, 132, 138	36.00	12.50
PS4	1984	161,602	KM60.2a, 74, 75.3, 77.2, 120.1, 132, 140	30.00	13.50
PS5	1985	157,037	KM60.2a, 74, 75.3, 77.2, 120.1, 132, 143	30.00	14.00
PS6	1986	175,745	KM60.2a, 74, 75.3, 77.2, 120.1, 132, 149	30.00	14.00
PS7	1987	179,004	KM60.2a, 74, 75.3, 77.2, 120.1, 132, 154	34.00	14.00
PS8	1988	175,259	KM60.2a, 74, 75.3, 77.2, 132, 157, 161	37.50	22.50
PS9	1989	170,928	KM60.2a, 74, 75.3, 77.2, 132, 157, 168	40.00	22.50
PS10	1989	6,823	KM125.2, 135-136, 153	1,190	800
PS11	1989	1,995	KM164-167	1,700	1,350
PS12	1989	2,550	KM125.2, 163, 167	1,530	1,200
PS13	1989	9,979	KM135, 163-164	165	155
PS14	1990	158,068	KM170, 181, 182, 183, 184, 185, 186	41.00	22.50
PS15	1990	2,629	KM174-177	1,720	1,250
PS16	1991	14,629	KM179, 181, 182, 183, 184, 185, 186	—	45.00
PS17	1991	873	KM198-201	1,760	1,250
PS18	1992	84,397	KM203a, 212a-214a, 218, 220a-223a, 231a-234a	—	60.00
PS19	1992	147,061	KM204-210	42.75	25.00
PS20	1992	3,500	KM226-229	1,680	1,250
PS21	1993	143,065	KM181, 182, 183, 184, 185, 186, 235	42.75	18.00
PS22	1993	3,500	KM240-243	1,329	1,250
PS23	1994	47,303	KM181-186, 248	47.50	28.00
PS24	1994	99,121	KM181, 182, 183, 184, 185, 186, 251	43.00	28.00
PS25	1994	1,500	KM252-255	915	1,450
PS26	1995	I.A.	KM181, 182, 183, 184, 185, 186, 259	37.45	25.00
PS27	1995	50,000	KM181, 182, 183, 184, 185, 258-259	49.45	22.00
PS28	1995	I.A.	KM261-264	42.00	60.00
PS29	1995	682	KM266-269	1,555	1,400
PS30	1995	I.A.	KM261-262	22.00	21.00
PS31	1995	I.A.	KM263-264	22.00	30.00
PS32	1996	423	KM278-281	1,555	1,400
PS33	1996	I.A.	KM181a, 182a, 183a, 184a, 185a, 186, 274	49.00	35.00
PS34	1996	I.A.	KM283-286	44.45	45.00
PS35	1997	I.A.	KM182a, 183a, 184a, 209, 270c, 282, 289,	60.00	30.00
PS36	1997	I.A.	KM292-295	44.45	35.00
PS37	1997	I.A.	KM300-303	1,530	1,400
PS38	1998	I.A.	KM182a, 183a, 184a, 186, 270b, 289, 290a, 306	59.45	50.00
PS39	1998	25,000	KM309-313	73.50	55.00
PS40	1998	61,000	KM316 w/China Y-727	72.50	30.00
PS41	1998	I.A.	KM318-321	44.45	38.00
PS42	1998	1,000	KM322-325	1,552	1,400
PS43	1998	25,000	KM310-313, 332	73.50	30.00
PS44	1999	I.A.	KM182a-184a, 186, 270c, 289, 290a,	59.45	60.00
PS45	1999	I.A.	KM335-338	39.95	40.00
PS46	1999	I.A.	KM342a-353a	99.45	75.00
PS47	1999	I.A.	KM359-362	1,425	1,450
PS48	2000	—	KM373a, 374a, 375a, 376a, 377a, 378a, 379a, 380a, 381a, 382a, 383a, 384.2a	101	90.00
PS49	2000	—	KM389-392	44.00	40.00
PS50	2000	600	KM405-408	1,416	1,420
PS51	2001	—	KM429, 430, 431, 432	—	1,420

PROOF-LIKE DOLLARS

KM	Date	Mintage	Identification	Issue Price	Mkt Val
D1.2	1951	I.A.	KM46, Arnprior		700
D2.1	1952	I.A.	KM46, water lines		1,200

KM	Date	Mintage	Identification	Issue Price	Mkt Val
D2.2	1952	I.A.	KM46, without water lines		175
D3	1953	1,200	KM54, Canoe w/shoulder fold	—	300
D4	1954	5,300	KM54, Canoe	1.25	125
D5	1955	7,950	KM54, Canoe	1.25	100
D5a	1955	I.A.	KM54, Arnprior	1.25	150
D6	1956	10,212	KM54, Canoe	1.25	50.00
D7	1957	16,241	KM54, Canoe	1.25	22.00
D10	1960	82,728	KM54, Canoe	1.25	7.00
D11	1961	120,928	KM54, Canoe	1.25	7.00
D12	1962	248,901	KM54, Canoe	1.25	6.00
D13	1963	963,525	KM54, Canoe	1.25	4.50
D14	1964	2,862,441	KM58, Charlottetown	1.25	4.50
D15	1965	2,904,352	KM64.1, Canoe	—	4.50
D16	1966	672,514	KM64.1, Canoe	—	4.50
D17	1967	1,036,176	KM70, Confederation	—	6.50

PROOF-LIKE SETS (PL)

KM	Date	Mintage	Identification	Issue Price	Mkt Val
PL3	1954	3,000	KM49-54	2.50	275
PL4	1954	I.A.	KM49 w/o shoulder fold, 50-54	2.50	550
PL5	1955	6,300	KM49, 50a, 51-54	2.50	165
PL6	1955	I.A.	KM49, 50a, 51-54, Arnprior	2.50	265
PL7	1956	6,500	KM49, 50a, 51-54	2.50	100
PL8	1957	11,862	KM49, 50a, 51-54	2.50	65.00
PL9	1958	18,259	KM49, 50a, 51-53, 55	2.50	45.00
PL10	1959	31,577	KM49, 50a, 51, 52, 54, 56	2.50	20.00
PL11	1960	64,097	KM49, 50a, 51, 52, 54, 56	3.00	14.00
PL12	1961	98,373	KM49, 50a, 51, 52, 54, 56	3.00	14.00
PL13	1962	200,950	KM49, 50a, 51, 52, 54, 56	3.00	10.00
PL14	1963	673,006	KM49, 51, 52, 54, 56, 57	3.00	7.00
PL15	1964	1,653,162	KM49, 51, 52, 56-58	3.00	7.00
PL16	1965	2,904,352	KM59.1-60.1, 61-63, 64.1	4.00	7.00
PL17	1966	672,514	KM59.1-60.1, 61-63, 64.1	4.00	7.00
PL18	1967	961,887	KM65-70 (pliofilm flat pack)	4.00	11.00
PL18A	1967	70,583	KM65-70 and Silver Medal (red box)	12.00	15.25
PL18B	1967	337,688	KM65-71 (black box)	40.00	200
PL19	1968	521,641	KM59.1-60.1, 62b, 72a, 75.1-76.1	4.00	2.25
PL20	1969	326,203	KM59.1-60.1, 62b, 75.1-77.1	4.00	2.75
PL21	1970	349,120	KM59.1-60.1, 62b, 75.1, 77.1, 78	4.00	3.25
PL22	1971	253,311	KM59.1-60.1, 62b, 75.1, 77.1, 79	4.00	2.75
PL23	1972	224,275	KM59.1-60.1, 62b-77.1	4.00	2.75
PL24	1973	243,695	KM59.1-60.1, 62b-75.1 obv. 120 beads, 77.1, 81.1, 82	4.00	4.00
PL25	1973	I.A.	KM59.1-60.1, 62b-75.1 obv. 132 beads, 77.1, 81.2, 82	4.00	110
PL26	1974	213,589	KM59.1-60.1, 62b-75.1, 77.1, 88	5.00	3.00
PL27.1	1975	197,372	KM59.1, 60.1, 62b-75.1, 76.2, 77.1	5.00	2.50
PL27.2	1975	I.A.	KM59.1, 60.1, 62b-75.1, 76.3, 77.1	5.00	5.00
PL28	1976	171,737	KM59.1, 60.1, 62b-75.1, 76.2, 77.1	5.15	2.75
PL29	1977	225,307	KM59.1, 60.1, 62b, 75.2, 77.1, 117.1	5.15	2.75
PL30	1978	260,000	KM59.1-60.1, 62b, 75.3, 77.1, 120.1	5.25	2.75
PL31	1979	187,624	KM59.2-60.2, 74, 75.3, 77.2, 120.1	6.25	2.75
PL32	1980	410,842	KM60.2, 74, 75.3, 77.2, 120.1, 127	6.50	4.50
PL33	1981	186,250	KM60.2, 74, 75.3, 77.2, 120.1, 123	5.00	3.25
PL34	1982	203,287	KM60.2, 74, 75.3, 77.2, 120.1, 123	6.00	2.50
PL36	1983	190,838	KM60.2a, 74, 75.3, 77.2, 120.1, 132	5.00	5.00
PL36.1	1983	I.A.	KM60.2a, 74, 75.3, 77.2, 120.1, 132; set in folder packaged by British Royal Mint Coin Club	—	—
PL37	1984	181,249	KM60.2a, 74, 75.3, 77.2, 120.1, 132	5.25	5.00
PL38	1985	173,924	KM60.2a, 74, 75.3, 77.2, 120.1, 132	5.25	6.00
PL39	1986	167,338	KM60.2a, 74, 75.3, 77.2, 120.1, 132	5.25	6.50
PL40	1987	212,136	KM60.2a, 74, 75.3, 77.2, 120.1, 132	5.25	5.00
PL41	1988	182,048	KM60.2a, 74, 75.3, 77.2, 132, 157	6.05	5.00
PL42	1989	173,622	KM60.2a, 74, 75.3, 77.2, 132, 157	6.60	8.00
PL43	1990	170,791	KM181-186	7.40	8.00
PL44	1991	147,814	KM181-186	7.40	25.00
PL45	1992	217,597	KM204-209	8.25	11.00
PL46	1993	171,680	KM181-186	8.25	4.50
PL47	1994	141,676	KM181-185, 258	8.50	6.00
PL48	1994	18,794	KM181-185, 258 (Oh Canada holder)	—	10.00
PL49	1995	143,892	KM181-186	6.95	6.50
PL50	1995	50,927	KM181-186 (Oh Canada holder)	14.65	10.00
PL51	1995	36,443	KM181-186 (Baby Gift holder)	—	11.00
PL52	1996	116,736	KM181-186	—	13.00
PL53	1996	29,747	KM181-186 (Baby Gift holder)	—	15.00
PL54	1996	I.A.	KM181a-185a, 186	8.95	15.00
PL55	1996	I.A.	KM181a-185a, 186 (Oh Canada holder)	14.65	12.00
PL56	1996	I.A.	KM181a-185a, 186 (Baby Gift holder)	—	12.00
PL57	1997	I.A.	KM182a-184a, 209, 270, 289-290	10.45	8.00
PL58	1997	I.A.	KM182a-184a, 270, 289-291 (Oh Canada holder)	16.45	20.00
PL59	1997	I.A.	KM182a-184a, 209, 270, 289-290 (Baby Gift holder)	18.50	10.00
PL60	1998	I.A.	KM182-184, 186, 270, 289-290	10.45	10.00
PL61	1998	I.A.	KM182-184, 186, 270, 289-290 (Oh Canada holder)	16.45	12.00
PL62	1998	I.A.	KM182-184, 186, 270, 289-290 (Tiny Treasures holder)	16.45	12.00
PL63	1999	I.A.	KM342-353	16.95	10.00
PL64	2000	—	KM373-384	16.95	10.00

SPECIMEN SETS (SS)

KM	Date	Mintage	Identification	Issue Price	Mkt Val
SS12	1902	100	KM8-12	—	25,000
SS13	1902	I.A.	KM9 (Large H), 10, 11	—	6,500
SS14	1903	—	KM10, 12, 13	—	7,000
SS15	1908	1,000	KM8, 10-13	—	2,200
SS16	1911	1,000	KM15-19	—	5,500
SS17	1911/12	5	KM15-20, 26-27	—	52,250
SS18	1921	I.A.	KM22-25, 28	—	120,000
SS19	1922	I.A.	KM28, 29	—	2,500
SS20	1923	I.A.	KM28, 29	—	5,000
SS21	1924	I.A.	KM28, 29	—	4,000
SS22	1925	I.A.	KM28, 29	—	7,000
SS23	1926	I.A.	KM28, 29 (Near 6)	—	5,000
SS24	1927	I.A.	KM24a, 28, 29	—	8,000
SS25	1928	I.A.	KM23a, 24a, 28, 29	—	12,000
SS26	1929	I.A.	KM23a,-25a, 28, 29	—	22,500
SS27	1930	I.A.	KM23a, 24a. 28, 29	—	16,000
SS28	1931	I.A.	KM23a-25a, 28, 29	—	26,500
SS29	1932	I.A.	KM23a-25a, 28, 29	—	20,000
SS30	1934	I.A.	KM23-25, 28, 29	—	23,000
SS31	1936	I.A.	KM23-25, 28, 29	—	12,000
SS32	1936	I.A.	KM23a(dot), 24a(dot), 25a, 28(dot), 29, 30	—	400,000
SS33	1937	1,025	KM32-37, Matte Finish	—	750
SS34	1937	I.A.	KM32-35, Mirror Fields	—	1,350
SS35	1937	75	KM32-37, Mirror Fields	—	3,900
SS36	1938	I.A.	KM32-37	—	18,250
SS-A36	1939	I.A.	KM32-35, 38, Matte Finish	—	—
SS-B36	1939	I.A.	KM32-35, 38, Mirror Fields	—	—
SS-C36	1942	I.A.	KM32, 33	—	1,000
SS-D36	1943	I.A.	KM32, 40	—	1,000
SS-A37	1944	I.A.	KM32, 40a	—	1,000
SS37	1944	3	KM32, 34-37, 40a	—	11,300
SS-A38	1945	I.A.	KM32, 40a	—	1,000
SS38	1945	6	KM32, 34-37, 40a	—	4,650
SS39	1946	15	KM32, 34-37, 39a	—	4,000
SS40	1947	I.A.	KM32, 34-37(7 curved), 37(7 pointed),	—	8,500
SS41	1947	I.A.	KM32, 34-36(7 curved), 37(blunt 7), 39a	—	6,200
SS42	1947	I.A.	KM32, 34-36(7 curved right), 37, 39a	—	4,250
SS43	1948	30	KM41-46	—	6,000
SS44	1949	20	KM41-45, 47	—	6,400
SS44A	1949	I.A.	KM47	—	1,550
SS45	1950	12	KM41-46	—	1,650
SS46	1950	I.A.	KM41-45, 46 (Arnprior)	—	3,175
SS47	1951	12	KM41, 48, 42a, 43-46 (w/water lines)	—	2,725
SS48	1952	2,317	KM41, 42a, 43-46 (water lines)	—	3,175
SS48A	1952	I.A.	KM41, 42a, 43-46 (w/o water lines)	—	3,175
SS49	1953	28	KM49 w/o straps, 50-54	—	1,850
SS50	1953	I.A.	KM49 w/ straps, 50-54	—	875
SS51	1964	I.A.	KM49, 51, 52, 56-58	—	850
SS52	1965	I.A.	KM59.1-60.1, 61-63, 64.1	—	850
SS56	1971	66,860	KM59.1-60.1, 62b-75.1, 77.1, 79 (2 pcs.); Double Dollar Prestige Sets	12.00	9.50
SS57	1972	36,349	KM59.1,-60.1, 62b-75.1, 76.1 (2 pcs.), 77; Double Dollar Prestige Sets	12.00	18.00
SS58	1973	119,819	KM59.1-60.1, 75.1, 77.1, 81.1, 82, 83; Double Dollar Prestige Sets	12.00	10.00
SS59	1973	I.A.	KM59.1-60.1, 75.1, 77.1, 81.2, 82, 83; Double Dollar Prestige Sets	—	125
SS60	1974	85,230	KM59.1-60.1, 62b-75.1, 77.1, 88, 88a; Double Dollar Prestige Sets	15.00	10.00
SS61	1975	97,263	KM59.1-60.1, 62b-75.1, 76.2, 77.1, 97; Double Dollar Prestige Sets	15.00	10.00
SS62	1976	87,744	KM59.1-60, 62b-75.1, 76.2, 77.1, 106; Double Dollar Prestige Sets	16.00	10.00
SS63	1977	142,577	KM59.1-60.1, 62b, 75.2, 77.1, 117.1, 118; Double Dollar Prestige Sets	16.50	10.00
SS64	1978	147,000	KM59.1-60.1, 62b, 75.3, 77.1, 120.1, 121; Double Dollar Prestige Sets	16.50	10.00
SS65	1979	155,698	KM59.2-60.2, 74, 75.3, 77.2, 120, 124; Double Dollar Prestige Sets	18.50	11.50
SS66	1980	162,875	KM60.2, 74-75.3, 77.2, 120, 127, 128; Double Dollar Prestige Sets	30.50	22.50
SS67	1981	71,300	KM60.2, 74, 75.3, 77.2, 120.1, 127; Regular Specimen Sets Resumed	10.00	6.00
SS68	1982	62,298	KM60.2a, 74, 75.3, 77.2, 120.1, 132; Regular Specimen Sets Resumed	11.50	6.00
SS69	1983	60,329	KM60.2a, 74, 75.3, 77.2, 120.1, 132; Regular Specimen Sets Resumed	12.75	6.00
SS70	1984	60,400	KM60.2a, 74, 75.3, 77.2, 120.1, 132; Regular Specimen Sets Resumed	10.00	6.00
SS71	1985	61,553	KM60.2a, 74, 75.3, 77.2, 120.1, 132; Regular Specimen Sets Resumed	10.00	6.50
SS72	1986	67,152	KM60.2a, 74, 75.3, 77.2, 120.1, 132; Regular Specimen Sets Resumed	10.00	6.50
SS72A	1987	75,194	KM60.2a, 74, 75.3, 77.2, 120.1, 132; Regular Specimen Sets Resumed	11.00	7.00
SS73	1988	70,205	KM60.2a, 74, 75.3, 77.2, 132, 157; Regular Specimen Sets Resumed	12.30	7.00
SS74	1989	75,306	KM60.2a, 74, 75.3, 77.2, 132, 157; Regular Specimen Sets Resumed	14.50	9.00
SS75	1990	76,611	KM181-186; Regular Specimen Sets Resumed	15.50	9.00
SS76	1991	68,552	KM181-186; Regular Specimen Sets Resumed	15.50	22.00
SS77	1992	78,328	KM204-209; Regular Specimen Sets Resumed	16.25	13.00
SS78	1993	77,351	KM181-186; Regular Specimen Sets Resumed	16.25	7.00
SS79	1994	77,349	KM181-186; Regular Specimen Sets Resumed	16.50	10.00
SS80	1995	I.A.	KM181-186; Regular Specimen Sets Resumed	13.95	10.00
SS82	1996	I.A.	KM181a-185a, 186; Regular Specimen Sets Resumed	18.95	12.00
SS83	1997	I.A.	KM182a-184a, 270, 289-291; Regular Specimen Sets Resumed	19.95	25.00
SS84	1998	I.A.	KM182-184, 186, 270, 289, 290; Regular Specimen Sets Resumed	19.95	12.00
SS85	1998	I.A.	KM182-184, 186, 270, 289a, 290; Regular Specimen Sets Resumed	19.95	12.00

V.I.P. SPECIMEN SETS (VS)

KM	Date	Mintage	Identification	Issue Price	Mkt Val
VS2	1970	100	KM59.1-60.1, 74.1-75.1, 77.1, 78	—	525
VS3	1971	69	KM59.1-60.1, 74.1-75.1, 77.1, 79(2 pcs.)	—	525
VS4	1972	25	KM59.1-60.1, 74.1-75.1, 76.1, (2 pcs.), 77.1	—	650
VS5	1973	26	KM59.1-60.1, 75.1, 77.1, 81.1, 82, 83	—	650
VS6	1974	72	KM59.1-60.1, 74.1-75.1, 77.1, 88, 88a	—	525
VS7	1975	94	KM59.1-60.1, 74.1-75.1, 76.2, 77.1, 97	—	525
VS8	1976	I.A.	KM59.1-60.1, 74.1-75.1, 76.2, 77.1, 106	—	525

CAPE VERDE

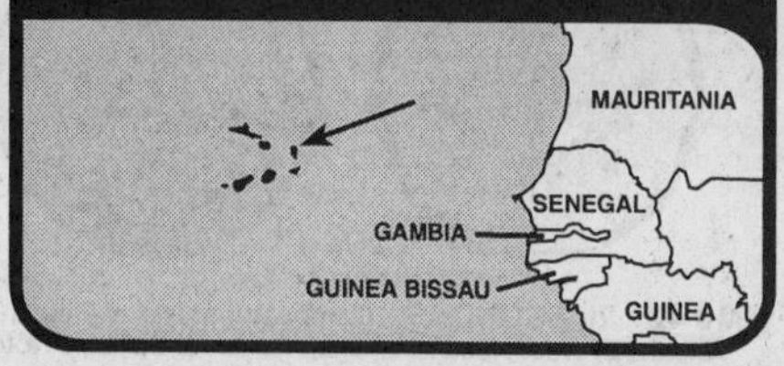

The Republic of Cape Verde, Africa's smallest republic, is located in the Atlantic Ocean, about 370 miles (595 km.) west of Dakar, Senegal, off the coast of Africa. The 14-island republic has an area of 1,557 sq. mi. (4,033 sq. km.) and a population of 435,983. Capital: Praia. The refueling of ships and aircraft is the chief economic function of the country. Fishing is important and agriculture is widely practiced, but the Cape Verdes are not self-sufficient in food. Fish products, salt, bananas, and shellfish are exported.

The date of discovery of the islands is uncertain. Possibly they were visited by Venetian captain Alvise Cadamosto in 1456. Portuguese navigator Diogo Gomes claimed them for Portugal in May of 1460. Settlement began two years later. The early importance and wealth of the islands, which caused them to be attacked by Sir Francis Drake and the Dutch, resulted from the monopoly of the Guinea slave trade granted the inhabitants in 1466. Poverty and famine occasioned by frequent periods of severe drought have marked the history of the country since abolition of the slave trade in 1876.

After 500 years of Portuguese rule, the Cape Verdes became independent on July 5, 1975. At the first general election, all seats of the new national assembly were won by the Party for the Independence of Guinea-Bissau and Cape Verde (PAIGC). The PAIGC linked the two former colonies into one state. Antonio Mascarenhas Monteiro won the first free presidential election in 1991.

RULERS
Portuguese, until 1975

MONETARY SYSTEM
100 Centavos = 1 Escudo

PORTUGUESE COLONY

COLONIAL COINAGE

KM# 1 5 CENTAVOS Composition: Bronze

Date	Mintage	F	VF	XF	Unc	BU
1930	1,000,000	0.75	1.50	3.00	7.00	—

KM# 2 10 CENTAVOS Composition: Bronze

Date	Mintage	F	VF	XF	Unc	BU
1930	1,500,000	0.75	1.50	3.50	10.00	—

KM# 3 20 CENTAVOS Composition: Bronze

Date	Mintage	F	VF	XF	Unc	BU
1930	1,500,000	1.00	2.00	4.00	11.50	—

KM# 4 50 CENTAVOS Composition: Nickel-Bronze

Date	Mintage	F	VF	XF	Unc	BU
1930	1,000,000	7.00	15.00	50.00	275	—

KM# 6 50 CENTAVOS Composition: Nickel-Bronze

Date	Mintage	F	VF	XF	Unc	BU
1949	1,000,000	0.50	1.00	2.50	6.00	—

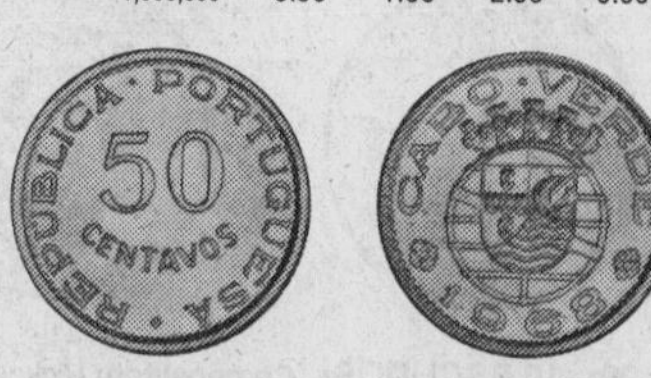

KM# 11 50 CENTAVOS Composition: Bronze

Date	Mintage	F	VF	XF	Unc	BU
1968	1,000,000	0.25	0.50	1.00	2.50	—

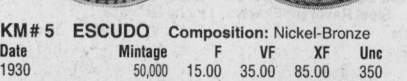

KM# 5 ESCUDO Composition: Nickel-Bronze

Date	Mintage	F	VF	XF	Unc	BU
1930	50,000	15.00	35.00	85.00	350	—

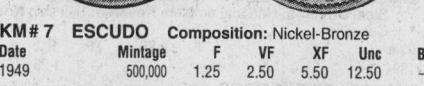

KM# 7 ESCUDO Composition: Nickel-Bronze

Date	Mintage	F	VF	XF	Unc	BU
1949	500,000	1.25	2.50	5.50	12.50	—

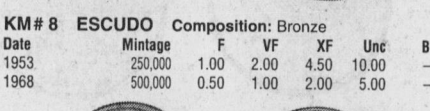

KM# 8 ESCUDO Composition: Bronze

Date	Mintage	F	VF	XF	Unc	BU
1953	250,000	1.00	2.00	4.50	10.00	—
1968	500,000	0.50	1.00	2.00	5.00	—

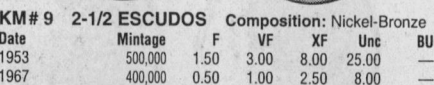

KM# 9 2-1/2 ESCUDOS Composition: Nickel-Bronze

Date	Mintage	F	VF	XF	Unc	BU
1953	500,000	1.50	3.00	8.00	25.00	—
1967	400,000	0.50	1.00	2.50	8.00	—

KM# 12 5 ESCUDOS Composition: Nickel-Bronze

Date	Mintage	F	VF	XF	Unc	BU
1968	200,000	0.75	1.50	3.50	10.00	—

KM# 10 10 ESCUDOS Weight: 5.0000 g. **Composition:** 0.7200 Silver .1158 oz. ASW

Date	Mintage	F	VF	XF	Unc	BU
1953	400,000	1.50	3.00	6.00	18.00	—

REPUBLIC

DECIMAL COINAGE

KM# 15 20 CENTAVOS Composition: Aluminum

Date	F	VF	XF	Unc	BU
1977	0.10	0.20	0.30	0.50	—
1980	0.10	0.20	0.30	0.50	—

KM# 16 50 CENTAVOS Composition: Aluminum

Date	F	VF	XF	Unc	BU
1977	0.15	0.25	0.40	0.75	—
1980	0.15	0.25	0.40	0.75	—

KM# 17 ESCUDO Composition: Nickel-Bronze **Series:** F.A.O.

Date	Mintage	F	VF	XF	Unc	BU
1977	1,000,000	0.25	0.50	0.85	1.75	—
1980	—	0.25	0.50	0.85	1.75	—

KM# 23 ESCUDO Composition: Brass Plated Steel **Subject:** 10th Anniversary of Independence

Date	F	VF	XF	Unc	BU
1985	—	—	0.85	1.75	—
1985 Proof	—	—	—	—	—

KM# 23a ESCUDO Weight: 4.0000 g. **Composition:** 0.9250 Silver .1190 oz. ASW **Subject:** 10th Anniversary of Indepencence

Date	Mintage	F	VF	XF	Unc	BU
1985 Proof	—	Value: 20.00				

KM# 23b ESCUDO Weight: 6.0000 g. **Composition:** 0.7500 Gold .1447 oz. AGW **Subject:** 10th Anniversary of Independence

Date	Mintage	F	VF	XF	Unc	BU
1985 Proof	50	Value: 250				

KM# 27 ESCUDO **Composition:** Brass Plated Steel **Reverse:** Tartaruga Sea Turtle

Date	F	VF	XF	Unc	BU
1994	—	—	—	1.00	—

KM# 18 2-1/2 ESCUDOS **Composition:** Nickel-Bronze **Series:** F.A.O.

Date	Mintage	F	VF	XF	Unc	BU
1977	1,200,000	0.25	0.50	0.85	1.75	—
1980	—	0.25	0.50	0.85	1.75	—
1982	—	0.25	0.50	0.85	1.75	—

KM# 28 5 ESCUDOS **Composition:** Copper Plated Steel **Reverse:** Osprey.

Date	F	VF	XF	Unc	BU
1994	—	—	—	1.50	—

KM# 31 5 ESCUDOS **Composition:** Copper Plated Steel **Reverse:** Flowers - Contra Bruxas

Date	F	VF	XF	Unc	BU
1994	—	—	—	1.00	—

KM# 36 5 ESCUDOS **Composition:** Copper Plated Steel **Reverse:** Sailboat - Belmira

Date	F	VF	XF	Unc	BU
1994	—	—	—	1.00	—

KM# 19 10 ESCUDOS **Composition:** Copper-Nickel **Reverse:** Eduardo Mondlane

Date	F	VF	XF	Unc	BU
1977	0.25	0.50	1.00	2.00	—
1980	0.25	0.50	1.00	2.00	—
1982	0.20	0.40	0.75	1.50	—

KM# 24 10 ESCUDOS **Composition:** Copper-Nickel **Subject:** 10th Anniversary of Independence

Date	F	VF	XF	Unc	BU
1985 Proof	—	—	—	—	—
1985	—	—	—	2.00	—

KM# 24a 10 ESCUDOS **Weight:** 9.0000 g. **Composition:** 0.9250 Silver .2677 oz. ASW **Subject:** 10th Anniversary of Independence

Date	F	VF	XF	Unc	BU
1985 Proof	—	Value: 25.00			

KM# 24b 10 ESCUDOS **Weight:** 9.0000 g. **Composition:** 0.7500 Gold .2170 oz. AGW **Subject:** 10th Anniversary of Independence

Date	Mintage	F	VF	XF	Unc	BU
1985 Proof	50	Value: 400				

KM# 29 10 ESCUDOS **Composition:** Nickel Plated Steel **Reverse:** Brown-headed Kingfisher.

Date	F	VF	XF	Unc	BU
1994	—	—	—	2.00	—

KM# 32 10 ESCUDOS **Composition:** Nickel Plated Steel **Reverse:** Flowers - Lingua De Vaca

Date	F	VF	XF	Unc	BU
1994	—	—	—	1.25	—

KM# 41 10 ESCUDOS **Composition:** Nickel Plated Steel **Obverse:** National emblem **Reverse:** Sail ship **Note:** Carvalho

Date	F	VF	XF	Unc	BU
1994	—	—	—	1.25	—

KM# 20 20 ESCUDOS **Composition:** Copper-Nickel **Reverse:** Domingos Ramos

Date	F	VF	XF	Unc	BU
1977	0.35	0.65	1.25	2.75	—
1980	0.35	0.65	1.25	2.75	—
1982	0.25	0.50	0.85	1.75	—

KM# 30 20 ESCUDOS **Composition:** Nickel Plated Steel **Reverse:** Brown Booby.

Date	F	VF	XF	Unc	BU
1994	—	—	—	3.00	—

KM# 33 20 ESCUDOS **Composition:** Nickel Plated Steel **Reverse:** Flowers - Carqueja

Date	F	VF	XF	Unc	BU
1994	—	—	—	2.00	—

KM# 42 20 ESCUDOS **Composition:** Nickel Plated Steel **Obverse:** National emblem **Reverse:** Sail ship **Note:** Novas de Alegria

Date	F	VF	XF	Unc	BU
1994	—	—	—	2.00	—

KM# 21 50 ESCUDOS **Composition:** Copper-Nickel **Reverse:** Amilcar Lopes Cabral

Date	F	VF	XF	Unc	BU
1977	1.00	1.50	2.50	4.50	—
1980	1.00	1.50	2.50	4.50	—

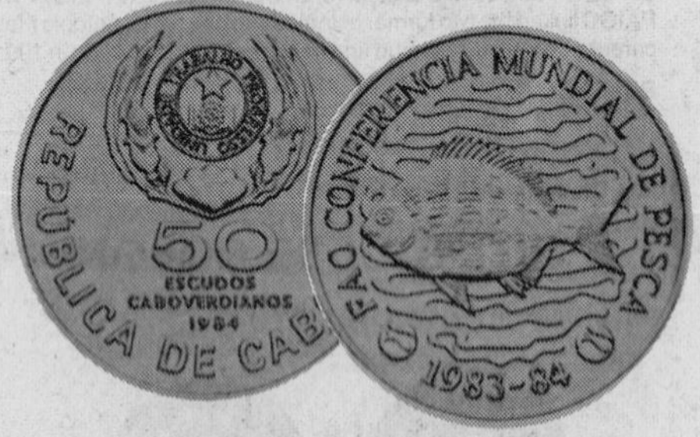

KM# 22 50 ESCUDOS **Composition:** Copper-Nickel **Series:** F.A.O. **Subject:** World Fisheries Conference

Date	F	VF	XF	Unc	BU
1984	—	—	—	7.50	—

KM# 22a 50 ESCUDOS **Weight:** 16.0000 g. **Composition:** 0.9250 Silver .4759 oz. ASW **Series:** F.A.O. **Subject:** World Fisheries Conference

Date	Mintage	F	VF	XF	Unc	BU
1984 Proof	Est. 20,000	Value: 47.50				

KM# 22b 50 ESCUDOS **Weight:** 27.0000 g. **Composition:** 0.9170 Gold .7958 oz. AGW **Series:** .F.A.O. **Subject:** World Fisheries Conference

Date	Mintage	F	VF	XF	Unc	BU
1984 Proof	Est. 100,000	Value: 1,500				

KM# 37 50 ESCUDOS **Weight:** 27.0000 g. **Composition:** 0.9170 Gold .7958 oz. AGW **Reverse:** Cape Verde Sparrow.

Date	F	VF	XF	Unc	BU
1994	—	—	—	7.50	—

KM# 44 50 ESCUDOS **Composition:** Nickel Plated Steel 8 oz. **Obverse:** National emblem **Reverse:** Macelina flowers

Date	F	VF	XF	Unc	BU
1994	—	—	—	5.00	—

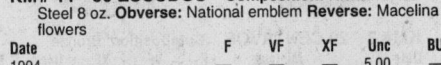

KM# 43 50 ESCUDOS **Composition:** Nickel Plated Steel 8 oz. **Obverse:** National emblem **Reverse:** Sail ship **Note:** Senhor das Areias

Date	F	VF	XF	Unc	BU
1994	—	—	—	5.00	—

KM# 25 100 ESCUDOS **Composition:** Copper-Nickel 8 oz. **Subject:** Papal Visit

Date	F	VF	XF	Unc	BU
1990	—	—	—	8.00	—

KM# 25a 100 ESCUDOS **Weight:** 33.4000 g. **Composition:** 0.9000 Gold .9666 oz. AGW **Subject:** Papal Visit

Date	F	VF	XF	Unc	BU
1990 Proof	—	—	—	—	—

KM# 38 100 ESCUDOS **Ring Composition:** Bronze **Center Composition:** Copper-Nickel **Reverse:** Saiao Flowers

Date	F	VF	XF	Unc	BU
1994	—	—	—	8.00	—

KM# 38a 100 ESCUDOS **Ring Composition:** Brass **Center Composition:** Copper-Nickel

Date	F	VF	XF	Unc	BU
1994	—	—	—	8.00	—

KM# 39 100 ESCUDOS **Ring Composition:** Bronze **Center Composition:** Copper-Nickel **Reverse:** Raza Lark.

Date	F	VF	XF	Unc	BU
1994	—	—	—	12.50	—

KM# 39a 100 ESCUDOS **Ring Composition:** Brass **Center Composition:** Copper-Nickel **Reverse:** Calhandra do Ilheu Raso bird

Date	F	VF	XF	Unc	BU
1994	—	—	—	12.50	—

KM# 40 100 ESCUDOS **Ring Composition:** Bronze **Center Composition:** Copper-Nickel **Reverse:** Sailship Medalan

Date	F	VF	XF	Unc	BU
1994	—	—	—	9.00	—

KM# 40a 100 ESCUDOS **Ring Composition:** Brass **Center Composition:** Copper-Nickel

Date	F	VF	XF	Unc	BU
1994	—	—	—	9.00	—

KM# 34 200 ESCUDOS **Composition:** Copper-Nickel **Series:** F.A.O. **Reverse:** Water

Date	F	VF	XF	Unc	BU
1995	—	—	—	8.00	—

KM# 35 200 ESCUDOS **Composition:** Copper-Nickel **Subject:** 20th Year of Independence

Date	F	VF	XF	Unc	BU
ND (1995)	—	—	—	8.00	—

KM# 13 250 ESCUDOS **Weight:** 16.4000 g. **Composition:** 0.9000 Silver .4745 oz. ASW **Subject:** 1st Anniversary of Independence

Date	Mintage	F	VF	XF	Unc	BU
1976	13,000	—	—	—	16.50	—
1976 Proof	3,525	Value: 32.50				

KM# 26 1000 ESCUDOS **Weight:** 28.1100 g. **Composition:** 0.9250 Silver .8361 oz. ASW **Subject:** Tordesilhas Treaty

Date	Mintage	F	VF	XF	Unc	BU
ND (1994)	—	—	—	—	25.00	—
ND (1994) Proof	Est. 10,000	Value: 45.00				

KM# 14 2500 ESCUDOS **Weight:** 8.0000 g. **Composition:** 0.9000 Gold .2315 oz. AGW **Subject:** 1st Anniversary of Independence

Date	Mintage	F	VF	XF	Unc	BU
1976 Proof	3,409	Value: 220				

PIEFORTS

KM#	Date	Mintage	Identification	Issue Price	Mkt Val
P1	1984	520	50 Escudos. 0.9250 Silver. KM22a	—	75.00

PROVAS

KM#	Date	Mintage	Identification	Issue Price	Mkt Val
Pr1	1930	—	5 Centavos. Stamped "PROVA" in field. KM1	—	35.00
Pr2	1930	—	10 Centavos. Stamped "PROVA" in field. KM2	—	35.00
Pr3	1930	—	20 Centavos. Stamped "PROVA" in field. KM3	—	35.00
Pr4	1930	—	50 Centavos. Stamped "PROVA" in field. KM4	—	75.00
Pr5	1930	—	Escudo. Stamped "PROVA" in field. KM5	—	100
Pr6	1949	—	50 Centavos. Stamped "PROVA" in field. KM6	—	30.00
Pr7	1949	—	Escudo. Stamped "PROVA" in field. KM7	—	35.00
Pr8	1953	—	Escudo. Stamped "PROVA" in field. KM8	—	35.00
Pr9	1953	—	2-1/2 Escudos. Stamped "PROVA" in field. KM9	—	30.00
Pr10	1953	—	10 Escudos. Stamped "PROVA" in field. KM10	—	35.00
Pr11	1954	—	Escudo. Stamped "PROVA" in field.	—	20.00
Pr12	1954	—	2-1/2 Escudos. Stamped "PROVA" in field.	—	30.00
Pr13	1955	—	Escudo. Stamped "PROVA" in field.	—	20.00
Pr14	1955	—	2-1/2 Escudos. Stamped "PROVA" in field.	—	30.00
Pr15	1956	—	Escudo. Stamped "PROVA" in field.	—	20.00
Pr16	1956	—	2-1/2 Escudos. Stamped "PROVA" in field.	—	30.00
Pr17	1957	—	Escudo. Stamped "PROVA" in field.	—	20.00
Pr18	1957	—	2-1/2 Escudos. Stamped "PROVA" in field.	—	30.00
Pr19	1958	—	Escudo. Stamped "PROVA" in field.	—	20.00
Pr20	1958	—	2-1/2 Escudos. Stamped "PROVA" in field.	—	30.00
Pr21	1959	—	Escudo. Stamped "PROVA" in field.	—	20.00
Pr22	1959	—	2-1/2 Escudos. Stamped "PROVA" in field.	—	30.00
Pr23	1960	—	Escudo. Stamped "PROVA" in field.	—	20.00
Pr24	1960	—	2-1/2 Escudos. Stamped "PROVA" in field.	—	30.00
Pr25	1961	—	Escudo. Stamped "PROVA" in field.	—	20.00
Pr26	1961	—	2-1/2 Escudos. Stamped "PROVA" in field.	—	30.00
Pr27	1962	—	Escudo. Stamped "PROVA" in field.	—	20.00
Pr28	1962	—	2-1/2 Escudos. Stamped "PROVA" in field.	—	30.00
Pr29	1963	—	Escudo. Stamped "PROVA" in field.	—	20.00
Pr30	1963	—	2-1/2 Escudos. Stamped "PROVA" in field.	—	30.00
Pr31	1964	—	Escudo. Stamped "PROVA" in field.	—	20.00
Pr32	1964	—	2-1/2 Escudos. Stamped "PROVA" in field.	—	30.00
Pr33	1965	—	Escudo. Stamped "PROVA" in field.	—	20.00
Pr34	1965	—	2-1/2 Escudos. Stamped "PROVA" in field.	—	30.00
Pr35	1966	—	Escudo. Stamped "PROVA" in field.	—	20.00
Pr36	1966	—	2-1/2 Escudos. Stamped "PROVA" in field.	—	30.00
Pr37	1967	—	Escudo. Stamped "PROVA" in field.	—	15.00
Pr38	1967	—	2-1/2 Escudos. Stamped "PROVA" in field. KM9	—	20.00
Pr39	1968	—	50 Centavos. Stamped "PROVA" in field. KM11	—	15.00
Pr40	1968	—	Escudo. Stamped "PROVA" in field. KM8	—	20.00
Pr41	1968	—	5 Escudos. Stamped "PROVA" in field. KM12	—	25.00

PROOF SETS

KM#	Date	Mintage	Identification	Issue Price	Mkt Val
PS1	(4)	—	KM13-14 1976, KM17-18	—	300
PS2	1985 (2)	—	KM23a, 24a	—	50.00

CAYMAN ISLANDS

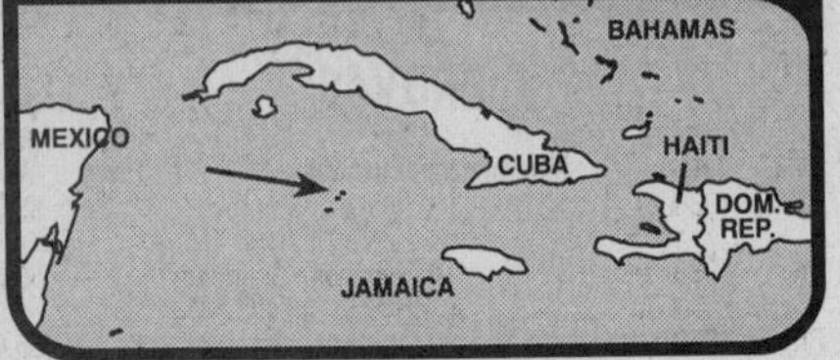

The Cayman Islands is a dependent territory of the United Kingdom with the British monarch as head of state. It is situated about 180 miles (290 km.) northwest of Jamaica, consists of three islands: Grand Cayman, Little Cayman, and Cayman Brac. The islands have an area of 102 sq. mi. (259 sq. km.) and a population of 33,200. Capital: George Town. Seafaring, commerce, banking, and tourism are the principal industries. Rope, turtle shells, and sharkskins are exported.

The islands were discovered by Columbus in 1503, and named by him Tortugas (Spanish for turtles') because of the great number of turtles in the nearby waters. Ceded to Britain in 1670, they were colonized from Jamaica by the British and remained dependencies of Jamaica until 1959, when they became a unit territory within the Federation of the West Indies. They became a separate colony when the Federation was dissolved in 1962. Since 1972 a form of self-government has existed, with the Governor responsible for defense and certain other affairs.

While the islands used Jamaican currency for much of their history, the Caymans issued its first national coinage in 1972. The $25 gold and silver commemorative coins issued in 1972 to celebrate the silver wedding anniversary of Queen Elizabeth II and Prince Philip are the first coins in 300 years of Commonwealth coinage to portray a member of the British royal family other than the reigning monarch.

RULERS
British

MINT MARKS
CHI - Valcambi
FM - Franklin Mint, U.S.A.*

MONETARY SYSTEM
100 Cents = 1 Dollar

BRITISH COLONY

DECIMAL COINAGE

100 Cents = 1 Dollar

KM# 1 CENT **Composition:** Bronze **Reverse:** Great Caiman Thrush

Date	Mintage	F	VF	XF	Unc	BU
1972	2,155,000	—	—	0.10	0.25	—
1972 Proof	11,000	Value: 0.50				
1973 Proof	9,988	Value: 0.50				
1974 Proof	30,000	Value: 0.50				
1975 Proof	7,175	Value: 0.50				
1976 Proof	3,044	Value: 0.50				
1977	1,800,000	—	—	0.10	0.25	—
1977 Proof	1,970	Value: 1.00				
1979FM Proof	4,247	Value: 0.50				
1980FM	—	—	—	0.10	0.25	—
1980FM Proof	1,215	Value: 1.25				
1981FM Proof	865	Value: 1.50				
1982FM Proof	589	Value: 1.50				
1982	—	—	—	0.10	0.25	—
1983FM Proof	—	Value: 1.50				
1984FM Proof	—	Value: 1.50				
1986	1,000	Value: 1.50				

KM# 26 CENT **Composition:** Bronze **Subject:** 25th Anniversary of Coronation

Date	Mintage	F	VF	XF	Unc	BU
1978 Proof	1,303	Value: 2.00				

KM# 87 CENT **Composition:** Bronze

Date		F	VF	XF	Unc	BU
1987		—	—	0.10	0.25	—
1987 Proof	317	Value: 3.00				
1988 Proof	318	Value: 3.00				
1990		—	—	0.10	0.25	—

KM# 87a CENT **Composition:** Bronze Clad Steel

Date	F	VF	XF	Unc	BU
1992	—	—	0.20	0.50	—
1996	—	—	0.10	0.25	—

KM# 131 CENT **Weight:** 2.5300 g. **Composition:** Bronze Plated Steel **Obverse:** Queen's head right **Reverse:** Great Caiman thrush **Edge:** Reeded **Size:** 17 mm.

Date	F	VF	XF	Unc	BU
1999	—	—	—	0.50	—

KM# 2 5 CENTS **Composition:** Copper-Nickel **Reverse:** Prawn **Note:** 1973 Uncirculates were not released to circulation.

Date	Mintage	F	VF	XF	Unc	BU
1972	300,000	—	—	0.10	0.25	—
1972 Proof	12,000	Value: 0.50				
1973	200,000	—	—	—	0.50	—

Note: 1973 Business strikes were not released to circulation

Date	Mintage	F	VF	XF	Unc	BU
1973 Proof	9,988	Value: 0.50				
1974 Proof	30,000	Value: 0.50				
1975 Proof	7,175	Value: 0.50				
1976 Proof	3,044	Value: 0.50				
1977	600,000	—	—	0.10	0.20	—
1977 Proof	1,980	Value: 0.50				
1979 Proof	4,247	Value: 0.50				
1980 Proof	—	Value: 2.00				
1981 Proof	—	Value: 2.50				
1982	—	—	—	0.10	0.20	—
1982 Proof	—	Value: 2.50				
1983 Proof	—	Value: 2.50				
1984 Proof	—	Value: 2.50				
1986	1,000	Value: 2.50				

KM# 27 5 CENTS **Composition:** Copper-Nickel **Subject:** 25th Anniversary of Coronation **Reverse:** Prawn

Date	Mintage	F	VF	XF	Unc	BU
1978 Proof	1,303	Value: 3.00				

KM# 88 5 CENTS **Composition:** Copper-Nickel

Date		F	VF	XF	Unc	BU
1987		—	—	0.10	0.25	—
1987 Proof	317	Value: 5.00				
1988 Proof	318	Value: 5.00				
1990		—	—	0.10	0.25	—

KM# 88a 5 CENTS **Composition:** Nickel Clad Steel

Date	F	VF	XF	Unc	BU
1992	—	—	0.20	0.50	—
1996	—	—	0.10	0.25	—

KM# 132 5 CENTS **Weight:** 2.0000 g. **Composition:** Nickel Clad Steel **Obverse:** Queen's head right **Reverse:** Prawn **Edge:** Plain **Size:** 18 mm.

Date	F	VF	XF	Unc	BU
1999	—	—	—	0.50	—

KM# 3 10 CENTS **Composition:** Copper-Nickel **Reverse:** Green Turtle

Date	Mintage	F	VF	XF	Unc	BU
1972	550,000	—	0.15	0.20	0.50	—
1972 Proof	11,000	Value: 1.00				
1973	200,000	—	—	—	1.00	—

Note: 1973 Business strikes were not released to circulation

Date	Mintage	F	VF	XF	Unc	BU
1973 Proof	9,988	Value: 1.00				
1974 Proof	30,000	Value: 1.00				
1975 Proof	7,175	Value: 1.00				
1976 Proof	3,044	Value: 1.00				
1977	960,000	—	0.15	0.20	0.50	—
1977 Proof	1,980	Value: 1.00				
1979FM Proof	4,247	Value: 1.00				
1980FM Proof	1,215	Value: 3.00				
1981FM Proof	865	Value: 3.00				
1982	—	—	0.15	0.20	0.50	—
1982FM Proof	589	Value: 3.00				
1983FM Proof	—	Value: 3.00				
1984FM Proof	—	Value: 3.00				
1986	1,000	Value: 3.00				

KM# 28 10 CENTS **Composition:** Copper-Nickel **Subject:** 25th Anniversary of Coronation

Date	Mintage	F	VF	XF	Unc	BU
1978 Proof	1,304	Value: 3.50				

KM# 89 10 CENTS **Composition:** Copper-Nickel

Date		F	VF	XF	Unc	BU
1987		—	0.15	0.20	0.50	—
1987 Proof	317	Value: 6.00				
1988 Proof	318	Value: 6.00				
1990		—	0.15	0.20	0.50	—

KM# 89a 10 CENTS **Composition:** Nickel Clad Steel

Date	F	VF	XF	Unc	BU
1992	—	0.25	0.40	1.00	—
1996	—	0.20	0.30	0.75	—

KM# 133 10 CENTS **Weight:** 3.4300 g. **Composition:** Nickel Clad Steel **Obverse:** Queen's head right **Reverse:** Green turtle **Edge:** Reeded **Size:** 21 mm.

Date	F	VF	XF	Unc	BU
1999	—	—	—	1.00	—

KM# 4 25 CENTS **Composition:** Copper-Nickel

Date	Mintage	F	VF	XF	Unc	BU
1972	350,000	—	0.35	0.50	1.00	—
1972 Proof	11,000	Value: 1.00				
1973	100,000	—	—	—	2.00	—

Date	Mintage	F	VF	XF	Unc	BU
Note: 1973 Business strikes were not released to circulation						
1973 Proof	9,988	Value: 1.00				
1974 Proof	30,000	Value: 1.00				
1975 Proof	7,175	Value: 1.00				
1976 Proof	3,044	Value: 1.00				
1977	520,000	—	0.35	0.50	1.00	—
1977 Proof	1,980	Value: 1.00				
1979FM Proof	4,247	Value: 1.00				
1980FM Proof	1,215	Value: 3.50				
1981FM Proof	865	Value: 4.00				
1982	—	—	0.35	0.50	1.00	—
1982FM Proof	589	Value: 4.00				
1983FM Proof	—	Value: 4.00				
1984FM Proof	—	Value: 4.00				
1986 Proof	1,000	Value: 4.00				

KM# 29 25 CENTS Composition: Copper-Nickel **Subject:** 25th Anniversary of Coronation **Reverse:** Similar to KM#4

Date	Mintage	F	VF	XF	Unc	BU
1978 Proof	1,303	Value: 4.00				

KM# 90 25 CENTS Composition: Copper-Nickel

Date	F	VF	XF	Unc	BU
1987	—	0.35	0.50	1.00	—
1987 Proof	317	Value: 8.00			
1988 Proof	318	Value: 8.00			
1990	—	0.35	0.50	1.00	—

KM# 90a 25 CENTS Composition: Nickel Clad Steel

Date	F	VF	XF	Unc	BU
1992	—	0.45	0.75	1.50	—
1996	—	0.35	0.60	1.25	—

KM# 134 25 CENTS Weight: 5.0400 g. **Composition:** Nickel-Clad Steel **Obverse:** Queen's head right **Reverse:** Sailboat **Edge:** Reeded **Size:** 24.2 mm.

Date	F	VF	XF	Unc	BU
1999	—	—	—	1.50	—

KM# 5 50 CENTS Weight: 10.3000 g. **Composition:** 0.9250 Silver .3063 oz. ASW **Reverse:** Caribbean Emperor Fish

Date	Mintage	F	VF	XF	Unc	BU
1972	500	—	—	—	12.50	—
1972 Proof	11,000	Value: 5.00				
1973 Proof	9,988	Value: 5.00				
1974 Proof	30,000	Value: 5.00				
1975 Proof	7,175	Value: 5.00				
1976 Proof	3,044	Value: 5.00				
1977 Proof	1,980	Value: 5.00				
1979FM Proof	4,247	Value: 5.00				
1980FM Proof	1,215	Value: 5.00				
1981FM Proof	865	Value: 6.50				
1982FM Proof	589	Value: 6.50				

KM# 30 50 CENTS Weight: 10.3000 g. **Composition:** 0.9250 Silver **Subject:** 25th Anniversary of Coronation

Date	Mintage	F	VF	XF	Unc	BU
1978 Proof	2,169	Value: 8.00				

KM# 73 50 CENTS Weight: 10.3000 g. **Composition:** 9.2500 Silver **Obverse:** Similar to KM#5 **Reverse:** Morning Glory

Date	Mintage	F	VF	XF	Unc	BU
1983FM Proof	—	Value: 15.00				
1984FM Proof	411	Value: 15.00				
1986 Proof	1,000	Value: 15.00				

KM# 91 50 CENTS Weight: 10.3000 g. **Composition:** 0.9250 Silver .3063 oz. ASW **Obverse:** Similar to 5 Dollars, KM#81

Date	Mintage	F	VF	XF	Unc	BU
1987 Proof	317	Value: 20.00				
1988 Proof	318	Value: 20.00				

KM# 6 DOLLAR Weight: 18.0000 g. **Composition:** 0.9250 Silver .5353 oz. ASW **Reverse:** Flamboyant

Date	Mintage	F	VF	XF	Unc	BU
1972	500	—	—	—	15.00	—
1972 Proof	11,000	Value: 4.50				
1973 Proof	9,988	Value: 4.50				
1974 Proof	30,000	Value: 4.50				
1975 Proof	7,175	Value: 5.00				
1976 Proof	3,044	Value: 7.00				
1977 Proof	1,980	Value: 7.00				
1979FM Proof	4,247	Value: 7.00				
1980FM Proof	1,215	Value: 9.00				
1981FM Proof	865	Value: 10.00				
1982FM Proof	589	Value: 10.00				

KM# 31 DOLLAR Weight: 18.0000 g. **Composition:** 0.9250 Silver .5353 oz. ASW **Subject:** 25th Anniversary of Coronation

Date	Mintage	F	VF	XF	Unc	BU
1978 Proof	2,168	Value: 12.00				

KM# 74 DOLLAR Weight: 18.0000 g. **Composition:** 0.9250 Silver .5353 oz. ASW **Obverse:** Similar to 50 Cents, KM#5 **Reverse:** Pineapple

Date	Mintage	F	VF	XF	Unc	BU
1983FM Proof	1,686	Value: 16.00				
1984FM Proof	456	Value: 16.00				
1986 Proof	1,000	Value: 16.00				

KM# 92 DOLLAR Weight: 18.0000 g. **Composition:** 0.9250 Silver .5353 oz. ASW **Obverse:** Similar to 5 Dollars, KM#81

Date	Mintage	F	VF	XF	Unc	BU
1987 Proof	317	Value: 22.00				
1988 Proof	318	Value: 22.00				

KM# 103 DOLLAR Weight: 18.1400 g. **Composition:** 0.9250 Silver .5395 oz. ASW **Reverse:** Green Turtle

Date	Mintage	F	VF	XF	Unc	BU
1990 Proof	Est. 5,000	Value: 65.00				

KM# 111 DOLLAR Weight: 18.1400 g. **Composition:** 0.9250 Silver .5395 oz. ASW **Reverse:** Rock Iquana

Date	Mintage	F	VF	XF	Unc	BU
1992 Proof	Est. 5,000	Value: 50.00				

KM# 116 DOLLAR Weight: 18.1400 g. **Composition:** 0.9250 Silver .5395 oz. ASW **Reverse:** Cayman Ironwood Tree

Date	Mintage	F	VF	XF	Unc	BU
1994 Proof	Est. 10,000	Value: 37.50				

KM# 118 DOLLAR **Weight:** 28.2800 g. **Composition:** 0.9250 Silver .8411 oz. ASW **Subject:** Royal Visit **Reverse:** Royal Couple above yacht "Britannia"

Date	Mintage	F	VF	XF	Unc	BU
1994 Proof	Est. 10,000	Value: 50.00				

KM# 120 DOLLAR **Weight:** 28.2800 g. **Composition:** 0.9250 Silver .8411 oz. ASW **Reverse:** Queen Mother's arms

Date	Mintage	F	VF	XF	Unc	BU
1994 Proof	Est. 20,000	Value: 28.50				

KM# 121 DOLLAR **Weight:** 28.2800 g. **Composition:** 0.9250 Silver .8411 oz. ASW **Reverse:** Sir Francis Drake

Date	Mintage	F	VF	XF	Unc	BU
1994 Proof	Est. 10,000	Value: 30.00				

KM# 125 DOLLAR **Weight:** 28.2800 g. **Composition:** 0.9250 Silver .8411 oz. ASW **Reverse:** Rock Iquana

Date	Mintage	F	VF	XF	Unc	BU
1995 Proof	Est. 10,000	Value: 55.00				

KM# 122 DOLLAR **Weight:** 18.1400 g. **Composition:** 0.9250 Silver .5394 oz. ASW **Reverse:** Amazona Leucocephala Caymanesis - Parrot

Date	Mintage	F	VF	XF	Unc	BU
1996 Proof	Est. 10,000	Value: 50.00				

KM# 124 DOLLAR **Weight:** 28.2800 g. **Composition:** 0.9250 Silver .8411 oz. ASW **Subject:** Olympics **Reverse:** Two sail boats

Date	Mintage	F	VF	XF	Unc	BU
1996 Proof	Est. 30,000	Value: 30.00				

KM# 7 2 DOLLARS **Weight:** 29.4500 g. **Composition:** 0.9250 Silver .8758 oz. ASW **Obverse:** Similar to 50 cents, KM#5 **Reverse:** Great Blue Heron

Date	Mintage	F	VF	XF	Unc	BU
1972	500	—	—	—	20.00	—
1972 Proof	11,000	Value: 7.50				
1973 Proof	9,988	Value: 7.50				
1974 Proof	30,000	Value: 7.50				
1975 Proof	5,390	Value: 8.50				
1976 Proof	3,044	Value: 12.50				
1977 Proof	1,980	Value: 12.50				
1979FM Proof	4,247	Value: 12.50				
1980FM Proof	1,215	Value: 18.00				
1981FM Proof	865	Value: 20.00				
1982FM Proof	589	Value: 20.00				
1986 Proof	1,000	Value: 18.00				

KM# 32 2 DOLLARS **Weight:** 29.4500 g. **Composition:** 0.9250 Silver .8758 oz. ASW **Subject:** 25th Anniversary of Coronation

Date	Mintage	F	VF	XF	Unc	BU
1978 Proof	2,169	Value: 22.50				

KM# 75 2 DOLLARS **Weight:** 29.4500 g. **Composition:** 0.9250 Silver .8758 oz. ASW **Obv. Legend:** Parrot

Date	Mintage	F	VF	XF	Unc	BU
1983FM Proof	409	Value: 45.00				
1984FM Proof	200	Value: 55.00				

KM# 93 2 DOLLARS **Weight:** 29.4500 g. **Composition:** 0.9250 Silver .8758 oz. ASW **Obverse:** Similar to 5 Dollars, KM#81 **Reverse:** Great Blue Heron

Date	Mintage	F	VF	XF	Unc	BU
1987 Proof	317	Value: 45.00				
1988 Proof	318	Value: 45.00				

KM# 114 2 DOLLARS **Weight:** 28.2800 g. **Composition:** 0.9250 Silver .8411 oz. ASW **Reverse:** Wreck of the "Ten Sails"

Date	Mintage	F	VF	XF	Unc	BU
1994 Proof	15,000	Value: 30.00				

KM# 127 2 DOLLARS **Weight:** 28.2800 g. **Composition:** 0.9250 Silver .8411 oz. ASW **Subject:** 25th Anniversary - Currency Board **Obverse:** Queen's portrait **Reverse:** Coins and arms in inner circle

Date	Mintage	F	VF	XF	Unc	BU
ND Proof	Est. 2,000	Value: 55.00				

KM# 128 2 DOLLARS **Weight:** 28.2800 g. **Composition:** 0.9250 Silver .8411 oz. ASW **Subject:** Queen's Golden Wedding Anniversary **Obverse:** Queen's portrait **Reverse:** Royal couple in carriage above gold-plated shield

Date	Mintage	F	VF	XF	Unc	BU
1997 Proof	Est. 30,000	Value: 57.00				

KM# 129 2 DOLLARS **Weight:** 28.2800 g. **Composition:** 0.9250 Silver .8411 oz. ASW **Obverse:** Queen's portrait **Reverse:** Schooners "Arbutus I" and "Goldfield" under sail

Date	Mintage	F	VF	XF	Unc	BU
1997 Proof	Est. 5,000	Value: 60.00				

KM# 130 2 DOLLARS **Weight:** 15.5520 g. **Composition:** 0.9990 Silver .4995 oz. ASW **Subject:** Millennium **Obverse:** Queen's portrait **Reverse:** Ornate clock above denomination **Edge:** Scalloped

Date	Mintage	F	VF	XF	Unc	BU
2000 Proof	30	Value: 47.50				

KM# 8 5 DOLLARS **Weight:** 35.5000 g. **Composition:** 0.9250 Silver 1.0557 oz. ASW

Date	Mintage	F	VF	XF	Unc	BU
1972	500	—	—	—	35.00	—
1972 Proof	11,000	Value: 7.50				
1973 Proof	17,000	Value: 7.50				
1974 Proof	26,000	Value: 7.50				
1975 Proof	7,753	Value: 9.00				
1976 Proof	5,177	Value: 9.00				
1977 Proof	3,525	Value: 10.00				
1979FM Proof	—	Value: 17.50				
1980FM Proof	—	Value: 20.00				
1981FM Proof	—	Value: 22.00				
1984FM Proof	—	Value: 22.00				
1986 Proof	1,000	Value: 22.00				

KM# 33 5 DOLLARS **Weight:** 35.5000 g. **Composition:** 0.9250 Silver 1.0557 oz. ASW **Subject:** 25th Anniversary of Coronation

Date	Mintage	F	VF	XF	Unc	BU
1978 Proof	2,168	Value: 27.50				

KM# 70 5 DOLLARS **Weight:** 35.5000 g. **Composition:** 0.9250 Silver 1.0557 oz. ASW **Subject:** 150th Anniversary of Parliamentary Government **Obverse:** Similar to 50 Cents, KM#5

Date	Mintage	F	VF	XF	Unc	BU
1982FM Proof	1,105	Value: 40.00				

KM# 76 5 DOLLARS **Weight:** 35.5000 g. **Composition:** 0.9250 Silver 1.0557 oz. ASW **Subject:** Royal Visit

Date	Mintage	F	VF	XF	Unc	BU
1983FM Proof	419	Value: 38.50				

KM# 81 5 DOLLARS **Weight:** 28.2800 g. **Composition:** 0.9250 Silver .8411 oz. ASW **Subject:** 250th Anniversary of Royal Land Grant

Date	Mintage	F	VF	XF	Unc	BU
1985 Proof	Est. 1,000	Value: 31.50				

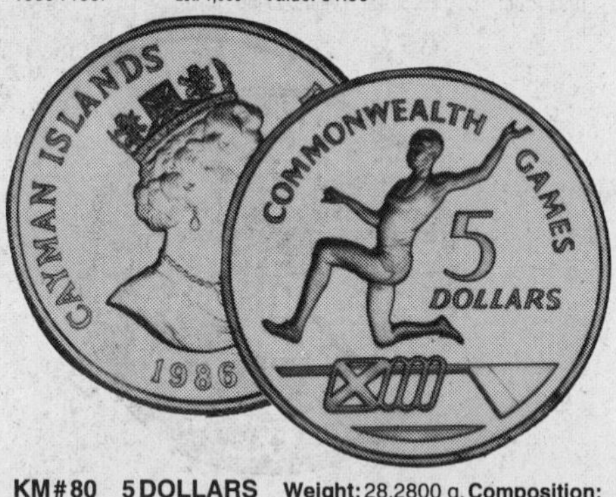

KM# 80 5 DOLLARS **Weight:** 28.2800 g. **Composition:** 0.5000 Silver .4547 oz. ASW **Subject:** Commonwealth Games

Date	Mintage	F	VF	XF	Unc	BU
1986	50,000	—	—	—	12.50	—

KM# 80a 5 DOLLARS **Weight:** 28.2800 g. **Composition:** 0.9250 Silver .8411 oz. ASW **Subject:** Commonwealth Games **Reverse:** Hurdler

Date	Mintage	F	VF	XF	Unc	BU
1986 Proof	Est. 20,000	Value: 25.00				

KM# 85 5 DOLLARS **Weight:** 28.2800 g. **Composition:** 0.9250 Silver .8411 oz. ASW **Subject:** Queen Elizabeth II and Philip's 40th Wedding Anniversary

Date	Mintage	F	VF	XF	Unc	BU
ND(1987) Proof	Est. 2,000	Value: 30.00				

KM# 85a 5 DOLLARS **Weight:** 35.6400 g. **Composition:** 0.9250 Silver 1.0560 oz. ASW **Subject:** Queen Elizabeth II and Philip's 40th Wedding Anniversary

Date	Mintage	F	VF	XF	Unc	BU
ND(1987) Proof	317	Value: 90.00				

KM# 95 5 DOLLARS **Weight:** 28.2800 g. **Composition:** 0.9250 Silver .8411 oz. ASW **Subject:** World Wildlife Fund **Reverse:** Cuban Amazon

Date		F	VF	XF	Unc	BU
1987 Proof	—	Value: 32.50				

KM# 94.2 5 DOLLARS **Weight:** 35.6400 g. **Composition:** 0.9250 Silver 1.0560 oz. ASW **Subject:** Seoul Olympics **Obverse:** Date below portrait

Date	Mintage	F	VF	XF	Unc	BU
1988 Proof	318	Value: 200				

KM# 94.1 5 DOLLARS **Weight:** 28.2800 g. **Composition:** 0.9250 Silver .8411 oz. ASW **Subject:** Seoul Olympics **Obverse:** Denomination below portrait

Date	Mintage	F	VF	XF	Unc	BU
1988 Proof	20,000	Value: 27.50				

KM# 96 5 DOLLARS **Weight:** 28.2800 g. **Composition:** 0.9250 Silver .8411 oz. ASW **Subject:** 50th Anniversary of Columbus' Discovery of America

Date	Mintage	F	VF	XF	Unc	BU
1988 Proof	10,000	Value: 27.50				

KM# 98 5 DOLLARS **Weight:** 28.2800 g. **Composition:** 0.9250 Silver .8411 oz. ASW **Subject:** Visit of Princess Alexandra **Note:** Similar to 250 Dollars, KM#99.

Date	Mintage	F	VF	XF	Unc	BU
1988 Proof	Est. 5,000	Value: 37.50				

KM# 100 5 DOLLARS **Weight:** 28.2800 g. **Composition:** 0.9250 Silver .8411 oz. ASW **Subject:** 100 Years of Postal Service

Date	Mintage	F	VF	XF	Unc	BU
ND(1989) Proof	10,000	Value: 40.00				

KM# 102 5 DOLLARS **Weight:** 28.2800 g. **Composition:** 0.9250 Silver .8411 oz. ASW **Subject:** Save the Children Fund **Reverse:** Two children sailing boats in water

Date	Mintage	F	VF	XF	Unc	BU
1989 Proof	Est. 20,000	Value: 20.00				

KM# 108 5 DOLLARS **Weight:** 28.2800 g. **Composition:** 0.9250 Silver .8411 oz. ASW **Subject:** Queen Mother's Birth Centennial

Date	Mintage	F	VF	XF	Unc	BU
ND (1990) Proof	Est. 10,000	Value: 25.00				
ND(1990) Proof	Est. 10,000	Value: 25.00				

KM# 109 5 DOLLARS **Weight:** 28.2800 g. **Composition:** 0.9250 Silver .8411 oz. ASW **Subject:** 20th Anniversary of the Currency Board

Date	Mintage	F	VF	XF	Unc	BU
ND(1991) Proof	Est. 2,500	Value: 40.00				

KM# 110 5 DOLLARS **Weight:** 28.2800 g. **Composition:** 0.9250 Silver .8411 oz. ASW **Subject:** 1992 Olympics - Barcelona

Date	Mintage	F	VF	XF	Unc	BU
1992 Proof	Est. 50,000	Value: 27.50				

KM# 112 5 DOLLARS **Weight:** 28.2800 g. **Composition:** 0.9250 Silver .8411 oz. ASW **Subject:** 40th Anniversary - Coronation of Queen Elizabeth

Date	Mintage	F	VF	XF	Unc	BU
ND (1993) Proof	Est. 10,000	Value: 32.50				
ND(1993) Proof	Est. 13,000	Value: 45.00				

KM# 126 5 DOLLARS **Weight:** 28.2800 g. **Composition:** 0.9250 Silver .8411 oz. ASW **Subject:** 70th Birthday of Queen Elizabeth II **Obverse:** Queen's portrait **Reverse:** The Queen on horseback

Date	Mintage	F	VF	XF	Unc	BU
ND (1996) Proof	Est. 13,000	Value: 45.00				

KM# 68 10 DOLLARS **Composition:** Copper-Nickel **Subject:** Wedding of Prince Charles and Lady Diana

Date	F	VF	XF	Unc	BU
1981	—	—	—	7.50	—

KM# 68a 10 DOLLARS **Weight:** 28.2800 g. **Composition:** 0.9250 Silver .8411 oz. ASW **Subject:** Wedding of Prince Charles and Lady Diana

Date	Mintage	F	VF	XF	Unc	BU
1981 Proof	40,000	Value: 17.50				

KM# 72 10 DOLLARS **Weight:** 27.8900 g. **Composition:** 0.9250 Silver .8295 oz. ASW **Subject:** International Year of the Child **Reverse:** Two children following sea turtle

Date	Mintage	F	VF	XF	Unc	BU
1982 Proof	6,616	Value: 21.50				

KM# 77 10 DOLLARS **Weight:** 23.4500 g. **Composition:** 0.9250 Silver .6975 oz. ASW **Subject:** Royal Visit

Date	Mintage	F	VF	XF	Unc	BU
1983FM Proof	10,000	Value: 30.00				

KM# 9 25 DOLLARS **Weight:** 51.3500 g. **Composition:** 0.9250 Silver 1.5271 oz. ASW **Subject:** Queen Elizabeth II and Philip's 25th Wedding Anniversary **Reverse:** Conjoined busts of royal couple facing right

Date	Mintage	F	VF	XF	Unc	BU
1972	186,000	—	—	—	25.00	—
1972 Proof	26,000	Value: 30.00				

KM# 9a 25 DOLLARS **Weight:** 15.7500 g. **Composition:** 0.5000 Gold .2222 oz. AGW **Subject:** Queen Elizabeth II and Philip's 25th Wedding Anniversary

Date	Mintage	F	VF	XF	Unc	BU
1972	7,706	—	—	—	120	—
1972 Proof	21,000	Value: 135				

KM# 10 25 DOLLARS **Weight:** 51.3500 g. **Composition:** 0.9250 Silver 1.5271 oz. ASW **Subject:** Churchill Centenary

Date	Mintage	F	VF	XF	Unc	BU
1974	1,200	—	—	—	32.50	—
1974 Proof	12,000	Value: 30.00				

Note: 4300 sets were issued in proof containing KM#10 and Turks & Caicos Islands 20 Crowns KM#2 with an issue price of $80.00

KM# 14 25 DOLLARS **Weight:** 51.3500 g. **Composition:** 0.9250 Silver 1.5271 oz. ASW **Subject:** Queen's Silver Jubliee

Date	Mintage	F	VF	XF	Unc	BU
1977	3,600	—	—	—	45.00	—
1977 Proof	7,854	Value: 45.00				

KM# 16 25 DOLLARS **Weight:** 51.3500 g. **Composition:** 0.9250 Silver 1.5271 oz. ASW **Obverse:** Portrait Queen Elizabeth right **Reverse:** Queen Mary I facing half left in inner circle

Date	Mintage	F	VF	XF	Unc	BU
1977 Proof	2,720	Value: 50.00				

KM# 17 25 DOLLARS **Weight:** 51.3500 g. **Composition:** 0.9250 Silver 1.5271 oz. ASW **Obverse:** Portrait Queen Elizabeth right **Reverse:** Queen Elizabeth I half right with ruffed collar in inner circle

Date	Mintage	F	VF	XF	Unc	BU
1977 Proof	2,677	Value: 50.00				

KM# 18 25 DOLLARS **Weight:** 51.3500 g. **Composition:** 0.9250 Silver 1.5271 oz. ASW **Obverse:** Portrait Queen Elizabeth right **Reverse:** Queen Mary II half right in inner circle

Date	Mintage	F	VF	XF	Unc	BU
1977 Proof	2,653	Value: 50.00				

KM# 19 25 DOLLARS **Weight:** 51.3500 g. **Composition:** 0.9250 Silver 1.5271 oz. ASW **Obverse:** Portrait Queen Elizabeth right **Reverse:** Queen Anne half left in inner circle

Date	Mintage	F	VF	XF	Unc	BU
1977 Proof	2,630	Value: 50.00				

KM# 20 25 DOLLARS **Weight:** 51.3500 g. **Composition:** 0.9250 Silver 1.5271 oz. ASW **Obverse:** Portrait Queen Elizabeth right **Reverse:** Queen Victoria 3/4 left in inner circle

Date	Mintage	F	VF	XF	Unc	BU
1977 Proof	2,623	Value: 50.00				

KM# 36 25 DOLLARS **Weight:** 51.3500 g. **Composition:** 0.9250 Silver 1.5271 oz. ASW **Subject:** 25th Anniversary of Coronation **Obverse:** Portrait Queen Elizabeth right **Reverse:** Ampulla

Date	Mintage	F	VF	XF	Unc	BU
1978 Proof	5,000	Value: 45.00				

KM# 37 25 DOLLARS **Weight:** 51.3500 g. **Composition:** 0.9250 Silver 1.5271 oz. ASW **Subject:** 25th Anniversary of Coronation **Obverse:** Portrait Queen Elizabeth right **Reverse:** Orb

Date	Mintage	F	VF	XF	Unc	BU
1978 Proof	5,000	Value: 45.00				

KM# 38 25 DOLLARS **Weight:** 51.3500 g. **Composition:** 0.9250 Silver 1.5271 oz. ASW **Subject:** 25th Anniversary of Coronation **Obverse:** Portrait Queen Elizabeth right **Reverse:** St. Edward's crown

Date	Mintage	F	VF	XF	Unc	BU
1978 Proof	5,000	Value: 45.00				

KM# 39 25 DOLLARS **Weight:** 51.3500 g. **Composition:** 0.9250 Silver 1.5271 oz. ASW **Subject:** 25th Anniversary of Coronation **Obverse:** Portrait Queen Elizabeth right **Reverse:** Coronation chair

Date	Mintage	F	VF	XF	Unc	BU
1978 Proof	5,000	Value: 45.00				

KM# 40 25 DOLLARS **Weight:** 51.3500 g. **Composition:** 0.9250 Silver 1.5271 oz. ASW **Subject:** 25th Anniversary of Coronation **Obverse:** Portrait Queen Elizabeth right **Reverse:** Royal scepter

Date	Mintage	F	VF	XF	Unc	BU
1978 Proof	5,000	Value: 45.00				

KM# 41 25 DOLLARS **Weight:** 51.3500 g. **Composition:** 0.9250 Silver 1.5271 oz. ASW **Subject:** 25th Anniversary of Coronation **Obverse:** Queen's portrait, date between dots **Reverse:** Spoon

Date	Mintage	F	VF	XF	Unc	BU
1978 Proof	5,000	Value: 45.00				

KM# 48 25 DOLLARS **Weight:** 35.6400 g. **Composition:** 0.5000 Silver .5729 oz. ASW **Obverse:** Portrait Queen Elizabeth right **Reverse:** Saxon Kings

Date	Mintage	F	VF	XF	Unc	BU
1980CHI Proof	12,000	Value: 35.00				

KM# 49 25 DOLLARS **Weight:** 35.6400 g. **Composition:** 0.5000 Silver .5729 oz. ASW **Obverse:** Portrait Queen Elizabeth right **Reverse:** Busts of Norman kings in a circle with names and dates

Date	Mintage	F	VF	XF	Unc	BU
1980CHI Proof	12,000	Value: 35.00				

KM# 50 25 DOLLARS **Weight:** 35.6400 g. **Composition:** 0.5000 Silver .5729 oz. ASW **Reverse:** House of Plantagenet - I

Date	Mintage	F	VF	XF	Unc	BU
1980CHI Proof	12,000	Value: 35.00				

KM# 51 25 DOLLARS **Weight:** 35.6400 g. **Composition:** 0.5000 Silver .5729 oz. ASW **Obverse:** Similar to KM#50 **Reverse:** House of Plantagenet - II

Date	Mintage	F	VF	XF	Unc	BU
1980CHI Proof	12,000	Value: 35.00				

KM# 52 25 DOLLARS **Weight:** 35.6400 g. **Composition:** 0.5000 Silver .5729 oz. ASW **Reverse:** House of Lancaster

Date	Mintage	F	VF	XF	Unc	BU
1980CHI Proof	12,000	Value: 35.00				

KM# 53 25 DOLLARS **Weight:** 35.6400 g. **Composition:** 0.5000 Silver .5729 oz. ASW **Obverse:** Similar to KM#52 **Reverse:** House of York

Date	Mintage	F	VF	XF	Unc	BU
1980CHI Proof	12,000	Value: 35.00				

KM# 54 25 DOLLARS **Weight:** 35.6400 g. **Composition:** 0.5000 Silver .5729 oz. ASW **Obverse:** Similar to KM#52 **Reverse:** House of Tudor

Date	Mintage	F	VF	XF	Unc	BU
1980CHI Proof	12,000	Value: 35.00				

KM# 55 25 DOLLARS **Weight:** 35.6400 g. **Composition:** 0.5000 Silver .5729 oz. ASW **Obverse:** Similar to KM#52 **Reverse:** House of Stuart & Orange

Date	Mintage	F	VF	XF	Unc	BU
1980CHI Proof	12,000	Value: 35.00				

KM# 56 25 DOLLARS **Weight:** 35.6400 g. **Composition:** 0.5000 Silver .5729 oz. ASW **Obverse:** Similar to KM#52 **Reverse:** House of Hanover

Date	Mintage	F	VF	XF	Unc	BU
1980CHI Proof	12,000	Value: 35.00				

KM# 57 25 DOLLARS **Weight:** 35.6400 g. **Composition:** 0.5000 Silver .5729 oz. ASW **Obverse:** Similar to KM#52 **Reverse:** House of Saxe-Coburg and Windsor

Date	Mintage	F	VF	XF	Unc	BU
1980CHI Proof	12,000	Value: 35.00				

KM# 78 25 DOLLARS **Weight:** 64.8000 g. **Composition:** 0.9250 Silver 1.9273 oz. ASW **Subject:** Royal Visit **Obverse:** Portrait Queen Elizabeth II right

Date	Mintage	F	VF	XF	Unc	BU
1983FM Proof	5,000	Value: 45.00				

KM# 104 25 DOLLARS **Weight:** 3.1340 g. **Composition:** 0.9990 Gold .1006 oz. AGW **Subject:** Winston Churchill - Evacuation of Dunkirk **Obverse:** Portrait Queen Elizabeth II right

Date	Mintage	F	VF	XF	Unc	BU
1990 Proof	Est. 500	Value: 100				

KM# 12 50 DOLLARS **Weight:** 64.9400 g. **Composition:** 0.9250 Silver 1.9314 oz. ASW **Subject:** Sovereign Queens of England **Obverse:** Portrait Queen Elizabeth II right **Reverse:** Portraits of sovereign queens in circle with names and dates

Date	Mintage	F	VF	XF	Unc	BU
1975	33,000	—	—	—	45.00	—
1975 Proof	7,800	Value: 50.00				
1976	1,292	—	—	—	55.00	—
1976 Proof	2,843	Value: 55.00				
1977	2,400	—	—	—	55.00	—
1977 Proof	Inc. above	Value: 55.00				

KM# 21 50 DOLLARS **Weight:** 11.3400 g. **Composition:** 0.5000 Gold .1823 oz. AGW **Reverse:** Bust of Queen Mary I half right

Date	Mintage	F	VF	XF	Unc	BU
1977 Proof	1,999	Value: 115				

KM# 22 50 DOLLARS **Weight:** 11.3400 g. **Composition:** 0.5000 Gold .1823 oz. AGW **Reverse:** Queen Elizabeth I

Date	Mintage	F	VF	XF	Unc	BU
1977 Proof	1,969	Value: 115				

KM# 23 50 DOLLARS **Weight:** 11.3400 g. **Composition:** 0.5000 Gold .1823 oz. AGW **Reverse:** Queen Mary II

Date	Mintage	F	VF	XF	Unc	BU
1977 Proof	1,961	Value: 115				

KM# 24 50 DOLLARS **Weight:** 11.3400 g. **Composition:** 0.5000 Gold .1823 oz. AGW **Reverse:** Bust of Queen Anne half left

Date	Mintage	F	VF	XF	Unc	BU
1977 Proof	1,938	Value: 115				

KM# 25 50 DOLLARS **Weight:** 11.3400 g. **Composition:** 0.5000 Gold .1823 oz. AGW **Reverse:** Bust of Queen Victoria 3/4 left

Date	Mintage	F	VF	XF	Unc	BU
1977 Proof	1,932	Value: 115				

KM# 34 50 DOLLARS **Weight:** 64.9400 g. **Composition:** 0.9250 Silver 1.9314 oz. ASW **Reverse:** Coronation Anniversary legend added to KM#12

Date	Mintage	F	VF	XF	Unc	BU
1978 Proof	5,775	Value: 60.00				

KM# 42 50 DOLLARS **Weight:** 11.3400 g. **Composition:** 0.5000 Gold .1823 oz. AGW **Subject:** 25th Anniversary of Coronation **Obv. Legend:** Ampulla

Date	Mintage	F	VF	XF	Unc	BU
1978 Proof	771	Value: 120				

KM# 43 50 DOLLARS **Weight:** 11.3400 g. **Composition:** 0.5000 Gold .1823 oz. AGW **Subject:** 25th Anniversary of Coronation **Obv. Legend:** Orb

Date	Mintage	F	VF	XF	Unc	BU
1978 Proof	771	Value: 120				

KM# 44 50 DOLLARS **Weight:** 11.3400 g. **Composition:** 0.5000 Gold .1823 oz. AGW **Subject:** 25th Anniversary of Coronation **Reverse:** St. Edward's Crown

Date	Mintage	F	VF	XF	Unc	BU
1978 Proof	771	Value: 120				

KM# 45 50 DOLLARS **Weight:** 11.3400 g. **Composition:** 0.5000 Gold .1823 oz. AGW **Subject:** 25th Anniversary of Coronation **Reverse:** Chair

Date	Mintage	F	VF	XF	Unc	BU
1978 Proof	771	Value: 120				

KM# 46 50 DOLLARS **Weight:** 11.3400 g. **Composition:** 0.5000 Gold .1823 oz. AGW **Subject:** 25th Anniversary of Coronation **Reverse:** Scepter

Date	Mintage	F	VF	XF	Unc	BU
1978 Proof	771	Value: 120				

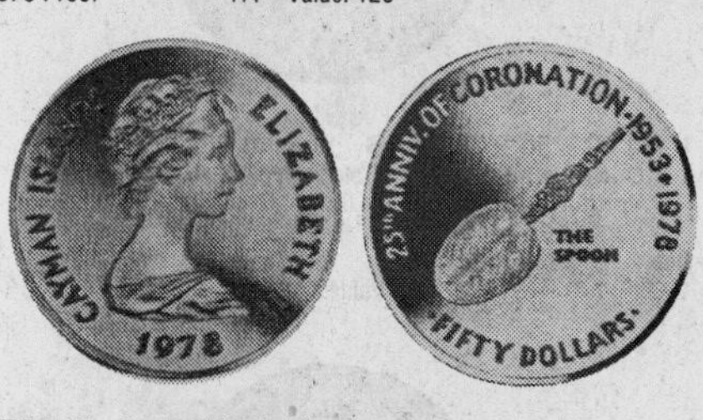

KM# 47 50 DOLLARS **Weight:** 11.3400 g. **Composition:** 0.5000 Gold .1823 oz. AGW **Subject:** 25th Anniversary of Coronation **Reverse:** Spoon

Date	Mintage	F	VF	XF	Unc	BU
1978 Proof	771	Value: 120				

KM# 58 50 DOLLARS **Weight:** 11.3400 g. **Composition:** 0.5000 Gold .1823 oz. AGW **Obverse:** Portrait Queen Elizabeth II right **Reverse:** Saxon Kings

Date	Mintage	F	VF	XF	Unc	BU
1980 Proof	10,000	Value: 110				

KM# 59 50 DOLLARS **Weight:** 11.3400 g. **Composition:** 0.5000 Gold .1823 oz. AGW **Obverse:** Portrait Queen Elizabeth II right **Reverse:** Norman Kings

Date	Mintage	F	VF	XF	Unc	BU
1980 Proof	10,000	Value: 110				

KM# 60 50 DOLLARS **Weight:** 11.3400 g. **Composition:** 0.5000 Gold .1823 oz. AGW **Obverse:** Portrait Queen Elizabeth II right **Reverse:** House of Plantagenet - I

Date	Mintage	F	VF	XF	Unc	BU
1980 Proof	11,000	Value: 110				

KM# 61 50 DOLLARS **Weight:** 11.3400 g. **Composition:** 0.5000 Gold .1823 oz. AGW **Obverse:** Portrait Queen Elizabeth II right **Reverse:** House of Plantagenet - II

Date	Mintage	F	VF	XF	Unc	BU
1980 Proof	11,000	Value: 110				

KM# 62 50 DOLLARS **Weight:** 11.3400 g. **Composition:** 0.5000 Gold .1823 oz. AGW **Obverse:** Portrait Queen Elizabeth II right **Reverse:** House of Lancaster

Date	Mintage	F	VF	XF	Unc	BU
1980 Proof	11,000	Value: 110				

KM# 63 50 DOLLARS **Weight:** 11.3400 g. **Composition:** 0.5000 Gold .1823 oz. AGW **Obverse:** Portrait Queen Elizabeth II right **Reverse:** House of York

Date	Mintage	F	VF	XF	Unc	BU
1980 Proof	11,000	Value: 110				

KM# 64 50 DOLLARS **Weight:** 11.3400 g. **Composition:** 0.5000 Gold .1823 oz. AGW **Obverse:** Portrait Queen Elizabeth II right **Reverse:** House of Tudor

Date	Mintage	F	VF	XF	Unc	BU
1980 Proof	11,000	Value: 110				

KM# 65 50 DOLLARS **Weight:** 11.3400 g. **Composition:** 0.5000 Gold .1823 oz. AGW **Obverse** Portrait Queen Elizabeth II right **Reverse:** House of Stuart and Oranage

Date	Mintage	F	VF	XF	Unc	BU
1980 Proof	11,000	Value: 110				

KM# 66 50 DOLLARS **Weight:** 11.3400 g. **Composition:** 0.5000 Gold .1823 oz. AGW **Obverse:** Portrait Queen Elizabeth II right **Reverse:** House of Hanover

Date	Mintage	F	VF	XF	Unc	BU
1980 Proof	11,000	Value: 110				

KM# 67 50 DOLLARS **Weight:** 11.3400 g. **Composition:** 0.5000 Gold .1823 oz. AGW **Obverse:** Portrait Queen Elizabeth II right **Reverse:** House of Saxe-Coburg and Windsor

Date	Mintage	F	VF	XF	Unc	BU
1980 Proof	11,000	Value: 110				

KM# 71 50 DOLLARS **Weight:** 5.0000 g. **Composition:** 0.9000 Gold .1447 oz. AGW **Subject:** 150th Anniversary of Parliamentary Government

Date	Mintage	F	VF	XF	Unc	BU
1982 Proof	585	Value: 115				

KM# 79 50 DOLLARS **Weight:** 5.1900 g. **Composition:** 0.9170 Gold .1530 oz. AGW **Subject:** Royal Visit

Date	Mintage	F	VF	XF	Unc	BU
1983	5,000	—	—	—	110	—

KM# 83 50 DOLLARS **Weight:** 129.6000 g. **Composition:** 0.9250 Silver 3.8547 oz. ASW **Subject:** Bird Conservation **Reverse:** Snowy Egret

Date	Mintage	F	VF	XF	Unc	BU
1985 Proof	10,000	Value: 90.00				

KM# 105 50 DOLLARS **Weight:** 7.8140 g. **Composition:** 0.9990 Gold .2509 oz. AGW **Reverse:** Winston Churchill - spitfires over Dover

Date	Mintage	F	VF	XF	Unc	BU
1990 Proof	Est. 500	Value: 200				

KM# 115 50 DOLLARS **Weight:** 15.9800 g. **Composition:** 0.9170 Gold .4708 oz. AGW **Reverse:** Wreck of the Ten Sails

Date	Mintage	F	VF	XF	Unc	BU
1994 Proof	Est. 200	Value: 500				

KM# 11 100 DOLLARS **Weight:** 22.6801 g. **Composition:** 0.5000 Gold .3646 oz. AGW **Subject:** Churchill Centenary

Date	Mintage	F	VF	XF	Unc	BU
1974	1,400	—	—	—	180	—
1974 Proof	6,300	Value: 200				

KM# 13 100 DOLLARS **Weight:** 22.6801 g. **Composition:** 0.5000 Gold .3646 oz. AGW **Obverse:** Portrait Queen Elizabeth II right **Reverse:** Sovereign Queens of England

Date	Mintage	F	VF	XF	Unc	BU
1975	8,053	—	—	—	175	—
1975 Proof	4,950	Value: 190				
1976	2,028	—	—	—	200	—
1976 Proof	3,560	Value: 225				
1977	—	—	—	—	200	—
1977 Proof	2,845	Value: 225				

KM# 15 100 DOLLARS **Weight:** 22.6801 g. **Composition:** 0.5000 Gold .3646 oz. AGW **Subject:** Queen's Silver Jubilee

Date	Mintage	F	VF	XF	Unc	BU
1977	562	—	—	—	185	—
1977 Proof	4,386	Value: 200				

KM# 35 100 DOLLARS **Weight:** 22.6801 g. **Composition:** 0.5000 Gold .3646 oz. AGW **Reverse:** Similar to KM#13, but with Coronation Anniversary legend

Date	Mintage	F	VF	XF	Unc	BU
1978 Proof	1,973	Value: 240				

KM# 69 100 DOLLARS **Weight:** 8.0352 g. **Composition:** 0.9170 Gold .2369 oz. AGW **Subject:** Wedding of Prince Charles and Lady Diana

Date	Mintage	F	VF	XF	Unc	BU
1981 Proof	11,000	Value: 150				

KM# 97 100 DOLLARS **Weight:** 15.9800 g. **Composition:** 0.9170 Gold .4708 oz. AGW **Subject:** 500th Anniversary of Columbus' Discovery of America

Date	Mintage	F	VF	XF	Unc	BU
1988 Proof	380	Value: 350				

KM# 101 100 DOLLARS **Weight:** 15.9800 g. **Composition:** 0.9170 Gold .4708 oz. AGW **Subject:** 100 Years of Postal Service **Reverse:** Similar to 5 Dollars, KM#100

Date	Mintage	F	VF	XF	Unc	BU
1989 Proof	93	Value: 475				

KM# 106 100 DOLLARS **Weight:** 15.6080 g. **Composition:** 0.9990 Gold .5013 oz. AGW **Obverse:** Portrait Queen Elizabeth II right **Reverse:** Winston Churchill - Evacuation of Dunkirk

Date	Mintage	F	VF	XF	Unc	BU
1990 Proof	500	Value: 375				

KM# 117 100 DOLLARS **Weight:** 30.5000 g. **Composition:** 0.9170 Gold .8974 oz. AGW **Obverse:** Portrait Queen Elizabeth right **Reverse:** Cayman Ironwood Tree

Date	Mintage	F	VF	XF	Unc	BU
1994 Proof	Est. 15,000	Value: 620				

KM# 123 100 DOLLARS **Weight:** 15.9800 g. **Composition:** 0.9170 Gold .4708 oz. AGW **Obverse:** Portrait Queen Elizabeth right **Reverse:** Amazona Leucocephala Caymanesis - Parrot

Date	Mintage	F	VF	XF	Unc	BU
1996 Proof	Est. 150	Value: 450				

KM# 82 250 DOLLARS **Weight:** 47.5400 g. **Composition:** 0.9170 Gold 1.4001 oz. AGW **Subject:** 250th Anniversary of Royal Land Grant **Note:** Similar to 5 Dollars, KM#81.

Date	Mintage	F	VF	XF	Unc	BU
1985 Proof	Est. 250	Value: 850				

KM# 84 250 DOLLARS **Weight:** 47.5400 g. **Composition:** 0.9170 Gold 1.4001 oz. AGW **Subject:** Commonwealth Games **Obverse:** Portrait Queen Elizabeth right **Reverse:** Long jumper

Date	Mintage	F	VF	XF	Unc	BU
1986 Proof	64	Value: 975				

KM# 86 250 DOLLARS **Weight:** 47.5400 g. **Composition:** 0.9170 Gold 1.4001 oz. AGW **Subject:** Queen Elizabeth II and Philip's 40th Wedding Anniversary **Obverse:** Portrait Queen Elizabeth right **Reverse:** E & P monogram

Date	Mintage	F	VF	XF	Unc	BU
ND Proof	75	Value: 950				

KM# 99 250 DOLLARS **Weight:** 47.5400 g. **Composition:** 0.9170 Gold 1.4001 oz. AGW **Subject:** Visit of Princess Alexander

Date	Mintage	F	VF	XF	Unc	BU
1988 Proof	86	Value: 950				

KM# 107 250 DOLLARS **Weight:** 31.2100 g. **Composition:** 0.9990 Gold 1.0014 oz. AGW **Obverse:** Portrait Queen Elizabeth right **Reverse:** Winston Churchill - Spitfires Over Dover

Date	Mintage	F	VF	XF	Unc	BU
1990 Proof	Est. 500	Value: 975				

KM# 113 250 DOLLARS **Weight:** 47.5400 g. **Composition:** 0.9170 Gold 1.4013 oz. AGW **Subject:** 40th Anniversary - Coronation of Queen Elizabeth II

Date	Mintage	F	VF	XF	Unc	BU
1993 Proof	Est. 100	Value: 1,000				

KM# 119 250 DOLLARS **Weight:** 47.5400 g. **Composition:** 0.9170 Gold 1.4013 oz. AGW **Subject:** Royal Visit **Obverse:** Portrait Queen Elizabeth **Reverse:** Royal couple above yacht "Britannia"

Date	Mintage	F	VF	XF	Unc	BU
1994 Proof	200	Value: 1,000				

PIEFORTS

KM#	Date	Mintage	Identification	Issue Price	Mkt Val
P1	1982	74	10 Dollars. KIM72	250	120

MINT SETS

KM#	Date	Mintage	Identification	Issue Price	Mkt Val
MS1	1987 (4)	—	KM87-90	—	5.00
MS2	1992 (4)	—	KM87a-90a	8.00	8.00
MS3	1996 (4)	—	KM87a-90a	—	12.00

PROOF SETS

KM#	Date	Mintage	Identification	Issue Price	Mkt Val
PS1	1972 (8)	10,757	KM1-8	40.00	25.00
PS2	1973 (8)	9,988	KM1-8	40.00	25.00
PS3	1974 (8)	15,387	KM1-8	40.00	25.00
PS4	1974 (2)	2,400	KM10-11	245	200
PS5	1975 (8)	5,390	KM1-8	54.50	28.00
PS6	1975 (6)	1,785	KM1-6	31.50	10.00
PS7	1975 (2)	3,650	KM12-13	293	235
PS8	1976 (8)	3,044	KM1-8	54.50	30.00
PS9	1976 (2)	1,531	KM12-13	293	265
PS11	1977 (8)	1,970	KM1-8	52.50	35.00
PS12	1977 (6)	2,445	KM12, 16-20	315	310
PS13	1977 (6)	1,932	KM13, 21-25	651	700
PS14	1977 (2)	223	KM14-15	290	250
PS15	1978 (8)	1,303	KM26-33	79.50	60.00
PS16	1978 (6)	5,000	KM36-41	306	270
PS17	1978 (6)	771	KM42-47	600	750
PS18	1979 (8)	4,427	KM1-8	117	50.00
PS19	1980 (8)	1,215	KM1-8	147	45.00
PS20	1980 (10)	—	KM48-57	—	350
PS21	1981 (8)	865	KM1-8	147	50.00
PS22	1982 (8)	589	KM1-7, 70	147	65.00
PS23	1983 (8)	348	KM1-4, 73-76	157	125
PS24	1984 (8)	—	KM1-4, 8, 73-75	159	120
PS25	1986 (8)	330	KM1-4, 7-8, 73-74	150	85.00
PS26	1987 (8)	317	KM85a, 87-93	160	200
PS27	1988 (8)	318	KM87-93, 94.2	170	300
PS28	1990 (4)	500	KM104-107	1,650	1,650

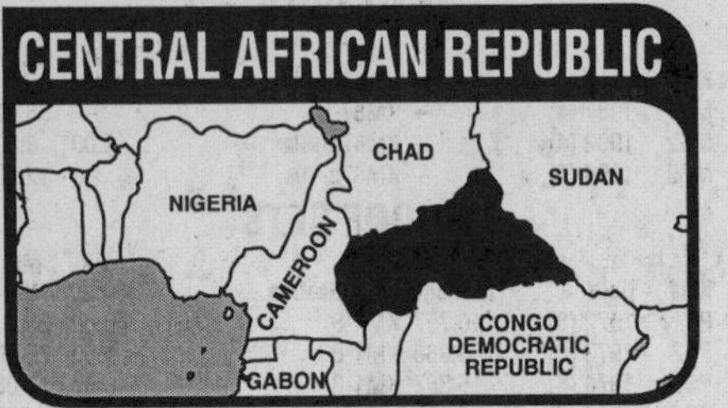

The Central African Republic, a landlocked country in Central Africa, bounded by Chad on the north, Cameroon on the west, Congo (Brazzaville) and Congo Democratic Republic, (formerly Zaire) on the south and the Sudan on the east, has an area of 240,324 sq. mi. (622,984 sq. km.) and a population of 3.2 million. Capital: Bangui. Deposits of uranium, iron ore, manganese and copper remain to be developed. Diamonds, cotton, timber and coffee are exported.

The area that is now the Central African Republic was constituted as the French territory of Ubangi-Shari in 1894. It was united with Chad in 1905 and joined with Middle Congo and Gabon in 1910, becoming one of the four territories of French Equatorial Africa. Upon dissolution of the federation on Dec. 1, 1958, the constituent territories became fully autonomous members of the French Community. Ubangi-Shari proclaimed its complete independence as the Central African Republic on Aug. 13, 1960.

On Jan. 1, 1966, Col. Jean-Bedel Bokassa, Chief of Staff of the Armed Forces, overthrew the government of President David Dacko and assumed power as president of the republic. President Bokassa abolished the constitution of 1959 and dissolved the National Assembly. In 1975 the Congress of the sole political party appointed Bokassa president for life. The republic became a constitutional monarchy on Dec. 4, 1976; President Bokassa was named Emperor Bokassa I. Bokassa was ousted as Central African emperor in a bloodless takeover of the government led by former president David Dacko on Sept. 20, 1979, and the African nation proclaimed once again a republic.

NOTE: For earlier coinage see French Equatorial Africa and Equatorial African States including later coinage as listed in Central African States.

RULERS
French, until 1960
Marshal Jean-Bedel Bokassa, 1976-1979

MINT MARKS
(a) - Paris, privy marks only

MONETARY SYSTEM
100 Centimes = 1 Franc

FIRST REPUBLIC

DECIMAL COINAGE

KM# 6 100 FRANCS **Composition:** Nickel **Obverse:** Three Giant Eland **Reverse:** Denomination

Date	Mintage	F	VF	XF	Unc	BU
1971	3,500,000	5.00	8.00	13.50	28.00	—
1972	—	5.00	8.00	13.50	28.00	—
1974	—	6.00	12.00	20.00	40.00	—

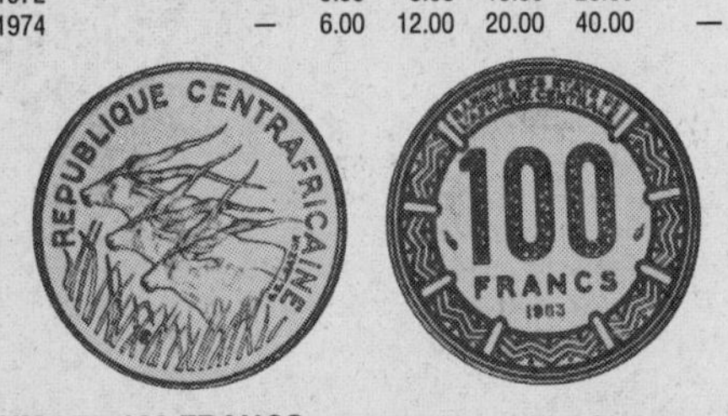

KM# 7 100 FRANCS **Composition:** Nickel **Obverse:** Three Giant Eland **Reverse:** Denomination

Date	F	VF	XF	Unc	BU
1975	4.50	7.50	12.50	22.50	—
1976	2.00	3.50	6.00	10.00	—
1979	6.00	13.50	20.00	35.00	—
1982	2.75	4.50	8.00	15.00	—
1983	2.75	4.50	9.00	20.00	—
1984	2.50	4.00	7.00	11.50	—
1985	2.50	4.00	7.00	11.50	—
1988	2.50	4.00	7.00	11.50	—
1990	2.00	3.50	6.00	10.00	—

KM# 1 1000 FRANCS **Weight:** 3.5000 g. **Composition:** 0.9000 Gold .1012 oz. AGW **Subject:** 10th Anniversary of Independence **Obverse:** Bust of President Jean Bedel Bokasso

Date	Mintage	F	VF	XF	Unc	BU
1970 Proof	4,000	Value: 90.00				

KM# 2 3000 FRANCS **Weight:** 10.5000 g. **Composition:** 0.9000 Gold .3038 oz. AGW **Subject:** 10th Anniversary of Independence

Date	Mintage	F	VF	XF	Unc	BU
1970 Proof	4,000	Value: 210				

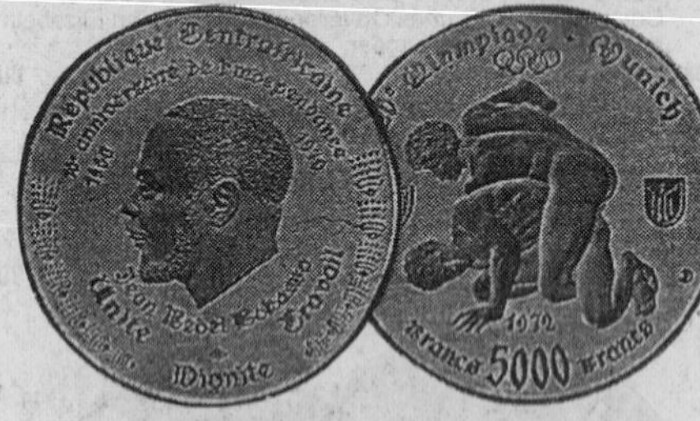

KM# 3 5000 FRANCS **Weight:** 17.5000 g. **Composition:** 0.9000 Gold .5064 oz. AGW **Subject:** 10th Anniversary of Independence; 1972 Munich Olympics **Obverse:** Similar to 3000 Francs, KM#2 **Reverse:** Wrestlers

Date	Mintage	F	VF	XF	Unc	BU
1970 Proof	4,000	Value: 350				

KM# 4 10000 FRANCS **Weight:** 35.0000 g. **Composition:** 0.9000 Gold 1.0128 oz. AGW **Subject:** 10th Anniversary of Independence; ONU 24th Anniversary **Obverse:** Similar to 3000 Francs, KM#2

Date	Mintage	F	VF	XF	Unc	BU
1970 Proof	4,000	Value: 700				

KM# 5 20000 FRANCS **Weight:** 70.0000 g. **Composition:** 0.9000 Gold 2.025728 oz. AGW **Subject:** 10th Anniversary of Independence; Operation Bohassa

Date	Mintage	F	VF	XF	Unc	BU
1970 Proof	4,000	Value: 1,420				

EMPIRE

DECIMAL COINAGE

KM# 8 100 FRANCS **Composition:** Nickel **Obverse:** Three Giant Eland **Rev. Legend:** EMPIRE CENTRAFRICAIN

Date	F	VF	XF	Unc	BU
1978(a)	30.00	60.00	160	450	—

Note: Although KM8 was never officially released for circulation, examples of this type exhibiting mild to heavy wear have become available in the numismatic market.

SECOND REPUBLIC

DECIMAL COINAGE

KM# 11 100 FRANCS **Composition:** Copper-Nickel

Date	F	VF	XF	Unc	BU
1985	7.50	15.00	30.00	55.00	—
1986	7.50	15.00	30.00	55.00	—

ESSAIS

KM#	Date	Mintage	Identification	Issue Price	Mkt Val
E1	1970	—	1000 Francs. Bronze. KM1.	—	100
E2	1971	1,450	100 Francs. KM6.	—	25.00
E3	1971	4	100 Francs. Gold. KM6.	—	1,250
E4	1975	1,700	100 Francs. KM7	—	22.00
E5	1978	1,900	100 Francs. KM8	—	150
E6	1985	1,700	500 Francs. KM11	—	45.00

PROOF SETS

KM#	Date	Mintage	Identification	Issue Price	Mkt Val
PS1	1970 (5)	40,000	KM1-5	375	2,765

CENTRAL AFRICAN STATES

The Central African States, a monetary union comprised of Equatorial Guinea (a former Spanish possession), the former French possessions and now independent states of the Republic of Congo (Brazzaville), Gabon, Central African Republic, Chad and Cameroon, issues a common currency for the member states from a common central bank. The monetary unit, the African Financial Community franc, is tied to and supported by the French franc.

In 1960, an attempt was made to form a union of the newly independent republics of Chad, Congo, Central Africa and Gabon. The proposal was discarded when Chad refused to become a constituent member. The four countries then linked into an Equatorial Customs Unit, to which Cameroon became an associate member in 1961. A more extensive cooperation of the five republics, identified as the Central African Customs and Economic Union, was entered into force at the beginning of 1966.

In 1974 the Central Bank of the Equatorial African States, which had issued coins and paper currency in its own name and with the names of the constituent member nations, changed its name to the Bank of the Central African States. Equatorial Guinea converted to the CFA currency system issuing its first 100 Franc in 1985.

For earlier coinage see French Equatorial Africa.

Country Code Letters

To observe the movement of coinage throughout the states, the country of origin in which the coin is intended to circulate is designated by the following additional code letters:

A = Chad
B = Central African Republic
C = Congo
D = Gabon
E = Cameroon

By 1996 this practice was discontinued as the strategy had proved to be inconclusive.

REPUBLIC OF CONGO

STANDARD COINAGE

KM# 8 FRANC **Composition:** Aluminum **Obverse:** Three giant eland. **Reverse:** Denomination

Date	F	VF	XF	Unc	BU
1974(a)	0.30	0.60	1.00	2.50	—
1976(a)	0.30	0.60	1.00	2.50	—
1978(a)	0.20	0.40	0.80	2.00	—
1979(a)	0.20	0.40	0.80	2.00	—
1982(a)	0.20	0.40	0.80	2.00	—
1985(a)	0.20	0.40	0.80	2.00	—
1986(a)	0.20	0.40	0.80	2.00	—
1988(a)	0.20	0.40	0.80	2.00	—
1990(a)	0.20	0.40	0.80	2.00	—
1992(a)	0.20	0.40	0.80	2.00	—

KM# 7 5 FRANCS **Composition:** Aluminum-Bronze **Obverse:** Three giant eland **Reverse:** Denomination

Date	F	VF	XF	Unc	BU
1973(a)	0.15	0.30	0.60	1.65	—
1975(a)	0.15	0.30	0.60	1.65	—
1976(a)	0.15	0.30	0.60	1.65	—
1977(a)	0.15	0.30	0.60	1.65	—
1978(a)	0.15	0.30	0.60	1.65	—
1979(a)	0.15	0.30	0.60	1.65	—
1980(a)	0.15	0.30	0.60	1.35	—
1981(a)	0.15	0.30	0.60	1.35	—
1982(a)	0.15	0.30	0.60	1.35	—
1983(a)	0.15	0.30	0.60	1.35	—
1984(a)	0.15	0.30	0.60	1.35	—
1985(a)	0.15	0.30	0.60	1.35	—
1992(a)	0.15	0.30	0.60	1.35	—

KM# 9 10 FRANCS **Composition:** Aluminum-Bronze **Obverse:** Three giant eland **Reverse:** Denomination

Date	F	VF	XF	Unc	BU
1974(a)	0.20	0.35	0.75	2.00	—
1975(a)	0.20	0.35	0.75	2.00	—
1976(a)	0.20	0.35	0.75	2.00	—
1977(a)	0.20	0.35	0.75	2.00	—
1978(a)	0.20	0.35	0.75	2.00	—
1979(a)	0.20	0.35	0.75	2.00	—
1980(a)	0.20	0.35	0.65	1.35	—
1981(a)	0.20	0.35	0.65	1.35	—
1982(a)	0.20	0.35	0.65	1.35	—
1983(a)	0.20	0.35	0.65	1.35	—
1984(a)	0.20	0.35	0.65	1.35	—
1985(a)	0.20	0.35	0.65	1.35	—
1992(a)	0.20	0.35	0.65	1.35	—
1996(a)	0.20	0.35	0.75	1.65	—

KM# 12 500 FRANCS **Composition:** Copper-Nickel

Date	Mintage	F	VF	XF	Unc	BU
1976(a) A	4,000,000	5.50	8.50	13.50	22.00	—
1976(a) B	Inc. above	5.50	8.50	13.50	22.00	—
1976(a) C	Inc. above	4.50	8.00	12.50	20.00	—
1976(a) D	Inc. above	4.50	8.00	12.50	20.00	—
1976(a) E	Inc. above	4.50	8.00	12.50	20.00	—
1977(a) A	—	5.50	8.50	15.00	25.00	—
1977(a) B	—	5.50	8.50	15.00	25.00	—
1977(a) C	—	4.50	8.00	12.50	25.00	—
1977(a) D	—	4.50	8.00	12.50	20.00	—
1977(a) E	—	3.00	6.00	10.00	16.50	—
1979(a) D	—	3.50	7.00	12.00	18.50	—
1982(a) D	—	3.50	7.00	12.00	18.50	—
1984(a) A	—	3.50	7.00	12.00	18.50	—
1984(a) B	—	3.50	7.00	12.00	18.50	—
1984(a) C	—	3.50	7.00	12.00	18.50	—
1984(a) E	—	3.50	7.00	12.00	18.50	—

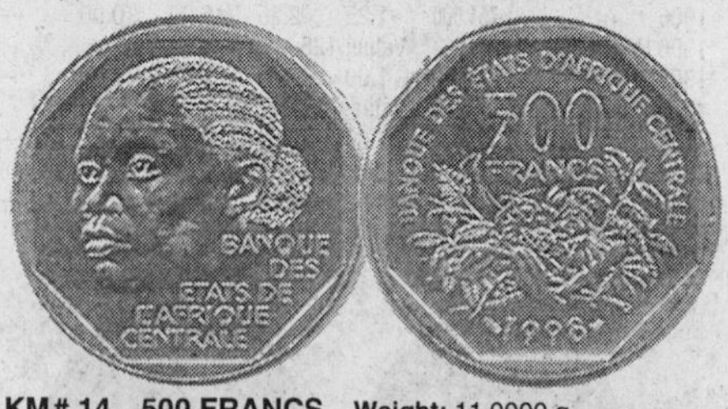

KM# 14 500 FRANCS **Weight:** 11.0000 g. **Composition:** Copper-Nickel **Subject:** Queen Elizabeth II - 50 Years of Reign **Obverse:** Native woman's head half left. **Reverse:** Denomination. **Edge:** Plain. **Size:** 30 mm.

Date	F	VF	XF	Unc	BU
1998 (a)	—	—	—	16.00	—

ESSAIS

Standard metals unless otherwise noted

KM#	Date	Mintage	Identification	Issue Price	Mkt Val
E1	1973(a)	1,550	5 Francs. KM7.	—	11.50
E3	1974(a)	1,550	KM9.	—	10.00

KM#	Date	Mintage	Identification	Issue Price	Mkt Val
E2	1974(a)	1,550	KM8.	—	10.00
EA4	1975	—	KM9.	—	10.00
E4	1975(a)	1,700	KM10.	—	10.00
E5	1976(a)	—	KM6	—	10.00
E9	1976 (a)	—	500 Francs. KM12	—	16.50
E6	1976(a)	—	KM7	—	10.00
E7	1976(a)	—	KM9	—	11.50
E8	1976(a)	—	KM11	—	12.50
E10	1979	—	KM9	—	10.00

KM#	Date	Mintage	Identification	Issue Price	Mkt Val
E11	1983	—	KM9	—	10.00

PATTERNS

Including off metal strikes

KM#	Date	Mintage	Identification	Issue Price	Mkt Val
Pn3	1956	33	40 Francs. Aluminum-Bronze.	—	375
Pn4	1956	33	40 Francs. Aluminum-Bronze.	—	375
Pn5	1956	33	40 Francs. Aluminum-Bronze.	—	375
Pn2	1956	33	40 Francs. Aluminum-Bronze.	—	375
Pn6	1956	33	40 Francs. Aluminum-Bronze.	—	375
Pn1	1956	33	40 Francs. Aluminum-Bronze.	—	375

CEYLON

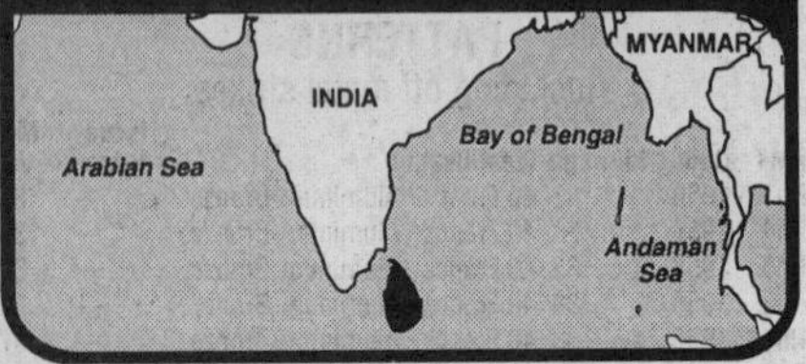

DUTCH OCCUPATION

The Dutch first sighted Ceylon in 1602. They made a treaty with the king of Kandy for trading rights and the Dutch would have to expel the Portuguese. Between 1638 and 1658 the Dutch had accomplished their purpose. The Portuguese were gone from Ceylon.

As the Dutch trade with Ceylon prospered the coins in use were local coins and countermarked coins of the Portuguese colonies. It was not until sometime after 1660 that the Dutch began striking anonymous copper coins.

In the second third of the 1700's, copper duits of the Netherlands provinces were sent to the East and used widely there. The VOC monogram on these coins became a familiar sight to the merchants of the sub-continent and the East Indies.

Local coinage started again in 1783.

Netherlands United East India Company

MONETARY SYSTEM

4 Duiten = 1 Stuiver
4 Stuivers = 1 Fanam
4-1/2 Stuivers = 1 Shahi
9-1/2 Stuivers = 1 Larin

BRITISH COLONIAL

DECIMAL COINAGE

100 Cents = 1 Rupee

KM# 90 1/4 CENT Composition: Copper

Date	Mintage	F	VF	XF	Unc	BU
1901	216,000	1.50	3.00	5.00	12.00	—
1901 Proof	—	Value: 100				

KM# 100 1/4 CENT Composition: Copper

Date	Mintage	F	VF	XF	Unc	BU
1904	103,000	2.50	5.00	10.00	22.00	—
1904 Proof	—	Value: 150				

KM# 100a 1/4 CENT Composition: Gold

Date		F	VF	XF	Unc	BU
1904	—	Value: 1,000				

KM# 91 1/2 CENT Composition: Copper

Date	Mintage	F	VF	XF	Unc	BU
1901	2,020,000	1.25	2.50	4.00	10.00	—

KM# 101 1/2 CENT Composition: Copper

Date	Mintage	F	VF	XF	Unc	BU
1904	2,012,000	1.00	2.00	5.00	12.00	—
1904 Proof	—	Value: 120				
1905	1,000,000	1.50	3.00	6.00	15.00	—
1905 Proof	—	Value: 120				
1906	3,056,000	1.00	2.00	5.00	12.00	—
1906 Proof	—	Value: 120				
1908	1,000,000	1.50	3.00	6.00	15.00	—
1908 Proof	—	Value: 200				
1909	3,000,000	1.00	2.00	5.00	12.00	—
1909 Proof	—	Value: 120				

KM# 106 1/2 CENT Composition: Copper

Date	Mintage	F	VF	XF	Unc	BU
1912	5,008,000	1.25	2.75	4.00	10.00	—
1912 Proof	—	Value: 120				
1914	2,000,000	1.25	2.75	6.00	12.00	—
1914 Proof	—	Value: 120				
1917	2,000,000	1.50	3.00	6.00	12.00	—
1917 Proof	—	Value: 120				
1926	5,000,000	0.50	1.00	2.00	5.00	—
1926 Proof	—	Value: 120				

KM# 110 1/2 CENT Composition: Copper

Date	Mintage	F	VF	XF	Unc	BU
1937	3,026,000	0.30	0.85	1.50	3.50	—
1937 Proof	—	Value: 175				
1940	5,080,000	0.25	0.65	1.25	3.00	—

KM# 92 CENT Composition: Copper

Date	Mintage	F	VF	XF	Unc	BU
1901	1,014,000	2.50	5.00	10.00	22.00	—

KM# 102 CENT Composition: Copper

Date	Mintage	F	VF	XF	Unc	BU
1904	2,529,000	1.00	2.00	4.00	8.00	—
1904 Proof	—	Value: 125				
1905	1,509,000	1.25	2.25	5.00	10.00	—
1905 Proof	—	Value: 125				
1906	1,751,000	1.25	2.25	5.00	10.00	—
1906 Proof	—	Value: 125				
1908	—	1.00	2.00	4.00	8.00	—
1908 Proof	—	Value: 225				
1909	2,500,000	1.00	2.00	4.00	8.00	—
1909 Proof	—	Value: 125				
1910	8,236,000	0.50	1.00	2.50	5.00	—
1910 Proof	—	Value: 125				

KM# 107 CENT Composition: Copper

Date	Mintage	F	VF	XF	Unc	BU
1912	5,855,000	0.50	1.00	2.00	4.00	—
1912 Proof	—	Value: 115				
1914	6,000,000	0.50	1.00	2.25	5.00	—
1914 Proof	—	Value: 115				
1917	1,000,000	1.00	1.75	3.00	8.00	—
1917 Proof	—	Value: 115				
1920	2,000,000	0.50	1.00	2.25	5.00	—
1920 Proof	—	Value: 115				
1922	2,930,000	0.50	1.00	2.25	5.00	—
1922 Proof	—	Value: 115				
1923	2,500,000	0.50	1.00	2.25	5.00	—
1923 Proof	—	Value: 115				
1925	7,490,000	0.35	0.75	1.50	3.50	—
1925 Proof	—	Value: 115				
1926	3,750,000	0.35	0.75	1.50	3.50	—
1926 Proof	—	Value: 115				
1928	2,500,000	0.35	0.75	1.50	4.00	—
1928 Proof	—	Value: 115				
1929	5,000,000	0.35	0.75	1.50	3.50	—
1929 Proof	—	Value: 115				

KM# 111 CENT Composition: Copper **Obverse:** PM below bust of George VI **Note:** High relief.

Date	Mintage	F	VF	XF	Unc	BU
1937	4,538,000	0.25	0.50	1.25	3.00	—
1937 Proof	—	Value: 100				
1940	10,190,000	0.15	0.30	1.00	2.00	—
1940 Proof	—	Value: 75.00				
1942	20,780,000	0.15	0.30	1.00	2.00	—

KM# 111a CENT Composition: Bronze **Obverse:** Without initials PM below bust of George VI **Note:** Low relief. Thin planchet.

Date	Mintage	F	VF	XF	Unc	BU
1942	Inc. above	0.15	0.30	0.75	1.75	—
1942 Proof	—	Value: 75.00				
1943	43,705,000	0.15	0.30	0.50	1.00	—
1945	34,100,000	0.15	0.35	0.60	1.20	—
1945 Proof	—	Value: 20.00				

Note: Frozen year 1945, restruck until 1962.

KM# 117 2 CENTS Composition: Nickel-Brass

Date	Mintage	F	VF	XF	Unc	BU
1944	30,165,000	0.10	0.25	0.50	1.25	—

KM# 119 2 CENTS Composition: Brass **Obv. Legend:** Without EMPEROR OF INDIA

Date	Mintage	F	VF	XF	Unc	BU
1951	15,000,000	0.10	0.25	0.75	1.75	—
1951 Proof	—	Value: 20.00				

KM# 124 2 CENTS Composition: Brass

Date	Mintage	F	VF	XF	Unc	BU
1955	37,131,000	0.10	0.15	0.25	0.65	—
1957	38,200,000	0.10	0.15	0.25	0.65	—
1957 Proof	—	Value: 75.00				

KM# 103 5 CENTS Composition: Copper-Nickel

Date	Mintage	F	VF	XF	Unc	BU
1909	2,000,000	1.50	3.00	5.00	17.00	—
1910	4,000,000	1.00	2.00	3.50	12.00	—

KM# 108 5 CENTS Composition: Copper-Nickel

Date	Mintage	F	VF	XF	Unc	BU
1912 H	4,000,000	0.75	1.50	3.00	10.00	—
1920	6,000,000	0.50	1.00	2.00	7.00	—
1926	3,000,000	0.75	1.50	4.00	12.50	—

KM# 113.1 5 CENTS **Composition:** Nickel-Brass

Date	Mintage	F	VF	XF	Unc	BU
1942	12,752,000	0.35	0.75	1.50	4.50	—
1942 Proof	—	Value: 50.00				
1943	Inc. above	0.35	0.75	1.50	4.50	—
1943 Proof	—	Value: 50.00				

KM# 113.2 5 CENTS **Composition:** Nickel-Brass **Note:** Thin planchet.

Date	Mintage	F	VF	XF	Unc	BU
1944	18,064,000	0.20	0.35	0.70	2.00	—
1945	31,192,000	0.15	0.30	0.60	1.75	—
1945 Proof	—	Value: 60.00				

Note: Varieties exist in bust, denomination and legend placement for 1945. The date was frozen at 1945 and these coins were struck until 1962.

KM# 120 5 CENTS **Composition:** Nickel-Brass **Obv. Legend:** Without EMPEROR OF INDIA

Date	Mintage	F	VF	XF	Unc	BU
1951 Proof	—	Value: 20.00				

KM# 97 10 CENTS **Weight:** 1.1664 g. **Composition:** 0.8000 Silver .03 oz. ASW

Date	Mintage	F	VF	XF	Unc	BU
1902	1,000,000	1.00	2.75	6.00	20.00	—
1902 Proof	—	Value: 150				
1903	1,000,000	1.00	2.75	6.00	20.00	—
1903 Proof	—	Value: 150				
1907	500,000	2.50	5.00	15.00	25.00	—
1908	1,500,000	1.00	2.75	6.00	15.00	—
1909	1,000,000	1.00	2.75	6.00	15.00	—
1910	2,000,000	1.00	2.75	6.00	15.00	—

KM# 104 10 CENTS **Weight:** 1.1664 g. **Composition:** 0.8000 Silver .03 oz. ASW

Date	Mintage	F	VF	XF	Unc	BU
1911	1,000,000	1.00	1.75	5.00	12.00	—
1912	1,000,000	1.25	2.00	6.00	15.00	—
1913	2,000,000	1.00	1.50	4.00	10.00	—
1914	2,000,000	1.00	1.50	4.00	10.00	—
1914 Proof	—	Value: 150				
1917	879,000	1.00	2.50	7.50	17.50	—
1917 Proof	—	Value: 150				

KM# 104a 10 CENTS **Weight:** 1.1664 g. **Composition:** 0.5500 Silver .0206 oz. ASW

Date	Mintage	F	VF	XF	Unc	BU
1919 B	750,000	1.50	3.50	10.00	20.00	—
1919 B Proof	—	Value: 150				
1920 B	3,059,000	1.00	2.50	6.00	15.00	—
1920 B Proof	—	Value: 150				
1921 B	1,583,000	0.75	1.75	5.00	10.00	—
1921 Proof	—	Value: 150				
1922	282,000	1.75	3.50	10.00	25.00	—
1922 Proof	—	Value: 150				
1924	1,508,000	0.75	1.75	4.00	10.00	—
1924 Proof	—	Value: 150				
1925	1,500,000	0.75	1.75	4.00	10.00	—
1925 Proof	—	Value: 150				
1926	1,500,000	0.75	1.75	4.00	10.00	—
1926 Proof	—	Value: 150				
1927	1,500,000	0.75	1.75	4.00	10.00	—
1927 Proof	—	Value: 150				
1928	1,500,000	0.75	1.75	4.00	10.00	—
1928 Proof	—	Value: 150				

KM# 112 10 CENTS **Weight:** 1.1664 g. **Composition:** 0.8000 Silver .03 oz. ASW

Date	Mintage	F	VF	XF	Unc	BU
1941	16,271,000	0.65	1.00	2.50	6.00	—

KM# 118 10 CENTS **Composition:** Nickel-Brass

Date	Mintage	F	VF	XF	Unc	BU
1944	30,500,000	0.25	0.50	1.00	3.00	—
1944 Proof	—	Value: 90.00				

KM# 121 10 CENTS **Composition:** Nickel-Brass **Obv. Legend:** Without EMPEROR OF INDIA

Date	Mintage	F	VF	XF	Unc	BU
1951		0.10	0.20	0.40	1.25	—
1951 Proof	—	Value: 15.00				
1951 Proof, restrike	Est. 3,000,000	Value: 4.00				

Note: Restrikes differ in the formation of native characters.

KM# 98 25 CENTS **Weight:** 2.9160 g. **Composition:** 0.8000 Silver .075 oz. ASW

Date	Mintage	F	VF	XF	Unc	BU
1902	400,000	4.00	8.00	20.00	40.00	—
1902 Proof	—	Value: 150				
1903	400,000	4.00	8.00	20.00	40.00	—
1903 Proof	—	Value: 150				
1907	120,000	7.50	20.00	30.00	50.00	—
1908	400,000	4.00	8.00	15.00	35.00	—
1909	400,000	4.00	8.00	15.00	35.00	—
1910	800,000	2.00	5.00	10.00	20.00	—

KM# 105 25 CENTS **Weight:** 2.9160 g. **Composition:** 0.8000 Silver .075 oz. ASW

Date	Mintage	F	VF	XF	Unc	BU
1911	400,000	3.00	6.00	12.00	30.00	—
1911 Proof	—	Value: 175				
1913	1,200,000	1.50	2.50	7.50	17.50	—
1913 Proof	—	Value: 175				
1914	400,000	3.00	6.00	12.00	25.00	—
1914 Proof	—	Value: 175				
1917	300,000	4.00	8.00	15.00	35.00	—
1917 Proof	—	Value: 175				

KM# 105a 25 CENTS **Weight:** 2.9160 g. **Composition:** 0.5500 Silver .0516 oz. ASW

Date	Mintage	F	VF	XF	Unc	BU
1919 B	1,400,000	1.25	3.00	7.50	15.00	—
1919 B Proof	—	Value: 150				
1920 B	1,600,000	1.25	3.00	7.50	15.00	—
1920 B Proof	—	Value: 150				
1921 B	600,000	3.50	7.50	15.00	30.00	—
1921 B Proof	—	Value: 150				
1922	1,211,000	1.25	3.25	7.50	15.00	—
1922 Proof	—	Value: 150				
1925	1,004,000	1.25	3.50	7.50	15.00	—
1925 Proof	—	Value: 150				
1926	1,000,000	1.25	3.50	7.50	15.00	—
1926 Proof	—	Value: 150				

KM# 115 25 CENTS **Composition:** Nickel-Brass **Note:** Frozen date 1943, restruck until 1951.

Date	Mintage	F	VF	XF	Unc	BU
1943	13,920,000	0.25	0.50	1.00	2.50	—

KM# 122 25 CENTS **Composition:** Nickel-Brass **Obv. Legend:** Without EMPEROR OF INDIA

Date	Mintage	F	VF	XF	Unc	BU
1951		0.10	0.30	0.60	1.75	—
1951 Proof	—	Value: 20.00				
1951 Proof, restrike	Est. 2,500,000	Value: 4.00				

Note: Numerals 9 and 5 differ on restrikes.

KM# 99 50 CENTS **Weight:** 5.8319 g. **Composition:** 0.8000 Silver .15 oz. ASW

Date	Mintage	F	VF	XF	Unc	BU
1902	200,000	5.00	10.00	30.00	70.00	—
1902 Proof	—	Value: 175				
1903	800,000	3.00	8.00	18.00	35.00	—
1903 Proof	—	Value: 175				
1910	200,000	7.00	13.00	30.00	60.00	—

KM# 109 50 CENTS **Weight:** 5.8319 g. **Composition:** 0.8000 Silver .15 oz. ASW

Date	Mintage	F	VF	XF	Unc	BU
1913	400,000	7.00	13.00	30.00	60.00	—
1913 Proof	—	Value: 175				
1914	200,000	5.00	15.00	30.00	60.00	—
1914 Proof	—	Value: 175				
1917	1,073,000	2.50	5.00	10.00	20.00	—
1917 Proof	—	Value: 175				

KM# 109a 50 CENTS **Weight:** 5.8319 g. **Composition:** 0.5500 Silver .1031 oz. ASW

Date	Mintage	F	VF	XF	Unc	BU
1919 B	750,000	1.00	3.00	7.00	16.00	—
1919 B Proof	—	Value: 120				
1920 B	800,000	1.00	3.00	7.00	16.00	—
1920 B Proof	—	Value: 120				
1921 B	800,000	1.00	3.00	7.00	16.00	—
1921 B Proof	—	Value: 120				
1922	1,040,000	1.00	3.00	7.00	16.00	—
1922 Proof	—	Value: 120				
1924	1,010,000	1.00	3.00	7.00	16.00	—
1924 Proof	—	Value: 120				
1925	500,000	2.00	5.00	10.00	20.00	—
1925 Proof	—	Value: 120				
1926	500,000	2.00	5.00	10.00	20.00	—
1926 Proof	—	Value: 120				
1927	500,000	2.00	5.00	10.00	20.00	—
1927 Proof	—	Value: 120				
1928	500,000	2.00	5.00	10.00	20.00	—
1928 Proof	—	Value: 120				
1929	500,000	2.00	5.00	10.00	20.00	—
1929 Proof	—	Value: 120				

KM# 114 50 CENTS **Weight:** 5.8319 g. **Composition:** 0.8000 Silver .15 oz. ASW

Date	Mintage	F	VF	XF	Unc	BU
1942	662,000	2.00	4.00	8.00	17.50	—

KM# 116 50 CENTS **Composition:** Nickel-Brass **Note:** Frozen date 1943, restruck until 1951.

Date	Mintage	F	VF	XF	Unc	BU
1943	8,600,000	0.35	0.75	1.50	3.50	—

KM# 123 50 CENTS **Composition:** Nickel-Brass **Obv. Legend:** Without EMPEROR OF INDIA

Date	Mintage	F	VF	XF	Unc	BU
1951		0.20	0.35	0.75	1.75	—
1951 Proof	—	Value: 20.00				
1951 Proof, restrike	Est. 1,500,000	Value: 5.00				

Note: Restrikes differ slightly in the formation of native inscriptions.

KM# 125 RUPEE **Composition:** Copper-Nickel **Subject:** 2,500 years of Buddhism

Date	Mintage	F	VF	XF	Unc	BU
1957	2,000,000	0.50	1.00	2.00	3.00	—
1957 Proof	1,800	Value: 12.00				

KM# 126 5 RUPEES **Weight:** 28.2757 g. **Composition:** 0.9250 Silver .8409 oz. ASW **Subject:** 2,500 years of Buddhism

Date	Mintage	F	VF	XF	Unc	BU
1957	500,000	8.00	12.50	17.50	30.00	—

Note: 258,000 returned in 1962 to be melted at The Royal Mint

Date	Mintage	
1957 Proof	1,800	Value: 65.00

REPUBLIC

DECIMAL COINAGE

KM# 127 CENT **Composition:** Aluminum

Date	Mintage	F	VF	XF	Unc	BU
1963		—	—	—	0.10	—
1965		—	—	0.10	0.15	—
1967		—	—	0.10	0.15	—
1968		—	—	—	0.10	—
1969		—	—	—	0.10	—
1970		—	—	—	0.10	—
1971		—	—	—	0.10	—
1971 Proof	20,000	Value: 0.50				

KM# 128 2 CENTS **Composition:** Aluminum

Date	Mintage	F	VF	XF	Unc	BU
1963		—	—	0.10	0.15	—
1965		—	—	0.10	0.15	—
1967		—	—	0.10	0.15	—
1968		—	—	0.10	0.15	—
1970		—	—	0.10	0.15	—
1971		—	—	0.10	0.15	—
1971 Proof	20,000	Value: 1.00				

KM# 129 5 CENTS **Composition:** Nickel-Brass

Date	Mintage	F	VF	XF	Unc	BU
1963		—	0.10	0.15	0.25	—
1965		—	0.10	0.15	0.25	—
1968		—	0.10	0.15	0.25	—
1969		—	0.10	0.20	0.40	—
1970		—	0.10	0.15	0.25	—
1971		—	0.10	0.15	0.25	—
1971 Proof	20,000	Value: 1.50				

KM# 130 10 CENTS **Composition:** Nickel-Brass

Date	Mintage	F	VF	XF	Unc	BU
1963		—	0.10	0.15	0.25	—
1965		—	0.10	0.15	0.35	—
1969		—	0.10	0.15	0.25	—
1971		—	0.10	0.15	0.20	—
1971 Proof	20,000	Value: 1.25				

KM# 131 25 CENTS **Composition:** Copper-Nickel

Date	Mintage	F	VF	XF	Unc	BU
1963		—	0.10	0.20	0.40	—
1965		—	0.10	0.25	0.50	—
1971		—	0.10	0.15	0.30	—
1971 Proof	20,000	Value: 1.50				

KM# 132 50 CENTS **Composition:** Copper-Nickel

Date	Mintage	F	VF	XF	Unc	BU
1963		0.10	0.20	0.35	0.75	—
1965		0.10	0.20	0.35	0.75	—
1971		0.25	0.50	0.75	1.50	—
1971 Proof	20,000	Value: 2.00				

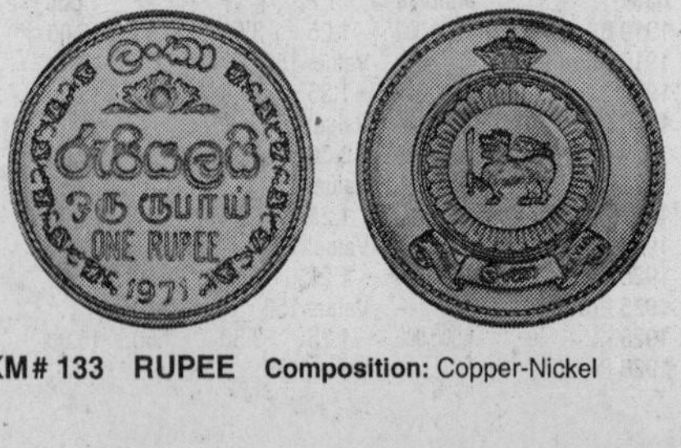

KM# 133 RUPEE **Composition:** Copper-Nickel

Date	Mintage	F	VF	XF	Unc	BU
1963		0.10	0.20	0.40	1.00	—
1965		0.15	0.25	0.50	1.25	—
1969		0.15	0.25	0.50	1.75	—
1971		0.15	0.25	0.50	1.50	—
1971 Proof	20,000	Value: 4.00				

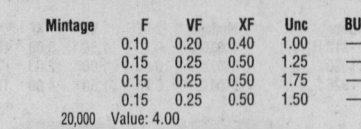

KM# 134 2 RUPEES **Composition:** Copper-Nickel **Series:** F.A.O.

Date	Mintage	F	VF	XF	Unc	BU
1968	500,000	0.50	1.50	2.25	3.00	—

PATTERNS

Including off metal strikes

KM#	Date	Mintage	Identification	Mkt Val
Pn8	1904	—	5 Cents. Copper.	3,500
pn9	1942	—	Cent. struck in Black Bakelite	—
Pn10	1943	—	50 Cents.	—
	1943	—	50 Cents.	—
pn11	1965	—	10 Cents. Nickel-Brass. similar to KM#130, with TRIAL in raised letters on obverse and reverse	—
pn12	1968	—	5 Cents. Nickel-Brass. similar to KM#129, with TRIAL in raised letters on obverse and reverse	—

PROOF SETS

KM#	Date	Mintage	Identification	Issue Price	Mkt Val
PS1	1951 (6)	150	KM111a (1945), 119-123 (1951). Restrikes exist.	—	40.00
PS2	1957 (2)	400	KM125-126	—	90.00
PS3	1957 (4)	700	KM125-126, 2 each	—	160
PS4	1971 (7)	20,000	KM127-133	—	10.00

CHAD

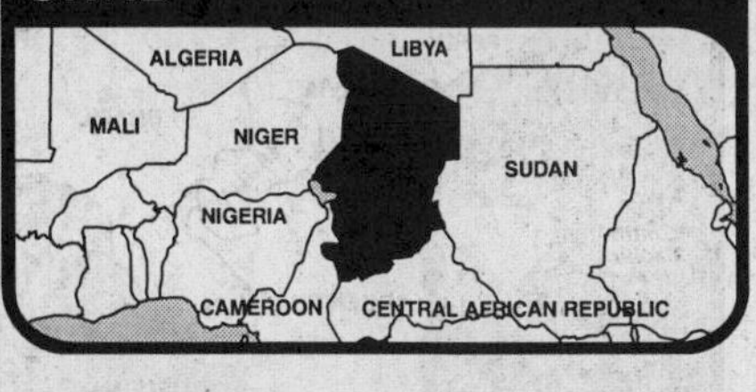

The Republic of Chad, a landlocked country of central Africa, is the largest country of former French Equatorial Africa. It has an area of 495,755 sq. mi. (1,284,000 sq. km.) and a population of *7.27 million. Capital: N'Djamena. An expanding livestock industry produces camels, cattle and sheep. Cotton (the chief product), ivory and palm oil are important exports.

Although supposedly known to Ptolemy, the Chad area was first visited by white men in 1823. Exaggerated estimates of its economic importance led to a race for its possession (1890-93), which resulted in the territory being divided by treaty between Great Britain, France and Germany. As a consequence of World War I, the German area was mandated to France in 1919. Chad was absorbed into the colony of French Equatorial Africa, as part of Ubangi-Shari, in 1910 and became a separate colony in 1920. Upon dissolution of French Equatorial Africa in 1959, the component states became autonomous members of the French Union. Chad became an independent republic on Aug. 11, 1960.

NOTE: For earlier and related coinage see French Equatorial Africa and the Equatorial African States. For later coinage see Central African States.

MINT MARKS
(a) - Paris, privy marks only
(b) = Brussels
NI - Numismatic Italiana, Arezzo, Italy

COMMEMORATIVE EDGE INSCRIPTIONS
1960 LIBERTE PROGRESS SOLIDARITE
1970/REPUBLIQUE DU TCHAD

REPUBLIC

DECIMAL COINAGE

KM# 1 100 FRANCS **Weight:** 5.0000 g. **Composition:** 0.9250 Silver .0957 oz. ASW **Subject:** 10th Anniversary of Independence **Reverse:** Robert Francis Kennedy

Date	Mintage	F	VF	XF	Unc	BU
1970(b) Proof	975	Value: 85.00				

KM# 2 100 FRANCS **Composition:** Nickel **Obverse:** Three Giant Eland **Reverse:** Denomination

Date	Mintage	F	VF	XF	Unc	BU
1971(a)	5,000,000	10.00	17.50	27.50	45.00	—
1972(a)	5,000,000	10.00	17.50	27.50	45.00	—

KM# 3 100 FRANCS **Composition:** Nickel

Date	F	VF	XF	Unc	BU
1975(a)	10.00	15.00	22.00	35.00	—
1978(a)	12.00	20.00	28.00	45.00	—
1980(a)	10.00	17.50	25.00	40.00	—
1982(a)	10.00	15.00	22.00	35.00	—
1984(a)	10.00	15.00	22.00	35.00	—
1985(a)	10.00	14.00	20.00	30.00	—
1988(a)	10.00	14.00	20.00	30.00	—
1990(a)	10.00	14.00	20.00	30.00	—
1991(a)	—	—	—	—	—

KM# 4 200 FRANCS **Weight:** 15.0000 g. **Composition:** 0.9250 Silver .4461 oz. ASW **Subject:** 10th Anniversary of Independence **Reverse:** Martin Luther King, Jr

Date	Mintage	F	VF	XF	Unc	BU
1970(b) Proof	952	Value: 165				

KM# 5 200 FRANCS **Weight:** 15.0000 g. **Composition:** 0.8000 Silver .3858 oz. ASW **Subject:** 10th Anniversary of Independence **Reverse:** Charles de Gaulle

Date	Mintage	F	VF	XF	Unc	BU
1970(b) Proof	442	Value: 185				

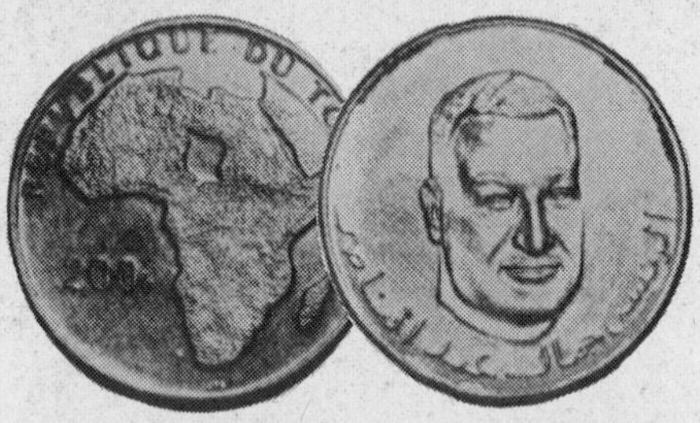

KM# 6 200 FRANCS **Weight:** 15.0000 g. **Composition:** 0.8000 Silver .3858 oz. ASW **Subject:** 10th Anniversary of Independence **Reverse:** Egypt's President Nasser

Date	Mintage	F	VF	XF	Unc	BU
1970(b) Proof	435	Value: 150				

KM# 7 300 FRANCS **Weight:** 25.0000 g. **Composition:** 0.9250 Silver .8922 oz. ASW **Subject:** 10th Anniversary of Independence **Reverse:** John Fitzgerald Kennedy

Date	Mintage	F	VF	XF	Unc	BU
1970(b) Proof	504	Value: 600				

KM# 13 500 FRANCS **Composition:** Copper-Nickel

Date	F	VF	XF	Unc	BU
1985(a)	15.00	22.00	35.00	50.00	—

KM# 8 1000 FRANCS **Weight:** 3.5000 g. **Composition:** 0.9000 Gold .1012 oz. AGW **Subject:** 10th Anniversary of Independence **Reverse:** Commandant Lamy

Date	Mintage	F	VF	XF	Unc	BU
ND(1970)(a)NI Proof	4,000	Value: 180				
ND(1970)(a)NI Proof	Inc. above	Value: 180				

KM# 16 1000 FRANCS **Weight:** 14.9700 g. **Composition:** 0.9850 Silver 0.4741 oz. ASW **Obverse:** Native portrait above denomination **Reverse:** Portrait of Galileo **Edge:** Plain **Size:** 35 mm.

Date	F	VF	XF	Unc	BU
1999 Proof	—	Value: 30.00			

KM# 9 3000 FRANCS **Weight:** 10.5000 g. **Composition:** 0.9000 Gold .3038 oz. AGW **Subject:** 10th Anniversary of Independence **Reverse:** Governor Eboue

Date	Mintage	F	VF	XF	Unc	BU
ND(1970)(a)NI	4,000	Value: 225				
ND(1970)NI	Inc. above	Value: 225				

KM# 10 5000 FRANCS **Weight:** 17.5000 g. **Composition:** 0.9000 Gold .5064 oz. AGW **Subject:** 10th Anniversary of Independence **Reverse:** General Leclerc

Date	Mintage	F	VF	XF	Unc	BU
ND(1970)(a)NI Proof	4,000	Value: 345				
ND(1970)NI Proof	Inc. above	Value: 345				

KM# 11 10000 FRANCS **Weight:** 36.0000 g. **Composition:** 0.9000 Gold 1.0128 oz. AGW **Subject:** 10th Anniversary of Independence **Reverse:** General De Gaulle

Date	Mintage	F	VF	XF	Unc	BU
ND(1970)(a)NI Proof	4,000	Value: 750				
ND (1970)NI Proof	Inc. above	Value: 750				

KM# 14 10000 FRANCS **Weight:** 36.0000 g. **Composition:** 0.9000 Gold 1.0128 oz. AGW **Subject:** 10th Anniversary of Independence **Reverse:** Egypt's President Nasser

Date	Mintage	F	VF	XF	Unc	BU
1970(b) Proof	205	Value: 1,175				

KM# 15 10000 FRANCS **Weight:** 36.0000 g. **Composition:** 0.9000 Gold 1.0128 oz. AGW **Subject:** 10th Anniversary of Independence **Obverse:** Map of Africa **Reverse:** Charles de Gaulle facing

Date	Mintage	F	VF	XF	Unc	BU
1970 Proof	90	Value: 1,350				

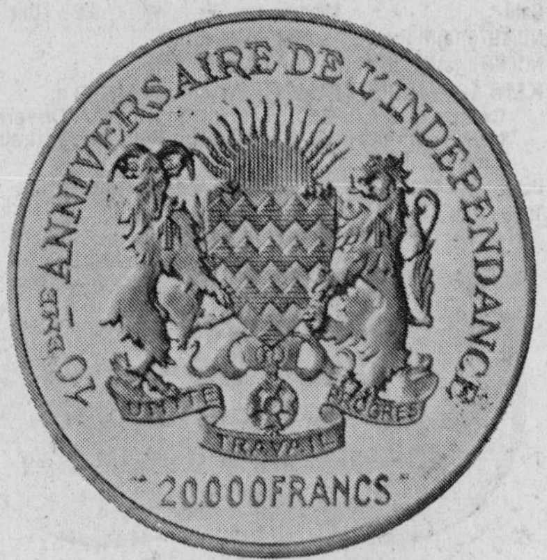

KM# 12 20000 FRANCS **Weight:** 70.0000 g. **Composition:** 0.9000 Gold 2.0257 oz. AGW **Subject:** 10th Anniversary of Independence **Reverse:** Francois Tombalbaye

Date	Mintage	F	VF	XF	Unc	BU
ND (1970)(a)NI Proof	Est. 4,000	Value: 1,650				
ND (1970)NI Proof	Inc. above	Value: 1,650				

ESSAIS

Standard metals unless otherwise noted

KM#	Date	Mintage	Identification	Issue Price	Mkt Val
E1	1970(a)	—	10000 Francs. Copper-Nickel-Aluminum. KM#11.	—	125

KM#	Date	Mintage	Identification	Issue Price	Mkt Val
E3	1971(a)	1,700	100 Francs. KM#2.	—	23.50
E4	1971	4	100 Francs. Gold. KM#2.	—	1,250
E5	1975(a)	1,700	100 Francs. KM#3.	—	22.50

KM#	Date	Mintage	Identification	Issue Price	Mkt Val
E6	1985(a)	1,700	500 Francs. KM#13.	—	70.00

PROOF SETS

KM#	Date	Mintage	Identification	Issue Price	Mkt Val
PS2	1970 (3)	—	KM1, 4, 7	33.00	735
PS1	1970 (5)	4,000	KM8-12	412	3,250

CHILE

The Republic of Chile, a ribbon-like country on the Pacific coast of southern South America, has an area of 292,135 sq. mi. (756,950 sq. km.) and a population of *15.21 million. Capital: Santiago. Historically, the economic base of Chile has been the rich mineral deposits of its northern provinces. Copper has accounted for more than 75 percent of Chile's export earnings in recent years. Other important mineral exports are iron ore, iodine and nitrate of soda. Fresh fruits and vegetables, as well as wine are increasingly significant in inter-hemispheric trade.

Diego de Almargo was the first Spaniard to attempt to wrest Chile from the Incas and Araucanian tribes in 1536. He failed, and was followed by Pedro de Valdivia, a favorite of Pizarro, who founded Santiago in 1541. When the Napoleonic Wars involved Spain, leaving the constituent parts of the Spanish Empire to their own devices, Chilean patriots formed a national government and proclaimed the country's independence, Sept. 18, 1810. Independence however, was not secured until Feb. 12, 1818, after a bitter struggle led by Bernardo O'Higgins and San Martin. Despite a long steady history of monetary devaluation, reflected in declining weight and fineness in its currency, Chile developed a strong democracy. This was displaced when rampant inflation characterized chaotic and subsequently repressive governments in the mid to late 20th century.

RULERS

Spanish until 1818

MINT MARKS

So - Santiago

MONETARY SYSTEM

16 Reales = 1 Escudo

REPUBLIC

DECIMAL COINAGE

KM# 161 CENTAVO **Composition:** Copper

Date	Mintage	VG	F	VF	XF	Unc
1904	970,000	0.25	0.50	1.50	3.00	7.00
1908	174,000	0.65	1.25	3.00	9.00	—
1919	173,000	0.50	1.00	2.50	8.50	—

KM# 164 2 CENTAVOS **Composition:** Copper

Date	Mintage	F	VF	XF	Unc	BU
1919	147,000	1.50	3.00	6.00	17.50	—

KM# 162 2-1/2 CENTAVOS (Dos I Medio) **Composition:** Copper

Date	Mintage	F	VF	XF	Unc	BU
1904	277,000	2.75	7.50	20.00	50.00	—
1906/4	161,000	3.50	10.00	22.00	55.00	—
1906	Inc. above	3.50	10.00	22.00	55.00	—
1907/4	262,000	2.75	7.50	20.00	45.00	—
1907	Inc. above	2.75	7.50	20.00	45.00	—

Note: Varieties exist for 1907 dated coins

Date	Mintage	F	VF	XF	Unc	BU
1908/4	201,000	2.50	7.00	19.00	45.00	—
1908	Inc. above	2.50	7.00	19.00	45.00	—

KM# 155.2 5 CENTAVOS **Weight:** 1.0000 g. **Composition:** 0.5000 Silver .0160 oz. ASW **Obverse:** 0.5 below condor **Note:** Varieties exist with 0.5, 0.5., 0/5.5., 0,5 or 05. below condor.

Date	Mintage	F	VF	XF	Unc	BU
1901/801	2,109,000	3.00	5.00	8.50	22.00	—
1901/891	Inc. above	3.00	5.00	8.50	22.00	—
1901/896	—	3.00	5.00	8.50	22.00	—
1901	Inc. above	2.00	4.00	8.00	20.00	—
1904/891/9	—	3.50	7.50	13.50	32.00	—
1904/894	2,527,000	3.50	7.50	13.50	32.00	—
1904/1	Inc. above	3.50	7.00	12.50	30.00	—

Note: With 0.5

Date	Mintage	F	VF	XF	Unc	BU
1904	Inc. above	2.00	4.00	8.00	20.00	—

Note: With 05.

Date	Mintage	F	VF	XF	Unc	BU
1906/4	713,000	5.00	10.00	20.00	35.00	—
1906	Inc. above	2.00	4.00	8.00	20.00	—
1907	2,791,000	2.00	3.00	7.00	18.00	—

Note: Exists with both 0.5 and 0.5. obverse varieties

Date	Mintage	F	VF	XF	Unc	BU
1909/899	—	2.50	5.00	10.00	22.00	—

KM# 155.2a 5 CENTAVOS **Weight:** 1.0000 g. **Composition:** 0.4000 Silver .0128 oz. ASW

Date	Mintage	F	VF	XF	Unc	BU
1908/1	—	2.50	5.00	10.00	20.00	—
1908/2	—	2.50	5.00	10.00	20.00	—
1908	3,642,000	2.00	3.00	7.00	15.00	—
1909/1	1,177,000	2.00	4.00	9.00	18.00	—
1909/2	—	2.00	4.00	9.00	18.00	—
1909/8	Inc. above	2.00	4.00	9.00	18.00	—
1909	Inc. above	2.00	5.00	9.00	18.00	—
1910/01	1,587,000	2.00	3.00	7.00	15.00	—
1910	Inc. above	2.00	3.00	7.00	15.00	—
1911	847,000	2.00	4.00	9.00	18.00	—
1913/1	—	2.50	5.00	10.00	20.00	—
1913/2	2,573,000	3.00	7.00	15.00	30.00	—

Note: Varieties exist with a dot below 1 in date for 1913

Date	Mintage	F	VF	XF	Unc	BU
1913	Inc. above	2.00	3.00	7.00	15.00	—

Note: Varieties exist with a dot below 1 in date for 1913

Date	Mintage	F	VF	XF	Unc	BU
1919	Inc. below	1.50	3.00	7.00	15.00	—

Note: With dash below second 9 in date

KM# 155.3 5 CENTAVOS **Weight:** 1.0000 g. **Composition:** 0.4500 Silver .0144 oz. ASW **Obverse:** 0.45 below condor

Date	Mintage	F	VF	XF	Unc	BU
1915/1	—	1.50	3.50	6.00	14.00	—
1915	2,250,000	1.50	3.00	5.00	12.00	—

Note: 1915 exists with flat and curved top on 5

Date	Mintage	F	VF	XF	Unc	BU
1916/1	4,337,000	1.50	3.50	6.00	14.00	—
1916/5	Inc. above	1.50	3.50	6.00	14.00	—
1916	Inc. above	1.50	3.00	5.00	12.00	—
1919/1	1,494,000	3.00	7.00	15.00	30.00	—

Note: With dash below second 9 in date

Date	Mintage	F	VF	XF	Unc	BU
1919/2	Inc. above	2.00	4.00	8.00	20.00	—
1919/5	Inc. above	2.00	4.00	8.00	20.00	—
1919	Inc. above	3.00	5.00	10.00	20.00	—

KM# 165 5 CENTAVOS **Composition:** Copper-Nickel **Obverse:** Without designer's name O. ROTY at bottom **Note:** Varieties exist.

Date	Mintage	F	VF	XF	Unc	BU
1920	718,000	1.00	1.50	3.00	10.00	—
1921	2,406,000	0.50	1.25	2.00	5.00	—
1922	3,872,000	0.50	1.25	2.00	5.00	—
1923	2,150,000	0.50	1.25	2.00	5.00	—

Date	Mintage	F	VF	XF	Unc	BU
1925	994,000	0.50	1.25	2.00	5.00	—

Note: Obverse variety known with dot to left of right wing tip.

Date	Mintage	F	VF	XF	Unc	BU
1926	594,000	1.50	2.50	3.00	6.50	—
1927	1,276,000	0.50	1.00	2.00	5.00	—
1928	5,197,000	0.50	1.00	2.00	5.00	—
1933	3,000,000	5.00	10.00	17.50	45.00	—
1934	Inc. above	0.25	0.50	1.00	2.00	—
1936	2,000,000	0.25	0.50	1.00	2.00	—
1937	2,000,000	0.25	0.50	1.00	2.00	—
1938	2,000,000	0.25	0.50	1.00	2.00	—

KM# 156.2 10 CENTAVOS **Weight:** 2.0000 g. **Composition:** 0.5000 Silver .0321 oz. ASW **Obverse:** 0.5 below condor **Note:** Obverse varieties exist with 0.5, 0,5, 0.5. or 0.5/9 below condor.

Date	Mintage	F	VF	XF	Unc	BU
1900	104,000	20.00	35.00	50.00	85.00	—
1901/801	Inc. above	10.00	20.00	35.00	90.00	—
1901/891	Inc. above	17.50	30.00	55.00	140	—
1901/896	—	17.50	30.00	55.00	140	—
1901	Inc. above	15.00	25.00	40.00	100	—
1904/896	—	2.00	3.50	7.00	16.50	—
1904/899	779,000	2.00	3.50	7.00	16.50	—
1904	Inc. above	2.50	4.50	9.00	20.00	—
1906	139,000	2.50	4.50	8.50	18.00	—
1907/807	—	2.50	4.50	8.50	18.00	—
1907	3,151,000	2.00	3.50	7.00	16.50	—

Note: Exists with both 0.5 and 0.5. obverse varieties

KM# 156.2a 10 CENTAVOS **Weight:** 1.5000 g. **Composition:** 0.4000 Silver .0192 oz. ASW **Note:** Varities exist.

Date	Mintage	F	VF	XF	Unc	BU
1908/1	—	1.50	3.00	6.00	15.00	—
1908	4,149,000	1.00	2.00	4.50	12.00	—
1908/inverted 6	—	1.50	3.00	6.00	15.00	—
1909/8	2,964,000	1.50	3.00	6.00	15.00	—
1909	Inc. above	1.00	2.00	4.50	12.00	—
1913	1,269,000	1.50	3.00	6.00	15.00	—
1919/8	—	3.00	6.00	12.00	25.00	—
1919	883,000	2.50	5.00	10.00	20.00	—
1920/5	—	1.50	3.00	6.00	18.00	—
1920	2,109,000	1.00	2.00	4.50	12.00	—

KM# 156.3 10 CENTAVOS **Weight:** 1.5000 g. **Composition:** 0.4500 Silver .0217 oz. ASW **Obverse:** 0.45 below condor

Date	Mintage	F	VF	XF	Unc	BU
1915	1,620,000	1.00	1.50	3.00	7.50	—
1916	2,855,000	1.00	1.50	3.00	7.50	—
1917/1	—	2.00	3.50	7.00	18.00	—
1917	736,000	1.50	2.50	5.00	14.00	—
1918/5	—	2.00	3.50	7.00	18.00	—
1918	Inc. above	1.50	2.50	5.00	14.00	—

KM# 166 10 CENTAVOS **Composition:** Copper-Nickel **Obverse:** Without designer's name O. ROTY at bottom **Edge:** Plain

Date	Mintage	F	VF	XF	Unc	BU
1920	451,000	1.50	3.50	5.00	10.00	—
1921	2,654,000	0.50	0.75	1.50	3.00	—
1922	4,017,000	0.50	0.75	1.50	3.00	—
1923	3,356,000	0.50	0.75	7.00	16.50	—
1924	1,445,000	0.50	0.75	1.50	3.00	—
1925	2,665,000	0.50	0.75	1.50	3.00	—
1927	523,000	1.00	2.00	3.50	7.00	—
1928	3,052,000	0.50	0.75	1.50	3.00	—
1932	1,500,000	0.75	1.00	2.00	4.00	—
1933/2	5,800,000	0.75	1.00	2.00	4.00	—
1933 Over reversed 3	—	0.50	1.00	2.00	5.00	—

Date	Mintage	F	VF	XF	Unc	BU
1933	Inc. above	0.25	0.50	1.00	2.00	—
1934	900,000	0.50	0.75	1.50	3.00	—
1935	1,500,000	0.50	0.75	1.50	3.00	—
1936	3,300,000	0.25	0.50	1.00	2.00	—
1937 Over reversed 3	—	0.50	1.00	2.00	5.00	—
1937	2,000,000	0.25	0.50	1.00	2.00	—
1938 Over reversed 3	—	0.50	1.00	2.00	5.00	—
1938	5,000,000	0.25	0.50	1.00	2.00	—
1939 Over reversed 3	—	0.50	1.00	2.00	5.00	—
1939	1,200,000	0.25	0.50	1.00	2.00	—
1940	6,100,000	0.25	0.50	1.00	2.00	—
1941	900,000	1.00	2.00	3.00	6.00	—

KM# 151.2 20 CENTAVOS **Weight:** 4.0000 g. **Composition:** 0.5000 Silver .0643 oz. ASW **Obverse:** 0.5 below condor **Note:** Obverse varieties with 0.5 or 0.5. exist.

Date	Mintage	F	VF	XF	Unc	BU
1900/899	334,000	60.00	80.00	—	—	—
1900	Inc. above	30.00	40.00	80.00	150	—
1906/806	—	2.50	6.00	12.00	25.00	—
1906/896	866,000	2.50	6.00	12.00	25.00	—
1906	Inc. above	2.00	5.00	10.00	20.00	—
1907/807	—	2.00	4.00	9.00	18.00	—
1907/895	7,625,000	2.00	4.00	9.00	18.00	—
1907	Inc. above	1.00	3.00	7.00	15.00	—

Note: Exists with both 0.5 and 0.5. obverse varieties

KM# 151.3 20 CENTAVOS **Weight:** 3.0000 g. **Composition:** 0.4000 Silver .0385 oz. ASW **Obverse:** Without 0.5 below condor

Date	Mintage	F	VF	XF	Unc	BU
1907/807	—	1.50	3.50	8.00	16.50	—
1907	1,201,000	1.00	3.00	7.00	15.00	—
1908/808	—	1.50	3.50	8.00	16.50	—
1908	5,869,000	0.75	3.00	6.00	12.00	—
1909	1,080,000	0.75	3.00	6.00	12.00	—
1913/1	3,507,000	0.75	3.00	6.00	12.00	—
1913/50	Inc. above	0.75	3.00	6.00	12.00	—
1913	Inc. above	1.50	4.00	8.00	20.00	—
1919	3,749,000	0.75	3.00	6.00	12.00	—
1920	4,189,000	0.75	3.00	6.00	12.00	—

KM# 151.4 20 CENTAVOS **Weight:** 3.0000 g. **Composition:** 0.4500 Silver .0434 oz. ASW **Obverse:** 0.45 below condor

Date	Mintage	F	VF	XF	Unc	BU
1916	3,377,000	2.00	4.00	8.00	20.00	—

KM# 167.1 20 CENTAVOS **Composition:** Copper-Nickel **Obverse:** Without designer's name O. ROTY at bottom **Reverse:** Large 20 **Edge:** Plain

Date	Mintage	F	VF	XF	Unc	BU
1920	499,000	1.00	2.50	5.50	15.00	—
1921	6,547,000	0.35	1.00	3.00	7.00	—
1922	8,261,000	0.35	1.00	3.00	7.00	—
1923	5,439,000	0.35	1.00	3.00	7.00	—
1924	16,096,000	0.35	1.00	3.00	7.00	—
1925	9,830,000	0.35	1.00	3.00	7.00	—

Note: Varieties exist with dot under 5 in date for 1925

Date	Mintage	F	VF	XF	Unc	BU
1929	9,685,000	0.35	1.00	3.00	7.00	—

KM# 167.2 20 CENTAVOS **Composition:** Copper-Nickel **Obverse:** Without designer's name **Reverse:** Small 20

Date	Mintage	F	VF	XF	Unc	BU
1925	—	—	—	—	—	—
1932 Over reversed 3	—	0.75	1.50	3.00	8.00	—
1932	—	0.50	1.00	2.00	6.00	—
1933 Over reversed 3X	—	0.50	1.00	2.00	5.00	—
1933/ Reversed 33	59,000,000	0.50	1.00	2.00	5.00	—
1933	Inc. above	0.35	0.75	1.25	3.50	—
1937	—	0.50	1.00	2.00	5.00	—

KM# 167.4 20 CENTAVOS **Composition:** Copper-Nickel **Obverse:** With designer's name O. ROTY at bottom

Date	F	VF	XF	Unc	BU
1929	1.00	2.50	5.00	10.00	—

KM# 167.3 20 CENTAVOS **Composition:** Copper-Nickel **Obverse:** With designer's name O. ROTY at bottom

Date	Mintage	F	VF	XF	Unc	BU
1932 Over reversed 3	—	0.50	1.00	2.00	6.50	—
1932	—	0.35	0.75	1.25	5.00	—
1933 Over reversed 3X	—	1.00	1.50	2.50	7.00	—
1933/ Reversed 33	1,000,000	1.00	1.50	2.50	7.00	—
1933	Inc. above	0.35	0.75	1.25	5.00	—
1937 Over reversed 3	—	1.00	1.50	2.50	7.00	—
1937	—	0.35	0.75	1.25	5.00	—
1938	3,043,000	0.35	0.75	1.25	5.00	—
1939 3/reversed 3	5,283,000	1.00	1.50	2.50	7.00	—
1939	Inc. above	0.35	0.75	1.25	3.50	—
1940	9,300,000	0.35	0.75	1.25	3.00	—
1941	3,000,000	0.35	0.75	1.25	3.50	—

KM# 177 20 CENTAVOS **Composition:** Copper **Obverse:** Bust of General Bernardo O'Higgins, Thenot on truncation

Date	Mintage	F	VF	XF	Unc	BU
1942	30,000,000	0.15	0.25	0.50	3.00	—
1943	396,000,000	0.15	0.25	0.50	3.00	—
1944	29,100,000	0.15	0.25	0.50	3.00	—
1945	11,400,000	0.15	0.25	0.50	3.00	—
1946	13,800,000	0.15	0.25	0.50	3.00	—
1947	15,700,000	0.15	0.25	0.50	3.00	—
1948	15,200,000	0.15	0.25	0.50	3.00	—
1949	14,700,000	0.15	0.25	0.50	3.00	—
1950	15,200,000	0.15	0.25	0.50	3.00	—
1951	14,700,000	0.15	0.25	0.50	3.00	—
1952	15,500,000	0.15	0.25	0.50	3.00	—
1953	7,800,000	0.15	0.25	0.50	3.00	—

KM# 163 40 CENTAVOS **Weight:** 6.0000 g. **Composition:** 0.4000 Silver .0771 oz. ASW

Date	Mintage	F	VF	XF	Unc	BU
1907	56,000	15.00	30.00	60.00	150	—
1908/6	—	7.00	14.00	28.00	55.00	—
1908	1,452,000	6.00	12.00	25.00	50.00	—

KM# 160 50 CENTAVOS **Weight:** 10.0000 g. **Composition:** 0.7000 Silver .2250 oz. ASW **Note:** Varieties with 0.7 or 0.7. exist.

Date	Mintage	F	VF	XF	Unc	BU
1902	2,022,000	5.00	10.00	20.00	40.00	—
1903	1,111,000	5.00	10.00	20.00	40.00	—
1905	1,075,000	5.00	10.00	20.00	40.00	—

KM# 178 50 CENTAVOS **Composition:** Copper **Obverse:** Bust of General Bernardo O'Higgins, Thenot on truncation **Edge:** Plain

Date	Mintage	F	VF	XF	Unc	BU
1942	4,715,000	1.00	2.00	5.00	10.00	—

KM# 152.2 PESO **Weight:** 20.0000 g. **Composition:** 0.7000 Silver .4501 oz. ASW **Obverse:** 0.7 below condor

Date	Mintage	F	VF	XF	Unc	BU
1902	178,000	12.00	25.00	60.00	125	—
1903	372,000	8.00	17.00	35.00	75.00	—
1905	429,000	8.00	17.00	35.00	75.00	—

KM# 152.3 PESO **Weight:** 12.0000 g. **Composition:** 0.9000 Silver .3472 oz. ASW **Obverse:** 0.9 below condor

Date	Mintage	F	VF	XF	Unc	BU
1910	2,166,000	4.00	6.00	12.00	25.00	—

KM# 152.4 PESO **Weight:** 9.0000 g. **Composition:** 0.7200 Silver .2083 oz. ASW **Obverse:** 0.72 below condor

Date	Mintage	F	VF	XF	Unc	BU
1915	6,032,000	3.75	5.00	6.50	15.00	—
1917	3,033,000	4.00	5.50	10.00	20.00	—

KM# 152.5 PESO **Weight:** 9.0000 g. **Composition:** 0.5000 Silver .1446 oz. ASW **Obverse:** 0.5 below condor

Date	Mintage	F	VF	XF	Unc	BU
1921	2,287,000	2.25	3.50	7.00	15.00	—
1922	2,718,000	2.25	3.50	7.00	15.00	—

KM# 152.6 PESO **Weight:** 9.0000 g. **Composition:** 0.5000 Silver .1446 oz. ASW **Note:** Struck with medal rotation.

Date	Mintage	F	VF	XF	Unc	BU
1924	1,748,000	2.25	3.50	7.00	15.00	—
1925	2,037,000	2.25	3.50	7.00	15.00	—

Note: Varieties of 1925 dated coins exist with flat and curved tops

KM# A171.1 PESO **Weight:** 9.0000 g. **Composition:** 0.5000 Silver .1446 oz. ASW **Obverse:** KM#152.5 **Reverse:** KM#171 **Note:** A mule, with 0.5 and without mint mark on obverse.

Date	F	VF	XF	Unc	BU
1927	15.00	30.00	45.00	90.00	—

KM# 171.1 PESO **Weight:** 9.0000 g. **Composition:** 0.5000 Silver .1446 oz. ASW **Reverse:** Thin 1 in denomination

Date	Mintage	F	VF	XF	Unc	BU
1927So	3,890,000	4.00	6.00	10.00	20.00	—

KM# 171.2 PESO **Weight:** 9.0000 g. **Composition:** 0.5000 Silver .1446 oz. ASW **Reverse:** Thick 1 in denomination **Note:** Varieties 0.5 and 0,5 exist. Total of 2,431,608 pieces dated 1921-1927 were melted down in 1932.

Date	F	VF	XF	Unc	BU
1927So	4.00	6.00	10.00	20.00	—

KM# 174 PESO **Weight:** 6.0000 g. **Composition:** 0.4000 Silver .0771 oz. ASW

Date	Mintage	F	VF	XF	Unc	BU
1932	4,000,000	1.75	2.75	5.00	10.00	—

KM# 176.1 PESO **Composition:** Copper-Nickel

Date	Mintage	F	VF	XF	Unc	BU
1933	29,976,000	0.35	0.75	1.75	3.50	—

KM# 176.2 PESO **Composition:** Copper-Nickel **Obverse:** O ROTY incuse on rock base

Date	Mintage	F	VF	XF	Unc	BU
1940	150,000	2.00	3.00	6.00	12.00	—

KM# 179 PESO **Composition:** Copper **Obverse:** General Bernardo O'Higgins

Date	Mintage	F	VF	XF	Unc	BU
1942	15,150,000	0.10	0.35	2.00	9.00	—
1943	16,900,000	0.10	0.35	2.00	9.00	—
1944	12,050,000	0.10	0.35	2.00	9.00	—
1945	7,600,000	0.10	0.35	2.00	9.00	—
1946	2,050,000	0.10	0.35	5.00	15.00	—
1947	2,200,000	0.10	0.35	5.00	15.00	—
1948	5,900,000	0.10	0.25	2.00	5.00	—
1949	7,100,000	0.10	0.20	1.00	4.00	—
1950	7,250,000	0.10	0.20	1.00	4.00	—
1951	8,150,000	0.10	0.20	1.00	4.00	—
1952	10,400,000	0.10	0.20	1.00	4.00	—
1953 Short top 5	17,200,000	0.10	0.20	1.00	3.00	—
1953 Long top 5	Inc. above	0.10	0.20	1.00	3.00	—
1954	7,566,000	0.10	0.20	1.00	3.00	—

KM# 179a PESO **Composition:** Aluminum

Date	Mintage	F	VF	XF	Unc	BU
1954	43,550,000	0.10	0.15	0.50	1.50	—
1955	69,050,000	0.10	0.15	0.50	1.50	—
1956	58,250,000	0.10	0.15	0.50	1.50	—
1956 Proof	—	—	—	—	—	—
1957	49,250,000	0.10	0.15	0.50	1.50	—
1958	29,900	0.10	0.15	0.50	1.50	—

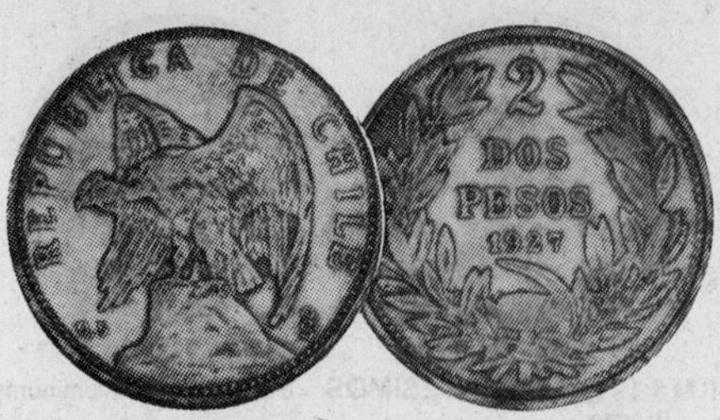

KM# 172 2 PESOS **Weight:** 18.0000 g. **Composition:** 0.5000 Silver .2893 oz. ASW **Note:** Obverse varieties 0.5 and 0,5 with curved top and flat top 5 exist. 459,510 pieces were melted down in 1932.

Date	Mintage	F	VF	XF	Unc	BU
1927	1,060,000	BV	4.00	9.00	20.00	—

KM# 159 5 PESOS **Weight:** 2.9955 g. **Composition:** 0.9170 Gold .0883 oz. AGW

Date	Mintage	F	VF	XF	Unc	BU
1900	1,265,000	50.00	90.00	120	150	—
1911	1,399	—	—	200	350	—

KM# 173.1 5 PESOS **Weight:** 25.0000 g. **Composition:** 0.9000 Silver .7234 oz. ASW **Reverse:** Wide 5

Date	Mintage	F	VF	XF	Unc	BU
1927	965,000	10.00	13.50	20.00	45.00	—

KM# 173.2 5 PESOS **Weight:** 25.0000 g. **Composition:** 0.9000 Silver .7234 oz. ASW **Reverse:** Narrow 5 **Note:** Varieties 0.9 and 0,9 exist. 436,510 pieces of KM#173.1 and #173.2 were melted down in 1932.

Date	Mintage	F	VF	XF	Unc	BU
1927	—	10.00	13.50	20.00	45.00	—

KM# 180 5 PESOS **Composition:** Aluminum

Date	Mintage	F	VF	XF	Unc	BU
1956	1,600,000	0.15	0.35	0.50	0.85	—

KM# 182 5 PESOS **Weight:** 22.5000 g. **Composition:** 0.9990 Silver .7228 oz. ASW **Subject:** 150th Anniversary of Naval Academy **Reverse:** Bust of Arturo Prat

Date	Mintage	F	VF	XF	Unc	BU
1968 Proof	1,200	Value: 25.00				

KM# 157 10 PESOS **Weight:** 5.9910 g. **Composition:** 0.9170 Gold .1766 oz. AGW

Date	Mintage	F	VF	XF	Unc	BU
1901	1,651,000	BV	100	125	200	—

KM# 181 10 PESOS **Composition:** Aluminum

Date	Mintage	F	VF	XF	Unc	BU
1956	13,100,000	0.15	0.35	0.50	0.75	—
1957	28,800,000	0.15	0.35	0.50	0.75	—
1958	44,500,000	0.15	0.35	0.50	0.75	—
1959	10,220,000	0.25	0.50	1.00	1.50	—

KM# 183 10 PESOS **Weight:** 45.0000 g. **Composition:** 0.9990 Silver 1.4455 oz. ASW **Subject:** Arrival of Liberation Fleet in 1820

Date	Mintage	F	VF	XF	Unc	BU
1968 Proof	1,215	Value: 85.00				

KM# 158 20 PESOS **Weight:** 11.9821 g. **Composition:** 0.9170 Gold .3532 oz. AGW

Date	Mintage	F	VF	XF	Unc	BU
1906	41,000	—	BV	165	275	—
1907	12,000	—	BV	165	275	—
1908	26,000	—	BV	165	275	—
1910	28,000	—	BV	165	275	—
1911	17,000	—	BV	165	275	—
1913/11	18,000	—	BV	165	275	—
1913	Inc. above	—	BV	165	275	—
1914	22,000	—	BV	165	275	—
1915	65,000	—	BV	165	275	—
1916	36,000	—	BV	165	275	—
1917	717,000	—	BV	165	275	—

KM# 168 20 PESOS **Weight:** 4.0679 g. **Composition:** 0.9000 Gold .1177 oz. AGW

Date	Mintage	F	VF	XF	Unc	BU
1926	85,000	—	BV	65.00	90.00	—
1958	500	BV	65.00	125	200	—
1959	25,000	—	—	BV	70.00	—
1961	20,000	—	—	BV	70.00	—
1964	—	—	—	BV	70.00	—

Date	Mintage	F	VF	XF	Unc	BU
1976	99,000	—	—	BV	70.00	—
1977	38,000	—	—	BV	70.00	—
1979	30,000	—	—	BV	70.00	—
1980	30,000	—	—	BV	70.00	—

KM# 188 20 PESOS **Weight:** 4.0679 g. **Composition:** 0.9000 Gold .1177 oz. AGW **Reverse:** Coat of arms on ornamental vines

Date	F	VF	XF	Unc	BU
1976	—	BV	65.00	90.00	—

KM# 169 50 PESOS **Weight:** 10.1698 g. **Composition:** 0.9000 Gold .2943 oz. AGW

Date	Mintage	F	VF	XF	Unc	BU
1926	126,000	—	BV	120	150	—
1958	10,000	—	—	BV	150	—
1961	20,000	—	—	BV	150	—
1962	30,000	—	—	BV	150	—
1965	—	—	—	BV	150	—
1966	—	—	—	BV	150	—
1967	—	—	—	BV	150	—
1968	—	—	—	BV	150	—
1969	—	—	—	BV	150	—
1970	—	—	—	—	650	—
1974	—	—	—	BV	150	—

KM# 184 50 PESOS **Weight:** 10.1698 g. **Composition:** 0.9000 Gold .2943 oz. AGW **Subject:** 150th Anniversary of Military Academy

Date	Mintage	F	VF	XF	Unc	BU
1968 Proof	2,515	Value: 185				

KM# 170 100 PESOS **Weight:** 20.3397 g. **Composition:** 0.9000 Gold .5886 oz. AGW

Date	Mintage	F	VF	XF	Unc	BU
1926	678,000	—	BV	200	285	—

KM# 175 100 PESOS **Weight:** 20.3397 g. **Composition:** 0.9000 Gold .5886 oz. AGW **Obverse:** Revised bust and legend style **Reverse:** Revised legend style

Date	Mintage	F	VF	XF	Unc	BU
1932	9,315	—	BV	325	425	—
1946	260,000	—	—	BV	265	—
1947	540,000	—	—	BV	265	—
1948	420,000	—	—	BV	265	—
1949	310,000	—	—	BV	265	—

Date	Mintage	F	VF	XF	Unc	BU
1950	20,000	—	—	BV	265	—
1951	145,000	—	—	BV	265	—
1952	245,000	—	—	BV	265	—
1953	175,000	—	—	BV	265	—
1954	190,000	—	—	BV	265	—
1955	150,000	—	—	BV	265	—
1956	60,000	—	—	BV	265	—
1957	40,000	—	—	BV	265	—
1958	157,000	—	—	BV	265	—
1959	90,000	—	—	BV	265	—
1960	200,000	—	—	BV	265	—
1961	295,000	—	—	BV	265	—
1962	260,000	—	—	BV	265	—
1963	210,000	—	—	BV	265	—
1964	—	—	—	BV	265	—
1968	—	—	—	BV	265	—
1969	—	—	—	BV	265	—
1970	—	—	—	BV	265	—
1971	—	—	—	BV	265	—
1972	—	—	—	BV	265	—
1973	—	—	—	BV	265	—
1974	—	—	—	BV	265	—
1976	172,000	—	—	BV	265	—
1977	25,000	—	—	BV	265	—
1979	100,000	—	—	BV	265	—
1980	50,000	—	—	BV	265	—

KM# 185 100 PESOS **Weight:** 20.3397 g. **Composition:** 0.9000 Gold .5886 oz. AGW **Subject:** 150th Anniversary of National Coinage

Date	Mintage	F	VF	XF	Unc	BU
1968 Proof	1,815	Value: 375				

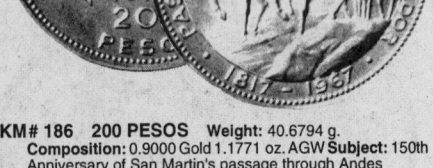

KM# 186 200 PESOS **Weight:** 40.6794 g. **Composition:** 0.9000 Gold 1.1771 oz. AGW **Subject:** 150th Anniversary of San Martin's passage through Andes Mountains

Date	Mintage	F	VF	XF	Unc	BU
1968 Proof	965	Value: 750				

KM# 187 500 PESOS **Weight:** 101.6985 g. **Composition:** 0.9000 Gold 2.9427 oz. AGW **Subject:** 150th Anniversary of National Flag

Date	F	VF	XF	Unc	BU
1968 Proof	—	Value: 1,950			

REFORM COINAGE

10 Pesos = 1 Centesimo; 100 Centesimos = 1 Escudo

KM# 192 1/2 CENTESIMO **Composition:** Aluminum

Date	Mintage	F	VF	XF	Unc	BU
1962	3,750,000	—	0.10	0.30	0.50	—
1962 Proof	—	—	—	—	—	—
1963	8,100,000	—	0.10	0.30	0.50	—

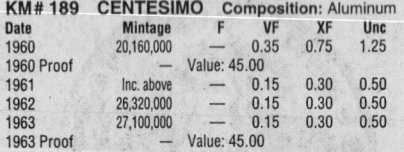

KM# 189 CENTESIMO **Composition:** Aluminum

Date	Mintage	F	VF	XF	Unc	BU
1960	20,160,000	—	0.35	0.75	1.25	—
1960 Proof	—	Value: 45.00				
1961	Inc. above	—	0.15	0.30	0.50	—
1962	26,320,000	—	0.15	0.30	0.50	—
1963	27,100,000	—	0.15	0.30	0.50	—
1963 Proof	—	Value: 45.00				

KM# 193 2 CENTESIMOS **Composition:** Aluminum-Bronze

Date	Mintage	F	VF	XF	Unc	BU
1960	2,050,000	—	—	—	50.00	—
Note: Not released for circulation						
1960 Proof	—	Value: 50.00				
1964	2,050,000	—	—	0.10	1.00	—
1965	32,550,000	—	—	0.10	1.00	—
1966	31,800,000	—	—	0.10	1.00	—
1967	34,750,000	—	—	0.10	1.00	—
1967 Proof	—	Value: 50.00				
1968	29,400,000	—	—	0.10	1.00	—
1969	—	—	—	—	2.50	—
1969 Proof	—	Value: 50.00				
1970	20,250,000	—	—	0.10	1.00	—

KM# 190 5 CENTESIMOS **Composition:** Aluminum-Bronze

Date	Mintage	F	VF	XF	Unc	BU
1960 Proof	—	Value: 100				
1961	12,000	—	2.50	5.00	10.00	—
1962	—	—	—	—	—	—
1964	16,628,000	—	0.10	0.15	1.00	—
1965	27,680,000	—	0.10	0.15	1.00	—
1966	32,360,000	—	0.10	0.15	1.00	—
1966 Proof	—	Value: 50.00				
1967	19,680,000	—	0.10	0.15	1.00	—
1968	4,400,000	—	0.10	0.15	1.00	—
1968 Proof	—	Value: 50.00				
1969	13,200,000	—	—	—	3.50	—
1969 Proof	—	Value: 50.00				
1970	30,680,000	—	0.10	0.15	1.00	—
1971	16,080,000	—	0.10	0.15	1.00	—

KM# 191 10 CENTESIMOS **Composition:** Aluminum-Bronze

Date	Mintage	F	VF	XF	Unc	BU
1960	—	—	2.00	3.50	6.50	—
1960 Proof	—	Value: 70.00				
1961	1,915,000	—	0.10	0.20	1.00	—
1962	1,480,000	—	0.10	0.20	1.00	—
1963 Small date	10,980,000	—	0.10	0.20	1.00	—
1964	27,070,000	—	0.10	0.20	1.00	—
1965	49,480,000	—	0.10	0.20	1.00	—
1966	60,680,000	—	0.10	0.20	1.00	—
1967	27,520,000	—	0.10	0.25	1.00	—
1967 Proof	—	Value: 50.00				
1968	8,040,000	—	0.10	0.20	1.00	—
1969	15,660,000	—	—	—	3.50	—
1970 Large date	42,080,000	—	0.10	0.20	1.00	—

KM# 194 10 CENTESIMOS **Composition:** Aluminum-Bronze **Obverse:** Bust of Bernardo O'Higgins

Date	Mintage	F	VF	XF	Unc	BU
1971	99,700,000	—	—	0.10	0.15	—

KM# 195 20 CENTESIMOS **Composition:** Aluminum-Bronze **Obverse:** Bust of Jose Manuel Balmaceda

Date	Mintage	F	VF	XF	Unc	BU
1971	89,200,000	—	—	0.10	0.20	—
1972	—	—	0.10	0.20	1.00	—

KM# 196 50 CENTESIMOS **Composition:** Aluminum-Bronze **Obverse:** Bust of Manuel Rodriguez

Date	Mintage	F	VF	XF	Unc	BU
1971	58,300,000	—	0.10	0.15	0.25	—

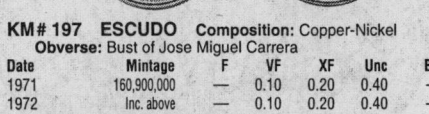

KM# 197 ESCUDO **Composition:** Copper-Nickel **Obverse:** Bust of Jose Miguel Carrera

Date	Mintage	F	VF	XF	Unc	BU
1971	160,900,000	—	0.10	0.20	0.40	—
1972	Inc. above	—	0.10	0.20	0.40	—
1972 Proof	—	Value: 50.00				

KM# 198 2 ESCUDOS **Composition:** Copper-Nickel **Obverse:** Caupolican, Chief of Araucanian Indians

Date	Mintage	F	VF	XF	Unc	BU
1971	106	—	—	—	125	—
Note: Not released for circulation						
1971 Proof	—	Value: 50.00				

KM# 199 5 ESCUDOS Composition: Copper-Nickel

Date	F	VF	XF	Unc	BU
1971	—	0.10	0.25	0.75	—
1972	—	0.10	0.25	0.75	—
1972 Proof	—	Value: 50.00			

KM# 199a 5 ESCUDOS Composition: Aluminum

Date	F	VF	XF	Unc	BU
1972	—	0.10	0.15	0.20	—

KM# 200 10 ESCUDOS Composition: Aluminum

Date	Mintage	F	VF	XF	Unc	BU
1974	33,750,000	—	0.10	0.15	0.35	—
1974 Proof	—	Value: 50.00				
1975	31,600,000	—	0.10	0.15	0.35	—

KM# 201 50 ESCUDOS Composition: Nickel-Brass

Date	Mintage	F	VF	XF	Unc	BU
1974	5,700,000	—	0.15	0.25	0.60	—
1975	20,300,000	—	0.15	0.20	0.50	—

KM# 202 100 ESCUDOS

Date	Mintage	F	VF	XF	Unc	BU
1974	32,100,000	—	0.20	0.35	0.75	—
1975	65,600,000	—	0.20	0.35	0.75	—

REFORM COINAGE

100 Centavos = 1 Peso; 1000 Old Escudos = 1 Peso

KM# 203 CENTAVO Composition: Aluminum

Date	Mintage	F	VF	XF	Unc	BU
1975	2,000,000	—	0.10	0.15	0.50	—

KM# 204 5 CENTAVOS Composition: Aluminum-Bronze

Date	Mintage	F	VF	XF	Unc	BU
1975	5,400,000	—	—	0.10	0.25	—
1976	6,600,000	—	—	—	—	—

Note: Although recorded with mintage, no examples are known with this date

KM# 204a 5 CENTAVOS Composition: Aluminum

Date	Mintage	F	VF	XF	Unc	BU
1976	5,000,000	—	—	0.10	0.25	—

KM# 205 10 CENTAVOS Composition: Aluminum-Bronze

Date	Mintage	F	VF	XF	Unc	BU
1975	8,600,000	—	—	0.10	0.25	—
1976	9,000,000	—	—	—	—	—

Note: Although recorded with mintage, no examples are known with this date

KM# 205a 10 CENTAVOS Composition: Aluminum

Date	Mintage	F	VF	XF	Unc	BU
1976	6,600,000	—	—	0.10	0.25	—
1977	57,800,000	—	—	0.10	0.25	—
1978	58,050,000	—	—	0.10	0.25	—
1979	101,950,000	—	—	0.10	0.25	—

KM# 206 50 CENTAVOS Composition: Copper-Nickel

Date	Mintage	F	VF	XF	Unc	BU
1975	38,000,000	—	—	0.10	0.25	—
1976	1,000,000	—	0.50	1.00	2.00	—
1977	10,000,000	—	—	0.10	0.25	—

KM# 206a 50 CENTAVOS Composition: Aluminum-Bronze

Date	Mintage	F	VF	XF	Unc	BU
1978	19,250,000	—	—	0.10	0.25	—
1979	28,000,000	—	—	0.10	0.25	—

KM# 207 PESO Composition: Copper-Nickel **Obverse:** Bust of Bernardo O'Higgins **Obv. Legend:** BERNARDO O'HIGGINS

Date	Mintage	F	VF	XF	Unc	BU
1975	51,000,000	—	0.10	0.15	0.25	—

KM# 208 PESO Composition: Copper-Nickel **Obverse:** Bust of Bernardo O'Higgins **Obv. Legend:** LIBERTADOR. B. O'HIGGINS

Date	Mintage	F	VF	XF	Unc	BU
1976	30,000,000	—	—	0.10	0.25	—
1977	20,000,000	—	—	0.10	0.25	—

KM# 208a PESO Composition: Aluminum-Bronze

Date	Mintage	F	VF	XF	Unc	BU
1978	39,706,000	—	—	0.10	0.25	—
1979	63,000,000	—	—	0.10	0.25	—

KM# 216.1 PESO Composition: Aluminum-Bronze **Note:** Reduced size, 17 millimeters. Wide date.

Date	Mintage	F	VF	XF	Unc	BU
1981	40,000,000	—	—	0.10	0.20	—
1984	60,000,000	—	—	0.10	0.20	—
1985	20,000,000	—	—	0.10	0.20	—
1986	45,000,000	—	—	0.10	0.20	—
1987	80,000,000	—	—	0.10	0.20	—

KM# 216.2 PESO Composition: Aluminum-Bronze **Note:** Narrow date.

Date	Mintage	F	VF	XF	Unc	BU
1988	105,000,000	—	—	0.10	0.20	—
1989	205,000,000	—	—	0.10	0.20	—
1990	140,000,000	—	—	0.10	0.20	—
1991	140,000,000	—	—	0.10	0.20	—
1992	—	—	—	0.10	0.20	—

KM# 231 PESO Composition: Aluminum **Note:** Varieties exist.

Date	F	VF	XF	Unc	BU
1992	—	—	—	0.10	—
1993	—	—	—	0.10	—
1994	—	—	—	0.10	—
1995	—	—	—	0.10	—
1996	—	—	—	0.10	—
1997	—	—	—	0.10	—
1998	—	—	—	0.10	—
1999	—	—	—	0.10	—
2000	—	—	—	0.10	—
2001	—	—	—	0.10	—
2002	—	—	—	0.10	—

KM# 209 5 PESOS Composition: Copper-Nickel **Subject:** 3rd Anniversary of New Government

Date	Mintage	F	VF	XF	Unc	BU
1976	2,100,000	—	0.15	0.25	2.00	—
1977	28,300,000	—	0.15	0.25	2.00	—
1978	11,704,000	—	0.15	0.25	2.00	—
1980	8,200,000	—	0.15	0.25	2.00	—

KM# 217.1 5 PESOS Composition: Nickel-Brass 19 oz. **Note:** Wide date, 19 millimeters.

Date	Mintage	F	VF	XF	Unc	BU
1981	17,000,000	—	—	0.10	0.50	—
1982	20,000,000	—	—	0.10	0.50	—
1984	12,000,000	—	—	0.10	0.50	—
1985	16,000,000	—	—	0.10	0.50	—
1986	16,000,000	—	—	0.10	0.50	—
1987	8,000,000	—	—	0.10	0.50	—

KM# 217.2 5 PESOS Composition: Nickel-Brass **Note:** Narrow date.

Date	Mintage	F	VF	XF	Unc	BU
1988	27,000,000	—	—	0.10	0.50	—
1989	32,000,000	—	—	0.10	0.50	—
1990	23,000,000	—	—	0.10	0.50	—

KM# 229 5 PESOS Composition: Nickel-Brass **Obverse:** Bust of Bernardo O'Higgins right **Reverse:** Denomination, date

Date	Mintage	F	VF	XF	Unc	BU
1990	8,000,000	—	—	0.10	0.50	—
1991	2,000,000	—	—	0.10	0.50	—
1992	—	—	—	0.10	0.50	—

KM# 232 5 PESOS Composition: Aluminum-Bronze **Note:** Varieties exist.

Date	F	VF	XF	Unc	BU
1992	—	—	0.10	0.35	—
1993	—	—	0.10	0.35	—
1994	—	—	0.10	0.35	—
1995	—	—	0.10	0.35	—
1996	—	—	0.10	0.35	—
1997	—	—	0.10	0.35	—
1998	—	—	0.10	0.35	—
1999	—	—	0.10	0.35	—
2000	—	—	0.10	0.35	—
2001	—	—	0.10	0.35	—
2001 (sa)	—	—	0.15	0.50	—
2002A	—	—	0.15	0.50	—
2002	—	—	0.10	0.35	—

KM# 210 10 PESOS **Composition:** Copper-Nickel **Subject:** 3rd Anniversary of New Government

Date	Mintage	F	VF	XF	Unc	BU
1976	2,100,000	—	0.10	0.20	1.25	—
1977	30,000,000	—	0.10	0.20	1.00	—
1978	20,004,000	—	0.10	0.20	1.00	—
1979	7,000,000	—	0.10	0.20	1.00	—
1980	20,000,000	—	0.10	0.20	1.00	—

KM# 211 10 PESOS **Weight:** 44.8000 g. **Composition:** 0.9990 Silver 1.4390 oz. ASW **Subject:** 3rd Anniversary of New Government

Date	Mintage	F	VF	XF	Unc	BU
ND(1976) Proof	1,000	Value: 115				

KM# 218.1 10 PESOS **Composition:** Nickel-Brass **Note:** Wide date, narrow rim.

Date	Mintage	F	VF	XF	Unc	BU
1981	55,000,000	—	0.10	0.20	0.50	—
1982	45,000,000	—	0.10	0.20	0.50	—
1984	30,000,000	—	0.10	0.20	0.50	—
1985	400,000	—	0.50	1.50	3.50	—
1986 Narrow date	25,000,000	—	0.10	0.20	0.50	—
1986 Wide date	Inc. above	—	0.10	0.20	0.50	—
1987	8,000,000	—	0.10	0.20	0.50	—

KM# 218.2 10 PESOS **Composition:** Nickel-Brass **Note:** Narrow date.

Date	Mintage	F	VF	XF	Unc	BU
1988	45,000,000	—	0.10	0.20	0.50	—
1989	73,000,000	—	0.10	0.20	0.50	—

KM# 218.3 10 PESOS **Composition:** Nickel-Brass **Note:** Wide rim.

Date	Mintage	F	VF	XF	Unc	BU
1990	10,000,000	—	0.10	0.20	0.50	—

KM# 228.1 10 PESOS **Composition:** Nickel-Brass **Obverse:** Small bust of Bernardo O'Higgins right, wide rim

Date	Mintage	F	VF	XF	Unc	BU
1990	5,000,000	—	0.10	0.20	0.50	—
1993	—	—	0.10	0.20	0.50	—

KM# 228.2 10 PESOS **Composition:** Nickel-Brass **Obverse:** Large bust of Bernardo O'Higgins right, normal rim

Date	Mintage	F	VF	XF	Unc	BU
1990	25,000,000	—	0.10	0.20	0.50	—
1991	—	—	0.10	0.20	0.50	—
1992	—	—	0.10	0.20	0.50	—
1993	—	—	0.10	0.20	0.50	—
1994	—	—	0.10	0.20	0.50	—
1995	—	—	0.10	0.20	0.50	—
1996	—	—	0.10	0.20	0.50	—
1997	—	—	0.10	0.20	0.50	—
1998	—	—	0.10	0.20	0.50	—
1999	—	—	0.10	0.20	0.50	—
2000	—	—	0.10	0.20	0.50	—

KM# 212 50 PESOS **Weight:** 10.1500 g. **Composition:** 0.9000 Gold .2937 oz. AGW **Subject:** 3rd Anniversary of New Government

Date	Mintage	F	VF	XF	Unc	BU
ND(1976)	1,900	—	—	—	200	—
ND(1976) Proof	Inc. above	Value: 225				

KM# 219.1 50 PESOS **Composition:** Aluminum-Bronze **Note:** Wide date.

Date	Mintage	F	VF	XF	Unc	BU
1981	12,000,000	—	0.25	0.50	1.25	—
1982	14,000,000	—	0.25	0.50	1.25	—
1985	400,000	—	0.60	1.50	3.50	—
1986	1,000,000	—	0.25	0.50	1.25	—
1987	4,000,000	—	0.25	0.50	1.25	—

KM# 219.2 50 PESOS **Composition:** Aluminum-Bronze **Note:** Narrow date.

Date	Mintage	F	VF	XF	Unc	BU
1988	4,800,000	—	0.25	0.50	1.25	—
1989	4,000,000	—	0.25	0.50	1.25	—
1991	10,845,000	—	0.25	0.50	1.25	—
1992	—	—	0.25	0.50	1.25	—
1993	—	—	0.25	0.50	1.25	—
1994	—	—	0.25	0.50	1.25	—
1995	—	—	0.25	0.50	1.25	—
1996	—	—	0.25	0.50	1.25	—
1997	—	—	0.25	0.50	1.25	—
1998	—	—	0.25	0.50	1.25	—
1999	—	—	0.25	0.50	1.25	—
2000	—	—	0.25	0.50	1.25	—
2001	—	—	0.25	0.50	1.25	—
2002	—	—	0.25	0.50	1.25	—

KM# 213 100 PESOS **Weight:** 20.3000 g. **Composition:** 0.9000 Gold .5874 oz. AGW **Subject:** 3rd Anniversary of New Government

Date	Mintage	F	VF	XF	Unc	BU
1976	2,900	—	—	—	350	—
1976 Proof	100	Value: 750				

KM# 226.1 100 PESOS **Composition:** Aluminum-Bronze **Note:** Wide date with pointed 9.

Date	Mintage	F	VF	XF	Unc	BU
1981	10,000,000	—	0.50	0.75	2.50	—
1984	8,000,000	—	0.50	0.75	2.50	—
1985	15,000,000	—	0.50	0.75	2.50	—
1986	11,000,000	—	0.50	0.75	2.50	—
1987	15,000,000	—	0.50	0.75	2.50	—

KM# 226.2 100 PESOS **Composition:** Aluminum-Bronze **Note:** Narrow date with curved 9.

Date	Mintage	F	VF	XF	Unc	BU
1989	20,000,000	—	0.50	0.75	2.50	—
1991	4,320,000	—	0.50	0.75	2.50	—
1992	—	—	0.50	0.75	2.50	—
1993	—	—	0.50	0.75	2.50	—
1994	—	—	0.50	0.75	2.50	—
1995	—	—	0.50	0.75	2.50	—
1996	—	—	0.50	0.75	2.50	—
1997	—	—	0.50	0.75	2.50	—
1998	—	—	0.50	0.75	2.50	—
1999	—	—	0.50	0.75	2.50	—
2000	—	—	0.50	0.75	2.50	—

KM# 236 100 PESOS **Ring Composition:** Brass **Center Weight:** 7.3000 g. **Center Composition:** Copper-Nickel **Subject:** Mapuche **Obverse:** Bust of Indian facing **Reverse:** National arms above denomination **Edge:** Reeded and striated sections **Size:** 23.5 mm.

Date	F	VF	XF	Unc	BU
2001	—	—	—	2.50	—

KM# 214 500 PESOS **Weight:** 102.2700 g. **Composition:** 0.9000 Gold 2.9595 oz. AGW **Subject:** 3rd Anniversary of New Government **Note:** Similar to 100 Pesos, KM#213.

Date	Mintage	F	VF	XF	Unc	BU
1976	500	—	—	—	1,850	—
1976 Proof	700	Value: 1,850				

KM# 235 500 PESOS **Ring Composition:** Copper-Nickel **Center Weight:** 6.5000 g. **Center Composition:** Aluminum-Bronze **Subject:** Cardenal Raul Silva Henrique **Obverse:** Bust of Henrique in inner ring facing left **Reverse:** Denomination with date below **Edge:** Reeded **Size:** 25.9 mm.

Date	F	VF	XF	Unc	BU
2000	—	—	—	6.00	—
2000 Proof	—	—	—	—	—
2001	—	—	—	6.00	—
2002 Narrow date	—	—	—	6.00	—
2002 Wide date	—	—	—	6.00	—

KM# 233 2000 PESOS **Weight:** 8.2000 g. **Composition:** 0.5000 Silver .1318 oz. ASW **Subject:** 250th Anniversary of the Mint

Date	Mintage	F	VF	XF	Unc	BU
1993	50,000	—	—	—	16.50	—

KM# 230 10000 PESOS **Weight:** 27.0000 g. **Composition:** 0.9250 Silver .8029 oz. ASW **Series:** Ibero - American

Date	Mintage	F	VF	XF	Unc	BU
1991 Proof	75,000	Value: 45.00				

SILVER BULLION COINAGE

KM# 223 1/4 ONZA **Weight:** 7.7770 g. **Composition:** 0.9990 Silver .2500 oz. ASW **Subject:** 10th Anniversary of National Liberation

Date	Mintage	F	VF	XF	Unc	BU
ND(1983) Proof	1,000	Value: 12.50				

KM# 224 1/2 ONZA **Weight:** 15.5530 g. **Composition:** 0.9990 Silver .5000 oz. ASW **Subject:** 10th Anniversary of National Liberation

Date	Mintage	F	VF	XF	Unc	BU
ND(1983) Proof	1,000	Value: 25.00				

KM# 225 ONZA **Weight:** 31.1070 g. **Composition:** 0.9990 Silver 1.0000 oz. ASW **Subject:** 10th Anniversary of National Liberation

Date	Mintage	F	VF	XF	Unc	BU
ND(1983) Proof	1,000	Value: 45.00				

GOLD BULLION COINAGE

KM# 220 1/4 ONZA **Weight:** 8.6400 g. **Composition:** 0.9000 Gold .2500 oz. AGW **Subject:** 10th Anniversary of National Liberation **Note:** Similar to KM#223.

Date	Mintage	F	VF	XF	Unc	BU
ND(1983)	1,000	—	—	—	175	—

KM# 221 1/2 ONZA **Weight:** 17.2800 g. **Composition:** 0.9000 Gold .5000 oz. AGW **Subject:** 10th Anniversary of National Liberation **Note:** Similar to KM#224.

Date	Mintage	F	VF	XF	Unc	BU
ND(1983)	1,000	—	—	—	350	—

KM# 227 ONZA **Weight:** 31.1000 g. **Composition:** 0.9990 Gold 1.0000 oz. AGW

Date	Mintage	F	VF	XF	Unc	BU
1948	1,950	—	—	—	800	—

KM# 215 ONZA **Weight:** 31.1000 g. **Composition:** 0.9990 Gold 1.0000 oz. AGW **Obverse:** Crowned arms **Reverse:** Crowned pillars and worlds

Date	Mintage	F	VF	XF	Unc	BU
1978	—	—	—	—	750	—
1979	1,580	—	—	—	600	—
1980	1,730	—	—	—	600	—
1981	200	—	—	—	700	—
1983	999	—	—	—	650	—
1983 Proof	1	—	—	—	—	—

KM# 222 ONZA **Weight:** 34.5590 g. **Composition:** 0.9000 Gold 1.0000 oz. AGW **Subject:** 10th Anniversary of National Liberation **Note:** Similar to KM#225.

Date	Mintage	F	VF	XF	Unc	BU
1983	1,000	—	—	—	675	—

PATTERNS

Including off metal strikes

KM#	Date	Mintage	Identification	Mkt Val
PnA26	1908	—	Copper-Nickel.	125
PnB26	1908	—	10 Centavos. Brass.	—
Pn26	1914	—	Peso. Silver.	600
PnA27	1914	—	2 Pesos. Silver. Piefort, large flan.	500
Pn27	1914	—	2 Pesos. Silver. Piefort, small flan.	500
Pn28	1916	—	20 Centavos. Silver. 4.0000 g.	—
Pn29	1916	—	20 Centavos. Silver. 4.0400 g.	—
Pn30	1917	—	10 Centavos. Silver. 1.9000 g.	—
Pn31	1917	—	10 Centavos. Silver. 2.5200 g.	—
Pn32	1919	—	Copper-Nickel.	—
Pn33	1919	—	Silver. 1.4900 g.	—
Pn34	1919	—	Silver. 1.5300 g.	—
Pn35	1919	—	10 Centavos. Copper-Nickel.	—
Pn36	1919	—	20 Centavos. Copper-Nickel.	—
Pn37	ND19xx	—	10 Centavos. Copper-Nickel. Center hole.	—
Pn38	1926	—	Peso. Silver.	550
Pn39	1926	—	Peso. Silver. Fineness added.	550
Pn40	1926	—	Peso. Silver. Coat of arms. Without fineness.	600
Pn41	1926	—	2 Pesos. Silver. Condor. Coat of arms. Without fineness.	1,000
Pn42	1926	—	2 Pesos. Silver. Indian. Star in wreath. "5" fineness, Pn#43.	600
Pn43	1926	—	2 Pesos. Silver. Indian. Star in wreath. "72" fineness, Pn44.	600
Pn44	1926	—	5 Pesos.	1,500
Pn45	1926	—	5 Pesos. Silver. Weak or no fineness (effaced from die).	1,500
Pn46	1926	—	5 Pesos. Silver.	1,250
Pn47	1927	—	Peso. Copper-Nickel.	250
Pn48	1927	—	Peso. Silver.	500
Pn49	1927	—	5 Pesos. Silver.	300
Pn50	1929	—	20 Centavos. Copper-Nickel. Center hole.	125
Pn51	1929	—	20 Centavos. Copper-Nickel. Pn49 but "CHILE" on reverse instead of "20"	125
Pn52	1929	—	Peso. Silver.	250
Pn53	ND(1929)	—	Peso. Silver. Without country, date or fineness.	250
Pn54	ND(1929)	—	Peso. Silver. Similar to Pn52, without mountains on obverse.	250
Pn55	1930	—	20 Centavos. Copper-Nickel. Center hole.	200
Pn56	1930	—	20 Centavos. Copper-Nickel. Pn54 but "20" instead of "CHILE" on obverse, with center hole.	200
Pn57	1930	—	Peso. Silver. Worker and factory. Value.	300
Pn58	1930	—	2 Pesos. Copper-Nickel. Condor. Value and date in wreath.	325
PnA59	1933	—	Peso. Nickel. KM#176.1.	—
Pn59	1933	—	Peso. Copper-Nickel. Condor. Value and date in wreath.	250
PnA60	1933	—	Peso. Copper-Nickel. Condor. Value and date in wreath. Mint punched cancelled.	250
PnA62	ND(1938)	—	5 Pesos. (No Composition). Plain edge. Aluminum-Bronze or Silver.	400
Pn62	ND(1938)	—	5 Pesos. Silver. Without date.	300
Pn60	1938	—	5 Pesos. Brass.	—
Pn61	1938	—	5 Pesos. Copper-Nickel.	—
PnA63	1941	—	20 Centavos. Bronze.	100
Pn63	1942	—	Peso. Copper. Like KM#179, but smaller diameter.	100
Pn64	1947	—	100 Pesos. Copper.	—
Pn65	1948	—	Onza. Silver.	75.00
Pn65a	1948	—	Onza. Copper.	25.00
PnA66	1951	—	10 Pesos. Aluminum-Bronze. Thick flan.	100
Pn66	1953	—	20 Centavos. Aluminum.	125
Pn67	1956	—	5 Pesos. Brass. KM#180.	—
Pn68	1959	—	10 Pesos. Brass. KM#181.	—
Pn69	1960	—	2 Centesimos. Brass. Uniface.	100
Pn70	1960	—	2 Centesimos. Copper-Nickel.	60.00
PnA70	1960	—	2 Centesimos. Aluminum-Bronze.	—
Pn71	1960	—	5 Centesimos. Copper. KM#190.	100
Pn72	1960	—	5 Centesimos. Copper-Nickel. Plain edge. KM#190.	90.00
Pn73	1960	—	5 Centesimos. Copper-Nickel. Milled edge. KM#190.	75.00
Pn74	1960	—	10 Centesimos. Copper. KM#191.	100
Pn75	1960	—	10 Centesimos. Copper-Nickel. KM#191.	40.00
Pn76	1960	—	10 Centesimos. Brass. KM#191.	—
Pn77	1960	—	10 Centesimos. Brass.	—
Pn78	1960	—	10 Centesimos. Aluminum-Bronze. Legend. Arms flanked by C-M.	65.00
Pn79	1960	—	10 Centesimos. Copper-Nickel. Legend. Arms flanked by C-M.	65.00
Pn80	1964	—	2 Centesimos. Copper-Nickel. KM#193.	75.00
Pn81	1968	—	100 Pesos. Copper. Center hole.	125
Pn82	1969	—	Peso. Copper-Nickel. Ten sided. Ten sided, arms with "C.M." below.	100
Pn83	1971	—	Peso. Nickel.	—
PnB84	1971	—	2 Escudos. Silver. KM#198.	—
PnC84	1972	—	5 Escudos. Silver. KM#199.	—
PnA84	1972	—	Escudo. Silver. KM197.	—
	1972	—	Escudo. Silver. KM197.	—
Pn84	1974	—	10 Escudos. Aluminum.	—
Pn85	1979	5	100 Pesos. 0.5000 Silver. Equestrian statue of O'Higgins.	—

PIEFORTS

KM#	Date	Mintage	Identification	Mkt Val
P4	1951	—	10 Pesos. Aluminum-Bronze. KM#181.	125

TRIAL STRIKES

KM#	Date	Mintage	Identification	Mkt Val
TS7	ND(1960)	—	10 Centesimos. Copper-Nickel. Coat of arms flanked by C-M. Coat of arms flanked by C-M.	60.00
TS8	ND(1960)	—	10 Centesimos. Aluminum-Bronze. Coat of arms flanked by C-M. Coat of arms flanked by C-M.	50.00

PROOF SETS

KM#	Date	Mintage	Identification	Issue Price	Mkt Val
PS1	1968 (6)	—	KM#182-187. Total of 12,000 coins struck for each denomination including those available singly	560	3,350
PS2	1968 (4)	—	KM#184-187. Total of 12,000 coins struck for each denomination including those available singly	528	3,250
PS3	1968 (2)	—	KM#182, 183. Total of 12,000 coins struck for each denomination including those available singly	31.50	100
PS4	1971/2 (3)	—	KM#197 (1972), KM#198 (1971), KM#199 (1972). Total of 12,000 coins struck for each denomination including those available singly	—	150

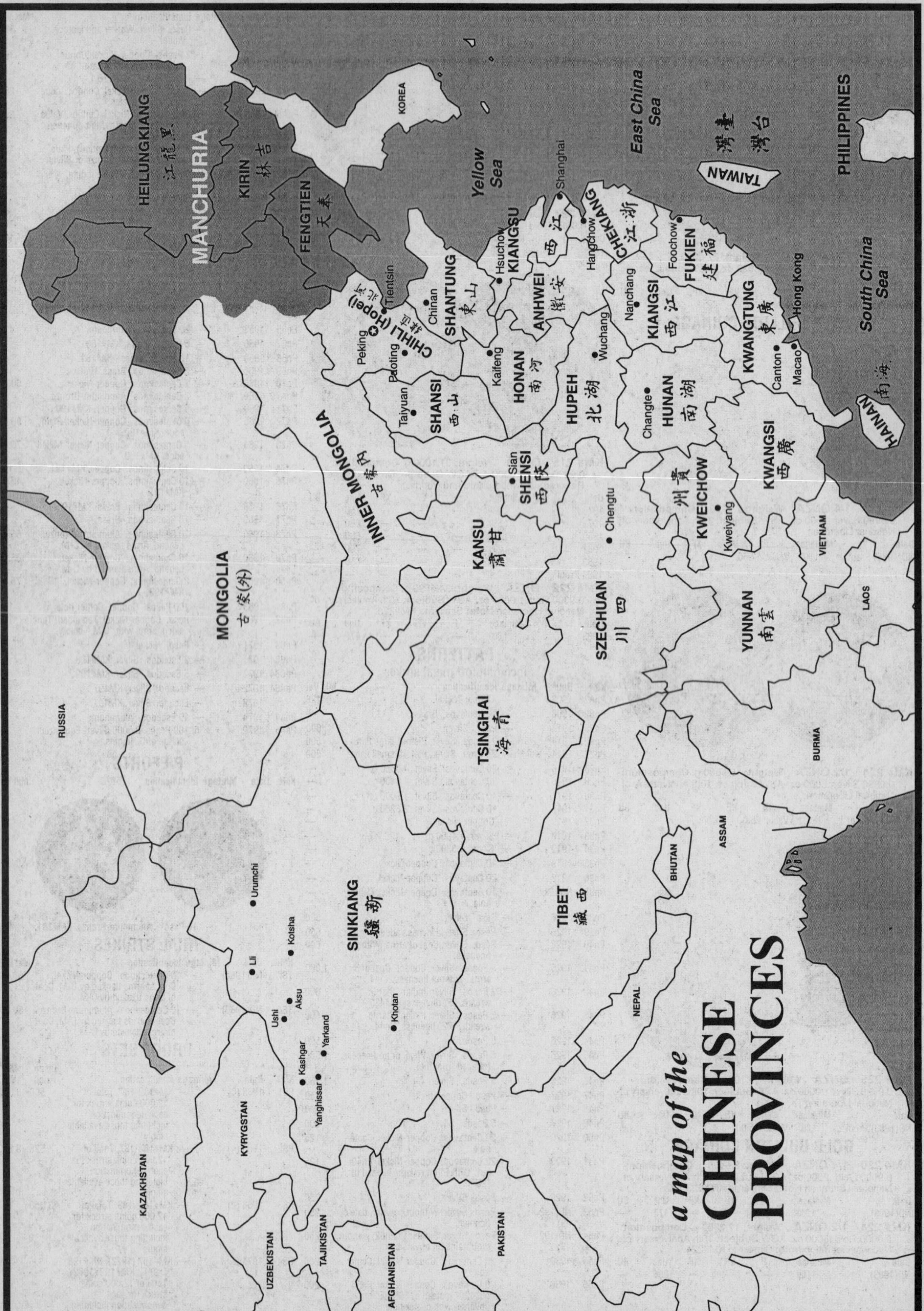
a map of the
CHINESE PROVINCES
MANCHURIA
HEILUNGKIANG
KIRIN
FENGTIEN
KOREA
Yellow Sea
East China Sea
TAIWAN
PHILIPPINES
South China Sea
HAINAN
CHIHLI (Hopei)
Peking
Tientsin
Paoting
SHANTUNG
Chinan
KIANGSU
Hsuchow
Shanghai
CHEKIANG
Hangchow
ANHWEI
FUKIEN
Foochow
KIANGSI
Nanchang
KWANGTUNG
Canton
Hong Kong
Macao
HONAN
Kaifeng
SHANSI
Taiyuan
HUPEH
Wuchang
HUNAN
Changte
KWANGSI
KWEICHOW
Kweiyang
SHENSI
Sian
SZECHUAN
Chengtu
YUNNAN
VIETNAM
LAOS
BURMA
ASSAM
BHUTAN
NEPAL
TIBET
TSINGHAI
KANSU
INNER MONGOLIA
MONGOLIA
SINKIANG
Urumchi
Kotsha
Lli
Aksu
Ushi
Khotan
Yarkand
Kashgar
Yanghissar
RUSSIA
KAZAKHSTAN
KYRGYSTAN
UZBEKISTAN
TAJIKISTAN
AFGHANISTAN
PAKISTAN

CHINA

Before 1912, China was ruled by an imperial government. The republican administration which replaced it was itself supplanted on the Chinese mainland by a communist government in 1949, but it has remained in control of Taiwan and other offshore islands in the China Sea with a land area of approximately 14,000 square miles and a population of more than 14 million. The People's Republic of China administers some 3.7 million square miles and an estimated 1.19 billion people. This communist government, officially established on October 1, 1949, was admitted to the United Nations, replacing its nationalist predecessor, the Republic of China, in 1971.

Cast coins in base metals were used in China many centuries before the Christian era, but locally struck coinages of the western type in gold, silver, copper and other metals did not appear until 1888.In spite of the relatively short time that modern coins have been in use, the number of varieties is exceptionally large.

Both Nationalist and Communist China, as well as the pre-revolutionary Imperial government and numerous provincial or other agencies, including some foreign-administered agencies and governments, have issued coins in China. Most of these have been in dollar (yuan) or dollar-fraction denominations, based on the internationally used dollar system, but coins in tael denominations were issued in the 1920's and earlier. The striking of coins nearly ceased in the late 1930's through the 1940's due to the war effort and a period of uncontrollable inflation while vast amounts of paper currency were issued by the Nationalist, Communist and Japanese occupation institutions.

EMPERORS

Obverse Types

KUANG-HSÜ

(Te Tsung) 德宗

1875-1908

Type A

光緒

Kuang-hsü T'ung-pao 光緒通寶

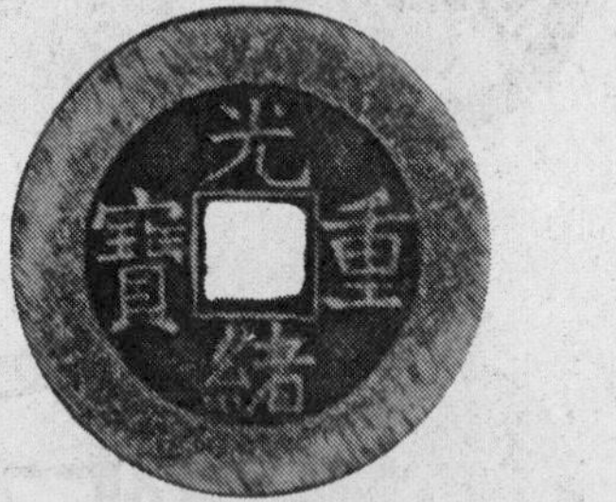

Type B

Kuang-hsü Chung-pao 光緒重寶

Type C

Kuang-hsü Yuan-pao 光緒元寶

Kuang-hsü - When the previous emperor died, his mother, the Empress Dowager Tz'u-hsi, chose her four-year-old nephew, born August 14, 1871, as emperor. She adopted the boy so that she could act as regent and on February 25, 1875, the young prince ascended the throne, taking the reign title of Kuang-hsü. In 1898 he tried to assert himself and collected a group of progressive officials around him. He issued a series of edicts for revamping of the military, abolition of civil service examinations, improvement of agriculture and restructuring of administrative procedures. During Kuang-hsü's reign (1875-1908) the Empress Dowager totally dominated the government. She confined the emperor to his palace and spread rumors that he was deathly ill. Foreign powers let it be known they would not take kindly to the Emperor's death. This saved his life but thereafter he had no power over the government. On November 15, 1908, Tz'u-hsi died under highly suspicious circumstances and the usually healthy emperor was announced as having died the previous day.

HSÜAN-T'UNG 宣統

1908-1911

Type A

Hsüan-t'ung T'ung-pao 宣統

Hsuan-t'ung - The last emperor of the Ch'ing dynasty in China and Japan's puppet emperor, under the assumed name of K'ang-te, in Manchoukuo from 1934 to 1945, was born on February 7, 1906. He succeeded to the throne at the age of three on November 14, 1908. He reigned under a regency for three years but on February 12, 1912, was forced to abdicate the throne. He was permitted to continue living in the palace in Peking until he left secretly in 1924. On March 9, 1932, he was installed as president, and from 1934 to 1945 was emperor of Manchoukuo under the reign title of K'ang-te. He was taken prisoner by the Russians in August of 1945 and returned to China as a war criminal in 1950. He was pardoned in 1959 and went to live in Peking where he worked in the repair shop of a botanical garden. He died peacefully in Peking in 1967.

Although Hsüan-t'ung became Emperor in 1908, all the coins of his reign are based on an Accession year of 1909.

憲洪

HUNG-HSIEN

(Yuan Shih-k'ai) 宣統 通

Dec. 15, 1915 - March 21, 1916

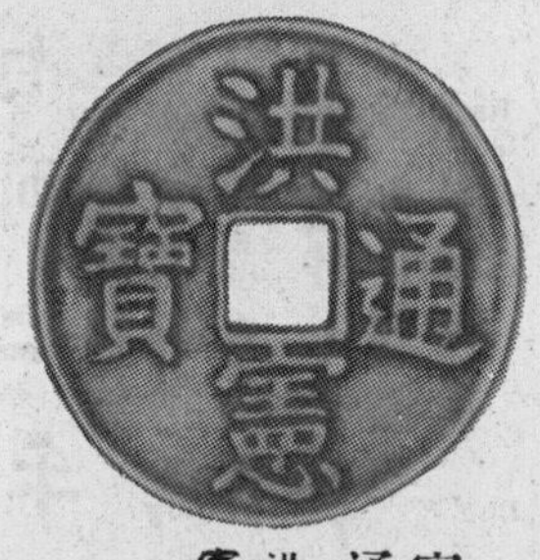

Hung-hsien T'ung-pao 憲洪 通寶

Hung-hsien (more popularly known as Yuan Shih-K'ai). Born in 1859 in Honan Province, he was the first Han Chinese to hold a viceroyalty and become a grand councillor without any academic qualifications. In 1885 he was made Chinese commissioner at Seoul. During the Boxer Rebellion of 1900, the division under his command was the only remnant of China's army to survive. He enjoyed the trust and support of the dowager empress, Tz'u-hsi, and at her death he was stripped of all his offices. However, when the tide of the revolution threatened to engulf the Manchus Yuan appeared as the only man who could lead the country to peace and unity. Both the Emperor and the provisional president recommended that Yuan be the first president of China. He contrived to make himself president for life and boldly tried to create a new imperial dynasty in 1915-1916. He died of uremia on June 6, 1916.

NOTE: For other legend types refer to Rebel Issues listed after Yunnan-Szechuan.

PROVINCIAL NAMES

(and other source indicators)

Provincial names throughout the catalog are based on the Wade-Giles transliteration of the Chinese word. Current spellings, known as the "Pinyin" form, are widely adopted by the printed media. Example: Sinkiang = Xinjiang.

	Single Character (1)	Full Name (Right to left reading)
ANHWEI Also An-hwi, Anhui,(Wan) now Anhui	皖	徽安
CHEKIANG Also Cheh-kiang,(Che) now Zhejiang	浙	江浙
CHIHLI Also Hopei (after 1928)(Chih) now Hebei	直	隸直
CH'ING DYNASTY Also Tsing Dynasty now Qing Dynasty		清大
CHING-KIANG Also Tsing-kiang(Huai now Qingjiang	淮	江清
FENGTIEN Also Fung-tien, Fun-tien Shengching, Manchurian Provinces,(Feng now Liaoning	奉	天奉
FUKIEN Also Foo-kien, F.K.,(Min) now Fujian	閩	建福
HEILUNGKIANG Also Hei Lung Kiang, now Heilongjiang	黑	江龍黑
HONAN Also Ho-nan,(Yu) now Henan	豫	南河
HOPEH Also Chihli, Hopei, (Chi) now Hebei	冀	北河
HUNAN Also Hu-nan, now/Hsiang Hunan	湘	南湖
HUPEH Also Hupei, Hu-peh,(O) now Hubei	鄂	北湖
HU PU (Board of Revenue) Also Hu Poo, Hoo Poo(Hu	户	部户
KANSU Now Gansu(Kan)	甘	肅甘
KIANGNAN Also Kiang Nan(Ning) Now Jiangnan	寗	南江
KIANGSI Also Kiang-si, Kiang-(Kan) see, now Jiangxi	贛	西江
KIANGSI (Alternate)(Kan)	贑	贛
KIANGSU Also Kiang-soo, now(Su) Jiangsu	蘇	蘇江
KIRIN Also Chi-lin Now Jilin(Chi)	吉	林吉
KWANGSI, KWANGSEA	桂	西廣

Also Kwang-si, now(Kuei)
Guangxi

KWANGTUNG 粵 東廣

Also Kwang-tung, now(Yueh)
Guangdong

KWEICHOW 黔 州貴

Also Kweichou, now(Ch'ien)
Guizhou

PEIYANG MINT (Tientsin) 洋北

Pei Yang

SHANSI 山 西山

Now Shanxi(Shan) or (Chin)

SHENSI 陝 西陝

Also Shen-si, now(Shan)
Shaanxi

SHANTUNG, SHAN-TUNG 東 東山

Also Shang-tung,(Tung)
now Shandong(Lu)

SIKANG 魯

SINKIANG (Chinese Turkestan) 新 疆新

Also Sin-kiang, Hsin kiang
Sungarei, now Xinjiang(Hsin)

SZECHUAN 川

Also Szechwan
Szechuen
Now Sichuan(Ch'uan)
or (Shu) 蜀 川四

TAIWAN 臺 弯臺

Also Tai-wan,(Tai)
now Taiwan

TAIWAN 灣台

(Alternate)(Tai

YUNNAN 雲 南雲

Also Yun-nan, now(Yun)
Yunnan

YUNNAN 滇 南雲

(Alternate)(Tien)

TUNG SAN SHENG 省三東

Manchuria

YUNNAN-SZECHUAN 滇川

GOVERNMENTAL NAMES
(and other source indicators)

Full Names
(Right to left reading)

CHITUNG
(Japanese puppet) 府政東冀

CHINESE SOVIET
REPUBLIC 國和共埃維蘇華中

MANCHOUKUO
(Japanese puppet)(2) 國洲滿大

MENGCHIANG
(Japanese puppet) 行銀疆蒙

PEOPLES REPUBLIC OF CHINA
(Communist)(3) 中華人民共和國

REPUBLIC OF CHINA
(Nationalist) 國民華中

NORTH CHINA
(Japanese puppet) 行銀備準合聯國中

(1) Single-character designators for provincial or regional mints are used primarily on copper coins of the Tai Ching Ti Kuo series.
(2) Vertical readings predominate.
(3) Reads left to right.
(4) For lists of mints in Sinkiang, see that section.

ADDITIONAL CHARACTERS

The additional characters illustrated and defined below are found on the reverse of cast bronze cash coins, usually above the square center hole. In the period covered by this catalog the following mints produced cash coins with these additional marks: Board of Revenue and Board of Works in Peking, Kweichow, Aksu and Ili in Sinkiang, Shantung, Szechuan, and all three mints listed in Yunnan.

CHARACTERS

一	I,Yi	十一	Shih i	心	Hsin
二	Erh	合	Ho	宇	Yu
三	San	工	Kung	宙	Chou
四	Szu	主	Chu	來	Lai
五	Wu	川	Ch'uan	往	Wang
六	Liu	之	Chih	晉	Chin
七	Ch'i	正	Cheng	村	Ts'un
八	Pa	又	Yu	日	Jih
九	Chiu	山	Shan	列	Lieh
十	Shih	大	Ta	仁	Jen
主	Chu	中	Chung	丰	Feng
上	Shang	順	Shun	云	Yun
手	Shou	天	T'ien	利	Li
Kung	穴	Fen	分	一	

MINT MARK IDENTIFIER

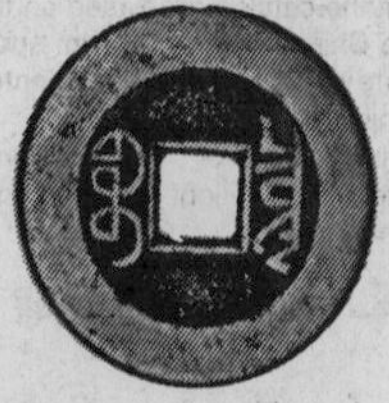

Boo-Clowan
(Peking)

Boo-Yuwan
(Peking)

Hu-PU BOARD OF REVENUE Kung-Pu BOARD OF PUBLIC WORKS

Boo Hu
Hu Mint
ANHWEI

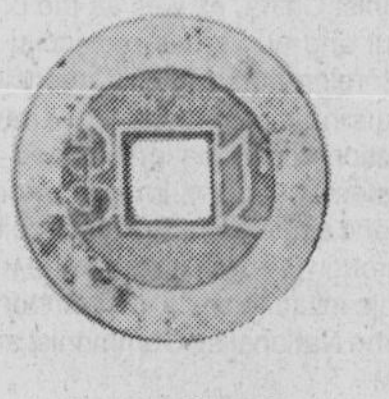

Boo Je
Che Mint
Hangchow
CHEKIANG

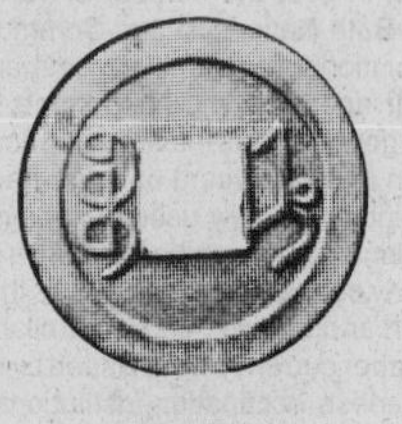

Boo Ji
Chihli Mint
Paoting
CHIHLI

Boo Gi
Chi Mint
Chichow
CHIHLI

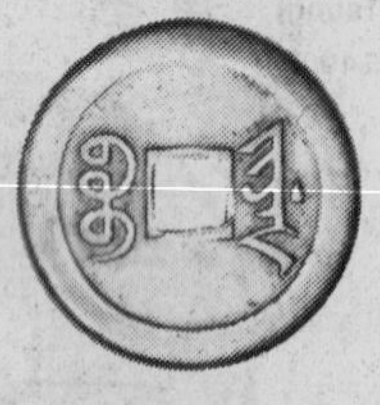

Boo Jiyen
Ching Mint
Tientsin
CHIHLI
(Through Hsien-Feng era)

Boo Fung
FENGTIEN

Boo Fu
Fu Mint
Fuchou
FUKIEN

Boo Ho
Ho Mint
K'aifeng
HONAN

Boo Nan
Nan Mint
Ch'ang-sha
HUNAN

Boo De
Teh Mint
Chengte
CHIHLI

Boo U
Wu Mint
Wuch'ang
HUPEH

Boo Gung
Kungchang
KANSU

Nanchang
KIANGSI

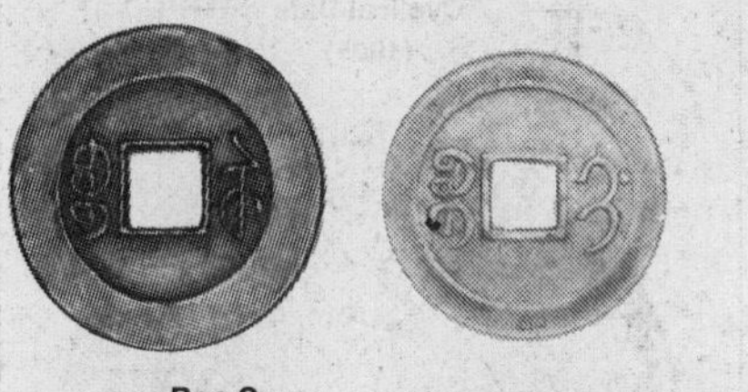

Boo Su
Su Mint
Soohow
KIANGSU

Boo Gi
Chi Mint
KIRIN

(Kuang-hsu era)

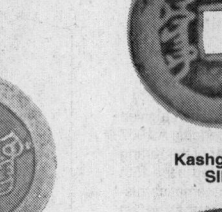

Boo Gui
Kuelin
KWANGSI

Boo Guwang
Canton
KWANGTUNG

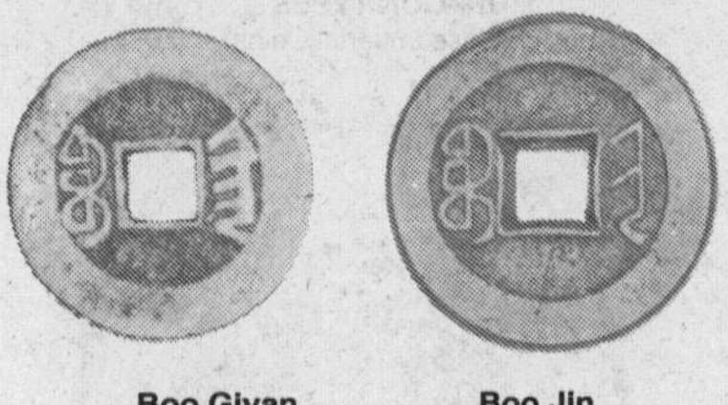

Boo Giyan
Kweiyang
KWEICHOW

Boo Jin
Taiyuan
SHANSI

Boo Ji
Chinan
SHANTUNG

Boo Cuwan
Chengtu
SZECHUAN

Boo San
Shan Mint
Sian
SHENSI

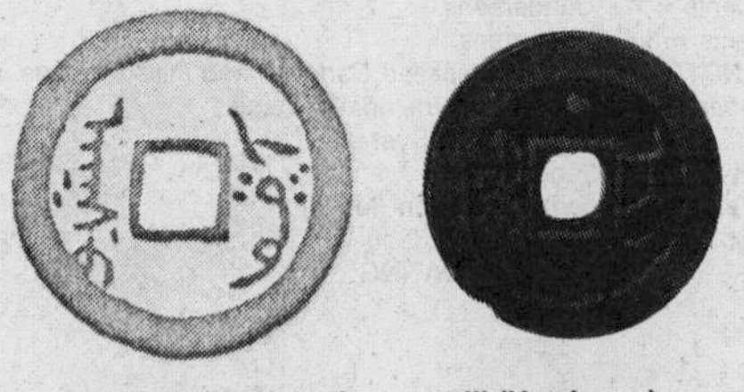

Aksu (Hocheng)
SINKIANG

Ili (Hweiyuan)
SINKIANG

Kotsha (Kuche)
SINKIANG

Kashgar (Shufu)
SINKIANG

Khotan (Hotien)
SINKIANG

Urumchi (Tihwa)
SINKIANG

Ushi (Wushih)
SINKIANG

Yarkand (Soche)
SINKIANG

Tai Mint
TAIWAN

Boo Yon
Yun Mint
Yunnanfu
YUNNAN

Boo Dong
Tung Mint
Tungch'uan
YUNNAN

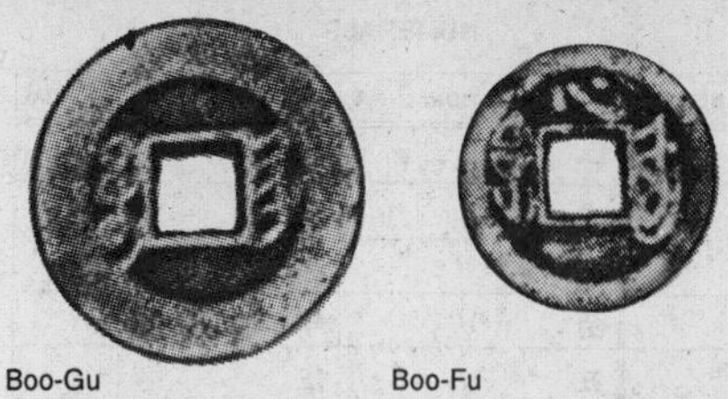

Boo-Gu
Ku Mint
Taku Arsenal
TIENTSIN, CHIHLI

Boo-Fu
Fu Mint
Fuchow
YUNNAN

Boo-Jing
Ching Mint
Chingchow
HUPEH

NON-CIRCULATING ISSUES:

Along with regular circulation coinage produced by the various mints certain cash types were cast in various sizes with the emperor's reign title on the obverse but with various characters and/or symbols not found in our mint identifiers. This listing is not complete but it will benefit the collector as an aid to proper identification.

PALACE ISSUES

(Palace Cash)

Usually 1-6 mace in weight, made of 60" copper and 40" zinc. Made for distribution in the palace during new year. Usually given to eunuchs and guards. Recipients hanged them under lamps - "lamp 'hanging' money."

Rev. leg: T'ien-hsia T'ai-p'ing
"Peace under Heaven."

The market value is about $60.00-100.00 in VF condition.

Obv: Kuang-hsu
Hsuan-t'ung
Rev: I-t'ung T'ien-hsia
"Unify the whole country".

The market value is about $50.00-70.00 in VF condition.

BIRTHDAY CASH

壽 福

These issues have the normal reign title on the obverse but the reverse has two Chinese characters *Fu* in normal or seal script (happiness), at right and *Shou* (birthday) at left. The market value is about $60.00-100.00 in F/VF condition. Some are palace issues, but most are made by private sources as good luck amulets.

Kuang-hsu

NUMERALS

NUMBER	CONVENTIONAL	FORMAL	COMMERCIAL
1	一 元	壹 弌	丨
2	二	弍 貳	〢
3	三	叁 弎	〣
4	四	肆	〤
5	五	伍	〥
6	六	陸	〦
7	七	柒	〧
8	八	捌	〨
9	九	玖	〩
10	十	拾 什	十
20	十 二 or 廿	拾貳	〢十
25	五 十 二 or 五廿	伍拾貳	〢十〥
30	十 三 or 卅	拾叁	〣十
100	百 一	佰壹	丨百
1,000	千 一	仟壹	丨千
10,000	萬 一	萬壹	丨万
100,000	萬十 億一	萬拾 億壹	十万
1,000,000	萬百一	萬佰壹	丨百万

NOTE: This table has been adapted from *Chinese Bank Notes* by Ward Smith and Brian Matravers.

MONETARY UNITS

Dollar Amounts		
DOLLAR (*Yuan*)	元 or 員	圓 or 圜
HALF DOLLAR (*Pan Yuan*)	圓 半	元中
50¢ (*Chiao/Hao*)	角伍	毫伍
10¢ (*Chiao/Hao*)	角壹	毫壹
1¢ (*Fen/Hsien*)	分壹	仙壹

Copper and Cash Coin Amounts			
COPPER (*Mei*)	枚	CASH (*Wen*)	文

Tael Amounts	
1 TAEL (*Liang*)	兩
HALF TAEL (*Pan Liang*)	兩半
5 MACE (*Wu Ch'ien*)	錢伍
1 MACE (*I Ch'ien*)	錢壹
1 CANDEREEN (*I Fen*)	分壹

Common Prefixes			
COPPER (*T'ung*)	銅	GOLD (*Chin*)	金
SILVER (*Yin*)	銀	Ku Ping (*Tael*)*	平庫

NOTE: This table has been adapted from Chinese Bank Notes by Ward Smith and Brian Matravers.

MONETARY SYSTEM

Cash Coin System

800-1600 Cash = 1 Tael
400 Sinkiang 'red' cash = 1 Tael

In theory, 1000 cash were equal to a tael of silver, but in actuality the rate varied from time to time and place to place.

Dollar System

10 Cash (Wen, Ch'ien) = 1 Cent (Fen, ¬¬Hsien)
10 Cents = 1 Chiao (Hao)
100 Cents = 1 Dollar (Yuan)
1 Dollar = 0.72 Tael

Imperial silver coins normally bore no denomination, but were inscribed with their weights as follows:
1 Dollar = 7 Mace and 2 Candareens
50 Cents = 3 Mace and 6 Candareens
20 Cents = 1 Mace and 4.4 Candareens
10 Cents = 7.2 Candareens
5 Cents = 3.6 Candareens

NOTE: *Candareen* is spelled *Candarin* and misspelled as *Caindarin* on Kirin Province Imperial coinage.

Tael System

10 Li = 1 Fen (Candareen)
10 Fen (Candareen) = 1 Ch'ien (Mace)
10 Ch'ien (Mace) = 1 Liang (Tael)

DATING

Most struck Chinese coins are dated by year within a given period, such as the regnal eras or the republican periods. A 1907 issue, for example, would be dated in the 33rd year of the Kuang Hsu era (1875 + 33 - 1 = 1907) or a 1926 issue is dated in the 15th year of the Republic (1912 + 15 - 1 = 1926). The mathematical discrepancy in both instances is accounted for by the fact that the first year is included in the elapsed time. Modern Chinese Communist coins are dated in western numerals using the western calendar, but earlier issues use conventional Chinese numerals. The coins of the Republic of China (Taiwan) are also dated in the year of the Republic, which is added to equal the calendar year. Still another method is a 60-year, repeating cycle, outlined in the table below. The date is shown by the combination of two characters, the first from the top row and the second from the column at left. In this catalog, when a cyclical date is used, the abbreviation CD appears before the AD date.

Dates not in parentheses are those which appear on the coins. For undated coins, dates appearing in parentheses are the years in which the coin was actually minted. Undated coins for which the year of minting is unknown are listed with ND (No Date) in the date or year column.

CYCLICAL DATES

	庚	辛	壬	癸	甲	乙	丙	丁	戊	己
戌	1850 1910		1862 1922		1874 1934		1886 1946		1838 1898	
亥		1851 1911		1863 1923		1875 1935		1887 1947		1839 1899
子	1840 1900		1852 1912		1864 1924		1876 1936		1888 1948	
丑		1841 1901		1853 1913		1865 1925		1877 1937		1889 1949
寅	1830 1890		1842 1902		1854 1914		1866 1926		1878 1938	
卯		1831 1891		1843 1903		1855 1915		1867 1927		1879 1939
辰	1880 1940		1832 1892		1844 1904		1856 1916		1868 1928	
巳		1881 1941		1833 1893		1845 1905		1857 1917		1869 1929
午	1870 1930		1882 1942		1834 1894		1846 1906		1858 1918	
未		1871 1931		1883 1943		1835 1895		1847 1907		1859 1919
申	1860 1920		1872 1932		1884 1944		1836 1896		1848 1908	
酉		1861 1921		1873 1933		1885 1945		1837 1897		1849 1909

NOTE: This table has been adapted from *Chinese Bank Notes* by Ward Smith and Brian Matravers.

GRADING

Chinese coins should not be graded entirely by western standards. In addition to Fine, Very Fine, Extremely Fine (XF), and Uncirculated, the type of strike should be considered weak, medium or sharp strike. China had no rigid minting rules as we know them. For instance, Kirin (Jilin) and Sinkiang (Xinjiang) Provinces used some dies made of iron - hence, they wore out rapidly. Some communist army issues were apparently struck by crude hand methods on soft dies (it is hard to find two coins of the same die!). In general, especially for some minor coins, dies were used until they were worn well beyond western standards. Subsequently, one could have an uncirculated coin struck from worn dies with little of the design or letters still visible, but still uncirculated! All prices quoted are for well-struck (sharp struck), well-centered specimens. Most silver coins can be found from very fine to uncirculated. Some copper coins are difficult to find except in poorer grades.

REFERENCES

The following references have been used for this section:
K - Edward Kann - *Illustrated Catalog of Chinese Coins.*
Hsu - T.K. Hsu - *Illustrated Catalog of Chinese Coins*, 1981 edition.
W - A.M. Tracey Woodward - *The Minted Ten-Cash Coins of China.*

NOTE: The die struck 10 and 20 Cash coins are often found silver plated. This was not done at the mint. They were apparently plated to be passed to the unwary as silver coins.

IDENTIFICATION

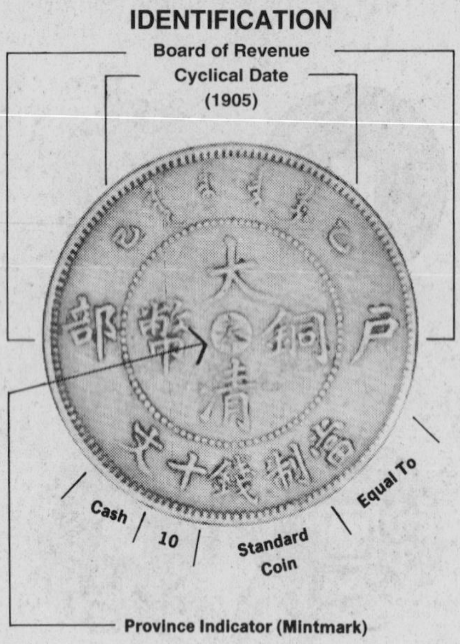

DRAGON TYPES
(Chinese Imperial Coins)

Side View Dragon-left (Silver Coins)

First used by the Kwangtung Mint in 1889. This was the standard (though not the only) dragon used on silver coins. Normally there is no circle around the dragon. Note the fireball beneath the dragon's chin. Normally there are seven flames on the fireball.

Side View Dragon-left (Copper Coins)

First used on copper coins in 1901 or 1902. The dragon may be circled or uncircled. Many varieties exist, with three to seven flames on the fireball.

Side View Dragon-right (Silver Coins)

First appears on the second series of Fukien. The dragon is redesigned with the dragon's body reversed.

Flying Dragon

Introduced in 1901. Copied from the dragon on Japanese coins. China used this dragon only on copper coins (with one rare exception). Note that the clouds around the dragon's body are curly and snake-like instead of puffy like those around the side view dragon. The fireball now appears as a pearl which the dragon is about to grasp, and normally has no flames. This dragon is normally circled.

Front View Dragon

Introduced about 1904, this type of dragon was not used by many mints. The dragon is usually uncircled and has few clouds around its body. Note the tiny mountain under the cloud beneath the fireball.

Tai Ch'ing Ti Kuo Dragon

In 1905 China carried out a coinage reform which standardized the designs of copper coins. All mints were ordered to use the same obverse and reverse designs, but to place a mint mark in the center of the obverse.

SYCEE (INGOTS)

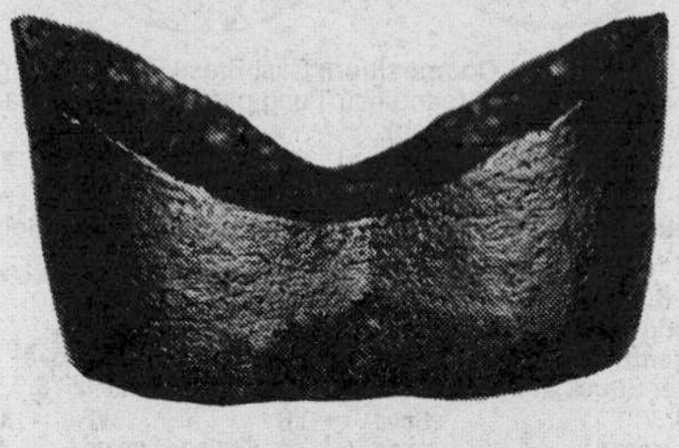

Prior to 1889 the general coinage issued by the Chinese government was the copper-alloy cash coin. Despite occasional short-lived experiments with silver and gold coinage, and disregarding paper money which tended to be unreliable, the government expected the people to get by solely with cash coins. This system worked well for individuals making purchases for themselves, but was unsatisfactory for trade and large business transactions, since a dollar's worth of cash coins weighed about four pounds. As a result, a private currency consisting of silver ingots, usually stamped by the firm which made them, came into use. These were the sycee ingots.

It is not known when these ingots first came into use. Some sources date them to the Yuan (Mongol) dynasty but they are certainly much older. Examples are known from as far back as the Han dynasty (206 BC - 220 AD) but prior to the Sung era (960 - 1280AD) they were used mainly for hoarding wealth. The development of commerce by the Sung dynasty, however, required the use of silver or gold to pay for large purchases. By the Mongol period (1280-1368) silver ingots and paper money had become the dominant currencies, especially for trade. The western explorers who traveled to China during this period (such as Marco Polo) mention both paper money and sycee but not a single one refers to cash coins.

During the Ming dynasty (1368-1644) trade fell off and the use of silver decreased. But toward the end of that dynasty, Dutch and British ships began a new China trade and sycee once again became common. During the 19th and early 20th centuries, the trade in sycee became enormous. Most of the sycee around today are from this period. In 1935 the Chinese government and in 1939 Sinkiang banned the use of sycee and it soon disappeared.

The word sycee (pronounced "sigh - see") is a western corruption of the Chinese word hsi-szu ("fine silk") or hsi yin ("fine silver") and is first known to have appeared in the English language in the late 1600's. By the early 1700's the word appeared regularly in the records of the British East India Company. Westerners also called these ingots "boat money" or "shoe money" owing to the fact that the most common type of ingot resembles a Chinese shoe. The Chinese, however, called the ingots by a variety of names, the most common of which were yuan pao, wen-yin (fine silver) and yin-ting (silver ingot).

The ingots were cast in molds (giving them their characteristic shapes) and while the metal was still semi-liquid, the inscription was impressed. It was due to this procedure that the sides of some sycee are higher than the center. The manufacturers were usually silver firms, often referred to as lu fang's, and after the sycee was finished it was occasionally tested and marked by the kung ku (public assayer).

Sycee were not circulated as we understand it. One didn't usually carry a sycee to market and spend it. Usually the ingots were used as a means of carrying a large amount of money on trips (as we would carry $100 bills instead of $5 bills) or for storing wealth. Large transactions between merchants or banks were paid by means of crates of sycee - each containing 60 fifty tael ingots.

Sycee are known in a variety of shapes the most common of which are the shoe or boat shaped, drum shaped, and loaf shaped (rectangular or hourglass-shaped, with a generally flat surface). Other shapes include one that resembles a double headed axe (this is the oldest type known), one that is square and flat, and others that are "fancy" (in the form of fish, butterflies, leaves, etc.).

Sycee have no denominations as they were simply ingots that passed by weight. Most are in more or less standard weights, however, the most common being 1, 5, 10 and 50 taels. Other weights known include 1/10, 1/5, 1/4, 1/3, 1/2, 2/3, 72/100 (this is the weight of a dollar), 3/4, 2, 3, 4, 6, 7, 8 and 25 taels. Most of the pieces weighing less than 5 taels were used as gifts or souvenirs.

The actual weight of any given value of sycee varied considerably due to the fact that the tael was not a single weight but a general term for a wide range of local weight standards. The weight of the tael varied depending upon location and type of tael in question. For example in one town, the weight of a tael of rice, of silver and of stones may each be different. In addition, the fineness of silver also varied depending upon location and type of tael in question. It was not true, as westerners often wrote, that sycee were made of pure silver. For most purposes, a weight of 37 grams may be used for the tael.

Weights and Current Market Value of Sycee
(Weights are approximate)

1/2 Tael	17-19 grams	26.00
72/100 Tael	25-27 grams	36.00
1 Tael	35-38 grams	46.00
2 Taels	70-75 grams	70.00
3 Taels	100-140 grams	85.00
5 Taels	175-190 grams	110.00
7 Taels	240-260 grams	125.00
10 Taels	350-380 grams	250.00
25 Taels	895-925 grams	3500.
50 Taels	1790-1850 grams	2000.
50 Taels, square	1790-1850 grams	1600.

SZECHUAN WARLORD ISSUE

200 Cash

Obv: Mirror image of normal coin, Y#459.

NOTE: Certain coins found with degenerate or reversed English legends are usually considered to be local warlord issues while some authorities insist on referring to them as contemporary counterfeits.

EMPIRE

GENERAL CAST COINAGE

NOTE: Coins of the Peking Hu Pu Mint in denominations of 6, 9, 20, 30, 300, 400, 600, 700, 900, 4000 and 5000 Cash are considered fantasy issues. Coins of the Peking Kung Pu Mint in denominations of 6, 9, 30, 80 and 90 Cash are considered fantasy issues.

C# 2-15 CASH **Composition:** Cast Brass **Ruler:** Kuang-hsü **Obverse:** Inscription: "Kuang-hsü T'ung-pao" **Note:** Struck at Board of Public Works (Peking).

Date	Good	VG	F	VF	XF
ND(1875-1908)Kung-pu	1.50	3.00	6.00	7.00	—

Note: For crude cast copper strikes, see Sinkiang General Coinage

C# 1-16.2 CASH Composition: Cast Brass **Ruler:** Kuang-hsü **Series:** Thousand Character Classic **Obv. Legend:** "Kuang-hsü T'ung-pao" **Reverse:** "Chou" above **Note:** Struck at Board of Revenue (Peking).

Date	Good	VG	F	VF	XF
ND(1875-1908)Hu-pu	6.00	9.00	13.50	20.00	—

C# 1-16.3 CASH Composition: Cast Brass **Ruler:** Kuang-hsü **Series:** Thousand Character Classic **Obv. Legend:** "Kuang-hsü T'ung-pao" **Reverse:** "Jih" above **Note:** Struck at Board of Revenue (Peking).

Date	Good	VG	F	VF	XF
ND(1875-1908)Hu-pu	6.00	9.00	13.50	20.00	—

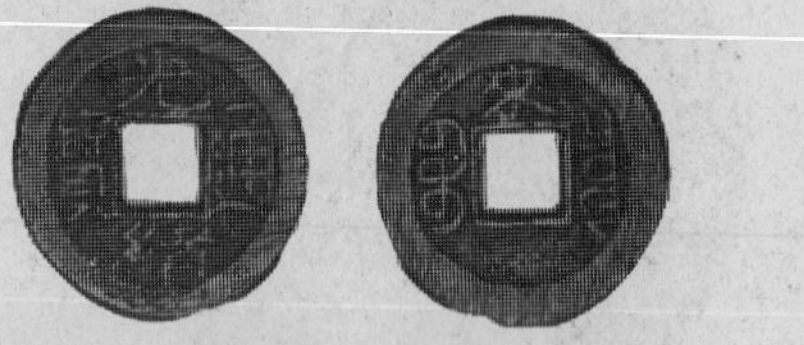

C# 1-16.4 CASH Composition: Cast Brass **Ruler:** Kuang-hsü **Series:** Thousand Character Classic **Obv. Legend:** "Kuang-hsü T'ung-pao" **Reverse:** "Lai" above **Note:** Struck at Board of Revenue (Peking).

Date	Good	VG	F	VF	XF
ND(1875-1908)Hu-pu	6.00	9.00	13.50	20.00	—

C# 1-16.5 CASH Composition: Cast Brass **Ruler:** Kuang-hsü **Series:** Thousand Character Classic **Obv. Legend:** "Kuang-hsü T'ung-pao" **Reverse:** "Lieh" above **Note:** Struck at Board of Revenue (Peking).

Date	Good	VG	F	VF	XF
ND(1875-1908)Hu-pu	6.00	9.00	13.50	20.00	—

C# 1-16.6 CASH Composition: Cast Brass **Ruler:** Kuang-hsü **Series:** Thousand Character Classic **Obv. Legend:** "Kuang-hsü T'ung-pao" **Reverse:** "Wang" above **Note:** Struck at Board of Revenue (Peking).

Date	Good	VG	F	VF	XF
ND(1875-1908)Hu-pu	6.00	9.00	13.50	20.00	—

C# 1-16.7 CASH Composition: Cast Brass **Ruler:** Kuang-hsü **Series:** Thousand Character Classic **Obv. Legend:** "Kuang-hsü T'ung-pao" **Reverse:** "Yu" above **Note:** Struck at Board of Revenue (Peking).

Date	Good	VG	F	VF	XF
ND(1875-1908)Hu-pu	6.00	9.00	13.50	20.00	—

C# 1-16.10 CASH Composition: Cast Brass **Ruler:** Kuang-hsü **Series:** Thousand Character Classic **Obv. Legend:** "Kuang-hsü T'ung-pao" **Reverse:** "Shou" above **Note:** Struck at Board of Revenue (Peking).

Date	Good	VG	F	VF	XF
ND(1875-1908)Hu-pu	6.00	9.00	13.50	20.00	—

C# 1-16 CASH Composition: Cast Brass **Ruler:** Kuang-hsü **Obv. Legend:** "Kuang-hsü T'ung-pao" **Note:** Struck at Board of Revenue (Peking).

Date	Good	VG	F	VF	XF
ND(1875-1908)Hu-pu	1.50	2.00	2.75	4.00	—

Note: For crude cast, red copper issues, see Sinkiang General coinage

C# 1-16.1 CASH Composition: Cast Brass **Ruler:** Kuang-hsü **Series:** Thousand Character Classic **Obv. Legend:** "Kuang-hsü T'ung-pao" **Reverse:** "Chih" above **Note:** Struck at Board of Revenue (Peking). Sch.#1578.

Date	Good	VG	F	VF	XF
ND(1875-1908)Hu-pu	6.00	9.00	13.50	20.00	—

C# 1-16.8 CASH Composition: Cast Brass **Ruler:** Kuang-hsü **Obv. Legend:** "Kuang-hsü T'ung-pao" **Reverse:** Dot below **Note:** Struck at Board of Revenue (Peking).

Date	Good	VG	F	VF	XF
ND(1899-1901)Hu-pu	1.75	3.00	4.00	6.00	—

C# 1-16.9 CASH Composition: Cast Brass **Ruler:** Kuang-hsü **Obv. Legend:** "Kuang-hsü T'ung-pao" **Reverse:** Dot above **Note:** Struck at Board of Revenue (Peking).

Date	Good	VG	F	VF	XF
ND(1899-1901)Hu-pu	1.75	3.00	4.00	6.00	—

C# 2-15.1 CASH Composition: Cast Brass **Ruler:** Kuang-hsü **Series:** Thousand Character Classic **Obv. Legend:** "Kuang-hsü T'ung-pao" **Reverse:** "Chou" above **Note:** Struck at Board of Public Works (Peking).

Date	Good	VG	F	VF	XF
ND(1899-1901Kung-pu	6.00	10.00	15.00	20.00	—

C# 2-15.2 CASH Composition: Cast Brass **Ruler:** Kuang-hsü **Series:** Thousand Character Classic **Obv. Legend:** "Kuang-hsü T'ung-pao" **Reverse:** "Lai" above **Note:** Struck at Board of Public Works (Peking).

Date	Good	VG	F	VF	XF
ND(1899-1901)Kung-pu	6.00	10.00	15.00	20.00	—

C# 2-15.3 CASH Composition: Cast Brass **Ruler:** Kuang-hsü **Series:** Thousand Character Classic **Obv. Legend:** "Kuang-hsü T'ung-pao" **Reverse:** "Lieh" above **Note:** Struck at Board of Public Works (Peking).

Date	Good	VG	F	VF	XF
ND(1899-1901Kung-pu	6.00	10.00	15.00	20.00	—

C# 2-15.4 CASH Composition: Cast Brass **Ruler:** Kuang-hsü **Series:** Thousand Character Classic **Obv. Legend:** "Kuang-hsü T'ung-pao" **Reverse:** "Yu" above **Note:** Struck at Board of Public Works (Peking).

Date	Good	VG	F	VF	XF
ND(1899-1901)Kung-pu	6.00	10.00	15.00	20.00	—

C# 2-15.5 CASH Composition: Cast Brass **Ruler:** Kuang-hsü **Series:** Thousand Character Classic **Obv. Legend:** "Kuang-hsü T'ung-pao" **Reverse:** "Jih" above **Note:** Struck at Board of Public Works (Peking).

Date	Good	VG	F	VF	XF
ND(1899-1901)Kung-pu	6.00	10.00	15.00	20.00	—

C# 2-15.6 CASH Composition: Cast Brass **Ruler:** Kuang-hsü **Series:** Thousand Character Classic **Obv. Legend:** "Kuang-hsü T'ung-pao" **Reverse:** "Wang" above **Note:** Struck at Board of Public Works (Peking).

Date	Good	VG	F	VF	XF
ND(1899-1901)Kung-pu	6.00	10.00	15.00	20.00	—

C# 2-15.7 CASH Composition: Cast Brass **Ruler:** Kuang-hsü **Series:** Thousand Character Classic **Obv. Legend:** "Kuang-hsü T'ung-pao" **Reverse:** "Jih" above, dot below **Note:** Struck at Board of Public Works (Peking).

Date	Good	VG	F	VF	XF
ND(1899-1901)Kung-pu	6.00	10.00	15.00	20.00	—

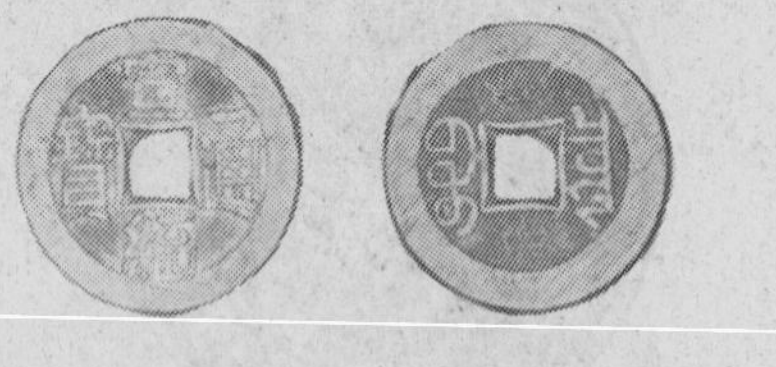

C# 1-19.1 CASH Composition: Cast Brass **Ruler:** Hsüan-t'ung **Obv. Legend:** "Hsüan-t'ung T'ung-pao" **Note:** Struck at Board of Revenue (Peking).

Date	Good	VG	F	VF	XF
ND(1909-11)Hu-pu	5.50	7.00	10.00	15.00	—

C# 1-19.2 CASH Composition: Cast Brass **Ruler:** Hsüan-t'ung **Obv. Legend:** "Hsüan-t'ung T'ung-pao" **Note:** Struck at Board of Revenue (Peking).

Date	Good	VG	F	VF	XF
ND(1909-11)Hu-pu	10.00	15.00	25.00	30.00	—

C# 1-19a CASH Composition: Iron **Ruler:** Hsüan-t'ung **Obv. Legend:** "Hsüan-t'ung T'ung-pao" **Note:** Struck at Board of Revenue (Peking).

Date	Good	VG	F	VF	XF
ND(1909-11)Hu-pu	12.00	20.00	30.00	50.00	—

C# 2-16 5 CASH Composition: Cast Brass **Ruler:** Kuang-hsü **Obv. Legend:** "Kuang-hsü Chung-pao" **Note:** Struck at Board of Public Works (Peking).

Date	Good	VG	F	VF	XF
ND(1875-1908)Kung-pu	200	350	500	700	—

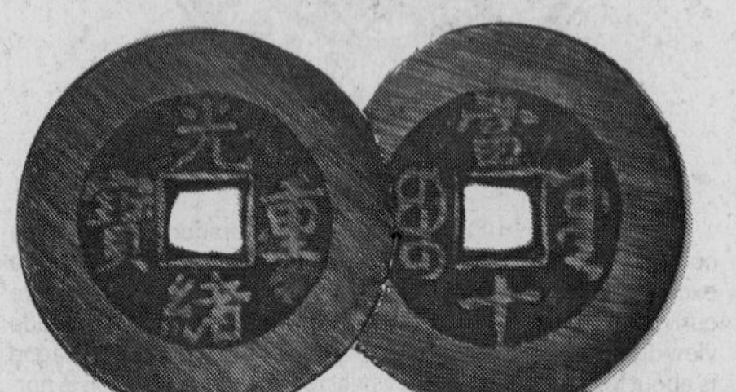

C# 2-17 10 CASH Composition: Cast Brass **Ruler:** Kuang-hsü **Obv. Legend:** "Kuang-hsü T'ung-pao" **Reverse:** Normal Shih(10) below **Note:** Struck at Board of Public Works (Peking). Size varies: 31-32 millimeters.

Date	Good	VG	F	VF	XF
ND(1875-1908)	4.50	7.50	10.00	25.00	—

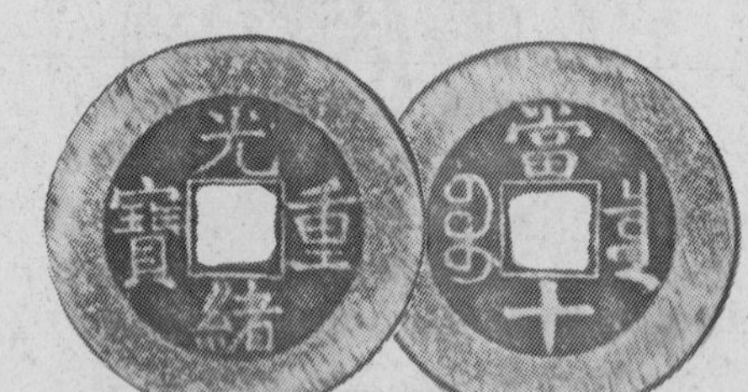

C# 1-17 10 CASH Composition: Cast Brass **Ruler:** Kuang-hsü **Obv. Legend:** "Kuang-hsü Chung-pao" **Reverse:** Normal "Shih" for 10 below **Size:** 30 mm. **Note:** Struck at Board of Revenue (Peking).

Date	Good	VG	F	VF	XF
ND(1875-1908)Hu-pu	3.00	5.00	8.00	10.00	—

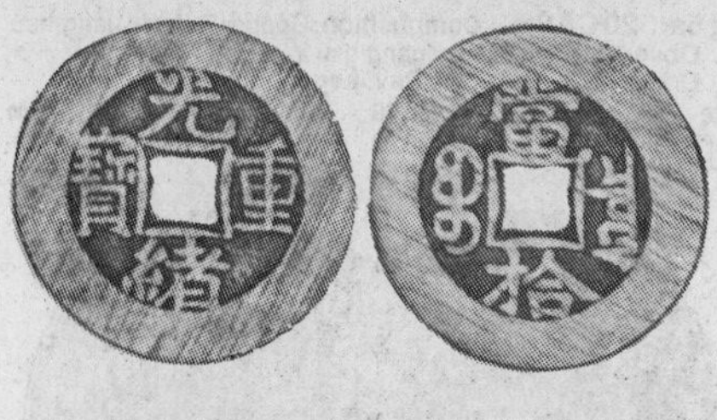

C# 1-18 10 CASH **Composition:** Cast Brass **Ruler:** Kuang-hsü **Obv. Legend:** "Kuang-hsü Chung-pao" **Reverse:** Official "Shih" for 10 below **Size:** 28 mm. **Note:** Struck at Board of Revenue (Peking).

Date	Good	VG	F	VF	XF
ND(1875-1908)Hu-pu	4.50	7.50	10.00	15.00	—

C# 1-18.1 10 CASH **Composition:** Cast Brass **Ruler:** Kuang-hsü **Obv. Legend:** "Kuang-hsü Chung-pao" **Reverse:** Official "Shih" for 10 below **Size:** 22 mm. **Note:** Struck at Board of Revenue (Peking).

Date	Good	VG	F	VF	XF
ND(1875-1908)Hu-pu	6.00	9.00	15.00	20.00	—

C# 2-18 10 CASH **Composition:** Cast Brass **Ruler:** Kuang-hsü **Obv. Legend:** "Kuang-hsü T'ung-pao" **Reverse:** Official Shih(10) below **Note:** Struck at Board of Public Works (Peking).

Date	Good	VG	F	VF	XF
ND(1880-1908)	6.00	10.00	15.00	35.00	—

STANDARD UNIFIED GENERAL COINAGE

A Central mint opened at Tientsin in 1905, was made responsible for producing most of the dies for the Tai Ch'ing Hu Poo coinage and for the 1910 and 1911 unified coinage. The mint was burned down in 1912 but resumed operations in 1914 with Yuan Shih-k'ai dollar issues. It continued producing dies for selected branch mints until 1921. It was superseded as the Central mint of China by Nanking in 1927 and by the new Nationalist Government mint at Shanghai in 1933.

Y# 7 CASH **Composition:** Brass **Ruler:** Kuang-hsü **Obv. Legend:** "Kuang-hsü" **Reverse:** Dragon **Note:** Struck.

Date	VG	F	VF	XF	Unc
CD(1908)	1.00	3.00	6.00	12.00	—

Y# 18 CASH **Composition:** Brass **Ruler:** Hsüan-t'ung **Obv. Legend:** "Hsüan-t'ung " **Reverse:** Dragon **Note:** Struck.

Date	VG	F	VF	XF	Unc
CD(1909)	25.00	50.00	85.00	135	—

Note: Inc. Y25

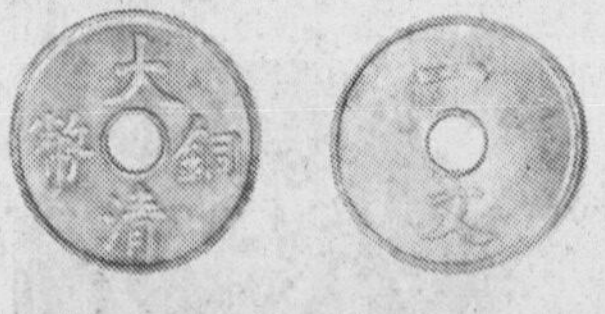

Y# 25 CASH **Obverse:** Inscription: Tai-ch'ing T'ung-pi

Date	Mintage	VG	F	VF	XF	Unc
ND(1909)	92,126,000	1.00	1.50	2.00	3.00	—

Y# 8 2 CASH **Composition:** Copper **Ruler:** Kuang-hsü **Obverse:** Inscription: Tai-ch'ing T'ung-pi **Reverse:** Dragon

Date	VG	F	VF	XF	Unc
CD(1905) Hu-pu	2.50	4.50	10.00	17.50	—
CD(1906) Hu-pu	3.00	6.00	10.00	25.00	—

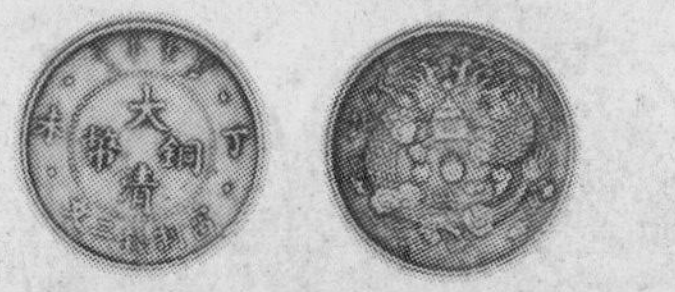

Y# 8.1 2 CASH **Composition:** Copper **Ruler:** Kuang-hsü **Obverse:** Inscription: Tai-ch'ing T'ung-pi; four dots divide legend **Reverse:** Dragon

Date	VG	F	VF	XF	Unc
CD(1907)	7.00	18.00	25.00	40.00	—

Y# A18 2 CASH **Composition:** Copper **Ruler:** Hsüan-t'ung **Obverse:** Inscription: Hsüan-t'ung

Date	Mintage	VG	F	VF	XF	Unc
CD(1909) Rare	13,353,000	—	—	—	—	—

Y# 3 5 CASH **Composition:** Copper **Ruler:** Kuang-hsü **Obverse:** Inscription: Kuang-hsü Yüan-pao **Reverse:** Dragon **Rev. Legend:** HU POO

Date	Mintage	VG	F	VF	XF	Unc
ND(1903-05) Hu-pu	3,671,000	7.00	14.00	21.00	35.00	—

Y# 9 5 CASH **Composition:** Copper **Ruler:** Kuang-hsü **Obverse:** Inscription: Tai-ch'ing T'ung-pi **Reverse:** Dragon; smaller legend **Rev. Legend:** Kuang-hsü

Date	VG	F	VF	XF	Unc
CD(1905)	5.00	10.00	20.00	35.00	—
CD(1906) Rare	—	—	—	—	—

Y# 9.1 5 CASH **Composition:** Copper **Ruler:** Kuang-hsü **Obverse:** Inscription: Tai-ch'ing T'ung-pi; four dots divide legend **Obv. Legend:** Kuang-hsü **Reverse:** Dragon

Date	VG	F	VF	XF	Unc
CD(1907)	16.50	40.00	75.00	125	—

Y# 19 5 CASH **Composition:** Copper **Ruler:** Hsüan-t'ung **Obv. Legend:** Hsüan-t'ung

Date	Mintage	VG	F	VF	XF	Unc
CD(1909)	2,170,000	—	—	850	1,200	—

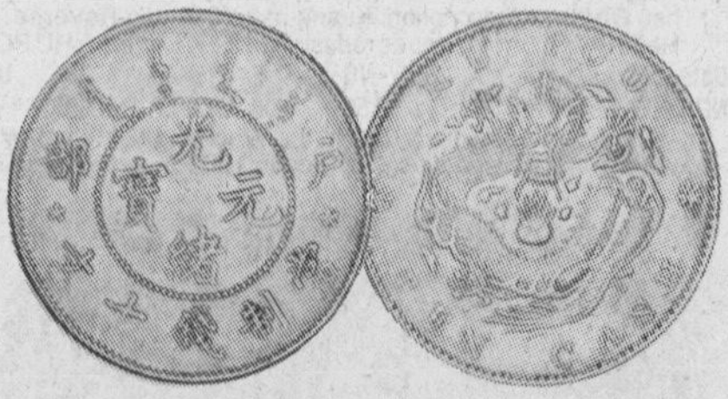

Y# 4 10 CASH **Composition:** Copper **Ruler:** Kuang-hsü **Obverse:** Inscription: Kuang-hsü Yüan-pao **Obv. Legend:** Hsüan-t'ung **Reverse:** Side view dragon **Rev. Legend:** HU POO

Date	Mintage	VG	F	VF	XF	Unc
ND(1903-05)	281,171,000	0.65	2.00	3.50	6.00	25.00

Y# 4.1 10 CASH **Composition:** Copper **Ruler:** Kuang-hsü **Reverse:** Side view dragon; different rosettes; smaller legend **Rev. Legend:** HU POO

Date	VG	F	VF	XF	Unc
ND(1903-05)	0.35	1.00	2.00	5.00	20.00

Y# 10 10 CASH **Composition:** Copper **Ruler:** Kuang-hsü **Obverse:** Inscription: Tai-ch'ing T'ung-pi **Reverse:** Side view dragon **Rev. Legend:** Kuang-hsü Nien-tsao TAI-CHING-TI-KUO...

Date	VG	F	VF	XF	Unc
CD(1905)	0.50	1.50	3.00	5.00	25.00

Y# 10.1 10 CASH **Composition:** Copper **Ruler:** Kuang-hsü **Obverse:** Inscription: Tai-ch'ing T'ung-pi **Reverse:** Different dragon; larger legend **Rev. Legend:** TAI-CHING-TI-KUO...

Date	VG	F	VF	XF	Unc
CD(1905)	10.00	25.00	65.00	110	200

Y# 10.2 10 CASH **Composition:** Copper **Ruler:** Kuang-hsü **Obverse:** Inscription: Tai-ch'ing T'ung-pi **Reverse:** Dragon **Rev. Legend:** Kuang-hsü Nien-tsao TAI-CHING-TI-KUO

Date	VG	F	VF	XF	Unc
CD(1906)	0.25	0.75	1.50	3.00	20.00

Y# 10.3 10 CASH **Composition:** Copper **Ruler:** Kuang-hsü **Obverse:** Inscription: Tai-ch'ing T'ung-pi; without dots **Reverse:** Dragon; legend without dot after KUO **Rev. Legend:** Kuang-hsü Nien-tsao TAI-CHING-TI-KUO

Date	VG	F	VF	XF	Unc
CD(1907)	0.35	1.00	2.00	4.50	18.00

Y# 10.4 10 CASH **Composition:** Copper **Ruler:** Kuang-hsü **Obverse:** Inscription: Tai-ch'ing T'ung-pi **Reverse:** Dragon; legend with dot after KUO **Rev. Legend:** Kuang-hsü Nien-tsao TAI-CHING-TI-KUO.

Date	VG	F	VF	XF	Unc
CD(1907)	0.35	1.00	2.00	4.50	18.00

Y# 10.4a 10 CASH **Composition:** Brass **Ruler:** Kuang-hsü **Obverse:** Inscription: Tai-ch'ing T'ung-pi; without dots **Reverse:** Dragon **Rev. Legend:** Kuang-hsü Nien-tsao TAI-CHING-TI-KUO.

Date	VG	F	VF	XF	Unc
CD(1907)	1.85	5.50	20.00	35.00	80.00

Y# 10.5 10 CASH **Composition:** Copper **Ruler:** Kuang-hsü **Obverse:** Inscription: Tai-ch'ing T'ung-pi; four dots divide legend **Reverse:** Dragon **Rev. Legend:** Kuang-hsü Nien-tsao TAI-CHING-TI-KUO.

Date	VG	F	VF	XF	Unc
CD(1907)	0.35	1.00	2.00	4.50	18.00

Y# 10.5a 10 CASH **Composition:** Brass **Ruler:** Kuang-hsü **Obverse:** Inscription: Tai-ch'ing T'ung-pi **Reverse:** Dragon **Rev. Legend:** Kuang-hsü Nien-tsao TAI-CHING-TI-KUO.

Date	VG	F	VF	XF	Unc
CD(1907)	1.85	5.50	15.00	30.00	85.00

Y# 20 10 CASH **Composition:** Copper **Ruler:** Hsüan-t'ung **Obverse:** Inscription: Tai-ch'ing T'ung-pi **Reverse:** Waves below dragon **Rev. Legend:** Hsüan-t'ung Nien-tsao TAI-CHING-TI-KUO.

Date	VG	F	VF	XF	Unc
CD(1909)	0.35	1.00	2.00	4.00	22.50

Y# 20.1 10 CASH **Composition:** Copper **Ruler:** Hsüan-t'ung **Obverse:** Inscription: Tai-ch'ing T'ung-pi **Reverse:** Rosette below dragon, U of KUO inverted A **Rev. Legend:** Hsüan-t'ung Nien-tsao TAI-CHING-TI-KUO.

Date	VG	F	VF	XF	Unc
CD(1909)	1.85	5.50	12.00	25.00	60.00

Note: Although this coin bears no indication of its origin, it was minted in the Manchurian Provinces ca.1922

Y# 20x 10 CASH **Composition:** Copper **Ruler:** Hsüan-t'ung **Obverse:** Inscription: Tai-ch'ing T'ung-pi; rosette in center **Reverse:** Dragon **Rev. Legend:** Hsüan-t'ung Nien-tsao TAI-CHING-TI-KUO.

Date	VG	F	VF	XF	Unc
CD(1909)	3.50	10.00	20.00	30.00	80.00

Note: Although this coin bears no indication of its origin, it was minted in Kirin Province

Y# 27 10 CASH **Composition:** Bronze **Ruler:** Hsüan-t'ung **Obverse:** Inscription: Tai-ch'ing T'ung-pi; dragon **Rev. Legend:** Hsüan-t'ung...

Date	Mintage	VG	F	VF	XF	Unc
3(1911)	95,585,000	0.85	2.50	4.00	8.00	40.00
3(1911) Rare	—	—	—	—	—	—

Y# 27a 10 CASH **Composition:** Brass **Ruler:** Hsüan-t'ung **Obverse:** Inscription: Tai-ch'ing T'ung-pi; dragon **Rev. Legend:** Hsüan-t'ung...

Date	VG	F	VF	XF	Unc
3(1911)	12.00	30.00	45.00	95.00	150

Y# 5 20 CASH **Composition:** Copper **Ruler:** Kuang-hsü **Obverse:** Inscription: Kuang-hsü Yüan-pao **Reverse:** Dragon **Rev. Legend:** HU POO

Date	VG	F	VF	XF	Unc
ND(1903) Restrike	0.50	1.00	2.00	3.00	—

Y# 5.1 20 CASH **Composition:** Copper **Ruler:** Kuang-hsü **Obverse:** Inscription: Kuang-hsü Yüan-pao; four-point rosette in center **Reverse:** Dragon **Rev. Legend:** HU POO

Date	VG	F	VF	XF	Unc
ND(1903) Restrike	2.50	6.00	12.00	25.00	—

Y# 5.2 20 CASH **Composition:** Copper **Ruler:** Kuang-hsü **Obverse:** Inscription: Kuang-hsü Yüan-pao **Reverse:** Head of dragon and clouds redesigned **Rev. Legend:** HU POO

Date	VG	F	VF	XF	Unc
ND(1903) Restrike	2.50	6.00	12.00	25.00	—

Note: Y#5-5.2 were struck at the Wuchang Mint in 1917 from unused dies prepared in 1903

Y# 5a 20 CASH **Composition:** Copper **Ruler:** Kuang-hsü **Obverse:** Inscription: Kuang-hsü Yüan-pao **Reverse:** Dragon in circle of dots **Rev. Legend:** HU POO

Date	VG	F	VF	XF	Unc
ND(1903-05)	30.00	50.00	85.00	125	—

Y# 11 20 CASH **Composition:** Copper **Ruler:** Kuang-hsü **Obverse:** Inscription: Tai-ch'ing T'ung-pi **Reverse:** Dragon **Rev. Legend:** Kuang-hsü Nien-tsao, TAI-CHING-TI-KUO

Date	VG	F	VF	XF	Unc
CD(1905)	12.50	30.00	50.00	75.00	—

Y# 11.1 20 CASH **Composition:** Copper **Ruler:** Kuang-hsü **Obverse:** Inscription: Tai-ch'ing T'ung-pi **Reverse:** Dragon **Rev. Legend:** Kuang-hsü Nien-tsao, TAI-CHING-TI-KUO

Date	VG	F	VF	XF	Unc
CD(1906)	12.50	30.00	50.00	75.00	—

Y# 11.3a 20 CASH **Composition:** Brass **Ruler:** Kuang-hsü **Obverse:** Inscription: Tai-ch'ing T'ung-pi **Reverse:** Dragon **Rev. Legend:** Kuang-hsü Nien-tsao, TAI-CHING-TI-KUO

Date	VG	F	VF	XF	Unc
CD(1907)	3.50	8.00	15.00	30.00	—

Y# 11.2 20 CASH **Composition:** Copper **Ruler:** Kuang-hsü **Obverse:** Inscription: Tai-ch'ing T'ung-pi; dots around date **Reverse:** Dragon **Rev. Legend:** Kuang-hsü Nien-tsao, TAI-CHING-TI-KUO **Note:** 1.2-1.7 millimeters thick.

Date	VG	F	VF	XF	Unc
CD(1907)	0.60	1.50	2.00	4.00	—

Y# 11.3 20 CASH **Composition:** Copper **Ruler:** Kuang-hsü **Obverse:** Inscription: Tai-ch'ing T'ung-pi **Reverse:** Dragon **Rev. Legend:** Kuang-hsü Nien-tsao, TAI-CHING-TI-KUO **Note:** 2.0-2.3 millimeters thick.

Date	VG	F	VF	XF	Unc
CD(1907)	2.50	6.00	12.00	25.00	—

Y# 21 20 CASH **Composition:** Brass **Ruler:** Hsüan-t'ung **Obverse:** Inscription: Tai-ch'ing T'ung-pi **Reverse:** With dot between KUO and COPPER; six waves beneath dragon **Rev. Legend:** Hsüan-t'ung Nien-tsao, TAI-CHING-TI-KUO...

Date	VG	F	VF	XF	Unc
CD(1909)	1.00	2.50	5.00	10.00	—

Y# 21.1 20 CASH **Composition:** Copper **Ruler:** Hsüan-t'ung **Obverse:** Inscription: Tai-ch'ing T'ung-pi **Reverse:** Without dot between KUO and COPPER; six waves beneath dragon **Rev. Legend:** Hsüan-t'ung Nien-tsao, TAI-CHING-TI-KUO... **Note:** 1.2-1.7 millimeters thick.

Date	VG	F	VF	XF	Unc
CD(1909)	1.25	3.00	6.00	10.00	—

Y# 21.2 20 CASH **Composition:** Copper **Ruler:** Hsüan-t'ung **Obverse:** Inscription: Tai-ch'ing T'ung-pi **Reverse:** Without dot between KUO and COPPER; six waves beneath dragon **Rev. Legend:** Hsüan-t'ung Nien-tsao, TAI-CHING-TI-KUO... **Note:** 2.0-2.3 millimeters thick.

Date	VG	F	VF	XF	Unc
CD(1909)	1.25	3.00	6.00	10.00	—

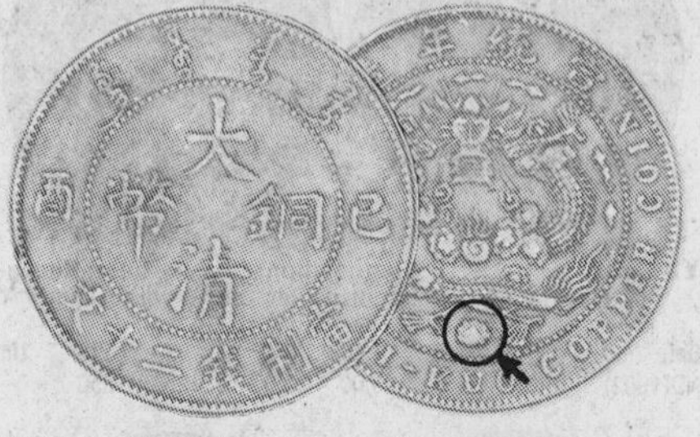

Y# 21.3 20 CASH **Composition:** Copper **Ruler:** Hsüan-t'ung **Obverse:** Inscription: Tai-ch'ing T'ung-pi **Reverse:** Without dot between KUO and COPPER; rosette beneath dragon **Rev. Legend:** Hsüan-t'ung Nien-tsao, TAI-CHING-TI-KUO...

Date	VG	F	VF	XF	Unc
CD(1909) (restrike)	6.00	15.00	40.00	70.00	—

Note: Although this coin bears no indication of its origin, it was minted in the Manchurian Provinces ca.1922

Y# 21.4 20 CASH **Composition:** Copper **Ruler:** Hsüan-t'ung **Obverse:** Inscription: Tai-ch'ing T'ung-pi **Reverse:** Without dot between KUO and COPPER; dot below dragon's chin **Rev. Legend:** Hsüan-t'ung Nien-tsao, TAI-CHING-TI-KUO...

Date	VG	F	VF	XF	Unc
CD(1909) (restrike)	3.50	8.50	16.00	30.00	—

Note: Although this coin bears no indication of its origin, it was minted in the Manchurian Provinces ca.1922

Y# 21.5 20 CASH **Composition:** Copper **Ruler:** Hsüan-t'ung **Obverse:** Inscription: Tai-ch'ing T'ung-pi; inner circle of large dots **Reverse:** Without dot between KUO and COPPER; five crude waves beneath dragon with redesigned forehead; inner circle of large dots **Rev. Legend:** Hsüan-t'ung Nien-tsao, TAI-CHING-TI-KUO...

Date	VG	F	VF	XF	Unc
CD(1909)	1.25	3.00	6.00	16.00	—

K# 215 10 CENTS **Weight:** 2.7000 g. **Composition:** 0.8200 Silver .0712 oz. ASW **Ruler:** Kuang-hsü **Obverse:** Inscription: Tai-ch'ing T'ung-pi **Reverse:** Dragon **Rev. Legend:** Kuang-hsü Nien-tsao, TAI-CHING-TI-KUO...

Date	VG	F	VF	XF	Unc
CD(1907)	28.00	85.00	150	250	400

Y# 12 10 CENTS **Weight:** 2.7000 g. **Composition:** 0.8200 Silver .0712 oz. ASW **Ruler:** Kuang-hsü **Obverse:** Inscription: Kuang-hsü Yüan-pao **Reverse:** Dragon **Rev. Legend:** Kuang-hsü Nien-tsao, TAI-CHING-TI-KUO...

Date	VG	F	VF	XF	Unc
ND(1908)	12.00	30.00	40.00	90.00	200

K# 222 10 CENTS **Weight:** 3.2000 g. **Composition:** 0.6500 Silver .0669 oz. ASW **Ruler:** Hsüan-t'ung **Obverse:** Inscription: Tai-ch'ing Yin-pi **Reverse:** Dragon **Rev. Legend:** Hsüan-t'ung Nien-tsao

Date	VG	F	VF	XF	Unc
ND(1910)	28.00	85.00	150	250	500
ND(1910) Proof	—	Value: 750			

Y#28 10 CENTS **Weight:** 2.7000 g. **Composition:** Silver **Ruler:** Hsüan-t'ung **Obverse:** Inscription: Tai-ch'ing Yin-pi **Obv. Legend:** Hsüan-t'ung **Reverse:** Dragon **Rev. Legend:** Hsüan-t'ung Nien-tsao

Date	VG	F	VF	XF	Unc
3(1911)	5.00	15.00	30.00	75.00	180

Note: Refer to Hunan Republic 10 Cents, K#762

K# 214 20 CENTS **Weight:** 5.5000 g. **Composition:** 0.8200 Silver .1450 oz. ASW **Ruler:** Kuang-hsü **Obverse:** Inscription: Tai-ch'ing Yin-pi **Reverse:** Dragon **Rev. Legend:** Kuang-hsü Nien-tsao, TAI-CHING-TI-KUO...

Date	VG	F	VF	XF	Unc
CD(1907)	35.00	100	150	250	450

Y# 13 20 CENTS **Weight:** 5.3000 g. **Composition:** 0.8200 Silver .1450 oz. ASW **Ruler:** Kuang-hsü **Obverse:** Inscription: Kuang-hsü Yüan-pao **Reverse:** Dragon **Rev. Legend:** Kuang-hsü Nien-tsao, TAI-CHING-TI-KUO...

Date	VG	F	VF	XF	Unc
ND(1908)	20.00	60.00	100	150	260

K# 217w 20 CENTS **Weight:** 5.3000 g. **Composition:** 0.8200 Silver .1450 oz. ASW **Ruler:** Kuang-hsü **Obverse:** Inscription: Kuang-hsü Yüan-pao **Reverse:** Dragon **Rev. Legend:** Kuang-hsü Nien-tsao, TAI-CHING-TI-KUO... with "COPPER COIN" (error)

Date	VG	F	VF	XF	Unc
ND(1908) Rare	—	—	—	—	—

Y# 29 20 CENTS **Weight:** 5.4000 g. **Composition:** 0.8200 Silver .1450 oz. ASW **Ruler:** Hsüan-t'ung **Obverse:** Inscription: Tai-ch'ing Yin-pi **Obv. Legend:** Hsüan-t'ung **Reverse:** Dragon

Date	VG	F	VF	XF	Unc
3(1911)	17.50	50.00	100	175	350

K# 221 25 CENTS **Weight:** 6.7000 g. **Composition:** 0.8000 Silver .1724 oz. ASW **Ruler:** Hsüan-t'ung **Obverse:** Inscription: Tai-ch'ing Yin-pi **Obv. Legend:** Hsüan-t'ung Nien-tsao **Reverse:** Dragon

Date	Mintage	VG	F	VF	XF	Unc
ND(1910)	1,410,000	65.00	200	400	750	1,200
ND(1910) Proof	—	Value: 2,000				

K# 213 50 CENTS **Weight:** 13.6000 g. **Composition:** 0.8600 Silver .3761 oz. ASW **Ruler:** Kuang-hsü **Obverse:** Inscription: Tai-ch'ing Yin-pi **Reverse:** Dragon **Rev. Legend:** Kuang-hsü Nien-tsao, TAI-CHING-TI-KUO...

Date	VG	F	VF	XF	Unc
CD(1907)	45.00	125	300	550	1,000

Y# 23 50 CENTS **Weight:** 13.4000 g. **Composition:** 0.8000 Silver .3447 oz. ASW **Ruler:** Hsüan-t'ung **Obverse:** Inscription: Tai-ch'ing Yin-pi **Reverse:** Dragon **Rev. Legend:** Hsüan-t'ung Nien-tsao

Date	Mintage	VG	F	VF	XF	Unc
ND(1910)	1,571,000	13.50	40.00	70.00	150	450
ND(1910) Proof	—	Value: 750				

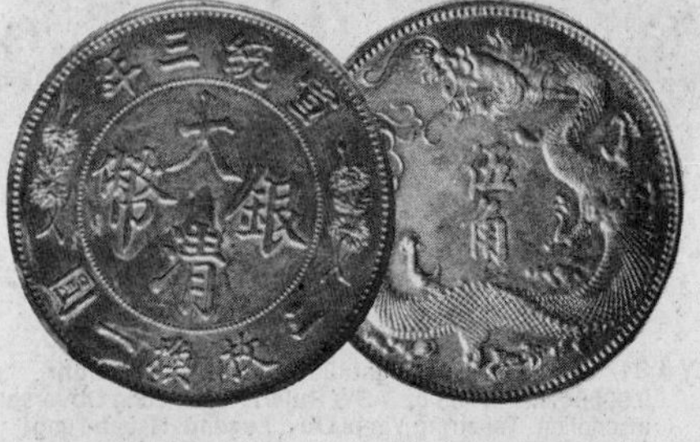

Y# 30 50 CENTS **Weight:** 13.4000 g. **Composition:** 0.8000 Silver .3447 oz. ASW **Ruler:** Hsüan-t'ung **Obverse:** Inscription: Tai-ch'ing Yin-pi **Obv. Legend:** Hsüan-t'ung **Reverse:** Dragon

Date	VG	F	VF	XF	Unc
3(1911)	85.00	250	500	800	1,500
3(1911) Proof	—	Value: 2,000			

K# 212 DOLLAR **Weight:** 26.9000 g. **Composition:** 0.9000 Silver .7785 oz. ASW **Ruler:** Kuang-hsü **Obverse:** Inscription: Tai-ch'ing Yin-pi **Reverse:** Dragon **Rev. Legend:** Kuang-hsü Nien-tsao, TAI-CHING-TI-KOU...

Date	VG	F	VF	XF	Unc
CD(1907)	65.00	200	350	700	1,400

Y# 14 DOLLAR **Weight:** 26.9000 g. **Composition:** 0.9000 Silver .7785 oz. ASW **Ruler:** Kuang-hsü **Obverse:** Inscription: Kuang-hsü Yüan-pao **Reverse:** Dragon **Rev. Legend:** Kuang-hsü Nien-tsao, TAI-CHING-TI-KOU...

Date	VG	F	VF	XF	Unc
ND(1908)	6.50	20.00	35.00	75.00	300

K# 219 DOLLAR **Weight:** 26.9000 g. **Composition:** 0.9000 Silver .7785 oz. ASW **Ruler:** Hsüan-t'ung **Obverse:** Inscription: Tai-ch'ing Yin-pi **Reverse:** Dragon **Rev. Legend:** Hsüan-t'ung Nien-tsao

Date	VG	F	VF	XF	Unc
ND(1910)	42.50	125	300	600	1,000
ND(1910) Proof	—	Value: 2,100			

Y# 31 DOLLAR **Weight:** 26.9000 g. **Composition:** 0.9000 Silver .7785 oz. ASW **Ruler:** Hsüan-t'ung **Obverse:** Inscription: Tai-ch'ing Yin-pi **Obv. Legend:** Hsüan-t'ung **Reverse:** Dragon

Date	Mintage	VG	F	VF	XF	Unc
3(1911)	77,153,000	6.00	18.00	25.00	50.00	300

Note: Struck at the Tientsin, Nanking, and Wuchang Mints without distinctive marks

Y# 31.1 DOLLAR **Weight:** 26.9000 g. **Composition:** 0.9000 Silver .7785 oz. ASW **Ruler:** Hsüan-t'ung **Obverse:** Inscription: Tai-ch'ing Yin-pi **Obv. Legend:** Hsüan-t'ung **Reverse:** Dragon; "dot" after DOLLAR

Date	VG	F	VF	XF	Unc
3(1911)	8.50	25.00	40.00	75.00	350

PATTERNS

Standard Unified General

KM#	Date	Mintage	Identification	Mkt Val
Pn253	ND	—	Cash. Brass. Hsu4	400
Pn254	ND	—	Cash. Brass. Hsu4a, square hole.	400
Pn255	ND	—	Cash. Brass. Hsu4b, without hole.	400
Pn256	ND	—	Cash. Copper. Y#7.	400
Pn257	ND	—	Cash. Brass. Y#25; without hole.	400
Pn258	CD(1907)	—	Dollar. Copper. K212.	—
Pn259	ND(1908)	—	20 Cents. Nickel. Milled edge. K217w.	—
Pn260	ND(1910)	—	10 Cents. Nickel. K222.	—
Pn262	ND(1910)	—	Li. Copper. Hsu33.	400
Pn263	ND(1910)	—	5 Li. Copper. Hsu34.	550
Pn264	ND(1910)	—	5 Li. Bronze.	550
Pn267	ND(1910)	—	Fen. Copper. Hsu35.	600
Pn268	ND(1910)	—	Fen. Bronze.	600
Pn269	ND(1910)	—	2 Fen. Copper. Hsu36.	1,000
Pn270	ND(1910)	—	2 Fen. Bronze.	1,000
Pn271	3(1911)	—	5 Cash. Copper. Y26; Hsu30.	600
Pn272	3(1911)	—	5 Cash. Bronze. Y26a.	600
Pn273	3(1911)	—	20 Cash. Copper. Hsu32.	700
Pn274	3(1911)	—	20 Cash. Bronze.	700
Pn294	3(1911)	—	Dollar. Silver. K223.	4,700
Pn295	3(1911)	—	Dollar. Silver. K223a.	1,800
Pn296	3(1911)	—	Dollar. Silver. K223b.	—
Pn297	3(1911)	—	Dollar. Silver. K224.	—
Pn298	3(1911)	—	Dollar. Silver. K225.	8,000
Pn299	3(1911)	—	Dollar. Silver. K226.	4,500

PATTERNS

Peking Tael Series

KM#	Date	Mintage	Identification	Mkt Val
Pn280	29(1903)	—	5 Fen. Silver. K931.	600
Pn281	29(1903)	—	Ch'len. Silver. K930.	750
Pn282	29(1903)	—	2 Ch'len. Silver. K929.	1,250
Pn283	29(1903)	—	2 Ch'len. Gold. K929v.	8,500
Pn284	29(1903)	—	5 Ch'len. Silver. K928.	3,000
Pn285	29(1903)	—	Liang. Silver. K927.	9,350
Pn286	29(1903)	—	Liang. Gold. K927v.	35,000
Pn287	CD(1906)	—	Ch'len. Silver. K937.	550
Pn288	CD(1906)	—	2 Ch'len. Silver. K936.	675
Pn289	CD(1906)	—	5 Ch'len. Silver. K935.	750
Pn290	CD(1906)	—	Liang. Silver. K934.	1,750
Pn291	CD(1906)	—	Liang. Gold. K1540.	24,750
Pn292	CD(1907)	—	Liang. Gold. K1541.	24,750
Pn293	CD(1907)	—	Liang. Silver. K1541y.	3,500
Pn300	ND(1908)	—	20 Cents. Nickel. K217y.	—
Pn301	ND(1910)	—	10 Cents. Nickel. K222y.	125

TRIAL STRIKES

KM#	Date	Mintage	Identification	Mkt Val
TS3	1(1910)	—	Fen. White Metal. Hsu35, KM#Pn267. Uniface.	125

PROOF SETS

KM#	Date	Mintage	Identification	Issue Price	Mkt Val
PS1	ND(1910) (4)	—	Y#23, K#219, 221, 222	—	—

ANHWEI PROVINCE

Anhui

A province located in eastern China. Made a separate province during the Manchu dynasty in the 17th century. Principally agricultural with some mining of coal and iron ore. Spanish-American 8 Reales saw wide circulation in this province until the end of World War I. The provincial mint at Anking began operations in 1897, closed in 1899, and later reopened in 1902. The primary production of the mint was cash coins but included a series of silver coinage.

EMPIRE

MILLED COINAGE

Y# 35 5 CASH **Composition:** Copper **Ruler:** Kuang-hsü **Obv. Legend:** Kuang-hsü Yüan-pao **Reverse:** Circled dragon **Rev. Legend:** AN-HWEI

Date	VG	F	VF	XF	Unc
ND(1902)	125	175	250	350	—

Y# 35.1 5 CASH **Composition:** Copper **Ruler:** Kuang-hsü **Obv. Legend:** Kuang-hsü Yüan-pao **Reverse:** Uncircled dragon **Rev. Legend:** AN-HUI

Date	VG	F	VF	XF	Unc
ND(c. 1902) Rare	—	—	—	—	—

Y# 36 10 CASH **Composition:** Copper **Ruler:** Kuang-hsü **Obverse:** Inscription: Kuang-hsü Yüan-pao **Reverse:** Letter "N" backwards in "AN-HWEI" and in "TEN"

Date	VG	F	VF	XF	Unc
ND(1902-1906)	6.00	12.00	20.00	40.00	—

Y# 34a 10 CASH **Composition:** Copper **Ruler:** Kuang-hsü **Obv. Legend:** Kuang-hsü Yüan-pao **Reverse:** Letter "A" inverted, denomination ONE SEN

Date	VG	F	VF	XF	Unc
ND(1902)	50.00	80.00	125	350	—

Y# 34a.1 10 CASH **Composition:** Copper **Ruler:** Kuang-hsü **Obv. Legend:** Kuang-hsü Yüan-pao **Reverse:** Letter "A" corrected, denomination ONE SEN

Date	VG	F	VF	XF	Unc
ND(1902)	40.00	65.00	100	250	—

Y# 36.1 10 CASH **Composition:** Copper **Ruler:** Kuang-hsü **Obverse:** Small Manchu in center, inscription: Kuang-hsü Yüan-pao **Reverse:** Rosettes close together, letter "N" corrected **Edge:** Plain

Date	VG	F	VF	XF	Unc
ND(1902-1906)	1.00	2.50	5.00	10.00	—

Y# 36.1a 10 CASH **Composition:** Copper **Ruler:** Kuang-hsü **Obverse:** Small Manchu in center, inscription: Kuang-hsü Yüan-pao **Reverse:** Rosettes close together, letter "N" corrected **Edge:** Milled

Date	VG	F	VF	XF	Unc
ND(1902-1906) Rare	—	—	—	—	—

Y# 34 10 CASH **Composition:** Copper **Ruler:** Kuang-hsü **Obv. Legend:** Kuang-hsü Yüan-pao **Reverse:** Denomination: ONE CEN **Note:** May show various stages of recutting of "C" in "CEN."

Date	VG	F	VF	XF	Unc
ND1902	35.00	50.00	85.00	150	—

Y# 36.2 10 CASH **Composition:** Copper **Ruler:** Kuang-hsü **Obverse:** Smaller, redesigned rosettes, larger Manchu words in center, inscription: Kuang-hsü Yüan-pao **Reverse:** Rosettes close together, larger clouds around redesigned dragon

Date	VG	F	VF	XF	Unc
ND(1902-1906)	1.50	4.00	6.00	10.00	—

Y# 36.3 10 CASH **Composition:** Copper **Ruler:** Kuang-hsü **Obverse:** Rosettes crude and heavy, inscription: Kuang-hsü Yüan-pao **Reverse:** Rosettes close together, dragon's head redesigned

Date	VG	F	VF	XF	Unc
ND(1902-1908)	5.00	12.00	17.50	35.00	—

Y# 36.4 10 CASH **Composition:** Copper **Ruler:** Kuang-hsü **Obverse:** Inscription: Kuang-hsü Yüan-pao **Reverse:** Rosettes far apart

Date	VG	F	VF	XF	Unc
ND(1902-1906)	1.00	2.50	5.00	10.00	—

Y# 36a 10 CASH **Composition:** Copper **Ruler:** Kuang-hsü **Obverse:** Small rosette at center, legend with 5 characters at bottom, inscription: Kuang-hsü Yüan-pao **Reverse:** Large English legend above dragon, without TEN CASH

Date	VG	F	VF	XF	Unc
ND(1902-1906)	1.00	2.50	5.00	12.00	—

Y# 36a.1 10 CASH **Composition:** Copper **Ruler:** Kuang-hsü **Obverse:** Small rosette, inscription: Kuang-hsu Yüan-pao **Reverse:** Small English legend above dragon

Date	VG	F	VF	XF	Unc
ND(1902-1906)	1.50	3.00	6.00	15.00	—

Y# 36a.2 10 CASH **Composition:** Copper **Ruler:** Kuang-hsü **Obverse:** Inscription: Kuang-hsü Yüan-pao **Reverse:** Small English legend with larger clouds around dragon and only one cloud below dragon's tail

Date	VG	F	VF	XF	Unc
ND(1902-1906)	2.00	5.00	8.00	18.00	—

Y# 36a.3 10 CASH **Composition:** Copper **Ruler:** Kuang-hsü **Obverse:** Large rosette at center, legend with 2 characters at bottom, inscription: Kuang-hsü Yüan-pao

Date	VG	F	VF	XF	Unc
ND(1902-1906)	1.00	2.50	5.00	10.00	—

Y# 36a.4 10 CASH **Composition:** Copper **Ruler:** Kuang-hsü **Obverse:** Large rosette at center, legend with 5 characters at bottom, inscription: Kuang-hsü Yüan-pao

Date	VG	F	VF	XF	Unc
ND(1902-1906)	1.25	2.50	5.00	10.00	—

Y# 36a.5 10 CASH **Composition:** Copper **Ruler:** Kuang-hsü **Obverse:** Legend with 2 characters at bottom, inscription: Kuang-hsü Yüan-pao **Reverse:** Small English legend above dragon

Date	VG	F	VF	XF	Unc
ND(1902-1906)	3.50	7.50	15.00	30.00	—

Y# 36a.6 10 CASH **Composition:** Copper **Ruler:** Kuang-hsü **Obverse:** Slightly smaller rosette at center with right Manchu word slightly higher than on Y#36a.5, inscription: Kuang-hsü Yüan-pao **Reverse:** Small English legend above dragon

Date	VG	F	VF	XF	Unc
ND(1902-1906)	1.00	2.50	5.00	10.00	—

Y# 38a 10 CASH **Composition:** Copper **Ruler:** Kuang-hsü **Obverse:** Legend with 2 characters at bottom, inscription: Kuang-hsü Yüan-pao **Reverse:** Ten spelled TOEN

Date	VG	F	VF	XF	Unc
ND(1902-1906)	8.00	15.00	30.00	50.00	—

Y# 38a.1 10 CASH **Composition:** Copper **Ruler:** Kuang-hsü **Obverse:** Legend with 5 characters at bottom, inscription: Kuang-hsü Yüan-pao **Reverse:** Ten spelled TOEN

Date	VG	F	VF	XF	Unc
ND(1902-1906)	35.00	70.00	150	250	—

Y# 38b 10 CASH **Composition:** Copper **Ruler:** Kuang-hsü **Obverse:** Legend with 2 characters at bottom, inscription: Kuang-hsü Yüan-pao **Reverse:** Without TEN CASH

Date	VG	F	VF	XF	Unc
ND(1902-1906)	5.00	12.00	25.00	65.00	—

Y# 38b.1 10 CASH **Composition:** Copper **Ruler:** Kuang-hsü **Obverse:** Legend with 5 characters at bottom, inscription: Kuang-hsü Yüan-pao

Date	VG	F	VF	XF	Unc
ND(1902-1906)	15.00	35.00	50.00	140	—

Y# 39 10 CASH **Composition:** Copper **Ruler:** Kuang-hsü **Obverse:** Legend with 7 characters at bottom, inscription: Kuang-hsü Yüan-pao **Reverse:** Rosettes at side and AN-HUI above dragon

Date	VG	F	VF	XF	Unc
ND(1902-1906) Rare	—	—	—	—	—

Y# 39.1 10 CASH **Composition:** Copper **Ruler:** Kuang-hsü **Obverse:** Inscription: Kuang-hsü Yüan-pao **Reverse:** Stars at sides and AN-HUI above dragon

Date	VG	F	VF	XF	Unc
ND(1902-1906) Rare	—	—	—	—	—

Y# 39.2 10 CASH **Composition:** Copper **Ruler:** Kuang-hsü **Obverse:** Inscription: Kuang-hsü Yüan-pao **Reverse:** AN-HUI, upright dragon **Note:** Square-holed center.

Date	VG	F	VF	XF	Unc
ND(1902-1906) Rare	—	—	—	—	—

Y# 10a 10 CASH **Composition:** Copper **Ruler:** Kuang-hsü **Obverse:** Large mint mark at center, inscription: Tai-ch'ing T'ung-pi **Rev. Legend:** Kuang-hsü Nien-tsao, TAI-CHING-TI-KUO ...

Date	VG	F	VF	XF	Unc
CD(1906)	1.00	2.50	5.00	10.00	—

Y# 10a.1 10 CASH **Composition:** Copper **Ruler:** Kuang-hsü **Obverse:** Small mint mark at center, inscription: Tai-ch'ing T'ung-pi **Rev. Legend:** Kuang-hsü Nien-tsao, TAI-CHING-TI-KUO ...

Date	VG	F	VF	XF	Unc
CD(1906)	1.50	3.00	6.00	12.00	—

Y# 10a.2 10 CASH **Composition:** Copper **Ruler:** Kuang-hsü **Obverse:** More finely engraved, cloud near dragon's lower foot shaped like a 3, inscription: Tai-ch'ing T'ung-pi **Reverse:** More finely engraved **Rev. Legend:** Kuang-hsü Nien-tsao, TAI-CHING-TI-KUO ...

Date	VG	F	VF	XF	Unc
CD(1906)	1.00	2.50	5.00	10.00	—

Y# 20a 10 CASH **Composition:** Copper **Ruler:** Hsüan-t'ung **Obverse:** Inscription: Tai-ch'ing T'ung-pi **Rev. Legend:** Hsüan-t'ung Nien-tsao, TAI-CHING-TI-KUO ...

Date	VG	F	VF	XF	Unc
CD(1909)	12.50	25.00	50.00	125	—

Y# 20a.1 10 CASH **Composition:** Copper **Ruler:** Hsüan-t'ung **Obverse:** Inscription: Tai-ch'ing T'ung-pi **Reverse:** Dot after COIN **Rev. Legend:** Hsüan-t'ung Nien-tsao, TAI-CHING-TI-KUO ...

Date	VG	F	VF	XF	Unc
CD(1909)	35.00	65.00	130	225	—

Y# 37 20 CASH **Composition:** Copper **Ruler:** Kuang-hsü **Obverse:** Inscription: Kuang-hsü Yüan-pao

Date	VG	F	VF	XF	Unc
ND(1902)	375	750	1,100	1,500	—

Y# 11a 20 CASH **Composition:** Copper **Ruler:** Kuang-hsü **Obverse:** Inscription: Tai-ch'ing T'ung-pi **Reverse:** Inscription: Kuang-hsü Nien-tsao, TAI-CHING-TI-KUO ...

Date	VG	F	VF	XF	Unc
CD(1906)	37.50	75.00	150	300	—

Y# 43.5 20 CENTS **Weight:** 5.3000 g. **Composition:** 0.9200 Silver .1397 oz. ASW **Ruler:** Kuang-hsü **Obverse:** Inscription: Kuang-hsü Yüan-pao **Reverse:** Dragon

Date	VG	F	VF	XF	Unc
ND 1 known	—	—	—	—	—

Note: D.K.E. Ching Sale 6-91 VF++ realized $2,420.

MILITARY TOKEN COINAGE

Given to An-hui Imperial troops by the Military Bureau for faithful and/or meritorious service.

KM# W45 10 CASH **Composition:** Copper **Ruler:** Kuang-hsü **Issuer:** Anhwei Military Bureau **Obverse:** Large central Chinese character "Cheang" (reward) **Obv. Legend:** An-hui Wu Dih Buh Yuen **Reverse:** Legend around dragon **Rev. Legend:** AN-HWEI***TEN CASH***

Date	VG	F	VF	XF	Unc
ND	125	225	375	550	—

KM# W46 10 CASH **Composition:** Copper **Ruler:** Kuang-hsü **Issuer:** Anhwei Military Bureau **Reverse:** Legend around Dragon **Rev. Legend:** AN-HWEI***TEN CASH***

Date	VG	F	VF	XF	Unc
ND	125	225	375	550	—

KM# W47 10 CASH **Composition:** Copper **Ruler:** Kuang-hsü **Issuer:** Anhwei Military Bureau **Reverse:** Legend without TEN CASH

Date	VG	F	VF	XF	Unc
ND	125	225	375	550	—

CHEKIANG PROVINCE

Zhejiang

A province located along the east coast of China. Although the smallest of the Chinese mainland provinces, it is one of the most densely populated. Economic interests are mostly agricultural with iron and coal mining and some fishing. A small mint opened in 1897. This was replaced by a larger mint which operated briefly 1898-99. Other mints opened in 1903 and 1905. These were merged with the Fukien Mint in 1906-07.

EMPIRE

PROVINCIAL CAST COINAGE

C# 4-19.1 CASH **Composition:** Cast Brass **Ruler:** Kuang-hsü **Reverse:** More angular mint mark

Date	Good	VG	F	VF	XF
ND(1875-1908)	2.00	3.00	4.00	6.00	—

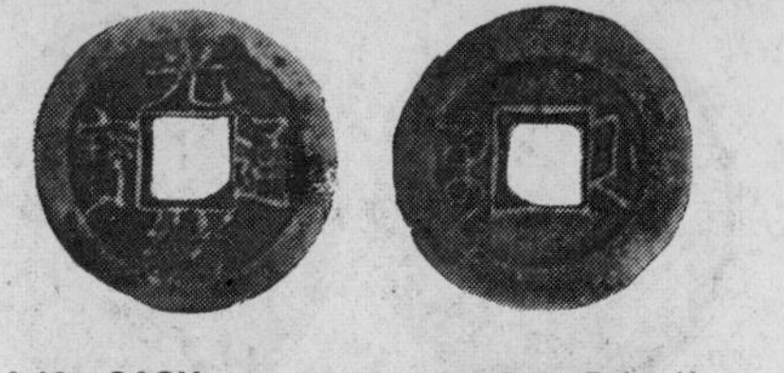

C# 4-19 CASH **Composition:** Cast Brass **Ruler:** Kuang-hsü **Obverse:** Type A **Reverse:** Mint mark as C#4-1

Date	Good	VG	F	VF	XF
ND(1875-1908)	3.00	4.50	6.50	12.00	—

MILLED COINAGE

Y# 8b 2 CASH **Composition:** Copper **Ruler:** Kuang-hsü **Obverse:** Inscription: Tai-ch'ing T'ung-pi **Reverse:** Dragon

Date	VG	F	VF	XF	Unc
CD(1906)	5.00	10.00	16.00	30.00	—

Y# 9b 5 CASH **Composition:** Copper **Ruler:** Kuang-hsü **Obverse:** Inscription: Tai-ch'ing T'ung-pi **Rev. Legend:** Kuang-hsü Nien-tsao, TAI-CHING-TI-KUO ...

Date	VG	F	VF	XF	Unc
CD(1906)	5.00	10.00	16.00	30.00	—

Y# 49 10 CASH **Composition:** Copper **Ruler:** Kuang-hsü **Obverse:** Ball in circle in center, inscription: Kuang-hsü Yüan-pao **Reverse:** Dragon

Date	VG	F	VF	XF	Unc
ND(1903-1906)	0.50	1.50	2.50	4.50	—

Y# 49.1 10 CASH **Composition:** Copper **Ruler:** Kuang-hsü **Obverse:** Rosette at center and large Manchu "Boo" at left, inscription: Kuang-hsü Yüan-pao **Reverse:** Dragon

Date	VG	F	VF	XF	Unc
ND(1903-1906)	0.50	1.50	2.50	4.50	—

Y# 49.1a 10 CASH **Composition:** Brass **Ruler:** Kuang-hsü **Obverse:** Rosette at center and large Manchu "Boo" at left, inscription: Kuang-hsü Yüan-pao **Reverse:** Dragon

Date	VG	F	VF	XF	Unc
ND(1903-1906)	2.00	4.00	8.00	15.00	—

Y# 49.2 10 CASH **Composition:** Copper **Ruler:** Kuang-hsü **Obverse:** Inscription: Kuang-hsü Yüan-pao **Reverse:** Dragon **Note:** Similar to Y#49.1a.

Date	VG	F	VF	XF	Unc
ND(1903-1906)	0.75	1.50	3.00	6.00	—

Y# 49.3 10 CASH **Composition:** Copper **Ruler:** Kuang-hsü **Obverse:** Rosette at center and small Manchu word at left, inscription: Kuang-hsü Yüan-pao **Reverse:** Small, cramped dragon with few clouds around body

Date	VG	F	VF	XF	Unc
ND(1903-1906)	0.75	1.50	3.00	6.00	—

Y# 49.4　10 CASH　Composition: Copper **Ruler:** Kuang-hsü **Obverse:** Inscription: Kuang-hsü Yüan-pao **Reverse:** Dragon without ball in center circle

Date	VG	F	VF	XF	Unc
ND(1903-1906)	1.25	2.50	5.00	10.00	—

Y# 49a　10 CASH　Composition: Brass **Ruler:** Kuang-hsü **Obverse:** Legend has 4 characters at bottom, inscription: Kuang-hsü Yüan-pao **Reverse:** Dragon

Date	VG	F	VF	XF	Unc
ND(1903-1906)	3.00	6.00	11.00	20.00	—

Y# 49b　10 CASH　Composition: Copper **Ruler:** Kuang-hsü **Obverse:** Inscription: Kuang-hsü Yüan-pao **Reverse:** Dragon

Date	VG	F	VF	XF	Unc
ND(1903-1906)	6.00	12.00	25.00	45.00	—

Y# 10b　10 CASH　Composition: Copper **Ruler:** Kuang-hsü **Obverse:** Inscription: Tai-ch'ing T'ung-pi **Reverse:** Dragon **Rev. Legend:** Kuang hsü Nien-tsao, TAI-CHING-TI-KUO with KUO spelled KIIO

Date	VG	F	VF	XF	Unc
CD(1906)	1.00	2.00	4.00	8.00	—

Y# 10b.1　10 CASH　Composition: Copper **Ruler:** Kuang-hsü **Obverse:** Inscription: Tai-ch'ing T'ung-pi **Reverse:** Dragon **Rev. Legend:** Kuang hsü Nien-tsao, TAI-CHING-TI-KUO with KUO spelled KUO

Date	VG	F	VF	XF	Unc
CD(1906)	2.50	5.00	10.00	20.00	—

Note: Chekiang and other 10 Cash coin types found struck over Korean 5 Fun coins are known. Why they were overstruck in China is unknown.

Y# 50　20 CASH　Composition: Copper **Ruler:** Kuang-hsü **Obverse:** Inscription: Kuang-hsü Yüan-pao **Reverse:** Dragon **Note:** Two planchet sizes exist.

Date	VG	F	VF	XF	Unc
ND(1903-1904)	100	200	350	600	—

Y# 11b　20 CASH　Composition: Copper **Ruler:** Kuang-hsü **Obverse:** Inscription: Tai-ch'ing T'ung-Pi **Rev. Legend:** Kuang-hsü Nien-tsao, TAI-CHING-TI-KUO ...

Date	VG	F	VF	XF	Unc
CD(1906)	60.00	100	200	350	—

REPUBLIC

MILLED COINAGE

Y# 371　10 CENTS　Weight: 2.6500 g. **Composition:** 0.6500 Silver .0554 oz. ASW **Obverse:** Crossed flags **Rev. Legend:** CHE-KIANG PROVINCE

Date	Mintage	VG	F	VF	XF	Unc
13(1924)	4,464,000	1.25	4.00	7.00	10.00	25.00

Y# 373　20 CENTS　Weight: 5.3000 g. **Composition:** Silver **Reverse:** Large value "20" **Rev. Legend:** CHE-KIANG PROVINCE

Date	VG	F	VF	XF	Unc
13(1924)	100	300	500	700	1,500

PATTERNS

Including off metal strikes

KM#	Date	Mintage	Identification	Mkt Val
Pn6	ND(1902)	—	20 Cents. Silver. CHE-KIANG. K121-I.	1,500
Pn4	ND(1902)	—	5 Cents. Silver. CHE-KIANG. K123-I.	2,100
Pn5	ND(1902)	—	10 Cents. Silver. CHE-KIANG. K122-I.	1,500
Pn7	ND(1902)	—	Dollar. Silver. CHE-KIANG. K 119-I.	20,000
Pn8	ND(1902)	—	Dollar. Copper. CHE-KIANG. K 119-I.	1,150
Pn9	ND(1903)	—	10 Cash. Copper. Y49.3a.	200
Pn10	ND(1903)	—	10 Cash. White copper. Y49.3a. W132.	—
Pn11	13(1924)	—	20 Cents. Silver. Crossed flags. Y372.	1,100

CHIHLI PROVINCE

Hebei, Hopei

A province located in northeastern China which contains the eastern end of the Great Wall. An important producer of coal and some iron ore. In 1928 the provincial name was changed from Chihli to Hopei. The Paoting mint was established in 1745 and only produced cast cash coins.

A mint for struck cash was established in 1888 and the mint for the Peiyang silver coinage was added in 1896. This was destroyed during the Boxer Rebellion. A replacement mint was built in 1902 for the provincial coinage and merged with the Tientsin (Tianjin) Central mint in 1910.

EMPIRE

PROVINCIAL CAST COINAGE

C# 8-1　CASH　Composition: Cast Brass **Ruler:** Kuang-hsü **Obverse:** Inscription: Kuang-hsü T'ung-pao **Reverse:** Inscription: Manchu Boo-jiyen **Note:** Struck at Chin Mint(Peiyang Arsenal), Tientsin.

Date	Good	VG	F	VF	XF
ND(1875-1908)	2.50	4.50	7.50	12.00	—

C# 3-1.1　CASH　Composition: Cast Brass **Ruler:** Kuang-hsü **Obverse:** Inscription: Kuang-hsü Tung-pao **Reverse:** Type 1 mint mark, inscription: Manchu, Boo-gu **Note:** Struck at Taku Naval Arsenal.

Date	Good	VG	F	VF	XF
ND(1875-1908)	120	180	275	400	—

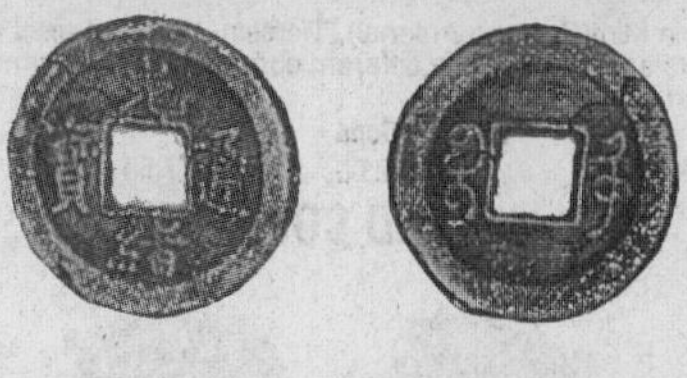

C# 3-1.2　CASH　Composition: Cast Brass **Ruler:** Kuang-hsü **Obverse:** Inscription: Kuang-hsü Tung-pao **Reverse:** Type 2 mint mark, inscription: Manchu, Boo-gu **Note:** Struck at Taku Naval Arsenal.

Date	Good	VG	F	VF	XF
ND(1875-1908)	20.00	30.00	50.00	75.00	—

C# 8-1.2　CASH　Composition: Cast Brass **Ruler:** Kuang-hsü **Obverse:** Inscription: Kuang-hsü T'ung-pao **Reverse:** Dot below, inscription: Manchu Boo-jiyen **Note:** Struck at Chin Mint(Peiyang Arsenal), Tientsin

Date	Good	VG	F	VF	XF
ND(1875-1908)	2.00	3.50	6.00	10.00	—

C# 8-1.1　CASH　Composition: Cast Brass **Ruler:** Kuang-hsü **Obverse:** Inscription: Kuang-hsü T'ung-pao **Reverse:** Dot above, inscription: Manchu Boo-jiyen **Note:** Struck at Chin Mint(Peiyang Arsenal), Tientsin

Date	Good	VG	F	VF	XF
ND(1875-1908)	2.75	4.50	7.50	15.00	—

C# 8-1.3　CASH　Composition: Cast Brass **Ruler:** Kuang-hsü **Obverse:** Inscription: Kuang-hsü T'ung-pao **Reverse:** 2 dots below, inscription: Manchu Boo-jiyen **Note:** Struck at Chin Mint(Peiyang Arsenal), Tientsin

Date	Good	VG	F	VF	XF
ND(1875-1908)	3.50	5.50	9.00	15.00	—

C# 8-1.4　CASH　Composition: Cast Brass **Ruler:** Kuang-hsü **Obverse:** Inscription: Kuang-hsü T'ung-pao **Reverse:** Circle above, inscription: Manchu Boo-jiyen **Note:** Struck at Chin Mint(Peiyang Arsenal), Tientsin

Date	Good	VG	F	VF	XF
ND(1875-1908)	3.50	5.50	9.00	18.00	—

C# 8-1.5　CASH　Composition: Cast Brass **Ruler:** Kuang-hsü **Obverse:** Inscription: Kuang-hsü T'ung-pao **Reverse:** Circle below, inscription: Manchu Boo-jiyen **Note:** Struck at Chin Mint(Peiyang Arsenal), Tientsin

Date	Good	VG	F	VF	XF
ND(1875-1908)	3.50	5.50	9.00	18.00	—

C# 8-1.6　CASH　Composition: Cast Brass **Ruler:** Kuang-hsü **Obverse:** Inscription: Kuang-hsü T'ung-pao **Reverse:** Crescent above, inscription: Manchu Boo-jiyen **Note:** Struck at Chin Mint(Peiyang Arsenal), Tientsin

Date	Good	VG	F	VF	XF
ND(1875-1908)	3.50	5.50	9.00	18.00	—

C# 8-1.7　CASH　Composition: Cast Brass **Ruler:** Kuang-hsü **Obverse:** Inscription: Kuang-hsü T'ung-pao **Reverse:** Crescent below, inscription: Manchu Boo-jiyen **Note:** Struck at Chin Mint(Peiyang Arsenal), Tientsin

Date	Good	VG	F	VF	XF
ND(1875-1908)	2.00	3.75	7.50	17.00	—

C# 8-1.8　CASH　Composition: Cast Brass **Ruler:** Kuang-hsü **Obverse:** Inscription: Kuang-hsü T'ung-pao **Reverse:** Dash below, inscription: Manchu Boo-jiyen **Note:** Struck at

Chin Mint(Peiyang Arsenal), Tientsin. Varieties exist with dots and crescents in different corners on reverse and also with incuse dots.

Date	Good	VG	F	VF	XF
ND(1875-1908)	2.00	3.75	7.50	15.00	—

MILLED COINAGE

Y# 66 CASH **Composition:** Brass **Ruler:** Kuang-hsü **Obverse:** Inscription: Kuang-hsü T'ung-pao **Note:** Struck at Chin Mint(Peiyang Arsenal), Tientsin

Date	VG	F	VF	XF	Unc
ND(1904-1907)	4.00	6.00	12.00	25.00	—

Y# 7c CASH **Composition:** Brass **Ruler:** Kuang-hsü **Obv. Legend:** Kuang-hsü **Reverse:** Dragon **Note:** Struck at Chin Mint(Peiyang Arsenal), Tientsin.

Date	VG	F	VF	XF	Unc
CD(1908)	2.50	4.50	7.50	13.50	—

Y# 8c (Y82) 2 CASH **Composition:** Copper **Ruler:** Kuang-hsü **Note:** Struck at Chin Mint(Peiyang Arsenal), Tientsin.

Date	VG	F	VF	XF	Unc
(1906) Rare	—	—	—	—	—

Y# 9c 5 CASH **Composition:** Copper **Ruler:** Kuang-hsü **Obverse:** Inscription: Tai-ch'ing T'ung-pi **Rev. Legend:** Kuang-hsü Nien-tsao, TAI-CHING-TI-KUO ... **Note:** Struck at Chin Mint(Peiyang Arsenal), Tientsin.

Date	VG	F	VF	XF	Unc
CD(1906)	10.00	20.00	35.00	48.00	—

Y# 67 10 CASH **Composition:** Copper **Ruler:** Kuang-hsü **Obverse:** Inscription: Kuang-hsü Yüan-pao **Reverse:** Side-view square-mouth dragon, hole in center of rosette **Rev. Legend:** PEI YANG **Note:** Struck at Chin Mint(Peiyang Arsenal), Tientsin.

Date	VG	F	VF	XF	Unc
ND(c. 1906)	1.00	2.00	2.50	4.00	—

Note: Mulings exist with obverse of Kwangtung (Guangdong) Y#192 and reverse of Chihli Y#67. Refer to Kwangtung listings.

Y# 67.1 10 CASH **Composition:** Copper **Ruler:** Kuang-hsü **Obverse:** Inscription: Kuang-hsü Yüan-pao **Reverse:** Dragon with round mouth **Note:** Struck at Chin Mint(Peiyang Arsenal), Tientsin.

Date	VG	F	VF	XF	Unc
ND(c. 1906)	1.00	2.00	2.50	4.00	—

Y# 67.2 10 CASH **Composition:** Copper **Ruler:** Kuang-hsü **Obverse:** Inscription: Kuang-hsü Yüan-pao **Reverse:** Dot in center of rosettes, dragon with square mouth **Note:** Struck at Chin Mint(Peiyang Arsenal), Tientsin.

Date	VG	F	VF	XF	Unc
ND(c. 1906)	1.00	2.00	2.50	4.00	—

Y# 67.3 10 CASH **Composition:** Copper **Ruler:** Kuang-hsü **Obverse:** Inscription: Kuang-hsü Yüan-pao **Reverse:** Dot in center of rosettes, dragon with round mouth **Note:** Struck at Chin Mint(Peiyang Arsenal), Tientsin.

Date	VG	F	VF	XF	Unc
ND(c. 1906)	1.00	2.00	2.50	4.00	—

Y# 67.4 10 CASH **Composition:** Copper **Ruler:** Kuang-hsü **Obverse:** Inscription: Kuang-hsü Yüan-pao **Reverse:** Redesigned dragon with smaller body and smaller English legends **Note:** Struck at Chin Mint(Peiyang Arsenal), Tientsin.

Date	VG	F	VF	XF	Unc
ND(c. 1906)	1.50	3.50	7.00	15.00	—

Y# 10c 10 CASH **Composition:** Copper **Ruler:** Kuang-hsü **Obverse:** Inscription: Tai-ch'ing T'ung-pi **Rev. Legend:** Kuang-hsü Nien-tsao, TAI-CHING-TI-KUO ... **Note:** Struck at Chin Mint (Peiyang Arsenal), Tientsin.

Date	VG	F	VF	XF	Unc
CD(1906)	1.00	2.00	3.00	5.00	—

Y# 68 20 CASH **Composition:** Copper **Ruler:** Kuang-hsü **Note:** Struck at Chin Mint (Peiyang Arsenal), Tientsin.

Date	VG	F	VF	XF	Unc
ND(c. 1906)	20.00	30.00	40.00	100	—

Y# 68a 20 CASH **Composition:** Brass **Ruler:** Kuang-hsü **Obverse:** Inscription: Kuang-hsü Yüan-pao **Reverse:** Side view dragon **Rev. Legend:** PEI YANG **Note:** Struck at Chin Mint (Peiyang Arsenal), Tientsin.

Date	VG	F	VF	XF	Unc
ND(c. 1906) Rare	—	—	—	—	—

Y# 68.1 20 CASH **Composition:** Copper **Ruler:** Kuang-hsü **Obverse:** Inscription: Kuang-hsü Yüan-pao **Reverse:** Smaller lettering **Note:** Struck at Chin Mint (Peiyang Arsenal), Tientsin.

Date	VG	F	VF	XF	Unc
ND(c. 1906)	25.00	35.00	50.00	120	—

Y# 11c 20 CASH **Composition:** Copper **Ruler:** Kuang-hsü **Obverse:** Inscription: Tai-ch'ing T'ung-pi **Rev. Legend:** Kuang-hsü Nien-tsao, TAI-CHING-TI-KUO ... **Note:** Struck at Chin Mint (Peiyang Arsenal), Tientsin.

Date	VG	F	VF	XF	Unc
CD(1906)	15.00	30.00	60.00	120	—

Y# 71a 20 CENTS **Weight:** 5.3000 g. **Composition:** 0.8200 Silver .1397 oz. ASW **Ruler:** Kuang-hsü **Obverse:** Inscription: Kuang-hsü Yüan-pao **Reverse:** Side view dragon, legend at bottom **Rev. Legend:** PEI YANG **Note:** Struck at Chin Mint (Peiyang Arsenal), Tientsin.

Date	Mintage	VG	F	VF	XF	Unc
31(1905)	161,000	12.00	35.00	75.00	150	350

Y# 73 DOLLAR **Weight:** 26.7000 g. **Composition:** 0.9000 Silver .7727 oz. ASW **Ruler:** Kuang-hsü **Obverse:** Similar to Y#73.2, inscription: Kuang-hsü Yüan-pao **Reverse:** Side view dragon, legend at bottom **Rev. Legend:** PEI YANG **Note:** Struck at Chin Mint (Peiyang Arsenal), Tientsin.

Date	Mintage	VG	F	VF	XF	Unc
29(1903)	22,018,000	4.00	12.00	17.00	35.00	150

Y# 73.1 DOLLAR **Weight:** 26.7000 g. **Composition:** 0.9000 Silver .7727 oz. ASW **Ruler:** Kuang-hsü **Obverse:** Inscription: Kuang-hsü Yüan-pao **Reverse:** Side view dragon, legend at bottom, period after legend **Rev. Legend:** PEI YANG **Note:** Struck at Chin Mint (Peiyang Arsenal), Tientsin.

Date	VG	F	VF	XF	Unc
29(1903)	4.00	12.50	17.00	40.00	200

Y# 73.2 DOLLAR **Weight:** 26.7000 g. **Composition:** 0.9000 Silver .7727 oz. ASW **Ruler:** Kuang-hsü **Obverse:** Inscription: Kuang-hsü Yüan-pao **Reverse:** Thinner side-view dragon, legend at bottom, year as "33rd" **Rev. Legend:** PEI YANG **Note:** Struck at Chin Mint (Peiyang Arsenal), Tientsin.

Date	Mintage	VG	F	VF	XF	Unc
33(1907)	2,341,000	5.00	15.00	25.00	50.00	250
34(1908)	—	4.00	12.50	20.00	38.00	175

Y# 73.3 DOLLAR **Weight:** 26.7000 g. **Composition:** 0.9000 Silver .7727 oz. ASW **Ruler:** Kuang-hsü **Obverse:** Inscription: Kuang-hsü Yüan-pao **Reverse:** Side view dragon, legend at bottom, short center spine to tail **Rev. Legend:** PEI YANG **Note:** Struck at Chin Mint (Peiyang Arsenal), Tientsin. Restruck during Republican times.

Date	VG	F	VF	XF	Unc
34(1908)	4.00	12.00	15.00	30.00	150

Y# 73.4 DOLLAR **Weight:** 26.7000 g. **Composition:** 0.9000 Silver .7727 oz. ASW **Ruler:** Kuang-hsü **Obverse:** Inscription: Kuang-hsü Yüan-pao **Reverse:** Side view dragon, legend at bottom, crosslet 4 in date **Rev. Legend:** PEI YANG **Note:** Struck at Chin Mint (Peiyang Arsenal), Tientsin. Restruck during Republican times.

Date	VG	F	VF	XF	Unc
34(1908)	16.50	50.00	125	250	600

Y# 74 TAEL **Weight:** 51.2000 g. **Composition:** Silver **Ruler:** Kuang-hsü **Obverse:** Inscription: Kuang-hsü Yüan-pao **Reverse:** Side view dragon, legend at bottom **Rev. Legend:** PEI YANG **Note:** Struck at Chin Mint (Peiyang Arsenal), Tientsin.

Date	VG	F	VF	XF	Unc
33(1907) (1907)	1,000	2,000	3,500	5,000	10,000

Y# 74.1 TAEL **Weight:** 51.2000 g. **Composition:** Silver **Ruler:** Kuang-hsü **Obverse:** Inscription: Kuang-hsü Yüan-pao **Reverse:** Side view dragon, legend at bottom, 3 dots on pearl arranged horizontally **Rev. Legend:** PEI YANG **Note:** Struck at Chin Mint (Peiyang Arsenal), Tientsin.

Date	VG	F	VF	XF	Unc
33(1907)	1,000	2,000	3,500	5,000	10,000

Y# 74.2 TAEL **Weight:** 51.2000 g. **Composition:** Silver **Ruler:** Kuang-hsü **Obverse:** Inscription: Kuang-hsü Yüan-pao **Reverse:** Side view dragon, legend at bottom, 3 dots on pearl arranged in arc **Rev. Legend:** PEI YANG **Note:** Struck at Chin Mint (Peiyang Arsenal), Tientsin.

Date	VG	F	VF	XF	Unc
33(1907)	1,000	2,000	3,500	5,000	10,000

PATTERNS

Including off metal strikes

KM#	Date	Mintage	Identification	Mkt Val
Pn6	29(1903)	—	Dollar. Brass. Y73.	—
Pn7	33(1907)	—	Tael. Gold. Y74.	—

FENGTIEN PROVINCE

(Fungtien)
Liaoning

The southernmost province of the Three Eastern Provinces was known by a variety of names including Fengtien, Shengching, and Liaoning. The modern Mukden (Fengtien Province) Mint operated from 1897 to 1931.

EMPIRE

PROVINCIAL CAST COINAGE

C# 9-1 CASH **Composition:** Cast Brass **Ruler:** Kuang-hsü **Obverse:** Type A, inscription: Kuang-hsü T'ung-pao **Reverse:** Inscription: Manchu Boo-fung **Note:** Struck at Fung (Fengtien) Mint.

Date	Good	VG	F	VF	XF
ND(1875-1908)	20.00	30.00	50.00	—	—

MILLED COINAGE

Y# 19e 5 CASH **Composition:** Copper **Ruler:** Hsüan-t'ung **Obverse:** Inscription: Tai-ching T'ung-pi **Rev. Legend:** Hsüan-t'ung Nien-tsao, TAI-CHING-TI-KUO ...

Date	VG	F	VF	XF	Unc
CD(1909)	37.50	75.00	125	200	—

Y# 81 10 CASH **Composition:** Copper **Ruler:** Kuang-hsü **Obverse:** Type A

Date	VG	F	VF	XF	Unc
ND(1902?)	40.00	60.00	90.00	200	—

Note: Seven varieties exist

Y# 88 10 CASH **Composition:** Brass **Ruler:** Kuang-hsü **Obverse:** Inscription: Kuang-hsü Yüan-pao **Rev. Legend:** Province named spelled FEN-TIEN

Date	VG	F	VF	XF	Unc
CD(1903)	50.00	90.00	135	225	—

Y# 89 10 CASH **Composition:** Brass **Ruler:** Kuang-hsü **Obverse:** Inscription: Kuang-hsü Yüan-pao **Rev. Legend:** FUNG-TIEN PROVINCE

Date	Mintage	VG	F	VF	XF	Unc
CD(1903)	—	3.75	7.50	25.00	40.00	—
CD(1904)	—	1.25	3.00	5.00	8.00	—
CD(1905)	—	1.50	4.50	10.00	12.00	—
CD(1906)	35,036,000	3.00	6.00	25.00	35.00	—

Y# 89.1 10 CASH **Composition:** Brass **Ruler:** Kuang-hsü **Obverse:** Manchu words in center reversed, inscription: Kuang-hsü Yüan-pao **Rev. Legend:** FUNG-TIEN PROVINCE

Date	VG	F	VF	XF	Unc
CD(1903)	28.00	85.00	150	250	—

Y# 89.2 10 CASH **Composition:** Brass **Ruler:** Kuang-hsü **Obverse:** Inscription: Kuang-hsü Yüan-pao **Reverse:** Large pearl **Rev. Legend:** FUNG-TIEN PROVINCE

Date	VG	F	VF	XF	Unc
CD(1905)	0.65	2.00	4.00	8.00	24.00

Y# 10e 10 CASH **Composition:** Copper **Ruler:** Kuang-hsü **Obverse:** Inscription: Tai-ch'ing T'ung-pi **Reverse:** Small pearl **Rev. Legend:** Kuang-hsü Nien-tsao, TAICHING TI KUO ...

Date	VG	F	VF	XF	Unc
CD(1905)	1.25	4.00	8.00	15.00	30.00

Y# 10e.1 10 CASH **Composition:** Copper **Ruler:** Kuang-hsü **Obverse:** Inscription: Tai-ch'ing T'ung-pi **Reverse:** Large pearl **Rev. Legend:** Kuang-hsü Nien-tsao, TAI-CHING-TI-KUO ...

Date	VG	F	VF	XF	Unc
CD(1905)	1.25	4.00	8.00	15.00	30.00

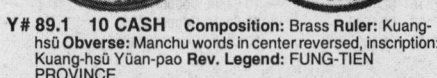

Y# 10e.2 10 CASH **Composition:** Copper **Ruler:** Kuang-hsü **Obverse:** Mint mark on spherical disc in center, inscription: Tai-ch'ing T'ung-pi **Reverse:** Large pearl **Rev. Legend:** Kuang-hsü Nien-tsao, TAI-CHING-TI KUO ...

Date	Mintage	VG	F	VF	XF	Unc
ND(1907)	130,000	1.00	3.00	6.00	20.00	—

Y# 10e.3 10 CASH **Composition:** Copper **Ruler:** Kuang-hsü **Obverse:** Mint mark on flat disc in center, inscription: Tai-ch'ing T'ung-pi **Rev. Legend:** Kuang-hsü Nien-tsao, TAI CHING TI KUO ...

Date	VG	F	VF	XF	Unc
CD(1907)	0.50	1.50	3.00	6.00	20.00

Y# 20e 10 CASH **Composition:** Copper **Ruler:** Hsüan-t'ung **Obverse:** Mint mark on flat disc in center, inscription: Tai-ch'ing T'ung-pi **Rev. Legend:** Hsüan-T'ung Nien-tsao, TAI-CHING-TI-KUO ...

Date	VG	F	VF	XF	Unc
CD(1909)	2.75	8.00	17.50	30.00	—

Y# W286 10 CASH **Composition:** Copper **Ruler:** Kuang-hsü **Obverse:** Inscription: Tai-ch'ing T'ung-pi **Rev. Legend:** Kuang-hsü Nien-tsao, TAI CHING TI KUO ... **Note:** Mule, obverse Y#20e, reverse Y#10e.

Date	VG	F	VF	XF	Unc
CD(1909) 6 known	—	—	—	—	—

Y# 90 20 CASH **Composition:** Brass **Ruler:** Kuang-hsü **Obverse:** Inscription: Kuang-hsü Yüan-pao **Rev. Legend:** FUNG TIEN PROVINCE

Date	VG	F	VF	XF	Unc
CD(1903)	75.00	100	125	175	—
CD(1904)	5.50	11.00	22.50	55.00	—
CD(1905)	9.00	18.00	25.00	60.00	—

Y# 11e 20 CASH **Composition:** Brass **Ruler:** Kuang-hsü **Obverse:** Inscription: Tai-ching T'ung-pi **Rev. Legend:** Kuang-hsü Nien-tsao, TAI-CHING-TI-KUO ...

Date	VG	F	VF	XF	Unc
CD(1905)	4.00	7.00	20.00	40.00	—
CD(1907)	6.00	12.00	25.00	50.00	—

Y# 21e 20 CASH **Composition:** Brass **Ruler:** Hsüan-t'ung **Obverse:** Inscription: Tai-ching T'ung-pi **Rev. Legend:** Hsüan-t'ung Nien-tsao, TAI-CHING-TI-KUO ...

Date	VG	F	VF	XF	Unc
CD(1909)	25.00	60.00	110	175	—

Y# 91 20 CENTS **Composition:** Silver **Ruler:** Kuang-hsü **Obverse:** Inscription: Kuang-hsü Yüan-pao **Reverse:** Side view dragon, 8 rows of scales on dragon **Rev. Legend:** FUNG-TIEN PROVINCE **Size:** 24 mm.

Date	VG	F	VF	XF	Unc
CD(1904)	2.75	8.00	14.00	25.00	70.00

Y# 91.1 20 CENTS Composition: Silver **Ruler:** Kuang-hsü **Obverse:** Inscription: Kuang-hsü Yüan-pao **Reverse:** Side view dragon, 5 rows of scales on dragon **Rev. Legend:** FUNG-TIEN PROVINCE

Date	VG	F	VF	XF	Unc
CD(1904)	3.00	9.00	16.00	30.00	80.00

Y# 92 DOLLAR Weight: 26.4000 g. **Composition:** 0.8500 Silver .7215 oz. ASW **Ruler:** Kuang-hsü **Obverse:** Inscription: Kuang-hsü Yüan-pao **Reverse:** Side view dragon **Rev. Legend:** FUNG-TIEN PROVINCE

Date	Mintage	VG	F	VF	XF	Unc
CD(1903)	262,000	40.00	120	200	500	1,500

Y# 92.1 DOLLAR Weight: 26.4000 g. **Composition:** 0.8500 Silver .7215 oz. ASW **Ruler:** Kuang-hsü **Obverse:** Manchu "Boo-funs" in center are reversed, inscription: Kuang-hsü Yüan-pao **Reverse:** Side view dragon **Rev. Legend:** FUNG-TIEN PROVINCE

Date	VG	F	VF	XF	Unc
CD(1903)	50.00	150	300	600	1,800

TOKEN COINAGE

KM# TnA1 10 CENTS Composition: Copper **Ruler:** Kuang-hsü **Obverse:** Dragon **Reverse:** Tang-shih (10)

Date	VG	F	VF	XF	Unc
ND(c. 1904)	—	—	900	1,500	2,500

KM# Tn1Y# W242 DOLLAR Composition: Copper **Ruler:** Kuang-hsü **Obverse:** Reverse of 10 Cash, Y#10e, small spiral on pearl **Reverse:** Inscription: Tang-yüan(1 Dollar)

Date	VG	F	VF	XF	Unc
ND(c. 1904)	—	—	550	900	1,500
ND(c. 1904)	—	—	550	900	1,500

KM# Tn1a DOLLAR Composition: Brass **Ruler:** Kuang-hsü **Obverse:** Reverse of 10 Cash, Y#10e, small spiral on pearl **Reverse:** Inscription: Tang-yüan(1 Dollar)

Date	VG	F	VF	XF	Unc
ND(c. 1904)	—	—	550	900	1,500

KM# Tn2Y# W243 100 CENTS Composition: Copper **Ruler:** Kuang-hsü **Obverse:** Dragon, large spiral on pearl **Obv. Legend:** FUNG TIEN PROVINCE **Reverse:** Inscription: Tang Pai **Note:** Silver forgeries exist.

Date	VG	F	VF	XF	Unc
ND(c. 1904)	—	—	550	900	1,500
ND(c. 1904)	—	—	550	900	1,500

KM# Tn3 100 CENTS Composition: Brass **Ruler:** Kuang-hsü **Obv. Legend:** FUNG-TIEN PROVINCE **Reverse:** Inscription: Tang Pai **Note:** Silver forgeries exist.

Date	VG	F	VF	XF	Unc
ND(c. 1904)	—	—	—	—	—

PATTERNS

Including off metal strikes

KM#	Date	Mintage	Identification	Mkt Val
Pn2A	ND(c.1902)	—	10 Cents. Brass. Regular provincial design.	—
Pn3	ND(c.1902)	—	20 Cents. Brass. Regular provincial design.	—
Pn4	ND(c.1902)	—	20 Cents. Brass. Error, TENG-TIEN.	—
Pn5	ND(c.1902)	—	20 Cents. Silver. FENG-TIEN.	—
Pn6	ND(c.1902)	—	50 Cents. Brass. Error, TENG-TIEN.	—
Pn7	ND(c.1902)	—	Dollar. Aluminum. Error, TENG-TIEN.	—
Pn8	ND(c.1902)	—	Dollar. Silver. Error, TENG-TIEN.	—
Pn9	ND(c.1902)	—	Dollar. Brass. Error, TENG-TIEN.	—
Pn10	ND(c.1902)	—	10 Cash. Copper.	—
Pn11	CD1903	—	10 Cash. Copper. Y88.	—
Pn12	CD1903	—	10 Cash. Copper. Y89.	—
Pn13	CD1903	—	10 Cash. Copper. Y89.1.	—
Pn14	CD1903	—	20 Cash. Copper. Y90.	200
Pn18	CD1903	—	Tael. Silver. K931-I.	—

Note: Superior Goodman sale 6-91 about XF realized $187,000.

KM#	Date	Mintage	Identification	Mkt Val
Pn15	CD1904	—	10 Cash. Copper. Y89.	—
Pn16	CD1905	—	10 Cash. Copper. Y89.	—
Pn17	CD1905	—	20 Cash. Copper. Y90.	—

FUKIEN PROVINCE

Fujian

A province located on the southeastern coast of China, including the island of Taiwan until it became its own separate province in 1885. Although known mainly as an agricultural area, forestry and some mining, particularly iron ore and coal, are also important to the economy. The Foochow Mint operated throughout the Manchu dynasty. The Viceroy's or City mint was opened in 1896 for struck coinage. Two other mints were established in 1905, the Mamoi Arsenal Mint which struck the Custom-House issues until it closed in 1906, and the West Mint which later became the main Fukien (Fujian) Mint. It closed between 1914 and 1920. Various subsidiary mints were in operation from 1924 to 1925.

EMPIRE

PROVINCIAL CAST COINAGE

C# 10-25 CASH Composition: Cast Brass **Ruler:** Kuang - hsü **Obverse:** Inscription: Kuang hsü T'ung-pao **Reverse:** Inscription: Manchu Boo-fu **Note:** Struck at Fu (Foochow). Sch. #1581.

Date	Good	VG	F	VF	XF
ND(1875-1908)	0.85	1.50	2.50	3.50	—

C# 10-25.1 CASH Composition: Cast Brass **Ruler:** Kuang - hsü **Obverse:** Inscription: Kuang hsü T'ung-pao **Reverse:** Dot at top of hole, inscription: Manchu "Boo-fu" **Note:** Struck at Fu (Foochow).

Date	Good	VG	F	VF	XF
ND(1875-1908)	2.50	4.00	6.50	10.00	—

C# 10-25.2 CASH Composition: Cast Brass **Ruler:** Kuang - hsü **Obverse:** Inscription: Kuang hsü T'ung-pao **Reverse:** Inverted, inscription: Manchu "Boo-fu" **Note:** Struck at Fu (Foochow).

Date	Good	VG	F	VF	XF
ND(1875-1908)	—	—	—	—	—

MILLED COINAGE

Y# 95 CASH Composition: Brass **Ruler:** Kuang - hsü **Obverse:** Inscription: Kuang hsü T'ung-pao **Reverse:** Inscription: Manchu Boo-fung **Note:** Struck at Fu (Foochow).

Date	VG	F	VF	XF	Unc
ND(1908)	6.00	10.00	15.00	30.00	—

Y# 7f CASH Composition: Brass **Ruler:** Kuang - hsü **Obverse:** Inscription: Kuang hsü **Reverse:** Dragon **Note:** Struck at Fu (Foochow).

Date	VG	F	VF	XF	Unc
CD(1908)	35.00	75.00	110	175	—

Y# 106 CASH Composition: Brass **Ruler:** Hsüan - T'ung **Obverse:** Inscription: Hsüan-t'ung T'ung-pao **Reverse:** Inscription: Manchu Boo-fu **Note:** Struck at Fu (Foochow).

Date	VG	F	VF	XF	Unc
ND(1909)	15.00	25.00	50.00	80.00	—

Y# 8f 2 CASH Composition: Brass **Obverse:** Inscription: Tai-ching T'ung-pi **Reverse:** Dragon **Note:** Struck at Fu (Foochow).

Date	VG	F	VF	XF	Unc
CD(1906)	3.00	8.00	14.00	25.00	—

Y# 99 5 CASH Composition: Copper **Ruler:** Kuang - hsü **Obverse:** Inscription: Kuang-hsü Yüan-pao **Reverse:** Dragon **Rev. Legend:** FOO-KIEN **Note:** Struck at Fu (Foochow).

Date	Mintage	VG	F	VF	XF	Unc
ND(1901-03)	590,000	18.00	25.00	37.50	60.00	—

Y# 99a 5 CASH Composition: Brass **Ruler:** Kuang - hsü **Obverse:** Inscription: Kuang-hsü Yüan-pao **Reverse:** Dragon **Rev. Legend:** FOO-KIEN **Note:** Struck at Fu (Foochow).

Date	VG	F	VF	XF	Unc
ND(1901-03)	12.00	25.00	50.00	75.00	—

Y# 97 10 CASH Composition: Copper **Ruler:** Kuang - hsü **Obverse:** Large characters at left and right, inscription: Kuang-hsü Yüan-pao **Reverse:** Dragon **Rev. Legend:** F.K. CUSTOM-HOUSE **Note:** Struck at Fu (Foochow).

Date	Mintage	VG	F	VF	XF	Unc
ND(1901-05)	417,031,000	0.50	1.50	2.50	8.00	25.00

Y# 97.1 10 CASH Composition: Copper **Ruler:** Kuang - hsü **Obverse:** Small characters at left and right sides, inscription: Kuang-hsü Yüan-pao **Reverse:** Dragon **Rev. Legend:** F.K. CUSTOM-HOUSE **Note:** Struck at Fu (Foochow).

Date	VG	F	VF	XF	Unc
ND(1901-05)	0.65	2.00	4.00	10.00	30.00

Y# 98 10 CASH **Composition:** Copper **Ruler:** Kuang - hsü **Obverse:** Inscription: Kuang-hsü Yüan-pao **Reverse:** Dragon **Rev. Legend:** FOO-KIEN CUSTOM **Note:** Struck at Fu (Foochow).

Date	VG	F	VF	XF	Unc
ND(1901-05)	35.00	100	150	250	—

Y# 100 10 CASH **Composition:** Copper **Ruler:** Kuang - hsü **Obverse:** Inscription: Kuang-hsü Yüan-pao **Reverse:** 1 cloud left of pearl, dragon **Rev. Legend:** FOO-KIEN **Note:** Struck at Fu (Foochow).

Date	VG	F	VF	XF	Unc
ND(1901-05)	1.00	3.00	6.00	9.00	30.00

Y# 100.1 10 CASH **Composition:** Copper **Ruler:** Kuang - hsü **Obverse:** Inscription: Kuang-hsü Yüan-pao **Reverse:** 3 clouds left of pearl and without cloud above tip of dragon's tail, dragon **Rev. Legend:** FOO-KIEN **Note:** Struck at Fu (Foochow).

Date	VG	F	VF	XF	Unc
ND(1901-05)	0.65	2.00	4.00	7.00	25.00

Y# 100.2 10 CASH **Composition:** Copper **Ruler:** Kuang - hsü **Obverse:** Inscription: Kuang-hsü Yüan-pao **Reverse:** 3 clouds left of pearl and a cloud above tip of dragon's tail, dragon **Rev. Legend:** FOO-KIEN **Note:** Struck at Fu (Foochow).

Date	VG	F	VF	XF	Unc
ND(1901-05)	0.35	1.00	2.00	4.00	25.00

Y# 100.3 10 CASH **Composition:** Copper **Ruler:** Kuang - hsü **Obverse:** Inscription: Kuang-hsü Yüan-pao **Reverse:** Dragon, denomination: 10 CASHES **Rev. Legend:** FOO-KIEN **Note:** Struck at Fu (Foochow).

Date	VG	F	VF	XF	Unc
ND(1901-05)	4.00	12.00	20.00	45.00	—

Y# 100.2a 10 CASH **Composition:** Brass **Ruler:** Kuang - hsü **Obverse:** Inscription: Kuang-hsü Yüan-pao **Reverse:** Dragon **Rev. Legend:** FOO-KIEN **Note:** Struck at Fu (Foochow).

Date	VG	F	VF	XF	Unc
ND(1901-05)	—	—	—	—	—

Y# 10f 10 CASH **Composition:** Copper **Ruler:** Kuang - hsü **Obverse:** Inscription: Tai-ch'ing T'ung-pi **Reverse:** Dragon, inscription: denomination 10 CASHES **Rev. Legend:** Kuang-hsü Nien-tsao, TAI-CHING-TI-KUO ... **Note:** Struck at Fu (Foochow).

Date	VG	F	VF	XF	Unc
CD(1906)	0.25	0.75	1.50	3.00	20.00

Y# 20f 10 CASH **Composition:** Copper **Ruler:** Hsüan - T'ung **Obverse:** Inscription: Tai-ch'ing T'ung-pi **Reverse:** Dragon **Rev. Legend:** Hsüan-tung Nien-tsao, TAI-CHING-TI-KUO ... **Note:** Struck at Fu (Foochow).

Date	VG	F	VF	XF	Unc
CD(1909)	16.50	50.00	85.00	125	—

Y# 101 20 CASH **Composition:** Copper **Ruler:** Kuang - hsü **Obverse:** Inscription: Kuang-hsü Yüan-pao **Reverse:** Dragon **Rev. Legend:** FOO-KIEN **Note:** Struck at Fu (Foochow).

Date	Mintage	VG	F	VF	XF	Unc
ND(1901-1902)	18,000	12.00	30.00	45.00	75.00	—

Y# 102 5 CENTS **Weight:** 1.3500 g. **Composition:** 0.8200 Silver .0356 oz. ASW **Ruler:** Kuang - hsü **Obverse:** Legend with 5 characters at top, inscription: Kuang-hsü Yüan-pao **Reverse:** Side view dragon left **Note:** Struck at Fu (Foochow).

Date	VG	F	VF	XF	Unc
ND(1896-1903)	2.25	7.00	13.00	22.50	60.00

Y# 102.1 5 CENTS **Weight:** 1.3500 g. **Composition:** 0.8200 Silver .0356 oz. ASW **Ruler:** Kuang - hsü **Obverse:** Legend with four characters at top, inscription: Kuang-hsü Yüan-pao **Reverse:** Rosette at either side of side view dragon right **Note:** Struck at Fu (Foochow).

Date	VG	F	VF	XF	Unc
ND(1903-08)	1.00	3.00	8.00	20.00	40.00

Y# 102.2 5 CENTS **Weight:** 1.3500 g. **Composition:** 0.8200 Silver .0356 oz. ASW **Ruler:** Kuang - hsü **Obverse:** Inscription: Kuang-hsü Yüan-pao **Reverse:** Rosette above dragon's head **Note:** Struck at Fu (Foochow).

Date	VG	F	VF	XF	Unc
ND(1903-08)	2.00	6.00	12.00	25.00	50.00

Y# 102.3 5 CENTS **Weight:** 1.3500 g. **Composition:** 0.8200 Silver .0356 oz. ASW **Ruler:** Kuang - hsü **Obverse:** Inscription: Kuang-hsü Yüan-pao **Rev. Legend:** PROVINCE FOO-KIRN **Note:** Struck at Fu (Foochow).

Date	VG	F	VF	XF	Unc
ND(1903-08)	—	—	—	—	—

Y# 103 10 CENTS **Weight:** 2.7000 g. **Composition:** 0.8200 Silver .0712 oz. ASW **Ruler:** Kuang - hsü **Obverse:** Legend with 5 characters at top, inscription: Kuang-hsü Yüan-pao **Reverse:** Rosette at either side of side view dragon left **Note:** Struck at Fu (Foochow).

Date	Mintage	VG	F	VF	XF	Unc
ND(1896-1903)	13,425,000	1.75	5.00	9.00	17.50	35.00

Y# 103.1 10 CENTS **Weight:** 2.7000 g. **Composition:** 0.8200 Silver .0712 oz. ASW **Ruler:** Kuang - hsü **Obverse:** Inscription: Kuang-hsü Yüan-pao **Reverse:** Dot at either side of side view dragon left **Note:** Struck at Fu (Foochow).

Date	VG	F	VF	XF	Unc
ND(1896-1903)	3.25	8.00	15.00	30.00	60.00

Y# 103.2 10 CENTS **Weight:** 2.7000 g. **Composition:** 0.8200 Silver .0712 oz. ASW **Ruler:** Kuang - hsü **Obverse:** Legend has 4 characters at top, inscription: Kuang-hsü Yüan-pao **Reverse:** Small side view dragon right **Note:** Struck at Fu (Foochow).

Date	VG	F	VF	XF	Unc
ND(1903-08)	1.00	3.00	6.00	12.00	30.00

Y# 103.3 10 CENTS **Weight:** 2.7000 g. **Composition:** 0.8200 Silver .0712 oz. ASW **Ruler:** Kuang - hsü **Obverse:** Legend has 4 characters at top, inscription: Kuang-hsü Yüan-pao **Reverse:** Large side view dragon right **Note:** Struck at Fu (Foochow).

Date	VG	F	VF	XF	Unc
ND(1903-08)	2.00	6.00	12.00	24.00	50.00

Y# 104 20 CENTS **Weight:** 5.4000 g. **Composition:** 0.8200 Silver .1424 oz. ASW **Ruler:** Kuang - hsü **Obverse:** Legend has 5 characters at top, inscription: Kuang-hsü Yüan-pao **Reverse:** Dot at either side of side view dragon left **Note:** Struck at Fu (Foochow).

Date	Mintage	VG	F	VF	XF	Unc
ND(1896-1903)	31,772,000	1.00	3.00	6.00	12.50	30.00

Y# 104.1 20 CENTS **Weight:** 5.4000 g. **Composition:** 0.8200 Silver .1424 oz. ASW **Ruler:** Kuang - hsü **Obverse:** Inscription: Kuang-hsü Yüan-pao **Reverse:** Rosette at either side of side view dragon left **Note:** Struck at Fu (Foochow).

Date	VG	F	VF	XF	Unc
ND(1898-1903)	1.00	3.00	6.00	12.50	30.00

Y# 104.2 20 CENTS **Weight:** 5.4000 g. **Composition:** 0.8200 Silver .1424 oz. ASW **Ruler:** Kuang - hsü **Obverse:** Legend has 4 characters at top, inscription: Kuang-hsü Yüan-pao **Reverse:** Side view dragon right **Note:** Struck at Fu (Foochow). Variety with large side view dragon right on reverse exists.

Date	VG	F	VF	XF	Unc
ND(1903-08)	1.00	3.00	6.00	12.50	30.00

REPUBLIC

PROVINCIAL CAST COINAGE

Y# 374 CASH Composition: Cast Brass **Obverse:** Inscription: Fu-chien T'ung-pao **Reverse:** 6 stripes on right flag

Date	VG	F	VF	XF	Unc
ND(c. 1912)	50.00	80.00	125	165	—

Y# 375 2 CASH Composition: Cast Brass **Obverse:** Inscription: Fu-chien T'ung-pao **Reverse:** 5 stripes on right flag

Date	VG	F	VF	XF	Unc
ND(c. 1912)	12.50	17.50	22.50	30.00	—

Y# 375.1 2 CASH Composition: Cast Brass **Obverse:** Inscription: Fu-chien T'ung-pao **Reverse:** 6 stripes on right flag

Date	VG	F	VF	XF	Unc
ND(c. 1912)	30.00	50.00	80.00	125	—

MILLED COINAGE

Y# 379 10 CASH Composition: Copper **Obverse:** Inscription: Chung-hua Yüan-pao **Rev. Legend:** FOO-KIEN COPPER COIN

Date	VG	F	VF	XF	Unc
ND(c. 1912)	1.25	4.00	8.00	15.00	35.00

Y# 379a 10 CASH Composition: Brass **Obverse:** Inscription: Chung-hua Yüan-pao **Rev. Legend:** FOO-KIEN COPPER COIN

Date	VG	F	VF	XF	Unc
ND(c. 1912)	18.50	37.50	50.00	87.50	125

Y# 380 10 CENTS Weight: 2.6000 g. **Composition:** Silver **Obverse:** Inscription: Chung-hua Yüan-pao

Date	VG	F	VF	XF	Unc
ND(c. 1912)	12.50	30.00	80.00	180	300

Y# 382 10 CENTS Weight: 2.6000 g. **Composition:** Silver **Obverse:** Inscription: Chung-hua Yüan-pao

Date	VG	F	VF	XF	Unc
ND(c. 1913)	0.85	2.50	5.00	9.00	20.00

Y# 380a 10 CENTS Weight: 2.6000 g. **Composition:** Silver **Obverse:** Different legend in center, inscription: Chung-hua Yüan-pao **Note:** Similar to Y#380.

Date	VG	F	VF	XF	Unc
CD1924	16.50	50.00	85.00	150	250

Y# 388 10 CENTS Weight: 2.6000 g. **Composition:** Silver **Subject:** Canton martyrs

Date	VG	F	VF	XF	Unc
17(1928)	2.50	7.50	15.00	30.00	50.00
20(1931)	3.50	10.00	25.00	50.00	75.00

Y# 390 10 CENTS Weight: 2.6000 g. **Composition:** Silver **Subject:** Canton martyrs

Date	VG	F	VF	XF	Unc
21(1932)	35.00	100	150	200	375

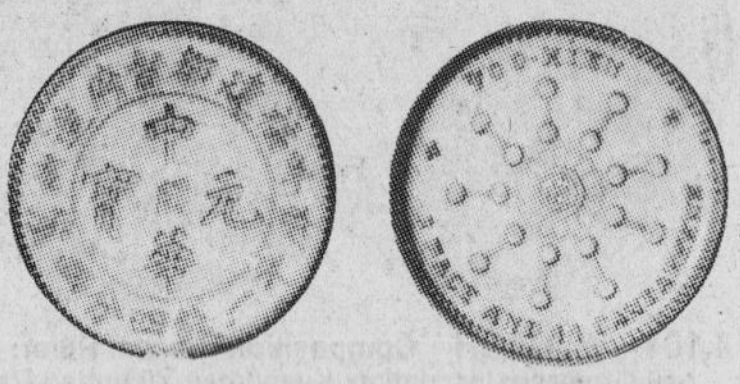

Y# 377 20 CENTS Weight: 5.0000 g. **Composition:** Silver **Obverse:** Inscription: Chung-hua Yüan-pao

Date	VG	F	VF	XF	Unc
CD1911	3.50	10.00	20.00	35.00	100

Y# A381 20 CENTS Weight: 5.4000 g. **Composition:** Silver **Obverse:** Inscription: Chung-hua Yüan-pao

Date	VG	F	VF	XF	Unc
ND(1912)	1.25	3.50	7.00	15.00	25.00

Y# 383 20 CENTS Weight: 5.2000 g. **Composition:** Silver

Date	VG	F	VF	XF	Unc
ND(1923)	1.00	3.00	5.00	10.00	20.00

Note: Kann dates this coin 1913, but evidence suggests that it was struck in 1923

Y# 381 20 CENTS Weight: 5.3000 g. **Composition:** Silver **Obverse:** Rosettes at sides, dot in middle of rosette center **Reverse:** Rosettes at sides

Date	VG	F	VF	XF	Unc
CD1923	1.25	3.50	7.00	10.00	25.00

Y# 381.1 20 CENTS Weight: 5.3000 g. **Composition:** Silver **Reverse:** MADE spelled MAIE in legend

Date	VG	F	VF	XF	Unc
CD1923	1.25	3.50	7.50	12.50	30.00

Y# 381.2 20 CENTS Weight: 5.3000 g. **Composition:** Silver **Rev. Legend:** MADEIN FOO-KIENMINT

Date	VG	F	VF	XF	Unc
CD1923	1.25	3.50	7.50	12.50	30.00

Y# 381.3 20 CENTS Weight: 5.3000 g. **Composition:** Silver **Obverse:** Without dot in middle of center rosette, 5-pointed star at sides in place of rosette

Date	VG	F	VF	XF	Unc
CD1923	3.50	10.00	12.50	17.50	35.00

Y# 381.4 20 CENTS Weight: 5.0000 g. **Composition:** Silver **Obverse:** Different legend in center

Date	VG	F	VF	XF	Unc
CD1924	1.75	5.00	8.00	15.00	35.00

Y# 383a 20 CENTS Weight: 5.7000 g. **Composition:** Silver

Date	VG	F	VF	XF	Unc
13(1924)	11.50	35.00	50.00	70.00	90.00

Y# 384 20 CENTS Weight: 5.0000 g. **Composition:** Silver **Subject:** Northern Expedition

Date	VG	F	VF	XF	Unc
16(1927)	65.00	200	300	400	600

Y# 385 20 CENTS Weight: 5.3000 g. **Composition:** Silver **Subject:** Northern Expedition

Date	VG	F	VF	XF	Unc
16(1927)	200	600	950	1,250	1,750

Y# 389.1 20 CENTS Weight: 5.3000 g. **Composition:** Silver **Subject:** Canton martyrs **Obverse:** Two rows of bricks at right of gate

Date	VG	F	VF	XF	Unc
17(1928)	1.75	5.00	7.50	12.50	30.00
20(1931)	2.50	7.50	12.00	20.00	60.00

Y# 389.2 20 CENTS Weight: 5.5000 g. **Composition:** Silver **Subject:** Canton martyrs **Obverse:** Half brick in 3rd row of bricks at right of gate

Date	VG	F	VF	XF	Unc
17(1928)	1.25	4.00	6.50	10.00	30.00
20(1931)	2.00	6.00	10.00	16.50	50.00

Y# 389.3 20 CENTS Weight: 5.5000 g. **Composition:** Silver **Subject:** Canton martyrs **Reverse:** 6-pointed star in legend

Date	VG	F	VF	XF	Unc
20(1931)	—	—	—	—	—

Y# 391 20 CENTS Weight: 5.3000 g. **Composition:** Silver **Subject:** Canton martyrs

Date	VG	F	VF	XF	Unc
21(1932)	13.50	40.00	65.00	100	250

PATTERNS

Including off metal strikes

KM#	Date	Mintage	Identification	Mkt Val
Pn3	ND(c.1912)	—	2 Cash. Cast Brass. "Fu-chien Sheng-tsao."	300
Pn4	ND(c.1912)	—	2 Cash. Cast Brass. "Fu-chien T'ung-pao."	300
Pn5	ND(c.1912)	—	2 Cash. Cast Brass. "Min-sheng T'ung-pao."	300
Pn6	16(1927)	—	20 Cents. Silver. 5.0000 g. Sun Yat-sen Memorial. K712.	600
Pn7	17(1928)	—	20 Cents. Brass. Y389.1.	—
Pn8	21(1932)	—	20 Cents. Brass. Y391.	—

HEILUNGKIANG PROVINCE

Heilongjiang

The northwesternmost of the former Three Eastern Provinces, bordering on Siberia. Though very large in extent, it is only sparsely populated, for wide areas are desert land. Economically the district was always backward. Heilungkiang (Heilongjiang) Province had no mint of its own, and seemingly no silver money bearing its name was ever placed in circulation although Imperial patterns in the standard dragon design exist for at least the dollar and 50 cent denominations. During the beginning of the 20th century it was suggested to contract for silver coins from the Berlin Mint.

PATTERNS

Including off metal strikes

KM#	Date	Mintage	Identification	Mkt Val
Pn1	ND(1903)	—	50 Cents. Brass. KM584x.	2,500
Pn2	ND(1903)	—	Dollar. Silver.	—
Pn3	ND(1903)	—	Dollar. Brass.	6,000
Pn4	ND(1903)	—	Dollar. Silver Plated Brass.	6,000

HONAN PROVINCE

Henan

A province in east-central China. As well as being one of the most densely populated provinces it is also one of the most important agriculturally. It is the area of earliest settlement in China and has housed the capital during various dynasties. The Kaifeng Mint issued coins from its opening in 1647 through most of the rulers of the Manchu dynasty. In 1905 a modern mint opened at Kaifeng but closed in 1914. A mint in Loyang opened in 1924.

EMPIRE

PROVINCIAL CAST COINAGE

C# 11-9 CASH Composition: Cast Brass **Ruler:** Kuang-hsü **Obverse:** Inscription: Kuang-hsü T'ung-pao **Reverse:** Inscription: Manchu Boo-ho **Note:** Struck at Ho (K'aifeng).

Date	Good	VG	F	VF	XF
ND(1875-1908)	4.00	8.00	10.00	12.00	—

C# 11-9.1 CASH Composition: Cast Brass **Ruler:** Kuang-hsü **Obverse:** Inscription: Kuang-hsü T'ung-pao **Reverse:** Circle above, inscription: Manchu Boo-ho **Note:** Struck at Ho (K'aifeng).

Date	Good	VG	F	VF	XF
ND(1875-1908)	5.00	9.00	13.50	35.00	—

C# 11-9.2 CASH Composition: Cast Brass **Ruler:** Kuang-hsü **Obverse:** Inscription: Kuang-hsü T'ung-pao **Reverse:** Circle below, inscription: Manchu Boo-ho **Note:** Struck at Ho (K'aifeng).

Date	Good	VG	F	VF	XF
ND(1875-1908)	5.00	9.00	13.50	25.00	—

C# 11-9.3 CASH Composition: Cast Brass **Ruler:** Kuang-hsü **Obverse:** Inscription: Kuang-hsü T'ung-pao **Reverse:** Crescent above, inscription: Manchu Boo-ho **Note:** Struck at Ho (K'aifeng).

Date	Good	VG	F	VF	XF
ND(1875-1908)	5.00	9.00	13.50	25.00	—

C# 11-9.4 CASH Composition: Cast Brass **Ruler:** Kuang-hsü **Obverse:** Inscription: Kuang-hsü T'ung-pao **Reverse:** Crescent below, inscription: Manchu Boo-ho **Note:** Struck at Ho (K'aifeng).

Date	Good	VG	F	VF	XF
ND(1875-1908)	5.00	9.00	13.50	25.00	—

C# 11-9.5 CASH Composition: Cast Brass **Ruler:** Kuang-hsü **Obverse:** Inscription: Kuang-hsü T'ung-pao **Reverse:** Crescent above, dot below, inscription: Manchu Boo-ho **Note:** Struck at Ho (K'aifeng). Sch. #1571.

Date	Good	VG	F	VF	XF
ND(1875-1908)	5.00	9.00	13.50	25.00	—

C# 11-9.6 CASH Composition: Cast Brass **Ruler:** Kuang-hsü **Obverse:** Inscription: Kuang-hsü T'ung-pao **Reverse:** Dot above, inscription: Manchu Boo-ho **Note:** Struck at Ho (K'aifeng).

Date	Good	VG	F	VF	XF
ND(1875-1908)	5.00	9.00	13.50	20.00	—

C# 11-9.7 CASH Composition: Cast Brass **Ruler:** Kuang-hsü **Obverse:** Inscription: Kuang-hsü T'ung-pao **Reverse:** Dot below, inscription: Manchu Boo-ho **Note:** Struck at Ho (K'aifeng).

Date	Good	VG	F	VF	XF
ND(1875-1908)	5.00	9.00	13.50	20.00	—

C# 11-9.8 CASH Composition: Cast Brass **Ruler:** Kuang-hsü **Obverse:** Inscription: Kuang-hsü T'ung-pao **Reverse:** Dot at upper left, inscription: Manchu Boo-ho **Note:** Struck at Ho (K'aifeng). Crescent and dot varieties exist.

Date	Good	VG	F	VF	XF
ND(1875-1908)	5.00	9.00	13.50	20.00	—

C# 3-1.1a CASH Composition: Cast Zinc **Ruler:** Kuang-hsü **Obverse:** Inscription: Kuang-hsü T'ung-pao **Reverse:** Dot at upper left, inscription: Manchu Boo-ho **Note:** Struck at Ho (K'aifeng).

Date	Good	VG	F	VF	XF
ND(1875-1908) Rare	—	—	—	—	—

MILLED COINAGE

Y# 7g CASH Composition: Brass **Ruler:** Kuang-hsü **Obv. Legend:** Kuang-hsü **Reverse:** Side view dragon

Date	VG	F	VF	XF	Unc
CD1908	10.00	25.00	42.50	75.00	—

Y# 7ga CASH Composition: Copper **Ruler:** Kuang-hsü **Obv. Legend:** Kuang-hsü **Reverse:** Side view dragon

Date	VG	F	VF	XF	Unc
CD1908	20.00	50.00	85.00	150	—

Y# 108 10 CASH Composition: Copper **Ruler:** Kuang-hsü **Obverse:** Inscription: Kuang-hsü Yüan-pao **Reverse:** Circled dragon without mountain below pearl with 3 flames

Date	VG	F	VF	XF	Unc
ND(1905)	4.00	10.00	20.00	45.00	—

Y# 108.1 10 CASH Composition: Copper **Ruler:** Kuang-hsü **Obverse:** Inscription: Kuang-hsü Yüan-pao **Reverse:** Circled dragon without mountain below pearl with 5 flames

Date	VG	F	VF	XF	Unc
ND(1905)	1.00	2.00	4.50	9.00	—

Y# 108.2 10 CASH Composition: Copper **Ruler:** Kuang-hsü **Obverse:** Inscription: Kuang-hsü Yüan-pao **Reverse:** Circled dragon, mountain below pearl, very small English lettering

Date	VG	F	VF	XF	Unc
ND(1905)	6.00	15.00	30.00	50.00	—

Y# 108.3 10 CASH Composition: Copper **Ruler:** Kuang-hsü **Obverse:** Inscription: Kuang-hsü Yüan-pao **Reverse:** Circled dragon, large English legend

Date	VG	F	VF	XF	Unc
ND(1905)	5.00	10.00	15.00	30.00	—

Y# 108a 10 CASH Composition: Brass **Ruler:** Kuang-hsü **Obverse:** Raised sphere yin-yang in center, inscription: Kuang-hsü Yüan-pao **Reverse:** Uncircled dragon, Honan spelled HOU-NAN **Note:** Dies made in Japan.

Date	VG	F	VF	XF	Unc
ND(1905) Rare	—	—	—	—	—

Y# 108a.1 10 CASH **Composition:** Copper **Ruler:** Kuang-hsü **Obverse:** Inscription: Kuang-hsü Yüan-pao **Reverse:** Uncircled dragon

Date	VG	F	VF	XF	Unc
ND(1905)	1.00	3.00	5.00	10.00	—

Y# 108a.2 10 CASH **Composition:** Copper **Ruler:** Kuang-hsü **Obverse:** Curved line on raised yin-yang slanted more, inscription: Kuang-hsü Yüan-pao **Reverse:** Uncircled dragon

Date	VG	F	VF	XF	Unc
ND(1905)	1.00	3.00	5.00	10.00	—

Y# 108a.3 10 CASH **Composition:** Copper **Ruler:** Kuang-hsü **Obverse:** Flat yin-yang slanted more, inscription: Kuang-hsü Yüan-pao **Reverse:** Circled dragon, plain pearl

Date	VG	F	VF	XF	Unc
ND(1905)	0.75	2.50	4.00	8.00	—

Note: Dies made in United States

Y# 108a.3a 10 CASH **Composition:** Brass **Ruler:** Kuang-hsü **Obverse:** Inscription: Kuang-hsü Yüan-pao **Reverse:** Dragon

Date	VG	F	VF	XF	Unc
ND(1905)	2.50	5.00	10.00	20.00	—

Y# 108a.4 10 CASH **Composition:** Copper **Ruler:** Kuang-hsü **Obverse:** Inscription: Kuang-hsü Yüan-pao **Reverse:** Dragon, incuse swirl in pearl

Date	VG	F	VF	XF	Unc
ND(1905)	1.00	3.00	5.00	12.00	—

Note: Dies made in United States

Y# 10g 10 CASH **Composition:** Copper **Ruler:** Kuang-hsü **Obverse:** Inscription: Tai-ch'ing T'ung-pi **Reverse:** Dragon, period after COIN in legend **Rev. Legend:** Kuang-hsü Nien-tsao, TAI-CHING-TI-KUO ...

Date	Mintage	VG	F	VF	XF	Unc
CD(1906)	132,000,000	0.85	2.00	5.00	10.00	—

Y# 10g.1 10 CASH **Composition:** Copper **Ruler:** Kuang-hsü **Obverse:** Inscription: Tai-ch'ing T'ung-pi **Reverse:** Dragon, period after COPPER in legend **Rev. Legend:** Kuang-hsü Nien-tsao, TAI-CHING-TI-KUO ...

Date	VG	F	VF	XF	Unc
CD(1906)	1.25	3.00	6.00	10.00	—

Y# 10g.2 10 CASH **Composition:** Copper **Ruler:** Kuang-hsü **Obverse:** Inscription: Tai-ch'ing T'ung-pi **Reverse:** Dragon **Rev. Legend:** Kuang-hsü Nien-tsao, TAI-CHING-TI-KUO ... **Note:** Cyclical dates at sides.

Date	VG	F	VF	XF	Unc
CD(1907) Rare	—	—	—	—	—

Y# 20g 10 CASH **Composition:** Copper **Ruler:** Hsüan-t'ung **Obverse:** Inscription: Tai-ch'ing T'ung-pi **Reverse:** Dragon **Rev. Legend:** Hsüan-t'ung Nien-tsao, TAI-CHING-TI-KUO ... **Note:** Normally encountered with weak legends.

Date	VG	F	VF	XF	Unc
CD(1909)	20.00	40.00	60.00	125	—
CD(1911)	5.00	15.00	25.00	50.00	—

REPUBLIC

MILLED COINAGE

Y# A392 10 CASH **Composition:** Copper

Date	VG	F	VF	XF	Unc
ND(1913-14)	0.35	1.00	2.00	6.00	20.00

Y# A392.1 10 CASH **Composition:** Copper **Obverse:** Without lines above and below rosettes

Date	VG	F	VF	XF	Unc
ND(1913-14)	0.35	1.00	2.00	6.00	20.00

Y# A392.2 10 CASH **Composition:** Copper **Reverse:** Letter "S" in CASH backwards

Date	VG	F	VF	XF	Unc
ND(c.1920)	6.00	17.50	30.00	60.00	—

Y# 392 10 CASH **Composition:** Copper **Reverse:** TEN CASH in legend in larger letters

Date	VG	F	VF	XF	Unc
ND(c.1920)	0.25	0.75	1.50	4.00	18.00

Y# 392.1 10 CASH **Composition:** Copper **Obverse:** Rosette in center higher in relation to heart-shaped leaves below

Date	VG	F	VF	XF	Unc
ND(c.1920)	0.65	2.00	3.50	6.00	20.00

Y# 393 20 CASH **Composition:** Copper **Reverse:** Legend has 6 characters at bottom

Date	Good	VG	F	VF	XF
ND(c. 1920)	1.25	2.50	5.00	10.00	30.00

Y# 393.1 20 CASH **Composition:** Copper **Reverse:** Legend has 5 characters at bottom

Date	Good	VG	F	VF	XF
ND(c. 1920)	1.00	2.00	4.00	6.00	20.00

Y# 393.2 20 CASH **Composition:** Copper **Reverse:** CHINA replaces HO-NAN in legend

Date	Good	VG	F	VF	XF
ND(c. 1921)	12.50	25.00	45.00	175	—

Y# A397 20 CASH **Composition:** Copper **Reverse:** Star above flags

Date	Good	VG	F	VF	XF
20(1931)	—	500	1,500	3,000	—

Y# 394 50 CASH **Composition:** Copper **Reverse:** Short flag poles

Date	Good	VG	F	VF	XF
ND(c. 1920)	2.00	5.00	10.00	20.00	60.00

Y# 394.1 50 CASH **Composition:** Copper **Reverse:** Long flag poles

Date	Good	VG	F	VF	XF
ND(c. 1920)	2.00	5.00	10.00	20.00	60.00

Y# 394b 50 CASH **Composition:** Brass

Date	Good	VG	F	VF	XF
ND(c. 1920)	10.00	20.00	40.00	80.00	225

Y# 394a 50 CASH **Composition:** Brass **Reverse:** CHINA replaces HONAN in legend

Date	Good	VG	F	VF	XF
ND(c. 1921)	6.50	12.50	25.00	60.00	175

Y# 397 50 CASH **Composition:** Brass

Date	VG	F	VF	XF	Unc
20(1931)	120	200	330	—	—

Y# 395 100 CASH **Composition:** Copper **Reverse:** Small star in right flag, tassels 4 millimeters long

Date	Good	VG	F	VF	XF
ND(c. 1928)	3.00	5.00	10.00	25.00	75.00

Y# 395.1 100 CASH **Composition:** Copper **Reverse:** Tassels 5 millimeters long

Date	Good	VG	F	VF	XF
ND(c. 1928)	3.75	6.50	12.50	30.00	90.00

Y# 395.2 100 CASH **Composition:** Copper **Reverse:** Large star in right flag

Date	Good	VG	F	VF	XF
ND(c. 1928)	—	—	—	—	—

Y# 398 100 CASH **Composition:** Copper

Date	VG	F	VF	XF	Unc
20(1931)	60.00	95.00	150	—	—

Y# 396 200 CASH **Composition:** Copper **Reverse:** Large square inside right flag

Date	Good	VG	F	VF	XF
ND(c. 1928)	3.00	5.00	10.00	25.00	75.00

Y# 396.1 200 CASH **Composition:** Copper **Reverse:** Small square and small star inside right flag

Date	Good	VG	F	VF	XF
ND(c. 1928)	2.50	4.50	9.00	25.00	75.00

Y# 396.2 200 CASH **Composition:** Copper **Reverse:** Small square and large star inside right flag

Date	Good	VG	F	VF	XF
ND(c. 1928)	2.50	4.50	9.00	25.00	75.00

Y# 396a 200 CASH **Composition:** Brass **Reverse:** Small square and large star inside right flag

Date	Good	VG	F	VF	XF
ND(c. 1928)	6.00	15.00	22.50	45.00	135

PATTERNS

Including off metal strikes

KM#	Date	Mintage	Identification	Mkt Val
Pn2	CD(1909)	—	5 Cash. Copper. Y19g.	—
Pn3	CD(1909)	—	20 Cash. Copper. Y21g.	—
Pn1	CD(1909)	—	2 Cash. Brass.	—

HUNAN PROVINCE

A province in south-central China. Mining of coal, antimony, tungsten and tin is important as well as raising varied agricultural products. The Changsha Mint produced Cash coins from early in the Manchu dynasty. Its facility for struck coinage opened in 1897, and two further copper mints were added in 1905. All three mints were closed down in 1907, but one mint was reopened at a later date and produced vast quantities of republican copper coinage until 1926.

EMPIRE

PROVINCIAL CAST COINAGE

C# 12-7 CASH **Composition:** Cast Brass **Ruler:** Kuang-hsü **Obverse:** Inscription: Kuang-hsü T'ung-pao **Reverse:** Inscription: Manchu Boo-nan **Note:** Cast at Nan (Ch'angsha)

Date	Good	VG	F	VF	XF
ND(1875-1908)	7.50	15.00	21.50	30.00	—

MILLED COINAGE

Y# 112 10 CASH **Composition:** Copper **Ruler:** Kuang-hsü **Obverse:** Inscription: Kuang-hsü Yüan-pao; rosette in ceetner with center of petals depressed; Manchu words at sides, "Tan Shih" at bottom **Reverse:** Narrow spacing in HU-NAN above dragon

Date	VG	F	VF	XF	Unc
ND(1902-06)	0.35	1.00	2.00	5.00	20.00

Y# 112.1 10 CASH **Composition:** Copper **Ruler:** Kuang-hsü **Obverse:** Inscription: Kuang-hsü Yüan-pao **Reverse:** Dragon; wide spacing in HU-NAN

Date	VG	F	VF	XF	Unc
ND(1902-06)	0.75	2.25	4.00	9.00	30.00

Y# 112.2 10 CASH **Composition:** Copper **Ruler:** Kuang-hsü **Obverse:** Inscription: Kuang-hsü Yüan-pao; petals of rosettes not depressed **Reverse:** Dragon

Date	VG	F	VF	XF	Unc
ND(1902-06)	0.50	1.50	2.50	6.00	20.00

Y# 112.3 10 CASH **Composition:** Copper **Ruler:** Kuang-hsü **Obverse:** Inscription: Kuang-hsü Yüan-pao; two Manchu words in center, "T'ung Yuan" at bottom **Reverse:** Dragon

Date	VG	F	VF	XF	Unc
ND(1902-06)	1.00	3.00	6.00	10.00	30.00

Y# 112.4 10 CASH **Composition:** Copper **Ruler:** Kuang-hsü **Obverse:** Inscription: Kuang-hsü Yüan-pao **Reverse:** Dragon; narrow spacing in HU-NAN

Date	VG	F	VF	XF	Unc
ND(1902-06)	0.50	1.50	2.50	6.00	20.00

Y# 112.5 10 CASH **Composition:** Copper **Ruler:** Kuang-hsü **Obverse:** Inscription: Kuang-hsü Yüan-pao; rosette in center, "Tang Shih" at bottom **Reverse:** Dragon; ring around pearl

Date	VG	F	VF	XF	Unc
ND(1902-06)	0.40	1.25	2.00	4.00	18.00

Y# 112.6 10 CASH **Composition:** Copper **Ruler:** Kuang-hsü **Obverse:** Inscription: Kuang-hsü Yüan-pao; centers of petals on rosette depressed **Reverse:** Dragon

Date	VG	F	VF	XF	Unc
ND(1902-06)	0.50	1.50	2.50	6.00	20.00

Y# 112.7 10 CASH **Composition:** Copper **Ruler:** Kuang-hsü **Obverse:** Inscription: Kuang-hsü Yüan-pao; two Manchu words in center, "T'ung Yüan" at bottom **Reverse:** Dragon; ring around pearl

Date	VG	F	VF	XF	Unc
ND(1902-06)	0.50	1.50	2.50	6.00	20.00

Y# 112.8 10 CASH **Composition:** Copper **Ruler:** Kuang-hsü **Obverse:** Inscription: Kuang-hsü Yüan-pao; larger characters at left and right, and different characters below **Reverse:** Dragon redesigned and small star at either side

Date	VG	F	VF	XF	Unc
ND(1902-06)	1.75	5.00	10.00	17.50	40.00

Y# 112.9 10 CASH **Composition:** Copper **Ruler:** Kuang-hsü **Obverse:** Inscription: Kuang-hsü Yüan-pao; rosette in center; legend: four characters at bottom **Reverse:** Redesigned dragon without pearl; rosette at either side

Date	VG	F	VF	XF	Unc
ND(1902-06)	2.50	7.50	15.00	30.00	75.00

Y# 112.10 10 CASH **Composition:** Copper **Rule** Kuang-hsü **Obverse:** Inscription: Kuang-hsü Yüan-pao; two Manchu words in center with dot between; "T'ung Yüan" at bottom **Reverse:** Dragon

Date	VG	F	VF	XF	Unc
ND(1902-06)	0.35	1.00	2.00	4.00	18.00

Y# 112.11 10 CASH **Composition:** Copper **Ruler:** Kuang-hsü **Obverse:** Inscription: Kuang-hsü Yüan-pao; without dot between Manchu words, "T'ung Yüan" at bottom **Reverse:** Dragon

Date	VG	F	VF	XF	Unc
ND(1902-06)	0.35	1.00	2.00	4.00	18.00

Y# 112.12 10 CASH **Composition:** Copper **Ruler:** Kuang-hsü **Obverse:** Inscription: Kuang-hsü Yüan-pao; smaller 15.5 millimeter inner circle, with larger beads, "T'ung Yüan" at bottom **Reverse:** Dragon

Date	VG	F	VF	XF	Unc
ND(1902-06)	0.35	1.00	2.00	4.00	18.00

Y# 112.13 10 CASH **Composition:** Copper **Ruler:** Kuang-hsü **Obverse:** Inscription: Kuang-hsü Yüan-pao; two Manchu words in center, 18.4 millimeter inner circle; "Huang T'ung" at bottom **Reverse:** Dragon

Date	VG	F	VF	XF	Unc
ND(1902-06)	8.50	25.00	45.00	80.00	—

Y# 112.14 10 CASH **Composition:** Copper **Ruler:** Kuang-hsü **Obverse:** Inscription: Kuang-hsü Yüan-pao; smaller 17.5 millimeter inner circle; "Huang T'ung Yüan" at bottom **Reverse:** Dragon

Date	VG	F	VF	XF	Unc
ND(1902-06)	8.50	25.00	45.00	80.00	—

Y# 113 10 CASH **Composition:** Copper **Ruler:** Kuang-hsü **Obverse:** Inscription: Kuang-hsü Yüan-pao **Obv. Legend:** Six characters at bottom **Reverse:** Flying dragon **Edge:** Reeded

Date	VG	F	VF	XF	Unc
ND(1902-06)	1.25	4.00	8.00	15.00	40.00

Y# 113.1 10 CASH **Composition:** Copper **Ruler:** Kuang-hsü **Obverse:** Inscription: Kuang-hsü Yüan-pao **Obv. Legend:** Inverted U in HU-NAN **Reverse:** Dragon **Edge:** Reeded

Date	VG	F	VF	XF	Unc
ND(1902-06)	4.50	12.50	25.00	45.00	—

Y# 113a 10 CASH **Composition:** Brass **Ruler:** Kuang-hsü **Obverse:** Inscription: Kuang-hsü Yüan-pao **Obv. Legend:** Three characters at bottom **Reverse:** Dragon

Date	VG	F	VF	XF	Unc
ND(1902-06)	1.25	3.50	6.00	12.50	35.00

Y# 10h 10 CASH **Composition:** Copper **Ruler:** Kuang-hsü **Obverse:** Inscription: Tai-ch'ing T'ung-pi; upper and lower parts of character "Hu" connected **Reverse:** Dragon; dot between Chinese characters above dragon **Rev. Legend:** Kuang-hsü Nien-tsao, TAI-CHING-TI-KUO...

Date	VG	F	VF	XF	Unc
CD(1906)	6.00	17.50	35.00	70.00	—

Y# 10h.1 10 CASH **Composition:** Copper **Ruler:** Kuang-hsü **Obverse:** Inscription: Tai-ch'ing T'ung-pi; upper and lower parts of character "Hu" not connected **Reverse:** Dragon; dot between Chinese characters at top **Rev. Legend:** Kuang-hsü Nien-tsao, TAI-CHING-TI-KUO...

Date	VG	F	VF	XF	Unc
CD(1906)	6.00	17.50	35.00	70.00	—

Y# 10h.2 10 CASH **Composition:** Copper **Ruler:** Kuang-hsü **Obverse:** Inscription: Tai-ch'ing T'ung-pi; similar to Y#10h.1 **Reverse:** Dragon; seven flames on pearl **Rev. Legend:** Kuang-hsü Nien-tsao, TAI-CHING-TI-KUO...

Date	VG	F	VF	XF	Unc
CD(1906)	0.65	2.00	4.00	8.00	22.00

Y# 10h.3 10 CASH **Composition:** Copper **Ruler:** Kuang-hsü **Obverse:** Inscription: Tai-ch'ing T'ung-pi **Reverse:** Dragon; seven-flame pearl ornamented with toothlike projections **Rev. Legend:** Kuang-hsü Nien-tsao, TAI-CHING-TI-KUO...

Date	VG	F	VF	XF	Unc
CD(1906)	0.65	2.00	3.50	6.00	18.00

Y# 10h.4 10 CASH **Composition:** Copper **Ruler:** Kuang-hsü **Obverse:** Inscription: Tai-ch'ing T'ung-pi **Reverse:** Dragon; four flames on pearl **Rev. Legend:** Kuang-hsü Nien-tsao, TAI-CHING-TI-KUO...

Date	VG	F	VF	XF	Unc
CD(1906)	1.00	3.00	6.00	10.00	22.00

Y# 10h.5 10 CASH **Composition:** Copper **Ruler:** Kuang-hsü **Obverse:** Inscription: Tai-ch'ing T'ung-pi **Reverse:** Redesigned dragon with high waves beneath **Rev. Legend:** Kuang-hsü Nien-tsao, TAI-CHING-TI-KUO...

Date	VG	F	VF	XF	Unc
CD(1906)	13.50	40.00	80.00	150	—

Y# 10h.6 10 CASH **Composition:** Copper **Ruler:** Kuang-hsü **Obverse:** Inscription: Tai-ch'ing T'ung-pi; character "Hu" connected **Reverse:** Redesigned dragon, dot between COPPER COIN **Rev. Legend:** Kuang-hsü Nien-tsao, TAI-CHING-TI-KUO...

Date	VG	F	VF	XF	Unc
CD(1906)	4.50	12.50	20.00	40.00	—

Y# 10h.7 10 CASH **Composition:** Copper **Ruler:** Kuang-hsü **Obverse:** Inscription: Tai-ch'ing T'ung-pi; character "Hu" connected **Reverse:** Redesigned dragon with five flames on pearl **Rev. Legend:** Kuang-hsü Nien-tsao, TAI-CHING-TI-KUO... **Note:** Cross-reference numbers: Woodward #342 and #343

Date	VG	F	VF	XF	Unc
CD(1906)	10.00	30.00	45.00	75.00	—

BULLION COINAGE

Mace/Tael Series

K# 951 CH'IEN (MACE) **Weight:** 3.7000 g. **Composition:** Silver **Obverse:** Two lines of two characters each **Reverse:** Two lines of one character each **Note:** Provincial type.

Date	VG	F	VF	XF	Unc
ND(ca.1906)	30.00	50.00	70.00	100	—

K# 971 CH'IEN (MACE) **Weight:** 3.7000 g. **Composition:** Silver **Obverse:** Three lines of two characters each **Reverse:** Two lines of three characters each **Note:** Merchant type.

Date	VG	F	VF	XF	Unc
ND(ca.1908)	30.00	50.00	70.00	120	—

K# 973 CH'IEN (MACE) **Weight:** 3.7000 g. **Composition:** Silver **Obverse:** Two lines of two characters each **Reverse:** Two lines of one character each **Note:** Merchant type.

Date	VG	F	VF	XF	Unc
ND(ca.1908)	30.00	50.00	70.00	120	—

K# 984/5 CH'IEN (MACE) **Weight:** 3.7000 g. **Composition:** Silver **Obverse:** Two lines of three characters each **Reverse:** Two lines of one character each **Note:** Merchant type.

Date	VG	F	VF	XF	Unc
ND(ca.1908)	30.00	50.00	70.00	120	—

K# 950 2 CH'IEN (MACE) **Weight:** 7.3000 g. **Composition:** Silver **Obverse:** Two lines of two characters each **Reverse:** Two lines of two characters each **Note:** Provincial type.

Date	VG	F	VF	XF	Unc
ND(ca.1906)	35.00	55.00	75.00	110	—

K# 960 2 CH'IEN (MACE) **Weight:** 7.3000 g. **Composition:** Silver **Obverse:** Three lines of two characters each **Reverse:** Two lines of two characters each **Note:** Provincial type.

Date	VG	F	VF	XF	Unc
ND(ca.1906)	35.00	55.00	75.00	110	—

K# 970 2 CH'IEN (MACE) **Weight:** 7.3000 g. **Composition:** Silver **Obverse:** Three lines of two characters each **Reverse:** Two lines of three characters each **Note:** Ta Ch'ing Bank type.

Date	VG	F	VF	XF	Unc
ND(ca.1908)	35.00	55.00	75.00	130	—

K# 972 2 CH'IEN (MACE) **Weight:** 7.3000 g. **Composition:** Silver **Obverse:** Two lines of two characters each **Reverse:** Two lines of two characters each **Note:** Merchant type.

Date	VG	F	VF	XF	Unc
ND(ca.1908)	35.00	55.00	75.00	130	—

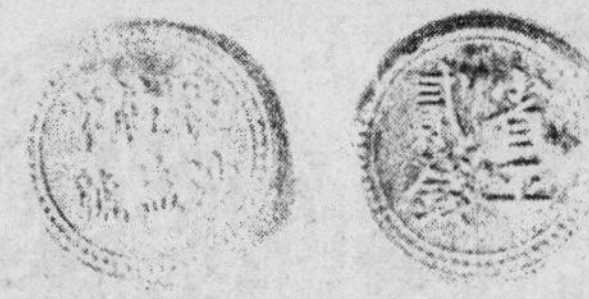

K# 982/3 2 CH'IEN (MACE) **Weight:** 7.3000 g. **Composition:** Silver **Obverse:** Two lines of three characters each **Reverse:** Two lines of two characters each **Note:** Merchant type.

Date	VG	F	VF	XF	Unc
ND(ca.1908)	35.00	55.00	75.00	110	—

K# 949 3 CH'IEN (MACE) **Weight:** 10.7000 g. **Composition:** Silver **Obverse:** Two lines of three characters each **Reverse:** Two lines of three characters each **Note:** Provincial type.

Date	VG	F	VF	XF	Unc
ND(ca.1906)	37.50	60.00	85.00	120	—

K# 959 3 CH'IEN (MACE) **Weight:** 10.7000 g. **Composition:** Silver **Obverse:** Three lines of two characters each **Reverse:** Two lines of three characters each **Note:** Provincial type.

Date	VG	F	VF	XF	Unc
ND(ca.1906)	37.50	60.00	85.00	120	—

K# 969 3 CH'IEN (MACE) **Weight:** 10.7000 g. **Composition:** Silver **Obverse:** Three lines of two characters each **Reverse:** Two lines of three characters each **Note:** Ta Ch'ing Bank type.

Date	VG	F	VF	XF	Unc
ND(ca.1908)	37.50	60.00	85.00	140	—

K# 981 3 CH'IEN (MACE) **Weight:** 10.7000 g. **Composition:** Silver **Obverse:** Two lines of three characters each **Reverse:** Two lines of three characters each **Note:** Merchant type.

Date	VG	F	VF	XF	Unc
ND(ca.1908)	37.50	60.00	85.00	140	—

K# 981a 3 CH'IEN (MACE) **Weight:** 10.7000 g. **Composition:** Silver **Note:** Merchant type; "official" character for three.

Date	VG	F	VF	XF	Unc
ND(ca.1908)	37.50	60.00	85.00	120	—

K# 948 4 CH'IEN (MACE) **Weight:** 14.3000 g. **Composition:** Silver **Obverse:** Two lines of three characters each **Reverse:** Two lines of three characters each **Note:** Provincial type.

Date	VG	F	VF	XF	Unc
ND(ca.1906)	40.00	65.00	90.00	125	—

K# 958 4 CH'IEN (MACE) **Weight:** 14.3000 g. **Composition:** Silver **Obverse:** Three lines of two characters each **Reverse:** Two lines of three characters each **Note:** Provincial type.

Date	VG	F	VF	XF	Unc
ND(ca.1906)	40.00	65.00	90.00	125	—

K# 968 4 CH'IEN (MACE) **Weight:** 14.3000 g. **Composition:** Silver **Obverse:** Three lines of two characters each **Reverse:** Two lines of three characters each **Note:** Ta Ch'ing Bank type.

Date	VG	F	VF	XF	Unc
ND(ca.1908)	40.00	65.00	90.00	135	—

K# 980 4 CH'IEN (MACE) **Weight:** 14.3000 g. **Composition:** Silver **Obverse:** Two lines of three characters each **Reverse:** Two lines of three characters each **Note:** Merchant type.

Date	VG	F	VF	XF	Unc
ND(ca.1908)	40.00	65.00	90.00	135	—

K# 947 5 CH'IEN (MACE) **Weight:** 18.3000 g. **Composition:** Silver **Obverse:** Two lines of three characters each **Reverse:** Two lines of three characters each **Note:** Provincial type.

Date	VG	F	VF	XF	Unc
ND(ca.1906)	42.50	70.00	100	140	—

K# 957 5 CH'IEN (MACE) **Weight:** 18.3000 g. **Composition:** Silver **Obverse:** Three lines of two characters each **Reverse:** Two lines of three characters each **Note:** Provincial type.

Date	VG	F	VF	XF	Unc
ND(ca.1906_)	42.50	70.00	100	140	—

K# 967 5 CH'IEN (MACE) **Weight:** 18.3000 g. **Composition:** Silver **Obverse:** Three lines of two characters each **Reverse:** Two lines of three characters each **Note:** Ta Ch'ing Bank type.

Date	VG	F	VF	XF	Unc
ND(ca.1908)	42.50	70.00	100	150	—

K# 979 5 CH'IEN (MACE) **Weight:** 18.3000 g. **Composition:** Silver **Obverse:** Two lines of three characters each **Reverse:** Two lines of three characters each **Note:** Merchant type.

Date	VG	F	VF	XF	Unc
ND(ca.1908)	42.50	70.00	100	150	—

K# 946 6 CH'IEN (MACE) **Weight:** 21.4000 g. **Composition:** Silver **Obverse:** Two lines of three characters each **Reverse:** Two lines of three characters each **Note:** Provincial type.

Date	VG	F	VF	XF	Unc
ND(ca.1906)	45.00	75.00	110	150	—

K# 956 6 CH'IEN (MACE) **Weight:** 21.4000 g. **Composition:** Silver **Obverse:** Three lines of two characters each **Reverse:** Two lines of three characters each **Note:** Provincial type.

Date	VG	F	VF	XF	Unc
ND(ca.1906)	45.00	75.00	110	150	—

K# 966 6 CH'IEN (MACE) **Weight:** 21.4000 g. **Composition:** Silver **Obverse:** Three lines of two characters each **Reverse:** Two lines of three characters each **Note:** Ta Ch'ing Bank type.

Date	VG	F	VF	XF	Unc
ND(ca.1908)	45.00	75.00	110	185	—

K# 978 6 CH'IEN (MACE) **Weight:** 21.4000 g. **Composition:** Silver **Obverse:** Two lines of three characters each **Reverse:** Two lines of three characters each **Note:** Merchant type.

Date	VG	F	VF	XF	Unc
ND(ca.1908)	45.00	75.00	110	185	—

K# 945 7 CH'IEN (MACE) **Weight:** 25.9000 g. **Composition:** Silver **Obverse:** Two lines of three characters each **Reverse:** Two lines of three characters each **Note:** Provincial type.

Date	VG	F	VF	XF	Unc
ND(ca.1906)	45.00	75.00	110	150	—

K# 955 7 CH'IEN (MACE) **Weight:** 25.9000 g. **Composition:** Silver **Obverse:** Three lines of two characters each **Reverse:** Two lines of three characters each **Note:** Provincial type.

Date	VG	F	VF	XF	Unc
ND(ca.1906)	45.00	75.00	110	150	—

K# 965 7 CH'IEN (MACE) **Weight:** 25.9000 g. **Composition:** Silver **Obverse:** Three lines of two characters each **Reverse:** Two lines of three characters each **Note:** Ta Ch'ing Bank type.

Date	VG	F	VF	XF	Unc
ND(ca.1908)	45.00	75.00	110	185	—

K# 977 7 CH'IEN (MACE) **Weight:** 25.9000 g. **Composition:** Silver **Obverse:** Two lines of three characters each **Reverse:** Two lines of three characters each **Note:** Merchant type.

Date	VG	F	VF	XF	Unc
ND(ca.1908)	45.00	75.00	110	185	—

K# 944 8 CH'IEN (MACE) **Weight:** 29.2000 g. **Composition:** Silver **Obverse:** Two lines of three characters each **Reverse:** Two lines of three characters each **Note:** Provincial type.

Date	VG	F	VF	XF	Unc
ND(ca.1906)	50.00	75.00	125	175	—

K# 954 8 CH'IEN (MACE) **Weight:** 29.2000 g. **Composition:** Silver **Obverse:** Three lines of two characters each **Reverse:** Two lines of three characters each **Note:** Provincial type.

Date	VG	F	VF	XF	Unc
ND(ca.1906)	50.00	75.00	125	175	—

K# 964 8 CH'IEN (MACE) **Weight:** 29.2000 g. **Composition:** Silver **Obverse:** Three lines of two characters each **Reverse:** Two lines of three characters each **Note:** Ta Ch'ing Bank type.

Date	VG	F	VF	XF	Unc
ND(ca.1908)	50.00	75.00	125	175	—

K# 976 8 CH'IEN (MACE) **Weight:** 29.2000 g. **Composition:** Silver **Obverse:** Two lines of three characters each **Reverse:** Two lines of three characters each **Note:** Merchant type.

Date	VG	F	VF	XF	Unc
ND(ca.1908)	50.00	75.00	125	175	—

K# 943 9 CH'IEN (MACE) **Weight:** 29.2000 g. **Composition:** Silver **Obverse:** Two lines of three characters each **Reverse:** Two lines of three characters each **Note:** Provincial type.

Date	VG	F	VF	XF	Unc
ND(ca.1906)	50.00	75.00	125	175	—

K# 953 9 CH'IEN (MACE) **Weight:** 29.2000 g. **Composition:** Silver **Obverse:** Three lines of two characters each **Reverse:** Two lines of three characters each **Note:** Provincial type.

Date	VG	F	VF	XF	Unc
ND(ca.1906)	50.00	75.00	125	175	—

K# 963 9 CH'IEN (MACE) **Weight:** 29.2000 g. **Composition:** Silver **Obverse:** Three lines of two characters each **Reverse:** Two lines of three characters each **Note:** Ta Ch'ing Bank type.

Date	VG	F	VF	XF	Unc
ND(ca.1908)	50.00	75.00	125	200	—

K# 975 9 CH'IEN (MACE) **Weight:** 29.2000 g. **Composition:** Silver **Obverse:** Two lines of three characters each **Reverse:** Two lines of three characters each **Note:** Merchant type.

Date	VG	F	VF	XF	Unc
ND(ca.1908)	50.00	75.00	125	200	—

K# 942 LIANG (Tael) **Weight:** 35.9000 g. **Composition:** Silver **Obverse:** Two lines of three characters each **Reverse:** Two lines of three characters each **Note:** Provincial type.

Date	VG	F	VF	XF	Unc
ND(ca.1906)	60.00	100	150	225	—

K# 952 LIANG (Tael) **Weight:** 35.9000 g. **Composition:** Silver **Obverse:** Three lines of two characters each **Reverse:** Two lines of three characters each **Note:** Provincial type.

Date	VG	F	VF	XF	Unc
ND(ca.1906)	60.00	100	140	200	—

K# 962 LIANG (Tael) **Weight:** 35.9000 g. **Composition:** Silver **Obverse:** Three lines of two characters each **Reverse:** Two lines of three characters each **Note:** Ta Ch'ing Bank type.

Date	VG	F	VF	XF	Unc
ND(ca.1908)	45.00	75.00	110	165	—

K# 942r LIANG (Tael) **Weight:** 35.9000 g. **Composition:** Silver **Obverse:** Three lines of four characters each

Date	VG	F	VF	XF	Unc
ND(ca.1908) Rare	—	—	—	—	—

K# 974 LIANG (Tael) **Weight:** 35.9000 g. **Composition:** Silver **Obverse:** Two lines of three characters each **Reverse:** Two lines of three characters each **Note:** Merchant type.

Date	VG	F	VF	XF	Unc
ND(ca.1908)	90.00	150	225	325	—

TRANSITIONAL COINAGE

Y# 401.1 10 CASH **Composition:** Copper **Ruler:** Hung-hsien **Obv. Legend:** THE FIRST YEAR OF HUNG SHUAN **Rev. Legend:** Hung-hsien Yüan-nien

Date	VG	F	VF	XF	Unc
1(1915)	35.00	60.00	100	150	—

Y# 401.2 10 CASH **Composition:** Copper **Ruler:** Hung-hsien **Obverse:** Wider space in legend

Date	VG	F	VF	XF	Unc
1(1915)	10.00	20.00	30.00	45.00	—

REPUBLIC

MILLED COINAGE

Y# 399 10 CASH **Composition:** Copper **Obverse:** Large rosette **Reverse:** Center of star convex

Date	VG	F	VF	XF	Unc
ND(1912)	0.65	2.00	4.00	7.50	24.00

Y# 399a 10 CASH **Composition:** Brass

Date	VG	F	VF	XF	Unc
ND(1912)	1.75	5.00	10.00	17.50	45.00

Y# 399.1 10 CASH **Composition:** Copper **Obverse:** Small rosette **Reverse:** Center of star convex

Date	VG	F	VF	XF	Unc
ND(1912)	0.67	2.00	4.00	7.00	24.00

Y# 399.2 10 CASH **Composition:** Copper **Reverse:** Center of star concave; star outlined

Date	VG	F	VF	XF	Unc
ND(1912)	0.75	2.25	4.50	8.50	26.00

Y# 399.3 10 CASH **Composition:** Copper **Reverse:** Star not outlined

Date	VG	F	VF	XF	Unc
ND(1912)	0.75	2.25	4.50	8.50	26.00

Y# 399.4 10 CASH **Composition:** Copper **Obverse:** Large rosette **Reverse:** Center of star concave

Date	VG	F	VF	XF	Unc
ND(1912)	0.75	2.25	4.50	8.50	26.00

Y# 399.5 10 CASH **Composition:** Copper **Note:** Mule. General Issue, Y#306.

Date	VG	F	VF	XF	Unc
ND(1912)	—	—	—	—	—

Y# 402 10 CASH **Composition:** Copper **Subject:** Provincial Constitution **Obverse:** Rosette above flags

Date	VG	F	VF	XF	Unc
11(1922)	15.00	25.00	38.00	60.00	—

Y# 402.1 10 CASH **Composition:** Copper **Obverse:** Star above flags

Date	VG	F	VF	XF	Unc
11(1922)	18.50	26.00	40.00	65.00	—

Y# 400b 20 CASH **Composition:** Brass

Date	VG	F	VF	XF	Unc
ND(1912)	1.65	4.00	10.00	20.00	—

Y# 400.2 20 CASH **Composition:** Copper

Date	VG	F	VF	XF	Unc
ND(1919)	0.60	1.00	3.00	6.00	—

Y# 400.3 20 CASH **Composition:** Copper **Obverse:** 25 small curls in ribbon at base of plant

Date	VG	F	VF	XF	Unc
ND(1919)	0.60	1.00	3.00	6.00	—

Y# 400.4 20 CASH **Composition:** Copper **Obverse:** Smaller rice grains **Reverse:** Floral ornament at left smaller

Date	VG	F	VF	XF	Unc
ND(1919)	0.60	1.00	3.00	6.00	—

Y# 400.5 20 CASH **Composition:** Copper **Obverse:** Thin ribbon at base of plant

Date	VG	F	VF	XF	Unc
ND(1919)	0.60	1.00	3.00	6.00	—

Y# 400.6 20 CASH **Composition:** Copper **Reverse:** Small pentagonal rosette above crossed flags

Date	VG	F	VF	XF	Unc
ND(1919)	0.60	1.00	3.00	6.00	—

Y# 400.7 20 CASH **Composition:** Copper **Reverse:** Larger star-shaped rosette above crossed flags

Date	VG	F	VF	XF	Unc
ND(1919)	1.00	2.50	4.00	7.00	—

Y# 400.7b 20 CASH **Composition:** Brass

Date	VG	F	VF	XF	Unc
ND(1919)	1.65	4.00	8.00	15.00	—

Y# 400.8 20 CASH **Composition:** Copper **Obverse:** Larger star-shaped rosette above flags

Date	VG	F	VF	XF	Unc
ND(1919)	1.00	2.50	4.00	7.00	—

Y# 400.9 20 CASH **Composition:** Copper **Reverse:** Sharp pointed star above crossed flags, long inner ribbons

Date	VG	F	VF	XF	Unc
ND(1919)	1.00	2.50	4.00	7.00	—

Y# 400.10 20 CASH **Composition:** Copper **Reverse:** Sharp 5-pointed star over crossed flags, short inner ribbons

Date	VG	F	VF	XF	Unc
ND(1919)	20.00	25.00	30.00	35.00	—

Y# 400.11 20 CASH **Composition:** Copper **Reverse:** Similar to Y#400.2; no dot in rosette above flags

Date	VG	F	VF	XF	Unc
ND(1919)	—	—	—	—	—

Y# 400a 20 CASH **Composition:** Copper **Obverse:** Denomination: 20 CASH

Date	VG	F	VF	XF	Unc
ND(1919)	50.00	75.00	100	150	—

Y# 400 20 CASH **Composition:** Copper **Reverse:** Rosette above flags, five characters at bottom in legend

Date	VG	F	VF	XF	Unc
ND(1919)	1.25	3.00	7.50	15.00	—

Y# 403.1 20 CASH **Composition:** Copper **Subject:** Provincial Constitution **Obverse:** Rosette above crossed flags **Obv. Legend:** THE REPUBLIC OF CHINA **Reverse:** 3 Horizontal bars in large sprays

Date	VG	F	VF	XF	Unc
11(1922)	22.50	35.00	65.00	90.00	—

Y# 403.2 20 CASH **Composition:** Copper **Subject:** Provincial Constitution **Obverse:** Rosette above crossed flags **Obv. Legend:** THE REPUBLIC OF CHINA **Reverse:** Three horizontal bars in smaller sprays

Date	VG	F	VF	XF	Unc
11(1922)	35.00	75.00	100	150	—

K# 762 10 CENTS **Composition:** Silver **Ruler:** Hung-hsien **Obverse:** Inscription: Chung-hua Yin-pi **Obv. Legend:** Hung-hsien Yüan-nien **Reverse:** "Flying" dragon

Date	VG	F	VF	XF	Unc
ND(1915)	85.00	250	550	900	1,400

Note: Though Kann calls this coin as Essay, contemporary reports indicate that the coin actually circulated briefly in 1915. Not to be confused with Y#28, the obverse of which has a different legend in Chinese. (See General Issues - Empire.)

Y# 404 DOLLAR **Weight:** 27.4000 g. **Composition:** Silver **Subject:** Provincial Constitution

Date	VG	F	VF	XF	Unc
11(1922)	45.00	125	250	400	800

PATTERNS

Including off metal strikes

KM#	Date	Mintage	Identification	Mkt Val
Pn4	ND(1902)	—	10 Cash. Copper. Three characters at bottom, Y#112.10.	850
Pn5	ND(1902)	—	10 Cash. Copper. Three characters at bottom, Y#112.12.	350

Note: Two Heaton (Birmingham) proof patterns for a proposed brass coinage which wasn't adopted. Dies were recut with only 2 characters for issue.

KM#	Date	Mintage	Identification	Mkt Val
Pn6	ND(1915)	—	10 Cents. Nickel. Plain edge. K#762x	—
Pn7	ND(1915)	—	10 Cents. Copper. Plain edge. K#762y	450
Pn9	11(1922)	—	Dollar. Silver. General Chao Heng-ti	—
Pn10	11(1922)	—	Dollar. Copper. General Chao Heng-ti	—

HUPEH PROVINCE

Hubei

A province located in east-central China. Hilly, with some lakes and swamps, it has rich coal and iron deposits plus a varied agricultural program. The Wuchang Mint had been active from early in the Manchu dynasty and its modern equipment began operations in 1895. It probably closed in 1929.

EMPIRE

PROVINCIAL CAST COINAGE

C# 13-11 CASH **Composition:** Cast Brass **Ruler:** Kuang-hsü **Obverse:** Inscription: Kuang-hsü T'ung-pao **Reverse:** Inscription: Manchu Boo-ching **Note:** Struck at Ching (Chingchow).

Date	Good	VG	F	VF	XF
ND(1875-1908)	12.50	20.00	30.00	45.00	—

C# 13-11.1 CASH **Composition:** Cast Brass **Ruler:** Kuang-hsü **Obverse:** Inscription: Kuang-hsü T'ung-pao **Reverse:** Inscription: Manchu Boo-ching **Note:** Struck at Ching (Chingchow). Attribution of this mint mark to Chingchow is uncertain. Some authorities claim the Taku (Dagu) Mint in Tientsin struck this coin.

Date	Good	VG	F	VF	XF
ND(1875-1908)	12.00	15.00	22.50	30.00	—

MILLED COINAGE

Y# 121 CASH **Composition:** Brass **Ruler:** Kuang-hsü **Obverse:** Inscription: Kuang-hsü Yüan-pao **Reverse:** Dragon **Note:** Struck at Ching (Chingchow).

Date	Mintage	VG	F	VF	XF	Unc
ND(1906)	66,474,000	8.00	12.00	18.00	25.00	—

Y# 7j CASH **Composition:** Brass **Ruler:** Kuang-hsü **Obverse:** Small mint mark on small disc in center **Obv. Legend:** Kuang-hsü **Reverse:** Dragon **Note:** Struck at Ching (Chingchow).

Date	VG	F	VF	XF	Unc
CD1908	3.50	8.00	15.00	25.00	—

Y# 7j.1 CASH **Composition:** Brass **Ruler:** Kuang-hsü **Obverse:** Large mint mark on small disc in center **Obv. Legend:** Kuang-hsü **Reverse:** Dragon **Note:** Struck at Ching (Chingchow).

Date	VG	F	VF	XF	Unc
CD1908	3.50	8.00	15.00	25.00	—

Y# 8j 2 CASH **Composition:** Copper **Ruler:** Kuang-hsü **Obverse:** Inscription: Tai-ch'ing T'ung-pi **Reverse:** Dragon **Note:** Struck at Ching (Chingchow).

Date	Mintage	VG	F	VF	XF	Unc
CD(1906)	844,000	50.00	80.00	125	200	—

Y# 9j 5 CASH **Composition:** Copper **Ruler:** Kuang-hsü **Obverse:** Inscription: Tai-ch'ing T'ung-pi **Rev. Legend:** Kuang-hsü Nien-tsao, TAI-CHING-TI-KUO ... **Size:** 24 mm. **Note:** Struck at Ching (Chingchow).

Date	Mintage	VG	F	VF	XF	Unc
CD(1906)	9,846,000	5.00	9.00	15.00	30.00	—

Y# 9j.1 5 CASH **Composition:** Copper **Ruler:** Kuang-hsü **Obverse:** Inscription: Tai-ch'ing T'ung-pi **Reverse:** Dragon redesigned **Rev. Legend:** Kuang-hsü Nien-tsao, TAI-CHING-TI-KUO ... **Size:** 23 mm. **Note:** Struck at Ching (Chingchow).

Date	VG	F	VF	XF	Unc
CD(1906)	6.00	11.00	17.50	35.00	—

Y# 120a.9 10 CASH **Composition:** Copper **Ruler:** Kuang-hsü **Obverse:** Square in circle, inscription: Kuang-hsü Yüan-pao **Reverse:** Dragon, hyphen in HU-PEH **Note:** Struck at Ching (Chingchow).

Date	VG	F	VF	XF	Unc
ND(1902-05)	1.25	4.00	7.50	15.00	30.00

Y# 120 10 CASH **Composition:** Copper **Ruler:** Kuang-hsü **Obverse:** 8-petalled rosette, inscription: Kuang-hsü Yüan-pao **Reverse:** Circled dragon **Note:** Struck at Ching (Chingchow).

Date	Mintage	VG	F	VF	XF	Unc
ND(1902-05)	4,475,000	1.75	5.00	8.00	15.00	35.00

Y# 120a 10 CASH **Composition:** Copper **Ruler:** Kuang-hsü **Obverse:** Inscription: Kuang-hsü Yüan-pao **Reverse:** Uncircled large dragon **Note:** Struck at Ching (Chingchow).

Date	VG	F	VF	XF	Unc
ND(1902-05)	1.00	3.50	7.00	13.50	30.00

Y# 120a.1 10 CASH **Composition:** Copper **Ruler:** Kuang-hsü **Obverse:** Inscription: Kuang-hsü Yüan-pao **Reverse:** Slightly larger English letters, wide face on dragon **Note:** Struck at Ching (Chingchow).

Date	VG	F	VF	XF	Unc
ND(1902-05)	0.35	1.00	2.00	3.00	20.00

Y# 120a.2 10 CASH **Composition:** Copper **Ruler:** Kuang-hsü **Obverse:** Inscription: Kuang-hsü Yüan-pao **Reverse:** Large pearl with many spines, narrower face on dragon **Note:** Struck at Ching (Chingchow).

Date	VG	F	VF	XF	Unc
ND(1902-05)	0.25	0.75	1.50	2.75	20.00

Y# 120a.3 10 CASH **Composition:** Copper **Ruler:** Kuang-hsü **Obverse:** Inscription: Kuang-hsü Yüan-pao **Reverse:** Smaller pearl with fewer spines on dragon **Note:** Struck at Ching (Chingchow). Commonly found with medal alignment but also exists with coin alignment.

Date	VG	F	VF	XF	Unc
ND(1902-05)	0.25	0.75	1.50	2.75	20.00

Y# 120a.3a 10 CASH **Composition:** Brass **Ruler:** Kuang-hsü **Obverse:** Inscription: Kuang-hsü Yüan-pao **Reverse:** Dragon **Note:** Struck at Ching (Chingchow).

Date	VG	F	VF	XF	Unc
ND(1902-05)	—	—	—	—	—

Y# 120a.4 10 CASH **Composition:** Copper **Ruler:** Kuang-hsü **Obverse:** 5-petalled rosette, small Manchu word at right, inscription: Kuang-hsü Yüan-pao **Reverse:** 4 dots in shape of cross at either side of dragon, PROVINCE spelled PHOVINCE, with "V" an inverted "A" **Note:** Struck at Ching (Chingchow).

Date	VG	F	VF	XF	Unc
ND(1902-05)	0.35	1.00	2.00	3.00	20.00

Y# 120a.5 10 CASH **Composition:** Copper **Ruler:** Kuang-hsü **Obverse:** Large Manchu at right, inscription: Kuang-hsü Yüan-pao **Reverse:** "R" in PROVINCE inverted, "V" an inverted "A", dragon **Note:** Struck at Ching (Chingchow).

Date	VG	F	VF	XF	Unc
ND(1902-05)	0.35	1.00	2.00	3.00	20.00

Y# 120a.6 10 CASH **Composition:** Copper **Ruler:** Kuang-hsü **Obverse:** Inscription: Kuang-hsü Yüan-pao **Reverse:** 6-pointed star at either side of dragon, hyphen in HU-PEH **Note:** Struck at Ching (Chingchow).

Date	VG	F	VF	XF	Unc
ND(1902-05)	0.35	1.00	2.00	3.00	20.00

Y# 120a.7 10 CASH **Composition:** Copper **Ruler:** Kuang-hsü **Obverse:** Inscription: Kuang-hsü Yüan-pao **Reverse:** 6-pointed star at either side of dragon, without hyphen in HU-PEH **Note:** Struck at Ching (Chingchow).

Date	VG	F	VF	XF	Unc
ND(1902-05)	0.50	1.50	3.00	6.00	22.00

Y# 120a.8 10 CASH **Composition:** Copper **Ruler:** Kuang-hsü **Obverse:** 5-petalled rosette and small Manchu, inscription: Kuang-hsü Yüan-pao **Reverse:** Dragon, very small pearl **Note:** Struck at Ching (Chingchow).

Date	VG	F	VF	XF	Unc
ND(1902-05)	1.00	3.50	6.00	12.00	25.00

Y# 120a.10 10 CASH **Composition:** Copper **Ruler:** Kuang-hsü **Obverse:** Square in circle, inscription: Kuang-hsü Yüan-pao **Reverse:** Dragon, without hyphen in HU-PEH **Note:** Struck at Ching (Chingchow).

Date	VG	F	VF	XF	Unc
ND(1902-05)	0.50	1.50	2.50	5.00	25.00

Y# 122 10 CASH **Composition:** Copper **Ruler:** Kuang-hsü **Obverse:** Second character from right at top is larger, 6-petalled rosette, inscription: Kuang-hsü Yüan-pao **Reverse:** Front view dragon **Note:** Struck at Ching (Chingchow).

Date	VG	F	VF	XF	Unc
ND(1902-05)	0.20	0.60	1.50	3.00	20.00

Y# 122.1 10 CASH **Composition:** Copper **Ruler:** Kuang-hsü **Obverse:** Second character from right "Pei" smaller, inscription: Kuang-hsü Yüan-pao **Reverse:** Dragon **Note:** Struck at Ching (Chingchow).

Date	VG	F	VF	XF	Unc
ND(1902-05)	0.20	0.50	1.50	3.00	20.00

Y# 122.3 10 CASH **Composition:** Copper **Ruler:** Kuang-hsü **Obverse:** Inscription: Kuang-hsü Yüan-pao **Reverse:** Clouds above dragon's head, 2 clouds below pearl instead of 1 **Note:** Struck at Ching (Chingchow).

Date	VG	F	VF	XF	Unc
ND(1902-05)	0.65	2.00	5.00	10.00	35.00

Y# 122.4 10 CASH **Composition:** Copper **Ruler:** Kuang-hsü **Obverse:** Inscription: Kuang-hsü Yüan-pao **Reverse:** Dragon, small circle around lower part of pearl, without dots on either side of mountain **Note:** Struck at Ching (Chingchow).

Date	VG	F	VF	XF	Unc
ND(1902-05)	0.65	2.00	5.00	10.00	35.00

Y# 122.5 10 CASH **Composition:** Copper **Ruler:** Kuang-hsü **Obverse:** Inscription: Kuang-hsü Yüan-pao **Reverse:** Dragon, larger circle around larger pearl, larger English letters **Note:** Struck at Ching (Chingchow).

Date	VG	F	VF	XF	Unc
ND(1902-05)	0.65	2.00	5.00	10.00	25.00

Y# 122a 10 CASH **Composition:** Copper **Ruler:** Kuang-hsü **Obverse:** Inscription: Kuang-hsü Yüan-pao **Reverse:** Circled front view of dragon **Note:** Struck at Ching (Chingchow).

Date	VG	F	VF	XF	Unc
ND(1902-05)	45.00	125	175	225	—

Y# 10j 10 CASH **Composition:** Copper **Ruler:** Kuang-hsü **Obverse:** Inscription: Tai-ch'ing T'ung-pi **Reverse:** Dragon, 7 flames on pearl **Rev. Legend:** Kuang hsü Nien-tsao, TAI-CHING-TI-KUO ... **Note:** Struck at Ching (Chingchow).

Date	Mintage	VG	F	VF	XF	Unc
CD(1906)	1,865,558,000	0.25	0.75	1.00	2.00	20.00

Y# 10j.1 10 CASH **Composition:** Copper **Ruler:** Kuang-hsü **Obverse:** Inscription: Tai-ch'ing T'ung-pi **Reverse:** Redesigned dragon with wide lips, cloud-shaped bar below pearl with 5 flames **Rev. Legend:** Kuang hsü Nien-tsao, TAI-CHING-TI-KUO ... **Note:** Struck at Ching (Chingchow). 28-29 millimeters.

Date	VG	F	VF	XF	Unc
CD(1906)	0.65	2.00	5.00	10.00	25.00

Y# 10j.2 10 CASH **Composition:** Copper **Ruler:** Kuang-hsü **Obverse:** Inscription: Tai-ch'ing T'ung-pi **Reverse:** Dragon **Rev. Legend:** Kuang hsü Nien-tsao, TAI-CHING-TI-KUO ... **Size:** 30 mm. **Note:** Struck at Ching (Chingchow).

Date	VG	F	VF	XF	Unc
CD(1906)	0.65	2.00	5.00	10.00	25.00

Y# 10j.3 10 CASH **Composition:** Copper **Ruler:** Kuang-hsü **Obverse:** Inscription: Tai-ch'ing T'ung-pi **Reverse:** Different dragon with hook-shaped cloud beneath, pearl with 4 flames, large incuse swirl on pearl **Rev. Legend:** Kuang hsü Nien-tsao, TAI-CHING-TI-KUO ... **Note:** Struck at Ching (Chingchow).

Date	VG	F	VF	XF	Unc
CD(1906)	0.35	1.00	2.00	3.00	20.00

Y# 10j.4 10 CASH **Composition:** Copper **Ruler:** Kuang-hsü **Obverse:** Inscription: Tai-ch'ing T'ung-pi **Reverse:** Dragon, small incuse swirl on pearl with 4 flames **Rev. Legend:** Kuang hsü Nien-tsao, TAI-CHING-TI-KUO ... **Note:** Struck at Ching (Chingchow).

Date	VG	F	VF	XF	Unc
CD(1906)	0.20	0.50	1.00	2.00	20.00

Y# 10j.5 10 CASH **Composition:** Copper **Ruler:** Kuang-hsü **Obverse:** Inscription: Tai-ch'ing T'ung-pi **Reverse:** Dragon, swirl on pearl in relief with 4 flames **Rev. Legend:** Kuang hsü Nien-tsao, TAI-CHING-TI-KUO ... **Note:** Struck at Ching (Chingchow).

Date	VG	F	VF	XF	Unc
CD(1906)	0.25	0.75	1.00	2.00	20.00

Y# 20j 10 CASH **Composition:** Copper **Ruler:** Hsüan-t'ung **Obverse:** Inscription: Tai-ch'ing T'ung-pi **Reverse:** Dragon, large incuse swirl on pearl **Rev. Legend:** Hsüan-t'ung Nien-tsao, TAI-CHING-TI-KUO ... **Note:** Struck at Ching (Chingchow).

Date	Mintage	VG	F	VF	XF	Unc
CD(1909)	371,577,000	0.50	1.50	3.00	6.00	25.00

Y# 20j.1 10 CASH **Composition:** Copper **Ruler:** Hsüan-t'ung **Obverse:** Inscription: Tai-ch'ing T'ung-pi **Reverse:** Dragon, small swirl in relief on pearl **Rev. Legend:** Hsüan-t'ung Nien-tsao, TAI-CHING-TI-KUO ... **Note:** Struck at Ching (Chingchow).

Date	VG	F	VF	XF	Unc
CD(1909)	0.50	1.50	3.00	6.00	25.00

Y# 20j.2 10 CASH **Composition:** Copper **Ruler:** Hsüan-t'ung **Obverse:** CD1909 over CD1906, inscription: Tai-ch'ing T'ung-pi **Reverse:** Dragon **Rev. Legend:** Hsüan-t'ung Nien-tsao, TAI-CHING-TI-KUO ... **Note:** Struck at Ching (Chingchow).

Date	VG	F	VF	XF	Unc
CD(1909/1906)	—	—	—	—	—

Y# 20j.3 10 CASH **Composition:** Copper **Ruler:** Hsüan-t'ung **Obverse:** Characters "Hsuan T'ung" re-engraved over characters "Kuang Hsu," inscription: Tai-ch'ing T'ung-pi **Reverse:** Dragon **Rev. Legend:** Hsüan-t'ung Nien-tsao, TAI-CHING-TI-KUO ... **Note:** Struck at Ching (Chingchow).

Date	VG	F	VF	XF	Unc
CD(1909) Rare	—	—	—	—	—

Y# 11j 20 CASH **Composition:** Copper **Ruler:** Kuang-hsü **Obverse:** Inscription: Tai-ch'ing T'ung-pi **Reverse:** Dragon **Rev. Legend:** Kuang-hsü Nien-tsao, TAI-CHING-TI-KUO ... **Note:** Struck at Ching (Chingchow).

Date	Mintage	VG	F	VF	XF	Unc
CD(1906)	3,710,000	100	250	375	625	—

Y# 127.1 DOLLAR **Weight:** 26.7000 g. **Composition:** 0.9000 Silver .7727 oz. ASW **Ruler:** Kuang-hsü **Obverse:** Inscription: Kuang-hsü Yüan-pao **Reverse:** Without "Pen Sheng" at either side of dragon **Note:** Struck at Ching (Chingchow).

Date	Mintage	VG	F	VF	XF	Unc
ND(1895-1907)	19,935,000	6.50	20.00	30.00	50.00	250

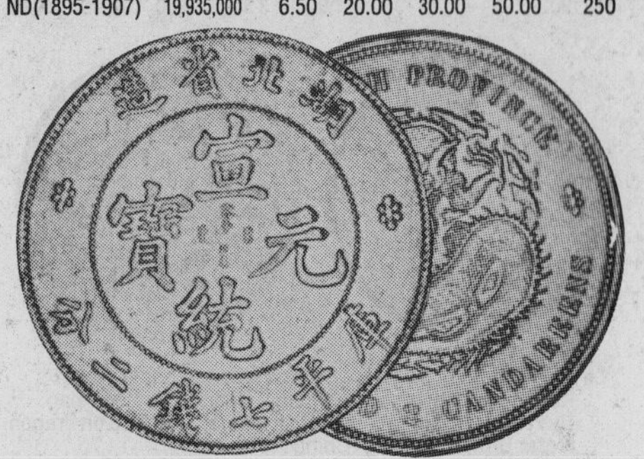

Y# 131 DOLLAR **Weight:** 27.0000 g. **Composition:** 0.9000 Silver .7814 oz. ASW **Ruler:** Hsüan-t'ung **Obverse:** Inscription: Hsüan-t'ung Yüan-pao **Reverse:** Dragon **Note:** Struck at Ching (Chingchow).

Date	Mintage	VG	F	VF	XF	Unc
ND(1909-1911)	2,703,000	6.50	20.00	30.00	50.00	200

Y# 123 5 CENTS **Weight:** 1.3500 g. **Composition:** 0.8200 Silver .0356 oz. ASW **Ruler:** Kuang-hsü **Obverse:** Inscription: Kuang-hsü Yüan-pao **Reverse:** Dragon **Rev. Legend:** Kuang-hsü Nien-tsao, TAI-CHING-TI-KUO ... **Note:** Struck at Ching (Chingchow).

Date	Mintage	VG	F	VF	XF	Unc
ND(1895-1905)	4,278,000	17.50	50.00	100	150	250

Y# 124.1 10 CENTS **Weight:** 2.7000 g. **Composition:** 0.8200 Silver .0712 oz. ASW **Ruler:** Kuang-hsü **Obverse:** Inscription: Kuang-hsü Yüan-pao **Reverse:** Without characters beside dragon, 2 varieties of edge milling **Rev. Legend:** Kuang-hsü Nien-tsao, TAI-CHING-TI-KUO ... **Note:** Struck at Ching (Chingchow).

Date	VG	F	VF	XF	Unc
ND(1895-1907)	0.65	2.00	4.00	7.50	20.00

Y# 129 10 CENTS **Composition:** Silver **Ruler:** Hsüan-t'ung **Obverse:** Inscription: Hsüan-t'ung Yüan-pao **Reverse:** Dragon **Rev. Legend:** Kuang-hsü Nien-tsao, TAI-CHING-TI-KUO ... **Note:** Struck at Ching (Chingchow).

Date	VG	F	VF	XF	Unc
ND(1909)	50.00	150	300	450	750

Y# 125.1 20 CENTS **Weight:** 5.3000 g. **Composition:** 0.8200 Silver .1397 oz. ASW **Ruler:** Kuang-hsü **Obverse:** Inscription: Kuang-hsü Yüan-pao **Reverse:** Without characters beside dragon **Note:** Struck at Ching (Chingchow).

Date	VG	F	VF	XF	Unc
ND(1895-1907)	1.75	5.00	10.00	15.00	30.00

Y# 130 20 CENTS **Composition:** Silver **Ruler:** Hsüan-t'ung **Obverse:** Inscription: Hsüan-t'ung Yüan-pao **Reverse:** Dragon **Note:** Struck at Ching (Chingchow).

Date	VG	F	VF	XF	Unc
ND(1909)	85.00	250	500	850	1,250

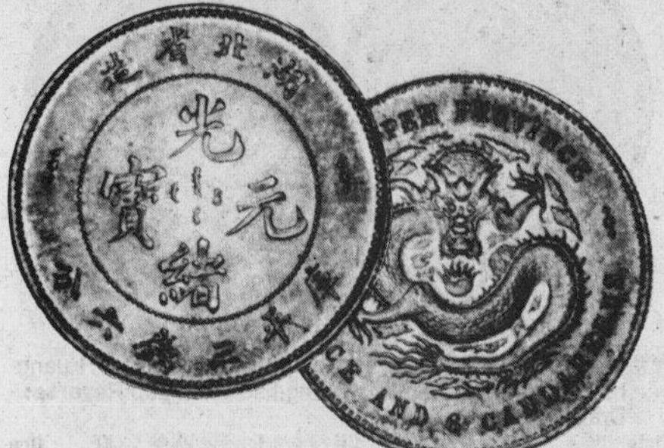

Y# 126 50 CENTS **Weight:** 13.5000 g. **Composition:** 0.8600 Silver .3733 oz. ASW **Ruler:** Hsüan-t'ung **Obverse:** Inscription: Kuang-hsü Yüan-pao **Reverse:** Dragon **Note:** Struck at Ching (Chingchow).

Date	VG	F	VF	XF	Unc
ND(1895-1905)	12.00	35.00	65.00	120	250

BULLION COINAGE/TAEL SYSTEM

Y# 128.1 TAEL **Weight:** 37.7000 g. **Composition:** 0.8770 Silver 1.0631 oz. ASW **Ruler:** Kuang-hsü **Obverse:** Large inscription: Kuang-hsü Yin-pi **Reverse:** Two dragons forming circle **Note:** Struck at Ching (Chingchow).

Date	Mintage	VG	F	VF	XF	Unc
30(1904)	648,000	110	325	600	1,800	3,000

Y# 128.2 TAEL **Weight:** 37.7000 g. **Composition:** 0.8770 Silver 1.0631 oz. ASW **Ruler:** Kuang-hsü **Obverse:** Smaller inscription: Kuang-hsü Yin-pi **Reverse:** Two dragons forming circle **Note:** Struck at Ching (Chingchow).

Date	VG	F	VF	XF	Unc
30(1904)	65.00	200	300	600	1,400

REPUBLIC

MILLED COINAGE

Y# A405 20 CASH **Composition:** Brass **Note:** Attribution is uncertain. Probably minted in Szechuan (Sichuan).

Date	VG	F	VF	XF	Unc
ND(c. 1914)	40.00	85.00	115	165	—

Y# 405 50 CASH **Composition:** Copper Or Brass **Note:** Crude strike. Similar coins dated Yr. 1 and Yr. 8 are known, but their status is uncertain.

Date	VG	F	VF	XF	Unc
3(1914)	575	850	1,100	—	—
7(1918)	400	600	850	—	—

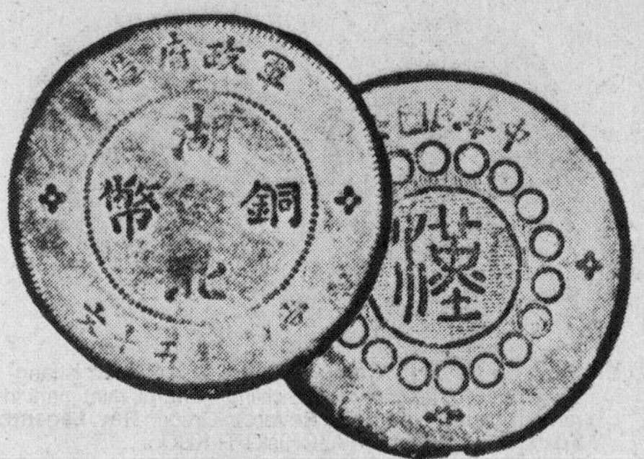

Y# 405.1 50 CASH **Composition:** Copper Or Brass **Note:** Machine strike. Not to be confused with Szechuan (Sichuan) Y#449.

Date	VG	F	VF	XF	Unc
7(1918)	575	850	1,100	—	—

Y# 406 20 CENTS **Weight:** 5.2000 g. **Composition:** Silver **Obverse:** Characters "Tsao" at left and "Hu" at right of military bust of Yuan Shih-k'ai left **Note:** Do not confuse with Y#327 (see Republic-general issues).

Date	VG	F	VF	XF	Unc
9(1920)	25.00	75.00	125	200	500

PATTERNS

Including off metal strikes

KM#	Date	Mintage	Identification	Mkt Val
PnA6	ND(1902)	—	10 Cash. White copper. Y122.5. W518.	—
Pn6	ND(1902)	—	10 Cash. Brass. W480.	—
PnA7	3(1911)	—	10 Cents. Pewter. K48y.	—
Pn7	1(1916)	—	10 Cents. White Metal. K764x.	—

KANSU PROVINCE

Gansu

A province located in north-central China with a contrast of mountains and sandy plains. The west end of the Great Wall with its branches lies in Kansu (Gansu). Kansu (Gansu) was the eastern end of the "Silk Road" that led to central and western Asia. Two mints issued Cash coins. It has been reported, but not confirmed, that the Lanchow Mint operated as late as 1949.

REPUBLIC

MILLED COINAGE

Y# C407 20 CASH **Composition:** Copper

Date	VG	F	VF	XF	Unc
ND(1920)	—	—	—	—	—

Y# D407 50 CASH **Composition:** Copper

Date	VG	F	VF	XF	Unc
ND(1920)	70.00	150	250	—	—

Y# 408 50 CASH **Composition:** Copper

Date	Mintage	VG	F	VF	XF	Unc
15(1926)	2,564,000	85.00	175	275	450	—

Y# A408 50 CASH **Composition:** Copper

Date	VG	F	VF	XF	Unc
ND(1927)	500	900	1,500	—	—

Y# 409 100 CASH **Composition:** Copper

Date	VG	F	VF	XF	Unc
15(1926)	35.00	50.00	100	150	—

Y# 407 DOLLAR **Weight:** 26.6000 g. **Composition:** Silver **Obverse:** Military bust of Yüan Shih-kai left, "Su" at left, "Kan" at right

Date	VG	F	VF	XF	Unc
3(1914)	45.00	125	200	350	800

Y# 410 DOLLAR **Weight:** 26.6000 g. **Composition:** Silver **Obverse:** Facing bust of Sun Yat-sen

Date	VG	F	VF	XF	Unc
17(1928)	60.00	175	300	500	1,000

PATTERNS

Including off metal strikes

KM#	Date	Mintage	Identification	Mkt Val
Pn1	ND(ca.1928)	—	5 Cash. Copper. Hsu#385.	650
Pn2	ND(ca.1928)	—	10 Cash. Copper.	—
Pn3	ND(1928)	—	5 Fen. Copper. Hsu#383.	300
Pn4	17(1928)	—	50 Cash. Copper.	—
Pn5	ND(ca.1928)	—	10 Fen. Copper. Hsu#384.	400

KIANGNAN

A district in eastern China made up of Anhwei (Anhui) and Kiangsu (Jiangsu) provinces. In 1667 the province of Kiangnan was divided into the present provinces of Anhwei (Anhui) and Kiangsu (Jiangsu). In 1723 Nanking, formerly the capital of Kiangnan, was made the capital of Liang-Chiang Chiang (an administrative area consisting of Anhwei (Anhui), Kiangsu (Jiangsu), and Kiangsi (Jiangxi) provinces).

Always highly regarded because of location, agriculture and manufacturing, Kiangnan has frequently been sought after by contending forces.

The Nanking Mint had been active during imperial times. Modern minting facilities began operations in 1897. A second mint was planned for the Kiangnan Arsenal in Shanghai in 1905. Mints for copper coins also operated in Chingkiang (Qingjiang) in central Kiangsu and at Soochow which is further south. A silver mint was planned for Shanghai in 1921. The Nanking Mint, the most important of the group, burned down in 1929. The Nationalist Government Central Mint was completed in Shanghai in 1930 and opened in 1933.

EMPIRE

MILLED COINAGE

The initials HAH, SY, CH and TH are those of mint officials and were placed on the coins as a guarantee of the coin's fineness. The 5-, 10-, and 20-cent coins are often found without a decimal point between the numbers on the reverse. The 1904 dated dollar was restruck during Republican times.

Y# 7k CASH **Composition:** Brass **Ruler:** Kuang-hsü **Obverse:** Bottom horizontal stroke in mint mark extends beyond outside vertical strokes **Obv. Legend:** Kuang-hsü **Reverse:** Dragon

Date	Mintage	VG	F	VF	XF	Unc
CD(1908)	25,450,000	2.50	4.50	8.50	16.00	—

Y# 7k.1 CASH **Composition:** Brass **Ruler:** Kuang-hsü **Obverse:** Bottom horizontal stroke in mint mark does not extend beyond outside vertical strokes **Obv. Legend:** Kuang-hsü **Reverse:** Dragon

Date	VG	F	VF	XF	Unc
CD(1908)	3.50	6.50	12.50	21.50	—

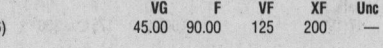

Y# 9k.1 5 CASH **Composition:** Copper **Ruler:** Kuang-hsü **Obverse:** Inscription: Tai-ch'ing T'ung-pi; mint mark incused on raised disk **Reverse:** Dragon **Rev. Legend:** Kuang-hsü Nien-tsao, TAI-CHING-TI-KUO...

Date	VG	F	VF	XF	Unc
CD(1906)	35.00	65.00	100	150	—

Y# 9k.1a 5 CASH **Composition:** Brass **Ruler:** Kuang-hsü **Obverse:** Inscription: Tai-ch'ing T'ung-pi **Reverse:** Dragon **Rev. Legend:** Kuang-hsü Nien-tsao, TAI-CHING-TI-KUO...

Date	VG	F	VF	XF	Unc
CD(1906)	45.00	90.00	125	200	—

Y# 9k.2 5 CASH **Composition:** Copper **Ruler:** Kuang-hsü **Obverse:** Inscription: Tai-ch'ing T'ung-pi; mint mark in relief at center without disk **Reverse:** Dragon **Rev. Legend:** Kuang-hsü Nien-tsao, TAI-CHING-TI-KUO...

Date	VG	F	VF	XF	Unc
CD(1906)	45.00	90.00	125	200	—

Y# 135 10 CASH **Composition:** Copper **Ruler:** Kuang-hsü **Obverse:** Inscription: Kuang-hsü Yüan-pao **Reverse:** Dragon **Edge:** Reeded

Date	VG	F	VF	XF	Unc
ND(ca.1902)	10.00	30.00	60.00	100	—

Y# 135.1 10 CASH **Composition:** Copper **Ruler:** Kuang-hsü **Obverse:** Inscription: Kuang-hsü Yüan-pao **Reverse:** Dragon **Edge:** Plain

Date	VG	F	VF	XF	Unc
ND(ca.1902)	10.00	30.00	60.00	100	—

Y# 135.3 10 CASH **Composition:** Copper **Ruler:** Kuang-hsü **Obverse:** Inscription: Kuang-hsü Yüan-pao; large Manchu words in center **Reverse:** Dragon

Date	VG	F	VF	XF	Unc
CD(ca.1902)	2.00	6.50	12.50	25.00	45.00

Y# 135.2 10 CASH **Composition:** Copper **Ruler:** Kuang-hsü **Obverse:** Inscription: Kuang-hsü Yüan-pao; small Manchu words in center **Reverse:** Dragon

Date	F	VF	XF	Unc	BU
CD(ca.1902)	1.50	3.00	5.00	20.00	—

Y# C140 10 CASH **Composition:** Copper **Ruler:** Kuang-hsü **Obverse:** Inscription: Kuang-hsü Yüan-pao; Kiang-nan **Reverse:** Dragon **Rev. Legend:** KIANG-SOO **Note:** Mule; often confused with Y#162.

Date	VG	F	VF	XF	Unc
CD(1902)	—	—	—	—	—
ND(ca.1902)	50.00	150	200	250	—

Y# 135.4 10 CASH **Composition:** Copper **Ruler:** Kuang-hsü **Obverse:** Inscription: Kuang-hsü Yüan-pao **Reverse:** Dragon

Date	VG	F	VF	XF	Unc
CD(1903)	1.25	4.00	5.00	7.00	24.00

Y# 135.5 10 CASH **Composition:** Copper **Ruler:** Kuang-hsü **Obverse:** Inscription: Kuang-hsü Yüan-pao **Reverse:** Dragon; cloud above letter T looks like number 3

Date	Mintage	VG	F	VF	XF	Unc
CD(1904)	351,974,000	0.35	1.00	2.00	5.00	20.00

Y# 135.6 10 CASH **Composition:** Copper **Ruler:** Kuang-hsü **Obverse:** Inscription: Kuang-hsü Yüan-pao **Reverse:** Dragon; cloud above T redesigned; CASH spelled GASH

Date	VG	F	VF	XF	Unc
CD(1904)	1.50	4.50	9.00	17.50	45.00

Y# 135.7 10 CASH **Composition:** Copper **Ruler:** Kuang-hsü **Obverse:** Inscription: Kuang-hsü Yüan-pao **Reverse:** Thin-tailed dragon; third design of cloud above letter T

Date	VG	F	VF	XF	Unc
CD(1904)	0.50	1.50	3.00	5.00	20.00

Y# 135.8 10 CASH **Composition:** Copper **Ruler:** Kuang-hsü **Obverse:** Inscription: Kuang-hsü Yüan-pao **Reverse:** Fewer clouds around dragon; scales on dragon's body different, pearl smaller

Date	VG	F	VF	XF	Unc
CD(1904)	1.50	4.50	9.00	17.50	45.00

Note: This coin is believed to be counterfeit

Y# 135.9 10 CASH **Composition:** Copper **Ruler:** Kuang-hsü **Obverse:** Inscription: Kuang-hsü Yüan-pao **Reverse:** Small rosette at either side of dragon

Date	Mintage	VG	F	VF	XF	Unc
CD(1905)	496,020,000	0.35	1.00	2.00	5.00	20.00

Y# 135.10 10 CASH **Composition:** Copper **Ruler:** Kuang-hsü **Obverse:** Inscription: Kuang-hsü Yüan-pao **Reverse:** Large oblong rosettes at either side of dragon

Date	VG	F	VF	XF	Unc
CD(1905)	0.50	1.50	3.00	5.00	20.00

Y# 138 10 CASH **Composition:** Copper **Ruler:** Kuang-hsü **Obverse:** Inscription: Kuang-hsü Yüan-pao **Reverse:** Dragon; denomination: TEN-CASH

Date	VG	F	VF	XF	Unc
CD(1905)	1.25	3.50	6.00	12.00	30.00

Y# 138.1 10 CASH **Composition:** Copper **Ruler:** Kuang-hsü **Obverse:** Inscription: Kuang-hsü Yüan-pao; rosette in center **Reverse:** Dragon; without hyphen in TEN CASH

Date	VG	F	VF	XF	Unc
CD(1905)	0.25	0.75	1.50	5.00	20.00

Y# 10k 10 CASH **Composition:** Copper **Ruler:** Kuang-hsü **Obverse:** Inscription: Tai-ch'ing T'ung-pi; mint mark in relief on raised disc **Reverse:** Dragon with wide face and incuse eyes **Rev. Legend:** Kuang-hsü Nien-tsao, TAI-CHING-TI-KUO...

Date	Mintage	VG	F	VF	XF	Unc
CD(1906)	504,800,000	0.45	1.25	2.50	5.00	20.00

Y# 10k.1 10 CASH **Composition:** Copper **Ruler:** Kuang-hsü **Obverse:** Inscription: Tai-ch'ing T'ung-pi **Reverse:** Dragon with narrower face and raised dots for eyes **Rev. Legend:** Kuang-hsü Nien-tsao, TAI-CHING-TI-KUO...

Date	VG	F	VF	XF	Unc
CD(1906)	0.45	1.25	2.50	5.00	20.00

Y# 10k.2 10 CASH **Composition:** Copper **Ruler:** Kuang-hsü **Obverse:** Inscription: Tai-ch'ing T'ung-pi; mint mark in relief without raised disc **Reverse:** Dragon with wide face and incuse eyes **Rev. Legend:** Kuang-hsü Nien-tsao, TAI-CHING-TI-KUO...

Date	VG	F	VF	XF	Unc
CD(1906)	0.35	1.00	2.50	5.00	20.00

Y# 10k.3 10 CASH **Composition:** Copper **Ruler:** Kuang-hsü **Obverse:** Inscription: Tai-ch'ing T'ung-pi **Reverse:** Dragon with narrow face and raised dots for eyes **Rev. Legend:** Kuang-hsü Nien-tsao, TAI-CHING-TI-KUO...

Date	VG	F	VF	XF	Unc
CD(1906)	0.35	1.00	2.50	5.00	20.00

Y# 10k.4 10 CASH **Composition:** Copper **Ruler:** Kuang-hsü **Obverse:** Inscription: Tai-ch'ing T'ung-pi; mint mark incuse on raised disc **Reverse:** Dragon **Rev. Legend:** Kuang-hsü Nien-tsao, TAI-CHING-TI-KUO...

Date	VG	F	VF	XF	Unc
CD(1906)	4.50	12.50	25.00	45.00	—

Y# 10k.4a 10 CASH **Composition:** Brass **Ruler:** Kuang-hsü **Obverse:** Inscription: Tai-ch'ing T'ung-pi **Reverse:** Dragon **Rev. Legend:** Kuang-hsü Nien-tsao, TAI-CHING-TI-KUO...

Date	VG	F	VF	XF	Unc
CD(1906)	—	—	—	—	—

Y# A140 10 CASH **Composition:** Copper **Ruler:** Kuang-hsü **Obverse:** Inscription: Tai-ch'ing T'ung-Pi; Y#10k.2 **Reverse:** Dragon; Y#138 **Note:** Mule

Date	VG	F	VF	XF	Unc
CD(1906)	8.50	25.00	40.00	60.00	—

Y# B140 10 CASH **Composition:** Copper **Ruler:** Kuang-hsü **Obverse:** Inscription: Kuang-hsü Yüan-pao; Y#138 **Reverse:** Dragon; Y#10k **Note:** Mule

Date	VG	F	VF	XF	Unc
CD(1905)	10.00	30.00	50.00	70.00	—

Y# D140 10 CASH **Composition:** Copper **Ruler:** Kuang-hsü **Obverse:** Inscription: Kuang-hsü Yüan-pao; Y#138.1 **Reverse:** Dragon; Y#135 **Note:** Mule

Date	VG	F	VF	XF	Unc
CD(1905)	35.00	100	150	200	—

Note: Other Kiangnan mules exist, dated 1902 and 1903

Y# E140 10 CASH **Composition:** Copper **Ruler:** Kuang-hsü **Obverse:** Inscription: Tai-ch'ing T'ung-pi; Y#10.5 **Reverse:** Dragon; Kiangnan Y#138.1 **Note:** Mule

Date	VG	F	VF	XF	Unc
CD(1907)	35.00	100	225	300	—

Y# 140.1 (Y140) 10 CASH **Composition:** Copper **Ruler:** Kuang-hsü **Obverse:** Inscription: Tai-ch'ing T'ung-Pi; Y#10k **Reverse:** Dragon; Y#138 **Note:** Mule; raised or incused mint mark.

Date	VG	F	VF	XF	Unc
CD(1906)	1.00	3.00	5.00	12.00	30.00

Y# 140.2 10 CASH **Composition:** Copper **Ruler:** Kuang-hsü **Obverse:** Inscription: Tai-ch'ing T'ung-pi, Y#10k **Reverse:** Dragon, Y#138 **Note:** Mule; mint mark incuse on raised disk.

Date	VG	F	VF	XF	Unc
CD(1906)	1.00	3.00	5.00	12.00	30.00

Y# 10k.5 10 CASH **Composition:** Copper **Ruler:** Kuang-hsü **Obverse:** Inscription: Tai-ch'ing T'ung-pi; mint mark incuse on raised disc **Reverse:** Dragon with wide face; seven flames on pearl **Rev. Legend:** Kuang-hsü Nien-tsao, TAI-CHING-TI-KUO...

Date	Mintage	VG	F	VF	XF	Unc
CD(1907)	552,000,000	0.50	1.50	3.00	5.00	20.00

Y# 10k.6 10 CASH **Composition:** Copper **Ruler:** Kuang-hsü **Obverse:** Inscription: Tai-ch'ing T'ung-pi **Reverse:** Different dragon with narrow face an small mouth; five flames on pearl; dot after COIN **Rev. Legend:** Kuang-hsü Nien-tsao, TAI-CHING-TI-KUO...

Date	VG	F	VF	XF	Unc
CD(1907)	0.35	1.00	2.00	4.50	20.00

Y# 10k.6a 10 CASH Composition: Brass **Ruler:** Kuang-hsü **Obverse:** Inscription: Tai-ch'ing T'ung-pi **Reverse:** Dragon **Rev. Legend:** Kuang-hsü Nien-tsao, TAI-CHING-TI-KUO...

Date	VG	F	VF	XF	Unc
CD(1907)	3.00	9.00	17.50	30.00	—

Y# 10k.7 10 CASH Composition: Copper **Ruler:** Kuang-hsü **Obverse:** Inscription: Tai-ch'ing T'ung-pi **Reverse:** Dragon with large mouth and redesigned head; flame below pearl has long tail which touches dragon's body; KUO spelled KIIO **Rev. Legend:** Kuang-hsü Nien-tsao, TAI-CHING-TI-KUO...

Date	VG	F	VF	XF	Unc
CD(1907)	0.35	1.00	2.50	5.00	20.00

Y# 10k.8 10 CASH Composition: Copper **Ruler:** Kuang-hsü **Obverse:** Inscription: Tai-ch'ing T'ung-pi **Reverse:** Tail of flame below pearl does not touch dragon's body; dash after word COIN; KUO spelled KUO **Rev. Legend:** Kuang-hsü Nien-tsao, TAI-CHING-TI-KUO...

Date	VG	F	VF	XF	Unc
CD(1907)	0.35	1.00	2.50	5.00	20.00

Y# 10k.9 10 CASH Composition: Copper **Ruler:** Kuang-hsü **Obverse:** Inscription: Tai-ch'ing T'ung-pi **Reverse:** Dragon with square mouth; letter K in KUO larger than other letters; without dot or dash after COIN **Rev. Legend:** Kuang-hsü Nien-tsao, TAI-CHING-TI-KUO...

Date	VG	F	VF	XF	Unc
CD(1907)	0.35	1.00	2.25	4.50	20.00

Y# 10k.9a 10 CASH Composition: Copper **Ruler:** Kuang-hsü **Obverse:** Inscription: Tai-ch'ing T'ung-pi **Reverse:** Large flat-faced dragon **Rev. Legend:** Kuang-hsü Nien-tsao, TAI-CHING-TI-KUO...

Date	VG	F	VF	XF	Unc
CD(1907)	—	—	—	—	—

Y# 10k.10 10 CASH Composition: Copper **Ruler:** Kuang-hsü **Obverse:** Inscription: Tai-ch'ing T'ung-pi: mint mark incuse on raised disc **Reverse:** Dragon with small moutn; five flame pearl; dot after COIN; KUO spelled KUO **Rev. Legend:** Kuang-hsü Nien-tsao, TAI-CHING-TI-KUO...

Date	Mintage	VG	F	VF	XF	Unc
CD(1908)	442,750,000	0.35	1.00	2.50	5.00	20.00

Y# 10k.11 10 CASH Composition: Copper **Ruler:** Kuang-hsü **Obverse:** Inscription: Tai-ch'ing T'ung-pi **Reverse:** Dragon has large mouth and redesigned head; tail on cloud beneath pearl touches dragon's body; KUO spelled KIIO **Rev. Legend:** Kuang-hsü Nien-tsao, TAI-CHING-TI-KUO...

Date	VG	F	VF	XF	Unc
CD(1908)	0.35	1.00	2.00	4.00	20.00

Y# 10k.12 10 CASH Composition: Copper **Ruler:** Kuang-hsü **Obverse:** Inscription: Tai-ch'ing T'ung-pi **Reverse:** Dragon; dash after COIN; KUO spelled KUO **Rev. Legend:** Kuang-hsü Nien-tsao, TAI-CHING-TI-KUO...

Date	VG	F	VF	XF	Unc
CD(1908)	0.50	1.50	3.00	5.00	20.00

Y# 10k.13 10 CASH Composition: Copper **Ruler:** Kuang-hsü **Obverse:** Inscription: Tai-ch'ing T'ung-pi **Reverse:** Dragon's head redesigned; without dot or dash after COIN; KUO spelled KIIO **Rev. Legend:** Kuang-hsü Nien-tsao, TAI-CHING-TI-KUO...

Date	VG	F	VF	XF	Unc
CD(1908)	0.35	1.00	2.00	4.00	20.00

Note: Most of the 1907 and 1908 ten cash above have copper spelled GOPPER

Y# 141a 5 CENTS Weight: 13.0000 g. **Composition:** 0.8200 Silver .0343 oz. ASW **Ruler:** Kuang-hsü **Obverse:** Inscription: Kuang-hsü Yüan-pao **Reverse:** Without circle around dragon

Date	Mintage	VG	F	VF	XF	Unc
ND(1898)	Inc. above	2.50	10.00	15.00	30.00	50.00
CD(1899)	3,812	17.50	50.00	100	150	300
CD(1900)	618,000	3.00	10.00	15.00	30.00	50.00
CD(1901)	—	17.50	50.00	75.00	150	275

Y# 142a.5 10 CENTS Weight: 2.6000 g. **Composition:** 0.8200 Silver .0343 oz. ASW **Ruler:** Kuang-hsü **Obverse:** Inscription: Kuang-hsü Yüan-pao; without initials **Reverse:** Large English letters

Date	Mintage	VG	F	VF	XF	Unc
CD(1901)	7,794,000	0.85	2.50	4.50	9.00	30.00

Y# 142a.6 10 CENTS Weight: 2.6000 g. **Composition:** 0.8200 Silver .0343 oz. ASW **Ruler:** Kuang-hsü **Obverse:** Inscription: Kuang-hsü Yüan-pao; without initials **Reverse:** Small English letters

Date	VG	F	VF	XF	Unc
CD(1901)	0.85	2.50	4.50	9.00	30.00

Y# 142a.7 10 CENTS Weight: 2.6000 g. **Composition:** 0.8200 Silver .0343 oz. ASW **Ruler:** Kuang-hsü **Obverse:** Inscription: Kuang-hsü Yüan-pao; initials "HAH" **Reverse:** Large rosettes beside dragon

Date	VG	F	VF	XF	Unc
CD(1901)	1.25	3.50	6.50	12.50	35.00

Y# 142a.8 10 CENTS Weight: 2.6000 g. **Composition:** 0.8200 Silver .0343 oz. ASW **Ruler:** Kuang-hsü **Obverse:** Inscription: Kuang-hsü Yüan-pao **Reverse:** Small rosettes beside dragon

Date	VG	F	VF	XF	Unc
CD(1901)	1.25	3.50	6.50	12.50	35.00

Y# 142a.9 10 CENTS Weight: 2.6000 g. **Composition:** 0.8200 Silver .0343 oz. ASW **Ruler:** Kuang-hsü **Obverse:** Inscription: Kuang-hsü Yüan-pao **Reverse:** Large stars beside dragon

Date	Mintage	VG	F	VF	XF	Unc
CD(1902)	3,778,000	1.00	3.00	5.50	10.00	30.00

Y# 142a.10 10 CENTS Weight: 2.6000 g. **Composition:** 0.8200 Silver .0343 oz. ASW **Ruler:** Kuang-hsü **Obverse:** Inscription: Kuang-hsü Yüan-pao **Reverse:** Small stars beside dragon

Date	VG	F	VF	XF	Unc
CD(1902)	1.25	4.00	7.00	12.00	50.00

Y# 142a.11 10 CENTS Weight: 2.6000 g. **Composition:** 0.8200 Silver .0343 oz. ASW **Ruler:** Kuang-hsü **Obverse:** Inscription: Kuang-hsü Yüan-pao; large rosette

Date	Mintage	VG	F	VF	XF	Unc
CD(1903)	1,161,000	3.00	10.00	25.00	50.00	90.00

Y# 142a.12 10 CENTS Weight: 2.6000 g. **Composition:** 0.8200 Silver .0343 oz. ASW **Ruler:** Kuang-hsü **Obverse:** Inscription: Kuang-hsü Yüan-pao; small rosette

Date	VG	F	VF	XF	Unc
CD(1903)	3.50	10.00	25.00	50.00	90.00

Y# 142a.13 10 CENTS Weight: 2.6000 g. **Composition:** 0.8200 Silver .0343 oz. ASW **Ruler:** Kuang-hsü **Obverse:** Inscription: Kuang-hsü Yüan-pao; initials "HAH TH"

Date	Mintage	VG	F	VF	XF	Unc
CD(1904)	897,000	1.75	5.00	10.00	25.00	75.00

Y# 142a.14 10 CENTS Weight: 2.6000 g. **Composition:** 0.8200 Silver .0343 oz. ASW **Ruler:** Kuang-hsü **Obverse:** Inscription: Kuang-hsü Yüan-pao; initials "SY" upside down

Date	Mintage	VG	F	VF	XF	Unc
CD(1905)	681,000	1.75	5.00	10.00	25.00	75.00

Y# 146 10 CENTS Weight: 2.6000 g. **Composition:** 0.8200 Silver .0343 oz. ASW **Ruler:** Hsüan-T'ung **Obverse:** Inscription: Hsüan-t'ung Yüan-pao **Reverse:** Dragon

Date	VG	F	VF	XF	Unc
ND(1911)	3.50	10.00	25.00	50.00	90.00

Note: Includes 590,000 pieces struck in debased silver in 1916

Y# 143 20 CENTS Weight: 5.3000 g. **Composition:** 0.8200 Silver .1397 oz. ASW **Ruler:** Kuang-hsü **Obverse:** Inscription: Kuang-hsü Yüan-pao; rosettes at 2 abd 10 o'clock **Reverse:** Circle around dragon

Date	Mintage	VG	F	VF	XF	Unc
ND(1898)	7,000,000	7.01	17.50	40.00	70.00	180

Y# 143a.6 20 CENTS Weight: 5.3000 g. **Composition:** 0.8200 Silver .1397 oz. ASW **Ruler:** Kuang-hsü **Obverse:** Inscription: Kuang-hsü Yüan-pao; without initials

Date	Mintage	VG	F	VF	XF	Unc
CD(1901)	47,114,000	1.50	4.50	8.00	15.00	50.00

Y# 143a.7 20 CENTS Weight: 5.3000 g. **Composition:** 0.8200 Silver .1397 oz. ASW **Ruler:** Kuang-hsü **Obverse:** Inscription: Kuang-hsü Yüan-pao; initials "HAH"

Date	VG	F	VF	XF	Unc
CD(1901)	1.25	3.50	5.00	10.00	50.00

Y# 143a.8 20 CENTS Weight: 5.3000 g. **Composition:** 0.8200 Silver .1397 oz. ASW **Ruler:** Kuang-hsü **Obverse:** Inscription: Kuang-hsü Yüan-pao

Date	Mintage	VG	F	VF	XF	Unc
CD(1902)	15,754,000	1.35	4.00	6.50	12.50	50.00

Y# 143a.9 20 CENTS **Weight:** 5.3000 g. **Composition:** 0.8200 Silver .1397 oz. ASW **Ruler:** Kuang-hsü **Obverse:** Inscription: Kuang-hsü Yüan-pao; rosette in outer legend

Date	Mintage	VG	F	VF	XF	Unc
CD(1903)	2,432,000	3.50	10.00	20.00	50.00	100

Y# 143a.10 20 CENTS **Weight:** 5.3000 g. **Composition:** 0.8200 Silver .1397 oz. ASW **Ruler:** Kuang-hsü **Obverse:** Inscription: Kuang-hsü Yüan-pao; without rosette

Date	VG	F	VF	XF	Unc
CD(1903)	4.50	12.50	25.00	50.00	150

Y# 143a.11 20 CENTS **Weight:** 5.3000 g. **Composition:** 0.8200 Silver .1397 oz. ASW **Ruler:** Kuang-hsü **Obverse:** Inscription: Kuang-hsü Yüan-pao; initials "HAH TH"

Date	Mintage	VG	F	VF	XF	Unc
CD(1904)	1,172,000	5.00	15.00	35.00	55.00	120

Y# 143a.12 20 CENTS **Weight:** 5.3000 g. **Composition:** 0.8200 Silver .1397 oz. ASW **Ruler:** Kuang-hsü **Obverse:** Inscription: Kuang-hsü Yüan-pao; without initials

Date	Mintage	VG	F	VF	XF	Unc
CD(1905)	828,000	3.50	10.00	25.00	45.00	120

Y# 143a.13 20 CENTS **Weight:** 5.3000 g. **Composition:** 0.8200 Silver .1397 oz. ASW **Ruler:** Kuang-hsü **Obverse:** Inscription: Kuang-hsü Yüan-pao; initials "SY"

Date	VG	F	VF	XF	Unc
CD(1905)	3.00	9.00	22.00	35.00	100

Y# 143a.14 20 CENTS **Weight:** 5.3000 g. **Composition:** 0.8200 Silver .1397 oz. ASW **Ruler:** Kuang-hsü **Obverse:** Inscription: Kuang-hsü Yüan-pao **Rev. Legend:** ...MACI...

Date	VG	F	VF	XF	Unc
CD(1901)	1.75	5.00	10.00	25.00	60.00

Y# 147 20 CENTS **Weight:** 5.3000 g. **Composition:** 0.8200 Silver .1397 oz. ASW **Ruler:** Hsüan-T'ung **Obverse:** Inscription: Hsüan-T'ung Yüan-pao **Reverse:** Dragon

Date	Mintage	VG	F	VF	XF	Unc
ND(1911)	2,320,000	6.50	20.00	50.00	80.00	150

Note: Includes 2,005,000 pieces struck in debased silver in 1916

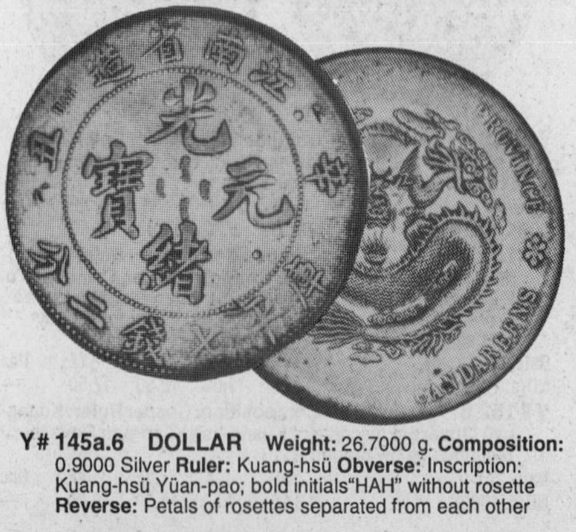

Y# 145a.6 DOLLAR **Weight:** 26.7000 g. **Composition:** 0.9000 Silver **Ruler:** Kuang-hsü **Obverse:** Inscription: Kuang-hsü Yüan-pao; bold initials"HAH" without rosette **Reverse:** Petals of rosettes separated from each other

Date	VG	F	VF	XF	Unc
CD(1901)	22.00	65.00	125	200	500

Y# 145a.7 DOLLAR **Weight:** 26.7000 g. **Composition:** 0.9000 Silver **Ruler:** Kuang-hsü **Obverse:** Inscription: Kuang-hsü Yüan-pao; initials "HAH" and rosette **Reverse:** Petals of rosettes run together

Date	VG	F	VF	XF	Unc
CD(1901)	6.50	20.00	35.00	75.00	275

Y# 145a.5 DOLLAR **Weight:** 26.7000 g. **Composition:** 0.9000 Silver **Ruler:** Kuang-hsü **Obverse:** Inscription: Kuang-hsü Yüan-pao; without initials **Note:** Cross-reference number K#86.

Date	Mintage	VG	F	VF	XF	Unc
CD(1901)	2,377,000	50.00	150	200	300	1,250

Y# 145a.21 DOLLAR **Weight:** 26.7000 g. **Composition:** 0.9000 Silver **Ruler:** Kuang-hsü **Obverse:** Inscription: Kuang-hsü Yüan-pao; fine initials"HAH" without rosette **Reverse:** Similar to Y#145a.6 **Note:** Cross-reference number K#90.

Date	VG	F	VF	XF	Unc
CD(1901)	22.00	65.00	125	200	500

Y# 145a.22 DOLLAR **Weight:** 26.7000 g. **Composition:** 0.9000 Silver **Ruler:** Kuang-hsü **Obverse:** Inscription: Kuang-hsü Yüan-pao; cross of six dots at upper right **Reverse:** Similar to Y#145a.6 **Note:** Cross-reference number K#90b.

Date	VG	F	VF	XF	Unc
CD(1901)	35.00	100	200	350	1,000

Y# 145a.8 DOLLAR **Weight:** 25.7000 g. **Composition:** 0.9000 Silver **Ruler:** Kuang-hsü **Obverse:** Inscription: Kuang-hsü Yüan-pao; small date, small "HAH" **Reverse:** Similar to Y#145a.4 **Note:** Cross-reference number K#94.

Date	Mintage	VG	F	VF	XF	Unc
CD(1902)	3,562,000	8.50	25.00	50.00	100	300

Y# 145a.9 DOLLAR **Weight:** 27.0000 g. **Composition:** 0.9000 Silver **Ruler:** Kuang-hsü **Obverse:** Inscription: Kuang-hsü Yüan-pao; larger date, larger "HAH"

Date	VG	F	VF	XF	Unc
CD(1902)	8.50	25.00	50.00	100	300

Y# 145a.10 DOLLAR **Weight:** 26.9000 g. **Composition:** 0.9000 Silver **Ruler:** Kuang-hsü **Obverse:** Inscription: Kuang-hsü Yüan-pao; "HAH" and rosettes in outer ring **Note:** Cross-reference number K#96.

Date	Mintage	VG	F	VF	XF	Unc
CD(1903)	1,489,000	13.00	40.00	85.00	175	400

Y# 145a.11 DOLLAR **Weight:** 27.0000 g. **Composition:** 0.9000 Silver **Ruler:** Kuang-hsü **Obverse:** Inscription: Kuang-hsü Yüan-pao; without rosette in outer ring **Note:** Cross-reference number K#96c.

Date	VG	F	VF	XF	Unc
CD(1903)	135	400	600	900	2,000

Y# 145a.12 DOLLAR **Weight:** 26.7000 g. **Composition:** 0.9000 Silver **Ruler:** Kuang-hsü **Obverse:** Inscription: Kuang-hsü Yüan-pao; initials "HAH" and "CH" without dots or rosettes **Reverse:** Similar to Y#145a.4 **Note:** Cross-reference number K#99.

Date	Mintage	VG	F	VF	XF	Unc
CD(1904)	44,725,000	5.00	15.00	25.00	40.00	200

Y# 145a.13 DOLLAR **Weight:** 27.0000 g. **Composition:** 0.9000 Silver **Ruler:** Kuang-hsü **Obverse:** Inscription: Kuang-hsü Yüan-pao; dot at either side

Date	VG	F	VF	XF	Unc
CD(1904)	5.00	15.00	25.00	40.00	200

Y# 145a.19 DOLLAR **Weight:** 27.0000 g. **Composition:** 0.9000 Silver **Ruler:** Kuang-hsü **Obverse:** Inscription: Kuang-hsü Yüan-pao; dot at either side, without four central characters

Date	VG	F	VF	XF	Unc
CD(1904)	—	—	—	—	—

Y# 145a.14 DOLLAR **Weight:** 27.0000 g. **Composition:** 0.9000 Silver **Ruler:** Kuang-hsü **Obverse:** Inscription: Kuang-hsü Yüan-pao **Reverse:** Dot to left of numeral 7

Date	VG	F	VF	XF	Unc
CD(1904)	5.00	15.00	25.00	40.00	150

Y# 145a.15 DOLLAR **Weight:** 27.0000 g. **Composition:** 0.9000 Silver **Ruler:** Kuang-hsü **Obverse:** Inscription: Kuang-hsü Yüan-pao; four-petalled rosette at either side "HAH" and "CH"

Date	VG	F	VF	XF	Unc
CD(1904)	17.50	50.00	125	200	500

Y# 145a.16 DOLLAR **Weight:** 27.0000 g. **Composition:** 0.9000 Silver **Ruler:** Kuang-hsü **Obverse:** Inscription: Kuang-hsü Yüan-pao; initials "HAH" and "TH"

Date	VG	F	VF	XF	Unc
CD(1904)	17.50	50.00	100	200	500

Y# 145a.17 DOLLAR **Weight:** 27.1000 g. **Composition:** 0.9000 Silver **Ruler:** Kuang-hsü **Obverse:** Inscription: Kuang-hsü Yüan-pao; initials "SY" **Reverse:** Similar to Y#145a.10

Date	Mintage	VG	F	VF	XF	Unc
CD(1905)	634,000	11.50	35.00	65.00	200	600

PATTERNS

Including off metal strikes

KM#	Date	Mintage	Identification	Mkt Val
Pn3	CD(1906)	—	2 Cash. Copper. Y#8k	2,000
Pn4	CD(1906)	—	20 Cash. Copper. Y#11k	—

KIANGSI PROVINCE

Jiangxi, Kiangsee

A province located in southeastern China. Mostly hilly with some mountains on the borders that produce coal and tungsten. Some of China's finest porcelain comes from this province. Kiangsi was visited by Marco Polo. A mint was opened in Nanchang in 1729, closed in 1733, reopened in 1736 and operated with reasonable continuity from that time. Modern machinery was introduced in 1901 although it only produced copper coins. The mint closed amidst internal problems in the 1920's.

EMPIRE

PROVINCIAL CAST COINAGE

C# 15-9 CASH **Composition:** Cast Brass **Ruler:** Kuang-hsü **Obverse:** Type A **Reverse:** Type 1 mint mark

Date	Good	VG	F	VF	XF
ND(1875-1908)	4.50	6.50	12.00	15.00	—

C# 15-10 10 CASH **Composition:** Cast Brass **Ruler:** Kuang-hsü **Obverse:** Type B

Date	Good	VG	F	VF	XF
ND(1875-1908) Rare	—	—	—	—	—

MILLED COINAGE

Many Kiangsi (Jiangxi) coins have a six-petalled rosette in the center of the obverse, arranged so that two sides of the rosette are formed by two petals in line with each other. The remainng two sides have a single petal, standing out from the rest. The direction that these

single petals point, determines whether the rosette is horizontal or vertical. A horizontal rosette has the single petals pointing left and right, while the single petals of the vertical rosette point up and down.

Y# 149 10 CASH Composition: Copper **Ruler:** Kuang-hsü **Obverse:** Vertical rosette at center, inscription: Kuang-hsü Yüan-pao **Reverse:** Province name spelled KIANG-SEE

Date	VG	F	VF	XF	Unc
ND(c. 1902)	3.50	8.00	12.50	22.50	—

Y# 149.1 10 CASH Composition: Copper **Ruler:** Kuang-hsü **Obverse:** Horizontal rosette at center, inscription: Kuang-hsü Yüan-pao

Date	VG	F	VF	XF	Unc
ND(c. 1902)	3.50	8.00	12.50	22.50	—

Y# 149.2 10 CASH Composition: Copper **Ruler:** Kuang-hsü **Obverse:** Different Manchu word at right, inscription: Kuang-hsü Yüan-pao **Reverse:** Circled dragon **Note:** May be a pattern.

Date	VG	F	VF	XF	Unc
ND(c. 1902) Rare	—	—	—	—	—

Y# 150 10 CASH Composition: Copper **Ruler:** Kuang-hsü **Obverse:** Manchu "Pao Yuan" at 3 and 9 o'clock, inscription: Kuang-hsü Yüan-pao **Reverse:** Province name spelled KIANG-SI, 2 stars at either side of dragon

Date	VG	F	VF	XF	Unc
ND(c. 1902)	2.00	6.00	11.00	17.50	35.00

Y# 150.1 10 CASH Composition: Copper **Ruler:** Kuang-hsü **Obverse:** Manchu "Pao Ch'ang" at center and Chinese reading "Ku P'ing" at 3 and 9 o'clock, inscription: Kuang-hsü Yüan-pao

Date	VG	F	VF	XF	Unc
ND(c. 1902)	1.00	3.00	6.00	12.00	25.00

Y# 150.2 10 CASH Composition: Copper **Ruler:** Kuang-hsü **Obverse:** Manchu "Pao Ch'ang" at 3 and 9 o'clock, horizontal rosette in center, inscription: Kuang-hsü Yüan-pao

Date	VG	F	VF	XF	Unc
ND(c. 1902)	0.35	1.00	2.00	5.00	20.00

Y# 150.2a 10 CASH Composition: Brass **Ruler:** Kuang-hsü **Obverse:** Inscription: Kuang-hsü Yüan-pao

Date	VG	F	VF	XF	Unc
ND(c. 1902)	1.75	5.00	10.00	20.00	40.00

Y# 150.3 10 CASH Composition: Copper **Ruler:** Kuang-hsü **Obverse:** Vertical rosette in center, inscription: Kuang-hsü Yüan-pao

Date	VG	F	VF	XF	Unc
ND(c. 1902)	0.35	1.00	2.00	5.00	20.00

Y# 150.4 10 CASH Composition: Copper **Ruler:** Kuang-hsü **Obverse:** Horizontal rosette, inscription: Kuang-hsü Yüan-pao **Reverse:** 1 star at either side of dragon, large English lettering

Date	VG	F	VF	XF	Unc
ND(c. 1902)	0.35	1.00	2.00	5.00	20.00

Y# 150.4a 10 CASH Composition: Brass **Ruler:** Kuang-hsü **Obverse:** Horizontal rosette, inscription: Kuang-hsü Yüan-pao **Reverse:** 1 star at either side of dragon, large English lettering

Date	VG	F	VF	XF	Unc
ND(c. 1902)	1.25	5.00	9.00	17.50	35.00

Y# 150.5 10 CASH Composition: Copper **Ruler:** Kuang-hsü **Obverse:** Vertical rosette, inscription: Kuang-hsü Yüan-pao

Date	VG	F	VF	XF	Unc
ND(c. 1902)	0.35	1.00	2.00	5.00	20.00

Y# 150.6 10 CASH Composition: Copper **Ruler:** Kuang-hsü **Obverse:** Inscription: Kuang-hsü Yüan-pao **Reverse:** Smaller English lettering, 1 star at either side of dragon

Date	VG	F	VF	XF	Unc
ND(c. 1902)	0.35	1.00	2.00	5.00	20.00

Y# 150.7 10 CASH Composition: Copper **Ruler:** Kuang-hsü **Obverse:** Small rosette center, inscription: Kuang-hsü Yüan-pao **Reverse:** 1 star at either side of dragon

Date	VG	F	VF	XF	Unc
ND(c. 1902)	2.00	6.00	11.00	17.50	35.00

Y# 150.8 10 CASH Composition: Copper **Ruler:** Kuang-hsü **Obverse:** Inscription: Kuang-hsü Yüan-pao **Reverse:** 3 stars at either side of dragon

Date	VG	F	VF	XF	Unc
ND(c. 1902)	4.50	12.50	20.00	30.00	60.00

Y# 152 10 CASH Composition: Copper **Ruler:** Kuang-hsü **Obverse:** Manchu "Pao Ch'ang" at 3 and 9 o'clock, inscription: Kuang-hsü Yüan-pao **Reverse:** Province name spelled KIANG-SI, front view dragon, mountain below pearl

Date	VG	F	VF	XF	Unc
ND(c. 1902)	2.50	4.00	6.00	12.00	—

Y# 152.1 10 CASH Composition: Copper **Ruler:** Kuang-hsü **Obverse:** Horizontal rosette in center, Manchu "Pao Ch'ang" at 3 and 9 o'clock, inscription: Kuang-hsü Yüan-pao

Date	VG	F	VF	XF	Unc
ND(c. 1902)	2.50	4.00	6.00	12.00	—

Y# 152.2 10 CASH Composition: Copper **Ruler:** Kuang-hsü **Obverse:** Horizontal rosette in center, Manchu "Pao Ch'ang" at 3 and 9 o'clock, small character "10," inscription: Kuang-hsü Yüan-pao

Date	VG	F	VF	XF	Unc
ND(c. 1902)	5.00	12.00	17.50	27.50	—

Y# 152.3 10 CASH Composition: Copper **Ruler:** Kuang-hsü **Obverse:** Horizontal rosette in center, Manchu "Pao Ch'ang" at 3 and 9 o'clock, large character "10," inscription: Kuang-hsü Yüan-pao **Reverse:** Without mountain below dragon

Date	VG	F	VF	XF	Unc
ND(c. 1902)	3.50	8.00	12.00	17.50	—

Y# 152.7 10 CASH Composition: Copper **Ruler:** Kuang-hsü **Obverse:** Vertical rosette in center, inscription: Kuang-hsü Yüan-pao

Date	VG	F	VF	XF	Unc
ND(c. 1902)	—	—	—	—	—

Y# 152.4 10 CASH Composition: Copper **Ruler:** Kuang-hsü **Obverse:** Horizontal rosette in center, small character "10," inscription: Kuang-hsü Yüan-pao

Date	VG	F	VF	XF	Unc
ND(c. 1902)	3.50	8.00	12.00	17.50	—

Y# 152.5 10 CASH Composition: Copper **Ruler:** Kuang-hsü **Obverse:** Manchu "Pao Ch'ang" in center, Chinese "K'u P'ing" at 3 and 9 o'clock, inscription: Kuang-hsü Yüan-pao **Reverse:** Without mountain below pearl, dragon's body repositioned

Date	VG	F	VF	XF	Unc
ND(c. 1902)	3.50	8.50	12.50	17.50	—

Y# 152.6 10 CASH Composition: Copper **Ruler:** Kuang-hsü **Obverse:** Inscription: Kuang-hsü Yüan-pao **Reverse:** Mountain below dragon

Date	VG	F	VF	XF	Unc
ND(c. 1902)	3.25	7.50	11.00	16.00	—

Y# 153 10 CASH Composition: Copper **Ruler:** Kuang-hsü **Obverse:** Inscription: Kuang-hsü Yüan-pao **Reverse:** Legend above front view dragon **Rev. Legend:** KIANG-SEE PROVINCE **Note:** Found with and without a swirl on the pearl below dragon's mouth.

Date	VG	F	VF	XF	Unc
ND(c. 1902)	2.00	4.50	7.00	11.00	—

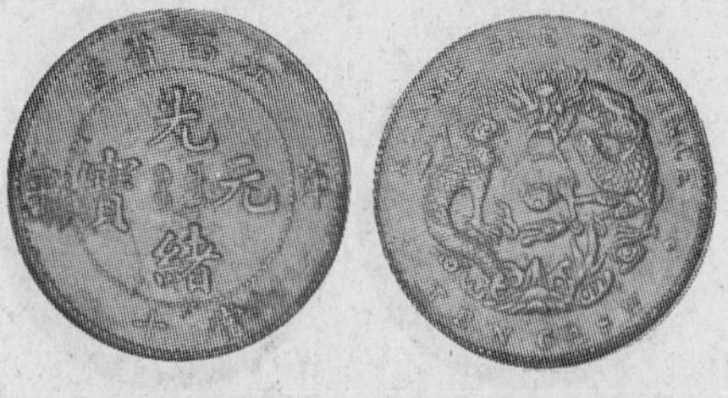

Y# 153.1 10 CASH Composition: Copper **Ruler:** Kuang-hsü **Obverse:** Manchu "Pao Ch'ang" at center and Chinese "K'u P'ing" at 3 and 9 o'clock, inscription: Kuang-hsü Yüan-pao **Note:** Found with and without a swirl on the pearl below dragon's mouth.

Date	VG	F	VF	XF	Unc
ND(c. 1902)	0.80	2.00	3.50	7.00	—

Y# 153.2 10 CASH Composition: Copper **Ruler:** Kuang-hsü **Obverse:** Small Manchu "Pao Ch'ang" at 3 and 9 o'clock, small horizontal rosette in center, inscription: Kuang-hsü Yüan-pao **Note:** Found with and without a swirl on the pearl below dragon's mouth.

Date	VG	F	VF	XF	Unc
ND(c. 1902)	0.80	2.00	3.50	7.00	—

Y# 153.3 10 CASH Composition: Copper **Ruler:** Kuang-hsü **Obverse:** Small vertical rosette in center, inscription: Kuang-hsü Yüan-pao **Note:** Found with and without a swirl on the pearl below dragon's mouth.

Date	VG	F	VF	XF	Unc
ND(c. 1902)	2.00	5.00	10.00	17.50	—

Y# 154 10 CASH Composition: Copper **Ruler:** Kuang-hsü **Obverse:** Inscription: Kuang-hsü Yüan-pao **Reverse:** Legend above flying dragon **Rev. Legend:** KIANG SI

Date	VG	F	VF	XF	Unc
ND(c. 1902)	40.00	60.00	80.00	100	—

Y# 10m 10 CASH Composition: Copper **Ruler:** Kuang-hsü **Obverse:** Inscription: Tai-ch'ing T'ung-pi **Reverse:** Dragon's eyes in relief **Rev. Legend:** Kuang-hsü Nien-tsao, TAI-CHING-TI-KUO ...

Date	VG	F	VF	XF	Unc
CD(1906)	1.25	3.00	6.00	12.00	—

Y# 10m.1 10 CASH Composition: Copper **Ruler:** Kuang-hsü **Obverse:** Inscription: Tai-ch'ing T'ung-pi **Reverse:** Dragon's eyes incuse **Rev. Legend:** Kuang-hsu Nien-tsao, TAI-CHING-TI-KUO ...

Date	VG	F	VF	XF	Unc
CD(1906)	1.25	3.00	6.00	12.00	—

Y# 10m.2 10 CASH Composition: Copper **Ruler:** Kuang-hsü **Obverse:** Inscription: Tai-ch'ing T'ung-pi **Reverse:** Dragon redesigned, small faint cloud beneath pearl **Rev. Legend:** Kuang-hsü Nien-tsao, TAI-CHING-TI-KUO ...

Date	VG	F	VF	XF	Unc
CD(1906)	5.00	12.00	17.50	30.00	—

REPUBLIC

MILLED COINAGE

Many Kiangsi (Jiangxi) coins have a six-petalled rosette in the center of the obverse, arranged so that two sides of the rosette are formed by two petals in line with each other. The remainng two sides have a single petal, standing out from the rest. The direction that these single petals point, determines whether the rosette is horizontal or vertical. A horizontal rosette has the single petals pointing left and right, while the single petals of the vertical rosette point up and down.

Y# 412 10 CASH Composition: Copper **Obverse:** Date appears at 3 and 9 o'clock **Obv. Legend:** Chiang-hsi Sheng-tsao **Reverse:** 9-pointed star inside circle and 5-petalled rosette at 3 and 9 o'clock

Date	VG	F	VF	XF	Unc
CD(1911)	200	300	450	650	—

Y# 412a 10 CASH Composition: Copper **Obverse:** Horizontal rosette in center with Chinese characters "Chiang Hsi" above and below **Reverse:** 6-petalled rosette at either side

Date	VG	F	VF	XF	Unc
CD1912	1.25	3.00	5.00	9.00	—

Y# 412a.1 10 CASH Composition: Copper **Obverse:** Small, vertical rosette in center

Date	VG	F	VF	XF	Unc
CD1912	1.25	3.00	5.00	9.00	—

Y# 412a.2 10 CASH Composition: Copper **Obverse:** Large, vertical rosette in center; thick, large-center characters **Reverse:** Small, 5-petalled rosettes at either side

Date	VG	F	VF	XF	Unc
CD(1912)	6.00	12.00	17.50	27.50	—

Y# 412a.3 10 CASH Composition: Copper **Obverse:** Large, vertical rosette in center; thin-center characters

Date	VG	F	VF	XF	Unc
CD(1912)	1.25	3.00	5.00	10.00	—

REBEL COINAGE

"Ta Han" was a rebel issue made before the revolution. Not only a symbol of defiance, this coin indicated secret membership. Ching law subjected those carrying these coins to execution.

Y# 411 10 CASH Composition: Copper **Obverse:** Mint mark incused on raised-disc center with Chinese characters on 4 sides, "Ta-Han T'ung-pi" character value in outer ring at bottom **Reverse:** Ring of 9 balls without inscription

Date	VG	F	VF	XF	Unc
CD(1911) Rare	—	—	—	—	—

KIANGSU-KIANGSOO PROVINCE

Jiangsu

A province located on the east coast of China. One of the smallest and most densely populated of all Chinese provinces. A mint opened in Soochow in 1667, but closed shortly after in 1670. A new mint opened in 1734 for producing cast coins and had continuous operation until about 1870. Modern equipment was introduced in 1898 and a second mint was opened in 1904. Both mints closed down production in 1906. Taels were produced in Shanghai by local silversmiths as early as 1856. These saw limited circulation in the immediate area.

EMPIRE

PROVINCIAL CAST COINAGE

C# 16-12 CASH Composition: Cast Brass **Ruler:** Kuang-hsü **Obverse:** Inscription: Kuang-hsü T'ung-pao **Reverse:** Inscription: Manchu Boo-su **Note:** Struck at Su (Soochow).

Date	Good	VG	F	VF	XF
ND(1875-1908)	2.25	4.50	8.00	13.00	—

C# 16-12.1 CASH Composition: Cast Brass **Ruler:** Kuang-hsü **Obverse:** Inscription: Kuang-hsü T'ung-pao **Reverse:** Circle above, inscription: Manchu Boo-su **Note:** Struck at Su (Soochow).

Date	Good	VG	F	VF	XF
ND(1875-1908)	3.00	6.00	10.00	16.00	—

C# 16-12.2 CASH Composition: Cast Brass **Ruler:** Kuang-hsü **Obverse:** Inscription: Kuang-hsü T'ung-pao **Reverse:** Crescent above, inscription: Manchu Boo-su **Note:** Struck at Su (Soochow).

Date	Good	VG	F	VF	XF
ND(1875-1908)	3.00	6.00	10.00	16.00	—

MILLED COINAGE

Y# 158 5 CASH Composition: Copper **Ruler:** Kuang-hsü **Obverse:** Inscription: Kuang-hsü Yüan-pao **Reverse:** Side view dragon, EIVE for FIVE

Date	VG	F	VF	XF	Unc
ND(1901)	12.00	32.50	55.00	100	—

Y# 9n 5 CASH Composition: Brass **Ruler:** Kuang-hsü **Obverse:** Inscription: Tai-ching T'ung-pi **Rev. Legend:** Kuang-hsü Nien-tasao, TAI-CHING-TI-KUO ...

Date	VG	F	VF	XF	Unc
CD(1906)	25.00	75.00	125	200	—

Y# 162 10 CASH Composition: Brass **Ruler:** Kuang-hsü **Obverse:** Manchu words at center, without rosettes, inscription: Kuang-hsü Yüan-pao **Edge:** Reeded

Date	VG	F	VF	XF	Unc
ND(c. 1902)	1.25	3.75	6.00	12.00	32.00

Y# 162.1 10 CASH Composition: Brass **Ruler:** Kuang-hsü **Obverse:** Manchu in center, rosettes at 2 and 10 o'clock, inscription: Kuang-hsü Yüan-pao

Date	VG	F	VF	XF	Unc
ND(c. 1902)	0.35	1.00	2.00	5.00	20.00

Y# 162.2 10 CASH Composition: Brass **Ruler:** Kuang-hsü **Obverse:** Inscription: Kuang-hsü Yüan-pao **Edge:** Plain

Date	VG	F	VF	XF	Unc
ND(c. 1902)	0.35	1.00	2.00	5.00	20.00

Y# 162.3 10 CASH Composition: Brass **Ruler:** Kuang-hsü **Obverse:** Tiny rosettes, inscription: Kuang-hsü Yüan-pao **Reverse:** Tiny rosettes **Edge:** Reeded

Date	VG	F	VF	XF	Unc
ND(c. 1902)	0.45	1.25	2.50	5.00	20.00

Y# 162.4 10 CASH Composition: Brass **Ruler:** Kuang-hsü **Obverse:** Rosette center, Manchu at 3 and 9 o'clock, inscription: Kuang-hsü Yüan-pao

Date	VG	F	VF	XF	Unc
ND(c. 1902)	0.35	1.00	2.00	5.00	20.00

Y# 162.5 10 CASH Composition: Brass **Ruler:** Kuang-hsü **Obverse:** Inscription: Kuang-hsü Yüan-pao **Edge:** Plain

Date	VG	F	VF	XF	Unc
ND(c. 1902)	0.35	1.00	2.00	5.00	20.00

Y# 162.6 10 CASH Composition: Brass **Ruler:** Kuang-hsü **Obverse:** Rosette center, large Manchu at 3 and 9 o'clock, higher than on Y#162.4, inscription: Kuang-hsü Yüan-pao **Edge:** Reeded

Date	VG	F	VF	XF	Unc
ND(c. 1902)	0.50	1.50	2.50	5.00	20.00

Y# 162.7 10 CASH Composition: Copper **Ruler:** Kuang-hsü **Obverse:** Inscription: Kuang-hsü Yüan-pao **Edge:** Plain

Date	VG	F	VF	XF	Unc
ND(c. 1902)	0.50	1.50	2.50	5.00	25.00

Y# 162.7a 10 CASH Composition: Brass **Ruler:** Kuang-hsü **Obverse:** Inscription: Kuang-hsü Yüan-pao

Date	VG	F	VF	XF	Unc
ND(c. 1902) Rare	—	—	—	—	—

Y# 162.8 10 CASH Composition: Copper **Ruler:** Kuang-hsü **Obverse:** Manchu "Boo-su" at center, inscription: Kuang-hsü Yüan-pao **Edge:** Reeded

Date	VG	F	VF	XF	Unc
CD(1902)	0.65	2.00	4.00	7.50	25.00

Y# 162.13 10 CASH Composition: Copper **Ruler:** Kuang-hsü **Obverse:** Inscription: Kuang-hsü Yüan-pao **Edge:** Plain

Date	VG	F	VF	XF	Unc
CD(1902)	—	—	—	—	—

Y# B162 10 CASH Composition: Copper **Ruler:** Kuang-hsü **Obverse:** Kiangsu Y#162.8, inscription: Kuang-hsü Yüan-pao **Reverse:** Kiangnan Y#135 **Note:** Mule.

Date	VG	F	VF	XF	Unc
CD(1902)	30.00	90.00	150	250	—

Y# 162.9 10 CASH Composition: Copper **Ruler:** Kuang-hsü **Obverse:** Manchu "Boo-su" at center, inscription: Kuang-hsü Yüan-pao **Edge:** Reeded

Date	VG	F	VF	XF	Unc
CD(1903)	1.75	5.00	7.50	12.00	32.00

Y# C162 10 CASH Composition: Copper **Ruler:** Kuang-hsü **Obverse:** Kiangsu Y#162.9, inscription: Kuang-hsü Yüan-pao **Reverse:** Kiangnan Y#135 **Note:** Mule.

Date	VG	F	VF	XF	Unc
CD(1903)	30.00	90.00	150	250	—

Y# 160 10 CASH Composition: Brass **Ruler:** Kuang-hsü **Obverse:** Inscription: Kuang-hsü Yüan-pao **Reverse:** Cloud below all 3 letters of SOO

Date	VG	F	VF	XF	Unc
ND(1904-05)	0.85	2.50	4.00	8.00	24.00

Y# 160.1 10 CASH Composition: Brass **Ruler:** Kuang-hsü **Obverse:** Inscription: Kuang-hsü Yüan-pao **Reverse:** Cloud below first 2 letters of SOO, Manchu "Boo" at 9 o'clock higher, dragon's body thinner

Date	VG	F	VF	XF	Unc
ND(1904-05)	0.85	2.50	4.00	8.00	24.00

Y# 162.10 10 CASH Composition: Copper **Ruler:** Kuang-hsü **Obverse:** Rosette center, small Manchu "Boo-su" at 3 and 9 o'clock, inscription: Kuang-hsü Yüan-pao **Edge:** Plain

Date	VG	F	VF	XF	Unc
CD(1905)	0.35	1.00	2.00	5.00	20.00

Y# 162.11 10 CASH Composition: Copper **Ruler:** Kuang-hsü **Obverse:** Larger Manchu "Boo-su", inscription: Kuang-hsü Yüan-pao

Date	VG	F	VF	XF	Unc
CD(1905)	0.85	2.50	5.00	8.00	25.00

Y# 162.12 10 CASH Composition: Copper **Ruler:** Kuang-hsü **Obverse:** Inscription: Kuang-hsü Yüan-pao **Reverse:** Kiangsu spelled KIANG-COO

Date	VG	F	VF	XF	Unc
CD(1905)	100	250	500	750	—

Note: Considered a contemporary counterfeit by some authorities

Y# A162 10 CASH Composition: Copper **Ruler:** Kuang-hsü **Obverse:** Kiangsu Y#162, inscription: Kuang-hsü Yüan-pao **Reverse:** Kiangnan Y#135 **Note:** Mule.

Date	VG	F	VF	XF	Unc
ND(c.1905)	30.00	90.00	150	250	—

Y# 10n 10 CASH **Composition:** Copper **Ruler:** Kuang-hsü **Obverse:** Mint mark incused on raised disc, inscription: Tai-ch'ing T'ung-pi **Rev. Legend:** Kuang-hsü Nien-tsao, TAI-CHING-TI-KUO ... **Edge:** Plain

Date	VG	F	VF	XF	Unc
CD(1906)	0.85	2.50	5.00	10.00	30.00

Y# 10n.1 10 CASH **Composition:** Copper **Ruler:** Kuang-hsü **Obverse:** Mint mark incused on raised disc, inscription: Tai-ch'ing T'ung-pi **Rev. Legend:** Kuang-hsü Nien-tsao, TAI-CHING-TI-KUO ... **Edge:** Reeded

Date	VG	F	VF	XF	Unc
CD(1906)	2.00	6.00	11.00	17.50	40.00

Y# 10n.2 10 CASH **Composition:** Copper **Ruler:** Kuang-hsü **Obverse:** Mint mark in relief in field at center without raised disc, inscription: Tai-ch'ing T'ung-pi **Rev. Legend:** Kuang-hsü Nien-tsao, TAI-CHING-TI-KUO ... **Edge:** Plain

Date	VG	F	VF	XF	Unc
CD(1906)	2.00	6.00	11.00	17.50	40.00

Y# 163 20 CASH **Composition:** Copper **Ruler:** Kuang-hsü **Obverse:** Inscription: Kuang-hsü Yüan-pao **Reverse:** Dragon

Date	VG	F	VF	XF	Unc
ND(c. 1902)	17.50	32.50	45.00	65.00	—

Y# 163a 20 CASH **Composition:** Brass **Ruler:** Kuang-hsü **Obverse:** Inscription: Kuang-hsü Yüan-pao **Reverse:** Dragon

Date	VG	F	VF	XF	Unc
ND(c. 1902)	30.00	45.00	70.00	110	—

Y# 11n.1 20 CASH **Composition:** Copper **Ruler:** Kuang-hsü **Obverse:** Inscription: Tai-ch'ing T'ung-pi **Rev. Legend:** Kuang-hsü Nien-tsao, TAI-CHING-TI-KUO ...

Date	VG	F	VF	XF	Unc
CD(1906)	25.00	40.00	60.00	90.00	—

Y# 11n.1a 20 CASH **Composition:** Brass **Ruler:** Kuang-hsü **Obverse:** Inscription: Tai-ch'ing T'ung-pi **Rev. Legend:** Kuang-hsü Nien-tsao, TAI-CHING-TI-KUO ...

Date	VG	F	VF	XF	Unc
CD(1906)	35.00	60.00	90.00	150	—

MILLED COINAGE

Chingkiang Series

Y# 77 10 CASH **Composition:** Copper **Ruler:** Kuang-hsü **Obverse:** Large character at 3 o'clock, inscription: Kuang-hsü Yüan-pao **Edge:** Reeded **Note:** Struck at Chingkiang.

Date	VG	F	VF	XF	Unc
ND(1905)	0.85	2.50	4.00	7.50	25.00

Y# 77.1 10 CASH **Composition:** Copper **Ruler:** Kuang-hsü **Obverse:** Large character at 3 o'clock, inscription: Kuang-hsü Yüan-pao **Edge:** Plain **Note:** Struck at Chingkiang.

Date	VG	F	VF	XF	Unc
ND(1905)	0.85	2.50	4.00	7.50	25.00

Y# 77.2 10 CASH **Composition:** Copper **Ruler:** Kuang-hsü **Obverse:** Ring around center dot in rosette, inscription: Kuang-hsü Yüan-pao **Edge:** Reeded **Note:** Struck at Chingkiang.

Date	VG	F	VF	XF	Unc
ND(1905)	1.00	3.00	5.00	10.00	30.00

Y# 77.3 10 CASH **Composition:** Copper **Ruler:** Kuang-hsü **Obverse:** Ring around center dot in rosette, inscription: Kuang-hsü Yüan-pao **Edge:** Plain **Note:** Struck at Chingkiang.

Date	VG	F	VF	XF	Unc
ND(1905)	3.00	9.00	12.00	15.00	35.00

Y# 77.4 10 CASH **Composition:** Copper **Ruler:** Kuang-hsü **Obverse:** Smaller character at 3 o'clock, inscription: Kuang-hsü Yüan-pao **Edge:** Reeded **Note:** Struck at Chingkiang.

Date	VG	F	VF	XF	Unc
ND(1905)	1.25	3.50	6.00	12.00	32.00

Y# 77.5 10 CASH **Composition:** Copper **Ruler:** Kuang-hsü **Obverse:** Smaller character at 3 o'clock, inscription: Kuang-hsü Yüan-pao **Edge:** Plain **Note:** Struck at Chingkiang.

Date	VG	F	VF	XF	Unc
ND(1905)	1.25	3.50	6.00	12.00	32.00

Y# 77.6 10 CASH **Composition:** Copper **Ruler:** Kuang-hsü **Obverse:** Without rosette, inscription: Kuang-hsü Yüan-pao **Edge:** Reeded **Note:** Struck at Chingkiang.

Date	VG	F	VF	XF	Unc
ND(1905)	1.00	3.00	5.00	10.00	30.00

Y# 77.7 10 CASH **Composition:** Copper **Ruler:** Kuang-hsü **Obverse:** Without rosette, inscription: Kuang-hsü Yüan-pao **Edge:** Plain **Note:** Struck at Chingkiang.

Date	VG	F	VF	XF	Unc
ND(1905)	2.75	8.00	10.00	15.00	35.00

Y# 78 10 CASH **Composition:** Copper **Ruler:** Kuang-hsü **Obverse:** Large character at 3 o'clock, inscription: Kuang-hsü Yüan-pao **Edge:** Reeded **Note:** Struck at Chingkiang,

Date	VG	F	VF	XF	Unc
ND(1905)	0.50	1.50	3.00	5.00	20.00

Y# 78.1 10 CASH **Composition:** Copper **Ruler:** Kuang-hsü **Obverse:** Large character at 3 o'clock, inscription: Kuang-hsü Yüan-pao **Edge:** Plain **Note:** Struck at Chingkiang.

Date	VG	F	VF	XF	Unc
ND(1905)	1.00	3.00	5.00	10.00	30.00

Y# 78.2 10 CASH **Composition:** Copper **Ruler:** Kuang-hsü **Obverse:** Small character at 3 o'clock, inscription: Kuang-hsü Yüan-pao **Edge:** Reeded **Note:** Struck at Chingkiang.

Date	VG	F	VF	XF	Unc
ND(1905)	0.35	1.00	2.00	5.00	20.00

Y# 78.3 10 CASH **Composition:** Copper **Ruler:** Kuang-hsü **Obverse:** Small character at 3 o'clock, inscription: Kuang-hsü Yüan-pao **Edge:** Plain **Note:** Struck at Chingkiang.

Date	VG	F	VF	XF	Unc
ND(1905)	0.35	1.00	2.00	5.00	20.00

Y# 78.4 10 CASH **Composition:** Copper **Ruler:** Kuang-hsü **Obverse:** Without rosette, inscription: Kuang-hsü Yüan-pao **Edge:** Reeded **Note:** Struck at Chingkiang.

Date	VG	F	VF	XF	Unc
ND(1905)	1.25	3.50	6.00	15.00	35.00

Y# 10d 10 CASH **Composition:** Copper **Ruler:** Kuang-hsü **Obverse:** Small mint mark in center, without center raised discInscription: Tai-ch'ing T-ung-pi **Reverse:** 5 flames on pearl **Rev. Legend:** Kuang-hsü Nien-tsao, TAI-CHING-TI-KUO ... **Note:** Struck at Chingkiang.

Date	VG	F	VF	XF	Unc
CD(1906)	8.50	25.00	50.00	100	—

Y# 10d.1 10 CASH **Composition:** Copper **Ruler:** Kuang-hsü **Obverse:** Small mint mark, inscription: Tai-ch'ing T-ung-pi **Reverse:** 7 flames on pearl **Rev. Legend:** Kuang-hsü Nien-tsao, TAI-CHING-TI-KUO ... **Note:** Struck at Chingkiang.

Date	VG	F	VF	XF	Unc
CD(1906)	0.50	1.50	2.50	5.00	20.00

Y# 10d.2 10 CASH **Composition:** Copper **Ruler:** Kuang-hsü **Obverse:** Inscription: Tai-ch'ing T-ung-pi **Reverse:** 9 flames on pearl **Rev. Legend:** Kuang-hsü Nien-tsao, TAI-CHING-TI-KUO ... **Note:** Struck at Chingkiang.

Date	VG	F	VF	XF	Unc
CD(1906)	0.35	1.00	2.00	5.00	20.00

Y# 10d.3 10 CASH **Composition:** Copper **Ruler:** Kuang-hsü **Obverse:** Large mint mark, inscription: Tai-ch'ing T-ung-pi **Reverse:** 5 flames on pearl **Rev. Legend:** Kuang-hsü Nien-tsao, TAI-CHING-TI-KUO ... **Note:** Struck at Chingkiang.

Date	VG	F	VF	XF	Unc
CD(1906)	0.50	1.50	2.50	5.00	20.00

Y#10d.4 10 CASH Composition: Copper **Ruler:** Kuang-hsü **Obverse:** Inscription: Tai-ch'ing T-ung-pi **Reverse:** 7 flames on pearl **Rev. Legend:** Kuang-hsü Nien-tsao, TAI-CHING-TI-KUO ... **Note:** Struck at Chingkiang.

Date	VG	F	VF	XF	Unc
CD(1906)	0.50	1.50	2.50	5.00	20.00

Y#10d.5 10 CASH Composition: Copper **Ruler:** Kuang-hsü **Obverse:** Inscription: Tai-ch'ing T-ung-pi **Reverse:** 9 flames on pearl **Rev. Legend:** Kuang-hsü Nien-tsao, TAI-CHING-TI-KUO ... **Note:** Struck at Chingkiang.

Date	VG	F	VF	XF	Unc
CD(1906)	0.50	1.50	2.50	5.00	20.00

Y#10d.6 10 CASH Composition: Copper **Ruler:** Kuang-hsü **Obverse:** Mint mark incused on raised disc, inscription: Tai-ch'ing T-ung-pi **Rev. Legend:** Kuang-hsü Nien-tsao, TAI-CHING-TI-KUO ... **Note:** Struck at Chingkiang. Trial piece.

Date	VG	F	VF	XF	Unc
CD(1906)	—	—	—	—	—

Note: 10 Cash coins of Kiangsu (Jiangsu) and Chingkiang are often found plated with a silvery material. This was not done at the mint. Apparently they were plated so they could be passed to the unwary as silver coins.

PATTERNS

Including off metal strikes

KM#	Date	Mintage	Identification	Mkt Val
Pn2	ND(c. 1901)	—	2 Cash. Brass. Y159.	200
Pn3	CD(1906)	—	2 Cash. Brass. Y8n.	200
Pn4	ND(c. 1906)	—	5 Cash. Brass. EIVE for FIVE. Y161.1.	300
Pn5	ND(c. 1906)	—	5 Cash. Copper. EIVE for FIVE. Y161.1a.	300
Pn6	ND(c. 1906)	—	10 Cash. White copper. Y162.5, W826.	—
Pn7	CD(1906)	—	20 Cash. Copper. Character "Huai" in center. Y11d.	—

KIRIN PROVINCE

Jilin

A province of northeast China that was formed in 1945. Before that it was one of the three original provinces of Manchuria. Besides growing corn, wheat and tobacco, there is also coal mining. An arsenal in Kirin (Jilin) opened in 1881 and was chosen as a source for coinage attempts. In 1884 Tael trials were struck and regular coinage began in 1895. Modern equipment was installed in a new mint in Kirin (Jilin) in 1901. The issues of this mint were very prolific and many varieties exist due to the use of hand cut dies for the earlier issues. The mint burned down in 1911.

EMPIRE

PROVINCIAL CAST COINAGE

C# 17-1 CASH Composition: Cast Brass **Ruler:** Kuang-hsü **Obv. Inscription:** Kuang-hsü T'ung-pao

Date	Good	VG	F	VF	XF
ND(1875-1908)	15.00	25.00	35.00	50.00	—

Note: This coin is sometimes erroneously attributed to Chi-chou (Chichow) in Chihli (Hebei) province, which used this mint mark in the Hsien-feng and earlier reigns

MILLED COINAGE

Errors in the English legends are very common in the Kirin coinage. It has been estimated there are over 2500 die varieties of Kirin (Jilin) silver coins and more than 1000 varieties of copper 10 Cash. Listed here are basic types and major varieties only.

Y#175 2 CASH Composition: Bronze **Ruler:** Kuang-hsü **Obverse:** Inscription: Kuang-hsü T'ung-pao **Note:** Struck at Chi (Chilin). Mint mark: Manchu Boo-gi.

Date	VG	F	VF	XF	Unc
ND(ca.1905)	80.00	120	160	250	—

SU# 481 10 CASH Composition: Brass **Ruler:** Kuang-hsü **Obverse:** Inscription: Kuang-hsü T'ung-pao **Note:** Four minor varieties exist.

Date	VG	F	VF	XF	Unc
ND(ca.1900)	10.00	30.00	50.00	75.00	100

Note: This coin is sometimes erroneously attributed to Chi-chou (Chichow) in Chihli (Hebei) province, which used this mint mark in the Hsien-feng and earlier reigns

Y# 176 10 CASH(ES) Composition: Copper **Ruler:** Kuang-hsü **Obverse:** Inscription: Kuang-hsü Yüan-pao **Reverse:** Dragon

Date	VG	F	VF	XF	Unc
ND(ca.1901)	35.00	60.00	90.00	125	—

Y# 176.1 10 CASH(ES) Composition: Copper **Ruler:** Kuang-hsü **Obverse:** Inscription: Kuang-hsü Yüan-pao **Reverse:** Thinner dragon

Date	VG	F	VF	XF	Unc
ND(ca.1901)	35.00	60.00	90.00	125	—

Y# 174 10 CASH(ES) Composition: Bronze **Ruler:** Kuang-hsü **Obverse:** Inscription: Kuang-hsü Yüan-pao **Note:** Struck at Chi (Chilin). Mint mark: Manchu Chi.

Date	VG	F	VF	XF	Unc
ND(1901) Rare	—	—	—	—	—

Y# 177 10 CASH(ES) Composition: Copper **Ruler:** Kuang-hsü **Obverse:** Inscription: Kuang-hsü Yüan-pao; small rosettes **Reverse:** Dragon; large rosettes

Date	VG	F	VF	XF	Unc
ND(ca.1903)	5.00	10.00	15.00	25.00	—

Y# 177.1 10 CASH(ES) Composition: Copper **Ruler:** Kuang-hsü **Obverse:** Inscription: Kuang-hsü Yüan-pao **Reverse:** Dragon; small stars

Date	VG	F	VF	XF	Unc
ND(ca.1903)	5.00	10.00	15.00	25.00	—

Y# 177.2 10 CASH(ES) Composition: Copper **Ruler:** Kuang-hsü **Obverse:** Inscription: Kuang-hsü Yüan-pao; small stars **Reverse:** Dragon; large rosettes

Date	VG	F	VF	XF	Unc
ND(ca.1903)	5.00	10.00	17.50	30.00	—

Y# 177.3 10 CASH(ES) Composition: Copper **Ruler:** Kuang-hsü **Obverse:** Inscription: Kuang-hsü Yüan-pao; small stars **Reverse:** Dragon; small stars

Date	VG	F	VF	XF	Unc
ND(ca.1903)	5.00	10.00	15.00	25.00	—

Y# 177.3a 10 CASH(ES) Composition: Brass **Ruler:** Kuang-hsü **Obverse:** Inscription: Kuang-hsü Yüan-pao **Reverse:** Dragon

Date	VG	F	VF	XF	Unc
ND(ca.1903)	5.00	10.00	17.50	30.00	—

Y# 177.4 10 CASH(ES) Composition: Brass **Ruler:** Kuang-hsü **Obverse:** Inscription: Kuang-hsü Yüan-pao; large stars **Reverse:** Dragon; large stars

Date	VG	F	VF	XF	Unc
ND(ca.1903)	4.00	7.00	12.00	17.50	—

Y# 177.5 10 CASH(ES) Composition: Brass **Ruler:** Kuang-hsü **Obverse:** Inscription: Kuang-hsü Yüan-pao; large stars **Reverse:** Dragon; large rosettes

Date	VG	F	VF	XF	Unc
ND(ca.1903)	4.00	7.00	12.00	17.50	—

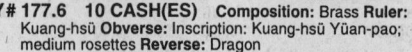

Y# 177.6 10 CASH(ES) Composition: Brass **Ruler:** Kuang-hsü **Obverse:** Inscription: Kuang-hsü Yüan-pao; medium rosettes **Reverse:** Dragon

Date	VG	F	VF	XF	Unc
ND(ca.1903)	4.00	7.00	12.00	17.50	—

Y# 177.7 10 CASH(ES) Composition: Brass **Ruler:** Kuang-hsü **Obverse:** Inscription: Kuang-hsü Yüan-pao **Reverse:** Dragon; CASHES spelled Cashis

Date	VG	F	VF	XF	Unc
ND(ca.1903)	60.00	100	160	250	—

Note: It is difficult to differentiate the stars and rosettes on worn coins; the rosettes have a raised dot in the center while the stars have a hole in the center; it has been estimated that 1000 varieties of Y#177 exist

Y# 20p 10 CASH(ES) **Composition:** Copper **Ruler:** Hsüan-t'ung **Obverse:** Inscription: Tai-ch'ing T'ung-pi; very small mint mark **Rev. Legend:** Hsüan-t'ung Nien-tsao, TAI-CHING-TI-KUO...

Date	VG	F	VF	XF	Unc
CD(1909)	8.00	15.00	25.00	40.00	—

Y# 20p.1 10 CASH(ES) **Composition:** Copper **Ruler:** Hsüan-t'ung **Obverse:** Inscription: Tai-ch'ing T'ung-pi; larger mint mark **Reverse:** Head of dragon, redesigned with more whiskers **Rev. Legend:** Hsüan-t'ung Nien-tsao, TAI-CHING-TI-KUO...

Date	VG	F	VF	XF	Unc
CD(1909)	10.00	17.50	30.00	45.00	—

Y# 20p.2 10 CASH(ES) **Composition:** Copper **Ruler:** Hsüan-t'ung **Obverse:** Inscription: Tai-ch'ing T'ung-pi; larger mint mark **Reverse:** Dragon similar to Y#20p **Rev. Legend:** Hsüan-t'ung Nien-tsao, TAI-CHING-TI-KUO...

Date	VG	F	VF	XF	Unc
CD(1909)	10.00	17.50	30.00	45.00	—

Note: For Y#20x refer to General Issues-Empire

Y# 20p.3 10 CASH(ES) **Composition:** Copper **Ruler:** Hsüan-t'ung **Obverse:** Inscription: Tai-ch'ing T'ung-pi; Y#20p **Reverse:** General Issue - Empire Y#20.1 **Rev. Legend:** Hsüan-t'ung Nien-tsao, TAI-CHING-TI-KUO... **Note:** Mule.

Date	VG	F	VF	XF	Unc
CD(1909) 2 known	—	—	—	3,500	—

Note: Though dated 1909, minted at Mukden ca.1922

Y# 178 20 CASH(ES) **Composition:** Copper **Ruler:** Kuang-hsü **Obverse:** Inscription: Kuang-hsü Yüan-pao **Reverse:** Dragon

Date	VG	F	VF	XF	Unc
ND(1903)	35.00	65.00	100	175	—

Y# A176 20 CASH(ES) **Composition:** Copper **Ruler:** Kuang-hsü **Obverse:** Inscription: Kuang-hsü Yüan-pao; Manchu in center, eight characters below **Reverse:** Dragon

Date	VG	F	VF	XF	Unc
ND(1903)	80.00	200	400	700	—

Y# A176.1 20 CASH(ES) **Composition:** Copper **Ruler:** Kuang-hsü **Obverse:** Inscription: Kuang-hsü Yüan-pao; rosette in center, three characters below **Reverse:** Dragon

Date	VG	F	VF	XF	Unc
ND(1903)	80.00	225	425	725	—

Y# 21p 20 CASH(ES) **Composition:** Copper **Ruler:** Kuang-hsü **Obverse:** Inscription: Tai-ch'ing T'ung-pi **Reverse:** Dragon **Rev. Legend:** Hsüan-t'ung Nien-tsao, TAI-CHING-TI-KUO...

Date	VG	F	VF	XF	Unc
CD(1909)	120	250	450	750	—

Y# E176 30 CASHES **Composition:** Brass **Ruler:** Kuang-hsü **Obverse:** Inscription: Kuang-hsü T'ung-pao **Reverse:** Side view dragon

Date	VG	F	VF	XF	Unc
CD(1901) Rare	—	—	—	—	—

Y# B176 50 CASHES **Composition:** Brass **Ruler:** Kuang-hsü **Obverse:** Inscription: Kuang-hsü T'ung-pao **Reverse:** Side view dragon

Date	Good	VG	F	VF	XF
CD(1901) 3 known	—	—	—	—	—

Note: D.K.E. Ching Sale 6-91 VG-F realized $3,410; a similar 20 Cashes and silver 50 Cent have been reported and are believed to be fantasies by some authorities

Y# F176 100 CASHES **Composition:** Brass **Ruler:** Kuang-hsü **Obverse:** Inscription: Kuang-hsü T'ung-pao **Reverse:** Side view dragon

Date	VG	F	VF	XF	Unc
CD(1901)	—	—	—	—	—

Y# C176 10 COPPERS **Composition:** Brass **Ruler:** Kuang-hsü **Obverse:** Inscription: Kuang-hsü Yüan-pao **Reverse:** Dragon **Note:** Similar to 50 Cashes, Y#B176

Date	VG	F	VF	XF	Unc
CD(1901)	—	—	—	—	—

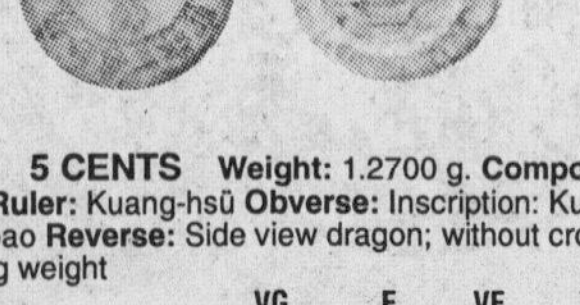

Y# 179.1 5 CENTS **Weight:** 1.2700 g. **Composition:** Silver **Ruler:** Kuang-hsü **Obverse:** Inscription: Kuang-hsü Yüan-pao **Reverse:** Side view dragon; without crosses flanking weight

Date	VG	F	VF	XF	Unc
ND(ca.1898)	1.75	5.00	10.00	20.00	50.00
CD(1899)	2.25	6.50	12.50	25.00	60.00
Note: Cross-reference number K#394					
CD(1900)	3.50	10.00	20.00	30.00	75.00
Note: Cross-reference number K#416					
CD(1906)	2.25	6.50	12.50	25.00	60.00
Note: Cross-reference number K#549					
CD(1907)	2.75	8.00	15.00	25.00	60.00
CD(1908) Rare	—	—	—	—	—

Y# 179a 5 CENTS **Weight:** 1.2700 g. **Composition:** Silver **Ruler:** Kuang-hsü **Obverse:** Inscription: Kuang-hsü Yüan-pao; Yin-yang in center **Reverse:** Side view dragon

Date	VG	F	VF	XF	Unc
CD(1900)	2.50	7.50	15.00	30.00	60.00
CD(1901)	1.85	5.50	11.50	25.00	50.00
Note: Cross-reference number K#444					
CD(1902)	2.25	6.50	12.50	25.00	60.00
Note: Cross-reference number K#465					
CD(1903)	4.50	12.50	25.00	50.00	100
Note: Cross-reference number K#481					
CD(1904)	3.50	10.00	15.00	30.00	70.00
Note: Cross-reference number K#510					
CD(1905)	2.50	7.50	15.00	30.00	65.00
Note: Cross-reference number K#533					

Y# 180.1 10 CENTS **Weight:** 2.5500 g. **Composition:** Silver **Ruler:** Kuang-hsü **Obverse:** Inscription: Kuang-hsü Yüan-pao; large flower vase center **Reverse:** Side view dragon; without crosses flanking weight

Date	VG	F	VF	XF	Unc
ND(ca.1898)	1.85	5.50	11.50	22.50	50.00
CD(1899)	2.25	6.50	12.50	25.00	60.00
Note: Cross-reference number K#393					
CD(1900)	2.25	6.50	12.50	25.00	60.00
Note: Cross-reference number K#416					
CD(1906)	2.25	6.50	12.50	25.00	60.00
Note: Cross-reference number K#546					
CD(1907)	15.00	45.00	90.00	150	250

Y# 180a 10 CENTS **Weight:** 2.5500 g. **Composition:** Silver **Ruler:** Kuang-hsü **Obverse:** Inscription: Kuang-hsü Yüan-pao; Yin-yang in center **Reverse:** Side view dragon

Date	VG	F	VF	XF	Unc
CD(1900)	2.50	7.50	15.00	30.00	75.00
CD(1901)	1.85	5.50	11.50	22.50	50.00
Note: Cross-reference number K#440					
CD(1902)	2.50	7.50	15.00	30.00	65.00
Note: Cross-reference number K#464					
CD(1903)	3.00	9.00	18.50	37.50	85.00
Note: Cross-reference number K#481					
CD(1904)	12.00	35.00	60.00	100	250
CD(1905)	2.25	6.50	11.50	22.50	50.00

Y# 180c 10 CENTS **Weight:** 2.5500 g. **Composition:** Silver **Ruler:** Kuang-hsü **Obverse:** Inscription: Kuang-hsü Yüan-pao; numeral 1 in center **Reverse:** Side view dragon

Date	VG	F	VF	XF	Unc
CD(1908)	22.50	70.00	125	175	350

Y# 181a 20 CENTS **Weight:** 5.1000 g. **Composition:** Silver **Ruler:** Kuang-hsü **Obverse:** Inscription: Kuang-hsü Yüan-pao; Yin-yang in center **Reverse:** Side view dragon

Date	Mintage	VG	F	VF	XF	Unc
CD(1901)	22,508,000	2.25	6.50	12.50	25.00	50.00
CD(1902)	Inc. above	2.25	6.50	12.50	25.00	50.00
CD(1903)	Inc. above	2.25	6.50	12.50	25.00	50.00
CD(1904)	Inc. above	2.25	6.50	12.50	25.00	50.00
CD(1905)	Inc. above	2.25	6.50	12.50	25.00	50.00

Y# 181 20 CENTS **Weight:** 5.1000 g. **Composition:** Silver **Ruler:** Kuang-hsü **Obverse:** Inscription: Kuang-hsü Yüan-pao; flower vase center **Reverse:** Side view dragon

Date	VG	F	VF	XF	Unc
CD(1906)	2.25	6.50	12.50	25.00	50.00
CD(1907)	2.25	6.50	12.50	25.00	50.00
CD(1908)	30.00	90.00	175	300	500

Y# 181b 20 CENTS **Weight:** 5.1000 g. **Composition:** Silver **Ruler:** Kuang-hsü **Obverse:** Inscription: Kuang-hsü Yüan-pao; Manchu words in center **Reverse:** Side view dragon

Date	VG	F	VF	XF	Unc
CD(1908)	17.50	50.00	100	150	275

Y# 181c 20 CENTS **Weight:** 5.1000 g. **Composition:** Silver **Ruler:** Kuang-hsü **Obverse:** Inscription: Kuang-hsü Yüan-pao; numeral 2 center **Reverse:** Side view dragon

Date	VG	F	VF	XF	Unc
CD(1908)	8.50	25.00	50.00	85.00	150

Y# 22 20 CENTS **Weight:** 5.1000 g. **Composition:** Silver **Ruler:** Hsüan-t'ung **Obverse:** Inscription: Hsüan-t'ung Yüan-pao; mint mark in relief on raised disc at center **Reverse:** Side view dragon

Date	VG	F	VF	XF	Unc
ND(1909)	12.00	35.00	70.00	125	225

Y# 22.2 20 CENTS **Weight:** 5.1000 g. **Composition:** Silver **Ruler:** Hsüan-t'ung **Obverse:** Inscription: Hsüan-t'ung Yüan-pao; mint mark in circle at center **Reverse:** Side view dragon

Date	VG	F	VF	XF	Unc
ND(1909)	12.00	35.00	70.00	125	225

Y# 182a.1 50 CENTS **Weight:** 13.1000 g. **Composition:** Silver **Ruler:** Kuang-hsü **Obverse:** Inscription: Kuang-hsü Yüan-pao; redesigned yin-yang in center **Reverse:** Side view dragon

Date	VG	F	VF	XF	Unc
CD(1901)	6.50	20.00	35.00	60.00	150
CD(1902)	6.50	20.00	35.00	60.00	150
CD(1903)	8.50	25.00	40.00	65.00	165
CD(1904)	6.50	20.00	35.00	60.00	150
CD(1905)	5.00	15.00	30.00	50.00	140

Y# 182.3 50 CENTS **Weight:** 13.1000 g. **Composition:** Silver **Ruler:** Kuang-hsü **Obverse:** Inscription: Kuang-hsü Yüan-pao **Reverse:** Side view dragon

Date	VG	F	VF	XF	Unc
CD(1906)	6.50	20.00	35.00	60.00	150
CD(1907)	6.50	20.00	35.00	60.00	150
CD(1908)	17.50	50.00	80.00	125	300

Y# 182b 50 CENTS **Weight:** 13.1000 g. **Composition:** Silver **Ruler:** Kuang-hsü **Obverse:** Inscription: Kuang-hsü Yüan-pao; Manchu words in center **Reverse:** Side view dragon

Date	VG	F	VF	XF	Unc
CD(1908)	25.00	75.00	150	275	450

Y# 183a.1 DOLLAR **Weight:** 26.1000 g. **Composition:** Silver **Ruler:** Kuang-hsü **Obverse:** Inscription: Kuang-hsü Yüan-pao; redesigned Yin-yang in center **Reverse:** Coarse-scaled, beady-eyed dragon

Date	VG	F	VF	XF	Unc
CD(1901)	25.00	75.00	125	200	550
CD(1902)	25.00	75.00	125	200	500

Y# 183a.2 DOLLAR **Weight:** 26.1000 g. **Composition:** Silver **Ruler:** Kuang-hsü **Obverse:** Inscription: Kuang-hsü Yüan-pao **Reverse:** Fine dot-scaled, beady-eyed dragon

Date	VG	F	VF	XF	Unc
CD(1902)	20.00	60.00	125	200	500
CD(1903)	25.00	75.00	125	200	400
CD(1904)	25.00	75.00	125	175	300
CD(1905)	25.00	75.00	125	175	300

Y# 183a.3 DOLLAR **Weight:** 26.1000 g. **Composition:** Silver **Ruler:** Kuang-hsü **Obverse:** Inscription: Kuang-hsü Yüan-pao **Reverse:** Fine oval-scaled, round-eyed dragon

Date	VG	F	VF	XF	Unc
CD(1905)	17.50	50.00	100	175	400

Y# 183.1 DOLLAR **Weight:** 26.1000 g. **Composition:** Silver **Ruler:** Kuang-hsü **Obverse:** Inscription: Kuang-hsü Yüan-pao; large rosettes **Reverse:** Side view dragon; without rosettes flanking weight

Date	VG	F	VF	XF	Unc
ND(ca.1905)	250	750	1,350	2,500	4,500

Y# 183.2 DOLLAR **Weight:** 26.1000 g. **Composition:** Silver **Ruler:** Kuang-hsü **Obverse:** Inscription: Kuang-hsü Yüan-pao **Reverse:** Side view dragon **Rev. Legend:** 3.2 CAINDARINS 2 (error)

Date	VG	F	VF	XF	Unc
CD(1906)	60.00	175	250	350	750

Y# 183.4 DOLLAR **Weight:** 26.1000 g. **Composition:** Silver **Ruler:** Kuang-hsü **Obverse:** Inscription: Kuang-hsü Yüan-pao; small leaves out of left basket **Reverse:** Side view dragon; similar to Y#183.2

Date	VG	F	VF	XF	Unc
ND(ca.1906)	20.00	60.00	100	150	400

Y# 183 DOLLAR **Weight:** 26.1000 g. **Composition:** Silver **Ruler:** Kuang-hsü **Obverse:** Inscription: Kuang-hsü Yüan-pao; flower vase center **Reverse:** Side view dragon; small rosettes before and after weight: 7 CANDARINS 2 or 7 CAINDARINS 2

Date	VG	F	VF	XF	Unc
CD(1906)	20.00	60.00	100	250	500
CD(1907)	45.00	125	175	300	650
CD(1908)	200	600	1,000	2,500	5,000

Y# 183.3 DOLLAR **Weight:** 26.1000 g. **Composition:** Silver **Ruler:** Kuang-hsü **Obverse:** Inscription: Kuang-hsü Yüan-pao; small rosettes **Reverse:** Side view dragon; small rosettes before and after weight 7 CANDARINS 2

Date	F	VF	XF	Unc	BU
ND(ca.1906)	100	135	175	500	—

Y# 183b DOLLAR **Weight:** 26.1000 g. **Composition:** Silver **Ruler:** Kuang-hsü **Obverse:** Inscription: Kuang-hsü Yüan-pao: Manchu words in center **Reverse:** Side view dragon

Date	VG	F	VF	XF	Unc
CD(1908)	175	500	1,000	2,000	3,500

Y# 183c DOLLAR **Weight:** 26.1000 g. **Composition:** Silver **Ruler:** Kuang-hsü **Obverse:** Inscription: Kuang-hsü Yüan-pao: numeral 11 in center **Reverse:** Side view dragon

Date	VG	F	VF	XF	Unc
CD(1908)	185	550	1,250	2,500	4,000

Note: The numeral 11 in center reflects the discount in subsidiary coinage; it took 11 dimes to equal the dollar

PATTERNS

Including off metal strikes

KM#	Date	Mintage	Identification	Mkt Val
Pn9	(1901)	—	20 Dollars. Gold.	21,500
Pn10	CD(1902)	—	50 Cents. Brass. Y#182a.1	—
Pn11	CD(1908)	—	20 Cents. Zinc. Y#181c	—
Pn12	ND(1909)	—	20 Cents. Silver. K#583, formerly Y#22.1	—

KWANGSI-KWANGSEA

Guangxi

A hilly region in southeast China with many forests. Large amounts of rice are grown adjacent to the many rivers. A mint opened in Kweilin in 1667, closed in 1670, reopened in 1679, closed again in 1681. It reopened in the mid-1700's and was a rather prolific issuer of Cash coins. In 1905 the government allowed modern mints to be established in Kwangsi (Guangxi) at Nanning (1905) and Kweilin (1905). The Nanning Mint began operation in 1919 and closed in 1923. In 1920 a new mint was opened at Wuchow and operated sporadically until 1929. In 1938 part of the Shanghai Central Mint was moved to Kweilin where it operated until at least 1945 and perhaps as late as 1949.

EMPIRE

PROVINCIAL CAST COINAGE

C# 18-9 CASH **Composition:** Cast Brass **Ruler:** Kuang-hsü **Obverse:** Inscription: Kuang-hsü T'ung-pao **Reverse:** Inscription: Manchu Boo-gui **Note:** Struck at Kue (Kuelin).

Date	Good	VG	F	VF	XF
ND(1875-1908)	5.50	8.50	13.50	25.00	—

REPUBLIC

MILLED COINAGE

Y# 413 CENT **Composition:** Brass **Obv. Legend:** KWANG-SEA

Date	VG	F	VF	XF	Unc
ND(1919)	50.00	150	250	400	—

Y# 413a CENT **Composition:** Brass **Obv. Legend:** KWANG-SI

Date	VG	F	VF	XF	Unc
8(1919)	15.00	40.00	75.00	150	—

Y# 347 CENT **Composition:** Brass **Reverse:** Large "Kuel" mint mark below Pu

Date	VG	F	VF	XF	Unc
28(1939) Rare	—	—	—	—	—

Y# 347.1 CENT **Composition:** Brass **Reverse:** Small "Kuel" mint mark below Pu

Date	VG	F	VF	XF	Unc
28(1939) Rare	—	—	—	—	—

Y# A415 5 CENTS **Composition:** Copper-Nickel **Reverse:** Large "5" in sprays

Date	VG	F	VF	XF	Unc
12(1923)	50.00	150	250	400	600

Y# 414 10 CENTS **Weight:** 2.7000 g. **Composition:** Silver

Date	VG	F	VF	XF	Unc
9(1920)	20.00	60.00	100	150	250

Y# 415 20 CENTS **Weight:** 5.3000 g. **Composition:** Silver **Rev. Legend:** KWANG-SEA

Date	VG	F	VF	XF	Unc
8(1919)	17.50	50.00	75.00	100	175
9(1920)	23.50	70.00	100	150	250

Y# 415a 20 CENTS **Weight:** 5.3000 g. **Composition:** Silver **Rev. Legend:** KWANG-SI

Date	VG	F	VF	XF	Unc
8(1919)	3.50	10.00	25.00	40.00	125
9(1920)	3.50	10.00	20.00	45.00	100
11(1922)	3.50	10.00	15.00	40.00	100
12(1923)	1.25	4.00	9.00	20.00	40.00
13(1924)	1.25	4.00	7.50	12.50	25.00
14(1925)	1.25	4.00	7.50	12.50	25.00

Y# 415a.1 20 CENTS **Weight:** 5.3000 g. **Composition:** Silver **Obverse:** Character "Kuei" in center instead of dot

Date	VG	F	VF	XF	Unc
13(1924)	27.50	80.00	100	150	250

Y# 415b 20 CENTS **Weight:** 5.3000 g. **Composition:** Silver **Obverse:** Tiny character "Hsi" on dot center **Reverse:** Wreath added around "20"

Date	VG	F	VF	XF	Unc
15(1926)	1.00	3.50	6.50	10.00	20.00
16(1927)	1.00	3.50	6.50	10.00	20.00

Y# 416 20 CENTS **Weight:** 5.3000 g. **Composition:** Silver **Reverse:** Elephant nose rock at Kueilin

Date	VG	F	VF	XF	Unc
38(1949)	30.00	90.00	150	200	350

PIEFORTS

KM#	Date	Mintage	Identification	Mkt Val
P1	19(1921)	—	10 Cents. Bronze. Y414c. KM#Pn5.	250
P2	10(1921)	—	10 Cents. Brass. 3.2900 g. Y414b. KM#Pn4.	150

PATTERNS

Including off metal strikes

KM#	Date	Mintage	Identification	Mkt Val
Pn1	ND(1905)	—	10 Cash. Copper.	—
Pn2	CD(1906)	—	10 Cash. Copper.	—
Pn3	10(1921)	—	10 Cents. Copper. 2.11-2.22 grams. Y414a, K746-IIx.	110
Pn4	10(1921)	—	10 Cents. Brass. Y414b.	—
Pn5	10(1921)	—	10 Cents. Bronze. Y414c.	140
Pn6	10(1921)	—	10 Cents. Silver. Y414f.	—
Pn7	10(1921)	—	20 Cents. Copper. 4.68-4.97 grams. Y415c, K746-Ix.	100
Pn8	10(1921)	—	20 Cents. Bronze. Y415d.	—
Pn9	10(1921)	—	20 Cents. Brass. Y415e.	—
Pn10	10(1921)	—	20 Cents. Silver. 4.8700 g. Y415f.	750

KWANGTUNG PROVINCE

Guangdong

A province located on the southeast coast of China. Kwangtung (Guangdong) lies mostly in the tropics and has both mountains and plains. Its coastline is nearly 800 miles long and provides many good harbors. Because of the location of Guangzhou (Canton) in the province, Kwangtung (Guangdong) was the first to be visited by seaborne foreign traders. Hong Kong was ceded to Great Britain after the First Opium War in 1841. Kowloon was later ceded to Britain in 1860 and the New Territories (100 year lease) in 1898 and Macao to Portugal in 1887, Kwangchowwan was leased to France in 1898 (a property was restored in 1946). A modern mint opened in Guangzhou (Canton) in 1889 with Edward Wyon as superintendent. The mint was a large issuer of coins until it closed in 1931. The Nationalists reopened the mint briefly in 1949, striking a few silver dollars, before abandoning the mainland for their retreat to Taiwan.

The large island of Hainan was split off from Kwangtung (Guangdong) Province in 1988 and established as a separate province.

Hong Kong was returned to China by Britain on July 1, 1997 and established as a special administrative region, retaining its own coinage.

EMPIRE

PROVINCIAL CAST COINAGE

C# 19-7 CASH **Composition:** Cast Brass **Ruler:** Kuang-hsü **Obverse:** Inscription: Kuang-hsü T'ung-pao **Reverse:** Inscription: Manchu Boo-guwang **Note:** Struck at Kwang (Canton).

Date	Good	VG	F	VF	XF
ND(1875-1908)	12.00	22.00	32.00	45.00	—

MILLED COINAGE

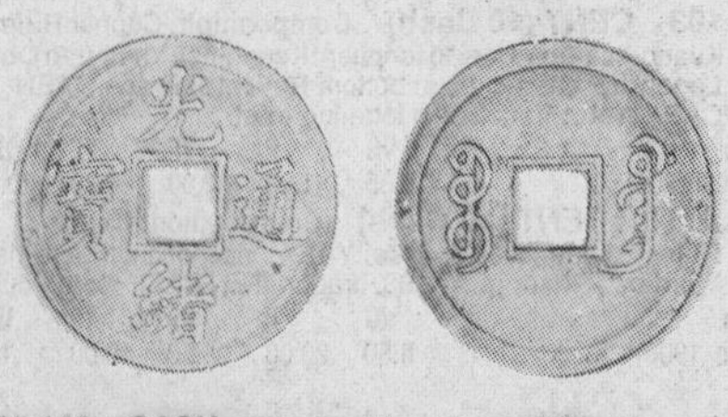

Y# 190 CASH **Composition:** Brass **Ruler:** Kuang-hsü **Obverse:** "Kuang" in a different style, inscription: Kuang-hsü T'ung-pao **Reverse:** Inscription: Manchu Boo-guwang **Note:** Struck at Kwang (Canton)

Date	Mintage	VG	F	VF	XF	Unc
ND(1890-1908)	1,059,253,000	—	0.10	0.25	1.00	2.00

Y# 191 CASH **Composition:** Brass **Ruler:** Kuang-hsü **Obverse:** Inscription: Kuang-hsü T'ung-pao **Reverse:** Inscription: Manchu Boo-guwang **Note:** Struck at Kwang (Canton).

Date	VG	F	VF	XF	Unc
ND(1906-08)	—	0.10	0.25	1.00	3.00

Y# 204 CASH **Composition:** Brass **Obverse:** Inscription: Hsüan-t'ung T'uang pao **Reverse:** Inscription: Manchu Boo-guwang **Note:** Struck at Kwang (Canton).

Date	VG	F	VF	XF	Unc
ND(1909-11)	0.20	0.50	1.00	2.00	5.00

Y# 20r 10 CASH **Composition:** Copper **Ruler:** Hsuan-T'ung **Obverse:** Inscription: Tai-ch'ing T'ung-pi **Reverse:** Dragon **Rev. Legend:** Hsüan-t'ung Nien-tsao, TAI-CHING-TI KUO ...

Date	VG	F	VF	XF	Unc
CD(1909)	0.50	1.50	3.00	5.00	25.00

Y# 192 CENT (10 Cash) **Composition:** Copper **Ruler:** Kuang-hsü **Obverse:** Inscription: Kuang-hsü Yuan-pao **Obv. Legend:** 6 characters at bottom **Reverse:** Dragon, ONE CENT

Date	VG	F	VF	XF	Unc
ND(1900-06)	0.25	0.75	1.50	3.00	20.00

Y# A192 CENT (10 Cash) **Composition:** Copper **Ruler:** Kuang-hsü **Obverse:** Y#192, inscription: Kuang-hsü Yuan-pao **Reverse:** Chihli 10 Cash, Y#67, dragon **Note:** Mule.

Date	VG	F	VF	XF	Unc
ND	8.50	25.00	35.00	50.00	125

Y# 193 CENT (10 Cash) **Composition:** Copper **Ruler:** Kuang-hsü **Obverse:** Inscription: Kuang-hsü Yuan-pao **Obv. Legend:** 7 characters at bottom **Reverse:** Dragon, TEN CASH **Note:** Varieties in lettering exist.

Date	VG	F	VF	XF	Unc
ND(1900-06)	0.35	1.00	2.00	4.00	20.00

Y# A193 CENT (10 Cash) **Composition:** Copper **Ruler:** Kuang-hsü **Obverse:** Y#192, inscription: Kuang-hsü Yuan-pao **Reverse:** Y#193, dragon, TEN CASH **Note:** Mule.

Date	VG	F	VF	XF	Unc
ND(c. 1906)	6.50	20.00	28.50	40.00	100

Y# 10r CENT (10 Cash) **Composition:** Copper **Ruler:** Kuang-hsü **Obverse:** Inscription: Tai-ch'ing T'ung-pi **Reverse:** Dragon **Rev. Legend:** Kuang-hsü Nien-tsao, TAI-CHING-TI KUO ...

Date	Mintage	VG	F	VF	XF	Unc
CD(1906)	79,000,000	0.35	1.00	2.00	4.00	20.00
CD(1907)	46,000,000	0.35	1.00	2.00	4.00	20.00
CD(1908)	62,736,000	0.35	1.00	2.00	4.00	20.00

Y# B193 CENT (10 Cash) **Composition:** Copper **Ruler:** Kuang-hsü **Obverse:** Y#193, inscription: Kuang-hsü Yuan-pao **Reverse:** Y#192, dragon **Note:** Mule.

Date	VG	F	VF	XF	Unc
ND(c. 1906)	6.50	20.00	28.50	40.00	100

KM# B192 (KM1) CENT **Composition:** Copper **Ruler:** Kuang-hsü **Obverse:** Inscription: Kuang-hsü Yüan-pao **Note:** Previous W#896.

Date	VG	F	VF	XF	Unc
ND(ca.1906)	22.50	65.00	100	150	225

Y# 199 5 CENTS **Weight:** 1.3000 g. **Composition:** 0.8200 Silver .0343 oz. ASW **Ruler:** Kuang-hsü **Obverse:** Inscription: Kuang-hsü Yüan-pao **Reverse:** English legend around dragon

Date	VG	F	VF	XF	Unc
ND(1890-1905)	1.00	3.50	6.00	10.00	30.00

Y# 200 10 CENTS **Weight:** 2.7000 g. **Composition:** 0.8200 Silver .0712 oz. ASW **Ruler:** Kuang-hsü **Obverse:** Inscription: Kuang-hsü Yüan-pao **Reverse:** English legends around dragon

Date	VG	F	VF	XF	Unc
ND(1890-1908)	0.65	2.00	4.00	6.00	15.00

Y# 201 20 CENTS **Weight:** 5.5000 g. **Composition:** 0.8000 Silver .1415 oz. ASW **Ruler:** Kuang-hsü **Obverse:** Inscription: Kuang-hsü Yüan-pao **Reverse:** Dragon

Date	VG	F	VF	XF	Unc
ND(1890-1908)	0.50	1.50	2.50	3.50	10.00
ND(1890-1908) Proof, 10 known	—	Value: 400			

Y# 205 20 CENTS **Weight:** 5.5000 g. **Composition:** 0.8000 Silver .1415 oz. ASW **Ruler:** Hsuan-T'ung **Obverse:** Inscription: Hsüan-t'ung Yüan-pao **Reverse:** Dragon **Note:** Two varieties of edge reeding known.

Date	Mintage	VG	F	VF	XF	Unc
ND(1909-11)	94,774,000	1.50	4.50	6.00	9.00	20.00

Y# 202 50 CENTS **Weight:** 13.5000 g. **Composition:** 0.8600 Silver .3733 oz. ASW **Ruler:** Kuang-hsü **Obverse:** Inscription: Kuang-hsü Yuan-pao **Reverse:** English legends around dragon

Date	VG	F	VF	XF	Unc
ND(1890-1905)	6.50	20.00	40.00	75.00	250
ND(1890-1905) Proof	—	Value: 650			

Y# 203 DOLLAR **Weight:** 27.0000 g. **Composition:** 0.9000 Silver .7814 oz. ASW **Ruler:** Kuang-hsü **Obverse:** Inscription: Kuang-hsü Yuan-pao **Reverse:** English legends around dragon

Date	VG	F	VF	XF	Unc
ND(1890-1908)	5.00	15.00	25.00	50.00	350
ND(1890-1908) Proof	—	Value: 1,000			

Y# 206 DOLLAR **Weight:** 27.0000 g. **Composition:** 0.9000 Silver .7814 oz. ASW **Obverse:** Inscription: Hsüan-t'ung Yüan-pao **Reverse:** Dragon

Date	VG	F	VF	XF	Unc
ND(1909-11)	5.00	15.00	25.00	50.00	300

REPUBLIC

MILLED COINAGE

Y# 417 CENT **Composition:** Bronze

Date	Mintage	VG	F	VF	XF	Unc
1(1912)	18,836,000	0.50	1.50	2.25	5.00	22.00
3(1914)	14,750,000	0.50	1.50	2.25	5.00	22.00
4(1915)	6,350,000	1.25	4.00	6.00	15.00	35.00
5(1916)	18,388,000	0.65	2.00	3.00	7.50	30.00
7(1918)	—	2.50	7.50	12.50	20.00	45.00

Y# 417a CENT **Composition:** Brass

Date	VG	F	VF	XF	Unc
1(1912)	—	—	—	—	—
3(1914)	0.65	2.00	5.00	10.00	25.00
4(1915)	1.00	3.00	7.50	15.00	30.00
5(1916)	0.45	1.25	3.00	6.00	20.00

Y# 418 2 CENTS **Composition:** Brass

Date	VG	F	VF	XF	Unc
7(1918)	10.00	30.00	50.00	90.00	175

Y# 418a 2 CENTS **Composition:** Copper

Date	VG	F	VF	XF	Unc
7(1918) Rare	—	—	—	—	—

Y# 420 5 CENTS **Composition:** Copper-Nickel **Reverse:** Large "5" in sprays

Date	Mintage	VG	F	VF	XF	Unc
8(1919)	916,000	0.35	1.00	2.00	3.00	5.00

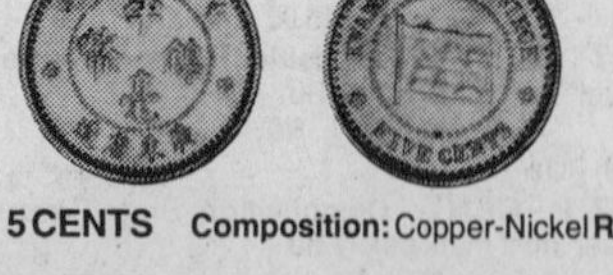

Y# 421 5 CENTS **Composition:** Copper-Nickel **Reverse:** Flag

Date	Mintage	VG	F	VF	XF	Unc
10(1921)	666,000	0.45	1.25	3.00	6.50	12.50

Y# 420a 5 CENTS **Composition:** Copper-Nickel **Reverse:** Large "5" in sprays

Date	Mintage	F	VF	XF	Unc	BU
12(1923)	480,000	1.00	2.00	3.00	5.00	—

Y# 422 10 CENTS **Weight:** 2.7000 g. **Composition:** Silver **Reverse:** Large "10"

Date	Mintage	VG	F	VF	XF	Unc
2(1913)	8,798,000	0.65	2.00	4.00	5.00	10.00
3(1914)	Inc. above	0.85	2.50	4.00	5.00	10.00
11(1922)	—	1.25	4.00	7.00	10.00	25.00

Y# 425 10 CENTS **Weight:** 2.5000 g. **Composition:** Silver **Reverse:** Bust of Sun Yat-sen

Date	Mintage	VG	F	VF	XF	Unc
18(1929)	48,960,000	0.50	1.50	3.00	5.00	8.00

Y# 423 20 CENTS **Weight:** 5.4000 g. **Composition:** Silver **Note:** The fineness of many of these 20-cent pieces, especially those dated Yr. 13 (1924), is as low as .500. In 1924 the Anhwei (Anhui) Mint secretly produced quantities of Kwangtung (Guangdong) 20-cent pieces that were only .400 fine.

Date	Mintage	VG	F	VF	XF	Unc
1(1912)	88,000,000	0.45	1.25	2.50	6.00	12.00
2(1913)	109,974,000	0.45	1.25	2.50	6.00	12.00
3(1914)	41,691,000	0.45	1.25	2.50	6.00	12.00
4(1915)	22,332,000	1.25	4.00	10.00	30.00	65.00
7(1918)	—	0.45	1.25	2.50	5.00	10.00
8(1919)	195,000,000	0.25	0.75	1.50	3.00	5.00
9(1920)	197,000,000	0.25	0.75	1.50	3.00	5.00
10(1921)	402,250,000	0.25	0.75	1.50	3.00	5.00
11(1922)	350,000,000	0.25	0.75	1.50	3.00	5.00
12(1923)	4,400,000	0.75	2.25	3.50	7.00	20.00
13(1924)	55,109,000	0.75	2.25	3.50	8.25	20.00

Y# 424 20 CENTS **Weight:** 5.3000 g. **Composition:** Silver **Reverse:** Bust of Sun Yat-sen

Date	VG	F	VF	XF	Unc
13(1924)	8.50	25.00	45.00	70.00	175

Y# 426 20 CENTS **Weight:** 5.3000 g. **Composition:** Silver **Obverse:** Value in sprays **Reverse:** Bust of Sun Yat-sen

Date	Mintage	VG	F	VF	XF	Unc
17(1928)	28,530,000	8.50	25.00	40.00	60.00	150
18(1929)	779,738,000	0.25	0.75	1.50	2.50	5.00
19(1930) 1 known	—	—	—	—	—	3,500

PATTERNS

Including off metal strikes

KM#	Date	Mintage	Identification	Mkt Val
Pn16	ND(c. 1902)	—	1/2 Cent. Copper. Circled "flying" dragon.	—
Pn17	ND(1904)	—	Tael. Silver. K932.	—

Note: Superior Goodman sale 6-91 proof realized $41,800.

KM#	Date	Mintage	Identification	Mkt Val
PnA18	ND(1904)	—	Tael. Pewter. 6 millimeters thick. K932x.	—
Pn18	ND(1904)	—	Tael. White Metal. K932y.	—
PnA19	ND(1906)	—	20 Cash. Copper. TCTK.	—
Pn19	3(1914)	—	10 Cents. Copper. Y422.	—
PnA20	4(1915)	—	Cent. Red Copper. Y417.	—
PnB20	5(1916)	—	Cent. Red Copper. Y417.	—
PnC20	7(1918)	—	Cent. Red Copper. Y417.	—
Pn20	8(1919)	—	20 Cents. Copper. Y423.	150
Pn21	9(1920)	—	20 Cents. Copper. Y423.	150
Pn22	10(1921)	—	20 Cents. Copper. Y423.	150
Pn-A23	11(1922)	—	20 Cents. Copper. Y423.	150
Pn23	13(1924)	—	20 Cents. Gold. Y424.	—
Pn24	17(1928)	—	20 Cents. Copper. Y426.	—
Pn25	18(1929)	—	20 Cents. Copper. Y426.	—
Pn26	ND(c. 1929)	—	20 Cents. Gold. Y426.	800
Pn27	25(1936)	—	Cent. Bronze. Sun Yat Sen.	3,000
Pn28	25(1936)	—	Cent. Copper.	700

KWEICHOW PROVINCE

Guizhou

A province located in southern China. It is basically a plateau region that is somewhat remote from the general traffic of China. The Kweichow Mint opened in 1730 and produced Cash coins until the end of the reign of Kuang Hsu. The Republic issues for this province are enigmatic as to their origin, as a mint supposedly did not exist in Kweichow (Guizhou) at this time.

EMPIRE

PROVINCIAL CAST COINAGE

The Kweichow (Guizhou) Provincial Cash Coinage obviously copied from contemporary Japanese coins, are still a mystery. Even as late as the 1920s, Kweichow (Guizhou) was a very primitive area. It is highly unlikely that the coins were made there in the 1880s and 1890s. It is possible that they were minted elsewhere, possibly in one of the central coastal provinces.

C# 20-9 CASH **Composition:** Cast Brass **Ruler:** Kuang-hsü **Obverse:** Inscription: Kuang-hsü T'ung-pao **Reverse:** Inscription: Manchu Boo-jiyan **Note:** Struck at Kweiyang.

Date	Good	VG	F	VF	XF
ND(1875-1908)	4.00	7.50	10.00	15.00	—

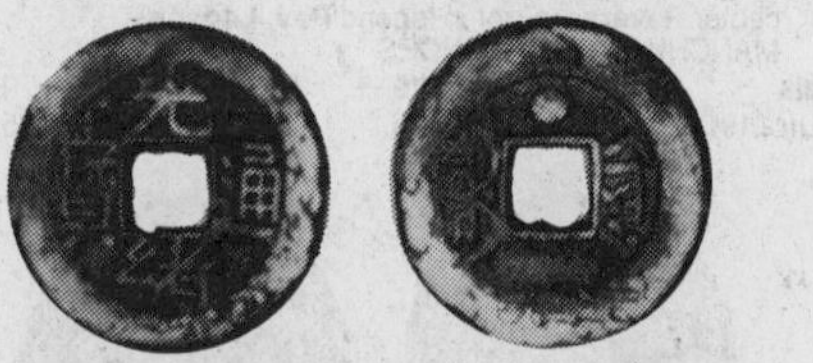

C# 20-9.1 CASH **Composition:** Cast Brass **Ruler:** Kuang-hsü **Obverse:** Inscription: Kuang-hsü T'ung-pao **Reverse:** Inscription: Manchu Boo-jiyan, dot above **Note:** Struck at Kweiyang.

Date	Good	VG	F	VF	XF
ND(1875-1908)	5.00	9.00	12.50	18.50	—

C# 20-9.2 CASH **Composition:** Cast Brass **Ruler:** Kuang-hsü **Obverse:** Inscription: Kuang-hsü T'ung-pao **Reverse:** Inscription: Manchu Boo-jiyan, Chinese "Kung" above **Note:** Struck at Kweiyang.

Date	Good	VG	F	VF	XF
ND(1875-1908)	8.50	11.50	16.50	25.00	—

REPUBLIC

MILLED COINAGE

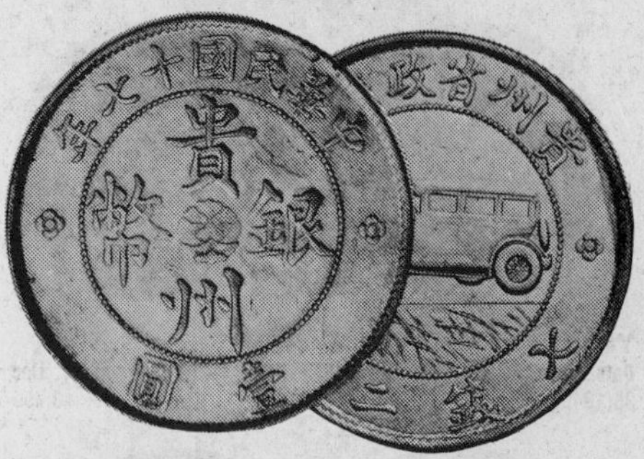

Y# 428 DOLLAR **Weight:** 25.8000 g. **Composition:** Silver **Subject:** First road in Kweichow

Date	Mintage	VG	F	VF	XF	Unc
17(1928)	648,000	125	350	550	1,200	3,000

Note: This coin is known as the "Auto Dollar" as it purports to portray the governor's automobile; minor varieties exist in Chinese legends and various automobile designs

Y# 433 DOLLAR **Weight:** 26.4000 g. **Composition:** Silver

Date	VG	F	VF	XF	Unc
38(1949)	135	400	700	1,250	3,000

Note: This coin is known as the "Bamboo Dollar"

Y# A429 1/2 CENT **Composition:** Copper

Date	VG	F	VF	XF	Unc
38(1949)	450	750	—	—	—

Y# A429a 1/2 CENT **Composition:** Brass

Date	VG	F	VF	XF	Unc
38(1949)	300	450	—	—	—

Y# A429a.2 1/2 CENT **Composition:** Brass **Obverse:** Narrow, thick characters

Date	VG	F	VF	XF	Unc
38(1949)	450	650	—	—	—

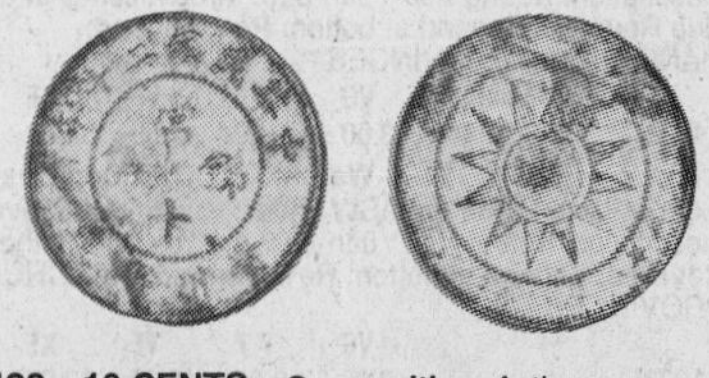

Y# 429 10 CENTS **Composition:** Antimony

Date	VG	F	VF	XF	Unc
20(1931)	250	450	650	900	—

Y# 430 20 CENTS Composition: Silver

Date	VG	F	VF	XF	Unc
38(1949)	45.00	125	200	300	425

Y# 431 20 CENTS Composition: Silver

Date	VG	F	VF	XF	Unc
38(1949)	—	—	—	—	3,750

Y# 432 50 CENTS Composition: Silver

Date	VG	F	VF	XF	Unc
38(1949)	—	—	1,750	3,000	5,300

MANCHURIAN PROVINCES

EMPIRE

MILLED COINAGE

Y# 209 10 CENTS Weight: 2.6000 g. Composition: 0.8900 Silver .0744 oz. ASW Ruler: Kuang-Hsü Obverse: Incscription: Kuang-hsü Yüan-pao Reverse: Legend at bottom Rev. Legend: MANCHURIAN PROVINCES

Date	Mintage	VG	F	VF	XF	Unc
33(1907)	1,079,000	3.50	10.00	25.00	40.00	100

Y# 210 20 CENTS Weight: 5.2000 g. Composition: 0.8900 Silver .1488 oz. ASW Ruler: Kuang-Hsü Obverse: Incscription: Kuang-hsü Yüan-pao; one dot at either side Reverse: Legend at bottom Rev. Legend: MANCHURIAN PROVINCES

Date	VG	F	VF	XF	Unc
33(1907)	6.50	20.00	30.00	60.00	120

Y# 210a.1 20 CENTS Weight: 5.2000 g. Composition: 0.8900 Silver .1388 oz. ASW Ruler: Kuang-Hsü Obverse: Incscription: Kuang-hsü Yüan-pao; three rosettes at either side Reverse: Legend at bottom Rev. Legend: MANCHURIAN PROVINCES

Date	Mintage	VG	F	VF	XF	Unc
33(ca.1908)	249,219,000	3.00	9.00	17.50	35.00	70.00

Y# 210a.2 20 CENTS Weight: 5.2000 g. Composition: 0.8900 Silver .1388 oz. ASW Ruler: Kuang-Hsü Obverse: Incscription: Kuang-hsü Yüan-pao; one rosette at either side Reverse: Legend at bottom Rev. Legend: MANCHURIAN PROVINCES

Date	VG	F	VF	XF	Unc
33(ca.1908)	2.00	6.00	12.00	20.00	60.00

Y# 213.2 20 CENTS Weight: 5.2000 g. Composition: 0.8900 Silver .1388 oz. ASW Ruler: Hsüan-t'ung Obverse: Incscription:Hsüan-t'ung Yüan-pao; one large-petalled rosette at either side Reverse: Legend at bottom; date as 1ST YEAR Rev. Legend: MANCHURIAN PROVINCES

Date	VG	F	VF	XF	Unc
1(1909)	1.25	4.00	8.50	15.00	40.00

Y# 213 20 CENTS Weight: 5.2000 g. Composition: 0.8900 Silver .1388 oz. ASW Ruler: Hsüan-t'ung Obverse: Incscription:Hsüan-t'ung Yüan-pao; two small stars flanking ond large star at either side Reverse: Legend at bottom; date given as FIRST YEAR Rev. Legend: MANCHURIAN PROVINCES

Date	VG	F	VF	XF	Unc
1(ca.1910)	1.25	4.00	7.50	12.50	30.00

Y# 213.1 20 CENTS Weight: 5.2000 g. Composition: 0.8900 Silver .1388 oz. ASW Ruler: Hsüan-t'ung Obverse: Incscription:Hsüan-t'ung Yüan-pao; one small star at either side Reverse: Legend at bottom Rev. Legend: MANCHURIAN PROVINCES

Date	VG	F	VF	XF	Unc
1(ca.1910)	1.25	4.00	8.50	15.00	35.00

Y# 213.3 20 CENTS Weight: 5.2000 g. Composition: 0.8900 Silver .1388 oz. ASW Ruler: Hsüan-t'ung Obverse: Incscription:Hsüan-t'ung Yüan-pao; one large star between two dots Reverse: Legend at bottom Rev. Legend: MANCHURIAN PROVINCES

Date	VG	F	VF	XF	Unc
1(ca.1910)	1.25	4.00	8.50	15.00	35.00

Y# 213a 20 CENTS Weight: 5.2000 g. Composition: 0.8900 Silver .1388 oz. ASW Ruler: Hsüan-t'ung Obverse: Incscription:Hsüan-t'ung Yüan-pao; Manchu "Boo-fu" at center Reverse: Error in legend Rev. Legend: MANCHURIAN PROVINCES

Date	VG	F	VF	XF	Unc
ND(ca.1911)	1.25	4.00	8.50	15.00	35.00

Y# 213a.6 20 CENTS Weight: 5.2000 g. Composition: 0.8900 Silver .1388 oz. ASW Ruler: Hsüan-t'ung Obverse: Incscription:Hsüan-t'ung Yüan-pao; without Manchu "Boo-fu" at center Reverse: Error in legend Rev. Legend: MANCHURIAN PROVINCES

Date	VG	F	VF	XF	Unc
ND(ca.1912)	1.75	5.00	10.00	20.00	40.00

Y# 213a.4 20 CENTS Weight: 5.2000 g. Composition: 0.7000 Silver .1170 oz. ASW Ruler: Hsüan-t'ung Obverse: Incscription:Hsüan-t'ung Yüan-pao; without Manchu "Boo-fu" at center Reverse: Legend at bottom Rev. Legend: MANCHURIAN PROVINCES

Date	VG	F	VF	XF	Unc
ND(ca.1913)	1.75	5.00	10.00	20.00	40.00

Y# 213a.1 20 CENTS Weight: 5.2000 g. Composition: 0.7000 Silver .1170 oz. ASW Ruler: Hsüan-t'ung Obverse: Incscription:Hsüan-t'ung Yüan-pao; five-pettaled rosette in center with dot in center of rosette; dot below side rosettes Reverse: Legend at bottom Rev. Legend: MANCHURIAN PROVINCES

Date	VG	F	VF	XF	Unc
ND(ca.1914-15)	1.25	4.00	8.50	15.00	30.00

Y# 213a.2 20 CENTS Weight: 5.2000 g. Composition: 0.7000 Silver .1170 oz. ASW Ruler: Hsüan-t'ung Obverse: Incscription:Hsüan-t'ung Yüan-pao; with dot below side rosettes Reverse: Legend at bottom Rev. Legend: MANCHURIAN PROVINCES

Date	VG	F	VF	XF	Unc
ND(ca.1914-15)	1.25	4.00	8.50	15.00	30.00

Y# 213a.3 20 CENTS Weight: 5.2000 g. Composition: 0.7000 Silver .1170 oz. ASW Ruler: Hsüan-t'ung Obverse: Incscription:Hsüan-t'ung Yüan-pao; with dot in center of five-pettaled rosette Reverse: Legend at bottom Rev. Legend: MANCHURIAN PROVINCES

Date	VG	F	VF	XF	Unc
ND(ca.1914-15)	1.25	4.00	8.50	15.00	30.00

Y# 211 50 CENTS Weight: 13.1000 g. Composition: 0.8900 Silver .3749 oz. ASW Ruler: Kuang-Hsü Obverse: Incscription: Kuang-Hsü Yüan-pao Reverse: Legend at bottom Rev. Legend: MANCHURIAN PROVINCES

Date	VG	F	VF	XF	Unc
33(1907)	50.00	150	300	500	1,000

Y# 212 DOLLAR Weight: 26.4000 g. Composition: 0.8900 Silver .7555 oz. ASW Ruler: Kuang-Hsü Obverse: Incscription: Kuang-Hsü Yüan-pao Reverse: Legend at bottom Rev. Legend: MANCHURIAN PROVINCES

Date	VG	F	VF	XF	Unc
33(1907)	65.00	200	400	700	1,500

REPUBLIC

MILLED COINAGE

Y# 434 CENT Composition: Copper Obv. Legend: Chung-hua Min-kuo... Reverse: Sunburst in floral sprays

Date	VG	F	VF	XF	Unc
18(1929)	0.65	2.00	3.00	5.00	25.00

Y# 434a CENT **Composition:** Brass **Obv. Legend:** Chung-hua Min-kuo... **Reverse:** Sunburst in floral sprays

Date	VG	F	VF	XF	Unc
18(1929)	—	—	—	—	—

PATTERNS

Including off metal strikes

KM#	Date	Mintage	Identification	Mkt Val
Pn2	18(1929)	—	Fen. Copper. Y#434 with formal Chinese "One Fen"	—
Pn1	18(1929)	—	Dollar. Silver.	—

Note: Superior Goodman sale 6-91 choice AU realized, $22,000

SHANSI PROVINCE

Shanxi

A province located in northeastern China that has some of the richest coal deposits in the world. Parts of the Great Wall cross the province. Extensive agriculture of early China started here. Cited as a "model province" in the new Chinese Republic. Intermittently active mints from 1645. The modern mint was established in 1919. It operated until the mid-1920's and closed because of the public's resistance against the coins that were being produced.

EMPIRE

PROVINCIAL CAST COINAGE

C# 21-8 CASH **Composition:** Cast Brass **Ruler:** Kuang-hsu **Obverse:** Inscription: Kuang-hsu T'ung-pao **Reverse:** Manchu "Boo-Jin" **Note:** Struck at Chin (Taiyuan).

Date	Good	VG	F	VF	XF
ND(1875-1908)	6.50	11.50	17.50	35.00	—

REPUBLIC

MILLED COINAGE

Y# A435 10 CASH ((1 Cent)) **Composition:** Copper **Obverse:** Crossed flags **Reverse:** Value in wheat sprays

Date	VG	F	VF	XF	Unc
ND(ca.1912)	35.00	100	150	220	—

Y# 217 20 CENTS **Weight:** 4.8000 g. **Composition:** Silver **Ruler:** Hsuan-Tung **Obverse:** Inscription: Hsuan-t'ung Yuan-pao **Reverse:** Side view dragon

Date	VG	F	VF	XF	Unc
ND(ca.1911)	100	175	300	450	—

Note: Several varieties exist similar to Y#217, but struck more crudely in base metal and with different Chinese legends at the top of the obverse. English legends are usually blundered. These were struck about 1913 and thought to be warlord issues. Do not confuse these with coins of Fengtien (Liaoning), from which this was copied.

PATTERNS

Including off metal strikes

KM#	Date	Mintage	Identification	Mkt Val
Pn2	14(1925)	—	5 Cents. Nickel. K823.	—

SHANTUNG PROVINCE

Shandong

A province located on the northeastern coast of China. Confucius was born in this province. Parts of the province were leased to Great Britain and to Germany. Farming, fishing and mining are the chief occupations. A mint was opened at Tsinan in 1647 and was an intermittent producer for the empire. A modern mint was opened at Tsinan in 1905, but closed in 1906. Patterns were prepared between 1926-1933 in anticipation of a new coinage, but none were struck for circulation.

EMPIRE

PROVINCIAL CAST COINAGE

C# 22-6 CASH **Composition:** Cast Brass **Ruler:** Kuang-hsü **Reverse:** Type 1 mint mark, inscription: Manchu Boo-ji **Note:** Struck at Chi (Chinan).

Date	Good	VG	F	VF	XF
ND(1875-1908)	10.00	18.50	27.50	40.00	—

Note: Refer to Tungchuan, Yünnan Province, for one-cash C#27 series coins previously listed here.

MILLED COINAGE

Y# 8a 2 CASH **Composition:** Copper **Ruler:** Kuang-hsü **Obverse:** Inscription: Tai-ch'ing T'ung-pi **Reverse:** Dragon

Date	VG	F	VF	XF	Unc
CD1906	12.00	25.00	35.00	70.00	—

Y# 220 10 CASH **Composition:** Copper **Ruler:** Kuang-hsü **Obverse:** Inscription: Kuang-hsü Yüan-pao **Reverse:** Side view dragon

Date	VG	F	VF	XF	Unc
ND(1904-1905)	3.25	8.00	15.00	30.00	55.00

Y# 221 10 CASH **Composition:** Copper **Ruler:** Kuang-hsü **Obverse:** Thin Manchu words in center, flying dragon, inscription: Kuang-hsü Yüan-pao **Reverse:** SHANTUNG

Date	VG	F	VF	XF	Unc
ND(1904-1905)	2.75	7.00	11.00	17.50	40.00

Y# 221.1 10 CASH **Composition:** Copper **Ruler:** Kuang-hsü **Obverse:** Thick Manchu in center, flying dragon, inscription: Kuang-hsü Yüan-pao

Date	VG	F	VF	XF	Unc
ND(1904-1905)	1.50	3.50	7.00	14.00	30.00

Y# 221.2 10 CASH **Composition:** Copper **Ruler:** Kuang-hsü **Obverse:** Smaller stars, flying dragon, inscription: Kuang-hsü Yüan-pao

Date	VG	F	VF	XF	Unc
ND(1904-1905)	1.50	3.50	7.00	14.00	30.00

Y# 221.3 10 CASH **Composition:** Copper **Ruler:** Kuang-hsü **Obverse:** Similar to Y#220, flying dragon, inscription: Kuang-hsü Yüan-pao **Reverse:** Similar to Y#221

Date	VG	F	VF	XF	Unc
ND(1904-1905)	62.50	125	200	300	—

Y# 221a 10 CASH **Composition:** Copper **Ruler:** Kuang-hsü **Obverse:** Thick Manchu in center, flying dragon, inscription: Kuang-hsü Yüan-pao **Reverse:** SHANG-TUNG

Date	VG	F	VF	XF	Unc
ND(1904-1905)	1.00	2.50	4.00	7.50	20.00

Y# 221a.1 10 CASH **Composition:** Copper **Ruler:** Kuang-hsü **Obverse:** Thin Manchu in center, flying dragon, inscription: Kuang-hsü Yüan-pao

Date	VG	F	VF	XF	Unc
ND(1904-1905)	2.00	5.00	10.00	17.50	40.00

Y# 10s 10 CASH **Composition:** Brass **Ruler:** Kuang-hsü **Obverse:** Inscription: Tai-ch'ing T'ung-pi **Reverse:** 6 large waves below dragon **Rev. Legend:** Kuang-hsü Nien-tsao, TAI-CHING-TI-KUO ...

Date	VG	F	VF	XF	Unc
CD(1906)	2.00	6.00	10.00	17.50	40.00

Y# 10s.1 10 CASH **Composition:** Copper **Ruler:** Kuang-hsü **Obverse:** Inscription: Tai-ch'ing T'ung-pi **Rev. Legend:** Kuang-hsü Nien-tsao, TAI-CHING-TI-KUO ...

Date	VG	F	VF	XF	Unc
CD(1906)	2.50	7.50	12.50	25.00	50.00

Y# 10s.1a 10 CASH **Composition:** Copper **Ruler:** Kuang-hsü **Obverse:** Inscription: Tai-ch'ing T'ung-pi **Reverse:** 5 small waves below dragon **Rev. Legend:** Kuang-hsü Nien-tsao, TAI-CHING-TI-KUO ...

Date	VG	F	VF	XF	Unc
CD(1906)	1.75	5.00	10.00	17.50	40.00

Y# 10s.2a 10 CASH **Composition:** Copper **Ruler:** Kuang-hsü **Obverse:** Inscription: Tai-ch'ing T'ung-pi **Reverse:** Dragon with larger forehead and narrower face, pearl redesigned **Rev. Legend:** Kuang-hsü Nien-tsao, TAI-CHING-TI-KUO ...

Date	VG	F	VF	XF	Unc
CD(1906)	2.75	8.00	15.00	30.00	60.00

PATTERNS

Including off metal strikes

KM#	Date	Mintage	Identification	Mkt Val
Pn2	ND(1851)	—	50 Cash. Cast Brass. C22-3.	—
Pn1	ND(1851)	—	10 Cash. Cast Brass. C22-7.	—
Pn3	ND(1851)	—	100 Cash. Cast Brass. C22-4.	—
Pn7	15(1926)	—	10 Dollars. Gold. K1536.	2,500
Pn8	15(1926)	—	10 Dollars. Pewter. K1536y.	—
Pn9	15(1926)	—	20 Dollars. Gold. K1535.	3,000
Pn10	15(1926)	—	20 Dollars. Pewter. K1535y.	—
Pn11	21(1932)	—	20 Cash. Copper. Wide flan.	—
Pn13	22(1933)	—	20 Cash. Copper.	—
Pn12	22(1933)	—	2 Cents. Nickel. K827.	—

SHENSI PROVINCE

Shaanxi

A province located in central China that is a rich agricultural area. A very important province in the early development of China. An active imperial mint was located at Sian (Xi'an).

EMPIRE

PROVINCIAL CASH COINAGE

C# 23-13 CASH Composition: Cast Brass **Ruler:** Kuang-hsü **Obverse:** Type A

Date	Good	VG	F	VF	XF
ND(1875-1908)	20.00	35.00	50.00	75.00	—

C# 23-14 10 CASH Composition: Cast Brass **Ruler:** Kuang-hsü **Obverse:** Type B

Date	Good	VG	F	VF	XF
ND(1875-1908) Rare	—	—	—	—	—

REPUBLIC

MILLED COINAGE

Y# 435 CENT Composition: Copper **Obverse:** Crossed flags **Obv. Legend:** IMTYPIF: "I Mei Ta Yuan Pi I (1) Fen" (One is 1/100 of Large Dollar Coin = 1 Cent) **Reverse:** Value above wheat sprays

Date	VG	F	VF	XF	Unc
ND(c. 1928)	25.00	40.00	70.00	150	—

Y# 436 2 CENTS Composition: Copper **Obverse:** Crossed flags, star between flags **Obv. Legend:** IMTYPEF: "I Mei Ta Yüan Pi Erh (2) Fen" **Reverse:** Value above wheat sprays **Note:** Dentilated borders.

Date	VG	F	VF	XF	Unc
ND(c. 1928)	35.00	60.00	90.00	150	—

Y# 436.1 2 CENTS Composition: Copper **Obverse:** Crossed flags, without star between flags **Obv. Legend:** IMTYPEF: "I Mei Ta Yüan Pi Erh (2) Fen" **Reverse:** Value above wheat sprays **Note:** Large Chinese legends.

Date	VG	F	VF	XF	Unc
ND(c. 1928)	15.00	25.00	40.00	75.00	—

Y# 436.2 2 CENTS Composition: Copper **Obverse:** Crossed flags, star in center **Obv. Legend:** IMTYPEF: "I Mei Ta Yüan Pi Erh (2) Fen" **Reverse:** Value above wheat sprays, star in center

Date	VG	F	VF	XF	Unc
ND(c. 1928)	40.00	75.00	120	225	—

Y# 436.3 2 CENTS Composition: Copper **Obverse:** Crossed flags, without star between flags **Obv. Legend:** IMTYPEF: "I Mei Ta Yüan Pi Erh (2) Fen" **Reverse:** Value above wheat sprays **Note:** Small Chinese legends.

Date	VG	F	VF	XF	Unc
ND(c. 1928)	25.00	50.00	80.00	125	—

Y# 436.4 2 CENTS Composition: Copper **Obverse:** Crossed flags **Obv. Legend:** IMTYPEF: "I Mei Ta Yüan Pi Erh (2) Fen" **Reverse:** Value above wheat sprays **Note:** Pearled borders.

Date	VG	F	VF	XF	Unc
ND(c. 1928)	50.00	80.00	120	200	—

Y# 436.5 2 CENTS Composition: Copper **Obverse:** Crossed flags, similar to Y#436.2 but with star between flags **Obv. Legend:** IMTYPEF: "I Mei Ta Yüan Pi Erh (2) Fen" **Reverse:** Value above wheat sprays **Note:** Large Chinese legends.

Date	VG	F	VF	XF	Unc
ND(c. 1928)	40.00	75.00	120	225	—

SIKANG PROVINCE

Created in 1928 from the western frontier region of Szechuan Province. It was dissolved in 1955, being divided between Szechuan (Sichuan) Province and Tibet.

REPUBLIC

MILLED COINAGE

KM# 1 100 CASH Composition: Copper

Date	VG	F	VF	XF	Unc
15(1926)	150	225	300	400	—
19(1930)	125	150	200	300	—

KM# 2 100 CASH Composition: Brass

Date	VG	F	VF	XF	Unc
19(1930)	125	150	225	375	—

Note: Previously listed in Szechuan (Sichuan) Province as Y466, 466a.

SINKIANG PROVINCE

Hsinkiang, Xinjiang

"New Dominion"

An autonomous region in western China, often referred to as Chinese Turkestan. High mountains surround 2000 ft. tableland on three sides with a large desert in center of this province. Many salt lakes, mining and some farming and oil. Inhabited by early man and was referred to as the "Silk Route" to the West. Sinkiang (Xinjiang) has been historically under the control of many factions, including Genghis Khan. It became a province in 1884. China has made claim to Sinkiang (Xinjiang) for many, many years. This rule has been more nominal than actual. Sinkiang (Xinjiang) had eight imperial mints, only three of which were in operation toward the end of the reign of Kuang Hsu. Only two mints operated during the early years of the republic. In 1949, due to a drastic coin shortage and lack of confidence in the inflated paper money, it was planned to mint some dollars in Sinkiang (Xinjiang). These did not see much circulation, however, due to the defeat of the nationalists, though they have recently appeared in considerable numbers in today's market.

PATTERNS

NOTE: A number of previously listed cast coins of Sinkiang Province are now known to be patterns - "mother" cash or "seed" cash for which no circulating issues are known. The following coins are, therefore, no longer listed. Most were probably manufactured in Beijing. They are generally made of brass rather than the purer copper usual to Sinkiang. The following coins are, therefore, no longer listed here: Craig #30-9, 30-11a, 30-12a, 30-14, 30-15a, 30-16, 30-17, 28-4.1, 28-8a, 28-9a, 28-9c, 28-10, 31-1a, 31-1v, 31-2, 32-4, 32-5, 33-12, 33-21, 34-2, 34-3, 35-5a and 35-6.

MONETARY SYSTEM

2 Pul = 1 Cash
2 Cash = 5 Li
4 Cash = 10 Li = 1 Fen
25 Cash = 10 Fen = 1 Miscal = 1 Ch'ien, Mace, Tanga
10 Miscals (Mace) = 1 Liang (Tael or Sar)
20 Miscals (Tangas) = 1 Tilla

MINT NAME

LOCAL MINT NAMES AND MARKS

Mint	Chinese	Turki	Manchu
Aksu	城阿	اقصو	
Ili, now Yining (Gulja)	犁伊	الي	
Kashgar, now Kashi	什喀	كشقر	
Khotan, now Hotan	闐和	خوتن	
Kuche, now Kuqa	車庫	كوچا	
Ushi, now Wushi (Uqturpan)	什烏	اوش	
Yarkand, now Shache (Yarkant)	羌爾葉	يارقند	

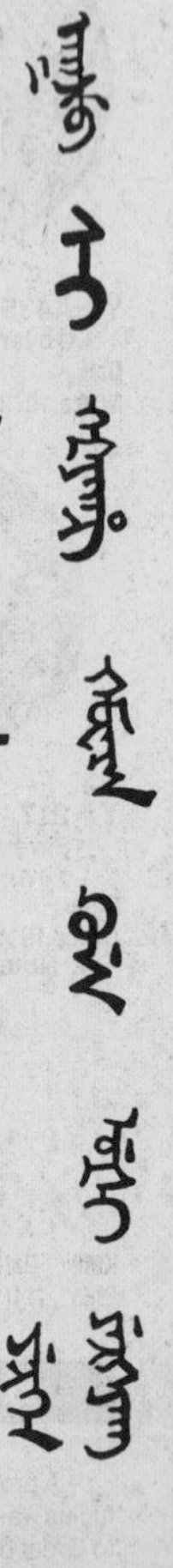

EMPIRE

PROVINCIAL CAST COINAGE

C# 33-23 CASH Composition: Cast Copper **Ruler:** Kuang-hsü **Obverse:** Inscription: "Kuang-hsü T'ung-pao" **Note:** Cast at Kuche (Kucha).

Date	Good	VG	F	VF	XF
ND(1875-1908)	6.00	8.00	12.00	20.00	—

C# 30-18 10 CASH Composition: Cast Copper **Ruler:** Kuang-hsü **Obverse:** Inscription: Kuang-hsü T'ung-pao **Reverse:** Character "A" (for Asku) above center hole, "Asku" in Turki at right, in Manchu at left **Note:** Cast at Aksu Mint.

Date	Good	VG	F	VF	XF
ND(1875-1908)	1.50	2.50	4.00	8.00	—

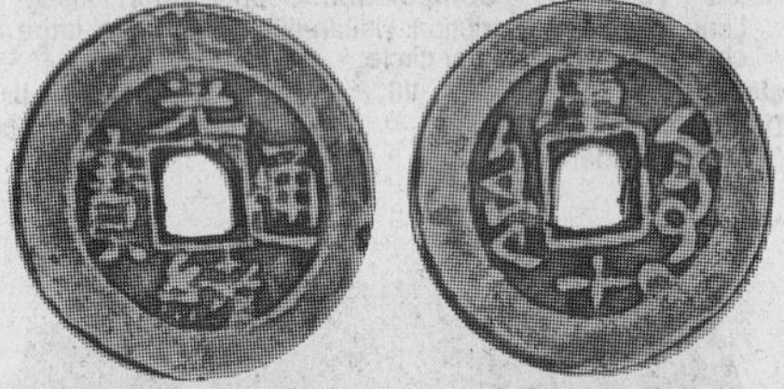

C# 30-18.1 10 CASH Composition: Cast Copper **Ruler:** Kuang-hsü **Reverse:** "Asku" in Manchu at right, in Turki at left **Note:** Cast at Aksu Mint.

Date	Good	VG	F	VF	XF
ND(1875-1908)	7.50	12.50	19.00	35.00	—

C# 32-6 10 CASH Composition: Cast Copper **Ruler:** Kuang-hsü **Obverse:** Inscription: Kuang-hsü T'ung-pao **Reverse:** "Kashgar" in Turki at left, in Manchu at right, "K'a" (Kashgar) above **Note:** Cast at the Kashgar Mint.

Date	Good	VG	F	VF	XF
ND(1875-1908)	5.00	9.50	15.00	25.00	—

C# 32-6.1 10 CASH Composition: Cast Copper **Ruler:** Kuang-hsü **Obverse:** Inscription: Kuang-hsü T'ung-pao **Reverse:** "Manchu Boo-Kashgar" (right-left) **Note:** Cast at the Kashgar Mint.

Date	Good	VG	F	VF	XF
ND(1875-1908)	5.00	9.50	15.00	25.00	—

C# 30-19 10 CASH Composition: Cast Copper **Ruler:** Kuang-hsü **Reverse:** Character "K'a" (for Kashgar) above **Note:** Cast at Aksu Mint.

Date	Good	VG	F	VF	XF
ND(1886-1908)	2.00	4.50	6.50	13.50	—

Note: Cast in the Aksu Mint for the Kashgar Mint, beginning in 1886 during the reign of Kuang-Hsu

C# 34-4 10 CASH Composition: Cast Copper **Ruler:** Hsüan-t'ung **Reverse:** "K'u" (Kuche) above, "Ushi" in Manchu and Turki right and left

Date	Good	VG	F	VF	XF
ND(1909-1911)	50.00	80.00	150	—	—

Note: Cast in Ushi to the order of the Kuche Mint; it is the last of the "red" copper cash

GENERAL CAST COINAGE

KM# 10 CASH Composition: Cast Copper **Ruler:** Kuang-hsü **Obverse:** Inscription: Kuang-hsü T'ung-pao **Reverse:** Inscription: Manchu "Boo Ciowan" for Hu-pu Board of Revenue **Note:** Cast at Kuche (Kucha) Mint.

Date	Good	VG	F	VF	XF
ND(1875-1908)	1.50	3.50	6.00	9.50	—

KM# 12 CASH Composition: Cast Copper **Ruler:** Kuang-hsü **Obverse:** Inscription: Kuang-hsü T'ung-pao **Reverse:** Similar to KM#11 **Note:** Cast at Kuche (Kucha) Mint.

Date	Good	VG	F	VF	XF
ND(1875-1908)	1.50	3.50	6.00	9.50	—

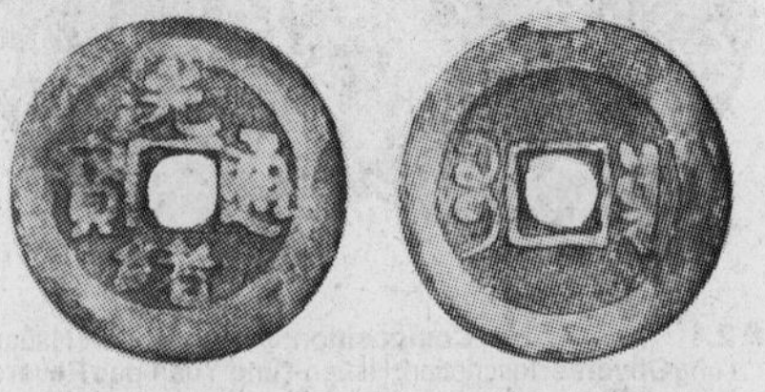

KM# 13 CASH Composition: Cast Copper **Ruler:** Kuang-hsü **Obverse:** Inscription: Kuang-hsü T'ung-pao **Reverse:** "Boo Chaun" or "Yuan" (illiterate Manchu) **Note:** Cast at Kuche (Kucha) Mint.

Date	Good	VG	F	VF	XF
ND(1875-1908)	1.50	3.50	6.00	9.50	—

KM# 14 CASH Composition: Cast Copper **Ruler:** Kuang-hsü **Obverse:** Inscription: Kuang-hsü T'ung-pao **Reverse:** "Boo Choan" (illiterate Manchu) **Note:** Cast at Kuche (Kucha) Mint.

Date	Good	VG	F	VF	XF
ND(1875-1908)	1.50	3.00	5.00	8.50	—

Note: The five one-cash varieties listed above could be confused with Beijing issues C1-16 or C2-15, but they are much more crudely cast, and are made of red copper rather than brass; see Landon Ross, 1986, Numismatics International Bulletin 20(3) for a more detailed review

KM# 11 CASH Composition: Cast Copper **Ruler:** Kuang-hsü **Reverse:** Similar to KM#10 but entire reverse is in inverted mirror image **Note:** Cast at Kuche (Kucha) Mint.

Date	Good	VG	F	VF	XF
ND(1875-1908)	3.50	6.00	9.00	13.50	—

KM# 7.1 10 CASH Composition: Cast Copper **Ruler:** Kuang-hsü **Obverse:** Inscription: "Kuang-hsü T'ung-pao" **Reverse:** "Pao Ku" with "K'u" (for Kuche) above **Note:** Cast at Kuche (Kucha) Mint.

Date	Good	VG	F	VF	XF
ND(1875-1908)	1.50	3.00	5.00	10.00	—

KM# 7.2 10 CASH Composition: Cast Copper **Ruler:** Kuang-hsü **Reverse:** "Pao" (for Kuche) at left reversed **Note:** Cast at Kuche (Kucha) Mint.

Date	Good	VG	F	VF	XF
ND(1875-1908)	7.50	13.50	22.50	35.00	—

KM# 8 10 CASH Composition: Cast Copper **Ruler:** Kuang-hsü **Obverse:** Inscription: "Kuang-hsü T'ung-pao" **Reverse:** "Manchu Boo Hsin" with "Hsin" (new, but here standing for the Tihwa (now Urumqi) Mint) above **Note:** Cast at Tihwa Mint.

Date	Good	VG	F	VF	XF
ND(1875-1908)	3.50	5.00	7.50	15.00	—

KM# 9 10 CASH Composition: Cast Copper **Ruler:** Kuang-hsü **Obverse:** Inscription: "Kuang-hsü T'ung-pao" **Reverse:** "Manchu Boo Hsin" (for Tihwa Mint) with "Hsin" (new) above **Note:** Cast at Tihwa Mint.

Date	Good	VG	F	VF	XF
ND(1875-1908)	3.00	4.50	7.00	15.00	—

C# 33-16 10 CASH Composition: Cast Copper **Ruler:** Kuang-hsü **Obverse:** Inscription: "Kuang-hsü T'ung-pao" **Note:** Cast at Kuche (Kucha) Mint.

Date	Good	VG	F	VF	XF
ND(1875-1908)	10.00	20.00	30.00	50.00	—

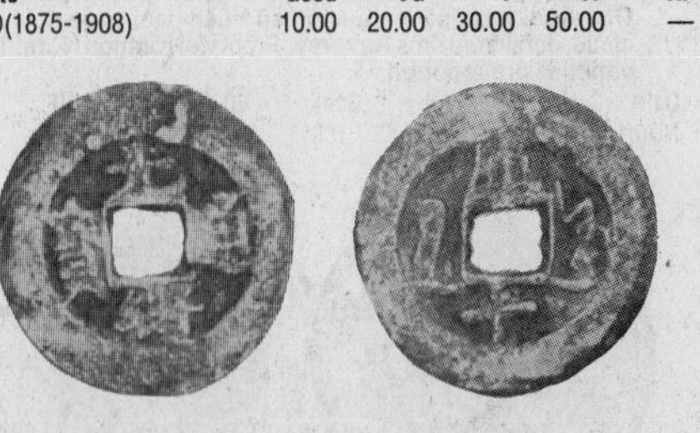

C# 33-18 10 CASH Composition: Cast Copper **Ruler:** Kuang-hsü **Reverse:** Character "K'u" above **Note:** Cast at Kuche (Kucha) Mint.

Date	Good	VG	F	VF	XF
ND1875-1908)	7.50	12.00	17.50	35.00	—

C# 33-18.1 10 CASH **Composition:** Cast Copper **Ruler:** Kuang-hsü **Reverse:** Semi-circle at lower right **Note:** Cast at Kuche (Kucha) Mint.

Date	Good	VG	F	VF	XF
ND(1875-1908)	7.50	13.50	22.50	35.00	—

C# 33-19 10 CASH **Composition:** Cast Copper **Ruler:** Kuang-hsü **Obverse:** Inscription: "Kuang-hsü T'ung-paoi" **Reverse:** Inscription: "Manchu Boo-kuce", kuce in simple style **Note:** Cast at Kuche (Kucha) Mint.

Date	Good	VG	F	VF	XF
ND(1875-1908)	2.00	3.00	10.00	18.00	—

KM# 16 10 CASH **Composition:** Cast Copper **Ruler:** Kuang-hsü **Obverse:** Inscription: Kuang-hsü Ting Wei **Reverse:** "Boo-yuan?" with "Hsin" (new) above

Date	Good	VG	F	VF	XF
CD(1907)	7.50	17.50	30.00	—	—

KM# 17 10 CASH **Composition:** Cast Copper **Ruler:** Kuang-hsü **Obverse:** Inscription: "Kuang-hsü Wu-shen"

Date	Good	VG	F	VF	XF
CD(1908)	11.50	25.00	45.00	—	—

MILLED COINAGE

Y# 1 FEN, 5 LI **Composition:** Copper **Ruler:** Kuang-hsü **Obverse:** Inscription: Kuang-hsü Yüan-pao; large dots in circle, dentilated rims **Reverse:** Front view dragon **Note:** Two varieties are reported.

Date	Good	VG	F	VF	XF
ND(ca.1906)	150	200	350	550	—

Y# 1a FEN, 5 LI **Composition:** Copper **Ruler:** Kuang-hsü **Obverse:** Inscription: Kuang-hsü Yüan-pao; small dots in circle, dotted rims **Reverse:** Front view dragon

Date	F	VF	XF	Unc	BU
ND(ca.1906) Modern copy	—	—	25.00	35.00	—

Note: The legend on this coin states that it is valued at 1 Fen 5 Li of silver (about 15 Cash); the coin is the size of a normal 10 Cash piece of Sinkiang (Xinjiang), but these pieces are usually larger than those of the other provinces; for this reason, it is assumed the coin was overvalued to benefit the government

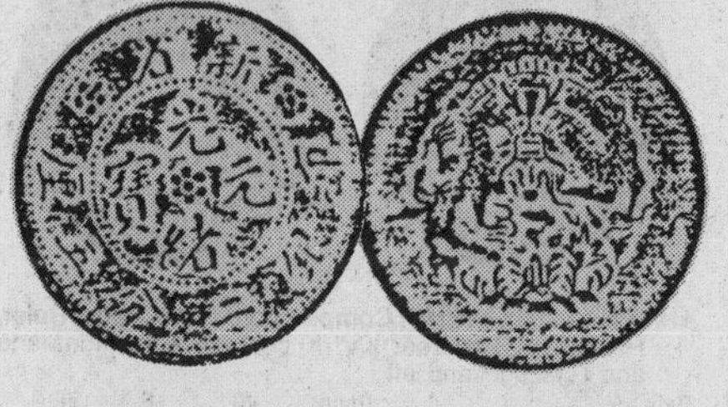

Y# A1 2 FEN 5 LI **Composition:** Copper **Ruler:** Kuang-hsü **Obverse:** Inscription: Kuang-hsü Yüan-pao **Reverse:** Front view dragon

Date	Good	VG	F	VF	XF
ND(ca.1906) Rare	—	—	—	—	—

Note: This denomination was recalled shortly after issue and the dies re-engraved 1 Fen and 5 Li to produce Y#1; do not confuse poorly re-engraved Chinese numeral "172" examples of Y#1 for Y#A1; note the difference in spacing of the Chinese characters below the rosettes between Y#1 and Y#A1

Y# B1 2 FEN 5 LI **Composition:** Copper **Ruler:** Kuang-hsü **Obverse:** Inscription: Kuang-hsü Yüan-pao **Reverse:** Side view dragon

Date	Good	VG	F	VF	XF
ND(ca.1906) Rare	—	—	—	—	—

Note: Status unknown

Y# 2.1 10 CASH **Composition:** Copper **Ruler:** Hsüan-t'ung **Obverse:** Inscription: Hsüan-t'ung Yüan-pao **Reverse:** Without Chinese legend above side-view dragon

Date	Good	VG	F	VF	XF
ND(ca.1909)	25.00	42.50	75.00	175	—

Y# 2.2 10 CASH **Composition:** Copper **Ruler:** Hsüan-t'ung **Obverse:** Inscription: Hsüan-t'ung Yüan-pao **Reverse:** Chinese legend with "Nien" (year) added above dragon

Date	Good	VG	F	VF	XF
CD(1910)	25.00	42.50	75.00	175	—
CD(1911)	30.00	50.00	100	200	—

Y# 2.3 10 CASH **Composition:** Copper **Ruler:** Hsüan-t'ung **Obverse:** Inscription: Hsüan-t'ung Yüan-pao; double ring around star in center

Date	Good	VG	F	VF	XF
CD(1911)	30.00	50.00	100	200	—

Y# 2a 10 CASH **Composition:** Copper **Ruler:** Hsüan-t'ung **Obverse:** Inscription: Hsüan-t'ung Yüan-pao; large characters within center circle

Date	VG	F	VF	XF	Unc
CD(1910)	—	—	—	25.00	35.00

Note: Modern copy

Y# A38.1 10 CASH **Composition:** Copper **Ruler:** Hung-hsien **Obverse:** Chinese legend "Hung-hsien T'ung-pi" in inner dotted circle **Note:** Struck at the Kashgar Mint.

Date	Good	VG	F	VF	XF
AH1334	120	180	250	—	—

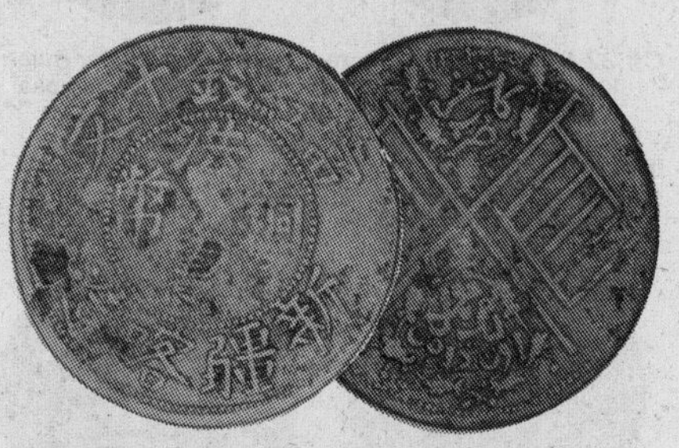

Y# A38.2 10 CASH **Composition:** Copper **Ruler:** Hung-hsien **Note:** Struck at the Kashgar Mint.

Date	Good	VG	F	VF	XF
AH1334	120	180	250	—	—

Note: Y#A38.1 and A38.2 were issued for the brief reign of Yuan Shih-kai as Emperor Hung-hsien (1916)

Y# B16 MISCAL (Mace) **Weight:** 3.5000 g. **Composition:** Silver **Ruler:** Kuang-hsü **Obverse:** Inscription: Kuang-hsü Yin-yüan; "Kashgar" at right, value at left **Note:** Struck at Kashgar Mint.

Date	VG	F	VF	XF	Unc
AH1331 Error for 1321	50.00	85.00	175	250	—
AH1322	50.00	85.00	175	250	—

Y# C16 MISCAL (Mace) **Weight:** 3.5000 g. **Composition:** Silver **Ruler:** Kuang-hsü **Obverse:** "Kashgar" in Chinese at right and left of value **Reverse:** Turki inscription in sprays **Note:** Struck at Kashgar Mint.

Date	VG	F	VF	XF	Unc
AH1322	45.00	70.00	125	200	—

Y# 3 MISCAL (Mace) **Weight:** 3.5000 g. **Composition:** Silver **Ruler:** Kuang-hsü **Obverse:** Outer legend: Turki without dot in center **Reverse:** Without Turki legend

Date	VG	F	VF	XF	Unc
ND(1905)	75.00	125	200	325	—

Y# 3.1 MISCAL (Mace) **Weight:** 3.5000 g. **Composition:** Silver **Ruler:** Kuang-hsü **Obverse:** Legend: Turki with dot in center **Reverse:** Without Turki legend

Date	VG	F	VF	XF	Unc
ND(1905)	75.00	125	200	325	—

Y# 3.2 MISCAL (Mace) **Weight:** 3.5000 g. **Composition:** Silver **Ruler:** Kuang-hsü **Obverse:** Without outer Turki legend **Reverse:** Turki legend

Date	VG	F	VF	XF	Unc
ND(1905)	325	550	900	1,500	—

Y# 3.3 MISCAL (Mace) **Weight:** 3.5000 g. **Composition:** Silver **Ruler:** Kuang-hsü **Obverse:** Without outer Turki legend **Reverse:** Without outer Turki legend

Date	VG	F	VF	XF	Unc
ND(1905)	90.00	150	250	400	—

Y# A20.1 MISCAL (Mace) **Weight:** 3.5000 g. **Composition:** Silver **Ruler:** Kuang-hsü **Obverse:** Turki at right and left of value, date at lower left **Reverse:** Side view dragon

Date	VG	F	VF	XF	Unc
AH1323	200	350	600	1,000	—

Y# A20.2 MISCAL (Mace) **Weight:** 3.5000 g. **Composition:** Silver **Ruler:** Kuang-hsü **Obverse:** Turki at right and left of value, date at lower right **Reverse:** Side view dragon **Note:** Struck at Kashgar Mint.

Date	VG	F	VF	XF	Unc
AH1323	200	350	600	1,000	—

Y# A20.3 MISCAL (Mace) **Weight:** 3.5000 g. **Composition:** Silver **Ruler:** Kuang-hsü **Obverse:** Inverted Turki legends at right and left of value **Note:** Struck at Kashgar Mint.

Date	VG	F	VF	XF	Unc
AH1323	200	350	600	1,000	—

Y# 10 MISCAL (Mace) **Weight:** 3.5000 g. **Composition:** Silver **Ruler:** Kuang-hsü **Obverse:** Without outer Turki legend **Reverse:** Legend above dragon, 1 MACE below **Rev. Legend:** SUNGAREI

Date	VG	F	VF	XF	Unc
ND(1906)	110	225	400	650	—

Y# 9 GOLD MISCAL (Mace) **Weight:** 7.8000 g. **Composition:** Gold **Ruler:** Kuang-hsü **Obverse:** Narrow-spaced Chinese "2" **Reverse:** Turki legend around uncircled dragon

Date	VG	F	VF	XF	Unc
ND(ca.1906)	250	750	1,350	2,000	2,800

Y# 9.1 GOLD MISCAL (Mace) **Weight:** 7.8000 g. **Composition:** Gold **Ruler:** Kuang-hsü **Obverse:** Wide-spaced Chinese "2" **Reverse:** Redesigned dragon

Date	VG	F	VF	XF	Unc
ND(ca.1906)	250	750	1,350	2,000	2,800

Y# 8 GOLD MISCAL (Mace) **Weight:** 3.9000 g. **Composition:** Gold **Ruler:** Kuang-hsü **Reverse:** Turki legend around uncircled dragon

Date	VG	F	VF	XF	Unc
ND(ca.1907)	135	400	650	950	1,350

Y# 8.1 GOLD MISCAL (Mace) **Weight:** 3.9000 g. **Composition:** Gold **Ruler:** Kuang-hsü **Reverse:** Without Turki legend around uncircled dragon

Date	VG	F	VF	XF	Unc
ND(ca.1907)	250	750	1,250	1,850	2,650

Y# 8.2 GOLD MISCAL (Mace) **Weight:** 3.9000 g. **Composition:** Gold **Ruler:** Kuang-hsü **Reverse:** Turki legend at left differs

Date	VG	F	VF	XF	Unc
ND(ca.1907)	150	450	750	1,150	1,650

Y# 8.3 GOLD MISCAL (Mace) **Weight:** 3.9000 g. **Composition:** Gold **Ruler:** Kuang-hsü **Reverse:** Turki legend in outer circle

Date	VG	F	VF	XF	Unc
ND(ca.1907)	185	550	950	1,350	2,000

Y# 17a 2 MISCALS (2 Mace) **Weight:** 7.2000 g. **Composition:** Silver **Ruler:** Kuang-hsü **Obverse:** Inscription: Kuang-hsü Yin-yüan between Kashgar and value **Note:** Struck at Kashgar Mint.

Date	VG	F	VF	XF	Unc
AH1311	—	—	—	—	—
Note: Error					
AH1312	12.50	22.50	32.50	50.00	—
AH1313	12.50	22.50	32.50	50.00	—
AH1314	12.50	22.50	32.50	50.00	—
AH1315	12.50	22.50	32.50	50.00	—
AH1317	12.50	22.50	32.50	50.00	—
AH1319	12.50	22.50	32.50	50.00	—
AH1320	17.50	30.00	45.00	75.00	—

Y# 17a.1 2 MISCALS (2 Mace) **Weight:** 7.2000 g. **Composition:** Silver **Ruler:** Kuang-hsü **Obverse:** Inscription: Kuang-hsü Yin-yüan between "K'a Tsao" at right, value at left **Note:** Struck at Kashgar Mint.

Date	VG	F	VF	XF	Unc
AH1320 Rare	—	—	—	—	—
AH1321	17.50	30.00	45.00	75.00	—
AH1322	20.00	35.00	55.00	100	—

Y# 33 2 MISCALS (2 Mace) **Composition:** Cast Copper **Ruler:** Kuang-hsü **Obverse:** Inscription: "Kuang-hsü Yin-yüan" between "Tihwa" and value with normal Erh (2) at left **Reverse:** Inscription: Turki in floral wreath **Note:** Struck at Tihwa Mint.

Date	VG	F	VF	XF	Unc
AH1321	15.00	22.00	55.00	90.00	—
AH1322	15.00	22.00	55.00	90.00	—
AH1323	17.50	30.00	55.00	90.00	—

Y# 33.1 2 MISCALS (2 Mace) **Composition:** Cast Copper **Ruler:** Kuang-hsü **Obverse:** Inscription: "Kuang-hsü Yin-yüan" between "Tihwa" and value with official Erh (2) at left **Reverse:** Inscription: Turki in floral wreath **Note:** Struck at Tihwa Mint.

Date	VG	F	VF	XF	Unc
AH1323	15.00	22.00	55.00	90.00	—
AH1324	15.00	22.00	55.00	90.00	—
AH1325	15.00	22.00	55.00	90.00	—

Y# B20.1 2 MISCALS (2 Mace) **Weight:** 7.2000 g. **Composition:** Silver **Obv. Legend:** Chinese and Turki around inscription Kuang-hsü Yüan-pao **Reverse:** Dragon **Note:** Struck at Kashgar Mint.

Date	VG	F	VF	XF	Unc
AH1323	175	300	500	850	—

Y# B20.2 2 MISCALS (2 Mace) **Weight:** 7.2000 g. **Composition:** Silver **Obv. Legend:** Chinese and Turki around inscription Kuang-hsü Yüan-pao **Reverse:** Dragon **Note:** Struck at Kashgar Mint.

Date	VG	F	VF	XF	Unc
AH1323	175	300	500	850	—

Y# 4 2 MISCALS (2 Mace) **Weight:** 7.2000 g. **Composition:** Silver **Ruler:** Kuang-hsü **Obverse:** Turki outer legend **Reverse:** Without Turki legend

Date	VG	F	VF	XF	Unc
ND(1905)	50.00	75.00	150	400	—

Y# 4.1 2 MISCALS (2 Mace) **Weight:** 7.2000 g. **Composition:** Silver **Ruler:** Kuang-hsü **Obverse:** Continuous Turki outer legend **Reverse:** Without Turki legend

Date	VG	F	VF	XF	Unc
ND(1905)	100	150	250	325	—

Y# 4.2 2 MISCALS (2 Mace) **Weight:** 7.2000 g. **Composition:** Silver **Ruler:** Kuang-hsü **Obverse:** Without outer Turki legend **Reverse:** Turki legend

Date	VG	F	VF	XF	Unc
ND(1905)	150	250	400	650	—

Y# 4.3 2 MISCALS (2 Mace) **Weight:** 7.2000 g. **Composition:** Silver **Ruler:** Kuang-hsü **Reverse:** Redesigned dragon without Turki legends

Date	VG	F	VF	XF	Unc
ND(1905)	150	250	400	650	—

Y# 4.4 2 MISCALS (2 Mace) **Weight:** 7.2000 g. **Composition:** Silver **Ruler:** Kuang-hsü **Obverse:** Turki outer legend **Reverse:** Circled dragon without Turki legend

Date	VG	F	VF	XF	Unc
ND(1905) Rare	—	—	—	—	—

Y# 11 2 MISCALS (2 Mace) **Weight:** 7.2000 g. **Composition:** Silver **Ruler:** Kuang-hsü **Reverse:** Legend above dragon, 2 MACE below **Rev. Legend:** SUNGAREI

Date	VG	F	VF	XF	Unc
ND(1906)	200	425	850	1,350	—

Y# 23 2 MISCALS (2 Mace) **Weight:** 7.2000 g. **Composition:** Silver **Obv. Legend:** Chinese and Turki around inscription Ta-Ch'ing Yin-pi **Reverse:** Dragon in circle surrounded by sprays

Date	VG	F	VF	XF	Unc
AH1324 Rare	—	—	—	—	—
AH1325	20.00	40.00	65.00	110	—
AH1326	20.00	40.00	65.00	110	—
AH1327	25.00	50.00	80.00	150	—
AH1329	35.00	65.00	110	175	—

Y# 29 2 MISCALS (2 Mace) **Weight:** 7.2000 g. **Composition:** Silver **Obverse:** Turki legend around Yin-Yüan Ërh-ch'ien within a beaded circle **Reverse:** Double ring around small dragon, floral pattern outside without legend **Note:** Struck at Kashgar Mint.

Date	VG	F	VF	XF	Unc
AH1329	55.00	90.00	150	250	—

Y# 29.1 2 MISCALS (2 Mace) **Weight:** 7.2000 g. **Composition:** Silver **Obverse:** Yin-yüan Ërh-ch'ien **Reverse:** Turki legend below larger dragon within single circle **Note:** Struck at Kashgar Mint.

Date	VG	F	VF	XF	Unc
AH1329	75.00	125	200	325	—

Y# 18a 3 MISCALS **Weight:** 10.5000 g. **Composition:** Silver **Ruler:** Kuang-hsü **Obverse:** Inscription: Kuang-hsü Yin-yüan between Kashgar and value **Reverse:** Turki in floral wreath **Note:** Struck at Kashgar Mint.

Date	VG	F	VF	XF	Unc
AH1319	10.00	20.00	32.50	65.00	—
AH1320	10.00	20.00	32.50	65.00	—

Y# 18a.1 3 MISCALS **Weight:** 10.5000 g. **Composition:** Silver **Ruler:** Kuang-hsü **Obverse:** Inscription: "Kuang-hsü Yin-yüan" between "K'a Tsao" and value **Reverse:** Turki in floral wreath **Note:** Struck at Kashgar Mint.

Date	VG	F	VF	XF	Unc
AH1320	10.00	20.00	32.50	65.00	—
AH1321	10.00	20.00	32.50	65.00	—
AH1322	10.00	20.00	32.50	65.00	—

Y# 34 3 MISCALS **Weight:** 10.3000 g. **Composition:** Silver **Ruler:** Kuang-hsü **Obverse:** Inscription: "Kuang-hsü Yin-yüan" between "Tihwa" and value with normal "San" (3) at left **Reverse:** Inscription: Turki in floral wreath **Note:** Struck at the Tihwa Mint.

Date	VG	F	VF	XF	Unc
AH1321	17.50	30.00	75.00	110	—
AH1322	17.50	30.00	75.00	110	—
AH1323	17.50	30.00	75.00	110	—

Y# 35 3 MISCALS **Weight:** 17.9000 g. **Composition:** Silver **Ruler:** Kuang-hsü **Obverse:** Inscription: "Kuang-hsü Yin-yüan" between "Tihwa" and value with normal "Wu" (5) at left **Reverse:** Inscription: Turki in floral wreath **Note:** Struck at the Tihwa Mint.

Date	VG	F	VF	XF	Unc
AH1321	20.00	35.00	70.00	125	—
AH1322	20.00	35.00	70.00	125	—
AH1323	20.00	35.00	70.00	125	—

Y# 35a 3 MISCALS **Weight:** 17.9000 g. **Composition:** Silver **Ruler:** Kuang-hsü **Obverse:** Inscription: "Kuang-hsü Yin-yüan" between "Tihwa" and value with official "Wu" (5) at left **Reverse:** Inscription: Turki in floral wreath **Note:** Struck at the Tihwa Mint.

Date	VG	F	VF	XF	Unc
AH1323	20.00	40.00	70.00	125	—
AH1324	15.00	30.00	60.00	100	—
AH1325	15.00	30.00	60.00	100	—

Y# 34a 3 MISCALS **Weight:** 10.3000 g. **Composition:** Silver **Ruler:** Kuang-hsü **Obverse:** Inscription: "Kuang-hsü Yin-yüan" between "Tihwa" and value with official "San" (3) at left **Reverse:** Inscription: Turki in floral wreath **Note:** Struck at the Tihwa Mint.

Date	VG	F	VF	XF	Unc
AH1323	10.00	20.00	32.50	65.00	—
AH1324	10.00	20.00	32.50	65.00	—
AH1325	10.00	20.00	32.50	65.00	—

Y# 20 3 MISCALS **Weight:** 10.5000 g. **Composition:** Silver **Ruler:** Kuang-hsü **Obv. Legend:** Turki and Chinese around inscription: "Ta-ch'ing Yüan-pao" with normal "San" (3) in Chinese at bottom **Note:** Struck at Kashgar Mint.

Date	VG	F	VF	XF	Unc
AH1323	85.00	175	275	450	—

Y# 20.1 3 MISCALS **Weight:** 10.5000 g. **Composition:** Silver **Ruler:** Kuang-hsü **Obv. Legend:** Turki and Chinese around inscription: "Ta-ch'ing Yüan-pao" with official "San" (3) in Chinese at bottom **Note:** Struck at Kashgar Mint.

Date	VG	F	VF	XF	Unc
AH1323	100	200	325	550	—

Y# 20.2 3 MISCALS **Weight:** 10.5000 g. **Composition:** Silver **Ruler:** Kuang-hsü **Obv. Legend:** Turki and Chinese around inscription: "Ta-ch'ing Yüan-pao" with official "San" (3) in Chinese at bottom, date at lower right **Note:** Struck at the Kashgar Mint.

Date	VG	F	VF	XF	Unc
AH1323	100	200	365	600	—

Y# 30 3 MISCALS **Weight:** 10.5000 g. **Composition:** Silver **Obverse:** Inscription: "Yin-yüan San-ch'ien" **Reverse:** Turki legend below snall, side view dragon in circle **Note:** Struck at the Kashgar Mint.

Date	VG	F	VF	XF	Unc
AH1329	200	350	600	1,000	—

Y# 5 4 MISCALS (4 Mace) **Weight:** 14.2000 g. **Composition:** Silver **Ruler:** Kuang-hsü

Date	VG	F	VF	XF	Unc
ND(1905)	85.00	125	200	400	—

Y# 19a 5 MISCALS **Weight:** 17.2000 g. **Composition:** Silver **Ruler:** Kuang-hsü **Obverse:** Inscription: "Kuang-hsü Yin-yüan" between "Kashgar" and value; Chinese characters "K'a Shih" at right **Reverse:** Inscription: Turki within sprays **Note:** Struck at the Kashgar Mint.

Date	VG	F	VF	XF	Unc
AH1311 Error	—	—	—	—	—
AH1313	17.50	25.00	40.00	70.00	—
AH1314	17.50	25.00	40.00	70.00	—
AH1315	17.50	25.00	40.00	70.00	—
AH1316	17.50	25.00	40.00	70.00	—
AH1317	17.50	25.00	40.00	70.00	—
AH1319	17.50	25.00	40.00	70.00	—
AH1320	17.50	25.00	40.00	70.00	—

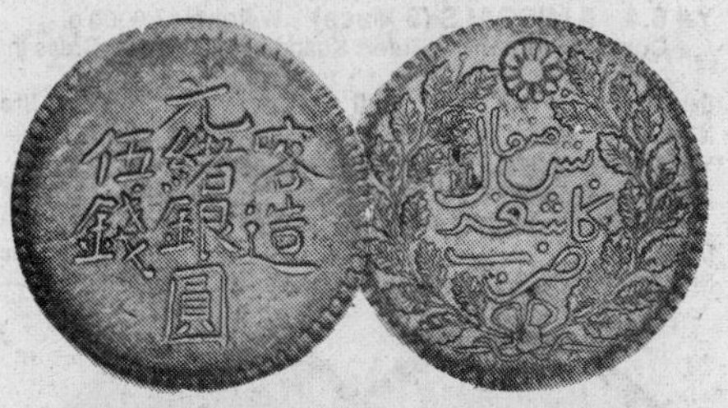

Y# 19a.1 5 MISCALS **Weight:** 17.2000 g. **Composition:** Silver **Ruler:** Kuang-hsü **Obverse:** Inscription: "Kuang-hsü Yin-yüan" between "K'a Tsao" at right, value at left **Note:** Struck at the Kashgar Mint.

Date	VG	F	VF	XF	Unc
AH1311 Error	—	—	—	—	—
AH1321	10.00	17.50	30.00	60.00	—
AH1322	10.00	17.50	30.00	60.00	—

Y# 21.1 5 MISCALS **Weight:** 17.2000 g. **Composition:** Silver **Obverse:** Simple 5 in Chinese, date at lower right. **Reverse:** Dragon's tail points to right **Note:** Struck at the Kashgar Mint.

Date	VG	F	VF	XF	Unc
AH1323	20.00	30.00	45.00	75.00	—

Y# 21.7 5 MISCALS **Weight:** 17.2000 g. **Composition:** Silver **Ruler:** Kuang-hsü **Obverse:** Date at upper right **Note:** Struck at the Kashgar Mint.

Date	VG	F	VF	XF	Unc
AH1323	20.00	30.00	45.00	75.00	—

Y# 21.2 5 MISCALS **Weight:** 17.2000 g. **Composition:** Silver **Ruler:** Kuang-hsü **Obverse:** Inverted Turki legend, date at lower right **Note:** Struck at the Kashgar Mint.

Date	VG	F	VF	XF	Unc
AH1323	22.50	35.00	60.00	100	—

Y# 21.3 5 MISCALS **Weight:** 17.2000 g. **Composition:** Silver **Ruler:** Kuang-hsü **Obverse:** Normal "Wu" (5) at bottom, date at lower right **Note:** Struck at the Kashgar Mint.

Date	VG	F	VF	XF	Unc
AH1323 Rare	—	—	—	—	—

Y# 21.4 5 MISCALS **Weight:** 17.2000 g. **Composition:** Silver **Ruler:** Kuang-hsü **Obverse:** Date at upper left **Reverse:** Side view dragon's tail points to left **Note:** Struck at the Kashgar Mint.

Date	VG	F	VF	XF	Unc
AH1323	15.00	25.00	50.00	90.00	—

Y# 21.5 5 MISCALS **Weight:** 17.2000 g. **Composition:** Silver **Ruler:** Kuang-hsü **Obverse:** Date at lower right **Note:** Struck at the Kashgar Mint.

Date	VG	F	VF	XF	Unc
AH1323	15.00	25.00	50.00	90.00	—

Y# 21.6 5 MISCALS **Weight:** 17.2000 g. **Composition:** Silver **Ruler:** Kuang-hsü **Obverse:** Inverted Turki legend, date at lower right **Note:** Struck at the Kashgar Mint.

Date	VG	F	VF	XF	Unc
AH1323	20.00	35.00	80.00	135	—

Y# 21 5 MISCALS **Weight:** 17.2000 g. **Composition:** Silver **Ruler:** Kuang-hsü **Obv. Legend:** Chinese and Turki around inscription: "Ta-ch'ing Yüan-pao", date at upper left **Reverse:** Side view dragon's tail points to right **Note:** Cross-reference number: K#1110. Struck at the Kashgar Mint.

Date	VG	F	VF	XF	Unc
AH1323	20.00	30.00	45.00	75.00	—

Y# 25 5 MISCALS **Weight:** 17.2000 g. **Composition:** Silver **Ruler:** Kuang-hsü **Obverse:** "Kashgar Tsao" at top between standard Turki legend; inscription: "Ta-ch'ing Yin-pi" **Note:** Struck at the Kashgar Mint.

Date	VG	F	VF	XF	Unc
ND(ca.1906)	22.50	40.00	85.00	150	—

Y# 25.1 5 MISCALS **Weight:** 17.2000 g. **Composition:** Silver **Obverse:** Date at left or upper left **Note:** Struck at the Kashgar Mint.

Date	VG	F	VF	XF	Unc
AH1325	22.50	40.00	85.00	150	—
AH1326	22.50	40.00	85.00	150	—
AH1327	22.50	40.00	85.00	150	—

Y# 25.3 5 MISCALS **Weight:** 17.2000 g. **Composition:** Silver **Obverse:** Inverted Turki legend, date at upper right, right, or lower right **Note:** Struck at the Kashgar Mint.

Date	VG	F	VF	XF	Unc
AH1325	17.50	25.00	75.00	110	—
AH1326	17.50	25.00	75.00	110	—
AH1328	17.50	25.00	75.00	110	—

Note: Error for 1326

Y# 25.4 5 MISCALS **Weight:** 17.2000 g. **Composition:** Silver **Obverse:** "Kashgar" at top between standard Turki legend with date at upper right **Note:** Struck at the Kashgar Mint.

Date	VG	F	VF	XF	Unc
AH1325	20.00	35.00	100	150	—

Y# 25.9 5 MISCALS **Weight:** 17.2000 g. **Composition:** Silver **Obverse:** Similar to Y#25.4 **Reverse:** Floral sprays reversed **Note:** Struck at the Kashgar Mint.

Date	VG	F	VF	XF	Unc
AH1325	50.00	100	165	275	—

Y# 25.10 5 MISCALS **Weight:** 17.2000 g. **Composition:** Silver **Obverse:** Date at upper left **Reverse:** Standard florals **Note:** Struck at the Kashgar Mint.

Date	VG	F	VF	XF	Unc
AH1325	50.00	100	165	275	—

Y# 25.11 5 MISCALS **Weight:** 17.2000 g. **Composition:** Silver **Obverse:** Date at upper left **Reverse:** Three rosettes at top **Note:** Struck at the Kashgar Mint.

Date	VG	F	VF	XF	Unc
AH1325	600	800	1,000	1,200	—

Y# 25.2 5 MISCALS **Weight:** 17.2000 g. **Composition:** Silver **Note:** Similar to Y#25.1. Varieties exist in date placement. Struck at the Kashgar Mint.

Date	VG	F	VF	XF	Unc
AH1325	22.50	40.00	85.00	150	—
AH1326	22.50	40.00	85.00	150	—
AH1327	22.50	40.00	85.00	150	—

Y# 25.8 5 MISCALS **Weight:** 17.2000 g. **Composition:** Silver **Obverse:** Date at upper left or left **Note:** Varieties exist. Struck at the Kashgar Mint.

Date	VG	F	VF	XF	Unc
AH1325	17.50	25.00	75.00	110	—

Y# 27 5 MISCALS **Weight:** 17.2000 g. **Composition:** Silver **Ruler:** Hsüan-t'ung **Obverse:** "Kashgar" at top, Turki below; inscription: "Hsüan-t'ung Yin-pi", star in center **Note:** Struck at the Kashgar Mint.

Date	VG	F	VF	XF	Unc
AH1327	20.00	30.00	65.00	110	—
AH1328	25.00	50.00	90.00	150	—

Y# 27.1 5 MISCALS **Weight:** 17.2000 g. **Composition:** Silver **Ruler:** Hsüan-t'ung **Obverse:** Official "Wu" (5) at right, dot in center **Note:** Struck at the Kashgar Mint.

Date	VG	F	VF	XF	Unc
AH1328	35.00	65.00	150	225	—

Y# 27.2 5 MISCALS **Weight:** 17.2000 g. **Composition:** Silver **Ruler:** Hsüan-t'ung **Obverse:** Rosette in center **Note:** Struck at the Kashgar Mint.

Date	VG	F	VF	XF	Unc
AH1329	50.00	100	200	275	—

Y# A28 (Y27.3) 5 MISCALS **Weight:** 17.2000 g. **Composition:** Silver **Ruler:** Hsüan-t'ung **Obverse:** "Kashgar" at top, normal "Wu" (5) at right, star in center; inscription: "Hsüan-t'ung Yüan-pao" **Reverse:** Side view dragon **Note:** Struck at the Kashgar Mint.

Date	VG	F	VF	XF	Unc
AH1329	17.50	25.00	75.00	110	—

Y# A28.1 (Y27.4) 5 MISCALS **Weight:** 17.2000 g. **Composition:** Silver **Ruler:** Hsüan-t'ung **Obverse:** Dot in center **Reverse:** Side view dragon **Note:** Struck at the Kashgar Mint.

Date	VG	F	VF	XF	Unc
AH1329	17.50	25.00	75.00	110	—

Y# A28.2 (Y27.5) 5 MISCALS **Weight:** 17.2000 g. **Composition:** Silver **Ruler:** Hsüan-t'ung **Obverse:** Rosette in center **Reverse:** Side view dragon **Note:** Struck at the Kashgar Mint.

Date	VG	F	VF	XF	Unc
AH1329	17.50	25.00	75.00	110	—

Y# A28.3 (Y27.6) 5 MISCALS **Weight:** 17.2000 g. **Composition:** Silver **Ruler:** Hsüan-t'ung **Obverse:** Official "Wu" (5) at right, star in center **Reverse:** Side view dragon **Note:** Struck at the Kashgar Mint.

Date	VG	F	VF	XF	Unc
AH1329	17.50	25.00	75.00	110	—

Y# 31.2 5 MISCALS **Weight:** 17.2000 g. **Composition:** Silver **Ruler:** Kuang-hsü **Obverse:** Rosettes in outer field **Note:** Struck at the Kashgar Mint.

Date	VG	F	VF	XF	Unc
AH1329	50.00	100	165	275	—

Y# 31.3 5 MISCALS **Weight:** 17.2000 g. **Composition:** Silver **Ruler:** Kuang-hsü **Reverse:** Rosettes in center **Note:** Struck at the Kashgar Mint.

Date	VG	F	VF	XF	Unc
AH1329	22.50	75.00	100	150	—

Y# 31 5 MISCALS **Weight:** 17.2000 g. **Composition:** Silver **Ruler:** Kuang-hsü **Obv. Legend:** Legend "Kashgar" at top, Turki below around side view dragon, star at center and at right **Reverse:** Inscription: "Hsiang-yin" (soldier's pay) between value **Note:** Varieties with two and three tail spines on dragon exist. Struck at the Kashgar Mint.

Date	VG	F	VF	XF	Unc
AH1329	20.00	40.00	100	150	—
AH1330	20.00	40.00	100	150	—
AH1321 Error for 1331	20.00	40.00	100	150	—
AH1331	20.00	40.00	100	150	—

Y# 6 5 MISCALS (5 Mace) **Weight:** 17.9000 g. **Composition:** Silver **Ruler:** Kuang-hsü **Obverse:** Without dot or rosette in center **Reverse:** Uncircled dragon

Date	VG	F	VF	XF	Unc
ND(1905)	15.00	25.00	60.00	175	—

Y# 6.1 5 MISCALS (5 Mace) **Weight:** 17.9000 g. **Composition:** Silver **Ruler:** Kuang-hsü **Reverse:** Circled dragon, without rosettes

Date	VG	F	VF	XF	Unc
ND(1905)	15.00	25.00	50.00	90.00	—

Y# 6.2 5 MISCALS (5 Mace) **Weight:** 17.9000 g. **Composition:** Silver **Ruler:** Kuang-hsü **Reverse:** Large rosettes at sides of dragon

Date	VG	F	VF	XF	Unc
ND(1905)	15.00	25.00	50.00	90.00	—

Y# 6.3 5 MISCALS (5 Mace) **Weight:** 17.9000 g. **Composition:** Silver **Ruler:** Kuang-hsü **Obverse:** Dot in center **Reverse:** Without rosettes, circled dragon

Date	VG	F	VF	XF	Unc
ND(1905)	15.00	25.00	50.00	90.00	—

Y# 6.4 5 MISCALS (5 Mace) **Weight:** 17.9000 g. **Composition:** Silver **Ruler:** Kuang-hsü **Obverse:** Cross in center

Date	VG	F	VF	XF	Unc
ND(1905)	15.00	25.00	50.00	90.00	—

Y# 6.5 5 MISCALS (5 Mace) **Weight:** 17.9000 g. **Composition:** Silver **Ruler:** Kuang-hsü **Obverse:** Large rosette in center, middle of which is depressed

Date	VG	F	VF	XF	Unc
ND(1905)	15.00	25.00	50.00	90.00	—

Y# 6.6 5 MISCALS (5 Mace) **Weight:** 17.9000 g. **Composition:** Silver **Ruler:** Kuang-hsü **Obverse:** Eight-petalled rosette in center, middle of which is raised **Reverse:** Small rosettes at sides of dragon

Date	VG	F	VF	XF	Unc
ND(1905)	15.00	25.00	50.00	90.00	—

Y# 6.7 5 MISCALS (5 Mace) **Weight:** 17.9000 g. **Composition:** Silver **Ruler:** Kuang-hsü **Reverse:** Bat above uncircled dragon's head

Date	VG	F	VF	XF	Unc
ND(1905)	175	300	450	700	—

Y# 6.8 5 MISCALS (5 Mace) **Weight:** 17.9000 g. **Composition:** Silver **Ruler:** Kuang-hsü **Reverse:** Turki legend around uncircled dragon

Date	VG	F	VF	XF	Unc
ND(1905)	400	600	—	—	—

Y# 6.9 5 MISCALS (5 Mace) **Weight:** 17.9000 g. **Composition:** Silver **Ruler:** Kuang-hsü **Reverse:** Legend above uncircled dragon, 5 MACE below **Rev. Legend:** SUNGAREI

Date	VG	F	VF	XF	Unc
ND(1906) Rare	—	—	—	—	—

Note: Some authorities consider this coin a fantasy

Y# 6.10 5 MISCALS (5 Mace) **Weight:** 17.9000 g. **Composition:** Silver **Ruler:** Kuang-hsü **Reverse:** Without SUNGREI, with four bats and many clouds around dragon

Date	VG	F	VF	XF	Unc
ND(1906) Rare	—	—	—	—	—

Y# 6.11 5 MISCALS (5 Mace) **Weight:** 17.9000 g. **Composition:** Silver **Ruler:** Kuang-hsü **Obverse:** Turki legend rotated **Reverse:** Bat above dragon's head

Date	VG	F	VF	XF	Unc
ND(1906) Rare	—	—	—	—	—

Y# 7 SAR (Tael) **Weight:** 35.5000 g. **Composition:** Silver **Ruler:** Kuang-hsü **Obverse:** Without Turki legend **Reverse:** Without Turki legend, rosettes at sides of uncircled dtagon

Date	VG	F	VF	XF	Unc
ND(1905)	25.00	40.00	60.00	140	—

Y# 7.1 SAR (Tael) **Weight:** 35.5000 g. **Composition:** Silver **Ruler:** Kuang-hsü **Reverse:** Turki legend around circled dragon, without rosettes

Date	VG	F	VF	XF	Unc
ND(1905)	40.00	65.00	100	300	—

Y# 7.2 SAR (Tael) **Weight:** 35.5000 g. **Composition:** Silver **Ruler:** Kuang-hsü **Reverse:** Turki legend around uncircled dragon

Date	VG	F	VF	XF	Unc
ND(1905)	500	850	1,250	1,600	—

Y# 7.3 SAR (Tael) **Weight:** 35.5000 g. **Composition:** Silver **Ruler:** Kuang-hsü **Obverse:** Outer Turki legend, rosette in center **Reverse:** Without Turki legend, with rosettes at sides of uncircled dragon

Date	VG	F	VF	XF	Unc
ND(1905)	35.00	50.00	70.00	150	—

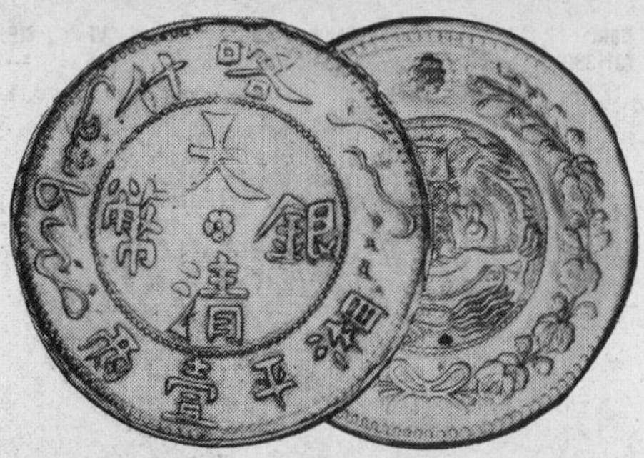

Y# 26 SAR (Tael) **Weight:** 35.2000 g. **Composition:** Silver **Obverse:** Chinese "Kashgar" at top wtih Turki "Kashgar" to left; inscription: "Ta-ch'ing Yin-pi" **Reverse:** Side view dragon in sprays **Note:** Struck at the Kashgar Mint.

Date	VG	F	VF	XF	Unc
AH1325	200	300	500	850	—

Y# 26.1 SAR (Tael) **Weight:** 35.2000 g. **Composition:** Silver **Obverse:** "Kashgar Tsao" at top **Note:** Struck at the Kashgar Mint.

Date	VG	F	VF	XF	Unc
AH1325	1,200	2,750	5,000	7,000	—

Y# 26.2 SAR (Tael) **Weight:** 35.2000 g. **Composition:** Silver **Obverse:** Chinese "Kashgar" at top wtih Turki "Kashgar" to right **Note:** Struck at the Kashgar Mint.

Date	VG	F	VF	XF	Unc
AH1325	300	500	700	1,200	—

REPUBLIC

PROVINCIAL CAST COINAGE

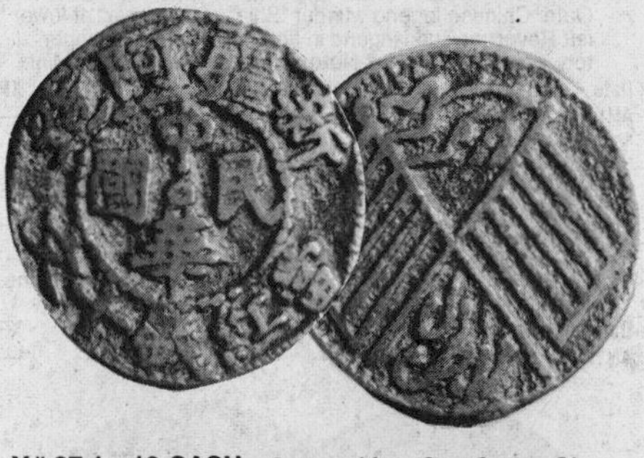

Y# 37.1 10 CASH **Composition:** Cast Copper **Obv. Inscription:** Chung Hua Min Kuo **Reverse:** Crossed flags **Size:** 32 mm. **Note:** Cast at the Aksu Mint.

Date	Good	VG	F	VF	XF
ND(ca.1912)	35.00	55.00	80.00	—	—

Y# 37.2 10 CASH **Composition:** Cast Copper **Obv. Inscription:** Chung Hua Min Kuo **Reverse:** Crossed flags **Size:** 29 mm. **Note:** Cast at the Aksu Mint.

Date	Good	VG	F	VF	XF
ND(ca.1912)	35.00	55.00	80.00	—	—

MILLED COINAGE

Y# A36.1 5 CASH **Composition:** Copper **Obverse:** Large Chinese inscription: "Chung-hua Min-kuo" between "T'ung-pi" **Rev. Legend:** Chinese outer, Turki inner, around flag **Note:** Struck at the Kashgar Mint.

Date	Good	VG	F	VF	XF
ND(ca.1912)	275	375	500	700	—

Y# A36.2 5 CASH **Composition:** Copper **Obverse:** Small Chinese inscription: "Chung-hua Min-kuo" between "T'ung-pi" **Rev. Legend:** Chinese outer, Turki inner, around flag **Note:** Struck at the Kashgar Mint.

Date	Good	VG	F	VF	XF
ND(ca.1912)	275	375	500	700	—

Y# 36 5 CASH **Composition:** Copper **Obv. Legend:** Chinese around inscription "Chung-hua Min-kuo" **Reverse:** Inscription: Turki above and below crossed flags **Note:** Struck at the Kashgar Mint.

Date	Good	VG	F	VF	XF
AH1331	100	135	225	350	—

寶

Y# B39.1 10 CASH **Composition:** Copper **Obverse:** Large character "Shih" (ten), normal "Pao"

Date	Good	VG	F	VF	XF
ND	8.50	15.00	25.00	37.50	65.00

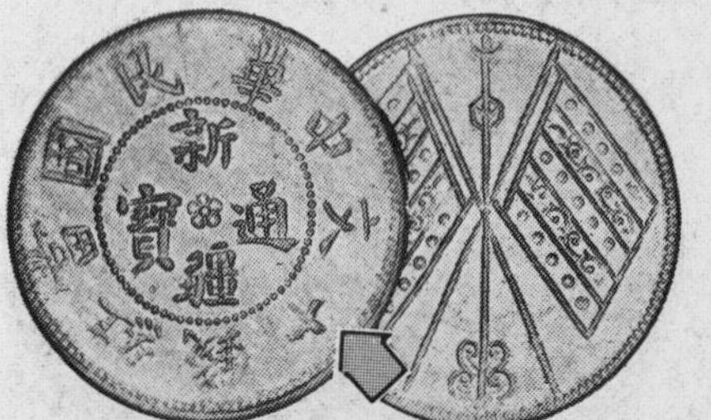

Y# B39.2 10 CASH **Composition:** Copper **Obverse:** Small character "Shih" (ten) **Reverse:** Small crossed flags

Date	Good	VG	F	VF	XF
ND	12.50	25.00	35.00	50.00	85.00

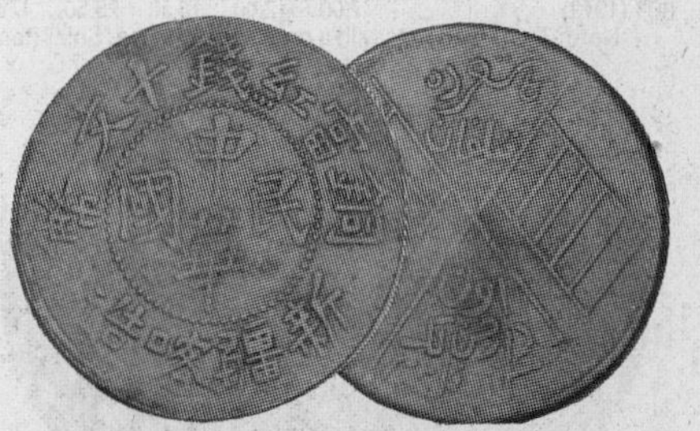

Y# 38.2 10 CASH **Composition:** Copper **Reverse:** Modified Turki legend with date at bottom **Note:** Struck at the Kashgar Mint.

Date	Good	VG	F	VF	XF
AH1331	8.50	12.50	17.50	30.00	—
AH1332	8.50	12.50	17.50	30.00	—
AH1334	8.50	12.50	17.50	30.00	—
AH1335	8.50	12.50	17.50	30.00	—

Y# B36.1 10 CASH **Composition:** Copper **Obverse:** Large Chinese inscription: "Chung-hua Min-kuo" between "T'ung-pi" **Rev. Legend:** Chinese outer, Turki inner, around flag **Note:** Struck at the Kashgar Mint.

Date	Good	VG	F	VF	XF
ND(ca.1912)	25.00	37.50	50.00	85.00	—

Y# B36.2 10 CASH Composition: Copper **Obverse:** Small Chinese inscription: "Chung-hua Min-kuo" between "T'ung-pi" **Rev. Legend:** Chinese outer, Turki inner, around flag **Note:** Struck at the Kashgar Mint.

Date	Good	VG	F	VF	XF
ND(ca.1912)	25.00	37.50	50.00	85.00	—

Y# A39.1 10 CASH Composition: Copper **Reverse:** Large crossed flags with vertical stirpes

Date	Good	VG	F	VF	XF
CD1 (1912)	7.50	13.50	18.50	28.50	49.50

Y# A39.2 10 CASH Composition: Copper **Reverse:** Small crossed flags with vertical stirpes

Date	Good	VG	F	VF	XF
CD1 (1912)	7.00	12.00	16.50	25.50	47.50

Note: This type exists with a great variety of the "Shih" (ten), and "Pao" characters

Y# 38.1 10 CASH Composition: Copper **Obverse:** Chinese legend: "Shih Wen" (10 Cash) at upper left **Reverse:** Date at upper center **Note:** Struck at the Kashgar Mint.

Date	Good	VG	F	VF	XF
ND(ca.1913)	7.50	15.00	20.00	35.00	—
AH1332	7.50	15.00	20.00	35.00	—
AH1333	7.50	15.00	20.00	35.00	—
AH1334	7.50	15.00	20.00	35.00	—

Y# F38 10 CASH Composition: Copper **Ruler:** Kuang-hsü **Obverse:** Chinese characters "Shih Wen" (10 Wen) at lower left **Reverse:** Upper Turki legend inverted

Date	Good	VG	F	VF	XF
AH1332	35.00	65.00	85.00	125	—

Y# 38.3 10 CASH Composition: Copper **Obverse:** Two lower right Chinese characters different **Reverse:** AH date at top **Note:** Struck at the Kashgar Mint.

Date	Good	VG	F	VF	XF
AH133-4 (1915)	50.00	75.00	125	200	—

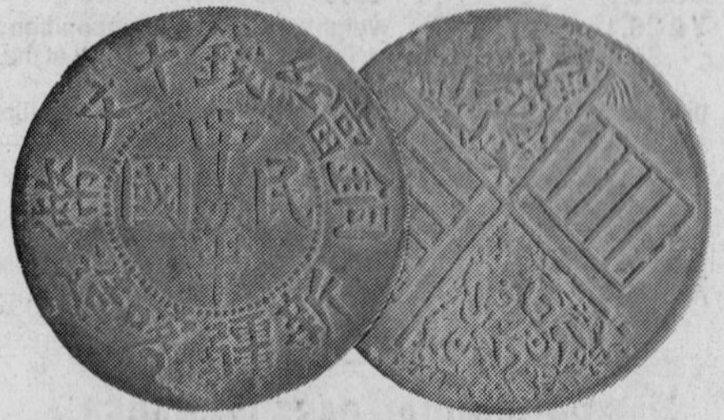

Y# 38.5 10 CASH Composition: Copper **Obverse:** Outer Chinese legend wtihout "Shih" of "Kashgar" at lower left **Reverse:** Turki legend in florals with "Zarb Kashgar" at top, similar to Y#A38.2 **Note:** Struck at the Kashgar Mint.

Date	Good	VG	F	VF	XF
AH1334 (1915)	37.50	60.00	100	150	—

Y# 38.6 10 CASH Composition: Copper **Reverse:** Single flower in lower Turki legend **Note:** Struck at the Kashgar Mint.

Date	Good	VG	F	VF	XF
AH1334	—	—	—	—	—

Y# 38.7 10 CASH Composition: Copper **Reverse:** Without flowers or florals in Turki legends **Note:** Struck at the Kashgar Mint.

Date	Good	VG	F	VF	XF
AH1334	—	—	—	—	—

Y# 38b.1 10 CASH Composition: Copper **Obverse:** Chinese legend "Min-kuo T'ung-yüan" in inner circle with "Kashgar" at right **Note:** Struck at the Kashgar Mint.

Date	Good	VG	F	VF	XF
AH1340	15.00	30.00	40.00	65.00	—

Y# 38b.2 10 CASH Composition: Copper **Obverse:** Outer Chinese legend rotated **Note:** Struck at the Kashgar Mint.

Date	Good	VG	F	VF	XF
AH134x	15.00	30.00	40.00	65.00	—

Y# C39 10 CASH Composition: Copper **Reverse:** Turki legend around crossed flags

Date	Good	VG	F	VF	XF
CD1921 Status unknown; rare	—	—	—	—	—

Y# 38a.3 10 CASH Composition: Copper **Reverse:** Turki legend rearranged **Note:** Struck at the Kashgar Mint.

Date	Good	VG	F	VF	XF
AH134x (1921)	5.00	10.00	15.00	25.00	—
AH1339 (1921)	5.00	10.00	15.00	25.00	—

Y# 38a.1 10 CASH Composition: Copper **Obverse:** Chinese date at upper right with rosette; Chinese legend in inner circle **Obv. Legend:** "Chung-hua Min-kuo: **Note:** Struck at the Kashgar Mint.

Date	Good	VG	F	VF	XF
AH1339 (1921)	5.00	10.00	15.00	25.00	—
AH1340 (1921)	5.00	10.00	15.00	25.00	—

Y# 38a.2 10 CASH Composition: Copper **Obverse:** Outer Chinese legend without "Shih" of "Kashgar" at upper left **Note:** Struck at the Kashgar Mint.

Date	Good	VG	F	VF	XF
AH134x (1921)	5.00	10.00	15.00	25.00	—

Y# 38a.5 10 CASH Composition: Copper **Obverse:** Crowded Chinese year "11" **Note:** Struck at Kashgar Mint.

Date	Good	VG	F	VF	XF
AH1340 (1921)	25.00	40.00	65.00	100	—

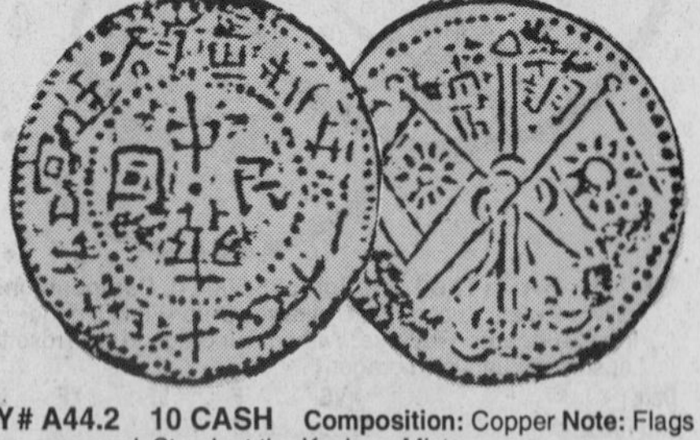

Y# A44.2 10 CASH Composition: Copper **Note:** Flags reversed; Struck at the Kashgar Mint.

Date	Good	VG	F	VF	XF
11(1922)	50.00	75.00	100	125	—

Y# A44.1 10 CASH **Composition:** Copper **Note:** Struck at the Kashgar Mint.

Date	Good	VG	F	VF	XF
11(1922)	50.00	75.00	100	125	—

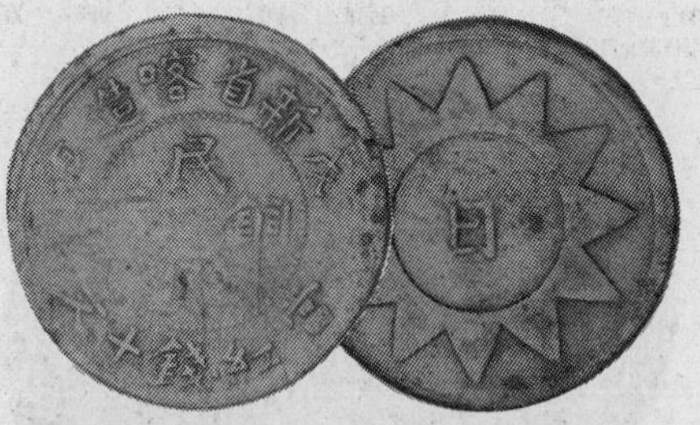

Y# B38c.1 10 CASH **Composition:** Copper **Obverse:** Chinese character "Jih" in solid sunburst

Date	Good	VG	F	VF	XF
CD(1928)	175	275	425	600	—

Y# B38c.4 10 CASH **Composition:** Copper **Obv. Legend:** Cyclic date at left and right like Y#B38.4

Date	Good	VG	F	VF	XF
CD(1928)	175	275	425	600	—

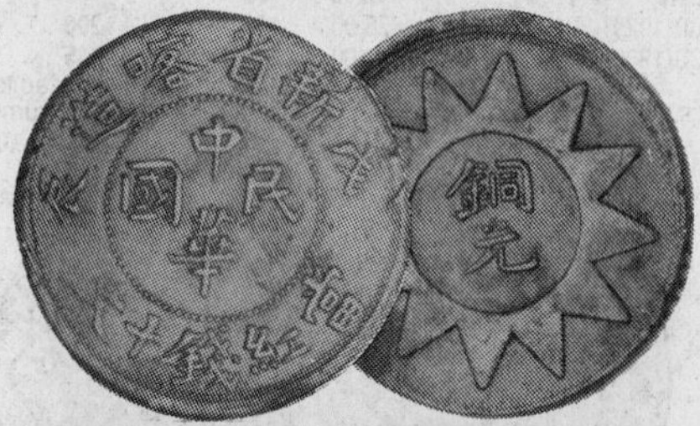

Y# B38.1 10 CASH **Composition:** Copper **Obverse:** Chinese legend in inner circle; Chinese date at left and right of upper legend **Obv. Legend:** "Chung Hua Min Kuo" **Reverse:** Chinese characters "T'ung Yüan" in solid sunburst

Date	Good	VG	F	VF	XF
CD(1928)	40.00	80.00	120	200	—

Y# B38c.2 10 CASH **Composition:** Copper **Obverse:** Like B38c.1 **Reverse:** Chinese character "Jih" in rayed sunburst **Note:** Struck at the Kashgar Mint.

Date	Good	VG	F	VF	XF
CD(1928)	175	275	425	600	—

Y# B38c.3 10 CASH **Composition:** Copper **Obverse:** Like Y#B38b.1 **Reverse:** Like Y#B38c.1 **Note:** Struck at the Kashgar Mint.

Date	Good	VG	F	VF	XF
CD(1928)	175	275	425	600	—

Y# B38d 10 CASH **Composition:** Copper **Obverse:** Chinese legend in inner circle **Obv. Legend:** "Min Kuo T'ung Yüan" **Reverse:** Chinese characters "T'ung Yüan" in solid sunburst **Note:** Struck at the Kashgar Mint.

Date	Good	VG	F	VF	XF
CD(1928)	125	175	300	400	—

Y# B38.2 10 CASH **Composition:** Copper **Obverse:** Upper legend **Obv. Legend:** "Hsinchiang Kashgar Tsao" **Reverse:** Small Chinese characters "T'ung-Yüan" in outlined sunburst **Note:** Struck at the Kashgar Mint.

Date	Good	VG	F	VF	XF
CD(1928)	30.00	70.00	100	180	—

Note: A similar coin with same upper legend and cyclical date 1929 at sides is reported

Y# B38.3 10 CASH **Composition:** Copper **Obverse:** Upper legend **Obv. Legend:** "Hsinchiang K'a Tsao" **Reverse:** Large Chinese characters "T'ung Yüan" in outlined sunburst **Note:** Struck at the Kashgar Mint.

Date	Good	VG	F	VF	XF
CD(1928)	15.00	23.00	30.00	50.00	—

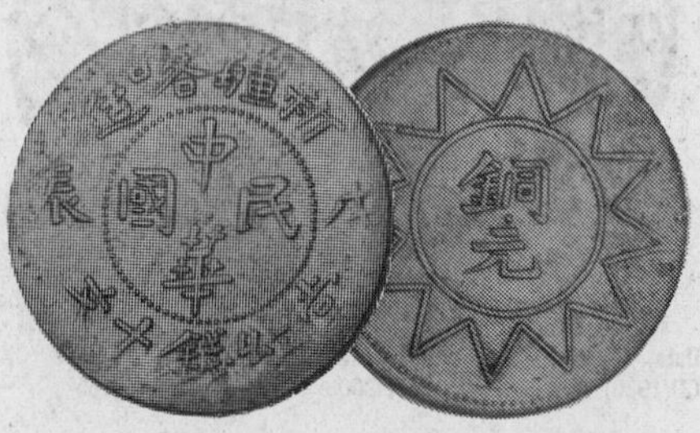

Y# B38.4 10 CASH **Composition:** Copper **Obverse:** Chinese date at left and right **Reverse:** Chinese characters "T'ung Yüan" in outlined sunburst **Note:** Struck at the Kashgar Mint.

Date	Good	VG	F	VF	XF
CD(1928)	3.00	5.50	8.00	16.00	—
CD(1929)	5.00	7.50	15.00	25.00	—

Y# B38.5 10 CASH **Composition:** Copper **Reverse:** Chinese characters "T'ung Yüan" in outlined finely rayed sunburst **Note:** Struck at the Kashgar Mint.

Date	Good	VG	F	VF	XF
CD(1928)	60.00	90.00	140	200	—

Y# B38b.1 10 CASH **Composition:** Copper **Obverse:** Legend in inner circle **Obv. Legend:** "Min-kuo T'ung Yüan" **Reverse:** Turki legend in solid sunburst **Note:** Struck at the Kashgar Mint.

Date	Good	VG	F	VF	XF
AH1346	125	175	300	400	—

Y# B38b.2 10 CASH **Composition:** Copper **Obverse:** Similar to Y#B838d **Reverse:** Similar to Y#B38b.1 **Note:** Struck at the Kashgar Mint.

Date	Good	VG	F	VF	XF
AH1346	150	200	350	500	—

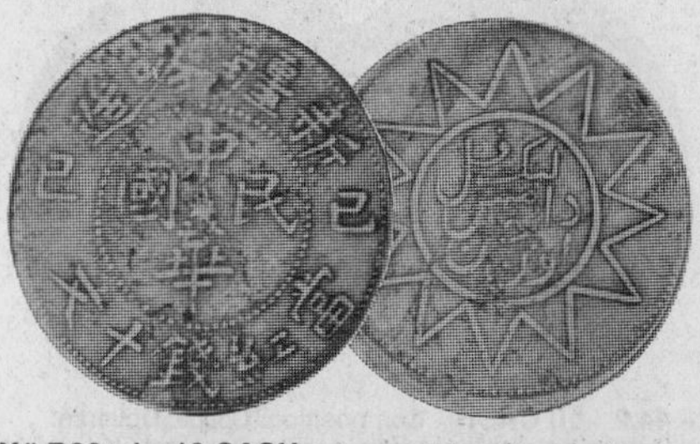

Y# B38a.1 10 CASH **Composition:** Copper **Obverse:** Chinese characters for date to left and right of "Chung Hua Min Kuo" in inner circle **Reverse:** Turki legend in oulined subnurst **Note:** Struck at the Kashgar Mint.

Date	Good	VG	F	VF	XF
CD(1929)	100	165	250	350	—

Y# B38a.2 10 CASH **Composition:** Copper **Obverse:** Upper legend **Obv. Legend:** "Hsinchiang K'ashih Tsao" **Note:** Struck at the Kashgar Mint.

Date	Good	VG	F	VF	XF
CD(1929)	75.00	100	125	150	—

Y# B38.6 10 CASH **Composition:** Copper **Obverse:** Upper legend **Reverse:** "Hsinchiang K'ashih Tsao" **Note:** Struck at the Kashgar Mint.

Date	Good	VG	F	VF	XF
CD(1929)	40.00	60.00	100	170	—

Y# 40.1 10 CASH **Composition:** Copper **Obverse:** Chinese legend in inner circle with "Hsin Chiang" at upper right **Obv. Legend:** Chung Hua Min Kuo **Reverse:** Flags with solid sunbursts with inner circles

Date	Good	VG	F	VF	XF
CD(1929)	7.00	12.00	16.50	25.00	40.00
CD(1930) Rare	—	—	—	—	—

Note: The cyclical date character at left exists closed, which is rare, and open for CD1929

Y# 44.6 10 CASH Composition: Copper **Reverse:** Reversed flags with large solid sunbursts **Note:** Struck at the Kashgar Mint.

Date	Good	VG	F	VF	XF
CD(1929)	3.00	7.00	13.00	18.00	—
CD(1930)	4.00	8.00	15.00	20.00	—

Y# 44.2 10 CASH Composition: Copper **Obverse:** Small eight-petalled rosette in center **Reverse:** Flag at right without inner circle **Note:** Struck at the Kashgar Mint.

Date	Good	VG	F	VF	XF
CD(1929) (1929)	4.50	7.50	12.00	16.00	—
CD(1930) (1930)	4.50	7.50	12.00	16.00	—

Y# 40.2 10 CASH Composition: Copper **Obverse:** Large starburst in center **Reverse:** Long streamers

Date	Good	VG	F	VF	XF
CD(1929) Rare	7.00	12.00	16.50	25.00	40.00

Note: Y#40 inscribed "Sheng Ch'eng" (provincial capital) in upper legend refers to Tihwa (Urumchi now Ürümqi)

Y# 40.3 10 CASH Composition: Copper **Obverse:** Cyclical date at upper right in legend **Note:** Struck at the Kashgar Mint.

Date	Good	VG	F	VF	XF
CD(1930) Rare	—	—	—	—	—

Y# 44.1 10 CASH Composition: Copper **Obverse:** Upper legend **Obv. Legend:** "Hsinchiang K'ashih Tsao" **Reverse:** Flags with wide outlined sungursts; flags at right with inner circle **Note:** Struck at the Kashgar Mint.

Date	Good	VG	F	VF	XF
CD(1929)	5.00	8.50	17.50	32.50	—

Y# 44.3 10 CASH Composition: Copper **Obverse:** Star with rays in center **Note:** Struck at the Kashgar Mint.

Date	Good	VG	F	VF	XF
CD(1930)	8.50	17.50	22.50	37.50	—

Y# 44.4 10 CASH Composition: Copper **Obverse:** Eight-petalled rosette in center **Reverse:** Flags with narrow outlined sunbursts **Note:** Struck at the Kashgar Mint.

Date	Good	VG	F	VF	XF
CD(1930)	10.00	20.00	35.00	55.00	—

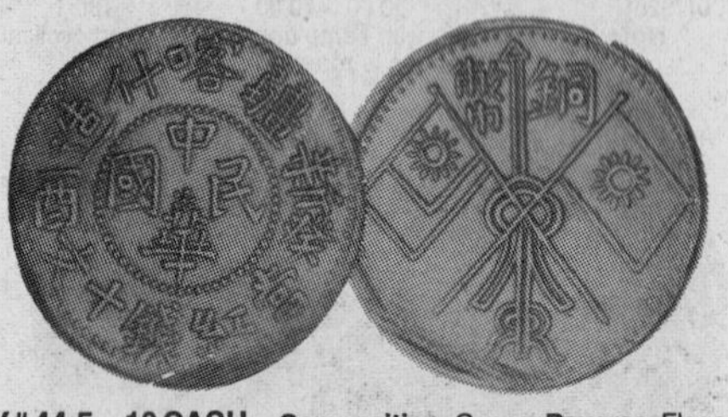

Y# 44.5 10 CASH Composition: Copper **Reverse:** Flags with solid sunbursts **Note:** Struck at the Kashgar Mint.

Date	Good	VG	F	VF	XF
CD(1933)	4.00	8.00	15.00	20.00	—

Y# 44.7 10 CASH Composition: Copper **Reverse:** Reversed flags with small solid sunbursts **Note:** Struck at the Kashgar Mint.

Date	Good	VG	F	VF	XF
CD(1930)	25.00	50.00	100	165	—

Y# 44.8 10 CASH Composition: Copper **Obverse:** Uper legend **Obv. Legend:** "Hsinchiang K'ashih Tsao" **Note:** Struck at the Kashgar Mint.

Date	Good	VG	F	VF	XF
CD(1929)	75.00	100	125	150	—

Y# 44.9 10 CASH Composition: Copper **Reverse:** Reversed flags with large "flower petal" outlined sunbursts **Note:** Struck at the Kashgar Mint.

Date	Good	VG	F	VF	XF
CD(1930)	4.00	8.00	15.00	20.00	—

Y# 44.10 10 CASH Composition: Copper **Reverse:** Flags reversed **Note:** Struck at the Kashgar Mint.

Date	Good	VG	F	VF	XF
CD(1930)	—	—	—	—	—

Y# 48 20 CASH Composition: Copper **Note:** Struck at the Kashgar Mint.

Date	Good	VG	F	VF	XF
AH133x (1921) Rare	—	—	—	—	—

Y# A41.1 20 CASH Composition: Copper **Obverse:** Chinese legend in inner circle with "Hsin Chiang" at upper right **Obv. Legend:** Chung-hua Min-kuo

Date	Good	VG	F	VF	XF
CD(1929)	75.00	125	200	300	—
CD(1930)	85.00	140	225	335	—

Note: Y#A41.1 inscribed "Sheng Ch'eng" (provincial capital) in upper legend refers to Tihwa (Urumchi now Urumqi)

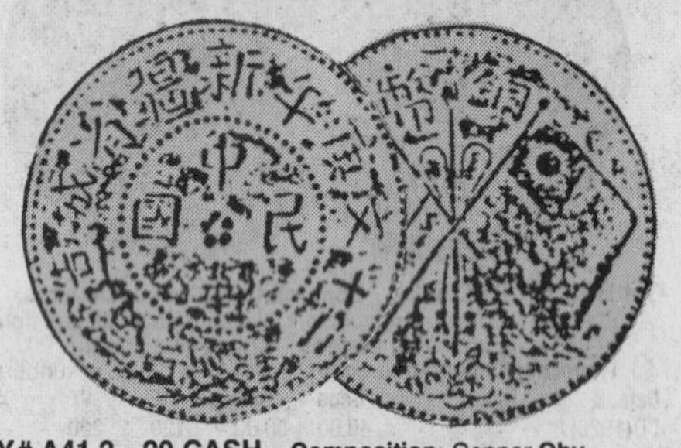

Y# A41.2 20 CASH Composition: Copper **Obv. Legend:** Cyclical date at upper right

Date	Good	VG	F	VF	XF
CD(1930) Rare	—	—	—	—	—

Y# 39.1 20 CASH Composition: Copper **Obverse:** Eight-petalled rosette in center **Reverse:** Two stripes in flags have arabesques

Date	VG	F	VF	XF	Unc
ND	10.00	16.50	20.00	27.50	—

Y# 39.2 20 CASH **Composition:** Copper **Obverse:** Five-petalled rosette in center

Date	VG	F	VF	XF	Unc
ND	50.00	100	150	225	—

Y# 39.3 20 CASH **Composition:** Copper **Reverse:** Without arabesques in flag

Date	VG	F	VF	XF	Unc
ND Restrike	—	—	—	50.00	75.00

Y# 43 5 MISCALS **Weight:** 17.3000 g. **Composition:** Silver **Obverse:** Stars dividing Chinese legends **Reverse:** Crossed flags dividing Turki legend **Note:** Struck at the Kashgar Mint.

Date	VG	F	VF	XF	Unc
AH1331	40.00	75.00	160	275	—
AH1332	40.00	75.00	160	275	—

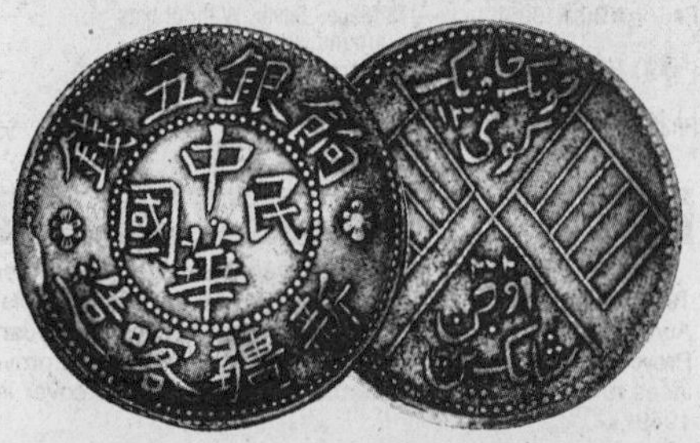

Y# 43.1 5 MISCALS **Weight:** 17.3000 g. **Composition:** Silver **Obverse:** Rosettes dividing Chinese legend **Note:** Varieties exist; Struck at the Kashgar Mint.

Date	VG	F	VF	XF	Unc
AH1330	35.00	65.00	135	225	—
AH1331	35.00	65.00	135	225	—
AH1332	35.00	65.00	135	225	—
AH13-32	35.00	65.00	135	225	—

Y# 43.3 5 MISCALS **Weight:** 17.3000 g. **Composition:** Silver **Obverse:** Rosette in center, floral arrangements dividing Chinese legend **Note:** Varieties exist; Struck at the Kashgar Mint.

Date	VG	F	VF	XF	Unc
AH13-32	40.00	75.00	160	275	—
AH133-4	45.00	85.00	185	325	—

Y# 43.2 5 MISCALS **Weight:** 17.3000 g. **Composition:** Silver **Obverse:** Rosettes dividing Chinese legend **Note:** Struck at the Kashgar Mint.

Date	VG	F	VF	XF	Unc
AH1334	45.00	85.00	185	325	—
AH133-4	45.00	85.00	185	325	—

Note: Varieties exist.

Y# 43.4 5 MISCALS **Weight:** 17.3000 g. **Composition:** Silver **Obverse:** Stars divide rotated outer Chinese legend **Note:** Struck at the Kashgar Mint.

Date	VG	F	VF	XF	Unc
AHx13x(ca.1916)	—	—	—	—	—

Note: Considered contemporary forgeries by some experts

Y# 41 5 MISCALS (5 Mace) **Weight:** 17.9000 g. **Composition:** Silver **Reverse:** Two stripes in flags have arabesques

Date	VG	F	VF	XF	Unc
1(1912)	40.00	65.00	150	200	—

Y# 41a 5 MISCALS (5 Mace) **Weight:** 17.9000 g. **Composition:** Silver **Reverse:** Four stripes in flags have arabesques

Date	VG	F	VF	XF	Unc
1(1912)	40.00	65.00	150	200	—

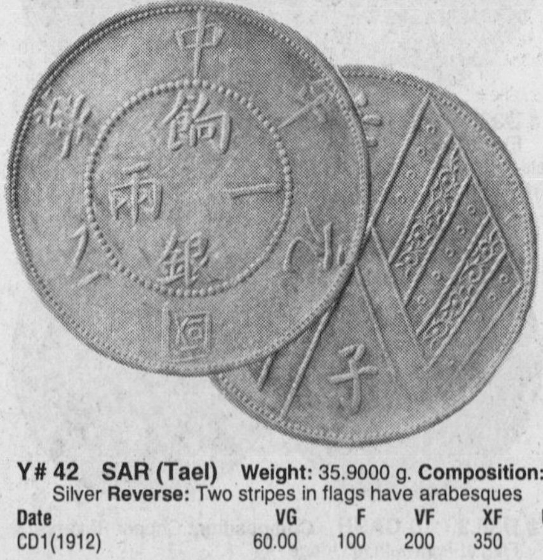

Y# 42 SAR (Tael) **Weight:** 35.9000 g. **Composition:** Silver **Reverse:** Two stripes in flags have arabesques

Date	VG	F	VF	XF	Unc
CD1(1912)	60.00	100	200	350	—

Y# 42a SAR (Tael) **Weight:** 35.9000 g. **Composition:** Silver **Obverse:** Similar to Y#42 **Reverse:** Four stripes in flags have arabesques

Date	VG	F	VF	XF	Unc
CD1(1912)	60.00	100	200	350	—

Y# 45 SAR (Tael) **Weight:** 35.0000 g. **Composition:** Silver **Obverse:** Large characters **Reverse:** Rosette at top between wheat ears

Date	VG	F	VF	XF	Unc
ND(1917)	15.00	20.00	32.50	50.00	—

Y# 45.1 SAR (Tael) **Weight:** 35.0000 g. **Composition:** Silver **Obverse:** Similar to Y#45 but with small characters **Reverse:** Without rosette at top

Date	VG	F	VF	XF	Unc
ND(1917)	15.00	20.00	32.50	50.00	—

Y# 45.2 SAR (Tael) **Weight:** 35.0000 g. **Composition:** Silver **Reverse:** Rosette at top between branches

Date	VG	F	VF	XF	Unc
ND(1918)	20.00	25.00	42.50	75.00	—

Y# 46 DOLLAR **Composition:** Silver **Obverse:** Similar to Y#46.2 but with larger Chinese characters **Reverse:** Think pointed base "1"

Date	VG	F	VF	XF	Unc
38(1949)	12.50	20.00	32.50	50.00	—

Y# 46.1 DOLLAR **Composition:** Silver **Obverse:** Similar to Y#46.2 but with larger Chinese characters **Reverse:** Think pointed base "1" with large serif

Date	VG	F	VF	XF	Unc
38(1949)	12.50	20.00	30.50	50.00	—

Y# 46.2 DOLLAR Composition: Silver **Obverse:** Smaller Chinese characters **Reverse:** Thin pointed base "1"

Date	VG	F	VF	XF	Unc
38(1949)	12.50	20.00	32.50	50.00	—

Y# 46.3 DOLLAR Composition: Silver **Reverse:** Square-based "1"

Date	VG	F	VF	XF	Unc
38(1949)	15.00	25.00	45.00	80.00	—

Y# 46.4 DOLLAR Composition: Silver **Obverse:** Outlined Chinese characters "Yüan" in center

Date	VG	F	VF	XF	Unc
38(1949)	15.00	25.00	60.00	100	—

Y# 46.5 DOLLAR Composition: Silver **Note:** 9-4-9-1 (1949) at bottom

Date	VG	F	VF	XF	Unc
1949	75.00	125	175	250	—

ISLAMIC REPUBLIC OF EASTERN TURKESTAN

MILLED COINAGE

Y# E38.1 20 CASH Composition: Copper **Note:** 32-34 millimeters.

Date	Good	VG	F	VF	XF
AH1352	60.00	120	200	300	—
AH1352 Retrograde	60.00	120	200	300	—

Y# E38.2 20 CASH Composition: Copper **Reverse:** Flags reversed

Date	Good	VG	F	VF	XF
AH1352	50.00	100	150	200	—

Note: Considered contemporary fantasies by some experts

Y# E39 MISCAL Composition: Silver **Obverse:** Turki legend around central Turki legend **Obv. Legend:** "Sharket Turkhestan Cumhuriyet Islamiyesi" around "Muskuk, sanah 1252" **Reverse:** Turki legend: "Zarb Kashgar"

Date	Good	VG	F	VF	XF
AH1352 Rare	—	—	—	—	—

Note: Varieties of sun with eight and nine rays exist

UIGHURISTAN REPUBLIC

Uighuristan was a rebel Islamic republic that sought independence from China. The rebellion was quickly crushed. Coins of the Republic were all made by over-striking on Kashgar Republic 10 Cash coins.

MILLED COINAGE

Y# D38.1 10 CASH Composition: Copper **Reverse:** Flag at right without fringe

Date	Good	VG	F	VF	XF
AH1352	50.00	100	160	250	—

Y# D38.2 10 CASH Composition: Copper **Reverse:** Flag at right with partial fringe

Date	Good	VG	F	VF	XF
AH1352	50.00	100	160	250	—

Y# D38.3 10 CASH Composition: Copper **Reverse:** Flag at right with full fringe

Date	Good	VG	F	VF	XF
AH1352	50.00	100	160	250	—

Note: Encountered overstruck on various earlier Republican Series 10 Cash

Y# G38 20 CASH Composition: Copper **Obverse:** Similar to 20 Cash, Y#E38.3 **Reverse:** Small flag at left

Date	Good	VG	F	VF	XF
AH1352	—	—	—	—	—

Y# E38.3 20 CASH Composition: Copper **Reverse:** Sun in partial frame in left flag, denomination given as two wen (sic) **Note:** Size varies 32-34 milimeters.

Date	Good	VG	F	VF	XF
AH1352 Rare	—	—	—	—	—

Y# E38.4 20 CASH Composition: Copper **Reverse:** Large sun in national flag at left **Note:** Varieties exist.

Date	Good	VG	F	VF	XF
AH1352	50.00	100	150	200	—

Note: Crudely cut Chinese denomination appears as 2 instead of 20; also encountered overstruck on 10 Cash, Y#44 varieties

PATTERNS

Including off metal strikes

KM#	Date	Mintage	Identification	Mkt Val
Pn1	ND(ca.1906)	—	Mace. Copper. SUNGAREI. Y#10	1,600
Pn2	ND(ca.1906)	—	2 Mace. Silver. SUNGAREI. Y#11	3,000
Pn3	ND(ca.1906)	—	2 Mace. Copper. SUNGAREI.	1,200
Pn4	ND(ca.1906)	—	4 Mace. Silver. SUNGAREI.	8,000
Pn5	ND(ca.1906)	—	4 Mace. Brass. SUNGAREI.	1,250
Pn6	ND(ca.1906)	—	5 Mace. Silver. Without bats around large dragon.	—
Pn7	ND(ca.1906)	—	7 Mace. Silver. SUNGAREI. 2 Candareens, Y#12.	—
Pn30	AH1324	—	Tael. Silver.	—

SUIYUAN PROVINCE

In November 1913, the central government grouped together 19 Mongolian and 12 Shansi districts to form the Suiyuan Special Administrative Zone. In 1928, the name was changed to Suiyuan Province. The province was joined with other Mongolian provinces to form Inner Mongolia after the communist takeover in 1949.

REPUBLIC

MILLED COINAGE

KM# 3 FEN Composition: Shell Casing Brass **Obverse:** White Tower **Reverse:** Ancient spade coin between Yi and Fen

Date	VG	F	VF	XF	Unc
38(1949)	175	250	350	550	—

KM# 5 5 FEN Composition: Shell Casing Brass **Obverse:** White Tower **Reverse:** Ancient spade coin between Wu(5) and Fen

Date	VG	F	VF	XF	Unc
38(1949)	600	750	1,000	1,350	—

SZECHUAN PROVINCE

Sichuan

A province located in south-central China. The largest of the traditional Chinese provinces, Szechuan (Sichuan) is a plateau region watered by many rivers. These rivers carry much trading traffic. Agriculture or mining are the occupational choices of most of the populace. In World War II the national capital was moved to Chungking in Szechuan (Sichuan). Chengtu was an active imperial mint that opened in 1732 and was in practically continuous operation until the advent of modern equipment. Modern minting was introduced in the province when Chengtu began milled coinage in 1898. A mint was authorized for Chungking in 1905 but it did not begin operations until 1913. The Chengtu Mint was looted by soldiers in 1925. The last republic issues from Szechuan (Sichuan) were dated 1932.

The machinery for the first Szechuan (Sichuan) Mint was produced in New Jersey and the dies were engraved in Philadelphia. The mint was opened in 1898, but closed within a few months and did not reopen until 1901. There is no doubt now that Y#234-238 (K#145-149) were the first issues of this mint, contrary to the Kann listings.

EMPIRE

PROVINCIAL CAST COINAGE

C# 24-9 CASH **Composition:** Cast Brass **Ruler:** Kuang-hsü **Obverse:** Inscription: Kuang-hsü T'ung-pao **Reverse:** Inscription: Manchu Boo-Cuwan **Note:** Struck at Chuan (Cheng tu)

Date	Good	VG	F	VF	XF
ND(1875-1908)	4.50	7.50	11.50	22.50	—

MILLED COINAGE

Y# 225 5 CASH **Composition:** Copper **Ruler:** Kuang-hsü **Obverse:** Inscription: Kuang-hsü Yüan-pao; Manchu at center **Reverse:** Side view dragon

Date	Mintage	VG	F	VF	XF	Unc
ND(1903-04)	85,000	50.00	70.00	100	150	—

Y# 225a 5 CASH **Composition:** Brass **Ruler:** Kuang-hsü **Obverse:** Inscription: Kuang-hsü Yüan-pao

Date	VG	F	VF	XF	Unc
ND(1903-04) Rare	—	—	—	—	—

Y# A229 (YA228) 5 CASH **Composition:** Brass **Ruler:** Kuang-hsü **Obverse:** Inscription: Kuang-hsü Yüan-pao; Y#228 **Reverse:** Y#225

Date	VG	F	VF	XF	Unc
ND(1903-04)	100	140	200	300	—

Y# 228 5 CASH **Composition:** Brass **Ruler:** Kuang-hsü **Obverse:** Inscription: Kuang-hsü Yüan-pao; flower at center **Reverse:** Flying dragon

Date	VG	F	VF	XF	Unc
ND(1903-04)	350	500	750	—	—

Y# 226 10 CASH **Composition:** Copper **Ruler:** Kuang-hsü **Obverse:** Inscription: Kuang-hsü Yüan-pao; with thick Manchu in center, large rosettes

Date	Mintage	VG	F	VF	XF	Unc
ND(1903-05)	95,960,000	12.50	25.00	35.00	60.00	—

Y# 226.1 10 CASH **Composition:** Copper **Ruler:** Kuang-hsü **Obverse:** Inscription: Kuang-hsü Yüan-pao; with thin Manchu in center, small rosettes

Date	VG	F	VF	XF	Unc
ND(1903-05)	22.50	45.00	70.00	125	—

Y# 226.2 10 CASH **Composition:** Copper **Ruler:** Kuang-hsü **Obverse:** Inscription: Kuang-hsü Yüan-pao; with large rosettes

Date	VG	F	VF	XF	Unc
ND(1903-05)	20.00	40.00	60.00	100	—

Y# 229 10 CASH **Composition:** Copper **Ruler:** Kuang-hsü **Obverse:** Inscription: Kuang-hsü Yüan-pao; legend with two characters at bottom, 6-9 milimeters apart **Reverse:** Trident-shaped flame on dragon's body below letters CHU

Date	VG	F	VF	XF	Unc
ND(1903-05)	4.00	6.50	10.00	17.50	—

Y# 229.1 10 CASH **Composition:** Copper **Ruler:** Kuang-hsü **Obverse:** Inscription: Kuang-hsü Yüan-pao; legend with characters at bottom, 4-5 milimeters apart

Date	VG	F	VF	XF	Unc
ND(1903-05)	4.00	6.50	10.00	17.50	—

Y# 229.2 10 CASH **Composition:** Copper **Ruler:** Kuang-hsü **Obverse:** Inscription: Kuang-hsü Yüan-pao; with Manchu at 3 o'clock is lower in relation to center characters

Date	VG	F	VF	XF	Unc
ND(1903-05)	4.00	6.50	10.00	17.50	—

Y# 229.3 10 CASH **Composition:** Copper **Ruler:** Kuang-hsü **Obverse:** Inscription: Kuang-hsü Yüan-pao; with characters 6-9 milimeters apart **Reverse:** Trident-shaped flame below letters HUE

Date	VG	F	VF	XF	Unc
ND(1903-05)	4.00	6.50	10.00	17.50	—

Y# 229.3a 10 CASH **Composition:** Brass **Ruler:** Kuang-hsü **Obverse:** Inscription: Kuang-hsü Yüan-pao

Date	VG	F	VF	XF	Unc
ND(1903-05)	4.00	6.50	10.00	17.50	—

Y# 229.4 10 CASH **Composition:** Brass **Ruler:** Kuang-hsü **Obverse:** Inscription: Kuang-hsü Yüan-pao; with characters 4-5 milimeters apart

Date	VG	F	VF	XF	Unc
ND(1903-05)	4.00	6.50	10.00	17.50	—

Y# 229.5 10 CASH **Composition:** Brass **Ruler:** Kuang-hsü **Obverse:** Inscription: Kuang-hsü Yüan-pao; with bottom characters 6-9 milimeters apart **Reverse:** Without trident-shaped flame, instead a cloud pointing to the letter U

Date	VG	F	VF	XF	Unc
ND(1903-05)	2.50	4.00	7.50	12.00	—

Y# 229.5a 10 CASH **Composition:** Copper **Ruler:** Kuang-hsü **Obverse:** Inscription: Kuang-hsü Yüan-pao

Date	VG	F	VF	XF	Unc
ND(1903-05)	3.00	5.00	10.00	15.00	—

Y# 229.6 10 CASH **Composition:** Brass **Ruler:** Kuang-hsü **Obverse:** Inscription: Kuang-hsü Yüan-pao; with characters 4-5 milimeters apart

Date	VG	F	VF	XF	Unc
ND(1903-05)	4.00	6.00	10.00	17.50	—

Y# 229.6a 10 CASH **Composition:** Copper **Ruler:** Kuang-hsü **Obverse:** Inscription: Kuang-hsü Yüan-pao

Date	VG	F	VF	XF	Unc
ND(1903-05)	2.00	3.00	5.50	10.00	—

Y# 229.7 10 CASH **Composition:** Brass **Ruler:** Kuang-hsü **Obverse:** Inscription: Kuang-hsü Yüan-pao; with Manchu at 3 o'clock is lower

Date	VG	F	VF	XF	Unc
ND(1903-05)	3.75	6.00	10.00	17.50	—

Y# 229.7a 10 CASH **Composition:** Copper **Ruler:** Kuang-hsü **Obverse:** Inscription: Kuang-hsü Yüan-pao

Date	VG	F	VF	XF	Unc
ND(1903-05)	2.00	3.50	6.00	9.00	—

Y# 229.8 10 CASH **Composition:** Brass **Ruler:** Kuang-hsü **Obverse:** Inscription: Kuang-hsü Yüan-pao; with characters 4-5 milimeters apart **Reverse:** Without cloud below CHU, high point of dragon's body below letter C, tail joins body above S in CASH

Date	VG	F	VF	XF	Unc
ND(1903-05)	4.00	6.00	9.00	17.50	—

Y# 229.8a 10 CASH **Composition:** Copper **Ruler:** Kuang-hsü **Obverse:** Inscription: Kuang-hsü Yüan-pao

Date	VG	F	VF	XF	Unc
ND(1903-05)	2.00	3.50	6.00	9.00	—

Y# 229.9 10 CASH **Composition:** Copper **Ruler:** Kuang-hsü **Obverse:** Inscription: Kuang-hsü Yüan-pao **Reverse:** High point of dragon's body below letter H, tail joins body above letter C in CASH

Date	VG	F	VF	XF	Unc
ND(1903-05)	2.00	3.50	6.00	9.00	—

Y# 231 10 CASH **Composition:** Copper **Ruler:** Kuang-hsü **Obverse:** Inscription: Kuang-hsü Yüan-pao

Date	VG	F	VF	XF	Unc
ND(1903-05)	150	200	225	275	—

Y# 10t 10 CASH **Composition:** Copper **Ruler:** Kuang-hsü **Obverse:** Inscription: Ta-ch'ing T'ung-pi **Rev. Legend:** Kuang-hsü Nien-tsao, TAI-CHING-TI-KUO...

Date	Mintage	VG	F	VF	XF	Unc
CD(1906)	337,748,000	1.00	1.50	3.00	6.00	—

Y# 20t.1 10 CASH **Composition:** Copper **Ruler:** Hsüan-t'ung **Obverse:** Inscription: Ta-ch'ing T'ung-pi; with bottom of Manchu word at 11 o'clock curls to left **Rev. Legend:** Hsüan-t'ung Nien-tsao, TAI-CHING-TI-KUO...

Date	Mintage	VG	F	VF	XF	Unc
CD(1909)	231,930,000	1.00	1.50	3.00	6.00	—

Y# 20t.1a 10 CASH **Composition:** Brass **Ruler:** Hsüan-t'ung **Obverse:** Inscription: Ta-ch'ing T'ung-pi **Rev. Legend:** Hsüan-t'ung Nien-tsao, TAI-CHING-TI-KUO...

Date	VG	F	VF	XF	Unc
CD(1909)	3.00	5.00	10.00	15.00	—

Y# 20t.2 10 CASH **Composition:** Copper **Ruler:** Hsüan-t'ung **Obverse:** Inscription: Ta-ch'ing T'ung-pi; with bottom of Manchu word at 11 o'clock curls to right **Rev. Legend:** Hsüan-t'ung Nien-tsao, TAI-CHING-TI-KUO...

Date	VG	F	VF	XF	Unc
CD(1909)	5.00	9.00	12.00	17.50	—

Y# 227 20 CASH **Composition:** Copper **Ruler:** Kuang-hsü **Obverse:** Inscription: Kuang-hsü Yüan-pao

Date	Mintage	VG	F	VF	XF	Unc
ND(1903-05)	25,319,000	100	125	175	250	—

Y# 230 20 CASH **Composition:** Copper **Ruler:** Kuang-hsü **Obverse:** Inscription: Kuang-hsü Yüan-pao; with small Manchu at 3 and 9 o'clock **Reverse:** Trident flame points to E of SZE

Date	VG	F	VF	XF	Unc
ND(1903-05)	10.00	15.00	30.00	50.00	—

Y# 230.1 20 CASH **Composition:** Copper **Ruler:** Kuang-hsü **Obverse:** Inscription: Kuang-hsü Yüan-pao; with large Manchu at 3 and 9 o'clock **Reverse:** Large trident flame points to C of CHUEN **Note:** Varieties exist.

Date	VG	F	VF	XF	Unc
ND(1903-05)	30.00	50.00	80.00	150	—

Y# 230.3 20 CASH **Composition:** Copper **Ruler:** Kuang-hsü **Obverse:** Inscription: Kuang-hsü Yüan-pao; with large Manchu **Reverse:** Trident flame below ZE

Date	VG	F	VF	XF	Unc
ND(1903-05)	15.00	30.00	50.00	80.00	—

Y# 230.4 20 CASH **Composition:** Copper **Ruler:** Kuang-hsü **Obverse:** Inscription: Kuang-hsü Yüan-pao **Reverse:** Trident flame below CHU of CHUEN, large letters

Date	VG	F	VF	XF	Unc
ND(1903-05)	30.00	60.00	100	160	—

Y# 230.5 20 CASH **Composition:** Copper **Ruler:** Kuang-hsü **Obverse:** Inscription: Kuang-hsü Yüan-pao **Reverse:** Trident flame points to E of CHUEN, small letters

Date	VG	F	VF	XF	Unc
ND(1903-05)	—	—	—	—	—

Y# 230.6 20 CASH **Composition:** Copper **Ruler:** Kuang-hsü **Obverse:** Inscription: Kuang-hsü Yüan-pao; with different small Manchu **Reverse:** Large 5-petalled rosettes, dragon differs

Date	VG	F	VF	XF	Unc
ND(1903-05)	12.50	20.00	35.00	60.00	—

Y# 230.7a 20 CASH **Composition:** Brass **Ruler:** Kuang-hsü **Obverse:** Inscription: Kuang-hsü Yüan-pao; with small Manchu **Reverse:** Larger cloud below CHUEN

Date	VG	F	VF	XF	Unc
ND(1903-05)	15.00	25.00	40.00	70.00	—

Y# 11t 20 CASH **Composition:** Copper **Obverse:** Inscription: Ta-ch'ing T'ung-pi

Date	Mintage	VG	F	VF	XF	Unc
CD(1906)	51,028,000	10.00	22.50	35.00	60.00	—

Y# 21t.1 20 CASH **Composition:** Copper **Obverse:** Inscription: Ta-ch'ing T'ung-pi; with bottom of Manchu word at 11 o'clock curls right

Date	Mintage	VG	F	VF	XF	Unc
CD(1909)	33,414,000	15.00	27.50	40.00	70.00	—

Y# 21t.1a 20 CASH **Composition:** Brass **Obverse:** Inscription: Ta-ch'ing T'ung-pi

Date	VG	F	VF	XF	Unc
CD(1909)	25.00	35.00	65.00	100	—

Y# 21t.2 20 CASH **Composition:** Copper **Obverse:** Inscription: Ta-ch'ing T'ung-pi; with bottom of Manchu word at 11 o'clock curls left

Date	VG	F	VF	XF	Unc
CD(1909)	15.00	27.50	40.00	70.00	—

Y# 234 5 CENTS **Weight:** 1.3000 g. **Composition:** 0.8200 Silver .0343 oz. ASW **Ruler:** Kuang-hsü **Obverse:** Inscription: Kuang-hsü Yüan-pao

Date	Mintage	VG	F	VF	XF	Unc
ND(1898; 1901-08)	671,000	4.50	12.50	17.50	30.00	80.00

Y# 234.1 5 CENTS **Weight:** 1.3000 g. **Composition:** 0.8200 Silver .0343 oz. ASW **Ruler:** Kuang-hsü **Obverse:** Inscription: Kuang-hsü Yüan-pao **Reverse:** With errors in the English legend

Date	VG	F	VF	XF	Unc
ND(1901-08)	5.00	15.00	25.00	40.00	90.00

Y# 239 5 CENTS **Weight:** 1.3000 g. **Composition:** 0.8200 Silver .0343 oz. ASW **Ruler:** Hsüan-t'ung **Obverse:** Inscription: Hsüan-t'ung Yüan-pao

Date	Mintage	VG	F	VF	XF	Unc
ND(1910)	566,000	6.50	20.00	30.00	55.00	120

Y# 235 10 CENTS **Weight:** 2.6000 g. **Composition:** 0.8200 Silver .0686 oz. ASW **Ruler:** Kuang-hsü **Obverse:** Inscription: Kuang-hsü Yüan-pao

Date	Mintage	VG	F	VF	XF	Unc
ND(1898; 1901-08)	1,274,000	3.50	10.00	20.00	30.00	90.00

Y# 240 10 CENTS **Weight:** 2.6000 g. **Composition:** 0.8200 Silver .0686 oz. ASW **Ruler:** Hsüan-t'ung **Obverse:** Inscription: Hsüan-t'ung Yüan-pao

Date	Mintage	VG	F	VF	XF	Unc
ND(1909-11)	278,000	8.50	25.00	30.00	55.00	120

Y# 236 20 CENTS **Weight:** 5.3000 g. **Composition:** 0.8200 Silver .1397 oz. ASW **Ruler:** Kuang-hsü **Obverse:** Inscription: Kuang-hsü Yüan-pao **Reverse:** Five flames on pearl

Date	Mintage	VG	F	VF	XF	Unc
ND(1898; 1901-08)	897,000	3.50	10.00	20.00	40.00	100

Y# 236.1 20 CENTS **Weight:** 5.3000 g. **Composition:** 0.8200 Silver .1397 oz. ASW **Ruler:** Kuang-hsü **Obverse:** Inscription: Kuang-hsü Yüan-pao **Reverse:** Six flames on pearl

Date	VG	F	VF	XF	Unc
ND(1898; 1901-08)	3.50	10.00	20.00	40.00	100

Y# 236.2 20 CENTS **Weight:** 5.3000 g. **Composition:** 0.8200 Silver .1397 oz. ASW **Ruler:** Kuang-hsü **Obverse:** Inscription: Kuang-hsü Yüan-pao **Reverse:** Seven flames on pearl

Date	VG	F	VF	XF	Unc
ND(1898; 1901-08)	3.50	10.00	20.00	40.00	100

Y# 236.3 20 CENTS **Weight:** 5.3000 g. **Composition:** 0.8200 Silver .1397 oz. ASW **Ruler:** Kuang-hsü **Obverse:** Inscription: Kuang-hsü Yüan-pao **Reverse:** Various errors in English legend

Date	VG	F	VF	XF	Unc
ND(1901-08)	5.00	15.00	25.00	50.00	125

Y# 241 20 CENTS **Weight:** 5.3000 g. **Composition:** 0.8200 Silver .1397 oz. ASW **Ruler:** Hsüan-t'ung **Obverse:** Inscription: Hsüan-t'ung Yüan-pao

Date	Mintage	VG	F	VF	XF	Unc
ND(1909-11) Rare	41,000	—	—	—	—	—

Y# 237 50 CENTS **Weight:** 13.2000 g. **Composition:** 0.8600 Silver .3650 oz. ASW **Ruler:** Kuang-hsü **Obverse:** Inscription: Kuang-hsü Yüan-pao **Reverse:** Dragon with narrow face, small cross at either side, large fireball

Date	Mintage	VG	F	VF	XF	Unc
ND(1898; 1901-08)	474,000	7.50	22.50	40.00	100	300

Y# 237.1 50 CENTS **Weight:** 13.2000 g. **Composition:** 0.8600 Silver .3650 oz. ASW **Ruler:** Kuang-hsü **Obverse:** Inscription: Kuang-hsü Yüan-pao **Reverse:** Various errors in English legend

Date	VG	F	VF	XF	Unc
ND(1901-08)	8.50	25.00	50.00	100	225

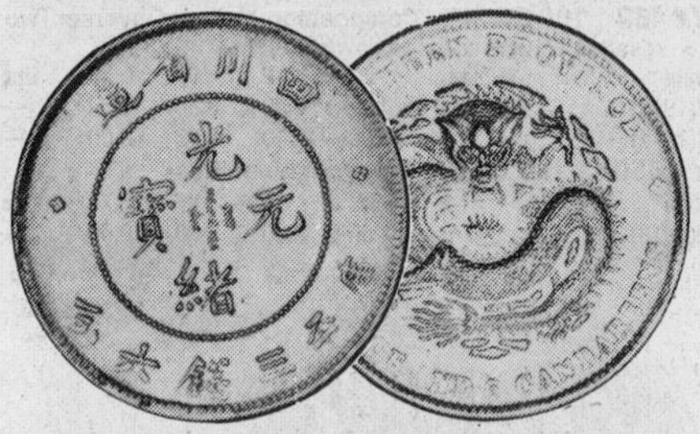

Y# 237.2 50 CENTS **Weight:** 13.2000 g. **Composition:** 0.8600 Silver .3650 oz. ASW **Ruler:** Kuang-hsü **Obverse:** Inscription: Kuang-hsü Yüan-pao **Reverse:** Dragon with tapering face and small chin, small fireball, small cross at either side of dragon

Date	VG	F	VF	XF	Unc
ND(1901-08)	11.50	—	40.00	100	200

Y# 237.3 50 CENTS **Weight:** 13.2000 g. **Composition:** 0.8600 Silver .3650 oz. ASW **Ruler:** Kuang-hsü **Obverse:** Inscription: Kuang-hsü Yüan-pao **Reverse:** Dragon with wide face and smaller fireball, thicker spines on top of dragon's head, small cross at either side of dragon

Date	VG	F	VF	XF	Unc
ND(1901-08)	7.50	22.50	40.00	100	200

Y# 242 50 CENTS **Weight:** 13.2000 g. **Composition:** 0.8600 Silver **Ruler:** Hsüan-t'ung **Obverse:** Inscription: Hsüan-t'ung Yüan-pao

Date	Mintage	VG	F	VF	XF	Unc
ND(1909-11)	38,000	25.00	75.00	130	180	325

Y# 242.1 50 CENTS **Weight:** 13.2000 g. **Composition:** 0.8600 Silver **Ruler:** Hsüan-t'ung **Obverse:** Inscription: Hsüan-t'ung Yüan-pao **Reverse:** Inverted A in place of V in PROVINCE in legend

Date	VG	F	VF	XF	Unc
ND(1901-11)	25.00	75.00	130	180	325

Y# 238 DOLLAR **Weight:** 26.8000 g. **Composition:** 0.9000 Silver .7756 oz. ASW **Ruler:** Kuang-hsü **Obverse:** Inscription: Kuang-hsü Yüan-pao **Reverse:** Dragon with narrow face and large fireball, small cross at either side of dragon

Date	Mintage	VG	F	VF	XF	Unc
ND(1901-08)	6,487,000	6.50	20.00	30.00	75.00	500

Y# 238.2 DOLLAR **Weight:** 26.8000 g. **Composition:** 0.9000 Silver .7756 oz. ASW **Ruler:** Kuang-hsü **Obverse:** Inscription: Kuang-hsü Yüan-pao **Reverse:** Dragon with wider face and flatter pearl, small cross at either side of dragon

Date	VG	F	VF	XF	Unc
ND(1901-08)	5.00	15.00	20.00	70.00	500

Y# 238.3 DOLLAR **Weight:** 26.8000 g. **Composition:** 0.9000 Silver .7756 oz. ASW **Ruler:** Kuang-hsü **Obverse:** Inscription: Kuang-hsü Yüan-pao **Reverse:** 7 MACE and 3 CANDAREENS instead of 2 CANDAREENS

Date	VG	F	VF	XF	Unc
ND(1901-08)	12.00	35.00	60.00	125	750

Y# 238.1 DOLLAR **Weight:** 26.8000 g. **Composition:** 0.9000 Silver .7756 oz. ASW **Ruler:** Kuang-hsü **Obverse:** Inscription: Kuang-hsü Yüan-pao **Reverse:** Inverted A instead of V in PROVINCE in legend

Date	VG	F	VF	XF	Unc
ND(1901-08)	6.00	17.50	25.00	70.00	500

Y# 243 DOLLAR **Weight:** 26.8000 g. **Composition:** 0.9000 Silver .7756 oz. ASW **Ruler:** Hsüan-t'ung **Obverse:** Inscription: Hsüan-t'ung Yüan-pao **Reverse:** Large spines on dragon's body

Date	Mintage	VG	F	VF	XF	Unc
ND(1909-11)	2,846,000	5.00	15.00	25.00	75.00	500

Y# 243.1 DOLLAR **Weight:** 26.8000 g. **Composition:** 0.9000 Silver .7756 oz. ASW **Ruler:** Hsüan-t'ung **Obverse:** Inscription: Hsüan-t'ung Yüan-pao **Reverse:** Inverted A instead of V in PROVINCE

Date	VG	F	VF	XF	Unc
ND(1909-11)	5.00	15.00	30.00	75.00	500

Y# 243.2 DOLLAR **Weight:** 26.8000 g. **Composition:** 0.9000 Silver .7756 oz. ASW **Ruler:** Hsüan-t'ung **Obverse:** Inscription: Hsüan-t'ung Yüan-pao **Reverse:** Small spines on dragon's body

Date	VG	F	VF	XF	Unc
ND(1909-11)	22.00	65.00	100	200	600

REPUBLIC

CUT MILLED COINAGE

Y# 459y 50 CASH **Composition:** Brass **Note:** 200 Cash, Y#459 cut into quarters.

Date	VG	F	VF	XF	Unc
2(1913)	30.00	35.00	40.00	50.00	—

Y# 459x 100 CASH **Composition:** Copper Or Brass **Note:** 200 Cash, Y#459 cut in half.

Date	VG	F	VF	XF	Unc
2(1913)	3.50	9.50	17.00	45.00	—

MILLED CASH COINAGE

Y# 441a 5 CASH **Composition:** Brass

Date	VG	F	VF	XF	Unc
1(1912)	—	—	—	—	—

Y# 441b 5 CASH **Composition:** Silver

Date	VG	F	VF	XF	Unc
1(1912)	—	—	1,000	1,500	—

Note: Modern forgeries of Y#441 in copper and of Y#441b in silver exist

Y# 443 5 CASH **Composition:** Copper

Date	VG	F	VF	XF	Unc
1(1912)	35.00	70.00	110	150	—

Y# 443a 5 CASH **Composition:** Brass

Date	VG	F	VF	XF	Unc
1(1912) Rare	—	—	—	—	—

Y# 446 5 CASH **Composition:** Copper

Date	VG	F	VF	XF	Unc
1(1912) Rare	—	—	—	—	—

Y# 446a 5 CASH **Composition:** Brass

Date	VG	F	VF	XF	Unc
1(1912) Rare	—	—	—	—	—

Y# 441 5 CASH **Composition:** Copper **Note:** Varieties exist.

Date	Mintage	VG	F	VF	XF	Unc
1(1912)	471,000	40.00	80.00	130	250	—

Y# 447 10 CASH **Composition:** Copper **Obverse:** Two rosettes

Date	Mintage	VG	F	VF	XF	Unc
1(1912)	108,618,000	1.75	3.00	10.00	20.00	—
2(1913)	Inc. above	6.00	15.00	25.00	50.00	—

Y# 447a 10 CASH **Composition:** Brass

Date	VG	F	VF	XF	Unc
1(1912)	0.80	1.50	2.50	5.00	—
2(1913)	1.65	4.00	8.00	20.00	—

Y# 447.1a 10 CASH **Composition:** Brass **Obverse:** Three rosettes

Date	VG	F	VF	XF	Unc
2(1913) Rare	—	—	—	—	—

DECIMAL COINAGE

Y# 475 10 CASH **Composition:** Red Copper **Obverse:** Characters in five-petalled flower **Reverse:** Denomination above sun

Date	VG	F	VF	XF	Unc
19(1930) Rare	—	—	—	—	—

Y# 448 20 CASH **Composition:** Copper **Obverse:** Two rosettes

Date	Mintage	VG	F	VF	XF	Unc
1(1912)	115,061,000	1.00	2.50	5.00	15.00	—

Note: Character for "first" instead of number one in date

Y# 448a 20 CASH **Composition:** Brass

Date	VG	F	VF	XF	Unc
1(1912)	0.75	1.50	2.50	6.00	—
2(1913)	1.00	2.00	3.50	7.00	—

Note: Character for "first" instead of number one in date

Y# 448.1 20 CASH **Composition:** Copper **Obverse:** Three rosettes

Date	VG	F	VF	XF	Unc
2(1913)	250	350	450	800	—
3(1914)	250	350	450	800	—

Y# 448.1a 20 CASH **Composition:** Brass

Date	VG	F	VF	XF	Unc
2(1913)	2.50	6.00	12.00	25.00	—
3(1914)	2.50	6.00	12.00	25.00	—

Note: There are many varieties of this 20 Cash; small and large rosettes; open and closed size characters and exaggerated size character with horns

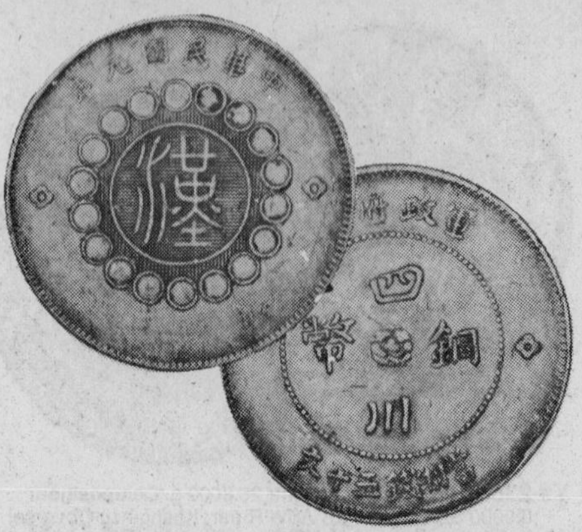

Y# 449 50 CASH **Composition:** Copper **Reverse:** Small flower in center

Date	Mintage	VG	F	VF	XF	Unc
1(1912)	489,382,000	2.00	4.00	7.00	15.00	—

Y# 449a 50 CASH **Composition:** Brass

Date	VG	F	VF	XF	Unc
1(1912)	1.50	3.50	6.00	10.00	—

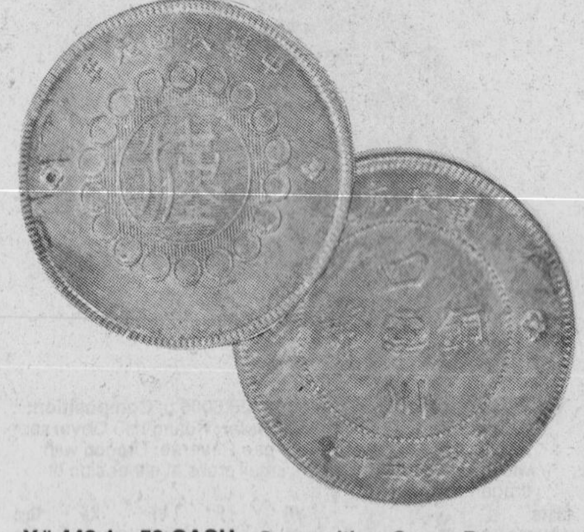

Y# 449.1 50 CASH **Composition:** Copper **Reverse:** Larger flower in center

Date	VG	F	VF	XF	Unc
1(1912)	2.00	5.00	10.00	20.00	—

Y# 449.1a 50 CASH **Composition:** Brass

Date	VG	F	VF	XF	Unc
1(1912)	2.50	6.00	12.50	25.00	—

Note: A Yr. 7 is reported, but its authenticity is not verified

Y# 449.2 50 CASH **Composition:** Copper **Obverse:** Three rosettes **Reverse:** Small flower in center

Date	VG	F	VF	XF	Unc
2(1913)	2.25	5.50	11.00	22.00	—

Y# 449.2a 50 CASH **Composition:** Brass

Date	VG	F	VF	XF	Unc
2(1913)	2.25	5.50	11.00	22.00	—
3(1914)	2.25	5.50	11.00	22.00	—

Y# 462 50 CASH **Composition:** Copper

Date	Mintage	VG	F	VF	XF	Unc
15(1926)	90,000	18.50	35.00	65.00	100	—

Y# 462a 50 CASH **Composition:** Brass

Date	VG	F	VF	XF	Unc
15(1926)	16.50	32.50	55.00	80.00	—

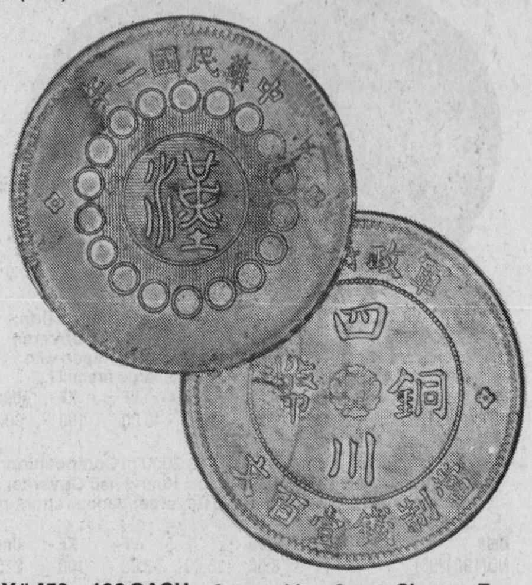

Y# 450 100 CASH **Composition:** Copper **Obverse:** Two rosettes **Reverse:** Large flower in center

Date	Mintage	VG	F	VF	XF	Unc
2(1913)	399,212,000	2.50	6.00	8.50	17.50	—
3(1914)	—	30.00	40.00	50.00	60.00	—

Y# 450a 100 CASH **Composition:** Brass

Date	VG	F	VF	XF	Unc
2(1913)	1.50	3.00	6.00	10.00	—

Y# 450.1 100 CASH **Composition:** Copper **Obverse:** Three rosettes **Reverse:** Small flower in center

Date	VG	F	VF	XF	Unc
2(1913)	3.50	9.00	15.00	25.00	—
3(1914)	—	—	—	—	—

Y# 463 100 CASH **Composition:** Copper

Date	Mintage	VG	F	VF	XF	Unc
15(1926)	7,055,000	3.50	9.00	15.00	25.00	—

Y# 463a 100 CASH **Composition:** Brass

Date	VG	F	VF	XF	Unc
15(1926)	3.25	8.00	12.50	20.00	—

Note: Two reverse varieties known; often struck over older 10 Cash coins

Y# 459a 200 CASH **Composition:** Brass

Date	VG	F	VF	XF	Unc
2(1913)	20.00	40.00	80.00	125	—

Y# 459.1 200 CASH **Composition:** Copper **Obverse:** Tassels draped over flag poles

Date	VG	F	VF	XF	Unc
2(1913)	6.00	10.00	25.00	40.00	—

Y# 459.1a 200 CASH **Composition:** Brass

Date	VG	F	VF	XF	Unc
2(1913)	4.50	8.00	20.00	35.00	—

Y# 459.2 200 CASH **Composition:** Copper **Reverse:** Smaller stars at sides

Date	VG	F	VF	XF	Unc
2(1913)	5.00	9.00	22.50	37.50	—

Note: For cut segments refer to 50 Cash, Y#459y and 100 Cash, Y#459x

Y# 464 200 CASH **Composition:** Copper **Edge:** Plain

Date	Mintage	VG	F	VF	XF	Unc
15(1926)	404,644,000	4.00	12.00	17.00	35.00	—

Y# 464.2 200 CASH **Composition:** Brass **Obverse:** Similar to Y#464 **Reverse:** Dot within first 0 of 200

Date	VG	F	VF	XF	Unc
15(1926)	—	—	—	—	—

Note: Many varieties: open and closed buds; overstruck on earlier pieces and on virgin flans; different sizes and thicknesses

Y# 464a 200 CASH **Composition:** Brass **Edge:** Plain

Date	VG	F	VF	XF	Unc
15(1926)	4.50	12.00	17.00	35.00	—

Y# 464.1 200 CASH **Composition:** Copper **Edge:** Reeded

Date	VG	F	VF	XF	Unc
15(1926)	6.00	15.00	25.00	45.00	—

Y# 464.1a 200 CASH **Composition:** Brass **Edge:** Reeded

Date	VG	F	VF	XF	Unc
15(1926)	—	—	—	—	—

Y# 476 2 CENTS **Composition:** Copper

Date	VG	F	VF	XF	Unc
19(1930) Rare	—	—	—	—	—

Y# 476a 2 CENTS **Composition:** Brass

Date	VG	F	VF	XF	Unc
19(1930)	—	—	—	—	—

Y# 453 10 CENTS **Weight:** 2.6000 g. **Composition:** Silver

Date	Mintage	VG	F	VF	XF	Unc
1(1912)	370,000	8.50	25.00	40.00	75.00	150

Y# 468 10 CENTS **Composition:** Copper-Nickel

Date	VG	F	VF	XF	Unc
ND(ca.1926)	4.50	12.50	20.00	45.00	70.00

Y# 468a 10 CENTS **Composition:** Silver

Date	VG	F	VF	XF	Unc
ND(ca.1926)	12.00	35.00	75.00	125	200

Y# 468b 10 CENTS **Composition:** Iron

Date	VG	F	VF	XF	Unc
ND(ca.1926)	6.50	20.00	50.00	70.00	125

Y# 454 20 CENTS **Weight:** 5.2000 g. **Composition:** Silver

Date	Mintage	VG	F	VF	XF	Unc
1(1912)	95,000	17.00	50.00	85.00	150	300

K# 795 20 CENTS **Weight:** 5.2000 g. **Composition:** Silver **Subject:** Tibetan War

Date	VG	F	VF	XF	Unc
1923	20.00	60.00	175	250	500

Note: Authenticity not established

Y# 455 50 CENTS **Weight:** 12.9000 g. **Composition:** Silver

Date	Mintage	VG	F	VF	XF	Unc
1(1912)	37,942,000	5.00	15.00	15.00	25.00	50.00
2(1913) Rare	Inc. above	—	—	—	—	—

Y# 473 50 CENTS **Weight:** 10.5000 g. **Composition:** Silver **Subject:** Sun Yat-sen

Date	VG	F	VF	XF	Unc
17(1928)	35.00	100	450	600	1,000

Y# 456 DOLLAR **Weight:** 25.6000 g. **Composition:** Silver

Date	Mintage	VG	F	VF	XF	Unc
1(1912)	55,670,000	4.50	12.50	20.00	55.00	125
2(1913) Rare	Inc. above	—	—	—	—	—

Y# 456.1 DOLLAR **Weight:** 25.6000 g. **Composition:** Silver **Reverse:** Right hand character with two dots instead of horizontal stroke

Date	VG	F	VF	XF	Unc
1(1912)	8.50	25.00	50.00	100	250

Note: Silver content ranged from 0.880 to 0.500 fine

Y# 474 DOLLAR **Weight:** 25.5000 g. **Composition:** Silver **Subject:** Sun Yat-sen

Date	VG	F	VF	XF	Unc
17(1928)	135	400	600	850	1,400

PATTERNS

Including off metal strikes

KM#	Date	Mintage	Identification	Mkt Val
Pn16	ND(ca.1901)	—	20 Cents. Aluminum. Dragon type.	—
Pn19	ND(1902)	—	20 Cents. Brass. K#147y	300
Pn18	ND(1902)	—	10 Cents. Brass. K#148y	250
Pn20	ND(1902)	—	50 Cents. Brass. K#146y	400
Pn17	ND(1902)	—	5 Cents. Brass. K#149y	200
Pn21	ND(1902)	—	Dollar. Brass. K#145y	800
Pn24	CD(1906)	—	2 Cash. Copper. Y#8t	—
Pn25	CD(1906)	—	5 Cash. Copper. Y#9t	—
Pn23	CD(1908)	—	5 Cash. Brass.	—
Pn22	CD(1908)	—	Cash. Brass. Y#7t	300
Pn27	1(1912)	—	50 Cents. Copper. Y#455	—
Pn26	ND(ca.1912)	—	10 Cents. Copper.	—
Pn28	ND(ca.1926)	—	10 Cents. Brass. Y#468	—
Pn29	17(1928)	—	Dollar. Copper. Y#474	—
Pn30	ND(1941)	—	50 Cents. Temple. Spade. World War II	—

YUNNAN PROVINCE

A province located in south China bordering Burma, Laos and Vietnam. It is very mountainous with many lakes. Yunnan was the home of various active imperial mints. A modern mint was established at Kunming in 1905 and the first struck copper coins were issued in 1906 and the first struck silver coins in 1908. General Tang Chi-yao issued coins in gold, silver and copper with his portrait in 1919. The last Republican coins were struck here in 1949.

EMPIRE

PROVINCIAL CAST COINAGE

C# 27-6 CASH **Composition:** Cast Brass **Ruler:** Kuang-hsü **Obverse:** Inscription: Kuang-hsü T'ung-pao **Reverse:** Inscription: Manchu Boo-dong **Note:** Struck at Tung Mint (Tungch'uan).

Date	Good	VG	F	VF	XF
ND(1875-1908)	4.00	6.50	9.00	15.00	—

C# 27-6.1 CASH **Composition:** Cast Brass **Ruler:** Kuang-hsü **Obverse:** Inscription: Kuang-hsü T'ung-pao **Reverse:** Inscription: Manchu Boo-dong; "Chin" above **Note:** Struck at Tung Tungch'uan.

Date	Good	VG	F	VF	XF
ND(1875-1908)	5.00	7.50	10.00	15.00	—

C# 27-6.2 CASH **Composition:** Cast Brass **Ruler:** Kuang-hsü **Obverse:** Inscription: Kuang-hsü T'ung-pao **Reverse:** Inscription: Manchu Boo-dong; "Ts'un" below **Note:** Struck at Tung Mint (Tungch'uan).

Date	Good	VG	F	VF	XF
ND(1875-1908)	5.00	7.50	10.00	15.00	—

C# 26-9 CASH **Composition:** Cast Brass **Ruler:** Kuang-hsü **Obverse:** Inscription: Kuang-hsü T'ung-pao **Reverse:** Inscription: Manchu Boo-yôn **Note:** Struck at Yün Mint (Yünnanfu).

Date	Good	VG	F	VF	XF
ND(1875-1908)	2.00	4.00	6.50	9.00	—

C# 26-9.1 CASH **Composition:** Cast Brass **Ruler:** Kuang-hsü **Obverse:** Inscription: Kuang-hsü T'ung-pao **Reverse:** Inscription: Manchu Boo-yôn; "Kung" above **Note:** Struck at Yün Mint (Yünnanfu).

Date	Good	VG	F	VF	XF
ND(1875-1908)	2.00	5.00	7.50	10.00	—

C# 26-9.2 CASH **Composition:** Cast Brass **Ruler:** Kuang-hsü **Obverse:** Inscription: Kuang-hsü T'ung-pao **Reverse:** Inscription: Manchu Boo-yôn; "Ssu" (four) above **Note:** Struck at Yün Mint (Yünnanfu).

Date	Good	VG	F	VF	XF
ND(1875-1908)	2.50	5.00	7.50	10.00	—

C# 26-9.3 CASH **Composition:** Cast Brass **Ruler:** Kuang-hsü **Obverse:** Inscription: Kuang-hsü T'ung-pao **Reverse:** Inscription: Manchu Boo-yôn; "Chin" above **Note:** Struck at Yün Mint (Yünnanfu).

Date	Good	VG	F	VF	XF
ND(1875-1908)	2.50	5.00	7.50	10.00	—

C# 26-9.4 CASH **Composition:** Cast Brass **Ruler:** Kuang-hsü **Obverse:** Inscription: Kuang-hsü T'ung-pao **Reverse:** Inscription: Manchu Boo-yôn; crescent above, dot below **Note:** Struck at Yün Mint (Yünnanfu).

Date	Good	VG	F	VF	XF
ND(1875-1908)	2.50	5.00	7.50	12.00	—

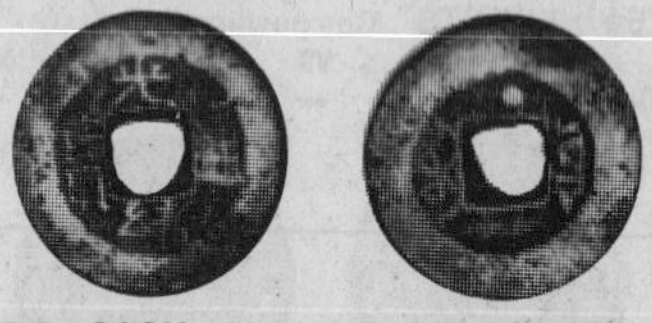

C# 26-9.5 CASH **Composition:** Cast Brass **Ruler:** Kuang-hsü **Obverse:** Inscription: Kuang-hsü T'ung-pao **Reverse:** Inscription: Manchu Boo-yôn; dot above hole **Note:** Struck at Yün Mint (Yünnanfu).

Date	Good	VG	F	VF	XF
ND(1875-1908)	2.50	5.00	7.50	12.00	—

C# 26-11 CASH **Composition:** Cast Brass **Ruler:** Hsüan-t'ung **Obverse:** Inscription: Hsuan-t'ung T'ung-pao **Reverse:** Inscription: Manchu Boo-yôn; "Kung" above hole **Note:** Struck at Yün Mint (Yünnanfu).

Date	Good	VG	F	VF	XF
ND(1909-11)	75.00	100	150	220	—

C# 27-7 CASH **Composition:** Cast Brass **Ruler:** Hsüan-t'ung **Obverse:** Inscription: Hsuan-t'ung T'ung-pao **Reverse:** Inscription: Manchu Boo-dong; "Ts'un" below **Note:** Struck at Tung Mint (Tungch'uan).

Date	Good	VG	F	VF	XF
ND(1909-11) Rare	—	—	—	—	—

C# 26-12 CASH **Composition:** Cast Brass **Ruler:** Hsüan-t'ung **Obverse:** Inscription: Hsuan-t'ung T'ung-pao **Reverse:** Inscription: Manchu Boo-yôn; "Shan" above hole **Note:** Struck at Yün Mint (Yünnanfu).

Date	Good	VG	F	VF	XF
ND(1909-11)	30.00	40.00	50.00	100	—

C# 26-13 CASH **Composition:** Cast Brass **Ruler:** Hsüan-t'ung **Obverse:** Inscription: Hsuan-t'ung T'ung-pao **Reverse:** Inscription: Manchu Boo-yôn; without character above hole **Note:** Struck at Yün Mint (Yünnanfu).

Date	Good	VG	F	VF	XF
ND(1909-11)	35.00	45.00	55.00	100	—

MILLED COINAGE

Y# 10u 10 CASH **Composition:** Copper **Obverse:** Inscription: Tai-ching T'ung-pi with large mint mark "Yun" in center **Reverse:** Side view dragon

Date	Mintage	VG	F	VF	XF	Unc
CD(1906)	36,701,000	10.00	22.00	35.00	60.00	—

Y# 10u.1 10 CASH **Composition:** Copper **Obverse:** Inscription: Tai-ching T'ung-pi with small mint mark "Yun" in center **Reverse:** Side view dragon

Date	VG	F	VF	XF	Unc
CD(1906)	25.00	55.00	85.00	125	—

Y# 10v 10 CASH **Composition:** Copper **Obverse:** Inscription: Tai-ching T'ung-pi with mint mark "Tien" in center **Reverse:** Side view dragon

Date	VG	F	VF	XF	Unc
CD(1906)	12.50	30.00	40.00	65.00	—

Y# 11u 20 CASH **Composition:** Copper **Obverse:** Inscription: Tai-ching T'ung-pi with large mint mark "Yun" in center **Reverse:** Side view dragon

Date	Mintage	VG	F	VF	XF	Unc
CD(1906)	645,000	125	175	225	275	—

Y# 11u.1 20 CASH **Composition:** Copper **Obverse:** Inscription: Tai-ching T'ung-pi with small mint mark "Yun" in center **Reverse:** Side view dragon

Date	VG	F	VF	XF	Unc
CD(1906)	150	275	400	550	—

Y# 11v.1 20 CASH **Composition:** Copper **Obverse:** Inscription: Tai-ching T'ung-pi with mint mark "Tien" in center **Reverse:** Side view dragon

Date	VG	F	VF	XF	Unc
CD(1906)	150	275	400	550	—

Y# 11v.1a 20 CASH **Composition:** Brass **Obverse:** Inscription: Tai-ching T'ung-pi **Reverse:** Side view dragon

Date	VG	F	VF	XF	Unc
CD(1906)	175	350	450	600	—

Y# 252 20 CENTS **Composition:** Brass **Ruler:** Kuang-hsü **Obverse:** Inscription: Kuang-hsü Yuan-pao **Reverse:** Side view dragon **Note:** Many minor varieties.

Date	Mintage	VG	F	VF	XF	Unc
ND(1908)	532,000	6.00	18.50	35.00	60.00	125

Y# 253 50 CENTS **Weight:** 13.2000 g. **Composition:** 0.8000 Silver .3395 oz. ASW **Ruler:** Kuang-hsü **Obverse:** Inscription: Kuang-hsü Yuan-pao **Reverse:** Side view dragon

Date	VG	F	VF	XF	Unc
ND(1908)	2.50	7.50	15.00	20.00	85.00

Y# 259 50 CENTS **Weight:** 13.2000 g. **Composition:** 0.8000 Silver .3395 oz. ASW **Ruler:** Hsüan-t'ung **Obverse:** Inscription: Hsüan-t'ung-pao **Reverse:** Side view dragon; seven flames on pearl

Date	VG	F	VF	XF	Unc
ND(1909-11)	2.25	7.00	13.50	22.50	90.00

Y# 259.1 50 CENTS **Weight:** 13.2000 g. **Composition:** 0.8000 Silver .3395 oz. ASW **Ruler:** Hsüan-t'ung **Obverse:** Inscription: Hsüan-t'ung-pao **Reverse:** Side view dragon; nine flames on pearl

Date	VG	F	VF	XF	Unc
ND(1909-11)	2.25	7.00	13.50	22.50	90.00

Y# 254 DOLLAR **Weight:** 26.8000 g. **Composition:** 0.9000 Silver .7755 oz. ASW **Ruler:** Kuang-hsü **Obverse:** Inscription: Kuang-hsü Yuan-pao **Reverse:** Side view dragon

Date	VG	F	VF	XF	Unc
ND(1908)	5.00	15.00	30.00	65.00	300

Y# 260 DOLLAR **Weight:** 26.8000 g. **Composition:** 0.9000 Silver .7755 oz. ASW **Ruler:** Hsüan-t'ung **Obverse:** Inscription: Hsüan-t'ung T'ung-pao **Obv. Legend:** Four characters at top **Reverse:** Side view dragon

Date	VG	F	VF	XF	Unc
ND(1909-11)	5.00	15.00	25.00	60.00	300

Y# 260.1 DOLLAR **Weight:** 26.8000 g. **Composition:** 0.9000 Silver .7755 oz. ASW **Ruler:** Hsüan-t'ung **Obverse:** Inscription: Hsüan-t'ung T'ung-pao **Obv. Legend:** Seven characters at top **Reverse:** Side view dragon

Date	VG	F	VF	XF	Unc
CD1910	—	—	—	—	32,500

REPUBLIC

TRANSITIONAL COINAGE

In the name of the Republic

KM# 5 CASH **Composition:** Cast Copper Or Brass **Obverse:** Inscription: Min-kuo T'ung-pao **Reverse:** Inscription: "Tung-ch'uan" **Note:** Struck at Tung (Tungch'uan) Mint.

Date	Good	VG	F	VF	XF
ND(1912)	20.00	30.00	40.00	65.00	—

KM# 5a CASH **Composition:** Cast Copper Or Brass **Obverse:** Inscription: Min-kuo T'ung-pao **Reverse:** Inscription: "Boo-yôn" **Note:** Struck at Yün Yünnan-fu.

Date	Good	VG	F	VF	XF
ND(1912)	100	125	180	—	—

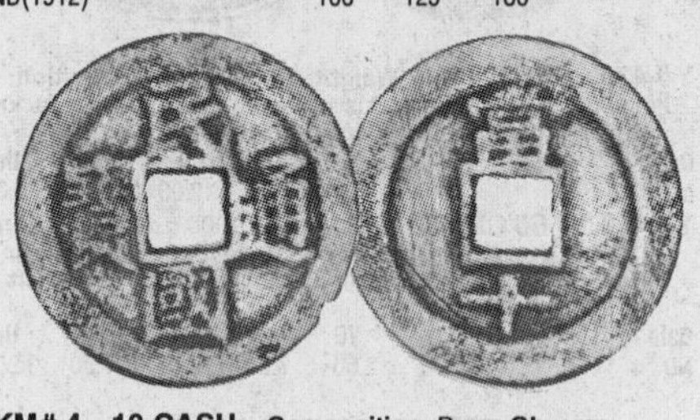

KM# 4 10 CASH **Composition:** Brass **Obverse:** Inscription: Min-kuo T'ung-pao

Date	Good	VG	F	VF	XF
ND(1912)	15.00	25.00	35.00	50.00	—

RESTRUCK IMPERIAL COINAGE

The following imperial coins are reign-dated 1875-1908. These coins were apparently restruck from previously unused dies at intervals from 1911 through to 1949, and with a progressively reduced silver content. The dates and silver content shown are approximate.

Y# 255 10 CENTS **Weight:** 2.6500 g. **Composition:** 0.6500 Silver .0554 oz. ASW **Obverse:** Inscription: Kuang-hsü Yüan-pao **Reverse:** Side view dragon with two circles beneath pearl

Date	Mintage	VG	F	VF	XF	Unc
ND(1911-15)	902,000	5.00	15.00	30.00	45.00	90.00

Y# 256 20 CENTS **Weight:** 5.3000 g. **Composition:** 0.8000 Silver .1363 oz. ASW **Obverse:** Inscription: Kuang-hsü Yüan-pao **Reverse:** Side view dragon with two circles beneath pearl

Date	VG	F	VF	XF	Unc
ND(1911-15)	4.50	12.50	17.50	32.50	75.00

Y# 256a 20 CENTS **Weight:** 5.3000 g. **Composition:** 0.6500 Silver .1108 oz. ASW **Obverse:** Inscription: Kuang-hsü Yüan-pao **Reverse:** Side view dragon with three circles beneath pearl

Date	VG	F	VF	XF	Unc
ND(1911-15)	4.50	12.50	22.50	37.50	75.00

Y# 256b 20 CENTS **Weight:** 5.3000 g. **Composition:** 0.4000 Silver .0682 oz. ASW **Obverse:** Inscription: Kuang-hsü Yüan-pao **Reverse:** Side view dragon with two or three circles beneath pearl

Date	VG	F	VF	XF	Unc
ND(1920-31)	—	—	—	—	—

Y# 257 50 CENTS **Weight:** 13.2000 g. **Composition:** 0.8000 Silver .3395 oz. ASW **Obverse:** Inscription: Kuang-hsü Yüan-pao **Reverse:** Side view dragon with two circles below pearl

Date	VG	F	VF	XF	Unc
ND(1911-15)	1.85	5.50	8.00	12.00	30.00

Y# 257.1 50 CENTS **Weight:** 13.2000 g. **Composition:** 0.8000 Silver .3395 oz. ASW **Obverse:** Inscription: Kuang-hsü Yüan-pao **Reverse:** Side view dragon with three circles below pearl

Date	VG	F	VF	XF	Unc
ND(1911-15)	1.75	5.00	7.00	10.00	20.00

Y# 257.2 50 CENTS **Weight:** 13.2000 g. **Composition:** 0.5000 Silver .2122 oz. ASW **Obverse:** Inscription: Kuang-hsü Yüan-pao **Reverse:** Side view dragon with four circles below pearl

Date	VG	F	VF	XF	Unc
ND(1920-31)	1.75	5.00	6.00	9.00	20.00

Note: There are more than 30 minor varieties of Y#257

Y# 257.3 50 CENTS **Weight:** 13.2000 g. **Composition:** 0.5000 Silver - Billon **Obverse:** Inscription: Kuang-hsü Yuan-pao **Reverse:** Side view dragon with two circles beneath pearl, large circle around center circle of rosettes

Date	VG	F	VF	XF	Unc
ND(1949)	—	—	—	—	—

Y# 258 DOLLAR **Weight:** 26.8000 g. **Composition:** 0.9000 Silver .7755 oz. ASW **Obverse:** Inscription: Kuang-hsü Yüan-pao **Reverse:** Side view dragon with one circle below pearl

Date	VG	F	VF	XF	Unc
ND(1911-15)	5.00	15.00	20.00	35.00	250

Y# 258.1 DOLLAR **Weight:** 26.8000 g. **Composition:** 0.9000 Silver .7755 oz. ASW **Obverse:** Inscription: Kuang-hsü Yüan-pao **Reverse:** Side view dragon with four circles below pearl

Date	VG	F	VF	XF	Unc
ND(1920-22)	5.00	15.00	20.00	35.00	250

STANDARD COINAGE

Y# 488 CENT **Composition:** Brass **Obv. Legend:** Chung-hua Min-kuo above crossed flags

Date	VG	F	VF	XF	Unc
21 (1932) Rare	—	—	—	—	—

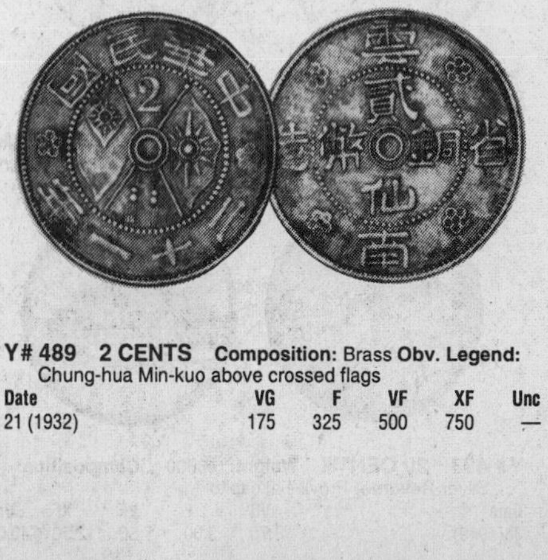

Y# 489 2 CENTS **Composition:** Brass **Obv. Legend:** Chung-hua Min-kuo above crossed flags

Date	VG	F	VF	XF	Unc
21 (1932)	175	325	500	750	—

Y# 478 50 CASH Composition: Brass **Obverse:** Bust of General T'ang Chi-yao facing **Note:** (ca.1919)

Date	VG	F	VF	XF	Unc
ND	10.00	20.00	40.00	70.00	—

Y# 478a 50 CASH Composition: Copper **Obverse:** Bust of General T'ang Chi-yao facing **Note:** (ca.1919)

Date	VG	F	VF	XF	Unc
ND	20.00	40.00	80.00	125	—

Y# 485 5 CENTS Composition: Copper-Nickel **Reverse:** Flag

Date	VG	F	VF	XF	Unc
12(1923)	22.50	32.50	47.50	75.00	—

Y# 490 5 CENTS Composition: Copper **Obv. Legend:** Chung-hua Min-kuo above crossed flags

Date	VG	F	VF	XF	Unc
21(1932)	125	175	250	350	—

Y# 486 10 CENTS Composition: Copper-Nickel **Reverse:** Flag **Edge:** Reeded

Date	VG	F	VF	XF	Unc
12(1923)	1.75	2.50	3.75	7.50	—

Y# 486.1 10 CENTS Composition: Copper-Nickel **Reverse:** Flag **Edge:** Unreeded

Date	VG	F	VF	XF	Unc
12(1923)	2.50	4.00	6.50	12.50	—

Y# 491 20 CENTS Weight: 5.6000 g. **Composition:** Silver **Obverse:** Crossed flags

Date	VG	F	VF	XF	Unc
21(1932)	1.00	3.00	5.00	8.00	20.00

Y# 493 20 CENTS Weight: 5.6000 g. **Composition:** Silver **Reverse:** Provincial capitol

Date	VG	F	VF	XF	Unc
38(1949)	1.75	5.00	7.50	12.50	40.00

Y# 480 50 CENTS Weight: 13.1000 g. **Composition:** 0.8500 Silver **Obverse:** Bust of General T'ang Chi-yao right **Reverse:** Crossed flags **Note:** (ca.1916)

Date	VG	F	VF	XF	Unc
ND	3.50	10.00	20.00	45.00	120

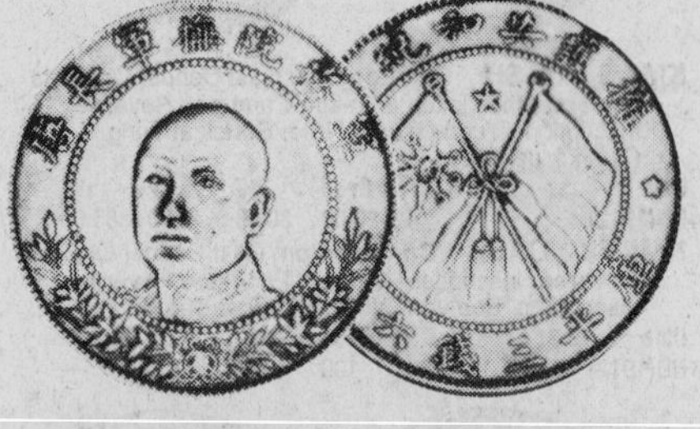

Y# 479 50 CENTS Weight: 13.1000 g. **Composition:** 0.8500 Silver **Obverse:** Bust of General T'ang Chi-yao facing **Reverse:** Crossed flags **Note:** (ca.1917)

Date	VG	F	VF	XF	Unc
ND	2.50	7.50	12.00	17.50	35.00

Y# 479.1 50 CENTS Weight: 13.1000 g. **Composition:** 0.8500 Silver **Obverse:** Bust of General T'ang Chi-yao facing **Reverse:** Crossed flags with circle in center of flag at left **Note:** (ca.1917)

Date	VG	F	VF	XF	Unc
ND	2.50	7.50	12.00	17.50	35.00

Y# 492 50 CENTS Weight: 13.1000 g. **Composition:** 0.5000 Silver

Date	VG	F	VF	XF	Unc
21	1.75	5.00	8.00	10.00	15.00

K# 1521 5 DOLLARS Composition: Gold **Obverse:** Inscription: "Equal to 5 (silver) Dollars" **Note:** Uniface; Similar to 10 Dollars, K#1520.

Date	VG	F	VF	XF	Unc
ND(1917) Rare	—	—	—	—	—

Y# 481 5 DOLLARS Weight: 4.5000 g. **Composition:** 0.7500 Gold **Obverse:** Bust of General T'ang Chi-yao facing **Reverse:** With numeral 2 below flag tassels

Date	VG	F	VF	XF	Unc
ND(1919)	65.00	200	300	400	600

K# 1529 5 DOLLARS Weight: 4.5000 g. **Composition:** 0.7500 Gold **Obverse:** Inscription: Wu(5)-Yüan Chin-pi **Reverse:** Tien in wheat sprays

Date	VG	F	VF	XF	Unc
ND(1925)	—	—	275	500	700

K# 1520 10 DOLLARS Composition: Gold **Obverse:** Inscription: "Equal to 10 Silver Dollars" **Note:** Uniface.

Date	VG	F	VF	XF	Unc
ND Rare	—	—	—	—	—

Y# 482 10 DOLLARS Weight: 8.5000 g. **Composition:** 0.7500 Gold **Obverse:** Bust of General T'ang Chi-yao facing **Reverse:** With numeral 1 below flag tassels

Date	Mintage	VG	F	VF	XF	Unc
ND(1919)	900,000	85.00	250	350	450	600

Y# 482.1 10 DOLLARS Weight: 8.5000 g. **Composition:** 0.7500 Gold **Obverse:** Bust of General T'ang Chi-yao facing **Reverse:** Without numeral 1 below flag tassels

Date	VG	F	VF	XF	Unc
ND(1919)	65.00	200	350	450	600

K# 1528 10 DOLLARS Weight: 8.5000 g. **Composition:** 0.7500 Gold **Obverse:** Inscription: Shih(10)-yüan Chin-pi **Reverse:** Tien in wheat sprays

Date	VG	F	VF	XF	Unc
ND(1925)	—	—	275	500	700

PATTERNS

Including off metal strikes

KM#	Date	Mintage	Identification	Mkt Val
Pn1	ND(ca.1902)	—	Cash. Brass. Tungch'uwan	—
Pn2	ND(1908)	—	10 Cash. Copper.	250
Pn3	ND(1908)	—	50 Cents. Copper. Y#253.	200
Pn4	ND(1908)	—	50 Cents. Brass. Y#253.	250
Pn5	ND(1908)	—	50 Cents. Copper. Y#257.	200
Pn6	ND(1908)	—	Dollar. Copper. Y#254.	350
Pn7	ND(1925)	—	5 Dollars. Silver.	200
Pn8	ND(1925)	—	10 Dollars. Silver.	300
Pn9	ND(1925)	—	10 Dollars. Pewter. K#1528y.	—

YUNNAN-SZECHUAN

Yunnan-Sichuan

These two coins have a 2-character mint mark in the center of the obverse, indicating the provinces of Yunnan and Szechuan (Sichuan).

EMPIRE

PROVINCIAL CAST COINAGE

Y# 10w 10 CASH Composition: Copper **Ruler:** Kuang-hsü **Obverse:** Inscription: Ta-ching T'ung-pi **Rev. Legend:** Kuang-hsu Nien Tsao, TAI-CHING-TI-KUO...

Date	VG	F	VF	XF	Unc
CD(1906)	20.00	40.00	60.00	110	—

Y# 11w 20 CASH Composition: Copper **Ruler:** Kuang-hsü **Obverse:** Inscription: Ta-ch'ing T'ung-pi **Rev. Legend:** Kuang-hsu Nien Tsao, TAI-CHING-TI-KUO...

Date	VG	F	VF	XF	Unc
CD(1906)	100	150	200	250	—

CHINA, REPUBLIC OF

EMPIRE

On December 15, 1915 Yuan Shih-K'ai had himself formally chosen and proclaimed emperor. Opposition developed within China and among various foreign powers. A rebellion broke out in Yünnan and spread to other southern provinces. Opposition was so great that Yuan rescinded the monarchy on March 21, 1916. On June 6th he died.

TRANSITIONAL COINAGE

KM# 1 5 CASH (5 Wen) **Composition:** Copper **Ruler:** Hung-hsien **Obverse:** Inscription: Hung-hsien T'ung-pao

Date	VG	F	VF	XF	Unc
ND(1916) (1916) Rare	—	—	—	—	—

Note: Questionable, believed to be a fantasy by some authorities

KM# 2 10 CASH (10 Wen) **Composition:** Bronze **Ruler:** Hung-hsien **Obverse:** Inscription: Hung-hsien T'ung-pao **Note:** Uniface.

Date	Good	VG	F	VF	XF
ND(1916) Rare	—	—	—	—	—

Note: Questionable, believed to be a fantasy by some authorities

STANDARD COINAGE

Y# 332 DOLLAR (Yuan) **Weight:** 26.8000 g. **Composition:** Silver **Ruler:** Hung-hsien **Subject:** Inauguration of Hung-hsien Regime **Obverse:** Bust of Hung-hsien in military uniform with plumed hat facing **Reverse:** Winged dragon left

Date	VG	F	VF	XF	Unc
ND (1916)	45.00	125	250	400	650

Y# 333 10 DOLLARS **Weight:** 7.0500 g. **Composition:** Red Gold **Ruler:** Hung-hsien **Obverse:** Bust of Hung-hsien left **Reverse:** Winged dragon left

Date	VG	F	VF	XF	Unc
1 (1916)	—	—	2,000	3,500	5,000

Y# 333a 10 DOLLARS **Weight:** 7.0500 g. **Composition:** Yellow Gold **Ruler:** Hung-hsien

Date	VG	F	VF	XF	Unc
1 (1916)	—	—	2,000	3,500	5,000

REPUBLIC

STANDARD COINAGE

Y# 301a 10 CASH (10 Wen) **Composition:** Brass

Date	VG	F	VF	XF	Unc
ND(ca.1912) (1912)	—	—	—	—	—

Y# 301 10 CASH (10 Wen) **Composition:** Copper **Reverse:** Double circle with small rosettes separating legend **Note:** Struck at Nanking.

Date	VG	F	VF	XF	Unc
ND(ca.1912) (1912)	0.20	0.50	0.75	1.50	15.00

Y# 301.1 10 CASH (10 Wen) **Composition:** Copper **Obverse:** Second character from right in bottom legend is rounded **Reverse:** Double circle with three dots separating legend **Note:** Unknown mint.

Date	VG	F	VF	XF	Unc
ND(ca.1912) (1912)	0.35	1.00	2.00	5.00	22.00

Y# 301.2 10 CASH (10 Wen) **Composition:** Copper **Obverse:** Second character from right in bottom legend is rounded **Reverse:** Double circle with two dots separating legend

Date	VG	F	VF	XF	Unc
ND(ca.1912) (1912)	0.20	0.50	1.00	2.50	16.00

Y# 301.3 10 CASH (10 Wen) **Composition:** Copper **Obverse:** Small star on flag **Reverse:** Double circle with six-pointed stars separating legend **Note:** Struck at Nanking.

Date	VG	F	VF	XF	Unc
ND(ca.1912) (1912)	0.25	0.75	1.50	3.00	18.00

Y# 301.4 10 CASH (10 Wen) **Composition:** Copper **Obverse:** Large star on flag extending to edges of flag **Reverse:** Double circle with six-pointed stars separating legend

Date	VG	F	VF	XF	Unc
ND(ca.1912) (1912)	3.50	10.00	15.00	25.00	65.00

Y# 301.4a 10 CASH (10 Wen) **Composition:** Brass

Date	VG	F	VF	XF	Unc
ND(ca.1912) (1912)	—	—	—	—	—

Y# 301.5 10 CASH (10 Wen) **Composition:** Copper **Obverse:** Flower wtih many stems **Reverse:** Single circle

Date	VG	F	VF	XF	Unc
ND(ca.1912) (1912)	0.25	0.75	1.50	3.00	20.00

Y# 301.6 10 CASH (10 Wen) **Composition:** Copper **Obverse:** Flower wtih fewer stems **Reverse:** Single circle

Date	VG	F	VF	XF	Unc
ND(ca.1912) (1912)	0.25	0.75	1.50	3.00	20.00

Y# 309 10 CASH (10 Wen) **Composition:** Copper **Note:** Struck at Tientsin.

Date	VG	F	VF	XF	Unc
ND(1914-17) (1914)	3.50	10.00	20.00	40.00	120

Note: Pieces with L. GIORGI near rim are patterns

Y# 324 10 CASH (10 Wen) **Composition:** Bronze **Note:** Struck at Tientsin.

Date	VG	F	VF	XF	Unc
5 (1916)	1.75	5.00	10.00	20.00	50.00

Note: Pieces with L. GIORGI near rim are patterns

Y# 307 10 CASH (10 Wen) **Composition:** Copper **Obverse:** One large rosette on either side **Reverse:** Slender leaves and short ribbon **Note:** Struck at Taiyüan, Shansi.

Date	Mintage	VG	F	VF	XF	Unc
ND(1919) (1919)	421,138,000	0.20	0.50	1.00	3.00	14.00

Y# 307a 10 CASH (10 Wen) **Composition:** Copper
Obverse: Three rosettes on either side, ornate right flag
Reverse: Long ribbon

Date	VG	F	VF	XF	Unc
ND(1919) (1919)	0.40	1.00	2.00	4.00	12.50

Y# 307a.1 10 CASH (10 Wen) **Composition:** Copper
Reverse: Short ribbon and smaller wheat ears

Date	VG	F	VF	XF	Unc
ND(1919) (1919)	3.50	10.00	20.00	40.00	100

Y# 307b 10 CASH (10 Wen) **Composition:** Brass

Date	VG	F	VF	XF	Unc
ND(1919) (1919)	—	—	—	—	—

Y# 307.1 10 CASH (10 Wen) **Composition:** Copper
Reverse: Larger leaves and longer ribbon

Date	VG	F	VF	XF	Unc
ND(1919) (1919)	3.50	10.00	20.00	40.00	100

Y# 302 10 CASH (10 Wen) **Composition:** Copper
Reverse: Vine above leaf at 12-o'clock; wreath tied at bottom; M-shaped leaves at base of wheat ears **Note:** Struck at Anhwei

Date	VG	F	VF	XF	Unc
ND(ca.1920) (1920)	0.20	0.60	1.50	3.00	18.00

Y# 302a 10 CASH (10 Wen) **Composition:** Brass

Date	VG	F	VF	XF	Unc
ND(ca.1920) (1920)	—	—	—	—	—

Y# 302.1 10 CASH (10 Wen) **Composition:** Copper
Reverse: Larger wheat ears

Date	VG	F	VF	XF	Unc
ND(ca.1920) (1920)	0.35	1.00	3.50	6.50	20.00

Y# 302.2 10 CASH (10 Wen) **Composition:** Copper
Reverse: Vine beneath leaf at 12-o'clock; wreath not tied at bottom; without M-shaped leaves at base of wheat ears

Date	VG	F	VF	XF	Unc
ND(ca.1920) (1920)	0.50	1.50	4.00	8.00	20.00

Y# 302.3 10 CASH (10 Wen) **Composition:** Copper
Reverse: Leaves pointing clockwise

Date	VG	F	VF	XF	Unc
ND(ca.1920) (1920)	10.00	30.00	40.00	60.00	100

Y# 303 10 CASH (10 Wen) **Composition:** Copper
Obverse: Small star-shaped rosettes **Reverse:** Small four-petalled rosettes separating legend

Date	VG	F	VF	XF	Unc
ND(ca.1920) (1920)	0.20	0.50	1.00	2.00	15.00

Y# 303a 10 CASH (10 Wen) **Composition:** Brass
Obverse: Stars replace rosettes

Date	VG	F	VF	XF	Unc
ND(ca.1920) (1920)	0.50	1.50	4.00	10.00	22.50

Y# 303.1 10 CASH (10 Wen) **Composition:** Copper
Obverse: Left flag's star in relief

Date	VG	F	VF	XF	Unc
ND(ca.1920) (1920)	0.20	0.50	1.00	2.00	15.00

Y# 303.3 10 CASH (10 Wen) **Composition:** Copper
Obverse: Large rosettes replace stars **Reverse:** Stars separating legend

Date	VG	F	VF	XF	Unc
ND(ca.1920) (1920)	1.00	3.00	6.25	12.50	25.00

Y# 303.4 10 CASH (10 Wen) **Composition:** Copper
Obverse: Very small pentagonal rosettes

Date	VG	F	VF	XF	Unc
ND(ca.1920) (1920)	0.25	0.75	1.50	3.00	15.00

Y# 303.4a 10 CASH (10 Wen) **Composition:** Brass

Date	VG	F	VF	XF	Unc
ND(ca.1920) (1920)	1.00	3.00	6.25	12.50	25.00

Y# 303.5 10 CASH (10 Wen) **Composition:** Brass
Obverse: Large rosettes **Note:** Similar to Y#307a.1.

Date	VG	F	VF	XF	Unc
ND(ca.1920) (1920)	—	—	—	—	—

Y# 304 10 CASH (10 Wen) **Composition:** Copper
Obverse: Circled flag flanked by pentagonal rosettes **Note:** Struck at Anhwei.

Date	VG	F	VF	XF	Unc
ND(ca.1920) (1920)	3.75	11.50	21.50	42.50	85.00

Y# 305 10 CASH (10 Wen) **Composition:** Copper
Reverse: Chrysanthemum **Note:** Struck at Changsha, Hunan.

Date	VG	F	VF	XF	Unc
ND(ca.1920) (1920)	5.00	15.00	25.00	50.00	115

Y# 306a 10 CASH (10 Wen) **Composition:** Copper
Obverse: Five characters in lower legend

Date	VG	F	VF	XF	Unc
ND(ca.1920) (1920)	1.75	5.00	12.00	25.00	65.00

Y# 306b 10 CASH (10 Wen) **Composition:** Brass

Date	VG	F	VF	XF	Unc
ND(ca.1920) (1920)	0.35	1.00	2.50	5.00	18.00

Y# 306.1 10 CASH (10 Wen) **Composition:** Copper
Note: Struck at Changsha, Hunan.

Date	VG	F	VF	XF	Unc
ND(ca.1920) (1920)	0.20	0.50	1.25	3.00	14.00

Y# 306.1b 10 CASH (10 Wen) **Composition:** Copper
Obverse: Y#306.1 **Reverse:** Y#306.4

Date	VG	F	VF	XF	Unc
ND(ca.1920) (1920)	1.75	5.00	7.50	14.00	30.00

Y# 306.2 10 CASH (10 Wen) **Composition:** Copper
Obverse: Dot on either side of upper legend

Date	VG	F	VF	XF	Unc
ND(ca.1920) (1920)	0.35	1.00	2.00	3.50	15.00

Y# 306.2b 10 CASH (10 Wen) **Composition:** Brass

Date	VG	F	VF	XF	Unc
ND(ca.1920) (1920)	0.45	1.25	3.00	5.00	15.00

Y# 306.3 10 CASH (10 Wen) **Composition:** Copper
Obverse: Star between flags

Date	VG	F	VF	XF	Unc
ND(ca.1920) (1920)	6.50	20.00	40.00	75.00	—

Y# 306.4 10 CASH (10 Wen) **Composition:** Copper
Obverse: Elongated rosettes, different characters in bottom legend **Reverse:** Thin leaf blade between lower wheat ears

Date	VG	F	VF	XF	Unc
ND(ca.1920) (1920)	9.00	27.50	55.00	85.00	210

Y# 311 10 CASH (10 Wen) **Composition:** Copper
Note: Struck at Kalgan.

Date	VG	F	VF	XF	Unc
13 (1924)	65.00	175	350	500	850

Y# 324a 10 CASH (10 Wen) **Composition:** Bronze

Date	VG	F	VF	XF	Unc
22 (1933)	2.75	8.00	15.00	30.00	100

Y# 347 10 CASH (10 Wen) **Composition:** Copper

Date	Mintage	VG	F	VF	XF	Unc
25 (1936)	311,780,000	0.15	0.40	0.75	1.75	2.50
26 (1937)	307,198,000	0.15	0.45	1.00	1.50	3.00
27 (1938)	12,000,000	1.00	3.00	5.00	8.00	16.00
28 (1939)	75,000,000	0.65	2.00	4.00	7.00	15.00

Y# 308 20 CASH (20 Wen) **Composition:** Copper
Obverse: Crossed flags **Reverse:** Value in sprays **Note:** Struck at Taiyüan, Shansi.

Date	Mintage	VG	F	VF	XF	Unc
8 (1919)	200,861,000	0.50	1.50	3.00	7.50	30.00

Y# 308b 20 CASH (20 Wen) **Composition:** Cast Brass
Obverse: Crossed flags **Reverse:** Value in sprays

Date	Good	VG	F	VF	XF
8(1919)	10.00	15.00	18.50	25.00	—

Note: A "warlord" issue; refer to note under Szechuan - Republic

Y# 308a 20 CASH (20 Wen) **Composition:** Copper
Obverse: Crossed flags **Reverse:** Value in sprays

Date	VG	F	VF	XF	Unc
10 (1921)	0.35	1.00	2.50	6.00	30.00

Y# 310 20 CASH (20 Wen) **Composition:** Copper
Obverse: Crossed flags **Reverse:** Value in sprays **Note:** Struck at Tientsin.

Date	VG	F	VF	XF	Unc
ND(ca.1921)	5.00	15.00	30.00	70.00	135

Note: Some sources date these 20 Cash pieces bearing crossed flags ca.1912, but many were not struck until the 1920s; this coin is usually found weakly struck and lightweight

Y# 312 20 CASH (20 Wen) **Composition:** Copper
Obverse: Crossed flags **Reverse:** Value in sprays **Note:** Struck at Kalgan.

Date	VG	F	VF	XF	Unc
13	3.50	10.00	30.00	70.00	135

Note: This coin is usually found weakly struck

HSU# 9 20 CASH (20 Wen) **Composition:** Copper
Obverse: Crossed flags **Reverse:** Value in sprays **Subject:** Nationalist commemorative.

Date	VG	F	VF	XF	Unc
ND(1927-28)	75.00	225	400	650	900

HSU# 445a 500 CASH (500 Wen) **Composition:** Copper **Subject:** Nationalist Commemorative **Obverse:** Crossed flags **Reverse:** Value in sprays

Date	Mintage	VG	F	VF	XF	Unc
ND(1927/8) Rare	12	—	—	—	—	—

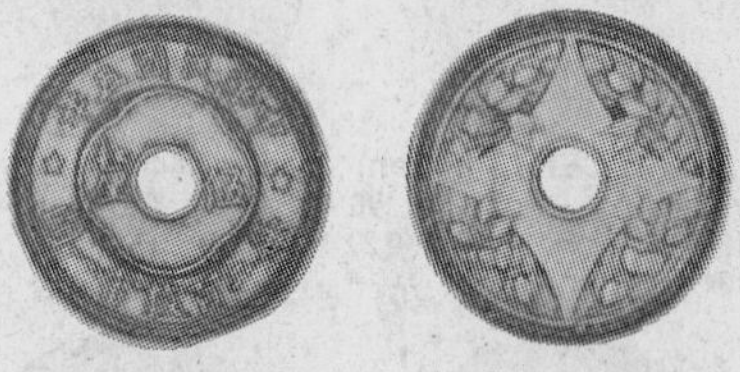

Y# 323 1/2 CENT (5 Li) **Composition:** Bronze **Note:** Struck at Tientsin.

Date	Mintage	VG	F	VF	XF	Unc
5 (1916)	1,789,000	1.75	5.00	10.00	20.00	45.00

Y# 346 1/2 CENT (1/2 Fen) **Composition:** Bronze

Date	Mintage	VG	F	VF	XF	Unc
25 (1936)	64,720,000	0.25	0.75	1.50	3.00	7.50
28 (1939) Rare	—	—	—	—	—	—

Y# 355 CENT (1 Fen) **Composition:** Aluminum

Date	Mintage	VG	F	VF	XF	Unc
29 (1940)	150,000,000	—	0.10	0.25	0.50	1.50

Y# 357 CENT (1 Fen) **Composition:** Brass

Date	Mintage	VG	F	VF	XF	Unc
29 (1940)	50,000,000	0.25	0.75	1.00	2.00	4.00

Y# 363 CENT (1 Fen) **Composition:** Bronze

Date	VG	F	VF	XF	Unc
37 (1948)	1.50	4.00	10.00	15.00	20.00

Y# 353 CENT (1 Hsien) **Composition:** Brass **Note:** Shi Kwan Cent.

Date	VG	F	VF	XF	Unc
28(1939)	13.50	40.00	60.00	120	200

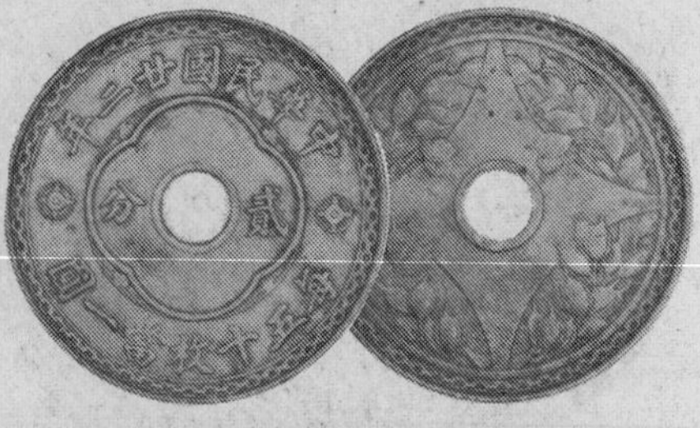

Y# 325a 2 CENTS (2 Fen) **Composition:** Bronze

Date	VG	F	VF	XF	Unc
22(1933)	13.50	40.00	60.00	95.00	150

Y# 358 2 CENTS (2 Fen) **Composition:** Brass

Date	VG	F	VF	XF	Unc
29(1940)	0.20	0.50	1.00	1.50	2.00
30(1941) Rare	—	—	—	—	—

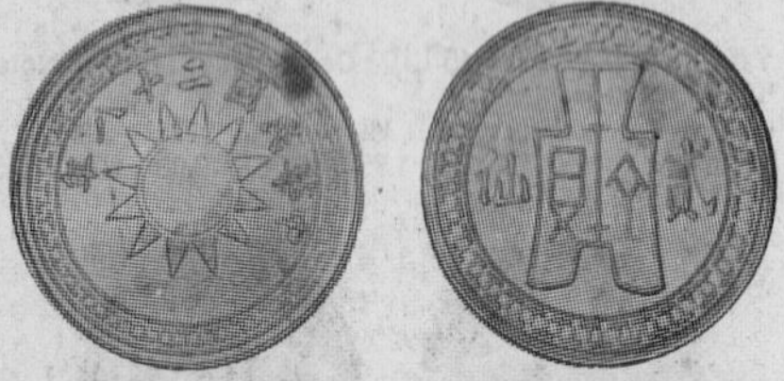

Y# 354 2 CENTS (2 Hsien) **Composition:** Brass

Date	Mintage	VG	F	VF	XF	Unc
28(1939)	300,000,000	3.50	10.00	15.00	25.00	50.00

Y# 348 5 CENTS (5 Fen) **Composition:** Nickel

Date	Mintage	VG	F	VF	XF	Unc
25(1936)	72,844,000	0.35	1.00	1.50	3.00	6.00
27(1938)	34,325,000	0.75	2.50	4.50	8.00	15.00
28(1939)	6,000,000	3.50	10.00	15.00	25.00	50.00

Y# 348.1 5 CENTS (5 Fen) **Composition:** Nickel
Reverse: A mint mark below spade (Vienna)

Date	Mintage	VG	F	VF	XF	Unc
25(1936)	20,000,000	0.35	1.00	2.00	3.50	15.00

Y# 348.2 5 CENTS (5 Fen) **Composition:** Nickel
Obverse: Character "P'ing" on both sides of portrait

Date	VG	F	VF	XF	Unc
25 (1936)	17.50	50.00	80.00	125	175

Y# 348.3 5 CENTS (5 Fen) **Composition:** Nickel
Obverse: Character "Ch'ing" on both sides of portrait

Date	VG	F	VF	XF	Unc
25 (1936)	17.50	50.00	80.00	125	175

Y# 356 5 CENTS (5 Fen) **Composition:** Aluminum

Date	Mintage	VG	F	VF	XF	Unc
29(1940)	350,000,000	0.20	0.50	1.00	2.50	4.00

Y# 359 5 CENTS (5 Fen) **Composition:** Copper-Nickel

Date	Mintage	VG	F	VF	XF	Unc
29(1940)	57,000,000	0.10	0.25	1.50	2.50	5.00
30(1941)	96,000,000	0.10	0.25	1.50	2.50	6.00

K# 602b 10 CENTS (1 Chiao) **Weight:** 2.3000 g. **Composition:** Silver **Note:** Engrailed with circles.

Date	VG	F	VF	XF	Unc
ND(1912)	—	—	700	850	1,500

K# 602 10 CENTS (1 Chiao) **Weight:** 2.3000 g. **Composition:** Silver **Note:** Similar to 1 Dollar, Y#318, vertical reeding.

Date	VG	F	VF	XF	Unc
ND(1912)	65.00	200	500	700	1,250

Y# 326 10 CENTS (1 Chiao) **Weight:** 2.7000 g. **Composition:** 0.7000 Silver .0607 oz. ASW

Date	VG	F	VF	XF	Unc
3 (1914)	1.75	5.00	10.00	17.50	40.00
5 (1916)	6.50	20.00	35.00	50.00	100

Y# 334 10 CENTS (1 Chiao) **Composition:** Silver
Subject: Pu Yi wedding

Date	VG	F	VF	XF	Unc
15 (1926)	1.75	5.00	12.00	25.00	60.00

Y# 339 10 CENTS (1 Chiao) **Weight:** 2.5000 g. **Composition:** Silver **Subject:** Death of Sun Yat-sen

Date	VG	F	VF	XF	Unc
16 (1927)	8.50	25.00	40.00	70.00	135

Y# 349 10 CENTS (1 Chiao) **Composition:** Nickel

Date	Mintage	VG	F	VF	XF	Unc
25(1936)	73,866,000	0.20	0.60	1.00	3.00	7.50
27(1938)	110,203,000	0.65	2.00	4.25	8.00	20.00
28(1939)	68,000,000	0.50	1.50	3.50	10.00	27.50

Y# 349a 10 CENTS (1 Chiao) **Composition:** Non-Magnetic Nickel Alloy

Date	Mintage	VG	F	VF	XF	Unc
25(1936)	1,000,000	6.00	18.00	30.00	35.00	65.00

Note: All of the Y#349 coins were supposed to have been minted in pure nickel at the Shanghai Mint. However, in 1936 a warloard had the Tientsin Mint produce about one million 10 Cent pieces of heavily alloyed nickel. The result is that the Shanghai pieces are attracted to a magnet while the Tientsin pieces are not.

Y# 349.1 10 CENTS (1 Chiao) **Composition:** Nickel
Reverse: Mint mark A below spade (Vienna Mint)

Date	Mintage	VG	F	VF	XF	Unc
25(1936)A	60,000,000	0.35	1.00	2.00	8.00	25.00

Y# 360 10 CENTS (1 Chiao) **Composition:** Copper-Nickel **Edge:** Reeded

Date	Mintage	VG	F	VF	XF	Unc
29(1940)	68,000,000	0.20	0.50	2.50	8.00	15.00
30(1941)	254,000,000	0.20	0.50	1.50	2.50	5.00
31(1942)	10,000,000	8.50	25.00	60.00	80.00	120

Y# 360.1 10 CENTS (1 Chiao) **Composition:** Copper-Nickel **Edge:** Plain

Date	VG	F	VF	XF	Unc
29(1940) Rare	—	—	—	—	—
30(1941)	0.65	2.00	7.50	10.00	15.00

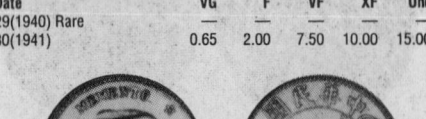

Y# 317 20 CENTS (2 Chiao) **Weight:** 5.2000 g. **Composition:** Silver **Subject:** Founding of the Republic

Date	Mintage	VG	F	VF	XF	Unc
ND(1912)	155,000	5.00	15.00	20.00	35.00	80.00

Y# 327 20 CENTS (2 Chiao) **Weight:** 5.4000 g. **Composition:** 0.7000 Silver .1215 oz. ASW

Date	VG	F	VF	XF	Unc
3 (1914)	1.00	3.00	5.00	9.00	35.00
5 (1916)	1.00	3.00	5.00	10.00	45.00
9 (1920)	35.00	100	250	300	500

Y# 335 20 CENTS (2 Chiao) **Weight:** 5.2000 g. **Composition:** Silver **Subject:** Pu Yi wedding

Date	VG	F	VF	XF	Unc
15 (1926)	3.50	10.00	15.00	30.00	80.00

Y# 340 20 CENTS (2 Chiao) **Weight:** 5.3000 g. **Composition:** Silver **Subject:** Death of Sun Yat-sen

Date	VG	F	VF	XF	Unc
16(1927)	5.00	15.00	25.00	40.00	100

Y# 350 20 CENTS (20 Fen) **Composition:** Nickel

Date	Mintage	VG	F	VF	XF	Unc
25(1936)	49,620,000	0.20	0.50	2.50	6.00	10.00
27(1938)	61,248,000	0.35	1.00	2.00	7.00	12.00
28(1939)	38,000,000	0.65	2.00	5.00	10.00	15.00

Y# 350.1 20 CENTS (20 Fen) **Composition:** Nickel **Reverse:** Mint mark A below spade (Vienna Mint)

Date	Mintage	VG	F	VF	XF	Unc
25(1936)A	40,000,000	0.35	1.00	2.00	3.50	6.00

Y# 361 20 CENTS (20 Fen) **Composition:** Copper-Nickel

Date	Mintage	VG	F	VF	XF	Unc
31(1942)	32,300,000	0.15	0.40	1.00	2.25	4.00

Y# 328 50 CENTS (1/2 Yuan) **Weight:** 13.6000 g. **Composition:** 0.7000 Silver .3060 oz. ASW

Date	VG	F	VF	XF	Unc
3 (1914)	6.50	20.00	30.00	50.00	100

Y# 362 50 CENTS (1/2 Yuan) **Composition:** Copper-Nickel

Date	Mintage	VG	F	VF	XF	Unc
31(1942)	57,000,000	0.50	1.50	3.00	7.50	15.00
32(1943)	4,000,000	1.25	3.50	9.50	17.50	30.00

Y# 318 DOLLAR (Yuan) **Weight:** 26.9000 g. **Composition:** 0.9000 Silver .7785 oz. ASW **Subject:** Sun Yat-sen Founding of the Republic **Reverse:** Two five-pointed stars dividing legend at top

Date	VG	F	VF	XF	Unc
ND(1912)	35.00	100	150	300	650

Y# 318.1 DOLLAR (Yuan) **Weight:** 26.9000 g. **Composition:** 0.9000 Silver .7785 oz. ASW **Obverse:** Dot below ear

Date	VG	F	VF	XF	Unc
ND(1912)	—	—	—	—	—

Note: For similar issue with rosettes see Y#318a.1 (1927)

Y# 319 DOLLAR (Yuan) **Weight:** 27.3000 g. **Composition:** 0.9000 Silver .7900 oz. ASW **Obverse:** Similar to Y#318

Date	VG	F	VF	XF	Unc
ND(1912)	27.50	80.00	125	200	450

Y# 320 DOLLAR (Yuan) **Weight:** 26.5000 g. **Composition:** Silver **Subject:** Li Yüan-hung Founding of Republic **Reverse:** Similar to Y#319

Date	VG	F	VF	XF	Unc
ND(1912)	45.00	125	250	400	700

Y# 320.1 DOLLAR (Yuan) **Weight:** 26.5000 g. **Composition:** Silver **Rev. Legend:** OE for OF

Date	VG	F	VF	XF	Unc
ND(1912)	50.00	150	275	450	750

Y# 320.2 DOLLAR (Yuan) **Weight:** 26.5000 g. **Composition:** Silver **Rev. Legend:** CIIINA for CHINA

Date	VG	F	VF	XF	Unc
ND(1912)	50.00	150	275	450	750

Y# 321 DOLLAR (Yuan) **Weight:** 26.5000 g. **Composition:** Silver **Subject:** Li Yüan-hung Founding of Republic

Date	VG	F	VF	XF	Unc
ND(1912)	17.50	50.00	100	150	250

Y# 321.1 DOLLAR (Yuan) **Weight:** 26.5000 g. **Composition:** Silver **Reverse:** H of "THE" in legend engraved as I I

Date	VG	F	VF	XF	Unc
ND(1912)	20.00	60.00	125	175	275

Y# 322 DOLLAR (Yuan) **Weight:** 26.7000 g. **Composition:** 0.9000 Silver .7474 oz. ASW **Subject:** Yüan Shih-kai Founding of Republic **Note:** 2.8 millimeters thickness.

Date	Mintage	VG	F	VF	XF	Unc
ND (1914)	20,000	20.00	60.00	125	250	375

Y# 329 DOLLAR (Yuan) **Weight:** 26.4000 g. **Composition:** 0.8900 Silver .7555 oz. ASW **Subject:** Yüan Shih-kai **Obverse:** Six characters above head **Note:** Vertical reeding.

Date	VG	F	VF	XF	Unc
3 (1914)	2.25	7.00	12.00	15.00	25.00

Y# 329.1 DOLLAR (Yuan) **Weight:** 26.4000 g. **Composition:** 0.8900 Silver .7555 oz. ASW **Note:** Edge engrailed with circles

Date	VG	F	VF	XF	Unc
3 (1914)	10.00	30.00	80.00	500	1,000

Y# 329.2 DOLLAR (Yuan) **Weight:** 26.4000 g. **Composition:** 0.8900 Silver .7555 oz. ASW **Edge:** Ornamented with alternating T's

Date	VG	F	VF	XF	Unc
3	10.00	30.00	80.00	500	1,000

Y# 329.3 DOLLAR (Yuan) **Weight:** 26.4000 g. **Composition:** 0.8900 Silver .7555 oz. ASW **Edge:** Plain

Date	VG	F	VF	XF	Unc
3 (1914)	6.50	20.00	40.00	300	500

Y# 329.4 DOLLAR (Yuan) **Weight:** 26.4000 g. **Composition:** 0.8900 Silver .7555 oz. ASW **Note:** Tiny circle in ribbon bow. This is a mint mark, but it is not clear what mint is indicated.

Date	VG	F	VF	XF	Unc
3 (1914)	5.00	15.00	30.00	70.00	125

Y# 322.1 DOLLAR (Yuan) **Weight:** 26.7000 g. **Composition:** 0.9000 Silver .7474 oz. ASW **Note:** 3.25 millimeters thickness.

Date	VG	F	VF	XF	Unc
ND(ca.1918)	20.00	60.00	125	250	375

Note: A restrike made about 1918 for collectors

Y# 330 DOLLAR (Yuan) **Weight:** 8.1500 g. **Composition:** 0.8500 Gold .2227 oz. AGW **Ruler:** Hung-hsien

Date	VG	F	VF	XF	Unc
8 (1919)	—	—	2,000	2,850	4,000

Y# 329.6 DOLLAR (Yuan) **Weight:** 26.4000 g. **Composition:** 0.8900 Silver .7555 oz. ASW **Obverse:** Seven characters above head

Date	VG	F	VF	XF	Unc
8 (1919)	3.50	10.00	15.00	35.00	100
9 (1920)	2.25	7.00	10.00	15.00	30.00
10 (1921)	2.25	7.00	10.00	15.00	30.00

Y# 329.5 DOLLAR (Yuan) **Weight:** 26.4000 g. **Composition:** 0.8900 Silver .7555 oz. ASW **Edge:** Oblique reeding

Date	VG	F	VF	XF	Unc
10 (1921)	6.00	17.50	30.00	35.00	50.00

K# 676 DOLLAR (Yuan) **Weight:** 26.5000 g. **Composition:** Silver **Subject:** President Hsu Shih-chang **Edge:** Reeded

Date	VG	F	VF	XF	Unc
10 (1921)	50.00	150	300	500	750

K# 676.1 DOLLAR (Yuan) **Weight:** 26.5000 g. **Composition:** Silver **Edge:** Plain

Date	VG	F	VF	XF	Unc
10 (1921)	100	300	600	800	1,200

K# 677 DOLLAR (Yuan) **Weight:** 26.7000 g. **Composition:** Silver **Obverse:** Bust of President Tsao Kun facing

Date	Mintage	VG	F	VF	XF	Unc
ND (1923)	50,000	35.00	100	200	300	450

K# 678 DOLLAR (Yuan) **Weight:** 26.7000 g. **Composition:** Silver **Obverse:** Bust of President Tsao Kun in military uniform

Date	VG	F	VF	XF	Unc
ND (1923)	—	—	200	300	450

Y# 336 DOLLAR (Yuan) **Weight:** 26.8000 g. **Composition:** Silver **Subject:** Pu Yi Wedding **Reverse:** Value in small characters

Date	VG	F	VF	XF	Unc
12 (1923)	60.00	175	350	600	1,200

Y# 336.1 DOLLAR (Yuan) **Weight:** 26.8000 g. **Composition:** Silver **Subject:** Pu Yi Wedding **Reverse:** Value in large characters

Date	VG	F	VF	XF	Unc
12 (1923)	100	300	600	1,000	2,400

K# 683 DOLLAR (Yuan) **Composition:** Silver **Obverse:** Bust of President Tuan Chi-jui facing

Date	VG	F	VF	XF	Unc
ND (1924)	35.00	100	200	300	600

K# 690 DOLLAR (Yuan) **Weight:** 26.5000 g. **Composition:** Silver **Obverse:** Bust of General Chu Yu-pu facing

Date	VG	F	VF	XF	Unc
ND (1927)	—	—	—	6,500	9,500

Y# 318a.1 DOLLAR (Yuan) **Weight:** 27.0000 g. **Composition:** 0.8900 Silver .7727 oz. ASW **Obverse:** Bust of Sun Yat-sen left **Reverse:** Two rosettes dividing legend at top; mausoleum in Nanking **Edge:** Incuse reeding

Date	VG	F	VF	XF	Unc
ND(1927)	2.25	7.00	9.00	12.50	22.50

Y# 318a.2 DOLLAR (Yuan) **Weight:** 27.0000 g. **Composition:** 0.8900 Silver .7727 oz. ASW **Edge:** Reeding in relief

Date	VG	F	VF	XF	Unc
ND(1927)	2.25	7.00	9.00	12.50	22.50

Note: Varieties exist with errors in the English legend. For similar coins with 5-pointed stars dividing legends, see Y#318 (1912). In 1949 the Canton Mint restruck Memento dollars. There are modern restrikes in red copper and brass.

K# 609 DOLLAR (Yuan) **Weight:** 27.0000 g. **Composition:** Silver **Obverse:** Bust of Sun Yat-sen **Reverse:** Sun Yat-sen Memorial

Date	Mintage	VG	F	VF	XF	Unc
16(1927)	480	250	700	1,500	2,750	5,000

Y# 344 DOLLAR (Yuan) **Weight:** 26.7000 g. **Composition:** 0.8800 Silver .7555 oz. ASW **Obverse:** Bust of Sun Yat-sen left **Reverse:** Birds above junk, rising sun

Date	Mintage	VG	F	VF	XF	Unc
21(1932)	2,260,000	45.00	125	200	300	600

Y# 345 DOLLAR (Yuan) **Weight:** 26.7000 g. **Composition:** 0.8800 Silver .7555 oz. ASW **Reverse:** Without birds above junk or rising sun

Date	Mintage	VG	F	VF	XF	Unc
23(1933)	46,400,000	4.00	12.50	15.00	20.00	45.00
24(1934)	128,740,000	3.00	9.00	12.50	15.00	25.00

Note: In 1949, three U.S. mints restruck a total of 30 million "Junk Dollars" dated Year 23

Y# 331 20 DOLLARS **Weight:** 16.3000 g. **Composition:** 0.8500 Gold .4456 oz. AGW **Ruler:** Hung-hsien

Date	VG	F	VF	XF	Unc
8 (1919)	—	—	—	4,500	7,500

TOKEN COINAGE

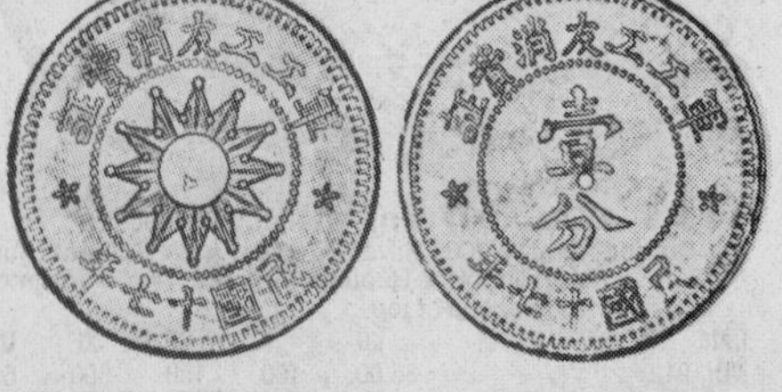

KM# Tn1 FEN **Composition:** Brass **Note:** Struck at Shansi Arsenal

Date	F	VF	XF	Unc	BU
17 (1928)	75.00	125	175	300	—

Note: This token is usually found with small punch marks near center on obverse and reverse

KM# Tn2 2 FEN **Composition:** Brass **Note:** Struck at Shansi Arsenal

Date	F	VF	XF	Unc	BU
17 (1928)	150	250	400	650	—

Note: This token has always been found with small punch marks near center on obverse and reverse

KM# Tn3 5 FEN **Composition:** Brass **Note:** Struck at Shansi Arsenal; similar to 2 Fen, KM#Tn2.

Date	F	VF	XF	Unc	BU
17 (1928)	450	750	1,250	—	—

Note: This token has always been found with small punch marks near center on obverse and reverse

KM# Tn4 10 FEN **Composition:** Brass **Note:** Struck at Shansi Arsenal; similar to 2 Fen, KM#Tn2.

Date	F	VF	XF	Unc	BU
17 (1928)	450	750	1,250	—	—

Note: This token has always been found with small punch marks near center on obverse and reverse

PATTERNS

Including off metal strikes

KM#	Date	Mintage	Identification	Mkt Val
Pn2	ND(1912)	—	Cash. Copper Or Brass.	—
Pn3	ND(1912)	—	Cash. Zinc.	—
Pn4	ND(1912)	—	Cash. Iron.	—
Pn5	ND(1912)	—	10 Cash. Copper. Hsu13	1,000
PnA6	ND(1912)	—	10 Cash. Copper. Similar to Pn5 but larger bust; W972.	—
Pn6	ND(1912)	—	10 Cash. Gold.	—
Pn7	ND(1912)	—	20 Cents. Gold. Y#317	1,500
Pn8	ND(1912)	—	Dollar. Gold. Y#318	—
Pn9	ND(1912)	—	Dollar. Gold. Y#318 - K#1550	6,500
PnA10	ND(1912)	—	Dollar. Silver. Li Yuan-hung	—
Pn10	ND(1912)	—	Dollar. Silver. Chin Teh-chuen, K#672	25,000
Pn11	ND(1912)	—	Dollar. Eyes in relief. Chin Teh-chuen, K#672a.	—

Note: Authenticity in doubt

KM#	Date	Mintage	Identification	Mkt Val
Pn12	ND(1912)	—	Dollar. Bronze. K#672x	4,000

Note: Authenticity in doubt

KM#	Date	Mintage	Identification	Mkt Val
PnA13	ND(1914)	—	10 Cash. Copper. With L. GEORGI; Y#309.	800
Pn13	3(1914)	—	5 Cents. Nickel. K#815	—
Pn14	3(1914)	—	5 Cents. Nickel. Plain edge. Essay, K#815a	—
Pn15	3(1914)	—	5 Cents. Nickel. Milled edge. Essay, K#815b; with G. L.	—
Pn16	3(1914)	—	5 Cents. Silver. Milled edge. Essay, K#815c; with G. L.	350
Pn17	3(1914)	—	5 Cents. Copper. Essay, K#815x	225
Pn18	3(1914)	—	5 Cents. Pewter. Plain edge. Essay, K#815y	—
Pn19	3(1914)	—	5 Cents. Copper. With G. L., essay, K#815z	—
Pn20	3(1914)	—	10 Cents. Silver. With G. L., K#659a	700
Pn21	3(1914)	—	10 Cents. Copper. Y#326	45.00
Pn22	3(1914)	—	10 Cents. Nickel. Y#326	350
Pn23	3(1914)	—	20 Cents. Silver. With G. L.; K#657a	900
Pn24	3(1914)	—	20 Cents. Copper. Y#327	65.00
Pn25	3(1914)	—	20 Cents. Nickel. Y#327	375
Pn26	3(1914)	—	20 Cents. Pewter. Y#327	300
Pn27	3(1914)	—	50 Cents. Silver. With L. GIORGI; Yuan Shih-kai, K#655a.	1,150
Pn28	ND(1914)	—	Dollar. Silver. With L. GIORGI; Yuan Shih-kai, K#642a.	1,250
Pn29	ND(1914)	—	Dollar. Gold. With L. GIORGI, Yuan Shih-kai; K#1558	8,500
Pn30	ND(1914)	—	Dollar. Silver. Yuan Shih-kai, plumes of hat touch rim; K#644.	2,500
Pn31	ND(1914)	—	Dollar. Silver. With L. GIORGI; Yuan Shih-kai, K#645	2,500
Pn32	3(1914)	—	Dollar. Silver. K#643	2,250
Pn33	3(1914)	—	Dollar. Silver. With L. GIORGI; K#643a	2,250
Pn34	ND(1914)	—	Dollar. Copper. Y#322	500
Pn35	ND(1914)	—	Dollar. Brass. Y#322	600
Pn36	ND(1914)	—	Dollar. Gold. Y#329	—
Pn37	ND(1914)	—	Dollar. Copper. Y#329	450
Pn38	ND(1914)	—	Dollar. Brass. Y#329	400
PnA39	ND(1914)	—	5 Dollars. K#1517	3,500
Pn39	5(1916)	—	1/2 Cent. Copper. Without center hole; Y#323	350
Pn40	5(1916)	—	10 Cash. Copper. Without center hole; Y#324	400
Pn41	5(1916)	—	10 Cash. Copper. With L. GIORGI; Y#324.3	—
Pn42	5(1916)	—	20 Cash. Copper. Hsu44	650
Pn43	5(1916)	—	20 Cents. Copper. Y#327	—
Pn44	ND(1916)	—	Dollar. Gold. Y#332	6,000
Pn45	ND(1916)	—	Dollar. White Metal. Y#332	—
Pn47	ND(1916)	—	Dollar. Silver. With L. GIORGI; plumes don't touch rim; K#663a.	17,500
Pn48	ND(1916)	—	Dollar. Silver. With L. GIORGI; K#663d	10,000
Pn50	1(1916)	—	10 Dollars. Gold. with L. G. Hung-hsien, near shoulder; K#1515a	—
Pn51	1(1916)	—	10 Dollars. Copper. with L. G. Hung-hsien, near shoulder; K#1515y	—
Pn52	ND(1916)	—	Dollar. Silver. Plumes of hat touch rim; K#664	3,750
Pn53	ND(1916)	—	Dollar. Gold. With L. GIORGI; K#1560	20,000
Pn54	1(1916)	—	10 Dollars. Silver. Y#333	—
Pn55	1(1916)	—	10 Dollars. Copper. Y#333	375
Pn56	8(1919)	—	10 Cash. Copper. Hsu29	1,000
Pn57	8(1919)	—	10 Cash. Copper. Hsu30	1,000
Pn59	8(1919)	—	10 Dollars. Copper. Y#330	325
Pn60	8(1919)	—	10 Dollars. Brass. Y#330	325
Pn61	8(1919)	—	20 Dollars. Copper. Y#331	485
PnA62	9(1920)	—	50 Cents. Gold. Ni Szu-ch'ung	6,000
PnB62	9(1920)	—	Dollar. Brass. K#666v. Ni Szu-ch'ung.	300
PnC62	9(1920)	—	Dollar. Pewter. K#666y. Ni Szu-ch'ung.	200
Pn62	10(1921)	—	Dollar. Gold. K#1570	6,500
Pn63	10(1921)	—	Dollar. Silver. Reeded edge. K#676a.1	900
Pn64	10(1921)	—	Dollar. Silver. Plain edge. K#676a.2	750
Pn65	10(1921)	—	Dollar. Gold. Reeded edge. K#1570	9,350
Pn66	10(1921)	—	Dollar. Gold. Plain edge. K#1570a	9,350
Pn67	ND(1923)	—	Dollar. Gold. K#1572	9,900
Pn68	ND(1923)	—	Dollar. Copper. K#677x	450
Pn69	ND(1923)	—	Dollar. Brass. K#677y	450
Pn70	12(1923)	—	Dollar. Gold. Y#336	8,500
Pn71	12(1923)	—	Dollar. Copper. Y#336	—
Pn72	12(1923)	—	Dollar. Gold. Y#336.1	—
Pn73	ND(1924)	—	Dollar. Gold. K#1577	7,000
Pn74	ND(1924)	—	Dollar. Copper. K#683x	700
Pn75	ND(1924)	—	Dollar. Pewter. K#683y	700
Pn76	15(1926)	—	10 Cents. Copper. Y#334	125
Pn77	15(1926)	—	10 Cents. Lead. Y#334	90.00
Pn78	15(1926)	—	20 Cents. Copper. Y#335	65.00
PnA79	15(1926)	—	Dollar. Silver. K#604	82,500
Pn79	15(1926)	—	Dollar. Silver. K#685	20,900
Pn80	16(1927)	—	10 Cents. Copper. Y#339	—
Pn81	16(1927)	—	10 Cents. Gold. Y#339	—
Pn82	ND(1927)	—	Dollar. Gold. Y#318	—
Pn83	ND(1927)	—	Dollar. Copper. Y#318	225
Pn84	ND(1927)	—	Dollar. Silver. K#687	25,000
Pn85	16(1927)	—	Dollar. Silver. K#686	27,500
Pn86	ND(1928)	—	20 Cash. Copper. Y#337	—
Pn87	ND(1928)	—	20 Cash. Copper. Similar to 1 Chiao.	—
Pn90	17(1928)	—	Dollar. Silver. K#688	4,500
Pn91	17(1928)	—	Dollar. Copper. K#688x	3,500
PnA92	17(1928)	—	Dollar. Gold. K#688z	19,800
Pn92	17(1928)	—	Dollar. Pewter. K#688y	6,500
Pn93	18(1929)	—	20 Cents. Silver. K#611	—
Pn94	18(1929)	—	10 Cents. Copper-Nickel. Vienna; K#617yVI	850
Pn95	18(1929)	—	20 Cents. Copper-Nickel. Vienna; K#617yV	—
Pn96	18(1929)	—	50 Cents. Copper-Nickel. Vienna; K#617yIV	—
Pn97	18(1929)	—	Dollar. Silver. Italian; K#614	1,250
Pn98	18(1929)	—	Dollar. Silver. With designer's name. K#614a	2,500
Pn99	18(1929)	—	Dollar. Silver. English; K#615	650
Pn100	18(1929)	—	Dollar. Silver. American; K#616	600
Pn101	18(1929)	—	Dollar. Silver. Austrian; K#61	600
Pn102	18(1929)	—	Dollar. Silver. Japanese; K#618	900

Note: In 1929 China invited several mints to submit designs for a new Sun Yat-sen Dollar, with his bust on one side and a junk on the other. All designs were very much alike, differing mainly in details of the portrait, the waves, and the junk.

KM#	Date	Mintage	Identification	Mkt Val
Pn103	18(1929)	—	10 Cents. Silver. K#617yIII	850
Pn104	18(1929)	—	20 Cents. Silver. K#617yII	850
Pn105	18(1929)	—	50 Cents. Silver. K#617yI	850
Pn106	18(1929)	—	Dollar. Silver. K#610	11,000
Pn107	18(1929)	—	20 Cents. Silver. K#611	5,000
Pn108	18(1929)	—	Dollar. Silver. Wreath. K#612	—
Pn109	ND(1929)	—	Dollar. Silver. Memento. K#620	—
Pn110	ND(1929)	—	Dollar. Copper. K#620x	—
Pn111	ND(1929)	—	Dollar. White Metal. K#620y	—
Pn112	ND(1929)	—	Dollar. Silver. Wreath. K#620k	—
Pn113	ND(1929)	—	Dollar. White Metal. K#620m	—
Pn114	21(1932)	—	Cent. Bronze.	—
Pn115	21(1932)	—	Cent. Bronze. Without center hole	—
Pn118	21(1932)	—	2 Cents. Nickel. Milled edge. K#830	1,200
Pn119	21(1932)	—	2 Cents. Nickel. Plain edge. K#830a	1,200
Pn120	21(1932)	—	2 Cents. Nickel. Without center hole; K#830b	2,000
Pn121	21(1932)	—	5 Cents. Nickel. Milled edge. K#829	550
Pn122	21(1932)	—	5 Cents. Nickel. Plain edge. K#829a	550
Pn123	21(1932)	—	5 Cents. Nickel. Without center; K#829b	550
Pn136	21(1932)	—	Dollar. Copper. K#628x	—
Pn137	21(1932)	—	Dollar. Copper. Y#344	275
Pn138	22(1933)	—	Dollar. Copper. Y#345	—
Pn139	23(1934)	—	Dollar. Copper. Y#345	—
Pn140	24(1935)	—	5 Cents. Nickel. K#833	400
Pn141	24(1935)	—	5 Cents. Copper. K#833x	—
Pn142	24(1935)	—	10 Cents. Nickel. K#832	400
Pn143	24(1935)	—	10 Cents. Copper. K#832x	—
Pn144	24(1935)	—	20 Cents. Nickel. K#831	400
Pn145	24(1935)	—	20 Cents. Copper. K#831x	—
PnA146	24(1935)	—	1/2 Dollar. Silver. K#625k	—
PnB146	24(1935)	—	1/2 Dollar. Copper. K#625x	—
Pn146	24(1935)	—	Dollar. Silver. K#625	—
Pn146a	24(1935)	—	Dollar. Copper Or Brass. Reduced size Pn146	1,550
Pn147	24(1935)	—	Dollar. Copper. Y#345	—
Pn148	25//1936	—	Mei. Copper. Character "Chin".	—
Pn149	25//1936	—	Mei. Copper.	—
Pn150	25//1936	—	2 Mei. Copper.	—
Pn151	25//1936	—	5 Mei. Copper.	—
Pn152	25//1936	—	10 Mei. Copper.	—
Pn153	25//1936	—	50 Mei. Copper.	—
Pn154	25//1936	—	20 Wen. Copper.	—
PnA155	25//1936	—	1/2 Fen. Copper. Character "P'ing" lower.	—

Note: This may also exist with character under spade on reverse

KM#	Date	Mintage	Identification	Mkt Val
Pn155	25//1936	—	Fen. Copper.	—
PnA156	25//1936	—	Fen. Copper. Character "P'ing" lower.	—
PnB156	25//1936	—	Fen. Copper. Character "P'ing" under spade.	—
PnC156	25//1936	—	Fen. Copper. Character "Ch'ing" lower.	—
PnD156	25//1936	—	Fen. Copper. Character "Ch'ing" under spade.	—
Pn156	25(1936)	—	5 Cents. Copper. Y#348	—
Pn157	25(1936)	—	10 Cents. Nickel. Character "Ch'ing" in field or on portrait.	450
Pn158	25(1936)	—	10 Cents. Nickel. Character "P'ing" in field or on portrait.	450
Pn159	25(1936)	—	10 Cents. Nickel. Character "Ch'ing" on side of portrait.	450
Pn160	25(1936)	—	10 Cents. Nickel. Character "P'ing" on side of portrait.	450
Pn161	25(1936)	—	10 Cents. Copper. Y#349	—
Pn162	25(1936)	—	10 Cents. Aluminum. Y#349	—
Pn163	25(1936)	—	10 Cents. Aluminum-Bronze. Y#349	—
Pn164	25(1936)	—	10 Cents. Lead. Y#349	—
Pn165	25(1936)	—	20 Cents. Copper. Y#350	—
Pn166	25(1936)	—	20 Cents. Aluminum. Y#350	—
Pn167	25(1936)	—	20 Cents. Aluminum-Bronze. Y#350	—
Pn168	25(1936)	—	20 Cents. Pewter. Y#350	75.00
Pn169	25(1936)	—	50 Cents. Silver. K#635	—
Pn170	25(1936)	—	50 Cents. Silver. K#633	—
Pn171	25(1936)	—	50 Cents. Silver. Similar to K#633 without Greek border.	—
Pn172	25(1936)	—	Dollar. Silver. K#634	—
Pn173	25(1936)	—	Dollar. Silver. Similar to K#632 without Greek border.	—
Pn174	25(1936)	—	Dollar. Silver. K#632	4,000
Pn175	25(1936)	—	Dollar. Copper. K#632x	—
Pn176	25(1936)	—	Dollar. Nickel. K#632y	—
Pn177	25(1936)	—	Dollar. Brass. K#632z	—
Pn178	25(1936)	—	Dollar. Silver. Chiang Kai-shek	25,000
Pn179	25(1936)	—	Dollar. Copper. Chiang Kai-shek	7,500
Pn180	26(1937)	—	5 Cents. Nickel. Y#348.2	—
Pn181	26(1937)	—	10 Cents. Nickel. "P'ing" on side of portrait; Y#349.7	—
Pn183	26(1937)	—	20 Cents. Nickel. Y#350.1	—
Pn184	26(1937) S	—	50 Cents. Silver. K#637	—
Pn185	26(1937) S	—	Dollar. Silver. K#636	—
Pn186	27(1938)	—	5 Cents. Copper. Y#348	—
Pn187	27(1938)	—	10 Cents. Copper. Y#349	—
Pn188	27(1938)	—	20 Cents. Copper. Y#350	—
Pn189	27(1938)	—	20 Cents. Pewter. Y#350	150
Pn190	28(1939)	—	5 Cents. Copper. Y#348	—
Pn191	28(1939)	—	5 Cents. Brass. Y#348	—
PnA192	28(1939)	—	20 Cents. Copper. K#857x	175
PnB192	29(1940)	—	1/2 Dollar. Copper.	250
Pn192	30(1941)	—	10 Cents. Copper. Y#360	250
Pn193	30(1941)	—	10 Cents. Brass. Y#360	—
PnA194	30(1941)	—	20 Cents. Nickel. K#863 IV	250
PnB194	30(1941)	—	1/2 Dollar. Silver. K#696x	—
PnC194	30(1941)	—	1/2 Dollar. Nickel. K#863 III	500
Pn194	31(1942)	—	10 Cents. Copper-Nickel. Character "Kuei" below the spade.	—
Pn195	31(1942)	—	10 Cents. Copper. Y#360	—
Pn196	31(1942)	—	10 Cents. Brass. Y#360	—
Pn197	31(1942)	—	20 Cents. Copper-Nickel. Character "Kuei" below spade.	—
Pn198	31(1942)	—	20 Cents. Copper. Y#361	—
Pn199	31(1942)	—	50 Cents. Copper-Nickel. Character "Kuei" between legs of space. K#866m	—
Pn200	31(1942)	—	50 Cents. Copper. Y#362	200
Pn201	31(1942)	—	50 Cents. Bronze. Y#362	200
Pn202	31(1942)	—	50 Cents. Silver. Y#362	500

KM#	Date	Mintage	Identification	Mkt Val
PnA203	32(1943)	—	50 Cents. Copper-Nickel. Character "Kuei" between legs of spade.	—
Pn203	32(1943)	—	50 Cents. Copper. Y#362	200
Pn204	32(1943)	—	50 Cents. Bronze. Y#362	200
PnA205	37(1948)	—	50 Cents. Silver. Ch'ing right; K#698	—
Pn205	37(1948)	—	Dollar. Silver. K#637yII	—
Pn206	37(1948)	—	2 Dollars. Silver. K#637yI; denomination	200

PATTERNS

Gold Standard

KM#Pn124-135 were intended to be a gold standard coinage, but was not adopted. Though inscribed One Yuan Dollar, the proposed unit was called a Sun.

KM#	Date	Mintage	Identification	Mkt Val
Pn124	21(1932)	—	10 Cents. Silver. K#631	—
Pn125	21(1932)	—	10 Cents. Silver. Plain edge. K#631a	—
Pn126	21(1932)	—	10 Cents. Copper. K#631	—
Pn127	21(1932)	—	20 Cents. Silver. Milled edge. K#630	—
Pn128	21(1932)	—	20 Cents. Silver. Plain edge. K#630a	—
Pn129	21(1932)	—	20 Cents. Copper. K#630x	—
Pn130	21(1932)	—	1/2 Dollar. Silver. Milled edge. K#629	4,000
Pn131	21(1932)	—	1/2 Dollar. Silver. Plain edge. K#629a	4,000
Pn132	21(1932)	—	1/2 Dollar. Copper. K#629x	—
Pn133	21(1932)	—	Dollar. Silver. Milled edge. K#628	—
Pn134	21(1932)	—	Dollar. Silver. Plain edge. K#628a	10,000
Pn135	21(1932)	—	Dollar. Silver. Cherry blossom edge	10,000

TRIAL STRIKES

KM#	Date	Mintage	Identification	Mkt Val
TS1	ND(1912)	—	Dollar. Silver. Uniface. Chin Te-chuan; K#672b	8,000

TS2	37(1948)	—	50 Cents. Silver. 4.9800 g. K#698w	750

TAIWAN

REPUBLIC

STANDARD COINAGE

Y# 531 CHIAO Composition: Bronze **Obverse:** Bust of Sun Yat-sen left

Date	Mintage	F	VF	XF	Unc	BU
38(1949)	157,600,000	0.10	0.30	1.00	4.00	—

Y# 533 CHIAO Composition: Aluminum

Date	Mintage	F	VF	XF	Unc	BU
44(1955)	583,980,000	—	0.10	0.15	1.00	—

Y# 545 CHIAO Composition: Aluminum

Date	Mintage	F	VF	XF	Unc	BU
56(1967)	89,999,000	—	0.10	0.15	0.75	—
59(1970)	30,000,000	—	0.10	0.25	1.00	—
60(1971)	19,925,000	—	0.20	0.40	1.50	—
61(1972)	11,141,000	0.10	0.40	0.60	2.00	—
62(1973)	111,400,000	—	—	0.10	0.75	—
63(1974)	71,930,000	—	0.10	0.25	1.00	—

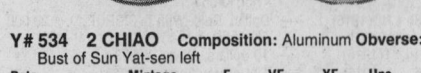

Y# 534 2 CHIAO Composition: Aluminum **Obverse:** Bust of Sun Yat-sen left

Date	Mintage	F	VF	XF	Unc	BU
39(1950)	327,495,000	—	0.10	0.50	3.00	—

Y# 532 5 CHIAO Weight: 5.0000 g. **Composition:** 0.7200 Silver .1157 oz. ASW **Obverse:** Bust of Sun Yat-sen left

Date	F	VF	XF	Unc	BU
38(1949)	1.50	2.00	3.50	5.00	—

Y# 535 5 CHIAO Composition: Brass

Date	Mintage	F	VF	XF	Unc	BU
43(1954)	279,624,000	—	0.10	0.25	1.00	—

Y# 546 5 CHIAO Composition: Brass

Date	Mintage	F	VF	XF	Unc	BU
56(1967)	109,999,000	—	0.10	0.15	0.50	—
59(1970)	6,010,000	0.15	0.30	0.60	1.25	—
60(1971)	4,434,000	0.20	0.40	0.80	1.50	—
61(1972)	21,171,000	—	0.10	0.20	1.00	—
62(1973)	88,840,000	—	0.10	0.20	1.00	—
69(1980)	3,972,000	—	0.10	0.20	1.00	—
70(1981)	100,000,000	—	0.10	0.20	1.00	—

Y# 550 5 CHIAO Composition: Bronze

Date	Mintage	F	VF	XF	Unc	BU
70(1981)	103,800,000	—	0.10	0.20	1.00	—
70(1981) Proof	—	Value: 10.00				
75(1986)	22,000,000	—	0.10	0.20	1.00	—
77(1988)	10,000,000	—	0.15	0.30	1.25	—

Y# 536 YUAN Composition: Copper-Nickel-Zinc

Date	Mintage	F	VF	XF	Unc	BU
49(1960)	321,717,000	—	0.10	0.20	0.50	—
59(1970)	48,800,000	0.10	0.20	0.50	1.00	—
60(1971)	41,532,000	0.10	0.20	0.50	1.00	—
61(1972)	105,309,000	—	0.10	0.20	0.50	—
62(1973)	353,924,000	—	0.10	0.20	0.50	—
63(1974)	535,605,000	—	0.10	0.20	0.50	—
64(1975)	456,874,000	—	0.10	0.20	0.50	—
65(1976)	634,497,000	—	0.10	0.20	0.50	—
66(1977)	116,900,000	—	0.10	0.20	0.50	—
67(1978)	104,245,000	—	0.10	0.20	0.50	—
68(1979)	—	0.10	0.20	0.50	0.80	—
69(1980)	113,900,000	—	0.10	0.20	0.50	—

Y# A537 YUAN Composition: Silver **Subject:** 50th Anniversary of the Republic **Obverse:** Chiang Kai-shek

Date	F	VF	XF	Unc	BU
50(1961)	—	—	—	280	—

Note: This coin was released accidentally or was released and quickly withdrawn and is very scarce today

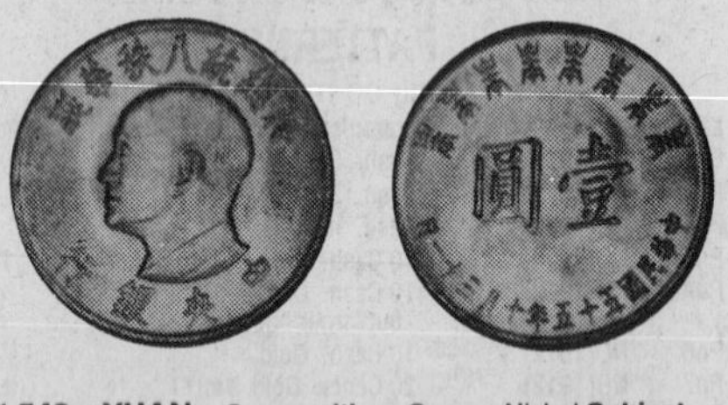

Y# 543 YUAN Composition: Copper-Nickel **Subject:** 80th Birthday of Chiang Kai-shek

Date	F	VF	XF	Unc	BU
55(1966)	0.15	0.25	0.40	1.00	—

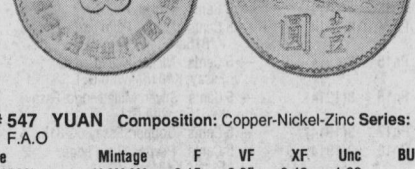

Y# 547 YUAN Composition: Copper-Nickel-Zinc **Series:** F.A.O

Date	Mintage	F	VF	XF	Unc	BU
58(1969)	10,000,000	0.15	0.25	0.40	1.00	—

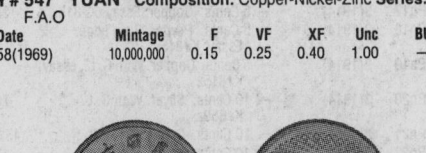

Y# 551 YUAN Composition: Bronze **Obverse:** Bust of Chiang Kai-shek left

Date	Mintage	F	VF	XF	Unc	BU
70(1981)	1,080,000,000	—	—	0.10	0.15	—
70(1981) Proof	—	Value: 12.50				
71(1982)	780,000,000	—	—	0.10	0.15	—
72(1983)	420,000,000	—	—	0.10	0.15	—
73(1984)	110,000,000	—	—	0.10	0.15	—
74(1985)	200,000,000	—	—	0.10	0.15	—
75(1986)	200,000,000	—	—	0.10	0.15	—
76(1987)	110,000,000	—	—	0.10	0.15	—
77(1988)	40,000,000	—	—	0.20	0.50	—
81(1992)	—	—	—	0.15	0.25	—
82(1993)	—	—	—	0.15	0.25	—
83(1994)	—	—	—	0.15	0.25	—
84(1995)	—	—	—	0.15	0.25	—
85(1996)	—	—	—	0.15	0.25	—
86(1997)	—	—	—	—	—	—

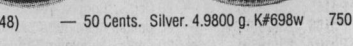

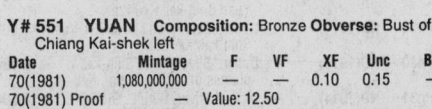

Y# 537 5 YUAN **Composition:** Copper-Nickel **Obverse:** Bust of Sun Yat-sen left

Date	F	VF	XF	Unc	BU
54(1965)	0.25	0.75	1.50	5.00	—

Y# 548 5 YUAN **Composition:** Copper-Nickel **Obverse:** Bust of Chiang Kai-shek left

Date	Mintage	F	VF	XF	Unc	BU
59(1970)	12,360,000	0.15	0.40	0.80	1.50	—
60(1971)	20,575,000	0.15	0.35	0.50	1.00	—
61(1972)	27,998,000	0.15	0.35	0.50	1.00	—
62(1973)	50,122,000	0.15	0.35	0.50	0.80	—
63(1974)	418,068,000	0.15	0.35	0.50	0.80	—
64(1975)	39,520,000	0.15	0.35	0.50	0.80	—
65(1976)	140,000,000	0.15	0.35	0.50	0.80	—
66(1977)	50,260,000	0.15	0.35	0.50	0.80	—
67(1978)	78,082,000	0.15	0.35	0.50	0.80	—
68(1979)	—	0.15	0.35	0.50	0.80	—
69(1980)	273,000,000	0.15	0.35	0.50	0.80	—
70(1981)	162,000,000	0.15	0.35	0.50	0.80	—

Y# 552 5 YUAN **Composition:** Copper-Nickel

Date	Mintage	F	VF	XF	Unc	BU
70(1981)	522,432,000	—	0.15	0.20	0.50	—
70(1981) Proof	—	Value: 12.50				
71(1982)	6,600,000	—	0.15	0.20	0.50	—
72(1983)	34,000,000	—	0.15	0.20	0.50	—
73(1984)	280,000,000	—	0.15	0.20	0.50	—
77(1988)	200,000,000	—	0.15	0.20	0.50	—
78(1989)	—	—	0.15	0.20	0.50	—

Y# 538 10 YUAN **Composition:** Copper-Nickel **Obverse:** Bust of Sun Yat-sen left

Date	F	VF	XF	Unc	BU
54(1965)	0.50	1.00	2.00	6.00	—

Y# 553 10 YUAN **Composition:** Copper-Nickel **Obverse:** Bust of Chiang Kai-shek left

Date	Mintage	F	VF	XF	Unc	BU
70(1981)	123,000,000	—	0.30	0.40	0.65	—
70(1981) Proof	—	Value: 15.00				
71(1982)	361,000,000	—	0.30	0.40	0.65	—
72(1983)	196,000,000	—	0.30	0.40	0.65	—
73(1984)	220,000,000	—	0.30	0.40	0.65	—

Date	Mintage	F	VF	XF	Unc	BU
74(1985)	200,000,000	—	0.30	0.40	0.65	—
75(1986)	100,000,000	—	0.30	0.40	0.65	—
76(1987)	90,000,000	—	0.30	0.40	0.65	—
77(1988)	100,000,000	—	0.30	0.40	0.65	—
78(1989)	—	—	0.30	0.40	0.65	—
79(1990)	—	—	0.30	0.40	0.65	—
80(1991)	—	—	0.30	0.40	0.65	—
81(1992)	—	—	0.30	0.40	0.65	—
82(1993)	—	—	0.30	0.40	0.65	—
83(1994)	—	—	0.30	0.40	0.65	—

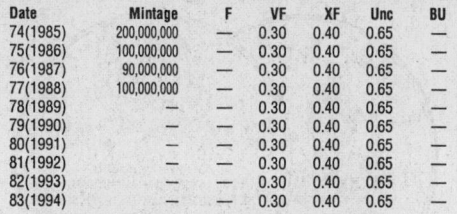

Y# 555 10 YUAN **Composition:** Copper-Nickel **Subject:** 50th Anniversary - Taiwan's Liberation from Japan

Date	F	VF	XF	Unc	BU
84(1995)	—	—	—	2.25	—

Y# 558 10 YUAN **Composition:** Copper-Nickel **Subject:** 50th Anniversary - Taiwan Yuan (Dollar) **Obverse:** Coins **Reverse:** Anniversary dates above denomination

Date	Mintage	F	VF	XF	Unc	BU
88(1999)	30,000,000	—	—	—	2.75	—

Y# 560 10 YUAN **Weight:** 7.5000 g. **Composition:** Copper-Nickel **Subject:** Year of the Dragon **Obverse:** Dragon **Reverse:** Stylized dragon above denomination

Date	F	VF	XF	Unc	BU
89(2000)	—	—	—	2.75	—

Y# 567 10 YUAN **Weight:** 7.4300 g. **Composition:** Copper-Nickel **Subject:** 90th Anniversary of the Republic **Obverse:** Bust of Sun Yat-sen facing. **Reverse:** Holographic design and denomination. **Edge:** Reeded. **Size:** 26 mm.

Date	F	VF	XF	Unc	BU
90 (2001)	—	—	—	2.50	—

Y# 565 20 YUAN **Ring Composition:** Brass**Center Weight:** 8.4000 g. **Center Composition:** Copper-Nickel **Obverse:** Male portrait. **Reverse:** Three boats. **Edge:** Reeded. **Size:** 26.8 mm.

Date	F	VF	XF	Unc	BU
90 (2001)	—	—	—	3.50	—

Y# 539 50 YUAN **Weight:** 17.1000 g. **Composition:** 0.7500 Silver .4123 oz. ASW **Obverse:** Bust of Sun Yat-sen left

Date	F	VF	XF	Unc	BU
54(1965)	—	—	10.00	20.00	—

Y# 554 50 YUAN **Composition:** Brass

Date	F	VF	XF	Unc	BU
81 (1992)	—	0.50	1.00	3.50	—
82 (1993)	—	0.50	1.00	3.50	—

Y# 556 50 YUAN **Ring Composition:** Copper-Nickel **Center Composition:** Brass **Obverse:** Parliament building

Date	F	VF	XF	Unc	BU
85 (1996)	—	—	—	5.75	—
86 (1997)	—	—	—	5.75	—

Y# 562 50 YUAN **Weight:** 15.5680 g. **Composition:** 0.9990 Silver .5004 oz. ASW **Subject:** Late President - Chiang Ching-Kuo **Obverse:** Bust of Ching-kuo facing. **Reverse:** Mausoleum above denomination. **Edge:** Reeded. **Size:** 33 mm.

Date	Mintage	F	VF	XF	Unc	BU
87 (1998)	70,000	—	—	—	25.00	—

Y# 559 50 YUAN **Weight:** 15.5500 g. **Composition:** 0.9250 Silver .4624 oz. ASW **Subject:** 50 Years - Taiwan Yuan (Dollar) **Obverse:** Coins **Reverse:** Denomination including coin design and date

Date	Mintage	F	VF	XF	Unc	BU
88(1999)	390,000	—	—	—	20.00	—

Y# 564 50 YUAN **Weight:** 15.5680 g. **Composition:** 0.9990 Silver .5004 oz. ASW **Subject:** Year 2000 **Obverse:** Celestial globe. **Reverse:** Dragon. **Edge:** Reeded. **Size:** 33 mm.

Date	Mintage	F	VF	XF	Unc	BU
89 (2000)	120,000	—	—	—	25.00	—

Y# 568 50 YUAN **Weight:** 10.0000 g. **Composition:** Brass **Obverse:** Bust **Reverse:** Denomination above latent image denomination **Edge:** Reeding and denomination **Size:** 28 mm.

Date	F	VF	XF	Unc	BU
91(2002)	—	—	—	—	7.75

Y# 540 100 YUAN **Weight:** 22.2100 g. **Composition:** 0.7500 Silver .5335 oz. ASW **Obverse:** Bust of Sun Yat-sen left

Date	F	VF	XF	Unc	BU
54(1965)	—	—	12.50	25.00	—

Y# 561 100 YUAN **Weight:** 15.5680 g. **Composition:** 0.9990 Silver .5000 oz. ASW **Subject:** 50th Anniversary - 2-28 Incident **Obverse:** Monument **Reverse:** Geometrical design **Edge:** Reeded **Size:** 33 mm.

Date	Mintage	F	VF	XF	Unc	BU
86(1997)	55,000	—	—	—	25.00	—

Y# 557 200 YUAN **Weight:** 31.1350 g. **Composition:** 0.9990 Silver 1.0000 oz. ASW **Subject:** First Popular Election Vote **Obverse:** Bust of President Lee Teng-hui and Vice President Lien Chan **Reverse:** National emblem above text

Date		F	VF	XF	Unc	BU
85(1996) Proof	—	Value: 65.00				

Y# 566 200 YUAN **Weight:** 31.3500 g. **Composition:** 0.9990 Silver 1.0069 oz. ASW **Subject:** Second Popular Vote Presidential Election **Obverse:** Bust of the President and Vice-president. **Reverse:** National emblem above inscription. **Edge:** Reeded. **Size:** 38 mm.

Date	F	VF	XF	Unc	BU
89 (2000)	—	—	—	75.00	—

Y# 541 1000 YUAN **Weight:** 15.0000 g. **Composition:** 0.9000 Gold .4340 oz. AGW **Obverse:** Bust of Sun Yat-sen left

Date	F	VF	XF	Unc	BU
54(1965)	—	—	—	285	385

Y# 563 1000 YUAN **Weight:** 15.5540 g. **Composition:** 0.9990 Gold .5000 oz. AGW **Subject:** Late President - Chiang Ching-kuo **Obverse:** Bust of Ching-kuo facing **Reverse:** Mausoleum **Edge:** Reeded **Size:** 25 mm.

Date	Mintage	F	VF	XF	Unc	BU
87(1998)	30,000	—	—	—	275	—

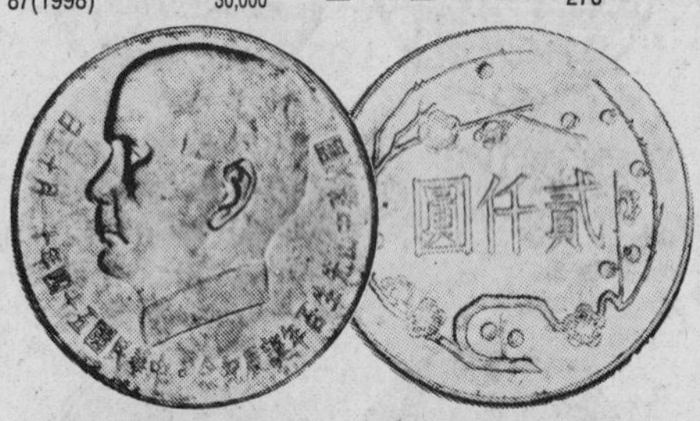

Y# 542 2000 YUAN **Weight:** 30.0000 g. **Composition:** 0.9000 Gold .8681 oz. AGW **Obverse:** Bust of Sun Yat-sen left

Date	F	VF	XF	Unc	BU
54(1965)	—	—	—	575	700

Y# 544 2000 YUAN **Weight:** 31.0600 g. **Composition:** 0.9000 Gold .8988 oz. AGW **Subject:** 80th Birthday of Chiang Kai-shek

Date	F	VF	XF	Unc	BU
55(1966)	—	—	—	600	725

PATTERNS

Yuan System; Including off metal strikes

KG numbers in reference to Coinage of the Chinese Emigre Government 1949-1957 by E. Kann and D. Graham.

KM#	Date	Mintage	Identification	Mkt Val
Pn1	ND38 (1949)	—	Chiao. Bronze. KG#12a	150
Pn2	38(1949)	—	Chiao. Aluminum. KG#12b	150
Pn3	38(1949)	—	Chiao. Copper. KG#12c	150
Pn4	38(1949)	—	Chiao. Copper. KG#12d	150
Pn5	38(1949)	—	Chiao. Aluminum. K#12e; without reeded edge	150
Pn6	38(1949)	—	Chiao. Copper. k#13	150
Pn7	38(1949)	—	Chiao. Copper. KG#14	150
Pn8	38(1949)	—	5 Chiao. Aluminum-Bronze. KG#15a	350
Pn9	38(1949)	—	5 Chiao. Aluminum. KG#15b	250
Pn10	38(1949)	—	5 Chiao. Silver. KG#16	400
Pn11	38(1949)	—	5 Chiao. Copper. KG#16a	300
Pn12	38(1949)	—	5 Chiao. Silver. KG#17	375
Pn13	38(1949)	—	5 Chiao. Silver. KG#18	600
Pn14	38(1949)	—	5 Chiao. Silver. KG#19	725
Pn15	38(1949)	—	5 Chiao. Silver. KG#20	400
Pn16	38(1949)	—	Yuan. Silver. KG#21i	400
PnA17	38(1949)	—	20 Yuan. Bronze.	1,200
Pn17	39(1950)	—	2 Chiao. Aluminum. Reeded edge. KG#21a	150
Pn18	39(1950)	—	2 Chiao. Aluminum-Bronze. KG#21b	150
Pn19	39(1950)	—	2 Chiao. Aluminum-Bronze. KG#21c; without reeded edge	150
Pn20	39(1950)	—	2 Chiao. Copper. KG#21d	150
Pn21	39(1950)	—	Yuan. Silver.	700
Pn22	39(1950)	—	Yuan. Copper-Nickel.	300
Pn23	39(1950)	—	Yuan. Copper-Nickel.	300
Pn24	39(1950)	—	Yuan. Aluminum-Bronze. KG#22a	200
Pn25	39(1950)	—	Yuan. Aluminum. KG#22b	350
Pn26	43(1954)	—	5 Chiao. Aluminum-Bronze. KG#23	300
Pn27	43(1954)	—	5 Chiao. Aluminum-Bronze. Reeded edge. KG#23a	300
Pn28	43(1954)	—	5 Chiao. Copper. KG#23b	300
Pn29	43(1954)	—	5 Chiao. Aluminum-Bronze. KG#23c	300
Pn30	43(1954)	—	5 Chiao. Aluminum-Bronze. KG#24	300
Pn31	43(1954)	—	5 Chiao. Aluminum-Bronze. KG#25	300
Pn32	43(1954)	—	5 Chiao. Aluminum-Bronze. KG#25a	300
Pn33	43(1954)	—	5 Chiao. Bronze. KG#26a	300
Pn34	44(1955)	—	Chiao. Aluminum. Simplified "TAI", KG#27a	175
Pn35	44(1955)	—	Chiao. Bronze. KG#27b	175
Pn36	45(1956)	—	2 Chiao. Copper-Nickel. Y#534	175
PnA37	45(1956)	—	Yuan. Copper-Nickel. Ocean unlined.	—
PnB37	45(1956)	—	Yuan. Aluminum-Bronze. Pn37 with simplified "TAI" character.	—
Pn37	45(1956)	—	Yuan. Copper-Nickel.	300
Pn38	48(1959)	—	Yuan. Nickel.	350
Pn39	48(1959)	—	Yuan. Nickel-Silver.	250
Pn40	49(1960)	—	Yuan. Nickel-Silver. Y#536	250
Pn41	49(1960)	—	Yuan. Nickel-Silver. Large flan	275
Pn42	49(1960)	—	Yuan. Nickel-Silver. With Taiwan-sheng	275
Pn43	49(1960)	—	Yuan. Nickel-Silver. With 1 Yuan	275
Pn44	49(1960)	—	Yuan. Nickel-Silver. With 1 Kinmen	275
Pn45	49(1960)	—	5 Yuan. Nickel.	—
Pn46	49(1960)	—	5 Yuan. Nickel. Ancient Chinese symbols	—
PnA47	50(1961)	—	Yuan. Copper-Nickel. Y#536	—
Pn47	50(1961)	—	Yuan. Nickel-Silver. Sun Yat-sen.	225
Pn48	50(1961)	—	Yuan. Nickel-Aluminum. Chiang Kai-shek.	225
Pn49	50(1961)	—	Yuan. Nickel-Silver. Similar to Pn48 but eleven characters above bust.	225
PnA49	50(1961)	—	Yuan. Nickel. Chiang Kai-shek	225
PnB49	50(1961)	—	Yuan. Nickel-Aluminum. Chiang Kai-shek	225
Pn50	51(1962)	—	5 Yuan. Nickel.	300
Pn51	53(1964)	—	5 Yuan. Copper-Nickel.	300
Pn52	54(1965)	—	10 Yuan. Copper-Nickel. Clouds replace mountains. Y#538	400
Pn53	54(1965)	—	10 Yuan. Copper-Nickel. Without clouds. Y#538	400
Pn54	55(1966)	—	2000 Yuan. Gilt Silver. Madam and President Chiang. Y#544	650
Pn65	62(1973)	—	5 Yuan. Gold. Y#548	1,250
Pn66	64(1975)	—	Yuan. Gold. Y#536	850
Pn67	64(1975)	—	Yuan. Aluminum. Y#536	200

PATTERNS

Tael System; Including off metal strikes

KG numbers in reference to Coinage of the Chinese Emigre Government 1949-1957 by E. Kann and D. Graham.

KM#	Date	Mintage	Identification	Mkt Val
Pn55	38(1949)	—	Chien. Aluminum-Bronze. KG#7b	350
Pn56	38(1949)	—	Chien. Silver. KG#6a	500
Pn57	38(1949)	—	Chien. Aluminum-Bronze. KG#6b	350
Pn58	38(1949)	—	2 Chien. Aluminum-Bronze. KG#4b	350
Pn59	38(1949)	—	2-1/2 Chien. Aluminum-Bronze. KG#3b	350
Pn60	38(1949)	—	5 Chien. Aluminum-Bronze. KG#2b	350
Pn62	45(1956)	—	2-1/2 Chien. Copper-Nickel.	250
Pn63	45(1956)	—	2-1/2 Chien. Aluminum-Bronze.	250
Pn64	45(1956)	—	2-1/2 Chien. Aluminum.	250

MINT SETS

KM#	Date	Mintage	Identification	Issue Price	Mkt Val
MS1	54(1965) (4)	—	Y#537-540	—	75.00
MS2	70(1981) (4)	—	Y#550-553	—	—
MS3	88(1999) (2)	260,000	Y#558-559	—	25.00

PROOF SETS

KM#	Date	Mintage	Identification	Issue Price	Mkt Val
PS1	70(1981) (4)	—	Y#550-553	—	50.00

CHINA-JAPANESE PUPPET STATES

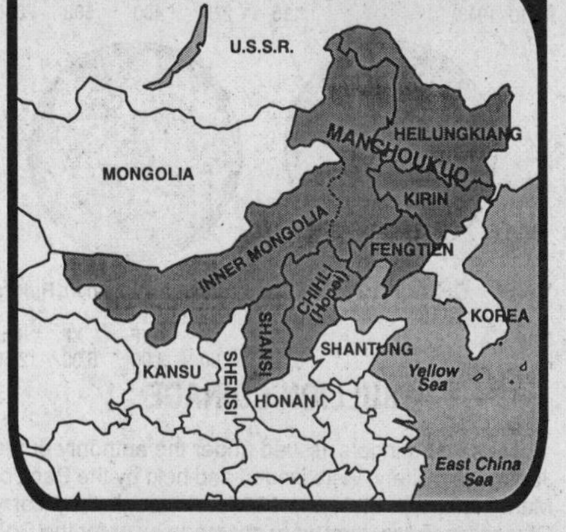

Shortly after World War I the greatest external threat to the territorial integrity of China was posed by Japan, which urgently needed room for an expanding population and raw materials for its industrial and military machines, and which recognized the necessity of controlling all of China if it was to realize its plan of dominating the rest of the Asiatic and South Sea countries. The Japanese had large investments in Manchuria (a name given by non-Chinese to the three northeastern provinces of China), which allowed them privileges that compromised Chinese sovereignty. The educated of China were not reconciled to Japan's growing power in Manchuria, and the resultant friction occasioned a series of vexing incidents, which Japan decided to circumvent by direct action. On the night of Sept. 18-19, 1931, with a contrived incident for an excuse, Japanese forces seized the city of Mukden (Shenyang), and within a few weeks completely demolished Chinese power north of the Great Wall.

In Feb. 1932, after the Japanese occupation of Manchuria, they set up Manchoukuo as an independent republic. Jehol (Rehe) was occupied by the Japanese in 1933 and added to Manchoukuo. Manchoukuo was established as an empire in 1934 with the deposed Manchu emperor Hsuan T'ung (the late Henry Pu Yi) as the puppet emperor K'ang Te. Lacking the means to face the Japanese armies in the field, the Chinese could only trade space for time.

Not content with confining its control of China to the areas north of the Great Wall, the Japanese launched a major campaign in 1937, and by the fall of 1938 had occupied in addition to Manchuria the provinces of Hopei (Hebei) and Chahar, most of the port cities, and the major cities as far west as Hankow (Hankou), now part of Wuhan. In addition, they dominated or threatened the provinces of Suiyuan, Shansi (Shanxi) and Shantung (Shandong).

Still the Chinese did not yield. The struggle was prolonged until the advent of World War II, which brought about the defeat of Japan and the return of the puppet states to Chinese control.

As the victorious Japanese armies swept deeper into China, Japan established central banks under control of the Bank of Japan in the conquered provinces for the purpose of establishing control over banking and finance in the puppet states, and eventually in all of China. These included the Chi Tung Bank, which had its main office in Tientsin (Tianjin) with branches in Peking (Beijing), Chinan (Jinan) and Tangshan, the Federal Reserve Bank of China with its main office in Peking (Beijing) and branches in 37 other cities; and the Hua Hsing Bank with its main office in Shanghai and two branches. The puppet states of Manchukuo, previously detailed in this introduction, and Mengchiang, which comprised a greater part of Inner Mongolia, were also major coin-issuing entities.

EAST HOPEI

AUTONOMOUS

The Chi Tung Bank was the banking institution of the "East Hopei Anti-Comintern Autonomous Government" established by the Japanese in 1936 to undermine the political position of China in the northwest provinces. It issued both coins and notes between 1937 and 1939 with a restraint uncharacteristic of the puppet banks of the China-Japanese puppet states.

ANTI-COMINTERN AUTONOMOUS GOVERNMENT

STANDARD COINAGE

Y# 516 5 LI **Composition:** Copper **Issuer:** Chi Tung Bank **Obverse:** Japanese character 'first" **Reverse:** Value in grain stalks

Date	VG	F	VF	XF	Unc
26(1937)	4.00	10.00	20.00	35.00	100

Y# 517 FEN **Composition:** Copper **Issuer:** Chi Tung Bank **Obverse:** Japanese character 'first" **Reverse:** Value in grain stalks

Date	VG	F	VF	XF	Unc
26(1937)	1.25	3.00	6.00	9.00	30.00

Y# 518 5 FEN **Composition:** Copper-Nickel **Issuer:** Chi Tung Bank **Obverse:** Japanese character 'first" **Reverse:** Value in grain stalks

Date	VG	F	VF	XF	Unc
26(1937)	1.00	2.50	4.50	6.50	25.00

Y# 519 CHIAO **Composition:** Copper-Nickel **Issuer:** Chi Tung Bank **Obverse:** T'ien-ning Pagoda in Peking **Reverse:** Value in grain stalks

Date	VG	F	VF	XF	Unc
26(1937)	1.00	2.50	4.50	6.50	22.50

Y# 520 2 CHIAO **Composition:** Copper-Nickel **Issuer:** Chi Tung Bank **Obverse:** T'ien-ning Pagoda in Peking **Reverse:** Value in grain stalks

Date	VG	F	VF	XF	Unc
26(1937)	1.25	3.00	6.00	10.00	35.00

MANCHUKUO

The former Japanese puppet state of Manchoukuo (largely Manchuria), comprising the northeastern Chinese provinces of Fengtien (Liaoning), Kirin (Jilin), Heilungkiang (Heilongjiang) and Jehol (Rehe), had an area of 503,143 sq. mi. (1,303,134 sq. km.) and a population of 43.3 million. Capital: Changchun, renamed Hsinking. The area is rich in fertile soil, timber and mineral resources, including coal, iron and gold.

Until the closing years of the 19th century when Chinese influence became predominant, Manchuria was chiefly a domain of the tribal Manchus and their Mongol allies. Coincident with the rise of Chinese influence, foreign imperialistic powers began to appreciate the value of the area to their expansionist philosophy. Japan, overpopulated and poor in resources, desired it as a source of raw materials and for increased living area. Russia wanted it as the eastern terminus of the Trans-Siberian railway that was to unite its Asian empire. The inevitable conflict of Japanese, Chinese and Russian interests required that one or more of the powers be eliminated. After eliminating Russia in their war of 1904-05, Japan eliminated China on the night of Sept. 18, 1931, when, on the pretext of a contrived incident, it moved militarily to seize control of the Three Eastern Provinces. Early in 1932 Japan declared Manchuria independent by virtue of a voluntary separatist movement and established the state of Manchoukuo. To give the puppet state an aura of legitimacy, the deposed emperor of the former Manchu dynasty was recalled from retirement and designated "chief executive". The area was restored to China at the end of World War II.

RULERS

Ta T'ung, 1932-1934
K'ang Te, 1934-1945

The puppet emperor under the assumed name of K'ang Te was previously the last emperor of China (P'u-yi, or Hsuan T'ung, 1909-11).

MONETARY SYSTEM

10 Li = 1 Fen
10 Fen = 1 Chiao

IDENTIFICATION OF REIGN CHARACTERS

'Nien' Year 1932-1934 Ta T'ung

'Nien' Year 1934-1945 K'ang Te

DATE ABBREVIATIONS

TT - Ta T'ung
KT - K'ang Te

NOTE: Uncirculated aluminum coins without any planchet defects are worth up to twice the market valuations given.

JAPANESE OCCUPATION

STANDARD COINAGE

Y# 1 5 LI **Composition:** Bronze **Ruler:** Ta-t'ung **Obverse:** Flag **Reverse:** Value in floral sprays

Date	VG	F	VF	XF	Unc
TT 2(1933)	8.00	20.00	35.00	50.00	100
TT 3(1934)	1.50	4.00	9.00	15.00	30.00

Y# 5 5 LI **Composition:** Bronze **Ruler:** K'ang-te **Obverse:** Character Yuan for "first", Flag **Reverse:** Value in floral sprays

Date	VG	F	VF	XF	Unc
KT 1(1934)	1.25	3.00	7.50	10.00	25.00
KT 2(1935)	1.25	3.00	7.50	10.00	25.00
KT 3(1936)	7.00	17.50	27.50	40.00	70.00
KT 4(1937)	1.50	4.00	10.00	12.50	27.50
KT 6(1939)	75.00	150	200	275	375

Y# 2 FEN **Composition:** Bronze **Ruler:** Ta-t'ung **Obverse:** Flag **Reverse:** Value in floral sprays

Date	VG	F	VF	XF	Unc
TT 3(1933)	0.80	2.00	4.00	8.00	25.00
TT 4(1934)	0.60	1.50	3.00	5.00	20.00

Y# 6 FEN **Composition:** Bronze **Ruler:** K'ang-te **Obverse:** Character Yuan for "first", Flag **Reverse:** Value in floral sprays

Date	VG	F	VF	XF	Unc
KT 1(1934)	0.40	1.00	3.00	6.00	15.00
KT 2(1935)	0.40	1.00	3.00	5.00	10.00
KT 3(1936)	0.40	1.00	3.00	5.00	10.00

Date	VG	F	VF	XF	Unc
KT 4(1937)	0.40	1.00	3.00	5.00	10.00
KT 5(1938)	0.40	1.00	3.00	5.00	10.00
KT 6(1939)	0.40	1.00	3.00	6.00	15.00

Y# 9 FEN Composition: Aluminum **Ruler:** K'ang-te **Obverse:** National symbol **Reverse:** Value in floral wreath

Date	VG	F	VF	XF	Unc
KT 6(1939)	0.15	0.40	0.75	2.00	5.00
KT 7(1940)	0.15	0.40	0.75	2.00	5.00
KT 8(1941)	0.15	0.40	0.75	2.00	5.00
KT 9(1942)	0.15	0.40	0.75	2.00	5.00
KT 10(1943)	0.15	0.40	0.75	2.00	5.00

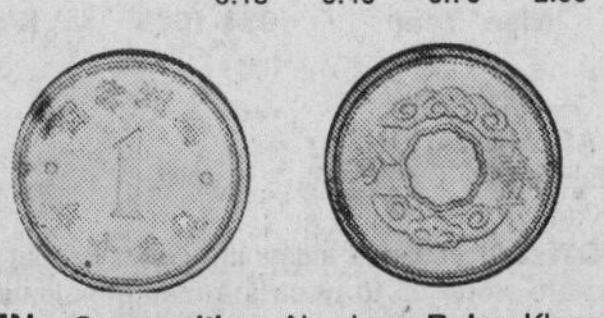

Y# 13 FEN Composition: Aluminum **Ruler:** K'ang-te **Obverse:** Legend around large "1" **Reverse:** Floral wreath

Date	VG	F	VF	XF	Unc
KT 10(1943)	0.35	0.75	2.00	5.00	10.00
KT 11(1944)	0.35	0.75	2.00	5.00	10.00

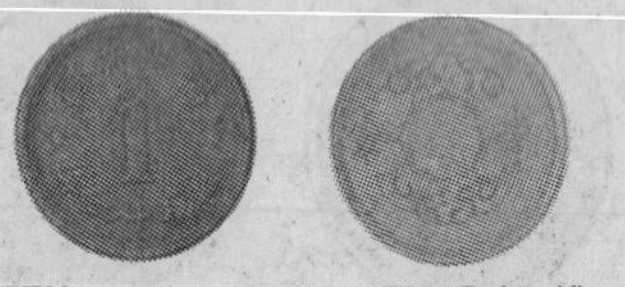

Y# 13a FEN Composition: Red Fiber **Ruler:** K'ang-te **Obverse:** Legend around large "1" **Reverse:** Floral wreath

Date	G	VG	F	VF	XF	Unc
KT 12(1945)	0.20	0.50	1.25	3.00	6.00	—

Y# 13a.1 FEN Composition: Brown Fiber **Ruler:** K'ang-te **Obverse:** Legend around large "1" **Reverse:** Floral wreath

Date	G	VG	F	VF	XF	Unc
KT 12(1945)	0.60	1.50	4.00	10.00	15.00	—

Y# 3 5 FEN Composition: Copper-Nickel **Ruler:** Ta-t'ung **Obverse:** Lotus flower **Reverse:** Pearl above value between facing dragons

Date	VG	F	VF	XF	Unc
TT 2(1933)	0.35	0.75	2.00	5.00	15.00
TT 3(1934)	0.15	0.40	1.00	2.00	10.00

Y# 7 5 FEN Composition: Copper-Nickel **Ruler:** K'ang-te **Obverse:** Character Yuan for "first" **Reverse:** Pearl above value between facing dragons

Date	VG	F	VF	XF	Unc
KT 1(1934)	0.25	0.60	1.50	3.00	6.00
KT 2(1935)	0.25	0.60	1.50	3.00	6.00
KT 3(1936)	0.25	0.60	1.50	3.00	6.00
Note: Narrow border design					
KT 3(1936)	0.50	1.25	3.00	6.00	12.00
Note: Wide border design					
KT 4(1937)	0.40	1.00	2.00	4.00	7.50
KT 6(1939)	0.40	1.00	2.00	4.00	7.50

Y# 11 5 FEN Composition: Aluminum **Ruler:** K'ang-te **Obverse:** Legend around large "5" **Reverse:** National symbol above value in floral sprays

Date	VG	F	VF	XF	Unc
KT 7 (1940)	0.25	0.60	1.50	3.00	6.00
KT 8 (1941)	0.15	0.40	0.75	2.00	4.00
KT 9 (1942)	0.15	0.40	0.75	2.00	4.00
KT 10 (1943)	0.15	0.40	0.75	2.00	4.00

Y# A13 5 FEN Composition: Aluminum **Ruler:** K'ang-te **Obverse:** Legend around small "5" **Reverse:** Wreath

Date	VG	F	VF	XF	Unc
KT 10 (1943)	0.40	1.00	2.50	5.00	12.50
KT 11 (1944)	0.40	1.00	2.50	5.00	12.50

Y# A13a 5 FEN Composition: Red Fiber **Ruler:** K'ang-te **Obverse:** Legend around small "5" **Reverse:** Wreath

Date	VG	F	VF	XF	Unc
KT 11 (1944)	1.00	2.00	3.50	7.00	—
KT 12 (1945)	60.00	75.00	100	—	—

Y# A13a.1 5 FEN Composition: Brown Fiber **Ruler:** K'ang-te **Obverse:** Legend around small "5" **Reverse:** Floral wreath

Date	VG	F	VF	XF	Unc
KT 11 (1944)	4.00	10.00	15.00	25.00	—

Y# 4 CHIAO (10 Fen) Composition: Copper-Nickel **Ruler:** Ta-t'ung **Obverse:** Lotus flower **Reverse:** Pearl above value between facing dragons

Date	VG	F	VF	XF	Unc
TT 2 (1933)	0.60	1.50	3.00	7.00	15.00
TT 3 (1934)	0.30	0.80	2.00	3.75	12.50

Y# 8 CHIAO (10 Fen) Composition: Copper-Nickel **Ruler:** K'ang-te **Obverse:** Character Yuan for "first" **Reverse:** Pearl above value between facing dragons

Date	VG	F	VF	XF	Unc
KT 1 (1934)	0.30	0.80	2.00	3.00	8.00
KT 2 (1935)	0.30	0.80	2.00	3.00	8.00
KT 5 (1938)	0.30	0.80	2.00	3.00	8.00
KT 6 (1939)	0.30	0.80	2.00	3.00	8.00
KT 6 (1939) Proof	—	—	—	—	—

Y# 10 CHIAO (10 Fen) Composition: Copper-Nickel **Ruler:** K'ang-te **Obverse:** Dragon head facing **Reverse:** National symbol above value in floral sprays

Date	VG	F	VF	XF	Unc
KT 7 (1940)	0.40	1.00	3.00	5.00	12.50

Y# 12 CHIAO (10 Fen) Composition: Aluminum **Ruler:** K'ang-te **Obverse:** Legend around "10" on "Fundo" weight outline **Reverse:** National symbol above value in floral sprays

Date	VG	F	VF	XF	Unc
KT 7 (1940)	0.35	0.80	2.00	3.00	8.00
KT 8 (1941)	0.35	0.80	2.00	3.00	8.00
KT 9 (1942)	0.35	0.80	2.00	3.00	8.00
KT 10 (1943)	115	275	400	500	600

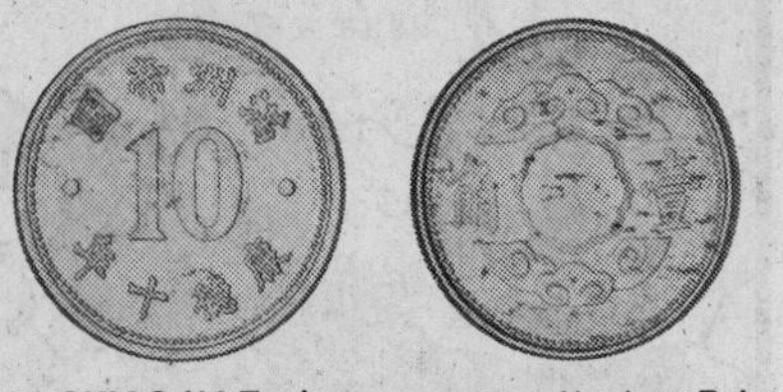

Y# 14 CHIAO (10 Fen) Composition: Aluminum **Ruler:** K'ang-te **Reverse:** Legend around large "10"

Date	VG	F	VF	XF	Unc
KT 10 (1943)	0.60	1.50	3.00	5.00	12.50

BULLION COINAGE

These gold ingots, issued under the authority of the Japanese military, were issued and held by the Bank of Manchoukuo in the early 1930s. Although they carry Chinese legends, they were not made by or for the Chinese market.

KM# 1.1 TAEL Weight: 31.2500 g. **Composition:** 1.0000 Gold 1.0048 oz. AGW **Obverse:** Character "Fu" "Happiness" **Reverse:** 24K/1000 all in outline **Size:** 30 mm.

Date	VG	F	VF	XF	Unc
ND(1932)	—	—	450	650	900

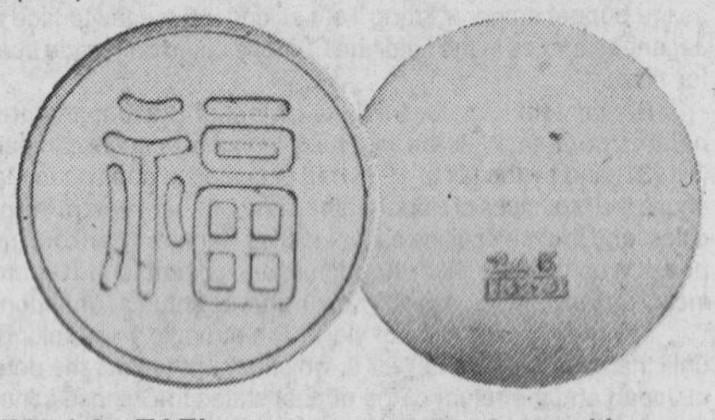

KM# 1.2 TAEL Weight: 31.2500 g. **Composition:** 1.0000 Gold 1.0048 oz. AGW **Obverse:** Character "Fu" (happiness) **Reverse:** 1000 in outline, 24K above

Date	VG	F	VF	XF	Unc
ND(1932)	—	—	450	650	900

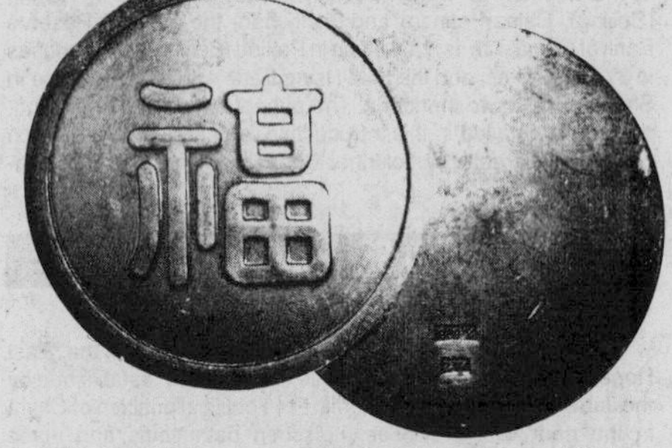

KM# 2 TAEL Composition: Gold 1.5000 oz. AGW **Obverse:** Character "Fu" (happiness) **Size:** 37 mm.

Date	VG	F	VF	XF	Unc
ND(1932)	—	—	950	1,250	1,500

KM# 3 TAEL Weight: 31.2500 g. **Composition:** 1.0000 Gold 1.0048 oz. AGW **Obverse:** Character "Shuang-hsi" (Double happiness) **Size:** 30 mm.

Date	VG	F	VF	XF	Unc
ND(1932)	—	—	1,200	1,550	1,950

KM# 4 TAEL **Weight:** 31.2500 g. **Composition:** 1.0000 Gold 1.0048 oz. AGW **Obverse:** Character "Fu" (happiness) in center, characters "Fu-kuei Wan-nien" top-bottom-right-left (Richness, honor (for) 10,000 years) **Reverse:** "24K/1000" over 4 characters in frame

Date	VG	F	VF	XF	Unc
ND(1932)	—	—	950	1,250	1,500

KM# 5 TAEL **Weight:** 31.2500 g. **Composition:** 1.0000 Gold 1.0048 oz. AGW **Obverse:** Character "Fu" (happiness) in center, characters "Fu-kuei Wan-nien" top-bottom-right-left (richness, honor (for) 10,000 years) **Reverse:** "24K/1000" over 4 characters in frame

Date	VG	F	VF	XF	Unc
ND(1932)	—	—	950	1,250	1,500

KM# 6 TAEL **Weight:** 31.2500 g. **Composition:** 1.0000 Gold 1.0048 oz. AGW **Obverse:** Character "Shou" (Longevity) **Reverse:** "24K" over "1000" in frame

Date	VG	F	VF	XF	Unc
ND(1932)	—	—	950	1,250	1,500

KM# 7 TAEL **Composition:** Gold 1.5000 oz. AGW **Obverse:** Character "Shou" (longevity) **Size:** 37 mm.

Date	VG	F	VF	XF	Unc
ND(1932)	—	—	1,450	1,850	2,250

KM# 8 TAEL **Weight:** 31.2500 g. **Composition:** 1.0000 Gold 1.0048 oz. AGW **Obverse:** Character "Lu" (Prosperity) **Size:** 30 mm.

Date	VG	F	VF	XF	Unc
ND(1932)	—	—	950	1,250	1,500

PATTERNS

Including off metal strikes

KM#	Date	Mintage	Identification	Mkt Val
Pn1	KT5 (1938)	—	5 Chiao. Copper-Nickel. Medieval emperor's bust. Portrait.	—
Pn2	KT5 (1938)	—	5 Chiao. Copper-Nickel. Two facing phoenix. Chinese characters.	—
Pn3	KT9 (1942)	—	Chiao. Silver. Specimen	400
Pn4	KT9 (1942)	—	Chiao. Copper-Nickel. Specimen	250
Pn5	KT9 (1942)	—	Chiao. Brass. Specimen	200
Pn6	KT9 (1942)	—	Chiao. Nickel-Bronze. Specimen	200
Pn7	KT12 (1945)	—	Fen. Copper Plated Steel. Y#13a	—

MENG CHIANG

As Japanese troops moved into North China in 1937, the political situation became fluid in several provinces bordering on Manchoukuo, which were sometimes referred to as Inner Mongolia. On September 27, 1937, the Chanan Bank was established. As the situation became more settled the Japanese effected the merger of two local banks with the Bank of Chanan under a new title, Meng Chiang (Mongolian Borderlands or Mongol Territory) Bank. The Meng Chiang Bank was organized on November 27 and opened on December 1, 1937, with headquarters in Kalgan (Zhangjiakou) and branch offices in about a dozen locations throughout the region. Its notes were declared the exclusive currency for the area. The bank closed at the end of the war.

JAPANESE OCCUPATION

STANDARD COINAGE

Y# 521 5 CHIAO **Composition:** Copper-Nickel **Obverse:** Legend in floral design **Reverse:** Value in facing dragons

Date	VG	F	VF	XF	Unc
27(1938)	1.50	3.50	6.50	10.00	25.00

PATTERNS

Including off metal strikes

Note: "KK" indicates Kublai Khan dating system

KM#	Date	Mintage	Identification	Mkt Val
Pn1	738(1943)	—	Fen. Aluminum. Ram's head.	—
Pn2	738(1943)	—	5 Fen. Aluminum. Ram's head.	1,650
Pn3	738(1943)	—	Chiao. Aluminum. Ram's head.	2,250

PROVISIONAL GOVT. OF CHINA

In late 1937 the Japanese North China Expeditionary Army established the "Provisional Government of China" at Peking (Beijing).

FEDERAL RESERVE BANK

The Federal Reserve Bank of China was opened in 1938 by Japanese military authorities in Peking (Beijing). It was the puppet financial agency of the Japanese in northeast China. The puppet bank issued both coins and currency, but in modest amounts.

JAPANESE OCCUPATION

STANDARD COINAGE

Y# 523 FEN **Composition:** Aluminum **Issuer:** Federal Reserve Bank **Obverse:** Legend around FR Bank symbol **Reverse:** Temple of Heaven

Date	VG	F	VF	XF	Unc
30 (1941)	0.20	0.50	1.00	2.50	7.00
31 (1942)	0.20	0.50	1.00	2.00	6.00
32 (1943)	1.25	3.00	6.00	10.00	30.00

Y# 524 5 FEN **Composition:** Aluminum **Issuer:** Federal Reserve Bank **Obverse:** Legend around FR Bank symbol **Reverse:** Temple of Heaven **Note:** The 5 Fen pieces were struck on thick (1 gram) and then (.8 gram) planchets.

Date	VG	F	VF	XF	Unc
30 (1941)	0.35	0.75	2.00	4.00	10.00
31 (1942)	0.40	1.00	2.50	5.00	15.00
32 (1943)	1.50	3.50	7.50	15.00	45.00

Y# 525 CHIAO **Composition:** Aluminum **Issuer:** Federal Reserve Bank **Obverse:** Legend around FR Bank symbol **Reverse:** Temple of Heaven **Note:** The 1 Chiao pieces were struck on thick (1.5 gram), thin (1.2 gram), and very thin (1.0 gram) planchets.

Date	VG	F	VF	XF	Unc
30 (1941)	0.15	0.40	1.00	2.00	6.00
31 (1942)	0.15	0.40	1.00	2.00	6.00
32 (1943)	0.60	1.50	3.00	6.50	20.00

PATTERNS

Including off metal strikes

KM#	Date	Mintage	Identification	Mkt Val
Pn2	30(1941)	—	5 Fen. Silver. KM#524, R.Y.30.	700
Pn1	30(1941)	—	Fen. Silver. KM#523, R.Y.30.	700

REFORMED GOVT. OF CHINA

On March 28, 1938 the Japanese Central China Expeditionary Army established the Reformed Government of the Republic of China at Nanking (Nanjing).

HUA HSING COMMERCIAL BANK

The Hua Hsing Commerce Bank was a financial agency created and established by the government of Japan and its puppet authorities in Shanghai in May 1939. Notes and coins were issued until sometime in 1941, with the quantities restricted by Chinese aversion to accepting them.

JAPANESE OCCUPATION

STANDARD COINAGE

Y# A522 FEN **Composition:** Bronze **Obverse:** Legend around character "Hua" above pair of wings **Reverse:** Stylized character divides value

Date	VG	F	VF	XF	Unc
29(1940)	50.00	100	200	300	400

Y# 522 10 FEN **Composition:** Copper-Nickel **Obverse:** Legend around character "Hua" above pair of wings **Reverse:** Floral bouquet divides value

Date	VG	F	VF	XF	Unc
29(1940)	0.40	1.00	2.00	3.50	7.00

Note: Metal Alloys vary

PATTERNS

Including off metal strikes

KM#	Date	Mintage	Identification	Mkt Val
Pn4	29(1940)	—	20 Fen. Copper-Nickel. Junk.	2,250
Pn3	29(1940)	—	5 Fen. Copper-Nickel. Liu-ho Pagoda.	650
Pn1	29(1940)	—	Fen. Copper-Nickel.	650
Pn2	29(1940)	—	Fen. Silver.	750

CHINESE SOVIET REPUBLIC

In November, 1931, the first congress of the Chinese Soviet proclaimed and established the "Chinese Soviet Republic" under the Chairmanship of Mao Tse-Tung.

CONSOLIDATED SOVIET REPUBLIC

STANDARD COINAGE

Y# 506 CENT Composition: Copper **Obverse:** Large "1" on hammer and sickle **Reverse:** Star above value in wheat stalks

Date	VG	F	VF	XF	Unc
ND(ca.1932)	10.00	20.00	30.00	50.00	—

Y# 506a CENT Composition: Copper **Obverse:** Large "1" on hammer and sickle **Reverse:** Star above value in wheat stalks

Date	F	VF	XF	Unc	BU
ND(ca.1960) Restrike	—	—	8.00	20.00	—

Y# 507 5 CENTS Comp.: Copper **Ruler:** Mao Tse-Tung **Obverse:** Hammer and sickle on map outline **Reverse:** Star over value in wheat stalks **Edge:** Plain **Note:** Varieties exist.

Date	VG	F	VF	XF	Unc
ND(ca.1932)	20.00	30.00	50.00	85.00	—

Y# 507.1 5 CENTS Composition: Copper **Ruler:** Mao Tse-Tung **Obverse:** Hammer and sickle on map outline **Reverse:** Star over value in wheat stalks **Edge:** Reeded **Note:** Varieties exist.

Date	VG	F	VF	XF	Unc
ND(ca.1932)	20.00	30.00	50.00	85.00	—

Y# 507a 5 CENTS Composition: Copper **Ruler:** Mao Tse-Tung **Obverse:** Hammer and sickle on map outline **Reverse:** Star over value in wheat stalks

Date	F	VF	XF	Unc	BU
ND(ca.1960) Restrike	—	—	10.00	25.00	—

Y# 508 20 CENTS Weight: 5.5000 g. **Composition:** Silver **Ruler:** Mao Tse-Tung **Obverse:** Star over hammer and sickle on globe in wheat stalks **Note:** Many minor varieties exist.

Date	VG	F	VF	XF	Unc
1932	15.00	25.00	40.00	75.00	—
1933	10.00	20.00	30.00	65.00	—

KM# 5 DOLLAR Composition: Silver **Ruler:** Mao Tse-Tung **Obverse:** Crude facing portrait of Lenin **Reverse:** Hammer, sickle, and value within ornamental wreath

Date	VG	F	VF	XF	Unc
1931 Rare	—	—	—	—	—

PATTERNS

Including off metal strikes

KM#	Date	Mintage	Identification	Mkt Val
Pn1	1932	—	20 Cents. Copper. Y#508.	265

HSIANG-O-HSI SOVIET

(Kiangsi-West Hupeh)

SOVIET CONTROLLED PROVINCE

STANDARD COINAGE

KM# 1 FEN Composition: Copper **Obverse:** Legend around large star **Reverse:** Denomination within wreath, legend around

Date	VG	F	VF	XF	Unc
ND(1931) Rare	—	—	—	—	—

HUNAN SOVIET

SOVIET CONTROLLED PROVINCE

STANDARD COINAGE

KM# 1.1 (KM1) DOLLAR Composition: Silver **Obverse:** Large star. **Obv. Legend:** "Hu-nan Sheng Su-wei-ai Cheng-fu"

Date	VG	F	VF	XF	Unc
1931	180	300	—	—	—
1931	180	300	—	—	—

KM# 1.2 DOLLAR Composition: Silver **Obverse:** Small star.

Date	VG	F	VF	XF	Unc
1931	80.00	180	300	—	—

HUPEH-HONAN-ANWHEI SOVIET

The Hupeh-Honan-Anwhei Soviet District was a large revolutionary base. It was formerly made up of three separate special districts: East Hupeh, South Honan and West Anwhei which united until after 1930. Between 1931 and 1932 this Bank has issued a quantity of copper and silver coins as well as banknotes.

SOVIET CONTROLLED PROVINCE

STANDARD COINAGE

Y# 503 DOLLAR Weight: 26.8000 g. **Composition:** Silver **Obverse:** Hammer and sickle on globe at center **Reverse:** Lower legend appears in crude Russian **Rev. Legend:** "SOVETS...."

Date	VG	F	VF	XF	Unc
1932	250	575	750	1,000	—

Note: Attribution of Y#503 to the Hupeh-Honan-Anhwei Soviet is not definite.

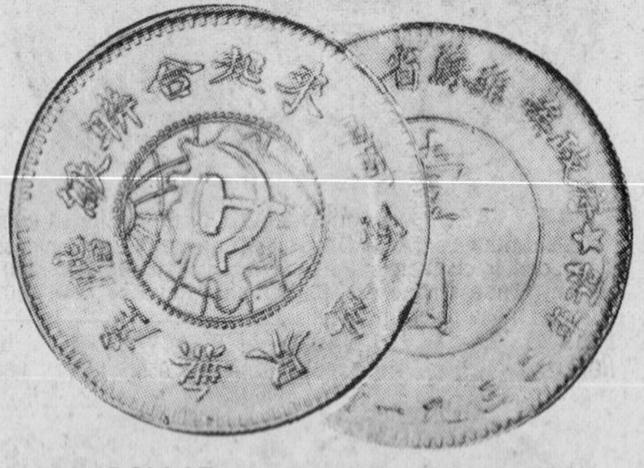

Y# 504 DOLLAR Weight: 27.2000 g. **Composition:** Silver **Obverse:** Hammer and sickle on globe at center

Date	VG	F	VF	XF	Unc
1932	175	275	400	700	—

MIN-CHE-KAN SOVIET

(Fukien-Chekiang-Kiangsi)

SOVIET CONTROLLED PROVINCE

STANDARD COINAGE

KM# 1 DOLLAR Composition: Silver **Obverse:** Profile bust of Lenin

Date	VG	F	VF	XF	Unc
1934	—	—	—	—	—

Note: Authenticity in doubt

KM# 2 DOLLAR Composition: Silver **Obverse:** 15 character legend around globe with hammer and sickle

Date	VG	F	VF	XF	Unc
1934	—	—	—	—	—

Note: Authenticity in doubt

P'ING CHIANG COUNTY SOVIET

SOVIET CONTROLLED PROVINCE

STANDARD COINAGE

KM# 1 DOLLAR **Composition:** Silver **Obverse:** Legend in 8 Chinese characters **Obv. Legend:** "P'ing Chiang..."

Date	VG	F	VF	XF	Unc
1931 Rare	—	—	—	—	—

SHENSI-NORTH SOVIET

SOVIET CONTROLLED PROVINCE

STANDARD COINAGE

Date is given in the 5th year of the Chinese Soviet Republic. They were issued after the Long March.

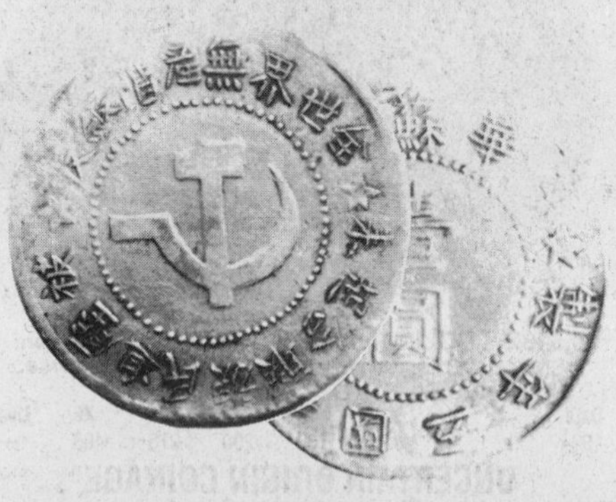

KM# 1.1 DOLLAR **Composition:** Silver **Obverse:** Large hammer and sickle **Reverse:** Value in plain field, yr.5 at bottom

Date	VG	F	VF	XF	Unc
5	1,750	2,250	2,850	—	—

KM# 1.2 DOLLAR **Composition:** Silver **Obverse:** Star at left, slightly lower **Reverse:** Legend rotated with yr.5 at top

Date	VG	F	VF	XF	Unc
5	1,750	2,250	2,850	—	—

KM# 2 DOLLAR **Composition:** Silver **Obverse:** Large hammer and sickle **Reverse:** Value within wheat stalks

Date	VG	F	VF	XF	Unc
5	2,500	3,000	3,500	—	—

SZECHUAN-SHENSI SOVIET

Sichuan

A province located in south-central China. The largest of the traditional Chinese provinces, Szechuan (Sichuan) is a plateau region watered by many rivers. These rivers carry much trading traffic. Agriculture or mining are the occupational choices of most of the populace. In World War II the national capital was moved to Chungking in Szechuan (Sichuan). Chengtu was an active imperial mint that opened in 1732 and was in practically continuous operation until the advent of modern equipment. Modern minting was introduced in the province when Chengtu began milled coinage in 1898. A mint was authorized for Chungking in 1905 but it did not begin operations until 1913. The Chengtu Mint was looted by soldiers in 1925. The last republic issues from Szechuan (Sichuan) were dated 1932.

The machinery for the first Szechuan (Sichuan) Mint was produced in New Jersey and the dies were engraved in Philadelphia. The mint was opened in 1898, but closed within a few months and did not reopen until 1901. There is no doubt now that Y#234-238 (K#145-149) were the first issues of this mint, contrary to the Kann listings.

SOVIET CONTROLLED PROVINCES

STANDARD COINAGE

Y# 510 200 CASH **Composition:** Copper **Obverse:** Three stars around hammer and sickle

Date	Good	VG	F	VF	XF
1933	25.00	50.00	80.00	140	—

Y# 510.1 200 CASH **Composition:** Copper **Obverse:** Three stars around hammer and sickle **Reverse:** Small "200" at center

Date	Good	VG	F	VF	XF
1933	25.00	50.00	80.00	140	—

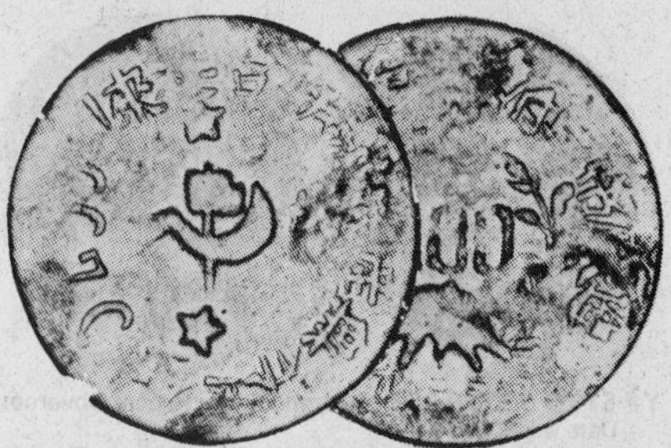

Y# 510.2 200 CASH **Composition:** Copper **Obverse:** Three stars around hammer and sickle **Reverse:** Large "200" at center

Date	Good	VG	F	VF	XF
1933	25.00	50.00	80.00	140	—

Y# 510.3 200 CASH **Composition:** Copper **Obverse:** Three stars around hammer and sickle **Reverse:** Square 0's in "200" at center

Date	Good	VG	F	VF	XF
1933	30.00	60.00	100	175	—

Y# 510.4 200 CASH **Composition:** Copper **Obverse:** Solid hammer and sickle reversed **Reverse:** 200 retrograde at center

Date	Good	VG	F	VF	XF
1933	35.00	70.00	115	200	—

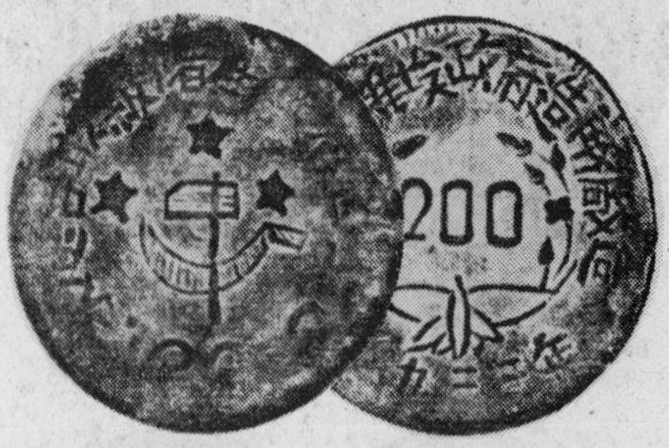

Y# 510.5 200 CASH **Composition:** Copper **Obverse:** Shaded hammer and sickle reversed **Note:** Varieties exist.

Date	Good	VG	F	VF	XF
1933	30.00	60.00	100	175	—

Y# 511.1 200 CASH **Composition:** Copper **Obverse:** Date with open 3 and backwards 4

Date	VG	F	VF	XF	Unc
1934	22.50	45.00	75.00	135	—

Y# 511.2 200 CASH **Composition:** Copper **Obverse:** Date with 4 corrected

Date	VG	F	VF	XF	Unc
1934	22.50	45.00	75.00	135	—

Y# 511 200 CASH **Composition:** Copper **Obverse:** Date with closed 3 and backwards 4 **Note:** Modern forgeries of this variety exist.

Date	VG	F	VF	XF	Unc
1934	22.50	45.00	75.00	135	—

Y# 511a 200 CASH **Composition:** Copper **Obverse:** Date with 4 corrected

Date	F	VF	XF	Unc	BU
1934 Restrike	—	—	12.50	25.00	—

Note: Many varieties of 200 Cash pieces exist; well struck, usually found in choice condition; unlisted varieties do not carry a premium

Y# 512 500 CASH **Composition:** Copper **Obverse:** Small stars flanking date

Date	VG	F	VF	XF	Unc
1934	75.00	100	175	275	—

Y# 512.1 500 CASH **Composition:** Copper **Obverse:** Large stars flanking date; hammer handle across lower leg of star

Date	VG	F	VF	XF	Unc
1934	50.00	100	160	250	—

Y# 512.2 500 CASH **Composition:** Copper **Obverse:** Hammer handle extends between right leg of star **Note:** 33-34 milimeters.

Date	VG	F	VF	XF	Unc
1934	50.00	100	150	225	—

Note: Many varieties of 500 Cash pieces exist; unlisted varieties do not carry a premium

Y# 513 DOLLAR **Weight:** 26.3000 g. **Composition:** Silver **Obverse:** Globe with hammer and sickle **Reverse:** Large, decorative, solid stars

Date	VG	F	VF	XF	Unc
1934	125	225	300	450	—

Y# 513.2 DOLLAR **Weight:** 26.3000 g. **Composition:** Silver **Obverse:** Globe with hammer and sickle **Reverse:** Small solid stars

Date	VG	F	VF	XF	Unc
1934	100	175	250	375	—
1933 Rare	—	—	—	—	—

Y# 513.3 DOLLAR **Weight:** 26.3000 g. **Composition:** Silver **Obverse:** Globe with hammer and sickle **Reverse:** Outlined stars

Date	VG	F	VF	XF	Unc
1934	100	200	275	400	—

Y# 513.1 DOLLAR **Weight:** 26.3000 g. **Composition:** Silver **Obverse:** Globe with hammer and sickle **Reverse:** Medium solid stars

Date	VG	F	VF	XF	Unc
1934	100	175	250	375	—

Y# 513.4 DOLLAR **Weight:** 26.3000 g. **Composition:** Silver **Obverse:** Globe with hammer and sickle **Reverse:** Pentagram stars **Note:** Many minor varieties exist.

Date	VG	F	VF	XF	Unc
1934	75.00	150	225	350	—

Y# 513.5 DOLLAR **Weight:** 26.3000 g. **Composition:** Silver **Obverse:** Globe with hammer and sickle **Reverse:** Large solid stars

Date	VG	F	VF	XF	Unc
1934	100	200	275	400	—

UNCERTAIN ORIGIN COINAGE

K# 650k DOLLAR **Weight:** 26.4000 g. **Composition:** Silver **Countermark:** Three Chinese characters in rectangular box **Obverse:** Countermark meaning <i>SOVIET</i> **Note:** Countermark on Y#329.

Date	VG	F	VF	XF	Unc
ND	125	200	325	600	—

WAN-HSI-PEI-SOVIET

(Northwest Anhwei)

SOVIET CONTROLLED PROVINCE

STANDARD COINAGE

KM# 1 50 CASH **Composition:** Brass **Obverse:** Legend around globe with hammer and sickle **Reverse:** Value in star within wreath, all within legend

Date	Good	VG	F	VF	XF
1931	37.50	75.00	125	200	—

KM# 2 50 CASH **Composition:** Copper **Obverse:** Legend around globe with hammer and sickle **Reverse:** Value in circle, Chinese legend above, Western legend below

Date	VG	F	VF	XF	Unc
ND(1931-32) Rare	—	—	—	—	—

CHINA, PEOPLE'S REPUBLIC

The Peoples Republic of China, located in eastern Asia, has an area of 3,696,100 sq. mi. (9,596,960 sq. km.) (including Manchuria and Tibet) and a population of *1.20 billion. Capital: Peking (Beijing). The economy is based on agriculture, mining, and manufacturing. Textiles, clothing, metal ores, tea and rice are exported.

China's ancient civilization began in east-central Henan's Huayang county, 2800-2300 B.C. The warring feudal states comprising early China were first united under Emperor Ch'in Shih (246-210 B.C.) who gave China its name and first central government. Subsequent dynasties alternated brilliant cultural achievements with internal disorder until the Empire was brought down by the revolution of 1911, and the Republic of China installed in its place. Chinese culture attained a pre-eminence in art, literature and philosophy, but a traditional backwardness in industry and administration ill prepared China for the demands of 19th century Western expansionism which exposed it to military and political humiliations, and mandated a drastic revision of political practice in order to secure an accommodation with the modern world.

The Republic of 1911 barely survived the stress of World War I, and was subsequently all but shattered by the rise of nationalism and the emergence of the Chinese Communist movement. Moscow, which practiced a policy of cooperation between Communists and other parties in movements for national liberation, sought to establish an entente between the Chinese Communist Party and the Kuomintang ('National Peoples Party') of Sun Yatsen. The ensuing cooperation was based on little more than the hope each had of using the other.

An increasingly uneasy association between the Kuomintang and the Chinese Communist Party developed and continued until April 12, 1927, when Chiang Kai-shek, Sun Yat-sen's political heir, instituted a bloody purge to stamp out the Communists within the Kuomintang and the government and virtually paralyzed their ranks throughout China. Some time after the mid-1927 purges, the Chinese Communist Party turned to armed force to resist Chiang Kai-shek and during the period of 1930-34 acquired control over large parts of Kiangsi (Jiangxi), Fukien (Fujian), Hunan and Hupeh (Hubei). The Nationalist Nanking government responded with a series of campaigns against the soviet power bases and, by October of 1934, succeeded in driving the remnants of the Communist army to a refuge in Shensi (Shaanxi) Province. There the Communists reorganized under the leadership of Mao Tse-tung, defeated the Nationalist forces, and on Sept. 21, 1949, established the Peoples Republic of China. Thereafter relations between Russia and Communist China steadily deteriorated until 1958, when China emerged as an independent center of Communist power.

SOVIET PERIOD

In November, 1931, the first congress of the Chinese Soviet proclaimed and established the "Chinese Soviet Republic" under the Chairmanship of Mao Tse-Tung.

Prior to 1949, the People's Republic of China did not exist as such, but the Communists did control areas known as Soviets. Most of the Soviets were established on the borders of two or more provinces and were named according to the provinces involved. Thus there were such soviets as the Kiangsi-Hunan Soviet, the Hunan-Hupeh-Kiangsi Soviet, the Hupeh-Honan-Anhwei Soviet and others. In 1931 some of the soviets in the southern Kiangsi area were consolidated into the Chinese Soviet Republic, which lasted until the Long March of 1934.

MONETARY SYSTEM

10 Cash (Wen) = 1 Cent (Fen)
100 Cents (Fen) = 1 Dollar (Yuan)

After 1949

10 Fen (Cents) = 1 Jiao
10 Jiao = 1 Renminbi Yuan

MINT MARKS

(b) - Beijing (Peking)
(s) - Shanghai
(y) - Shenyang (Mukden)

PEOPLES REPUBLIC

STANDARD COINAGE

Y# 1 FEN **Composition:** Aluminum

Date	Mintage	F	VF	XF	Unc	BU
1955	—	0.20	0.50	1.50	5.00	—
1956	—	0.40	1.00	2.50	7.50	—
1957	—	0.60	1.50	3.50	10.00	—
1958	—	0.10	0.25	0.75	2.50	—
1959	—	0.10	0.25	0.75	2.50	—
1961	—	0.10	0.25	0.75	2.50	—
1963	—	0.10	0.25	0.50	1.50	—
1964	—	0.10	0.25	0.50	1.00	—
1971	—	0.10	0.25	0.50	1.00	—
1972	—	0.10	0.25	0.50	1.00	—
1973	—	0.10	0.25	0.50	1.50	—
1974	—	0.10	0.25	0.50	1.00	—

Date	Mintage	F	VF	XF	Unc	BU
1975	500,000	0.10	0.25	0.50	1.00	—
1976	—	—	0.10	0.25	0.50	—
1977	—	—	0.10	0.25	0.50	—
1978	—	—	0.10	0.25	0.50	—
1979	—	—	0.10	0.25	0.50	—
1980	—	—	0.10	0.25	0.50	—
1980 Proof	—	Value: 1.00				
1981	—	—	0.10	0.25	0.50	—
1981 Proof	—	Value: 1.00				
1982	—	—	—	0.25	0.50	—
1982 Proof	—	Value: 1.00				
1983	2,412,000	—	—	0.10	0.25	—
1984	3,283,000	—	—	0.10	0.25	—
1985	—	—	—	0.10	0.25	—
1985 Proof	—	Value: 1.00				
1986	—	—	—	0.10	0.25	—
1986 Proof	—	Value: 1.00				
1987	—	—	—	0.10	0.25	—
1991	—	—	—	0.10	0.25	—
1991 Proof	—	Value: 1.00				
1992	—	—	—	0.10	0.25	—
1992 Proof	—	Value: 1.00				
1993 In sets only	—	—	—	—	0.75	—
1993 Proof	—	Value: 1.00				
1994 In sets only	—	—	—	—	0.75	—
1994 Proof	—	Value: 1.00				
1995 In sets only	—	—	—	—	0.75	—
1995 Proof	—	Value: 1.00				
1996 In sets only	—	—	—	—	0.75	—
1996 Proof	—	Value: 1.00				
1997	—	—	—	0.10	0.25	—

Y# 2 2 FEN **Composition:** Aluminum

Date	Mintage	F	VF	XF	Unc	BU
1956	—	0.10	0.25	0.75	1.50	—
1959	—	0.20	0.50	1.00	4.00	—
1960	—	0.20	0.50	1.00	4.00	—
1961	—	0.10	0.25	0.75	1.50	—
1962	—	0.10	0.25	0.75	1.50	—
1963	—	0.10	0.25	0.75	1.50	—
1964	—	0.10	0.25	0.50	1.25	—
1974	—	0.10	0.25	0.50	1.50	—
1975	—	0.10	0.25	0.50	1.00	—
1976	—	0.10	0.25	0.50	1.00	—
1977	360,000	0.10	0.25	0.50	0.75	—
1978	—	0.10	0.20	0.40	0.60	—
1979	—	0.10	0.20	0.40	0.60	—
1980	—	0.10	0.20	0.40	0.60	—
1980 Proof	—	Value: 1.00				
1981	—	0.10	0.20	0.40	0.60	—
1981 Proof	—	Value: 1.00				
1982	—	0.10	0.20	0.40	0.60	—
1982 Proof	—	Value: 1.00				
1983	1,790,000	—	0.10	0.20	0.35	—
1984	1,963,000	—	0.10	0.20	0.35	—
1985	—	—	0.10	0.20	0.35	—
1985 Proof	—	Value: 1.00				
1986	—	—	0.15	0.35	0.75	—
1986 Proof	—	Value: 1.00				
1987	—	—	0.10	0.20	0.35	—
1988	—	—	0.10	0.20	0.35	—
1989	—	—	0.10	0.20	0.35	—
1990	—	—	0.10	0.20	0.35	—
1991	—	—	0.10	0.20	0.35	—
1991 Proof	—	Value: 1.00				
1992	—	—	0.10	0.20	0.35	—
1992 Proof	—	Value: 1.00				
1993 In sets only	—	—	—	—	0.75	—
1993 Proof	—	Value: 1.00				
1994 In sets only	—	—	—	—	0.75	—
1994 Proof	—	Value: 1.00				
1995 In sets only	—	—	—	—	0.75	—
1995 Proof	—	Value: 1.00				
1996 In sets only	—	—	—	—	0.75	—
1996 Proof	—	Value: 1.00				

Y# 3 5 FEN **Composition:** Aluminum

Date	Mintage	F	VF	XF	Unc	BU
1955	—	0.30	0.75	2.00	10.00	—
1956	—	0.15	0.35	0.75	2.00	—
1957	—	0.15	0.35	0.75	2.50	—

Date	Mintage	F	VF	XF	Unc	BU
1974	—	0.15	0.25	0.50	1.50	—
1975	—	0.15	0.25	0.50	1.50	—
1976	350,000	0.15	0.25	0.50	0.75	—
1979	—	0.15	0.35	0.75	2.00	—
1980	—	0.15	0.25	0.50	0.75	—
1980 Proof	—	Value: 1.00				
1981	—	0.15	0.25	0.50	0.75	—
1981 Proof	—	Value: 1.00				
1982	—	0.15	0.25	0.50	0.75	—
1982 Proof	—	Value: 1.00				
1983	484,000	—	0.15	0.25	0.45	—
1984	600,000	—	0.15	0.25	0.45	—
1985	—	—	0.15	0.25	0.45	—
1985 Proof	—	Value: 1.00				
1986	—	—	0.15	0.25	0.45	—
1986 Proof	—	Value: 1.00				
1987	—	—	0.15	0.25	0.45	—
1988	—	—	0.15	0.25	0.45	—
1989	—	—	0.15	0.25	0.45	—
1990	—	—	0.15	0.25	0.45	—
1991	—	—	0.15	0.25	0.45	—
1991 Proof	—	Value: 1.00				
1992	—	—	0.15	0.25	0.45	—
1992 Proof	—	Value: 1.00				
1993 In sets only	—	—	—	—	0.75	—
1993 Proof	—	Value: 1.00				
1994 In sets only	—	—	—	—	0.75	—
1994 Proof	—	Value: 1.00				
1995 In sets only	—	—	—	—	0.75	—
1995 Proof	—	Value: 1.00				
1996 In sets only	—	—	—	—	0.75	—
1996 Proof	—	Value: 1.00				

Y# 24 JIAO Composition: Copper-Zinc

Date	Mintage	F	VF	XF	Unc	BU
1980	—	—	—	—	0.50	—
1980 Proof	—	Value: 1.00				
1981	—	—	—	—	0.50	—
1981 Proof	—	Value: 1.00				
1982 Proof	—	Value: 1.00				
1983	3,100,000	—	—	—	0.50	—
1984	3,500,000	—	—	—	0.50	—
1985 Proof	—	Value: 1.00				
1986 Proof	—	Value: 1.00				

Y# 148 JIAO Composition: Brass **Series:** 6th National Games **Subject:** Gymnast

Date	Mintage	F	VF	XF	Unc	BU
1987	10,570,000	—	—	1.00	2.00	—

Y# 149 JIAO Composition: Brass **Series:** 6th National Games **Subject:** Soccer

Date	F	VF	XF	Unc	BU
1987	—	—	1.00	2.00	—

Y# 150 JIAO Composition: Brass **Series:** 6th National Games **Subject:** Volleyball

Date	F	VF	XF	Unc	BU
1987	—	—	1.00	2.00	—

Y# 328 JIAO Composition: Aluminum **Reverse:** Peony blossom

Date	F	VF	XF	Unc	BU
1991	—	—	—	0.50	—
1991 Proof	— Value: 1.00				
1992	—	—	—	0.50	—
1992 Proof	— Value: 1.00				
1993	—	—	—	0.50	—
1993 Proof	— Value: 1.00				
1994	—	—	—	0.50	—
1994 Proof	— Value: 1.00				
1995	—	—	—	0.50	—
1995 Proof	— Value: 1.00				
1996	—	—	—	0.50	—
1996 Proof	— Value: 1.00				
1997	—	—	—	0.50	—
1999	—	—	—	—	—
1999 Proof	—	—	—	—	—

Y#1068 JIAO Composition: Aluminum 1.9 oz. **Obverse:** Denomination **Reverse:** Orchid **Edge:** Plain **Size:** 18.9 mm.

Date	F	VF	XF	Unc	BU
1999	—	—	—	0.50	—
2000	—	—	—	0.50	—

Y# 25 2 JIAO Composition: Copper-Zinc

Date	Mintage	F	VF	XF	Unc	BU
1980	—	—	—	—	0.60	—
1980 Proof	—	Value: 1.25				
1981	—	—	—	—	0.60	—
1981 Proof	—	Value: 1.25				
1982 Proof	—	Value: 1.25				
1983	4,200,000	—	—	—	0.60	—
1984	2,500,000	—	—	—	0.60	—
1985 Proof	—	Value: 1.25				
1986 Proof	—	Value: 1.25				

Y# 26 5 JIAO Composition: Copper-Zinc

Date	Mintage	F	VF	XF	Unc	BU
1980	—	—	—	—	0.75	—
1980 Proof	—	Value: 1.50				
1981	—	—	—	—	0.75	—
1981 Proof	—	Value: 1.50				
1982 Proof	—	Value: 1.50				
1983	3,000,000	—	—	—	0.75	—
1984	3,500,000	—	—	—	0.75	—
1985	—	—	—	—	0.75	—
1985 Proof	—	Value: 1.50				
1986 Proof	—	Value: 1.50				

Y# 53 5 JIAO Weight: 2.2000 g. **Composition:** 0.9000 Silver .0637 oz. ASW **Reverse:** Marco Polo

Date	Mintage	F	VF	XF	Unc	BU
1983 Proof	7,050	Value: 90.00				

Y# 205 5 JIAO Weight: 2.0000 g. **Composition:** 0.9990 Silver .0643 oz. ASW **Reverse:** Phoenix and dragon representing good luck.

Date	Mintage	F	VF	XF	Unc	BU
1990 Proof	55,000	Value: 10.00				
1990 Proof	55,000	Value: 10.00				

Y# 329 5 JIAO Composition: Brass

Date	F	VF	XF	Unc	BU
1991	—	—	—	1.00	—
1991 Proof	— Value: 1.50				
1992	—	—	—	1.00	—
1992 Proof	— Value: 1.50				
1993	—	—	—	1.00	—
1993 Proof	— Value: 1.50				
1994	—	—	—	1.00	—
1994 Proof	— Value: 1.50				
1995	—	—	—	1.00	—
1995 Proof	— Value: 1.50				
1996	—	—	—	1.00	—
1996 Proof	— Value: 1.50				
1997	—	—	—	1.00	—
1998	—	—	—	1.00	—

Y# 1106 5 JIAO Weight: 3.8000 g. **Composition:** Brass **Obverse:** Denomination **Reverse:** Flower **Edge:** Reeded and plain sections **Size:** 20.5 mm.

Date	F	VF	XF	Unc	BU
2002	—	—	—	1.50	—

Y# 10 YUAN Composition: Brass **Series:** 1980 Olympics **Subject:** Archery

Date	Mintage	F	VF	XF	Unc	BU
1980 Proof	40,000	Value: 11.50				

Y# 11 YUAN Composition: Brass **Series:** 1980 Olympics **Subject:** Wrestling

Date	Mintage	F	VF	XF	Unc	BU
1980 Proof	40,000	Value: 11.50				

Y# 12 YUAN Composition: Brass **Series:** 1980 Olympics **Subject:** Equestrian **Obverse:** Similar to Y#14

Date	Mintage	F	VF	XF	Unc	BU
1980 Proof	40,000	Value: 11.50				

Y#13 YUAN **Composition:** Brass **Series:** 1980 Olympics **Subject:** Soccer **Obverse:** State seal

Date	Mintage	F	VF	XF	Unc	BU
1980 Proof	40,000	Value: 11.50				

Y#14 YUAN **Composition:** Brass **Series:** 1980 Olympics **Subject:** Alpine Skiing

Date	Mintage	F	VF	XF	Unc	BU
1980 Proof	29,000	Value: 13.50				

Y#15 YUAN **Composition:** Brass **Series:** 1980 Olympics **Subject:** Speed Skating

Date	Mintage	F	VF	XF	Unc	BU
1980 Proof	29,000	Value: 13.50				

Y#16 YUAN **Composition:** Brass **Series:** 1980 Olympics **Subject:** Figure Skating

Date	Mintage	F	VF	XF	Unc	BU
1980 Proof	29,000	Value: 13.50				

Y#17 YUAN **Composition:** Brass **Series:** 1980 Olympics **Subject:** Biathlon

Date	Mintage	F	VF	XF	Unc	BU
1980 Proof	29,000	Value: 13.50				

Y# 27 YUAN **Composition:** Copper-Nickel

Date	Mintage	F	VF	XF	Unc	BU
1980	—	—	—	—	2.00	—
1980 Proof	—	Value: 3.00				
1981	—	—	—	—	2.00	—
1981 Proof	—	Value: 3.00				
1982 Proof	—	Value: 3.00				
1983	3,100,000	—	—	—	2.00	—
1984	4,100,000	—	—	—	2.00	—
1985	—	—	—	—	2.00	—
1985 Proof	—	Value: 3.00				
1986 Proof	—	Value: 3.00				

Y# 34 YUAN **Composition:** Brass **Subject:** World Cup Soccer

Date	Mintage	F	VF	XF	Unc	BU
1982 Proof	20,000	Value: 12.50				

Y# 58 YUAN **Composition:** Brass **Reverse:** Panda

Date	Mintage	F	VF	XF	Unc	BU
1983 Proof	30,000	Value: 15.00				
1984 Proof	30,000	Value: 15.00				

Y# 85 YUAN **Composition:** Copper-Nickel **Subject:** 35th Anniversary - Peoples Republic

Date	Mintage	F	VF	XF	Unc	BU
ND(1984)	20,410,000	—	—	—	6.00	—
ND(1984) Proof	—	Value: 7.50				

Y# 86 YUAN **Composition:** Copper-Nickel **Subject:** 35th Anniversary - Peoples Republic

Date		F	VF	XF	Unc	BU
ND(1984)		—	—	—	6.00	—
ND(1984) Proof		—	Value: 7.50			

Y# 87 YUAN **Composition:** Copper-Nickel **Subject:** 35th Anniversary - Peoples Republic

Date		F	VF	XF	Unc	BU
ND(1984)		—	—	—	6.00	—
ND(1984) Proof		—	Value: 7.50			

Y# 96 YUAN **Composition:** Copper-Nickel **Subject:** 20th Anniversary - Tibet Autonomous Region

Date	Mintage	F	VF	XF	Unc	BU
1985	2,612,000	—	—	3.00	8.50	—
1985 Proof	10,000	Value: 12.00				

Y# 109 YUAN **Composition:** Copper-Nickel **Subject:** 30th Anniversary - Xinjiang Autonomous Region

Date	Mintage	F	VF	XF	Unc	BU
1985	4,500,000	—	—	2.00	6.00	—
1985 Proof	10,000	Value: 7.50				

Y# 151 YUAN **Composition:** Copper-Nickel **Subject:** Year of Peace

Date	Mintage	F	VF	XF	Unc	BU
1986	27,048,000	—	—	—	6.50	—

Y# 140 YUAN **Composition:** Copper-Nickel **Subject:** 40th Anniversary - Mongolian Autonomous Region

Date	Mintage	F	VF	XF	Unc	BU
1987	9,054,000	—	—	2.00	6.00	—

Y# 198 YUAN **Composition:** Copper-Nickel **Subject:** 30th Anniversary - Kwangsi Autonomous Region

Date	Mintage	F	VF	XF	Unc	BU
1988	4,072,000	—	—	—	7.00	—

Y# 211 YUAN **Composition:** Copper-Nickel **Subject:** 30th Anniversary - Ningxia Autonomous Region

Date	Mintage	F	VF	XF	Unc	BU
1988	1,560,000	—	—	—	7.50	—

Y# 212 YUAN **Composition:** Copper-Nickel **Subject:** 40th Anniversary - Peoples Bank

Date	Mintage	F	VF	XF	Unc	BU
1988	2,068,000	—	—	5.00	14.00	—

Y# 204 YUAN **Composition:** Copper-Nickel **Subject:** 40th Anniversary - Peoples Republic

Date	Mintage	F	VF	XF	Unc	BU
1989	2,000,000	—	—	—	5.00	—

Y# 264 YUAN **Composition:** Nickel Clad Steel **Series:** XI Asian Games **Reverse:** Sword Dancer

Date	Mintage	F	VF	XF	Unc	BU
1990	25,608,000	—	—	—	4.00	—

Y# 265 YUAN **Composition:** Nickel Clad Steel **Series:** XI Asian Games **Reverse:** Female Archer

Date	F	VF	XF	Unc	BU
1990	—	—	—	4.00	—

Y# 279 YUAN **Composition:** Nickel Clad Steel **Subject:** Planting Trees Festival **Reverse:** Head of young woman

Date	Mintage	F	VF	XF	Unc	BU
1991	10,000,000	—	—	—	2.25	—

Y# 280 YUAN **Composition:** Nickel Clad Steel **Subject:** Planting Trees Festival **Reverse:** Globe

Date	Mintage	F	VF	XF	Unc	BU
1991	10,000,000	—	—	—	2.25	—

Y# 281 YUAN **Composition:** Nickel Clad Steel **Subject:** Planting Trees Festival **Reverse:** Seedling

Date	Mintage	F	VF	XF	Unc	BU
1991	10,000,000	—	—	—	2.25	—

Y# 284 YUAN **Composition:** Nickel Plated Steel **Subject:** 1st Meeting of Chinese Communist Party **Reverse:** House of Shanghai

Date	Mintage	F	VF	XF	Unc	BU
1991	30,000,000	—	—	—	2.25	—

Y# 285 YUAN **Composition:** Nickel Plated Steel **Subject:** Party Meeting During Long March in 1935 **Reverse:** House in Zunyi, Kweichow Province

Date	Mintage	F	VF	XF	Unc	BU
1991	30,000,000	—	—	—	2.25	—

Y# 286 YUAN **Composition:** Nickel Plated Steel **Subject:** 1978 Party Conference - Tiananmen Square

Date	Mintage	F	VF	XF	Unc	BU
1991	30,000,000	—	—	—	2.25	—

Y# 316 YUAN **Composition:** Nickel Plated Steel **Subject:** Women's World Soccer Championship **Reverse:** Goalie

Date	Mintage	F	VF	XF	Unc	BU
1991	10,000,000	—	—	—	2.50	—

Y# 317 YUAN **Composition:** Nickel Plated Steel **Subject:** Women's World Soccer Championship **Reverse:** Player

Date	Mintage	F	VF	XF	Unc	BU
1991	10,000,000	—	—	—	2.50	—

Y# 330 YUAN **Composition:** Nickel Clad Steel

Date		F	VF	XF	Unc	BU
1991		—	—	—	1.50	—
1991 Proof	— Value: 2.50					
1992		—	—	—	1.50	—
1992 Proof	— Value: 2.50					
1993		—	—	—	1.50	—
1993 Proof	— Value: 2.50					
1994		—	—	—	1.50	—
1994 Proof	— Value: 2.50					
1995		—	—	—	1.50	—
1995 Proof	— Value: 2.50					
1996		—	—	—	1.50	—
1996 Proof	— Value: 2.50					
1997		—	—	—	1.50	—
1997 Proof	— Value: 2.50					
1998		—	—	—	—	—
1998 Proof		—	—	—	—	—
1999		—	—	—	—	—
1999 Proof		—	—	—	—	—

Y# 364 YUAN **Composition:** Nickel Clad Steel **Subject:** 10th Anniversary - Constitution

Date	Mintage	F	VF	XF	Unc	BU
1992	10,000,000	—	—	—	2.50	—

Y# 365 YUAN **Composition:** Nickel Clad Steel **Subject:** 100th Birthday of Ching Ling - Second Wife of Sun Yat-sen

Date	Mintage	F	VF	XF	Unc	BU
1993	10,448,000	—	—	—	3.50	—

Y# 399 YUAN **Composition:** Nickel Clad Steel **Subject:** 100th Anniversary - Birth of Chairman Mao

Date	Mintage	F	VF	XF	Unc	BU
1993	20,000,000	—	—	—	3.50	—
1993 Prooflike	—	—	—	—	5.00	—

Y# 455 YUAN **Composition:** Nickel Clad Steel **Series:** Children's Year **Reverse:** Two children

Date	F	VF	XF	Unc	BU
1994	—	—	—	2.50	—

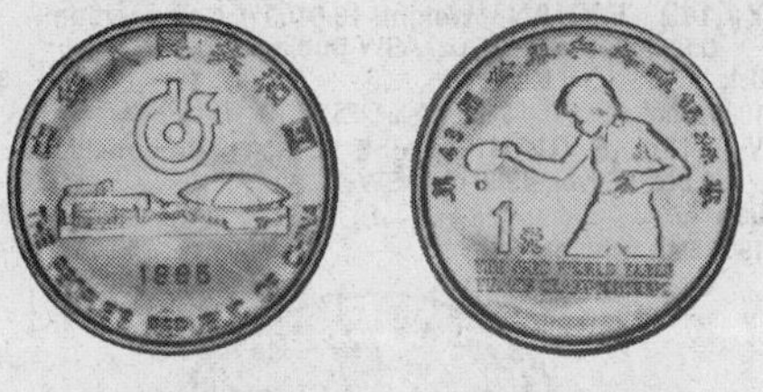

Y# 487 YUAN **Composition:** Nickel Plated Steel **Subject:** Table Tennis

Date	Mintage	F	VF	XF	Unc	BU
1995	10,000,000	—	—	—	3.50	—
1995 Proof	20,000	Value: 6.50				

Y# 528 YUAN **Composition:** Nickel Plated Steel **Subject:** 50th Anniversary - Defeat of Fascism and Japan

Date	Mintage	F	VF	XF	Unc	BU
1995	10,000,000	—	—	—	3.50	—

Y# 529 YUAN **Composition:** Nickel Plated Steel **Subject:** 50th Anniversary - United Nations

Date	Mintage	F	VF	XF	Unc	BU
1995	10,000,000	—	—	—	3.00	—

Y# 530 YUAN **Composition:** Nickel Plated Steel **Subject:** 4th UN Women's Conference

Date	Mintage	F	VF	XF	Unc	BU
1995	10,000,000	—	—	—	3.00	—

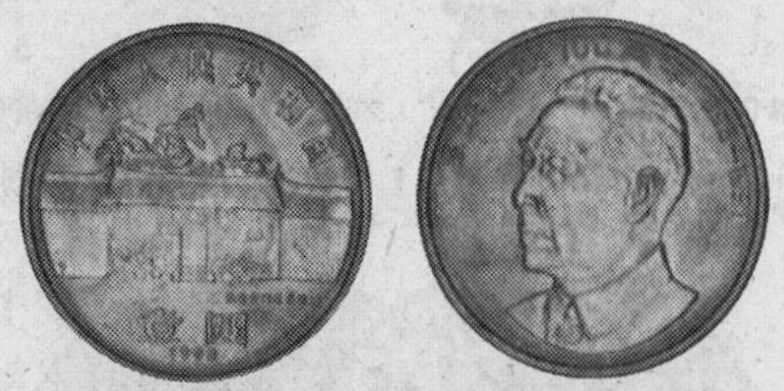

Y# 721 YUAN **Composition:** Nickel Clad Steel **Subject:** 100th Birthday - Chou (Zhou) Enlai **Obverse:** Chou (Zhou) birth place **Reverse:** Chou (Zhou) bust left

Date	F	VF	XF	Unc	BU
1998	—	—	—	3.00	—

Y# 1057 YUAN **Weight:** 6.1000 g. **Composition:** Nickel Clad Steel **Subject:** Liu Shao-chi **Obverse:** Building, denomination and date **Reverse:** Bust of Liu left **Edge Lettering:** ZHONGGUO twice **Size:** 24.9 mm.

Date	F	VF	XF	Unc	BU
1998	—	—	—	3.75	—

Y# 1058 YUAN **Weight:** 6.1000 g. **Composition:** Nickel Clad Steel **Subject:** 50th Anniversary - People's Political Consultative Conference **Obverse:** Building. **Reverse:** Coat of arms. **Size:** 24.9 mm.

Date	F	VF	XF	Unc	BU
1999	—	—	—	3.75	—

Y# 1069 YUAN **Composition:** Nickel Clad Steel 6.03 oz. **Obverse:** Denomination **Reverse:** Flower **Edge:** "RMB" three times **Size:** 24.9 mm.

Date	F	VF	XF	Unc	BU
2000	—	—	—	3.50	—

Y# 1037 YUAN **Weight:** 6.1000 g. **Composition:** Nickel Clad Steel **Subject:** Dunhuang Cave **Obverse:** Pagoda **Reverse:** Standing and floating figures **Edge:** "RMB" 3 times

Date	F	VF	XF	Unc	BU
2000	—	—	—	4.00	—

Y# 307 3 YUAN **Weight:** 1.0000 g. **Composition:** 0.9990 Gold .0321 oz. AGW **Obverse:** Temple of Heaven

Date	F	VF	XF	Unc	BU
1991 Proof	—	Value: 30.00			

Y# 362 3 YUAN **Weight:** 15.0000 g. **Composition:** 0.9000 Silver .4340 oz. ASW **Subject:** Ancient Chinese Coins

Date	Mintage	F	VF	XF	Unc	BU
1992 Proof	23,000	Value: 16.50				

Y# 363 3 YUAN **Weight:** 15.0000 g. **Composition:** 0.9000 Silver .4340 oz. ASW **Subject:** Ancient Chinese Paper

Date		F	VF	XF	Unc	BU
1992 Proof	Est. 20,000	Value: 16.50				

Y# 403 3 YUAN **Weight:** 15.0000 g. **Composition:** 0.9000 Silver .4340 oz. ASW **Reverse:** Chinese gods Fu, Lu and Shu **Note:** Similar to 500 Yuan, Y#407.

Date	Mintage	F	VF	XF	Unc	BU
1993 Proof	20,000	Value: 18.50				

Y# 733 3 YUAN **Weight:** 15.0000 g. **Composition:** 0.9000 Silver .4340 oz. ASW **Subject:** Yin and Yang Concept **Obverse:** Great Wall tower **Reverse:** Chinese gods Fu, Lu and Shu with Yin Yang symbol

Date	F	VF	XF	Unc	BU
1995 Proof	—	Value: 16.50			

Y# 734 3 YUAN **Weight:** 15.0000 g. **Composition:** 0.9000 Silver .4340 oz. ASW **Subject:** Great Wall of China **Obverse:** Great Wall view **Reverse:** Great Wall construction scene

Date	F	VF	XF	Unc	BU
1995 Proof	—	Value: 16.50			

Y# 1081 3 YUAN **Weight:** 15.0000 g. **Composition:** 0.9000 Silver 0.434 oz. ASW **Subject:** World Wildlife Federation **Obverse:** State emblem. **Reverse:** Panda seated right eating leaves. **Edge:** Reeded. **Size:** 30 mm.

Date	Mintage	F	VF	XF	Unc	BU
1997 Proof	50,000	Value: 20.00				

Y# 48 5 YUAN **Weight:** 1.5552 g. **Composition:** 0.9990 Gold .0500 oz. AGW

Date	Mintage	F	VF	XF	Unc	BU
1983 Proof	58,000	Value: 65.00				

Y# 54 5 YUAN **Weight:** 22.2200 g. **Composition:** 0.9000 Silver .6430 oz. ASW **Reverse:** Marco Polo

Date	Mintage	F	VF	XF	Unc	BU
1983 Proof	15,000	Value: 55.00				

Y# 61 5 YUAN **Weight:** 8.4500 g. **Composition:** 0.8000 Silver .2173 oz. ASW **Series:** 1984 Summer and Winter Olympics **Reverse:** High Jumper

Date	Mintage	F	VF	XF	Unc	BU
1984 Proof	10,000	Value: 25.00				

Y# 68 5 YUAN **Weight:** 22.2200 g. **Composition:** 0.9000 Silver .6430 oz. ASW **Reverse:** Soldier statue from archaeological discovery

Date	Mintage	F	VF	XF	Unc	BU
1984 Proof	14,000	Value: 20.00				

Y# 69 5 YUAN **Weight:** 22.2200 g. **Composition:** 0.9000 Silver .6430 oz. ASW **Reverse:** Soldier statue from archaeological discovery

Date	Mintage	F	VF	XF	Unc	BU
1984 Proof	14,000	Value: 20.00				

Y# 70 5 YUAN **Weight:** 22.2200 g. **Composition:** 0.9000 Silver .6430 oz. ASW **Reverse:** Soldier statue from archaeological discovery

Date	Mintage	F	VF	XF	Unc	BU
1984 Proof	14,000	Value: 20.00				

Y# 71 5 YUAN **Weight:** 22.2200 g. **Composition:** 0.9000 Silver .6430 oz. ASW **Reverse:** Soldier statue from archaeological discovery

Date	Mintage	F	VF	XF	Unc	BU
1984 Proof	14,000	Value: 20.00				

Y# 73 5 YUAN **Weight:** 1.5552 g. **Composition:** 0.9990 Gold .0500 oz. AGW

Date	Mintage	F	VF	XF	Unc	BU
1984 Proof	86,000	Value: 40.00				

Y# 80 5 YUAN **Weight:** 1.5552 g. **Composition:** 0.9990 Gold .0500 oz. AGW

Date	Mintage	F	VF	XF	Unc	BU
1985 Proof	217,000	Value: 55.00				

Y# 90 5 YUAN **Weight:** 22.2200 g. **Composition:** 0.9000 Silver .6430 oz. ASW **Subject:** Founders of Chinese Culture **Obverse:** State seal **Reverse:** Lao-Tse riding water buffalo

Date	Mintage	F	VF	XF	Unc	BU
1985 Proof	8,175	Value: 28.50				

Y# 91 5 YUAN **Weight:** 22.2200 g. **Composition:** 0.9000 Silver .6430 oz. ASW **Subject:** Founders of Chinese Culture **Reverse:** Qu Yuan

Date	Mintage	F	VF	XF	Unc	BU
1985 Proof	8,175	Value: 28.50				

Y# 92 5 YUAN **Weight:** 22.2200 g. **Composition:** 0.9000 Silver .6430 oz. ASW **Subject:** Founders of Chinese Culture **Reverse:** Sun Wu

Date	Mintage	F	VF	XF	Unc	BU
1985 Proof	8,175	Value: 28.50				

Y# 93 5 YUAN **Weight:** 22.2200 g. **Composition:** 0.9000 Silver .6430 oz. ASW **Subject:** Founders of Chinese Culture **Reverse:** Chen Sheng and Wu Guang

Date	Mintage	F	VF	XF	Unc	BU
1985 Proof	8,175	Value: 28.50				

Y# 101 5 YUAN **Weight:** 1.5552 g. **Composition:** 0.9990 Gold .0500 oz. AGW

Date	Mintage	F	VF	XF	Unc	BU
1986	53,000	—	—	—	35.00	—
1986 P Proof	98,000	Value: 40.00				

Y# 106 5 YUAN **Weight:** 22.2200 g. **Composition:** 0.9000 Silver .6430 oz. ASW **Subject:** Wildlife **Reverse:** Giant panda

Date	Mintage	F	VF	XF	Unc	BU
1986	20,000	—	—	—	35.00	—
1986 Proof	20,000	Value: 50.00				

Y# 112 5 YUAN **Weight:** 18.6100 g. **Composition:** 0.9250 Silver .5535 oz. ASW **Subject:** Soccer

Date	Mintage	F	VF	XF	Unc	BU
1986 Proof	8,500	Value: 25.00				

Y# 112a 5 YUAN **Weight:** 17.0600 g. **Composition:** 0.8000 Silver .4388 oz. ASW

Date	F	VF	XF	Unc	BU
1986 Satin finish	—	—	—	40.00	—

Y# 113 5 YUAN **Weight:** 22.2200 g. **Composition:** 0.9000 Silver .6367 oz. ASW **Subject:** Chinese Culture **Reverse:** Cai Lun - paper making

Date	Mintage	F	VF	XF	Unc	BU
1986 Proof	9,675	Value: 22.50				

Y# 114 5 YUAN **Weight:** 22.2200 g. **Composition:** 0.9000 Silver .6367 oz. ASW **Subject:** Chinese Culture **Reverse:** Zhang Heng, astronomer

Date	Mintage	F	VF	XF	Unc	BU
1986 Proof	9,675	Value: 22.50				

Y# 115 5 YUAN Weight: 22.2200 g. **Composition:** 0.9000 Silver .6367 oz. ASW **Subject:** Chinese Culture **Reverse:** Zu Chong Zhi, mathematician

Date	Mintage	F	VF	XF	Unc	BU
1986 Proof	9,675	Value: 22.50				

Y# 116 5 YUAN Weight: 22.2200 g. **Composition:** 0.9000 Silver .6367 oz. ASW **Subject:** Chinese Culture **Reverse:** Sima Qian, historian

Date	Mintage	F	VF	XF	Unc	BU
1986 Proof	9,675	Value: 22.50				

Y# 119 5 YUAN Weight: 18.6100 g. **Composition:** 0.9250 Silver .5535 oz. ASW **Subject:** Year of Peace

Date	Mintage	F	VF	XF	Unc	BU
1986 Proof	1,350	Value: 200				

Y# 132 5 YUAN Weight: 22.2200 g. **Composition:** 0.9000 Silver .6367 oz. ASW **Obverse:** Great Wall **Reverse:** The Ship Empress of China

Date	Mintage	F	VF	XF	Unc	BU
1986	75,000	—	—	—	20.00	35.00

Y# 197 5 YUAN Weight: 18.6100 g. **Composition:** 0.9250 Silver .5535 oz. ASW **Subject:** Soccer **Reverse:** Two players

Date	Mintage	F	VF	XF	Unc	BU
1986	1,000	—	—	—	65.00	90.00

Y# 197a 5 YUAN Weight: 16.8300 g. **Composition:** 0.8000 Silver .4328 oz. ASW

Date	Mintage	F	VF	XF	Unc	BU
1986 Proof	4,000	Value: 30.00				

Y# 124 5 YUAN Weight: 1.5552 g. **Composition:** 0.9990 Gold .0500 oz. AGW

Date	Mintage	F	VF	XF	Unc	BU
1987(s)	99,000	—	—	—	35.00	—
1987(y)	39,000	—	—	—	35.00	—
1987 P Proof	10,000	Value: 40.00				

Y# 135 5 YUAN Weight: 31.4700 g. **Composition:** 0.9000 Silver .9107 oz. ASW **Reverse:** Poet Li Bai

Date	Mintage	F	VF	XF	Unc	BU
1987 Proof	4,000	Value: 23.50				

Y# 136 5 YUAN Weight: 31.4700 g. **Composition:** 0.9000 Silver .9107 oz. ASW **Reverse:** Poet Du Fu

Date	Mintage	F	VF	XF	Unc	BU
1987 Proof	4,000	Value: 23.50				

Y# 137 5 YUAN Weight: 31.4700 g. **Composition:** 0.9000 Silver .9107 oz. ASW **Subject:** Bridge Builder - Li Chun

Date	Mintage	F	VF	XF	Unc	BU
1987 Proof	4,000	Value: 24.00				

Y# 138 5 YUAN Weight: 31.4700 g. **Composition:** 0.9000 Silver .9107 oz. ASW **Reverse:** Princess Chen Wen and Song Zan Gan Bu strolling to left

Date	Mintage	F	VF	XF	Unc	BU
1987 Proof	4,000	Value: 24.00				

Y# 129 5 YUAN Weight: 31.4700 g. **Composition:** 0.9000 Silver .9107 oz. ASW **Series:** Winter Olympics **Reverse:** Downhill Skier

Date	Mintage	F	VF	XF	Unc	BU
1988 Proof	17,000	Value: 60.00				

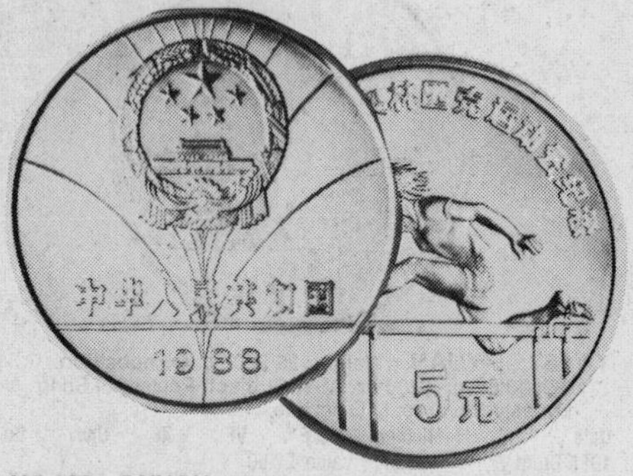

Y# 130 5 YUAN Weight: 31.4700 g. **Composition:** 0.9000 Silver .9107 oz. ASW **Series:** Summer Olympics **Reverse:** Woman hurdler

Date	Mintage	F	VF	XF	Unc	BU
1988 Proof	20,000	Value: 32.50				

Y# 152 5 YUAN Weight: 1.5552 g. **Composition:** 0.9990 Gold .0500 oz. AGW **Reverse:** Panda pawing bamboo

Date	Mintage	F	VF	XF	Unc	BU
1988	482,000	—	—	—	35.00	—
1988 Proof	11,000	Value: 40.00				

Y# 160 5 YUAN Weight: 22.2200 g. **Composition:** 0.9000 Silver .6430 oz. ASW **Subject:** Military Hero of Song Dynasty - Yue Fei

Date	Mintage	F	VF	XF	Unc	BU
1988 Proof	13,000	Value: 22.50				

Y# 161 5 YUAN Weight: 22.2200 g. **Composition:** 0.9000 Silver .6430 oz. ASW **Subject:** Inventor of Movable-type Printing **Reverse:** Bi Sheng

Date	Mintage	F	VF	XF	Unc	BU
1988 Proof	14,000	Value: 22.50				

Y# 162 5 YUAN **Weight:** 22.2200 g. **Composition:** 0.9000 Silver .6430 oz. ASW **Subject:** Song Dynasty Poet **Reverse:** Su Shi

Date	Mintage	F	VF	XF	Unc	BU
1988 Proof	9,500	Value: 22.50				

Y# 163 5 YUAN **Weight:** 22.2200 g. **Composition:** 0.9000 Silver .6430 oz. ASW **Subject:** Poetess of Song Dynasty **Reverse:** Li Qingzhao

Date	Mintage	F	VF	XF	Unc	BU
1988 Proof	13,000	Value: 22.50				

Y# 171 5 YUAN **Weight:** 27.0000 g. **Composition:** 0.9000 Silver .7812 oz. ASW **Series:** Olympics **Reverse:** Sailboat racing

Date	Mintage	F	VF	XF	Unc	BU
1988 Proof	20,000	Value: 32.50				

Y# 172 5 YUAN **Weight:** 27.0000 g. **Composition:** 0.9000 Silver .7812 oz. ASW **Series:** Olympics **Subject:** Fencing

Date	Mintage	F	VF	XF	Unc	BU
1988 Proof	20,000	Value: 30.00				

Y# 213 5 YUAN **Weight:** 22.2200 g. **Composition:** 0.9000 Silver .6431 oz. ASW **Reverse:** Kublai Khan, emperor

Date	Mintage	F	VF	XF	Unc	BU
1989 Proof	10,000	Value: 35.00				

Y# 214 5 YUAN **Weight:** 22.2200 g. **Composition:** 0.9000 Silver .6431 oz. ASW **Reverse:** Guan Hanqing, playwright

Date	Mintage	F	VF	XF	Unc	BU
1989 Proof	8,000	Value: 27.50				

Y# 215 5 YUAN **Weight:** 22.2200 g. **Composition:** 0.9000 Silver .6431 oz. ASW **Reverse:** Guo Shoujing, scientist

Date	Mintage	F	VF	XF	Unc	BU
1989 Proof	8,500	Value: 27.50				

Y# 216 5 YUAN **Weight:** 22.2200 g. **Composition:** 0.9000 Silver .6431 oz. ASW **Reverse:** Huang Daopo, inventor of water wheel

Date	Mintage	F	VF	XF	Unc	BU
1989 Proof	8,000	Value: 27.50				

Y# 230 5 YUAN **Weight:** 22.2200 g. **Composition:** 0.9000 Silver .6431 oz. ASW **Series:** Save The Children Fund

Date	Mintage	F	VF	XF	Unc	BU
1989	20,000	—	—	—	30.00	—

Y# 243 5 YUAN **Weight:** 27.0000 g. **Composition:** 0.9250 Silver .8030 oz. ASW **Subject:** Soccer **Reverse:** 2 Players

Date	Mintage	F	VF	XF	Unc	BU
1989 Proof	30,000	Value: 25.00				

Y# 187 5 YUAN **Weight:** 1.5552 g. **Composition:** 0.9990 Gold .0500 oz. AGW **Series:** Olympics **Note:** Similar to 100 Yuan, Y#191.

Date	Mintage	F	VF	XF	Unc	BU
1989	334,000	—	—	—	35.00	—
1989 Proof	—	Value: 45.00				

Y# 238 5 YUAN **Weight:** 1.5552 g. **Composition:** 0.9990 Gold .0500 oz. AGW **Note:** Similar to 100 Yuan, Y#242.

Date	Mintage	F	VF	XF	Unc	BU
1990	—	—	—	—	35.00	—
1990 Proof	5,000	Value: 45.00				

Y# 257 5 YUAN **Weight:** 15.0000 g. **Composition:** 0.9000 Silver .4341 oz. ASW **Subject:** Bronze Archaeological Finds **Reverse:** Elephant Pitcher

Date	Mintage	F	VF	XF	Unc	BU
1990 Proof	5,000	Value: 28.50				

Y# 258 5 YUAN **Weight:** 15.0000 g. **Composition:** 0.9000 Silver .4341 oz. ASW **Subject:** Bronze Archaeological Finds **Reverse:** Mythical Creature

Date	Mintage	F	VF	XF	Unc	BU
1990 Proof	5,000	Value: 28.50				

Y# 259 5 YUAN **Weight:** 15.0000 g. **Composition:** 0.9000 Silver .4341 oz. ASW **Subject:** Bronze Archaeological Finds **Reverse:** Rhinoceros

Date	Mintage	F	VF	XF	Unc	BU
1990 Proof	5,000	Value: 28.50				

Y# 260 5 YUAN **Weight:** 15.0000 g. **Composition:** 0.9000 Silver .4341 oz. ASW **Subject:** Bronze Archaeological Finds **Reverse:** Leopard

Date	Mintage	F	VF	XF	Unc	BU
1990 Proof	5,000	Value: 28.50				

Y# 297 5 YUAN **Weight:** 27.0000 g. **Composition:** 0.9250 Silver .8030 oz. ASW **Subject:** Soccer **Reverse:** 2 Players

Date	Mintage	F	VF	XF	Unc	BU
1990 Proof	30,000	Value: 27.50				

Y# 298 5 YUAN **Weight:** 27.0000 g. **Composition:** 0.9250 Silver .8030 oz. ASW **Subject:** Soccer **Reverse:** Goalie

Date	Mintage	F	VF	XF	Unc	BU
1990 Proof	30,000	Value: 27.50				

Y# 302 5 YUAN **Weight:** 22.2200 g. **Composition:** 0.9000 Silver .6431 oz. ASW **Reverse:** Luo Guanzhong, historian

Date	F	VF	XF	Unc	BU
1990	—	—	—	18.50	—

Y# 303 5 YUAN **Weight:** 22.2200 g. **Composition:** 0.9000 Silver .6431 oz. ASW **Reverse:** Li Zicheng, revolutionary

Date	F	VF	XF	Unc	BU
1990	—	—	—	20.00	—

Y# 304 5 YUAN **Weight:** 22.2200 g. **Composition:** 0.9000 Silver .6431 oz. ASW **Reverse:** Li Shi Zhen, herbalist

Date	F	VF	XF	Unc	BU
1990	—	—	—	20.00	—

Y# 305 5 YUAN **Weight:** 22.2200 g. **Composition:** 0.9000 Silver .6431 oz. ASW **Reverse:** Zheng He, seafarer

Date	F	VF	XF	Unc	BU
1990	—	—	—	20.00	—

Y# 322 5 YUAN **Weight:** 22.2200 g. **Composition:** 0.9000 Silver .6431 oz. ASW **Reverse:** Song Yingxing, scientist

Date	Mintage	F	VF	XF	Unc	BU
1991 Proof	25,000	Value: 22.50				

Y# 323 5 YUAN **Weight:** 22.2200 g. **Composition:** 0.9000 Silver .6431 oz. ASW **Reverse:** Cao Xueqin, writer

Date	Mintage	F	VF	XF	Unc	BU
1991 Proof	Est. 25,000	Value: 22.50				

Y# 324 5 YUAN **Weight:** 22.2200 g. **Composition:** 0.9000 Silver .6431 oz. ASW **Reverse:** Lin Zexu, high ranking official

Date	Mintage	F	VF	XF	Unc	BU
1991 Proof	25,000	Value: 22.50				

Y# 325 5 YUAN **Weight:** 22.2200 g. **Composition:** 0.9000 Silver .6431 oz. ASW **Reverse:** Hong Xuquan, revolutionary

Date	Mintage	F	VF	XF	Unc	BU
1991 Proof	25,000	Value: 22.50				

Y# 309 5 YUAN **Weight:** 1.5552 g. **Composition:** 0.9990 Gold .0500 oz. AGW **Note:** Similar to 100 Yuan, Y#313.

Date	F	VF	XF	Unc	BU
1991	—	—	—	45.00	—
1991 Proof	—	Value: 50.00			

Y# 341 5 YUAN **Weight:** 1.5552 g. **Composition:** 0.9990 Gold .0500 oz. AGW **Note:** Similar to 100 Yuan, Y#345.

Date	F	VF	XF	Unc	BU
1992	—	—	—	45.00	—
1992 Proof	—	Value: 50.00			

Y# 331 5 YUAN **Weight:** 22.2200 g. **Composition:** 0.9000 Silver .6431 oz. ASW **Subject:** Archaeological Finds **Obverse:** Great Wall **Reverse:** Ancient Ships and Shipbuilding

Date	Mintage	F	VF	XF	Unc	BU
1992 Proof	15,000	Value: 27.50				

Y# 332 5 YUAN **Weight:** 22.2200 g. **Composition:** 0.9000 Silver .6431 oz. ASW **Subject:** First Compass

Date	Mintage	F	VF	XF	Unc	BU
1992 Proof	15,000	Value: 25.00				

Y# 333 5 YUAN **Weight:** 22.2200 g. **Composition:** 0.9000 Silver .6431 oz. ASW **Subject:** First Seismograph

Date	Mintage	F	VF	XF	Unc	BU
1992 Proof	15,000	Value: 25.00				

Y# 334 5 YUAN **Weight:** 22.2200 g. **Composition:** 0.9000 Silver .6431 oz. ASW **Subject:** Ancient Kite Flying

Date	Mintage	F	VF	XF	Unc	BU
1992 Proof	15,000	Value: 25.00				

Y# 335 5 YUAN Weight: 22.2200 g. **Composition:** 0.9000 Silver .6431 oz. ASW **Reverse:** Bronze Age Metal Working Scene

Date	Mintage	F	VF	XF	Unc	BU
1992 Proof	15,000	Value: 25.00				

Y# 548 5 YUAN Weight: 22.2200 g. **Composition:** 0.9000 Silver .6430 oz. ASW **Subject:** United Nations Environmental Protection **Obverse:** State seal **Reverse:** Woman drawing water from stream

Date	Mintage	F	VF	XF	Unc	BU
1992 Proof	20,000	Value: 40.00				

Y# 549 5 YUAN Weight: 22.2200 g. **Composition:** 0.9000 Silver .6430 oz. ASW **Obverse:** State seal **Reverse:** Zheng Chenggong portrait.

Date		F	VF	XF	Unc	BU
1992 Proof	—	Value: 17.50				

Y# 550 5 YUAN Weight: 22.2200 g. **Composition:** 0.9000 Silver .6430 oz. ASW **Obverse:** State seal **Reverse:** Cai Wenji, writer

Date		F	VF	XF	Unc	BU
1992 Proof	Est. 7,000	Value: 20.00				

Y# 551 5 YUAN Weight: 22.2200 g. **Composition:** 0.9000 Silver .6430 oz. ASW **Obverse:** State seal **Reverse:** Hua Mulan, soldier

Date		F	VF	XF	Unc	BU
1992 Proof	Est. 7,000	Value: 28.00				

Y# 552 5 YUAN Weight: 22.2200 g. **Composition:** 0.9000 Silver .6430 oz. ASW **Obverse:** State seal **Reverse:** Wang Zhaojun, princess, peacemaker.

Date		F	VF	XF	Unc	BU
1992 Proof	Est. 7,000	Value: 20.00				

Y# 676 5 YUAN Weight: 15.0000 g. **Composition:** 0.9000 Silver .4350 oz. ASW **Subject:** Taiwan Scenery Series **Obverse:** Great Wall **Reverse:** Tall, narrow building

Date	Mintage	F	VF	XF	Unc	BU
1992 Proof	2,000	Value: 32.00				

Y# 677 5 YUAN Weight: 15.0000 g. **Composition:** 0.9000 Silver .4350 oz. ASW **Reverse:** Pondside building

Date	Mintage	F	VF	XF	Unc	BU
1992 Proof	2,000	Value: 32.00				

Y# 678 5 YUAN Weight: 15.0000 g. **Composition:** 0.9000 Silver .4350 oz. ASW **Reverse:** Hillside building

Date	Mintage	F	VF	XF	Unc	BU
1992 Proof	2,000	Value: 32.00				

Y# 679 5 YUAN Weight: 15.0000 g. **Composition:** 0.9000 Silver .4350 oz. ASW **Reverse:** 3 buildings joined by bridges

Date	Mintage	F	VF	XF	Unc	BU
1992 Proof	2,000	Value: 32.00				

Y# 750 5 YUAN Weight: 15.0000 g. **Composition:** 0.9000 Silver .4340 oz. ASW **Subject:** Archaeological Finds **Obverse:** National emblem **Reverse:** Resting deer with long antlers

Date	Mintage	F	VF	XF	Unc	BU
1992 Proof	3,000	Value: 35.00				

Y# 393 5 YUAN Weight: 15.0000 g. **Composition:** 0.9000 Silver .4341 oz. ASW **Reverse:** Marco Polo

Date	Mintage	F	VF	XF	Unc	BU
1992 Proof	12,000	Value: 20.00				

Y# 751 5 YUAN Weight: 15.0000 g. **Composition:** 0.9000 Silver .4340 oz. ASW **Subject:** Archeological Finds **Obverse:** National emblem **Reverse:** Panther sculpture **Note:** Similar to Y#556.

Date	Mintage	F	VF	XF	Unc	BU
1992 Proof	3,000	Value: 35.00				

Y# 752 5 YUAN Weight: 15.0000 g. **Composition:** 0.9000 Silver .4340 oz. ASW **Subject:** Archaeological Finds **Obverse:** National emblem **Reverse:** Big horn sheep **Note:** Similar to Y#555.

Date	Mintage	F	VF	XF	Unc	BU
1992 Proof	3,000	Value: 35.00				

Y# 753 5 YUAN Weight: 15.0000 g. **Composition:** 0.9000 Silver .4340 oz. ASW **Subject:** Archaeological Finds **Obverse:** National emblem **Reverse:** Changzin court lantern

Date	Mintage	F	VF	XF	Unc	BU
1992 Proof	3,000	Value: 35.00				

Y# 553 5 YUAN Weight: 22.2200 g. **Composition:** 0.9000 Silver .6430 oz. ASW **Obverse:** State seal **Reverse:** Xiao Zhuo, strategist

Date		F	VF	XF	Unc	BU
1993 Proof	Est. 7,000	Value: 28.00				

Y# 558 5 YUAN Weight: 22.2200 g. **Composition:** 0.9000 Silver .6430 oz. ASW **Subject:** Mathematical Definition of Zero **Obverse:** State seal **Reverse:** Mathematicians, abacus

Date	Mintage	F	VF	XF	Unc	BU
1993 Proof	15,000	Value: 22.00				

Y# 559 5 YUAN Weight: 22.2200 g. **Composition:** 0.9000 Silver .6430 oz. ASW **Subject:** Invention of the Stirrup **Obverse:** Great Wall **Reverse:** Early polo game

Date	Mintage	F	VF	XF	Unc	BU
1993 Proof	15,000	Value: 22.00				

Y# 560 5 YUAN **Weight:** 22.2200 g. **Composition:** 0.9000 Silver .6430 oz. ASW **Subject:** The Terracotta Army **Obverse:** Great Wall **Reverse:** The unearthing of the terracotta figurines

Date	Mintage	F	VF	XF	Unc	BU
1993 Proof	15,000	Value: 22.00				

Y# 359 5 YUAN **Composition:** Copper **Reverse:** 2 Pandas eating bamboo

Date	Mintage	F	VF	XF	Unc	BU
1993	2,000,000	—	—	—	15.00	—

Y# 377 5 YUAN **Weight:** 22.2200 g. **Composition:** 0.9000 Silver .6431 oz. ASW **Subject:** Chin-Yin Yang

Date	Mintage	F	VF	XF	Unc	BU
1993 Proof	15,000	Value: 35.00				

Y# 392 5 YUAN **Weight:** 15.5517 g. **Composition:** 0.9990 Silver .5000 oz. ASW **Reverse:** Panda facing forward

Date	F	VF	XF	Unc	BU
1993	—	—	—	17.50	—

Y# 400 5 YUAN **Weight:** 22.2200 g. **Composition:** 0.9000 Silver .6431 oz. ASW **Subject:** Invention of the Umbrella

Date	Mintage	F	VF	XF	Unc	BU
1993 Proof	15,000	Value: 18.00				

Y# 483 5 YUAN **Weight:** 1.5552 g. **Composition:** 0.9995 Platinum .0500 oz. APW **Reverse:** Panda seated on rock

Date	F	VF	XF	Unc	BU
1993 Proof	—	Value: 50.00			

Y# 498 5 YUAN **Weight:** 1.5552 g. **Composition:** 0.9990 Gold .0500 oz. AGW **Subject:** Goddess of Mercy

Date	Mintage	F	VF	XF	Unc	BU
1993 Prooflike	15,000	—	—	—	35.00	—

Y# 500 5 YUAN **Weight:** 1.5552 g. **Composition:** 0.9990 Gold .0500 oz. AGW **Reverse:** Goddess Kuan Yin - Seated in Flowers

Date	Mintage	F	VF	XF	Unc	BU
1993 Proof	1,000	Value: 55.00				

Y# 534 5 YUAN **Weight:** 22.2200 g. **Composition:** 0.9000 Silver .6431 oz. ASW **Obverse:** State emblem **Reverse:** Chou En-Lai

Date	Mintage	F	VF	XF	Unc	BU
1993 Proof	25,000	Value: 22.50				

Y# 535 5 YUAN **Weight:** 22.2200 g. **Composition:** 0.9000 Silver .6431 oz. ASW **Reverse:** Liu Shaoqi

Date	Mintage	F	VF	XF	Unc	BU
1993 Proof	25,000	Value: 22.50				

Y# 536 5 YUAN **Weight:** 22.2200 g. **Composition:** 0.9000 Silver .6431 oz. ASW **Reverse:** Chu Teh

Date	Mintage	F	VF	XF	Unc	BU
1993 Proof	25,000	Value: 20.00				

Y# 537 5 YUAN **Weight:** 22.2200 g. **Composition:** 0.9000 Silver .6431 oz. ASW **Reverse:** Li Da-Chao

Date	Mintage	F	VF	XF	Unc	BU
1993 Proof	25,000	Value: 20.00				

Y# 610 5 YUAN **Weight:** 1.5552 g. **Composition:** 0.9990 Gold .0500 oz. AGW **Obverse:** Panda pawing bamboo

Date	F	VF	XF	Unc	BU
1993	—	—	—	37.50	—
1993 Proof	—	Value: 50.00			

Y# 768 5 YUAN **Weight:** 15.0000 g. **Composition:** 0.9000 Silver .4340 oz. ASW **Subject:** Archeological Finds **Obverse:** State seal **Reverse:** Ox lantern

Date	Mintage	F	VF	XF	Unc	BU
1993 Proof	3,000	Value: 35.00				

Y# 769 5 YUAN **Weight:** 15.0000 g. **Composition:** 0.9000 Silver .4340 oz. ASW **Subject:** Archeological Finds **Obverse:** National emblem **Reverse:** Human figure lantern

Date	Mintage	F	VF	XF	Unc	BU
1993 Proof	3,000	Value: 35.00				

Y# 770 5 YUAN **Weight:** 15.0000 g. **Composition:** 0.9000 Silver .4340 oz. ASW **Subject:** Archeological Finds **Obverse:** National emblem **Reverse:** Horse statue

Date	Mintage	F	VF	XF	Unc	BU
1993 Proof	3,000	Value: 35.00				

Y# 771 5 YUAN **Weight:** 15.0000 g. **Composition:** 0.9000 Silver .4340 oz. ASW **Subject:** Archeological Finds **Obverse:** National emblem **Reverse:** Pig statue

Date	Mintage	F	VF	XF	Unc	BU
1993 Proof	2,000	Value: 35.00				

Y# 441 5 YUAN **Weight:** 15.0000 g. **Composition:** 0.9000 Silver .4341 oz. ASW **Obverse:** Great Wall **Reverse:** Taiwan Temple Buddha Statue **Note:** Similar to 50 Yuan, Y#445.

Date	Mintage	F	VF	XF	Unc	BU
1993 Proof	1,000	Value: 35.00				

Y# 442 5 YUAN **Weight:** 15.0000 g. **Composition:** 0.9000 Silver .4341 oz. ASW **Subject:** Taiwan Temple **Obverse:** Great Wall **Reverse:** Large temple **Note:** Similar to 50 Yuan, Y#446.

Date	Mintage	F	VF	XF	Unc	BU
1993 Proof	1,000	Value: 35.00				

Y# 443 5 YUAN **Weight:** 15.0000 g. **Composition:** 0.9000 Silver .4341 oz. ASW **Subject:** Taiwan Temple **Obverse:** Great Wall **Reverse:** Small temple **Note:** Similar to 50 Yuan, Y#447.

Date	Mintage	F	VF	XF	Unc	BU
1993 Proof	1,000	Value: 35.00				

Y# 444 5 YUAN **Weight:** 15.0000 g. **Composition:** 0.9000 Silver .4341 oz. ASW **Subject:** Taiwan Temple **Obverse:** Great Wall **Reverse:** Tower temple **Note:** Similar to 50 Yuan, Y#448.

Date	Mintage	F	VF	XF	Unc	BU
1993 Proof	1,000	Value: 35.00				

Y# 773 5 YUAN **Weight:** 1.5552 g. **Composition:** 0.9990 Gold .0500 oz. AGW **Subject:** Mount Song **Obverse:** Great Wall **Reverse:** Temple **Note:** Similar to 10 Yuan, Y#420.

Date	Mintage	F	VF	XF	Unc	BU
1993 Proof	8,888	Value: 35.00				

Y# 419 5 YUAN **Weight:** 1.5552 g. **Composition:** 0.9990 Gold .0500 oz. AGW **Reverse:** Unicorn

Date	Mintage	F	VF	XF	Unc	BU
1994 Proof	31,000	Value: 60.00				

Y# 431 5 YUAN **Weight:** 1.5552 g. **Composition:** 0.9990 Gold .0500 oz. AGW

Date	Mintage	F	VF	XF	Unc	BU
1994	35,000	—	—	—	45.00	—
1994 Proof	—	Value: 50.00				

Y# 436 5 YUAN **Weight:** 15.5517 g. **Composition:** 0.9990 Silver .5000 oz. ASW **Reverse:** Panda approaching water

Date	F	VF	XF	Unc	BU
1994	—	—	—	20.00	—

Y# 506 5 YUAN **Weight:** 15.5517 g. **Composition:** 0.9990 Silver .5000 oz. ASW **Reverse:** Goddess Kuan Yin - with child

Date	Mintage	F	VF	XF	Unc	BU
1994 Proof	3,000	Value: 27.50				

Y# 507 5 YUAN **Weight:** 15.5517 g. **Composition:** 0.9990 Silver .5000 oz. ASW **Reverse:** Goddess Kuan Yin - with bottle

Date	Mintage	F	VF	XF	Unc	BU
1994 Proof	3,000	Value: 27.50				

Y# 508 5 YUAN **Weight:** 15.5517 g. **Composition:** 0.9990 Silver .5000 oz. ASW **Reverse:** Goddess Kuan Yin - standing

Date	Mintage	F	VF	XF	Unc	BU
1994 Proof	3,000	Value: 27.50				

Y# 509 5 YUAN **Weight:** 15.5517 g. **Composition:** 0.9990 Silver .5000 oz. ASW **Reverse:** Goddess Kuan Yin - seated

Date	Mintage	F	VF	XF	Unc	BU
1994 Proof	3,000	Value: 27.50				

Y# 616 5 YUAN **Weight:** 22.2200 g. **Composition:** 0.9000 Silver .6430 oz. ASW **Subject:** Oriental Inventions **Obverse:** Great Wall **Reverse:** First tuned bells

Date	Mintage	F	VF	XF	Unc	BU
1994 Proof	15,000	Value: 18.00				

Y# 617 5 YUAN **Weight:** 22.2200 g. **Composition:** 0.9000 Silver .6430 oz. ASW **Subject:** Oriental Inventions **Obverse:** Great Wall **Reverse:** First silken fabric

Date	Mintage	F	VF	XF	Unc	BU
1994 Proof	15,000	Value: 20.00				

Y# 618 5 YUAN **Weight:** 22.2200 g. **Composition:** 0.9000 Silver .6430 oz. ASW **Subject:** Oriental Invention **Obverse:** Great Wall **Reverse:** First records of comets

Date	Mintage	F	VF	XF	Unc	BU
1994 Proof	15,000	Value: 20.00				

Y# 619 5 YUAN **Weight:** 22.2200 g. **Composition:** 0.9000 Silver .6430 oz. ASW **Subject:** Oriental Inventions **Obverse:** Great Wall **Reverse:** First masts for sailing

Date	Mintage	F	VF	XF	Unc	BU
1994 Proof	15,000	Value: 20.00				

Y# 620 5 YUAN **Weight:** 22.2200 g. **Composition:** 0.9000 Silver .6430 oz. ASW **Subject:** Oriental Inventions **Obverse:** Great Wall **Reverse:** First chain pumps used to draw water

Date	Mintage	F	VF	XF	Unc	BU
1994 Proof	15,000	Value: 18.00				

Y# 481 5 YUAN **Weight:** 22.2200 g. **Composition:** 0.9000 Silver .6430 oz. ASW **Reverse:** Sea Goddess

Date	Mintage	F	VF	XF	Unc	BU
1995 Proof	8,000,000	Value: 23.50				

Y# 516 5 YUAN **Weight:** 22.2200 g. **Composition:** 0.9000 Silver .6430 oz. ASW **Reverse:** Goddess Kuan Yin - with Lotus flower

Date	Mintage	F	VF	XF	Unc	BU
1995 Proof	3,000	Value: 27.50				

Y# 517 5 YUAN **Weight:** 22.2200 g. **Composition:** 0.9000 Silver .6430 oz. ASW **Reverse:** Goddess Kuan Yin - with wheel

Date	Mintage	F	VF	XF	Unc	BU
1995 Proof	3,000	Value: 27.50				

Y# 518 5 YUAN **Weight:** 22.2200 g. **Composition:** 0.9000 Silver .6430 oz. ASW **Reverse:** Goddess Kuan Yin - with sceptre

Date	Mintage	F	VF	XF	Unc	BU
1995 Proof	3,000	Value: 27.50				

Y# 519 5 YUAN **Weight:** 22.2200 g. **Composition:** 0.9000 Silver .6430 oz. ASW **Reverse:** Goddess Kuan Yin - with bowl

Date	Mintage	F	VF	XF	Unc	BU
1995 Proof	3,000	Value: 27.50				

Y# 547 5 YUAN **Composition:** Bronze **Reverse:** Golden Monkey

Date	F	VF	XF	Unc	BU
1995	—	—	—	10.00	—

Y# 600 5 YUAN **Weight:** 22.2200 g. **Composition:** 0.9000 Silver .6430 oz. ASW **Reverse:** 2 men leading camel

Date	Mintage	F	VF	XF	Unc	BU
1995 Proof	15,000	Value: 30.00				

Y# 601 5 YUAN **Weight:** 22.2200 g. **Composition:** 0.9000 Silver .6430 oz. ASW **Reverse:** Dancer

Date	Mintage	F	VF	XF	Unc	BU
1995 Proof	15,000	Value: 27.50				

Y# 602 5 YUAN **Weight:** 22.2200 g. **Composition:** 0.9000 Silver .6430 oz. ASW **Reverse:** Silk merchant and customer

Date	Mintage	F	VF	XF	Unc	BU
1995 Proof	15,000	Value: 25.00				

Y# 603 5 YUAN **Weight:** 22.2200 g. **Composition:** 0.9000 Silver .6430 oz. ASW **Reverse:** Silk spinner

Date	Mintage	F	VF	XF	Unc	BU
1995 Proof	Est. 15,000	Value: 25.00				

Y# 628 (Y629) 5 YUAN **Weight:** 22.2200 g. **Composition:** 0.9000 Silver .6430 oz. ASW **Subject:** Oriental Inventions **Obverse:** Great Wall **Reverse:** Individual block printing

Date	Mintage	F	VF	XF	Unc	BU
1995 Proof	15,000	Value: 18.00				

Y# 630 5 YUAN **Weight:** 22.2200 g. **Composition:** 0.9000 Silver .6430 oz. ASW **Subject:** Oriental Inventions **Obverse:** Great Wall **Reverse:** Potter

Date	Mintage	F	VF	XF	Unc	BU
1995 Proof	15,000	Value: 20.00				

Y# 640 5 YUAN **Weight:** 1.5552 g. **Composition:** 0.9990 Gold .0500 oz. AGW **Reverse:** Panda holding bamboo stick

Date	F	VF	XF	Unc	BU
1995	—	—	—	45.00	—

Y# 736 5 YUAN **Weight:** 1.5552 g. **Composition:** 0.9990 Gold .0500 oz. AGW **Obverse:** Eastern unicorn **Reverse:** Western unicorn with offspring

Date	Mintage	F	VF	XF	Unc	BU
1995 Proof	20,000	Value: 70.00				

Y# 791 5 YUAN **Weight:** 15.7717 g. **Composition:** 0.9990 Silver .5000 oz. ASW **Obverse:** Temple of Heaven **Reverse:** Panda climbing tree branch

Date	Mintage	F	VF	XF	Unc	BU
1995 Proof	—	Value: 32.50				

Y# 794 5 YUAN **Weight:** 22.2223 g. **Composition:** 0.9000 Silver .6430 oz. ASW **Subject:** Chinese Culture Series **Obverse:** Great Wall seen through arch **Reverse:** Pagoda of Six Harmonies

Date	Mintage	F	VF	XF	Unc	BU
1995 Proof	20,000	Value: 37.50				

Y# 795 5 YUAN **Weight:** 22.2223 g. **Composition:** 0.9000 Silver .6430 oz. ASW **Subject:** Chinese Culture Series **Obverse:** Great Wall seen through arch **Reverse:** Mencius seated at table

Date	Mintage	F	VF	XF	Unc	BU
1995 Proof	20,000	Value: 37.50				

Y# 796 5 YUAN **Weight:** 22.2223 g. **Composition:** 0.9000 Silver .6430 oz. ASW **Subject:** Chinese Culture Series **Obverse:** Great Wall seen through arch **Reverse:** Tang Taizong seated

Date	Mintage	F	VF	XF	Unc	BU
1995 Proof	20,000	Value: 37.50				

Y# 797 5 YUAN **Weight:** 22.2223 g. **Composition:** 0.9000 Silver .6430 oz. ASW **Subject:** Chinese Culture Series **Obverse:** Great Wall seen through arch **Reverse:** Lion dance

Date	Mintage	F	VF	XF	Unc	BU
1995 Proof	20,000	Value: 37.50				

Y# 798 5 YUAN **Weight:** 22.2223 g. **Composition:** 0.9000 Silver .6430 oz. ASW **Subject:** Chinese Culture Series **Obverse:** Great Wall seen through arch **Reverse:** Female opera role

Date	Mintage	F	VF	XF	Unc	BU
1995 Proof	20,000	Value: 37.50				

Y# 629 5 YUAN **Weight:** 20.0000 g. **Composition:** 0.9000 Silver **Subject:** Oriental Inventions **Obverse:** The Great Wall. **Size:** 36 mm.

Date	F	VF	XF	Unc	BU
1995 Proof	—	Value: 22.50			

Y# 627 5 YUAN **Weight:** 22.2200 g. **Composition:** 0.9000 Silver .6430 oz. ASW **Subject:** Oriental Inventions **Obverse:** Great Wall **Reverse:** Soldiers with cannon and gunpowder **Note:** Similar to 50 Yuan, Y#632.

Date	Mintage	F	VF	XF	Unc	BU
1995 Proof	15,000	Value: 18.00				

Y# 631 5 YUAN **Weight:** 22.2200 g. **Composition:** 0.9000 Silver .6430 oz. ASW **Subject:** Oriental Inventions **Obverse:** Great Wall **Reverse:** Teacher with chart of human body **Note:** Similar to 50 Yuan, Y#636.

Date	Mintage	F	VF	XF	Unc	BU
1995 Proof	15,000	Value: 18.00				

Y# 581 5 YUAN **Weight:** 1.5552 g. **Composition:** 0.9990 Gold .0500 oz. AGW **Reverse:** Panda in tree looking down

Date	F	VF	XF	Unc	BU
1996	—	—	—	50.00	—

Y# 581a 5 YUAN **Weight:** 1.5552 g. **Composition:** 0.9990 Platinum .0500 oz. APW

Date	Mintage	F	VF	XF	Unc	BU
1996	5,000	—	—	—	75.00	—

Y# 604 5 YUAN **Weight:** 22.2200 g. **Composition:** 0.9000 Silver .6430 oz. ASW **Reverse:** Caravan route market scene

Date	Mintage	F	VF	XF	Unc	BU
1996 Proof	15,000	Value: 45.00				

Y# 605 5 YUAN **Weight:** 22.2200 g. **Composition:** 0.9000 Silver .6430 oz. ASW **Reverse:** Fairy above Magao Sanctuary

Date	Mintage	F	VF	XF	Unc	BU
1996 Proof	15,000	Value: 45.00				

Y# 606 5 YUAN **Weight:** 22.2200 g. **Composition:** 0.9000 Silver .6430 oz. ASW **Reverse:** Various historic sculptures

Date	Mintage	F	VF	XF	Unc	BU
1996 Proof	15,000	Value: 45.00				

Y# 607 5 YUAN **Weight:** 22.2200 g. **Composition:** 0.9000 Silver .6430 oz. ASW **Reverse:** Musicians on camel

Date	Mintage	F	VF	XF	Unc	BU
1996 Proof	15,000	Value: 45.00				

Y# 729 5 YUAN **Composition:** Bronze **Obverse:** State emblem **Reverse:** Tiger

Date	F	VF	XF	Unc	BU
1996	—	—	—	12.00	—

Y# 730 5 YUAN **Composition:** Bronze **Obverse:** State emblem **Reverse:** Pair of dolphins

Date	F	VF	XF	Unc	BU
1996	—	—	—	12.00	—

Y# 740 5 YUAN **Weight:** 1.5552 g. **Composition:** 0.9990 Gold .0500 oz. AGW **Obverse:** Eastern unicorn **Reverse:** Head of western unicorn

Date	Mintage	F	VF	XF	Unc	BU
1996		—	—	—	40.00	—
1996 Proof	5,000	Value: 80.00				

Y# 740a 5 YUAN **Weight:** 1.5552 g. **Composition:** 0.9990 Platinum .0500 oz. APW

Date	F	VF	XF	Unc	BU
1996	—	—	—	75.00	—

Y# 847 5 YUAN **Weight:** 15.5517 g. **Composition:** 0.9990 Silver .5000 oz. ASW **Obverse:** Temple of Heaven **Reverse:** Panda seated on shore

Date	F	VF	XF	Unc	BU
1996	—	—	—	12.50	15.00

Y# 871 5 YUAN **Weight:** 22.2223 g. **Composition:** 0.9000 Silver .6430 oz. ASW **Subject:** Chinese Inventions and Discoveries Series **Obverse:** Great Wall **Reverse:** Three musicians

Date	Mintage	F	VF	XF	Unc	BU
1996 Proof	15,000	Value: 30.00				

Y# 872 5 YUAN **Weight:** 22.2223 g. **Composition:** 0.9000 Silver .6430 oz. ASW **Subject:** Chinese Inventions and Discoveries Series **Obverse:** Great Wall **Reverse:** Suspension bridge

Date	Mintage	F	VF	XF	Unc	BU
1996 Proof	15,000	Value: 30.00				

Y# 873 5 YUAN **Weight:** 22.2223 g. **Composition:** 0.9000 Silver .6430 oz. ASW **Subject:** Chinese Inventions and Discoveries Series **Obverse:** Great Wall **Reverse:** Astronomical clock

Date	Mintage	F	VF	XF	Unc	BU
1996 Proof	15,000	Value: 30.00				

Y# 874 5 YUAN **Weight:** 22.2223 g. **Composition:** 0.9000 Silver .6430 oz. ASW **Subject:** Chinese Inventions and Discoveries Series **Obverse:** Great Wall **Reverse:** Sailing ship

Date	Mintage	F	VF	XF	Unc	BU
1996 Proof	15,000	Value: 30.00				

Y# 875 5 YUAN **Weight:** 22.2223 g. **Composition:** 0.9000 Silver .6430 oz. ASW **Subject:** Chinese Inventions and Discoveries Series **Obverse:** Great Wall **Reverse:** Horse cart

Date	Mintage	F	VF	XF	Unc	BU
1996 Proof	15,000	Value: 30.00				

Y# 883 5 YUAN **Weight:** 15.5517 g. **Composition:** 0.9990 Silver .5000 oz. ASW **Obverse:** Eastern unicorn **Reverse:** Western unicorn

Date	F	VF	XF	Unc	BU
1996 Proof	—	Value: 25.00			

Y# 885 5 YUAN **Weight:** 1.5552 g. **Composition:** 0.9990 Gold .0500 oz. AGW **Subject:** Goddess Guanyin **Obverse:** Temple **Reverse:** Goddess holding flower

Date	F	VF	XF	Unc	BU
1996 Proof	—	Value: 35.00			

Y# 953 5 YUAN **Weight:** 1.5551 g. **Composition:** 0.9990 Platinum .0500 oz. APW **Obverse:** Eastern unicorn **Reverse:** Western unicorn

Date	Mintage	F	VF	XF	Unc	BU
1996 Prooflike	8,000	—	—	—	75.00	—
1996 Proof	5,000	Value: 65.00				

Y# 982 5 YUAN **Weight:** 1.5552 g. **Composition:** 0.9990 Gold .0500 oz. AGW **Subject:** Pu Tuo Mountain

Date	Mintage	F	VF	XF	Unc	BU
1997	35,000	—	—	—	30.00	—

Y# 728 5 YUAN **Weight:** 15.6300 g. **Composition:** 0.9990 Silver .5020 oz. ASW **Obverse:** Temple of Heaven **Reverse:** Panda crossing stream

Date	F	VF	XF	Unc	BU
1997 Proof	—	Value: 20.00			

Y# 731 5 YUAN **Composition:** Bronze **Obverse:** State emblem **Reverse:** Crested Ibis

Date	F	VF	XF	Unc	BU
1997	—	—	—	14.00	—

Y# 732 5 YUAN **Composition:** Bronze **Obverse:** State emblem **Reverse:** Red Crested Crane

Date	F	VF	XF	Unc	BU
1997	—	—	—	14.00	—

Y# 892 5 YUAN **Weight:** 15.5517 g. **Composition:** 0.9990 Silver .5000 oz. ASW **Obverse:** Temple of Heaven **Reverse:** Panda on branch

Date	F	VF	XF	Unc	BU
1997 Proof	—	Value: 15.00			

Y# 893 5 YUAN **Weight:** 15.5517 g. **Composition:** 0.9990 Silver .5000 oz. ASW **Obverse:** Similar to Y#892 with additional legend on Hong Kong's return **Reverse:** Panda crossing stream

Date	Mintage	F	VF	XF	Unc	BU
1997	30,000	—	—	—	15.00	18.00

Y# 911 5 YUAN **Weight:** 15.5517 g. **Composition:** 0.9990 Silver .5000 oz. ASW **Obverse:** 2 Eastern unicorns **Reverse:** 1 Western unicorn

Date	F	VF	XF	Unc	BU
1997 Proof	—	Value: 30.00			

Y# 916 5 YUAN **Weight:** 15.5517 g. **Composition:** 0.9990 Silver .5000 oz. ASW **Subject:** Traditional Chinese Mascot **Obverse:** Ornamental column **Reverse:** Child holding carp

Date	Mintage	F	VF	XF	Unc	BU
1997	80,000	—	—	—	20.00	—

Y# 958 5 YUAN **Weight:** 1.5551 g. **Composition:** 0.9990 Platinum .0500 oz. APW **Obverse:** 2 Eastern unicorns **Reverse:** 1 Western unicorn

Date	Mintage	F	VF	XF	Unc	BU
1997 Proof	5,000	Value: 50.00				

Y# 962 5 YUAN **Weight:** 15.6000 g. **Composition:** 0.9990 Silver .5000 oz. ASW **Subject:** Panda **Obverse:** Temple of Heaven **Reverse:** Multicolor panda and flora. **Edge:** Reeded. **Size:** 36 mm.

Date	Mintage	F	VF	XF	Unc	BU
1997	100,000	—	—	—	20.00	—

Y# 716 5 YUAN **Weight:** 1.5552 g. **Composition:** 0.9990 Gold .0500 oz. AGW **Obverse:** Temple of Heaven **Reverse:** Panda on branch **Note:** Similar to 100 Yuan, Y#720.

Date	F	VF	XF	Unc	BU
1997	—	—	—	40.00	—

Note: Exists in large and small date varieties

Y# 940 5 YUAN **Composition:** Bronze **Subject:** Brown-eared Pheasant **Obverse:** State seal **Reverse:** Denomination above pheasant

Date	F	VF	XF	Unc	BU
1998	—	—	—	10.00	—

Y# 941 5 YUAN **Composition:** Bronze **Subject:** Chinese Alligator **Obverse:** State seal **Reverse:** Denomination above alligator

Date	F	VF	XF	Unc	BU
1998	—	—	—	10.00	—

Y# 964 5 YUAN **Weight:** 15.5517 g. **Composition:** 0.9990 Silver .5000 oz. ASW **Reverse:** Multicolor panda

Date	Mintage	F	VF	XF	Unc	BU
1998	100,000	—	—	—	20.00	—

Y# 990 5 YUAN **Weight:** 1.5600 g. **Composition:** 0.9990 Gold .0500 oz. AGW **Obverse:** Temple of Heaven **Reverse:** Panda seated on rock

Date	F	VF	XF	Unc	BU
1998	—	—	—	35.00	—

Note: Exists in large and small date varieties

Y# 981 5 YUAN **Weight:** 1.5600 g. **Composition:** 0.9990 Gold .0500 oz. AGW **Obverse:** Temple of Heaven **Reverse:** Panda on ledge

Date	F	VF	XF	Unc	BU
1999	—	—	—	35.00	—

Note: Exists in large and small date varieties

Y# 945 5 YUAN **Weight:** 1.5600 g. **Composition:** 0.9990 Gold .0500 oz. AGW **Obverse:** Temple of Heaven **Reverse:** Panda seated on leaves **Note:** Similar to 100 Yuan, KM#949.

Date	F	VF	XF	Unc	BU
2000	—	—	—	35.00	—

Note: Domestic Chinese examples struck with mirror fields, overseas examples struck with frosted fields

Y# 1107 5 YUAN **Weight:** 12.9000 g. **Composition:** Brass **Subject:** The Great Wall **Obverse:** State arms. Microscopic inscription "SHI JIE WEN HUA YI CHAN" repeated four times on the inner raised rim. **Reverse:** Two views of the Great Wall **Edge:** Reeded **Size:** 29.9 mm.

Date	F	VF	XF	Unc	BU
2002	—	—	—	7.00	—

Y# 1108 5 YUAN **Weight:** 12.9000 g. **Composition:** Base Silver **Subject:** Terra Cotta Army **Obverse:** State arms and the microscopic inscription "SHI JIE WEN HUA YI CHAN" repeated four times on the raised inner rim. **Reverse:** Terra Cotta Soldier close-up with many more in background **Edge:** Reeded **Size:** 29.9 mm.

Date	F	VF	XF	Unc	BU
2002	—	—	—	7.00	—

Y# 44 10 YUAN **Weight:** 15.0000 g. **Composition:** 0.8500 Silver .4099 oz. ASW **Subject:** Year of the Pig

Date	Mintage	F	VF	XF	Unc	BU
1983 Proof	6,790	Value: 300				

Y# 49 10 YUAN **Weight:** 3.1103 g. **Composition:** 0.9990 Gold .1000 oz. AGW

Date	Mintage	F	VF	XF	Unc	BU
1983	74,000	—	—	—	55.00	—

Y# 55 10 YUAN **Weight:** 1.2000 g. **Composition:** 0.9000 Gold .0347 oz. AGW **Reverse:** Marco Polo

Date	Mintage	F	VF	XF	Unc	BU
1983 Proof	50,000	Value: 50.00				

Y# 57 10 YUAN **Weight:** 27.0000 g. **Composition:** 0.9000 Silver .7813 oz. ASW **Reverse:** Pandas

Date	Mintage	F	VF	XF	Unc	BU
1983 Proof	10,000	Value: 175				
1983 Frosted Proof	Inc. above	Value: 200				

Y# 59 10 YUAN **Weight:** 15.0000 g. **Composition:** 0.8500 Silver .4099 oz. ASW **Subject:** Year of the Rat **Reverse:** Rat eating squash

Date	Mintage	F	VF	XF	Unc	BU
1984 Proof	11,000	Value: 100				

Y# 62 10 YUAN **Weight:** 16.8100 g. **Composition:** 0.9250 Silver .5000 oz. ASW **Subject:** Women's Decade

Date	Mintage	F	VF	XF	Unc	BU
ND(1984) Proof	4,000	Value: 50.00				

Y# 63 10 YUAN **Weight:** 16.8100 g. **Composition:** 0.9250 Silver .5000 oz. ASW **Series:** Olympics **Reverse:** Volleyball player serving

Date	Mintage	F	VF	XF	Unc	BU
1984	1,000	—	—	—	70.00	—

Y# 63a 10 YUAN **Weight:** 17.0600 g. **Composition:** 0.8000 Silver .4388 oz. ASW

Date	Mintage	F	VF	XF	Unc	BU
1984 Proof	4,500	Value: 30.00				

Y# 64 10 YUAN **Weight:** 17.0600 g. **Composition:** 0.8000 Silver .4388 oz. ASW **Series:** Olympics **Reverse:** Speed skater

Date	Mintage	F	VF	XF	Unc	BU
1984 Proof	6,000	Value: 40.00				

Y# 67 10 YUAN **Weight:** 27.0000 g. **Composition:** 0.9250 Silver .8031 oz. ASW **Obverse:** Temple of Heaven **Reverse:** Pandas

Date	Mintage	F	VF	XF	Unc	BU
1984 Proof	10,000	Value: 80.00				

Y# 74 10 YUAN **Weight:** 3.1103 g. **Composition:** 0.9990 Gold .1000 oz. AGW **Obverse:** Temple of Heaven **Reverse:** Panda holding bamboo branch

Date	Mintage	F	VF	XF	Unc	BU
1984	85,000	—	—	—	60.00	—

Y# 88 10 YUAN **Weight:** 27.0000 g. **Composition:** 0.9000 Silver .7813 oz. ASW **Subject:** 110th Anniversary - Birth of Dr. Cheng Jiageng

Date	Mintage	F	VF	XF	Unc	BU
1984 Proof	6,000	Value: 55.00				

Y# 78 10 YUAN **Weight:** 15.0000 g. **Composition:** 0.9000 Silver .4341 oz. ASW **Subject:** Year of the Ox **Reverse:** Ox

Date	Mintage	F	VF	XF	Unc	BU
1985 Proof	22,000	Value: 45.00				

Y# 81 10 YUAN **Weight:** 3.1103 g. **Composition:** 0.9990 Gold .1000 oz. AGW

Date	Mintage	F	VF	XF	Unc	BU
1985	150,000	—	—	—	60.00	—

Y# 95 10 YUAN **Weight:** 27.0000 g. **Composition:** 0.9000 Silver .7813 oz. ASW **Reverse:** Pandas

Date	Mintage	F	VF	XF	Unc	BU
1985 Proof	10,000	Value: 80.00				

Y# 97 10 YUAN **Weight:** 34.5600 g. **Composition:** 0.9000 Silver 1.0000 oz. ASW **Subject:** 20th Anniversary - Tibet Autonomous Region

Date	Mintage	F	VF	XF	Unc	BU
1985 Proof	3,000	Value: 50.00				

Y# 110 10 YUAN **Weight:** 34.5600 g. **Composition:** 0.9000 Silver 1.0000 oz. ASW **Subject:** 30th Anniversary - Xinjiang Autonomous Region

Date	Mintage	F	VF	XF	Unc	BU
1985 Proof	1,400	Value: 60.00				

Y# 98 10 YUAN **Weight:** 15.0000 g. **Composition:** 0.9000 Silver .4341 oz. ASW **Subject:** Year of the Tiger **Reverse:** Tiger

Date	Mintage	F	VF	XF	Unc	BU
1986 Proof	15,000	Value: 55.00				

Y# 102 10 YUAN **Weight:** 3.1103 g. **Composition:** 0.9990 Gold .1000 oz. AGW

Date	Mintage	F	VF	XF	Unc	BU
1986	45,000	—	—	—	55.00	—
1986 P Proof	10,000	Value: 60.00				

Y# 111 10 YUAN **Weight:** 29.1900 g. **Composition:** 0.9250 Silver .8682 oz. ASW **Subject:** 120th Anniversary - Birth of Sun Yat-sen **Reverse:** Sun Yat-sen's residence

Date	Mintage	F	VF	XF	Unc	BU
1986 Proof	8,450	Value: 50.00				

Y# 121 10 YUAN **Weight:** 15.0000 g. **Composition:** 0.9000 Silver .4341 oz. ASW **Subject:** Year of the Rabbit **Obverse:** Yellow Crane Pavilion above legend **Reverse:** 2 rabbits above denomination

Date	Mintage	F	VF	XF	Unc	BU
1987 Proof	14,000	Value: 110				

Y# 125 10 YUAN **Weight:** 3.1103 g. **Composition:** 0.9990 Gold .1000 oz. AGW

Date	Mintage	F	VF	XF	Unc	BU
1987(s)	99,000	—	—	—	55.00	—
1987(y)	37,000	—	—	—	60.00	—
1987 P Proof	10,000	Value: 65.00				

Y# 133 10 YUAN **Weight:** 31.1000 g. **Composition:** 0.9990 Silver 1.0000 oz. ASW **Obverse:** Temple of Heaven **Reverse:** Panda climbing tree

Date	Mintage	F	VF	XF	Unc	BU
1987 Proof	31,000	Value: 40.00				

Y# 141 10 YUAN **Weight:** 15.0000 g. **Composition:** 0.9000 Silver .4341 oz. ASW **Subject:** Year of the Dragon

Date	Mintage	F	VF	XF	Unc	BU
1988 Proof	15,000	Value: 65.00				

Y# 153 10 YUAN **Ring Weight:** 31.1035 g. **Ring Composition:** 0.9990 Silver 1.0000 oz. ASW **Center Weight:** 3.1103 g. **Center Composition:** 0.9990 Gold .1000 oz. AGW **Reverse:** Panda pawing bamboo

Date	Mintage	F	VF	XF	Unc	BU
1988	290,000	—	—	—	55.00	—
1988 Proof	11,000	Value: 60.00				

Y# 165 10 YUAN **Weight:** 27.0000 g. **Composition:** 0.9250 Silver .5056 oz. ASW **Subject:** Rare Animal Protection **Reverse:** Crested Ibis

Date	Mintage	F	VF	XF	Unc	BU
1988 Proof	35,000	Value: 30.00				

Y# 166 10 YUAN **Weight:** 27.0000 g. **Composition:** 0.9250 Silver .5056 oz. ASW **Subject:** Rare Animal Protection **Reverse:** Baiji Dolphins

Date	Mintage	F	VF	XF	Unc	BU
1988 Proof	35,000	Value: 32.50				

Y# 174 10 YUAN **Weight:** 31.1000 g. **Composition:** 0.9990 Silver 1.0000 oz. ASW **Subject:** Year of the Dragon

Date	Mintage	F	VF	XF	Unc	BU
1988 Proof	20,000	Value: 65.00				

Y# 177 10 YUAN **Weight:** 15.0000 g. **Composition:** 0.8500 Silver .4100 oz. ASW **Subject:** Year of the Snake **Obverse:** Shanhaiguan City Gate

Date	Mintage	F	VF	XF	Unc	BU
1989 Proof	15,000	Value: 40.00				

Y# 183 10 YUAN **Weight:** 31.1000 g. **Composition:** 0.9990 Silver 1.0000 oz. ASW **Subject:** Year of the Snake **Obverse:** State seal **Reverse:** Snake

Date	Mintage	F	VF	XF	Unc	BU
1989 Proof	6,000	Value: 135				

Y# 186 10 YUAN **Weight:** 31.1000 g. **Composition:** 0.9990 Silver 1.0000 oz. ASW **Reverse:** Baby Panda

Date	Mintage	F	VF	XF	Unc	BU
1989	250,000	—	—	—	18.50	22.50
1989 Proof	25,000	Value: 32.50				

Y# 199 10 YUAN **Weight:** 27.0000 g. **Composition:** 0.9250 Silver .8031 oz. ASW **Subject:** 1990 Asian Games **Obverse:** Monument, stadium, Great Wall segment and sun **Reverse:** Weight lifter

Date	Mintage	F	VF	XF	Unc	BU
1989 Proof	20,000	Value: 30.00				

Y# 200 10 YUAN **Weight:** 27.0000 g. **Composition:** 0.9250 Silver .8031 oz. ASW **Subject:** 1990 Asian Games **Obverse:** Monument, stadium, Great Wall segment and sun **Reverse:** Diver

Date	Mintage	F	VF	XF	Unc	BU
1989 Proof	20,000	Value: 30.00				

Y# 201 10 YUAN **Weight:** 27.0000 g. **Composition:** 0.9250 Silver .8031 oz. ASW **Subject:** 1990 Asian Games **Obverse:** Monument, stadium, Great Wall segment and sun **Reverse:** Tennis player

Date	Mintage	F	VF	XF	Unc	BU
1989 Proof	20,000	Value: 30.00				

Y# 202 10 YUAN **Weight:** 27.0000 g. **Composition:** 0.9250 Silver .8031 oz. ASW **Subject:** 1990 Asian Games **Obverse:** Monument, stadium, Great Wall segment and sun **Reverse:** Bicyclist

Date	Mintage	F	VF	XF	Unc	BU
1989 Proof	20,000	Value: 30.00				

Y# 235 10 YUAN **Weight:** 27.0000 g. **Composition:** 0.9250 Silver .8031 oz. ASW **Subject:** 40th Anniversary of Peoples Republic **Reverse:** Tiananmen Square

Date	Mintage	F	VF	XF	Unc	BU
ND(1989) Proof	5,000	Value: 35.00				

Y# 236 10 YUAN **Weight:** 27.0000 g. **Composition:** 0.9250 Silver .8031 oz. ASW **Subject:** 40th Anniversary of Peoples Republic **Reverse:** Great Wall with eagles in flight above

Date	Mintage	F	VF	XF	Unc	BU
ND(1989) Proof	5,000	Value: 35.00				

Y# 248 10 YUAN **Weight:** 27.0000 g. **Composition:** 0.9250 Silver .8031 oz. ASW **Subject:** Endangered Animals **Obverse:** State seal **Reverse:** Japanese deer

Date	Mintage	F	VF	XF	Unc	BU
1989 Proof	10,000	Value: 32.50				

Y# 249 10 YUAN **Weight:** 27.0000 g. **Composition:** 0.9250 Silver .8031 oz. ASW **Subject:** Endangered Animals **Obverse:** State seal **Reverse:** Red-crowned crane

Date	Mintage	F	VF	XF	Unc	BU
1989 Proof	10,000	Value: 32.50				

Y# 188 10 YUAN **Weight:** 3.1103 g. **Composition:** 0.9990 Gold .1000 oz. AGW **Note:** Similar to 100 Yuan, Y#191.

Date	Mintage	F	VF	XF	Unc	BU
1989	128,000	—	—	—	55.00	—
1989 Proof	8,000	Value: 60.00				

Y# 206 10 YUAN **Weight:** 1.0000 g. **Composition:** 0.9990 Gold .0322 oz. AGW **Reverse:** Phoenix and dragon

Date	Mintage	F	VF	XF	Unc	BU
1990 Proof	34,000	Value: 35.00				

Y# 221 10 YUAN **Weight:** 15.0000 g. **Composition:** 0.8500 Silver .4100 oz. ASW **Subject:** Year of the Horse **Obverse:** Temple of Confucius

Date	Mintage	F	VF	XF	Unc	BU
1990 Proof	15,000	Value: 45.00				

Y# 222 10 YUAN **Weight:** 31.1000 g. **Composition:** 0.9990 Silver 1.0000 oz. ASW **Subject:** Year of the Horse

Date	Mintage	F	VF	XF	Unc	BU
1990 Proof	12,000	Value: 40.00				

Y# 237 10 YUAN **Weight:** 31.1000 g. **Composition:** 0.9990 Silver 1.0000 oz. ASW **Reverse:** Panda

Date	Mintage	F	VF	XF	Unc	BU
1990	200,000	—	—	—	20.00	25.00
1990 Proof	20,000	Value: 35.00				

Y# 239 10 YUAN **Weight:** 3.1100 g. **Composition:** 0.9990 Gold .0322 oz. AGW **Reverse:** Panda

Date	Mintage	F	VF	XF	Unc	BU
1990	—	—	—	—	55.00	—
1990 Proof	5,000	Value: 65.00				

Y# 244 10 YUAN Weight: 27.0000 g. **Composition:** 0.9250 Silver .8031 oz. ASW **Reverse:** Homer, poet

Date	Mintage	F	VF	XF	Unc	BU
1990 Proof	30,000	Value: 21.50				

Y# 245 10 YUAN Weight: 27.0000 g. **Composition:** 0.9250 Silver .8031 oz. ASW **Reverse:** William Shakespeare

Date	Mintage	F	VF	XF	Unc	BU
1990 Proof	30,000	Value: 21.50				

Y# 246 10 YUAN Weight: 27.0000 g. **Composition:** 0.9250 Silver .8031 oz. ASW **Reverse:** Ludwig Van Beethoven

Date	Mintage	F	VF	XF	Unc	BU
1990 Proof	30,000	Value: 21.50				

Y# 247 10 YUAN Weight: 27.0000 g. **Composition:** 0.9250 Silver .8031 oz. ASW **Reverse:** Thomas Alva Edison

Date	Mintage	F	VF	XF	Unc	BU
1990 Proof	30,000	Value: 25.00				

Y# 251 10 YUAN Weight: 27.0000 g. **Composition:** 0.9250 Silver .8031 oz. ASW **Subject:** XI Asian Games **Reverse:** Javelin Thrower

Date	Mintage	F	VF	XF	Unc	BU
1990 Proof	20,000	Value: 35.00				

Y# 252 10 YUAN Weight: 27.0000 g. **Composition:** 0.9250 Silver .8031 oz. ASW **Subject:** XI Asian Games **Reverse:** Baseball player

Date	Mintage	F	VF	XF	Unc	BU
1990 Proof	20,000	Value: 35.00				

Y# 253 10 YUAN Weight: 27.0000 g. **Composition:** 0.9250 Silver .8031 oz. ASW **Subject:** XI Asian Games **Reverse:** Gymnast on rings

Date	Mintage	F	VF	XF	Unc	BU
1990 Proof	20,000	Value: 35.00				

Y# 254 10 YUAN Weight: 27.0000 g. **Composition:** 0.9250 Silver .8031 oz. ASW **Subject:** XI Asian Games **Reverse:** Soccer player

Date	Mintage	F	VF	XF	Unc	BU
1990 Proof	20,000	Value: 35.00				

Y# 261 10 YUAN Weight: 31.1000 g. **Composition:** 0.9990 Silver 1.0000 oz. ASW **Obverse:** Great Wall **Reverse:** Phoenix and dragon

Date	Mintage	F	VF	XF	Unc	BU
1990 Proof	12,000	Value: 35.00				

Y# 267 10 YUAN Weight: 3.1100 g. **Composition:** 0.9995 Platinum .1000 oz. APW **Reverse:** Panda with branch

Date	Mintage	F	VF	XF	Unc	BU
1990 Proof	2,500	Value: 90.00				

Y# 283 10 YUAN Weight: 27.0000 g. **Composition:** 0.9000 Silver .7814 oz. ASW **Series:** Summer Olympics **Reverse:** Bicycle racers

Date	Mintage	F	VF	XF	Unc	BU
1990 Proof	30,000	Value: 22.50				

Y# 300 10 YUAN Weight: 27.0000 g. **Composition:** 0.9000 Silver .7814 oz. ASW **Series:** Summer Olympics **Reverse:** High jumper

Date	Mintage	F	VF	XF	Unc	BU
1990 Proof	30,000	Value: 27.50				

Y# 366 10 YUAN Weight: 30.0000 g. **Composition:** 0.9000 Silver .8682 oz. ASW **Series:** Olympics **Reverse:** High diver

Date	Mintage	F	VF	XF	Unc	BU
1990 Proof	30,000	Value: 27.50				

Y# 270 10 YUAN Weight: 15.0000 g. **Composition:** 0.9000 Silver .4340 oz. ASW **Subject:** Year of the Goat **Obverse:** Chinese building and legend

Date	Mintage	F	VF	XF	Unc	BU
1991 Proof	15,000	Value: 40.00				

Y# 271 10 YUAN Weight: 31.1000 g. **Composition:** 0.9990 Silver 1.0000 oz. ASW **Subject:** Year of the Goat

Date	Mintage	F	VF	XF	Unc	BU
1991 Proof	8,000	Value: 75.00				

Y# 308.1 10 YUAN Weight: 31.1000 g. **Composition:** 0.9990 Silver 1.0000 oz. ASW **Obverse:** Date with bottom serifs **Reverse:** Panda - hind feet in water

Date	Mintage	F	VF	XF	Unc	BU
1991	100,000	—	—	—	18.50	22.50

Y# 308.2 10 YUAN Weight: 31.1000 g. **Composition:** 0.9990 Silver 1.0000 oz. ASW **Reverse:** P behind panda

Date	Mintage	F	VF	XF	Unc	BU
1991 Proof	20,000	Value: 30.00				

Y# 308.3 10 YUAN Weight: 31.1000 g. **Composition:** 0.9990 Silver 1.0000 oz. ASW **Obverse:** Date without bottom serifs

Date	F	VF	XF	Unc	BU
1991	—	—	—	16.00	20.00

Y# 314 10 YUAN Weight: 62.2000 g. **Composition:** 0.9990 Silver 2.0000 oz. ASW **Reverse:** Panda - Climbing bamboo branch

Date	Mintage	F	VF	XF	Unc	BU
1991 Proof	10,000	Value: 50.00				

Y# 318 10 YUAN Weight: 27.0800 g. **Composition:** 0.9250 Silver .8030 oz. ASW **Subject:** 1st World Women's Football Championships **Obverse:** 5 story building **Reverse:** Women's soccer, 2 players

Date	Mintage	F	VF	XF	Unc	BU
1991 Proof	2,800	Value: 35.00				

Y# 319 10 YUAN Weight: 27.0800 g. **Composition:** 0.9250 Silver .8030 oz. ASW **Subject:** 1st World Women's Football Championships **Obverse:** 5 story building **Reverse:** Women's soccer, 3 players

Date	Mintage	F	VF	XF	Unc	BU
1991 Proof	2,800	Value: 35.00				

Y# 347 10 YUAN Weight: 27.0800 g. **Composition:** 0.9250 Silver .8030 oz. ASW **Reverse:** Mozart seated at piano

Date	F	VF	XF	Unc	BU
1991 Proof	—	Value: 25.00			

Y# 348 10 YUAN Weight: 27.0800 g. **Composition:** 0.9250 Silver .8030 oz. ASW **Reverse:** Columbus

Date	F	VF	XF	Unc	BU
1991 Proof	—	Value: 25.00			

Y# 349 10 YUAN Weight: 27.0800 g. **Composition:** 0.9250 Silver .8030 oz. ASW **Reverse:** Einstein

Date	F	VF	XF	Unc	BU
1991 Proof	—	Value: 25.00			

Y# 350 10 YUAN Weight: 27.0800 g. **Composition:** 0.9250 Silver .8030 oz. ASW **Reverse:** Mark Twain

Date	F	VF	XF	Unc	BU
1991 Proof	—	Value: 25.00			

Y# 367 10 YUAN Weight: 30.0000 g. **Composition:** 0.9000 Silver .8682 oz. ASW **Series:** Olympics **Reverse:** Downhill skier

Date	Mintage	F	VF	XF	Unc	BU
1991 Proof	30,000	Value: 25.00				

Y# 456 10 YUAN Weight: 30.0000 g. **Composition:** 0.9000 Silver .8682 oz. ASW **Series:** Olympics **Reverse:** Woman playing table tennis

Date	Mintage	F	VF	XF	Unc	BU
1991 Proof	30,000	Value: 35.00				

Y# 476 10 YUAN Weight: 31.1035 g. **Composition:** 0.9990 Silver 1.0000 oz. ASW **Subject:** 80th Anniversary - 1911 Revolution **Reverse:** Sun Yat Sen in civilian clothes

Date	Mintage	F	VF	XF	Unc	BU
ND(1991) Proof	2,500	Value: 50.00				

Y# 310 10 YUAN Weight: 3.1100 g. **Composition:** 0.9990 Gold .10000 oz. AGW **Note:** Similar to 100 Yuan, KM#313.

Date	F	VF	XF	Unc	BU
1991	—	—	—	60.00	—
1991 Proof	—	Value: 70.00			

Y# 342 10 YUAN Weight: 3.1103 g. **Composition:** 0.9990 Gold .1000 oz. AGW **Note:** Similar to Y#346.

Date	F	VF	XF	Unc	BU
1992	—	—	—	65.00	—
1992 Proof	—	Value: 75.00			

Y# 288 10 YUAN Weight: 15.0000 g. **Composition:** 0.9000 Silver .4340 oz. ASW **Subject:** Year of the Monkey

Date	F	VF	XF	Unc	BU
1992 Proof	—	Value: 50.00			

Y# 294 10 YUAN Weight: 31.1000 g. **Composition:** 0.9990 Silver 1.0000 oz. ASW **Subject:** Year of the Monkey

Date	Mintage	F	VF	XF	Unc	BU
1992 Proof	8,000	Value: 60.00				

Y# 346 10 YUAN Weight: 31.1000 g. **Composition:** 0.9990 Silver 1.0000 oz. ASW **Reverse:** Panda climbing right on eucalyptus branch

Date	Mintage	F	VF	XF	Unc	BU
1992	100,000	—	—	—	18.50	22.50
1992 Proof	5,202	Value: 35.00				

Y# 351 10 YUAN Weight: 26.8300 g. **Composition:** 0.9000 Silver .7764 oz. ASW **Series:** 1994 Winter Olympics **Subject:** Slalom **Obverse:** State seal

Date	Mintage	F	VF	XF	Unc	BU
1992 Proof	7,500	Value: 37.50				

Y# 368 10 YUAN Weight: 26.8300 g. **Composition:** 0.9000 Silver .7764 oz. ASW **Series:** 1994 Winter Olympics **Subject:** Cross Country Skiing **Obverse:** State seal

Date	Mintage	F	VF	XF	Unc	BU
1992 Proof	7,500	Value: 30.00				

Y# 391 10 YUAN Weight: 3.1103 g. **Composition:** 0.9990 Silver .1000 oz. ASW **Reverse:** Panda on branch

Date	Mintage	F	VF	XF	Unc	BU
1992 Proof	30,000	Value: 120				

Y# 486 10 YUAN Weight: 27.0000 g. **Composition:** 0.9250 Silver .8031 oz. ASW **Subject:** Wildlife **Reverse:** White Storks

Date	Mintage	F	VF	XF	Unc	BU
1992 Proof	7,260	Value: 38.50				

Y# 490 10 YUAN Weight: 26.9500 g. **Composition:** 0.9000 Silver .7798 oz. ASW **Series:** 1994 Winter Olympics **Reverse:** Ski jumper

Date	Mintage	F	VF	XF	Unc	BU
1992 Proof	30,000	Value: 30.00				

Y# 584 10 YUAN Weight: 26.9500 g. **Composition:** 0.9000 Silver .7798 oz. ASW **Reverse:** Snow leopard

Date	Mintage	F	VF	XF	Unc	BU
1992 Proof	7,260	Value: 32.50				

Y# 709 10 YUAN Weight: 27.1100 g. **Composition:** 0.9000 Silver .7844 oz. ASW **Obverse:** State seal **Reverse:** Tschaikovsky leaning against piano

Date	Mintage	F	VF	XF	Unc	BU
1992 Proof	—	Value: 32.50				

Y# 755 10 YUAN Weight: 27.0000 g. **Composition:** 0.9250 Silver .8030 oz. ASW **Subject:** International Celebrities **Obverse:** State seal **Reverse:** Leonardo Da Vinci

Date	Mintage	F	VF	XF	Unc	BU
1992 Proof	30,000	Value: 25.00				

Y# 756 10 YUAN Weight: 27.0000 g. **Composition:** 0.9250 Silver .8030 oz. ASW **Subject:** International Celebrities **Obverse:** State seal **Reverse:** Wolfgang Von Goethe

Date	Mintage	F	VF	XF	Unc	BU
1992 Proof	30,000	Value: 27.50				

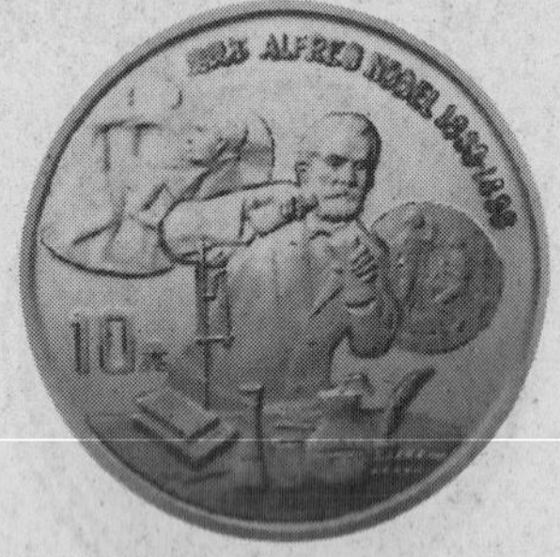

Y# 757 10 YUAN Weight: 27.0000 g. **Composition:** 0.9250 Silver .8030 oz. ASW **Subject:** International Celebrities **Obverse:** State seal **Reverse:** Alfred Nobel

Date	Mintage	F	VF	XF	Unc	BU
1992 Proof	30,000	Value: 27.50				

Y# 942 10 YUAN Weight: 31.1035 g. **Composition:** 0.9990 Silver 1.0000 oz. ASW **Subject:** Environmental Protection **Obverse:** National arms **Reverse:** Kneeling woman fetching water at stream

Date	Mintage	F	VF	XF	Unc	BU
1992	60,000	—	—	—	30.00	—

Y# 352 10 YUAN Weight: 31.1000 g. **Composition:** 0.9990 Silver 1.0000 oz. ASW **Obverse:** Temple of Heaven **Reverse:** Peacocks

Date	Mintage	F	VF	XF	Unc	BU
1992 Proof	—	Value: 40.00				
1993 Proof	7,000	Value: 40.00				
1997 Prooflike	—	—	—	—	—	—

Y# 360 10 YUAN Weight: 31.1000 g. **Composition:** 0.9990 Silver 1.0000 oz. ASW **Obverse:** Similar to KM#361 **Reverse:** Mother panda nurturing cub

Date	Mintage	F	VF	XF	Unc	BU
1993 Proof	20,000	Value: 35.00				

Y# 361 10 YUAN Weight: 31.1000 g. **Composition:** 0.9990 Silver 1.0000 oz. ASW **Reverse:** Panda on flat rock

Date	Mintage	F	VF	XF	Unc	BU
1993	120,000	—	—	—	18.50	22.50

Y# 412.1 10 YUAN Weight: 27.0000 g. **Composition:** 0.9250 Silver .8031 oz. ASW **Subject:** Bust of Mao

Date	Mintage	F	VF	XF	Unc	BU
1993	30,000	—	—	—	40.00	—

Y# 412.2 10 YUAN Weight: 27.0000 g. **Composition:** 0.9250 Silver .8031 oz. ASW **Reverse:** Revised bust of Mao

Date	F	VF	XF	Unc	BU
1993	—	—	—	40.00	—

Y# 418 10 YUAN Weight: 24.2550 g. **Composition:** 0.9000 Silver .7799 oz. ASW **Subject:** World Cup Soccer - 1994

Date	Mintage	F	VF	XF	Unc	BU
1993 Proof	30,000	Value: 35.00				

Y# 474 10 YUAN Weight: 3.1103 g. **Composition:** 0.9990 Gold .1000 oz. AGW **Obverse:** Temple of Harmony **Reverse:** 2 peacocks

Date	F	VF	XF	Unc	BU
1993 Prooflike	—	—	—	65.00	—

Y# 480 10 YUAN Weight: 20.7500 g. **Composition:** 0.9990 Silver .6640 oz. ASW **Subject:** Year of the Rooster **Edge:** Scalloped

Date	Mintage	F	VF	XF	Unc	BU
1993 Proof	6,800	Value: 95.00				

Y# 484 10 YUAN Weight: 3.1103 g. **Composition:** 0.9990 Gold .1000 oz. AGW

Date	F	VF	XF	Unc	BU
1993	—	—	—	65.00	—
1993 Proof	—	Value: 75.00			

Y# 484a 10 YUAN Weight: 3.1100 g. **Composition:** 0.9995 Platinum .1000 oz. APW **Reverse:** Panda seated on rock

Date	F	VF	XF	Unc	BU
1993	—	—	—	75.00	—

Y# 492 10 YUAN Weight: 30.0000 g. **Composition:** 0.9000 Silver .8682 oz. ASW **Series:** Olympics **Reverse:** Runners

Date	Mintage	F	VF	XF	Unc	BU
1993 Proof	30,000	Value: 30.00				

Y# 493 10 YUAN Weight: 30.0000 g. **Composition:** 0.9000 Silver .8682 oz. ASW **Subject:** Olympics **Reverse:** Fencing

Date	Mintage	F	VF	XF	Unc	BU
1993 Proof	30,000	Value: 30.00				

Y# 499 10 YUAN Weight: 3.1103 g. **Composition:** 0.9990 Gold .1000 oz. AGW **Reverse:** Goddess of Mercy - holding flower

Date	Mintage	F	VF	XF	Unc	BU
1993 Prooflike	10,000	—	—	—	40.00	—

Y# 501 10 YUAN Weight: 3.1103 g. **Composition:** 0.9990 Gold .1000 oz. AGW **Reverse:** Goddess Guanyin - seated in flowers

Date	Mintage	F	VF	XF	Unc	BU
1993 Proof	1,000	Value: 60.00				

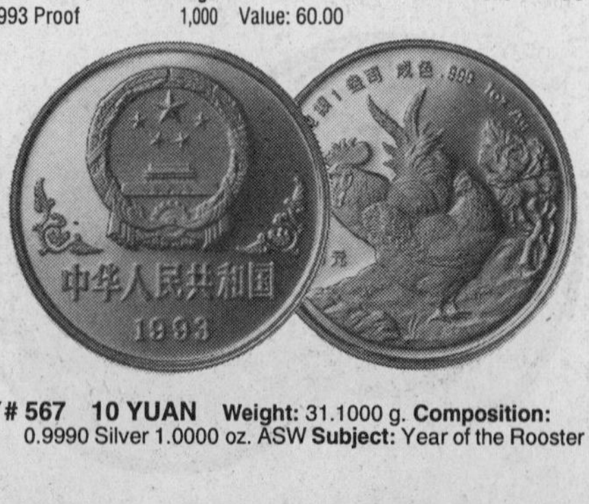

Y# 567 10 YUAN Weight: 31.1000 g. **Composition:** 0.9990 Silver 1.0000 oz. ASW **Subject:** Year of the Rooster

Date	Mintage	F	VF	XF	Unc	BU
1993 Proof	Est. 9,000	Value: 60.00				

Y# 758 10 YUAN Weight: 30.0000 g. **Composition:** 0.9000 Silver .8681 oz. ASW **Obverse:** National emblem **Reverse:** Song Qingling

Date	Mintage	F	VF	XF	Unc	BU
1993 Proof	20,000	Value: 35.00				

Y# 759 10 YUAN Weight: 30.0000 g. **Composition:** 0.9000 Silver .8681 oz. ASW **Obverse:** National emblem **Reverse:** Song Qingling

Date	Mintage	F	VF	XF	Unc	BU
1993 Proof	20,000	Value: 35.00				

Y# 774 10 YUAN Weight: 3.1030 g. **Composition:** 0.9990 Gold .1000 oz. AGW **Obverse:** Great Wall **Reverse:** Mount Heng

Date	Mintage	F	VF	XF	Unc	BU
1993 Proof	8,888	Value: 40.00				

Y# 779 10 YUAN Weight: 27.0000 g. **Composition:** 0.9250 Silver .8030 oz. ASW **Subject:** World Cup Soccer **Obverse:** National emblem **Reverse:** 3 soccer players

Date	Mintage	F	VF	XF	Unc	BU
1993 Proof	30,000	Value: 32.50				

Y# 932 10 YUAN Weight: 31.2000 g. **Composition:** 0.9990 Silver 1.0021 oz. ASW **Subject:** Mt. Heng **Obverse:** Great Wall **Reverse:** Large building, islands in background

Date	Mintage	F	VF	XF	Unc	BU
1993 Proof	60,000	Value: 35.00				

Y# 933 10 YUAN **Weight:** 31.2000 g. **Composition:** 0.9990 Silver 1.0021 oz. ASW **Subject:** Mt. Tai **Obverse:** Great Wall **Reverse:** Small building with long staircase

Date	Mintage	F	VF	XF	Unc	BU
1993 Proof	60,000	Value: 35.00				

Y# 934 10 YUAN **Weight:** 31.2000 g. **Composition:** 0.9990 Silver 1.0021 oz. ASW **Subject:** Mt. Hua **Obverse:** Great Wall **Reverse:** Bird's eye view of mountain tops, shelter

Date	Mintage	F	VF	XF	Unc	BU
1993 Proof	60,000	Value: 35.00				

Y# 935 10 YUAN **Weight:** 31.2000 g. **Composition:** 0.9990 Silver 1.0021 oz. ASW **Subject:** Mt. Song **Obverse:** Great Wall **Reverse:** Tall domed building

Date	Mintage	F	VF	XF	Unc	BU
1993 Proof	60,000	Value: 35.00				

Y# 611 10 YUAN **Composition:** Gold **Reverse:** Panda on flat rock

Date		F	VF	XF	Unc	BU
1993 Proof	—	Value: 65.00				

Y# 1077 10 YUAN **Weight:** 30.0000 g. **Composition:** 0.9000 Silver .8681 oz. ASW **Subject:** Yin and Yang Concept **Obverse:** Great Wall blockhouse. **Reverse:** Four men studying the symbol. **Edge:** Reeded. **Size:** 40 mm.

Date		F	VF	XF	Unc	BU
1993		—	—	—	32.50	40.00

Note: Probably minted at a much later date.

Y# 432 10 YUAN **Weight:** 3.1103 g. **Composition:** 0.9990 Gold .1000 oz. AGW **Reverse:** Seated panda eating **Note:** Similar to Y#416.

Date		F	VF	XF	Unc	BU
1994		—	—	—	55.00	—
1994 Prof	—	Value: 75.00				

Y# 494 10 YUAN **Weight:** 31.1035 g. **Composition:** 0.9990 Silver 1.0000 oz. ASW **Series:** Olympics **Reverse:** Basketball player

Date	Mintage	F	VF	XF	Unc	BU
1994 Proof	30,000	Value: 32.50				

Y# 396 10 YUAN **Weight:** 31.1000 g. **Composition:** 0.9990 Silver 1.0000 oz. ASW **Subject:** Year of the Dog

Date	Mintage	F	VF	XF	Unc	BU
1994 Proof	8,000	Value: 55.00				

Y# 416 10 YUAN **Weight:** 31.1000 g. **Composition:** 0.9990 Silver 1.0000 oz. ASW **Reverse:** Seated panda eating

Date	Mintage	F	VF	XF	Unc	BU
1994	120,000	—	—	—	22.50	—

Y# 420 10 YUAN **Weight:** 31.1000 g. **Composition:** 0.9990 Silver 1.0000 oz. ASW **Reverse:** Unicorn

Date	Mintage	F	VF	XF	Unc	BU
1994	50,000	—	—	—	27.50	—
1994 Proof	4,000	Value: 40.00				

Y# 421 10 YUAN **Weight:** 3.1103 g. **Composition:** 0.9990 Gold .1000 oz. AGW **Reverse:** Unicorn looking back towards right

Date	Mintage	F	VF	XF	Unc	BU
1994 Proof	5,100	Value: 95.00				

Y# 432a 10 YUAN **Weight:** 3.1103 g. **Composition:** 0.9990 Platinum .1000 oz. APW

Date	Mintage	F	VF	XF	Unc	BU
1994	2,500	—	—	—	125	—

Y# 437 10 YUAN **Weight:** 31.1000 g. **Composition:** 0.9990 Silver 1.0000 oz. ASW **Reverse:** Panda sitting on branch of tree

Date	Mintage	F	VF	XF	Unc	BU
1994 Proof	20,000	Value: 35.00				

Y# 438 10 YUAN **Weight:** 27.0000 g. **Composition:** 0.9250 Silver .8031 oz. ASW **Subject:** 12th Asian Games **Reverse:** Swimming

Date	Mintage	F	VF	XF	Unc	BU
1994 Proof	5,000	Value: 30.00				

Y# 439 10 YUAN **Weight:** 27.0000 g. **Composition:** 0.9250 Silver .8031 oz. ASW **Subject:** 12th Asian Games **Reverse:** Runners

Date	Mintage	F	VF	XF	Unc	BU
1994 Proof	5,000	Value: 30.00				

Y# 457 10 YUAN **Weight:** 31.1035 g. **Composition:** 0.9990 Silver 1.0000 oz. ASW **Subject:** Children at Play **Reverse:** 2 children and cat

Date	Mintage	F	VF	XF	Unc	BU
1994 Proof	6,000,000	Value: 30.00				

Y# 458 10 YUAN **Weight:** 31.1035 g. **Composition:** 0.9990 Silver 1.0000 oz. ASW **Subject:** Children at Play **Reverse:** 3 children and toy boat

Date	Mintage	F	VF	XF	Unc	BU
1994 Proof	6,000,000	Value: 30.00				

Y# 463 10 YUAN **Weight:** 3.1103 g. **Composition:** 0.9990 Silver .1000 oz. ASW **Reverse:** Phoenix and dragon

Date	Mintage	F	VF	XF	Unc	BU
1994	2,500	—	—	—	125	—

Y# 482 10 YUAN **Weight:** 31.1035 g. **Composition:** 0.9990 Silver 1.0000 oz. ASW **Reverse:** Guanyin - Goddess of Mercy, holding child

Date	Mintage	F	VF	XF	Unc	BU
1994 Proof	30,000	Value: 30.00				

Y# 495 10 YUAN **Weight:** 31.1035 g. **Composition:** 0.9990 Silver 1.0000 oz. ASW **Series:** Olympics **Reverse:** Female archer

Date	Mintage	F	VF	XF	Unc	BU
1994 Proof	30,000	Value: 32.50				

Y# 496 10 YUAN **Weight:** 31.1035 g. **Composition:** 0.9990 Silver 1.0000 oz. ASW **Series:** Olympics **Reverse:** Boxing match

Date	Mintage	F	VF	XF	Unc	BU
1994 Proof	30,000	Value: 30.00				

Y# 510 10 YUAN **Weight:** 3.1103 g. **Composition:** 0.9990 Gold .1000 oz. AGW **Reverse:** Guanyin-Goddess of Mercy, holding child

Date	Mintage	F	VF	XF	Unc	BU
1994 Prooflike	8,000	—	—	—	50.00	—

Y# 539 10 YUAN **Weight:** 27.0000 g. **Composition:** 0.9250 Silver .8031 oz. ASW **Obverse:** State emblem **Reverse:** Confucius

Date		F	VF	XF	Unc	BU
1994 Proof	—	Value: 30.00				

Y# 540 10 YUAN **Weight:** 27.0000 g. **Composition:** 0.9250 Silver .8031 oz. ASW **Reverse:** Socrates

Date		F	VF	XF	Unc	BU
1994 Proof	—	Value: 30.00				

Y# 541 10 YUAN **Weight:** 27.0000 g. **Composition:** 0.9250 Silver .8031 oz. ASW **Reverse:** Rembrandt

Date		F	VF	XF	Unc	BU
1994 Proof	—	Value: 30.00				

Y# 542 10 YUAN **Weight:** 27.0000 g. **Composition:** 0.9250 Silver .8031 oz. ASW **Reverse:** Verdi

Date		F	VF	XF	Unc	BU
1994 Proof	—	Value: 30.00				

Y# 579 10 YUAN **Weight:** 27.0000 g. **Composition:** 0.9250 Silver .8031 oz. ASW **Reverse:** 2 Bactrian camels

Date	Mintage	F	VF	XF	Unc	BU
1994 Proof	4,825	Value: 35.00				

Y# 580 10 YUAN **Weight:** 27.0000 g. **Composition:** 0.9250 Silver .8031 oz. ASW **Reverse:** Pere David deer

Date	Mintage	F	VF	XF	Unc	BU
1994 Proof	4,825	Value: 35.00				

Y# 615 10 YUAN **Weight:** 27.2000 g. **Composition:** 0.9250 Silver .8089 oz. ASW **Obverse:** State emblem **Reverse:** Soccer player

Date		F	VF	XF	Unc	BU
1994 Prof	—	Value: 40.00				

Y# 680 10 YUAN **Weight:** 3.1103 g. **Composition:** 0.9990 Silver .1000 oz. ASW **Reverse:** Panda tugging bamboo sprig

Date	Mintage	F	VF	XF	Unc	BU
1994 Proof	2,500	Value: 125				

Y# 681 10 YUAN **Weight:** 20.7360 g. **Composition:** 0.9000 Silver .6013 oz. ASW **Reverse:** Magpies on branch **Shape:** 12-sided

Date	Mintage	F	VF	XF	Unc	BU
1994 Proof	3,900	Value: 40.00				

Y# 710 10 YUAN **Weight:** 31.1035 g. **Composition:** 0.9990 Silver 1.0000 oz. ASW **Subject:** Sino - Singapore Friendship **Obverse:** Great Wall **Reverse:** City view of Singapore

Date	Mintage	F	VF	XF	Unc	BU
1994 Proof	30,000	Value: 40.00				

Y# 783 10 YUAN **Weight:** 31.1035 g. **Composition:** 0.9990 Silver 1.0000 oz. ASW **Subject:** Children at Play

Obverse: Imperial Palace, corner building **Reverse:** Three children carrying tray

Date	Mintage	F	VF	XF	Unc	BU
1994 Proof	2,500	Value: 35.00				

Y# 784 10 YUAN **Weight:** 31.1035 g. **Composition:** 0.9990 Silver 1.0000 oz. ASW **Subject:** Children at Play **Obverse:** Imperial Palace, corner building **Reverse:** Three children playing on ground

Date	Mintage	F	VF	XF	Unc	BU
1994 Proof	2,500	Value: 35.00				

Y# 450 10 YUAN **Weight:** 31.2400 g. **Composition:** 0.9990 Silver 1.0045 oz. ASW **Subject:** Year of the Pig

Date	Mintage	F	VF	XF	Unc	BU
1995 Proof	8,000	Value: 75.00				

Y# 452 10 YUAN **Weight:** 20.7500 g. **Composition:** 0.9990 Silver .6640 oz. ASW **Subject:** Year of the Pig **Reverse:** 2 pigs

Date	Mintage	F	VF	XF	Unc	BU
1995 Proof	6,800	Value: 100				

Y# 469 10 YUAN **Weight:** 27.0000 g. **Composition:** 0.9250 Silver .8022 oz. ASW **Subject:** Dinosaurs **Reverse:** Pterodactylus

Date	Mintage	F	VF	XF	Unc	BU
1995 Proof	Est. 5,000	Value: 45.00				

Y# 470 10 YUAN **Weight:** 27.0000 g. **Composition:** 0.9250 Silver .8022 oz. ASW **Subject:** Dinosaurs **Reverse:** Stegosaurus

Date	Mintage	F	VF	XF	Unc	BU
1995 Proof	Est. 5,000	Value: 45.00				

Y# 485.1 10 YUAN **Weight:** 31.1035 g. **Composition:** 0.9990 Silver 1.0000 oz. ASW **Subject:** Shanghai Mint **Obverse:** Temple of Heaven **Reverse:** Panda sitting on branch eating large twig

Date	F	VF	XF	Unc	BU
1995	—	—	—	18.50	22.50

Y# 485.2 10 YUAN **Weight:** 31.1035 g. **Composition:** 0.9990 Silver 1.0000 oz. ASW **Subject:** Shenyang Mint **Reverse:** Panda eating small twig

Date	F	VF	XF	Unc	BU
1995	—	—	—	20.00	—

Y# 489 10 YUAN **Weight:** 31.1035 g. **Composition:** 0.9990 Silver 1.0000 oz. ASW **Reverse:** Guanyin, Goddess of Mercy with sceptre

Date	Mintage	F	VF	XF	Unc	BU
1995 Prooflike	30,000	—	—	—	30.00	—

Y# 520 10 YUAN **Weight:** 3.1103 g. **Composition:** 0.9990 Gold .1000 oz. AGW **Reverse:** Guanyin - Goddess of Mercy with Lotus flower

Date	Mintage	F	VF	XF	Unc	BU
1995 Proof	3,000	Value: 75.00				

Y# 521 10 YUAN **Weight:** 3.1103 g. **Composition:** 0.9990 Gold .1000 oz. AGW **Reverse:** Guanyin, Goddess of Mercy with wheel

Date	Mintage	F	VF	XF	Unc	BU
1995 Proof	3,000	Value: 75.00				

Y# 522 10 YUAN **Weight:** 3.1103 g. **Composition:** 0.9990 Gold .1000 oz. AGW **Reverse:** Guanyin - Goddess of Mercy with sceptre

Date	Mintage	F	VF	XF	Unc	BU
1995 Proof	3,000	Value: 75.00				

Y# 523 10 YUAN **Weight:** 3.1103 g. **Composition:** 0.9990 Gold .1000 oz. AGW **Reverse:** Guanyinm, Goddess of Mercy with bowl

Date	Mintage	F	VF	XF	Unc	BU
1995 Proof	3,000	Value: 75.00				

Y# 531 10 YUAN **Weight:** 31.1035 g. **Composition:** 0.9990 Silver 1.0000 oz. ASW **Subject:** Return of Hong Kong to China **Obverse:** Tiananmen **Reverse:** Deng Xiao Ping

Date	Mintage	F	VF	XF	Unc	BU
1995 Proof	88,000	Value: 80.00				

Y# 571 10 YUAN **Ring Weight:** 1.1108 g. **Ring Composition:** 0.9990 Silver .0356 oz. ASW **Center Weight:** 3.1103 g. **Center Composition:** 0.9990 Gold .1000 oz. AGW **Reverse:** Panda at stream

Date	Mintage	F	VF	XF	Unc	BU
1995 Proof set	2,000	Value: 100				

Y# 588 10 YUAN **Weight:** 27.0000 g. **Composition:** 0.9250 Silver .8031 oz. ASW **Obverse:** Dragon in inner circle **Reverse:** Huang Di in chariot

Date	Mintage	F	VF	XF	Unc	BU
1995 Proof	5,000	Value: 40.00				

Y# 589 10 YUAN **Weight:** 27.0000 g. **Composition:** 0.9250 Silver .8031 oz. ASW **Obverse:** Dragon in inner circle **Reverse:** Yan Di, wearing skins

Date	Mintage	F	VF	XF	Unc	BU
1995 Proof	5,000	Value: 40.00				

Y# 590 10 YUAN **Weight:** 27.0000 g. **Composition:** 0.9250 Silver .8031 oz. ASW **Obverse:** Dragon in inner circle **Reverse:** Yao holding feathers

Date	Mintage	F	VF	XF	Unc	BU
1995 Proof	5,000	Value: 40.00				

Y# 591 10 YUAN **Weight:** 27.0000 g. **Composition:** 0.9250 Silver .8031 oz. ASW **Obverse:** Dragon in inner circle **Reverse:** Shun with urn

Date	Mintage	F	VF	XF	Unc	BU
1995 Proof	5,000	Value: 40.00				

Y# 641 10 YUAN **Weight:** 3.1103 g. **Composition:** 0.9990 Gold .1000 oz. AGW **Obverse:** Temple of Heaven **Reverse:** Panda eating bamboo

Date	F	VF	XF	Unc	BU
1995	—	—	—	55.00	—

Y# 641a 10 YUAN **Weight:** 3.1103 g. **Composition:** 0.9990 Platinum .1000 oz. APW

Date	Mintage	F	VF	XF	Unc	BU
1995 Proof	5,000	Value: 100				

Y# 647 10 YUAN **Weight:** 27.0000 g. **Composition:** 0.9250 Silver .8031 oz. ASW **Reverse:** Dragon boat

Date	Mintage	F	VF	XF	Unc	BU
1995 Proof	10,000	Value: 75.00				

Y# 650 10 YUAN **Weight:** 27.0000 g. **Composition:** 0.9250 Silver .8031 oz. ASW **Reverse:** Junk

Date	Mintage	F	VF	XF	Unc	BU
1995 Proof	10,000	Value: 75.00				

Y# 682 10 YUAN **Weight:** 27.0000 g. **Composition:** 0.9250 Silver .8031 oz. ASW **Series:** 50th Anniversary - United Nations **Obverse:** UN logo **Reverse:** UN building

Date	Mintage	F	VF	XF	Unc	BU
1995 Proof	115,000	Value: 30.00				

Y# 683 10 YUAN **Weight:** 31.1003 g. **Composition:** 0.9990 Silver 1.0001 oz. ASW **Reverse:** Unicorn with offspring

Date		F	VF	XF	Unc	BU
1995 Proof	—	Value: 30.00				

Y# 684 10 YUAN **Weight:** 31.1003 g. **Composition:** 0.9990 Silver 1.0001 oz. ASW **Subject:** 50th Anniversary of Anti-Japanese War **Obverse:** State seal **Reverse:** Chou and Mao above soldiers

Date	Mintage	F	VF	XF	Unc	BU
1995 Proof	3,750	Value: 35.00				

Y# 685 10 YUAN **Weight:** 31.1003 g. **Composition:** 0.9990 Silver 1.0001 oz. ASW **Obverse:** State seal **Reverse:** Attacking soldiers above bridge guarded by lion

Date	Mintage	F	VF	XF	Unc	BU
1995 Proof	3,750	Value: 35.00				

Y# 713 10 YUAN **Weight:** 27.0000 g. **Composition:** 0.9250 Silver .8022 oz. ASW **Series:** 1996 Olympics **Obverse:** State seal **Reverse:** Handball player

Date		F	VF	XF	Unc	BU
1995 Proof	—	Value: 27.50				

Y# 714 10 YUAN **Weight:** 27.0000 g. **Composition:** 0.9250 Silver .8022 oz. ASW **Series:** 1996 Olympics **Obverse:** State seal **Reverse:** Kick boxer

Date		F	VF	XF	Unc	BU
1995 Proof	—	Value: 27.50				

Y# 737 10 YUAN **Weight:** 3.1100 g. **Composition:** 0.9990 Gold .0999 oz. AGW **Obverse:** Eastern unicorn **Reverse:** Western unicorn with offspring

Date	Mintage	F	VF	XF	Unc	BU
1995 Proof	5,000	Value: 95.00				

Y# 787 10 YUAN **Weight:** 31.1035 g. **Composition:** 0.9990 Silver 1.0000 oz. ASW **Obverse:** Temple of Heaven **Reverse:** Panda approaching water from right

Date		F	VF	XF	Unc	BU
1995 Proof only	—	Value: 40.00				

Y# 792 10 YUAN **Weight:** 31.1035 g. **Composition:** 0.9990 Silver 1.0000 oz. ASW **Subject:** Beijing Stamp Fair **Obverse:** Temple of Heaven with additional legend below **Reverse:** Similar to Y#787

Date	Mintage	F	VF	XF	Unc	BU
1995 Proof	18,000	Value: 40.00				

Y# 799 10 YUAN **Weight:** 3.1103 g. **Composition:** 0.9990 Gold .1000 oz. AGW **Subject:** Chinese Culture Series **Obverse:** Great Wall seen through arch **Reverse:** Pagoda of six harmonies

Date	Mintage	F	VF	XF	Unc	BU
1995 Proof	25,000	Value: 55.00				

Y# 800 10 YUAN **Weight:** 3.1103 g. **Composition:** 0.9990 Gold .1000 oz. AGW **Subject:** Chinese Culture Series **Obverse:** Great Wall seen through arch **Reverse:** Mencius seated at table

Date	Mintage	F	VF	XF	Unc	BU
1995 Proof	25,000	Value: 55.00				

Y# 801 10 YUAN **Weight:** 3.1103 g. **Composition:** 0.9990 Gold .1000 oz. AGW **Subject:** Chinese Culture Series **Obverse:** Great Wall seen through arch **Reverse:** Tang Taizong seated

Date	Mintage	F	VF	XF	Unc	BU
1995 Proof	25,000	Value: 55.00				

Y# 802 10 YUAN **Weight:** 3.1103 g. **Composition:** 0.9990 Gold .1000 oz. AGW **Subject:** Chinese Culture Series **Obverse:** Great Wall seen through arch **Reverse:** Lion dance

Date	Mintage	F	VF	XF	Unc	BU
1995 Proof	25,000	Value: 55.00				

Y# 803 10 YUAN **Weight:** 3.1103 g. **Composition:** 0.9990 Gold .1000 oz. AGW **Subject:** Chinese Culture Series **Obverse:** Great Wall seen through arch **Reverse:** Female opera role

Date	Mintage	F	VF	XF	Unc	BU
1995 Proof	25,000	Value: 55.00				

Y# 809 10 YUAN **Weight:** 20.7333 g. **Composition:** 0.9000 Silver .5999 oz. ASW **Obverse:** Great Wall **Reverse:** Eagle in flight **Shape:** 12-sided

Date	Mintage	F	VF	XF	Unc	BU
1995 Proof	3,900	Value: 65.00				

Y# 811 10 YUAN **Weight:** 31.1035 g. **Composition:** 0.9990 Silver 1.0000 oz. ASW **Subject:** 50th Anniversary - Return of Taiwan to China **Obverse:** Great Wall **Reverse:** Taiwan and China maps

Date	Mintage	F	VF	XF	Unc	BU
1995 Proof	5,000	Value: 200				

Y# 812 10 YUAN **Weight:** 31.1035 g. **Composition:** 0.9990 Silver 1.0000 oz. ASW **Subject:** 50th Anniversary - Return of Taiwan to China **Obverse:** Great Wall **Reverse:** Zhongshan Hall

Date	Mintage	F	VF	XF	Unc	BU
1995 Proof	5,000	Value: 200				

Y# 819 10 YUAN **Weight:** 27.0000 g. **Composition:** 0.9250 Silver .8030 oz. ASW **Subject:** Painter Zu Beihong **Obverse:** Portrait **Reverse:** Cat stalking

Date	Mintage	F	VF	XF	Unc	BU
1995 Proof	8,000	Value: 50.00				

Y# 820 10 YUAN **Weight:** 27.0000 g. **Composition:** 0.9250 Silver .8030 oz. ASW **Subject:** Painter Zu Beihong **Obverse:** Portrait **Reverse:** Horse running left

Date	Mintage	F	VF	XF	Unc	BU
1995 Proof	8,000	Value: 50.00				

Y# 825 10 YUAN **Weight:** 27.0000 g. **Composition:** 0.9250 Silver .8030 oz. ASW **Subject:** Romance of the Three Kingdoms Series **Obverse:** Luo Guanzhong bust **Reverse:** Liu Bei standing holding rod

Date	Mintage	F	VF	XF	Unc	BU
1995 Proof	7,000	Value: 60.00				

Y# 826 10 YUAN **Weight:** 27.0000 g. **Composition:** 0.9250 Silver .8030 oz. ASW **Subject:** Romance of the Three Kingdoms Series **Obverse:** Luo Guanzhong bust **Reverse:** Guan Yo reading

Date	Mintage	F	VF	XF	Unc	BU
1995 Proof	7,000	Value: 60.00				

Y# 827 10 YUAN **Weight:** 27.0000 g. **Composition:** 0.9250 Silver .8030 oz. ASW **Subject:** Romance of the Three Kingdoms Series **Obverse:** Luo Guanzhong bust **Reverse:** Zhang Fei on horse

Date	Mintage	F	VF	XF	Unc	BU
1995 Proof	7,000	Value: 60.00				

Y# 828 10 YUAN **Weight:** 27.0000 g. **Composition:** 0.9250 Silver .8030 oz. ASW **Subject:** Romance of the Three Kingdoms Series **Obverse:** Luo Guanzhong bust **Reverse:** Zhuge Liang on throne

Date	Mintage	F	VF	XF	Unc	BU
1995 Proof	7,000	Value: 60.00				

Y# 836 10 YUAN **Weight:** 31.1035 g. **Composition:** 0.9990 Silver 1.0000 oz. ASW **Subject:** Table Tennis **Obverse:** Tianjing Stadium **Reverse:** Table tennis player

Date	Mintage	F	VF	XF	Unc	BU
1995 Proof	3,000	Value: 75.00				

Y# 837 10 YUAN **Weight:** 31.1035 g. **Composition:** 0.9990 Silver 1.0000 oz. ASW **Subject:** Table Tennis **Obverse:** Tianjing Stadium **Reverse:** Two table tennis players

Date	Mintage	F	VF	XF	Unc	BU
1995 Proof	3,000	Value: 75.00				

Y# 841 10 YUAN **Weight:** 31.1035 g. **Composition:** 0.9990 Silver 1.0000 oz. ASW **Series:** Olympics **Obverse:** National emblem **Reverse:** Gymnast

Date	Mintage	F	VF	XF	Unc	BU
1995	30,000	—	—	—	27.50	—

Y# 842 10 YUAN **Weight:** 31.1035 g. **Composition:** 0.9990 Silver 1.0000 oz. ASW **Series:** 1996 Olympics **Obverse:** State seal **Reverse:** Female shooter

Date	Mintage	F	VF	XF	Unc	BU
1995	30,000	—	—	—	27.50	—

Y# 686 10 YUAN **Weight:** 31.1003 g. **Composition:** 0.9990 Silver 1.0001 oz. ASW **Subject:** 4th UN World Women's Congress **Obverse:** Logo above building. **Reverse:** Three women with flowers and birds. **Note:** Similar to 50 Yuan, Y#691.

Date	Mintage	F	VF	XF	Unc	BU
1995 Proof	30,500	Value: 35.00				

Y# 575 10 YUAN **Weight:** 3.1103 g. **Composition:** 0.9990 Gold .1000 oz. AGW **Reverse:** Panda in tree **Note:** Similar to 100 Yuan, Y#578.

Date	F	VF	XF	Unc	BU
1996	—	—	—	55.00	—

Y# 1096 10 YUAN **Weight:** 31.2300 g. **Composition:** 0.9990 Silver 1.0031 oz. ASW **Subject:** Panda Bullion **Obverse:** Temple of Heaven **Reverse:** Seated panda facing left. **Edge:** Reeded **Size:** 39.8 mm.

Date	F	VF	XF	Unc	BU
1996 Prooflike	—	—	—	30.00	—

Y# 575a 10 YUAN **Weight:** 3.1103 g. **Composition:** 0.9990 Platinum .1000 oz. APW

Date	Mintage	F	VF	XF	Unc	BU
1996	2,500	—	—	—	125	—

Y# 583 10 YUAN **Weight:** 31.1035 g. **Composition:** 0.9990 Silver 1.0000 oz. ASW **Obverse:** Temple of Heaven **Reverse:** Seated panda mother and cub

Date	F	VF	XF	Unc	BU
1996 Prooflike	—	—	—	22.50	25.00

Y# 585 10 YUAN **Weight:** 31.1035 g. **Composition:** 0.9990 Silver 1.0000 oz. ASW **Subject:** Year of the Rat

Date	Mintage	F	VF	XF	Unc	BU
1996 Proof	8,000	Value: 65.00				

Y# 741 10 YUAN **Weight:** 31.1700 g. **Composition:** 0.9990 Silver 1.0011 oz. ASW **Obverse:** Eastern unicorn **Reverse:** Western unicorn in wreath

Date	Mintage	F	VF	XF	Unc	BU
1996 Proof	8,000	Value: 65.00				

Y# 742 10 YUAN **Weight:** 3.1100 g. **Composition:** 0.9990 Gold .0999 oz. AGW **Obverse:** Eastern unicorn **Reverse:** Western unicorn in wreath

Date	Mintage	F	VF	XF	Unc	BU
1996 Proof	5,000	Value: 80.00				

Y# 845 10 YUAN **Weight:** 27.0000 g. **Composition:** 0.9250 Silver .8030 oz. ASW **Subject:** Ninth Asian Stamp Exhibition **Obverse:** Temple of Heaven with additional legend **Reverse:** Seated panda eating with cub

Date	Mintage	F	VF	XF	Unc	BU
1996 Proof	2,000	Value: 50.00				

Y# 846 10 YUAN **Weight:** 27.0000 g. **Composition:** 0.9250 Silver .8030 oz. ASW **Subject:** Beijing Coin Fair **Obverse:** Similar to Y#845 with additional legend **Reverse:** Similar to Y#845 with gold insert

Date	Mintage	F	VF	XF	Unc	BU
1996 Proof	2,000	Value: 50.00				

Y# 848 10 YUAN **Weight:** 3.1103 g. **Composition:** 0.9990 Gold .1000 oz. AGW **Subject:** 15th Anniversary - Gold Panda Coins **Obverse:** Temple of Heaven with additional legend **Reverse:** Panda in tree

Date	Mintage	F	VF	XF	Unc	BU
1996 Proof	20,000	Value: 60.00				

Y# 851 10 YUAN **Ring Weight:** 1.1108 g. **Ring Composition:** 0.9990 Silver .0357 oz. ASW **Center Weight:** 3.1103 g. **Center Composition:** 0.9990 Gold .1000 oz. AGW **Obverse:** Temple of Heaven **Reverse:** Panda seated in rock

Date	Mintage	F	VF	XF	Unc	BU
1996 Proof	2,500	Value: 100				

Y# 854 10 YUAN **Weight:** 23.0375 g. **Composition:** 0.9000 Silver .6666 oz. ASW **Subject:** Year of the Rat **Obverse:** Dengdu Pavilion **Reverse:** Rat eating corn cob **Shape:** Scalloped

Date	Mintage	F	VF	XF	Unc	BU
1996 Proof	6,800	Value: 75.00				

Y# 858 10 YUAN **Weight:** 31.1035 g. **Composition:** 0.9990 Silver 1.0000 oz. ASW **Obverse:** Building **Reverse:** Sun Yat-Sen

Date	Mintage	F	VF	XF	Unc	BU
1996 Proof	20,000	Value: 50.00				

Y# 860 10 YUAN **Weight:** 31.1035 g. **Composition:** 0.9990 Silver 1.0000 oz. ASW **Subject:** Return of Hong Kong to China **Obverse:** Tiananmen Square **Reverse:** Law book above Hong Kong harbor view

Date	Mintage	F	VF	XF	Unc	BU
1996 Proof	88,000	Value: 75.00				

Y# 861 10 YUAN **Weight:** 31.1035 g. **Composition:** 0.9990 Silver 1.0000 oz. ASW **Subject:** 45th Anniversary - Chinese Aviation Industry **Obverse:** National emblem **Reverse:** Propeller airplane

Date	Mintage	F	VF	XF	Unc	BU
1996 Proof	20,000	Value: 50.00				

Y# 862 10 YUAN **Weight:** 31.1035 g. **Composition:** 0.9990 Silver 1.0000 oz. ASW **Subject:** 45th Anniversary - Chinese Aviation Industry **Obverse:** National emblem **Reverse:** Jet airplane

Date	Mintage	F	VF	XF	Unc	BU
1996 Proof	20,000	Value: 50.00				

Y# 863 10 YUAN **Weight:** 31.1035 g. **Composition:** 0.9990 Silver 1.0000 oz. ASW **Subject:** 40th Anniversary - Chinese Aviation Industry **Obverse:** National emblem above Great Wall **Reverse:** Satellites

Date	Mintage	F	VF	XF	Unc	BU
1996 Proof	20,000	Value: 50.00				

Y# 864 10 YUAN **Weight:** 31.1035 g. **Composition:** 0.9990 Silver 1.0000 oz. ASW **Subject:** 40th Anniversary - Chinese Aviation Industry **Obverse:** National emblem above Great Wall **Reverse:** Rocket and satellites

Date	Mintage	F	VF	XF	Unc	BU
1996 Proof	20,000	Value: 50.00				

Y# 865 10 YUAN **Weight:** 31.1035 g. **Composition:** 0.9990 Silver 1.0000 oz. ASW **Subject:** Centennial of Chinese Post Office **Obverse:** Modern stamp **Reverse:** Imperial stamp

Date	Mintage	F	VF	XF	Unc	BU
1996 Proof	20,000	Value: 50.00				

Y# 866 10 YUAN **Weight:** 31.1035 g. **Composition:** 0.9990 Silver 1.0000 oz. ASW **Subject:** 9th Asian Stamp Exhibition **Obverse:** Similar to Y#866 **Reverse:** Similar to Y#866 with additional legend

Date	Mintage	F	VF	XF	Unc	BU
1996 Proof	20,000	Value: 55.00				

Y# 868 10 YUAN **Weight:** 31.1035 g. **Composition:** 0.9990 Silver 1.0000 oz. ASW **Subject:** 60th Anniversary - Long March **Obverse:** Flag above building **Reverse:** Chairman Mao on horse

Date	Mintage	F	VF	XF	Unc	BU
1996 Proof	20,000	Value: 50.00				

Y# 869 10 YUAN **Weight:** 31.1035 g. **Composition:** 0.9990 Silver 1.0000 oz. ASW **Subject:** 60th Anniversary - Long March **Obverse:** Flag above Baota Mountain **Reverse:** Two armies enjoined in battle

Date	Mintage	F	VF	XF	Unc	BU
1996 Proof	20,000	Value: 50.00				

Y# 876 10 YUAN **Weight:** 27.0000 g. **Composition:** 0.9250 Silver .8030 oz. ASW **Subject:** Romance of the Three Kingdoms Series **Obverse:** Luo Guanzhong portrait **Reverse:** Cao Cao standing with spear

Date	Mintage	F	VF	XF	Unc	BU
1996 Proof	7,000	Value: 50.00				

Y# 877 10 YUAN **Weight:** 27.0000 g. **Composition:** 0.9250 Silver .8030 oz. ASW **Subject:** Romance of the Three Kingdoms Series **Obverse:** Luo Guanzhong portrait **Reverse:** Cao Pi seated at desk

Date	Mintage	F	VF	XF	Unc	BU
1996 Proof	7,000	Value: 50.00				

Y# 878 10 YUAN **Weight:** 27.0000 g. **Composition:** 0.9250 Silver .8030 oz. ASW **Subject:** Romance of the Three Kingdoms Series **Obverse:** Luo Guanzhong portrait **Reverse:** Cao Zhi standing with scroll and flags

Date	Mintage	F	VF	XF	Unc	BU
1996 Proof	7,000	Value: 50.00				

Y# 879 10 YUAN **Weight:** 27.0000 g. **Composition:** 0.9250 Silver .8030 oz. ASW **Subject:** Romance of the Three Kingdoms Series **Obverse:** Luo Guanzhong portrait **Reverse:** Sima Yi on horse with spear

Date	Mintage	F	VF	XF	Unc	BU
1996 Proof	7,000	Value: 50.00				

Y# 886 10 YUAN **Weight:** 31.1035 g. **Composition:** 0.9990 Silver 1.0000 oz. ASW **Subject:** Goddess of Mercy - Guanyin **Obverse:** Temple **Reverse:** Goddess holding flower

Date	Mintage	F	VF	XF	Unc	BU
1996 Proof	30,000	Value: 27.50				

Y# 887 10 YUAN **Weight:** 3.1101 g. **Composition:** 0.9990 Gold .1000 oz. AGW **Subject:** Goddess Guanyin **Obverse:** Temple **Reverse:** Goddess holding flower

Date		F	VF	XF	Unc	BU
1996 Proof	—	Value: 75.00				

Y# 890 10 YUAN **Weight:** 27.0000 g. **Composition:** 0.9250 Silver .8030 oz. ASW **Series:** Olympics **Obverse:** National emblem **Reverse:** Sailboarder

Date	Mintage	F	VF	XF	Unc	BU
1996 Proof	30,000	Value: 45.00				

Y# 711 10 YUAN **Weight:** 31.1035 g. **Composition:** 0.9990 Silver 1.0000 oz. ASW **Subject:** Sino - Thailand Friendship **Obverse:** Forbidden City and Thai Royal Palace **Reverse:** Two Buddha statues

Date	Mintage	F	VF	XF	Unc	BU
1997 Proof	45,000	Value: 22.50				

Y# 715 10 YUAN **Weight:** 31.1035 g. **Composition:** 0.9990 Silver 1.0000 oz. ASW **Obverse:** Temple of Heaven **Reverse:** Panda on thick branch

Date	F	VF	XF	Unc	BU
1997 Prooflike	—	—	—	32.50	—

Y# 717a 10 YUAN **Weight:** 3.1100 g. **Composition:** 0.9990 Platinum .1000 oz. APW

Date	Mintage	F	VF	XF	Unc	BU
1997	2,500	—	—	—	125	—

Y# 722 10 YUAN **Ring Composition:** Brass **Center Composition:** Copper-Nickel **Subject:** Return of Hong Kong **Obverse:** Stylized flower **Reverse:** City view in inner ring

Date	F	VF	XF	Unc	BU
1997	—	—	—	6.50	—

Note: 5,000 pieces were struck and issued in boxes with certificates and are valued at $350

Y# 723 10 YUAN **Ring Composition:** Copper-Nickel **Center Composition:** Brass **Subject:** Hong Kong - Constitution **Obverse:** Stylized flower **Reverse:** Document with state emblem

Date	F	VF	XF	Unc	BU
1997	—	—	—	6.50	—

Y# 726 10 YUAN **Weight:** 31.2200 g. **Composition:** 0.9990 Silver 1.0027 oz. ASW **Obverse:** Temple of Heaven **Reverse:** Panda on large tree branch

Date	Mintage	F	VF	XF	Unc	BU
1997	50,000	—	—	—	18.50	22.50

Y# 894 10 YUAN **Weight:** 31.1035 g. **Composition:** 0.9990 Silver 1.0000 oz. ASW **Obverse:** Temple of Heaven **Reverse:** Panda on branch

Date	Mintage	F	VF	XF	Unc	BU
1997 Proof	50,000	Value: 45.00				

Y# 894a 10 YUAN **Weight:** 3.1100 g. **Composition:** 0.9995 Platinum .1000 oz. APW **Reverse:** Panda on branch

Date	Mintage	F	VF	XF	Unc	BU
1997 Proof	2,500	Value: 125				

Y# 895 10 YUAN **Weight:** 31.1035 g. **Composition:** 0.9990 Silver 1.000 oz. ASW **Obverse:** Similar to Y#894 with legend variety **Reverse:** Similar to Y#8945 with gold insert

Date	Mintage	F	VF	XF	Unc	BU
1997 Proof	30,000	Value: 30.00				

Y# 896 10 YUAN **Weight:** 23.0375 g. **Composition:** 0.9000 Silver .6666 oz. ASW **Subject:** Year of the Ox **Obverse:** Mingyuan Pavilion **Reverse:** Bull **Shape:** Scalloped

Date	Mintage	F	VF	XF	Unc	BU
1997 Proof	6,800	Value: 70.00				

Y# 899.1 10 YUAN **Weight:** 31.1035 g. **Composition:** 0.9990 Silver 1.0000 oz. ASW **Subject:** Year of the Ox **Obverse:** State seal **Reverse:** Water buffalo

Date	Mintage	F	VF	XF	Unc	BU
1997 Proof	8,000	Value: 65.00				

Y# 901 10 YUAN **Weight:** 3.1103 g. **Composition:** 0.9990 Gold .1000 oz. AGW **Subject:** Year of the Ox **Obverse:** Mingyuan Pavilion **Reverse:** Calf

Date	Mintage	F	VF	XF	Unc	BU
1997 Proof	48,000	Value: 90.00				

Y# 902 10 YUAN **Weight:** 31.1035 g. **Composition:** 0.9990 Silver 1.0000 oz. ASW **Subject:** Return of Hong Kong to China **Obverse:** Tiananmen Square **Reverse:** Flag and fireworks over city

Date	Mintage	F	VF	XF	Unc	BU
1997	800,000	—	—	—	40.00	—
1997 Proof	88,000	Value: 75.00				

Y# 905 10 YUAN **Weight:** 31.1035 g. **Composition:** 0.9990 Silver 1.0000 oz. ASW **Subject:** Return of Macao to China **Obverse:** Tiananmen Square **Reverse:** Deng Xiaoping viewing Macao

Date	F	VF	XF	Unc	BU
1997 Proof	—	Value: 60.00			

Y# 908 10 YUAN **Weight:** 31.1035 g. **Composition:** 0.9990 Silver 1.0000 oz. ASW **Subject:** Peoples Liberation Army **Obverse:** Radiant star above Great Wall **Reverse:** Founding of PLA scene

Date	Mintage	F	VF	XF	Unc	BU
1997 Proof	30,000	Value: 40.00				

Y# 909 10 YUAN **Weight:** 31.1035 g. **Composition:** 0.9990 Silver 1.0000 oz. ASW **Obverse:** Radiant star above Great Wall **Reverse:** Three members of the PRC Army, Air Force and Navy. Airplanes, boats and missile in background.

Date	Mintage	F	VF	XF	Unc	BU
1997 Proof	30,000	Value: 40.00				

Y# 912 10 YUAN **Weight:** 31.1035 g. **Composition:** 0.9990 Silver 1.0000 oz. ASW **Obverse:** Eastern unicorn **Reverse:** Western unicorn

Date	Mintage	F	VF	XF	Unc	BU
1997 Proof	8,000	Value: 27.50				

Y# 912a 10 YUAN **Weight:** 3.1100 g. **Composition:** 0.9990 Gold .1000 oz. AGW **Obverse:** Eastern unicorn **Reverse:** Western unicorn

Date	Mintage	F	VF	XF	Unc	BU
1997 Proof	5,000	Value: 95.00				

Y# 913 10 YUAN **Weight:** 3.1100 g. **Composition:** 0.9990 Gold .1000 oz. AGW **Subject:** Goddess Guanyin **Obverse:** Putuo Hill Temple **Reverse:** Goddess holding jug of dew

Date	Mintage	F	VF	XF	Unc	BU
1997 Proof	30,000	Value: 40.00				

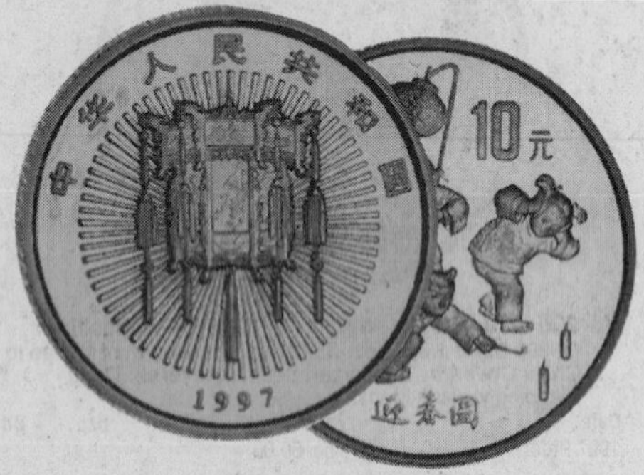

Y# 914.1 10 YUAN **Weight:** 31.1035 g. **Composition:** 0.9990 Silver 1.0000 oz. ASW **Subject:** Celebrating Spring **Obverse:** Lantern **Reverse:** Children setting off firecrackers

Date	Mintage	F	VF	XF	Unc	BU
1997	20,000	—	—	—	60.00	—
1997 Proof	60,000	Value: 40.00				

Y# 1079 10 YUAN **Weight:** 20.7333 g. **Composition:** 0.9000 Silver 0.5999 oz. ASW **Subject:** Wildlife of China **Obverse:** The Great Wall **Reverse:** Two penguins **Edge:** Plain **Shape:** 12-sided **Size:** 35 mm.

Date	F	VF	XF	Unc	BU
1997 Proof	—	Value: 75.00			

Y# 1092 10 YUAN **Weight:** 31.4400 g. **Composition:** 0.9990 Silver 1.0098 oz. ASW **Subject:** Forbidden City **Obverse:** Exterior view of the Forbidden City **Reverse:** Main interior approach and gatehouse to the palaces **Edge:** Reeded **Size:** 39.8 mm.

Date	F	VF	XF	Unc	BU
1997 Proof	—	Value: 40.00			

Y# 1093 10 YUAN **Weight:** 31.4400 g. **Composition:** 0.9990 Silver 1.0098 oz. ASW **Subject:** Forbidden City **Obverse:** Exterior view of the Forbidden City **Reverse:** Causeway to palace **Edge:** Reeded **Size:** 39.8 mm.

Date	F	VF	XF	Unc	BU
1997 Proof	—	Value: 40.00			

Y# 1094 10 YUAN **Weight:** 31.4400 g. **Composition:** 0.9990 Silver 1.0098 oz. ASW **Subject:** Forbidden City **Obverse:** Exterior view of the Forbidden City **Reverse:** Bronze lion statue **Edge:** Reeded **Size:** 39.8 mm.

Date	F	VF	XF	Unc	BU
1997 Proof	—	Value: 40.00			

Y# 1095 10 YUAN **Weight:** 31.4400 g. **Composition:** 0.9990 Silver 1.0098 oz. ASW **Subject:** Forbidden City **Obverse:** Exterior view of the Forbidden City **Reverse:** Interior view **Edge:** Reeded **Size:** 39.8 mm.

Date	F	VF	XF	Unc	BU
1997 Proof	—	Value: 40.00			

Y# 1099 10 YUAN **Weight:** 27.0000 g. **Composition:** 0.9250 Silver 0.803 oz. ASW **Subject:** Ancient Chinese Culture Series **Obverse:** Dragon seal **Reverse:** Bronze wares **Edge:** Reeded **Size:** 38 mm.

Date	Mintage	F	VF	XF	Unc	BU
1997 Proof	10,000	Value: 45.00				

Y# 1100 10 YUAN **Weight:** 27.0000 g. **Composition:** 0.9250 Silver 0.803 oz. ASW **Subject:** Ancient Chinese Culture Series **Obverse:** Dragon seal **Reverse:** Pottery **Edge:** Reeded **Size:** 38 mm.

Date	Mintage	F	VF	XF	Unc	BU
1997 Proof	10,000	Value: 45.00				

Y# 1101 10 YUAN **Weight:** 27.0000 g. **Composition:** 0.9250 Silver 0.803 oz. ASW **Subject:** Ancient Chinese Culture Series **Obverse:** Dragon seal **Reverse:** Calligraphy **Edge:** Reeded **Size:** 38 mm.

Date	Mintage	F	VF	XF	Unc	BU
1997 Proof	10,000	Value: 45.00				

Y# 1102 10 YUAN **Weight:** 27.0000 g. **Composition:** 0.9250 Silver 0.803 oz. ASW **Subject:** Ancient Chinese Culture Series **Obverse:** Dragon seal **Reverse:** Coinage **Edge:** Reeded **Size:** 38 mm.

Date	Mintage	F	VF	XF	Unc	BU
1997 Proof	10,000	Value: 45.00				

Y# 717 10 YUAN **Weight:** 3.1103 g. **Composition:** 0.9990 Gold .1000 oz. AGW **Subject:** Panda Bullion **Note:** Similar to 100 Yuan, Y#720.

Date	F	VF	XF	Unc	BU
1997	—	—	—	50.00	—

Note: Exists in large and small date varieties

Y# 899.2 10 YUAN **Weight:** 31.1035 g. **Composition:** 0.9990 Silver 1.0000 oz. ASW **Subject:** Year of the Ox **Size:** 40 mm. **Note:** Increased size.

Date	Mintage	F	VF	XF	Unc	BU
1997	50,000	—	—	—	45.00	—

Y# 1060 10 YUAN **Weight:** 31.1035 g. **Composition:** 0.9990 Silver 1.0000 oz. ASW **Subject:** Panda **Obverse:** Temple of Heaven **Reverse:** Multi-colored panda and flora **Edge:** Reeded **Size:** 40 mm.

Date	F	VF	XF	Unc	BU
1997	—	—	—	35.00	—

Y# 983 10 YUAN **Weight:** 3.1103 g. **Composition:** 0.9990 Gold .1000 oz. AGW **Subject:** Celebrating Spring **Obverse:** Lantern **Reverse:** Children setting off firecrackers

Date	Mintage	F	VF	XF	Unc	BU
1997	100,000	—	—	—	40.00	—

Y# 917.1 10 YUAN **Weight:** 31.1035 g. **Composition:** 0.9990 Silver 1.0000 oz. ASW **Subject:** Traditional Chinese Mascot **Obverse:** Monument in Tiananmen Square, sprays below. **Reverse:** Child holding carp

Date	Mintage	F	VF	XF	Unc	BU
1997 Proof	8,000	Value: 40.00				

Y# 917.2 10 YUAN **Weight:** 31.1035 g. **Composition:** 0.9990 Silver 1.0000 oz. ASW **Subject:** Traditional Chinese Mascot **Obverse:** Monument in Tiananmen Square, sprays below **Reverse:** Multicolor version of child holding carp

Date	Mintage	F	VF	XF	Unc	BU
1997 Proof	100,000	Value: 35.00				
1998 Proof	—	Value: 35.00				

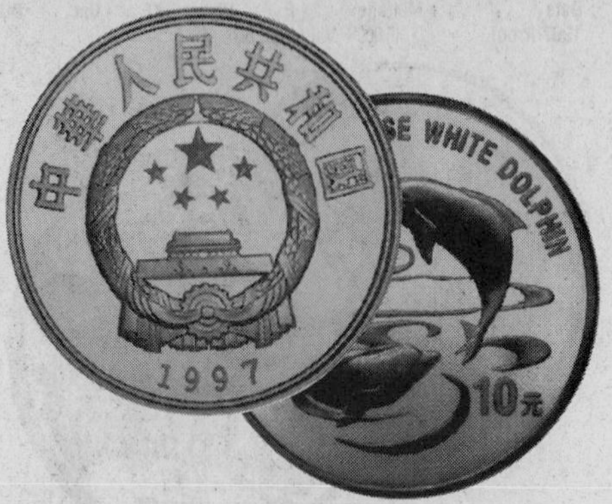

Y# 919 10 YUAN **Weight:** 31.1035 g. **Composition:** 0.9990 Silver 1.0000 oz. ASW **Subject:** Wildlife of China **Obverse:** State seal **Reverse:** Two white dolphins

Date	Mintage	F	VF	XF	Unc	BU
1997 Proof	68,000	Value: 40.00				

Y# 920 10 YUAN **Weight:** 31.1035 g. **Composition:** 0.9990 Silver 1.0000 oz. ASW **Subject:** Wildlife of China **Obverse:** State seal **Reverse:** Swan with young.

Date	Mintage	F	VF	XF	Unc	BU
1997 Proof	68,000	Value: 40.00				

Y# 936 10 YUAN **Weight:** 31.2000 g. **Composition:** 0.9990 Silver 1.0021 oz. ASW **Subject:** Gesal, King of Tibet **Obverse:** Towered building **Reverse:** King on horseback

Date	Mintage	F	VF	XF	Unc	BU
1997 Proof	28,000	Value: 37.50				

Y# 937 10 YUAN **Weight:** 31.2000 g. **Composition:** 0.9990 Silver 1.0021 oz. ASW **Subject:** Gadamellin of Mongolia **Obverse:** Towered building **Reverse:** Cavalry attack with swords

Date	Mintage	F	VF	XF	Unc	BU
1997 Proof	28,000	Value: 37.50				

Y# 938 10 YUAN **Weight:** 31.2000 g. **Composition:** 0.9990 Silver 1.0021 oz. ASW **Subject:** Yi Nationality **Obverse:** Towered building **Reverse:** Madame She Ziang with sword

Date	Mintage	F	VF	XF	Unc	BU
1997 Proof	28,000	Value: 28.00				

Y# 939 10 YUAN **Weight:** 31.2000 g. **Composition:** 0.9990 Silver 1.0021 oz. ASW **Subject:** Li Nationality **Obverse:** Towered building **Reverse:** Madame Zian reading scroll

Date	Mintage	F	VF	XF	Unc	BU
1997 Proof	28,000	Value: 30.00				

Y# 984 10 YUAN **Weight:** 3.1103 g. **Composition:** 0.9990 Gold .1000 oz. AGW **Obverse:** Forbidden city **Reverse:** Bronze chinze

Date	Mintage	F	VF	XF	Unc	BU
1997 Proof	11,000	Value: 65.00				

Y# 985 10 YUAN **Weight:** 3.1103 g. **Composition:** 0.9990 Gold .1000 oz. AGW **Subject:** Goddess of Mercy - Guanyin

Date	Mintage	F	VF	XF	Unc	BU
1997	10,000	—	—	—	55.00	—

Y# 986 10 YUAN **Ring Weight:** 1.5552 g. **Ring Composition:** 0.9990 Silver .0500 oz. ASW **Center Weight:** 3.1103 g. **Center Composition:** 0.9990 Gold .1000 oz. AGW **Reverse:** Panda climbing tree

Date	Mintage	F	VF	XF	Unc	BU
1997 Proof	2,800	Value: 75.00				

Y# 963 10 YUAN **Weight:** 31.1035 g. **Composition:** 0.9990 Silver 1.0000 oz. ASW **Reverse:** Multi-colored panda

Date	Mintage	F	VF	XF	Unc	BU
1997	100,000	—	—	—	35.00	—

Y# 724 10 YUAN **Weight:** 31.0220 g. **Composition:** 0.9990 Silver .9963 oz. ASW **Subject:** 100th Birthday - Zhou Enlai **Obverse:** Zhou Enlai Memorial Hall **Reverse:** Zhou on horseback

Date	Mintage	F	VF	XF	Unc	BU
1998 Proof	38,000	Value: 40.00				

Y# 725 10 YUAN **Weight:** 31.0220 g. **Composition:** 0.9990 Silver .9963 oz. ASW **Subject:** 100th Birthday - Zhou Enlai **Obverse:** Zhou Enlai Memorial Hall **Reverse:** Zhou standing facing 3/4 right

Date	Mintage	F	VF	XF	Unc	BU
1998 Proof	38,000	Value: 40.00				

Y# 727 10 YUAN **Weight:** 31.3900 g. **Composition:** 0.9990 Silver 1.0082 oz. ASW **Obverse:** State emblem **Reverse:** Portrait of Dr. Norman Bethune with surgery scene

Date	Mintage	F	VF	XF	Unc	BU
1998 In Proof sets only	61,000	Value: 20.00				

Y# 744 10 YUAN **Weight:** 31.4700 g. **Composition:** 0.9990 Silver 1.0110 oz. ASW **Subject:** Celebrating Spring **Obverse:** Radiant lantern **Reverse:** Three children about to fly kites

Date	F	VF	XF	Unc	BU
1998 Proof	—	Value: 40.00			

Y# 922 10 YUAN **Weight:** 31.1035 g. **Composition:** 0.9990 Silver 1.0000 oz. ASW **Subject:** Year of the Tiger **Obverse:** National emblem **Reverse:** Tiger on rock

Date	Mintage	F	VF	XF	Unc	BU
1998	50,000	—	—	—	40.00	—

Y# 923 10 YUAN **Weight:** 31.1035 g. **Composition:** 0.9990 Silver 1.0000 oz. ASW **Subject:** Year of the Tiger **Obverse:** Badaling building **Reverse:** Multicolor tiger cub

Date	Mintage	F	VF	XF	Unc	BU
1998	100,000	—	—	—	50.00	—

Y# 924 10 YUAN **Weight:** 3.1103 g. **Composition:** 0.9990 Gold .1000 oz. AGW **Subject:** Year of the Tiger **Obverse:** Badaling building **Reverse:** Tiger cub

Date	Mintage	F	VF	XF	Unc	BU
1998 Proof	48,000	Value: 80.00				

Y# 925 10 YUAN **Weight:** 3.1103 g. **Composition:** 0.9990 Gold .1000 oz. AGW **Subject:** Year of the Tiger **Obverse:** Badaling building **Reverse:** Multicolor tiger head

Date	Mintage	F	VF	XF	Unc	BU
1998 Proof	30,000	Value: 80.00				

Y# 926 10 YUAN **Weight:** 23.0375 g. **Composition:** 0.9000 Silver .6666 oz. ASW **Subject:** Year of the Tiger **Obverse:** Badaling building **Reverse:** Tiger **Shape:** Scalloped

Date	Mintage	F	VF	XF	Unc	BU
1998 Proof	6,800	Value: 65.00				

Y# 969 10 YUAN **Weight:** 31.1035 g. **Composition:** 0.9990 Silver 1.0000 oz. ASW **Reverse:** Panda

Date	Mintage	F	VF	XF	Unc	BU
1998	250,000	—	—	—	25.00	—

Y# 970 10 YUAN **Weight:** 31.1035 g. **Composition:** 0.9990 Silver 1.0000 oz. ASW **Reverse:** Multicolor panda

Date	Mintage	F	VF	XF	Unc	BU
1998	100,000	—	—	—	35.00	—

Y# 987 10 YUAN **Weight:** 3.1103 g. **Composition:** 0.9990 Gold .1000 oz. AGW **Subject:** Culture of Dragons

Date	F	VF	XF	Unc	BU
1998 Proof	—	Value: 60.00			

Y# 988 10 YUAN **Weight:** 3.1103 g. **Composition:** 0.9990 Gold .1000 oz. AGW **Obverse:** Temple of Heaven **Reverse:** Panda seated on rock

Date	F	VF	XF	Unc	BU
1998	—	—	—	55.00	—

Note: Exists in large and small date varieties

Y# 1063 10 YUAN **Weight:** 31.1035 g. **Composition:** 0.9990 Silver 1.0000 oz. ASW **Subject:** World Wildlife Fund **Obverse:** National arms **Reverse:** Clouded leopard. **Edge:** Reeded **Size:** 38 mm.

Date	F	VF	XF	Unc	BU
1998 Proof	—	Value: 50.00			

Y# 1064 10 YUAN **Weight:** 31.1035 g. **Composition:** 0.9990 Silver 1.0000 oz. ASW **Obverse:** Denomination, inscription and ornamental design **Reverse:** Old cash coin characters **Edge:** Reeded **Size:** 40 mm. **Note:** Square holed cash coin design.

Date	F	VF	XF	Unc	BU
1998 Proof	—	Value: 40.00			

Y# 1065 10 YUAN **Weight:** 3.1100 g. **Composition:** 0.9990 Gold .0999 oz. AGW **Obverse:** Denomination, inscription and ornamental design. **Reverse:** Old cash coin characters. **Edge:** Reeded. **Size:** 18 mm. **Note:** Square holed cash coin design.

Date	F	VF	XF	Unc	BU
1998 Proof	—	Value: 50.00			

Y# 1055 10 YUAN **Ring Weight:** 7.6500 g. **Ring Composition:** Brass**Center Weight:** 7.6500 g. **Center Composition:** Copper Nickel **Subject:** Return of Macau **Obverse:** Stylized water lilly **Reverse:** Junk and building **Edge:** Reeded and plain sections **Size:** 25.5 mm.

Date	F	VF	XF	Unc	BU
1999	—	—	—	8.00	—

Y# 1056 10 YUAN **Ring Weight:** 7.6500 g. **Ring Composition:** Brass **Center Composition:** Copper Nickel **Subject:** Return of Macau **Obverse:** Stylized water lilly **Reverse:** Modern harbor and city view with document background **Edge:** Reeded and plain sections **Size:** 25.5 mm.

Date	F	VF	XF	Unc	BU
1999	—	—	—	8.00	—

Y# 1059 10 YUAN **Ring Composition:** Copper-Nickel**Center Weight:** 7.8000 g. **Center Composition:** Brass **Subject:** 50th Anniversary - People's Republic **Obverse:** Fireworks above building **Reverse:** Birds above "50" **Edge:** Reeded and plain sections **Size:** 25.5 mm.

Date	F	VF	XF	Unc	BU
1999	—	—	—	6.50	—

Y# 980 10 YUAN **Weight:** 3.1103 g. **Composition:** 0.9990 Gold .1000 oz. AGW **Subject:** Year of the Rabbit

Date	Mintage	F	VF	XF	Unc	BU
1999 Proof	48,000	Value: 80.00				

Y# 1078 10 YUAN **Weight:** 30.9200 g. **Composition:** 0.9990 Silver .9931 oz. ASW **Subject:** Yin and Yang Concept **Obverse:** Gate **Reverse:** Gold plated standing goddess **Edge:** Reeded **Size:** 40 mm.

Date	F	VF	XF	Unc	BU
1999	—	Value: 50.00			

Y# 989 10 YUAN **Weight:** 3.1103 g. **Composition:** 0.9990 Gold .1000 oz. AGW **Obverse:** Temple of Heaven **Reverse:** Panda on ledge

Date	F	VF	XF	Unc	BU
1999	—	—	—	55.00	—

Note: Exists in large and small date varieties

Y# 991 10 YUAN **Weight:** 3.1103 g. **Composition:** 0.9990 Gold .1000 oz. AGW **Reverse:** Multicolor rabbit

Date	Mintage	F	VF	XF	Unc	BU
1999 Proof	30,000	Value: 80.00				

Y# 931.1 10 YUAN **Weight:** 31.1035 g. **Composition:** 0.9990 Silver 1.0000 oz. ASW **Obverse:** Temple of Heaven **Reverse:** Panda on rock

Date	F	VF	XF	Unc	BU
1999 Large date; Proof	—	Value: 50.00			

Y# 931.2 10 YUAN **Weight:** 31.1035 g. **Composition:** 0.9990 Silver 1.0000 oz. ASW **Obverse:** Temple of Heaven **Reverse:** Panda on rock

Date	F	VF	XF	Unc	BU
1999 Small date; Proof	—	Value: 50.00			

Y# 943 10 YUAN **Weight:** 31.1035 g. **Composition:** 0.9990 Silver 1.0000 oz. ASW **Obverse:** Wan Chun Pavilion **Reverse:** Gold plated Chinese roses

Date	Mintage	F	VF	XF	Unc	BU
1999	100,000	—	—	—	50.00	—

Y# 944 10 YUAN **Weight:** 31.1035 g. **Composition:** 0.9990 Silver 1.0000 oz. ASW **Obverse:** Da Guan Tower in Kunming **Reverse:** Multi-colored camellias

Date	Mintage	F	VF	XF	Unc	BU
1999 Proof	100,000	Value: 50.00				

Y# 973 10 YUAN **Weight:** 31.1035 g. **Composition:** 0.9990 Silver 1.0000 oz. ASW **Reverse:** Panda

Date	Mintage	F	VF	XF	Unc	BU
1999	250,000	—	—	—	20.00	—

Y# 974 10 YUAN **Weight:** 31.1035 g. **Composition:** 0.9990 Silver 1.0000 oz. ASW **Reverse:** Multi-colored panda

Date	Mintage	F	VF	XF	Unc	BU
1999	100,000	—	—	—	35.00	—

Y# 914.2 10 YUAN **Weight:** 31.2600 g. **Composition:** 0.9990 Silver 1.0040 oz. ASW **Subject:** Celebrating Spring **Obverse:** Radiant lantern **Reverse:** Multicolor, children lighting firecrackers

Date	F	VF	XF	Unc	BU
1999 Proof	—	Value: 42.50			

Y# 978 10 YUAN **Weight:** 23.0375 g. **Composition:** 0.9000 Silver .6666 oz. ASW **Subject:** Year of the Dragon **Obverse:** Building **Reverse:** Dragon **Shape:** Scalloped

Date	Mintage	F	VF	XF	Unc	BU
2000 Proof	6,800	Value: 65.00				

Y# 992 10 YUAN **Weight:** 3.1103 g. **Composition:** 0.9990 Gold .1000 oz. AGW **Subject:** Year of the Dragon

Date	Mintage	F	VF	XF	Unc	BU
2000 Proof	48,000	Value: 75.00				

Y# 993 10 YUAN **Weight:** 23.0375 g. **Composition:** 0.9000 Silver .6666 oz. ASW **Reverse:** Multi-colored dragon **Size:** 40 mm.

Date	Mintage	F	VF	XF	Unc	BU
2000	100,000	—	—	—	25.00	—
2000 Proof	30,000	Value: 75.00				

Y# 979 10 YUAN **Weight:** 31.1035 g. **Composition:** 0.9990 Silver 1.0000 oz. ASW **Obverse:** Temple of Heaven **Reverse:** Panda seated holding bamboo branch

Date	F	VF	XF	Unc	BU
2000	—	—	—	25.00	—

Note: Domestic Chinese examples struck with mirror fields, overseas examples struck with frosted fields

Y# 994 10 YUAN **Weight:** 3.1103 g. **Composition:** 0.9990 Gold .1000 oz. AGW **Subject:** Y2K

Date	Mintage	F	VF	XF	Unc	BU
2000	50,000	—	—	—	50.00	—

Y# 995 10 YUAN **Weight:** 3.1103 g. **Composition:** 0.9990 Gold .1000 oz. AGW **Subject:** Chinese Grotto Art

Date	Mintage	F	VF	XF	Unc	BU
2000	50,000	—	—	—	50.00	—

Y# 996 10 YUAN **Weight:** 3.1103 g. **Composition:** 0.9990 Gold .1000 oz. AGW **Subject:** Goddess Guanyin

Date	Mintage	F	VF	XF	Unc	BU
2000	33,000	—	—	—	50.00	—

Y# 1048 10 YUAN **Weight:** 20.7357 g. **Composition:** 0.9000 Silver .6000 oz. ASW **Subject:** Dragons **Note:** Scalloped edge.

Date	Mintage	F	VF	XF	Unc	BU
2000 Proof	6,800	Value: 75.00				

Y# 946 10 YUAN **Weight:** 3.1103 g. **Composition:** 0.9990 Gold .1000 oz. AGW **Obverse:** Temple of Heaven **Reverse:** Panda seated on leaves **Note:** Similar to 100 Yuan, Y#949.

Date		F	VF	XF	Unc	BU
2000 Proof	—	Value: 60.00				

Y# 1041 10 YUAN **Weight:** 30.8400 g. **Composition:** 0.9990 Silver .9905 oz. ASW **Subject:** Year of the Snake **Obverse:** Traditional style building **Reverse:** Snake **Edge:** Scalloped **Size:** 39.9 mm.

Date	Mintage	F	VF	XF	Unc	BU
2001 Proof	6,800,000	Value: 65.00				

Y# 1103 10 YUAN **Weight:** 31.1035 g. **Composition:** 0.9990 Silver 0.999 oz. ASW **Subject:** 2008 Olympics to be in Beijing **Obverse:** Gold-plated "v" design **Reverse:** Radiant Temple of Heaven **Edge:** Reeded **Size:** 40 mm.

Date	Mintage	F	VF	XF	Unc	BU
2001 Proof	60,000	Value: 50.00				

Y# 1042 10 YUAN **Weight:** 31.1035 g. **Composition:** 0.9990 Silver 1.0000 oz. ASW **Subject:** Year of the Snake **Shape:** Fan-like

Date	Mintage	F	VF	XF	Unc	BU
2001	66,000	—	—	—	35.00	—

Y# 1043 10 YUAN **Weight:** 3.1104 g. **Composition:** 0.9990 Gold .1000 oz. AGW **Subject:** Year of the Snake

Date	Mintage	F	VF	XF	Unc	BU
2001	48,000	—	—	—	60.00	—

Y# 1097 10 YUAN **Weight:** 31.2300 g. **Composition:** 0.9990 Silver 1.0031 oz. ASW **Subject:** Panda Bullion **Obverse:** Temple of Heaven, incuse legend **Reverse:** Two tone gold plated panda walking in bamboo **Edge:** Slanted reeding **Size:** 40 mm.

Date		F	VF	XF	Unc	BU
2002 Proof	—	Value: 50.00				

Y# 1098 10 YUAN **Weight:** 31.2300 g. **Composition:** 0.9990 Silver 1.0031 oz. ASW **Subject:** Panda Bullion **Obverse:** Temple of Heaven, incuse legend **Reverse:** Multicolor panda walking in bamboo **Edge:** Slanted reeding **Size:** 40 mm.

Date		F	VF	XF	Unc	BU
2002 Proof	—	Value: 40.00				

Y# 745 15 YUAN **Weight:** 10.0000 g. **Composition:** 0.8000 Silver .2572 oz. ASW **Series:** Olympics **Obverse:** State seal **Reverse:** Ancient archers

Date	Mintage	F	VF	XF	Unc	BU
1980	15,000	—	—	—	75.00	—

Y# 18 20 YUAN **Weight:** 10.3500 g. **Composition:** 0.8500 Silver .2829 oz. ASW **Series:** 1980 Olympics **Subject:** Wrestling **Obverse:** Similar to 1 Yuan, Y#10

Date	Mintage	F	VF	XF	Unc	BU
1980 Proof	29,000	Value: 16.50				

Y# 38 20 YUAN **Weight:** 15.0000 g. **Composition:** 0.8500 Silver .4099 oz. ASW **Subject:** Year of the Dog **Obverse:** Temple of Heaven **Reverse:** Dog

Date	Mintage	F	VF	XF	Unc	BU
1982 Proof	8,825	Value: 125				

Y# 207 20 YUAN **Weight:** 62.2060 g. **Composition:** 0.9990 Silver 2.0000 oz. ASW **Reverse:** Phoenix and dragon

Date	Mintage	F	VF	XF	Unc	BU
1989 Proof	7,325	Value: 90.00				

Y# 888 20 YUAN **Weight:** 62.2060 g. **Composition:** 0.9990 Silver 2.0000 oz. ASW **Obverse:** Great Wall **Reverse:** Horse and dragon

Date	Mintage	F	VF	XF	Unc	BU
1992 Proof	6,000	Value: 100				

Note: Issued in 1996

Y# 595 20 YUAN **Weight:** 62.2060 g. **Composition:** 0.9990 Silver 2.0000 oz. ASW **Obverse:** Bai Di city gate **Reverse:** Yangtze River scene **Shape:** Rectangular

Date	Mintage	F	VF	XF	Unc	BU
1996 Proof	8,000	Value: 60.00				

Y# 596 20 YUAN **Weight:** 62.2060 g. **Composition:** 0.9990 Silver 2.0000 oz. ASW **Obverse:** Qu Yuan Temple **Shape:** Rectangular

Date	Mintage	F	VF	XF	Unc	BU
1996 Proof	8,000	Value: 60.00				

Y# 597 20 YUAN **Weight:** 62.2060 g. **Composition:** 0.9990 Silver 2.0000 oz. ASW **Obverse:** Zhang Fei Temple **Shape:** Rectangular

Date	Mintage	F	VF	XF	Unc	BU
1996 Proof	8,000	Value: 60.00				

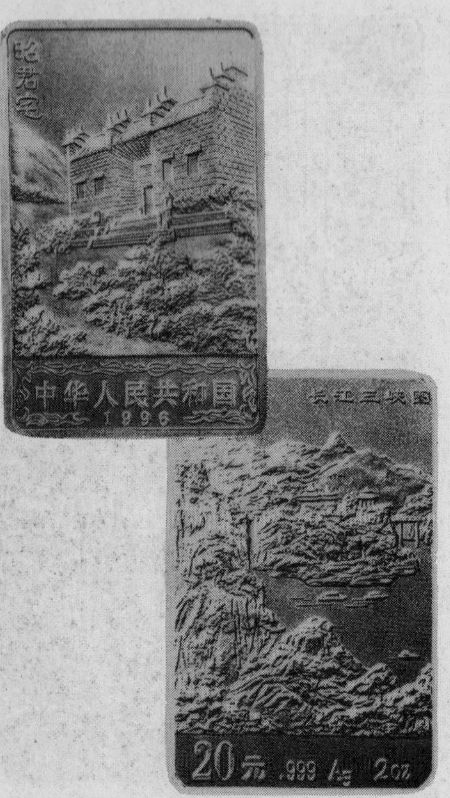

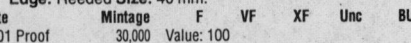

Y# 598 20 YUAN **Weight:** 62.2060 g. **Composition:** 0.9990 Silver 2.0000 oz. ASW **Obverse:** Zhao Jun Temple **Shape:** Rectangular

Date	Mintage	F	VF	XF	Unc	BU
1996 Proof	8,000	Value: 60.00				

Y# 1082 20 YUAN **Weight:** 62.2070 g. **Composition:** 0.9990 Silver 1.998 oz. ASW **Subject:** Mogao Grottos **Obverse:** 8-story building **Reverse:** Buddha-like statue **Edge:** Reeded **Size:** 40 mm.

Date	Mintage	F	VF	XF	Unc	BU
2001 Proof	30,000	Value: 100				

Y# 35 25 YUAN **Weight:** 19.4400 g. **Composition:** 0.8000 Silver .5000 oz. ASW **Subject:** World Soccer Cup

Date	Mintage	F	VF	XF	Unc	BU
1982 Proof	40,000	Value: 27.50				

Y# 36 25 YUAN **Weight:** 19.4400 g. **Composition:** 0.8000 Silver .5000 oz. ASW **Subject:** World Soccer Cup

Date	Mintage	F	VF	XF	Unc	BU
1982 Proof	40,000	Value: 27.50				

Y# 50 25 YUAN **Weight:** 7.7758 g. **Composition:** 0.9990 Gold .2500 oz. AGW **Obverse:** Temple of Heaven **Reverse:** Panda walking right in inner circle

Date	Mintage	F	VF	XF	Unc	BU
1983	39,000	—	—	—	150	—

Y# 75 25 YUAN **Weight:** 7.7758 g. **Composition:** 0.9990 Gold .2500 oz. AGW **Obverse:** Temple of Heaven **Reverse:** Lounging Panda with bamboo

Date	Mintage	F	VF	XF	Unc	BU
1984	38,000	—	—	—	150	—

Y# 82 25 YUAN **Weight:** 7.7758 g. **Composition:** 0.9990 Gold .2500 oz. AGW **Obverse:** Temple of Heaven **Reverse:** Panda hanging onto bamboo branch

Date	Mintage	F	VF	XF	Unc	BU
1985	95,000	—	—	—	175	—

Y# 103 25 YUAN **Weight:** 7.7758 g. **Composition:** 0.9990 Gold .2500 oz. AGW **Obverse:** Temple of Heaven **Reverse:** Facing panda standing

Date	Mintage	F	VF	XF	Unc	BU
1986	33,000	—	—	—	95.00	—
1986 P Proof	11,000	Value: 110				

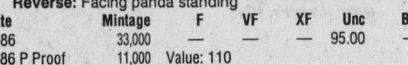

Y# 126 25 YUAN **Weight:** 7.7758 g. **Composition:** 0.9990 Gold .2500 oz. AGW **Obverse:** Temple of Heaven **Reverse:** Panda drinking

Date	Mintage	F	VF	XF	Unc	BU
1987(s)	73,000	—	—	—	95.00	—
1987(y)	31,000	—	—	—	95.00	—
1987 P Proof	10,000	Value: 100				

Y# 154 25 YUAN **Weight:** 7.7758 g. **Composition:** 0.9990 Gold .2500 oz. AGW **Obverse:** Temple of Heaven **Reverse:** Panda pawing bamboo

Date	Mintage	F	VF	XF	Unc	BU
1988	122,000	—	—	—	125	—
1988 Proof	10,000	Value: 135				

Y# 189 25 YUAN **Weight:** 7.7758 g. **Composition:** 0.9990 Gold .2500 oz. AGW **Note:** Similar to 100 Yuan, Y#191.

Date	Mintage	F	VF	XF	Unc	BU
1989	71,000	—	—	—	125	—
1989 Proof	—	Value: 150				

Y# 240 25 YUAN **Weight:** 7.7758 g. **Composition:** 0.9990 Gold .2500 oz. AGW **Reverse:** Panda

Date	Mintage	F	VF	XF	Unc	BU
1990	—	—	—	—	135	—
1990 Proof	5,000	Value: 150				

Y# 268 25 YUAN **Weight:** 7.7758 g. **Composition:** 0.9995 Platinum .2500 oz. APW **Reverse:** Panda climbing tree

Date	Mintage	F	VF	XF	Unc	BU
1990 Proof	2,500	Value: 185				

Y# 301 25 YUAN **Ring Weight:** 3.3879 g. **Ring Composition:** 0.9990 Silver .1250 oz. ASW **Center Weight:** 7.7758 g. **Center Composition:** 0.9990 Gold .2500 oz. AGW **Reverse:** Seated panda in inner circle

Date	Mintage	F	VF	XF	Unc	BU
1991 Proof	2,000	Value: 250				

Y# 311 25 YUAN **Weight:** 7.7758 g. **Composition:** 0.9990 Gold .2500 oz. AGW **Edge:** reeded **Size:** 22mm mm. **Note:** design similar to Y#301.

Date	F	VF	XF	Unc	BU
1991	—	—	—	135	—
1991 Proof	—	Value: 165			

Y# 343 25 YUAN **Weight:** 7.7758 g. **Composition:** 0.9990 Gold .2500 oz. AGW **Reverse:** Panda on limb **Note:** Similar to 100 Yuan, Y#345.

Date	F	VF	XF	Unc	BU
1992	—	—	—	125	—
1992 Proof	—	Value: 165			

Y# 555 25 YUAN **Weight:** 8.4800 g. **Composition:** 0.9170 Gold .2500 oz. AGW **Subject:** Bronze Age Sculptures **Obverse:** State seal **Reverse:** Ram

Date	Mintage	F	VF	XF	Unc	BU
1992 Proof	Est. 500	Value: 250				

Y# 556 25 YUAN **Weight:** 8.4800 g. **Composition:** 0.9170 Gold .2500 oz. AGW **Subject:** Bronze Age Sculptures **Reverse:** Panther

Date	Mintage	F	VF	XF	Unc	BU
1992 Proof	Est. 500	Value: 250				

Y# 889 25 YUAN **Weight:** 7.7759 g. **Composition:** 0.9990 Gold .2500 oz. AGW **Obverse:** Great Wall **Reverse:** Horse and dragon

Date	Mintage	F	VF	XF	Unc	BU
1992 Proof	5,000	Value: 120				

Note: Issued in 1996

Y# 404 25 YUAN **Weight:** 7.7759 g. **Composition:** 0.9990 Gold .2500 oz. AGW **Reverse:** Chinese Gods: Fu, Lu, and Shu

Date		F	VF	XF	Unc	BU
1993		—	—	—	175	—

Y# 408 25 YUAN **Weight:** 8.4900 g. **Composition:** 0.9170 Gold .2500 oz. AGW **Subject:** Bronze Age Sculptures **Obverse:** State seal **Reverse:** Horse

Date	Mintage	F	VF	XF	Unc	BU
1993 Proof	500	Value: 175				

Y# 475 25 YUAN **Weight:** 7.7758 g. **Composition:** 0.9990 Gold .2500 oz. AGW **Obverse:** Temple of Heaven **Reverse:** Two peacocks

Date		F	VF	XF	Unc	BU
1993 Prooflike		—	—	—	150	—

Y# 502 25 YUAN **Weight:** 7.7758 g. **Composition:** 0.9990 Gold .2500 oz. AGW **Reverse:** Koddess Kuan Yin seated in flower

Date	Mintage	F	VF	XF	Unc	BU
1993 Proof	1,000	Value: 175				

Y# 930 25 YUAN **Ring Weight:** 3.3879 g. **Ring Composition:** 0.9990 Silver .1250 oz. ASW **Center Weight:** 7.7758 g. **Center Composition:** 0.9990 Gold .2500 oz. AGW **Reverse:** Panda on rock

Date	Mintage	F	VF	XF	Unc	BU
1993 Proof	2,500	Value: 200				

Y# 775 25 YUAN **Weight:** 7.7758 g. **Composition:** 0.9990 Gold .2500 oz. AGW **Subject:** Mount Heng **Obverse:** Great Wall **Reverse:** Large temple

Date	Mintage	F	VF	XF	Unc	BU
1993 Proof	8,888	Value: 200				

Y# 409 25 YUAN **Weight:** 8.4900 g. **Composition:** 0.9170 Gold .2500 oz. AGW **Subject:** Bronze Age Sculptures **Obverse:** State seal **Reverse:** Pig

Date	Mintage	F	VF	XF	Unc	BU
1993 Proof	500	Value: 175				

Y# 612 25 YUAN **Weight:** 7.7758 g. **Composition:** 0.9990 Gold .2500 oz. AGW **Note:** Similar to Y#544.

Date	Mintage	F	VF	XF	Unc	BU
1993		—	—	—	125	—
1993 Proof	—	Value: 150				

Y# 1072 25 YUAN **Weight:** 7.7758 g. **Composition:** 0.9995 Platinum .2500 oz. APW **Series:** Chinese Inventions and Discoveries **Obverse:** Great Wall **Reverse:** Stirrup and equestrians **Edge:** Reeded **Size:** 21.95 mm.

Date	Mintage	F	VF	XF	Unc	BU
1993 Proof	100	Value: 375				

Y# 1073 25 YUAN **Weight:** 7.7758 g. **Composition:** 0.9995 Platinum .2500 oz. APW **Series:** Chinese Inventions and Discoveries **Obverse:** Great Wall **Reverse:** Umbrella use and repair scene

Date	Mintage	F	VF	XF	Unc	BU
1993 Proof	100	Value: 375				

Y# 1074 25 YUAN **Weight:** 7.7758 g. **Composition:** 0.9995 Platinum .2500 oz. APW **Series:** Chinese Inventions and Discoveries **Obverse:** Great Wall **Reverse:** Mathematicians using an abacus

Date	Mintage	F	VF	XF	Unc	BU
1993 Proof	100	Value: 375				

Y# 1075 25 YUAN **Weight:** 7.7758 g. **Composition:** 0.9995 Platinum .2500 oz. APW **Series:** Chinese Inventions and Discoveries **Obverse:** Great Wall **Reverse:** Two men and Yin and Yang symbol

Date	Mintage	F	VF	XF	Unc	BU
1993 Proof	100	Value: 375				

Y# 1076 25 YUAN **Weight:** 7.7758 g. **Composition:** 0.9995 Platinum .2500 oz. APW **Series:** Chinese Inventions and Discoveries **Obverse:** Great Wall **Reverse:** Excavating the Terracotta army

Date	Mintage	F	VF	XF	Unc	BU
1993 Proof	100	Value: 375				

Y# 422 25 YUAN **Ring Weight:** 3.3879 g. **Ring Composition:** 0.9990 Silver .1250 oz. ASW **Center Weight:** 7.7758 g. **Center Composition:** 0.9990 Gold .2500 oz. AGW **Reverse:** Unicorn **Note:** Similar to 10 Yuan, Y#420.

Date	Mintage	F	VF	XF	Unc	BU
1994 Proof	1,100	Value: 175				

Y# 423 25 YUAN **Weight:** 7.7758 g. **Composition:** 0.9990 Gold .2500 oz. AGW **Reverse:** Unicorn

Date	Mintage	F	VF	XF	Unc	BU
1994 Proof	5,100	Value: 200				

Y# 433 25 YUAN **Weight:** 7.7758 g. **Composition:** 0.9990 Gold .2500 oz. AGW **Reverse:** Panda tugging on bamboo sprig

Date	Mintage	F	VF	XF	Unc	BU
1994	35,000	—	—	—	125	—
1994 Proof	—	Value: 175				

Y# 544 25 YUAN **Ring Weight:** 3.3879 g. **Ring Composition:** 0.9990 Silver .1250 oz. ASW **Center Weight:** 7.7758 g. **Center Composition:** 0.9990 Gold .2500 oz. AGW **Reverse:** Panda tugging on bamboo sprig

Date	Mintage	F	VF	XF	Unc	BU
1994 Proof	2,000	Value: 200				

Y# 511 25 YUAN **Weight:** 3.1103 g. **Composition:** 0.9990 Gold .1000 oz. AGW **Reverse:** Goddess Kuan Yin holding child

Date	Mintage	F	VF	XF	Unc	BU
1994 Proof	1,000	Value: 200				

Y# 512 25 YUAN **Weight:** 3.1103 g. **Composition:** 0.9990 Gold .1000 oz. AGW **Reverse:** Goddess Kuan Yin with bottle

Date	Mintage	F	VF	XF	Unc	BU
1994 Proof	1,000	Value: 200				

Y# 513 25 YUAN **Weight:** 3.1103 g. **Composition:** 0.9990 Gold .1000 oz. AGW **Reverse:** Goddess Kuan Yin standing

Date	Mintage	F	VF	XF	Unc	BU
1994 Proof	1,000	Value: 200				

Y# 514 25 YUAN **Weight:** 3.1103 g. **Composition:** 0.9990 Gold .1000 oz. AGW **Reverse:** Goddess Kuan Yin seated

Date	Mintage	F	VF	XF	Unc	BU
1994 Proof	1,000	Value: 200				

Y# 524 25 YUAN **Weight:** 7.7758 g. **Composition:** 0.9990 Gold .2500 oz. AGW **Obverse:** Pu-Tow temple **Reverse:** Goddess of Mercy - with Lotus flower

Date	Mintage	F	VF	XF	Unc	BU
1995 Proof	1,000	Value: 175				

Y# 525 25 YUAN **Weight:** 7.7758 g. **Composition:** 0.9990 Gold .2500 oz. AGW **Reverse:** Goddess of Mercy with wheel

Date	Mintage	F	VF	XF	Unc	BU
1995 Proof	1,000	Value: 175				

Y# 526 25 YUAN **Weight:** 7.7758 g. **Composition:** 0.9990 Gold .2500 oz. AGW **Reverse:** Goddess of Mercy with sceptre

Date	Mintage	F	VF	XF	Unc	BU
1995 Proof	1,000	Value: 175				

Y# 527 25 YUAN **Weight:** 7.7758 g. **Composition:** 0.9990 Gold .2500 oz. AGW **Reverse:** Goddess of Mercy with bowl

Date	Mintage	F	VF	XF	Unc	BU
1995 Proof	1,000	Value: 175				

Y# 572 25 YUAN **Ring Weight:** 3.8879 g. **Ring Composition:** 0.9990 Silver .1250 oz. ASW **Center Weight:** 7.7758 g. **Center Composition:** 0.9990 Gold .2500 oz. AGW **Reverse:** Panda at stream

Date	Mintage	F	VF	XF	Unc	BU
1995 Proof set	Est. 2,000	Value: 210				

Y# 687 25 YUAN Ring **Weight:** 3.8879 g. Ring **Composition:** 0.9990 Silver .1250 oz. ASW **Center Weight:** 7.7758 g. **Center Composition:** 0.9990 Gold .2500 oz. AGW **Reverse:** Unicorn with offspring

Date	Mintage	F	VF	XF	Unc	BU
1995 Proof	1,600	Value: 175				

Y# 738 25 YUAN **Weight:** 7.8300 g. **Composition:** 0.9990 Gold .2515 oz. AGW **Obverse:** Eastern unicorn **Reverse:** Western unicorn with offspring

Date	Mintage	F	VF	XF	Unc	BU
1995 Proof	5,000	Value: 250				

Y# 835 25 YUAN **Weight:** 7.8300 g. **Composition:** 0.9990 Gold .2515 oz. AGW **Subject:** Sea Goddess Mazhu **Obverse:** Mazhu Temple **Reverse:** Mazhu's portrayal

Date	Mintage	F	VF	XF	Unc	BU
1995 Proof	3,000	Value: 150				

Y# 642 25 YUAN **Weight:** 7.7600 g. **Composition:** 0.9990 Gold .2500 oz. AGW **Reverse:** Panda **Note:** Similar to 10 Yuan, Y#641.

Date	F	VF	XF	Unc	BU
1995	—	—	—	120	—

Y# 1061 25 YUAN Ring **Weight:** 3.8879 g. Ring **Composition:** 0.9990 Silver .1250 oz. ASW **Center Weight:** 7.7758 g. **Center Composition:** 0.9990 Gold .2500 oz. AGW **Obverse:** Eastern unicorn **Reverse:** Western unicorn with offspring **Edge:** Reeded **Size:** 30 mm.

Date	F	VF	XF	Unc	BU
1995 Proof	—	Value: 220			

Y# 955 25 YUAN **Weight:** 7.7758 g. **Composition:** 0.9995 Platinum .2500 oz. APW **Subject:** Unicorn **Obverse:** Eastern unicorn, full body **Reverse:** Western unicorn head **Edge:** Reeded **Size:** 21.9 mm.

Date	F	VF	XF	Unc	BU
1996 Proof	—	Value: 225			

Y# 849 25 YUAN **Weight:** 7.7759 g. **Composition:** 0.9990 Gold .2500 oz. AGW **Subject:** 15th Anniversary - Gold Panda Coinage **Obverse:** Temple of Heaven with additional legend **Reverse:** Panda in tree

Date	Mintage	F	VF	XF	Unc	BU
1996 Proof	8,000	Value: 200				

Y# 852 25 YUAN Ring **Weight:** 3.8879 g. Ring **Composition:** 0.9990 Silver .1250 oz. ASW **Center Weight:** 7.7759 g. **Center Composition:** 0.9990 Gold .2500 oz. AGW **Obverse:** Temple of Heaven **Reverse:** Panda seated on rock

Date	Mintage	F	VF	XF	Unc	BU
1996 Proof	2,500	Value: 220				

Y# 867 25 YUAN **Weight:** 7.7759 g. **Composition:** 0.9990 Gold .2500 oz. AGW **Subject:** Centennial of Chinese Post Office **Obverse:** Modern postal stamp **Reverse:** Imperial postal stamp

Date	Mintage	F	VF	XF	Unc	BU
1996 Proof	3,000	Value: 125				

Y# 576 25 YUAN **Weight:** 7.8300 g. **Composition:** 0.9990 Gold .2515 oz. AGW **Reverse:** Panda **Note:** Similar to 100 Yuan, Y#578.

Date	F	VF	XF	Unc	BU
1996	—	—	—	140	—

Y# 743 25 YUAN **Weight:** 7.7759 g. **Composition:** 0.9990 Gold .2500 oz. AGW **Obverse:** Eastern unicorn **Reverse:** Western unicorn and maiden

Date	Mintage	F	VF	XF	Unc	BU
1996 Proof	3,000	Value: 225				

Y# 743a 25 YUAN **Weight:** 7.7759 g. **Composition:** 0.9990 Platinum .2500 oz. APW

Date	Mintage	F	VF	XF	Unc	BU
1996 Proof	500	Value: 250				

Y# 718 25 YUAN **Weight:** 7.7759 g. **Composition:** 0.9990 Gold .2500 oz. AGW **Subject:** Panda Bullion **Obverse:** Temple of Heaven **Reverse:** Panda on branch **Note:** Similar to 100 Yuan, Y#720.

Date	F	VF	XF	Unc	BU
1997	—	—	—	125	—

Note: Exists in large and small date varietes

Y# 915 25 YUAN **Weight:** 7.7759 g. **Composition:** 0.9990 Gold .2500 oz. AGW **Subject:** Celebrating Spring **Obverse:** Radiant lantern **Reverse:** Children setting off firecrackers

Date	Mintage	F	VF	XF	Unc	BU
1997 Proof	10,000	Value: 100				

Y# 997 25 YUAN **Weight:** 7.7759 g. **Composition:** 0.9990 Gold .2500 oz. AGW **Subject:** China Palace Museum **Obverse:** Forbidden City **Reverse:** Imperial Gardens

Date	Mintage	F	VF	XF	Unc	BU
1997 Proof	4,000	Value: 125				

Y# 998 25 YUAN **Weight:** 7.7759 g. **Composition:** 0.9990 Gold .2500 oz. AGW **Subject:** China Palace Museum **Obverse:** Forbidden City **Reverse:** Jin Shui

Date	Mintage	F	VF	XF	Unc	BU
1997 Proof	4,000	Value: 125				

Y# 999 25 YUAN **Weight:** 7.7759 g. **Composition:** 0.9990 Gold .2500 oz. AGW **Subject:** China Palace Museum **Obverse:** Forbidden City **Reverse:** Quan Quin Palace

Date	Mintage	F	VF	XF	Unc	BU
1997 Proof	4,000	Value: 125				

Y# 1000 25 YUAN **Weight:** 7.7759 g. **Composition:** 0.9990 Gold .2500 oz. AGW **Subject:** China Palace Museum **Obverse:** Forbidden City **Reverse:** Inner view of palace

Date	Mintage	F	VF	XF	Unc	BU
1997 Proof	4,000	Value: 125				

Y# 1001 25 YUAN Ring **Weight:** 3.3879 g. Ring **Composition:** 0.9990 Silver .1250 oz. ASW **Center Weight:** 7.7758 g. **Center Composition:** 0.9990 Gold .2500 oz. AGW **Reverse:** Panda climbing tree

Date	Mintage	F	VF	XF	Unc	BU
1997 Proof	2,800	Value: 220				

Y# 1002 25 YUAN **Weight:** 7.7758 g. **Composition:** 0.9990 Gold .2500 oz. AGW **Obverse:** Temple of Heaven **Reverse:** Panda seated on rock

Date	F	VF	XF	Unc	BU
1998	—	—	—	95.00	—

Note: Exists in both large and small date varieties

Y# 1003 25 YUAN **Weight:** 7.7758 g. **Composition:** 0.9990 Gold .2500 oz. AGW **Obverse:** Temple of Heaven **Reverse:** Panda on ledge

Date	F	VF	XF	Unc	BU
1999	—	—	—	95.00	—

Note: Exists in both large and small date varieties

Y# 947 25 YUAN **Weight:** 7.7758 g. **Composition:** 0.9990 Gold .2500 oz. AGW **Obverse:** Temple of Heaven **Reverse:** Panda seated on leaves **Note:** Similar to 100 Yuan, Y#949.

Date	F	VF	XF	Unc	BU
2000 Proof	—	Value: 125			

Note: Domestic Chinese examples struck with mirror fields, overseas examples struck with frosted fields

Y# 19 30 YUAN **Weight:** 15.0000 g. **Composition:** 0.8500 Silver .4099 oz. ASW **Series:** 1980 Olympics **Subject:** Equestrian **Obverse:** State seal **Reverse:** Horse racing

Date	Mintage	F	VF	XF	Unc	BU
1980 Proof	29,000	Value: 17.50				

Y# 20 30 YUAN **Weight:** 15.0000 g. **Composition:** 0.8500 Silver .4099 oz. ASW **Series:** 1980 Olympics **Obverse:** State seal **Reverse:** Soccer

Date	Mintage	F	VF	XF	Unc	BU
1980 Proof	29,000	Value: 17.50				

Y# 21 30 YUAN **Weight:** 15.0000 g. **Composition:** 0.8500 Silver .4099 oz. ASW **Series:** 1980 Olympics **Obverse:** State seal **Reverse:** Speed skater

Date	Mintage	F	VF	XF	Unc	BU
1980 Proof	20,000	Value: 18.50				

Y# 746 30 YUAN **Weight:** 16.0000 g. **Composition:** Silver .4373 oz. ASW **Series:** 1980 Olympics **Obverse:** State seal **Reverse:** Downhill skier

Date	Mintage	F	VF	XF	Unc	BU
1980 Proof	20,000	Value: 18.50				

Y# 747 30 YUAN **Weight:** 16.0000 g. **Composition:** Silver .4373 oz. ASW **Series:** 1980 Olympics **Obverse:** State seal **Reverse:** Figure skater

Date	Mintage	F	VF	XF	Unc	BU
1980 Proof	20,000	Value: 18.50				

Y# 748 30 YUAN **Weight:** 16.0000 g. **Composition:** Silver .4373 oz. ASW **Series:** 1980 Olympics **Obverse:** State seal **Reverse:** Biathalon skier

Date	Mintage	F	VF	XF	Unc	BU
1980 Proof	20,000	Value: 18.50				

Y# 32 30 YUAN **Weight:** 15.0000 g. **Composition:** 0.8500 Silver .4099 oz. ASW **Subject:** Year of the Rooster **Obverse:** Shoreline temple **Reverse:** Rooster

Date	Mintage	F	VF	XF	Unc	BU
1981 Proof	10,000	Value: 225				

Y# 8 35 YUAN **Weight:** 19.4400 g. **Composition:** 0.8000 Silver .5000 oz. ASW **Subject:** UNICEF and IYC **Obverse:** State seal above sprays **Reverse:** Children planting a flower

Date	Mintage	F	VF	XF	Unc	BU
1979 Matte	1,000	—	—	—	150	—
1979 Proof	14,000	Value: 65.00				

Y# 46 35 YUAN **Weight:** 33.5800 g. **Composition:** 0.8000 Silver .8638 oz. ASW **Subject:** 70th Anniversary - 1911 Revolution **Obverse:** Staue of Sun Yat-sen **Reverse:** Mausoleum

Date	Mintage	F	VF	XF	Unc	BU
1981 Proof	3,885	Value: 200				

Y# 51 50 YUAN **Weight:** 15.5517 g. **Composition:** 0.9990 Gold .5000 oz. AGW **Obverse:** Temple of Heaven **Reverse:** Panda walking right in inner circle

Date	Mintage	F	VF	XF	Unc	BU
1983 Proof	23,000	Value: 250				

Y# 76 50 YUAN **Weight:** 15.5517 g. **Composition:** 0.9990 Gold .5000 oz. AGW **Obverse:** Temple of Heaven **Reverse:** Lounging panda with bamboo sprig

Date	Mintage	F	VF	XF	Unc	BU
1984 Proof	17,000	Value: 275				

Y# 83 50 YUAN **Weight:** 15.5517 g. **Composition:** 0.9990 Gold .5000 oz. AGW **Obverse:** Temple of Heaven **Reverse:** Panda hanging onto bamboo branch

Date	Mintage	F	VF	XF	Unc	BU
1985 Proof	76,000	Value: 250				

Y# 104 50 YUAN **Weight:** 15.5517 g. **Composition:** 0.9990 Gold .5000 oz. AGW **Obverse:** Temple of Heaven **Reverse:** Facing panda standing

Date	Mintage	F	VF	XF	Unc	BU
1986	28,000	—	—	—	225	—
1986 P Proof	10,000	Value: 250				

Y# 108 50 YUAN **Weight:** 155.5000 g. **Composition:** 0.9990 Silver 5.0000 oz. ASW **Subject:** 120th Anniversary - Birth of Sun Yat-sen **Reverse:** Sun Yat-sen standing facing **Size:** 70 mm. **Note:** Illustration reduced.

Date	Mintage	F	VF	XF	Unc	BU
1986 Proof	3,000	Value: 175				

Y# 134 50 YUAN **Weight:** 155.5000 g. **Composition:** 0.9990 Silver 5.0000 oz. ASW **Obverse:** Temple of Heaven **Reverse:** Panda clinging to tree trunk **Size:** 70 mm. **Note:** Illustration reduced.

Date	Mintage	F	VF	XF	Unc	BU
1987 Proof	8,540	Value: 80.00				

Y# 122 50 YUAN **Weight:** 155.5000 g. **Composition:** 0.9990 Silver 5.0000 oz. ASW **Subject:** Year of the Rabbit **Note:** Similar to 150 Yuan, Y#123.

Date	Mintage	F	VF	XF	Unc	BU
1987 Proof	4,000	Value: 250				

Y# 127 50 YUAN **Weight:** 15.5517 g. **Composition:** 0.9990 Gold .5000 oz. AGW **Obverse:** Temple of Heaven **Reverse:** Panda drinking water

Date	Mintage	F	VF	XF	Unc	BU
1987(s)	78,000	—	—	—	225	—
1987(y)	17,000	—	—	—	225	—
1987 P Proof	10,000	Value: 250				

Y# 155 50 YUAN **Weight:** 15.5517 g. **Composition:** 0.9990 Gold .5000 oz. AGW **Reverse:** Panda pawing bamboo

Date	Mintage	F	VF	XF	Unc	BU
1988	104,000	—	—	—	225	—
1988 Proof	10,000	Value: 250				

Y# 168 50 YUAN **Weight:** 155.5000 g. **Composition:** 0.9990 Silver 5.0000 oz. ASW **Obverse:** Temple of Heaven **Reverse:** Two pandas in tree

Date	Mintage	F	VF	XF	Unc	BU
1988 Proof	11,000	Value: 95.00				

Y# 142 50 YUAN **Weight:** 155.5000 g. **Composition:** 0.9990 Silver 5.0000 oz. ASW **Subject:** Year of the Dragon **Obverse:** Great Wall **Size:** 70 mm. **Note:** Illustration reduced.

Date	Mintage	F	VF	XF	Unc	BU
1988 Proof	5,000	Value: 250				

Y# 170 50 YUAN **Weight:** 155.5000 g. **Composition:** 0.9990 Silver 5.0000 oz. ASW **Series:** 1988 Summer Olympics **Reverse:** Volleyball game **Size:** 70 mm. **Note:** Illustration reduced.

Date	Mintage	F	VF	XF	Unc	BU
1988 Proof	3,898	Value: 250				

Y# 178 50 YUAN **Weight:** 155.5000 g. **Composition:** 0.9990 Silver 5.0000 oz. ASW **Subject:** Year of the Snake **Obverse:** Shanhaiguan Pass Gate **Size:** 70 mm. **Note:** Illustration reduced.

Date	Mintage	F	VF	XF	Unc	BU
1989 Proof	1,000	Value: 350				

Y# 190 50 YUAN **Weight:** 15.5517 g. **Composition:** 0.9990 Gold .5000 oz. AGW **Obverse:** Temple of Heaven **Reverse:** Grid behind panda **Note:** Similar to Y#220.

Date	Mintage	F	VF	XF	Unc	BU
1989	46,000	—	—	—	235	—
1989 Proof	—	Value: 250				

Y# 218 50 YUAN **Weight:** 155.5000 g. **Composition:** 0.9990 Silver 5.0000 oz. ASW **Obverse:** Temple of Heaven **Reverse:** Mother panda with cub

Date	Mintage	F	VF	XF	Unc	BU
1989 Proof	9,599	Value: 100				

Y# 220 50 YUAN **Weight:** 31.1030 g. **Composition:** 0.9990 Palladium 1.0000 oz.

Date	Mintage	F	VF	XF	Unc	BU
1989	5,000	—	—	—	BV+10%	—

Y# 241 50 YUAN **Weight:** 15.5517 g. **Composition:** 0.9990 Gold .5000 oz. AGW **Reverse:** Panda

Date	Mintage	F	VF	XF	Unc	BU
1990	—	—	—	—	250	—
1990 Proof	5,000	Value: 275				

Y# 262 50 YUAN **Weight:** 155.5000 g. **Composition:** 0.9990 Silver 5.0000 oz. ASW **Obverse:** Temple of Heaven **Reverse:** Two pandas, one in tree

Date	Mintage	F	VF	XF	Unc	BU
1990 Proof	4,000	Value: 100				

Y# 266 50 YUAN **Ring Weight:** 6.2207 g. **Ring Composition:** 0.9990 Silver .2000 oz. ASW **Center Weight:** 15.5517 g. **Center Composition:** 0.9990 Gold .5000 oz. AGW **Reverse:** Panda walking

Date	Mintage	F	VF	XF	Unc	BU
1990 Proof	2,000	Value: 275				

Y# 269 50 YUAN **Weight:** 15.5517 g. **Composition:** 0.9995 Platinum .5000 oz. APW **Reverse:** Panda eating bamboo on rock

Date	Mintage	F	VF	XF	Unc	BU
1990 Proof	2,500	Value: 370				

Y# 704 50 YUAN **Weight:** 15.5517 g. **Composition:** 0.9990 Gold .5000 oz. AGW **Subject:** Taiwan Scenery Series **Obverse:** Great Wall **Reverse:** Pagoda

Date	Mintage	F	VF	XF	Unc	BU
1990 Proof	2,000	Value: 250				

Y# 705 50 YUAN **Weight:** 15.5517 g. **Composition:** 0.9990 Gold .5000 oz. AGW **Subject:** Taiwan Scenery Series **Obverse:** Great Wall **Reverse:** Pondside building

Date	Mintage	F	VF	XF	Unc	BU
1990 Proof	2,000	Value: 250				

Y# 706 50 YUAN **Weight:** 15.5517 g. **Composition:** 0.9990 Gold .5000 oz. AGW **Subject:** Taiwan Scenery Series **Obverse:** Great Wall **Reverse:** Hillside building

Date	Mintage	F	VF	XF	Unc	BU
1990 Proof	2,000	Value: 250				

Y# 707 50 YUAN **Weight:** 15.5517 g. **Composition:** 0.9990 Gold .5000 oz. AGW **Obverse:** Great Wall **Reverse:** Three buildings joined by docks and bridge

Date	Mintage	F	VF	XF	Unc	BU
1990 Proof	2,000	Value: 250				

Y# 223 50 YUAN **Weight:** 155.5000 g. **Composition:** 0.9990 Silver 5.0000 oz. ASW **Subject:** Year of the Horse **Obverse:** Temple of Confucius **Reverse:** Two horses drinking at stream **Size:** 70 mm. **Note:** Illustration reduced.

Date	Mintage	F	VF	XF	Unc	BU
1990 Proof	2,000	Value: 200				

Y# 321 50 YUAN **Weight:** 155.6800 g. **Composition:** 0.9990 Silver 5.0053 oz. ASW **Series:** 1992 Olympics **Reverse:** Speed skaters **Note:** Illustration reduced.

Date	Mintage	F	VF	XF	Unc	BU
1990 Proof	10,000	Value: 165				

Y# 272 50 YUAN **Weight:** 155.5000 g. **Composition:** 0.9990 Silver 5.0000 oz. ASW **Subject:** Year of the Goat **Obverse:** Chinese building and legend **Size:** 60 mm. **Note:** Illustration reduced.

Date	Mintage	F	VF	XF	Unc	BU
1991 Proof	2,000	Value: 250				

Y# 315 50 YUAN **Weight:** 31.1035 g. **Composition:** 0.9990 Gold 1.0000 oz. AGW **Subject:** 10th Anniversary of Panda Coinage **Reverse:** Panda climbing bamboo branch **Note:** Double thick.

Date	Mintage	F	VF	XF	Unc	BU
1991 Proof	2,500	Value: 375				

Y# 312 50 YUAN **Weight:** 15.5517 g. **Composition:** 0.9990 Gold .5000 oz. AGW **Note:** Similar to 100 Yuan, Y#313.

Date	F	VF	XF	Unc	BU
1991	—	—	—	250	—
1991 Proof	—	Value: 275			

Y# 373 50 YUAN **Weight:** 155.5000 g. **Composition:** 0.9990 Silver 5.0000 oz. ASW **Reverse:** Panda

Date	Mintage	F	VF	XF	Unc	BU
1991 Proof	5,000	Value: 120				

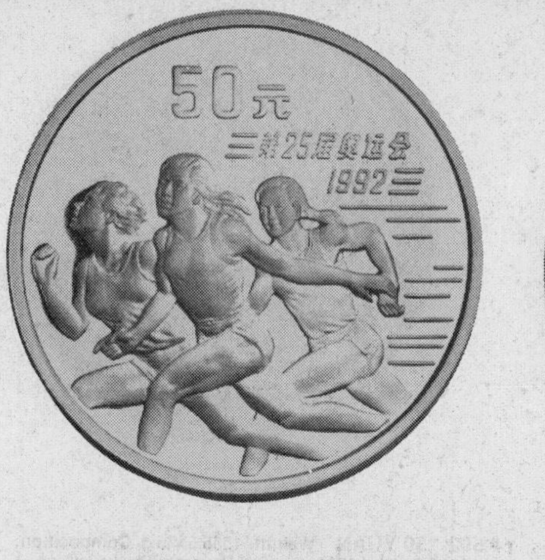

Y# 472 50 YUAN **Weight:** 155.5000 g. **Composition:** 0.9990 Silver 5.0000 oz. ASW **Series:** 1992 Olympics **Obverse:** State seal **Reverse:** Female runners

Date	Mintage	F	VF	XF	Unc	BU
1991 Proof	10,000	Value: 175				

Y# 477 50 YUAN **Weight:** 155.5000 g. **Composition:** 0.9990 Silver 5.0000 oz. ASW **Subject:** 80th Anniversary - 1911 Revolution **Obverse:** Similar to 10 Yuan, Y#476 **Reverse:** Sun Yat Sen in uniform

Date	Mintage	F	VF	XF	Unc	BU
1991 Proof	1,000	Value: 350				

Y# 374 50 YUAN **Weight:** 155.5000 g. **Composition:** 0.9990 Silver 5.0000 oz. ASW **Reverse:** Pandas

Date	Mintage	F	VF	XF	Unc	BU
1992 Proof	4,000	Value: 120				

Y# 557 50 YUAN **Weight:** 16.9600 g. **Composition:** 0.9170 Gold .5000 oz. AGW **Subject:** Bronze Age Sculptures **Obverse:** State seal **Reverse:** Kneeling figure

Date	Mintage	F	VF	XF	Unc	BU
1992 Proof	Est. 500	Value: 350				

Y# 344 50 YUAN **Weight:** 15.5660 g. **Composition:** 0.9990 Gold .5000 oz. AGW **Reverse:** Panda on tree branch **Note:** Similar to 100 Yuan, Y#345.

Date	Mintage	F	VF	XF	Unc	BU
1992		—	—	—	250	—
1992 Proof	—	Value: 300				

Y# 289 50 YUAN **Weight:** 155.5000 g. **Composition:** 0.9990 Silver 5.0000 oz. ASW **Subject:** Year of the Monkey **Obverse:** Building **Reverse:** Monkey **Note:** Similar to 50 Yuan, Y#292.

Date	Mintage	F	VF	XF	Unc	BU
1992 Proof	1,000	Value: 300				

Y# 405 50 YUAN **Weight:** 155.5175 g. **Composition:** 0.9990 Silver 5.0000 oz. ASW **Subject:** Chinese Gods, Fu, Lu and Shu **Note:** Similar to 500 Yuan, Y#407.

Date	Mintage	F	VF	XF	Unc	BU
1993 Proof	1,000	Value: 325				

Y# 413 50 YUAN **Weight:** 155.5175 g. **Composition:** 0.9990 Silver 5.0000 oz. ASW **Reverse:** Chairman Mao writing **Size:** 70 mm. **Note:** Illustration reduced.

Date	Mintage	F	VF	XF	Unc	BU
1993	1,500	—	—	—	300	—

Y# 353 50 YUAN **Weight:** 155.5000 g. **Composition:** 0.9990 Silver 5.0000 oz. ASW **Obverse:** Temple of Heaven **Reverse:** Two peacocks

Date	Mintage	F	VF	XF	Unc	BU
1993 Proof	888	Value: 275				

Y# 378 50 YUAN **Weight:** 15.5517 g. **Composition:** 0.9990 Gold .5000 oz. AGW **Reverse:** Chin with Yin Yang

Date	Mintage	F	VF	XF	Unc	BU
1993 Proof	1,200	Value: 275				

Y# 379 50 YUAN **Weight:** 155.5000 g. **Composition:** 0.9990 Silver 5.0000 oz. ASW **Obverse:** Temple of Heaven **Reverse:** Pandas

Date	Mintage	F	VF	XF	Unc	BU
1993 Proof	Est. 3,000	Value: 135				

Y# 381 50 YUAN **Weight:** 155.5000 g. **Composition:** 0.9990 Silver 5.0000 oz. ASW **Subject:** Year of the Rooster

Date	Mintage	F	VF	XF	Unc	BU
1993 Proof	1,000	Value: 275				

Y# 394 50 YUAN **Weight:** 155.5000 g. **Composition:** 0.9990 Silver 5.0000 oz. ASW **Reverse:** Marco Polo

Date	Mintage	F	VF	XF	Unc	BU
1993 Proof	500	Value: 285				

Y# 401 50 YUAN **Weight:** 15.5517 g. **Composition:** 0.9990 Gold .5000 oz. AGW **Subject:** Invention of the Umbrella **Obverse:**-Great Wall

Date	Mintage	F	VF	XF	Unc	BU
1993 Proof	1,200	Value: 275				

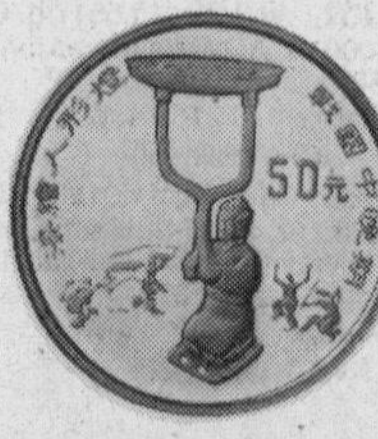

Y# 410 50 YUAN **Weight:** 16.9800 g. **Composition:** 0.9170 Gold .5000 oz. AGW **Subject:** Bronze Age Sculptures **Obverse:** State seal **Reverse:** Kneeling man lantern

Date	Mintage	F	VF	XF	Unc	BU
1993 Proof	500	Value: 300				

Y# 414 50 YUAN **Weight:** 15.5517 g. **Composition:** 0.9990 Gold .5000 oz. AGW **Subject:** Chairman Mao

Date	Mintage	F	VF	XF	Unc	BU
1993	2,500	—	—	—	425	—

Y# 445 50 YUAN **Weight:** 15.5517 g. **Composition:** 0.9990 Gold .5000 oz. AGW **Subject:** Taiwan Temples **Obverse:** Great Wall **Reverse:** Buddha statue

Date	Mintage	F	VF	XF	Unc	BU
1993 Proof	500	Value: 250				

Y# 446 50 YUAN **Weight:** 15.5517 g. **Composition:** 0.9990 Gold .5000 oz. AGW **Subject:** Taiwan Temples **Obverse:** Great Wall **Reverse:** Large temple

Date	Mintage	F	VF	XF	Unc	BU
1993 Proof	500	Value: 250				

Y# 447 50 YUAN **Weight:** 15.5517 g. **Composition:** 0.9990 Gold .5000 oz. AGW **Subject:** Taiwan Temples **Obverse:** Great Wall **Reverse:** Small temple

Date	Mintage	F	VF	XF	Unc	BU
1993 Proof	500	Value: 250				

Y# 448 50 YUAN **Weight:** 15.5517 g. **Composition:** 0.9990 Gold .5000 oz. AGW **Subject:** Taiwan Temples **Obverse:** Great Wall **Reverse:** Tower temple

Date	Mintage	F	VF	XF	Unc	BU
1993 Proof	500	Value: 250				

Y# 503 50 YUAN **Weight:** 15.5517 g. **Composition:** 0.9990 Gold .5000 oz. AGW **Obverse:** Great Wall **Reverse:** Goddess Kuan Yin - seated in flower

Date	Mintage	F	VF	XF	Unc	BU
1993 Proof	1,000	Value: 275				

Y# 613 50 YUAN **Weight:** 15.5517 g. **Composition:** 0.9990 Gold .5000 oz. AGW **Obverse:** Temple of Heaven **Reverse:** Pandas

Date		F	VF	XF	Unc	BU
1993		—	—	—	250	—
1993 Proof	—	Value: 300				

Y# 765 50 YUAN **Weight:** 15.5517 g. **Composition:** 0.9990 Gold .5000 oz. AGW **Subject:** Chinese Inventions and Discoveries **Obverse:** Great Wall **Reverse:** Stirrup

Date	Mintage	F	VF	XF	Unc	BU
1993 Proof	1,200	Value: 275				

Y# 766 50 YUAN **Weight:** 15.5517 g. **Composition:** 0.9990 Gold .5000 oz. AGW **Subject:** Chinese Inventions and Discoveries **Obverse:** Great Wall **Reverse:** Excavation of the Terra Cotta Army

Date	Mintage	F	VF	XF	Unc	BU
1993 Proof	1,200	Value: 275				

Y# 767 50 YUAN **Weight:** 15.5517 g. **Composition:** 0.9990 Gold .5000 oz. AGW **Subject:** Chinese Inventions and Discoveries **Obverse:** Great Wall **Reverse:** Discovery of mathematical zero

Date	Mintage	F	VF	XF	Unc	BU
1993 Proof	1,200	Value: 275				

Y# 772 50 YUAN **Weight:** 155.5518 g. **Composition:** 0.9990 Silver 5.0000 oz. ASW **Subject:** Chinese Wildlife **Obverse:** State seal **Reverse:** Brown bear and cub

Date	Mintage	F	VF	XF	Unc	BU
1993 Proof	4,500	Value: 350				

Y# 776 50 YUAN **Weight:** 155.5518 g. **Composition:** 0.9990 Silver 5.0000 oz. ASW **Obverse:** Great Wall **Reverse:** Mount Hau and river

Date	Mintage	F	VF	XF	Unc	BU
1993 Proof	8,888	Value: 275				

Y# 386 50 YUAN **Weight:** 155.5000 g. **Composition:** 0.9990 Silver 5.0000 oz. ASW **Subject:** Year of the Dog

Date	Mintage	F	VF	XF	Unc	BU
1994 Proof	1,000	Value: 225				

Y# 460 50 YUAN **Weight:** 15.5517 g. **Composition:** 0.9990 Gold .5000 oz. AGW **Subject:** Children At Play **Obverse:** Temple of Heaven **Reverse:** Three children with toy boat

Date	Mintage	F	VF	XF	Unc	BU
1994 Proof	1,888	Value: 250				

Y# 461 50 YUAN **Weight:** 155.5000 g. **Composition:** 0.9990 Silver 5.0000 oz. ASW **Subject:** Children At Play **Obverse:** Temple of Heaven **Reverse:** Two children with cat

Date	Mintage	F	VF	XF	Unc	BU
1994 Proof	500	Value: 375				

Y# 621 50 YUAN **Weight:** 15.5517 g. **Composition:** 0.9990 Gold .5000 oz. AGW **Subject:** Oriental Inventions **Obverse:** Great Wall **Reverse:** First tuned bells

Date	Mintage	F	VF	XF	Unc	BU
1994 Proof	1,200	Value: 275				

Y# 623 50 YUAN **Weight:** 15.5517 g. **Composition:** 0.9990 Gold .5000 oz. AGW **Subject:** Oriental Inventions - Astronomy **Obverse:** Great Wall **Reverse:** First records of comets

Date	Mintage	F	VF	XF	Unc	BU
1994 Proof	1,200	Value: 275				

Y# 625 50 YUAN **Weight:** 15.5517 g. **Composition:** 0.9990 Gold .5000 oz. AGW **Subject:** Oriental Inventions **Obverse:** Great Wall **Reverse:** First chain pumps used to draw water

Date	Mintage	F	VF	XF	Unc	BU
1994 Proof	1,200	Value: 275				

Y# 638 50 YUAN **Weight:** 155.5000 g. **Composition:** 0.9990 Silver 5.0000 oz. ASW **Obverse:** Temple of Heaven **Reverse:** Two pandas, one in tree

Date	Mintage	F	VF	XF	Unc	BU
1994 Proof	3,000	Value: 175				

Y# 708 50 YUAN **Weight:** 155.5175 g. **Composition:** 0.9990 Silver 5.0000 oz. ASW **Reverse:** Taiwan temple

Date	Mintage	F	VF	XF	Unc	BU
1994 Proof	500	Value: 250				

Y# 785 50 YUAN **Weight:** 155.5175 g. **Composition:** 0.9990 Silver 5.0000 oz. ASW **Subject:** Sino-Singapore Friendship **Obverse:** Great Wall **Reverse:** Singapore harbor view

Date	Mintage	F	VF	XF	Unc	BU
1994 Proof	300	Value: 800				

Y# 459 50 YUAN **Weight:** 15.5517 g. **Composition:** 0.9990 Gold .5000 oz. AGW **Subject:** Children At Play **Reverse:** Two children with cat **Note:** Similar to 500 Yuan, Y#462.

Date	Mintage	F	VF	XF	Unc	BU
1994 Proof	1,888	Value: 250				

Y# 624 50 YUAN **Weight:** 15.5517 g. **Composition:** 0.9990 Gold .5000 oz. AGW **Subject:** Oriental Inventions **Obverse:** Great Wall **Reverse:** First masts for sailing **Note:** Similar to 5 Yuan, Y#619.

Date	Mintage	F	VF	XF	Unc	BU
1994 Proof	1,200	Value: 275				

Y# 434 50 YUAN **Weight:** 15.5517 g. **Composition:** 0.9990 Gold .5000 oz. AGW **Obverse:** Temple of Heaven **Reverse:** Panda **Note:** Similar to 100 Yuan, Y#435.

Date	Mintage	F	VF	XF	Unc	BU
1994	35,000	—	—	—	250	—
1994 Proof	—	Value: 300				

Y# 424 50 YUAN **Weight:** 155.5000 g. **Composition:** 0.9990 Silver 5.0000 oz. ASW **Reverse:** Unicorn **Note:** Similar to 10 Yuan, Y#420.

Date	Mintage	F	VF	XF	Unc	BU
1994 Proof	1,100	Value: 150				

Y# 425 50 YUAN **Weight:** 15.5517 g. **Composition:** 0.9990 Gold .5000 oz. AGW **Note:** Similar to 10 Yuan, Y#420.

Date	Mintage	F	VF	XF	Unc	BU
1994 Proof	1,100	Value: 300				

Y# 648 50 YUAN **Weight:** 15.5517 g. **Composition:** 0.9990 Gold .5000 oz. AGW **Reverse:** Dragon boat **Note:** Similar to 10 Yuan, Y#647.

Date	Mintage	F	VF	XF	Unc	BU
1995 Proof	1,000	Value: 450				

Y# 651 50 YUAN **Weight:** 15.5517 g. **Composition:** 0.9990 Gold .5000 oz. AGW **Reverse:** Junk **Note:** Similar to 10 Yuan, Y#650.

Date	Mintage	F	VF	XF	Unc	BU
1995 Proof	1,000	Value: 450				

Y# 633 50 YUAN **Weight:** 11.3180 g. **Composition:** 0.9160 Gold .3333 oz. AGW **Subject:** Oriental Inventions **Obverse:** Great Wall **Reverse:** Individual block printing **Note:** Similar to 5 Yuan, Y#629.

Date	Mintage	F	VF	XF	Unc	BU
1995 Proof	1,200	Value: 275				

Y# 592 50 YUAN **Weight:** 1555.5175 g. **Composition:** 0.9990 Silver 5.0000 oz. ASW **Reverse:** Da Yu walking through water **Size:** 70 mm. **Note:** Illustration reduced.

Date	Mintage	F	VF	XF	Unc	BU
1995 Proof	500	Value: 325				

Y# 688 50 YUAN **Weight:** 155.5000 g. **Composition:** 0.9990 Silver 5.0000 oz. ASW **Reverse:** Unicorn with offspring **Size:** 69 mm. **Note:** Illustration reduced.

Date		F	VF	XF	Unc	BU
1995 Proof	—	Value: 150				

Y# 689 50 YUAN **Weight:** 155.5000 g. **Composition:** 0.9990 Silver 5.0000 oz. ASW **Reverse:** Junk **Size:** 70 mm. **Note:** Illustration reduced.

Date	Mintage	F	VF	XF	Unc	BU
1995 Proof	1,000	Value: 300				

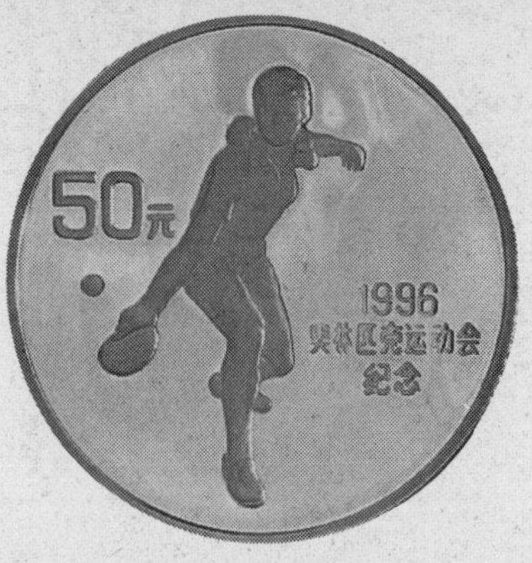

Y# 891 50 YUAN **Weight:** 155.5175 g. **Composition:** 0.9990 Silver 5.0000 oz. ASW **Series:** 1996 Summer Olympics **Obverse:** State seal **Reverse:** Table tennis player **Note:** Illustration reduced.

Date	Mintage	F	VF	XF	Unc	BU
1995 Proof	—	Value: 110				
1996 Proof	3,000	Value: 125				

Y# 464 50 YUAN **Weight:** 155.5175 g. **Composition:** 0.9990 Silver 5.0000 oz. ASW **Subject:** Year of the Pig **Obverse:** Traditional building **Reverse:** Sow and 4 piglets

Date	Mintage	F	VF	XF	Unc	BU
1995 Proof	1,000	Value: 225				

Y# 471 50 YUAN **Weight:** 15.5517 g. **Composition:** 0.9990 Gold .5000 oz. AGW **Subject:** Dinosaur **Reverse:** Brontosaurus

Date	Mintage	F	VF	XF	Unc	BU
1995 Proof	Est. 2,000	Value: 250				

Y# 488 50 YUAN **Weight:** 15.5517 g. **Composition:** 0.9990 Gold .5000 oz. AGW **Series:** 50th Anniversary - United Nations

Date	Mintage	F	VF	XF	Unc	BU
1995 Proof	8,500	Value: 275				

Y# 532 50 YUAN **Weight:** 15.5517 g. **Composition:** 0.9990 Gold .5000 oz. AGW **Subject:** Return of Hong Kong to China - Series I **Obverse:** Tiananmen building and monument **Reverse:** Deng Xiaoping's portrait above Hong Kong skyline

Date	Mintage	F	VF	XF	Unc	BU
1995 Proof	12,000	Value: 300				

Y# 573 50 YUAN **Ring Weight:** 6.2207 g. **Ring Composition:** 0.9990 Silver .2000 oz. ASW **Center Weight:** 21.7724 g. **Center Composition:** 0.9990 Gold .5000 oz. AGW **Reverse:** Panda at stream

Date	Mintage	F	VF	XF	Unc	BU
1995 Proof set	Est. 2,000	Value: 300				

Y# 593 50 YUAN **Weight:** 15.5517 g. **Composition:** 0.9990 Gold .5000 oz. AGW **Reverse:** Nu Wa Rising

Date	Mintage	F	VF	XF	Unc	BU
1995 Proof	2,500	Value: 350				

Y# 632 50 YUAN **Weight:** 11.3180 g. **Composition:** 0.9160 Gold .3333 oz. AGW **Subject:** Oriental Inventions **Obverse:** Great Wall **Reverse:** Soldiers with cannon and gunpowder

Date	Mintage	F	VF	XF	Unc	BU
1995 Proof	1,200	Value: 275				

Y# 636 50 YUAN **Weight:** 11.3180 g. **Composition:** 0.9160 Gold .3333 oz. AGW **Subject:** Oriental Inventions **Obverse:** Great Wall **Reverse:** Teacher with anatomy chart of human body

Date	Mintage	F	VF	XF	Unc	BU
1995 Proof	1,200	Value: 275				

Y# 643 50 YUAN **Weight:** 15.5517 g. **Composition:** 0.9990 Gold .5000 oz. AGW **Obverse:** Temple of Heaven **Reverse:** Panda eating bamboo

Date	F	VF	XF	Unc	BU
1995	—	—	—	250	—

Y# 645 50 YUAN **Weight:** 155.5000 g. **Composition:** 0.9990 Silver 5.0000 oz. ASW **Obverse:** Temple of Heaven **Reverse:** Two pandas on river bank

Date	Mintage	F	VF	XF	Unc	BU
1995 Proof	3,000	Value: 175				

Y# 690 50 YUAN **Weight:** 155.5517 g. **Composition:** 0.9990 Gold .5000 oz. AGW **Subject:** 50th Anniversary - Anti-Japanese War **Obverse:** State seal **Reverse:** Zhou and Mao above soldiers

Date	Mintage	F	VF	XF	Unc	BU
1995 Proof	2,500	Value: 300				

Y# 691 50 YUAN **Ring Weight:** 5.1800 g. **Ring Composition:** 0.9990 Silver .1667 oz. ASW **Center Weight:** 10.3600 g. **Center Composition:** 0.9990 Gold .3335 oz. AGW **Subject:** World Women's Conference

Date	Mintage	F	VF	XF	Unc	BU
1995 Proof	3,000	Value: 250				

Y# 739 50 YUAN **Weight:** 15.5517 g. **Composition:** 0.9990 Gold .5000 oz. AGW **Obverse:** Eastern unicorn **Reverse:** Western unicorn with offspring

Date	Mintage	F	VF	XF	Unc	BU
1995 Proof	2,000	Value: 300				

Y# 739a 50 YUAN **Weight:** 15.5517 g. **Composition:** 0.9995 Platinum .5000 oz. APW **Subject:** Unicorn **Obverse:** Eastern unicorn. **Reverse:** Western unicorn with offspring. **Edge:** Reeded. **Size:** 26.8 mm.

Date	F	VF	XF	Unc	BU
1995 Proof					

Y# 789 50 YUAN **Ring Weight:** 6.2207 g. **Ring Composition:** 0.9990 Silver .2000 oz. ASW **Center Weight:** 15.5517 g. **Center Composition:** 9990.0000 Gold .5000 oz. AGW **Obverse:** Temple of Heaven **Reverse:** Panda approaching water from right

Date	F	VF	XF	Unc	BU
1995 Proof only	—	—	—	300	—

Y# 813 50 YUAN **Weight:** 155.5175 g. **Composition:** 0.9990 Silver 5.000 oz. ASW **Subject:** 50th Anniversary - For the return of Taiwan to China **Obverse:** Great Wall **Reverse:** Taiwan and China maps

Date	Mintage	F	VF	XF	Unc	BU
1995 Proof	999	Value: 575				

Y# 814 50 YUAN **Weight:** 15.5517 g. **Composition:** 0.9990 Gold .5000 oz. AGW **Subject:** 50th Anniversary - For the return of Taiwan to China **Obverse:** Great Wall **Reverse:** Taiwan and China maps

Date	Mintage	F	VF	XF	Unc	BU
1995 Proof	3,000	Value: 250				

Y# 815 50 YUAN **Weight:** 15.5517 g. **Composition:** 0.9990 Gold .5000 oz. AGW **Subject:** 50th Anniversary - For the return of Taiwan to China **Obverse:** Great Wall **Reverse:** Zhongshan Hall

Date	Mintage	F	VF	XF	Unc	BU
1995 Proof	3,000	Value: 250				

Y# 821 50 YUAN **Weight:** 7.9020 g. **Composition:** 0.9160 Gold .2327 oz. AGW **Obverse:** Bust of painter Xu Beihong **Reverse:** Lion

Date	Mintage	F	VF	XF	Unc	BU
1995 Proof	3,000	Value: 150				

Y# 822 50 YUAN **Weight:** 155.5175 g. **Composition:** 0.9990 Silver 5.0000 oz. ASW **Obverse:** Chiqian building **Reverse:** Zheng Chenggong standing with flag and ships

Date	Mintage	F	VF	XF	Unc	BU
1995 Proof	250	Value: 475				

Y# 829 50 YUAN **Weight:** 155.5175 g. **Composition:** 0.9990 Silver 5.0000 oz. ASW **Subject:** Three Shu Han Heroes **Obverse:** Luo Guanzhong **Reverse:** Three figures

Date	Mintage	F	VF	XF	Unc	BU
1995 Proof	7,000	Value: 475				

Y# 829a 50 YUAN **Weight:** 155.5517 g. **Composition:** 0.9990 Gold .5000 oz. AGW

Date	Mintage	F	VF	XF	Unc	BU
1995 Proof	2,000	Value: 275				

Y# 838 50 YUAN **Weight:** 10.3678 g. **Composition:** 0.9990 Gold .3333 oz. AGW **Subject:** Table Tennis **Obverse:** Tianjing Stadium **Reverse:** Table tennis player

Date	Mintage	F	VF	XF	Unc	BU
1995 Proof	2,000	Value: 250				

Y# 577 50 YUAN **Weight:** 15.5517 g. **Composition:** 0.9990 Gold .5000 oz. AGW **Reverse:** Panda in tree

Date	F	VF	XF	Unc	BU
1996	—	—	—	250	—

Y# 599 50 YUAN **Weight:** 15.5517 g. **Composition:** 0.9990 Gold .5000 oz. AGW **Obverse:** Yangtze River scene **Reverse:** Large dam **Shape:** Rectangular

Date	Mintage	F	VF	XF	Unc	BU
1996 Proof	6,000	Value: 350				

Y# 608 50 YUAN **Weight:** 11.3180 g. **Composition:** 0.9160 Gold .3333 oz. AGW **Reverse:** Man riding camel

Date	Mintage	F	VF	XF	Unc	BU
1996 Proof	Est. 10,000	Value: 200				

Y# 609 50 YUAN **Weight:** 11.3180 g. **Composition:** 0.9160 Gold .3333 oz. AGW **Reverse:** Water vendor

Date	Mintage	F	VF	XF	Unc	BU
1996 Proof	10,000	Value: 200				

Y# 853 50 YUAN **Ring Weight:** 6.2207 g. **Ring Composition:** 0.9990 Silver .2000 oz. ASW **Center Weight:** 15.5517 g. **Center Composition:** 0.9990 Gold .5000 oz. AGW **Obverse:** Temple of Heaven **Reverse:** Panda seated on rock

Date	Mintage	F	VF	XF	Unc	BU
1996 Proof	2,500	Value: 325				

Y# 855 50 YUAN **Weight:** 155.5175 g. **Composition:** 0.9990 Silver 5.0000 oz. ASW **Subject:** Year of the Rat **Obverse:** Dengdu Pavilion **Reverse:** Rat and grapes

Date	Mintage	F	VF	XF	Unc	BU
1996 Proof	1,000	Value: 240				

Y# 859 50 YUAN **Weight:** 155.5517 g. **Composition:** 0.9990 Gold .5000 oz. AGW **Obverse:** Building **Reverse:** Sun Yat-sen bust facing, fan sprays

Date	Mintage	F	VF	XF	Unc	BU
1996 Proof	3,000	Value: 300				

Y# 870 50 YUAN **Weight:** 155.5517 g. **Composition:** 0.9990 Gold .5000 oz. AGW **Subject:** 60th Anniversary - Long March **Obverse:** Flag above building **Reverse:** Chairman Mao portrait

Date	Mintage	F	VF	XF	Unc	BU
1996 Proof	6,000	Value: 275				

Y# 881 50 YUAN **Weight:** 15.5517 g. **Composition:** 0.9990 Gold .5000 oz. AGW **Subject:** Romance of the Three Kingdoms Series **Obverse:** Luo Guanzhong portrait **Reverse:** Guand Du leading his troops

Date	Mintage	F	VF	XF	Unc	BU
1996 Proof	2,000	Value: 225				

Y# 658 50 YUAN **Weight:** 15.5517 g. **Composition:** 0.9990 Gold .5000 oz. AGW **Subject:** Return of Hong Kong to China Series II **Obverse:** Hong Kong Harbor

Date	F	VF	XF	Unc	BU
1996 Proof	—	Value: 275			

Y# 1039 50 YUAN **Weight:** 15.5517 g. **Composition:** 0.9990 Gold .5000 oz. AGW **Subject:** Unicorn **Obverse:** Eastern unicorn, full body. **Reverse:** Western unicorn in wreath. **Edge:** Reeded. **Size:** 27 mm.

Date	F	VF	XF	Unc	BU
1996 Proof	—	Value: 275			

Y# 1038 50 YUAN **Weight:** 155.5175 g. **Composition:** 0.9990 Silver 5.0000 oz. ASW **Subject:** Unicorn **Obverse:** Eastern unicorn, full body. **Reverse:** Western unicorn with maiden. **Edge:** Reeded. **Size:** 70.2 mm. **Note:** Illustration reduced.

Date	F	VF	XF	Unc	BU
1996 Proof	—	Value: 325			

Y# 1091 50 YUAN **Weight:** 15.5518 g. **Composition:** 0.9990 Gold 0.4995 oz. AGW **Subject:** Unicorns **Obverse:** Eastern unicorn. **Reverse:** Western unicorn. **Edge:** Reeded. **Size:** 27 mm.

Date	Mintage	F	VF	XF	Unc	BU
1996 Proof	1,000	Value: 400				

Y# 880 50 YUAN **Weight:** 155.5175 g. **Composition:** 0.9990 Silver 5.0000 oz. ASW **Subject:** Romance of the Three Kingdoms Series **Obverse:** Bust of Luo Guanzhong **Reverse:** Battle scene **Size:** 80 mm. **Note:** Illustration reduced.

Date	Mintage	F	VF	XF	Unc	BU
1996 Proof	500	Value: 325				

Y# 897 50 YUAN **Weight:** 155.5175 g. **Composition:** 0.9990 Silver 5.0000 oz. ASW **Subject:** Year of the Ox **Obverse:** Mingyuan Pavilion **Reverse:** Bull **Size:** 80 mm. **Note:** Illustration reduced.

Date	Mintage	F	VF	XF	Unc	BU
1997 Proof	1,000	Value: 300				

Y# 906 50 YUAN **Weight:** 155.5175 g. **Composition:** 0.9990 Silver 5.0000 oz. ASW **Subject:** Return of Macao to China **Obverse:** Tiananmen Square - Forbidden City **Reverse:** Deng Xiaoping viewing Macao **Size:** 80 mm. **Note:** Illustration reduced.

Date	F	VF	XF	Unc	BU
1997 Proof	—	Value: 200			

Y# 719 50 YUAN **Weight:** 15.5517 g. **Composition:** 0.9990 Gold .5000 oz. AGW **Reverse:** Panda on large tree branch **Note:** Similar to 100 Yuan, Y#720.

Date	F	VF	XF	Unc	BU
1997	—	—	—	225	—

Note: Exists in large and small date varieties

Y# 903 50 YUAN **Weight:** 15.5517 g. **Composition:** 0.9990 Gold .5000 oz. AGW **Subject:** Return of Hong Kong to China - Series III **Obverse:** Tiananmen Square - Forbidden City **Reverse:** Flag and fireworks above Hong Kong

Date	Mintage	F	VF	XF	Unc	BU
1997 Proof	12,000	Value: 250				

Y# 1004 50 YUAN **Weight:** 15.5517 g. **Composition:** 0.9990 Gold .5000 oz. AGW **Subject:** Huang (Yellow) River Culture **Obverse:** Archer **Reverse:** Dragon

Date	Mintage	F	VF	XF	Unc	BU
1997 Proof	3,000	Value: 250				

Y# 906a 50 YUAN **Weight:** 155.5517 g. **Composition:** 0.9990 Gold .5000 oz. AGW

Date	Mintage	F	VF	XF	Unc	BU
1997 Proof	5,000	Value: 325				

Y# 910 50 YUAN **Weight:** 155.5517 g. **Composition:** 0.9990 Gold .5000 oz. AGW **Subject:** People's Liberation Army **Obverse:** Radiant star above Great Wall **Reverse:** Youthful Chairman Mao standing

Date	Mintage	F	VF	XF	Unc	BU
1997 Proof	12,000	Value: 250				

Y# 918 50 YUAN **Weight:** 155.5175 g. **Composition:** 0.9990 Silver 5.0000 oz. ASW **Subject:** Traditional Chinese Mascot **Obverse:** Ornamental column **Reverse:** Child holding carp

Date	Mintage	F	VF	XF	Unc	BU
1997 Proof	3,800	Value: 120				

Y# 1009 50 YUAN **Ring Weight:** 6.2207 g. **Ring Composition:** 0.9990 Silver .2000 oz. ASW **Center Weight:** 15.5517 g. **Center Composition:** 0.9990 Gold .5000 oz. AGW **Reverse:** Panda climbing tree

Date	Mintage	F	VF	XF	Unc	BU
1997 Proof	2,800	Value: 325				

Y# 921 50 YUAN **Weight:** 15.5517 g. **Composition:** 0.9990 Gold .50000 oz. AGW **Subject:** Chinese Wildlife **Obverse:** State seal **Reverse:** Two white dolphins

Date	Mintage	F	VF	XF	Unc	BU
1997 Proof	30,000	Value: 225				

Y# 1005 50 YUAN **Weight:** 15.5517 g. **Composition:** 0.9990 Gold .50000 oz. AGW **Obverse:** Portrait of Qi Bashi **Reverse:** Squirrels eating grapes **Shape:** Rectangular

Date	Mintage	F	VF	XF	Unc	BU
1997 Proof	5,000	Value: 375				

Y# 927 50 YUAN **Weight:** 155.5175 g. **Composition:** 0.9990 Silver 5.0000 oz. ASW **Subject:** Year of the Tiger **Obverse:** Badaling building **Reverse:** Tiger

Date	Mintage	F	VF	XF	Unc	BU
1998 Proof	1,000	Value: 300				

Y# 1007 50 YUAN **Weight:** 15.5517 g. **Composition:** 0.9990 Gold .5000 oz. AGW **Subject:** Zhou Enlai

Date	Mintage	F	VF	XF	Unc	BU
1998 Proof	8,000	Value: 300				

Y# 1010 50 YUAN **Weight:** 15.5517 g. **Composition:** 0.9990 Gold .5000 oz. AGW **Obverse:** Temple of Heaven **Reverse:** Panda seated on rock

Date	F	VF	XF	Unc	BU
1998	—	—	—	175	—

Note: Exists in large and small date varieties

Y# 1011 50 YUAN **Weight:** 15.5517 g. **Composition:** 0.9990 Gold .5000 oz. AGW **Obverse:** Temple of Heaven **Reverse:** Panda on ledge

Date	F	VF	XF	Unc	BU
1999	—	—	—	175	—

Note: Exists in large and small date varieties

Y# 1008 50 YUAN **Weight:** 15.5517 g. **Composition:** 0.9990 Gold .5000 oz. AGW **Subject:** 50th Anniversary of Peoples Republic

Date	Mintage	F	VF	XF	Unc	BU
1999 Proof	22,000	Value: 300				

Y# 1044 50 YUAN **Weight:** 15.5518 g. **Composition:** 0.9990 Gold .5000 oz. AGW **Subject:** Year of the Snake

Date	Mintage	F	VF	XF	Unc	BU
2000	6,600	—	—	—	285	—

Y# 1049 50 YUAN **Weight:** 155.5175 g. **Composition:** 0.9990 Silver 5.0000 oz. ASW **Reverse:** Dragons **Shape:** Rectangle

Date	Mintage	F	VF	XF	Unc	BU
2000 Proof	1,888	Value: 325				

Y# 948 50 YUAN **Weight:** 15.5518 g. **Composition:** 0.9990 Gold .5000 oz. AGW **Obverse:** Temple of Heaven **Reverse:** Panda seated on leaves **Note:** Similar to 100 Yuan, Y#949.

Date	F	VF	XF	Unc	BU
2000 Proof	—	Value: 215			

Note: Domestic Chinese examples struck with mirror fields, overseas examples struck with frosted fields

Y# 1006 50 YUAN **Weight:** 15.5518 g. **Composition:** 0.9990 Gold .5000 oz. AGW **Subject:** Year of the Dragon **Note:** Fan shape.

Date	Mintage	F	VF	XF	Unc	BU
2000	6,600	—	—	—	350	—

Y# 1050 50 YUAN **Weight:** 15.5518 g. **Composition:** 0.9990 Gold .5000 oz. AGW **Reverse:** Dragons **Note:** Fan shape.

Date	Mintage	F	VF	XF	Unc	BU
2000	6,600	—	—	—	350	—

Y# 1040 50 YUAN **Weight:** 155.4400 g. **Composition:** 0.9990 Silver 4.9925 oz. ASW **Subject:** Year of the Snake

Obverse: Traditional style building. **Reverse:** Snake. **Edge:** Plain. **Size:** 80.6 x 50.5 mm. **Note:** Illustration reduced.

Date	Mintage	F	VF	XF	Unc	BU
2001 Proof	1,888,000	Value: 235				

Y# 1083 50 YUAN **Weight:** 155.5175 g. **Composition:** 0.9990 Silver 4.995 oz. ASW **Subject:** Mogao Grottoes **Obverse:** Eight story building. **Reverse:** Four musicians. **Edge:** Reeded. **Size:** 70 mm.

Date	Mintage	F	VF	XF	Unc	BU
2001 Proof	8,000	Value: 200				

Y# 1084 50 YUAN **Weight:** 3.1104 g. **Composition:** 0.9990 Gold 0.0999 oz. AGW **Subject:** Mogao Grottoes **Obverse:** Eight story building. **Reverse:** Buddha-like statue. **Edge:** Reeded.

Date	Mintage	F	VF	XF	Unc	BU
2001 Proof	50,000	Value: 75.00				

Y# 1104 50 YUAN **Weight:** 155.5175 g. **Composition:** 0.9990 Silver 4.995 oz. ASW **Subject:** Han Xizai's Dinner Party **Obverse:** Tang dynasty buildings **Reverse:** Multicolor "Five Dynasties" painting **Edge:** Plain **Shape:** Rectangular **Note:** Illustration reduced. Actual size: 90x40mm.

Date	Mintage	F	VF	XF	Unc	BU
2001 Proof	18,800	Value: 175				

Y# 52 100 YUAN **Weight:** 31.1320 g. **Composition:** 0.9990 Gold 1.0000 oz. AGW **Obverse:** Temple of Heaven **Reverse:** Panda half right

Date	Mintage	F	VF	XF	Unc	BU
1983	22,000	—	—	—	500	—

Y# 56 100 YUAN **Weight:** 11.0000 g. **Composition:** 0.9000 Gold .3183 oz. AGW **Reverse:** Marco Polo

Date	Mintage	F	VF	XF	Unc	BU
1983 Proof	1,030	Value: 700				

Y# 72 100 YUAN **Weight:** 11.3180 g. **Composition:** 0.9170 Gold .3337 oz. AGW **Reverse:** Emperor Huang Di

Date	Mintage	F	VF	XF	Unc	BU
1984 Proof	10,000	Value: 210				

Y# 77 100 YUAN **Weight:** 31.1320 g. **Composition:** 0.9990 Gold 1.0000 oz. AGW **Reverse:** Seated panda holding bamboo sprig

Date	Mintage	F	VF	XF	Unc	BU
1984	23,000	—	—	—	450	—

Y# 84 100 YUAN **Weight:** 31.1320 g. **Composition:** 0.9990 Gold 1.0000 oz. AGW

Date	Mintage	F	VF	XF	Unc	BU
1985	164,000	—	—	—	375	—

Y# 94 100 YUAN **Weight:** 11.3180 g. **Composition:** 0.9170 Gold .3337 oz. AGW **Subject:** Founders of Chinese Culture **Reverse:** Confucius

Date	Mintage	F	VF	XF	Unc	BU
1985 Proof	7,000	Value: 250				

Y# 105 100 YUAN **Weight:** 31.1320 g. **Composition:** 0.9990 Gold 1.0000 oz. AGW **Reverse:** Pand amongst bamboo plants

Date	Mintage	F	VF	XF	Unc	BU
1986	97,000	—	—	—	375	—
1986 P Proof	10,000	Value: 400				

Y# 107 100 YUAN **Weight:** 11.3180 g. **Composition:** 0.9170 Gold .3337 oz. AGW **Subject:** Wildlife **Reverse:** Wild Yak

Date	Mintage	F	VF	XF	Unc	BU
1986 Proof	3,000	Value: 275				

Y# 117 100 YUAN **Weight:** 11.3180 g. **Composition:** 0.9170 Gold .3337 oz. AGW **Subject:** Chinese Culture **Reverse:** Revolutionary Soldier, Liu Bang

Date	Mintage	F	VF	XF	Unc	BU
1986 Proof	7,000	Value: 210				

Y# 120 100 YUAN **Weight:** 11.3180 g. **Composition:** 0.9170 Gold .3337 oz. AGW **Subject:** Year of Peace **Reverse:** Statue of seated female **Note:** Similar to 5 Yuan, Y#119.

Date	Mintage	F	VF	XF	Unc	BU
1986 Proof	—	Value: 475				

Y# 131 100 YUAN **Weight:** 373.2360 g. **Composition:** 0.9990 Silver 12.0000 oz. ASW **Subject:** 125th Anniversary - Birth of Zhan Tianyou **Obverse:** State seal **Reverse:** Bust of Zhan Tianyou facing above steam locomotive crossing bridge **Size:** 80 mm. **Note:** Illustration reduced.

Date	Mintage	F	VF	XF	Unc	BU
1987 Proof	2,911	Value: 250				

Y# 158 100 YUAN **Weight:** 31.1030 g. **Composition:** 0.9995 Platinum 1.0000 oz. APW **Note:** Similar to 100 Yuan, Y#128.

Date	Mintage	F	VF	XF	Unc	BU
1987 Proof	2,000	—	—	—	—	—

Y# 128 100 YUAN **Weight:** 31.1320 g. **Composition:** 0.9990 Gold 1.0000 oz. AGW **Reverse:** Panda drinking at stream

Date	Mintage	F	VF	XF	Unc	BU
1987(s)	84,000	—	—	—	375	—
1987(y)	47,000	—	—	—	375	—
1987 P Proof	10,000	Value: 400				

Y# 139 100 YUAN **Weight:** 11.3180 g. **Composition:** 0.9170 Gold .3337 oz. AGW **Obverse:** State seal **Reverse:** Emperor Li Shih on horseback

Date	Mintage	F	VF	XF	Unc	BU
1987 Proof	7,000	Value: 210				

Y# 156 100 YUAN **Weight:** 31.1320 g. **Composition:** 0.9990 Gold 1.0000 oz. AGW **Reverse:** Panda pawing bamboo

Date	Mintage	F	VF	XF	Unc	BU
1988	167,000	—	—	—	375	—
1988 Proof	10,000	Value: 400				

Y# 164 100 YUAN **Weight:** 11.3180 g. **Composition:** 0.9170 Gold .3337 oz. AGW **Reverse:** Emperor Zhao Kuangyin

Date	Mintage	F	VF	XF	Unc	BU
1988 Proof	Est. 7,000	Value: 275				

Y# 167 100 YUAN **Weight:** 8.0000 g. **Composition:** 0.9170 Gold .2359 oz. AGW **Subject:** Rare Animal Protection **Reverse:** Golden Monkey

Date	Mintage	F	VF	XF	Unc	BU
1988 Proof	29,000	Value: 175				

Y# 173 100 YUAN **Weight:** 15.5500 g. **Composition:** 0.9990 Gold .5000 oz. AGW **Series:** Olympics **Reverse:** Sword dancer

Date	Mintage	F	VF	XF	Unc	BU
1988 Proof	5,500	Value: 250				

Y# 175 100 YUAN **Weight:** 31.1320 g. **Composition:** 0.9990 Gold 1.0000 oz. AGW **Subject:** Year of the Dragon **Obverse:** Temple of Heaven **Reverse:** 2 floating dragons

Date	Mintage	F	VF	XF	Unc	BU
1988 Proof	10,000	Value: 475				

Y# 159 100 YUAN **Weight:** 31.1030 g. **Composition:** 0.9995 Platinum 1.0000 oz. APW **Obverse:** Temple of Heaven **Reverse:** Panda grasping bamboo shoot **Note:** Similar to 100 Yuan, Y#156.

Date	Mintage	F	VF	XF	Unc	BU
1988 Proof	2,000	—	—	—	—	—

Note: Value is determined at current bullion value + 20%

Y# 176 100 YUAN **Weight:** 31.1030 g. **Composition:** 0.9995 Platinum 1.0000 oz. APW **Subject:** Year of the Dragon **Obverse:** Temple of Heaven **Reverse:** 2 floating dragons

Date	Mintage	F	VF	XF	Unc	BU
1988 Proof	2,000	—	—	—	—	—

Note: Value is determined at current bullion value + 20%

Y# 143 100 YUAN **Weight:** 373.2360 g. **Composition:** 0.9990 Silver 12.0000 oz. ASW **Subject:** Year of the Dragon **Obverse:** Similar to 10 Yuan, Y#141 **Reverse:** Two dragons facing **Size:** 80 mm. **Note:** Illustration reduced.

Date	Mintage	F	VF	XF	Unc	BU
1988 Proof	3,000	Value: 450				

Y# 169 100 YUAN **Weight:** 373.2360 g. **Composition:** 0.9990 Silver 12.0000 oz. ASW **Obverse:** Temple of Heaven **Reverse:** Two pandas in tree **Size:** 70 mm. **Note:** Illustration reduced.

Date	Mintage	F	VF	XF	Unc	BU
1988 Proof	5,000	Value: 190				

Y# 179 100 YUAN **Weight:** 373.2360 g. **Composition:** 0.9990 Silver 12.0000 oz. ASW **Subject:** Year of the Snake **Obverse:** Shanhaiguan Pass Gate, similar to 10 Yuan, Y#177 **Note:** Illustration reduced.

Date	Mintage	F	VF	XF	Unc	BU
1989 Proof	400	Value: 800				

Y# 185 100 YUAN **Weight:** 31.1030 g. **Composition:** 0.9995 Platinum 1.0000 oz. APW **Subject:** Year of the Snake **Obverse:** State seal

Date	Mintage	F	VF	XF	Unc	BU
1989 Proof	1,000	—	—	—	—	—

Note: Value is determined at current bullion value + 20%

Y# 184 100 YUAN **Weight:** 31.1320 g. **Composition:** 0.9990 Gold 1.0000 oz. AGW **Subject:** Year of the Snake **Obverse:** State seal

Date	Mintage	F	VF	XF	Unc	BU
1989 Proof	3,000	Value: 475				

Y# 191 100 YUAN **Weight:** 31.1320 g. **Composition:** 0.9990 Gold 1.0000 oz. AGW **Obverse:** Temple of Heaven **Reverse:** Panda reclining, grid behind

Date	F	VF	XF	Unc	BU
1989	—	—	—	400	—
1989 Proof	—	Value: 425			

Y# 191a 100 YUAN **Weight:** 31.1030 g. **Composition:** 0.9995 Platinum 1.0000 oz. APW **Obverse:** Temple of Heaven **Reverse:** Panda reclining, grid behind

Date	Mintage	F	VF	XF	Unc	BU
1989 Proof	5,000	—	—	—	—	—

Note: Value is determined at current bullion value + 20%

Y# 203 100 YUAN **Weight:** 8.0000 g. **Composition:** 0.9170 Gold .2359 oz. AGW **Subject:** 1990 Asian Games **Obverse:** Stadium **Reverse:** Ribbon dancer

Date	Mintage	F	VF	XF	Unc	BU
1989 Proof	Est. 7,000	Value: 125				

Y# 217 100 YUAN **Weight:** 11.3180 g. **Composition:** 0.9170 Gold .3337 oz. AGW **Obverse:** State seal **Reverse:** Genghis Khan on horseback

Date	Mintage	F	VF	XF	Unc	BU
1989 Proof	Est. 7,000	Value: 250				

Y# 219 100 YUAN **Weight:** 373.2360 g. **Composition:** 0.9990 Silver 12.0000 oz. ASW **Obverse:** Temple of Heaven **Reverse:** Panda with two cubs

Date	Mintage	F	VF	XF	Unc	BU
1989 Proof	3,670	Value: 200				

Y# 231 100 YUAN Weight: 11.3180 g. **Composition:** 0.9170 Gold .3337 oz. AGW **Series:** Save the Children Fund **Obverse:** State seal **Reverse:** Child running flying kites

Date	Mintage	F	VF	XF	Unc	BU
1989 Proof	5,000	Value: 200				

Y# 250 100 YUAN Weight: 8.0000 g. **Composition:** 0.9170 Gold .2359 oz. AGW **Series:** Endangered Animals **Obverse:** State seal **Reverse:** Chinese tiger

Date	Mintage	F	VF	XF	Unc	BU
1989 Proof	14,000	Value: 150				

Y# 299 100 YUAN Weight: 7.7750 g. **Composition:** 0.9990 Gold .2500 oz. AGW **Subject:** 40th Anniversary of Peoples Republic **Obverse:** State seal **Reverse:** Pair of flying cranes

Date	Mintage	F	VF	XF	Unc	BU
1989 Proof	1,000	Value: 250				

Y# 225 100 YUAN Weight: 31.1320 g. **Composition:** 0.9990 Gold 1.0000 oz. AGW **Subject:** Year of the Horse **Obverse:** State seal **Reverse:** Prancing horse

Date	Mintage	F	VF	XF	Unc	BU
1990 Proof	6,000	Value: 450				

Y# 242 100 YUAN Weight: 31.1320 g. **Composition:** 0.9990 Gold 1.0000 oz. AGW **Obverse:** Temple of Heaven **Reverse:** Panda climbing rock

Date	Mintage	F	VF	XF	Unc	BU
1990	5,000	—	—	—	425	—
1990 Proof	—	Value: 475				

Y# 256 100 YUAN Weight: 8.0000 g. **Composition:** 0.9170 Gold .2359 oz. AGW **Subject:** XI Asian Games **Obverse:** Stadium **Reverse:** Swimmer

Date	Mintage	F	VF	XF	Unc	BU
1990 Proof	10,000	Value: 125				

Y# 263 100 YUAN Weight: 373.2360 g. **Composition:** 0.9990 Silver 12.0000 oz. ASW **Obverse:** Temple of Heaven **Reverse:** Three curious pandas

Date	Mintage	F	VF	XF	Unc	BU
1990 Proof	2,500	Value: 225				

Y# 287 100 YUAN Weight: 10.3700 g. **Composition:** 0.9170 Gold .3054 oz. AGW **Obverse:** State seal **Reverse:** First emperor, Huang Di standing

Date	Mintage	F	VF	XF	Unc	BU
1990 Proof	20,000	Value: 250				

Y# 306 100 YUAN Weight: 11.3180 g. **Composition:** 0.9170 Gold .3333 oz. AGW **Obverse:** State seal **Reverse:** Emperor Zhu Yuanzhang seated

Date	F	VF	XF	Unc	BU
1990	—	—	—	275	—

Y# 327 100 YUAN Weight: 11.3180 g. **Composition:** 0.9170 Gold .3333 oz. AGW **Series:** 1990 Summer Olympics **Obverse:** State seal **Reverse:** Women playing basketball

Date	Mintage	F	VF	XF	Unc	BU
1990	10,000	—	—	—	175	—

Y# 735 100 YUAN Weight: 31.1400 g. **Composition:** 0.9995 Platinum 1.0077 oz. APW **Obverse:** Temple of Heaven **Reverse:** Panda on rock

Date	Mintage	F	VF	XF	Unc	BU
1990 Proof	778	Value: 750				

Y# 225a 100 YUAN Weight: 31.1030 g. **Composition:** 0.9995 Platinum 1.0000 oz. APW **Subject:** Year of the Horse **Obverse:** State seal **Reverse:** Prancing horse

Date	Mintage	F	VF	XF	Unc	BU
1990 Proof	2,000	—	—	—	—	—

Note: Value is determined at current bullion value + 20%

Y# 224 100 YUAN Weight: 373.2360 g. **Composition:** 0.9990 Silver 12.0000 oz. ASW **Subject:** Year of the Horse **Obverse:** Temple of Confucius **Size:** 80 mm. **Note:** Illustration reduced.

Date	Mintage	F	VF	XF	Unc	BU
1990 Proof	1,000	Value: 375				

Y# 273 100 YUAN Weight: 373.2360 g. **Composition:** 0.9990 Silver 12.0000 oz. ASW **Subject:** Year of the Goat **Reverse:** Two goats **Size:** 80 mm. **Note:** Illustration reduced.

Date	Mintage	F	VF	XF	Unc	BU
1991 Proof	1,000	Value: 375				

Y# 274 100 YUAN Weight: 31.1320 g. **Composition:** 0.9990 Gold 1.0000 oz. AGW **Subject:** Year of the Goat **Obverse:** State seal **Reverse:** Two goats butting

Date	Mintage	F	VF	XF	Unc	BU
1991 Proof	1,800	Value: 1,000				

Y# 274a 100 YUAN **Weight:** 31.1030 g. **Composition:** 0.9995 Platinum 1.0000 oz. APW **Subject:** Year of the Goat **Obverse:** State seal **Reverse:** Two goats butting heads

Date	Mintage	F	VF	XF	Unc	BU
1991 Proof	500	Value: 1,100				

Y# 313 100 YUAN **Weight:** 31.1320 g. **Composition:** 0.9990 Gold 1.0000 oz. AGW **Obverse:** Temple of Heaven **Reverse:** Panda with hind feet in water eating bamboo

Date		F	VF	XF	Unc	BU
1991		—	—	—	475	—
1991 Proof	—	Value: 550				

Y# 320 100 YUAN **Weight:** 8.0000 g. **Composition:** 0.9160 Gold .2357 oz. AGW **Subject:** Women's Soccer **Obverse:** Stadium **Reverse:** Woman kicking ball

Date	Mintage	F	VF	XF	Unc	BU
1991 Proof	1,400	Value: 150				

Y# 326 100 YUAN **Weight:** 8.0000 g. **Composition:** 0.9160 Gold .2357 oz. AGW **Subject:** Emperor Kang Xi **Obverse:** State seal

Date	Mintage	F	VF	XF	Unc	BU
1991 Proof	Est. 7,000	Value: 275				

Y# 375 100 YUAN **Weight:** 373.2360 g. **Composition:** 0.9990 Silver 12.0000 oz. ASW **Obverse:** Temple of Heaven **Reverse:** Pandas

Date	Mintage	F	VF	XF	Unc	BU
1991 Proof	Est. 2,500	Value: 250				

Y# 473 100 YUAN **Weight:** 11.3180 g. **Composition:** 0.9170 Gold .3334 oz. AGW **Series:** 1992 Olympics **Obverse:** State seal **Reverse:** Pairs figure skating

Date	Mintage	F	VF	XF	Unc	BU
1991 Proof	10,000	Value: 175				

Y# 478 100 YUAN **Weight:** 8.6000 g. **Composition:** 0.9170 Gold .2533 oz. AGW **Subject:** 80th Anniversary - 1911 Revolution **Obverse:** Building **Reverse:** Sun Yat-sen writing

Date	Mintage	F	VF	XF	Unc	BU
1991 Proof	2,500	Value: 285				

Y# 479 100 YUAN **Weight:** 31.1035 g. **Composition:** 0.9990 Gold 1.0000 oz. AGW **Obverse:** Building **Reverse:** Sun Yat-sen in uniform

Date	Mintage	F	VF	XF	Unc	BU
ND(1991) Proof	1,000	Value: 800				

Y# 545 100 YUAN **Weight:** 11.3180 g. **Composition:** 0.9170 Gold .3337 oz. AGW **Reverse:** Emperor Yan Di

Date		F	VF	XF	Unc	BU
1991 Proof	—	Value: 285				

Y# 295 100 YUAN **Weight:** 31.1035 g. **Composition:** 0.9990 Gold 1.0000 oz. AGW **Subject:** Year of the Monkey **Reverse:** Monkey seated on branch

Date	Mintage	F	VF	XF	Unc	BU
1992 Proof	1,800	Value: 900				

Y# 295a 100 YUAN **Weight:** 31.1030 g. **Composition:** 0.9995 Platinum 1.0000 oz. APW **Subject:** Year of the Monkey **Reverse:** Monkey seated on branch

Date	Mintage	F	VF	XF	Unc	BU
1992 Proof	300	Value: 950				

Y# 336 100 YUAN **Weight:** 31.1035 g. **Composition:** 0.9990 Gold 1.0000 oz. AGW **Subject:** Chinese inventions **Obverse:** Great Wall **Reverse:** Ancient ships and shipbuilding

Date	Mintage	F	VF	XF	Unc	BU
1992 Proof	1,000	Value: 500				

Y# 337 100 YUAN **Weight:** 31.1035 g. **Composition:** 0.9990 Gold 1.0000 oz. AGW **Subject:** Chinese inventions **Reverse:** First compass

Date	Mintage	F	VF	XF	Unc	BU
1992 Proof	1,000	Value: 500				

Y# 338 100 YUAN **Weight:** 31.1035 g. **Composition:** 0.9990 Gold 1.0000 oz. AGW **Subject:** Chinese inventions **Reverse:** First seismograph

Date	Mintage	F	VF	XF	Unc	BU
1992 Proof	1,000	Value: 500				

Y# 339 100 YUAN **Weight:** 31.1035 g. **Composition:** 0.9990 Gold 1.0000 oz. AGW **Subject:** Chinese inventions **Reverse:** First Kite

Date	Mintage	F	VF	XF	Unc	BU
1992 Proof	1,000	Value: 500				

Y# 340 100 YUAN **Weight:** 31.1035 g. **Composition:** 0.9990 Gold 1.0000 oz. AGW **Obverse:** Great Wall **Reverse:** Bronze Age Metal Working, large urn

Date	Mintage	F	VF	XF	Unc	BU
1992 Proof	1,000	Value: 500				

Y# 345 100 YUAN **Weight:** 31.1035 g. **Composition:** 0.9990 Gold 1.0000 oz. AGW **Obverse:** Temple of Heaven **Reverse:** Panda on branch

Date		F	VF	XF	Unc	BU
1992		—	—	—	425	—
1992 Proof	—	Value: 525				

Y# 376 100 YUAN **Weight:** 373.2360 g. **Composition:** 0.9990 Silver 12.0000 oz. ASW **Reverse:** Pandas **Size:** 80 mm.

Date	Mintage	F	VF	XF	Unc	BU
1992 Proof	Est. 2,500	Value: 250				

Y# 546 100 YUAN **Weight:** 10.3700 g. **Composition:** 0.9170 Gold .3054 oz. AGW **Obverse:** State seal **Reverse:** Emperor Da Yu

Date	Mintage	F	VF	XF	Unc	BU
1992 Proof	—	Value: 285				

Y# 554 100 YUAN **Weight:** 11.3180 g. **Composition:** 0.9170 Gold .3334 oz. AGW **Obverse:** State seal **Reverse:** Wu Zetian "The Iron Lady"

Date	Mintage	F	VF	XF	Unc	BU
1992 Proof	Est. 7,000	Value: 275				

Y# 692 100 YUAN **Weight:** 11.3180 g. **Composition:** 0.9170 Gold .3334 oz. AGW **Series:** 1994 Olympics **Reverse:** Male figure skater

Date	Mintage	F	VF	XF	Unc	BU
1992 Proof	10,000	Value: 150				

Y# 693 100 YUAN **Weight:** 8.0000 g. **Composition:** 0.9170 Gold .2356 oz. AGW **Series:** Endangered Wildlife **Reverse:** Mountain sheep

Date	Mintage	F	VF	XF	Unc	BU
1992 Proof	1,500	Value: 225				

Y# 290 100 YUAN **Weight:** 373.2360 g. **Composition:** 0.9990 Silver 12.0000 oz. ASW **Subject:** Year of the Monkey **Obverse:** Building **Reverse:** Family of monkeys **Note:** Similar to 1000 Yuan, Y#293.

Date	Mintage	F	VF	XF	Unc	BU
1992 Proof	500	Value: 475				

Y# 754 100 YUAN **Weight:** 33.9600 g. **Composition:** 0.9160 Gold .2356 oz. AGW **Subject:** Archeological Finds **Obverse:** State seal **Reverse:** Resting deer with long antlers

Date	Mintage	F	VF	XF	Unc	BU
1992 Proof	500	Value: 700				

Y# 406 100 YUAN **Weight:** 31.1035 g. **Composition:** 0.9990 Gold 1.0000 oz. AGW **Reverse:** Chinese Gods: Fu, Lu, and Shu **Note:** Similar to 500 Yuan, Y#407.

Date	Mintage	F	VF	XF	Unc	BU
1993 Proof	888	Value: 800				

Y# 354 100 YUAN **Weight:** 31.1320 g. **Composition:** 0.9990 Gold 1.0000 oz. AGW **Obverse:** Temple **Reverse:** Two peacocks

Date	Mintage	F	VF	XF	Unc	BU
1993 Proof	1,200	Value: 625				

Y# 380 100 YUAN **Weight:** 373.2360 g. **Composition:** 0.9990 Silver 12.0000 oz. ASW **Obverse:** Temple of Heaven **Reverse:** Pandas

Date	Mintage	F	VF	XF	Unc	BU
1993 Proof	Est. 2,500	Value: 250				

Y# 382 100 YUAN **Weight:** 31.1030 g. **Composition:** 0.9995 Platinum 1.0000 oz. APW **Subject:** Year of the Rooster

Date	Mintage	F	VF	XF	Unc	BU
1993 Proof	300	Value: 950				

Y# 383 100 YUAN **Weight:** 373.2360 g. **Composition:** 0.9990 Silver 12.0000 oz. ASW **Subject:** Year of the Rooster

Date	Mintage	F	VF	XF	Unc	BU
1993 Proof	500	Value: 425				

Y# 411 100 YUAN **Weight:** 33.9500 g. **Composition:** 0.9170 Gold 1.0000 oz. AGW **Subject:** Bronze Age Sculptures **Obverse:** State seal **Reverse:** Bull lantern

Date	Mintage	F	VF	XF	Unc	BU
1993 Proof	500	Value: 700				

Y# 491 100 YUAN **Weight:** 10.3600 g. **Composition:** 0.9170 Gold .3053 oz. AGW **Subject:** World Cup Soccer **Obverse:** State seal **Reverse:** Player kicking ball

Date	Mintage	F	VF	XF	Unc	BU
1993 Proof	5,000	Value: 175				

Y# 504 100 YUAN **Weight:** 31.1035 g. **Composition:** 0.9990 Gold 1.0000 oz. AGW **Obverse:** Great Wall **Reverse:** Guanyin, Goddess of Mercy, seated in flower

Date	Mintage	F	VF	XF	Unc	BU
1993 Proof	1,000	Value: 625				

Y# 538 100 YUAN **Weight:** 11.3180 g. **Composition:** 0.9170 Gold .3337 oz. AGW **Obverse:** State seal **Reverse:** Bust of Chairman Mao Zedong

Date	Mintage	F	VF	XF	Unc	BU
1993 Proof	Est. 7,000	Value: 300				

Y# 568 100 YUAN **Weight:** 15.5517 g. **Composition:** 0.9170 Gold .5000 oz. AGW **Subject:** Year of the Rooster **Obverse:** City gate **Reverse:** Rooster, sunflowers **Shape:** Scalloped

Date	Mintage	F	VF	XF	Unc	BU
1993 Proof	Est. 2,300	Value: 500				

Y# 569 100 YUAN **Weight:** 373.2420 g. **Composition:** 0.9990 Silver 12.0000 oz. ASW **Subject:** Year of the Rooster **Obverse:** State seal

Date	Mintage	F	VF	XF	Unc	BU
1993 Proof	Est. 500	Value: 500				

Y# 570 100 YUAN **Weight:** 31.1035 g. **Composition:** 0.9990 Gold 1.0000 oz. AGW **Subject:** Year of the Rooster **Obverse:** State seal **Reverse:** Rooster and hen

Date	Mintage	F	VF	XF	Unc	BU
1993 Proof	19,000	Value: 700				

Y# 614 100 YUAN **Weight:** 31.1035 g. **Composition:** 0.9990 Gold 1.0000 oz. AGW **Obverse:** Temple of Heaven **Reverse:** Panda seated on rock

Date	F	VF	XF	Unc	BU
1993	—	—	—	450	—

Y# 760 100 YUAN **Weight:** 8.0000 g. **Composition:** 0.9160 Gold .2356 oz. AGW **Obverse:** State seal **Reverse:** Bust of Song Qingling

Date	Mintage	F	VF	XF	Unc	BU
1993 Proof	2,000	Value: 200				

Y# 763 100 YUAN **Weight:** 31.1035 g. **Composition:** 0.9990 Gold 1.0000 oz. AGW **Obverse:** Home of Sun Yat-sen **Reverse:** Bust of Sun Yat-sen

Date	Mintage	F	VF	XF	Unc	BU
1993 Proof	8,888	Value: 725				

Y# 777 100 YUAN **Weight:** 31.1035 g. **Composition:** 0.9990 Gold 1.0000 oz. AGW **Subject:** Mount Tai **Obverse:** Great Wall **Reverse:** Temple

Date	Mintage	F	VF	XF	Unc	BU
1993 Proof	8,888	Value: 500				

Y# 388 100 YUAN **Weight:** 373.2360 g. **Composition:** 0.9990 Silver 12.0000 oz. ASW **Subject:** Year of the Dog

Date	Mintage	F	VF	XF	Unc	BU
1994 Proof	500	Value: 425				

Y# 397 100 YUAN **Weight:** 31.1320 g. **Composition:** 0.9990 Gold 1.0000 oz. AGW **Subject:** Year of the Dog

Date	Mintage	F	VF	XF	Unc	BU
1994 Proof	1,800	Value: 700				

Y# 397a 100 YUAN **Weight:** 31.1030 g. **Composition:** 0.9995 Platinum 1.0000 oz. APW **Subject:** Year of the Dog

Date	Mintage	F	VF	XF	Unc	BU
1994 Proof	300	Value: 950				

Y# 427 100 YUAN **Weight:** 31.1035 g. **Composition:** 0.9990 Gold 1.0000 oz. AGW **Obverse:** Equestrian **Reverse:** Unicorn

Date	Mintage	F	VF	XF	Unc	BU
1994 Proof	1,100	Value: 525				

Y# 435 100 YUAN **Weight:** 31.1035 g. **Composition:** 0.9990 Gold 1.0000 oz. AGW **Reverse:** Panda seated, eating bamboo shoots

Date	F	VF	XF	Unc	BU
1994	—	—	—	550	—

Y# 440 100 YUAN **Weight:** 8.0000 g. **Composition:** 0.9170 Gold .2356 oz. AGW **Subject:** 12th Asian Games **Obverse:** State seal **Reverse:** Gymnast on bars

Date	Mintage	F	VF	XF	Unc	BU
1994 Proof	3,000	Value: 200				

Y# 497 100 YUAN **Weight:** 10.3600 g. **Composition:** 0.9170 Gold .3053 oz. AGW **Series:** 1994 Olympics **Reverse:** Female torch runner

Date	Mintage	F	VF	XF	Unc	BU
1994 Proof	5,000	Value: 150				

Y# 543 100 YUAN **Weight:** 10.3600 g. **Composition:** 0.9170 Gold .3053 oz. AGW **Obverse:** State seal **Reverse:** Emperor Zhou Wenwang

Date	F	VF	XF	Unc	BU
1994 Proof	—	Value: 275			

Y# 652 100 YUAN **Weight:** 373.2360 g. **Composition:** 0.9990 Silver 12.0000 oz. ASW **Obverse:** Temple of Heaven **Reverse:** Panda with two cubs at waters edge

Date	Mintage	F	VF	XF	Unc	BU
1994 Proof	2,500	Value: 250				

Y# 694 100 YUAN **Weight:** 8.0000 g. **Composition:** 0.9160 Gold .2361 oz. AGW **Obverse:** State seal **Reverse:** Panda climbing tree

Date	F	VF	XF	Unc	BU
1994 Proof	—	Value: 200			

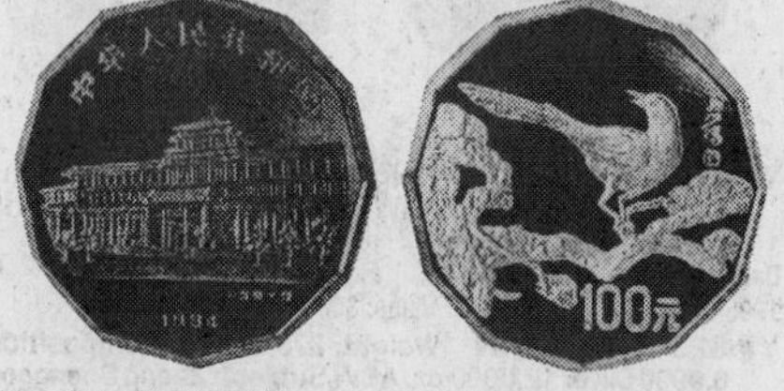

Y# 695 100 YUAN **Weight:** 15.5500 g. **Composition:** 0.9160 Gold .4579 oz. AGW **Obverse:** Building **Reverse:** Black-billed Magpie on branch **Shape:** 12-sided

Date	Mintage	F	VF	XF	Unc	BU
1994 Proof	1,300	Value: 300				

Y#780 100 YUAN **Weight:** 16.3980 g. **Composition:** 0.9160 Gold .5000 oz. AGW **Subject:** Year of the Dog **Obverse:** Phoenix Pavilion **Reverse:** Lap dog **Shape:** Scalloped

Date	Mintage	F	VF	XF	Unc	BU
1994 Proof	2,300	Value: 375				

Y# 781 100 YUAN **Weight:** 373.2420 g. **Composition:** 0.9990 Silver 12.0000 oz. ASW **Subject:** Year of the Dog **Obverse:** Phoenix Pavilion **Reverse:** Large dog

Date	Mintage	F	VF	XF	Unc	BU
1994 Proof	500	Value: 575				

Y# 426 100 YUAN **Weight:** 373.2360 g. **Composition:** 0.9990 Silver 12.0000 oz. ASW **Reverse:** Unicorn with offspring **Size:** 85 mm. **Note:** Illustration reduced.

Date	Mintage	F	VF	XF	Unc	BU
1994 Proof	2,000	Value: 300				

Y# 698 100 YUAN **Weight:** 373.2360 g. **Composition:** 0.9990 Silver 20.0000 oz. ASW **Reverse:** Unicorn with offspring **Size:** 98 mm. **Note:** Illustration reduced.

Date	F	VF	XF	Unc	BU
1995 Proof	—	Value: 300			

Y# 644 100 YUAN **Weight:** 31.1030 g. **Composition:** 0.9990 Gold 1.0000 oz. AGW **Obverse:** Temple of Heaven **Reverse:** Panda eating bamboo **Note:** Similar to 10 Yuan, Y#641.

Date	F	VF	XF	Unc	BU
1995	—	—	—	450	—

Y# 646 100 YUAN **Weight:** 373.2360 g. **Composition:** 0.9990 Silver 12.0000 oz. ASW **Obverse:** Temple of Heaven **Reverse:** Panda family

Date	Mintage	F	VF	XF	Unc	BU
1995 Proof	500	Value: 400				

Y# 1062 100 YUAN **Weight:** 31.1035 g. **Composition:** 0.9990 Gold 1.0000 oz. AGW **Subject:** Unicorn **Obverse:** Eastern unicorn. **Reverse:** Western unicorn with offspring. **Edge:** Reeded. **Size:** 32 mm.

Date	F	VF	XF	Unc	BU
1995 Proof	—	Value: 500			

Y# 843 100 YUAN **Weight:** 10.3678 g. **Composition:** 0.9990 Gold .3330 oz. AGW **Series:** 1996 Olympics **Obverse:** State seal **Reverse:** High diver

Date	Mintage	F	VF	XF	Unc	BU
1995 Proof	10,000	Value: 150				

Y# 844 100 YUAN **Weight:** 10.3678 g. **Composition:** 0.9990 Gold .3330 oz. AGW **Series:** Olympics **Obverse:** State seal **Reverse:** Rhythmic gymnast

Date	Mintage	F	VF	XF	Unc	BU
1995 Proof	10,000	Value: 150				

Y# 466 100 YUAN **Weight:** 373.2420 g. **Composition:** 0.9990 Silver 12.0000 oz. ASW **Subject:** Year of the Pig **Reverse:** Sow and five piglets **Size:** 80 mm. **Note:** Illustration reduced.

Date	Mintage	F	VF	XF	Unc	BU
1995 Proof	500	Value: 400				

Y# 451 100 YUAN **Weight:** 31.1030 g. **Composition:** 0.9990 Gold 1.0000 oz. AGW **Subject:** Year of the Pig **Reverse:** Pig

Date	Mintage	F	VF	XF	Unc	BU
1995 Proof	1,800	Value: 700				

Y# 453 100 YUAN **Weight:** 15.5557 g. **Composition:** 0.9990 Gold .5000 oz. AGW **Subject:** Year of the Pig **Reverse:** Two pigs **Shape:** Scalloped

Date	Mintage	F	VF	XF	Unc	BU
1995 Proof	2,300	Value: 375				

Y# 465 100 YUAN **Weight:** 31.1030 g. **Composition:** 0.9995 Platinum 1.0000 oz. APW **Subject:** Year of the Pig

Date	Mintage	F	VF	XF	Unc	BU
1995 Proof	300	Value: 950				

Y# 1012 100 YUAN **Weight:** 31.1030 g. **Composition:** 0.9990 Gold 1.0000 oz. AGW **Reverse:** Unicorn

Date	Mintage	F	VF	XF	Unc	BU
1995 Proof	1,500	Value: 525				

Y# 696 100 YUAN **Weight:** 31.1035 g. **Composition:** 0.9990 Gold 1.0000 oz. AGW **Subject:** 50th Anniversary - Anti-Japanese War **Reverse:** People at wall

Date	Mintage	F	VF	XF	Unc	BU
1995 Proof	1,400	Value: 600				

Y# 697 100 YUAN **Weight:** 31.1035 g. **Composition:** 0.9990 Gold 1.0000 oz. AGW **Reverse:** Soldiers above bridge guarded by chinze

Date	Mintage	F	VF	XF	Unc	BU
1995 Proof	1,400	Value: 600				

Y# 790 100 YUAN **Weight:** 31.0103 g. **Composition:** 0.9990 Gold 1.0000 oz. AGW **Obverse:** Temple of Heaven **Reverse:** Panda approaching water from right

Date	Mintage	F	VF	XF	Unc	BU
1995 Proof only	2,000	Value: 700				

Y# 804 100 YUAN **Weight:** 31.0103 g. **Composition:** 0.9990 Gold 1.0000 oz. AGW **Subject:** Chinese Culture Series **Obverse:** Great Wall seen through arch **Reverse:** Pagoda of Six Harmonies

Date	Mintage	F	VF	XF	Unc	BU
1995 Proof	25,000	Value: 375				

Y# 805 100 YUAN **Weight:** 31.0103 g. **Composition:** 0.9990 Gold 1.0000 oz. AGW **Subject:** Chinese Culture Series **Obverse:** Great Wall seen through arch **Reverse:** Mencius seated at table

Date	Mintage	F	VF	XF	Unc	BU
1995 Proof	25,000	Value: 375				

Y# 806 100 YUAN **Weight:** 31.0103 g. **Composition:** 0.9990 Gold 1.0000 oz. AGW **Subject:** Chinese Culture Series **Obverse:** Great Wall seen through arch **Reverse:** Tang Taizong seated

Date	Mintage	F	VF	XF	Unc	BU
1995 Proof	25,000	Value: 375				

Y# 807 100 YUAN **Weight:** 31.0103 g. **Composition:** 0.9990 Gold 1.0000 oz. AGW **Subject:** Chinese Culture Series **Obverse:** Great Wall seen through arch **Reverse:** Lion dance

Date	Mintage	F	VF	XF	Unc	BU
1995 Proof	25,000	Value: 375				

Y# 808 100 YUAN **Weight:** 31.0103 g. **Composition:** 0.9990 Gold 1.0000 oz. AGW **Subject:** Chinese Culture Series **Obverse:** Great Wall seen through arch **Reverse:** Female opera role

Date	Mintage	F	VF	XF	Unc	BU
1995 Proof	25,000	Value: 375				

Y# 810 100 YUAN **Weight:** 16.9779 g. **Composition:** 0.9160 Gold .5000 oz. AGW **Obverse:** Great Wall **Reverse:** Perched eagle **Shape:** 12-sided

Date	Mintage	F	VF	XF	Unc	BU
1995 Proof	1,300	Value: 300				

Y# 823 100 YUAN **Weight:** 373.2420 g. **Composition:** 0.9990 Silver 12.0000 oz. ASW **Subject:** Zheng Chenggong **Obverse:** Chiqian building **Reverse:** Standing figure with flag and ships

Date	Mintage	F	VF	XF	Unc	BU
1995 Proof	150	Value: 900				

Y# 830 100 YUAN **Weight:** 373.2420 g. **Composition:** 0.9990 Silver 12.0000 oz. ASW **Subject:** Romance of the Three Kingdoms **Obverse:** Luo Guanzhong **Reverse:** Standing Liu Bei with flags

Date	Mintage	F	VF	XF	Unc	BU
1995 Proof	1,500	Value: 700				

Y# 831 100 YUAN **Weight:** 373.2420 g. **Composition:** 0.9990 Silver 12.0000 oz. ASW **Subject:** Romance of the Three Kingdoms **Obverse:** Luo Guanzhong **Reverse:** Seated Guan Yu reading

Date	Mintage	F	VF	XF	Unc	BU
1995 Proof	1,500	Value: 700				

Y# 832 100 YUAN **Weight:** 373.2420 g. **Composition:** 0.9990 Silver 12.0000 oz. ASW **Subject:** Romance of the Three Kingdoms **Obverse:** Luo Guanzhong **Reverse:** Zhang Fei on horseback

Date	Mintage	F	VF	XF	Unc	BU
1995 Proof	1,500	Value: 700				

Y# 833 100 YUAN **Weight:** 373.2420 g. **Composition:** 0.9990 Silver 12.0000 oz. ASW **Subject:** Romance of the Three Kingdoms **Obverse:** Luo Guanzhong **Reverse:** Zhuge Liang seated on throne

Date	Mintage	F	VF	XF	Unc	BU
1995 Proof	1,500	Value: 700				

Y# 578 100 YUAN **Weight:** 31.1035 g. **Composition:** 0.9990 Gold 1.0000 oz. AGW **Obverse:** Temple of Heaven **Reverse:** Panda in tree

Date	F	VF	XF	Unc	BU
1996	—	—	—	425	—

Y# 1013 100 YUAN **Weight:** 31.1035 g. **Composition:** 0.9990 Gold 1.0000 oz. AGW **Obverse:** Temple of Heaven **Reverse:** Panda sitting on rock

Date	Mintage	F	VF	XF	Unc	BU
1996 Proof	1,500	Value: 700				

Y# 586 100 YUAN **Weight:** 31.1035 g. **Composition:** 0.9990 Gold 1.0000 oz. AGW **Subject:** Year of the Rat **Reverse:** Rat by oil lamp

Date	Mintage	F	VF	XF	Unc	BU
1996 Proof	1,800	Value: 700				

Y# 586a 100 YUAN **Weight:** 31.1035 g. **Composition:** 0.9995 Platinum 1.0000 oz. APW **Subject:** Year of the Rat **Reverse:** Rat by oil lamp

Date	Mintage	F	VF	XF	Unc	BU
1996 Proof	300	Value: 950				

Y# 850 100 YUAN **Weight:** 31.1035 g. **Composition:** 0.9990 Gold 1.0000 oz. AGW **Subject:** 15th Anniversary - Gold Panda Coins **Obverse:** Temple of Heaven with additional legend **Reverse:** Panda in tree

Date	Mintage	F	VF	XF	Unc	BU
1996 Proof	1,500	Value: 550				

Y# 956 100 YUAN **Weight:** 31.1035 g. **Composition:** 0.9990 Gold 1.0000 oz. AGW **Obverse:** Eastern unicorn **Reverse:** Western unicorn on wreath **Edge:** Reeded **Size:** 32 mm.

Date	Mintage	F	VF	XF	Unc	BU
1996 Proof	1,250	Value: 575				

Y# 956a 100 YUAN **Weight:** 31.1035 g. **Composition:** 0.9990 Platinum 1.0000 oz. APW **Subject:** Unicorn **Obverse:** Eastern unicorn, full body. **Reverse:** Western unicorn and maiden. **Edge:** Reeded. **Size:** 32 mm.

Date	Mintage	F	VF	XF	Unc	BU
1996 Proof	500	Value: 850				

Y# 856 100 YUAN **Weight:** 16.9779 g. **Composition:** 0.9160 Gold .5000 oz. AGW **Subject:** Year of the Rat **Obverse:** Dengdu Pavilion **Reverse:** Rat on corn cob **Shape:** Scalloped

Date	Mintage	F	VF	XF	Unc	BU
1996 Proof	2,300	Value: 400				

Y# 1014 100 YUAN **Weight:** 31.1035 g. **Composition:** 0.9990 Gold 1.0000 oz. AGW **Subject:** Unicorn **Obverse:** Eastern unicorn, full body. **Reverse:** Western unicorn. **Edge:** Reeded. **Size:** 32.1 mm.

Date	Mintage	F	VF	XF	Unc	BU
1996 Proof	1,250	Value: 500				

Y# 1080 100 YUAN **Weight:** 16.9779 g. **Composition:** 0.9160 Gold 0.5 oz. AGW **Subject:** Wildlife of China **Obverse:** The Great Wall. **Reverse:** Penguin. **Edge:** Plain. **Size:** 26.5 mm.

Date	Mintage	F	VF	XF	Unc	BU
1997 Proof	2,800	Value: 400				

Y# 669 100 YUAN **Weight:** 373.2360 g. **Composition:** 0.9990 Silver 12.0000 oz. ASW **Subject:** Year of the Ox

Date	Mintage	F	VF	XF	Unc	BU
1997	500	—	—	—	450	—

Y# 670 100 YUAN **Weight:** 15.5557 g. **Composition:** 0.9990 Gold .5000 oz. AGW **Subject:** Year of the Ox **Shape:** Scalloped

Date	Mintage	F	VF	XF	Unc	BU
1997 Proof	2,300	Value: 400				

Y# 720 100 YUAN **Weight:** 31.1035 g. **Composition:** 0.9990 Gold 1.0000 oz. AGW **Obverse:** Temple of Heaven **Reverse:** Panda on large branch

Date	F	VF	XF	Unc	BU
1997	—	—	—	375	—

Note: Exists in large and small date varieties

Y# 898 100 YUAN **Weight:** 373.2420 g. **Composition:** 0.9990 Silver 12.0000 oz. ASW **Subject:** Year of the Ox **Obverse:** Minguan Pavilion **Reverse:** Cow nursing calf

Date	Mintage	F	VF	XF	Unc	BU
1997 Proof	500	Value: 475				

Y# 900 100 YUAN **Weight:** 31.1035 g. **Composition:** 0.9990 Gold 1.0000 oz. AGW **Subject:** Year of the Ox **Obverse:** State seal **Reverse:** Water buffalo

Date	Mintage	F	VF	XF	Unc	BU
1997 Proof	1,600	Value: 600				

Y# 900a 100 YUAN **Weight:** 31.1035 g. **Composition:** 0.9995 Platinum 1.0000 oz. APW **Subject:** Year of the Ox **Obverse:** State seal **Reverse:** Water buffalo

Date	Mintage	F	VF	XF	Unc	BU
1997 Proof	300	Value: 950				

Y# 966 100 YUAN **Weight:** 31.1035 g. **Composition:** 0.9995 Platinum 1.0000 oz. APW **Obverse:** Eastern unicorn **Reverse:** Western unicorn

Date	Mintage	F	VF	XF	Unc	BU
1997 Proof	500	Value: 800				

Y# 928 100 YUAN **Weight:** 373.2420 g. **Composition:** 0.9990 Silver 12.0000 oz. ASW **Subject:** Year of the Tiger **Obverse:** Badaling building **Reverse:** Tiger

Date	Mintage	F	VF	XF	Unc	BU
1998 Proof	500	Value: 600				

Y# 929 100 YUAN **Weight:** 31.1035 g. **Composition:** 0.9990 Gold 1.0000 oz. AGW **Subject:** Year of the Tiger **Obverse:** State seal **Reverse:** Tiger

Date	Mintage	F	VF	XF	Unc	BU
1998 Proof	1,600	Value: 700				

Y# 929a 100 YUAN **Weight:** 31.1035 g. **Composition:** 0.9990 Platinum 1.0000 oz. APW **Subject:** Year of the Tiger **Obverse:** State seal **Reverse:** Tiger

Date	Mintage	F	VF	XF	Unc	BU
1998 Proof	300	Value: 1,150				

Y# 1015 100 YUAN **Weight:** 15.5557 g. **Composition:** 0.9990 Gold .5000 oz. AGW **Subject:** Year of the Tiger **Shape:** Scalloped

Date	Mintage	F	VF	XF	Unc	BU
1998 Proof	2,300	Value: 400				

Y# 1016 100 YUAN **Weight:** 31.1320 g. **Composition:** 0.9990 Gold 1.0000 oz. AGW **Obverse:** Temple of Heaven **Reverse:** Panda seated on rock **Note:** Exists in large and small date varieties.

Date	F	VF	XF	Unc	BU
1998	—	—	—	350	—
1999	—	—	—	350	—

Y# 1017 100 YUAN **Weight:** 31.1320 g. **Composition:** 0.9990 Gold 1.0000 oz. AGW **Obverse:** Temple of Heaven **Reverse:** Panda on ledge

Date	F	VF	XF	Unc	BU
1999	—	—	—	325	—

Note: Exists in large and small date varieties

Y# 1018 100 YUAN **Weight:** 31.1035 g. **Composition:** 0.9990 Gold 1.0000 oz. AGW **Subject:** Year of the Rabbit

Date	F	VF	XF	Unc	BU
1999 Proof	—	Value: 600			

Y# 1018a 100 YUAN **Weight:** 31.1035 g. **Composition:** 0.9990 Platinum 1.0000 oz. APW **Subject:** Year of the Rabbit

Date	F	VF	XF	Unc	BU
1999 Proof	—	Value: 1,150			

Y# 1019 100 YUAN **Weight:** 15.5551 g. **Composition:** 0.9990 Gold .5000 oz. AGW **Subject:** Year of the Rabbit **Shape:** Scalloped

Date	F	VF	XF	Unc	BU
1999 Prof	—	Value: 400			

Y# 949 100 YUAN **Weight:** 31.1036 g. **Composition:** 0.9990 Gold 1.0000 oz. AGW **Obverse:** Temple of Heaven **Reverse:** Panda seated on leaves

Date	F	VF	XF	Unc	BU
2000 Proof	—	Value: 420			

Note: Domestic Chinese examples struck with mirror fields, overseas examples struck with frosted fields

Y# 1051 100 YUAN **Weight:** 15.5518 g. **Composition:** 0.9160 Gold .4580 oz. AGW **Reverse:** Dragons **Shape:** Scalloped

Date	Mintage	F	VF	XF	Unc	BU
2000 Proof	2,300	Value: 450				

Y# 45 150 YUAN **Weight:** 8.0000 g. **Composition:** 0.9170 Gold .2359 oz. AGW **Subject:** Year of the Pig **Obverse:** Hillside pagoda, waterfront **Reverse:** Two pigs

Date	Mintage	F	VF	XF	Unc	BU
1983 Proof	2,035	Value: 1,250				

Y# 60 150 YUAN **Weight:** 8.0000 g. **Composition:** 0.9170 Gold .2359 oz. AGW **Subject:** Year of the Rat **Obverse:** Fortress **Reverse:** Rat, squash

Date	Mintage	F	VF	XF	Unc	BU
1984 Proof	2,248	Value: 1,750				

Y# 79 150 YUAN **Weight:** 8.0000 g. **Composition:** 0.9170 Gold .2359 oz. AGW **Subject:** Year of the Ox **Obverse:** Houseboat in harbor **Reverse:** Ox left

Date	Mintage	F	VF	XF	Unc	BU
1985 Proof	16,000	Value: 200				

Note: 5,000 pieces were struck and issued in boxes with certificates and are valued at $400

Y# 99 150 YUAN **Weight:** 8.0000 g. **Composition:** 0.9170 Gold .2359 oz. AGW **Subject:** Year of the Tiger **Obverse:** Qing Dynasty Palace **Reverse:** Tiger growling

Date	Mintage	F	VF	XF	Unc	BU
1986 Proof	5,480	Value: 450				

Y# 123 150 YUAN **Weight:** 8.0000 g. **Composition:** 0.9170 Gold .2359 oz. AGW **Subject:** Year of the Rabbit **Obverse:** Pagoda **Reverse:** Two rabbits

Date	Mintage	F	VF	XF	Unc	BU
1987 Proof	4,780	Value: 300				

Y# 144 150 YUAN **Weight:** 8.0000 g. **Composition:** 0.9170 Gold .2359 oz. AGW **Subject:** Year of the Dragon **Obverse:** Great Wall of China **Reverse:** Dragon attacking

Date	Mintage	F	VF	XF	Unc	BU
1988 Proof	7,600	Value: 300				

Y# 180 150 YUAN **Weight:** 8.0000 g. **Composition:** 0.9170 Gold .2359 oz. AGW **Subject:** Year of the Snake **Obverse:** Shanhaiguan Pass Gate

Date	Mintage	F	VF	XF	Unc	BU
1989 Proof	7,500	Value: 200				

Y# 208 150 YUAN **Weight:** 622.0400 g. **Composition:** 0.9990 Silver 20.0000 oz. ASW **Reverse:** Phoenix and dragon

Date	Mintage	F	VF	XF	Unc	BU
1990 Proof	1,500	Value: 650				

Y# 227 150 YUAN **Weight:** 8.0000 g. **Composition:** 0.9170 Gold .2359 oz. AGW **Subject:** Year of the Horse **Obverse:** Temple of Confucius **Reverse:** Horse galloping

Date	Mintage	F	VF	XF	Unc	BU
1990 Proof	7,500	Value: 275				

Y# 276 150 YUAN **Weight:** 8.0000 g. **Composition:** 0.9170 Gold .2359 oz. AGW **Subject:** Year of the Goat **Obverse:** Chinese building and legend **Reverse:** Goat reclining

Date	Mintage	F	VF	XF	Unc	BU
1991 Proof	7,500	Value: 220				

Y# 291 150 YUAN **Weight:** 8.0000 g. **Composition:** 0.9170 Gold .2359 oz. AGW **Subject:** Year of the Monkey **Obverse:** Pavilion of Emperor Teng **Reverse:** Monkey sitting

Date	Mintage	F	VF	XF	Unc	BU
1992 Proof	5,000	Value: 285				

Y# 355 150 YUAN **Weight:** 373.2360 g. **Composition:** 0.9990 Silver 12.0000 oz. ASW **Obverse:** Temple of Harmony **Reverse:** Two peacocks

Date	Mintage	F	VF	XF	Unc	BU
1993 Proof	500	Value: 650				

Y# 428 150 YUAN **Weight:** 622.0400 g. **Composition:** 0.9990 Silver 20.0000 oz. ASW **Obverse:** Equestrian **Reverse:** Unicorn **Note:** Similar to 10 Yuan, Y#420.

Date	Mintage	F	VF	XF	Unc	BU
1994 Proof	500	Value: 500				

Y# 699 150 YUAN **Weight:** 622.0400 g. **Composition:** 0.9990 Silver 20.0000 oz. ASW **Obverse:** Mythical animal **Reverse:** Unicorn with offspring **Size:** 98 mm. **Note:** Illustration reduced.

Date	F	VF	XF	Unc	BU
1995	—	—	—	450	—

Y# 884 150 YUAN **Weight:** 622.0400 g. **Composition:** 0.9990 Silver 20.0000 oz. ASW **Obverse:** Eastern unicorn **Reverse:** Western unicorn

Date	Mintage	F	VF	XF	Unc	BU
1996 Proof	500	Value: 600				

Y# 28 200 YUAN **Weight:** 8.4700 g. **Composition:** 0.9170 Gold .2497 oz. AGW **Subject:** Chinese Bronze Age Finds **Obverse:** State seal **Reverse:** Leopard

Date	Mintage	F	VF	XF	Unc	BU
1981 Proof	1,000	Value: 350				

Y# 29 200 YUAN **Weight:** 8.4700 g. **Composition:** 0.9170 Gold .2497 oz. AGW **Subject:** Chinese Bronze Age Finds **Obverse:** State seal **Reverse:** Winged creature

Date	Mintage	F	VF	XF	Unc	BU
1981 Proof	1,000	Value: 550				

Y# 37 200 YUAN **Weight:** 8.4700 g. **Composition:** 0.9170 Gold .2497 oz. AGW **Subject:** World Cup Soccer **Obverse:** State seal above floral sprays **Reverse:** Player kicking

Date	Mintage	F	VF	XF	Unc	BU
1982 Proof	1,261	Value: 350				

Y# 39 200 YUAN **Weight:** 8.4700 g. **Composition:** 0.9170 Gold .2497 oz. AGW **Subject:** Year of the Dog **Obverse:** Temple of Heaven

Date	Mintage	F	VF	XF	Unc	BU
1982 Proof	2,500	Value: 600				

Y# 209 200 YUAN **Weight:** 62.2060 g. **Composition:** 0.9990 Gold 2.0000 oz. AGW **Reverse:** Phoenix and dragon

Date	Mintage	F	VF	XF	Unc	BU
1990 Proof	2,538	Value: 850				
1990 Proof	2,538	Value: 850				

Y# 700 200 YUAN **Weight:** 1000.0000 g. **Composition:** 0.9990 Silver 32.1895 oz. ASW **Subject:** Completion of 150 Yuan Lunar - Animal Coin Series **Size:** 120 mm. **Note:** Illustration reduced.

Date	Mintage	F	VF	XF	Unc	BU
1992 Proof	185	Value: 1,250				

Y# 816 200 YUAN **Weight:** 1000.0000 g. **Composition:** 0.9990 Silver 32.1895 oz. ASW **Subject:** 50th Anniversary - Return of Taiwan to China **Obverse:** Great Wall **Reverse:** Taiwan and China maps **Size:** 100 mm.

Date	Mintage	F	VF	XF	Unc	BU
1995 Proof	100	Value: 2,100				

Y# 712 200 YUAN **Weight:** 1000.0000 g. **Composition:** 0.9990 Silver 32.1895 oz. ASW **Subject:** Sino - Thailand Friendship **Obverse:** Forbidden City and Thai Royal Palace **Reverse:** 2 Buddha statues **Note:** Similar to 10 Yuan, Y#711.

Date	Mintage	F	VF	XF	Unc	BU
1997 Proof	880	Value: 1,000				

Y# 968 200 YUAN **Weight:** 1000.0000 g. **Composition:** 0.9990 Silver 32.1895 oz. ASW **Obverse:** Temple of Heaven **Reverse:** Panda

Date	Mintage	F	VF	XF	Unc	BU
1998 Proof	1,998	Value: 650				

Y# 976 200 YUAN **Weight:** 1000.2108 g. **Composition:** 0.9990 Silver 32.1253 oz. ASW **Subject:** Completion of 12 Year Lunar Cycle

Date	Mintage	F	VF	XF	Unc	BU
1999 Proof	1,000	Value: 1,200				

Y# 971 200 YUAN **Weight:** 1000.2108 g. **Composition:** 0.9990 Silver 32.1253 oz. ASW **Obverse:** Temple of Heaven **Reverse:** Panda on rock **Size:** 100 mm. **Note:** Illustration reduced.

Date	F	VF	XF	Unc	BU
1999 Proof	—	Value: 750			

Y# 1085 200 YUAN **Weight:** 15.5518 g. **Composition:** 0.9990 Gold 0.4995 oz. AGW **Subject:** Mogao Grottoes **Obverse:** Eight story building. **Reverse:** Dancing drummer. **Edge:** Reeded. **Size:** 27 mm.

Date	Mintage	F	VF	XF	Unc	BU
2001 Proof	8,800	Value: 300				

Y# 1087 200 YUAN **Weight:** 15.5518 g. **Composition:** 0.9990 Gold 0.4995 oz. AGW **Subject:** 50th Anniversary Chinese Occupation of Tibet **Obverse:** Five stars. **Reverse:** Denomination in flower. **Edge:** Reeded. **Size:** 27 mm.

Date	Mintage	F	VF	XF	Unc	BU
2001 Proof	15,000	Value: 300				

Y# 1105 200 YUAN **Weight:** 15.5518 g. **Composition:** 0.9990 Gold 0.4995 oz. AGW **Subject:** Panda Bullion **Obverse:** Temple of Heaven **Reverse:** Panda in bamboo forest. **Edge:** Slanted reeding. **Size:** 27 mm. **Note:** Illustration reduced. Actual size: 27mm.

Date	F	VF	XF	Unc	BU
2001 Proof	—	Value: 320			

Y# 1045 200 YUAN **Weight:** 15.5518 g. **Composition:** 0.9990 Gold .5000 oz. AGW **Subject:** Year of the Snake **Shape:** Scalloped

Date	Mintage	F	VF	XF	Unc	BU
2001 Proof	2,300	Value: 320				

Y# 22 250 YUAN **Weight:** 8.0000 g. **Composition:** 0.9170 Gold .2358 oz. AGW **Subject:** 1980 Winter Olympics **Obverse:** State seal **Reverse:** Alpine Skiing

Date	Mintage	F	VF	XF	Unc	BU
1980 Proof	10,000	Value: 135				

Y# 33 250 YUAN **Weight:** 8.0000 g. **Composition:** 0.9170 Gold .2358 oz. AGW **Subject:** Year of the Rooster **Obverse:** Monument

Date	Mintage	F	VF	XF	Unc	BU
1981 Proof	5,015	Value: 375				

Y# 23 300 YUAN **Weight:** 10.0000 g. **Composition:** 0.9170 Gold .2948 oz. AGW **Series:** 1980 Olympics **Subject:** Archery **Obverse:** State seal above floral sprays **Reverse:** Two archers

Date	Mintage	F	VF	XF	Unc	BU
1980 Proof	15,000	Value: 175				

Y# 515 300 YUAN **Weight:** 103.1250 g. **Composition:** 0.9990 Gold 3.3155 oz. AGW **Obverse:** Great Wall **Reverse:** Guanyin, Goddess of Mercy, holding child

Date	Mintage	F	VF	XF	Unc	BU
1994 Proof	128	Value: 2,800				

Y# 1071 300 YUAN **Weight:** 999.9775 g. **Composition:** 0.9990 Silver 32.1500 oz. ASW **Subject:** Panda Billion. **Obverse:** Temple of Heaven. **Reverse:** Panda seated on leaves. **Edge:** Plain. **Size:** 100 mm. **Note:** Illustration reduced.

Date	Mintage	F	VF	XF	Unc	BU
2000 Proof	2,000	Value: 750				

Y# 4 400 YUAN **Weight:** 16.9500 g. **Composition:** 0.9170 Gold .4997 oz. AGW **Obverse:** State seal **Reverse:** 30th Anniversary of Peoples Republic - Tiananmen

Date	Mintage	F	VF	XF	Unc	BU
ND(1979) Proof	23,000	Value: 225				

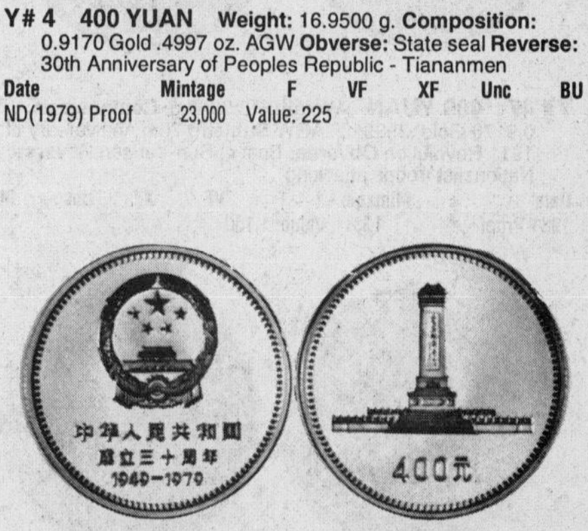

Y# 5 400 YUAN **Weight:** 16.9500 g. **Composition:** 0.9170 Gold .4997 oz. AGW **Subject:** 30th Anniversary of Peoples Republic **Obverse:** State seal **Reverse:** Peoples Heroes Monument

Date	Mintage	F	VF	XF	Unc	BU
ND(1979) Proof	23,000	Value: 225				

Y# 6 400 YUAN **Weight:** 16.9500 g. **Composition:** 0.9170 Gold .4997 oz. AGW **Subject:** 30th Anniversary of Peoples Republic **Obverse:** State seal **Reverse:** Chairman Mao Memorial Hall

Date	Mintage	F	VF	XF	Unc	BU
ND(1979) Proof	23,000	Value: 225				

Y# 7 400 YUAN **Weight:** 16.9500 g. **Composition:** 0.9170 Gold .4997 oz. AGW **Subject:** 30th Anniversary of Peoples Republic **Obverse:** State seal **Reverse:** Great Hall of the People

Date	Mintage	F	VF	XF	Unc	BU
ND(1979) Proof	23,000	Value: 225				

Y# 30 400 YUAN **Weight:** 16.9500 g. **Composition:** 0.9170 Gold .4997 oz. AGW **Subject:** Chinese Bronze Age Finds **Obverse:** State seal **Reverse:** Rhinoceros

Date	Mintage	F	VF	XF	Unc	BU
1981 Proof	1,000	Value: 650				

Y# 47 400 YUAN **Weight:** 13.3600 g. **Composition:** 0.9170 Gold .3939 oz. AGW **Subject:** 70th Anniversary of 1911 Revolution **Obverse:** Bust of Sun-Yat-sen **Reverse:** Nationalist troops attacking

Date	Mintage	F	VF	XF	Unc	BU
1981 Proof	1,338	Value: 1,150				

Y# 9 450 YUAN **Weight:** 17.1700 g. **Composition:** 0.9000 Gold .4968 oz. AGW **Series:** International Year of the Child **Obverse:** State seal above floral sprays **Reverse:** Two children planting flower

Date	Mintage	F	VF	XF	Unc	BU
1979 Proof	12,000	Value: 250				

Y# 147 500 YUAN **Weight:** 155.5150 g. **Composition:** 0.9990 Gold 5.0000 oz. AGW **Subject:** International Year of the Child **Obverse:** Temple of Heaven **Reverse:** Panda with cub **Size:** 60 mm. **Note:** Illustration reduced.

Date	Mintage	F	VF	XF	Unc	BU
1987 Proof	Est. 3,000	Value: 2,400				

Y# 145 500 YUAN **Weight:** 155.5150 g. **Composition:** 0.9990 Gold 5.0000 oz. AGW **Subject:** Year of the Dragon **Obverse:** Great Wall **Reverse:** Three dragons **Size:** 60 mm. **Note:** Illustration reduced.

Date	Mintage	F	VF	XF	Unc	BU
1988 Proof	3,000	Value: 3,200				

Y# 233 500 YUAN **Weight:** 155.5150 g. **Composition:** 0.9990 Gold 5.0000 oz. AGW **Obverse:** Temple of Heaven **Reverse:** Two pandas in tree

Date	Mintage	F	VF	XF	Unc	BU
1988 Proof	3,000	Value: 2,500				

Y# 181 500 YUAN **Weight:** 155.5150 g. **Composition:** 0.9990 Gold 5.0000 oz. AGW **Subject:** Year of the Snake **Obverse:** State seal **Size:** 60 mm. **Note:** Illustration reduced.

Date	Mintage	F	VF	XF	Unc	BU
1989 Proof	500	Value: 3,000				

Y# 228 500 YUAN **Weight:** 155.5150 g. **Composition:** 0.9990 Gold 5.0000 oz. AGW **Subject:** Two horses drinking water **Obverse:** Temple of Confucius **Reverse:** Two goats, on nursing offspring **Size:** 60 mm. **Note:** Illustration reduced.

Date	Mintage	F	VF	XF	Unc	BU
1990 Proof	500	Value: 3,000				

Y# 277 500 YUAN **Weight:** 155.5150 g. **Composition:** 0.9990 Gold 5.0000 oz. AGW **Subject:** Year of the Goat **Obverse:** Two goats, one nursing offspring **Size:** 60 mm. **Note:** Illustration reduced.

Date	Mintage	F	VF	XF	Unc	BU
1991 Proof	250	Value: 3,200				

Y# 292 500 YUAN **Weight:** 155.5150 g. **Composition:** 0.9990 Gold 5.0000 oz. AGW **Subject:** Year of the Monkey **Obverse:** Chinese building **Reverse:** Monkey seated **Size:** 60 mm. **Note:** Illustration reduced.

Date	Mintage	F	VF	XF	Unc	BU
1992 Proof	99	Value: 4,800				

Y# 369 500 YUAN **Weight:** 155.5150 g. **Composition:** 0.9990 Gold 5.0000 oz. AGW **Reverse:** Pandas

Date	Mintage	F	VF	XF	Unc	BU
1992 Proof	99	Value: 3,500				

Y# 384 500 YUAN **Weight:** 155.5150 g. **Composition:** 0.9990 Gold 5.0000 oz. AGW **Subject:** Year of the Rooster

Date	Mintage	F	VF	XF	Unc	BU
1993 Proof	99	Value: 3,900				

Y# 761 500 YUAN **Weight:** 155.5150 g. **Composition:** 0.9990 Gold 5.0000 oz. AGW **Obverse:** Temple of Heaven **Reverse:** Two pandas climbing tree stumps

Date	Mintage	F	VF	XF	Unc	BU
1993 Proof	99	Value: 3,500				

Y# 764 500 YUAN **Weight:** 155.5150 g. **Composition:** 0.9990 Gold 5.0000 oz. AGW **Subject:** Sun Yat-sen **Obverse:** Home of Sun Yat-sen **Reverse:** Bust of Sun Yat-sen facing

Date	Mintage	F	VF	XF	Unc	BU
1993 Proof	99	Value: 4,500				

Y# 778 500 YUAN **Weight:** 155.5150 g. **Composition:** 0.9990 Gold 5.0000 oz. AGW **Subject:** Tomb of Emperor Huang **Obverse:** Great Wall **Reverse:** Tomb

Date	Mintage	F	VF	XF	Unc	BU
1993 Proof	99	Value: 3,000				

Y# 395 500 YUAN **Weight:** 155.5150 g. **Composition:** 0.9990 Gold 5.0000 oz. AGW **Subject:** Marco Polo **Size:** 60 mm. **Note:** Illustration reduced.

Date	Mintage	F	VF	XF	Unc	BU
1993 Proof	100	Value: 2,400				

Y# 407 500 YUAN **Weight:** 155.5150 g. **Composition:** 0.9990 Gold 5.0000 oz. AGW **Subject:** Chinese Gods Fu, Lu and Shu **Size:** 60 mm. **Note:** Illustration reduced.

Date	Mintage	F	VF	XF	Unc	BU
1993 Proof	99	Value: 2,900				

Y# 415 500 YUAN **Weight:** 155.5150 g. **Composition:** 0.9990 Gold 5.0000 oz. AGW **Subject:** Chairman Mao **Size:** 60 mm. **Note:** Illustration reduced.

Date	Mintage	F	VF	XF	Unc	BU
1993 Proof	100	Value: 4,250				

Y# 417 500 YUAN **Weight:** 155.5150 g. **Composition:** 0.9990 Gold 5.0000 oz. AGW **Subject:** Yandi, Semi-mythical First Emperor **Obverse:** State seal **Size:** 60 mm. **Note:** Illustration reduced.

Date	Mintage	F	VF	XF	Unc	BU
1993 Proof	99	Value: 2,800				

Y# 356 500 YUAN **Weight:** 155.5150 g. **Composition:** 0.9990 Gold 5.0000 oz. AGW **Obverse:** Temple of Harmony **Reverse:** Two peacocks **Note:** Similar to 100 Yuan, Y#356.

Date	Mintage	F	VF	XF	Unc	BU
1993 Proof	99	Value: 4,000				

Y# 429 500 YUAN **Weight:** 155.5150 g. **Composition:** 0.9990 Gold 5.0000 oz. AGW **Reverse:** Unicorn **Note:** Similar to 10 Yuan, Y#420.

Date	Mintage	F	VF	XF	Unc	BU
1994 Proof	99	Value: 3,900				

Y# 449 500 YUAN **Weight:** 155.5150 g. **Composition:** 0.9990 Gold 5.0000 oz. AGW **Obverse:** Taiwan Temple **Reverse:** Buddha Statue **Size:** 60 mm. **Note:** Illustration reduced.

Date	Mintage	F	VF	XF	Unc	BU
1994 Proof	76	Value: 3,750				

Y# 462 500 YUAN **Weight:** 155.5150 g. **Composition:** 0.9990 Gold 5.0000 oz. AGW **Subject:** Children At Play **Reverse:** Two children with cat **Size:** 60 mm. **Note:** Illustration reduced.

Date	Mintage	F	VF	XF	Unc	BU
1994 Proof	99	Value: 3,200				

Y# 701 500 YUAN **Weight:** 155.5150 g. **Composition:** 0.9990 Gold 5.0000 oz. AGW **Subject:** Sino-Singapore Friendship **Obverse:** Great Wall **Note:** Illustration reduced.

Date	Mintage	F	VF	XF	Unc	BU
1994 Proof	91	Value: 3,250				

Y# 389 500 YUAN **Weight:** 155.5150 g. **Composition:** 0.9990 Gold 5.0000 oz. AGW **Subject:** Year of the Dog

Date	Mintage	F	VF	XF	Unc	BU
1994 Proof	99	Value: 3,900				

Y# 639 500 YUAN **Weight:** 155.5150 g. **Composition:** 0.9990 Gold 5.0000 oz. AGW **Obverse:** Temple of Heaven **Reverse:** Two pandas, one in tree

Date	Mintage	F	VF	XF	Unc	BU
1994 Proof	99	Value: 3,500				

Y# 467 500 YUAN **Weight:** 155.5150 g. **Composition:** 0.9990 Gold 5.0000 oz. AGW **Subject:** Year of the Pig

Date	Mintage	F	VF	XF	Unc	BU
1995 Proof	99	Value: 3,900				

Y# 656 500 YUAN **Weight:** 155.5150 g. **Composition:** 0.9990 Gold 5.0000 oz. AGW **Subject:** Unicorn **Obverse:** Eastern unicorn. **Reverse:** Unicorn mother and baby **Edge:** Reeded. **Size:** 60 mm.

Date	Mintage	F	VF	XF	Unc	BU
1995 Proof	99	Value: 3,900				

Y# 793 500 YUAN **Ring Weight:** 62.2070 g. **Ring Composition:** 0.9990 Silver 2.0000 oz. ASW **Center Weight:** 155.5175 g. **Center Composition:** 0.9999 Gold 5.0000 oz. AGW **Obverse:** Temple of Heaven **Reverse:** Two pandas sitting on rock

Date	Mintage	F	VF	XF	Unc	BU
1995 Proof	199	Value: 2,750				

Y# 817 500 YUAN **Weight:** 155.5175 g. **Composition:** 0.9999 Gold 5.0000 oz. AGW **Subject:** 50th Anniversary - Taiwan's Return to China **Obverse:** Great Wall **Reverse:** Taiwan and China maps

Date	Mintage	F	VF	XF	Unc	BU
1995 Proof	99	Value: 3,000				

Y# 824 500 YUAN **Weight:** 155.5175 g. **Composition:** 0.9999 Gold 5.0000 oz. AGW **Subject:** Zheng Chenggong **Obverse:** Chiqian Building **Reverse:** Standing figure with flag, war ships in background

Date	Mintage	F	VF	XF	Unc	BU
1995 Proof	99	Value: 2,400				

Y# 834 500 YUAN **Weight:** 155.5175 g. **Composition:** 0.9999 Gold 5.0000 oz. AGW **Subject:** Romance of the Three Kingdoms Series **Obverse:** Bust of Luo Guanzhong **Reverse:** Three heroes of Shu Han

Date	Mintage	F	VF	XF	Unc	BU
1995 Proof	99	Value: 2,400				

Y# 594 500 YUAN **Weight:** 155.5150 g. **Composition:** 0.9990 Gold 5.0000 oz. AGW **Reverse:** Nu Wa Rising **Size:** 60 mm. **Note:** Illustration reduced.

Date	Mintage	F	VF	XF	Unc	BU
1995 Proof	99	Value: 3,250				

Y# 649 500 YUAN **Weight:** 155.5150 g. **Composition:** 0.9990 Gold 5.0000 oz. AGW **Reverse:** Dragon boat **Size:** 60 mm. **Note:** Illustration reduced.

Date	Mintage	F	VF	XF	Unc	BU
1995 Proof	99	Value: 6,000				

Y# 533 500 YUAN **Weight:** 155.5150 g. **Composition:** 0.9990 Gold 5.0000 oz. AGW **Subject:** Return of Hong Kong to China - Series I **Obverse:** Bust of Deng Xiaoping over Hong Kong city view **Note:** Similar to 10 Yuan, Y#531.

Date	Mintage	F	VF	XF	Unc	BU
1995 Proof	228	Value: 4,250				

Y# 657 500 YUAN **Weight:** 155.5175 g. **Composition:** 0.9999 Gold 5.0000 oz. AGW **Obverse:** Western unicorn on hind legs, surrounded by roses **Reverse:** Eastern unicorn standing

Date	Mintage	F	VF	XF	Unc	BU
1996 Proof	108	Value: 3,900				

Y# 659 500 YUAN **Weight:** 155.5175 g. **Composition:** 0.9999 Gold 5.0000 oz. AGW **Subject:** Return of Hong Kong to China - Series II

Date	Mintage	F	VF	XF	Unc	BU
1996 Proof	228	Value: 3,000				

Y# 663 500 YUAN **Weight:** 155.5175 g. **Composition:** 0.9999 Gold 5.0000 oz. AGW **Subject:** Year of the Rat **Reverse:** Rat eating grapes

Date	Mintage	F	VF	XF	Unc	BU
1996 Proof	99	Value: 4,000				

Y# 882 500 YUAN **Weight:** 155.5175 g. **Composition:** 0.9990 Gold 5.0000 oz. AGW **Subject:** Romance of the Three Kingdoms Series **Obverse:** Bust of Luo Guanzhong **Reverse:** Guan Du on horseback leading troops

Date	Mintage	F	VF	XF	Unc	BU
1996 Proof	99	Value: 2,400				

Y# 1020 500 YUAN **Ring Weight:** 62.2070 g. **Ring Composition:** 0.9990 Silver 2.0000 oz. ASW **Center Weight:** 155.5175 g. **Center Composition:** 0.9990 Gold 5.0000 oz. AGW **Reverse:** Panda

Date	Mintage	F	VF	XF	Unc	BU
1996 Proof	199	Value: 2,750				

Y# 672 500 YUAN **Weight:** 155.5175 g. **Composition:** 0.9990 Gold 5.0000 oz. AGW **Subject:** Year of the Ox

Date	Mintage	F	VF	XF	Unc	BU
1997 Proof	99	Value: 3,900				

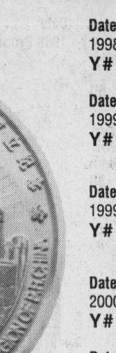

Y# 904 500 YUAN **Weight:** 155.5175 g. **Composition:** 0.9990 Gold 5.0000 oz. AGW **Subject:** Return of Hong Kong to China - Series III **Obverse:** Tiananmen Square **Reverse:** Bust of Deng Xiaoping above city

Date	Mintage	F	VF	XF	Unc	BU
1997 Proof	228	Value: 3,500				

Y# 907 500 YUAN **Weight:** 155.5175 g. **Composition:** 0.9990 Gold 5.0000 oz. AGW **Subject:** Return of Macao to China **Obverse:** Tiananmen Square **Reverse:** Deng Xiaoping standing viewing Macao

Date	Mintage	F	VF	XF	Unc	BU
1997 Proof	228	Value: 3,500				

Y# 1021 500 YUAN **Ring Weight:** 62.2070 g. **Ring Composition:** 0.9990 Silver 2.0000 oz. ASW **Center Weight:** 155.5175 g. **Center Composition:** 0.9990 Gold 5.0000 oz. AGW **Obverse:** Temple of Heaven **Reverse:** Two pandas resting near stream

Date	Mintage	F	VF	XF	Unc	BU
1997 Proof	199	Value: 2,750				

Y# 1022 500 YUAN **Weight:** 155.5175 g. **Composition:** 0.9990 Gold 5.0000 oz. AGW **Subject:** Greeting Spring **Obverse:** Lantern **Reverse:** Children lighting firecrackers

Date	Mintage	F	VF	XF	Unc	BU
1997 Proof	108	Value: 2,250				

Y# 1029 500 YUAN **Weight:** 155.5175 g. **Composition:** 0.9990 Gold 5.0000 oz. AGW **Obverse:** Bust of Qi Bashi **Reverse:** Squirrels eating grapes

Date	Mintage	F	VF	XF	Unc	BU
1997 Proof	99	Value: 3,500				

Y# 1023 500 YUAN **Weight:** 155.5175 g. **Composition:** 0.9990 Gold 5.0000 oz. AGW **Subject:** Greeting Spring **Obverse:** Lantern **Reverse:** Children making kites

Date	Mintage	F	VF	XF	Unc	BU
1998 Proof	128	Value: 2,500				

Y# 1024 500 YUAN **Weight:** 155.5175 g. **Composition:** 0.9990 Gold 5.0000 oz. AGW **Subject:** Year of the Tiger

Date	Mintage	F	VF	XF	Unc	BU
1998 Proof	99	Value: 3,900				

Y# 1025 500 YUAN **Weight:** 155.5175 g. **Composition:** 0.9990 Gold 5.0000 oz. AGW **Subject:** Year of the Rabbit

Date	Mintage	F	VF	XF	Unc	BU
1999 Proof	99	Value: 3,900				

Y# 1026 500 YUAN **Weight:** 155.5175 g. **Composition:** 0.9990 Gold 5.0000 oz. AGW **Subject:** 50th Anniversary of Peoples Republic Founding Ceremony **Note:** Rectangular.

Date	Mintage	F	VF	XF	Unc	BU
1999 Proof	990	Value: 3,500				

Y# 1027 500 YUAN **Weight:** 155.5175 g. **Composition:** 0.9990 Gold 5.0000 oz. AGW **Subject:** Year of the Dragon **Note:** Rectangular.

Date	Mintage	F	VF	XF	Unc	BU
2000 Proof	108	Value: 4,500				

Y# 1028 500 YUAN **Weight:** 155.5175 g. **Composition:** 0.9990 Gold 5.0000 oz. AGW **Subject:** Y2K

Date	Mintage	F	VF	XF	Unc	BU
2000 Proof	—	—	—	—	—	—

Y# 1088 500 YUAN **Weight:** 31.1035 g. **Composition:** 0.9990 Gold 0.999 oz. AGW **Subject:** Panda Bullion **Obverse:** Temple of Heaven. **Reverse:** Panda walking through bamboo. **Edge:** Reeded. **Size:** 32 mm.

Date	Mintage	F	VF	XF	Unc	BU
2001	150,000	—	—	—	350	—

Y# 31 800 YUAN **Weight:** 33.2000 g. **Composition:** 0.9170 Gold .9789 oz. AGW **Subject:** Chinese Bronze Age Finds **Obverse:** State seal **Reverse:** Elephant

Date	Mintage	F	VF	XF	Unc	BU
1981 Proof	1,000	Value: 1,000				

Y# 66 1000 YUAN **Weight:** 373.2360 g. **Composition:** 0.9990 Gold 12.0000 oz. AGW **Obverse:** Temple of Heaven **Reverse:** Panda seated **Size:** 70 mm. **Note:** Illustration reduced.

Date	Mintage	F	VF	XF	Unc	BU
1984 Proof	250	Value: 10,000				

Note: A typical sealed proof exhibits some scuffing and is valued as above, while perfect examples can bring up to a 50% premium

Y# 118.1 1000 YUAN Weight: 373.2360 g. **Composition:** 0.9990 Gold 12.0000 oz. AGW **Obverse:** Temple of Heaven **Reverse:** Panda eating bamboo shoot with cub **Size:** 70 mm. **Note:** Illustration reduced.

Date	Mintage	F	VF	XF	Unc	BU
1986 Proof	2,550	Value: 4,500				

Y# 118.2 1000 YUAN Weight: 373.2360 g. **Composition:** 0.9990 Gold 12.0000 oz. AGW **Obverse:** Temple of Heaven **Reverse:** Panda eating bamboo shoot with cub **Edge:** Plain

Date		F	VF	XF	Unc	BU
1986 2 known; Proof	—	Value: 45,000				

Y# 157 1000 YUAN Weight: 373.2360 g. **Composition:** 0.9990 Gold 12.0000 oz. AGW **Obverse:** Temple of Heaven **Reverse:** Panda with cub **Shape:** 70 **Note:** Illustration reduced.

Date	Mintage	F	VF	XF	Unc	BU
1987 Proof	2,445	Value: 4,500				

Y# 146 1000 YUAN Weight: 373.2360 g. **Composition:** 0.9990 Gold 12.0000 oz. AGW **Subject:** Year of the Dragon **Obverse:** Great Wall **Reverse:** Two facing dragons **Size:** 70 mm. **Note:** Illustration reduced.

Date	Mintage	F	VF	XF	Unc	BU
1988 Proof	518	Value: 7,000				

Y# 234 1000 YUAN Weight: 373.2360 g. **Composition:** 0.9990 Gold 12.0000 oz. AGW **Obverse:** Temple of Heaven **Reverse:** Pandas in tree **Note:** Similar to 500 Yuan, KM#233.

Date	Mintage	F	VF	XF	Unc	BU
1988 Proof	1,650	Value: 5,000				

Y# 182 1000 YUAN Weight: 373.2360 g. **Composition:** 0.9990 Gold 12.0000 oz. AGW **Subject:** Year of the Snake **Obverse:** State seal **Size:** 70 mm. **Note:** Illustration reduced.

Date	Mintage	F	VF	XF	Unc	BU
1989 Proof	200	Value: 6,000				

Y# 229 1000 YUAN Weight: 373.2360 g. **Composition:** 0.9990 Gold 12.0000 oz. AGW **Subject:** Year of the Horse **Obverse:** Temple of Confucius **Reverse:** Two horses running **Size:** 70 mm. **Note:** Illustration reduced.

Date	Mintage	F	VF	XF	Unc	BU
1990 Proof	500	Value: 5,500				

Y# 282 1000 YUAN Weight: 373.2360 g. **Composition:** 0.9990 Gold 12.0000 oz. AGW **Obverse:** Temple of Heaven **Reverse:** Three pandas **Size:** 70 mm.

Date	Mintage	F	VF	XF	Unc	BU
1990 Proof	500	Value: 5,250				

Y# 371 1000 YUAN Weight: 373.2360 g. **Composition:** 0.9990 Gold 12.0000 oz. AGW **Reverse:** Pandas

Date	Mintage	F	VF	XF	Unc	BU
1991 Proof	400	Value: 5,250				

Y# 278 1000 YUAN Weight: 373.2360 g. **Composition:** 0.9990 Gold 12.0000 oz. AGW **Subject:** Year of the Goat **Obverse:** Chinese building and legend **Reverse:** Three goats **Note:** Illustration reduced.

Date	Mintage	F	VF	XF	Unc	BU
1991 Proof	200	Value: 5,500				

Y# 293 1000 YUAN Weight: 373.2360 g. **Composition:** 0.9990 Gold 12.0000 oz. AGW **Subject:** Year of the Monkey **Obverse:** Chinese building **Reverse:** Five monkeys **Note:** Illustration reduced.

Date	Mintage	F	VF	XF	Unc	BU
1992 Proof	99	Value: 7,000				

Y# 372 1000 YUAN Weight: 373.2360 g. **Composition:** 0.9990 Gold 12.0000 oz. AGW **Obverse:** Temple of Heaven **Reverse:** Pandas

Date	Mintage	F	VF	XF	Unc	BU
1992 Proof	99	Value: 5,750				

Y# 385 1000 YUAN Weight: 373.2360 g. **Composition:** 0.9990 Gold 12.0000 oz. AGW **Subject:** Year of the Rooster

Date	Mintage	F	VF	XF	Unc	BU
1993 Proof	99	Value: 6,500				

Y# 762 1000 YUAN Weight: 373.2360 g. **Composition:** 0.9990 Gold 12.0000 oz. AGW **Obverse:** Temple of Heaven **Reverse:** Panda family of three

Date	Mintage	F	VF	XF	Unc	BU
1993 Proof	99	Value: 5,750				

Y# 390 1000 YUAN Weight: 373.2360 g. **Composition:** 0.9990 Gold 12.0000 oz. AGW **Subject:** Year of the Dog

Date	Mintage	F	VF	XF	Unc	BU
1994 Proof	99	Value: 6,500				

Y# 1089 1000 YUAN Weight: 373.2420 g. **Composition:** 0.9990 Gold 11.988 oz. AGW **Subject:** Panda Bullion **Obverse:** Temple of Heaven. **Reverse:** Panda and two cubs at waters edge. **Edge:** Reeded. **Size:** 70 mm. **Note:** Illustration reduced. Actual size: 70mm.

Date	Mintage	F	VF	XF	Unc	BU
1994 Proof	99	Value: 7,500				

Y# 468 1000 YUAN Weight: 373.2360 g. **Composition:** 0.9990 Gold 12.0000 oz. AGW **Subject:** Year of the Pig

Date	Mintage	F	VF	XF	Unc	BU
1995 Proof	99	Value: 6,500				

Y# 664 1000 YUAN Weight: 373.2360 g. **Composition:** 0.9990 Gold 12.0000 oz. AGW **Subject:** Year of the Rat

Date	Mintage	F	VF	XF	Unc	BU
1996 Proof	99	Value: 6,500				

Y# 673 1000 YUAN Weight: 373.2360 g. **Composition:** 0.9990 Gold 12.0000 oz. AGW **Subject:** Year of the Ox

Date	Mintage	F	VF	XF	Unc	BU
1997 Proof	99	Value: 6,500				

Y# 1030 1000 YUAN Weight: 373.2360 g. **Composition:** 0.9990 Gold 12.0000 oz. AGW **Subject:** Year of the Tiger

Date	Mintage	F	VF	XF	Unc	BU
1998 Proof	99	Value: 6,500				

Y# 1031 1000 YUAN Weight: 373.2360 g. **Composition:** 0.9990 Gold 12.0000 oz. AGW **Subject:** Year of the Rabbit

Date	Mintage	F	VF	XF	Unc	BU
1999 Proof	99	Value: 6,500				

Y# 210 1500 YUAN Weight: 622.6000 g. **Composition:** 0.9990 Gold 20.0000 oz. AGW **Obverse:** Great Wall **Reverse:** Phoenix and dragon

Date	Mintage	F	VF	XF	Unc	BU
1989 Proof	250	Value: 11,000				

Y# 232 1500 YUAN **Weight:** 622.6000 g. **Composition:** 0.9990 Gold 20.0000 oz. AGW **Subject:** Anniversary of Peoples Republic **Obverse:** State seal above city view with fireworks in sky **Size:** 90 mm. **Note:** Illustration reduced.

Date	Mintage	F	VF	XF	Unc	BU
1989 Proof	100	Value: 30,000				

Y# 505 1500 YUAN **Weight:** 562.5068 g. **Composition:** 0.9990 Gold 18.0850 oz. AGW **Reverse:** Guanyin, Goddess of Mercy, seated in flower **Size:** 85 mm. **Note:** Illustration reduced.

Date	Mintage	F	VF	XF	Unc	BU
1993 Proof	88	Value: 12,500				

Y# 357 1500 YUAN **Weight:** 622.6000 g. **Composition:** 0.9990 Gold 20.0000 oz. AGW **Obverse:** Temple of Harmony **Reverse:** Two peacocks

Date	Mintage	F	VF	XF	Unc	BU
1993 Proof	66	Value: 12,500				

Y# 749 2000 YUAN **Weight:** 1000.0000 g. **Composition:** 0.9990 Gold 32.1500 oz. AGW **Subject:** Chinese Inventions and Discoveries **Obverse:** Great Wall **Reverse:** Seismograph, similar to 100 Yuan, KM#338

Date	Mintage	F	VF	XF	Unc	BU
1992 Proof	16	—	—	—	—	—

Y# 402 2000 YUAN **Weight:** 1000.0000 g. **Composition:** 0.9990 Gold 32.1500 oz. AGW **Subject:** Chinese inventions **Reverse:** First compass **Size:** 100 mm. **Note:** Illustration reduced.

Date	Mintage	F	VF	XF	Unc	BU
1992 Proof	16	—	—	—	—	—

Y# 702 2000 YUAN **Weight:** 1000.0000 g. **Composition:** 0.9990 Gold 32.1500 oz. AGW **Subject:** Completion of 150 Yuan Lunar Animal Coin Series **Size:** 100 mm. **Note:** Illustration reduced.

Date	Mintage	F	VF	XF	Unc	BU
1992 Proof	21	—	—	—	—	—

Y# 703 2000 YUAN **Weight:** 1000.0000 g. **Composition:** 0.9990 Gold 32.1500 oz. AGW **Subject:** Sino-Singapore Friendship **Obverse:** Great Wall **Reverse:** Singapore Harbor **Size:** 112 mm. **Note:** Illustration reduced.

Date	Mintage	F	VF	XF	Unc	BU
1994	15	—	—	—	18,000	—

Y# 430 2000 YUAN **Weight:** 1000.0000 g. **Composition:** 0.9990 Gold 32.1500 oz. AGW **Obverse:** Equestrian **Reverse:** Unicorn **Note:** Similar to 10 Yuan, Y#420.

Date	Mintage	F	VF	XF	Unc	BU
1994 Proof	20	Value: 25,000				

Y# 660 2000 YUAN **Weight:** 1000.0000 g. **Composition:** 0.9990 Gold 32.1500 oz. AGW **Subject:** Year of the Pig **Edge:** Scalloped

Date	Mintage	F	VF	XF	Unc	BU
1995 Proof	15	Value: 25,000				

Y# 818 2000 YUAN **Weight:** 1000.0000 g. **Composition:** 0.9990 Gold 32.1500 oz. AGW **Subject:** 50th Anniversary - Taiwan's Return to China **Obverse:** Great Wall **Reverse:** Taiwan and China maps

Date	Mintage	F	VF	XF	Unc	BU
1995 Proof	25	Value: 20,000				

Y# 665 2000 YUAN **Weight:** 1000.0000 g. **Composition:** 0.9990 Gold 32.1500 oz. AGW **Subject:** Year of the Rat **Shape:** Scalloped

Date	Mintage	F	VF	XF	Unc	BU
1996 Proof	15	Value: 25,000				

Y# 957 2000 YUAN **Weight:** 1000.0000 g. **Composition:** 0.9990 Gold 32.1500 oz. AGW **Obverse:** Eastern unicorn **Reverse:** Western unicorn with maiden

Date	Mintage	F	VF	XF	Unc	BU
1996 Proof	18	Value: 20,000				

Y# 961 2000 YUAN **Weight:** 1000.0000 g. **Composition:** 0.9990 Gold 32.1500 oz. AGW **Obverse:** Temple of Heaven **Reverse:** Panda

Date	Mintage	F	VF	XF	Unc	BU
1997 Proof	58	Value: 15,000				

Y# 674 2000 YUAN **Weight:** 1000.0000 g. **Composition:** 0.9990 Gold 32.1500 oz. AGW **Subject:** Year of the Ox

Date	Mintage	F	VF	XF	Unc	BU
1997 Proof	15	Value: 25,000				

Y# 1036 2000 YUAN **Weight:** 1000.0000 g. **Composition:** 0.9990 Gold 32.1500 oz. AGW **Obverse:** Temple of Heaven **Reverse:** Panda

Date	Mintage	F	VF	XF	Unc	BU
1998 Proof	58	Value: 15,000				

Y# 967 2000 YUAN **Weight:** 1000.0000 g. **Composition:** 0.9990 Gold 32.1500 oz. AGW **Subject:** Year of the Tiger **Shape:** Scalloped

Date	Mintage	F	VF	XF	Unc	BU
1998 Proof	15	Value: 25,000				

Y# 975 2000 YUAN **Weight:** 1000.0000 g. **Composition:** 0.9990 Gold 32.1500 oz. AGW **Subject:** Year of the Rabbit **Shape:** Scalloped

Date	Mintage	F	VF	XF	Unc	BU
1999 Proof	15	Value: 25,000				

Y# 972 2000 YUAN **Weight:** 1000.2108 g. **Composition:** 0.9990 Gold 32.1253 oz. AGW **Obverse:** Temple of Heaven **Reverse:** Panda on rock **Note:** Similar to 200 Yuan, KM#971.

Date	Mintage	F	VF	XF	Unc	BU
1999 Proof	68	Value: 15,000				

Y# 977 2000 YUAN **Weight:** 1000.2108 g. **Composition:** 0.9990 Gold 32.1253 oz. AGW **Subject:** Year of the Dragon **Size:** Scalloped mm.

Date	Mintage	F	VF	XF	Unc	BU
2000 Proof	15	Value: 30,000				

Y# 1046 2000 YUAN **Weight:** 155.5175 g. **Composition:** 0.9990 Gold 5.0000 oz. AGW **Subject:** Year of the Snake **Shape:** Rectangle

Date	Mintage	F	VF	XF	Unc	BU
2001 Proof	118	Value: 3,500				

Y# 1086 2000 YUAN **Weight:** 155.5175 g. **Composition:** 0.9990 Gold 4.995 oz. AGW **Subject:** Mogao Grottoes **Obverse:** Eight story building. **Reverse:** Two dancers. **Edge:** Reeded. **Size:** 60 mm.

Date	F	VF	XF	Unc	BU
2001 Proof	288 Value: 2,500				

Y# 358 10000 YUAN **Weight:** 4851.6001 g. **Composition:** 0.9990 Gold 156.000 oz. AGW **Subject:** 10th Anniversary of Gold Panda Issue **Obverse:** Temple of Heaven **Reverse:** Panda on branch in center of 10 panda coin designs

Date	Mintage	F	VF	XF	Unc	BU
1991 Proof	10	Value: 120,000				

Y# 1090 10000 YUAN **Weight:** 373.2420 g. **Composition:** 0.9990 Gold 11.988 oz. AGW **Subject:** Panda Bullion **Obverse:** Temple of Heaven. **Reverse:** Two adult pandas with cub. **Edge:** Reeded. **Size:** 70 mm. **Note:** Illustration reduced. Actual size: 70mm.

Date	Mintage	F	VF	XF	Unc	BU
1995 Proof	99	Value: 7,500				

Y# 1052 10000 YUAN **Weight:** 1000.2108 g. **Composition:** 0.9990 Gold 32.1575 oz. AGW **Reverse:** Dragons **Shape:** Scalloped

Date	Mintage	F	VF	XF	Unc	BU
2000 Proof	15	Value: 30,000				

Y# 1047 10000 YUAN **Weight:** 1000.2108 g. **Composition:** 0.9990 Gold 32.1575 oz. AGW **Subject:** Year of the Snake **Shape:** Scalloped

Date	Mintage	F	VF	XF	Unc	BU
2001 Proof	15	Value: 25,000				

Y# 1070 30000 YUAN **Weight:** 8228.4492 g. **Composition:** 0.9999 Gold 264.5506 oz. AGW **Subject:** Third Millennium - House of Borbon - Philip V **Obverse:** China Centenary Altar. **Reverse:** Denominations. **Edge:** Plain. **Size:** 180 mm. **Note:** Illustration reduced.

Date	Mintage	F	VF	XF	Unc	BU
2000 Proof	20	—	—	—	—	—

GOLD BULLION COINAGE

Y# 40 1/10 OUNCE **Weight:** 3.1103 g. **Composition:** 0.9990 Gold .1000 oz. AGW **Obverse:** Temple of Heaven **Reverse:** Panda with bamboo shoot

Date	Mintage	F	VF	XF	Unc	BU
1982	75,000	—	—	—	—	85.00

Y# 41 1/4 OUNCE **Weight:** 7.7758 g. **Composition:** 0.9990 Gold .2500 oz. AGW **Obverse:** Temple of Heaven **Reverse:** Panda with bamboo shoot

Date	Mintage	F	VF	XF	Unc	BU
1982	40,000	—	—	—	—	165

Y# 42 1/2 OUNCE **Weight:** 15.5517 g. **Composition:** 0.9990 Gold .5000 oz. AGW **Obverse:** Temple of Heaven **Reverse:** Panda with bamboo shoot

Date	Mintage	F	VF	XF	Unc	BU
1982	13,000	—	—	—	—	375

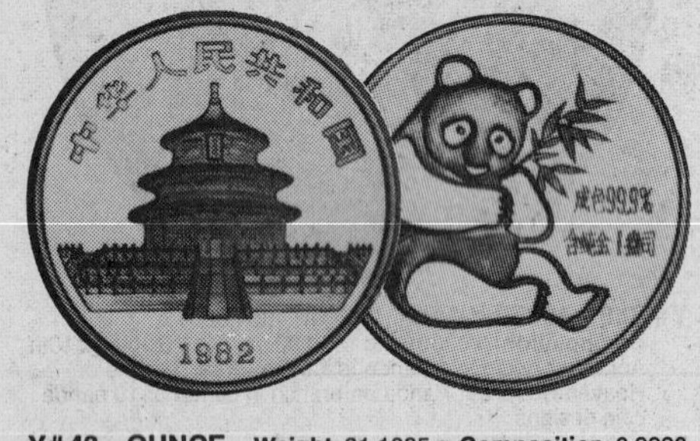

Y# 43 OUNCE **Weight:** 31.1035 g. **Composition:** 0.9990 Gold 1.0000 oz. AGW **Obverse:** Temple of Heaven **Reverse:** Panda with bamboo shoot

Date	Mintage	F	VF	XF	Unc	BU
1982	16,000	—	—	—	—	850

PATTERNS

Including off metal strikes

KM#	Date	Mintage	Identification	Issue Price	Mkt Val
Pn1	1983	—	5 Yuan. (No Composition). Silvered base metal, Marco Polo.	—	600
Pn2	1983	—	100 Yuan. Gilt Bronze.	—	600
Pn3	1985	—	200 Yuan. Gold. Decade for Women, KM#89.	—	—
Pn4	1991	—	Yuan. Nickel Plated Steel. Raised character "pattern". Y#284.	—	100
Pn5	1991	—	Yuan. Nickel Plated Steel. Raised character "pattern". Y#285.	—	100
Pn6	1991	—	Yuan. Nickel Plated Steel. Raised character "pattern". Y#287.	—	100
Pn7	1991	—	Yuan. Nickel Plated Steel. Raised character "pattern". Y#315.	—	150
Pn8	1991	—	Yuan. Nickel Plated Steel. Raised character "pattern". Y#317.	—	150
Pn9	1991	—	10000 Yuan. Gold. Y#358.	—	—

PIEFORTS

KM#	Date	Mintage	Identification	Issue Price	Mkt Val
P2	1979	500	450 Yuan. 0.9000 Gold. Y#9.	—	2,250
P1	1979	3,500	35 Yuan. 0.8000 Silver. Y#8.	—	200
P6	1980	2,500	Yuan. Copper. Y#13.	—	15.00
P7	1980	1,000	Yuan. Copper. Y#14.	—	15.00
P11	1980	2,000	15 Yuan. 0.8000 Silver. Archery.	—	85.00
P12	1980	2,000	20 Yuan. 0.8000 Silver. Y#18, Wrestling.	—	85.00
P13	1980	1,000	30 Yuan. 0.8000 Silver. Equestrian, Y#19.	248	80.00
P17	1980	2,000	30 Yuan. 0.8000 Silver. Biathalon.	—	80.00
P18	1980	2,000	30 Yuan. 0.8000 Silver. Figure skating.	—	80.00
P19	1980	360	250 Yuan. 0.9170 Gold. Alpine skiing, Y#22.	1,750	850
P20	1980	500	300 Yuan. 0.9170 Gold. Archery, Y#23.	—	1,250
P3	1980	2,500	Yuan. Copper. Y#10.	—	15.00
P4	1980	2,500	Yuan. Copper. Y#11.	—	15.00
P8	1980	1,000	Yuan. Copper. Y#15.	—	15.00
P9	1980	1,000	Yuan. Copper. Y#16.	—	15.00
P10	1980	1,000	Yuan. Copper. Y#17.	—	15.00
P14	1980	1,000	30 Yuan. 0.8000 Silver. Soccer.	248	80.00
P5	1980	2,500	Yuan. Copper. Y#12.	—	15.00
P15	1980	2,000	30 Yuan. 0.8000 Silver. Speed skating, Y#21.	248	80.00
P16	1980	2,000	30 Yuan. 0.8000 Silver. Alpine skiing.	—	80.00
PA21	1991	—	10 Yuan. 0.9990 Silver. 62.2000 g. Panda - Hind feet in water.	—	200
P21	1992	—	5 Yuan. 0.9000 Silver. Ancient ship building, Y#331.	—	60.00
P22	1992	—	5 Yuan. 0.9000 Silver. First compass, Y#332.	—	60.00
P23	1992	—	5 Yuan. 0.9000 Silver. First seismograph, Y#333.	—	60.00
P24	1992	—	5 Yuan. 0.9000 Silver. Ancient kite flying, Y#334.	—	60.00
P25	1992	—	5 Yuan. 0.9000 Silver. Bronze metal working, Y#335.	—	60.00
P26	1997	80,000	5 Yuan. 0.9990 Silver. Y#916.	—	30.00
P27	1998	—	10 Yuan. 0.9990 Silver. Y#922.	—	60.00
P28	1998	100,000	10 Yuan. 0.9990 Silver. Y#917.	—	40.00

MINT SETS

KM#	Date	Mintage	Identification	Issue Price	Mkt Val
MS1	1979 (s) (3)	—	Y#1-3, Medal	—	7.50
MS2	1980(b) (7)	—	Y#1-3, 24-27	—	8.50
MS3	1982 (4)	—	Y#40-43	750	3,400
MS4	1986 (2)	—	KM#151 (2)	—	12.50
MS5	1990 (2)	—	Y#264-265	—	8.00
MS7	1991 (2)	—	Y#316-317	—	5.00
MS6	1991 (6)	—	Y#1-3, 328-330	—	5.50
MS8	1992 (6)	—	Y#1-3, 328-330	—	5.50
MS9	1993 (6)	—	Y#1-3, 328-330	—	5.50
MS10	1994 (6)	—	Y#1-3, 328-330	—	5.50
MS11	1995 (6)	—	Y#1-3, 328-330	—	5.50
MS12	1996 (6)	—	Y#1-3, 328-330	—	5.50

PROOF SETS

KM#	Date	Mintage	Identification	Issue Price	Mkt Val
PS1	1979 (4)	70,000	Y#4-7	1,695	800
PS2	1980 (14)	1,000	Y#10-23	1,750	425
PS4	1980 (4)	—	Y#10-13	—	40.00
PS5	1980 (4)	—	Y#14-17	—	45.00
PS6	1980 (3)	1,000	Y#18-20	—	50.00
PS3	1980 (7)	—	Y#1-3, 24-27	—	10.00
PS8	1981 (4)	1,000	Y#28-31	2,950	2,550
PS7	1981(s) (7)	10,000	Y#1-3, 24-27 Medal	—	12.00
PS9	1982(s) (7)	—	Y#1-3, 24-27 Medal	—	10.00
PS10	1983(s) (7)	—	Y#1-3, 24-27 Book	—	12.50
PS11	1983(s) (7)	—	Y#1-3, 24-27 Medal (paper cover)	—	140
PS13	1984 (4)	—	Y#68-71	—	90.00
PS12	1984(y) (7)	—	Y#1-3, 24-27 Medal	—	12.50
PS14	1984 (3)	—	Y#85-87	—	22.50
PS15	1985 (2)	—	Y#96-97	45.00	60.00
PS16	1985(y) (7)	—	Y#1-3, 24-27 Medal	—	12.00
PS17	1985 (2)	—	Y#109-110	45.00	65.00
PS18	1985 (4)	—	Y#90-93	—	115
PS19	1986(y) (7)	—	Y#1-3, 24-27 Medal	10.00	15.00
PS21	1986 (4)	—	Y#113-116	—	110
PS20	1986 (5)	10,000	Y#101-105	—	800
PS23	1987 (2)	—	Y#133-134	278	115
PS24	1987 (4)	—	Y#135-138	—	120
PS22	1987 (5)	10,000	Y#124-128	—	800
PS25	1988 (4)	—	Y#160-163	200	110
PS26	1988 (5)	10,000	Y#152-156	—	900
PS28	1989 (4)	—	Y#213-216	—	130
PS27	1989 (5)	8,000	Y#187-191	—	850
PS30	1990 (3)	2,500	Y#267-269	1,095	750
PS31	1990 (2)	2,000	Y#266 and medal	995	500
PS29	1990 (5)	5,000	Y#238-242	—	1,000
PS33	1991 (2)	2,000	Y#301 and medal	575	350
PS32	1991 (6)	—	Y#1-3, 328-330	—	6.50
PS34	1991 (5)	350	Y#309-313	—	1,000
PS37	1992 (5)	1,000	Y#331-335	—	4,500
PS35	1992 (6)	—	Y#1-3, 328-330	—	6.50
PS38	1992 (5)	—	Y#341-345	—	1,000
PS39	1993 (4)	2,000	Y#441-444	200	140
PS40	1993 (4)	1,000	Y#445-448	1,600	1,300
PS41	1993 (3)	—	Y#352-354	—	925
PS42	1993 (5)	—	Y#610-614	—	600
PS44	1993 (5)	100	Y#1072-1076	1,875	1,875
PS43	1993 (6)	—	Y#1-3, 328-330	—	8.00
PS45	1994 (12)	50	Y#419, 420 Unc/Proof, 421-429	—	5,860
PS46	1994 (11)	50	Y#419, 420 Unc/Proof, 421-428	—	4,360
PS47	1994 (5)	1,000	Y#419, 421-423, 425	—	1,385
PS48	1994 (4)	2,500	Y#419-421, 423	645	655
PS49	1994 (3)	1,000	Y#420-424, 426	—	845
PS50	1994 (2)	400	Y#420, 428	—	1,270
PS51	1994 (5)	—	Y#431-434, 544	—	600
PS52	1994 (6)	—	Y#1-3, 328-330	—	8.00
PS53	1995 (3)	2,000	Y#469-471	485	500
PS54	1995 (3)	2,000	Y#571-573	—	710
PS55	1995 (2)	3,000	Y#469-470	89.00	90.00
PS56	1995 (4)	15,000	Y#600-603	—	150
PS57	1995 (4)	9,000	Y#588-591	—	160
PS59	1995 (5)	1,000	Y#687, 736-739	—	1,385
PS58	1995 (6)	—	Y#1-3, 328-330	—	8.00
PS60	1996 (4)	15,000	Y#604-607	—	180
PS61	1996 (4)	8,000	Y#595-598	—	240
PS63	1996 (4)	750	Y#740-743 Plus bottle	—	625
PS62	1996 (6)	—	Y#1-3, 328-330	—	8.00
PS64	1997 (4)	28,000	Y#936-939	—	200
PS65	1997 (4)	10,000	Y#1099-1102	—	180
PS66	1998 (2)	61,000	China Y#727 and Canadian KM#316	72.50	70.00

COLOMBIA

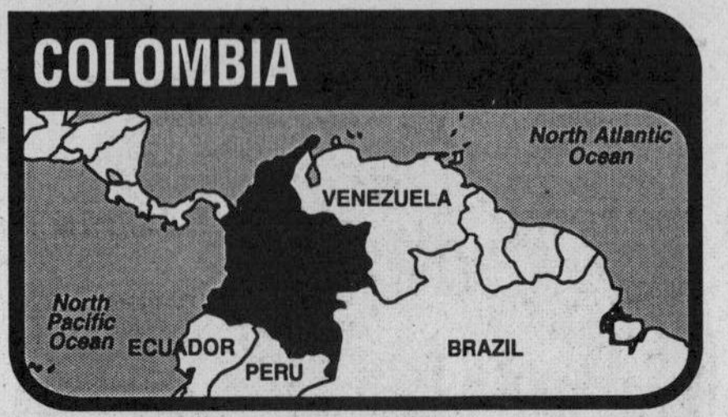

The Republic of Colombia, in the northwestern corner of South America, has an area of 440,831 sq. mi. (1,138,910 sq. km.) and a population of*42.3 million. Capital: Bogota. The economy is primarily agricultural with a mild, rich coffee being the chief crop. Colombia has the world's largest platinum deposits and important reserves of coal, iron ore, petroleum and limestone; other precious metals and emeralds are also mined. Coffee, crude oil, bananas, sugar and emeralds are exported.

The northern coast of present Colombia was one of the first parts of the American continent to be visited by Spanish navigators. At Darien in Panama is the site of the first permanent European settlement on the American mainland in 1510. New Granada, as Colombia was known until 1861, stemmed from the settlement of Santa Marta in 1525. New Granada was established as a Spanish colony in 1549. Independence was declared in 1810, and secured in 1819 when Simon Bolivar united Colombia, Venezuela, Panama and Ecuador as the Republic of Gran Colombia. Venezuela withdrew from the Republic in 1829; Ecuador in 1830; and Panama in 1903.

MINT MARKS

A, M – Medellin (capital), Antioquia (state)
B - BOGOTA
(D) Denver, USA
H – Birmingham (Heaton & Sons)
(m) - Medellin, w/o mint mark
(Mo) - Mexico City
NI - Numismatica Italiana, Arezzo, Italy mint marks stylized in wreath
(P) - Philadelphia
(S) - San Francisco, USA.
(W) - Waterbury, CT (USA, Scoville mint)

REPUBLIC

DECIMAL COINAGE

100 Centavos = 1 Peso

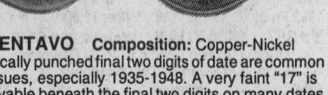

KM# 275 CENTAVO **Composition:** Copper-Nickel **Note:** Erratically punched final two digits of date are common on these issues, especially 1935-1948. A very faint "17" is often observable beneath the final two digits on many dates of this type.

Date	Mintage	F	VF	XF	Unc	BU
1918	430,000	6.00	15.00	35.00	125	—
1919	Inc. above	8.00	25.00	60.00	140	—
1920(D)	7,540,000	4.00	12.50	30.00	125	—
1921(D)	12,460,000	2.00	6.00	20.00	60.00	—
1933(P)	3,000,000	0.50	3.00	5.00	10.00	—
1935(P)	5,000,000	0.50	3.00	5.00	10.00	—
1936	1,540,000	2.00	5.00	15.00	50.00	—
1938(P)	7,920,000	0.25	0.50	2.00	6.00	—
1941B	1,000,000	0.50	1.00	3.00	10.00	—
1946B	2,096,000	0.35	0.75	2.50	6.50	—
1947/17B	1,835,000	1.00	3.50	6.00	12.00	—
1947/37B	Inc. above	1.00	3.50	6.00	12.00	—
1947/6B	Inc. above	1.00	3.50	6.00	12.00	—
1947B	Inc. above	0.50	1.00	2.00	5.00	—
1948/38B	1,139,000	1.00	3.50	6.00	12.00	—
1948B	Inc. above	0.50	1.00	2.00	5.00	—

KM# 205 CENTAVO **Composition:** Bronze **Note:** Several date varieties exist.

Date	Mintage	F	VF	XF	Unc	BU
1942	1,000,000	1.00	2.00	4.50	12.50	—
1942B	Inc. above	1.00	3.50	9.00	28.00	—
1943	—	0.50	1.00	2.50	7.00	—
1943B	4,515,000	0.50	1.00	2.50	7.00	—
1944B	4,515,000	0.35	0.65	1.50	5.00	—
1945B	3,769,000	0.50	1.00	2.50	7.00	—
1945B over reversed B	—	0.35	0.65	1.50	5.00	—
1948B	585,000	0.50	1.00	3.00	10.00	—

Date	Mintage	F	VF	XF	Unc	BU
1949B	4,255,000	0.35	0.65	1.50	5.00	—
1950B	5,827,000	0.45	0.75	2.50	8.00	—
1951B	Inc. above	0.35	0.65	1.75	5.50	—
1957	2,500,000	0.25	0.45	0.75	2.00	—
1958	590,000	0.25	0.45	1.00	2.25	—
1959	2,677,000	0.15	0.25	0.50	1.25	—
1960	2,500,000	0.15	0.25	0.50	1.25	—
1961 Widely spaced date	3,673,000	0.15	0.25	0.50	1.25	—
1961 Narrowly spaced date	Inc. above	0.15	0.25	0.45	1.00	—
1962	4,065,000	0.15	0.25	0.50	1.25	—
1963	1,845,000	0.15	0.25	0.75	2.00	—
1964/44	3,165,000	0.50	1.50	2.50	5.00	—
1964	Inc. above	0.15	0.25	0.50	1.25	—
1965 Large date	5,510,000	0.15	0.25	0.45	1.00	—
1965 Small date	Inc. above	0.15	0.25	0.45	1.00	—
1966	3,910,000	0.15	0.25	0.50	1.25	—

KM# 275a CENTAVO **Composition:** Nickel Clad Steel **Note:** Erratically punched final two digits of date are common on these issues.

Date	Mintage	F	VF	XF	Unc	BU
1952/12B	—	0.20	0.50	1.50	3.50	—
1952B	Inc. above	0.10	0.15	0.75	2.50	—
1954B	5,080,000	0.10	0.15	0.50	1.75	—
1956	1,315,000	0.10	0.20	1.00	2.00	—
1957	900,000	0.35	0.75	2.50	7.50	—
1958/48	—	0.35	0.75	2.00	6.00	—
1958	1,596,000	0.20	0.45	1.00	2.00	—

KM# 218 CENTAVO **Composition:** Bronze **Subject:** Uprising Sesquicentennial **Note:** This and the other issues in the uprising commemorative series offer the usual design of the period with the dates 1810-1960 added at the bottom of the obverse.

Date	Mintage	F	VF	XF	Unc	BU
ND(1960)	500,000	0.60	1.50	3.00	6.50	—

KM# 205a CENTAVO **Composition:** Copper Clad Steel **Note:** Several date varieties exist.

Date	Mintage	F	VF	XF	Unc	BU
1967	5,730,000	—	0.10	0.15	0.45	—
1968	7,390,000	—	0.10	0.15	0.45	—
1969	6,870,000	—	0.10	0.15	0.45	—
1970	3,839,000	—	0.10	0.20	0.60	—
1971	3,020,000	—	0.10	0.20	0.60	—
1972	3,100,000	—	0.10	0.20	0.60	—
1973	—	—	—	0.10	0.35	—
1974	2,000,000	—	—	0.10	0.35	—
1975	1,000,000	—	—	0.10	0.35	—
1976	1,000,000	—	—	0.10	0.35	—
1977	900,000	—	0.10	0.15	0.45	—
1978	224,000	—	0.10	0.20	0.65	—

KM# 198 2 CENTAVOS **Composition:** Copper-Nickel **Note:** Erratically punched final two digits exist for 1946-1947. A very faint "17" is often observable beneath the final two digits on many dates of this type.

Date	Mintage	F	VF	XF	Unc	BU
1918	930,000	10.00	20.00	40.00	90.00	—
1919	Inc. above	20.00	40.00	70.00	150	—
1920	3,855,000	3.50	7.50	20.00	55.00	—
1921(D)	11,145,000	2.50	5.00	15.00	40.00	—
1922 10 pieces known	—	1,350	2,800	—	—	—
1933(P)	3,500,000	0.50	1.50	4.00	10.00	—
1935(P)	2,500,000	0.35	1.00	3.50	8.00	—
1938(P)	3,872,000	0.35	1.00	3.25	7.00	—
1941B	500,000	1.00	2.00	7.00	15.00	—
1942B	500,000	1.50	2.50	8.00	16.50	—
1946/36B	2,593,000	1.00	2.50	6.00	12.50	—
1946B	Inc. above	0.75	1.50	4.75	11.00	—
1947/3B	1,337,000	0.75	1.50	4.00	10.00	—
1947/36B	Inc. above	0.75	1.50	4.00	10.00	—
1947B	Inc. above	0.35	1.00	3.00	6.50	—

KM# 210 2 CENTAVOS **Composition:** Bronze

Date	Mintage	F	VF	XF	Unc	BU
1948B	2,648,000	0.35	1.00	4.00	7.50	—
1949B	1,278,000	0.75	2.00	5.00	10.00	—
1950B	2,285,000	0.75	1.50	4.50	9.00	—

KM# 211 2 CENTAVOS **Composition:** Aluminum-Bronze **Obverse:** Divided legend

Date	Mintage	F	VF	XF	Unc	BU
1952B Small date	5,038,000	0.15	0.25	0.50	1.50	—
1965/3	1,830,000	0.10	0.20	0.40	1.00	—
1965 Large date	Inc. above	0.15	0.25	0.50	1.25	—

KM# 214 2 CENTAVOS **Composition:** Aluminum-Bronze **Obverse:** Continuous legend

Date	Mintage	F	VF	XF	Unc	BU
1955 Large date	2,513,000	0.10	0.25	1.00	3.00	—
1955B Large date	Inc. above	0.10	0.25	0.75	2.00	—
1959 Small date	4,609,000	0.10	0.20	0.50	1.50	—

KM# 219 2 CENTAVOS **Composition:** Aluminum-Bronze **Subject:** Uprising Sesquicentennial

Date	Mintage	F	VF	XF	Unc	BU
ND(1960)	250,000	1.00	2.00	3.00	8.00	—

KM# 190 2-1/2 CENTAVOS **Composition:** Copper-Nickel

Date	Mintage	F	VF	XF	Unc	BU
1902(W)	400,000	—	—	500	900	—

KM# 184 5 CENTAVOS **Composition:** Copper-Nickel

Date	Mintage	F	VF	XF	Unc	BU
1902(W)	400,000	—	—	650	1,000	—

KM# 191 5 CENTAVOS **Weight:** 1.2500 g. **Composition:** 0.6660 Silver .0268 oz. ASW **Edge:** Plain

Date	Mintage	F	VF	XF	Unc	BU
1902(P)	400,000	0.50	1.50	3.50	7.50	—

KM# 199 5 CENTAVOS **Composition:** Copper-Nickel **Note:** Varieties exist. Erratically punched final two digits of date are common on these issues, especially 1935-1950. A very faint "17" is often observable beneath the final two digits on many dates of this type.

Date	Mintage	F	VF	XF	Unc
1918	767,000	5.50	15.00	45.00	85.00
1919	1,926,000	3.00	12.50	25.00	55.00
1920	2,062,000	2.50	12.50	25.00	60.00
1920H	—	3.50	13.50	27.50	65.00
1921	1,574,000	2.00	10.00	20.00	50.00
1921H	—	2.00	10.00	20.00	50.00
1922	2,623,000	2.50	11.50	22.50	55.00
1922H	—	3.50	12.50	30.00	65.00
1924	120,000	6.50	15.00	35.00	75.00
1933(P)	2,000,000	0.75	1.75	3.50	10.00
1935/24	1,616,000	5.00	12.00	30.00	60.00
1935(P)	10,000,000	0.75	1.75	3.50	10.00
1936	—	6.50	15.00	32.50	65.00
1938B	2,000,000	1.00	2.50	5.50	12.50
1938	3,867,000	2.00	3.75	8.00	15.00
1938 Large 38 in date	Inc. above	2.00	4.50	10.00	20.00
1939/5	2,000,000	1.75	3.00	6.00	12.50
1939	Inc. above	0.75	1.50	3.50	7.50
1941	—	2.50	5.50	9.00	22.50
1941B	500,000	3.00	6.00	10.00	25.00
1946(P) (S) Small date	40,000,000	0.20	0.50	1.00	3.00
1946(m) Large date	3,330,000	2.00	4.00	8.50	22.50
1949B	2,750,000	0.45	1.00	2.50	6.00
1950B Large 50 in date	3,611,000	6.00	12.00	25.00	45.00
1950B Small 50 in date	Inc. above	0.45	1.00	3.00	6.00

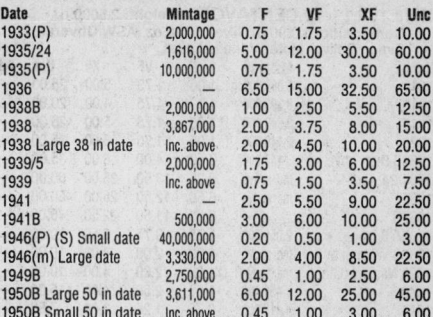

KM# 206 5 CENTAVOS **Composition:** Bronze **Note:** Some coins of 1942-1956 have weak "B" mint mark.

Date	Mintage	F	VF	XF	Unc	BU
1942	—	2.00	4.00	12.00	30.00	—
1942B	800,000	1.00	2.50	4.50	12.00	—
1943	—	5.00	9.00	18.00	35.00	—
1943B	6,053,000	0.75	1.50	3.00	10.00	—
1944	—	0.75	1.50	3.00	10.00	—
1944B	9,013,000	0.75	1.50	3.00	10.00	—
1945/4	—	0.75	1.50	3.00	10.00	—
1945	—	0.75	1.50	3.00	10.00	—
1945B	11,101,000	0.25	0.75	1.25	4.00	—
1946/5	—	1.25	3.50	4.50	12.50	—
1946	—	0.50	1.25	2.00	7.00	—
1952	—	1.25	2.50	3.50	10.00	—
1952B	3,985,000	0.15	0.40	1.00	2.50	—
1953B	5,180,000	0.10	0.25	0.75	2.00	—
1954B	1,159,000	0.10	0.25	0.75	2.00	—
1955B	6,819,000	0.10	0.25	0.75	2.00	—
1956	8,772,000	0.10	0.25	0.50	1.00	—
1956B	—	0.75	1.50	4.50	12.50	—
1957	8,912,000	0.10	0.25	0.75	2.00	—
1958	15,016,000	0.10	0.25	0.50	1.50	—
1959	14,271,000	0.10	0.25	0.50	1.50	—
1960/660	11,716,000	0.25	0.75	1.00	2.25	—
1960/70	Inc. above	0.25	0.75	1.00	2.25	—
1960	Inc. above	0.10	0.25	0.50	1.25	—
1961	11,200,000	0.10	0.25	0.50	1.25	—
CD1962	10,928,000	—	0.10	0.35	1.00	—
1963/53	15,113,000	—	—	—	—	—
1963	Inc. above	—	0.10	0.35	1.00	—
1964	9,336,000	—	0.10	0.35	1.00	—
1965	6,460,000	—	0.10	0.35	1.00	—
1966	7,170,000	—	0.10	0.35	1.00	—

KM# 206a 5 CENTAVOS **Composition:** Bronze **Note:** Varieties exist for 1967, 1970, and 1973.

Date	Mintage	F	VF	XF	Unc	BU
1967	10,280,000	—	—	0.10	0.35	—
1968	8,900,000	—	—	0.10	0.35	—
1969	17,800,000	—	—	0.10	0.35	—
1970	14,842,000	—	—	0.10	0.35	—
1971	10,730,000	—	—	0.10	0.35	—
1972	10,170,000	—	—	0.10	0.35	—
1973	10,525,000	—	—	0.10	0.35	—
1974	5,310,000	—	—	0.10	0.50	—
1975	5,631,000	—	—	0.10	0.50	—
1976	3,009,000	—	—	0.10	0.50	—
1977	2,000,000	—	—	0.10	0.50	—
1978	468,000	—	—	0.10	0.50	—
1979	8,087,000	—	—	—	—	—

KM# 220 5 CENTAVOS **Composition:** Bronze **Subject:** Uprising Sesquicentennial

Date	Mintage	F	VF	XF	Unc	BU
ND(1960)	400,000	1.75	3.50	7.50	25.00	—

KM# 196.1 10 CENTAVOS **Weight:** 2.5000 g. **Composition:** 0.9000 Silver .0723 oz. ASW **Obverse:** Simon Bolivar **Note:** Varieties exist.

Date	Mintage	F	VF	XF	Unc	BU
1911	5,065,000	1.00	1.75	5.00	25.00	—
1913	8,305,000	1.00	1.75	4.00	20.00	—
1914	3,840,000	1.00	1.75	5.00	25.00	—
1920	2,149,000	1.00	1.75	5.00	25.00	—
1934B B on obverse	140,000	2.50	4.00	8.00	35.00	—
1934/24	Inc. above	6.25	13.50	28.00	60.00	—
1934	Inc. above	6.50	12.50	25.00	50.00	—
1937B	—	5.00	11.50	22.50	45.00	—
1938/7B	2,055,000	1.75	3.75	6.50	20.00	—
1938B Wide date	Inc. above	1.00	2.00	4.00	10.00	—
1938 Narrow date	Inc. above	1.00	2.00	4.00	10.00	—
1940	450,000	1.50	2.50	4.50	15.00	—
1941	4,415,000	0.75	1.25	3.00	7.50	—
1942	3,140,000	5.00	10.00	16.50	37.50	—
1942B B on reverse	Inc. above	0.75	1.25	3.00	7.50	—

KM# 196.2 10 CENTAVOS **Weight:** 2.5000 g. **Composition:** 0.9000 Silver .0723 oz. ASW **Obverse:** Simon Bolivar **Reverse:** National arms recut

Date	F	VF	XF	Unc	BU
1920	1.50	2.50	7.00	27.50	—

KM# 207.1 10 CENTAVOS **Weight:** 2.5000 g. **Composition:** 0.5000 Silver .0401 oz. ASW **Obverse:** Francisco de Paula Santander **Reverse:** Mint mark at bottom

Date	Mintage	F	VF	XF	Unc	BU
1945B	4,830,000	0.75	1.50	3.50	8.50	—
1945 B-B	—	—	—	—	—	—
1945 Backwards B	—	1.00	2.00	4.00	10.00	—
1946/5B	—	0.60	1.50	4.50	12.50	—
1946B	—	0.60	1.50	4.50	12.50	—
1947/5B	7,366,000	1.50	3.00	5.00	15.00	—
1947/6B	Inc. above	1.50	3.00	5.00	15.00	—
1947B	Inc. above	1.50	3.00	5.00	15.00	—

KM# 207.2 10 CENTAVOS **Weight:** 2.5000 g. **Composition:** 0.5000 Silver .0401 oz. ASW **Obverse:** Francisco de Paula Santander **Reverse:** Mint mark at top **Note:** Varieties exist. Almost all dies for 1946-1951 show at least faint traces of overdating from 1945. Coins with absolutely no underdate, and those with very bold underdate, are generally worth more to advanced specialists.

Date	Mintage	F	VF	XF	Unc	BU
1947/5B	Inc. above	2.00	4.00	7.50	20.00	—
1947B	Inc. above	2.00	4.00	7.50	20.00	—
1948/5B	3,629,000	0.60	1.50	3.00	10.00	—
1948B	Inc. above	0.50	1.00	2.25	8.00	—
1949/5B	5,923,000	3.00	6.50	12.50	28.00	—
1949B	Inc. above	0.65	1.25	2.25	7.50	—
1950B	6,783,000	0.65	1.50	2.75	8.50	—
1951/5B	5,185,000	0.65	1.50	2.75	8.50	—
1951B	Inc. above	0.65	1.25	2.25	7.50	—
1952B	1,060,000	1.25	2.25	4.50	12.50	—

KM# 212.1 10 CENTAVOS **Composition:** Copper-Nickel **Reverse:** Head of Chief Calarca right **Note:** 18mm.

Date	Mintage	F	VF	XF	Unc	BU
1952B	6,035,000	0.35	1.00	3.50	15.00	—
1953B	6,985,000	0.25	0.50	1.50	4.50	—

KM# 212.2 10 CENTAVOS **Composition:** Copper-Nickel **Note:** 18.5mm. Varieties exist.

Date	Mintage	F	VF	XF	Unc	BU
1954B	13,006,000	0.20	0.50	1.25	3.00	—
1955B	9,968,000	0.20	0.50	1.25	3.00	—
1956	36,010,000	0.10	0.20	0.50	1.50	—
1956B	—	0.10	0.20	0.50	1.50	—
1958	41,695,000	—	—	—	—	—
1959	36,653,000	0.10	0.20	0.50	1.50	—
1960	32,290,000	0.10	0.20	0.50	2.00	—
1961	17,780,000	0.10	0.20	0.50	2.00	—
1962	8,930,000	0.10	0.20	0.50	2.00	—
1963	37,540,000	0.10	0.20	0.50	1.50	—
1964	61,672,000	0.10	0.20	0.50	1.50	—
1965	12,804,000	0.10	0.25	0.75	3.00	—
1966 Large date	23,544,000	0.10	0.20	0.50	1.50	—

KM# 221 10 CENTAVOS **Composition:** Copper-Nickel **Subject:** Uprising Sesquicentennial

Date	Mintage	F	VF	XF	Unc	BU
ND(1960)	1,000,000	1.00	2.00	3.50	8.00	—

KM# 226 10 CENTAVOS **Composition:** Nickel Clad Steel **Obverse:** Francisco de Paula Santander

Date	Mintage	F	VF	XF	Unc	BU
1967	26,980,000	—	0.10	0.20	0.75	—
1968	23,670,000	—	0.10	0.20	0.75	—
1969	29,450,000	—	0.10	0.20	0.75	—

KM# 236 10 CENTAVOS **Composition:** Nickel Clad Steel **Issuer:** Francisco de Paula Santander **Obverse:** Legend divided after REPUBLICA DE.

Date	Mintage	F	VF	XF	Unc	BU
1969	Inc. above	—	0.10	0.20	0.65	—
1970	38,935,000	—	0.10	0.20	0.50	—
1971	53,314,000	—	0.10	0.20	0.50	—

KM# 243 10 CENTAVOS **Composition:** Nickel Clad Steel **Obverse:** Legend divided after REPUBLICA

Date	F	VF	XF	Unc	BU
1970	—	—	—	—	—
1971	—	—	—	—	—

KM# 253 10 CENTAVOS **Composition:** Nickel Clad Steel **Obverse:** Continuous legend **Note:** Varieties exist.

Date	Mintage	F	VF	XF	Unc	BU
1972	58,000,000	—	0.10	0.15	0.35	—
1973	46,549,000	—	0.10	0.15	0.35	—
1974	49,740,000	—	0.10	0.15	0.35	—
1975	46,037,000	—	0.10	0.15	0.35	—
1976	46,084,000	—	0.10	0.15	0.35	—
1977	8,127,000	—	0.10	0.15	0.35	—
1978	97,081,000	—	0.10	0.15	0.35	—
1980	18,929,000	—	0.10	0.15	0.35	—

KM# 197 20 CENTAVOS **Weight:** 5.0000 g. **Composition:** 0.9000 Silver .1446 oz. ASW **Obverse:** Bust of Simon Bolivar right **Reverse:** Arms

Date	Mintage	F	VF	XF	Unc	BU
1911	1,206,000	1.50	3.50	7.50	17.50	—
1913	1,630,000	1.50	3.50	7.50	22.50	—
1914	2,560,000	1.50	3.50	9.00	25.00	—
1920 Wide date	1,242,000	2.50	6.00	12.50	32.50	—
1920 Narrow date	Inc. above	2.50	6.00	12.50	32.50	—
1921	372,000	7.00	15.00	35.00	85.00	—
1922	45,000	30.00	55.00	85.00	225	—
1933B Mint mark on obverse	330,000	3.50	7.50	15.00	35.00	—
1933B Mint mark on reverse	Inc. above	12.50	25.00	45.00	125	—
1933B Mint mark on both sides	Inc. above	5.00	10.00	20.00	50.00	—
1938/1	1,410,000	4.00	8.00	17.00	35.00	—
1938	Inc. above	1.75	5.00	10.00	22.00	—
1941	—	2.00	6.00	12.00	28.00	—
1942	155,000	9.00	20.00	32.50	65.00	—
1942B Mint mark on reverse	Inc. above	1.50	3.50	7.50	20.00	—

KM# 208.1 20 CENTAVOS **Weight:** 5.0000 g. **Composition:** 0.5000 Silver .0803 oz. ASW **Obverse:** Francisco de Paula Santander **Reverse:** Mint mark in field below CENTAVOS

Date	Mintage	F	VF	XF	Unc	BU
1945B	1,675,000	1.00	3.00	7.00	15.00	—
1945BB	Inc. above	4.25	8.00	15.00	32.50	—

Note: 1945BB has extra B on wreath at bottom

Date	Mintage	F	VF	XF	Unc	BU
1946/5B	6,599,000	1.00	2.50	6.50	15.00	—
1946B	Inc. above	1.50	3.00	9.00	20.00	—
1947/5B	9,708,000	3.00	6.00	12.00	28.00	—
1947B	—	3.00	6.00	12.00	28.00	—

KM# 208.3 20 CENTAVOS **Weight:** 5.0000 g. **Composition:** 0.5000 Silver .0803 oz. ASW **Obverse:** Francisco de Paula Santander **Reverse:** Without mint mark

Date	Mintage	F	VF	XF	Unc	BU
1946(m)	—	3.00	7.50	15.00	32.50	—
1946/5(m)	—	3.75	9.50	16.50	37.50	—
1947(m)	1,748,000	5.00	8.50	15.00	35.00	—

KM# 208.2 20 CENTAVOS **Weight:** 5.0000 g. **Composition:** 0.5000 Silver .0803 oz. ASW **Obverse:** Francisco de Paula Santander **Reverse:** Mint mark on wreath at top **Note:** Almost all dies for 1946-1951 show at least faint traces of overdating from 1945. Coins with absolutely no underdate, and those with very bold underdate, are generally worth more to advanced specialists. Varieties exist.

Date	Mintage	F	VF	XF	Unc	BU
1947/5B	Inc. above	5.00	10.00	20.00	50.00	—
1948/5B	Inc. above	1.00	3.00	5.00	12.00	—
1948B	Inc. above	1.50	3.00	5.00	14.00	—
1949/5B	403,000	3.75	8.50	17.50	45.00	—
1949B	Inc. above	2.50	5.00	10.00	32.50	—
1950/45B	1,899,000	2.75	6.75	15.00	50.00	—
1950B	Inc. above	2.75	6.00	13.50	37.50	—
1951/45B	7,498,000	1.00	3.00	6.50	13.50	—
1951B	Inc. above	1.00	3.00	6.00	12.50	—

KM# 213 20 CENTAVOS **Weight:** 5.0000 g. **Composition:** 0.3000 Silver .0482 oz. ASW **Obverse:** Arms **Reverse:** Bust of Simon Bolivar left

Date	Mintage	F	VF	XF	Unc	BU
1952B Rare	3,887	—	—	—	—	—
1953B	17,819,000	0.50	1.00	2.50	7.00	—

KM# 215.1 20 CENTAVOS **Composition:** Copper-Nickel **Obverse:** Bust of Simon Bolivar right, small date

Date	Mintage	F	VF	XF	Unc	BU
1956	39,778,000	0.10	0.15	0.50	1.50	—
1959	44,779,000	0.10	0.15	0.50	1.50	—
1961	10,740,000	0.15	0.25	0.75	2.50	—

KM# 215.2 20 CENTAVOS **Composition:** Copper-Nickel **Obverse:** Bust of Simon Bolivar right, large date

Date	Mintage	F	VF	XF	Unc	BU
1963	12,035,000	—	0.10	0.50	1.50	—
1964	29,075,000	—	0.10	0.50	1.50	—
1965	19,180,000	0.10	0.25	0.75	2.50	—

KM# 215.3 20 CENTAVOS **Composition:** Copper-Nickel **Obverse:** Bust of Simon Bolivar right, medium date

Date	Mintage	F	VF	XF	Unc	BU
1966	23,060,000	0.10	0.15	0.50	1.50	—

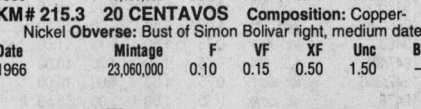

KM# 222 20 CENTAVOS **Composition:** Copper-Nickel **Subject:** Uprising Sesquicentennial

Date	Mintage	F	VF	XF	Unc	BU
ND(1960)	500,000	0.75	1.50	3.00	8.00	—

KM# 224 20 CENTAVOS **Composition:** Copper-Nickel **Reverse:** Jorge Eliecer Gaitan

Date	Mintage	F	VF	XF	Unc	BU
1965	1,000,000	—	0.10	0.50	1.50	—

KM# 227 20 CENTAVOS **Composition:** Nickel Clad Steel **Obverse:** Francisco de Paula Santander

Date	Mintage	F	VF	XF	Unc	BU
1967	15,720,000	—	0.10	0.20	1.00	—
1968	26,680,000	—	0.10	0.20	1.00	—
1969	22,470,000	—	0.10	0.20	1.00	—

KM# 237 20 CENTAVOS **Composition:** Nickel Clad Steel **Obverse:** Francisco de Paula Santander, legend divided after REPUBLICA

Date	Mintage	F	VF	XF	Unc	BU
1969	Inc. above	—	—	—	—	—
1970	44,358,000	—	0.10	0.20	1.00	—

KM# 245 20 CENTAVOS **Composition:** Nickel Clad Steel **Obverse:** Legend divided after REPUBLICA DE

Date	Mintage	F	VF	XF	Unc	BU
1971	77,526,000	—	—	0.10	0.35	—

KM# 246.1 20 CENTAVOS **Composition:** Nickel Clad Steel **Obverse:** Legend continuous **Note:** Varieties exist with and without dots.

Date	Mintage	F	VF	XF	Unc	BU
1971	Inc. above	—	—	0.10	0.35	—
1972	41,891,000	—	—	0.10	0.35	—
1973/1	41,440,000	—	—	0.10	0.35	—
1973	Inc. above	—	—	0.15	0.50	—
1974/1	45,941,000	—	—	0.35	1.00	—
1974	Inc. above	—	—	0.10	0.35	—
1975	28,635,000	—	—	0.10	0.35	—
1976	29,590,000	—	—	0.10	0.35	—
1977	2,054,000	—	—	0.15	0.50	—
1978	10,630,000	—	—	0.10	0.35	—

KM# 246.2 20 CENTAVOS **Composition:** Nickel Clad Steel **Obverse:** Smaller letters in legend **Reverse:** Wreath with larger 20 and smaller CENTAVOS

Date	Mintage	F	VF	XF	Unc	BU
1979	16,655,000	—	—	0.10	0.20	—

KM# 267 25 CENTAVOS **Composition:** Aluminum-Bronze **Obverse:** Simon Bolivar bust right

Date	Mintage	F	VF	XF	Unc	BU
1979	88,874,000	—	0.10	0.15	0.25	—
1980	46,168,000	—	0.10	0.15	0.25	—

KM# 186.2 50 CENTAVOS **Weight:** 12.5000 g. **Composition:** 0.8350 Silver .3356 oz. ASW **Obverse:** Liberty head, incuse lettering on head band **Edge Lettering:** DIOS LEI LIBERTAD **Note:** Similar to KM#186.1a. Struck at the Bogota Mint.

Date	Mintage	VG	F	VF	XF	Unc
1906	446,000	7.00	15.00	25.00	50.00	100
1907	1,126,000	5.00	10.00	18.50	40.00	75.00
1908/7	871,000	20.00	40.00	70.00	150	200
1908	Inc. above	10.00	17.50	27.50	75.00	150

KM# 192 50 CENTAVOS **Weight:** 12.5000 g. **Composition:** 0.8350 Silver .3356 oz. ASW **Obverse:** Liberty head **Reverse:** Arms

Date	Mintage	F	VF	XF	Unc	BU
1902(P)	960,000	15.00	30.00	60.00	120	—

KM# 193.1 50 CENTAVOS **Weight:** 12.5000 g. **Composition:** 0.9000 Silver .3617 oz. ASW **Obverse:** Simon Bolivar, sharper featured bust **Reverse:** Left wing and flags far from legend **Note:** Struck at Birmingham and Bogota mints. Many date varieties exist.

Date	Mintage	F	VF	XF	Unc	BU
1912	1,207,000	6.00	12.50	35.00	75.00	—
1912 Proof; rare	—	—	—	—	—	—
1913	417,000	6.00	12.50	35.00	75.00	—
1914 Closed 4	769,000	7.00	15.00	40.00	85.00	—
1915 Small date	946,000	6.00	12.50	30.00	70.00	—
1915 Small date; Proof; rare	—	—	—	—	—	—
1915 Large date	Inc. above	—	—	—	—	—
1915 Proof; rare	—	—	—	—	—	—
1916 Small date	1,060,000	5.00	10.00	22.50	50.00	—
1917 Normal 7	99,000	10.00	20.00	45.00	90.00	—
1917 Foot on 7	Inc. above	10.00	20.00	45.00	90.00	—
1917 Curved top	Inc. above	10.00	20.00	50.00	100	—
1918	400,000	5.00	10.00	25.00	75.00	—
1919	Inc. above	15.00	25.00	40.00	85.00	—
1922	150,000	10.00	15.00	30.00	75.00	—
1923	150,000	10.00	15.00	30.00	75.00	—
1931/21B	—	5.00	10.00	22.50	50.00	—
1931B	700,000	5.00	10.00	22.50	50.00	—
1931	Inc. above	65.00	120	185	350	—
1932/12B	300,000	8.00	14.00	30.00	75.00	—
1932/22B	Inc. above	7.00	15.00	35.00	80.00	—
1932B	Inc. above	5.00	10.00	22.50	50.00	—
1932 Flat top 3, no B	Inc. above	20.00	30.00	45.00	90.00	—
1933/13B	1,000,000	5.00	10.00	20.00	45.00	—

Date	Mintage	F	VF	XF	Unc	BU
1933/23B	Inc. above	5.00	10.00	25.00	50.00	—
1933B	Inc. above	3.00	5.00	10.00	28.00	—

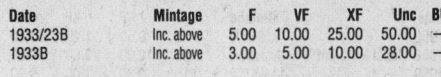

KM# 193.2 50 CENTAVOS **Weight:** 12.5000 g. **Composition:** 0.9000 Silver .3617 oz. ASW **Obverse:** Simon Bolivar, sharper featured bust **Reverse:** Larger letters, left wing and flags close to legend **Note:** Many date varieties exist. Struck at the Medellin Mint.

Date	Mintage	F	VF	XF	Unc	BU
1914 Open 4	—	5.00	10.00	30.00	80.00	—
1915/4 Large date	—	45.00	75.00	125	200	—
1915 Large date	—	55.00	100	150	250	—
1918/4	—	10.00	20.00	35.00	75.00	—
1918	—	5.00	10.00	25.00	65.00	—
1919/8	—	7.50	15.00	30.00	70.00	—
1919	—	7.50	15.00	30.00	70.00	—
1921	300,000	7.50	15.00	30.00	70.00	—
1922	—	5.00	10.00	25.00	65.00	—
1932/22M	1,200,000	20.00	40.00	70.00	145	—
1932M	Inc. above	3.00	5.00	15.00	30.00	—
1932 Round top 3, no M	Inc. above	18.00	35.00	60.00	125	—
1933M	800,000	3.50	7.50	25.00	50.00	—
1933/23 Round top 3s, no M	Inc. above	15.00	25.00	35.00	75.00	—

KM# 274 50 CENTAVOS **Weight:** 12.5000 g. **Composition:** 0.9000 Silver .3617 oz. ASW **Obverse:** Simon Bolivar, rounded featured bust

Date	Mintage	F	VF	XF	Unc	BU
1916(P)	1,300,000	BV	7.50	25.00	50.00	—
1917(P)	142,000	6.00	18.00	37.50	75.00	—
1921(P)	1,000,000	BV	5.00	20.00	45.00	—
1922(P)	3,000,000	BV	5.00	15.00	40.00	—
1934(S)	10,000,000	BV	5.00	15.00	40.00	—

KM# 209 50 CENTAVOS **Weight:** 12.5000 g. **Composition:** 0.5000 Silver .2009 oz. ASW **Obverse:** Simon Bolivar

Date	Mintage	F	VF	XF	Unc	BU
1947/6B	1,240,000	4.50	7.00	20.00	50.00	—
1947B	Inc. above	10.00	15.00	30.00	75.00	—
1948/6B	707,000	4.50	7.00	20.00	50.00	—
1948B/B inverted B	Inc. above	25.00	40.00	60.00	120	—
1948B	Inc. above	7.50	12.50	25.00	65.00	—

KM# 217 50 CENTAVOS **Composition:** Copper-Nickel **Obverse:** Arms **Reverse:** Simon Bolivar **Note:** Various sizes of date exist.

Date	Mintage	F	VF	XF	Unc
1958	3,596,000	0.15	0.50	1.25	3.50
1958 Medal Rotation	Inc. above	6.00	12.00	22.00	40.00
1959	13,466,000	0.15	0.30	1.00	3.00
1959 Medal Rotation	Inc. above	2.00	3.50	6.00	10.00
1960	4,360,000	0.15	0.30	1.50	4.00
1961	3,260,000	0.15	0.30	1.50	4.00
1962	2,336,000	0.15	0.30	1.50	4.00
1963	4,098,000	0.15	0.30	1.00	3.00
1964	9,274,000	0.15	0.30	1.00	3.00
1965	5,800,000	0.15	0.30	1.00	3.00
1966	2,820,000	0.15	0.30	1.00	3.00

KM# 223 50 CENTAVOS Composition: Copper-Nickel **Subject:** Uprising Sesquicentennial

Date	Mintage	F	VF	XF	Unc	BU
ND(1960)	200,000	1.50	3.00	7.50	15.00	—

KM# 225 50 CENTAVOS Composition: Copper-Nickel **Reverse:** Jorge Eliecer Gaitan

Date	Mintage	F	VF	XF	Unc	BU
1965	600,000	0.10	0.20	0.50	1.50	—

KM# 228 50 CENTAVOS Composition: Nickel Clad Steel **Obverse:** Francisco de Paula Santander

Date	Mintage	F	VF	XF	Unc	BU
1967	3,460,000	0.10	0.15	0.25	1.00	—
1968	5,460,000	0.10	0.15	0.25	1.00	—
1969	1,590,000	0.10	0.15	0.25	1.00	—

KM# 244.1 50 CENTAVOS Composition: Nickel Clad Steel **Obverse:** Flat truncation **Reverse:** 5 far from wreath **Note:** Date varieties exist.

Date	Mintage	F	VF	XF	Unc	BU
1970	30,906,000	—	0.10	0.15	0.50	—
1971	32,650,000	—	0.10	0.15	0.50	—
1972	25,290,000	—	0.10	0.15	0.50	—
1973	8,060,000	—	0.10	0.15	0.50	—
1974	19,541,000	—	0.10	0.15	0.50	—
1975	4,325,000	—	0.10	0.15	0.60	—
1976	13,181,000	—	0.10	0.15	0.45	—
1977	10,413,000	—	0.10	0.15	0.45	—
1978	10,736,000	—	0.10	0.15	0.45	—

KM# 244.2 50 CENTAVOS Composition: Nickel Clad Steel **Obverse:** Angled truncation **Reverse:** 5 close to wreath **Note:** Various sizes of dates exist.

Date	Mintage	F	VF	XF	Unc	BU
1979	22,584,000	—	0.10	0.15	0.45	—
1980	16,433,000	—	0.10	0.15	0.45	—
1982	10,107,000	—	0.10	0.15	0.45	—

KM# 244.3 50 CENTAVOS Composition: Nickel Clad Steel **Obverse:** 244.2 **Reverse:** 244.1 **Note:** Mule.

Date	F	VF	XF	Unc	BU
1979	10.00	20.00	30.00	50.00	—

KM# 216 PESO Weight: 25.0000 g. **Composition:** 0.9000 Silver .7234 oz. ASW **Subject:** 200th Anniversary of Popayan Mint

Date	Mintage	F	VF	XF	Unc	BU
ND(1956)(Mo)	12,000	6.00	9.00	15.00	25.00	—

KM# 229 PESO Composition: Copper-Nickel **Obverse:** Simon Bolivar

Date	Mintage	F	VF	XF	Unc	BU
1967	4,000,000	0.15	0.30	0.50	1.00	—

KM# 258.1 PESO Composition: Copper-Nickel **Obverse:** Simon Bolivar, small date

Date	Mintage	F	VF	XF	Unc	BU
1974	56,020,000	—	0.10	0.15	0.50	—
1975 medium date	117,714,000	—	0.10	0.15	0.40	—
1976	98,728,000	—	0.10	0.15	0.40	—

KM# 258.2 PESO Composition: Copper-Nickel **Obverse:** Simon Bolivar, large date

Date	Mintage	F	VF	XF	Unc	BU
1976	Inc. above	—	0.10	0.15	0.40	—
1977	62,083,000	—	0.10	0.15	0.40	—
1978	48,624,000	—	0.10	0.15	0.40	—
1979	83,908,000	—	0.10	0.15	0.40	—
1980	93,406,000	—	0.10	0.15	0.40	—
1981	65,219,000	—	0.10	0.15	0.40	—

KM# 263 2 PESOS Composition: Bronze **Obverse:** Simon Bolivar **Note:** Varieties exist.

Date	Mintage	F	VF	XF	Unc	BU
1977	76,661,000	0.10	0.15	0.25	0.50	—
1978	69,575,000	0.10	0.15	0.25	0.50	—
1979	56,537,000	0.10	0.15	0.25	0.50	—
1980	108,521,000	0.10	0.15	0.25	0.50	—
1981	40,368,000	0.10	0.15	0.25	0.50	—
1983	8,358,000	0.10	0.15	0.25	0.50	—
1987	—	0.10	0.15	0.25	0.50	—
1988	16,200,000	0.10	0.15	0.25	0.50	—

KM# 194 2-1/2 PESOS Weight: 3.9940 g. **Composition:** 0.9170 Gold .1177 oz. AGW

Date	Mintage	F	VF	XF	Unc	BU
1913	18,000	—	BV	75.00	125	—

KM# 200 2-1/2 PESOS Weight: 3.9940 g. **Composition:** 0.9170 Gold .1177 oz. AGW **Obverse:** Simon Bolivar, large head

Date	Mintage	F	VF	XF	Unc	BU
1919A	—	—	BV	60.00	100	—
1919B	—	—	—	—	—	—
1919	34,000	—	BV	60.00	100	—
1920/19A	—	—	BV	60.00	100	—
1920A	—	—	BV	60.00	100	—
1920	34,000	—	BV	85.00	150	—

KM# 203 2-1/2 PESOS Weight: 3.9940 g. **Composition:** 0.9170 Gold .1177 oz. AGW **Obverse:** Simon Bolivar, small head, MEDELLIN below bust

Date	Mintage	F	VF	XF	Unc	BU
1924	—	—	BV	60.00	100	—
1925 Rare	—	—	—	—	—	—
1927	—	—	BV	75.00	125	—
1928	14,000	—	BV	100	175	—
1929 Rare	—	—	—	—	—	—

KM# 195.2 5 PESOS Weight: 7.9881 g. **Composition:** 0.9170 Gold .2355 oz. AGW **Note:** Medallic die rotation.

Date	Mintage	F	VF	XF	Unc	BU
1913	Inc. above	—	BV	100	150	—
1917	43,000	—	BV	100	150	—
1918	Inc. above	—	BV	100	175	—
1919	Inc. above	—	BV	100	150	—

KM# 195.1 5 PESOS **Weight:** 7.9881 g. **Composition:** 0.9170 Gold .2355 oz. AGW **Note:** Various rotations of dies exist.

Date	Mintage	F	VF	XF	Unc	BU
1913	17,000	—	BV	125	200	—
1918/3	423,000	—	BV	100	175	—
1918	Inc. above	—	BV	100	175	—
1919	2,181,000	—	—	BV	125	—
1919 Long-tail 9	Inc. above	—	—	BV	130	—
1919 Dot over 9	Inc. above	—	BV	100	175	—

KM# 201.1 5 PESOS **Weight:** 7.9881 g. **Composition:** 0.9170 Gold .2355 oz. AGW **Obverse:** Simon Bolivar, large head **Note:** 1920A dated coins come with mint mark centered or on right side of coat of arms; 1923B dated coins come with B on the left or right of coat of arms. The 1923B mint mark to right carries a 25% premium in value. Various rotations of dies exist.

Date	Mintage	F	VF	XF	Unc	BU
1919 Long-tail 9	Inc. above	—	BV	90.00	125	—
1919A	Inc. above	—	BV	90.00	125	—
1919B	—	—	BV	100	145	—
1920	870,000	—	BV	90.00	125	—
1920A	Inc. above	—	BV	90.00	125	—
1920B	108,000	—	BV	100	145	—
1921A	—	—	—	—	—	—
1922B	29,000	—	BV	90.00	125	—
1923B	74,000	—	BV	90.00	125	—
1924B	705,000	—	BV	90.00	125	—

KM# 201.2 5 PESOS **Weight:** 7.9881 g. **Composition:** 0.9170 Gold .2355 oz. AGW **Obverse:** Simon Bolivar, large head **Note:** Medallic die rotation.

Date	F	VF	XF	Unc	BU
1920	100	145	—	—	—

KM# 204 5 PESOS **Weight:** 7.9881 g. **Composition:** 0.9170 Gold .2355 oz. AGW **Obverse:** Simon Bolivar, small head, MEDELLIN below bust **Note:** 1924 dated coins have several varieties in size of 2 and 4. 1925 dated coins exist with an Arabic and a Spanish style 5. 1930 dated coins have three varieties in size and placement of 3.

Date	Mintage	F	VF	XF	Unc	BU
1924 Large 2	120,000	—	BV	100	145	—
1924 Large 4	Inc. above	—	BV	85.00	115	—
1924 Small 4	Inc. above	—	BV	90.00	125	—
1925/4	668,000	—	BV	85.00	115	—
1925	Inc. above	—	BV	85.00	115	—
1926	383,000	—	BV	90.00	125	—
1927	365,000	—	BV	90.00	125	—
1928	314,000	—	BV	85.00	115	—
1929	321,000	—	BV	100	145	—
1930	502,000	—	BV	90.00	125	—

KM# 230 5 PESOS **Composition:** Copper-Nickel **Subject:** International Eucharistic Congress

Date	Mintage	F	VF	XF	Unc	BU
1968B	660,000	0.25	0.50	0.75	1.75	—

KM# 247 5 PESOS **Composition:** Nickel Clad Steel **Subject:** 6th Pan-American Games

Date	Mintage	F	VF	XF	Unc	BU
1971	2,000,000	0.15	0.35	0.60	1.50	—

KM# 268 5 PESOS **Composition:** Bronze

Date	Mintage	F	VF	XF	Unc	BU
1980	146,268,000	0.15	0.35	0.60	1.25	—
1.981	9,148,000	0.15	0.35	0.60	1.25	—
1.982	—	0.15	0.35	0.75	1.50	—
1983	84,107,000	0.15	0.35	0.60	1.25	—
1985	—	0.15	0.35	0.60	1.25	—
1986	14,700,000	0.15	0.35	0.60	1.25	—
1987	—	0.15	0.35	0.60	1.25	—
1988 Small date	45,000,000	0.15	0.35	0.60	1.25	—
1988 Large inverted date	Inc. above	0.15	0.35	0.60	1.25	—
1989	—	0.15	0.35	0.60	1.25	—

KM# 280 5 PESOS **Composition:** Copper-Aluminum-Nickel **Note:** Varieties exist, such as 1989 where some have 72 beads on the obverse and reverse and some have 66 beads.

Date	F	VF	XF	Unc	BU
1989	—	—	—	0.50	—
1990	—	—	—	0.50	—
1991	—	—	—	0.50	—
1992	—	—	—	0.35	—
1993	—	—	—	0.35	—

KM# 202 10 PESOS **Weight:** 15.9761 g. **Composition:** 0.9170 Gold .4710 oz. AGW **Obverse:** Simon Bolivar

Date	Mintage	F	VF	XF	Unc	BU
1919	101,000	—	BV	225	350	—
1924B	55,000	—	BV	225	350	—

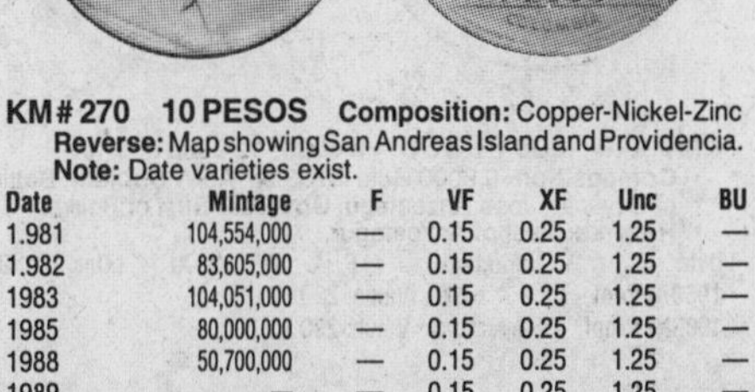

KM# 270 10 PESOS **Composition:** Copper-Nickel-Zinc **Reverse:** Map showing San Andreas Island and Providencia. **Note:** Date varieties exist.

Date	Mintage	F	VF	XF	Unc	BU
1.981	104,554,000	—	0.15	0.25	1.25	—
1.982	83,605,000	—	0.15	0.25	1.25	—
1983	104,051,000	—	0.15	0.25	1.25	—
1985	80,000,000	—	0.15	0.25	1.25	—
1988	50,700,000	—	0.15	0.25	1.25	—
1989	—	—	0.15	0.25	1.25	—

KM# 281.1 10 PESOS **Composition:** Copper-Nickel-Zinc **Obverse:** Flags and arms **Reverse:** Wide 10 (5mm) **Note:** Varieties exist.

Date	F	VF	XF	Unc	BU
1989	—	—	—	0.75	—
1990	—	—	—	0.75	—
1991	—	—	—	0.75	—
1992	—	—	—	0.50	—
1993	—	—	—	0.50	—
1994	—	—	—	0.50	—

KM# 281.2 10 PESOS **Composition:** Copper-Nickel-Zinc **Obverse:** Flags and arms **Reverse:** Narrow 10 (4.5mm)

Date	F	VF	XF	Unc	BU
1993	—	—	3.00	7.00	—
1994	—	—	3.00	7.00	—

KM# 271 20 PESOS **Composition:** Aluminum-Bronze **Note:** 1985 and 1988 coins exist with large and small dates.

Date	Mintage	F	VF	XF	Unc	BU
1982	—	—	0.15	0.20	0.30	—
1984	64,066,000	—	0.15	0.20	0.30	—
1985	100,690,000	—	0.15	0.20	0.30	—
1986	18,300,000	—	0.15	0.20	0.30	—
1987	—	—	0.15	0.20	0.30	—
1988	72,000,000	—	0.15	0.20	0.30	—
1989	—	—	0.15	0.20	0.30	—

KM# 282.1 20 PESOS **Composition:** Copper-Aluminum-Nickel **Obverse:** 72 beads circle around the rim **Note:** Varieties exist.

Date	F	VF	XF	Unc	BU
1989	—	—	—	0.75	—
1990	—	—	—	0.75	—
1991	—	—	—	0.75	—
1992	—	—	—	0.75	—
1993	—	—	—	0.75	—
1994	—	—	—	0.75	—

KM# 282.2 20 PESOS **Composition:** Copper-Aluminum-Nickel **Obverse:** 68 beads circle around the rim

Date	F	VF	XF	Unc	BU
1994	—	—	—	0.50	—

KM# 272 50 PESOS **Composition:** Copper-Nickel **Subject:** National Constitution

Date	Mintage	F	VF	XF	Unc	BU
1986	14,900,000	—	—	—	1.25	—
1987 Large date	—	—	—	—	1.25	—
1988 Small date	100,000,000	—	—	—	1.25	—
1989	—	—	—	—	1.25	—

KM# 283.1 50 PESOS **Composition:** Copper-Nickel-Zinc **Reverse:** 66 beads circle around rim. **Note:** Varieties exist.

Date	F	VF	XF	Unc	BU
1989	—	—	—	1.00	—
1990	—	—	—	1.00	—
1991	—	—	—	1.00	—
1992	—	—	—	1.00	—
1993	—	—	—	1.00	—
1994	—	—	—	1.00	—

KM# 283.2 50 PESOS Composition: Copper-Nickel-Zinc **Reverse:** 72 beads circle around rim.

Date	F	VF	XF	Unc	BU
1990	—	—	—	1.00	—
1994	—	—	—	1.00	—

KM# 231 100 PESOS Weight: 4.3000 g. **Composition:** 0.9000 Gold .1244 oz. AGW **Subject:** Interntional Eucharistic Congress

Date	Mintage	F	VF	XF	Unc	BU
1968	—	—	—	—	65.00	—
1968 Proof	8,000	Value: 85.00				

KM# 238 100 PESOS Weight: 4.3000 g. **Composition:** 0.9000 Gold .1244 oz. AGW **Subject:** Battle of Boyaca - Joachim Paris **Obverse:** Bust of Bolivar **Reverse:** Bust of Paris

Date	Mintage	F	VF	XF	Unc	BU
1969B Proof	6,000	Value: 90.00				
1969NI Proof	Inc. above	Value: 90.00				

KM# 248 100 PESOS Weight: 4.3000 g. **Composition:** 0.9000 Gold .1244 oz. AGW **Subject:** 6th Pan-American Games

Date	Mintage	F	VF	XF	Unc	BU
1971 Proof	6,000	Value: 100				

KM# 285.1 100 PESOS Composition: Brass **Reverse:** Numerals 4.5mm talll

Date	F	VF	XF	Unc	BU
1992	—	—	—	1.75	—
1993	—	—	—	1.75	—
1994	—	—	—	1.75	—
1995	—	—	—	1.75	—

KM# 285.2 100 PESOS Composition: Brass **Reverse:** Numerals 6mm talll **Note:** Edge varieties exist.

Date	F	VF	XF	Unc	BU
1994	—	—	—	1.75	—
1995	—	—	—	1.75	—

KM# 232 200 PESOS Weight: 8.6000 g. **Composition:** 0.9000 Gold .2488 oz. AGW **Subject:** International Eucharistic Congress **Reverse:** Arms and value

Date	Mintage	F	VF	XF	Unc	BU
1968	—	—	—	—	130	—
1968 Proof	8,000	Value: 150				

KM# 239 200 PESOS Weight: 8.6000 g. **Composition:** 0.9000 Gold .2488 oz. AGW **Subject:** Battle of Boyaca - Carlos Soublette **Obverse:** Bust of Bolivar **Reverse:** Bust of Soublette

Date	Mintage	F	VF	XF	Unc	BU
1969B Proof	6,000	Value: 165				
1969NI Proof	Inc. above	Value: 165				

KM# 249 200 PESOS Weight: 8.6000 g. **Composition:** 0.9000 Gold .2488 oz. AGW **Subject:** 6th Pan-American Games

Date	Mintage	F	VF	XF	Unc	BU
1971 Proof	6,000	Value: 175				

KM# 287 200 PESOS Composition: Copper-Zinc-Nickel **Reverse:** Quimbaya artwork

Date	F	VF	XF	Unc	BU
1994	—	—	—	1.50	—
1995	—	—	—	1.50	—
1996	—	—	—	1.50	—

KM# 233 300 PESOS Weight: 12.9000 g. **Composition:** 0.9000 Gold .3733 oz. AGW **Subject:** International Eucharistic Congress

Date	Mintage	F	VF	XF	Unc	BU
1968	—	—	—	—	185	—
1968 Proof	8,000	Value: 225				

KM# 240 300 PESOS Weight: 12.9000 g. **Composition:** 0.9000 Gold .3733 oz. AGW **Subject:** Battle of Boyaca - Jose Anzoategui **Obverse:** Bust of Bolivar **Reverse:** Bust of Anzoategui

Date	Mintage	F	VF	XF	Unc	BU
1969B Proof	6,000	Value: 220				
1969NI Proof	Inc. above	Value: 220				

KM# 250 300 PESOS Weight: 12.9000 g. **Composition:** 0.9000 Gold .3733 oz. AGW **Subject:** 6th Pan-American Games

Date	Mintage	F	VF	XF	Unc	BU
1971 Proof	6,000	Value: 245				

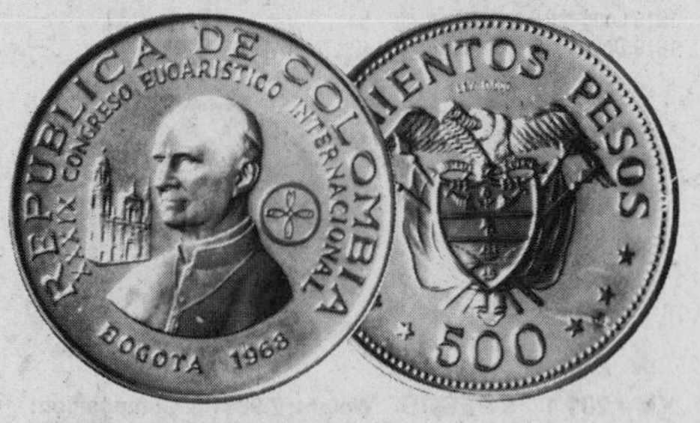

KM# 234 500 PESOS Weight: 21.5000 g. **Composition:** 0.9000 Gold .6221 oz. AGW **Subject:** International Eucharistic Congress **Reverse:** Arms and value

Date	Mintage	F	VF	XF	Unc	BU
1968	—	—	—	—	325	—
1968 Proof	8,000	Value: 350				

KM# 241 500 PESOS Weight: 21.5000 g. **Composition:** 0.9000 Gold .6221 oz. AGW **Subject:** Battle of Boyaca **Obverse:** Simon Bolivar **Reverse:** Juan Jose Rondon

Date	Mintage	F	VF	XF	Unc	BU
ND(1969)B Proof	6,000	Value: 350				
ND(1969)NI Proof	Inc. above	Value: 350				

KM# 251 500 PESOS Weight: 21.5000 g. **Composition:** 0.9000 Gold .6221 oz. AGW **Subject:** 6th Pan-American Games

Date	Mintage	F	VF	XF	Unc	BU
1971 Proof	6,000	Value: 420				

KM# 264 500 PESOS **Weight:** 28.2800 g. **Composition:** 0.9250 Silver .8411 oz. ASW **Subject:** Conservation **Reverse:** Orinoco Crocodile

Date	Mintage	F	VF	XF	Unc	BU
1978	—	—	—	—	25.00	—
1978 Proof	3,233	Value: 35.00				
1979 Proof	—	Value: 35.00				

KM# 286 500 PESOS **Ring Composition:** Copper-Nickel **Center Composition:** Aluminum-Bronze **Reverse:** Guacari Tree

Date	F	VF	XF	Unc	BU
1993	—	—	—	4.00	—
1994	—	—	—	4.00	—
1995	—	—	—	4.00	—
1996	—	—	—	4.00	—

KM# 265 750 PESOS **Weight:** 35.0000 g. **Composition:** 0.9250 Silver 1.0409 oz. ASW **Subject:** Conservation **Obverse:** Similar to 500 Pesos, KM#264 **Reverse:** Chestnut-bellied Humingbird

Date	Mintage	F	VF	XF	Unc	BU
1978	—	—	—	—	28.00	—
1978 Proof	3,100	Value: 38.00				
1979 Proof	—	Value: 38.00				

KM# 254 1000 PESOS **Weight:** 4.3000 g. **Composition:** 0.9000 Gold .1244 oz. AGW **Subject:** 100th Anniversary - Birth of Guillermo Valencia

Date	Mintage	F	VF	XF	Unc	BU
1973 Proof	10,003	Value: 65.00				

KM# 259 1000 PESOS **Weight:** 4.3000 g. **Composition:** 0.9000 Gold .1244 oz. AGW **Subject:** 450th Anniversary - City of Santa Marta

Date	Mintage	F	VF	XF	Unc	BU
ND(1975) Proof	2,500	Value: 75.00				

KM# 260 1000 PESOS **Weight:** 4.3000 g. **Composition:** 0.9000 Gold .1244 oz. AGW **Subject:** Tricentennial - City of Medellin **Shape:** Square

Date	Mintage	F	VF	XF	Unc	BU
ND(1975) Proof	4,000	Value: 75.00				

KM# 288 1000 PESOS **Composition:** Copper-Aluminum-Nickel **Edge:** Reeded and lettered **Edge Lettering:** CULTURA SINU MIL PESOS

Date	F	VF	XF	Unc	BU
1996	—	—	—	3.75	—
1997	—	—	—	3.75	—
1998	—	—	—	3.75	—

KM# 235 1500 PESOS **Weight:** 64.5000 g. **Composition:** 0.9000 Gold 1.8664 oz. AGW **Subject:** International Eucharistic Congress **Obverse:** Similar to 300 Pesos, KM#233

Date	Mintage	F	VF	XF	Unc	BU
1968	—	—	—	—	1,000	—
1968 Proof	8,000	Value: 1,200				

KM# 242 1500 PESOS **Weight:** 64.5000 g. **Composition:** 0.9000 Gold 1.8664 oz. AGW **Subject:** Battle of Boyaca **Obverse:** Bust of Bolivar **Reverse:** Portrait of Santander

Date	Mintage	F	VF	XF	Unc	BU
ND(1969)B Proof	6,000	Value: 1,200				
ND(1969)NI Proof	Inc. above	Value: 1,200				

KM# 252 1500 PESOS **Weight:** 64.5000 g. **Composition:** 0.9000 Gold 1.8664 oz. AGW **Subject:** 6th Pan-American Games **Obverse:** Similar to 300 Pesos, KM#250

Date	Mintage	F	VF	XF	Unc	BU
1971 Proof	6,000	Value: 1,400				

KM# 255 1500 PESOS **Weight:** 19.1000 g. **Composition:** 0.9000 Gold .5527 oz. AGW **Subject:** 50th Anniversary - Gold Museum of Central Bank of Bogota

Date	Mintage	F	VF	XF	Unc	BU
ND(1973) Proof	4,911	Value: 275				

KM# 257 2000 PESOS **Weight:** 12.9000 g. **Composition:** 0.9000 Gold .3733 oz. AGW **Subject:** 100th Anniversary - Birth of Guillermo Valencia

Date	Mintage	F	VF	XF	Unc	BU
1973 Proof	5,003	Value: 225				

KM# 261 2000 PESOS **Weight:** 8.6000 g. **Composition:** 0.9000 Gold .2488 oz. AGW **Subject:** 450th Anniversary - City of Santa Marta

Date	Mintage	F	VF	XF	Unc	BU
ND(1975) Proof	2,500	Value: 150				

KM# 262 2000 PESOS **Weight:** 8.6000 g. **Composition:** 0.9000 Gold .2488 oz. AGW **Subject:** Tricentennial - City of Medellin

Date	Mintage	F	VF	XF	Unc	BU
ND(1975) Proof	4,000	Value: 150				

KM# 293 5000 PESOS **Weight:** 15.3000 g. **Composition:** Nickel **Subject:** 50th Anniversary - Organization of American States **Obverse:** Denomination **Reverse:** Circle of flags

Date	F	VF	XF	Unc	BU
1998	—	—	—	5.50	—

KM# 284 10000 PESOS **Weight:** 27.0000 g. **Composition:** 0.9250 Silver .8029 oz. ASW **Series:** Ibero - American **Subject:** Bogota Mint

Date	Mintage	F	VF	XF	Unc	BU
1991 Proof	70,000	Value: 55.00				

KM# 266 15000 PESOS **Weight:** 33.4370 g. **Composition:** 0.9000 Gold .9676 oz. AGW **Subject:** Conservation **Reverse:** Ocelot

Date	Mintage	F	VF	XF	Unc	BU
1978		—	—	—	650	—
1978 Proof	148	Value: 2,000				

KM# 276 15000 PESOS **Weight:** 17.2900 g. **Composition:** 0.9000 Gold .5000 oz. AGW **Subject:** 150th Anniversary - Death of Antonio Jose De Sucre

Date	Mintage	F	VF	XF	Unc	BU
1980 Proof	250	Value: 285				

KM# 278 15000 PESOS **Weight:** 17.2900 g. **Composition:** 0.9000 Gold .5000 oz. AGW **Subject:** 150th Anniversary - Death of Jose Maria Cordova

Date	Mintage	F	VF	XF	Unc	BU
1980 Proof	250	Value: 285				

KM# 289 20000 PESOS **Weight:** 8.6400 g. **Composition:** 0.9000 Gold .2500 oz. AGW **Subject:** Birth Centennial **Obverse:** Alfonso Lopez-Pumarejo **Reverse:** Building

Date	Mintage	F	VF	XF	Unc	BU
ND(1986) Proof	1,351	Value: 200				

KM# 269 30000 PESOS **Weight:** 34.5800 g. **Composition:** 0.9000 Gold 1.0007 oz. AGW **Subject:** Death of Bolivar

Date	Mintage	F	VF	XF	Unc	BU
1980 Proof	500	Value: 550				

KM# 273 35000 PESOS **Weight:** 8.6400 g. **Composition:** 0.9000 Gold .2500 oz. AGW **Subject:** 100th Anniversary - Birth of President Santos

Date	Mintage	F	VF	XF	Unc	BU
ND(1988) Proof	900	Value: 200				

KM# 292 40000 PESOS **Weight:** 17.2800 g. **Composition:** 0.9000 Gold .5000 oz. AGW **Subject:** Centennial - Birthday of Alfonso Lopez-Pumarejo **Note:** Similar to 20,000 Pesos, KM#289

Date	Mintage	F	VF	XF	Unc	BU
ND(1986) Proof	1,351	Value: 400				

KM# 290 50000 PESOS **Weight:** 8.6400 g. **Composition:** 0.9000 Gold .2500 oz. AGW **Subject:** Centennial - Birthday of Mariano Ospina P **Obverse:** Portrait **Reverse:** Inscription and wreath

Date	F	VF	XF	Unc	BU
ND(1991) Proof	—	Value: 200			

KM# 291 100000 PESOS **Weight:** 17.2800 g. **Composition:** 0.9000 Gold .5000 oz. AGW **Subject:** Centennial - Birthday of Mariano Ospina P **Obverse:** Portrait **Reverse:** Inscription and wreath

Date	F	VF	XF	Unc	BU
ND(1991) Proof	—	Value: 400			

INFLATIONARY COINAGE

P/M - Papel Moneda

Beginning about 1886, Colombia fell victim to rampant printing press inflation and a debased, vanishing coinage. Left without solid backing, the peso gradually fell until it was worth 1 centavo of the old silver-based currency. The copper-nickel 1, 2, and 5 peso p/m coins reflected this inflation, and later circulated at par with the newer 1, 2, and 5 centavo coins.

KM# A279 PESO (Papel Moneda) **Composition:** Copper-Nickel

Date	Mintage	F	VF	XF	Unc
1907 AM	2,860,000	0.75	1.75	5.00	22.50
1907 AM Proof	—	Value: 80.00			
1910 AM	1,205,000	1.25	2.50	7.00	25.00
1911 AM	2,816,000	1.75	2.50	8.00	27.50
1912 AM	6,094,000	1.25	2.00	6.00	20.00
1912 H Without crossbar	2,000,000	1.25	2.00	6.00	20.00
1912 H With crossbar	Inc. above	1.25	2.00	6.00	20.00
1913 AM	306,000	3.00	7.50	13.50	30.00
1914 AM	552,000	3.50	8.50	20.00	47.50
1916/4 AM	234,000	4.25	9.00	18.50	45.00
1916 AM	Inc. above	4.25	9.00	18.50	45.00

KM# B279 2 PESOS (Papel Moneda) **Composition:** Copper-Nickel **Note:** Date varieties exist.

Date	Mintage	F	VF	XF	Unc	BU
1907 AM	4,161,000	1.50	2.75	7.50	27.50	—
1907 AM Proof	—	Value: 90.00				
1910/07 AM	649,000	3.25	5.75	12.50	37.50	—
1910 AM	Inc. above	3.00	5.00	9.00	30.00	—
1911	458,000	3.50	8.50	16.50	55.00	—
1913 Reported, not confirmed	82,000	—	—	—	—	—
1914 AM	1,000,000	3.00	5.00	12.00	32.50	—

KM# 279 5 PESOS (Papel Moneda) **Composition:** Copper-Nickel

Date	Mintage	F	VF	XF	Unc	BU
1907 AM	6,143,000	0.75	2.50	7.00	25.00	—
1907 AM Proof	—	Value: 110				
1909 AM	4,000,000	1.00	2.75	7.50	22.50	—
1912 H	2,000,000	1.00	2.75	7.50	22.50	—
1912 AM	1,897,000	2.25	5.00	12.50	27.50	—
1913 AM	Inc. above	5.00	15.00	40.00	—	—
1914 AM	Inc. above	12.50	27.50	50.00	80.00	—

LEPROSARIUM COINAGE

Bogota Mint

Special coinage for use in the three government leper colonies of Agua de Dios, Cano de Lord, and Contrataction. The hospitals were closed in the late 1950s and patients were allowed to exchange these special coins for regular currency at any bank.

KM# L9 CENTAVO **Composition:** Copper-Nickel

Date	Mintage	Good	VG	F	VF	XF
1921 RH	300,000	0.75	1.50	3.50	7.00	—

KM# L10 2 CENTAVOS **Composition:** Copper-Nickel

Date	Mintage	Good	VG	F	VF	XF
1921 RH	350,000	0.75	1.50	4.00	8.00	—

KM# L1 2-1/2 CENTAVOS **Composition:** Brass

Date	Mintage	Good	VG	F	VF	XF
1901 Rare	20,000	—	—	—	—	3,500

Note: Only a few examples of this type are currently known to have survived.

KM# L2 5 CENTAVOS **Composition:** Brass

Date	Mintage	Good	VG	F	VF	XF
1901 B	15,000	6.00	12.50	22.00	45.00	—

KM# L11 5 CENTAVOS **Composition:** Copper-Nickel

Date	Mintage	Good	VG	F	VF	XF
1921 H	200,000	1.00	2.00	4.50	9.00	—

KM# L3 10 CENTAVOS **Composition:** Brass

Date	Mintage	Good	VG	F	VF	XF
1901 B	10,000	10.00	15.00	28.00	50.00	—

KM# L12 10 CENTAVOS **Composition:** Copper-Nickel

Date	Mintage	Good	VG	F	VF	XF
1921 RH	200,000	1.00	2.00	4.50	9.00	—

KM# L4 20 CENTAVOS **Composition:** Brass

Date	Mintage	Good	VG	F	VF	XF
1901 B	30,000	10.00	15.00	28.00	50.00	—

KM# L5 50 CENTAVOS **Composition:** Brass

Date	Mintage	Good	VG	F	VF	XF
1901 B	26,000	13.50	20.00	35.00	65.00	—

KM# L5a 50 CENTAVOS **Composition:** Copper

Date	Good	VG	F	VF	XF
1901 2 known	—	—	—	—	—

KM# L13 50 CENTAVOS **Composition:** Copper-Nickel

Date	Mintage	Good	VG	F	VF	XF
1921 RH	120,000	2.00	4.00	7.50	16.00	—

KM# L14 50 CENTAVOS **Composition:** Brass

Date	Mintage	Good	VG	F	VF	XF
1928 RH	50,000	2.00	4.50	9.00	18.00	—

KM# L14a 50 CENTAVOS **Composition:** Copper

Date	Good	VG	F	VF	XF
1928 Proof; Rare	—	—	—	—	—

INFLATIONARY LEPROSARIUM COINAGE

P/M - Papel Moneda

1 Peso was equal in value to 1 Centavo of the old silver currency. It later circulated at par with the newer 1 Centavo coins.

KM# L6 PESO (Papel Moneda) **Composition:** Copper-Nickel

Date	Mintage	Good	VG	F	VF	XF
1907/0	792,000	—	—	—	—	—
1907	Inc. above	5.00	10.00	20.00	45.00	—

KM# L7 5 PESOS (Papel Moneda) **Composition:** Copper-Nickel

Date	Mintage	Good	VG	F	VF	XF
1907	159,000	30.00	60.00	100	200	—

KM# L8 10 PESOS (Papal Moneda) **Composition:** Copper-Nickel

Date	Mintage	Good	VG	F	VF	XF
1907	129,000	40.00	75.00	125	250	—

PROVINCE OF SANTANDER

CIVIL WAR COINAGE

KM# A1 10 CENTAVOS **Composition:** Brass **Note:** Uniface.

Date	F	VF	XF	Unc	BU
ND(1902)	15.00	25.00	55.00	—	—

KM# A2 20 CENTAVOS **Composition:** Brass **Note:** Uniface.

Date	F	VF	XF	Unc	BU
1902	32.50	45.00	75.00	—	—

KM# A3 50 CENTAVOS **Composition:** Brass **Note:** Uniface. Varieties exist in shape of "0" in denomination: a fully rounded zero commands double the listed values. Later 20th Century counterfeits are known.

Date	F	VF	XF	Unc	BU
1902	4.00	9.00	20.00	—	—

Note: Varieties exist with round or elliptical 0 in denomination

PATTERNS

Including off metal strikes

KM#	Date	Mintage	Identification	Mkt Val
Pn79	1900	—	10 Centavos. Copper-Nickel. Quartefoil.	100
Pn76	1900	—	5 Centavos. Copper-Nickel.	275
Pn77	1900	—	10 Centavos. Copper-Nickel.	175
Pn81	1900	—	20 Centavos. Silver. Reeded edge.	—
Pn78	1900	—	10 Centavos. Copper-Nickel. ESSAI MONETAIRE.	100
Pn80	1900	—	10 Centavos. Silver. Reeded edge.	—
Pn82	1900	—	50 Centavos. 0.8350 Silver. Plain edge.	—
Pn83	1900	—	50 Centavos. 0.8350 Silver. Reeded edge.	—
Pn84	1909	—	5 Centavos. Copper-Nickel.	—
Pn86	1913	—	5 Decimos. Thin Bolivar head, canceled obverse die.	—
Pn87	1913	—	2-1/2 Pesos. Gold. ENSAYO; KM#194.	—
Pn88	1913	—	5 Pesos. Gold. ENSAYO; KM#195.	—
Pn85	1913	—	5 Decimos. Thin Bolivar head.	—
Pn89	1915	—	2-1/2 Pesos. Gold. ENSAYO; KM#194.	—
Pn90	1917	—	5 Centavos. Copper-Nickel. PAZ on cap band, similar to KM#199.	—
Pn91	1917	—	5 Centavos. Copper-Nickel. KM#199.	—
Pn94	1923	—	5 Pesos. ENSAYO, KM#204.	—
Pn93	1923	—	2-1/2 Pesos. Silver. ESSAI; KM#203.	—
Pn95	1923	—	5 Pesos. Silver. ESSAI; KM#204.	—
Pn92	1923	—	2-1/2 Pesos. ENSAYO; KM#203.	2,450
Pn96	1941	—	5 Centavos. Copper-Nickel. KM#199.	—
Pn97	1946	—	50 Centavos. Copper-Nickel. 10-sided planchet.	—
Pn98	1946	—	50 Centavos. 0.5000 Silver. Reeded edge.	—
Pn102	1950	—	50 Centavos. 0.9000 Silver.	—
Pn99	1950	—	20 Centavos. 0.5000 Silver.	100
Pn100	1950	—	50 Centavos. 0.9000 Silver. Bolivar military bust, condor over large shield.	100
Pn101	1950	—	50 Centavos. 0.9000 Silver. Condor over small shield.	100
Pn103	1951	—	50 Centavos. Silver.	100
Pn104	1952	—	50 Centavos. Silver.	100
Pn105	1956	—	50 Centavos. Copper-Nickel.	125
Pn106	1956	—	Peso. Gold.	—
Pn107	1957	—	50 Centavos. Copper-Nickel.	125
Pn108	1963	—	Peso. Copper-Nickel. Previous KM#Pn57.	125
Pn109	1968	—	Peso. Copper-Nickel. Previous KM#Pn58.	125
Pn110	1969	—	50 Centavos. Copper-Nickel. Previous KM#Pn59.	75.00
Pn111	1969	—	50 Centavos. Copper-Nickel. Previous KM#Pn60.	75.00
Pn114	1969	—	Peso. Copper-Nickel. Previous KM#Pn63.	125
Pn112	1969	—	Peso. Copper-Nickel. Previous KM#Pn61.	125
Pn113	1969	—	Peso. Copper-Nickel. Previous KM#Pn62.	125
Pn115	1970	—	Centavo. Aluminum. Previous KM#Pn64.	25.00
Pn116	1970	—	5 Centavos. Aluminum. Previous KM#Pn65.	25.00
Pn117	1971	—	10 Centavos. Aluminum. Previous KM#Pn66.	30.00
Pn118	1971	—	50 Centavos. Copper-Nickel. Previous KM#Pn67.	65.00
Pn119	1974	—	Peso. Silver. 6.7000 g. Previous KM#Pn68.	150
Pn120	1979	—	5 Pesos. Inverted date. Previous KM#Pn69.	—

PIEFORTS

KM#	Date	Mintage	Identification	Mkt Val
P3	1913	—	50 Centavos. 0.9000 Silver. Ensayo	2,500

KM#	Date	Mintage	Identification	Mkt Val
P4	1915	—	10 Centavos. 0.9000 Silver. Ensayo	—
P5	1915	—	20 Centavos. 0.9000 Silver. Ensayo	—

TRIAL STRIKES

KM#	Date	Mintage	Identification	Mkt Val
TS15	1911	—	10 Centavos. Lead. Uniface.	—
TS16	1911	—	20 Centavos. Lead. Uniface.	—
TS14	ND	—	50 Centavos. Lead.	—

PROOF SETS

KM#	Date	Mintage	Identification	Issue Price	Mkt Val
PS1	1968 (5)	8,000	KM#231-235	340	1,950
PS2	1969 (5)	6,000	KM#238-242	—	2,000
PS3	1971 (5)	6,000	KM#248-252	—	2,300
PS4	1973 (3)	—	KM#254, 256, 257	—	450
PS5	1975 (2)	2,500	KM#260, 262	195	235
PS6	1975 (2)	4,000	KM#259, 261	195	245
PS7	1979 (2)	—	KM#264-265	—	75.00

COMOROS

The Federal Islamic Republic of the Comoros, a volcanic archipelago located in the Mozambique Channel of the Indian Ocean 300 miles (483 km.) northwest of Madagascar, has an area of 719 sq. mi. (2,171 sq. km.) and a population of *714,000. Capital: Moroni. The economy of the islands is based on agriculture. There are practically no mineral resources. Vanilla, essence for perfumes, copra, and sisal are exported.

Ancient Phoenician traders were probably the first visitors to the Comoro Islands, but the first detailed knowledge of the area was gathered by Arab sailors. Arab dominion and culture were firmly established when the Portuguese, Dutch, and French arrived in the 16th century. In 1843 a Malagasy ruler ceded the island of Mayotte to France; the other three principal islands of the archipelago-Anjouan, Moheli, and Grand Comore came under French protection in 1886. The islands were joined administratively with Madagascar in 1912. The Comoros became partially autonomous, with the status of a French overseas territory, in 1946, and achieved complete internal autonomy in 1961. On Dec. 31, 1975, after 133 years of French association, the Comoro Islands became the independent Republic of the Comoros.

Mayotte retained the option of determining its future ties and in 1976 voted to remain French. Its present status is that of a French Territorial Collectivity. French currency now circulates there.

TITLES

Daulat Anjazanchiyah

دولة انجزنجية

RULERS

French, 1886-1975

MINT MARKS

(a) - Paris, privy marks only

A - Paris

MONETARY SYSTEM

100 Centimes = 1 Franc

FRENCH COLONIAL

DECIMAL COINAGE

KM# 4 FRANC **Composition:** 0.9000 Aluminum

Date	Mintage	F	VF	XF	Unc	BU
1964(a)	500,000	0.15	0.25	0.40	1.25	—

KM# 5 2 FRANCS **Composition:** Aluminum

Date	Mintage	F	VF	XF	Unc	BU
1964(a)	600,000	0.15	0.25	0.50	1.50	—

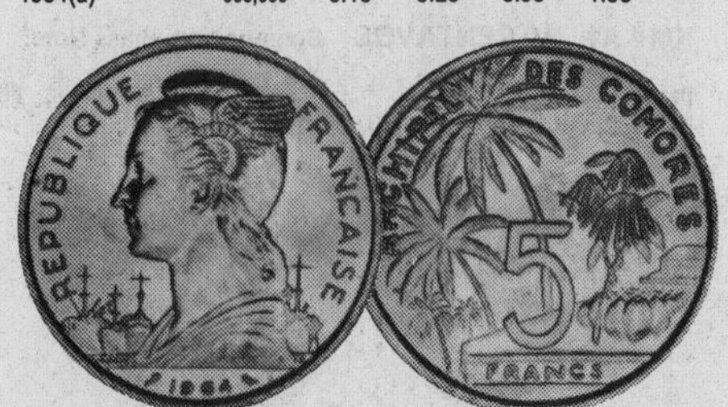

KM# 6 5 FRANCS **Composition:** Aluminum

Date	Mintage	F	VF	XF	Unc	BU
1964(a)	1,000,000	0.20	0.40	0.65	2.00	—

KM# 7 10 FRANCS **Composition:** Aluminum-Bronze

Date	Mintage	F	VF	XF	Unc	BU
1964(a)	600,000	0.20	0.50	1.00	2.50	—

KM# 8 20 FRANCS **Composition:** Aluminum-Bronze

Date	Mintage	F	VF	XF	Unc	BU
1964(a)	500,000	0.30	0.65	1.25	3.00	—

TOKEN COINAGE

KM# Tn1 25 CENTIMES **Weight:** 1.2000 g. **Composition:** Aluminum **Issuer:** Societe Anonyme

Date	F	VF	XF	Unc	BU
ND(1915)	30.00	60.00	125	250	—

KM# Tn1a 25 CENTIMES **Weight:** 4.6000 g. **Composition:** Brass **Issuer:** Societe Anonyme

Date	F	VF	XF	Unc	BU
ND(1922)	—	—	150	—	—

KM# Tn2 50 CENTIMES **Composition:** Aluminum **Note:** Similar to 25 Centimes, Tn#1.

Date	F	VF	XF	Unc	BU
ND(1915)	35.00	70.00	120	—	—

KM# Tn2a 50 CENTIMES **Composition:** Brass

Date	F	VF	XF	Unc	BU
ND(1915)	—	—	350	—	—

KM# Tn3 FRANC **Weight:** 1.3000 g. **Composition:** Aluminum **Note:** Similar to 25 Centimes, Tn#1.

Date	F	VF	XF	Unc	BU
ND(1915)	40.00	80.00	135	—	—

KM# Tn3a FRANC **Composition:** Brass

Date	F	VF	XF	Unc	BU
ND(1922)	—	—	215	—	—

KM# Tn4 2 FRANCS **Composition:** Aluminum 1.7 oz. **Note:** Similar to 25 Centimes, Tn#1.

Date	F	VF	XF	Unc	BU
ND(1915)	50.00	90.00	155	—	—

KM# Tn5 2 FRANCS **Composition:** Aluminum 1.7 oz. **Note:** Uniface.

Date	F	VF	XF	Unc	BU
1915	50.00	100	165	—	—

FEDERAL ISLAMIC REPUBLIC

STANDARD COINAGE

KM# 15 5 FRANCS **Composition:** Aluminum **Issuer:** Banque Central **Subject:** World Fisheries Conference **Obverse:** Coelacanth fish

Date	Mintage	F	VF	XF	Unc	BU
1984(a)	1,010,000	0.25	0.50	1.50	4.00	6.00
1992(a)	—	0.25	0.50	1.50	4.00	6.00

KM# 17 10 FRANCS **Composition:** Aluminum-Bronze **Issuer:** Banque Central

Date	F	VF	XF	Unc	BU
1992(a)	—	—	—	1.65	—

KM# 14 25 FRANCS **Composition:** Nickel **Issuer:** Banque Central **Series:** F.A.O **Obverse:** Chickens

Date	Mintage	F	VF	XF	Unc	BU
1981(a)	1,000,000	1.50	3.00	6.00	16.00	—
1982(a)	2,007,000	0.20	0.40	0.80	2.00	—

KM# 9 50 FRANCS **Composition:** Nickel **Issuer:** Institut d' Emmission **Subject:** Independence of Republic

Date	Mintage	F	VF	XF	Unc	BU
1975(a)	1,200,000	0.40	0.75	1.25	2.25	—

KM# 16 50 FRANCS **Composition:** Nickel Plated Steel **Issuer:** Institut d' Emission

Date	F	VF	XF	Unc	BU
1990(a)	0.50	0.80	1.50	2.50	—
1994(a)	0.50	0.80	1.50	2.50	—

KM# 13 100 FRANCS **Composition:** Nickel **Issuer:** Institut d' Emmission **Series:** F.A.O

Date	Mintage	F	VF	XF	Unc	BU
1977(a)	1,500,000	0.60	1.00	2.00	3.75	—

KM# 18 100 FRANCS **Weight:** 10.0000 g. **Composition:** Nickel Plated Steel **Subject:** Circulation Type **Obverse:** Denomination. **Reverse:** Boat and fish. **Edge:** Plain. **Size:** 28 mm.

Date	F	VF	XF	Unc	BU
1999	—	—	—	3.50	—

KM# 10 5000 FRANCS **Weight:** 44.8300 g. **Composition:** 0.9250 Silver 1.3332 oz. ASW **Issuer:** Etat Comorien **Obverse:** Flowers **Reverse:** Similar to 20,000 Francs, KM#12

Date	Mintage	F	VF	XF	Unc	BU
1976	700	—	—	—	70.00	—
1976 Proof	1,000	Value: 90.00				

KM# 11 10000 FRANCS **Weight:** 3.0700 g. **Composition:** 0.9000 Gold .0888 oz. AGW **Issuer:** Etat Comorien **Obverse:** Hummingbird, similar to 20,000 Francs, KM#12

Date	Mintage	F	VF	XF	Unc	BU
1976	500	—	—	—	100	—
1976 Proof	500	Value: 125				

KM# 12 20000 FRANCS **Weight:** 6.1400 g. **Composition:** 0.9000 Gold .1776 oz. AGW **Issuer:** Etat Comorien **Obverse:** Coelacanth fish **Reverse:** Said Mohamed Cheikh

Date	Mintage	F	VF	XF	Unc	BU
1976	500	—	—	—	200	—
1976 Proof	500	Value: 225				

ESSAIS

Standard metals unless otherwise noted

KM#	Date	Mintage	Identification	Issue Price	Mkt Val
E1	1964(a)	1,700	Franc. KM4.	—	15.00
E2	1964(a)	1,700	2 Francs. KM5.	—	15.00
E3	1964(a)	1,700	5 Francs. KM6.	—	15.00
E4	1964(a)	1,700	10 Francs. KM7.	—	15.00
E5	1964(a)	1,700	20 Francs. KM8.	—	17.50
E6	1975(a)	1,800	50 Francs. KM9.	—	22.50
E7	1977(a)	1,900	100 Francs. KM13.	—	25.00
E8	1982(a)	1,900	25 Francs.	—	20.00
E9	1984(a)	1,700	5 Francs. KM15.	—	17.50

"FDC" SETS

This fleur-de-coin set was issued with New Caledonia and French Polynesia 1967 sets.

KM#	Date	Mintage	Identification	Issue Price	Mkt Val
SS1	1964 (5)	—	KM4-8. Issued with reunion set.	—	15.00

MINT SETS

KM#	Date	Mintage	Identification	Issue Price	Mkt Val
MS1	1976 (3)	500	KM10-12	—	370

PROOF SETS

KM#	Date	Mintage	Identification	Issue Price	Mkt Val
PS1	1976 (3)	500	KM10-12	229	435

CONGO FREE STATE

ROYAL DOMAIN

1865-1909

STANDARD COINAGE

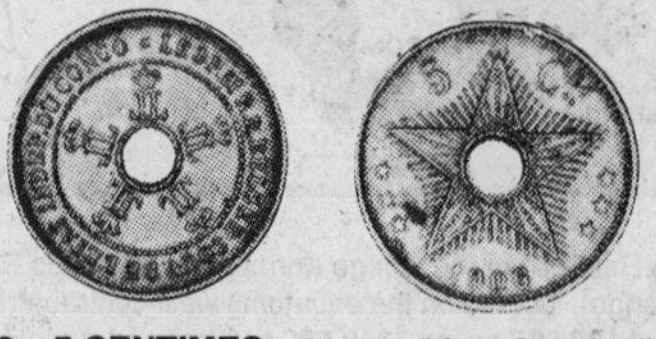

KM# 9 5 CENTIMES **Composition:** Copper-Nickel **Ruler:** Leopold II

Date	Mintage	F	VF	XF	Unc	BU
1906	100,000	5.00	10.00	25.00	60.00	—
1908	180,000	4.00	8.00	20.00	50.00	—

KM# 10 10 CENTIMES **Composition:** Copper-Nickel **Ruler:** Leopold II

Date	Mintage	F	VF	XF	Unc	BU
1906	100,000	5.00	12.00	35.00	85.00	—
1908	800,000	3.00	8.00	30.00	80.00	—

KM# 11 20 CENTIMES **Composition:** Copper-Nickel **Ruler:** Leopold II

Date	Mintage	F	VF	XF	Unc	BU
1906	100,000	5.00	12.00	40.00	110	—
1908	400,000	4.00	8.00	35.00	95.00	—

CONGO REPUBLIC

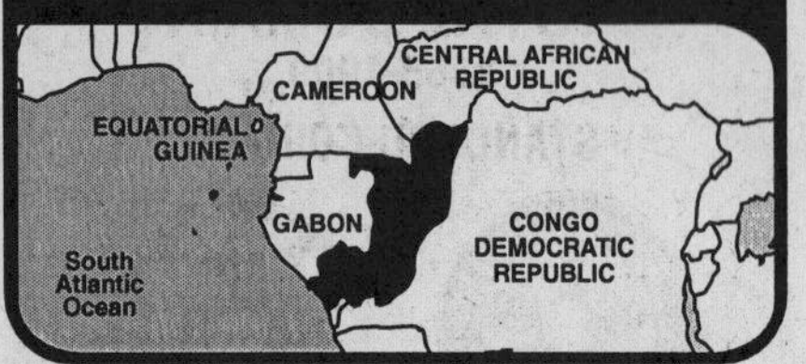

The Republic of the Congo (formerly the Peoples Republic of the Congo), located on the equator in west-central Africa, has an area of 132,047 sq. mi. (342,000 sq. km.) and a population of *2.98 million. Capital: Brazzaville. Agriculture forestry, mining, and food processing are the principal industries. Timber, industrial diamonds, potash, peanuts, and cocoa beans are exported.

The Portuguese were the first Europeans to explore the Congo (Brazzaville) area, 14th century. They conducted a slave trade with the tribal kingdoms of Teke, Loango, and Kongo without attempting developmental colonization. French influence was established in 1883 when the king of Teke signed a treaty with Savorgnan de Brazza, thereby placing his kingdom under the protection of France. While a French protectorate, the area was known as Middle Congo. In 1910 Middle Congo became a part of French Equatorial Africa, which also included Gabon, Ubangi-Shari (now the Central African Republic), and Chad. Following World War II, during which it was an important center of Free French activities, the Middle Congo was given a large measure of internal autonomy, and its inhabitants were made French citizens. Upon approval of the constitution of the Fifth French Republic, 1958, it became a member of the new French Community. On Aug. 15, 1960, Middle Congo became the independent Republic of the Congo-Brazzaville. In Jan. 1970 the country's name was changed to Peoples Republic of the Congo. A new constitution which asserts the government's advocacy of socialism was adopted in 1973.

In June and July of 1992, a new 125-member National Assembly was elected. Later that year a new president, Pascal Lissouba was elected. In November, President Lissouba dismissed the previous government and dissolved the National Assembly. A new 23-member government, including members of the opposition, was formed in December, 1992, and the name was changed to Republique du Congo.

NOTE: For earlier and related coinage see French Equatorial Africa and the Equatorial African States. For later coinage see Central African States.

RULERS

French until 1960

MINT MARKS

(a) - Paris, privy marks only

MONETARY SYSTEM

100 Centimes = 1 Franc

PEOPLE'S REPUBLIC

Republique Populaire du Congo

DECIMAL COINAGE

KM# 1 100 FRANCS **Composition:** Nickel

Date	Mintage	F	VF	XF	Unc	BU
1971(a)	2,500,000	8.00	15.00	25.00	40.00	—
1972(a)	—	8.00	15.00	25.00	40.00	—

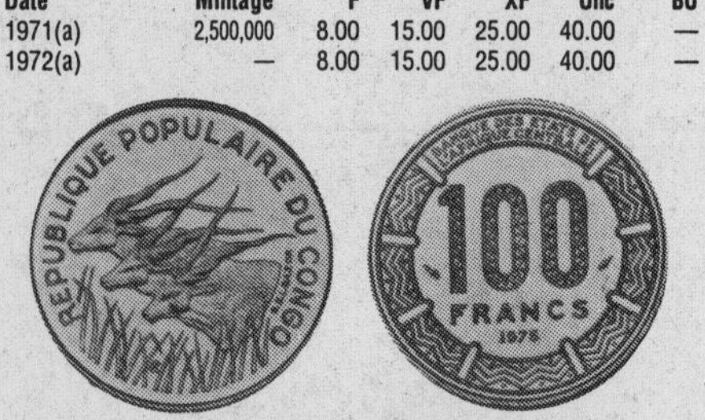

KM# 2 100 FRANCS **Composition:** Nickel

Date	F	VF	XF	Unc	BU
1975(a)	4.00	8.00	16.50	30.00	—
1982(a)	2.50	4.50	8.00	12.50	—
1983(a)	2.50	5.00	8.00	12.50	—
1985(a)	2.00	3.00	6.00	10.00	—
1990(a)	2.00	3.00	4.00	6.00	—

KM# 3 100 FRANCS **Composition:** Copper-Nickel **Subject:** International Games **Reverse:** Handball

Date	F	VF	XF	Unc	BU
1984 Proof	—	Value: 16.50			

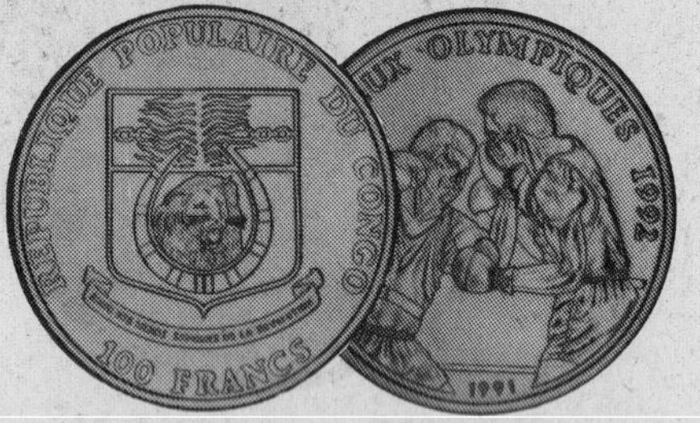

KM# 7 100 FRANCS **Composition:** Nickel Plated Steel **Subject:** Olympics **Reverse:** Boxing

Date	Mintage	F	VF	XF	Unc	BU
1991	5,000	—	—	—	15.00	—

KM# 8 100 FRANCS **Composition:** Nickel Plated Steel **Subject:** Olympics **Reverse:** Hurdler

Date	Mintage	F	VF	XF	Unc	BU
1991	5,000	—	—	—	15.00	—

KM# 10 100 FRANCS **Composition:** Nickel Plated Steel **Series:** Old Ships **Reverse:** Spanish galleon

Date	F	VF	XF	Unc	BU
1991	—	—	—	14.00	—

KM# 30 100 FRANCS **Composition:** Copper **Series:** Old ships **Obverse:** National arms, "Republique Populaire du Congo" in legend **Reverse:** Spanish galleon

Date	Mintage	F	VF	XF	Unc	BU
1991 Proof	100	Value: 55.00				

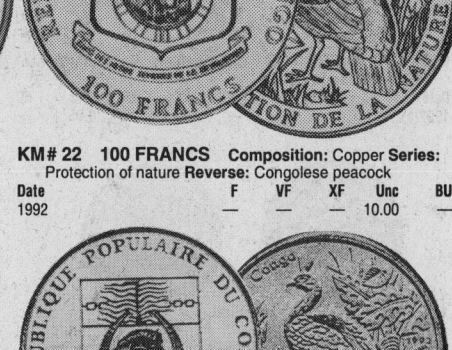

KM# 22 100 FRANCS **Composition:** Copper **Series:** Protection of nature **Reverse:** Congolese peacock

Date	F	VF	XF	Unc	BU
1992	—	—	—	10.00	—

KM# 31 100 FRANCS **Composition:** Copper-Nickel **Series:** Protection of nature **Obverse:** National arms, "Republic Populaire du Congo" in legend **Reverse:** Congolese peacock

Date	Mintage	F	VF	XF	Unc	BU
1992	333	—	—	—	50.00	—

KM# 4 500 FRANCS **Composition:** Copper-Nickel

Date	F	VF	XF	Unc	BU
1985(a)	3.50	6.50	10.00	18.50	—
1986(a)	3.50	6.50	10.00	18.50	—

KM# 5 500 FRANCS **Weight:** 16.0000 g. **Composition:** 0.9990 Silver .5144 oz. ASW **Series:** Old ships **Reverse:** Spanish galleon

Date	F	VF	XF	Unc	BU
1991 Proof	—	Value: 30.00			

KM# 6 500 FRANCS **Weight:** 12.0000 g. **Composition:** 0.9990 Silver .3858 oz. ASW **Subject:** World Cup Soccer

Date	F	VF	XF	Unc	BU
1991	—	—	—	27.50	—

KM# 9 500 FRANCS **Weight:** 16.0700 g. **Composition:** 0.9990 Silver .517 oz. ASW **Subject:** Olympics **Reverse:** Hurdler

Date	F	VF	XF	Unc	BU
1991 Proof	—	Value: 25.00			

KM# 9a 500 FRANCS **Weight:** 20.0000 g. **Composition:** 0.9990 Silver .6425 oz. ASW **Subject:** Olympics **Reverse:** Hurdler

Date	Mintage	F	VF	XF	Unc	BU
1991	5,000	—	—	—	27.50	—

KM# 11 500 FRANCS **Weight:** 20.0000 g. **Composition:** 0.9990 Silver .643 oz. ASW **Subject:** World Cup Soccer **Reverse:** Player and Statue of Liberty

Date	F	VF	XF	Unc	BU
1992 Proof	—	Value: 25.00			

KM# 12 500 FRANCS **Weight:** 19.9500 g. **Composition:** 0.9990 Silver .6415 oz. ASW **Subject:** Protection of nature **Reverse:** Congolese peacock

Date	F	VF	XF	Unc	BU
1992 Proof	—	Value: 32.50			

KM# 38 500 FRANCS **Composition:** Silver **Series:** 2000 Olympics **Subject:** Basketball

Date	F	VF	XF	Unc	BU
1998 Proof	—	Value: 22.00			

REPUBLIC

Republique du Congo

DECIMAL COINAGE

KM# 18 100 FRANCS **Composition:** Copper Nickel **Obverse:** Female writing on tablets **Reverse:** Four-masted sailing ship "Herzogin Cecilie"

Date	F	VF	XF	Unc	BU
1993	—	—	—	10.00	—

KM# 20 100 FRANCS **Composition:** Copper **Subject:** Preservation of nature **Reverse:** Four elephants

Date	F	VF	XF	Unc	BU
1993	—	—	—	12.00	—

KM# 32 100 FRANCS **Composition:** Copper **Obverse:** Woman writing on tablets **Reverse:** Four-masted sailing ship "Herzogin Cecilie"

Date	Mintage	F	VF	XF	Unc	BU
1993 Proof	100	Value: 50.00				

KM# 33 100 FRANCS **Composition:** Copper **Subject:** Prehistoric animals **Obverse:** Woman writing on tablets **Reverse:** Brachiosaurus

Date	Mintage	F	VF	XF	Unc	BU
1993 Proof	100	Value: 50.00				

KM# 16 100 FRANCS **Composition:** Copper Nickel **Subject:** Prehistoric animals **Obverse:** Woman writing on tablets **Reverse:** Polacanthus

Date	F	VF	XF	Unc	BU
1994	—	—	—	18.00	—

KM# 19 100 FRANCS **Composition:** Copper Nickel **Subject:** Prehistoric animals **Obverse:** Woman writing on tablets **Reverse:** Spinosaurus

Date	F	VF	XF	Unc	BU
1994	—	—	—	25.00	—

KM# 34 100 FRANCS **Composition:** Copper Nickel **Subject:** Prehistoric animals **Obverse:** Woman writing on tablets **Reverse:** Mammuthus

Date	Mintage	F	VF	XF	Unc	BU
1994 Proof	100	Value: 50.00				

KM# 21 100 FRANCS **Composition:** Copper Nickel **Reverse:** Junkers JU52 trimotor airplane **Note:** Multicolored.

Date	Mintage	F	VF	XF	Unc	BU
1995	25,000	—	—	—	25.00	—

KM# 35 (KM45) 100 FRANCS **Composition:** Copper Nickel **Subject:** XXVII Olympiade **Obverse:** Woman seated with tablet **Reverse:** Shot putter

Date	Mintage	F	VF	XF	Unc	BU
1999	10,000	—	—	—	7.00	9.00
1999	10,000	—	—	—	7.00	9.00

KM# 13 1000 FRANCS **Weight:** 20.0000 g. **Composition:** 0.9990 Silver .643 oz. ASW **Subject:** Preservation of nature **Reverse:** Elephants

Date	F	VF	XF	Unc	BU
1993 Proof	—	Value: 35.00			

KM# 14 1000 FRANCS **Weight:** 15.9000 g. **Composition:** 0.9990 Silver .5107 oz. ASW **Subject:** Prehistoric animals **Reverse:** Brachiosaurus

Date	F	VF	XF	Unc	BU
1993 Proof	—	Value: 37.50			

KM# 15 1000 FRANCS **Weight:** 20.1000 g. **Composition:** 0.9990 Silver .6456 oz. ASW **Reverse:** 4 masted sailing ship "Herzogin Cecilie"

Date	Mintage	F	VF	XF	Unc	BU
1993	100	—	—	—	100	—
1993 Proof	—	Value: 40.00				

KM# 17 1000 FRANCS **Weight:** 15.8800 g. **Composition:** 0.9990 Silver .5106 oz. ASW **Subject:** Prehistoric animals **Reverse:** Mammoth

Date	F	VF	XF	Unc	BU
1994 Proof	—	Value: 35.00			

KM# 23 1000 FRANCS **Weight:** 20.0000 g. **Composition:** 0.9990 Silver .6430 oz. ASW **Subject:** 1996 Olympics **Reverse:** Discus throwing

Date	Mintage	F	VF	XF	Unc	BU
1995 Proof	15,000	Value: 30.00				

KM# 24 1000 FRANCS **Weight:** 20.0000 g. **Composition:** 0.9990 Silver .6430 oz. ASW **Reverse:** Swiss airliner - Junkers JU 52 **Note:** Multicolored.

Date	Mintage	F	VF	XF	Unc	BU
1995 Proof	15,000	Value: 60.00				

KM# 25 1000 FRANCS **Weight:** 20.0000 g. **Composition:** 0.9990 Silver .6430 oz. ASW **Reverse:** Panther **Note:** Multicolored.

Date	F	VF	XF	Unc	BU
1996 Proof	—	Value: 60.00			

KM# 27 1000 FRANCS **Weight:** 20.0000 g. **Composition:** 0.9990 Silver .6430 oz. ASW **Subject:** World Cup Soccer **Obverse:** Woman writing on tablets **Reverse:** Eiffel Tower, soccer ball, French flag **Note:** Multicolored.

Date	F	VF	XF	Unc	BU
1996 Proof	—	Value: 45.00			

KM# 26 1000 FRANCS **Weight:** 20.0000 g. **Composition:** 0.9990 Silver .6430 oz. ASW **Subject:** World Cup Soccer **Obverse:** Woman writing on tablets **Reverse:** Two soccer players

Date	Mintage	F	VF	XF	Unc	BU
1996	100	—	—	—	75.00	—
1996 Proof	—	Value: 45.00				

KM# 29 1000 FRANCS **Weight:** 15.0000 g. **Composition:** 0.9990 Silver .4818 oz. ASW **Obverse:** Woman writing on tablets **Reverse:** Ancient Roman ship

Date	Mintage	F	VF	XF	Unc	BU
1997 Proof	5,000	Value: 40.00				

KM# 28.1 1000 FRANCS **Weight:** 20.0000 g. **Composition:** 0.9990 Silver .6430 oz. ASW **Subject:** XXVII Olympiade **Obverse:** Woman writing on tablets **Reverse:** Two boxers **Note:** Multicolored.

Date	Mintage	F	VF	XF	Unc	BU
1997	100	—	—	—	100	—
1997 Proof	500	Value: 55.00				

KM# 107 1000 FRANCS **Weight:** 15.0000 g. **Composition:** 0.9990 Silver 0.4818 oz. ASW **Subject:** Graf Zeppelin **Obverse:** Woman with tablet **Reverse:** Multicolor New York City view with Zeppelin in flight and a cameo insert at lower right of Count Zeppelin **Edge:** Plain **Size:** 34.9 mm.

Date	F	VF	XF	Unc	BU
ND Proof	—	Value: 45.00			

KM# 28.2 1000 FRANCS **Weight:** 15.8800 g. **Composition:** 0.9990 Silver .5106 oz. ASW **Subject:** XXVII Olympiade **Obverse:** Woman writing on tablets **Reverse:** Two boxers **Note:** Multicolored.

Date	Mintage	F	VF	XF	Unc	BU
1998	100	—	—	—	100	—
1998 Proof	5,000	Value: 45.00				

KM# 36 (KM46) 1000 FRANCS **Weight:** 20.1000 g. **Composition:** 0.9990 Silver .6456 oz. ASW **Subject:** XXVII Olympiade **Obverse:** Woman seated with tablet **Reverse:** Shot putter

Date	Mintage	F	VF	XF	Unc	BU
1999 Proof	5,000	Value: 32.50				
1999 Proof	5,000	Value: 32.50				

ESSAIS

Standard metals unless otherwise noted

KM#	Date	Mintage	Identification	Mkt Val
E1	1971(a)	1,450	100 Francs.	25.00
E2	1971(a)	4	100 Francs. Gold.	1,250
E3	1975(a)	1,700	100 Francs.	20.00

KM#	Date	Mintage	Identification	Mkt Val
E5	1985(a)	1,700	500 Francs. KM4.	35.00

PIEFORTS

KM#	Date	Mintage	Identification	Mkt Val
P1	1991	110	500 Francs. 0.9990 Silver. KM5.	110

TRIAL STRIKES

KM#	Date	Mintage	Identification	Mkt Val
TS1	1984	3	10 Francs. Silver. Fencing. Uniface.	600
TS2	1984	3	50 Francs. Silver. Shot put. Uniface.	600

CONGO DEMOCRATIC REPUBLIC

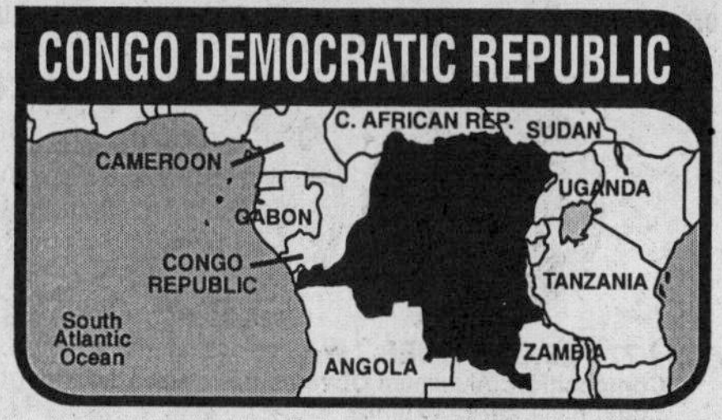

The Democratic Republic of the Congo (formerly the Republic of Zaire, and earlier the Belgian Congo), located in the south-central part of Africa, has an area of 905,568 sq. mi. (2,345,410 sq. km.) and a population of *47.4 million. Capital: Kinshasa. The mineral-rich country produces copper, tin, diamonds, gold, zinc, cobalt and uranium.

In ancient times the territory comprising former Zaire was occupied by Negrito peoples (Pygmies) pushed into the mountains by Bantu and Nilotic invaders. The interior was first explored by the American correspondent Henry Stanley, who was subsequently commissioned by King Leopold II of Belgium to conclude development treaties with the local chiefs. The Berlin conference of 1885 awarded the area to Leopold, who administered and exploited it as his private property until it was annexed to Belgium in 1908. Belgium received the mandate for the German territory of Ruanda-Urundi as a result of the international treaties after WWI. During World War II, Belgian Congolese troops fought on the side of the Allies, notably in Ethiopia. Following the eruption of bloody independence riots in 1959, Belgium granted the Belgian Congo independence as the Republic of the Congo on June 30, 1960. The nation officially changed its name to Zaire on Oct. 27, 1971, and following a Civil War in 1997 changed its name to the "Democratic Republic of the Congo."

REPUBLIC, 1960-1971

DECIMAL COINAGE

KM# 1 10 FRANCS Composition: Aluminum **Note:** Most recalled and melted.

Date	F	VF	XF	Unc	BU
1965(b)	0.60	1.50	3.00	7.00	—

KM# 2 10 FRANCS Weight: 3.2260 g. **Composition:** 0.9000 Gold .0934 oz. AGW **Subject:** 5th Anniversary of Independence **Obverse:** President Joseph Kasa-Vubu **Note:** Approximately 70 percent melted.

Date	Mintage	F	VF	XF	Unc	BU
1965 Proof	Est. 3,000	Value: 70.00				

KM# 3 20 FRANCS Weight: 6.4520 g. **Composition:** 0.9000 Gold .1867 oz. AGW **Subject:** 5th Anniversary of Independence **Obverse:** President Joseph Kasa-Vubu **Reverse:** Palm trees **Note:** Approximately 70 percent melted.

Date	Mintage	F	VF	XF	Unc	BU
1965 Proof	Est. 3,000	Value: 125				

KM# 4 25 FRANCS Weight: 8.0640 g. **Composition:** 0.9000 Gold .2334 oz. AGW **Subject:** 5th Anniversary of Independence **Reverse:** Elephant left **Note:** Approximately 70 percent melted.

Date	Mintage	F	VF	XF	Unc	BU
1965 Proof	Est. 3,000	Value: 160				

KM# 4a 25 FRANCS Composition: Silver **Subject:** 5th Anniversary of Independence

Date	F	VF	XF	Unc	BU
1965 Proof	—	Value: 60.00			

KM# 5 50 FRANCS Weight: 16.1290 g. **Composition:** 0.9000 Gold .4668 oz. AGW **Subject:** 5th Anniversary of Independence **Note:** Approximately 70 percent melted.

Date	Mintage	F	VF	XF	Unc	BU
1965 Proof	Est. 3,000	Value: 325				

KM# 6 100 FRANCS Weight: 32.2580 g. **Composition:** 0.9000 Gold .9335 oz. AGW **Subject:** 5th Anniversary of Independence **Obverse:** President Joseph Kasa-Vubu **Reverse:** Elephant left **Note:** Approximately 70 percent melted.

Date	Mintage	F	VF	XF	Unc	BU
1965 Proof	Est. 3,000	Value: 550				

KM# 6a 100 FRANCS Composition: Silver **Subject:** 5th Anniversary of Independence **Obverse:** President Joseph Kasa-Vubu **Reverse:** Elephant left

Date	F	VF	XF	Unc	BU
1965 Proof	—	Value: 100			

REFORM COINAGE

100 Sengis = 1 Likuta; 100 Makuta (plural of Likuta) = 1 Zaire

KM# 7 10 SENGIS Composition: Aluminum **Obverse:** Denomination **Reverse:** Leopard crouching on branch

Date	Mintage	F	VF	XF	Unc	BU
1967	90,996,000	—	0.15	0.45	1.00	—

KM# 10 10 SENGIS Weight: 3.2000 g. **Composition:** 0.9000 Gold .0926 oz. AGW **Subject:** 5th Year of Mobutu Presidency **Obverse:** Arms **Reverse:** Bust of President Joseph Desire Mobutu

Date	Mintage	F	VF	XF	Unc	BU
1970	1,000	—	—	—	55.00	—
1970 Proof	1,000	Value: 85.00				

KM# 10a 10 SENGIS Composition: Gilt Brass **Subject:** 5th Year of Mobutu Presidency **Obverse:** Arms **Reverse:** Bust of President Joseph Desire Mobutu

Date	F	VF	XF	Unc	BU
1970 Proof	—	Value: 70.00			

KM# 8 LIKUTA Composition: Aluminum **Obverse:** Denomination **Reverse:** Arms

Date	Mintage	F	VF	XF	Unc	BU
1967	49,180,000	—	0.15	0.50	1.25	—

KM# 9 5 MAKUTA **Composition:** Copper-Nickel **Reverse:** Bust of President Mobutu left

Date	Mintage	F	VF	XF	Unc	BU
1967	2,470,000	0.25	0.50	1.00	3.00	—

KM# 11 25 MAKUTAS **Composition:** Gilt Brass **Subject:** 5th year of Mobutu presidency

Date	F	VF	XF	Unc	BU
1970 Proof	—	Value: 100			

KM# 11a 25 MAKUTAS **Weight:** 8.0000 g. **Composition:** 0.9000 Gold .2315 oz. AGW **Subject:** 5th year of Mobutu presidency

Date	Mintage	F	VF	XF	Unc	BU
1970	1,000	—	—	—	100	—
1970 Proof	1,000	Value: 155				

KM# 12 50 MAKUTAS **Composition:** Gilt Brass **Subject:** 5th year of Mobutu presidency

Date	F	VF	XF	Unc	BU
1970 Proof	—	Value: 125			

KM# 12a 50 MAKUTAS **Weight:** 16.0000 g. **Composition:** 0.9000 Gold .4630 oz. AGW **Subject:** 5th year of Mobutu presidency

Date	Mintage	F	VF	XF	Unc	BU
1970	1,000	—	—	—	200	—
1970 Proof	1,000	Value: 275				

KM# 13 ZAIRE **Composition:** Gilt Brass **Subject:** 5th year of Mobutu presidency

Date	F	VF	XF	Unc	BU
1970 Proof	—	Value: 150			

KM# 13a ZAIRE **Weight:** 32.0000 g. **Composition:** 0.9000 Gold .9261 oz. AGW **Subject:** 5th year of Mobutu presidency

Date	Mintage	F	VF	XF	Unc	BU
1970	1,000	—	—	—	400	—
1970 Proof	1,000	Value: 500				

REPUBLIC, 1998-

REFORM COINAGE

Congo Francs replace Zaire; July 1998

KM# 76 25 CENTIMES **Weight:** 0.8500 g. **Composition:** Aluminum **Obverse:** Lion. **Reverse:** Weasel. **Edge:** Plain. **Size:** 20 mm.

Date	F	VF	XF	Unc	BU
2002	—	—	—	0.75	—

KM# 77 25 CENTIMES **Weight:** 0.8500 g. **Composition:** Aluminum **Obverse:** Lion. **Reverse:** Ram. **Edge:** Plain. **Size:** 20 mm.

Date	F	VF	XF	Unc	BU
2002	—	—	—	0.75	—

KM# 83 25 CENTIMES **Weight:** 1.3000 g. **Composition:** Aluminum **Obverse:** Lion **Reverse:** Dog **Edge:** Plain **Size:** 20 mm.

Date	F	VF	XF	Unc	BU
2002	—	—	—	—	0.50

KM# 75 50 CENTIMES **Weight:** 2.1600 g. **Composition:** Aluminum **Obverse:** Lion. **Reverse:** Soccer player. **Edge:** Plain. **Size:** 27 mm.

Date	F	VF	XF	Unc	BU
2002	—	—	—	1.25	—

KM# 78 50 CENTIMES **Weight:** 2.1600 g. **Composition:** Aluminum **Obverse:** Lion. **Reverse:** Giraffe. **Edge:** Plain. **Size:** 27 mm.

Date	F	VF	XF	Unc	BU
2002	—	—	—	1.00	—

KM# 79 50 CENTIMES **Weight:** 2.1600 g. **Composition:** Aluminum **Obverse:** Lion. **Reverse:** Gorilla. **Edge:** Plain. **Size:** 27 mm.

Date	F	VF	XF	Unc	BU
2002	—	—	—	1.00	—

KM# 80 50 CENTIMES **Weight:** 2.1600 g. **Composition:** Aluminum **Obverse:** Lion. **Reverse:** Butterfly. **Edge:** Plain. **Size:** 27 mm.

Date	F	VF	XF	Unc	BU
2002	—	—	—	1.50	—

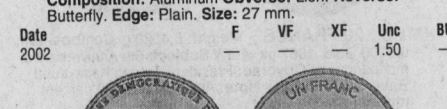

KM# 81 FRANC **Weight:** 4.5700 g. **Composition:** Brass **Obverse:** Lion. **Reverse:** Turtle. **Edge:** Plain. **Size:** 22 mm.

Date	F	VF	XF	Unc	BU
2002	—	—	—	1.25	—

KM# 82 FRANC **Weight:** 4.5700 g. **Composition:** Brass **Obverse:** Lion. **Reverse:** Chicken. **Edge:** Plain. **Size:** 22 mm.

Date	F	VF	XF	Unc	BU
2002	—	—	—	1.25	—

KM# 73 5 FRANCS **Weight:** 24.3000 g. **Composition:** Copper Nickel **Subject:** Royals of Europe **Obverse:** Lion **Reverse:** Multicolored portrait of Queen Juliana (1948-80) and crowned arms **Edge:** Reeded **Size:** 38.5 mm.

Date	F	VF	XF	Unc	BU
1999 Proof	—	—	—	10.00	—

KM# 63 5 FRANCS **Weight:** 28.7500 g. **Composition:** Copper-Nickel **Subject:** Lady Diana - Visit to India **Obverse:** Lion **Reverse:** Lady Diana at left, Taj Mahal at right, cameo of Queen Mother top center **Edge:** Reeded **Size:** 38 mm. **Note:** Prev. KM#86.

Date	F	VF	XF	Unc	BU
ND(2000) Proof	—	Value: 45.00			

KM# 64 5 FRANCS **Weight:** 28.7500 g. **Composition:** Copper-Nickel **Subject:** Lady Diana - Meeting with Pope John Paul II **Obverse:** Lion **Reverse:** Lady Diana front left, Pope John Paul II facing left, cameo of Queen Mother top center **Edge:** Reeded **Size:** 38 mm. **Note:** Prev. KM#87.

Date	F	VF	XF	Unc	BU
ND(2000) Proof	—	Value: 45.00			

KM# 24 5 FRANCS **Composition:** Copper-Nickel **Subject:** Panama Canal **Obverse:** Lion **Reverse:** Sailing ship above map **Note:** Prev. KM#47.

Date	F	VF	XF	Unc	BU
2000	—	—	—	9.00	—

KM# 39 5 FRANCS **Weight:** 27.1600 g. **Composition:** Copper Nickel **Series:** Wild Life Protection **Obverse:** Lion. **Reverse:** Multicolor holographic parrot with folded wings. **Edge:** Reeded. **Size:** 37.3 mm. **Note:** Prev. KM#62.

Date		F	VF	XF	Unc	BU
2000 Proof	—	Value: 25.00				

KM# 40 5 FRANCS **Composition:** Copper Nickel **Series:** Wild Life Protection **Obverse:** Lion. **Reverse:** Multicolor holographic parrot with open wings. **Edge:** Reeded. **Size:** 37.3 mm. **Note:** Prev. KM#63.

Date		F	VF	XF	Unc	BU
2000 Proof	—	Value: 25.00				

KM# 41 5 FRANCS **Weight:** 27.1600 g. **Composition:** Copper Nickel **Series:** Wild Life Protection **Obverse:** Lion. **Reverse:** Multicolor holographic toucan. **Note:** Prev. KM#64.

Date		F	VF	XF	Unc	BU
2000 Proof	—	Value: 25.00				

KM# 56 5 FRANCS **Weight:** 22.4000 g. **Composition:** Copper Nickel **Series:** Wild Life Protection **Obverse:** Lion. **Reverse:** Multicolor swallowtail butterfly hologram. **Edge:** Reeded. **Size:** 39.8 mm. **Note:** Prev. KM#79.

Date	F	VF	XF	Unc	BU
2002(2001)	—	—	—	27.50	—

KM# 57 5 FRANCS **Weight:** 22.4000 g. **Composition:** Copper Nickel **Series:** Wild Life Protection **Obverse:** Lion. **Reverse:** Multicolor dark greenish butterfly hologram. **Edge:** Reeded. **Size:** 39.8 mm. **Note:** Prev. KM#80.

Date	F	VF	XF	Unc	BU
2002(2001)	—	—	—	27.50	—

KM# 58 5 FRANCS **Weight:** 22.4000 g. **Composition:** Copper Nickel **Series:** Wild Life Protection **Obverse:** Lion. **Reverse:** Multicolor red and black butterfly hologram. **Edge:** Reeded. **Size:** 39.8 mm. **Note:** Prev. KM#81.

Date	F	VF	XF	Unc	BU
2002(2001)	—	—	—	27.50	—

KM# 17 10 FRANCS **Weight:** 20.0000 g. **Composition:** 0.9250 Silver .5948 oz. ASW **Series:** Endangered Wildlife **Obverse:** National arms **Reverse:** Water chevrotain **Note:** Prev. KM#38.

Date	Mintage	F	VF	XF	Unc	BU
1999 Proof	10,000	Value: 35.00				

KM# 14 10 FRANCS **Weight:** 20.0000 g. **Composition:** 0.9250 Silver .5948 oz. ASW **Series:** Endangered Wildlife **Obverse:** National arms **Reverse:** Bonobos, chimpanzee mother and child **Note:** Prev. KM#35.

Date	Mintage	F	VF	XF	Unc	BU
1999 Proof	10,000	Value: 35.00				

KM# 15 10 FRANCS **Weight:** 20.0000 g. **Composition:** 0.9250 Silver .5948 oz. ASW **Series:** Endangered Wildlife **Obverse:** National arms **Reverse:** Pygmy hippopotamus **Note:** Prev. KM#36.

Date	Mintage	F	VF	XF	Unc	BU
1999 Proof	10,000	Value: 35.00				

KM# 16 10 FRANCS **Weight:** 20.0000 g. **Composition:** 0.9250 Silver .5948 oz. ASW **Series:** Endangered Wildlife **Obverse:** National arms **Reverse:** Crocodile **Note:** Prev. KM#37.

Date	Mintage	F	VF	XF	Unc	BU
1999 Proof	10,000	Value: 35.00				

KM# 18 10 FRANCS **Weight:** 20.0000 g. **Composition:** 0.9250 Silver .5948 oz. ASW **Series:** Endangered Wildlife **Obverse:** National arms **Reverse:** Ground pangolin **Note:** Prev. KM#39.

Date	Mintage	F	VF	XF	Unc	BU
1999 Proof	10,000	Value: 35.00				

KM# 19 10 FRANCS **Weight:** 20.0000 g. **Composition:** 0.9250 Silver .5948 oz. ASW **Series:** Endangered Wildlife **Obverse:** National arms **Reverse:** Poto **Note:** Prev. KM#40.

Date	Mintage	F	VF	XF	Unc	BU
1999 Proof	10,000	Value: 35.00				

KM# 20 10 FRANCS **Weight:** 25.3100 g. **Composition:** 0.9250 Silver .7524 oz. ASW **Subject:** Explorers of Africa **Obverse:** National arms **Reverse:** Dr. David Livingstone **Note:** Prev. KM#41.

Date	Mintage	F	VF	XF	Unc	BU
1999 Proof	10,000	Value: 37.50				

KM# 21 10 FRANCS Weight: 25.3100 g. **Composition:** 0.9250 Silver .7524 oz. ASW **Subject:** Explorers of Africa **Obverse:** National arms **Reverse:** Sir Henry Morton Stanley **Note:** Prev. KM#42.

Date	Mintage	F	VF	XF	Unc	BU
1999 Proof	10,000	Value: 37.50				

KM# 22 10 FRANCS Weight: 25.3100 g. **Composition:** 0.9250 Silver .7524 oz. ASW **Subject:** 30th Anniversary of the Lunar Landing **Obverse:** National arms **Reverse:** First lunar landing scene **Note:** Prev. KM#43.

Date	Mintage	F	VF	XF	Unc	BU
1999 Proof	10,000	Value: 37.50				

KM# 23 10 FRANCS Weight: 25.3100 g. **Composition:** 0.9250 Silver .7524 oz. ASW **Subject:** Sydney 2000 **Obverse:** National arms **Reverse:** Diver and opera house **Note:** Prev. KM#44.

Date	Mintage	F	VF	XF	Unc	BU
1999 Proof	10,000	Value: 37.50				

KM# 25 10 FRANCS Weight: 25.1300 g. **Composition:** 0.9250 Silver .7474 oz. ASW **Subject:** Panama Canal **Obverse:** Lion **Reverse:** Sailing ship above map **Note:** Prev. KM#48.

Date	F	VF	XF	Unc	BU
2000 Proof	—	Value: 35.00			

KM# 44 10 FRANCS Weight: 19.9200 g. **Composition:** 0.9250 Silver .5924 oz. ASW **Series:** Olympics **Obverse:** Lion. **Reverse:** Long jumper. **Edge:** Reeded. **Size:** 41.1 mm. **Note:** Prev. KM#67.

Date	F	VF	XF	Unc	BU
2000 Proof	—	Value: 40.00			

KM# 45 10 FRANCS Weight: 19.9200 g. **Composition:** 0.9250 Silver .5924 oz. ASW **Series:** Olympics **Obverse:** Lion. **Reverse:** Two divers. **Edge:** Reeded. **Size:** 41.1 mm. **Note:** Prev. KM#68.

Date	F	VF	XF	Unc	BU
2000 Proof	—	Value: 40.00			

KM# 46 10 FRANCS Weight: 19.9200 g. **Composition:** 0.9250 Silver .5924 oz. ASW **Series:** Olympics **Obverse:** Lion. **Reverse:** Tennis player. **Edge:** Reeded. **Size:** 41.1 mm. **Note:** Prev. KM#69.

Date	F	VF	XF	Unc	BU
2000 Proof	—	Value: 40.00			

KM# 47 10 FRANCS Weight: 19.9200 g. **Composition:** 0.9250 Silver .5924 oz. ASW **Series:** Olympics **Edge:** Reeded. **Size:** 41.1 mm. **Note:** Prev. KM#70.

Date	F	VF	XF	Unc	BU
2000 Proof	—	Value: 40.00			

KM# 48 10 FRANCS Weight: 19.9200 g. **Composition:** 0.9250 Silver .5924 oz. ASW **Series:** Olympics **Obverse:** Lion. **Reverse:** Two fencers. **Edge:** Plain. **Size:** 41.1 mm. **Note:** Prev. KM#71.

Date	F	VF	XF	Unc	BU
2000 Proof	—	Value: 40.00			

KM# 49 10 FRANCS Weight: 19.9200 g. **Composition:** 0.9250 Silver .5924 oz. ASW **Series:** Olympics **Obverse:** Lion. **Reverse:** Two boxers. **Edge:** Reeded. **Size:** 41.1 mm. **Note:** Prev. KM#72.

Date	F	VF	XF	Unc	BU
2000 Proof	—	Value: 40.00			

KM# 50 10 FRANCS Weight: 19.9200 g. **Composition:** 0.9250 Silver .5924 oz. ASW **Series:** Olympics **Obverse:** Lion. **Reverse:** Rowing. **Edge:** Reeded. **Size:** 41.1 mm. **Note:** Prev. KM#73.

Date	F	VF	XF	Unc	BU
2000 Proof	—	Value: 40.00			

KM# 51 10 FRANCS Weight: 19.9200 g. **Composition:** 0.9250 Silver .5924 oz. ASW **Series:** Olympics **Obverse:** Lion. **Reverse:** Archer. **Edge:** Reeded. **Size:** 41.1 mm. **Note:** Prev. KM#74.

Date	F	VF	XF	Unc	BU
2000 Proof	—	Value: 40.00			

KM# 52 10 FRANCS Weight: 19.9200 g. **Composition:** 0.9250 Silver .5924 oz. ASW **Series:** Olympics **Obverse:** Lion. **Reverse:** Judo match. **Edge:** Reeded. **Size:** 41.1 mm. **Note:** Prev. KM#75.

Date	F	VF	XF	Unc	BU
2000 Proof	—	Value: 40.00			

KM# 53 10 FRANCS **Weight:** 19.9200 g. **Composition:** 0.9250 Silver .5924 oz. ASW **Series:** Olympics **Obverse:** Lion. **Reverse:** Ribbon dancer. **Edge:** Reeded. **Size:** 41.1 mm. **Note:** Prev. KM#76.

Date	F	VF	XF	Unc	BU
2000 Proof	—	Value: 40.00			

KM# 54 10 FRANCS **Weight:** 19.9200 g. **Composition:** 0.9250 Silver .5924 oz. ASW **Series:** Olympics **Obverse:** Lion. **Reverse:** Badminton player. **Edge:** Reeded. **Size:** 41.1 mm. **Note:** Prev. KM#77.

Date	F	VF	XF	Unc	BU
2000 Proof	—	Value: 40.00			

KM# 55 10 FRANCS **Weight:** 25.4500 g. **Composition:** 0.9250 Silver .7569 oz. ASW **Series:** Wild Life Protection **Obverse:** Lion **Reverse:** Multicolored toucan hologram **Edge:** Reeded **Size:** 37.2 mm. **Note:** Prev. KM#78.

Date	F	VF	XF	Unc	BU
2000 Proof	—	Value: 60.00			

KM# 37 10 FRANCS **Weight:** 20.0000 g. **Composition:** 0.9250 Silver .5948 oz. ASW **Subject:** Millennium - Jesus **Obverse:** Lion. **Reverse:** Portrait of Jesus **Edge:** Plain. **Size:** 38 mm. **Note:** Prev. KM#60.

Date	F	VF	XF	Unc	BU
2000 Proof	—	Value: 40.00			

KM# 30 10 FRANCS **Weight:** 25.4500 g. **Composition:** 0.9250 Silver .7569 oz. ASW **Subject:** Wild Life Protection **Obverse:** Lion above denomination **Reverse:** Multicolored parrot with open wings **Edge:** Reeded **Size:** 37.3 mm. **Note:** Prev. KM#53.

Date	F	VF	XF	Unc	BU
2000 Proof	—	Value: 45.00			

KM# 31 10 FRANCS **Weight:** 25.4500 g. **Composition:** 0.9250 Silver .7569 oz. ASW **Subject:** Wild Life Protection **Obverse:** Lion above denomination **Reverse:** Multicolored parrot with folded wings **Edge:** Reeded **Size:** 37.3 mm. **Note:** Prev. KM#54.

Date	F	VF	XF	Unc	BU
2000 Proof	—	Value: 45.00			

KM# 32 10 FRANCS **Weight:** 31.2600 g. **Composition:** 0.9990 Silver 1.004 oz. ASW **Subject:** Millennium - space travel **Obverse:** Lion above denomination **Reverse:** Footprint on the moon **Edge:** Plain **Note:** Rectangle; 47.7 x 27.1 millimeters. Prev. KM#55.

Date	F	VF	XF	Unc	BU
2000 Proof	—	Value: 32.50			

KM# 33 10 FRANCS **Weight:** 31.2600 g. **Composition:** 0.9990 Silver 1.004 oz. ASW **Subject:** Animal Protection **Obverse:** Lion above denomination **Reverse:** Chimpanzee hanging from branches **Edge:** Plain **Note:** Triangle; 45.1 x 23.4 millimeters. Prev. KM#56.

Date	F	VF	XF	Unc	BU
2000 Proof	—	Value: 32.50			

KM# 34 10 FRANCS **Weight:** 31.2600 g. **Composition:** 0.9990 Silver 1.004 oz. ASW **Subject:** Animal Protection **Obverse:** Lion above denomination **Reverse:** 2 chimpanzees in trees **Edge:** Plain **Note:** Triangle; 45.1 x 23.4 millimeters. Prev. KM#57.

Date	F	VF	XF	Unc	BU
2000 Proof	—	Value: 32.50			

KM# 35 10 FRANCS **Weight:** 31.2600 g. **Composition:** 0.9990 Silver 1.004 oz. ASW **Subject:** Animal Protection **Obverse:** Lion above denomination **Reverse:** Female chimpanzee with young one **Edge:** Plain **Note:** Triangle; 45.1 x 23.4 millimeters. Prev. KM#58.

Date	F	VF	XF	Unc	BU
2000 Proof	—	Value: 32.50			

KM# 36 10 FRANCS **Weight:** 31.2600 g. **Composition:** 0.9990 Silver 1.004 oz. ASW **Subject:** Animal Protection **Obverse:** Lion above denomination **Reverse:** 2 chimpanzees on the ground **Edge:** Plain **Note:** Triangle; 45.1 x 23.4 millimeters. Prev. KM#59.

Date	F	VF	XF	Unc	BU
2000 Proof	—	Value: 32.50			

KM# 26 10 FRANCS **Weight:** 25.1300 g. **Composition:** 0.9250 Silver .7474 oz. ASW **Subject:** Panama Canal **Obverse:** Lion **Reverse:** Cargo ship over map of Panama **Note:** Prev. KM#49.

Date	F	VF	XF	Unc	BU
2000 Proof	—	Value: 35.00			

KM# 27 10 FRANCS **Weight:** 25.1300 g. **Composition:** 0.9250 Silver .7474 oz. ASW **Subject:** 25th Anniversary - Visit of Pope John Paul II **Obverse:** Lion **Reverse:** Bust right of Pope John Paul II **Note:** Prev. KM#50.

Date	F	VF	XF	Unc	BU
2000 Proof	—	Value: 35.00			

KM# 28 10 FRANCS **Weight:** 25.1300 g. **Composition:** 0.9250 Silver .7474 oz. ASW **Subject:** 25th Anniversary - Visit of Pope John Paul II **Obverse:** Lion **Reverse:** Half-length bust of Pope John Paul II facing **Note:** Prev. KM#51.

Date	F	VF	XF	Unc	BU
2000 Proof	—	Value: 35.00			

KM# 72 10 FRANCS **Weight:** 20.0000 g. **Composition:** 0.9250 Silver 0.5948 oz. ASW **Series:** Airplanes. **Obverse:** Lion. **Reverse:** Mikoyan - Gurevich Mig 21 fighter. **Edge:** Reeded. **Size:** 40.1 mm.

Date	F	VF	XF	Unc	BU
2001 Proof	—	Value: 40.00			

KM# 74 10 FRANCS **Weight:** 31.1035 g. **Composition:** 0.9990 Silver 0.999 oz. ASW **Subject:** Olympics **Obverse:** Lion. **Reverse:** Convex chariot. **Edge:** Reeded. **Size:** 40 mm.

Date	Mintage	F	VF	XF	Unc	BU
2001 Antique Finish	15,000	—	—	—	50.00	—

KM# 65 10 FRANCS **Weight:** 20.0000 g. **Composition:** 0.9250 Silver 0.5948 oz. ASW **Series:** Airplanes **Obverse:** Lion. **Reverse:** Vickers Vimy twin engine biplane. **Edge:** Reeded. **Size:** 40.1 mm. **Note:** Prev. KM#88.

Date	F	VF	XF	Unc	BU
2001 Proof	—	Value: 40.00			

KM# 66 10 FRANCS **Weight:** 20.0000 g. **Composition:** 0.9250 Silver 0.5948 oz. ASW **Series:** Airplanes. **Obverse:** Lion. **Reverse:** Fokker DR1 triplane. **Edge:** Reeded. **Size:** 40.1 mm. **Note:** Prev. KM#89.

Date	F	VF	XF	Unc	BU
2001 Proof	—	Value: 40.00			

KM# 67 10 FRANCS **Weight:** 20.0000 g. **Composition:** 0.9250 Silver 0.5948 oz. ASW **Series:** Airplanes. **Obverse:** Lion. **Reverse:** Lockheed Vega. **Edge:** Reeded. **Size:** 40.1 mm. **Note:** Prev. KM#90.

Date	F	VF	XF	Unc	BU
2001 Proof	—	Value: 40.00			

KM# 68 10 FRANCS **Weight:** 20.0000 g. **Composition:** 0.9250 Silver 0.5948 oz. ASW **Series:** Airplanes. **Obverse:** Lion. **Reverse:** Boeing 314 Clipper. **Edge:** Reeded. **Size:** 40.1 mm. **Note:** Prev. KM#91.

Date	F	VF	XF	Unc	BU
2001 Proof	—	Value: 40.00			

KM# 69 10 FRANCS **Weight:** 20.0000 g. **Composition:** 0.9250 Silver 0.5948 oz. ASW **Series:** Airplanes. **Obverse:** Lion. **Reverse:** Junkers JU-87 Stuka in a dive. **Edge:** Reeded. **Size:** 40.1 mm. **Note:** Prev. KM#92.

Date	F	VF	XF	Unc	BU
2001 Proof	—	Value: 40.00			

KM# 70 10 FRANCS **Weight:** 20.0000 g. **Composition:** 0.9250 Silver 0.5948 oz. ASW **Series:** Airplanes. **Obverse:** Lion. **Reverse:** B-29 Enola Gay. **Edge:** Reeded. **Size:** 40.1 mm. **Note:** Prev. KM#93.

Date	F	VF	XF	Unc	BU
2001 Proof	—	Value: 40.00			

KM# 71 10 FRANCS **Weight:** 20.0000 g. **Composition:** 0.9250 Silver 0.5948 oz. ASW **Series:** Airplanes **Obverse:** Lion. **Reverse:** Bell X-1 rocket plane. **Edge:** Reeded. **Size:** 40.1 mm. **Note:** Prev. KM#94.

Date	F	VF	XF	Unc	BU
2001 Proof	—	Value: 40.00			

KM# 59 10 FRANCS **Weight:** 25.9500 g. **Composition:** 0.9250 Silver .7717 oz. ASW **Series:** Wild Life Protection **Obverse:** Lion. **Reverse:** Multicolored swallowtail butterfly hologram **Edge:** Reeded. **Size:** 39.9 mm. **Note:** Prev. KM#82.

Date	F	VF	XF	Unc	BU
2002 (2001) Proof	—	Value: 65.00			

KM# 60 10 FRANCS **Weight:** 25.9500 g. **Composition:** 0.9250 Silver .7717 oz. ASW **Series:** Wild Life Protection **Obverse:** Lion. **Reverse:** Multicolored dark greenish butterfly hologram **Edge:** Reeded. **Size:** 39.9 mm. **Note:** Prev. KM#83.

Date		F	VF	XF	Unc	BU
2002 (2001) Proof	—	Value: 65.00				

KM# 61 10 FRANCS **Weight:** 25.9500 g. **Composition:** 0.9250 Silver .7717 oz. ASW **Series:** Wild Life Protection **Obverse:** Lion. **Reverse:** Multicolored red and black butterfly hologram **Edge:** Reeded. **Size:** 39.9 mm. **Note:** Prev. KM#84.

Date		F	VF	XF	Unc	BU
2002 (2001) Proof	—	Value: 65.00				

KM# 38 10 FRANCS **Weight:** 31.3000 g. **Composition:** 0.9250 Silver .9308 oz. ASW **Subject:** Illusion **Obverse:** Lion. **Reverse:** Multicolored couple in flower picture **Edge:** Plain. **Shape:** Rectangular **Size:** 27 x 47.1 mm. **Note:** Prev. KM#61.

Date		F	VF	XF	Unc	BU
2001 Proof	—	Value: 50.00				

KM# 29 20 FRANCS **Weight:** 1.5300 g. **Composition:** 0.9990 Gold .0492 oz. AGW **Subject:** 25th Anniversary - Visit of Pope John Paul II **Obverse:** Lion **Reverse:** Bust right of Pope John Paul II **Note:** Prev. KM#52.

Date		F	VF	XF	Unc	BU
2000 Proof	—	Value: 40.00				

KM# 62 20 FRANCS **Weight:** 62.2000 g. **Composition:** 0.9999 Silver 1.9996 oz. ASW **Subject:** Japanese New 500 Yen Coin **Obverse:** Lion above denomination. **Reverse:** Japanese 500 yen coin Y-125, embedded over the obverse and reverse design of the Y-99 500 yen coin. **Edge:** Reeded. **Size:** 40 mm. **Note:** Prev. KM#85.

Date	Mintage	F	VF	XF	Unc	BU
2000	1,500	—	—	—	65.00	—

KM# 42 100 FRANCS **Weight:** 31.5400 g. **Composition:** 0.9999 Gold 1.0139 oz. AGW **Subject:** Wild Life Protection **Obverse:** Lion. **Reverse:** Multicolored holographic parrot with folded wings **Edge:** Reeded. **Size:** 37.3 mm. **Note:** Prev. KM#65.

Date	Mintage	F	VF	XF	Unc	BU
2000 Proof	25	Value: 1,200				

KM# 43 100 FRANCS **Weight:** 31.5400 g. **Composition:** 0.9999 Gold 1.0139 oz. AGW **Subject:** Wild Life Protection **Obverse:** Lion. **Rev. Designer:** Multicolor holographic parrot with open wings. **Edge:** Reeded. **Size:** 37.3 mm. **Note:** Prev. KM#66.

Date	Mintage	F	VF	XF	Unc	BU
2000 Proof	25	Value: 1,200				

ESSAIS

KM#	Date	Mintage	Identification	Mkt Val
E1	1965	—	10 Francs. Silver.	—
E2	1965(b)	—	10 Francs. Gold.	—

Note: Aluminum and copper-nickel essais of the 10 Francs are valued at $175 and $250 respectively. These are considered off-metal pieces created as die trials or set-up strikes in the process of producing the official silver and gold coins.

KM#	Date	Mintage	Identification	Mkt Val
E3	1970	—	50 Makutas. Pewter. KM12.	250

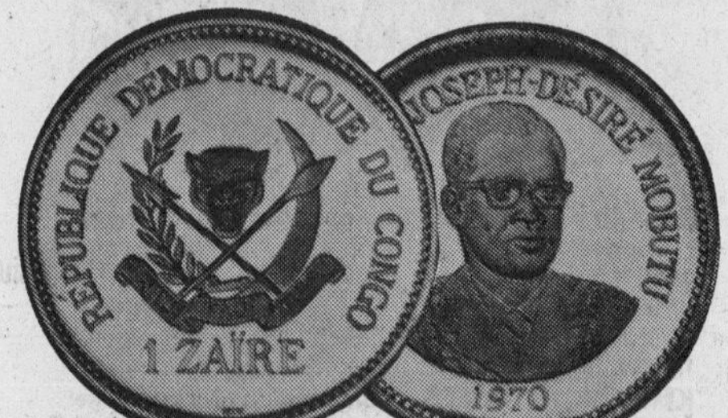

KM#	Date	Mintage	Identification	Mkt Val
E4	1970	—	Zaire. Pewter. KM13.	325
E5	1970	—	Zaire. Silver. KM13.	165
E6	1970	10	Zaire. Gold. ESSAI.	1,000

PIEFORTS WITH ESSAI

KM#	Date	Mintage	Identification	Mkt Val
PE1	1970	10	Zaire. Silver. 2.4 millimeters thick.	250
PE2	1970	10	Zaire. Silver. 4.7 millimeters thick.	365

MINT SETS

KM#	Date	Mintage	Identification	Issue Price	Mkt Val
MS1	1970 (4)	1,000	KM10-13	1,300	900

PROOF SETS

KM#	Date	Mintage	Identification	Issue Price	Mkt Val
PS1	1965 (5)	3,000	KM2-6. Approximately 70 percent melted.	490	1,290
PS2	1970 (4)	1,000	KM10-13	—	1,100

COOK ISLANDS

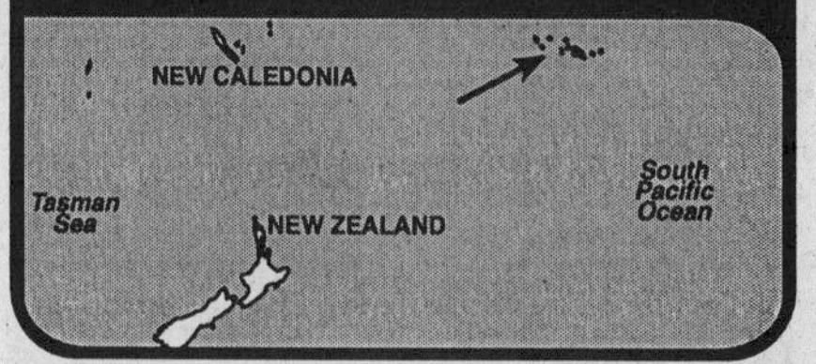

Cook Islands, a self-governing dependency of New Zealand consisting of 15 islands, is located in the South Pacific Ocean about 2,000 miles (3,218 km.) northeast of New Zealand. It has an area of 93 sq. mi. (234 sq. km.) and a population of 17,185. Capital: Avarua. The United States claims the islands of Danger, Manahiki, Penrhyn, and Rakahanga atolls. Citrus and canned fruits and juices, copra, clothing, jewelry, and mother-of-pearl shell are exported.

Spanish navigator Alvaro de Mendada first sighted the islands in 1595. Portuguese navigator Pedro Fernandes de Quieros landed on Rakahanga in 1606. English navigator Capt. James Cook sailed to the islands on three occasions: 1773, 1774 and 1777. He named them Hervey Islands, in honor of Augustus John Hervey, a lord of the Admiralty. The islands were declared a British protectorate in 1888, and were annexed to New Zealand in 1901. They were granted internal self-government in 1965. New Zealand provides an annual subsidy and retains responsibility for defense and foreign affairs.

RULERS

British

MINT MARKS

(b) - British Royal Mint
FM - Franklin Mint, U.S.A. *
PM - Pobjoy Mint

***NOTE:** From 1975-1985 the Franklin Mint produced coinage in up to three different qualities. Qualities of issue are designated in () after each date and are defined as follows:

(M) MATTE - Normal circulation strike or a dull finish produced by sandblasting special uncirculated (polish finish) or proof quality dies.

(U) SPECIAL UNCIRCULATED - Polished or proof-like in appearance without any frosted features.

(P) PROOF - The highest quality obtainable having mirror-like fields and frosted features.

MONETARY SYSTEM

(Until 1967)

12 Pence = 1 Shilling
20 Shillings = 1 Pound

(Commencing 1967)

100 Cents = 1 Dollar

DEPENDENCY OF NEW ZEALAND

DECIMAL COINAGE

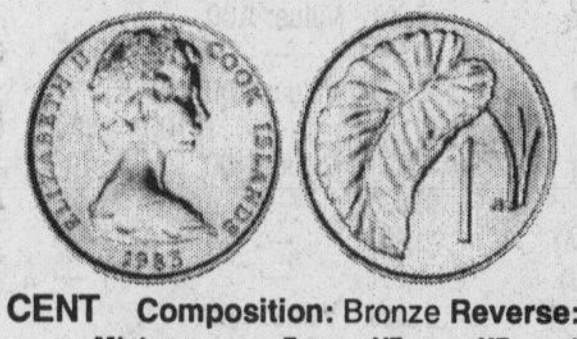

KM# 1 CENT **Composition:** Bronze **Reverse:** Taro leaf

Date	Mintage	F	VF	XF	Unc	BU
1972	117,000	—	—	0.10	0.20	—
1972 Proof	17,000	Value: 0.50				
1973	8,500	—	—	0.10	0.20	—
1973 Proof	13,000	Value: 0.50				
1974	300,000	—	—	0.10	0.20	—
1974 Proof	7,300	Value: 0.50				
1975	429,000	—	—	0.10	0.20	—
1975FM (M)	1,000	—	—	—	0.50	—
1975FM (U)	2,251	—	—	—	0.20	—
1975FM (P)	21,000	Value: 0.50				
1976FM (M)	1,001	—	—	—	0.50	—
1976FM (U)	1,066	—	—	—	0.20	—
1976FM (P)	18,000	Value: 0.50				
1977FM (M)	1,171	—	—	—	0.50	—
1977FM (U)	1,002	—	—	—	0.20	—
1977FM (P)	5,986	Value: 0.50				
1979FM (M)	1,000	—	—	—	0.50	—
1979FM (U)	500	—	—	—	1.00	—
1979FM (P)	4,058	Value: 0.50				
1983	—	—	—	0.10	0.20	—
1983 Proof	10,000	Value: 0.50				

KM# 1a CENT **Composition:** Bronze **Edge Lettering:** 1728 CAPTAIN COOK 1978

Date	Mintage	F	VF	XF	Unc	BU
1978FM (M)	1,000	—	—	—	1.00	—
1978FM (U)	767	—	—	—	1.00	—
1978FM (P)	6,287	Value: 0.50				

KM# 1b CENT **Composition:** Bronze **Subject:** Wedding of Prince Charles and Lady Diana **Edge Lettering:** THE ROYAL WEDDING 29 JULY 1981

Date	Mintage	F	VF	XF	Unc	BU
1981FM (M)	1,000	—	—	—	0.50	—
1981FM (U)	1,100	—	—	—	0.50	—
1981FM (P)	9,205	Value: 0.40				

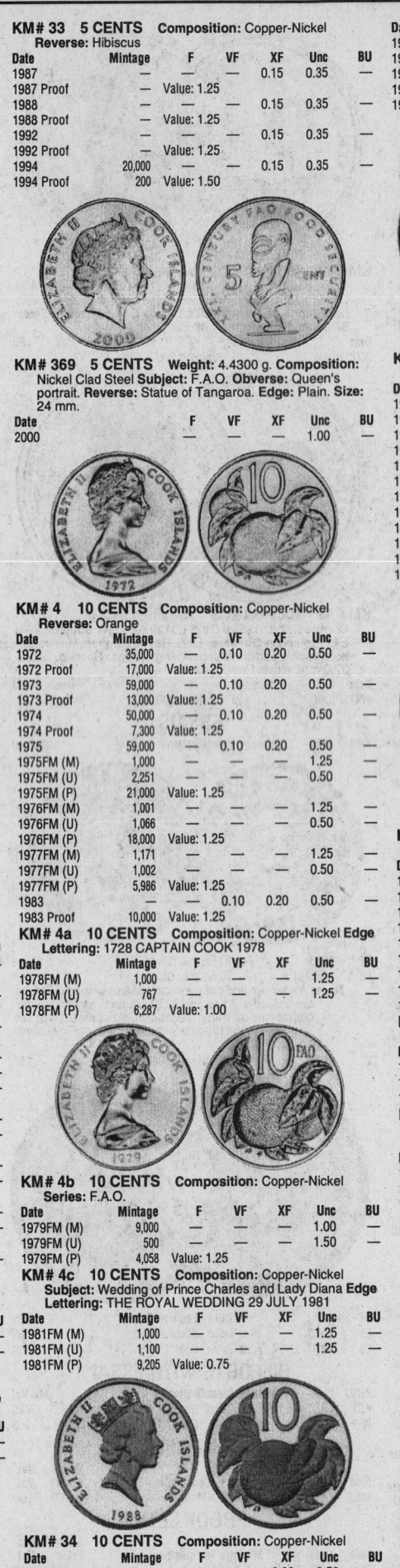

KM# 2 2 CENTS **Composition:** Bronze **Reverse:** Pineapple

Date	Mintage	F	VF	XF	Unc	BU
1972	63,000	—	0.10	0.15	0.30	—
1972 Proof	17,000	Value: 0.75				
1973	8,500	—	0.15	0.20	0.40	—
1973 Proof	13,000	Value: 0.75				
1974	120,000	—	0.10	0.15	0.30	—
1974 Proof	7,300	Value: 0.75				
1975	129,000	—	0.10	0.15	0.25	—
1975FM (M)	1,000	—	—	—	0.75	—
1975FM (U)	2,251	—	—	—	0.30	—
1975FM (P)	21,000	Value: 0.75				
1976FM (M)	1,001	—	—	—	0.75	—
1976FM (U)	1,066	—	—	—	0.30	—
1976FM (P)	18,000	Value: 0.75				
1977FM (M)	1,171	—	—	—	0.75	—
1977FM (U)	1,002	—	—	—	0.30	—
1977FM (P)	5,986	Value: 0.75				
1979FM (M)	1,000	—	—	—	0.75	—
1979FM (U)	500	—	—	—	0.30	—
1979FM (P)	4,058	Value: 0.75				
1983	—	—	0.10	0.15	0.25	—
1983 Proof	10,000	Value: 0.75				

KM# 2a 2 CENTS **Composition:** Bronze **Edge Lettering:** 1798 CAPTAIN COOK 1978

Date	Mintage	F	VF	XF	Unc	BU
1978FM (M)	1,000	—	—	—	0.75	—
1978FM (U)	767	—	—	—	0.75	—
1978FM (P)	6,287	Value: 0.50				

KM# 2b 2 CENTS **Composition:** Bronze **Subject:** Wedding of Prince Charles and Lady Diana **Edge Lettering:** THE ROYAL WEDDING 29 JULY 1981

Date	Mintage	F	VF	XF	Unc	BU
1981FM (M)	1,000	—	—	—	0.75	—
1981FM (U)	1,100	—	—	—	0.75	—
1981FM (P)	9,205	Value: 0.50				

KM# 3 5 CENTS **Composition:** Copper-Nickel **Reverse:** Hibiscus

Date	Mintage	F	VF	XF	Unc	BU
1972	32,000	—	0.10	0.20	0.40	—
1972 Proof	17,000	Value: 1.00				
1973	8,500	—	0.15	0.25	0.50	—
1973 Proof	13,000	Value: 1.00				
1974	80,000	—	0.10	0.20	0.40	—
1974 Proof	7,300	Value: 1.00				
1975	89,000	—	0.10	0.20	0.40	—
1975FM (M)	1,000	—	—	—	1.00	—
1975FM (U)	2,251	—	—	—	0.40	—
1975FM (P)	21,000	Value: 1.00				
1976FM (M)	1,001	—	—	—	1.00	—
1976FM (U)	1,066	—	—	—	0.40	—
1976FM (P)	18,000	Value: 1.00				
1977FM (M)	1,171	—	—	—	1.00	—
1977FM (U)	1,002	—	—	—	0.40	—
1977FM (P)	5,986	Value: 1.00				
1979FM (M)	1,000	—	—	—	1.00	—
1979FM (U)	500	—	—	—	0.40	—
1979FM (P)	4,058	Value: 1.00				
1983	—	—	0.10	0.20	0.40	—
1983 Proof	10,000	Value: 1.00				

KM# 3a 5 CENTS **Composition:** Copper-Nickel **Edge Lettering:** 1728 CAPTAIN COOK 1978

Date	Mintage	F	VF	XF	Unc	BU
1978FM (M)	1,000	—	—	—	1.00	—
1978FM (U)	767	—	—	—	0.75	—
1978FM (P)	6,287	Value: 0.50				

KM# 3b 5 CENTS **Composition:** Copper-Nickel **Subject:** Wedding of Prince Charles and Lady Diana **Edge Lettering:** THE ROYAL WEDDING 29 JULY 1981

Date	Mintage	F	VF	XF	Unc	BU
1981FM (M)	1,000	—	—	—	1.00	—
1981FM (U)	1,100	—	—	—	1.00	—
1981FM (P)	9,205	Value: 0.50				

KM# 33 5 CENTS **Composition:** Copper-Nickel **Reverse:** Hibiscus

Date	Mintage	F	VF	XF	Unc	BU
1987	—	—	—	0.15	0.35	—
1987 Proof	—	Value: 1.25				
1988	—	—	—	0.15	0.35	—
1988 Proof	—	Value: 1.25				
1992	—	—	—	0.15	0.35	—
1992 Proof	—	Value: 1.25				
1994	20,000	—	—	0.15	0.35	—
1994 Proof	200	Value: 1.50				

KM# 369 5 CENTS **Weight:** 4.4300 g. **Composition:** Nickel Clad Steel **Subject:** F.A.O. **Obverse:** Queen's portrait. **Reverse:** Statue of Tangaroa. **Edge:** Plain. **Size:** 24 mm.

Date	F	VF	XF	Unc	BU
2000	—	—	—	1.00	—

KM# 4 10 CENTS **Composition:** Copper-Nickel **Reverse:** Orange

Date	Mintage	F	VF	XF	Unc	BU
1972	35,000	—	0.10	0.20	0.50	—
1972 Proof	17,000	Value: 1.25				
1973	59,000	—	0.10	0.20	0.50	—
1973 Proof	13,000	Value: 1.25				
1974	50,000	—	0.10	0.20	0.50	—
1974 Proof	7,300	Value: 1.25				
1975	59,000	—	0.10	0.20	0.50	—
1975FM (M)	1,000	—	—	—	1.25	—
1975FM (U)	2,251	—	—	—	0.50	—
1975FM (P)	21,000	Value: 1.25				
1976FM (M)	1,001	—	—	—	1.25	—
1976FM (U)	1,066	—	—	—	0.50	—
1976FM (P)	18,000	Value: 1.25				
1977FM (M)	1,171	—	—	—	1.25	—
1977FM (U)	1,002	—	—	—	0.50	—
1977FM (P)	5,986	Value: 1.25				
1983	—	—	0.10	0.20	0.50	—
1983 Proof	10,000	Value: 1.25				

KM# 4a 10 CENTS **Composition:** Copper-Nickel **Edge Lettering:** 1728 CAPTAIN COOK 1978

Date	Mintage	F	VF	XF	Unc	BU
1978FM (M)	1,000	—	—	—	1.25	—
1978FM (U)	767	—	—	—	1.25	—
1978FM (P)	6,287	Value: 1.00				

KM# 4b 10 CENTS **Composition:** Copper-Nickel **Series:** F.A.O.

Date	Mintage	F	VF	XF	Unc	BU
1979FM (M)	9,000	—	—	—	1.00	—
1979FM (U)	500	—	—	—	1.50	—
1979FM (P)	4,058	Value: 1.25				

KM# 4c 10 CENTS **Composition:** Copper-Nickel **Subject:** Wedding of Prince Charles and Lady Diana **Edge Lettering:** THE ROYAL WEDDING 29 JULY 1981

Date	Mintage	F	VF	XF	Unc	BU
1981FM (M)	1,000	—	—	—	1.25	—
1981FM (U)	1,100	—	—	—	1.25	—
1981FM (P)	9,205	Value: 0.75				

KM# 34 10 CENTS **Composition:** Copper-Nickel

Date	Mintage	F	VF	XF	Unc	BU
1987	—	—	—	0.20	0.50	—
1987 Proof	—	Value: 1.25				
1988	—	—	—	0.20	0.50	—
1988 Proof	—	Value: 1.25				
1992	—	—	—	0.20	0.50	—
1992 Proof	—	Value: 1.25				
1994	20,000	—	—	0.20	0.50	—
1994 Proof	200	Value: 1.50				

KM# 5 20 CENTS **Composition:** Copper-Nickel **Reverse:** Fairy Tern

Date	Mintage	F	VF	XF	Unc	BU
1972	31,000	—	0.20	0.40	0.75	—
1972 Proof	17,000	Value: 1.50				
1973	49,000	—	0.20	0.40	0.75	—
1973 Proof	13,000	Value: 1.50				
1974	5,500	—	0.20	0.45	0.85	—
1974 Proof	7,300	Value: 1.50				
1975	60,000	—	0.20	0.40	0.75	—
1975FM (M)	1,000	—	—	—	1.50	—
1975FM (U)	2,251	—	—	—	0.85	—
1975FM (P)	21,000	Value: 1.50				
1983	—	—	0.20	0.40	0.85	—
1983 Proof	10,000	Value: 1.50				

KM# 14 20 CENTS **Composition:** Copper-Nickel **Reverse:** Two Pacific Triton shells

Date	Mintage	F	VF	XF	Unc	BU
1976FM (M)	1,001	—	—	—	1.50	—
1976FM (U)	1,066	—	—	—	1.00	—
1976FM (P)	18,000	Value: 1.50				
1977FM (M)	1,171	—	—	—	1.50	—
1977FM (U)	1,002	—	—	—	1.00	—
1977FM (P)	5,986	Value: 1.50				
1979FM (M)	1,000	—	—	—	1.50	—
1979FM (U)	500	—	—	—	2.00	—
1979FM (P)	4,058	Value: 1.50				

KM# 14a 20 CENTS **Composition:** Copper-Nickel **Edge Lettering:** 1728 CAPTAIN COOK 1978

Date	Mintage	F	VF	XF	Unc	BU
1978FM (M)	1,000	—	—	—	1.50	—
1978FM (U)	767	—	—	—	2.00	—
1978FM (P)	6,287	Value: 1.00				

KM# 14b 20 CENTS **Composition:** Copper-Nickel **Subject:** Wedding of Prince Charles and Lady Diana **Edge Lettering:** THE ROYAL WEDDING 29 JULY 1981

Date	Mintage	F	VF	XF	Unc	BU
1981FM (M)	1,000	—	—	—	1.50	—
1981FM (U)	1,100	—	—	—	1.50	—
1981FM (P)	9,205	Value: 1.00				

KM# 35 20 CENTS **Composition:** Copper-Nickel **Reverse:** Fairy Tern

Date	Mintage	F	VF	XF	Unc	BU
1987	—	—	—	0.25	0.65	—
1987 Proof	—	Value: 1.50				
1988	—	—	—	0.25	0.65	—
1988 Proof	—	Value: 1.50				
1992	—	—	—	0.25	0.65	—
1992 Proof	—	Value: 1.50				
1994	20,000	—	—	0.25	0.65	—
1994 Proof	200	Value: 2.00				

KM# 6.1 50 CENTS **Composition:** Copper-Nickel **Obverse:** Bust of Queen Elizabeth II **Obv. Designer:** Machin **Reverse:** Bonito fish, denomination

Date	Mintage	F	VF	XF	Unc	BU
1972	31,000	—	0.40	0.75	1.50	—
1972 Proof	17,000	Value: 3.00				
1973	19,000	—	0.40	0.75	1.50	—
1973 Proof	13,000	Value: 3.00				
1974	10,000	—	0.40	0.75	1.50	—
1974 Proof	7,300	Value: 3.00				
1975	19,000	—	0.40	0.75	1.50	—
1975FM (M)	1,000	—	—	—	2.00	—
1975FM (U)	2,251	—	—	—	1.50	—
1975FM (P)	21,000	Value: 3.00				
1976FM (M)	1,001	—	—	—	2.00	—
1976FM (U)	1,066	—	—	—	1.50	—
1976FM (P)	18,000	Value: 3.00				
1977FM (M)	1,171	—	—	—	2.00	—
1977FM (U)	1,002	—	—	—	1.50	—
1977FM (P)	5,986	Value: 3.00				
1983	—	—	0.40	0.75	1.50	—
1983 Proof	10,000	Value: 3.50				

KM# 6.2 50 CENTS **Composition:** Copper-Nickel **Edge Lettering:** 1728 CAPTAIN COOK 1978

Date	Mintage	F	VF	XF	Unc	BU
1978FM (M)	1,000	—	—	—	2.00	—
1978FM (U)	767	—	—	—	2.00	—
1978FM (P)	6,287	Value: 2.00				

KM# 6.3 50 CENTS **Composition:** Copper-Nickel **Series:** F.A.O. **Reverse:** FAO logo, fish, denomination

Date	Mintage	F	VF	XF	Unc	BU
1979FM (M)	9,000	—	0.50	1.00	2.00	—
1979FM (U)	500	—	—	—	2.50	—
1979FM (P)	4,058	Value: 2.25				

KM# 6.4 50 CENTS **Composition:** Copper-Nickel **Subject:** Wedding of Prince Charles and Lady Diana **Edge Lettering:** THE ROYAL WEDDING 29 JULY 1981

Date	Mintage	F	VF	XF	Unc	BU
1981FM (M)	1,000	—	—	—	2.00	—
1981FM (U)	1,100	—	—	—	2.00	—
1981FM (P)	9,205	Value: 1.50				

KM# 36 50 CENTS **Composition:** Copper-Nickel **Obverse:** Mature portrait of Queen Elizabeth **Reverse:** Bonito fish, denomination

Date		F	VF	XF	Unc	BU
1987		—	0.40	0.75	1.50	—
1987 Proof	—	Value: 2.00				
1992		—	0.40	0.75	1.50	—

KM# 307 50 CENTS **Composition:** Copper-Nickel **Obverse:** Queen's portrait **Reverse:** Princess Diana's portrait, dates

Date		F	VF	XF	Unc	BU
1997 Proof	—	Value: 12.00				

KM# 338 50 CENTS **Weight:** 26.9000 g. **Composition:** Copper-Nickel **Obverse:** Queen's head right **Reverse:** Multicolored cartoon cat "Garfield" **Edge:** Reeded

Date		F	VF	XF	Unc	BU
1999 Proof	—	Value: 17.50				

KM# 41 50 TENE **Composition:** Copper-Nickel **Reverse:** Sea turtle

Date	Mintage	F	VF	XF	Unc	BU
1988	60,000	—	—	—	2.50	—
1988 Proof	1,000	Value: 3.00				
1992	—	—	—	—	2.50	—
1992 Proof	—	Value: 3.00				
1994	20,000	—	—	—	2.50	—
1994 Proof	200	Value: 3.50				

KM# 7 DOLLAR **Composition:** Copper-Nickel **Reverse:** Tangaroa, Polynesian God of Creation

Date	Mintage	F	VF	XF	Unc	BU
1972	31,000	—	1.25	2.00	4.00	—
1972 Proof	27,000	Value: 5.00				
1973	49,000	—	1.25	2.00	4.00	—
1973 Proof	13,000	Value: 6.00				
1974	20,000	—	1.25	2.00	4.00	—
1974 Proof	7,300	Value: 6.00				
1975	29,000	—	1.25	2.00	4.00	—
1975FM (M)	1,000	—	—	—	5.00	—
1975FM (U)	2,251	—	—	—	4.00	—
1975FM (P)	21,000	Value: 6.00				
1976FM (M)	1,001	—	—	—	5.00	—
1976FM (U)	1,066	—	—	—	5.00	—
1976FM (P)	18,000	Value: 6.00				
1977FM (M)	1,171	—	—	—	5.00	—
1977FM (U)	1,002	—	—	—	5.00	—
1977FM (P)	5,986	Value: 8.00				
1979FM (M)	1,000	—	—	—	5.00	—
1979FM (U)	500	—	—	—	6.00	—
1979FM (P)	4,058	Value: 8.00				
1983	—	—	1.25	2.00	4.00	—
1983 Proof	10,000	Value: 6.00				

KM# 7a DOLLAR **Composition:** Copper-Nickel **Edge Lettering:** 1728 CAPTAIN COOK 1978

Date	Mintage	F	VF	XF	Unc	BU
1978FM (M)	1,000	—	—	—	6.00	—
1978FM (U)	767	—	—	—	6.00	—
1978FM (P)	6,287	Value: 5.00				

KM# 7b DOLLAR **Composition:** Copper-Nickel **Subject:** Wedding of Prince Charles and Lady Diana **Edge Lettering:** THE ROYAL WEDDING 29 JULY 1981

Date	Mintage	F	VF	XF	Unc	BU
1981FM (M)	1,000	—	—	—	6.00	—
1981FM (U)	1,100	—	—	—	6.00	—
1981FM (P)	9,205	Value: 5.00				

KM# 30 DOLLAR **Composition:** Copper-Nickel **Subject:** 16th Forum, 2nd P.I.C. and Mini Games **Reverse:** Tangaroa, Polynesian God of Creation

Date		F	VF	XF	Unc	BU
1985		—	—	—	4.50	—

KM# 30a DOLLAR **Weight:** 27.2200 g. **Composition:** 0.9250 Silver .8096 oz. ASW **Subject:** 16th Forum, 2nd P.I.C. and Mini Games **Reverse:** Tangaroa, Polynesian God of Creation

Date	Mintage	F	VF	XF	Unc	BU
1985 Proof	Est. 2,500	Value: 37.50				

KM# 30b DOLLAR **Weight:** 39.8000 g. **Composition:** 0.9170 Gold 1.1735 oz. AGW **Subject:** 16th Forum, 2nd P.I.C. and Mini Games **Reverse:** Tangaroa, Polynesian God of Creation

Date	Mintage	F	VF	XF	Unc	BU
1985 Proof	Est. 25	Value: 3,000				

KM# 31 DOLLAR **Composition:** Copper-Nickel **Subject:** 60th Birthday of Queen Elizabeth II **Reverse:** Cameos of family members in circle

Date	Mintage	F	VF	XF	Unc	BU
1986	20,000	—	—	—	4.50	—

KM# 32 DOLLAR **Composition:** Copper-Nickel **Subject:** Prince Andrew's Wedding **Reverse:** Busts of Andrew and Sarah facing each other in wreath

Date		F	VF	XF	Unc	BU
1986		—	—	—	4.50	—

KM# 31a DOLLAR **Weight:** 27.2200 g. **Composition:** 0.9250 Silver .8096 oz. ASW **Subject:** 60th Birthday of Queen Elizabeth II **Reverse:** Busts of Andrew and Sarah facing each other in wreath

Date	Mintage	F	VF	XF	Unc	BU
1986 Proof	Est. 2,500	Value: 15.00				

KM# 32a DOLLAR **Weight:** 27.2200 g. **Composition:** 0.9250 Silver .8096 oz. ASW **Reverse:** Busts of Andrew and Sarah facing each other in wreath

Date	Mintage	F	VF	XF	Unc	BU
1986 Proof	Est. 2,500	Value: 15.00				

KM# 31b DOLLAR **Weight:** 44.0000 g. **Composition:** 0.9170 Gold 1.2969 oz. AGW **Subject:** 60th Birthday of Queen Elizabeth II **Reverse:** Busts of Andrew and Sarah facing each other in wreath

Date	Mintage	F	VF	XF	Unc	BU
1986 Proof	Est. 60	Value: 1,500				

KM# 32b DOLLAR **Weight:** 44.0000 g. **Composition:** 0.9170 Gold 1.2969 oz. AGW **Subject:** Prince Andrew's Wedding **Reverse:** Busts of Andrew and Sarah facing each other in wreath

Date	Mintage	F	VF	XF	Unc	BU
1986 Proof	Est. 75	Value: 825				

KM# 37 DOLLAR **Composition:** Copper-Nickel **Obverse:** Head of Queen Elizabeth II right **Reverse:** Tangaroa, head of Queen Elizabeth II right

Date	Mintage	F	VF	XF	Unc	BU
1987	—	—	—	1.50	3.50	—
1987 Proof	—	Value: 5.00				
1988	—	—	—	1.50	3.50	—
1988 Proof	—	Value: 5.00				
1992	—	—	—	1.50	3.50	—
1992 Proof	—	Value: 5.00				
1994	20,000	—	—	1.50	3.50	—
1994 Proof	200	Value: 6.00				

KM# 147 DOLLAR **Composition:** Copper-Nickel **Obverse:** Portrait of Queen Elizabeth **Reverse:** Tangaroa, Polynesian God of Fertility

Date	F	VF	XF	Unc	BU
1992	—	—	—	4.00	—

KM# 266 DOLLAR **Composition:** Copper-Nickel **Reverse:** Queen Mother and daughters

Date	Mintage	F	VF	XF	Unc	BU
1995 Proof	Est. 30,000	Value: 8.00				

KM# 268 DOLLAR **Composition:** Copper-Nickel **Reverse:** Sir Francis Drake and sailing ship right

Date	Mintage	F	VF	XF	Unc	BU
1996 Proof	Est. 25,000	Value: 11.50				

KM# 277 DOLLAR **Composition:** Copper-Nickel **Subject:** Yellowstone National Park **Reverse:** Multicolored Grizzly Bear and cub

Date	F	VF	XF	Unc	BU
1996	—	—	—	7.50	—

KM# 278 DOLLAR **Composition:** Copper-Nickel **Subject:** Olympic National Park **Reverse:** Multicolored Bald Eagle in flight

Date	F	VF	XF	Unc	BU
1996	—	—	—	7.50	—

KM# 341 DOLLAR **Composition:** Copper-Nickel **Subject:** Endangered Wildlife **Reverse:** Senegalese lion

Date	F	VF	XF	Unc	BU
1996	—	—	—	10.00	—

KM# 267 DOLLAR **Weight:** 10.0000 g. **Composition:** 0.5000 Silver .1607 oz. ASW **Subject:** 1996 Summer Olympics **Reverse:** Horse jumping

Date	Mintage	F	VF	XF	Unc	BU
1996 Proof	Est. 10,000	Value: 14.50				

KM# 311 DOLLAR **Weight:** 9.9700 g. **Composition:** 0.5000 Silver .1603 oz. ASW **Subject:** Endangered Wildlife **Obverse:** Queen's portrait **Reverse:** Mother elephant with calf

Date	Mintage	F	VF	XF	Unc	BU
1996 Proof	—	Value: 15.00				

KM# 326 DOLLAR **Weight:** 31.1035 g. **Composition:** 0.9990 Silver 1.0000 oz. ASW **Subject:** Lunar Year of the Mouse **Obverse:** Queen's portrait **Reverse:** Mouse in basket

Date	Mintage	F	VF	XF	Unc	BU
1996 Proof	—	Value: 35.00				

KM# 387 DOLLAR **Weight:** 28.4000 g. **Composition:** Copper-Nickel **Subject:** Endangered Wildlife **Obverse:** Bust of Queen Elizabeth II right **Reverse:** Alpine Ibex on mountain **Edge:** Reeded **Size:** 38.6 mm.

Date	F	VF	XF	Unc	BU
1996	—	—	—	10.00	—

KM# 342 DOLLAR **Composition:** Copper-Nickel **Subject:** Endangered Wildlife **Obverse:** Queen's portrait right **Reverse:** European otters

Date	F	VF	XF	Unc	BU
1996	—	—	—	10.00	—

KM# 343 DOLLAR **Composition:** Copper-Nickel **Subject:** Endangered Wildlife **Obverse:** Queen's portrait right **Reverse:** Jackass penguins

Date	F	VF	XF	Unc	BU
1996	—	—	—	10.00	—

KM# 344 DOLLAR **Composition:** Copper-Nickel **Subject:** Endangered Wildlife **Obverse:** Queen's portrait right **Reverse:** Fallow deer

Date	F	VF	XF	Unc	BU
1996	—	—	—	10.00	—

KM# 345 DOLLAR **Composition:** Copper-Nickel **Subject:** Endangered Wildlife **Obverse:** Queen's portrait right **Reverse:** Heaviside's dolphins

Date	F	VF	XF	Unc	BU
1996	—	—	—	10.00	—

KM# 346 DOLLAR **Composition:** Copper-Nickel **Subject:** Endangered Wildlife **Obverse:** Queen's portrait right **Reverse:** Cougar and cub

Date	F	VF	XF	Unc	BU
1996	—	—	—	10.00	—

KM# 347 DOLLAR **Composition:** Copper-Nickel **Subject:** Endangered Wildlife **Obverse:** Queen's portrait right **Reverse:** Lowland gorilla

Date	F	VF	XF	Unc	BU
1996	—	—	—	10.00	—

KM# 348 DOLLAR **Composition:** Copper-Nickel **Subject:** Endangered Wildlife **Obverse:** Queen's portrait right **Reverse:** Peregrine falcon

Date	F	VF	XF	Unc	BU
1996	—	—	—	10.00	—

KM# 349 DOLLAR **Composition:** Copper-Nickel **Subject:** Endangered Wildlife **Obverse:** Queen's portrait right **Reverse:** Kangaroo

Date	F	VF	XF	Unc	BU
1996	—	—	—	10.00	—

KM# 350 DOLLAR **Composition:** Copper-Nickel **Subject:** Endangered Wildlife **Obverse:** Queen's portrait right **Reverse:** Bee hummingbird

Date	F	VF	XF	Unc	BU
1996	—	—	—	10.00	—

KM# 351 DOLLAR **Composition:** Copper-Nickel **Subject:** Endangered Wildlife **Obverse:** Queen's portrait right **Reverse:** Butterfly and thistle

Date	F	VF	XF	Unc	BU
1996	—	—	—	10.00	—

KM# 352 DOLLAR **Composition:** Copper-Nickel **Subject:** Endangered Wildlife **Obverse:** Queen's portrait right **Reverse:** Ring-tailed lemurs

Date	F	VF	XF	Unc	BU
1996	—	—	—	10.00	—

KM# 353 DOLLAR **Composition:** Copper-Nickel **Subject:** Endangered Wildlife **Obverse:** Queen's portrait right **Reverse:** Szechuan takins

Date	F	VF	XF	Unc	BU
1996	—	—	—	10.00	—

KM# 354 DOLLAR **Composition:** Copper-Nickel **Subject:** Endangered Wildlife **Obverse:** Queen's portrait right **Reverse:** Eagle owl

Date	F	VF	XF	Unc	BU
1996	—	—	—	10.00	—

KM# 355 DOLLAR **Composition:** Copper-Nickel **Subject:** Endangered Wildlife **Obverse:** Queen's portrait right **Reverse:** White-tailed deer

Date	F	VF	XF	Unc	BU
1996	—	—	—	10.00	—

KM# 356 DOLLAR **Composition:** Copper-Nickel **Subject:** Endangered Wildlife **Obverse:** Queen's portrait right **Reverse:** Drill

Date	F	VF	XF	Unc	BU
1996	—	—	—	10.00	—

KM# 327 DOLLAR **Weight:** 31.1035 g. **Composition:** 0.9990 Silver 1.0000 oz. ASW **Obverse:** Queen's portrait **Reverse:** Carnation **Note:** Multicolor.

Date		F	VF	XF	Unc	BU
1996 Proof	—	Value: 45.00				

KM# 308.1 DOLLAR **Weight:** 31.4600 g. **Composition:** 0.9990 Silver 1.0104 oz. ASW **Obverse:** Queen's portrait right **Reverse:** Princess Diana's portrait, dates **Note:** Polished fields with matte portraits.

Date		F	VF	XF	Unc	BU
1997 Proof	—	Value: 32.50				

KM# 308.2 DOLLAR **Weight:** 34.4600 g. **Composition:** 0.9990 Silver 1.0104 oz. ASW **Note:** Matte fields with polished portraits.

Date	F	VF	XF	Unc	BU
1997 Matte Proof	—	—	—	22.50	—

KM# 314 DOLLAR **Weight:** 31.6350 g. **Composition:** 0.9990 Silver 1.0160 oz. ASW **Subject:** Australian Fauna **Obverse:** Queen's portrait right **Reverse:** Multicolored ring-tailed gecko

Date	Mintage	F	VF	XF	Unc	BU
1998 Proof	Est. 4,000	Value: 45.00				

KM# 315 DOLLAR **Weight:** 31.6350 g. **Composition:** 0.9990 Silver 1.0160 oz. ASW **Subject:** Australian Fauna **Obverse:** Queen's portrait right **Reverse:** Multicolored bilby (mouse)

Date	Mintage	F	VF	XF	Unc	BU
1998 Proof	Est. 4,000	Value: 45.00				

KM# 316 DOLLAR **Weight:** 31.6350 g. **Composition:** 0.9990 Silver 1.0160 oz. ASW **Subject:** Australian Fauna **Obverse:** Queen's portrait right **Reverse:** Multicolored platypus

Date	Mintage	F	VF	XF	Unc	BU
1998 Proof	Est. 4,000	Value: 45.00				

KM# 317 DOLLAR **Weight:** 31.6350 g. **Composition:** 0.9990 Silver 1.0160 oz. ASW **Subject:** Australian Fauna **Obverse:** Queen's portrait right **Reverse:** Multicolored ghost bat

Date	Mintage	F	VF	XF	Unc	BU
1998 Proof	Est. 4,000	Value: 45.00				

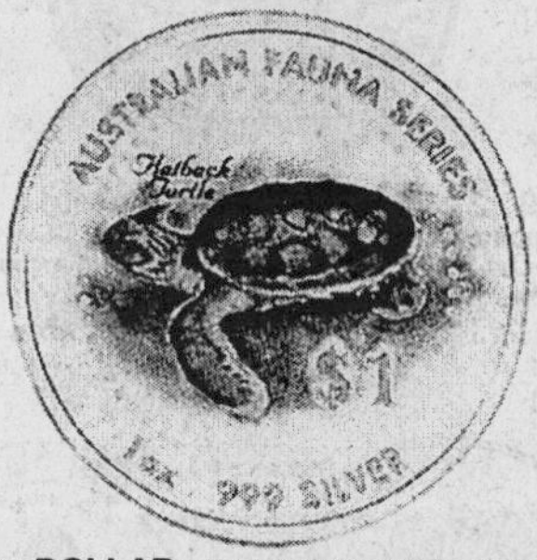

KM# 318 DOLLAR **Weight:** 31.6350 g. **Composition:** 0.9990 Silver 1.0160 oz. ASW **Subject:** Australian Fauna **Obverse:** Queen's portrait right **Reverse:** Multicolored hatback turtle

Date	Mintage	F	VF	XF	Unc	BU
1998 Proof	Est. 4,000	Value: 45.00				

KM# 361 DOLLAR **Weight:** 31.6800 g. **Composition:** 0.9990 Silver 1.0000 oz. ASW **Subject:** Tropical Fish **Obverse:** Queens portrait right **Reverse:** Multicolored Lemonpeel angelfish **Edge:** Reeded

Date		F	VF	XF	Unc	BU
1999 Proof	—	Value: 45.00				

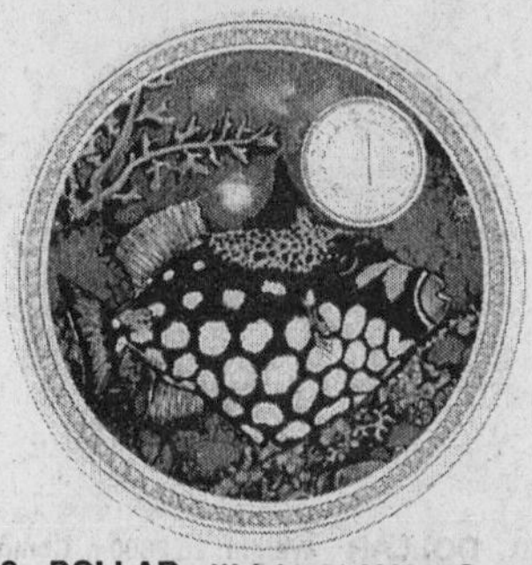

KM# 362 DOLLAR **Weight:** 31.6800 g. **Composition:** 0.9990 Silver 1.0000 oz. ASW **Subject:** Tropical Fish **Obverse:** Queen's portrait right **Reverse:** Multicolored Clown triggerfish **Edge:** Reeded

Date		F	VF	XF	Unc	BU
1999 Proof	—	Value: 45.00				

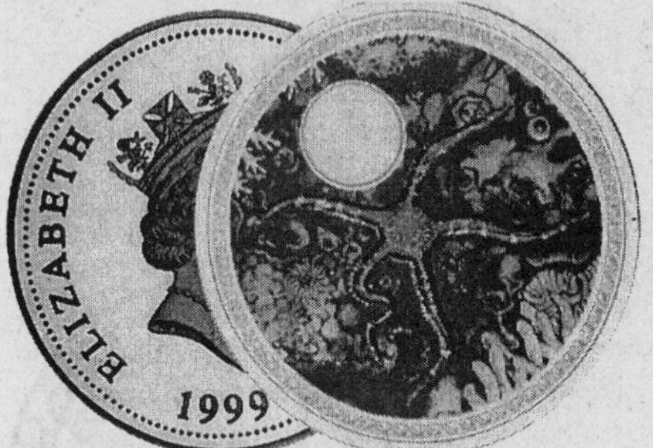

KM# 364 DOLLAR **Center Weight:** 31.6800 g. **Center Composition:** 0.9990 Silver 1.0000 oz. ASW **Subject:** Tropical Fish **Obverse:** Queen's portrait right **Reverse:** Multicolored serpent starfish **Edge:** Reeded

Date		F	VF	XF	Unc	BU
1999 Proof	—	Value: 45.00				

KM# 363 DOLLAR **Weight:** 31.6800 g. **Composition:** 0.9990 Silver 1.0000 oz. ASW **Subject:** Tropical Fish **Obverse:** Queen's portrait right **Reverse:** Multicolored Regal angelfish **Edge:** Reeded

Date		F	VF	XF	Unc	BU
1999 Proof	—	Value: 45.00				

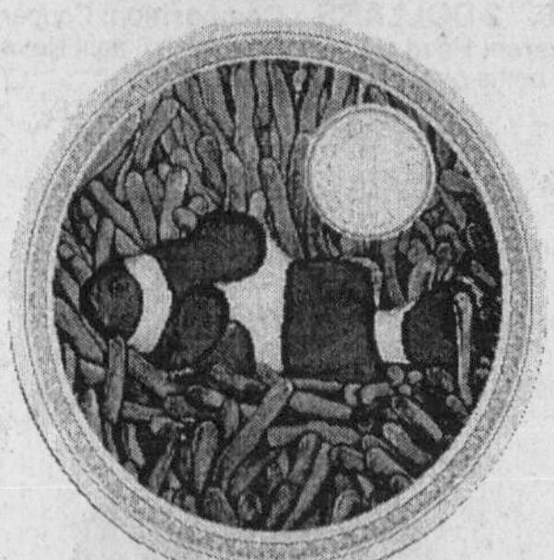

KM# 365 DOLLAR **Weight:** 31.6800 g. **Composition:** 0.9990 Silver 1.0000 oz. ASW **Subject:** Tropical Fish **Obverse:** Queen's portrait right **Reverse:** Multicolored clown anemone fish **Edge:** Reeded

Date		F	VF	XF	Unc	BU
1999 Proof	—	Value: 45.00				

KM# 380 DOLLAR **Weight:** 28.2800 g. **Composition:** 0.9250 Silver 0.841 oz. ASW **Subject:** Queen's Golden Jubilee **Obverse:** Bust of Queen Elizabeth II right **Reverse:** Flags over roof tops **Edge:** Reeded **Size:** 38.6 mm.

Date		F	VF	XF	Unc	BU
2000 Proof	15,000	Value: 50.00				

KM# 8 2 DOLLARS **Weight:** 25.7000 g. **Composition:** 0.9250 Silver .7646 oz. ASW **Subject:** 20th Anniversary of Coronation **Obverse:** Queen's portrait right

Date	Mintage	F	VF	XF	Unc	BU
1973	16,000	—	—	—	8.00	—
1973 Proof	46,000	Value: 8.00				

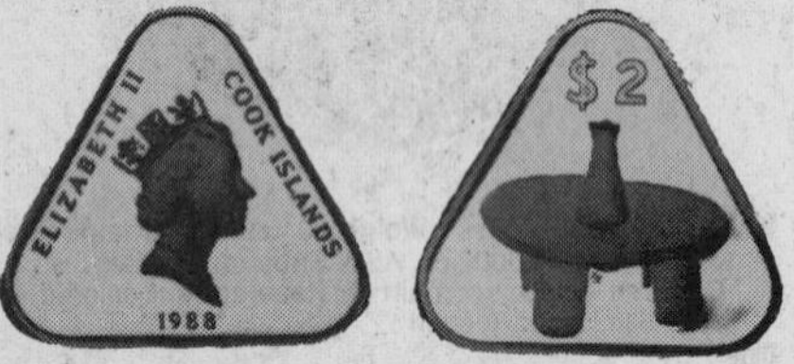

KM# 38 2 DOLLARS **Composition:** Copper-Nickel **Obverse:** Head of Queen Elizabeth II right **Reverse:** Table with bottle on top **Shape:** Triangular

Date	Mintage	F	VF	XF	Unc	BU
1987	—	—	—	2.25	3.75	—
1987 Proof	—	Value: 7.50				
1988	—	—	—	2.25	3.75	—
1988 Proof	—	Value: 7.50				
1992	—	—	—	2.25	3.75	—
1992 Proof	—	Value: 7.50				
1994	20,000	—	—	2.25	3.75	—
1994 Proof	200	Value: 8.50				

KM# 279 2 DOLLARS **Weight:** 10.0000 g. **Composition:** 0.5000 Silver .1607 oz. ASW **Subject:** Yellowstone National Park **Reverse:** Grizzly bears

Date		F	VF	XF	Unc	BU
1996 Proof	—	Value: 13.50				

KM# 280 2 DOLLARS **Weight:** 10.0000 g. **Composition:** 0.5000 Silver .1607 oz. ASW **Subject:** Olympic National Park **Reverse:** Eagle flying in the mountain tops

Date		F	VF	XF	Unc	BU
1996 Proof	—	Value: 13.50				

KM# 328 2 DOLLARS **Weight:** 10.0000 g. **Composition:** 0.5000 Silver .160736 oz. ASW **Subject:** Petrified Forest National Park **Obverse:** Queen's portrait right **Reverse:** Pronghorn

Date		F	VF	XF	Unc	BU
1997 Proof		—	—	—	—	—
1998 Proof	—	Value: 13.50				

KM# 329 2 DOLLARS **Weight:** 10.0000 g. **Composition:** 0.5000 Silver .160736 oz. ASW **Subject:** Crater Lake National Park **Obverse:** Queen's portrait right **Reverse:** White-tailed deer

Date		F	VF	XF	Unc	BU
1997 Proof		—	—	—	—	—
1998 Proof	—	Value: 13.50				

KM# 376 2 DOLLARS **Weight:** 15.8400 g. **Composition:** 0.9990 Silver 14.3400 oz. ASW **Subject:** British Queen Mother **Obverse:** Queen's portrait **Reverse:** Queen Mother and daughters, circa 1936 **Edge:** Reeded **Size:** 28.3 mm.

Date		F	VF	XF	Unc	BU
1997 Proof	—	Value: 25.00				

KM# 371 2 DOLLARS **Weight:** 10.0000 g. **Composition:** 0.5000 Silver .1608 oz. ASW **Subject:** Great Smoky Mountains National Park **Obverse:** Queen's portrait **Reverse:** Red wolf and two cubs **Edge:** Reeded **Size:** 30 mm.

Date		F	VF	XF	Unc	BU
1997 Proof	—	Value: 15.00				

KM# 372 2 DOLLARS **Weight:** 10.0000 g. **Composition:** 0.5000 Silver .1608 oz. ASW **Subject:** Theodore Roosevelt National Park **Obverse:** Queen's portrait **Reverse:** Bison **Edge:** Reeded **Size:** 30 mm.

Date		F	VF	XF	Unc	BU
1997 Proof	—	Value: 15.00				

KM# 373 2 DOLLARS **Weight:** 10.0000 g. **Composition:** 0.5000 Silver .1608 oz. ASW **Subject:** Yosemite National Park **Obverse:** Queen's portrait **Reverse:** Peregrine falcon **Edge:** Reeded **Size:** 30 mm.

Date		F	VF	XF	Unc	BU
1997 Proof	—	Value: 15.00				

KM# 374 2 DOLLARS **Weight:** 10.0000 g. **Composition:** 0.5000 Silver .1608 oz. ASW **Subject:** North Cascades National Park **Obverse:** Queen's portrait **Reverse:** Spotted owl **Edge:** Reeded **Size:** 30 mm.

Date		F	VF	XF	Unc	BU
1998 Proof	—	Value: 15.00				

KM# 321 2 DOLLARS **Weight:** 42.4139 g. **Composition:** 0.9250 Silver 1.3636 oz. ASW **Obverse:** Queen's portrait right **Reverse:** Denomination, Cook Islands attractions and features **Shape:** 1/3 circular segment

Date	Mintage	F	VF	XF	Unc	BU
1998 Proof	Est. 20,000	Value: 65.00				

Note: This coin is part of a tri-national, three coin matching set with Fiji and Western Samoa

KM# 339 2 DOLLARS **Weight:** 31.1035 g. **Composition:** 0.9990 Silver 1.0000 oz. ASW **Obverse:** Queen's portrait right **Reverse:** Multicolored cartoon cat, Garfield, flipping coin **Edge:** Reeded

Date	F	VF	XF	Unc	BU
1999 Proof	—	Value: 45.00			

KM# 340 2 DOLLARS **Weight:** 31.1035 g. **Composition:** 0.9990 Silver 1.0000 oz. ASW **Obverse:** Queen's portrait right **Reverse:** Multicolored cartoon cat, Garfield, tricking Odie **Edge:** Reeded

Date	F	VF	XF	Unc	BU
1999 Proof	—	Value: 45.00			

KM# 9 2-1/2 DOLLARS **Weight:** 27.3500 g. **Composition:** 0.9250 Silver .8133 oz. ASW **Subject:** Captain James Cook's 2nd Pacific Voyage **Obverse:** Queen's portrait right **Reverse:** Sailing ships above world globe

Date	Mintage	F	VF	XF	Unc	BU
1973	6,000	—	—	—	12.50	—
1973 Proof	12,000	Value: 10.00				
1974	2,000	—	—	—	20.00	—
1974 Proof	12,000	Value: 10.00				

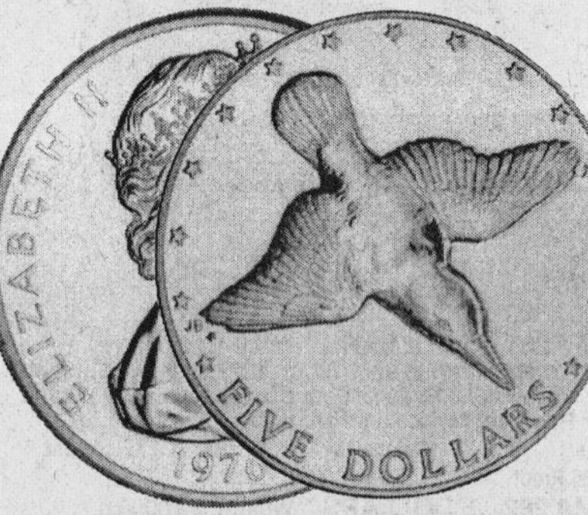

KM# 15 5 DOLLARS **Weight:** 27.3000 g. **Composition:** 0.5000 Silver .4388 oz. ASW **Subject:** Wildlife Conservation **Obverse:** Queen's portrait right **Reverse:** Mangara kingfisher

Date	Mintage	F	VF	XF	Unc	BU
1976FM (M)	251	—	—	—	25.00	—
1976FM (U)	2,192	—	—	—	12.50	—
1976FM (P)	28,000	Value: 10.50				

KM# 17 5 DOLLARS **Weight:** 27.3000 g. **Composition:** 0.5000 Silver .4388 oz. ASW **Obverse:** Queen's portrait right **Reverse:** Atiu swiftlet **Edge Lettering:** Wildlife Conservation

Date	Mintage	F	VF	XF	Unc	BU
1977FM (M)	252	—	—	—	35.00	—
1977FM (U)	4,032	—	—	—	12.50	—
1977FM (P)	11,000	Value: 10.00				

KM# 20 5 DOLLARS **Weight:** 27.3000 g. **Composition:** 0.5000 Silver .4388 oz. ASW **Subject:** Wildlife Conservation **Obverse:** Queen's portrait right **Reverse:** Polynesian warblers by nest in branches

Date	Mintage	F	VF	XF	Unc	BU
1978FM (M)	250	—	—	—	25.00	—
1978FM (U)	3,659	—	—	—	12.50	—
1978FM (P)	11,000	Value: 10.00				

KM# 24 5 DOLLARS **Weight:** 27.3000 g. **Composition:** 0.5000 Silver .4388 oz. ASW **Subject:** Wildlife Conservation **Obverse:** Queen's portrait right **Reverse:** Rarotongan fruit doves on branch

Date	Mintage	F	VF	XF	Unc	BU
1979FM (U)	2,500	—	—	—	16.50	—
1979FM (P)	8,612	Value: 18.50				

KM# 39 5 DOLLARS **Composition:** Aluminum-Bronze **Reverse:** Conch shell **Shape:** 12-sided

Date	Mintage	F	VF	XF	Unc	BU
1987	—	—	—	5.00	10.00	—
1987 Proof	—	Value: 15.00				
1988	—	—	—	5.00	10.00	—
1988 Proof	—	Value: 15.00				
1992	—	—	—	5.00	10.00	—
1992 Proof	—	Value: 15.00				
1994	20,000	—	—	5.00	10.00	—
1994 Proof	200	Value: 16.00				

KM# 39a 5 DOLLARS **Composition:** Copper-Nickel **Shape:** 12-sided **Note:** Mint error, struck on Australian 50 cents planchet.

Date	F	VF	XF	Unc	BU
1988	—	—	—	—	—

KM# 181 5 DOLLARS **Composition:** Copper-Nickel **Subject:** Endangered World Wildlife **Reverse:** Tiger

Date	F	VF	XF	Unc	BU
1990	—	—	—	12.00	—

KM# 149 5 DOLLARS **Weight:** 9.9500 g. **Composition:** 0.5000 Silver .1600 oz. ASW **Subject:** World Cup Soccer **Reverse:** Three soccer players

Date	Mintage	F	VF	XF	Unc	BU
1991 Proof	150,000	Value: 7.50				

KM# 217 5 DOLLARS **Weight:** 9.8500 g. **Composition:** 0.5000 Silver .1600 oz. ASW **Obverse:** Queen's portrait **Reverse:** Christopher Columbus

Date	F	VF	XF	Unc	BU
1991	—	—	—	12.50	—

KM# 218 5 DOLLARS **Weight:** 9.9500 g. **Composition:** 500.0000 Silver .1600 oz. ASW **Subject:** Endangered Wildlife **Obverse:** Queen's portrait **Reverse:** European Otters

Date	F	VF	XF	Unc	BU
1991	—	—	—	11.50	—

KM# 219 5 DOLLARS **Weight:** 9.9500 g. **Composition:** 0.5000 Silver .1600 oz. ASW **Subject:** Endangered Wildlife **Obverse:** Queen's portrait **Reverse:** Penguins

Date	F	VF	XF	Unc	BU
1991	—	—	—	11.50	—

KM# 220 5 DOLLARS **Weight:** 9.9500 g. **Composition:** 0.5000 Silver .1600 oz. ASW **Subject:** Endangered Wildlife **Obverse:** Queen's portrait **Reverse:** Deer

Date	F	VF	XF	Unc	BU
1991	—	—	—	11.50	—

KM# 221 5 DOLLARS **Weight:** 9.9500 g. **Composition:** 0.5000 Silver .1600 oz. ASW **Subject:** Endangered Wildlife **Obverse:** Queen's portrait **Reverse:** Cape dolphins

Date	F	VF	XF	Unc	BU
1991	—	—	—	11.50	—

KM# 222 5 DOLLARS **Weight:** 9.9500 g. **Composition:** 0.5000 Silver .1600 oz. ASW **Subject:** Endangered Wildlife **Obverse:** Queen's portrait **Reverse:** Cougar

Date	F	VF	XF	Unc	BU
1991	—	—	—	11.50	—

KM# 223 5 DOLLARS **Weight:** 9.9500 g. **Composition:** 0.5000 Silver .1600 oz. ASW **Subject:** Endangered Wildlife **Obverse:** Queen's portrait **Reverse:** Ibex

Date	F	VF	XF	Unc	BU
1991	—	—	—	11.50	—

KM#224 5 DOLLARS **Weight:** 9.9500 g. **Composition:** 0.5000 Silver .1600 oz. ASW **Subject:** Endangered Wildlife **Obverse:** Queen's portrait **Reverse:** Eagle owl

Date	F	VF	XF	Unc	BU
1991	—	—	—	11.50	—

KM#225 5 DOLLARS **Weight:** 9.9500 g. **Composition:** 0.5000 Silver .1600 oz. ASW **Subject:** Endangered Wildlife **Obverse:** Queen's portrait **Reverse:** Peregrine falcon

Date	F	VF	XF	Unc	BU
1991	—	—	—	11.50	—

KM#226 5 DOLLARS **Weight:** 9.9500 g. **Composition:** 0.5000 Silver .1600 oz. ASW **Subject:** Endangered Wildlife **Obverse:** Queen's portrait **Reverse:** African lion

Date	F	VF	XF	Unc	BU
1991	—	—	—	11.50	—

KM#227 5 DOLLARS **Weight:** 9.9500 g. **Composition:** 0.5000 Silver .1600 oz. ASW **Subject:** Endangered Wildlife **Obverse:** Queen's portrait **Reverse:** Bee hummingbird

Date	F	VF	XF	Unc	BU
1991	—	—	—	11.50	—

KM#228 5 DOLLARS **Weight:** 9.9500 g. **Composition:** 0.5000 Silver .1600 oz. ASW **Subject:** Endangered Wildlife **Obverse:** Queen's portrait **Reverse:** Kangaroo

Date	F	VF	XF	Unc	BU
1991	—	—	—	11.50	—

KM#229 5 DOLLARS **Weight:** 9.9500 g. **Composition:** 0.5000 Silver .1600 oz. ASW **Subject:** Endangered Wildlife **Obverse:** Queen's portrait **Reverse:** Persian fallow deer

Date	F	VF	XF	Unc	BU
1991	—	—	—	11.50	—

KM#230 5 DOLLARS **Weight:** 9.9500 g. **Composition:** 0.5000 Silver .1600 oz. ASW **Subject:** Endangered Wildlife **Obverse:** Queen's portrait **Reverse:** Lowland gorilla

Date	F	VF	XF	Unc	BU
1991	—	—	—	11.50	—

KM# 253 5 DOLLARS **Weight:** 10.1300 g. **Composition:** 0.5000 Silver .1628 oz. ASW **Obverse:** Queen's portrait **Reverse:** First man on the moon

Date	F	VF	XF	Unc	BU
1991 Proof	—	Value: 10.00			

KM# 137 5 DOLLARS **Weight:** 10.0000 g. **Composition:** 0.5000 Silver .1607 oz. ASW **Subject:** Environmental Protection **Obverse:** Queen's portrait **Reverse:** Child watching butterfly

Date	Mintage	F	VF	XF	Unc	BU
1992 Proof	Est. 25,000	Value: 8.00				

KM# 150 5 DOLLARS **Weight:** 10.0000 g. **Composition:** 0.5000 Silver .1607 oz. ASW **Obverse:** Queen's portrait **Reverse:** Johann Sebastian Bach

Date	F	VF	XF	Unc	BU
1992 Proof	—	Value: 10.00			

KM# 160 5 DOLLARS **Weight:** 10.0000 g. **Composition:** 0.5000 Silver .1607 oz. ASW **Obverse:** Queen's portrait **Reverse:** Sailing ship Astrolabe

Date	F	VF	XF	Unc	BU
1992 Proof	—	Value: 10.00			

KM# 231 5 DOLLARS **Weight:** 10.0000 g. **Composition:** 0.5000 Silver .1607 oz. ASW **Subject:** Endangered Wildlife **Obverse:** Queen's portrait **Reverse:** Drill

Date	F	VF	XF	Unc	BU
1992	—	—	—	13.50	—

KM# 232 5 DOLLARS **Weight:** 10.0000 g. **Composition:** 0.5000 Silver .1607 oz. ASW **Subject:** Endangered Wildlife **Obverse:** Queen's portrait **Reverse:** Butterfly

Date	F	VF	XF	Unc	BU
1992	—	—	—	13.50	—

KM# 233 5 DOLLARS **Weight:** 10.0000 g. **Composition:** 0.5000 Silver .1607 oz. ASW **Subject:** Endangered Wildlife **Obverse:** Queen's portrait **Reverse:** Takin

Date	F	VF	XF	Unc	BU
1992	—	—	—	13.50	—

KM#252 5 DOLLARS **Weight:** 9.9500 g. **Composition:** 0.5000 Silver .1600 oz. ASW **Subject:** 1992 Olympics **Obverse:** Queen's portrait **Reverse:** High jump

Date	Mintage	F	VF	XF	Unc	BU
1992 Proof	150,000	Value: 12.50				

KM# 255 5 DOLLARS **Weight:** 31.4700 g. **Composition:** 0.9250 Silver .9359 oz. ASW **Subject:** Queen Elizabeth II's 25th Wedding Anniversary **Obverse:** Queen's portrait **Reverse:** St. Paul's Cathedral

Date	Mintage	F	VF	XF	Unc	BU
1995 Proof	Est. 30,000	Value: 21.50				

KM# 234 5 DOLLARS **Weight:** 10.0000 g. **Composition:** 0.5000 Silver .1607 oz. ASW **Subject:** Endangered Wildlife **Obverse:** Queen's portrait **Reverse:** African elephant

Date	Mintage	F	VF	XF	Unc	BU
1995 Proof	Est. 25,000	Value: 15.00				

KM# 269 5 DOLLARS **Weight:** 31.4700 g. **Composition:** 0.9250 Silver .9359 oz. ASW **Subject:** Endangered Wildlife **Obverse:** Queen's portrait **Reverse:** Cheetah

Date	Mintage	F	VF	XF	Unc	BU
1996 Proof	Est. 15,000	Value: 25.00				

KM# 281 5 DOLLARS **Weight:** 28.0000 g. **Composition:** 0.9250 Silver .8327 oz. ASW **Subject:** Yellowstone National Park **Obverse:** Queen's portrait **Reverse:** Multicolored grizzly bear and cub

Date	Mintage	F	VF	XF	Unc	BU
1996 Proof	25,000	Value: 25.00				

KM# 282 5 DOLLARS **Weight:** 28.0000 g. **Composition:** 0.9250 Silver .8327 oz. ASW **Subject:** Olympic National Park **Obverse:** Queen's portrait **Reverse:** Multicolored bald eagle in flight

Date	Mintage	F	VF	XF	Unc	BU
1996 Proof	25,000	Value: 25.00				

KM# 301 5 DOLLARS **Weight:** 28.0000 g. **Composition:** 0.9250 Silver .8327 oz. ASW **Subject:** Endangered Wildlife Series **Obverse:** Queen's portrait **Reverse:** Crocodile on river bank

Date	F	VF	XF	Unc	BU
1996 Proof	—	Value: 40.00			

KM# 302 5 DOLLARS **Weight:** 28.0000 g. **Composition:** 0.9250 Silver .8327 oz. ASW **Subject:** Endangered Wildlife Series **Obverse:** Queen's portrait **Reverse:** Lion, lioness and cubs

Date	F	VF	XF	Unc	BU
1996 Proof	—	Value: 25.00			

KM# 303 5 DOLLARS **Weight:** 28.0000 g. **Composition:** 0.9250 Silver .8327 oz. ASW **Subject:** Endangered Wildlife Series **Obverse:** Queen's portrait **Reverse:** Female gorilla and offspring

Date	F	VF	XF	Unc	BU
1996 Proof	—	Value: 25.00			

KM# 304 5 DOLLARS **Weight:** 28.0000 g. **Composition:** 0.9250 Silver .8327 oz. ASW **Subject:** Endangered Wildlife Series **Obverse:** Queen's portrait **Reverse:** Penguin family

Date	F	VF	XF	Unc	BU
1996 Proof	—	Value: 40.00			

KM# 368 5 DOLLARS **Weight:** 28.0000 g. **Composition:** 0.9250 Silver .8327 oz. ASW **Subject:** Great Smoky Mountains National Park **Obverse:** Queen's head right **Reverse:** Red wolf and two cubs **Edge:** Reeded

Date	F	VF	XF	Unc	BU
1996 Proof	—	Value: 25.00			

KM# 366 5 DOLLARS **Weight:** 31.4700 g. **Composition:** 0.9250 Silver .9353 oz. ASW **Subject:** Protect Our World **Obverse:** Queen's head right **Reverse:** Charles Darwin bust at right, map and tortoise **Edge:** Reeded

Date	F	VF	XF	Unc	BU
1996 Proof	—	Value: 45.00			

KM# 377 5 DOLLARS **Weight:** 31.5000 g. **Composition:** 0.9250 Silver 0.9368 oz. ASW **Subject:** Endangered Wildlife **Obverse:** Bust of Queen Elizabeth II right **Reverse:** Two adult polar bears with cub **Edge:** Reeded **Size:** 38.6 mm.

Date	F	VF	XF	Unc	BU
1996 Proof	—	Value: 45.00			

KM# 379 5 DOLLARS **Weight:** 31.4700 g. **Composition:** 0.9250 Silver 0.9359 oz. ASW **Subject:** Queen Mother **Obverse:** Bust of Queen Elizabeth II right **Reverse:** Queen Mother and daughters, circa 1936 **Edge:** Reeded **Size:** 38.6 mm.

Date	F	VF	XF	Unc	BU
1996 Proof	—	Value: 35.00			

KM# 370 5 DOLLARS **Weight:** 31.5000 g. **Composition:** 0.9250 Silver .9368 oz. ASW **Subject:** Olympics **Obverse:** Queen's portrait **Reverse:** Pole vaulter and runner **Edge:** Reeded **Size:** 38.6 mm.

Date	F	VF	XF	Unc	BU
1996 Proof	—	Value: 35.00			

KM# 335 5 DOLLARS **Weight:** 15.5200 g. **Composition:** 0.9990 Silver .4985 oz. ASW **Subject:** Japanese Samurai **Obverse:** Queen's head right **Reverse:** 3/4 bust Yoshinobu Tokugawa facing **Edge:** Reeded

Date	F	VF	XF	Unc	BU
1997FM Proof	—	Value: 25.00			

KM# 312 5 DOLLARS **Weight:** 1.2441 g. **Composition:** 0.9999 Gold .400 oz. AGW **Obverse:** Queen's portrait **Reverse:** Portrait of Princess Diana, dates

Date	F	VF	XF	Unc	BU
1997 Proof	—	Value: 40.00			

KM# 367 5 DOLLARS **Weight:** 31.4500 g. **Composition:** 0.9250 Silver .9353 oz. ASW **Subject:** Millennium - 2000 A.D. **Obverse:** Queen's head right **Reverse:** Christian symbol above Tangaroa, Pagan God of Creation **Edge:** Plain **Shape:** 7-sided

Date	F	VF	XF	Unc	BU
1999 Proof	—	Value: 30.00			

KM# 378 5 DOLLARS **Weight:** 31.5000 g. **Composition:** 0.9250 Silver 0.9368 oz. ASW **Subject:** Takitumu Conservation Area **Obverse:** Bust of Queen Elizabeth II right **Reverse:** Rarotongan Monarch Flycatcher **Edge:** Reeded **Size:** 38.6 mm.

Date	F	VF	XF	Unc	BU
1999 Proof	—	Value: 45.00			

KM# 375 5 DOLLARS **Weight:** 28.1000 g. **Composition:** 0.9250 Silver .8357 oz. ASW **Ring Composition:** Gold Plated **Subject:** Queen Mother's 100th Birthday **Obverse:** Queen's portrait **Reverse:** Queen Mother and daughters, circa 1980 **Edge:** Reeded **Size:** 38.6 mm.

Date	Mintage	F	VF	XF	Unc	BU
2000 Proof	1,000	Value: 60.00				

KM# 10 7-1/2 DOLLARS **Weight:** 33.8000 g. **Composition:** 0.9250 Silver 1.0052 oz. ASW **Subject:** Capt. James Cook's 2nd Pacific Voyage **Obverse:** Queen's portrait right

Date	Mintage	F	VF	XF	Unc	BU
1973	6,000	—	—	—	18.50	—
1973 Proof	12,000	Value: 13.50				
1974	2,000	—	—	—	25.00	—
1974 Proof	13,000	Value: 13.50				

KM# 21 10 DOLLARS **Weight:** 27.9000 g. **Composition:** 0.9250 Silver .8297 oz. ASW **Subject:** 25th Anniversary of Coronation **Obverse:** Queen's portrait right

Date	Mintage	F	VF	XF	Unc	BU
1978FM (U)	5,350	—	—	—	17.50	—
1978FM Proof	11,000	Value: 13.50				

KM# 72 10 DOLLARS **Weight:** 10.0000 g. **Composition:** 0.9250 Silver .2974 oz. ASW **Subject:** Endangered World Wildlife **Obverse:** Queen's portrait right **Reverse:** Elephant's head left

Date	Mintage	F	VF	XF	Unc	BU
1990 Proof	25,000	Value: 15.00				

KM# 73 10 DOLLARS **Weight:** 10.0000 g. **Composition:** 0.9250 Silver .2974 oz. ASW **Subject:** Endangered World Wildlife **Obverse:** Queen's portrait right **Reverse:** Tiger

Date	Mintage	F	VF	XF	Unc	BU
1990 Proof	Est. 25,000	Value: 15.00				

KM# 79 10 DOLLARS **Weight:** 10.0000 g. **Composition:** 0.9250 Silver .2974 oz. ASW **Subject:** Olympics **Obverse:** Queen's portrait right **Reverse:** Runner

Date	Mintage	F	VF	XF	Unc	BU
1990 Proof	150,000	Value: 6.50				

KM# 80 10 DOLLARS **Weight:** 10.0000 g. **Composition:** 0.9250 Silver .2974 oz. ASW **Subject:** Endangered World Wildlife **Obverse:** Queen's portrait right **Reverse:** African elephants

Date	Mintage	F	VF	XF	Unc	BU
1990 Proof	Est. 25,000	Value: 15.00				

KM# 81 10 DOLLARS **Weight:** 28.0000 g. **Composition:** 0.9250 Silver .8327 oz. ASW **Subject:** Save the Children **Obverse:** Queen's portrait right **Reverse:** Grass-skirted dancers

Date	Mintage	F	VF	XF	Unc	BU
1990 Proof	20,000	Value: 22.50				

KM# 90 10 DOLLARS **Weight:** 10.0000 g. **Composition:** 0.9250 Silver .2974 oz. ASW **Subject:** 500 Years of America **Obverse:** Queen's portrait right

Date	Mintage	F	VF	XF	Unc	BU
1990 Proof	Est. 150,000	Value: 7.50				

KM# 91 10 DOLLARS **Weight:** 10.0000 g. **Composition:** 0.9250 Silver .2974 oz. ASW **Subject:** 1991 Winter Olympics **Obverse:** Queen's portrait right **Reverse:** Cross-country skier

Date	Mintage	F	VF	XF	Unc	BU
1990 Proof	150,000	Value: 15.00				

KM# 121 10 DOLLARS **Weight:** 10.0000 g. **Composition:** 0.9250 Silver .2974 oz. ASW **Subject:** 500 Years of America **Obverse:** Queen's portrait right **Reverse:** Columbus and ship

Date	Mintage	F	VF	XF	Unc	BU
1990 Proof	Est. 150,000	Value: 7.50				

KM# 136 10 DOLLARS **Weight:** 31.4700 g. **Composition:** 0.9250 Silver .9359 oz. ASW **Obverse:** Queen's portrait right **Reverse:** Bust of Nicolaus Copernicus with planet earth revolving around radiant sun in background

Date	F	VF	XF	Unc	BU
1992 Proof	—	Value: 22.50			

KM# 254 10 DOLLARS **Weight:** 31.4700 g. **Composition:** 0.9250 Silver .9359 oz. ASW **Subject:** Soccer **Obverse:** Queen's portrait right **Reverse:** Goalie catching ball

Date	Mintage	F	VF	XF	Unc	BU
1992 Proof	Est. 20,000	Value: 25.00				

KM# 358 10 DOLLARS **Weight:** 14.8000 g. **Composition:** 0.9250 Silver .4401 oz. ASW **Subject:** Captain Cook **Obverse:** Queen's portrait right **Reverse:** Captain Cook wading ashore **Edge:** Reeded

Date	F	VF	XF	Unc	BU
1994FM Proof	—	Value: 17.50			

KM# 283 10 DOLLARS **Weight:** 28.0000 g. **Composition:** 0.9250 Silver .8327 oz. ASW **Subject:** Olympic National Park **Obverse:** Queen's portrait right **Reverse:** Multicolored Bald eagle in flight over mountain tops

Date	Mintage	F	VF	XF	Unc	BU
1996 Proof	10,000	Value: 30.00				

KM# 284 10 DOLLARS **Weight:** 28.0000 g. **Composition:** 0.9250 Silver .8327 oz. ASW **Subject:** Yellowstone National Park **Obverse:** Queen's portrait right **Reverse:** Multicolored Grizzly bear and cub

Date	Mintage	F	VF	XF	Unc	BU
1996 Proof	10,000	Value: 30.00				

KM# 359 10 DOLLARS **Weight:** 28.0000 g. **Composition:** 0.9250 Silver .8327 oz. ASW **Subject:** Theodore Roosevelt National Park **Obverse:** Queen's portrait right **Reverse:** Multicolored bison **Edge:** Reeded

Date	F	VF	XF	Unc	BU
1996 Proof	—	Value: 32.50			
1997 Proof	—	Value: 30.00			

KM# 285 10 DOLLARS **Weight:** 1.2441 g. **Composition:** 0.9990 Gold .0399 oz. AGW **Subject:** Olympic National Park

Date	F	VF	XF	Unc	BU
1996 Proof	—	Value: 42.50			

KM# 286 10 DOLLARS **Weight:** 1.2441 g. **Composition:** 0.9990 Gold .0399 oz. AGW **Subject:** Yellowstone National Park

Date	F	VF	XF	Unc	BU
1996 Proof	—	Value: 42.50			

KM# 330 10 DOLLARS **Weight:** 28.0000 g. **Composition:** 0.9250 Silver .8327 oz. ASW **Subject:** Great Smoky Mountains National Park **Obverse:** Queen's portrait right **Reverse:** Multicolored red wolf with two cubs

Date	F	VF	XF	Unc	BU
1997 Proof	—	Value: 35.00			

KM# 331 10 DOLLARS **Weight:** 28.0000 g. **Composition:** 0.9250 Silver .8327 oz. ASW **Subject:** Yosemite National Park **Obverse:** Queen's portrait right **Reverse:** Multicolored Peregrine falcon

Date	F	VF	XF	Unc	BU
1997 Proof	—	Value: 35.00			

KM# 360 10 DOLLARS **Weight:** 28.0000 g. **Composition:** 0.9250 Silver .8327 oz. ASW **Subject:** Glacier Bay National Park **Obverse:** Queen's portrait right **Reverse:** Multicolored Humpback whale breaking the water

Date	F	VF	XF	Unc	BU
1997 Proof	—	Value: 32.50			

KM# 332 10 DOLLARS **Weight:** 28.0000 g. **Composition:** 0.9250 Silver .8327 oz. ASW **Subject:** Grand Teton National park **Obverse:** Queen's portrait right **Reverse:** Multicolored Whooping crane

Date	F	VF	XF	Unc	BU
1998 Proof	—	Value: 35.00			

KM# 333 10 DOLLARS **Weight:** 28.0000 g. **Composition:** 0.9250 Silver .8327 oz. ASW **Subject:** Grand Canyon National Park **Obverse:** Queen's portrait right **Reverse:** Multicolored California condor in flight over canyon

Date	F	VF	XF	Unc	BU
1998 Proof	—	Value: 35.00			

KM# 28 20 DOLLARS **Weight:** 28.2800 g. **Composition:** 0.9250 Silver .8411 oz. ASW **Subject:** International Year of the Scout **Obverse:** Queen's portrait right

Date	Mintage	F	VF	XF	Unc	BU
1983	10,000	—	—	—	45.00	—
1983 Proof	10,000	Value: 50.00				

KM# 151 20 DOLLARS **Weight:** 31.4700 g. **Composition:** 0.9250 Silver .9359 oz. ASW **Obverse:** Queen's portrait right **Reverse:** Friedrich von Schiller

Date	F	VF	XF	Unc	BU
1993 Proof	—	Value: 35.00			

KM# 152 20 DOLLARS **Weight:** 31.4700 g. **Composition:** 0.9250 Silver .9359 oz. ASW **Obverse:** Queen's portrait right **Reverse:** Bust of Charles Darwin facing left

Date	Mintage	F	VF	XF	Unc	BU
1993 Proof	10,000	Value: 35.00				

KM# 161 20 DOLLARS **Weight:** 31.4700 g. **Composition:** 0.9250 Silver .9359 oz. ASW **Subject:** 1996 Olympics **Obverse:** Queen's portrait right **Reverse:** Pole vaulter and sprinter

Date	Mintage	F	VF	XF	Unc	BU
1993 Proof	50,000	Value: 22.50				

KM# 235 20 DOLLARS **Weight:** 31.4700 g. **Composition:** 0.9250 Silver .9359 oz. ASW **Obverse:** Queen's portrait right **Reverse:** Catamaran

Date	Mintage	F	VF	XF	Unc	BU
1995 Proof	Est. 15,000	Value: 30.00				

KM# 236 20 DOLLARS **Weight:** 1.2441 g. **Composition:** 0.9990 Gold .400 oz. AGW **Subject:** 500 Years of America **Obverse:** Queen's portrait right **Reverse:** Columbus claims the New World

Date	F	VF	XF	Unc	BU
1995	—	—	—	40.00	—

KM# 237 20 DOLLARS **Weight:** 1.2441 g. **Composition:** 0.9990 Gilt Silver .400 oz. **Subject:** 500 Years of America **Obverse:** Queen's portrait right **Reverse:** Washington crossing the Delaware

Date	F	VF	XF	Unc	BU
1995	—	—	—	40.00	—

KM# 256 20 DOLLARS **Weight:** 31.4700 g. **Composition:** 0.9250 Silver .9359 oz. ASW **Obverse:** Queen's portrait right **Reverse:** Queen Mother and daughters

Date	Mintage	F	VF	XF	Unc	BU
1995 Proof	Est. 30,000	Value: 30.00				

KM# 257 20 DOLLARS **Weight:** 1.2441 g. **Composition:** 0.9999 Gold .0400 oz. AGW **Subject:** 500 Years of America **Obverse:** Queen's portrait right **Reverse:** Statue of Liberty

Date	F	VF	XF	Unc	BU
1995	—	—	—	40.00	—

KM# 258 20 DOLLARS **Weight:** 1.2441 g. **Composition:** 0.9999 Gold .0400 oz. AGW **Subject:** 500 Years of America **Obverse:** Queen's portrait right **Reverse:** Capt. James Cook

Date	Mintage	F	VF	XF	Unc	BU
1995 Proof	Est. 25,000	Value: 40.00				

KM# 270 20 DOLLARS **Weight:** 1.2441 g. **Composition:** 0.9999 Gold .0400 oz. AGW **Subject:** 500 Years of America **Obverse:** Queen's portrait right **Reverse:** Astronaut on moon

Date	Mintage	F	VF	XF	Unc	BU
1995 Proof	Est. 25,000	Value: 40.00				

KM# 287 20 DOLLARS **Weight:** 155.5175 g. **Composition:** 0.9990 Silver 4.9950 oz. ASW **Subject:** Olympic National Park **Obverse:** Queen's portrait right **Reverse:** Bald eagle

Date	Mintage	F	VF	XF	Unc	BU
1996 Proof	1,000	Value: 85.00				

KM# 288 20 DOLLARS **Weight:** 155.5175 g. **Composition:** 0.9990 Silver 4.9950 oz. ASW **Subject:** Yellowstone National Park **Obverse:** Queen's portrait right **Reverse:** Grizzly bear

Date	Mintage	F	VF	XF	Unc	BU
1996 Proof	1,000	Value: 85.00				

KM# 298 20 DOLLARS **Weight:** 3.0000 g. **Composition:** 0.9999 Gold .0964 oz. AGW **Subject:** Year of the Mouse **Obverse:** Queen's portrait right **Reverse:** Multicolored Mickey Mouse portrait

Date	F	VF	XF	Unc	BU
1996 Proof	—	Value: 70.00			

KM# 334 20 DOLLARS **Weight:** 32.0200 g. **Composition:** 0.9250 Silver .9517 oz. ASW **Subject:** 12th Century **Obverse:** Queen's portrait right **Reverse:** Genghis Khan on horse left, soldier on camel at right

Date	F	VF	XF	Unc	BU
1997 Proof	—	Value: 20.00			

KM# 336 20 DOLLARS **Weight:** 31.8800 g. **Composition:** 0.9250 Silver .9481 oz. ASW **Subject:** 18th Century **Obverse:** Queen's portrait right **Reverse:** Signing of the Declaration of Independence **Edge:** Reeded

Date	F	VF	XF	Unc	BU
1997FM Proof	—	Value: 20.00			

KM# 337 20 DOLLARS **Weight:** 31.8800 g. **Composition:** 0.9250 Silver .9481 oz. ASW **Subject:** 19th Century **Obverse:** Queen's portrait right **Reverse:** Waving driver with two passengers in horseless carriage, bicycle at right in back **Edge:** Reeded

Date	F	VF	XF	Unc	BU
1997FM Proof	—	Value: 20.00			

KM# 18 25 DOLLARS **Weight:** 48.8500 g. **Composition:** 0.9250 Silver 1.4527 oz. ASW **Subject:** Queen's Silver Jubilee **Obverse:** Queen's portrait right **Reverse:** Crowned EIIR monogram between flowers

Date	Mintage	F	VF	XF	Unc	BU
1977FM (M)	100	—	—	—	75.00	—
1977FM (U)	4,068	—	—	—	27.50	—
1977FM Proof	17,000	Value: 16.50				

KM# 42 25 DOLLARS **Weight:** 37.0000 g. **Composition:** 0.9250 Silver 1.1005 oz. ASW **Subject:** 100th Anniversary of British Rule **Obverse:** Queen's portrait right

Date	Mintage	F	VF	XF	Unc	BU
1988 Proof	3,000	Value: 37.50				

KM# 83 25 DOLLARS **Weight:** 1.2144 g. **Composition:** 0.9990 Gold .0400 oz. AGW **Subject:** Endangered Wildlife **Obverse:** Queen's portrait right **Reverse:** Bison

Date	Mintage	F	VF	XF	Unc	BU
1990 Proof	100,000	Value: 42.50				

KM# 84 25 DOLLARS **Weight:** 1.2144 g. **Composition:** 0.9990 Gold .0400 oz. AGW **Subject:** Endangered Wildlife **Obverse:** Queen's portrait right **Reverse:** Longhorn sheep

Date	Mintage	F	VF	XF	Unc	BU
1990 Proof	Est. 100,000	Value: 42.5C				

KM# 85 25 DOLLARS **Weight:** 1.2144 g. **Composition:** 0.9990 Gold .0400 oz. AGW **Subject:** Endangered Wildlife **Obverse:** Queen's portrait right **Reverse:** Tiger

Date	F	VF	XF	Unc	BU
1990 Proof	—	Value: 42.50			

KM# 86 25 DOLLARS **Weight:** 1.2144 g. **Composition:** 0.9990 Gold .0400 oz. AGW **Subject:** Endangered Wildlife **Obverse:** Queen's portrait right **Reverse:** Eagle

Date	Mintage	F	VF	XF	Unc	BU
1990 Proof	Est. 100,000	Value: 42.50				

KM# 87 25 DOLLARS **Weight:** 1.2144 g. **Composition:** 0.9990 Gold .0400 oz. AGW **Subject:** Endangered Wildlife **Obverse:** Queen's portrait right **Reverse:** Elephant

Date	Mintage	F	VF	XF	Unc	BU
1990 Proof	Est. 100,000	Value: 42.50				

KM# 88 25 DOLLARS **Weight:** 1.2144 g. **Composition:** 0.9990 Gold .0400 oz. AGW **Subject:** Endangered Wildlife **Obverse:** Queen's portrait right **Reverse:** Lynx

Date	Mintage	F	VF	XF	Unc	BU
1990 Proof	Est. 100,000	Value: 42.50				

KM# 239 25 DOLLARS **Weight:** 1.2144 g. **Composition:** 0.9990 Gold .0400 oz. AGW **Subject:** Endangered Wildlife **Obverse:** Queen's portrait right **Reverse:** Bee hummingbird

Date	Mintage	F	VF	XF	Unc	BU
1990 Proof	Est. 100,000	Value: 42.50				

KM# 240 25 DOLLARS **Weight:** 1.2144 g. **Composition:** 0.9990 Gold .0400 oz. AGW **Subject:** Endangered Wildlife **Obverse:** Queen's portrait right **Reverse:** Koala bear

Date	Mintage	F	VF	XF	Unc	BU
1991 Proof	Est. 100,000	Value: 42.50				

KM# 241 25 DOLLARS **Weight:** 1.2144 g. **Composition:** 0.9990 Gold .0400 oz. AGW **Subject:** Endangered Wildlife **Obverse:** Queen's portrait right **Reverse:** Panda bear

Date	Mintage	F	VF	XF	Unc	BU
1991 Proof	Est. 100,000	Value: 42.50				

KM# 138 25 DOLLARS **Weight:** 1.2144 g. **Composition:** 0.9990 Gold .0400 oz. AGW **Subject:** Endangered Wildlife **Obverse:** Queen's portrait right **Reverse:** Przewalski's horse galloping right

Date	F	VF	XF	Unc	BU
1992 Proof-like	—	—	—	—	—

KM# 242 25 DOLLARS **Weight:** 1.2144 g. **Composition:** 0.9990 Gold .0400 oz. AGW **Subject:** Endangered Wildlife **Obverse:** Queen's portrait right **Reverse:** African lion

Date	Mintage	F	VF	XF	Unc	BU
1992 Proof	Est. 100,000	Value: 42.50				

KM# 243 25 DOLLARS **Weight:** 1.2144 g. **Composition:** 0.9990 Gold .0400 oz. AGW **Subject:** Endangered Wildlife **Obverse:** Queen's portrait right **Reverse:** Butterfly

Date	Mintage	F	VF	XF	Unc	BU
1992 Proof	Est. 100,000	Value: 42.50				

KM# 238 25 DOLLARS **Weight:** 6.2200 g. **Composition:** 0.5830 Gold .1166 oz. AGW **Subject:** 1996 Olympics **Obverse:** Queen's portrait right **Reverse:** Ancient archer

Date	Mintage	F	VF	XF	Unc	BU
1995 Proof	Est. 5,000	Value: 65.00				

KM# 271 25 DOLLARS **Weight:** 155.5175 g. **Composition:** 0.9990 Silver 5.000 oz. ASW **Subject:** Endangered Wildlife **Obverse:** Queen's portrait right **Reverse:** Koala bear and baby

Date	Mintage	F	VF	XF	Unc	BU
1996 Proof	Est. 10,000	Value: 85.00				

KM# 272 25 DOLLARS **Weight:** 155.5175 g. **Composition:** 0.9990 Silver 5.000 oz. ASW **Subject:** Endangered Wildlife **Obverse:** Queen's portrait right **Reverse:** Family of chimpanzees

Date	Mintage	F	VF	XF	Unc	BU
1996 Proof	Est. 10,000	Value: 85.00				

KM# 273 25 DOLLARS **Weight:** 155.5175 g. **Composition:** 0.9990 Silver 5.000 oz. ASW **Subject:** Endangered Wildlife **Obverse:** Queen's portrait right **Reverse:** Family of elephants

Date	Mintage	F	VF	XF	Unc	BU
1996 Proof	Est. 10,000	Value: 85.00				

KM# 274 25 DOLLARS **Weight:** 155.5175 g. **Composition:** 0.9990 Silver 5.000 oz. ASW **Subject:** Endangered Wildlife **Obverse:** Queen's portrait right **Reverse:** Family of whooping cranes

Date	Mintage	F	VF	XF	Unc	BU
1996 Proof	Est. 10,000	Value: 85.00				

KM# 289 25 DOLLARS **Weight:** 155.5175 g. **Composition:** 0.9990 Silver 5.000 oz. ASW **Subject:** Olympic National Park **Obverse:** Queen's portrait right **Reverse:** Multicolored bald eagle in flight

Date	Mintage	F	VF	XF	Unc	BU
1996 Proof	1,000	Value: 100				

KM# 290 25 DOLLARS **Weight:** 155.5175 g. **Composition:** 0.9990 Silver 5.000 oz. ASW **Subject:** Yellowstone National Park **Obverse:** Queen's portrait right **Reverse:** Multicolored grizzly bear and cub

Date	Mintage	F	VF	XF	Unc	BU
1996 Proof	1,000	Value: 100				

KM# 291 25 DOLLARS **Weight:** 3.1103 g. **Composition:** 0.9990 Gold .1000 oz. AGW **Subject:** Olympic National Park **Obverse:** Queen's portrait right **Reverse:** Bald eagle

Date		F	VF	XF	Unc	BU
1996 Proof	—	Value: 85.00				

KM# 292 25 DOLLARS **Weight:** 3.1103 g. **Composition:** 0.9990 Gold .1000 oz. AGW **Subject:** Yellowstone National Park **Obverse:** Queen's portrait right **Reverse:** Grizzly bear

Date		F	VF	XF	Unc	BU
1996 Proof	—	Value: 85.00				

KM# 309 25 DOLLARS **Weight:** 10000.0996 g. **Composition:** 0.9990 Silver 32.1218 oz. ASW **Obverse:** Queen's portrait right **Reverse:** Princess Diana's portrait, dates

Date		F	VF	XF	Unc	BU
1997 Matte Proof	—	Value: 400				

KM# 11 50 DOLLARS **Weight:** 97.2000 g. **Composition:** 0.9250 Silver 2.8907 oz. ASW **Subject:** Winston Churchill Centenary **Obverse:** Queen's portrait right

Date	Mintage	F	VF	XF	Unc	BU
1974	1,202	—	—	—	30.00	35.00
1974 Proof	2,502	Value: 35.00				

KM# 11a 50 DOLLARS **Weight:** 97.2000 g. **Composition:** 0.9250 Silver Gilt 2.8907 oz. ASW **Subject:** Winston Churchill Centenary **Obverse:** Queen's portrait right

Date	Mintage	F	VF	XF	Unc	BU
1974 Proof	2,002	Value: 47.50				

KM# 203 50 DOLLARS Weight: 3.9450 g. **Composition:** 0.5000 Gold 0.634 oz. AGW **Obverse:** Queen's portrait right

Date		F	VF	XF	Unc	BU
1980 Proof	—	Value: 90.00				

KM# 27 50 DOLLARS Weight: 3.9450 g. **Composition:** 0.5000 Gold 0.634 oz. AGW **Subject:** Wedding of Prince Charles and Lady Diana **Obverse:** Queen's portrait right

Date	Mintage	F	VF	XF	Unc	BU
1981	220	—	—	—	75.00	—
1981 Proof	1,309	Value: 90.00				

KM# 40 50 DOLLARS Weight: 28.2800 g. **Composition:** 0.9250 Silver .8411 oz. ASW **Subject:** 1988 Olympics **Obverse:** Queen's portrait right **Reverse:** Torch bearer

Date	Mintage	F	VF	XF	Unc	BU
1987PM Proof	20,000	Value: 27.50				

KM# 61 50 DOLLARS Weight: 20.9400 g. **Composition:** 0.9250 Silver .6228 oz. ASW **Subject:** Great Explorers **Obverse:** Queen's portrait right **Reverse:** Stanley and Livingstone

Date		F	VF	XF	Unc	BU
1988FM (P)	—	Value: 25.00				

KM# 62 50 DOLLARS Weight: 20.9400 g. **Composition:** 0.9250 Silver .6228 oz. ASW **Subject:** Great Explorers **Obverse:** Queen's portrait right **Reverse:** Capt. James Cook

Date		F	VF	XF	Unc	BU
1988FM (P)	—	Value: 27.50				

KM# 63 50 DOLLARS Weight: 20.9400 g. **Composition:** 0.9250 Silver .6228 oz. ASW **Subject:** Great Explorers **Obverse:** Queen's portrait right **Reverse:** Vasco Nunez de Balboa

Date		F	VF	XF	Unc	BU
1988FM (P)	—	Value: 22.50				

KM# 64 50 DOLLARS Weight: 20.9400 g. **Composition:** 0.9250 Silver .6228 oz. ASW **Subject:** Great Explorers **Obverse:** Queen's portrait right **Reverse:** Ferdinand Magellan

Date		F	VF	XF	Unc	BU
1988FM (P)	—	Value: 20.00				

KM# 65 50 DOLLARS Weight: 20.9400 g. **Composition:** 0.9250 Silver .6228 oz. ASW **Subject:** Great Explorers **Obverse:** Queen's portrait right **Reverse:** Marco Polo

Date		F	VF	XF	Unc	BU
1988FM (P)	—	Value: 20.00				

KM# 66 50 DOLLARS Weight: 20.9400 g. **Composition:** 0.9250 Silver .6228 oz. ASW **Subject:** Great Explorers **Obverse:** Queen's portrait right **Reverse:** Vasco da Gama

Date		F	VF	XF	Unc	BU
1988FM (P)	—	Value: 20.00				

KM# 67 50 DOLLARS Weight: 20.9400 g. **Composition:** 0.9250 Silver .6228 oz. ASW **Subject:** Great Explorers **Obverse:** Queen's portrait right **Reverse:** Christopher Columbus

Date		F	VF	XF	Unc	BU
1988FM (P)	—	Value: 20.00				

KM# 68 50 DOLLARS Weight: 20.9400 g. **Composition:** 0.9250 Silver .6228 oz. ASW **Subject:** Great Explorers **Obverse:** Queen's portrait right **Reverse:** Sir Francis Drake

Date		F	VF	XF	Unc	BU
1988FM (P)	—	Value: 20.00				

KM# 69 50 DOLLARS Weight: 20.9400 g. **Composition:** 0.9250 Silver .6228 oz. ASW **Subject:** Great Explorers **Obverse:** Queen's portrait right **Reverse:** Sieur de la Salle

Date		F	VF	XF	Unc	BU
1988FM (P)	—	Value: 22.50				

KM# 96 50 DOLLARS Weight: 20.9400 g. **Composition:** 0.9250 Silver .6228 oz. ASW **Subject:** Great Explorers **Obverse:** Queen's portrait right **Reverse:** Alexander the Great

Date		F	VF	XF	Unc	BU
1988FM (P)	—	Value: 22.50				

KM# 97 50 DOLLARS Weight: 20.9400 g. **Composition:** 0.9250 Silver .6228 oz. ASW **Subject:** Great

Explorers **Obverse:** Queen's portrait right **Reverse:** Leif Ericson

Date	F	VF	XF	Unc	BU
1988FM (P)	—	Value: 22.50			

KM# 98 50 DOLLARS **Weight:** 20.9400 g. **Composition:** 0.9250 Silver .6228 oz. ASW **Subject:** Great Explorers **Obverse:** Queen's portrait right **Reverse:** Amerigo Vespucci

Date	F	VF	XF	Unc	BU
1988FM (P)	—	Value: 20.00			

KM# 99 50 DOLLARS **Weight:** 20.9400 g. **Composition:** 0.9250 Silver .6228 oz. ASW **Subject:** Great Explorers **Obverse:** Queen's portrait right **Reverse:** Bartolomeu Diaz

Date	F	VF	XF	Unc	BU
1988FM (P)	—	Value: 25.00			

KM# 100 50 DOLLARS **Weight:** 20.9400 g. **Composition:** 0.9250 Silver .6228 oz. ASW **Subject:** Great Explorers **Obverse:** Queen's portrait right **Reverse:** Juan Ponce de Léon

Date	F	VF	XF	Unc	BU
1988FM (P)	—	Value: 27.50			

KM# 101 50 DOLLARS **Weight:** 20.9400 g. **Composition:** 0.9250 Silver .6228 oz. ASW **Subject:** Great Explorers **Obverse:** Queen's portrait right **Reverse:** Hernando Cortés

Date	F	VF	XF	Unc	BU
1988FM (P)	—	Value: 20.00			

KM# 102 50 DOLLARS **Weight:** 20.9400 g. **Composition:** 0.9250 Silver .6228 oz. ASW **Subject:** Great Explorers **Obverse:** Queen's portrait right **Reverse:** Francisco Coronado

Date	F	VF	XF	Unc	BU
1988FM (P)	—	Value: 22.50			

KM# 103 50 DOLLARS **Weight:** 20.9400 g. **Composition:** 0.9250 Silver .6228 oz. ASW **Subject:** Great Explorers **Obverse:** Queen's portrait right **Reverse:** Francisco Pizarro

Date	F	VF	XF	Unc	BU
1988FM (P)	—	Value: 20.00			

KM# 104 50 DOLLARS **Weight:** 20.9400 g. **Composition:** 0.9250 Silver .6228 oz. ASW **Subject:** Great Explorers **Obverse:** Queen's portrait right **Reverse:** Samuel de Champlain

Date	F	VF	XF	Unc	BU
1988FM (P)	—	Value: 20.00			

KM# 105 50 DOLLARS **Weight:** 20.9400 g. **Composition:** 0.9250 Silver .6228 oz. ASW **Subject:** Great Explorers **Obverse:** Queen's portrait right **Reverse:** John Cabot

Date	F	VF	XF	Unc	BU
1988FM (P)	—	Value: 20.00			

KM# 106 50 DOLLARS **Weight:** 20.9400 g. **Composition:** 0.9250 Silver .6228 oz. ASW **Subject:** Great Explorers **Obverse:** Queen's portrait right **Reverse:** Abel Janszoon Tasman

Date	F	VF	XF	Unc	BU
1988FM (P)	—	Value: 22.50			

KM# 107 50 DOLLARS **Weight:** 20.9400 g. **Composition:** 0.9250 Silver .6228 oz. ASW **Subject:** Great Explorers **Obverse:** Queen's portrait right **Reverse:** Lewis and Clark

Date	F	VF	XF	Unc	BU
1988FM (P)	—	Value: 22.50			

KM# 108 50 DOLLARS **Weight:** 20.9400 g. **Composition:** 0.9250 Silver .6228 oz. ASW **Subject:** Great Explorers **Obverse:** Queen's portrait right **Reverse:** Fridtjof Nansen

Date	F	VF	XF	Unc	BU
1988FM (P)	—	Value: 27.50			

KM# 109 50 DOLLARS **Weight:** 20.9400 g. **Composition:** 0.9250 Silver .6228 oz. ASW **Subject:** Great Explorers **Obverse:** Queen's portrait right **Reverse:** Robert Peary

Date	F	VF	XF	Unc	BU
1988FM (P)	—	Value: 20.00			

KM# 110 50 DOLLARS **Weight:** 20.9400 g. **Composition:** 0.9250 Silver .6228 oz. ASW **Subject:** Great Explorers **Obverse:** Queen's portrait right **Reverse:** Roald Amundsen

Date		F	VF	XF	Unc	BU
1988FM (P); Proof	—	Value: 20.00				

KM# 111 50 DOLLARS **Weight:** 20.9400 g. **Composition:** 0.9250 Silver .6228 oz. ASW **Subject:** Great Explorers **Reverse:** Richard Byrd

Date		F	VF	XF	Unc	BU
1988FM (P)	—	Value: 27.50				

KM# 47 50 DOLLARS **Weight:** 29.9000 g. **Composition:** 0.9250 Silver .8892 oz. ASW **Subject:** 500 Years of America **Obverse:** Queen's portrait right **Reverse:** Christopher Columbus **Edge Lettering:** CHRISTOPHER COLUMBUS WITH THE SANTA MARIA

Date	Mintage	F	VF	XF	Unc	BU
1989 Proof	Est. 15,000	Value: 30.00				

Note: Prior to the 27th edition, the illustration for KM#47 was incorrect. Please see KM182 for correct listing

KM# 49 50 DOLLARS **Weight:** 31.1000 g. **Composition:** 0.9250 Silver .9250 oz. ASW **Subject:** 500 Years of America **Obverse:** Queen's portrait right **Reverse:** Ferdinand Magellan

Date	Mintage	F	VF	XF	Unc	BU
1989 Proof	15,000	Value: 22.50				
1991 Proof	Est. 60,000	Value: 20.00				

KM# 45 50 DOLLARS **Weight:** 19.4000 g. **Composition:** 0.9250 Silver .5770 oz. ASW **Subject:** 500 Years of America **Obverse:** Queen's portrait right **Reverse:** Sir Francis Drake

Date	Mintage	F	VF	XF	Unc	BU
1989 Proof	15,000	Value: 30.00				
1990 Proof	—	Value: 22.50				

KM# 46 50 DOLLARS **Weight:** 31.1000 g. **Composition:** 0.9990 Silver 1.0000 oz. ASW **Subject:** 500 Years of America **Obverse:** Queen's portrait right **Reverse:** Capt. James Cook

Date	Mintage	F	VF	XF	Unc	BU
1989 Proof	15,000	Value: 22.50				

KM# 60 50 DOLLARS **Weight:** 28.2800 g. **Composition:** 0.9250 Silver .8411 oz. ASW **Subject:** 1990 Olympics **Obverse:** Queen's portrait right **Reverse:** Runners and biathalon

Date	Mintage	F	VF	XF	Unc	BU
1989 Proof	40,000	—	—	—	22.50	—

KM# 70 50 DOLLARS **Weight:** 28.2800 g. **Composition:** 0.9250 Silver .8411 oz. ASW **Subject:** Soccer World Championship **Obverse:** Queen's portrait right

Date		F	VF	XF	Unc	BU
1989 Proof	—	Value: 22.50				

KM# 43 50 DOLLARS **Weight:** 31.1000 g. **Composition:** 0.9250 Silver .9250 oz. ASW **Subject:** 500 Years of America **Obverse:** Queen's portrait right **Reverse:** Jacques Cartier

Date	Mintage	F	VF	XF	Unc	BU
1990 Proof	60,000	Value: 20.00				
1991 Proof	—	Value: 25.00				

KM# 44 50 DOLLARS **Weight:** 31.1000 g. **Composition:** 0.9990 Silver 1.0000 oz. ASW **Subject:** 500 Years of America **Obverse:** Queen's portrait right **Reverse:** Vasco Nunez de Balboa

Date	Mintage	F	VF	XF	Unc	BU
1990 Proof	15,000	Value: 20.00				
1991 Proof	—	Value: 20.00				

KM# 52 50 DOLLARS **Weight:** 19.4000 g. **Composition:** 0.9250 Silver .5770 oz. ASW **Subject:** Endangered World Wildlife **Obverse:** Queen's portrait right **Reverse:** Grizzly bear

Date	Mintage	F	VF	XF	Unc	BU
1990PM Matte	550	Value: 75.00				
1990PM Proof	2,500	Value: 22.50				

KM# 48 50 DOLLARS **Weight:** 31.1000 g. **Composition:** 0.9990 Silver 1.0000 oz. ASW **Subject:** 500 Years of America **Obverse:** Queen's portrait right **Reverse:** President Abraham Lincoln in foreground of capitol

Date	Mintage	F	VF	XF	Unc	BU
1990 Proof	15,000	Value: 20.00				
1991 Proof	—	Value: 20.00				

KM# 53 50 DOLLARS **Weight:** 19.4000 g. **Composition:** 0.9250 Silver 5770 oz. ASW **Subject:** Endangered World Wildlife **Obverse:** Queen's portrait right **Reverse:** African elephant

Date	Mintage	F	VF	XF	Unc	BU
1990 Matte	1,000	Value: 60.00				
1990 Proof	25,000	Value: 22.50				

KM# 54 50 DOLLARS **Weight:** 19.4000 g. **Composition:** 0.9250 Silver 5770 oz. ASW **Subject:** Endangered World Wildlife **Obverse:** Queen's portrait right **Reverse:** Lynx

Date	Mintage	F	VF	XF	Unc	BU
1990 Proof	25,000	Value: 22.50				

KM# 55 50 DOLLARS **Weight:** 19.4000 g. **Composition:** 0.9250 Silver 5770 oz. ASW **Subject:** Endangered World Wildlife **Obverse:** Queen's portrait right **Reverse:** Black rhinoceros

Date	Mintage	F	VF	XF	Unc	BU
1990 Proof	Est. 25,000	Value: 22.50				

KM# 56 50 DOLLARS **Weight:** 19.4000 g. **Composition:** 0.9250 Silver 5770 oz. ASW **Subject:** Endangered World Wildlife **Obverse:** Queen's portrait right **Reverse:** Bighorn sheep

Date	Mintage	F	VF	XF	Unc	BU
1990 Proof	Est. 25,000	Value: 22.50				

KM# 57 50 DOLLARS **Weight:** 19.4000 g. **Composition:** 0.9250 Silver 5770 oz. ASW **Subject:** Endangered World Wildlife **Obverse:** Queen's portrait right **Reverse:** Koala bear

Date	Mintage	F	VF	XF	Unc	BU
1990 Proof	Est. 25,000	Value: 25.00				

KM# 58 50 DOLLARS **Weight:** 19.4000 g. **Composition:** 0.9250 Silver 5770 oz. ASW **Subject:** Endangered World Wildlife **Obverse:** Queen's portrait right **Reverse:** Buffalo

Date	Mintage	F	VF	XF	Unc	BU
1990	600	—	—	—	60.00	—
1990 Proof	25,000	Value: 24.00				

KM# 59 50 DOLLARS **Weight:** 19.4000 g. **Composition:** 0.9250 Silver 5770 oz. ASW **Subject:** Endangered World Wildlife **Obverse:** Queen's portrait right **Reverse:** Chimpanzee

Date	Mintage	F	VF	XF	Unc	BU
1990 Proof	Est. 25,000	Value: 22.50				

KM# 89 50 DOLLARS **Weight:** 31.1000 g. **Composition:** 0.9250 Silver .9250 oz. ASW **Subject:** 500 Years of America **Obverse:** Queen's portrait right **Reverse:** Henry Hudson

Date	Mintage	F	VF	XF	Unc	BU
1990 Proof	60,000	Value: 25.00				

KM# 134 50 DOLLARS **Weight:** 31.1000 g. **Composition:** 0.9250 Silver .9250 oz. ASW **Subject:** 500 Years of America **Obverse:** Queen's portrait right **Reverse:** Cabral

Date	Mintage	F	VF	XF	Unc	BU
1990 Proof	Est. 60,000	Value: 20.00				

KM# 135 50 DOLLARS **Weight:** 31.1000 g. **Composition:** 0.9250 Silver .9250 oz. ASW **Subject:** 500 Years of America **Obverse:** Queen's portrait right **Reverse:** Bolivar

Date	Mintage	F	VF	XF	Unc	BU
1990 Proof	Est. 60,000	Value: 22.50				

KM# 139 50 DOLLARS **Weight:** 31.2600 g. **Composition:** 0.9250 Silver .9296 oz. ASW **Subject:** 500 Years of America **Obverse:** Queen's portrait right **Reverse:** Samuel Clemens

Date	Mintage	F	VF	XF	Unc	BU
1990 Proof	Est. 60,000	Value: 25.00				

KM# 182 50 DOLLARS **Weight:** 31.3500 g. **Composition:** 0.9250 Silver .9324 oz. ASW **Subject:** 500 Years of America **Obverse:** Queen's portrait right **Reverse:** Columbus' portrait w/Santa Maria in background

Date	F	VF	XF	Unc	BU
1990 Proof	—	Value: 27.50			

KM# 184 50 DOLLARS **Weight:** 31.3500 g. **Composition:** 0.9250 Silver .9324 oz. ASW **Subject:** 500 Years of America **Obverse:** Queen's portrait right **Reverse:** Inca Prince

Date	Mintage	F	VF	XF	Unc	BU
1990 Proof	Est. 60,000	Value: 22.50				

KM# 185 50 DOLLARS **Weight:** 31.3500 g. **Composition:** 0.9250 Silver .9324 oz. ASW **Subject:** 500 Years of America **Obverse:** Queen's portrait right **Reverse:** Cortez and Montezuma

Date	Mintage	F	VF	XF	Unc	BU
1990 Proof	Est. 60,000	Value: 22.50				

KM# 186 50 DOLLARS **Weight:** 31.3500 g. **Composition:** 0.9250 Silver .9324 oz. ASW **Subject:** 500 Years of America **Obverse:** Queen's portrait right **Reverse:** Samuel de Champalin

Date	Mintage	F	VF	XF	Unc	BU
1990 Proof	Est. 60,000	Value: 20.00				

KM# 116 50 DOLLARS **Weight:** 19.8000 g. **Composition:** 0.9250 Silver .5888 oz. ASW **Subject:** Endangered World Wildlife **Obverse:** Queen's portrait right **Reverse:** European mouflon

Date	F	VF	XF	Unc	BU
1990 Proof	—	Value: 30.00			

KM# 206 50 DOLLARS **Weight:** 19.2000 g. **Composition:** 0.9250 Silver .5768 oz. ASW **Subject:** Endangered World Wildlife **Obverse:** Queen's portrait right **Reverse:** Tiger

Date	Mintage	F	VF	XF	Unc	BU
1990 Proof	Est. 25,000	Value: 25.00				

KM# 188 50 DOLLARS **Weight:** 31.3500 g. **Composition:** 0.9250 Silver .9324 oz. ASW **Subject:** 500 Years of America **Obverse:** Queen's portrait right **Reverse:** Sir Walter Raleigh

Date	Mintage	F	VF	XF	Unc	BU
1990 Proof	Est. 60,000	Value: 25.00				

KM# 117 50 DOLLARS **Weight:** 19.8000 g. **Composition:** 0.9250 Silver .5888 oz. ASW **Subject:** Endangered World Wildlife **Obverse:** Queen's portrait right **Reverse:** Whooping crane

Date	F	VF	XF	Unc	BU
1990 Proof	—	Value: 27.50			

KM# 207 50 DOLLARS **Weight:** 19.2000 g. **Composition:** 0.9250 Silver .5768 oz. ASW **Subject:** Endangered World Wildlife **Obverse:** Queen's portrait right **Reverse:** Dama gazelles

Date	Mintage	F	VF	XF	Unc	BU
1990 Proof	Est. 25,000	Value: 22.50				

KM# 112 50 DOLLARS **Weight:** 19.2000 g. **Composition:** 0.9250 Silver .5768 oz. ASW **Subject:** 1992 Olympics **Obverse:** Queen's portrait right **Reverse:** Runner

Date	Mintage	F	VF	XF	Unc	BU
1990 Proof	40,000	Value: 25.00				

KM# 144 50 DOLLARS **Weight:** 19.4000 g. **Composition:** 0.9250 Silver .5768 oz. ASW **Subject:** Endangered World Wildlife **Obverse:** Queen's portrait right **Reverse:** European hedgehog

Date		F	VF	XF	Unc	BU
1990 Proof	Est. 25,000	Value: 27.50				

KM# 208 50 DOLLARS **Weight:** 19.2000 g. **Composition:** 0.9250 Silver .5768 oz. ASW **Subject:** Endangered World Wildlife **Obverse:** Queen's portrait right **Reverse:** Cougars

Date	F	VF	XF	Unc	BU
1990PM Proof	—	Value: 42.50			

KM# 115 50 DOLLARS **Weight:** 19.8000 g. **Composition:** 0.9250 Silver .5888 oz. ASW **Subject:** Endangered World Wildlife **Obverse:** Queen's portrait right **Reverse:** Blackbuck

Date	F	VF	XF	Unc	BU
1990 Proof	—	Value: 27.50			

KM# 205 50 DOLLARS **Weight:** 19.2000 g. **Composition:** 0.9250 Silver .5768 oz. ASW **Subject:** Endangered World Wildlife **Obverse:** PM mint mark below truncaton **Reverse:** European bison and calf

Date	Mintage	F	VF	XF	Unc	BU
1990PM Proof	Est. 25,000	Value: 35.00				

KM# 209 50 DOLLARS **Weight:** 19.2000 g. **Composition:** 0.9250 Silver .5768 oz. ASW **Subject:** Endangered World Wildlife **Obverse:** Queen's portrait right **Reverse:** Eagle Owl

Date	F	VF	XF	Unc	BU
1990(b) Proof	—	Value: 42.50			

KM# 210 50 DOLLARS Weight: 19.2000 g. **Composition:** 0.9250 Silver .5768 oz. ASW **Subject:** Endangered World Wildlife **Obverse:** Queen's portrait right **Reverse:** Heaviside's dolphins

Date	F	VF	XF	Unc	BU
1990(b) Proof	— Value: 45.00				

KM# 211 50 DOLLARS Weight: 19.2000 g. **Composition:** 0.9250 Silver .5768 oz. ASW **Subject:** Endangered World Wildlife **Obverse:** Queen's portrait right **Reverse:** European otters

Date	F	VF	XF	Unc	BU
1990 Proof	— Value: 42.50				

KM# 357 50 DOLLARS Weight: 19.2000 g. **Composition:** 0.9250 Silver .5768 oz. ASW **Subject:** Endangered World Wildlife **Obverse:** Queen's portrait right **Reverse:** Peregrine falcon

Date	F	VF	XF	Unc	BU
1990(b) Proof	— Value: 42.50				

KM# 212 50 DOLLARS Weight: 19.2000 g. **Composition:** 0.9250 Silver .5768 oz. ASW **Subject:** Endangered World Wildlife **Obverse:** Queen's portrait right **Reverse:** Alpine ibex

Date	F	VF	XF	Unc	BU
1990 Proof	— Value: 37.50				

KM# 213 50 DOLLARS Weight: 19.2000 g. **Composition:** 0.9250 Silver .5768 oz. ASW **Subject:** Endangered World Wildlife **Obverse:** Queen's portrait right **Reverse:** Senegalese lion

Date	F	VF	XF	Unc	BU
1990 Proof	— Value: 42.50				

KM# 214 50 DOLLARS Weight: 19.2000 g. **Composition:** 0.9250 Silver .5768 oz. ASW **Subject:** Endangered World Wildlife **Obverse:** Queen's portrait right **Reverse:** Fallow deer

Date	F	VF	XF	Unc	BU
1990 Proof	— Value: 40.00				

KM# 215 50 DOLLARS Weight: 19.2000 g. **Composition:** 0.9250 Silver .5768 oz. ASW **Subject:** Endangered World Wildlife **Obverse:** Queen's portrait right **Reverse:** Bee hummingbird

Date	F	VF	XF	Unc	BU
1990 Proof	— Value: 42.50				

KM# 216 50 DOLLARS Weight: 19.2000 g. **Composition:** 0.9250 Silver .5768 oz. ASW **Subject:** Endangered World Wildlife **Obverse:** Queen's portrait right **Reverse:** Jackass penguins

Date	F	VF	XF	Unc	BU
1990 Proof	— Value: 37.50				

KM# 265 50 DOLLARS Weight: 28.3000 g. **Composition:** 0.9250 Silver .8416 oz. ASW **Subject:** World Cup Soccer

Date	F	VF	XF	Unc	BU
1990 Proof	— Value: 22.50				

KM# 93 50 DOLLARS Weight: 19.8000 g. **Composition:** 0.9250 Silver .5888 oz. ASW **Subject:** Endangered World Wildlife **Obverse:** Queen's portrait right **Reverse:** Eagle owl

Date	Mintage	F	VF	XF	Unc	BU
1991 Proof	Est. 25,000	Value: 30.00				

KM# 95 50 DOLLARS Weight: 19.2000 g. **Composition:** 0.9250 Silver .5768 oz. ASW **Subject:** Endangered World Wildlife **Obverse:** Queen's portrait right **Reverse:** Heavisdie's dolphins

Date	Mintage	F	VF	XF	Unc	BU
1991 Proof	Est. 25,000	Value: 30.00				

KM# 118 50 DOLLARS Weight: 19.2000 g. **Composition:** 0.9250 Silver .5768 oz. ASW **Subject:** Endangered World Wildlife **Obverse:** Queen's portrait right **Reverse:** European otters

Date	F	VF	XF	Unc	BU
1991 Proof	— Value: 30.00				

KM# 119 50 DOLLARS Weight: 19.2000 g. **Composition:** 0.9250 Silver .5768 oz. ASW **Subject:** Endangered World Wildlife **Obverse:** Queen's portrait right **Reverse:** Peregrine falcon

Date	Mintage	F	VF	XF	Unc	BU
1991 Proof	Est. 25,000	Value: 30.00				

KM# 120 50 DOLLARS Weight: 19.2000 g. **Composition:** 0.9250 Silver .5768 oz. ASW **Subject:** Endangered World Wildlife **Obverse:** Queen's portrait right **Reverse:** Alpine ibex

Date	Mintage	F	VF	XF	Unc	BU
1991 Proof	Est. 25,000	Value: 25.00				

KM# 122 50 DOLLARS **Weight:** 19.2000 g. **Composition:** 0.9250 Silver .5768 oz. ASW **Subject:** Endangered World Wildlife **Obverse:** Queen's portrait right **Reverse:** Senegalese lion

Date	Mintage	F	VF	XF	Unc	BU
1991 Proof	Est. 25,000	Value: 30.00				

KM# 123 50 DOLLARS **Weight:** 19.2000 g. **Composition:** 0.9250 Silver .5768 oz. ASW **Subject:** Endangered World Wildlife **Obverse:** Queen's portrait right **Reverse:** White-tailed deer

Date	Mintage	F	VF	XF	Unc	BU
1991 Proof	Est. 25,000	Value: 30.00				

KM# 124 50 DOLLARS **Weight:** 19.2000 g. **Composition:** 0.9250 Silver .5768 oz. ASW **Subject:** Endangered World Wildlife **Obverse:** Queen's portrait right **Reverse:** Kangaroo

Date	Mintage	F	VF	XF	Unc	BU
1991 Proof	Est. 25,000	Value: 22.50				

KM# 125 50 DOLLARS **Weight:** 19.2000 g. **Composition:** 0.9250 Silver .5768 oz. ASW **Subject:** Endangered World Wildlife **Obverse:** Queen's portrait right **Reverse:** Cougar and cub

Date	Mintage	F	VF	XF	Unc	BU
1991 Proof	Est. 25,000	Value: 25.00				

KM# 126 50 DOLLARS **Weight:** 19.2000 g. **Composition:** 0.9250 Silver .5768 oz. ASW **Subject:** Endangered World Wildlife **Obverse:** Queen's portrait right **Reverse:** Fallow deer

Date	Mintage	F	VF	XF	Unc	BU
1991 Proof	Est. 25,000	Value: 22.50				

KM# 127 50 DOLLARS **Weight:** 19.2000 g. **Composition:** 0.9250 Silver .5768 oz. ASW **Subject:** Endangered World Wildlife **Obverse:** Queen's portrait right **Reverse:** Bee hummingbird

Date		F	VF	XF	Unc	BU
1991 Proof	Est. 25,000	Value: 30.00				

KM# 128 50 DOLLARS **Weight:** 19.2000 g. **Composition:** 0.9250 Silver .5768 oz. ASW **Subject:** Endangered World Wildlife **Obverse:** Queen's portrait right **Reverse:** Jackass penguins

Date	Mintage	F	VF	XF	Unc	BU
1991 Proof	Est. 25,000	Value: 30.00				

KM# 94 50 DOLLARS **Weight:** 31.1000 g. **Composition:** 0.9250 Silver .9250 oz. ASW **Subject:** 500 Years of America **Obverse:** Queen's portrait right **Reverse:** Sitting Bull

Date	Mintage	F	VF	XF	Unc	BU
1991 Proof	Est. 15,000	Value: 27.50				

KM# 140 50 DOLLARS **Weight:** 31.2600 g. **Composition:** 0.9250 Silver .9296 oz. ASW **Subject:** 500 Years of America **Obverse:** Queen's portrait right **Reverse:** Mayflower and pilgrims

Date	Mintage	F	VF	XF	Unc	BU
1991 Proof	—	Value: 20.00				
1992 Proof	60,000	Value: 20.00				

KM# 141 50 DOLLARS **Weight:** 31.2600 g. **Composition:** 0.9250 Silver .9296 oz. ASW **Subject:** 500 Years of America **Obverse:** Queen's portrait right **Reverse:** Alexander Mackenzie

Date	Mintage	F	VF	XF	Unc	BU
1991 Proof	60,000	Value: 20.00				

KM# 145 50 DOLLARS **Weight:** 7.7750 g. **Composition:** 0.5833 Gold .1458 oz. AGW **Subject:** 500 Years of America **Obverse:** Queen's portrait right **Reverse:** Columbus kneeling

Date	Mintage	F	VF	XF	Unc	BU
1991 Proof	Est. 60,000	Value: 85.00				

KM# 148 50 DOLLARS **Weight:** 31.1000 g. **Composition:** 0.9250 Silver .9250 oz. ASW **Subject:** 500 Years of America **Obverse:** Queen's portrait right **Reverse:** Aztec Priest

Date	Mintage	F	VF	XF	Unc	BU
1991 Proof	Est. 15,000	Value: 20.00				

KM# 189 50 DOLLARS **Weight:** 31.1000 g. **Composition:** 0.9250 Silver .9250 oz. ASW **Subject:** 500

Years of America **Obverse:** Queen's portrait right **Reverse:** Franicsco Pizarro

Date	Mintage	F	VF	XF	Unc	BU
1991 Proof	Est. 60,000	Value: 20.00				

KM# 190 50 DOLLARS Weight: 31.1000 g. **Composition:** 0.9250 Silver .9250 oz. ASW **Subject:** 500 Years of America **Obverse:** Queen's portrait right **Reverse:** Jesuit Church in Cuzco

Date	Mintage	F	VF	XF	Unc	BU
1991 Proof	Est. 60,000	Value: 20.00				

KM# 191 50 DOLLARS Weight: 31.1000 g. **Composition:** 0.9250 Silver .9250 oz. ASW **Subject:** 500 Years of America **Obverse:** Queen's portrait right **Reverse:** Peter Minuit's purchase of Manhattan Island

Date	Mintage	F	VF	XF	Unc	BU
1991 Proof	Est. 60,000	Value: 20.00				

KM# 192 50 DOLLARS Weight: 31.1000 g. **Composition:** 0.9250 Silver .9250 oz. ASW **Subject:** 500 Years of America **Obverse:** Queen's portrait right **Reverse:** Boston Tea Party

Date	Mintage	F	VF	XF	Unc	BU
1991 Proof	Est. 60,000	Value: 20.00				

KM# 193 50 DOLLARS Weight: 31.1000 g. **Composition:** 0.9250 Silver .9250 oz. ASW **Subject:** 500 Years of America **Obverse:** Queen's portrait right **Reverse:** Marquis de Lafayette

Date	Mintage	F	VF	XF	Unc	BU
1991 Proof	Est. 60,000	Value: 20.00				

KM# 194 50 DOLLARS Weight: 31.1000 g. **Composition:** 0.9250 Silver .9250 oz. ASW **Subject:** 500 Years of America **Obverse:** Queen's portrait right **Reverse:** Robert Fulton

Date	Mintage	F	VF	XF	Unc	BU
1991 Proof	Est. 60,000	Value: 20.00				

KM# 195 50 DOLLARS Weight: 31.1000 g. **Composition:** 0.9250 Silver .9250 oz. ASW **Subject:** 500 Years of America **Obverse:** Queen's portrait right **Reverse:** First U.S. transcontinental railroad

Date	Mintage	F	VF	XF	Unc	BU
1991 Proof	Est. 60,000	Value: 20.00				

KM# 196 50 DOLLARS Weight: 31.1000 g. **Composition:** 0.9250 Silver .9250 oz. ASW **Subject:** 500 Years of America **Obverse:** Queen's portrait right **Reverse:** Emperior Maximilian of Mexico

Date	Mintage	F	VF	XF	Unc	BU
1991 Proof	Est. 60,000	Value: 20.00				

KM# 305 50 DOLLARS Weight: 31.1000 g. **Composition:** 0.9250 Silver .9250 oz. ASW **Subject:** 500 Years of America **Obverse:** Queen's portrait right **Reverse:** Capt. James Cook

Date	Mintage	F	VF	XF	Unc	BU
1991 Proof	Est. 60,000	Value: 20.00				

KM# 44a 50 DOLLARS Weight: 31.1000 g. **Composition:** 0.9250 Silver .9250 oz. ASW **Subject:** 500 Years of America **Obverse:** Queen's portrait right **Reverse:** Vasco Nunez de Balboa

Date	Mintage	F	VF	XF	Unc	BU
1991 Proof	60,000	Value: 35.00				

KM# 46a 50 DOLLARS Weight: 31.1000 g. **Composition:** 0.9250 Silver .9250 oz. ASW **Subject:** 500 Years of America **Obverse:** Queen's portrait right **Reverse:** Capt. James Cook

Date	Mintage	F	VF	XF	Unc	BU
1991 Proof	Est. 60,000	Value: 25.00				

KM# 261 50 DOLLARS Weight: 19.2000 g. **Composition:** 0.9250 Silver .5768 oz. ASW **Subject:** Endangered Wildlife **Obverse:** Queen's portrait right **Reverse:** Szechuan Takins

Date	Mintage	F	VF	XF	Unc	BU
1992 Proof	25,000	Value: 25.00				

KM# 262 50 DOLLARS Weight: 19.2000 g. **Composition:** 0.9250 Silver .5768 oz. ASW **Subject:** Endangered Wildlife **Obverse:** Queen's portrait right **Reverse:** Ring-tailed lemurs

Date	Mintage	F	VF	XF	Unc	BU
1992 Proof	25,000	Value: 25.00				

KM# 263 50 DOLLARS Weight: 19.2000 g. **Composition:** 0.9250 Silver .5768 oz. ASW **Subject:** Endangered Wildlife **Obverse:** Queen's portrait right **Reverse:** Drill

Date	Mintage	F	VF	XF	Unc	BU
1992 Proof	25,000	Value: 25.00				

KM# 264 50 DOLLARS Weight: 19.2000 g. **Composition:** 0.9250 Silver .5768 oz. ASW **Subject:** Endangered Wildlife **Obverse:** Queen's portrait right **Reverse:** Lowland gorilla

Date	Mintage	F	VF	XF	Unc	BU
1992 Proof	25,000	Value: 25.00				

KM# 310 50 DOLLARS Weight: 31.0000 g. **Composition:** 0.9250 Silver .9219 oz. ASW **Obverse:** Queen's portrait right **Reverse:** Aztec kneels before Alvarado **Edge Lettering:** PEDRO DE ALVARADO CONQUEROR of the AZTEC EMPIRE

Date		F	VF	XF	Unc	BU
1992 Proof	—	Value: 22.50				

KM# 114 50 DOLLARS **Weight:** 31.1000 g. **Composition:** 0.9250 Silver .9250 oz. ASW **Subject:** 500 Years of America **Obverse:** Queen's portrait right **Reverse:** Coronado's discovery of the Grand Canyon

Date	Mintage	F	VF	XF	Unc	BU
1992 Proof	Est. 15,000	Value: 27.50				

KM# 129 50 DOLLARS **Weight:** 7.7760 g. **Composition:** 0.5830 Gold .1458 oz. AGW **Subject:** Endangered Wildlife **Obverse:** Queen's portrait right **Reverse:** Eagle's head

Date		F	VF	XF	Unc	BU
1992 Proof	—	Value: 85.00				

KM# 131 50 DOLLARS **Weight:** 7.7760 g. **Composition:** 0.5830 Gold .1458 oz. AGW **Subject:** Endangered Wildlife **Obverse:** Queen's portrait right **Reverse:** Elephant head

Date		F	VF	XF	Unc	BU
1992 Proof	—	Value: 85.00				

KM# 132 50 DOLLARS **Weight:** 7.7760 g. **Composition:** 0.5830 Gold .1458 oz. AGW **Subject:** Endangered Wildlife **Obverse:** Queen's portrait right **Reverse:** Tiger head

Date		F	VF	XF	Unc	BU
1992 Proof	—	Value: 85.00				

KM# 142 50 DOLLARS **Weight:** 31.2600 g. **Composition:** 0.9250 Silver .9296 oz. ASW **Subject:** 500 Years of America **Obverse:** Queen's portrait right **Reverse:** John Davis' strait marked on map, ship at right

Date	Mintage	F	VF	XF	Unc	BU
1992 Proof	Est. 60,000	Value: 20.00				

KM# 143 50 DOLLARS **Weight:** 31.2600 g. **Composition:** 0.9250 Silver .9296 oz. ASW **Subject:** 500 Years of America **Obverse:** Queen's portrait right **Reverse:** Vitus Bering

Date	Mintage	F	VF	XF	Unc	BU
1992 Proof	Est. 60,000	Value: 20.00				

KM# 156 50 DOLLARS **Weight:** 31.1035 g. **Composition:** 0.9250 Silver .9250 oz. ASW **Subject:** 500 Years of America **Obverse:** Queen's portrait right **Reverse:** Pedro de Valdivia

Date		F	VF	XF	Unc	BU
1992 Proof	—	Value: 20.00				

KM# 157 50 DOLLARS **Weight:** 31.1035 g. **Composition:** 0.9250 Silver .9250 oz. ASW **Subject:** 500 Years of America **Obverse:** Queen's portrait right **Reverse:** Diego de Almagro

Date		F	VF	XF	Unc	BU
1992 Proof	—	Value: 20.00				

KM# 162 50 DOLLARS **Weight:** 31.1035 g. **Composition:** 0.9250 Silver .9250 oz. ASW **Subject:** 500 Years of America **Obverse:** Queen's portrait right **Reverse:** Francisco de Coronado

Date		F	VF	XF	Unc	BU
1992 Proof	—	Value: 20.00				

KM# 176 50 DOLLARS **Weight:** 7.7760 g. **Composition:** 0.5833 Gold .1458 oz. AGW **Subject:** 500 Years of America **Obverse:** Queen's portrait right **Reverse:** Robert de La Salle

Date		F	VF	XF	Unc	BU
1992 Proof	—	Value: 85.00				

KM# 183 50 DOLLARS **Weight:** 31.1035 g. **Composition:** 0.9250 Silver .9250 oz. ASW **Subject:** 500 Years of America **Obverse:** Queen's portrait right **Reverse:** Giovanni da Verrazano

Date	Mintage	F	VF	XF	Unc	BU
1992 Proof	Est. 60,000	Value: 20.00				

KM# 197 50 DOLLARS **Weight:** 31.1035 g. **Composition:** 0.9250 Silver .9250 oz. ASW **Subject:** 500 Years of America **Obverse:** Queen's portrait right **Reverse:** Juan Ponce de Leon

Date	Mintage	F	VF	XF	Unc	BU
1992 Proof	Est. 60,000	Value: 20.00				

KM# 198 50 DOLLARS **Weight:** 31.1035 g. **Composition:** 0.9250 Silver .9250 oz. ASW **Subject:** 500 Years of America **Obverse:** Queen's portrait right **Reverse:** 3/4 bust of Pedro de Mendoza at left, historic monuments at right

Date	Mintage	F	VF	XF	Unc	BU
1992 Proof	Est. 60,000	Value: 20.00				

KM# 199 50 DOLLARS **Weight:** 31.1035 g. **Composition:** 0.9250 Silver .9250 oz. ASW **Subject:** 500 Years of America **Obverse:** Queen's portrait right **Reverse:** Pedro Menendez de Aviles on horseback at lower right, monument at left

Date		F	VF	XF	Unc	BU
1992 Proof	—	Value: 20.00				

KM# 200 50 DOLLARS **Weight:** 31.1035 g. **Composition:** 0.9250 Silver .9250 oz. ASW **Subject:** 500 Years of America **Obverse:** Queen's portrait right **Reverse:** Independence Hall

Date		F	VF	XF	Unc	BU
1992 Proof	—	Value: 20.00				

KM# 201 50 DOLLARS **Weight:** 31.1035 g. **Composition:** 0.9250 Silver .9250 oz. ASW **Subject:** 500 Years of America **Obverse:** Queen's portrait right **Reverse:** Sacagawea guiding Lewis and Clark

Date	Mintage	F	VF	XF	Unc	BU
1992 Proof	Est. 60,000	Value: 20.00				

KM# 202 50 DOLLARS **Weight:** 31.1035 g. **Composition:** 0.9250 Silver .9250 oz. ASW **Subject:** 500 Years of America **Obverse:** Queen's portrait right **Reverse:** Oregon Trail, conestoga wagon in front of U.S. map outline

Date	Mintage	F	VF	XF	Unc	BU
1992 Proof	Est. 60,000	Value: 20.00				

KM# 204 50 DOLLARS **Weight:** 7.7760 g. **Composition:** 0.5833 Gold .1458 oz. AGW **Subject:** 500 Years of America **Obverse:** Queen's portrait right **Reverse:** Bust of John Cabot at left, ship at right

Date	Mintage	F	VF	XF	Unc	BU
1992 Proof	5,000	Value: 85.00				

KM# 249 50 DOLLARS **Weight:** 7.7760 g. **Composition:** 0.5830 Gold .1458 oz. AGW **Subject:** 500 Years of America **Obverse:** Queen's portrait right **Reverse:** Ferdinand and Isabella

Date	Mintage	F	VF	XF	Unc	BU
1992 Proof	Est. 5,000	Value: 85.00				

KM# 259 50 DOLLARS **Weight:** 7.7760 g. **Composition:** 0.5830 Gold .1458 oz. AGW **Subject:** 500 Years of America **Obverse:** Queen's portrait right **Reverse:** Paul de Maisonneuve, map and city view

Date	Mintage	F	VF	XF	Unc	BU
1992 Proof	Est. 5,000	Value: 85.00				

KM# 260 50 DOLLARS **Weight:** 7.7760 g. **Composition:** 0.5830 Gold .1458 oz. AGW **Subject:** 500 Years of America **Obverse:** Queen's portrait right **Reverse:** Jakob le Maire, ship and map

Date	Mintage	F	VF	XF	Unc	BU
1992 Proof	Est. 5,000	Value: 85.00				

KM# 244 50 DOLLARS **Weight:** 19.2000 g. **Composition:** 0.9250 Silver .5768 oz. ASW **Reverse:** Poplar Admiral Butterfly and thistle

Date	Mintage	F	VF	XF	Unc	BU
1992 Proof	Est. 25,000	Value: 35.00				

KM# 155 50 DOLLARS **Weight:** 31.1035 g. **Composition:** 0.9250 Silver .9250 oz. ASW **Subject:** 500 Years of America **Obverse:** Queen's portrait right **Reverse:** Father Jacques Marquette

Date	F	VF	XF	Unc	BU
1993 Proof	—	Value: 22.50			

KM# 163 50 DOLLARS **Weight:** 31.1035 g. **Composition:** 0.9250 Silver .9250 oz. ASW **Subject:** 500 Years of America **Obverse:** Queen's portrait right **Reverse:** Francisco de Orellana

Date	F	VF	XF	Unc	BU
1993 Proof	—	Value: 22.50			

KM# 153 50 DOLLARS **Weight:** 7.7760 g. **Composition:** 0.5833 Gold .1453 oz. AGW **Subject:** Endangered Wildlife **Obverse:** Queen's portrait right **Reverse:** Ibex

Date	F	VF	XF	Unc	BU
1993 Proof	—	Value: 85.00			

KM# 154 50 DOLLARS **Weight:** 7.7760 g. **Composition:** 0.5833 Gold .1453 oz. AGW **Subject:** Endangered Wildlife **Obverse:** Queen's portrait right **Reverse:** Owl and parrot

Date	F	VF	XF	Unc	BU
1993 Proof	—	Value: 85.00			

KM# 164 50 DOLLARS **Weight:** 31.1035 g. **Composition:** 0.9250 Silver .9250 oz. ASW **Subject:** 500 Years of America **Obverse:** Queen's portrait right **Reverse:** Pinzon Brothers

Date	F	VF	XF	Unc	BU
1993 Proof	—	Value: 22.50			

KM# 165 50 DOLLARS **Weight:** 31.1035 g. **Composition:** 0.9250 Silver .9250 oz. ASW **Subject:** 500 Years of America **Obverse:** Queen's portrait right **Reverse:** Juan de la Cosa

Date	F	VF	XF	Unc	BU
1993 Proof	—	Value: 21.50			

KM# 166 50 DOLLARS **Weight:** 31.1035 g. **Composition:** 0.9250 Silver .9250 oz. ASW **Subject:** 500 Years of America **Obverse:** Queen's portrait right **Reverse:** William Penn

Date	F	VF	XF	Unc	BU
1993 Proof	—	Value: 22.50			

KM# 167 50 DOLLARS **Weight:** 31.1035 g. **Composition:** 0.9250 Silver .9250 oz. ASW **Subject:** 500 Years of America **Obverse:** Queen's portrait right **Reverse:** Diego de Velasquez

Date	F	VF	XF	Unc	BU
1993 Proof	—	Value: 22.50			

KM# 168 50 DOLLARS **Weight:** 31.1035 g. **Composition:** 0.9250 Silver .9250 oz. ASW **Subject:** 500 Years of America **Obverse:** Queen's portrait right **Reverse:** Miner panning for gold

Date	F	VF	XF	Unc	BU
1993 Proof	—	Value: 22.50			

KM# 169 50 DOLLARS **Weight:** 31.1035 g. **Composition:** 0.9250 Silver .9250 oz. ASW **Subject:** 500 Years of America **Obverse:** Queen's portrait right **Reverse:** Sir Martin Frobisher

Date	F	VF	XF	Unc	BU
1993 Proof	—	Value: 21.50			

KM# 170 50 DOLLARS **Weight:** 31.1035 g. **Composition:** 0.9250 Silver .9250 oz. ASW **Subject:** 500 Years of America **Obverse:** Queen's portrait right **Reverse:** George Vancouver

Date	F	VF	XF	Unc	BU
1993 Proof	—	Value: 22.50			

KM# 171 50 DOLLARS **Weight:** 31.1035 g. **Composition:** 0.9250 Silver .9250 oz. ASW **Subject:** 500 Years of America **Obverse:** Queen's portrait right **Reverse:** John Hawkins

Date		F	VF	XF	Unc	BU
1993 Proof	—	Value: 22.50				

KM# 172 50 DOLLARS **Weight:** 31.1035 g. **Composition:** 0.9250 Silver .9250 oz. ASW **Subject:** 500 Years of America **Obverse:** Queen's portrait right **Reverse:** Amerigo Vespucci

Date		F	VF	XF	Unc	BU
1993 Proof	—	Value: 22.50				

KM# 173 50 DOLLARS **Weight:** 7.7760 g. **Composition:** 0.5833 Gold .1458 oz. AGW **Subject:** 500 Years of America **Obverse:** Queen's portrait right **Reverse:** George Washington

Date		F	VF	XF	Unc	BU
1993 Proof	—	Value: 85.00				

KM# 174 50 DOLLARS **Weight:** 7.7760 g. **Composition:** 0.5833 Gold .1458 oz. AGW **Subject:** 500 Years of America **Obverse:** Queen's portrait right **Reverse:** Alonso de Hojeda

Date		F	VF	XF	Unc	BU
1993 Proof	—	Value: 85.00				

KM# 175 50 DOLLARS **Weight:** 7.7760 g. **Composition:** 0.5833 Gold .1458 oz. AGW **Subject:** 500 Years of America **Obverse:** Queen's portrait right **Reverse:** Thomas Jefferson

Date		F	VF	XF	Unc	BU
1993 Proof	—	Value: 85.00				

KM# 177 50 DOLLARS **Weight:** 7.7760 g. **Composition:** 0.5833 Gold .1458 oz. AGW **Subject:** 500 Years of America **Obverse:** Queen's portrait right **Reverse:** Captain James Cook

Date		F	VF	XF	Unc	BU
1993 Proof	—	Value: 85.00				

KM# 178 50 DOLLARS **Weight:** 7.7760 g. **Composition:** 0.5833 Gold .1458 oz. AGW **Subject:** 500 Years of America **Obverse:** Queen's portrait right **Reverse:** Christopher Columbus

Date		F	VF	XF	Unc	BU
1993 Proof	—	Value: 85.00				

KM# 179 50 DOLLARS **Weight:** 7.7760 g. **Composition:** 0.5833 Gold .1458 oz. AGW **Subject:** 500 Years of America **Obverse:** Queen's portrait right **Reverse:** Statue of Liberty

Date		F	VF	XF	Unc	BU
1993 Proof	—	Value: 85.00				

KM# 180 50 DOLLARS **Weight:** 7.7760 g. **Composition:** 0.5833 Gold .1458 oz. AGW **Subject:** 1996 Olympics **Obverse:** Queen's portrait right **Reverse:** Gymnastics

Date	Mintage	F	VF	XF	Unc	BU
1993 Proof	Est. 5,000	Value: 85.00				

KM# 245 50 DOLLARS **Weight:** 7.7760 g. **Composition:** 0.5833 Gold .1458 oz. AGW **Subject:** Endangered Wildlife **Obverse:** Queen's portrait right **Reverse:** African lion

Date	Mintage	F	VF	XF	Unc	BU
1993 Proof	Est. 10,000	Value: 85.00				

KM# 248 50 DOLLARS **Weight:** 31.1035 g. **Composition:** 0.9250 Silver .9250 oz. ASW **Subject:** 500 Years of America **Obverse:** Queen's portrait right **Reverse:** Jose de San Martin

Date	Mintage	F	VF	XF	Unc	BU
1993 Proof	Est. 60,000	Value: 32.50				

KM# 246 50 DOLLARS **Weight:** 7.7760 g. **Composition:** 0.5830 Gold .1458 oz. AGW **Subject:** Endangered Wildlife **Obverse:** Queen's portrait right **Reverse:** Sea otter

Date	Mintage	F	VF	XF	Unc	BU
1994 Proof	Est. 10,000	Value: 75.00				

KM# 247 50 DOLLARS **Weight:** 7.7760 g. **Composition:** 0.5830 Gold .1458 oz. AGW **Subject:** Endangered Wildlife **Obverse:** Queen's portrait right **Reverse:** Przewalski's horse

Date	Mintage	F	VF	XF	Unc	BU
1994 Proof	Est. 10,000	Value: 75.00				

KM# 275 50 DOLLARS **Weight:** 7.7760 g. **Composition:** 0.5830 Gold .1458 oz. AGW **Subject:** Endangered Wildlife **Obverse:** Queen's portrait right **Reverse:** Poplar Admiral butterflies

Date	Mintage	F	VF	XF	Unc	BU
1994 Proof	Est. 10,000	Value: 80.00				

KM# 276 50 DOLLARS **Weight:** 7.7760 g. **Composition:** 0.5830 Gold .1458 oz. AGW **Obverse:** Queen's portrait right **Reverse:** The Queen Mother and daughters

Date	Mintage	F	VF	XF	Unc	BU
1995 Proof	Est. 5,000	Value: 85.00				

KM# 299 50 DOLLARS **Weight:** 8.0000 g. **Composition:** 0.9999 Gold .2572 oz. AGW **Subject:** Year of the Mouse **Obverse:** Queen's portrait right **Reverse:** Mickey and Minnie Mouse portrait

Date		F	VF	XF	Unc	BU
1996 Proof	—	Value: 185				

KM# 322 50 DOLLARS **Weight:** 32.2225 g. **Composition:** 0.9250 Silver .9583 oz. ASW **Subject:** 2nd Century **Obverse:** Queen's portrait right **Reverse:** Chinese paper maker

Date		F	VF	XF	Unc	BU
1997 Proof	—	Value: 47.50				

KM# 323 50 DOLLARS **Weight:** 32.2225 g. **Composition:** 0.9250 Silver .9583 oz. ASW **Subject:** 8th Century **Obverse:** Queen's portrait right **Reverse:** Coronation of Charlemagne

Date		F	VF	XF	Unc	BU
1997 Proof	—	Value: 47.50				

KM# 324 50 DOLLARS **Weight:** 32.2225 g. **Composition:** 0.9250 Silver .9583 oz. ASW **Subject:** 12th Century **Obverse:** Queen's portrait right **Reverse:** Genghis Khan

Date		F	VF	XF	Unc	BU
1997 Proof	—	Value: 47.50				

KM# 325 50 DOLLARS **Weight:** 32.2225 g. **Composition:** 0.9250 Silver .9583 oz. ASW **Subject:** 13th Century **Obverse:** Queen's portrait right **Reverse:** Marco Polo and Kublai Khan

Date		F	VF	XF	Unc	BU
1997 Proof	—	Value: 47.50				

KM# 306 50 DOLLARS **Ring Weight:** 3.8879 g. **Ring Composition:** 0.9999 Gold .1250 oz. AGW **Center Weight:** 3.8879 g. **Center Composition:** 0.9995 Platinum .1250 oz. APW **Obverse:** Queen's portrait right **Reverse:** Mother seal with pup

Date		F	VF	XF	Unc	BU
1997 Proof	—	Value: 200				

KM# 381 50 DOLLARS **Weight:** 4.6000 g. **Composition:** 0.5833 Gold 0.0863 oz. AGW **Subject:** Explorers Series **Obverse:** Bust of Queen Elizabeth II right **Reverse:** Lief Ericson with battle ax **Edge:** Reeded **Size:** 20.9 mm.

Date		F	VF	XF	Unc	BU
1997 Proof	—	Value: 50.00				
1997FM Proof	—	Value: 50.00				

KM# 382 50 DOLLARS **Weight:** 4.6000 g. **Composition:** 0.5833 Gold 0.0863 oz. AGW **Subject:** Explorers Series **Obverse:** Bust of Queen Elizabeth II right **Reverse:** Marco Polo on camel **Edge:** Reeded **Size:** 20.9 mm.

Date		F	VF	XF	Unc	BU
1997FM Proof	—	Value: 50.00				

KM# 383 50 DOLLARS **Weight:** 4.6000 g. **Composition:** 0.5833 Gold 0.0863 oz. AGW **Subject:** Explorers Series **Obverse:** Bust of Queen Elizabeth II right **Reverse:** Vasco Da Gama **Edge:** Reeded **Size:** 20.9 mm.

Date		F	VF	XF	Unc	BU
1997FM Proof	—	Value: 50.00				

KM# 384 50 DOLLARS **Weight:** 4.6000 g. **Composition:** 0.5833 Gold 0.0863 oz. AGW **Subject:** Explorers Series **Obverse:** Bust of Queen Elizabeth II right **Reverse:** Vasco de Nunez Balboa **Edge:** Reeded

Date		F	VF	XF	Unc	BU
1997FM Proof	—	Value: 50.00				

KM# 385 50 DOLLARS **Weight:** 4.6000 g. **Composition:** 0.5833 Gold 0.0863 oz. AGW **Subject:** Explorers Series **Obverse:** Bust of Queen Elizabeth II right **Reverse:** Hernando Cortes **Edge:** Reeded **Size:** 20.9 mm.

Date		F	VF	XF	Unc	BU
1997FM Proof	—	Value: 50.00				

KM# 386 50 DOLLARS **Weight:** 4.6000 g. **Composition:** 0.5833 Gold 0.0863 oz. AGW **Subject:** Explorers Series **Obverse:** Bust of Queen Elizabeth II right **Reverse:** Magellan's ships **Edge:** Reeded **Size:** 20.9 mm.

Date		F	VF	XF	Unc	BU
1997FM Proof	—	Value: 50.00				

KM# 12 100 DOLLARS **Weight:** 16.7185 g. **Composition:** 0.9170 Gold .4929 oz. AGW **Subject:** Winston Churchill Centenary

Date	Mintage	F	VF	XF	Unc	BU
1974	368	—	—	—	325	—
1974 Proof	1,453	Value: 250				

KM# 13 100 DOLLARS **Weight:** 9.6000 g. **Composition:** 0.9000 Gold .2778 oz. AGW **Subject:** Bicentennial - Return of Captain James Cook from Second Pacific Voyage

Date	Mintage	F	VF	XF	Unc	BU
1975FM (M)	100	—	—	—	400	—
1975FM (U)	7,447	—	—	—	125	—
1975FM Proof	17,000	Value: 150				

KM# 16 100 DOLLARS **Weight:** 9.6000 g. **Composition:** 0.9000 Gold .2778 oz. AGW **Subject:** U.S. Bicentennial **Reverse:** Conjoined busts of Benjamin Franklin and George Washington

Date	Mintage	F	VF	XF	Unc	BU
1976FM (M)	50	—	—	—	350	—
1976FM (U)	852	—	—	—	150	—
1976FM Proof	9,373	Value: 180				

KM# 19 100 DOLLARS **Weight:** 9.6000 g. **Composition:** 0.9000 Gold .2778 oz. AGW **Subject:** Queen's Silver Jubilee **Reverse:** Crowned EIIR monogram

Date	Mintage	F	VF	XF	Unc	BU
1977FM (M)	50	—	—	—	350	—
1977FM (P)	562	—	—	—	150	—
1977FM Proof	9,364	Value: 200				

KM# 25 100 DOLLARS **Weight:** 9.6000 g. **Composition:** 0.9000 Gold .2778 oz. AGW **Subject:** Membership in Commonwealth of Nations

Date	Mintage	F	VF	XF	Unc	BU
1979FM (U)	400	—	—	—	175	—
1979FM Proof	3,367	Value: 165				

KM# 74 100 DOLLARS **Weight:** 1.2441 g. **Composition:** 0.9990 Gold .0400 oz. AGW **Subject:** Endangered World Wildlife **Obverse:** Queen's portrait right **Reverse:** American bald eagle

Date	Mintage	F	VF	XF	Unc	BU
1990 Prooflike	1,320	—	—	—	—	—

KM# 75 100 DOLLARS **Weight:** 1.2441 g. **Composition:** 0.9990 Gold .0400 oz. AGW **Subject:** Endangered World Wildlife **Obverse:** Queen's portrait right **Reverse:** Bison

Date	Mintage	F	VF	XF	Unc	BU
1990 Prooflike	320	—	—	—	—	—

KM# 76 100 DOLLARS **Weight:** 1.2441 g. **Composition:** 0.9990 Gold .0400 oz. AGW **Subject:** Endangered World Wildlife **Obverse:** Queen's portrait right **Reverse:** Elephant

Date	Mintage	F	VF	XF	Unc	BU
1990 Prooflike	720	—	—	—	—	—

KM# 77 100 DOLLARS **Weight:** 1.2441 g. **Composition:** 0.9990 Gold .0400 oz. AGW **Subject:** Endangered World Wildlife **Obverse:** Queen's portrait right **Reverse:** Tiger

Date	Mintage	F	VF	XF	Unc	BU
1990 Prooflike	420	—	—	—	—	—

KM# 78 100 DOLLARS **Weight:** 1.2441 g. **Composition:** 0.9990 Gold .0400 oz. AGW **Subject:** Endangered World Wildlife **Obverse:** Queen's portrait right **Reverse:** Mouflon

Date	Mintage	F	VF	XF	Unc	BU
1990 Prooflike	320	—	—	—	—	—

KM# 92 100 DOLLARS **Weight:** 3.4550 g. **Composition:** 0.9000 Gold .09999 oz. AGW **Subject:** 1992 Summer Olympics **Obverse:** Queens' portrait right **Reverse:** Bicyclists

Date	Mintage	F	VF	XF	Unc	BU
1990 Proof	Est. 5,000	Value: 100				

KM# 113 100 DOLLARS **Weight:** 172.1100 g. **Composition:** Silver **Subject:** 500 Years of America **Obverse:** Queen's portrait right **Reverse:** Ferdinand Magellan **Note:** Illustration reduced.

Date	Mintage	F	VF	XF	Unc	BU
1990 Proof	Est. 3,000	Value: 120				

KM# 319 100 DOLLARS Weight: 170.6000 g. **Composition:** 0.9250 Silver 5.0735 oz. ASW **Subject:** 500 Years of America **Obverse:** Queen's portrait right **Reverse:** Mt. Rushmore **Note:** Illustration reduced.

Date	F	VF	XF	Unc	BU
1991 Proof	—	Value: 115			

KM# 297 100 DOLLARS Weight: 155.6500 g. **Composition:** 0.9990 Silver 4.992 oz. ASW **Subject:** Endangered Wildlife **Reverse:** Three elephants **Note:** Illustration reduced.

Date	F	VF	XF	Unc	BU
1991 Proof	—	Value: 130			

KM# 320 100 DOLLARS Weight: 170.6000 g. **Composition:** 0.9250 Silver 5.0735 oz. ASW **Subject:** 500 Years of America **Obverse:** Queen's portrait right **Reverse:** Columbus' portrait with three ships **Note:** Illustration reduced.

Date	F	VF	XF	Unc	BU
1992 Proof	—	Value: 125			

KM# 159 100 DOLLARS Weight: 155.5175 g. **Composition:** 0.9990 Silver 5.0000 oz. ASW **Subject:** 500 Years of America **Obverse:** Queen's portrait right **Reverse:** Hudson's "Half Moon" and New York City skyline **Note:** Illustration reduced.

Date	F	VF	XF	Unc	BU
1993 Proof	—	Value: 125			

KM# 158 100 DOLLARS Weight: 155.5176 g. **Composition:** 0.9990 Silver 5.0000 oz. ASW **Subject:** Endangered Wildlife **Obverse:** Queen's portrait right **Reverse:** Manchurian cranes **Note:** Illustration reduced.

Date	F	VF	XF	Unc	BU
1993 Proof	—	Value: 200			

KM# 250 100 DOLLARS Weight: 7.7761 g. **Composition:** 0.9990 Platinum .1458 oz. APW **Obverse:** Queen's portrait right **Reverse:** Javelin throwing

Date	F	VF	XF	Unc	BU
1995 Proof	Est. 1,000	Value: 150			

KM# 294 100 DOLLARS Weight: 7.7800 g. **Composition:** 0.9990 Gold .2501 oz. AGW **Subject:** Yellowstone National Park **Obverse:** Queen's portrait right

Date	F	VF	XF	Unc	BU
1996 Proof	—	Value: 165			

KM# 300 100 DOLLARS Weight: 15.0000 g. **Composition:** 0.9999 Gold .4822 oz. AGW **Subject:** Year of the Mouse **Obverse:** Queen's portrait right **Reverse:** Mickey Mouse sailboarding

Date	F	VF	XF	Unc	BU
1996 Proof	—	Value: 350			

KM# 293 100 DOLLARS Weight: 7.7800 g. **Composition:** 0.9990 Gold .2501 oz. AGW **Obverse:** Queen's portrait right **Note:** Olympic National Park.

Date	F	VF	XF	Unc	BU
1996 Proof	—	Value: 165			

KM# 388 100 DOLLARS Weight: 7.7800 g. **Composition:** 0.9990 Gold 0.2499 oz. AGW **Subject:** Yellowstone National Park **Obverse:** Queen's portrait **Reverse:** Bear on tree branch **Edge:** Reeded **Size:** 22 mm.

Date	F	VF	XF	Unc	BU
1996	—	Value: 165			

KM# 22 200 DOLLARS Weight: 16.6000 g. **Composition:** 0.9000 Gold .4803 oz. AGW **Subject:** Bicentennial - Discovery of Hawaii by Capt. James Cook **Obverse:** Queen's portrait right

Date	Mintage	F	VF	XF	Unc	BU
1978FM (M)	26	—	—	—	600	—
1978FM (U)	621	—	—	—	275	—
1978FM Proof	3,216	Value: 225				

KM# 26 200 DOLLARS Weight: 16.6000 g. **Composition:** 0.9000 Gold .4803 oz. AGW **Subject:** Legacy of Capt. James Cook **Obverse:** Queen's portrait right

Date	Mintage	F	VF	XF	Unc	BU
1979FM (U)	271	—	—	—	290	—
1979FM Proof	1,939	Value: 275				

KM# 29 200 DOLLARS Weight: 15.9800 g. **Composition:** 0.9170 Gold .4712 oz. AGW **Subject:** International Year of the Scout **Obverse:** Queen's portrait right

Date	F	VF	XF	Unc	BU
1983 Proof	—	Value: 450			

KM# 251 200 DOLLARS Weight: 15.5520 g. **Composition:** 0.9990 Platinum .2916 oz. APW **Obverse:** Queen's portrait right **Reverse:** Wrestling

Date	Mintage	F	VF	XF	Unc	BU
1995 Proof	1,000	Value: 300				

KM# 23 250 DOLLARS Weight: 17.9000 g. **Composition:** 0.9000 Gold .5180 oz. AGW **Subject:** 250th Anniversary - Birth of James Cook **Obverse:** Queen's portrait right

Date	Mintage	F	VF	XF	Unc	BU
1978FM (M)	25	—	—	—	600	—
1978FM (U)	200	—	—	—	275	—
1978FM Proof	1,757	Value: 250				

KM# 50 250 DOLLARS **Weight:** 7.7750 g. **Composition:** 0.9990 Gold .2500 oz. AGW **Subject:** 500 Years of America **Obverse:** Queen's portrait right **Reverse:** Cameos of Captain James Cook and Benjamin Franklin flanking a sailing ship

Date	Mintage	F	VF	XF	Unc	BU
1989 Proof	3,000	Value: 225				

KM# 51 250 DOLLARS **Weight:** 7.7750 g. **Composition:** 0.9990 Gold .2500 oz. AGW **Subject:** 500 Years of America **Obverse:** Queen's portrait right **Reverse:** Amerigo Vespucci

Date	Mintage	F	VF	XF	Unc	BU
1990 Proof	Est. 3,000	Value: 225				

KM# 82 250 DOLLARS **Weight:** 9.6000 g. **Composition:** 0.9000 Gold .2778 oz. AGW **Subject:** Save the Children **Obverse:** Queen's portrait right

Date	Mintage	F	VF	XF	Unc	BU
1990 Proof	3,000	Value: 265				

KM# 71 250 DOLLARS **Weight:** 7.7750 g. **Composition:** 0.9990 Gold .2500 oz. AGW **Subject:** 1992 Olympics **Obverse:** Queen's portrait right **Reverse:** Torch

Date	Mintage	F	VF	XF	Unc	BU
1991 Proof	Est. 5,000	Value: 225				

KM# 295 250 DOLLARS **Weight:** 31.1035 g. **Composition:** 0.9990 Gold 1.0000 oz. AGW **Subject:** Olympic National Park **Obverse:** Queen's portrait right **Reverse:** Multicolored bald eagle in flight

Date	Mintage	F	VF	XF	Unc	BU
1996 Proof	1,000	Value: 525				

KM# 296 250 DOLLARS **Weight:** 31.1035 g. **Composition:** 0.9990 Gold 1.0000 oz. AGW **Subject:** Yellowstone National Park **Obverse:** Queen's portrait right **Reverse:** Multicolored grizzly bear and cub

Date	Mintage	F	VF	XF	Unc	BU
1996 Proof	1,000	Value: 525				

KM# 313 500 DOLLARS **Weight:** 14.7400 g. **Composition:** 0.9990 Platinum .4734 oz. APW **Obverse:** Queen's portrait right **Reverse:** Marco Polo, oriental building in background

Date	Mintage	F	VF	XF	Unc	BU
1995 Proof	Est. 1,000	Value: 500				

KM# 389 500 DOLLARS **Weight:** 1723.1259 g. **Composition:** 0.9990 Silver 55.3443 oz. ASW **Subject:** Moby Dick **Obverse:** Queen's portrait **Reverse:** Whale jumping over a six-man row boat **Edge:** Plain **Size:** 115.2 mm.

Date		F	VF	XF	Unc	BU
2001 Proof	—	Value: 1,000				

PIEFORTS

KM#	Date	Mintage	Identification	Mkt Val
P1	1985	250	Dollar. 0.9250 Silver.	200
P2	1986	500	Dollar. 0.9250 Silver.	45.00
P3	1986	500	Dollar. 0.9250 Silver.	45.00

TRIAL STRIKES

KM#	Date	Mintage	Identification	Mkt Val
TS1	ND	—	20 Cents. Copper Nickel. KM#14. Reverse of KM#14	—

MINT SETS

KM#	Date	Mintage	Identification	Issue Price	Mkt Val
MS1	1972 (7)	11,045	KM1-5, 6.1, 7	7.50	5.00
MS2	1973 (9)	3,652	KM1-5, 6.1, 7, 9, 10	52.50	40.00
MS3	1973 (7)	3,023	KM1-5, 6.1, 7	10.00	8.00
MS4	1973 (2)	2,348	KM9, 10	45.00	35.00
MS5	1974 (9)	913	KM1-5, 6.1, 7. 9. 10	5,250	50.00
MS6	1974 (7)	2,087	KM1-5, 6.1, 7	10.00	6.00
MS7	1974 (2)	587	KM9, 10	45.00	45.00
MS8	1975 (7)	2,251	KM1-5, 6.1, 7	10.00	6.00
MS9	1976 (8)	1,066	KM1-4, 6.1,7, 14, 15	20.00	25.00
MS10	1977 (8)	1,171	KM1-4, 6.1, 7, 14, 17	20.00	25.00
MS11	1978 (8)	767	KM1a-4a, 6.2, 7a, 14a, 20	20.00	30.00
MS12	1979 (8)	500	KM1-3, 4b, 6.3 7, 14, 24	—	30.00
MS13	1981 (7)	1,100	KM1b-3b, 4c, 6.4, 7b, 14b	—	1,500
MS14	1983	—	KM1-5, 6.1, 7	—	6.00
MS15	1987 (7)	—	KM33-39	—	15.00
MS16	1988 (7)	—	KM33-35, 37-39, 41	—	16.00
MS17	1992 (7)	—	KM33-35, 37-39, 41	—	16.00

PROOF SETS

KM#	Date	Mintage	Identification	Issue Price	Mkt Val
PS1	1972 (7)	17,101	KM1-5, 6.1, 7	20.00	9.00
PS2	1973 (9)	7,395	KM1-5, 6.1, 7, 9-10	89.50	45.00
PS3	1973 (7)	5,136	KM1-5, 6.1, 7	29.50	10.00
PS4	1973 (2)	4,754	KM9-10	60.00	35.00
PS5	1974 (9)	4,444	KM1-5, 6.1, 7, 9-10	95.00	50.00
PS6	1974 (7)	5,300	KM1-5, 6.1, 7	32.50	10.00
PS7	1974 (2)	2,856	KM9-10	65.00	35.00
PS8	1975 (7)	21,290	KM-15, 6.1, 7	31.50	10.00
PS9	1976 (8)	17,658	KM1-4, 6.1, 7, 14-15	40.00	22.50
PS10	1977 (8)	5,986	KM1-4, 6.1, 7, 14, 17	42.00	25.00
PS11	1978 (8)	6,287	KM1a-4a, 6.2, 7a, 14a, 20	42.00	25.00
PS12	1979 (8)	4,058	KM1-3,4b, 6.3, 7, 14, 24	44.00	25.00
PS13	1981 (7)	9,205	KM1b-3b, 4c, 6.4, 7b, 14b	39.50	12.50
PS14	1983 (7)	10,000	KM1-5, 6.1, 7	29.95	10.00
PS15	1987 (7)	—	KM33-39	—	32.50
PS16	1988 (7)	—	KM33-35, 37-39, 41	—	32.50
PS17	1991 (12)	1,000	KM93, 95, 118-120, 122-128	—	300
PS18	1992 (7)	—	KM33-35, 37-39, 41	—	32.50
PS19	1994 (7)	200	KM33-35, 37-39, 41	—	37.50
PS20	1996 (3)	—	KM298-300	—	600
PS21	1996 (6)	—	KM284, 286, 288, 292, 294, 296	—	935
PS22	1998 (5)	4,000	KM314-318	185	225
PS23	1999 (3)	—	KM338-340	98.00	110
PS24	1999 (5)	4,000	KM361-365	122	225

PROOF-LIKE SETS (PL)

KM#	Date	Mintage	Identification	Issue Price	Mkt Val
PLS1	1990 (5)	—	KM74-78	325	350

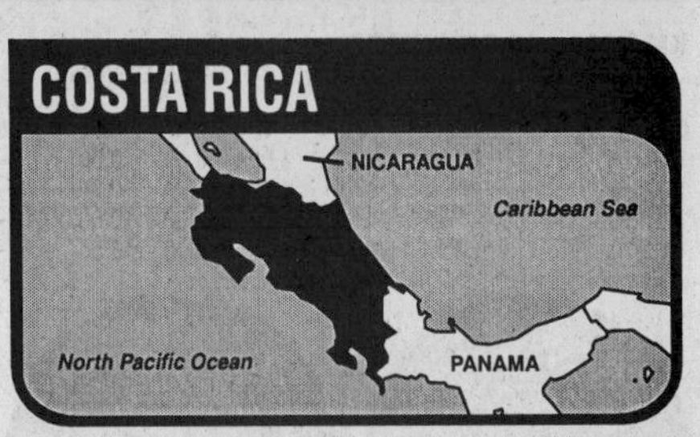

The Republic of Costa Rica, located in southern Central America between Nicaragua and Panama, has an area of 19,730 sq. mi. (51,100 sq. km.) and a population of 3.4 million. Capital: San Jose. Agriculture predominates; tourism and coffee, bananas, beef and sugar contribute heavily to the country's export earnings.

Costa Rica was discovered by Christopher Columbus in 1502, during his last voyage to the New World, and was a colony of Spain from 1522 until independence in 1821. Columbus named the territory Nueva Cartago; the name Costa Rica wasn't generally applied until 1540. Bartholomew Columbus attempted the first settlement but was driven off by Indian attacks and the country wasn't subdued until 1530. After centuries, as part of the Spanish Captaincy-General of Guatemala, Costa Rica was absorbed into the Mexican Empire of Augustin de Iturbide from 1821-1823. From 1823 to 1848, it was a constituent state of the Central American Republic (q.v.). Established as a republic in 1848, Costa Rica adopted democratic reforms in the 1870's and 80's. Today, Costa Rica remains a model of orderly democracy in Latin America, although, like most of the hemisphere - its economy is in stress.

NOTE: Also see Central American Republic.

MINT MARKS

CR - San Jose 1825-1947
HEATON - Heaton, Birmingham, England, 1889-93
BIRMm - Heaton, Birmingham, England, 1889-93
(P) – Philadelphia, 1905-1961
(L) – London, 1937, 1948

ISSUING BANK INITIALS - MINTS

BCCR - Philadelphia 1951-1958,1961
BICR - Philadelphia 1935
BNCR - London 1937,1948
BNCR - San Jose 1942-1947
GCR - Philadelphia 1905-1908,1929
GCR - San Jose 1917-1941

ASSAYERS INITIALS

MM – Miguel Mora, 1842
JB – Juan Barth, 1847-1864
GW - Guillermo Witting, 1854-1890
CB – Carlos Blanco, 1889
CY – Carlos Iglesias, 1902
JCV – Jesus Cubero Vargas, 1903

MONETARY SYSTEM

8 Reales = 1 Peso
16 Pesos = 8 Escudos = 1 Onza

REPUBLIC

REFORM COINAGE

1897, 100 Centimos = 1 Colon

KM# 144 2 CENTIMOS **Weight:** 1.0000 g. **Composition:** Copper-Nickel **Edge:** Plain

Date	Mintage	F	VF	XF	Unc	BU
1903	360,000	0.50	1.00	2.25	5.00	—

KM# 145 5 CENTIMOS **Weight:** 1.0000 g. **Composition:** 0.9000 Silver .0289 oz. ASW **Obverse:** Ornate arms **Edge:** Reeded

Date	Mintage	F	VF	XF	Unc	BU
1905(P)	500,000	BV	0.75	2.00	6.00	—
1910(P)	400,000	BV	0.75	2.00	7.50	—
1912(P)	540,000	BV	0.75	1.50	5.00	—
1914(P)	510,000	BV	0.75	1.50	5.50	—

KM# 146 10 CENTIMOS **Weight:** 2.0000 g. **Composition:** 0.9000 Silver .0578 oz. ASW **Obverse:** Ornate arms

Date	Mintage	F	VF	XF	Unc	BU
1905(P)	400,000	0.55	1.00	3.00	10.00	—
1910(P)	400,000	0.55	1.00	3.00	10.00	—
1912(P)	270,000	0.55	1.00	3.00	10.00	—
1914(P)	150,000	0.75	1.25	4.00	13.50	—

KM# 143 50 CENTIMOS **Weight:** 10.0000 g. **Composition:** 0.9000 Silver .2893 oz. ASW **Obverse:** Ornate arms

Date	Mintage	F	VF	XF	Unc	BU
1902 CY	120,000	15.00	27.50	45.00	110	—
1903 JCV	380,000	10.00	18.00	32.50	75.00	—

Note: Of the total minatge for this date, San Jose Mint struck 132,140 in 1903 and Philadelphia Mint struck an additional 250,000 in 1904 with the 1903 date. The two strikings are indistinguishable.

Date	Mintage	F	VF	XF	Unc	BU
1914(P) GCR	200,000	300	500	850	1,200	—

Note: Most coins dated 1914 were later counterstamped UN COLON/ 1923. See KM#164

KM# 139 2 COLONES **Weight:** 1.5560 g. **Composition:** 0.9000 Gold .0456 oz. AGW **Obverse:** Ornate arms **Reverse:** Bust of Christopher Colombus

Date	Mintage	F	VF	XF	Unc	BU
1897 Proof	500	Value: 750				
1915(P)	5,000	40.00	60.00	75.00	100	—
1916(P)	5,000	40.00	60.00	75.00	100	—
1921(P)	3,000	50.00	75.00	100	140	—
1922(P)	13,000	30.00	40.00	60.00	80.00	—
1926(P)	15,000	30.00	40.00	60.00	80.00	—
1928(P)	25,000	25.00	37.50	60.00	80.00	—

REFORM COINAGE

1917, 100 Centavos = 1 Colon

KM# 147 5 CENTAVOS **Weight:** 1.0000 g. **Composition:** Brass **Obverse:** Ornate arms **Edge:** Plain

Date	Mintage	F	VF	XF	Unc	BU
1917	400,000	2.00	4.50	12.50	35.00	—
1918	1,000,000	1.25	4.00	10.00	28.50	—
1919	500,000	2.00	4.50	11.00	32.50	—

KM# 148 10 CENTAVOS **Weight:** 2.0000 g. **Composition:** 0.5000 Silver .0321 oz. ASW **Obverse:** Ornate arms **Edge:** Reeded

Date	Mintage	F	VF	XF	Unc	BU
1917	100,000	1.00	2.00	3.00	6.50	—

KM# 149.1 10 CENTAVOS **Weight:** 2.0000 g. **Composition:** Brass **Obverse:** Ornate arms **Reverse:** GCR at lower right

Date	Mintage	F	VF	XF	Unc	BU
1917 GCR	500,000	1.50	3.50	10.00	32.50	—

KM# 149.2 10 CENTAVOS **Weight:** 2.0000 g. **Composition:** Brass **Obverse:** Ornate arms **Reverse:** GCR at bottom center

Date	Mintage	F	VF	XF	Unc	BU
1917 GCR	Inc. above	2.75	6.00	15.00	38.50	—
1918 GCR	900,000	1.25	3.00	8.00	27.50	—
1919 GCR	250,000	1.75	5.00	13.50	35.00	—

KM# 150 50 CENTAVOS **Weight:** 10.0000 g. **Composition:** 0.5000 Silver .1607 oz. ASW **Obverse:** Ornate arms **Note:** All but 10 examples of the 1917 issue and the complete 1918 mintage were counterstamped UN COLON/1923. See KM#165.

Date	Mintage	F	VF	XF	Unc	BU
1917 GCR	9,400	—	—	800	1,000	—
1918 GCR	30,000	—	—	—	—	—

REFORM COINAGE

1920, 100 Centimos = 1 Colon

KM# 151 5 CENTIMOS **Weight:** 1.0000 g. **Composition:** Brass **Edge:** Plain

Date	Mintage	F	VF	XF	Unc	BU
1920	500,000	1.25	4.00	12.50	25.00	—
1921	500,000	1.25	4.00	10.00	27.50	—
1922	500,000	1.75	5.00	13.50	35.00	—
1936	1,500,000	0.40	0.75	1.50	6.50	—
1938	1,000,000	0.50	1.25	3.25	10.00	—
1940	1,300,000	0.40	0.75	1.50	7.00	—
1941	1,000,000	0.50	1.25	3.50	10.00	—

KM# 169 5 CENTIMOS **Weight:** 1.0000 g. **Composition:** Bronze **Obverse:** Ornate arms

Date	Mintage	F	VF	XF	Unc	BU
1929	1,500,000	0.60	1.25	3.25	7.50	—

KM# 178 5 CENTIMOS **Weight:** 1.0000 g. **Composition:** Copper-Nickel **Obverse:** Ornate arms

Date	Mintage	F	VF	XF	Unc	BU
1942	274,000	0.55	1.25	3.50	10.00	—

Note: Struck over 2 Centimos, KM#144. Overstrikes with clear evidence of the undertype command a 10-15% premium

KM# 179 5 CENTIMOS **Composition:** Brass **Obverse:** Ornate arms

Date	Mintage	F	VF	XF	Unc	BU
1942	1,730,000	0.20	0.60	1.25	4.50	—
1942 Prooflike	—	Value: 22.50				
1943	1,000,000	0.20	0.60	2.00	6.00	—
1946	1,000,000	0.35	0.90	2.25	6.50	—
1946 Proof	—	Value: 60.00				
1947	3,000,000	0.15	0.45	1.00	3.50	—

KM# A184 (KM184.1) 5 CENTIMOS **Weight:** 1.0000 g. **Composition:** Copper-Nickel **Obverse:** Ornate arms **Reverse:** Large lettering B.C. - C.R. divided at bottom

Date	Mintage	F	VF	XF	Unc	BU
1951(P)	3,000,000	0.35	0.75	1.50	4.50	—
1951(P)	3,000,000	0.35	0.75	1.50	4.50	—

KM# 184.1 (KM184.2) 5 CENTIMOS **Weight:** 1.0000 g. **Composition:** Copper-Nickel **Obverse:** Ornate arms **Reverse:** Small lettering B.C.C.R. not divided

Date	Mintage	F	VF	XF	Unc	BU
1951(P)	7,000,000	0.10	0.15	0.40	1.00	—
1951(P)	7,000,000	0.10	0.15	0.40	1.00	—

KM# 184.1a (KM184.2a) 5 CENTIMOS **Weight:** 0.8750 g. **Composition:** Stainless Steel **Obverse:** Ornate arms

Date	Mintage	F	VF	XF	Unc	BU
1953(P)	9,040,000	—	—	0.10	0.25	—
1953(P)	9,040,000	—	—	0.10	0.25	—
1958(P)	19,940,000	—	—	0.10	0.15	—

Note: Struck in 1959

Date	Mintage	F	VF	XF	Unc	BU
1958(P)	19,940,000	—	—	0.10	0.15	—

Note: Struck in 1959

Date	Mintage	F	VF	XF	Unc	BU
1967	6,020,000	—	—	0.10	0.20	—
1967	6,020,000	—	—	0.10	0.20	—

KM# 184.2 (KM184.3) 5 CENTIMOS **Composition:** Copper-Nickel **Obverse:** Small ships, 7 stars on arms, no flag on near ship **Note:** Varieties exist for shields of each date.

Date	Mintage	F	VF	XF	Unc	BU
1969	20,000,000	—	—	0.10	0.15	—
1969	20,000,000	—	—	0.10	0.15	—
1976	—	—	—	0.10	0.15	—
1976	—	—	—	0.10	0.15	—
1976 Proof	—	Value: 0.75				
1976 Proof	—	Value: 0.75				
1978	7,520,000	—	—	0.10	0.15	—
1978	7,520,000	—	—	0.10	0.15	—

KM# 184.3 (KM184.4) 5 CENTIMOS **Composition:** Copper-Nickel **Obverse:** Large ships, 7 stars on arms, flag on near ship **Note:** Dies vary for each date.

Date	Mintage	F	VF	XF	Unc	BU
1972	12,550,000	—	—	0.10	0.15	—
1972	12,550,000	—	—	0.10	0.15	—
1973	20,000,000	—	—	0.10	0.15	—
1973	20,000,000	—	—	0.10	0.15	—
1976	33,270,000	—	—	0.10	0.15	—
1976	33,270,000	—	—	0.10	0.15	—

KM# 184.3a (KM184.4a) 5 CENTIMOS **Composition:** Brass **Obverse:** Large date, flag, no sun

Date	Mintage	F	VF	XF	Unc	BU
1979	3,060,000	—	—	0.10	0.15	—
1979	3,060,000	—	—	0.10	0.15	—

KM# 152 10 CENTIMOS **Composition:** Brass **Obverse:** Ornate arms **Reverse:** GCR at lower right

Date	Mintage	F	VF	XF	Unc	BU
1920 GCR	850,000	0.75	2.00	6.50	28.50	—
1921 GCR	750,000	1.00	2.50	8.00	35.00	—
1922 GCR	750,000	0.75	2.00	6.50	27.50	—

KM# 170 10 CENTIMOS **Weight:** 2.0000 g. **Composition:** Bronze **Obverse:** Ornate arms **Reverse:** GCR at bottom

Date	Mintage	F	VF	XF	Unc	BU
1929(P) GCR	500,000	1.25	3.00	7.25	20.00	—

KM# 174 10 CENTIMOS **Composition:** Brass **Obverse:** Ornate arms

Date	Mintage	F	VF	XF	Unc	BU
1936	750,000	0.35	0.65	2.50	8.50	—
1941	500,000	0.50	1.50	4.25	15.00	—

KM# 180 10 CENTIMOS **Composition:** Brass **Obverse:** Ornate arms **Reverse:** B.N. - C.R. divided at bottom

Date	Mintage	F	VF	XF	Unc	BU
1942	1,000,000	0.30	0.60	2.00	6.50	—
1943	500,000	0.35	0.75	3.50	9.00	—
1946	500,000	0.50	1.00	3.50	10.00	—
1947	1,500,000	0.25	0.50	1.50	5.50	—

Note: Edge varieties exist on 1947 strikes

KM# 185.1 10 CENTIMOS **Weight:** 2.0000 g. **Composition:** Copper-Nickel **Obverse:** Small ships, 5 stars in shield **Reverse:** B.C.C.R. at bottom

Date	Mintage	F	VF	XF	Unc	BU
1951(P)	2,500,000	0.10	0.20	0.70	1.25	—

Note: Struck in 1952

KM# 185.1a 10 CENTIMOS **Weight:** 1.7500 g. **Composition:** Stainless Steel **Obverse:** Ornate arms

Date	Mintage	F	VF	XF	Unc	BU
1953(P)	5,290,000	—	—	0.10	0.75	—
1958(P)	10,470,000	—	—	0.10	0.25	—

Note: Struck in 1959

Date	Mintage	F	VF	XF	Unc	BU
1967	5,500,000	—	—	0.10	0.25	—

KM# 185.2 10 CENTIMOS **Composition:** Copper-Nickel **Obverse:** Small ships, 7 stars in field **Reverse:** Small 10 **Note:** Dies vary for each date

Date	Mintage	F	VF	XF	Unc	BU
1969	10,000,000	—	—	0.10	0.15	—
1976	40,000,000	—	—	0.10	0.15	—
1976 Proof	—	Value: 0.75				

KM# 185.3 10 CENTIMOS **Composition:** Copper-Nickel **Obverse:** Large ships, 7 stars in field **Reverse:** Large 10

Date	Mintage	F	VF	XF	Unc	BU
1972	20,000,000	—	—	0.10	0.15	—
1975	5,000,000	—	—	0.10	0.15	—

KM# 185.2b 10 CENTIMOS **Composition:** Nickel Clad Steel

Date	Mintage	F	VF	XF	Unc	BU
1979	10,000,000	—	—	0.10	0.15	—

KM# 185.2a 10 CENTIMOS **Composition:** Aluminum **Obverse:** Small ships, 7 stars in field

Date	Mintage	F	VF	XF	Unc	BU
1982	40,000,000	—	—	0.10	0.15	—

KM# 168 25 CENTIMOS **Weight:** 3.4500 g. **Composition:** 0.6500 Silver .0721 oz. ASW **Obverse:** Ornate arms **Edge:** Reeded

Date	Mintage	F	VF	XF	Unc	BU
1924	1,340,000	1.25	2.25	5.00	15.00	—

Note: Typical examples of KM#168 are weak at centers, fully struck up XF and Unc pieces command a 50% premium

KM# 171 25 CENTIMOS **Weight:** 3.4500 g. **Composition:** Copper-Nickel **Obverse:** Ornate arms **Reverse:** BICR at bottom **Edge:** Incuse lettered

Date	Mintage	F	VF	XF	Unc	BU
1935(P)	1,200,000	0.25	0.75	2.50	15.00	—

KM# 175 25 CENTIMOS **Composition:** Copper-Nickel **Obverse:** Ornate arms **Reverse:** B.N.C.R. at bottom

Date	Mintage	F	VF	XF	Unc	BU
1937(L)	1,600,000	0.25	0.75	1.75	8.00	—
1937(L) Proof	—	Value: 100				
1948(L)	9,200,000	0.10	0.20	0.40	1.25	—
1948(L) Proof	—	—	—	—	—	—

KM# 181 25 CENTIMOS **Composition:** Yellow Brass **Obverse:** Ornate arms **Reverse:** B.N. * C.R. at bottom **Edge:** Reeded

Date	Mintage	F	VF	XF	Unc	BU
1944	800,000	0.50	1.25	3.50	14.50	—
1945	1,200,000	0.50	1.00	2.75	12.50	—
1946	1,200,000	0.50	1.00	2.50	10.00	—

KM# 181a 25 CENTIMOS **Composition:** Red Brass **Edge:** Reeded

Date	F	VF	XF	Unc	BU
1945	1.00	2.00	4.00	20.00	—

KM# 188.1 25 CENTIMOS **Composition:** Copper-Nickel **Obverse:** Small ships, 7 stars on arms **Reverse:** B.C.C.R. at bottom **Note:** Dies vary for each date.

Date	Mintage	F	VF	XF	Unc	BU
1967	4,000,000	—	—	0.10	0.50	—
1969	4,000,000	—	—	0.10	0.50	—
1974	—	—	—	0.10	0.30	—
1976	12,000,000	—	—	0.10	0.30	—
1978	—	—	—	0.10	0.30	—

KM# 188.1a 25 CENTIMOS **Composition:** Nickel Clad Steel **Obverse:** Small ships **Note:** Beaded rims.

Date	Mintage	F	VF	XF	Unc	BU
1980	30,000,000	—	—	0.10	0.25	—

KM# 188.1b 25 CENTIMOS **Composition:** Aluminum **Edge:** Plain

Date	Mintage	F	VF	XF	Unc	BU
1982	30,000,000	—	—	0.10	0.25	—

KM# 188.2 25 CENTIMOS **Composition:** Aluminum **Obverse:** Large ships, 7 stars on arms, flag

Date	Mintage	F	VF	XF	Unc	BU
1972	8,000,000	—	—	0.10	0.25	—

KM# 188.3 25 CENTIMOS **Composition:** Aluminum **Edge:** Reeded **Size:** 17 mm. **Note:** Reduced size. Dies vary for each date.

Date	F	VF	XF	Unc	BU
1983	—	—	0.10	0.20	—
1986	—	—	0.10	0.20	—
1989	—	—	0.10	0.20	—

KM# 172 50 CENTIMOS **Weight:** 6.2500 g. **Composition:** Copper-Nickel **Obverse:** Ornate arms **Reverse:** B.I.C.R. at bottom

Date	Mintage	F	VF	XF	Unc	BU
1935(P)	700,000	0.50	1.25	5.00	22.50	—

KM# 176 50 CENTIMOS **Composition:** Copper-Nickel **Obverse:** Ornate arms **Reverse:** B.N.C.R. at bottom

Date	Mintage	F	VF	XF	Unc	BU
1937(L)	600,000	0.30	1.00	3.00	14.00	—
1937(L) Proof	—	Value: 125				

KM# 182 50 CENTIMOS **Composition:** Copper-Nickel **Obverse:** Ornate arms

Date	Mintage	F	VF	XF	Unc	BU
1948(L)	4,000,000	0.15	0.25	0.50	2.00	—
1948(L) Proof	—	—	—	—	—	—

KM# 189.1 50 CENTIMOS **Composition:** Copper-Nickel **Obverse:** Small ships, 7 stars in shield, small 50

Date	Mintage	F	VF	XF	Unc	BU
1965	1,000,000	—	0.10	0.25	1.00	—

KM# 189.3 50 CENTIMOS **Composition:** Copper-Nickel **Reverse:** Large 50 and B.C.C.R **Note:** Dies vary for each date.

Date	Mintage	F	VF	XF	Unc	BU
1968	2,000,000	—	0.10	0.15	0.50	—
1970	4,000,000	—	0.10	0.15	0.35	—
1976	6,000,000	—	0.10	0.15	0.35	—
1976 Proof	—	Value: 1.50				
1978	—	—	0.10	0.15	0.35	—

KM# 189.2 50 CENTIMOS **Composition:** Copper-Nickel **Obverse:** Large ships, 7 stars in shield

Date	Mintage	F	VF	XF	Unc	BU
1972 Small date	Inc. above	—	0.10	0.15	0.35	—
1975 Large date	524,000	—	0.10	0.15	0.35	—
1975 Small date	Inc. above	—	0.10	0.15	0.35	—
1972 Large date	4,000,000	—	0.10	0.15	0.35	—

KM# 209.1 50 CENTIMOS **Composition:** Stainless Steel **Obverse:** Large ships, letters incuse on ribbon

Date	Mintage	F	VF	XF	Unc	BU
1982	12,000,000	—	—	0.10	0.25	—
1983	—	—	—	0.10	0.25	—
1990	—	—	—	0.10	0.25	—

KM# 209.2 50 CENTIMOS **Composition:** Stainless Steel **Obverse:** Small ships, letters in relief on ribbon

Date	F	VF	XF	Unc	BU
1984	—	—	0.10	0.25	—

KM# 173 COLON **Weight:** 10.0000 g. **Composition:** Copper-Nickel **Obverse:** Ornate arms **Reverse:** B.I.C.R at bottom **Edge:** Incuse BICR; plain **Note:** Beaded rims.

Date	Mintage	F	VF	XF	Unc	BU
1935(P)	350,000	0.75	2.00	7.00	32.50	—

Note: Struck in 1936

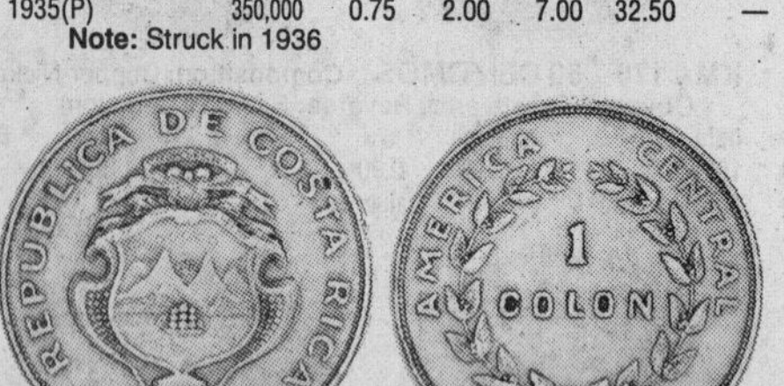

KM# 177 COLON **Composition:** Copper-Nickel **Obverse:** Ornate arms **Reverse:** B.N.C.R. at bottom

Date	Mintage	F	VF	XF	Unc	BU
1937(L)	300,000	0.50	1.25	4.50	20.00	—
1937(L) Proof	—	Value: 150				
1948(L)	1,350,000	0.20	0.40	0.75	2.00	—
1948(L) Proof	—	—	—	—	—	—

KM# 186.1 COLON **Weight:** 8.6670 g. **Composition:** Stainless Steel **Obverse:** Small ships, 5 stars in shield

Date	Mintage	F	VF	XF	Unc	BU
1954(P)	987,000	0.20	0.35	1.00	7.50	—

KM# 186.1a COLON **Weight:** 10.0000 g. **Composition:** Copper-Nickel

Date	Mintage	F	VF	XF	Unc	BU
1961(P)	1,000,000	0.10	0.20	0.50	2.00	—

KM# 186.2 COLON **Composition:** Copper-Nickel **Obverse:** Small ships, 7 stars in shield **Reverse:** Small 1

Date	Mintage	F	VF	XF	Unc	BU
1965	1,000,000	0.10	0.20	0.40	1.00	—
1968	2,000,000	0.10	0.20	0.30	0.65	—
1970	2,000,000	0.10	0.20	0.30	0.65	—
1974	—	0.10	0.20	0.30	0.65	—
1978	—	0.10	0.20	0.30	0.65	—

KM# 186.3 COLON **Composition:** Copper-Nickel **Obverse:** Large ships, 7 stars in shield

Date	Mintage	F	VF	XF	Unc	BU
1972	2,000,000	0.10	0.20	0.30	0.65	—
1975	1,028,000	0.10	0.20	0.30	0.65	—

KM# 186.4 COLON **Composition:** Copper-Nickel **Obverse:** Small ships, 7 stars in shield **Reverse:** Large 1 **Note:** Dies vary for each date.

Date	Mintage	F	VF	XF	Unc	BU
1976	12,000,000	0.10	0.20	0.30	0.65	—
1976 Proof	—	Value: 2.50				
1977	22,000,000	0.10	0.20	0.30	0.65	—

KM# 210.1 COLON **Composition:** Stainless Steel **Obverse:** Large ships, letters incuse on ribbon

Date	Mintage	F	VF	XF	Unc	BU
1982	12,000,000	—	—	0.15	0.35	—
1983	—	—	—	0.15	0.35	—
1984	—	—	—	0.15	0.35	—
1991	—	—	—	0.15	0.35	—

KM# 210.2 COLON **Composition:** Stainless Steel **Obverse:** Small ships, letters in relief on ribbon

Date	F	VF	XF	Unc	BU
1984	—	—	0.15	0.35	—
1989	—	—	0.15	0.35	—
1993	—	—	0.15	0.35	—
1994	—	—	0.15	0.35	—

KM# 233 COLON **Composition:** Brass **Obverse:** National arms **Reverse:** Denomination

Date	F	VF	XF	Unc	BU
1998	—	—	0.10	0.35	—

KM# 183 2 COLONES **Composition:** Copper-Nickel **Obverse:** Ornate arms

Date	Mintage	F	VF	XF	Unc	BU
1948(L)	1,380,000	0.50	0.75	1.25	3.00	—
1948(L) Proof	—	—	—	—	—	—

KM# 187.1 2 COLONES **Weight:** 12.0000 g. **Composition:** Stainless Steel **Obverse:** Ornate arms with small ships, 5 stars in shield

Date	Mintage	F	VF	XF	Unc	BU
1954(P)	1,028,000	0.25	0.50	2.00	10.00	—

KM# 187.1a 2 COLONES **Composition:** Copper-Nickel

Date	Mintage	F	VF	XF	Unc	BU
1961(P)	1,000,000	0.15	0.30	0.50	1.25	—

KM# 187.2 2 COLONES **Composition:** Copper-Nickel **Obverse:** Small ships, 7 stars in shield **Note:** Dies vary for each date.

Date	Mintage	F	VF	XF	Unc	BU
1968	2,000,000	0.15	0.30	0.45	1.00	—
1970	1,000,000	0.15	0.30	0.45	1.25	—
1972	2,000,000	0.15	0.30	0.45	1.00	—
1976	—	0.15	0.30	0.45	1.00	—
1978	—	0.15	0.30	0.45	1.00	—

KM# 190 2 COLONES **Weight:** 4.3000 g. **Composition:** 0.9990 Silver .1381 oz. ASW **Subject:** 20th Anniversary of the Central Bank

Date	Mintage	F	VF	XF	Unc	BU
1970 Proof	5,157	Value: 15.00				

Note: Also exists with a small oval with 1000 inside above the S in COLONES

KM# 211.1 2 COLONES **Composition:** Stainless Steel **Obverse:** Large ships, letters incuse on ribbon

Date	Mintage	F	VF	XF	Unc	BU
1982	12,000,000	—	—	0.20	0.60	—
1983	—	—	—	0.20	0.60	—

KM# 211.2 2 COLONES **Composition:** Stainless Steel **Obverse:** Small ship, letters in relief on ribbon

Date	F	VF	XF	Unc	BU
1984	—	—	0.20	0.60	—

KM# 191 5 COLONES **Weight:** 10.7800 g. **Composition:** 0.9990 Silver .3463 oz. ASW **Subject:** 400th Year - The Founding of New Carthage **Reverse:** Raised 1000 hallmark in oval below "o" of "Cartago" **Edge:** Reeded

Date	Mintage	F	VF	XF	Unc	BU
1970 Proof	5,157	Value: 20.00				

KM# 203 5 COLONES **Composition:** Nickel **Subject:** 25th Anniversary of the Central Bank

Date	Mintage	F	VF	XF	Unc	BU
ND(1975)	2,000,000	—	0.15	0.35	1.25	—
ND(1975) Proof	5,000,000	Value: 2.00				

KM# 214.1 5 COLONES **Composition:** Stainless Steel **Obverse:** Small ship, letters in relief on ribbon

Date	F	VF	XF	Unc	BU
1983	—	0.10	0.25	0.75	—
1989	—	0.10	0.25	0.75	—
1993	—	0.10	0.25	0.75	—

KM# 214.2 5 COLONES **Composition:** Stainless Steel **Obverse:** Large ship, letters incuse on ribbon

Date	F	VF	XF	Unc	BU
1985	—	0.10	0.25	0.75	—

KM# 227 5 COLONES **Composition:** Brass Plated Steel **Obverse:** National arms **Reverse:** Denomination

Date	F	VF	XF	Unc	BU
1995	—	—	0.25	0.75	—
1997	—	—	0.25	0.75	—
1999	—	—	0.25	0.75	—

KM# 192 10 COLONES **Weight:** 21.7000 g. **Composition:** 0.9990 Silver .6976 oz. ASW **Subject:** Attempt of Unification of Middle America **Obverse:** Similar to 5 Colones, KM#191

Date	Mintage	F	VF	XF	Unc	BU
1970 Proof	5,157	Value: 28.00				

KM# 204 10 COLONES **Composition:** Nickel **Subject:** 25th Anniversary of the Central Bank

Date	Mintage	F	VF	XF	Unc	BU
ND(1975)	500,000	0.25	0.50	1.00	2.00	—
ND(1975) Proof	5,000	Value: 4.00				

KM# 215.1 10 COLONES **Composition:** Stainless Steel **Obverse:** Small ship, letters in relief on ribbon

Date	F	VF	XF	Unc	BU
1983	—	0.20	0.35	1.25	—
1992	—	0.20	0.35	1.25	—

KM# 215.2 10 COLONES **Composition:** Stainless Steel **Obverse:** Large ship, letters incuse on ribbon

Date	F	VF	XF	Unc	BU
1985	—	0.20	0.35	1.25	—

KM# 228 10 COLONES **Composition:** Brass Plated Steel **Obverse:** National arms **Reverse:** Denomination

Date	F	VF	XF	Unc	BU
1995	—	—	0.35	1.25	—
1996	—	—	0.35	1.25	—
1997	—	—	0.35	1.25	—

KM# 193 20 COLONES **Weight:** 43.7000 g. **Composition:** 0.9990 Silver 1.4050 oz. ASW **Reverse:** Venus de Milo statue, raised 1000 hallmark in oval below "O" in "MILO"

Date	Mintage	F	VF	XF	Unc	BU
1970 Proof	7,500	Value: 40.00				

KM# 205 20 COLONES **Composition:** Nickel **Subject:** 25th Anniversary of the Central Bank **Reverse:** Flowers

Date	Mintage	F	VF	XF	Unc	BU
ND(1975)	250,000	0.50	1.00	2.00	4.00	—
ND(1975) Proof	5,000	Value: 9.00				

KM# 216.1 20 COLONES **Composition:** Stainless Steel **Obverse:** Letters in relief on ribbon

Date	F	VF	XF	Unc	BU
1983	—	0.35	0.65	1.75	—
1989	—	0.35	0.65	1.75	—
1994	—	0.35	0.65	1.75	—

KM# 216.2 20 COLONES **Composition:** Stainless Steel **Obverse:** Letters incuse on ribbon

Date	F	VF	XF	Unc	BU
1985	—	0.35	0.65	1.75	—
1994	—	0.35	0.65	1.75	—
1996	—	0.35	0.65	1.75	—

KM# 194 25 COLONES **Weight:** 53.9000 g. **Composition:** 0.9990 Silver 1.7312 oz. ASW **Subject:** 25 Years of Social Legislation **Obverse:** Similar to 5 Colones, KM#191 **Reverse:** "Materidad" Sculpture by F. Zuniga.

Date	Mintage	F	VF	XF	Unc	BU
1970 Proof	6,800	Value: 47.50				

KM# 229 25 COLONES **Composition:** Brass Plated Steel **Obverse:** National arms **Reverse:** Denomination

Date	F	VF	XF	Unc	BU
1995	—	—	—	2.50	—

KM# 195.1 50 COLONES **Weight:** 7.4500 g. **Composition:** 0.9000 Gold .2155 oz. AGW **Subject:** Inter-American Human Rights Convention

Date	Mintage	F	VF	XF	Unc	BU
1970 Proof	3,507	Value: 125				

KM# 195.2 50 COLONES **Weight:** 7.4500 g. **Composition:** 0.9000 Gold .2155 oz. AGW **Reverse:** "1 AR" countermark above fineness statement

Date	Mintage	F	VF	XF	Unc	BU
1970 Proof	Inc. above	Value: 150				

KM# 200 50 COLONES **Weight:** 25.5500 g. **Composition:** 0.5000 Silver .4107 oz. ASW **Subject:** Conservation **Reverse:** Green turtle

Date	Mintage	F	VF	XF	Unc	BU
1974	7,599	—	—	—	16.50	—

KM# 200a 50 COLONES **Weight:** 28.2800 g. **Composition:** 0.9250 Silver .8411 oz. ASW **Subject:** Conservation **Obv. Legend:** Green Turtle

Date	Mintage	F	VF	XF	Unc	BU
1974 Proof	11,000	Value: 24.00				

KM# 231 50 COLONES **Composition:** Brass **Obverse:** National arms **Reverse:** Denomination

Date	F	VF	XF	Unc	BU
1997	—	—	—	3.00	—
1999	—	—	—	3.00	—

KM# 196 100 COLONES **Weight:** 14.9000 g. **Composition:** 0.9000 Gold .4311 oz. AGW

Date	Mintage	F	VF	XF	Unc	BU
1970 Proof	3,507	Value: 245				

KM# 201 100 COLONES **Weight:** 32.1000 g. **Composition:** 0.5000 Silver .5160 oz. ASW **Subject:** Conservation **Obverse:** Similar to 1500 Colones, KM#202 **Reverse:** Manatee

Date	Mintage	F	VF	XF	Unc	BU
1974	7,599	—	—	—	22.50	—

KM# 201a 100 COLONES **Weight:** 35.0000 g. **Composition:** 0.9250 Silver 1.0409 oz. ASW **Subject:** Conservation **Reverse:** Manatee

Date	Mintage	F	VF	XF	Unc	BU
1974 Proof	11,000	Value: 30.00				

KM# 206 100 COLONES **Weight:** 35.0000 g. **Composition:** 0.9250 Silver 1.0409 oz. ASW **Subject:** International Year of the Child **Reverse:** Three birds in nest

Date	Mintage	F	VF	XF	Unc	BU
1979	9,500	—	—	—	10.00	—
1979 Proof	5,000	Value: 27.50				

KM# 224 100 COLONES **Composition:** Nickel **Reverse:** President Dr. Oscar Arias S.

Date	Mintage	F	VF	XF	Unc	BU
1987	25,000	—	—	—	7.50	—

KM# 230 100 COLONES **Composition:** Brass Plated Steel **Obverse:** National arms **Reverse:** Denomination

Date	F	VF	XF	Unc	BU
1995	—	—	—	4.50	—

KM# 230a 100 COLONES **Composition:** Brass

Date	F	VF	XF	Unc	BU
1997	—	—	—	4.50	—
1998	—	—	—	4.50	—
1999	—	—	—	4.50	—

KM# 197 200 COLONES **Weight:** 29.8000 g. **Composition:** 0.9000 Gold .8623 oz. AGW **Reverse:** Juan Santamaria and canon

Date	Mintage	F	VF	XF	Unc	BU
1970 Proof	3,507	Value: 500				

KM# 212 250 COLONES **Weight:** 30.3300 g. **Composition:** 0.9250 Silver .9020 oz. ASW **Subject:** Conservation **Reverse:** Jaguar head facing

Date	Mintage	F	VF	XF	Unc	BU
1982(P) FM Proof	1,109	Value: 95.00				

KM# 217 250 COLONES **Weight:** 30.3300 g. **Composition:** 0.9250 Silver .9020 oz. ASW **Reverse:** National flower

Date	Mintage	F	VF	XF	Unc	BU
1983(P) FM Proof	393	Value: 75.00				

KM# 207 300 COLONES **Weight:** 10.9700 g. **Composition:** 0.9250 Silver .3262 oz. ASW **Subject:** 125th Anniversary - Death of Juan Santamaria **Reverse:** Juan Santamaria standing with flag and rifle

Date	Mintage	F	VF	XF	Unc	BU
1981 Proof	10,000	Value: 12.50				

KM# 223 300 COLONES **Weight:** 10.9700 g. **Composition:** 0.9250 Silver .3262 oz. ASW **Subject:** 200th Anniversary - Founding of Alajuela

Date	F	VF	XF	Unc	BU
1981 Proof	—	Value: 12.50			

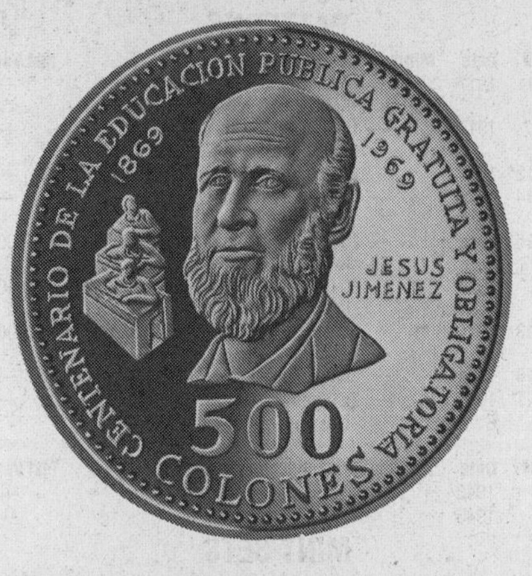

KM# 198 500 COLONES **Weight:** 74.5200 g. **Composition:** 0.9000 Gold 2.1565 oz. AGW **Subject:** 100th Anniversary of Public Education **Obverse:** Similar to 100 Colones, KM#196 **Reverse:** Jesus Jimenez and students at desks

Date	Mintage	F	VF	XF	Unc	BU
1970 Proof	3,507	Value: 1,200				

KM# 236 500 COLONES **Composition:** Brass **Subject:** 50 Years - Central Bank **Obverse:** National arms **Reverse:** Bank building

Date	Mintage	F	VF	XF	Unc	BU
2000	5,000	—	—	—	2.50	—

KM# 199 1000 COLONES **Weight:** 149.0400 g. **Composition:** 0.9000 Gold 4.3126 oz. AGW **Subject:** 150th Anniversary of Central American Independence **Obverse:** Similar to 100 Colones, KM#196

Date	Mintage	F	VF	XF	Unc	BU
1970 Proof	3,507	Value: 3,150				

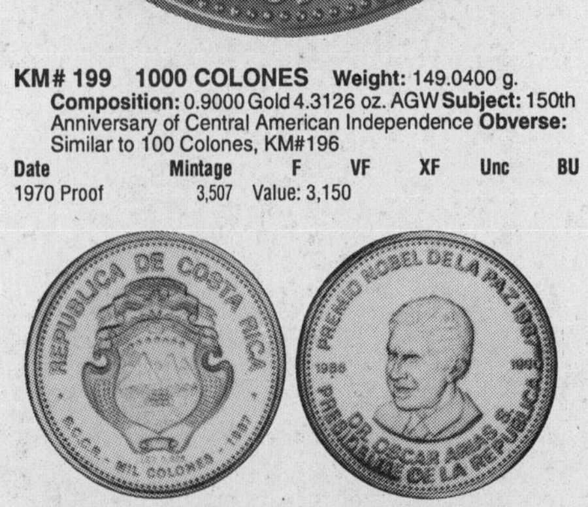

KM# 225 1000 COLONES **Weight:** 10.9700 g. **Composition:** 0.9250 Silver .3272 oz. ASW **Reverse:** President Dr. Oscar Arias S.

Date	Mintage	F	VF	XF	Unc	BU
1987	10,000	—	—	—	30.00	—

KM# 202 1500 COLONES **Weight:** 33.4370 g. **Composition:** 0.9000 Gold .9676 oz. AGW **Subject:** Conservation **Reverse:** Giant anteater

Date	Mintage	F	VF	XF	Unc	BU
1974	2,418	—	—	—	420	—
1974 Proof	726	Value: 650				

KM# 213 1500 COLONES **Weight:** 6.9800 g. **Composition:** 0.5000 Gold .1122 oz. AGW **Reverse:** Francisco Coronado and Christopher Columbus

Date	Mintage	F	VF	XF	Unc	BU
1982FM (P)	724	Value: 125				

KM# 218 1500 COLONES **Weight:** 6.9800 g. **Composition:** 0.5000 Gold .1122 oz. AGW

Date	Mintage	F	VF	XF	Unc	BU
1983FM (P)	272	Value: 275				

KM# 234 3000 COLONES **Weight:** 25.3600 g. **Composition:** 0.9250 Silver .7542 oz. ASW **Subject:** 150th Anniversary San Juan de Dios Hospital **Obverse:** National arms **Reverse:** Hospital building

Date	F	VF	XF	Unc	BU
1994 Proof	—	—	—	—	—

KM# 208 5000 COLONES **Weight:** 15.0000 g. **Composition:** 0.9000 Gold .4341 oz. AGW **Subject:** 125th Anniversary - Death of Juan Santamaria

Date	Mintage	F	VF	XF	Unc	BU
1981	—	—	—	—	185	—
1981 Proof	2,000	Value: 225				

KM# 232 5000 COLONES **Weight:** 15.0000 g. **Composition:** 0.9000 Gold .4341 oz. AGW **Subject:** Founding of Alajuela **Obverse:** National arms **Reverse:** Portrait of Ramirez

Date	Mintage	F	VF	XF	Unc	BU
1981 Proof	2,000	Value: 235				

KM# 235 5000 COLONES **Weight:** 25.0600 g. **Composition:** 0.9250 Silver .7453 oz. ASW **Subject:** Centennial of the Colon **Obverse:** National arms **Reverse:** Bust of Columbus right

Date	F	VF	XF	Unc	BU
1997 Proof	—	Value: 50.00			

KM# 237 5000 COLONES **Weight:** 31.1000 g. **Composition:** 0.9250 Silver .9429 oz. ASW **Subject:** 50 Years - Central Bank **Obverse:** National arms **Reverse:** Man working screw press

Date	Mintage	F	VF	XF	Unc	BU
2000 Proof	7,500	Value: 30.00				

KM# 226 25000 COLONES **Weight:** 15.0000 g. **Composition:** 0.9000 Gold .4341 oz. AGW **Reverse:** President Dr. Oscar Arias S.

Date	Mintage	F	VF	XF	Unc	BU
1987 Proof	5,000	Value: 225				

KM# 238 100000 COLONES **Weight:** 15.5500 g. **Composition:** 0.9000 Gold .4499 oz. AGW **Subject:** 50 Years - Central Bank **Obverse:** National arms **Reverse:** Three standing citizens

Date	Mintage	F	VF	XF	Unc	BU
2000 Proof	2,500	Value: 350				

COUNTERSTAMPED COINAGE

Type VIII • 1923

Obverse counterstamp: 1923 in 11mm circle.

Reverse counterstamp: 50/CENTIMOS in 11mm circle.

NOTE: The total mintage for KM#154-159 was 1,866,000 pieces

KM# 156 50 CENTIMOS **Weight:** 6.2500 g. **Composition:** 0.7500 Silver .1507 oz. ASW **Counterstamp:** Type VIII **Note:** Counterstamped on 25 Centavos, KM#106.

CS Date	Host Date	Good	VG	F	VF	XF
1923	1864 GW	—	225	400	650	—
1923	1865 GW	—	35.00	58.00	80.00	125
1923	1875 GW	—	22.50	42.00	65.00	100

KM# 157 50 CENTIMOS **Weight:** 6.2500 g. **Composition:** 0.7500 Silver .1507 oz. ASW **Counterstamp:** Type VIII **Note:** Counterstamped on 25 Centavos, KM#127.1.

CS Date	Host Date	Good	VG	F	VF	XF
1923	1886 GW	—	3.00	5.00	9.00	15.00
1923	1887 GW	—	3.00	5.00	9.00	15.00

KM# 158 50 CENTIMOS **Weight:** 6.2500 g. **Composition:** 0.7500 Silver .1507 oz. ASW **Counterstamp:** Type VIII **Reverse:** 9Ds GW **Note:** Counterstamped on 25 Centavos, KM#127.2.

CS Date	Host Date	Good	VG	F	VF	XF
1923	1886 GW	—	4.00	8.00	15.00	25.00
1923	1887 GW	—	3.00	5.00	9.00	15.00

KM# 159 50 CENTIMOS **Weight:** 6.3000 g. **Composition:** 0.7500 Silver .1519 oz. ASW **Counterstamp:** Type VIII **Note:** Counterstamped on 25 Centavos, KM#130.

CS Date	Host Date	Good	VG	F	VF	XF
1923	1889HEATON	—	1.50	2.75	5.00	8.50
1923	1890/80HEATON	—	2.50	3.75	7.00	10.00
1923	1890HEATON	—	1.50	2.75	5.00	8.50
1923	1892HEATON	—	1.50	2.75	5.00	8.50
1923	1893HEATON	—	1.25	2.50	4.50	7.50

KM# 154 50 CENTIMOS **Weight:** 6.4000 g. **Composition:** 0.9030 Silver .1858 oz. ASW **Counterstamp:** Type VIII **Note:** Counterstamped on 1/4 Peso, KM#103.

CS Date	Host Date	Good	VG	F	VF	XF
1923	1850 JB	—	500	700	1,000	1,250

KM# 155 50 CENTIMOS **Weight:** 6.2500 g. **Composition:** 0.0750 Silver .1507 oz. ASW **Counterstamp:** Type VIII **Note:** Counterstamped on 25 Centavos, KM#105.

CS Date	Host Date	Good	VG	F	VF	XF
1923	1864 GW	—	325	550	900	—

COUNTERSTAMPED COINAGE

Type IX • 1923

Obverse counterstamp: 1923 in 14mm circle

Reverse counterstamp: UN/COLON in 14mm circle

NOTE: The total mintage for KM#162-164 was 421,810 pieces. Host dates of 1867 GW, 1870 GW and 1872 GW are listed, but no examples are currently known to exist.

KM# 162 COLON **Weight:** 12.5000 g. **Composition:** 0.7500 Silver **Counterstamp:** Type IX **Note:** Counterstamped on 50 Centavos, KM#112.

CS Date	Host Date	Good	VG	F	VF	XF
1923	1865 GW	—	35.00	50.00	75.00	125
1923	1866/5 GW	—	37.50	55.00	85.00	150
1923	1867 GW	—	—	—	—	—
1923	1870 GW	—	—	—	—	—
1923	1872 GW	—	—	—	—	—
1923	1875 GW	—	32.50	45.00	70.00	125

KM# 165 COLON **Weight:** 10.0000 g. **Composition:** 0.5000 Silver **Counterstamp:** Type IX **Note:** Counterstamped on 50 Centimos, KM#150. For KM#165 the mintage were: 1917 host 9,390 pieces; 1918 host 28,800 pieces.

CS Date	Host Date	Good	VG	F	VF	XF
1923	1917 GCR	—	6.00	12.00	17.50	25.00
1923	1918 GCR	—	4.50	8.50	13.50	20.00

KM# 163 COLON (Un) **Weight:** 12.5000 g. **Composition:** 0.7500 Silver **Counterstamp:** Type IX **Note:** Counterstamped on 50 Centavos, KM#124.

CS Date	Host Date	Good	VG	F	VF	XF
1923	1880 GW	—	6.50	10.00	25.00	50.00
1923	1885 GW	—	6.50	10.00	25.00	50.00
1923	1886 GW	—	9.00	17.50	30.00	60.00
1923	1887 GW	—	6.50	10.00	27.50	55.00
1923	1890 GW	—	6.50	10.00	27.50	55.00

KM# 164 COLON (Un) **Weight:** 10.0000 g. **Composition:** 0.9000 Silver **Counterstamp:** Type IX **Note:** Counterstamped on 50 Centimos, KM#143.

CS Date	Host Date	Good	VG	F	VF	XF
1923	1902 CY	—	4.00	8.00	13.50	22.50
1923	1903 JCV	—	3.00	6.00	10.00	17.50
1923	1914 GCR	—	4.00	8.00	13.50	20.00

LEPROSARIUM COINAGE

KM# L1 5 CENTIMOS **Composition:** Copper Nickel **Note:** 4 millimeter hole punched through 5 Centimos, KM#178.

Date	Mintage	VG	F	VF	XF	Unc
1942 (1944) Rare	2,000	—	—	—	—	—

KM# L2 25 CENTIMOS **Composition:** Copper Nickel **Note:** 6 millimeter hole punched through 25 Centimos, KM#171.

Date	Mintage	VG	F	VF	XF	Unc
1935 (1944) Rare	2,000	—	—	—	—	—

KM# L3 25 CENTIMOS **Note:** 6 millimeter hole punched through 25 Centimos, KM#175.

Date	VG	F	VF	XF	Unc
1937 (1944) Rare	—	—	—	—	—

KM# L4 50 CENTIMOS **Composition:** Copper Nickel **Note:** 8 millimeter hole punched through 50 Centimos, KM#172.

Date	Mintage	VG	F	VF	XF	Unc
1935 (1944) Rare	800	—	—	—	—	—

KM# L5 50 CENTIMOS **Composition:** Copper Nickel **Note:** 8 millimeter hole punched throuth 50 Centimos, KM#176.

Date	VG	F	VF	XF	Unc
1937 (1944) Rare	—	—	—	—	—

KM# L6 COLON **Composition:** Copper Nickel **Note:** 9 millimeter hole punched through 1 Colon, KM#173.

Date	Mintage	VG	F	VF	XF	Unc
1935 (1944) Rare	1,000	—	—	—	—	—

KM# L7 COLON **Composition:** Copper Nickel **Note:** 9 millimeter hole punched through 1 Colon, KM#177.

Date	VG	F	VF	XF	Unc
1937 (1944) Rare	—	—	—	—	—

PATTERNS

KM#	Date	Mintage	Identification	Mkt Val
Pn11	1917	—	10 Centavos. Silver. Similar to KM#129. As KM#148.	—
	1917	—	10 Centavos. Silver. Similar to KM#129. As KM#148.	—
Pn12	1924	—	25 Centimos. Brass. KM#168.	—
Pn14	19xx	—	5 Centimos. Brass. Similar to 1929 issues.	—
Pn15	19xx	—	10 Centimos. Copper-Nickel. Similar to 1929 issue.	60.00
	19xx	—	10 Centimos. Copper-Nickel. Similar to 1929 issue.	60.00
Pn13	19xx	—	5 Centimos. Copper Nickel. Similar to 1929 issue	50.00
Pn16	1944	—	25 Centimos. Silver.	—
Pn17	1944	—	25 Centimos. Brass. Polished dies.	—

PIEFORTS

KM#	Date	Mintage	Identification	Mkt Val
P5	1946	—	25 Centimos. Brass.	—
P6	1946	—	25 Centimos. Nickel.	—

MINT SETS

KM#	Date	Mintage	Identification	Issue Price	Mkt Val
MS1	1972 (6)	—	KM#184.4, 185.3-186.3, 187.2, 188.2-189.2	—	10.00
MS2	1975 (3)	—	KM#203-205	—	7.50

PROOF SETS

KM#	Date	Mintage	Identification	Issue Price	Mkt Val
PS2	1937 (3)	—	KM#175-177	—	375
PS3	1970 (10)	570	KM#190-199	—	5,375
PS4	1970 (5)	4,650	KM#190-194	52.00	150
PS5	1970 (5)	3,000	KM#195-199	832	5,225
PS6	1974 (2)	30,000	KM#200a-201a	50.00	50.00
PS7	1975 (3)	—	KM#203-205	—	15.00
PS8	1976 (5)	5,000	KM#184.3, 185.2, 186.4, 188.1, 189.1	10.00	7.50

CRETE

The island of Crete (Kriti), located 60 miles southeast of the Peloponnesus, was the center of a brilliant civilization that flourished before the advent of Greek culture. After being conquered by the Romans, Byzantines, Moslems and Venetians, Crete became part of the Turkish Empire in 1669. As a consequence of the Greek Revolution of the1820s, it was ceded to Egypt. Egypt returned the island to the Turks in 1840, and they ceded it to Greece in 1913, after the Second Balkan War.

RULERS

Prince George, 1898-1906

MINT MARKS

A - Paris

(a) - Paris (privy marks only)

TURKISH EMPIRE

STANDARD COINAGE

KM# 1.1 LEPTON Composition: Bronze

Date	Mintage	F	VF	XF	Unc	BU
1901A	1,711,000	5.00	10.00	25.00	60.00	—

KM# 1.2 LEPTON Composition: Bronze

Date	F	VF	XF	Unc	BU
1901A	6.00	12.00	27.50	65.00	—

KM# 2 2 LEPTA Composition: Bronze

Date	Mintage	F	VF	XF	Unc	BU
1901A	707,000	6.00	12.50	30.00	70.00	—

KM# 6 50 LEPTA Weight: 2.5000 g. **Composition:** 0.8350 Silver .0671 oz. ASW

Date	Mintage	F	VF	XF	Unc	BU
1901(a)	600,000	25.00	55.00	125	300	—

KM# 7 DRACHMA Weight: 5.0000 g. **Composition:** 0.8350 Silver .1342 oz. ASW **Obverse:** Bust of Prince George right **Reverse:** Arms

Date	Mintage	F	VF	XF	Unc	BU
1901(a)	500,000	35.00	60.00	200	1,000	—

KM# 8 2 DRACHMAI Weight: 10.0000 g. **Composition:** 0.8350 Silver .2685 oz. ASW **Obverse:** Bust of Prince George right **Reverse:** Arms

Date	Mintage	F	VF	XF	Unc	BU
1901(a)	175,000	75.00	150	400	2,000	—

KM# 9 5 DRACHMAI Weight: 25.0000 g. **Composition:** 0.9000 Silver .7234 oz. ASW **Obverse:** Bust of Prince George right **Reverse:** Arms

Date	Mintage	F	VF	XF	Unc	BU
1901(a)	150,000	100	200	700	4,000	—

CROATIA

The Republic of Croatia, (Hrvatska) bordered on the west by the Adriatic Sea and the northeast by Hungary, has an area of 21,829 sq. mi. (56,538 sq. km.) and a population of 4.7 million. Capital: Zagreb.

The country was attached to the Kingdom of Hungary until Dec. 1, 1918, when it joined with the Serbs and Slovenes to form the Kingdom of the Serbs, Croats and Slovenes, which changed its name to the Kingdom of Yugoslavia on Oct. 3, 1929. On April 6, 1941, Hitler, angered by the coup d'etat that overthrew the pro-Nazi regime of regent Prince Paul, sent the Nazi armies crashing across the Yugoslav borders from Germany, Hungary, Romania and Bulgaria. Within a week the army of the Balkan Kingdom was prostrate and broken. Yugoslavia was dismembered to reward Hitler's Balkan allies. Croatia, reconstituted as a nominal kingdom, was given to the administration of an Italian princeling, who wisely decided to remain in Italy. By 1947 it was again totally part of the 6 Yugoslav Socialist Republics.

Croatia proclaimed their independence from Yugoslavia on Oct. 8, 1991.

Local Serbian forces, supported by the Yugoslav Federal Army, had developed a military stronghold and proclaimed an independent "SRPSKEKRAJINA" State in the area around Knin, located in southern Croatia having an estimated population of 350,000 Croat Serbs. In September 1995, Croat forces overwhelmed Croat Serb forces ending the short life of their proclaimed Serbian Republic.

MONETARY SYSTEM

100 Banica = 1 Kuna

The word kunas', related to the Russian Kunitsa, which means marten, reflects the use of furs for money in medieval Eastern Europe.

KINGDOM

DECIMAL COINAGE

KM# 1 KUNA Composition: Zinc **Note:** Similar to 2 Kune, KM#2.

Date	F	VF	XF	Unc	BU
1941 Rare	—	—	—	—	—

KM# 2 2 KUNE Composition: Zinc

Date	F	VF	XF	Unc	BU
1941	3.00	7.00	15.00	35.00	—
1941 Proof	—	Value: 80.00			

KM# A3 500 KUNA Weight: 9.9500 g. **Composition:** 0.9000 Gold .2821 oz. AGW

Date	Mintage	F	VF	XF	Unc	BU
1941	170	—	1,750	2,250	3,000	—

KM# B3 500 KUNA Weight: 9.9500 g. **Composition:** 0.9000 Gold .2821 oz. AGW

Date	F	VF	XF	Unc	BU
1941	—	—	—	3,000	—

REPUBLIC

REFORM COINAGE

May 30, 1994 - 1000 Dinara = 1 Kuna; 100 Lipa = 1 Kuna

KM# 3 LIPA Composition: Aluminum **Reverse:** Ears of corn

Date	Mintage	F	VF	XF	Unc	BU
1993	—	—	—	0.20	0.50	—
1993 Proof	17,000	Value: 1.00				
1995 With dot	—	—	—	0.20	0.50	—
1995 With dot, Proof	4,000	Value: 1.00				
1999	—	—	—	0.20	0.50	—
2000	—	—	—	0.20	0.50	—

KM# 3a LIPA Composition: Silver **Reverse:** Ears of corn

Date	Mintage	F	VF	XF	Unc	BU
1993 Proof, Rare	10	—	—	—	—	—

KM# 3b LIPA Composition: Gold **Reverse:** Ears of corn

Date	Mintage	F	VF	XF	Unc	BU
1993 Proof, Rare	5	—	—	—	—	—

KM# 12 LIPA Composition: Aluminum **Reverse:** Ears of corn **Rev. Legend:** ZEA MAYS

Date	Mintage	F	VF	XF	Unc	BU
1994	—	—	—	0.30	0.60	—
1994 Proof	4,000	Value: 1.00				
1996	—	—	—	0.30	0.60	—
1996 Proof	5,000	Value: 1.00				

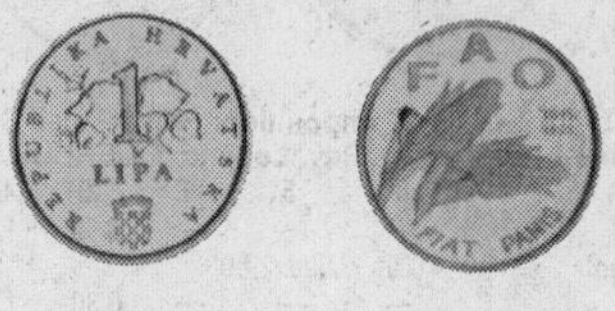

KM# 13 LIPA Composition: Aluminum **Reverse:** Ears of corn **Rev. Legend:** FAO

Date	Mintage	F	VF	XF	Unc	BU
ND(1995)	1,000,000	—	—	0.30	1.00	—
ND(1995) Proof	5,000	Value: 1.50				

KM# 4 2 LIPE Composition: Aluminum **Reverse:** Grape vine

Date	Mintage	F	VF	XF	Unc	BU
1993	—	—	—	0.40	1.00	—
1993 Proof	17,000	Value: 2.00				
1995 With dot	—	—	—	0.40	1.00	—
1995 With dot, Proof	4,000	Value: 2.00				
1999	—	—	—	0.40	1.00	—

KM# 4a 2 LIPE Composition: Silver **Reverse:** Grape vine

Date	Mintage	F	VF	XF	Unc	BU
1993 Proof, Rare	10	—	—	—	—	—

KM# 4b 2 LIPE Composition: Gold **Reverse:** Grape vine

Date	Mintage	F	VF	XF	Unc	BU
1993 Proof, Rare	5	—	—	—	—	—

KM# 14 2 LIPE Composition: Aluminum **Reverse:** Grape vine **Rev. Legend:** VIIIS VINIFERA

Date	Mintage	F	VF	XF	Unc	BU
1994	—	—	—	0.50	1.50	—
1994 Proof	4,000	Value: 2.00				
1996	—	—	—	0.50	1.50	—
1996 Proof	5,000	Value: 2.00				
1999	—	—	—	0.50	1.50	—
2000	—	—	—	0.50	1.50	—

KM# 36 2 LIPE Composition: Aluminum **Subject:** Olympics **Obverse:** Denomination **Reverse:** Olympic rings, flame

Date	Mintage	F	VF	XF	Unc	BU
1996	—	—	—	0.30	0.60	—
1996 Proof	5,000	Value: 1.00				

KM# 5 5 LIPA Composition: Brass Plated Steel **Reverse:** Oak leaves

Date	Mintage	F	VF	XF	Unc	BU
1993	—	—	—	0.40	1.50	—
1993 Proof	17,000	Value: 2.00				
1995 With dot	—	—	—	0.40	1.00	—
1995 Proof	4,000	Value: 3.00				
1997	—	—	—	0.40	1.00	—
1999	—	—	—	0.40	1.00	—

KM# 5a 5 LIPA Composition: Silver **Reverse:** Oak leaves

Date	Mintage	F	VF	XF	Unc	BU
1993 Proof, Rare	10	—	—	—	—	—

KM# 5b 5 LIPA Composition: Gold **Reverse:** Oak leaves

Date	Mintage	F	VF	XF	Unc	BU
1993 Proof, Rare	5	—	—	—	—	—

KM# 15 5 LIPA Composition: Brass Plated Steel **Reverse:** Oak leaves **Rev. Legend:** QUERCUS ROBUR

Date	Mintage	F	VF	XF	Unc	BU
1994	—	—	—	0.30	1.00	—
1994 Proof	4,000	Value: 2.00				
1996	—	—	—	0.30	1.00	—
1996 Proof	5,000	Value: 2.50				
1997	—	—	—	0.30	1.00	—

KM# 37 5 LIPA Composition: Brass Plated Steel **Subject:** Olympics **Obverse:** Denomination **Reverse:** Olympic rings, flame

Date	Mintage	F	VF	XF	Unc	BU
1996	—	—	—	0.60	1.20	—
1996 Proof	5,000	Value: 2.00				

KM# 6 10 LIPA Composition: Brass Plated Steel **Reverse:** Tobacco plant

Date	Mintage	F	VF	XF	Unc	BU
1993	—	—	—	0.40	1.50	—
1993 Proof	17,000	Value: 3.00				
1995 With dot	—	—	—	0.40	1.50	—
1995 With dot, Proof	4,000	Value: 4.00				
1997	—	—	—	0.40	1.50	—
1999	—	—	—	0.40	1.50	—
2001	—	—	—	0.40	1.50	—

KM# 6a 10 LIPA Composition: Silver **Reverse:** Tobacco plant

Date	Mintage	F	VF	XF	Unc	BU
1993 Proof, Rare	10	—	—	—	—	—

KM# 6b 10 LIPA Composition: Gold **Reverse:** Oak leaves

Date	Mintage	F	VF	XF	Unc	BU
1993 Proof, Rare	5	—	—	—	—	—

KM# 16 10 LIPA Composition: Brass Plated Steel **Reverse:** Tobacco plant **Rev. Legend:** NICOTIANA TABACUM

Date	Mintage	F	VF	XF	Unc	BU
1994	—	—	—	0.35	1.50	—
1994 Proof	4,000	Value: 4.00				
1996	—	—	—	0.30	1.50	—
1996 Proof	5,000	Value: 3.50				

KM# 38 10 LIPA Composition: Brass **Subject:** 50th Anniversary - UN **Obverse:** Denomination **Reverse:** UN logo

Date	Mintage	F	VF	XF	Unc	BU
ND(1995)	—	—	—	0.50	1.00	—
ND(1995)	5,000	Value: 4.00				

KM# 7 20 LIPA Composition: Nickel Plated Steel **Reverse:** Olive branch

Date	Mintage	F	VF	XF	Unc	BU
1993	—	—	—	0.50	1.50	—
1993 Proof	17,000	Value: 3.00				
1995 With dot	—	—	—	0.50	1.50	—
1995 Proof	4,000	Value: 4.00				
1996	—	—	—	0.45	1.50	—
1997	—	—	—	0.45	1.50	—
1998	—	—	—	0.45	1.50	—
2001	—	—	—	0.45	1.50	—

KM# 7a 20 LIPA Composition: Silver **Reverse:** Olive branch

Date	Mintage	F	VF	XF	Unc	BU
1993 Proof, Rare	10	—	—	—	—	—

KM# 7b 20 LIPA Composition: Gold **Reverse:** Olive branch

Date	Mintage	F	VF	XF	Unc	BU
1993 Proof, Rare	5	—	—	—	—	—

KM# 17 20 LIPA Composition: Nickel Plated Steel **Reverse:** Olive branch **Rev. Legend:** OLEA EUROPAEA

Date	Mintage	F	VF	XF	Unc	BU
1994	—	—	—	0.50	1.50	—
1994 Proof	4,000	Value: 3.00				
1996	—	—	—	0.45	1.50	—
1996 Proof	5,000	Value: 4.00				
1998	—	—	—	0.50	1.50	—

KM# 18 20 LIPA Composition: Nickel Plated Steel **Reverse:** Olive branch **Rev. Legend:** FAO

Date	Mintage	F	VF	XF	Unc	BU
ND(1995)	1,000,000	—	—	0.50	1.50	—
ND(1995) Proof	5,000	Value: 4.50				

KM# 8 50 LIPA Composition: Nickel Plated Steel **Reverse:** Flowers

Date	Mintage	F	VF	XF	Unc	BU
1993	—	—	—	0.60	1.50	—
1993 Proof	17,000	Value: 4.00				
1995 With dot	—	—	—	0.60	1.50	—
1995 With dot, Proof	4,000	Value: 4.50				
1999	—	—	—	0.60	1.50	—

KM# 8a 50 LIPA Composition: Silver **Reverse:** Flowers

Date	Mintage	F	VF	XF	Unc	BU
1993 Proof, Rare	10	—	—	—	—	—

KM# 8b 50 LIPA Composition: Gold **Reverse:** Flowers

Date	Mintage	F	VF	XF	Unc	BU
1993 Proof, Rare	5	—	—	—	—	—

KM# 19 50 LIPA Composition: Nickel Plated Steel **Reverse:** Flowers **Rev. Legend:** DEGENIA VELEBITICA

Date	Mintage	F	VF	XF	Unc	BU
1994	—	—	—	0.60	1.60	—
1994 Proof	4,000	Value: 4.00				
1996	—	—	—	0.60	1.50	—
1996 Proof	5,000	Value: 4.00				

KM# 39 50 LIPA Composition: Nickel Plated Steel **Subject:** European soccer **Obverse:** Denomination **Reverse:** Checkered shield, soccer ball

Date	Mintage	F	VF	XF	Unc	BU
1996	—	—	—	0.40	1.50	—
1996 Proof	5,000	Value: 4.00				

KM# 9.1 KUNA Composition: Copper-Nickel **Reverse:** Nightingale

Date	Mintage	F	VF	XF	Unc	BU
1993	—	—	—	0.75	1.50	—
1993 Proof	17,000	Value: 3.00				
1995 With dot	—	—	—	0.75	1.50	—
1995 With dot, Proof	5,000	Value: 3.50				

KM# 9.1a KUNA Composition: Silver **Reverse:** Nightingale

Date	F	VF	XF	Unc	BU
1993 Proof, Rare					

KM# 9.1b KUNA Composition: Gold **Reverse:** Nightingale

Date	F	VF	XF	Unc	BU
1993 Proof, Rare	—	—	—	—	—

KM# 20 KUNA Composition: Copper-Nickel **Reverse:** Nightingale **Rev. Legend:** LUSCINNIA MEGARHYNCHOS

Date	Mintage	F	VF	XF	Unc	BU
1994	—	—	—	0.50	1.75	—
1994 Proof	4,000	Value: 4.00				
1996	—	—	—	0.50	1.50	—
1996 Proof	5,000	Value: 3.00				
1997	—	—	—	0.50	1.50	—
1998	—	—	—	0.50	1.50	—

KM# 40 KUNA Composition: Copper-Nickel **Subject:** Olympics **Obverse:** Denomination **Reverse:** Olympic flame, rings

Date	Mintage	F	VF	XF	Unc	BU
1996	—	—	—	0.40	1.50	—
1996 Proof	5,000	Value: 3.00				

KM# 9.2 KUNA Weight: 4.9300 g. **Composition:** Copper-Nickel **Obverse:** Denomination **Reverse:** "1994" above bird in field **Edge:** Reeded **Size:** 22.5 mm.

Date	F	VF	XF	Unc	BU
1999	—	—	0.75	1.50	—

KM# 10 2 KUNE Composition: Copper-Nickel **Reverse:** Tuna

Date	Mintage	F	VF	XF	Unc	BU
1993	—	—	—	1.00	2.00	—
1993 Proof	17,000	Value: 4.50				
1995 With dot	—	—	—	1.00	2.00	—
1995 With dot, Proof	4,000	Value: 5.50				
1997	—	—	—	1.00	2.00	—
1999	—	—	—	1.00	2.00	—

KM# 10a 2 KUNE Composition: Silver **Reverse:** Tuna

Date	Mintage	F	VF	XF	Unc	BU
1993 Proof, Rare	10	—	—	—	—	—

KM# 10b 2 KUNE Composition: Gold **Reverse:** Tuna

Date	Mintage	F	VF	XF	Unc	BU
1993 Proof, Rare	5	—	—	—	—	—

KM# 21 2 KUNE Composition: Copper-Nickel **Reverse:** Tuna **Rev. Legend:** THUNNUS - THYNNUS

Date	Mintage	F	VF	XF	Unc	BU
1994	500,000	—	—	0.75	2.00	—
1994 Proof	4,000	Value: 5.00				
1996	—	—	—	0.70	2.00	—
1996 Proof	5,000	Value: 4.50				
1997	—	—	—	0.75	2.00	—

KM# 22 2 KUNE Composition: Copper-Nickel **Reverse:** Tuna **Rev. Legend:** FAO

Date	Mintage	F	VF	XF	Unc	BU
ND(1995)	—	—	—	0.60	2.00	—
ND(1995) Proof	5,000	Value: 5.50				

KM# 11 5 KUNA Composition: Copper-Nickel **Reverse:** Bear

Date	Mintage	F	VF	XF	Unc	BU
1993	—	—	—	1.50	3.50	—
1993 Proof	17,000	Value: 6.50				
1995 With dot	—	—	—	1.50	3.50	—
1995 With dot, Proof	4,000	Value: 7.00				
1997	—	—	—	—	—	—
1997 Proof	—	—	—	—	—	—

KM# 11a 5 KUNA Composition: Silver **Reverse:** Bear

Date	Mintage	F	VF	XF	Unc	BU
1993 Proof, Rare	10	—	—	—	—	—

KM# 11b 5 KUNA Composition: Gold **Reverse:** Bear

Date	Mintage	F	VF	XF	Unc	BU
1993 Proof, Rare	5	—	—	—	—	—

KM# 23 5 KUNA Composition: Copper-Nickel **Reverse:** Bear **Rev. Legend:** URSUS ARCTOS

Date	Mintage	F	VF	XF	Unc	BU
1994	—	—	—	1.00	4.00	—
1994 Proof	4,000	Value: 7.50				
1996	—	—	—	1.00	4.00	—
1996 Proof	5,000	Value: 7.50				

KM# 24 5 KUNA Composition: Copper-Nickel **Subject:** 500th Anniversary - Senj

Date	Mintage	F	VF	XF	Unc	BU
1994	—	—	—	—	3.50	—
1994 Proof	5,000	Value: 8.00				

KM# 24a 5 KUNA Composition: Silver **Subject:** 500th Anniversary - Senj

Date	Mintage	F	VF	XF	Unc	BU
1994 Proof	500	Value: 270				

KM# 24b 5 KUNA Composition: Gold **Subject:** 500th Anniversary - Senj

Date	Mintage	F	VF	XF	Unc	BU
1994 Proof	250	Value: 390				

KM# 47 25 KUNA Ring Composition: Copper-Nickel **Center Composition:** Brass **Subject:** Danube Border Region **Obverse:** Denomination in inner circle **Reverse:** Regional map

Date	F	VF	XF	Unc	BU
1997	—	—	—	11.00	—

KM# 48 25 KUNA Ring Composition: Copper-Nickel **Center Composition:** Brass **Subject:** 5th Anniversary - UN Membership **Obverse:** National arms **Reverse:** UN emblem

Date	F	VF	XF	Unc	BU
1997	—	—	—	11.00	—

KM# 49 25 KUNA Ring Composition: Copper-Nickel **Center Composition:** Brass **Subject:** First Croatian Esperanto Congress **Obverse:** Denomination **Reverse:** Logo

Date	F	VF	XF	Unc	BU
1997	—	—	—	11.00	—

KM# 63 25 KUNA Ring Composition: Copper-Nickel **Center Composition:** Brass **Subject:** Lisbon Expo **Obverse:** Denomination **Reverse:** Sailboat

Date	F	VF	XF	Unc	BU
1998	—	—	—	11.00	—

KM# 64 25 KUNA Ring Composition: Copper-Nickel**Center Weight:** 12.5600 g. **Center Composition:** Brass **Subject:** European Union **Obverse:** Denomination **Reverse:** 12 stars on a large "E" **Edge:** Plain **Shape:** 12-sided **Size:** 31 mm.

Date	F	VF	XF	Unc	BU
1999	—	—	—	11.00	—

KM# 65 25 KUNA Ring Composition: Copper-Nickel**Center Weight:** 12.6500 g. **Center Composition:** Brass **Obverse:** Denomination. **Reverse:** Human fetus **Edge:** Plain **Shape:** 12-sided **Size:** 31 mm.

Date	F	VF	XF	Unc	BU
2000	—	—	—	11.00	—

KM# 66 25 KUNA Ring Composition: Copper-Nickel **Center Weight:** 12.6400 g. **Center Composition:** Brass **Subject:** 10th Anniversary of Independence **Obverse:** Denomination **Reverse:** National map **Edge:** Plain **Shape:** 12-sided **Size:** 31 mm.

Date	F	VF	XF	Unc	BU
ND(2001)	—	—	—	8.50	—

KM# 25.1 100 KUNA Weight: 15.0000 g. **Composition:** Silver **Subject:** 900th Anniversary - St. Blaza Church **Reverse:** Altar at St. Blaza

Date	Mintage	F	VF	XF	Unc	BU
ND(1994) Proof	3,000	Value: 47.50				

KM# 25.2 100 KUNA Weight: 15.0000 g. **Composition:** Silver **Subject:** 900th Anniversary - St. Blaza Church **Obverse:** Series II mark added **Reverse:** Altar at St. Blaza

Date	Mintage	F	VF	XF	Unc	BU
ND(1994) Proof	1,000	Value: 75.00				

KM# 26 100 KUNA Weight: 33.6300 g. **Composition:** Silver **Reverse:** Half-length bust of Pope John Paul II

Date	Mintage	F	VF	XF	Unc	BU
1994 Proof	10,000	Value: 65.00				

KM# 27 100 KUNA Weight: 20.0000 g. **Composition:** 0.9250 Silver .5947 oz. ASW **Subject:** 5th Anniversary of Independence

Date	Mintage	F	VF	XF	Unc	BU
ND(1995) Proof	6,000	Value: 35.00				

KM# 50 100 KUNA Weight: 20.0000 g. **Composition:** 0.9250 Silver .5947 oz. ASW **Subject:** City of Split **Obverse:** Towered building **Reverse:** Ancient depiction of king on throne

Date	Mintage	F	VF	XF	Unc	BU
ND(1995) Proof	5,000	Value: 32.00				

KM# 41 100 KUNA Weight: 20.0000 g. **Composition:** 0.9250 Silver .5947 oz. ASW **Subject:** Olympics **Obverse:** Sailboat racing **Reverse:** Wheelchair-bound javelin thrower

Date	Mintage	F	VF	XF	Unc	BU
1996 Proof	2,000	Value: 40.00				

KM# 42 100 KUNA Weight: 20.0000 g. **Composition:** 0.9250 Silver .5947 oz. ASW **Subject:** Olympics **Obverse:** Rowing **Reverse:** Water polo player

Date	Mintage	F	VF	XF	Unc	BU
1996 Proof	2,000	Value: 40.00				

KM# 28 150 KUNA Weight: 24.0000 g. **Composition:** 0.9250 Silver .7136 oz. ASW **Subject:** 5th Anniversary of Independence

Date	Mintage	F	VF	XF	Unc	BU
1995 Proof	5,000	Value: 42.50				

KM# 43 150 KUNA Weight: 24.0000 g. **Composition:** 0.9250 Silver .7136 oz. ASW **Subject:** Olympics **Obverse:** Gymnast **Reverse:** Basketball players

Date	Mintage	F	VF	XF	Unc	BU
1996 Proof	2,000	Value: 42.50				

KM# 44 150 KUNA Weight: 24.0000 g. **Composition:** 0.9250 Silver .7136 oz. ASW **Subject:** Olympics **Obverse:** Table tennis and paddle **Reverse:** Marksmanship eye design

Date	Mintage	F	VF	XF	Unc	BU
1996	2,000	Value: 42.50				

KM# 56 150 KUNA Weight: 24.0000 g. **Composition:** 0.9250 Silver .7136 oz. ASW **Subject:** 800th Anniversary - City of Osijek **Obverse:** National arms above denomination **Reverse:** City view

Date	Mintage	F	VF	XF	Unc	BU
ND(1996) Proof	1,000	Value: 40.00				

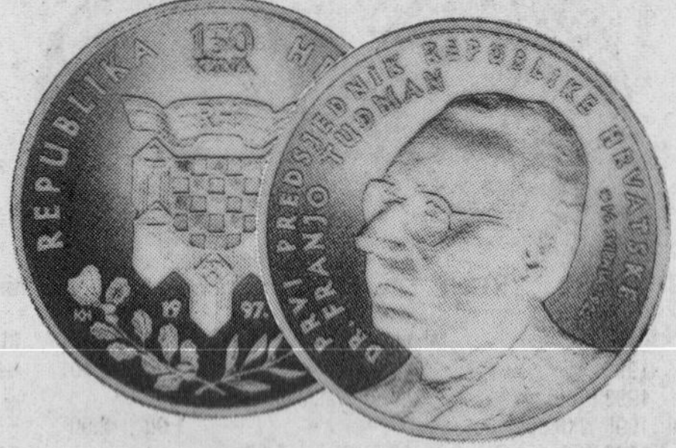

KM# 59 150 KUNA Weight: 24.0000 g. **Composition:** 0.9250 Silver .7136 oz. ASW **Obverse:** Denomination above national arms **Reverse:** Bust of President Tudman left

Date	Mintage	F	VF	XF	Unc	BU
1997 Proof	10,000	Value: 40.00				

KM# 29.1 200 KUNA Weight: 33.6300 g. **Composition:** 0.9250 Silver .9999 oz. ASW **Obverse:** St. Marka Church **Reverse:** Portal of St. Marka Church

Date	Mintage	F	VF	XF	Unc	BU
ND(1994) Proof	3,000	Value: 75.00				

KM# 29.2 200 KUNA Weight: 33.6300 g. **Composition:** 0.9250 Silver .9999 oz. ASW **Obverse:** St. Marka Church, Series II mark added **Reverse:** Portal of St. Marka Church

Date	Mintage	F	VF	XF	Unc	BU
ND(1994) Proof	1,000	Value: 90.00				

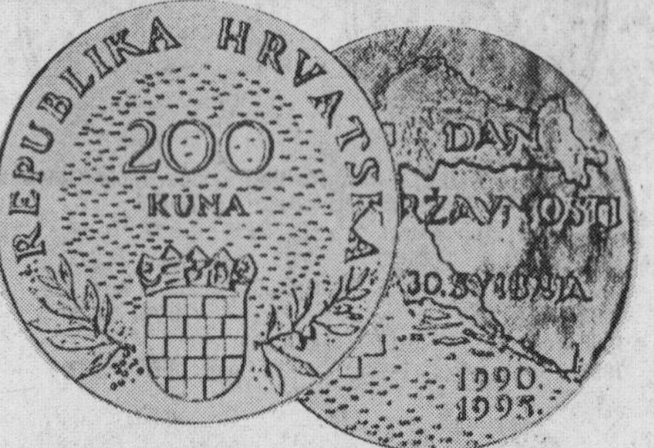

KM# 30 200 KUNA Weight: 33.6300 g. **Composition:** 0.9250 Silver .9999 oz. ASW **Subject:** 5th Anniversary of Independence

Date	Mintage	F	VF	XF	Unc	BU
ND(1995) Proof	4,000	Value: 75.00				

KM# 51 200 KUNA Weight: 33.6300 g. **Composition:** 0.9250 Silver .9999 oz. ASW **Subject:** Spalatum **Obverse:** Diocletian's palace **Reverse:** Sarcophagus

Date	Mintage	F	VF	XF	Unc	BU
ND(1995) Proof	5,000	Value: 45.00				

KM# 45 200 KUNA **Weight:** 33.6300 g. **Composition:** 0.9250 Silver .9999 oz. ASW **Subject:** Olympics **Obverse:** High jumper **Reverse:** Tennis player

Date	Mintage	F	VF	XF	Unc	BU
ND Proof	2,000	Value: 45.00				

KM# 46 200 KUNA **Weight:** 33.6300 g. **Composition:** 0.9250 Silver .9999 oz. ASW **Subject:** Olympics **Obverse:** Diving swimmers **Reverse:** Basketball game

Date	Mintage	F	VF	XF	Unc	BU
1996 Proof	2,000	Value: 45.00				

KM# 54 200 KUNA **Weight:** 33.6300 g. **Composition:** 0.9250 Silver .9999 oz. ASW **Subject:** University in Zadar **Obverse:** Circle of arches **Reverse:** Saint reading

Date	Mintage	F	VF	XF	Unc	BU
ND(1996) Proof	1,000	Value: 55.00				

KM# 57 200 KUNA **Weight:** 33.6300 g. **Composition:** 0.9250 Silver .9999 oz. ASW **Subject:** 800th Anniversary - City of Osijek **Obverse:** National arms above denomination **Reverse:** City view

Date	Mintage	F	VF	XF	Unc	BU
ND(1996) Proof	1,000	Value: 52.00				

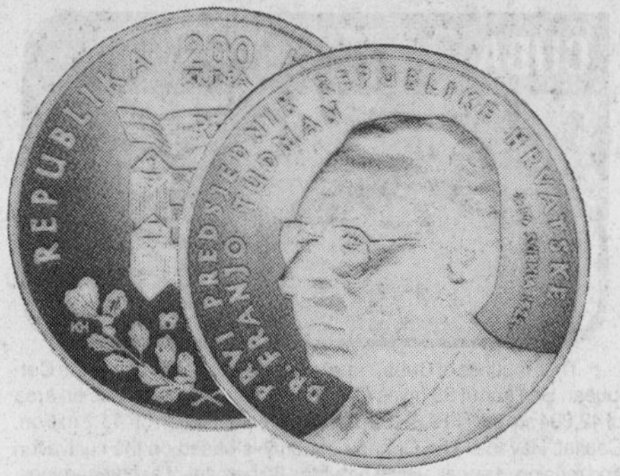

KM# 60 200 KUNA **Weight:** 33.6300 g. **Composition:** 0.9250 Silver .9999 oz. ASW **Obverse:** Denomination above national arms **Reverse:** Bust of President Tudman left

Date	Mintage	F	VF	XF	Unc	BU
1997 Proof	5,000	Value: 45.00				

KM# 31.1 500 KUNA **Weight:** 3.5000 g. **Composition:** 0.9860 Gold .1109 oz. AGW **Obverse:** Izborna Cathedral

Date	Mintage	F	VF	XF	Unc	BU
1994 Proof	1,000	Value: 200				

KM# 31.2 500 KUNA **Weight:** 3.5000 g. **Composition:** 0.9860 Gold .1109 oz. AGW **Obverse:** Izborna Cathedral, Series II added

Date	Mintage	F	VF	XF	Unc	BU
1994 Proof	1,000	Value: 175				

KM# 32 500 KUNA **Weight:** 3.5000 g. **Composition:** 0.9860 Gold .1109 oz. AGW **Subject:** 5th Anniversary of Independence

Date	Mintage	F	VF	XF	Unc	BU
1995 Proof	4,000	Value: 175				

KM# 52 500 KUNA **Weight:** 3.5000 g. **Composition:** 0.9860 Gold .1109 oz. AGW **Subject:** City of Split **Obverse:** Towered building **Reverse:** Ancient depiction of king on throne

Date	Mintage	F	VF	XF	Unc	BU
ND(1995) Proof	6,000	Value: 150				

KM# 55 500 KUNA **Weight:** 3.5000 g. **Composition:** 0.9860 Gold .1109 oz. AGW **Subject:** University of Zadar **Obverse:** Circle of arches **Reverse:** Saint reading

Date	Mintage	F	VF	XF	Unc	BU
ND(1996) Proof	1,000	Value: 175				

KM# 58 500 KUNA **Weight:** 3.5000 g. **Composition:** 0.9860 Gold .1109 oz. AGW **Subject:** 800th Anniversary - City of Osijek **Obverse:** National arms **Reverse:** City view

Date	Mintage	F	VF	XF	Unc	BU
ND(1996) Proof	1,000	Value: 175				

KM# 33 1000 KUNA **Weight:** 7.0000 g. **Composition:** 0.9860 Gold .2218 oz. AGW **Reverse:** Half-length portrait of Pope John Paul II

Date	Mintage	F	VF	XF	Unc	BU
1994 Proof	4,000	Value: 285				

KM# 34 1000 KUNA **Weight:** 7.0000 g. **Composition:** 0.9860 Gold .2218 oz. AGW **Subject:** 5th Anniversary of Independence

Date	Mintage	F	VF	XF	Unc	BU
ND(1995) Proof	3,000	Value: 285				

KM# 53 1000 KUNA **Weight:** 7.0000 g. **Composition:** 0.9860 Gold .2218 oz. AGW **Subject:** Spalatum **Obverse:** Diocletian's palace **Reverse:** Sarcophagus

Date	Mintage	F	VF	XF	Unc	BU
ND(1995) Proof	3,000	Value: 285				

TRADE COINAGE

KM# 35 DUCAT **Weight:** 3.5000 g. **Composition:** 0.9860 Gold .1109 oz. AGW **Reverse:** Ruder Boskovic

Date	Mintage	F	VF	XF	Unc	BU
1994 Proof	5,000	Value: 150				

KM# 62 DUCAT **Weight:** 3.5000 g. **Composition:** 0.9860 Gold .1109 oz. AGW **Subject:** Liberation of Knin **Obverse:** Crowned arms **Reverse:** Regional view

Date	Mintage	F	VF	XF	Unc	BU
ND(1995)	3,000	—	—	—	145	—

PATTERNS

Including off metal strikes

KM#	Date	Mintage	Identification	Mkt Val
Pn5	1934	—	5 Kuna. Bronze.	350
Pn6	1934	—	5 Kuna. Copper Nickel.	400
Pn7	1934	—	5 Kuna. 0.9000 Silver.	450
Pn8	1934	—	5 Kuna. Zinc.	—
Pn9	1941	—	25 Banica. Zinc. With initials. 16 or 17 mm.	—
Pn10	1941	—	25 Banica. Zinc. Without initials. 16 or 17 mm.	—
Pn11	1941	—	25 Banica. Nickel. 16 or 17 mm.	—
Pn12	1941	—	25 Banica. Gold. 16 or 17 mm.	3,500
Pn13	1941	—	50 Banica. Nickel.	—
Pn14	1941	—	50 Banica. Zinc.	—
Pn15	1941	—	50 Banica. Silver.	—
Pn16	1941	—	50 Banica. Gold.	4,500
Pn17	1941	—	Kuna. Zinc.	—
Pn18	1941	—	Kuna. Copper.	—
Pn19	1941	—	Kuna. Aluminum.	175
Pn20	1941	—	Kuna. Nickel.	—
Pn21	1941	—	Kuna. Silver.	450
Pn22	1941	—	Kuna. Gold.	3,500

KM#	Date	Mintage	Identification	Mkt Val
Pn23	1941	—	Kuna. Silver. 4.3800 g. 20 mm. Without undulating background.	—
Pn24	1941	—	2 Kune. Aluminum.	—
Pn25	1941	—	2 Kune. Nickel.	—
Pn26	1941	—	2 Kune. Silver. 4.8900 g. 22 mm.	—
Pn27	1941	—	2 Kune. Gold.	4,500
Pn28	1941	—	10 Kuna. Similar to Pn 19. 10 Kuna above shield within wheat border. Reported, not confirmed.	—
Pn29	1941	—	500 Kuna. Aluminum. Pn 26. Similar to B3.	—
Pn30	1941	—	500 Kuna. Copper Nickel. Pn 26. Similar to B3.	—
Pn31	1941	—	500 Kuna. Aluminum. Chain.	—
Pn32	1941	—	500 Kuna. Aluminum-Bronze.	—
Pn33	1941	—	500 Kuna. Copper.	—
Pn34	1941	—	500 Kuna. Copper Nickel.	—
Pn35	1941	—	500 Kuna. Silver.	—
Pn36	1941	—	500 Kuna. Aluminum. 1.6700 g. 22 mm. Wheat chain. Similar to KMA3.	600
Pn37	1941	—	500 Kuna. Gold. 27 mm. Chain. KMA3.	—
Pn38	1941	—	500 Kuna. Nickel. 22 mm. KMA3.	—
Pn39	1941	—	500 Kuna. Aluminum. KMA3.	—
Pn40	1941	—	500 Kuna. Brass. 7.1100 g. 23 mm. KMA3.	400
Pn41	1943	—	5 Kuna.	—
Pn42	1943	—	10 Kuna.	—

MINT SETS

KM#	Date	Mintage	Identification	Issue Price	Mkt Val
MS1	1993 (9)	50,000	KM3-11	8.00	14.00

PROOF SETS

KM#	Date	Mintage	Identification	Issue Price	Mkt Val
PS1	1993 (9)	17,000	KM3-11	15.20	28.50
PS2	1993 (9)	10	KM3a-11a, rare	—	—
PS3	1993 (9)	5	KM3b-11b, rare	—	—
PS7	1994 (2)	1,000	KM26, 33	240	350
PS8	ND (1994) (3)	250	KM25.1, 29.1, 31.1	154	325
PS10	1994-95 (2)	1,000	KM22, 25.2	—	85.00
PS11	1994-95 (4)	—	KM13, 18, 22, 24	—	40.00
PS12	1994-96 (9)	5,000	KM13, 18, 22, 24, 36-40	8.00	33.50
PS4	1994 (9)	4,000	KM12, 14-17, 19-21, 23	15.20	32.50
PS9	ND (1994) (3)	500	KM25.2, 29.2, 31.2	154	340
PS5	1994 (3)	500	KM21, 23, 24a	—	280
PS6	1994 (3)	250	KM21, 23, 24b	—	400
PS14	1995 (5)	—	KM27, 28, 30, 32, 34	—	550
PS20	ND (1995) (5)	1,000	KM 27, 28, 30, 32, 34	406	620
PS21	ND (1995) (3)	2,000	KM 27, 30, 34	270	400
PS22	1995 (2)	2,000	KM28, 32	135	225
PS13	1995 (9)	4,000	KM3-11	15.20	34.50
PS15	ND (1995) (4)	1,000	KM50-53	375	500
PS16	ND (1995) (2)	1,000	KM50, 51	62.50	75.00
PS17	ND (1995) (2)	1,000	KM50, 52	125	180
PS18	ND (1995) (2)	1,000	KM51, 53	250	325
PS19	ND (1995) (2)	1,000	KM52, 53	312	430
PS23	1996 (6)	1,000	KM41-46	187	265
PS24	1996 (9)	5,000	KM12, 14-17, 19-21, 23	8.00	32.00
PS25	ND (1996) (2)	500	KM54-55	146	230
PS26	ND (1996) (3)	300	KM56-58	177	265
PS27	1997 (3)	300	KM59-61	281	370

CUBA

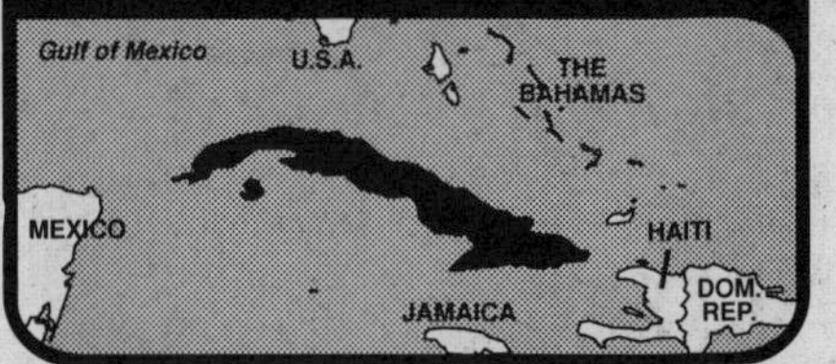

The Republic of Cuba, situated at the northern edge of the Caribbean Sea about 90 miles (145 km.) south of Florida, has an area of 42,804 sq. mi. (110,860 sq. km.) and a population of *11.2 million. Capital: Havana. The Cuban economy is based on the cultivation and refining of sugar, which provides 80 percent of export earnings.

Discovered by Columbus in 1492 and settled by Diego Velasquez in the early 1500s, Cuba remained a Spanish possession until 1898, except for a brief British occupancy of Havana in 1762-63. Cuban attempts to gain freedom were crushed, even while Spain was granting independence to its other American possessions. Ten years of warfare, 1868-78, between Spanish troops and Cuban rebels exacted guarantees of rights which were never implemented. The final revolt, begun in 1895, evoked American sympathy, and with the aid of U.S. troops independence was proclaimed on May 20, 1902. Fulgencio Batista seized the government in 1952 and established a dictatorship. Opposition to Batista, led by Fidel Castro, drove him into exile on Jan. 1, 1959. A communist-type, 25-member collective leadership headed by Castro was inaugurated in March, 1962.

RULERS
Spanish, until 1898

MINT MARKS
Key - Havana, 1977--

MONETARY SYSTEM
100 Centavos = 1 Peso

FIRST REPUBLIC
1902 - 1962

DECIMAL COINAGE

KM# 9.1 CENTAVO Composition: Copper-Nickel **Reverse:** 2.5 G. 250M

Date	Mintage	F	VF	XF	Unc	BU
1915	9,396,000	—	1.00	2.00	40.00	80.00
1915 Proof	200	Value: 175				
1916	9,318,000	—	1.00	2.00	50.00	100
1916 Proof	104	Value: 750				
1920	19,378,000	—	1.50	3.00	50.00	110
1938	2,000,000	—	2.50	6.00	55.00	140

KM# 9.2a CENTAVO Composition: Brass **Reverse:** 2.3 GR. 300M

Date	Mintage	F	VF	XF	Unc	BU
1943	20,000,000	—	0.40	1.25	7.00	15.00

KM# 9.2 CENTAVO Composition: Copper-Nickel **Reverse:** 2.5 GR. 250M

Date	Mintage	F	VF	XF	Unc	BU
1946	50,000,000	—	0.20	1.00	4.00	12.50
1961	100,000,000	—	0.25	0.60	1.50	2.50

KM# 26 CENTAVO Composition: Brass **Subject:** Birth of Jose Marti Centennial

Date	Mintage	F	VF	XF	Unc	BU
1953	50,000,000	—	0.15	0.75	12.00	30.00
1953 Proof; Rare	100	—	—	—	—	—

KM# 30 CENTAVO Composition: Copper-Nickel **Reverse:** Bust of Jose Marti

Date	Mintage	F	VF	XF	Unc	BU
1958	50,000,000	—	0.15	0.75	45.00	75.00

KM# A10 2 CENTAVOS Composition: Copper-Nickel

Date	Mintage	F	VF	XF	Unc	BU
1915	6,090,000	—	1.25	3.00	40.00	100
1915 Proof	150	Value: 150				
1916	5,322,000	—	1.25	3.50	45.00	110
1916 Proof	100	Value: 750				

KM# 11.1 5 CENTAVOS Composition: Copper-Nickel **Reverse:** 5.0 G. 250M

Date	Mintage	F	VF	XF	Unc	BU
1915	5,096,000	—	1.50	4.00	50.00	125
1915 Proof	150	Value: 175				
1916	1,714,000	—	1.50	5.00	50.00	150
1916 Proof	100	Value: 800				
1920	10,000,000	—	1.50	4.50	60.00	135

KM# 11.3a (KM11.2a) 5 CENTAVOS Composition: Brass **Reverse:** 4.6 GR. 300M

Date	Mintage	F	VF	XF	Unc	BU
1943	6,000,000	—	1.00	3.50	15.00	25.00
1943	6,000,000	—	1.00	3.50	15.00	25.00

KM# 11.2 5 CENTAVOS Reverse: 5.0 G 250M

Date	F	VF	XF	Unc	BU
1920	—	1.75	5.00	100	200

KM# 11.3 (KM11.2) 5 CENTAVOS Composition: Copper-Nickel **Reverse:** 5 GR. 250M

Date	Mintage	F	VF	XF	Unc	BU
1946	40,000,000	—	0.50	0.75	5.00	8.50
1946	40,000,000	—	0.50	0.75	5.00	8.50
1960	20,000,000	—	0.75	1.25	15.00	40.00
1960	20,000,000	—	0.75	1.25	15.00	40.00
1961	70,000,000	—	0.15	0.40	1.00	2.00
1961	70,000,000	—	0.15	0.40	1.00	2.00

KM# A12 10 CENTAVOS Weight: 2.5000 g. **Composition:** 0.9000 Silver .723 oz. ASW

Date	Mintage	F	VF	XF	Unc	BU
1915	5,690,000	—	4.00	12.00	100	200
1915 Proof	125	Value: 850				
1916	560,000	—	20.00	75.00	450	1,400
1916 Proof	50	Value: 1,400				
1920	3,090,000	—	6.00	20.00	200	450
1948	5,120,000	—	1.25	2.00	4.00	10.00
1949	9,880,000	—	1.25	1.75	4.00	10.00

KM# 23 10 CENTAVOS Weight: 2.5000 g. **Composition:** 0.9000 Silver .0723 oz. ASW **Subject:** 50th Year of Republic

Date	Mintage	F	VF	XF	Unc	BU
1952	10,000,000	—	0.50	1.00	4.00	10.00

KM# 13.1 20 CENTAVOS Weight: 5.0000 g. **Composition:** 0.9000 Silver .1446 oz. ASW **Reverse:** High relief star

Date	Mintage	F	VF	XF	Unc	BU
1915 Fine reeding	—	—	8.00	35.00	225	500
1915 Coarse reeding	—	—	225	450	—	—
1915 Proof	125	Value: 825				

KM# 13.2 20 CENTAVOS **Weight:** 5.0000 g. **Composition:** 0.9000 Silver .1446 oz. ASW **Reverse:** Low relief star **Note:** Coins with high relief stars normally exhibit a weak key and palm tree on the reverse. Coins with low relief stars tend to exhibit much more distinct lines running towards the center of the star.

Date	Mintage	F	VF	XF	Unc	BU
1915 Fine reeding	Inc. above	—	50.00	175	1,200	1,700
1915 Course reeding	Inc. above	—	5.00	15.00	60.00	100
1916	2,535,000	—	6.50	18.00	225	500
1916 Proof	50	Value: 1,900				
1920	6,130,000	—	3.00	8.00	50.00	100
1932	184,000	—	75.00	300	1,000	1,500
1948	6,830,000	—	1.50	3.00	6.00	12.50
1949	13,170,000	—	1.50	3.00	6.00	12.50

KM# 24 20 CENTAVOS **Weight:** 5.0000 g. **Composition:** 0.9000 Silver .1446 oz. ASW **Subject:** 50th Year of Republic

Date	Mintage	F	VF	XF	Unc	BU
1952	8,700,000	—	1.00	2.50	6.50	17.50

KM# 27 25 CENTAVOS **Weight:** 6.2500 g. **Composition:** 0.9000 Silver .1808 oz. ASW **Subject:** Centennial - Birth of Jose Marti

Date	Mintage	F	VF	XF	Unc	BU
1953	19,000,000	—	1.75	3.50	7.00	15.00
1953 Proof; Rare	—	—	—	—	—	—

KM# 14.1 40 CENTAVOS **Weight:** 10.0000 g. **Composition:** 0.9000 Silver .2893 oz. ASW **Reverse:** High relief star

Date	Mintage	F	VF	XF	Unc	BU
1915	2,633,000	—	12.00	25.00	225	400
1915 Proof	100	Value: 850				
1920	540,000	—	45.00	100	450	1,250
1920 Proof; Rare	—	—	—	—	—	—

KM# 14.2 40 CENTAVOS **Weight:** 10.0000 g. **Composition:** 0.9000 Silver .2893 oz. ASW **Reverse:** Medium relief star

Date	F	VF	XF	Unc	BU
1915	—	100	275	1,250	1,750

KM# 14.3 40 CENTAVOS **Weight:** 10.0000 g. **Composition:** 0.9000 Silver .2893 oz. ASW **Reverse:** Low relief star **Note:** Coins with high relief stars normally exhibit a weak key and palm tree on the reverse. Coins with low relief stars tend to exhibit much more distinct lines running towards the center of the star.

Date	Mintage	F	VF	XF	Unc	BU
1915	Inc. above	—	15.00	35.00	150	350
1916	188,000	—	65.00	350	1,250	2,500
1916 Proof	50	Value: 2,500				
1920	Inc. above	—	75.00	175	700	1,500

KM# 25 40 CENTAVOS **Weight:** 10.0000 g. **Composition:** 0.9000 Silver .2893 oz. ASW **Subject:** 50th Year of Republic

Date	Mintage	F	VF	XF	Unc	BU
1952	1,250,000	—	2.50	5.00	25.00	55.00

KM# 28 50 CENTAVOS **Weight:** 12.5000 g. **Composition:** 0.9000 Silver .3617 oz. ASW **Subject:** Centennial - Birth of Jose Marti

Date	Mintage	F	VF	XF	Unc	BU
ND(1953)	2,000,000	—	3.50	7.50	20.00	35.00
ND(1953) Proof; Rare	—	—	—	—	—	—

KM# 15.1 PESO **Weight:** 26.7295 g. **Composition:** 0.9000 Silver .7735 oz. ASW **Reverse:** High relief star

Date	Mintage	F	VF	XF	Unc	BU
1915	1,976,000	—	20.00	60.00	300	650
1915 Proof	100	Value: 2,000				

KM# 16 PESO **Weight:** 1.6718 g. **Composition:** 0.9000 Gold .0483 oz. AGW **Obverse:** Arms **Reverse:** Bust of Jose Marti

Date	Mintage	F	VF	XF	Unc	BU
1915	6,850	50.00	100	150	250	—
1915 Proof	140	Value: 1,500				
1916	11,000	50.00	100	150	250	—
1916 Proof	100	Value: 1,700				

KM# 15.2 PESO **Weight:** 26.7295 g. **Composition:** 0.9000 Silver .7735 oz. ASW **Reverse:** Low relief star **Note:** Coins with high relief stars normally exhibit a weak key and palm tree on the reverse. Coins with low relief stars tend to exhibit much more distinct lines running towards the center of the star.

Date	Mintage	F	VF	XF	Unc	BU
1915	Inc. above	—	225	600	2,000	4,000
1916	843,000	—	20.00	70.00	1,000	1,750
1916 Proof	50	Value: 3,000				
1932	3,550,000	—	9.00	28.00	175	450
1933	6,000,000	—	9.00	20.00	125	200
1934	3,000,000	—	9.00	20.00	100	175

KM# 22 PESO **Weight:** 26.7295 g. **Composition:** 0.9000 Silver .7735 oz. ASW **Note:** Known as the "ABC" Peso.

Date	Mintage	F	VF	XF	Unc	BU
1934	7,000,000	—	25.00	60.00	175	325
1934 Matte proof	—	Value: 5,250				
1935	12,500,000	—	25.00	55.00	200	300
1936	16,000,000	—	25.00	65.00	250	525
1937	11,500,000	—	250	550	1,000	1,750
1938	10,800,000	—	22.50	45.00	125	250
1939	9,200,000	—	22.50	40.00	100	140

KM# 29 PESO **Weight:** 26.7295 g. **Composition:** 0.9000 Silver .7735 oz. ASW **Subject:** Centennial of Jose Marti

Date	Mintage	F	VF	XF	Unc	BU
ND(1953)	1,000,000	—	4.50	7.00	35.00	75.00
ND(1953) Proof; Rare	—	—	—	—	—	—

KM# 17 2 PESOS **Weight:** 3.3436 g. **Composition:** 0.9000 Gold .0967 oz. AGW **Obverse:** Arms **Reverse:** Bust of Jose Marti

Date	Mintage	F	VF	XF	Unc	BU
1915	10,000	65.00	85.00	115	200	—
1915 Proof	100	Value: 2,000				
1916	150,000	60.00	70.00	85.00	120	—
1916 Proof; Rare	8	—	—	—	—	—

KM# 18 4 PESOS **Weight:** 6.6872 g. **Composition:** 0.9000 Gold .1935 oz. AGW **Obverse:** Arms **Reverse:** Bust of Jose Marti

Date	Mintage	F	VF	XF	Unc	BU
1915	6,300	125	175	275	600	—
1915 Proof	100	Value: 3,000				
1916	129,000	100	120	150	250	—
1916 Proof	90	Value: 4,500				

KM# 19 5 PESOS **Weight:** 8.3592 g. **Composition:** 0.9000 Gold .2419 oz. AGW **Obverse:** Arms **Reverse:** Bust of Jose Marti

Date	Mintage	F	VF	XF	Unc	BU
1915	696,000	—	BV	125	165	—
1915 Proof	—	Value: 3,200				
1916	1,132,000	—	BV	125	150	—
1916 Proof	—	Value: 6,500				

KM# 20 10 PESOS **Weight:** 16.7185 g. **Composition:** 0.9000 Gold .4838 oz. AGW **Obverse:** Arms **Reverse:** Bust of Jose Marti

Date	Mintage	F	VF	XF	Unc	BU
1915	95,000	—	—	250	300	—
1915 Proof	—	Value: 7,500				
1916	1,169,000	—	—	220	275	—
1916 Proof, Rare	—	—	—	—	—	—

Note: David Akers John Jay Pittman sale 8-99 very choice Proof realized $19,550, choice Proof realized $14,950

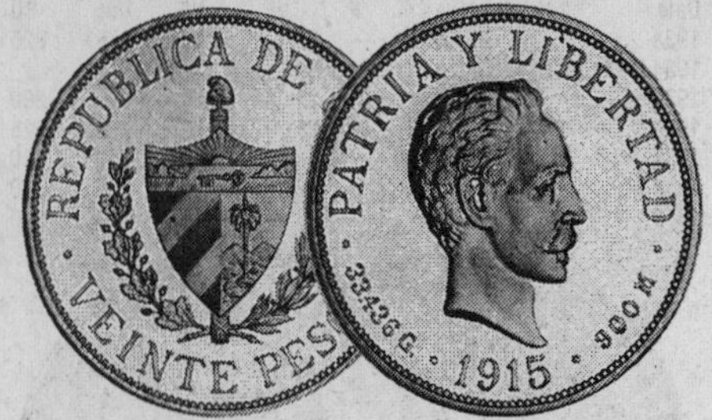

KM# 21 20 PESOS **Weight:** 33.4370 g. **Composition:** 0.9000 Gold .9676 oz. AGW **Subject:** Jose Marti

Date	Mintage	F	VF	XF	Unc	BU
1915	57,000	BV	475	550	750	—
1915 Proof; Rare		—	—	—	—	—

Note: David Akers John Jay Pittman sale 8-99 very choice proof 1915 realized $11,500

Date	Mintage	F	VF	XF	Unc	BU
1916 Proof; Rare	10	—	—	—	—	—

Note: David Akers John Jay Pittman sale 8-99 nearly choice Proof 1916 realized $43,125

SECOND REPUBLIC
1962 - Present
DECIMAL COINAGE

KM# 33.1 CENTAVO **Composition:** Aluminum **Rev. Legend:** PATRIA Y LIBERTAD

Date	Mintage	F	VF	XF	Unc	BU
1963	200,020,000	—	0.10	0.30	0.60	1.25
1966	50,000,000	—	0.10	0.40	0.80	1.75
1967	—	—	—	—	—	—
1969	50,000,000	—	0.10	0.40	0.80	1.75
1970	50,000,000	—	0.10	0.40	0.80	1.75
1971	49,960,000	—	0.40	0.80	1.50	3.00
1972	100,000,000	—	0.10	0.40	0.80	1.75
1978	50,000,000	—	0.10	0.40	0.80	1.75
1979	100,000,000	—	0.10	0.40	0.80	1.75
1981	—	—	0.10	0.40	0.80	1.75
1982	—	—	0.10	0.40	0.80	1.75

KM# 33.2 CENTAVO **Composition:** Aluminum **Rev. Legend:** PATRIA O MUERTE

Date		F	VF	XF	Unc	BU
1983		—	0.10	0.40	0.80	1.75
1984		—	0.10	0.40	0.80	1.75
1985		—	0.10	0.40	0.80	1.75
1986		—	0.10	0.40	0.80	1.75
1987		—	0.10	0.40	0.80	1.75
1988		—	0.10	0.40	0.80	1.75

KM# 33.3 CENTAVO **Composition:** Aluminum **Obverse:** Cuban arms **Reverse:** Wide "1" in star

Date		F	VF	XF	Unc	BU
1998		—	0.10	0.40	0.80	1.75

KM# 729 CENTAVO **Weight:** 1.7000 g. **Composition:** Copper Plated Steel **Obverse:** National arms **Reverse:** Tower and denomination **Edge:** Reeded **Size:** 15 mm.

Date		F	VF	XF	Unc	BU
2000		—	—	—	3.00	—

KM# 104.1 2 CENTAVOS **Composition:** Aluminum **Obverse:** Small lettered legends, long edge denticles **Reverse:** Small lettered legends, long edge denticles

Date	Mintage	F	VF	XF	Unc	BU
1983	3,996,000	—	0.10	0.25	1.00	2.00

KM# 104.2 2 CENTAVOS **Composition:** Aluminum **Obverse:** Large lettered legends, short edge denticles **Reverse:** Large lettered legends, short edge denticles

Date		F	VF	XF	Unc	BU
1983		—	0.10	0.20	0.50	1.00
1984		—	0.10	0.25	1.00	2.00
1985		—	0.10	0.20	0.50	1.00
1986		—	0.10	0.20	0.50	1.00

KM# 34 5 CENTAVOS **Composition:** Aluminum

Date	Mintage	F	VF	XF	Unc	BU
1963	80,000,000	—	0.10	0.25	0.75	1.50
1966	50,000,000	—	0.15	0.35	1.50	3.00
1968	—	—	0.15	0.35	1.50	3.00
1969	—	—	0.25	0.50	2.50	5.00
1971	100,020,000	—	0.10	0.25	0.75	1.50
1972	100,000,000	—	0.10	0.25	0.75	1.50

KM# 31 20 CENTAVOS **Composition:** Copper-Nickel **Subject:** Jose Marti

Date	Mintage	F	VF	XF	Unc	BU
1962	83,860,000	—	1.00	1.50	3.00	6.00
1968	25,750,000	—	1.25	2.00	4.00	8.00

KM# 35 20 CENTAVOS **Composition:** Aluminum

Date	Mintage	F	VF	XF	Unc	BU
1969	25,000,000	—	1.00	1.50	2.50	5.00
1970	29,560,000	0.35	1.25	1.75	4.00	—
1971	25,000,000	—	1.00	1.50	2.50	5.00
1972	—	—	1.00	1.50	2.50	5.00

KM#360 25 CENTAVOS **Composition:** Copper-Nickel **Reverse:** Bust of Carlos Finlay at lower right

Date		F	VF	XF	Unc	BU
ND		—	—	3.00	6.00	9.00

KM#361 25 CENTAVOS **Composition:** Copper-Nickel **Subject:** Alexander von Humboldt

Date		F	VF	XF	Unc	BU
1989		—	—	3.00	6.00	9.00

KM# 32 40 CENTAVOS **Composition:** Copper-Nickel **Subject:** Camilo Cienfuegos Gornaran

Date	Mintage	F	VF	XF	Unc	BU
1962	15,250,000	—	3.00	5.00	7.00	12.00

KM# 186 PESO **Composition:** Copper-Nickel **Subject:** Carlos Manuel de Cespedes

Date	Mintage	F	VF	XF	Unc	BU
ND(1977)	3,000	—	—	—	7.00	—

KM# 187 PESO **Composition:** Copper-Nickel **Subject:** Ignacio Agramonte

Date	Mintage	F	VF	XF	Unc	BU
1977	3,000	—	—	—	7.00	—

KM# 188 PESO **Composition:** Copper-Nickel **Subject:** Maximo Gomez

Date	Mintage	F	VF	XF	Unc	BU
1977	3,000	—	—	—	7.00	—

KM# 189 PESO **Composition:** Copper-Nickel **Subject:** Antonio Maceo

Date	Mintage	F	VF	XF	Unc	BU
1977	3,000	—	—	—	7.00	—

KM# 190 PESO **Composition:** Copper-Nickel **Subject:** 60th Anniversary of Socialist Revolution - Lenin

Date	Mintage	F	VF	XF	Unc	BU
ND(1977)	6,000	—	—	—	15.00	—

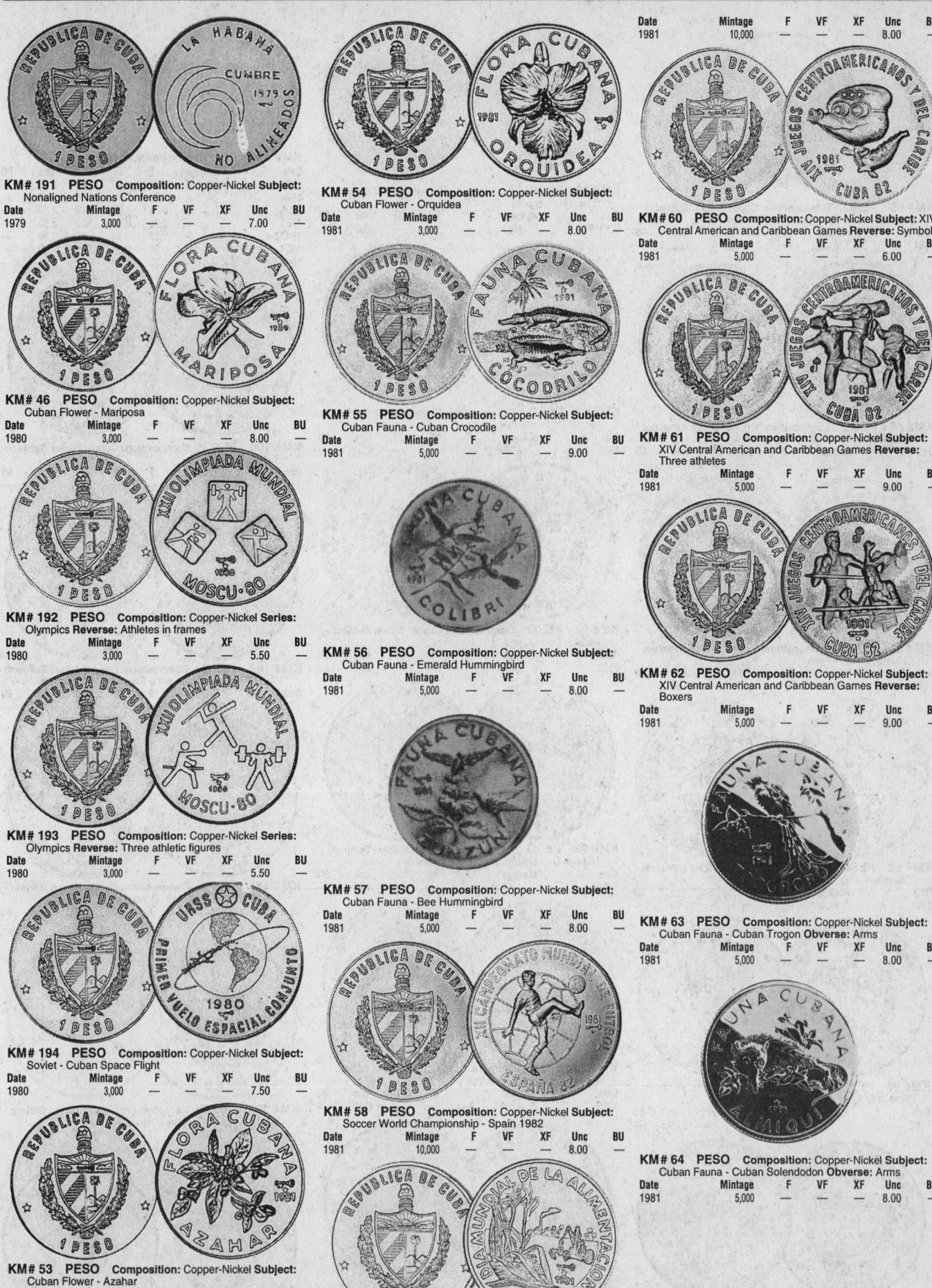

KM# 191 PESO Composition: Copper-Nickel **Subject:** Nonaligned Nations Conference

Date	Mintage	F	VF	XF	Unc	BU
1979	3,000	—	—	—	7.00	—

KM# 46 PESO Composition: Copper-Nickel **Subject:** Cuban Flower - Mariposa

Date	Mintage	F	VF	XF	Unc	BU
1980	3,000	—	—	—	8.00	—

KM# 192 PESO Composition: Copper-Nickel **Series:** Olympics **Reverse:** Athletes in frames

Date	Mintage	F	VF	XF	Unc	BU
1980	3,000	—	—	—	5.50	—

KM# 193 PESO Composition: Copper-Nickel **Series:** Olympics **Reverse:** Three athletic figures

Date	Mintage	F	VF	XF	Unc	BU
1980	3,000	—	—	—	5.50	—

KM# 194 PESO Composition: Copper-Nickel **Subject:** Soviet - Cuban Space Flight

Date	Mintage	F	VF	XF	Unc	BU
1980	3,000	—	—	—	7.50	—

KM# 53 PESO Composition: Copper-Nickel **Subject:** Cuban Flower - Azahar

Date	Mintage	F	VF	XF	Unc	BU
1981	3,000	—	—	—	8.00	—

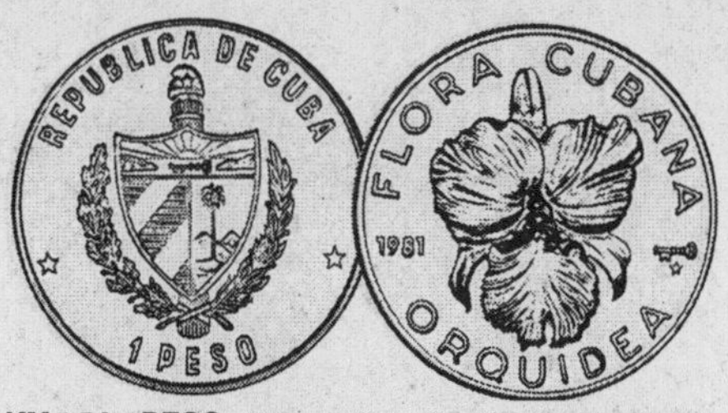

KM# 54 PESO Composition: Copper-Nickel **Subject:** Cuban Flower - Orquidea

Date	Mintage	F	VF	XF	Unc	BU
1981	3,000	—	—	—	8.00	—

KM# 55 PESO Composition: Copper-Nickel **Subject:** Cuban Fauna - Cuban Crocodile

Date	Mintage	F	VF	XF	Unc	BU
1981	5,000	—	—	—	9.00	—

KM# 56 PESO Composition: Copper-Nickel **Subject:** Cuban Fauna - Emerald Hummingbird

Date	Mintage	F	VF	XF	Unc	BU
1981	5,000	—	—	—	8.00	—

KM# 57 PESO Composition: Copper-Nickel **Subject:** Cuban Fauna - Bee Hummingbird

Date	Mintage	F	VF	XF	Unc	BU
1981	5,000	—	—	—	8.00	—

KM# 58 PESO Composition: Copper-Nickel **Subject:** Soccer World Championship - Spain 1982

Date	Mintage	F	VF	XF	Unc	BU
1981	10,000	—	—	—	8.00	—

KM# 59 PESO Composition: Copper-Nickel **Subject:** World Food Day - Sugar Production

Date	Mintage	F	VF	XF	Unc	BU
1981	10,000	—	—	—	8.00	—

KM# 60 PESO Composition: Copper-Nickel **Subject:** XIV Central American and Caribbean Games **Reverse:** Symbols

Date	Mintage	F	VF	XF	Unc	BU
1981	5,000	—	—	—	6.00	—

KM# 61 PESO Composition: Copper-Nickel **Subject:** XIV Central American and Caribbean Games **Reverse:** Three athletes

Date	Mintage	F	VF	XF	Unc	BU
1981	5,000	—	—	—	9.00	—

KM# 62 PESO Composition: Copper-Nickel **Subject:** XIV Central American and Caribbean Games **Reverse:** Boxers

Date	Mintage	F	VF	XF	Unc	BU
1981	5,000	—	—	—	9.00	—

KM# 63 PESO Composition: Copper-Nickel **Subject:** Cuban Fauna - Cuban Trogon **Obverse:** Arms

Date	Mintage	F	VF	XF	Unc	BU
1981	5,000	—	—	—	8.00	—

KM# 64 PESO Composition: Copper-Nickel **Subject:** Cuban Fauna - Cuban Solendodon **Obverse:** Arms

Date	Mintage	F	VF	XF	Unc	BU
1981	5,000	—	—	—	8.00	—

KM# 65 PESO **Composition:** Copper-Nickel **Subject:** Cuban Fauna - Giant Gar Fish **Obverse:** Arms

Date	Mintage	F	VF	XF	Unc	BU
1981	5,000	—	—	—	8.00	—

KM# 66 PESO **Composition:** Copper-Nickel **Reverse:** Columbus' ship - Nina

Date	Mintage	F	VF	XF	Unc	BU
1981	10,000	—	—	—	12.00	—

KM# 67 PESO **Composition:** Copper-Nickel **Reverse:** Columbus' ship - Pinta

Date	Mintage	F	VF	XF	Unc	BU
1981	10,000	—	—	—	12.00	—

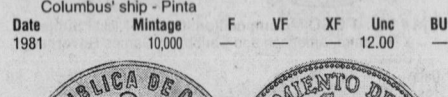

KM# 68 PESO **Composition:** Copper-Nickel **Reverse:** Columbus' ship - Santa Maria

Date	Mintage	F	VF	XF	Unc	BU
1981	10,000	—	—	—	12.00	—

KM# 88 PESO **Composition:** Copper-Nickel **Reverse:** Bust of Ernest Hemingway facing

Date	Mintage	F	VF	XF	Unc	BU
1982	7,000	—	—	—	15.00	—

KM# 89 PESO **Composition:** Copper-Nickel **Subject:** Ernest Hemingway - Fishing Yacht

Date	Mintage	F	VF	XF	Unc	BU
1982	7,000	—	—	—	15.00	—

KM# 90 PESO **Composition:** Copper-Nickel **Subject:** Ernest Hemingway - Small Boat

Date	Mintage	F	VF	XF	Unc	BU
ND(1982)	7,000	—	—	—	15.00	—

KM# 91 PESO **Composition:** Copper-Nickel **Subject:** Miquel De Cervantes

Date	Mintage	F	VF	XF	Unc	BU
1982	7,000	—	—	—	6.50	—

KM# 92 PESO **Composition:** Copper-Nickel **Subject:** Hidalgo Don Quijote

Date	Mintage	F	VF	XF	Unc	BU
1982	7,000	—	—	—	6.50	—

KM# 93 PESO **Composition:** Copper-Nickel **Subject:** Hidalgo Don Quijote and Sancho Panza

Date	Mintage	F	VF	XF	Unc	BU
1982	7,000	—	—	—	6.50	—

KM# 94 PESO **Composition:** Copper-Nickel **Series:** F.A.O. **Reverse:** Citrus fruit

Date	Mintage	F	VF	XF	Unc	BU
1982	6,609	—	—	—	6.50	—

KM# 95 PESO **Composition:** Copper-Nickel **Series:** F.A.O. **Reverse:** Cow

Date	Mintage	F	VF	XF	Unc	BU
1982	5,684	—	—	—	7.00	—

KM# 105 PESO **Composition:** Brass

Date	Mintage	F	VF	XF	Unc	BU
1983	10,000,000	0.25	0.50	1.00	2.50	—
1984	—	0.25	0.50	1.00	2.50	—
1985	—	0.25	0.50	1.00	2.50	—
1986	—	0.25	0.50	1.00	2.50	—
1987	—	0.25	0.50	1.00	2.50	—
1988	—	0.25	0.50	1.00	2.50	—
1989	—	0.25	0.50	1.00	2.50	—

KM# 106 PESO **Composition:** Copper-Nickel **Subject:** Railroad

Date	Mintage	F	VF	XF	Unc	BU
1983	7,000	—	—	—	7.50	—

KM# 107 PESO **Composition:** Copper-Nickel **Subject:** World Fisheries Conference **Reverse:** Spiny lobster

Date	Mintage	F	VF	XF	Unc	BU
1983	5,000	—	—	—	6.50	—

KM# 173 PESO **Composition:** Copper-Nickel **Series:** 1984 Olympics **Reverse:** Runner

Date	Mintage	F	VF	XF	Unc	BU
1983	3,000	—	—	—	4.50	—

KM# 174 PESO **Composition:** Copper-Nickel **Series:** 1984 Olympics **Reverse:** Discus thrower

Date	Mintage	F	VF	XF	Unc	BU
1983	3,000	—	—	—	4.50	—

KM# 175 PESO **Composition:** Copper-Nickel **Series:** 1984 Olympics **Reverse:** Judo

Date	Mintage	F	VF	XF	Unc	BU
1983	3,000	—	—	—	4.50	—

KM# 195 PESO **Composition:** Copper-Nickel **Series:** Olympics **Reverse:** Woman holding torch

Date	Mintage	F	VF	XF	Unc	BU
1983	3,000	—	—	—	4.50	—

KM# 196 PESO **Composition:** Copper-Nickel **Series:** Olympics **Reverse:** Two hockey players

Date	Mintage	F	VF	XF	Unc	BU
1983	3,000	—	—	—	4.50	—

KM# 197 PESO **Composition:** Copper-Nickel **Series:** Olympics **Reverse:** Downhill skier

Date	Mintage	F	VF	XF	Unc	BU
1983	3,000	—	—	—	4.50	—

KM# 118 PESO **Composition:** Copper-Nickel **Subject:** Santisima Trinidad **Obverse:** Arms

Date	Mintage	F	VF	XF	Unc	BU
1984	3,000	—	—	—	8.00	—

KM# 130 PESO **Composition:** Copper-Nickel **Subject:** Transportation **Reverse:** Volanta coach

Date	Mintage	F	VF	XF	Unc	BU
1984	5,000	—	—	—	8.00	—

KM# 140 PESO **Composition:** Copper-Nickel **Subject:** Castillos - El Morro La Habana **Obverse:** Arms

Date	Mintage	F	VF	XF	Unc	BU
1984	5,000	—	—	—	8.00	—

KM# 142 PESO **Composition:** Copper-Nickel **Subject:** Castillos - La Fuerza La Habana **Obverse:** Arms

Date	Mintage	F	VF	XF	Unc	BU
1984	5,000	—	—	—	10.00	—

KM# 144 PESO **Composition:** Copper-Nickel **Subject:** Castillos - El Morro Santiago De Cuba **Obverse:** Arms

Date	Mintage	F	VF	XF	Unc	BU
1984	5,000	—	—	—	8.00	—

KM# 172 PESO **Composition:** Copper-Nickel **Subject:** Transportation **Reverse:** Hot air balloon

Date	Mintage	F	VF	XF	Unc	BU
1984	23	—	—	—	1,400	—

KM# 116 PESO **Composition:** Copper-Nickel **Subject:** Transportation **Reverse:** Freighter **Note:** Similar to 5 Pesos, KM#117.

Date	Mintage	F	VF	XF	Unc	BU
1984	5,000	—	—	—	8.00	—

KM# 120 PESO **Composition:** Copper-Nickel **Subject:** International Year of Music **Reverse:** Bust of Bach at left, musical score at right

Date	Mintage	F	VF	XF	Unc	BU
1985	2,000	—	—	—	9.00	—

KM# 124 PESO **Composition:** Copper-Nickel **Subject:** Wildlife Preservation **Reverse:** Cuban crocodile (head only)

Date	Mintage	F	VF	XF	Unc	BU
1985	5,000	—	—	—	12.00	—

KM# 126 PESO **Composition:** Copper-Nickel **Subject:** Wildlife Preservation **Reverse:** Cuban rock iguana (half body)

Date	Mintage	F	VF	XF	Unc	BU
1985	5,000	—	—	—	13.00	—

KM# 128 PESO **Composition:** Copper-Nickel **Subject:** Wildlife Preservation **Reverse:** Cuban amazon parrot (head)

Date	Mintage	F	VF	XF	Unc	BU
1985	5,000	—	—	—	15.00	—

KM# 132 PESO **Composition:** Copper-Nickel **Subject:** 40th Anniversary of F.A.O. **Reverse:** Sugar cane, lobster, palm tree, and F.A.O. logo

Date	Mintage	F	VF	XF	Unc	BU
ND(1985)	5,000	—	—	—	8.00	—

KM# 133 PESO **Composition:** Copper-Nickel **Series:** F.A.O. **Reverse:** Two people amid forest

Date	Mintage	F	VF	XF	Unc	BU
1985	5,000	—	—	—	6.50	—

KM# 181 PESO **Composition:** Copper-Nickel **Subject:** Wildlife Preservation **Reverse:** Crocodile (full body)

Date	F	VF	XF	Unc	BU
1985	—	—	—	35.00	—

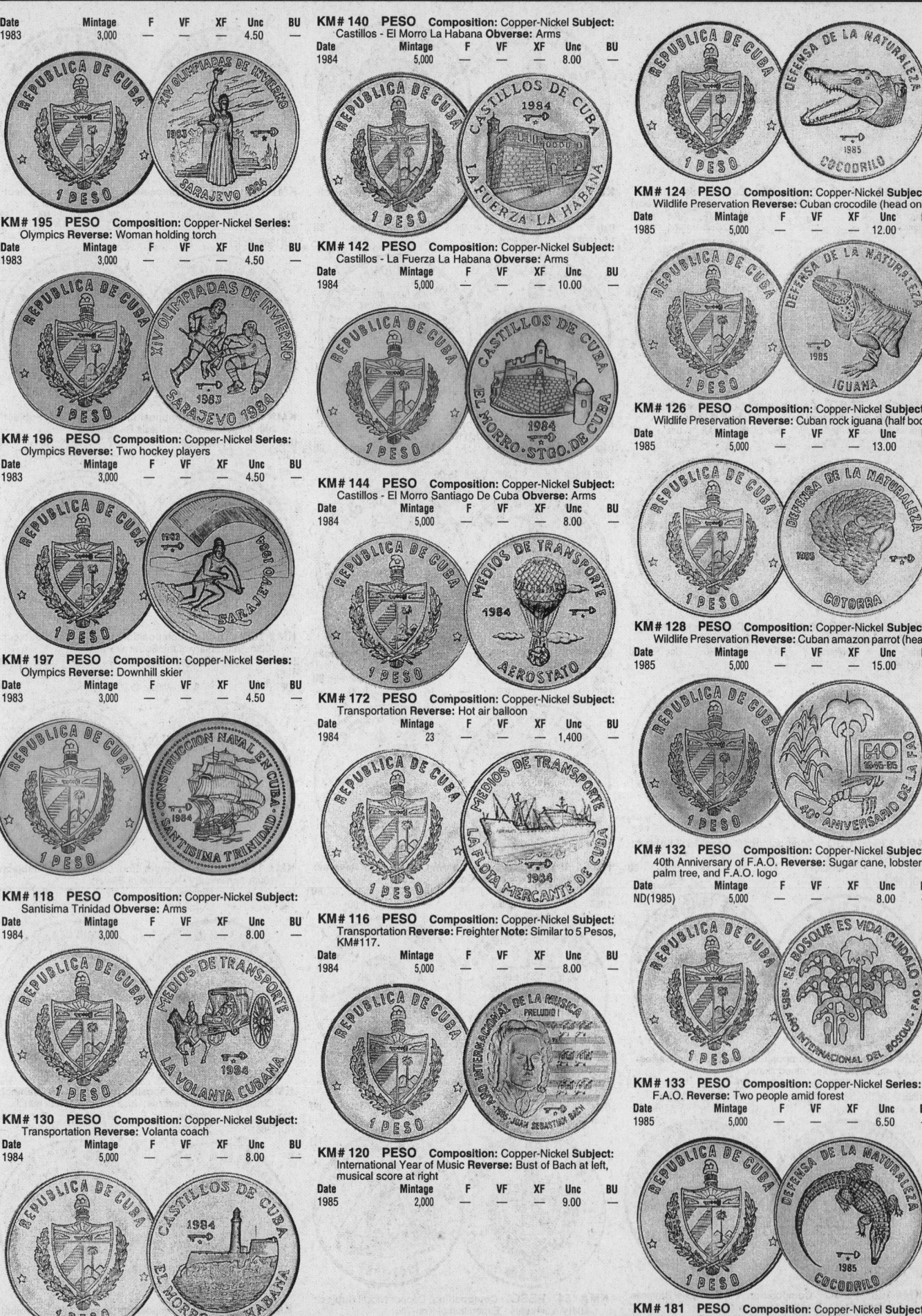

KM# 182 PESO **Composition:** Copper-Nickel **Subject:** Wildlife Preservation **Reverse:** Cuban rock iguana (full body)

Date	F	VF	XF	Unc	BU
1985	—	—	—	35.00	—

KM# 183 PESO **Composition:** Copper-Nickel **Subject:** Wildlife Preservation **Reverse:** Parrot (full body)

Date	F	VF	XF	Unc	BU
1985	—	—	—	32.50	—

KM# 134 PESO **Composition:** Copper-Nickel **Subject:** 100th Anniversary of Automobile **Reverse:** Mercedes

Date	Mintage	F	VF	XF	Unc	BU
ND(1986)	3,000	—	—	—	8.00	—

KM# 136 PESO **Composition:** Copper-Nickel **Subject:** 30th Anniversary - Voyage of the Granma

Date	Mintage	F	VF	XF	Unc	BU
ND(1986)	3,000	—	—	—	8.00	—

KM# 138 PESO **Composition:** Copper-Nickel **Series:** Olympics **Reverse:** Speed skater

Date	Mintage	F	VF	XF	Unc	BU
1986	1,000	—	—	—	12.50	—

KM# 198 PESO **Composition:** Copper-Nickel **Reverse:** Similar to KM#138, without rings above skater

Date	Mintage	F	VF	XF	Unc	BU
1986	3,000	—	—	—	4.50	—

KM# 122 PESO **Composition:** Copper-Nickel **Subject:** Soccer World Championship - Mexico '85 **Reverse:** Two soccer players

Date	Mintage	F	VF	XF	Unc	BU
ND(1986)	5,000	—	—	—	8.00	—

KM# 156 PESO **Composition:** Copper-Nickel **Subject:** International Year of Peace **Reverse:** Dove

Date	Mintage	F	VF	XF	Unc	BU
1986	5,000	—	—	—	8.00	—
1986 Proof	5,000	Value: 15.00				

KM# 148 PESO **Composition:** Copper-Nickel **Reverse:** Cathedral in Santiago

Date	Mintage	F	VF	XF	Unc	BU
1987	3,000	—	—	—	8.00	—

KM# 150 PESO **Composition:** Copper-Nickel **Reverse:** Cathedral in Caridad del Cobre

Date	Mintage	F	VF	XF	Unc	BU
1987	3,000	—	—	—	8.00	—

KM# 152 PESO **Composition:** Copper-Nickel **Reverse:** Cathedral in Trinidad

Date	Mintage	F	VF	XF	Unc	BU
1987	3,000	—	—	—	8.00	—

KM# 154 PESO **Composition:** Copper Nickel **Subject:** 40th Anniversary - Expedition of Kon-Tiki

Date	Mintage	F	VF	XF	Unc	BU
ND(1987)	3,000	—	—	—	12.00	—

KM# 158 PESO **Composition:** Copper-Nickel **Subject:** 20th Anniversary - Demise of Ernesto Che Guevara

Date	Mintage	F	VF	XF	Unc	BU
ND(1987)	6,000	—	—	—	15.00	—
ND(1987) Proof	200	Value: 40.00				

KM# 160 PESO **Composition:** Copper-Nickel **Subject:** 70th Anniversary of Bolshevik Revolution

Date	Mintage	F	VF	XF	Unc	BU
1987	5,000	—	—	—	7.50	—

KM# 165 PESO **Composition:** Copper-Nickel **Subject:** 100th Anniversary of the Souvenir Peso

Date	Mintage	F	VF	XF	Unc	BU
1987	3,000	—	—	—	10.00	—
1987 Proof	3,000	Value: 45.00				

KM# 167 PESO **Composition:** Copper-Nickel **Subject:** 100th Anniversary - Abolition of Slavery

Date	Mintage	F	VF	XF	Unc	BU
1987	2,000	—	—	—	12.50	—

KM# 179 PESO **Composition:** Copper-Nickel **Subject:** Chess Centennial **Reverse:** Jose Capablanca at match

Date	Mintage	F	VF	XF	Unc	BU
ND(1988)	1,000	—	—	—	13.50	—

KM# 184 PESO **Composition:** Copper-Nickel **Subject:** Soccer - 1986 Mexico

Date	Mintage	F	VF	XF	Unc	BU
1988	1,000	—	—	—	13.50	—

KM# 200 PESO **Composition:** Copper-Nickel **Subject:** Chess Centennial **Reverse:** Chess pieces

Date	Mintage	F	VF	XF	Unc	BU
ND(1988)	6,000	—	—	—	10.00	—

KM# 244 PESO **Composition:** Copper-Nickel **Subject:** Soccer World Championship - Italy 1990

Date	Mintage	F	VF	XF	Unc	BU
1988	2,000	—	—	—	12.00	—

KM# 245 PESO **Composition:** Copper-Nickel **Subject:** European World Soccer Championship - Federal Republic of Germany **Reverse:** Three players

Date	Mintage	F	VF	XF	Unc	BU
1988	2,000	—	—	—	12.00	—

KM# 246 PESO **Composition:** Copper-Nickel **Subject:** European World Soccer Championship - Federal Republic of Germany **Reverse:** Four players

Date	Mintage	F	VF	XF	Unc	BU
1988	2,000	—	—	—	14.50	—

KM# 276 PESO **Composition:** Copper-Nickel **Subject:** 40th Anniversary of Cuban National Ballet

Date	Mintage	F	VF	XF	Unc	BU
ND(1988)	2,000	—	—	—	10.00	—

KM# 277 PESO **Composition:** Copper-Nickel **Subject:** 150th Anniversary of Havana Grand Theater

Date	Mintage	F	VF	XF	Unc	BU
ND(1977)	2,000	—	—	—	10.00	—

KM# 282 PESO **Composition:** Copper-Nickel **Reverse:** Carlos J. Finlay

Date	Mintage	F	VF	XF	Unc	BU
ND(1988)	2,000	—	—	—	11.50	—

KM# 512 PESO **Composition:** Copper **Reverse:** Bust of Carlos J. Finlay at lower right

Date	Mintage	F	VF	XF	Unc	BU
ND(1988)	2,500	—	—	—	6.00	—

KM# 258 PESO **Composition:** Copper **Subject:** World Health Organization

Date	Mintage	F	VF	XF	Unc	BU
1988	2,000	—	—	—	10.00	—

KM# 269 PESO **Composition:** Copper **Subject:** Transportation **Reverse:** Zeppelin

Date	Mintage	F	VF	XF	Unc	BU
1988	1,000	—	—	—	25.00	—

KM# 324 PESO **Composition:** Copper-Nickel **Subject:** Assault of the Moncada Garrison **Reverse:** Battle scene

Date	Mintage	F	VF	XF	Unc	BU
1988	2,000	—	—	—	10.00	—

KM# 363 PESO **Composition:** Brass **Reverse:** Bust of Jose Marti right

Date	F	VF	XF	Unc	BU
1988	—	—	—	12.00	—

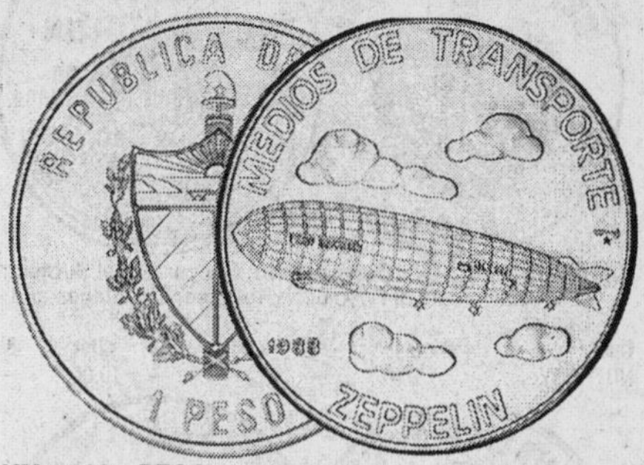

KM# 513 PESO **Composition:** Copper **Subject:** Transportation **Reverse:** Zeppelin

Date	Mintage	F	VF	XF	Unc	BU
1988	2,500	—	—	—	10.00	—

KM# 247 PESO **Composition:** Copper-Nickel **Subject:** World Soccer Championship - Italy 1990 **Reverse:** Three players

Date	Mintage	F	VF	XF	Unc	BU
1989	4,000	—	—	—	12.00	—

KM# 248 PESO **Composition:** Copper-Nickel **Subject:** World Soccer Championship - Italy 1990 **Reverse:** Colosseum

Date	Mintage	F	VF	XF	Unc	BU
1989	2,000	—	—	—	12.00	—

KM# 253 PESO **Composition:** Copper-Nickel **Subject:** 30th Anniversary of Revolution **Reverse:** Castro with gun standing before radiant sun

Date	Mintage	F	VF	XF	Unc	BU
ND(1989)	5,000	—	—	—	10.00	—

KM# 254 PESO **Composition:** Copper-Nickel **Subject:** 30th Anniversary of Revolution **Reverse:** Facing busts of Jose Marti and Castro

Date	Mintage	F	VF	XF	Unc	BU
1989	5,000	—	—	—	12.00	—

KM# 255 PESO Composition: Copper-Nickel **Subject:** 30th Anniversary of Revolution **Reverse:** Cienfuegos and Castro

Date	Mintage	F	VF	XF	Unc	BU
ND(1989)	5,000	—	—	—	10.00	—

KM# 257 PESO Composition: Copper-Nickel **Subject:** Triumph of the Revolution

Date	Mintage	F	VF	XF	Unc	BU
1989	2,000	—	—	—	12.00	—

KM# 259 PESO Composition: Copper-Nickel **Subject:** Cuban Tobacco

Date	Mintage	F	VF	XF	Unc	BU
1989	1,000	—	—	—	14.00	—

KM# 260 PESO Composition: Copper-Nickel **Subject:** 160th Anniversary of First Railroad in England

Date	Mintage	F	VF	XF	Unc	BU
1989	2,000	—	—	—	12.00	—

KM# 261 PESO Composition: Copper-Nickel **Subject:** 500th Anniversary - Discovery of America

Date	Mintage	F	VF	XF	Unc	BU
1989	3,145	—	—	—	12.00	—

KM# 270 PESO Composition: Copper-Nickel **Subject:** 30th Anniversary - The March to Victory

Date	Mintage	F	VF	XF	Unc	BU
1989	2,000	—	—	—	10.00	—

KM# 271 PESO Composition: Copper-Nickel **Subject:** 200th Anniversary of French Revolution - Female Allegory of Revolution

Date	Mintage	F	VF	XF	Unc	BU
ND(1989)	2,000	—	—	—	10.00	—

KM# 272 PESO Composition: Copper-Nickel **Subject:** 200th Anniversary of French Revolution - Bastille

Date	Mintage	F	VF	XF	Unc	BU
ND(1989)	2,000	—	—	—	8.00	—

KM# 274 PESO Composition: Copper-Nickel **Subject:** First Spanish Railroad

Date	Mintage	F	VF	XF	Unc	BU
1989	2,000	—	—	—	10.00	—

KM# 275 PESO Composition: Copper-Nickel **Subject:** First Cuban Railroad

Date	Mintage	F	VF	XF	Unc	BU
1989	2,000	—	—	—	15.00	—

KM# 278 PESO Composition: Copper-Nickel **Subject:** 5th Centennial - Discovery of America

Date	Mintage	F	VF	XF	Unc	BU
1989	2,000	—	—	—	10.00	—

KM# 283 PESO Composition: Copper-Nickel **Subject:** Alexander von Humboldt **Reverse:** Cameo of Alexander von Humboldt, birds on branch

Date	Mintage	F	VF	XF	Unc	BU
1989	2,000	—	—	—	12.50	—

KM# 284 PESO Composition: Copper-Nickel **Series:** 1992 Olympics **Reverse:** Two boxers

Date	Mintage	F	VF	XF	Unc	BU
1989	1,000	—	—	—	13.50	—

KM# 285 PESO Composition: Copper-Nickel **Reverse:** Facing bust of Camilo Cienfuegos

Date	Mintage	F	VF	XF	Unc	BU
1989	2,000	—	—	—	10.00	—

KM# 286 PESO Composition: Copper-Nickel **Reverse:** Profile of Ernesto Che Guevara

Date	Mintage	F	VF	XF	Unc	BU
1989	2,000	—	—	—	18.00	—

KM# 287 PESO Composition: Copper-Nickel **Reverse:** Bust of Tania La Guerrillera

Date	Mintage	F	VF	XF	Unc	BU
1989	2,000	—	—	—	10.00	—

KM# 436 PESO Composition: Copper **Reverse:** Cameo of Alexander von Humboldt, birds

Date	F	VF	XF	Unc	BU
1989	—	—	—	10.00	—

KM# 250 PESO Composition: Copper **Reverse:** Esperanto at right, world globe at left

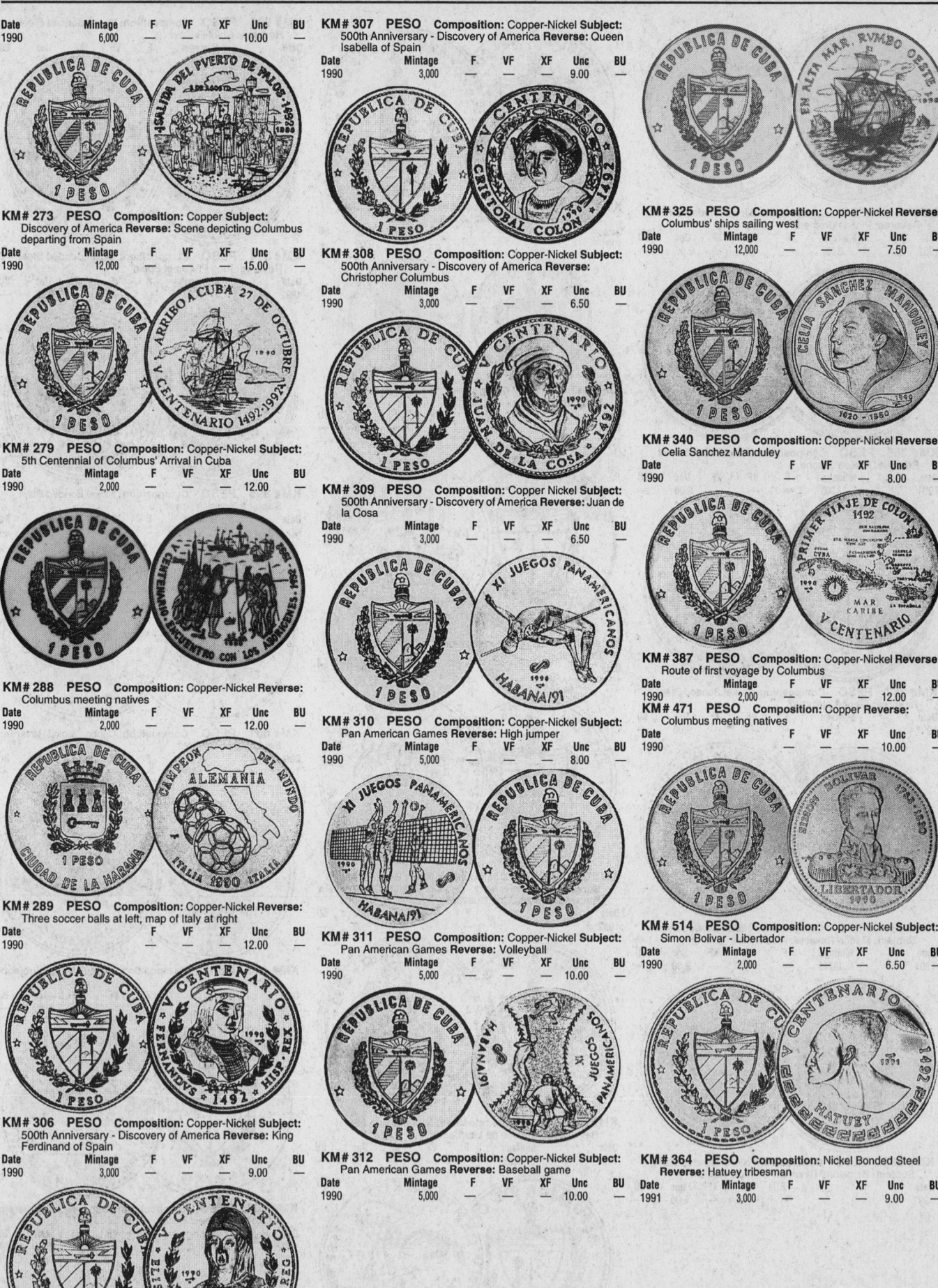

Date	Mintage	F	VF	XF	Unc	BU
1990	6,000	—	—	—	10.00	—

KM# 273 PESO Composition: Copper **Subject:** Discovery of America **Reverse:** Scene depicting Columbus departing from Spain

Date	Mintage	F	VF	XF	Unc	BU
1990	12,000	—	—	—	15.00	—

KM# 279 PESO Composition: Copper-Nickel **Subject:** 5th Centennial of Columbus' Arrival in Cuba

Date	Mintage	F	VF	XF	Unc	BU
1990	2,000	—	—	—	12.00	—

KM# 288 PESO Composition: Copper-Nickel **Reverse:** Columbus meeting natives

Date	Mintage	F	VF	XF	Unc	BU
1990	2,000	—	—	—	12.00	—

KM# 289 PESO Composition: Copper-Nickel **Reverse:** Three soccer balls at left, map of Italy at right

Date	F	VF	XF	Unc	BU
1990	—	—	—	12.00	—

KM# 306 PESO Composition: Copper-Nickel **Subject:** 500th Anniversary - Discovery of America **Reverse:** King Ferdinand of Spain

Date	Mintage	F	VF	XF	Unc	BU
1990	3,000	—	—	—	9.00	—

KM# 307 PESO Composition: Copper-Nickel **Subject:** 500th Anniversary - Discovery of America **Reverse:** Queen Isabella of Spain

Date	Mintage	F	VF	XF	Unc	BU
1990	3,000	—	—	—	9.00	—

KM# 308 PESO Composition: Copper-Nickel **Subject:** 500th Anniversary - Discovery of America **Reverse:** Christopher Columbus

Date	Mintage	F	VF	XF	Unc	BU
1990	3,000	—	—	—	6.50	—

KM# 309 PESO Composition: Copper Nickel **Subject:** 500th Anniversary - Discovery of America **Reverse:** Juan de la Cosa

Date	Mintage	F	VF	XF	Unc	BU
1990	3,000	—	—	—	6.50	—

KM# 310 PESO Composition: Copper-Nickel **Subject:** Pan American Games **Reverse:** High jumper

Date	Mintage	F	VF	XF	Unc	BU
1990	5,000	—	—	—	8.00	—

KM# 311 PESO Composition: Copper-Nickel **Subject:** Pan American Games **Reverse:** Volleyball

Date	Mintage	F	VF	XF	Unc	BU
1990	5,000	—	—	—	10.00	—

KM# 312 PESO Composition: Copper-Nickel **Subject:** Pan American Games **Reverse:** Baseball game

Date	Mintage	F	VF	XF	Unc	BU
1990	5,000	—	—	—	10.00	—

KM# 325 PESO Composition: Copper-Nickel **Reverse:** Columbus' ships sailing west

Date	Mintage	F	VF	XF	Unc	BU
1990	12,000	—	—	—	7.50	—

KM# 340 PESO Composition: Copper-Nickel **Reverse:** Celia Sanchez Manduley

Date	F	VF	XF	Unc	BU
1990	—	—	—	8.00	—

KM# 387 PESO Composition: Copper-Nickel **Reverse:** Route of first voyage by Columbus

Date	Mintage	F	VF	XF	Unc	BU
1990	2,000	—	—	—	12.00	—

KM# 471 PESO Composition: Copper **Reverse:** Columbus meeting natives

Date	F	VF	XF	Unc	BU
1990	—	—	—	10.00	—

KM# 514 PESO Composition: Copper-Nickel **Subject:** Simon Bolivar - Libertador

Date	Mintage	F	VF	XF	Unc	BU
1990	2,000	—	—	—	6.50	—

KM# 364 PESO Composition: Nickel Bonded Steel **Reverse:** Hatuey tribesman

Date	Mintage	F	VF	XF	Unc	BU
1991	3,000	—	—	—	9.00	—

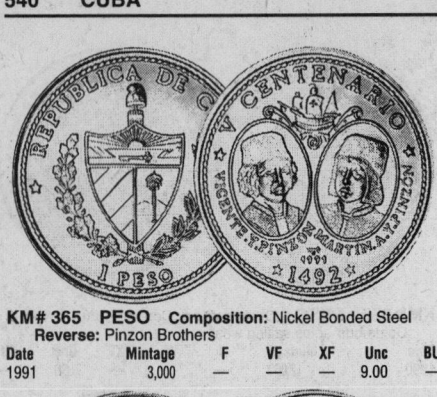

KM# 365 PESO **Composition:** Nickel Bonded Steel **Reverse:** Pinzon Brothers

Date	Mintage	F	VF	XF	Unc	BU
1991	3,000	—	—	—	9.00	—

KM# 366 PESO **Composition:** Nickel Bonded Steel **Reverse:** Queen Joanna

Date	Mintage	F	VF	XF	Unc	BU
1991	3,000	—	—	—	9.00	—

KM# 367 PESO **Composition:** Nickel Bonded Steel **Reverse:** Diego Velazquez

Date	Mintage	F	VF	XF	Unc	BU
1991	3,000	—	—	—	9.00	—

KM# 388 PESO **Composition:** Nickel Bonded Steel **Subject:** Madrid **Reverse:** Alcala Gate

Date	Mintage	F	VF	XF	Unc	BU
1991	10,000	—	—	—	9.00	—

KM# 389 PESO **Composition:** Nickel Bonded Steel **Subject:** Barcelona **Reverse:** Olympic stadium

Date		F	VF	XF	Unc	BU
1991		—	—	—	5.00	—

KM# 390 PESO **Composition:** Nickel Bonded Steel **Subject:** Seville **Reverse:** La Giralda Tower

Date		F	VF	XF	Unc	BU
1991		—	—	—	9.00	—

KM# 347 PESO **Composition:** Brass Plated Steel **Subject:** Jose Marti

Date		F	VF	XF	Unc	BU
1992		—	—	1.00	2.00	—
1994		—	—	1.00	2.00	—

KM# 368 PESO **Composition:** Copper-Nickel **Subject:** Postal Ship

Date		F	VF	XF	Unc	BU
1992		—	—	—	12.00	—

KM# 391 PESO **Composition:** Nickel Bonded Steel **Subject:** 25th Anniversary - Death of Ernesto Che Guevara **Reverse:** Ernesto Che Guevara

Date		F	VF	XF	Unc	BU
1992		—	—	—	9.00	—

KM# 392 PESO **Composition:** Nickel Bonded Steel **Reverse:** Bartolome de Las Casas

Date	Mintage	F	VF	XF	Unc	BU
1992	3,000	—	—	—	9.00	—

KM# 393 PESO **Composition:** Nickel Bonded Steel **Reverse:** Chief Guama

Date	Mintage	F	VF	XF	Unc	BU
1992	3,000	—	—	—	9.00	—

KM# 394 PESO **Composition:** Nickel Bonded Steel **Reverse:** King Philipp of Spain

Date	Mintage	F	VF	XF	Unc	BU
1992	3,000	—	—	—	9.00	—

KM# 395 PESO **Composition:** Nickel Bonded Steel **Subject:** Spanish Royalty

Date	Mintage	F	VF	XF	Unc	BU
ND(1992)	3,000	—	—	—	9.00	—

KM# 401 PESO **Composition:** Copper-Nickel **Reverse:** Seville Tower of Gold

Date		F	VF	XF	Unc	BU
1992		—	—	—	5.00	—

KM# 402 PESO **Composition:** Copper-Nickel **Subject:** El Escorial

Date		F	VF	XF	Unc	BU
1992		—	—	—	5.00	—

KM# 403 PESO **Composition:** Copper-Nickel **Reverse:** St. Jorge Palace

Date	Mintage	F	VF	XF	Unc	BU
1992	10,000	—	—	—	5.00	—

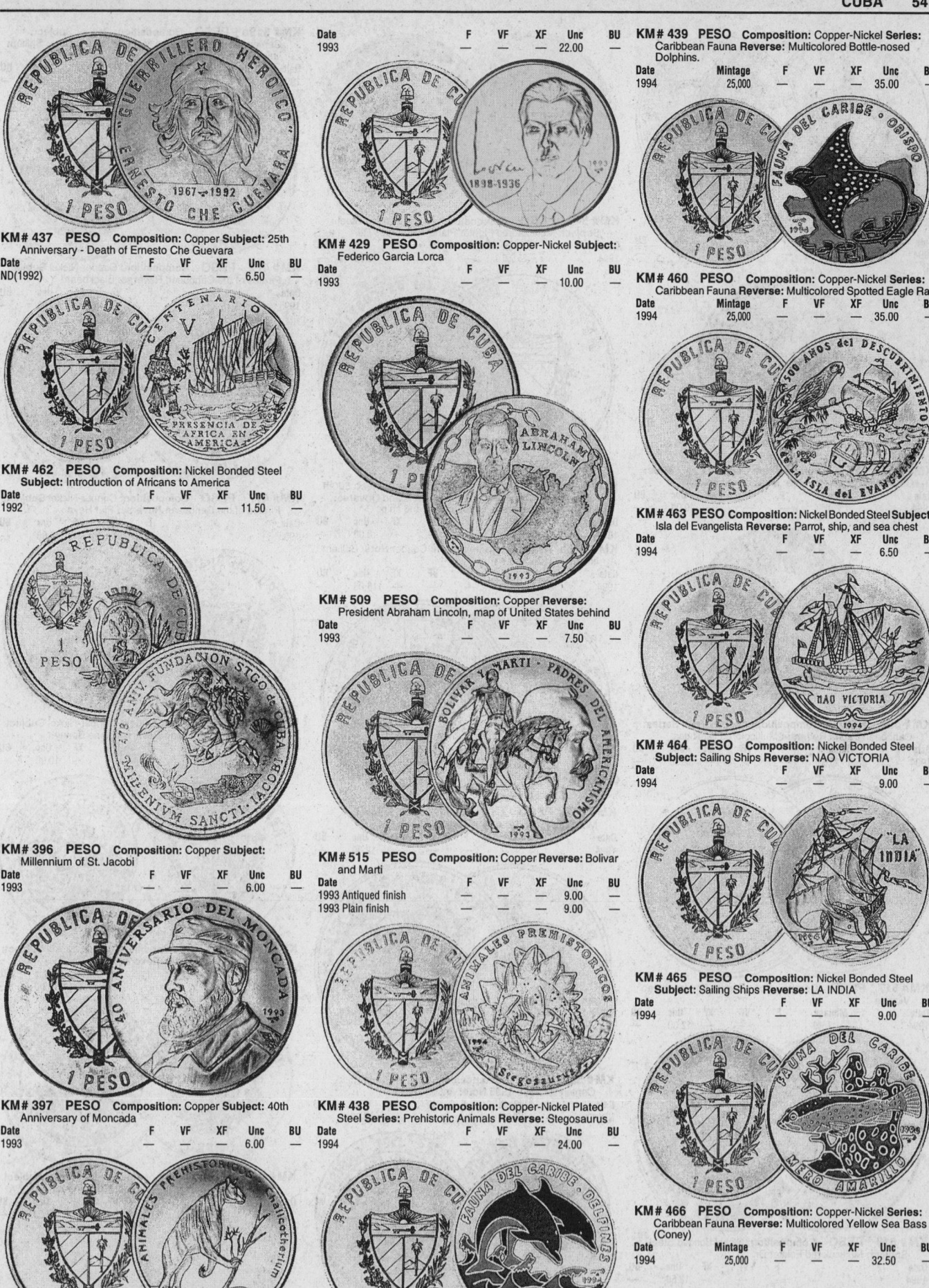

KM# 437 PESO Composition: Copper **Subject:** 25th Anniversary - Death of Ernesto Che Guevara

Date	F	VF	XF	Unc	BU
ND(1992)	—	—	—	6.50	—

KM# 462 PESO Composition: Nickel Bonded Steel **Subject:** Introduction of Africans to America

Date	F	VF	XF	Unc	BU
1992	—	—	—	11.50	—

KM# 396 PESO Composition: Copper **Subject:** Millennium of St. Jacobi

Date	F	VF	XF	Unc	BU
1993	—	—	—	6.00	—

KM# 397 PESO Composition: Copper **Subject:** 40th Anniversary of Moncada

Date	F	VF	XF	Unc	BU
1993	—	—	—	6.00	—

KM# 404 PESO Composition: Copper-Nickel **Series:** Prehistoric Animals **Reverse:** Chalicotherium

Date	F	VF	XF	Unc	BU
1993	—	—	—	22.00	—

KM# 429 PESO Composition: Copper-Nickel **Subject:** Federico Garcia Lorca

Date	F	VF	XF	Unc	BU
1993	—	—	—	10.00	—

KM# 509 PESO Composition: Copper **Reverse:** President Abraham Lincoln, map of United States behind

Date	F	VF	XF	Unc	BU
1993	—	—	—	7.50	—

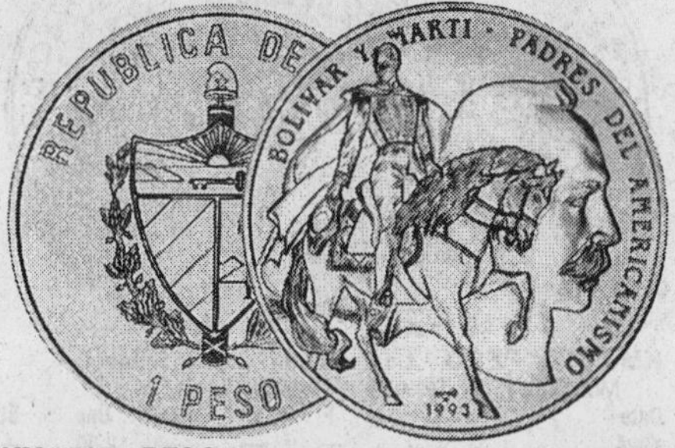

KM# 515 PESO Composition: Copper **Reverse:** Bolivar and Marti

Date	F	VF	XF	Unc	BU
1993 Antiqued finish	—	—	—	9.00	—
1993 Plain finish	—	—	—	9.00	—

KM# 438 PESO Composition: Copper-Nickel Plated Steel **Series:** Prehistoric Animals **Reverse:** Stegosaurus

Date	F	VF	XF	Unc	BU
1994	—	—	—	24.00	—

KM# 439 PESO Composition: Copper-Nickel **Series:** Caribbean Fauna **Reverse:** Multicolored Bottle-nosed Dolphins.

Date	Mintage	F	VF	XF	Unc	BU
1994	25,000	—	—	—	35.00	—

KM# 460 PESO Composition: Copper-Nickel **Series:** Caribbean Fauna **Reverse:** Multicolored Spotted Eagle Ray

Date	Mintage	F	VF	XF	Unc	BU
1994	25,000	—	—	—	35.00	—

KM# 463 PESO Composition: Nickel Bonded Steel **Subject:** Isla del Evangelista **Reverse:** Parrot, ship, and sea chest

Date	F	VF	XF	Unc	BU
1994	—	—	—	6.50	—

KM# 464 PESO Composition: Nickel Bonded Steel **Subject:** Sailing Ships **Reverse:** NAO VICTORIA

Date	F	VF	XF	Unc	BU
1994	—	—	—	9.00	—

KM# 465 PESO Composition: Nickel Bonded Steel **Subject:** Sailing Ships **Reverse:** LA INDIA

Date	F	VF	XF	Unc	BU
1994	—	—	—	9.00	—

KM# 466 PESO Composition: Copper-Nickel **Series:** Caribbean Fauna **Reverse:** Multicolored Yellow Sea Bass (Coney)

Date	Mintage	F	VF	XF	Unc	BU
1994	25,000	—	—	—	32.50	—

KM# 467 PESO Composition: Copper-Nickel **Series:** Caribbean Fauna **Reverse:** Multicolored Swordfish

Date	Mintage	F	VF	XF	Unc	BU
1994	25,000	—	—	—	35.00	—

KM# 497 PESO Composition: Copper-Nickel **Series:** Caribbean Fauna **Reverse:** Multicolored pelican

Date	Mintage	F	VF	XF	Unc	BU
1994	25,000	—	—	—	40.00	—

KM# 498 PESO Composition: Copper-Nickel **Series:** Caribbean Fauna **Reverse:** Multicolored flamingos

Date	Mintage	F	VF	XF	Unc	BU
1994	25,000	—	—	—	32.50	—

KM# 517 PESO Composition: Copper **Reverse:** Nao Victoria

Date	Mintage	F	VF	XF	Unc	BU
1994	2,500	—	—	—	12.00	—

KM# 518 PESO Composition: Nickel Bonded Steel **Subject:** Multicolored Fokker Dr. I

Date	F	VF	XF	Unc	BU
1994	—	—	—	18.50	—

KM# 547 PESO Composition: Nickel Bonded Steel **Subject:** Multicolored Fighter Plane - Albatross DII

Date	Mintage	F	VF	XF	Unc	BU
1994	25,000	—	—	—	18.50	—

KM# 606 PESO Composition: Copper **Subject:** 500th Anniversary - Discovery of Evangelista Island **Obverse:** Cuban arms **Reverse:** Parrot, chest, and ship

Date	F	VF	XF	Unc	BU
1994	—	—	—	8.00	—

KM# 516a PESO Composition: Copper **Note:** Brilliant finish

Date	F	VF	XF	Unc	BU
1994	—	—	—	15.00	—

KM# 516 PESO Composition: Copper **Subject:** Montecristi Manifesto **Note:** Antique finish.

Date	F	VF	XF	Unc	BU
1994	—	—	—	12.00	—

KM# 520 PESO Composition: Copper **Subject:** Centennial 1895-1995 **Note:** Antique finish.

Date	Mintage	F	VF	XF	Unc	BU
ND(1995)	2,000	—	—	—	12.00	—

KM# 473 PESO Composition: Copper-Nickel **Subject:** Pirates of the Caribbean **Reverse:** Sir Henry Morgan

Date	Mintage	F	VF	XF	Unc	BU
1995	25,000	—	—	—	10.00	—

KM# 519a PESO Composition: Copper **Subject:** Centennial - Death of Jose Marti in Combat **Note:** Brilliant finish.

Date	F	VF	XF	Unc	BU
1995	—	—	—	15.00	—

KM# 472 PESO Composition: Copper-Nickel **Subject:** Pirates of the Caribbean **Reverse:** Blackbeard

Date	F	VF	XF	Unc	BU
1995	—	—	—	10.00	—

KM# 477 PESO Composition: Copper-Nickel **Subject:** Pirates of the Caribbean **Reverse:** Piet Heyn

Date	F	VF	XF	Unc	BU
1995	—	—	—	10.00	—

KM# 474 PESO Composition: Copper-Nickel **Subject:** Pirates of the Caribbean **Reverse:** Anne Bonny

Date	F	VF	XF	Unc	BU
1995	—	—	—	10.00	—

KM# 475 PESO Composition: Copper-Nickel **Subject:** Pirates of the Caribbean **Reverse:** Mary Read

Date	F	VF	XF	Unc	BU
1995	—	—	—	10.00	—

KM# 476 PESO Composition: Copper-Nickel **Subject:** Pirates of the Caribbean **Reverse:** Captain Kidd

Date	F	VF	XF	Unc	BU
1995	—	—	—	10.00	—

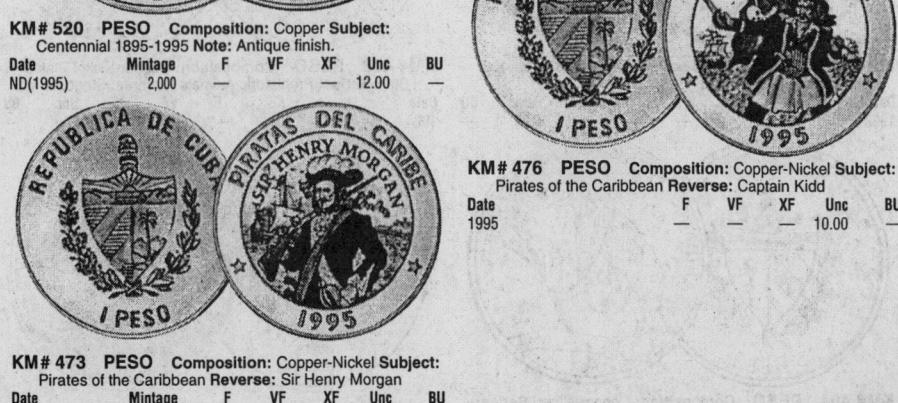

KM# 519 PESO **Composition:** Copper **Subject:** Centennial - Death of Jose Marti in combat

Date	Mintage	F	VF	XF	Unc	BU
1995 Antiqued finish	3,000	—	—	—	12.00	—
1995 Plain finish	—	—	—	—	12.00	—

KM# 521 PESO **Composition:** Nickel Bonded Steel **Subject:** Centennial - Jose Marti in combat

Date	F	VF	XF	Unc	BU
1995	—	—	—	7.50	—

KM# 522 PESO **Composition:** Nickel-Bonded Steel **Reverse:** Multicolored SIAI Marchetti Seaplane

Date	F	VF	XF	Unc	BU
1995	—	—	—	18.50	—

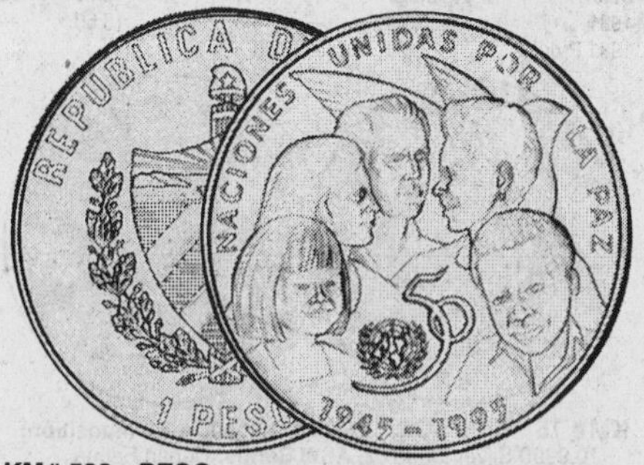

KM# 523 PESO **Composition:** Copper-Nickel **Subject:** 50th Anniversary - United Nations

Date	F	VF	XF	Unc	BU
ND(1995)	—	—	—	15.00	—

KM# 607 PESO **Composition:** Nickel Bonded Steel **Subject:** 50th Anniversary - F.A.O. **Obverse:** Cuban arms **Reverse:** Farmer plowing behind two oxen

Date	F	VF	XF	Unc	BU
ND(1995)	—	—	—	7.50	—

KM# 549 PESO **Composition:** Nickel-Bonded Steel **Series:** Caribbean Fauna **Reverse:** Multicolored Ruby Throated Hummingbird

Date	Mintage	F	VF	XF	Unc	BU
1996	10,000	—	—	—	22.50	—

KM# 550 PESO **Composition:** Nickel Bonded Steel **Series:** Caribbean Fauna **Reverse:** Multicolored Yellow Perch

Date	Mintage	F	VF	XF	Unc	BU
1996	10,000	—	—	—	22.50	—

KM# 551 PESO **Composition:** Nickel Bonded Steel **Series:** Caribbean Fauna **Reverse:** Multicolored Cuban Tody Bird

Date	Mintage	F	VF	XF	Unc	BU
1996	10,000	—	—	—	25.00	—

KM# 552 PESO **Composition:** Nickel Bonded Steel **Series:** Caribbean Fauna **Reverse:** Multicolored Wood Duck

Date	Mintage	F	VF	XF	Unc	BU
1996	10,000	—	—	—	22.50	—

KM# 562 PESO **Composition:** Nickel Bonded Steel **Series:** Caribbean Fauna **Reverse:** Multicolored Vaca Anil Fish **Note:** Similar to 10 Pesos, KM#563.

Date	Mintage	F	VF	XF	Unc	BU
1996	10,000	—	—	—	27.50	—

KM# 565 PESO **Composition:** Nickel Bonded Steel **Series:** Caribbean Fauna **Reverse:** Multicolored Papilio butterfly

Date	Mintage	F	VF	XF	Unc	BU
1996	10,000	—	—	—	32.50	—

KM# 731 PESO **Weight:** 25.8300 g. **Composition:** Copper-Nickel **Series:** F.A.O. **Obverse:** National arms **Reverse:** Woman picking fruit **Edge:** Plain **Size:** 37.9 mm.

Date	F	VF	XF	Unc	BU
1996	—	—	—	18.50	—

KM# 614 PESO **Composition:** 25.9100 Copper-Nickel **Subject:** 40th Anniversary of the "Granma" Landing **Obverse:** National arms **Reverse:** Portrait above ship **Edge:** Plain **Size:** 37.9 mm.

Date	F	VF	XF	Unc	BU
ND(1996)	—	Value: 15.00			

KM# 722 PESO **Composition:** Copper-Nickel 12.9 oz. **Subject:** Hibiscus Elatus **Obverse:** National arms **Reverse:** Multicolored flower **Size:** 32.5 mm.

Date	Mintage	F	VF	XF	Unc	BU
1997	5,000	Value: 10.00				

KM# 617 PESO **Composition:** Copper-Nickel **Subject:** 30th Anniversary - Death of Ernesto Che Guevara **Reverse:** Full figure of Guevara with rifle walking down road between anniversary dates, mountains behind **Size:** 37 mm.

Date	F	VF	XF	Unc	BU
1997	—	—	—	15.00	—

KM# 612 PESO **Composition:** Copper-Nickel **Subject:** Fidel Castro's visit to the Vatican **Obverse:** Cuban arms **Reverse:** Pope and Castro meeting

Date	F	VF	XF	Unc	BU
1997	—	—	—	15.00	—

KM# 622 PESO **Composition:** Copper-Nickel **Subject:** AIDS **Obverse:** Cuban arms **Reverse:** AIDS ribbon on silhouette before world map

Date	Mintage	F	VF	XF	Unc	BU
1998	50,000	—	—	—	15.00	—

KM# 732 PESO **Weight:** 25.8300 g. **Composition:** Copper-Nickel **Subject:** Papal Visit **Obverse:** National arms **Reverse:** Pope John Paul II and cathedral **Edge:** Plain **Size:** 37.9 mm.

Date	F	VF	XF	Unc	BU
1998	—	—	—	16.50	—

KM# 662 PESO **Composition:** Copper-Nickel **Subject:** 40th Anniversary - The Triumph of the Revolution

Date	F	VF	XF	Unc	BU
1999	—	—	—	15.00	—

KM# 346 3 PESOS **Composition:** Copper-Nickel **Subject:** Ernesto Che Guevara

Date	Mintage	F	VF	XF	Unc	BU
1990	4,050,000	—	—	3.00	6.00	—

KM# 346a 3 PESOS **Composition:** Nickel Clad Steel

Date	Mintage	F	VF	XF	Unc	BU
1992	—	—	—	3.00	6.00	—
1992	500	Value: 12.50				
1995	—	—	—	3.00	6.00	—

KM# 36 5 PESOS **Weight:** 13.3300 g. **Composition:** 0.9000 Silver .3857 oz. ASW **Subject:** 25th Anniversary - National Bank of Cuba

Date	Mintage	F	VF	XF	Unc	BU
ND(1975) Proof	50,000	Value: 15.00				

KM# 47 5 PESOS **Weight:** 12.0000 g. **Composition:** 0.9990 Silver .3855 oz. ASW **Subject:** First Soviet-Cuban Space Flight

Date	Mintage	F	VF	XF	Unc	BU
1980	10,000	—	—	—	11.50	—
1980 Proof	5,000	Value: 50.00				

KM# 48 5 PESOS **Weight:** 12.0000 g. **Composition:** 0.9990 Silver .3855 oz. ASW **Subject:** Moscow Olympics

Date	Mintage	F	VF	XF	Unc	BU
1980	10,000	—	—	—	10.00	—

KM# 49 5 PESOS **Weight:** 12.0000 g. **Composition:** 0.9990 Silver .3855 oz. ASW **Reverse:** Cuban flower - Mariposa

Date	Mintage	F	VF	XF	Unc	BU
1980	10,000	—	—	—	12.50	—
1980 Proof	2,000	Value: 25.00				

KM# 69 5 PESOS **Weight:** 12.0000 g. **Composition:** 0.9990 Silver .3855 oz. ASW **Reverse:** Cuban flower - Mariposa

Date	Mintage	F	VF	XF	Unc	BU
1981	10,000	—	—	—	12.50	—
1981 Proof	2,000	Value: 25.00				

KM# 70 5 PESOS **Weight:** 12.0000 g. **Composition:** 0.9990 Silver .3855 oz. ASW **Reverse:** Cuban flower - Orquidea

Date	Mintage	F	VF	XF	Unc	BU
1981	10,000	—	—	—	12.50	—
1981 Proof	2,000	Value: 25.00				

KM# 71 5 PESOS **Weight:** 12.0000 g. **Composition:** 0.9990 Silver .3855 oz. ASW **Reverse:** Columbus' ship - Nina

Date	Mintage	F	VF	XF	Unc	BU
1981	10,000	—	—	—	22.50	—
1981 Proof	1,000	Value: 37.50				

KM# 72 5 PESOS **Weight:** 12.0000 g. **Composition:** 0.9990 Silver .3855 oz. ASW **Reverse:** Columbus' ship - Pinta

Date	Mintage	F	VF	XF	Unc	BU
1981	10,000	—	—	—	22.50	—
1981 Proof	1,000	Value: 37.50				

KM# 73 5 PESOS **Weight:** 12.0000 g. **Composition:** 0.9990 Silver .3855 oz. ASW **Reverse:** Columbus' ship - Santa Maria

Date	Mintage	F	VF	XF	Unc	BU
1981	10,000	—	—	—	22.50	—
1981 Proof	1,000	Value: 37.50				

KM# 74 5 PESOS **Weight:** 12.0000 g. **Composition:** 0.9990 Silver .3855 oz. ASW **Series:** Cuban Fauna **Reverse:** Crocodile

Date	Mintage	F	VF	XF	Unc	BU
1981	5,000	—	—	—	18.50	—
1981 Proof	1,000	Value: 35.00				

KM# 75 5 PESOS **Weight:** 12.0000 g. **Composition:** 0.9990 Silver .3855 oz. ASW **Series:** Cuban Fauna **Reverse:** Emerald Hummingbird

Date	Mintage	F	VF	XF	Unc	BU
1981	5,000	—	—	—	18.50	—
1981 Proof	1,000	Value: 35.00				

KM# 76 5 PESOS **Weight:** 12.0000 g. **Composition:** 0.9990 Silver .3855 oz. ASW **Series:** Cuban Fauna **Reverse:** Bee Hummingbird

Date	Mintage	F	VF	XF	Unc	BU
1981	5,000	—	—	—	18.50	—
1981 Proof	1,000	Value: 35.00				

KM# 77 5 PESOS **Weight:** 12.0000 g. **Composition:** 0.9990 Silver .3855 oz. ASW **Subject:** Soccer Games - Spain 1982 **Reverse:** Soccer player

Date	Mintage	F	VF	XF	Unc	BU
1981 Proof	4,000	Value: 22.50				

KM# 78 5 PESOS **Weight:** 12.0000 g. **Composition:** 0.9990 Silver .3855 oz. ASW **Subject:** World Food Day - Sugar Production

Date	Mintage	F	VF	XF	Unc	BU
1981	7,000	—	—	—	20.00	—
1981 Proof	1,560	Value: 25.00				

KM# 79 5 PESOS **Weight:** 12.0000 g. **Composition:** 0.9990 Silver .3855 oz. ASW **Subject:** XIV Central American and Caribbean Games **Reverse:** Animated Mascot

Date	Mintage	F	VF	XF	Unc	BU
1981	5,000	—	—	—	12.50	—
1981 Proof	2,000	Value: 32.50				

KM# 80 5 PESOS **Weight:** 12.0000 g. **Composition:** 0.9990 Silver .3855 oz. ASW **Subject:** XIV Central American and Caribbean Games **Reverse:** Three athletes

Date	Mintage	F	VF	XF	Unc	BU
1981	5,000	—	—	—	11.50	—
1981 Proof	2,000	Value: 35.00				

KM# 81 5 PESOS **Weight:** 12.0000 g. **Composition:** 0.9990 Silver .3855 oz. ASW **Subject:** XIV Central American and Caribbean Games **Reverse:** Boxers

Date	Mintage	F	VF	XF	Unc	BU
1981	5,000	—	—	—	11.50	—
1981 Proof	2,000	Value: 35.00				

KM# 82 5 PESOS **Weight:** 12.0000 g. **Composition:** 0.9990 Silver .3855 oz. ASW **Series:** Cuban Fauna **Reverse:** Cuban Trogon

Date	Mintage	F	VF	XF	Unc	BU
1981	5,000	—	—	—	14.00	—
1981 Proof	1,000	Value: 30.00				

KM# 83 5 PESOS **Weight:** 12.0000 g. **Composition:** 0.9990 Silver .3855 oz. ASW **Series:** Cuban Fauna **Reverse:** Cuban Solenodon

Date	Mintage	F	VF	XF	Unc	BU
1981	5,000	—	—	—	12.50	—
1981 Proof	1,000	Value: 28.00				

KM# 84 5 PESOS **Weight:** 12.0000 g. **Composition:** 0.9990 Silver .3855 oz. ASW **Series:** Cuban Fauna **Reverse:** Giant Garfish

Date	Mintage	F	VF	XF	Unc	BU
1981	5,000	—	—	—	12.50	—
1981 Proof	1,000	Value: 30.00				

KM# 96 5 PESOS **Weight:** 12.0000 g. **Composition:** 0.9990 Silver .3855 oz. ASW **Reverse:** Bust of Ernest Hemingway

Date	Mintage	F	VF	XF	Unc	BU
1982	5,000	—	—	—	20.00	—
1982 Proof	1,000	Value: 40.00				

KM# 97 5 PESOS **Weight:** 12.0000 g. **Composition:** 0.9990 Silver .3855 oz. ASW **Reverse:** Ernest Hemingway's fishing yacht

Date	Mintage	F	VF	XF	Unc	BU
1982	5,000	—	—	—	20.00	—
1982 Proof	1,000	Value: 40.00				

KM# 98 5 PESOS **Weight:** 12.0000 g. **Composition:** 0.9990 Silver .3855 oz. ASW **Reverse:** Ernest Hemingway - small boat

Date	Mintage	F	VF	XF	Unc	BU
1982	5,000	—	—	—	20.00	—
1982 Proof	1,000	Value: 40.00				

KM# 99 5 PESOS **Weight:** 12.0000 g. **Composition:** 0.9990 Silver .3855 oz. ASW **Reverse:** Miguel De Cervantes

Date	Mintage	F	VF	XF	Unc	BU
1982	7,000	—	—	—	11.50	—
1982 Proof	2,000	Value: 30.00				

KM# 100 5 PESOS **Weight:** 12.0000 g. **Composition:** 0.9990 Silver .3855 oz. ASW **Reverse:** Hidalgo Don Quijote on horse

Date	Mintage	F	VF	XF	Unc	BU
1982	7,000	—	—	—	11.50	—
1982 Proof	2,000	Value: 30.00				

KM# 101 5 PESOS **Weight:** 12.0000 g. **Composition:** 0.9990 Silver .3855 oz. ASW **Subject:** Hidalgo Don Quijote and Sancho Panza

Date	Mintage	F	VF	XF	Unc	BU
1982	7,000	—	—	—	11.50	—
1982 Proof	2,000	Value: 30.00				

KM# 102 5 PESOS **Weight:** 12.0000 g. **Composition:** 0.9990 Silver .3855 oz. ASW **Series:** F.A.O. **Reverse:** Citrus fruit **Note:** Similar to 1 Peso, KM#94.

Date	Mintage	F	VF	XF	Unc	BU
1982	3,125	—	—	—	22.00	—
1982 Proof	1,040	Value: 32.50				

KM# 103 5 PESOS **Weight:** 12.0000 g. **Composition:** 0.9990 Silver .3855 oz. ASW **Series:** F.A.O. **Reverse:** Cow **Note:** Similar to 1 Peso, KM#95.

Date	Mintage	F	VF	XF	Unc	BU
1982	4,177	—	—	—	22.00	—
1982 Proof	1,000	Value: 32.50				

KM# 108 5 PESOS **Weight:** 12.0000 g. **Composition:** 0.9990 Silver .3855 oz. ASW **Series:** 1984 Winter Olympics - Hockey **Obverse:** Similar to KM#99

Date	Mintage	F	VF	XF	Unc	BU
1983 Proof	5,000	Value: 13.50				

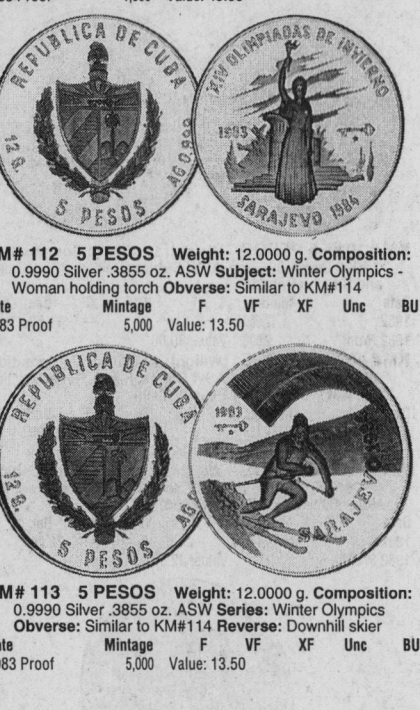

KM# 109 5 PESOS **Weight:** 12.0000 g. **Composition:** 0.9990 Silver .3855 oz. ASW **Series:** 1984 Summer Olympics - Runner **Obverse:** Similar to KM#99

Date	Mintage	F	VF	XF	Unc	BU
1983 Proof	5,000	Value: 13.50				

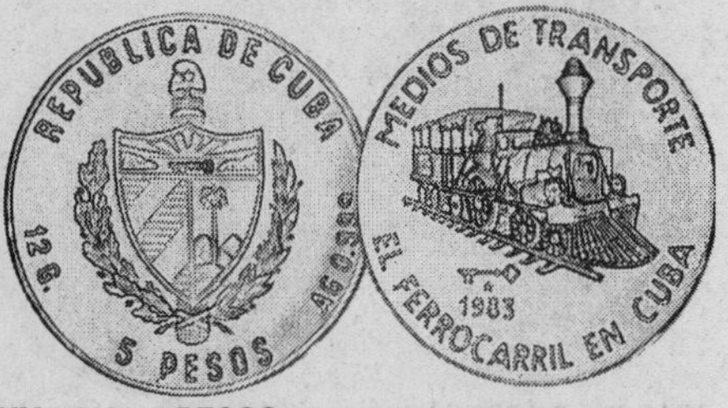

KM# 110 5 PESOS **Weight:** 12.0000 g. **Composition:** 0.9990 Silver .3855 oz. ASW **Reverse:** Railroad

Date	Mintage	F	VF	XF	Unc	BU
1983	5,000	—	—	—	15.00	—
1983 Proof	2,000	Value: 30.00				

KM# 111 5 PESOS **Weight:** 12.0000 g. **Composition:** 0.9990 Silver .3855 oz. ASW **Subject:** World Fisheries **Reverse:** Spiny lobster

Date	Mintage	F	VF	XF	Unc	BU
1983	5,000	—	—	—	22.50	—
1983 Proof	1,000	Value: 45.00				

KM# 112 5 PESOS **Weight:** 12.0000 g. **Composition:** 0.9990 Silver .3855 oz. ASW **Subject:** Winter Olympics - Woman holding torch **Obverse:** Similar to KM#114

Date	Mintage	F	VF	XF	Unc	BU
1983 Proof	5,000	Value: 13.50				

KM# 113 5 PESOS **Weight:** 12.0000 g. **Composition:** 0.9990 Silver .3855 oz. ASW **Series:** Winter Olympics **Obverse:** Similar to KM#114 **Reverse:** Downhill skier

Date	Mintage	F	VF	XF	Unc	BU
1983 Proof	5,000	Value: 13.50				

KM# 114 5 PESOS **Weight:** 12.0000 g. **Composition:** 0.9990 Silver .3855 oz. ASW **Series:** Summer Olympics **Reverse:** Discus thrower

Date	Mintage	F	VF	XF	Unc	BU
1983 Proof	5,000	Value: 12.50				

KM# 115 5 PESOS **Weight:** 12.0000 g. **Composition:** 0.9990 Silver .3855 oz. ASW **Series:** Summer Olympics **Reverse:** Judo match

Date	Mintage	F	VF	XF	Unc	BU
1983 Proof	5,000	Value: 15.00				

KM# 117 5 PESOS **Weight:** 12.0000 g. **Composition:** 0.9990 Silver .3855 oz. ASW **Subject:** Transportation **Reverse:** Freighter

Date	Mintage	F	VF	XF	Unc	BU
1984	5,000	—	—	—	20.00	—
1984 Proof	1,000	Value: 40.00				

KM# 119 5 PESOS **Weight:** 12.0000 g. **Composition:** 0.9990 Silver .3855 oz. ASW **Reverse:** Santisimo Trinidad

Date	Mintage	F	VF	XF	Unc	BU
1984	5,000	—	—	—	16.50	—

KM# 131 5 PESOS **Weight:** 12.0000 g. **Composition:** 0.9990 Silver .3855 oz. ASW **Subject:** Transportation **Reverse:** Volanta coach

Date	Mintage	F	VF	XF	Unc	BU
1984	5,000	—	—	—	11.50	—
1984 Proof	1,000	Value: 40.00				

KM# 666 5 PESOS **Weight:** 12.0000 g. **Composition:** 0.9990 Silver .3855 oz. ASW **Subject:** Transportation **Reverse:** Hot air balloon

Date	Mintage	F	VF	XF	Unc	BU
1984	2	—	—	—	4,000	—

KM# 141 5 PESOS **Weight:** 12.0000 g. **Composition:** 0.9990 Silver .3855 oz. ASW **Subject:** Fortress - El Morro La Habana

Date	Mintage	F	VF	XF	Unc	BU
1984	5,000	—	—	—	11.50	—
1984 Proof	1,000	Value: 45.00				

KM# 143 5 PESOS **Weight:** 12.0000 g. **Composition:** 0.9990 Silver .3855 oz. ASW **Subject:** Fortress - La Fuerza La Habana

Date	Mintage	F	VF	XF	Unc	BU
1984	5,000	—	—	—	11.50	—
1984 Proof	1,000	Value: 45.00				

KM# 145 5 PESOS **Weight:** 12.0000 g. **Composition:** 0.9990 Silver .3855 oz. ASW **Subject:** Fortress - El Morro Santiago De Cuba

Date	Mintage	F	VF	XF	Unc	BU
1984	5,000	—	—	—	11.50	—
1984 Proof	1,000	Value: 45.00				

KM# 121 5 PESOS **Weight:** 12.0000 g. **Composition:** 0.9990 Silver .3855 oz. ASW **Subject:** International Year of Music - Bach

Date	Mintage	F	VF	XF	Unc	BU
1985	2,000	—	—	—	32.50	—
1985 Proof	—	Value: 45.00				

KM# 125 5 PESOS **Weight:** 12.0000 g. **Composition:** 0.9990 Silver .3855 oz. ASW **Subject:** Wildlife Preservation **Reverse:** Cuban crocodile

Date	Mintage	F	VF	XF	Unc	BU
1985	5,000	—	—	—	45.00	—

KM# 127 5 PESOS **Weight:** 12.0000 g. **Composition:** 0.9990 Silver .3855 oz. ASW **Subject:** Wildlife Preservation **Reverse:** Cuban Rock Iquana

Date	Mintage	F	VF	XF	Unc	BU
1985	5,000	—	—	—	35.00	—

KM# 129 5 PESOS **Weight:** 12.0000 g. **Composition:** 0.9990 Silver .3855 oz. ASW **Subject:** Wildlife Preservation **Reverse:** Cuban Amazon Parrot

Date	Mintage	F	VF	XF	Unc	BU
1985	5,000	—	—	—	30.00	—

KM# 146 5 PESOS **Weight:** 12.0000 g. **Composition:** 0.9990 Silver .3855 oz. ASW **Subject:** 40th Anniversary of F.A.O. **Obverse:** Similar to KM#129 **Reverse:** Lobster, palm tree, and sugar cane

Date	Mintage	F	VF	XF	Unc	BU
ND(1985)	4,500	—	—	—	11.50	—
ND(1985) Proof	500	Value: 45.00				

KM# 147 5 PESOS **Weight:** 12.0000 g. **Composition:** 0.9990 Silver .3855 oz. ASW **Series:** F.A.O. **Subject:** Forestry **Obverse:** Similar to KM#129 **Reverse:** Stylized forest

Date	Mintage	F	VF	XF	Unc	BU
ND(1985)	4,500	—	—	—	22.50	—
ND(1985) Proof	500	Value: 40.00				

KM# 123 5 PESOS **Weight:** 12.0000 g. **Composition:** 0.9990 Silver .3855 oz. ASW **Subject:** Soccer **Note:** Similar to 1 Peso, KM#122.

Date	Mintage	F	VF	XF	Unc	BU
1985	5,000	—	—	—	22.00	—
1985 Proof	—	Value: 35.00				

KM# 135 5 PESOS **Weight:** 12.0000 g. **Composition:** 0.9990 Silver .3855 oz. ASW **Subject:** 100th Anniversary of the Automobile

Date	Mintage	F	VF	XF	Unc	BU
ND(1986)	2,500	—	—	—	22.50	—

KM# 137 5 PESOS **Weight:** 12.0000 g. **Composition:** 0.9990 Silver .3855 oz. ASW **Subject:** 30th Anniversary - Voyage of the Granma

Date	Mintage	F	VF	XF	Unc	BU
ND(1986)	2,500	—	—	—	20.00	—

KM# 139 5 PESOS **Weight:** 12.0000 g. **Composition:** 0.9990 Silver .3855 oz. ASW **Series:** Olympics **Reverse:** Skater

Date	Mintage	F	VF	XF	Unc	BU
1986	2,500	—	—	—	25.00	—

KM# 157 5 PESOS **Weight:** 12.0000 g. **Composition:** 0.9990 Silver .3855 oz. ASW **Series:** F.A.O. **Subject:** International Year of Peace

Date	Mintage	F	VF	XF	Unc	BU
1986	10,000	—	—	—	22.50	—
1986 Proof	2,000	Value: 32.50				

KM# 199 5 PESOS **Weight:** 12.0000 g. **Composition:** 0.9990 Silver .3855 oz. ASW **Series:** Olympics **Reverse:** Without rings above skater

Date	Mintage	F	VF	XF	Unc	BU
1986	10,000	—	—	—	10.00	—

KM# 149 5 PESOS **Weight:** 12.0000 g. **Composition:** 0.9990 Silver .3855 oz. ASW **Subject:** Cathedral in Santiago

Date	Mintage	F	VF	XF	Unc	BU
1987	2,500	—	—	—	25.00	—

KM# 151 5 PESOS **Weight:** 12.0000 g. **Composition:** 0.9990 Silver .3855 oz. ASW **Subject:** Cathedral in Caridad del Cobre

Date	Mintage	F	VF	XF	Unc	BU
1987	2,500	—	—	—	25.00	—

KM# 153 5 PESOS **Weight:** 12.0000 g. **Composition:** 0.9990 Silver .3855 oz. ASW **Subject:** Cathedral in Trinidad

Date	Mintage	F	VF	XF	Unc	BU
1987	2,500	—	—	—	25.00	—

KM# 155 5 PESOS **Weight:** 12.0000 g. **Composition:** 0.9990 Silver .3855 oz. ASW **Subject:** 40th Anniversary - Expedition of Kon-Tiki

Date	Mintage	F	VF	XF	Unc	BU
ND(1987)	5,000	—	—	—	20.00	—

KM# 159 5 PESOS **Weight:** 12.0000 g. **Composition:** 0.9990 Silver .3855 oz. ASW **Subject:** 20th Anniversary - Demise of Ernesto Che Guevara

Date	Mintage	F	VF	XF	Unc	BU
ND(1987)	5,000	—	—	—	30.00	—
ND(1987) Proof	200	Value: 75.00				

KM# 161 5 PESOS **Weight:** 12.0000 g. **Composition:** 0.9990 Silver .3855 oz. ASW **Subject:** 70th Anniversary - Bolshevik Revolution

Date	Mintage	F	VF	XF	Unc	BU
1987	3,000	—	—	—	22.50	—
1987 Proof	1,000	Value: 45.00				

KM# 166 5 PESOS **Weight:** 12.0000 g. **Composition:** 0.9990 Silver .3855 oz. ASW **Subject:** 100th Anniversary - Souvenir Peso

Date	Mintage	F	VF	XF	Unc	BU
1987	3,000	—	—	—	25.00	—

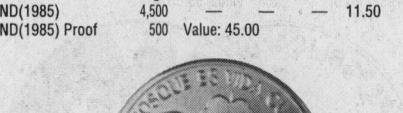

KM# 326 5 PESOS **Weight:** 12.0000 g. **Composition:** 0.9990 Silver .3855 oz. ASW **Subject:** Abolition of Slavery

Date	Mintage	F	VF	XF	Unc	BU
1987	2,000	—	—	—	32.50	—

KM# 180 5 PESOS **Weight:** 12.0000 g. **Composition:** 0.9990 Silver .3855 oz. ASW **Subject:** Jose Capablanca Chess Championship - Player

Date	Mintage	F	VF	XF	Unc	BU
ND	5,000	—	—	—	22.50	—

KM# 185 5 PESOS **Weight:** 12.0000 g. **Composition:** 0.9990 Silver .3855 oz. ASW **Subject:** Soccer - Mexico 1986

Date	Mintage	F	VF	XF	Unc	BU
1988	5,000	—	—	—	16.50	—
1988 Proof	—	Value: 30.00				

KM# 216 5 PESOS **Weight:** 6.0000 g. **Composition:** 0.9990 Silver .1927 oz. ASW **Subject:** Soccer - Italy 1990

Date	F	VF	XF	Unc	BU
1988	—	—	—	16.50	—

KM# 216a 5 PESOS **Weight:** 12.0000 g. **Composition:** 0.9990 Silver .3855 oz. ASW **Subject:** Soccer - Italy 1990

Date	Mintage	F	VF	XF	Unc	BU
1988	5,000	—	—	—	20.00	—

KM# 217 5 PESOS **Weight:** 12.0000 g. **Composition:** 0.9990 Silver .3855 oz. ASW **Subject:** Soccer - West Germany **Reverse:** Three players

Date	Mintage	F	VF	XF	Unc	BU
1988	5,000	—	—	—	18.50	—

KM# 218 5 PESOS **Weight:** 12.0000 g. **Composition:** 0.9990 Silver .3855 oz. ASW **Subject:** Soccer - West Germany **Reverse:** Four players

Date	Mintage	F	VF	XF	Unc	BU
1988	5,000	—	—	—	18.50	—

KM# 219 5 PESOS **Weight:** 16.0000 g. **Composition:** 0.9990 Silver .5145 oz. ASW **Subject:** 40th Anniversary - Cuban National Ballet

Date	Mintage	F	VF	XF	Unc	BU
ND(1988) Proof	2,000	Value: 47.50				

KM# 220.1 5 PESOS **Weight:** 16.0000 g. **Composition:** 0.9990 Silver .5145 oz. ASW **Reverse:** Graf Zeppelin

Date	Mintage	F	VF	XF	Unc	BU
1988 Proof	3,000	Value: 250				

KM# 220.2 5 PESOS **Weight:** 15.9400 g. **Composition:** 0.9990 Silver .5119 oz. ASW **Obverse:** Thicker wreath **Reverse:** Graf Zeppelin

Date		F	VF	XF	Unc	BU
1988 Proof	—	Value: 37.50				

KM# 221 5 PESOS **Weight:** 16.0000 g. **Composition:** 0.9990 Silver .5119 oz. ASW **Reverse:** Carlos J. Finlay

Date	Mintage	F	VF	XF	Unc	BU
ND(1988) Proof	2,000	Value: 47.50				

KM# 222 5 PESOS **Weight:** 16.0000 g. **Composition:** 0.9990 Silver .5119 oz. ASW **Subject:** World Health Organization

Date	Mintage	F	VF	XF	Unc	BU
ND(1988) Proof	2,000	Value: 47.50				

KM# 223 5 PESOS **Weight:** 16.0000 g. **Composition:** 0.9990 Silver .5119 oz. ASW **Subject:** 150th Anniversary - Grand National Theater in Havana

Date	Mintage	F	VF	XF	Unc	BU
ND(1988) Proof	2,000	Value: 55.00				

KM# 224 5 PESOS **Weight:** 16.0000 g. **Composition:** 0.9990 Silver .5119 oz. ASW **Series:** Olympics - Barcelona **Reverse:** Boxing

Date	Mintage	F	VF	XF	Unc	BU
1989 Proof	10,000	Value: 25.00				

KM# 225 5 PESOS **Weight:** 16.0000 g. **Composition:** 0.9990 Silver .5119 oz. ASW **Series:** Olympics - Italy **Reverse:** Three players

Date	Mintage	F	VF	XF	Unc	BU
1989 Proof	10,000	Value: 52.50				

KM# 226 5 PESOS **Weight:** 16.0000 g. **Composition:** 0.9990 Silver .5119 oz. ASW **Series:** Olympics - Italy **Reverse:** Colosseum

Date	Mintage	F	VF	XF	Unc	BU
1989 Proof	10,000	Value: 52.50				

KM# 227 5 PESOS **Weight:** 16.0000 g. **Composition:** 0.9990 Silver .5119 oz. ASW **Subject:** Cuban tobacco

Date	Mintage	F	VF	XF	Unc	BU
1989 Proof	2,000	Value: 52.50				

KM# 231 5 PESOS **Weight:** 16.0000 g. **Composition:** 0.9990 Silver .5119 oz. ASW **Subject:** Alexander von Humboldt

Date	Mintage	F	VF	XF	Unc	BU
1989 Proof	3,000	Value: 50.00				

KM# 251 5 PESOS **Weight:** 16.0000 g. **Composition:** 0.9990 Silver .5119 oz. ASW **Subject:** Universal Congress of Esperanto

Date	Mintage	F	VF	XF	Unc	BU
1990 Proof	6,000	Value: 45.00				

KM# 290 5 PESOS **Weight:** 16.0000 g. **Composition:** 0.9990 Silver .5119 oz. ASW **Subject:** Soccer **Reverse:** Map of Italy and soccer balls

Date	Mintage	F	VF	XF	Unc	BU
1990 Proof	10,000	Value: 55.00				

KM# 338 5 PESOS **Weight:** 12.0000 g. **Composition:** 0.9990 Silver .3855 oz. ASW **Subject:** Soccer Championship **Reverse:** Two players

Date	Mintage	F	VF	XF	Unc	BU
1991 Proof	10,000	—	—	—	52.50	—

KM# 405 5 PESOS **Weight:** 6.0000 g. **Composition:** 0.9990 Silver .1927 oz. ASW **Series:** Prehistoric Animals **Reverse:** Apatosaurus

Date	Mintage	F	VF	XF	Unc	BU
1993 Proof	30,000	Value: 22.50				

KM# 524 5 PESOS **Weight:** 15.0000 g. **Composition:** 0.9990 Silver .4818 oz. ASW **Subject:** Historia Postal de Cuba Steamship

Date	Mintage	F	VF	XF	Unc	BU
1993 Proof	25,000	Value: 16.50				

KM# 440 5 PESOS **Weight:** 16.0000 g. **Composition:** 0.9990 Silver .5145 oz. ASW **Series:** Prehistoric Animals **Reverse:** Triceratops

Date	Mintage	F	VF	XF	Unc	BU
1994 Proof	10,000	Value: 50.00				

KM# 573 5 PESOS **Weight:** 16.0000 g. **Composition:** 0.9990 Silver .5145 oz. ASW **Series:** Prehistoric Animals **Reverse:** Maiasaura

Date	Mintage	F	VF	XF	Unc	BU
1994 Proof	—	Value: 50.00				

KM# 581 5 PESOS **Weight:** 7.0000 g. **Composition:** 0.9990 Silver .2248 oz. ASW **Subject:** Hibiscus Elatus Flower **Obverse:** Cuban arms **Reverse:** Multicolored hibiscus

Date	Mintage	F	VF	XF	Unc	BU
1997 Proof	—	Value: 20.00				

KM# 623 5 PESOS **Weight:** 11.3000 g. **Composition:** 0.9990 Silver .3633 oz. ASW **Subject:** AIDS **Obverse:** Cuban arms **Reverse:** AIDS ribbon on silhouette before world map

Date	Mintage	F	VF	XF	Unc	BU
1998 Proof	50,000	Value: 18.50				

KM# 655 5 PESOS **Weight:** 11.3000 g. **Composition:** 0.9990 Silver .3633 oz. ASW **Subject:** Expo 2000 - Philadelphia **Obverse:** Cuban arms **Reverse:** Cartoon above building

Date	Mintage	F	VF	XF	Unc	BU
1999 Proof	31,000	Value: 16.50				

KM# 656 5 PESOS **Weight:** 11.3000 g. **Composition:** 0.9990 Silver .3633 oz. ASW **Subject:** Expo 2000 - Hannover **Obverse:** Cuban arms **Reverse:** Cartoon above city hall

Date	Mintage	F	VF	XF	Unc	BU
1999 Proof	31,000	Value: 16.50				

KM# 657 5 PESOS **Weight:** 11.3000 g. **Composition:** 0.9990 Silver .3633 oz. ASW **Subject:** Expo 2000 - Osaka **Obverse:** Cuban arms **Reverse:** Cartoon above city view

Date	Mintage	F	VF	XF	Unc	BU
1999 Proof	31,000	Value: 16.50				

KM# 658 5 PESOS **Weight:** 11.3000 g. **Composition:** 0.9990 Silver .3633 oz. ASW **Subject:** Expo 2000 - Montreal **Obverse:** Cuban arms **Reverse:** Cartoon above sports buildings

Date	Mintage	F	VF	XF	Unc	BU
1999 Proof	31,000	Value: 16.50				

KM# 660 5 PESOS **Weight:** 11.3000 g. **Composition:** 0.9990 Silver .3633 oz. ASW **Subject:** Expo 2000 **Obverse:** Cuban arms **Reverse:** World map with logo center square

Date	Mintage	F	VF	XF	Unc	BU
1999 Proof	31,000	Value: 16.50				

KM# 673 5 PESOS **Composition:** 0.9990 Gold .0500 oz. AGW **Subject:** Zunzuncita **Reverse:** Hummingbird

Date		F	VF	XF	Unc	BU
1999 Proof	—	Value: 75.00				

KM# 659 5 PESOS **Weight:** 11.3000 g. **Composition:** 0.9990 Silver .3633 oz. ASW **Subject:** Expo 2000 - Twipsy **Obverse:** Cuban arms **Reverse:** "Twipsy" in square **Note:** Similar to 50 Pesos, KM#654

Date	Mintage	F	VF	XF	Unc	BU
1999 Proof	31,000	Value: 16.50				

KM# 37 10 PESOS **Weight:** 26.6600 g. **Composition:** 0.9000 Silver .7715 oz. ASW **Subject:** 25th Anniversary - National Bank of Cuba

Date	Mintage	F	VF	XF	Unc	BU
1975 Proof	55,000	Value: 40.00				

KM# 50 10 PESOS **Weight:** 18.0000 g. **Composition:** 0.9990 Silver .5782 oz. ASW **Subject:** First Soviet-Cuban Space Flight

Date	Mintage	F	VF	XF	Unc	BU
1980	10,000	—	—	—	20.00	—
1980 Proof	5,000	Value: 35.00				
1980 Matte proof	—	—	—	—	45.00	—

KM# 51 10 PESOS Weight: 18.0000 g. **Composition:** 0.9990 Silver .5782 oz. ASW **Subject:** Moscow Olympics

Date	Mintage	F	VF	XF	Unc	BU
1980	10,000	—	—	—	12.50	—
1980 Matte proof	—	Value: 65.00				

KM# 162 10 PESOS Weight: 31.1000 g. **Composition:** 0.9990 Silver 1.0000 oz. ASW **Subject:** Triumph of the Revolution

Date	Mintage	F	VF	XF	Unc	BU
1987 Proof	2,000	Value: 47.50				
1988 Proof	4,000	Value: 37.50				
1989 Proof	2,000	Value: 47.50				

KM# 163 10 PESOS Weight: 31.1000 g. **Composition:** 0.9990 Silver 1.0000 oz. ASW **Subject:** 60th Anniversary - Birth of Ernesto Che Guevara

Date	Mintage	F	VF	XF	Unc	BU
1987 Proof	2,000	Value: 47.50				
1988 Proof	4,000	Value: 37.50				
1989 Proof	2,000	Value: 47.50				

KM# 164 10 PESOS Weight: 31.1000 g. **Composition:** 0.9990 Silver 1.0000 oz. ASW **Subject:** 30th Anniversary - The March to Victory

Date	Mintage	F	VF	XF	Unc	BU
1987 Proof	2,000	Value: 47.50				
1988 Proof	4,000	Value: 37.50				
1989 Proof	2,000	Value: 47.50				

KM# 205 10 PESOS Weight: 31.1000 g. **Composition:** 0.9990 Silver 1.0000 oz. ASW **Subject:** 150th Anniversary - First Railroad in Spanish Cuba

Date	Mintage	F	VF	XF	Unc	BU
1988 Proof	5,000	Value: 37.50				

KM# 206 10 PESOS Weight: 31.1000 g. **Composition:** 0.9990 Silver 1.0000 oz. ASW **Subject:** 140th Anniversary - First Railroad in Spain

Date	Mintage	F	VF	XF	Unc	BU
1988 Proof	5,000	Value: 37.50				

KM# 207 10 PESOS Weight: 31.1000 g. **Composition:** 0.9990 Silver 1.0000 oz. ASW **Subject:** 160th Anniversary - First Railroad in England

Date	Mintage	F	VF	XF	Unc	BU
1988 Proof	5,000	Value: 37.50				

KM# 211 10 PESOS Weight: 3.1100 g. **Composition:** 0.9990 Gold .1000 oz. AGW **Reverse:** Jose Marti

Date	Mintage	F	VF	XF	Unc	BU
1988	50	—	—	—	75.00	—
1988 Proof	10	Value: 125				
1989	2,250	—	—	—	60.00	—
1989 Proof	15	Value: 125				
1990	15	—	—	—	100	—
1990 Proof	12	Value: 125				

KM# 228 10 PESOS Weight: 31.1000 g. **Composition:** 0.9990 Silver 1.0000 oz. ASW **Reverse:** Tania La Guerrillera

Date	Mintage	F	VF	XF	Unc	BU
1988 Proof	5,000	Value: 42.50				

KM# 229 10 PESOS Weight: 31.1000 g. **Composition:** 0.9990 Silver 1.0000 oz. ASW **Reverse:** Camilo Cienfuegos

Date	Mintage	F	VF	XF	Unc	BU
1988 Proof	5,000	Value: 42.50				

KM# 230 10 PESOS Weight: 31.1000 g. **Composition:** 0.9990 Silver 1.0000 oz. ASW **Subject:** 35th Anniversary - Assault of the Moncada Garrison

Date	Mintage	F	VF	XF	Unc	BU
ND(1988) Proof	5,000	Value: 42.50				

KM# 238 10 PESOS Weight: 20.0000 g. **Composition:** 0.9990 Silver .6431 oz. ASW **Subject:** 5th Centennial - Discovery of America

Date	Mintage	F	VF	XF	Unc	BU
1989	3,145	—	—	—	47.50	—

KM# 239 10 PESOS Weight: 26.7200 g. **Composition:** 0.9990 Silver .8592 oz. ASW **Subject:** 200th Anniversary of French Revolution - Lady Justice

Date	Mintage	F	VF	XF	Unc	BU
ND(1989)	500	—	—	—	40.00	—
ND(1989) Proof	2,000	Value: 60.00				

KM# 240 10 PESOS **Weight:** 26.7200 g. **Composition:** 0.9990 Silver .8592 oz. ASW **Subject:** 200th Anniversary of French Revolution **Reverse:** Bastille

Date	Mintage	F	VF	XF	Unc	BU
ND(1989)	500	—	—	—	45.00	—
ND(1989) Proof	2,000	Value: 65.00				

KM# 241 10 PESOS **Weight:** 31.1000 g. **Composition:** 0.9990 Silver 1.0000 oz. ASW **Subject:** 30th Anniversary of Revolution **Reverse:** Castro

Date	Mintage	F	VF	XF	Unc	BU
ND(1989)	5,000	—	—	—	35.00	—
ND(1989) Proof	5,000	Value: 45.00				

KM# 242 10 PESOS **Weight:** 31.1000 g. **Composition:** 0.9990 Silver 1.0000 oz. ASW **Subject:** 30th Anniversary of Revolution **Reverse:** Jose Marti and Castro

Date	Mintage	F	VF	XF	Unc	BU
1989	5,000	—	—	—	30.00	—
1989 Proof	5,000	Value: 40.00				

KM# 243 10 PESOS **Weight:** 31.1000 g. **Composition:** 0.9990 Silver 1.0000 oz. ASW **Subject:** 30th Anniversary of Revolution **Reverse:** Camilo Cienfuegos and Fidel Castro

Date	Mintage	F	VF	XF	Unc	BU
ND(1989)	5,000	—	—	—	35.00	—
ND(1989) Proof	5,000	Value: 45.00				

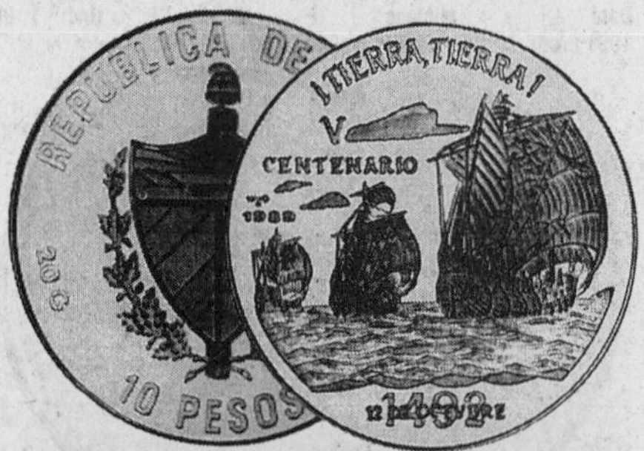

KM# 249 10 PESOS **Weight:** 20.0000 g. **Composition:** 0.9990 Silver .6431 oz. ASW **Subject:** Discovery of America **Reverse:** Three sailing ships

Date	Mintage	F	VF	XF	Unc	BU
1989 Proof	8,855	Value: 32.50				

KM# 383 10 PESOS **Weight:** 3.1100 g. **Composition:** 0.9990 Gold .1000 oz. AGW **Reverse:** Alexander von Humboldt

Date	Mintage	F	VF	XF	Unc	BU
1989	500	—	—	—	50.00	—
1989 Proof	—	Value: 55.00				

KM# 252 10 PESOS **Weight:** 20.0000 g. **Composition:** 0.9990 Silver .6431 oz. ASW **Subject:** Discovery of America **Reverse:** Ship and map of Cuba

Date	Mintage	F	VF	XF	Unc	BU
1990 Proof	10,000	Value: 32.50				

KM# 256 10 PESOS **Weight:** 20.0000 g. **Composition:** 0.9990 Silver .6431 oz. ASW **Subject:** 500th Anniversary of Columbus Meeting Native Americans

Date	Mintage	F	VF	XF	Unc	BU
1990 Proof	10,000	Value: 32.50				

KM# 262 10 PESOS **Weight:** 31.1030 g. **Composition:** 0.9990 Silver 1.0000 oz. ASW **Reverse:** Celia Sanchez Manduley

Date	Mintage	F	VF	XF	Unc	BU
1990 Proof	2,000	Value: 55.00				

KM# 263 10 PESOS **Weight:** 31.1030 g. **Composition:** 0.9990 Silver 1.0000 oz. ASW **Subject:** Discovery of America **Reverse:** King Ferdinand

Date	Mintage	F	VF	XF	Unc	BU
1990 Proof	5,000	Value: 50.00				

KM# 264 10 PESOS **Weight:** 31.1030 g. **Composition:** 0.9990 Silver 1.0000 oz. ASW **Subject:** Discovery of America **Reverse:** Queen Isabella

Date	Mintage	F	VF	XF	Unc	BU
1990 Proof	5,000	Value: 50.00				

KM# 265 10 PESOS **Weight:** 31.1030 g. **Composition:** 0.9990 Silver 1.0000 oz. ASW **Subject:** Discovery of America **Reverse:** Christopher Columbus

Date	Mintage	F	VF	XF	Unc	BU
1990 Proof	5,000	Value: 50.00				

KM# 266 10 PESOS **Weight:** 31.1030 g. **Composition:** 0.9990 Silver 1.0000 oz. ASW **Subject:** Discovery of America **Reverse:** Juan de la Casa

Date	Mintage	F	VF	XF	Unc	BU
1990 Proof	5,000	Value: 50.00				

KM# 267 10 PESOS **Weight:** 20.0000 g. **Composition:** 0.9990 Silver .6438 oz. ASW **Subject:** Discovery of America **Reverse:** Map of Columbus' route

Date	Mintage	F	VF	XF	Unc	BU
1990 Proof	10,000	Value: 32.50				

KM# 280 10 PESOS **Weight:** 25.0000 g. **Composition:** 0.9990 Silver .9037 oz. ASW **Reverse:** Simon Bolivar

Date	Mintage	F	VF	XF	Unc	BU
1990 Proof	3,300	Value: 47.50				

KM# 291 10 PESOS **Weight:** 31.1000 g. **Composition:** 0.9990 Silver 1.0000 oz. ASW **Subject:** Pan American Games **Reverse:** High jumper

Date	Mintage	F	VF	XF	Unc	BU
1990 Proof	3,000	Value: 55.00				

KM# 292 10 PESOS **Weight:** 31.1000 g. **Composition:** 0.9990 Silver 1.0000 oz. ASW **Subject:** Pan American Games **Reverse:** Volleyball

Date	Mintage	F	VF	XF	Unc	BU
1990 Proof	3,000	Value: 55.00				

KM# 293 10 PESOS **Weight:** 31.1000 g. **Composition:** 0.9990 Silver 1.0000 oz. ASW **Subject:** Pan American Games **Reverse:** Baseball

Date	Mintage	F	VF	XF	Unc	BU
1990 Proof	3,000	Value: 57.50				

KM# 336 10 PESOS **Weight:** 28.0000 g. **Composition:** 0.9250 Silver .8327 oz. ASW **Series:** Summer Olympics **Reverse:** Hurdler

Date	Mintage	F	VF	XF	Unc	BU
1990 Proof	25,000	Value: 25.00				

KM# 342 10 PESOS **Weight:** 3.1100 g. **Composition:** 0.9990 Gold .1000 oz. AGW **Series:** Olympics **Reverse:** Basketball

Date	Mintage	F	VF	XF	Unc	BU
1990 Proof	Est. 5,000	Value: 75.00				

KM# 344 10 PESOS **Weight:** 28.0000 g. **Composition:** 0.9250 Silver .8327 oz. ASW **Series:** Summer Olympics **Reverse:** Volleyball

Date	Mintage	F	VF	XF	Unc	BU
1990 Proof	25,000	Value: 25.00				

KM# 345 10 PESOS **Weight:** 28.0000 g. **Composition:** 0.9250 Silver .8327 oz. ASW **Series:** Summer Olympics **Reverse:** High jumper

Date	Mintage	F	VF	XF	Unc	BU
1990 Proof	25,000	Value: 27.50				

KM# 362 10 PESOS **Weight:** 28.0000 g. **Composition:** 0.9250 Silver .8327 oz. ASW **Series:** Olympics **Reverse:** Basketball

Date	Mintage	F	VF	XF	Unc	BU
1990 Proof	25,000	Value: 25.00				

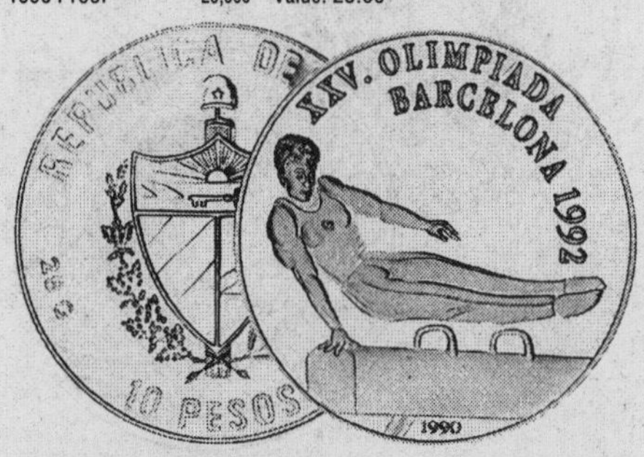

KM# 369 10 PESOS **Weight:** 28.0000 g. **Composition:** 0.9990 Silver .8994 oz. ASW **Series:** Olympics **Reverse:** Pommel horse

Date	Mintage	F	VF	XF	Unc	BU
1990 Proof	Est. 25,000	Value: 25.00				

KM# 327 10 PESOS **Weight:** 31.1000 g. **Composition:** 0.9990 Silver 1.0000 oz. ASW **Reverse:** Vicente and Martin Pinzon

Date	Mintage	F	VF	XF	Unc	BU
1991 Proof	3,000	Value: 55.00				

KM# 328 10 PESOS **Weight:** 31.1000 g. **Composition:** 0.9990 Silver 1.0000 oz. ASW **Reverse:** Hatuey tribesman

Date	Mintage	F	VF	XF	Unc	BU
1991 Proof	3,000	Value: 55.00				

KM# 329 10 PESOS **Weight:** 25.0000 g. **Composition:** 0.9990 Silver .8031 oz. ASW **Subject:** American International Monetary Conference

Date	Mintage	F	VF	XF	Unc	BU
ND(1991) Proof	3,300	Value: 55.00				

KM# 337 10 PESOS **Weight:** 27.0000 g. **Composition:** 0.9990 Silver .8673 oz. ASW **Subject:** Ibero - American - Columbus at Gardenas

Date	Mintage	F	VF	XF	Unc	BU
1991 Proof	51,000	Value: 40.00				

KM# 348 10 PESOS **Weight:** 31.1000 g. **Composition:** 0.9990 Silver 1.0000 oz. ASW **Subject:** Madrid **Reverse:** Alcala Gate

Date	Mintage	F	VF	XF	Unc	BU
1991 Proof	Est. 3,250	Value: 55.00				

KM# 349 10 PESOS **Weight:** 31.1000 g. **Composition:** 0.9990 Silver 1.0000 oz. ASW **Subject:** Seville **Reverse:** La Giralda Tower

Date	Mintage	F	VF	XF	Unc	BU
1991 Proof	Est. 3,250	Value: 55.00				

KM# 350 10 PESOS **Weight:** 31.1000 g. **Composition:** 0.9990 Silver 1.0000 oz. ASW **Subject:** Barcelona **Reverse:** Olympic Stadium

Date	Mintage	F	VF	XF	Unc	BU
1991 Proof	3,250	Value: 42.50				

KM# 525 10 PESOS **Weight:** 31.1000 g. **Composition:** 0.9990 Silver 1.0000 oz. ASW **Reverse:** Diego Velazquez

Date	Mintage	F	VF	XF	Unc	BU
1991 Proof	3,000	Value: 55.00				

KM# 526 10 PESOS **Weight:** 31.1000 g. **Composition:** 0.9990 Silver 1.0000 oz. ASW **Reverse:** Queen Joanna

Date	Mintage	F	VF	XF	Unc	BU
1991 Proof	3,000	Value: 55.00				

KM# 341.1 10 PESOS **Weight:** 20.0000 g. **Composition:** 0.9990 Silver .6430 oz. ASW **Subject:** Postal History of Cuba **Obverse:** 1992 style national arms **Reverse:** Spanish galleon sailship, 1765 date

Date	Mintage	F	VF	XF	Unc	BU
1992 Proof	10,000	Value: 35.00				

KM# 341.2 10 PESOS **Weight:** 20.0000 g. **Composition:** 0.9990 Silver .6430 oz. ASW **Subject:** Postal History **Obverse:** Pre-1990 detailed, styled arms **Reverse:** Sailing ship

Date		F	VF	XF	Unc	BU
1992 Proof	—	Value: 32.50				

KM# 351 10 PESOS **Weight:** 31.1000 g. **Composition:** 0.9990 Silver 1.0000 oz. ASW **Subject:** Seville **Reverse:** Tower of Gold

Date	Mintage	F	VF	XF	Unc	BU
1992 Proof	2,050	Value: 55.00				

KM# 352 10 PESOS **Weight:** 31.1000 g. **Composition:** 0.9990 Silver 1.0000 oz. ASW **Reverse:** El Escorial

Date	Mintage	F	VF	XF	Unc	BU
1992 Proof	2,050	Value: 55.00				

KM# 353 10 PESOS **Weight:** 31.1000 g. **Composition:** 0.9990 Silver 1.0000 oz. ASW **Subject:** 500th Anniversary of Philipp's rule **Reverse:** Philip I

Date	Mintage	F	VF	XF	Unc	BU
1992 Proof	3,000	Value: 55.00				

KM# 354.1 10 PESOS **Weight:** 20.0000 g. **Composition:** 0.9990 Silver .6430 oz. ASW **Subject:** Ptolomeo and Toscanelli

Date		F	VF	XF	Unc	BU
1992 Proof	—	Value: 37.50				

KM# 354.2 10 PESOS **Weight:** 20.0000 g. **Composition:** 0.9990 Silver .6430 oz. ASW **Obverse:** Arms with thick wreath of the pre-1990 style

Date		F	VF	XF	Unc	BU
1992 Proof	—	Value: 35.00				

KM# 355 10 PESOS **Weight:** 31.1000 g. **Composition:** 0.9990 Silver 1.0000 oz. ASW **Reverse:** Guama tribesman

Date	Mintage	F	VF	XF	Unc	BU
1992 Proof	2,050	Value: 55.00				

KM# 370 10 PESOS **Weight:** 20.0000 g. **Composition:** 0.9990 Silver .6430 oz. ASW **Subject:** Postal History **Reverse:** Steam powered sailing ship

Date	Mintage	F	VF	XF	Unc	BU
1992 Proof	10,000	Value: 32.50				

KM# 372 10 PESOS **Weight:** 31.0000 g. **Composition:** 0.9990 Silver 1.0000 oz. ASW **Reverse:** Bartolome de Las Casas

Date	Mintage	F	VF	XF	Unc	BU
1992 Proof	2,050	Value: 50.00				

KM# 373 10 PESOS Weight: 31.0000 g. **Composition:** 0.9990 Silver 1.0000 oz. ASW **Subject:** Spanish Kings and Queens **Obverse:** Coat of arms

Date	Mintage	F	VF	XF	Unc	BU
ND(1992) Proof	2,050	Value: 55.00				

KM# 374 10 PESOS Weight: 31.0000 g. **Composition:** 0.9990 Silver 1.0000 oz. ASW **Subject:** San Jorge Palace

Date	Mintage	F	VF	XF	Unc	BU
1992 Proof	2,050	Value: 40.00				

KM# 527 10 PESOS Weight: 20.0000 g. **Composition:** 0.9990 Silver .6430 oz. ASW **Subject:** 25th Anniversary - Death of Ernesto Che Guevara

Date	Mintage	F	VF	XF	Unc	BU
ND(1992) Proof	10,000	Value: 35.00				

KM# 561 10 PESOS Weight: 20.0000 g. **Composition:** 0.9990 Silver .6430 oz. ASW **Subject:** Postal History **Reverse:** Old steam and sail ship

Date	F	VF	XF	Unc	BU
1992 Proof	—	Value: 32.50			

KM# 458.1 10 PESOS Weight: 20.0000 g. **Composition:** 0.9990 Silver .6430 oz. ASW **Subject:** World Cup Soccer **Note:** Thick letters and numbers.

Date	F	VF	XF	Unc	BU
1992 Proof	—	Value: 35.00			

KM# 458.2 10 PESOS Weight: 20.0000 g. **Composition:** 0.9990 Silver .6430 oz. ASW **Note:** Thin letters and numbers.

Date	F	VF	XF	Unc	BU
1992 Proof	—	Value: 35.00			

KM# 371.1 10 PESOS Weight: 20.0000 g. **Composition:** 0.9990 Silver .6430 oz. ASW **Subject:** Introduction of Africans into America **Note:** Thin wreath.

Date	Mintage	F	VF	XF	Unc	BU
1992 Proof	10,000	Value: 42.50				

KM# 371.2 10 PESOS Weight: 20.0000 g. **Composition:** 0.9990 Silver .6430 oz. ASW **Note:** Thick wreath.

Date	F	VF	XF	Unc	BU
1992 Proof	—	Value: 42.50			

KM# 406.1 10 PESOS Weight: 31.1035 g. **Composition:** 0.9990 Silver 1.0000 oz. ASW **Obverse:** Lower left division of the arms has two slanting bars on a solid field **Reverse:** Bolivar and Mari

Date	F	VF	XF	Unc	BU
1993 Proof	—	Value: 40.00			

KM# 406.2 10 PESOS Weight: 31.1035 g. **Composition:** 0.9990 Silver 1.0000 oz. ASW **Obverse:** Lower left division of the arms has two slanting bars on a horizontally lined field **Reverse:** Bolivar and Marti

Date	F	VF	XF	Unc	BU
1993 Proof	—	Value: 60.00			

KM# 375 10 PESOS Weight: 20.0000 g. **Composition:** 0.9990 Silver .6430 oz. ASW **Reverse:** President Abraham Lincoln

Date	F	VF	XF	Unc	BU
1993 Proof	—	Value: 32.50			

KM# 398.1 10 PESOS Weight: 31.1000 g. **Composition:** 0.9990 Silver 1.0000 oz. ASW **Reverse:** Frosted bust of Fidel Castro

Date	Mintage	F	VF	XF	Unc	BU
1993 Proof	5,000	Value: 45.00				

KM# 398.2 10 PESOS Weight: 31.1000 g. **Composition:** 0.9990 Silver 1.0000 oz. ASW **Reverse:** Polished bust of Fidel Castro

Date	Mintage	F	VF	XF	Unc	BU
1993 Proof	Inc. above	Value: 45.00				

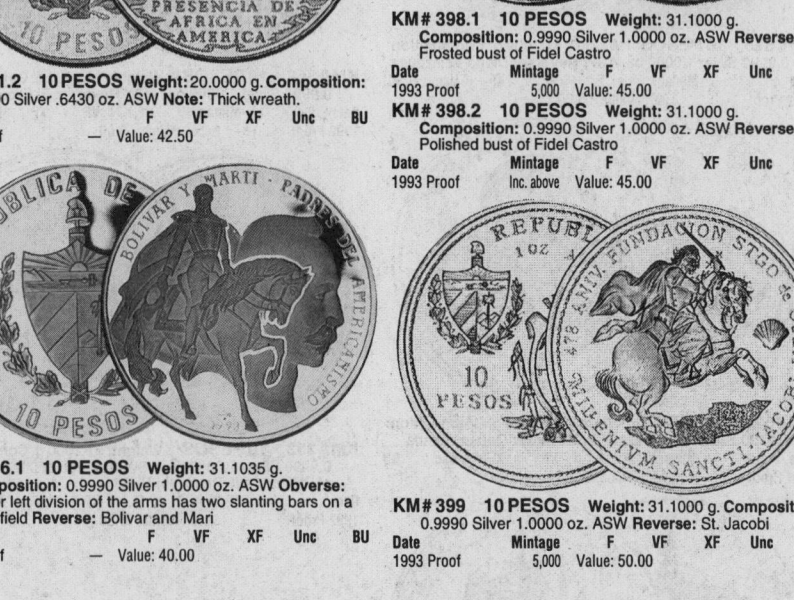

KM# 399 10 PESOS Weight: 31.1000 g. **Composition:** 0.9990 Silver 1.0000 oz. ASW **Reverse:** St. Jacobi

Date	Mintage	F	VF	XF	Unc	BU
1993 Proof	5,000	Value: 50.00				

KM# 406 10 PESOS Weight: 31.1000 g. **Composition:** 0.9990 Silver 1.0000 oz. ASW **Reverse:** Bolivar and Marti

Date	Mintage	F	VF	XF	Unc	BU
1993 Proof	3,000	Value: 40.00				

KM# 407 10 PESOS Weight: 31.1000 g. **Composition:** 0.9990 Silver 1.0000 oz. ASW **Reverse:** Frederico Garcia Lorca

Date	Mintage	F	VF	XF	Unc	BU
1993 Proof	3,300	Value: 45.00				

KM# 496 10 PESOS Weight: 19.9600 g. **Composition:** 0.9990 Silver .6411 oz. ASW **Subject:** Postal History **Reverse:** Steamship Almen Dares

Date	F	VF	XF	Unc	BU
1993 Proof	—	Value: 45.00			

KM# 408 10 PESOS Weight: 19.9600 g. **Composition:** 0.9990 Silver .6411 oz. ASW **Subject:** Montecristi Manifesto

Date	Mintage	F	VF	XF	Unc	BU
1994 Proof	3,300	Value: 45.00				

KM# 427 10 PESOS Weight: 20.0000 g. **Composition:** 0.9990 Silver .6430 oz. ASW **Reverse:** Sailing ship - LA INDIA

Date	Mintage	F	VF	XF	Unc	BU
1994 Proof	10,000	Value: 32.50				

KM# 428 10 PESOS Weight: 20.0000 g. **Composition:** 0.9990 Silver .6430 oz. ASW **Reverse:** Sailing ship - NAO VICTORIA

Date	Mintage	F	VF	XF	Unc	BU
1994 Proof	10,000	Value: 32.50				

KM# 441 10 PESOS Weight: 20.0000 g. **Composition:** 0.9990 Silver .6430 oz. ASW **Subject:** Evangelista Island

Date	F	VF	XF	Unc	BU
1994 Proof	—	Value: 32.50			

KM# 442 10 PESOS Weight: 20.0000 g. **Composition:** 0.9990 Silver .6430 oz. ASW **Series:** Caribbean Fauna **Reverse:** Multicolored flamingos

Date	Mintage	F	VF	XF	Unc	BU
1994 Proof	10,000	Value: 40.00				

KM# 443 10 PESOS Weight: 20.0000 g. **Composition:** 0.9990 Silver .6430 oz. ASW **Series:** Caribbean Fauna **Reverse:** Multicolored Yellow Sea Bass (Coney)

Date	Mintage	F	VF	XF	Unc	BU
1994 Proof	10,000	Value: 50.00				

KM# 468 10 PESOS Weight: 20.0000 g. **Composition:** 0.9990 Silver .6430 oz. ASW **Subject:** Environmental Protection **Reverse:** Scale

Date	Mintage	F	VF	XF	Unc	BU
1994 Proof	Est. 5,000	Value: 45.00				

KM# 469 10 PESOS Weight: 20.0000 g. **Composition:** 0.9990 Silver .6430 oz. ASW **Series:** 1996 Olympics **Reverse:** Boxers

Date	Mintage	F	VF	XF	Unc	BU
1994 Proof	Est. 30,000	Value: 27.50				

KM# 470 10 PESOS Weight: 20.0000 g. **Composition:** 0.9990 Silver .6430 oz. ASW **Reverse:** Red Baron Plane - Multicolored Fokker Dr. I

Date	F	VF	XF	Unc	BU
1994 Proof	—	Value: 55.00			

KM# 499 10 PESOS Weight: 20.0000 g. **Composition:** 0.9990 Silver .6424 oz. ASW **Series:** Caribbean Fauna **Reverse:** Multicolored bottle-nosed dolphins

Date	Mintage	F	VF	XF	Unc	BU
1994 Proof	Est. 10,000	Value: 50.00				

KM# 500 10 PESOS Weight: 20.0000 g. **Composition:** 0.9990 Silver .6424 oz. ASW **Series:** Caribbean Fauna **Reverse:** Multicolored swordfish

Date	Mintage	F	VF	XF	Unc	BU
1994 Proof	10,000	Value: 40.00				

KM# 501 10 PESOS **Weight:** 20.0000 g. **Composition:** 0.9990 Silver .6424 oz. ASW **Series:** Caribbean Fauna **Reverse:** Multicolored Brown Pelican

Date	Mintage	F	VF	XF	Unc	BU
1994 Proof	10,000	Value: 50.00				

KM# 502 10 PESOS **Weight:** 20.0000 g. **Composition:** 0.9990 Silver .6424 oz. ASW **Series:** Caribbean Fauna **Reverse:** Multicolored Spotted Eagle Ray

Date	Mintage	F	VF	XF	Unc	BU
1994 Proof	10,000	Value: 50.00				

KM# 510.1 10 PESOS **Weight:** 20.0000 g. **Composition:** 0.9990 Silver .6424 oz. ASW **Subject:** World Cup Soccer **Obverse:** Thin letters **Reverse:** Two players with bridge in background, thick letters and date

Date	Mintage	F	VF	XF	Unc	BU
1994 Proof	Est. 10,000	Value: 50.00				

KM# 510.2 10 PESOS **Weight:** 20.0000 g. **Composition:** 0.9990 Silver .6424 oz. ASW **Subject:** World Cup Soccer **Obverse:** Thick letters **Reverse:** Two players with bridge in background, thin letters and date

Date	Mintage	F	VF	XF	Unc	BU
1994 Proof	Inc. above	Value: 350				

KM# 528 10 PESOS **Weight:** 20.0000 g. **Composition:** 0.9990 Silver .6424 oz. ASW **Reverse:** Multicolored Albatross DII fighter plane

Date	F	VF	XF	Unc	BU
1994 Proof —	Value: 42.50				

KM# 541 10 PESOS **Weight:** 27.0000 g. **Composition:** 0.9250 Silver .8030 oz. ASW **Subject:** Environmental Protection **Reverse:** Ivory-billed Woodpecker

Date	Mintage	F	VF	XF	Unc	BU
1994 Proof	20,000	Value: 45.00				

KM# 478 10 PESOS **Weight:** 20.0000 g. **Composition:** 0.9990 Silver .6430 oz. ASW **Subject:** Pirates of the Caribbean **Reverse:** Blackbeard

Date	Mintage	F	VF	XF	Unc	BU
1995 Proof	Est. 10,000	Value: 60.00				

KM# 479 10 PESOS **Weight:** 20.0000 g. **Composition:** 0.9990 Silver .6430 oz. ASW **Subject:** Pirates of the Caribbean **Reverse:** Sir Henry Morgan

Date	Mintage	F	VF	XF	Unc	BU
1995 Proof	Est. 10,000	Value: 60.00				

KM# 480 10 PESOS **Weight:** 20.0000 g. **Composition:** 0.9990 Silver .6430 oz. ASW **Subject:** Pirates of the Caribbean **Reverse:** Anne Bonny

Date	Mintage	F	VF	XF	Unc	BU
1995 Proof	Est. 10,000	Value: 60.00				

KM# 481 10 PESOS **Weight:** 20.0000 g. **Composition:** 0.9990 Silver .6430 oz. ASW **Subject:** Pirates of the Caribbean **Reverse:** Mary Read

Date	Mintage	F	VF	XF	Unc	BU
1995 Proof	Est. 10,000	Value: 60.00				

KM# 482 10 PESOS **Weight:** 20.0000 g. **Composition:** 0.9990 Silver .6430 oz. ASW **Subject:** Pirates of the Caribbean **Reverse:** Captain Kidd

Date	Mintage	F	VF	XF	Unc	BU
1995 Proof	Est. 10,000	Value: 60.00				

KM# 483 10 PESOS **Weight:** 20.0000 g. **Composition:** 0.9990 Silver .6430 oz. ASW **Subject:** Pirates of the Caribbean **Reverse:** Piet Heyn

Date	Mintage	F	VF	XF	Unc	BU
1995 Proof	Est. 10,000	Value: 60.00				

KM# 511 10 PESOS **Weight:** 20.0000 g. **Composition:** 0.9990 Silver .6430 oz. ASW **Reverse:** Arnaldo Tamayo Mendez

Date	Mintage	F	VF	XF	Unc	BU
1995 Proof	Est. 5,000	Value: 45.00				

KM# 529 10 PESOS **Weight:** 20.0000 g. **Composition:** 0.9990 Silver .6430 oz. ASW **Subject:** F.A.O. 50th Anniversary **Reverse:** Farmer plowing with two oxen

Date	Mintage	F	VF	XF	Unc	BU
ND(1995) Proof	3,000	Value: 40.00				

KM# 530 10 PESOS **Weight:** 31.1000 g. **Composition:** 0.9990 Silver 1.0000 oz. ASW **Subject:** Centennial 1895-1995

Date	Mintage	F	VF	XF	Unc	BU
ND(1995) Proof	500	Value: 60.00				

KM# 540 10 PESOS **Weight:** 28.2800 g. **Composition:** 0.9250 Silver .8411 oz. ASW **Subject:** 50th Anniversary - United Nations

Date	Mintage	F	VF	XF	Unc	BU
ND(1995) Proof	Est. 105,000	Value: 40.00				

KM# 574 10 PESOS **Weight:** 20.0000 g. **Composition:** 0.9990 Silver .6430 oz. ASW **Subject:** Death of Jose Marti

Date	F	VF	XF	Unc	BU
1995	—	—	—	45.00	—

KM# 548 10 PESOS **Composition:** Silver **Subject:** Seaplane **Reverse:** Multicolored SIAI Marchetti S55

Date	Mintage	F	VF	XF	Unc	BU
1995 Proof	15,000	Value: 45.00				

KM# 600 10 PESOS **Weight:** 15.0000 g. **Composition:** 0.9990 Silver .6423 oz. ASW **Subject:** Caribbean Flora **Obverse:** Cuban arms **Reverse:** Multicolor flower, Ruelia tuberosa

Date	Mintage	F	VF	XF	Unc	BU
ND(1995) Proof	3,000	Value: 40.00				

KM# 553 10 PESOS **Weight:** 20.0000 g. **Composition:** 0.9990 Silver .6430 oz. ASW **Series:** Caribbean Fauna **Reverse:** Multicolored Ruby-throated Hummingbird

Date	Mintage	F	VF	XF	Unc	BU
1996 Proof	5,000	Value: 50.00				

KM# 554 10 PESOS **Composition:** Silver **Series:** Caribbean Fauna **Reverse:** Multicolored Yellow Perch

Date	Mintage	F	VF	XF	Unc	BU
1996 Proof	5,000	Value: 40.00				

KM# 555 10 PESOS **Weight:** 20.0000 g. **Composition:** 0.9990 Silver .6430 oz. ASW **Series:** Caribbean Fauna **Reverse:** Multicolored Cuban Tody Bird

Date	Mintage	F	VF	XF	Unc	BU
1996 Proof	5,000	Value: 50.00				

KM# 556 10 PESOS **Weight:** 20.0000 g. **Composition:** 0.9990 Silver .6430 oz. ASW **Series:** Caribbean Fauna **Reverse:** Multicolored Wood Duck

Date	Mintage	F	VF	XF	Unc	BU
1996 Proof	5,000	—	—	—	50.00	—

KM# 566 10 PESOS **Weight:** 20.0000 g. **Composition:** 0.9990 Silver .6430 oz. ASW **Series:** Caribbean Fauna **Reverse:** Multicolored Papilio Butterfly

Date	Mintage	F	VF	XF	Unc	BU
1996	5,000	Value: 75.00				

KM# 563.1 10 PESOS **Weight:** 20.0000 g. **Composition:** 0.9990 Silver .6430 oz. ASW **Series:** Caribbean Fauna **Reverse:** Multicolored Vaca Anil (Blue Cow) Fish

Date	Mintage	F	VF	XF	Unc	BU
1996 Proof	5,000	Value: 50.00				

KM# 582 10 PESOS **Weight:** 15.0000 g. **Composition:** 0.9990 Silver .6423 oz. ASW **Subject:** First Railroads - Germany **Obverse:** Cuban arms **Reverse:** First German locomotive, date 1835-1996

Date		F	VF	XF	Unc	BU
1996 Proof	—	Value: 32.50				

KM# 583 10 PESOS **Weight:** 15.0000 g. **Composition:** 0.9990 Silver .6423 oz. ASW **Subject:** First Railroads - Austria **Obverse:** Cuban arms **Reverse:** First Austrian locomotive, date 1848-1996

Date		F	VF	XF	Unc	BU
1996 Proof	—	Value: 32.50				

KM# 584 10 PESOS **Weight:** 15.0000 g. **Composition:** 0.9990 Silver .6423 oz. ASW **Subject:** First Railroads - Switzerland **Obverse:** Cuban arms **Reverse:** First Swiss locomotive, date 1847-1997

Date		F	VF	XF	Unc	BU
1996 Proof	—	Value: 32.50				

KM# 585 10 PESOS **Weight:** 15.0000 g. **Composition:** 0.9990 Silver .6423 oz. ASW **Subject:** El Mundo de la Aventura **Obverse:** Cuban arms **Reverse:** Multicolored submarine and cameo portrait of Capt. Nemo

Date		F	VF	XF	Unc	BU
1996 Proof	—	Value: 40.00				

KM# 586 10 PESOS **Weight:** 20.0000 g. **Composition:** 0.9990 Silver .6430 oz. ASW **Subject:** Campeonato Mundial de Futbol - Francia **Obverse:** Cuban arms **Reverse:** Joan of Arc with France's flag before soccer ball

Date	F	VF	XF	Unc	BU
1996 Proof	—	Value: 45.00			

KM# 587 10 PESOS Weight: 20.0000 g. **Composition:** 0.9990 Silver .6430 oz. ASW **Subject:** America - El Nuevo Mundo **Obverse:** Cuban arms **Reverse:** Ship and cameo portrait of America Vespucci

Date	F	VF	XF	Unc	BU
1996 Proof	—	Value: 35.00			

KM# 588 10 PESOS Weight: 20.0000 g. **Composition:** 0.9990 Silver .6430 oz. ASW **Subject:** World Food Summit **Obverse:** Cuban arms **Reverse:** Woman picking fruit, F.A.O. logo, dates

Date	F	VF	XF	Unc	BU
1996 Proof	—	Value: 45.00			

KM# 589 10 PESOS Weight: 31.1035 g. **Composition:** 0.9990 Silver 1.0000 oz. ASW **Subject:** 40th Anniversary of the Granma's Landing **Obverse:** Cuban arms **Reverse:** Castro's portrait above the Granma

Date	F	VF	XF	Unc	BU
1996 Proof	—	Value: 50.00			

KM# 590 10 PESOS Weight: 20.0000 g. **Composition:** 0.9990 Silver .6430 oz. ASW **Subject:** Circumnavigation of Cuba - Pinzon **Obverse:** Cuban arms **Reverse:** Sailship and cameo portrait of Vincente Pizon

Date	F	VF	XF	Unc	BU
1997 Proof	—	Value: 35.00			

KM# 591 10 PESOS Weight: 15.0000 g. **Composition:** 0.9990 Silver .6423 oz. ASW **Subject:** XXVII Olympics **Obverse:** Cuban arms **Reverse:** Two fencers

Date	F	VF	XF	Unc	BU
1997 Proof	—	Value: 35.00			

KM# 592 10 PESOS Weight: 15.0000 g. **Composition:** 0.9990 Silver .6423 oz. ASW **Subject:** XXVII Olympics **Obverse:** Cuban arms **Reverse:** Multicolored baseballl player at bat

Date	F	VF	XF	Unc	BU
1997 Proof	—	Value: 40.00			

KM# 593 10 PESOS Weight: 15.0000 g. **Composition:** 0.9990 Silver .6423 oz. ASW **Subject:** Wonders of the Ancient World **Obverse:** Cuban arms **Reverse:** Hanging Gardens of Babylon

Date	F	VF	XF	Unc	BU
1997 Proof	—	Value: 32.50			

KM# 594 10 PESOS Weight: 15.0000 g. **Composition:** 0.9990 Silver .6423 oz. ASW **Subject:** Wonders of the Ancient World **Obverse:** Cuban arms **Reverse:** Temple of Artemis

Date	F	VF	XF	Unc	BU
1997 Proof	—	Value: 32.50			

KM# 595 10 PESOS Weight: 15.0000 g. **Composition:** 0.9990 Silver .6423 oz. ASW **Subject:** Wonders of the Ancient World **Obverse:** Cuban arms **Reverse:** Lighthouse of Alexandria

Date	F	VF	XF	Unc	BU
1997 Proof	—	Value: 32.50			

KM# 596 10 PESOS Weight: 15.0000 g. **Composition:** 0.9990 Silver .6423 oz. ASW **Subject:** Wonders of the Ancient World **Obverse:** Cuban arms **Reverse:** Statue of Colossus of Rhodes over breakwater

Date	F	VF	XF	Unc	BU
1997 Proof	—	Value: 32.50			

KM# 597 10 PESOS Weight: 15.0000 g. **Composition:** 0.9990 Silver .6423 oz. ASW **Subject:** Wonders of the Ancient World **Obverse:** Cuban arms **Reverse:** Painting above Egyptian pyramids and excavation

Date	F	VF	XF	Unc	BU
1997 Proof	—	Value: 32.50			

KM# 598 10 PESOS Weight: 15.0000 g. **Composition:** 0.9990 Silver .6423 oz. ASW **Subject:** Wonders of the Ancient World - Temple of Jupiter **Obverse:** Cuban arms **Reverse:** Statue of Jupiter inside temple

Date	F	VF	XF	Unc	BU
1997 Proof	—	Value: 32.50			

KM# 601 10 PESOS Weight: 15.0000 g. **Composition:** 0.9990 Silver .6423 oz. ASW **Subject:** Caribbean Flora **Obverse:** Cuban arms **Reverse:** Multicolored flower, "Cordia sebestena"

Date	F	VF	XF	Unc	BU
1997 Proof	—	Value: 32.50			

KM# 602 10 PESOS Weight: 15.0000 g. **Composition:** 0.9990 Silver .6423 oz. ASW **Subject:** Caribbean Flora **Obverse:** Cuban arms **Reverse:** Multicolored flower, "Lochnera rosea"

Date	F	VF	XF	Unc	BU
1997 Proof	—	Value: 32.50			

KM# 603 10 PESOS **Weight:** 15.0000 g. **Composition:** 0.9990 Silver .6423 oz. ASW **Subject:** Caribbean Flora **Obverse:** Cuban arms **Reverse:** Multicolored flower, "Turnera ulmifolia"

Date	F	VF	XF	Unc	BU
1997 Proof	—	Value: 32.50			

KM# 604 10 PESOS **Weight:** 15.0000 g. **Composition:** 0.9990 Silver .6423 oz. ASW **Subject:** Caribbean Flora **Obverse:** Cuban arms **Reverse:** Multicolored flower, "Bidens pilosa"

Date	F	VF	XF	Unc	BU
1997 Proof	—	Value: 32.50			

KM# 609 10 PESOS **Weight:** 15.0000 g. **Composition:** 0.9990 Silver .4818 oz. ASW **Subject:** Sesquicentennial of First Steam/Sail Powered Ship **Obverse:** Cuban arms **Reverse:** Ship, date

Date	Mintage	F	VF	XF	Unc	BU
1997 Proof	5,000	Value: 42.50				

KM# 613 10 PESOS **Weight:** 31.1035 g. **Composition:** 0.9990 Silver 1.0000 oz. ASW **Subject:** Castro Visit to Vatican **Obverse:** Cuban arms **Reverse:** Pope and Castro meeting

Date	F	VF	XF	Unc	BU
1997	—	—	—	55.00	—

KM# 667 10 PESOS **Weight:** 15.0000 g. **Composition:** 0.9990 Silver .4818 oz. ASW **Subject:** 450th Anniversary - Birth of Cervantes

Date	F	VF	XF	Unc	BU
1997 Proof	—	Value: 50.00			

KM# 625 10 PESOS **Weight:** 27.0000 g. **Composition:** 0.9250 Silver .8030 oz. ASW **Subject:** Ibero - American **Reverse:** Two rumba dancers

Date	F	VF	XF	Unc	BU
1997	—	—	—	50.00	—

KM# 723 10 PESOS **Weight:** 31.1035 g. **Composition:** 0.9990 Silver 1.0000 oz. ASW **Subject:** 25th Anniversary - Ernesto Che Guevara's Death **Obverse:** National arms and inscription **Reverse:** Ernesto Che Guevara walking **Edge:** Edge **Size:** 42 mm.

Date	Mintage	F	VF	XF	Unc	BU
ND(1997) Proof	10,000	Value: 50.00				

KM# 724 10 PESOS **Weight:** 31.1035 g. **Composition:** 0.9990 Silver 1.0000 oz. ASW **Subject:** 30th Anniversary - Ernesto Che Guevara's Death **Reverse:** Ernest Cheo Guevara's portrait **Edge:** Reeded **Size:** 42 mm.

Date	Mintage	F	VF	XF	Unc	BU
ND(1997) Proof	10,000	Value: 50.00				

KM# 599 10 PESOS **Weight:** 15.0000 g. **Comp.:** 0.9990 Silver .6423 oz. ASW **Subject:** Wonders of the Ancient World **Obverse:** Cuban Arms **Reverse:** Mausoleum of Halicarnas

Date	F	VF	XF	Unc	BU
1997 Proof	—	Value: 32.50			

KM# 670 10 PESOS **Weight:** 31.1800 g. **Composition:** 0.9990 Silver 1.0015 oz. ASW **Subject:** Havana Puzzle - Sailing Ship San Genaro **Obverse:** Cuban arms **Reverse:** Three sailing ships **Edge:** Plain **Shape:** Rectangular **Size:** 45.2 x 35.1 mm. **Note:** Rectangular shaped.

Date	Mintage	F	VF	XF	Unc	BU
1998 Proof	3,000	Value: 50.00				

KM# 610 10 PESOS **Weight:** 15.0000 g. **Composition:** 0.9990 Silver .4818 oz. ASW **Subject:** Mississippi **Obverse:** Cuban arms **Reverse:** Riverboat

Date	Mintage	F	VF	XF	Unc	BU
1998 Proof	5,000	Value: 37.50				

KM# 611 10 PESOS **Weight:** 15.0000 g. **Composition:** 0.9990 Silver .4818 oz. ASW **Obverse:** Cuban arms **Reverse:** The ship Rio Bravo

Date	F	VF	XF	Unc	BU
1998 Proof	—	Value: 35.00			

KM# 644 10 PESOS **Weight:** 31.1035 g. **Composition:** 0.9990 Silver 1.0000 oz. ASW **Subject:** Centenary - Explosion del Maine **Obverse:** Cuban arms **Reverse:** Explosion scene

Date	Mintage	F	VF	XF	Unc	BU
1998 Proof	5,000	Value: 65.00				

KM# 645 10 PESOS **Weight:** 31.1035 g. **Composition:** 0.9990 Silver 1.0000 oz. ASW **Subject:** Centenary - Naval battle of Santiago **Obverse:** Cuban arms **Reverse:** Cameo of Admiral Cervera and burning ship

Date	Mintage	F	VF	XF	Unc	BU
1998 Proof	5,000	Value: 65.00				

KM# 646 10 PESOS **Weight:** 31.1035 g. **Composition:** 0.9990 Silver 1.0000 oz. ASW **Subject:** Centenary - Calixto Garcia - Combate en Oriente **Obverse:** Cuban arms **Reverse:** Portrait above three Cuban cavalry troopers

Date	Mintage	F	VF	XF	Unc	BU
1998 Proof	5,000	Value: 65.00				

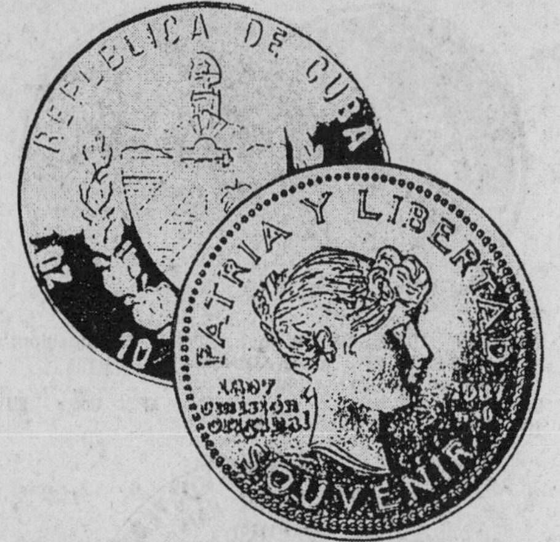

KM# 647 10 PESOS **Weight:** 31.1035 g. **Composition:** 0.9990 Silver 1.0000 oz. ASW **Reverse:** Souvenir peso design, bust of Leonor Molina

Date	Mintage	F	VF	XF	Unc	BU
1998 Proof	5,000	Value: 55.00				

KM# 648 10 PESOS **Weight:** 31.1035 g. **Composition:** 0.9990 Silver 1.0000 oz. ASW **Subject:** Expo 2000 - Twipsy **Obverse:** Cuban arms **Reverse:** "Twipsy" cartoon logo

Date	Mintage	F	VF	XF	Unc	BU
1998 Proof	19,000	Value: 35.00				

KM# 649 10 PESOS **Weight:** 31.1035 g. **Composition:** 0.9990 Silver 1.0000 oz. ASW **Subject:** Expo 2000 - Germany **Obverse:** Cuban arms **Reverse:** German map

Date	Mintage	F	VF	XF	Unc	BU
1998 Proof	19,000	Value: 35.00				

KM# 650 10 PESOS **Weight:** 31.1035 g. **Composition:** 0.9990 Silver 1.0000 oz. ASW **Subject:** Expo 2000 - London **Obverse:** Cuban arms **Reverse:** Cartoon over exhibit hall

Date	Mintage	F	VF	XF	Unc	BU
1998 Proof	19,000	Value: 35.00				

KM# 651 10 PESOS **Weight:** 31.1035 g. **Composition:** 0.9990 Silver 1.0000 oz. ASW **Subject:** Expo 2000 - Paris **Obverse:** Cuban arms **Reverse:** Cartoon and Eiffel Tower

Date	Mintage	F	VF	XF	Unc	BU
1998 Proof	19,000	Value: 35.00				

KM# 652 10 PESOS **Weight:** 31.1035 g. **Composition:** 0.9990 Silver 1.0000 oz. ASW **Subject:** Expo 2000 - Brussels **Obverse:** Cuban arms **Reverse:** Cartoon and Atomium structure

Date	Mintage	F	VF	XF	Unc	BU
1998 Proof	19,000	Value: 35.00				

KM# 653 10 PESOS **Weight:** 31.1035 g. **Composition:** 0.9990 Silver 1.0000 oz. ASW **Subject:** Expo 2000 - Postrimerias **Obverse:** Cuban arms **Reverse:** Cartoon on tree bearing world globe

Date	Mintage	F	VF	XF	Unc	BU
1998 Proof	19,000	Value: 35.00				

KM# 668 10 PESOS **Weight:** 31.1035 g. **Composition:** 0.9990 Silver 1.0015 oz. ASW **Subject:** Havana Puzzle - Frigate Oquendo **Obverse:** Cuban arms **Reverse:** Two sailing ships **Edge:** Plain **Shape:** Rectangular **Size:** 45.2 x 35.1 mm.

Date	F	VF	XF	Unc	BU
1998 Proof	—	Value: 50.00			

KM# 669 10 PESOS **Weight:** 31.1035 g. **Composition:** 0.9990 Silver 1.0015 oz. ASW **Subject:** Havana Puzzle - City of Havana **Obverse:** Cuban arms **Reverse:** Havana city view **Edge:** Plain **Shape:** Rectangular **Size:** 45.2 x 35.1 mm.

Date	Mintage	F	VF	XF	Unc	BU
1998 Proof	3,000	Value: 50.00				

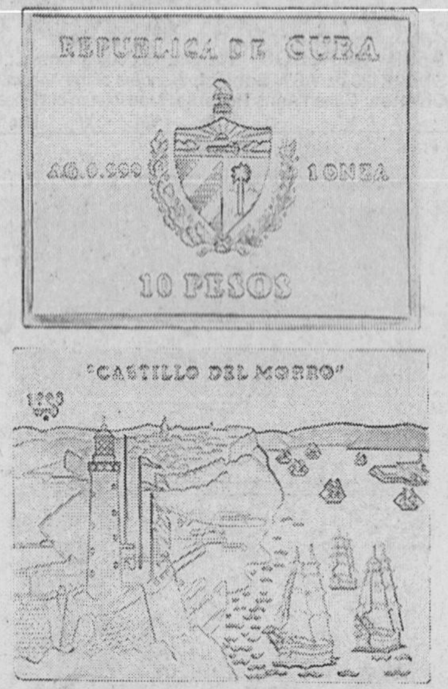

KM# 671 10 PESOS **Weight:** 31.1800 g. **Composition:** 0.9990 Silver 1.0015 oz. ASW **Subject:** Hava Puzzle - El Morro **Obverse:** Cuban arms **Reverse:** Light house and sailing ships **Edge:** Plain **Shape:** Rectangular **Size:** 45.2 x 35.1 mm.

Date	Mintage	F	VF	XF	Unc	BU
1998 Proof	3,000	Value: 50.00				

KM# 672 10 PESOS **Weight:** 31.1035 g. **Composition:** 0.9990 Silver 1.0000 oz. ASW **Subject:** 40th Anniversary - Triumph of the Revolution

Date	F	VF	XF	Unc	BU
1999 Proof	—	Value: 45.00			

KM# 674 10 PESOS **Weight:** 31.1035 g. **Composition:** 0.9990 Silver 1.0000 oz. ASW **Subject:** Spanish Royal Visit - Fidel Castro receives King Juan Carlos I

Date	F	VF	XF	Unc	BU
1999 Proof	—	Value: 75.00			

KM# 676 10 PESOS **Weight:** 31.1035 g. **Composition:** 0.9990 Silver 1.0000 oz. ASW **Subject:** Spanish Royal Visit - 2 Peoples United

Date	F	VF	XF	Unc	BU
1999 Proof	—	Value: 75.00			

KM# 677 10 PESOS **Weight:** 31.1035 g. **Composition:** 0.9990 Silver 1.0000 oz. ASW **Subject:** Spanish Royal Visit - Homage to the Spanish Soldier

Date	F	VF	XF	Unc	BU
1999 Proof	—	Value: 75.00			

KM# 661 10 PESOS **Weight:** 31.1035 g. **Composition:** 0.9990 Silver 1.0000 oz. ASW **Subject:** Zunzuncito **Obverse:** National arms **Reverse:** Hummingbird **Edge:** Plain

Date	F	VF	XF	Unc	BU
1999 Proof	—	Value: 50.00			

KM# 725 10 PESOS **Weight:** 3.1100 g. **Composition:** 0.9990 Gold .1000 oz. AGW **Subject:** Zunzuncito **Obverse:** National arms **Reverse:** Hummingbird **Edge:** Reeded **Size:** 18 mm.

Date	Mintage	F	VF	XF	Unc	BU
1999 Proof	1,000	Value: 100				

KM# 212 15 PESOS **Weight:** 3.8800 g. **Composition:** 0.9990 Gold .1250 oz. AGW **Reverse:** Jose Marti

Date	Mintage	F	VF	XF	Unc	BU
1988	50	—	—	—	100	—
1988 Proof	15	Value: 150				
1989	50	—	—	—	100	—
1989 Proof	15	Value: 150				
1990	15	—	—	—	125	—
1990 Proof	12	Value: 150				

KM# 38 20 PESOS **Weight:** 26.0000 g. **Composition:** 0.9250 Silver .7732 oz. ASW **Reverse:** Ignacio Agramonte

Date	Mintage	F	VF	XF	Unc	BU
1977 Proof	25,000	Value: 32.50				

KM# 39 20 PESOS **Weight:** 26.0000 g. **Composition:** 0.9250 Silver .7732 oz. ASW **Reverse:** Maximo Gomez

Date	Mintage	F	VF	XF	Unc	BU
1977 Proof	75,000	Value: 28.00				

KM# 40 20 PESOS **Weight:** 26.0000 g. **Composition:** 0.9250 Silver .7732 oz. ASW **Reverse:** Antonio Maceo

Date	Mintage	F	VF	XF	Unc	BU
1977 Proof	75,000	Value: 28.00				

KM# 41 20 PESOS Weight: 26.0000 g. **Composition:** 0.9250 Silver .7732 oz. ASW **Subject:** 60th Anniversary Socialist Revolution - Lenin

Date	Mintage	F	VF	XF	Unc	BU
1977 Proof	100	Value: 1,400				

KM# 44 20 PESOS Weight: 26.0000 g. **Composition:** 0.9250 Silver .7732 oz. ASW **Subject:** Nonaligned Nations Conference

Date	Mintage	F	VF	XF	Unc	BU
1979	20,000	—	—	—	12.50	—
1979 Proof	—	Value: 60.00				
1980 Matte Proof	—	Value: 100				

KM# 169 20 PESOS Weight: 62.2000 g. **Composition:** 0.9990 Silver 2.0000 oz. ASW **Subject:** Triumph of the Revolution

Date	Mintage	F	VF	XF	Unc	BU
1987 Proof	500	Value: 85.00				
1988 Proof	1,000	Value: 75.00				
1989 Proof	500	Value: 85.00				

KM# 170 20 PESOS Weight: 62.2000 g. **Composition:** 0.9990 Silver 2.0000 oz. ASW **Subject:** 60th Anniversary - Birth of Ernesto Che Guevara

Date	Mintage	F	VF	XF	Unc	BU
1987 Proof	500	Value: 85.00				
1988 Proof	1,000	Value: 75.00				
1989 Proof	500	Value: 85.00				

KM# 171 20 PESOS Weight: 62.2000 g. **Composition:** 0.9990 Silver 2.0000 oz. ASW **Subject:** 30th Anniversary - The March to Victory **Reverse:** Soldiers on the march

Date	Mintage	F	VF	XF	Unc	BU
1987 Proof	333	Value: 85.00				
1988 Proof	1,000	Value: 75.00				
1989 Proof	500	Value: 85.00				

KM# 232 20 PESOS Weight: 62.2000 g. **Composition:** 0.9990 Silver 2.0000 oz. ASW **Subject:** 150th Anniversary - First Railroad in Cuba

Date	Mintage	F	VF	XF	Unc	BU
1988 Proof	Est. 1,000	Value: 80.00				

KM# 233 20 PESOS Weight: 62.2000 g. **Composition:** 0.9990 Silver 2.0000 oz. ASW **Subject:** 140th Anniversary - First Railroad in Spain **Obverse:** Star behind arms

Date	Mintage	F	VF	XF	Unc	BU
ND(1988) Proof	Est. 1,000	Value: 80.00				

KM# 234 20 PESOS Weight: 62.2000 g. **Composition:** 0.9990 Silver 2.0000 oz. ASW **Subject:** 160th Anniversary - First Railroad in England

Date	Mintage	F	VF	XF	Unc	BU
1988 Proof	Est. 1,000	Value: 80.00				

KM# 235 20 PESOS Weight: 62.2000 g. **Composition:** 0.9990 Silver 2.0000 oz. ASW **Reverse:** Tania La Guerrillera

Date	Mintage	F	VF	XF	Unc	BU
1988 Proof	1,000	Value: 75.00				

KM# 236 20 PESOS Weight: 62.2000 g. **Composition:** 0.9990 Silver 2.0000 oz. ASW **Reverse:** Camilo Cienfuegos

Date	Mintage	F	VF	XF	Unc	BU
1988 Proof	1,000	Value: 75.00				

KM# 237 20 PESOS Weight: 62.2000 g. **Composition:** 0.9990 Silver 2.0000 oz. ASW **Subject:** 35th Anniversary - Assault of the Moncada Garrison

Date	Mintage	F	VF	XF	Unc	BU
ND(1988) Proof	1,000	Value: 75.00				

KM# 531 20 PESOS Weight: 62.2000 g. **Composition:** 0.9990 Silver 2.0000 oz. ASW **Reverse:** Jose Raul playing chess

Date	Mintage	F	VF	XF	Unc	BU
ND(1988) Proof	1,000	Value: 90.00				

KM# 532 20 PESOS **Weight:** 62.2000 g. **Composition:** 0.9990 Silver 2.0000 oz. ASW **Subject:** 25th Anniversary - Death of Ernesto Che Guevara **Obverse:** Arms

Date	Mintage	F	VF	XF	Unc	BU
ND(1992) Proof	1,000	Value: 80.00				

KM# 471.1 20 PESOS **Weight:** 62.2000 g. **Composition:** 0.9990 Silver 2.0000 oz. ASW **Subject:** Fidel Castro - 40th Anniversary of Moncada

Date	F	VF	XF	Unc	BU
1993 Proof	—	Value: 90.00			

KM# 459 20 PESOS **Weight:** 62.2000 g. **Composition:** 0.9990 Silver 2.0000 oz. ASW **Subject:** Cuban Railroad **Obverse:** Arms

Date	F	VF	XF	Unc	BU
1994 Proof	—	Value: 90.00			

KM# 533 20 PESOS **Weight:** 62.2000 g. **Composition:** 0.9990 Silver 2.0000 oz. ASW **Subject:** Transportation **Obverse:** Arms **Reverse:** Zeppelin

Date	Mintage	F	VF	XF	Unc	BU
1995 Proof	1,000	Value: 95.00				

KM# 213 25 PESOS **Weight:** 7.7700 g. **Composition:** 0.9990 Gold .2500 oz. AGW

Date	Mintage	F	VF	XF	Unc	BU
1988	50	—	—	—	200	—
1988 Proof	15	Value: 300				
1989	50	—	—	—	200	—
1989 Proof	15	Value: 300				
1990	12	—	—	—	250	—
1990 Proof	12	Value: 300				

Y# 726 25 PESOS **Weight:** 7.7759 g. **Composition:** 0.9990 Gold .2500 oz. AGW **Subject:** Zunzuncito **Obverse:** National arms **Reverse:** Hummingbird **Edge:** Reeded **Size:** 20 mm.

Date	Mintage	F	VF	XF	Unc	BU
1999 Proof	1,000	Value: 135				

KM# 422 30 PESOS **Weight:** 93.2500 g. **Composition:** 0.9990 Silver 2.9951 oz. ASW **Reverse:** Vincente and Martin Pinzon

Date	Mintage	F	VF	XF	Unc	BU
1991 Proof	1,000	Value: 125				

KM# 423 30 PESOS **Weight:** 93.2500 g. **Composition:** 0.9990 Silver 2.9951 oz. ASW **Reverse:** Hatuey People

Date	Mintage	F	VF	XF	Unc	BU
1991 Proof	1,000	Value: 125				

KM# 430 30 PESOS **Weight:** 93.3000 g. **Composition:** 0.9990 Silver 2.9970 oz. ASW **Subject:** 500th Anniversary **Obverse:** Arms **Reverse:** Queen Joanna

Date	Mintage	F	VF	XF	Unc	BU
1991 Proof	1,000	Value: 165				

KM# 431 30 PESOS **Weight:** 93.3000 g. **Composition:** 0.9990 Silver 2.9970 oz. ASW **Obverse:** Arms **Reverse:** Diego Velazquez

Date	Mintage	F	VF	XF	Unc	BU
1991 Proof	1,000	Value: 165				

KM# 376 30 PESOS **Weight:** 93.2500 g. **Composition:** 0.9990 Silver 2.9951 oz. ASW **Subject:** 500th Anniversary **Obverse:** Arms **Reverse:** Guama native

Date	Mintage	F	VF	XF	Unc	BU
1992 Proof	550	Value: 125				

KM# 377 30 PESOS **Weight:** 93.2500 g. **Composition:** 0.9990 Silver 2.9951 oz. ASW **Subject:** 500th Anniversary **Obverse:** Arms **Reverse:** Bartolome de Las Casas

Date	Mintage	F	VF	XF	Unc	BU
1992 Proof	550	Value: 125				

KM# 378 30 PESOS **Weight:** 93.2500 g. **Composition:** 0.9990 Silver 2.9951 oz. ASW **Subject:** 500th Anniversary **Obverse:** Arms **Reverse:** King Philipp

Date	Mintage	F	VF	XF	Unc	BU
1992 Proof	550	Value: 125				

KM# 379 30 PESOS **Weight:** 93.2500 g. **Composition:** 0.9990 Silver 2.9951 oz. ASW **Subject:** 500th anniversary **Obverse:** Arms **Reverse:** Spanish kings and queens

Date	Mintage	F	VF	XF	Unc	BU
ND(1992) Proof	550	Value: 125				

KM# 208 50 PESOS **Weight:** 15.5500 g. **Composition:** 0.9990 Gold .5000 oz. AGW **Subject:** 30th Anniversary - The March to Victory

Date	Mintage	F	VF	XF	Unc	BU
1988 Proof	150	Value: 300				

KM# 209 50 PESOS **Weight:** 15.5500 g. **Composition:** 0.9990 Gold .5000 oz. AGW **Subject:** 60th Anniversary - Birth of Ernesto Che Guevara

Date	Mintage	F	VF	XF	Unc	BU
1988 Proof	150	Value: 300				

KM# 210 50 PESOS **Weight:** 15.5500 g. **Composition:** 0.9990 Gold .5000 oz. AGW **Subject:** Triumph of the Revolutionary

Date	Mintage	F	VF	XF	Unc	BU
1988 Proof	150	Value: 300				

KM# 214 50 PESOS **Weight:** 15.5500 g. **Composition:** 0.9990 Gold .5000 oz. AGW **Reverse:** Jose Marti

Date	Mintage	F	VF	XF	Unc	BU
1988	12	—	—	—	450	—
1988 Proof	15	Value: 600				
1989	150	—	—	—	300	—
1989 Proof	15	Value: 600				
1990	15	—	—	—	450	—
1990 Proof	12	Value: 600				

KM# 313 50 PESOS **Weight:** 15.5500 g. **Composition:** 0.9990 Gold .5000 oz. AGW **Subject:** 160th Anniversary - First Train in England **Reverse:** Train, Liverpool - Manchester

Date	Mintage	F	VF	XF	Unc	BU
1989 Proof	150	Value: 260				

KM# 314 50 PESOS **Weight:** 15.5500 g. **Composition:** 0.9990 Gold .5000 oz. AGW **Subject:** 150th Anniversary - First Train in Spanish America **Reverse:** Train **Rev. Legend:** HABANA-BEJUCAL

Date	Mintage	F	VF	XF	Unc	BU
1989 Proof	150	Value: 260				

KM# 315 50 PESOS **Weight:** 15.5500 g. **Composition:** 0.9990 Gold .5000 oz. AGW **Subject:** 140th Anniversary - First Train in Spain **Reverse:** Train **Rev. Legend:** BARCELONA-MATARD

Date	Mintage	F	VF	XF	Unc	BU
1989 Proof	150	Value: 260				

KM# 331 50 PESOS **Weight:** 15.5500 g. **Composition:** 0.9990 Gold .5000 oz. AGW **Subject:** Camilo Cienfuegos Gomaran **Reverse:** Portrait of Camilo Cienfuegos

Date	Mintage	F	VF	XF	Unc	BU
1989 Proof	150	Value: 375				

KM# 332 50 PESOS **Weight:** 15.5500 g. **Composition:** 0.9990 Gold .5000 oz. AGW **Subject:** Assualt of the Moncada Garrison **Reverse:** Battle scene

Date	Mintage	F	VF	XF	Unc	BU
1989 Proof	150	Value: 375				

KM# 330 50 PESOS **Weight:** 15.5500 g. **Composition:** 0.9990 Gold .5000 oz. AGW **Subject:** Tania La Guerrillera **Reverse:** Portrait of female guerilla fighter

Date	Mintage	F	VF	XF	Unc	BU
1989 Proof	150	Value: 375				

KM# 281 50 PESOS **Weight:** 15.5500 g. **Composition:** 0.9990 Gold .5000 oz. AGW **Subject:** Simon Bolivar **Reverse:** Portrait of Simon Bolivar

Date	Mintage	F	VF	XF	Unc	BU
1990 Proof	50	Value: 325				

KM# 294 50 PESOS **Weight:** 155.5150 g. **Composition:** 0.9990 Silver 5.0000 oz. ASW **Subject:** 500th Anniversary - Discovery of America **Obverse:** Arms **Reverse:** Christopher Columbus

Date	Mintage	F	VF	XF	Unc	BU
1990 Proof	2,000	Value: 110				

KM# 295 50 PESOS **Weight:** 155.5150 g. **Composition:** 0.9990 Silver 5.0000 oz. ASW **Subject:** 500th Anniversary - Discovery of America **Reverse:** King Ferdinand of Spain

Date	Mintage	F	VF	XF	Unc	BU
1990 Proof	2,000	Value: 110				

KM# 296 50 PESOS **Weight:** 155.5150 g. **Composition:** 0.9990 Silver 5.0000 oz. ASW **Subject:** 500th Anniversary - Discovery of America **Reverse:** Queen Isabella of Spain

Date	Mintage	F	VF	XF	Unc	BU
1990 Proof	2,000	Value: 110				

KM# 297 50 PESOS **Weight:** 155.5150 g. **Composition:** 0.9990 Silver 5.0000 oz. ASW **Subject:** 500th Anniversary - Discovery of America **Reverse:** Juan de la Cosa

Date	Mintage	F	VF	XF	Unc	BU
1990 Proof	2,000	Value: 110				

KM# 298 50 PESOS **Weight:** 15.5500 g. **Composition:** 0.9990 Gold .5000 oz. AGW **Subject:** 500th Anniversary - Discovery of America **Reverse:** Portrait of Christopher Columbus

Date	Mintage	F	VF	XF	Unc	BU
1990 Proof	250	Value: 300				

KM# 299 50 PESOS **Weight:** 15.5500 g. **Composition:** 0.9990 Gold .5000 oz. AGW **Subject:** 500th Anniversary - Discovery of America **Reverse:** Portrait of King Ferdinand V

Date	Mintage	F	VF	XF	Unc	BU
1990 Proof	250	Value: 300				

KM# 300 50 PESOS **Weight:** 15.5500 g. **Composition:** 0.9990 Gold .5000 oz. AGW **Subject:** 500th Anniversary - Discovery of America **Reverse:** Portrait of Queen Isabella of Spain

Date	Mintage	F	VF	XF	Unc	BU
1990 Proof	250	Value: 300				

KM# 301 50 PESOS **Weight:** 15.5500 g. **Composition:** 0.9990 Gold .5000 oz. AGW **Subject:** 500th Anniversary - Discovery of America **Reverse:** Portrait of Juan de la Cosa

Date	Mintage	F	VF	XF	Unc	BU
1990 Proof	250	Value: 300				

KM# 321 50 PESOS **Weight:** 15.5500 g. **Composition:** 0.9990 Gold .5000 oz. AGW **Subject:** Pan American Games - Baseball **Reverse:** Baseball players

Date	Mintage	F	VF	XF	Unc	BU
1990 Proof	15	Value: 400				

KM# 322 50 PESOS **Weight:** 15.5500 g. **Composition:** 0.9990 Gold .5000 oz. AGW **Subject:** Pan American Games - High Jump **Reverse:** High jumper clearing pole

Date	Mintage	F	VF	XF	Unc	BU
1990 Proof	15	Value: 400				

KM# 323 50 PESOS **Weight:** 15.5500 g. **Composition:** 0.9990 Gold .5000 oz. AGW **Subject:** Pan American Games - Volleyball **Reverse:** Volleyball players

Date	Mintage	F	VF	XF	Unc	BU
1990 Proof	15	Value: 400				

KM# 339 50 PESOS **Weight:** 15.5500 g. **Composition:** 0.9990 Gold .5000 oz. AGW **Reverse:** Hatuey tribesman

Date	Mintage	F	VF	XF	Unc	BU
1991 Proof	200	Value: 300				

KM# 343 50 PESOS **Weight:** 155.5000 g. **Composition:** 0.9990 Silver 5.0000 oz. ASW **Series:** Olympics **Obverse:** Arms **Reverse:** Stadium

Date	Mintage	F	VF	XF	Unc	BU
1991 Proof	1,050	Value: 240				

KM# 356 50 PESOS **Weight:** 155.5000 g. **Composition:** 0.9990 Silver 5.0000 oz. ASW **Subject:** Madrid - Alcala Gate **Obverse:** Arms

Date	Mintage	F	VF	XF	Unc	BU
1991 Proof	550	Value: 285				

KM# 357 50 PESOS **Weight:** 155.5000 g. **Composition:** 0.9990 Silver 5.0000 oz. ASW **Subject:** Seville - La Giralda Tower **Obverse:** Arms

Date	Mintage	F	VF	XF	Unc	BU
1991 Proof	550	Value: 285				

KM# 432 50 PESOS **Weight:** 155.5000 g. **Composition:** 0.9990 Silver 5.0000 oz. ASW **Subject:** 500th Anniversary - Queen Joanna **Obverse:** Arms

Date	Mintage	F	VF	XF	Unc	BU
1991	1,000	—	—	—	—	—

KM# 433 50 PESOS **Weight:** 155.5000 g. **Composition:** 0.9990 Silver 5.0000 oz. ASW **Subject:** 500th Anniversary **Obverse:** Arms **Reverse:** Diego Valezquez

Date	Mintage	F	VF	XF	Unc	BU
1991	1,000	—	—	—	—	—

KM# 434 50 PESOS **Weight:** 155.5000 g. **Composition:** 0.9990 Silver 5.0000 oz. ASW **Subject:** 500th Anniversary - Pinzon Brothers

Date	Mintage	F	VF	XF	Unc	BU
1991 Proof	1,000	Value: 165				

KM# 435 50 PESOS **Weight:** 155.5000 g. **Composition:** 0.9990 Silver 5.0000 oz. ASW **Subject:** 500th Anniversary - Hatuey Tribesman

Date	Mintage	F	VF	XF	Unc	BU
1991 Proof	1,000	Value: 165				

KM# 444 50 PESOS **Weight:** 15.5500 g. **Composition:** 0.9990 Gold .5000 oz. AGW **Subject:** Queen Joanna

Date	Mintage	F	VF	XF	Unc	BU
1991 Proof	200	Value: 300				

KM# 445 50 PESOS **Weight:** 15.5500 g. **Composition:** 0.9990 Gold .5000 oz. AGW **Subject:** Diego Valezquez

Date	Mintage	F	VF	XF	Unc	BU
1991 Proof	200	Value: 300				

KM# 446 50 PESOS **Weight:** 15.5500 g. **Composition:** 0.9990 Gold .5000 oz. AGW **Subject:** Pinzon Brothers

Date	Mintage	F	VF	XF	Unc	BU
1991 Proof	200	Value: 300				

KM# 358 50 PESOS **Weight:** 155.5000 g. **Composition:** 0.9990 Silver 5.0000 oz. ASW **Obverse:** Arms **Reverse:** Philip I

Date	Mintage	F	VF	XF	Unc	BU
1992 Proof	550	Value: 185				

KM# 359 50 PESOS **Weight:** 155.5000 g. **Composition:** 0.9990 Silver 5.0000 oz. ASW **Obverse:** Arms **Reverse:** Chief Guama

Date	Mintage	F	VF	XF	Unc	BU
1992 Proof	550	Value: 185				

KM# 380 50 PESOS **Weight:** 155.7300 g. **Composition:** 0.9990 Silver 5.0019 oz. ASW **Obverse:** Arms **Reverse:** Bartolome de Las Casas

Date	Mintage	F	VF	XF	Unc	BU
1992 Proof	550	Value: 185				

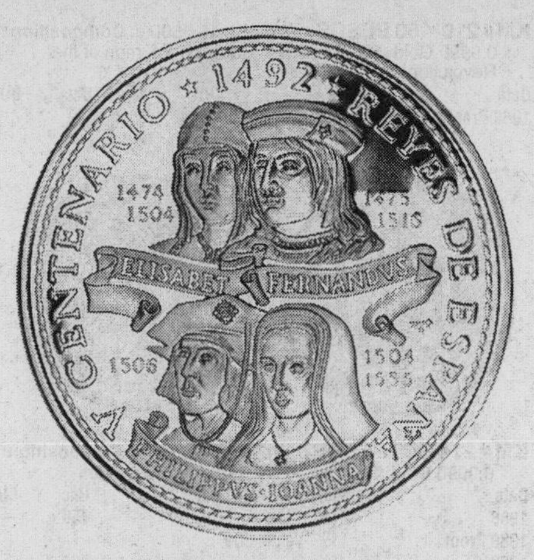

KM# 381 50 PESOS **Weight:** 155.7300 g. **Composition:** 0.9990 Silver 5.0019 oz. ASW **Subject:** Spanish Kings and Queens **Obverse:** Arms

Date	Mintage	F	VF	XF	Unc	BU
ND(1992) Proof	550	Value: 185				

KM# 382 50 PESOS **Weight:** 155.7300 g. **Composition:** 0.9990 Silver 5.0019 oz. ASW **Obverse:** Arms **Reverse:** San Jorge Palace

Date	Mintage	F	VF	XF	Unc	BU
1992 Proof	550	Value: 185				

KM# 568 50 PESOS **Weight:** 155.7300 g. **Composition:** 0.9990 Silver 5.0019 oz. ASW **Subject:** Cuban Fauna **Reverse:** Multicolored Papilio butterfly

Date	F	VF	XF	Unc	BU
1992 Proof	—	Value: 175			

KM# 641 50 PESOS **Weight:** 155.7300 g. **Composition:** 0.9990 Silver 5.0019 oz. ASW **Subject:** 1982 - Ano de Espana **Obverse:** Cuban arms **Reverse:** Seville's Tower of Gold

Date	Mintage	F	VF	XF	Unc	BU
1992 Proof	—	Value: 200				

KM# 400 50 PESOS **Weight:** 155.5150 g. **Composition:** 0.9990 Silver 5.0000 oz. ASW **Obverse:** Similar to 10 Pesos, KM#399 **Reverse:** St. Jacobi

Date	Mintage	F	VF	XF	Unc	BU
1993 Proof	1,000	Value: 175				

KM# 693 50 PESOS **Weight:** 15.5518 g. **Composition:** 0.9990 Gold .4990 oz. AGW **Subject:** 40th Anniversary - Assault on Moncada Garrison

Date	Mintage	F	VF	XF	Unc	BU
1993 Proof	—	Value: 350				

KM# 503 50 PESOS **Weight:** 155.5150 g. **Composition:** 0.9990 Silver 5.0000 oz. ASW **Subject:** Caribbean Fauna **Obverse:** Arms **Reverse:** Multicolored Bottle-nosed dophins **Edge:** Reeded

Date	Mintage	F	VF	XF	Unc	BU
1994 Proof	2,500	Value: 225				

KM# 504 50 PESOS **Weight:** 155.5150 g. **Composition:** 0.9990 Silver 5.0000 oz. ASW **Subject:** Caribbean Fauna **Obverse:** Arms **Reverse:** Multicolored Swordfish

Date	Mintage	F	VF	XF	Unc	BU
1994 Proof	2,500	Value: 200				

KM# 505 50 PESOS **Weight:** 155.5150 g. **Composition:** 0.9990 Silver 5.0000 oz. ASW **Subject:** Caribbean Fauna **Obverse:** Arms **Reverse:** Multicolored brown pelican

Date	Mintage	F	VF	XF	Unc	BU
1994 Proof	2,500	Value: 225				

KM# 506 50 PESOS **Weight:** 155.5150 g. **Composition:** 0.9990 Silver 5.0000 oz. ASW **Subject:** Caribbean Fauna **Obverse:** Arms **Reverse:** Multicolored flamingos

Date	Mintage	F	VF	XF	Unc	BU
1994 Proof	2,500	Value: 200				

KM# 507 50 PESOS **Weight:** 155.5150 g. **Composition:** 0.9990 Silver 5.0000 oz. ASW **Subject:** Caribbean Fauna **Obverse:** Arms **Reverse:** Multicolored yellow sea bass (Coney)

Date	Mintage	F	VF	XF	Unc	BU
1994 Proof	2,500	Value: 200				

KM# 508 50 PESOS **Weight:** 155.5150 g. **Composition:** 0.9990 Silver 5.0000 oz. ASW **Subject:** Caribbean Fauna **Obverse:** Arms **Reverse:** Multicolored spotted eagle ray

Date	Mintage	F	VF	XF	Unc	BU
1994 Proof	2,500	Value: 250				

KM# 484 50 PESOS **Weight:** 155.5150 g. **Composition:** 0.9990 Silver 5.0000 oz. ASW **Subject:** Pirate of the Caribbean **Reverse:** Blackbeard

Date	Mintage	F	VF	XF	Unc	BU
1995 Proof	Est. 3,000	Value: 265				

KM# 485 50 PESOS **Weight:** 155.5150 g. **Composition:** 0.9990 Silver 5.0000 oz. ASW **Subject:** Pirates of the Caribbean **Reverse:** Sir Henry Morgan

Date	Mintage	F	VF	XF	Unc	BU
1995 Proof	Est. 3,000	Value: 265				

KM# 488 50 PESOS **Weight:** 155.5150 g. **Composition:** 0.9990 Silver 5.0000 oz. ASW **Subject:** Pirates of the Caribbean **Reverse:** Captain Kidd

Date	Mintage	F	VF	XF	Unc	BU
1995 Proof	Est. 3,000	Value: 265				

KM# 486 50 PESOS **Weight:** 155.5150 g. **Composition:** 0.9990 Silver 5.0000 oz. ASW **Subject:** Pirates of the Caribbean **Reverse:** Anne Bonny

Date	Mintage	F	VF	XF	Unc	BU
1995 Proof	Est. 3,000	Value: 265				

KM# 489 50 PESOS **Weight:** 155.5150 g. **Composition:** 0.9990 Silver 5.0000 oz. ASW **Subject:** Pirates of the Caribbean **Reverse:** Piet Heyn

Date	Mintage	F	VF	XF	Unc	BU
1995 Proof	Est. 3,000	Value: 265				

KM# 487 50 PESOS **Weight:** 155.5150 g. **Composition:** 0.9990 Silver 5.0000 oz. ASW **Subject:** Pirates of the Caribbean **Reverse:** Mary Read

Date	Mintage	F	VF	XF	Unc	BU
1995 Proof	Est. 3,000	Value: 265				

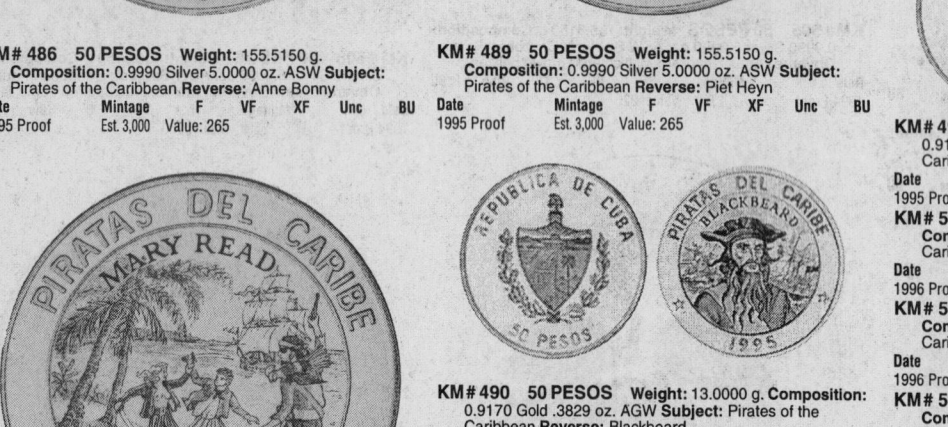

KM# 490 50 PESOS **Weight:** 13.0000 g. **Composition:** 0.9170 Gold .3829 oz. AGW **Subject:** Pirates of the Caribbean **Reverse:** Blackbeard

Date	Mintage	F	VF	XF	Unc	BU
1995 Proof	Est. 1,000	Value: 275				

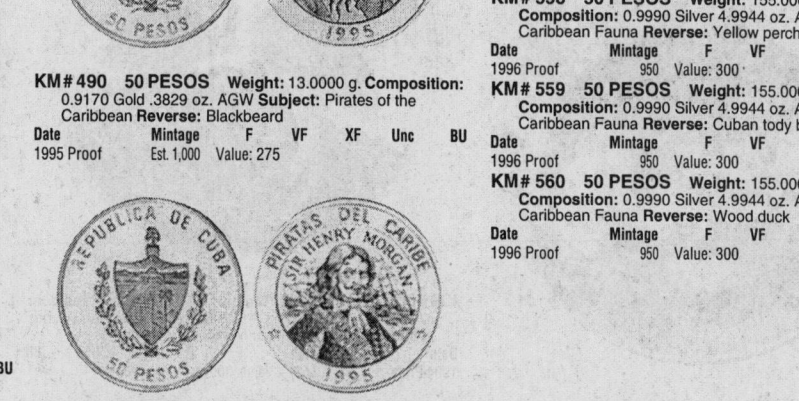

KM# 491 50 PESOS **Weight:** 13.0000 g. **Composition:** 0.9170 Gold .3829 oz. AGW **Subject:** Pirates of the Caribbean **Reverse:** Sir Henry Morgan

Date	Mintage	F	VF	XF	Unc	BU
1995 Proof	Est. 1,000	Value: 275				

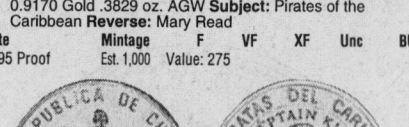

KM# 492 50 PESOS **Weight:** 13.0000 g. **Composition:** 0.9170 Gold .3829 oz. AGW **Subject:** Pirates of the Caribbean **Reverse:** Anne Bonny

Date	Mintage	F	VF	XF	Unc	BU
1995 Proof	Est. 1,000	Value: 275				

KM# 493 50 PESOS **Weight:** 13.0000 g. **Composition:** 0.9170 Gold .3829 oz. AGW **Subject:** Pirates of the Caribbean **Reverse:** Mary Read

Date	Mintage	F	VF	XF	Unc	BU
1995 Proof	Est. 1,000	Value: 275				

KM# 494 50 PESOS **Weight:** 13.0000 g. **Composition:** 0.9170 Gold .3829 oz. AGW **Subject:** Pirates of the Caribbean **Reverse:** Captain Kidd

Date	Mintage	F	VF	XF	Unc	BU
1995 Proof	Est. 1,000	Value: 275				

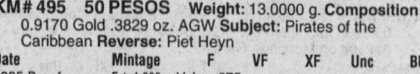

KM# 495 50 PESOS **Weight:** 13.0000 g. **Composition:** 0.9170 Gold .3829 oz. AGW **Subject:** Pirates of the Caribbean **Reverse:** Piet Heyn

Date	Mintage	F	VF	XF	Unc	BU
1995 Proof	Est. 1,000	Value: 275				

KM# 557 50 PESOS **Weight:** 155.0000 g. **Composition:** 0.9990 Silver 4.9944 oz. ASW **Series:** Caribbean Fauna **Reverse:** Ruby-throated hummingbird

Date	Mintage	F	VF	XF	Unc	BU
1996 Proof	950	Value: 300				

KM# 558 50 PESOS **Weight:** 155.0000 g. **Composition:** 0.9990 Silver 4.9944 oz. ASW **Series:** Caribbean Fauna **Reverse:** Yellow perch

Date	Mintage	F	VF	XF	Unc	BU
1996 Proof	950	Value: 300				

KM# 559 50 PESOS **Weight:** 155.0000 g. **Composition:** 0.9990 Silver 4.9944 oz. ASW **Series:** Caribbean Fauna **Reverse:** Cuban tody bird

Date	Mintage	F	VF	XF	Unc	BU
1996 Proof	950	Value: 300				

KM# 560 50 PESOS **Weight:** 155.0000 g. **Composition:** 0.9990 Silver 4.9944 oz. ASW **Series:** Caribbean Fauna **Reverse:** Wood duck

Date	Mintage	F	VF	XF	Unc	BU
1996 Proof	950	Value: 300				

KM# 564 50 PESOS Weight: 155.0000 g. **Composition:** 0.9990 Silver 4.9944 oz. ASW **Series:** Caribbean Fauna **Reverse:** Vaca anil fish

Date	Mintage	F	VF	XF	Unc	BU
1996 Proof	950	Value: 300				

KM# 567 50 PESOS Weight: 155.0000 g. **Composition:** 0.9990 Silver 4.9944 oz. ASW **Series:** Caribbean Fauna **Reverse:** Papilio butterfly

Date	Mintage	F	VF	XF	Unc	BU
1996 Proof	950	Value: 300				

KM# 694 50 PESOS Weight: 155.0000 g. **Composition:** 0.9990 Silver 4.9944 oz. ASW **Subject:** Caribbean Flora **Reverse:** Multicolored flower, "Bidens Romerillo"

Date		F	VF	XF	Unc	BU
1997 Proof	—	Value: 300				

KM# 695 50 PESOS Weight: 155.0000 g. **Composition:** 0.9990 Silver 4.9944 oz. ASW **Subject:** Caribbean Flora **Reverse:** Multicolored flower, "Cordia Vomitel"

Date		F	VF	XF	Unc	BU
1997 Proof	—	Value: 300				

KM# 697 50 PESOS Weight: 155.0000 g. **Composition:** 0.9990 Silver 4.9944 oz. ASW **Subject:** Wonders of the Ancient World **Reverse:** Temple of Artemisa

Date		F	VF	XF	Unc	BU
1997 Proof	—	Value: 250				

KM# 698 50 PESOS Weight: 155.0000 g. **Composition:** 0.9990 Silver 4.9944 oz. ASW **Subject:** Wonders of the Ancient World **Reverse:** Pyramids

Date		F	VF	XF	Unc	BU
1997 Proof	—	Value: 250				

KM# 699 50 PESOS Weight: 155.0000 g. **Composition:** 0.9990 Silver 4.9944 oz. ASW **Subject:** Wonders of the Ancient World **Reverse:** Hanging Gardens of Babylon

Date		F	VF	XF	Unc	BU
1997 Proof	—	Value: 250				

KM# 700 50 PESOS Weight: 155.0000 g. **Composition:** 0.9990 Silver 4.9944 oz. ASW **Subject:** Wonders of the Ancient World **Reverse:** Statue of Jupiter at Olympus

Date		F	VF	XF	Unc	BU
1997 Proof	—	Value: 250				

KM# 701 50 PESOS Weight: 155.0000 g. **Composition:** 0.9990 Silver 4.9944 oz. ASW **Subject:** Wonders of the Ancient World **Reverse:** Colossus of Rhodes

Date		F	VF	XF	Unc	BU
1997 Proof	—	Value: 250				

KM# 702 50 PESOS Weight: 155.0000 g. **Composition:** 0.9990 Silver 4.9944 oz. ASW **Subject:** Wonders of the Ancient World **Reverse:** Mausoleum at Halicarnasos

Date		F	VF	XF	Unc	BU
1997 Proof	—	Value: 250				

KM# 654 50 PESOS Weight: 15.5500 g. **Composition:** 0.9990 Gold .4999 oz. AGW **Subject:** Expo 2000 **Obverse:** Cuban arms **Reverse:** Twipsy cartoon logo

Date	Mintage	F	VF	XF	Unc	BU
1998 Proof	3,125	Value: 275				

KM# 638 50 PESOS Weight: 15.5500 g. **Composition:** 0.9990 Gold .4999 oz. AGW **Subject:** AIDS **Obverse:** Cuban arms **Reverse:** AIDS ribbon on silhouette before world map

Date	Mintage	F	VF	XF	Unc	BU
1998 Proof	2,000	Value: 320				

KM# 703 50 PESOS Weight: 15.5500 g. **Composition:** 0.9990 Gold .4999 oz. AGW **Subject:** 40th Anniversary - Triumph of the Revolution

Date		F	VF	XF	Unc	BU
1999 Proof	—	Value: 450				

KM# 704 50 PESOS Weight: 15.5500 g. **Composition:** 0.9990 Gold .4999 oz. AGW **Reverse:** Hummingbird

Date		F	VF	XF	Unc	BU
1999 Proof	—	Value: 400				

Y# 727 50 PESOS Weight: 15.5518 g. **Composition:** 0.9990 Gold .5000 oz. AGW **Obverse:** National arms **Reverse:** Hummingbird **Edge:** Reeded **Size:** 32.5 mm.

Date	Mintage	F	VF	XF	Unc	BU
1999 Proof	1,000	Value: 200				

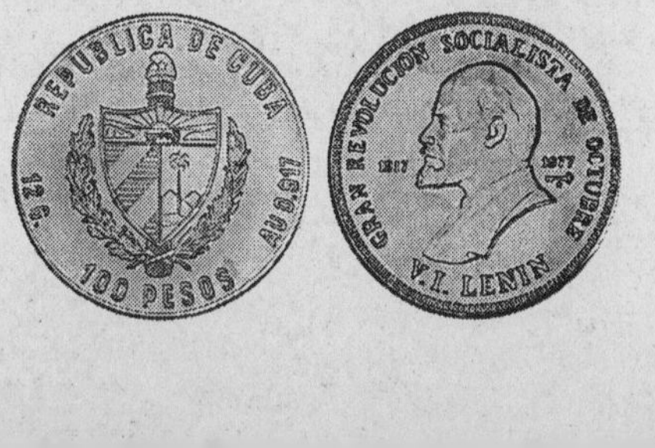

KM# 42 100 PESOS Weight: 12.0000 g. **Composition:** 0.9170 Gold .3538 oz. AGW **Subject:** 60th Anniversary of Socialist Revolution Lenin

Date	Mintage	F	VF	XF	Unc	BU
ND(1977) Proof	10	Value: 10,000				

KM# 43 100 PESOS Weight: 12.0000 g. **Composition:** 0.9170 Gold .3538 oz. AGW **Reverse:** Carlos Manuel de Cespedes

Date	Mintage	F	VF	XF	Unc	BU
ND(1977) Proof	25,000	Value: 200				

KM# 45 100 PESOS Weight: 12.0000 g. **Composition:** 0.9170 Gold .3538 oz. AGW **Subject:** Nonaligned Nations Conference

Date	Mintage	F	VF	XF	Unc	BU
1979	2,000	—	—	—	350	—
1979 Proof	20,000	Value: 275				

KM# 52 100 PESOS Weight: 12.0000 g. **Composition:** 0.9170 Gold .3538 oz. AGW **Subject:** First Soviet-Cuban space flight

Date	Mintage	F	VF	XF	Unc	BU
1980	1,000	—	—	—	350	—

KM# 85 100 PESOS Weight: 12.0000 g. **Composition:** 0.9170 Gold .3538 oz. AGW **Obverse:** Arms **Reverse:** Columbus' ship - Nina

Date	Mintage	F	VF	XF	Unc	BU
1981	2,000	—	—	—	200	—

KM# 86 100 PESOS Weight: 12.0000 g. **Composition:** 0.9170 Gold .3538 oz. AGW **Obverse:** Arms **Reverse:** Columbus' ship - Pinta

Date	Mintage	F	VF	XF	Unc	BU
1981	2,000	—	—	—	200	—

KM# 87 100 PESOS Weight: 12.0000 g. **Composition:** 0.9170 Gold .3538 oz. AGW **Obverse:** Arms **Reverse:** Columbus' ship - Santa Maria

Date	Mintage	F	VF	XF	Unc	BU
1981	2,000	—	—	—	200	—

KM# 202 100 PESOS Weight: 31.1030 g. **Composition:** 0.9990 Gold 1.0000 oz. AGW **Subject:** 30th Anniversary of March to Victory **Obverse:** Star behind arms

Date	Mintage	F	VF	XF	Unc	BU
1988 Proof	100	Value: 650				

KM# 203 100 PESOS Weight: 31.1030 g. **Composition:** 0.9990 Gold 1.0000 oz. AGW **Subject:** 60th Anniversary - Birth of Ernesto Che Guevara **Obverse:** Star behind arms

Date	Mintage	F	VF	XF	Unc	BU
1988 Proof	100	Value: 650				

KM# 204 100 PESOS Weight: 31.1030 g. **Composition:** 0.9990 Gold 1.0000 oz. AGW **Subject:** 30th Anniversary - Triumph of the Revolution **Obverse:** Star behind arms

Date	Mintage	F	VF	XF	Unc	BU
1988 Proof	100	Value: 650				

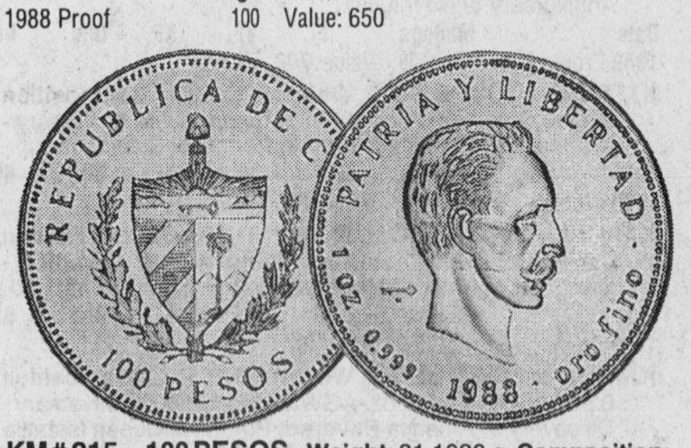

KM# 215 100 PESOS Weight: 31.1030 g. **Composition:** 0.9990 Gold 1.0000 oz. AGW **Reverse:** Jose Marti

Date	Mintage	F	VF	XF	Unc	BU
1988	50	—	—	—	800	—
1988 Proof	15	Value: 1,200				
1989	150	—	—	—	650	—
1989 Proof	15	Value: 1,200				
1990	15	—	—	—	1,000	—
1990 Proof	12	Value: 1,250				

KM# 316 100 PESOS Weight: 31.1030 g. **Composition:** 0.9990 Gold 1.0000 oz. AGW **Subject:** 160th Anniversary - First train in England **Reverse:** Train **Rev. Legend:** LIVERPOOL-MANCHESTER

Date	Mintage	F	VF	XF	Unc	BU
1989 Proof	150	Value: 650				

KM# 317 100 PESOS Weight: 31.1030 g. **Composition:** 0.9990 Gold 1.0000 oz. AGW **Subject:** 150th Anniversary - First train in Spanish America **Reverse:** Train **Rev. Legend:** HABANA-BEJUCAL

Date	Mintage	F	VF	XF	Unc	BU
1989 Proof	150	Value: 650				

KM# 318 100 PESOS Weight: 31.1030 g. **Composition:** 0.9990 Gold 1.0000 oz. AGW **Subject:** 140th Anniversary - First train in Spain **Reverse:** Train **Rev. Legend:** BARCELONA-MATARO

Date	Mintage	F	VF	XF	Unc	BU
1989 Proof	150	Value: 650				

KM# 319 100 PESOS **Weight:** 31.1030 g. **Composition:** 0.9990 Gold 1.0000 oz. AGW **Subject:** 200th Anniversary of French Revolution - Lady Justice **Reverse:** Female revolutionary raising flag

Date	Mintage	F	VF	XF	Unc	BU
1989 Proof	150	Value: 800				

KM# 320 100 PESOS **Weight:** 31.1030 g. **Composition:** 0.9990 Gold 1.0000 oz. AGW **Subject:** 200th Anniversary of French Revolution - Bastille **Reverse:** Bastille, soldiers in foreground

Date	Mintage	F	VF	XF	Unc	BU
1989	150	—	—	—	800	—

KM# 333 100 PESOS **Weight:** 31.1030 g. **Composition:** 0.9990 Gold 1.0000 oz. AGW **Subject:** Tania La Guerrillera **Reverse:** Portrait of female guerilla fighter

Date	Mintage	F	VF	XF	Unc	BU
1989 Proof	150	Value: 800				

KM# 334 100 PESOS **Weight:** 31.1030 g. **Composition:** 0.9990 Gold 1.0000 oz. AGW **Subject:** Camilo Cienfuegos Gornaran **Reverse:** Portrait of Camilo Cienfuegos

Date	Mintage	F	VF	XF	Unc	BU
1989 Proof	150	Value: 800				

KM# 335 100 PESOS **Weight:** 31.1030 g. **Composition:** 0.9990 Gold 1.0000 oz. AGW **Subject:** 35th Anniversary - Assault of the Moncada Garrison **Reverse:** Battle scene

Date	Mintage	F	VF	XF	Unc	BU
1989 Proof	150	Value: 800				

KM# 447 100 PESOS **Weight:** 31.1030 g. **Composition:** 0.9990 Gold 1.0000 oz. AGW **Subject:** 30th Anniversary of Revolution

Date	Mintage	F	VF	XF	Unc	BU
1989 Proof	250	Value: 700				

KM# 448 100 PESOS **Weight:** 31.1030 g. **Composition:** 0.9990 Gold 1.0000 oz. AGW **Subjec**: 30th Anniversary of Revolution

Date	Mintage	F	VF	XF	Unc	BU
1989 Proof	250	Value: 700				

KM# 449 100 PESOS **Weight:** 31.1030 g. **Composition:** 0.9990 Gold 1.0000 oz. AGW **Subject:** 30th Anniversary of Revolution

Date	Mintage	F	VF	XF	Unc	BU
1989 Proof	250	Value: 700				

KM# 302 100 PESOS **Weight:** 31.1030 g. **Composition:** 0.9990 Gold 1.0000 oz. AGW **Subject:** 500th Anniversary - Discovery of America **Reverse:** Portrait of Columbus

Date	Mintage	F	VF	XF	Unc	BU
1990 Proof	250	Value: 825				

KM# 303 100 PESOS **Weight:** 31.1030 g. **Composition:** 0.9990 Gold 1.0000 oz. AGW **Subject:** 500th Anniversary - Discovery of America **Reverse:** Portrait of King Ferdinand V

Date	Mintage	F	VF	XF	Unc	BU
1990 Proof	250	Value: 825				

KM# 304 100 PESOS **Weight:** 31.1030 g. **Composition:** 0.9990 Gold 1.0000 oz. AGW **Subject:** 500th Anniversary - Discovery of America **Reverse:** Portrait of Queen Isabella

Date	Mintage	F	VF	XF	Unc	BU
1990 Proof	250	Value: 825				

KM# 305 100 PESOS **Weight:** 31.1030 g. **Composition:** 0.9990 Gold 1.0000 oz. AGW **Subject:** 500th Anniversary - Discovery of America **Reverse:** Portrait of Juan de la Cosa

Date	Mintage	F	VF	XF	Unc	BU
1990 Proof	250	Value: 825				

KM# 450 100 PESOS **Weight:** 31.1030 g. **Composition:** 0.9990 Gold 1.0000 oz. AGW **Subject:** Pinzon Brothers

Date	Mintage	F	VF	XF	Unc	BU
1991 Proof	200	Value: 750				

KM# 451 100 PESOS **Weight:** 31.1030 g. **Composition:** 0.9990 Gold 1.0000 oz. AGW **Subject:** 500th Anniversary **Reverse:** Queen Joanna

Date	Mintage	F	VF	XF	Unc	BU
1991 Proof	200	Value: 750				

KM# 452 100 PESOS **Weight:** 31.1030 g. **Composition:** 0.9990 Gold 1.0000 oz. AGW **Subject:** 500th Anniversary **Reverse:** Diego Velazquez

Date	Mintage	F	VF	XF	Unc	BU
1991 Proof	200	Value: 750				

KM# 534 100 PESOS **Weight:** 31.1030 g. **Composition:** 0.9990 Gold 1.0000 oz. AGW **Series:** Olympics **Reverse:** Stadium

Date	Mintage	F	VF	XF	Unc	BU
1991 Proof	225	Value: 800				

KM# 535 100 PESOS **Weight:** 31.1030 g. **Composition:** 0.9990 Gold 1.0000 oz. AGW **Subject:** Madrid - Alcala Gate

Date	Mintage	F	VF	XF	Unc	BU
1991 Proof	225	Value: 800				

KM# 569 100 PESOS **Weight:** 31.1030 g. **Composition:** 0.9990 Gold 1.0000 oz. AGW **Subject:** Hatuey People

Date		F	VF	XF	Unc	BU
1991 Proof	—	Value: 800				

KM# 384 100 PESOS **Weight:** 31.1030 g. **Composition:** 0.9990 Gold 1.0000 oz. AGW **Subject:** Seville - Tower of Gold **Reverse:** Tower of Gold in Seville

Date	Mintage	F	VF	XF	Unc	BU
1992 Proof	225	Value: 825				

KM# 385 100 PESOS **Weight:** 31.1030 g. **Composition:** 0.9990 Gold 1.0000 oz. AGW **Subject:** El Escorial **Reverse:** El Escorial palace

Date	Mintage	F	VF	XF	Unc	BU
1992 Proof	225	Value: 825				

KM# 453 100 PESOS **Weight:** 31.1030 g. **Composition:** 0.9990 Gold 1.0000 oz. AGW **Subject:** 500th Anniversary **Reverse:** Bartolome de las Casas

Date	Mintage	F	VF	XF	Unc	BU
1992 Proof	100	Value: 750				

KM# 454 100 PESOS **Weight:** 31.1030 g. **Composition:** 0.9990 Gold 1.0000 oz. AGW **Subject:** 500th Anniversary **Reverse:** Guama Tribesman

Date	Mintage	F	VF	XF	Unc	BU
1992 Proof	100	Value: 750				

KM# 455 100 PESOS **Weight:** 31.1030 g. **Composition:** 0.9990 Gold 1.0000 oz. AGW **Subject:** 500th anniversary **Reverse:** King Philipp

Date	Mintage	F	VF	XF	Unc	BU
1992 Proof	100	Value: 750				

KM# 456 100 PESOS **Weight:** 31.1030 g. **Composition:** 0.9990 Gold 1.0000 oz. AGW **Subject:** 500th Anniversary **Reverse:** Spanish kings and queens

Date	Mintage	F	VF	XF	Unc	BU
1992 Proof	100	Value: 750				

KM# 536 100 PESOS **Weight:** 31.1030 g. **Composition:** 0.9990 Gold 1.0000 oz. AGW **Subject:** San Jorge Palace

Date	Mintage	F	VF	XF	Unc	BU
1992 Proof	225	Value: 800				

KM# 570 100 PESOS **Weight:** 31.1030 g. **Composition:** 0.9990 Gold 1.0000 oz. AGW **Subject:** Ernesto Che Guevara

Date		F	VF	XF	Unc	BU
1992 Proof	—	Value: 700				

KM# 537 100 PESOS **Weight:** 31.1030 g. **Composition:** 0.9990 Gold 1.0000 oz. AGW **Subject:** 40th Anniversary of Moncada **Reverse:** Fidel Castro

Date	Mintage	F	VF	XF	Unc	BU
1993 Proof	100	Value: 775				

KM# 538 100 PESOS **Weight:** 31.1030 g. **Composition:** 0.9990 Gold 1.0000 oz. AGW **Reverse:** St. Jacobi

Date	Mintage	F	VF	XF	Unc	BU
1993 Proof	100	Value: 775				

KM# 539 100 PESOS **Weight:** 31.1030 g. **Composition:** 0.9990 Gold 1.0000 oz. AGW **Reverse:** Federico Garcia Lorca

Date	Mintage	F	VF	XF	Unc	BU
1993 Proof	100	Value: 775				

KM# 571 100 PESOS **Weight:** 31.1030 g. **Composition:** 0.9990 Gold 1.0000 oz. AGW **Reverse:** Jose Marti

Date		F	VF	XF	Unc	BU
1994 Proof	—	Value: 650				

KM# 572 100 PESOS **Weight:** 31.1030 g. **Composition:** 0.9990 Gold 1.0000 oz. AGW **Subject:** Centennial of the Necessary War

Date		F	VF	XF	Unc	BU
1995 Proof	—	Value: 650				

KM# 708 100 PESOS **Weight:** 31.1030 g. **Composition:** 0.9990 Gold 1.0000 oz. AGW **Subject:** Meeting of Fidel Castro and Pope John Paul II in the Vatican

Date		F	VF	XF	Unc	BU
1997 Proof	—	Value: 800				

KM# 709 100 PESOS **Weight:** 31.1030 g. **Composition:** 0.9990 Gold 1.0000 oz. AGW **Subject:** Papal visit to Cuba

Date		F	VF	XF	Unc	BU
1997 Proof	—	Value: 800				

KM# 710 100 PESOS **Weight:** 31.1030 g. **Composition:** 0.9990 Gold 1.0000 oz. AGW **Subject:** 90th Anniversary - Triumph of the Revolution

Date		F	VF	XF	Unc	BU
1999 Proof	—	Value: 700				

KM# 719 100 PESOS **Weight:** 31.1030 g. **Composition:** 0.9990 Gold 1.0000 oz. AGW **Reverse:** Hummingbird

Date		F	VF	XF	Unc	BU
1999 Proof	—	Value: 800				

Y# 728 100 PESOS **Weight:** 31.1035 g. **Composition:** 0.9990 Gold 1.0000 oz. AGW **Obverse:** National arms **Reverse:** Hummingbird **Edge:** Reeded **Size:** 38 mm.

Date	Mintage	F	VF	XF	Unc	BU
1999 Proof	1,000	Value: 450				

KM# 642 150 PESOS **Weight:** 411.4225 g. **Composition:** 0.9990 Silver 13.2275 oz. ASW **Series:** Cuban Fauna **Obverse:** Cuban arms **Reverse:** Multicolored Tocororo bird

Date	Mintage	F	VF	XF	Unc	BU
1996 Proof	Est. 420	Value: 600				

KM# 542 200 PESOS **Weight:** 31.1000 g. **Composition:** Gold **Reverse:** Bolivar and Marti

Date	Mintage	F	VF	XF	Unc	BU
1993	100	—	—	—	750	—
1993 Proof	100	Value: 800				

KM# 543 200 PESOS **Weight:** 31.1000 g. **Composition:** Gold **Series:** Prehistoric Animals **Reverse:** Apatosaurus

Date	Mintage	F	VF	XF	Unc	BU
1993 Proof	100	Value: 900				

KM# 544 200 PESOS **Weight:** 31.1000 g. **Composition:** Gold **Series:** Prehistoric Animals **Reverse:** Chalicotherium

Date	Mintage	F	VF	XF	Unc	BU
1993 Proof	100	Value: 900				

KM# 545 200 PESOS **Weight:** 31.1000 g. **Composition:** Gold **Subject:** Montecristi Manifesto

Date	Mintage	F	VF	XF	Unc	BU
1994 Proof	100	Value: 800				

KM# 643 300 PESOS **Weight:** 822.8449 g. **Composition:** 0.9990 Silver 27.5661 oz. ASW **Series:** Cuban Fauna **Obverse:** Cuban arms **Reverse:** Multicolored Mariposa butterfly

Date	F	VF	XF	Unc	BU
1996 Proof	Est. 420	Value: 975			

KM# 457 500 PESOS **Weight:** 155.5500 g. **Composition:** 0.9990 Gold 5,0000 oz. AGW **Reverse:** Christopher Columbus

Date	Mintage	F	VF	XF	Unc	BU
1990 Proof	15	Value: 4,000				

KM# 386 500 PESOS **Weight:** 155.5500 g. **Composition:** 0.9990 Gold 5,0000 oz. AGW **Subject:** 500th Anniversary **Obverse:** Coat of arms **Reverse:** Four portraits of Spanish kings and queens

Date	Mintage	F	VF	XF	Unc	BU
ND(1992) Proof	15	Value: 4,000				

KM# 605 500 PESOS **Weight:** 155.5500 g. **Composition:** 0.9990 Platinum 5,0000 oz. APW **Subject:** Cuban Flora **Reverse:** Multicolored Turnera Ulmifolia (Yellow Alder)

Date	F	VF	XF	Unc	BU
1993 Proof	—	—	—	—	—

VISITOR'S COINAGE

KM# 409 CENTAVO **Composition:** Copper-Nickel

Date	F	VF	XF	Unc	BU
1988	—	0.50	1.50	3.00	—

KM# 410 CENTAVO **Composition:** Aluminum

Date	F	VF	XF	Unc	BU
1988	—	0.50	1.50	5.00	—

KM# 411 5 CENTAVOS **Composition:** Copper-Nickel

Date	F	VF	XF	Unc	BU
1981	0.45	0.75	2.00	4.00	—

KM# 412.1 5 CENTAVOS **Composition:** Copper-Nickel **Reverse:** Large, thick 5

Date	F	VF	XF	Unc	BU
1981	0.45	0.75	2.00	4.00	—

KM# 412.2 5 CENTAVOS **Composition:** Copper-Nickel **Reverse:** Large, thin 5

Date	F	VF	XF	Unc	BU
1981	0.45	0.75	2.00	4.00	—

KM# 413 5 CENTAVOS **Composition:** Aluminum

Date	F	VF	XF	Unc	BU
1988	0.50	1.00	3.00	5.00	—

KM# 412.3 5 CENTAVOS **Composition:** Copper-Nickel **Reverse:** Small 5

Date	F	VF	XF	Unc	BU
1989	0.35	0.50	1.50	3.00	—

KM# 412.3a 5 CENTAVOS **Composition:** Stainless Steel

Date	F	VF	XF	Unc	BU
1989	—	1.00	3.00	6.00	—

KM# 414 10 CENTAVOS **Composition:** Copper-Nickel

Date	F	VF	XF	Unc	BU
1981	—	0.65	2.00	4.00	—

KM# 416 10 CENTAVOS **Composition:** Aluminum

Date	F	VF	XF	Unc	BU
1988	—	0.65	2.00	4.00	—

KM# 415.1 10 CENTAVOS **Composition:** Copper-Nickel **Note:** Large 10

Date	F	VF	XF	Unc	BU
1989	0.50	1.00	3.00	5.00	—

KM# 415.3 10 CENTAVOS **Composition:** Copper-Nickel **Note:** Reduced size.

Date	F	VF	XF	Unc	BU
1989	—	1.25	4.50	10.00	—

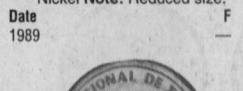

KM# 415.2 10 CENTAVOS **Composition:** Copper-Nickel **Note:** Small 10

Date	F	VF	XF	Unc	BU
1989	—	0.65	2.00	4.00	—

KM# 415.2a 10 CENTAVOS **Composition:** Stainless Steel **Note:** Small 10.

Date	F	VF	XF	Unc	BU
1989	—	1.25	4.00	9.00	—

KM# 417 25 CENTAVOS **Composition:** Copper-Nickel

Date	F	VF	XF	Unc	BU
1981	0.50	1.00	2.50	6.00	—

KM# 418.1 25 CENTAVOS **Composition:** Copper-Nickel **Reverse:** Large 25

Date	F	VF	XF	Unc	BU
1981	—	1.00	3.00	7.00	—

KM# 419 25 CENTAVOS **Composition:** Aluminum

Date	F	VF	XF	Unc	BU
1988	—	0.75	2.50	5.00	—

KM# 418.2a 25 CENTAVOS **Composition:** Stainless Steel

Date	F	VF	XF	Unc	BU
1989	—	2.00	5.50	12.00	—

KM# 418.2 25 CENTAVOS **Composition:** Copper-Nickel **Reverse:** Small 25

Date	F	VF	XF	Unc	BU
1989	—	1.00	3.00	7.00	—

KM# 420 50 CENTAVOS **Composition:** Copper-Nickel

Date	F	VF	XF	Unc	BU
1981	—	2.50	7.50	15.00	—

Note: Varieties exist in the number of lines below the palm tree

KM# 461 50 CENTAVOS **Composition:** Copper-Nickel **Obverse:** Palm tree **Reverse:** Denomination and logo

Date	F	VF	XF	Unc	BU
1989	—	2.00	7.00	14.00	—

KM# 421 PESO **Composition:** Copper-Nickel **Obverse:** Lighthouse **Reverse:** Denomination and logo

Date	F	VF	XF	Unc	BU
1981	—	4.00	12.00	24.00	—

KM# 580 PESO **Composition:** Copper-Nickel **Obverse:** Lighthouse **Reverse:** Denomination and logo

Date	F	VF	XF	Unc	BU
1989	—	4.00	12.00	24.00	—

PESO CONVERTIBLE SERIES

KM# 733 CENTAVO **Weight:** 0.7300 g. **Composition:** Aluminum **Obverse:** National arms **Reverse:** Tower and denomination **Edge:** Plain **Size:** 16.8 mm.

Date	F	VF	XF	Unc	BU
2001	—	—	—	2.00	—

KM# 575.1 5 CENTAVOS **Composition:** Stainless Steel **Obverse:** National arms **Reverse:** Casa Colonial **Note:** Medal alignment

Date	F	VF	XF	Unc	BU
1994	—	—	—	1.00	—

KM# 575.2 5 CENTAVOS **Composition:** Stainless Steel **Obverse:** National arms **Reverse:** Casa Colonial **Note:** Coin alignment, recut designs

Date	F	VF	XF	Unc	BU
1996	—	—	—	1.00	—
1998	—	—	—	1.00	—
1999	—	—	—	1.00	—

KM# 576.1 10 CENTAVOS **Composition:** Stainless Steel **Obverse:** National arms **Reverse:** Castillo de la Fuerza **Note:** Medal alignment

Date	F	VF	XF	Unc	BU
1994	—	—	—	2.00	—

KM# 576.2 10 CENTAVOS **Composition:** Stainless Steel **Obverse:** National arms **Reverse:** Castillo de la Fuerza **Note:** Coin alignment, recut designs

Date	F	VF	XF	Unc	BU
1996	—	—	—	2.00	—
1999	—	—	—	2.00	—

KM# 577.1 (KM577) 25 CENTAVOS **Composition:** Stainless Steel **Obverse:** National arms **Reverse:** Trinidad **Note:** Medal alignment.

Date	F	VF	XF	Unc	BU
1994	—	—	—	3.00	—
1994	—	—	—	3.00	—

KM# 577.2 25 CENTAVOS **Composition:** Stainless Steel **Obverse:** National arms **Reverse:** Trinidad **Note:** Coin alignment.

Date	F	VF	XF	Unc	BU
1998	—	—	—	3.00	—
2000	—	—	—	3.00	—

KM# 578 50 CENTAVOS **Composition:** Stainless Steel **Obverse:** Cuban arms **Reverse:** Cathedral of Havana

Date	F	VF	XF	Unc	BU
1994	—	—	—	5.00	—

KM# 579 PESO **Composition:** Stainless Steel **Obverse:** National arms **Reverse:** Guama

Date	F	VF	XF	Unc	BU
1994	—	—	—	7.00	—

KM# 730 5 PESOS **Ring Composition:** Brass Plated Steel **Center Weight:** 4.4600 g. **Center Composition:** Stainless Steel **Obverse:** National arms **Reverse:** Bust of Che Guevara right in inner circle **Edge:** Reeded **Size:** 23 mm. **Note:** Medal alignment

Date	F	VF	XF	Unc	BU
1999	—	—	—	56.00	—

TRIAL STRIKES

KM#	Date	Mintage	Identification	Mkt Val
TS5	1977	—	20 Pesos. Brass. Antonio Maceo, KM40.	300
TS6	1977	—	20 Pesos. Brass. Maximo Gomez, KM39.	300
TS8	1977	—	20 Pesos. Copper-Nickel. Antonio Maceo, KM40.	500
TS9	1977	—	100 Pesos. Brass. de Cespedes, KM43.	300
TS7	1977	—	20 Pesos. Brass. Ignacio Aramonte, KM38.	300
TS2	1994	10	100 Pesos. Gold. Reverse of KM467, uniface.	2,000
TS3	1994	1	50 Pesos. Silver. KM503; dolphins green and red.	—
TS4	1994	1	50 Pesos. Silver. KM503, dolphins green and red.	—

PIEFORTS

KM#	Date	Mintage	Identification	Mkt Val
P25	1989	12	50 Pesos. Gold. KM314.	1,650
P26	1989	12	50 Pesos. Gold. KM315.	1,650
P27	1989	15	100 Pesos. Silver. KM215.	—
P32	1989	12	100 Pesos. Gold. KM318.	1,600
P33	1989	12	100 Pesos. Gold. KM319.	2,000
P24	1989	12	50 Pesos. Gold. KM313.	1,650
P34	1989	12	100 Pesos. Gold. KM320.	2,000
P28	1989	10	100 Pesos. Gold. KM215.	2,000
P29	1989	15	100 Pesos. Gold. KM215.	2,000
P30	1989	12	100 Pesos. Gold. KM316.	1,500
P31	1989	12	100 Pesos. Gold. KM317.	1,600
P22	1989	10	50 Pesos. Gold. KM214.	2,000
P23	1989	15	50 Pesos. Gold. KM214.	2,000
P36	1990	15	10 Pesos. Silver. KM280.	160
P41	1990	12	10 Pesos. Gold. KM211.	1,000
P47	1990	12	50 Pesos. Gold. KM214.	2,000
P35	1990	50	10 Pesos. Silver. Ship and Cub; KM252.	—
P37	1990	100	10 Pesos. Silver. KM291.	160
P42	1990	12	15 Pesos. Gold. KM212.	1,000
P43	1990	12	15 Pesos. Gold. KM212.	1,000
P48	1990	12	50 Pesos. Gold. KM321.	2,000
P49	1990	12	50 Pesos. Gold. KM322.	2,000
P50	1990	12	50 Pesos. Gold. KM323.	2,000
P38	1990	100	10 Pesos. Silver. KM292.	160
P39	1990	100	10 Pesos. Silver. KM293.	160
P51	1990	12	100 Pesos. Gold. KM215.	2,000
P52	1990	15	100 Pesos. Gold. KM215.	2,000
P40	1990	12	10 Pesos. Gold. KM211.	1,000
P44	1990	12	25 Pesos. Gold. 15.5400 g. KM213.	—
P45	1990	12	25 Pesos. Gold. 15.5400 g. KM213.	—
P46	1990	12	50 Pesos. Gold. KM214.	2,000
P53	1992	50	10 Pesos. Silver. KM341.	150
P58	1993	—	100 Pesos. Gold. Similar to 200 Pesos; KM542.	—
P54	1993	150	5 Pesos. Silver. KM405.	150
P55	1993	—	10 Pesos. Silver. KM406.	150
P56	1993	15	200 Pesos. Gold. KM542.	2,000
P57	1994	10	100 Pesos. Gold. KM545.	1,600
PA65	ND(1995)	100	50 Pesos. Gold Plated Brass.	—
P65	1999	—	10 Pesos. Silver. KM672.	200

PATTERNS

Including off metal strikes

KM#	Date	Mintage	Identification	Mkt Val
Pn10	1915	—	Centavo. Bronze.	—
PnB10	1915	—	2 Centavos. Bronze.	2,000
PnB11	1970	—	Peso. 0.9990 Silver. KM158.	500
PnA11	1970	—	Peso. 0.9990 Silver. KM158.	500
PnE11	1986	—	5 Pesos. 0.0500 Gold. KM326.	—
PnD11	1986	—	5 Pesos. 0.0500 Silver. KM326.	—
PnC11	1986	—	5 Pesos. 0.9000 Copper. KM326.	—
PnG11	1987	—	5 Pesos. Copper. .900 Copper, 050 Silver, .050 Gold, KM#26.	—
PnF11	1987	—	5 Pesos. Copper. KM166.	—
Pn11	1987	3	5 Pesos. 0.9990 Gold. KM159.	6,000
PnB13	1988	—	100 Pesos. 0.9990 Gold.	5,000
Pn13	1988	6	100 Pesos. Gold.	—
PnA12	1988	6	5 Pesos. 0.9990 Silver.	1,150
Pn12	1988	6	5 Pesos. Silver.	1,150
PnA13	1988	6	100 Pesos. 0.9990 Gold.	5,000
Pn14	1993	34	10 Pesos. Silver. Mirror bust with frosted field. KM398.	500
Pn15	1994	25	10 Pesos. Silver. KM510.	385
Pn25	ND(1995)	100	10 Pesos. Brass In Silver. Proof.	65.00
Pn105	1995	50	10 Pesos. Aluminum. Mariposas del Caribe, pink bckground, Proof.	65.00
Pn38	1995	50	10 Pesos. Brass In Silver. Mariposas del Caribe, green background; Proof.	80.00
Pn16	1995	22	10 Pesos. Silver. Date, mint mark, in proof relief.	385
Pn17	1995	100	Peso. Copper Nickel. Pirates del Carib, Sir Francis Drake, proof.	50.00
Pn22	ND(1995)	100	10 Pesos. Brass. Similar to Pn25 Proof.	65.00
Pn106	1999	—	Peso. Copper-Nickel. KM662.	100
Pn107	1999	—	10 Pesos. Silver. KM672.	200
Pn108	1999	—	100 Pesos. Gold. KM710.	1,200

MINT SETS

KM#	Date	Mintage	Identification	Issue Price	Mkt Val
MS1	1953 (4)	—	KM#26-29	—	125
MS2	1994 (5)	—	KM#575.1-576.1, 577-579	—	35.00

PROOF SETS

KM#	Date	Mintage	Identification	Issue Price	Mkt Val
PS1	1915 (7)	20	KM#9-15	—	3,600
PS2	1915 (6)	24	KM#16-21; Rare	—	—
PS4	1916 (6)	—	KM#16-21; Rare	—	—
PS3	1916 (7)	20	KM#9-15	—	6,250
PS5	1953 (4)	—	KM#26-29; Rare	—	—
PS6	1975 (2)	—	KM#36, 37	—	30.00
PS7	1977 (4)	—	KM#38-40, 43	290	335
PSA7	1977 (3)	—	KM#38-40	—	110
PS8	1979 (2)	—	KM#44, 45	240	260
PS9	1988 (5)	15	KM#211-215	—	1,650
PS10	1998 (4)	—	KM#668-671	—	200
PS11	1999 (5)	—	KM#671, 673, 692, 704, 719	—	1,250

CURACAO

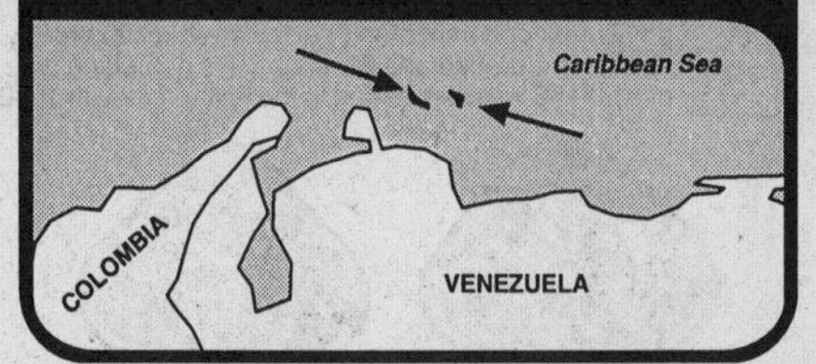

The island of Curacao, the largest of the Netherlands Antilles, which is an autonomous part of the Kingdom of the Netherlands located in the Caribbean Sea 40 miles off the coast of Venezuela, has an area of 173 sq. mi. (472 sq. km.) and a population of 127,900. Capital: Willemstad. The chief industries are banking and tourism. Salt, phosphates and cattle are exported.

Curacao was discovered by Spanish navigator Alonsode Ojeda in 1499 and was settled by Spain in 1527. The Dutch West India Company took the island from Spain in 1634 and administered it until 1787, when it was surrendered to the United Netherlands. The Dutch held it there-after except for two periods during the Napoleonic Wars, 1800-1803 and 1807-16, when it was occupied by the British. During World War II, Curacao refined 60 percent of the oil used by the Allies; the refineries were protected by U.S. troops after Germany invaded the Netherlands in1940.

During the second occupation of the Napoleonic period, the British created an emergency coinage for Curacao by cutting the Spanish dollar into 5 equal segments and countermarking each piece with a rosette indent.

MINT MARKS

D - Denver
P - Philadelphia
(u) - Utrecht

NETHERLANDS RESTORED

MODERN COINAGE

100 Cents = 1 Gulden

KM# 39 CENT **Composition:** Bronze

Date	Mintage	F	VF	XF	Unc	BU
1942P	2,500,000	1.25	2.50	5.00	10.00	—

Note: This coin was also circulated in Surinam. For similar coins dated 1943P & 1957-1960, see Surinam

KM# 41 CENT **Composition:** Bronze

Date	Mintage	F	VF	XF	Unc	BU
1944D	3,000,000	0.75	1.50	3.00	6.50	—
1947 (u)	1,500,000	1.25	2.50	4.00	8.50	—
1947 (u) Proof	80	Value: 25.00				

KM# 42 2-1/2 CENTS **Composition:** Bronze

Date	Mintage	F	VF	XF	Unc	BU
1944D	1,000,000	1.00	1.50	3.00	6.50	—
1947 (u)	500,000	1.25	2.50	5.00	10.00	—
1947 (u) Proof	80	Value: 25.00				
1948 (u)	1,000,000	0.75	1.50	3.00	6.50	—
1948 (u) Proof	75	Value: 25.00				

KM# 40 5 CENTS **Composition:** Copper-Nickel

Date	Mintage	F	VF	XF	Unc	BU
1943	8,595,000	1.25	2.50	4.00	8.50	—

Note: The above piece does not bear either a palm tree privy mark or a mint mark, but it was struck expressly for use in Curacao and Surinam. This homeland type of KM#153 was last issued in the Netherlands in 1940

KM# 47 5 CENTS Composition: Copper-Nickel

Date	Mintage	F	VF	XF	Unc	BU
1948	1,000,000	1.00	2.00	4.00	8.50	—
1948 Proof	75	Value: 45.00				

KM# 37 10 CENTS Weight: 1.4000 g. **Composition:** 0.6400 Silver .0288 oz. ASW

Date	Mintage	F	VF	XF	Unc	BU
1941P	800,000	3.75	8.00	17.50	35.00	—
1943P	4,500,000	2.50	6.00	15.00	30.00	—

Note: Both these coins were also circulated in Surinam. For coins dated 1942P, see Surinam

KM# 38 25 CENTS Weight: 3.5800 g. **Composition:** 0.6400 Silver .0736 oz. ASW

Date	Mintage	F	VF	XF	Unc	BU
1941P	1,100,000	2.50	5.50	12.00	25.00	—
1943/1P	2,500,000	4.00	8.00	17.50	35.00	—
1943P	Inc. above	1.50	4.00	8.50	17.50	—

Note: Both coins were also circulated in Surinam. For similar coins dated 1943, 1944 & 1945-P with acorn mint mark see Netherlands

KM# 36 1/10 GULDEN Weight: 1.4000 g. **Composition:** 0.6400 Silver .0288 oz. ASW

Date	Mintage	F	VF	XF	Unc	BU
1901	300,000	10.00	20.00	40.00	90.00	—
1901 Proof	40	Value: 250				

KM# 43 1/10 GULDEN Weight: 1.4000 g. **Composition:** 0.6400 Silver .0288 oz. ASW

Date	Mintage	F	VF	XF	Unc	BU
1944D	1,500,000	1.00	1.50	3.00	6.50	—
1947	1,000,000	1.00	1.50	3.00	6.50	—
1947 Proof	80	Value: 60.00				

KM# 48 1/10 GULDEN Weight: 1.4000 g. **Composition:** 0.6400 Silver .0288 oz. ASW

Date	Mintage	F	VF	XF	Unc	BU
1948	1,000,000	1.00	1.50	3.00	6.50	—
1948 Proof	75	Value: 60.00				

KM# 44 1/4 GULDEN Weight: 3.5800 g. **Composition:** 0.6400 Silver .0736 oz. ASW

Date	Mintage	F	VF	XF	Unc	BU
1944D	1,500,000	1.00	2.00	3.50	7.50	—
1947 (u)	1,000,000	1.00	2.00	3.50	7.50	—
1947 (u) Proof	80	Value: 80.00				

KM# 45 GULDEN Weight: 10.0000 g. **Composition:** 0.7200 Silver .2315 oz. ASW

Date	Mintage	F	VF	XF	Unc	BU
1944D	500,000	2.50	5.00	11.50	25.00	—

KM# 46 2-1/2 GULDEN Weight: 25.0000 g. **Composition:** 0.7200 Silver .5787 oz. ASW

Date	Mintage	F	VF	XF	Unc	BU
1944D	200,000	—	—	4.50	10.00	—

PROOF SETS

KM#	Date	Mintage	Identification	Issue Price	Mkt Val
PS1	1901 (2)	40	KM36(1901), KM35(1900)	—	400
PS2	1947 (4)	80	KM41-44	—	185
PS3	1948 (3)	75	KM42, 47-48	—	125

CYPRUS

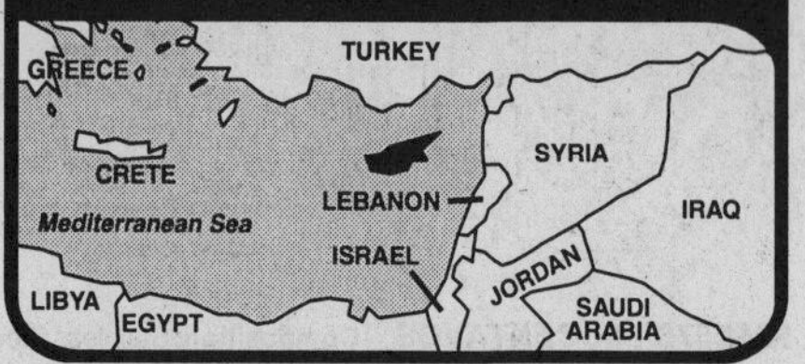

The Republic of Cyprus lies in the eastern Mediterranean Sea 44 miles (71 km.) south of Turkey and 60 miles (97 km.) west of Syria. It is the third largest island in the Mediterranean Sea, having an area of 3,572 sq. mi. (9,251 sq. km.) and a population of 736,636. Capital: Nicosia. Agriculture, light manufacturing and tourism are the chief industries. Citrus fruit, potatoes, footwear and clothing are exported

The importance of Cyprus dates from the Bronze Age when it was desired as a principal source of copper (from which the island derived its name) and as a strategic trading center. It was during this period that large numbers of Greeks settled on the island and gave it the predominantly Greek character. Its role as an international marketplace made it a prime disseminator of the then prevalent cultures, a role that still influences the civilization of Western man. Because of its fortuitous position and influential role, Cyprus was conquered by a succession of empires: the Assyrian, Egyptian, Persian, Macedonian, Ptolemaic, Roman and Byzantine. It was taken from Isaac Comnenus by Richard the Lion-Heart in 1191, sold to the Templar Knights and for the following 7 centuries was ruled by the Franks, the Venetians and the Ottomans. During the Ottoman period Cyprus acquired its Turkish community (18 percent of its population). In 1878 the island fell into British hands and was made a crown colony of Britain in 1925. Finally, on Aug. 16, 1960, it became an independent republic.

In 1964, the ethnic Turks withdrew from active participation in the government. Turkish forces invaded Cyprus in 1974, gained control of 40 percent of the island and forcibly separated the Greek and Turkish communities. In 1983, Turkish Cypriots proclaimed their own state in northern Cyprus, which remains without international recognition.

Cyprus is a member of the Commonwealth of Nations. The president is Chief of State and Head of Government.

RULERS

British, until 1960

MINT MARKS

no mint mark - Royal Mint, London, England
H - Birmingham, England

MONETARY SYSTEM

9 Piastres = 1 Shilling
20 Shillings = 1 Pound

BRITISH COLONY

PIASTRE COINAGE

KM# 1.2 1/4 PIASTRE Composition: Bronze **Obverse:** Bust of King Edward VII **Reverse:** Denomination **Size:** 21 mm.

Date	Mintage	F	VF	XF	Unc	BU
1901	72,000	10.00	25.00	60.00	140	—

KM# 8 1/4 PIASTRE Composition: Bronze **Reverse:** Denomination

Date	Mintage	F	VF	XF	Unc	BU
1902	72,000	5.00	12.50	30.00	125	—
1905	422,000	4.00	12.50	27.50	100	—
1908	36,000	35.00	100	150	350	—

KM# 16 1/4 PIASTRE Composition: Bronze

Date	Mintage	F	VF	XF	Unc	BU
1922	72,000	5.00	15.00	30.00	80.00	—
1926	360,000	3.50	7.50	15.00	65.00	—
1926 Proof	—	Value: 365				

KM# 11 1/2 PIASTRE Composition: Bronze **Obverse:** Bust of King Edward VII right **Reverse:** Denomination

Date	Mintage	F	VF	XF	Unc	BU
1908	36,000	50.00	150	350	600	—

KM# 17 1/2 PIASTRE Composition: Bronze **Obverse:** Bust of King George left **Reverse:** Denomination

Date	Mintage	F	VF	XF	Unc	BU
1922	36,000	20.00	50.00	125	250	—
1927	108,000	3.50	10.00	35.00	80.00	—
1927 Proof	—	Value: 375				
1930	180,000	3.00	8.00	30.00	75.00	—
1930 Proof	—	Value: 365				
1931	90,000	5.00	15.00	40.00	100	—
1931 Proof	—	Value: 425				

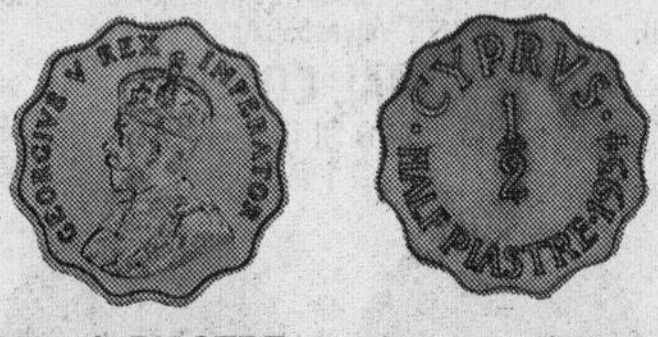

KM# 20 1/2 PIASTRE Composition: Copper-Nickel **Obverse:** Bust of King George V left **Reverse:** Denomination **Shape:** Scalloped

Date	Mintage	F	VF	XF	Unc	BU
1934	1,440,000	0.75	2.50	6.50	16.50	—
1934 Proof	—	Value: 325				

KM# 22 1/2 PIASTRE Composition: Copper-Nickel **Obverse:** Bust of King George VI left **Reverse:** Denomination **Shape:** Scalloped

Date	Mintage	F	VF	XF	Unc	BU
1938	1,080,000	0.35	1.00	4.00	12.50	—
1938 Proof	—	Value: 325				

KM# 22a 1/2 PIASTRE Composition: Bronze **Obverse:** Bust of King George VI left **Reverse:** Denomination **Shape:** Scalloped

Date	Mintage	F	VF	XF	Unc	BU
1942	1,080,000	0.25	1.00	2.50	12.50	—
1942 Proof	—	Value: 200				
1943	1,620,000	0.25	1.00	2.50	12.50	—
1944	2,160,000	0.25	1.00	2.50	12.50	—
1945	1,080,000	0.25	1.00	2.50	12.50	—
1945 Proof	—	Value: 200				

KM# 29 1/2 PIASTRE Composition: Bronze **Obverse:** Bust of King George VI left **Reverse:** Denomination **Shape:** Scalloped

Date	Mintage	F	VF	XF	Unc	BU
1949	1,080,000	0.15	0.35	1.00	3.50	—
1949 Proof	—	Value: 150				

KM# 3.2 PIASTRE Composition: Bronze **Obverse:** Bust of Queen Victoria left **Reverse:** Thick "1" in denomination

Date	Mintage	F	VF	XF	Unc	BU
1881 Proof	Inc. above	Value: 1,000				
1881H Proof	—	Value: 900				
1882H	18,000	135	225	450	1,250	—
1882H Proof	—	Value: 2,000				
1884	18,000	135	225	450	1,250	—
1884 Proof	—	Value: 1,800				
1885	54,000	25.00	70.00	115	275	—
1885 Proof	—	Value: 1,220				
1886	227,000	10.00	30.00	85.00	175	—
1887	45,000	10.00	32.50	100	200	—
1889	27,000	30.00	90.00	250	500	—
1890	90,000	20.00	70.00	150	350	—
1891	54,000	25.00	80.00	200	400	—
1891 Proof	—	Value: 780				
1895	54,000	25.00	80.00	200	400	—
1896	54,000	25.00	80.00	200	400	—
1900	27,000	35.00	100	250	500	—
1900 Proof	—	Value: 1,900				

KM# 12 PIASTRE Composition: Bronze **Obverse:** Bust of King Edward VII right **Reverse:** Denomination in inner circle

Date	Mintage	F	VF	XF	Unc	BU
1908	27,000	100	200	350	700	—

KM# 18 PIASTRE Composition: Bronze **Obverse:** Bust of King George V left **Reverse:** Denomination in inner circle

Date	Mintage	F	VF	XF	Unc	BU
1922	54,000	10.00	35.00	125	250	—
1927	127,000	5.00	20.00	60.00	150	—
1927 Proof	—	Value: 400				
1930	96,000	6.00	22.50	70.00	175	—
1930 Proof	—	Value: 400				
1931	45,000	15.00	35.00	75.00	200	—
1931 Proof	—	Value: 725				

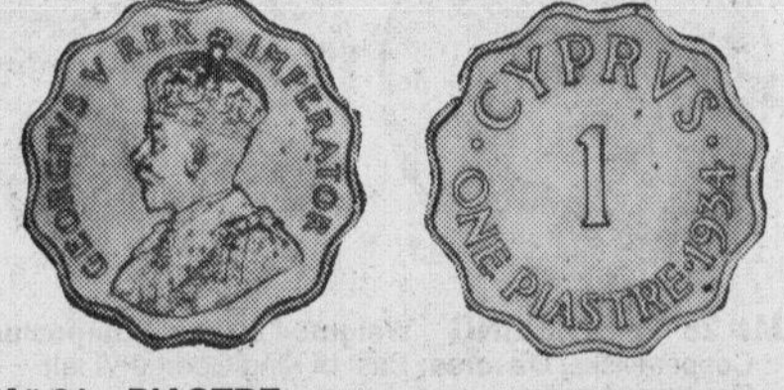

KM# 21 PIASTRE Composition: Copper-Nickel **Obverse:** Bust of King George V left **Reverse:** Denomination **Shape:** Scalloped

Date	Mintage	F	VF	XF	Unc	BU
1934	1,440,000	1.00	2.50	6.50	16.50	—
1934 Proof	—	Value: 325				

KM# 23 PIASTRE Composition: Copper-Nickel **Obverse:** Bust of King George VI left **Reverse:** Denomination **Shape:** Scalloped

Date	Mintage	F	VF	XF	Unc	BU
1938	2,700,000	0.60	1.50	3.00	12.50	—
1938 Proof	—	Value: 325				

KM# 23a PIASTRE Composition: Bronze

Date	Mintage	F	VF	XF	Unc	BU
1942	1,260,000	0.50	1.00	2.50	10.00	—
1942 Proof	—	Value: 225				
1943	2,520,000	0.50	1.00	2.50	10.00	—
1944	3,240,000	0.50	1.00	2.50	10.00	—
1945	1,080,000	0.60	1.50	3.00	12.00	—
1945 Proof	—	Value: 200				
1946	1,080,000	0.60	1.50	3.00	12.00	—
1946 Proof	—	Value: 200				

KM# 30 PIASTRE Composition: Bronze **Obverse:** Bust of King George VI left **Obv. Legend:** ends ...DEI GRATIA REX **Reverse:** Denomination **Shape:** Scalloped

Date	Mintage	F	VF	XF	Unc	BU
1949	1,080,000	0.25	0.75	2.00	4.00	—
1949 Proof	—	Value: 150				

KM# 4 3 PIASTRES Weight: 1.8851 g. **Composition:** 0.9250 Silver .0561 oz. ASW **Obverse:** Bust of Queen Victoria left **Reverse:** Denomination

Date	Mintage	F	VF	XF	Unc	BU
1901	300,000	8.00	20.00	40.00	100	—
1901 Proof	—	Value: 800				

KM# 5 4-1/2 PIASTRES Weight: 2.8276 g. **Composition:** 0.9250 Silver .0841 oz. ASW **Obverse:** Bust of Queen Victoria left **Reverse:** Denomination, arms

Date	Mintage	F	VF	XF	Unc	BU
1901	400,000	5.00	15.00	40.00	100	—
1901 Proof	—	Value: 950				

KM# 15 4-1/2 PIASTRES Weight: 2.8276 g. **Composition:** 0.9250 Silver .0841 oz. ASW **Obverse:** Bust of Queen Victoria left **Reverse:** Denomination, arms

Date	Mintage	F	VF	XF	Unc	BU
1921	600,000	3.50	10.00	30.00	80.00	—

KM# 24 4-1/2 PIASTRES Weight: 2.8276 g. **Composition:** 0.9250 Silver .0841 oz. ASW **Obverse:** Bust of King George VI left **Reverse:** Denomination

Date	Mintage	F	VF	XF	Unc	BU
1938	192,000	2.00	4.00	12.00	30.00	—
1938 Proof	—	Value: 400				

KM# 6 9 PIASTRES **Weight:** 5.6552 g. **Composition:** 0.9250 Silver .1682 oz. ASW **Obverse:** Bust of Queen Victoria left **Reverse:** Arms

Date	Mintage	F	VF	XF	Unc	BU
1901	600,000	15.00	40.00	100	200	—
1901 Proof	—	Value: 1,250				

KM# 9 9 PIASTRES **Weight:** 5.6552 g. **Composition:** 0.9250 Silver .1682 oz. ASW **Obverse:** Bust of King Edward VII right **Reverse:** Arms

Date	Mintage	F	VF	XF	Unc	BU
1907	60,000	35.00	100	275	500	—

KM# 13 9 PIASTRES **Weight:** 5.6552 g. **Composition:** 0.9250 Silver .1682 oz. ASW **Obverse:** Bust of King George V left **Reverse:** Arms

Date	Mintage	F	VF	XF	Unc	BU
1913	50,000	40.00	125	300	600	—
1919	400,000	2.50	10.00	30.00	100	—
1921	490,000	2.50	10.00	30.00	100	—

KM# 25 9 PIASTRES **Weight:** 5.6552 g. **Composition:** 0.9250 Silver .1682 oz. ASW **Obverse:** Bust of King George VI left **Reverse:** Arms

Date	Mintage	F	VF	XF	Unc	BU
1938	504,000	2.00	3.50	8.00	30.00	—
1938 Proof	—	Value: 400				
1940	800,000	1.50	3.00	7.00	27.50	—
1940 Proof	—	Value: 400				

KM# 27 SHILLING **Composition:** Copper-Nickel **Obverse:** Bust of King George VI left **Reverse:** Arms

Date	Mintage	F	VF	XF	Unc	BU
1947	1,440,000	0.50	1.00	5.00	30.00	—
1947 Proof	—	Value: 300				

KM# 31 SHILLING **Composition:** Copper-Nickel **Obverse:** Bust of King George VI left **Obv. Legend:** ends ... DEI GRATIA REX **Reverse:** Arms

Date	Mintage	F	VF	XF	Unc	BU
1949	1,440,000	0.50	1.00	5.00	30.00	—
1949 Proof	—	Value: 300				

KM# 7 18 PIASTRES **Weight:** 11.3104 g. **Composition:** 0.9250 Silver .3364 oz. ASW **Obverse:** Bust of Queen Victoria left **Reverse:** Arms

Date	Mintage	F	VF	XF	Unc	BU
1901	200,000	40.00	150	300	500	—
1901 Proof	—	Value: 2,500				

KM# 10 18 PIASTRES **Weight:** 11.3104 g. **Composition:** 0.9250 Silver .3364 oz. ASW **Obverse:** Bust of King Edward VII right **Reverse:** Arms

Date	Mintage	F	VF	XF	Unc	BU
1907	20,000	55.00	225	485	1,250	—

KM# 14 18 PIASTRES **Weight:** 11.3104 g. **Composition:** 0.9250 Silver .3364 oz. ASW **Obverse:** Bust of King George V left **Reverse:** Denomination

Date	Mintage	F	VF	XF	Unc	BU
1913	25,000	35.00	140	350	650	—
1921	155,000	25.00	60.00	150	350	—

KM# 26 18 PIASTRES **Weight:** 11.3104 g. **Composition:** 0.9250 Silver .3364 oz. ASW **Obverse:** Bust of King George VI left **Reverse:** Arms

Date	Mintage	F	VF	XF	Unc	BU
1938	200,000	3.50	5.00	10.00	40.00	—
1938 Proof	—	Value: 450				
1940	100,000	4.00	6.50	15.00	50.00	—
1940 Proof	—	Value: 450				

KM# 28 2 SHILLING **Weight:** 4.0000 g. **Composition:** Copper-Nickel **Obverse:** Bust of King George VI left **Reverse:** Arms

Date	Mintage	F	VF	XF	Unc	BU
1947	720,000	1.00	2.50	7.50	35.00	—
1947 Proof	—	Value: 400				

KM# 32 2 SHILLING **Composition:** Copper-Nickel **Obverse:** ends ...DEI GRATIA REX **Reverse:** Arms

Date	Mintage	F	VF	XF	Unc	BU
1949	720,000	1.00	2.50	7.50	35.00	—
1949 Proof	—	Value: 400				

KM# 19 45 PIASTRES **Weight:** 28.2759 g. **Composition:** 0.9250 Silver .8409 oz. ASW **Subject:** 50th Anniversary of British Rule **Obverse:** Bust of King George V left **Reverse:** Arms

Date	Mintage	F	VF	XF	Unc	BU
ND		15.00	25.00	45.00	135	—
ND(1928)	517	Value: 550				

DECIMAL COINAGE

50 Mils = 1 Shilling; 20 Shillings = 1 Pound; 1000 Mils = 1 Pound

KM# 33 3 MILS **Composition:** Bronze **Reverse:** Flying fish

Date	Mintage	F	VF	XF	Unc	BU
1955	6,250,000	—	—	0.10	0.25	—
1955 Proof	2,000	Value: 2.50				

KM# 34 5 MILS **Composition:** Bronze

Date	Mintage	F	VF	XF	Unc	BU
1955	10,000,000	—	0.15	0.25	0.40	—
1955 Proof	2,000	Value: 3.00				
1956	2,950,000	—	0.15	0.30	0.50	—
1956 Proof	—	Value: 300				

KM# 35 25 MILS **Composition:** Copper-Nickel **Reverse:** Head of bull

Date	Mintage	F	VF	XF	Unc	BU
1955	2,500,000	—	0.25	0.35	0.50	—
1955 Proof	2,000	Value: 3.00				

KM# 36 50 MILS **Composition:** Copper-Nickel **Reverse:** Fern leaves

Date	Mintage	F	VF	XF	Unc	BU
1955	4,000,000	—	0.35	0.50	1.00	—
1955 Proof	2,000	Value: 3.00				

KM# 37 100 MILS Composition: Copper-Nickel

Date	Mintage	F	VF	XF	Unc	BU
1955		—	0.50	0.75	1.50	—
1955 Proof	2,000	Value: 4.50				
1957		—	10.00	15.00	50.00	—
1957 Proof	—	Value: 440				

Note: All but 10,000 of 1957 issue were melted down

REPUBLIC

DECIMAL COINAGE

50 Mils = 1 Shilling; 20 Shillings = 1 Pound; 1000 Mils = 1 Pound

KM# 38 MIL Composition: Aluminum **Shape:** Scalloped

Date	Mintage	F	VF	XF	Unc	BU
1963	5,000,000	—	—	—	0.15	—
1963 Proof	25,000	Value: 1.00				
1971	500,000	—	—	0.10	0.25	—
1972	500,000	—	—	0.10	0.25	—
1972 Proof	—	Value: 2.00				

KM# 39 5 MILS Composition: Bronze

Date	Mintage	F	VF	XF	Unc	BU
1963	12,000,000	—	—	0.10	0.35	—
1963 Proof	25,000	Value: 1.25				
1970	2,500,000	—	—	0.10	0.35	—
1971	2,500,000	—	—	0.10	0.35	—
1972	2,500,000	—	—	0.10	0.35	—
1973	5,000,000	—	—	0.10	0.35	—
1974	2,500,000	—	—	0.10	0.35	—
1976	2,000,000	—	—	0.10	0.35	—
1977	2,000,000	—	—	0.10	0.35	—
1978	2,000,000	—	—	0.10	0.35	—
1979	2,000,000	—	—	0.10	0.35	—
1980	4,000,000	—	—	0.10	0.35	—
1980 Proof	—	Value: 2.50				

KM# 50.1 5 MILS Composition: Aluminum **Obverse:** Small date

Date	Mintage	F	VF	XF	Unc	BU
1981	12,500,000	—	—	—	0.25	—

KM# 50.2 5 MILS Composition: Aluminum **Obverse:** Large date and legends

Date	Mintage	F	VF	XF	Unc	BU
1982	15,000,000	—	—	—	0.25	—
1982 Proof	—	Value: 2.00				

KM# 40 25 MILS Composition: Copper-Nickel **Reverse:** Cedar of Lebanon

Date	Mintage	F	VF	XF	Unc	BU
1963	2,500,000	—	0.10	0.15	0.45	—
1963 Proof	25,000	Value: 1.50				
1968	1,500,000	—	0.10	0.15	0.45	—
1971	1,000,000	—	0.10	0.15	0.45	—
1972	500,000	—	0.10	0.15	0.50	—
1973	1,000,000	—	0.10	0.15	0.45	—
1974	1,000,000	—	0.10	0.15	0.45	—
1976	2,000,000	—	0.10	0.15	0.45	—
1977	500,000	—	0.10	0.15	0.45	—
1978	500,000	—	0.10	0.15	0.45	—
1979	1,000,000	—	0.10	0.15	0.45	—
1980	2,000,000	—	0.10	0.15	0.45	—
1981	3,000,000	—	0.10	0.15	0.45	—
1982	1,000,000	—	0.10	0.15	0.45	—
1982 Proof	—	Value: 3.00				

KM# 41 50 MILS Composition: Copper-Nickel **Reverse:** Bunch of grapes

Date	Mintage	F	VF	XF	Unc	BU
1963	2,800,000	—	0.20	0.30	1.00	—
1963 Proof	25,000	Value: 1.75				
1970	500,000	—	0.20	0.35	1.25	—
1971	500,000	—	0.20	0.35	1.25	—
1972	750,000	—	0.20	0.30	1.00	—
1973	750,000	—	0.20	0.30	1.00	—
1974	1,500,000	—	0.20	0.30	1.00	—
1976	1,500,000	—	0.20	0.30	1.00	—
1977	500,000	—	0.20	0.30	1.00	—
1978	500,000	—	0.20	0.30	1.00	—
1979	1,000,000	—	0.20	0.30	1.00	—
1980	3,000,000	—	0.20	0.30	1.00	—
1981	4,000,000	—	0.20	0.30	1.00	—
1982	2,000,000	—	0.20	0.30	1.00	—
1982 Proof	—	Value: 3.50				

KM# 42 100 MILS Composition: Copper-Nickel **Reverse:** Cyprus Mouflon

Date	Mintage	F	VF	XF	Unc	BU
1963	1,750,000	—	0.40	0.70	2.00	—
1963 Proof	25,000	Value: 2.50				
1971	500,000	—	0.50	0.75	2.00	—
1973	750,000	—	0.40	0.70	2.00	—
1974	1,000,000	—	0.50	0.75	2.00	—
1976	1,500,000	—	0.40	0.70	2.00	—
1977	500,000	—	0.50	0.75	2.00	—
1978	1,000,000	—	0.50	0.75	2.00	—
1979	1,000,000	—	0.40	0.70	2.00	—
1980	1,000,000	—	0.40	0.70	2.00	—
1981	2,000,000	—	0.40	0.70	2.00	—
1982	2,000,000	—	0.40	0.70	2.00	—
1982 Proof	—	Value: 5.00				

KM# 43 500 MILS Composition: Copper-Nickel **Series:** F.A.O. **Reverse:** Woman holding tray of fruit

Date	Mintage	F	VF	XF	Unc	BU
1970	80,000	—	1.25	2.75	7.50	—

KM# 43a 500 MILS Weight: 22.6200 g. **Composition:** 0.8000 Silver .5818 oz. ASW **Series:** F.A.O **Reverse:** Woman holding tray of fruit

Date	Mintage	F	VF	XF	Unc	BU
1970 Proof	5,000	Value: 50.00				

KM# 44 500 MILS Composition: Copper-Nickel **Reverse:** Hercules

Date	Mintage	F	VF	XF	Unc	BU
1975	500,000	—	1.25	1.75	3.50	—
1977	300,000	—	1.25	1.75	3.50	—
1977 Proof	—	Value: 15.00				

KM# 44a 500 MILS Weight: 14.1400 g. **Composition:** 0.8000 Silver .3637 oz. ASW

Date	Mintage	F	VF	XF	Unc	BU
1975 Proof	10,000	Value: 22.50				

KM# 45 500 MILS Composition: Copper-Nickel **Subject:** Refugees

Date	Mintage	F	VF	XF	Unc	BU
1976	25,000	—	1.25	2.00	4.00	—

KM# 45a 500 MILS Weight: 14.1400 g. **Composition:** 0.9250 Silver .4205 oz. ASW **Reverse:** Refugees

Date	Mintage	F	VF	XF	Unc	BU
1976 Proof	25,000	Value: 25.00				

KM# 48 500 MILS Composition: Copper-Nickel **Subject:** Human Rights

Date	Mintage	F	VF	XF	Unc	BU
ND(1978)	50,000	—	1.25	2.00	4.00	—

KM# 48a 500 MILS Weight: 14.1400 g. **Composition:** 0.9250 Silver .4205 oz. ASW **Subject:** Human Rights

Date	Mintage	F	VF	XF	Unc	BU
ND Proof	5,000	Value: 65.00				

KM# 49 500 MILS Composition: Copper-Nickel **Series:** Summer Olympic Games **Reverse:** Rings logo

Date	Mintage	F	VF	XF	Unc	BU
1980	50,000	—	1.25	2.50	6.50	—

KM# 49a 500 MILS Weight: 14.1400 g. **Composition:** 0.9250 Silver .4205 oz. ASW

Date	Mintage	F	VF	XF	Unc	BU
1980 Proof	7,500	Value: 45.00				

KM# 51a 500 MILS Weight: 14.1400 g. **Composition:** 0.9250 Silver .4205 oz. ASW **Reverse:** Swordfish and grain

Date	Mintage	F	VF	XF	Unc	BU
ND(1978) Proof	7,500	Value: 45.00				

KM# 51 500 MILS **Composition:** Copper-Nickel **Subject:** World Food Day **Reverse:** Swordfish and grain

Date	Mintage	F	VF	XF	Unc	BU
ND(1978)	50	—	1.25	2.00	6.00	—

KM# 46 POUND **Composition:** Copper-Nickel **Note:** Refugee Commemorative.

Date	Mintage	F	VF	XF	Unc	BU
1976	25,000	—	2.00	2.50	5.50	—

KM# 46a POUND **Weight:** 28.2800 g. **Composition:** 0.9250 Silver .8411 oz. ASW **Note:** Refugee Commemorative.

Date	Mintage	F	VF	XF	Unc	BU
1976 Proof	25,000	Value: 40.00				

KM# 47 50 POUNDS **Weight:** 15.9800 g. **Composition:** 0.9170 Gold .4711 oz. AGW **Reverse:** Archbishop Makarios

Date	Mintage	F	VF	XF	Unc	BU
1977	39,000	—	—	—	275	—
1977 Proof	51,000	Value: 300				

REFORM COINAGE

100 Cents = 1 Pound

KM# 52 HALF CENT **Composition:** Aluminum **Reverse:** Cyclamen **Shape:** Scalloped

Date	Mintage	F	VF	XF	Unc	BU
1983	10,000,000	—	—	0.10	0.15	—
1983 Proof	6,250	Value: 1.50				

KM# 53.1 CENT **Composition:** Nickel-Brass **Reverse:** Stylized bird on a branch; value number surrounded by single line

Date	Mintage	F	VF	XF	Unc	BU
1983	15,000,000	—	—	0.10	0.20	—
1983 Proof	6,250	Value: 1.50				

KM# 53.2 CENT **Composition:** Nickel-Brass **Reverse:** Stylized bird on a branch; value number surrounded by double line

Date	Mintage	F	VF	XF	Unc	BU
1985	5,000,000	—	—	0.10	0.20	—
1987	5,000,000	—	—	0.10	0.20	—
1988	5,000,000	—	—	0.10	0.20	—

Date	Mintage	F	VF	XF	Unc	BU
1989	—	—	—	0.10	0.20	—
1990	—	—	—	0.10	0.20	—
1994	—	—	—	0.10	0.20	—

KM# 53.3 CENT **Composition:** Nickel-Brass **Reverse:** Stylized bird on a branch; altered wreath around arms

Date	F	VF	XF	Unc	BU
1991	—	—	0.10	0.20	—
1992	—	—	0.10	0.20	—
1993	—	—	0.10	0.20	—
1994	—	—	0.10	0.20	—
1996	—	—	0.10	0.20	—
1998	—	—	0.10	0.20	—

KM# 54.1 2 CENTS **Composition:** Nickel-Brass **Reverse:** Stylized goats; value number surrounded by single line

Date	Mintage	F	VF	XF	Unc	BU
1983	12,000,000	—	—	0.15	0.25	—
1983 Proof	6,250	Value: 1.50				

KM# 54.2 2 CENTS **Composition:** Nickel-Brass **Reverse:** Stylized goats; value number surrounded by double line

Date	Mintage	F	VF	XF	Unc	BU
1985	8,000,000	—	—	0.15	0.25	—
1987	—	—	—	0.15	0.25	—
1988	5,150,000	—	—	0.15	0.25	—
1989	—	—	—	0.15	0.25	—
1990	—	—	—	0.15	0.25	—

KM# 54.3 2 CENTS **Composition:** Nickel-Brass **Obverse:** Stylized goats, altered wreath around arms

Date	F	VF	XF	Unc	BU
1991	—	—	0.15	0.25	—
1992	—	—	0.15	0.25	—
1993	—	—	0.15	0.25	—
1994	—	—	0.15	0.25	—
1996	—	—	0.15	0.25	—

KM# 55.1 5 CENTS **Composition:** Nickel-Brass **Reverse:** Value number surrounded by single line

Date	Mintage	F	VF	XF	Unc	BU
1983	15,000,000	—	—	0.20	0.50	—
1983 Proof	6,250	Value: 2.00				

KM# 55.2 5 CENTS **Composition:** Nickel-Brass **Reverse:** Value number surrounded by double line

Date	Mintage	F	VF	XF	Unc	BU
1985	5,000,000	—	—	0.20	0.50	—
1987	5,000,000	—	—	0.20	0.50	—
1988	5,060,000	—	—	0.20	0.50	—
1989	—	—	—	0.20	0.50	—
1990	—	—	—	0.20	0.50	—

KM# 55.3 5 CENTS **Composition:** Nickel-Brass **Obverse:** Altered wreath around arms

Date	F	VF	XF	Unc	BU
1991	—	—	0.20	0.50	—
1992	—	—	0.20	0.50	—
1993	—	—	0.20	0.50	—
1994	—	—	0.20	0.50	—
1998	—	—	0.20	0.50	—

KM# 56.1 10 CENTS **Composition:** Nickel-Brass **Reverse:** Value number surrounded by single line

Date	Mintage	F	VF	XF	Unc	BU
1983	10,000,000	—	—	0.35	0.75	—
1983 Proof	6,250	Value: 3.00				

KM# 56.2 10 CENTS **Composition:** Nickel-Brass **Reverse:** Value number surrounded by double line

Date	Mintage	F	VF	XF	Unc	BU
1985	5,000,000	—	—	0.35	0.75	—
1987	—	—	—	0.35	0.75	—
1988	5,035,000	—	—	0.35	0.75	—
1989	—	—	—	0.35	0.75	—
1990	—	—	—	0.35	0.75	—

KM# 56.3 10 CENTS **Composition:** Nickel-Brass **Obverse:** Altered wreath around arms

Date	F	VF	XF	Unc	BU
1991	—	—	0.35	0.75	—
1992	—	—	0.35	0.75	—
1993	—	—	0.35	0.75	—
1994	—	—	0.35	0.75	—

KM# 57.1 20 CENTS **Composition:** Nickel-Brass **Reverse:** Value number framed by single line

Date	Mintage	F	VF	XF	Unc	BU
1983	10,000,000	—	—	0.50	1.50	—
1983 Proof	6,200	Value: 5.00				

KM# 57.2 20 CENTS **Composition:** Nickel-Brass **Reverse:** Value number framed by double line

Date	Mintage	F	VF	XF	Unc	BU
1985	5,040,000	—	—	0.50	1.50	—
1987	—	—	—	0.50	1.50	—
1988	1,000,000	—	—	0.50	1.50	—

KM# 62.1 20 CENTS **Composition:** Bronze **Reverse:** Zamon D. Keteus head left

Date	F	VF	XF	Unc	BU
1989	—	—	—	1.00	—
1989 Proof	— Value: 18.00				
1990	—	—	—	1.00	—

KM# 62.2 20 CENTS **Comp.:** Nickel-Brass **Obverse:** Zamon D. Keteus head left, altered wreath around arms

Date	F	VF	XF	Unc	BU
1991	—	—	—	1.00	—
1992	—	—	—	1.00	—

Date	F	VF	XF	Unc	BU
1993	—	—	—	1.00	—
1994	—	—	—	1.00	—

KM# 58 50 CENTS Composition: Copper-Nickel **Series:** F.A.O. **Subject:** Forestry **Reverse:** Stylized tree

Date	Mintage	F	VF	XF	Unc	BU
1985	33,000	—	1.50	3.50	10.00	—

KM# 58a 50 CENTS Weight: 14.1400 g. **Composition:** 0.9250 Silver .4205 oz. ASW **Series:** F.A.O. **Reverse:** Stylized tree

Date	Mintage	F	VF	XF	Unc	BU
1985 Proof	4,000	Value: 50.00				

KM# 60 50 CENTS Composition: Copper-Nickel **Subject:** Olympics **Reverse:** Symbols

Date	Mintage	F	VF	XF	Unc	BU
1988	14,000	—	—	—	3.50	—

KM# 60a 50 CENTS Weight: 14.1400 g. **Composition:** 0.9250 Silver .4205 oz. ASW

Date	Mintage	F	VF	XF	Unc	BU
1988 Proof	4,000	Value: 45.00				

KM# 66a 50 CENTS Weight: 7.0000 g. **Composition:** 0.9250 Silver .2082 oz. ASW

Date	Mintage	F	VF	XF	Unc	BU
1991 Proof	5,000	Value: 35.00				

KM# 66 50 CENTS Composition: Copper-Nickel **Subject:** Abduction of Europe

Date	Mintage	F	VF	XF	Unc	BU
1991 narrow date	3,005,000	—	—	—	2.50	—
1993 wide date	—	—	—	—	2.50	—
1994 wide date	—	—	—	—	2.50	—
1996	—	—	—	—	2.50	—

KM# 59 POUND Composition: Copper-Nickel **Subject:** World Wildlife Fund **Obverse:** National arms **Reverse:** Cyprian wild sheep

Date	Mintage	F	VF	XF	Unc	BU
1986	39,000	—	—	—	6.50	—

KM# 59a POUND Composition: 0.9250 Silver

Date	Mintage	F	VF	XF	Unc	BU
1986 Proof	13,000	Value: 40.00				

KM# 61 POUND Composition: Copper-Nickel **Series:** Olympics **Reverse:** Symbols

Date	Mintage	F	VF	XF	Unc	BU
1988	14,000	—	—	—	6.50	—

KM# 61a POUND Weight: 28.2800 g. **Composition:** 0.9250 Silver .8411 oz. ASW

Date	Mintage	F	VF	XF	Unc	BU
1988 Proof	4,000	Value: 55.00				

KM# 63 POUND Composition: Copper-Nickel **Subject:** Small European States Games

Date	F	VF	XF	Unc	BU
1989	—	—	—	5.50	—

KM# 64 POUND Composition: Copper-Nickel **Series:** Save the Children Fund

Date	F	VF	XF	Unc	BU
1989	—	—	—	5.50	—

KM# 63a POUND Weight: 28.2800 g. **Composition:** 0.9250 Silver .8411 oz. ASW **Subject:** Small European States Games

Date	Mintage	F	VF	XF	Unc	BU
1989 Proof	4,000	Value: 50.00				

KM# 64a POUND Weight: 28.2800 g. **Composition:** 0.9250 Silver .8411 oz. ASW **Series:** Save the Children Fund

Date	Mintage	F	VF	XF	Unc	BU
1989 Proof	4,000	Value: 42.50				

KM# 67 POUND Composition: Copper-Nickel **Series:** Olympics **Reverse:** Relay Racing

Date	Mintage	F	VF	XF	Unc	BU
1992	8,000	—	—	—	8.50	—

KM# 67a POUND Weight: 28.2800 g. **Composition:** 0.9250 Silver .8411 oz. ASW **Series:** Olympics

Date	Mintage	F	VF	XF	Unc	BU
1992 Proof	4,000	Value: 50.00				

KM# 69 POUND Composition: Copper-Nickel **Subject:** 50th Anniversary - United Nations **Obverse:** National arms **Reverse:** Tree of flag shields, denomination and logo

Date	F	VF	XF	Unc	BU
1995	—	—	—	8.50	—

KM# 70 POUND Composition: Copper-Nickel **Series:** F.A.O. **Subject:** 50th Anniversary - United Nations **Obverse:** National arms **Reverse:** Bovine portrait, wheat and denominaton

Date	F	VF	XF	Unc	BU
1995	—	—	—	12.50	—

KM# 69a POUND Weight: 28.2800 g. **Composition:** 0.9250 Silver .8411 oz. ASW **Series:** 50th Anniversary - United Nations **Obverse:** National Arms **Reverse:** Tree of flags, denomination amd logo

Date	Mintage	F	VF	XF	Unc	BU
1995	Est. 100,000	Value: 42.00				

KM# 70a POUND Weight: 28.2800 g. **Composition:** 0.9250 Silver .8411 oz. ASW **Series:** 50th Anniversary - F.A.O. **Obverse:** National Arms **Reverse:** Bovine Portrait, wheat and denomination

Date	Mintage	F	VF	XF	Unc	BU
1995	4,000	Value: 55.00				

KM# 71 POUND Composition: Copper-Nickel **Subject:** 1996 Olympics **Obverse:** National arms **Reverse:** Olympic rings, stylized flames, olive branch

Date	Mintage	F	VF	XF	Unc	BU
1996 Proof	2,000	Value: 45.00				

KM# 71a POUND Weight: 28.2800 g. **Composition:** 0.9250 Silver .8410 oz. ASW **Series:** 1996 Olympics **Obverse:** National Arms **Reverse:** Olympic rings, stylized flames, olive branch

Date	Mintage	F	VF	XF	Unc	BU
1996	4,000	Value: 45.00				

KM# 72 POUND Composition: Copper-Nickel **Subject:** World Wildlife Fund - Conserving Nature **Obverse:** National arms **Reverse:** Green turtle

Date	F	VF	XF	Unc	BU
1997	—	—	—	15.00	—

KM# 72a POUND **Weight:** 28.2800 g. **Composition:** 0.9250 Silver .8411 oz. ASW

Date	Mintage	F	VF	XF	Unc	BU
1997 Proof	Est. 15,000	Value: 50.00				

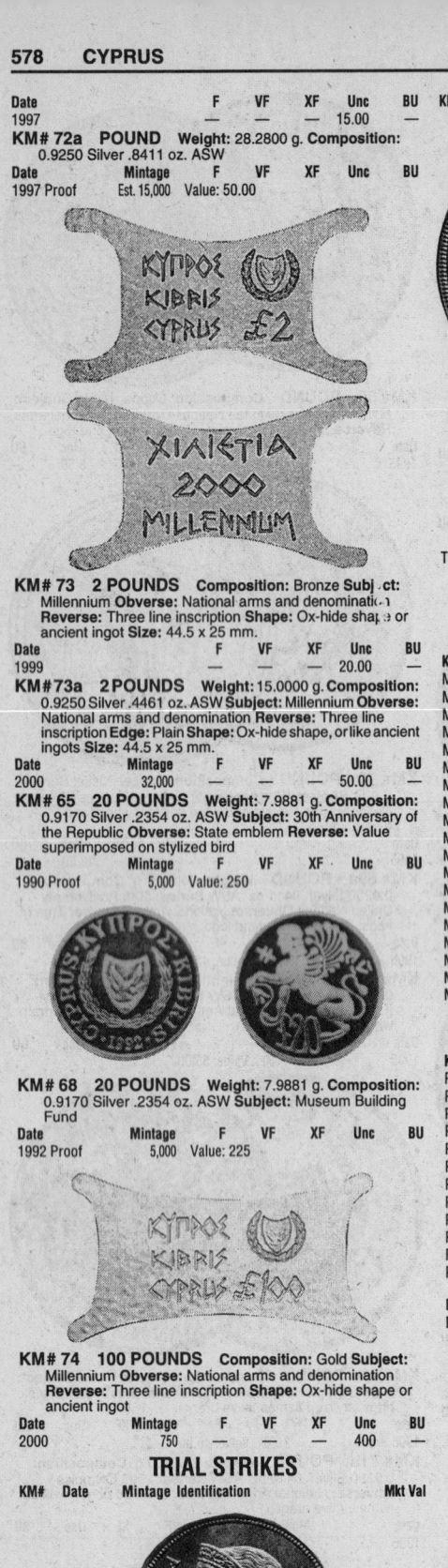

KM# 73 2 POUNDS **Composition:** Bronze **Subject:** Millennium **Obverse:** National arms and denomination **Reverse:** Three line inscription **Shape:** Ox-hide shape or ancient ingot **Size:** 44.5 x 25 mm.

Date	F	VF	XF	Unc	BU
1999	—	—	—	20.00	—

KM# 73a 2 POUNDS **Weight:** 15.0000 g. **Composition:** 0.9250 Silver .4461 oz. ASW **Subject:** Millennium **Obverse:** National arms and denomination **Reverse:** Three line inscription **Edge:** Plain **Shape:** Ox-hide shape, or like ancient ingots **Size:** 44.5 x 25 mm.

Date	Mintage	F	VF	XF	Unc	BU
2000	32,000	—	—	—	50.00	—

KM# 65 20 POUNDS **Weight:** 7.9881 g. **Composition:** 0.9170 Silver .2354 oz. ASW **Subject:** 30th Anniversary of the Republic **Obverse:** State emblem **Reverse:** Value superimposed on stylized bird

Date	Mintage	F	VF	XF	Unc	BU
1990 Proof	5,000	Value: 250				

KM# 68 20 POUNDS **Weight:** 7.9881 g. **Composition:** 0.9170 Silver .2354 oz. ASW **Subject:** Museum Building Fund

Date	Mintage	F	VF	XF	Unc	BU
1992 Proof	5,000	Value: 225				

KM# 74 100 POUNDS **Composition:** Gold **Subject:** Millennium **Obverse:** National arms and denomination **Reverse:** Three line inscription **Shape:** Ox-hide shape or ancient ingot

Date	Mintage	F	VF	XF	Unc	BU
2000	750	—	—	—	400	—

TRIAL STRIKES

KM#	Date	Mintage	Identification	Mkt Val
TS1	1879	—	Piastre. 0.9170 Gold. 40.0000 g. Uniface.	2,500
TS2	ND	—	45 Piastres. 0.9170 Gold. 40.0000 g. Uniface.	3,000

Note: 1 known

MINT SETS

KM#	Date	Mintage	Identification	Issue Price	Mkt Val
MS1	1955 (5)	2,550	KM33-37	2.20	6.50
MS2	1963 (5)	8,050	KM38-42	1.95	5.00
MS3	1971 (5)	3,000	KM38-42	1.65	5.00
MS4	1972 (4)	30,000	KM38-41	2.35	5.00
MS5	1973 (4)	5,000	KM39-42	2.75	5.00
MS6	1974 (4)	5,000	KM39-42	3.25	5.00
MS7	1976 (3)	5,000	KM40-42	1.25	4.50
MS8	1976 (2)	25,000	KM45-46	6.50	6.00
MS9	1977 (5)	10,000	KM39-42, 44	—	6.50
MS10	1978 (5)	—	KM39-42, 48	5.50	6.50
MS11	1979 (4)	—	KM39-42	—	6.50
MS12	1980 (4)	—	KM39-42	—	6.50
MS13	1981 (5)	—	KM40-42, 50.1, 51	5.00	6.50
MS14	1981 (4)	—	KM40-42, 50.1	5.00	6.50
MS15	1982 (4)	5,000	KM40-42, 50.2	5.00	6.50
MS16	1983 (6)	11,400	KM52,53.1-57.1	15.00	10.00
MS17	1988 (5)	—	KM53.2-57.2	—	10.00
MS18	1989 (5)	—	KM53.2-56.2, 62.1	—	10.00
MS19	1990 (5)	—	KM53.2-56.2, 62.1	10.00	10.00

PROOF SETS

KM#	Date	Mintage	Identification	Issue Price	Mkt Val
PS3	1900 (3)	—	KM1.1, 2, 3.2	—	3,500
PS4	1901 (4)	—	KM4-7	—	5,500
PS5	1931 (2)	—	KM17-18	—	1,175
PS6	1934 (2)	—	KM20-21	—	650
PS7	1938 (5)	—	KM-22-26	—	2,000
PS8	1947 (2)	—	KM27-28	—	700
PS10	1949 (4)	—	KM29-32	—	950
PS9	1949 (2)	—	KM31-32	—	700
PS11	1955 (5)	2,000	KM33-37	5.50	16.00
PS12	1963 (5)	24,501	KM38-42	9.00	8.50
PS13	1963 (5)	500	KM38-42	8.70	8.00
PS15	0 (7)	—	KM38(72), 39(80), 40-42(82), 50.2(82)	30.00	30.00
PS14	1976 (2)	25,000	KM45a-46a	50.00	35.00
PS16	1983 (6)	6,250	KM52, 53.1-57.1	40.00	15.00

CZECH REPUBLIC

The Czech Republic was formerly united with Slovakia as Czechoslovakia. It is bordered in the west by Germany, to the north by Poland, to the east by Slovakia and to the south by Austria. It consists of 3 major regions: Bohemia, Moravia and Silesia and has an area of 30,450 sq. mi. (78,864 sq. km.) and a population of 10.4 million. Capital: Prague (Praha). Agriculture and livestock are chief occupations while coal deposits are the main mineral resources.

The Czech lands were united with the Slovaks to form the Czechoslovak State, which came into existence on Oct. 28, 1918 upon the dissolution of the Austrian-Hungarian Empire. In 1938, this territory was broken up for the benefit of Germany, Poland, and Hungary by the Munich (Munchen) Agreement. In March 1939 the German influenced Slovak government proclaimed Slovakia independent. Germany incorporated the Czech lands into the Third Reich as the "Protectorate of Bohemia and Moravia." A Czech government-in-exile was set up in London in July 1940. The Soviets and USA forces liberated the area by May 1945. Communist influence increased steadily while pressure for liberalization culminated in the overthrow of the Stalinist leader Antonin Novotny and his associates in 1968. The Communist Party then introduced far reaching reforms which resulted in warnings from Moscow (Moskva), followed by occupation and stationing of Soviet forces. Mass demonstrations for reform began again in Nov. 1989 and the Federal Assembly abolished the Communist Party's sole right to govern. The new government formed was the Czech and Slovak Federal Republic. A movement for Democratic Slovakia was apparent in the June 1992 elections and on December 31, 1992, the CSFR was dissolved and the two new republics came into being on Jan. 1, 1993.

NOTE: For earlier issues see Czechoslovakia, Bohemia and Moravia or Slovakia listings.

MINT MARKS

(c) - castle = Hamburg
(cr) - cross = British Royal Mint
(l) - leaf = Royal Canadian
(m) - crowned *b* and *CM* = Jablonec nad Nisou
(mk) - *MK* in circle = Kremnica
(o) - broken circle = Vienna (Wien)

MONETARY SYSTEM

1 Czechoslovak Koruna (Kcs) = 1 Czech Koruna (Kc)
1 Koruna = 100 Haleru

REPUBLIC

STANDARD COINAGE

KM# 6 10 HALERU **Composition:** 0.9900 Aluminum 0.6 oz. **Obverse:** Crowned Czech lion **Reverse:** Value and stylized river **Edge:** Plain **Size:** 15.5 mm. **Note:** Two varieties of mint marks exist for 1994.

Date	F	VF	XF	Unc	BU
1993(c)	—	—	—	0.20	—
1993(m)	—	—	—	0.20	—
1994(c) In Sets only	—	—	—	2.50	—
1994(m)	—	—	—	0.20	—
1994(m) Proof, dull	—	—	—	—	—
1994(m) Proof, bright	—	—	—	—	—
1995(m)	—	—	—	0.20	—
1996(m)	—	—	—	0.20	—
1997(m)	—	—	—	0.20	—
1997(m) Proof	1,500	Value: 3.50			
1998(m)	—	—	—	0.20	—
1998(m) Proof	2,600	Value: 2.00			
1999(m)	—	—	—	0.20	—
1999(m) Proof	2,000	Value: 2.00			
2000(m)	—	—	—	0.20	—
2000(m) Proof	3,000	Value: 2.00			
2001(m)	—	—	—	0.20	—
2001(m) Proof	3,000	Value: 2.00			
2002(m)	—	—	—	0.20	—
2002(m) Proof	—	Value: 2.00			

KM# 2.1 20 HALERU **Weight:** 0.7400 g. **Composition:** Aluminum **Obverse:** Crowned Czech lion **Reverse:** Linden leaf within value; Closed 2, "h" above flat line **Edge:** Milled **Size:** 17 mm. **Note:** Medallic coin alignment.

Date	Mintage	F	VF	XF	Unc	BU
1993(c)	80,000,000	—	—	—	0.30	—
1993(m)	30,558,000	—	—	—	0.30	—
1994(c)	9,310,000	—	—	—	0.30	—
1994(m)	81,289,000	—	—	—	0.30	—
1994(m) Proof, dull	2,500	—	—	—	3.00	—
1994(m) Proof, bright	17,500	—	—	—	1.00	—
1995(m)	80,960,374	—	—	—	0.30	—
1995(c)	450,000	—	—	—	1.75	—
1996(m)	61,086,142	—	—	—	0.30	—
1997(m)	51,013,450	—	—	—	0.30	—
1997(m) Proof	1,500	Value: 5.00				
2000(m)	—	—	—	—	0.30	—
2002(m)	—	—	—	—	0.30	—

KM# 2.3 20 HALERU **Composition:** Aluminum **Reverse:** Open 2 in denomination, "h" above angle line **Note:** Medallic coin alignment.

Date	Mintage	F	VF	XF	Unc	BU
1998(m)	51,135,904	—	—	—	0.30	—
1998(m) Proof	2,510	Value: 3.00				
1999(m)	20,820,612	—	—	—	0.30	—
1999(m) Proof	2,000	Value: 3.00				
2000(m)	30,000,000	—	—	—	—	—
2000(m) Proof	3,000	—	—	—	—	—
2001(m)	40,000,000	—	—	—	0.30	—
2001(m) Proof	3,000	Value: 3.00				
2002(m)	—	—	—	—	0.30	—
2002(m) Proof	—	Value: 3.00				

(KM2.2) 20 HALERU **Composition:** Aluminum **Reverse:** H above flat line

Date	Mintage	F	VF	XF	Unc	BU
1998		—	—	—	0.30	—
1998 Proof	—	Value: 3.00				
1999		—	—	—	0.30	—
1999 Proof	—	Value: 3.00				

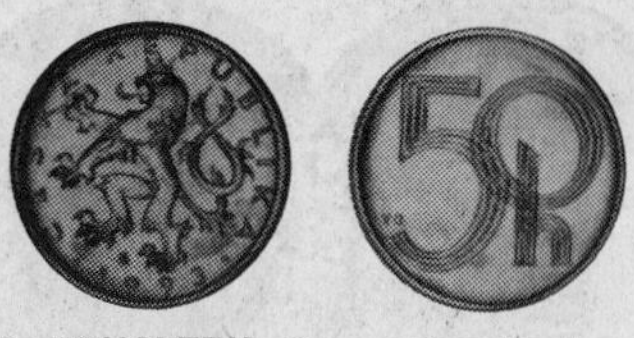

KM# 3 50 HALERU **Composition:** Aluminum 0.9 oz. **Obverse:** Crowned Czech lion **Reverse:** Large value **Edge:** Part plain, part milled repeated **Size:** 19 mm. **Note:** Two styles of "9" exist for 1994.

Date	Mintage	F	VF	XF	Unc	BU
1993(c)		—	—	—	0.50	—
1993(m)		—	—	—	0.50	—
1994(m)		—	—	—	0.50	—
1994(m) Proof, dull		—	—	—	3.00	—
1994(m) Proof, bright		—	—	—	1.00	—
1995(m)		—	—	—	0.50	—
1996(m)		—	—	—	0.50	—
1997(m)		—	—	—	0.50	—
1997(m) Proof	1,500	Value: 5.00				
1998(m)		—	—	—	0.50	—
1998(m) Proof	2,510	Value: 3.00				
1999(m)		—	—	—	0.50	—
1999(m) Proof	2,000	Value: 3.00				
2000(m)		—	—	—	0.50	—
2000(m) Proof		—	—	—	—	—
2001(m)		—	—	—	0.50	—
2001(m) Proof	3,000	Value: 3.00				
2002(m)		—	—	—	0.50	—
2002(m) Proof	—	Value: 3.00				

KM# 7 KORUNA **Composition:** Nickel Clad Steel **Obverse:** Crowned Czech lion **Reverse:** Value above crown **Edge:** Milled **Size:** 20 mm. **Note:** Two varieties of mint marks exist for 1996.

Date	Mintage	F	VF	XF	Unc	BU
1993(l)	102,431,000	—	—	—	0.60	—
1994(m)	52,162,620	—	—	—	0.60	—
1995(m)	668,280	—	—	—	0.60	—
1996(m)	35,344,913	—	—	—	0.60	—
1997(m)	15,055,501	—	—	—	0.60	—
1997(m) Proof	1,500	Value: 6.50				
1998(m)	25,000	—	—	—	0.60	—
1998(m) Proof	2,510	Value: 4.00				
1999(m)	24,904	—	—	—	0.60	—
1999(m) Proof	2,000	Value: 4.00				
2000(m)	20,000,000	—	—	—	0.60	—
2000(m) Proof	3,000	Value: 4.00				
2001(m)	10,000,000	—	—	—	0.60	—
2001(m) Proof	3,000	Value: 4.00				
2002(m)	—	—	—	—	0.60	—
2002(m) Proof	—	Value: 4.00				

KM# 9 2 KORUN **Composition:** Nickel Clad Steel 3.7 oz. **Obverse:** Crowned Czech lion **Edge:** Plain **Size:** 21.5 mm.

Date	Mintage	F	VF	XF	Unc	BU
1993(l)	80,001,000	—	—	—	0.65	—
1994(m)	30,310,000	—	—	—	0.65	—
1994(l)	18,360,000	—	—	—	0.65	—
1995(m)	30,520,405	—	—	—	0.65	—
1996(m)	15,201,750	—	—	—	0.65	—
1997(m)	15,040,245	—	—	—	0.65	—
1997(m) Proof	1,500	Value: 8.50				
1998(m)	10,455,480	—	—	—	0.65	—
1998(m) Proof	2,510	Value: 5.00				
1999(m)	28,768	—	—	—	0.65	—
1999(m) Proof	2,000	Value: 5.00				
2000	30,000	—	—	—	0.65	—
2000(m) Proof	3,000	Value: 5.00				
2001(m)	25,000,000	—	—	—	0.65	—
2001(m) Proof	3,000	Value: 5.00				
2002(m)	—	—	—	—	0.65	—
2002(m) Proof	—	Value: 5.00				

KM# 8 5 KORUN **Weight:** 4.8000 g. **Composition:** Nickel Plated Steel **Obverse:** Crowned Czech lion **Reverse:** Large value, Charles bridge and linden leaf **Edge:** Plain **Size:** 23 mm.

Date	Mintage	F	VF	XF	Unc	BU
1993(l)	70,001,000	—	—	—	1.00	—
1994(m)	30,475,491	—	—	—	1.00	—
1994(l)	14,400,000	—	—	—	1.00	—
1995(m)	20,155,218	—	—	—	1.00	—
1996(m)	5,053,730	—	—	—	1.00	—
1997(m)	40,000	—	—	—	1.00	—
1997(m) Proof	1,500	Value: 10.00				
1998(m)	25,000	—	—	—	1.00	—
1998(m) Proof	2,510	Value: 6.00				
1999(m)	29,490	—	—	—	1.00	—
1999(m) Proof	2,000	Value: 6.00				
2000(m)	30,000	—	—	—	1.00	—
2000(m) Proof	3,000	Value: 6.00				
2001(m)	25,000	—	—	—	1.00	—
2001(m) Proof	3,000	Value: 6.00				
2002(m)	25,000	—	—	—	1.00	—
2002(m) Proof	—	Value: 6.00				

KM# 4 10 KORUN **Weight:** 7.6200 g. **Composition:** Copper Plated Steel **Obverse:** Crowned Czech lion **Reverse:** Brno Cathedral **Edge:** Milled **Size:** 24.5 mm. **Note:** Position of designer's initials on reverse change during the 1995 strike.

Date	Mintage	F	VF	XF	Unc	BU
1993(c)	70,001,000	—	—	—	2.00	—
1993(c) Small 10	1,000	25.00	75.00	150	250	—
1994(m) bright	30,000	—	—	—	2.00	—
1994(m)	20,677,220	—	—	—	1.50	—
1995(m)	152,388	—	—	—	1.50	—
1995(m) LK below	20,530,459	—	—	—	1.50	—
1996(m)	20,644,143	—	—	—	1.50	—
1997(m)	48,215	—	—	—	1.50	—
1997(m) Proof	1,500	Value: 12.00				
1998(m)	25,000	—	—	—	1.50	—
1998(m) Proof	2,510	Value: 7.00				
1999(m)	29,490	—	—	—	1.50	—
1999(m) Proof	2,000	Value: 7.00				
2000(m)	30,000	—	—	—	1.50	—
2000(m) Proof	3,000	Value: 7.00				
2001(m)	25,000	—	—	—	1.50	—
2001(m) Proof	3,000	Value: 7.00				
2002(m)	—	—	—	—	1.50	—
2002(m) Proof	—	Value: 7.00				

KM# 42 10 KORUN **Weight:** 7.5200 g. **Composition:** Copper Plated Steel **Subject:** Year 2000 **Obverse:** Crowned Czech lion **Reverse:** Clockworks above denomination **Edge:** Reeded **Size:** 24.5 mm.

Date	Mintage	F	VF	XF	Unc	BU
2000	10,000,000	—	—	—	1.50	—
2000 Proof	3,000	Value: 7.50				

KM# 5 20 KORUN **Composition:** Brass Plated Steel **Obverse:** Crowned Czech lion **Reverse:** St. Wenceslas (Duke Vaclav) on horse **Edge:** Plain **Size:** 26 mm. **Note:** Two varieties of mint marks and style of 9s exist for 1997.

Date	Mintage	F	VF	XF	Unc	BU
1993(c)	55,001,000	—	—	1.00	3.00	—
1994(c)	100,000	—	—	—	3.50	—
1995(m)	101,837	—	—	—	2.50	—
1996(m)	101,152	—	—	—	2.50	—
1997(m)	8,091,219	—	—	—	2.50	—
1997(m) Proof	1,500	Value: 16.50				
1998(m)	15,725,000	—	—	—	2.50	—
1998(m) Proof	2,510	Value: 10.00				
1999(m)	26,274,900	—	—	—	2.50	—
1999(m) Proof	2,000	Value: 10.00				
2000(m)	5,000,000	—	—	—	—	—
2000(m) Proof	3,000	—	—	—	—	—
2001(m)	25,000	—	—	—	2.50	—
2001(m) Proof	3,000	Value: 10.00				
2002(m)	—	—	—	—	2.50	—
2002(m) Proof	—	Value: 10.00				

KM# 43 20 KORUN **Weight:** 8.6000 g. **Composition:** Brass Plated Steel **Subject:** Year 2000 **Obverse:** Crowned Czech lion **Reverse:** Astrolab and denomination **Edge:** Plain **Size:** 26 mm. **Note:** 13-sided.

Date	Mintage	F	VF	XF	Unc	BU
2000	10,000,000	—	—	—	2.50	—
2000 Proof	3,000	Value: 10.00				

KM# 1 50 KORUN **Ring Composition:** Copper Plated Steel **Obverse:** Crowned Czech lion **Reverse:** Prague city view **Edge:** Plain **Size:** 27.5 mm.

Date	Mintage	F	VF	XF	Unc	BU
1993(c)	35,001,000	—	—	2.50	7.50	—
1994(c)	100,000	—	—	—	9.00	—
1995(m)	102,977	—	—	—	9.00	—
1996(m)	103,073	—	—	—	9.00	—
1997(m)	40,002	—	—	—	9.00	—
1997(m) Proof	1,500	Value: 35.00				
1998(m)	25,000	—	—	—	9.00	—
1998(m) Proof	2,510	Value: 20.00				
1999(m)	29,490	—	—	—	9.00	—
1999(m) Proof	2,000	Value: 20.00				

Date	Mintage	F	VF	XF	Unc	BU
2000(m)	30,000	—	—	—	—	—
2000(m) Proof	3,000	—	—	—	—	—
2001(m)	25,000	—	—	—	9.00	—
2001(m) Proof	3,000	Value: 20.00				
2002(m)	—	—	—	—	9.00	—
2002(m) Proof	—	Value: 20.00				

KM# 10 200 KORUN **Weight:** 13.0000 g. **Composition:** 0.9000 Silver .3440 oz. ASW **Subject:** 1st Anniversary of Constitution **Size:** 31 mm. **Note:** 22 pieces, Unc and Proof, were melted by the Czech National Bank in 1977.

Date	Mintage	F	VF	XF	Unc	BU
1993(o)	30,000	—	—	—	12.50	14.50
Note: Milled edge						
1993(o) Proof	5,000	Value: 30.00				
Note: Edge: CESKA NARODNI BANKA						

KM# 11.1 200 KORUN **Weight:** 13.0000 g. **Composition:** 0.9000 Silver .3440 oz. ASW **Subject:** 650th Anniversary **Reverse:** St. Vitus Cathedral and Archbishop's arms **Edge:** Reeded **Size:** 31 mm. **Note:** See note with KM#11.2.

Date	Mintage	F	VF	XF	Unc	BU
ND(1994)(o)	28,000	—	—	—	12.50	14.50

KM# 11.2 200 KORUN **Weight:** 13.0000 g. **Composition:** 0.9000 Silver .3440 oz. ASW **Subject:** 650th Anniversary **Reverse:** St. Vitus Cathedral and Prague Archbishop's Arms **Edge:** Plain **Size:** 31 mm. **Note:** 22 pieces, Unc and Proof of KM#11.1 and 11.2, were melted by the Czech National Bank in 1997.

Date	Mintage	F	VF	XF	Unc	BU
ND(1994)(o)	5,000	Value: 50.00				

KM# 12 200 KORUN **Weight:** 13.0000 g. **Composition:** 0.9000 Silver .3440 oz. ASW **Subject:** 50th Anniversary - Normandy Invasion **Reverse:** Spitfires in formation **Size:** 31 mm. **Note:** 6,445 pieces, Unc and Proof, were melted by the Czech National Bank in 1997.

Date	Mintage	F	VF	XF	Unc	BU
1994(cr)	29,980	—	—	—	16.50	18.50
Note: Milled edge						
1994(cr)	5,000	Value: 45.00				
Note: Plain edge with CESKA NARODNI BANKA *0.900*						

KM# 13.1 200 KORUN **Weight:** 13.0000 g. **Composition:** 0.9000 Silver .3440 oz. ASW **Subject:** 125th Anniversary of Brno Tramway **Edge:** Reeded **Size:** 31 mm. **Note:** See note with KM#13.2.

Date	Mintage	F	VF	XF	Unc	BU
1994(mk)	25,000	—	—	—	14.00	16.00

KM# 13.2 200 KORUN **Weight:** 13.0000 g. **Composition:** 0.9000 Silver .3440 oz. ASW **Subject:** 125th Anniversary Brno Tramway **Edge:** Plain **Size:** 31 mm. **Note:** 22 pieces, Unc and Proof, were melted by the Czech National Bank in 1997. Beginning with KM#14, all 200 Korun strikes come either reeded, or plain edges with the inscription, "CESKA NARODNI BANKA".

Date	Mintage	F	VF	XF	Unc	BU
1994	2,000	Value: 35.00				

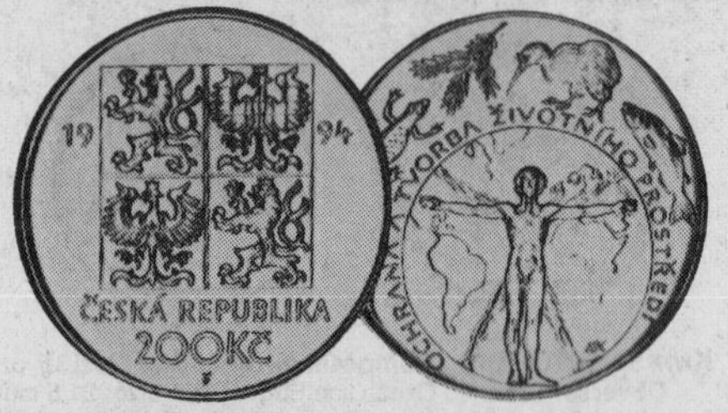

KM# 14 200 KORUN **Weight:** 13.0000 g. **Composition:** 0.9000 Silver .3440 oz. ASW **Subject:** Environmental Protection **Size:** 31 mm. **Note:** 22 pieces, Unc and Proof, were melted by the Czech National Bank in 1997.

Date	Mintage	F	VF	XF	Unc	BU
1994(m)	25,000	—	—	—	14.00	16.00
Note: Milled edge						
1994(m) Proof	2,000	Value: 45.00				
Note: Edge: Plain with CESKA NARODNI BANKA *0.900*						

KM# 15 200 KORUN **Weight:** 13.0000 g. **Composition:** 0.9000 Silver .3440 oz. ASW **Subject:** 50th Anniversary - Victory Over Fascism **Size:** 31 mm. **Note:** 22 pieces, Unc and Proof, were melted by the Czech National Bank in 1997.

Date	Mintage	F	VF	XF	Unc	BU
ND(1995)	25,000	—	—	—	14.00	16.00
Note: Plain edge						
ND(1995) Proof	2,000	Value: 55.00				
Note: Plain edge with CESKA NARODNI BANKA *0.900*						

KM# 16 200 KORUN **Weight:** 13.0000 g. **Composition:** 0.9000 Silver .3440 oz. ASW **Subject:** 200th Anniversary - Birth of Pavel Josef Safarik **Size:** 31 mm. **Note:** 22 pieces, Unc and Proof, were melted by the Czech National Bank in 1997.

Date	Mintage	F	VF	XF	Unc	BU
1995	25,000	—	—	—	14.00	16.00
Note: Plain edge						
1995 Proof	2,000	Value: 42.00				
Note: Plain edge with CESKA NARODNI BANKA *0.900*						

KM# 17 200 KORUN **Weight:** 13.0000 g. **Composition:** 0.9000 Silver .3440 oz. ASW **Subject:** 50th Anniversary - United Nations **Size:** 31 mm. **Note:** 25 pieces, Unc and Proof, were melted by the Czech National Bank in 1997.

Date	Mintage	F	VF	XF	Unc	BU
ND(1995)	25,000	—	—	—	14.00	16.00
Note: Milled edge						
ND(1995) Proof	2,500	Value: 40.00				
Note: Plain edge with CESKA NARODNI BANKA *0.900*						

KM# 22 200 KORUN **Weight:** 13.0000 g. **Composition:** 0.9000 Silver .3440 oz. ASW **Subject:** Czech Philharmonic **Reverse:** Building and musical instruments **Size:** 31 mm. **Note:** 25 pieces, Unc and Proof, were melted by the Czech National Bank in 1997.

Date	Mintage	F	VF	XF	Unc	BU
1996 Proof	2,500	Value: 45.00				
Note: Plain edge with CESKA NARODNI BANKA *0.900*						

KM# 23 200 KORUN **Weight:** 13.0000 g. **Composition:** 0.9000 Silver .3440 oz. ASW **Subject:** Karel Svolinsky **Size:** 31 mm. **Note:** 25 pieces, Unc and Proof, were melted by the Czech National Bank in 1997.

Date	Mintage	F	VF	XF	Unc	BU
ND(1996)	24,500	—	—	—	14.00	16.00
Note: Milled edge						
ND(1996) Proof	2,000	Value: 45.00				
Note: Plain edge with CESKA NARODNI BANKA *0.900*						

KM# 24 200 KORUN **Weight:** 13.0000 g. **Composition:** 0.9000 Silver .3440 oz. ASW **Subject:** Jean-Baptiste Gaspard Deburau **Size:** 31 mm.

Date	Mintage	F	VF	XF	Unc	BU
1996	24,500	—	—	—	14.00	16.00
Note: Milled edge						
1996 Proof	2,000	Value: 35.00				
Note: Plain edge with CESKA NARODNI BANKA *0.900*						

KM# 25 200 KORUN **Weight:** 13.0000 g. **Composition:** 0.9000 Silver .3761 oz. ASW **Subject:** 200th Anniversary - Czech Christmas Mass by Jakub J. Ryba **Size:** 31 mm.

Date	Mintage	F	VF	XF	Unc	BU
ND(1996)	25,000	—	—	—	14.00	16.00
Note: Milled edge						
ND(1996) Proof	2,500	Value: 40.00				
Note: Plain edge with CESKA NARODNI BANKA *0.900*						

KM# 26 200 KORUN **Weight:** 13.0000 g. **Composition:** 0.9000 Silver .3761 oz. ASW **Subject:** Centennial - First Automobile in Bohemia **Obverse:** National arms **Reverse:** Sideview of antique automobile - Prasident **Size:** 31 mm.

Date	Mintage	F	VF	XF	Unc	BU
ND(1997)	22,500	—	—	—	14.00	16.00

Note: Milled edge

Date	Mintage	Value
ND(1997) Proof	3,000	Value: 32.00

Note: Plain edge with CESKA NARODNI BANKA *0.900*

KM# 30 200 KORUN **Weight:** 13.0000 g. **Composition:** 0.9000 Silver .3761 oz. ASW **Subject:** 650th Anniversary - Charles University in Prague **Obverse:** National arms **Reverse:** Charles IV portrait and document seal **Size:** 31 mm.

Date	Mintage	F	VF	XF	Unc	BU
ND(1998)	27,000	—	—	—	14.00	16.00

Note: Milled edge

Date	Mintage	Value
ND(1998) Proof	2,000	Value: 35.00

Note: Plain edge with CESKA NARODNI BANKA *0.900*

KM# 34 200 KORUN **Weight:** 13.0000 g. **Composition:** 0.9000 Silver .3761 oz. ASW **Subject:** 50th Anniversary - NATO **Obverse:** Undivided national arms **Reverse:** NATO style cross **Edge Lettering:** CESKA REPUBLIKA CLENSKA ZEME NATO 1996 **Size:** 31 mm.

Date	Mintage	F	VF	XF	Unc	BU
ND(1999)	20,000	—	—	—	14.00	16.00

Note: Edge: CESKA REPUBLIKA...

Date	Mintage	Value
ND(1999) Proof	3,000	Value: 30.00

Note: Plain edge with CESKA NARODNI BANKA *0.900*

KM# 27 200 KORUN **Weight:** 13.0000 g. **Composition:** 0.9000 Silver .3761 oz. ASW **Subject:** Millennium - St. Adalbert's Death **Obverse:** Unbordered arms **Reverse:** Bishop's portrait **Size:** 31 mm.

Date	Mintage	F	VF	XF	Unc	BU
ND(1997)	23,000	—	—	—	14.00	16.00

Note: Milled edge

Date	Mintage	Value
ND(1997) Proof	3,000	Value: 32.00

Note: Plain edge with CESKA NARODNI BANKA *0.900*

KM# 31 200 KORUN **Weight:** 13.0000 g. **Composition:** 0.9000 Silver .3761 oz. ASW **Subject:** 200th Aniversary - Birth of Frantisek Palacky **Obverse:** National arms **Reverse:** Head of Palacky left **Size:** 31 mm.

Date	Mintage	F	VF	XF	Unc	BU
ND(1998)	20,000	—	—	—	14.00	16.00

Note: Milled edge

Date	Mintage	Value
ND(1998) Proof	2,500	Value: 30.00

Note: Plain edge with CESKA NARODNI BANKA *0.900*

KM# 35 200 KORUN **Weight:** 13.0000 g. **Composition:** 0.9000 Silver .3761 oz. ASW **Subject:** 200 Years - Prague Fine Arts Academy **Obverse:** Stylized national arms **Reverse:** Stylized design **Edge:** Reeded **Size:** 31 mm.

Date	Mintage	F	VF	XF	Unc	BU
ND(1999)	20,000	—	—	—	14.00	16.00

Note: Milled edge

Date	Mintage	Value
ND(1999) Proof	3,000	Value: 28.00

Note: Plain edge with CESKA NARODNI BANKA *0.900*

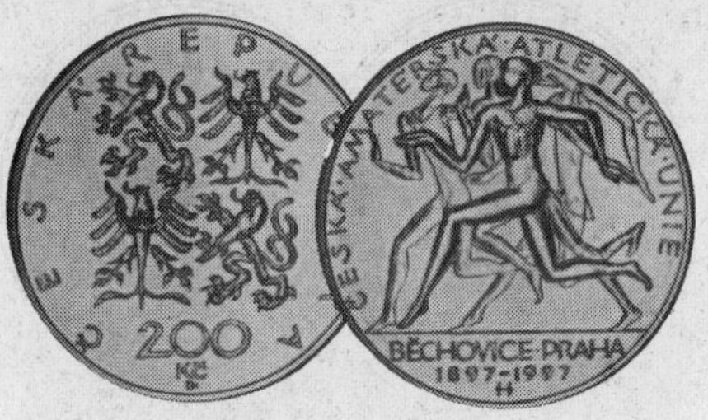

KM# 28 200 KORUN **Weight:** 13.0000 g. **Composition:** 0.9000 Silver .3761 oz. ASW **Subject:** Czech Amateur Athletic Union **Obverse:** Unbordered arms **Reverse:** Runners **Size:** 31 mm.

Date	Mintage	F	VF	XF	Unc	BU
ND(1997)	23,000	—	—	—	14.00	16.00
ND(1997) Proof	3,000	Value: 35.00				

KM# 32 200 KORUN **Weight:** 13.0000 g. **Composition:** 0.9000 Silver .3761 oz. ASW **Subject:** 800th Anniversary - Coronation of King Premysl I. Otakar **Obverse:** National arms **Reverse:** Half facing head of the king at right, coin design at left **Size:** 31 mm.

Date	Mintage	F	VF	XF	Unc	BU
ND(1998)(m)	20,000	—	—	—	14.00	16.00

Note: Milled edge

Date	Mintage	Value
ND(1998) Proof	3,000	Value: 30.00

Note: Plain edge with CESKA NARODNI BANKA *0.900*

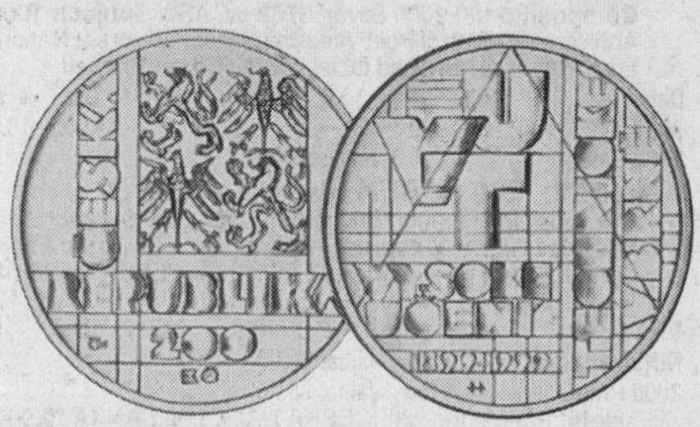

KM# 36 200 KORUN **Weight:** 13.0000 g. **Composition:** 0.9000 Silver .3761 oz. ASW **Subject:** 100 Years - Brno University of Technology **Obverse:** Undivided national arms **Reverse:** Stylized design **Size:** 31 mm.

Date	Mintage	F	VF	XF	Unc	BU
ND(1999)	20,000	—	—	—	14.00	16.00

Note: Milled edge

Date	Mintage	Value
ND(1999) Proof	3,200	Value: 28.00

Note: Plain edge with CESKA NARODNI BANKA *0.900*

KM# 29 200 KORUN **Weight:** 13.0000 g. **Composition:** 0.9000 Silver .3761 oz. ASW **Subject:** 650th Anniversary - Na Slovanech-Emauzy Monastery **Obverse:** National arms **Reverse:** Seated saintly figure **Size:** 31 mm.

Date	Mintage	F	VF	XF	Unc	BU
ND(1997)	22,500	—	—	—	14.00	16.00

Note: Milled edge

Date	Mintage	Value
ND(1997) Proof	3,000	Value: 32.00

Note: Plain edge with CESKA NARODNI BANKA *0.900*

KM# 33 200 KORUN **Weight:** 13.0000 g. **Composition:** 0.9000 Silver .3761 oz. ASW **Subject:** 200th Anniversary - Birth of Frantisek Kmoch **Obverse:** National arms **Reverse:** Head of Kmoch facing left, dates **Size:** 31 mm.

Date	Mintage	F	VF	XF	Unc	BU
ND(1998)(m)	20,000	—	—	—	11.50	13.50

Note: Milled edge

Date	Mintage	Value
ND(1998)(m)	3,000	Value: 28.00

Note: Plain edge with CESKA NARODNI BANKA *0.900*

KM# 37 200 KORUN **Weight:** 13.0000 g. **Composition:** 0.9000 Silver .3761 oz. ASW **Subject:** 100th Birthday - Ondrej Sekora **Obverse:** National arms **Reverse:** Ant holding flowers **Size:** 31 mm.

Date	Mintage	F	VF	XF	Unc	BU
ND(1999)	20,000	—	—	—	14.00	16.00

Note: Milled edge

Date	Mintage	Value
ND(1999) Proof	3,200	Value: 28.00

Note: Plain edge with CESKA NARODNI BANKA *0.900*

KM# 46.1 (KM46) 200 KORUN **Weight:** 13.0000 g. **Composition:** 0.9000 Silver .3762 oz. ASW **Subject:** 700th Anniversary - Prague Groschen - Currency Reform **Obverse:** National arms above coin design **Reverse:** Seated king between two coin designs **Edge:** Reeded **Size:** 31 mm.

Date	Mintage	F	VF	XF	Unc	BU
2000	20,000	—	—	—	14.00	16.00
2000 Proof	3,500	Value: 28.00				

KM# 46.2 200 KORUN **Weight:** 13.0000 g. **Composition:** 0.9000 Silver .3762 oz. ASW **Subject:** 700th Anniversary - Prague Groschen **Obverse:** National arms above coin design **Reverse:** Seated king between two coin designs **Edge Lettering:** "CESKA NARODNI BANK" **Size:** 31 mm.

Date	Mintage	F	VF	XF	Unc	BU
ND(2000) Proof	3,500	Value: 30.00				
2000 Proof	—	—	—	—	25.00	—

Note: Plain edge with CESKA NARODNI BANKA *0.900*

KM# 47.1 (KM47) 200 KORUN **Weight:** 13.0000 g. **Composition:** 0.9000 Silver .3762 oz. ASW **Subject:** 100th Anniversary - Birth of Poet Vitezslav Nezval **Obverse:** National arms **Reverse:** Stylized facial portrait **Edge:** Reeded

Date	Mintage	F	VF	XF	Unc	BU
2000	20,000	—	—	—	14.00	16.00
2000 Proof	3,200	Value: 28.00				

KM# 47.2 200 KORUN **Weight:** 13.0000 g. **Composition:** 0.9000 Silver .3762 oz. ASW **Subject:** Vitezslav Nezval **Obverse:** National arms **Reverse:** Facial portrait **Edge:** Reeded **Edge Lettering:** "CESKA NARODNI BANK" **Size:** 31 mm.

Date	Mintage	F	VF	XF	Unc	BU
ND(2000) Proof	3,500	Value: 30.00				
2000 Proof	3,200	Value: 25.00				

Note: Plain edge with CESKA NARODNI BANKA *0.900*

KM# 48 200 KORUN **Weight:** 13.0000 g. **Composition:** 0.9000 Silver .3762 oz. ASW **Subject:** 150th Anniversary - Birth of Zdenek Fibich, Musical Composer **Obverse:** National arms **Reverse:** Portrait **Size:** 31 mm.

Date	Mintage	F	VF	XF	Unc	BU
2000	17,000	—	—	—	14.00	16.00

Note: Milled edge

Date	Mintage	F	VF	XF	Unc	BU
2000 Proof	3,200	Value: 28.00				

Note: Plain edge with CESKA NARODNI BANKA *0.900*

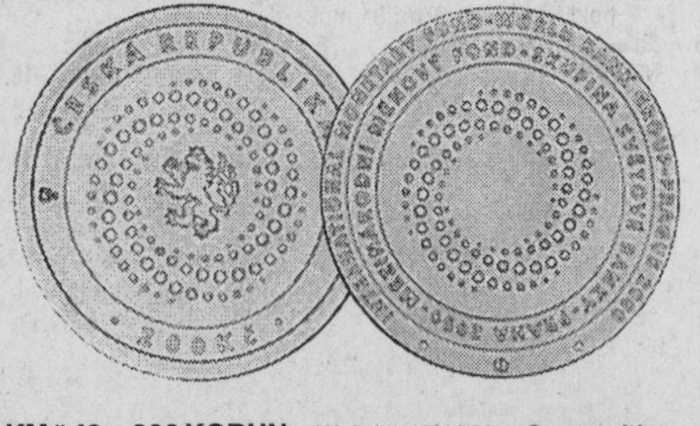

KM# 49 200 KORUN **Weight:** 13.0000 g. **Composition:** 0.9000 Silver .3762 oz. ASW **Subject:** International Monetary Fund and Prague World Bank Group **Obverse:** Crowned lion in swirling dots **Reverse:** Circle of swirling dots **Size:** 31 mm.

Date	Mintage	F	VF	XF	Unc	BU
2000	18,000	—	—	—	14.00	16.00

Note: Milled edge

Date	Mintage	F	VF	XF	Unc	BU
2000 Proof	5,000	Value: 28.00				

Note: Plain edge with CESKA NARODNI BANKA *0.900*

KM# 50 200 KORUN **Weight:** 13.0000 g. **Composition:** 0.9000 Silver .3762 oz. ASW **Subject:** New Millennium **Obverse:** National arms **Reverse:** Stylized phoenix design **Size:** 31 mm.

Date	Mintage	F	VF	XF	Unc	BU
2000	17,000	—	—	—	14.00	16.00

Note: Milled edge

Date	Mintage	F	VF	XF	Unc	BU
2000 Proof	3,500	Value: 28.00				

Note: Plain edge with CESKA NARODNI BANKA *0.900*

KM# 58 200 KORUN **Weight:** 13.0000 g. **Composition:** 0.9000 Silver 0.3762 oz. ASW **Subject:** Frantisek Skroup **Obverse:** National arms **Reverse:** Portrait and name **Size:** 31 mm.

Date	F	VF	XF	Unc	BU
ND(2001)	—	—	—	15.00	—

Note: Milled edge

Date	F	VF	XF	Unc	BU
ND(2001) Proof	—	—	—	—	—

Note: Plain edge with CESKA NARODNI BANKA *0.900*

KM# 51 200 KORUN **Weight:** 13.0000 g. **Composition:** 0.9000 Silver 0.3762 oz. ASW **Subject:** Jaroslav Seifert **Obverse:** National arms **Reverse:** Head of Jaroslav Seifert right **Size:** 31 mm.

Date	F	VF	XF	Unc	BU
ND(2001)	—	—	—	15.00	—

Note: Milled edge

Date	F	VF	XF	Unc	BU
ND(2001) Proof	—	—	—	—	—

Note: Plain edge with CESKA NARODNI BANKA *0.900*

KM# 52 200 KORUN **Weight:** 13.0000 g. **Composition:** 0.9000 Silver 0.3762 oz. ASW **Subject:** Soccer **Obverse:** National arms **Reverse:** Rampant lion on soccer ball **Size:** 31 mm.

Date	F	VF	XF	Unc	BU
ND(2001) Proof	—	—	—	—	—

Note: Plain edge with CESKA NARODNI BANKA *0.900*

KM# 53 200 KORUN **Weight:** 13.0000 g. **Composition:** 0.9000 Silver 0.3762 oz. ASW **Subject:** Kilian Ignac Dientzenhofer **Obverse:** National arms. **Reverse:** Doorway and caliper. **Edge:** Reeded. **Size:** 31 mm.

Date	F	VF	XF	Unc	BU
ND(2001)	—	—	—	15.00	—
ND(2001) Proof	—	—	—	—	—

KM# 54 200 KORUN **Weight:** 13.0000 g. **Composition:** 0.9000 Silver 0.3762 oz. ASW **Subject:** Euro Currency System **Obverse:** National arms **Reverse:** Prague gros coin design **Size:** 31 mm.

Date	F	VF	XF	Unc	BU
ND(2001)	—	—	—	15.00	—

Note: Milled edge

Date	F	VF	XF	Unc	BU
ND(2001) Proof	—	—	—	—	—

Note: Plain edge with CESKA NARODNI BANKA *0.900*

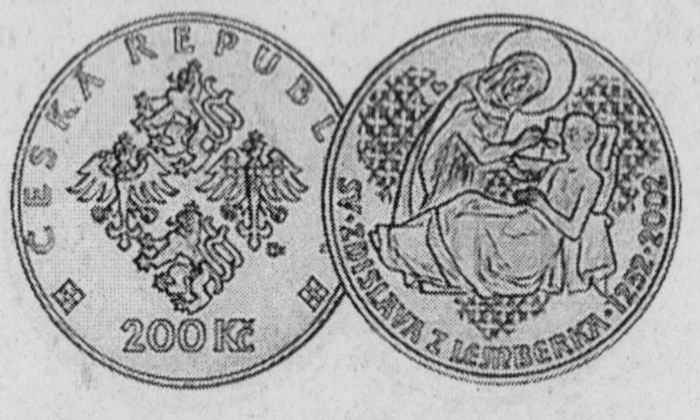

KM# 55 200 KORUN **Weight:** 13.0000 g. **Composition:** 0.9000 Silver 0.3762 oz. ASW **Subject:** St. Zdislava **Obverse:** National arms **Reverse:** Saint feeding sick person **Size:** 31 mm.

Date	F	VF	XF	Unc	BU
ND(2002)	—	—	—	15.00	—

Note: Milled edge

Date	F	VF	XF	Unc	BU
ND(2002) Proof	—	—	—	—	—

Note: Plain edge with CESKA NARODNI BANKA *0.900*

KM# 56 200 KORUN **Weight:** 13.0000 g. **Composition:** 0.9000 Silver 0.3762 oz. ASW **Subject:** Emil Holub **Obverse:** National arms **Reverse:** Traveller and African dancers **Size:** 30.9 mm.

Date	F	VF	XF	Unc	BU
ND(2002)	—	—	—	15.00	—

Note: Milled edge

Date	F	VF	XF	Unc	BU
ND(2002) Proof	—	—	—	—	—

Note: Plain edge with CESKA NARODNI BANKA *0.900*

Date	F	VF	XF	Unc	BU
ND(2002)	—	—	—	15.00	—
Note: Milled edge					
ND(2002) Proof	—	—	—	—	—
Note: Plain edge with CESKA NARODNI BANKA *0.900*					

KM# 57 200 KORUN **Weight:** 13.0000 g. **Composition:** 0.9000 Silver 0.3762 oz. ASW **Subject:** George of Podebrad **Obverse:** Overlapped arms **Reverse:** Head of Podebrad **Edge:** Reeded **Size:** 30.9 mm.

Date	F	VF	XF	Unc	BU
ND(2002)	—	—	—	15.00	—

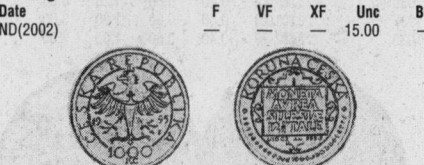

KM# 18 1000 KORUN **Weight:** 3.1103 g. **Composition:** 0.9999 Gold .1000 oz. AGW **Subject:** Historic Coins **Size:** 16 mm. **Note:** Tolar of Silesian Estates 12-1/2 tolar 1620.

Date	Mintage	F	VF	XF	Unc	BU
1995	2,000	—	—	—	90.00	100
1996	3,256	—	—	—	90.00	100
1996 Proof	744	Value: 145				
1997 Proof	2,250	Value: 120				

KM# 38 1000 KORUN **Weight:** 3.1103 g. **Composition:** 0.9999 Gold .1000 oz. AGW **Size:** 16 mm. **Note:** Karlstejn Castle.

Date	Mintage	F	VF	XF	Unc	BU
1998	2,300	—	—	—	65.00	75.00
Note: Milled edge						
1998 Proof	2,210	Value: 80.00				
Note: Plain edge						
1999 Proof	2,000	Value: 80.00				

KM# 44 2000 KORUN **Weight:** 34214.0000 g. **Composition:** 0.9990 Silver .9990 oz. ASW **Subject:** Millennium **Obverse:** National arm hologram on gold inlay **Reverse:** Stylized 2000 **Edge Lettering:** *CNB* Ag 0.999* 31.103 g *CNB* AU 999.9 *3. 111 g* **Size:** 40 mm. **Note:** With a 3.1110 gram, .999 gold, .0999 ounce actual gold weight gold inlay.

Date	Mintage	F	VF	XF	Unc	BU
ND(1999)(m)	17,000	—	—	—	75.00	85.00
ND(1999)(m)	3,000	Value: 150				

KM# 19 2500 KORUN **Weight:** 7.7759 g. **Composition:** 0.9999 Gold .2500 oz. AGW **Subject:** Historic Coins - 1620 Tolar of Moravian Estates **Size:** 22 mm.

Date	Mintage	F	VF	XF	Unc	BU
1995	2,000	—	—	—	235	250
1996	1,256	—	—	—	235	250
1996 Proof	744	Value: 300				
1997 Proof	3,000	Value: 265				

KM# 39 2500 KORUN **Weight:** 7.7759 g. **Composition:** 0.9999 Gold .2500 oz. AGW **Reverse:** Seal of Karel IV with legal document **Size:** 22 mm.

Date	Mintage	F	VF	XF	Unc	BU
1998	2,000	—	—	—	155	165
Note: Milled edge						
1998 Proof	2,000	Value: 200				
Note: Plain edge						
1999 Proof	1,500	Value: 170				
Note: Plain edge						

KM# 20 5000 KORUN **Weight:** 15.5517 g. **Composition:** 0.9999 Gold .5000 oz. AGW **Subject:** Historic Coins **Reverse:** Bohemian Maley Gros of 1587 **Size:** 28 mm.

Date	Mintage	F	VF	XF	Unc	BU
1995	1,000	—	—	—	540	560
1996	1,256	—	—	—	540	560
1996 Proof	744	Value: 625				
1997 Proof	1,500	Value: 575				

KM# 40 5000 KORUN **Weight:** 15.5530 g. **Composition:** 0.9999 Gold .5000 oz. AGW **Reverse:** Karel IV, Charles University founder **Size:** 28 mm.

Date	Mintage	F	VF	XF	Unc	BU
1998	2,000	—	—	—	285	300
Note: Milled edge						
1998 Proof	2,000	Value: 350				
Note: Edge: CESKA NARODNI BANKA 18.553 g.						
1999 Proof	1,500	Value: 285				
Note: Edge: CESKA NARODNI BANKA 18.553 g.						

KM# 21 10000 KORUN **Weight:** 31.1035 g. **Composition:** 0.9999 Gold 1.0000 oz. AGW **Subject:** Historic Coins **Reverse:** Lion holding Prague Groschen **Size:** 34 mm.

Date	Mintage	F	VF	XF	Unc	BU
1995	1,000	—	—	—	945	965
1996	1,256	—	—	—	945	965
1996 Proof	744	Value: 1,100				
1997 Proof	1,500	Value: 1,000				

KM# 41 10000 KORUN **Weight:** 31.1070 g. **Composition:** 0.9999 Gold 1.0000 oz. AGW **Reverse:** Karel IV and seals of Nove Mesto **Size:** 34 mm.

Date	Mintage	F	VF	XF	Unc	BU
1998	2,000	—	—	—	550	575
Note: Milled edge						
1998 Proof	2,000	Value: 650				
Note: Edge: CESKA NARODNI BANKA 31.107 g.						
1999 Proof	1,300	Value: 550				
Note: Edge: CESKA NARODNI BANKA 31.107 g.						

MINT SETS

KM#	Date	Mintage	Identification	Issue Price	Mkt Val
MS1	1993 (9)	20,000	KM1, 2.1, 3-9	—	14.00
MS3	1995 (9)	21,000	KM1, 2.1, 3-9	—	14.00
MS4	1996 (9)	14,000	KM1, 2.1, 3-9	—	14.00
MS5	1996 (9)	11,000	KM1, 2.1, 3-9 w/EURO 96 medal	—	15.50
MS6	1997 (9)	15,000	KM1, 2.1, 3-9	—	14.00
MS7	1998 (9)	5,000	KM1, 2.3, 3-9, Olympic Hockey Folder	—	14.00
MS10	1999 (9)	2,500	KM1, 2.3, 3-9, Childrens Motif Folder	—	14.00
MS8	1999 (9)	5,000	KM1, 2.3, 3-9, Parler Folder	—	14.00
MS9	1999 (9)	2,500	KM1, 2.3, 3-9, Nato Folder	—	14.00
MS11	2001 (9)	6,000	KM#1, 2.3, 3-9	—	14.00

PROOF SETS

KM#	Date	Mintage	Identification	Issue Price	Mkt Val
PS1	1994 (3)	2,000	KM2.1, 3, 6	—	—
PS2	1997 (9)	1,500	KM1, 2.1, 3-9, plus silver medal	35.00	300
PS3	1998 (9)	2,500	KM1, 2.3, 3-9, plus silver medal	35.00	60.00
PS4	1999 (9)	2,000	KM1, 2.3, 3-9, plus silver medal	35.00	60.00
PS5	2001 (9)	2,500	KM#1, 2.3, 3-9	35.00	50.00

CZECHOSLOVAKIA

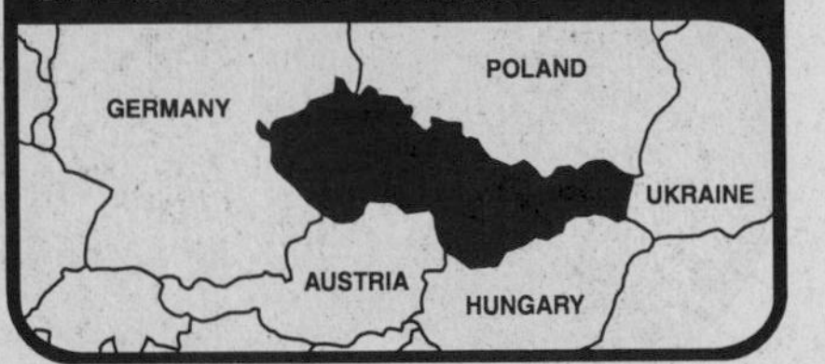

The Republic of Czechoslovakia, founded at the end of World War I, was part of the old Austrian-Hungarian Empire. It had an area of 49,371 sq. mi. (127,870 sq. km.) and a population of 15.6 million. Capital: Prague (Praha).

Czechoslovakia proclaimed itself a republic on Oct. 28, 1918, with Tomas G. Masaryk as President. Hitler's rise to power in Germany provoked Czechoslovakia's German minority in the Sudetenland to agitate for autonomy. At Munich (Munchen) in Sept. of 1938, France and Britain, seeking to avoid World War II, forced the cession of the Sudetenland to Germany. In March, 1939, Germany invaded Czechoslovakia and established the "protectorate of Bohemia and Moravia". Bohemia is a historic province in northwest Czechoslovakia that includes the city of Prague, one of the oldest continually occupied sites in Europe. Moravia is an area of considerable mineral wealth in central Czechoslovakia. Slovakia, a province in southeastern Czechoslovakia under Nazi influence was constituted as a republic. The end of World War II saw the re-established independence of Czechoslovakia, while bringing it within the Russian sphere of influence. On Feb. 23-25, 1948, the Communists seized control of the government in a coup d'etat, and adopted a constitution making the country a 'people's republic'. A new constitution adopted June 11, 1960, converted the country into a 'socialist republic', which lasted until 1989. On Nov. 11, 1989, demonstrations against the communist government began and in Dec. of that same year, communism was overthrown, and the Czech and Slovak Federal Republic was formed. In 1993 the CSFR split into the Czech Republic and The Republic of Slovakia.

NOTE: For additional listings see Bohemia and Moravia, Czech Republic and Slovakia.

MINT MARKS

(k) - Kremnica

(l) - Leningrad

MONETARY SYSTEM

100 Haleru = 1 Koruna

REPUBLIC

DECIMAL COINAGE

KM# 5 2 HALERE **Weight:** 2.0000 g. **Composition:** Zinc **Obverse:** State emblem: Czech lion with Slovak shield **Reverse:** Bridge of Karel in Praha, value below **Edge:** Plain **Size:** 17 mm.

Date	Mintage	F	VF	XF	Unc	BU
1923	2,700,000	3.00	5.00	10.00	16.00	—
1924	17,300,000	2.25	3.50	5.00	9.00	—
1925	2,000,000	3.00	5.00	7.50	17.00	—

KM# 6 5 HALERU **Weight:** 1.6600 g. **Composition:** Bronze **Obverse:** State emblem: Czech lion with Slovak shield **Reverse:** Karels Bridge in Praha, value below **Edge:** Plain **Size:** 16 mm.

Date	Mintage	F	VF	XF	Unc	BU
1923	37,800,000	0.20	0.30	0.50	2.00	—
1924	10	—	—	—	1,500	—
Note: There are two varieteis of the number 4 in 1924 dated coins: with and without seraphs						
1925	12,000,000	0.20	0.30	0.50	2.50	—
1926	1,084,000	1.50	4.00	9.00	20.00	—
1927	8,916,000	0.25	0.35	0.75	2.50	—
1928	5,320,000	0.30	0.45	0.75	2.50	—
1929	12,680,000	0.25	0.35	0.75	2.50	—
1930	5,000,000	0.35	1.25	3.00	10.00	—
1931	7,448,000	0.25	0.35	0.75	2.50	—
1932	3,556,000	0.65	1.50	3.00	9.00	—
1938	14,244,000	0.25	0.35	0.75	2.00	—

KM# 3 10 HALERU **Composition:** Bronze **Reverse:** Karels Bridge of Praha, value below **Edge:** Plain **Size:** 18 mm.

Date	Mintage	F	VF	XF	Unc	BU
1922	6,000,000	0.30	0.45	1.00	2.75	—
1923	24,000,000	0.25	0.35	0.75	2.00	—
1924	5,320,000	0.30	0.45	1.00	3.00	—
1925	24,680,000	0.25	0.35	0.60	2.25	—
1926	10,000,000	0.25	0.35	0.75	2.25	—
1927	10,000,000	0.25	0.35	0.75	2.25	—
1928	14,290,000	0.25	0.35	0.75	2.25	—
1929	5,710,000	1.25	2.50	5.50	10.00	—
1930	6,980,000	0.30	0.45	1.00	2.50	—
1931	6,740,000	0.30	0.45	1.00	2.50	—
1932	11,280,000	0.25	0.35	0.75	2.00	—
1933	4,190,000	0.35	0.60	1.25	5.00	—
1934	13,200,000	0.25	0.35	0.75	2.00	—
1935	3,420,000	0.50	0.75	1.50	5.00	—
1936	8,560,000	0.25	0.35	0.75	2.00	—
1937	20,200,000	0.25	0.35	0.75	2.00	—
1938	21,400,000	0.25	0.35	0.75	2.00	—

KM# 1 20 HALERU **Weight:** 3.3300 g. **Composition:** Copper-Nickel **Obverse:** State emblem: Czech lion with Slovak shield, date **Reverse:** Sheaf with sickle, lime spring **Edge:** Plain **Size:** 20 mm.

Date	Mintage	F	VF	XF	Unc	BU
1921	40,000,000	0.25	0.35	0.60	2.50	—
1922	9,100,000	0.25	0.35	0.60	2.50	—
1924	20,931,000	0.25	0.35	0.60	2.50	—
1925	4,244,000	0.60	1.00	2.00	6.00	—
1926	14,825,000	0.25	0.35	0.60	2.50	—
1927	11,757,000	0.25	0.35	0.60	2.50	—
1928	14,018,000	0.25	0.35	0.60	2.50	—
1929	4,225,000	0.30	0.50	1.25	3.50	—
1930	—	0.30	0.40	0.75	3.00	—
1931	5,000,000	0.30	0.40	0.75	3.00	—
1933	Inc. above	9.00	18.00	35.00	75.00	—
1937	8,208,000	0.25	0.35	0.60	2.50	—
1938	18,787,000	0.25	0.35	0.60	2.50	—

KM# 16 25 HALERU **Weight:** 4.0000 g. **Composition:** Copper-Nickel **Obverse:** State emblem: Czech lion with Slovak shield **Reverse:** 25 **Edge:** Milled **Size:** 21 mm.

Date	Mintage	F	VF	XF	Unc	BU
1932	—	—	1,250	2,250	3,000	—
1933	22,711,000	0.50	1.00	2.00	4.00	—

KM# 2 50 HALERU **Weight:** 5.0000 g. **Composition:** Copper-Nickel **Obverse:** State emblem: Czech lion with Slovak shield, date **Reverse:** Lime springs and ears, value **Edge:** Milled **Size:** 22 mm.

Date	Mintage	F	VF	XF	Unc	BU
1921	3,000,000	0.25	0.50	1.00	3.00	—
1922	37,000,000	0.20	0.40	0.60	2.50	—
1924	10,000,000	0.20	0.40	0.60	3.00	—
1925	1,415,000	0.50	1.00	2.50	10.00	—
1926	1,585,000	3.50	9.00	20.00	45.00	—
1927	2,000,000	0.50	1.00	2.00	9.00	—
1931	6,000,000	0.25	0.50	1.00	2.50	—

KM# 4 KORUNA **Weight:** 6.6600 g. **Composition:** Copper-Nickel **Obverse:** State emblem: Czech lion with Slovak shield, date **Reverse:** Woman with sheaf and sickle **Edge:** Milled **Size:** 25 mm.

Date	Mintage	F	VF	XF	Unc	BU
1922	50,000,000	0.30	0.50	0.75	2.00	—
1923	15,385,000	0.30	0.50	0.75	2.00	—
1924	21,041,000	0.30	0.50	0.75	2.00	—
1925	8,574,000	0.40	0.60	1.25	4.00	—
1929	5,000,000	0.50	0.75	1.25	3.50	—
1930	5,000,000	0.40	0.60	1.25	5.00	—
1937	3,806,000	0.40	0.60	1.00	3.00	—
1938	8,582,000	0.40	0.60	1.00	3.00	—

KM# 10 5 KORUN **Weight:** 10.0000 g. **Composition:** Copper-Nickel **Obverse:** State emblem: Czech lion with Slovak shield **Reverse:** Industrial factory and large value **Size:** 30 mm.

Date	Mintage	F	VF	XF	Unc	BU
1925	16,474,500	1.50	2.50	3.50	9.00	—
1926	8,912,000	1.75	2.75	4.00	10.00	—
1927	4,613,500	2.50	10.00	35.00	60.00	—

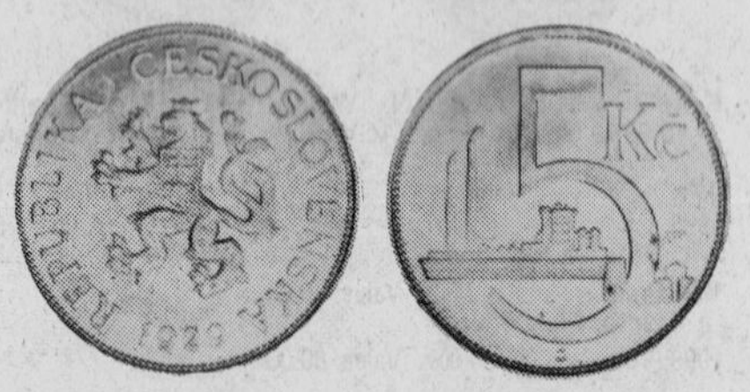

KM# 11 5 KORUN **Weight:** 7.0000 g. **Composition:** 0.5000 Silver .125 oz. ASW **Obverse:** Czech lion with Slovak shield **Reverse:** Industrial factory and large value **Edge:** Plain with crosses and waves **Size:** 27 mm.

Date	Mintage	F	VF	XF	Unc	BU
1928	1,710,000	2.00	3.00	5.00	10.00	—
Note: Edge varieties exist for 1928						
1929	12,861,000	1.00	2.00	4.00	8.50	—
1930	10,429,000	1.00	2.00	4.00	8.50	—
1931	2,000,000	3.00	5.00	8.00	32.00	—
1932	1,000,000	5.00	7.50	10.00	35.00	—

KM# 11a 5 KORUN **Weight:** 8.0000 g. **Composition:** Nickel **Obverse:** Czech lion with Slovak shield **Reverse:** Industrial factory and large value **Size:** 27 mm.

Date	Mintage	F	VF	XF	Unc	BU
1937	36,000	150	350	675	1,400	—
1938	17,200,000	1.25	2.50	4.00	6.50	—

KM# 12 10 KORUN **Weight:** 10.0000 g. **Composition:** 0.7000 Silver .2250 oz. ASW **Subject:** 10th Anniversary of

Independence **Obverse:** Value above state shield, date **Reverse:** President Tomas G. Masaryk bust right **Edge:** Milled **Size:** 30 mm.

Date	Mintage	F	VF	XF	Unc	BU
ND(1928)	1,000,000	2.50	4.50	6.50	11.00	—

KM# 15 10 KORUN Weight: 10.0000 g. **Composition:** 0.7000 Silver .2250 oz. ASW **Obverse:** State emblem, date **Reverse:** Republic, lime tree, value, artist Jaroslav Horejc **Edge:** Milled **Size:** 30 mm.

Date	Mintage	F	VF	XF	Unc	BU
1930	4,949,000	2.50	4.00	7.00	11.50	—
1931	6,689,000	2.50	3.75	6.00	10.00	—
1932	11,447,500	2.00	3.50	5.00	9.00	—
1933	915,000	25.00	135	275	450	—

KM# 17 20 KORUN Weight: 12.0000 g. **Composition:** 0.7000 Silver .2700 oz. ASW **Obverse:** State emblem, date **Reverse:** Three figures: Industry, Agriculture, Business; value, artist Jaroslav Horejc **Edge:** Plain with crosses and waves **Size:** 34 mm.

Date	Mintage	F	VF	XF	Unc	BU
1933	2,280,000	—	4.00	7.50	14.00	—
1934	3,280,000	—	4.00	7.50	14.00	—

KM# 18 20 KORUN Weight: 12.0000 g. **Composition:** 0.7000 Silver .2700 oz. ASW **Subject:** Death of President Masaryk **Obverse:** Value, state emblem **Obv. Designer:** J. Horejc **Reverse:** President Tomas G. Masaryk bust right **Rev. Designer:** O. Spaniel **Edge:** Plain with crosses and waves **Size:** 34 mm.

Date	Mintage	F	VF	XF	Unc	BU
ND(1937)	1,000,000	—	3.50	6.50	11.00	—

TRADE COINAGE

KM# 7 DUKAT Weight: 3.4900 g. **Composition:** 0.9860 Gold .1106 oz. AGW **Subject:** 5th Anniversary of the Republic **Obverse:** Shield with Czech lion and Slovak shield **Obv. Designer:** J. Benda **Reverse:** Duke Wenceslas (Vaclav) half-length figure facing **Rev. Designer:** O. Spaniel **Edge:** Milled

Date	Mintage	F	VF	XF	Unc	BU
1923	1,000	—	450	1,250	2,250	—

Note: The above coins are serially numbered below the duke

KM# 8 DUKAT Weight: 3.4900 g. **Composition:** 0.9860 Gold .1106 oz. AGW **Obverse:** Shield with Czech lion and Slovak shield **Obv. Designer:** J. Benda **Reverse:** Duke Wenceslas (Vaclav) half-length figure facing **Rev. Designer:** O. Spaniel **Edge:** Milled **Note:** Similar to KM#7 but w/o serial numbers.

Date	Mintage	F	VF	XF	Unc	BU
1923	61,861	—	55.00	75.00	125	—
1924	32,814	—	55.00	75.00	125	—
1925	66,279	—	55.00	75.00	125	—
1926	58,669	—	55.00	75.00	125	—
1927	25,774	—	55.00	75.00	125	—
1928	18,983	—	55.00	75.00	135	—

Date	Mintage	F	VF	XF	Unc	BU
1929	10,253	—	60.00	80.00	165	—
1930	11,338	—	60.00	80.00	165	—
1931	43,482	—	55.00	75.00	125	—
1932	26,617	—	55.00	75.00	125	—
1933	57,597	—	55.00	75.00	125	—
1934	9,729	—	80.00	100	175	—
1935	13,178	—	55.00	75.00	135	—
1936	14,566	—	55.00	75.00	135	—
1937	324	—	275	650	1,000	—
1938	56	—	800	1,750	3,500	—
1939	276	—	400	1,250	2,000	—

Note: Czech reports show mintage of 20 for Czechoslovakia and 256 for state of Slovakia

Date	Mintage	F	VF	XF	Unc	BU
1951	500	—	325	725	1,500	—

KM# 9 2 DUKATY Weight: 6.9800 g. **Composition:** 0.9860 Gold .2212 oz. AGW **Obverse:** Shield with Czech lion and Slovak shield **Obv. Designer:** J. Benda **Reverse:** Duke Wenceslas (Vaclav) half-length figure facing **Rev. Designer:** O. Spaniel **Edge:** Milled **Size:** 25 mm.

Date	Mintage	F	VF	XF	Unc	BU
1923	4,000	—	150	225	350	—
1929	3,262	—	150	225	350	—
1930	Inc. above	—	150	250	400	—
1931	2,994	—	150	225	350	—
1932	5,496	—	150	225	350	—
1933	4,671	—	150	225	350	—
1934	2,403	—	150	225	350	—
1935	2,577	—	150	225	350	—
1936	819	—	300	400	750	—
1937	8	—	2,000	3,500	6,500	—
1938	186	—	600	1,650	2,250	—

Note: Czech reports show mintage of 14 for Czechoslovakia and 172 for state of Slovakia

Date	Mintage	F	VF	XF	Unc	BU
1951	200	—	500	1,500	2,250	—

KM# 13 5 DUKATU Weight: 17.4500 g. **Composition:** 0.9860 Gold .5532 oz. AGW **Obverse:** Value, state emblem, date **Obv. Designer:** J. Benda **Reverse:** Duke Wenceslas (Vaclav) on horseback right **Rev. Designer:** O. Spaniel **Edge:** Milled **Size:** 34 mm.

Date	Mintage	F	VF	XF	Unc	BU
1929	1,827	—	350	450	725	—
1930	543	—	500	700	1,250	—
1931	1,528	—	350	450	725	—
1932	1,827	—	350	450	725	—
1933	1,752	—	350	450	725	—
1934	1,101	—	350	450	725	—
1935	1,037	—	350	450	725	—
1936	728	—	500	850	1,200	—
1937	4	—	—	—	9,500	—
1938	56	—	1,500	3,500	5,000	—

Note: Czech reports show mintage of 12 for Czechoslovakia and 44 for state of Slovakia

Date	Mintage	F	VF	XF	Unc	BU
1951	100	—	1,200	2,250	4,500	—

KM# 14 10 DUKATU Weight: 34.9000 g. **Composition:** 0.9860 Gold 1.1064 oz. AGW **Obverse:** State emblem, value, date **Obv. Designer:** J. Benda **Reverse:** Duke Wenceslas (Vaclav) on horseback right **Rev. Designer:** O. Spaniel **Size:** 42 mm.

Date	Mintage	F	VF	XF	Unc	BU
1929	1,564	—	700	1,100	1,650	—
1930	394	—	1,000	1,900	3,000	—
1931	1,239	—	700	1,100	1,750	—
1932	1,035	—	700	1,100	1,750	—
1933	1,780	—	700	1,100	1,750	—
1934	1,298	—	700	1,100	1,750	—
1935	600	—	750	1,350	2,100	—
1936	633	—	750	1,350	2,100	—
1937	34	—	—	—	12,000	—
1938	192	—	2,000	2,800	5,000	—
1951	100	—	2,500	4,500	9,000	—

Note: Czech reports show mintage of 20 for Czechoslovakia and 172 for state of Slovakia.

POST WAR COINAGE

KM# 20 20 HALERU Composition: Bronze **Obverse:** State emblem: Czech lion with Slovak shield, date **Reverse:** Sheaf with sickle, lime spring **Edge:** Plain **Size:** 18 mm.

Date	Mintage	F	VF	XF	Unc	BU
1947	—	65.00	125	200	300	—
1948	24,340,000	0.10	0.15	0.40	1.50	—
1949	25,660,000	0.10	0.15	0.40	1.50	—
1950	11,132,000	0.10	0.15	0.40	2.00	—

KM# 31 20 HALERU Composition: Aluminum **Obverse:** Czech lion with Slovak shield **Reverse:** Wheat ears, sickle, linden branch **Edge:** Plain **Size:** 16 mm.

Date	Mintage	F	VF	XF	Unc	BU
1951	46,800,000	0.10	0.15	0.25	1.00	—
1952	80,340,000	0.10	0.15	0.25	1.00	—

KM# 21 50 HALERU Composition: Bronze **Obverse:** Czech lion with Slovak shield **Reverse:** Value above linden branch and wheat wreath **Edge:** Plain **Size:** 20 mm.

Date	Mintage	F	VF	XF	Unc	BU
1947	50,000,000	0.15	0.25	0.40	1.50	—
1948	20,000,000	0.15	0.25	0.40	1.50	—
1949	12,715,000	0.15	0.25	0.40	2.00	—
1950	17,415,000	0.15	0.25	0.40	1.80	—

KM# 32 50 HALERU Composition: Aluminum **Obverse:** Czech lion with Slovak shield **Reverse:** Value above linden branch and wheat wreath **Edge:** Plain **Size:** 18 mm.

Date	Mintage	F	VF	XF	Unc	BU
1951	60,000,000	0.15	0.35	0.50	0.75	—
1952	60,000,000	0.25	0.45	0.60	1.00	—
1953	34,920,000	1.00	2.50	6.00	10.00	—

KM# 19 KORUNA Composition: Copper-Nickel **Obverse:** State emblem: Czech lion with Slovak shield, date **Reverse:** Woman with sheaf and sickle **Edge:** Milled **Size:** 21 mm.

Date	Mintage	F	VF	XF	Unc	BU
1946	88,000,000	0.15	0.25	0.50	1.00	—
1947	12,550,000	1.50	2.50	3.75	6.50	—

Note: Varieties exist for "4" in 1946 strikes

KM# 22 KORUNA Composition: Aluminum **Obverse:** Czech lion with Slovak shield **Reverse:** Female harvesting wheat **Edge:** Milled **Size:** 21 mm.

Date	Mintage	F	VF	XF	Unc	BU
1947	—	50.00	185	375	600	—
1950	62,190,000	0.20	0.35	0.45	1.00	—
1951	61,395,000	0.20	0.35	0.45	1.25	—
1952	101,105,000	0.20	0.30	0.40	0.80	—
1953	73,905,000	0.40	0.75	1.75	4.50	—

KM# 23 2 KORUNY Composition: Copper-Nickel **Obverse:** Czech lion with Slovak shield **Reverse:** Juraj Janesik bust right, wearing hat **Edge:** Milled **Size:** 23.5 mm.

Date	Mintage	F	VF	XF	Unc	BU
1947	20,000,000	0.20	0.40	0.60	1.25	—
1948	20,476,000	0.20	0.40	0.60	1.50	—

KM# 34 5 KORUN Composition: Aluminum **Obverse:** Czech lion with Slovak shield **Reverse:** Industrial factory and large value **Size:** 23 mm.

Date	Mintage	F	VF	XF	Unc	BU
1951	—	—	300	700	1,500	—
Note: Not released for circulation. Almost the entire mintage was melted						
1952	40,715,000	17.50	25.00	40.00	75.00	—

KM# 24 50 KORUN Weight: 10.0000 g. **Composition:** 0.5000 Silver .1607 oz. ASW **Subject:** 1944 Slovak Uprising **Obverse:** Crowned lion, value **Obv. Designer:** O. Spaniel **Reverse:** Veiled female standing holding linden sprig **Rev. Designer:** R. Pribis **Edge:** Plain with stars and waves **Size:** 28 mm.

Date	Mintage	F	VF	XF	Unc	BU
ND(1947)	1,000,000	—	2.75	4.50	6.50	—

KM# 25 50 KORUN Weight: 10.0000 g. **Composition:** 0.5000 Silver .1607 oz. ASW **Subject:** 3rd Anniverary - Prague Uprising **Obverse:** Czech lion with Slovak shield **Reverse:** Liberator, value **Edge:** Plain with stars and waves **Size:** 28 mm.

Date	Mintage	F	VF	XF	Unc	BU
ND(1948)	1,000,000	—	2.75	4.50	6.50	—

KM# 28 50 KORUN Weight: 10.0000 g. **Composition:** 0.5000 Silver .1607 oz. ASW **Subject:** 70th Birthday - Josef Stalin **Obverse:** Czech lion with Slovak shield, value **Reverse:** Josef Stalin head left **Edge:** Plain with stars and waves **Size:** 28 mm.

Date	Mintage	F	VF	XF	Unc	BU
ND(1949)	1,000,000	—	2.75	4.50	7.00	—

KM# 26 100 KORUN Weight: 14.0000 g. **Composition:** 0.5000 Silver .2250 oz. ASW **Subject:** 600th Anniversary - Charles University **Obverse:** Shield of Czech lion with Slovak shield **Reverse:** Kg. Charles kneeling before Duke Wenceslas **Size:** 31 mm.

Date	Mintage	F	VF	XF	Unc	BU
1948	1,000,000	—	2.75	4.50	7.00	—

KM# 27 100 KORUN Weight: 14.0000 g. **Composition:** 0.5000 Silver .2250 oz. ASW **Subject:** 30th Anniversary of Independence **Obverse:** Shield of Czech lion with Slovak shield **Reverse:** Man with flag and lauer branch **Edge:** Plain with stars and waves **Size:** 31 mm.

Date	Mintage	F	VF	XF	Unc	BU
ND(1948)	1,000,000	—	2.75	4.50	7.00	—

KM# 29 100 KORUN Weight: 14.0000 g. **Composition:** 0.5000 Silver .2250 oz. ASW **Subject:** 700th Anniversary - Jihlava Mining Privileges **Obverse:** Shield of Czech lion with Slovak shield, date **Reverse:** King Karel I and St. Vaclav **Edge:** Plain with stars and waves **Size:** 31 mm.

Date	Mintage	F	VF	XF	Unc	BU
1949	1,000,000	—	2.75	4.50	7.00	—

KM# 30 100 KORUN Weight: 14.0000 g. **Composition:** 0.5000 Silver .2250 oz. ASW **Subject:** 70th Birthday - Josef V. Stalin **Obverse:** Shield of Czech lion with Slovak shield **Reverse:** Josef Stalin bust left **Edge:** Plain with stars and waves **Size:** 28 mm.

Date	Mintage	F	VF	XF	Unc	BU
ND(1949)	1,000,000	—	2.75	4.50	7.00	—

KM# 33 100 KORUN Weight: 14.0000 g. **Composition:** 0.5000 Silver .2250 oz. ASW **Subject:** 30th Anniversary - Communist party **Obverse:** Shield of Czech lion with Slovak shield **Reverse:** Klement Gottwald, Party Chairman, bust right **Edge:** Plain with stars and waves **Size:** 31 mm.

Date	Mintage	F	VF	XF	Unc	BU
ND(1951)	1,000,000	—	2.75	4.50	7.00	—

PEOPLES REPUBLIC

DECIMAL COINAGE

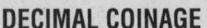

KM# 35 HALER Composition: Aluminum **Obverse:** Czech lion with Slovak shield **Reverse:** Value within linden wreath, star above **Edge:** Plain **Size:** 16 mm.

Date	Mintage	F	VF	XF	Unc	BU
1953	188,885,000	—	—	0.10	0.25	—
1954	—	—	—	0.10	0.25	—
1955	—	—	—	0.15	0.50	—
1956	—	—	—	0.10	0.25	—
1957	—	—	—	0.10	0.25	—
1958	—	0.10	0.25	0.35	0.75	—
1959	—	—	—	0.15	0.50	—
1960	—	—	—	0.10	0.25	—

KM# 36 3 HALERE Composition: Aluminum **Obverse:** Czech lion with Slovak shield **Reverse:** Value within linden wreath, star above **Edge:** Plain **Size:** 18 mm.

Date	Mintage	F	VF	XF	Unc	BU
1953	90,001,000	—	0.10	0.15	0.30	—
1954	Inc. above	—	0.10	0.15	0.30	—

KM# 37 5 HALERU Composition: Aluminum **Obverse:** Czech lion with Slovak shield **Reverse:** Value within linden wreath, star above **Edge:** Plain **Size:** 20 mm.

Date	Mintage	F	VF	XF	Unc	BU
1953	160,233,000	0.10	0.15	0.25	0.50	—
1954	Inc. above	0.10	0.15	0.25	0.50	—
1955	Inc. above	0.50	2.00	6.00	20.00	—

KM# 38 10 HALERU Composition: Aluminum **Obverse:** Czech lion with Slovak shield **Reverse:** Value within linden wreath, star above **Size:** 22 mm.

Date	Mintage	F	VF	XF	Unc	BU
1953	—	0.10	0.15	1.00	5.00	—
Note: Unknown Mint-125 notches in milled edge						
1953	160,000	0.10	0.15	1.00	5.00	—
Note: Leningrad Mint-133 notches in milled edge						
1954	—	0.25	0.50	2.00	7.00	—
1955	—	0.50	0.75	3.50	12.00	—
1956	—	0.10	0.15	1.00	5.00	—
1958	—	0.50	0.75	2.50	9.00	—

KM# 39 25 HALERU **Composition:** Aluminum **Obverse:** Czech lion with Slovak shield **Reverse:** Value within linden wreath, star above **Size:** 24 mm.

Date	Mintage	F	VF	XF	Unc	BU
1953	215,002,000	0.10	0.20	0.30	4.00	—
Note: Kremnica Mint-134 notches in milled edge						
1953	Inc. above	0.30	0.50	0.60	6.00	—
Note: Leningrad Mint-145 notches in milled edge						
1954	Inc. above	4.00	8.00	16.00	38.00	—

KM# 46 KORUNA **Composition:** Aluminum-Bronze **Obverse:** Czech lion with Slovak shield **Reverse:** Female kneeling planting linden sprig, value **Rev. Designer:** M. Uchitilova-Kucova **Edge:** Milled **Size:** 23 mm.

Date	Mintage	F	VF	XF	Unc	BU
1957	137,000,000	0.20	0.30	0.45	5.00	—
1958	Inc. above	0.20	0.30	0.45	7.00	—
1959	Inc. above	0.15	0.25	0.35	4.50	—
1960	Inc. above	0.15	0.25	0.35	4.50	—

KM# 40 10 KORUN **Weight:** 12.0000 g. **Composition:** 0.5000 Silver .1929 oz. ASW **Subject:** 10th Anniversary - Slovak Uprising **Obverse:** Shield with Czech lion and Slovak shield **Obv. Designer:** O. Spaniel **Reverse:** Soldier standing right, train and construction site in background **Rev. Designer:** R. Pribis **Edge:** Milled **Size:** 30 mm. **Note:** 61,010 pieces, Unc and Proof, were melted by the Czech National Bank in 1997.

Date	Mintage	F	VF	XF	Unc	BU
ND(1954)	250,000	—	2.00	3.00	5.00	—
ND(1954) Proof	5,000	Value: 12.00				

KM# 42 10 KORUN **Weight:** 12.0000 g. **Composition:** 0.5000 Silver .1929 oz. ASW **Subject:** 10th Anniversary - Liberation from Germany **Obverse:** Czech lion with Slovak shield **Reverse:** Soldier kneeling left holding child **Edge:** Milled **Size:** 30 mm. **Note:** 90,552 pieces Unc and Proof, were melted by the Czech National Bank in 1997.

Date	Mintage	F	VF	XF	Unc	BU
ND(1955)	300,000	—	2.50	3.50	6.00	—
ND(1955) Proof	5,000	Value: 14.50				

KM# 48 10 KORUN **Weight:** 12.0000 g. **Composition:** 0.5000 Silver .1929 oz. ASW **Obverse:** Czech lion with Slovak shield **Reverse:** J. A. Komensky bust right **Edge:** Milled **Size:** 30 mm. **Note:** 6,454 pieces Unc and 1,800 Proof, were melted by the Czech National Bank in 1997.

Date	Mintage	F	VF	XF	Unc	BU
1957	150,000	—	2.50	3.50	6.50	—
1957 Proof	5,000	Value: 14.50				

KM# 47.1 10 KORUN **Weight:** 12.0000 g. **Composition:** 0.5000 Silver .1929 oz. ASW **Subject:** 250th Anniversary - Technical College **Obverse:** Czech lion with Slovak shield, value **Reverse:** C. J. Willenberg bust left **Edge:** Plain with stars and waves **Size:** 30 mm. **Note:** Raised designer initials.

Date	Mintage	F	VF	XF	Unc	BU
1957	75,000	—	2.50	3.50	7.50	—
Note: See note below KM#47.2						

KM# 47.2 10 KORUN **Weight:** 12.0000 g. **Composition:** 0.5000 Silver .1929 oz. ASW **Obverse:** Czech lion with Slovak shield **Reverse:** C. J. Willenberg bust left **Size:** 30 mm. **Note:** Incuse designer initials.

Date	Mintage	F	VF	XF	Unc	BU
1957 Proof	Est. 5,000	Value: 14.50				
Note: 138 pieces, Unc and Proof, were melted by the Czech National Bank in 1997						

KM# 41 25 KORUN **Weight:** 16.0000 g. **Composition:** 0.5000 Silver .2572 oz. ASW **Subject:** 10th Anniversary - Slovak Unprising **Obverse:** Shield with Czech lion and Slovak shield **Obv. Designer:** O. Spaniel **Reverse:** Soldier standing right, train and construction site in background **Rev. Designer:** R. Pribis **Edge:** Milled **Size:** 34 mm. **Note:** 106,433 Unc and 800 Proof, were melted by the Czech National Bank in 1997.

Date	Mintage	F	VF	XF	Unc	BU
ND(1954)	—	—	5.00	7.50	—	
ND(1954) Proof	Est. 5,000	Value: 25.00				

KM# 43 25 KORUN **Weight:** 16.0000 g. **Composition:** 0.5000 Silver .2572 oz. ASW **Subject:** 10th Anniversary - Liberation from Germany **Obverse:** Czech lion with Slovak shield **Reverse:** Mother and child greeting soldier **Edge:** Milled **Size:** 34 mm. **Note:** 76,143 pieces, Unc and Proof, were melted by the Czech National Bank in 1997.

Date	Mintage	F	VF	XF	Unc	BU
ND(1955)	200,000	—	—	5.00	7.50	—
ND(1955) Proof	5,000	Value: 25.00				

KM# 44 50 KORUN **Weight:** 20.0000 g. **Composition:** 0.9000 Silver .5787 oz. ASW **Subject:** 10th Anniversary - Liberation from Germany **Obverse:** Czech lion with Slovak shield **Reverse:** Soldier standing wearing cloak, raising rifle **Edge:** Milled **Size:** 37 mm. **Note:** 36,050 pieces were melted by the Czech National Bank in 1997.

Date	Mintage	F	VF	XF	Unc	BU
1955	120,000	—	5.00	9.00	16.50	—

KM# 45 100 KORUN **Weight:** 24.0000 g. **Composition:** 0.9000 Silver .6945 oz. ASW **Subject:** 10th Anniversary - Liberation from Germany **Obverse:** Czech lion with Slovak shield **Reverse:** Father and young boy greeting two returning soldiers **Size:** 40 mm. **Note:** 22,044 pieces were melted by the Czech National Bank in 1997.

Date	F	VF	XF	Unc	BU
ND(1955)	—	10.00	16.50	32.50	40.00

SOCIALIST REPUBLIC

DECIMAL COINAGE

KM# 51 HALER **Composition:** Aluminum **Obverse:** Czech lion with socialist shield **Reverse:** Value within linden wreath, star above **Edge:** Plain **Size:** 16 mm.

Date	Mintage	F	VF	XF	Unc	BU
1962	20,056,000	—	—	0.10	0.15	—
1963	Inc. above	—	—	0.10	0.15	—
1986	3,360,000	—	—	—	1.00	—

KM# 52 3 HALERE **Composition:** Aluminum **Obverse:** Czech lion with socialist shield **Reverse:** Value within linden wreath, star above **Edge:** Plain **Size:** 18 mm.

Date	Mintage	F	VF	XF	Unc	BU
1962	Inc. below	100	150	200	280	—
1963	5,130,000	—	—	0.10	0.15	—

KM# 53 5 HALERU **Composition:** Aluminum **Obverse:** Czech lion with socialist shield **Reverse:** Value within linden wreath, star above **Edge:** Plain **Size:** 20 mm.

Date	Mintage	F	VF	XF	Unc	BU
1962	55,150,000	—	0.10	0.15	0.25	—
1963	Inc. above	—	0.10	0.15	0.25	—
1966	Inc. above	—	0.10	0.15	0.25	—
1967	20,770,000	—	0.10	0.15	0.25	—
1970	5,090,000	—	0.10	0.15	0.20	—
1972	10,090,000	—	0.10	0.15	0.20	—
1973	10,140,000	—	0.10	0.15	0.20	—
1974	15,510,000	—	0.10	0.15	0.20	—
1975	15,510,000	—	0.10	0.15	0.20	—
1976	15,550,000	—	0.10	0.15	0.20	—

KM# 86 5 HALERU **Composition:** Aluminum **Obverse:** Czech lion with socialist shield **Reverse:** Value, star above **Edge:** Plain **Size:** 16.2 mm.

Date	Mintage	F	VF	XF	Unc	BU
1977	26,710,000	—	—	0.10	0.25	—
1978	51,110,000	—	—	0.10	0.25	—
1979	72,380,000	—	—	0.10	0.25	—
1980 In mint set only	50,600	—	—	—	0.25	—

Date	Mintage	F	VF	XF	Unc	BU
1981 In mint set only	66,160	—	—	—	0.50	—
1982 In mint set only	53,847	—	—	—	1.00	—
1983 In mint set only	60,000	—	—	—	0.50	—
1984 In mint set only	39,957	—	—	—	0.75	—
1985 In mint set only	39,791	—	—	—	0.75	—
1986	20,020,000	—	—	0.10	0.25	—
1987	520,000	—	—	0.10	0.35	—
1988	8,029,999	—	—	0.10	0.25	—
1989	110,000	—	—	0.10	0.50	—
1990	13,950,000	—	—	0.10	0.25	—

KM# 49.1 10 HALERU **Composition:** Aluminum

Date	Mintage	F	VF	XF	Unc	BU
1961	314,480,000	—	0.10	0.20	0.35	—
1962	Inc. above	—	0.10	0.20	0.35	—
1963	Inc. above	—	0.10	0.20	0.35	—
1964	Inc. above	—	0.10	0.20	0.35	—
1965	Inc. above	—	0.10	0.20	0.35	—
1966	Inc. above	—	0.10	0.20	0.35	—
1967	46,990,000	—	0.10	0.20	0.35	—
1968	37,275,000	—	0.10	0.20	0.35	—
1969	80,000,000	—	0.10	0.15	0.35	—
1970	50,005,000	—	0.10	0.20	0.35	—
1971	30,450,000	—	0.10	0.20	0.35	—

KM# 49.2 10 HALERU **Composition:** Aluminum **Obverse:** Czech lion with socialist shield, flat-top 3 in date **Reverse:** Value within linden wreath, star above **Size:** 22 mm. **Note:** Obverse muled from 50 Haleru, KM 55.1.

Date	F	VF	XF	Unc	BU
1963	12.50	25.00	37.50	65.00	—

KM# 80 10 HALERU **Composition:** Aluminum **Obverse:** Czech lion with socialist shield **Reverse:** Value, star above **Size:** 18.2 mm. **Note:** Varieties exist.

Date	Mintage	F	VF	XF	Unc	BU
1974	11,470,000	—	—	0.10	0.25	—
1975	41,002,000	—	—	0.10	0.25	—
1976	182,000,000	—	—	0.10	0.25	—
1977	151,760,000	—	—	0.10	0.25	—
1978	62,620,000	—	—	0.10	0.25	—
1979	30,240,000	—	—	0.10	0.25	—
1980	31,280,000	—	—	0.10	0.25	—
1981	43,616,160	—	—	0.10	0.25	—
1982	74,568,847	—	—	0.10	0.25	—
1983	50,560,000	—	—	0.10	0.25	—
1984	40,369,957	—	—	0.10	0.25	—
1985	92,929,791	—	—	0.10	0.25	—
1986	87,260,000	—	—	0.10	0.25	—
1987	30,030,000	—	—	0.10	0.25	—
1988	47,479,999	—	—	0.10	0.25	—
1989	50,300,000	—	—	0.10	0.25	—
1990	25,220,000	—	—	0.10	0.25	—

KM# 74 20 HALERU **Composition:** Brass **Obverse:** Czech lion with socialist shield **Reverse:** Value, star above **Size:** 19.5 mm. **Note:** Varieties exist.

Date	Mintage	F	VF	XF	Unc	BU
1972	25,820,000	—	0.10	0.20	0.40	—
1973	39,095,000	—	0.10	0.20	0.40	—
1974	24,795,000	—	0.10	0.20	0.40	—
1975	30,025,000	—	0.10	0.20	0.40	—
1976	30,540,000	—	0.10	0.20	0.40	—
1977	30,655,000	—	0.10	0.20	0.40	—
1978	30,095,000	—	0.10	0.20	0.40	—
1979	12,120,000	—	0.10	0.20	0.40	—
1980	52,301,000	—	0.10	0.15	0.30	—
1981	35,126,160	—	0.10	0.15	0.30	—
1982	41,238,847	—	0.10	0.15	0.30	—

Date	Mintage	F	VF	XF	Unc	BU
1983	50,160,000	—	0.10	0.15	0.30	—
1984	33,684,957	—	0.10	0.15	0.30	—
1985	40,454,791	—	0.10	0.15	0.30	—
1986	37,055,000	—	0.10	0.15	0.30	—
1987	26,975,000	—	0.10	0.15	0.30	—
1988	18,259,999	—	0.10	0.15	0.30	—
1989	29,980,000	—	0.10	0.15	0.30	—
1990	15,030,000	—	0.10	0.15	0.30	—

KM# 54 25 HALERU **Composition:** Aluminum **Obverse:** Czech lion with socialist shield **Reverse:** Value within linden wreath, star above **Edge:** Milled **Size:** 24 mm. **Note:** This denomination ceased to be legal tender in 1972.

Date	Mintage	F	VF	XF	Unc	BU
1962	69,880,000	0.10	0.15	0.20	0.35	—
1963	Inc. above	0.10	0.15	0.20	0.35	—
1964	Inc. above	0.10	0.15	0.20	0.35	—

KM# 55.1 50 HALERU **Composition:** Bronze **Obverse:** Czech lion with socialist shield **Reverse:** Value within linden wreath, star above **Size:** 21.5 mm.

Date	Mintage	F	VF	XF	Unc	BU
1963	80,560,000	0.10	0.20	0.30	0.45	—
1964	Inc. above	0.10	0.20	0.30	0.45	—
1965	Inc. above	0.10	0.20	0.30	0.45	—
1969	9,876,000	0.10	0.20	0.30	0.45	—
1970	31,536,000	0.10	0.20	0.30	0.40	—
1971	20,800,000	0.10	0.20	0.30	0.40	—

KM# 55.2 50 HALERU **Composition:** Bronze **Obverse:** Czech lion with socialist shield, small date, without dots **Reverse:** Value within linden wreath, star above **Size:** 21.5 mm. **Note:** Obverse muled with 10 Haleru, KM 49.1.

Date	F	VF	XF	Unc	BU
1969	12.50	22.50	40.00	75.00	—

KM# 89 50 HALERU **Composition:** Copper-Nickel **Obverse:** Czech lion with socialist shield **Reverse:** Value, star above **Edge:** Milled **Size:** 20.8 mm. **Note:** Date varieties exist.

Date	Mintage	F	VF	XF	Unc	BU
1978	40,480,000	—	—	0.10	0.50	—
1979	76,116,000	—	—	0.10	0.50	—
1980 In mint sets only	51,000	—	—	—	1.50	—
1981 In mint sets only	66,000	—	—	—	1.50	—
1982	14,261,847	—	—	0.10	0.50	—
1983	16,168,000	—	—	0.10	0.50	—
1984	16,207,957	—	—	0.10	0.50	—
1985	10,467,791	—	—	0.10	0.50	—
1986	10,020,000	—	—	0.10	0.50	—
1987	5,138,000	—	—	0.10	0.50	—
1988	5,089,999	—	—	0.10	0.50	—
1989	13,030,000	—	—	0.10	0.50	—
1990	7,742,000	—	—	0.10	0.50	—

KM# 50 KORUNA **Composition:** Aluminum-Bronze **Obverse:** Czech lion with socialist shield **Reverse:** Female planting linden sprig **Rev. Designer:** Marie Uchytilova-Kucova **Edge:** Milled **Size:** 23 mm. **Note:** Date varieties exist.

Date	Mintage	F	VF	XF	Unc	BU
1961	146,964,000	—	0.15	0.30	0.60	—
1962	Inc. above	—	0.15	0.30	0.60	—
1963	Inc. above	—	0.15	0.30	0.60	—
1964	Inc. above	—	0.15	0.30	0.60	—
1965	Inc. above	—	0.15	0.30	0.60	—
1966	Inc. above	0.40	0.65	0.90	1.25	—

Date	Mintage	F	VF	XF	Unc	BU
1967	7,924,000	—	0.15	0.30	0.60	—
1968	10,696,000	—	0.15	0.30	0.60	—
1969	21,820,000	—	0.15	0.30	0.60	—
1970	31,036,000	—	0.15	0.30	0.60	—
1971	10,152,000	—	0.15	0.30	0.60	—
1975	6,657,000	—	0.15	0.30	0.60	—
1976	14,211,000	—	0.15	0.30	0.60	—
1977	10,434,000	—	0.15	0.30	0.75	—
1979	Inc. below	—	0.15	0.30	0.75	—
1980	24,513,000	—	0.15	0.30	0.75	—
1981	7,179,000	—	0.15	0.30	0.75	—
1982	17,162,847	—	0.15	0.30	0.75	—
1983	4,758,000	—	0.15	0.30	0.75	—
1984	9,732,957	—	0.15	0.30	0.75	—
1985	10,545,751	—	0.15	0.30	0.75	—
1986	2,789,000	—	0.15	0.30	0.75	—
1987 In mint sets only	30,000	—	—	—	2.50	—
1988 In mint sets only	29,999	—	—	—	2.50	—
1989	1,038,000	—	0.15	0.30	0.75	—
1990	19,368,000	—	0.15	0.30	0.75	—

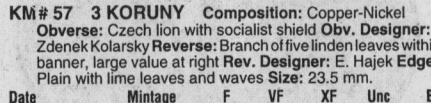

KM# 75 2 KORUNY **Composition:** Copper-Nickel **Obverse:** Czech lion with socialist shield **Reverse:** Star above hammer and sickle, large value at right **Edge:** Plain with crosses and waves **Size:** 24 mm.

Date	Mintage	F	VF	XF	Unc	BU
1972	20,344,000	—	0.25	0.45	1.00	—
1973	21,087,000	—	0.25	0.45	1.00	—

Note: 1973 date exists with edge of 5 Korun KM#60, value: 15.00

Date	Mintage	F	VF	XF	Unc	BU
1974	27,957,000	—	0.25	0.45	1.00	—
1975	35,094,000	—	0.25	0.45	1.00	—
1976	1,100,000	—	0.25	0.45	1.00	—
1977	4,201,000	—	0.25	0.65	1.50	—
1980	14,943,000	—	0.25	0.35	0.75	—
1981	17,264,000	—	0.25	0.35	0.75	—
1982	8,108,000	—	0.25	0.35	0.75	—
1983	10,190,000	—	0.25	0.35	0.75	—
1984	8,634,000	—	0.25	0.35	0.75	—
1985	6,772,000	—	0.25	0.35	0.75	—
1986	10,262,000	—	0.25	0.35	0.75	—
1987 In mint sets only	30,000	—	—	—	2.50	—
1988 In mint sets only	30,000	—	—	—	2.50	—
1989	9,092,000	—	0.25	0.35	0.75	—
1990	10,672,000	—	0.25	0.35	0.75	—

KM# 57 3 KORUNY **Composition:** Copper-Nickel **Obverse:** Czech lion with socialist shield **Obv. Designer:** Zdenek Kolarsky **Reverse:** Branch of five linden leaves within banner, large value at right **Rev. Designer:** E. Hajek **Edge:** Plain with lime leaves and waves **Size:** 23.5 mm.

Date	Mintage	F	VF	XF	Unc	BU
1965	15,000,000	—	0.50	1.00	2.50	—
1966	Inc. above	—	0.50	1.00	2.50	—
1968	7,000,000	—	0.45	0.85	2.00	—
1969	10,080,000	—	0.40	0.75	1.50	—

KM# 60 5 KORUN **Composition:** Copper-Nickel **Obverse:** Czech lion with socialist shield **Reverse:** Geometric design and large value **Edge:** Plain with rhombs and waves **Size:** 26 mm.

Date	Mintage	F	VF	XF	Unc	BU
1966	6,383,000	—	0.75	1.00	2.00	—

Note: 1966 varieties on obverse of coin: large date: no space between letter B in REPUBLIC and coat of arms; small date: space between letter B in REPUBLIC and coat of arms; plain edge: no ornamental inscription on edge (error coin). So far there has been no indication of any of the varieties as being scarce

Date	Mintage	F	VF	XF	Unc	BU
1967	4,544,000	—	—	0.75	1.50	—

Date	Mintage	F	VF	XF	Unc	BU
1968	14,120,000	—	—	0.75	1.50	—
1969 Straight date	5,486,000	—	—	0.75	1.50	—
1969 Date in semi-circle	Inc. above	0.75	1.50	5.00	9.00	—
1970	10,073,000	—	—	0.75	1.50	—
1973	15,620,000	—	—	0.75	1.25	—
Note: Two variations in 3 of date						
1974	20,053,000	—	—	0.75	1.25	—
Note: Three variations in 4 of date						
1975	17,158,000	—	—	0.75	1.25	—
1978	5,317,000	—	—	0.75	1.25	—
1979	9,219,000	—	—	0.75	1.25	—
1980	12,559,000	—	—	0.75	1.25	—
1981	8,620,160	—	—	0.75	1.25	—
1982	6,903,847	—	—	0.75	1.25	—
1983	6,704,000	—	—	0.75	1.25	—
1984	6,856,957	—	—	0.75	1.25	—
1985	6,763,791	—	—	0.75	1.25	—
1986 In mint sets only	20,000	—	—	—	15.00	—
1987 In mint sets only	30,000	—	—	—	7.00	—
1988	29,999	—	—	—	5.00	—
1989	5,039,000	—	—	0.75	1.25	—
1990	2,783,000	—	—	0.75	1.25	—

KM# 56 10 KORUN **Weight:** 12.0000 g. **Composition:** 0.5000 Silver .1929 oz. ASW **Subject:** 20th Anniversary - 1944 Slovak Uprising **Obverse:** Czech lion with socialist shield **Obv. Designer:** A. Havelka **Reverse:** Three hands and linden sprig **Rev. Designer:** Z. Kolarsky **Edge Lettering:** SLOVENSKE NARODNE POVSTANIE **Size:** 30 mm. **Note:** 7,876 pieces were melted by the Czech National Bank in 1997.

Date	Mintage	F	VF	XF	Unc	BU
ND(1964)	120,000	—	—	3.00	5.00	—

KM# 58 10 KORUN **Weight:** 12.0000 g. **Composition:** 0.5000 Silver .1929 oz. ASW **Subject:** 550th Anniversary - Death of Jan Hus **Obverse:** Czech lion with socialist shield, value **Obv. Designer:** Z. Kolarsky **Reverse:** Jan Hus bust right **Rev. Designer:** K. Lidicky **Edge Lettering:** 550 LET UPALENI M, JANA HUSA **Size:** 30 mm. **Note:** 80 pieces, Unc and Proof, were melted by the Czech National Bank in 1997.

Date	Mintage	F	VF	XF	Unc	BU
ND(1965)	55,000	—	—	7.00	15.00	—
ND(1965) Proof	5,000	Value: 20.00				

KM# 61 10 KORUN **Weight:** 12.0000 g. **Composition:** 0.5000 Silver .1929 oz. ASW **Subject:** 1100th Anniversary of Great Moravia **Obverse:** Czech lion with socialist shield **Obv. Designer:** L. Ruzicka **Reverse:** Medal with horseman with falcon and plot of church **Rev. Designer:** Lubos Ruzicka and Jan Solpera **Edge:** Plain with ellipse and rings **Size:** 30 mm. **Note:** 3,146 pieces, Unc and Proof, were melted by the Czech National Bank in 1997.

Date	Mintage	F	VF	XF	Unc	BU
1966	115,000	—	—	4.00	6.50	—
1966 Proof	5,000	Value: 12.50				

KM# 62 10 KORUN **Weight:** 12.0000 g. **Composition:** 0.5000 Silver .1929 oz. ASW **Subject:** 500th Anniversary - Bratislava University **Obverse:** Czech lion with socialist shield above stylized three mountains and river **Reverse:** University seal and building **Edge:** Plain with Rhombs and waves **Size:** 30 mm. **Note:** 103 pieces, Unc and Proof, were melted by the Czech National Bank in 1997.

Date	Mintage	F	VF	XF	Unc	BU
ND(1967)	45,000	—	—	10.00	20.00	—
ND(1967) Proof	500	Value: 22.50				

KM# 63 10 KORUN **Weight:** 12.0000 g. **Composition:** 0.5000 Silver .1929 oz. ASW **Subject:** Centennial - Prague (Praha) National Theater **Obverse:** Czech lion with socialist shield, value **Reverse:** Female goddess in three-horse chariot **Edge:** Plain with crosses and waves **Size:** 30 mm. **Note:** 50 pieces, Unc and Proof, were melted by the Czech National Bank in 1997.

Date	Mintage	F	VF	XF	Unc	BU
ND(1968)	55,000	—	—	15.00	20.00	—
ND(1968) Proof	5,000	Value: 40.00				

KM# 76 20 KORUN **Weight:** 9.0000 g. **Composition:** 0.5000 Silver .1446 oz. ASW **Subject:** Centennial - Death of Andrej Sladkovic **Obverse:** Czech lion with socialist shield **Reverse:** Andrej Sladkovic head left **Size:** 29 mm. **Note:** 2,642 pieces, 2,600 Unc and 42 Proof, were melted by the Czech National Bank in 1997.

Date	Mintage	F	VF	XF	Unc	BU
ND(1972)	55,000	—	—	3.00	5.00	—
ND(1972) Proof	5,000	Value: 12.50				

KM# 59 25 KORUN **Weight:** 16.0000 g. **Composition:** 0.5000 Silver .2572 oz. ASW **Subject:** 20th Anniversary - Czechoslovakian Liberation **Obverse:** Czech lion with socialist shield **Reverse:** Female head, dove with linden branch **Edge Lettering:** 20 LET OSVOBOZENI CSSR **Size:** 34 mm. **Note:** 21,114 pieces, Unc and Proof, were melted by the Czech National Bank in 1997.

Date	Mintage	F	VF	XF	Unc	BU
ND(1965)	150,000	—	—	4.00	6.50	—
ND(1965) Proof	5,000	Value: 12.50				

KM# 64 25 KORUN **Weight:** 16.0000 g. **Composition:** 0.5000 Silver .2572 oz. ASW **Subject:** 150th Anniversary - Prague (Praha) National Museum **Obverse:** Czech lion with socialist shield **Reverse:** National Museum building **Edge:** Plain with crosses and waves **Size:** 34 mm. **Note:** 51 pieces, Unc and Proof, were melted by the Czech National Bank in 1997.

Date	Mintage	F	VF	XF	Unc	BU
ND(1968)	51,000	—	—	4.50	9.00	—
ND(1968) Proof	5,000	Value: 40.00				

KM# 66 25 KORUN **Weight:** 16.0000 g. **Composition:** 0.5000 Silver .2572 oz. ASW **Subject:** 100th Anniversary - Death of J. E. Purkyne **Obverse:** Czech lion with socialist shield **Obv. Designer:** J. Dostal **Reverse:** Jan E. Purkyne head right **Rev. Designer:** J. Harcuba **Edge Lettering:** FYSIOLOG, FILOSOF, BUDITEL, BASNIK **Size:** 34 mm. **Note:** Edge varieties exist; 40 pieces, Unc and Proof, were melted by the Czech National Bank in 1997.

Date	Mintage	F	VF	XF	Unc	BU
ND(1969)	45,000	—	—	4.00	8.00	—
ND(1969) Proof	5,000	Value: 28.00				

KM# 67 25 KORUN **Weight:** 16.0000 g. **Composition:** 0.5000 Silver .2572 oz. ASW **Subject:** 25th Anniversary - 1944 Slovak Uprising **Obverse:** Czech lion with socialist shield **Reverse:** Three mountians and plant **Edge Lettering:** 25. VYROCIE SLOVENSKEHO NARODNEHO POVSTANIA **Size:** 34 mm. **Note:** Edge varieties exist; 40 pieces, Unc and Proof, were melted by the Czech National Bank in 1997.

Date	Mintage	F	VF	XF	Unc	BU
ND(1969)	25,000	—	—	20.00	40.00	—
ND(1969) Proof	5,000	Value: 50.00				

KM# 68 25 KORUN **Weight:** 10.0000 g. **Composition:** 0.5000 Silver .1607 oz. ASW **Subject:** 50th Anniversary - Slovak National Theater **Obverse:** Czech lion with socialist shield **Obv. Designer:** Z. Kolarsky **Reverse:** Stylized head of muse **Rev. Designer:** I. Strnad **Size:** 30 mm. **Note:** 2,323 pieces, Unc and Proof, were melted by the Czech National Bank in 1997.

Date	Mintage	F	VF	XF	Unc	BU
ND(1970)	45,000	—	—	5.00	10.00	—
ND(1970) Proof	5,000	Value: 60.00				

KM# 69 25 KORUN **Weight:** 10.0000 g. **Composition:** 0.5000 Silver .1607 oz. ASW **Subject:** 25th Anniversary of Liberation **Obverse:** Czech lion with socialist shield **Obv. Designer:** I. Strnad **Reverse:** Sun of Liberation, landscape **Rev. Designer:** Z. Kovarsky **Edge:** - x - **Size:** 30 mm. **Note:** 18,052 pieces, Unc and Proof, were melted by the Czech National Bank in 1997.

Date	Mintage	F	VF	XF	Unc	BU
ND(1970)	95,000	—	—	4.00	6.00	—
ND(1970) Proof	5,000	Value: 15.00				

KM# 65 50 KORUN **Weight:** 20.0000 g. **Composition:** 0.9000 Silver .5787 oz. ASW **Subject:** 50th Anniversary of Czechoslovakia 20th Anniversary - People's Republic **Obverse:** Czech lion with socialist shield **Obv. Designer:** Imra Svitana and Jan Zoricak **Reverse:** Female head left wearing linden and floral wreath **Rev. Designer:** J. Harcuba **Size:** 37 mm. **Note:** 50 pieces, Unc and Proof, were melted by the Czech National Bank in 1997.

Date	Mintage	F	VF	XF	Unc	BU
ND(1968)	58,000	—	—	18.00	32.00	40.00
ND(1968) Proof	2,000	Value: 75.00				

KM# 70 50 KORUN **Weight:** 13.0000 g. **Composition:** 0.7000 Silver .2926 oz. ASW **Subject:** Centennial - Birth of Lenin **Obverse:** Czech lion with socialist shield **Reverse:** V. I. Lenin head right **Size:** 31 mm. **Note:** 51 pieces, Unc and Proof, were melted by the Czech National Bank in 1997.

Date	Mintage	F	VF	XF	Unc	BU
ND(1970)	44,000	—	—	4.00	8.00	—
ND(1970) Proof	6,200	Value: 30.00				

KM# 71 50 KORUN **Weight:** 13.0000 g. **Composition:** 0.7000 Silver .2926 oz. ASW **Subject:** 50th Anniversary - Czechoslovak Communist Party **Obverse:** Czech lion with socialist shield **Reverse:** Five figures standing within hammer and sickle, star above **Edge:** Wave, star, wave **Size:** 31 mm. **Note:** 4,450 pieces, 4,400 Unc and 50 Proof, were melted by the Czech National Bank in 1997.

Date	Mintage	F	VF	XF	Unc	BU
ND(1971)	45,000	—	—	4.00	8.00	—
ND(1971) Proof	5,000	Value: 22.00				

KM# 72 50 KORUN **Weight:** 13.0000 g. **Composition:** 0.7000 Silver .2926 oz. ASW **Subject:** 50th Anniversary - Death of Pavol Orsagh-Hviezdoslav **Obverse:** Czech lion with socialist shield **Reverse:** Pavol Orsagh-Hviezdoslav head left **Size:** 31 mm. **Note:** 3,900 pieces, 3,800 Unc and 100 Proof, were melted by the Czech National Bank in 1997.

Date	Mintage	F	VF	XF	Unc	BU
ND(1971)	45,000	—	—	4.00	7.00	—
ND(1971) Proof	5,000	Value: 20.00				

KM# 77 50 KORUN **Weight:** 13.0000 g. **Composition:** 0.7000 Silver .2926 oz. ASW **Subject:** 50th Anniversary - Death of J. V. Myslbek **Obverse:** Czech lion with socialist shield **Obv. Designer:** A. Peter **Reverse:** J. V. Myslbek head left **Rev. Designer:** L. Picha **Edge Lettering:** J. V. MYSLBEK *1922-1972* **Size:** 31 mm. **Note:** 6,039 pieces, 6,000 Unc and 39 Proof, were melted by the Czech National Bank in 1997.

Date	Mintage	F	VF	XF	Unc	BU
ND(1972)	45,000	—	—	4.00	7.00	—
ND(1972) Proof	5,000	Value: 20.00				

KM# 78 50 KORUN **Weight:** 13.0000 g. **Composition:** 0.7000 Silver .2926 oz. ASW **Subject:** 25th Anniversary - Victory of Communist Party **Obverse:** Czech lion with socialist shield **Obv. Designer:** F. David **Reverse:** Soldier standing before large star, hammer and sickle at right **Rev. Designer:** I. Liptak **Edge Lettering:** 25. VYROCI VITEZNEHO UNORA* **Size:** 31 mm. **Note:** 4,740 pieces, 4,637 Unc and 103 Proof, were melted by the Czech National Bank in 1997.

Date	Mintage	F	VF	XF	Unc	BU
ND(1973)	55,000	—	—	4.00	7.00	—
ND(1973) Proof	5,000	Value: 20.00				

KM# 79 50 KORUN **Weight:** 13.0000 g. **Composition:** 0.7000 Silver .2926 oz. ASW **Subject:** 200th Anniversary - Birth of Josef Jungmann **Obverse:** Czech lion with socialist shield **Reverse:** J. Jungmann head right **Size:** 31 mm. **Note:** 1,584 pieces, 1,500 Unc and 84 Proof, were melted by the Czech National Bank in 1997.

Date	Mintage	F	VF	XF	Unc	BU
ND(1973)	45,000	—	—	4.00	7.00	—
ND(1973) Proof	5,000	Value: 11.50				

KM# 81 50 KORUN **Weight:** 13.0000 g. **Composition:** 0.7000 Silver .2926 oz. ASW **Subject:** Centennial - Birth of Janko Jesensky **Obverse:** Czech lion with socialist shield **Reverse:** Jan Jesensky head 3/4 facing right **Edge:** Plain with wave star wave **Size:** 31 mm. **Note:** 10,738 pieces, 9,700 Unc and 1,038 Proof, were melted by the Czech National Bank in 1997.

Date	Mintage	F	VF	XF	Unc	BU
ND(1974)	55,000	—	—	4.00	6.50	—
ND(1974) Proof	5,000	Value: 11.50				

KM# 83 50 KORUN **Weight:** 13.0000 g. **Composition:** 0.7000 Silver .2926 oz. ASW **Subject:** Centennial - Birth of S. K. Neumann **Obverse:** Czech lion with socialist shield **Reverse:** S. K. Neumann head right **Edge:** Milled **Size:** 31 mm. **Note:** 11,037 pieces, 9,000 Unc and 2,037 Proof, were melted by the Czech National Bank in 1997.

Date	Mintage	F	VF	XF	Unc	BU
ND(1975)	55,000	—	—	4.00	6.50	—
ND(1975) Proof	5,000	Value: 11.50				

KM# 87 50 KORUN **Weight:** 13.0000 g. **Composition:** 0.7000 Silver .2926 oz. ASW **Subject:** 125th Anniversary - Death of Jan Kollar **Obverse:** Czech lion with socialist shield **Reverse:** Jan Kollar head facing **Edge:** Milled **Size:** 31 mm. **Note:** 19,043 pieces, 18,143 Unc and 900 Proof, were melted by the Czech National Bank in 1997.

Date	Mintage	F	VF	XF	Unc	BU
ND(1977)	75,000	—	—	4.00	6.50	—
ND(1977) Proof	5,000	Value: 11.50				

KM# 90 50 KORUN **Weight:** 13.0000 g. **Composition:** 0.7000 Silver .2926 oz. ASW **Subject:** Centennial - Birth of Zdenek Nejedly **Obverse:** Czech lion with socialist shield **Reverse:** Z. Nejedly bust right **Edge:** Milled **Size:** 31 mm. **Note:** 18,938 pieces, Unc and 1,100 Proof, were melted by the Czech National Bank in 1997.

Date	Mintage	F	VF	XF	Unc	BU
ND(1978)	75,000	—	—	4.00	6.50	—
ND(1978) Proof	5,000	Value: 11.50				

KM# 91 50 KORUN **Weight:** 13.0000 g. **Composition:** 0.7000 Silver .2926 oz. ASW **Subject:** 650th Anniversary of Kremnica Mint **Obverse:** Czech lion with socialist shield **Reverse:** Montage of five coin designs **Size:** 31 mm. **Note:** 21,537 pieces, 19,837 Unc and 1,700 Proof, were melted by the Czech National Bank in 1997.

Date	Mintage	F	VF	XF	Unc	BU
ND(1978)	93,000	—	—	4.00	6.50	—
ND(1978) Proof	7,000	Value: 11.50				

KM# 98 50 KORUN **Weight:** 13.0000 g. **Composition:** 0.7000 Silver .2926 oz. ASW **Subject:** 30th Anniversary of 9th Congress **Obverse:** Czech lion with socialist shield, linden leaves flanking **Reverse:** Hammer and sickle in gear at center, linden leaves at left **Edge:** Milled **Size:** 31 mm. **Note:** 26,239 pieces, 24,039 Unc and 2,200 Proof, were melted by the Czech National Bank in 1997.

Date	Mintage	F	VF	XF	Unc	BU
ND(1979)	94,000	—	—	4.00	6.50	—
ND(1979) Proof	6,000	Value: 11.50				

KM# 121 50 KORUN **Weight:** 7.0000 g. **Composition:** 0.5000 Silver .1125 oz. ASW **Obverse:** Czech lion with socialist shield **Reverse:** Prague (Praha) city view **Size:** 27 mm. **Note:** 3,738 pieces, 3,700 Unc and 38 Proof, were melted by the Czech National Bank in 1997.

Date	Mintage	F	VF	XF	Unc	BU
1986	90,000	—	—	—	6.00	—
1986 Proof	10,000	Value: 12.50				

KM# 122 50 KORUN **Weight:** 7.0000 g. **Composition:** 0.5000 Silver .1125 oz. ASW **Obverse:** Czech lion with socialist shield **Reverse:** Levoca city view above three statues **Size:** 27 mm. **Note:** 4,338 pieces 4,300 Unc and 38 Proof, were melted by the Czech National Bank in 1997.

Date	Mintage	F	VF	XF	Unc	BU
1986	69,000	—	—	—	6.00	—
1986 Proof	10,000	Value: 11.50				

KM# 124 50 KORUN **Weight:** 7.0000 g. **Composition:** 0.5000 Silver .1125 oz. ASW **Obverse:** Czech lion with socialist shield **Reverse:** Three building facades in Telc **Size:** 27 mm. **Note:** 5,938 pieces 5,900 Unc and 38 Proof, were melted by the Czech National Bank in 1997.

Date	Mintage	F	VF	XF	Unc	BU
1986	69,000	—	—	—	6.00	—
1986 Proof	10,000	Value: 11.50				

KM# 125 50 KORUN **Weight:** 7.0000 g. **Composition:** 0.5000 Silver .1125 oz. ASW **Obverse:** Czech lion with socialist shield **Reverse:** Bratislava city view **Size:** 27 mm. **Note:** 5,738 pieces 5,700 Unc and 38 Proof, were melted by the Czech National Bank in 1997.

Date	Mintage	F	VF	XF	Unc	BU
1986	69,000	—	—	—	6.00	—
1986 Proof	10,000	Value: 11.50				

KM# 126 50 KORUN **Weight:** 7.0000 g. **Composition:** 0.5000 Silver .1125 oz. ASW **Obverse:** Czech lion with socialist shield **Reverse:** Cesky Krumlov city view **Size:** 27 mm. **Note:** 4,538 pieces 4,500 Unc and 38 Proof, were melted by the Czech National Bank in 1997.

Date	Mintage	F	VF	XF	Unc	BU
1986	69,000	—	—	—	6.00	—
1986 Proof	10,000	Value: 11.50				

KM# 127 50 KORUN **Weight:** 7.0000 g. **Composition:** 0.5000 Silver .1125 oz. ASW **Subject:** Environmental Protection **Obverse:** Czech lion with socialist shield **Reverse:** Two Przewalski's horses **Size:** 27 mm. **Note:** 38 pieces Unc and Proof, were melted by the Czech National Bank in 1997.

Date	Mintage	F	VF	XF	Unc	BU
1987	55,000	—	—	—	15.00	—
1987 Proof	5,000	Value: 24.00				

KM# 129 50 KORUN **Weight:** 7.0000 g. **Composition:** 0.5000 Silver .1125 oz. ASW **Subject:** 300th Anniversary - Birth of Juraj Janosik **Obverse:** Czech lion with socialist shield **Reverse:** Caped male standing, bird at left **Size:** 27 mm. **Note:** 35 pieces Unc and Proof, were melted by the Czech National Bank in 1997.

Date	Mintage	F	VF	XF	Unc	BU
ND(1988)	53,000	—	—	—	7.00	—
ND(1988) Proof	5,000	Value: 15.00				

KM# 133 50 KORUN **Weight:** 7.0000 g. **Composition:** 0.5000 Silver .1125 oz. ASW **Subject:** 150th Anniversary - Breclav to Brno Railroad **Obverse:** Czech lion with socialist shield **Reverse:** Early steam locomotive **Size:** 27 mm. **Note:** 35 pieces Unc and Proof, were melted by the Czech National Bank in 1997.

Date	Mintage	F	VF	XF	Unc	BU
ND(1989)	67,000	—	—	—	7.00	—
ND(1989) Proof	3,000	Value: 16.00				

KM# 73 100 KORUN **Weight:** 15.0000 g. **Composition:** 0.7000 Silver .3376 oz. ASW **Subject:** Centennial - Death of Josef Manes **Obverse:** Czech lion with socialist shield **Obv. Designer:** J. Kulich **Reverse:** J. Manes bust right **Rev. Designer:** P. Formanek **Size:** 33 mm. **Note:** 6,403 pieces 6,300 Unc and 103 Proof, were melted by the Czech National Bank in 1997.

Date	Mintage	F	VF	XF	Unc	BU
ND(1971)	45,000	—	—	10.00	13.50	—
ND(1971) Proof	5,000	Value: 17.50				

KM# 82 100 KORUN **Weight:** 15.0000 g. **Composition:** 0.7000 Silver .3376 oz. ASW **Subject:** Sesquicentennial - Birth of Bedrich Smetana **Obverse:** Czech lion with socialist shield **Reverse:** B. Smetana head right **Edge:** Plain with 150 LET OD NAROZENI **Size:** 33 mm. **Note:** 5,061 pieces 3,561 Unc and 1,500 Proof, were melted by the Czech National Bank in 1997.

Date	Mintage	F	VF	XF	Unc	BU
ND(1974)	75,000	—	—	10.00	12.00	—
ND(1974) Proof	5,000	Value: 17.50				

KM# 84 100 KORUN **Weight:** 15.0000 g. **Composition:** 0.7000 Silver .3376 oz. ASW **Subject:** Centennial - Death of Janko Kral **Obverse:** Czech lion with socialist shield **Reverse:** J. Kral bust right **Edge Lettering:** BASNIK * REVOLUCIONAR **Size:** 33 mm. **Note:** 19,039 pieces 13,500 Unc and 5,539 Proof, were melted by the Czech National Bank in 1997.

Date	Mintage	F	VF	XF	Unc	BU
ND(1976)	75,000	—	—	10.00	12.00	—
ND(1976) Proof	5,000	Value: 17.50				

KM# 85 100 KORUN **Weight:** 15.0000 g. **Composition:** 0.7000 Silver .3376 oz. ASW **Subject:** Centennial - Birth of Viktor Kaplan **Obverse:** Czech lion with socialist shield **Reverse:** V. Kaplan bust right **Edge:** - * - **Size:** 33 mm. **Note:** 21,339 pieces 19,638 Unc and 1,701 Proof, were melted by the Czech National Bank in 1997.

Date	Mintage	F	VF	XF	Unc	BU
ND(1976)	75,000	—	—	10.00	12.00	—
ND(1976) Proof	5,000	Value: 17.50				

KM# 88 100 KORUN **Weight:** 15.0000 g. **Composition:** 0.7000 Silver .3376 oz. ASW **Subject:** 300th Anniversary - Death of Vaclav Hollar **Obverse:** Czech lion with socialist shield **Reverse:** V. Hollar bust left **Edge:** Plain with waves and dots **Size:** 33 mm. **Note:** 29,739 pieces, 27,240 Unc and 2,499 Proof, were melted by the Czech National Bank in 1997.

Date	Mintage	F	VF	XF	Unc	BU
ND(1977)	95,000	—	—	10.00	12.00	—
ND(1977) Proof	5,000	Value: 17.50				

KM# 92 100 KORUN **Weight:** 15.0000 g. **Composition:** 0.7000 Silver .3376 oz. ASW **Subject:** 75th Anniversary - Birth of Julius Fucik **Obverse:** Czech lion with socialist shield **Reverse:** J. Fucik head left **Edge Lettering:** LIDE, MEL JSEM VAS RAD, BDETE! **Size:** 33 mm. **Note:** 24,240 pieces, 22,040 Unc and 2,200 Proof, were melted by the Czech National Bank in 1997.

Date	Mintage	F	VF	XF	Unc	BU
ND(1978)	75,000	—	—	10.00	12.00	—
ND(1978) Proof	5,000	Value: 17.50				

KM# 93 100 KORUN **Weight:** 15.0000 g. **Composition:** 0.7000 Silver .3376 oz. ASW **Subject:** 600th Anniversary - Death of Charles IV **Obverse:** Czech lion with socialist shield **Reverse:** Charles IV bust right **Size:** 33 mm. **Note:** 32,238 pieces, 30,200 Unc and 2,038 Proof, were melted by the Czech National Bank in 1997.

Date	Mintage	F	VF	XF	Unc	BU
1978	90,000	—	—	10.00	12.00	—
1978 Proof	10,000	Value: 17.50				

KM# 99 100 KORUN **Weight:** 15.0000 g. **Composition:** 0.7000 Silver .3376 oz. ASW **Subject:** 150th Anniversary - Birth of Jan Botto **Obverse:** Czech lion with socialist shield **Reverse:** J. Botto bust 3/4 facing left **Edge:** ooo star ooo **Size:** 33 mm. **Note:** 24,240 pieces, 22,540 Unc and 1,800 Proof, were melted by the Czech National Bank in 1997.

Date	Mintage	F	VF	XF	Unc	BU
ND(1979)	75,000	—	—	10.00	12.00	—
ND(1979) Proof	5,000	Value: 17.50				

KM# 100 100 KORUN **Weight:** 15.0000 g. **Composition:** 0.7000 Silver .3376 oz. ASW **Subject:** 150th Anniversary - Birth of Peter Parler **Obverse:** Czech lion with socialist shield, medieval arches in background **Reverse:** P. Parler bust facing, medieval arches in background **Edge:** Plain with waves and dots **Size:** 33 mm. **Note:** 54,738 pieces, 50,038 Unc and 4,600 Proof, were melted by the Czech National Bank in 1997.

Date	Mintage	F	VF	XF	Unc	BU
ND(1980)	91,000	—	—	10.00	12.00	—
ND(1980) Proof	9,000	Value: 17.50				

KM# 101 100 KORUN **Weight:** 9.0000 g. **Composition:** 0.5000 Silver .1446 oz. ASW **Subject:** Fifth Spartakiade Games **Obverse:** Czech lion with socialist shield **Reverse:** Seven female gymnastic figures **Size:** 29 mm. **Note:** 45,541 pieces, 39,541 Unc and 6,000 Proof, were melted by the Czech National Bank in 1997.

Date	Mintage	F	VF	XF	Unc	BU
1980	110,000	—	—	—	12.00	—
1980 Proof	10,000	Value: 18.50				

KM# 102 100 KORUN **Weight:** 9.0000 g. **Composition:** 0.5000 Silver .1446 oz. ASW **Subject:** Centennial - Birth of Bohumir Smeral **Obverse:** Czech lion with socialist shield **Reverse:** B. Smeral bust 3/4 facing **Edge:** Milled **Size:** 29 mm. **Note:** 26,443 pieces, 23,443 Unc and 3,000 Proof, were melted by the Czech National Bank in 1997.

Date	Mintage	F	VF	XF	Unc	BU
ND(1980)	74,000	—	—	—	12.00	—
ND(1980) Proof	6,000	Value: 17.50				

KM# 103 100 KORUN **Weight:** 9.0000 g. **Composition:** 0.5000 Silver .1446 oz. ASW **Subject:** 20th Anniversary - Manned Space Flight **Obverse:** Czech lion with socialist shield **Reverse:** Cosmonaut Gagarin **Edge:** Milled **Size:** 29 mm. **Note:** 24,739 pieces, 24,539 Unc and 200 Proof, were melted by the Czech National Bank in 1997.

Date	Mintage	F	VF	XF	Unc	BU
ND(1981)	95,000	—	—	—	9.00	—
ND(1981) Proof	5,000	Value: 17.50				

KM# 104 100 KORUN **Weight:** 9.0000 g. **Composition:** 0.5000 Silver .1446 oz. ASW **Subject:** Centennial - Birth of Prof. Otakar Spaniel **Obverse:** Czech lion with socialist shield **Reverse:** O. Spaniel head left **Edge:** Milled **Size:** 29 mm. **Note:** 45,139 pieces, 42,239 Unc and 2,900 Proof, were melted by the Czech National Bank in 1997.

Date	Mintage	F	VF	XF	Unc	BU
ND(1981)	115,000	—	—	—	9.00	—
ND(1981) Proof	5,000	Value: 17.50				

KM# 107 100 KORUN **Weight:** 9.0000 g. **Composition:** 0.5000 Silver .1446 oz. ASW **Subject:** 150th Anniversary - Ceske Budejovice Horse Drawn Railway **Obverse:** Czech lion with socialist shield **Reverse:** Horse-drawn carriage **Size:** 29 mm. **Note:** 9,139 pieces, 6,739 Unc and 2,400 Proof, were melted by the Czech National Bank in 1997.

Date	Mintage	F	VF	XF	Unc	BU
ND(1982)	76,000	—	—	—	12.00	—
ND(1982) Proof	7,000	Value: 17.50				

KM# 106 100 KORUN **Weight:** 9.0000 g. **Composition:** 0.5000 Silver .1446 oz. ASW **Subject:** Centennial - Birth of Ivan Olbracht **Obverse:** Czech lion with socialist shield **Reverse:** I. Olbracht head left, wearing hat **Edge:** Milled **Size:** 29 mm. **Note:** 16,140 pieces, 15,340 Unc and 800 Proof, were melted by the Czech National Bank in 1997.

Date	Mintage	F	VF	XF	Unc	BU
ND(1982)	76,000	—	—	—	12.00	—
ND(1982) Proof	4,000	Value: 20.00				

KM# 108 100 KORUN **Weight:** 9.0000 g. **Composition:** 0.5000 Silver .1446 oz. ASW **Subject:** 100th Anniversary - Death of Karl Marx **Obverse:** Czech lion with socialist shield **Reverse:** K. Marx head facing **Edge:** Milled **Size:** 29 mm. **Note:** 15,343 pieces, 14,543 Unc and 800 Proof, were melted by the Czech National Bank in 1997.

Date	Mintage	F	VF	XF	Unc	BU
ND(1983)	76,000	—	—	—	12.00	—
ND(1983) Proof	4,000	Value: 20.00				

KM# 109 100 KORUN **Weight:** 9.0000 g. **Composition:** 0.5000 Silver .1446 oz. ASW **Subject:** Centennial - Birth of Jaroslav Hasek **Obverse:** Czech lion with socialist shield

Reverse: J. Hasek bust facing **Edge:** Milled **Size:** 29 mm. **Note:** 15,638 pieces, 14,838 Unc and 800 Proof, were melted by the Czech National Bank in 1997.

Date	Mintage	F	VF	XF	Unc	BU
ND(1983)	76,000	—	—	—	12.00	—
ND(1983) Proof	4,000	Value: 20.00				

KM# 110 100 KORUN **Weight:** 9.0000 g. **Composition:** 0.5000 Silver .1446 oz. ASW **Subject:** Centennial - Death of Samo Chalupka **Obverse:** Czech lion with socialist shield **Reverse:** S. Chalupka bust 3/4 facing **Edge:** Milled **Size:** 29 mm. **Note:** 21,538 pieces, 19,938 Unc and 1,600 Proof, were melted by the Czech National Bank in 1997.

Date	Mintage	F	VF	XF	Unc	BU
ND(1983)	76,000	—	—	—	12.00	—
ND(1983) Proof	4,000	Value: 20.00				

KM# 111 100 KORUN **Weight:** 9.0000 g. **Composition:** 0.5000 Silver .1446 oz. ASW **Subject:** 100th Anniversary of National Theater of Prague **Obverse:** Czech lion with socialist shield **Reverse:** View of the National Theater in Prague **Edge:** Milled **Size:** 29 mm. **Note:** 13,338 pieces, 7,738 Unc and 5,600 Proof, were melted by the Czech National Bank in 1997.

Date	Mintage	F	VF	XF	Unc	BU
ND(1983)	140,000	—	—	—	9.00	—
ND(1983) Proof	10,000	Value: 17.50				

KM# 113 100 KORUN **Weight:** 9.0000 g. **Composition:** 0.5000 Silver .1446 oz. ASW **Subject:** 300th Anniversary - Birth of Matej Bel **Obverse:** Czech lion with socialist shield **Reverse:** Figure seated **Edge:** Milled **Size:** 29 mm. **Note:** 438 pieces, 400 Unc and 38 Proof, were melted by the Czech National Bank in 1997.

Date	Mintage	F	VF	XF	Unc	BU
ND(1984)	57,000	—	—	—	12.00	—
ND(1984) Proof	3,000	Value: 20.00				

KM# 114 100 KORUN **Weight:** 9.0000 g. **Composition:** 0.5000 Silver .1446 oz. ASW **Subject:** 150th Anniversary - Birth of Jan Neruda **Obverse:** Czech lion with socialist shield **Reverse:** J. Neruda head 3/4 facing left, house at left **Edge:** Milled **Size:** 29 mm. **Note:** 3,539 pieces, 2,739 Unc and 800 Proof, were melted by the Czech National Bank in 1997.

Date	Mintage	F	VF	XF	Unc	BU
ND(1984)	76,000	—	—	—	12.00	—
ND(1984) Proof	4,000	Value: 20.00				

KM# 115 100 KORUN **Weight:** 9.0000 g. **Composition:** 0.5000 Silver .1446 oz. ASW **Subject:** Centennial - Birth of Antonin Zapotocky **Obverse:** Czech lion with socialist shield **Reverse:** A. Zapocky head 3/4 facing right **Edge:** Milled **Size:** 29 mm. **Note:** 13,038 pieces, 12,238 Unc and 800 Proof, were melted by the Czech National Bank in 1997.

Date	Mintage	F	VF	XF	Unc	BU
ND(1984)	76,000	—	—	—	12.00	—
ND(1984) Proof	4,000	Value: 20.00				

KM# 119 100 KORUN **Weight:** 9.0000 g. **Composition:** 0.5000 Silver .1446 oz. ASW **Subject:** 10th Anniversary of Helsinki Conference **Obverse:** Czech lion with socialist shield **Reverse:** Stylized dove embracing European map **Edge:** Milled **Size:** 29 mm. **Note:** 11,938 pieces, 9,538 Unc and 2,400 Proof, were melted by the Czech National Bank in 1997.

Date	Mintage	F	VF	XF	Unc	BU
ND(1985)	75,000	—	—	—	10.00	—
ND(1985) Proof	5,000	Value: 20.00				

KM# 116 100 KORUN **Weight:** 9.0000 g. **Composition:** 0.5000 Silver .1446 oz. ASW **Subject:** 200th Anniversary - Birth of Jan Holly **Obverse:** Czech lion with socialist shield **Reverse:** J. Holly bust facing **Edge:** Milled **Size:** 29 mm. **Note:** 4,438 pieces, 4,400 Unc and 38 Proof, were melted by the Czech National Bank in 1997.

Date	Mintage	F	VF	XF	Unc	BU
ND(1985)	62,000	—	—	—	12.00	—
ND(1985) Proof	3,000	Value: 20.00				

KM# 117 100 KORUN **Weight:** 9.0000 g. **Composition:** 0.5000 Silver .1446 oz. ASW **Subject:** 1985 Ice Hockey Championships **Obverse:** Czech lion with socialist shield **Reverse:** Hockey player skating left **Edge:** Milled **Size:** 29 mm. **Note:** 38 pieces, Unc and Proof, were melted by the Czech National Bank in 1997.

Date	Mintage	F	VF	XF	Unc	BU
1985	66,000	—	—	—	12.00	—
1985 Proof	4,000	Value: 20.00				

KM# 120 100 KORUN **Weight:** 9.0000 g. **Composition:** 0.5000 Silver .1446 oz. ASW **Subject:** 250th Anniversary - Death of Petr Brandl **Obverse:** Czech lion with socialist shield **Reverse:** P. Brandl bust facing **Edge:** Milled **Size:** 29 mm. **Note:** 8,938 pieces, 8,900 Unc and 38 Proof, were melted by the Czech National Bank in 1997.

Date	Mintage	F	VF	XF	Unc	BU
ND(1985)	71,000	—	—	—	10.00	—
ND(1985) Proof	4,000	Value: 20.00				

KM# 118 100 KORUN **Weight:** 9.0000 g. **Composition:** 0.5000 Silver .1446 oz. ASW **Subject:** 125th Anniversary - Birth of Martin Kukucin **Obverse:** Czech lion with socialist shield **Reverse:** M. Kukucin bust facing **Edge:** Milled **Size:** 29 mm. **Note:** 6,238 pieces, 5,438 Unc and 800 Proof, were melted by the Czech National Bank in 1997.

Date	Mintage	F	VF	XF	Unc	BU
ND(1985)	62,000	—	—	—	12.00	—
ND(1985) Proof	3,000	Value: 20.00				

KM# 123 100 KORUN **Weight:** 13.0000 g. **Composition:** 0.5000 Silver .2090 oz. ASW **Subject:** 150th Anniversary - Death of Karel Hynek Macha **Obverse:** Czech lion with socialist shield **Reverse:** M. Macha bust facing 3/4 left **Edge:** Milled **Size:** 31 mm. **Note:** 4,338 pieces, 4,300 Unc and 38 Proof, were melted by the Czech National Bank in 1997.

Date	Mintage	F	VF	XF	Unc	BU
ND(1986)	63,000	—	—	—	10.00	—
ND(1986) Proof	5,000	Value: 20.00				

KM# 128 100 KORUN **Weight:** 13.0000 g. **Composition:** 0.5000 Silver .2090 oz. ASW **Subject:** 225th Anniversary of Mining Academy **Obverse:** Czech lion with socialist shield **Reverse:** Mining equipment **Edge:** Milled **Size:** 31 mm. **Note:** 2,438 pieces, 2,400 Unc and 38 Proof, were melted by the Czech National Bank in 1997.

Date	Mintage	F	VF	XF	Unc	BU
ND(1987)	55,000	—	—	—	12.00	—
ND(1987) Proof	5,000	Value: 22.50				

KM# 130 100 KORUN **Weight:** 13.0000 g. **Composition:** 0.5000 Silver .2090 oz. ASW **Subject:** Prague Philatelic Exposition **Obverse:** Czech lion with socialist shield **Reverse:** City views of Prague presented as four stamps **Edge:** Milled **Size:** 31 mm. **Note:** 7,035 pieces, 7,000 Unc and 35 Proof, were melted by the Czech National Bank in 1997.

Date	Mintage	F	VF	XF	Unc	BU
1988	66,000	—	—	—	12.00	—
1988 Proof	5,000	Value: 25.00				

KM# 132 100 KORUN Weight: 13.0000 g. **Composition:** 0.5000 Silver .2090 oz. ASW **Subject:** Centennial - Birth of Martin Benka **Obverse:** Czech lion with socialist shield **Reverse:** M. Benka in national costume standing with dove **Edge:** Milled **Size:** 31 mm. **Note:** 7,035 pieces, 7,000 Unc and 35 Proof, were melted by the Czech National Bank in 1997.

Date	Mintage	F	VF	XF	Unc	BU
ND(1988)	55,000	—	—	—	12.00	—
ND(1988) Proof	5,000	Value: 28.00				

KM# 135 100 KORUN Weight: 13.0000 g. **Composition:** 0.5000 Silver .2090 oz. ASW **Subject:** 50th Anniversary of Student Organization Against Occupation and Fascism **Obverse:** Czech lion with socialist shield **Reverse:** Barbed wire and medieval document seal **Edge:** Milled **Size:** 31 mm. **Note:** 35 pieces, Unc and Proof, were melted by the Czech National Bank in 1997.

Date	Mintage	F	VF	XF	Unc	BU
ND(1989)		—	—	—	14.00	—
ND(1989) Proof	Est. 3,000	Value: 25.00				

KM# 137 100 KORUN Weight: 13.0000 g. **Composition:** 0.5000 Silver .2090 oz. ASW **Subject:** 100th Anniversary - Birth of Karel Capek **Obverse:** Czech lion with socialist shield, value **Reverse:** K. Capek bust left **Edge:** Milled **Size:** 31 mm. **Note:** 3,020 pieces, 2,020 Unc and 1,000 Proof, were melted by the Czech National Bank in 1997.

Date	Mintage	F	VF	XF	Unc	BU
ND(1990)	67,000	—	—	—	14.00	—
ND(1990) Proof	3,500	Value: 25.00				

KM# 138 100 KORUN Weight: 13.0000 g. **Composition:** 0.5000 Silver .2090 oz. ASW **Subject:** 250th Anniversary - Death of Jan Kupecky **Obverse:** Czech lion with socialist shield **Reverse:** J. Kupecky half-length figure right **Edge:** Milled **Size:** 31 mm. **Note:** 4,020 pieces, 4,000 Unc and 20 Proof, were melted by the Czech National Bank in 1997.

Date	Mintage	F	VF	XF	Unc	BU
ND(1990)	58,000	—	—	—	14.00	—
ND(1990) Proof	2,500	Value: 28.00				

KM# 105 500 KORUN Weight: 24.0000 g. **Composition:** 0.9000 Silver .6944 oz. ASW **Subject:** 125th Anniversary - Death of Ludovit Stur **Obverse:** Czech lion with socialist shield, value **Reverse:** L. Stur head facing **Edge Lettering:** 125 ROKOV OD SMRTI L' STURA **Size:** 40 mm. **Note:** 5,657 pieces, 4,057 Unc and 1,600 Proof, were melted by the Czech National Bank in 1997.

Date	Mintage	F	VF	XF	Unc	BU
ND(1981)	51,000	—	—	—	35.00	—
ND(1981) Proof	4,000	Value: 65.00				

KM# 112 500 KORUN Weight: 24.0000 g. **Composition:** 0.9000 Silver .6944 oz. ASW **Subject:** 100th Anniversary of Prague Theater **Obverse:** Czech lion with socialist shield, value **Reverse:** Female with book, theater facade at right **Edge Lettering:** NAROD SOBE **Size:** 40 mm. **Note:** 3,640 pieces, 2,040 Unc and 1,600 Proof, were melted by the Czech National Bank in 1997.

Date	Mintage	F	VF	XF	Unc	BU
ND(1983)	55,000	—	—	—	40.00	—
ND(1983) Proof	5,000	Value: 75.00				

KM# 136 500 KORUN Weight: 24.0000 g. **Composition:** 0.9000 Silver .6944 oz. ASW **Subject:** 100th Anniversary - Birth of Josef Lada **Obverse:** Czech lion with socialist shield, value **Reverse:** Town view, children building snowman **Edge Lettering:** CESKY MALIR NARODNI UMELEC **Size:** 40 mm. **Note:** 838 pieces, 800 Unc and 38 Proof, were melted by the Czech National Bank in 1997.

Date	Mintage	F	VF	XF	Unc	BU
ND(1987)	45,000	—	—	—	45.00	—
ND(1987) Proof	5,000	Value: 70.00				

KM# 131 500 KORUN Weight: 24.0000 g. **Composition:** 0.9000 Silver .6944 oz. ASW **Subject:** 20th Anniversary of National Federation **Obverse:** Czech lion with socialist shield, value **Reverse:** Stylized linden tree encircled by ribbon in shape of country **Edge Lettering:** 20. VYROCIE CESKOSLOVENSKEJ FEDERACIE oj **Size:** 40 mm. **Note:** 5,035 pieces, 5,000 Unc and 35 Proof, were melted by the Czech National Bank in 1997.

Date	Mintage	F	VF	XF	Unc	BU
ND(1988)	46,000	—	—	—	40.00	—
ND(1988) Proof	3,000	Value: 75.00				

KM# 134 500 KORUN Weight: 24.0000 g. **Composition:** 0.9000 Silver .6944 oz. ASW **Subject:** 125th Anniversary of Matica Slovenska Institute **Obverse:** Czech lion with socialist shield, value **Reverse:** Female standing in national costume holding book and linden sprig **Edge Lettering:** HOJ VLAST MOJA TY ZEM DRAHA **Size:** 40 mm. **Note:** 5,038 pieces, 5,000 Unc and 38 Proof, were melted by the Czech National Bank in 1997.

Date	Mintage	F	VF	XF	Unc	BU
ND(1988)	44,000	—	—	—	40.00	—
ND(1988) Proof	5,000	Value: 70.00				

CZECH SLOVAK FEDERAL REPUBLIC

DECIMAL COINAGE

KM# 149 HALER Composition: Aluminum **Obverse:** CSFR above shield, linden leaves flanking, date below **Reverse:** Value within linden wreath **Edge:** Plain **Size:** 16 mm.

Date	Mintage	F	VF	XF	Unc	BU
1991	55,000	—	—	—	2.50	—
1992	50,000	—	—	—	2.50	—

KM# 150 5 HALERU Weight: 0.7500 g. **Composition:** Aluminum **Obverse:** CSFR above shield, linden leaves flanking, date below **Obv. Designer:** Miroslav Ronai **Reverse:** Value **Rev. Designer:** Frantisek David **Edge:** Plain **Size:** 16.2 mm.

Date	Mintage	F	VF	XF	Unc	BU
1991	10,055,000	—	—	0.10	0.25	—
1992 In mint set only	50,000	—	—	—	2.00	—

KM# 146 10 HALERU Composition: Aluminum **Obverse:** CSFR above shield, linden leaves flanking, date below **Obv. Designer:** Miroslav Ronai **Reverse:** Value **Rev. Designer:** Frantisek David **Size:** 18.2 mm.

Date	Mintage	F	VF	XF	Unc	BU
1991 In mint sets only	55,000	—	—	—	0.50	—
1992 In mint sets only	50,000	—	—	—	0.50	—

KM# 143 20 HALERU Composition: Aluminum-Bronze **Obverse:** CSFR above shield, linden leaves flanking, date below **Obv. Designer:** Miroslav Ronai **Reverse:** Value **Rev. Designer:** Frantisek David **Edge:** Milled **Size:** 19.5 mm.

Date	Mintage	F	VF	XF	Unc	BU
1991	41,105,000	—	—	0.20	0.50	—
1992	35,050,000	—	—	0.20	0.50	—

KM# 144 50 HALERU Composition: Copper-Nickel **Obverse:** CSFR above shield, linden leaves flanking, date below **Obv. Designer:** Miroslav Ronai **Reverse:** Value **Rev. Designer:** Frantisek David **Edge:** Milled **Size:** 20.8 mm.

Date	Mintage	F	VF	XF	Unc	BU
1991	24,463,000	—	—	0.35	0.75	—
1992	15,062,000	—	—	0.35	0.75	—

KM# 151 KORUNA Composition: Copper-Aluminum **Obverse:** CSFR above shield, linden leaves flanking, date below **Obv. Designer:** Miroslav Ronai **Reverse:** Female planting linden sprig **Rev. Designer:** Marie Uchytilova-Kucova **Edge:** Milled **Size:** 23 mm.

Date	Mintage	F	VF	XF	Unc	BU
1991	20,056,000	—	—	0.50	1.00	—
1992	20,387,000	—	—	0.50	1.00	—

KM# 148 2 KORUNY Composition: Copper-Nickel **Obverse:** CSFR above shield, linden leaves flanking, date below **Obv. Designer:** Miroslav Ronai **Reverse:** Linden leaf, large value at right **Rev. Designer:** Josef Nalep . **Edge:** Plain with wave x wave **Size:** 24 mm.

Date	Mintage	F	VF	XF	Unc	BU
1991(k)	25,201,000	—	—	0.60	1.25	—
1991(l)	20,000,000	—	—	0.60	1.25	—
1992	1,051,000	—	—	—	1.25	—

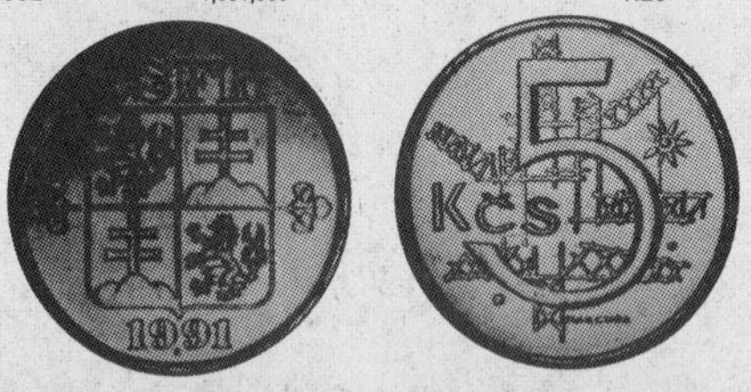

KM# 152 5 KORUN Composition: Copper-Nickel **Obverse:** CSFR above shield, linden leaves flanking, date below **Obv. Designer:** Jarmila Truhlikova-Spevakova **Reverse:** Geometric design, large value **Rev. Designer:** Drahomir Zobek **Edge:** Eight plain and eight milled areas **Size:** 26 mm.

Date	Mintage	F	VF	XF	Unc	BU
1991(k)	18,564,000	—	—	0.75	2.00	—
1991(l)	10,000,750	—	—	—	—	—
1992 In mint sets only	50,000	—	—	2.50	6.00	—

KM# 139.1 10 KORUN Composition: Nickel-Bronze **Obverse:** CSFR above shield, date below **Obv. Designer:** J. Truhlikova-Spevakova **Reverse:** Tomas G. Masaryk bust right **Rev. Designer:** M. Ronai **Edge:** Eight plain and eight milled areas **Size:** 24.5 mm. **Note:** Designer initials (MR) below bust, four varieties exist.

Date	Mintage	F	VF	XF	Unc	BU
1990	9,990,000	—	—	2.00	7.00	—
1993	2,500,000	—	—	2.00	6.00	—

KM# 139.2 10 KORUN Composition: Nickel-Bronze **Obverse:** CSFR above shield, date below **Obv. Designer:** J. Truhlikova-Spevakova **Reverse:** Tomas G. Masaryk bust right **Rev. Designer:** M. Ronai **Size:** 24.5 mm. **Note:** Designer name below bust: RONAI.

Date	F	VF	XF	Unc	BU
1990	—	2.00	5.00	10.00	—

KM# 153 10 KORUN Composition: Nickel-Bronze **Obverse:** CSFR above shield, date below **Obv. Designer:** J. Truhlikova-Spevakova **Reverse:** M. R. Stefanik bust left **Rev. Designer:** D. Zobek **Size:** 24.5 mm.

Date	Mintage	F	VF	XF	Unc	BU
1991	10,036,000	—	—	2.00	5.00	—
1993	2,500,000	—	—	2.50	6.00	—

KM# 159 10 KORUN Composition: Nickel-Bronze **Obverse:** Value, CSFR above shield, date below **Obv. Designer:** J. Truhlikova-Spevakova **Reverse:** A. Rasin bust right **Rev. Designer:** J. Uprka **Edge:** Eight plain and eight milled areas **Size:** 24.5 mm.

Date	Mintage	F	VF	XF	Unc	BU
1992	5,050,000	—	—	2.00	5.00	—

KM# 140.1 50 KORUN Weight: 7.0000 g. **Composition:** 0.5000 Silver .1125 oz. ASW **Obverse:** CSFR shield w/designer's initials (LK) below **Obv. Designer:** Ladislav Kolar **Reverse:** St. Agnes (Anezka) veiled head left **Rev. Designer:** Michal Vitanovsky **Edge:** Milled **Size:** 27 mm. **Note:** See note with KM#140.2. Designer emblem exists with and without initials.

Date	Mintage	F	VF	XF	Unc	BU
1990	147,000	—	—	—	7.00	—
1990 Proof	3,000	Value: 18.00				

KM# 140.2 50 KORUN Weight: 7.0000 g. **Composition:** 0.5000 Silver .1125 oz. ASW **Obverse:** CSFR shield, w/o designer initials (LK) **Reverse:** St. Agnes (Anezka) veiled head left **Size:** 27 mm. **Note:** 20 pieces, Unc and Proof of either KM#140.1 or 140.2, were melted by the Czech National Bank in 1977.

Date	F	VF	XF	Unc	BU
1990	—	—	—	10.00	—

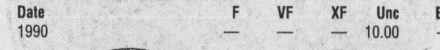

KM# 145 50 KORUN Weight: 7.0000 g. **Composition:** 0.5000 Silver .1125 oz. ASW **Obverse:** CSFR shield **Reverse:** Steamship Bohemia **Edge:** Milled **Size:** 27 mm. **Note:** 20 pieces, Unc and Proof, were melted by the Czech National Bank in 1977.

Date	Mintage	F	VF	XF	Unc	BU
ND(1991)	77,000	—	—	—	7.00	—
ND(1991) Proof	3,000	Value: 18.00				

KM# 155 50 KORUN Weight: 7.0000 g. **Composition:** 0.7000 Silver .1575 oz. ASW **Obverse:** CSFR shield **Reverse:** Piestany Spa building **Rev. Designer:** V. Oppl **Edge:** Milled **Size:** 27 mm. **Note:** 13,520 pieces, 12,020 Unc and 2,000 Proof, were melted by the Czech National Bank in 1977.

Date	Mintage	F	VF	XF	Unc	BU
1991		—	—	—	7.50	—
1991	Est. 5,000	Value: 16.50				

KM# 156 50 KORUN Weight: 7.0000 g. **Composition:** 0.7000 Silver .1575 oz. ASW **Obverse:** CSFR shield, value, date **Reverse:** Marianske Lazne Spa buildings **Rev. Designer:** J. Truhlikova-Spevakova **Edge:** Milled **Size:** 27 mm. **Note:** 13,520 pieces, 12,020 Unc and 1,500 Proof, were melted by the Czech National Bank in 1977.

Date	Mintage	F	VF	XF	Unc	BU
1991	75,000	—	—	—	7.50	—
1991 Proof	5,000	Value: 16.50				

KM# 157 50 KORUN Weight: 7.0000 g. **Composition:** 0.7000 Silver .1575 oz. ASW **Obverse:** CSFR shield, value, date **Reverse:** Chamois on rock, Karlovy Vary Spa buildings **Rev. Designer:** J. Truhlikova-Spevakova **Edge:** Milled **Size:** 27 mm. **Note:** 11,020, pieces, 10,020 Unc and 1,000 Proof, were melted by the Czech National Bank in 1977.

Date	Mintage	F	VF	XF	Unc	BU
1991	75,000	—	—	—	7.50	—
1991 Proof	5,000	Value: 16.50				

KM# 141 100 KORUN Weight: 13.0000 g. **Composition:** 0.5000 Silver .2090 oz. ASW **Subject:** Two horsemen right **Obverse:** CSFR shield, value **Edge:** Milled **Size:** 31 mm. **Note:** 20 pieces, Unc and Proof, were melted by the Czech National Bank in 1977.

Date	Mintage	F	VF	XF	Unc	BU
1990	67,000	—	—	—	15.00	—
1990 Proof	3,000	Value: 25.00				

KM# 142 100 KORUN Weight: 13.0000 g. **Composition:** 0.5000 Silver .2090 oz. ASW **Subject:** 100th Anniversary - Birth of Bohuslav Martinu **Obverse:** CSFR shield **Reverse:** B. Martinu head facing **Edge:** Milled **Size:** 31 mm. **Note:** 20 pieces, Unc and Proof, were melted by the Czech National Bank in 1977.

Date	Mintage	F	VF	XF	Unc	BU
ND(1990)	53,000	—	—	—	15.00	—
ND(1990)	53,000	—	—	—	15.00	—
ND(1990) Proof	2,000	Value: 22.00				

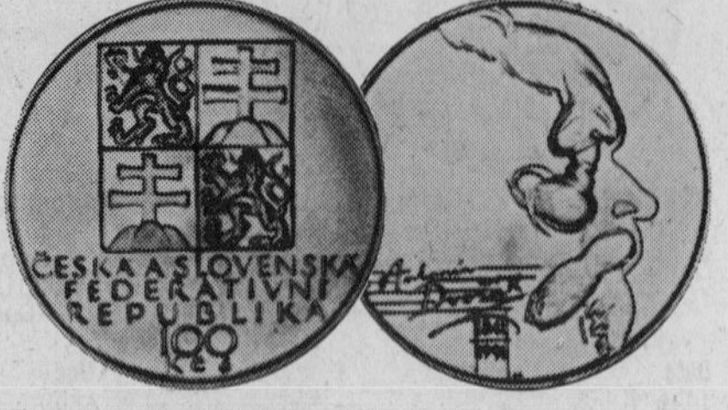

KM# 147 100 KORUN **Weight:** 13.0000 g. **Composition:** 0.5000 Silver .2926 oz. ASW **Subject:** 150th Anniversary - Birth of A. Dvorak **Obverse:** State emblem, value **Reverse:** A. Dvorak head right **Edge:** Milled **Size:** 31 mm. **Note:** 12,020 pieces, 10,029 Unc and 2,000 Proof, were melted by the Czech National Bank in 1977.

Date	Mintage	F	VF	XF	Unc	BU
1991	75,000	—	—	—	12.00	—
1991 Proof	5,000	Value: 20.00				

KM# 154 100 KORUN **Weight:** 13.0000 g. **Composition:** 0.7000 Silver .2926 oz. ASW **Subject:** 200th Anniversary - Death of Wolfgang A. Mozart **Obverse:** CSFR shield, value **Reverse:** Mozart bust right **Edge:** Milled **Size:** 31 mm. **Note:** 1,020 pieces, 1,000 Unc and 20 Proof, were melted by the Czech National Bank in 1977.

Date	Mintage	F	VF	XF	Unc	BU
ND(1991)	75,000	—	—	—	12.00	—
ND(1991) Proof	5,000	Value: 20.00				

KM# 160 100 KORUN **Weight:** 13.0000 g. **Composition:** 0.5000 Silver .2926 oz. ASW **Obverse:** CSFR shield, value **Reverse:** Moravian Museum, Moravian eagle **Edge:** Milled **Size:** 31 mm. **Note:** 23,877 pieces, Unc and Proof, were melted by the Czech National Bank in 1977.

Date	Mintage	F	VF	XF	Unc	BU
1992	73,000	—	—	—	10.00	—
1992 Proof	5,000	Value: 22.00				

KM# 161 100 KORUN **Weight:** 13.0000 g. **Composition:** 0.5000 Silver .2926 oz. ASW **Subject:** Nazi Massacres at Lidice and Lezaky **Obverse:** CSFR shield, value **Reverse:** Cross with barbed wire loop **Edge:** Milled **Size:** 31 mm. **Note:** 22,020 pieces, 22,000 Unc and 20 Proof, were melted by the Czech National Bank in 1977.

Date	Mintage	F	VF	XF	Unc	BU
1992	70,000	—	—	—	10.00	—
1992 Proof	3,000	Value: 22.00				

KM# 162 100 KORUN **Weight:** 13.0000 g. **Composition:** 0.5000 Silver .2926 oz. ASW **Subject:** 1000 Years of Brevnovsky Monastery **Obverse:** CSFR shield, value **Reverse:** Church and cloiser columns **Edge:** Milled **Size:** 31 mm. **Note:** 24,132 pieces, 24,000 Unc and 132 Proof, were melted by the Czech National Bank in 1977.

Date	Mintage	F	VF	XF	Unc	BU
ND(1993)	70,000	—	—	—	8.00	—
ND(1993) Proof	3,000	Value: 22.00				

KM# 163 100 KORUN **Weight:** 13.0000 g. **Composition:** 0.5000 Silver .2926 oz. ASW **Subject:** Society for Slovakian Museum **Obverse:** CSFR shield, value **Reverse:** Historic folk art designs **Edge:** Milled **Size:** 31 mm. **Note:** 30,132 pieces, 30,000 Unc and 132 Proof, were melted by the Czech National Bank in 1977.

Date	Mintage	F	VF	XF	Unc	BU
ND(1993)	70,000	—	—	—	8.00	—
ND(1993) Proof	3,000	Value: 22.00				

KM# 158 500 KORUN **Weight:** 24.0000 g. **Composition:** 0.9000 Silver .6944 oz. ASW **Subject:** 400th Anniversary - Birth of J. A. Komensky **Obverse:** CSFR shield, value **Reverse:** J. A. Komensky standing **Edge:** Milled **Size:** 40 mm. **Note:** 12,020 pieces, 10,020 Unc and 2000 Proof, were melted by the Czech National Bank in 1977.

Date	Mintage	F	VF	XF	Unc	BU
1992	60,000	—	—	—	32.50	—
1992 Proof	5,000	Value: 55.00				

KM# 164 500 KORUN **Weight:** 24.0000 g. **Composition:** 0.9000 Silver .6944 oz. ASW **Subject:** 100th year of Czech Tennis **Obverse:** CSFR shield, value **Reverse:** Male tennis player, stadium at left **Edge:** Milled **Size:** 40 mm. **Note:** 18,174 pieces, 18,042 Unc and 132 Proof, were melted by the Czech National Bank in 1977.

Date	Mintage	F	VF	XF	Unc	BU
ND(1993)	62,000	—	—	—	35.00	—
ND(1993) Proof	3,000	Value: 65.00				

PROBA

KM#	Date	Mintage	Identification	Mkt Val
Pr1	1922	—	Koruna. Aluminum.	—
Pr2	1922	—	Koruna. Copper-Nickel.	—
Pr5	1932	2	25 Haleru. Copper-Nickel. Thin notches.	—
Pr4	1932	2	25 Haleru. Copper-Nickel. W/dense notches.	—
Pr6	1932	10	25 Haleru. Copper-Nickel.	—
Pr3	1951	—	5 Koruna. Aluminum-Copper Magnesium.	—
Pr7	1976	—	3 Koruny.	—
Pr8	ND	2,500	100 Korun.	100

MINT SETS

KM#	Date	Mintage	Identification	Issue Price	Mkt Val
MS1	1980 (7)	50,000	KM50, 60, 74-75, 80, 86, 89	5.00	3.50
MS3	1982 (7)	53,000	KM50, 60, 74-75, 80, 86, 89	—	5.50
MS4	1983 (7)	50,000	KM50, 60, 74-75, 80, 86, 89	—	4.50
MS5	1984 (7)	39,000	KM50, 60, 74-75, 80, 86, 89	—	6.50
MS6	1985 (7)	39,000	KM50, 60, 74-75, 80, 86, 89	—	6.50
MS7	1986 (7)	20,000	KM50, 60, 74-75, 80, 86, 89	—	30.00
MS8	1987 (7)	30,000	km50, 60, 74-75, 80, 86, 89	—	15.00
MS9	1988 (7)	29,000	KM50, 60, 74-75, 80, 86, 89	—	10.00
MS10	1989 (7)	30,000	KM50, 60, 74-75, 80, 86, 89	—	10.00
MS11	1990 (7)	30,000	KM50, 60, 74-75, 80, 86, 89	—	10.00
MS12	1991 (9)	25,000	KM143-144, 146, 148-153	—	12.50
MS13	1991 (8)	30,000	KM143-144, 146, 148-152	—	12.50
MS14	1992 (9)	49,000	KM143-144, 146, 148-152, 159	—	15.00
MS15	1992 (8)	49,000	KM143-144,146, 148-152	—	10.00

DAHOMEY (Benin)

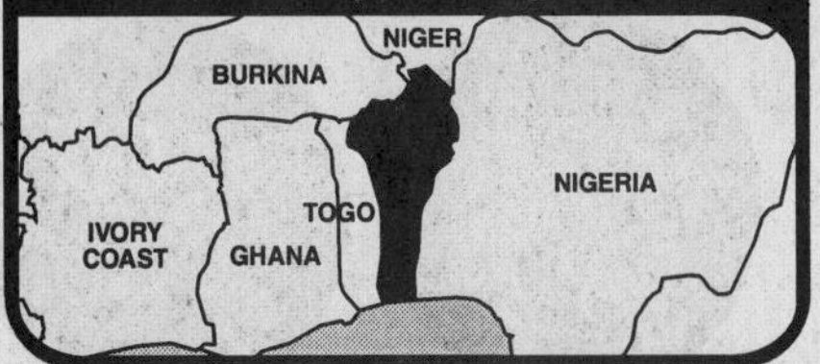

Porto-Novo, on the Bight of Benin, was founded as a trading post by the Portuguese in the 17th century. At that time, Dahomey (Benin) was composed of an aggregation of mutually suspicious tribes, the majority of which were tributary to the powerful northern Kingdom of Abomey. In 1863, the King of Porto-Novo petitioned France for protection from Abomey. The French subjugated other militant tribes as well, and in 1892 organized the area as a protectorate of France; in 1904 it was incorporated into French West Africa as the Territory of Dahomey. After the establishment of the Fifth French Republic, the Territory at Dahomey became an autonomous state within the French community. On Aug. 1, 1960, it became the fully independent Republic of Dahomey. In 1974, the republic began a transition to a socialist society with Marxism-Leninism as its revolutionary philosophy under Col. Ahmed Kerekow. On Nov. 30, 1975, the name of the Republic of Dahomey was changed to the Peoples Republic of Benin. As a result of Benin's first free presidential election in 30 years, Nicephore Soglo defeated Colonel Kerekou.

MINT MARKS

1 AR - Uno-A-Erre, Arezzo, Italy

REPUBLIC

STANDARD COINAGE

KM# 1.1 100 FRANCS Weight: 5.1000 g. **Composition:** 0.9990 Silver .1638 oz. ASW **Subject:** 10th Anniversary of Independence **Obverse:** Hallmark "999.9" above denomination

Date	Mintage	F	VF	XF	Unc	BU
1971 Proof	4,650	Value: 17.50				

KM# 1.2 100 FRANCS Weight: 5.1000 g. **Composition:** 0.9990 Silver .1638 oz. ASW **Obverse:** Hallmark "999.9" right of denomination

Date	Mintage	F	VF	XF	Unc	BU
1971 Proof	Inc. above	Value: 17.50				

KM# 1.3 100 FRANCS Weight: 5.1000 g. **Composition:** 0.9990 Silver .1638 oz. ASW **Obverse:** Hallmark "1000" lower right S in FRANCS

Date	Mintage	F	VF	XF	Unc	BU
1971 Proof	Inc. above	Value: 17.50				

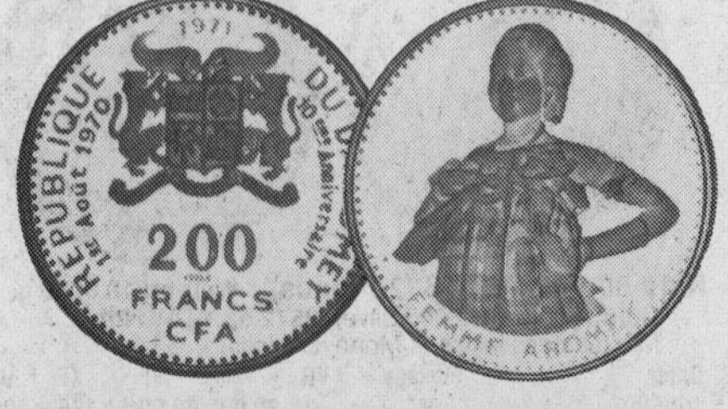

KM# 2.1 200 FRANCS Weight: 10.2500 g. **Composition:** 0.9990 Silver .3292 oz. ASW **Subject:** 10th Anniversary of Independence **Obverse:** Hallmark "999.9" between 200 and FRANCS

Date	Mintage	F	VF	XF	Unc	BU
1971 Proof	5,150	Value: 27.50				

KM# 2.2 200 FRANCS Weight: 10.2500 g. **Composition:** 0.9990 Silver .3292 oz. ASW **Obverse:** Hallmark "1000" lower right of S in FRANCS

Date	Mintage	F	VF	XF	Unc	BU
1971 Proof	Inc. above	Value: 27.50				

KM# 2.3 200 FRANCS Weight: 10.2500 g. **Composition:** 0.9990 Silver .3292 oz. ASW **Obverse:** Hallmark "999.9" lower right of S in FRANCS

Date	Mintage	F	VF	XF	Unc	BU
1971 Proof	Inc. above	Value: 27.50				

KM# 2.4 200 FRANCS Weight: 10.2500 g. **Composition:** 0.9990 Silver .3292 oz. ASW **Obverse:** Hallmark "999.9" in oval below "F" in "CFA".

Date	Mintage	F	VF	XF	Unc	BU
1971 Proof	Inc. above	Value: 60.00				

KM# 3.1 500 FRANCS Weight: 25.2000 g. **Composition:** 0.9990 Silver .8094 oz. ASW **Subject:** 10th Anniversary of Independence **Obverse:** "1000" in oval below "S" in FRANCS

Date	Mintage	F	VF	XF	Unc	BU
1971 Proof	5,550	Value: 75.00				

KM# 3.2 500 FRANCS Weight: 25.2000 g. **Composition:** 0.9990 Silver .8094 oz. ASW **Obverse:** "1 AR" and "1000" to right of CFA

Date	Mintage	F	VF	XF	Unc	BU
1971 Proof	Inc. above	Value: 75.00				

KM# 4.1 1000 FRANCS Weight: 51.5000 g. **Composition:** 0.9990 Silver 1.6542 oz. ASW **Subject:** 10th Anniversary of Independence **Obverse:** Similar to 500 Francs, KM#3.1

Date	Mintage	F	VF	XF	Unc	BU
1971 Proof	6,500	Value: 125				

KM# 4.2 1000 FRANCS Weight: 51.5000 g. **Composition:** 0.9990 Silver 1.6542 oz. ASW **Obverse:** Similar to 500 Francs, KM#3.2

Date	Mintage	F	VF	XF	Unc	BU
1971 Proof	Inc. above	Value: 125				

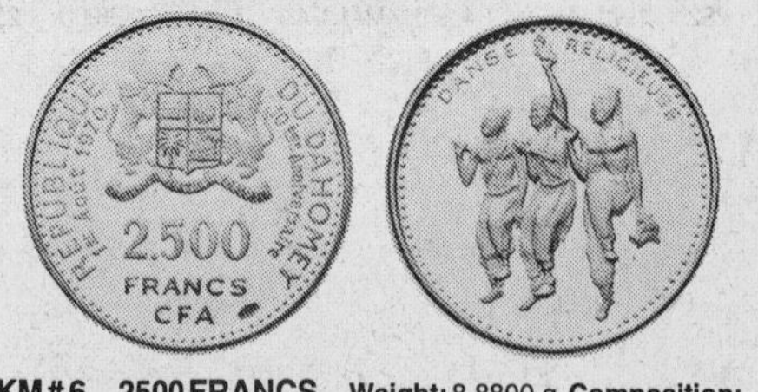

KM# 6 2500 FRANCS Weight: 8.8800 g. **Composition:** 0.9000 Gold .2569 oz. AGW **Subject:** 10th Anniversary of Independence **Reverse:** Dancers

Date	Mintage	F	VF	XF	Unc	BU
1971 Proof	960	Value: 220				

KM# 7 5000 FRANCS Weight: 17.7700 g. **Composition:** 0.9000 Gold .5142 oz. AGW **Subject:** 10th Anniversary of Independence **Obverse:** Similar to 2500 Francs, KM#6 **Reverse:** Water Buffalos

Date	Mintage	F	VF	XF	Unc	BU
1971 Proof	610	Value: 425				

KM# 8 10000 FRANCS **Weight:** 35.5500 g. **Composition:** 0.9000 Gold 1.0287 oz. AGW **Subject:** 10th Anniversary of Independence **Obverse:** Similar to 2500 Francs, KM#6 **Reverse:** Hippopotamuses

Date	Mintage	F	VF	XF	Unc	BU
1971 Proof	470	Value: 825				

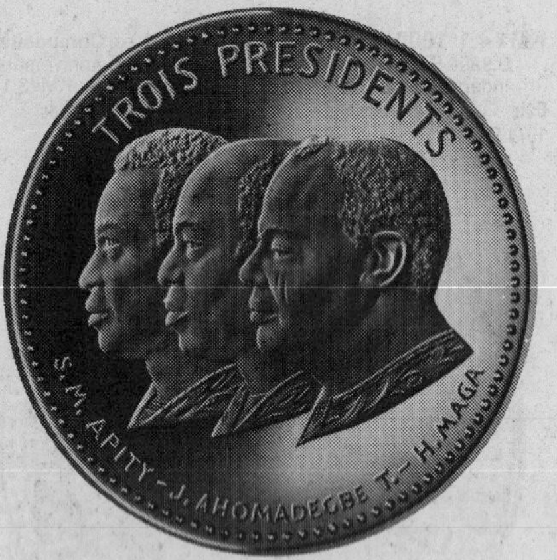

KM# 9 25000 FRANCS **Weight:** 88.8800 g. **Composition:** 0.9000 Gold 2.5720 oz. AGW **Subject:** 10th Anniversary of Independence **Obverse:** Similar to 2500 Francs, KM#6 **Reverse:** Presidents

Date	Mintage	F	VF	XF	Unc	BU
1971 Proof	380	Value: 1,450				

PROOF SETS

KM#	Date	Mintage	Identification	Issue Price	Mkt Val
PS1	1971 (8)	380	KM#1.1-4.1, 6-9	—	3,175
PS2	1971 (4)	4,270	KM#1.1-4.1	36.00	250

DANISH WEST INDIES

The Danish West Indies (now the U.S. organized unincorporated territory of the Virgin Islands of the United States) consisted of the islands of St. Thomas, St. John, St. Croix, and 62 islets in the Caribbean Sea roughly 40 miles (64 km.) east of Puerto Rico. The islands have a combined area of 133 sq. mi. (352 sq. km.) and a population of *106,000. Capital: Charlotte Amalie. Tourism is the principal industry. Watch movements, costume jewelry, pharmaceuticals, and rum are exported.

The Virgin Islands were discovered by Columbus, in 1493, during his second voyage to America. During the 17th century, individual islands, actually the peaks of a submerged mountain range, were held by Spain, Holland, England, France and Denmark. These islands were also the favorite resorts of the buccaneers operating in the Caribbean and the coastal waters of eastern North America. Control of most of the 100-island group finally passed to Denmark, with England securing the easterly remainder. The Danish islands had their own coinage from the early 18th century, based on but unequal to, Denmark's homeland system. In the late 18th and early 19th centuries, Danish minor copper and silver coinage augmented the islands currency. The Danish islands were purchased by the United States in 1917 for $25 million, mainly to forestall their acquisition by Germany and because they command the Anegada Passage into the Caribbean Sea, a strategic point on the defense perimeter of the Panama Canal.

RULERS

Danish, until 1917

MINTMASTERS INITIALS

Letter	Date	Name
P, VBP	1893-1918	Vilhelm Buchard Poulsen

MONEYERS INITIALS

Letter	Date	Name
GJ	1901-1933	Knud Gunnar Jensen
AH	1908-1924	Andreas Frederik Vilhelm Hansen

MONETARY SYSTEM

(1904-1934)
5 Bit = 1 Cent
100 Bit = 1 Franc
5 Francs = 1 Daler

DANISH COLONY

DECIMAL COINAGE

20 Cents = 1 Franc

KM# 74 1/2 CENT (2-1/2 Bit) **Composition:** Bronze **Note:** Mintmaster's initial: P. Moneyer's initials: GJ.

Date	Mintage	VG	F	VF	XF	Unc
1905(h)	190,000	—	3.50	5.50	12.50	25.00
1905(h) Prooflike, rare	—	—	—	—	—	—

KM# 75 CENT (5 Bit) **Composition:** Bronze **Note:** Mintmaster's initial: P. Moneyer's initials: GJ.

Date	Mintage	VG	F	VF	XF	Unc
1905(h)	500,000	—	3.50	7.50	18.50	40.00

KM# 83 CENT (5 Bit) **Composition:** Bronze **Note:** Mintmaster's initials: VBP. Moneyer's initials: AH-GJ.

Date	Mintage	VG	F	VF	XF	Unc
1913(h)	200,000	—	10.00	17.50	40.00	70.00

KM# 76 2 CENTS (10 Bit) **Composition:** Bronze **Note:** Mintmaster's initial: P. Moneyer's initials: GJ.

Date	Mintage	VG	F	VF	XF	Unc
1905(h)	150,000	—	5.00	13.50	30.00	55.00
1905(h) Prooflike, rare	20	—	—	—	—	—

KM# 77 5 CENTS (25 Bit) **Composition:** Nickel **Note:** Mintmaster's initial: P. Moneyer's initials: GJ.

Date	Mintage	VG	F	VF	XF	Unc
1905(h)	199,000	—	3.00	7.50	18.50	50.00
1905(h) Prooflike, rare	20	—	—	—	—	—

KM# 78 10 CENTS (50 Bit) **Weight:** 2.5000 g. **Composition:** 0.8000 Silver .0643 oz. ASW **Note:** Mintmaster's initial: P. Moneyer's initials: GJ.

Date	Mintage	VG	F	VF	XF	Unc
1905(h)	175,000	—	4.00	8.50	18.50	50.00
1905(h) Prooflike, rare	20	—	—	—	—	—

KM# 79 20 CENTS (1 Franc) **Weight:** 5.0000 g. **Composition:** 0.8000 Silver .1286 oz. ASW **Note:** Mintmaster's initial: P. Moneyer's initials: GJ.

Date	Mintage	VG	F	VF	XF	Unc
1905(h)	150,000	—	12.50	27.50	65.00	115
1905(h) Prooflike, rare	20	—	—	—	—	—

KM# 81 20 CENTS (1 Franc) **Weight:** 5.0000 g. **Composition:** 0.8000 Silver .1286 oz. ASW **Note:** Mintmaster's initial: P. Moneyer's initials: GJ.

Date	Mintage	VG	F	VF	XF	Unc
1907(h)	101,000	—	15.00	32.50	82.50	140
1907(h) Prooflike, rare	10	—	—	—	—	—

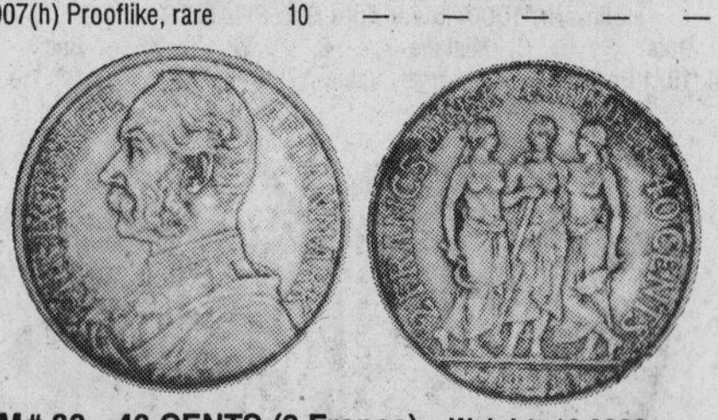

KM# 80 40 CENTS (2 Francs) **Weight:** 10.0000 g. **Composition:** 0.8000 Silver .2572 oz. ASW **Note:** Mintmaster's initial: P. Moneyer's initials: GJ.

Date	Mintage	VG	F	VF	XF	Unc
1905(h)	38,000	—	30.00	60.00	135	265
1905(h) Prooflike, rare	20	—	—	—	—	—

KM# 82 40 CENTS (2 Francs) **Weight:** 10.0000 g. **Composition:** 0.8000 Silver .2572 oz. ASW **Note:** Mintmaster's initial: P. Moneyer's initials: GJ.

Date	Mintage	VG	F	VF	XF	Unc
1907(h)	25,000	—	52.50	115	190	365
1907(h)	10	—	—	—	—	—

KM# 72 4 DALER (20 Francs) **Weight:** 6.4516 g. **Composition:** 0.9000 Gold .1867 oz. AGW **Note:** Mintmaster's initial: P. Moneyer's initials: GJ.

Date	Mintage	F	VF	XF	Unc	BU
1904(h)	121,000	150	250	350	575	—
1905(h)	Inc. above	150	275	400	675	—

KM# 73 10 DALER (50 Francs) **Weight:** 16.1290 g. **Composition:** 0.9000 Gold .4667 oz. AGW **Note:** Mintmaster's initial: P. Moneyer's initials: GJ.

Date	Mintage	F	VF	XF	Unc	BU
1904(h)	2,005	1,250	2,000	4,250	6,775	—

TRIAL STRIKES

KM#	Date	Mintage	Identification	Mkt Val
TS1	1904	—	20 Francs. Copper. 10.8000 g. KM#72.	—
TS2	1904	—	20 Francs. Copper. 10.8000 g. KM#72.	—

PROOF-LIKE SETS (PL)

KM#	Date	Mintage	Identification	Issue Price	Mkt Val
PL4	1905 (5)	20	KM#76-80	—	—
PL5	1907 (2)	10	KM#81-82	—	—

DENMARK

The Kingdom of Denmark (Danmark), a constitutional monarchy located at the mouth of the Baltic Sea, has an area of 16,639 sq. mi. (43,070 sq. km.) and a population of 5.2 million. Capital: Copenhagen. Most of the country is arable. Agriculture is conducted by large farms served by cooperatives. The largest industries are food processing, iron and metal, and shipping. Machinery, meats (chiefly bacon), dairy products and chemicals are exported.

Denmark, a great power during the Viking period of the 9th-11th centuries, conducted raids on western Europe and England, and in the 11th century united England, Denmark and Norway under the rule of King Canute. Despite a struggle between the crown and the nobility (13th-14th centuries) which forced the King to grant a written constitution, Queen Margaret (Margrethe) (1387-1412) succeeded in uniting Denmark, Norway, Sweden, Finland and Greenland under the Danish crown, placing all of the Nordic countries under the rule of Denmark. An unwise alliance with Napoleon caused the loss of Norway to Sweden in 1814. In the following years a liberal movement was fostered, which succeeded in making Denmark a constitutional monarchy in 1849.

In 1864, Denmark lost Schleswig and Holstein to Prussia. In 1920, Denmark regained North-Schleswig by plebiscite.

The present decimal system of currency was introduced in 1874. As a result of a referendum held September 28, 2000, the currency of the European Monetary Union, the Euro, will not be introduced in Denmark in the foreseeable future.

RULERS

Christian IX, 1863-1906
Frederik VIII, 1906-1912
Christian X, 1912-1947
Frederik IX, 1947-1972
Margrethe II, 1972—

MINT MARKS

(h) - Copenhagen, heart

MINTMASTERS INITIALS

Copenhagen

Letter	Date	Name
*P, VBP	1893-1918	Vilhelm Buchard Poulsen
HCN	1919-1927	Hans Christian Nielsen
N	1927-1955	Niels Peter Nielsen
C	1956-1971	Alfred Frederik Christiansen
S	1971-1978	Vagn Sorensen
B	1978-1981	Peter M Bjarno
R, NR	1982-1989	N. Norregaard Rasmussen
LG	1989-	Laust Grove

NOTE: The letter P was only used on Danish West Indies coins.

MONEYERS INITIALS

Copenhagen

Letter	Date	Name
GI, GJ	1901-1933	Knud Gunnar Jensen
AH	1908-1924	Andreas Frederik Vilhelm Hansen
HS, S	1933-1968	Harald Salomon
B	1968-1983	Frode Bahnsen
A	1986-	Johan Alkjaer (designer)
HV	1986-	Hanne Varming (sculptor)
JP	1989-	Jan Petersen

MONETARY SYSTEM

100 Øre = 1 Krone

KINGDOM

DECIMAL COINAGE

100 Øre = 1 Krone

KM# 792.2 ØRE **Weight:** 2.0000 g. **Composition:** Bronze **Ruler:** Christian IX **Obverse:** Crowned CIX monogram, date lower left, initials lower right **Reverse:** Value above porpoise and barley ear

Date	Mintage	F	VF	XF	Unc	BU
1902/802(h) VBP	2,977,000	2.75	4.50	10.00	25.00	—
1902(h) VBP	Inc. above	1.75	2.75	6.50	20.00	—
1904/804(h) VBP	4,962,000	1.75	3.50	6.00	17.50	—
1904(h) VBP	Inc. above	1.25	2.25	3.50	12.50	—

KM# 804 ØRE **Weight:** 2.0000 g. **Composition:** Bronze **Ruler:** Frederik VIII **Obverse:** Value within legend, date and initials **Reverse:** Crowned F VIII monogram, initials lower right **Rev. Legend:** "THE KINGDOM OF DENMARK"

Date	Mintage	F	VF	XF	Unc	BU
1907(h) VBP, GJ	5,975,000	1.25	2.75	5.50	14.00	—
1909(h) VBP, GJ	2,985,000	1.25	2.75	5.50	15.00	—
1910(h) VBP; GJ	2,994,000	1.75	4.50	10.00	22.00	—
1912(h) VBP; GJ	3,006,000	1.25	3.75	7.00	18.50	—

KM# 812.1 ØRE **Weight:** 2.0000 g. **Composition:** Bronze **Ruler:** Christian X **Obverse:** Crowned CX monogram, initials and mint mark lower left, date and initials lower right **Reverse:** Value, ornament flanking

Date	Mintage	F	VF	XF	Unc	BU
1913(h) VBP; GJ	5,011,000	1.00	1.50	2.00	6.00	—
1915(h) VBP; GJ	4,940,000	1.35	2.25	3.75	8.00	—
1916(h) VBP; GJ	2,439,000	1.35	2.75	4.50	11.00	—
1917(h) VBP; GJ	4,564,000	16.00	25.00	37.50	70.00	—

KM# 812.1a ØRE **Weight:** 1.7400 g. **Composition:** Iron **Ruler:** Christian X **Obverse:** Crowned CX monogram, initials and mint mark lower left, date and initials lower right **Reverse:** Value, ornament flanking

Date	Mintage	F	VF	XF	Unc	BU
1918(h) VBP; GJ	6,776,000	1.75	3.75	11.50	37.50	—

KM# 812.2 ØRE **Weight:** 2.0000 g. **Composition:** Bronze **Ruler:** Christian X **Obverse:** Crowned F VIII monogram, initials and mint mark lower left, date and initials lower right **Reverse:** Value, ornament flanking

Date	Mintage	F	VF	XF	Unc	BU
1919(h) HCN; GJ	4,586,000	1.00	1.75	4.00	8.50	—
1920(h) HCN; GJ	2,367,000	6.00	12.00	22.50	50.00	—
1921(h) HCN; GJ	3,121,000	1.35	2.25	3.25	8.50	—
1922(h) HCN; GJ	3,267,000	1.75	2.50	4.00	9.50	—
1923(h) HCN; GJ	2,938,000	1.75	2.50	3.75	8.50	—

KM# 812.2a ØRE **Weight:** 1.7400 g. **Composition:** Iron **Ruler:** Christian X **Obverse:** Crowned F VIII monogram, initials and mint mark lower left, date and initials lower right **Reverse:** Value, ornament flanking

Date	Mintage	F	VF	XF	Unc	BU
1919(h) HCN; GJ	931,000	4.50	14.00	32.00	65.00	—

KM# 826.1 ØRE **Weight:** 1.9000 g. **Composition:** Bronze **Ruler:** Christian X **Obverse:** Country name and date above center hole, denomination, mint mark, and initials below **Reverse:** Crowned CX monogram within title "KING OF DENMARK"

Date	Mintage	F	VF	XF	Unc	BU
1926(h) HCN; GJ	1,572,000	2.75	5.50	18.50	50.00	—
1927(h) HCN; GJ	Inc. above	0.10	0.30	3.50	17.50	—

KM# 826.2 ØRE **Weight:** 1.9000 g. **Composition:** Bronze **Ruler:** Christian X **Obverse:** Date above center hole, value, mint mark and initials below **Reverse:** Date above center hole, value, mint mark, initials **Note:** For coins dated 1941 refer to Faeroe Islands listings at the end of Denmark.

Date	Mintage	F	VF	XF	Unc	BU
1927(h) N; GJ	Inc. above	3.75	9.50	25.00	80.00	—
1928(h) N; GJ	29,691,000	0.10	0.25	2.75	12.50	—
1929(h) N; GJ	5,172,000	0.10	0.25	2.75	16.50	—
1930(h) N; GJ	5,306,000	0.10	0.20	2.75	19.50	—
1932(h) N; GJ	5,089,000	0.10	0.20	2.75	16.50	—
1933(h) N; GJ	2,095,000	0.25	1.00	4.00	27.50	—
1934(h) N; GJ	3,665,000	—	0.10	1.00	9.00	—
1935(h) N; GJ	5,668,000	—	0.10	1.00	6.50	—
1936(h) N; GJ	5,584,000	—	0.10	0.50	3.50	—
1937(h) N; GJ	6,877,000	—	0.10	0.50	2.75	—
1938(h) N; GJ	3,850,000	—	0.10	0.50	2.25	—
1939(h) N; GJ	5,662,000	—	0.10	0.35	2.25	—
1940(h) N; GJ	1,965,000	—	0.10	0.35	1.75	—

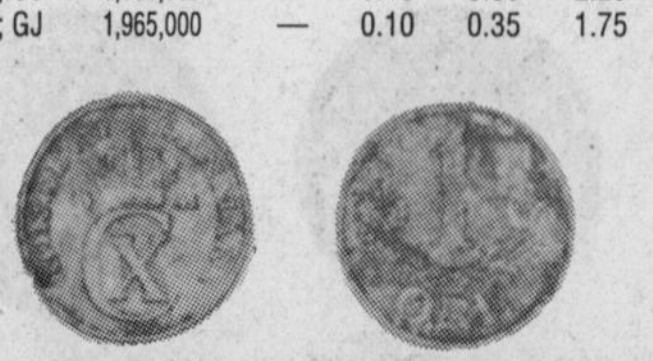

KM# 832 ØRE **Weight:** 1.6000 g. **Composition:** Zinc **Ruler:** Christian X **Obverse:** Crowned CX monogram and date within title: "KING OF DENMARK"; mint mark and initials below **Reverse:** Value between oak and beach leaves

Date	Mintage	F	VF	XF	Unc	BU
1941(h) N; S	21,570,000	0.10	0.35	6.50	28.00	—
1942(h) N; S	6,997,000	0.10	0.35	6.50	28.00	—
1943(h) N; S	15,082,000	0.10	0.35	6.50	28.00	—
1944(h) N; S	11,981,000	0.10	0.35	6.50	28.00	—
1945(h) N; S	916,000	1.00	2.00	13.50	37.50	—
1946(h) N; S	712,000	3.00	6.50	18.50	50.00	—

KM# 839.1 ØRE Weight: 1.6000 g. **Composition:** Zinc **Ruler:** Frederik IX **Obverse:** Crowned F IX monogram and date **Reverse:** Mint mark, initials below value

Date	Mintage	F	VF	XF	Unc	BU
1948(h) N; S	460,000	1.25	2.25	9.50	40.00	—
1949(h) N; S	2,513,000	0.35	1.00	3.50	40.00	—
1950(h) N; S	9,453,000	0.25	0.50	3.25	30.00	—
1951(h) N; S	2,931,000	0.35	1.00	3.50	40.00	—
1952(h) N; S	7,626,000	0.10	0.35	2.25	20.00	—
1953(h) N; S	11,994,000	0.10	0.25	2.25	20.00	—
1954(h) N; S	12,642,000	0.10	0.25	2.25	18.00	—
1955(h) N; S	14,177,000	0.10	0.25	1.75	18.00	—

KM# 839.2 ØRE Weight: 1.6000 g. **Composition:** Zinc **Ruler:** Frederik IX **Obverse:** Crowned F IX monogram, date **Reverse:** Mint mark, initial C below value

Date	Mintage	F	VF	XF	Unc	BU
1956(h) C; S	20,211,000	0.10	0.25	1.00	4.50	—
1957(h) C; S	20,900,000	0.10	0.25	1.00	4.50	—
1958(h) C; S	16,021,000	—	0.10	0.75	3.75	—
1959(h) C; S	15,929,000	—	0.10	0.75	3.75	—
1960(h) C; S	23,982,000	—	0.10	0.75	2.75	—
1961(h) C; S	18,986,000	—	0.10	0.60	2.25	—
1962(h) C; S	16,992,000	—	0.10	0.50	1.50	—
1963(h) C; S	28,986,000	—	0.10	0.50	1.50	—
1964(h) C; S	21,971,000	—	0.10	0.35	1.50	—
1965(h) C; S	29,943,000	—	0.10	0.25	1.50	—
1966(h) C; S	35,907,000	—	0.10	0.25	1.50	—
1967(h) C; S	32,959,000	—	0.10	0.25	1.50	—
1968(h) C; S	21,889,000	—	—	0.10	0.85	—
1969(h) C; S	29,243,000	—	—	0.10	0.88	—
1970(h) C; S	22,970,000	—	—	0.10	0.50	—
1971(h) C; S	21,983,000	—	—	0.10	0.50	—

KM# 846 ØRE Weight: 1.8000 g. **Composition:** Bronze **Ruler:** Frederik IX **Obverse:** Crowned F IX monogram, date **Reverse:** Two barley stalks around value, initials below **Note:** Never released for circulation, see note 2 Ore, KM#847.

Date	Mintage	F	VF	XF	Unc	BU
1960(h) C; S	8,990,000	—	—	—	3.00	—
1962(h) C; S	Inc. above	—	—	—	3.00	—
1963(h) C; S	9,980,000	—	—	—	3.00	—
1964(h) C; S	2,990,000	—	—	—	3.00	—

KM# 839.3 ØRE Composition: Zinc **Ruler:** Frederik IX **Obverse:** Crowned F IX monogram, date **Reverse:** Mint mark, initial S below value

Date	Mintage	F	VF	XF	Unc	BU
1972(h) S; S	13,000,000	—	—	0.10	0.60	—

KM# 793.2 2 ØRE Composition: Bronze **Ruler:** Christian IX **Obverse:** Crowned CIX monogram, date lower left, initials lower right **Reverse:** Value above porpoise and barley ear

Date	Mintage	F	VF	XF	Unc	BU
1902/802(h) VBP	3,502,000	1.75	4.00	6.50	42.00	—
1902(h) VBP	Inc. above	1.35	2.75	5.00	32.00	—
1906(h) VBP	2,498,000	3.25	7.00	11.50	42.00	—

KM# 805 2 ØRE Weight: 4.0000 g. **Composition:** Bronze **Ruler:** Frederik VIII **Obverse:** Value within legend, date, initials **Reverse:** Crowned F VIII monogram, initials lower right

Date	Mintage	F	VF	XF	Unc	BU
1907(h) VBP; GJ	2,502,000	1.50	3.00	7.50	22.00	—
1909(h) VBP; GJ	2,485,000	2.00	4.00	16.50	50.00	—
1912(h) VBP; GJ	2,480,000	2.00	4.00	10.00	30.00	—

KM# 813.1 2 ØRE Weight: 4.0000 g. **Composition:** Bronze **Ruler:** Christian X **Obverse:** Crowned CX monogram, initials and mint mark at lower left, date and initials at lower right **Reverse:** Value, ornament flanking

Date	Mintage	F	VF	XF	Unc	BU
1913(h) VBP; GJ	373,000	27.50	45.00	75.00	175	—
1914(h) VBP; GJ	2,126,000	2.25	4.00	6.50	25.00	—
1915(h) VBP; GJ	2,485,000	1.75	4.00	6.50	22.50	—
1916(h) VBP; GJ	1,383,000	2.75	4.00	7.50	27.50	—
1917(h) VBP; GJ	1,837,000	14.00	27.50	45.00	80.00	—

KM# 813.1a 2 ØRE Weight: 3.4700 g. **Composition:** Iron **Ruler:** Christian X **Obverse:** Crowned CX monogram, initials and mint mark lower left, date and initials lower right **Reverse:** Value, ornament flanking

Date	Mintage	F	VF	XF	Unc	BU
1918(h) VBP; GJ	4,160,999	2.00	4.00	14.00	55.00	—

KM# 813.2 2 ØRE Weight: 4.0000 g. **Composition:** Bronze **Ruler:** Christian X **Obverse:** Crowned F VIII monogram, initials and mint mark lower left, date and initials lower right **Reverse:** Value, ornament flanking

Date	Mintage	F	VF	XF	Unc	BU
1919(h) HCN; GJ	5,503,000	5.50	10.00	22.50	50.00	—
1920(h) HCN; GJ	2,528,000	1.00	1.50	3.50	20.00	—
1921(h) HCN; GJ	2,158,000	3.25	5.00	7.50	17.50	—
1923(h) HCN; GJ	2,625,000	2.25	4.00	6.00	17.50	—

KM# 813.2a 2 ØRE Weight: 3.4700 g. **Composition:** Iron **Ruler:** Christian X **Obverse:** Crowned F VIII monogram, initials and mint mark lower left, date and initials lower right **Reverse:** Value, ornament flanking

Date	Mintage	F	VF	XF	Unc	BU
1919(h) HCN; GJ	1,944,000	16.50	37.50	70.00	175	—

KM# 827.1 2 ØRE Weight: 3.8000 g. **Composition:** Bronze **Ruler:** Christian X **Obverse:** Country name and date above center hole, denomination, mint mark, and initials below **Reverse:** Crowned CX monogram within title "KING OF DENMARK"

Date	Mintage	F	VF	XF	Unc	BU
1926(h) HCN; GJ	301,000	37.50	55.00	180	550	—
1927(h) HCN; GJ	15,359,000	0.10	0.20	2.75	18.50	—

KM# 827.2 2 ØRE Weight: 3.8000 g. **Composition:** Bronze **Ruler:** Christian X **Obverse:** Date above center hole, value, mint mark and initials below **Reverse:** Date above center hole, value, mint mark, initials **Note:** For coins dated 1941 refer to Faeore Islands listings.

Date	Mintage	F	VF	XF	Unc	BU
1927(h) N; GJ	Inc. above	1.25	2.25	37.50	150	—
1928(h) N; GJ	5,758,000	0.10	0.20	2.25	16.00	—
1929(h) N; GJ	6,817,000	0.10	0.20	2.25	32.00	—
1930(h) N; GJ	2,327,000	0.60	1.25	5.50	60.00	—
1931(h) N; GJ	5,135,000	0.10	0.20	2.25	25.00	—
1932(h) N; GJ	Inc. above	1.25	2.25	18.50	90.00	—
1934(h) N; GJ	756,000	0.50	1.00	7.00	37.50	—
1935(h) N; GJ	1,391,000	0.10	0.20	1.50	18.50	—
1936(h) N; GJ	2,973,000	0.10	0.20	1.00	18.50	—
1937(h) N; GJ	3,437,000	0.10	0.20	1.00	9.50	—
1938(h) N; GJ	2,177,000	—	0.10	0.55	4.50	—
1939(h) N; GJ	3,165,000	—	0.10	0.55	2.75	—
1940(h) N; GJ	1,582,000	—	0.10	0.50	2.00	—

KM# 833 2 ØRE Weight: 1.2000 g. **Composition:** Aluminum **Ruler:** Christian X **Obverse:** Crowned CX monogram and date within title: "KING OF DENMARK"; mint mark and initials below **Reverse:** Value between oak and beach leaves

Date	Mintage	F	VF	XF	Unc	BU
1941(h) N; S	26,205,000	0.10	0.60	2.25	12.50	—
1941(h) N; S Proof	—	Value: 150				

KM# 833a 2 ØRE Weight: 3.2000 g. **Composition:** Zinc **Ruler:** Christian X **Obverse:** Crowned CX monogram and date within title: "KING OF DENMARK"; mint mark and initials below **Reverse:** Value between oak and beach leaves

Date	Mintage	F	VF	XF	Unc	BU
1942(h) N; S	12,934,000	0.10	0.50	5.50	35.00	—
1943(h) N; S	9,603,000	0.10	0.50	5.50	35.00	—
1944(h) N; S	6,069,000	0.10	0.50	5.50	35.00	—
1945(h) N; S	329,000	3.75	7.50	27.50	90.00	—
1947(h) N; S	589,000	1.35	2.25	14.00	70.00	—

KM# 840.1 2 ØRE Weight: 3.2000 g. **Composition:** Zinc **Ruler:** Frederik IX **Obverse:** Crowned F IX monogram and date **Reverse:** Mint mark, initials below value

Date	Mintage	F	VF	XF	Unc	BU
1948(h) N; S	1,927,000	0.40	1.00	4.50	27.50	—
1949(h) N; S	1,603,000	3.75	14.50	40.00	165	—
1950(h) N; S	4,544,000	0.75	1.35	4.50	32.00	—
1951(h) N; S	3,766,000	1.50	2.50	9.50	55.00	—
1952(h) N; S	4,874,000	0.10	0.20	2.25	27.50	—
1953(h) N; S	8,112,000	0.10	0.20	2.25	20.00	—
1954(h) N; S	6,497,000	0.10	0.20	2.25	18.00	—
1955(h) N; S	6,968,000	—	0.10	1.50	11.50	—

KM# 840.2 2 ØRE Weight: 3.2000 g. **Composition:** Zinc **Ruler:** Frederik IX **Obverse:** Crowned F IX monogram and date **Reverse:** Mint mark, initials below value

Date	Mintage	F	VF	XF	Unc	BU
1956(h) C; S	10,004,000	—	0.10	1.25	5.50	—
1957(h) C; S	15,329,000	—	0.10	1.00	4.50	—
1958(h) C; S	8,119,999	—	0.10	1.00	4.00	—
1959(h) C; S	10,462,000	—	0.10	1.00	3.75	—
1960(h) C; S	16,504,000	—	0.10	0.80	2.75	—
1961(h) C; S	15,504,000	—	0.10	0.80	2.25	—
1962(h) C; S	10,980,000	—	0.10	0.80	2.25	—
1963(h) C; S	19,470,000	—	0.10	0.35	1.50	—
1964(h) C; S	15,411,000	—	0.10	0.35	1.25	—
1965(h) C; S	20,173,000	—	0.10	0.20	1.00	—
1966(h) C; S	21,949,000	—	0.10	0.20	1.00	—
1967(h) C; S	22,439,000	—	0.10	0.20	1.00	—
1968(h) C; S	17,632,000	—	—	0.10	0.80	—
1969(h) C; S	29,276,000	—	—	0.10	0.80	—
1970(h) C; S	23,864,000	—	—	0.10	0.50	—
1971(h) C; S	35,811,000	—	—	0.10	0.50	—

KM# 847 2 ØRE Weight: 3.6000 g. **Composition:** Bronze **Ruler:** Frederik IX **Obverse:** Crowned F IX monogram, date **Reverse:** Two barley stalks around value, initials below **Note:** KM#847 was never released for circulation. Together with the 4 dates of 1 Ore, KM#846, they were sold as a 10 coin set to collectors by the mint. Approximately 100,000 sets were sold, remaining coins were melted.

Date	Mintage	F	VF	XF	Unc	BU
1960(h) C; S	Inc. above	—	—	—	3.00	—
1962(h) C; S	Inc. above	—	—	—	3.00	—
1963(h) C; S	100,000	—	—	—	3.00	—
1964(h) C; S	3,990,000	—	—	—	3.00	—
1965(h) C; S	11,980,000	—	—	—	3.00	—
1966(h) C; S	12,000,000	—	—	—	3.00	—

KM# 840.3 2 ØRE Weight: 3.2000 g. **Composition:** Zinc **Ruler:** Frederik IX **Obverse:** Crowned F IX monogram and date **Reverse:** Mint mark, initials below value

Date	Mintage	F	VF	XF	Unc	BU
1972(h) S; S	6,496,000	—	0.15	0.35	0.85	—

KM# 794.2 5 ØRE Weight: 8.0000 g. **Composition:** Bronze **Ruler:** Frederik IX **Obverse:** Crowned CIX monogram, date lower left, initials lower right **Reverse:** Value above porpoise and barley ear

Date	Mintage	F	VF	XF	Unc	BU
1902(h) VBP	601,000	10.00	17.50	37.50	125	—
1904(h) VBP	397,000	20.00	37.50	75.00	185	—
1906(h) VBP	1,000,000	10.00	17.50	37.50	110	—

KM# 806 5 ØRE Weight: 8.0000 g. **Composition:** Bronze **Ruler:** Frederik VIII **Obverse:** Value within legend, date and initials **Reverse:** Crowned F VIII monogram, initials lower right

Date	Mintage	F	VF	XF	Unc	BU
1907(h) VBP; GJ	1,000,000	5.50	10.00	18.00	55.00	—
1908(h) VBP; GJ	1,198,000	6.00	12.00	20.00	60.00	—
1912(h) VBP; GJ	999,000	6.50	13.00	22.50	65.00	—

KM# 814.1 5 ØRE **Weight:** 8.0000 g. **Composition:** Bronze **Ruler:** Christian X **Obverse:** Crowned CX monogram, initials and mint mark lower left, date and initials lower right **Reverse:** Value, ornament flanking

Date	Mintage	F	VF	XF	Unc	BU
1913(h) VBP; GJ	216,000	60.00	100	165	285	—
1914(h) VBP; GJ	785,000	7.00	13.50	18.50	40.00	—
1916(h) VBP; GJ	887,000	8.50	17.50	25.00	50.00	—
1917(h) VBP; GJ	494,000	9.00	18.00	35.00	70.00	—

KM# 814.1a 5 ØRE **Weight:** 6.9400 g. **Composition:** Iron **Ruler:** Christian X **Obverse:** Crowned CX monogram, initials and mint mark lower left, date and initials lower right **Reverse:** Value, ornament flanking

Date	Mintage	F	VF	XF	Unc	BU
1918(h) VBP; GJ	1,918,000	5.50	9.50	22.50	80.00	—

KM# 814.2 5 ØRE **Weight:** 8.0000 g. **Composition:** Bronze **Ruler:** Christian X **Obverse:** Crowned F VIII monogram, initials and mint mark lower left, date and initials lower right **Reverse:** Value, ornament flanking

Date	Mintage	F	VF	XF	Unc	BU
1919(h) HCN; GJ	994,000	3.25	5.50	8.50	18.50	—
1920(h) HCN; GJ	2,618,000	7.00	13.50	22.50	40.00	—
1921(h) HCN; GJ	3,248,000	4.50	8.00	11.50	22.50	—
1923(h) HCN; GJ	369,000	85.00	175	235	400	—

KM# 814.2a 5 ØRE **Weight:** 6.9400 g. **Composition:** Iron **Ruler:** Christian X **Obverse:** Crowned F VIII monogram, initials and mint mark lower left, date and initials lower right **Reverse:** Value, ornament flanking

Date	Mintage	F	VF	XF	Unc	BU
1919(h) HCN; GJ	1,034,999	15.00	30.00	55.00	160	—

KM# 828.1 5 ØRE **Weight:** 7.6000 g. **Composition:** Bronze **Ruler:** Christian X **Obverse:** Country name and date above center hole, value, mint mark and initials below **Reverse:** Crowned CX monogram within title "KING OF DENMARK"

Date	Mintage	F	VF	XF	Unc	BU
1926(h) HCN; GJ Unique	—	—	—	—	—	—
Note: Thomas Hoiland Sale 11-00 $8,600. Beware of counterfeits						
1927(h) HCN; GJ	7,129,000	0.10	0.20	2.75	20.00	—

KM# 828.2 5 ØRE **Weight:** 7.6000 g. **Composition:** Bronze **Ruler:** Christian X **Obverse:** Date above center hole, value, mint mark and initials below **Reverse:** Date above center hole, value, mint mark, initials **Note:** For coins dated 1941 refer to Faeroe Islands.

Date	Mintage	F	VF	XF	Unc	BU
1927(h) N; GJ	Inc. above	3.75	7.00	70.00	500	—
1928(h) N; GJ	4,685,000	0.10	0.50	3.25	22.50	—
1929(h) N; GJ	1,387,000	0.35	0.75	4.50	65.00	—
1930(h) N; GJ	1,339,000	0.45	0.80	10.00	70.00	—
1932(h) N; GJ	1,010,999	0.35	0.75	8.50	65.00	—
1932(h) N; GJ Proof	—	Value: 90.00				
1934(h) N; GJ	524,000	0.35	0.75	7.00	60.00	—
1935(h) N; GJ	1,124,000	1.75	3.75	20.00	100	—
1936(h) N; GJ	1,091,000	0.25	0.50	2.75	27.50	—
1937(h) N; GJ	1,209,000	0.25	0.50	1.35	20.00	—
1938(h) N; GJ	1,093,000	0.45	0.80	1.75	10.00	—
1939(h) N; GJ	1,402,000	0.15	0.25	0.50	3.75	—
1940(h) N; GJ	2,735,000	0.15	0.25	0.50	3.75	—

KM# 834 5 ØRE **Weight:** 2.4000 g. **Composition:** Aluminum **Ruler:** Christian X **Obverse:** Crowned CX monogram and date within title: "KING OF DENMARK"; mint mark and initials below **Reverse:** Value between oak and beach leaves

Date	Mintage	F	VF	XF	Unc	BU
1941(h) N; S	16,984,000	0.10	1.00	3.75	16.50	—
1941(h) N; S Proof	—	Value: 150				

KM# 834a 5 ØRE **Weight:** 6.4000 g. **Composition:** Zinc **Ruler:** Christian X **Obverse:** Crowned CX monogram and date within title: "KING OF DENMARK"; mint mark and initials below **Reverse:** Value between oak and beach leaves

Date	Mintage	F	VF	XF	Unc	BU
1942(h) N; S	2,963,000	1.25	2.50	18.50	60.00	—
1943(h) N; S	4,522,000	0.50	1.50	11.50	50.00	—
1944(h) N; S	3,744,000	0.60	1.75	11.50	50.00	—
1945(h) N; S	864,000	3.50	8.50	27.50	87.50	—

KM# 843.1 5 ØRE **Weight:** 6.4000 g. **Composition:** Zinc **Ruler:** Frederik IX **Obverse:** Crowned F IX monogram and date **Reverse:** Mint mark, initials below value

Date	Mintage	F	VF	XF	Unc	BU
1950(h) N; S	657,000	6.00	10.00	32.50	87.50	—
1951(h) N; S Straight 5	1,858,000	1.25	2.50	10.00	40.00	—
1951(h) N; S Slant 5	Inc. above	1.25	2.25	9.50	37.50	—
1952(h) N; S	3,562,000	0.60	1.25	4.50	25.00	—
1953(h) N; S	5,944,000	0.60	1.25	3.75	20.00	—
1954(h) N; S	3,060,000	0.40	1.00	2.75	16.50	—
1955(h) N; S	2,314,000	1.00	1.75	4.00	16.50	—

KM# 843.2 5 ØRE **Weight:** 6.4000 g. **Composition:** Zinc **Ruler:** Frederik IX **Obverse:** Crowned F IX monogram and date **Reverse:** Mint mark, initials below value

Date	Mintage	F	VF	XF	Unc	BU
1956(h) C; S	5,888,000	0.50	1.00	2.25	9.50	—
1957(h) C; S	8,606,000	0.25	0.50	1.50	5.50	—
1958(h) C; S	9,598,000	0.25	0.50	1.50	4.50	—
1959(h) C; S	6,110,000	0.10	0.25	1.00	4.50	—
1960(h) C; S	11,800,000	0.10	0.25	1.00	2.75	—
1961(h) C; S	8,995,000	0.20	0.45	1.00	2.25	—
1962(h) C; S	9,729,000	0.10	0.25	0.80	2.25	—
1963(h) C; S	8,980,000	0.10	0.25	0.80	2.25	—
1964(h) C; S	6,738,000	0.75	1.25	2.75	5.50	—

KM# 848.1 5 ØRE **Weight:** 6.0000 g. **Composition:** Bronze **Ruler:** Frederik IX **Obverse:** Crowned F IX monogram, date **Reverse:** Two barley stalks around value, initials below

Date	Mintage	F	VF	XF	Unc	BU
1960(h) C; S	3,760,000	0.10	0.25	1.00	4.50	—
1962(h) C; S	5,873,000	0.25	0.50	1.75	14.00	—
1963(h) C; S	23,287,000	—	0.10	0.60	2.75	—
1964(h) C; S	41,521,000	—	0.10	0.60	2.75	—
1965(h) C; S	14,229,000	—	0.10	0.60	2.75	—
1966(h) C; S	23,410,000	—	0.10	0.60	2.75	—
1967(h) C; S	15,094,000	—	0.10	0.60	2.75	—
1968(h) C; S	16,105,000	—	0.10	0.50	1.75	—
1969(h) C; S	23,594,000	—	0.10	0.35	1.00	—
1970(h) C; S	26,176,000	—	—	0.10	1.00	—
1971(h) C; S	10,076,000	—	—	0.10	1.00	—

KM# 848.2 5 ØRE **Weight:** 6.0000 g. **Composition:** Bronze **Ruler:** Frederik IX **Obverse:** Crowned F IX monogram, date **Reverse:** Two barley stalks around value, initials below

Date	Mintage	F	VF	XF	Unc	BU
1972(h) S; S	27,938,000	—	—	0.10	1.00	—

KM# 859.1 5 ØRE **Weight:** 1.6000 g. **Composition:** Copper Clad Iron **Ruler:** Margrethe II **Obverse:** Crowned MIIR monogram divides date; mint mark, initials **Reverse:** "DANMARK" above value

Date	Mintage	F	VF	XF	Unc	BU
1973(h) S; B	75,138,000	—	—	0.10	0.70	—
1974(h) S; B	71,796,000	—	—	0.10	0.70	—
1975(h) S; B	45,004,000	—	—	0.10	0.70	—
1976(h) S; B	73,296,000	—	—	0.10	0.70	—
1977(h) S; B	74,066,000	—	—	0.10	0.70	—
1978(h) S; B	52,425,000	—	—	0.10	0.70	—

KM# 859.2 5 ØRE **Weight:** 1.6000 g. **Composition:** Copper Clad Iron **Ruler:** Margrethe II **Obverse:** "DANMARK" above value **Reverse:** Crowned MIIR monogram divides date; mint mark, initials

Date	Mintage	F	VF	XF	Unc	BU
1979(h) B; B	58,953,000	—	—	0.10	0.70	—
1980(h) B; B	54,362,000	—	—	0.10	0.70	—
1981(h) B; B	52,201,000	—	—	0.10	0.35	—

KM# 859.3 5 ØRE **Weight:** 1.6000 g. **Composition:** Copper Clad Iron **Ruler:** Margrethe II **Obverse:** "DANMARK" above value **Reverse:** Crowned MIIR monogram divides date; mint mark, initials

Date	Mintage	F	VF	XF	Unc	BU
1982(h) R; B	74,296,000	—	—	0.10	0.35	—
1983(h) R; B	70,655,000	—	—	0.10	0.35	—
1984(h) R; B	27,599,000	—	—	0.10	0.35	—
1985(h) R; B	56,676,000	—	—	0.10	0.35	—
1986(h) R; B	62,496,000	—	—	0.10	0.35	—
1987(h) R; B	71,798,000	—	—	0.10	0.35	—
1988(h) R; B	48,925,000	—	—	0.10	0.35	—

KM# 795.2 10 ØRE **Weight:** 1.4500 g. **Composition:** 0.4000 Silver .0186 oz. ASW **Ruler:** Christian IX **Obverse:** Head of Christian IX, date, mint mark

Date	Mintage	F	VF	XF	Unc	BU
1903/803(h) VBP	3,007,000	3.75	6.00	10.00	32.00	—
1903(h) VBP	Inc. above	2.25	4.50	9.00	22.50	—
1904(h) VBP	2,449,000	16.00	27.50	35.00	70.00	—
1905(h) VBP	1,571,000	2.00	4.00	8.00	18.50	—

KM# 807 10 ØRE **Weight:** 1.4500 g. **Composition:** 0.4000 Silver .0186 oz. ASW **Ruler:** Frederik VIII **Obverse:** Head of Frederik VIII, initials below **Reverse:** Value, date, mint mark, initials within lily ornamentation

Date	Mintage	F	VF	XF	Unc	BU
1907(h) VBP; GJ	3,068,000	2.75	4.50	9.00	18.50	—
1910(h) VBP; GJ	2,530,000	3.25	5.50	10.00	21.50	—
1911(h) VBP; GJ	579,000	27.50	45.00	67.50	100	—
1912(h) VBP; GJ	1,951,000	3.75	6.50	10.00	21.50	—

KM# 818.1 10 ØRE **Weight:** 1.4500 g. **Composition:** 0.4000 Silver .0186 oz. ASW **Ruler:** Christian X **Obverse:** Crowned CX monogram, initials and mint mark lower left, date and initials lower right **Reverse:** Value, ornament flanking

Date	Mintage	F	VF	XF	Unc	BU
1914(h) VBP; GJ	2,128,000	4.00	6.00	9.00	16.50	—
1915(h) VBP; GJ	915,000	5.50	9.00	13.50	20.00	—
1916(h) VBP; GJ	2,699,000	4.00	6.50	10.00	16.50	—
1917(h) VBP; GJ	6,003,000	2.25	3.50	5.50	9.00	—
1918(h) VBP; GJ	5,042,000	1.35	2.25	3.75	6.00	—

KM# 818.2 10 ØRE **Weight:** 1.4500 g. **Composition:** 0.4000 Silver .0186 oz. ASW **Ruler:** Christian X **Obverse:** Crowned CX monogram, initials and mint mark lower left, date and initials lower right **Reverse:** Value, ornament flanking

Date	Mintage	F	VF	XF	Unc	BU
1919(h) HCN; GJ	10,184,000	1.00	1.50	2.25	3.50	—

KM# 818.2a 10 ØRE **Weight:** 1.5000 g. **Composition:** Copper-Nickel **Ruler:** Christian X **Obverse:** Crowned CX monogram, initials and mint mark lower left, date and initials lower right **Reverse:** Value, ornament flanking

Date	Mintage	F	VF	XF	Unc	BU
1920(h) HCN; GJ	10,234,000	2.75	4.00	9.50	32.50	—
1921(h) HCN; GJ	8,064,000	2.75	3.75	8.00	28.00	—
1922(h) HCN; GJ	3,065,000	18.50	27.50	36.00	65.00	—
1923(h) HCN; GJ	1,790,000	250	385	500	700	—

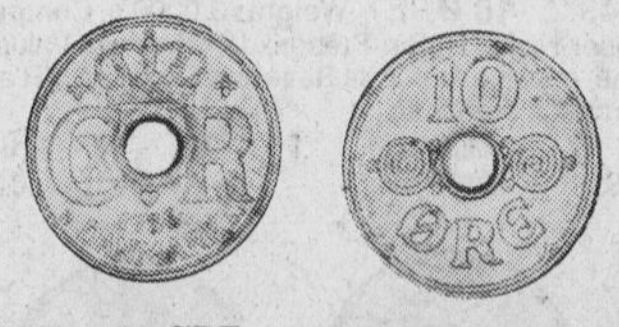

KM# 822.1 10 ØRE **Weight:** 3.0000 g. **Composition:** Copper-Nickel **Ruler:** Christian X **Obverse:** Crowned CXR monogram around center hole, date, mint mark and initials below hole **Reverse:** Value above, ornaments flanking center hole

Date	Mintage	F	VF	XF	Unc	BU
1924(h) HCN; GJ	14,661,000	0.20	0.75	2.25	11.50	—
1925(h) HCN; G	8,678,000	0.25	0.75	7.00	27.50	—
1926(h) HCN; GJ	4,107,000	0.25	0.75	7.00	32.50	—

KM# 822.2 10 ØRE **Weight:** 3.0000 g. **Composition:** Copper-Nickel **Ruler:** Christian X **Obverse:** Crowned CXR monogram around center hole, date, mint mark and initials below hole **Reverse:** Value above, ornaments flanking center hole **Note:** For coins dated 1941 without mint mark or initials refer to Faeroe Islands listings.

Date	Mintage	F	VF	XF	Unc	BU
1929(h) N; GJ	5,037,000	0.75	1.25	7.00	36.50	—
1931(h) N; GJ	3,054,000	1.35	2.25	9.50	45.00	—
1933(h) N; GJ	1,274,000	6.50	12.00	27.00	75.00	—
1934(h) N; GJ	2,013,000	1.25	2.25	7.00	25.00	—
1935(h) N; GJ	2,848,000	1.35	2.25	6.00	22.50	—
1936(h) N; GJ	3,320,000	1.35	2.25	5.50	36.50	—
1937(h) N; GJ	2,234,000	1.00	1.50	5.50	18.50	—
1938(h) N; GJ	2,991,000	1.75	2.75	4.50	16.50	—
1939(h) N; GJ	2,973,000	1.00	1.75	4.50	16.50	—
1940(h) N; GJ	2,998,000	0.60	1.25	2.00	10.00	—
1941(h) N; GJ	748,000	2.75	4.50	7.00	20.00	—
1946(h) N; GJ	460,000	2.00	3.75	5.00	8.50	—
1947(h) N; GJ	1,292,000	85.00	110	165	220	—

KM# 822.2a 10 ØRE **Weight:** 2.4000 g. **Composition:** Zinc **Ruler:** Christian X **Obverse:** Crowned CXR monogram around center hole, date, mint mark and initials below hole **Reverse:** Value above, ornaments flanking center hole

Date	Mintage	F	VF	XF	Unc	BU
1941(h) N; GJ	7,706,000	1.00	2.00	9.00	30.00	—
1942(h) N; GJ	8,676,000	1.00	2.00	9.00	30.00	—
1943(h) N; GJ	2,181,000	1.75	3.25	11.50	32.50	—
1944(h) N; GJ	7,994,000	1.35	2.50	7.50	23.50	—
1945(h) N; GJ	1,280,000	40.00	60.00	90.00	185	250

KM# 841.1 10 ØRE **Weight:** 3.0000 g. **Composition:** Copper-Nickel **Ruler:** Frederik IX **Obverse:** Value, country name, mint mark, initials **Reverse:** Crowned IXR above oak and beech branches

Date	Mintage	F	VF	XF	Unc	BU
1948(h) N; S	5,317,000	0.25	0.75	3.25	16.50	—
1949(h) N; S	7,595,000	0.10	0.25	2.75	14.50	—
1950(h) N; S	6,886,000	0.10	0.25	2.75	14.50	—
1951(h) N; S	8,763,000	0.10	0.25	3.25	22.50	—
1952(h) N; S	6,810,000	0.10	0.25	2.75	14.50	—
1953(h) N; S	11,946,000	0.10	0.25	2.75	13.50	—
1954(h) N; S	19,739,000	—	0.10	1.50	8.50	—
1955(h) N; S	17,623,000	—	0.10	1.50	8.50	—

KM# 841.2 10 ØRE **Weight:** 3.0000 g. **Composition:** Copper-Nickel **Ruler:** Frederik IX **Obverse:** Value, country name, mint mark, initials **Reverse:** Crowned IXR above oak and beech branches

Date	Mintage	F	VF	XF	Unc	BU
1956(h) C; S	12,323,000	—	0.10	2.25	11.50	—
1957(h) C; S	13,227,000	—	0.10	1.00	5.50	—
1958(h) C; S	10,870,000	—	0.10	1.00	5.50	—
1959(h) C; S	1,255,000	27.50	40.00	55.00	115	—
1960(h) C; S	5,107,000	0.10	0.30	1.00	3.75	—

KM# 849.1 10 ØRE **Weight:** 3.0000 g. **Composition:** Copper-Nickel **Ruler:** Frederik IX **Obverse:** Value, country name, mint mark, initials **Reverse:** Crowned IXR above oak and beech branches

Date	Mintage	F	VF	XF	Unc	BU
1960(h) C; S	Inc. above	0.10	0.30	0.75	3.75	—
1961(h) C; S	20,258,000	—	0.15	0.50	4.50	—
1962(h) C; S	12,785,000	—	0.15	0.50	4.50	—
1963(h) C; S	17,171,000	—	0.15	0.50	3.75	—
1964(h) C; S	14,282,000	—	0.15	0.50	3.25	—
1965(h) C; S	21,857,000	—	0.15	0.50	3.25	—
1966(h) C; S	24,160,000	—	0.15	0.25	2.75	—
1967(h) C; S	21,544,000	—	0.15	0.25	1.75	—
1968(h) C; S	7,586,000	—	0.15	0.25	1.50	—
1969(h) C; S	31,534,000	—	—	0.10	1.00	—
1970(h) C; S	37,813,000	—	—	0.10	0.35	—
1971(h) C; S	17,719,000	—	—	0.10	0.35	—

KM# 849.2 10 ØRE **Weight:** 3.0000 g. **Composition:** Copper-Nickel **Ruler:** Frederik IX **Obverse:** Value, country name, mint mark, initials **Reverse:** Crowned IXR above oak and beech branches

Date	Mintage	F	VF	XF	Unc	BU
1972(h) S; S	46,959,000	—	—	0.10	0.35	—

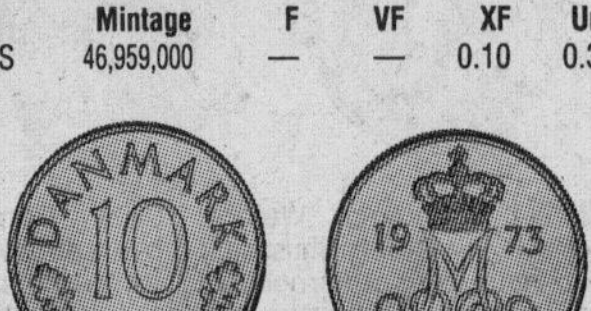

KM# 860.1 10 ØRE **Weight:** 3.0000 g. **Composition:** Copper-Nickel **Ruler:** Margrethe II **Obverse:** Value flanked by oak leaves **Reverse:** Crowned MIIR monogram divides date, mint mark and initials below

Date	Mintage	F	VF	XF	Unc	BU
1973(h) S; B	37,538,000	—	—	0.10	0.35	—
1974(h) S; B	38,570,000	—	—	0.10	0.35	—
1975(h) S; B	62,633,000	—	—	0.10	0.35	—
1976(h) S; B	64,358,999	—	—	0.10	0.35	—
1977(h) S; B	61,994,000	—	—	0.10	0.35	—
1978(h) S; B	30,302,000	—	—	0.10	0.35	—

KM# 860.2 10 ØRE **Weight:** 3.0000 g. **Composition:** Copper-Nickel **Ruler:** Margrethe II **Obverse:** Value flanked by oak leaves **Reverse:** Crowned MIIR monogram divides date, mint mark and initials below

Date	Mintage	F	VF	XF	Unc	BU
1979(h) B; B	10,224,000	—	—	0.10	0.35	—
1980(h) B; B	37,233,000	—	—	0.10	0.35	—
1981(h) B; B	51,565,000	—	—	0.10	0.25	—

KM# 860.3 10 ØRE **Weight:** 3.0000 g. **Composition:** Copper-Nickel **Ruler:** Margrethe II **Obverse:** Value flanked by oak leaves **Reverse:** Crowned MIIR monogram divides date, mint mark and initials below

Date	Mintage	F	VF	XF	Unc	BU
1982(h) R; B	40,195,000	—	—	0.10	0.25	—
1983(h) R; B	35,634,000	—	—	0.10	0.25	—
1984(h) R; B	17,828,000	—	—	0.10	0.25	—
1985(h) R; B	29,317,000	—	—	0.10	0.25	—
1986(h) R; B	46,254,000	—	—	0.10	0.25	—
1987(h) R; B	27,898,000	—	—	0.10	0.25	—
1988(h) R; B	29,400,000	—	—	0.10	0.25	—

KM# 796.2 25 ØRE **Weight:** 2.4200 g. **Composition:** 0.6000 Silver .0467 oz. ASW **Ruler:** Christian IX **Obverse:** Head of Christian IX, date, mint mark

Date	Mintage	F	VF	XF	Unc	BU
1900/800(h) VBP	1,206,000	15.00	30.00	40.00	90.00	—
1900(h) VBP	Inc. above	13.00	27.50	37.50	85.00	—
1904(h) VBP	1,922,000	14.00	25.00	37.50	82.50	—
1905/805(h) VBP	1,722,000	7.00	12.00	27.50	50.00	—
1905(h) VBP	Inc. above	5.50	10.00	22.50	45.00	—

KM# 808 25 ØRE **Weight:** 2.4200 g. **Composition:** 0.6000 Silver .0467 oz. ASW **Ruler:** Frederik VIII **Obverse:** Head of Frederik VIII, initials below **Reverse:** Value, date, mint mark, initials within lily ornamentation

Date	Mintage	F	VF	XF	Unc	BU
1907(h) VBP; GJ	2,009,000	5.50	10.00	16.50	32.50	—
1911(h) VBP; GJ	2,015,000	5.50	10.00	16.50	32.50	—

KM# 815.1 25 ØRE **Weight:** 2.4200 g. **Composition:** 0.6000 Silver .0467 oz. ASW **Ruler:** Frederik VIII **Obverse:** Crowned CX monogram, initials and mint mark lower left, date and initials lower right **Reverse:** Value, ornament flanking

Date	Mintage	F	VF	XF	Unc	BU
1913(h) VBP; GJ	2,016,000	4.00	7.50	11.50	22.50	—
1914(h) VBP; GJ	347,000	85.00	135	175	245	—
1915(h) VBP; GJ	2,862,000	3.25	6.00	9.00	16.50	—
1916(h) VBP; GJ	938,000	10.00	16.00	22.50	37.50	—
1917(h) VBP; GJ	1,354,000	40.00	65.00	85.00	135	—
1918(h) VBP; GJ	2,089,999	6.00	9.50	14.50	23.50	—

KM# 815.2 25 ØRE **Weight:** 2.4200 g. **Composition:** 0.6000 Silver .0467 oz. ASW **Ruler:** Christian X **Obverse:** Crowned CX monogram, initials and mint mark lower left, date and initials lower right **Reverse:** Value, ornament flanking

Date	Mintage	F	VF	XF	Unc	BU
1919(h) HCN; GJ	9,295,000	1.25	1.75	2.75	5.00	—

KM# 815.2a 25 ØRE **Weight:** 2.4000 g. **Composition:** Copper-Nickel **Ruler:** Christian X **Obverse:** Crowned CX monogram, initials and mint mark lower left, date and initials lower right **Reverse:** Value, ornament flanking

Date	Mintage	F	VF	XF	Unc	BU
1920(h) HCN; GJ	12,288,000	2.75	4.50	13.50	38.00	—
1921(h) HCN; GJ	9,444,000	2.25	3.75	13.50	38.00	—
1922(h) HCN; GJ	5,701,000	25.00	35.00	50.00	90.00	—

KM# 823.1 25 ØRE **Weight:** 4.5000 g. **Composition:** Copper-Nickel **Ruler:** Christian X **Obverse:** Crowned CXR monogram around center hole, date, mint mark and initials below hole **Reverse:** Value above, ornaments flanking center hole

Date	Mintage	F	VF	XF	Unc	BU
1924(h) HCN; GJ	8,035,000	0.35	1.75	4.00	16.50	—
1925(h) HCN; GJ	1,906,000	4.50	8.00	18.50	60.00	—
1926(h) HCN; GJ	2,659,000	1.75	2.75	7.50	42.50	—

KM# 823.2 25 ØRE **Weight:** 4.5000 g. **Composition:** Copper-Nickel **Ruler:** Christian X **Obverse:** Crowned CXR monogram around center hole, date, mint mark and initials below hole **Reverse:** Value above, ornaments flanking center hole **Note:** For coins dated 1941 refer to Faeroe Islands listings.

Date	Mintage	F	VF	XF	Unc	BU
1929(h) N; GJ	886,000	1.75	3.75	9.50	45.00	—
1930(h) N; GJ	3,423,000	2.25	4.50	14.00	55.00	—
1932(h) N; GJ	846,000	8.50	12.50	22.50	65.00	—
1933(h) N; GJ	479,000	25.00	36.50	52.50	120	—
1934(h) N; GJ	1,660,000	2.25	3.75	9.50	37.50	—
1935(h) N; GJ	1,032,000	11.00	20.00	37.50	85.00	—
1936(h) N; GJ	1,453,000	1.75	2.75	7.50	32.50	—
1937(h) N; GJ	1,612,000	3.25	5.50	9.50	22.50	—
1938(h) N; GJ	1,794,000	2.75	4.00	8.00	25.00	—
1939(h) N; GJ	1,972,000	11.00	18.50	30.00	60.00	—
1940(h) N; GJ	1,356,000	1.35	2.25	4.00	11.50	—
1946(h) N; GJ	2,323,000	1.25	2.75	4.00	9.50	—
1947(h) N; GJ	1,751,000	4.00	7.00	9.00	14.00	—

KM# 823.2a 25 ØRE **Weight:** 3.6000 g. **Composition:** Zinc **Ruler:** Christian X **Obverse:** Crowned CXR monogram around center hole, date, mint mark and initials below hole **Reverse:** Value above, ornaments flanking center hole

Date	Mintage	F	VF	XF	Unc	BU
1941(h) N; GJ	15,332,000	3.75	7.00	12.50	32.50	—
1942(h) N; GJ	997,000	1.35	2.75	6.50	27.50	—
1943(h) N; GJ	5,784,000	3.75	7.50	14.00	35.00	—
1944(h) N; GJ	10,665,000	1.35	3.25	6.50	25.00	—
1945(h) N; GJ	4,543,000	2.25	4.00	7.50	25.00	35.00

KM# 842.1 25 ØRE **Weight:** 4.5000 g. **Composition:** Copper-Nickel **Ruler:** Frederik IX **Obverse:** Value, country name, mint mark, initials **Reverse:** Crowned IXR above oak and beech branches

Date	Mintage	F	VF	XF	Unc	BU
1948(h) N; S	1,853,000	2.25	5.00	10.00	37.50	—
1949(h) N; S	15,000,000	0.10	0.35	2.25	11.50	—
1950(h) N; S	13,771,000	0.10	0.35	3.75	20.00	—
1951(h) N; S	5,045,000	0.10	0.35	4.50	22.50	—
1952(h) N; S	2,017,999	0.75	1.50	11.50	35.00	—
1953(h) N; S	9,553,000	0.10	0.35	2.25	8.50	—
1954(h) N; S	11,337,000	0.10	0.30	1.50	5.50	—
1955(h) N; S	6,385,000	0.20	0.35	1.50	5.50	—

KM# 842.2 25 ØRE **Weight:** 4.5000 g. **Composition:** Copper-Nickel **Ruler:** Frederik IX **Obverse:** Value, country name, mint mark, initials **Reverse:** Crowned IXR above oak and beech branches

Date	Mintage	F	VF	XF	Unc	BU
1956(h) C; S	10,228,000	0.10	0.25	1.00	4.50	—
1957(h) C; S	7,421,000	0.10	0.25	0.75	3.75	—
1958(h) C; S	3,600,000	0.30	0.50	1.00	4.00	—
1959(h) C; S	2,211,000	1.75	3.75	6.00	9.50	—
1960(h) C; S	3,453,000	0.30	0.50	1.25	4.50	—

KM# 850 25 ØRE **Weight:** 4.5000 g. **Composition:** Copper-Nickel **Ruler:** Frederik IX **Obverse:** Value, country name, mint mark, initials **Reverse:** Crowned IXR above oak and beech branches

Date	Mintage	F	VF	XF	Unc	BU
1960(h) C; S	Inc. above	5.50	9.50	13.50	20.00	—
1961(h) C; S	20,860,000	0.10	0.25	0.75	4.00	—
1962(h) C; S	12,563,000	0.10	0.25	0.75	3.25	—
1964(h) C; S	6,175,000	0.10	0.25	0.75	3.25	—
1965(h) C; S	13,492,000	0.10	0.25	0.75	3.25	—

Date	Mintage	F	VF	XF	Unc	BU
1966(h) C; S	50,220,000	0.10	0.25	0.75	3.25	—
1967(h) C; S	87,468,000	4.50	9.50	13.50	20.00	—

KM# 855.1 25 ØRE Weight: 4.3000 g. **Composition:** Copper-Nickel **Ruler:** Frederik IX **Obverse:** Value, country name and two stalks of barley around center hole **Reverse:** Crowned F IX R monogram and date to left of center hole, beech branch to right, initials and mint mark at bottom

Date	Mintage	F	VF	XF	Unc	BU
1966(h) C; S	Inc. above	—	0.10	0.40	2.25	—
1967(h) C; S	Inc. above	—	0.10	0.40	1.75	—
1968(h) C; S	39,142,000	—	0.10	0.40	1.35	—
1969(h) C; S	16,974,000	—	0.10	0.40	1.00	—
1970(h) C; S	5,393,000	—	—	0.15	0.75	—
1971(h) C; S	12,725,000	—	—	0.15	0.60	—

KM# 855.2 25 ØRE Weight: 4.3000 g. **Composition:** Copper-Nickel **Ruler:** Frederik IX **Obverse:** Value, country name and two stalks of barley around center hole **Reverse:** Crowned F IX R monogram and date to left of center hole, beech branch to right, initials and mint mark at bottom

Date	Mintage	F	VF	XF	Unc	BU
1972(h) S; S	31,422,000	—	—	0.10	0.45	—

KM# 861.1 25 ØRE Weight: 4.3000 g. **Composition:** Copper-Nickel **Ruler:** Margrethe II **Reverse:** Crowned MIIR monogram to left, oak branch to right of center hole, date above, mint mark and initials below

Date	Mintage	F	VF	XF	Unc	BU
1973(h) S; B	30,834,000	—	—	0.10	0.45	—
1974(h) S; B	22,178,000	—	—	0.10	0.45	—
1975(h) S; B	28,798,000	—	—	0.10	0.45	—
1976(h) S; B	48,388,000	—	—	0.10	0.45	—
1977(h) S; B	32,238,999	—	—	0.10	0.45	—
1978(h) S; B	17,444,000	—	—	0.10	0.35	—

KM# 861.2 25 ØRE Weight: 4.3000 g. **Composition:** Copper-Nickel **Ruler:** Margrethe II **Obverse:** Crowned MIIR monogram to left, oak branch to right of center hole, date above, mint mark and initials below

Date	Mintage	F	VF	XF	Unc	BU
1979(h) B; B	24,261,000	—	—	0.10	0.35	—
1980(h) B; B	30,448,000	—	—	0.10	0.35	—
1981(h) B; B	1,427,000	—	—	0.10	0.35	—

KM# 861.3 25 ØRE Weight: 4.3000 g. **Composition:** Copper-Nickel **Ruler:** Margrethe II **Reverse:** Crowned MIIR monogram to left, oak branch to right of center hole, date above, mint mark and initials below

Date	Mintage	F	VF	XF	Unc	BU
1982(h) R; B	24,671,000	—	—	0.10	0.35	—
1983(h) R; B	32,706,000	—	—	0.10	0.35	—
1984(h) R; B	22,882,000	—	—	0.10	0.35	—
1985(h) R; B	29,048,000	—	—	0.10	0.35	—
1986(h) R; B	53,496,000	—	—	0.10	0.35	—
1987(h) R; B	30,575,000	—	—	0.10	0.35	—
1988(h) R; B	23,370,000	—	—	0.10	0.35	—

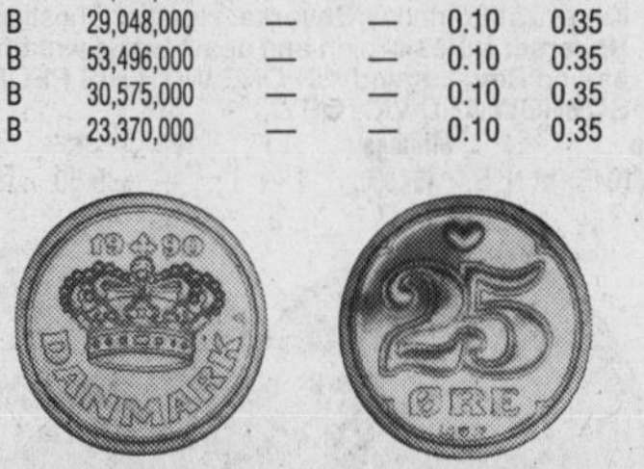

KM# 868 25 ØRE Weight: 2.8000 g. **Composition:** Bronze **Ruler:** Margrethe II **Obverse:** Date above large crown, country name below, initial to right **Reverse:** Large heart above value, mint mark and initials below **Note:** Beginning in 1996 and ending with 1998, the words "DANMARK" and "ØRE" have raised edges. Heart mint mark under "ØRE".

Date	Mintage	F	VF	XF	Unc	BU
1990 LG; JP; A	109,084,000	—	—	—	0.15	—
1991 LG; JP; A	102,162,000	—	—	—	0.15	—
1992 LG; JP; A	6,293,000	—	—	—	0.15	—
1993 LG; JP; A	14,756,000	—	—	—	0.15	—
1994 LG; JP; A	35,750,000	—	—	—	0.15	—
1995 LG; JP; A	40,000,000	—	—	—	0.15	—
1996 LG; JP; A	46,760,000	—	—	—	0.15	—
1997 LG; JP; A	30,306,000	—	—	—	0.15	—
1998 LG; JP; A	17,200,000	—	—	—	0.15	—
1999 LG; JP; A	18,748,000	—	—	—	0.15	—
2000 LG; JP; A	14,500,000	—	—	—	0.15	—

Date	Mintage	F	VF	XF	Unc	BU
2001 LG; JP; A	10,530,000	—	—	—	0.15	—
2002 LG; JP; A	—	—	—	—	0.15	—

KM# 866.1 50 ØRE Weight: 4.3000 g. **Composition:** Bronze **Ruler:** Margrethe II **Obverse:** Date above large crown, country name below, initial to right **Reverse:** Large heart above value, mint mark and initials below **Note:** Heart mint mark under the word "Øre".

Date	Mintage	F	VF	XF	Unc	BU
1989 NR; JP and A	92,236,000	—	—	—	0.20	—
1989	92,236,000	—	—	—	0.20	—

KM# 866.2 50 ØRE Weight: 4.3000 g. **Composition:** Bronze **Ruler:** Margrethe II **Obverse:** Date above large crown, country name below, initial to right **Reverse:** Large heart above value, mint mark and initials below **Note:** Beginning in 1996 and ending with 1998, the words "DANMARK" and "ØRE" have raised edges. Heart mint mark under the word "ØRE".

Date	Mintage	F	VF	XF	Unc	BU
1990 LG; JP; A	63,518,000	—	—	—	0.20	—
1991 LG; JP; A	11,115,000	—	—	—	0.20	—
1992 LG; JP; A	14,397,000	—	—	—	0.20	—
1993 LG; JP; A	14,328,000	—	—	—	0.20	—
1994 LG; JP; A	25,055,000	—	—	—	0.20	—
1995 LG; JP; A	15,988,000	—	—	—	0.20	—
1996 LG; JP; A	11,536,000	—	—	—	0.20	—
1997 LG; JP; A	15,574,000	—	—	—	0.20	—
1998 LG; JP; A	13,120,000	—	—	—	0.20	—
1999 LG; JP; A	14,186,000	—	—	—	0.20	—
2000 LG; JP; A	15,500,000	—	—	—	0.20	—
2001 LG; JP; A	12,270,000	—	—	—	0.20	—
2002 LG; JP; A	—	—	—	—	0.20	—

KM# 831.1 1/2 KRONE Weight: 3.0000 g. **Composition:** Aluminum-Bronze **Ruler:** Christian X **Obverse:** Value above, country name below large crown **Reverse:** Crowned CX monogram, date, mint mark, and initials

Date	Mintage	F	VF	XF	Unc	BU
1924(h) HCN; GJ	2,150,000	4.00	8.00	14.50	42.50	—
1925(h) HCN; GJ	3,432,000	4.00	8.00	16.50	47.50	—
1926(h) HCN; GJ	716,000	11.50	20.00	32.00	65.00	—

KM# 831.2 1/2 KRONE Weight: 3.0000 g. **Composition:** Aluminum-Bronze **Ruler:** Christian X **Obverse:** Value above, country name below large crown **Reverse:** Crowned CX monogram, date, mint mark, and initials

Date	Mintage	F	VF	XF	Unc	BU
1939(h) N; GJ	226,000	60.00	85.00	115	150	—
1940(h) N; GJ	1,871,000	4.00	8.00	11.00	17.50	—

KM# 819 KRONE Weight: 7.5000 g. **Composition:** 0.8000 Silver .1929 oz. ASW **Ruler:** Christian X **Obverse:** Head of Christian X with titles, date, mint mark and initials **Reverse:** Crowned royal arms with porpoise to left, barley stalk to right, value below

Date	Mintage	F	VF	XF	Unc	BU
1915(h) VBP; AH	1,410,000	2.25	4.50	7.50	18.50	—
1916(h) VBP; AH	992,000	3.75	8.00	14.00	22.00	—

KM# 824.1 KRONE Weight: 6.5000 g. **Composition:** Aluminum-Bronze **Ruler:** Christian X **Obverse:** Value above, country name below large crown **Reverse:** Crowned CX monogram, date, mint mark, and initials

Date	Mintage	F	VF	XF	Unc	BU
1924(h) HCN; GJ	999,000	135	285	750	2,000	—
1925(h) HCN; GJ	6,314,000	1.50	7.00	30.00	82.00	—
1926(h) HCN; GJ	2,706,000	1.50	7.00	32.50	90.00	—

KM# 824.2 KRONE Weight: 6.5000 g. **Composition:** Aluminum-Bronze **Ruler:** Christian X **Obverse:** Value above, country name below large crown **Reverse:** Crowned CX monogram, date, mint mark, and initials

Date	Mintage	F	VF	XF	Unc	BU
1929(h) N; GJ	501,000	5.50	12.50	60.00	185	—
1930(h) N; GJ	540,000	16.00	27.50	80.00	290	—
1931(h) N; GJ	540,000	5.50	12.00	45.00	155	—
1934(h) N; GJ	529,000	3.75	8.00	35.00	125	—
1935(h) N; GJ	505,000	25.00	40.00	72.50	185	—
1936(h) N; GJ	558,000	8.00	15.00	36.50	135	—
1938(h) N; GJ	407,000	14.00	22.00	36.50	130	—
1939(h) N; GJ	1,517,000	1.75	2.75	8.50	40.00	—
1940(h) N; GJ	1,496,000	1.75	3.25	8.00	42.50	—
1941(h) N; GJ	661,000	7.00	14.00	36.50	185	—

KM# 835 KRONE Weight: 6.5000 g. **Composition:** Aluminum-Bronze **Ruler:** Christian X **Obverse:** Head of Christian X with titles, mint mark, initials **Reverse:** Value divided by stalk of wheat and stalk of oats, date

Date	Mintage	F	VF	XF	Unc	BU
1942(h) N; S	3,952,000	1.00	2.75	8.50	36.00	—
1943(h) N; S	798,000	7.00	16.00	82.50	285	—
1944(h) N; S	1,760,000	1.35	2.25	14.00	47.50	—
1945(h) N; S	2,581,000	1.35	2.25	7.00	35.00	—
1946(h) N; S	4,321,000	1.00	1.75	4.50	20.00	—
1947(h) N; S	5,060,000	1.00	1.50	2.25	9.50	—

KM# 837.1 KRONE Weight: 6.5000 g. **Composition:** Aluminum-Bronze **Ruler:** Frederik IX **Obverse:** Head of Frederic IX, titles, mint mark, initials **Reverse:** Crowned royal arms dividing date, value above

Date	Mintage	F	VF	XF	Unc	BU
1947(h) N; S	Inc. above	2.00	3.75	6.50	16.00	—
1948(h) N; S	4,248,000	1.00	2.00	3.75	10.00	—
1949(h) N; S	1,300,000	3.25	6.00	12.50	30.00	—
1952(h) N; S	2,124,000	1.75	3.25	6.50	16.00	—
1953(h) N; S	573,000	2.75	5.50	93.50	18.50	—
1954(h) N; S	584,000	11.50	20.00	28.00	45.00	—
1955(h) N; S	1,359,000	4.00	7.00	10.00	18.50	—

KM# 837.2 KRONE Weight: 6.5000 g. **Composition:** Aluminum-Bronze **Ruler:** Frederik IX **Obverse:** Head of Frederic IX, titles, mint mark, initials **Reverse:** Crowned royal arms dividing date, value above

Date	Mintage	F	VF	XF	Unc	BU
1956(h) C; S	2,858,000	1.75	2.75	4.00	6.50	—
1957(h) C; S	10,896,000	0.65	1.00	1.50	3.25	—
1958(h) C; S	1,507,000	1.00	1.75	2.25	3.75	—
1959(h) C; S	243,000	14.00	22.50	27.50	37.50	—
1960(h) C; S	100	—	—	2,900	3,250	—

Note: 1960 dated coins were not released into circulation, however, approximately 50 pieces did eventually make their way into the collector maket.

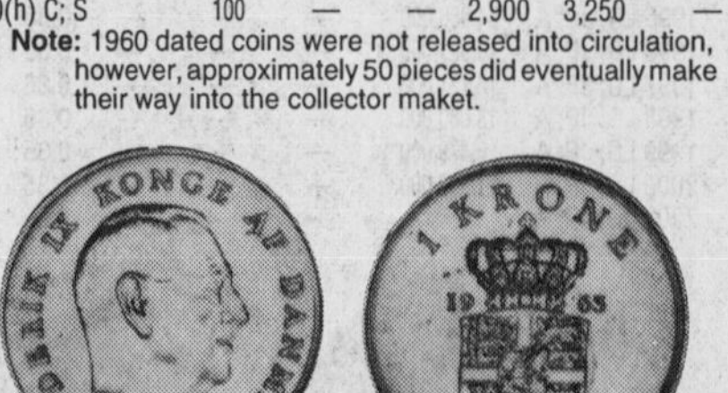

KM# 851.1 KRONE Weight: 6.8000 g. **Composition:** Copper-Nickel **Ruler:** Frederik IX **Obverse:** Older head of Frederic IX, titles, mint mark, initials **Reverse:** Crowned royal arms dividing date, value at top

Date	Mintage	F	VF	XF	Unc	BU
1960(h) C; S	1,000,000	0.75	1.35	2.75	7.00	—
1961(h) C; S	10,348,000	—	0.35	1.75	11.50	—
1962(h) C; S	27,068,000	—	0.25	1.75	10.00	—
1963(h) C; S	32,083,000	—	0.25	1.35	5.00	—
1964(h) C; S	5,984,000	—	0.25	1.35	5.00	—
1965(h) C; S	13,799,000	—	0.25	1.00	5.50	—
1966(h) C; S	10,890,000	—	0.25	1.00	4.50	—
1967(h) C; S	18,304,000	—	0.25	1.00	4.50	—

Date	Mintage	F	VF	XF	Unc	BU
1968(h) C; S	8,212,999	—	0.25	0.75	3.75	—
1969(h) C; S	9,597,000	—	0.25	0.65	1.75	—
1970(h) C; S	9,460,000	—	—	0.45	1.35	—
1971(h) C; S	13,985,000	—	—	0.25	0.75	—

KM# 851.2 KRONE **Weight:** 6.8000 g. **Composition:** Copper-Nickel **Ruler:** Frederik IX **Obverse:** Older head of Frederic IX, titles, mint mark, initials **Reverse:** Crowned royal arms dividing date, value at top

Date	Mintage	F	VF	XF	Unc	BU
1972(h) S; S	21,019,000	—	—	0.25	0.50	—

KM# 862.1 KRONE **Weight:** 6.8000 g. **Composition:** Copper-Nickel **Ruler:** Margrethe II **Obverse:** Head of Margrethe II with titles, mint mark, initials **Reverse:** Crowned royal arms dividing date, value at bottom

Date	Mintage	F	VF	XF	Unc	BU
1973(h) S; B Narrow rim (0.7mm)	18,268,000	—	—	0.25	0.75	—
1973(h) S; B Wide rim (1.1mm)	Inc. above	—	—	0.30	0.75	—
1974(h) S; B	17,742,000	—	—	0.30	0.75	—
1975(h) S; B	20,136,000	—	—	0.30	0.75	—
1976(h) S; B	28,049,000	—	—	0.30	0.75	—
1977(h) S; B	25,685,000	—	—	0.30	0.75	—
1978(h) S; B	11,286,000	—	—	0.30	0.75	—

KM# 862.2 KRONE **Weight:** 6.8000 g. **Composition:** Copper-Nickel **Ruler:** Margrethe II **Obverse:** Head of Margrethe II with titles, mint mark, initials **Reverse:** Crowned royal arms dividing date, value at bottom

Date	Mintage	F	VF	XF	Unc	BU
1979(h) B; B	25,216,000	—	—	0.25	0.75	—
1980(h) B; B	25,825,000	—	—	0.25	0.75	—
1981(h) B; B	8,889,000	—	—	0.25	0.75	—

KM# 862.3 KRONE **Weight:** 6.8000 g. **Composition:** Copper-Nickel **Ruler:** Margrethe II **Obverse:** Head of Margrethe II with titles, mint mark, initials **Reverse:** Crowned royal arms dividing date, value at bottom

Date	Mintage	F	VF	XF	Unc	BU
1982(h) R; B	5,011,000	—	—	0.25	0.50	—
1983(h) R; B	13,946,000	—	—	0.20	0.50	—
1984(h) R; B	36,439,000	—	—	0.20	0.40	—
1985(h) R; B	10,843,000	—	—	0.20	0.40	—
1986(h) R; B	12,556,000	—	—	0.20	0.40	—
1987(h) R; B	20,120,000	—	—	0.20	0.40	—
1988(h) R; B	32,073,999	—	—	0.20	0.40	—
1989(h) R; B	15,704,000	—	—	0.20	0.40	—

KM# 873 KRONE **Weight:** 3.6000 g. **Composition:** Copper-Nickel **Ruler:** Margrethe II **Obverse:** Value, country name, ornaments around center hole **Reverse:** Crowned MII monograms

Date	Mintage	F	VF	XF	Unc	BU
1992 LG; JP; A	81,621,000	—	—	—	0.35	—
1993 LG; JP; A	15,844,000	—	—	—	0.35	—
1994 LG; JP; A	23,658,000	—	—	—	0.35	—
1995 LG; JP; A	34,966,000	—	—	—	0.35	—
1996 LG; JP; A	10,081,000	—	—	—	0.35	—
1997 LG; JP; A	10,121,000	—	—	—	0.35	—
1998 LG; JP; A	13,080,000	—	—	—	0.35	—
1999 LG; JP; A	6,479,000	—	—	—	0.35	—
2000 LG; JP; A	21,500,000	—	—	—	0.35	—
2002 LG; JP; A	—	—	—	—	0.35	—

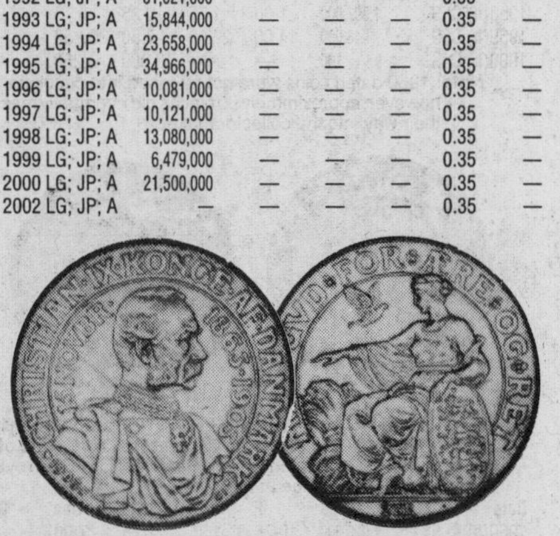

KM# 802 2 KRONER **Weight:** 15.0000 g. **Composition:** 0.8000 Silver .3858 oz. ASW **Ruler:** Christian IX **Subject:** 40th Anniversary of Reign **Obverse:** Christian IX with titles, date **Reverse:** Seated figure with motto and value

Date	Mintage	F	VF	XF	Unc	BU
1903(h) P; GJ	103,000	5.50	14.00	25.00	40.00	—

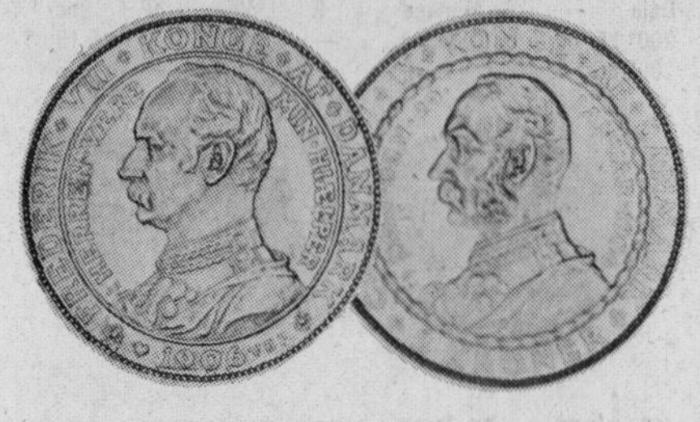

KM# 803 2 KRONER **Weight:** 15.0000 g. **Composition:** 0.8000 Silver .3858 oz. ASW **Ruler:** Christian IX **Subject:** Death of Christian IX and Accession of Frederik VIII **Obverse:** Frederik VIII with titles, motto, date, initials **Reverse:** Christian IX, titles, date of death, value

Date	Mintage	F	VF	XF	Unc	BU
1906(h) VBP GJ	151,000	3.00	7.00	16.00	27.50	—

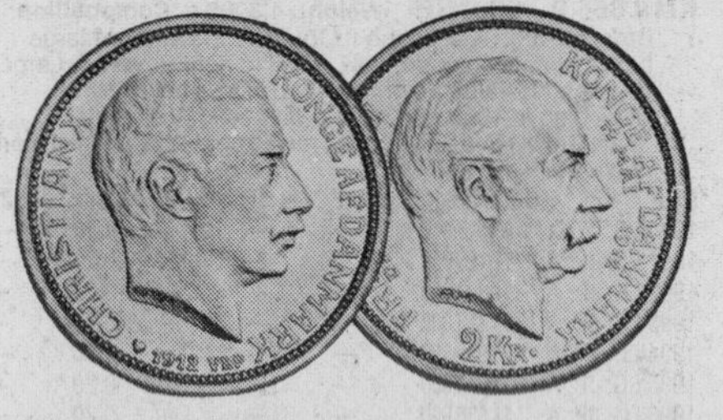

KM# 811 2 KRONER **Weight:** 15.0000 g. **Composition:** 0.8000 Silver .3858 oz. ASW **Ruler:** Frederik VIII **Subject:** Death of Frederik VIII and Accession of Christian X **Obverse:** Head of Christian X right **Reverse:** Head of Frederik VIII right, value below

Date	Mintage	F	VF	XF	Unc	BU
1912(h) VBP; AH	102,000	5.50	14.00	25.00	45.00	—

KM# 820 2 KRONER **Weight:** 15.0000 g. **Composition:** 0.8000 Silver .3858 oz. ASW **Ruler:** Christian X **Obverse:** Head of Christian X right **Reverse:** Crowned royal arms, porpoise and barley stalk flanking, value below

Date	Mintage	F	VF	XF	Unc	BU
1915(h) AH	657,000	9.50	20.00	32.00	55.00	—
1916(h) AH	402,000	5.50	11.50	16.50	32.50	—

KM# 821 2 KRONER **Weight:** 15.0000 g. **Composition:** 0.8000 Silver .3858 oz. ASW **Ruler:** Christian X **Subject:** Silver Wedding Anniversary **Obverse:** Heads of Christian X and Queen Alexanreine right **Reverse:** Crowned arms

Date	Mintage	F	VF	XF	Unc	BU
1923(h) HCN; GJ	203,000	—	—	11.50	20.00	—

KM# 825.1 2 KRONER **Weight:** 13.0000 g. **Composition:** Aluminum-Bronze **Ruler:** 3 Christian X **Obverse:** Value above, country name below large crown **Reverse:** Crowned CX monogram, date, mint mark, and initials

Date	Mintage	F	VF	XF	Unc	BU
1924(h) HCN; GJ	1,138,000	18.50	90.00	430	1,500	—
1925(h) HCN; GJ	3,248,000	1.35	9.50	27.50	87.50	—
1926(h) HCN; GJ	1,126,000	1.35	9.50	35.00	120	—

KM# 829 2 KRONER **Weight:** 15.0000 g. **Composition:** 0.8000 Silver .3858 oz. ASW **Ruler:** Christian X **Subject:** King's 60th Birthday **Obverse:** Head of Christian X right, date, mint mark, initials **Reverse:** Draped and supported national arms, value below

Date	Mintage	F	VF	XF	Unc	BU
1930(h) N; AH/HS	303,000	—	—	5.00	9.50	—

KM# 825.2 2 KRONER **Weight:** 13.0000 g. **Composition:** Aluminum-Bronze **Ruler:** Christian X **Obverse:** Value above, country name below large crown **Reverse:** Crowned CX monogram, date, mint mark, and initials

Date	Mintage	F	VF	XF	Unc	BU
1936(h) N; GJ	400,000	5.50	13.00	60.00	290	—
1938(h) N; GJ	191,000	14.00	22.50	67.50	200	—
1939(h) N; GJ	723,000	2.00	3.75	9.50	35.00	—
1940(h) N; GJ	743,000	6.00	10.00	20.00	55.00	—
1941(h) N; GJ	129,000	35.00	50.00	160	450	—

KM# 830 2 KRONER **Weight:** 15.0000 g. **Composition:** 0.8000 Silver .3858 oz. ASW **Ruler:** Christian X **Subject:** 25th Anniversary of Reign **Obverse:** Head of Christian X right **Reverse:** Crowned royal arms, value below

Date	Mintage	F	VF	XF	Unc	BU
ND(1937)(h) N; S	209,000	—	—	6.50	14.00	—

KM# 836 2 KRONER **Weight:** 15.0000 g. **Composition:** 0.8000 Silver .3858 oz. ASW **Ruler:** Christian X **Subject:** King's 75th Birthday **Obverse:** Head of Christian X right **Reverse:** Dates of birth and death within wreath, legend around **Rev. Legend:** "IN ONE WITH HIS PEOPLE IN SORROW AND VICTORY"

Date	Mintage	F	VF	XF	Unc	BU
ND(1945)(h) N; S	157,000	—	—	8.50	16.00	—

KM# 838.1 2 KRONER **Weight:** 13.0000 g. **Composition:** Aluminum-Bronze **Ruler:** Frederik IX **Reverse:** Crowned royal arms divide date, value above

Date	Mintage	F	VF	XF	Unc	BU
1947(h) N; S	1,151,000	2.25	4.00	10.00	20.00	—
1948(h) N; S	857,000	1.75	2.75	6.50	14.50	—
1949(h) N; S	272,000	4.50	9.50	18.50	36.00	—
1951(h) N; S	1,576,000	1.35	2.25	4.50	15.00	—
1952(h) N; S	1,958,000	1.00	2.00	4.00	11.50	—
1953(h) N; S	432,000	2.25	4.50	9.50	25.00	—
1954(h) N; S	716,000	2.25	4.00	8.00	16.50	—
1955(h) N; S	457,000	3.75	6.50	9.50	17.50	—

KM# 838.2 2 KRONER **Weight:** 13.0000 g. **Composition:** Aluminum-Bronze **Ruler:** Frederik IX **Obverse:** Head of Frederic IX right **Reverse:** Crowned royal arms divide date, value above

Date	Mintage	F	VF	XF	Unc	BU
1956(h) C; S	1,444,000	1.75	2.75	4.50	8.50	—
1957(h) C; S	2,610,000	1.00	1.65	2.25	4.50	—
1958(h) C; S	2,605,000	1.25	1.85	2.75	5.50	—
1959(h) C; S	192,000	14.50	21.50	28.00	42.50	—

KM# 844 2 KRONER **Weight:** 15.0000 g. **Composition:** 0.8000 Silver .3858 oz. ASW **Ruler:** Frederik IX **Obverse:** Heads of Frederik IX and Queen Ingrid right **Reverse:** Map of Greenland, country name, value **Note:** Greenland Commemorative.

Date	Mintage	F	VF	XF	Unc	BU
1953(h) N; S	152,000	—	4.50	14.00	25.00	—

KM# 845 2 KRONER **Weight:** 15.0000 g. **Composition:** 0.8000 Silver .3858 oz. ASW **Ruler:** Frederik IX **Subject:** Princess Margrethe's 18th Birthday **Obverse:** Head of Frederik IX right with titles **Reverse:** Head of Princess Margrethe left, date of 18th birthday

Date	Mintage	F	VF	XF	Unc	BU
ND(1958)(h) C; S	301,000	—	—	7.00	11.50	—

KM# 874 2 KRONER **Composition:** Copper-Nickel **Ruler:** Margrethe II **Obverse:** Value, country name, ornaments around center hole **Reverse:** Crowned MII monograms

Date	Mintage	F	VF	XF	Unc	BU
1992 LG; JP; A	41,648,000	—	—	—	0.60	—
1993 LG; JP; A	43,864,000	—	—	—	0.60	—
1994 LG; JP; A	27,629,000	—	—	—	0.60	—
1995 LG; JP; A	19,850,000	—	—	—	0.60	—
1996 LG; JP; A	2,884,000	—	—	—	0.60	—
1997 LG; JP; A	25,874,000	—	—	—	0.60	—
1998 LG; JP; A	4,360,000	—	—	—	0.60	—
1999 LG; JP; A	20,608,000	—	—	—	0.60	—
2000 LG; JP; A	10,400,000	—	—	—	0.60	—
2001 LG; JP; A	11,180,000	—	—	—	0.60	—
2002 LG; JP; A	—	—	—	—	0.60	—

KM# 852 5 KRONER **Weight:** 17.0000 g. **Composition:** 0.8000 Silver .4372 oz. ASW **Ruler:** Frederik IX **Subject:** Silver Wedding Anniversary **Obverse:** Heads of Frederik IX and Queen Ingrid right **Reverse:** Crowned double F✱I monogram

Date	Mintage	F	VF	XF	Unc	BU
ND(1960)(h) C; S	410,000	—	3.50	5.50	9.50	—

KM# 853.1 5 KRONER **Weight:** 15.0000 g. **Composition:** Copper-Nickel **Ruler:** Frederik IX **Obverse:** Head of Frederik IX right, mint mark **Reverse:** Crowned arms divide date within two oak branches, value above

Date	Mintage	F	VF	XF	Unc	BU
1960(h) C; S	6,418,000	—	1.50	2.50	9.50	—
1961(h) C; S	9,744,000	—	1.50	3.25	15.00	—
1962(h) C; S	2,073,999	—	2.50	4.00	15.00	—
1963(h) C; S	709,000	—	2.00	3.00	18.50	—
1964(h) C; S	1,443,000	—	1.50	4.00	16.00	—
1965(h) C; S	2,574,000	—	1.50	2.50	14.00	—
1966(h) C; S	4,370,000	—	1.35	1.85	8.50	—
1967(h) C; S	1,864,000	—	1.35	1.85	5.50	—
1968(h) C; S	4,131,999	—	1.35	1.85	4.50	—
1969(h) C; S	72,000	2.00	4.50	7.50	10.00	—
1970(h) C; S	2,246,000	—	—	1.35	2.25	—
1971(h) C; S	4,767,000	—	—	1.35	1.85	—

KM# 853.2 5 KRONER **Weight:** 15.0000 g. **Composition:** Copper-Nickel **Ruler:** Frederik IX **Obverse:** Head of Frederik IX right, mint mark **Reverse:** Crowned MII monogram

Date	Mintage	F	VF	XF	Unc	BU
1972(h) S; S	2,599,000	—	—	1.25	1.75	—

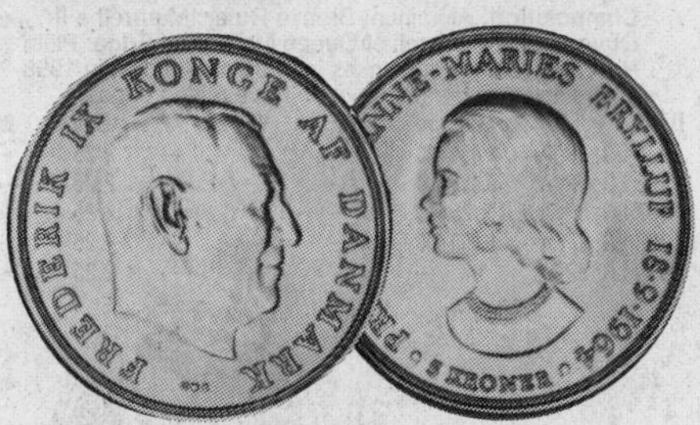

KM# 854 5 KRONER **Weight:** 17.0000 g. **Composition:** 0.8000 Silver .4372 oz. ASW **Ruler:** Frederik IX **Subject:** Wedding of Princess Anne Marie

Date	Mintage	F	VF	XF	Unc	BU
1964(h) C; S	359,000	—	—	5.50	9.50	—

KM# 863.1 5 KRONER **Weight:** 15.0000 g. **Composition:** Copper-Nickel **Ruler:** Margrethe II **Obverse:** Head of Margrethe right **Reverse:** Crowned national arms divide date and oak leaves, value below

Date	Mintage	F	VF	XF	Unc	BU
1973(h) S; B Narrow rim (1.0mm)	3,774,000	—	—	1.25	2.25	—
1973(h) S; B Wide rim (1.5mm)	Inc. above	—	—	1.25	2.25	—
1974(h) S; B	5,239,000	—	—	1.25	2.25	—
1975(h) S; B	5,810,000	—	—	2.25	5.50	—
1976(h) S; B	7,651,000	—	—	1.35	2.75	—
1977(h) S; B	6,885,000	—	—	1.35	2.75	—
1978(h) S; B	2,984,000	—	—	1.35	2.75	—

KM# 863.2 5 KRONER **Weight:** 15.0000 g. **Composition:** Copper-Nickel **Ruler:** Margrethe II **Obverse:** Head of Margrethe right **Reverse:** Crowned national arms divide date and oak leaves, value below

Date	Mintage	F	VF	XF	Unc	BU
1979(h) B; B	2,861,000	—	—	1.35	2.25	—
1980(h) B; B	3,622,000	—	—	2.25	4.00	—
1981(h) B; B	1,057,000	—	—	1.35	2.25	—

KM# 863.3 5 KRONER **Weight:** 15.0000 g. **Composition:** Copper-Nickel **Ruler:** Margrethe II **Obverse:** Head of Margrethe right **Reverse:** Crowned national arms divide date and oak leaves, value below

Date	Mintage	F	VF	XF	Unc	BU
1982(h) R; B	1,002,000	—	—	2.25	4.00	—
1983(h) R; B	1,044,000	—	—	1.25	2.25	—
1984(h) R; B	713,000	—	—	1.25	2.25	—
1985(h) R; B	621,000	—	—	1.25	2.25	—
1986(h) R; B	1,042,000	—	—	1.25	2.25	—
1987(h) R; B	611,000	—	—	1.25	2.25	—
1988(h) R; B	648,000	—	—	1.25	2.25	—

KM# 869 5 KRONER **Weight:** 9.2000 g. **Composition:** Copper-Nickel **Ruler:** Margrethe II **Obverse:** Value, country name, ornaments around center hole **Reverse:** Crowned MII monograms

Date	Mintage	F	VF	XF	Unc	BU
1990 LG; JP; A	46,745,000	—	—	—	1.25	—
1991 LG; JP; A	3,752,000	—	—	—	1.25	—
1992 LG; JP; A	2,426,000	—	—	—	1.25	—
1993 LG; JP; A	1,538,000	—	—	—	1.25	—
1994 LG; JP; A	7,920,000	—	—	—	1.25	—
1995 LG; JP; A	5,850,000	—	—	—	1.25	—
1997 LG; JP; A	5,258,000	—	—	—	1.25	—
1998 LG; JP; A	6,450,000	—	—	—	1.25	—
1999 LG; JP; A	4,786,000	—	—	—	1.25	—
2000 LG; JP; A	2,800,000	—	—	—	1.25	—
2001 LG; JP; A	5,700,000	—	—	—	1.25	—
2002 LG; JP; A	—	—	—	—	1.25	—

KM# 809 10 KRONER **Weight:** 4.4803 g. **Composition:** 0.9000 Gold .1296 oz. AGW **Ruler:** Frederik VIII **Obverse:** Head of Frederik VIII with titles **Reverse:** Draped crowned national arms above date, value, mint mark and initials

Date	Mintage	F	VF	XF	Unc	BU
1908(h) VBP; GJ	308,000	—	BV	50.00	80.00	—
1909(h) VBP; GJ	153,000	—	BV	55.00	85.00	—

KM# 816 10 KRONER **Weight:** 4.4803 g. **Composition:** 0.9000 Gold .1296 oz. AGW **Ruler:** Christian X **Obverse:** Head of Christian X with title, date, mint mark, initials **Reverse:** Draped crowned national arms above date, value, mint mark and initials

Date	Mintage	F	VF	XF	Unc	BU
1913(h) AH/ GJ	312,000	—	BV	50.00	80.00	—
1917(h) AH/ GJ	132,000	—	BV	60.00	90.00	—

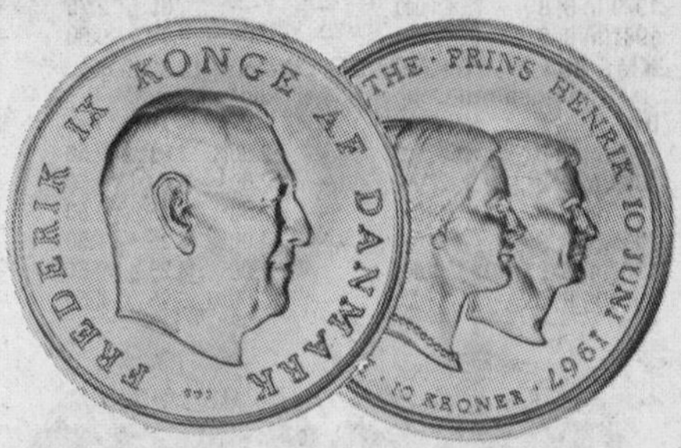

KM# 856 10 KRONER **Weight:** 20.4000 g. **Composition:** 0.8000 Silver .5247 oz. ASW **Ruler:** Frederik IX **Subject:** Wedding of Princess Margrethe **Obverse:** Head of Frederik IX with titles, mint mark, initials **Reverse:** Head of Princess Margrethe and Prince Henrik right, value below

Date	Mintage	F	VF	XF	Unc	BU
ND(1967)(h) C; S	419,000	—	—	5.50	9.50	—

Note: 78,383 were melted

KM# 857 10 KRONER **Weight:** 20.4000 g. **Composition:** 0.8000 Silver .5247 oz. ASW **Ruler:** Frederik IX **Subject:** Wedding of Princess Benediktes **Obverse:** Head of Frederik IX right **Reverse:** Head of Princess Benediktes left, value below

Date	Mintage	F	VF	XF	Unc	BU
ND(1968)(h) C; S	254,000	—	—	6.00	11.50	—

Note: 42,923 were melted

KM# 858 10 KRONER **Weight:** 20.4000 g. **Composition:** 0.8000 Silver .5247 oz. ASW **Ruler:** Frederik IX **Subject:** Death of Frederik IX and Accession of Margrethe II **Obverse:** Head of Margrethe right, motto, titles, mint mark **Reverse:** Head of Frederik IX with titles, value below

Date	Mintage	F	VF	XF	Unc	BU
1972(h) S; S	402,000	—	—	5.50	7.50	—

KM# 864.1 10 KRONER **Weight:** 12.5000 g. **Composition:** Copper-Nickel **Ruler:** Margrethe II **Obverse:** Head of Margrethe right **Reverse:** Large 10 on horizontal grid, two rye stalks flanking, date above

Date	Mintage	F	VF	XF	Unc	BU
1979(h) B; B	76,801,000	—	—	1.35	2.75	—
1981(h) B; B	10,520,000	—	2.00	4.00	9.50	—

KM# 864.2 10 KRONER **Weight:** 12.5000 g. **Composition:** Copper-Nickel **Ruler:** Margrethe II

Date	Mintage	F	VF	XF	Unc	BU
1982(h) R; B	1,065,000	—	2.00	4.00	9.50	—
1983(h) R; B	1,123,000	—	2.00	4.00	9.50	—
1984(h) R; B	748,000	—	2.00	3.25	9.50	—
1985(h) R; B	720,000	—	2.00	3.25	11.50	—
1987(h) R; B	719,000	—	2.00	3.25	9.50	—
1988(h) R; B	718,000	—	2.00	3.25	8.50	—

KM# 865 10 KRONER **Weight:** 12.5000 g. **Composition:** Copper-Nickel **Ruler:** Margrethe II **Subject:** Crown Prince's 18th Birthday **Obverse:** Head of Margrethe II with crown right **Reverse:** Head of Crown Prince Frederik left, value below

Date	Mintage	F	VF	XF	Unc	BU
ND(1986)(h) R; A	1,090,000	—	—	—	2.75	—
ND(1986)(h) R; A Proof	2,000	Value: 200				

KM# 865a 10 KRONER **Weight:** 14.3000 g. **Composition:** 0.8000 Silver .3678 oz. ASW **Ruler:** Margrethe II

Date	Mintage	F	VF	XF	Unc	BU
1986(h) R; A Proof	24,000	Value: 52.50				

KM# 867.1 10 KRONER **Weight:** 7.0000 g. **Composition:** Aluminum-Bronze **Ruler:** Margrethe II **Obverse:** Head of Margrethe II, titles, date, initials **Reverse:** Crowned arms within ornaments, value below

Date	Mintage	F	VF	XF	Unc	BU
1989 NR; JP; A	38,346,000	—	—	—	2.25	—

KM# 867.2 10 KRONER **Weight:** 7.0000 g. **Composition:** Aluminum-Bronze **Ruler:** Margrethe II

Date	Mintage	F	VF	XF	Unc	BU
1990 LG; JP; A	12,193,000	—	—	—	2.25	—
1991 LG; JP; A	1,065,000	—	—	—	3.00	—
1992 LG; JP; A	484,000	—	—	—	4.50	—
1993 LG; JP; A	1,069,000	—	—	—	3.50	—

KM# 877 10 KRONER **Weight:** 7.0000 g. **Composition:** Aluminum-Bronze **Ruler:** Margrethe II **Obverse:** New portrait of Queen Margrethe **Edge:** Plain **Note:** Beginning with strikes in 1995 and ending in 1998, letters and numbers on reverse have raised edges.

Date	Mintage	F	VF	XF	Unc	BU
1994 LG; JP; A	4,058,000	—	—	—	2.25	—
1995 LG; JP; A	9,461,000	—	—	—	2.25	—
1997 LG; JP; A	3,725,000	—	—	—	2.25	—
1998 LG; JP; A	6,000,000	—	—	—	2.25	—
1999 LG; JP; A	—	—	—	—	2.25	—

KM# 887 10 KRONER **Weight:** 7.0000 g. **Composition:** Copper-Aluminum-Nickel **Ruler:** Margrethe II **Obverse:** Queen's new portrait **Reverse:** Crowned arms above denomination **Edge:** Plain

Date	Mintage	F	VF	XF	Unc	BU
2001 LG; JP; A	4,800,000	—	—	—	2.25	—
2002 LG; JP; A	—	—	—	—	2.25	—

KM# 810 20 KRONER **Weight:** 8.9606 g. **Composition:** 0.9000 Gold .2592 oz. AGW **Ruler:** Frederik VIII **Obverse:** Head of Frederik VIII with titles **Reverse:** Draped crowned national arms above date, value, mint mark and initials

Date	Mintage	F	VF	XF	Unc	BU
1908(h) VBP; GJ	243,000	BV	85.00	110	170	—
1909(h) VBP; GJ	365,000	BV	95.00	120	180	—
1910(h) VBP; GJ	200,000	BV	100	125	190	—
1911(h) VBP; GJ	183,000	BV	90.00	115	170	—
1912(h) VBP; GJ	184,000	BV	90.00	115	170	—

KM# 817.1 20 KRONER **Weight:** 8.9606 g. **Composition:** 0.9000 Gold .2592 oz. AGW **Ruler:** Frederik VIII **Obverse:** Head of Christian X with title, date, mint mark, initials **Reverse:** Draped crowned national arms above date, value, mint mark and initials

Date	Mintage	F	VF	XF	Unc	BU
1913(h) AH/GJ	815,000	BV	85.00	110	150	—
1914(h) AH/GJ	920,000	BV	85.00	110	150	—
1915(h) AH/GJ	532,000	BV	85.00	115	155	—
1916(h) AH/GJ	1,401,000	BV	90.00	120	170	—
1917(h) AH/GJ	Inc. above	BV	90.00	115	160	—

KM# 817.2 20 KRONER **Weight:** 8.9606 g. **Composition:** 0.9000 Gold .2592 oz. AGW **Ruler:** Christian X **Note:** 1926-1931 dated 20 Kroners were not released for circulation.

Date	Mintage	F	VF	XF	Unc	BU
1926(h) HCN	358,000	—	—	2,750	4,500	—
1927(h) HCN	Inc. above	—	—	2,750	4,500	—

KM# 817.3 20 KRONER **Weight:** 8.9606 g. **Composition:** 0.9000 Gold .2592 oz. AGW **Ruler:** Christian X **Note:** The 1926-1931 dated 20 Kroners were not released for circulation.

Date	Mintage	F	VF	XF	Unc	BU
1930(h) N	1,285,000	—	—	2,750	4,500	—
1931(h) N	Inc. above	—	—	2,750	4,500	—

KM# 870 20 KRONER **Composition:** Aluminum-Bronze **Ruler:** Margrethe II **Subject:** 50th Birthday of Queen Margrethe **Obverse:** Head of Margrethe II with hat **Reverse:** Large crown above daisy-like flower, value below

Date	Mintage	F	VF	XF	Unc	BU
ND(1990)(h) LG	1,101,000	—	—	—	4.50	—

KM# 871 20 KRONER **Weight:** 9.3000 g. **Composition:** Aluminum-Bronze **Ruler:** Margrethe II **Obverse:** Head of Margrethe II, titles, date, initials **Reverse:** Crowned arms within ornaments, value below **Note:** Date varieties exist.

Date	Mintage	F	VF	XF	Unc	BU
1990(h) LG; JP and A	34,368,000	—	—	—	4.25	—
1991(h) LG; JP and A	11,563,000	—	—	—	4.25	—
1993(h) LG; JP and A	674,000	—	—	—	5.00	—

KM# 875 20 KRONER **Weight:** 9.3000 g. **Composition:** Aluminum-Bronze **Ruler:** Margrethe II **Subject:** Silver Wedding Anniversary **Obverse:** Heads of Prince Henrik and Margrethe II facing each other **Reverse:** Fairy tale house

Date	Mintage	F	VF	XF	Unc	BU
ND(1992)(h) LG	994,000	—	—	—	4.50	—

KM# 878 20 KRONER **Composition:** Aluminum-Bronze **Ruler:** Margrethe II **Obverse:** New portrait of Queen Margrethe **Edge:** Alternating reeded and plain sections **Note:** Strikes dated 1996 and 1998 have letters and numbers on reverse with raised edges.

Date	Mintage	F	VF	XF	Unc	BU
1994(h) LG, JP and A	2,565,000	—	—	—	4.50	—
1996(h) LG, JP and A	8,651,000	—	—	—	4.50	—
1998(h) LG, JP and A	4,000,000	—	—	—	4.50	—
1999(h) LG, JP and A	4,133,363	—	—	—	4.50	—

KM# 879 20 KRONER **Weight:** 9.3000 g. **Composition:** Aluminum-Bronze **Ruler:** Margrethe II **Subject:** 1000 Years of Danish Coinage **Obverse:** Head of Margrethe II left **Reverse:** Large crown on cross

Date	Mintage	F	VF	XF	Unc	BU
ND(1995)(h) LG; JP; A	1,000,000	—	—	—	4.50	—

KM# 881 20 KRONER **Weight:** 9.3000 g. **Composition:** Aluminum-Bronze **Ruler:** Margrethe II **Subject:** Wedding of Prince Joachim

Date	Mintage	F	VF	XF	Unc	BU
1995(h) LJ, JP and A	1,000,000	—	—	—	4.50	—

Note: Although dated 1995, minted at the end of the year and included in a 1996 mint set

KM# 883 20 KRONER **Weight:** 9.3000 g. **Composition:** Aluminum-Bronze **Ruler:** Margrethe II **Subject:** 25th Anniversary - Queen's Reign **Obverse:** Full-length portrait **Reverse:** Crowned arms

Date	F	VF	XF	Unc	BU
ND(1997)(h) LG; JP; A	—	—	—	4.50	—

KM# 885 20 KRONER **Weight:** 9.3600 g. **Composition:** Brass **Ruler:** Margrethe II **Subject:** 60th Birthday of Queen Margrethe II **Obverse:** Bust of Queen Margrethe II right **Reverse:** Crown above flowers **Edge:** Alternating reeded and plain sections

Date	F	VF	XF	Unc	BU
ND(2000)	—	—	4.00	5.50	—

KM# 888 20 KRONER **Weight:** 9.3000 g. **Composition:** Copper-Aluminum-Nickel **Ruler:** Margrethe II **Obverse:** Queen's new portrait **Reverse:** Crowned arms above denomination **Edge:** Alternating reeded and plain sections

Date	Mintage	F	VF	XF	Unc	BU
2001(h) LG; JP; A	2,900,000	—	—	—	5.00	—
2002(h) LG; JP; A	—	—	—	—	5.00	—

KM# 889 20 KRONER **Weight:** 9.3000 g. **Composition:** Brass **Ruler:** Margrethe II **Subject:** Arhus City Hall **Obverse:** Queen's portrait **Reverse:** Tower **Edge:** Reeded and plain sections **Size:** 26.8 mm.

Date	F	VF	XF	Unc	BU
2002	—	—	—	5.00	—

KM# 872 200 KRONER **Weight:** 31.1000 g. **Composition:** 0.8000 Silver .8000 oz. ASW **Ruler:** Margrethe II **Subject:** 50th Birthday of Queen Margrethe

Date	Mintage	F	VF	XF	Unc	BU
ND(1990)(h)	128,000	—	—	—	37.50	—

KM# 876 200 KRONER **Weight:** 31.1000 g. **Composition:** 0.9990 Silver 1.0000 oz. ASW **Ruler:** Margrethe II **Subject:** Silver Wedding Anniversary

Date	Mintage	F	VF	XF	Unc	BU
ND(1992)(h)	58,000	—	—	—	37.50	—

KM# 880 200 KRONER **Weight:** 31.1000 g. **Composition:** 0.9990 Silver 1.0000 oz. ASW **Ruler:** Margrethe II **Subject:** 1000 Year of Danish Coinage **Obverse:** Head of Margrethe II left **Reverse:** Large crown on cross

Date	Mintage	F	VF	XF	Unc	BU
ND(1995)(h)	27,000	—	—	—	42.50	—

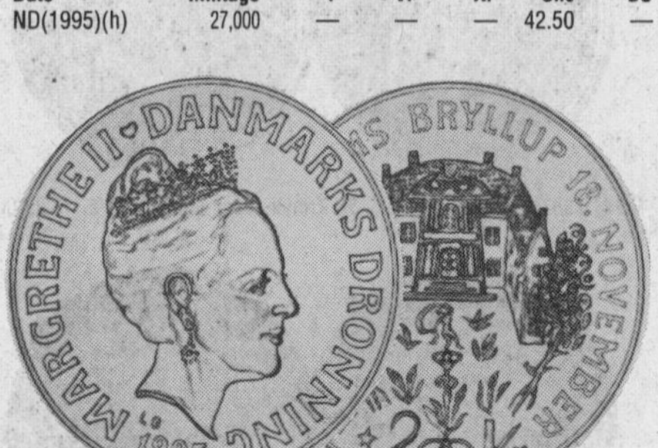

KM# 882 200 KRONER **Weight:** 31.1000 g. **Composition:** 0.9990 Silver 1.0000 oz. ASW **Ruler:** Margrethe II **Subject:** Wedding of Prince Joachim **Reverse:** Palace

Date	Mintage	F	VF	XF	Unc	BU
1995(h)	55,000	—	—	—	37.50	—

KM# 884 200 KRONER **Weight:** 31.1000 g. **Composition:** 0.9990 Silver 1.0000 oz. ASW **Ruler:** Margrethe II **Subject:** 25th Anniversary - Queen's Reign **Obverse:** Full-length portrait **Reverse:** National arms and date of 25th anniversary

Date	Mintage	F	VF	XF	Unc	BU
ND(1997)(h)	60,000	—	—	—	45.00	—

KM# 886 200 KRONER **Weight:** 31.1000 g. **Composition:** 0.9990 Silver 1.0000 oz. ASW **Ruler:** Margrethe II **Subject:** 60th Birthday of Queen Margrethe II **Obverse:** Bust of Queen Margrethe II right **Reverse:** Crown above flowers **Edge:** Plain **Size:** 38 mm.

Date	Mintage	F	VF	XF	Unc	BU
ND(2000)(h)	60,000	—	—	—	45.00	—

PATTERNS

Including off metal strikes

KM#	Date	Mintage	Identification	Mkt Val
PnB63	1940	—	25 Ore. Zinc. KM#823.	—
PnA64	1941	—	2 Ore. Zinc. KM#833.	—
PnB64	1941	—	5 Ore. Zinc. KM#834.	—
Pn63	1941	—	Ore. Aluminum. KM#832.	4,850
Pn65	1947	—	5 Kroner. Nickel. Without denomination.	3,650
Pn66	1948N	—	5 Ore. Zinc. KM#843.	—
Pn64	19xxC	—	Krone. Copper-Nickel. KM#837.2.	1,000

PROVAS

KM#	Date	Mintage	Identification	Mkt Val

KM#	Date	Mintage	Identification	Mkt Val
Pr1	1900 (1984-1986)	9	10 Kroner. Aluminum-Bronze. I.	1,050

KM#	Date	Mintage	Identification	Mkt Val
Pr2	1900 (1984-1986)	16	20 Kroner. Aluminum-Bronze. II.	660

KM#	Date	Mintage	Identification	Mkt Val
Pr3	1983	6	25 Ore. Bronze. Crowned MIIR monogram. Value on circular grid. I.	2,900

KM# Date Mintage Identification Mkt Val

Pr4 1983 5 25 Ore. Bronze. II. 3,000

Pr5 1983 7 50 Ore. Bronze. II. 2,900

Pr6 1983 6 50 Ore. Bronze. II. 2,900

Pr7 1983 — 50 Ore. Bronze. Without Roman numeral. —

Pr8 1983 4 50 Ore. Bronze. 22.5 mm. Wide rim. —

Pr9 1983 4 Krone. Copper-Nickel. Head of Margrethe II. Crowned arms, date, value. Similar to Pr11. —

Pr10 1983 4 2 Kroner. Copper-Nickel. Similar to Pr11. —

Pr12 1983 6 10 Kroner. Aluminum-Bronze. Supported national arms, date, value. I. 2,000

Pr13 1983 7 10 Kroner. Aluminum-Bronze. II. 1,575

Pr14 1983 7 10 Kroner. Aluminum-Bronze. III. 2,400

Pr15 1983 6 10 Kroner. Aluminum-Bronze. IIII. 2,400

Pr16 1983 — 10 Kroner. Aluminum-Bronze. Without Roman numeral. —

Pr17 1983 7 20 Kroner. Aluminum-Bronze. I. 2,400

KM# Date Mintage Identification Mkt Val

Pr18 1983 7 20 Kroner. Aluminum-Bronze. II. 2,400

Pr19 1983 7 20 Kroner. Aluminum-Bronze. III. 2,400

Pr20 1983 6 20 Kroner. Aluminum-Bronze. IIII. 2,650

Pr21 1983 — 20 Kroner. Aluminum-Bronze. Without Roman numeral. —

Pr23 1983 7 50 Kroner. Aluminum-Bronze. II. 2,100

Pr24 1983 7 50 Kroner. Aluminum-Bronze. III. 2,100

Pr25 1983 6 50 Kroner. Aluminum-Bronze. IIII. 2,400

Pr26 1983 22 50 Kroner. Aluminum-Bronze. Without Roman numeral. 1,475

KM# Date Mintage Identification Mkt Val

Pr11 1983 3 5 Kroner. Copper-Nickel. —

PrA11 1983 4 5 Kroner. Copper-Nickel. 27.2 mm. 1,800

PrB11 1983 6 5 Kroner. Copper-Nickel. 1,500

Pr27 1984 81 25 Ore. Bronze. 17.25 mm. Large crown. 85.00

Pr28 1984 81 50 Ore. Bronze. 19.75 mm. Value below heart. 85.00

Pr29 1984 99 Krone. Copper-Nickel. Three crowned MIIR monograms. Ornaments around center hole. 70.00

Pr30 1984 118 Krone. Copper-Nickel. Large crown above date divided by center hole, MIIR below. 50.00

Pr31 1984 203 Krone. Copper-Nickel. Reverse of 1988. 40.00

Pr32 1984 — Krone. Copper-Nickel. Similar to Pr30 but without hole. 450

Pr33 1984 191 2 Kroner. Copper-Nickel. Triple monogram. Ornaments around center hole, value above. 40.00

Pr34 1984 103 2 Kroner. Copper-Nickel. Milled edge. 75.00

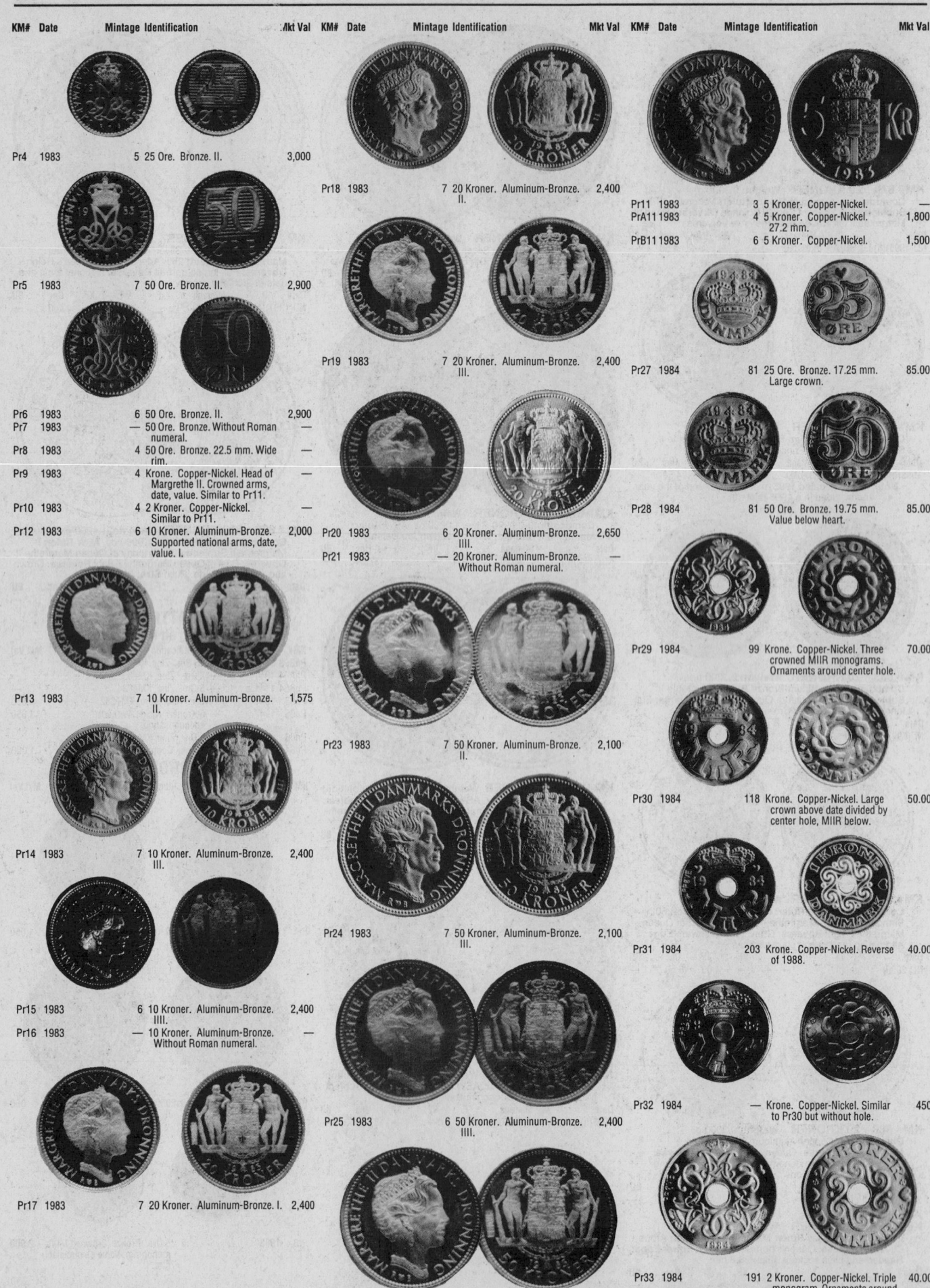

KM# Date Mintage Identification Mkt Val

Pr35 1984 201 2 Kroner. Copper-Nickel. Interrupted milling 6 or 7 notches. 40.00

Pr36 1984 85 5 Kroner. Copper-Nickel. Triple monogram. Ornament around center hole, value. 70.00

Pr37 1984 108 5 Kroner. Copper-Nickel. Milled edge. 75.00

Pr38 1984 202 5 Kroner. Copper-Nickel. Milled edge. 40.00

Pr39 1984 6 5 Kroner. Copper-Nickel. As Pr36 except for added date at top and country name at bottom. Large 5 above ornament and denomination. 2,000

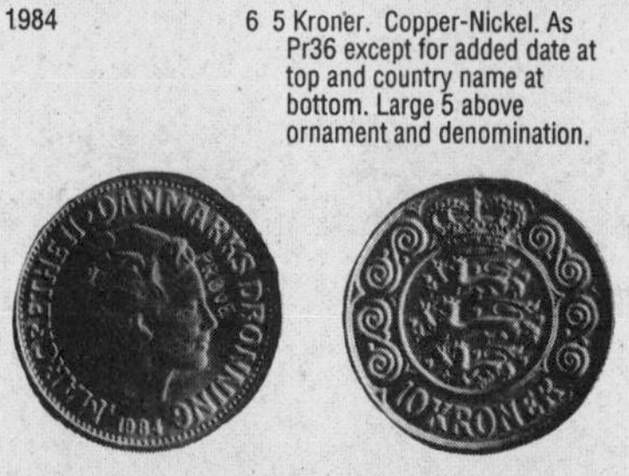

Pr40 1984 85 10 Kroner. Aluminum-Bronze. Crowned arms, ornament, value. 100

PrA41 1984 4 10 Kroner. Aluminum-Bronze. Without "Prove". —

PrB41 1984 3 10 Kroner. Aluminum-Bronze. Different ornaments and value style. Without "Prove". —

Pr41 1984 112 20 Kroner. Aluminum-Bronze. 80.00

Pr42 1984 4 20 Kroner. Aluminum-Bronze. Without "PROVE". —

PrA43 1984 51 20 Kroner. Aluminum-Bronze. Without "Prove". 150

KM# Date Mintage Identification Mkt Val

Pr43 1986 183 25 Ore. Bronze. 17.5 mm. 40.00

Pr44 1986 210 25 Ore. Bronze. 18 mm. 30.00

Pr45 19(86) 23 50 Ore. Bronze. 19.75 mm. 215

Pr46 1986 181 50 Ore. Bronze. 40.00

Pr47 19(86) 10 Krone. Copper-Nickel. Crowned MIIR monogram, date. Ornaments around center hole, value, country name. Crown lacks lower rim. 500

Pr48 19(86) 10 Krone. Copper-Nickel. Full crown (miscolored). 625

Pr49 198(6) 6 Krone. Copper-Nickel. Three digits in date. 1,400

Pr50 18(6) 9 Krone. Copper-Nickel. Without hole. 850

Pr51 1986 185 Krone. Copper-Nickel. Full date. 40.00

PrA52 1986 2 Krone. Copper-Nickel. Without hole. —

KM# Date Mintage Identification Mkt Val

Pr52a 1986 91 2 Kroner. Copper-Nickel. Two crowned MIIR monograms, date. Ornaments around center hole, value, country name. With hole interrupted milling 7x5 grooves. 100

Pr52b 1986 196 2 Kroner. Copper-Nickel. Without hole, interrupted milling, 6x6 grooves. 20.00

Pr52c 1986 196 2 Kroner. Copper-Nickel. Without hole, interrupted milling, 8x7 grooves, widely spaced notches. 20.00

Pr52d 1986 196 2 Kroner. Copper-Nickel. Without hole, interrupted milling, 8x9 grooves. 20.00

Pr52e 1986 196 2 Kroner. Copper-Nickel. Without hole, interrupted milling, 8x8 grooves, no notches. 20.00

Pr52f 1986 196 2 Kroner. Copper-Nickel. Without hole, interrupted milling, 8x8 grooves, with notches. 20.00

Pr52g 1986 196 2 Kroner. Copper-Nickel. Without hole, interrupted milling, 6x7 grooves. 20.00

Pr52h 1986 196 2 Kroner. Copper-Nickel. Interrupted milling, 8x7 grooves, narrowly spaced notches. 20.00

Pr53 1986 2 2 Kroner. Copper-Nickel. Three crowned MIIR monograms, date. Ornaments around center hole, denomination. Without hole. —

Pr54 1986 190 2 Kroner. Copper-Nickel. With hole. 20.00

Pr55 1986 102 5 Kroner. Copper-Nickel. Three crowned MIIr monograms, mint mark, date. Ornaments with value and country name. 120

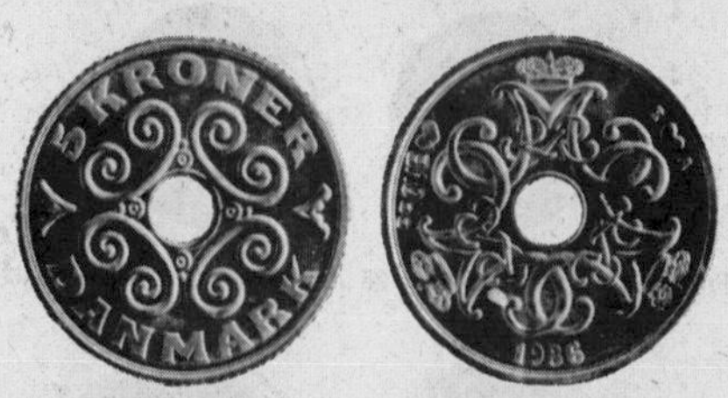

Pr56 1986 212 5 Kroner. Copper-Nickel. Turned 120 degrees. 25.00

Pr57 1986 5 5 Kroner. Copper-Nickel. Without hole. 2,100

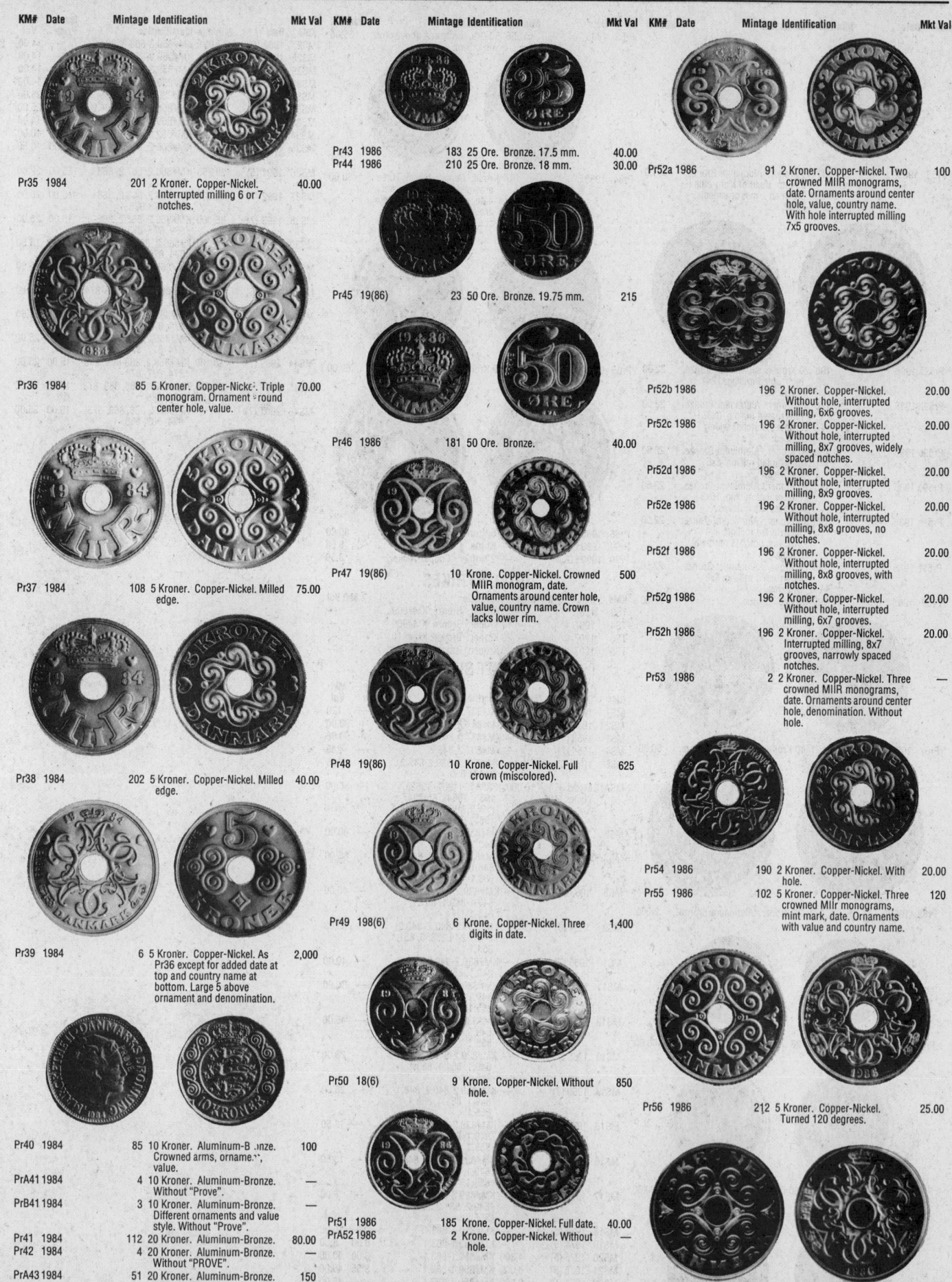

KM#	Date	Mintage	Identification	Mkt Val

KM#	Date	Mintage	Identification	Mkt Val
Pr58	1986	302	10 Kroner. Aluminum-Bronze. 23 mm. Head of Margrethe II. Crowned arms, ornaments, value.	55.00

KM#	Date	Mintage	Identification	Mkt Val
Pr59a	1986	198	20 Kroner. Aluminum-Bronze. Interrupted milling, 12x4 grooves.	22.50
Pr59b	1986	198	20 Kroner. Aluminum-Bronze. Interrupted milling, 8x8 grooves, notches widely spaced.	22.50
Pr59c	1986	198	20 Kroner. Aluminum-Bronze. Interrupted milling, 8x6 grooves.	22.50
Pr59d	1986	198	20 Kroner. Aluminum-Bronze. Interrupted milling, 16x3 grooves, no notches.	22.50
Pr59e	1986	198	20 Kroner. Aluminum-Bronze. Interrupted milling, 8x8 grooves, notches narrowly spaced.	22.50
Pr59f	1986	198	20 Kroner. Aluminum-Bronze. Interrupted milling, 8x8 grooves.	22.50
Pr60	1987	190	50 Ore. Bronze.	22.50

KM#	Date	Mintage	Identification	Mkt Val
Pr67	1988	171	10 Kroner. Aluminum-Bronze.	50.00

KM#	Date	Mintage	Identification	Mkt Val
Pr68	1988	171	20 Kroner. Aluminum-Bronze.	28.00

KM#	Date	Mintage	Identification	Mkt Val
Pr61	1988	171	25 Ore. Bronze.	60.00

KM#	Date	Mintage	Identification	Mkt Val
Pr62	1988	178	50 Ore. Bronze.	60.00

KM#	Date	Mintage	Identification	Mkt Val
Pr63	1988	56	50 Ore. Bronze. A above cross on crown.	65.00

KM#	Date	Mintage	Identification	Mkt Val
Pr64	1988	187	Krone. Copper-Nickel. Three crowned MIIR monograms, date, mint mark. Ornaments around center hole, value, country name.	60.00

KM#	Date	Mintage	Identification	Mkt Val
Pr65	1988	175	2 Kroner. Copper-Nickel.	60.00

KM#	Date	Mintage	Identification	Mkt Val
Pr66	1988	174	5 Kroner. Copper-Nickel.	60.00
Pr69	1990 LG-JP	—	Krone. Copper-Nickel.	8.50
Pr70	1990 LG-JP	—	2 Kroner. Copper-Nickel.	8.50

TRIAL STRIKES

KM#	Date	Mintage	Identification	Mkt Val
TS3	1907	—	10 Kroner. Bronze. KM#809.	—
TS4	1907	—	10 Kroner. Bronze. KM#809.	—
TS5	1907	—	20 Kroner. Bronze. KM#810.	—
TS6	1907	—	20 Kroner. Bronze. KM#810.	—

MINT SETS

KM#	Date	Mintage	Identification	Issue Price	Mkt Val
MS1	1956 (7)	—	KM#837.2-843.2	—	120
MS2	1957 (7)	—	KM#837.2-843.2	—	90.00
MS3	1958 (7)	—	KM#837.2-843.2	—	90.00
MS4	1959 (7)	—	KM#837.2-843.2	—	245
MS5	1960 (8)	—	KM#837.2, 839.2-843.2, 849.1, 850	—	135
MSA12	Mixed dates (10)	10,000	KM#846 (1960, 1962, 1963, 1964), KM#847 (1960, 1962, 1963, 1964, 1965, 1966)	—	30.00
MS6	1961 (7)	—	KM#839.2-840.2, 843.2, 849.1, 850, 851.1, 853.1	—	80.00
MS7	1962 (8)	—	KM#839.2-840.2, 843.2, 848.1-849.1, 850, 851.1, 853.1	—	65.00
MS8	1963 (7)	—	KM#839.2-840.2, 843.2, 848.1-849.1, 851.1, 853.1	—	40.00
MS9	1964 (8)	—	KM#839.2-840.2, 843.2, 848.1-849.1, 850, 851.1, 853.1	—	40.00
MS10	1965 (7)	—	KM#839.2-840.2, 848.1-849.1, 850, 851.1, 853.1	—	40.00
MS11	1966 (8)	—	KM#839.2-840.2, 848.1-849.1, 850, 851.1, 853.1, 855.1	—	30.00
MS12	1967 (8)	—	KM#839.2-840.2, 848.1-849.1, 850, 851.1, 853.1, 855.1	—	45.00
MS13	1968 (7)	—	KM#839.2-840.2, 848.1-849.1, 851.1, 853.1, 855.1	—	28.00
MS14	1969 (7)	—	KM#839.2-840.2, 848.1-849.1, 851.1, 853.1, 855.1	—	28.00
MS15	1970 (7)	—	KM#839.2-840.2, 848.1-849.1, 851.1, 853.1, 855.1	—	13.50
MS16	1971 (7)	—	KM#839.2-840.2, 848.1-849.1, 851.1, 853.1, 855.1	—	13.50
MS17	1972 (7)	—	KM#839.3-840.3, 848.2-849.2, 851.2, 853.2, 855.2	—	8.00
MS18	1973 (5)	—	KM#859.1-863.1	—	10.00
MS19	1974 (5)	—	KM#859.1-863.1	6.00	8.00
MS20	1975 (5)	4,300	KM#859.1-863.1	6.00	90.00
MS21	1976 (5)	6,000	KM#859.1-863.1	3.55	45.00
MS22	1977 (5)	6,000	KM#859.1-863.1	—	45.00
MS23	1978 (5)	6,000	KM#859.1-863.1	—	20.00
MS24	1979 (6)	6,000	KM#859.2-863.2, 864.1	—	18.00
MS25	1980 (5)	4,000	KM#859.2-863.2	—	150
MS26	1981 (6)	15,767	KM#859.2-863.2, 864.1	—	16.50
MS27	1982 (6)	17,031	KM#859.3-863.3, 864.2	—	14.00
MS28	1983 (6)	14,595	KM#859.3-863.3, 864.2	—	14.00
MS29	1984 (6)	14,041	KM#859.3-863.3, 864.2	—	14.00
MS30	1985 (6)	14,000	KM#859.3-863.3, 864.2	—	14.00
MS31	1986 (6)	20,000	KM#859.3-863.3, 865	—	25.00
MS32	1987 (6)	15,000	KM#859.3-863.3, 864.2	—	25.00
MS33	1988 (6)	19,692	KM#859.3-863.3, 864.2	—	14.00
MS34	1989 (3)	27,123	KM#862.3, 866.1, 867.1	12.00	10.00
MS35	1990 (6)	39,258	KM#866.2, 867.2, 868-871	15.00	16.50
MS36	1991 (5)	33,258	KM#866.2, 867.2, 868-869, 871	15.00	22.50
MS37	1992 (7)	40,000	KM#866.2, 867.2, 868-869, 873-875	15.00	25.00
MS38	1993 (7)	35,000	KM#866.2, 867.2, 868-869, 871, 873-874	15.00	25.00
MS39	1994 (7)	30,000	K#866.2, 868-869, 873-874, 877-878	15.00	16.50
MS40	1995 (7)	25,000	KM#866.2, 868-869, 873-874, 877, 879	15.00	16.50
MS41	1996 (6)	25,000	KM#866.2, 868, 873-874, 878, 881 (1995 date)	15.00	16.50
MS42	1997 (7)	25,000	KM#866.2, 868-869, 873-874, 877, 883	15.00	30.00
MS43	1998 (7)	28,000	KM#866.2, 868, 869, 873-874, 877, 878	15.00	25.00
MS44	1999 (7)	30,100	KM#866.2, 868-869, 873-874, 877, 878	15.00	25.00
MS45	2000 (6)	28,000	KM#866.2, 868, 869, 873, 874, 885	15.00	50.00
MS46	2001 (7)	—	KM866.2, 868, 869, 873, 874, 887, 888	15.00	25.00

DJIBOUTI

The Republic of Djibouti (formerly French Somaliland and the French Overseas Territory of Afars and Issas), located in northeast Africa at the Bab el Mandeb Strait connecting the Suez Canal and the Red Sea with the Gulf of Aden and the Indian Ocean, has an area of 8,950 sq. mi. (22,000 sq. km.) and a population of 421,320. Capital: Djibouti. The tiny nation has less than one sq. mi. of arable land, and no natural resources except salt, sand, and camels. The commercial activities of the transshipment port of Djibouti and the Addis Abada-Djibouti railroad are the basis of the economy. Salt, fish and hides are exported.

French interest in former French Somaliland began in 1839 with concessions obtained by a French naval lieutenant from the provincial sultans. French Somaliland was made a protectorate in 1884 and its boundaries were delimited by the Franco-British and Ethiopian accords of 1887 and 1897. It became a colony in 1896 and a territory within the French Union in 1946. In 1958 it voted to join the new French Community as an overseas territory, and reaffirmed that choice by a referendum in March, 1967. Its name was changed from French Somaliland to the French Territory of Afars and Issas on July 5, 1967.

The French Tricolor, which had flown over the strategically important territory for 115 years, was lowered for the last time on June 27, 1977, when French Afars and Issas became Africa's 49th independent state, under the name of the Republic of Djibouti.

Djibouti, a seaport and capital city of the Republic of Djibouti (and formerly of French Somaliland and French Afars and Issas) is located on the east coast of Africa at the southernmost entrance to the Red Sea. The capital was moved from Obok to Djibouti in 1892 and established as the transshipment point for Ethiopia's foreign trade via the Franco-Ethiopian railway linking Djibouti and Addis Ababa.

RULERS
French, until 1977

COLONY

COUNTERMARKED COINAGE

Rupee-Taler (Riyal) Coinage Series

KM# 2.4 RUPEE SIZE **Composition:** 0.9170 Silver
Note: Countermark on India Rupee, KM#473.

CM Date	Host Date	Good	VG	F	VF	XF
	1862-1901	—	35.00	65.00	125	250

TOKEN COINAGE

KM# Tn1 5 CENTIMES **Composition:** Zinc **Issuer:** Chamber of Commerce

Date	VG	F	VF	XF	Unc
1920	4.50	10.00	35.00	85.00	175

KM# Tn5 5 CENTIMES **Composition:** Aluminum **Issuer:** Chamber of Commerce

Date	VG	F	VF	XF	Unc
1921	3.00	7.50	28.00	65.00	140

KM# Tn2 10 CENTIMES **Composition:** Zinc **Issuer:** Chamber of Commerce

Date	VG	F	VF	XF	Unc
1920	6.00	18.00	45.00	100	225

KM# Tn6 10 CENTIMES **Composition:** Aluminum **Issuer:** Chamber of Commerce

Date	VG	F	VF	XF	Unc
1921	4.50	10.00	30.00	70.00	150

KM# Tn7 25 CENTIMES **Composition:** Aluminum **Issuer:** Chamber of Commerce

Date	VG	F	VF	XF	Unc
1921	6.00	12.00	38.00	90.00	195

KM# Tn3 50 CENTIMES **Composition:** Zinc **Issuer:** Chamber of Commerce

Date	VG	F	VF	XF	Unc
1920	7.50	20.00	55.00	110	240

KM# Tn8 50 CENTIMES **Composition:** Bronze-Aluminum **Issuer:** Chamber of Commerce

Date	VG	F	VF	XF	Unc
1921	6.00	15.00	32.00	85.00	180

KM# Tn9 50 CENTIMES **Composition:** Bronze **Issuer:** Chamber of Commerce

Date	VG	F	VF	XF	Unc
1921	7.50	20.00	48.00	100	225

KM# Tn10 50 CENTIMES **Composition:** Aluminum **Issuer:** Chamber of Commerce

Date	VG	F	VF	XF	Unc
1922	10.00	28.00	65.00	125	275

KM# Tn4 FRANC **Composition:** Aluminum **Issuer:** Chamber of Commerce

Date	VG	F	VF	XF	Unc
1920	15.00	35.00	75.00	150	330

REPUBLIC

STANDARD COINAGE

KM# 20 FRANC **Composition:** Aluminum

Date	Mintage	F	VF	XF	Unc	BU
1977(a)	300,000	0.50	0.75	1.50	3.00	—
1996	—	0.50	0.75	1.50	3.00	—

KM# 21 2 FRANCS **Composition:** Aluminum

Date	Mintage	F	VF	XF	Unc	BU
1977(a)	200,000	0.75	1.00	1.75	3.50	—

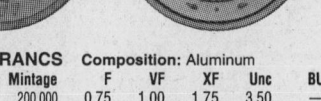

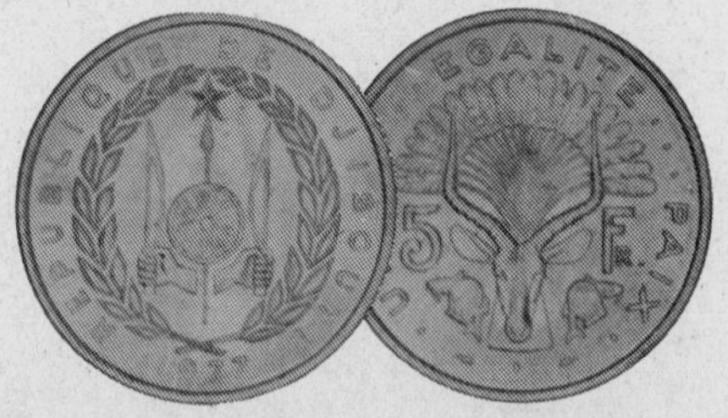

KM# 22 5 FRANCS **Composition:** Aluminum

Date	Mintage	F	VF	XF	Unc	BU
1977(a)	400,000	0.75	1.25	2.00	4.00	—
1986(a)	—	0.75	1.00	1.75	3.50	—

Date	Mintage	F	VF	XF	Unc	BU
1989(a)	—	0.75	1.00	1.75	3.50	—
1991(a)	—	0.75	1.00	1.75	3.50	—

KM# 23 10 FRANCS **Composition:** Aluminum-Bronze
Note: Varieties exist.

Date	Mintage	F	VF	XF	Unc	BU
1977(a)	600,000	0.45	0.85	1.50	3.00	—
1983(a)	—	0.50	1.00	1.75	3.50	—
1989(a)	—	0.45	0.75	1.25	2.50	—
1991(a)	—	0.45	0.75	1.25	2.50	—
1996(a)	—	0.45	0.75	1.25	2.50	—

KM# 24 20 FRANCS **Composition:** Aluminum-Bronze
Note: Varieties exist.

Date	Mintage	F	VF	XF	Unc	BU
1977(a)	700,000	0.50	1.00	1.50	3.00	—
1982(a)	—	0.50	1.00	1.75	3.50	—
1983(a)	—	0.50	1.00	1.50	3.00	—
1986(a)	—	0.45	0.75	1.25	2.50	—
1991(a)	—	0.45	0.75	1.25	2.50	—
1996(a)	—	0.45	0.75	1.25	2.50	—

KM# 25 50 FRANCS **Composition:** Copper-Nickel
Reverse: Pair of dromedary camels, denomination

Date	Mintage	F	VF	XF	Unc	BU
1977(a)	1,500,000	0.75	1.50	3.00	6.00	—
1982(a)	—	0.75	1.50	3.00	6.00	—
1983(a)	—	0.50	1.00	2.25	4.50	—
1986(a)	—	0.50	1.00	2.25	4.50	—
1989(a)	—	0.50	1.00	2.25	4.50	—
1991(a)	—	0.50	1.00	2.25	4.50	—

KM# 26 100 FRANCS **Composition:** Copper-Nickel
Reverse: Pair of dromedary camels, denomination

Date	Mintage	F	VF	XF	Unc	BU
1977(a)	1,500,000	1.00	2.00	3.00	6.50	—
1983(a)	—	1.00	2.50	3.50	7.00	—
1991(a)	—	1.00	1.75	2.75	5.50	—

KM# 29 100 FRANCS **Weight:** 31.4700 g. **Composition:** 0.9250 Silver **Subject:** World Cup Soccer

Date	Mintage	F	VF	XF	Unc	BU
1994 Proof	Est. 15,000	Value: 35.00				

KM# 30 100 FRANCS **Weight:** 31.4700 g. **Composition:** 0.9250 Silver **Subject:** 1996 Olympic Games **Reverse:** Runner

Date	Mintage	F	VF	XF	Unc	BU
1994 Proof	Est. 30,000	Value: 32.50				

KM# 31 100 FRANCS **Weight:** 31.4700 g. **Composition:** 0.9250 Silver **Reverse:** Frigate "Bateau"

Date	Mintage	F	VF	XF	Unc	BU
1994 Proof	Est. 15,000	Value: 45.00				

KM# 32 100 FRANCS **Weight:** 31.4700 g. **Composition:** 0.9250 Silver **Subject:** Endangered Wildlife **Reverse:** Grevy zebras

Date	Mintage	F	VF	XF	Unc	BU
1994 Proof	Est. 15,000	Value: 42.50				

KM# 33 100 FRANCS **Weight:** 31.4700 g. **Composition:** 0.9250 Silver **Reverse:** Portuguese "Nao" ship

Date	Mintage	F	VF	XF	Unc	BU
1996 Proof	Est. 15,000	Value: 45.00				

KM# 27 500 FRANCS **Composition:** Aluminum-Bronze

Date	F	VF	XF	Unc	BU
1989(a)	3.00	4.00	6.00	10.00	—
1991(a)	3.00	4.00	6.00	10.00	—

KM# 28 15000 FRANCS **Weight:** 24.3000 g. **Composition:** 0.9990 Silver .7710 oz. ASW **Note:** Republic of Djibouti.

Date	F	VF	XF	Unc	BU
1991	—	—	—	125	—

ESSAIS

Standard metals unless otherwise noted

KM#	Date	Mintage	Identification	Issue Price	Mkt Val
E4	1977(a)	—	10 Francs. KM23.	—	14.50
E1	1977(a)	—	Franc. KM20.	—	12.50
E2	1977(a)	—	2 Francs. KM21.	—	12.50
E3	1977(a)	—	5 Francs. KM22.	—	12.50
E5	1977(a)	—	20 Francs. KM24.	—	14.50
E6	1977(a)	—	50 Francs. KM25.	—	16.50
E7	1977(a)	—	100 Francs. KM26.	—	17.50

DOMINICA

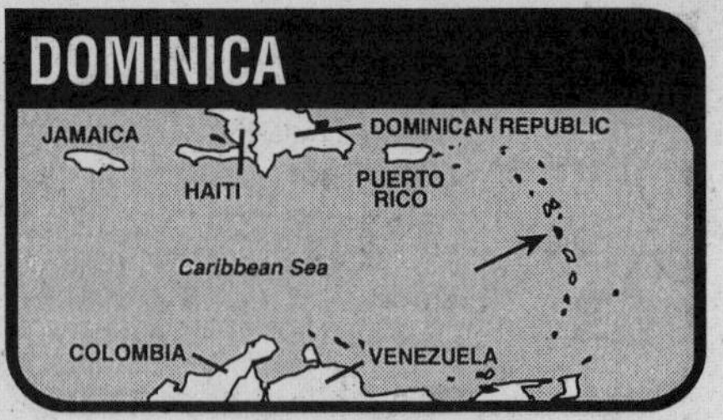

The Commonwealth of Dominica, situated in the Lesser Antilles midway between Guadeloupe to the north and Martinique to the south, has an area of 290 sq. mi. (750 sq. km.) and a population of 82,608. Capital: Roseau. Agriculture is the chief economic activity of the mountainous island. Bananas are the chief export.

Columbus discovered and named the island on Nov. 3, 1493. Spain neglected it and it was finally colonized by the French in 1632. The British drove the French from the island in 1756. Thereafter it changed hands between the French and British a dozen or more times before becoming permanently British in 1805. Around 1761, pierced or mutilated silver from Martinique was used on the island. A council in 1798 acknowledged and established value for these mutilated coins and ordered other cut and countermarked to be made in Dominica. These remained in use until 1862, when they were demonetized and sterling became the standard. Throughout the greater part of its British history, Dominica was a presidency of the Leeward Islands. In 1940 its administration was transferred to the Windward Islands and it was established as a separate colony with considerable local autonomy. From 1955, Dominica was a member of the currency board of the British Caribbean Territories (Eastern Group), which issued its own coins until 1965. Dominica became a West Indies associated state with a built in option for independence in 1967. Full independence was attained on Nov. 3, 1978. Dominica, which has a republican form of government, is a member of the Commonwealth of Nations.

RULERS

British, until 1978

MINT MARKS

CHI in circle - Valcambi, Chiasso, Italy
(ml) - maple leaf - Canadian Royal Mint

MONETARY SYSTEM

(Commencing 1813)
16 Bits = 12 Shillings = 1 Dollar (Spanish)
100 Cents = 1 Dollar (Dominican)

COLONY

TOKEN COINAGE

KM# Tn1 10 CENTS **Composition:** Brass **Obverse:** Denomination **Reverse:** Denomination

Date	VG	F	VF	XF	Unc
ND	7.00	15.00	30.00	50.00	—

MODERN COINAGE

KM# 11 4 DOLLARS **Composition:** Copper-Nickel **Series:** F.A.O **Obverse:** Arms **Reverse:** Sugar cane and banana tree branch **Note:** This 4-dollar F.A.O. commemorative coin is part of a group. The others are listed individually under their respective country names: Antigua, Barbados, Dominica, Grenada, Montserrat, St. Kitts, St. Lucia, and St. Vincent.

Date	Mintage	F	VF	XF	Unc	BU
1970	13,000	—	4.00	6.50	12.00	—
1970 Proof	2,000	Value: 17.50				

COMMONWEALTH

MODERN COINAGE

KM# 12.1 10 DOLLARS Weight: 20.5000 g. **Composition:** 0.9250 Silver .6097 oz. ASW **Subject:** Independence - History of Carnival **Obverse:** Queen Elizabeth **Reverse:** With mint mark

Date	Mintage	F	VF	XF	Unc	BU
ND(1978)CHI	1,500	—	—	7.50	18.50	—
ND(1978)CHI Proof	2,000	Value: 25.00				

KM# 12.2 10 DOLLARS Weight: 20.5000 g. **Composition:** 0.9250 Silver .6097 oz. ASW **Subject:** Independence - History of Carnival **Obverse:** Queen Elizabeth **Reverse:** Without mint mark

Date	F	VF	XF	Unc	BU
ND(1978)	—	—	7.50	18.50	—

KM# 12.3 10 DOLLARS Weight: 20.5000 g. **Composition:** 0.9250 Silver .6097 oz. ASW **Subject:** Independence - History of Carnival **Obverse:** Queen Elizabeth **Reverse:** Canadian mint mark and fineness

Date	Mintage	F	VF	XF	Unc	BU
ND(1978)(ml)	18	—	—	—	—	—
ND(1978)(ml) Proof	233	—	—	—	—	—

KM# 16 10 DOLLARS Weight: 20.5000 g. **Composition:** 0.9250 Silver .6097 oz. ASW **Subject:** Visit of Pope John Paul II **Obverse:** Queen Elizabeth II **Reverse:** Pope John Paul II

Date	Mintage	F	VF	XF	Unc	BU
ND(1979)	1,150	—	—	7.50	20.00	—
ND(1979) Proof	3,450	Value: 25.00				

KM# 20 10 DOLLARS Composition: Copper Nickel **Subject:** Royal Visit **Obverse:** Mature portrait of Queen Elizabeth II **Reverse:** Arms in inner circle

Date	F	VF	XF	Unc	BU
1985	—	—	5.00	8.00	—

KM# 20a 10 DOLLARS Weight: 28.2800 g. **Composition:** 0.9250 Silver .8409 oz. ASW **Subject:** Royal Visit **Obverse:** Mature portrait of Queen Elizabeth II **Reverse:** Arms in inner circle

Date	Mintage	F	VF	XF	Unc	BU
1985 Proof	Est. 5,000	Value: 27.50				

KM# 20b 10 DOLLARS Weight: 47.5400 g. **Composition:** 0.9170 Gold 1.4013 oz. AGW **Subject:** Royal Visit **Obverse:** Mature portrait of Queen Elizabeth II **Reverse:** Arms in inner circle

Date	Mintage	F	VF	XF	Unc	BU
1985 Proof	Est. 250	Value: 850				

KM# 13.1 20 DOLLARS Weight: 40.9100 g. **Composition:** 0.9250 Silver 1.2167 oz. ASW **Subject:** Independence and 50th Anniversary of Graf Zeppelin **Obverse:** Similar to 300 Dollars, KM#15 **Reverse:** Blimp

Date	Mintage	F	VF	XF	Unc	BU
ND(1978)CHI	500	—	—	30.00	65.00	—
ND(1978)CHI Proof	1,000	Value: 80.00				

KM# 13.2 20 DOLLARS Weight: 40.9100 g. **Composition:** 0.9250 Silver 1.2167 oz. ASW **Subject:** Independence and 50th Anniversary of Graf Zeppelin **Obverse:** Similar to 300 Dollars, KM#15 **Reverse:** Blimp; Canadian mint mark and .925 fineness stamp added

Date	Mintage	F	VF	XF	Unc	BU
ND(1978)(ml)	—	—	—	—	—	—
ND(1978)(ml) Proof	233	—	—	—	—	—

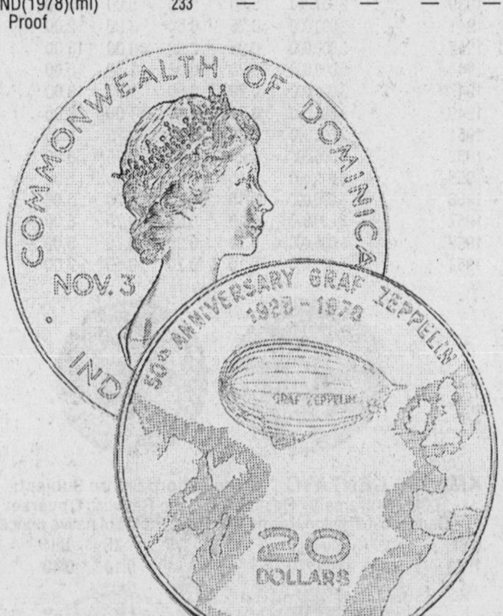

KM# 13.3 20 DOLLARS Composition: Silver **Edge:** Reeded **Size:** 45.2 mm. **Note:** No mintmarks or fineness.

Date	F	VF	XF	Unc	BU
ND(1978) Proof	— Value: 150				

KM# 17 20 DOLLARS Weight: 40.9100 g. **Composition:** 0.9250 Silver 1.2167 oz. ASW **Subject:** Israel and Egypt Peace Treaty **Obverse:** Queen Elizabeth II **Reverse:** Portrait of Sadat, Begin, and Carter

Date	Mintage	F	VF	XF	Unc	BU
ND(1979)	200	—	—	35.00	75.00	—
ND(1979) Proof	200	Value: 95.00				

KM# 21 100 DOLLARS Weight: 129.5900 g. **Composition:** 0.9250 Silver 3.8543 oz. ASW **Subject:** Tropical Birds - Imperial Parrots **Obverse:** Arms in inner circle **Reverse:** Parrots in trees **Size:** 63 mm. **Note:** Illustration reduced.

Date	Mintage	F	VF	XF	Unc	BU
1988 Proof	Est. 10,000	Value: 150				

KM# 14.1 150 DOLLARS Weight: 9.6000 g. **Composition:** 0.9000 Gold .2778 oz. AGW **Subject:** Independence - Imperial Parrot **Obverse:** Queen Elizabeth II **Reverse:** Map of Dominica and parrot, without fineness

Date	Mintage	F	VF	XF	Unc	BU
ND(1978)	300	—	—	—	200	—
ND(1978) Proof	400	Value: 240				

KM# 14.2 150 DOLLARS Weight: 9.6000 g. **Composition:** 0.9000 Gold .2778 oz. AGW **Subject:** Independence - Imperial Parrot **Obverse:** Queen Elizabeth II **Reverse:** Canadian mint mark and .900 fineness added

Date	Mintage	F	VF	XF	Unc	BU
ND(1978)	18	—	—	—	—	—
ND(1978) Proof	116	Value: 265				

KM# 18 150 DOLLARS **Weight:** 9.6000 g. **Composition:** 0.9000 Gold .2778 oz. AGW **Subject** Israel and Egypt Peace Treaty

Date	Mintage	F	VF	XF	Unc	BU
ND(1979)(ml)	100	—	—	—	500	—
ND(1979)(ml) Proof	100	Value: 550				

KM# 15.1 300 DOLLARS **Weight:** 19.2000 g. **Composition:** 0.9000 Gold .5556 oz. AGW **Subject:** Independence - Arms **Obverse:** Queen Elizabeth II **Reverse:** Dominican arms and parrots, without fineness

Date	Mintage	F	VF	XF	Unc	BU
ND(1978)	500	—	—	—	350	—
ND(1978) Proof	800	Value: 400				

KM# 15.2 300 DOLLARS **Weight:** 19.2000 g. **Composition:** 0.9000 Gold .5556 oz. AGW **Subject:** Independence - Arms **Obverse:** Queen Elizabeth II **Reverse:** Canadian mint mark and .900 fineness added

Date	Mintage	F	VF	XF	Unc	BU
ND(1978)(ml)	18	—	—	—	—	—
ND(1978)(ml) Proof	82	Value: 450				

KM# 19 300 DOLLARS **Weight:** 19.2000 g. **Composition:** 0.9000 Gold .5556 oz. AGW **Subject:** Visit of Pope John Paul II

Date	Mintage	F	VF	XF	Unc	BU
ND(1979)	5,000	—	—	—	300	—
ND(1979)	300	—	—	—	525	—

DOMINICAN REPUBLIC

The Dominican Republic, which occupies the eastern two-thirds of the island of Hispaniola, has an area of 18,704 sq. mi. (48,734 sq. km.) and a population of 7.9 million. Capital: Santo Domingo. The largely agricultural economy produces sugar, coffee, tobacco and cocoa. Tourism and casino gaming are also a rising source of revenue.

Columbus discovered Hispaniola in 1492, and named it La Isla Espanola - 'the Spanish Island'. Santo Domingo, the oldest white settlement in the Western Hemisphere, was the base from which Spain conducted its exploration of the New World. Later, French buccaneers settled the western third of Hispaniola, naming the colony St. Dominique, which in 1697, was ceded to France by Spain. In 1804, following a bloody revolt by former slaves, the French colony became the Republic of Haiti - mountainous country'. The Spanish called their part of Hispaniola Santo Domingo. In 1822, the Haitians conquered the entire island and held it until 1844, when Juan Pablo Duarte, the national hero of the Dominican Republic, drove them out of Santo Domingo and established an independent Dominican Republic. The republic returned voluntarily to Spanish dominion from 1861 to 1865, after being rejected by France, Britain and the United States. Independence was reclaimed in 1866.

MINT MARKS

(c) - Stylized maple leaf, Royal Canadian Mint
Mo – Mexico City
(o) - CHI in oval - Valcambi, Chiasso, Italy
(t) - Tower, Tower Mint, London

MONETARY SYSTEM

100 Centavos = 1 Peso Oro

REPUBLIC

REFORM COINAGE

1937

100 Centavos = 1 Peso Oro

KM# 17 CENTAVO **Composition:** Bronze **Obverse:** Banner over national arms **Reverse:** Palm tree, denomination

Date	Mintage	F	VF	XF	Unc	BU
1937	1,000,000	0.50	1.50	7.50	75.00	—
1937	—	Value: 350				
1939	2,000,000	0.50	1.25	5.00	40.00	—
1941	2,000,000	0.25	0.50	3.00	12.00	—
1942	2,000,000	0.25	0.50	3.00	15.00	—
1944	5,000,000	0.20	0.50	1.50	10.00	—
1947	3,000,000	0.20	0.50	1.00	8.00	—
1949	3,000,000	0.20	0.40	1.00	8.00	—
1951	3,000,000	0.20	0.35	0.75	8.00	—
1952	3,000,000	0.20	0.35	0.75	8.00	—
1955	3,000,000	0.15	0.35	0.75	6.00	—
1956	3,000,000	0.15	0.35	0.75	6.00	—
1957	5,000,000	0.10	0.25	0.75	5.00	—
1959	5,000,000	0.10	0.25	0.75	5.00	—
1961	5,000,000	0.10	0.20	0.50	2.00	—

KM# 25 CENTAVO **Composition:** Bronze **Subject:** 100th Anniversary - Restoration of the Republic **Obverse:** Banner over national arms **Reverse:** Profile of native princess

Date	Mintage	F	VF	XF	Unc	BU
1963	13,000,000	—	—	0.10	0.40	—

KM# 31 CENTAVO **Composition:** Bronze **Obverse:** Banner over national arms **Reverse:** Profile of native princess

Date	Mintage	F	VF	XF	Unc	BU
1968	5,000,000	—	—	0.10	0.20	—
1971	6,000,000	—	—	0.10	0.20	—
1972	3,000,000	—	—	0.10	0.20	—
1972 Proof	500	Value: 15.00				
1975	500,000	—	—	0.10	0.20	—

KM# 32 CENTAVO **Composition:** Bronze **Series:** F.A.O. **Obverse:** Banner over national arms **Reverse:** Profile of native princess

Date	Mintage	F	VF	XF	Unc	BU
1969	5,000,000	—	—	0.10	0.30	—

KM# 40 CENTAVO **Composition:** Bronze **Subject:** Centennial - Death of Juan Pablo Duarte **Obverse:** Banner over national arms **Reverse:** Portrait of Duarte

Date	Mintage	F	VF	XF	Unc	BU
1976	3,995,000	—	—	0.10	0.20	—
1976 Proof	5,000	Value: 1.00				

KM# 48 CENTAVO **Composition:** Bronze **Obverse:** Without memorial legend

Date	Mintage	F	VF	XF	Unc	BU
1978	2,995,000	—	—	0.10	0.15	—
1978 Proof	5,000	Value: 2.00				
1979	2,985,000	—	—	0.10	0.15	—
1979 Proof	500	Value: 15.00				
1980	200,000	—	—	0.10	0.15	—
1980 Proof	3,000	Value: 1.00				
1981 Proof	3,000	Value: 1.00				

Note: KM#48a previously listed here has been moved to the Pattern section

KM# 64 CENTAVO **Composition:** Copper Plated Zinc **Subject:** Human Rights **Obverse:** Banner over national arms **Reverse:** Bust of Coanabo

Date	Mintage	F	VF	XF	Unc	BU
1984Mo	10,000,000	—	—	—	0.25	—
1984Mo Proof	1,600	Value: 1.50				
1986	18,067,000	—	—	—	0.25	—
1986 Proof	1,600	Value: 1.50				
1987	15,000,000	—	—	—	0.25	—
1987 Proof	1,600	Value: 1.50				

KM# 64a CENTAVO **Weight:** 2.0000 g. **Composition:** 0.9000 Silver .0578 oz. ASW **Subject:** Human Rights **Obverse:** Banner over national arms **Reverse:** Bust of Coanabo

Date	Mintage	F	VF	XF	Unc	BU
1984Mo Proof	100	Value: 20.00				
1986 Proof	100	Value: 20.00				

KM# 72 CENTAVO **Composition:** Copper Plated Zinc **Obverse:** Banner over national arms **Reverse:** Triangular artifact

Date	Mintage	F	VF	XF	Unc	BU
1989	1,115	—	—	—	1.25	—

KM# 72a CENTAVO **Weight:** 3.7000 g. **Composition:** 0.9250 Silver .1100 oz. ASW **Obverse:** Banner over national arms **Reverse:** Triangular artifact

Date	Mintage	F	VF	XF	Unc	BU
1989 Proof	2,600	—	—	—	—	—

KM# 18 5 CENTAVOS Composition: Copper-Nickel **Obverse:** Banner over national arms **Reverse:** Profile of native princess

Date	Mintage	F	VF	XF	Unc	BU
1937	2,000,000	1.00	1.75	5.00	50.00	—
1937 Proof	—	Value: 600				
1939	200,000	3.50	8.00	40.00	350	—
1951	2,000,000	0.75	1.25	2.00	20.00	—
1956	1,000,000	0.20	0.50	0.80	3.50	—
1959	1,000,000	0.20	0.50	0.80	3.50	—
1961	4,000,000	0.10	0.20	0.35	0.75	—
1971	440,000	0.10	0.15	0.20	0.50	—
1972	2,000,000	0.10	0.15	0.20	0.40	—
1972 Proof	500	Value: 15.00				
1974	5,000,000	—	—	0.10	0.40	—
1974 Proof	500	Value: 15.00				

KM# 18a 5 CENTAVOS Weight: 5.0000 g. **Composition:** 0.3500 Silver .0563 oz. ASW **Obverse:** Banner over national arms **Reverse:** Profile of native princess

Date	Mintage	F	VF	XF	Unc	BU
1944	2,000,000	1.50	3.50	7.50	30.00	—

KM# 26 5 CENTAVOS Composition: Copper-Nickel **Subject:** 100th Anniversary - Restoration of the Republic **Obverse:** Banner over national arms **Reverse:** Profile of native princess

Date	Mintage	F	VF	XF	Unc	BU
1963	4,000,000	—	0.10	0.15	0.60	—

KM# 41 5 CENTAVOS Composition: Copper-Nickel **Subject:** Centennial - Death of Juan Pablo Duarte **Obverse:** Banner over national arms **Reverse:** Portrait of Duarte

Date	Mintage	F	VF	XF	Unc	BU
1976	5,595,000	—	—	0.10	0.50	—
1976 Proof	5,000	Value: 2.00				

KM# 49 5 CENTAVOS Composition: Copper-Nickel **Reverse:** Without memorial legend

Date	Mintage	F	VF	XF	Unc	BU
1978	1,996,000	—	—	0.10	0.35	—
1978 Proof	5,000	Value: 1.50				
1979	2,988,000	—	—	0.10	0.35	—
1979 Proof	500	Value: 15.00				
1980	5,300,000	—	—	0.10	0.35	—
1980 Proof	3,000	Value: 2.00				
1981	4,500,000	—	—	0.10	0.35	—
1981 Proof	3,000	Value: 2.00				

Note: KM#49a previously listed here has been moved to the Pattern section

KM# 59 5 CENTAVOS Composition: Copper Nickel **Subject:** Human Rights **Obverse:** Banner over national arms **Reverse:** Conjoined busts of Sanchez and Mello

Date	Mintage	F	VF	XF	Unc	BU
1983	3,998,000	—	—	0.10	0.30	—
1983(t) Proof	1,600	Value: 2.00				
1984Mo	10,000,000	—	—	0.10	0.30	—
1984Mo Proof	1,600	Value: 2.00				
1986	12,898,000	—	—	0.10	0.30	—
1986 Proof	1,600	Value: 2.00				
1987	10,000,000	—	—	0.10	0.30	—
1987 Proof	1,700	Value: 2.00				

KM# 59a 5 CENTAVOS Weight: 5.0000 g. **Composition:** 0.9000 Silver .1447 oz. ASW **Subject:** Human Rights **Obverse:** Banner over national arms **Reverse:** Conjoined busts of Sanchez and Mello

Date	Mintage	F	VF	XF	Unc	BU
1983 Proof	100	Value: 30.00				
1984Mo Proof	100	Value: 30.00				
1986 Proof	100	Value: 30.00				

KM# 69 5 CENTAVOS Composition: Nickel Clad Steel **Subject:** Native Culture **Obverse:** Banner over national arms **Reverse:** Native drummer

Date	Mintage	F	VF	XF	Unc	BU
1989	50,000,000	—	—	—	0.35	—

KM# 69a 5 CENTAVOS Weight: 5.8300 g. **Composition:** 0.9250 Silver .1734 oz. ASW **Subject:** Native Culture **Obverse:** Banner over national arms **Reverse:** Native drummer

Date	Mintage	F	VF	XF	Unc	BU
1989 Proof	2,600	—	—	—	—	—

KM# 19 10 CENTAVOS Weight: 2.5000 g. **Composition:** 0.9000 Silver .0723 oz. ASW **Obverse:** Banner over national arms **Reverse:** Profile of native princess

Date	Mintage	F	VF	XF	Unc	BU
1937	1,000,000	BV	2.00	5.00	40.00	—
1937 Proof	—	Value: 700				
1939	150,000	3.00	6.00	20.00	300	—
1942	2,000,000	1.00	2.00	3.00	30.00	—
1944	1,000,000	1.00	2.00	4.00	50.00	—
1951	500,000	1.00	2.00	3.00	10.00	—
1952	500,000	1.00	2.00	3.00	10.00	—
1953	750,000	1.00	2.00	3.00	8.00	—
1956	1,000,000	0.75	1.50	2.50	8.00	—
1959	2,000,000	BV	1.25	2.25	7.00	—
1961	2,000,000	BV	1.00	2.00	6.00	—

KM# 27 10 CENTAVOS Weight: 2.5000 g. **Composition:** 0.6500 Silver .0522 oz. ASW **Subject:** 100th Anniversary - Restoration of the Republic **Obverse:** Banner over national arms **Reverse:** Profile of native princess

Date	Mintage	F	VF	XF	Unc	BU
1963	4,000,000	—	BV	1.00	2.00	—

KM# 19a 10 CENTAVOS Composition: Copper-Nickel **Obverse:** Banner over national arms **Reverse:** Profile of native princess **Edge:** Plain

Date	Mintage	F	VF	XF	Unc	BU
1967	10,000,000	—	—	0.15	0.50	—
1973	8,000,000	—	—	0.15	0.50	—
1973 Proof	500	Value: 20.00				
1975	8,000,000	—	—	0.15	0.50	—

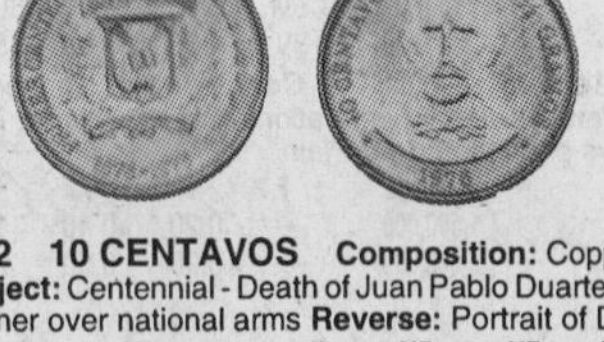

KM# 42 10 CENTAVOS Composition: Copper-Nickel **Subject:** Centennial - Death of Juan Pablo Duarte **Obverse:** Banner over national arms **Reverse:** Portrait of Duarte

Date	Mintage	F	VF	XF	Unc	BU
1976	5,595,000	—	—	0.10	0.75	—
1976 Proof	5,000	Value: 2.00				

KM# 50 10 CENTAVOS Composition: Copper-Nickel

Date	Mintage	F	VF	XF	Unc	BU
1978	3,000,000	—	—	0.10	0.50	—
1978 Proof	5,000	Value: 2.00				
1979	4,020,000	—	—	0.10	0.50	—
1979 Proof	500	Value: 20.00				
1980	4,400,000	—	—	0.10	0.35	—
1980 Proof	3,000	Value: 3.00				
1981	6,000,000	—	—	0.10	0.35	—
1981 Proof	3,000	Value: 3.00				

Note: KM#50a previously listed here has been moved to the Pattern section

KM# 60 10 CENTAVOS Composition: Copper-Nickel **Subject:** Human Rights **Obverse:** Banner over national arms **Reverse:** Profile of Duarte

Date	Mintage	F	VF	XF	Unc	BU
1983	4,998,000	—	—	0.10	0.35	—
1983(t)	4,000,000	—	—	0.10	0.35	—
1983(t) Proof	1,600	Value: 2.50				
1984Mo	15,000,000	—	—	0.10	0.25	—
1984Mo Proof	1,600	Value: 2.50				
1986	15,515,000	—	—	0.10	0.25	—
1986 Proof	1,600	Value: 2.50				
1987	20,000,000	—	—	0.10	0.25	—
1987 Proof	1,700	Value: 2.50				

KM# 60a 10 CENTAVOS Weight: 2.5000 g. **Composition:** 0.9000 Silver .0723 oz. ASW **Subject:** Human Rights **Obverse:** Banner over national arms **Reverse:** Profile of Duarte

Date	Mintage	F	VF	XF	Unc	BU
1983(t) Proof	100	Value: 30.00				
1984 Proof	100	Value: 30.00				
1986 Proof	100	Value: 30.00				

KM# 70 10 CENTAVOS Composition: Nickel Clad Steel **Obverse:** Banner over national arms **Reverse:** Indigenous fruits and vegetables

Date	Mintage	F	VF	XF	Unc	BU
1989	40,000,000	—	—	—	0.40	—
1991	3,500,000	—	—	—	0.40	—

KM# 70a 10 CENTAVOS Weight: 2.9000 g. **Composition:** 925.0000 Silver .0863 oz. ASW **Obverse:** Banner over national arms **Reverse:** Indigenous fruits and vegetables

Date	Mintage	F	VF	XF	Unc	BU
1989 Proof	2,600	—	—	—	—	—

KM# 20 25 CENTAVOS Weight: 6.2500 g. **Composition:** 0.9000 Silver .1808 oz. ASW **Obverse:** Banner over national arms **Reverse:** Profile of native princess

Date	Mintage	F	VF	XF	Unc	BU
1937	560,000	BV	5.00	15.00	65.00	—
1937 Proof	—	Value: 1,000				
1939	160,000	4.00	8.00	25.00	500	—
1942	560,000	2.00	4.00	10.00	100	—
1944	400,000	2.00	4.00	8.00	80.00	—
1947	400,000	2.00	4.00	8.00	80.00	—
1951	400,000	2.00	4.00	8.00	80.00	—
1952	400,000	2.00	3.00	5.00	12.50	—
1956	400,000	2.00	2.50	4.00	10.00	—
1960	600,000	2.00	2.50	4.00	10.00	—
1961	800,000	2.00	2.50	4.00	10.00	—

KM# 20a.1 25 CENTAVOS Composition: Copper Nickel **Obverse:** Banner over national arms **Reverse:** Profile of native princess **Edge:** Plain

Date	Mintage	F	VF	XF	Unc	BU
1967	5,000,000	—	0.10	0.20	0.75	—

Date	Mintage	F	VF	XF	Unc	BU
1972	800,000	—	0.10	0.40	1.00	—
1972 Proof	500	Value: 20.00				

KM# 20a.2 25 CENTAVOS Composition: Copper-Nickel **Obverse:** Banner over national arms **Reverse:** Profile of native princess **Edge:** Reeded

Date	Mintage	F	VF	XF	Unc	BU
1974	2,000,000	—	0.10	0.40	1.00	—
1974 Proof	500	Value: 20.00				

KM# 28 25 CENTAVOS Weight: 6.2500 g. **Composition:** 0.6500 Silver .1306 oz. ASW **Subject:** 100th Anniversary - Restoration of the Republic **Obverse:** Banner over national arms **Reverse:** Profile of native princess

Date	Mintage	F	VF	XF	Unc	BU
1963	2,400,000	—	BV	1.50	3.00	—

KM# 43 25 CENTAVOS Composition: Copper-Nickel **Subject:** Centennial - Death of Juan Pablo Duarte **Obverse:** Banner over national arms **Reverse:** Portrait of Duarte

Date	Mintage	F	VF	XF	Unc	BU
1976	3,195,000	—	0.10	0.40	1.00	—
1976 Proof	5,000	Value: 2.50				

KM# 51 25 CENTAVOS Composition: Copper-Nickel **Reverse:** Without memorial legend

Date	Mintage	F	VF	XF	Unc	BU
1978	996,000	—	—	0.35	0.75	—
1978 Proof	5,000	Value: 3.00				
1979	2,089,000	—	—	0.15	0.50	—
1979 Proof	500	Value: 25.00				
1980	2,600,000	—	—	0.15	0.50	—
1980 Proof	3,000	Value: 3.00				
1981	3,200,000	—	—	0.15	0.50	—
1981 Proof	3,000	Value: 3.00				

Note: KM#51a previously listed here has been mov -d to the Pattern section

KM# 61a 25 CENTAVOS Weight: 6.2500 g. **Composition:** 0.9000 Silver .1808 oz. ASW **Subject:** Human Rights **Obverse:** Banner over national arms **Reverse:** Profile of the Mirabel sisters

Date	Mintage	F	VF	XF	Unc	BU
1983(t) Proof	100	Value: 40.00				
1984Mo Proof	100	Value: 40.00				
1986 Proof	100	Value: 40.00				

KM# 61 25 CENTAVOS Composition: Copper-Nickel **Subject:** Human Rights **Obverse:** Banner over national arms **Reverse:** Profile of the Mirabel sisters **Note:** Coin and medal rotations and edge-reeding varieties exist.

Date	Mintage	F	VF	XF	Unc	BU
1983	793,000	—	0.10	0.20	0.50	—
1983(t)	5,000	—	—	—	2.50	—
1983(t) Proof	1,600	Value: 8.00				
1984Mo	6,400,000	—	—	0.15	0.40	—
1984Mo Proof	1,600	Value: 8.00				
1986	10,132,000	—	—	0.15	0.40	—
1986 Proof	1,600	Value: 8.00				
1987	6,000,000	—	—	0.15	0.40	—
1987 Proof	1,700	Value: 8.00				

KM# 71.2 25 CENTAVOS Composition: Nickel Clad Steel **Subject:** Native Culture **Obverse:** Banner over national arms. **Reverse:** Two oxen pulling cart **Note:** Obverse and reverse legends and designs in beaded circle. Varieties exist.

Date	Mintage	F	VF	XF	Unc	BU
1989	Inc. above	—	—	—	0.60	—
1990	20,000,000	—	—	—	0.60	—

KM# 71.1 25 CENTAVOS Composition: Nickel Clad Steel **Subject:** Native Culture **Obverse:** Banner over national arms **Reverse:** Two oxen pulling cart

Date	Mintage	F	VF	XF	Unc	BU
1989	16,000,000	—	—	—	0.60	—
1991	38,000,000	—	—	—	0.60	—

KM# 71.1a 25 CENTAVOS Weight: 6.7400 g. **Composition:** 0.9250 Silver .2005 oz. ASW **Subject:** Native Culture **Obverse:** Banner over national arms. **Reverse:** Two oxen pulling cart

Date	Mintage	F	VF	XF	Unc	BU
1989 Proof	2,600	—	—	—	—	—

KM# 21a.2 1/2 PESO Composition: Copper-Nickel **Obverse:** Banner over national arms **Reverse:** Profile of native princess **Edge:** Reeded

Date	Mintage	F	VF	XF	Unc	BU
1973	600,000	—	0.20	0.40	1.50	—
1973 Proof	500	Value: 30.00				
1975	600,000	—	0.20	0.40	1.50	—

KM# 21 1/2 PESO Weight: 12.5000 g. **Composition:** 0.9000 Silver .3617 oz. ASW **Obverse:** Banner over national arms. **Reverse:** Profile of native princess

Date	Mintage	F	VF	XF	Unc	BU
1937	500,000	BV	7.50	12.50	70.00	—
1937 Proof	—	Value: 1,500				
1944	100,000	BV	10.00	25.00	300	—
1947	200,000	BV	7.50	15.00	200	—
1951	200,000	BV	7.50	15.00	150	—
1952	140,000	BV	7.50	12.50	70.00	—
1959	100,000	BV	6.00	10.00	40.00	—
1960	100,000	BV	6.00	9.00	30.00	—
1961	400,000	BV	4.00	6.00	25.00	—

KM# 21a.1 1/2 PESO Composition: Copper-Nickel **Obverse:** Banner over national arms **Reverse:** Profile of native princess **Edge:** Plain

Date	Mintage	F	VF	XF	Unc	BU
1967	1,500,000	—	0.20	0.40	1.50	—
1968	600,000	—	0.30	0.50	2.50	—

KM# 29 1/2 PESO Weight: 12.5000 g. **Composition:** 0.6500 Silver .2612 oz. ASW **Subject:** 100th Anniversary - Restoration of the Republic **Obverse:** Banner over national arms **Reverse:** Profile of native princess

Date	Mintage	F	VF	XF	Unc	BU
1963	300,000	—	BV	4.00	7.50	—

KM# 44 1/2 PESO Composition: Copper-Nickel **Subject:** Centennial - Death of Juan Pablo Duarte **Obverse:** Banner over national arms **Reverse:** Portrait of Duarte

Date	Mintage	F	VF	XF	Unc	BU
1976	195,000	—	0.20	0.40	1.50	—
1976 Proof	5,000	Value: 3.00				

KM# 52 1/2 PESO Composition: Copper-Nickel **Reverse:** Without memorial legend

Date	Mintage	F	VF	XF	Unc	BU
1978	296,000	—	0.20	0.40	1.50	—
1978 Proof	5,000	Value: 4.00				
1979	967,000	—	0.20	0.40	1.50	—
1979 Proof	500	Value: 30.00				
1980	1,000,000	—	0.20	0.40	1.50	—
1980 Proof	3,000	Value: 5.00				
1981	1,300,000	—	0.20	0.40	1.50	—
1981 Proof	3,000	Value: 5.00				

Note: KM#52a previously listed here has been moved to the Pattern section

KM# 62a 1/2 PESO Weight: 12.5000 g. **Composition:** 0.9000 Silver .3617 oz. ASW **Subject:** Human Rights **Obverse:** Banner over national arms **Reverse:** Profiles of Bono, Espaillat and Rojas

Date	Mintage	F	VF	XF	Unc	BU
1983(t) Proof	100	Value: 50.00				
1984Mo Proof	100	Value: 50.00				
1986 Proof	100	Value: 50.00				

KM# 62 1/2 PESO Composition: Copper-Nickel **Subject:** Human Rights **Obverse:** Banner over national arms **Reverse:** Profiles of Bono, Espaillat and Rojas **Note:** Coin and medal rotations exist.

Date	Mintage	F	VF	XF	Unc	BU
1983	393,000	—	0.20	0.40	1.50	—
1983(t)	5,000	—	—	—	4.00	—
1983(t) Proof	1,600	Value: 15.00				
1984Mo	3,200,000	—	0.20	0.40	1.50	—
1984Mo Proof	1,600	Value: 15.00				
1986	5,225,000	—	0.20	0.40	1.50	—
1986 Proof	1,600	Value: 15.00				
1987	3,000,000	—	0.20	0.40	1.50	—
1987 Proof	1,700	Value: 15.00				

KM# 73.1 1/2 PESO Composition: Nickel Clad Steel **Subject:** National Culture **Obverse:** Banner over national arms **Reverse:** Beacon at Colon

Date	Mintage	F	VF	XF	Unc	BU
1989	8,000,000	—	—	—	2.00	—

KM# 73.1a 1/2 PESO Weight: 14.6500 g. **Composition:** 0.9250 Silver .4357 oz. ASW **Subject:** National Culture **Obverse:** Banner over national arms **Reverse:** Beacon at Colon

Date	Mintage	F	VF	XF	Unc	BU
1989 Proof	2,600	—	—	—	—	—

KM# 73.2 1/2 PESO Composition: Nickel-Clad Steel **Subject:** National Culture **Obverse:** Banner over national arms, legend and design in inner circle **Reverse:** Beacon at Colon

Date	Mintage	F	VF	XF	Unc	BU
1990	1,500,000	—	—	—	2.00	—

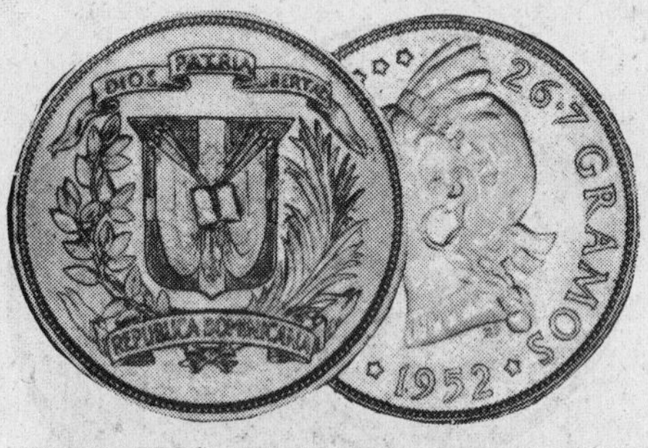

KM# 22 PESO Weight: 26.7000 g. **Composition:** 0.9000 Silver .7725 oz. ASW **Obverse:** Banner over national arms **Reverse:** HP below bust of native princess

Date	Mintage	F	VF	XF	Unc	BU
1939	15,000	15.00	45.00	200	1,500	—
1939 Proof	—	Value: 2,250				
1952	20,000	BV	7.00	10.00	15.00	—

KM# 23 PESO Weight: 26.7000 g. **Composition:** 0.9000 Silver .7725 oz. ASW **Subject:** 25th Anniversary of Trujillo Regime **Obverse:** Banner over national arms **Reverse:** Profile bust of Trujillo **Note:** 30,550 officially melted following Trujillo's assassination in 1961.

Date	Mintage	F	VF	XF	Unc	BU
1955	50,000	7.50	10.00	15.00	25.00	—

KM# 30 PESO Weight: 26.7000 g. **Composition:** 0.6500 Silver .5579 oz. ASW **Subject:** 100th Anniversary - Restoration of the Republic **Obverse:** Memorial legend around national arms **Reverse:** Profile of native princess

Date	Mintage	F	VF	XF	Unc	BU
1963	20,000	—	—	5.00	9.00	—
1963 Proof	—	—	—	—	—	—

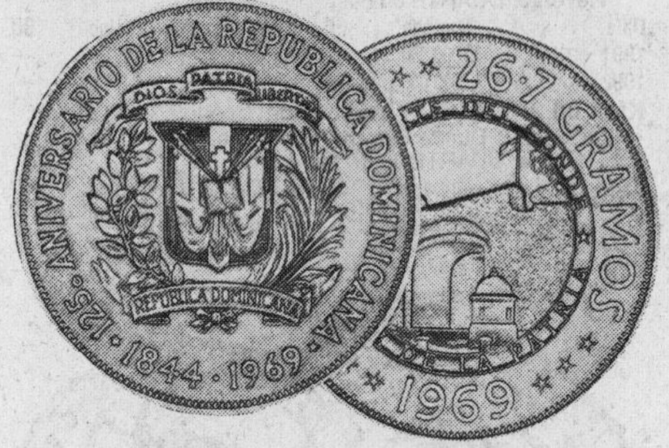

KM# 33 PESO Composition: Copper-Nickel **Subject:** 125th Anniversary of the Republic **Obverse:** Memorial legend around national arms **Reverse:** Pueblo entrance

Date	Mintage	F	VF	XF	Unc	BU
1969	30,000	—	—	2.00	4.50	—

KM# 34 PESO Weight: 26.7000 g. **Composition:** 0.9000 Silver .7725 oz. ASW **Subject:** 25th Anniversary - Central Bank **Obverse:** Memorial legend around national arms **Reverse:** Bank door in inner circle

Date	Mintage	F	VF	XF	Unc	BU
1972	27,000	—	—	—	9.00	—
1972 Proof	3,000	Value: 15.00				

KM# 35 PESO Weight: 26.7000 g. **Composition:** 0.9000 Silver .7725 oz. ASW **Subject:** 12th Central American and Caribbean Games **Obverse:** Without memorial legend **Reverse:** Map and coat of arms

Date	Mintage	F	VF	XF	Unc	BU
1974	50,000	—	—	—	9.00	—
1974 Proof	5,000	Value: 15.00				

KM# 45 PESO Composition: Copper-Nickel **Subject:** Centennial - Death of Juan Pablo Duarte **Obverse:** Banner over national arms **Reverse:** Portrait of Duarte

Date	Mintage	F	VF	XF	Unc	BU
1976	25,000	—	—	1.00	2.00	—
1976 Proof	5,000	Value: 7.50				

KM# 53 PESO Composition: Copper-Nickel **Obverse:** Without memorial legend **Reverse:** Portrait of Duarte

Date	Mintage	F	VF	XF	Unc	BU
1978	35,000	—	—	1.00	2.00	—
1978 Proof	5,000	Value: 7.50				
1979	45,000	—	—	1.00	2.00	—
1979 Proof	500	Value: 35.00				
1980	20,000	—	—	1.00	2.00	—
1980 Proof	3,000	Value: 6.00				
1981 Proof	3,000	Value: 6.00				

Note: KM#53a previously listed here has been moved to the Pattern section

KM# 63 PESO Composition: Copper Nickel **Subject:** Human Rights - Montesinos, Enriquillo and Lemba **Obverse:** Denomination, national arms **Reverse:** Profile portraits of Montesinos, Enriquillo and Lemba **Shape:** 10 sided **Note:** Coin and medal rotations exist.

Date	Mintage	F	VF	XF	Unc	BU
1983(t)	93,000	—	—	1.00	2.50	—
1983	5,000	—	—	—	6.00	—
1983(t) Proof	1,600	Value: 15.00				
1984Mo	120,000	—	—	1.00	2.50	—
1984Mo Proof	1,600	Value: 15.00				
1986	—	—	—	1.00	2.50	—

KM# 63a PESO Weight: 17.0000 g. **Composition:** 0.9000 Silver .4919 oz. ASW **Subject:** Human Rights **Obverse:** Denomination, national arms **Reverse:** Profile portraits of Montesinos, Enriquillo and Lemba **Shape:** 10 sided **Note:** 10-sided.

Date	Mintage	F	VF	XF	Unc	BU
1983 Proof	100	Value: 100				
1984 Proof	100	Value: 100				

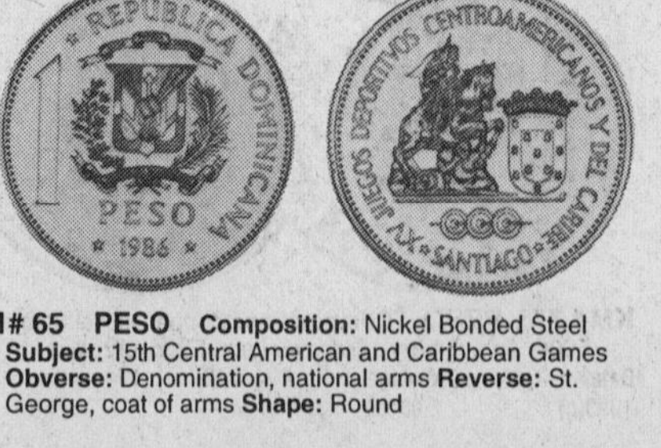

KM# 65 PESO Composition: Nickel Bonded Steel **Subject:** 15th Central American and Caribbean Games **Obverse:** Denomination, national arms **Reverse:** St. George, coat of arms **Shape:** Round

Date	Mintage	F	VF	XF	Unc	BU
1986	100,000	—	—	1.00	3.00	—
1986 Proof	1,700	Value: 15.00				

KM# 65a PESO **Weight:** 6.5000 g. **Composition:** Copper-Nickel **Subject:** 15th Central American and Caribbean Games **Obverse:** Denomination, national arms **Reverse:** St. George, coat of arms **Shape:** Round

Date	Mintage	F	VF	XF	Unc	BU
1986	548	—	—	—	40.00	—
1986 Proof	48	—	—	—	—	—

KM# 65b PESO **Weight:** 10.0000 g. **Composition:** Copper-Nickel **Subject:** 15th Central American and Caribbean Games **Obverse:** Denomination, national arms **Reverse:** St. George, coat of arms **Shape:** Round

Date	Mintage	F	VF	XF	Unc	BU
1986	550	—	—	—	40.00	—
1986 Proof	50	—	—	—	—	—

KM# 66 PESO **Weight:** 19.8400 g. **Composition:** Copper-Nickel **Subject:** 500th Anniversary - Discovery and Evangelization **Obverse:** Denomination, national arms **Reverse:** 3 ships at sea

Date	Mintage	F	VF	XF	Unc	BU
1988(c)	150,000	—	—	—	2.50	—
1988(c) Proof	1,500	Value: 12.50				

KM# 66a PESO **Weight:** 21.1035 g. **Composition:** 0.9990 Silver 1 oz. ASW **Subject:** 500th Anniversary - Discovery and Evangelization **Obverse:** Denomination, national arms **Reverse:** 3 ships at sea

Date	Mintage	F	VF	XF	Unc	BU
1988 Proof	10,000	Value: 18.50				

KM# 66b PESO **Weight:** 31.1035 g. **Composition:** 0.9990 Gold 1 oz. AGW **Subject:** 500th Anniversary - Discovery and Evangelization **Obverse:** Denomination, national arms **Reverse:** 3 ships at sea

Date		F	VF	XF	Unc	BU
1988 Proof	—	Value: 1,250				

KM# 74 PESO **Composition:** Copper-Nickel **Subject:** 500th Anniversary - Discovery and Evangelization **Obverse:** Denomination, national arms **Reverse:** Sailship landing

Date		F	VF	XF	Unc	BU
1989(c)		—	—	—	2.50	—

KM# 74a PESO **Weight:** 31.1035 g. **Composition:** 0.9990 Silver 1 oz. ASW **Subject:** 500th Anniversary - Discovery and Evangelization **Obverse:** Denomination, national arms **Reverse:** Sailship landing

Date	Mintage	F	VF	XF	Unc	BU
1989 Proof	10,000	Value: 18.50				

KM# 74b PESO **Weight:** 31.1035 g. **Composition:** 0.9990 Gold 1 oz. AGW **Subject:** 500th Anniversary - Discovery and Evangelization **Obverse:** Denomination, national arms **Reverse:** Sailship landing

Date	Mintage	F	VF	XF	Unc	BU
1989(c) Proof	30	Value: 1,250				

KM# 77 PESO **Composition:** Copper-Nickel **Subject:** 500th Anniversary - Discovery and Evangelization

Date	Mintage	F	VF	XF	Unc	BU
1990(c)	30,000	—	—	—	2.50	—

KM# 77a PESO **Weight:** 31.1035 g. **Composition:** 0.9990 Silver 1 oz. ASW **Subject:** 500th Anniversary - Discovery and Evangelization

Date	Mintage	F	VF	XF	Unc	BU
1990 Proof	10,000	Value: 18.00				

KM# 77b PESO **Weight:** 31.1035 g. **Composition:** 0.9990 Gold 1 oz. AGW **Subject:** 500th Anniversary - Discovery and Evangelization

Date	Mintage	F	VF	XF	Unc	BU
1990 Proof	50	—	—	—	1,000	—

KM# 80.1 PESO **Composition:** Copper-Zinc **Subject:** Juan Pablo Duarte **Obverse:** Denomination, national arms **Reverse:** DUARTE on bust

Date	Mintage	F	VF	XF	Unc	BU
1991	40,000,000	—	—	—	2.00	—
1992	35,000,000	—	—	—	2.00	—

KM# 80.2 PESO **Composition:** Copper-Zinc **Subject:** Juan Pablo Duarte **Obverse:** Denomination, national arms **Reverse:** DUARTE below bust

Date	Mintage	F	VF	XF	Unc	BU
1992	35,000,000	—	—	—	2.00	—
1993	40,000,000	—	—	—	2.00	—
1997	—	—	—	—	2.00	—

Note: Medal alignment.

KM# 81 PESO **Composition:** Copper-Nickel **Obverse:** Denomination, national arms **Reverse:** Pinzon brothers on ship at sea

Date	Mintage	F	VF	XF	Unc	BU
1991(c)	50,000	—	—	—	2.50	—

KM# 81a PESO **Weight:** 31.1035 g. **Composition:** 0.9990 Silver 1 oz. ASW **Obverse:** Denomination, national arms **Reverse:** Pinzon Brothers on ship at sea

Date	Mintage	F	VF	XF	Unc	BU
1991 Proof	10,000	Value: 20.00				

KM# 81b PESO **Weight:** 31.1035 g. **Composition:** 0.9990 Gold 1 oz. AGW **Obverse:** Denomination, national arms **Reverse:** Pinzon Brothers on ship at sea

Date	Mintage	F	VF	XF	Unc	BU
1991 Proof	35	Value: 1,150				

KM# 82 PESO **Composition:** Copper-Nickel **Subject:** Christopher Columbus **Obverse:** Denomination, national arms **Reverse:** Portrait of Columbus

Date	Mintage	F	VF	XF	Unc	BU
1992(c)	50,000	—	—	—	2.50	—

KM# 82a PESO **Weight:** 31.1035 g. **Composition:** 0.9990 Silver 1 oz. ASW **Subject:** Christopher Columbus **Obverse:** Denomination, national arms **Reverse:** Portrait of Columbus

Date	Mintage	F	VF	XF	Unc	BU
1992 Proof	10,000	Value: 20.00				

KM# 82b PESO **Weight:** 31.1035 g. **Composition:** 0.9990 Gold 1 oz. AGW **Subject:** Christopher Columbus **Obverse:** Denomination, national arms **Reverse:** Portrait of Columbus

Date	Mintage	F	VF	XF	Unc	BU
1992(c) Proof	35	Value: 1,150				

KM# 87 PESO **Composition:** Copper-Nickel **Subject:** UN - Peace **Obverse:** Denomination, arms, stars **Reverse:** UN logo, two doves

Date		F	VF	XF	Unc	BU
1995		—	—	—	8.00	—

KM# 87a PESO **Weight:** 28.4400 g. **Composition:** 0.9250 Silver .8458 oz. ASW **Subject:** UN - Peace **Obverse:** Denomination, arms, stars **Reverse:** UN logo, two doves

Date		F	VF	XF	Unc	BU
1995 Proof	—	Value: 35.00				

KM# 88 5 PESOS **Ring Composition:** Brass Center **Composition:** Stainless Steel **Subject:** 50th Anniversary - Central Bank **Obverse:** Denomination and national arms **Reverse:** Portrait, dates

Date		F	VF	XF	Unc	BU
1997		—	—	—	2.00	—

KM# 37 10 PESOS **Weight:** 28.0000 g. **Composition:** 0.9000 Silver .8102 oz. ASW **Subject:** International Bankers' Conference - First Hispaniola Coinage of Carlos and Johanna **Obverse:** National arms, denomination **Reverse:** Arms of Castille in inner ring

Date	Mintage	F	VF	XF	Unc	BU
1975	—	—	—	—	10.00	—
1975 Proof	4,000	Value: 17.50				

KM# 38 10 PESOS **Weight:** 30.0000 g. **Composition:** 0.9000 Silver .8681 oz. ASW **Subject:** Taino Art **Obverse:** National arms **Reverse:** Ancient figurine "Pueblo Viejo Mine"

Date	Mintage	F	VF	XF	Unc	BU
1975	45,000	—	—	—	8.50	—
1975 Proof	5,000	Value: 13.50				

KM# 57 10 PESOS **Weight:** 23.3300 g. **Composition:** 0.9250 Silver .6938 oz. ASW **Subject:** International Year of the Child **Obverse:** Banner over national arms

Date	Mintage	F	VF	XF	Unc	BU
1982(o) Proof	8,712	Value: 12.50				

KM# 54 25 PESOS **Weight:** 65.0000 g. **Composition:** 0.9250 Silver .9332 oz. ASW **Subject:** Pope John Paul II's Visit

Date	Mintage	F	VF	XF	Unc	BU
ND(1979)	3,000	—	—	—	37.50	—
ND(1979) Proof	6,000	Value: 45.00				

KM# 24 30 PESOS **Weight:** 29.6220 g. **Composition:** 0.9000 Gold .8572 oz. AGW **Subject:** 25th Anniversary of Trujillo regime

Date	Mintage	F	VF	XF	Unc	BU
1955	33,000	—	—	BV	385	—

KM# 36 30 PESOS **Weight:** 11.7000 g. **Composition:** 0.9000 Gold .3385 oz. AGW **Subject:** 12th Central American and Caribbean Games

Date	Mintage	F	VF	XF	Unc	BU
1974	25,000	—	—	—	150	—
1974 Proof	5,000	Value: 175				

KM# 46 30 PESOS **Weight:** 78.0000 g. **Composition:** 0.9250 Silver 2.3199 oz. ASW **Subject:** 30th Anniversary of Central Bank

Date	Mintage	F	VF	XF	Unc	BU
1977	5,000	—	—	—	27.50	—
1977 Proof	2,000	Value: 40.00				

KM# 39 100 PESOS **Weight:** 10.0000 g. **Composition:** 0.9000 Gold .2893 oz. AGW **Subject:** Taino Art

Date	Mintage	F	VF	XF	Unc	BU
1975	18,000	—	—	—	125	—
1975 Proof	2,000	Value: 150				

KM# 55 100 PESOS **Weight:** 12.0000 g. **Composition:** 0.9000 Gold .3472 oz. AGW **Subject:** Pope John Paul II's Visit

Date	Mintage	F	VF	XF	Unc	BU
ND(1979)	1,000	—	—	—	155	—
ND(1979) Proof	3,000	Value: 175				

KM# 67 100 PESOS **Weight:** 155.5000 g. **Composition:** 0.9990 Silver 5 oz. ASW **Subject:** Discovery of America - Native Americans **Size:** 65 mm. **Note:** Illustration reduced.

Date	Mintage	F	VF	XF	Unc	BU
1988 Proof	5,300	Value: 85.00				

KM# 75 100 PESOS **Weight:** 155.5000 g. **Composition:** 0.9990 Silver 5 oz. ASW **Subject:** 500th Anniversary of Discovery and Evangelization of America - Columbus and Crew **Obverse:** Arms

Date	Mintage	F	VF	XF	Unc	BU
1989(c) (c) Proof	1,500	Value: 125				

KM# 75a 100 PESOS **Weight:** 155.5000 g. **Composition:** 0.9990 Gold 5 oz. AGW **Subject:** 500th Anniversary of Discovery and Evangelization of America - Columbus and Crew **Obverse:** Arms

Date	Mintage	F	VF	XF	Unc	BU
1989 Proof	30	Value: 3,500				

KM# 78 100 PESOS **Weight:** 155.5000 g. **Composition:** 0.9990 Silver 5 oz. ASW **Subject:** 500th Anniversary of Discovery and Evangelization of America - Building a Stockade **Size:** 65 mm. **Note:** Illustration reduced.

Date	Mintage	F	VF	XF	Unc	BU
1990 Proof	1,000	Value: 145				

KM# 78a 100 PESOS **Weight:** 155.5300 g. **Composition:** 0.9990 Gold 5 oz. AGW **Subject:** 500th Anniversary of Discovery and Evangelization of America - Building a Stockade **Size:** 65 mm. **Note:** Illustration reduced.

Date	Mintage	F	VF	XF	Unc	BU
1990 Proof	50	Value: 3,000				

KM# 83 100 PESOS Weight: 155.5300 g. **Composition:** 0.9990 Silver 5 oz. ASW **Subject:** 500th Anniversary of Discovery and Evangelization of America - Columbus Presenting Native American to Court **Obverse:** Similar to KM#78 **Size:** 65 mm. **Note:** Illustration reduced.

Date	Mintage	F	VF	XF	Unc	BU
1991 Proof	1,500	Value: 125				

KM# 83a 100 PESOS Weight: 155.5300 g. **Composition:** 0.9990 Gold 5 oz. AGW **Subject:** 500th Anniversary of Discovery and Evangelization of America - Columbus Presenting Native American to Court **Size:** 65 mm. **Note:** Illustration reduced.

Date	Mintage	F	VF	XF	Unc	BU
1991 Proof	35	Value: 3,200				

KM# 84 100 PESOS Weight: 155.5300 g. **Composition:** 0.9990 Silver 5 oz. ASW **Subject:** 500th Anniversary - Discovery and Evangelization of America - Columbus and Anchored Ship **Obverse:** Similar to KM#78 **Size:** 65 mm. **Note:** Illustration reduced.

Date	Mintage	F	VF	XF	Unc	BU
1992 Proof	1,500	Value: 135				

KM# 84a 100 PESOS Weight: 155.5300 g. **Composition:** 0.9990 Gold 5 oz. AGW **Subject:** 500th Anniversary - Discovery and Evangelization of America - Columbus and Anchored Ship **Obverse:** Similar to KM#78 **Size:** 65 mm. **Note:** Illustration reduced.

Date	Mintage	F	VF	XF	Unc	BU
1992 Proof	35	Value: 3,200				

KM# 47 200 PESOS Weight: 31.0000 g. **Composition:** 0.8000 Gold .7974 oz. AGW **Subject:** Centennial - Death of Juan Pablo Duarte **Note:** Large quantities of both varieties were melted for bullion.

Date	Mintage	F	VF	XF	Unc	BU
1977	1,000	—	—	—	450	—
1977 Proof	2,000	Value: 500				

KM# 58 200 PESOS Weight: 17.1700 g. **Composition:** 0.9000 Gold .4969 oz. AGW **Subject:** International Year of the Child

Date	Mintage	F	VF	XF	Unc	BU
1982 Proof	4,303	Value: 250				

KM# 56 250 PESOS Weight: 31.1000 g. **Composition:** 0.9000 Gold .9000 oz. AGW **Subject:** Visit of Pope John Paul II

Date	Mintage	F	VF	XF	Unc	BU
1979	1,000	—	—	—	475	—
1979 Proof	3,000	Value: 525				

KM# 68 500 PESOS Weight: 31.1000 g. **Composition:** 0.9990 Gold .9989 oz. AGW **Subject:** Discovery of America - Columbus

Date	Mintage	F	VF	XF	Unc	BU
1988 Proof	2,600	Value: 650				

KM# 76 500 PESOS Weight: 31.1000 g. **Composition:** 0.9990 Gold .9989 oz. AGW **Subject:** 500th Anniversary - Discovery and Evangelization of America **Obverse:** National arms **Reverse:** Portraits of Ferdinand and Isabella

Date	Mintage	F	VF	XF	Unc	BU
1989 Proof	600	Value: 825				

KM# 76a 500 PESOS Weight: 31.1000 g. **Composition:** 0.9990 Platinum .9989 oz. APW **Subject:** 500th Anniversary - Discovery and Evangelization of America **Obverse:** National arms **Reverse:** Portraits of Ferdinand and Isabella

Date	F	VF	XF	Unc	BU
1989 Proof	— Value: 850				

KM# 79 500 PESOS Weight: 16.9600 g. **Composition:** 0.9170 Gold .5 oz. AGW **Subject:** 500th Anniversary - Discovery and Evangelization of America **Obverse:** National arms **Reverse:** Santa Maria and landing crew

Date	Mintage	F	VF	XF	Unc	BU
1990 Proof	1,500	Value: 350				

KM# 79a 500 PESOS Weight: 15.5500 g. **Composition:** 0.9990 Platinum .5 oz. APW **Subject:** 500th Anniversary - Discovery and Evangelization of America **Obverse:** National arms **Reverse:** Santa Maria and landing crew

Date	Mintage	F	VF	XF	Unc	BU
1990 Proof	50	Value: 650				

KM# 85 500 PESOS Weight: 16.9600 g. **Composition:** 0.9170 Gold .5 oz. AGW **Subject:** 500th Anniversary - Discovery and Evangelization of America **Obverse:** National arms **Reverse:** American fruits

Date	Mintage	F	VF	XF	Unc	BU
1991 Proof	1,500	Value: 350				

KM# 85a 500 PESOS Weight: 15.5500 g. **Composition:** 0.9990 Platinum .5 oz. APW **Subject:** 500th Anniversary - Discovery and Evangelization of America **Obverse:** National arms **Reverse:** American fruits

Date	Mintage	F	VF	XF	Unc	BU
1991 Proof	35	Value: 700				

KM# 86 500 PESOS Weight: 16.9600 g. **Composition:** 0.9170 Gold .5 oz. AGW **Subject:** 500th Anniversary - Discovery and Evangelization of America **Obverse:** National arms **Reverse:** Enshrined tomb of Christopher Columbus

Date	Mintage	F	VF	XF	Unc	BU
1992 Proof	2,000	Value: 325				

KM# 86a 500 PESOS Weight: 15.5000 g. **Composition:** 0.9990 Platinum .5 oz. APW **Subject:** 500th Anniversary - Discovery and Evangelization of America **Obverse:** National arms **Reverse:** Enshrined tomb of Christopher Columbus

Date	Mintage	F	VF	XF	Unc	BU
1992 Proof	35	Value: 700				

PATTERNS

Including off metal strikes

KM#	Date	Mintage	Identification	Mkt Val
Pn7	1937	—	50 Centavos. Copper. Obverse only.	—
Pn8	1937	—	50 Centavos. Silver. Reverse only.	—
Pn9	1961	—	5 Centavos. Copper-Bonded Steel.	—
Pn12	1961	—	10 Centavos. Copper-Bonded Steel.	—
Pn13	1961	—	25 Centavos. Chrome Plated Steel.	—
Pn11	1961	—	5 Centavos. Copper-Bonded Steel. Same design both sides.	—
Pn10	1961	—	5 Centavos. Copper-Bonded Steel.	—
Pn14	1968	3	50 Centavos. Reeded edge.	—
Pn15	1972	1	25 Centavos. Reeded edge.	—
Pn16	1975	1	10 Pesos. Silver.	—
Pn17	1975	11	10 Pesos. 0.5000 Gold.	—
Pn18	1975	1	10 Pesos. 0.2940 Gold.	—
Pn19	1975	1	10 Pesos. 0.4000 Gold.	—
Pn20	1975	1	10 Pesos. 0.8000 Gold.	—
Pn21	1975	1	100 Pesos. 0.9000 Gold. without matte details.	—
Pn22	1975	1	100 Pesos. 0.8000 Gold. alloyed with .050 Silver and .150 Copper.	—
Pn23	1975	5	100 Pesos. 0.8000 Gold. alloyed with .150 Silver.	—
Pn24	1975	5	100 Pesos. 0.8000 Gold. alloyed with .150 Silver and .050 Copper, Proof.	—
Pn25	1976	3	10 Centavos. Plain rim.	—
Pn26	1977	5	30 Pesos. Gold. Proof.	—
Pn27	1978	3	Centavo. Aluminum.	—
Pn28	1978	3	Centavo. Copper And Zinc.	100
Pn29	1978	—	Centavo. 0.9000 Silver. 3.5800 g.	125
Pn30	1978	—	5 Centavos. 0.9000 Silver. 5.8600 g. Without memorial legend.	125
Pn31	1978	—	10 Centavos. 0.9000 Silver. 2.9500 g. Without memorial legend.	125
Pn32	1978	3	25 Centavos. 6-1/2 Gramos.	—
Pn33	1978	—	25 Centavos. 0.9000 Silver. 7.3200 g. Without memorial legend.	150
Pn34	1978	—	1/2 Peso. 0.9000 Silver. 14.5500 g. Without memorial legend.	150
Pn35	1978	—	Peso. 0.9000 Silver. 30.9200 g. Without memorial legend. Portrait of Duarte.	300
Pn36	1979	—	Centavo. 0.9000 Silver. 3.5800 g.	125
Pn37	1979	—	5 Centavos. 0.9000 Silver. 5.8600 g. Without memorial legend.	125
Pn38	1979	—	10 Centavos. 0.9000 Silver. 2.9500 g. Without memorial legend.	125
Pn39	1979	3	25 Centavos. 6-1/2 Gramos.	—
Pn40	1979	—	25 Centavos. 0.9000 Silver. 7.3200 g. Without memorial legend.	150

KM#	Date	Mintage	Identification	Mkt Val
Pn41	1979	—	1/2 Peso. 0.9000 Silver. 14.5500 g. Without memorial legend.	150
Pn42	1979	—	Peso. 0.9000 Silver. 30.9200 g. Without memorial legend. Portrait of Duarte.	300
Pn43	1980	—	Centavo. 0.9000 Silver. 3.5800 g.	125
Pn44	1980	—	5 Centavos. 0.9000 Silver. 5.8600 g. Without memorial legend.	125
Pn45	1980	—	10 Centavos. 0.9000 Silver. 2.9500 g. Without memorial legend.	125
Pn46	1980	—	25 Centavos. 0.9000 Silver. 7.3200 g. Without memorial legend.	150
Pn47	1980	—	1/2 Peso. 0.9000 Silver. 14.5500 g. Without memorial legend.	150
Pn48	1980	—	Peso. 0.9000 Silver. 30.9200 g. Without memorial legend. Portrait of Duarte.	300
Pn49	1981	—	Centavo. 0.9000 Silver. 3.5800 g.	125
Pn50	1981	—	5 Centavos. 0.9000 Silver. 5.8600 g. Without memorial legend.	125
Pn51	1981	—	10 Centavos. 0.9000 Silver. 2.9500 g. Without memorial legend.	125
Pn52	1981	—	25 Centavos. 0.9000 Silver. 7.3200 g. Without memorial legend.	150
Pn53	1981	—	1/2 Peso. 0.9000 Silver. 14.5500 g. Without memorial legend.	150
Pn54	1981	—	Peso. 0.9000 Silver. 30.9200 g. Without memorial legend. Portrait of Duarte.	300
Pn55	1982	80	10 Pesos. KM#57.	—
Pn56	1983	15	25 Centavos. Nickel Bonded Steel.	200
Pn57	1984	3	25 Centavos. Nickel Bonded Steel.	200
Pn58	1984	5	Peso. Nickel Bonded Steel.	—
Pn59	1986	500	Peso. Copper-Nickel.	—

Note: Several issues previously listed under Patterns have now been correctly identified as commercially inspired, privately contracted Medallic Issues and have been moved to that section. The remaining patterns have been renumbered

ESSAIS

KM#	Date	Mintage	Identification	Mkt Val
E13	1878	—	2 Centavos. Nickel.	—

PIEFORTS

KM#	Date	Mintage	Identification	Mkt Val
P1	1977	5	30 Pesos. Gold. Piefort.	—
P3	1982	42	200 Pesos.	2,250
P2	1982	262	10 Pesos.	150
P8	1983	300	1/2 Peso. KM#62.	40.00
P9	1983	300	Peso. KM#63.	50.00
P7	1983 H	300	25 Centavos. Copper-Nickel	35.00
P4	1983 H	300	5 Centavos.	20.00
P5	1983 H	300	10 Centavos. Nickel Bonded Steel.	30.00
P6	1983	300	25 Centavos. KM#61.	35.00
P12	1984	300	10 Centavos.	5.00
P13	1984	300	25 Centavos.	8.00
P14	1984	300	1/2 Peso.	10.00
P15	1984	300	Peso.	12.00
P10	1984	300	Centavo.	5.00
P11	1984	300	5 Centavos.	5.00
P17	1986	50	Peso. Copper Nickel. 20.0000 g.	—
P22	1986	300	1/2 Peso. Copper-Nickel.	12.00
P16	1986	300	Peso. Nickel Bonded Steel.	15.00
P18	1986	300	Centavo. Copper Plated Zinc.	5.00
P19	1986	300	5 Centavos. Copper-Nickel.	5.00
P20	1986	300	10 Centavos. Copper-Nickel.	8.00
P21	1986	300	25 Centavos. Copper-Nickel.	10.00
P26	1987	300	25 Centavos. 0.9250 Silver.	—
P27	1987	300	1/2 Peso. 0.9250 Silver.	—
P24	1987	300	5 Centavos. 0.9250 Silver.	—
P23	1987	300	Centavo. 0.9250 Silver.	—
P25	1987	300	10 Centavos. 0.9250 Silver.	—
P29	1988	100	100 Pesos. 0.9990 Silver. KM#67.	325
P28	1988	100	Peso. 0.9990 Silver. KM#67.	50.00
	1988	100	Peso. 0.9990 Silver. KM#67.	50.00
P33	1989	300	25 Centavos. 0.9250 Silver. KM#71a.	—
P35	1989	10,000	Peso. 0.9990 Silver. KM#74.	40.00

KM#	Date	Mintage	Identification	Mkt Val
P36	1989	200	100 Pesos. 0.9990 Silver. KM#75.	375
P34	1989	300	1/2 Peso. 0.9250 Silver. KM#73a.	—
P30	1989	300	Centavo. 0.9250 Silver. KM#72a.	—
P31	1989	300	5 Centavos. 0.9250 Silver. KM#69a.	—
P32	1989	300	10 Centavos. 0.9250 Silver. KM#70a.	—
P37	1990	10,000	Peso. 0.9990 Silver. KM#77.	40.00
P38	1990	200	100 Pesos. 0.9990 Silver. KM#78.	300

KM#	Date	Mintage	Identification	Mkt Val
P39	1991	10,000	Peso. 0.9990 Silver. KM#81.	40.00
P40	1992	10,000	Peso. 0.9990 Silver. KM#82.	40.00

MINT SETS

KM#	Date	Mintage	Identification	Issue Price	Mkt Val
MS1	1983 (5)	2,000	KM#59-63	10.00	15.00
MS2	1984	2,000	KM#59-64	—	15.00
MS3	1986 (5)	2,000	KM#59-62, 64	10.00	14.00
MS4	1987 (5)	1,000	KM#59-62, 64	10.00	14.00
MS5	1989 (5)	1,000	KM#69-73	—	14.00

PROOF SETS

KM#	Date	Mintage	Identification	Issue Price	Mkt Val
PS1	1937 (5)	—	KM#17-21	—	5,000
PS2	1972 (4)	500	KM#18, 20a.1, 31, 34	20.00	65.00
PS3	1973 (2)	500	KM#19a, 21a.2	5.00	50.00
PS4	1974 (2)	500	KM#18, 20a.2	5.00	35.00
PS5	1974 (2)	500	KM#35-36	120	190
PS6	1975 (2)	500	KM#38-39	200	165
PS7	1976 (6)	5,000	KM#40-45	10.00	20.00
PS9	1978 (6)	15	KM#Pn29-31, Pn33-35	175	900
PS8	1978 (6)	5,000	KM#48-53	10.00	20.00
PS11	1979 (6)	15	KM#Pn36-38, Pn40-42	255	900
PS10	1979 (6)	500	KM#48-53	15.00	135
PS13	1980 (6)	15	KM#Pn43-48	255	900
PS12	1980 (6)	3,000	KM#48-53	15.00	20.00
PS14	1981 (6)	3,000	KM#48-53	15.00	20.00
PS15	1981 (6)	15	KM#Pn49-54	300	900
PS17	1983 (2)	300	KM-P4, P5	25.00	50.00
PS18	1983 (2)	100	KM#59a, 60a	45.00	45.00
PS20	1983 (3)	270	KM-P7, 8, 9	45.00	115
PS21	1983 (3)	70	KM#61a-63a	125	125
PS16	1983 (2)	1,600	KM#59-60	10.00	10.00
PS19	1983 (3)	1,570	KM#61-63	20.00	20.00
PS23	1984 (6)	270	KM-P10, 11, 12, 13, 14, 15	30.00	30.00
PS24	1984 (6)	70	KM#59a-64a	250	250
PS22	1984 (6)	1,570	KM#59-64	20.00	45.00
PS26	1986 (5)	270	KM-P17, 19, 20, 21, 22	40.00	40.00
PS27	1986 (5)	70	KM#59a-62a, 64a	150	150
PS25	1986 (5)	1,570	KM#59-62, 64	30.00	20.00
PS29	1987 (5)	300	KM-P23, 24, 25, 26, 27	—	75.00
PS28	1987 (5)	1,600	KM#59-62, 64	—	30.00
PS30	1989 (5)	2,500	KM#69a-70a, 71.1a, 72a, 73.1a	—	—
PS31	1989 (5)	300	KM-P30, 31, 32, 33, 34	—	—

SPECIAL SETS

KM#	Date	Mintage	Identification	Issue Price	Mkt Val
SS1	1983 (15)	30	KM#61-63, 61a-63a, all mint marks, including Piefort	200	200
SS2	1984 (24)	30	KM#59-64, including Piefort	400	400
SS3	1986 (20)	30	KM#59-64	300	300
SS4	1986 (2)	1,700	KM65	35.00	25.00
SS5	1986 (3)	300	KM#65, KM-P16	75.00	75.00
SS6	1986 (2)	23	KM#65a	—	—
SS7	1986 (3)	25	KM#65a, KM-P17	—	—
SS8	1986 (2)	25	KM#65b	—	—
SS9	1986 (3)	25	KM#65b, KM-P17	—	—
SS10	1987 (15)	100	KM#59-62, 64, KM-P23, 24, 25, 26, 27	—	125
SS11	1989 (15)	100	KM#69-73, KM-P31, 32, 33, 34, 35	—	—

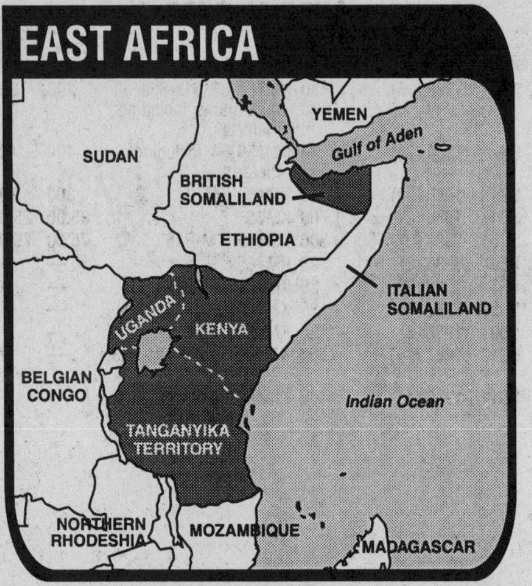

East Africa was an administrative grouping of five separate British territories: Kenya, Tanganyika (now part of Tanzania), the Sultanate of Zanzibar and Pemba (now part of Tanzania), Uganda and British Somaliland (now part of Somalia). See individual entries for specific statistics and history.

The common interest of Kenya, Tanganyika and Uganda invited cooperation in economic matters and consideration of political union. The territorial governors, organized as the East Africa High Commission, met periodically to administer such common activities as taxation, industrial development and education. The authority of the Commission did not infringe upon the constitution and internal autonomy of the individual colonies. A common coinage and banknotes, which were also legal tender in Aden, were provided for use of the member colonies by the East Africa Currency Board. The coinage through 1919 had the legend "East Africa and Uganda Protectorate". From 1920 on, the legend has read, "East Africa". The East African coinage includes two denominations of 1936 which bear the style and titles of Edward VIII.

NOTE: For later coinage see Kenya, Tanzania and Uganda.

RULERS
British

MINT MARKS
A - Ackroyd & Best, Morley
I - Bombay Mint
H - Heaton Mint, Birmingham, England
K, KN - King's Norton Mint, Birmingham, England
SA - Pretoria Mint, South Africa
no mint mark – British Royal Mint, London

EAST AFRICA AND UGANDA PROTECTORATES

100 Cents = 1 Rupee

DECIMAL COINAGE

KM# 6 1/2 CENT Composition: Aluminum **Ruler:** Edward VII

Date	Mintage	F	VF	XF	Unc	BU
1907	5	400	750	1,500	3,000	—
1908	900,000	15.00	25.00	50.00	90.00	—

KM# 6a 1/2 CENT Composition: Copper-Nickel **Ruler:** Edward VII

Date	Mintage	F	VF	XF	Unc	BU
1909	900,000	6.00	12.00	25.00	60.00	—

KM# 5 CENT Composition: Aluminum **Ruler:** Edward VII

Date	Mintage	F	VF	XF	Unc	BU
1906	—	500	750	1,500	2,000	—
1907	6,948,000	5.00	10.00	30.00	50.00	—
1907 Proof	—	Value: 200				
1908	2,871,000	8.00	16.00	30.00	60.00	—

KM# 5a CENT Composition: Copper-Nickel **Ruler:** Edward VII

Date	Mintage	F	VF	XF	Unc	BU
1908 Unique	—	—	—	—	—	—
1909	25,000,000	0.50	1.25	3.00	7.00	—
1910	6,000,000	0.50	1.25	4.00	12.00	—

KM# 7 CENT Composition: Copper-Nickel **Ruler:** George V

Date	Mintage	F	VF	XF	Unc	BU
1911H	25,000,000	0.25	1.00	2.50	15.00	—
1912H	20,000,000	0.25	1.00	2.00	8.00	—
1913	4,529,000	0.75	1.50	3.75	20.00	—
1914	6,000,000	0.75	1.75	5.00	15.00	—
1914H	2,500,000	1.00	3.00	7.50	20.00	—
1916H	1,824,000	1.25	4.00	6.00	25.00	—
1917H	3,176,000	0.75	2.00	5.00	15.00	—
1918H	10,000,000	0.50	1.00	3.25	12.00	—

KM# A11 5 CENTS Composition: Copper-Nickel **Ruler:** Edward VII

Date	F	VF	XF	Unc	BU
1907 Rare	—	—	—	—	—

KM# 11 5 CENTS Composition: Copper-Nickel **Ruler:** George V

Date	Mintage	F	VF	XF	Unc	BU
1913H	300,000	1.50	4.00	15.00	35.00	—
1914K	1,240,000	0.75	3.25	6.00	22.50	—
1914K Proof	—	Value: 200				

Note: The 1914K was issued with British West Africa KM#8 in a double (4 pieces) Specimen Set

Date	Mintage	F	VF	XF	Unc	BU
1919H	200,000	10.00	15.00	40.00	120	—

KM# 2 10 CENTS Composition: Copper-Nickel **Ruler:** Edward VII

Date	Mintage	F	VF	XF	Unc	BU
1906	—	1,000	1,500	2,000	3,000	—
1907	1,000,000	1.50	4.00	10.00	30.00	—
1910	500,000	4.00	8.00	25.00	60.00	—

KM# 8 10 CENTS Composition: Copper-Nickel **Ruler:** George V

Date	Mintage	F	VF	XF	Unc	BU
1911H	1,250,000	2.00	5.00	10.00	40.00	—
1912H	1,050,000	2.00	5.00	12.50	55.00	—
1913	50,000	75.00	150	250	500	—
1918H	400,000	10.00	20.00	50.00	150	—

KM# 3 25 CENTS Weight: 2.9160 g. **Composition:** 0.8000 Silver .0750 oz. ASW **Ruler:** Edward VII

Date	Mintage	F	VF	XF	Unc	BU
1906	400,000	3.00	7.00	22.00	60.00	—
1910H	200,000	4.00	8.00	30.00	90.00	—

KM# 10 25 CENTS Weight: 2.9160 g. **Composition:** 0.8000 Silver .0750 oz. ASW **Ruler:** George V

Date	Mintage	F	VF	XF	Unc	BU
1912	180,000	4.00	8.00	25.00	80.00	—
1913	300,000	3.50	7.50	22.50	60.00	—
1914H	80,000	20.00	35.00	60.00	100	—
1914H Proof	—	Value: 400				
1918H	40,000	150	300	500	900	—

KM# 4 50 CENTS Weight: 5.8319 g. **Composition:** 0.8000 Silver .1500 oz. ASW **Ruler:** Edward VII

Date	Mintage	F	VF	XF	Unc	BU
1906	200,000	4.50	12.50	30.00	140	—
1906 Proof	—	Value: 400				
1909	100,000	15.00	30.00	85.00	300	—
1910	100,000	10.00	22.00	60.00	225	—

KM# 9 50 CENTS Weight: 5.8319 g. **Composition:** 0.8000 Silver .1500 oz. ASW **Ruler:** George V

Date	Mintage	F	VF	XF	Unc	BU
1911	150,000	7.50	15.00	35.00	140	—
1911 Proof	—	Value: 250				
1912	100,000	8.00	20.00	60.00	200	—
1913	200,000	5.00	12.50	30.00	135	—
1914H	180,000	5.00	12.50	30.00	135	—
1918H	60,000	60.00	150	250	500	—
1919	100,000	250	350	600	1,500	—

BRITISH COLONY

DECIMAL COINAGE

KM# 12 CENT Composition: Copper-Nickel **Ruler:** George V

Date	F	VF	XF	Unc	BU
1920H	30.00	60.00	100	225	—

Note: Only about 30% of the total mintage was released into circulation

Date	F	VF	XF	Unc	BU
1920	—	—	—	750	—
1921	—	—	—	3,000	—

Note: Not released for circulation

KM# 13 5 CENTS Composition: Copper-Nickel **Ruler:** George V

Date	F	VF	XF	Unc	BU
1920H	75.00	150	200	400	—

Note: Only about 30% of the total mintage was released into circulation

KM# 14 10 CENTS Composition: Copper-Nickel **Ruler:** George V

Date		F	VF	XF	Unc	BU
1920H		120	150	225	375	—
1920H Proof; 20-30 pcs	—	Value: 600				

KM# 15 25 CENTS Weight: 2.9160 g. **Composition:** 0.5000 Silver .0469 oz. ASW **Ruler:** George V

Date	Mintage	F	VF	XF	Unc	BU
1920H	748,000	25.00	35.00	75.00	150	—
1920H 20-30 pieces; Proof	—	Value: 250				

KM# 16 50 CENTS Weight: 5.8319 g. **Composition:** 0.5000 Silver .0937 oz. ASW **Ruler:** George V **Note:** Not released for circulation.

Date	Mintage	F	VF	XF	Unc	BU
1920A	12,000	1,500	2,000	3,000	4,000	—
1920H	62,000	500	1,000	1,500	2,000	—
1920H 20-30 pieces; Proof	—	Value: 600				

KM# 17 FLORIN Weight: 11.6638 g. **Composition:** 0.5000 Silver .1875 oz. ASW **Ruler:** George V

Date	Mintage	F	VF	XF	Unc	BU
1920	1,479,000	15.00	35.00	100	325	—
1920A	542,000	200	300	600	2,000	—
1920H	9,689,000	12.50	25.00	75.00	275	—
1920H 20-30 pieces; Proof	—	Value: 800				
1921	2	—	—	—	4,500	—

REFORM COINAGE

Commencing May 1921

100 Cents = 1 Shilling

KM# 22 CENT Composition: Bronze **Ruler:** George V

Date	Mintage	F	VF	XF	Unc	BU
1922	8,250,000	0.25	1.00	3.00	15.00	—
1922H	43,750,000	0.25	0.50	1.50	6.50	—
1923	50,000,000	0.25	0.50	1.50	6.50	—
1924	Inc. above	0.25	0.75	3.25	10.00	—
1924H	17,500,000	0.25	0.75	3.25	8.00	—
1924KN	10,720,000	0.25	0.75	3.25	8.00	—
1924KN Proof	—	Value: 125				
1925	6,000,000	50.00	100	175	350	—
1925KN	6,780,000	2.00	4.00	15.00	35.00	—
1927	10,000,000	0.25	0.75	3.00	10.00	—
1927 Proof	—	Value: 125				
1928H	12,000,000	0.25	0.75	3.25	8.00	—
1928KN	11,764,000	0.50	2.00	5.00	12.00	—
1928KN Proof	—	Value: 125				
1930	15,000,000	0.25	0.75	2.00	5.00	—
1930 Proof	—	Value: 125				
1935	10,000,000	0.25	0.50	1.25	3.50	—

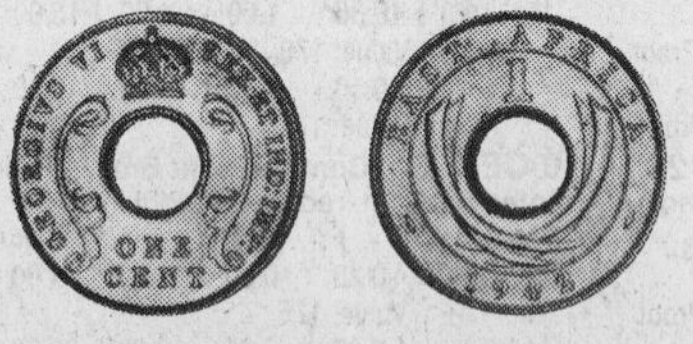

KM# 29 CENT Composition: Bronze **Ruler:** George VI

Date	Mintage	F	VF	XF	Unc	BU
1942	25,000,000	0.10	0.25	0.85	2.50	—
1942I	15,000,000	0.15	0.30	1.00	3.00	—

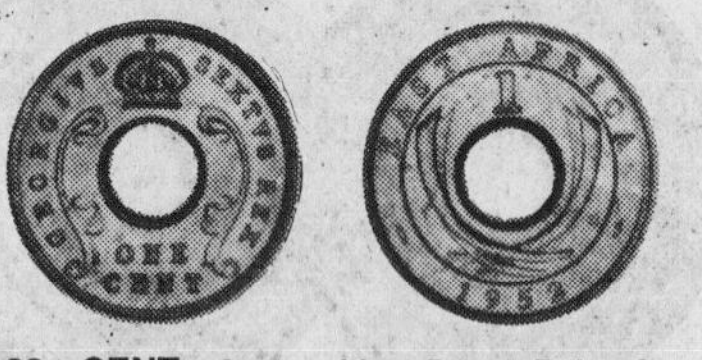

KM# 32 CENT Composition: Bronze **Ruler:** George VI **Obverse:** ET IND. IMP. dropped from legend

Date	Mintage	F	VF	XF	Unc	BU
1949	4,000,000	0.35	0.75	2.00	4.00	—
1949 Proof	—	Value: 125				
1950	16,000,000	0.10	0.25	0.85	2.50	—
1950 Proof	—	Value: 150				
1951H	9,000,000	0.10	0.25	0.85	2.50	—
1951H Proof	—	Value: 125				
1951KN	11,140,000	0.10	0.25	0.85	2.50	—
1951KN Proof	—	Value: 125				
1952	7,000,000	0.10	0.25	0.85	2.50	—
1952 Proof	—	Value: 150				
1952H	13,000,000	0.10	0.25	0.85	2.50	—
1952H Proof	—	Value: 125				
1952KN	5,230,000	0.10	0.35	1.25	5.00	—

KM# 35 CENT Composition: Bronze **Ruler:** Elizabeth II

Date	Mintage	F	VF	XF	Unc	BU
1954	8,000,000	0.10	0.25	0.85	2.50	—
1954 Proof	—	Value: 150				
1955	5,000,000	0.10	0.25	0.50	1.75	—
1955H	6,384,000	0.10	0.20	0.65	1.75	—
1955KN	4,000,000	0.10	0.20	0.65	1.75	—
1956H	15,616,000	0.10	0.15	0.30	1.25	—
1956KN	9,680,000	0.10	0.20	0.40	1.25	—
1957	15,000,000	0.10	0.20	0.65	1.75	—
1957H	5,000,000	1.50	3.00	6.00	15.00	—
1957KN	Inc. above	0.10	0.20	0.65	1.75	—
1959H	10,000,000	0.10	0.20	0.40	1.25	—
1959KN	10,000,000	0.10	0.20	0.40	1.25	—
1961	1,800,000	0.15	0.40	2.00	3.50	—
1961 Proof	—	Value: 100				
1961H	1,800,000	0.15	0.40	2.00	3.50	—
1962H	10,320,000	0.10	0.20	0.40	1.25	—

KM# 18 5 CENTS Composition: Bronze **Ruler:** George V

Date	Mintage	F	VF	XF	Unc	BU
1921	1,000,000	2.00	4.00	10.00	32.00	—
1922	2,500,000	0.50	1.25	4.50	12.50	—
1923	2,400,000	0.50	1.25	4.50	12.50	—
1923 Proof	—	Value: 150				
1924	4,800,000	0.50	1.00	3.00	15.00	—
1925	6,600,000	0.50	1.00	3.00	10.00	—
1925 Proof	—	Value: 125				
1928	1,200,000	1.50	3.00	5.00	25.00	—
1928 Proof	—	Value: 150				
1933	5,000,000	0.50	1.00	2.50	10.00	—
1934	3,910,000	0.50	1.00	3.50	15.00	—
1934 Proof	—	Value: 150				
1935	5,800,000	0.50	1.00	3.00	10.00	—
1935 Proof	—	Value: 150				
1936	1,000,000	2.00	6.00	10.00	50.00	—

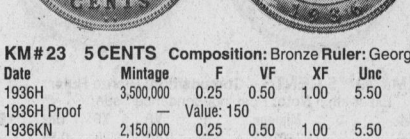

KM# 23 5 CENTS Composition: Bronze **Ruler:** George V

Date	Mintage	F	VF	XF	Unc	BU
1936H	3,500,000	0.25	0.50	1.00	5.50	—
1936H Proof	—	Value: 150				
1936KN	2,150,000	0.25	0.50	1.00	5.50	—
1936KN Proof	—	Value: 150				

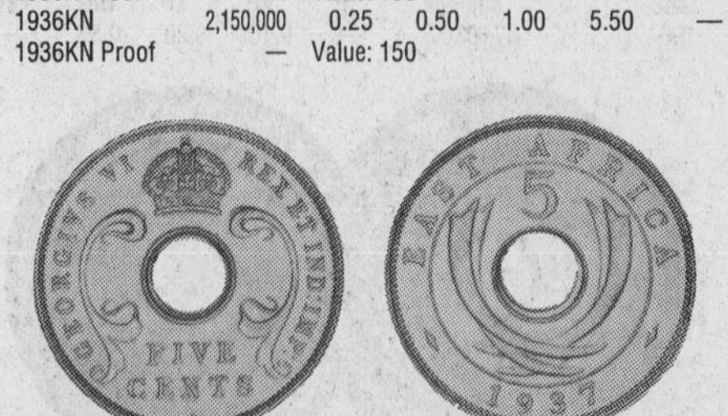

KM# 25.1 5 CENTS Composition: Bronze **Ruler:** George VI **Note:** Thick flan.

Date	Mintage	F	VF	XF	Unc	BU
1937H	3,000,000	0.50	1.00	2.00	4.00	—
1937KN	3,000,000	0.50	1.00	2.00	6.00	—
1939H	2,000,000	0.50	1.00	3.00	13.50	—
1939KN	2,000,000	0.50	1.00	3.00	13.50	—
1941	—	3.00	7.50	15.00	40.00	—
1941I	20,000,000	0.50	1.00	2.00	5.00	—

KM# 25.2 5 CENTS Composition: Bronze **Ruler:** George VI **Note:** Thin flan, reduced weight.

Date	Mintage	F	VF	XF	Unc	BU
1941I	Inc. above	0.50	1.00	2.00	5.00	—
1942	16,000,000	0.50	1.00	2.00	4.00	—
1942SA	4,120,000	1.00	2.00	10.00	30.00	—
1943SA	17,880,000	0.50	1.00	5.00	10.00	—

KM# 25.3 5 CENTS Composition: Bronze **Ruler:** George VI **Note:** Similar to KM#25.2, but hole not punched.

Date	F	VF	XF	Unc	BU
1942	—	—	—	100	—

KM# 33 5 CENTS Composition: Bronze **Ruler:** George VI **Obverse:** ET IND. IMP. dropped from legend

Date	Mintage	F	VF	XF	Unc	BU
1949	4,000,000	0.25	0.50	3.00	6.00	—
1949 Proof	—	Value: 175				
1951H	6,000,000	0.25	0.50	2.00	5.00	—
1951H Proof	—	Value: 175				
1952	11,200,000	0.20	0.40	1.00	3.00	—
1952 Proof	—	Value: 200				

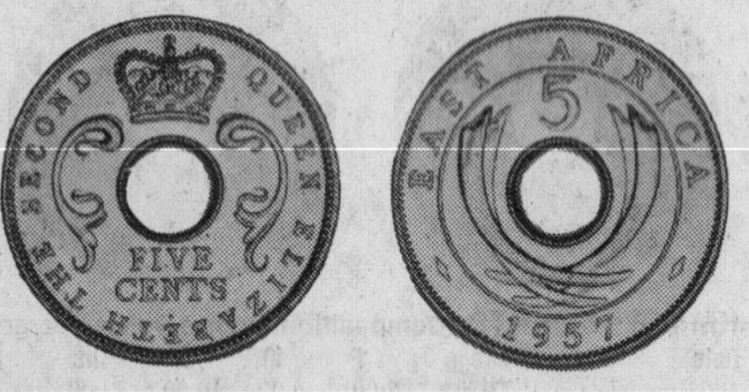

KM# 37 5 CENTS Composition: Bronze **Ruler:** Elizabeth II

Date	Mintage	F	VF	XF	Unc	BU
1955	2,000,000	0.10	0.25	0.75	2.00	—
1955 Proof	—	Value: 150				
1955H	4,000,000	0.20	0.50	1.25	3.50	—
1955H Proof	—	Value: 150				
1955KN	2,000,000	0.35	0.80	2.50	5.00	—
1956H	3,000,000	0.15	0.35	1.00	3.00	—
1956KN	3,000,000	3.00	5.00	8.00	10.00	—
1956KN Proof	—	Value: 125				
1957H	5,000,000	0.10	0.25	0.75	2.00	—
1957KN	5,000,000	0.10	0.25	0.75	2.00	—
1961H	4,000,000	0.15	0.35	1.00	3.00	—
1963	12,600,000	—	0.10	0.30	0.75	—
1963 Proof	—	Value: 150				

KM# 39 5 CENTS Composition: Bronze **Ruler:** Elizabeth II **Note:** Post-independence issue.

Date	Mintage	F	VF	XF	Unc	BU
1964	7,600,000	—	0.10	0.20	0.50	—

KM# 19 10 CENTS Composition: Bronze **Ruler:** George V

Date	Mintage	F	VF	XF	Unc	BU
1921	130,000	5.00	10.00	25.00	80.00	—
1922	7,120,000	1.00	3.00	8.00	20.00	—
1923	1,200,000	1.25	4.00	12.50	40.00	—
1924	4,900,000	0.65	2.25	6.00	25.00	—
1925	4,800,000	0.65	2.25	6.00	25.00	—
1927	2,000,000	0.75	2.50	6.50	20.00	—
1928	3,800,000	0.75	2.50	6.50	30.00	—
1928 Proof	—	Value: 175				
1933	6,260,000	0.75	2.50	6.50	17.50	—
1934	3,649,000	0.75	2.50	6.50	30.00	—

Date	Mintage	F	VF	XF	Unc	BU
1935	7,300,000	0.65	2.00	5.00	18.00	—
1936	500,000	1.50	5.00	15.00	50.00	—

KM# 24 10 CENTS Composition: Bronze **Ruler:** George V **Note:** For listing of mule dated 1936H with obverse of KM#24 and reverse of British West Africa KM#16 refer to British West Africa listings.

Date	Mintage	F	VF	XF	Unc	BU
1936	2,000,000	1.00	3.50	8.00	25.00	40.00
1936 Proof	—	Value: 200				
1936H	4,330,000	0.25	0.50	1.50	6.50	10.00
1936H Proof	—	Value: 325				
1936KN	4,142,000	0.25	0.50	1.50	6.50	10.00
1936KN Proof	—	Value: 145				

KM# 24a 10 CENTS Composition: Copper-Nickel **Ruler:** George V

Date	F	VF	XF	Unc	BU
1936KN	—	—	—	—	—

KM# 26.1 10 CENTS Composition: Bronze **Ruler:** George VI **Note:** Thick flan.

Date	Mintage	F	VF	XF	Unc	BU
1937	2,000,000	0.25	0.75	2.50	6.00	—
1937 Proof	—	Value: 175				
1937H	2,500,000	0.25	0.75	2.50	8.00	—
1937H Proof	—	Value: 175				
1937KN	2,500,000	0.25	0.75	2.50	8.00	—
1937KN Proof	—	Value: 175				
1939H	2,000,000	0.25	0.70	3.50	15.00	—
1939KN	2,029,999	0.25	0.70	3.50	12.50	—
1939KN Proof	—	Value: 175				
1941I	15,682,000	0.35	1.00	4.00	15.00	—
1941I Proof	—	Value: 175				
1941	—	0.50	1.50	4.50	16.00	—
1941 Proof	—	Value: 175				

KM# 26.2 10 CENTS Composition: Bronze **Ruler:** George VI **Note:** Thin flan, reduced weight.

Date	Mintage	F	VF	XF	Unc	BU
1942	12,000,000	0.20	0.50	1.75	4.00	—
1942 Proof	—	Value: 175				
1942I	4,317,000	3.00	5.00	10.00	20.00	—
1943SA	14,093,000	0.25	0.50	4.50	10.00	—
1945SA	5,000,000	0.25	0.50	3.00	12.50	—

KM# 34 10 CENTS Composition: Bronze **Ruler:** George VI **Obverse:** ET IND. IMP. dropped from legend

Date	Mintage	F	VF	XF	Unc	BU
1949	4,000,000	0.25	0.50	2.00	5.00	—
1949 Proof	—	Value: 175				
1950	8,000,000	0.20	0.40	1.75	4.00	—
1950 Proof	—	Value: 200				
1951	14,500,000	0.20	0.40	1.25	3.00	—
1951 Proof	—	Value: 175				
1952	15,800,000	0.20	0.40	1.25	3.00	—
1952 Proof	—	Value: 250				
1952H	2,000,000	3.00	5.00	10.00	20.00	—

KM# 38 10 CENTS Composition: Bronze **Ruler:** Elizabeth II

Date	Mintage	F	VF	XF	Unc	BU
1956	6,001,000	0.35	1.00	2.50	10.00	—
1956 Proof	—	Value: 175				
1964H	—	—	—	—	1,250	—

KM# 40 10 CENTS Composition: Bronze **Ruler:** Elizabeth II **Note:** Post-independence issue.

Date	Mintage	F	VF	XF	Unc	BU
1964H	10,002,000	0.10	0.15	0.30	1.00	—

KM# 20 50 CENTS Weight: 3.8879 g. **Composition:** 0.2500 Silver .0312 oz. ASW **Ruler:** George V **Reverse:** Fifty Cents - Half Shilling

Date	Mintage	F	VF	XF	Unc	BU
1921	6,200,000	1.00	2.00	7.50	30.00	—
1922	Inc. above	1.00	2.00	6.00	27.50	—
1923	396,000	5.00	8.00	40.00	80.00	—
1924	1,000,000	2.00	4.00	10.00	40.00	—

KM# 27 50 CENTS Weight: 3.8879 g. **Composition:** 0.2500 Silver .0312 oz. ASW **Ruler:** George VI

Date	Mintage	F	VF	XF	Unc	BU
1937H	4,000,000	0.75	1.25	3.50	12.50	—
1937H Proof	—	Value: 275				
1942H	5,000,000	0.75	1.25	4.00	20.00	—
1943I	2,000,000	1.50	3.00	7.50	30.00	—
1944SA	1,000,000	2.00	4.00	9.00	32.50	—

KM# 30 50 CENTS Composition: Copper-Nickel **Ruler:** George VI **Obverse:** ET INDIA IMPERATOR dropped from legend

Date	Mintage	F	VF	XF	Unc	BU
1948	7,290,000	0.20	0.40	2.00	6.00	—
1948 Proof	—	Value: 250				
1949	12,960,000	0.15	0.30	1.50	4.00	—
1949 Proof	—	Value: 325				
1952KN	2,000,000	0.20	0.40	2.00	7.50	—

KM# 36 50 CENTS Composition: Copper-Nickel **Ruler:** Elizabeth II **Note:** The KHN mint marks above exist because the master dies were produced with both the KN and H mint marks for use at either mint. Each mint was required to remove the others mint mark before striking, but this was not always meticulously done. When one or the other mint mark was not fully removed a weak trace would remain creating the appearance of a wide space K N with a weak H in the middle or an H flanked by a weak K and N, in the field below the lion.

Date	Mintage	F	VF	XF	Unc	BU
1954	3,700,000	0.15	0.35	1.00	3.00	—
1954 Proof	—	Value: 225				
1955H	1,600,000	1.00	3.00	6.00	15.00	—
1955H Proof	—	Value: 225				
1955KHN	—	10.00	20.00	35.00	65.00	—
1955KN	—	0.15	0.35	1.75	4.50	—
1956H	2,000,000	0.15	0.25	1.25	3.00	—
1956H Proof	—	Value: 225				
1956KHN	—	10.00	20.00	35.00	65.00	—
1956KN	2,000,000	0.15	0.35	1.75	4.00	—
1958H	2,600,000	0.15	0.40	2.00	5.00	—
1960	4,000,000	0.10	0.25	1.25	3.25	—
1962KN	4,000,000	0.15	0.35	1.75	4.50	—
1963	6,000,000	0.10	0.25	1.25	3.00	—

KM# 21 SHILLING Weight: 7.7759 g. **Composition:** 0.2500 Silver .0625 oz. ASW **Ruler:** George V

Date	Mintage	F	VF	XF	Unc	BU
1921	6,141,000	1.50	2.75	10.00	30.00	—
1921H	4,240,000	1.75	3.00	15.00	40.00	—
1922	18,858,000	1.25	2.25	9.00	28.00	—
1922H	20,052,000	1.25	2.25	9.00	28.00	—
1923	4,000,000	5.00	10.00	25.00	45.00	—
1924	44,604,000	1.00	2.00	7.00	18.00	—
1925	28,405,000	1.00	2.00	7.00	20.00	—
1925 Proof	—	Value: 250				

KM# 28.1 SHILLING Weight: 7.7759 g. **Composition:** 0.2500 Silver .0625 oz. ASW **Ruler:** George VI **Obverse:** Bust of King George VI **Reverse:** Type I, thin rim and short milling, EAST AFRICA further from edge than Type II, larger loop on right side of coin below diamond in legend. Edge reeding spaced out

Date	Mintage	F	VF	XF	Unc	BU
1937H	7,672,000	1.00	2.00	7.50	22.00	—
1937H Proof	—	Value: 300				
1941I	7,000,000	1.25	2.00	8.00	28.00	—
1942H	4,430,000	1.25	2.00	8.00	28.00	—
1942H Proof	—	Value: 300				
1944H	10,000,000	1.25	2.00	10.00	32.00	—

KM# 28.2 SHILLING Weight: 7.7759 g. **Composition:** 0.2500 Silver .0625 oz. ASW **Ruler:** George VI **Reverse:** Type II, thicker rim and larger milling, EAST AFRICA and leaves very near the edge, small leaf (loop) under diamond on right side

Date	F	VF	XF	Unc	BU
1941I Rare	—	—	—	—	—

KM# 28.3 SHILLING Weight: 7.7759 g. **Composition:** 0.2500 Silver .0625 oz. ASW **Ruler:** George VI **Reverse:** Type III, retouched central image, especially tuft of grass in front of lion

Date	Mintage	F	VF	XF	Unc	BU
1942I	3,900,000	1.00	2.00	7.00	25.00	—
1943I 25-50 pieces	—	500	750	1,000	1,500	—

KM# 28.4 SHILLING Weight: 7.7759 g. **Composition:** 0.2500 Silver .0625 oz. ASW **Ruler:** George VI **Note:** Obverse and reverse as KM#28.1, edge reeding close. For more in-depth comparison of these reverse variety types, see The Guidebook and Catalogue of British Commonwealth Coins, 1649-1971, 3rd Edition, Remick, J. Winnipeg, Regency Coin and Stamp, 1971.

Date	Mintage	F	VF	XF	Unc	BU
1944SA	5,820,000	1.25	2.00	7.00	30.00	—
1945SA	10,080,000	1.25	2.00	7.00	27.50	—
1946SA	18,260,000	1.25	2.00	5.00	20.00	—

KM# 31 SHILLING Composition: Copper-Nickel **Ruler:** George VI **Obverse:** ET INDIA IMPERATOR dropped from legend

Date	Mintage	F	VF	XF	Unc	BU
1948	19,704,000	0.50	0.90	2.00	6.50	—
1949	38,318,000	0.50	0.90	2.00	6.50	—
1949 Proof	—	Value: 250				
1949H	12,584,000	0.50	0.90	2.25	7.50	—
1949KN	15,060,000	0.50	0.90	2.25	7.50	—
1950	56,362,000	0.35	0.60	1.50	3.00	—
1950 Proof	—	Value: 250				
1950H	12,416,000	0.50	0.90	2.25	6.00	—
1950KN	10,040,000	0.40	0.70	2.00	5.00	—
1952	55,605,000	0.35	0.60	1.50	3.00	—
1952 Proof	—	Value: 175				
1952H	8,023,999	0.35	0.60	1.75	3.50	—
1952KN	9,360,000	0.35	0.60	1.75	3.50	—

PATTERNS

Including off metal strikes

KM#	Date	Mintage	Identification	Mkt Val
Pn6	1906	—	Cent. Aluminum. KM#5.	1,500
Pn7	1907	—	1/2 Cent. Aluminum. KM#6.	2,000
Pn8	1907	—	5 Cents. Copper-Nickel. KM#11.	2,500
Pn9	1908	—	Cent. Copper-Nickel. KM#5.	—
Pn11	1920 (a)	—	Florin. Aluminum. KM#17.	2,000
Pn10	1920 (a)	—	50 Cents. Aluminum. KM#16.	3,000

MINT SETS

KM#	Date	Mintage	Identification	Issue Price	Mkt Val
MS1	1921-1922 (5)	—	KM#18-22. The 5 cent coin is dated 1921, all others are 1922.	—	2,000

PROOF SETS

KM#	Date	Mintage	Identification	Issue Price	Mkt Val
PS1	1906-1907 (4)	—	KM#2-5, Pn7-8; Rare	—	—
PSA1	1920H (6)	—	KM#12-17; 20-30 pieces	—	3,000
PS2	1949 (5)	—	KM#30-34	—	1,000
PS3	1950 (3)	—	KM#31, 32, 34	—	600
PS4	1952 (3)	—	KM#32, 33, 34	—	600

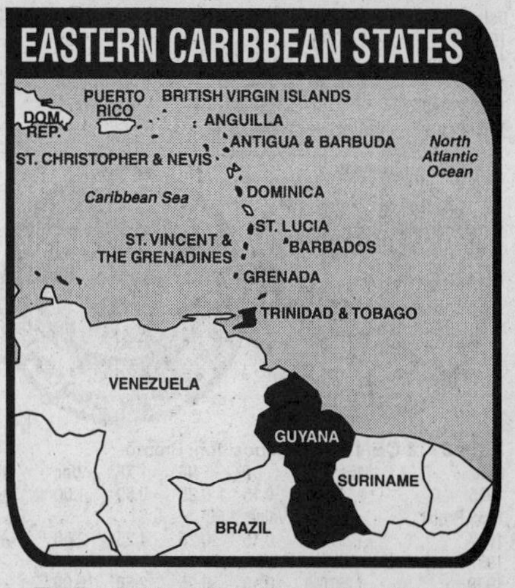

The East Caribbean States, formerly the British Caribbean Territories (Eastern group), formed a currency board in 1950 to provide the constituent territories of Trinidad & Tobago, Barbados, British Guiana (now Guyana), British Virgin Islands, Anguilla, St. Kitts, Nevis, Antigua, Dominica, St. Lucia, St. Vincent and Grenada with a common currency, thereby permitting withdrawal of the regular British Pound currency. This was dissolved in 1965 and after the breakup, the East Caribbean Territories, a grouping including Barbados, the Leeward and Windward Islands, came into being. Coinage of the dissolved 'Eastern Group' continues to circulate. Paper currency of the East Caribbean Authority was first issued in 1965 and although Barbados withdrew from the group they continued using them prior to 1973 when Barbados issued a decimal coinage.

A series of 4-dollar coins tied to the FAO coinage program were released in 1970 under the name of the Caribbean Development Bank by eight loosely federated island groupings in the eastern Caribbean. These issues are listed individually in this volume under Antigua, Barbados, Dominica, Grenada, Montserrat, St. Kitts, St. Lucia and St. Vincent.

RULERS

British

BRITISH EAST CARIBBEAN TERRITORIES

100 Cents = 1 Br. W. Indies Dollar

STANDARD COINAGE

100 Cents = 1 British West Indies Dollar

KM# 1 1/2 CENT Composition: Bronze

Date	Mintage	F	VF	XF	Unc	BU
1955	500,000	0.30	0.50	1.00	2.50	—
1955 Proof	2,000	Value: 3.00				
1958	200	0.50	0.75	1.50	3.00	—
1958 Proof	20	Value: 145				

KM# 2 CENT Composition: Bronze

Date	Mintage	F	VF	XF	Unc	BU
1955	8,000,000	0.15	0.25	0.60	1.00	—
1955 Proof	2,000	Value: 3.00				
1957	3,000,000	0.15	0.25	1.75	3.00	—
1957 Proof	—	Value: 100				
1958	1,500,000	0.35	0.50	4.50	7.50	—
1958 Proof	20	Value: 165				
1959	500,000	0.40	0.60	6.00	20.00	—
1959 Proof	—	Value: 100				
1960	2,500,000	0.15	0.25	0.60	1.25	—
1960 Proof	—	Value: 100				
1961	2,280,000	0.25	0.35	0.75	1.25	—
1961 Proof	—	Value: 100				
1962	2,000,000	0.15	0.25	0.50	1.25	—
1962 Proof	—	Value: 100				
1963	750,000	0.45	0.70	1.20	2.50	—
1963 Proof	—	Value: 100				

Date	Mintage	F	VF	XF	Unc	BU
1964	2,500,000	—	—	0.20	0.35	—
1964 Proof	—	Value: 100				
1965	4,800,000	—	—	0.20	0.35	—
1965 Prooflike	—	—	—	—	0.75	—
1965 Proof	—	Value: 5.00				

KM# 3 2 CENTS Composition: Bronze

Date	Mintage	F	VF	XF	Unc	BU
1955	5,500,000	0.15	0.25	0.50	1.00	—
1955 Proof	2,000	Value: 3.00				
1957	1,250,000	0.15	0.25	1.25	2.50	—
1957 Proof	—	Value: 110				
1958	1,250,000	0.15	0.25	2.50	5.00	—
1958 Proof	20	Value: 185				
1960	750,000	0.15	0.25	1.75	3.50	—
1960 Proof	—	Value: 110				
1961	788,000	0.15	0.25	1.75	3.50	—
1961 Proof	—	Value: 110				
1962	1,060,000	0.10	0.20	0.30	0.85	—
1962 Proof	—	Value: 110				
1963	250,000	0.50	0.75	1.50	5.00	—
1963 Proof	—	Value: 110				
1964	1,188,000	0.10	0.20	0.30	0.75	—
1964 Proof	—	Value: 110				
1965	2,001,000	—	0.10	0.20	0.45	—
1965 Prooflike	—	—	—	—	0.75	—
1965 Proof	—	Value: 5.00				

KM# 4 5 CENTS Composition: Nickel-Brass

Date	Mintage	F	VF	XF	Unc	BU
1955	8,600,000	0.15	0.25	0.60	1.25	—
1955 Proof	2,000	Value: 4.50				
1956	2,000,000	0.15	0.25	0.60	1.00	—
1956 Proof	—	Value: 300				
1960	1,000,000	0.20	0.30	0.90	1.50	—
1960 Proof	—	Value: 150				
1962	1,300,000	0.15	0.25	0.50	1.00	—
1962 Proof	—	Value: 150				
1963	200,000	0.25	0.35	1.20	2.00	—
1963 Proof	—	Value: 150				
1964	1,350,000	—	0.10	0.30	0.75	—
1964 Proof	—	Value: 150				
1965	2,400,000	—	0.10	0.20	0.50	—
1965 Prooflike	—	—	—	—	0.75	—
1965 Proof	—	Value: 5.00				

KM# 5 10 CENTS Composition: Copper-Nickel

Date	Mintage	F	VF	XF	Unc	BU
1955	5,000,000	0.15	0.25	0.45	0.75	—
1955 Proof	2,000	Value: 4.50				
1956	4,000,000	0.15	0.25	0.45	0.75	—
1956 Proof	—	Value: 175				
1959	2,000,000	0.15	0.25	0.60	1.00	—
1959 Proof	—	Value: 175				
1961	1,260,000	0.20	0.30	0.50	1.00	—
1961 Proof	—	Value: 175				
1962	1,200,000	0.15	0.25	0.50	1.00	—
1962 Proof	—	Value: 175				
1964	1,400,000	0.10	0.20	0.35	0.65	—
1965	3,200,000	0.10	0.20	0.30	0.50	—
1965 Prooflike	—	—	—	—	0.75	—
1965 Proof	—	Value: 5.00				

KM# 6 25 CENTS Composition: Copper-Nickel

Date	Mintage	F	VF	XF	Unc	BU
1955	7,000,000	0.35	0.50	0.70	1.00	—
1955 Proof	2,000	Value: 6.50				
1957	800,000	0.75	1.00	2.25	4.50	—
1957 Proof	—	Value: 225				
1959	1,000,000	0.35	0.50	1.25	2.25	—
1959 Proof	—	Value: 225				
1961	744,000	0.50	0.75	2.50	5.00	—
1961 Proof	—	Value: 225				
1962	480,000	0.25	0.50	1.25	2.50	—
1962 Proof	—	Value: 225				
1963	480,000	0.25	0.50	1.25	2.50	—
1963 Proof	—	Value: 225				
1964	480,000	0.25	0.50	1.00	1.75	—
1964 Proof	—	Value: 225				
1965	1,280,000	0.25	0.50	0.75	1.00	—
1965 Prooflike	—	—	—	—	1.50	—
1965 Proof	—	Value: 7.50				

KM# 7 50 CENTS Composition: Copper-Nickel

Date	Mintage	F	VF	XF	Unc	BU
1955	1,500,000	1.00	1.50	2.00	3.50	—
1955 Proof	2,000	Value: 12.50				
1965	100,000	2.00	5.00	7.50	15.00	—
1965 Prooflike	—	—	—	—	7.50	—
1965 Proof	—	Value: 10.00				

EAST CARIBBEAN TERRITORIES

100 Cents = 1 Dollar

STANDARD COINAGE

100 Cents = 1 Dollar

KM# 8 10 DOLLARS Composition: Copper-Nickel **Subject:** 10th Anniversary of Caribbean Development Bank **Note:** Previous KM#1

Date	F	VF	XF	Unc	BU
1980	—	—	—	7.00	—

KM# 8a 10 DOLLARS Weight: 28.2800 g. **Composition:** 0.9250 Silver .8411 oz. ASW **Note:** Previous KM#1a

Date	Mintage	F	VF	XF	Unc	BU
1980 Proof	10,000	Value: 45.00				

KM# 9 10 DOLLARS Composition: Copper-Nickel **Subject:** Wedding of Prince Charles and Lady Diana **Note:** Previous KM#2.

Date	Mintage	F	VF	XF	Unc	BU
1981	50,000	—	—	—	7.00	—

KM# 9a 10 DOLLARS Weight: 28.2800 g. **Composition:** 0.9250 Silver .8411 oz. ASW **Note:** Previous KM#2a.

Date	Mintage	F	VF	XF	Unc	BU
1981 Proof	30,000	Value: 30.00				

EAST CARIBBEAN STATES

British Administration

STANDARD COINAGE

100 Cents = 1 Dollar

KM# 10 CENT Composition: Bronze **Note:** Previous KM#1.

Date	Mintage	F	VF	XF	Unc	BU
1981	—	—	—	—	0.20	—
1981 Proof	5,000	Value: 1.25				
1983	—	—	—	—	0.20	—
1984	—	—	—	—	0.20	—
1986	—	—	—	—	0.20	—
1986 Proof	2,500	Value: 1.25				
1987	—	—	—	—	0.20	—
1989	—	—	—	—	0.20	—
1991	—	—	—	—	0.20	—
1992	—	—	—	—	0.20	—
1993	—	—	—	—	0.20	—
1994	—	—	—	—	0.20	—
1995	—	—	—	—	0.20	—
1996	—	—	—	—	0.20	—
1997	—	—	—	—	0.20	—
1998	—	—	—	—	0.20	—
1999	—	—	—	—	0.20	—
2000	—	—	—	—	0.20	—

KM# 34 CENT Weight: 1.0300 g. **Composition:** Aluminum **Obverse:** Queen's new portrait **Reverse:** Denomination **Edge:** Plain **Size:** 18.42 mm.

Date	F	VF	XF	Unc	BU
2002	—	—	—	0.20	—

KM# 11 2 CENTS Composition: Aluminum **Shape:** Square **Note:** Previous KM#2.

Date	Mintage	F	VF	XF	Unc	BU
1981	—	—	—	0.10	0.25	—
1981 Proof	5,000	Value: 1.50				
1984	—	—	—	0.10	0.25	—
1986	—	—	—	0.10	0.25	—
1986 Proof	2,500	Value: 1.50				
1987	—	—	—	0.10	0.25	—
1989	—	—	—	0.10	0.25	—
1991	—	—	—	0.10	0.25	—
1992	—	—	—	0.10	0.25	—
1993	—	—	—	0.10	0.25	—
1994	—	—	—	0.10	0.25	—
1995	—	—	—	0.10	0.25	—
1996	—	—	—	0.10	0.25	—
1997	—	—	—	0.10	0.25	—

Date	Mintage	F	VF	XF	Unc	BU
1999	—	—	—	0.10	0.25	—
2000	—	—	—	0.10	0.25	—

KM# 35 2 CENTS **Weight:** 1.4200 g. **Composition:** Aluminum **Obverse:** Queen's new portrait **Reverse:** Denomination **Edge:** Plain **Size:** 21.46 mm.

Date	F	VF	XF	Unc	BU
2002	—	—	—	0.25	—

KM# 12 5 CENTS **Composition:** Aluminum **Shape:** Scalloped **Note:** Previous KM#3.

Date	Mintage	F	VF	XF	Unc	BU
1981	—	—	—	0.10	0.30	—
1981 Proof	5,000	Value: 2.25				
1984	—	—	—	0.10	0.30	—
1986	—	—	—	0.10	0.30	—
1986 Proof	2,500	Value: 2.25				
1987	—	—	—	0.10	0.30	—
1989	—	—	—	0.10	0.30	—
1991	—	—	—	0.10	0.30	—
1992	—	—	—	0.10	0.30	—
1993	—	—	—	0.10	0.30	—
1994	—	—	—	0.10	0.30	—
1995	—	—	—	0.10	0.30	—
1996	—	—	—	0.10	0.30	—
1997	—	—	—	0.10	0.30	—
1998	—	—	—	0.10	0.30	—
1999	—	—	—	0.10	0.30	—
2000	—	—	—	0.10	0.30	—

KM# 36 5 CENTS **Weight:** 1.7400 g. **Composition:** Aluminum **Obverse:** Queen's new portrait **Reverse:** Denomination **Edge:** Plain **Size:** 23.11 mm.

Date	F	VF	XF	Unc	BU
2002	—	—	—	0.30	—

KM# 13 10 CENTS **Composition:** Copper-Nickel **Note:** Previous KM#4.

Date	Mintage	F	VF	XF	Unc	BU
1981	—	—	0.10	0.15	0.40	—
1981 Proof	5,000	Value: 3.00				
1986	—	—	0.10	0.15	0.40	—
1986 Proof	2,500	Value: 3.00				
1987	—	—	0.10	0.15	0.40	—
1989	—	—	0.10	0.15	0.40	—
1991	—	—	0.10	0.15	0.40	—
1992	—	—	0.10	0.15	0.35	—
1993	—	—	0.10	0.15	0.40	—
1994	—	—	0.10	0.15	0.40	—
1995	—	—	0.10	0.15	0.40	—
1996	—	—	0.10	0.15	0.40	—
1997	—	—	0.10	0.15	0.40	—
1998	—	—	0.10	0.15	0.40	—
1999	—	—	0.10	0.15	0.40	—
2000	—	—	0.10	0.15	0.40	—

KM# 37 10 CENTS **Obverse:** Queen's new portrait **Reverse:** Ship and denomination **Edge:** Reeded **Size:** 18.06 mm.

Date	F	VF	XF	Unc	BU
2002	—	—	—	0.40	—

KM# 14 25 CENTS **Composition:** Copper-Nickel **Note:** Previous KM#5.

Date	Mintage	F	VF	XF	Unc	BU
1981	—	—	0.15	0.20	0.50	—
1981 Proof	5,000	Value: 4.00				
1986	—	—	0.15	0.20	0.50	—
1986 Proof	2,500	Value: 4.00				
1987	—	—	0.15	0.20	0.50	—
1989	—	—	0.15	0.20	0.50	—
1991	—	—	0.15	0.20	0.50	—
1992	—	—	0.15	0.20	0.50	—
1993	—	—	0.15	0.20	0.50	—
1994	—	—	0.15	0.20	0.50	—
1995	—	—	0.15	0.20	0.50	—
1996	—	—	0.15	0.20	0.50	—
1997	—	—	0.15	0.20	0.50	—

Date	Mintage	F	VF	XF	Unc	BU
1998	—	—	0.15	0.20	0.50	—
1999	—	—	0.15	0.20	0.50	—
2000	—	—	0.15	0.20	0.50	—

KM# 38 25 CENTS **Weight:** 6.4800 g. **Composition:** Copper-Nickel **Obverse:** Queen's new portrait **Reverse:** Ship and denomination **Edge:** Reeded **Size:** 23.98 mm.

Date	F	VF	XF	Unc	BU
2002	—	—	—	0.50	—

KM# 15 DOLLAR **Composition:** Aluminum-Bronze **Note:** Previous KM#6.

Date	Mintage	F	VF	XF	Unc	BU
1981	—	—	0.50	0.75	1.50	—
1981 Proof	5,000	Value: 8.00				
1986	—	—	0.50	0.75	1.50	—
1986 Proof	2,500	Value: 8.00				

KM# 20 DOLLAR **Composition:** Copper-Nickel **Shape:** 10-sided **Note:** Previous KM#11.

Date	F	VF	XF	Unc	BU
1989	—	—	—	2.25	—
1991	—	—	—	2.25	—
1992	—	—	—	2.25	—
1993	—	—	—	2.25	—
1994	—	—	—	2.25	—
1995	—	—	—	2.25	—
1996	—	—	—	2.25	—
1997	—	—	—	2.00	—
1998	—	—	—	2.00	—
1999	—	—	—	2.00	—
2000	—	—	—	2.00	—

KM# 39 DOLLAR **Weight:** 7.9800 g. **Composition:** Copper-Nickel **Obverse:** Queen's new portrait **Reverse:** Ship and denomination **Edge:** Reeded **Size:** 26.5 mm.

Date	F	VF	XF	Unc	BU
2002	—	—	—	2.00	—

KM# 24 2 DOLLARS **Composition:** Copper-Nickel **Subject:** 10th Anniversary of Central Bank **Note:** Previous KM#15.

Date	F	VF	XF	Unc	BU
ND(1993)	—	—	—	9.50	—

KM# 16 10 DOLLARS **Composition:** Copper-Nickel **Series:** F.A.O. **Subject:** World Food Day **Note:** Previous KM#7.

Date	F	VF	XF	Unc	BU
1981	—	—	—	14.50	—

KM#16a 10 DOLLARS **Weight:** 28.2800 g. **Composition:** 0.5000 Silver .4546 oz. ASW **Note:** Previous KM#7a.

Date	Mintage	F	VF	XF	Unc	BU
1981	10,000	—	—	—	17.50	—
1981 Proof	5,000	Value: 47.50				

KM# 22 10 DOLLARS **Weight:** 28.2800 g. **Composition:** 0.9250 Silver .8411 oz. ASW **Subject:** Queen Mother's 90th Birthday **Note:** Previous KM#13.

Date	F	VF	XF	Unc	BU
ND(1990) Proof	—	Value: 50.00			

KM# 23 10 DOLLARS **Weight:** 28.2800 g. **Composition:** 0.9250 Silver .8411 oz. ASW **Subject:** 40th Anniversary - Coronation of Queen Elizabeth **Note:** Previous KM#14.

Date	Mintage	F	VF	XF	Unc	BU
ND(1993) Proof	10,000	Value: 47.50				

KM# 25 10 DOLLARS **Weight:** 28.2800 g. **Composition:** 0.9250 Silver .8411 oz. ASW **Subject:** 10th Anniversary of Central Bank **Note:** Previous KM#16.

Date	Mintage	F	VF	XF	Unc	BU
ND(1993) Proof	2,500	Value: 55.00				

KM# 27 10 DOLLARS **Weight:** 31.4700 g. **Composition:** 0.9250 Silver .9359 oz. ASW **Subject:** World Cup Soccer **Note:** Previous KM#18.

Date	Mintage	F	VF	XF	Unc	BU
1994 Proof	10,000	Value: 45.00				

KM# 33 10 DOLLARS **Weight:** 28.5000 g. **Composition:** 0.9250 Silver 0.8476 oz. ASW **Subject:** Reeded **Obverse:** Queen's portrait **Reverse:** The Royal Launch **Edge:** Reeded **Size:** 38.5 mm.

Date	F	VF	XF	Unc	BU
1996 Proof	—	Value: 50.00			

KM# 32 10 DOLLARS **Weight:** 28.5000 g. **Composition:** 0.9250 Silver 0.8476 oz. ASW **Subject:** Queen Elizabeth and Philip's Golden Wedding Anniversary **Obverse:** Bust of Queen Elizabeth II right. **Reverse:** The royal couple waving behind gold inset shield. **Edge:** Reeded. **Size:** 38.5 mm.

Date	F	VF	XF	Unc	BU
1997 Proof	—	Value: 45.00			

KM# 30 10 DOLLARS **Weight:** 28.2800 g. **Composition:** 0.9250 Silver .8410 oz. ASW **Subject:** Montserrat Volcano Appeal Fund **Obverse:** Queen Elizabeth II **Reverse:** Multicolor rainbow and volcano **Note:** Previous KM#30.

Date	Mintage	F	VF	XF	Unc	BU
1998 Proof	10,000	Value: 60.00				

KM# 28 10 DOLLARS **Weight:** 28.2800 g. **Composition:** 0.9250 Silver .8410 oz. ASW **Subject:** 50th Anniversary - University of the West Indies **Obverse:** Portrait **Reverse:** University arms **Note:** Previous KM#19.

Date	Mintage	F	VF	XF	Unc	BU
ND(1999) Proof	1,000	Value: 60.00				

KM# 31 2000 CENTS **Weight:** 7.9800 g. **Composition:** 0.9170 Gold .2353 oz. AGW **Series:** Millennium **Subject:** British Royal Mint **Obverse:** Queen's head right **Reverse:** Ship, palm trees and radiant sun **Edge:** Reeded **Note:** Previous KM#22.

Date	F	VF	XF	Unc	BU
2000	—	—	—	115	—

KM# 19 50 DOLLARS **Weight:** 28.2800 g. **Composition:** 0.9250 Silver .8411 oz. ASW **Series:** International Year of Disabled Persons **Note:** Previous KM#10.

Date	Mintage	F	VF	XF	Unc	BU
1981	10,000	—	—	—	30.00	—
1981 Proof	10,000	Value: 45.00				

KM# 17 50 DOLLARS **Weight:** 28.2800 g. **Composition:** 0.9250 Silver .8411 oz. ASW **Series:** International Year of the Scout **Note:** Previous KM#8.

Date	Mintage	F	VF	XF	Unc	BU
ND(1983)	10,000	—	—	—	30.00	—
ND(1983) Proof	10,000	Value: 47.50				

KM# 26 100 DOLLARS **Weight:** 15.9760 g. **Composition:** 0.9170 Gold .4708 oz. AGW **Subject:** 10th Anniversary of Central Bank **Obverse:** Bank **Reverse:** Portrait of Sir Arthur Lewis **Note:** Similar to 10 Dollars, KM#25; Previous KM#17.

Date	Mintage	F	VF	XF	Unc	BU
1993 Proof	150	Value: 500				

KM# 29 100 DOLLARS **Weight:** 15.9760 g. **Composition:** 0.9170 Gold .4708 oz. AGW **Subject:** 50th Anniversary - University of West Indies **Obverse:** Portrait **Reverse:** University arms **Note:** Similar to 10 Dollars, KM#28; Previous KM#20.

Date	Mintage	F	VF	XF	Unc	BU
ND(1999) Proof	300	Value: 530				

KM# 21 500 DOLLARS **Weight:** 15.9800 g. **Composition:** 0.9170 Gold .4712 oz. AGW **Series:** International Year of Disabled Persons **Note:** Previous KM#12.

Date	F	VF	XF	Unc	BU
1981	—	—	—	500	—
1981 Proof	—	Value: 750			

KM# 18 500 DOLLARS **Weight:** 15.9800 g. **Composition:** 0.9170 Gold .4712 oz. AGW **Series:** International Year of the Scout **Obverse:** Bust of Elizabeth II right **Reverse:** One scout standing, pointing; one scout kneeling with map **Note:** Previous KM#9.

Date	Mintage	F	VF	XF	Unc	BU
ND(1983)	2,000	—	—	—	375	—
ND(1983) Proof	2,000	Value: 550				

PIEFORTS

KM#	Date	Mintage	Identification	Mkt Val
P2	1981	—	500 Dollars. KM#12.	1,600
P1	1981	1,000	50 Dollars. KM#10.	65.00

MINT SETS

KM#	Date	Mintage	Identification	Issue Price	Mkt Val
MS1	1986 (6)	—	KM#10-15	—	7.50
MS2	1991 (6)	—	KM#10-14, 20	19.95	20.00
MS3	1992 (6)	—	KM#10-14, 20	—	15.00
MS4	1995-97 (6)	—	KM#10-11 (1995), 12-14, 20 (1997)	25.00	25.00
MS5	1999 (6)	—	KM#10-14, 20	25.00	25.00
MS6	2000 (7)	—	KM#10-14, 20, 31	139	145

PROOF SETS

KM#	Date	Mintage	Identification	Issue Price	Mkt Val
PS1	1955 (7)	2,000	KM#1-7	—	30.00
PS2	1958 (3)	20	KM#1-3	—	500
PS3	1965 (6)	—	KM#2-7	—	35.00
PS5	1981 (6)	5,000	KM#10-15	29.00	20.00
PS6	1986 (6)	2,500	KM#10-15	30.75	20.00

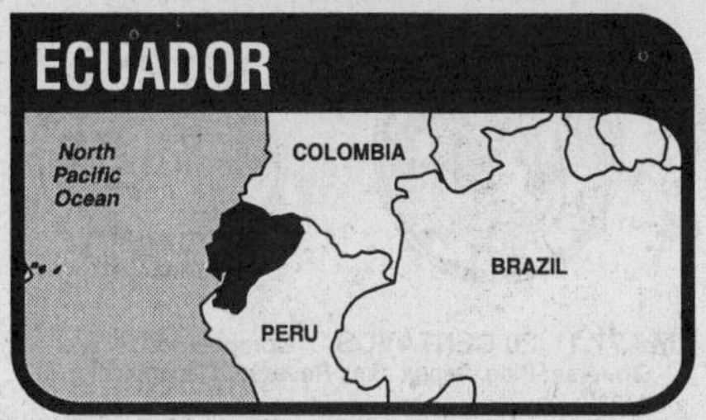

The Republic of Ecuador, located astride the equator on the Pacific Coast of South America, has an area of 105,037 sq. mi. (283,560 sq. km.) and a population of 10.9 million. Capital: Quito. Agriculture is the mainstay of the economy but there are appreciable deposits of minerals and petroleum. It is one of the world's largest exporters of bananas and balsa wood. Coffee, cacao, sugar and petroleum are also valuable exports.

Ecuador was first sighted in 1526 by Francisco Pizarro. Conquest was undertaken by Sebastian de Benalcazar, who founded Quito in 1534. Ecuador was part of the Viceroyalty of New Granada through the 16th and 17th centuries. After previous attempts to attain independence were crushed, Antonio Sucre, the able lieutenant of Bolivar, secured Ecuador's freedom in the Battle of Pinchincha, May 24, 1822. It then joined Venezuela and Colombia in a confederation known as Gran Colombia, and became an independent republic when it left the confederacy in 1830.

MINT MARKS

BIRMm - Birmingham, Heaton
Birmingham - Birmingham
D - Denver
H - Heaton, Birmingham
HF - LeLocle (Swiss)
LIMA - Lima
Mo - Mexico
PHILA.U.S.A. - Philadelphia
PHILADELPHIA - Philadelphia
PHILA - Philadelphia

MONETARY SYSTEM

10 Centavos = 1 Decimo
10 Decimos = 1 Sucre
25 Sucres = 1 Condor

REPUBLIC

DECIMAL COINAGE

10 Centavos = 1 Decimo; 10 Decimos = 1 Sucre; 25 Sucres = 1 Condor

KM# 57 1/2 CENTAVO (Medio) **Composition:** Copper-Nickel **Obverse:** Flag draped arms **Reverse:** Denomination in laurels

Date	Mintage	F	VF	XF	Unc	BU
1909H	4,000,000	4.00	9.00	20.00	40.00	—

KM# 58 CENTAVO (Un) **Composition:** Copper-Nickel **Obverse:** Flag draped arms **Reverse:** Denomination in laurels

Date	Mintage	F	VF	XF	Unc	BU
1909H	3,000,000	4.50	10.00	22.00	45.00	—

KM# 67 CENTAVO (Un) **Composition:** Bronze **Obverse:** Flag draped arms **Reverse:** Denomination in laurels

Date	Mintage	F	VF	XF	Unc	BU
1928	2,016,000	1.00	2.00	7.50	25.00	—

KM# 104 CENTAVO (Un) **Weight:** 2.5200 g. **Composition:** Brass **Obverse:** Map of the Americas **Reverse:** Denomination **Edge:** Plain **Size:** 19 mm.

Date	F	VF	XF	Unc	BU
2000	—	—	—	0.20	—

KM# 59 2 CENTAVOS (Dos) **Composition:** Copper-Nickel **Obverse:** Flag draped arms **Reverse:** Denomination in laurels

Date	Mintage	F	VF	XF	Unc	BU
1909H	2,500,000	5.00	12.00	25.00	60.00	—
1909H Proof	—	Value: 175				

KM# 61 2-1/2 CENTAVOS **Composition:** Copper-Nickel **Obverse:** Flag draped arms **Reverse:** Denomination in laurels

Date	Mintage	F	VF	XF	Unc	BU
1917	1,600,000	6.00	15.00	55.00	175	—

KM# 68 2-1/2 CENTAVOS **Composition:** Nickel **Obverse:** Flag draped arms **Reverse:** Denomination in laurels

Date	Mintage	F	VF	XF	Unc	BU
1928	4,000,000	2.00	4.00	20.00	50.00	—

KM# 55.1 1/2 DECIMO (Medio) **Weight:** 1.2500 g. **Composition:** 0.9000 Silver .0361 oz. ASW **Obverse:** Denomination in laurels **Reverse:** Flag draped arm

Date	Mintage	F	VF	XF	Unc	BU
1902/892LIMA JF	1,000,000	1.00	2.00	8.50	17.50	—
1902/802LIMA JF	Inc. above	1.00	2.00	8.50	17.50	—
1902LIMA JF	Inc. above	0.75	1.50	6.00	12.50	—
1905/805LIMA JF	500,000	3.00	5.00	15.00	40.00	—
1905/2LIMA JF	Inc. above	3.50	6.00	18.00	50.00	—
1905LIMA JF	Inc. above	0.75	1.50	7.00	15.00	—
1912/05LIMA FG	20,000	3.00	6.00	18.00	50.00	—
1912LIMA FG	Inc. above	0.75	1.50	6.00	12.50	—
1912LIMA FG	Inc. above	2.00	3.00	8.50	17.50	—

Note: FCUADOR (obverse error)

KM# 55.2 1/2 DECIMO (Medio) **Weight:** 1.2500 g. **Composition:** 0.9000 Silver .0361 oz. ASW **Obverse:** Head of Sucre **Reverse:** Modified flag draped arm

Date	Mintage	F	VF	XF	Unc	BU
1915BIRMm	2,000,000	0.75	1.25	3.00	8.00	—
1915BIRMm Proof	—	Value: 150				

KM# 60.1 5 CENTAVOS (Cinco) **Composition:** Copper-Nickel **Obverse:** Flag draped arms with tails on flagpoles pointing outward **Reverse:** Denomination in laurels

Date	Mintage	F	VF	XF	Unc	BU
1909H	2,000,000	4.50	10.00	30.00	80.00	—

KM# 60.2 5 CENTAVOS (Cinco) **Composition:** Copper-Nickel **Obverse:** Flag draped arms with tails on flagpoles pointing downward **Reverse:** Denomination in laurels **Note:** Thin planchet.

Date	Mintage	F	VF	XF	Unc	BU
1917	1,200,000	8.50	25.00	80.00	185	—
1918	7,980,000	4.00	8.50	17.50	65.00	—

KM# 63 5 CENTAVOS (Cinco) **Composition:** Copper-Nickel **Obverse:** Flag draped arms **Reverse:** Denomination in laurels

Date	Mintage	F	VF	XF	Unc	BU
1919	12,000,000	1.00	2.00	8.00	15.00	—
Note: 3 berries to left of "C" on reverse						
1919	Inc. above	1.25	2.50	10.00	20.00	—
Note: 4 berries loose to left of "C" on reverse						
1919	Inc. above	1.25	2.50	10.00	20.00	—
Note: 4 berries tight to left of "C" on reverse						

KM# 65 5 CENTAVOS (Cinco) **Composition:** Copper-Nickel

Date	Mintage	F	VF	XF	Unc	BU
1924H	10,000,000	2.00	5.00	10.00	30.00	—

KM# 69 5 CENTAVOS (Cinco) **Composition:** Nickel

Date	Mintage	F	VF	XF	Unc	BU
1928	16,000,000	1.00	2.00	3.00	6.50	—

KM# 75 5 CENTAVOS (Cinco) **Composition:** Nickel **Obverse:** Flag draped arms **Reverse:** Denomination in wreath

Date	Mintage	F	VF	XF	Unc	BU
1937HF	15,000,000	0.10	0.20	0.75	2.00	—

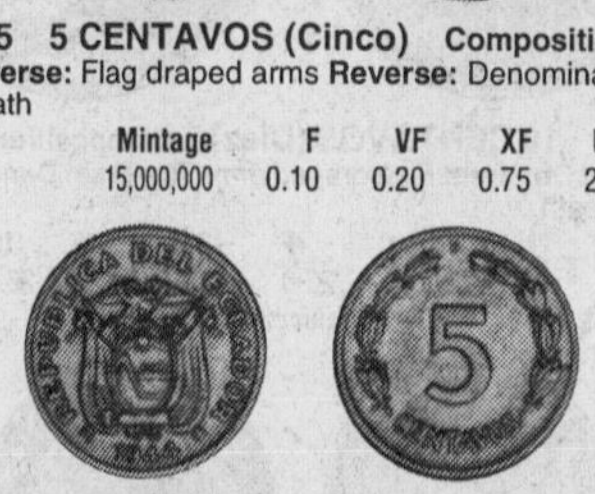

KM# 75a 5 CENTAVOS (Cinco) **Composition:** Brass **Obverse:** Flag draped arms **Reverse:** Denomination in wreath

Date	Mintage	F	VF	XF	Unc	BU
1942	2,000,000	1.00	2.00	6.00	15.00	—
1944D	3,000,000	1.00	2.00	5.00	10.00	—

KM# 75b 5 CENTAVOS (Cinco) **Composition:** Copper-Nickel **Obverse:** Flag draped arms **Reverse:** Denomination in wreath

Date	Mintage	F	VF	XF	Unc	BU
1946	40,000,000	—	—	0.40	1.00	—

KM# 75c 5 CENTAVOS (Cinco) **Composition:** Nickel Clad Steel

Date	F	VF	XF	Unc	BU
1970	—	—	0.15	0.50	—
1970	—	—	—	—	—

Note: ECADOR (obverse legend error)

KM# 105 5 CENTAVOS (Cinco) **Weight:** 5.0000 g. **Composition:** Steel **Subject:** Juan Montalvo **Obverse:** Portrait and arms **Reverse:** Denomination **Edge:** Plain **Size:** 21.2 mm.

Date	F	VF	XF	Unc	BU
2000	—	—	—	0.50	—

KM# 50.3 DECIMO (Un) **Weight:** 2.5000 g. **Composition:** 0.9000 Silver .0723 oz. ASW **Obverse:** Head of Sucre left, legend without LEY **Rev. Legend:** Flag draped arms

Date	Mintage	VG	F	VF	XF	Unc
1902LIMA JF	519,000	—	1.50	4.50	10.00	22.00
Note: With JR below fasces on reverse						
1902LIMA JF	Inc. above	—	1.50	4.50	10.00	22.00
Note: Without JR below fasces on reverse						
1902LIMA JF/TF	—	—	1.00	3.00	6.00	15.00
1905LIMA JF	250,000	—	1.00	3.00	6.00	15.00
1912LIMA FG	30,000	—	3.00	6.00	12.50	28.00

KM# 50.4 DECIMO (Un) **Weight:** 2.5000 g. **Composition:** 0.9000 Silver .0723 oz. ASW **Obverse:** Head of Sucre left **Reverse:** Flag draped arms

Date	Mintage	VG	F	VF	XF	Unc
1915BIRMm	1,000,000	—	BV	1.25	2.00	7.00
1915BIRMm Proof	—	Value: 200				

KM# 50.5 DECIMO (Un) **Weight:** 2.5000 g. **Composition:** 0.9000 Silver .0723 oz. ASW **Obverse:** Head of Sucre left **Reverse:** Flag draped arms

Date	Mintage	VG	F	VF	XF	Unc
1916PHILA	2,000,000	—	BV	1.25	2.00	7.00

KM# 62 10 CENTAVOS (Diez) **Composition:** Copper-Nickel **Obverse:** Flag draped arms **Reverse:** Denomination in wreath

Date	Mintage	F	VF	XF	Unc	BU
1918	1,000,000	7.50	15.00	35.00	85.00	—

KM# 64 10 CENTAVOS (Diez) **Composition:** Copper-Nickel **Obverse:** Flag draped arms **Reverse:** Denomination in wreath

Date	Mintage	F	VF	XF	Unc	BU
1919	2,000,000	2.00	4.00	10.00	25.00	—
1919 Proof	—	Value: 200				

KM# 66 10 CENTAVOS (Diez) **Composition:** Copper-Nickel **Obverse:** Flag draped arms **Reverse:** Bust of Bolivar **Note:** The H mint mark is very small and is located above the date.

Date	Mintage	F	VF	XF	Unc	BU
1924H	5,000,000	1.25	2.50	7.50	20.00	—
1924H Proof	—	Value: 80.00				

KM# 70 10 CENTAVOS (Diez) **Composition:** Nickel **Obverse:** Flag draped arms **Reverse:** Bolivar head right

Date	Mintage	F	VF	XF	Unc	BU
1928	16,000,000	1.00	2.00	6.50	20.00	—

KM# 76 10 CENTAVOS (Diez) **Composition:** Nickel **Obverse:** Flag draped arms **Reverse:** Denomination in wreath

Date	Mintage	F	VF	XF	Unc	BU

KM# 76a 10 CENTAVOS (Diez) **Composition:** Brass **Obverse:** Flag draped arms **Reverse:** Denomination in wreath

Date	Mintage	F	VF	XF	Unc	BU
1942	5,000,000	0.60	1.00	5.00	15.00	—

KM# 76b 10 CENTAVOS (Diez) **Composition:** Copper-Nickel **Obverse:** Flag draped arms **Reverse:** Denomination in wreath

Date	Mintage	F	VF	XF	Unc	BU
1946	40,000,000	0.10	0.15	0.25	1.00	—

KM# 76c 10 CENTAVOS (Diez) **Composition:** Nickel Clad Steel **Note:** Varieties exist.

Date	Mintage	F	VF	XF	Unc	BU
1964	20,000,000	—	—	0.20	0.75	—
1968	15,000,000	—	—	0.20	0.75	—
1972	20,000,000	—	—	0.15	0.65	—

KM# 76d 10 CENTAVOS (Diez) **Composition:** Copper-Nickel Clad Steel

Date	Mintage	F	VF	XF	Unc	BU
1976	10,000,000	—	—	0.15	0.65	—

KM# 106 10 CENTAVOS (Diez) **Weight:** 2.2400 g. **Composition:** Steel **Subject:** Eugenio Espejo **Obverse:** Portrait and arms **Reverse:** Denomination **Edge:** Plain **Size:** 17.9 mm.

Date	F	VF	XF	Unc	BU
2000	—	—	—	0.75	—

KM# 51.3 2 DECIMOS (Dos) **Weight:** 5.0000 g. **Composition:** 0.9000 Silver .1446 oz. ASW **Obverse:** Head of Sucre left **Reverse:** Flag draped arms; legend without LEY

Date	Mintage	F	VF	XF	Unc	BU
1912/18 FG	50,000	5.00	12.50	20.00	50.00	—
1912 FG	Inc. above	2.00	6.00	12.50	35.00	—
1914 FG LIMA.	110,000	3.00	7.00	14.50	40.00	—
1914 FG LIMA	Inc. above	2.00	5.50	11.50	30.00	—
1915 FG	157,000	5.00	12.50	25.00	60.00	—
Note: Small "R" below fasces on reverse						

KM# 51.4 2 DECIMOS (Dos) **Weight:** 5.0000 g. **Composition:** 0.9000 Silver .1446 oz. ASW **Obverse:** Head of Sucre **Reverse:** Flag draped arms

Date	Mintage	F	VF	XF	Unc	BU
1914PHILADELPHIA TF	2,500,000	1.50	3.00	7.00	15.00	—
1916PHILADELPHIA TF	1,000,000	1.50	3.00	7.00	15.00	—

KM# 77.1 20 CENTAVOS **Composition:** Nickel **Obverse:** Flag draped arms **Reverse:** Denomination in wreath

Date	Mintage	F	VF	XF	Unc	BU
1937HF	7,500,000	0.25	0.50	1.00	5.00	—

KM# 77.1a 20 CENTAVOS **Composition:** Brass **Obverse:** Flag draped arms **Reverse:** Denomination in wreath

Date	Mintage	F	VF	XF	Unc	BU
1942	5,000,000	0.60	1.00	6.00	15.00	—
1944 D	15,000,000	0.40	0.75	4.00	10.00	—

KM# 77.1b 20 CENTAVOS **Composition:** Copper Nickel **Obverse:** Flag draped arms **Reverse:** Denomination in wreath

Date	Mintage	F	VF	XF	Unc	BU
1946	30,000,000	0.25	0.75	1.50	3.50	—

KM# 77.1c 20 CENTAVOS **Composition:** Nickel Clad Steel **Obverse:** Flag draped arms **Reverse:** Denomination in wreath

Date	Mintage	F	VF	XF	Unc	BU
1959	14,400,000	—	—	0.20	0.75	—
1962	14,400,000	—	—	0.20	0.75	—
1966	24,000,000	—	—	0.20	0.75	—
1969	24,000,000	—	—	0.20	0.75	—
1971	12,000,000	—	—	0.20	0.75	—
1972	48,432,000	—	—	0.20	0.75	—

KM# 77.2 20 CENTAVOS **Composition:** Copper-Nickel **Obverse:** Modified coat of arms

Date	Mintage	F	VF	XF	Unc	BU
1974	19,562,000	—	—	0.15	0.50	—

KM# 77.2a 20 CENTAVOS **Composition:** Nickel Coated Steel

Date	Mintage	F	VF	XF	Unc	BU
1975	52,437,000	—	—	0.15	0.35	—
1978	37,500,000	—	—	0.15	0.35	—
1980	18,000,000	—	—	0.15	0.35	—
1981	21,000,000	—	—	0.15	0.35	—

KM# 107 25 CENTAVOS **Weight:** 5.6500 g. **Composition:** Steel **Subject:** Jose Joaquin De Olmedo **Obverse:** Portrait and arms **Reverse:** Denomination **Edge:** Reeded **Size:** 24.2 mm.

Date	F	VF	XF	Unc	BU
2000	—	—	—	1.00	—

KM# 71 50 CENTAVOS (Cinquenta) **Weight:** 2.5000 g. **Composition:** 0.7200 Silver .0579 oz. ASW **Obverse:** Head of Sucre left **Reverse:** Flag draped arms

Date	Mintage	F	VF	XF	Unc	BU
1928PHILA•U•S•A.	1,000,000	1.50	3.00	12.00	30.00	—
1930PHILA•U•S•A.	155,000	2.00	5.00	18.00	40.00	—

KM# 81 50 CENTAVOS (Cinquenta) **Composition:** Nickel Clad Steel

Date	Mintage	F	VF	XF	Unc	BU
1963	20,000,000	—	0.15	0.25	0.85	—
1971	5,000,000	—	0.15	0.25	0.85	—
1974	—	—	0.15	0.25	0.85	—
1975	—	—	0.15	0.25	0.85	—
1977	40,000,000	—	0.10	0.20	0.75	—
1979	25,000,000	—	0.10	0.20	0.75	—
1982	20,000,000	—	0.10	0.20	0.75	—

KM# 87 50 CENTAVOS (Cinquenta) Composition: Nickel Clad Steel **Obverse:** Modified coat of arms

Date	Mintage	F	VF	XF	Unc	BU
1985	30,000,000	—	0.10	0.20	0.40	—

KM# 90 50 CENTAVOS (Cinquenta) Composition: Nickel Clad Steel **Note:** The circulation strikes were withdrawn from circulation and remelted. Approximately 100,000 pieces were released.

Date	F	VF	XF	Unc	BU
1988	—	—	—	0.30	—
1988 Proof	—	—	—	—	—

KM# 108 50 CENTAVOS (Cinquenta) Weight: 11.3200 g. **Composition:** Steel **Subject:** Eloy Alfaro **Obverse:** Portrait and arms **Reverse:** Denomination **Edge:** Reeded **Size:** 30.6 mm.

Date	F	VF	XF	Unc	BU
2000	—	—	2.00	5.00	—

KM# 72 SUCRE (Un) Weight: 5.0000 g. **Composition:** 0.7200 Silver .1157 oz. ASW **Obverse:** Head of Sucre left **Reverse:** Flag draped arms

Date	Mintage	F	VF	XF	Unc	BU
1928PHILA•U•S•A.	3,000,000	1.75	3.50	12.50	35.00	—
1930PHILA•U•S•A.	400,000	3.00	10.00	30.00	70.00	—
1934PHILA•U•S•A.	2,000,000	BV	2.00	5.00	15.00	—

KM# 78.1 SUCRE (Un) Composition: Nickel **Obverse:** Flag draped arms **Reverse:** Head of Sucre left **Size:** 26.5 mm.

Date	Mintage	F	VF	XF	Unc	BU
1937 HF	9,000,000	0.50	1.00	2.00	7.00	—

KM# 78.2 SUCRE (Un) Composition: Nickel **Obverse:** Flag draped arms **Reverse:** Head of Sucre left **Size:** 25.9 mm.

Date	Mintage	F	VF	XF	Unc	BU
1946	18,000,000	0.40	0.60	0.80	2.00	—

KM# 78a SUCRE (Un) Composition: Copper-Nickel **Obverse:** Different ship in coat of arms **Reverse:** Head of Sucre left

Date	Mintage	F	VF	XF	Unc	BU
1959	8,400,000	0.25	0.50	0.65	1.00	—
1959 Proof	—	Value: 250				

KM# 78b SUCRE (Un) Composition: Nickel Clad Steel **Obverse:** Ship in arms similar to KM#78

Date	Mintage	F	VF	XF	Unc	BU
1964	20,000,000	—	0.10	0.25	0.75	—
1970	24,000,000	—	0.10	0.25	0.75	—
1971	8,092,000	—	0.10	0.25	0.75	—
1974	40,308,000	—	0.10	0.25	0.50	—
1978	32,000,000	—	0.10	0.25	0.50	—
1979	32,000,000	—	0.10	0.25	0.50	—
1980	110,000,000	—	0.10	0.25	0.50	—
1981	70,000,000	—	0.10	0.25	0.50	—

KM# 83 SUCRE (Un) Composition: Nickel Clad Steel **Obverse:** Modified coat of arms, ship similar to KM#78a

Date	Mintage	F	VF	XF	Unc	BU
1974	32,000,000	—	0.10	0.20	0.40	—
1975	32,000,000	—	0.10	0.20	0.40	—
1975 Proof	—	Value: 150				
1977	32,000,000	—	0.10	0.20	0.35	—

KM# 85.1 SUCRE (Un) Composition: Nickel Clad Steel **Obverse:** Modified coat of arms **Reverse:** Large head

Date	F	VF	XF	Unc	BU
1985	—	—	—	0.50	—

KM# 85.2 SUCRE (Un) Composition: Nickel Clad Steel **Reverse:** Small head

Date	F	VF	XF	Unc	BU
1986	—	—	—	0.50	—

KM# 89 SUCRE (Un) Composition: Nickel Clad Steel **Note:** The 1988 circulation strikes were reportedly withdrawn from circulation and remelted. Approximately 100,000 pieces were released.

Date	F	VF	XF	Unc	BU
1988	—	—	—	0.40	—
1988 Proof	—	—	—	—	—
1990	—	—	—	0.40	—
1992	—	—	—	0.40	—

KM# 73 2 SUCRES (Dos) Weight: 10.0000 g. **Composition:** 0.7200 Silver .2315 oz. ASW **Obverse:** Head of Sucre **Reverse:** Flag draped arms

Date	Mintage	F	VF	XF	Unc	BU
1928PHILA•U•S•A.	500,000	3.00	10.00	25.00	55.00	—
1930PHILA•U•S•A.	100,000	7.00	20.00	40.00	75.00	—

KM# 80 2 SUCRES (Dos) Weight: 10.0000 g. **Composition:** 0.7200 Silver .2315 oz. ASW **Obverse:** Head of Sucre **Reverse:** Flag draped arms

Date	Mintage	F	VF	XF	Unc	BU
1944Mo	1,000,000	2.50	3.50	6.50	15.00	—

KM# 82 2 SUCRES (Dos) Composition: Copper-Nickel **Note:** Not released to circulation. All but approximatley 35 pieces remelted.

Date	Mintage	F	VF	XF	Unc	BU
1973	2,000,000	—	—	200	300	—

KM# 79 5 SUCRES (Cinco) Weight: 25.0000 g. **Composition:** 0.7200 Silver .5787 oz. ASW **Obverse:** Head of Sucre left **Reverse:** Flag draped arms

Date	Mintage	F	VF	XF	Unc	BU
1943Mo	1,000,000	—	BV	6.00	10.00	—
1944Mo	2,600,000	—	BV	5.00	8.00	—

KM# 91 5 SUCRES (Cinco) Composition: Nickel Clad Steel **Note:** The 1988 circulation strikes were reportedly withdrawn from circulation and remelted. Approximately 100,000 pieces released.

Date	F	VF	XF	Unc	BU
1988	—	—	—	0.50	—
1988 Proof	—	—	—	—	—
1991	—	—	—	0.50	—

KM# 92.1 10 SUCRES (Diez) Composition: Nickel Clad Steel **Note:** Similar to KM#92.2 but small arms and letters. The circulation strikes were withdrawn from circulation and remelted. Approximately 100,000 pieces were released.

Date	F	VF	XF	Unc	BU
1988	—	—	—	1.00	—
1988 Proof	—	—	—	—	—

KM# 92.2 10 SUCRES (Diez) Composition: Nickel Clad Steel **Obverse:** Large arms and letters

Date	F	VF	XF	Unc	BU
1991	—	—	—	1.00	—

KM# 94.1 20 SUCRES Composition: Nickel Clad Steel **Note:** The circulation strikes were withdrawn from circulation and remelted. Approximately 100,000 pieces released.

Date	Mintage	F	VF	XF	Unc	BU
1988	—	—	—	—	1.75	—
1988 Proof	25	—	—	—	—	—

KM# 94.2 20 SUCRES **Composition:** Nickel Clad Steel **Obverse:** Modified coat of arms

Date	F	VF	XF	Unc	BU
1991	—	—	—	1.75	—

KM# 93 50 SUCRES **Composition:** Nickel Clad Steel **Note:** The 1988 circulation strikes were withdrawn from circulation and remelted. Approximately 100,000 pieces released.

Date	Mintage	F	VF	XF	Unc	BU
1988 narrow date	—	—	—	—	3.00	—
Note: 141 denticles in obverse border.						
1988 Proof	25	—	—	—	—	—
1991 wide date	—	—	—	—	3.00	—
Note: 141 denticles in obverse border.						
1991 narrow date	—	—	—	—	3.00	—
Note: 161 denticles in obverse border.						

KM# 96 100 SUCRES **Ring Composition:** Nickel Plated Steel **Center Composition:** Bronze Plated Steel **Subject:** National Bicentennial **Size:** 19 mm.

Date	F	VF	XF	Unc	BU
1995	—	0.35	0.55	2.00	—

KM# 101 100 SUCRES **Ring Composition:** Stainless Steel **Center Composition:** Brass Clad Steel **Subject:** 70th Anniversary - Central Bank **Obverse:** Portrait of Antonio Jose de Sucre left **Reverse:** Denomination **Size:** 19 mm.

Date	F	VF	XF	Unc	BU
ND(1997)	—	0.25	0.50	2.00	—

KM# 97 500 SUCRES **Ring Composition:** Nickel Plated Steel **Center Composition:** Bronze Plated Steel **Subject:** State Reform **Reverse:** Isidro Ayora

Date	F	VF	XF	Unc	BU
1995	—	—	—	3.00	—

KM# 102 500 SUCRES **Ring Composition:** Copper-Nickel **Center Composition:** Aluminum-Bronze **Subject:** 70th Anniversary - Central Bank **Obverse:** Portrait of Isidro Ayora **Reverse:** Denomination

Date	F	VF	XF	Unc	BU
ND(1997)	—	—	—	3.00	—

KM# 86 1000 SUCRES **Weight:** 23.3300 g. **Composition:** 0.9250 Silver .6938 oz. ASW **Subject:** Championship Soccer

Date	Mintage	F	VF	XF	Unc	BU
1986 Proof	8,125	Value: 50.00				

KM# 88 1000 SUCRES **Weight:** 23.3300 g. **Composition:** 0.9250 Silver .6938 oz. ASW **Subject:** Championship Soccer

Date	Mintage	F	VF	XF	Unc	BU
1986 Proof	Est. 10,000	Value: 50.00				

KM# 99 1000 SUCRES **Ring Composition:** Stainless Steel **Center Composition:** Brass **Reverse:** Portrait of Eugenio Espejo right

Date	F	VF	XF	Unc	BU
1996	—	—	—	5.00	—

KM# 103 1000 SUCRES **Ring Composition:** Copper-Nickel **Center Composition:** Aluminum-Bronze **Subject:** 70th Anniversary - Central Bank **Obverse:** Portrait of Eugenio Espejo right **Reverse:** Denomination

Date	F	VF	XF	Unc	BU
ND(1997)	—	—	—	5.00	—

KM# 95 5000 SUCRES **Weight:** 27.0000 g. **Composition:** 0.9250 Silver .8029 oz. ASW **Subject:** Ibero - American Series

Date	Mintage	F	VF	XF	Unc	BU
1991 Proof	50,000	Value: 75.00				

KM# 98 5000 SUCRES **Weight:** 27.0000 g. **Composition:** 0.9250 Silver .8029 oz. ASW **Subject:** Environmental Protection - Galapagos Penguins

Date	Mintage	F	VF	XF	Unc	BU
1994 Proof	20,000	Value: 70.00				

KM# 100 5000 SUCRES **Weight:** 27.0000 g. **Composition:** 0.9250 Silver .8029 oz. ASW **Subject:** Ibero-American Series - Native Costumes

Date	Mintage	F	VF	XF	Unc	BU
1997 Proof	20,000	Value: 60.00				

KM# 109 5000 SUCRES **Weight:** 27.1000 g. **Composition:** 0.9250 Silver 0.8059 oz. ASW **Subject:** Ibero-America Series **Obverse:** National arms in a circle of arms **Reverse:** Man on horse with condor in background **Edge:** Reeded **Size:** 40 mm.

Date	F	VF	XF	Unc	BU
1999 Proof	—	Value: 60.00			

KM# 74 CONDOR (Un) **Weight:** 8.3592 g. **Composition:** 0.9000 Gold .2419 oz. AGW **Obverse:** Head of Bolivar **Reverse:** Flag draped arms **Note:** 5,000 were released into circulation; the remainder are held as the Central Bank gold reserve.

Date	Mintage	F	VF	XF	Unc	BU
1928Birmingham	20,000	90.00	140	200	350	—

PATTERNS

Including off metal strikes

KM#	Date	Mintage	Identification	Mkt Val
Pn11	1928	—	Condor. Copper-Nickel. KM#74.	—
Pn12	1928	—	Condor. Copper. KM#74.	—
Pn13	1974	—	20 Centavos. Brass. 3.6000 g. KM#77.2	150
Pn15	1975	—	Sucre. Brass. 6.7900 g. KM#83.	150
Pn14	1975	—	50 Centavos. Brass. 5.2100 g. KM#81.	150
Pn16	1976	—	10 Centavos. Brass. 2.9100 g. KM#76d.	150

PIEFORTS

KM#	Date	Mintage	Identification	Mkt Val
P1	1915H	—	1/2 Decimo. Copper Nickel.	—
P2	1915H	—	Decimo. Copper Nickel.	—

MINT SETS

KM#	Date	Mintage	Identification	Issue Price	Mkt Val
MS35	1975	10,000	8 circulating coins and 1 commemorative dollar	30.00	42.00
MS36	2000 (5)	—	KM#104-108	30.00	—

PROOF SETS

KM#	Date	Mintage	Identification	Issue Price	Mkt Val
PS2	1988 (6)	25	KM#89-94	—	—

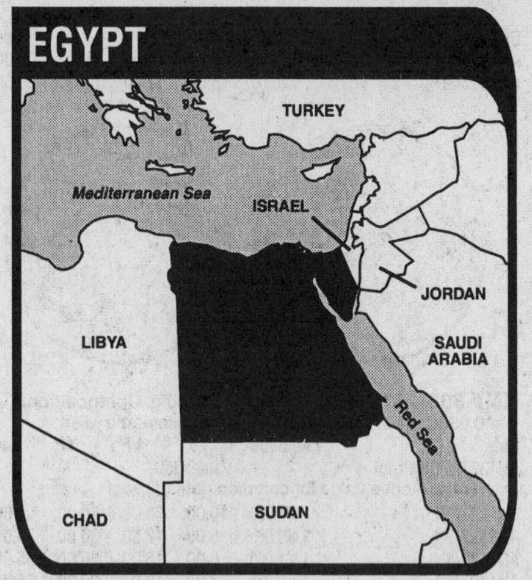

The Arab Republic of Egypt, located on the northeastern corner of Africa, has an area of 385,229 sq. mi. (1,1001,450 sq. km.) and a population of 62.4 million. Capital: Cairo. Although Egypt is an almost rainless expanse of desert, its economy is predominantly agricultural. Cotton, rice and petroleum are exported. Other main sources of income are revenues from the Suez Canal, remittances of Egyptian workers abroad and tourism.

Egyptian history dates back to about 3000 B.C. when the empire was established by uniting the upper and lower kingdoms. Following its 'Golden Age' (16th to 13th centuries B.C.), Egypt was conquered by Persia (525 B.C.) and Alexander the Great (332 B.C.). The Ptolemies, descended from one of Alexander's generals, ruled until the suicide of Cleopatra (30 B.C.) when Egypt became the private domain of the Roman emperor, and subsequently part of the Byzantine world. Various Muslim dynasties ruled Egypt from 641 on, including Ayyubid Sultans to 1250 and Mamluks to 1517, when it was conquered by the Ottoman Turks, interrupted by the occupation of Napoleon (1798-1801). A semi-independent dynasty was founded by Muhammad Ali in 1805 which lasted until 1952. Turkish rule became increasingly casual, permitting Great Britain to inject its influence by purchasing shares in the Suez Canal. British troops occupied Egypt in 1882, becoming the de facto rulers. On Dec. 14, 1914, Egypt was made a protectorate of Britain. British occupation ended on Feb. 28, 1922, when Egypt became a sovereign, independent kingdom. The monarchy was abolished and a republic proclaimed on June 18, 1953.

On Feb. 1, 1958, Egypt and Syria formed the United Arab Republic. Yemen joined on March 8 in an association known as the United Arab States. Syria withdrew from the United Arab Republic on Sept. 29, 1961, and on Dec. 26 Egypt dissolved its ties with Yemen in the United Arab States. On Sept. 2, 1971, Egypt finally shed the name United Arab Republic in favor of the Arab Republic of Egypt.

RULERS

British, 1882-1922

Local Khedives

Mohammed Tewfik Pasha, 1882--
Abbas II Hilmi, 1892-1914

Local Sultans

Hussein Kamil, 1914-1917
Ahmed Fuad I, 1917-1922

Kingdom, 1922-1953

Ahmed Fuad I, 1922-1936
Farouk, 1936-1952
Fuad II, 1952-1953

Republic, 1953-

MONETARY SYSTEM

(1885-1916)

10 Ushr-al-Qirsh = 1 Piastre

(Commencing 1916)

10 Milliemes = 1 Piastre (Qirsh)
100 Piastres = 1 Pound (Gunayh)

MINT MARKS

Egyptian coins issued prior to the advent of the British Protectorate series of Sultan Hussein Kamil introduced in 1916 were very similar to Turkish coins of the same period. They can best be distinguished by the presence of the Arabic word *Misr* Egypt) on the reverse, which generally appears immediately above the Muslim accession date of the ruler, which is presented in Arabic numerals. Each coin is individually dated according to the regnal years.

BP - Budapest, Hungary
H - Birmingham, England
KN - King's Norton, England

ENGRAVER

W - Emil Weigand, Berlin

INITIAL LETTERS

Letters, symbols and numerals were placed on coins during the reigns of Mustafa II (1695) until Selim III (1789). They have been observed in various positions but the most common position being over *bin* in the third row of the obverse. In Egypt these letters and others used on the Paras (Medins) above the word *duribe* on the reverse during this period.

REGNAL YEAR IDENTIFICATION

4
Duriba fi

Misr Accession Date

DENOMINATIONS

Para

Qirsh

NOTE: The unit of value on coins of this period is generally presented on the obverse immediately below the toughra, as shown in the illustrations above.

Piastres 1916-1933

Milliemes

Piastres 1934 –

TITLES

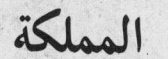

المملكة المصرية

al-Mamlaka al-Misriya
(The Kingdom of Egypt)

U.A.R. EGYPT

The legend illustrated is *Jumhuriyat Misr* al-*Arabiyya* which translates to 'The Arab Republic of Egypt'. Similar legends are found on the modern issues of Syria.

OTTOMAN EMPIRE

Abdul Hamid II

AH1293-1327/1876-1909AD

OTTOMAN COINAGE

KM# 287 1/40 QIRSH Composition: Bronze **Note:** Mintname Misr.

Date	Mintage	VG	F	VF	XF	Unc
AH1293/27	1,200,000	—	1.50	3.00	7.00	18.00
AH1293/29	2,000,000	—	1.00	2.00	4.00	15.00
AH1293/31H	2,400,000	—	1.00	2.00	4.00	15.00
AH1293/32H	Inc. below	—	1.00	2.00	4.00	15.00
AH1293/33H	1,200,000	—	1.00	2.00	4.00	12.00
AH1293/35H	1,200,000	—	2.00	5.00	7.00	15.00

KM# 288 1/20 QIRSH Composition: Bronze **Note:** Mintname Misr.

Date	Mintage	F	VF	XF	Unc
AH1293/27 (1901)	1,402,000	1.00	2.00	3.00	12.00
AH1293/29 (1903)	3,200,000	1.00	2.00	3.00	12.00
AH1293/31 (1905) H	3,000,000	1.00	2.00	3.00	10.00
AH1293/32 (1906) H	Inc. below	1.00	2.00	3.00	10.00
AH1293/33 (1907) H	1,400,000	2.00	3.00	5.00	15.00
AH1293/35 (1909) H	1,400,000	3.00	6.00	10.00	20.00

KM# 289 1/10 QIRSH Composition: Copper-Nickel **Note:** Mintname Misr.

Date	Mintage	VG	F	VF	XF	Unc
AH1293/27-35 Proof	—	Value: 100				
Note: Above value for common date proof						
AH1293/27	3,010,000	—	1.00	1.50	3.00	10.00
AH1293/28	6,000,000	—	1.00	1.50	3.00	10.00
AH1293/29	1,500,000	—	1.00	2.00	4.00	15.00
AH1293/30	1,000,000	—	1.00	1.50	3.00	12.50
AH1293/31H	3,000,000	—	1.00	1.50	4.00	15.00
AH1293/32H	Inc. below	—	1.00	1.50	3.00	12.50
AH1293/33H	2,000,000	—	1.00	1.50	2.50	8.50
AH1293/35H	2,000,000	—	1.25	3.00	6.00	20.00

KM# 290 2/10 QIRSH Composition: Copper-Nickel **Note:** Mintname Misr.

Date	Mintage	VG	F	VF	XF	Unc
AH1293/27	1,002,000	—	1.00	3.00	6.00	20.00
AH1293/28	2,000,000	—	1.00	3.00	6.00	20.00
AH1293/29	1,500,000	—	1.00	3.00	6.00	20.00
AH1293/30	—	—	3.00	6.00	12.00	40.00
AH1293/31H	1,000,000	—	1.00	3.00	6.00	20.00
AH1293/33H	1,500,000	—	1.00	3.00	6.00	20.00
AH1293/35H	750,000	—	2.00	6.00	10.00	35.00

KM# 291 5/10 QIRSH Composition: Copper-Nickel **Note:** Mintname Misr.

Date	Mintage	VG	F	VF	XF	Unc
AH1293/27-33 Proof	—	Value: 145				
Note: Above value for common date proof						
AH1293/27	4,999,000	—	0.30	1.50	5.00	20.00
AH1293/29	12,000,000	—	0.30	1.50	5.00	20.00
AH1293/30	2,000,000	—	0.50	2.00	6.00	25.00
AH1293/33H	1,000,000	—	2.00	6.00	12.50	40.00

KM# 292 QIRSH Weight: 1.4000 g. **Composition:** 0.8330 Silver .0375 oz. ASW **Note:** Mintname Misr.

Date	Mintage	VG	F	VF	XF	Unc
AH1293/27-33 Proof	—	Value: 135				
Note: Above value for common date proof						
AH1293/27 W	200,000	—	1.25	4.00	10.00	27.50
AH1293/29 W	100,000	—	1.50	4.00	10.00	30.00
AH1293/29H	100,000	—	1.25	3.00	7.50	25.00
AH1293/33H	100,000	—	1.25	3.00	7.50	25.00

KM# 299 QIRSH Composition: Copper-Nickel **Note:** Mintname Misr.

Date	Mintage	VG	F	VF	XF	Unc
AH1293/27	999,000	—	2.00	6.00	20.00	50.00
AH1293/29	3,500,000	—	2.00	5.00	15.00	40.00
AH1293/30	500,000	—	2.50	6.00	20.00	55.00
AH1293/33H	1,000,000	—	2.00	5.00	15.00	40.00

KM# 293 2 QIRSH **Weight:** 2.8000 g. **Composition:** 0.8330 Silver **Obverse:** Flower to right of toughra **Note:** Mintname Misr.

Date	Mintage	VG	F	VF	XF	Unc
AH1293/17-33 Proof	—	Value: 145				
Note: Above value for common date of proof						
AH1293/27 W	1,000,000	—	2.00	4.00	10.00	35.00
AH1293/29 W	450,000	—	2.00	4.00	10.00	35.00
AH1293/29H	1,250,000	—	2.00	4.00	10.00	35.00
AH1293/30H	500,000	—	3.00	6.00	15.00	40.00
AH1293/31H	Inc. above	—	3.00	6.00	15.00	40.00
AH1293/33H	450,000	—	2.00	4.00	10.00	35.00

KM# 295 10 QIRSH **Weight:** 14.0000 g. **Composition:** 0.8330 Silver .3749 oz. ASW **Obverse:** Flower at right of toughra **Note:** Mintname Misr.

Date	VG	F	VF	XF	Unc
AH1293/27-33 Proof	—	Value: 435			
Note: Above value for common date of proof					
AH1293/27 W	—	15.00	25.00	60.00	150
AH1293/29 W	—	8.00	15.00	40.00	100
AH1293/29H	—	8.00	15.00	35.00	100
AH1293/30H	—	8.00	15.00	35.00	100
AH1293/31H	—	10.00	20.00	45.00	150
AH1293/32H	—	8.00	15.00	35.00	100
AH1293/33H	—	8.00	12.50	35.00	100

KM# 282 10 QIRSH **Weight:** 0.8544 g. **Composition:** 0.8750 Gold .0240 oz. AGW **Obverse:** Al-Ghazi at right of toughra **Note:** Mintname Misr.

Date	Mintage	VG	F	VF	XF	Unc
AH1293/34	5,000	—	40.00	70.00	110	—

KM# 296 20 QIRSH **Weight:** 28.0000 g. **Composition:** 0.8330 Silver .7499 oz. ASW **Note:** Mintname Misr.

Date	Mintage	VG	F	VF	XF	Unc
AH1293/27-33 Proof	—	Value: 825				
Note: Above value for common date of proof						
AH1293/27 W	25,000	—	17.50	50.00	150	500
AH1293/29 W	50,000	—	15.00	40.00	100	425
AH1293/29H	425,000	—	12.00	30.00	80.00	400
AH1293/30H	200,000	—	12.00	30.00	80.00	400
AH1293/31H	250,000	—	12.00	30.00	80.00	400
AH1293/32H	Inc. below	—	12.00	30.00	85.00	400
AH1293/33H	300,000	—	12.00	30.00	85.00	400

Muhammad V

AH1327-1332/1909-1914AD

OTTOMAN COINAGE

KM# 300 1/40 QIRSH **Composition:** Bronze **Note:** Mintname Misr.

Date	Mintage	VG	F	VF	XF	Unc
AH1327/2H	2,000,000	—	1.50	3.00	7.50	25.00
AH1327/3H	2,000,000	—	1.50	3.00	7.50	25.00
AH1327/4H	1,200,000	—	1.50	3.00	7.50	25.00
AH1327/6H	1,200,000	—	1.00	2.00	5.00	20.00

KM# 301 1/20 QIRSH **Composition:** Bronze **Note:** Mintname Misr.

Date	Mintage	VG	F	VF	XF	Unc
AH1327/2H	2,000,000	—	1.00	3.00	6.00	18.00
AH1327/3H	2,000,000	—	1.50	4.00	8.00	25.00
AH1327/4H	2,400,000	—	1.00	3.00	6.00	18.00
AH1327/6H	1,400,000	—	0.75	2.00	6.00	18.00

KM# 302 1/10 QIRSH **Composition:** Copper-Nickel **Note:** Mintname Misr.

Date	Mintage	VG	F	VF	XF	Unc
AH1327/2-6H Proof	—	Value: 110				
Note: Above value for common date of proof						
AH1327/2H	3,000,000	—	3.00	6.00	10.00	25.00
AH1327/3	1,000,000	—	5.00	12.00	20.00	50.00
AH1327/4H	3,000,000	—	1.00	2.00	4.00	12.50
AH1327/6H	3,000,000	—	0.75	1.50	3.00	12.50

KM# 303 2/10 QIRSH **Composition:** Copper-Nickel **Note:** Mintname Misr

Date	Mintage	F	VF	XF	Unc
AH1327/2 (1910) H	1,000,000	2.00	4.00	7.00	25.00
AH1327/3 (1911)	500,000	3.00	10.00	15.00	35.00
AH1327/4 (1911) H	1,000,000	2.00	4.00	7.00	25.00
AH1327/6 (1913) H	1,000,000	1.25	3.00	7.00	25.00
AH1327/2-6 (1914) H Proof	—	Value: 120			
Note: Above value for common date of proof					

KM# 304 5/10 QIRSH **Composition:** Copper-Nickel **Note:** Mintname Misr.

Date	Mintage	VG	F	VF	XF	Unc
AH1327/2H	2,131,000	—	2.50	6.00	15.00	50.00
AH1327/3	1,000,000	—	5.00	15.00	35.00	75.00
AH1327/4H	3,327,000	—	1.00	2.50	6.00	25.00
AH1327/6H	3,000,000	—	1.00	2.50	6.00	25.00

KM# 305 QIRSH **Weight:** 1.4000 g. **Composition:** 0.8330 Silver .0375 oz. ASW **Note:** Mintname Misr.

Date	Mintage	VG	F	VF	XF	Unc
AH1327/2H	251,000	—	2.00	4.00	15.00	28.00
AH1327/3H	171,000	—	2.25	4.50	16.00	35.00

KM# 306 QIRSH **Composition:** Copper-Nickel **Note:** Mintname Misr.

Date	Mintage	VG	F	VF	XF	Unc
AH1327/2H	1,000,000	—	2.00	5.00	12.00	35.00
AH1327/3	300,000	—	20.00	40.00	75.00	150
AH1327/4H	500,000	—	4.00	8.00	22.50	65.00
AH1327/6H	2,500,000	—	2.00	4.00	8.00	28.00

KM# 307 2 QIRSH **Weight:** 2.8000 g. **Composition:** 0.8330 Silver .0750 oz. ASW **Note:** Mintname Misr.

Date	Mintage	F	VF	XF	Unc
AH1327/2H	250,000	5.00	12.50	28.00	90.00
AH1327/3H	300,000	5.00	12.50	28.00	90.00

KM# 308 5 QIRSH **Weight:** 7.0000 g. **Composition:** 0.8330 Silver .1875 oz. ASW **Note:** Mintname Misr.

Date	Mintage	F	VF	XF	Unc
AH1327/2-6H Proof	—	Value: 350			
Note: Above value for common date of proof					
AH1327/2H	574,000	10.00	30.00	60.00	150
AH1327/3H	2,400,000	5.00	12.50	30.00	70.00
AH1327/4H	1,351,000	6.00	15.00	35.00	85.00
AH1327/6H	7,400,000	4.00	10.00	20.00	55.00

KM# 309 10 QIRSH **Weight:** 14.0000 g. **Composition:** 0.8330 Silver .3749 oz. ASW **Note:** Mintname Misr.

Date	Mintage	F	VF	XF	Unc
AH1327/2-6H Proof	—	Value: 475			
Note: Above value for common date of proof					
AH1327/2H	300,000	20.00	30.00	60.00	200
AH1327/3H	1,300,000	8.00	15.00	30.00	115
AH1327/4H	300,000	10.00	25.00	40.00	200
AH1327/6H	4,212,000	6.00	12.50	25.00	100

KM# 310 20 QIRSH **Weight:** 28.0000 g. **Composition:** 0.8330 Silver .7499 oz. ASW **Note:** Mintname Misr.

Date	Mintage	F	VF	XF	Unc
AH1327/2-6H Proof	—	Value: 950			
Note: Above value for common date of proof					
AH1327/2H	75,000	25.00	45.00	160	500
AH1327/3H	600,000	12.50	25.00	75.00	325
AH1327/4H	100,000	20.00	35.00	90.00	425
AH1327/6H	875,000	11.50	22.50	60.00	300

BRITISH OCCUPATION

AH1333-1341/1914-1922AD

Hussein Kamil

As Sultan, AH1333-1336/1914-1917AD

OCCUPATION COINAGE

British

KM# 312 1/2 MILLIEME **Composition:** Bronze

Date	Mintage	F	VF	XF	Unc
AH1335-1917	4,000,000	1.35	3.50	7.50	25.00

KM# 313 MILLIEME **Composition:** Copper-Nickel

Date	Mintage	F	VF	XF	Unc
AH1335-1917	4,002,000	1.25	3.00	6.00	20.00
AH1335-1917H	12,000,000	0.40	1.00	3.00	12.00

KM# 314 2 MILLIEMES **Composition:** Copper-Nickel

Date	Mintage	F	VF	XF	Unc
AH1335-1916H	300,000	1.25	3.00	7.50	30.00
AH1335-1917	3,006,000	1.00	2.50	6.50	22.00
AH1335-1917H	9,000,000	0.40	1.00	3.00	14.00

KM# 315 5 MILLIEMES **Composition:** Copper-Nickel

Date	Mintage	F	VF	XF	Unc
AH1335-1916	3,000,000	2.00	5.00	10.00	25.00
AH1335-1916H	3,000,000	1.35	3.50	8.00	20.00
AH1335-1917	6,776,000	1.00	2.50	6.00	15.00
AH1335-1917H	37,000,000	0.60	1.50	2.50	8.00

KM# 316 10 MILLIEMES **Composition:** Copper-Nickel

Date	Mintage	F	VF	XF	Unc
AH1335-1916	1,006,999	2.00	5.00	10.00	35.00
AH1335-1916H	1,000,000	1.50	4.00	8.00	25.00
AH1335-1917	1,010,999	2.00	5.00	15.00	40.00
AH1335-1917H	6,000,000	0.75	2.00	4.00	15.00
AH1335-1917KN	4,000,000	1.25	3.00	6.00	20.00

KM# 317.1 2 PIASTRES **Weight:** 2.8000 g. **Composition:** 0.8330 Silver .0749 oz. ASW

Date	Mintage	F	VF	XF	Unc
AH1335-1916	2,505,000	1.50	4.00	10.00	30.00
AH1335-1917	4,461,000	1.00	2.50	5.00	20.00

KM# 317.2 2 PIASTRES **Weight:** 2.8000 g. **Composition:** 0.8330 Silver .0749 oz. ASW **Obverse:** Without inner circle **Reverse:** Without inner circle

Date	Mintage	F	VF	XF	Unc
AH1335-1917H	2,180,000	1.00	2.50	5.00	15.00

KM# 318.1 5 PIASTRES **Weight:** 7.0000 g. **Composition:** 0.8330 Silver .1874 oz. ASW

Date	Mintage	F	VF	XF	Unc
AH1335-1916	6,000,000	2.00	5.00	15.00	35.00
AH1335-1917	9,218,000	1.50	4.00	12.50	32.00

KM# 318.2 5 PIASTRES **Weight:** 7.0000 g. **Composition:** 0.8330 Silver .1874 oz. ASW **Obverse:** Without inner circle **Reverse:** Without inner circle

Date	Mintage	F	VF	XF	Unc
AH1335-1917H	5,036,000	2.00	5.00	15.00	45.00
AH1335-1917H Proof	—	Value: 325			

KM# 319 10 PIASTRES **Weight:** 14.0000 g. **Composition:** 0.8330 Silver .3749 oz. ASW

Date	Mintage	F	VF	XF	Unc
AH1335-1916	2,900,000	4.00	10.00	25.00	95.00
AH1335-1917	4,859,000	4.00	10.00	20.00	85.00

KM# 320 10 PIASTRES **Weight:** 14.0000 g. **Composition:** 0.8330 Silver .3749 oz. ASW **Obverse:** Without inner circle **Reverse:** Without inner circle

Date	Mintage	F	VF	XF	Unc
AH1335-1917H	2,000,000	4.00	10.00	28.00	100

KM# 321 20 PIASTRES **Weight:** 28.0000 g. **Composition:** 0.8330 Silver .7499 oz. ASW

Date	Mintage	F	VF	XF	Unc
AH1335-1916	1,500,000	6.50	16.00	35.00	160
AH1335-1917	840,000	6.50	16.00	35.00	180
AH1335-1917 Proof	—	Value: 750			

KM# 322 20 PIASTRES **Weight:** 28.0000 g. **Composition:** 0.8330 Silver .7499 oz. ASW **Obverse:** Without inner circle **Reverse:** Without inner circle

Date	Mintage	F	VF	XF	Unc
AH1335-1917H	250,000	20.00	40.00	70.00	300

KM# 324 100 PIASTRES **Weight:** 8.5000 g. **Composition:** 0.8750 Gold .2391 oz. AGW

Date	Mintage	F	VF	XF	Unc
AH1335-1916	10,000	50.00	90.00	140	265
AH1335-1916 Proof	—	Value: 1,500			

Note: Restrikes may exist

Fuad I

As Sultan, AH1335-1341/1917-1922AD

OCCUPATION COINAGE

British

KM# 325 2 PIASTRES **Weight:** 2.8000 g. **Composition:** 0.8330 Silver .0749 oz. ASW

Date	Mintage	F	VF	XF	Unc
AH1338-1920H	2,820,000	37.50	75.00	150	365

KM# 326 5 PIASTRES **Weight:** 7.0000 g. **Composition:** 0.8330 Silver .1874 oz. ASW

Date	Mintage	F	VF	XF	Unc
AH1338-1920H	1,000,000	17.50	35.00	80.00	340

KM# 327 10 PIASTRES **Weight:** 14.0000 g. **Composition:** 0.8330 Silver .3749 oz. ASW

Date	Mintage	F	VF	XF	Unc
AH1338-1920H	500,000	17.50	35.00	85.00	350

KM# 328 20 PIASTRES **Weight:** 28.0000 g. **Composition:** 0.8330 Silver .7499 oz. ASW

Date	Mintage	F	VF	XF	Unc
AH1338-1920H Rare	2	—	—	—	—

KINGDOM

AH1341-1372/1922-1952AD

Fuad I

As King, AH1341-1355/1922-1936AD

DECIMAL COINAGE

KM# 330 1/2 MILLIEME **Composition:** Bronze

Date	Mintage	F	VF	XF	Unc
AH1342-1924H	3,000,000	2.00	5.00	10.00	25.00
AH1342-1924H Proof	—	Value: 120			

KM# 343 1/2 MILLIEME **Composition:** Bronze

Date	Mintage	F	VF	XF	Unc
AH1348-1929BP	1,000,000	6.00	15.00	25.00	50.00
AH1351-1932H	1,000,000	3.00	7.50	15.00	30.00
AH1351-1932H Proof	—	Value: 160			

KM# 331 MILLIEME **Composition:** Bronze

Date	Mintage	F	VF	XF	Unc
AH1342-1924H	6,500,000	1.25	3.00	6.00	15.00

KM# 344 MILLIEME **Composition:** Bronze

Date	Mintage	F	VF	XF	Unc
AH1348-1929BP	4,500,000	1.50	4.00	8.00	20.00
AH1351-1932H	2,500,000	0.50	1.25	3.00	15.00
AH1351-1932H Proof	—	Value: 120			
AH1352-1933H	5,110,000	1.25	3.00	6.00	15.00
AH1354-1935H	18,000,000	0.20	0.50	2.00	8.00

KM# 332 2 MILLIEMES **Composition:** Copper-Nickel

Date	Mintage	F	VF	XF	Unc
AH1342-1924H	4,500,000	1.25	3.00	8.00	20.00
AH1342-1924H Proof	—	Value: 120			

KM# 345 2 MILLIEMES **Composition:** Copper-Nickel

Date	F	VF	XF	Unc
AH1348-1929BP	0.40	1.00	3.00	10.00

KM# 356 2-1/2 MILLIEMES **Composition:** Copper-Nickel

Date	Mintage	F	VF	XF	Unc
AH1352-1933	4,000,000	1.25	3.00	8.00	30.00

KM# 333 5 MILLIEMES **Composition:** Copper-Nickel

Date	Mintage	F	VF	XF	Unc
AH1342-1924	6,000,000	1.25	3.00	7.50	28.00

KM# 346 5 MILLIEMES **Composition:** Copper-Nickel

Date	Mintage	F	VF	XF	Unc
AH1348-1929BP	4,000,000	0.75	2.00	8.00	25.00
AH1352-1933H	3,000,000	1.50	4.00	12.00	35.00
AH1354-1935H	8,000,000	0.80	1.00	5.00	12.50
AH1354-1935H Proof	—	Value: 120			

KM# 334 10 MILLIEMES **Composition:** Copper-Nickel

Date	Mintage	F	VF	XF	Unc
AH1342-1924	2,000,000	2.00	5.00	15.00	50.00

KM# 347 10 MILLIEMES **Composition:** Copper-Nickel

Date	Mintage	F	VF	XF	Unc
AH1348-1929BP	1,500,000	1.35	3.50	10.00	38.00
AH1352-1933H	1,500,000	1.35	3.50	10.00	45.00
AH1354-1935H	4,000,000	0.75	2.00	7.50	20.00

KM# 335 2 PIASTRES **Weight:** 2.8000 g. **Composition:** 0.8330 Silver .0749 oz. ASW

Date	Mintage	F	VF	XF	Unc
AH1342-1923H	2,500,000	1.75	4.50	11.50	35.00

KM# 348 2 PIASTRES **Weight:** 2.8000 g. **Composition:** 0.8330 Silver .0749 oz. ASW

Date	Mintage	F	VF	XF	Unc
AH1348-1929BP	500,000	1.75	2.00	6.00	20.00

Note: Edge varieties exist

KM# 336 5 PIASTRES **Weight:** 7.0000 g. **Composition:** 0.8330 Silver .1874 oz. ASW

Date	Mintage	F	VF	XF	Unc
AH1341-1923	800,000	4.00	10.00	27.00	60.00
AH1341-1923H	1,800,000	2.50	6.00	25.00	60.00
AH1341-1923H Proof	—	Value: 250			

KM# 349 5 PIASTRES **Weight:** 7.0000 g. **Composition:** 0.8330 Silver .1874 oz. ASW

Date	Mintage	F	VF	XF	Unc
AH1348-1929BP	800,000	4.00	10.00	35.00	65.00
AH1352-1933	1,300,000	3.00	7.50	25.00	55.00
AH1352-1933 Proof	—	Value: 250			

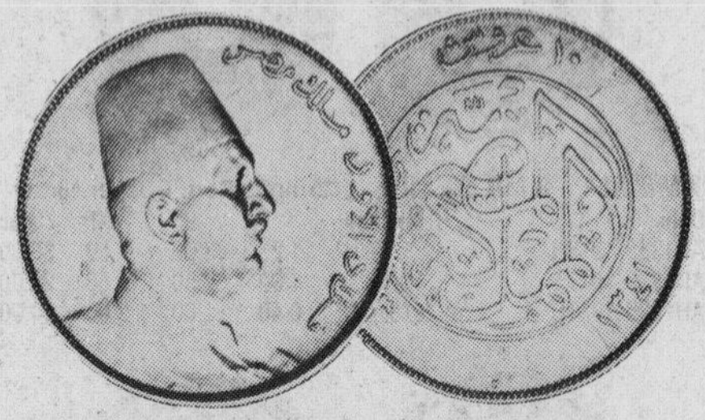

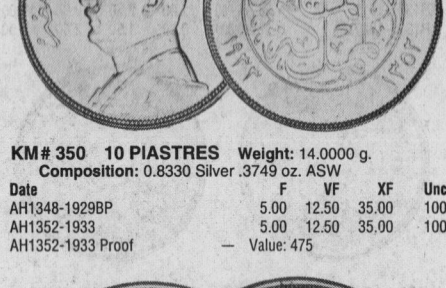

KM# 337 10 PIASTRES **Weight:** 14.0000 g. **Composition:** 0.8330 Silver .3749 oz. ASW

Date	Mintage	F	VF	XF	Unc
AH1341-1923	400,000	5.00	12.50	40.00	120
AH1341-1923H	1,000,000	5.00	12.50	40.00	120
AH1341-1923H Proof	—	Value: 450			

KM# 350 10 PIASTRES **Weight:** 14.0000 g. **Composition:** 0.8330 Silver .3749 oz. ASW

Date	F	VF	XF	Unc
AH1348-1929BP	5.00	12.50	35.00	100
AH1352-1933	5.00	12.50	35.00	100
AH1352-1933 Proof	—	Value: 475		

KM# 338 20 PIASTRES **Weight:** 28.0000 g. **Composition:** 0.8330 Silver .7499 oz. ASW

Date	Mintage	F	VF	XF	Unc
AH1341-1923	100,000	20.00	40.00	90.00	425
AH1341-1923H	50,000	20.00	40.00	90.00	425
AH1341-1923H Proof	—	Value: 875			

KM# 339 20 PIASTRES **Weight:** 1.7000 g. **Composition:** 0.8750 Gold .0478 oz. AGW

Date	Mintage	F	VF	XF	Unc
AH1341-1923	65,000	25.00	40.00	60.00	115

KM# 352 20 PIASTRES **Weight:** 28.0000 g. **Composition:** 0.8330 Silver .7499 oz. ASW

Date	Mintage	F	VF	XF	Unc
AH1348-1929BP	50,000	15.00	30.00	65.00	350
AH1352-1933	25,000	12.50	25.00	50.00	300
AH1352-1933 Proof	—	—	—	—	—

KM# 351 20 PIASTRES **Weight:** 1.7000 g. **Composition:** 0.8750 Gold .0478 oz. AGW **Obverse:** Bust left

Date	F	VF	XF	Unc
AH1348 Proof	—	—	—	—
AH1348-1929	25.00	40.00	55.00	110
AH1349-1930	25.00	40.00	55.00	110
AH1349-1930 Proof	—	—	—	—

KM# 340 50 PIASTRES **Weight:** 4.2500 g. **Composition:** 0.8750 Gold .1195 oz. AGW

Date	Mintage	F	VF	XF	Unc
AH1341-1923	18,000	40.00	70.00	90.00	145

KM# 353 50 PIASTRES **Weight:** 4.2500 g. **Composition:** 0.8750 Gold .1195 oz. AGW

Date	F	VF	XF	Unc
AH1348-1929	47.50	80.00	100	160
AH1348-1929 Proof	—	—	—	—
AH1349-1930	42.50	70.00	80.00	130
AH1349-1930 Proof	—	—	—	—

KM# 341 100 PIASTRES **Weight:** 8.5000 g. **Composition:** 0.8750 Gold .2391 oz. AGW

Date	Mintage	F	VF	XF	Unc
AH1340-1922	25,000	BV	115	135	245

KM# 354 100 PIASTRES **Weight:** 8.5000 g. **Composition:** 0.8750 Gold .2391 oz. AGW **Obverse:** Bust of Fuad I left

Date	F	VF	XF	Unc
AH1348-1929	BV	120	140	255
AH1349-1930	BV	115	135	245
AH1349-1930 Proof	—	—	—	—

KM# 342 500 PIASTRES **Weight:** 42.5000 g. **Composition:** 0.8750 Gold 1.1957 oz. AGW

Date	Mintage	F	VF	XF	Unc
AH1340-1922	1,800	—	—	800	1,400
AH1340-1922 Proof	—	Value: 1,500			

Note: Circulation coins were struck in both red and yellow gold

KM# 355 500 PIASTRES **Weight:** 42.5000 g. **Composition:** 0.8750 Gold 1.1957 oz. AGW

Date	F	VF	XF	Unc
AH1348-1929	—	—	675	1,250
AH1349-1930	—	—	675	1,250
AH1351-1932	—	—	675	1,250
AH1351-1932 Proof	—	Value: 1,450		

Farouk
AH1355-1372/1936-1952AD
DECIMAL COINAGE

KM# 357 1/2 MILLIEME **Composition:** Bronze

Date	Mintage	F	VF	XF	Unc
AH1357-1938	4,000,000	1.50	4.00	6.00	18.00
AH1357-1938 Proof	—	Value: 100			

KM# 358 MILLIEME **Composition:** Bronze

Date	Mintage	F	VF	XF	Unc
AH1357-1938	26,240,000	0.20	0.50	2.00	7.00
AH1357-1938 Proof	—	Value: 120			
AH1364-1945	10,000,000	1.25	3.00	10.00	50.00
AH1366-1947	—	1.25	3.00	10.00	50.00
AH1369-1950	5,000,000	0.40	1.00	3.00	10.00
AH1369-1950 Proof	—	Value: 85.00			

KM# 362 MILLIEME **Composition:** Copper-Nickel

Date	Mintage	F	VF	XF	Unc
AH1357-1938	3,500,000	1.00	2.50	5.00	15.00

KM# 359 2 MILLIEMES **Composition:** Copper-Nickel

Date	Mintage	F	VF	XF	Unc
AH1357-1938	2,500,000	1.50	4.00	10.00	25.00
AH1357-1938 Proof	—	Value: 140			

KM# 360 5 MILLIEMES **Composition:** Bronze

Date	F	VF	XF	Unc
AH1357-1938	0.40	1.00	3.00	10.00
AH1357-1938 Proof	—	Value: 65.00		
AH1362-1943	0.40	1.00	3.00	10.00

KM# 363 5 MILLIEMES **Composition:** Copper-Nickel

Date	Mintage	F	VF	XF	Unc
AH1357-1938	7,000,000	0.40	1.00	3.00	10.00
AH1357-1938 Proof	—	Value: 75.00			
AH1360-1941	11,500,000	0.20	0.50	2.50	8.00

KM# 361 10 MILLIEMES **Composition:** Bronze

Date	F	VF	XF	Unc
AH1357-1938	0.40	1.00	3.00	10.00
AH1357-1938 Proof	—	Value: 140		
AH1362-1943	—	0.75	3.00	10.00

KM# 364 10 MILLIEMES **Composition:** Copper-Nickel

Date	Mintage	F	VF	XF	Unc
AH1357-1938	3,500,000	0.40	1.00	3.00	12.50
AH1357-1938 Proof	—	Value: 85.00			
AH1360-1941	5,322,000	0.40	1.00	3.00	12.50

KM# 365 2 PIASTRES **Weight:** 2.8000 g. **Composition:** 0.8330 Silver .0749 oz. ASW

Date	Mintage	F	VF	XF	Unc
AH1356-1937	500,000	0.60	1.50	3.00	8.00
AH1356-1937 Proof	—	Value: 300			
AH1358-1939	500,000	1.50	4.00	10.00	75.00
AH1358-1939 Proof	—	Value: 200			
AH1361-1942	10,000,000	0.60	1.50	4.00	10.00

Note: Normal and flat rim varieties exist for AH1361 coins

KM# 369 2 PIASTRES **Weight:** 2.8000 g. **Composition:** 0.5000 Silver .0450 oz. ASW

Date	Mintage	F	VF	XF	Unc
AH1363-1944	32,000	0.40	1.00	2.00	4.50

KM# 366 5 PIASTRES **Weight:** 7.0000 g. **Composition:** 0.8330 Silver .1874 oz. ASW

Date	Mintage	F	VF	XF	Unc
AH1356-1937	—	1.25	3.00	6.00	15.00
AH1356-1937 Proof	—	Value: 275			
AH1358-1939	8,000,000	1.25	3.00	6.00	15.00
AH1358-1939 Proof	—	Value: 275			

KM# 367 10 PIASTRES **Weight:** 14.0000 g. **Composition:** 0.8330 Silver .3749 oz. ASW

Date	Mintage	F	VF	XF	Unc
AH1356-1937	2,800,000	3.00	7.50	10.00	32.00
AH1356-1937 Proof	—	Value: 375			
AH1358-1939	2,850,000	3.00	7.50	10.00	32.00
AH1358-1939 Proof	—	Value: 300			

KM# 368 20 PIASTRES **Weight:** 28.0000 g. **Composition:** 0.8330 Silver .7499 oz. ASW

Date	F	VF	XF	Unc
AH1356-1937	6.00	15.00	35.00	85.00
AH1356-1937 Proof	—	Value: 1,000		
AH1358-1939	6.00	15.00	35.00	85.00
AH1358-1939 Proof	—	Value: 1,200		

KM# 370 20 PIASTRES **Weight:** 1.7000 g. **Composition:** 0.8750 Gold .0478 oz. AGW **Subject:** Royal Wedding

Date	Mintage	F	VF	XF	Unc
AH1357-1938	20,000	—	28.00	40.00	85.00

KM# 371 50 PIASTRES **Weight:** 4.2500 g. **Composition:** 0.8750 Gold .1195 oz. AGW **Subject:** Royal Wedding

Date	Mintage	F	VF	XF	Unc
AH1357-1938	10,000	—	70.00	120	200

KM# 372 100 PIASTRES **Weight:** 8.5000 g. **Composition:** 0.8750 Gold .2391 oz. AGW **Subject:** Royal Wedding

Date	Mintage	F	VF	XF	Unc
AH1357-1938	5,000	—	125	165	285

Note: Circulation coins were struck in both red and yellow gold

KM# 373 500 PIASTRES **Weight:** 42.5000 g. **Composition:** 0.8750 Gold 1.1957 oz. AGW **Subject:** Royal Wedding

Date	F	VF	XF	Unc
AH1357-1938	—	—	1,250	2,000
AH1357-1938 Proof	—	Value: 2,250		

REPUBLIC
AH1373-1378/1953-1958AD
DECIMAL COINAGE

KM# 375 MILLIEME **Composition:** Aluminum-Bronze **Reverse:** Small sphinx with outlined base

Date	F	VF	XF	Unc
AH1373-1954	—	50.00	100	200
AH1374-1954	—	3.00	6.00	25.00
AH1374-1955	—	2.00	5.00	15.00
AH1375-1955	—	2.00	5.00	15.00
AH1375-1956	—	2.00	5.00	15.00

KM# 376 MILLIEME **Composition:** Aluminum-Bronze **Reverse:** Small sphinx without base outlined

Date	F	VF	XF	Unc
AH1373-1954	—	—	—	—
AH1374-1954	—	2.00	5.00	15.00
AH1374-1955	—	1.00	2.00	5.00
AH1375-1955	—	1.00	2.00	5.00
AH1375-1956	—	1.50	2.50	10.00
AH1376-1957	—	—	—	—

KM# 377 MILLIEME **Composition:** Aluminum-Bronze **Reverse:** Large sphinx

Date	F	VF	XF	Unc
AH1375-1956	—	0.50	1.00	4.00
AH1376-1957	—	0.75	1.50	5.00
AH1377-1958	—	0.75	1.50	5.00

KM# 378 5 MILLIEMES **Composition:** Aluminum-Bronze **Reverse:** Small sphinx with outlined base

Date	F	VF	XF	Unc
AH1373-1954	—	5.00	10.00	35.00
AH1374-1954	—	4.00	8.00	25.00
AH1374-1955	—	10.00	20.00	50.00
AH1375-1956	—	3.00	6.00	15.00

KM# 379 5 MILLIEMES **Composition:** Aluminum-Bronze **Reverse:** Large sphinx

Date	F	VF	XF	Unc
AH1376-1957	—	2.00	4.00	10.00
AH1377-1957	—	2.00	4.00	10.00
AH1377-1958	—	2.00	4.00	10.00

Thin *milliemes*

Thick *milliemes*

KM# 380 10 MILLIEMES **Composition:** Aluminum-Bronze **Reverse:** Small sphinx without base outlined

Date	F	VF	XF	Unc
AH1373-1954	—	5.00	10.00	25.00
Note: Thin milliemes				
AH1374-1954	—	4.00	8.00	20.00
AH1374-1955	—	3.00	6.00	15.00
Note: Thick milliemes				

KM# 381 10 MILLIEMES **Composition:** Aluminum-Bronze **Reverse:** Large sphinx

Date	F	VF	XF	Unc
AH1374-1955	—	50.00	85.00	150
AH1375-1956	—	3.00	6.00	15.00
AH1376-1957	—	2.00	5.00	12.00
AH1377-1958	—	2.00	5.00	12.00

KM# 382 5 PIASTRES **Weight:** 3.5000 g. **Composition:** 0.7200 Silver .0810 oz. ASW

Date	F	VF	XF	Unc
AH1375-1956	—	1.50	3.00	8.00
AH1376-1956	—	3.00	5.00	10.00
AH1376-1957	—	1.50	3.00	8.00

KM# 383 10 PIASTRES **Weight:** 7.0000 g. **Composition:** 0.6250 Silver .1406 oz. ASW

Date	Mintage	F	VF	XF	Unc
AH1374-1955	1,408,000	—	3.50	7.00	18.00

Note: Varieties in date sizes exist

KM# 383a 10 PIASTRES **Weight:** 7.0000 g. **Composition:** 0.7200 Silver .1620 oz. ASW

Date	F	VF	XF	Unc
AH1375-1956	—	3.50	7.00	15.00
AH1376-1957	—	3.50	6.00	12.00

KM# 384 20 PIASTRES **Weight:** 14.0000 g. **Composition:** 0.7200 Silver .3241 oz. ASW

Date	F	VF	XF	Unc
AH1375-1956	—	5.00	9.00	18.00

KM# 385 25 PIASTRES **Weight:** 17.5000 g. **Composition:** 0.7200 Silver .4051 oz. ASW **Subject:** Suez Canal Nationalization

Date	Mintage	F	VF	XF	Unc
AH1375-1956	258,000	—	6.00	10.00	20.00

KM# 389 25 PIASTRES **Weight:** 17.5000 g. **Composition:** 0.7200 Silver .4051 oz. ASW **Subject:** National Assembly Inauguration

Date	Mintage	F	VF	XF	Unc
AH1376-1957	246,000	—	6.00	9.00	17.00

KM# 386 50 PIASTRES **Weight:** 28.0000 g. **Composition:** 0.9000 Silver .8102 oz. ASW **Subject:** Evacuation of the British

Date	Mintage	F	VF	XF	Unc
AH1375-1956	250,000	—	7.50	13.50	22.00

KM# 387 POUND **Weight:** 8.5000 g. **Composition:** 0.8750 Gold .2391 oz. AGW **Subject:** 3rd and 5th Anniversaries of Revolution **Reverse:** Horse, chariot, and archer

Date	Mintage	F	VF	XF	Unc
AH1374-1955	16,000	—	—	125	200
AH1377-1957	10,000	—	—	140	220

Note: Struck in red and yellow gold

KM# 388 5 POUNDS **Weight:** 42.5000 g. **Composition:** 0.8750 Gold 1.1957 oz. AGW **Subject:** 3rd and 5th Anniversaries of Revolution **Reverse:** Horse, chariot, and archer

Date	F	VF	XF	Unc
AH1374-1955	—	—	650	1,250
AH1377-1957	—	—	675	1,300

Note: Struck in red and yellow gold

UNITED ARAB REPUBLIC
AH1378-1391/1958-1971AD

DECIMAL COINAGE

KM# 393 MILLIEME **Composition:** Aluminum-Bronze

Date	F	VF	XF	Unc
AH1380-1960	—	0.10	0.15	0.30
AH1386-1966 Proof	—	Value: 3.00		

KM# 403 2 MILLIEMES **Composition:** Aluminum-Bronze

Date	F	VF	XF	Unc
AH1381-1962	—	0.15	0.35	0.60
AH1386-1966 Proof	—	Value: 3.00		

KM# 394 5 MILLIEMES **Composition:** Aluminum-Bronze

Date	F	VF	XF	Unc
AH1380-1960	—	0.15	0.45	0.80
AH1386-1966 Proof	—	Value: 3.00		

KM# 410 5 MILLIEMES **Composition:** Aluminum

Date	F	VF	XF	Unc
AH1386-1967	—	0.15	0.40	0.65

KM# 395 10 MILLIEMES **Composition:** Aluminum-Bronze **Obverse:** Legend above denomination **Obv. Legend:** Misr

Date	Mintage	F	VF	XF	Unc
AH1377-1958	—	—	15.00	20.00	40.00
AH1380-1960	16,079,999	—	0.80	1.20	2.25
AH1386-1966 Proof	—	Value: 4.00			

KM# 396 10 MILLIEMES **Composition:** Aluminum-Bronze **Obverse:** Without Misr above denomination

Date	F	VF	XF	Unc
AH1377-1958	—	15.00	20.00	40.00

KM# 411 10 MILLIEMES **Composition:** Aluminum

Date	F	VF	XF	Unc
AH1386-1967	—	0.10	0.25	0.65

KM# 390 20 MILLIEMES **Composition:** Aluminum-Bronze **Subject:** Agriculture and Industrial Fair

Date	F	VF	XF	Unc
AH1378-1958	—	0.75	1.50	5.00

KM# 397 5 PIASTRES **Weight:** 3.5000 g. **Composition:** 0.7200 Silver .810 oz. ASW

Date	F	VF	XF	Unc
AH1380-1960	—	1.75	3.00	5.00
AH1386-1966	—	Value: 8.00		

KM# 404 5 PIASTRES **Weight:** 2.5000 g. **Composition:** 0.7200 Silver .0578 oz. ASW **Subject:** Diversion of the Nile **Reverse:** Nile River basin scene

Date	Mintage	F	VF	XF	Unc
AH1384-1964	500,000	—	1.25	2.50	4.00
AH1384-1964 Proof	2,000	Value: 8.00			

KM# 412 5 PIASTRES **Composition:** Copper-Nickel

Date	Mintage	F	VF	XF	Unc
AH1387-1967	10,800,000	—	0.50	0.75	1.50

Note: Edge varieties, narrow and gapped milling, exist

KM# 414 5 PIASTRES **Composition:** Copper-Nickel **Subject:** International Industrial Fair **Reverse:** Globe with cogwheel section around

Date	Mintage	F	VF	XF	Unc
AH1388-1968	500,000	—	0.75	1.00	2.50

KM# 417 5 PIASTRES Composition: Copper-Nickel
Subject: 50th Anniversary - International Labor Organization
Reverse: Hands holding open-ended wrenches

Date	Mintage	F	VF	XF	Unc
AH1389-1969	500,000	—	0.75	1.00	2.50

KM# 392 10 PIASTRES Weight: 7.0000 g.
Composition: 0.7200 Silver .1620 oz. ASW **Subject:** First Anniversary of U.A.R. Founding

Date	F	VF	XF	Unc
AH1378-1959	—	3.25	6.00	17.50

KM# 398 10 PIASTRES Weight: 7.0000 g.
Composition: 0.7200 Silver .1620 oz. ASW

Date	Mintage	F	VF	XF	Unc
AH1380-1960	500,000	—	3.00	4.50	7.50
AH1386-1966 Proof	—	Value: 12.50			

KM# 405 10 PIASTRES Weight: 5.0000 g.
Composition: 0.7200 Silver .1157 oz. ASW **Subject:** Diversion of the Nile **Reverse:** Nile River basin scene

Date	Mintage	F	VF	XF	Unc
AH1384-1964	500,000	—	2.50	3.50	5.50
AH1384-1964 Proof	2,000	Value: 12.50			

KM# 413 10 PIASTRES Composition: Copper-Nickel

Date	Mintage	F	VF	XF	Unc
AH1387-1967	13,200,000	—	0.60	0.90	2.00

KM# 419 10 PIASTRES Composition: Copper-Nickel
Subject: Cairo International Agricultural Fair

Date	Mintage	F	VF	XF	Unc
AH1389-1969	1,000,000	—	0.75	1.25	3.00

KM# 418 10 PIASTRES Composition: Copper-Nickel
Series: F.A.O.

Date	Mintage	F	VF	XF	Unc
ND(1970)	500,000	—	0.75	1.25	3.50

KM# 420 10 PIASTRES Composition: Copper-Nickel
Subject: 50 Years - Banque Misr

Date	Mintage	F	VF	XF	Unc
AH1390-1970	500,000	—	0.60	1.00	2.00

KM# 421.1 10 PIASTRES Composition: Copper-Nickel **Subject:** Cairo International Industrial Fair

Date	Mintage	F	VF	XF	Unc
AH1390-1970	500,000	—	0.60	1.00	3.25

KM# 421.2 10 PIASTRES Composition: Copper-Nickel **Subject:** Cairo International Industrial Fair **Obverse:** New shorter Arabic inscriptions

Date	Mintage	F	VF	XF	Unc
AH1391-1971	500,000	—	0.60	1.00	2.75

KM# 399 20 PIASTRES Weight: 14.0000 g.
Composition: 0.7200 Silver .3241 oz. ASW

Date	Mintage	F	VF	XF	Unc
AH1380-1960	400,000	—	6.00	10.00	25.00
AH1386-1966 Proof	—	Value: 32.50			

KM# 400 25 PIASTRES Weight: 17.5000 g.
Composition: 0.7200 Silver .4051 oz. ASW **Subject:** 3rd Year of National Assembly

Date	Mintage	F	VF	XF	Unc
AH1380-1960	250,000	—	5.00	8.00	18.00

KM# 406 25 PIASTRES Weight: 10.0000 g.
Composition: 0.7200 Silver .2315 oz. ASW **Subject:** Diversion of the Nile **Reverse:** Nile River basin scene

Date	Mintage	F	VF	XF	Unc
AH1384-1964	250,000	—	3.00	4.50	7.00
AH1384-1964 Proof	2,000	Value: 20.00			

KM# 422 25 PIASTRES Weight: 6.0000 g.
Composition: 0.7200 Silver .1388 oz. ASW **Subject:** President Nasser **Obverse:** Head of President Nasser right

Date	Mintage	F	VF	XF	Unc
AH1390-1970	700,000	—	2.50	4.00	6.50

KM# 407 50 PIASTRES Weight: 20.0000 g.
Composition: 0.7200 Silver .4630 oz. ASW **Subject:** Diversion of the Nile **Reverse:** Nile River basin scene

Date	Mintage	F	VF	XF	Unc
AH1384-1964	250,000	—	4.50	5.50	7.50
AH1384-1964 Proof	2,000	Value: 40.00			

KM# 423 50 PIASTRES Weight: 12.5000 g.
Composition: 0.7200 Silver .2893 oz. ASW **Subject:** President Nasser **Obverse:** Head of President Nasser right

Date	Mintage	F	VF	XF	Unc
AH1390-1970	400,000	—	3.00	5.00	7.50

KM# 391 1/2 POUND Weight: 4.2500 g. **Composition:** 0.8750 Gold .1195 oz. AGW **Subject:** U.A.R. Founding

Date	Mintage	F	VF	XF	Unc
AH1377-1958	30,000	—	—	—	185

KM# 401 POUND Weight: 8.5000 g. **Composition:** 0.8750 Gold .2391 oz. AGW **Reverse:** Aswan Dam

Date	Mintage	F	VF	XF	Unc
AH1379-1960	252,000	—	—	—	160

KM# 415 POUND **Weight:** 25.0000 g. **Composition:** 0.7200 Silver .5787 oz. ASW **Reverse:** Power station for Aswan Dam

Date	Mintage	F	VF	XF	Unc
AH1387-1968	100,000	—	5.00	6.00	8.00

KM# 424 POUND **Weight:** 25.0000 g. **Composition:** 0.7200 Silver .5787 oz. ASW **Subject:** 1000th Anniversary - Al Azhar Mosque **Reverse:** Al Azhar Mosque

Date	Mintage	F	VF	XF	Unc
AH1359-1361 - 1970-1972	100,000	—	5.50	7.00	10.00

KM# 425 POUND **Weight:** 25.0000 g. **Composition:** 0.7200 Silver .5787 oz. ASW **Subject:** President Nasser **Obverse:** Head of President Nasser right

Date	Mintage	F	VF	XF	Unc
AH1390-1970	400,000	—	5.00	6.00	8.50

KM# 426 POUND **Weight:** 8.0000 g. **Composition:** 0.8750 Gold .2251 oz. AGW **Subject:** President Nasser **Obverse:** Head of President Nasser right

Date	Mintage	F	VF	XF	Unc
AH1390-1970	10,000	—	—	—	140

KM# 402 5 POUNDS **Weight:** 42.5000 g. **Composition:** 0.8750 Gold 1.1957 oz. AGW **Reverse:** Aswan Dam

Date	Mintage	F	VF	XF	Unc
AH1379-1960	5,000	—	—	—	600

KM# 408 5 POUNDS **Weight:** 26.0000 g. **Composition:** 0.8750 Gold .7315 oz. AGW **Subject:** Diversion of the Nile **Reverse:** Nile River basin scene

Date	F	VF	XF	Unc
AH1384-1964	—	—	—	375

KM# 416 5 POUNDS **Weight:** 26.0000 g. **Composition:** 0.8750 Gold .7315 oz. AGW **Subject:** 1400th Anniversary of the Koran **Reverse:** Open Koran book above globe with radiant sun in back

Date	Mintage	F	VF	XF	Unc
AH1388-1968	10,000	—	—	—	335

KM# 427 5 POUNDS **Weight:** 26.0000 g. **Composition:** 0.8750 Gold .7315 oz. AGW **Subject:** 1000th Anniversary - Al Azhar Mosque **Reverse:** Al Azhar Mosque

Date	F	VF	XF	Unc
AH1390-1970	—	—	—	350

KM# 428 5 POUNDS **Weight:** 26.0000 g. **Composition:** 0.8750 Gold .7315 oz. AGW **Subject:** President Nasser **Obverse:** Head of President Nasser right

Date	Mintage	F	VF	XF	Unc
AH1390-1970	3,000	—	—	—	335

KM# 409 10 POUNDS **Weight:** 52.0000 g. **Composition:** 0.8750 Gold 1.4630 oz. AGW **Subject:** Diversion of the Nile **Reverse:** Nile River basin scene

Date	Mintage	F	VF	XF	Unc
AH1384-1964	2,000	—	—	—	675

ARAB REPUBLIC

AH1391- /1971- AD

DECIMAL COINAGE

KM# A423 MILLIEME **Composition:** Aluminum

Date	F	VF	XF	Unc
AH1392-1972	—	0.10	0.30	0.50

KM# A425 5 MILLIEMES **Composition:** Aluminum

Date	Mintage	F	VF	XF	Unc
AH1392-1972	16,000,000	—	0.20	0.50	2.50

KM# A424 5 MILLIEMES **Composition:** Aluminum **Obverse:** KM#A425 **Reverse:** KM#433 **Note:** Mule.

Date	F	VF	XF	Unc
AH1392-1972	—	10.00	20.00	45.00

KM# A433 5 MILLIEMES **Composition:** Aluminum **Obverse:** KM#433 **Reverse:** KM#A425 **Note:** Mule.

Date	F	VF	XF	Unc
AH1393-1973	—	10.00	20.00	45.00

KM# 434 5 MILLIEMES **Composition:** Brass **Obverse:** KM#432 **Reverse:** KM#445 **Note:** Mule

Date	F	VF	XF	Unc
AH1393-1973	—	5.00	10.00	20.00

KM# 432 5 MILLIEMES **Composition:** Brass

Date	F	VF	XF	Unc
AH1393-1973	—	0.10	0.15	0.30

KM# 433 5 MILLIEMES **Composition:** Aluminum **Series:** F.A.O.

Date	Mintage	F	VF	XF	Unc
AH1393-1973	10,000,000	—	0.10	0.20	0.35

KM# 445 5 MILLIEMES Composition: Brass **Series:** International Women's Year

Date	Mintage	F	VF	XF	Unc
AH1395-1975	10,000,000	—	0.10	0.15	0.30

KM# 462 5 MILLIEMES Composition: Brass **Series:** F.A.O.

Date	Mintage	F	VF	XF	Unc
AH1397-1977	5,000,000	—	0.10	0.20	0.50

KM# 463 5 MILLIEMES Composition: Brass **Subject:** 1971 Corrective Revolution

Date	Mintage	F	VF	XF	Unc
AH1397-1977	2,500,000	—	0.10	0.20	0.50
AH1399-1979	2,500,000	—	0.10	0.20	0.50

KM# A426 10 MILLIEMES Composition: Aluminum

Date	Mintage	F	VF	XF	Unc
AH1392-1972	20,000,000	—	0.50	2.00	6.00

Note: Two varieties of edge letterings exist

KM# 435 10 MILLIEMES Composition: Brass

Date	F	VF	XF	Unc
AH1393-1973	—	0.10	0.25	0.50
AH1396-1976	—	0.75	1.50	3.00

KM# 446 10 MILLIEMES Composition: Brass **Series:** F.A.O.

Date	Mintage	F	VF	XF	Unc
AH1395-1975	10,000,000	—	0.10	0.20	0.35

KM# 449 10 MILLIEMES Composition: Brass **Series:** F.A.O.

Date	Mintage	F	VF	XF	Unc
AH1396-1976	10,000,000	—	0.10	0.20	0.30

KM# 464 10 MILLIEMES Composition: Brass **Series:** F.A.O.

Date	Mintage	F	VF	XF	Unc
AH1397-1977	10,000,000	—	0.10	0.20	0.85

KM# 465 10 MILLIEMES Composition: Brass **Subject:** 1971 Corrective Revolution

Date	Mintage	F	VF	XF	Unc
AH1397-1977	2,500,000	—	0.10	0.20	0.65
AH1399-1979	2,500,000	—	0.20	0.40	1.00

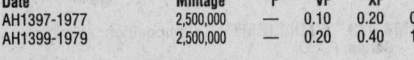

KM# 476 10 MILLIEMES Composition: Brass **Series:** F.A.O.

Date	Mintage	F	VF	XF	Unc
AH1398-1978	2,000,000	—	0.10	0.20	0.80

KM# 483 10 MILLIEMES Composition: Brass **Series:** International Year of the Child

Date	Mintage	F	VF	XF	Unc
AH1399-1979	2,000,000	—	0.10	0.20	0.65

KM# 498 10 MILLIEMES Composition: Aluminum-Bronze **Subject:** Sadat's Corrective Revolution

Date	Mintage	F	VF	XF	Unc
AH1400-1980	2,500,000	—	0.10	0.25	1.00

KM# 499 10 MILLIEMES Composition: Aluminum-Bronze **Series:** F.A.O.

Date	Mintage	F	VF	XF	Unc
AH1400-1980	2,000,000	—	0.10	0.20	0.60

KM# 553.1 PIASTRE Composition: Aluminum-Bronze **Obverse:** Christian date left of denomination

Date	F	VF	XF	Unc
AH1404-1984	—	—	0.15	0.35

KM# 553.2 PIASTRE Composition: Aluminum-Bronze **Obverse:** Islamic date left of denomination

Date	F	VF	XF	Unc
AH1404-1984	—	—	0.15	0.35

KM# 500 2 PIASTRES Composition: Aluminum-Bronze

Date	F	VF	XF	Unc
AH1400-1980	—	0.20	0.30	0.60

KM# 554.1 2 PIASTRES Composition: Aluminum-Bronze **Obverse:** Christian date left of denomination

Date	F	VF	XF	Unc
AH1404-1984	—	—	0.20	0.50

KM# 554.2 2 PIASTRES Composition: Aluminum-Bronze **Obverse:** Islamic date left of denomination

Date	F	VF	XF	Unc
AH1404-1984	—	—	0.20	0.50

KM# A427 5 PIASTRES Composition: Copper-Nickel **Subject:** 25th Anniversary of UNICEF

Date	Mintage	F	VF	XF	Unc
AH1392-1972	500,000	—	0.75	1.00	3.00

Note: Error in spelling "UNICFE".

KM# A428 5 PIASTRES Composition: Copper-Nickel **Reverse:** Islamic falcon

Date	F	VF	XF	Unc
AH1392-1972	—	0.50	0.75	2.00

KM# 436 5 PIASTRES Composition: Copper-Nickel **Subject:** Cairo State Fair

Date	Mintage	F	VF	XF	Unc
AH1393-1973	500,000	—	0.60	0.75	2.25

KM# 437 5 PIASTRES Composition: Copper-Nickel **Subject:** 75th Anniversary - National Bank of Egypt **Reverse:** Bank building in front of globe at left

Date	Mintage	F	VF	XF	Unc
AH1393-1973	1,000,000	—	0.60	0.75	2.00

KM# A441 5 PIASTRES **Composition:** Copper-Nickel **Subject:** First Anniversary - October War **Reverse:** Soldier with gun facing right

Date	Mintage	F	VF	XF	Unc
AH1394-1974	2,000,000	—	0.60	0.75	2.00

KM# 447 5 PIASTRES **Composition:** Copper-Nickel **Series:** International Women's Year **Reverse:** Bust of Nefertiti right, sheaf of grain at left

Date	Mintage	F	VF	XF	Unc
AH1395-1975	2,000,000	—	0.50	0.65	1.25

KM# 451 5 PIASTRES **Composition:** Copper-Nickel **Subject:** 1976 Cairo Trade Fair

Date	Mintage	F	VF	XF	Unc
AH1396-1976	500,000	—	0.60	0.75	2.00

KM# 450 5 PIASTRES **Composition:** Copper-Nickel **Obverse:** KM#451 **Reverse:** KM#A428 **Note:** Mule

Date	F	VF	XF	Unc
AH1396-1976	—	5.00	10.00	20.00

KM# 466 5 PIASTRES **Composition:** Copper-Nickel **Subject:** 1971 Corrective Revolution

Date	Mintage	F	VF	XF	Unc
AH1397-1977	1,000,000	—	0.50	0.60	1.50
AH1399-1979	—	—	0.50	0.60	1.25

KM# 467 5 PIASTRES **Composition:** Copper-Nickel **Subject:** 50th Anniversary - Textile Industry

Date	Mintage	F	VF	XF	Unc
AH1397-1977	1,000,000	—	0.50	0.75	1.65

KM# 468 5 PIASTRES **Composition:** Copper-Nickel **Series:** F.A.O.

Date	F	VF	XF	Unc
AH1397-1977	—	0.50	0.75	1.65

Note: Edge varieties exist

KM# 477 5 PIASTRES **Composition:** Copper-Nickel **Subject:** Portland Cement

Date	Mintage	F	VF	XF	Unc
AH1398-1978	500,000	—	0.50	0.75	1.65

KM# 478 5 PIASTRES **Composition:** Copper-Nickel **Series:** F.A.O.

Date	Mintage	F	VF	XF	Unc
AH1398-1978	1,000,000	—	0.50	0.75	1.65

KM# 484 5 PIASTRES **Composition:** Copper-Nickel **Series:** International Year of the Child

Date	Mintage	F	VF	XF	Unc
AH1399-1979	1,000,000	—	0.50	0.75	1.65

KM# 501 5 PIASTRES **Composition:** Copper-Nickel **Subject:** Applied Professions

Date	Mintage	F	VF	XF	Unc
AH1400-1980	500,000	—	0.50	0.75	1.35

KM# 502 5 PIASTRES **Composition:** Copper-Nickel **Subject:** Sadat's Corrective Revolution of May 15, 1971 **Reverse:** Raised clenched fist holding stalk of grain

Date	Mintage	F	VF	XF	Unc
AH1400-1980	1,000,000	—	0.50	0.75	1.75

KM# 555.1 5 PIASTRES **Composition:** Aluminum-Bronze **Obverse:** Christian date left of denomination

Date	F	VF	XF	Unc
AH1404-1984	—	—	0.25	0.75

Note: Varieties exist with wide and narrow rims

KM# 555.2 5 PIASTRES **Composition:** Aluminum-Bronze **Obverse:** Islamic date left of denomination

Date	F	VF	XF	Unc
AH1404-1984	—	—	0.25	0.75

KM# 622.1 5 PIASTRES **Composition:** Aluminum-Bronze **Obverse:** Denomination not shaded

Date	F	VF	XF	Unc
AH1404-1984	—	—	0.25	0.85

KM# 622.2 5 PIASTRES **Composition:** Aluminum-Bronze **Obverse:** Denomination shaded

Date	F	VF	XF	Unc
AH1404-1984	—	—	0.25	0.85

KM# 731 5 PIASTRES **Composition:** Brass **Reverse:** Decorated vase

Date	F	VF	XF	Unc
AH1413-1992	—	—	—	0.85

KM# 429 10 PIASTRES **Composition:** Copper-Nickel **Subject:** Cairo International Fair

Date	Mintage	F	VF	XF	Unc
AH1392-1972	500,000	—	0.60	1.00	2.50

KM# 430 10 PIASTRES **Composition:** Copper-Nickel **Reverse:** Islamic falcon

Date	F	VF	XF	Unc
AH1392-1972	—	0.60	1.00	2.50

KM# 431 10 PIASTRES **Composition:** Copper-Nickel **Obverse:** KM#452 **Reverse:** KM#430 **Note:** Mule.

Date	F	VF	XF	Unc
AH1392-1972	—	5.50	12.50	27.50

Note: Wide and narrow inscriptions exist for obverse

KM# 442 10 PIASTRES **Composition:** Copper-Nickel **Subject:** First Anniversary - October War

Date	Mintage	F	VF	XF	Unc
AH1394-1974	2,000,000	—	0.60	1.00	3.50

KM# 448 10 PIASTRES **Composition:** Copper-Nickel
Series: F.A.O.

Date	Mintage	F	VF	XF	Unc
AH1395-1975	2,000,000	—	0.60	1.00	3.50

KM# 452 10 PIASTRES **Composition:** Copper-Nickel
Subject: Reopening of the Suez Canal

Date	Mintage	F	VF	XF	Unc
AH1396-1976	5,000,000	—	0.60	1.00	3.50

Note: Wide and narrow inscriptions exist for the obverse

KM# 469 10 PIASTRES **Composition:** Copper-Nickel
Series: F.A.O.

Date	Mintage	F	VF	XF	Unc
AH1397-1977	1,000,000	—	0.60	1.00	2.25

KM# 470 10 PIASTRES **Composition:** Copper-Nickel
Subject: 1971 Corrective Revolution

Date	Mintage	F	VF	XF	Unc
AH1397-1977	1,000,000	—	0.50	0.85	2.50
AH1399-1979	1,000,000	—	0.50	0.85	2.50

KM# 471 10 PIASTRES **Composition:** Copper-Nickel
Subject: 20th Anniversary - Economic Union

Date	Mintage	F	VF	XF	Unc
AH1397-1977	1,000,000	—	0.50	0.85	2.25

KM# 479 10 PIASTRES **Composition:** Copper-Nickel
Subject: Cairo International Fair

Date	F	VF	XF	Unc
AH1398-1978	—	0.50	0.85	2.75

KM# 485 10 PIASTRES **Composition:** Copper-Nickel
Subject: 25th Anniversary of Abbasia Mint

Date	Mintage	F	VF	XF	Unc
AH1399-1979	1,000,000	—	0.50	0.85	2.25

KM# 486 10 PIASTRES **Composition:** Copper-Nickel
Subject: National Education Day

Date	Mintage	F	VF	XF	Unc
AH1399-1979	1,000,000	—	0.50	0.85	2.25

KM# 503 10 PIASTRES **Composition:** Copper-Nickel
Subject: Doctor's Day **Reverse:** Seated Egyptian healer with staff left

Date	Mintage	F	VF	XF	Unc
AH1400-1980	1,000,000	—	0.50	0.85	2.50

KM# 504 10 PIASTRES **Composition:** Copper-Nickel
Subject: Egyptian-Israeli Peace Treaty **Reverse:** Anwar Sadat facing left at right, dove of peace, hand with quill signing treaty

Date	Mintage	F	VF	XF	Unc
AH1400-1980	1,000,000	—	1.00	2.00	3.50

KM# 505 10 PIASTRES **Composition:** Copper-Nickel
Series: F.A.O.

Date	Mintage	F	VF	XF	Unc
AH1400-1980	1,000,000	—	0.50	0.85	2.25

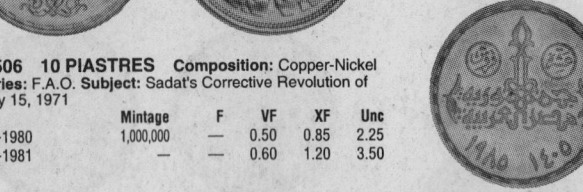

KM# 506 10 PIASTRES **Composition:** Copper-Nickel
Series: F.A.O. **Subject:** Sadat's Corrective Revolution of May 15, 1971

Date	Mintage	F	VF	XF	Unc
AH1400-1980	1,000,000	—	0.50	0.85	2.25
AH1401-1981	—	—	0.60	1.20	3.50

KM# 520 10 PIASTRES **Composition:** Copper-Nickel
Subject: Scientist's Day

Date	F	VF	XF	Unc
AH1401-1981	—	0.50	0.85	2.25

KM# 521 10 PIASTRES **Composition:** Copper-Nickel
Subject: 25th Anniversary - Trade Unions

Date	F	VF	XF	Unc
AH1402-1981	—	1.00	2.00	3.50

KM# 599 10 PIASTRES **Composition:** Copper-Nickel
Subject: 50th Anniversary of Egyptian Products Co.

Date	F	VF	XF	Unc
AH1402-1982	—	0.50	0.85	2.25

KM# 556 10 PIASTRES **Composition:** Copper-Nickel
Subject: Circulation Coinage

Date	F	VF	XF	Unc
AH1404-1984	—	—	0.50	0.85

KM# 570 10 PIASTRES **Composition:** Copper-Nickel
Subject: 25th Anniversary - National Planning Institute

Date	Mintage	F	VF	XF	Unc
AH1405-1985	100,000	—	—	—	1.75

KM# 573 10 PIASTRES **Composition:** Copper-Nickel
Subject: 60th Anniversary - Egyptian Parliament

Date	Mintage	F	VF	XF	Unc
AH1405-1985	250,000	—	—	—	1.75

KM# 675 10 PIASTRES Composition: Copper-Nickel
Subject: 1973 October War

Date	Mintage	F	VF	XF	Unc
AH1410-1989	250,000	—	—	—	1.75

KM# 732 10 PIASTRES Composition: Brass

Date	F	VF	XF	Unc
AH1413-1992	—	—	—	1.25

KM# 507 20 PIASTRES Composition: C· pper-Nickel

Date	F	VF	XF	Unc
AH1400-1980	—	0.75	1.00	2.35

KM# 557 20 PIASTRES Composition: Copper-Nickel
Subject: Circulation Coinage

Date	F	VF	XF	Unc
AH1404-1984	—	—	0.70	1.65

KM# 596 20 PIASTRES Composition: Copper-Nickel
Subject: 25th Anniversary - Cairo International Airport

Date	Mintage	F	VF	XF	Unc
AH1405-1985	50,000	—	—	—	2.25

KM# 597 20 PIASTRES Composition: Copper-Nickel
Subject: Professions

Date	Mintage	F	VF	XF	Unc
AH1406-1985	100,000	—	—	—	2.50

KM# 606 20 PIASTRES Composition: Copper-Nickel
Subject: Soldiers

Date	Mintage	F	VF	XF	Unc
AH1406-1986	50,000	—	—	—	2.50

KM# 607 20 PIASTRES Composition: Copper-Nickel
Subject: Census

Date	Mintage	F	VF	XF	Unc
AH1407-1986	500,000	—	—	—	2.25

KM# 652 20 PIASTRES Composition: Copper-Nickel
Subject: Investment Bank

Date	Mintage	F	VF	XF	Unc
AH1407-1987	250,000	—	—	—	2.50

KM# 646 20 PIASTRES Composition: Copper-Nickel
Subject: Police Day

Date	Mintage	F	VF	XF	Unc
AH1408-1988	250,000	—	—	—	2.75

KM# 650 20 PIASTRES Composition: Copper-Nickel
Subject: Dedication of Cairo Opera House

Date	Mintage	F	VF	XF	Unc
AH1409-1988	250,000	—	—	—	2.50

KM# 676 20 PIASTRES Composition: Copper-Nickel
Subject: 1973 October War

Date	Mintage	F	VF	XF	Unc
AH1410-1989	250,000	—	—	—	2.50

KM# 685 20 PIASTRES Composition: Copper-Nickel
Subject: National Health Insurance

Date	Mintage	F	VF	XF	Unc
AH1409-1989	250,000	—	—	—	2.50

KM# 690 20 PIASTRES Composition: Copper-Nickel
Subject: Cairo Subway

Date	Mintage	F	VF	XF	Unc
AH1409-1989	250,000	—	—	—	2.75

KM# 733 20 PIASTRES Composition: Copper-Nickel
Subject: Mosque

Date	F	VF	XF	Unc
AH1413-1992	—	—	—	2.50

KM# 438 25 PIASTRES Weight: 6.0000 g. **Composition:** 0.7200 Silver .1388 oz. ASW **Subject:** 75th Anniversary - National Bank of Egypt **Reverse:** National Bank building at right, globe at left in back

Date	Mintage	F	VF	XF	Unc
AH1393-1973	100,000	—	4.00	6.00	9.00

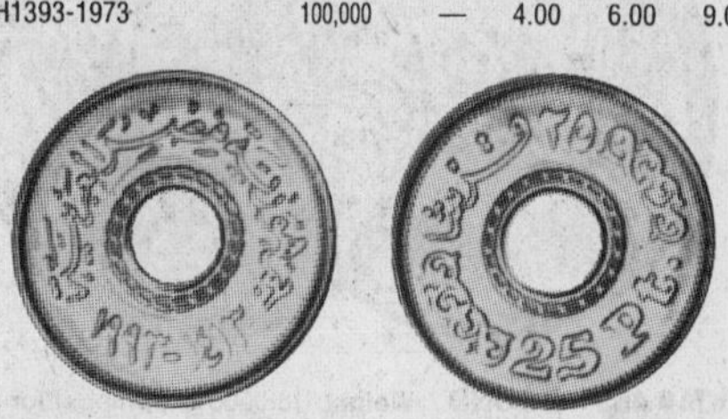

KM# 734 25 PIASTRES Composition: Copper-Nickel

Date	F	VF	XF	Unc
AH1413-1993	—	—	—	2.75

KM# 834 1/2 POUND Weight: 4.0000 g. **Composition:** 0.8750 Gold .1125 oz. AGW **Subject:** El Akkad **Obverse:** Legend and vase **Reverse:** Portrait

Date	Mintage	F	VF	XF	Unc
AH1413-1992	600	—	—	—	250

KM# 809 1/2 POUND Weight: 4.0000 g. **Composition:** 0.8750 Gold .1125 oz. AGW **Subject:** 20th Anniversary - October War **Obverse:** Smoking chimney text **Reverse:** Soldier with flag

Date	F	VF	XF	Unc
AH1414-1993	—	—	—	250

KM# 760 1/2 POUND Weight: 4.0000 g. **Composition:** 0.8750 Gold .1125 oz. AGW **Subject:** Salah El Din El-Ayubi **Obverse:** Denomination **Reverse:** Portrait

Date	Mintage	F	VF	XF	Unc
AH1414-1994	500	—	—	—	250

KM# 439 POUND **Weight:** 25.0000 g. **Composition:** 0.7200 Silver .5787 oz. ASW **Series:** F.A.O. **Reverse:** Aswan Dam

Date	Mintage	F	VF	XF	Unc
AH1393-1973	50,000	—	5.00	6.00	9.00

KM# 440 POUND **Weight:** 8.0000 g. **Composition:** 0.8750 Gold .2250 oz. AGW **Subject:** 75th Anniversary - National Bank of Egypt **Reverse:** National Bank of Egypt building

Date	Mintage	F	VF	XF	Unc
AH1393-1973	7,000	—	—	—	125

KM# 443 POUND **Weight:** 15.0000 g. **Composition:** 0.7200 Silver .3472 oz. ASW **Subject:** First Anniversary - October War

Date	Mintage	F	VF	XF	Unc
AH1394-1974	50,000	—	—	—	7.50

KM# 453 POUND **Weight:** 15.0000 g. **Composition:** 0.7200 Silver .3472 oz. ASW **Series:** F.A.O.

Date	Mintage	F	VF	XF	Unc
AH1396-1976	50,000	—	—	—	7.50

KM# 454 POUND **Weight:** 15.0000 g. **Composition:** 0.7200 Silver .3472 oz. ASW **Subject:** Reopening of Suez Canal

Date	Mintage	F	VF	XF	Unc
AH1396-1976	250,000	—	—	—	7.50

KM# 455 POUND **Weight:** 15.0000 g. **Composition:** 0.7200 Silver .3472 oz. ASW **Reverse:** Om Kalsoum right

Date	Mintage	F	VF	XF	Unc
AH1396-1976	250,000	—	—	—	7.50

KM# 456 POUND **Weight:** 8.0000 g. **Composition:** 0.8750 Gold .2250 oz. AGW **Reverse:** Om Kalsoum right

Date	Mintage	F	VF	XF	Unc
AH1396-1976	5,000	—	—	—	150

KM# 457 POUND **Weight:** 15.0000 g. **Composition:** 0.7200 Silver .3472 oz. ASW **Reverse:** Bust of King Faisal half right

Date	Mintage	F	VF	XF	Unc
AH1396-1976	100,000	—	—	—	7.50

KM# 458 POUND **Weight:** 8.0000 g. **Composition:** 0.8750 Gold .2250 oz. AGW **Reverse:** Bust of King Faisal half right

Date	Mintage	F	VF	XF	Unc
AH1396-1976	8,000	—	—	—	145

KM# 472 POUND **Weight:** 15.0000 g. **Composition:** 0.7200 Silver .3472 oz. ASW **Series:** F.A.O.

Date	Mintage	F	VF	XF	Unc
AH1397-1977	50,000	—	—	—	7.50

KM# 473 POUND **Weight:** 15.0000 g. **Composition:** 0.7200 Silver .3472 oz. ASW **Subject:** 1971 Corrective Revolution

Date	Mintage	F	VF	XF	Unc
AH1397-1977	50,000	—	—	—	7.50
AH1399-1979	49,000	—	—	—	7.50
AH1399-1979 Proof	1,500	Value: 11.50			

KM# 474 POUND **Weight:** 15.0000 g. **Composition:** 0.7200 Silver .3472 oz. ASW **Subject:** 20th Anniversary - Economic Union

Date	Mintage	F	VF	XF	Unc
AH1397-1977	50,000	—	—	—	7.50

KM# 475 POUND **Weight:** 8.0000 g. **Composition:** 0.8750 Gold .2250 oz. AGW **Subject:** 20th Anniversary - Economic Union

Date	Mintage	F	VF	XF	Unc
AH1397-1977	5,000	—	—	—	150

KM# 480 POUND **Weight:** 15.0000 g. **Composition:** 0.7200 Silver .3472 oz. ASW **Subject:** Portland Cement

Date	Mintage	F	VF	XF	Unc
AH1398-1978	50,000	—	—	—	7.50

KM# 481 POUND **Weight:** 15.0000 g. **Composition:** 0.7200 Silver .3472 oz. ASW **Subject:** 25th Anniversary - Ain Shams University

Date	Mintage	F	VF	XF	Unc
AH1398-1978	50,000	—	—	—	7.50

KM# 482 POUND **Weight:** 15.0000 g. **Composition:** 0.7200 Silver .3472 oz. ASW **Series:** F.A.O.

Date	Mintage	F	VF	XF	Unc
AH1398-1978	50,000	—	—	—	7.50

KM# 488 POUND **Weight:** 15.0000 g. **Composition:** 0.7200 Silver .3472 oz. ASW **Subject:** 25th Anniversary - Abbasia Mint

Date	Mintage	F	VF	XF	Unc
AH1399-1979	23,000	—	—	—	7.50
AH1399-1979 Proof	2,000	Value: 10.00			

KM# 489 POUND **Weight:** 15.0000 g. **Composition:** 0.7200 Silver .3472 oz. ASW **Series:** F.A.O. and I.Y.C.

Date	Mintage	F	VF	XF	Unc
AH1399-1979	48,000	—	—	—	7.50
AH1399-1979 Proof	2,500	Value: 10.00			

KM# 490 POUND **Weight:** 15.0000 g. **Composition:** 0.7200 Silver .3472 oz. ASW **Subject:** National Education Day

Date	Mintage	F	VF	XF	Unc
AH1399-1979	98,000	—	—	—	7.50
AH1399-1979 Proof	2,000	Value: 10.00			

KM# 491 POUND **Weight:** 15.0000 g. **Composition:** 0.7200 Silver .3472 oz. ASW **Subject:** 100th Anniversary - Bank of Land Reform

Date	Mintage	F	VF	XF	Unc
AH1399-1979	98,000	—	—	—	7.50
AH1399-1979 Proof	2,000	Value: 10.00			

KM# 492 POUND **Weight:** 8.0000 g. **Composition:** 0.8750 Gold .2250 oz. AGW **Subject:** 100th Anniversary - Bank of Land Reform

Date	Mintage	F	VF	XF	Unc
AH1399-1979	4,200	—	—	—	145
AH1399-1979 Proof	800	Value: 225			

KM# 493 POUND **Weight:** 15.0000 g. **Composition:** 0.7200 Silver .3472 oz. ASW **Subject:** 1400th Anniversary - Mohammed's Flight

Date	Mintage	F	VF	XF	Unc
AH1400-1979	97,000	—	—	—	7.50
AH1400-1979 Proof	3,000	Value: 10.00			

KM# 494 POUND **Weight:** 8.0000 g. **Composition:** 0.8750 Gold .2250 oz. AGW **Subject:** 1400th Anniversary - Mohammed's Flight

Date	Mintage	F	VF	XF	Unc
AH1400-1979	2,000	—	—	—	150
AH1400-1979 Proof	2,000	Value: 200			

KM# 508 POUND **Weight:** 15.0000 g. **Composition:** 0.7200 Silver .3472 oz. ASW **Subject:** Egyptian-Israeli Peace Treaty **Reverse:** Head of Anwar Sadat at right facing left with dove of peace at left

Date	Mintage	F	VF	XF	Unc
AH1400-1980	95,000	—	—	—	7.50
AH1400-1980	5,000	Value: 11.50			

KM# 509 POUND **Weight:** 8.0000 g. **Composition:** 0.8750 Gold .2250 oz. AGW **Subject:** Egyptian-Israeli Peace Treaty **Reverse:** Head of Anwar Sadat left with dove of peace at right

Date	Mintage	F	VF	XF	Unc
AH1400-1980	9,500	—	—	—	110
AH1400-1980 Proof	500	Value: 185			

KM# 510 POUND **Weight:** 15.0000 g. **Composition:** 0.7200 Silver .3472 oz. ASW **Subject:** Applied Professions in Egypt **Reverse:** Different professions depicted

Date	Mintage	F	VF	XF	Unc
AH1400-1980	22,000	—	—	—	6.50
AH1400-1980 Proof	3,000	Value: 9.00			

KM# 511 POUND **Weight:** 15.0000 g. **Composition:** 0.7200 Silver .3472 oz. ASW **Subject:** Doctor's Day **Reverse:** Seated healer with staff facing left

Date	Mintage	F	VF	XF	Unc
AH1400-1980	97,000	—	—	—	6.50
AH1400-1980 Proof	3,000	Value: 9.00			

KM# 512 POUND **Weight:** 8.0000 g. **Composition:** 0.8750 Gold .2250 oz. AGW **Subject:** Doctor's Day **Reverse:** Seated healer with staff facing left

Date	Mintage	F	VF	XF	Unc
AH1400-1980 Proof	5,000	Value: 185			

KM# 513 POUND **Weight:** 15.0000 g. **Composition:** 0.7200 Silver .3472 oz. ASW **Series:** F.A.O.

Date	Mintage	F	VF	XF	Unc
AH1400-1980	97,000	—	—	—	6.50
AH1400-1980 Proof	3,000	Value: 9.00			

KM# 514 POUND **Weight:** 15.0000 g. **Composition:** 0.7200 Silver .3472 oz. ASW **Subject:** Sadat's Corrective Revolution of May 15, 1971 **Reverse:** Raised clenched fist holding grain sprig

Date	Mintage	F	VF	XF	Unc
AH1400-1980	47,000	—	—	—	8.00
AH1400-1980 Proof	3,000	Value: 14.00			

KM# 515 POUND **Weight:** 15.0000 g. **Composition:** 0.7200 Silver .3472 oz. ASW **Reverse:** Cairo University Law facility

Date	Mintage	F	VF	XF	Unc
AH1400-1980	47,000	—	—	—	8.00
AH1400-1980 Proof	3,000	Value: 14.00			

KM# 516 POUND **Weight:** 8.0000 g. **Composition:** 0.8750 Gold .2250 oz. AGW **Reverse:** Cairo University Law facility

Date	Mintage	F	VF	XF	Unc
AH1400-1980	2,000	—	—	—	150
AH1400-1980 Proof	—	Value: 225			

KM# 522 POUND **Weight:** 15.0000 g. **Composition:** 0.7200 Silver .3472 oz. ASW **Subject:** Scientist's Day

Date	Mintage	F	VF	XF	Unc
AH1401-1981	25,000	—	—	—	9.00

KM# 523 POUND **Weight:** 15.0000 g. **Composition:** 0.7200 Silver .3472 oz. ASW **Series:** World Food Day

Date	Mintage	F	VF	XF	Unc
AH1401-1981	50,000	—	—	—	7.50
AH1401-1981 Proof	1,500	Value: 16.00			

KM# 524 POUND **Weight:** 15.0000 g. **Composition:** 0.7200 Silver .3472 oz. ASW **Subject:** 3rd Anniversary - Suez Canal Reopening

Date	Mintage	F	VF	XF	Unc
AH1401-1981	50,000	—	—	—	9.00
AH1401-1981 Proof	2,000	Value: 13.50			

KM# 525 POUND **Weight:** 8.0000 g. **Composition:** 0.8750 Gold .2250 oz. AGW **Subject:** 3rd Anniversary - Suez Canal Reopening

Date	Mintage	F	VF	XF	Unc
AH1401-1981 Proof	150	Value: 250			

KM# 528 POUND **Weight:** 15.0000 g. **Composition:** 0.7200 Silver .3472 oz. ASW **Subject:** 25th Anniversary - Nationalization of Suez Canal

Date	Mintage	F	VF	XF	Unc
AH1401-1981	25,000	—	—	—	10.00
AH1401-1981 Proof	1,500	Value: 25.00			

KM# 529 POUND **Weight:** 8.0000 g. **Composition:** 0.8750 Gold .2250 oz. AGW **Subject:** 25th Anniversary - Nationalization of Suez Canal

Date	Mintage	F	VF	XF	Unc
AH1401-1981	3,000	—	—	—	175

KM# 532 POUND **Weight:** 15.0000 g. **Composition:** 0.7200 Silver .3472 oz. ASW **Series:** F.A.O.

Date	Mintage	F	VF	XF	Unc
AH1401-1981	50,000	—	—	—	7.50

KM# 526 POUND **Weight:** 15.0000 g. **Composition:** 0.7200 Silver .3472 oz. ASW **Subject:** 25th Anniversary - Egyptian Industry

Date	Mintage	F	VF	XF	Unc
AH1402-1981	25,000	—	—	—	8.50

KM# 527 POUND **Weight:** 15.0000 g. **Composition:** 0.7200 Silver .3472 oz. ASW **Subject:** 25th Anniversary - Trade Unions

Date	Mintage	F	VF	XF	Unc
AH1402-1981	25,000	—	—	—	8.50

KM# 530 POUND **Weight:** 15.0000 g. **Composition:** 0.7200 Silver .3472 oz. ASW **Subject:** 100th Anniversary - Revolt by Arabi Pasha **Reverse:** Pasha mounted on horse in front of his followers

Date	Mintage	F	VF	XF	Unc
AH1402-1981	50,000	—	—	—	10.00
AH1402-1981 Proof	1,500	Value: 25.00			

KM# 531 POUND **Weight:** 8.0000 g. **Composition:** 0.8750 Gold .2250 oz. AGW **Subject:** 100th Anniversary - Revolt by Arabi Pasha **Reverse:** Pasha mounted on horse in front of his followers

Date	Mintage	F	VF	XF	Unc
AH1402-1981	3,000	—	—	—	175

KM# 539 POUND **Weight:** 15.0000 g. **Composition:** 0.7200 Silver .3472 oz. ASW **Subject:** Golden Jubilee - Egypt Air

Date	Mintage	F	VF	XF	Unc
AH1402-1982	20,000	—	—	—	12.00

KM# 540 POUND **Weight:** 15.0000 g. **Composition:** 0.7200 Silver .3472 oz. ASW **Subject:** 1000th Anniversary - Al Azhar Mosque **Reverse:** Mosque

Date	Mintage	F	VF	XF	Unc
AH1402-1982	23,000	—	—	—	10.00
AH1402-1982 Proof	4,000	Value: 15.00			

KM# 541 POUND **Weight:** 8.0000 g. **Composition:** 0.8750 Gold .2250 oz. AGW **Subject:** 1000th Anniversary - Al Azhar Mosque **Reverse:** Mosque

Date	Mintage	F	VF	XF	Unc
AH1402-1982 Proof	2,000	Value: 175			

KM# 544 POUND **Weight:** 15.0000 g. **Composition:** 0.7200 Silver .3472 oz. ASW **Subject:** 50th Anniversary - Egyptian Products Co.

Date	Mintage	F	VF	XF	Unc
AH1402-1982	5,000	—	—	—	20.00
AH1402-1982 Proof	2,000	Value: 25.00			

KM# 545 POUND **Weight:** 15.0000 g. **Composition:** 0.7200 Silver .3472 oz. ASW **Subject:** Return of Sinai to Egypt

Date	Mintage	F	VF	XF	Unc
AH1402-1982(1983)	50,000	—	—	—	10.00
AH1402-1982(1983) Proof	2,000	Value: 20.00			

KM# 542 POUND **Weight:** 15.0000 g. **Composition:** 0.7200 Silver .3472 oz. ASW **Subject:** 50th Anniversary of Air Force **Reverse:** Air Force insignia within wreath

Date	Mintage	F	VF	XF	Unc
AH1403-1982	10,000	—	—	—	13.50
AH1403-1982 Proof	2,260	Value: 25.00			

KM# 543 POUND **Weight:** 8.0000 g. **Composition:** 0.8750 Gold .2250 oz. AGW **Subject:** 50th Anniversary of Air Force **Reverse:** Air Force insignia within wreath

Date	Mintage	F	VF	XF	Unc
AH1403-1982 Proof	2,000	Value: 175			

KM# 549 POUND **Weight:** 15.0000 g. **Composition:** 0.7200 Silver .3472 oz. ASW **Subject:** 50th Anniversary - Deaths of Shawky and Hafez

Date	Mintage	F	VF	XF	Unc
AH1403-1983	25,000	—	—	—	12.00

KM# 551 POUND **Weight:** 15.0000 g. **Composition:** 0.7200 Silver .3472 oz. ASW **Subject:** Misr Insurance Company

Date	Mintage	F	VF	XF	Unc
AH1404-1984	20,000	—	—	—	12.00

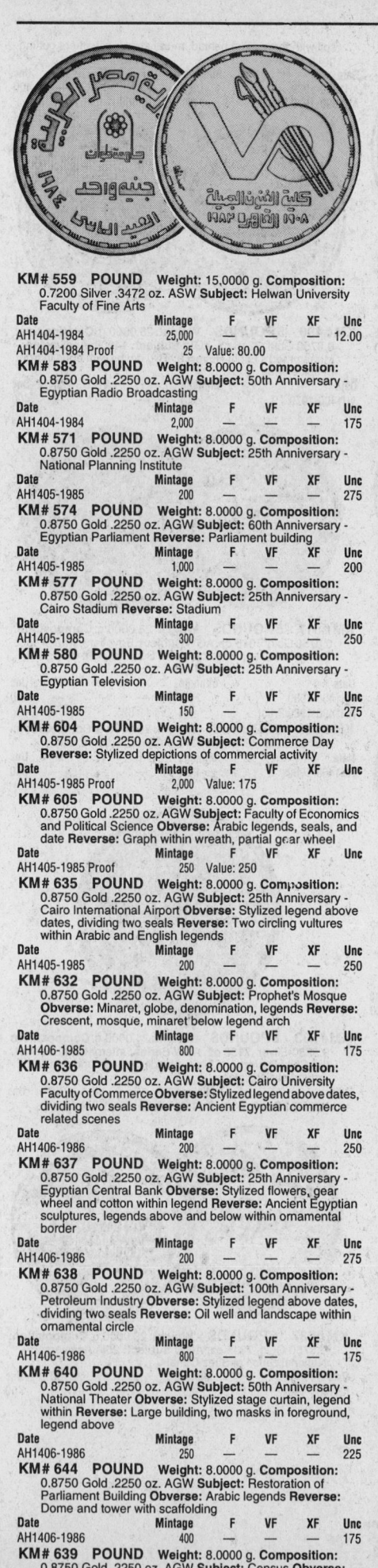

KM# 559 POUND **Weight:** 15.0000 g. **Composition:** 0.7200 Silver .3472 oz. ASW **Subject:** Helwan University Faculty of Fine Arts

Date	Mintage	F	VF	XF	Unc
AH1404-1984	25,000	—	—	—	12.00
AH1404-1984 Proof	25	Value: 80.00			

KM# 583 POUND **Weight:** 8.0000 g. **Composition:** 0.8750 Gold .2250 oz. AGW **Subject:** 50th Anniversary - Egyptian Radio Broadcasting

Date	Mintage	F	VF	XF	Unc
AH1404-1984	2,000	—	—	—	175

KM# 571 POUND **Weight:** 8.0000 g. **Composition:** 0.8750 Gold .2250 oz. AGW **Subject:** 25th Anniversary - National Planning Institute

Date	Mintage	F	VF	XF	Unc
AH1405-1985	200	—	—	—	275

KM# 574 POUND **Weight:** 8.0000 g. **Composition:** 0.8750 Gold .2250 oz. AGW **Subject:** 60th Anniversary - Egyptian Parliament **Reverse:** Parliament building

Date	Mintage	F	VF	XF	Unc
AH1405-1985	1,000	—	—	—	200

KM# 577 POUND **Weight:** 8.0000 g. **Composition:** 0.8750 Gold .2250 oz. AGW **Subject:** 25th Anniversary - Cairo Stadium **Reverse:** Stadium

Date	Mintage	F	VF	XF	Unc
AH1405-1985	300	—	—	—	250

KM# 580 POUND **Weight:** 8.0000 g. **Composition:** 0.8750 Gold .2250 oz. AGW **Subject:** 25th Anniversary - Egyptian Television

Date	Mintage	F	VF	XF	Unc
AH1405-1985	150	—	—	—	275

KM# 604 POUND **Weight:** 8.0000 g. **Composition:** 0.8750 Gold .2250 oz. AGW **Subject:** Commerce Day **Reverse:** Stylized depictions of commercial activity

Date	Mintage	F	VF	XF	Unc
AH1405-1985 Proof	2,000	Value: 175			

KM# 605 POUND **Weight:** 8.0000 g. **Composition:** 0.8750 Gold .2250 oz. AGW **Subject:** Faculty of Economics and Political Science **Obverse:** Arabic legends, seals, and date **Reverse:** Graph within wreath, partial gear wheel

Date	Mintage	F	VF	XF	Unc
AH1405-1985 Proof	250	Value: 250			

KM# 635 POUND **Weight:** 8.0000 g. **Composition:** 0.8750 Gold .2250 oz. AGW **Subject:** 25th Anniversary - Cairo International Airport **Obverse:** Stylized legend above dates, dividing two seals **Reverse:** Two circling vultures within Arabic and English legends

Date	Mintage	F	VF	XF	Unc
AH1405-1985	200	—	—	—	250

KM# 632 POUND **Weight:** 8.0000 g. **Composition:** 0.8750 Gold .2250 oz. AGW **Subject:** Prophet's Mosque **Obverse:** Minaret, globe, denomination, legends **Reverse:** Crescent, mosque, minaret below legend arch

Date	Mintage	F	VF	XF	Unc
AH1406-1985	800	—	—	—	175

KM# 636 POUND **Weight:** 8.0000 g. **Composition:** 0.8750 Gold .2250 oz. AGW **Subject:** Cairo University Faculty of Commerce **Obverse:** Stylized legend above dates, dividing two seals **Reverse:** Ancient Egyptian commerce related scenes

Date	Mintage	F	VF	XF	Unc
AH1406-1986	200	—	—	—	250

KM# 637 POUND **Weight:** 8.0000 g. **Composition:** 0.8750 Gold .2250 oz. AGW **Subject:** 25th Anniversary - Egyptian Central Bank **Obverse:** Stylized flowers, gear wheel and cotton within legend **Reverse:** Ancient Egyptian sculptures, legends above and below within ornamental border

Date	Mintage	F	VF	XF	Unc
AH1406-1986	200	—	—	—	275

KM# 638 POUND **Weight:** 8.0000 g. **Composition:** 0.8750 Gold .2250 oz. AGW **Subject:** 100th Anniversary - Petroleum Industry **Obverse:** Stylized legend above dates, dividing two seals **Reverse:** Oil well and landscape within ornamental circle

Date	Mintage	F	VF	XF	Unc
AH1406-1986	800	—	—	—	175

KM# 640 POUND **Weight:** 8.0000 g. **Composition:** 0.8750 Gold .2250 oz. AGW **Subject:** 50th Anniversary - National Theater **Obverse:** Stylized stage curtain, legend within **Reverse:** Large building, two masks in foreground, legend above

Date	Mintage	F	VF	XF	Unc
AH1406-1986	250	—	—	—	225

KM# 644 POUND **Weight:** 8.0000 g. **Composition:** 0.8750 Gold .2250 oz. AGW **Subject:** Restoration of Parliament Building **Obverse:** Arabic legends **Reverse:** Dome and tower with scaffolding

Date	Mintage	F	VF	XF	Unc
AH1406-1986	400	—	—	—	175

KM# 639 POUND **Weight:** 8.0000 g. **Composition:** 0.8750 Gold .2250 oz. AGW **Subject:** Census **Obverse:** Arabic legends, seals, date **Reverse:** City view with paper doll cutout human figures

Date	Mintage	F	VF	XF	Unc
AH1407-1986	200	—	—	—	200

KM# 643 POUND **Weight:** 8.0000 g. **Composition:** 0.8750 Gold .2250 oz. AGW **Subject:** 40th Anniversary - Engineer's Syndicate **Obverse:** Arabic legends, seals, dates **Reverse:** Three triangles, legend, ornamentation

Date	Mintage	F	VF	XF	Unc
AH1407-1986	400	—	—	—	175

KM# 645 POUND **Weight:** 8.0000 g. **Composition:** 0.8750 Gold .2250 oz. AGW **Subject:** Parliament Museum **Obverse:** Arabic legends, seals, dates **Reverse:** Documents, quill, carriage, building with national emblem

Date	Mintage	F	VF	XF	Unc
AH1407-1987	400	—	—	—	175

KM# 653 POUND **Weight:** 8.0000 g. **Composition:** 0.8750 Gold .2250 oz. AGW **Subject:** Investment Bank **Obverse:** Toughra, legends above and below, dates **Reverse:** Symbol within stylized circle, legend around

Date	Mintage	F	VF	XF	Unc
AH1407-1987	600	—	—	—	175

KM# 673 POUND **Weight:** 8.0000 g. **Composition:** 0.8750 Gold .2250 oz. AGW **Subject:** First African Subway **Obverse:** Stylized legends and denomination **Reverse:** Subway emerging from tunnel emerging from tunnel with legend around rim

Date	Mintage	F	VF	XF	Unc
AH1408-1987 Proof	500	Value: 225			

KM# 647 POUND **Weight:** 8.0000 g. **Composition:** 0.8750 Gold .2250 oz. AGW **Subject:** Police Day **Obverse:** Arabic and English legends, seals, dates **Reverse:** Police emblem - eagle in wreath, legends

Date	Mintage	F	VF	XF	Unc
AH1408-1988	500	—	—	—	175

KM# 654 POUND **Weight:** 8.0000 g. **Composition:** 0.8750 Gold .2250 oz. AGW **Subject:** Dedication of Cairo Opera House **Obverse:** Arabic legends, seals, dates **Reverse:** Opera house, legends above and below

Date	Mintage	F	VF	XF	Unc
AH1409-1988	1,500	—	—	—	225

KM# 661 POUND **Weight:** 8.0000 g. **Composition:** 0.8750 Gold .2250 oz. AGW **Subject:** Naquib Mahfouz, Nobel Laureate **Obverse:** Stylized quill ink and paper design with legend above **Reverse:** Head of Mahfouz left

Date	Mintage	F	VF	XF	Unc
AH1409-1988 Proof	1,000	Value: 175			

KM# 664 POUND **Weight:** 8.0000 g. **Composition:** 0.8750 Gold .2250 oz. AGW **Subject:** United Parliamentary Union **Obverse:** Kufic legend above denomination and dates **Reverse:** Anniversary dates, map in wreath above domed building, and legend

Date	Mintage	F	VF	XF	Unc
AH1409-1989 Proof	200	Value: 275			

KM# 666 POUND **Weight:** 8.0000 g. **Composition:** 0.8750 Gold .2250 oz. AGW **Subject:** First Arab Olympics **Obverse:** Kufic legend above denomination and dates **Reverse:** 5 Olympic rings and map as part of torch held by hand within wreath and legend

Date	Mintage	F	VF	XF	Unc
AH1409-1989 Proof	300	Value: 250			

KM# 668 POUND **Weight:** 8.0000 g. **Composition:** 0.8750 Gold .2250 oz. AGW **Subject:** National Research Center **Obverse:** Kufic legend above denomination and dates **Reverse:** Stylized ancient and modern research elements

Date	Mintage	F	VF	XF	Unc
AH1409-1989 Proof	250	Value: 250			

KM# 677 POUND **Weight:** 8.0000 g. **Composition:** 0.8750 Gold .2250 oz. AGW **Subject:** University of Cairo, School of Agriculture **Obverse:** Denomination between wheat ears above legend **Reverse:** Ancient farming scene and coat of arms, building in background

Date	Mintage	F	VF	XF	Unc
AH1410-1989 Proof	200	Value: 275			

KM# 695 POUND **Weight:** 8.0000 g. **Composition:** 0.8750 Gold .2250 oz. AGW **Subject:** Export Trade Show **Obverse:** Toughra, inscription above **Reverse:** Display of symbols

Date	Mintage	F	VF	XF	Unc
AH1410-1989 Proof	200	Value: 275			

KM# 696 POUND **Weight:** 8.0000 g. **Composition:** 0.8750 Gold .2250 oz. AGW **Subject:** Union of African Parliament **Obverse:** Toughra, denomination, date within circle and legend **Reverse:** Map of Africa, laurel branch and Parliament building

Date	Mintage	F	VF	XF	Unc
AH1410-1990 Proof	200	Value: 275			

KM# 699 POUND **Weight:** 8.0000 g. **Composition:** 0.8750 Gold .2250 oz. AGW **Subject:** 5th African Games - Cairo **Obverse:** Torch with legend and inscription **Reverse:** Logo above rings within legend

Date	Mintage	F	VF	XF	Unc
AH1411-1991 Proof	200	Value: 275			

KM# 832 POUND **Weight:** 8.0000 g. **Composition:** 0.8750 Gold .2250 oz. AGW **Subject:** Library of Alexandria **Obverse:** Legend and inscription **Reverse:** Waterfront building with tower

Date	Mintage	F	VF	XF	Unc
AH1411-1991	300	—	—	—	400

KM# 726 POUND **Weight:** 8.0000 g. **Composition:** 0.8750 Gold .2250 oz. AGW **Subject:** Mohamed Abdel Wahab **Reverse:** Bust of Mohamed Abdel Wahab left with music sheet in background

Date	Mintage	F	VF	XF	Unc
AH1412-1991	1,000	—	—	—	175

KM# 835 POUND **Weight:** 15.0000 g. **Composition:** 0.7200 Silver .3472 oz. ASW **Subject:** Gorgui Zidane **Obverse:** Legend and vase **Reverse:** Portrait **Edge:** Reeded

Date	Mintage	F	VF	XF	Unc
AH1413-1992	3,000	—	—	—	20.00

KM# 836 POUND **Weight:** 8.0000 g. **Composition:** 0.8750 Gold .2250 oz. AGW **Subject:** Rifa'a El Tahtaoui **Obverse:** Legend and vase **Reverse:** Portrait

Date	Mintage	F	VF	XF	Unc
AH1413-1992	800	—	—	—	400

KM# 810 POUND **Weight:** 15.0000 g. **Composition:** 0.7200 Silver .3472 oz. ASW **Subject:** 20th Anniversary - October War **Obverse:** Smoking chimney text **Reverse:** Soldier with flag

Date		F	VF	XF	Unc
AH1414-1993		—	—	—	30.00

KM# 811 POUND **Weight:** 8.0000 g. **Composition:** 0.8750 Gold .2250 oz. AGW **Subject:** 20th Anniversary - October War **Obverse:** Smoking chimney text **Reverse:** Soldier with flag

Date		F	VF	XF	Unc
AH1414-1993		—	—	—	400

KM# 761 POUND **Weight:** 15.0000 g. **Composition:** 0.7200 Silver .3472 oz. ASW **Subject:** Salah El Din El-Ayubi **Obverse:** Denomination **Reverse:** Portrait

Date	Mintage	F	VF	XF	Unc
AH1414-1994	5,000	—	—	—	25.00

KM# 762 POUND **Weight:** 8.0000 g. **Composition:** 0.8750 Gold .2250 oz. AGW **Subject:** Salah El Din El-Ayubi **Obverse:** Denomination **Reverse:** Portrait

Date	Mintage	F	VF	XF	Unc
AH1414-1994	300	—	—	—	400

KM# 764 POUND **Weight:** 15.0000 g. **Composition:** 0.7200 Silver .3472 oz. ASW **Subject:** 125 Years - Suez Canal **Obverse:** Toughra **Reverse:** Building and canal scenes

Date	Mintage	F	VF	XF	Unc
AH1415-1994	3,000	—	—	—	20.00

KM# 766 POUND **Weight:** 15.0000 g. **Composition:** 0.7200 Silver .3472 oz. ASW **Subject:** 75 Years - Bank of Misr **Obverse:** Inscription **Reverse:** Bank building and emblem

Date	Mintage	F	VF	XF	Unc
AH1415-1994	2,500	—	—	—	30.00

KM# 839 POUND **Weight:** 15.0000 g. **Composition:** 0.7200 Silver .3472 oz. ASW **Subject:** Abd Al Halem Hafez **Obverse:** Denomination **Reverse:** Portrait

Date	Mintage	F	VF	XF	Unc
AH1416-1995	3,000	—	—	—	20.00

KM# 767 POUND **Weight:** 8.0000 g. **Composition:** 0.8750 Gold .2250 oz. AGW **Subject:** 75 Years - Bank of Misr

Date	Mintage	F	VF	XF	Unc
AH1415-1995	1,000	—	—	—	400

KM# 769 POUND **Weight:** 15.0000 g. **Composition:** 0.7200 Silver .3472 oz. ASW **Series:** F.A.O. **Reverse:** Workers

Date	Mintage	F	VF	XF	Unc
AH1415-1995	3,000	—	—	—	40.00

KM# 771 POUND **Weight:** 8.0000 g. **Composition:** 0.8750 Gold .2250 oz. AGW **Subject:** Pediatrics International Conference

Date	Mintage	F	VF	XF	Unc
AH1416-1995	300	—	—	—	400

KM# 840 POUND **Weight:** 8.0000 g. **Composition:** 0.8750 Gold .2250 oz. AGW **Subject:** Abd Al Halem Hafez **Obverse:** Denomination **Reverse:** Abd Al Halem Hafez

Date	Mintage	F	VF	XF	Unc
AH1416-1995	500	—	—	—	400

KM# 844 POUND **Weight:** 15.0000 g. **Composition:** 0.7200 Silver .3472 oz. ASW **Subject:** Centennial - Electrification **Obverse:** Legend and inscription **Reverse:** Electric bolt on Pyramid

Date	Mintage	F	VF	XF	Unc
AH1417-1996	3,000	—	—	—	15.00

KM# 845 POUND **Weight:** 15.0000 g. **Composition:** 0.7200 Silver .3472 oz. ASW **Subject:** 65 Years - Egyptian Air Force **Obverse:** Denomination **Reverse:** Flying eagle in wreath

Date	Mintage	F	VF	XF	Unc
AH1418-1997	226	—	—	—	85.00

KM# 847 POUND **Weight:** 15.0000 g. **Composition:** 0.7200 Silver .3472 oz. ASW **Subject:** 50 Years Arab Land Bank **Obverse:** Denomination **Reverse:** Domed building

Date	F	VF	XF	Unc
AH1418-1997	—	—	—	35.00

KM# 849 POUND **Weight:** 15.0000 g. **Composition:** 0.7200 Silver .3472 oz. ASW **Subject:** 95th Interparliamentary Union Conference **Obverse:** Circular design above inscription **Reverse:** Pyramids in wreath

Date	Mintage	F	VF	XF	Unc
AH1418-1997	375	—	—	—	85.00

KM# 851 POUND **Weight:** 15.0000 g. **Composition:** 0.7200 Silver .3472 oz. ASW **Series:** Centennial - Chemical Office **Obverse:** Denomination **Reverse:** Symbolic design

Date	F	VF	XF	Unc
AH1419-1998	—	—	—	35.00

KM# 855 POUND **Weight:** 15.0000 g. **Composition:** 0.7200 Silver .3472 oz. ASW **Series:** Centennial - National Bank **Obverse:** Denomination **Reverse:** Large "100"

Date	Mintage	F	VF	XF	Unc
AH1419-1998	200	—	—	—	85.00

KM# 857 POUND **Weight:** 15.0000 g. **Composition:** 0.7200 Silver .3472 oz. ASW **Subject:** 25th Anniversary - October War **Obverse:** Denomination **Reverse:** Symbolic design

Date	F	VF	XF	Unc
AH1419-1998	—	—	—	40.00

KM# 859 POUND **Weight:** 15.0000 g. **Composition:** 0.7200 Silver .3472 oz. ASW **Subject:** Imam Metwaly El Sharawi **Obverse:** Open book **Reverse:** Portrait

Date	F	VF	XF	Unc
AH1419-1998	—	—	—	40.00

KM# 861 POUND **Weight:** 15.0000 g. **Composition:** 0.7200 Silver .3472 oz. ASW **Series:** Centennial - Land Surveying **Obverse:** Denomination **Reverse:** "100" above ancient surveyors

Date	F	VF	XF	Unc
AH1419-1998	—	—	—	35.00

KM# 863 POUND **Weight:** 15.0000 g. **Composition:** 0.7200 Silver .3472 oz. ASW **Series:** Centennial - Solidarity **Obverse:** Denomination **Reverse:** Symbolic design

Date	F	VF	XF	Unc
AH1419-1998	—	—	—	35.00

KM# 865 POUND **Weight:** 15.0000 g. **Composition:** 0.7200 Silver .3472 oz. ASW **Subject:** Golden Jubilee of Ash Shanns University **Obverse:** Denomination **Reverse:** Monument

Date	F	VF	XF	Unc
AH1420-1999	—	—	—	35.00

KM# 441 5 POUNDS **Weight:** 26.0000 g. **Composition:** 0.8750 Gold .7315 oz. AGW **Subject:** 75th Anniveresary - National Bank of Egypt **Reverse:** World globe with bank building at right

Date	Mintage	F	VF	XF	Unc
AH1393-1973	1,000	—	—	—	400
AH1393-1973 Proof	—	Value: 600			

KM# 444 5 POUNDS **Weight:** 26.0000 g. **Composition:** 0.8750 Gold .7315 oz. AGW **Subject:** 1973 October War

Date	Mintage	F	VF	XF	Unc
AH1394-1974	1,000	—	—	—	420

KM# 459 5 POUNDS **Weight:** 26.0000 g. **Composition:** 0.8750 Gold .7315 oz. AGW **Subject:** King Faisal of Saudi Arabia **Reverse:** Head of King Faisal half right

Date	Mintage	F	VF	XF	Unc
AH1396-1976	2,500	—	—	—	550

KM# 460 5 POUNDS **Weight:** 26.0000 g. **Composition:** 0.8750 Gold .7315 oz. AGW **Subject:** Reopening of Suez Canal

Date	Mintage	F	VF	XF	Unc
AH1396-1976	2,000	—	—	—	400

KM# 461 5 POUNDS **Weight:** 26.0000 g. **Composition:** 0.8750 Gold .7315 oz. AGW **Subject:** Om Kalsoum **Reverse:** Head of Om Kalsoum right

Date	Mintage	F	VF	XF	Unc
AH1396-1976	1,000	—	—	—	800

KM# 495 5 POUNDS **Weight:** 26.0000 g. **Composition:** 0.8750 Gold .7315 oz. AGW **Subject:** 100th Anniversary - Bank of Land Reform **Reverse:** Seated man, farmer tilling soil with three oxen behind, mural showing workers cutting grain sheaves

Date	Mintage	F	VF	XF	Unc
AH1399-1979	1,750	—	—	—	400
AH1399-1979 Proof	250	Value: 550			

KM# 496 5 POUNDS **Weight:** 26.0000 g. **Composition:** 0.8750 Gold .7315 oz. AGW **Subject:** 1400th Anniversary - Mohammed's Flight **Reverse:** Two doves with eggs in front of spider web

Date	Mintage	F	VF	XF	Unc
AH1400-1979	2,000	—	—	—	400

KM# 517 5 POUNDS **Weight:** 26.0000 g. **Composition:** 0.8750 Gold .7315 oz. AGW **Subject:** Egyptian-Israeli Peace Treaty **Reverse:** Head of Anwar Sadat at right facing left, dove of peace at right behind

Date	Mintage	F	VF	XF	Unc
AH1400-1980	2,375	—	—	—	400
AH1400-1980 Proof	125	Value: 625			

KM# 518 5 POUNDS **Weight:** 26.0000 g. **Composition:** 0.8750 Gold .7315 oz. AGW **Subject:** Doctors' Day

Date	Mintage	F	VF	XF	Unc
AH1400-1980	1,000	—	—	—	550

KM# 533 5 POUNDS **Weight:** 24.0000 g. **Composition:** 0.9250 Silver .7138 oz. ASW **Series:** International Year of the Child **Reverse:** Children holding hands and dancing around stylistic globe

Date	Mintage	F	VF	XF	Unc
AH1401-1981 Proof	10,000	Value: 30.00			

KM# 537 5 POUNDS **Weight:** 26.0000 g. **Composition:** 0.8750 Gold .7315 oz. AGW **Subject:** 25th Anniversary - Nationalization of Suez Canal

Date	Mintage	F	VF	XF	Unc
AH1401-1981	1,000	—	—	—	400

KM#535 5 POUNDS **Weight:** 26.0000 g. **Composition:** 0.8750 Gold .7315 oz. AGW **Subject:** 25th Anniversary - Ministry of Industry

Date	Mintage	F	VF	XF	Unc
AH1402-1981 Proof	1,500	Value: 400			

KM#536 5 POUNDS **Weight:** 26.0000 g. **Composition:** 0.8750 Gold .7315 oz. AGW **Subject:** 100th Anniversary - Revolt by Arabi Pasha **Reverse:** Pasha mounted on horse in front of his followers

Date	Mintage	F	VF	XF	Unc
AH1402-1981	1,000	—	—	—	400

KM#534 5 POUNDS **Weight:** 26.0000 g. **Composition:** 0.8750 Gold .7315 oz. AGW **Subject:** 3rd Anniversary - Suez Canal Reopening

Date	Mintage	F	VF	XF	Unc
AH1401-1981	925	—	—	—	400
AH1401-1981 Proof	75	Value: 650			

KM#546 5 POUNDS **Weight:** 26.0000 g. **Composition:** 0.8750 Gold .7315 oz. AGW **Subject:** 1000th Anniversary - Al Azhar Mosque **Reverse:** Mosque

Date	Mintage	F	VF	XF	Unc
AH1402-1982	1,500	—	—	—	400

KM#547 5 POUNDS **Weight:** 26.0000 g. **Composition:** 0.8750 Gold .7315 oz. AGW **Subject:** 50th Anniversary - Air Force **Reverse:** Air Force insignia within wreath

Date	Mintage	F	VF	XF	Unc
AH1403-1982	1,000	—	—	—	400

KM#552 5 POUNDS **Weight:** 17.5000 g. **Composition:** 0.7200 Silver .4051 oz. ASW **Subject:** 75th Anniversary - Cairo University

Date	Mintage	F	VF	XF	Unc
AH1404-1983	25,000	—	—	—	18.00

KM#558 5 POUNDS **Weight:** 17.5000 g. **Composition:** 0.7200 Silver .4051 oz. ASW **Subject:** Los Angeles Olympics

Date	Mintage	F	VF	XF	Unc
AH1404-1984	20,000	—	—	—	13.50

KM#560 5 POUNDS **Weight:** 17.5000 g. **Composition:** 0.7200 Silver .4051 oz. ASW **Subject:** Academy of Arabic Languages

Date	Mintage	F	VF	XF	Unc
AH1404-1984	25,000	—	—	—	13.50

KM#561 5 POUNDS **Weight:** 17.5000 g. **Composition:** 0.7200 Silver .4051 oz. ASW **Subject:** 50th Anniversary - Egyptian Radio Broadcasting

Date	Mintage	F	VF	XF	Unc
AH1404-1984	25,000	—	—	—	13.50

KM#565 5 POUNDS **Weight:** 17.5000 g. **Composition:** 0.7200 Silver .4051 oz. ASW **Subject:** Sculptor Mahmoud Mokhtar **Reverse:** Bust of Mokhtar left

Date	Mintage	F	VF	XF	Unc
AH1404-1984	10,000	—	—	—	12.50

KM#566 5 POUNDS **Weight:** 17.5000 g. **Composition:** 0.7200 Silver .4051 oz. ASW **Subject:** Golden Jubilee of Petroleum Industry

Date	Mintage	F	VF	XF	Unc
AH1404-1984	10,000	—	—	—	13.50

KM#567 5 POUNDS **Weight:** 17.5000 g. **Composition:** 0.7200 Silver .4051 oz. ASW **Subject:** Diamond Jubilee of Cooperation **Reverse:** Seven joined hexagons with different scenes

Date	Mintage	F	VF	XF	Unc
AH1404-1984	10,000	—	—	—	12.50

KM#671 5 POUNDS **Weight:** 26.0000 g. **Composition:** 0.8750 Gold .7315 oz. AGW **Subject:** 50th Anniversary - Egyptian Radio **Obverse:** Arabic legends **Reverse:** Tall buildings with transmitter

Date	Mintage	F	VF	XF	Unc
AH1404-1984 Proof	500	Value: 450			

KM#563 5 POUNDS **Weight:** 17.5000 g. **Composition:** 0.7205 Silver .4051 oz. ASW **Subject:** 100th Anniversary - Moharram Printing Press Co.

Date	Mintage	F	VF	XF	Unc
AH1405-1985	20,000	—	—	—	14.50

KM#564 5 POUNDS **Weight:** 40.0000 g. **Composition:** 0.8750 Gold 1.1253 oz. AGW **Subject:** 100th Anniversary - Moharram Printing Press Co.

Date	Mintage	F	VF	XF	Unc
AH1405-1985	200	—	—	—	1,850

KM#572 5 POUNDS **Weight:** 17.5000 g. **Composition:** 0.7200 Silver .4051 oz. ASW **Subject:** 25th Anniversary - National Planning Institute

Date	Mintage	F	VF	XF	Unc
AH1405-1985	15,000	—	—	—	12.50

KM#575 5 POUNDS **Weight:** 17.5000 g. **Composition:** 0.7200 Silver .4051 oz. ASW **Subject:** 60th Anniversary - Egyptian Parliament **Reverse:** Parliament building

Date	Mintage	F	VF	XF	Unc
AH1405-1985	25,000	—	—	—	12.50

KM# 576 5 POUNDS **Weight:** 26.0000 g. **Composition:** 0.8750 Gold .7315 oz. AGW **Subject:** 60th Anniversary - Egyptian Parliament **Reverse:** Parliament building

Date	Mintage	F	VF	XF	Unc
AH1405-1985	500	—	—	—	1,750

KM# 578 5 POUNDS **Weight:** 17.5000 g. **Composition:** 0.7200 Silver .4051 oz. ASW **Subject:** 25th Anniversary - Cairo Stadium **Reverse:** Stadium

Date	Mintage	F	VF	XF	Unc
AH1405-1985	25,000	—	—	—	12.50

KM# 581 5 POUNDS **Weight:** 17.5000 g. **Composition:** 0.7200 Silver .4051 oz. ASW **Subject:** 25th Anniversary - Egyptian Television

Date	Mintage	F	VF	XF	Unc
AH1405-1985	5,000	—	—	—	12.50

KM# 585 5 POUNDS **Weight:** 17.5000 g. **Composition:** 0.7200 Silver .4051 oz. ASW **Subject:** 25th Anniversary - Cairo International Airport

Date	Mintage	F	VF	XF	Unc
AH1405-1985	20,000	—	—	—	12.50

KM# 592 5 POUNDS **Weight:** 17.5000 g. **Composition:** 0.7200 Silver .4051 oz. ASW **Subject:** Tutankhamen **Reverse:** Bust of Tutankhamen left

Date	Mintage	F	VF	XF	Unc
AH1405-1985	6,000	—	—	—	18.00
AH1405-1985 Proof	2,000	Value: 30.00			

KM# 593 5 POUNDS **Weight:** 17.5000 g. **Composition:** 0.7200 Silver .4051 oz. ASW **Subject:** XV UIA Congress **Reverse:** Pyramid

Date	Mintage	F	VF	XF	Unc
AH1405-1985	—	—	—	—	13.50
AH1405-1985 Proof	Est. 500	Value: 25.00			

KM# 598 5 POUNDS **Weight:** 17.5000 g. **Composition:** 0.7200 Silver .4051 oz. ASW **Subject:** Faculty of Economics and Political Science

Date	Mintage	F	VF	XF	Unc
AH1405-1985	8,000	—	—	—	14.00

KM# 600 5 POUNDS **Weight:** 17.5000 g. **Composition:** 0.7200 Silver .4051 oz. ASW **Subject:** Commerce Day

Date	Mintage	F	VF	XF	Unc
AH1405-1985	20,000	—	—	—	11.50
AH1405-1985 Proof	1,000	Value: 22.50			

KM# 584 5 POUNDS **Weight:** 17.5000 g. **Composition:** 0.7200 Silver .4051 oz. ASW **Subject:** The Prophet's Mosque **Reverse:** Mosque

Date	Mintage	F	VF	XF	Unc
AH1406-1985	25,000	—	—	—	11.50
AH1406-1985 Proof	1,000	Value: 22.50			

KM# 587 5 POUNDS **Weight:** 17.5000 g. **Composition:** 0.7200 Silver .4051 oz. ASW **Subject:** Professions **Reverse:** Different professions illustrated on coin

Date	Mintage	F	VF	XF	Unc
AH1406-1985	8,000	—	—	—	13.50

KM# 633 5 POUNDS **Weight:** 26.0000 g. **Composition:** 0.8750 Gold .7315 oz. AGW **Subject:** Prophet's Mosque **Obverse:** Minaret, globe, denomination, legends **Reverse:** Crescent, mosque, minaret below legend arch

Date	Mintage	F	VF	XF	Unc
AH1406-1985	400	—	—	—	450

KM# 579 5 POUNDS **Weight:** 26.0000 g. **Composition:** 0.8750 Gold .7315 oz. AGW **Subject:** 25th Anniversary - Cairo Stadium **Reverse:** Stadium

Date	Mintage	F	VF	XF	Unc
AH1405-1985	200	—	—	—	1,800

KM# 582 5 POUNDS **Weight:** 26.0000 g. **Composition:** 0.8750 Gold .7315 oz. AGW **Subject:** 25th Anniversary - Egyptian Television

Date	Mintage	F	VF	XF	Unc
AH1405-1985	100	—	—	—	1,100

KM# 609a 5 POUNDS **Weight:** 26.0000 g. **Composition:** 0.8750 Gold .7315 oz. AGW **Subject:** Mecca

Date	Mintage	F	VF	XF	Unc
AH1406-1986 Proof	1,400	Value: 400			

KM# 586 5 POUNDS **Weight:** 17.5000 g. **Composition:** 0.7200 Silver .4051 oz. ASW **Subject:** Cairo University Faculty of Commerce

Date	Mintage	F	VF	XF	Unc
AH1406-1986	20,000	—	—	—	13.50

KM# 588 5 POUNDS **Weight:** 17.5000 g. **Composition:** 0.7200 Silver .4051 oz. ASW **Subject:** 25th Anniversary - Egyptian National Bank

Date	Mintage	F	VF	XF	Unc
AH1406-1986	6,000	—	—	—	13.50

KM# 589 5 POUNDS **Weight:** 17.6800 g. **Composition:** 0.7200 Silver .4093 oz. ASW **Subject:** World Soccer Championships **Reverse:** Soccer ball, three pyramids

Date	Mintage	F	VF	XF	Unc
AH1406-1986 Proflike	5,000	—	—	—	15.00
AH1406-1986 Proof	2,150	Value: 30.00			

KM# 590 5 POUNDS **Weight:** 17.5000 g. **Composition:** 0.7200 Silver .4051 oz. ASW **Subject:** African Soccer Championship Games **Reverse:** Two soccer players at right

Date	Mintage	F	VF	XF	Unc
AH1406-1986	15,000	—	—	—	14.00
AH1406-1986 Proof	2,000	Value: 30.00			

KM# 594 5 POUNDS **Weight:** 17.5000 g. **Composition:** 0.7200 Silver .4051 oz. ASW **Subject:** 50th Anniversary - Ministry of Health

Date	Mintage	F	VF	XF	Unc
AH1406-1986	—	—	—	—	14.00
AH1406-1986 Proof	Est. 500	Value: 30.00			

KM# 601 5 POUNDS **Weight:** 17.5000 g. **Composition:** 0.7200 Silver .4051 oz. ASW **Reverse:** Crossed swords within wreath

Date	Mintage	F	VF	XF	Unc
AH1406-1986	16,000	—	—	—	13.50

KM# 602 5 POUNDS **Weight:** 17.5000 g. **Composition:** 0.7200 Silver .4051 oz. ASW **Subject:** 100th Anniversary - Petroleum Industry **Reverse:** Oil derrick with building behind

Date	Mintage	F	VF	XF	Unc
AH1406-1986	6,000	—	—	—	15.00

KM# 608 5 POUNDS **Weight:** 17.5000 g. **Composition:** 0.7200 Silver .4051 oz. ASW **Subject:** 50th Anniversary - National Theater

Date	Mintage	F	VF	XF	Unc
AH1406-1986	6,000	—	—	—	15.00

KM# 609 5 POUNDS **Weight:** 17.5000 g. **Composition:** 0.7200 Silver .4051 oz. ASW **Subject:** Mecca

Date	Mintage	F	VF	XF	Unc
AH1406-1986	30,000	—	—	—	12.50
AH1406-1986 Proof	—	Value: 22.50			

KM# 614 5 POUNDS **Weight:** 17.5000 g. **Composition:** 0.7200 Silver .4051 oz. ASW **Subject:** Restoration of Parliament Building **Obverse:** Arabic legends **Reverse:** Dome and tower with scaffolding

Date	Mintage	F	VF	XF	Unc
AH1406-1986	5,000	—	—	—	15.00

KM# 614a 5 POUNDS **Weight:** 26.0000 g. **Composition:** 0.8750 Gold .7315 oz. AGW **Subject:** Restoration of Parliament Building **Obverse:** Arabic legends **Reverse:** Dome and tower with scaffolding

Date	Mintage	F	VF	XF	Unc
AH1406-1986	300	—	—	—	350

KM# 615 5 POUNDS **Weight:** 17.5000 g. **Composition:** 0.7200 Silver .4051 oz. ASW **Subject:** 30th Anniversary - Atomic Energy Organization

Date	Mintage	F	VF	XF	Unc
AH1406-1986	5,000	—	—	—	15.00

KM# 603 5 POUNDS **Weight:** 17.5000 g. **Composition:** 0.7200 Silver .4051 oz. ASW **Subject:** Census

Date	Mintage	F	VF	XF	Unc
AH1407-1986	6,000	—	—	—	15.00

KM# 610 5 POUNDS **Weight:** 17.5000 g. **Composition:** 0.7200 Silver .4051 oz. ASW **Subject:** 40th Anniversary - Engineer's Syndicate

Date	Mintage	F	VF	XF	Unc
AH1407-1986	6,000	—	—	—	15.00

KM# 616 5 POUNDS **Weight:** 17.5000 g. **Composition:** 0.7200 Silver .4051 oz. ASW **Subject:** 30th Anniversary - Egyptian Industry

Date	Mintage	F	VF	XF	Unc
AH1407-1986	5,000	—	—	—	15.00

KM# 611 5 POUNDS **Weight:** 17.5000 g. **Composition:** 0.7200 Silver .4051 oz. ASW **Subject:** Aida Opera

Date	Mintage	F	VF	XF	Unc
ND(1407-1987)	25,000	—	—	—	35.00

KM# 617 5 POUNDS **Weight:** 17.5000 g. **Composition:** 0.7200 Silver .4051 oz. ASW **Subject:** Parliament Museum **Obverse:** Arabic legends, seals and dates **Reverse:** Documents, quill, carriage, building with national emblem

Date	Mintage	F	VF	XF	Unc
AH1407-1987	5,000	—	—	—	15.00

KM# 618 5 POUNDS **Weight:** 17.5000 g. **Composition:** 0.7200 Silver .4051 oz. ASW **Subject:** Veterinarian Day

Date	Mintage	F	VF	XF	Unc
AH1407-1987	5,000	—	—	—	12.50

KM# 619 5 POUNDS **Weight:** 17.5000 g. **Composition:** 0.7200 Silver .4051 oz. ASW **Subject:** 75th Anniversary - Misr Petroleum Company

Date	Mintage	F	VF	XF	Unc
AH1407-1987	10,000	—	—	—	13.50

KM# 630 5 POUNDS **Weight:** 17.5000 g. **Composition:** 0.7200 Silver .4051 oz. ASW **Subject:** Faculty of Fine Arts

Date	Mintage	F	VF	XF	Unc
AH1407-1987	5,000	—	—	—	13.50

KM# 651 5 POUNDS **Weight:** 17.7800 g. **Composition:** 0.7200 Silver .4052 oz. ASW **Subject:** Investment Bank

Date	Mintage	F	VF	XF	Unc
AH1407-1987	8,000	—	—	—	12.50

KM# 620 5 POUNDS **Weight:** 17.5000 g. **Composition:** 0.7200 Silver .4051 oz. ASW **Subject:** First African Subway

Date	Mintage	F	VF	XF	Unc
AH1408-1987	15,000	—	—	—	12.50

KM# 623 5 POUNDS **Weight:** 17.5000 g. **Composition:** 0.7200 Silver .4051 oz. ASW **Subject:** 25th Anniversary - Hellwan Company

Date	Mintage	F	VF	XF	Unc
AH1408-1987	8,000	—	—	—	13.50

KM# 617a 5 POUNDS **Weight:** 26.0000 g. **Composition:** 0.8750 Gold .7315 oz. AGW **Subject:** Parliament Museum **Obverse:** Arabic legends, seals and dates **Reverse:** Documents, quill, carriage, building with national emblem

Date	Mintage	F	VF	XF	Unc
AH1407-1987	300	—	—	—	350

KM# 674 5 POUNDS **Weight:** 26.0000 g. **Composition:** 0.8750 Gold .7315 oz. AGW **Subject:** First African Subway **Obverse:** Stylized legends and denomination **Reverse:** Subway emerging from tunnel with legend around rim

Date	Mintage	F	VF	XF	Unc
AH1408-1987 Proof	200	Value: 550			

KM# 670 5 POUNDS **Weight:** 26.0000 g. **Composition:** 0.8750 Gold .7315 oz. AGW **Subject:** National Research Center **Obverse:** Kufic legend above denomination and date **Reverse:** Stylized ancient and modern research elements

Date	Mintage	F	VF	XF	Unc
AH1408-1988 Proof	—	Value: 550			
AH1409-1989 Proof	200	Value: 550			

KM# 655 5 POUNDS **Weight:** 26.0000 g. **Composition:** 0.8750 Gold .7315 oz. AGW **Subject:** Dedication of Cairo Opera House **Obverse:** Arabic legends, seals, dates **Reverse:** Opera house, legends above and below

Date	Mintage	F	VF	XF	Unc
AH1409-1988	200	—	—	—	525

KM# 621 5 POUNDS **Weight:** 17.5000 g. **Composition:** 0.7200 Silver .4051 oz. ASW **Subject:** Police Day

Date	Mintage	F	VF	XF	Unc
AH1408-1988	35,000	—	—	—	13.50

KM# 624 5 POUNDS **Weight:** 17.5000 g. **Composition:** 0.7200 Silver .4051 oz. ASW **Series:** Summer Olympics **Reverse:** Pharoah and athletes

Date	Mintage	F	VF	XF	Unc
AH1408-1988	30,000	—	—	—	13.50
AH1408-1988 Matte	—	—	—	—	55.00
AH1408-1988 Proof	2,000	Value: 27.50			

KM# 626 5 POUNDS **Weight:** 17.5000 g. **Composition:** 0.7200 Silver .4051 oz. ASW **Series:** Summer Olympics **Reverse:** Athletes and mythological figures

Date	Mintage	F	VF	XF	Unc
AH1408-1988	24,000	—	—	—	13.50
AH1408-1988 Matte	—	—	—	—	55.00
AH1408-1988 Proof	5,000	Value: 30.00			

KM# 628 5 POUNDS **Weight:** 17.5000 g. **Composition:** 0.7200 Silver .4051 oz. ASW **Series:** Winter Olympics **Reverse:** Ski jumper and figure skater

Date	Mintage	F	VF	XF	Unc
AH1408-1988	8,000	—	—	—	13.50
AH1408-1988 Matte	—	—	—	—	55.00
AH1408-1988 Proof	2,000	Value: 30.00			

KM# 631 5 POUNDS **Weight:** 17.5000 g. **Composition:** 0.7200 Silver .4051 oz. ASW **Subject:** 50th Anniversary of Air Travel

Date	Mintage	F	VF	XF	Unc
AH1408-1988	5,000	—	—	—	13.50

KM# 649 5 POUNDS **Weight:** 17.5000 g. **Composition:** 0.7200 Silver .4051 oz. ASW **Subject:** Dedication of Cairo Opera House

Date	Mintage	F	VF	XF	Unc
AH1409-1988	30,000	—	—	—	12.50

KM# 660 5 POUNDS **Weight:** 17.5000 g. **Composition:** 0.7200 Silver .4051 oz. ASW **Subject:** Ministry of Agriculture

Date	Mintage	F	VF	XF	Unc
AH1409-1988	5,000	—	—	—	12.50

KM# 662 5 POUNDS **Weight:** 17.5000 g. **Composition:** 0.7200 Silver .4051 oz. ASW **Subject:** Naguib Mahfouz, Nobel Laureate **Reverse:** Head of Mahfouz left

Date	Mintage	F	VF	XF	Unc
AH1409-1988	15,000	—	—	—	12.50

KM# 663 5 POUNDS **Weight:** 17.5000 g. **Composition:** 0.7200 Silver .4051 oz. ASW **Subject:** Advista Arabia II

Date	Mintage	F	VF	XF	Unc
AH1409-1989	5,000	—	—	—	12.50

KM# 665 5 POUNDS **Weight:** 17.5000 g. **Composition:** 0.7200 Silver .4051 oz. ASW **Subject:** United Parliamentary Union

Date	Mintage	F	VF	XF	Unc
AH1409-1989	5,000	—	—	—	12.50

KM# 667 5 POUNDS **Weight:** 17.5000 g. **Composition:** 0.7200 Silver .4051 oz. ASW **Subject:** First Arab Olympics **Obverse:** Kufic legend above denomination and date

Date	Mintage	F	VF	XF	Unc
AH1409-1989	8,000	—	—	—	12.50

KM# 669 5 POUNDS **Weight:** 17.5000 g. **Composition:** 0.7200 Silver .4051 oz. ASW **Subject:** National Research Center **Reverse:** Stylized ancient and modern research elements

Date	Mintage	F	VF	XF	Unc
AH1409-1989	5,000	—	—	—	12.50

KM# 686 5 POUNDS **Weight:** 17.5000 g. **Composition:** 0.7200 Silver .4051 oz. ASW **Subject:** National Health Insurance

Date	Mintage	F	VF	XF	Unc
AH1409-1989	3,000	—	—	—	15.00

KM# 678 5 POUNDS **Weight:** 17.5000 g. **Composition:** 0.7200 Silver .4051 oz. ASW **Subject:** University of Cairo - School of Agriculture

Date	Mintage	F	VF	XF	Unc
AH1410-1989	4,000	—	—	—	22.00

KM# 679 5 POUNDS **Weight:** 17.5000 g. **Composition:** 0.7200 Silver .4051 oz. ASW **Series:** Soccer World Championship - Italy **Reverse:** Ancient Gods in front of pyramid with soccer ball above

Date	Mintage	F	VF	XF	Unc
AH1410-1990	600	—	—	—	35.00
AH1410-1990 Proof	8,000	Value: 25.00			

KM# 682 5 POUNDS **Weight:** 17.5000 g. **Composition:** 0.7200 Silver .4051 oz. ASW **Series:** Soccer World Championship - Italy **Reverse:** Player chasing ball

Date	Mintage	F	VF	XF	Unc
AH1410-1990 Matte	400	—	—	—	40.00
AH1410-1990 Proof	4,000	Value: 30.00			

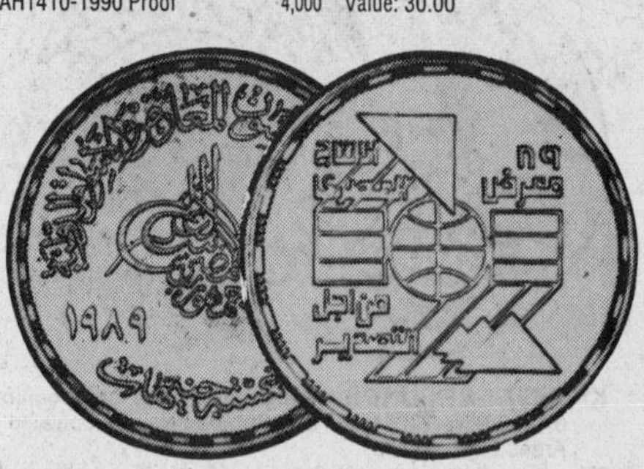

KM# 687 5 POUNDS **Weight:** 17.5000 g. **Composition:** 0.7200 Silver .4051 oz. ASW **Subject:** Export Drive

Date	Mintage	F	VF	XF	Unc
AH1410-1990	4,000	—	—	—	15.00

KM# 688 5 POUNDS **Weight:** 17.5000 g. **Composition:** 0.7200 Silver .4051 oz. ASW **Subject:** National Population Center

Date	Mintage	F	VF	XF	Unc
AH1410-1990	5,000	—	—	—	13.50

KM# 689 5 POUNDS **Weight:** 17.5000 g. **Composition:** 0.7200 Silver .4051 oz. ASW **Subject:** Union of African Parliaments

Date	Mintage	F	VF	XF	Unc
AH1410-1990	5,000	—	—	—	13.50

KM# 691 5 POUNDS **Weight:** 17.8200 g. **Composition:** 0.9000 Silver .5156 oz. ASW **Subject:** Dar-el-Eloun Faculty

Date	Mintage	F	VF	XF	Unc
AH1410-1990	5,000	—	—	—	13.50

KM# 697 5 POUNDS **Weight:** 17.5000 g. **Composition:** 0.7200 Silver .4051 oz. ASW **Subject:** Newly Populated Areas Organization

Date	Mintage	F	VF	XF	Unc
AH1410-1990	2,000	—	—	—	45.00

KM# 698 5 POUNDS **Weight:** 17.5000 g. **Composition:** 0.7200 Silver .4051 oz. ASW **Subject:** Alexandria Sports Club

Date	Mintage	F	VF	XF	Unc
AH1411-1990	5,000	—	—	—	20.00

KM# 692 5 POUNDS **Weight:** 17.8200 g. **Composition:** 0.9000 Silver .5156 oz. ASW **Subject:** Islamic Development Bank

Date	Mintage	F	VF	XF	Unc
AH1411-1991	5,000	—	—	—	13.50

KM# 700 5 POUNDS **Weight:** 17.8200 g. **Composition:** 0.9000 Silver .5156 oz. ASW **Subject:** 5th African Games - Cairo

Date	Mintage	F	VF	XF	Unc
AH1411-1991	3,000	—	—	—	30.00

KM# 727 5 POUNDS **Weight:** 17.5000 g. **Composition:** 0.7200 Silver .4051 oz. ASW **Subject:** Muhamed Abdel Wahab **Obverse:** Arabic legends and inscriptions **Reverse:** Bust of Wahab left with music sheet in background

Date	Mintage	F	VF	XF	Unc
AH1412-1991	30,000	—	—	—	13.50

KM# 728 5 POUNDS **Weight:** 26.0000 g. **Composition:** 0.8750 Gold .7314 oz. AGW **Subject:** Muhamed Abdel Wahab **Obverse:** Arabic legends and inscriptions **Reverse:** Bust of Wahab left with music sheet in background

Date	Mintage	F	VF	XF	Unc
AH1412-1991 Proof	400	—	—	—	500

KM# 791 5 POUNDS **Weight:** 17.4200 g. **Composition:** 0.7200 Silver .4032 oz. ASW **Subject:** National Zoo **Obverse:** Zoo entrance, dates **Reverse:** Zoo animals

Date	F	VF	XF	Unc
AH1411-1991	—	—	—	25.00

KM# 804 5 POUNDS **Weight:** 17.5000 g. **Composition:** 0.7200 Silver .4051 oz. ASW **Subject:** Atomic Energy **Obverse:** Denomination **Reverse:** Ancient statue and pyramid within rings

Date	F	VF	XF	Unc
AH1411-1991	—	—	—	15.00

KM# 805 5 POUNDS **Weight:** 17.5000 g. **Composition:** 0.7200 Silver .4051 oz. ASW **Subject:** Library of Alexandria **Obverse:** Arabic inscription **Reverse:** Library building complex

Date	F	VF	XF	Unc
AH1411-1991	—	—	—	15.00

KM# 805a 5 POUNDS **Weight:** 26.0000 g. **Composition:** 0.8750 Gold .7314 oz. AGW **Subject:** Library of Alexandria **Obverse:** Arabic inscription **Reverse:** Library building complex **Edge:** Reeded **Note:** Struck at Cairo.

Date	Mintage	F	VF	XF	Unc
AH1411-1991 Proof	200	—	—	—	500

KM# 833 5 POUNDS **Weight:** 26.0000 g. **Composition:** 0.8750 Gold .7315 oz. AGW **Subject:** Library of Alexandria **Obverse:** Legend and inscription **Reverse:** Waterfront building with tower

Date	Mintage	F	VF	XF	Unc
AH1411-1991	200	—	—	—	500

KM# 701 5 POUNDS **Weight:** 17.5000 g. **Composition:** 0.7200 Silver .4051 oz. ASW **Series:** Summer Olympics **Reverse:** Two men fencing

Date	Mintage	F	VF	XF	Unc
AH1412-1992	999	—	—	—	42.50
AH1412-1992 Proof	2,999	Value: 40.00			

KM# 702 5 POUNDS **Weight:** 17.5000 g. **Composition:** 0.7200 Silver .4051 oz. ASW **Series:** Summer Olympics **Reverse:** Two men wrestling

Date	Mintage	F	VF	XF	Unc
AH1412-1992	999	—	—	—	42.50
AH1412-1992 Proof	2,999	Value: 40.00			

KM# 703 5 POUNDS **Weight:** 17.5000 g. **Composition:** 0.7200 Silver .4051 oz. ASW **Series:** Summer Olympics **Reverse:** Archery demonstrated

Date	Mintage	F	VF	XF	Unc
AH1412-1992	999	—	—	—	42.50
AH1412-1992 Proof	2,999	Value: 40.00			

KM# 704 5 POUNDS **Weight:** 17.5000 g. **Composition:** 0.7200 Silver .4051 oz. ASW **Series:** Summer Olympics **Reverse:** Many men wrestling an ox

Date	Mintage	F	VF	XF	Unc
AH1412-1992	999	—	—	—	42.50
AH1412-1992 Proof	2,999	Value: 40.00			

KM# 705 5 POUNDS **Weight:** 17.5000 g. **Composition:** 0.7200 Silver .4051 oz. ASW **Series:** Summer Olympics **Reverse:** Swimmer stalking a duck

Date	Mintage	F	VF	XF	Unc
AH1412-1992	999	—	—	—	42.50
AH1412-1992 Proof	2,999	Value: 40.00			

KM# 706 5 POUNDS **Weight:** 17.5000 g. **Composition:** 0.7200 Silver .4051 oz. ASW **Series:** Summer Olympics **Reverse:** Handball player

Date	Mintage	F	VF	XF	Unc
AH1412-1992	999	—	—	—	42.50
AH1412-1992 Proof	25,000	Value: 20.00			

KM# 707 5 POUNDS **Weight:** 17.5000 g. **Composition:** 0.7200 Silver .4051 oz. ASW **Series:** Summer Olympics **Reverse:** Field hockey player

Date	Mintage	F	VF	XF	Unc
AH1412-1992	999	—	—	—	42.50
AH1412-1992 Proof	25,000	Value: 20.00			

KM# 708 5 POUNDS **Weight:** 17.5000 g. **Composition:** 0.7200 Silver .4051 oz. ASW **Series:** Summer Olympics **Reverse:** Soccer player

Date	Mintage	F	VF	XF	Unc
AH1412-1992	999	—	—	—	42.50
AH1412-1992 Proof	25,000	Value: 20.00			

KM# 806 5 POUNDS **Weight:** 17.5000 g. **Composition:** 0.7200 Silver .4051 oz. ASW **Subject:** Lighthouse of Alexandria **Obverse:** Denomination **Reverse:** Ancient tower and Egyptian

Date	F	VF	XF	Unc
AH1412-1992	—	—	—	17.50

KM# 807 5 POUNDS **Weight:** 17.5000 g. **Composition:** 0.7200 Silver .4051 oz. ASW **Subject:** 50 Years - University of Alexandria **Obverse:** Arabic inscription **Reverse:** University emblem

Date	F	VF	XF	Unc
AH1413-1992	—	—	—	18.50

KM# 808 5 POUNDS **Weight:** 17.5000 g. **Composition:** 0.7200 Silver .4051 oz. ASW **Subject:** Naguib Mahfouz, Nobel Laureate **Obverse:** Vase and inscriptions **Reverse:** Bust of Naguib Mahfouz right

Date	F	VF	XF	Unc
AH1413-1992	—	—	—	15.00

KM# 735 5 POUNDS **Weight:** 22.5000 g. **Composition:** 0.9990 Silver .7227 oz. ASW **Subject:** Cleopatra **Reverse:** Bust of Cleopatra left

Date	Mintage	F	VF	XF	Unc
AH1413-1993 Proof	50,000	Value: 36.50			

KM# 759 5 POUNDS **Weight:** 17.5000 g. **Composition:** 0.7200 Silver .4051 oz. ASW **Subject:** Beram El Tunsi, Poet **Reverse:** Bust of Beram El Tunsi facing left

Date	Mintage	F	VF	XF	Unc
AH1413-1993	3,000	—	—	—	25.00

KM# 740 5 POUNDS **Weight:** 22.5000 g. **Composition:** 0.9990 Silver .7227 oz. ASW **Subject:** Pyramids **Reverse:** Three pyramids

Date	Mintage	F	VF	XF	Unc
AH1414-1993 Proof	50,000	Value: 36.50			

KM# 741 5 POUNDS **Weight:** 22.5000 g. **Composition:** 0.9990 Silver .7227 oz. ASW **Subject:** Sphinx

Date	Mintage	F	VF	XF	Unc
AH1414-1993 Proof	50,000	Value: 36.50			

KM# 742 5 POUNDS **Weight:** 22.5000 g. **Composition:** 0.9990 Silver .7227 oz. ASW **Subject:** King Narmur Smiting a Foe

Date	Mintage	F	VF	XF	Unc
AH1414-1993 Proof	50,000	Value: 30.00			

KM# 743 5 POUNDS **Weight:** 22.5000 g. **Composition:** 0.9990 Silver .7227 oz. ASW **Subject:** Guardian Goddess Serket

Date	Mintage	F	VF	XF	Unc
AH1414-1993 Proof	50,000	Value: 30.00			

KM# 744 5 POUNDS **Weight:** 22.5000 g. **Composition:** 0.9990 Silver .7227 oz. ASW **Subject:** Amulet of Hathor

Date	Mintage	F	VF	XF	Unc
AH1414-1993 Proof	50,000	Value: 30.00			

KM# 745 5 POUNDS **Weight:** 22.5000 g. **Composition:** 0.9990 Silver .7227 oz. ASW **Subject:** Standing Ramses II

Date	Mintage	F	VF	XF	Unc
AH1414-1993 Proof	50,000	Value: 30.00			

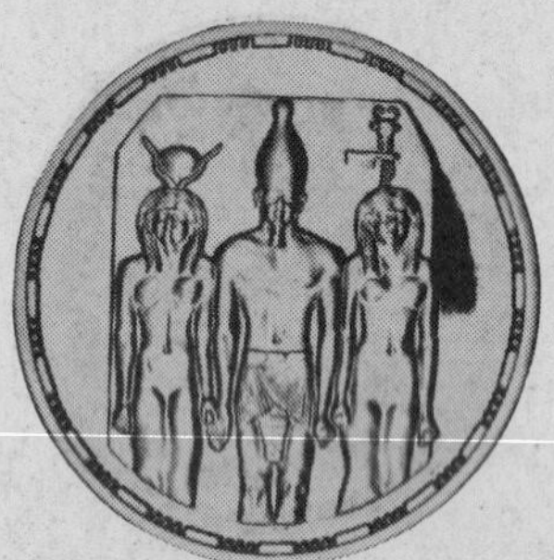

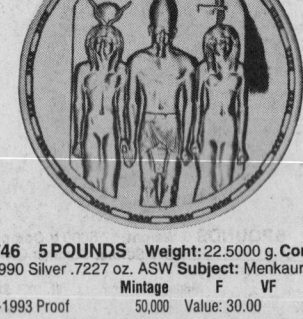

KM# 746 5 POUNDS **Weight:** 22.5000 g. **Composition:** 0.9990 Silver .7227 oz. ASW **Subject:** Menkaure Triad

Date	Mintage	F	VF	XF	Unc
AH1414-1993 Proof	50,000	Value: 30.00			

KM# 747 5 POUNDS **Weight:** 22.5000 g. **Composition:** 0.9990 Silver .7227 oz. ASW **Subject:** Symbol of Unification **Reverse:** Two females representing the upper and lower Nile

Date	Mintage	F	VF	XF	Unc
AH1414-1993 Proof	50,000	Value: 30.00			

KM# 793 5 POUNDS **Weight:** 22.5000 g. **Composition:** 0.9990 Silver .7227 oz. ASW **Obverse:** Vulture **Reverse:** Tutankhamen's burial mask

Date	F	VF	XF	Unc
AH1414-1993 Proof	—	Value: 37.50		

KM# 812 5 POUNDS **Weight:** 17.5000 g. **Composition:** 0.7200 Silver .4051 oz. ASW **Subject:** 20th Anniversary - October War **Obverse:** Smoking chimney text **Reverse:** Soldier with flag

Date	F	VF	XF	Unc
AH1414-1993	—	—	—	15.00

KM# 837 5 POUNDS **Weight:** 17.5000 g. **Composition:** 0.7200 Silver .4051 oz. ASW **Subject:** 125th Anniversary of Taalat Harb Birth **Obverse:** Denomination and date in circle above inscription **Reverse:** Taalat Harb wearing fez **Edge:** Reeded

Date	Mintage	F	VF	XF	Unc
AH1413-1993	5,000	—	—	—	25.00

KM# 869 5 POUNDS **Weight:** 22.5500 g. **Composition:** 0.9990 Silver .7243 oz. ASW **Subject:** King Kha-Sekhem **Obverse:** Vulture **Reverse:** Seated figure **Edge:** Reeded

Date	Mintage	F	VF	XF	Unc
AH1414-1993 Proof	15,000	—	—	—	45.00

KM# 748 5 POUNDS **Weight:** 22.5000 g. **Composition:** 0.9990 Silver .7227 oz. ASW **Series:** World Cup Soccer **Reverse:** Kneeling King Pepi I facing

Date	Mintage	F	VF	XF	Unc
AH1414-1993 Proof	—	Value: 32.50			
AH1415-1994 Proof	50,000	Value: 30.00			

KM# 879 5 POUNDS **Weight:** 26.0000 g. **Composition:** 0.8750 Gold .7315 oz. AGW **Subject:** Symbol of Unification **Reverse:** Two females representing the upper and lower Nile

Date	Mintage	F	VF	XF	Unc
AH1414-1993 Proof	3,000	—	—	—	275

KM# 880 5 POUNDS **Weight:** 26.0000 g. **Composition:** 0.8750 Gold .7315 oz. AGW **Reverse:** Kneeling King Pepi I facing

Date	Mintage	F	VF	XF	Unc
AH1415-1994 Proof	3,000	—	—	—	275

KM# 881 5 POUNDS **Weight:** 26.0000 g. **Composition:** 0.8750 Gold .7315 oz. AGW **Reverse:** Statue of King Amenemhat III

Date	Mintage	F	VF	XF	Unc
AH1415-1994 Proof	3,000	—	—	—	275

KM# 785 5 POUNDS **Weight:** 22.5000 g. **Composition:** 0.9990 Silver .7227 oz. ASW **Obverse:** Ancient style vulture **Reverse:** Five birds

Date	Mintage	F	VF	XF	Unc
AH1415-1994 Proof	50,000	Value: 40.00			

KM# 786 5 POUNDS **Weight:** 22.5000 g. **Composition:** 0.9990 Silver .7227 oz. ASW **Obverse:** Ancient style vulture **Reverse:** Hippopotamus right

Date	Mintage	F	VF	XF	Unc
AH1415-1994 Proof	50,000	Value: 40.00			

KM# 787 5 POUNDS **Weight:** 22.5000 g. **Composition:** 0.9990 Silver .7227 oz. ASW **Obverse:** Ancient style vulture **Reverse:** Ruins of Karnak

Date	Mintage	F	VF	XF	Unc
AH1415-1994 Proof	50,000	Value: 30.00			

KM# 788 5 POUNDS **Weight:** 22.5000 g. **Composition:** 0.9990 Silver .7227 oz. ASW **Obverse:** Ancient style vulture **Reverse:** Standing goddess Neith wearing the Red Crown

Date	Mintage	F	VF	XF	Unc
AH1415-1994 Proof	50,000	Value: 30.00			

KM# 789 5 POUNDS **Weight:** 22.5000 g. **Composition:** 0.9990 Silver .7227 oz. ASW **Obverse:** Ancient style vulture **Reverse:** Statue of King Amenemhat III

Date	Mintage	F	VF	XF	Unc
AH1415-1994 Proof	50,000	Value: 30.00			

KM# 790 5 POUNDS **Weight:** 22.5000 g. **Composition:** 0.9990 Silver .7227 oz. ASW **Obverse:** Ancient style vulture **Reverse:** Ritual mask of Queen Hatshepsut

Date	Mintage	F	VF	XF	Unc
AH1415-1994 Proof	50,000	Value: 30.00			

KM# 792 5 POUNDS **Weight:** 15.0000 g. **Composition:** 0.7200 Silver .3472 oz. ASW **Subject:** ICPD Cairo **Obverse:** Inscription and seals **Reverse:** Stylized design

Date	F	VF	XF	Unc
AH1415-1994	—	—	—	17.50

KM# 794 5 POUNDS **Weight:** 22.5950 g. **Composition:** 0.9990 Silver .7264 oz. ASW **Obverse:** Ancient style vulture **Reverse:** Seated, jeweled cat

Date	F	VF	XF	Unc
AH1415-1994 Proof	—	Value: 40.00		

KM# 795 5 POUNDS **Weight:** 22.5950 g. **Composition:** 0.9990 Silver .7264 oz. ASW **Obverse:** Ancient style vulture **Reverse:** Sacred falcon at Edfu

Date	F	VF	XF	Unc
AH1415-1994 Proof	—	Value: 40.00		

KM# 797 5 POUNDS **Weight:** 22.5950 g. **Composition:** 0.9990 Silver .7264 oz. ASW **Obverse:** Ancient style vulture **Reverse:** Tutankhamon's throne

Date	F	VF	XF	Unc
AH1415-1994 Proof	—	Value: 31.50		

KM# 798 5 POUNDS **Weight:** 22.5950 g. **Composition:** 0.9990 Silver .7264 oz. ASW **Obverse:** Ancient style vulture **Reverse:** King Au as high priest

Date	F	VF	XF	Unc
AH1415-1994 Proof	—	Value: 31.50		

KM# 799 5 POUNDS **Weight:** 22.5950 g. **Composition:** 0.9990 Silver .7264 oz. ASW **Obverse:** Ancient style vulture **Reverse:** Akhnaton

Date	F	VF	XF	Unc
AH1415-1994 Proof	—	Value: 40.00		

KM# 800 5 POUNDS **Weight:** 22.5950 g. **Composition:** 0.9990 Silver .7264 oz. ASW **Obverse:** Ancient style vulture **Reverse:** Osiris seated right

Date	F	VF	XF	Unc
AH1415-1994 Proof	—	Value: 30.00		

KM# 801 5 POUNDS **Weight:** 22.5950 g. **Composition:** 0.9990 Silver .7264 oz. ASW **Obverse:** Ancient style vulture **Reverse:** RE, the sun god walking left

Date	F	VF	XF	Unc
AH1415-1994 Proof	—	Value: 30.00		

KM# 823 5 POUNDS **Weight:** 22.5000 g. **Composition:** 0.9990 Silver .7227 oz. ASW **Obverse:** Ancient style vulture, denomination **Reverse:** Temple of Ramses II

Date	F	VF	XF	Unc
AH1415-1994 Proof	—	Value: 36.50		

KM# 827 5 POUNDS **Weight:** 22.5000 g. **Composition:** 0.9990 Silver .7227 oz. ASW **Obverse:** Ancient style vulture, denomination **Reverse:** Seated King Khufu

Date	F	VF	XF	Unc
AH1415-1994 Proof	—	Value: 30.00		

KM# 802 5 POUNDS **Weight:** 22.5950 g. **Composition:** 0.9990 Silver .7264 oz. ASW **Obverse:** Ancient style vulture **Reverse:** The god Khnoum walking right

Date	F	VF	XF	Unc
AH1415-1994 Proof	—	Value: 37.50		

KM# 824 5 POUNDS **Weight:** 22.5000 g. **Composition:** 0.9990 Silver .7227 oz. ASW **Obverse:** Ancient style vulture, denomination **Reverse:** Ancient ruins

Date	F	VF	XF	Unc
AH1415-1994 Proof	—	Value: 30.00		

KM# 828 5 POUNDS **Weight:** 22.5000 g. **Composition:** 0.9990 Silver .7227 oz. ASW **Obverse:** Ancient style vulture, denomination **Reverse:** Standing goddess Hathor left

Date	F	VF	XF	Unc
AH1415-1994 Proof	—	Value: 30.00		

KM# 803 5 POUNDS **Weight:** 22.5950 g. **Composition:** 0.9990 Silver .7264 oz. ASW **Obverse:** Ancient style vulture **Reverse:** Sobek, crocodile god, walking left

Date	F	VF	XF	Unc
AH1415-1994 Proof	—	Value: 37.50		

KM# 825 5 POUNDS **Weight:** 22.5000 g. **Composition:** 0.9990 Silver .7227 oz. ASW **Obverse:** Ancient style vulture, denomination **Reverse:** Goat right

Date	F	VF	XF	Unc
AH1415-1994 Proof	—	Value: 36.50		

KM# 829 5 POUNDS **Weight:** 22.5000 g. **Composition:** 0.9990 Silver .7227 oz. ASW **Obverse:** Ancient style vulture, denomination **Reverse:** Standing god Ptah of Memphis right

Date	F	VF	XF	Unc
AH1415-1994 Proof	—	Value: 30.00		

KM# 813 5 POUNDS **Weight:** 22.5500 g. **Composition:** 0.9990 Silver .7243 oz. ASW **Obverse:** Ancient style vulture, denomination **Reverse:** Seated ancient scribe **Edge:** Reeded

Date	F	VF	XF	Unc
AH1415-1994 Proof	—	Value: 37.50		

KM# 826 5 POUNDS **Weight:** 22.5000 g. **Composition:** 0.9990 Silver .7227 oz. ASW **Obverse:** Ancient style vulture, denomination **Reverse:** King Thoutmosis III kneeling left

Date	F	VF	XF	Unc
AH1415-1994 Proof	—	Value: 30.00		

KM# 830 5 POUNDS **Weight:** 22.5000 g. **Composition:** 0.9990 Silver .7227 oz. ASW **Obverse:** Ancient style vulture, denomination **Reverse:** Seated goddess Isis nursing child

Date	F	VF	XF	Unc
AH1415-1994 Proof	—	Value: 30.00		

KM# 831 5 POUNDS **Weight:** 22.5000 g. **Composition:** 0.9990 Silver .7227 oz. ASW **Obverse:** Ancient style vulture, denomination **Reverse:** Dwarf Seneb and family

Date	F	VF	XF	Unc
AH1415-1994 Proof	—	Value: 30.00		

KM# 878 5 POUNDS **Weight:** 26.0000 g. **Composition:** 0.8750 Gold .7315 oz. AGW **Obverse:** Ancient style vulture, denomination **Reverse:** Dwarf Seneb and family

Date	Mintage	F	VF	XF	Unc
AH1415-1994 Proof	3,000	—	—	—	275

KM# 874 5 POUNDS **Weight:** 26.0000 g. **Composition:** 0.8750 Gold .7315 oz. AGW **Reverse:** Sphinx and pyramids

Date	Mintage	F	VF	XF	Unc
AH1415-1994 Proof	5,000	—	—	—	275

KM# 877 5 POUNDS **Weight:** 26.0000 g. **Composition:** 0.8750 Gold .7315 oz. AGW **Reverse:** Seated scribe

Date	Mintage	F	VF	XF	Unc
AH1415-1994 Proof	3,000	Value: 275			

KM# 876 5 POUNDS **Weight:** 26.0000 g. **Composition:** 0.8750 Gold .7315 oz. AGW **Reverse:** 3/4-length standing Sheikh El Balad

Date	Mintage	F	VF	XF	Unc
AH1415-1994 Proof	3,000	Value: 275			

KM# 750 5 POUNDS **Weight:** 22.5000 g. **Composition:** 0.9990 Silver .7227 oz. ASW **Reverse:** King Djoser wearing the Red Crown right

Date	Mintage	F	VF	XF	Unc
AH1415-1994 Proof	50,000	Value: 30.00			

KM# 751 5 POUNDS **Weight:** 22.5000 g. **Composition:** 0.9990 Silver .7227 oz. ASW **Reverse:** King Khonsu facing

Date	Mintage	F	VF	XF	Unc
AH1415-1994 Proof	50,000	Value: 30.00			

KM# 752 5 POUNDS **Weight:** 22.5000 g. **Composition:** 0.9990 Silver .7227 oz. ASW **Reverse:** RE (Sun God) presenting the Ankh (Symbol of Life) to Sesostris I wearing Double Crown

Date	Mintage	F	VF	XF	Unc
AH1415-1994 Proof	50,000	Value: 30.00			

KM# 753 5 POUNDS **Weight:** 22.5000 g. **Composition:** 0.9990 Silver .7227 oz. ASW **Reverse:** God Horus wearing Double Crown

Date	Mintage	F	VF	XF	Unc
AH1415-1994 Proof	50,000	Value: 30.00			

KM# 754 5 POUNDS **Weight:** 22.5000 g. **Composition:** 0.9990 Silver .7227 oz. ASW **Reverse:** Standing god Seth left

Date	Mintage	F	VF	XF	Unc
AH1415-1994 Proof	50,000	Value: 30.00			

KM# 757 5 POUNDS **Weight:** 22.5000 g. **Composition:** 0.9990 Silver .7227 oz. ASW **Reverse:** Queen Nofretari, wife of Ramses II kneeling right

Date	Mintage	F	VF	XF	Unc
AH1415-1994 Proof	Est. 25,000	Value: 37.50			

KM# 783 5 POUNDS **Weight:** 22.5000 g. **Composition:** 0.9990 Silver .7227 oz. ASW **Obverse:** Ancient style vulture **Reverse:** Bust of Nefertiti right

Date	Mintage	F	VF	XF	Unc
AH1415-1994 Proof	50,000	Value: 36.50			

KM# 784 5 POUNDS **Weight:** 22.5000 g. **Composition:** 0.9990 Silver .7227 oz. ASW **Obverse:** Ancient style vulture **Reverse:** Archer in chariot

Date	Mintage	F	VF	XF	Unc
AH1415-1994 Proof	50,000	Value: 37.50			

KM# 749 5 POUNDS **Weight:** 22.5000 g. **Composition:** 0.9990 Silver .7227 oz. ASW **Reverse:** Sphinx and pyramids

Date	Mintage	F	VF	XF	Unc
AH1414-1994 Proof	50,000	Value: 32.50			

KM# 763 5 POUNDS **Weight:** 17.5000 g. **Composition:** 0.7200 Silver .4051 oz. ASW **Subject:** Salah El Din El-Ayubi **Reverse:** Bust of El-Ayubi center, mosque behind at left, mounted rider with sword at right

Date	Mintage	F	VF	XF	Unc
AH1414-1994	5,000	—	—	—	25.00

KM# 736 5 POUNDS **Weight:** 17.5000 g. **Composition:** 0.9250 Silver .5205 oz. ASW **Series:** World Cup Soccer **Reverse:** Two players, pyramid with Statue of Liberty at left

Date	Mintage	F	VF	XF	Unc
AH1415-1994	499	—	—	—	45.00
AH1415-1994 Proof	15,000	Value: 40.00			

KM# 738 5 POUNDS **Weight:** 17.5000 g. **Composition:** 0.9250 Silver .5205 oz. ASW **Series:** World Cup Soccer **Reverse:** Stylized player

Date	Mintage	F	VF	XF	Unc
AH1415-1994	499	—	—	—	45.00
AH1415-1994 Proof	15,000	Value: 40.00			

KM# 875 5 POUNDS **Weight:** 22.5000 g. **Composition:** 0.9990 Silver .7227 oz. ASW **Reverse:** 3/4-length standing Sheikh El Balad

Date	Mintage	F	VF	XF	Unc
AH1415-1994 Proof	15,000	Value: 40.00			

KM# 883 5 POUNDS **Weight:** 22.5000 g. **Composition:** 0.9990 Silver .7227 oz. ASW **Reverse:** Seated King Horemheb

Date	Mintage	F	VF	XF	Unc
AH1415-1994 Proof	15,000	Value: 40.00			

KM# 889 5 POUNDS **Weight:** 22.5000 g. **Composition:** 0.9990 Silver .7227 oz. ASW **Reverse:** Akhnaton and family

Date	Mintage	F	VF	XF	Unc
AH1415-1994 Proof	15,000	Value: 40.00			

KM# 894 5 POUNDS **Weight:** 22.5000 g. **Composition:** 0.9990 Silver .7227 oz. ASW **Reverse:** Bust amulet of Hathor

Date	Mintage	F	VF	XF	Unc
AH1415-1994 Proof	15,000	Value: 40.00			

KM# 896 5 POUNDS **Weight:** 22.5000 g. **Composition:** 0.9990 Silver .7227 oz. ASW **Reverse:** Pair of geese

Date	Mintage	F	VF	XF	Unc
AH1415-1994 Proof	15,000	Value: 40.00			

KM# 765 5 POUNDS **Weight:** 17.5000 g. **Composition:** 0.7200 Silver .4051 oz. ASW **Subject:** 50 Years - Arab League

Date	Mintage	F	VF	XF	Unc
AH1415-1995	5,000	—	—	—	22.50

KM# 768 5 POUNDS **Weight:** 17.5000 g. **Composition:** 0.7200 Silver .4051 oz. ASW **Subject:** 75 Years - Bank of Misr

Date	Mintage	F	VF	XF	Unc
AH1415-1995	2,500	—	—	—	28.00

KM# 770 5 POUNDS **Weight:** 17.5000 g. **Composition:** 0.7200 Silver .4051 oz. ASW **Series:** F.A.O. **Reverse:** People working

Date	Mintage	F	VF	XF	Unc
AH1415-1995	5,000	—	—	—	50.00

KM# 772 5 POUNDS **Weight:** 17.5000 g. **Composition:** 0.7200 Silver .4051 oz. ASW **Subject:** Pediatrics International Conference

Date	Mintage	F	VF	XF	Unc
AH1416-1995	4,000	—	—	—	22.00

KM# 773 5 POUNDS **Weight:** 17.5000 g. **Composition:** 0.7200 Silver .4051 oz. ASW **Subject:** 75 Years - Architects Association

Date	Mintage	F	VF	XF	Unc
AH1416-1995	3,000	—	—	—	50.00

KM# 838 5 POUNDS **Weight:** 17.5000 g. **Composition:** 0.7200 Silver .4051 oz. ASW **Subject:** 75 Years - American University in Cairo

Date	Mintage	F	VF	XF	Unc
AH1415-1995	3,000	—	—	—	25.00

KM# 841 5 POUNDS **Weight:** 17.5000 g. **Composition:** 0.7200 Silver .4051 oz. ASW **Obverse:** Denomination **Reverse:** Abd Al Halem Hafez

Date	Mintage	F	VF	XF	Unc
AH1416-1995	5,000	—	—	—	45.00

KM# 774 5 POUNDS **Weight:** 26.0000 g. **Composition:** 0.8750 Gold .7315 oz. AGW **Subject:** 75 Years - Architects Association

Date	Mintage	F	VF	XF	Unc
AH1416-1995	300	—	—	—	500

KM# 842 5 POUNDS **Weight:** 26.0000 g. **Composition:** 0.8750 Gold .7315 oz. AGW **Reverse:** Abd Al Halem Hafez

Date	Mintage	F	VF	XF	Unc
AH1416-1995	500	—	—	—	500

KM# 843 5 POUNDS **Weight:** 17.5000 g. **Composition:** 0.9000 Silver .5084 oz. ASW **Subject:** Centennial - Mining and Geology

Date	Mintage	F	VF	XF	Unc
AH1416-1996	700	—	—	—	75.00

KM# 846 5 POUNDS **Weight:** 17.5000 g. **Composition:** 0.9000 Silver .5084 oz. ASW **Subject:** 65 Years - Egyptian Air Force **Reverse:** Flying eagle in wreath

Date	Mintage	F	VF	XF	Unc
AH1418-1997	300	—	—	—	85.00

KM# 848 5 POUNDS **Weight:** 17.5000 g. **Composition:** 0.9000 Silver .5084 oz. ASW **Subject:** 50 Years Arab Land Bank **Reverse:** Domed building

Date	F	VF	XF	Unc
AH1418-1997	—	—	—	37.50

KM# 850 5 POUNDS **Weight:** 17.5000 g. **Composition:** 0.9000 Silver .5084 oz. ASW **Subject:** 95th Interparliamentary Union Conference **Obverse:** Circular design above inscription **Reverse:** Pyramids in wreath

Date	Mintage	F	VF	XF	Unc
AH1418-1997	375	—	—	—	85.00

KM# 852 5 POUNDS **Weight:** 17.5000 g. **Composition:** 0.9000 Silver .5084 oz. ASW **Subject:** Centennial - 100 Years Chemical Office **Reverse:** Symbolic design

Date	F	VF	XF	Unc
AH1419-1998	—	—	—	40.00

KM# 853 5 POUNDS **Weight:** 17.5000 g. **Composition:** 0.9000 Silver .5084 oz. ASW **Subject:** Restoration of Al Azhar Mosque

Date	F	VF	XF	Unc
AH1419-1998	—	—	—	37.50

KM# 856 5 POUNDS **Weight:** 17.5000 g. **Composition:** 0.9000 Silver .5084 oz. ASW **Subject:** Centennial of National Bank **Reverse:** Large "100"

Date	Mintage	F	VF	XF	Unc
AH1419-1998	300	—	—	—	85.00

KM# 858 5 POUNDS **Weight:** 17.5000 g. **Composition:** 0.9000 Silver .5084 oz. ASW **Subject:** 25th Anniversary - October War **Reverse:** Symbolic design

Date	F	VF	XF	Unc
AH1419-1998	—	—	—	40.00

KM# 860 5 POUNDS **Weight:** 17.5000 g. **Composition:** 0.9000 Silver .5084 oz. ASW **Reverse:** Imam Metwaly El Sharawi

Date	F	VF	XF	Unc
AH1419-1998	—	—	—	40.00

KM# 862 5 POUNDS **Weight:** 17.5000 g. **Composition:** 0.9000 Silver .5084 oz. ASW **Subject:** Centennial - Land Surveying **Reverse:** "100" above ancient surveyors

Date	F	VF	XF	Unc
AH1419-1998	—	—	—	40.00

KM# 864 5 POUNDS **Weight:** 17.5000 g. **Composition:** 0.9000 Silver .5084 oz. ASW **Subject:** Centennial - Solidarity **Reverse:** Symbolic design

Date	F	VF	XF	Unc
AH1419-1998	—	—	—	37.50

KM# 854 5 POUNDS **Weight:** 17.5000 g. **Composition:** 0.9000 Silver .5084 oz. ASW **Subject:** 16th Men's World Handball Championship

Date	F	VF	XF	Unc
AH1420-1999	—	—	—	45.00

KM# 867 5 POUNDS **Weight:** 17.5000 g. **Composition:** 0.9000 Silver .5084 oz. ASW **Subject:** 50 Years Cairo Metropolitan Mass Transit System **Reverse:** Water above subway train

Date	F	VF	XF	Unc
AH1420-1999	—	—	—	40.00

KM# 897 5 POUNDS **Weight:** 17.5000 g. **Composition:** 0.9000 Silver .5084 oz. ASW **Subject:** 75 Years - Dar El-Eloum University

Date	F	VF	XF	Unc
AH1420-1999	—	—	—	40.00

KM# 898 5 POUNDS **Weight:** 17.3300 g. **Composition:** 0.9750 Silver 0.5432 oz. ASW **Subject:** Sacred Falcon **Obverse:** Denomination and inscription **Reverse:** Ancient sacred falcon **Edge:** Reeded **Size:** 37 mm.

Date	F	VF	XF	Unc
AH1420-1999 Proof	—	Value: 50.00		

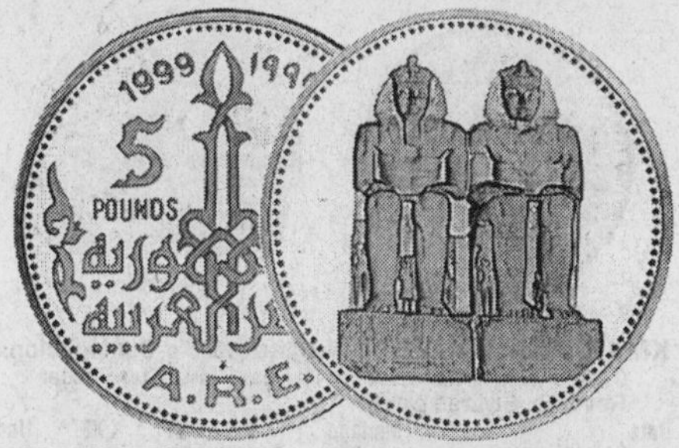

KM#899 5 POUNDS **Weight:** 17.3300 g. **Composition:** 0.9750 Silver 0.5432 oz. ASW **Obverse:** Denomination and inscription **Reverse:** Two statues of Ramses II **Edge:** Reeded **Size:** 37 mm.

Date		F	VF	XF	Unc
AH1420-1999 Proof	—	Value: 50.00			

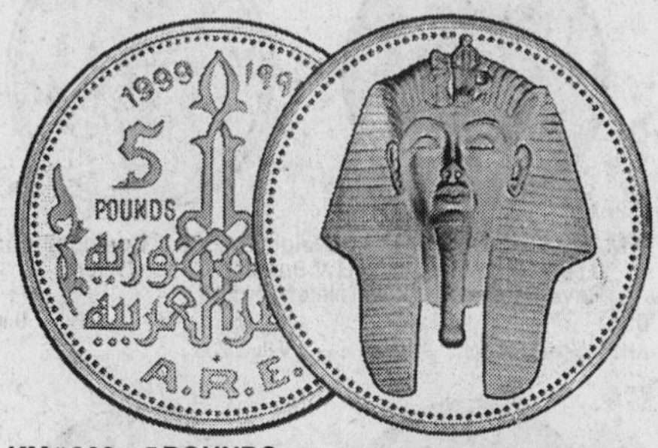

KM#900 5 POUNDS **Weight:** 17.3300 g. **Composition:** 0.9750 Silver 0.5432 oz. ASW **Obverse:** Denomination and inscription **Reverse:** Tutankhamen's Death Mask **Edge:** Reeded **Size:** 37 mm.

Date		F	VF	XF	Unc
AH1420-1999 Proof	—	Value: 50.00			

KM#901 5 POUNDS **Weight:** 17.3300 g. **Composition:** 0.9750 Silver 0.5432 oz. ASW **Obverse:** Denomination and inscription **Reverse:** Bust of Nefertiti right **Edge:** Reeded **Size:** 37 mm.

Date		F	VF	XF	Unc
AH1420-1999 Proof	—	Value: 50.00			

KM#902 5 POUNDS **Weight:** 17.3300 g. **Composition:** 0.9750 Silver 0.5432 oz. ASW **Obverse:** Denomination and inscription **Reverse:** Imaginary bust of Cleopatra left **Edge:** Reeded **Size:** 37 mm.

Date		F	VF	XF	Unc
AH1420-1999 Proof	—	Value: 50.00			

KM# 519 10 POUNDS **Weight:** 40.0000 g. **Composition:** 0.8750 Gold 1.1254 oz. AGW **Subject:** Egyptian-Israeli Peace Treaty

Date	Mintage	F	VF	XF	Unc
AH1400-1980	950	—	—	—	900
AH1400-1980 Proof	50	Value: 1,150			

KM# 538 10 POUNDS **Weight:** 40.0000 g. **Composition:** 0.8750 Gold 1.1254 oz. AGW **Subject:** 25th Anniversary - Ministry of Industry

Date	Mintage	F	VF	XF	Unc
AH1402-1981	18	—	—	—	1,500
AH1402-1981 Proof	1,000	Value: 700			

KM# 548 10 POUNDS **Weight:** 40.0000 g. **Composition:** 0.8750 Gold 1.1254 oz. AGW **Subject:** 1000th Anniveresary - Al Azhar Mosque

Date	Mintage	F	VF	XF	Unc
AH1402-1982 Proof	1,322	Value: 700			

KM# 634 10 POUNDS **Weight:** 40.0000 g. **Composition:** 0.8750 Gold 1.1254 oz. AGW **Subject:** Prophet's Mosque **Obverse:** Minaret, globe, denomination, legends **Reverse:** Crescent, mosque, minaret below legend arch

Date	Mintage	F	VF	XF	Unc
AH1406-1985 Proof	300	Value: 600			

KM#672 50 POUNDS **Weight:** 8.5000 g. **Composition:** 0.9000 Gold .2460 oz. AGW **Series:** World Soccer Championships **Obverse:** Stylized flowers, denomination, date and legends **Reverse:** Soccer ball on road between Mexican and Egyptian pyramids

Date	Mintage	F	VF	XF	Unc
AH1406-1986	250	—	—	—	250
AH1406-1986 Proof	250	Value: 300			

KM#641 50 POUNDS **Weight:** 8.5000 g. **Composition:** 0.9000 Gold .2460 oz. AGW **Subject:** Mecca **Obverse:** Arabic legend, ornamentation **Reverse:** Interior view of the Kaaba

Date	Mintage	F	VF	XF	Unc
AH1406-1986	14,000	—	—	—	200

KM#612 50 POUNDS **Weight:** 8.5000 g. **Composition:** 0.9000 Gold .2460 oz. AGW **Subject:** Aida Opera **Obverse:** Radiant sun, pillars and inscriptions **Reverse:** Ancient figures among ruins

Date	Mintage	F	VF	XF	Unc
AH1407-1987	40,000	—	—	—	225

KM#625 50 POUNDS **Weight:** 8.5000 g. **Composition:** 0.9000 Gold .2460 oz. AGW **Series:** Summer Olympics **Obverse:** Arabic legend and ornamentation within English legend **Reverse:** Pharoah and athletes

Date	Mintage	F	VF	XF	Unc
AH1408-1988	150	—	—	—	300
AH1408-1988 Proof	50	Value: 350			

KM#627 50 POUNDS **Weight:** 8.5000 g. **Composition:** 0.9000 Gold .2460 oz. AGW **Series:** Summer Olympics **Reverse:** Athletes and mythological figures

Date	Mintage	F	VF	XF	Unc
AH1408-1988	750	—	—	—	250
AH1408-1988 Proof	250	Value: 275			

KM#629 50 POUNDS **Weight:** 8.5000 g. **Composition:** 0.9000 Gold .2460 oz. AGW **Series:** Winter Olympics **Obverse:** Winged design, English legend, Arabic inscription **Reverse:** Ski jumper and figure skater within Arabic legend

Date	Mintage	F	VF	XF	Unc
AH1408-1988	150	—	—	—	300
AH1408-1988 Proof	50	Value: 350			

KM#680 50 POUNDS **Weight:** 8.5000 g. **Composition:** 0.9000 Gold .2460 oz. AGW **Subject:** Soccer World Championship - Italy **Reverse:** Ancient gods

Date	Mintage	F	VF	XF	Unc
AH1410-1990 Proof	225	Value: 450			

KM#683 50 POUNDS **Weight:** 8.5000 g. **Composition:** 0.9000 Gold .2460 oz. AGW **Subject:** Soccer World Championship **Reverse:** Player chasing ball

Date	Mintage	F	VF	XF	Unc
AH1410-1990 Proof	75	Value: 500			

KM#709 50 POUNDS **Weight:** 8.5000 g. **Composition:** 0.9000 Gold .2460 oz. AGW **Series:** Summer Olympics **Reverse:** Fencing

Date	Mintage	F	VF	XF	Unc
AH1412-1992	49	—	—	—	425
AH1412-1992 Proof	99	Value: 425			

KM#710 50 POUNDS **Weight:** 8.5000 g. **Composition:** 0.9000 Gold .2460 oz. AGW **Series:** Summer Olympics **Reverse:** Wrestling

Date	Mintage	F	VF	XF	Unc
AH1412-1992	49	—	—	—	425
AH1412-1992 Proof	99	Value: 425			

KM#711 50 POUNDS **Weight:** 8.5000 g. **Composition:** 0.9000 Gold .2460 oz. AGW **Series:** Summer Olympics **Reverse:** Archery

Date	Mintage	F	VF	XF	Unc
AH1412-1992	49	—	—	—	425
AH1412-1992 Proof	99	Value: 425			

KM#712 50 POUNDS **Weight:** 8.5000 g. **Composition:** 0.9000 Gold .2460 oz. AGW **Series:** Summer Olympics **Reverse:** Many men wrestling an ox

Date	Mintage	F	VF	XF	Unc
AH1412-1992	49	—	—	—	425
AH1412-1992 Proof	99	Value: 425			

KM# 713 50 POUNDS **Weight:** 8.5000 g. **Composition:** 0.9000 Gold .2460 oz. AGW **Series:** Summer Olympics **Reverse:** Swimmer stalking a duck

Date	Mintage	F	VF	XF	Unc
AH1412-1992	49	—	—	—	425
AH1412-1992 Proof	99	Value: 425			

KM# 714 50 POUNDS **Weight:** 8.5000 g. **Composition:** 0.9000 Gold .2460 oz. AGW **Series:** Summer Olympics **Reverse:** Handball player

Date	Mintage	F	VF	XF	Unc
AH1412-1992	49	—	—	—	425
AH1412-1992 Proof	99	Value: 425			

KM# 715 50 POUNDS **Weight:** 8.5000 g. **Composition:** 0.9000 Gold .2460 oz. AGW **Series:** Summer Olympics **Reverse:** Field hockey player

Date	Mintage	F	VF	XF	Unc
AH1412-1992	49	—	—	—	425
AH1412-1992 Proof	99	Value: 425			

KM# 716 50 POUNDS **Weight:** 8.5000 g. **Composition:** 0.9000 Gold .2460 oz. AGW **Series:** Summer Olympics **Reverse:** Soccer player

Date	Mintage	F	VF	XF	Unc
AH1412-1992	49	—	—	—	425
AH1412-1992 Proof	115	Value: 425			

KM# 755 50 POUNDS **Weight:** 8.5000 g. **Composition:** 0.9000 Gold .2460 oz. AGW **Reverse:** King Tutankhamen's burial mask

Date		F	VF	XF	Unc
AH1414-1993 Proof		—	Value: 260		

KM# 756 50 POUNDS **Weight:** 8.5000 g. **Composition:** 0.9000 Gold .2460 oz. AGW **Subject:** Cleopatra **Reverse:** Bust of Cleopatra left

Date		F	VF	XF	Unc
AH1414-1993 Proof		—	Value: 240		

KM# 776 50 POUNDS **Weight:** 8.5000 g. **Composition:** 0.9000 Gold .2460 oz. AGW **Reverse:** Sphinx head

Date		F	VF	XF	Unc
AH1414-1993 Proof		—	Value: 200		

KM# 777 50 POUNDS **Weight:** 8.5000 g. **Composition:** 0.9000 Gold .2460 oz. AGW **Reverse:** Standing Ramses II

Date		F	VF	XF	Unc
AH1414-1993 Proof		—	Value: 200		

KM# 778 50 POUNDS **Weight:** 8.5000 g. **Composition:** 0.9000 Gold .2460 oz. AGW **Reverse:** Crowned falcon left

Date		F	VF	XF	Unc
AH1414-1993 Proof		—	Value: 220		

KM# 868 50 POUNDS **Weight:** 8.5000 g. **Composition:** 0.9000 Gold .2460 oz. AGW **Subject:** King Narmer Palette **Obverse:** Vulture **Reverse:** King Narmer killing a wounded foe

Date	Mintage	F	VF	XF	Unc
AH1414-1993 Proof	3,000	Value: 250			

KM# 870 50 POUNDS **Weight:** 8.5000 g. **Composition:** 0.9000 Gold .2460 oz. AGW **Subject:** King Kna-Sekhem **Reverse:** Seated king

Date	Mintage	F	VF	XF	Unc
AH1414-1993 Proof	3,000	Value: 250			

KM# 873 50 POUNDS **Weight:** 8.5000 g. **Composition:** 0.9000 Gold .2460 oz. AGW **Subject:** Menkaure Triad **Reverse:** Three carved figurines

Date	Mintage	F	VF	XF	Unc
AH1414-1993 Proof	3,000	Value: 250			

KM# 885 50 POUNDS **Weight:** 8.5000 g. **Composition:** 0.9000 Gold .2460 oz. AGW **Subject:** Thoutmosis III **Reverse:** Kneeling figure holding jar

Date	Mintage	F	VF	XF	Unc
AH1414-1993 Proof	3,000	Value: 250			

KM# 775 50 POUNDS **Weight:** 8.5000 g. **Composition:** 0.9000 Gold .2460 oz. AGW **Reverse:** Three pyramids

Date		F	VF	XF	Unc
AH1414-1993 Proof		—	Value: 200		

KM# 737 50 POUNDS **Weight:** 8.5000 g. **Composition:** 0.9000 Gold .2460 oz. AGW **Series:** World Cup Soccer **Reverse:** Two players, pyramid and Statue of Liberty

Date	Mintage	F	VF	XF	Unc
AH1415-1994	99	—	—	—	300
AH1415-1994 Proof	99	Value: 300			

KM# 739 50 POUNDS **Weight:** 8.5000 g. **Composition:** 0.9000 Gold .2460 oz. AGW **Series:** World Cup Soccer **Reverse:** Stylized player

Date	Mintage	F	VF	XF	Unc
AH1415-1994	99	—	—	—	300
AH1415-1994 Proof	99	Value: 300			

KM# 779 50 POUNDS **Weight:** 8.5000 g. **Composition:** 0.9000 Gold .2460 oz. AGW **Subject:** Queen Nefertiti **Reverse:** Bust of Queen Nefertiti right

Date		F	VF	XF	Unc
AH1415-1994 Proof		—	Value: 200		

KM# 780 50 POUNDS **Weight:** 8.5000 g. **Composition:** 0.9000 Gold .2460 oz. AGW **Reverse:** Seated cat right

Date		F	VF	XF	Unc
AH1415-1994 Proof		—	Value: 200		

KM# 781 50 POUNDS **Weight:** 8.5000 g. **Composition:** 0.9000 Gold .2460 oz. AGW **Reverse:** Archer in chariot

Date		F	VF	XF	Unc
AH1415-1994 Proof		—	Value: 220		

KM# 782 50 POUNDS **Weight:** 8.5000 g. **Composition:** 0.9000 Gold .2460 oz. AGW **Reverse:** Standing god Seth left

Date		F	VF	XF	Unc
AH1415-1994 Proof		—	Value: 165		

KM# 814 50 POUNDS **Weight:** 8.5000 g. **Composition:** 0.9000 Gold .2460 oz. AGW **Reverse:** Hippopotamus

Date		F	VF	XF	Unc
AH1415-1994 Proof		—	Value: 165		

KM# 815 50 POUNDS **Weight:** 8.5000 g. **Composition:** 0.9000 Gold .2460 oz. AGW **Reverse:** Egyptian gazelle

Date		F	VF	XF	Unc
AH1415-1994 Proof		—	Value: 165		

KM# 816 50 POUNDS **Weight:** 8.5000 g. **Composition:** 0.9000 Gold .2460 oz. AGW **Reverse:** Phoenix birds

Date		F	VF	XF	Unc
AH1415-1994 Proof		—	Value: 165		

KM# 817 50 POUNDS **Weight:** 8.5000 g. **Composition:** 0.9000 Gold .2460 oz. AGW **Reverse:** Egyptian geese

Date		F	VF	XF	Unc
AH1415-1994 Proof		—	Value: 165		

KM# 818 50 POUNDS **Weight:** 8.5000 g. **Composition:** 0.9000 Gold .2460 oz. AGW **Reverse:** King Taharqa

Date		F	VF	XF	Unc
AH1415-1994 Proof		—	Value: 165		

KM# 819 50 POUNDS **Weight:** 8.5000 g. **Composition:** 0.9000 Gold .2460 oz. AGW **Reverse:** Amenhotep Temple

Date	F	VF	XF	Unc
AH1415-1994 Proof	—	Value: 165		

KM# 820 50 POUNDS **Weight:** 8.5000 g. **Composition:** 0.9000 Gold .2460 oz. AGW **Reverse:** Karnak Temple

Date	F	VF	XF	Unc
AH1415-1994 Proof	—	Value: 165		

KM# 821 50 POUNDS **Weight:** 8.5000 g. **Composition:** 0.9000 Gold .2460 oz. AGW **Reverse:** Philae Temple

Date	F	VF	XF	Unc
AH1415-1994 Proof	—	Value: 165		

KM# 822 50 POUNDS **Weight:** 8.5000 g. **Composition:** 0.9000 Gold .2460 oz. AGW **Reverse:** Khonsu Temple

Date	F	VF	XF	Unc
AH1415-1994 Proof	—	Value: 165		

KM# 871 50 POUNDS **Weight:** 8.5000 g. **Composition:** 0.9000 Gold .2460 oz. AGW **Reverse:** King Djoser wearing the Red Crown

Date	Mintage	F	VF	XF	Unc
AH1415-1994 Proof	3,000	Value: 250			

KM# 872 50 POUNDS **Weight:** 8.5000 g. **Composition:** 0.9000 Gold .2460 oz. AGW **Reverse:** Seated King Khufu with flat-top hat

Date	Mintage	F	VF	XF	Unc
AH1415-1994 Proof	3,000	Value: 250			

KM# 882 50 POUNDS **Weight:** 8.5000 g. **Composition:** 0.9000 Gold .2460 oz. AGW **Subject:** King Sesostris I **Reverse:** RE (sun god) presenting the ANKH (symbol of life) to the king wearing the double crown

Date	Mintage	F	VF	XF	Unc
AH1415-1994 Proof	3,000	Value: 275			

KM# 884 50 POUNDS **Weight:** 8.5000 g. **Composition:** 0.9000 Gold .2460 oz. AGW **Subject:** King Horemheb **Reverse:** Seated King Horemheb

Date	Mintage	F	VF	XF	Unc
AH1415-1994 Proof	3,000	Value: 275			

KM# 886 50 POUNDS **Weight:** 8.5000 g. **Composition:** 0.9000 Gold .2460 oz. AGW **Subject:** King Khonsu **Reverse:** 1/2-length King Khonsu

Date	Mintage	F	VF	XF	Unc
AH1415-1994 Proof	3,000	Value: 275			

KM# 887 50 POUNDS **Weight:** 8.5000 g. **Composition:** 0.9000 Gold .2460 oz. AGW **Subject:** Tutankhamon's Throne **Reverse:** King Tut seated on throne with servant

Date	Mintage	F	VF	XF	Unc
AH1415-1994 Proof	3,000	Value: 300			

KM# 888 50 POUNDS **Weight:** 8.5000 g. **Composition:** 0.9000 Gold .2460 oz. AGW **Subject:** Queen Hatshepsut **Reverse:** Queen's facial sculpture

Date	Mintage	F	VF	XF	Unc
AH1415-1994 Proof	3,000	Value: 275			

KM# 890 50 POUNDS **Weight:** 8.5000 g. **Composition:** 0.9000 Gold .2460 oz. AGW **Subject:** Akhnaton and Family **Reverse:** Family scene

Date	Mintage	F	VF	XF	Unc
AH1415-1994 Proof	3,000	Value: 275			

KM# 891 50 POUNDS **Weight:** 8.5000 g. **Composition:** 0.9000 Gold .2460 oz. AGW **Reverse:** Akhnaton

Date	Mintage	F	VF	XF	Unc
AH1415-1994 Proof	3,000	Value: 275			

KM# 892 50 POUNDS **Weight:** 8.5000 g. **Composition:** 0.9000 Gold .2460 oz. AGW **Subject:** Queen Nefertari **Reverse:** Kneeling Queen Nefertari

Date	Mintage	F	VF	XF	Unc
AH1415-1994 Proof	5,000	Value: 275			

KM# 893 50 POUNDS **Weight:** 8.5000 g. **Composition:** 0.9000 Gold .2460 oz. AGW **Subject:** Ramses III **Reverse:** 3/4-length Ramses III

Date	Mintage	F	VF	XF	Unc
AH1415-1994 Proof	3,000	Value: 300			

KM# 895 50 POUNDS **Weight:** 8.5000 g. **Composition:** 0.9000 Gold .2460 oz. AGW **Reverse:** Amulet of Hathor

Date	Mintage	F	VF	XF	Unc
AH1415-1994 Proof	3,000	Value: 275			

KM# 550 100 POUNDS **Weight:** 17.1500 g. **Composition:** 0.9000 Gold .4963 oz. AGW **Reverse:** Queen Nefertiti

Date	Mintage	F	VF	XF	Unc
1983 Proof	16,000	Value: 700			

KM# 562 100 POUNDS **Weight:** 17.1500 g. **Composition:** 0.9000 Gold .4963 oz. AGW **Reverse:** Cleopatra VII

Date	Mintage	F	VF	XF	Unc
1984 Proof	2,121	Value: 750			

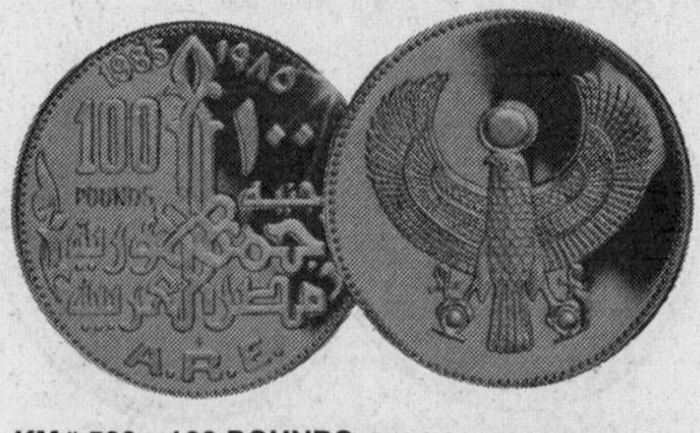

KM# 569 100 POUNDS **Weight:** 17.1500 g. **Composition:** 0.9000 Gold .4963 oz. AGW **Reverse:** The golden falcon

Date	Mintage	F	VF	XF	Unc
1985 Proof	1,800	Value: 450			

KM# 591 100 POUNDS **Weight:** 17.1500 g. **Composition:** 0.9000 Gold .4963 oz. AGW **Reverse:** Tutankhamen

Date	Mintage	F	VF	XF	Unc
1986 Proof	7,500	Value: 700			

KM# 642 100 POUNDS **Weight:** 17.0000 g. **Composition:** 0.9000 Gold .4918 oz. AGW **Subject:** Mecca **Obverse:** Arabic legend, ornamentation **Reverse:** Interior view of the Kaaba

Date	Mintage	F	VF	XF	Unc
AH1406-1986	700	—	—	—	350

KM# 613 100 POUNDS **Weight:** 17.0000 g. **Composition:** 0.9000 Gold .4918 oz. AGW **Reverse:** The golden ram

Date	Mintage	F	VF	XF	Unc
1987 Proof	7,500	Value: 450			

KM# 648 100 POUNDS **Weight:** 17.0000 g. **Composition:** 0.9000 Gold .4918 oz. AGW **Reverse:** The golden warrior

Date	Mintage	F	VF	XF	Unc
1988 Proof	5,500	Value: 475			

KM# 656 100 POUNDS **Weight:** 17.1500 g. **Composition:** 0.9000 Gold .4963 oz. AGW **Reverse:** The golden cat

Date	Mintage	F	VF	XF	Unc
1989 FM Proof	Est. 7,500	Value: 450			

KM# 681 100 POUNDS **Weight:** 17.0000 g. **Composition:** 0.9000 Gold .4918 oz. AGW **Series:** World Soccer Championship - Italy **Reverse:** Ancient gods

Date	Mintage	F	VF	XF	Unc
AH1410-1990 Proof	125	Value: 775			

KM# 684 100 POUNDS **Weight:** 17.0000 g. **Composition:** 0.9000 Gold .4918 oz. AGW **Series:** World Soccer Championship - Italy **Reverse:** Player chasing ball

Date	Mintage	F	VF	XF	Unc
AH1410-1990 Proof	75	Value: 800			

KM# 693 100 POUNDS **Weight:** 17.0000 g. **Composition:** 0.9000 Gold .4918 oz. AGW **Series:** Ancient Egyptian Culture **Reverse:** Sphinx

Date	Mintage	F	VF	XF	Unc
1990 FM Proof	Est. 5,000	Value: 550			

KM# 729 100 POUNDS **Weight:** 17.0000 g. **Composition:** 0.9000 Gold .4918 oz. AGW **Series:** Ancient Egyptian Culture **Reverse:** Pyramids of Giza

Date	Mintage	F	VF	XF	Unc
1991 Proof	Est. 5,000	Value: 550			

KM# 717 100 POUNDS **Weight:** 17.0000 g. **Composition:** 0.9000 Gold .4918 oz. AGW **Series:** Summer Olympics **Reverse:** Fencing

Date	Mintage	F	VF	XF	Unc
AH1412-1992	49	—	—	—	800
AH1412-1992 Proof	99	Value: 800			

KM# 718 100 POUNDS Weight: 17.0000 g. **Composition:** 0.9000 Gold .4918 oz. AGW **Series:** Summer Olympics **Reverse:** Two men wrestling

Date	Mintage	F	VF	XF	Unc
AH1412-1992	49	—	—	—	800
AH1412-1992 Proof	99	Value: 800			

KM# 720 100 POUNDS Weight: 17.0000 g. **Composition:** 0.9000 Gold .4918 oz. AGW **Series:** Summer Olympics **Reverse:** Many men wrestling an ox

Date	Mintage	F	VF	XF	Unc
AH1412-1992	49	—	—	—	800
AH1412-1992 Proof	99	Value: 800			

KM# 721 100 POUNDS Weight: 17.0000 g. **Composition:** 0.9000 Gold .4918 oz. AGW **Series:** Summer Olympics **Reverse:** Swimmer stalking a duck

Date	Mintage	F	VF	XF	Unc
AH1412-1992	49	—	—	—	800
AH1412-1992 Proof	99	Value: 800			

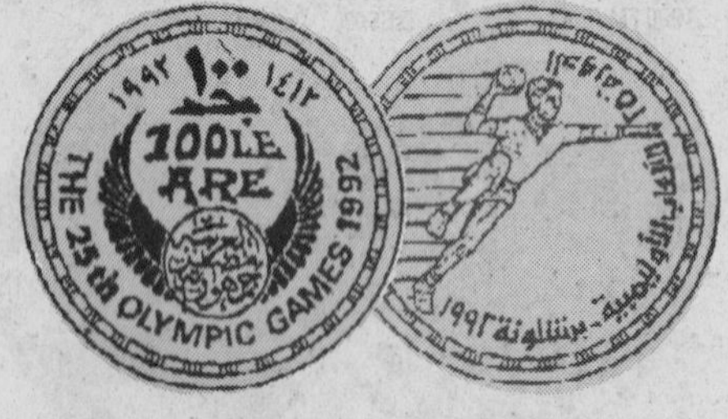

KM# 722 100 POUNDS Weight: 17.0000 g. **Composition:** 0.9000 Gold .4918 oz. AGW **Series:** Summer Olympics **Reverse:** Handball player

Date	Mintage	F	VF	XF	Unc
AH1412-1992	49	—	—	—	800
AH1412-1992 Proof	99	Value: 800			

KM# 723 100 POUNDS Weight: 17.0000 g. **Composition:** 0.9000 Gold .4918 oz. AGW **Series:** Summer Olympics **Reverse:** Field hockey player

Date	Mintage	F	VF	XF	Unc
AH1412-1992	49	—	—	—	800
AH1412-1992 Proof	99	Value: 800			

KM# 724 100 POUNDS Weight: 17.0000 g. **Composition:** 0.9000 Gold .4918 oz. AGW **Series:** Summer Olympics **Reverse:** Soccer player

Date	Mintage	F	VF	XF	Unc
AH1412-1992	49	—	—	—	800
AH1412-1992 Proof	115	Value: 800			

KM# 730 100 POUNDS Weight: 17.1500 g. **Composition:** 0.9000 Gold .4963 oz. AGW **Subject:** The Golden Guardians

Date	Mintage	F	VF	XF	Unc
1992 Proof	Est. 5,000	Value: 525			

KM# 719 100 POUNDS Weight: 17.0000 g. **Composition:** 0.9000 Gold .4918 oz. AGW **Series:** Summer Olympics **Reverse:** Archery demonstration

Date	Mintage	F	VF	XF	Unc
AH1412-1992	49	—	—	—	800
AH1412-1992 Proof	99	Value: 800			

PATTERNS

Including off metal strikes

KM#	Date	Mintage	Identification	Mkt Val
Pn26	1917	—	1/2 Millieme. Copper-Nickel.	125
Pn27	1361-1942	—	2 Piastres. Platinum. KM#365	—
Pn28	1960	—	25 Piastres. Silver. KM#400 but with hand pointing to right	—
Pn29	1962	—	5 Piastres. Bronze. ESSAY	—
Pn30	1382-1962	—	5 Piastres. Brass Or Aluminum-Bronze. 7.3400 g.	1,600
Pn31	1964	—	10 Piastres. Copper-Nickel.	—

PIEFORTS

KM#	Date	Mintage	Identification	Mkt Val
P1	1981	152	5 Pounds. 0.9000 Gold. KM533	165

PROOF SETS

KM#	Date	Mintage	Identification	Issue Price	Mkt Val
PS1	1938 (4)	—	KM#370, 371, 372, 373	4,200	4,500
PS3	1966 (7)	2,500	KM#393, 394, 395, 397, 398, 399, 403	9.00	75.00
PS2	1964 (4)	2,000	KM#404, 405, 406, 407	18.00	90.00
PS4	1980 (4)	—	KM#508, 509, 517, 519	—	1,875
PS5	1980 (3)	—	KM#509, 517, 519	—	1,850

SPECIMEN SETS (SS)

KM#	Date	Mintage	Identification	Issue Price	Mkt Val
SS1	1916/7 (10)	—	KM#312-316, 317.1, 318.1, 319, 321, 324	—	1,700

EL SALVADOR

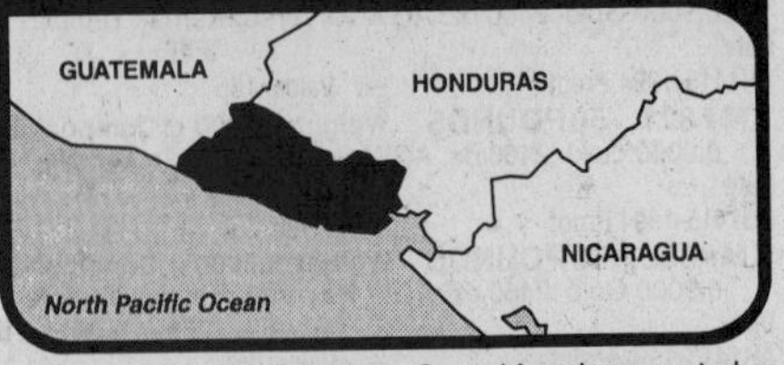

The Republic of El Salvador, a Central American country bordered by Guatemala, Honduras and the Pacific Ocean, has an area of 8,124 sq. mi. (21,040 sq. km.) and a population of 6.0 million. Capital: San Salvador. This most intensely cultivated of Latin America countries produces coffee (the major crop), sugar and balsam for export. Gold, silver and other metals are largely unexploited.

The first Spanish attempt to subjugate the area was undertaken in 1523 by Pedro de Alvarado, Cortes' lieutenant. He was forced to retreat by Indian forces, but returned in 1525 and succeeded in bringing the region under control of the Captaincy General of Guatemala. In 1821, El Salvador and the other Central American provinces jointly declared independence from Spain. In 1823, the Republic of Central America was formed by the five Central American states; this federation dissolved in 1839. El Salvador then became an independent republic in 1841.

Since 1960, El Salvador has been a part of the Central American Common Market. During the 1980's El Salvador went through a 12 year Civil War that ended in 1992 with the signing of a United Nations-sponsored Peace Accord. Free elections, with full participation of all political parties, were held in 1994, 1997 and 1999. Armando Calderon-Sol was elected president in 1994 for a 5-year term and Francisco Flores was elected in 1999 for a 5-year term as well.

MINT MARKS

C.A.M. - Central American Mint, San Salvador
H - Heaton Mint, Birmingham
S - San Francisco
Mo - Mexico
(a) - British Royal Mint, England
(b) - Denver Mint, USA
(c) - Deutsche Nickel A.G., Germany
(d) - Guatemala City Mint, Guatemala
(e) - Mexico City Mint, Mexico
(f) - San Francisco Mint, USA
(g) - Sherrit Mint, Canada
(h) - Vereingte Deutsche Metall, Germany
(i) - Royal Canadian Mint, Canada
(P) – Philadelphia Mint, USA

REPUBLIC OF EL SALVADOR

DECIMAL COINAGE

100 Centavos = 1 Peso

KM# 120 1/4 REAL Weight: 3.2000 g. **Composition:** Bronze **Note:** The decimal value of this coin was about 3 Centavos. It was apparently struck in response to the continuing use of the Reales monetary system in rural areas.

Date	F	VF	XF	Unc	BU
1909	20.00	30.00	60.00	120	—

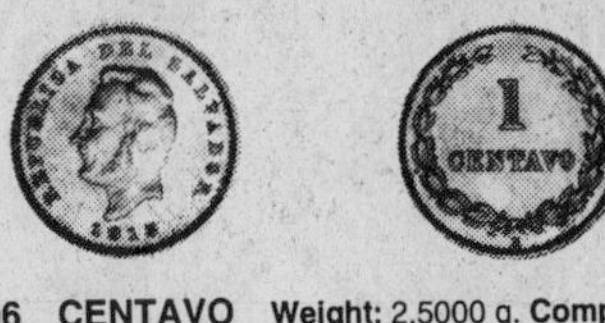

KM# 106 CENTAVO Weight: 2.5000 g. **Composition:** Copper-Nickel **Obverse:** Francisco Morazan

Date	Mintage	F	VF	XF	Unc	BU
1889H	1,500,000	1.00	2.50	4.50	13.50	—
1913H	2,500,000	1.50	3.50	6.00	35.00	—

KM# 127 CENTAVO Weight: 2.5000 g. **Composition:** Copper **Obverse:** Francisco Morazan **Reverse:** Denomination

Date	Mintage	F	VF	XF	Unc	BU
1915(P)	5,000,000	1.25	4.50	12.50	35.00	—
1919(P)	1,000,000	2.25	7.00	18.50	55.00	—
1920(P)	1,490,000	1.50	6.00	15.00	40.00	—

Date	Mintage	F	VF	XF	Unc	BU
1925(f)	200,000	4.00	12.00	25.00	60.00	—
1926(f)	400,000	3.00	10.00	20.00	55.00	—
1928S	5,000,000	1.25	7.00	16.00	40.00	—
Note: Varieties exist with Large or small S						
1936(P)	2,500,000	1.25	4.50	12.50	35.00	—

KM# 107 3 CENTAVOS **Weight:** 3.3000 g. **Composition:** Copper-Nickel **Obverse:** Francisco Morazan

Date	Mintage	F	VF	XF	Unc	BU
1913H	1,000,000	2.00	8.00	20.00	60.00	—

KM# 128 3 CENTAVOS **Weight:** 3.5000 g. **Composition:** Copper Nickel **Obverse:** Francisco Morazan **Reverse:** Denomination

Date	Mintage	F	VF	XF	Unc	BU
1915(P)	2,700,000	2.00	8.00	20.00	60.00	—

KM# 121 5 CENTAVOS **Weight:** 1.2500 g. **Composition:** 0.8350 Silver .0336 oz. ASW

Date	Mintage	F	VF	XF	Unc	BU
1911	1,000,000	3.00	10.00	20.00	45.00	—

KM# 124 5 CENTAVOS **Weight:** 1.2500 g. **Composition:** 0.8350 Silver .0336 oz. ASW

Date	Mintage	F	VF	XF	Unc	BU
1914(P)	2,000,000	2.00	5.00	10.00	30.00	—
1914(P) Proof	20	Value: 200				

KM# 129 5 CENTAVOS **Weight:** 5.0000 g. **Composition:** Copper-Nickel **Obverse:** Francisco Morazan **Reverse:** Denomination

Date	Mintage	F	VF	XF	Unc	BU
1915(P)	2,500,000	2.25	6.00	15.00	60.00	—
1916(P)	1,500,000	2.50	7.00	17.50	65.00	—
1917(P)	1,000,000	3.00	8.00	20.00	70.00	—
1918/7(P)	1,000,000	2.50	7.00	17.50	60.00	—
1918(P)	Inc. above	2.50	7.00	17.50	70.00	—
1919/8(P)	—	2.50	7.00	17.50	70.00	—
1919(P)	2,000,000	2.50	7.00	17.50	70.00	—
1920(P)	2,000,000	1.75	4.50	10.00	50.00	—
1921(f)	1,780,000	2.00	5.00	12.00	55.00	—
1925(f)	4,000,000	1.25	3.50	7.50	45.00	—

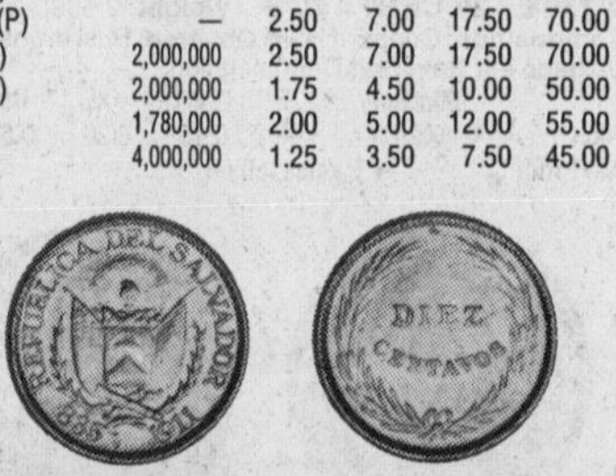

KM# 122 10 CENTAVOS **Weight:** 2.5000 g. **Composition:** 0.8350 Silver **Obverse:** Arms **Reverse:** Denomination

Date	Mintage	F	VF	XF	Unc	BU
1911	1,000,000	3.00	7.00	15.00	65.00	—

KM# 125 10 CENTAVOS **Weight:** 2.5000 g. **Composition:** 0.8350 Silver **Obverse:** Triangular arms **Reverse:** Denomination

Date	Mintage	F	VF	XF	Unc	BU
1914(P)	1,500,000	2.50	6.50	12.50	45.00	—
1914(P) Proof	20	Value: 250				

KM# 123 25 CENTAVOS **Weight:** 6.2500 g. **Composition:** 0.8350 Silver .1678 oz. ASW **Obverse:** Arms **Reverse:** Denomination

Date	Mintage	F	VF	XF	Unc	BU
1911	600,000	5.00	9.00	18.00	50.00	—

KM# 126 25 CENTAVOS **Weight:** 6.2500 g. **Composition:** 0.8350 Silver .1678 oz. ASW **Obverse:** Triangular arms **Reverse:** Denomination

Date	Mintage	F	VF	XF	Unc	BU
1914(P) 15 DE SEPT DE 1821	1,400,000	5.50	6.50	10.00	30.00	—
1914(P) 15 SET DE 1821	Inc. above	5.50	6.50	10.00	30.00	—
1914(P) Proof	20	Value: 600				

KM# 115.2 PESO (Colon) **Weight:** 25.0000 g. **Composition:** 0.9000 Silver .7234 oz. ASW **Reverse:** Heavier portrait (wider right shoulder) **Note:** Struck at United States mints.

Date	Mintage	F	VF	XF	Unc	BU
1904C.A.M. (f)		9.00	20.00	40.00	175	—
1909C.A.M. (f)		8.50	16.50	32.50	160	—
1911C.A.M. (P) (S)		7.50	15.00	30.00	150	—
Note: Of the total mintage, 510, 993 struck at Philadelphia Mint (P), and 511,108 were struck at San Francisco Mint (f)						
1914C.A.M. (P)		7.50	15.00	30.00	150	—
1914C.A.M. Proof	Est. 20	Value: 1,800				

KM# 115.1 PESO (Colon) **Weight:** 25.0000 g. **Composition:** 0.9000 Silver .7234 oz. ASW **Obverse:** Arms **Reverse:** Columbus **Note:** Struck in San Salvador and European mints.

Date	Mintage	F	VF	XF	Unc	BU
1904C.A.M.	600,000	7.50	15.00	30.00	160	—
1908C.A.M.	1,600,000	7.50	13.50	28.00	140	—
1911C.A.M.	500,000	7.50	15.00	30.00	150	—
1914C.A.M.	700,000	—	—	—	625	—
Note: 1914 struck at the Brussels mint, but then remelted for the striking of 1914 minor coinage.						

REFORM COINAGE

100 Centavos = 1 Colon

KM# 133 CENTAVO **Weight:** 2.5000 g. **Composition:** Copper-Nickel **Obverse:** Francisco Morazan **Reverse:** Denomination

Date	Mintage	F	VF	XF	Unc	BU
1940(P)	1,000,000	2.00	6.00	15.00	45.00	—

KM# 135.1 (135) CENTAVO **Weight:** 2.5000 g. **Composition:** Bronze **Obverse:** Francisco Morazan **Reverse:** Denomination

Date	Mintage	F	VF	XF	Unc	BU
1942(f)	5,000,000	0.20	0.50	1.00	4.50	—
Note: Struck in 1943						
1942(f)	5,000,000	0.20	0.50	1.00	4.50	—
Note: Struck in 1943						
1943(f)	5,000,000	0.20	0.50	1.00	4.50	—
Note: Struck in 1944						
1943(f)	5,000,000	0.20	0.50	1.00	4.50	—
Note: Struck in 1944						
1945(P)	5,000,000	0.20	0.40	0.75	3.50	—
1945(P)	5,000,000	0.20	0.40	0.75	3.50	—
1947(f)	5,000,000	0.20	0.50	1.00	4.00	—
1947(f)	5,000,000	0.20	0.50	1.00	4.00	—
1951(f)	10,000,000	0.10	0.30	0.75	2.50	—
1951(f)	10,000,000	0.10	0.30	0.75	2.50	—
1952(f)	10,000,000	0.10	0.20	0.40	2.00	—
Note: Struck in 1953						
1952(f)	10,000,000	0.10	0.20	0.40	2.00	—
Note: Struck in 1953						
1956(P)	10,000,000	0.10	0.20	0.40	2.00	—
Note: Struck in 1957						
1956(P)	10,000,000	0.10	0.20	0.40	2.00	—
Note: Struck in 1957						
1966	5,000,000	—	—	0.10	0.75	—
1966	5,000,000	—	—	0.10	0.75	—
1968 (f)	5,000,000	—	—	0.10	0.75	—
1968 (f)	5,000,000	—	—	0.10	0.75	—
1969 (b)	5,000,000	—	—	0.10	0.75	—
1969 (b)	5,000,000	—	—	0.10	0.75	—
1972 (f)	20,000,000	—	—	0.10	0.50	—
1972 (f)	20,000,000	—	—	0.10	0.50	—

KM# 135.1a CENTAVO **Weight:** 2.5000 g. **Composition:** Bronze Clad Steel **Obverse:** Francisco Morazan **Reverse:** Denomination **Note:** Previously KM#135d.

Date	Mintage	F	VF	XF	Unc	BU
1989(h)	36,000,000	—	—	0.10	0.20	—
1992(h)	—	—	—	0.10	0.20	—

KM# 135.2 CENTAVO **Weight:** 2.5000 g. **Composition:** Brass **Obverse:** Francisco Morazan **Reverse:** Denomination **Note:** Previously KM#135a.

Date	Mintage	F	VF	XF	Unc	BU
1976(g)	20,000,000	—	—	0.10	0.20	—
1977(g)	40,000,000	—	—	0.10	0.20	—

KM# 135.2a CENTAVO **Weight:** 2.5000 g. **Composition:** Copper-Zinc **Obverse:** DH monogram at truncation, smaller Morazan portrait **Reverse:** Denomination in wreath, SM at right base of 1 **Note:** Previously KM#135c.

Date	Mintage	F	VF	XF	Unc	BU
1981(d)	50,000,000	—	—	0.10	0.20	—

KM# 135.2b CENTAVO **Weight:** 2.5000 g. **Composition:** Copper Clad Steel **Obverse:** DH monogram at truncation, smaller Morazan portrait **Reverse:** Denomination in wreath, SM at right base of 1 **Note:** Previously KM#135b.

Date	Mintage	F	VF	XF	Unc	BU
1986 (a)	30,000,000	—	—	0.10	0.20	—

KM# 135.2c CENTAVO **Weight:** 2.5000 g. **Composition:** Brass Clad Steel **Obverse:** DH monogram at truncation, smaller Morazan portrait **Reverse:** Denomination in wreath, SM at right base of 1

Date	F	VF	XF	Unc	BU
1995(a)	—	—	0.10	0.20	—

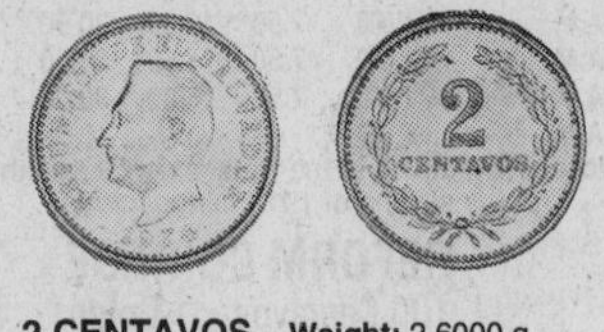

KM# 147 2 CENTAVOS **Weight:** 2.6000 g. **Composition:** Nickel-Brass **Obverse:** Francisco Morazan **Reverse:** Denomination

Date	Mintage	F	VF	XF	Unc	BU
1974(a)	10,002,000	—	0.10	0.15	0.50	—
1974(a) In proof sets only	2,000	Value: 30.00				

KM# 148 3 CENTAVOS **Weight:** 4.0000 g. **Composition:** Nickel-Brass **Obverse:** Francisco Morazan **Reverse:** Denomination

Date	Mintage	F	VF	XF	Unc	BU
1974(a)	10,002,000	0.10	0.15	0.20	0.75	—
1974(a) In proof sets only	2,000	Value: 35.00				

KM# 134 5 CENTAVOS **Weight:** 5.0000 g. **Composition:** Copper-Nickel **Obverse:** Francisco Morazan **Reverse:** Denomination

Date	Mintage	F	VF	XF	Unc	BU
1940(P)	800,000	1.00	3.00	10.00	30.00	—
1951	2,000,000	0.75	2.00	6.00	15.00	—
1956	8,000,000	0.10	0.15	0.25	1.00	—
1959	6,000,000	0.10	0.15	0.25	1.00	—
1963	10,000,000	—	0.10	0.15	0.50	—
1966	6,000,000	0.10	0.15	0.25	0.75	—
1967 (f)	10,000,000	—	0.10	0.15	0.50	—
1972 (f)	10,000,000	—	0.10	0.15	0.50	—
1974 (g)	10,002,000	—	0.10	0.15	0.50	—
1974 (g) In proof sets only	2,000	Value: 35.00				

KM# 134a 5 CENTAVOS **Weight:** 5.0000 g. **Composition:** Nickel-Silver **Obverse:** Francisco Morazan **Reverse:** Denomination

Date	Mintage	F	VF	XF	Unc	BU
1944(f)	5,000,000	0.25	0.50	1.50	5.00	—
1948(f)	3,000,000	0.25	0.50	1.00	2.50	—
1950(f)	2,000,000	0.25	0.50	1.50	5.00	—
1952(f)	4,000,000	0.20	0.35	0.75	4.00	—

Note: Half the totlal mintage was struck in 1952, the remainder in 1953

KM# 149 (149.1) 5 CENTAVOS **Weight:** 5.0000 g. **Composition:** Copper-Nickel Clad Steel **Obverse:** Francisco Morazan **Reverse:** Denomination

Date	Mintage	F	VF	XF	Unc	BU
1975 (a)	15,000,000	—	0.10	0.15	0.30	—
1975 (a)	15,000,000	—	0.10	0.15	0.30	—
1975 In proof sets only	2,000	Value: 40.00				
1975 In proof sets only	2,000	Value: 40.00				
1986 (h)	30,000,000	—	0.10	0.15	0.30	—
1986 (h)	30,000,000	—	0.10	0.15	0.30	—

KM# 149a (149.2) 5 CENTAVOS **Weight:** 5.0000 g. **Composition:** Nickel Clad Steel **Obverse:** Francisco Morazan **Reverse:** Denomination

Date	Mintage	F	VF	XF	Unc	BU
1976 (g)	15,000,000	—	0.10	0.15	0.30	—
1976 (g)	15,000,000	—	0.10	0.15	0.30	—
1984 (a)	15,000,000	—	0.10	0.15	0.30	—
1984 (a)	15,000,000	—	0.10	0.15	0.30	—

KM# 149b 5 CENTAVOS **Weight:** 5.0000 g. **Composition:** Copper-Nickel-Zinc **Obverse:** Francisco Morazan **Reverse:** Denomination **Note:** Previously KM#149a.

Date	Mintage	F	VF	XF	Unc	BU
1977(h)	26,000,000	—	0.10	0.15	0.30	—

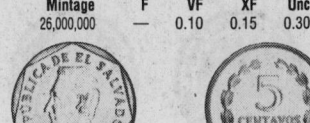

KM# 154 5 CENTAVOS **Weight:** 2.0000 g. **Composition:** Stainless Steel **Obverse:** Francisco Morazan

Date	Mintage	F	VF	XF	Unc	BU
1987(h)	30,000,000	—	0.10	0.15	0.30	—
1987(h) Proof	—	Value: 50.00				
1999(h)	—	—	0.10	0.15	0.30	—

KM# 154a 5 CENTAVOS **Weight:** 2.0000 g. **Composition:** Copper-Nickel Clad Steel **Obverse:** Francisco Morazan

Date	F	VF	XF	Unc	BU
1991 (h)	—	0.10	0.15	0.30	—
1998 (c)	—	0.10	0.15	0.30	—

KM# 154b 5 CENTAVOS **Weight:** 2.0000 g. **Composition:** Nickel Clad Steel **Obverse:** Francisco Morazan

Date	F	VF	XF	Unc	BU
1992 (g)	—	0.10	0.15	0.30	—
1993 (g)	—	0.10	0.15	0.30	—
1994 (h)	—	0.10	0.15	0.30	—
1994(h) Proof	—	Value: 40.00			
1995 (g)	—	0.10	0.15	0.30	—
1998	—	0.10	0.15	0.30	—
1999	—	0.10	0.15	0.30	—

KM# 130 10 CENTAVOS **Weight:** 7.0000 g. **Composition:** Copper-Nickel **Obverse:** Francisco Morazan **Reverse:** Denomination

Date	Mintage	F	VF	XF	Unc	BU
1921(f)	2,000,000	4.50	10.00	30.00	75.00	—
1925(f)	2,000,000	5.00	12.50	35.00	—	—
1940(f)	500,000	6.50	15.00	40.00	90.00	—
1951(f)	1,000,000	1.00	3.50	12.50	30.00	—
1967(f)	2,000,000	—	0.10	0.50	2.00	—
1968(b)	3,000,000	—	0.10	0.40	1.25	—
1969(b)	3,000,000	—	0.10	0.40	1.25	—
1972(f)	7,000,000	—	0.10	0.25	1.00	—

KM# 130a 10 CENTAVOS **Weight:** 7.0000 g. **Composition:** Copper-Nickel-Zinc

Date	Mintage	F	VF	XF	Unc	BU
1952(f)	2,000,000	0.15	0.25	0.75	4.00	—

Note: Of the 2,000,000 struck, 336,000 were struck in 1952 and the remaining 1,664,000 struck in 1953

Date	Mintage	F	VF	XF	Unc	BU
1985 Mo	15,000,000	—	0.10	0.15	0.30	—

KM# 150 10 CENTAVOS **Weight:** 7.0000 g. **Composition:** Copper-Nickel Clad Steel **Obverse:** Francisco Morazan **Reverse:** Denomination

Date	Mintage	F	VF	XF	Unc	BU
1975(a)	15,000,000	—	0.15	0.25	0.50	—
1975(a) Proof sets only	2,000	Value: 35.00				

KM# 150a 10 CENTAVOS **Composition:** Copper-Nickel-Zinc **Obverse:** Francisco Morazan **Reverse:** Denomination

Date	Mintage	F	VF	XF	Unc	BU
1977(h)	24,000,000	—	0.10	0.20	0.45	—
1977(h) Proof	—	Value: 40.00				

KM# 155 10 CENTAVOS **Weight:** 7.0000 g. **Composition:** Stainless Steel **Obverse:** Francisco Morazan

Date	Mintage	F	VF	XF	Unc	BU
1987 (h)	30,000,000	—	0.10	0.20	0.40	—
1987(h) Proof	—	Value: 40.00				
1999 (i)	—	—	0.10	0.20	0.40	—

KM# 155a 10 CENTAVOS **Composition:** Nickel Clad Steel

Date	F	VF	XF	Unc	BU
1992 (a)	—	0.10	0.20	0.40	—
1993 (g)	—	0.10	0.20	0.40	—
1994 (h)	—	0.10	0.20	0.40	—
1994 Proof	—	Value: 40.00			

KM# 155b 10 CENTAVOS **Composition:** Copper-Nickel Clad Steel

Date	F	VF	XF	Unc	BU
1995 (c)	—	0.10	0.20	0.40	—
1998 (c)	—	0.10	0.20	0.40	—
1999	—	0.10	0.20	0.40	—

KM# 136 25 CENTAVOS **Weight:** 7.5000 g. **Composition:** 0.9000 Silver .217 oz. ASW **Obverse:** Francisco Morazan **Reverse:** Denomination

Date	Mintage	F	VF	XF	Unc	BU
1943	1,000,000	2.00	3.00	7.00	15.00	—
1944	1,000,000	2.00	3.00	7.00	15.00	—

KM# 137 25 CENTAVOS **Weight:** 2.5000 g. **Composition:** 0.9000 Silver .0723 oz. ASW **Obverse:** Bust of Jose Matias Delgado left **Reverse:** Denomination

Date	Mintage	F	VF	XF	Unc	BU
1953	14,000,000	0.50	1.00	2.00	4.00	—

KM# 139 25 CENTAVOS **Weight:** 2.5000 g. **Composition:** Nickel **Obverse:** Bust of Jose Matias Delgado left **Reverse:** Denomination

Date	Mintage	F	VF	XF	Unc	BU
1970 (a)	14,000,000	—	0.10	0.20	0.60	—
1973 (g)	28,000,000	—	0.10	0.20	0.50	—
1975 (g)	20,000,000	—	0.10	0.20	0.50	—
1977 (a)	22,400,000	—	0.10	0.20	0.50	—

KM# 139a 25 CENTAVOS **Weight:** 2.5000 g. **Composition:** Copper-Nickel **Obverse:** Bust of Jose Matias Delgado left **Reverse:** Denomination

Date	Mintage	F	VF	XF	Unc	BU
1986Mo	21,000,000	—	0.10	0.20	0.50	—
1986Mo Proof	—	Value: 50.00				

KM# 157 25 CENTAVOS **Weight:** 4.0000 g. **Composition:** Stainless Steel **Obverse:** Bust of Jose Matias Delgado left **Reverse:** Denomination

Date	Mintage	F	VF	XF	Unc	BU
1988 (h)	20,000,000	—	0.10	0.20	0.50	—
1988(h) Proof	—	Value: 50.00				
1999 (i)	—	—	0.10	0.20	0.50	—

KM# 157a 25 CENTAVOS **Weight:** 4.0000 g. **Composition:** Copper-Nickel Clad Steel **Obverse:** Bust of Jose Matias Delgado left **Reverse:** Denomination

Date	F	VF	XF	Unc	BU
1992(c)	—	0.10	0.20	0.50	—
1995(c)	—	0.10	0.20	0.50	—

KM# 157b 25 CENTAVOS **Weight:** 4.0000 g. **Composition:** Nickel Clad Steel **Obverse:** Bust of Jose Matias Delgado left **Reverse:** Denomination

Date	F	VF	XF	Unc	BU
1993 (a)	—	0.10	0.20	0.50	—
1994 (g)	—	0.10	0.20	0.50	—
1998	—	0.10	0.20	0.50	—
1999	—	0.10	0.20	0.50	—

KM# 138 50 CENTAVOS **Weight:** 5.0000 g. **Composition:** 0.9000 Silver .1446 oz. ASW **Obverse:** Bust of Jose Matias Delgado left

Date	Mintage	F	VF	XF	Unc	BU
1953	3,000,000	1.00	2.00	3.00	7.00	—

KM# 140.1 50 CENTAVOS **Weight:** 5.0000 g. **Composition:** Nickel **Obverse:** Bust of Jose Matias Delgado left **Note:** 1.65 millimeters thick.

Date	Mintage	F	VF	XF	Unc	BU
1970(a)	3,000,000	—	0.20	0.30	0.60	—

KM# 140.2 50 CENTAVOS **Weight:** 5.1000 g. **Composition:** Nickel **Obverse:** Bust of Jose Matias Delgado left **Note:** Two millimeters thick.

Date	Mintage	F	VF	XF	Unc	BU
1977(a)	1,500,000	—	0.20	0.30	0.60	—

KM# 131 COLON **Weight:** 25.0000 g. **Composition:** 0.9000 Silver .7234 oz. ASW **Subject:** 400th Anniversary - San Salvador **Obverse:** Coat of arms **Reverse:** Alvarado and Quinonez

Date	Mintage	F	VF	XF	Unc	BU
ND(1925)Mo	2,000	50.00	90.00	125	200	—

KM# 141 COLON **Weight:** 2.3000 g. **Composition:** 0.9990 Silver .0738 oz. ASW **Subject:** 150th Anniversary of Independence **Obverse:** Coat of arms **Reverse:** Dali

Date	Mintage	F	VF	XF	Unc	BU
1971 Proof	21,000	Value: 7.50				

KM# 153 COLON **Weight:** 9.2500 g. **Composition:** Copper-Nickel **Obverse:** Christopher Columbus

Date	Mintage	F	VF	XF	Unc	BU
1984Mo	10,000,000	—	0.50	1.00	2.50	—
1984Mo Proof	—	Value: 125				
1985Mo	20,000,000	—	0.50	1.00	2.50	—
1985Mo Proof	—	Value: 200				

KM# 156 COLON **Weight:** 6.0000 g. **Composition:** Stainless Steel **Obverse:** Christopher Columbus

Date	Mintage	F	VF	XF	Unc	BU
1988 (h)	30,000,000	—	0.40	0.80	2.25	—
1988 Proof	—	Value: 40.00				
1999 (i)	—	—	—	0.80	2.25	—

KM# 156a COLON **Weight:** 6.0000 g. **Composition:** Copper-Nickel Clad Steel **Obverse:** Christopher Columbus

Date	F	VF	XF	Unc	BU
1991(h)	—	0.40	0.80	2.25	—

KM# 156b COLON **Weight:** 6.0000 g. **Composition:** Nickel Clad Steel **Obverse:** Christopher Columbus

Date	F	VF	XF	Unc	BU
1993 (a)	—	0.40	0.80	2.25	—
1994 (g)	—	0.40	0.80	2.25	—
1995 (h)	—	0.40	0.80	2.25	—
1998	—	0.40	0.80	2.25	—
1999	—	0.40	0.80	2.25	—

KM# 142 5 COLONES **Weight:** 11.5000 g. **Composition:** 0.9990 Silver .3694 oz. ASW **Subject:** 150th Anniversary of Independence **Obverse:** Coat of arms **Reverse:** Liberty and Cañas

Date	Mintage	F	VF	XF	Unc	BU
1971 Proof	18,000	Value: 12.50				

KM# 132 20 COLONES **Weight:** 15.5600 g. **Composition:** 0.9000 Gold .4502 oz. AGW **Subject:** 400th Anniversary - San Salvador **Obverse:** Coat of arms **Reverse:** Alvarado and Quinonez

Date	Mintage	F	VF	XF	Unc	BU
ND(1925)Mo	200	—	800	1,600	2,500	—

KM# 143 25 COLONES **Weight:** 2.9400 g. **Composition:** 0.9000 Gold .0850 oz. AGW **Subject:** 150th Anniversary of Independence **Obverse:** Coat of arms **Reverse:** Dali

Date	Mintage	F	VF	XF	Unc	BU
1971 Proof	7,650	Value: 75.00				

KM# 151 25 COLONES **Weight:** 25.0000 g. **Composition:** 0.9000 Silver .7234 oz. ASW **Subject:** 18th Annual Governors' Assembly **Obverse:** Coat of arms **Reverse:** First coin of C.A. Federation 1874

Date	Mintage	F	VF	XF	Unc	BU
1977	2,000	—	—	—	27.50	—
1977 Proof	20,000	Value: 36.00				

KM# 144 50 COLONES **Weight:** 5.9000 g. **Composition:** 0.9000 Gold .1707 oz. AGW **Subject:** 150th Anniversary of Independence **Obverse:** Coat of arms **Reverse:** Liberty and Cañas

Date	Mintage	F	VF	XF	Unc	BU
1971 Proof	3,530	Value: 100				

KM# 145 100 COLONES **Weight:** 11.8000 g. **Composition:** 0.9000 Gold .3414 oz. AGW **Subject:** 150th Anniversary of Independence **Obverse:** Coat of arms **Reverse:** Map of El Salvador

Date	Mintage	F	VF	XF	Unc	BU
1971 Proof	2,750	Value: 200				

KM# 158 150 COLONES **Weight:** 25.0000 g. **Composition:** 0.9000 Silver .7235 oz. ASW **Subject:** Union for Peace **Obverse:** Four clasped hands

Date	F	VF	XF	Unc	BU
1992	—	—	—	42.50	—

KM# 160 150 COLONES **Weight:** 25.0000 g. **Composition:** 0.9000 Silver .7235 oz. ASW **Subject:** Discovery of America **Obverse:** Columbus' ships and world map

Date	F	VF	XF	Unc	BU
1992	—	—	—	47.50	—

KM# 146 200 COLONES **Weight:** 23.6000 g. **Composition:** 0.9000 Gold .6829 oz. AGW **Subject:** 150th Anniversary of Independence **Obverse:** Coat of arms **Reverse:** Panchimalco Church

Date	Mintage	F	VF	XF	Unc	BU
1971 Proof	2,245	Value: 375				

KM# 152 250 COLONES **Weight:** 16.0000 g. **Composition:** 0.9170 Gold .4717 oz. AGW **Subject:** 18th Annual Governors' Assembly **Obverse:** Coat of arms **Reverse:** First coin of C.A. Federation 1824

Date	Mintage	F	VF	XF	Unc	BU
1977	4,000	—	—	—	275	—
1977 Proof	400	Value: 350				

KM# 159 2500 COLONES **Weight:** 16.0000 g. **Composition:** 0.9170 Gold .4715 oz. AGW **Subject:** Union for Peace **Obverse:** Four clasped hands

Date	F	VF	XF	Unc	BU
1992	—	—	—	350	—

KM# 161 2500 COLONES **Weight:** 16.0000 g. **Composition:** 0.9170 Gold .4715 oz. AGW **Subject:** Discovery of America **Obverse:** Columbus' ships and world map

Date	F	VF	XF	Unc	BU
1992	—	—	—	350	—

PATTERNS

Including off metal strikes

KM#	Date	Mintage	Identification	Mkt Val
Pn15	1997	—	5 Colones. Nickel-Plated Steel ring. 7.4000 g. 25.9 mm. Columbus' ships and world map. Denomination.	275

PROOF SETS

KM#	Date	Mintage	Identification	Issue Price	Mkt Val
PS3	1914 (4)	—	KM#115.2, 124-126	—	4,000
PS4	1971 (6)	—	KM#141-146	—	770
PS5	1971 (4)	—	KM#143-146	250	750
PS6	1971 (2)	—	KM#141-142	6.00	20.00
PS7	1974 (3)	2,000	KM#134, 147-148	—	100
PS8	1975 (2)	2,000	KM#149.1, 150	—	70.00

EQUATORIAL AFRICAN STATES

For historical background, see the introduction to Central African States.

CURRENCY UNION

DECIMAL COINAGE

100 Centimes = 1 Franc

KM# 6 FRANC **Composition:** Aluminum **Obverse:** Three giant eland **Reverse:** Denomination

Date	Mintage	F	VF	XF	Unc	BU
1969(a)	2,500,000	0.25	0.65	1.00	2.25	—
1971(a)	3,000,000	0.25	0.65	1.00	2.25	—

KM# 24 5 FRANCS **Composition:** Aluminum-Bronze **Obverse:** Three giant eland **Reverse:** Denomination

Date	Mintage	F	VF	XF	Unc	BU
1958(a)	30,000,000	0.25	0.50	1.00	3.00	—

KM# 1 5 FRANCS **Composition:** Aluminum-Bronze **Obverse:** Three giant eland **Reverse:** Denomination

Date	Mintage	F	VF	XF	Unc	BU
1961(a)	10,000,000	0.35	1.00	1.50	2.50	—
1962(a)	5,000,000	0.35	1.00	1.50	2.50	—

KM# 1a 5 FRANCS **Composition:** Aluminum-Nickel-Bronze **Obverse:** Three giant eland **Reverse:** Denomination

Date	Mintage	F	VF	XF	Unc	BU
1965(a)	2,010,000	0.35	1.00	1.50	3.00	—
1967(a)	5,795,000	0.35	1.00	1.25	2.50	—
1968(a)	5,000,000	0.35	1.00	1.25	2.50	—
1969(a)	—	0.35	1.00	1.25	2.50	—
1970(a)	9,000,000	0.35	1.00	1.25	2.50	—
1972(a)	31,010,000	0.35	1.00	1.25	2.50	—
1973(a)	5,010,000	0.35	1.00	1.25	2.50	—

KM# 25 10 FRANCS **Composition:** Aluminum-Bronze **Obverse:** Three giant eland **Reverse:** Denomination

Date	Mintage	F	VF	XF	Unc	BU
1958(a)	25,000,000	0.25	0.50	1.50	4.00	—

KM# 2 10 FRANCS **Composition:** Aluminum-Bronze **Obverse:** Three giant eland **Reverse:** Denomination

Date	Mintage	F	VF	XF	Unc	BU
1961(a)	10,000,000	0.40	1.00	1.75	3.00	—
1962(a)	5,000,000	0.40	1.00	1.75	3.00	—

KM# 2a 10 FRANCS **Composition:** Aluminum-Nickel-Bronze **Obverse:** Three giant eland **Reverse:** Denomination

Date	Mintage	F	VF	XF	Unc	BU
1965(a)	7,000,000	1.00	1.75	2.75	5.00	—
1967(a)	8,000,000	0.40	1.00	1.75	3.00	—
1968(a)	2,000,000	1.50	2.25	3.50	6.00	—
1969(a)	10,000,000	0.40	1.00	1.75	3.00	—
1972(a)	23,500,000	0.40	1.00	1.75	3.00	—
1973(a)	5,000,000	0.75	1.50	2.50	4.50	—

KM# 26 25 FRANCS **Composition:** Aluminum-Bronze **Obverse:** Three giant eland **Reverse:** Denomination

Date	Mintage	F	VF	XF	Unc	BU
1958(a)	12,000,000	0.50	1.00	2.00	6.00	—

KM# 4 25 FRANCS **Composition:** Aluminum-Bronze **Obverse:** Three giant eland **Reverse:** Denomination

Date	Mintage	F	VF	XF	Unc	BU
1962(a)	6,000,000	0.50	1.25	2.25	4.00	—

KM# 4a 25 FRANCS **Composition:** Aluminum-Nickel-Bronze **Obverse:** Three giant eland **Reverse:** Denomination

Date	Mintage	F	VF	XF	Unc	BU
1968(a)	—	1.25	2.50	4.00	7.50	—
1969(a)	—	1.25	2.50	4.00	7.50	—
1970(a)	3,019,000	0.50	1.25	2.25	4.00	—
1972(a)	18,516,000	0.50	1.25	2.00	3.00	—
1973(a)	—	1.25	2.50	4.00	7.50	—

KM# 3 50 FRANCS **Composition:** Copper-Nickel **Obverse:** Three giant eland **Reverse:** Denomination

Date	Mintage	F	VF	XF	Unc	BU
1961(a)	5,000,000	2.00	4.00	6.00	10.00	—
1963(a)	5,000,000	2.00	4.00	6.00	10.00	—

KM# 5 100 FRANCS **Composition:** Nickel **Obverse:** Three giant eland **Reverse:** Denomination

Date	Mintage	F	VF	XF	Unc	BU
1966(a)	9,948,000	2.00	4.00	7.00	12.00	—
1967(a)	11,000,000	2.00	4.00	7.00	12.00	—
1968(a)	—	2.00	4.00	7.00	12.00	—

ESSAIS

Standard metals unless otherwise noted

KM#	Date	Mintage	Identification	Issue Price	Mkt Val
E1	1961(a)	—	5 Francs. KM#1.	—	10.00
E2	1961(a)	—	10 Francs. KM#2.	—	15.00
E3	1961(a)	—	50 Francs. KM#3.	—	30.00
E4	1961(a)	—	50 Francs. Gold. KM#4.	—	1,250
E5	1962(a)	—	25 Francs. KM#4. This is a mule, having an old reverse die with a wing privy mark.	—	15.00
E6	1966(a)	—	100 Francs. KM#5.	—	20.00
E7	1969(a)	—	Franc. KM#6.	—	12.00

PIEFORTS

KM#	Date	Mintage	Identification	Issue Price	Mkt Val
P1	1965(a)	—	100 Francs. Gold. 23.4800 g. KM#5. With ESSAI.	—	775

EQUATORIAL GUINEA

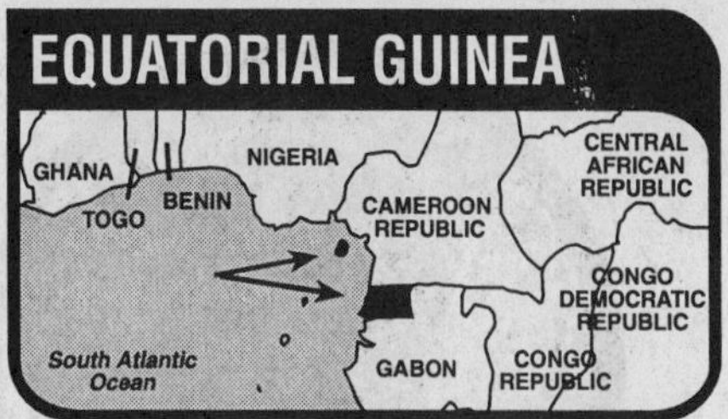

The Republic of Equatorial Guinea (formerly Spanish Guinea) consists of Rio Muni, located on the coast of West-Central Africa between Cameroon and Gabon, and the off-shore islands of Fernando Po, Annobon, Corisco, Elobey Grande and Elobey Chico. The equatorial country has an area of 10,831 sq. mi. (28,050 sq. km.) and a population of 420,293. Capital: Malabo. The economy is based on agriculture and forestry. Cacao, wood and coffee are exported.

Fernando Po was discovered between 1474 and 1496 by Portuguese navigators charting a route to the spice islands of the Far East. Portugal retained control of it and the adjacent islands until 1778 when they, together with trading rights to the African coast between the Ogooue and Niger Rivers, were ceded to Spain. Fernando Po was administered, with Spanish consent, by the British from 1827 to 1844 when it was reclaimed by Spain. Mainland Rio Muni was granted to Spain by the Berlin Conference of 1885. The name of the colony was changed from Spanish Guinea to Equatorial Guinea in Dec. of 1963. Independence was attained on Oct. 12, 1968.

Equatorial Guinea converted to the CFA currency system as issued for the Central African States issuing its first 100 Franc denomination in 1985.

NOTE: The 1969 coinage carries the actual minting date in the stars at the sides of the large date.

MINT MARKS

(a) - Paris, privy marks only

REPUBLIC

PESETA COINAGE

KM# 1 PESETA **Composition:** Aluminum-Bronze

Date	F	VF	XF	Unc	BU
1969(69)	0.35	0.75	1.25	2.00	—

KM# 2 5 PESETAS **Composition:** Copper-Nickel

Date	F	VF	XF	Unc	BU
1969(69)	0.75	1.50	2.50	8.00	—

KM# 3 25 PESETAS **Composition:** Copper-Nickel

Date	F	VF	XF	Unc	BU
1969(69)	1.50	2.50	6.50	12.00	—

KM# 5 25 PESETAS **Weight:** 5.0000 g. **Composition:** 0.9990 Silver .1606 oz. ASW **Subject:** World Bank

Date	Mintage	F	VF	XF	Unc	BU
1970 Proof	2,475	Value: 9.00				

KM# 6 25 PESETAS **Weight:** 5.0000 g. **Composition:** 0.9990 Silver .1606 oz. ASW **Subject:** United Nations

Date	Mintage	F	VF	XF	Unc	BU
1970 Proof	2,475	Value: 9.00				

KM# 4 50 PESETAS **Composition:** Copper-Nickel

Date	F	VF	XF	Unc	BU
1969(69)	2.00	3.00	7.50	15.00	—

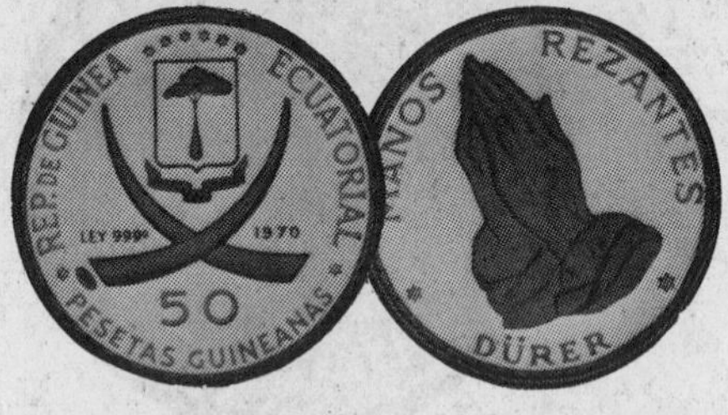

KM# 7 50 PESETAS **Weight:** 10.0000 g. **Composition:** 0.9990 Silver .3212 oz. ASW **Reverse:** Durer's Praying Hands

Date	Mintage	F	VF	XF	Unc	BU
1970 Proof	3,840	Value: 12.00				

KM# 8 75 PESETAS **Weight:** 15.0000 g. **Composition:** 0.9990 Silver .4818 oz. ASW **Obverse:** Arms **Reverse:** Pope John XXIII

Date	Mintage	F	VF	XF	Unc	BU
1970 Proof	4,000	Value: 21.50				

KM# 9 75 PESETAS **Weight:** 15.0000 g. **Composition:** 0.9990 Silver .4818 oz. ASW **Subject:** Centennial - Birth of Vladimir Ilyich Lenin **Reverse:** Bust of Lenin

Date	Mintage	F	VF	XF	Unc	BU
1970 Proof	4,000	Value: 21.50				

KM# 10.1 75 PESETAS **Weight:** 15.0000 g. **Composition:** 0.9990 Silver .4818 oz. ASW **Obverse:** Hallmark "1000" in oval at left tusk base **Reverse:** President Abraham Lincoln

Date	Mintage	F	VF	XF	Unc	BU
1970 Proof	4,390	Value: 16.50				

KM# 10.2 75 PESETAS **Weight:** 15.0000 g. **Composition:** 0.9990 Silver .4818 oz. ASW **Obverse:** "1 AR" Hallmark above "E" in "Pesetas"

Date	Mintage	F	VF	XF	Unc	BU
1970 Proof	Inc. above	Value: 30.00				

KM# 11 75 PESETAS **Weight:** 15.0000 g. **Composition:** 0.9990 Silver .4818 oz. ASW **Subject:** Centennial - Birth of Mahatma Gandhi **Obverse:** Arms **Reverse:** Portrait of Gandhi

Date	Mintage	F	VF	XF	Unc	BU
1970 Proof	4,000	Value: 21.50				

KM# 12.1 100 PESETAS **Weight:** 20.0000 g. **Composition:** 0.9990 Silver .6430 oz. ASW **Obverse:** Arms **Reverse:** Durer's Praying Hands

Date	Mintage	F	VF	XF	Unc	BU
1970 Proof	4,000	Value: 16.50				

KM# 12.2 100 PESETAS **Weight:** 20.0000 g. **Composition:** 0.9990 Silver .6430 oz. ASW **Obverse:** "1 AR" hallmark **Reverse:** Durer's Praying Hands

Date	Mintage	F	VF	XF	Unc	BU
1970 Proof	Inc. above	Value: 27.50				

KM# 13.1 100 PESETAS **Weight:** 20.0000 g. **Composition:** 0.9990 Silver .6430 oz. ASW **Reverse:** Goya's Naked Maja

Date	Mintage	F	VF	XF	Unc	BU
1970 Proof	30,000	Value: 35.00				

KM# 13.2 100 PESETAS **Weight:** 20.0000 g. **Composition:** 0.9990 Silver .6430 oz. ASW **Obverse:** Fineness stamp at base of right tusk **Reverse:** Goya's Naked Maja

Date	Mintage	F	VF	XF	Unc	BU
1970 Proof	Inc. above	Value: 35.00				

KM# 13.3 100 PESETAS **Weight:** 20.0000 g. **Composition:** 0.9990 Silver .6430 oz. ASW **Obverse:**

Fineness stamp below base of right tusk **Reverse:** Goya's Naked Maja

Date	Mintage	F	VF	XF	Unc	BU
1970 Proof	Inc. above	Value: 35.00				

KM# 13.4 100 PESETAS Weight: 20.0000 g. **Composition:** 0.9990 Silver .6430 oz. ASW **Obverse:** Fineness stamp above letters AN **Reverse:** Goya's Naked Maja

Date	Mintage	F	VF	XF	Unc	BU
1970 Proof	Inc. above	Value: 35.00				

KM# 13.5 100 PESETAS Weight: 20.0000 g. **Composition:** 0.9990 Silver .6430 oz. ASW **Obverse:** 1000 in oval counterstamp at base of right tusk **Reverse:** Goya's Naked Maja

Date	Mintage	F	VF	XF	Unc	BU
1970 Proof	Inc. above	Value: 35.00				

KM# 14 150 PESETAS Weight: 30.0000 g. **Composition:** 0.9990 Silver .9636 oz. ASW **Subject:** Centennial of the Capital Rome **Reverse:** Roma **Size:** 30 mm.

Date	Mintage	F	VF	XF	Unc	BU
1970 Proof	3,520	Value: 27.50				

KM# 15 150 PESETAS Weight: 30.0000 g. **Composition:** 0.9990 Silver .9636 oz. ASW **Subject:** Centennial of the Capital Rome **Reverse:** Colisseum

Date	Mintage	F	VF	XF	Unc	BU
1970 Proof	3,520	Value: 27.50				

KM# 16 150 PESETAS Weight: 30.0000 g. **Composition:** 0.9990 Silver .9636 oz. ASW **Subject:** Centennial of the Capital Rome **Reverse:** Athena

Date	Mintage	F	VF	XF	Unc	BU
1970 Proof	3,520	Value: 27.50				

KM# 17 150 PESETAS Weight: 30.0000 g. **Composition:** 0.9990 Silver .9636 oz. ASW **Subject:** Centennial of the Capital Rome **Reverse:** Mercury

Date	Mintage	F	VF	XF	Unc	BU
1970 Proof	3,520	Value: 27.50				

KM# 18.1 200 PESETAS Weight: 40.0000 g. **Composition:** 0.9990 Silver 1.2848 oz. ASW **Subject:** World Soccer Championship in Mexico **Obverse:** Similar to 100 Pesetas, KM#13

Date	Mintage	F	VF	XF	Unc	BU
1970 Proof	4,200	Value: 45.00				

KM# 18.2 200 PESETAS Weight: 40.0000 g. **Composition:** 0.9990 Silver 1.2848 oz. ASW **Subject:** World Soccer Championship in Mexico **Obverse:** Similar to 100 Pesetas, KM#13 **Reverse:** Fineness stamp in oval at base of right tusk; mint mark stamp "1 AR" at base of left tusk; incuse serial number below denomination

Date	Mintage	F	VF	XF	Unc	BU
1970 Proof	Inc. above	Value: 75.00				

KM# 19 200 PESETAS Weight: 40.0000 g. **Composition:** 0.9990 Silver 1.2848 oz. ASW **Subject:** First President Francisco Macias

Date	Mintage	F	VF	XF	Unc	BU
1970 Proof	4,000	Value: 37.50				

KM# 20.1 (KM20) 250 PESETAS Weight: 3.5200 g. **Composition:** 0.9000 Gold .1018 oz. AGW **Reverse:** Goya's Naked Maja; fineness countermark at 8 o'clock by tusk base

Date	Mintage	F	VF	XF	Unc	BU
1970 Proof	3,500	Value: 120				
1970 Proof	3,500	Value: 120				

KM# 20.2 250 PESETAS Weight: 3.5200 g. **Composition:** 0.9000 Gold 0.1019 oz. AGW **Reverse:** Fineness countermark at 4 o'clock by tusk base

Date	Mintage	F	VF	XF	Unc	BU
1970 Proof	—	Value: 120				

KM# 21 250 PESETAS Weight: 3.5200 g. **Composition:** 0.9000 Gold .1018 oz. AGW **Reverse:** Durer's Praying Hands **Note:** Similar to 100 pesetas, KM#12.

Date	Mintage	F	VF	XF	Unc	BU
1970 Proof	2,000	Value: 75.00				

KM# 23 500 PESETAS Weight: 7.0500 g. **Composition:** 0.9000 Gold .2040 oz. AGW **Reverse:** Vladimir Illyich Lenin **Note:** Similar to 75 Pesetas, KM#9.

Date	Mintage	F	VF	XF	Unc	BU
1970 Proof	1,680	Value: 135				

KM# 22 500 PESETAS Weight: 7.0500 g. **Composition:** 0.9000 Gold .2040 oz. AGW **Reverse:** Bust of Pope John XXIII

Date	Mintage	F	VF	XF	Unc	BU
1970 Proof	1,680	Value: 130				

KM# 24 500 PESETAS Weight: 7.0500 g. **Composition:** 0.9000 Gold .2040 oz. AGW **Reverse:** President Abraham Lincoln

Date	Mintage	F	VF	XF	Unc	BU
1970 Proof	1,700	Value: 125				

KM# 25 500 PESETAS Weight: 7.0500 g. **Composition:** 0.9000 Gold .2040 oz. AGW **Subject:** Centennial - Birth of Mahatma Gandhi **Reverse:** Portrait of Gandhi

Date	Mintage	F	VF	XF	Unc	BU
1970 Proof	1,680	Value: 135				

KM# 26 750 PESETAS Weight: 10.5700 g. **Composition:** 0.9000 Gold .3058 oz. AGW **Subject:** Centennial of the Capital Rome - Roma **Note:** Similar to 150 Pesetas, KM#14.

Date	Mintage	F	VF	XF	Unc	BU
1970 Proof	1,650	Value: 185				

KM# 27 750 PESETAS Weight: 10.5700 g. **Composition:** 0.9000 Gold .3058 oz. AGW **Subject:** Centennial of the Capital Rome - Colisseum **Note:** Similar to 150 Pesetas, KM#15.

Date	Mintage	F	VF	XF	Unc	BU
1970 Proof	1,550	Value: 200				

KM# 28 750 PESETAS Weight: 10.5700 g. **Composition:** 0.9000 Gold .3058 oz. AGW **Subject:** Centennial of the Capital Rome - Athena **Note:** Similar to 150 Pesetas, KM#16.

Date	Mintage	F	VF	XF	Unc	BU
1970 Proof	1,550	Value: 185				

KM# 29 750 PESETAS Weight: 10.5700 g. **Composition:** 0.9000 Gold .3058 oz. AGW **Subject:** Centennial of the Capital Rome - Mercury **Note:** Similar to 150 Pesetas, KM#17.

Date	Mintage	F	VF	XF	Unc	BU
1970 Proof	1,550	Value: 185				

KM# 30 1000 PESETAS Weight: 14.100‿ g. **Composition:** 0.9000 Gold .4080 oz. AGW **Subject:** World Soccer Championship in Mexico **Note:** Similar to 200 Pesetas, KM#18.

Date	Mintage	F	VF	XF	Unc	BU
1970 Proof	1,190	Value: 250				

KM# 31 5000 PESETAS Weight: 70.5200 g. **Composition:** 0.9000 Gold 2.0407 oz. AGW **Subject:** First President - Francisco Macias **Note:** Similar to 200 Pesetas, KM#19.

Date	Mintage	F	VF	XF	Unc	BU
1970 Proof	330	Value: 1,350				

REFORM COINAGE

1975-1980

KM# 32 EKUELE Composition: Brass **Note:** Withdrawn from circulation.

Date	Mintage	F	VF	XF	Unc	BU
1975	3,000,000	1.00	2.00	3.00	5.00	—

KM# 33 5 EKUELE Composition: Copper-Nickel **Note:** Withdrawn from circulation.

Date	Mintage	F	VF	XF	Unc	BU
1975	2,800,000	1.00	2.00	3.50	6.00	—

KM# 34 10 EKUELE Composition: Copper-Nickel **Note:** Withdrawn from circulation.

Date	Mintage	F	VF	XF	Unc	BU
1975	1,300,000	1.50	2.50	4.50	9.00	—

KM# 35 1000 EKUELE Weight: 21.4300 g. **Composition:** 0.9250 Silver .6373 oz. ASW **Reverse:** President Masie Nguema Biyogo

Date	Mintage	F	VF	XF	Unc	BU
1978 Proof	31,000	Value: 17.50				

KM# 55 2000 EKUELE Weight: 31.0000 g. **Composition:** 0.9270 Silver .9270 oz. ASW **Reverse:** Burchell's zebra

Date	Mintage	F	VF	XF	Unc	BU
1980 (1983) Proof	1,000	Value: 30.00				

KM# 56 2000 EKUELE Weight: 31.0000 g. **Composition:** 0.9270 Silver .9270 oz. ASW **Reverse:** Impalas

Date	Mintage	F	VF	XF	Unc	BU
1980 (1983) Proof	1,000	Value: 30.00				

KM# 38 2000 EKUELE Weight: 42.8700 g. **Composition:** 0.9250 Silver 1.2749 oz. ASW **Subject:** Soccer Games - Argentina 1978

Date	Mintage	F	VF	XF	Unc	BU
ND(1979) Proof	195	Value: 80.00				

KM# 36 2000 EKUELE Weight: 42.8700 g. **Composition:** 0.9250 Silver 1.2749 oz. ASW **Reverse:** President Masie Nguema Biyogo

Date	Mintage	F	VF	XF	Unc	BU
1978 Proof	31,000	Value: 30.00				

KM# 37 2000 EKUELE Weight: 31.1000 g. **Composition:** 0.9270 Silver .9270 oz. ASW **Subject:** XXII Olympics

Date	Mintage	F	VF	XF	Unc	BU
ND(1979) Proof	11,000	Value: 16.50				

KM# 57 2000 EKUELE Weight: 31.0000 g. **Composition:** 0.9270 Silver .9270 oz. ASW **Reverse:** Tiger's head

Date	Mintage	F	VF	XF	Unc	BU
1980 (1983) Proof	1,000	Value: 35.00				

KM# 58 2000 EKUELE Weight: 31.0000 g. **Composition:** 0.9270 Silver .9270 oz. ASW **Reverse:** Cheetah running left

Date	Mintage	F	VF	XF	Unc	BU
1980 (1983) Proof	1,000	Value: 30.00				

KM# 39 5000 EKUELE Weight: 6.9600 g. **Composition:** 0.9170 Gold .2052 oz. AGW **Reverse:** President Nguema Biyogo

Date	Mintage	F	VF	XF	Unc	BU
1978 Proof	31,000	Value: 150				

KM# 40 10000 EKUELE Weight: 13.9200 g. **Composition:** 0.9170 Gold .4104 oz. AGW **Reverse:** President Nguema Biyogo

Date	Mintage	F	VF	XF	Unc	BU
1978 Proof	31,000	Value: 300				

KM# 41 10000 EKUELE **Weight:** 13.9200 g. **Composition:** 0.9170 Gold .4104 oz. AGW **Subject:** Soccer Games - Argentina 1978

Date	Mintage	F	VF	XF	Unc	BU
ND(1979) Proof	121	Value: 500				

REFORM COINAGE

1980-1982

KM# 50 EKUELE **Composition:** Aluminum-Bronze **Obverse:** T.E. Nkogo

Date	F	VF	XF	Unc	BU
1980	—	—	—	55.00	—

KM# 54 EKUELE **Weight:** 62.2900 g. **Composition:** 0.9990 Gold 2.0009 oz. AGW **Obverse:** Coat of arms **Reverse:** Pope John Paul II

Date	F	VF	XF	Unc	BU
1982	—	—	—	1,200	—

KM# 51 5 BIPKWELE **Composition:** Copper-Nickel **Obverse:** T.E. Nkogo right **Reverse:** Value and arms

Date	F	VF	XF	Unc	BU
1980	—	60.00	100	150	—

KM# 52 25 BIPKWELE **Composition:** Copper-Nickel **Obverse:** T.E. Nkogo

Date	F	VF	XF	Unc	BU
1980	—	12.00	18.00	30.00	—
1981	—	—	—	—	—

KM# 53 50 BIPKWELE **Composition:** Copper-Nickel **Obverse:** T.E. Nkogo right **Reverse:** Value and arms

Date	F	VF	XF	Unc	BU
1980	—	—	—	37.50	—
1981	—	—	—	—	—

KM# 114 7000 FRANCOS **Weight:** 9.9300 g. **Composition:** 0.7400 Silver .2362 oz. ASW **Subject:** Endangered Wildlife **Obverse:** National arms **Reverse:** Giraffe family **Edge:** Reeded **Size:** 34.8 mm.

Date	F	VF	XF	Unc	BU
1993 Proof	—	Value: 50.00			

KM# 107 30000 FRANCOS **Weight:** 33.9300 g. **Composition:** 0.9170 Gold 1.0003 oz. AGW **Subject:** Elephant Protection **Obverse:** National arms **Reverse:** Elephant **Edge:** Reeded **Size:** 32.8 mm.

Date	Mintage	F	VF	XF	Unc	BU
1993 Proof	700	Value: 600				

Note: 400 pieces remelted at mint

REFORM COINAGE

1985-

KM# 62 5 FRANCOS **Composition:** Aluminum-Bronze **Obverse:** Three eland facing **Reverse:** Value

Date	F	VF	XF	Unc	BU
1985(a)	—	2.50	4.50	8.00	—

KM# 60 25 FRANCOS **Composition:** Aluminum-Bronze **Obverse:** Three eland facing **Reverse:** Value

Date	F	VF	XF	Unc	BU
1985(a)	—	3.50	7.00	15.00	—

KM# 64 50 FRANCOS **Composition:** Nickel **Obverse:** Three eland facing **Reverse:** Value

Date	F	VF	XF	Unc	BU
1985(a)	—	8.00	16.00	28.00	—
1986(a)	—	6.00	12.00	20.00	—

KM# 59 100 FRANCOS **Composition:** Nickel

Date	F	VF	XF	Unc	BU
1985(a)	—	10.00	20.00	35.00	—
1986(a)	—	7.00	14.00	25.00	—

KM# 68 1000 FRANCOS **Composition:** Copper-Nickel **Reverse:** Brandenburg Gate

Date	Mintage	F	VF	XF	Unc	BU
1991 Proof	6,000	Value: 10.00				

KM# 81 1000 FRANCOS **Composition:** Copper-Nickel **Subject:** Jurassic Dinosaurs **Reverse:** Diplodocus **Note:** Multicolored.

Date	F	VF	XF	Unc	BU
1993	—	—	—	27.50	—

KM# 115 1000 FRANCOS **Weight:** 25.5600 g. **Composition:** Copper-Nickel **Subject:** Jurassic Dinosaurs **Obverse:** National arms. **Reverse:** Multicolor stegosaurus. **Edge:** Reeded. **Size:** 38 mm.

Date	F	VF	XF	Unc	BU
1993	—	—	—	20.00	—

KM# 82 1000 FRANCOS **Composition:** Copper-Nickel **Subject:** Jurassic Dinosaurs **Reverse:** Styracosaurus

Date	F	VF	XF	Unc	BU
1993	—	—	—	25.00	—

KM# 83 1000 FRANCOS **Composition:** Copper-Nickel **Subject:** Jurassic Dinosaurs **Reverse:** Tyrannosaurus

Date	F	VF	XF	Unc	BU
1993	—	—	—	32.50	—

KM# 87 1000 FRANCOS **Composition:** Copper-Nickel **Subject:** Jurassic Dinosaurs **Reverse:** Allosaurus

Date	F	VF	XF	Unc	BU
1993	—	—	—	27.50	—

KM# 88 1000 FRANCOS **Composition:** Copper-Nickel **Subject:** Jurassic Dinosaurs **Reverse:** Plateosaurus

Date	F	VF	XF	Unc	BU
1993	—	—	—	27.50	—

KM# 90 1000 FRANCOS **Composition:** Copper-Nickel **Subject:** World Soccer Championship - 1994

Date	F	VF	XF	Unc	BU
1994	—	—	—	27.50	—

KM# 89 1000 FRANCOS **Composition:** Copper-Nickel **Subject:** African Bird Wildlife - Kingfisher **Note:** Similar to 7000 Francos, KM#98.

Date	F	VF	XF	Unc	BU
1994	—	—	—	25.00	—

KM# 91 1000 FRANCOS **Composition:** Copper-Nickel **Subject:** World's Famous Dogs - St. Bernard **Note:** Multicolored.

Date	F	VF	XF	Unc	BU
1994	—	—	—	22.50	—

KM# 92 1000 FRANCOS **Composition:** Copper-Nickel **Subject:** 25th Anniversary - Moon Landing

Date	F	VF	XF	Unc	BU
1994	—	—	—	22.50	—

KM# 93 1000 FRANCOS **Composition:** Copper-Nickel **Subject:** Famous Stamps of the World - Swiss

Date	F	VF	XF	Unc	BU
1994	—	—	—	20.00	—

KM# 84.1 1000 FRANCOS **Composition:** Copper-Nickel **Subject:** 150th Anniversary - Basel "Taube" Stamp **Note:** Multicolored.

Date	Mintage	F	VF	XF	Unc	BU
1995	15,000	—	—	—	20.00	—

KM# 84.2 1000 FRANCOS **Composition:** Copper-Nickel **Subject:** 150th Anniversary - Basel "Taube" Stamp **Rev. Legend:** Error, "TAUBER" **Note:** Multicolored.

Date	F	VF	XF	Unc	BU
1995	—	—	—	35.00	—

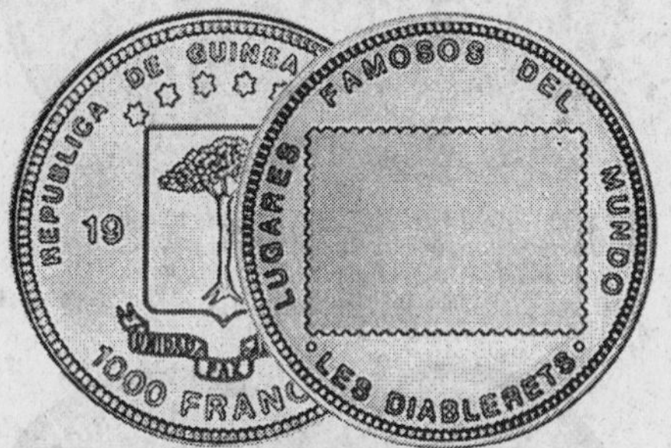

KM# 118 1000 FRANCOS **Weight:** 29.5000 g. **Composition:** Copper-Nickel **Subject:** Famous Places - les Diablerets **Obverse:** National arms. **Reverse:** Multicolor stamp design. **Edge:** Reeded. **Size:** 38 mm.

Date	F	VF	XF	Unc	BU
1996	—	—	—	—	—

KM# 95 1000 FRANCOS **Composition:** Copper-Nickel **Subject:** Famous Places in the World - Altdorf-Wilhelm Tell **Obverse:** State arms **Reverse:** Multicolored applique of Wilhelm Tell

Date	F	VF	XF	Unc	BU
1996 Proof	—	Value: 27.50			

KM# 96 1000 FRANCOS **Composition:** Copper-Nickel **Subject:** Famous Stamps of the World - Pintores Famosos dei Mundo - Rolf Knie **Obverse:** State arms **Reverse:** Multicolored applique of Swiss circus stamp design

Date	F	VF	XF	Unc	BU
1996 Proof	—	Value: 35.00			

KM# 97 1000 FRANCOS **Composition:** Copper-Nickel **Subject:** Famous Stamps of the World - XXVI Juegos Olimpicos de Verano **Obverse:** State arms **Reverse:** Stamp with downhill skier

Date	F	VF	XF	Unc	BU
1996 Proof	—	Value: 35.00			

KM# 66 7000 FRANCOS **Weight:** 26.3000 g. **Composition:** 0.9990 Silver .8455 oz. ASW **Reverse:** President Mbasogo bust above three shields

Date	F	VF	XF	Unc	BU
1991 Proof	—	Value: 42.50			

KM# 67 7000 FRANCOS **Weight:** 25.7000 g. **Composition:** 0.9990 Silver .8263 oz. ASW **Subject:** Soccer - Italy 1990

Date	Mintage	F	VF	XF	Unc	BU
1991 Proof	6,000	Value: 45.00				

KM# 69 7000 FRANCOS **Weight:** 20.0000 g. **Composition:** 0.9990 Silver .6430 oz. ASW **Subject:** Discovery of America **Reverse:** Santa Maria

Date	Mintage	F	VF	XF	Unc	BU
1991 Proof	15,000	Value: 40.00				

KM# 70 7000 FRANCOS **Weight:** 20.0000 g. **Composition:** 0.9990 Silver .6430 oz. ASW **Subject:** Seville Expo

Date	Mintage	F	VF	XF	Unc	BU
1991 Proof	15,000	Value: 40.00				

KM# 71 7000 FRANCOS **Weight:** 20.0000 g. **Composition:** 0.9990 Silver .6430 oz. ASW **Subject:** Barcelona Olympics **Reverse:** Athletes on rings

Date	Mintage	F	VF	XF	Unc	BU
1991 Proof	15,000	Value: 42.50				

KM# 76 7000 FRANCOS **Weight:** 510.3000 g. **Composition:** 0.9990 Silver 16.4062 oz. ASW **Subject:** Endangered Wildlife **Reverse:** Lions **Size:** 75.1 mm. **Note:** Illustration reduced.

Date	F	VF	XF	Unc	BU
1992 Proof	—	Value: 250			

KM# 105 7000 FRANCOS **Weight:** 7.7700 g. **Composition:** 0.9000 Gold .2248 oz. AGW **Subject:** Endangered Wildlife **Reverse:** Lions

Date	Mintage	F	VF	XF	Unc	BU
1992 Proof	450	Value: 200				

KM# 80 7000 FRANCOS **Weight:** 10.4800 g. **Composition:** 0.9990 Silver .3366 oz. ASW **Subject:** Barcelona Olympics **Reverse:** Female runner

Date	Mintage	F	VF	XF	Unc	BU
1992 Proof	25,000	Value: 22.50				

KM# 77 7000 FRANCOS **Weight:** 10.5100 g. **Composition:** 0.9990 Silver .3379 oz. ASW **Subject:** African Elephant Protection

Date	Mintage	F	VF	XF	Unc	BU
1993 Proof	Est. 25,000	Value: 27.50				

KM# 119 7000 FRANCOS **Weight:** 20.0000 g. **Composition:** 0.9990 Silver 0.6424 oz. ASW **Subject:** Zebras

Date	F	VF	XF	Unc	BU
1993 Proof	—	Value: 27.50			

KM# 78 7000 FRANCOS **Weight:** 20.0000 g. **Composition:** 0.9990 Silver .6430 oz. ASW **Subject:** Barcelona Olympics **Reverse:** Athletes on Olympic rings

Date	F	VF	XF	Unc	BU
1993 Proof	—	Value: 65.00			

KM# 94 7000 FRANCOS **Weight:** 20.1700 g. **Composition:** 0.9990 Silver .6478 oz. ASW **Subject:** Jurassic Dinosaurs **Obverse:** National arms **Reverse:** Multicolored stegosaurus scene applique

Date	F	VF	XF	Unc	BU
1993 Proof	—	Value: 65.00			

KM# 86 7000 FRANCOS **Weight:** 20.1700 g. **Composition:** 0.9990 Silver .6651 oz. ASW **Subject:** World Cup Soccer

Date	F	VF	XF	Unc	BU
1994 Proof	—	Value: 40.00			

KM# 98 7000 FRANCOS **Weight:** 20.3500 g. **Composition:** 0.9990 Silver .6536 oz. ASW **Subject:** African Bird Wildlife - Kingfisher **Obverse:** National arms **Reverse:** Pair of multicolored kingfishers

Date	F	VF	XF	Unc	BU
1994 Proof	—	Value: 42.50			

KM# 99 7000 FRANCOS **Weight:** 20.3500 g. **Composition:** 0.9990 Silver .6536 oz. ASW **Subject:** World Famous Dogs - St. Bernard **Obverse:** National arms **Reverse:** Pair of multicolored St. Bernards

Date	F	VF	XF	Unc	BU
1994 Proof	—	Value: 42.50			

KM# 108 7000 FRANCOS **Weight:** 20.3500 g. **Composition:** 0.9990 Silver .6536 oz. ASW **Subject:** 25th Anniversary - Moon Landing **Reverse:** Multicolored moon-landing scene

Date	F	VF	XF	Unc	BU
1994 Proof	—	Value: 42.50			

KM# 109 7000 FRANCOS **Weight:** 20.3500 g. **Composition:** 0.9990 Silver .6536 oz. ASW **Subject:** 150th Anniversary - Basel "Taube" Stamp **Reverse:** Multicolored stamp

Date	F	VF	XF	Unc	BU
1995 Proof	—	Value: 30.00			

KM# 85 7000 FRANCOS **Weight:** 21.0000 g. **Composition:** 0.9990 Silver .6752 oz. ASW **Subject:** 50th Anniversary - United Nations

Date	F	VF	XF	Unc	BU
1995 Proof	—	Value: 37.50			

KM# 100 7000 FRANCOS **Weight:** 157.5500 g. **Composition:** 0.9990 Silver 5.0603 oz. ASW **Subject:** Endangered wildlife **Obverse:** Topical map of Africa, similar to KM#76 **Reverse:** Elephant head **Size:** 64.9 mm. **Note:** Illustration reduced.

Date	Mintage	F	VF	XF	Unc	BU
1995 Proof	555	Value: 100				

KM# 101 7000 FRANCOS **Weight:** 157.5500 g. **Composition:** 0.9990 Silver 5.0603 oz. ASW **Subject:** Endangered wildlife **Obverse:** Topical map of Africa **Reverse:** Mother elephant with calf

Date	Mintage	F	VF	XF	Unc	BU
1995 Proof	555	Value: 100				

KM# 102 7000 FRANCOS **Weight:** 157.5500 g. **Composition:** 0.9990 Silver 5.0603 oz. ASW **Subject:** Endangered wildlife **Obverse:** Topical map of Africa **Reverse:** Elephant at watering hole

Date	Mintage	F	VF	XF	Unc	BU
1995 Proof	555	Value: 100				

KM# 103 7000 FRANCOS **Weight:** 157.5500 g. **Composition:** 0.9990 Silver 5.0603 oz. ASW **Subject:** Endangered wildlife **Obverse:** Topical map of Africa **Reverse:** Elephant family

Date	Mintage	F	VF	XF	Unc	BU
1995 Proof	555	Value: 100				

KM# 104 7000 FRANCOS **Weight:** 157.5500 g. **Composition:** 0.9990 Silver 5.0603 oz. ASW **Subject:** Endangered wildlife **Obverse:** Topical map of Africa **Reverse:** Adolescent elephant with adult

Date	Mintage	F	VF	XF	Unc	BU
1995 Proof	555	Value: 100				

KM# 116 8000 FRANCOS **Weight:** 7.7700 g. **Composition:** 0.9990 Gold 0.2496 oz. AGW **Subject:** World's Famous Dogs **Obverse:** National arms. **Reverse:** Pekingese dog and Chinese building. **Edge:** Reeded. **Size:** 26.9 mm.

Date	F	VF	XF	Unc	BU
1994 Proof	—	Value: 250			

KM# 72 15000 FRANCOS **Weight:** 7.0000 g. **Composition:** 0.9170 Gold .2063 oz. AGW **Subject:** Discovery of America - Columbus **Obverse:** Coat of arms above denomination

Date	Mintage	F	VF	XF	Unc	BU
1991 Proof	1,500	Value: 155				

KM# 73 15000 FRANCOS **Weight:** 7.0000 g. **Composition:** 0.9170 Gold .2063 oz. AGW **Subject:** Expo Seville - Ship and Space Shuttle **Obverse:** Coat of arms above denomination

Date	Mintage	F	VF	XF	Unc	BU
1991 Proof	1,500	Value: 155				

KM# 74 15000 FRANCOS **Weight:** 7.0000 g. **Composition:** 0.9170 Gold .2063 oz. AGW **Series:** Barcelona Olympics **Obverse:** Coat of arms above denomination **Reverse:** Equestrian jumping

Date	Mintage	F	VF	XF	Unc	BU
1991 Proof	1,500	Value: 165				

KM# 74a 15000 FRANCOS **Weight:** 20.3300 g. **Composition:** 0.9990 Silver .6350 oz. ASW **Series:** Barcelona Olympics **Obverse:** Coat of arms above denomination **Reverse:** Equestrian jumping

Date	F	VF	XF	Unc	BU
1992 Proof	—	Value: 50.00			

KM# 79 15000 FRANCOS **Weight:** 855.3422 g. **Composition:** 0.9990 Silver 27.49 oz. ASW **Subject:** Endangered wildlife **Obverse:** Similar to KM#76 **Reverse:** Elephant **Size:** 106 mm. **Note:** Illustration reduced.

Date	F	VF	XF	Unc	BU
1992 Proof	—	Value: 275			

KM# 106 15000 FRANCOS **Weight:** 15.5500 g. **Composition:** 0.9000 Gold .4499 oz. AGW **Subject:** Endangered wildlife **Reverse:** Elephant

Date	Mintage	F	VF	XF	Unc	BU
1992 Proof	450	Value: 325				

ESSAIS

KM#	Date	Mintage	Identification	Issue Price	Mkt Val
E14	1980	—	1000 Bipkwele. Copper. M5.	—	18.00
E1	1978	25	1000 Ekuele. Aluminum. KM#35.	—	45.00
E2	1978	20	1000 Ekuele. Copper. KM#35.	—	50.00
E3	1978	25	2000 Ekuele. Aluminum. KM#36.	—	55.00
E4	1978	—	2000 Ekuele. Copper. KM#36.	—	60.00
E5	1978	—	5000 Ekuele. Aluminum. KM#39.	—	35.00
E6	1978	—	5000 Ekuele. Copper. KM#39.	—	40.00
E7	1978	—	10000 Ekuele. Aluminum. KM#40.	—	45.00
E8	1978	—	10000 Ekuele. Copper. KM#40.	—	50.00
E9	ND(1979)	—	2000 Ekuele. Aluminum. KM#38.	—	25.00

KM#	Date	Mintage	Identification	Issue Price	Mkt Val
E10	ND(1979)	—	2000 Ekuele. Copper. KM#38.	—	90.00
E11	ND(1979)	—	10000 Ekuele. Aluminum. KM#41.	—	25.00
E12	ND(1979)	—	10000 Ekuele. Copper. KM#41.	—	60.00
E13	1980	—	Bipkwele. Copper. M1.	—	20.00
E15	1980	—	2000 Bipkwele. Aluminum. M2.	—	20.00
E16	1980	—	2000 Bipkwele. Copper. M2.	—	30.00
E17	1980	—	2000 Bipkwele. Aluminum. M6.	—	17.50
E18	1980	—	2000 Bipkwele. Copper. M6.	—	27.50
E19	1980	—	5000 Bipkwele. Aluminum. M3.	—	12.50
E20	1980	—	5000 Bipkwele. Copper. M3.	—	16.50
E21	1980	—	5000 Bipkwele. Aluminum. M7.	—	10.00
E22	1980	—	5000 Bipkwele. Copper. M7.	—	14.50
E23	1980	—	10000 Bipkwele. Aluminum. KM#48.	—	18.50
E24	1980	—	10000 Bipkwele. Copper. M4.	—	22.50
E25	1980	—	10000 Bipkwele. 0.9250 Silver. M4.	—	65.00
E26	1980	—	10000 Bipkwele. Aluminum. M8.	—	14.50
E27	1980	—	10000 Bipkwele. Copper. M8.	—	18.50

KM#	Date	Mintage	Identification	Issue Price	Mkt Val
E28	1985	—	5 Francos. Aluminum-Bronze. KM#62.	—	17.50

KM#	Date	Mintage	Identification	Issue Price	Mkt Val
E29	1985	—	25 Francos. KM#60.	—	22.50

KM#	Date	Mintage	Identification	Issue Price	Mkt Val
E31	1985	—	100 Francos. KM#59.	—	27.50
E30	1985	—	50 Francos. KM#64.	—	25.00

PATTERNS

Including off metal strikes

KM#	Date	Mintage	Identification	Mkt Val
Pn1	1980	—	5000 Bipkwele. Silver. Similar to M1.	55.00
Pn2	1980	—	5000 Bipkwele. Goldine. Similar to M1.	45.00
Pn3	1980	—	5000 Bipkwele. Silver. Similar to M5.	50.00
Pn4	1980	—	5000 Bipkwele. Goldine. Similar to M5.	40.00
Pn5	1980	—	10000 Bipkwele. Silver. Reeded edge. Similar to M2.	110
Pn6	1980	—	10000 Bipkwele. Silver. Plain edge. Similar to M2.	110
Pn7	1980	—	10000 Bipkwele. Goldine. Plain edge. Similar to M2.	85.00
Pn8	1980	—	10000 Bipkwele. Silver. Reeded edge. Similar to M6.	100
Pn9	1980	—	10000 Bipkwele. Silver. Plain edge. Similar to M6.	100
Pn10	1980	—	10000 Bipkwele. Goldine. Plain edge. Similar to M6.	75.00
Pn11	1992	—	15000 Francos. 0.9990 Gold Plated Silver. 12.6700 g.	—
Pn12	1993	—	1000 Francos. Copper Nickel. Soccer scene.	45.00
Pn13	1993	—	1000 Francos. Copper Nickel. Soccer players through net.	45.00
Pn14	1994	—	1000 Francos. Copper Nickel. Hands holding FIFA cup.	35.00
Pn15	1994	—	1000 Francos. Copper Nickel. Three players holding cup.	35.00
Pn16	1994	—	7000 Francos. 0.9990 Silver. 19.9100 g.	—
Pn18	1995	—	1000 Francos. Copper-Nickel. 26.4000 g. 38.2 mm. National arms.. "UN" letters with German inscription and the UN logo in background.. Reeded. edge.	—
Pn17	1996	—	1000 Francos. Brass. 28.5000 g. 38 mm. National arms. French postage stamp design. Reeded edge.	300

PIEFORTS

KM#	Date	Mintage	Identification	Issue Price	Mkt Val
P1	1978	—	1000 Ekuele. Copper. KM#35.	—	200
P2	1978	—	1000 Ekuele. 0.9250 Silver. KM#35.	—	250
P3	1978	—	2000 Ekuele. Copper. 6.8 mm. Plain edge. KM#36.	—	300
P4	1978	—	5000 Ekuele. Copper. 2.6 mm. Milled edge. KM#39.	—	175
P5	1978	—	5000 Ekuele. Copper. 4.1 mm. Plain edge.	—	150
P6	1978	—	10000 Ekuele. Copper. 3.4 mm. Milled edge. KM#41.	—	110
P7	ND(1979)	—	2000 Ekuele. Copper. KM#38.	—	215
P11	ND(1979)	—	10000 Ekuele. Gold. KM#41.	—	1,200
P8	ND(1979)	—	2000 Ekuele. 0.9250 Silver. KM#38.	—	300
P9	ND(1979)	—	2000 Ekuele. Gilt Copper.	—	215
P10	ND(1979)	—	10000 Ekuele. Copper. KM#41.	—	225
P12	ND(1979)	—	10000 Ekuele. Gilt Copper. KM#41.	—	200
P13	1980	—	1000 Bipkwele. Gilt Copper. M1.	—	45.00
P33	1980	750	10000 Bipkwele. M4.	—	400
P35	1980	750	10000 Bipkwele. M8.	—	400
P14	1980	—	1000 Bipkwele. 0.9250 Silver. 25.4900 g. M1.	—	65.00
P25	1980	750	5000 Bipkwele. M3.	—	200
P27	1980	750	5000 Bipkwele. M7.	—	200
P29	1980	—	5000 Bipkwele. Goldine. Plain edge. Similar to M1.	—	85.00
P15	1980	—	1000 Bipkwele. Gold. 25.5000 g.	—	475
P16	1980	—	1000 Bipkwele. Copper. M5.	—	35.00
P17	1980	—	1000 Bipkwele. Silver. M5.	—	55.00
P18	1980	—	2000 Bipkwele. Copper. Plain edge. M2.	—	65.00
P19	1980	—	2000 Bipkwele. Silver. Reeded edge. M2.	—	125
P20	1980	—	2000 Bipkwele. Silver. Plain edge. M2.	—	125
P21	1980	—	2000 Bipkwele. Copper. Plain edge. M6.	—	55.00
P22	1980	—	2000 Bipkwele. Silver. Reeded edge. M6.	—	115
P23	1980	—	2000 Bipkwele. Silver. Plain edge. M6.	—	115
P24	1980	—	5000 Bipkwele. Copper. M3.	—	45.00
P26	1980	—	5000 Bipkwele. Copper. M7.	—	40.00
P28	1980	—	5000 Bipkwele. Silver. Plain edge. Similar to M1.	—	110
P30	1980	—	5000 Bipkwele. Silver. Plain edge. Similar to M5.	—	100
P31	1980	—	5000 Bipkwele. Goldine. Plain edge. Similar to M5.	—	75.00
P32	1980	—	10000 Bipkwele. Copper. M4.	—	65.00
P34	1980	—	10000 Bipkwele. Copper. M8.	—	65.00

TRIAL STRIKES

KM#	Date	Mintage	Identification	Issue Price	Mkt Val
TS8	1978(80)	—	2000 Bipkwele. 0.9250 Silver. 25.2100 g. PRUEBA. M3.	—	150

KM#	Date	Mintage	Identification	Issue Price	Mkt Val
TS5	1978	—	10000 Ekuele. Copper. 3.6 mm. KM40. PRUEBA.	—	75.00
TS1	1978	—	2000 Ekuele. Copper. 3.9 mm. KM#36. PRUEBA.	—	150
TS2	1978	—	2000 Ekuele. Copper. 3.9 mm. PRUEBA. KM#36.	—	150

KM#	Date	Mintage	Identification	Issue Price	Mkt Val
TS3	1978	—	5000 Ekuele. Copper. 2.8 mm. KM39. PRUEBA.	—	75.00
TS4	1978	—	5000 Ekuele. Copper. 2.8 mm. KM39. PRUEBA.	—	75.00

KM#	Date	Mintage	Identification	Issue Price	Mkt Val
TS6	1978	—	10000 Ekuele. Copper. PRUEBA. KM#40.	—	75.00

KM#	Date	Mintage	Identification	Issue Price	Mkt Val
TS7	1978(80)	—	2000 Bipkwele. 0.9250 Silver. 25.2100 g. M3. PRUEBA.	—	150

MINT SETS

KM#	Date	Mintage	Identification	Issue Price	Mkt Val
MS1	1975 (3)	—	KM#32-34	—	22.00

PROOF SETS

KM#	Date	Mintage	Identification	Issue Price	Mkt Val
PS1	1970 (27)	330	KM#5-31	—	3,500
PS2	1970 (15)	2,475	KM#5-19	126	350
PS3	1970 (12)	330	KM#20-31	—	3,150

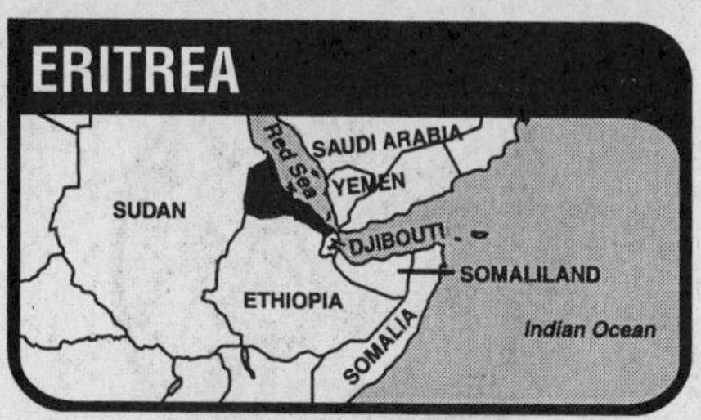

The State of Eritrea, a former Ethiopian province fronting on the Red Sea, has an area of 45,300 sq. mi. (117,600 sq. km.) and a population of 3.6 million. It was an Italian colony from 1889 until its incorporation into Italian East Africa in 1936. It was under the British Military Administration from 1941 to Sept. 15, 1952, when the United Nations designated it an autonomous unit within the federation of Ethiopia and Eritrea. On Nov. 14, 1962, it was annexed with Ethiopia. In 1991 the Eritrean Peoples Liberation Front extended its control over the entire territory of Eritrea. Following 2 years of provisional government, Eritrea held a referendum on independence in May 1993. Overwhelming popular approval led to the proclamation of an independent Republic of Eritrea on May 24.

RULERS
Umberto I, 1889-1900
Vittorio Emanuele III, 1900-1945

MINT MARKS
M - Milan
PM - Pobjoy
R – Rome

MONETARY SYSTEM
100 Centesimi = 1 Lira
5 Lire = 1 Tallero
100 Cents = 1 Nakfa (from 1997)

ITALIAN COLONY

COLONIAL COINAGE

KM# 5 TALLERO **Weight:** 28.0668 g. **Composition:** 0.8350 Silver .7535 oz. ASW

Date	Mintage	F	VF	XF	Unc	BU
1918R	510,000	25.00	55.00	125	425	—

REPUBLIC

DECIMAL COINAGE

100 Cents = 1 Dollar

KM# 43 CENT **Composition:** Nickel Clad Steel **Obverse:** Antelope **Reverse:** Soldiers with flag

Date	F	VF	XF	Unc	BU
1997	—	—	—	0.50	—

KM# 44 5 CENTS **Composition:** Nickel Clad Steel **Obverse:** Leopard on log **Reverse:** Soldiers with flag

Date	F	VF	XF	Unc	BU
1997	—	—	—	0.75	—

KM# 45 10 CENTS **Composition:** Nickel Clad Steel **Obverse:** Ostrich **Reverse:** Soldiers with flag

Date	F	VF	XF	Unc	BU
1997	—	—	—	1.00	—

KM# 46 25 CENTS **Composition:** Nickel Clad Steel **Obverse:** Grevy's zebra **Reverse:** Soldiers with flag

Date	F	VF	XF	Unc	BU
1997	—	—	—	1.25	—

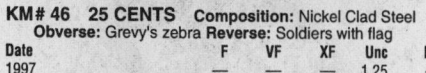

KM# 47 50 CENTS **Composition:** Nickel Clad Steel **Obverse:** Antelope **Reverse:** Soldiers with flag

Date	F	VF	XF	Unc	BU
1997	—	—	—	1.50	—

KM# 48 100 CENTS **Composition:** Nickel Clad Steel **Obverse:** Elephant and calf **Reverse:** Soldiers with flag

Date	F	VF	XF	Unc	BU
1997	—	—	—	2.00	—

KM# 6 DOLLAR **Composition:** Copper-Nickel **Subject:** Independence Day

Date	F	VF	XF	Unc	BU
1993	—	—	—	8.50	—

KM# 10 DOLLAR **Composition:** Copper-Nickel **Subject:** Preserve Planet Earth **Reverse:** Triceratops

Date	F	VF	XF	Unc	BU
1993	—	—	—	9.00	—

KM# 13 DOLLAR **Composition:** Copper-Nickel **Subject:** Preserve Planet Earth **Reverse:** Ankylosaurus

Date	F	VF	XF	Unc	BU
1993	—	—	—	9.00	—

KM# 14 DOLLAR **Composition:** Copper-Nickel **Subject:** Preserve Planet Earth **Reverse:** Pteranodon

Date	F	VF	XF	Unc	BU
1993	—	—	—	9.00	—

KM# 15 DOLLAR **Composition:** Copper-Nickel **Subject:** Preserve Planet Earth **Reverse:** Cheetah

Date	F	VF	XF	Unc	BU
1994	—	—	—	8.50	—

KM# 16 DOLLAR **Composition:** Copper-Nickel **Subject:** Preserve Planet Earth **Reverse:** Black Rhinoceros

Date	F	VF	XF	Unc	BU
1994	—	—	—	9.00	—

KM# 17 DOLLAR **Composition:** Copper-Nickel **Subject:** Preserve Planet Earth **Reverse:** Black and White Colobus Monkey

Date	F	VF	XF	Unc	BU
1994	—	—	—	8.50	—

KM# 28 DOLLAR **Composition:** Copper-Nickel **Subject:** Preserve Planet Earth **Reverse:** Lions **Note:** Similar to 10 Dollars, KM#29.

Date	F	VF	XF	Unc	BU
1995PM	—	—	—	9.00	—

KM# 31 DOLLAR **Composition:** Copper-Nickel **Subject:** Preserve Planet Earth **Reverse:** Cape Eagle owl **Note:** Similar to 10 Dollars, KM#32.

Date	F	VF	XF	Unc	BU
1995PM	—	—	—	9.00	—

KM# 34 DOLLAR **Composition:** Copper-Nickel **Subject:** Preserve Planet Earth **Reverse:** Wattled Cranes **Note:** Similar to 10 Dollars, KM#35.

Date	F	VF	XF	Unc	BU
1996	—	—	—	8.50	—

KM# 37 DOLLAR **Composition:** Copper-Nickel **Subject:** Preserve Planet Earth **Reverse:** Laner falcon **Note:** Similar to 10 Dollars, KM#38.

Date	F	VF	XF	Unc	BU
1996	—	—	—	9.00	—

KM# 40 DOLLAR **Composition:** Copper-Nickel **Subject:** Jurassic Park **Obverse:** National emblem **Reverse:** Triceratops, Jurassic Park logo **Note:** Similar to 10 Dollars, KM#41

Date	F	VF	XF	Unc	BU
1997	—	—	—	9.00	—

KM# 7 10 DOLLARS **Weight:** 31.1030 g. **Composition:** 0.9999 Silver 1.0000 oz. ASW **Subject:** Independence Day

Date	Mintage	F	VF	XF	Unc	BU
1993 Proof	Est. 30,000	Value: 45.00				

KM# 11 10 DOLLARS **Weight:** 28.2800 g. **Composition:** 0.9250 Silver .8411 oz. ASW **Subject:** Preserve Planet Earth **Reverse:** Triceratops

Date	Mintage	F	VF	XF	Unc	BU
1993 Proof	Est. 30,000	Value: 42.50				

KM# 24 10 DOLLARS **Weight:** 28.2800 g. **Composition:** 0.9250 Silver .8411 oz. ASW **Subject:** Preserve Planet Earth **Reverse:** Ankylosaurus **Note:** Similar to 1 Dollar, KM#13.

Date	Mintage	F	VF	XF	Unc	BU
1993 Proof	Est. 30,000	Value: 42.50				

KM# 25 10 DOLLARS **Weight:** 28.2800 g. **Composition:** 0.9250 Silver .8411 oz. ASW **Subject:** Preserve Planet Earth **Reverse:** Pteranodon **Note:** Similar to 1 Dollar, KM#14.

Date	Mintage	F	VF	XF	Unc	BU
1993 Proof	Est. 30,000	Value: 42.50				

KM# 18 10 DOLLARS **Weight:** 28.2800 g. **Composition:** 0.9250 Silver .8411 oz. ASW **Subject:** Preserve Planet Earth **Reverse:** Cheetah

Date	Mintage	F	VF	XF	Unc	BU
1994 Proof	Est. 30,000	Value: 42.50				

KM# 19 10 DOLLARS **Weight:** 28.2800 g. **Composition:** 0.9250 Silver .8411 oz. ASW **Subject:** Preserve Planet Earth **Reverse:** Black rhinoceros

Date	Mintage	F	VF	XF	Unc	BU
1994 Proof	Est. 30,000	Value: 42.50				

KM# 20 10 DOLLARS **Weight:** 28.2800 g. **Composition:** 0.9250 Silver .8411 oz. ASW **Subject:** Preserve Planet Earth **Reverse:** Colobus monkey

Date	Mintage	F	VF	XF	Unc	BU
1994 Proof	Est. 30,000	Value: 42.50				

KM# 29 10 DOLLARS **Weight:** 28.2800 g. **Composition:** 0.9250 Silver .8411 oz. ASW **Subject:** Preserve Planet Earth **Reverse:** Lions

Date	Mintage	F	VF	XF	Unc	BU
1995PM Proof	5,000	Value: 42.50				

KM# 32 10 DOLLARS **Weight:** 28.2800 g. **Composition:** 0.9250 Silver .8411 oz. ASW **Subject:** Preserve Planet Earth **Reverse:** Cape Eagle owl

Date	Mintage	F	VF	XF	Unc	BU
1995PM Proof	Est. 30,000	Value: 42.50				

KM# 35 10 DOLLARS **Weight:** 28.2800 g. **Composition:** 0.9250 Silver .8411 oz. ASW **Subject:** Preserve Planet Earth **Reverse:** Wattled cranes

Date	Mintage	F	VF	XF	Unc	BU
1996 Proof	Est. 30,000	Value: 42.50				

KM# 38 10 DOLLARS **Weight:** 28.2800 g. **Composition:** 0.9250 Silver .8411 oz. ASW **Subject:** Preserve Planet Earth **Reverse:** Laner falcon

Date	Mintage	F	VF	XF	Unc	BU
1996 Proof	Est. 30,000	Value: 42.50				

KM# 41 10 DOLLARS **Weight:** 28.2800 g. **Composition:** 0.9250 Silver .8411 oz. ASW **Subject:** Jurassic Park **Obverse:** National emblem **Reverse:** Triceratops, Jurassic Park logo

Date	Mintage	F	VF	XF	Unc	BU
1997 Proof	Est. 10,000	Value: 47.50				

KM# 8 50 DOLLARS **Weight:** 3.1100 g. **Composition:** 0.9990 Gold .1000 oz. AGW **Subject:** Independence Day **Note:** Similar to 1 Dollar, KM#6.

Date	Mintage	F	VF	XF	Unc	BU
1993 Proof	Est. 20,000	Value: 100				

KM# 26 100 DOLLARS **Weight:** 6.2200 g. **Composition:** 0.9990 Gold .2000 oz. AGW **Subject:** Preserve Planet Earth **Reverse:** Ankylosaurus **Note:** Similar to 1 Dollar KM#13.

Date	Mintage	F	VF	XF	Unc	BU
1993 Proof	Est. 5,000	Value: 175				

KM# 27 100 DOLLARS **Weight:** 6.2200 g. **Composition:** 0.9990 Gold .2000 oz. AGW **Subject:** Preserve Planet Earth **Reverse:** Pteranodon **Note:** Similar to 1 Dollar KM#14.

Date	Mintage	F	VF	XF	Unc	BU
1993 Proof	Est. 5,000	Value: 175				

KM# 9 100 DOLLARS **Weight:** 6.2200 g. **Composition:** 0.9990 Gold .2000 oz. AGW **Subject:** Independence Day

Date	Mintage	F	VF	XF	Unc	BU
1993 Proof	Est. 5,000	Value: 200				

KM# 12 100 DOLLARS **Weight:** 6.2200 g. **Composition:** 0.9990 Gold .2000 oz. AGW **Subject:** Preserve Planet Earth **Reverse:** Triceratops

Date	Mintage	F	VF	XF	Unc	BU
1993 Proof	Est. 5,000	Value: 175				

KM# 21 100 DOLLARS **Weight:** 6.2200 g. **Composition:** 0.9990 Gold .2000 oz. AGW **Subject:** Preserve Planet Earth **Obverse:** State emblem **Reverse:** Mother and by cheetah **Note:** Similar to 1 Dollar KM#18.

Date	Mintage	F	VF	XF	Unc	BU
1994 Proof	5,000	Value: 175				

KM# 22 100 DOLLARS **Weight:** 6.2200 g. **Composition:** 0.9990 Gold .2000 oz. AGW **Subject:** Preserve Planet Earth **Obverse:** State emblem **Reverse:** Rhinoceros head right **Note:** Similar to 1 Dollar KM#19.

Date	Mintage	F	VF	XF	Unc	BU
1994 Proof	5,000	Value: 175				

KM# 23 100 DOLLARS **Weight:** 6.2200 g. **Composition:** 0.9990 Gold .2000 oz. AGW **Subject:** Preserve Planet Earth **Obverse:** State emblem **Reverse:** Colobus monkey **Note:** Similar to 1 Dollar, KM#20.

Date	Mintage	F	VF	XF	Unc	BU
1994 Proof	5,000	Value: 175				

KM# 30 100 DOLLARS **Weight:** 6.2200 g. **Composition:** 0.9990 Gold .2000 oz. AGW **Subject:** Preserve Planet Earth **Obverse:** State emblem **Reverse:** Female lion and cub **Note:** Similar to 1 Dollar, KM#29.

Date	Mintage	F	VF	XF	Unc	BU
1995 Proof	Est. 5,000	Value: 185				

KM# 33 100 DOLLARS **Weight:** 6.2200 g. **Composition:** 0.9990 Gold .2000 oz. AGW **Subject:** Preserve Planet Earth **Obverse:** State emblem **Reverse:** Cape eagle owl **Note:** Similar to 1 Dollar, KM#32.

Date	Mintage	F	VF	XF	Unc	BU
1995 Proof	Est. 5,000	Value: 175				

KM# 36 100 DOLLARS **Weight:** 6.2200 g. **Composition:** 0.9990 Gold .2000 oz. AGW **Subject:** Preserve Planet Earth **Reverse:** Wattled cranes **Note:** Similar to 1 Dollar, KM#35.

Date	Mintage	F	VF	XF	Unc	BU
1996 Proof	Est. 5,000	Value: 175				

KM# 39 100 DOLLARS **Weight:** 6.2200 g. **Composition:** 0.9990 Gold .2000 oz. AGW **Subject:** Preserve Planet Earth **Reverse:** Laner falcon **Note:** Similar to 1 Dollar, KM#38.

Date	Mintage	F	VF	XF	Unc	BU
1996 Proof	Est. 5,000	Value: 175				

KM# 42 100 DOLLARS **Weight:** 6.2200 g **Composition:** 0.9990 Gold .2000 oz. AGW **Subject:** Jurassic Park **Obverse:** National emblem **Reverse:** Triceratops, Jurassic Park logo

Date	Mintage	F	VF	XF	Unc	BU
1997 Proof	Est. 2,500	Value: 185				

PROVAS

KM#	Date	Mintage	Identification	Mkt Val
PR1	1918R	—	Tallero. KM5.	550

ESTONIA

The Republic of Estonia (formerly the Estonian Soviet Socialist Republic of the U.S.S.R.) is the northernmost of the three Baltic States in Eastern Europe. It has an area of 17,462 sq. mi. (45,100 sq. km.) and a population of 1.6 million. Capital: Tallinn. Agriculture and dairy farming are the principal industries. Butter, eggs, bacon, timber and petroleum are exported.

This small and ancient Baltic state had enjoyed but two decades of independence since the 13th century until the present time. After having been conquered by the Danes, the Livonian Knights, the Teutonic Knights of Germany (who reduced the people to serfdom), the Swedes, the Poles and Russia, Estonia declared itself an independent republic on Feb. 24, 1918 but was not freed until Feb. 1919. The peace treaty was signed Feb. 2, 1920. Shortly after the start of World War II, it was again occupied by Russia and incorporated as the 16th state of the U.S.S.R Germany occupied the tiny state from 1941 to 1944, after which it was retaken by Russia. Most of the nations of the world, including the United States and Great Britain, did not recognize Estonia's incorporation into the Soviet Union.

The coinage, issued during the country's brief independence, is obsolete.

On August 20, 1991, the Parliament of the Estonian Soviet Socialist Republic voted to reassert the republic's independence.

REPUBLIC
1918-1941
REPUBLIC COINAGE

KM# 1 MARK **Composition:** Copper-Nickel **Edge:** Milled **Size:** 18 mm.

Date	Mintage	F	VF	XF	Unc	BU
1922	5,025,000	1.50	2.50	5.50	12.50	—

KM# 1a MARK **Weight:** 2.6000 g. **Composition:** Nickel-Bronze **Edge:** Milled **Size:** 18 mm.

Date	Mintage	F	VF	XF	Unc	BU
1924	1,985,000	2.00	4.00	7.50	15.00	—

KM# 5 MARK **Composition:** Nickel-Bronze

Date	Mintage	F	VF	XF	Unc	BU
1926-	3,979,000	3.50	6.50	12.00	30.00	—

KM# 2 3 MARKA **Composition:** Copper-Nickel

Date	Mintage	F	VF	XF	Unc	BU
1922-	2,089,000	2.00	4.00	6.00	12.50	—

KM# 2a 3 MARKA **Composition:** Nickel-Bronze

Date	Mintage	F	VF	XF	Unc	BU
1925-	1,134,000	4.00	7.00	12.50	30.00	—

KM# 6 3 MARKA **Composition:** Nickel-Bronze

Date	Mintage	F	VF	XF	Unc	BU
1926-	903,000	25.00	50.00	80.00	150	—

KM# 3 5 MARKA **Weight:** 5.0000 g. **Composition:** Copper-Nickel **Edge:** Milled **Size:** 23 mm.

Date	Mintage	F	VF	XF	Unc	BU
1922	3,983,000	3.00	5.00	8.00	20.00	—

KM# 3a 5 MARKA **Weight:** 5.0000 g. **Composition:** Nickel-Bronze **Edge:** Milled **Size:** 23 mm.

Date	Mintage	F	VF	XF	Unc	BU
1924	1,335,000	3.50	6.00	9.00	25.00	—

KM# 7 5 MARKA **Composition:** Nickel-Bronze

Date	Mintage	F	VF	XF	Unc	BU
1926-	1,038,000	75.00	150	200	350	—

KM# 4 10 MARKA **Weight:** 6.0000 g. **Composition:** Nickel-Bronze **Edge:** Milled **Size:** 26 mm.

Date	Mintage	F	VF	XF	Unc	BU
1925	2,200,000	3.50	7.50	12.50	37.50	—

KM# 8 10 MARKA **Composition:** Nickel-Bronze

Date	Mintage	F	VF	XF	Unc	BU
1926-	2,789,000	650	1,000	1,500	2,000	—

Note: Most of this issue were melted down. Not released to circulation

REFORM COINAGE
100 Senti = 1 Kroon

KM# 10 SENT **Weight:** 2.0000 g. **Composition:** Bronze **Edge:** Plain **Size:** 17 mm.

Date	Mintage	F	VF	XF	Unc	BU
1929-	23,553,000	0.50	1.00	2.00	4.00	—

KM# 19.1 SENT **Weight:** 2.0000 g. **Composition:** Bronze **Edge:** Plain **Size:** 16 mm. **Note:** 1 millimeter thick planchet.

Date	Mintage	F	VF	XF	Unc	BU
1939	5,000,000	4.00	8.00	15.00	35.00	—

KM# 19.2 SENT **Composition:** Bronze **Note:** 0.9 millimeter thick planchet.

Date		F	VF	XF	Unc	BU
1939		4.00	8.00	15.00	35.00	—

KM# 15 2 SENTI **Weight:** 3.5000 g. **Composition:** Bronze **Edge:** Plain **Size:** 19 mm.

Date	Mintage	F	VF	XF	Unc	BU
1934	5,838,000	1.50	2.50	4.50	10.00	—

KM# 11 5 SENTI **Weight:** 3.5000 g. **Composition:** Bronze **Edge:** Plain **Size:** 23.3 mm.

Date	Mintage	F	VF	XF	Unc	BU
1931	11,000,000	1.50	2.50	4.50	10.00	—

KM# 12 10 SENTI **Composition:** Nickel-Bronze **Edge:** Plain **Size:** 18 mm.

Date	Mintage	F	VF	XF	Unc	BU
1931	4,089,000	1.50	2.50	4.50	12.00	—

KM# 17 20 SENTI **Composition:** Nickel-Bronze **Edge:** Plain **Size:** 21 mm.

Date	Mintage	F	VF	XF	Unc	BU
1935-	4,250,000	2.00	3.50	5.50	15.00	—

KM# 9 25 SENTI **Composition:** Nickel-Bronze

Date	Mintage	F	VF	XF	Unc	BU
1928-	2,025,000	3.00	6.00	10.00	25.00	—

KM# 18 25 SENTI **Weight:** 7.5000 g. **Composition:** Nickel-Bronze **Edge:** Plain **Size:** 27.5 mm.

Date	Mintage	F	VF	XF	Unc	BU
1936-	1,256,000	3.00	6.00	12.00	30.00	—

KM# 14 KROON **Weight:** 6.0000 g. **Composition:** 0.5000 Silver .0965 oz. ASW **Subject:** 10th Singing Festival

Date	Mintage	F	VF	XF	Unc	BU
1933-	350,000	7.00	14.00	30.00	50.00	70.00

KM# 16 KROON **Composition:** Aluminum-Bronze **Obverse:** State emblem **Reverse:** Ship of Vikings **Edge:** Plain **Size:** 25 mm. **Note:** 1990 restrikes which exist are private issues.

Date	Mintage	F	VF	XF	Unc	BU
1934	3,304,000	3.50	6.00	14.00	40.00	60.00

KM# 20 2 KROONI **Weight:** 12.0000 g. **Composition:** 0.5000 Silver .1929 oz. ASW **Subject:** Toompea Fortress at Tallinn **Obverse:** State emblem **Reverse:** Castle, value **Edge:** Milled **Size:** 30 mm.

Date	Mintage	F	VF	XF	Unc	BU
1930	1,276,000	3.50	6.50	13.50	35.00	55.00

KM# 13 2 KROONI **Weight:** 12.0000 g. **Composition:** 0.5000 Silver .1929 oz. ASW **Subject:** Tercentenary - University of Tartu **Obverse:** State emblem **Edge:** Plain **Size:** 30 mm.

Date	Mintage	F	VF	XF	Unc	BU
1932	100,000	10.00	20.00	30.00	50.00	70.00

NEW REPUBLIC
1991 - present
STANDARD COINAGE

KM# 21 5 SENTI **Composition:** Brass

Date	F	VF	XF	Unc	BU
1991	—	—	—	0.25	—
1992	—	—	—	0.25	—
1993	—	—	—	0.25	—
1995	—	—	—	0.25	—

KM# 22 10 SENTI **Composition:** Brass

Date	F	VF	XF	Unc	BU
1991	—	—	—	0.50	—
1992	—	—	—	0.50	—
1994	—	—	—	0.50	—
1996	—	—	—	0.50	—
1997	—	—	—	0.50	—
1998	—	—	—	0.50	—

KM# 23 20 SENTI **Composition:** Brass

Date	F	VF	XF	Unc	BU
1992	—	—	—	0.75	—
1996	—	—	—	0.75	—
1999	—	—	—	0.75	—

KM# 23a 20 SENTI **Composition:** Nickel Plated Steel

Date	F	VF	XF	Unc	BU
1997	—	—	—	0.75	—
1999	—	—	—	0.75	—

KM# 24 50 SENTI **Composition:** Brass

Date	F	VF	XF	Unc	BU
1992	—	—	—	1.00	—

KM# 28 KROON **Composition:** Copper-Nickel **Edge:** Plain.

Date	Mintage	F	VF	XF	Unc	BU
1992 In sets only	20,000	—	—	—	—	—
1993	—	—	—	—	1.50	—
1995	—	—	—	—	1.50	—

KM# 35 KROON **Composition:** Brass **Edge:** Three reeded and plain sections.

Date	F	VF	XF	Unc	BU
1998	—	—	—	1.25	—
2001	—	—	—	—	—

KM# 36 KROON **Composition:** Brass **Obverse:** Bird above date **Reverse:** Festival building and denomination

Date	Mintage	F	VF	XF	Unc	BU
1999	100,000	—	—	—	5.00	—

KM# 29 5 KROONI **Composition:** Brass **Subject:** 75th Anniversary - Declaration of Independence

Date	F	VF	XF	Unc	BU
1993	—	—	—	2.25	—
1993 Prooflike	—	Value: 4.50			

KM# 30 5 KROONI **Composition:** Brass **Subject:** 75th Anniversary - Estonian National Bank

Date	F	VF	XF	Unc	BU
1994	—	—	—	2.00	—

KM# 25 10 KROONI **Weight:** 28.2800 g. **Composition:** 0.9250 Silver .8411 oz. ASW **Series:** Olympics

Date	Mintage	F	VF	XF	Unc	BU
1992 Proof	Est. 20,000	Value: 47.50				

KM# 26 10 KROONI **Weight:** 28.2800 g. **Composition:** 0.9250 Silver .8411 oz. ASW **Reverse:** Barn Swallow

Date	Mintage	F	VF	XF	Unc	BU
1992 Proof	Est. 10,000	Value: 50.00				

KM# 32 10 KROONI **Weight:** 16.0000 g. **Composition:** 0.9250 Silver .4758 oz. ASW **Subject:** 80th Anniversary of Nation **Obverse:** Framed dates **Reverse:** Farmer plowing field

Date	F	VF	XF	Unc	BU
ND(1998) Prooflike	—	—	—	20.00	—

KM# 37 15.65 KROONI **Weight:** 1.7300 g. **Composition:** 0.9000 Gold .0501 oz. AGW **Subject:** Estonia's Euro Equivalent **Obverse:** National arms **Reverse:** Cross and stars design

Date	Mintage	F	VF	XF	Unc	BU
1999 Proof	Est. 5,000	Value: 37.50				

KM# 27 100 KROONI **Weight:** 24.0000 g. **Composition:** 0.9250 Silver .7135 oz. ASW **Reverse:** Barn Swallows

Date	Mintage	F	VF	XF	Unc	BU
1992 Proof	Est. 50,000	Value: 30.00				

KM# 31 100 KROONI **Weight:** 28.2800 g. **Composition:** 0.9250 Silver .8411 oz. ASW **Reverse:** Olympics - Nike crowning Wrestler

Date	Mintage	F	VF	XF	Unc	BU
1996	—	—	—	—	30.00	—
1996 Proof	10,000	Value: 40.00				

KM# 33 100 KROONI **Weight:** 27.0000 g. **Composition:** 0.9250 Silver .8030 oz. ASW **Subject:** 80th Anniversary of Nation **Obverse:** Framed dates **Reverse:** Male figure and stylized eagle head

Date	Mintage	F	VF	XF	Unc	BU
ND(1998) Proof	Est. 12,000	Value: 42.50				

KM# 34 500 KROONI **Weight:** 8.6400 g. **Composition:** 0.9000 Gold .2500 oz. AGW **Subject:** 80th Anniversary of Nation **Obverse:** Framed dates **Reverse:** Male figure on horse

Date	Mintage	F	VF	XF	Unc	BU
ND(1998) Proof	Est. 3,000	Value: 185				

MINT SETS

KM#	Date	Mintage	Identification	Issue Price	Mkt Val
MS1	1992 (5)	20,000	KM#21-24, 28	—	38.50

ETHIOPIA

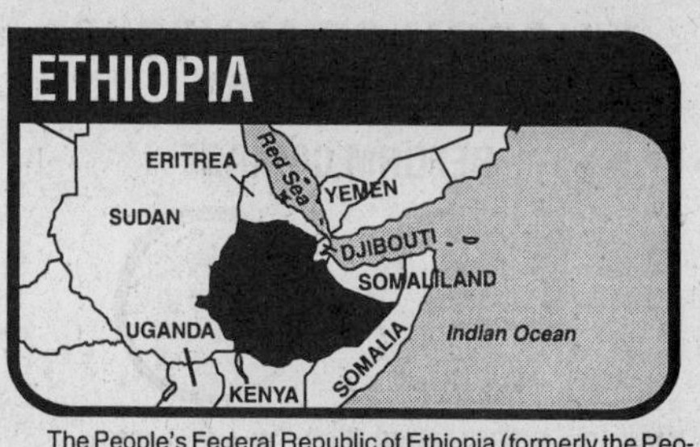

The People's Federal Republic of Ethiopia (formerly the Peoples Democratic Republic and the Empire of Ethiopia), Africa's oldest independent nation, faces the Red Sea in East-Central Africa. The country has an area of 424,214 sq. mi. (1,004,390 sq. km.) and a population of 56 million people who are divided among 40 tribes that speak some 270 languages and dialects. Capital: Addis Ababa. The economy is predominantly agricultural and pastoral. Gold and platinum are mined and petroleum fields are being developed. Coffee, oilseeds, hides and cereals are exported.

Legend claims that Menelik I, the son born to Solomon, King of Israel, by the Queen of Sheba, settled in Axum in North Ethiopia to establish the dynasty, which reigned with only brief interruptions until 1974. Modern Ethiopian history began with the reign of Emperor Menelik II (1889-1913) under whose guidance the country emerged from medieval isolation. Progress continued throughout the reigns of Menelik's daughter, Empress Zauditu, and her successor Emperor Haile Selassie I who was coronated in 1930. Ethiopia was invaded by Italy in 1935, and together with Italian Somaliland and Eritrea became part of Italian East Africa. Victor Emmanuel III, as declared by Mussolini, would be Ethiopia's emperor as well as a king of Italy. Liberated by British and Ethiopian troops in 1941, Ethiopia reinstated Haile Selassie I to the throne. The 225th consecutive Solomonic ruler was deposed by a military committee on Sept 12, 1974. In July 1976 Ethiopia's military provisional government referred to the country as Socialist Ethiopia. After establishing a new regime in 1991, Ethiopia became a federated state and is now the Federal Republic of Ethiopia. Following 2 years of provisional government, the province of Eritrea held a referendum on independence in May 1993 leading to the proclamation of its independence on May 24.

No coins, patterns or presentation pieces are known bearing Emperor Lij Yasu's likeness or titles. Coins of Menelik II were struck during this period with dates frozen.

RULERS

Menelik II, 1889-1913
Lij Yasu, 1913-1916
Zauditu, Empress, 1916-1930
Haile Selassie I
1930-36, 1941-1974
Victor Emmanuel III, of Italy
1936-1941

MINT MARKS

A - Paris
- Paris, privy marks only

Coinage of Menelik II, 1889-1913

NOTE: The first national issue coinage, dated 1887 and 1888 E.E., carried a cornucopia, A, and fasces on the reverse. Subsequent dates have a torch substituted for the fasces, the A being dropped. All issues bearing these marks were struck at the Paris Mint. Coins without mint marks were struck in Addis Ababa.

MONETARY SYSTEM

(Until about 1903)

40 Besa = 20 Gersh = 1 Birr

(After 1903)

32 Besa = 16 Gersh = 1 Birr

DATING

Ethiopian coinage is dated by the Ethiopian Era calendar (E.E.), which commenced 7 years and 8 months after the advent of A.D. dating.

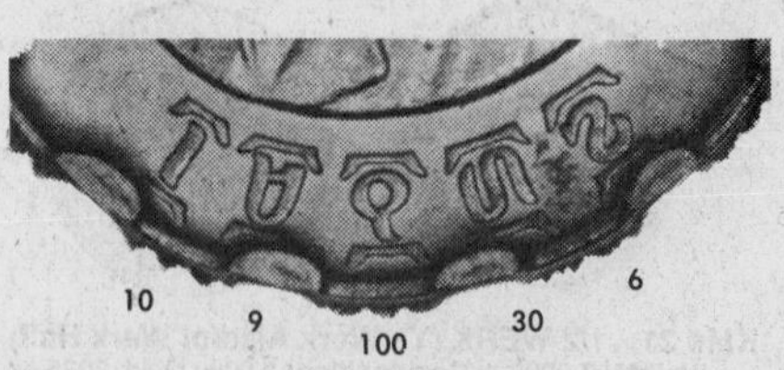

EXAMPLE

1900 (10 and 9 = 19 x 100)
36 (Add 30 and 6)
1936 E.E.
8 (Add)
1943/4 AD

KINGDOM OF ABYSSINIA (ETHIOPIA)

REFORM COINAGE

KM# 12 GERSH (1/20 Birr) **Weight:** 1.4038 g. **Composition:** 0.8350 Silver .0377 oz. ASW **Reverse:** Lion's left foreleg raised

Date	Mintage	F	VF	XF	Unc	BU
EE1895A	44,789,000	2.00	3.50	6.00	15.00	—

Note: Struck between 1903-1928

KM# 3 1/4 BIRR (Ya Birr Rub/of Birr Fourth) **Weight:** 7.1088 g. **Composition:** 0.8350 Silver .1884 oz. ASW **Reverse:** Lion's left foreleg raised

Date	Mintage	F	VF	XF	Unc	BU
EE1895A	821,000	4.00	8.00	20.00	80.00	—

Note: Struck between 1903 and 1925

KM# 19 BIRR **Weight:** 28.0750 g. **Composition:** 0.8350 Silver .7537 oz. ASW **Reverse:** Lion's right foreleg raised

Date	Mintage	F	VF	XF	Unc	BU
EE1895	459,000	12.50	25.00	85.00	250	—
Note: Struck in 1901, 1903 and 1904						
EE1895 Proof	—	Value: 500				

KM# 20 1/2 WERK (Ya Werk Alad/of Werk Half) **Weight:** 3.5000 g. **Composition:** 0.9000 Gold .1012 oz. AGW

Date	F	VF	XF	Unc	BU
EE1923	175	325	500	850	—

KM# 21 1/2 WERK (Ya Werk Alad/of Werk Half) **Weight:** 7.0000 g. **Composition:** 0.9000 Gold .2025 oz. AGW

Date	F	VF	XF	Unc	BU
EE1923	225	450	700	1,200	—

EMPIRE OF ETHIOPIA

DECIMAL COINAGE

100 Matonas = 100 Santeems

100 Santeems (Cents) = 1 Birr (Dollar)

KM# 27 MATONA **Composition:** Copper

Date	Mintage	F	VF	XF	Unc	BU
EE1923	1,250,000	1.50	2.50	5.00	15.00	20.00

Note: Struck by ICI in Birmingham, England. Other denominations in the Matona series were struck in Addis Ababa

KM# 32 CENT (Ande Santeem) **Composition:** Copper

Date	Mintage	F	VF	XF	Unc	BU
EE1936	20,000	—	0.10	0.20	0.50	1.00

Note: Coins in the one cent to fifty cent denominations were struck at Philadelphia, Birmingham and the Royal Mint, London between 1944 and 1975 with the date EE1936 frozen

KM# 28.1 5 MATONAS **Composition:** Copper **Edge:** Plain

Date	Mintage	F	VF	XF	Unc	BU
EE1923	1,363,000	2.00	3.50	6.00	20.00	25.00

KM# 28.2 5 MATONAS **Composition:** Copper **Edge:** Reeded

Date	F	VF	XF	Unc	BU
EE1923	2.00	3.50	7.00	25.00	40.00

KM# 33 5 CENTS (Amist Santeem) **Composition:** Copper

Date	Mintage	F	VF	XF	Unc	BU
EE1936	219,000,000	—	0.10	0.20	0.50	1.25

Note: Struck between 1944-1962 in Philadelphia and 1964-1966 in Birmingham

KM# 29 10 MATONAS **Composition:** Nickel

Date	Mintage	F	VF	XF	Unc	BU
EE1923	936,000	1.50	2.50	4.50	12.50	—

KM# 34 10 CENTS (Assir Santeem) **Composition:** Copper

Date	Mintage	F	VF	XF	Unc	BU
EE1936	348,998,000	—	0.10	0.25	0.75	1.50

Note: Struck between 1945-1963 in Philadelphia, 1964-1966 in Birmingham and 1974-1975 in London

KM# 30 25 MATONAS **Composition:** Nickel

Date	Mintage	F	VF	XF	Unc	BU
EE1923	2,742,000	1.25	2.00	3.25	10.00	—

KM# 35 25 CENTS (Haya Amist Santeem) **Composition:** Copper

Date	Mintage	F	VF	XF	Unc	BU
EE1936	10,000,000	5.00	10.00	20.00	45.00	—

Note: 421,500 issued and 1952 withdrawn and replaced by KM#36

KM# 36 25 CENTS (Haya Amist Santeem) **Composition:** Copper

Date	Mintage	F	VF	XF	Unc	BU
EE1936	30,000,000	0.25	0.50	1.00	3.50	5.00

Note: Issued in 1952 and 1953. Crude and refined edges

KM# 31 50 MATONAS **Composition:** Nickel

Date	Mintage	F	VF	XF	Unc	BU
EE1923	1,621,000	1.50	2.50	4.50	11.50	—

KM# 37 50 CENTS (Hamsa Santeem) **Weight:** 7.0307 g. **Composition:** 0.8000 Silver .1808 oz. ASW

Date	Mintage	F	VF	XF	Unc	BU
EE1936	30,000,000	2.00	3.50	7.50	20.00	—

Note: Struck in 1944-1945

KM# 37a 50 CENTS (Hamsa Santeem) **Weight:** 7.0307 g. **Composition:** 0.7000 Silver .1582 oz. ASW

Date	Mintage	F	VF	XF	Unc	BU
EE1936	20,434,000	2.00	3.50	7.50	20.00	—

Note: Struck in 1947

KM# 48 5 DOLLARS **Weight:** 20.0000 g. **Composition:** 0.9250 Silver .5948 oz. ASW **Reverse:** Theodros II

Date	Mintage	F	VF	XF	Unc	BU
EE1964 (1972) F-NI	—	—	—	—	75.00	—
EE1964 (1972) NI Proof	55,000	Value: 40.00				

KM#49 5 DOLLARS **Weight:** 20.0000 g. **Composition:** 0.9250 Silver .5948 oz. ASW **Reverse:** Yohannes Iv

Date	Mintage	F	VF	XF	Unc	BU
EE1964 (1972) F-NI	—	—	—	—	75.00	—
EE1964 (1972) NI Proof	55,000	Value: 40.00				

KM#50 5 DOLLARS **Weight:** 20.0000 g. **Composition:** 0.9250 Silver .5948 oz. ASW **Reverse:** Menelik II

Date	Mintage	F	VF	XF	Unc	BU
EE1964 (1972) F-NI	—	—	—	—	85.00	—
EE1964 (1972) NI Proof	60,000	Value: 40.00				

KM#51 5 DOLLARS **Weight:** 20.0000 g. **Composition:** 0.9250 Silver .5948 oz. ASW **Reverse:** Zauditu bust veiled left

Date	Mintage	F	VF	XF	Unc	BU
EE1964 (1972) F-NI	—	—	—	—	90.00	—
EE1964 (1972) NI Proof	60,000	Value: 42.50				

KM#52 5 DOLLARS **Weight:** 25.0000 g. **Composition:** 0.9999 Silver .8030 oz. ASW **Obverse:** Haile Selassie bust right

Date	Mintage	F	VF	XF	Unc	BU
EE1972 (1972) HF Proof	100,000	Value: 15.00				

KM#38 10 DOLLARS **Weight:** 4.0000 g. **Composition:** 0.9000 Gold .1157 oz. AGW **Subject:** 75th Anniverary of Birth and 50th Jubilee of Reign of Emperor Haile Selassie I

Date	Mintage	F	VF	XF	Unc	BU
EE1958 (1966) NI Proof	28,000	Value: 95.00				

KM# 53 10 DOLLARS **Weight:** 40.0000 g. **Composition:** 0.9250 Silver 1.1895 oz. ASW **Obverse:** Emperor Haile Selassie I

Date	Mintage	F	VF	XF	Unc	BU
EE1964 (1972) F-NI	—	—	—	—	175	—
EE1964 (1972) NI Proof	50,000	Value: 85.00				

KM#39 20 DOLLARS **Weight:** 8.0000 g. **Composition:** 0.9000 Gold .2315 oz. AGW **Subject:** 75th Anniversary of Birth and 50th Jubilee of Reign of Emperor Haile Selassie I

Date	Mintage	F	VF	XF	Unc	BU
EE1958 (1966) NI Proof	25,000	Value: 165				

KM# 40 50 DOLLARS **Weight:** 20.0000 g. **Composition:** 0.9000 Gold .5787 oz. AGW **Subject:** 75th Anniversary of Birth and 50th Jubilee of Reign of Emperor Haile Selassie I

Date	Mintage	F	VF	XF	Unc	BU
EE1958 (1966) NI Proof	15,000	Value: 300				

KM# 55 50 DOLLARS **Weight:** 20.0000 g. **Composition:** 0.9000 Gold .5787 oz. AGW **Obverse:** Bust of Theodros II **Reverse:** Lion

Date	Mintage	F	VF	XF	Unc	BU
EE1964 (1972) NI Proof	12,000	Value: 375				

KM# 56 50 DOLLARS **Weight:** 20.0000 g. **Composition:** 0.9000 Gold .5787 oz. AGW **Obverse:** Bust of Yohannes IV

Date	Mintage	F	VF	XF	Unc	BU
EE1964 (1972) NI Proof	12,000	Value: 375				

KM# 57 50 DOLLARS **Weight:** 20.0000 g. **Composition:** 0.9000 Gold .5787 oz. AGW **Obverse:** Bust of Menelik II

Date	Mintage	F	VF	XF	Unc	BU
EE1964 (1972) NI Proof	20,000	Value: 375				

KM# 58 50 DOLLARS **Weight:** 20.0000 g. **Composition:** 0.9000 Gold .5787 oz. AGW **Obverse:** Bust of Empress Zauditu

Date	Mintage	F	VF	XF	Unc	BU
EE1964 (1972) NI Proof	16,000	Value: 375				

KM# 41 100 DOLLARS **Weight:** 40.0000 g. **Composition:** 0.9000 Gold 1.1575 oz. AGW **Subject:** 75th Anniversary of Birth and 50th Jubilee of Reign of Emperor Haile Selassie I

Date	Mintage	F	VF	XF	Unc	BU
EE1958 (1966) NI Proof	11,000	Value: 550				

KM# 59 100 DOLLARS **Weight:** 40.0000 g. **Composition:** 0.9000 Gold 1.1575 oz. AGW **Obverse:** Emperor Haile Selassie I **Note:** Similar to 10 Dollars, KM#53

Date	Mintage	F	VF	XF	Unc	BU
EE1964 (1972) NI Proof	10,000	Value: 750				

KM# 42 200 DOLLARS **Weight:** 80.0000 g. **Composition:** 0.9000 Gold 2.3151 oz. AGW **Subject:** 75th Anniversary of Birth and 50th Jubilee of Reign of Emperor Haile Selassie I

Date	Mintage	F	VF	XF	Unc	BU
EE1958 (1966) NI Proof	8,823	Value: 1,175				

TOKEN COINAGE

KM# Tn1 PIASTRE (1/16 Thaler) **Composition:** Aluminum

Date	VG	F	VF	XF	Unc
1922	12.00	25.00	40.00	60.00	—

Note: Issued by a commercial syndicate in Dire Dawa

KM# Tn2 PIASTRE (1/16 Thaler) **Composition:** Aluminum

Date	VG	F	VF	XF	Unc
ND	10.00	20.00	35.00	55.00	—

Note: Issued by P. P. Trohalis in Addis Ababa

KM# Tn3 PIASTRE (1/16 Thaler) Composition: Copper-Nickel-Zinc

Date	VG	F	VF	XF	Unc
ND	25.00	40.00	65.00	85.00	—

Note: Issued by Magdalinos Freres in Addis Ababa

KM# Tn4 PIASTRE (1/16 Thaler) Composition: Aluminum

Date	VG	F	VF	XF	Unc
ND	20.00	35.00	60.00	80.00	—

Note: Issued by Prasso Concessions En Abyssinie

KM# Tn5 PIASTRE (1/16 Thaler) Composition: Aluminum **Note:** Uniface

Date	VG	F	VF	XF	Unc
ND	25.00	45.00	75.00	90.00	—

Note: Issued by F. L. in Addis Abada

PEOPLES DEMOCRATIC REPUBLIC

We have two varieties for KM#43.1 to KM#46.1. One was minted at the British Royal Mint, the other at the Berlin Mint. The main difference is where the lion's chin whiskers end above the date (easiest to see on the 2nd, 3rd and 4th characters).

British Royal Mint

Berlin Mint

DECIMAL COINAGE

100 Matonas = 100 Santeems

100 Santeems (Cents) = 1 Birr (Dollar)

KM# 43.2 CENT Composition: Aluminum **Obverse:** Small lion head, two long chin whiskers at left nearly touch date **Note:** Struck at Berlin Mint.

Date	F	VF	XF	Unc	BU
EE1969	0.25	0.35	0.65	1.25	—

KM# 43.3 (KM43.2) CENT Composition: Aluminum **Obverse:** Large lion head

Date	Mintage	F	VF	XF	Unc	BU
EE1969 FM Proof	12,000	Value: 2.50				
EE1969 FM Proof	12,000	Value: 2.50				

KM# 43.1 CENT Composition: Aluminum **Series:** F.A.O. **Obverse:** Small lion head, uniform chin whiskers **Note:** Struck at British Royal Mint.

Date	Mintage	F	VF	XF	Unc	BU
EE1969	35,034,000	0.20	0.30	0.50	1.00	—

KM# 44.2 5 CENTS Composition: Copper-Zinc **Note:** Struck at Berlin Mint.

Date	F	VF	XF	Unc	BU
EE1969	0.25	0.35	0.65	1.25	—

KM# 44.3 (KM44.2) 5 CENTS Composition: Copper-Zinc **Obverse:** Large lion head

Date	Mintage	F	VF	XF	Unc	BU
EE1969 FM Proof	12,000	Value: 2.50				
EE1969 FM Proof	12,000	Value: 2.50				

KM# 44.1 5 CENTS Composition: Copper-Zinc **Obverse:** Small lion head, uniform chin whiskers **Note:** Struck at British Royal Mint.

Date	Mintage	F	VF	XF	Unc	BU
EE1969	201,275,000	0.20	0.30	0.50	1.00	—

KM# 45.2 10 CENTS Composition: Copper-Zinc **Obverse:** Small lion head, two long chin whiskers at left nearly touch date **Note:** Struck at Berlin Mint.

Date	F	VF	XF	Unc	BU
EE1969	0.25	0.40	0.75	1.75	—

KM# 45.3 (KM45.2) 10 CENTS Composition: Copper-Zinc **Obverse:** Large lion head

Date	Mintage	F	VF	XF	Unc	BU
EE1969 FM	—	—	—	—	2.00	2.00
EE1969 FM	—	—	—	—	2.00	2.00
EE1969 FM Proof	12,000	Value: 4.00				
EE1969 FM Proof	12,000	Value: 4.00				

KM# 45.1 10 CENTS Composition: Copper-Zinc **Obverse:** Small lion head, uniform chin whiskers **Reverse:** Mountain Nyala **Note:** Struck at British Royal Mint.

Date	Mintage	F	VF	XF	Unc	BU
EE1969	202,722,000	0.20	0.30	0.60	1.50	2.00

KM# 46.3 (KM46.2) 25 CENTS Composition: Copper-Nickel **Obverse:** Large lion head

Date	Mintage	F	VF	XF	Unc	BU
EE1969 FM Proof	12,000	Value: 4.50				
EE1969 FM Proof	12,000	Value: 4.50				

KM# 46.1 25 CENTS Composition: Copper-Nickel **Obverse:** Small lion head, uniform chin whiskers **Note:** Struck at British Royal Mint.

Date	Mintage	F	VF	XF	Unc	BU
EE1969	44,983,000	0.20	0.30	0.60	1.25	—

KM# 47.2 50 CENTS Composition: Copper-Nickel **Obverse:** Small lion head, two long chin whiskers at left nearly touch date **Note:** Struck at Berlin Mint.

Date	F	VF	XF	Unc	BU
EE1969	0.50	0.85	1.50	3.00	—

KM# 47.3 (KM47.2) 50 CENTS Composition: Copper-Nickel **Obverse:** Large lion head

Date	Mintage	F	VF	XF	Unc	BU
EE1969 FM Proof	12,000	Value: 7.50				
EE1969 FM Proof	12,000	Value: 7.50				

KM# 47.1 50 CENTS Composition: Copper-Nickel **Obverse:** Small lion head, uniform chin whiskers **Note:** Struck at British Royal Mint.

Date	Mintage	F	VF	XF	Unc	BU
EE1969	27,772,000	0.40	0.75	1.25	2.50	—

KM# 64 2 BIRR Composition: Copper-Nickel **Subject:** World Soccer Games 1982

Date	Mintage	F	VF	XF	Unc	BU
EE1964 (error)	7	—	—	—	145	—
EE1974	—	—	—	—	9.00	—

KM# 61 10 BIRR Weight: 25.3100 g. **Composition:** 0.9250 Silver .7527 oz. ASW **Subject:** Conservation **Reverse:** Bearded Vulture

Date	Mintage	F	VF	XF	Unc	BU
EE1970	4,002	—	—	—	25.00	—

KM# 61a 10 BIRR Weight: 28.2800 g. **Composition:** 0.9250 Silver .8411 oz. ASW

Date	Mintage	F	VF	XF	Unc	BU
EE1970 Proof	3,460	Value: 35.00				

KM# 54 20 BIRR **Weight:** 23.3300 g. **Composition:** 0.9250 Silver .6938 oz. ASW **Subject:** International Year of the Child

Date	Mintage	F	VF	XF	Unc	BU
EE1972 Proof	16,000	Value: 20.00				

KM# 65 20 BIRR **Weight:** 23.3300 g. **Composition:** 0.9250 Silver .6938 oz. ASW **Subject:** World Soccer Games 1982 **Obverse:** Similar to 2 Birr, KM#64

Date	Mintage	F	VF	XF	Unc	BU
EE1974 Proof	10,000	Value: 40.00				

KM# 73 20 BIRR **Weight:** 23.3300 g. **Composition:** 0.9250 Silver .6938 oz. ASW **Subject:** Decade for Women

Date	Mintage	F	VF	XF	Unc	BU
1984 Proof	372	Value: 85.00				

KM# 74 20 BIRR **Weight:** 23.3300 g. **Composition:** 0.9250 Silver .6938 oz. ASW **Subject:** 50th Anniversary UNICEF - Folk Dance

Date	Mintage	F	VF	XF	Unc	BU
1998 Proof	—	Value: 28.00				

KM# 62 25 BIRR **Weight:** 31.6500 g. **Composition:** 0.9250 Silver .9413 oz. ASW **Subject:** Conservation **Obverse:** Similar to 10 Birr, KM#61 **Reverse:** Mountain nyala

Date	Mintage	F	VF	XF	Unc	BU
EE1970	4,002	—	—	—	30.00	—

KM# 62a 25 BIRR **Weight:** 35.0000 g. **Composition:** 0.9250 Silver 1.0409 oz. ASW

Date	Mintage	F	VF	XF	Unc	BU
EE1970 Proof	3,295	Value: 40.00				

KM# 66 50 BIRR **Weight:** 28.2800 g. **Composition:** 0.9250 Silver .8411 oz. ASW **Subject:** International Year of Disabled Persons

Date	Mintage	F	VF	XF	Unc	BU
EE1974	11,000	—	—	—	32.50	—
EE1974 Proof	10,000	Value: 45.00				

KM# 67 200 BIRR **Weight:** 7.1300 g. **Composition:** 0.9000 Gold .2063 oz. AGW **Subject:** World Soccer Games 1982

Date	Mintage	F	VF	XF	Unc	BU
1982 Proof	1,310	Value: 175				

KM# 72 200 BIRR **Weight:** 7.1300 g. **Composition:** 0.9000 Gold .2063 oz. AGW **Subject:** Decade forWomen

Date	Mintage	F	VF	XF	Unc	BU
1984 Proof	298	Value: 250				

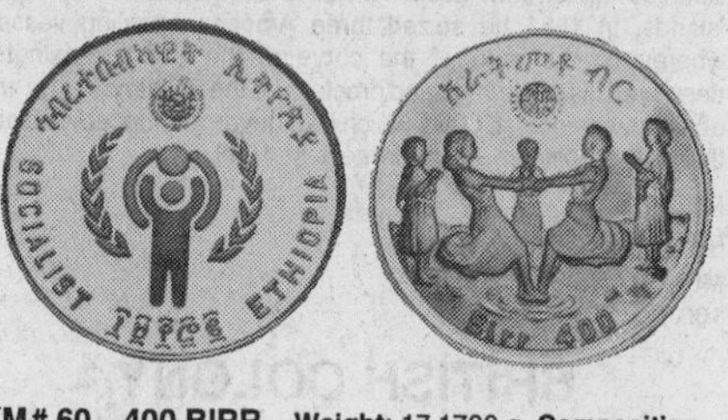

KM# 60 400 BIRR **Weight:** 17.1700 g. **Composition:** 0.9000 Gold .4968 oz. AGW **Subject:** International Year ofthe Child

Date	Mintage	F	VF	XF	Unc	BU
EE1972 Proof	3,387	Value: 185				

KM# 68 500 BIRR **Weight:** 15.9800 g. **Composition:** 0.9170 Gold .5006 oz. AGW **Subject:** International Year of the Disabled Persons

Date	Mintage	F	VF	XF	Unc	BU
EE1974	2,007	—	—	—	245	—
EE1974 Proof	2,042	Value: 275				

KM# 63 600 BIRR **Weight:** 33.4370 g. **Composition:** 0.9000 Gold .9676 oz. AGW **Subject:** Conservation **Reverse:** Walia Ibex

Date	Mintage	F	VF	XF	Unc	BU
EE1970	547	—	—	—	450	—
EE1970 Proof	160	Value: 750				

PATTERNS

Including off metal strikes

KM#	Date	Mintage	Identification	Mkt Val
Pn8	EE1921	—	Werk. Gold. Similar to KM21 (proof)	—
Pn7	EE1921	—	1/2 Werk. Gold. Similar to KM20 (proof)	—

TRIAL STRIKES

KM#	Date	Mintage	Identification	Mkt Val
TS9	EE1917	—	1/2 Birr. Pewter. KM M3. (thin)	300
TS10	EE1917	—	Birr. Pewter. KM M4. (thin)	500
TS15	1966	—	200 Dollars. Gilt Bronze. KM42	450

Note: Issued in cased set of five pieces

KM#	Date	Mintage	Identification	Mkt Val
TS12	1966	—	20 Dollars. Gilt Bronze. KM39	80.00
TS13	1966	—	50 Dollars. Gilt Bronze. KM40	130
TS14	1966	—	100 Dollars. Gilt Bronze. KM41	240
TS11	1966	—	10 Dollars. Gilt Bronze. KM38	50.00

PIEFORTS

KM#	Date	Mintage	Identification	Issue Price	Mkt Val
P2	1980	8	400 Birr. KM60	—	775
P1	1980	39	20 Birr. KM54	—	115
P3	1981	1,100	50 Birr. KM66	—	65.00
P4	1982	520	500 Birr. KM68	—	800

MINT SETS

KM#	Date	Mintage	Identification	Issue Price	Mkt Val
MS1	1972 (5)	—	KM48-51, 53	—	475

PROOF SETS

KM#	Date	Mintage	Identification	Issue Price	Mkt Val
PS2	1966 (5)	8,823	KM38-42	—	2,285
PS3	1972 (10)	—	KM48-51, 53, 55-59	—	2,500
PS5	1972 (5)	10,000	KM55-59	—	2,250
PS6	1972 (5)	50,000	KM48-51, 53	46.00	220
PS7	1977 (5)	11,724	KM43.2-47.2	25.00	21.50
PS8	1979 (2)	—	KM61a-62a	—	75.00

FAEROE ISLANDS

The Faeroe Islands, a self-governing community within the kingdom of Denmark, are situated in the North Atlantic between Iceland and the Shetland Islands. The 17 inhabited islands and numerous islets and reefs have an area of 540 sq. mi. (1,400 sq. km.)and a population of 46,000. Capital: Thorshavn. The principal industries are fishing and livestock. Fish and fish products are exported.

While it is thought that Irish hermits lived on the islands in the 7th and 8th centuries, the present inhabitants are descended from 6th century Norse settlers. The Faeroe Islands became a Norwegian fief in 1035 and became Danish in 1380 when Norway and Denmark were united. They have ever since remained in Danish possession and were granted self-government (except for an appointed governor-general) with their own legislature, executive and flag in 1948.

The islands were occupied by British troops during World War II, after the German occupation of Denmark. The Faeroe island coinage was struck in London during World War II.

RULER
Danish

MONETARY SYSTEM
100 Øre = 1 Krone

DANISH STATE

DECIMAL COINAGE

KM# 1 ØRE Composition: Bronze

Date	F	VF	XF	Unc	BU
1941	20.00	40.00	60.00	85.00	—

Note: Also struck in 1942 with 1941 dies

Date		
1941 Proof	—	Value: 550

KM# 2 2 ØRE Composition: Bronze

Date	F	VF	XF	Unc	BU
1941	5.00	10.00	22.50	50.00	—

Note: Also struck in 1942 with 1941 dies

Date		
1941 Proof	—	Value: 550

KM# 3 5 ØRE Composition: Bronze

Date	F	VF	XF	Unc	BU
1941	4.00	8.00	18.50	50.00	—

Note: Also struck in 1942 with 1941 dies

Date		
1941 Proof	—	Value: 550

KM# 4 10 ØRE Composition: Copper-Nickel

Date	F	VF	XF	Unc	BU
1941	5.50	11.00	27.50	75.00	—

Note: Also struck in 1942 with 1941 dies

Date		
1941 Proof	—	Value: 575

KM# 5 25 ØRE Composition: Copper-Nickel

Date	F	VF	XF	Unc	BU
1941	7.00	12.50	30.00	85.00	—

Note: Also struck in 1942 with 1941 dies

Date		
1941 Proof	—	Value: 575

PROOF SETS

KM#	Date	Mintage	Identification	Issue Price	Mkt Val
PS1	1941 (5)	—	KM1-5	—	2,800

FALKLAND ISLANDS

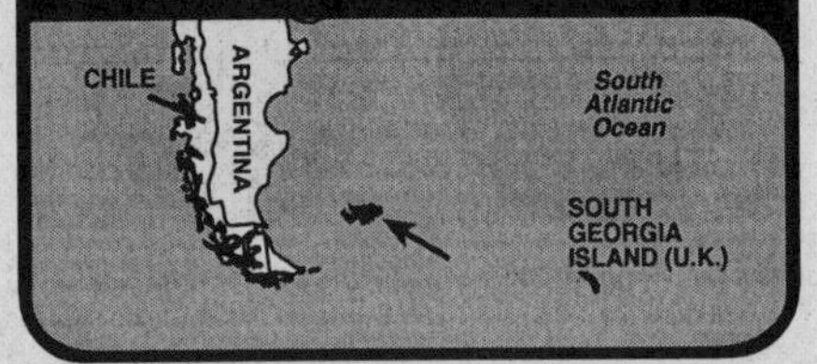

The Colony of the Falkland Islands and Dependencies, a British colony located in the South Atlantic about 500 miles northeast of Cape Horn, has an area of 4,700 sq. mi. (12,170 sq. km.) and a population of 2,121. East Falkland, West Falkland, South Georgia, and South Sandwich are the largest of the 200 islands. Capital: Stanley. Sheep grazing is the main industry. Wool, whale oil, and seal oil are exported.

The Falklands were discovered by British navigator John Davis (Davys) in 1592, and named by Capt. John Strong - for Viscount Falkland, treasurer of the British navy - in 1690. French navigator Louis De Bougainville established the first settlement, at Port Louis, in 1764. The following year Capt. John Byron claimed the islands for Britain and left a small party at Saunders Island. Spain later forced the French and British to abandon their settlements but did not implement its claim to the islands. In 1829 the Republic of Buenos Aires, which claimed to have inherited the Spanish rights, sent Louis Vernet to develop a colony on the islands. In 1831 he seized three American sealing vessels, whereupon the men of the corvette, the U.S.S. Lexington, destroyed his settlement and proclaimed the Falklands to be 'free of all governance'. Britain, which had never renounced its claim, then re-established its settlement in 1833.

RULERS
British

MONETARY SYSTEM
100 Pence = 1 Pound

BRITISH COLONY

DECIMAL COINAGE

KM# 1 1/2 PENNY Composition: Bronze **Reverse:** Salmon

Date	Mintage	F	VF	XF	Unc	BU
1974	140,000	—	—	0.10	0.25	—
1974 Proof	23,000	Value: 1.50				
1980	—	—	—	0.10	0.15	—
1980 Proof	10,000	Value: 1.50				
1982	—	—	—	0.10	0.15	—
1982 Proof	—	Value: 1.50				
1983	—	—	—	0.10	0.15	—

KM# 2 PENNY Composition: Bronze **Reverse:** Gentee penguins

Date	Mintage	F	VF	XF	Unc	BU
1974	96,000	—	0.10	0.20	0.60	—
1974 Proof	23,000	Value: 2.00				
1980	—	—	0.10	0.20	0.60	—
1980 Proof	10,000	Value: 2.00				
1982	—	—	0.10	0.20	0.60	—
1982 Proof	—	Value: 2.00				
1983	—	—	0.10	0.20	0.60	—
1985	—	—	0.10	0.20	0.45	—
1987	111,000	—	—	0.20	0.45	—
1987 Proof	—	Value: 2.50				
1992	—	—	0.10	0.20	0.45	—
1992 Proof	—	Value: 2.50				

KM# 2a PENNY Composition: Copper Plated Steel

Date	Mintage	F	VF	XF	Unc	BU
1998	2,500	—	—	—	0.40	—
1999		—	—	—	0.40	—
1999 Proof	2,500	Value: 2.00				

KM# 3 2 PENCE Composition: Bronze **Reverse:** Upland goose

Date	Mintage	F	VF	XF	Unc	BU
1974	72,000	—	0.10	0.15	0.50	0.85
1974 Proof	23,000	Value: 3.00				
1980	—	—	0.10	0.15	0.40	0.75
1980 Proof	10,000	Value: 3.00				
1982	—	—	0.10	0.15	0.40	0.75
1982 Proof	—	Value: 3.00				
1983	—	—	0.10	0.15	0.40	0.75
1985	—	—	0.10	0.15	0.40	0.75
1987	106,000	—	—	0.15	0.40	0.75
1987 Proof	—	Value: 3.50				
1992	—	—	0.10	0.15	0.40	0.75
1992 Proof	—	Value: 3.50				

KM# 3a 2 PENCE Composition: Copper Plated Steel

Date	Mintage	F	VF	XF	Unc	BU
1998	—	—	—	—	0.35	0.75
1999	—	—	—	—	0.35	0.75
1999 Proof	2,500	Value: 3.00				

KM# 4.1 5 PENCE Composition: Copper-Nickel **Reverse:** Blackbrowed albatross

Date	Mintage	F	VF	XF	Unc	BU
1974	67,000	—	0.10	0.25	0.75	—
1974 Proof	23,000	Value: 3.50				
1980	—	—	0.10	0.25	0.75	—
1980 Proof	10,000	Value: 4.00				
1982	—	—	0.10	0.25	0.75	—
1982 Proof	—	Value: 4.00				
1983	—	—	0.10	0.25	0.75	—
1985	—	—	0.10	0.20	0.75	—
1987	5,000	—	—	0.25	0.75	—
1987 Proof	—	Value: 4.50				
1992	—	—	0.10	0.25	0.75	—
1992 Proof	—	Value: 4.50				

KM# 4.2 5 PENCE Composition: Copper-Nickel

Date	Mintage	F	VF	XF	Unc	BU
1998	—	—	—	—	0.75	—
1999	—	—	—	—	0.75	—
1999 Proof	2,500	Value: 4.00				

KM# 5.1 10 PENCE Composition: Copper-Nickel **Reverse:** Ursine seal

Date	Mintage	F	VF	XF	Unc	BU
1974	87,000	—	0.20	0.40	1.50	2.50
1974 Proof	23,000	Value: 4.50				
1980	—	—	0.20	0.40	1.50	2.50
1980 Proof	10,000	Value: 5.00				
1982	—	—	0.20	0.40	1.50	2.50
1982 Proof	—	Value: 5.00				
1983	—	—	0.20	0.40	1.50	2.50
1985	—	—	0.20	0.40	1.50	2.50
1987	4,000	—	—	0.40	1.50	2.50
1987 Proof	—	Value: 5.50				
1992	—	—	0.20	0.40	1.50	2.50
1992 Proof	—	Value: 5.50				

KM# 5.2 10 PENCE Composition: Copper-Nickel

Date	Mintage	F	VF	XF	Unc	BU
1998	—	—	—	—	1.50	2.50
1999	—	—	—	—	1.50	2.50
1999 Proof	2,500	Value: 5.00				

KM# 17 20 PENCE Composition: Copper-Nickel
Reverse: Romney marsh sheep

Date	Mintage	F	VF	XF	Unc	BU
1982	—	—	0.40	0.65	2.00	—
1982 Proof	—	Value: 5.00				
1983	—	—	0.40	0.65	2.00	—
1985	—	—	0.40	0.65	2.00	—
1987	4,250	—	0.40	0.65	2.00	—
1987 Proof	—	Value: 5.50				
1992	—	—	0.40	0.65	2.00	—
1992 Proof	—	Value: 5.50				
1999	—	—	—	—	2.00	—
1999 Proof	2,500	Value: 5.00				

KM# 10 50 PENCE Composition: Copper-Nickel
Subject: Queen's Silver Jubilee

Date	Mintage	F	VF	XF	Unc	BU
ND(1977)	100,000	—	1.00	1.50	3.00	—

KM# 10a 50 PENCE Weight: 28.2800 g. **Composition:** 0.9250 Silver .8411 oz. ASW

Date	Mintage	F	VF	XF	Unc	BU
ND(1977) Proof	22,000	Value: 13.50				

KM# 14.1 50 PENCE Composition: Copper-Nickel
Reverse: Falkland Island fox (extinct)

Date	Mintage	F	VF	XF	Unc	BU
1980 Proof	—	Value: 6.00				
1980	—	—	1.00	2.00	5.00	—
1982	—	—	1.00	2.00	5.00	—
1982 Proof	—	Value: 6.00				
1983	—	—	1.00	2.00	5.00	—
1985	—	—	1.00	2.00	5.00	—
1987	4,000	—	1.00	2.00	5.00	—
1987 Proof	—	Value: 6.50				
1992	—	—	1.00	2.00	5.00	—
1992 Proof	—	Value: 6.50				
1995	—	—	—	2.00	5.00	—

KM# 14.2 50 PENCE Composition: Copper-Nickel
Reverse: Falkland Island fox (extinct). **Size:** 27.5 mm. **Note:** Reduced size.

Date	Mintage	F	VF	XF	Unc	BU
1998	—	—	—	2.00	5.00	—
Note: Reduced size: 27 mm						
1999	—	—	—	2.00	5.00	—
1999 Proof	2,500	Value: 6.00				

KM# 15 50 PENCE Composition: Copper-Nickel
Subject: 80th Anniversary - Birth of Queen Mother

Date	F	VF	XF	Unc	BU
ND(1980)	—	1.00	1.50	3.00	—

KM# 15a 50 PENCE Weight: 28.2800 g. **Composition:** 0.9250 Silver .8411 oz. ASW

Date	F	VF	XF	Unc	BU
ND(1980) Proof	—	Value: 12.50			

KM# 16 50 PENCE Composition: Copper-Nickel
Subject: Wedding of Prince Charles and Lady Diana

Date	F	VF	XF	Unc	BU
1981	—	1.00	1.50	3.00	—

KM# 16a 50 PENCE Weight: 28.2800 g. **Composition:** 0.9250 Silver .8411 oz. ASW

Date	Mintage	F	VF	XF	Unc	BU
1981 Proof	40,000	Value: 20.00				

KM# 18 50 PENCE Composition: Copper-Nickel
Subject: Liberation From Argentina Forces

Date	F	VF	XF	Unc	BU
ND(1982)	—	1.00	1.50	3.00	—

KM# 18a 50 PENCE Weight: 28.2800 g. **Composition:** 0.9250 Silver .8411 oz. ASW

Date	F	VF	XF	Unc	BU
ND(1982) Proof	Est. 25,000	Value: 15.00			

KM# 18b 50 PENCE Weight: 47.5000 g. **Composition:** 0.9170 Gold 1.4005 oz. AGW **Subject:** Liberation From Argentina Forces

Date	Mintage	F	VF	XF	Unc	BU
ND(1982) Proof	25	Value: 5,500				

KM# 19 50 PENCE Composition: Copper-Nickel
Subject: 150th Anniversary of British Rule

Date	F	VF	XF	Unc	BU
ND(1983)	—	1.00	2.00	5.00	—

KM# 19a 50 PENCE Weight: 28.2800 g. **Composition:** 0.9250 Silver .8411 oz. ASW

Date	Mintage	F	VF	XF	Unc	BU
ND(1983) Proof	Est. 10,000	Value: 18.50				

KM# 19b 50 PENCE Weight: 47.5400 g. **Composition:** 0.9170 Gold 1.4017 oz. AGW **Subject:** 150th Anniversary of British Rule

Date	Mintage	F	VF	XF	Unc	BU
ND(1983) Proof	150	Value: 1,350				

KM# 21 50 PENCE Composition: Copper-Nickel
Subject: Opening of Mount Pleasant Airport

Date	F	VF	XF	Unc	BU
ND(1985)	—	—	—	3.00	—

KM# 21a 50 PENCE Weight: 28.2750 g. **Composition:** 0.9250 Silver .8410 oz. ASW

Date	Mintage	F	VF	XF	Unc	BU
ND (1985) Proof	Est. 5,000	Value: 15.00				

KM# 25 50 PENCE Composition: Copper-Nickel
Subject: World Wildlife Fund **Reverse:** King penguins

Date	F	VF	XF	Unc	BU
1987	—	—	—	7.00	—

KM# 25a 50 PENCE Weight: 28.2800 g. **Composition:** 0.9250 Silver .8411 oz. ASW

Date	Mintage	F	VF	XF	Unc	BU
1987 Proof	Est. 25,000	Value: 32.50				

KM# 26 50 PENCE Composition: Copper-Nickel
Subject: Children's Fund

Date	F	VF	XF	Unc	BU
1990	—	—	—	4.50	—

KM# 26a 50 PENCE Weight: 28.2800 g. **Composition:** 0.9250 Silver .8411 oz. ASW

Date	F	VF	XF	Unc	BU
1990 Proof	—	Value: 37.50			

KM# 34 50 PENCE **Composition:** Copper-Nickel **Subject:** 40th Anniversary - Reign of Queen Elizabeth II

Date	F	VF	XF	Unc	BU
ND(1992)	—	—	—	4.50	—

KM# 34a 50 PENCE **Weight:** 28.2800 g. **Composition:** 0.9250 Silver .8411 oz. ASW

Date	Mintage	F	VF	XF	Unc	BU
ND(1992) Proof	5,000	Value: 50.00				

KM# 34b 50 PENCE **Weight:** 47.5400 g. **Composition:** 0.9170 Gold 1.4011 oz. AGW **Subject:** 40th Anniversary - Reign of Queen Elizabeth

Date	Mintage	F	VF	XF	Unc	BU
ND(1992) Proof	150	Value: 950				

KM# 43 50 PENCE **Composition:** Copper-Nickel **Subject:** 40th Anniversary - Coronation of Queen Elizabeth II

Date	F	VF	XF	Unc	BU
ND(1993)	—	—	—	6.50	—

KM# 43a 50 PENCE **Weight:** 28.2800 g. **Composition:** 0.9250 Silver .8411 oz. ASW

Date	Mintage	F	VF	XF	Unc	BU
ND(1993) Proof	Est. 10,000	Value: 55.00				

KM# 72 50 PENCE **Weight:** 28.1600 g. **Composition:** Silver **Subject:** Queen Elizabeth, the Queen Mother - Birth of Princess Elizabeth II **Obverse:** Bust of Queen Elizabeth II right **Reverse:** The Queen Mother holding the princess **Size:** 39 mm.

Date	F	VF	XF	Unc	BU
1995 Proof	—	—	—	—	—

KM# 45 50 PENCE **Composition:** Copper-Nickel **Subject:** V. E. Day - 50th Anniversary

Date	F	VF	XF	Unc	BU
1995	—	—	—	5.50	—

KM# 45a 50 PENCE **Weight:** 28.2800 g. **Composition:** 0.9250 Silver .8411 oz. ASW

Date	Mintage	F	VF	XF	Unc	BU
1995 Proof	Est. 10,000	Value: 50.00				

KM# 45b 50 PENCE **Weight:** 47.5400 g. **Composition:** 0.9170 Gold 1.4011 oz. AGW **Subject:** V.E. Day - 50th Anniversary

Date	Mintage	F	VF	XF	Unc	BU
1995 Proof	Est. 100	Value: 1,100				

KM# 46 50 PENCE **Composition:** Copper-Nickel **Subject:** Queen Elizabeth II's 70th Birthday **Obverse:** Queen's portrait **Reverse:** Queen and Prince Philip as young adults

Date	F	VF	XF	Unc	BU
1996	—	—	—	8.00	—

KM# 46a 50 PENCE **Weight:** 28.2800 g. **Composition:** 0.9250 Silver .8411 oz. ASW

Date	F	VF	XF	Unc	BU
1996 Proof	—	Value: 50.00			

KM# 59 50 PENCE **Composition:** Copper-Nickel **Subject:** WWF - Conserving Nature **Obverse:** Bust of Queen Elizabeth II right **Reverse:** Pair of Black-browed Albatross

Date	F	VF	XF	Unc	BU
1997	—	—	—	8.50	—

KM# 59a 50 PENCE **Weight:** 28.2800 g. **Composition:** 0.9250 Silver .8410 oz. ASW **Subject:** WWF - Conserving Nature **Obverse:** Bust of Queen Elizabeth II right **Reverse:** Pair of Black-browed Albatross

Date	Mintage	F	VF	XF	Unc	BU
1997 Proof	Est. 15,000	Value: 40.00				

KM# 60 50 PENCE **Composition:** Copper-Nickel **Subject:** WWF - Conserving Nature **Obverse:** Bust of Queen Elizabeth II right **Reverse:** Peale's dolphin

Date	F	VF	XF	Unc	BU
1998	—	—	—	8.00	—

KM# 66 50 PENCE **Weight:** 28.2800 g. **Composition:** Copper-Nickel **Subject:** Winston Churchill **Obverse:** Queen's head right **Reverse:** Churchill in Admiral's uniform

Date	F	VF	XF	Unc	BU
1999	—	—	—	8.00	—

KM# 66a 50 PENCE **Weight:** 28.2800 g. **Composition:** 0.9250 Silver .8410 oz. ASW **Subject:** Winston Churchill **Obverse:** Queen's head right **Reverse:** Churchill in Admiral's uniform

Date	Mintage	F	VF	XF	Unc	BU
1999 Proof	2,500	Value: 40.00				

KM# 66b 50 PENCE **Weight:** 47.5400 g. **Composition:** 0.9160 Gold 1.4010 oz. AGW

Date	Mintage	F	VF	XF	Unc	BU
1999 Proof	125	Value: 1,500				

KM# 73 50 PENCE **Weight:** 28.1300 g. **Composition:** Copper-Nickel **Subject:** Queen's Golden Jubilee **Obverse:** Bust of Queen Elizabeth II right **Reverse:** Queen Elizabeth II on throne in inner circle **Edge:** Reeded **Size:** 38.6 mm.

Date	F	VF	XF	Unc	BU
2002(2001) Proof	—	Value: 6.00			

KM# 74 50 PENCE **Weight:** 28.1300 g. **Composition:** Copper-Nickel **Subject:** Queen's Golden Jubilee **Obverse:** Bust of Queen Elizabeth II right **Reverse:** Queen on horse half left in inner circle **Edge:** Reeded **Size:** 38.6 mm.

Date	F	VF	XF	Unc	BU
2002(2001) Proof	—	Value: 6.00			

KM# 75 50 PENCE **Weight:** 28.1300 g. **Composition:** Copper-Nickel **Subject:** Queen's Golden Jubilee **Obverse:** Bust of Queen Elizabeth II right **Reverse:** Queen Elizabeth II talking into microphone **Edge:** Reeded **Size:** 38.6 mm.

Date	F	VF	XF	Unc	BU
2002(2001) Proof	—	Value: 6.00			

KM# 76 50 PENCE **Weight:** 28.1300 g. **Composition:** Copper-Nickel **Subject:** Queen's Golden Jubilee **Obverse:** Bust of Queen Elizabeth II right **Reverse:** Queen walking to left in front of a crowd **Edge:** Reeded **Size:** 38.6 mm.

Date	F	VF	XF	Unc	BU
2002(2001) Proof	—	Value: 6.00			

KM# 77 50 PENCE **Weight:** 28.1300 g. **Composition:** Copper-Nickel **Subject:** Queen's Golden Jubilee **Obverse:** Bust of Queen Elizabeth II right **Reverse:** Conjoined busts of Queen Elizabeth, Prince Charles, Prince William facing left in inner circle **Edge:** Reeded **Size:** 38.6 mm.

Date	F	VF	XF	Unc	BU
2002(2001) Proof	—	Value: 6.00			

KM# 70 50 PENCE **Weight:** 29.1000 g. **Composition:** Copper-Nickel **Subject:** Centennial of Queen Victoria's Death **Obverse:** Queen Elizabeth's portrait **Reverse:** Queen Victoria's portrait **Edge:** Reeded **Size:** 38.6 mm.

Date	F	VF	XF	Unc	BU
2001	—	—	—	6.00	—

KM# 71 50 PENCE **Weight:** 29.1000 g. **Composition:** Copper-Nickel **Subject:** Queen Elizabeth's 75th Birthday **Obverse:** Queen's crowned portrait **Reverse:** Uncrowned portrait **Edge:** Reeded **Size:** 38.6 mm.

Date	F	VF	XF	Unc	BU
2001	—	—	—	6.00	—

KM# 78 50 PENCE **Weight:** 28.1300 g. **Composition:** Copper-Nickel **Subject:** Queen's Golden Jubilee **Obverse:** Bust of Queen Elizabeth right **Reverse:** Royal coach **Edge:** Reeded **Size:** 38.6 mm.

Date	F	VF	XF	Unc	BU
2002 Proof	—	Value: 6.00			

KM# 79 50 PENCE **Weight:** 28.1300 g. **Composition:** Copper-Nickel **Subject:** Queen's Golden Jubilee **Obverse:** Bust of Queen Elizabeth right **Reverse:** Scepter and orb **Edge:** Reeded **Size:** 38.6 mm.

Date	F	VF	XF	Unc	BU
2002 Proof	—	Value: 6.00			

KM# 80 50 PENCE **Weight:** 28.1300 g. **Composition:** Copper-Nickel **Subject:** Queen's Golden Jubilee **Obverse:** Bust of Queen Elizabeth right **Reverse:** Crown **Edge:** Reeded **Size:** 38.6 mm.

Date	F	VF	XF	Unc	BU
2002 Proof	—	Value: 6.00			

KM# 81 50 PENCE **Weight:** 28.1300 g. **Composition:** Copper-Nickel **Subject:** Queen's Golden Jubilee **Obverse:** Bust of Queen Elizabeth right **Reverse:** Throne **Edge:** Reeded **Size:** 38.6 mm.

Date	F	VF	XF	Unc	BU
2002 Proof	—	Value: 6.00			

KM# 82 50 PENCE **Weight:** 28.1300 g. **Composition:** Copper-Nickel **Subject:** Queen's Golden Jubilee **Obverse:** Bust of Queen Elizabeth right **Reverse:** Queen on throne **Edge:** Reeded **Size:** 38.6 mm.

Date	F	VF	XF	Unc	BU
2002 Proof	—	—	—	6.00	—

KM# 83 50 PENCE **Weight:** 28.1300 g. **Composition:** Copper-Nickel **Subject:** Queen's Golden Jubilee **Obverse:** Bust of Queen Elizabeth right **Reverse:** Queen and young family **Edge:** Reeded **Size:** 38.6 mm.

Date	F	VF	XF	Unc	BU
2002 Proof	—	—	—	6.00	—

KM# 84 50 PENCE **Weight:** 28.1300 g. **Composition:** Copper-Nickel **Subject:** Queen's Golden Jubilee **Obverse:** Bust of Queen Elizabeth right **Reverse:** Queen and tree house **Edge:** Reeded **Size:** 38.6 mm.

Date	F	VF	XF	Unc	BU
2002 Proof	—	Value: 6.00			

KM# 6 1/2 POUND **Weight:** 3.9900 g. **Composition:** 0.9170 Gold .1176 oz. AGW **Reverse:** Romney marsh sheep

Date	Mintage	F	VF	XF	Unc	BU
1974 Proof	2,673	Value: 150				

KM# 7 POUND **Weight:** 7.9900 g. **Composition:** 0.9170 Gold .2356 oz. AGW **Reverse:** Romney marsh sheep

Date	Mintage	F	VF	XF	Unc	BU
1974 Proof	2,675	Value: 250				

KM# 24 POUND **Composition:** Nickel-Brass

Date	Mintage	F	VF	XF	Unc	BU
1987	—	—	—	—	3.50	—
1987 Proof	2,500	Value: 12.50				
1992	—	—	—	—	3.50	—
1992 Proof	—	Value: 12.50				
1999	—	—	—	—	3.50	—
1999 Proof	2,500	Value: 12.50				

KM# 24a POUND **Weight:** 9.5000 g. **Composition:** 0.9250 Silver .2825 oz. ASW

Date	Mintage	F	VF	XF	Unc	BU
1987 Proof	Est. 5,000	Value: 22.50				

KM# 24b POUND **Weight:** 19.6500 g. **Composition:** 0.9170 Gold .5791 oz. AGW **Reverse:** Romney marsh sheep

Date	Mintage	F	VF	XF	Unc	BU
1987 Proof	Est. 200	Value: 600				

KM# 8 2 POUNDS **Weight:** 15.9800 g. **Composition:** 0.9170 Gold .4712 oz. AGW **Reverse:** Romney marsh sheep

Date	Mintage	F	VF	XF	Unc	BU
1974 Proof	2,158	Value: 500				

KM# 22 2 POUNDS **Weight:** 28.2800 g. **Composition:** 0.5000 Silver .4546 oz. ASW **Subject:** Commonweatlth Games

Date	F	VF	XF	Unc	BU
1986	—	—	—	32.00	—

KM# 22a 2 POUNDS **Weight:** 28.2800 g. **Composition:** 0.9250 Silver .8411 oz. ASW

Date	Mintage	F	VF	XF	Unc	BU
1986	Est. 20,000	Value: 45.00				

KM# 32 2 POUNDS **Weight:** 28.2800 g. **Composition:** 0.9250 Silver .8411 oz. ASW **Subject:** 10th Wedding Anniversary - Prince Charles and Lady Diana

Date	Mintage	F	VF	XF	Unc	BU
1991 Proof	Est. 10,000	Value: 40.00				

KM# 35 2 POUNDS **Composition:** Copper-Nickel **Subject:** Heritage Year

Date	F	VF	XF	Unc	BU
1992	—	—	—	11.50	—

KM# 35a 2 POUNDS **Weight:** 28.2800 g. **Composition:** 0.9250 Silver .8411 oz. ASW

Date	Mintage	F	VF	XF	Unc	BU
1992 Proof	Est. 7,500	Value: 37.50				

KM# 47 2 POUNDS **Weight:** 28.2800 g. **Composition:** 0.9250 Silver .8410 oz. ASW **Subject:** Royal Heritage - Egbert of Wessex **Obverse:** Bust of Queen Elizabeth II right **Reverse:** Egbert in archway, dates

Date	Mintage	F	VF	XF	Unc	BU
1996 Proof	10,000	Value: 50.00				

KM# 47a 2 POUNDS **Weight:** 28.2800 g. **Composition:** 0.9250 Silver .8411 oz. ASW **Obverse:** Bust of Queen Elizabeth II right

Date	Mintage	F	VF	XF	Unc	BU
1996 Proof	Est. 10,000	Value: 45.00				

KM# 48 2 POUNDS **Weight:** 28.2800 g. **Composition:** 0.9250 Silver .8410 oz. ASW **Subject:** Royal Heritage - Alfred the Great **Obverse:** Bust of Queen Elizabeth II right **Reverse:** Alfred with axe, scroll, ancient coin, dates

Date	Mintage	F	VF	XF	Unc	BU
1996 Proof	10,000	Value: 50.00				

KM# 48a 2 POUNDS **Center Weight:** 28.2800 g. **Center Composition:** 0.9250 Silver .8411 oz. ASW **Subject:** Royal Heritage - Alfred the Great **Obverse:** Bust of Queen Elizabeth II right **Reverse:** Alfred with axe, scroll, ancient coin, dates

Date	Mintage	F	VF	XF	Unc	BU
1996 Proof	Est. 10,000	Value: 35.00				

KM# 49 2 POUNDS **Weight:** 28.2800 g. **Composition:** 0.9250 Silver .8410 oz. ASW **Subject:** Royal Heritage - Edward the Confessor **Obverse:** Bust of Queen Elizabeth II right **Reverse:** Edward with halo offering miniature church; dates

Date	Mintage	F	VF	XF	Unc	BU
1996 Proof	10,000	Value: 50.00				

KM# 49a 2 POUNDS **Center Weight:** 28.2800 g. **Center Composition:** 0.9250 Silver .8411 oz. ASW **Subject:** Royal Heritage - Edward the Confessor **Obverse:** Bust of Queen Elizabeth II right **Reverse:** Edward with halo offering miniature church; dates

Date	Mintage	F	VF	XF	Unc	BU
1996 Proof	Est. 10,000	Value: 35.00				

KM# 50 2 POUNDS **Weight:** 28.2800 g. **Composition:** 0.9250 Silver .8410 oz. ASW **Subject:** Royal Heritage - William I **Obverse:** Bust of Queen Elizabeth II right **Reverse:** Seated William with shield, miniature church, Domesday Book, dates

Date	Mintage	F	VF	XF	Unc	BU
1996 Proof	10,000	Value: 50.00				

KM# 50a 2 POUNDS **Center Weight:** 28.2800 g. **Center Composition:** 0.9250 Silver .8411 oz. ASW **Subject:** Royal Heritage - William I **Obverse:** Bust of Queen Elizabeth II right **Reverse:** Seated William with shield, miniature church, Domesday Book, dates

Date	Mintage	F	VF	XF	Unc	BU
1996 Proof	Est. 10,000	Value: 35.00				

KM# 51 2 POUNDS **Weight:** 28.2800 g. **Composition:** 0.9250 Silver .8410 oz. ASW **Subject:** Royal Heritage - Henry II **Obverse:** Bust of Queen Elizabeth II right **Reverse:** Crowned bust of Henry II; dates

Date	Mintage	F	VF	XF	Unc	BU
1996 Proof	10,000	Value: 50.00				

KM# 51a 2 POUNDS **Center Weight:** 28.2800 g. **Center Composition:** 0.9250 Silver .8411 oz. ASW **Subject:** Royal Heritage - William I **Obverse:** Bust of Queen Elizabeth II right **Reverse:** Seated William with shield, miniature church, Domesday Book, dates

Date	Mintage	F	VF	XF	Unc	BU
1996 Proof	Est. 10,000	Value: 35.00				

KM# 52 2 POUNDS **Weight:** 28.2800 g. **Composition:** 0.9250 Silver .8410 oz. ASW **Subject:** Royal Heritage - Richard I The Lionheart **Obverse:** Bust of Queen Elizabeth II right **Reverse:** Seated Richard flanked by sun and crescent moon; dates

Date	Mintage	F	VF	XF	Unc	BU
1996 Proof	10,000	Value: 50.00				

KM# 52a 2 POUNDS **Center Weight:** 28.2800 g. **Center Composition:** 0.9250 Silver .8411 oz. ASW **Subject:** Royal Heritage - Richard I The Lionheart **Obverse:** Bust of Queen Elizabeth II right **Reverse:** Seated Richard flanked by sun and crescent moon; dates

Date	Mintage	F	VF	XF	Unc	BU
1996 Proof	Est. 10,000	Value: 35.00				

KM# 53 2 POUNDS **Weight:** 28.2800 g. **Composition:** 0.9250 Silver .8410 oz. ASW **Subject:** Royal Heritage - Henry IV **Obverse:** Bust of Queen Elizabeth II right **Reverse:** Portrait of Henry in crown and cape; dates

Date	Mintage	F	VF	XF	Unc	BU
1996 Proof	10,000	Value: 50.00				

KM# 53a 2 POUNDS **Center Weight:** 28.2800 g. **Center Composition:** 0.9250 Silver .8411 oz. ASW **Subject:** Royal Heritage - Henry IV **Obverse:** Bust of Queen Elizabeth II right **Reverse:** Portrait of Henry in crown and cape; dates

Date	Mintage	F	VF	XF	Unc	BU
1996 Proof	Est. 10,000	Value: 35.00				

KM# 54 2 POUNDS **Weight:** 28.2800 g. **Composition:** 0.9250 Silver .8410 oz. ASW **Subject:** Royal Heritage - Edward IV **Obverse:** Bust of Queen Elizabeth II right **Reverse:** Youthful Edward portrait

Date	Mintage	F	VF	XF	Unc	BU
1996 Proof	10,000	Value: 50.00				

KM#54a 2 POUNDS **Center Weight:** 28.2800 g. **Center Composition:** 0.9250 Silver .8411 oz. ASW **Subject:** Royal Heritage - Edward IV **Obverse:** Bust of Queen Elizabeth II right **Reverse:** Youthful Edward portrait

Date	Mintage	F	VF	XF	Unc	BU
1996 Proof	Est. 10,000	Value: 35.00				

KM# 55 2 POUNDS **Weight:** 28.2800 g. **Composition:** 0.9250 Silver .8410 oz. ASW **Subject:** Royal Heritage - Henry VIII **Obverse:** Bust of Queen Elizabeth II right **Reverse:** Standing Henry with shield; dates

Date	Mintage	F	VF	XF	Unc	BU
1996 Proof	10,000	Value: 50.00				

KM#55a 2 POUNDS **Center Weight:** 28.2800 g. **Center Composition:** 0.9250 Silver .8411 oz. ASW **Subject:** Royal Heritage - Henry VIII **Obverse:** Bust of Queen Elizabeth II right **Reverse:** Standing Henry with shield; dates

Date	Mintage	F	VF	XF	Unc	BU
1996 Proof	Est. 10,000	Value: 35.00				

KM# 56 2 POUNDS **Weight:** 28.2800 g. **Composition:** 0.9250 Silver .8410 oz. ASW **Subject:** Royal Heritage - Elizabeth I **Obverse:** Bust of Queen Elizabeth II right **Reverse:** Bust of Queen Elizabeth I; dates

Date	Mintage	F	VF	XF	Unc	BU
1996 Proof	10,000	Value: 50.00				

KM#56a 2 POUNDS **Center Weight:** 28.2800 g. **Center Composition:** 0.9250 Silver .8411 oz. ASW **Subject:** Royal Heritage - Elizabeth I **Obverse:** Bust of Queen Elizabeth II right **Reverse:** Bust of Queen Elizabeth I; dates

Date	Mintage	F	VF	XF	Unc	BU
1996 Proof	Est. 10,000	Value: 35.00				

KM# 57 2 POUNDS **Weight:** 28.2800 g. **Composition:** 0.9250 Silver .8410 oz. ASW **Subject:** Royal Heritage - Charles I **Obverse:** Bust of Queen Elizabeth II right **Reverse:** Smiling portrait of Charles, shield, dates

Date	Mintage	F	VF	XF	Unc	BU
1996 Proof	10,000	Value: 50.00				

KM#57a 2 POUNDS **Center Weight:** 28.2800 g. **Center Composition:** 0.9250 Silver .8411 oz. ASW **Subject:** Royal Heritage - Charles I **Obverse:** Bust of Queen Elizabeth II right **Reverse:** Smiling portrait of Charles, shield, dates

Date	Mintage	F	VF	XF	Unc	BU
1996 Proof	Est. 10,000	Value: 35.00				

KM# 58 2 POUNDS **Weight:** 28.2800 g. **Composition:** 0.9250 Silver .8410 oz. ASW **Subject:** Royal Heritage - Victoria **Obverse:** Bust of Queen Elizabeth II right **Reverse:** Seated Queen Victoria with sceptre, shield

Date	Mintage	F	VF	XF	Unc	BU
1996 Proof	10,000	Value: 50.00				

KM#58a 2 POUNDS **Center Weight:** 28.2800 g. **Center Composition:** 0.9250 Silver .8411 oz. ASW **Subject:** Royal Heritage - Victoria **Obverse:** Bust of Queen Elizabeth II right **Reverse:** Seated Queen Victoria with sceptre, shield

Date	Mintage	F	VF	XF	Unc	BU
1996 Proof	Est. 10,000	Value: 35.00				

KM#61a 2 POUNDS **Center Weight:** 28.2800 g. **Center Composition:** 0.9250 Silver .8411 oz. ASW **Subject:** Flying Doctor Service **Obverse:** Bust of Queen Elizabeth II right **Reverse:** Two airplanes in flight

Date	Mintage	F	VF	XF	Unc	BU
1998 Proof	Est. 10,000	Value: 50.00				

KM# 61 2 POUNDS **Composition:** Copper-Nickel **Subject:** Flying Doctor Service **Obverse:** Bust of Queen Elizabeth II right **Reverse:** Two airplanes in flight

Date	F	VF	XF	Unc	BU
1998	—	—	—	8.50	—

KM# 64 2 POUNDS **Composition:** Copper-Nickel **Subject:** Sir Ernest Henry Shackleton **Obverse:** Bust of Queen Elizabeth II right **Reverse:** Cameo portrait and icebound ship "Endurance"

Date	F	VF	XF	Unc	BU
1999	—	—	—	8.50	—

KM#64a 2 POUNDS **Center Weight:** 28.2800 g. **Center Composition:** 0.9250 Silver .8411 oz. ASW **Subject:** Sir Ernest Henry Shackleton **Obverse:** Bust of Queen Elizabeth II right **Reverse:** Cameo portrait and icebound ship "Endurance"

Date	Mintage	F	VF	XF	Unc	BU
1999 Proof	Est. 10,000	Value: 50.00				

KM# 69 2 POUNDS **Ring Composition:** Nickel-Brass **Center Weight:** 28.2800 g. **Center Composition:** Copper-Nickel **Obverse:** Queen's head right **Reverse:** Island map, radiant sun in circle of wildlife **Edge:** Plain

Date	Mintage	F	VF	XF	Unc	BU
1999	—	—	—	—	10.00	—
1999 Proof	2,500	Value: 20.00				

KM# 85 2 POUNDS **Weight:** 28.4000 g. **Composition:** 0.9250 Silver 0.8446 oz. ASW **Subject:** Queen Mother **Obverse:** Queen's portrait **Reverse:** Queen Mother holding baby **Edge:** Reeded **Size:** 38.4 mm.

Date	Mintage	F	VF	XF	Unc	BU
2000 Proof	10,000	Value: 50.00				

KM# 67 2 POUNDS **Weight:** 28.2800 g. **Composition:** Copper-Nickel **Subject:** The Gold Rush - "Vicar of Bray" Ship **Obverse:** Queen's head right **Reverse:** "Vicar of Bray" in harbor **Edge:** Reeded

Date	F	VF	XF	Unc	BU
2000	—	—	—	8.50	—

KM#67a 2 POUNDS **Center Weight:** 28.2800 g. **Center Composition:** 0.9250 Silver .8411 oz. ASW **Subject:** The Gold Rush - "Vicar of Bray" Ship **Obverse:** Queen's head right **Reverse:** "Vicar of Bray" in harbor **Edge:** Reeded

Date	Mintage	F	VF	XF	Unc	BU
2000 Proof	10,000	Value: 47.50				

KM# 9 5 POUNDS **Weight:** 39.9400 g. **Composition:** 0.9170 Gold 1.1773 oz. AGW **Obverse:** Queen's portrait **Reverse:** Romney marsh sheep

Date	Mintage	F	VF	XF	Unc	BU
1974 Proof	2,158	Value: 1,100				

KM# 11 5 POUNDS **Weight:** 28.2800 g. **Composition:** 0.9250 Silver .8411 oz. ASW **Subject:** Conservation **Obverse:** Portrait of Queen Elizabeth II **Reverse:** Humpback whale

Date	Mintage	F	VF	XF	Unc	BU
1979	3,998	—	—	—	30.00	—
1979 Proof	3,432	Value: 45.00				

KM# 27 5 POUNDS **Composition:** Copper-Nickel **Subject:** 90th Birthday of Queen Mother

Date	F	VF	XF	Unc	BU
1990	—	—	—	17.50	—

KM# 27a 5 POUNDS **Weight:** 28.2800 g. **Composition:** 0.9250 Silver .8411 oz. ASW **Subject:** 90th Birthday of Queen Mother

Date	Mintage	F	VF	XF	Unc	BU
1990 Proof	Est. 10,000	Value: 37.50				

KM# 33 5 POUNDS **Weight:** 39.9400 g. **Composition:** 0.9170 Gold 1.1773 oz. AGW **Subject:** 10th Wedding Anniversary - Prince Charles and Lady Diana **Obverse:** Portrait of Queen **Reverse:** Facing cameo portraits of Prince Charles and Princess Diana

Date	Mintage	F	VF	XF	Unc	BU
1991 Proof	Est. 200	Value: 850				

KM# 36 5 POUNDS **Composition:** Copper-Nickel **Subject:** 10th Anniversary of Liberation

Date	F	VF	XF	Unc	BU
1992	—	—	—	15.00	—

KM# 36a 5 POUNDS **Weight:** 28.2800 g. **Composition:** 0.9250 Silver .8411 oz. ASW **Subject:** 10th Anniversary of Liberation

Date	Mintage	F	VF	XF	Unc	BU
1992 Proof	Est. 5,000	Value: 42.50				

KM# 36b 5 POUNDS **Weight:** 39.9400 g. **Composition:** 0.9170 Gold 1.1773 oz. AGW **Subject:** 10th Anniversary of Liberation

Date	Mintage	F	VF	XF	Unc	BU
1992 Proof	100	Value: 1,000				

KM# 37 5 POUNDS **Weight:** 28.2800 g. **Composition:** 0.9250 Silver .8411 oz. ASW **Subject:** 400th Anniversary of Discovery - Ship "Desire"

Date	Mintage	F	VF	XF	Unc	BU
ND(1992) Proof	Est. 20,000	Value: 40.00				

KM# 63 5 POUNDS **Composition:** Copper-Nickel **Subject:** Queen's Golden Wedding Anniversary **Obverse:** Bust of Queen Elizabeth II right **Reverse:** Royal couple with gold inlay shield

Date	F	VF	XF	Unc	BU
1997	—	—	—	20.00	—

KM# 12 10 POUNDS **Weight:** 35.0000 g. **Composition:** 0.9250 Silver 1.0409 oz. ASW **Subject:** Conservation **Obverse:** Bust of Queen Elizabeth II right **Reverse:** Flightless steamer duck

Date	Mintage	F	VF	XF	Unc	BU
1979	3,996	—	—	—	35.00	—
1979 Proof	3,247	Value: 50.00				

KM# 28 10 POUNDS **Weight:** 3.1300 g. **Composition:** 0.9990 Gold .1000 oz. AGW **Subject:** 90th Birthday of Queen Mother **Obverse:** Portrait of Queen Elizabeth

Date	Mintage	F	VF	XF	Unc	BU
ND(1990) Proof	Est. 750	Value: 75.00				

KM# 38 10 POUNDS **Weight:** 3.1300 g. **Composition:** 0.9990 Gold .1000 oz. AGW **Subject:** 400th Anniversary of Discovery - Ship "Desire" **Note:** Similar to 5 Pounds, KM#37.

Date	Mintage	F	VF	XF	Unc	BU
ND(1992) Proof	Est. 400	Value: 65.00				

KM# 62 20 POUNDS **Weight:** 6.2200 g. **Composition:** 0.9990 Gold .2000 oz. AGW **Subject:** Flying Doctor Service **Obverse:** Bust of Queen Elizabeth II right **Reverse:** Two airplanes in flight

Date	Mintage	F	VF	XF	Unc	BU
1998 Proof	Est. 1,000	Value: 175				

KM# 65 20 POUNDS **Weight:** 6.2200 g. **Composition:** 0.9990 Gold .2000 oz. AGW **Subject:** Sir Ernest H. Shackleton **Obverse:** Queen's portrait **Reverse:** Cameo portrait and icebound ship

Date	Mintage	F	VF	XF	Unc	BU
1999 Proof	Est. 1,000	Value: 175				

KM# 68 20 POUNDS **Weight:** 6.2200 g. **Composition:** 0.9990 Gold .2000 oz. AGW **Subject:** The Gold Rush **Obverse:** Queen's head right **Reverse:** "Vicar of Bray" in harbor **Edge:** Reeded

Date	Mintage	F	VF	XF	Unc	BU
2000 Proof	1,000	Value: 175				

KM# 20 25 POUNDS **Weight:** 150.0000 g. **Composition:** 0.9250 Silver 4.4614 oz. ASW **Subject:** 100 Years of Self Sufficiency

Date	Mintage	F	VF	XF	Unc	BU
ND(1985) Proof	Est. 20,000	Value: 55.00				

KM# 23 25 POUNDS **Weight:** 150.0000 g. **Composition:** 0.9250 Silver 4.4614 oz. ASW **Subject:** Prince Andrew's Wedding **Reverse:** Profiles of Andrew and Fergie facing

Date	Mintage	F	VF	XF	Unc	BU
1986 Proof	Est. 20,000	Value: 45.00				

KM# 29 25 POUNDS **Weight:** 7.8100 g. **Composition:** 0.9990 Gold .2500 oz. AGW **Subject:** 90th Birthday of Queen Mother **Obverse:** Bust of Queen Elizabeth II right

Date	Mintage	F	VF	XF	Unc	BU
ND(1990) Proof	Est. 750	Value: 200				

KM# 40 25 POUNDS **Weight:** 7.8100 g. **Composition:** 0.9990 Gold .2500 oz. AGW **Subject:** 100th Anniversary of Christchurch Cathedral **Reverse:** Cathedral and cross

Date	Mintage	F	VF	XF	Unc	BU
1992 Proof	Est. 400	Value: 160				

KM# 39 25 POUNDS **Weight:** 155.5800 g. **Composition:** 0.9990 Silver 4.9970 oz. ASW **Subject:** 400th Anniversary - First Sighting of Falkland Islands

Date	Mintage	F	VF	XF	Unc	BU
ND(1992) Proof	Est. 3,000	Value: 200				

KM# 30 50 POUNDS **Weight:** 15.6100 g. **Composition:** 0.9990 Gold .5000 oz. AGW **Subject:** 90th Birthday of Queen Mother **Obverse:** Bust of Queen Elizabeth II right

Date	Mintage	F	VF	XF	Unc	BU
ND(1990) Proof	Est. 750	Value: 325				

KM# 41 50 POUNDS **Weight:** 15.6100 g. **Composition:** 0.9990 Gold .5000 oz. AGW **Subject:** 100th Anniversary of Defense **Reverse:** Soldier

Date	Mintage	F	VF	XF	Unc	BU
ND(1992) Proof	Est. 400	Value: 300				

KM# 44 50 POUNDS **Weight:** 47.5400 g. **Composition:** 0.9170 Gold 1.4013 oz. AGW **Subject:** 40th Anniversary - Coronation of Queen Elizabeth II

Date	Mintage	F	VF	XF	Unc	BU
ND(1993) Proof	Est. 100	Value: 1,150				

KM# 31 100 POUNDS **Weight:** 31.2100 g. **Composition:** 0.9990 Gold 1.0000 oz. AGW **Subject:** 90th Birthday of Queen Mother **Obverse:** Portrait of Queen Elizabeth

Date	Mintage	F	VF	XF	Unc	BU
ND(1990) Proof	Est. 750	Value: 550				

KM# 42 100 POUNDS **Weight:** 31.2100 g. **Composition:** 0.9990 Gold 1.0000 oz. AGW **Subject:** 400th Anniversary of Discovery - SHip "Desire' **Note.** Similar to 5 Pounds, KM#37.

Date	Mintage	F	VF	XF	Unc	BU
ND(1992) Proof	Est. 400	Value: 525				

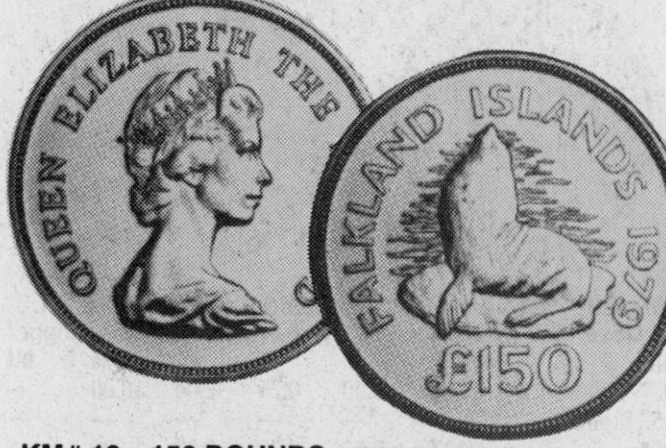

KM# 13 150 POUNDS **Weight:** 33.4370 g. **Composition:** 0.9000 Gold .9676 oz. AGW **Subject:** Conservation **Obverse:** Bust of Queen Elizabeth II right **Reverse:** Falkland Fur Seal

Date	Mintage	F	VF	XF	Unc	BU
1979	488	—	—	—	625	—
1979 Proof	164	Value: 1,350				

PIEFORTS

KM#	Date	Mintage	Identification	Mkt Val
P1	1987	2,500	Pound. 0.9250 Silver. KM24a.	45.00
P2	1992	750	50 Pence. 0.9250 Silver. KM34a	60.00
P3	1995	—	50 Pence. 0.9250 Silver. KM48a	85.00

MINT SETS

KM#	Date	Mintage	Identification	Issue Price	Mkt Val
MS1	1987 (7)	—	KM2-3, 4.1-5.1, 14.1, 17, 24	10.00	12.00
MS2	1992 (8)	—	KM2-3, 4.1-5.1, 14.1, 17, 24, 35	24.50	25.00
MS3	1999 (8)	—	KM2a-3a, 4.2-5.2, 14.2, 17, 24, 69	20.00	22.50

PROOF SETS

KM#	Date	Mintage	Identification	Issue Price	Mkt Val
PS1	1974 (5)	20,000	KM1-3, 4.1-5.1	12.00	15.50
PS2	1974 (4)	2,000	KM6-9	1,100	2,000
PS3	1979 (2)	10,000	KM11-12	—	115
PS4	1980 (6)	10,000	KM1-3, 4.1-5.1, 14.1	35.00	20.00
PS5	1982 (8)	5,000	KM1-3, 4.1-5.1, 14.1, 17, 18a	—	45.00
PS6	1982 (7)	5,000	KM1-3, 4.1-5.1, 14.1, 17	—	26.50
PS7	1987 (7)	2,500	KM2-3, 4.1-5.1, 14.1, 17, 24	35.00	40.00
PS8	1990 (4)	750	KM28-31	1,595	1,150
PS10	1992 (4)	400	KM38, 40-42	1,595	1,075
PS9	1992 (8)	2,500	KM2-3, 4.1-5.1, 14.1, 17, 24, 35a	89.50	90.00
PS11	1999 (8)	2,500	KM2a-3a, 4.2-5.2, 14.2, 17, 24, 69	50.00	55.00

FIJI ISLANDS

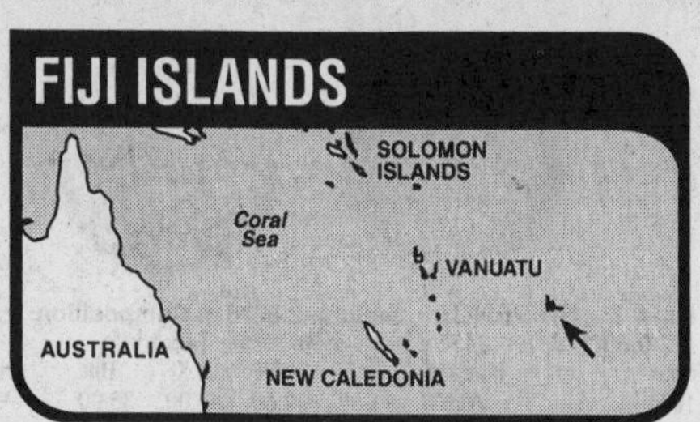

The Republic of Fiji, consists of about 320 islands located in the southwestern Pacific 1,100 miles (1,770 km.) north of New Zealand. The islands have a combined area of 7,056 sq. mi. (18,274 sq. km.) and a population of 772,891. Capital: Suva. Fiji's economy is based on agriculture and mining. Sugar, coconut products, manganese, and gold are exported.

The first European to sight Fiji was the Dutch navigator Abel Tasman in 1643 and the islands were visited by British naval captain James Cook in 1774. The first complete survey of the island was conducted by the United States in 1840. Settlement by mercenaries from Tonga, and traders attracted by the sandalwood trade, began in 1801. Following a lengthy period of intertribal warfare, the islands were unconditionally ceded to Great Britain in 1874 by King Cakobau. Fiji became a sovereign and independent nation on Oct. 10, 1970, the 96th anniversary of the cession of the islands to Queen Victoria.

Fiji was declared a Republic in 1987 following two military coups. It left the British Commonwealth and Queen Elizabeth ceased to be the Head of State. A new constitution was introduced in 1991. The country returned to the Commonwealth in 1997 with a revised constitution.

RULERS
British until 1970

MINT MARKS
(c) - Australian Mint, Canberra
(o) - Royal Canadian Mint, Ottawa
S - San Francisco, U.S.A.

MONETARY SYSTEM
12 Pence = 1 Shilling
2 Shillings = 1 Florin
20 Shillings = 1 Pound

REPUBLIC
(British administration until 1970)
POUND STERLING COINAGE

KM# 1 1/2 PENNY **Composition:** Copper-Nickel

Date	Mintage	F	VF	XF	Unc	BU
1934	96,000	1.00	3.00	6.00	17.50	—
1934 Proof	—	—	—	—	—	—

KM# 14 1/2 PENNY **Composition:** Copper-Nickel

Date	Mintage	F	VF	XF	Unc	BU
1940	24,000	5.00	10.00	20.00	30.00	—
1940 Proof	—	Value: 350				
1941	96,000	0.75	1.50	4.00	12.50	—
1941 Proof	—	Value: 200				

KM# 14a 1/2 PENNY **Composition:** Brass

Date	Mintage	F	VF	XF	Unc	BU
1942S	250,000	0.25	0.50	3.50	15.00	—
1943S	250,000	0.25	0.50	3.50	17.50	—

KM# 16 1/2 PENNY **Composition:** Copper-Nickel **Obverse:** EMPEROR dropped from legend

Date	Mintage	F	VF	XF	Unc	BU
1949	96,000	0.50	1.00	2.00	6.00	—
1949	—	Value: 210				

Date	Mintage	F	VF	XF	Unc	BU
1950	115,000	0.25	0.50	1.50	5.00	—
1950 Proof	—	Value: 230				
1951	115,000	0.25	0.50	1.50	5.00	—
1951 Proof	—	Value: 190				
1952	228,000	0.15	0.35	0.75	2.00	—
1952 Proof	—	—	—	—	—	—

KM# 20 1/2 PENNY **Composition:** Copper-Nickel

Date	Mintage	F	VF	XF	Unc	BU
1954	228,000	0.15	0.25	0.50	1.00	—
1954 Proof	—	Value: 180				

KM# 2 PENNY **Composition:** Copper-Nickel

Date	Mintage	F	VF	XF	Unc	BU
1934	480,000	0.50	1.00	5.00	12.50	—
1934 Proof	—	—	—	—	—	—
1935	240,000	0.65	1.25	5.50	17.50	—
1935 Proof	—	—	—	—	—	—
1936	240,000	0.65	1.25	5.50	20.00	—
1936 Proof	—	—	—	—	—	—

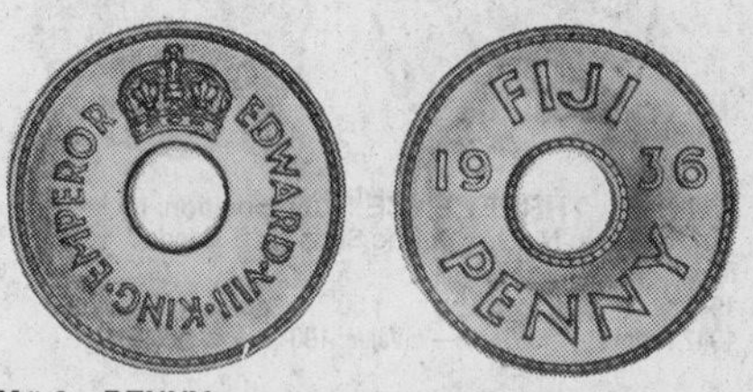

KM# 6 PENNY **Composition:** Copper-Nickel

Date	Mintage	F	VF	XF	Unc	BU
1936	120,000	0.50	1.00	2.00	4.00	—
1936 Proof	—	Value: 225				

KM# 7 PENNY **Composition:** Copper-Nickel

Date	Mintage	F	VF	XF	Unc	BU
1937	360,000	0.50	1.00	3.00	9.00	—
1937 Proof	—	Value: 225				
1940	144,000	2.00	3.00	15.00	45.00	—
1940 Proof	—	Value: 225				
1941	228,000	0.50	1.00	2.00	9.00	—
1941 Proof	—	Value: 225				
1945	240,000	2.00	3.00	8.00	25.00	—
1945 Proof	—	Value: 225				

KM# 7a PENNY **Composition:** Brass

Date	Mintage	F	VF	XF	Unc	BU
1942S	1,000,000	0.50	1.00	3.50	17.50	—
1943S	1,000,000	0.50	1.00	3.50	20.00	—

KM# 17 PENNY **Composition:** Copper-Nickel **Obverse:** EMPEROR dropped from legend

Date	Mintage	F	VF	XF	Unc	BU
1949	120,000	0.25	0.50	1.00	6.00	—
1949 Proof	—	Value: 325				
1950	58,000	2.00	4.50	12.50	75.00	—
1950 Proof	—	Value: 200				

Date	Mintage	F	VF	XF	Unc	BU
1952	230,000	0.25	0.50	1.00	5.00	—
1952 Proof	—	Value: 175				

KM# 21 PENNY **Composition:** Copper-Nickel

Date	Mintage	F	VF	XF	Unc	BU
1954	511,000	0.20	0.50	1.00	3.00	—
1954 Proof	—	Value: 175				
1955	230,000	0.25	0.50	1.25	8.50	—
1955 Proof	—	Value: 175				
1956	230,000	0.25	0.50	1.25	6.00	—
1956 Proof	—	Value: 175				
1957	360,000	0.10	0.25	0.75	5.00	—
1957 Proof	—	Value: 175				
1959	864,000	0.10	0.20	0.35	2.00	—
1959 Proof	—	Value: 175				
1961	432,000	0.20	0.35	0.50	1.25	—
1961 Proof	—	Value: 175				
1963	432,000	0.20	0.35	0.50	1.25	—
1963 Proof	—	Value: 175				
1964	864,000	0.10	0.15	0.25	0.85	—
1964 Proof	—	Value: 150				
1965	1,440,000	0.10	0.15	0.25	0.75	—
1966	720,000	0.10	0.15	0.25	0.85	—
1967	720,000	0.10	0.15	0.25	0.75	—
1968	720,000	0.10	0.15	0.25	0.75	—

KM# 15 THREEPENCE **Composition:** Nickel-Brass **Reverse:** Native dwelling **Shape:** 12-sided

Date	Mintage	F	VF	XF	Unc	BU
1947	450,000	1.50	2.50	6.00	17.50	—
1947 Proof	—	Value: 190				

KM# 18 THREEPENCE **Composition:** Nickel-Brass **Obverse:** EMPEROR dropped from legend **Shape:** 12-sided

Date	Mintage	F	VF	XF	Unc	BU
1950	450,000	0.50	1.00	4.00	15.00	—
1950 Proof	—	Value: 190				
1952	400,000	0.50	1.00	5.00	22.50	—
1952 Proof	—	Value: 190				

KM# 22 THREEPENCE **Composition:** Nickel-Brass **Shape:** 12-sided

Date	Mintage	F	VF	XF	Unc	BU
1955	400,000	0.50	1.00	4.00	17.50	—
1955 Proof	—	Value: 130				
1956	200,000	0.50	1.00	4.00	22.50	—
1956 Proof	—	Value: 155				
1958	200,000	0.50	1.00	4.00	22.50	—
1958 Proof	—	Value: 140				
1960	240,000	0.25	0.50	3.00	8.50	—
1960 Proof	—	Value: 125				
1961	240,000	0.25	0.50	1.25	6.00	—
1961 Proof	—	Value: 125				
1963	240,000	0.15	0.30	0.75	5.00	—
1963 Proof	—	Value: 115				
1964	240,000	0.15	0.30	0.50	2.00	—
1965	800,000	0.10	0.15	0.25	1.50	—
1967	800,000	0.10	0.15	0.25	1.50	—

KM# 3 SIXPENCE **Weight:** 2.8276 g. **Composition:** 0.5000 Silver .0455 oz. ASW **Reverse:** Sea turtle

Date	Mintage	F	VF	XF	Unc	BU
1934	160,000	1.00	2.50	10.00	35.00	—
1934 Proof	—	Value: 450				
1935	120,000	1.50	3.50	12.50	47.50	—
1935 Proof	—	—	—	—	—	—
1936	40,000	2.00	4.00	15.00	55.00	—
1936 Proof	—	—	—	—	—	—

KM# 8 SIXPENCE **Weight:** 2.8276 g. **Composition:** 0.5000 Silver .0455 oz. ASW

Date	Mintage	F	VF	XF	Unc	BU
1937	40,000	2.00	4.00	16.00	60.00	—
1937 Proof	—	Value: 400				

KM# 11 SIXPENCE **Weight:** 2.8276 g. **Composition:** 0.5000 Silver .0455 oz. ASW **Obverse:** Smaller head

Date	Mintage	F	VF	XF	Unc	BU
1938	40,000	2.00	4.00	13.50	50.00	—
1938 Proof	—	—	—	—	—	—
1940	40,000	2.00	4.00	13.50	50.00	—
1940 Proof	—	—	—	—	—	—
1941	40,000	3.00	8.00	20.00	75.00	—
1941 Proof	—	—	—	—	—	—

KM# 11a SIXPENCE **Weight:** 2.8276 g. **Composition:** 0.9000 Silver .0818 oz. ASW

Date	Mintage	F	VF	XF	Unc	BU
1942	400,000	—	1.00	2.50	6.50	—
1943	400,000	—	1.00	2.50	6.50	—

KM# 19 SIXPENCE **Composition:** Copper-Nickel

Date	Mintage	F	VF	XF	Unc	BU
1953	800,000	0.15	0.30	1.00	3.00	4.00
1953 Proof	—	Value: 210				
1958	400,000	0.25	0.50	1.50	4.50	6.00
1958 Proof	—	Value: 200				
1961	400,000	0.25	0.50	1.00	3.50	5.00
1961 Proof	—	Value: 200				
1962	400,000	0.25	0.50	1.00	3.00	4.00
1962 Proof	—	Value: 200				
1965	800,000	0.15	0.30	0.75	2.00	3.50
1967	800,000	0.15	0.30	0.75	2.00	3.50

KM# 4 SHILLING **Weight:** 5.6552 g. **Composition:** 0.5000 Silver .0909 oz. ASW **Reverse:** Outrigger

Date	Mintage	F	VF	XF	Unc	BU
1934	360,000	1.50	4.00	14.50	60.00	—
1934 Proof	—	Value: 650				
1935	180,000	1.50	4.00	14.50	80.00	—
1935 Proof	—	—	—	—	—	—
1936	140,000	1.50	6.00	15.50	80.00	—
1936 Proof	—	—	—	—	—	—

KM# 9 SHILLING **Weight:** 5.6552 g. **Composition:** 0.5000 Silver .0909 oz. ASW

Date	Mintage	F	VF	XF	Unc	BU
1937	40,000	1.50	7.00	17.50	90.00	—
1937 Proof	—	Value: 500				

KM# 12 SHILLING **Weight:** 5.6552 g. **Composition:** 0.5000 Silver .0909 oz. ASW **Obverse:** Smaller head

Date	Mintage	F	VF	XF	Unc	BU
1938	40,000	1.50	7.00	17.50	85.00	—
1938 Proof	—	—	—	—	—	—
1941	40,000	1.50	7.00	17.50	80.00	—
1941 Proof	—	—	—	—	—	—

KM# 12a SHILLING **Weight:** 5.6552 g. **Composition:** 0.9000 Silver .1636 oz. ASW

Date	Mintage	F	VF	XF	Unc	BU
1942	500,000	—	1.25	3.00	7.50	—
1943	500,000	—	1.25	3.00	7.50	—

KM# 23 SHILLING **Composition:** Copper-Nickel **Obverse:** Young Queen Elizabeth II right **Reverse:** Outrigger

Date	Mintage	F	VF	XF	Unc	BU
1957	400,000	0.50	0.75	2.00	10.00	—
1957 Proof	—	—	—	—	—	—
1958	400,000	0.50	0.75	2.25	10.00	—
1958 Proof	—	—	—	—	—	—
1961	200,000	0.75	1.00	2.25	7.50	—
1961 Proof	—	Value: 275				
1962	400,000	0.35	0.75	1.25	4.00	—
1962 Proof	—	Value: 250				
1965	800,000	0.25	0.50	0.75	2.00	—

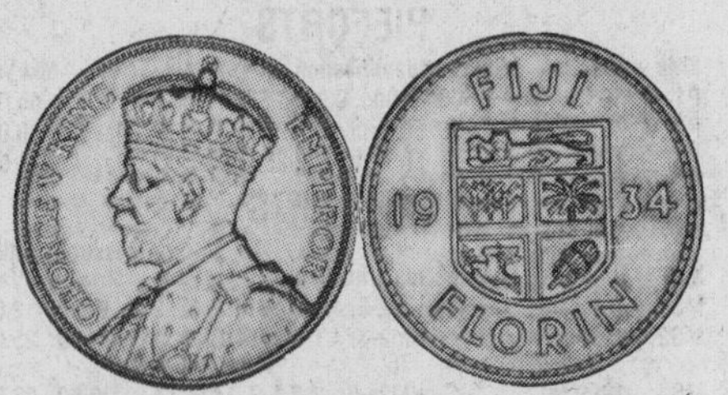

KM# 5 FLORIN **Weight:** 11.3104 g. **Composition:** 0.5000 Silver .1818 oz. ASW **Obverse:** Bust of King George V left **Reverse:** Shield of arms

Date	Mintage	F	VF	XF	Unc	BU
1934	200,000	1.50	4.50	17.50	125	—
1934 Proof	—	Value: 750				
1935	50,000	2.00	9.00	20.00	190	—
1935 Proof	—	—	—	—	—	—
1936	65,000	2.00	9.00	20.00	170	—
1936 Proof	—	—	—	—	—	—

KM# 10 FLORIN **Weight:** 11.3104 g. **Composition:** 0.5000 Silver .1818 oz. ASW **Obverse:** Head of King George VI left

Date	Mintage	F	VF	XF	Unc	BU
1937	30,000	2.50	7.00	17.50	150	—
1937 Proof	—	Value: 750				

KM# 13 FLORIN **Weight:** 11.3104 g. **Composition:** 0.5000 Silver .1818 oz. ASW **Obverse:** Smaller head

Date	Mintage	F	VF	XF	Unc	BU
1938	20,000	4.00	12.00	25.00	185	—
1938 Proof	—	—	—	—	—	—
1941	20,000	4.00	12.00	25.00	185	—
1941 Proof	—	—	—	—	—	—
1945	100,000	9.00	20.00	35.00	230	—
1945 Proof	—	—	—	—	—	—

KM# 13a FLORIN **Weight:** 11.3104 g. **Composition:** 0.9000 Silver .3273 oz. ASW

Date	Mintage	F	VF	XF	Unc	BU
1942	250,000	—	2.50	5.00	15.00	—
1943	250,000	—	2.50	5.00	17.50	—

KM# 24 FLORIN **Composition:** Copper-Nickel **Obverse:** Bust of young Queen Elizabeth II right

Date	Mintage	F	VF	XF	Unc	BU
1957	300,000	0.50	1.00	4.00	15.00	—
1957 Proof	—	Value: 375				
1958	220,000	0.50	1.00	4.00	15.00	—
1958 Proof	—	Value: 375				
1962	200,000	0.25	0.50	2.00	10.00	—
1962 Proof	—	Value: 375				
1964	200,000	0.25	0.50	1.50	5.00	—
1964 Proof	—	Value: 400				
1965	400,000	0.25	0.50	1.00	3.00	—

DECIMAL COINAGE

100 Cents = 1 Dollar

KM# 27 CENT **Composition:** Bronze **Reverse:** Tanoa kava dish

Date	Mintage	F	VF	XF	Unc	BU
1969	11,000,000	—	—	0.10	0.20	—
1969 Proof	10,000	Value: 0.50				
1973	3,000,000	—	—	0.10	1.00	—
1975	2,064,000	—	—	0.10	0.50	—
1976	2,005,000	—	—	0.10	0.50	—
1983	—	—	—	0.10	0.50	—
1983 Proof	3,000	Value: 1.00				
1984	2,295,000	—	—	0.10	0.35	—
1985	—	—	—	0.10	0.35	—

KM# 27a CENT **Weight:** 2.2600 g. **Composition:** 0.9250 Silver .0672 oz. ASW

Date	Mintage	F	VF	XF	Unc	BU
1976 Proof	3,012	Value: 3.50				

KM# 39 CENT **Composition:** Bronze **Series:** F.A.O **Reverse:** Rice

Date	Mintage	F	VF	XF	Unc	BU
1977	3,000,000	—	—	0.10	0.50	—
1978	3,032,000	—	—	0.10	0.50	—
1978 Proof	2,000	Value: 2.50				
1979	2,500,000	—	—	0.15	2.00	—
1980	314,000	—	—	0.10	0.50	—
1980 Proof	2,500	Value: 1.50				
1981	4,040,000	—	—	0.10	0.50	—
1982	5,000,000	—	—	0.10	1.00	—
1982 Proof	3,000	Value: 1.00				

KM# 49 CENT **Composition:** Bronze

Date	Mintage	F	VF	XF	Unc	BU
1986(c)	3,400,000	—	—	0.10	0.50	—
1987(c)	3,400,000	—	—	0.15	1.00	—

KM# 49a CENT **Composition:** Copper Plated Zinc

Date	Mintage	F	VF	XF	Unc	BU
1990	8,500,000	—	—	0.10	0.25	—
1992	—	—	—	0.10	0.25	—
1994	—	—	—	—	0.50	—
1995	—	—	—	—	0.50	—
1997	—	—	—	—	0.50	—

KM# 28 2 CENTS **Composition:** Bronze **Reverse:** Palm fan

Date	Mintage	F	VF	XF	Unc	BU
1969	8,000,000	—	—	0.10	0.50	—
1969 Proof	10,000	Value: 0.75				
1973	2,110,000	—	0.10	0.15	0.75	—
1975	1,500,000	—	0.10	0.15	0.50	—
1976	1,004,999	—	0.10	0.15	0.50	—
1977	1,250,000	—	—	0.10	0.50	—
1978	1,502,000	—	—	0.10	0.50	—
1978 Proof	2,000	Value: 3.50				
1979	500,000	—	0.10	0.20	2.50	—
1980	4,019,999	—	—	0.10	0.50	—
1980 Proof	2,500	Value: 2.50				
1981	3,250,000	—	—	0.10	0.50	—
1982	4,000,000	—	—	0.10	0.50	—
1982 Proof	3,000	Value: 2.00				
1983	—	—	—	0.10	0.50	—
1983 Proof	3,000	Value: 1.50				
1984	1,845,000	—	—	0.10	0.40	—
1985	1,700,000	—	—	0.10	0.40	—

KM# 28a 2 CENTS **Weight:** 4.5300 g. **Composition:** 0.9250 Silver .1347 oz. ASW

Date	Mintage	F	VF	XF	Unc	BU
1976 Proof	3,012	Value: 4.50				

KM# 50 2 CENTS **Composition:** Bronze

Date	Mintage	F	VF	XF	Unc	BU
1986(c)	1,700,000	—	—	0.15	1.00	—
1987(c)	1,700,000	—	—	0.15	1.00	—

KM# 50a 2 CENTS **Composition:** Copper Plated Zinc

Date	Mintage	F	VF	XF	Unc	BU
1990(o)	5,500,000	—	—	—	1.00	—
1992(o)	—	—	—	—	0.50	—
1994	—	—	—	—	0.35	—

KM# 29 5 CENTS **Composition:** Copper-Nickel **Reverse:** Fijian drum

Date	Mintage	F	VF	XF	Unc	BU
1969	9,200,000	—	0.10	0.20	0.75	—
1969 Proof	10,000	Value: 0.75				
1973	600,000	—	0.10	0.30	1.50	—
1974	608,000	—	0.10	0.30	1.25	—
1975	1,008,000	—	0.10	0.20	0.75	—
1976	1,205,000	—	0.10	0.20	0.75	—
1977	960,000	—	0.10	0.20	0.75	—
1978	880,000	—	0.10	0.20	0.75	—
1978 Proof	2,000	Value: 5.00				
1979	1,500,000	—	0.10	0.25	2.00	—
1980	2,506,000	—	0.10	0.15	0.75	—
1980 Proof	2,500	Value: 3.50				
1981	1,980,000	—	0.10	0.15	0.50	—
1982	2,700,000	—	0.10	0.15	1.00	—
1982 Proof	3,000	Value: 3.00				
1983	—	—	0.10	0.15	0.50	—
1983 Proof	3,000	Value: 2.00				
1984	5,000	—	0.10	0.20	0.75	—

KM# 29a 5 CENTS **Weight:** 3.2800 g. **Composition:** 0.9250 Silver .0975 oz. ASW **Series:** F.A.O.

Date	Mintage	F	VF	XF	Unc	BU
1976 Proof	3,012	Value: 6.00				

KM# 51 5 CENTS **Composition:** Copper-Nickel

Date	Mintage	F	VF	XF	Unc	BU
1986(c)	1,200,000	—	0.10	0.20	1.00	—
1987(c)	1,200,000	—	0.10	0.20	1.00	—

KM# 51a 5 CENTS **Composition:** Nickel Bonded Steel

Date	Mintage	F	VF	XF	Unc	BU
1990	4,000,000	—	—	—	0.50	—
1992	—	—	—	—	0.35	—
1994	—	—	—	—	0.75	—

KM# 77 5 CENTS **Composition:** Nickel Bonded Steel **Series:** F.A.O. **Subject:** Harvest from the Sea **Obverse:** Queen's portrait **Reverse:** Fish, F.A.O. logo

Date	F	VF	XF	Unc	BU
1995	—	—	—	0.75	—

KM# 30 10 CENTS **Composition:** Copper-Nickel **Reverse:** Throwing club

Date	Mintage	F	VF	XF	Unc	BU
1969	3,500,000	—	0.20	0.40	1.00	—
1969 Proof	10,000	Value: 1.00				
1973	750,000	—	0.25	0.65	2.00	—
1975	752,000	—	0.20	0.50	1.25	—
1976	805,000	—	0.20	0.50	1.25	—
1977	240,000	—	0.25	0.65	1.25	—
1978	664,000	—	0.20	0.50	1.25	—
1978 Proof	2,000	Value: 6.00				
1979	702,000	—	0.20	0.50	1.25	—
1980	1,000,000	—	0.15	0.30	1.25	—
1980 Proof	2,500	Value: 4.50				
1981	1,200,000	—	0.20	0.50	1.25	—
1982	1,500,000	—	0.20	0.50	1.50	—
1982 Proof	3,000	Value: 4.00				
1983	3,000	—	0.25	.65	2.00	—
1983 Proof	3,000	Value: 3.00				
1984	5,000	—	0.25	0.65	1.75	—
1985	660,000	—	0.20	0.50	1.50	—

KM# 30a 10 CENTS **Weight:** 6.5500 g. **Composition:** 0.9250 Silver .1948 oz. ASW **Reverse:** Throwing club

Date	Mintage	F	VF	XF	Unc	BU
1976 Proof	3,012	Value: 6.50				

KM# 52 10 CENTS **Composition:** Copper-Nickel **Reverse:** Throwing club

Date	Mintage	F	VF	XF	Unc	BU
1986(c)	740,000	—	0.20	0.40	2.00	—
1987(c)	740,000	—	0.20	0.40	2.00	—

KM# 52a 10 CENTS **Composition:** Nickel Bonded Steel **Reverse:** Throwing club

Date	Mintage	F	VF	XF	Unc	BU
1990	2,000,000	—	—	—	1.00	—
1992	—	—	—	—	1.00	—
1994	—	—	—	—	1.00	—

Date	Mintage	F	VF	XF	Unc	BU
1995	—	—	—	—	1.00	—
1996	—	—	—	—	1.00	—

KM# 31 20 CENTS **Composition:** Copper-Nickel **Reverse:** Tabua on braided sennit cord

Date	Mintage	F	VF	XF	Unc	BU
1969	2,000,000	—	0.30	0.80	1.50	—
1969 Proof	10,000	Value: 1.75				
1973	250,000	—	0.35	1.00	2.25	—
1974	252,000	—	0.35	0.75	2.00	—
1975	352,000	—	0.35	0.75	2.50	—
1976	405,000	—	0.25	0.65	1.75	—
1977	200,000	—	0.35	0.75	3.50	—
1978	406,000	—	0.25	0.50	1.75	—
1978 Proof	2,000	Value: 8.00				
1979	500,000	—	0.25	0.60	1.75	—
1980	1,014,000	—	0.25	0.60	1.75	—
1980 Proof	2,500	Value: 6.50				
1981	1,200,000	—	0.25	0.60	1.75	—
1982	1,500,000	—	0.25	0.60	1.50	—
1982 Proof	3,000	Value: 6.00				
1983	3,000	—	0.35	0.75	2.50	—
1983 Proof	3,000	Value: 5.00				
1984	5,000	—	0.35	0.75	2.25	—
1985	240,000	—	0.20	0.35	2.00	—

KM# 31a 20 CENTS **Weight:** 13.0900 g. **Composition:** 0.9250 Silver .3893 oz. ASW

Date	Mintage	F	VF	XF	Unc	BU
1976 Proof	3,012	Value: 8.50				

KM# 53 20 CENTS **Composition:** Copper-Nickel **Reverse:** Throwing club

Date	Mintage	F	VF	XF	Unc	BU
1986(c)	360,000	—	0.25	0.60	2.50	—
1987(c)	360,000	—	0.25	0.60	2.50	—

KM# 53a 20 CENTS **Composition:** Nickel Bonded Steel **Reverse:** Throwing club

Date	Mintage	F	VF	XF	Unc	BU
1990	1,500,000	—	0.20	0.35	1.50	—
1992	—	—	0.20	0.35	1.50	—
1994	—	—	0.20	0.35	1.00	—
1995	—	—	0.20	0.35	1.00	—

KM# 36 50 CENTS **Composition:** Copper-Nickel **Reverse:** Sailing canoe - Takia

Date	Mintage	F	VF	XF	Unc	BU
1975	1,000,000	—	0.75	1.50	5.00	—
1976	805,000	—	0.75	1.00	3.00	—
1978	4,006	—	1.25	2.50	6.00	—
1978 Proof	2,000	Value: 13.00				
1980	316,000	—	0.75	1.00	3.00	—
1980 Proof	2,500	Value: 11.50				
1981	511,000	—	0.75	1.00	5.00	—
1982	1,000,000	—	0.75	1.00	4.00	—
1982 Proof	3,000	Value: 10.00				
1983	3,000	—	0.65	1.00	3.50	—
1983 Proof	3,000	Value: 9.00				
1984	5,000	—	0.65	1.00	3.25	—

KM# 36a 50 CENTS **Weight:** 18.0000 g. **Composition:** 0.9250 Silver .5353 oz. ASW **Reverse:** Sailing canoe - Takia

Date	Mintage	F	VF	XF	Unc	BU
1976 Proof	3,012	Value: 13.50				

KM# 44 50 CENTS **Composition:** Copper-Nickel **Series:** F.A.O. **Subject:** First Indians in Fiji Centennial

Date	Mintage	F	VF	XF	Unc	BU
1979	258,000	—	—	—	2.50	—
1979 Proof	6,004	Value: 7.50				

KM# 45 50 CENTS **Composition:** Copper-Nickel **Subject:** 10th Anniversary of Independence **Reverse:** Prince Charles

Date	Mintage	F	VF	XF	Unc	BU
1980	10,000	—	—	—	2.50	—

KM# 54 50 CENTS **Composition:** Copper-Nickel **Reverse:** Sailing canoe - Takia

Date	Mintage	F	VF	XF	Unc	BU
1986(c)	160,000	—	0.75	1.00	3.50	—
1987(c)	160,000	—	0.50	0.75	2.00	—

KM# 54a 50 CENTS **Composition:** Nickel Bonded Steel **Reverse:** Sailing canoe - Takia

Date	Mintage	F	VF	XF	Unc	BU
1990(o)	800,000	—	—	0.60	1.50	—
1992(o)	—	—	—	0.60	1.50	—
1994(o)	—	—	—	0.60	1.50	—

KM# 32 DOLLAR **Composition:** Copper-Nickel **Obverse:** Bust of young Queen Elizabeth II right **Reverse:** Arms

Date	Mintage	F	VF	XF	Unc	BU
1969 Proof	10,000	Value: 5.00				
1969	70,000	—	1.00	2.00	4.50	—
1976	5,007	—	1.50	3.00	6.50	—

KM# 32a DOLLAR **Weight:** 28.2800 g. **Composition:** 0.9250 Silver .8411 oz. ASW **Obverse:** Bust of young Queen Elizabeth II right **Reverse:** Arms

Date	Mintage	F	VF	XF	Unc	BU
1976 Proof	3,012	Value: 20.00				

KM# 33a DOLLAR **Weight:** 28.2800 g. **Composition:** 0.9250 Silver .8411 oz. ASW

Date	Mintage	F	VF	XF	Unc	BU
1970 Proof	1,000	Value: 45.00				

KM# 33 DOLLAR **Composition:** Copper-Nickel **Subject:** Independence Commemorative

Date	Mintage	F	VF	XF	Unc	BU
1970	15,000	—	—	—	5.00	—
1970 Proof	15,000	Value: 6.00				

Note: Variety with medallic alignment exists; Value: $100

KM# 71 DOLLAR **Composition:** Copper-Nickel **Subject:** Move to Buckingham Palace **Reverse:** Buckingham Palace and soldier

Date	F	VF	XF	Unc	BU
1995	—	—	—	10.00	—

KM# 73 DOLLAR **Composition:** Brass **Reverse:** Native rattle

Date	F	VF	XF	Unc	BU
1995	—	—	1.00	3.00	—

KM# 78 2 DOLLARS **Weight:** 42.4139 g. **Composition:** 0.9250 Silver 1.3636 oz. ASW **Subject:** Soft Coral Capital of the World **Obverse:** Queen's portrait **Reverse:** Denominatoin, coral industry scenes **Shape:** 1/3 circle segment

Date	Mintage	F	VF	XF	Unc	BU
1998 Proof	Est. 20,000	Value: 30.00				

Note: Part of a tri-nation, three coin matching set with Cook Islands and Western Samoa

KM# 81 5 DOLLARS **Weight:** 20.0000 g. **Composition:** 0.5000 Silver .3215 oz. ASW **Subject:** Protect Our World **Obverse:** Bust of young Queen Elizabeth II right **Reverse:** Heron, fish and tree **Edge:** Reeded

Date	Mintage	F	VF	XF	Unc	BU
1993 Proof	25,000	Value: 15.00				

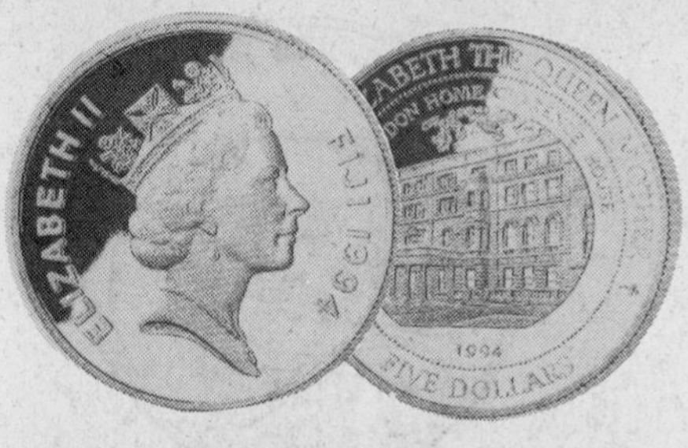

KM# 69 5 DOLLARS **Weight:** 20.0000 g. **Composition:** 0.5000 Silver .3215 oz. ASW **Subject:** Queen Mother's London House **Obverse:** Bust of young Queen Elizabeth II right **Reverse:** Clarence House

Date	Mintage	F	VF	XF	Unc	BU
1994 Proof	Est. 50,000	Value: 15.00				

KM# 80 5 DOLLARS **Weight:** 31.4400 g. **Composition:** 0.9250 Silver .9350 oz. ASW **Subject:** Millennium 2000 **Obverse:** Bust of young Queen Elizabeth II right **Reverse:** Native, map and branch **Shape:** 5-sided

Date	F	VF	XF	Unc	BU
1999 Proof	—	Value: 25.00			

KM# 40 10 DOLLARS **Weight:** 30.3000 g. **Composition:** 0.9250 Silver .9012 oz. ASW **Subject:** Queen's Silver Jubilee

Date	Mintage	F	VF	XF	Unc	BU
1977 Proof	3,010	Value: 18.50				

KM# 41 10 DOLLARS **Weight:** 28.2800 g. **Composition:** 0.5000 Silver .4547 oz. ASW **Subject:** Conservation **Reverse:** Pink-billed parrot finch

Date	Mintage	F	VF	XF	Unc	BU
1978	3,582	—	—	—	22.50	—

KM# 41a 10 DOLLARS **Weight:** 28.2800 g. **Composition:** 0.9250 Silver .8411 oz. ASW **Subject:** Conservation **Reverse:** Pink-billed parrot finch

Date	Mintage	F	VF	XF	Unc	BU
1978 Proof	4,026	Value: 30.00				

KM# 46 10 DOLLARS **Weight:** 28.4400 g. **Composition:** 0.5000 Silver .4572 oz. ASW **Subject:** 10th Anniversary of Independence **Reverse:** Prince Charles

Date	Mintage	F	VF	XF	Unc	BU
1980	5,001	—	—	—	12.50	—

KM# 46a 10 DOLLARS **Weight:** 30.4800 g. **Composition:** 0.9250 Silver .9066 oz. ASW **Subject:** 10th Anniversary of Independence **Reverse:** Prince Charles

Date	Mintage	F	VF	XF	Unc	BU
1980 Proof	3,001	Value: 20.00				

KM# 48 10 DOLLARS **Weight:** 30.0000 g. **Composition:** 0.9250 Silver .8922 oz. ASW **Subject:** Wedding of Prince Charles and Lady Diana **Obverse:** Queen's portrait right

Date	Mintage	F	VF	XF	Unc	BU
1981 Proof	5,000	Value: 20.00				

KM# 55 10 DOLLARS **Weight:** 28.2800 g. **Composition:** 0.9250 Silver .8411 oz. ASW **Subject:** 25th Anniversary - World Wildlife Fund **Obverse:** Queen's portrait right **Reverse:** Fijian ground frog

Date	Mintage	F	VF	XF	Unc	BU
1986 Proof	Est. 25,000	Value: 27.50				

KM# 60 10 DOLLARS **Weight:** 28.2800 g. **Composition:** 0.9250 Silver .8411 oz. ASW **Subject:** Save the Children Fund **Reverse:** Children reading by lantern light

Date	Mintage	F	VF	XF	Unc	BU
1991 Proof	20,000	Value: 20.00				

KM# 62 10 DOLLARS **Weight:** 28.2800 g. **Composition:** 0.9250 Silver .8411 oz. ASW **Subject:** 40th Anniversary - Coronation of Queen Elizabeth II

Date	Mintage	F	VF	XF	Unc	BU
1993 Proof	Est. 10,000	Value: 20.00				

KM# 63 10 DOLLARS **Weight:** 31.1035 g. **Composition:** 0.9250 Silver .9250 oz. ASW **Subject:** Discovery of Fiji **Reverse:** Cameo of Abel J. Tasman upper right, ships below

Date	Mintage	F	VF	XF	Unc	BU
1993 Proof	10,000	Value: 20.00				

KM# 64 10 DOLLARS **Weight:** 31.1035 g. **Composition:** 0.9250 Silver .9250 oz. ASW **Subject:** Discovery of Fiji **Reverse:** Cameo of William Bligh upper right, long boat with sailors

Date	Mintage	F	VF	XF	Unc	BU
1993 Proof	10,000	Value: 20.00				

KM# 66 10 DOLLARS **Weight:** 31.4600 g. **Composition:** 0.9250 Silver .9357 oz. ASW **Subject:** Protect Our World

Date	F	VF	XF	Unc	BU
1993 Proof	—	Value: 20.00			

KM# 67 10 DOLLARS **Weight:** 31.4600 g. **Composition:** 0.9250 Silver .9357 oz. ASW **Series:** 1996 Olympics **Reverse:** Judo match

Date	Mintage	F	VF	XF	Unc	BU
1993 Proof	20,000	Value: 20.00				

KM# 68 10 DOLLARS **Weight:** 31.6400 g. **Composition:** 0.9250 Silver .9409 oz. ASW **Subject:** World Cup Soccer **Reverse:** Soccer player

Date	F	VF	XF	Unc	BU
1993 Proof	— Value: 22.50				

KM# 70 10 DOLLARS **Weight:** 31.4700 g. **Composition:** 0.9250 Silver .9359 oz. ASW **Subject:** Lunar Module "Eagle" **Obverse:** Queen's portrait right **Reverse:** Lunar module on moon

Date	Mintage	F	VF	XF	Unc	BU
1994 Proof	Est. 10,000	Value: 27.50				

KM# 74 10 DOLLARS **Weight:** 31.3700 g. **Composition:** 0.9250 Silver .9329 oz. ASW **Subject:** Endangered Wildlife **Obverse:** Queen's portrait right **Reverse:** Fantail on branch

Date	F	VF	XF	Unc	BU
1995 Proof	— Value: 30.00				

KM# 75 10 DOLLARS **Weight:** 34.4600 g. **Composition:** 0.9250 Silver .9357 oz. ASW **Subject:** Silver Jubilee of Independence **Obverse:** Queen's portrait right **Reverse:** Coat of arms

Date	F	VF	XF	Unc	BU
1995 Proof	— Value: 22.50				

KM# 79 10 DOLLARS **Weight:** 31.5200 g. **Composition:** 0.9250 Silver .9368 oz. ASW **Series:** Olympic Games 1996 **Obverse:** Queen's portrait right **Reverse:** Two sailboarders

Date	F	VF	XF	Unc	BU
1995 Proof	— Value: 27.50				

KM# 86 10 DOLLARS **Weight:** 31.3500 g. **Composition:** 0.9250 Silver 0.9323 oz. ASW **Subject:** Queen Elizabeth II and The Queen Mother - Move to Buckingham Palace **Obverse:** Bust of Queen Elizabeth II right **Reverse:** 1/2 bust of soldier at right in front of Buckingham Palace **Edge:** Reeded **Size:** 38.7 mm.

Date	F	VF	XF	Unc	BU
1995 Proof	— Value: 22.50				

KM# 90 10 DOLLARS **Weight:** 28.5000 g. **Composition:** 0.9250 Silver 0.8476 oz. ASW **Subject:** Queen's 70th Birthday **Obverse:** Queen's portrait **Reverse:** Native dancer **Edge:** Reeded **Size:** 38.5 mm.

Date	F	VF	XF	Unc	BU
1996 Proof	— Value: 50.00				

KM# 85 10 DOLLARS **Weight:** 28.2800 g. **Composition:** 0.9250 Silver 0.841 oz. ASW **Subject:** UNICEF **Obverse:** Bust of Queen Elizabeth II right **Reverse:** Two young folk dancers **Edge:** Reeded **Size:** 38.6 mm.

Date	Mintage	F	VF	XF	Unc	BU
1997 Proof	25,000	Value: 17.50				

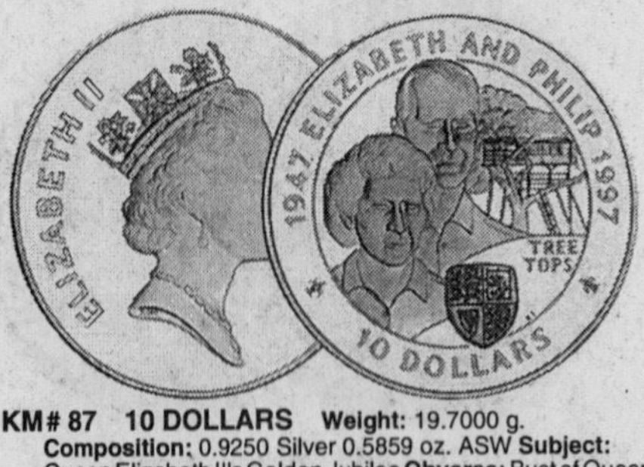

KM# 87 10 DOLLARS **Weight:** 19.7000 g. **Composition:** 0.9250 Silver 0.5859 oz. ASW **Subject:** Queen Elizabeth II's Golden Jubilee **Obverse:** Bust of Queen Elizabeth II right **Reverse:** Queen Elizabeth II left front, Philip behind, Tree Tops in background, gold-plated arms bottom right **Edge:** Reeded **Size:** 33.9 mm.

Date	F	VF	XF	Unc	BU
1997 Proof	— Value: 22.50				

KM# 76 10 DOLLARS **Weight:** 31.3300 g. **Composition:** 0.9250 Silver .9317 oz. ASW **Subject:** Endangered Wildlife **Obverse:** Queen's portrait right **Reverse:** Banded iguana

Date	F	VF	XF	Unc	BU
1997 Proof	— Value: 30.00				

KM# 82 10 DOLLARS **Weight:** 31.6200 g. **Composition:** 0.9250 Silver .9404 oz. ASW **Subject:** HMS Providence **Obverse:** Queen's portrait **Reverse:** Sail powered war ship **Edge:** Reeded **Size:** 38.6 mm.

Date	F	VF	XF	Unc	BU
2001 Proof	— Value: 22.50				

KM# 83 10 DOLLARS **Weight:** 28.2800 g. **Composition:** 0.9250 Silver 0.841 oz. ASW **Subject:** Queen Elizabeth II - 50 Years of Reign **Obverse:** Queen's head right **Reverse:** Cloth draped sword hilt, legend and denomination **Rev. Legend:** Defender of the Faith... **Edge:** Reeded **Size:** 38.6 mm.

Date	Mintage	F	VF	XF	Unc	BU
2002 Proof	15,000	Value: 22.50				

KM# 84 10 DOLLARS **Weight:** 28.2800 g. **Composition:** 0.9250 Silver 0.841 oz. ASW **Subject:** Queen Elizabeth II - 50th Year of Reign **Obverse:** Queen's head right **Reverse:** Four man chorus, legend, and denomination **Rev. Legend:** Westminster Abbey June 1953. **Edge:** Reeded **Size:** 38.6 mm.

Date	Mintage	F	VF	XF	Unc	BU
2002 Proof	15,000	Value: 22.50				

KM# 42 20 DOLLARS **Weight:** 35.0000 g. **Composition:** 0.5000 Silver .5627 oz. ASW **Subject:** Conservation **Obverse:** Queen's portrait right **Reverse:** Golden cowrie

Date	Mintage	F	VF	XF	Unc	BU
1978	3,584	—	—	—	30.00	—

KM# 42a 20 DOLLARS **Weight:** 35.0000 g. **Composition:** 0.9250 Silver 1.0409 oz. ASW **Subject:** Conservation **Obverse:** Queen's portrait right **Reverse:** Golden cowrie

Date	Mintage	F	VF	XF	Unc	BU
1978 Proof	3,869	Value: 35.00				

KM# 34 25 DOLLARS **Weight:** 48.6000 g. **Composition:** 0.9250 Silver 1.4455 oz. ASW **Subject:** 100th Anniversary - Cession to Great Britian **Obverse:** Queen's portrait right

Date	Mintage	F	VF	XF	Unc	BU
1974	2,400	—	—	—	32.50	—
1974 Proof	8,299	Value: 18.50				

KM# 37 25 DOLLARS **Weight:** 48.6000 g. **Composition:** 0.9250 Silver 1.4455 oz. ASW **Obverse:** Queen's portrait right **Reverse:** King Cakobau

Date	Mintage	F	VF	XF	Unc	BU
1975	836	—	—	—	45.00	—
1975 Proof	5,157	Value: 25.00				

KM#57 25 DOLLARS **Weight:** 7.7750 g. **Composition:** 0.7500 Gold .1875 oz. AGW **Reverse:** Balikula mint mark of Pacific Sovereign Mint, Fijian thatched temple **Note:** Dates are privy marks; 1990 - Boar Tusks; 1991 - War Fan; 1992 - ?.

Date	Mintage	F	VF	XF	Unc	BU
ND(1990)	443	—	—	—	150	—
ND(1991)	512	—	—	—	150	—
ND(1992)	50	—	—	—	200	—

KM# 58 50 DOLLARS **Weight:** 15.5500 g. **Composition:** 0.7500 Gold .3750 oz. AGW **Reverse:** Balikula mint mark of Pacific Sovereign Mint, Fijian warrior **Note:** Dates are privy marks; 1990 - Boar Tusks; 1991 - War Fan; 1992 - ?.

Date	Mintage	F	VF	XF	Unc	BU
ND(1990)	168	—	—	—	275	—
ND(1991)	141	—	—	—	275	—
ND(1992)	43	—	—	—	350	—

KM# 88 50 DOLLARS **Weight:** 1000.0000 g. **Composition:** 0.9990 Silver 32.1186 oz. ASW **Subject:** 70th Birthday of Queen Elizabeth II **Obverse:** Bust of Queen Elizabeth II right. **Reverse:** Standing 3/4 Queen Mother at left, Queen Elizabeth II at right. **Edge:** Reeded. **Size:** 100 mm. **Note:** Illustration reduced. Actual size: 100mm.

Date	Mintage	F	VF	XF	Unc	BU
1996 Proof	99	Value: 600				

KM#72 50 DOLLARS **Weight:** 7.7760 g. **Composition:** 0.5833 Gold .1458 oz. AGW **Subject:** Olympics **Reverse:** Two field hockey players

Date	F	VF	XF	Unc	BU
1996	—	—	—	80.00	—

KM# 35 100 DOLLARS **Weight:** 31.3600 g. **Composition:** 0.5000 Gold .5042 oz. AGW **Subject:** 100th Anniversary - Cession to Great Britain **Obverse:** Similar to 250 Dollars KM#43

Date	Mintage	F	VF	XF	Unc	BU
1974	1,109	—	—	—	200	—
1974 Proof	2,321	Value: 235				

KM# 38 100 DOLLARS **Weight:** 31.3000 g. **Composition:** 0.5000 Gold .5032 oz. AGW **Obverse:** Similar to 250 Dollars KM#43 **Reverse:** King Cakobau

Date	Mintage	F	VF	XF	Unc	BU
1975	593	—	—	—	240	—
1975 Proof	3,197	Value: 255				

KM# 59 100 DOLLARS **Weight:** 31.1000 g. **Composition:** 0.7500 Gold .7500 oz. AGW **Reverse:** Balikula mint mark of Pacific Sovereign Mint **Note:** Dates are privy marks; 1990 - Boar Tusks; 1991 - War Fan; 1992 - ?.

Date	Mintage	F	VF	XF	Unc	BU
ND(1990)	161	—	—	—	550	—
ND(1991)	131	—	—	—	550	—
ND(1992)	41	—	—	—	650	—

KM# 65 100 DOLLARS **Weight:** 7.5000 g. **Composition:** 0.9170 Gold .2209 oz. AGW **Subject:** Discovery of Fiji **Reverse:** James Cook

Date	Mintage	F	VF	XF	Unc	BU
1993 Proof	3,000	Value: 150				

KM# 47 200 DOLLARS **Weight:** 15.9800 g. **Composition:** 0.9170 Gold .4712 oz. AGW **Subject:** 10th Anniversary of Independence **Reverse:** Prince Charles

Date	Mintage	F	VF	XF	Unc	BU
1980	500	—	—	—	245	—
1980 Proof	1,166	Value: 200				

KM# 56 200 DOLLARS Weight: 15.9800 g. **Composition:** 0.9170 Gold .4712 oz. AGW **Subject:** 25th Anniversary - World Wildlife Fund **Obverse:** Similar to 10 cents, KM#31 **Reverse:** Ogmodon

Date	Mintage	F	VF	XF	Unc	BU
1986 Proof	5,000	Value: 300				

KM# 61 200 DOLLARS Weight: 10.0000 g. **Composition:** 0.9170 Gold .2948 oz. AGW **Subject:** Save the Children Fund

Date	Mintage	F	VF	XF	Unc	BU
1991 Proof	32,000	Value: 200				

KM# 43 250 DOLLARS Weight: 33.4370 g. **Composition:** 0.9000 Gold .9676 oz. AGW **Subject:** Conservation **Reverse:** Banded iguana

Date	Mintage	F	VF	XF	Unc	BU
1978	810	—	—	—	500	—
1978 Proof	252	Value: 800				

TRIAL STRIKES

KM#	Date	Mintage	Identification	Mkt Val
TS1	1974	—	100 Dollars. Bronze. KM35.	750
TS2	1974	—	Cent. Bronze. Fijian planting taro.	200
TS3	1974	—	Cent. Copper-Nickel. Fijian planting taro.	250

MINT SETS

KM#	Date	Mintage	Identification	Issue Price	Mkt Val
MSA1	1934 (3)	—	KM3-5	—	600
MSB1	1969 (6)	—	KM27-32	—	6.00
MS1	1976 (7)	5,001	KM27-32, 36	9.00	12.50
MS2	1976 (6)	—	KM27-31, 36	—	6.50
MS3	1978 (6)	4,006	KM28-31, 36, 39	4.50	8.00
MS4	1978 (3)	—	KM41-43	444	550
MS5	1978 (2)	—	KM41-42	44.00	50.00
MS6	1983 (6)	3,000	KM27-31, 36	5.00	4.50
MS7	1984 (6)	5,000	KM27-31, 36	3.60	4.50
MS8	1990 (8)	—	KM49a-54a	—	5.00
MS9	1990 (3)	—	KM57-59	905	975

PROOF SETS

KM#	Date	Mintage	Identification	Issue Price	Mkt Val
PS1	1969 (6)	10,000	KM#27-32	7.20	7.00
PS2	1976 (7)	3,023	KM#27a-32a, 36a	87.50	40.00
PS3	1978 (6)	2,000	KM#28-31, 36, 39	31.00	20.00
PS4	1978 (2)	—	KM#41a, 42a	76.00	55.00
PS5	1978 (3)	—	KM#41a, 42a, 43	726	865
PS6	1980 (6)	2,500	KM#28-31, 36, 39	45.00	20.00
PS7	1982 (6)	3,000	KM#28-31, 36, 39	32.00	20.00
PS8	1983 (6)	3,000	KM#27-31, 36	27.00	20.00
PS9	1993 (3)	—	KM#63-65	370	350

FINLAND

The Republic of Finland, the third most northerly state of the European continent, has an area of 130,559 sq. mi. (338,127 sq. km.) and a population of 5.1 million. Capital: Helsinki. Lumbering, shipbuilding, metal and woodworking are the leading industries. Paper, timber, woodpulp, plywood and metal products are exported.

The Finns, who probably originated in the Volga region of Russia, took Finland from the Lapps late in the 7th century. They were conquered in the 12th century by Eric IX of Sweden, and brought into contact with Western Christendom. In 1809, Sweden was conquered by Alexander I of Russia, and the peace terms gave Finland to Russia which became a grand duchy within the Russian Empire until Dec. 6, 1917, when, shortly after the Bolshevik revolution it declared its independence. After a brief but bitter civil war between the Russian sympathizers and Finnish nationalists in which the Whites (nationalists) were victorious, a new constitution was adopted, and on Dec. 6, 1917 Finland was established as a republic. In 1939 Soviet troops invaded Finland over disputed territorial concessions which were later granted in the peace treaty of 1940. When the Germans invaded Russia, Finland became involved and in the Armistice of 1944 lost the Petsamo area to the Soviets.

RULERS

Alexander II, 1855-1881
Alexander III, 1881-1894

Nicholas II, 1894-1917

MONETARY SYSTEM

100 Pennia = 1 Markka

Commencing 1963

100 Old Markka = 1 New Markka

MINT MARKS

H - Birmingham 1921
Heart (h) - Copenhagen 1922
No mm – Helsinki

MINTMASTERS INITIALS

Letter	Date	Name
H	1948-1958	Peippo Uolevi Helle
H-M	1990`	Raimo Heino & Raimo Makkonen
K	1976-1983	Timo Koivuranta
K-H	1977, 1979	Timo Koivuranta & Heikki Haivaoja (Designer)
K-M	1983	Timo Koivuranta & Pertti Makinen
K-N	1978	Timo Koivuranta & Antti Neuvonen
K-T	1982	Timo Koivuranta & Erja Tielinen
L	1885-1912	Johan Conrad Lihr
L	1948	Vesa Uolevi Liuhto
L-M	1991	Arto Lappalainen & Raimo Makkonen
L-M	2000	Maija Lavonen & Raimo Makkonen
M	1987	Raimo Makkonen
M-G	1998	Raimo Makkonen & Henrik Gummerus
M-L	1997	Raimo Makkonen & Tero Lounas
M-L-L	1995	Raimo Makkonen & Arto Lappalainen & Marita Lappalainen
M-L-M	1989	Marjo Lahtinen & Raimo Makkonen
M-O	1998	Raimo Makkonen & Harri Ojala
M-S	1992, 1997	Raimo Makkonen & Erkki Salmela
N	1983-1987	Tapio Nevalainen
P-M	1989-1991, 1994-1995, 1997, 2000	Reijo Paavilainen & Raimo Makkonen
P-N	1985	Reijo Paavilainen & Tapio Nevalainen
P-V-M	1999	Juhani Pallasmaa, Jukka Veistola & Raimo Makkonen
R-M	1999	Jarkko Roth & Raimo Makkonen
S	1912-1947	Isak Gustaf Sundell
S	1958-1975	Allan Alarik Soiniemi
S-H	1967-1971	Allan Alarik Soiniemi & Heikki Haivaoja (Designer)
S-J	1960	Allan Alarik Soiniemi & Toivo Jaatinen
S-M	1995	Terho Sakki & Raimo Makkonen
T-M	1996, 2000	Erja Tielinen & Raimo Makkonen

GRAND DUCHY

DECIMAL COINAGE

KM# 13 PENNI Weight: 1.2800 g. **Composition:** Copper **Obverse:** Monogram of Nicholas II **Reverse:** Value, date **Size:** 15 mm.

Date	Mintage	F	VF	XF	Unc	BU
1901	1,520,000	0.75	1.25	2.50	8.00	—
1902	1,000,000	0.75	1.25	2.50	10.00	—
1903 Small 3	1,145,000	0.75	1.25	2.50	10.00	—
1903 Large 3	Inc. above	1.50	2.50	5.00	12.00	—
1904	500,000	2.50	5.00	10.00	20.00	—
1905	1,390,000	0.50	1.00	2.00	6.00	—
1906	1,020,000	0.50	1.00	2.00	5.00	—
1907 Normal 7	2,490,000	0.75	1.25	2.50	4.00	—
1907 Without serif on 7 arm	Inc. above	0.30	0.75	1.75	4.00	—
1908	950,000	0.50	1.00	3.00	7.00	—
1909	3,060,000	0.25	0.65	1.25	2.50	—
1911	2,550,000	0.25	0.65	1.25	2.50	—
1912	2,450,000	0.25	0.65	1.25	2.50	—
1913	1,650,000	0.25	0.65	1.25	3.00	—
1914	1,900,000	0.25	0.65	1.25	3.50	—
1915	2,250,000	0.25	0.65	1.25	2.50	—
1916	3,040,000	0.25	0.50	1.00	2.00	—

KM# 15 5 PENNIA Weight: 6.4000 g. **Composition:** Copper **Obverse:** Monogram of Nicholas II **Reverse:** Value, date **Size:** 25 mm.

Date	Mintage	F	VF	XF	Unc	BU
1901	990,000	1.00	5.00	15.00	80.00	—
1905	620,000	2.00	10.00	30.00	100	—
1906	960,000	1.00	5.00	15.00	80.00	—
1907	770,000	2.00	10.00	40.00	120	—
1908	1,660,000	0.75	2.50	10.00	40.00	—
1910	60,000	25.00	50.00	100	200	—
1911	1,050,000	0.75	2.50	6.00	30.00	—
1912	460,000	1.50	5.00	25.00	75.00	—
1913	1,060,000	0.65	1.25	4.00	15.00	—
1914	820,000	0.65	1.25	3.00	15.00	—
1915	2,080,000	0.30	0.75	3.00	10.00	—
1916	4,470,000	0.30	0.75	3.00	10.00	—
1917	4,070,000	0.30	0.75	3.00	10.00	—

KM# 14 10 PENNIA Weight: 12.8000 g. **Composition:** Copper **Obverse:** Monogram of Nicholas II **Reverse:** Value and date in wreath **Size:** 30 mm.

Date	Mintage	F	VF	XF	Unc	BU
1905	500,000	2.00	10.00	50.00	150	—
1907	503,000	2.00	10.00	50.00	150	—
1908	320,000	1.50	10.00	30.00	100	—
1909	180,000	3.00	20.00	80.00	200	—
1910	241,000	1.50	7.50	25.00	80.00	—
1911	370,000	1.00	5.00	15.00	50.00	—
1912	191,000	1.50	7.50	20.00	80.00	—
1913	150,000	2.50	10.00	50.00	150	—
1914	605,000	0.75	1.50	10.00	30.00	—
1915	420,000	0.50	1.00	5.00	15.00	—
1916	1,952,000	0.50	1.00	3.00	10.00	—
1917	1,600,000	0.75	1.50	4.00	12.00	—

KM# 6.2 25 PENNIA Weight: 1.2747 g. **Composition:** 0.7500 Silver .0307 oz. ASW **Obverse:** Coat of arms **Reverse:** Value and date in wreath **Size:** 16 mm. **Note:** Dentilated border.

Date	Mintage	F	VF	XF	Unc	BU
1901 L	993,000	1.00	2.00	8.00	35.00	—
1902 L	210,000	3.00	10.00	30.00	100	—
1906 L	281,000	2.00	5.00	15.00	60.00	—
1907 L	590,000	1.00	2.00	5.00	25.00	—
1908 L	340,000	1.00	2.50	15.00	40.00	—
1909 L	1,099,000	0.75	1.50	5.00	15.00	—

Date	Mintage	F	VF	XF	Unc	BU
1910 L	392,000	2.50	5.00	15.00	50.00	—
1913 S	832,000	0.50	1.00	1.50	3.00	—
1915 S	2,400,000	0.50	0.75	1.00	1.50	—
1916 S	6,392,000	0.50	0.75	1.00	1.50	—
1917 S	5,820,000	0.50	0.75	1.00	1.50	—

KM# 2.2 50 PENNIA **Weight:** 2.5494 g. **Composition:** 0.7500 Silver .0615 oz. ASW **Obverse:** Coat of arms **Reverse:** Value and date in wreath **Size:** 18.6 mm. **Note:** Dentilated border.

Date	Mintage	F	VF	XF	Unc	BU
1907 L	260,000	1.00	3.00	30.00	90.00	—
1908 L	353,000	0.75	2.00	10.00	30.00	—
1911 L	616,000	0.75	1.25	2.50	5.00	—
1914 S	600,000	0.75	1.00	1.50	4.00	—
1915 S	1,000,000	0.75	1.00	1.50	2.50	—
1916 S	4,752,000	0.75	1.00	1.50	2.50	—
1917 S	3,972,000	0.75	1.00	1.50	2.50	—

KM# 3.2 MARKKA **Weight:** 5.1828 g. **Composition:** 0.8680 Silver .1446 oz. ASW **Obverse:** Coat of arms, fineness around (text in Finnish) **Size:** 24 mm. **Note:** Obverse text translates to: "94.48 pieces from one pound of fine silver." Dentilated border.

Date	Mintage	F	VF	XF	Unc	BU
1907 L	350,000	2.00	3.00	8.00	25.00	—
1908 L	153,000	4.00	10.00	25.00	50.00	—
1915 S	1,212,000	2.00	3.00	6.00	10.00	—

KM# 7.2 2 MARKKAA **Weight:** 10.3657 g. **Composition:** 0.8680 Silver .2893 oz. ASW **Obverse:** Coat of arms, fineness around (Finnish text) **Size:** 27.5 mm. **Note:** Obverse text translates to: "47.24 pieces from one pound of fine silver." Dentilated border.

Date	Mintage	F	VF	XF	Unc	BU
1905 L	24,000	60.00	100	300	850	—
1906 L	225,000	5.00	8.00	40.00	80.00	—
1907 L	125,000	10.00	20.00	60.00	100	—
1908 L	124,000	5.00	15.00	30.00	60.00	—

KM# 8.2 10 MARKKAA **Weight:** 3.2258 g. **Composition:** 0.9000 Gold .0933 oz. AGW **Obverse:** Wide eagle coat of arms **Reverse:** Value and date, fineness around **Size:** 18.9 mm. **Note:** Regal issues; similar to 20 Markkaa, KM#9.2.

Date	Mintage	F	VF	XF	Unc	BU
1904 L	102,000	225	250	300	350	—
1905 L	43,000	1,000	1,200	1,400	1,700	—
1913 L	396,000	50.00	60.00	70.00	85.00	—

KM# 9.2 20 MARKKAA **Weight:** 6.4516 g. **Composition:** 0.9000 Gold .1867 oz. AGW **Obverse:** Wide eagle coat of arms **Reverse:** Value and date, fineness around **Size:** 21.3 mm. **Note:** Regal issues.

Date	Mintage	F	VF	XF	Unc	BU
1903 L	112,000	75.00	85.00	110	140	—
1904 L	188,000	75.00	85.00	110	130	—
1910 L	201,000	75.00	85.00	110	130	—
1911 L	161,000	75.00	85.00	110	140	—
1912 L	881,000	1,000	1,500	2,500	4,000	—
1912 S	Inc. above	70.00	80.00	100	115	—
1913 S	214,000	70.00	80.00	100	115	—

CIVIL WAR COINAGE

Kerenski Government Issue

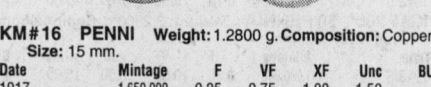

KM# 16 PENNI **Weight:** 1.2800 g. **Composition:** Copper **Size:** 15 mm.

Date	Mintage	F	VF	XF	Unc	BU
1917	1,650,000	0.25	0.75	1.00	1.50	—

KM# 17 5 PENNIA **Weight:** 6.4000 g. **Composition:** Copper **Size:** 25 mm.

Date	F	VF	XF	Unc	BU
1917	0.30	0.75	2.50	5.00	—

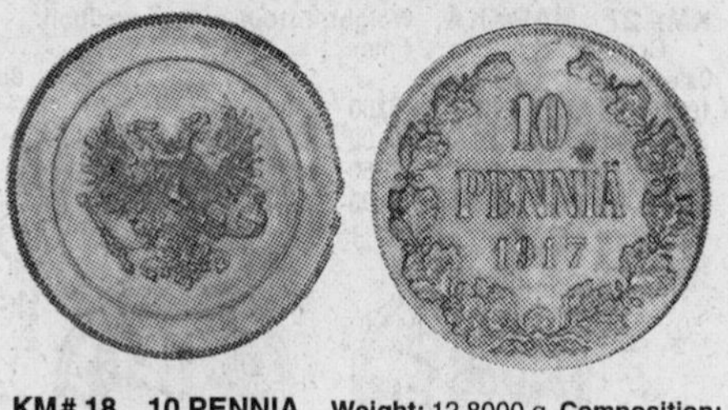

KM# 18 10 PENNIA **Weight:** 12.8000 g. **Composition:** Copper **Size:** 30 mm.

Date	F	VF	XF	Unc	BU
1917	0.50	1.00	2.50	7.50	—

KM# 19 25 PENNIA **Weight:** 1.2747 g. **Composition:** 0.7500 Silver .0307 oz. ASW **Obverse:** Crown above eagle removed **Size:** 16 mm.

Date	Mintage	F	VF	XF	Unc	BU
1917 S	2,310,000	—	BV	1.00	1.50	—

KM# 20 50 PENNIA **Weight:** 2.5494 g. **Composition:** 0.7500 Silver .0615 oz. ASW **Obverse:** Crown above eagle removed **Size:** 18.6 mm.

Date	Mintage	F	VF	XF	Unc	BU
1917 S	570,000	—	BV	1.25	2.00	—

CIVIL WAR COINAGE

Liberated Finnish Government Issue

KM# 21.1 5 PENNIA **Weight:** 2.5000 g. **Composition:** Copper **Obverse:** Wreath knot centered between 9 and 1 of date

Date	Mintage	F	VF	XF	Unc	BU
1918	35,000	20.00	30.00	45.00	60.00	—

KM# 21.2 5 PENNIA **Weight:** 2.5000 g. **Composition:** Copper **Obverse:** Wreath knot above second 1 in 1918

Date	F	VF	XF	Unc	BU
1918	50.00	100	175	350	—

Note: This type was unofficially struck outside of Finland in the early 1920's

REPUBLIC

DECIMAL COINAGE

KM# 23 PENNI **Weight:** 1.0000 g. **Composition:** Copper **Size:** 14 mm.

Date	Mintage	F	VF	XF	Unc	BU
1919	1,200,000	0.25	0.65	1.75	3.00	—
1920	720,000	0.25	0.65	1.75	3.00	—
1921	510,000	0.35	1.00	2.00	4.00	—
1922	1,060,000	0.25	0.65	1.75	3.00	—
1923	990,000	0.25	0.65	1.75	3.00	—
1924	2,180,000	0.25	0.65	1.75	3.00	—

KM# 22 5 PENNIA **Weight:** 2.5000 g. **Composition:** Copper **Size:** 18 mm.

Date	Mintage	F	VF	XF	Unc	BU
1918	4,270,000	0.10	0.25	1.00	4.00	—
1919	4,640,000	0.10	0.25	1.00	4.00	—
1920	7,710,000	0.10	0.25	1.00	3.00	—
1921	5,910,000	0.10	0.25	1.00	3.00	—
1922	8,540,000	0.10	0.25	1.00	3.00	—
1927	1,520,000	0.75	1.50	3.50	15.00	—
1928	2,110,000	0.25	0.50	1.50	8.00	—
1929	1,500,000	0.25	0.50	1.50	8.00	—
1930	2,140,000	0.75	1.25	3.00	12.00	—
1932	2,130,000	0.15	0.50	1.00	4.00	—
1934	2,180,000	0.15	0.50	1.00	4.00	—
1935	1,610,000	0.15	0.35	1.00	3.00	—
1936	2,610,000	0.15	0.35	1.00	3.00	—
1937	3,830,000	0.10	0.25	1.00	3.00	—
1938	4,300,000	0.10	0.25	1.00	3.00	—
1939	2,270,000	0.10	0.25	1.00	3.00	—
1940	1,610,000	0.25	0.50	1.50	5.00	—

KM# 64.1 5 PENNIA **Weight:** 1.2700 g. **Composition:** Copper **Size:** 16 mm. **Note:** Punched center hole.

Date	Mintage	F	VF	XF	Unc	BU
1941	5,950,000	0.10	0.20	0.50	1.25	—
1942	4,280,000	0.10	0.20	0.50	1.25	—
1943	1,530,000	0.10	0.50	1.25	2.50	—

KM# 64.2 5 PENNIA **Composition:** Copper **Size:** 16 mm. **Note:** Without punched center hole. These issues were not authorized by the government and any that exist were illegally removed from the mint.

Date	F	VF	XF	Unc	BU
1941	25.00	30.00	70.00	100	—
1942	25.00	30.00	70.00	100	—
1943	50.00	70.00	100	125	—

KM# 24 10 PENNIA **Weight:** 5.0000 g. **Composition:** Copper **Size:** 22 mm.

Date	Mintage	F	VF	XF	Unc	BU
1919	3,670,000	0.10	0.25	1.00	5.00	—
1920	2,380,000	0.10	0.25	1.00	5.00	—
1921	3,970,000	0.10	0.25	1.00	5.00	—
1922	2,180,000	0.10	0.25	2.00	7.00	—
1923	910,000	1.00	2.00	10.00	30.00	—
1924	1,350,000	0.25	0.50	3.00	12.00	—
1926	1,690,000	0.25	0.50	2.00	10.00	—
1927	1,330,000	0.50	1.00	5.00	15.00	—
1928	1,006,000	0.50	1.00	2.50	10.00	—
1929	1,560,000	0.35	0.85	2.00	7.00	—
1930	650,000	0.75	1.50	7.00	15.00	—
1931	1,040,000	1.00	2.00	10.00	30.00	—
1934	1,680,000	0.35	0.85	2.00	7.00	—
1935	1,690,000	0.15	0.25	1.00	5.00	—

Date	Mintage	F	VF	XF	Unc	BU
1936	2,009,999	0.15	0.25	1.00	5.00	—
1937	2,420,000	0.10	0.25	0.50	3.50	—
1938	2,940,000	0.10	0.25	0.50	3.50	—
1939	2,100,000	0.10	0.25	0.50	3.50	—
1940	2,009,999	0.25	0.50	1.00	5.00	—

KM# 33.1 10 PENNIA Weight: 2.5500 g. Composition: Copper Size: 18.5 mm.

Date	Mintage	F	VF	XF	Unc	BU
1941	3,610,000	0.10	0.25	0.50	1.25	—
1942	4,970,000	0.10	0.25	0.50	1.25	—
1943	1,860,000	0.25	0.75	1.50	2.50	—

KM# 33.2 10 PENNIA Weight: 2.6000 g. Composition: Copper Size: 18.5 mm. Note: Without punched center hole. These issues were not authorized by the government and any that exist were illegally removed from the mint.

Date	F	VF	XF	Unc	BU
1941	20.00	30.00	50.00	75.00	—
1942	20.00	30.00	50.00	75.00	—
1943	30.00	50.00	70.00	100	—

KM# 34.2 10 PENNIA Composition: Iron Note: Without punched center hole. These issues were not authorized by the government and any that exist were illegally removed from the mint.

Date	F	VF	XF	Unc	BU
1943	30.00	50.00	70.00	100	—
1944	30.00	50.00	70.00	100	—
1945	50.00	70.00	100	150	—

KM# 34.1 10 PENNIA Weight: 1.1200 g. Composition: Iron Size: 16 mm. Note: Reduced planchet size.

Date	Mintage	F	VF	XF	Unc	BU
1943	1,430,000	0.10	0.25	1.00	5.00	—
1944	3,040,000	0.10	0.25	1.00	5.00	—
1945	1,810,000	0.25	0.50	2.00	10.00	—

KM# 25 25 PENNIA Weight: 1.2700 g. Composition: Copper-Nickel Size: 16 mm.

Date	Mintage	F	VF	XF	Unc	BU
1921 H	20,096,000	0.10	0.25	1.00	3.00	—
1925 S	1,250,000	0.50	1.50	10.00	20.00	—
1926 S	2,820,000	0.40	1.25	5.00	12.00	—
1927 S	1,120,000	0.50	1.50	10.00	20.00	—
1928 S	2,920,000	0.40	1.00	5.00	12.00	—
1929 S	200,000	2.00	4.00	20.00	40.00	—
1930 S	1,090,000	0.50	1.50	5.00	15.00	—
1934 S	1,260,000	0.40	0.75	2.00	7.00	—
1935 S	2,190,000	0.30	0.50	1.50	6.00	—
1936 S	2,300,000	0.20	0.40	1.00	3.00	—
1937 S	4,019,999	0.20	0.40	1.00	3.00	—
1938 S	4,500,000	0.20	0.40	1.00	3.00	—
1939 S	2,712,000	0.20	0.40	1.00	3.00	—
1940 S	4,840,000	0.15	0.30	0.75	2.00	—

KM# 25a 25 PENNIA Weight: 1.2700 g. Composition: Copper Size: 16 mm.

Date	Mintage	F	VF	XF	Unc	BU
1940 S	72,000	0.50	1.00	3.00	12.00	—
1941 S	5,980,000	0.10	0.35	2.00	5.00	—
1942 S	6,464,000	0.10	0.35	2.00	5.00	—
1943 S	4,912,000	0.25	0.50	2.00	7.00	—

KM# 25b 25 PENNIA Composition: Iron Size: 16 mm.

Date	Mintage	F	VF	XF	Unc	BU
1943 S	2,700,000	0.15	0.50	2.00	10.00	—
1944 S Small closed 4's	5,480,000	0.15	0.50	1.50	7.00	—
1944 S Large open 4's	Inc. above	0.15	0.50	1.50	7.00	—
1945 S	6,810,000	0.25	0.75	2.00	8.00	—

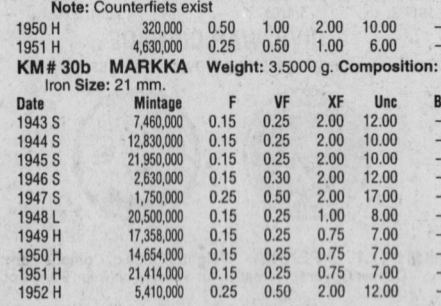

KM# 26 50 PENNIA Weight: 2.5500 g. Composition: Copper-Nickel Size: 18.5 mm.

Date	Mintage	F	VF	XF	Unc	BU
1921 H	10,072,000	0.15	0.30	1.00	3.00	—
1923 S	6,000,000	0.25	1.00	3.00	12.00	—
1929 S	984,000	0.75	1.50	10.00	35.00	—
1934 S	612,000	1.00	2.50	10.00	35.00	—
1935 S	610,000	1.00	2.50	7.50	30.00	—
1936 S	1,520,000	0.30	0.50	2.00	7.50	—
1937 S	2,350,000	0.15	0.25	1.00	5.00	—
1938 S	2,330,000	0.15	0.25	1.00	5.00	—
1939 S	1,280,000	0.15	0.25	1.00	5.00	—
1940 S	3,152,000	0.15	0.25	1.00	3.00	—

KM# 26a 50 PENNIA Weight: 2.5500 g. Composition: Copper Size: 18.5 mm.

Date	Mintage	F	VF	XF	Unc	BU
1940 S	480,000	1.25	2.50	5.00	15.00	—
1941 S	3,860,000	0.15	0.40	2.00	5.00	—
1942 S	5,900,000	0.15	0.40	2.00	5.00	—
1943 S	3,140,000	0.25	0.50	2.00	5.00	—

KM# 26b 50 PENNIA Weight: 2.2500 g. Composition: Iron Size: 18.5 mm.

Date	Mintage	F	VF	XF	Unc	BU
1943 S	1,580,000	0.25	0.50	2.50	15.00	—
1944 S	7,600,000	0.15	0.40	2.00	12.00	—
1945 S	4,700,000	0.15	0.40	2.00	12.00	—
1946 S	2,632,000	0.30	0.50	2.00	12.00	—
1947 S	1,748,000	0.50	1.50	5.00	20.00	—
1948 L	1,112,000	3.00	5.00	12.00	25.00	—

KM# 27 MARKKA Weight: 5.1000 g. Composition: Copper-Nickel Size: 24 mm.

Date	Mintage	F	VF	XF	Unc	BU
1921 H	10,048,000	0.50	1.00	2.50	5.00	—
1922 Heart	10,000,000	1.00	2.00	5.00	15.00	—
1923 S	1,780,000	7.50	15.00	25.00	50.00	—
1924 S	3,270,000	3.00	7.00	15.00	30.00	—

KM# 30 MARKKA Weight: 4.0000 g. Composition: Copper-Nickel Size: 21 mm. Note: Reduced size.

Date	Mintage	F	VF	XF	Unc	BU
1928 S	3,000,000	0.15	0.30	3.00	20.00	—
1929 S	3,862,000	0.15	0.30	3.00	20.00	—
1930 S	10,284,000	0.15	0.30	1.00	12.00	—
1931 S	2,830,000	0.15	0.30	1.00	12.00	—
1932 S	4,140,000	0.15	0.30	1.00	10.00	—
1933 S	4,032,000	0.15	0.30	1.00	10.00	—
1936 S	562,000	0.50	1.50	7.00	30.00	—
1937 S	4,930,000	0.15	0.30	1.00	6.00	—
1938 S	4,410,000	0.15	0.25	1.00	6.00	—
1939 S	3,070,000	0.15	0.25	1.00	6.00	—
1940 S	3,372,000	0.15	0.25	1.00	6.00	—

Note: Coins dated 1928S, 1929S and 1930S are known to be restruck on 1921-24, KM#27 coins. (1928S: 2 or 3 known

KM# 30a MARKKA Weight: 4.0000 g. Composition: Copper Size: 21 mm.

Date	Mintage	F	VF	XF	Unc	BU
1940 S	84,000	1.50	3.50	8.00	20.00	—
1941 S	8,970,000	0.15	0.50	1.25	6.00	—
1942 S	11,200,000	0.15	0.50	1.00	4.00	—
1943 S	7,460,000	0.15	0.50	1.25	5.00	—
1949 H	250	2,000	3,500	5,000	7,000	
Note: Counterfeits exist						
1950 H	320,000	0.50	1.00	2.00	10.00	—
1951 H	4,630,000	0.25	0.50	1.00	6.00	—

KM# 30b MARKKA Weight: 3.5000 g. Composition: Iron Size: 21 mm.

Date	Mintage	F	VF	XF	Unc	BU
1943 S	7,460,000	0.15	0.25	2.00	12.00	—
1944 S	12,830,000	0.15	0.25	2.00	10.00	—
1945 S	21,950,000	0.15	0.25	2.00	10.00	—
1946 S	2,630,000	0.15	0.30	2.00	12.00	—
1947 S	1,750,000	0.25	0.50	2.00	17.00	—
1948 L	20,500,000	0.15	0.25	1.00	8.00	—
1949 H	17,358,000	0.15	0.25	0.75	7.00	—
1950 H	14,654,000	0.15	0.25	0.75	7.00	—
1951 H	21,414,000	0.15	0.25	0.75	7.00	—
1952 H	5,410,000	0.25	0.50	2.00	12.00	—

KM# 36 MARKKA Weight: 1.1500 g. Composition: Iron Size: 16 mm.

Date	Mintage	F	VF	XF	Unc	BU
1952	22,050,000	0.15	0.35	1.00	7.00	—
1953	28,618,000	0.15	0.35	1.00	7.00	—

KM# 36a MARKKA Weight: 1.1500 g. Composition: Nickel Plated Iron Size: 16 mm.

Date	Mintage	F	VF	XF	Unc	BU
1953	6,000,000	5.00	8.00	12.50	20.00	—
1954	36,400,000	—	0.10	0.25	0.50	—
1955	38,100,000	—	0.10	0.25	0.50	—
1956	35,600,000	—	0.10	0.25	1.00	—
1957	29,100,000	—	0.10	0.25	0.50	—
1958	19,940,000	0.10	0.20	0.35	0.70	—
1959 Thick letters	23,920,000	—	0.10	0.25	0.50	—
1959 Thin letters	Inc. above	—	0.10	0.25	1.00	—
1960	22,020,000	—	0.10	0.25	0.50	—
1961	32,220,000	—	0.10	0.25	0.50	—
1962	29,040,000	—	0.10	0.25	0.50	—

KM# 31 5 MARKKAA Weight: 4.5000 g. Composition: Aluminum-Bronze Size: 23 mm.

Date	Mintage	F	VF	XF	Unc	BU
1928 S	580,000	30.00	50.00	120	250	—
1929 S	Inc. above	30.00	50.00	100	220	—
1930 S	592,000	0.75	1.75	10.00	50.00	—
1931 S	3,090,000	0.50	1.00	6.00	30.00	—
1932 S	964,000	5.00	10.00	100	200	—
1933 S	1,050,000	0.50	1.00	10.00	40.00	—
1935 S	440,000	1.50	3.00	12.00	50.00	—
1936 S	470,000	1.50	3.00	12.00	50.00	—
1937 S	1,032,000	0.50	1.00	6.00	20.00	—
1938 S	912,000	0.50	1.00	6.00	20.00	—
1939 S	752,000	0.50	1.00	6.00	20.00	—
1940 S	820,000	1.25	2.75	10.00	30.00	—
1941 S	1,452,000	0.50	1.00	5.00	12.00	—
1942 S	1,390,000	0.50	1.00	7.00	15.00	—
1946 S	618,000	3.50	7.00	20.00	60.00	—

KM# 31a 5 MARKKAA Weight: 4.5500 g. Composition: Brass Size: 23 mm.

Date	Mintage	F	VF	XF	Unc	BU
1946 S	5,538,000	0.20	0.50	1.50	3.50	—
1947 S	6,550,000	0.25	0.75	2.00	6.00	—
1948 L	8,210,000	0.25	0.50	1.50	5.00	—
1949 H Thin H	11,014,000	0.50	1.00	3.00	5.00	—
1949 H Wide H	Inc. above	0.20	0.50	1.50	3.50	—
1950 H	4,760,000	0.20	0.50	1.50	3.50	—
1951 H	7,800,000	0.20	0.50	1.50	3.50	—
1952 H	1,210,000	2.50	6.00	12.00	25.00	—

KM# 37 5 MARKKAA Weight: 2.5500 g. Composition: Iron Size: 18 mm.

Date	Mintage	F	VF	XF	Unc	BU
1952	10,820,000	0.20	0.35	2.00	8.00	—
1953	9,772,000	0.20	0.35	3.00	10.00	—

KM# 37a 5 MARKKAA Weight: 2.5500 g. Composition: Nickel Plated Iron Size: 18 mm.

Date	Mintage	F	VF	XF	Unc	BU
1953	Inc. above	45.00	75.00	100	150	—
1954	6,696,000	—	0.20	0.35	1.50	—
1955	9,894,000	—	0.20	0.35	1.50	—
1956	8,220,000	—	0.20	0.35	1.00	—
1957	4,276,000	—	0.20	0.35	1.00	—
1958	3,300,000	—	0.20	0.35	2.00	—
1959	5,874,000	—	0.20	0.35	1.00	—
1960	3,066,000	0.10	0.25	0.35	2.00	—
1961	7,254,000	0.10	0.25	0.35	1.50	—
1962	4,542,000	0.50	1.00	3.00	6.00	—

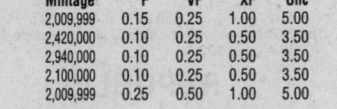

KM# 63 10 MARKKAA **Weight:** 8.0000 g. **Composition:** Aluminum-Bronze **Size:** 27 mm.

Date	Mintage	F	VF	XF	Unc	BU
1928 S	730,000	2.50	5.00	25.00	130	—
1929 S	Inc. above	2.00	4.00	20.00	100	—
1930 S	260,000	1.00	2.50	15.00	80.00	—
1931 S	1,530,000	1.00	2.50	10.00	70.00	—
1932 S	1,010,000	1.00	2.50	8.00	55.00	—
1934 S	154,000	1.50	3.00	20.00	100	—
1935 S	81,000	3.00	5.00	20.00	100	—
1936 S	304,000	2.00	4.00	20.00	80.00	—
1937 S	181,000	1.50	2.50	10.00	70.00	—
1938 S	631,000	0.75	1.50	10.00	60.00	—
1939 S	133,000	4.00	8.00	15.00	60.00	—

KM# 38 10 MARKKAA **Weight:** 3.0000 g. **Composition:** Aluminum-Bronze **Size:** 20 mm.

Date	Mintage	F	VF	XF	Unc	BU
1952 H	6,390,000	0.20	0.50	2.00	7.00	—
1953 H	22,650,000	0.15	0.35	1.00	5.00	—
1954 H	2,452,000	0.50	1.00	5.00	15.00	—
1955 H	2,342,000	0.20	0.50	3.00	10.00	—
1956 H	4,240,000	0.20	0.40	2.00	7.00	—
1958 H Thin 1	3,292,000	2.00	5.00	12.00	30.00	—
1958 H Wide 1	Inc. above	0.20	0.40	1.00	5.00	—
1960 S	740,000	1.00	2.00	7.00	15.00	—
1961 S	3,580,000	0.20	0.50	1.50	5.00	—
1961 S Wide 1	Inc. above	2.00	4.00	10.00	20.00	—
1962 S	1,852,000	0.30	0.60	1.75	5.00	—

Note: The "1" in the denomination on all 1952 to 1956 issues is the thin variety. 1960 issues are the wide variety, and 1961's and 1962's are thin. Varieties exist in root length of tree

KM# 32 20 MARKKAA **Weight:** 13.0000 g. **Composition:** Aluminum-Bronze **Size:** 31 mm.

Date	Mintage	F	VF	XF	Unc	BU
1931 S	16,000	25.00	35.00	50.00	80.00	—
1932 S	14,000	30.00	40.00	60.00	100	—
1934 S	390,000	2.00	10.00	25.00	80.00	—
1935 S	250,000	2.00	10.00	25.00	80.00	—
1936 S	110,000	3.00	10.00	30.00	120	—
1937 S	510,000	1.50	2.00	15.00	50.00	—
1938 S	360,000	1.50	2.00	15.00	50.00	—
1939 S	960,000	1.00	2.00	6.00	20.00	—

KM# 39 20 MARKKAA **Weight:** 4.5000 g. **Composition:** Aluminum-Bronze **Size:** 25.5 mm.

Date	Mintage	F	VF	XF	Unc	BU
1952 H	83,000	7.00	10.00	20.00	40.00	—
1953 H	2,880,000	0.25	0.50	3.00	15.00	—
1954 H	17,034,000	0.15	0.50	2.00	10.00	—
1955 H	2,800,000	0.25	0.50	3.00	15.00	—
1956 H	2,540,000	0.25	0.50	3.00	15.00	—
1957 H	1,050,000	0.50	1.00	5.00	17.00	—
1958 H	515,000	2.50	5.00	15.00	30.00	—
1959 S	1,580,000	0.25	0.50	3.00	15.00	—
1960 S	3,850,000	0.15	0.50	2.00	8.00	—
1961 S	4,430,000	0.15	0.50	2.00	8.00	—
1962 S	2,280,000	0.15	0.50	1.50	6.00	—

KM# 40 50 MARKKAA **Weight:** 5.5000 g. **Composition:** Aluminum-Bronze **Size:** 25 mm.

Date	Mintage	F	VF	XF	Unc	BU
1952 H	991,000	2.00	5.00	15.00	30.00	—
1953 H	10,300,000	0.25	0.50	3.00	10.00	—
1954 H	1,170,000	2.00	5.00	15.00	30.00	—
1955 H	583,000	2.50	5.00	20.00	40.00	—
1956 H	792,000	2.00	5.00	15.00	30.00	—
1958 H	242,000	25.00	30.00	40.00	60.00	—
1960 S	110,000	25.00	35.00	50.00	70.00	—
1961 S	1,811,000	1.00	2.00	5.00	10.00	—
1962 S	405,000	2.00	4.00	10.00	17.00	—

KM# 28 100 MARKKAA **Weight:** 4.2105 g. **Composition:** 0.9000 Gold .1218 oz. AGW **Size:** 18.5 mm.

Date	Mintage	F	VF	XF	Unc	BU
1926 S	50,000	—	450	650	850	—

KM# 41 100 MARKKAA **Weight:** 5.2000 g. **Composition:** 0.5000 Silver .0836 oz. ASW **Size:** 24 mm.

Date	Mintage	F	VF	XF	Unc	BU
1956 H	3,012,000	—	BV	1.50	3.00	—
1957 H	3,012,000	—	BV	1.50	3.00	—
1958 H	1,704,000	BV	1.50	2.50	4.00	—
1959 H	1,270,000	3.00	5.00	10.00	15.00	—
1960 S	290,000	3.50	5.50	8.00	12.00	—

KM# 29 200 MARKKAA **Weight:** 8.4210 g. **Composition:** 0.9000 Gold .2436 oz. AGW **Size:** 22.5 mm.

Date	Mintage	F	VF	XF	Unc	BU
1926 S	50,000	—	650	900	1,100	—

KM# 42 200 MARKKAA **Weight:** 8.3000 g. **Composition:** 0.5000 Silver .1334 oz. ASW **Size:** 27.5 mm.

Date	Mintage	F	VF	XF	Unc	BU
1956 H	1,552,000	—	BV	2.50	5.00	—
1957 H	2,157,000	—	BV	2.50	5.00	—
1958 H	1,477,000	BV	2.50	4.00	7.00	—
1958 S	34,000	400	500	600	700	—
1959 S	70,000	25.00	30.00	40.00	60.00	—

KM# 35 500 MARKKAA **Weight:** 12.0000 g. **Composition:** 0.5000 Silver .1929 oz. ASW **Size:** 32 mm.

Date	Mintage	F	VF	XF	Unc	BU
1951 H	19,000	200	250	325	400	—
1952 H	586,000	20.00	25.00	35.00	45.00	—

KM# 43 1000 MARKKAA **Weight:** 14.0000 g. **Composition:** 0.8750 Silver .3938 oz. ASW **Subject:** Markka Currency System Centennial - Snellman **Size:** 30 mm.

Date	Mintage	F	VF	XF	Unc	BU
1960 S-J	201,000	7.00	10.00	15.00	20.00	—

REFORM COINAGE

100 Old Markka = 1 New Markka 1963

KM# 44 PENNI **Weight:** 1.6000 g. **Composition:** Copper **Size:** 15.8 mm.

Date	Mintage	F	VF	XF	Unc	BU
1963	171,333,000	—	0.10	0.25	1.50	—

Note: Struck at Leningrad Mint

Date	Mintage	F	VF	XF	Unc	BU
1964	49,300,000	—	0.10	0.50	2.00	—
1965	43,112,000	—	0.10	0.50	2.00	—
1966	36,880,000	—	0.10	0.50	2.00	—
1967	62,792,000	—	0.10	0.50	2.00	—
1968	73,416,000	—	—	0.50	2.00	—
1969	51,748,000	—	—	0.50	2.00	—

KM# 44a PENNI **Weight:** 0.4500 g. **Composition:** Aluminum **Size:** 15.8 mm.

Date	Mintage	F	VF	XF	Unc	BU
1969	28,524,000	—	—	0.50	2.00	—
1970	85,140,000	—	—	0.20	1.00	—
1971	70,240,000	—	—	0.20	1.00	—
1972	95,096,000	—	—	0.20	1.00	—
1973	115,532,000	—	—	0.20	0.50	—
1974	100,132,000	—	—	0.20	0.50	—
1975	111,906,000	—	—	0.20	0.50	—
1976	34,965,000	—	—	0.20	0.50	—
1977	61,393,000	—	—	0.20	0.50	—
1978	90,132,000	—	—	0.20	0.50	—
1979	33,388,000	—	—	0.20	0.50	—

KM# 45 5 PENNIA **Weight:** 2.6000 g. **Composition:** Copper **Size:** 18.5 mm.

Date	Mintage	F	VF	XF	Unc	BU
1963	60,320,000	—	0.10	0.50	1.50	—
1964	4,634,000	0.50	1.00	2.00	7.50	—
1965	10,264,000	—	0.10	0.50	1.50	—
1966	8,064,000	—	0.10	0.50	1.50	—
1967	9,968,000	—	0.10	0.50	1.50	—
1968	6,144,000	—	0.10	0.50	1.50	—
1969	3,598,000	—	0.15	0.50	2.00	—
1970	13,772,000	—	0.10	0.25	1.00	—

Date	Mintage	F	VF	XF	Unc	BU
1971	20,010,000	—	—	0.25	1.00	—
1972	24,122,000	—	—	0.25	1.00	—
1973	25,644,000	—	—	0.25	1.00	—
1974	21,530,000	—	—	0.25	1.00	—
1975	25,010,000	—	—	0.25	1.00	—
1976	25,551,000	—	—	0.25	1.00	—
1977	1,489,000	—	0.10	0.50	1.50	—

KM# 45a 5 PENNIA **Weight:** 0.8000 g. **Composition:** Aluminum **Size:** 18 mm.

Date	Mintage	F	VF	XF	Unc	BU
1977	30,552,000	—	—	0.15	0.50	—
1978	26,112,000	—	—	0.15	0.50	—
1979	40,042,000	—	—	0.15	0.50	—
1980	60,026,000	—	—	0.15	0.50	—
1981	2,044,000	—	0.20	0.40	1.00	—
1982	10,012,000	—	—	0.25	0.75	—
1983	33,885,000	—	—	—	0.25	—
1984	25,001,000	—	—	—	0.25	—
1985	25,000,000	—	—	—	0.25	—
1986	20,000,000	—	—	—	0.25	—
1987	2,020,000	—	—	—	0.25	—
1988	33,005,000	—	—	—	0.15	—
1989	2,200,000	—	—	—	0.25	—
1990	2,506,000	—	—	—	0.25	—

KM# 46 10 PENNIA **Weight:** 3.0000 g. **Composition:** Aluminum-Bronze **Size:** 20 mm.

Date	Mintage	F	VF	XF	Unc	BU
1963 S	38,420,000	—	0.10	0.25	1.50	—
1964 S	6,926,000	—	0.10	0.50	2.00	—
1965 S	4,524,000	—	0.10	0.25	1.50	—
1966 S	3,094,000	—	0.10	0.25	1.50	—
1967 S	1,050,000	0.10	0.20	2.00	5.00	—
1968 S	3,004,000	—	0.10	0.20	1.50	—
1969 S	5,046,000	—	—	0.20	1.50	—
1970 S	3,996,000	—	—	0.20	1.50	—
1971 S	15,026,000	—	—	0.10	1.00	—
1972 S	19,900,000	—	—	0.10	1.00	—
1973 S	9,196,000	—	—	0.10	1.00	—
1974 S	8,930,000	—	—	0.10	1.00	—
1975 S	15,064,000	—	—	0.10	0.50	—
1976 K	10,063,000	—	—	0.10	0.50	—
1977 K	10,043,000	—	—	0.10	0.50	—
1978 K	10,062,000	—	—	0.10	0.50	—
1979 K	13,072,000	—	—	0.10	0.50	—
1980 K	23,654,000	—	—	0.10	0.50	—
1981 K	30,036,000	—	—	0.10	0.50	—
1982 K	35,548,000	—	—	0.10	0.50	—

KM# 46a 10 PENNIA **Weight:** 1.0000 g. **Composition:** Aluminum **Size:** 20 mm.

Date	Mintage	F	VF	XF	Unc	BU
1983 K	6,320,000	—	—	0.25	1.00	—
1983 N	4,191,000	—	—	0.25	1.00	—
1984 N	20,061,000	—	—	0.10	0.50	—
1985 N	20,000,000	—	—	0.10	0.50	—
1986 N	15,000,000	—	—	0.10	0.50	—
1987 N	1,400,000	—	—	0.25	1.00	—
1987 M	8,654,000	—	—	0.25	1.00	—
1988 M	23,197,000	—	—	0.10	0.50	—
1989 M	2,400,000	—	—	0.25	0.50	—
1990 M	2,254,000	—	—	0.25	0.50	—

KM# 65 10 PENNIA **Weight:** 1.8000 g. **Composition:** Copper-Nickel **Obverse:** Flower pods and stems **Size:** 16.3 mm.

Date	Mintage	F	VF	XF	Unc	BU
1990 M	338,100,000	—	—	0.10	0.15	—
1991 M	263,899,000	—	—	0.10	0.15	—
1992 M	136,131,000	—	—	0.10	0.15	—
1993 M	56,206,000	—	—	0.10	0.15	—
1994 M	59,946,000	—	—	0.10	0.15	—
1994 M Proof	5,000	Value: 7.00				
1995 M	85,000,000	—	—	0.10	0.15	—
1995 M Proof	3,000	Value: 7.00				
1996 M	123,000,000	—	—	0.10	0.15	—
1996 M Proof	1,200	Value: 7.00				
1997 M	43,406,000	—	—	0.10	0.15	—
1997 M Proof	2,000	Value: 7.00				
1998 M	95,000,000	—	—	0.10	0.15	—
1998 M Proof	2,000	Value: 7.00				
1999 M	—	—	—	0.10	0.15	—
1999 M Proof	—	Value: 7.00				
2000 M	—	—	—	—	0.15	—
2000 M Proof	—	Value: 7.00				
2001 M	Inc. above	—	—	—	1.00	—
2001 M Proof	Inc. above	Value: 7.00				

KM# 47 20 PENNIA **Weight:** 4.5000 g. **Composition:** Aluminum-Bronze **Size:** 22.5 mm.

Date	Mintage	F	VF	XF	Unc	BU
1963 S	39,970,000	—	0.10	0.20	1.50	—
1964 S	4,248,000	0.50	1.00	2.50	5.00	—
1965 S	5,704,000	0.10	0.50	1.00	2.00	—
1966 S	4,085,000	0.10	0.50	1.00	2.00	—
1967 S	1,716,000	0.10	0.50	1.00	2.00	—
1968 S	1,330,000	0.10	0.50	1.00	2.00	—
1969 S	201,000	0.50	1.00	1.50	3.50	—
1970 S	230,000	0.50	1.00	1.50	3.50	—
1971 S	5,150,000	—	0.25	0.50	1.00	—

Note: Some coins dated 1971 are magnetic and command a higher premium

Date	Mintage	F	VF	XF	Unc	BU
1972 S	10,001,000	—	0.25	0.50	1.00	—
1973 S	9,462,000	—	0.25	0.50	1.00	—
1974 S	12,705,000	—	0.25	0.50	1.00	—
1975 S	12,068,000	—	0.25	0.50	1.00	—
1976 K	20,058,000	—	0.25	0.50	1.00	—
1977 K	10,063,000	—	0.25	0.50	1.00	—
1978 K	10,014,000	—	0.25	0.50	1.00	—
1979 K	7,513,000	—	0.25	0.50	1.00	—
1980 K	20,047,000	—	—	0.25	0.50	—
1981 K	30,002,000	—	—	0.25	0.50	—
1982 K	35,050,000	—	—	0.25	0.50	—
1983 K	7,113,000	—	—	0.25	0.50	—
1983 N	12,889,000	—	—	0.25	0.50	—
1984 N	20,029,000	—	—	0.25	0.50	—
1985 N	15,004,000	—	—	0.25	0.50	—
1986 N	20,001,000	—	—	0.25	0.50	—
1987 N	1,200,000	—	0.25	0.50	1.00	—
1987 M	25,670,000	—	—	0.25	0.50	—
1988 M	13,853,000	—	—	0.25	0.50	—
1989 M	40,695,000	—	—	0.25	0.50	—
1990 M	9,168,000	—	—	0.25	0.50	—

KM# 48 50 PENNIA **Weight:** 5.5000 g. **Composition:** Aluminum-Bronze **Size:** 25.0 mm.

Date	Mintage	F	VF	XF	Unc	BU
1963 S	17,316,000	—	0.20	0.50	3.00	—
1964 S	3,101,000	—	0.25	2.00	8.00	—
1965 S	1,667,000	—	0.20	1.00	4.00	—
1966 S	1,051,000	—	0.20	1.00	4.00	—
1967 S	400,000	0.25	0.50	2.00	5.00	—
1968 S	816,000	—	0.25	1.00	4.00	—
1969 S	1,341,000	—	0.20	0.50	3.00	—
1970 S	2,250,000	—	0.20	0.50	2.00	—
1971 S	10,003,000	—	0.20	0.50	1.50	—

Note: Some coins dated 1971 are magnetic and command a higher premium

Date	Mintage	F	VF	XF	Unc	BU
1972 S	7,892,000	—	0.20	0.50	1.50	—
1973 S	5,428,000	—	0.20	0.50	1.50	—
1974 S	5,049,000	—	0.20	0.50	1.50	—
1975 S	4,305,000	—	0.20	0.50	1.50	—
1976 K	7,022,000	—	0.20	0.50	1.50	—
1977 K	8,077,000	—	0.20	0.50	1.50	—
1978 K	8,048,000	—	0.20	0.50	1.50	—
1979 K	8,004,000	—	0.20	0.50	1.50	—
1980 K	5,349,000	—	0.20	0.50	1.50	—
1981 K	20,031,000	—	0.20	0.50	1.00	—
1982 K	5,042,000	—	0.20	0.50	1.00	—
1983 K	4,043,999	—	—	0.25	1.00	—
1983 N	1,016,000	—	0.20	0.50	1.50	—
1984 N	3,006,000	—	—	0.25	1.00	—
1985 N	10,000,000	—	—	0.25	1.00	—
1986 N	9,002,000	—	—	0.25	1.00	—
1987 N	700,000	—	0.30	0.75	1.50	—
1987 M	4,305,000	—	—	0.25	1.00	—
1988 M	14,735,000	—	—	0.25	1.00	—
1989 M	10,651,000	—	—	0.25	1.00	—
1990 M	5,391,000	—	—	0.50	2.00	—

KM# 66 50 PENNIA **Weight:** 3.3000 g. **Composition:** Copper-Nickel **Obverse:** Polar bear **Size:** 19.7 mm.

Date	Mintage	F	VF	XF	Unc	BU
1990 M	70,459,000	—	—	0.20	0.75	—
1991 M	90,480,000	—	—	0.20	0.75	—
1992 M	58,996,000	—	—	0.20	0.75	—
1993 M	10,066,000	—	—	0.20	0.75	—
1994 M	3,005,000	—	—	0.20	0.75	—
1994 M Proof	5,000	Value: 8.00				
1995 M	1,048,000	—	—	0.20	0.75	—
1995 M Proof	3,000	Value: 8.00				
1996 M	17,000,000	—	—	0.20	0.75	—
1996 M Proof	1,200	Value: 8.00				
1997 M	524,000	—	—	0.20	0.75	—
1997 M Proof	2,000	Value: 8.00				
1998 M	12,000,000	—	—	0.20	0.75	—
1998 M Proof	2,000	Value: 8.00				
1999 M	—	—	—	0.20	0.75	—
1999 M Proof	—	Value: 8.00				
2000 M	—	—	—	0.20	0.75	—
2000 M Proof	—	Value: 8.00				
2001 M	Inc. above	—	—	0.20	0.75	—
2001 M Proof	Inc. above	Value: 8.00				

KM# 49 MARKKA **Weight:** 6.4000 g. **Composition:** 0.3500 Silver .0720 oz. ASW **Size:** 24 mm.

Date	Mintage	F	VF	XF	Unc	BU
1964 S	9,999,000	BV	1.00	2.00	5.00	—
1965 S	15,107,000	BV	0.50	1.50	4.00	—
1966 S	15,183,000	BV	0.50	1.50	3.00	—
1967 S	6,249,000	BV	0.50	1.50	3.00	—
1968 S	3,063,000	BV	0.50	1.50	3.00	—

KM# 49A MARKKA **Weight:** 6.1000 g. **Composition:** Copper-Nickel **Size:** 24 mm.

Date	Mintage	F	VF	XF	Unc	BU
1969 S	1,308,000	0.25	0.50	1.00	2.00	—
1970 S	12,255,000	—	0.35	0.50	1.00	—
1971 S	19,676,000	—	0.35	0.50	1.00	—
1972 S	19,885,000	—	0.35	0.50	1.00	—
1973 S	17,060,000	—	0.35	0.50	1.00	—
1974 S	18,065,000	—	0.35	0.50	1.00	—
1975 S	11,523,000	—	0.35	0.50	1.00	—
1976 K	12,048,000	—	0.35	0.50	1.00	—
1977 K	10,077,000	—	0.35	0.50	1.00	—
1978 K	10,022,000	—	0.35	0.50	1.00	—
1979 K	11,311,000	—	0.35	0.50	1.00	—
1980 K	19,306,000	—	—	0.35	0.75	—
1981 K	32,003,000	—	—	0.35	0.75	—
1982 K	30,001,000	—	—	0.35	0.75	—
1983 K	8,074,999	—	—	0.35	0.75	—
1983 N	11,927,000	—	—	0.35	0.75	—
1984 N	15,000,000	—	—	0.35	0.75	—
1985 N	19,001,000	—	—	0.35	0.75	—
1986 N	10,000,000	—	—	0.35	0.75	—
1987 N	700,000	—	0.50	1.00	2.00	—
1987 M	9,303,000	—	—	0.35	0.75	—
1988 M	27,535,000	—	—	0.35	0.75	—
1989 M	37,520,000	—	—	0.35	0.75	—
1990 M	50,305,000	—	—	0.35	0.75	—
1991 M	15,026,000	—	—	0.35	0.75	—
1992 M	3,628,000	—	—	0.35	0.75	—
1993 M	1,036,000	—	—	0.50	1.00	—

KM# 76 MARKKA **Weight:** 4.9000 g. **Composition:** Aluminum-Bronze **Size:** 22 mm.

Date	Mintage	F	VF	XF	Unc	BU
1993 M	91,588,000	—	—	0.35	0.75	—
1994 M	152,011,000	—	—	0.35	0.75	—
1994 M Proof	5,000	Value: 10.00				
1995 M	40,008,000	—	—	0.35	0.75	—
1995 M Proof	3,000	Value: 10.00				
1996 M	21,000,000	—	—	0.35	0.75	—
1996 M Proof	1,200	Value: 10.00				
1997 M	23,775,200	—	—	0.35	0.75	—
1997 M Proof	2,000	Value: 10.00				
1998 M	—	—	—	0.35	0.75	—
1998 M Proof	2,000	Value: 10.00				
1999 M	—	—	—	0.35	0.75	—
1999 M Proof	—	Value: 10.00				
2000 M	—	—	—	0.35	0.75	—
2000 M Proof	—	Value: 10.00				
2001 M	Inc. above	—	—	0.35	0.75	—
2001 M Proof	Inc. above	Value: 10.00				

KM# 76a MARKKA **Composition:** Copper-Nickel

Date	Mintage	F	VF	XF	Unc	BU
1993 M In sets only	100,000	—	—	—	—	—

KM# 95 MARKKA **Weight:** 8.6400 g. **Composition:** 0.7500 Gold .2083 oz. AGW **Subject:** Last Markka Coin **Obverse:** National arms **Reverse:** Stylized tree with roots **Edge:** Reeded **Size:** 22 mm.

Date	Mintage	F	VF	XF	Unc	BU
2001 Proof	55,000	Value: 250				

KM# 106 MARKKA **Composition:** Copper Nickel **Subject:** Remebrance Markka **Obverse:** National arms **Reverse:** Denomination and pine tree **Edge:** Plain **Size:** 24.2 mm. **Note:** This coin is encased in acrylic resin and sealed in a display card.

Date	Mintage	F	VF	XF	Unc	BU
2001	500,000	—	—	—	5.00	—

KM# 53 5 MARKKAA **Weight:** 8.0000 g. **Composition:** Aluminum-Bronze **Obverse:** Icebreaker "Varma" **Size:** 26.3 mm.

Date	Mintage	F	VF	XF	Unc	BU
1972 S	400,000	1.50	2.00	2.50	4.00	—
1973 S	2,188,000	—	1.25	2.00	3.00	—
1974 S	300,000	—	1.25	2.00	3.00	—
1975 S	300,000	—	1.25	2.00	3.00	—
1976 K	400,000	—	1.25	2.00	3.00	—
1977 K	300,000	—	1.25	2.00	3.00	—
1978 K	300,000	—	1.25	2.00	3.00	—

KM# 57 5 MARKKAA **Weight:** 8.0000 g. **Composition:** Aluminum-Bronze **Obverse:** Icebreaker "Urho" **Size:** 26.3 mm.

Date	Mintage	F	VF	XF	Unc	BU
1979 K	2,005,000	—	—	1.50	2.25	—
1980 K	501,000	—	1.50	2.00	3.00	—
1981 K	1,009,000	—	—	1.50	2.25	—
1982 K	3,004,000	—	—	1.50	2.25	—
1983 K	8,776,000	—	—	1.50	2.25	—
1983 N	11,230,000	—	—	1.50	2.25	—
1984 N	15,001,000	—	—	1.50	2.25	—
1985 N	8,005,000	—	—	1.50	2.25	—
1986 N	5,006,000	—	—	1.50	2.25	—
1987 N	660,000	—	1.50	2.00	3.00	—
1987 M	2,348,000	—	—	1.50	2.25	—
1988 M	3,042,000	—	—	1.50	2.25	—
1989 M	10,175,000	—	—	1.50	2.25	—
1990 M	9,925,000	—	—	1.50	2.25	—
1991 M	9,910,000	—	—	2.00	3.00	—
1992 M	547,000	—	—	2.00	3.00	—
1993 M	911,000	—	—	2.00	3.00	—

KM# 73 5 MARKKAA **Weight:** 5.5000 g. **Composition:** Copper-Aluminum-Nickel **Obverse:** Lake Saimaa ringed seal **Size:** 24.5 mm.

Date	Mintage	F	VF	XF	Unc	BU
1992 M	800,000	—	—	—	3.50	—
1993 M	46,034,000	—	—	—	2.00	—
1994 M	19,003,000	—	—	—	2.00	—
1994 M Proof	5,000	Value: 12.00				
1995 M	9,016,000	—	—	—	2.50	—
1995 M Proof	3,000	Value: 12.00				
1996 M	7,000,000	—	—	—	2.50	—
1996 M Proof	1,200	Value: 12.00				
1997 M	537,700	—	—	2.00	3.00	—
1997 M Proof	2,000	Value: 12.00				
1998 M	—	—	—	—	2.50	—
1998 M Proof	2,000	Value: 12.00				
1999 M	—	—	—	—	2.50	—
1999 M Proof	—	Value: 12.00				
2000 M	—	—	—	—	2.50	—
2000 M Proof	—	Value: 12.00				
2001 M	Inc. above	—	—	—	2.50	—
2001 M	Inc. above	Value: 12.00				

KM# 50 10 MARKKAA **Weight:** 23.7500 g. **Composition:** 0.9000 Silver .6872 oz. ASW **Subject:** 50th Anniversary of Independence **Size:** 35 mm.

Date	Mintage	F	VF	XF	Unc	BU
1967 S-H	1,000,000	—	—	4.00	7.50	9.50

KM# 51 10 MARKKAA **Weight:** 22.7500 g. **Composition:** 0.5000 Silver .3657 oz. ASW **Subject:** Centennial - Birth of President Paasikivi **Size:** 35 mm.

Date	Mintage	F	VF	XF	Unc	BU
1970 S-H	600,000	—	—	3.00	5.00	7.00

KM# 52 10 MARKKAA **Weight:** 24.2000 g. **Composition:** 0.5000 Silver .3890 oz. ASW **Subject:** 10th European Athletic Championships **Size:** 35 mm.

Date	Mintage	F	VF	XF	Unc	BU
1971 S-H	1,000,000	—	—	3.00	5.00	7.00

KM# 54 10 MARKKAA **Weight:** 23.5000 g. **Composition:** 0.5000 Silver .3778 oz. ASW **Subject:** 75th Birthday of President Kekkonen **Size:** 35 mm.

Date	Mintage	F	VF	XF	Unc	BU
1975 S-H	1,000,000	—	—	3.00	5.00	7.00

KM# 55 10 MARKKAA **Weight:** 21.7800 g. **Composition:** 0.5000 Silver .3501 oz. ASW **Subject:** 60th Anniversary of Independence **Size:** 35 mm.

Date	Mintage	F	VF	XF	Unc	BU
1977 K-H	400,000	—	—	3.00	5.00	7.00

KM# 77 10 MARKKAA **Ring Composition:** Copper-Nickel **Center Composition:** Bi-Metallic Brass **Obverse:** Capercaillie bird **Size:** 27.25 mm. **Note:** Total weight 8.800 grams.

Date	Mintage	F	VF	XF	Unc	BU
1993 M	30,002,000	—	—	2.50	5.50	—
1994 M	19,979,000	—	—	2.50	5.50	—
1994 M Proof	5,000	Value: 18.00				
1995 M	4,008,000	—	—	2.75	6.00	—
1995 M Proof	3,000	Value: 18.00				
1996 M	3,300,000	—	—	3.00	6.50	—
1996 M Proof	1,200	Value: 18.00				
1997 M	—	—	—	3.00	6.50	—
1997 M Proof	2,000	Value: 18.00				
1998 M	—	—	—	3.00	6.50	—
1998 M Proof	2,000	Value: 18.00				
1999 M	—	—	—	3.00	6.50	—
1999 M Proof	—	Value: 18.00				
2000 M	—	—	—	3.00	6.50	—
2000 M Proof	—	Value: 18.00				
2001 M	Inc. above	—	—	3.00	6.50	—
2001 M Proof	Inc. above	Value: 18.00				

KM# 82 10 MARKKAA **Ring Composition:** Copper-Nickel **Center Composition:** Bi-Metallic Brass **Subject:** European Unity **Obverse:** Swan in flight **Size:** 27.25 mm. **Note:** Total weight 8.000 grams.

Date	Mintage	F	VF	XF	Unc	BU
1995 M	500,000	—	—	4.00	7.50	—

KM# 82a 10 MARKKAA **Ring Composition:** 0.9250 Silver **Center Composition:** 0.5850 Gold **Subject:** European Unity **Obverse:** Swan in flight **Size:** 27.25 mm. **Note:** Total weight 12.200 grams.

Date	Mintage	F	VF	XF	Unc	BU
1995 M Proof	2,000	Value: 750				

KM# 91a 10 MARKKAA **Ring Composition:** 0.7500 Gold**Center Weight:** 13.2000 g. **Center Composition:** 0.9250 Silver **Edge:** Lettered **Size:** 27.25 mm. **Note:** Total weight 13.200 grams.

Date	Mintage	F	VF	XF	Unc	BU
1999	3,000	—	—	—	450	550

KM# 91 10 MARKKAA **Ring Composition:** Copper-Nickel**Center Weight:** 8.8200 g. **Center Composition:** Brass **Obverse:** Fire breathing face **Reverse:** Denomination, pine branch **Size:** 27.25 mm. **Note:** Finnish Presidency of the EU. Total weight 12.200 grams.

Date	Mintage	F	VF	XF	Unc	BU
1999	100,000	—	—	5.00	8.50	—

KM# 56 25 MARKKAA **Weight:** 26.3000 g. **Composition:** 0.5000 Silver .4228 oz. ASW **Subject:** Winter Games in Lahti **Size:** 37 mm.

Date	Mintage	F	VF	XF	Unc	BU
1978 K-N	500,000	—	—	6.00	8.00	—

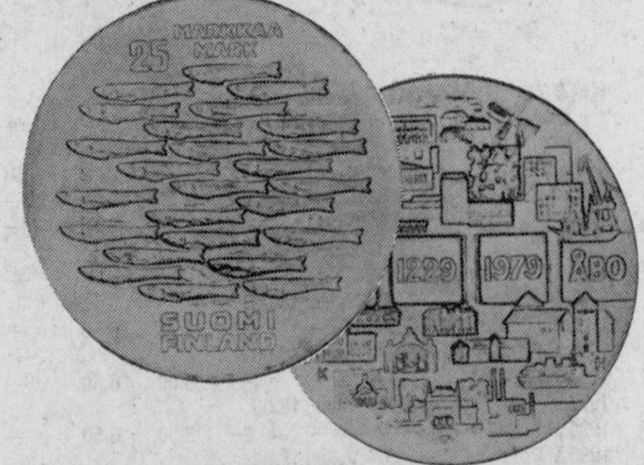

KM# 58 25 MARKKAA **Weight:** 26.3000 g. **Composition:** 0.5000 Silver .4228 oz. ASW **Subject:** 750th Anniversary of Turku **Size:** 37 mm.

Date	Mintage	F	VF	XF	Unc	BU
1979 K-H	300,000	—	—	6.00	8.00	—

KM# 85 25 MARKKAA **Ring Composition:** Copper-Nickel **Center Composition:** Brass **Subject:** 80th Anniversary of Independenceersary of Turku **Obverse:** Stylized landscape **Reverse:** Stylized city view **Size:** 35 mm. **Note:** Total weight 20.200 grams.

Date	Mintage	F	VF	XF	Unc	BU
ND(1997) M-L	100,000	—	—	—	12.00	—
ND(1997) M-L Proof	2,000	Value: 16.50				

KM# 96 25 MARKKAA **Ring Composition:** Copper-Nickel**Center Weight:** 20.2000 g. **Center Composition:** Brass **Subject:** First Nordic Ski Championship, "Lahti 2001" **Obverse:** Stylized woman's face **Reverse:** Female torso, landscape **Edge:** Plain **Size:** 35 mm.

Date	Mintage	F	VF	XF	Unc	BU
2001 Prooflike	100,000	—	—	—	25.00	—

KM# 59 50 MARKKAA **Weight:** 20.0000 g. **Composition:** 0.5000 Silver .3216 oz. ASW **Subject:** 80th Birthday of President Kekkonen **Size:** 30 mm.

Date	Mintage	F	VF	XF	Unc	BU
1981 K	500,000	—	—	10.00	12.00	14.50

KM# 60 50 MARKKAA **Weight:** 23.1000 g. **Composition:** 0.5000 Silver .3698 oz. ASW **Subject:** World Ice Hockey Championship Games **Size:** 35 mm.

Date	Mintage	F	VF	XF	Unc	BU
1982 K-T	400,000	—	—	12.00	14.00	16.50

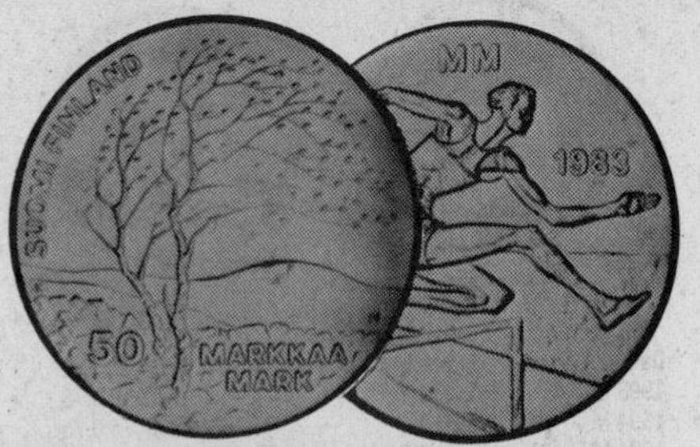

KM# 61 50 MARKKAA **Weight:** 21.8000 g. **Composition:** 0.5000 Silver .3537 oz. ASW **Subject:** 1st World Athletics Championships **Size:** 35 mm.

Date	Mintage	F	VF	XF	Unc	BU
1983 K-M	450,000	—	—	12.00	14.00	16.50

KM# 62 50 MARKKAA **Weight:** 19.9000 g. **Composition:** 0.5000 Silver .3216 oz. ASW **Subject:** National Epic - The Kalevala **Size:** 35 mm.

Date	Mintage	F	VF	XF	Unc	BU
1985 P-N	300,000	—	—	13.00	15.00	18.00

KM# 74 100 MARKKAA **Weight:** 24.0000 g. **Composition:** 0.8300 Silver .6405 oz. ASW **Subject:** World Ski Championship

Date	Mintage	F	VF	XF	Unc	BU
1989 M-L-M	100,000	—	—	25.00	35.00	—

KM# 75 100 MARKKAA **Weight:** 24.0000 g. **Composition:** 0.8300 Silver .6405 oz. ASW **Subject:** Pictorial Arts of Finland

Date	Mintage	F	VF	XF	Unc	BU
1989 P-M	100,000	—	—	25.00	35.00	40.00

KM# 67 100 MARKKAA **Weight:** 24.0000 g. **Composition:** 0.8300 Silver .6405 oz. ASW **Subject:** 50th Anniversary of Disabled War Veterans Association

Date	Mintage	F	VF	XF	Unc	BU
1990 P-M	100,000	—	—	25.00	35.00	40.00

KM# 68 100 MARKKAA Weight: 24.0000 g. **Composition:** 0.8300 Silver .6405 oz. ASW **Subject:** 350th Anniversary - University of Helsinki

Date	Mintage	F	VF	XF	Unc	BU
1990 H-M	150,000	—	—	25.00	40.00	45.00

KM# 69 100 MARKKAA Weight: 24.0000 g. **Composition:** 0.8300 Silver .6405 oz. ASW **Subject:** Ice Hockey World Championship Games

Date	Mintage	F	VF	XF	Unc	BU
1991 L-M	150,000	—	—	25.00	35.00	40.00
1991 L-M	200	Value: 350				

Note: Struck w/polished dies to prooflike quality and encapsulated in hard plastic 60 mm x 83 mm square. These pieces were given out as business gifts to selected mint visitors

KM# 70 100 MARKKAA Weight: 24.0000 g. **Composition:** 0.9250 Silver .7137 oz. ASW **Subject:** 70th Anniversary - Autonomy of Aland

Date	Mintage	F	VF	XF	Unc	BU
1991 P-M	—	—	—	25.00	35.00	40.00
1991 P-M	Est. 700	Value: 300				

Note: Encapsulated as KM#69 above, but struck to higher prooflike quality

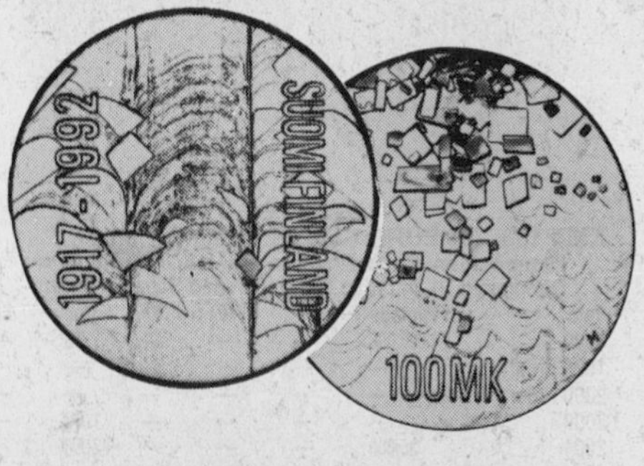

KM# 71 100 MARKKAA Weight: 24.0000 g. **Composition:** 0.9250 Silver .7137 oz. ASW **Subject:** 75th Anniversary of Independence

Date	Mintage	F	VF	XF	Unc	BU
1992 M-S	300,000	—	—	25.00	35.00	40.00

KM# 78 100 MARKKAA Weight: 24.0000 g. **Composition:** 0.9250 Silver .7137 oz. ASW **Subject:** Stadium of Friendship

Date	Mintage	F	VF	XF	Unc	BU
1994 P-M	80,000	—	—	—	35.00	40.00

Note: Encapsulated as KM#69 above, but struck to higher proof quality

Date	Mintage	F	VF	XF	Unc	BU
1994 P-M Proof	15,000	Value: 65.00				

KM# 80 100 MARKKAA Weight: 24.0000 g. **Composition:** 0.9250 Silver .7137 oz. ASW **Subject:** 100th Birthday - Artturi Ilmari Virtanen

Date	Mintage	F	VF	XF	Unc	BU
1995 S-M	40,000	—	—	—	35.00	40.00
1995 S-M Proof	3,000	Value: 65.00				

KM# 81 100 MARKKAA Weight: 24.0000 g. **Composition:** 0.9250 Silver .7137 oz. ASW **Subject:** 50th Anniversary - United Nations

Date	Mintage	F	VF	XF	Unc	BU
1995 P-M	40,000	—	—	—	35.00	40.00
1995 P-M Proof	3,000	Value: 65.00				

KM# 83 100 MARKKAA Weight: 24.0000 g. **Composition:** 0.9250 Silver .7137 oz. ASW **Subject:** Helene Schjerfbeck - Painter

Date	Mintage	F	VF	XF	Unc	BU
1996 T-M	300,000	—	—	—	35.00	40.00
1996 T-M Proof	3,000	Value: 65.00				

KM# 84 100 MARKKAA Weight: 22.0000 g. **Composition:** 0.9250 Silver .6543 oz. ASW **Subject:** 100th Birthday - Paavo Nurmi **Obverse:** Two gymnasts **Reverse:** Facial portrait and running Paavo Nurmi

Date	Mintage	F	VF	XF	Unc	BU
1997 M-S	45,000	—	—	—	35.00	40.00
1997 M-S Proof	6,500	Value: 65.00				

KM# 87 100 MARKKAA Weight: 22.0000 g. **Composition:** 0.9250 Silver .6543 oz. ASW **Subject:** 100th Birthday - Alvar Aalto **Obverse:** Walls above cliffs and denominations **Reverse:** Mature rye plants

Date	F	VF	XF	Unc	BU
1998 M-G	—	—	—	35.00	40.00
1998 M-G Proof	4,000	Value: 65.00			

KM# 88 100 MARKKAA Weight: 22.0000 g. **Composition:** 0.9250 Silver .6543 oz. ASW **Subject:** Suomenlinna Fortress **Obverse:** Stylized island view **Reverse:** Sailship and fortress gate

Date	Mintage	F	VF	XF	Unc	BU
1998 M-O	30,000	—	—	—	35.00	40.00
1998 M-O Proof	3,300	Value: 65.00				

KM# 89 100 MARKKAA Weight: 22.0000 g. **Composition:** 0.9250 Silver .6543 oz. ASW **Subject:** Jean Sibelius - Composer **Obverse:** Finlandia musical score **Reverse:** Sibelius head left

Date	Mintage	F	VF	XF	Unc	BU
1999 P-V-M	30,000	—	—	—	35.00	40.00
1999 P-V-M Proof	6,000	Value: 65.00				

KM# 92 100 MARKKAA Weight: 22.0000 g. **Composition:** 0.9250 Silver .6543 oz. ASW **Subject:** Jubilee Year 2000 **Obverse:** Turku Cathedral vault ceiling design **Reverse:** Leaf **Edge:** Plain

Date	Mintage	F	VF	XF	Unc	BU
2000 L-M	15,000	—	—	—	35.00	40.00
2000 L-M Proof	3,000	Value: 65.00				

KM# 93 100 MARKKAA **Weight:** 22.0000 g. **Composition:** 0.9250 Silver .6543 oz. ASW **Subject:** 450th Anniversary - Helsinki Cultural Capital **Obverse:** Symbolic column design **Reverse:** Carved city view **Edge:** Plain

Date	Mintage	F	VF	XF	Unc	BU
2000 P-M	10,000	—	—	—	35.00	40.00
2000 P-M Proof	8,000	Value: 65.00				

KM# 94 100 MARKKAA **Weight:** 22.0000 g. **Composition:** 0.9250 Silver .6543 oz. ASW **Subject:** Aleksis Kivi **Obverse:** Books on shelves **Reverse:** Portrait on partial disc **Edge:** Plain **Size:** 35 mm.

Date	Mintage	F	VF	XF	Unc	BU
2000 Proof	12,000	Value: 30.00				

KM# 97 100 MARKKAA **Weight:** 31.0000 g. **Composition:** 0.9250 Silver 0.9219 oz. ASW **Subject:** Aino Ackte **Obverse:** Partial portrait **Reverse:** High heel shoe and trouser bottom **Edge:** Plain **Size:** 35 mm.

Date	Mintage	F	VF	XF	Unc	BU
2001	45,000	—	—	—	35.00	—

KM# 72 1000 MARKKAA **Weight:** 9.0000 g. **Composition:** 0.9000 Gold .2604 oz. AGW **Subject:** 75th Anniversary of Independence **Size:** 22.1 mm.

Date	Mintage	F	VF	XF	Unc	BU
1992 M-S	35,000	—	—	—	—	275

KM# 86 1000 MARKKAA **Weight:** 8.6400 g. **Composition:** 0.9000 Gold .2500 oz. AGW **Subject:** 80th Anniversary of Independence **Obverse:** New shoot growing from tree stump **Reverse:** Symbolic design separating dates

Date	Mintage	F	VF	XF	Unc	BU
ND (1997) M-P Proof	20,000	Value: 285				

KM# 90 1000 MARKKAA **Weight:** 8.6400 g. **Composition:** 0.9000 Gold .2500 oz. AGW **Subject:** Jean Sibelius - Composer **Obverse:** Sibelius head left **Reverse:** Finlandia musical score, denomination above, date below

Date	Mintage	F	VF	XF	Unc	BU
1999 P-V-M Proof	25,000	Value: 275				

KM# 79 2000 MARKKAA **Weight:** 16.9700 g. **Composition:** 0.9000 Gold .4910 oz. AGW **Subject:** 50 Years of Peace **Size:** 28 mm.

Date	Mintage	F	VF	XF	Unc	BU
1995 M-L-L Proof	6,900	Value: 450				

EURO COINAGE

European Economic Community Issues

KM# 98 EURO CENT **Weight:** 2.2700 g. **Composition:** Copper Plated Steel **Obverse:** Rampant lion **Reverse:** Denomination and globe **Edge:** Plain **Size:** 16.3 mm.

Date	Mintage	F	VF	XF	Unc	BU
1999	2,000,000	—	—	—	1.25	—
1999 Proof	—	—	—	—	—	—
2000 Proof	—	—	—	—	—	—
2000	—	—	—	—	1.75	—
2001	35,000	—	—	—	10.00	—
2001 Proof	—	—	—	—	—	—
2002 Proof	—	Value: 25.00				
2002	80,000	—	—	—	5.00	—

KM# 99 2 EURO CENTS **Weight:** 3.0000 g. **Composition:** Copper Plated Steel **Obverse:** Rampant lion **Reverse:** Denomination and globe **Edge:** Grooved **Size:** 18.7 mm.

Date	Mintage	F	VF	XF	Unc	BU
1999	2,000,000	—	—	—	1.25	—
1999 Proof	—	—	—	—	—	—
2000 Proof	—	—	—	—	—	—
2000	—	—	—	—	1.25	—
2001	35,000	—	—	—	10.00	—
2001 Proof	—	—	—	—	—	—
2002 Proof	—	Value: 25.00				
2002	80,000	—	—	—	5.00	—

KM# 100 5 EURO CENTS **Weight:** 3.8600 g. **Composition:** Copper Plated Steel **Obverse:** Rampant lion **Reverse:** Denomination and globe **Edge:** Plain **Size:** 21.2 mm.

Date	F	VF	XF	Unc	BU
1999 Proof	—	—	—	—	—
2000 Proof	—	—	—	—	—
2000	—	—	—	1.00	—
2001	—	—	—	0.50	—
2001 Proof	—	—	—	—	—
2002 Proof	—	Value: 25.00			

KM# 101 10 EURO CENTS **Weight:** 4.0000 g. **Composition:** Brass **Obverse:** Rampant lion **Reverse:** Denomination and map **Edge:** Reeded **Size:** 19.7 mm.

Date	Mintage	F	VF	XF	Unc	BU
1999	296,000,000	—	—	—	1.25	—
1999 Proof	—	—	—	—	—	—
2000 Proof	—	—	—	—	—	—
2000	—	—	—	—	1.75	—
2001	—	—	—	—	1.75	—
2001 Proof	—	—	—	—	—	—
2002 Proof	—	Value: 30.00				
2002	366,000,000	—	—	—	1.00	—

KM# 102 20 EURO CENTS **Weight:** 5.7300 g. **Composition:** Brass **Obverse:** Rampant lion **Reverse:** Denomination and map **Edge:** Notched **Size:** 22.2 mm.

Date	Mintage	F	VF	XF	Unc	BU
1999	211,000,000	—	—	—	1.25	—
1999 Proof	—	—	—	—	—	—
2000 Proof	—	—	—	—	—	—
2000	35,000	—	—	—	12.00	—
2001	—	—	—	—	1.75	—
Note: Mintage included in 1999						
2001 Proof	—	—	—	—	—	—
2002 Proof	—	Value: 35.00				
2002	158,000,000	—	—	—	1.75	—

KM# 103 50 EURO CENTS **Weight:** 7.8100 g. **Composition:** Brass **Obverse:** Rampant lion **Reverse:** Denomination and map **Edge:** Reeded **Size:** 24.2 mm.

Date	Mintage	F	VF	XF	Unc	BU
1999	71,000,000	—	—	—	1.75	—
1999 Proof	—	—	—	—	—	—
2000 Proof	—	—	—	—	—	—
2000	—	—	—	—	1.50	—
2001	35,000	—	—	—	12.50	—
2001 Proof	—	—	—	—	—	—
2002 Proof	—	Value: 40.00				
2002	—	—	—	—	1.50	—

KM# 104 EURO **Weight:** 7.5000 g. **Composition:** Bi-Metallic **Obverse:** Flying geese **Reverse:** Denomination and map **Edge:** Reeded and plain sections **Size:** 23.2 mm.

Date	Mintage	F	VF	XF	Unc	BU
1999	60,000,000	—	—	—	3.00	—
1999 Proof	—	—	—	—	—	—
2000 Proof	—	—	—	—	—	—
2000	—	—	—	—	2.50	—
2001	—	—	—	—	2.50	—
2001 Proof	—	—	—	—	—	—
2002 Proof	—	Value: 45.00				
2002	—	—	—	—	2.50	—

KM# 105 2 EURO **Weight:** 8.5200 g. **Composition:** Bi-Metallic **Obverse:** Flowers **Reverse:** Denomination and map **Edge:** Reeded and lettered **Size:** 25.6 mm.

Date	Mintage	F	VF	XF	Unc	BU
1999	50,000,000	—	—	—	3.75	—
1999 Proof	—	—	—	—	—	—
2000 Proof	—	—	—	—	—	—
2000	—	—	—	—	4.00	—
2001	—	—	—	—	3.75	—
2001 Proof	—	—	—	—	—	—
2002 Proof	—	Value: 50.00				
2002	—	—	—	—	4.00	—

KM# 107 10 EURO **Weight:** 27.4000 g. **Composition:** 0.9250 Silver 0.8149 oz. ASW **Subject:** Helsinki Olympics 50th Anniversary **Obverse:** Flames and denomination above globe with map of Finland **Reverse:** Tower and partial coin design **Edge:** Plain **Size:** 38.6 mm.

Date	Mintage	F	VF	XF	Unc	BU
2002	50,000	—	—	—	35.00	—
2002 Proof	—	Value: 65.00				

KM# 108 10 EURO **Weight:** 27.0000 g. **Composition:** 0.9250 Silver 0.803 oz. ASW **Subject:** Elias Lonnrot **Obverse:** Ribbon with stars **Reverse:** Quill and signature **Edge:** Plain **Size:** 38.6 mm.

Date	Mintage	F	VF	XF	Unc	BU
2002	80,000	—	—	—	35.00	—
2002 Proof	—	Value: 65.00				

KM# 109 100 EURO **Weight:** 8.6400 g. **Composition:** 0.9000 Gold 0.25 oz. AGW **Subject:** Lapland **Obverse:** Small tree and mountain stream **Reverse:** Lake landscape beneath the midnight sun **Edge:** Plain with serial number **Size:** 22 mm.

Date	Mintage	F	VF	XF	Unc	BU
2002 Proof	25,000	Value: 275				

PATTERNS

Including off metal strikes

KM#	Date	Mintage	Identification	Mkt Val
Pn53	1956	—	500 Markkaa. Silver. With waves.	—
Pn54	1956	—	500 Markkaa. Silver. With plain field.	—
Pn48	1954	—	Iron. With pearls.	1,700
Pn42	1953	—	Markka. Aluminum. With pearls.	—
Pn11	1918	—	5 Pennia. Silver.	3,500
Pn12	1919	—	Penni. Nickel.	—
Pn13	1921	—	10 Pennia. Iron.	—
Pn14	1922	—	5 Pennia. Silver.	—
Pn15	1923	—	50 Pennia. Copper.	—
Pn16	1923	—	Copper.	—
Pn17	1924	—	10 Pennia. Nickel.	—
Pn18	1926	—	200 Markkaa. Copper.	—
Pn19	1927	—	10 Pennia. Copper.	—
Pn20	1936	—	25 Pennia. Copper.	—
Pn21	1936	—	Iron.	—
Pn22	1941	—	10 Pennia. Iron.	250
Pn23	1942	—	25 Pennia. Aluminum.	—
Pn26	1942	—	Markka. Iron - Blued.	—
Pn27	1942	—	5 Markkaa. Brass.	—
Pn25	1942	—	Aluminum.	—
Pn24	1942	—	50 Pennia. Aluminum.	—
Pn28	1945	—	Brass.	3,000
Pn29	1946	—	5 Markkaa. Nickel.	—
Pn30	1947	—	5 Markkaa. Iron.	—
Pn31	1948	—	Aluminum.	—
Pn33	1948	—	5 Markkaa. Nickel.	—
Pn32	1948	—	Bronze.	—
Pn34	1949	—	Copper.	5,000
Pn35	1949	—	5 Markkaa. Iron.	—
Pn36	1950 H	—	Brass.	2,500
Pn37	1951	—	500 Markkaa. Aluminum - Blued.	—
Pn38	1952	—	Iron - Blued.	—
Pn40	1952	—	10 Markkaa. Iron.	500
Pn41	1952	—	10 Markkaa. Copper.	—
Pn39	1952	—	5 Markkaa. Iron - Blued.	—
Pn44	1953	—	Markka. Iron. With pearls.	—
Pn45	1953	—	5 Markkaa. Iron - Blued.	—
Pn46	1953	—	50 Markkaa. Nickel.	—
Pn43	1953	—	Markka. Iron. Lion head.	—
Pn50	1954	—	20 Markkaa. Nickel.	—
Pn48	1954	—	Iron. With pearls.	—
Pn47	1954	—	Nickel Plated Iron.	1,000
Pn49	1954	—	5 Markkaa. Iron. With pearls.	—
Pn51	1956	—	20 Markkaa. Nickel.	—
Pn52	1956	—	20 Markkaa. Silver.	—
Pn55	1969	—	5 Markkaa. Copper-Nickel.	—

TRIAL STRIKES

KM#	Date	Mintage	Identification	Mkt Val
TS6	1918	—	5 Pennia. Iron.	2,000
TS8	1960	—	(1000 Markkaa). Brass.	—
TS7	1960	—	(1000 Markkaa). Brass.	—

MINT SETS

KM#	Date	Mintage	Identification	Issue Price	Mkt Val
MS1	1973 (7)	10,029	KM44a, 45-48, 49a, 53	5.00	25.00
MS2	1973 (7)	9,978	KM44a, 45-48, 49a, 53	10.00	60.00
MS3	1974	79,258	KM44a, 45-48, 49a, 53	3.75	8.00
MS4	1975 (7)	58,820	KM44a, 45-48, 49a, 53	3.75	8.00
MS5	1976 (7)	45,263	KM44a, 45-48, 49a, 53	3.75	8.00
MS6	1977 (7)	40,392	KM44a, 45-48, 49a, 53	4.00	10.00
MS7	1978 (7)	39,745	KM44a-45a, 46-48, 49a, 53	4.45	8.00
MS8	1979 (7)	36,000	KM44a-45a, 46-48, 49a, 57	4.85	10.00
MS9	1980 (6)	33,805	KM45a, 46-48, 49a, 57	5.00	8.00
MS10	1981 (6)	63,100	KM45a, 46-48, 49a, 57	5.25	8.00
MS11	1982 (6)	35,500	KM45a, 46-48, 49a, 57	5.50	8.00
MS12	1983 (6)	30,100	KM45a-46a, 47-48, 49a, 57	3.25	8.00
MS13	1983 (6)	9,250	KM45a-46a, 47-48, 49a, 57	3.25	20.00
MS14	1984 (6)	30,500	KM45a-46a, 47-48, 49a, 57	3.25	6.00
MS15	1984 (6)	600	KM45a-46a, 47-48, 49a, 57	3.75	50.00
MS16	1985 (6)	38,385	KM45a-46a, 47-48, 49a, 57	3.25	6.00
MS17	1985 (6)	1,500	KM45a-46a, 47-48, 49a, 57	4.65	20.00
MS18	1985 (6)	1,560	KM45a-46a, 47-48, 49a, 57	3.75	20.00
MS19	1986 (6)	37,100	KM45a-46a, 47-48, 49a, 57	3.25	6.00
MS20	1986 (6)	1,300	KM45a-46a, 47-48, 49a, 57	5.00	20.00
MS21	1986 (6)	1,780	KM45a-46a, 47-48, 49a, 57	4.25	20.00
MS22	1987 (6)	34,300	KM45a-46a, 47-48, 49a, 57	—	6.00
MS23	1987 (6)	1,120	KM45a-46a, 47-48, 49a, 57	—	20.00
MS24	1987 (6)	1,400	KM45a-46a, 47-48, 49a, 57	—	20.00
MS25	1987 (6)	15,900	KM45a-46a, 47-48, 49a, 57	—	10.00
MS26	1987 (6)	300	KM45a-46a, 47-48, 57	—	50.00
MS27	1987 (6)	180	KM45a-46a, 47-48, 49a, 57	—	50.00
MS28	1988 (6)	35,750	KM45a-46a, 47-48, 49a, 57	—	6.00
MS29	1988 (6)	1,450	KM45a-46a, 47-48, 49a, 57	—	15.00
MS30	1988 (6)	1,220	KM45a-46a, 47-48, 49a, 57	—	15.00
MS31	1989 (6)	33,000	KM45a-46a, 47-48, 49a, 57	—	6.00
MS32	1989 (6)	1,450	KM45a-46a, 47-48, 49a, 57	—	10.00
MS33	1989 (6)	1,700	KM45a-46a, 47-48, 49a, 57	—	10.00
MS34	1989 (6)	15,982	KM45a-46a, 47-48, 49a, 57	—	22.00
MS35	1989 (6)	1,000	KM45a-46a, 47-48, 49a, 57	—	35.00
MS36	1989 (6)	1,150	KM45a-46a, 47-48, 49a, 57	—	35.00
MS37	1990 (6)	29,400	KM45a-46a, 47-48, 49a, 57	—	6.00
MS38	1990 (6)	1,000	KM45a-46a, 47-48, 49a, 57	—	10.00
MS39	1990 (6)	1,500	KM45a-46a, 47-48, 49a, 57	—	10.00
MS40	1990 (4)	41,750	KM49a, 57, 65-66	—	9.00
MS41	1990 (4)	3,500	KM49a, 57, 65-66	—	10.00
MS42	1991 (4)	30,000	KM49a, 57, 65-66	—	10.00
MS43	1991 (4)	5,000	KM49a, 57, 65-66	—	10.00
MS44	1992 (5)	28,000	KM49a, 57, 65-55, 73	—	12.50
MS45	1993 (6)	100,000	KM49a, 65-66, 73, 76a, 77	—	21.50
MS46	1993 (5)	—	Km65-66, 73, 76-77	13.30	13.50
MS47	1993 (4)	20,000	Km49a, 65-66, 73	—	15.00
MS48	1994 (5)	25,000	Km65-66, 73, 76-77	—	18.00
MS49	1995 (5)	23,190	KM65-66, 73, 76-77	—	20.00
MS50	1995 (5)	15,000	KM65-66, 73, 76-77	—	20.00
MS51	1996 (5)	16,300	KM65-66, 73, 76-77	—	20.00
MS52	1997 (5)	18,000	KM65-66, 73, 76-77	—	20.00
MS56	2000 (5)	—	KM65-66, 73, 76-77	12.50	20.00
MS53	1998 (5)	18,000	KM65-66, 73, 76-77	—	20.00
MS54	1999 (5)	—	KM65-66, 73, 76-77	—	20.00
MS55	1999 (5)	—	KM65-66, 73, 76-77	12.50	20.00
MS57	2000 (5)	—	KM65-66, 73, 76-77	12.50	20.00
MS58	2001 (5)	20,000	KM#65, 66, 73, 76, 77	18.00	20.00
MS59	2001 (5)	—	KM#65, 66, 73, 76, 77, medal	—	22.50
MS60	2002 (8)	—	KM#98-105, medal	—	35.00

PROOF SETS

KM#	Date	Mintage	Identification	Issue Price	Mkt Val
PS1	1994 (5)	1,000	KM65-66, 73, 76-77	—	150
PS2	1995 (2)	500	KM80, 80a	802	700
PS3	1995 (5)	1,810	KM65-66, 73, 76-77	—	55.00
PS4	1996 (5)	1,200	KM65-66, 73, 76-77	—	55.00
PS5	1997 (6)	2,000	KM65-66, 73, 76-77, 85	67.50	70.00
PS6	1998 (5)	1,600	KM65-66, 73, 76-77	—	55.00
PS7	1999 (5)	—	KM65-66, 73, 76-77	—	55.00
PS8	2000 (5)	—	KM65-66, 73, 76-77, medal	—	55.00
PS9	2001 (5)	—	KM#65, 66, 73, 76, 77, medal	—	60.00
PS10	2002 (8)	8,000	KM#98-105, gold medal	—	500

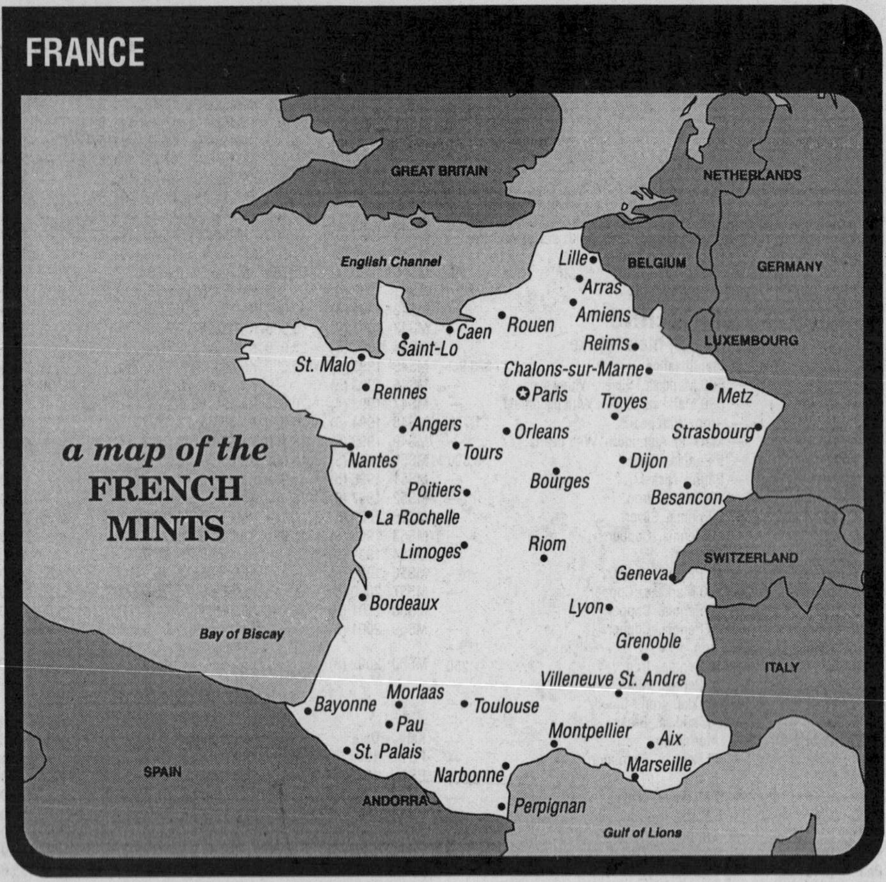

The French Republic, largest of the West European nations, has an area of 210,026 sq. mi. (547,030 sq. km.) and a population of 58.1 million. Capital: Paris. Agriculture, manufacturing, tourist industry and financial services are the most important elements of France's diversified economy. Textiles and clothing, steel products, machinery and transportation equipment, chemicals, pharmaceuticals, nuclear electricity, agricultural products and wine are exported.

France, the Gaul of ancient times, emerged from the Renaissance as a modern centralized national state which reached its zenith during the reign of Louis XIV (1643-1715) when it became an absolute monarchy and the foremost power in Europe. Although his reign marks the golden age of French culture, the domestic abuses and extravagance of Louis XIV plunged France into a series of costly wars. This, along with a system of special privileges granted the nobility and other favored groups, weakened the monarchy and brought France to bankruptcy. This laid the way for the French Revolution of 1789-99 that shook Europe and affected the whole world.

The monarchy was abolished and the First Republic formed in 1793. The new government fell in 1799 to a coup led by Napoleon Bonaparte who, after declaring himself First Consul for life, in 1804 had himself proclaimed Emperor of France and King of Italy.

Napoleon's military victories made him master of much of Europe, but his disastrous Russian campaign of 1812 initiated a series of defeats that led to his abdication in 1814 and exile to the island of Elba. The monarchy was briefly restored under Louis XVIII. Napoleon returned to France in March 1815, but his efforts to uphold his power were totally crushed at the battle of Waterloo. He was exiled to the island of St. Helena where he died in 1821.

The monarchy under Louis XVIII was again restored in 1815, but the ultra reactionary regime of Charles X (1824-30) was overthrown by a liberal revolution and Louis Philippe of Orleans replaced him as monarch. The monarchy was ousted by the Revolution of 1848 and the Second Republic proclaimed. Louis Napoleon Bonaparte (nephew of Napoleon I) was elected president of the Second Republic. He was proclaimed emperor in 1852. As Napoleon III, he gave France two decades of prosperity under a stable, autocratic regime, but led it to defeat in the Franco-Prussian War of 1870, after which the Third Republic was established.

The Third Republic endured until 1940 and the capitulation of France to the swiftly maneuvering German forces. Marshal Philippe Petain formed a puppet government that sued for peace and ruled unoccupied France until 1942 from Vichy. Meanwhile, General Charles de Gaulle escaped to London where he formed a wartime government in exile and the Free French army. De Gaulle's provisional exile government was officially recognized by the Allies after the liberation of Paris in 1944, and De Gaulle, who had been serving as head of the provisional government, tacitly maintained that position. In October 1945, the people overwhelmingly rejected a return to the prewar government, thus paving the way for the formation of the Fourth Republic in 1947 just after the dismissal of De Gaulle, at grips with a coalition of rival parties, the Communists especially.

In actual operation, the Fourth Republic was remarkably like the Third, with the National Assembly the focus of power causing a constant governmental instability. The later years of the Fourth Republic were marked by a burst of industrial expansion unmatched in modern French history. The growth rate, however, was marred by a two colonial wars, nagging inflationary trend that weakened the franc and undermined the betterment of the people's buying power. This and the Algerian conflict led to the recall of De Gaulle to power, the adoption of a new constitution vesting strong powers in the executive, and the establishment in 1959 of the current Fifth Republic.

RULERS

Third Republic, 1871-1940
Vichy State, 1940-1944
De Gaulle's Provisional Govt., 1944-1946
Fourth Republic, 1947-1958
Fifth Republic, 1959—

MINT MARKS AND PRIVY MARKS

In addition to the date and mint mark which are customary on western civilization coinage, most coins manufactured by the French Mints contain two or three small 'Marks or Differents' as the French call them. These privy marks represent the men responsible for the dies which struck the coins. One privy mark is sometimes for the Engraver General (since 1880 the title is Chief Engraver). The other privy mark is the signature of the Mint Director of each mint; another one is the different' of the local engraver. Three other marks appeared at the end of Louis XIV's reign: one for the Director General of Mints, one for the General Engineer of Mechanical edge-marking, one identifying over struck coins in 1690-1705 and in 1715-1723. Equally amazing and unique is that sometimes the local assayer's or Judge-custody's 'different' or 'secret pellet' appears. Since 1880 this privy mark has represented the office rather than the personage of both the Administration of Coins & Medals and the Mint Director, and a standard privy mark has been used (cornucopia).

For most dates these privy marks are important though minor features for advanced collectors or local researchers. During some issue dates, however, the marks changed. To be even more accurate sometimes the marks changed when the date didn't, even though it should have. These coins can be attributed to the proper mintage report only by considering the privy marks. Previous references (before G. Sobin and F. Droulers) have by and large ignored these privy marks. It is entirely possible that unattributed varieties may exist for any privy mark transition. All transition years which may have two or three varieties or combinations of privy marks have the known attribution indicated after the date (if it has been confirmed).

ENGRAVER GENERAL'S PRIVY MARKS

Mark		Date
	Torch	1896-1926
	Wing	1927-58
	Owl	1958-74
	Fish	1974-94
	Bee	1994-

MINT DIRECTOR'S PRIVY MARKS

Some modern coins struck from dies produced at the Paris Mint have the 'A' mint mark. In the absence of a mint mark, the cornucopia privy mark serves to attribute a coin to Paris design.

A – Paris, Central Mint

B – Beaumont – Le Roger

Mark		Date
	Cornucopia	1943-58

(b) – Brussels

Legend ending BD, see PAU

C - Castelsarrasin

Mark		Date
C	Cornucopia	1914, 1943-46

Thunderbolt (tb) - Poissy

Mark		Date
	Cornucopia	1922-24

Star (s) - Madrid

Mark	Date
*	1916

MONETARY SYSTEM

(Commencing 1960)

1 Old Franc = 1 New Centime
100 New Centimes = 1 New Franc

MODERN REPUBLICS
1870-
DECIMAL COINAGE

KM# 840 CENTIME **Composition:** Bronze **Note:** Without mint mark or privy mark. Struck at Paris Mint.

Date	Mintage	F	VF	XF	Unc	BU
1901	1,000,000	1.00	2.00	15.00	35.00	—
1902	1,000,000	0.75	1.50	4.00	15.00	—
1903	2,000,000	0.50	1.50	3.00	15.00	—
1904	1,000,000	0.75	1.50	4.00	15.00	—
1908	4,500,000	2.00	4.00	10.00	20.00	—
1909	1,500,000	3.00	5.00	12.00	30.00	—
1910	1,500,000	10.00	20.00	40.00	80.00	—
1911	5,000,000	0.25	0.75	1.50	5.00	—
1912	2,000,000	0.50	1.00	2.00	7.00	—
1913	1,500,000	0.50	1.00	2.00	7.00	—
1914	1,000,000	0.75	1.50	3.00	9.50	—
1916	1,996,000	0.50	1.00	2.00	6.50	—
1919	2,407,000	0.25	0.75	1.50	4.00	—
1920	2,594,000	0.25	0.75	1.50	4.00	—

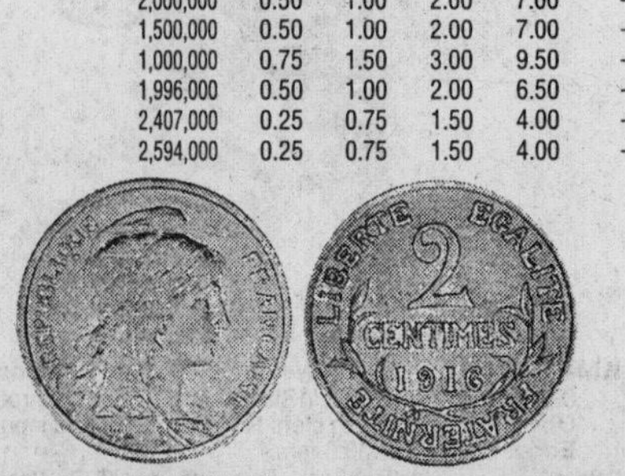

KM# 841 2 CENTIMES **Composition:** Bronze **Note:** Without mark mark or privy mark. Struck at Paris Mint.

Date	Mintage	F	VF	XF	Unc	BU
1901	1,000,000	1.00	2.50	4.00	11.50	—
1902	750,000	1.50	3.50	5.50	15.00	—

Date	Mintage	F	VF	XF	Unc	BU
1903	750,000	1.50	3.50	5.50	16.50	—
1904	500,000	2.00	4.50	7.50	18.50	—
1907	250,000	10.00	25.00	55.00	130	—
1908	3,500,000	0.35	0.75	2.00	6.00	—
1909	1,750,000	6.00	12.00	30.00	50.00	—
1910	1,750,000	0.50	1.00	5.00	12.50	—
1911	5,000,000	0.15	0.50	1.25	5.00	—
1912	1,500,000	0.25	1.00	2.00	7.00	—
1913	1,750,000	0.25	1.00	2.00	7.00	—
1914	2,000,000	0.15	0.50	1.25	5.00	—
1916	500,000	0.75	1.50	3.00	9.00	—
1919	902,000	0.50	1.00	2.00	6.00	—
1920	598,000	0.75	1.50	3.00	8.00	—

KM# 842 5 CENTIMES Composition: Bronze **Note:** Without mint mark. Struck at Paris Mint.

Date	Mintage	F	VF	XF	Unc	BU
1901 (c)	6,000,000	1.75	3.50	15.00	60.00	—
1902	7,900,000	1.75	3.50	10.00	50.00	—
1903	2,879,000	5.00	10.00	25.00	80.00	—
1904	8,000,000	1.00	3.00	6.50	25.00	—
1905	2,100,000	6.00	16.00	45.00	115	—
1906	8,394,000	0.75	2.50	6.00	24.00	—
1907	7,900,000	0.75	2.50	6.00	24.00	—
1908	6,090,000	2.00	4.00	12.00	32.00	—
1909	8,000,000	0.75	2.50	6.00	25.00	—
1910	4,000,000	1.50	2.50	9.00	50.00	—
1911	15,386,000	0.25	0.75	1.75	9.00	—
1912	20,000,000	0.25	0.75	1.75	9.00	—
1913	12,603,000	0.25	0.75	1.75	9.00	—
1914	7,000,000	0.25	0.75	1.75	9.00	—
1915	6,032,000	0.25	0.75	1.75	9.00	—
1916	41,531,000	0.25	0.75	1.75	7.50	—
1916 (s)	Inc. above	0.25	0.75	1.75	7.50	—
1917	16,963,000	0.25	0.75	1.75	7.50	—
1920	8,151,999	2.00	4.00	9.00	28.00	—
1921	142,000	250	450	850	1,350	—

KM# 865 5 CENTIMES Composition: Copper-Nickel

Date	Mintage	F	VF	XF	Unc	BU
1914 Rare	—	—	—	—	—	—
1917	10,458,000	1.00	1.75	4.00	18.00	—
1918	35,592,000	0.25	0.75	1.75	4.50	—
1919	43,848,000	0.25	0.75	1.75	4.00	—
1920	51,321,000	0.25	0.50	1.75	3.50	—

KM# 875 5 CENTIMES Weight: 2.0000 g. Composition: Copper-Nickel

Date	Mintage	F	VF	XF	Unc	BU
1920	Inc. above	5.00	15.00	28.00	75.00	—
1921	32,908,000	0.25	0.50	1.75	4.00	—
1922	31,700,000	0.25	0.50	1.75	4.00	—
1922 (t)	17,717,000	1.50	2.50	5.00	13.50	—
1923	23,322,000	0.50	1.50	2.00	6.50	—
1923 (t)	45,097,000	0.25	0.50	1.00	3.50	—
1924	47,018,000	0.25	0.50	1.00	3.50	—
1924 (t)	21,210,000	0.50	1.50	2.00	5.50	—
1925	66,837,999	0.25	0.50	1.00	2.50	—
1926	19,820,000	0.25	1.50	2.00	5.50	—
1927	6,066,000	2.50	8.50	25.00	70.00	—
1930	31,902,000	0.20	0.50	1.00	2.25	—
1931	34,711,000	0.20	0.50	1.00	2.25	—
1932	31,112,000	0.20	0.50	1.00	2.25	—
1933	12,970,000	1.00	1.75	4.00	10.00	—
1934	27,144,000	0.30	0.65	2.00	5.00	—
1935	57,221,000	0.25	0.50	1.00	2.25	—
1936	64,340,999	0.15	0.25	0.75	2.25	—
1937	26,329,000	0.15	0.25	0.75	2.25	—
1938	21,614,000	0.15	0.25	0.75	2.25	—

KM# 875a 5 CENTIMES Weight: 1.5000 g. Composition: Nickel-Bronze

Date	Mintage	F	VF	XF	Unc	BU
.1938. star	Inc. above	100	200	300	425	—
.1939.	52,673,000	0.10	0.25	0.75	2.00	—
.1938.	26,330,000	0.15	0.50	1.00	3.00	—

KM# 843 10 CENTIMES Composition: Bronze **Note:** Without mint mark. Struck at Paris Mint.

Date	Mintage	F	VF	XF	Unc	BU
1898	4,000,000	1.00	3.00	8.00	20.00	—
1898 Matte Proof	—	Value: 450				
1899	4,000,000	1.00	3.00	8.00	20.00	—
1900 (n)	5,000,000	1.00	3.00	8.00	20.00	—
1900 (n) Proof	—	Value: 425				
1901 (c)	2,700,000	1.50	3.00	20.00	55.00	—
1902	3,800,000	0.75	1.75	6.50	25.00	—
1903	3,650,000	0.75	1.75	6.50	25.00	—
1904	3,800,000	0.75	1.75	6.50	25.00	—
1905	950,000	25.00	50.00	125	275	—
1906	3,000,000	2.00	5.00	12.00	40.00	—
1907	4,000,000	0.75	1.75	4.50	20.00	—
1908	3,500,000	0.75	1.75	4.50	20.00	—
1909	2,933,000	0.75	1.75	4.50	25.00	—
1910	3,567,000	0.75	1.75	4.50	20.00	—
1911	7,903,000	0.50	1.25	2.75	12.00	—
1912	9,500,000	0.50	1.25	2.75	12.00	—
1913	9,000,000	0.50	1.25	2.75	12.00	—
1914	6,000,000	0.75	1.75	3.50	14.00	—
1915	4,362,000	0.50	1.25	2.75	12.00	—
1916	22,477,000	0.25	0.75	1.50	7.00	—
1916 (s)	Inc. above	0.25	0.75	1.50	7.00	—
1917	11,914,000	0.25	0.75	1.50	7.00	—
1920	4,119,000	1.50	3.00	10.00	40.00	—
1921	1,896,000	8.00	16.00	40.00	85.00	—

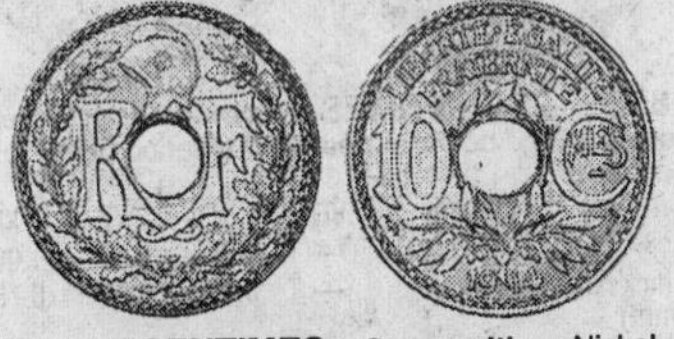

KM# 866 10 CENTIMES Composition: Nickel

Date	Mintage	F	VF	XF	Unc	BU
1914 dash	3,972	400	700	1,000	1,600	—

KM# 866a 10 CENTIMES Composition: Copper-Nickel

Date	Mintage	F	VF	XF	Unc	BU
1917	8,170,999	0.75	1.50	3.50	20.00	—
1918	30,605,000	0.25	0.50	1.00	3.50	—
1919	33,488,999	0.25	0.50	1.00	3.50	—
1920	38,845,000	0.25	0.50	1.00	3.50	—
1921	42,768,000	0.10	0.35	0.75	2.50	—
1922	23,033,000	0.35	0.75	1.25	4.00	—
1922 (t)	12,412,000	0.75	1.50	2.50	6.50	—
1923	18,701,000	0.50	1.00	2.00	4.50	—
1923 (t)	30,016,000	0.25	0.50	1.00	3.00	—
1924	43,949,000	0.10	0.35	0.75	2.00	—
1924 (t)	13,591,000	1.50	4.50	12.50	38.00	—
1925	46,266,000	0.10	0.35	0.75	2.00	—
1926	25,660,000	0.25	0.50	1.00	3.00	—
1927	16,203,000	0.40	0.75	1.25	4.00	—
1928	6,967,000	1.00	2.50	8.00	28.00	—
1929	24,531,000	0.10	0.35	1.00	2.00	—
1930	22,146,000	0.10	0.35	1.00	2.00	—
1931	49,107,000	0.10	0.35	1.00	2.00	—
1932	30,317,000	0.10	0.35	1.00	2.00	—
1933	13,042,000	0.35	0.75	1.50	4.00	—
1934	24,067,000	0.10	0.50	1.00	2.00	—
1935	47,487,000	0.10	0.50	1.00	2.00	—
1936	57,738,000	0.10	0.50	1.00	2.00	—
1937	25,308,000	0.10	0.50	1.00	2.00	—
1938	17,063,000	0.25	0.75	1.75	4.50	—

KM# 889.1 10 CENTIMES Composition: Nickel-Bronze

Date	Mintage	F	VF	XF	Unc	BU
.1938.	24,151,000	0.25	0.50	1.00	2.00	—
.1.938.	Inc. above	—	—	—	—	—
.1939.	62,269,000	0.15	0.30	0.65	1.75	—

KM# 889.2 10 CENTIMES Composition: Nickel-Bronze **Note:** Thin flan.

Date	F	VF	XF	Unc	BU
.1939.	0.10	0.20	0.50	1.25	—

KM# 898.1 10 CENTIMES Composition: Zinc **Note:** Issued for Vichy French State, thickness 1.5mm.

Date	Mintage	F	VF	XF	Unc	BU
1941	70,860,000	0.35	0.65	1.50	6.00	—
1942	139,598,000	0.30	0.60	1.25	4.00	—
1943	21,520,000	1.00	2.00	4.00	15.00	—

KM# 898.2 10 CENTIMES Composition: Zinc **Note:** Without mint mark. Thin flan, 1.3mm. Struck at Paris Mint.

Date	F	VF	XF	Unc	BU
1941	0.25	0.50	1.25	3.00	—
1942	0.20	0.40	1.00	2.25	—
1943	0.75	1.50	2.75	6.00	—

KM# 895 10 CENTIMES Composition: Zinc **Reverse:** Without dash below MES in C MES

Date	Mintage	F	VF	XF	Unc	BU
1941	235,875,000	1.00	2.00	6.00	15.00	—

KM# 896 10 CENTIMES Composition: Zinc **Reverse:** Dash below MES in C MES

Date	F	VF	XF	Unc	BU
1941	0.75	1.25	4.00	10.00	—

KM# 897 10 CENTIMES Composition: Zinc **Reverse:** Dot before and after date, or just after

Date	F	VF	XF	Unc	BU
.1941.	0.25	0.50	1.00	4.00	—
1941.	0.25	0.50	1.00	4.00	—

KM# 903 10 CENTIMES Composition: Zinc

Date	Mintage	F	VF	XF	Unc	BU
1943	22,008,000	0.25	0.75	2.50	7.00	—
1944	58,463,000	0.25	0.50	2.00	5.00	—

KM# 906.1 10 CENTIMES Composition: Zinc

Date	Mintage	F	VF	XF	Unc	BU
1945	38,174,000	1.00	1.75	3.25	12.00	—
1946 Rare	—	—	—	—	—	—

KM# 906.2 10 CENTIMES Composition: Zinc

Date	Mintage	F	VF	XF	Unc	BU
1945B	7,246,000	1.50	3.00	6.00	16.00	—
1946B	10,566,000	2.50	5.00	10.00	25.00	—

KM# 906.3 10 CENTIMES Composition: Zinc

Date	Mintage	F	VF	XF	Unc	BU
1945C	8,379,000	2.00	4.00	8.00	20.00	—

KM# 899 20 CENTIMES Composition: Zinc **Note:** Issued for Vichy French State.

Date	Mintage	F	VF	XF	Unc	BU
1941	54,044,000	1.00	2.00	4.00	17.00	—

KM# 900.1 20 CENTIMES Weight: 3.5000 g. **Composition:** Zinc **Note:** Thick flan.

Date	Mintage	F	VF	XF	Unc	BU
1941	31,397,000	1.00	2.00	4.00	15.00	—
1942	112,868,000	0.50	1.00	2.00	7.00	—
1943	64,138,000	0.75	1.50	2.50	8.50	—

KM# 900.2 20 CENTIMES Weight: 3.0000 g. **Composition:** Zinc **Note:** Without mint mark. Thin flan. Struck at Paris Mint.

Date	Mintage	F	VF	XF	Unc	BU
1941	Inc. above	0.50	0.75	2.00	8.50	—
1943	Inc. above	0.50	0.75	2.00	6.50	—
1944	5,250,000	15.00	30.00	80.00	165	—

KM# 900.2a 20 CENTIMES Composition: Iron

Date	Mintage	F	VF	XF	Unc	BU
1944	695,000	25.00	50.00	150	185	—

KM# 907.2 20 CENTIMES Composition: Zinc

Date	Mintage	F	VF	XF	Unc	BU
1945B	100,000	85.00	165	285	470	—
1946B	5,525,000	75.00	150	260	450	—

KM# 907.1 20 CENTIMES Composition: Zinc **Note:** Fourth Republic.

Date	Mintage	F	VF	XF	Unc	BU
1945	6,003,000	2.00	4.00	9.00	22.00	—
1946	2,662,000	8.00	18.00	35.00	70.00	—

KM# 907.3 20 CENTIMES Composition: Zinc

Date	Mintage	F	VF	XF	Unc	BU
1945C	299,000	20.00	40.00	85.00	150	—

KM# 902.3 20 CENTIMES (Vingt) Composition: Aluminum

Date	Mintage	F	VF	XF	Unc	BU
1944 Large C	74,859,000	0.25	0.75	1.50	5.50	—
1944 Small C	Inc. above	15.00	30.00	70.00	325	—

KM# 855 25 CENTIMES Composition: Nickel **Note:** Without mint mark. Struck at Paris Mint.

Date	Mintage	F	VF	XF	Unc	BU
1903	16,000,000	0.25	1.00	2.00	11.50	—

KM# 856 25 CENTIMES Composition: Nickel

Date	Mintage	F	VF	XF	Unc	BU
1904	16,000,000	0.25	0.75	2.00	13.50	—
1905	8,000,000	0.50	1.50	3.50	20.00	—

KM# 867 25 CENTIMES Composition: Nickel **Reverse:** Dash under MES in denomination

Date	Mintage	F	VF	XF	Unc	BU
1914	941,000	1.50	3.00	7.00	22.50	—
1915	535,000	2.50	4.00	8.00	32.00	—
1916	100,000	15.00	30.00	60.00	120	—
1917	65,000	30.00	50.00	85.00	185	—

KM# 867a 25 CENTIMES Composition: Copper-Nickel **Reverse:** Without dash under MES in denomination

Date	Mintage	F	VF	XF	Unc	BU
1917	3,085,000	2.00	4.00	12.00	22.00	—
1918	18,330,000	0.25	0.50	1.50	3.50	—
1919	5,106,000	1.00	2.00	3.00	7.00	—
1920	18,108,000	0.15	0.50	1.00	3.00	—
1921	18,531,000	0.15	0.50	1.00	3.00	—
1922	17,766,000	0.15	0.50	1.00	3.00	—
1923	19,718,000	0.15	0.50	1.00	3.00	—
1924	24,535,000	0.15	0.50	1.00	3.00	—
1925	17,807,000	0.15	0.50	1.00	3.00	—
1926	13,226,000	0.15	0.50	1.00	3.00	—
1927	13,465,000	0.15	0.50	1.00	3.00	—
1928	9,960,000	0.25	0.50	1.50	3.50	—
1929	12,887,000	0.15	0.50	1.00	2.50	—
1930	28,363,000	0.15	0.50	1.00	2.50	—
1931	22,121,000	0.15	0.50	1.00	2.50	—
1932	30,364,000	0.15	0.50	1.00	2.50	—
1933	28,562,000	0.15	0.50	1.00	2.50	—
1936	4,657,000	1.50	3.00	8.00	18.00	—
1937	7,780,000	0.25	0.50	1.50	3.50	—

KM# 867b 25 CENTIMES Composition: Nickel-Bronze **Note:** Listings below appear with a period before and after the date.

Date	Mintage	VG	F	VF	XF	Unc
1938	5,170,000	—	0.25	0.50	1.00	2.50
1939 Thick flan (1.55mm)	42,964,000	—	0.15	0.35	0.75	1.50
1939 Thin flan (1.35mm)	Inc. above	—	0.15	0.35	0.75	1.50
1940	3,446,000	—	6.00	12.00	18.00	35.00

KM# 854 50 CENTIMES Weight: 2.5000 g. **Composition:** 0.8350 Silver .0671 oz. ASW **Note:** Without mint mark. Struck at Paris Mint.

Date	Mintage	F	VF	XF	Unc	BU
1897	88,000	30.00	75.00	125	200	—
1897 Proof	—	Value: 300				
1898	30,000,000	1.00	2.00	10.00	20.00	—
1898 Proof	—	Value: 300				
1899	18,000,000	1.50	3.00	8.00	35.00	—
1900	9,195,000	3.00	6.00	15.00	45.00	—
1900 Proof	—	Value: 300				
1901	4,960,000	2.00	4.00	12.00	45.00	—
1902	3,778,000	2.50	5.00	15.00	55.00	—
1903	2,222,000	12.00	25.00	50.00	150	—
1904	4,000,000	1.50	3.50	10.00	45.00	—
1905	2,381,000	5.00	9.00	20.00	100	—
1906	2,679,000	2.50	5.00	15.00	55.00	—
1907	7,332,000	1.50	3.50	10.00	30.00	—
1908	14,304,000	0.75	1.50	4.00	15.00	—
1909	9,900,000	0.75	1.50	4.00	15.00	—
1910	15,923,000	BV	1.00	3.00	10.00	—
1911	1,330,000	20.00	50.00	110	200	—
1912	16,000,000	BV	0.75	1.50	5.00	—
1913	14,000,000	BV	0.75	1.50	5.00	—
1914	9,657,000	BV	0.75	1.50	6.00	—
1915	20,893,000	BV	0.75	1.25	3.00	—
1916	52,963,000	BV	0.75	1.25	2.50	—
1917	48,629,000	BV	0.75	1.25	2.50	—
1918	36,492,000	BV	0.75	1.25	2.50	—
1919	24,299,000	BV	0.75	1.25	2.50	—
1920	8,509,000	0.75	1.50	3.00	6.00	—

KM# 884 50 CENTIMES Composition: Aluminum-Bronze

Date	Mintage	F	VF	XF	Unc	BU
1921	8,692,000	0.75	2.00	6.00	18.00	—
1922	86,226,000	0.15	0.25	1.00	4.00	—
1923	119,584,000	0.15	0.25	0.75	2.50	—
1924	97,036,000	0.15	0.25	1.00	3.00	—
1925	48,017,000	0.25	0.50	1.25	5.00	—
1926	46,447,000	0.25	0.50	1.25	5.00	—
1927	23,703,000	0.75	1.50	3.00	8.50	—
1928	10,329,000	0.75	2.00	5.00	16.00	—
1929	6,669,000	2.50	6.00	12.50	25.00	—

KM# 894.1 50 CENTIMES Composition: Aluminum-Bronze

Date	F	VF	XF	Unc	BU
1931	0.15	0.25	1.00	3.00	—
1932	0.15	0.25	0.50	2.00	—
1932 Closed date	0.15	0.25	0.50	2.00	—
1933	0.15	0.25	0.75	3.00	—
1933 Closed date	0.15	0.25	0.75	3.00	—
1936	0.50	1.00	2.00	5.00	—
1937	0.15	0.25	0.75	3.00	—
1938	0.15	0.25	0.75	3.00	—
1939	0.15	0.25	0.50	2.00	—
1940	0.50	1.00	2.00	5.00	—
1941	0.15	0.25	1.00	3.00	—
1947	60.00	125	225	350	—

Note: 1947 date was struck for colonial use in Africa

KM# 894.1a 50 CENTIMES Composition: Aluminum **Note:** Without mint mark. Struck at Paris Mint. Thick and thin planchets exist.

Date	Mintage	F	VF	XF	Unc	BU
1941	129,758,000	0.15	0.25	0.50	2.00	—
1944	9,898,000	0.50	1.00	2.50	6.00	—
1945	26,224,000	0.15	0.25	1.00	3.00	—
1946	24,605,000	0.15	0.25	1.00	3.00	—
1947	51,744,000	0.15	0.25	0.60	2.00	—

KM# 894.2a 50 CENTIMES Composition: Aluminum

Date	Mintage	F	VF	XF	Unc	BU
1944B Reported, not confirmed	20,000	—	—	—	—	—
1945B	6,357,000	0.50	1.00	3.00	8.00	—
1946B	29,344,000	0.15	0.25	1.00	4.00	—
1947B	18,504,000	2.00	5.00	10.00	20.00	—

KM# 894.3a 50 CENTIMES Composition: Aluminum

Date	Mintage	F	VF	XF	Unc	BU
1944C Reported, not confirmed	17,220,000	—	—	—	—	—
1945C	2,968,000	1.00	3.00	6.00	12.00	

KM# 894.2 50 CENTIMES Composition: Aluminum-Bronze

Date	Mintage	F	VF	XF	Unc	BU
1939B	6,200,000	0.50	1.00	2.50	10.00	—

KM# 914.2 50 CENTIMES Composition: Aluminum

Date	Mintage	F	VF	XF	Unc	BU
1943B	21,916,000	5.00	10.00	28.00	50.00	—
1944B	27,334,000	1.50	3.00	7.00	15.00	—

KM# 914.3 50 CENTIMES Composition: Aluminum

Date	Mintage	F	VF	XF	Unc	BU
1944C Small C	27,213,000	2.00	4.00	8.00	26.00	—
1944C Large C	Inc. above	—	—	—	—	—

KM# 914.4 50 CENTIMES Composition: Aluminum **Note:** Without mint mark. Thin flan. Struck at Paris Mint.

Date	F	VF	XF	Unc	BU
1942	0.15	0.25	1.00	2.50	—
1943	0.15	0.25	0.50	1.25	—

KM# 914.1 50 CENTIMES Composition: Aluminum **Note:** Without mint mark. Vichy French State. Struck at Paris Mint. Thick and thin planchets exist.

Date	Mintage	F	VF	XF	Unc	BU
1942	50,134,000	0.15	0.25	0.75	2.00	—
1943	84,462,000	0.15	0.25	0.75	1.50	—
1944	57,410,000	1.50	3.00	6.00	18.00	—

KM# 844.1 FRANC Weight: 5.0000 g. **Composition:** 0.8350 Silver .1342 oz. ASW **Note:** Without mint mark. Struck at Paris Mint.

Date	Mintage	F	VF	XF	Unc	BU
1898	15,000,000	1.50	2.50	5.00	30.00	—
1898 Proof	—	Value: 400				
1899	11,000,000	1.50	3.00	7.00	35.00	—
1900	99,000	125	225	450	850	—
1900 Proof	—	Value: 425				
1901	6,200,000	2.00	4.00	20.00	75.00	—
1902	6,000,000	2.00	4.00	20.00	75.00	—
1903	472,000	40.00	80.00	325	650	—
1904	7,000,000	2.00	4.00	17.50	75.00	—
1905	6,004,000	2.00	4.00	15.00	65.00	—
1906	1,908,000	6.00	20.00	40.00	100	—
1907	2,563,000	4.00	9.00	30.00	90.00	—
1908	3,961,000	2.50	5.00	20.00	65.00	—
1909	10,924,000	1.25	2.50	5.00	22.00	—
1910	7,725,000	1.25	2.50	5.00	22.00	—
1911	5,542,000	1.75	3.00	12.00	45.00	—
1912	10,001,000	1.25	2.50	5.00	22.00	—
1913	13,654,000	1.25	2.50	4.00	18.00	—
1914	14,361,000	1.25	2.50	3.50	15.00	—
1915	47,955,000	BV	1.25	2.00	5.50	—
1916	92,029,000	BV	1.00	1.50	3.50	—
1917	57,153,000	BV	1.00	1.50	3.50	—
1918	50,112,000	BV	1.00	1.50	3.50	—
1919	46,112,000	BV	1.00	1.50	3.50	—
1920	19,322,000	BV	1.50	2.50	5.50	—

KM# 844.2 FRANC **Weight:** 5.0000 g. **Composition:** 0.8350 Silver .1342 oz. ASW

Date	Mintage	F	VF	XF	Unc	BU
1914C	43,000	135	250	325	450	—

KM# 876 FRANC **Composition:** Aluminum-Bronze **Note:** Without mint mark. Chamber of Commerce. Struck at Paris Mint.

Date	Mintage	F	VF	XF	Unc	BU
1920	590,000	3.00	5.00	12.50	32.00	—
1921	54,572,000	0.25	0.50	1.50	5.50	—
1922	111,343,000	0.15	0.25	1.00	4.50	—
1923	140,138,000	0.15	0.25	1.00	3.50	—
1924 Open 4	87,715,000	0.15	0.25	1.00	4.50	—
1924 Closed 4	Inc. above	0.35	0.60	2.00	6.50	—
1925	36,523,000	0.25	0.50	1.50	5.50	—
1926	1,580,000	3.00	8.00	20.00	45.00	—
1927	11,330,000	0.50	1.50	3.50	8.50	—

KM# 885 FRANC **Composition:** Aluminum-Bronze

Date	Mintage	F	VF	XF	Unc	BU
1931	15,504,000	0.25	0.50	2.00	6.50	—
1932	29,768,000	0.15	0.25	1.00	4.00	—
1933	15,356,000	0.25	0.50	2.00	6.50	—
1934	17,286,000	0.25	0.50	2.00	5.00	—
1935	1,166,000	6.00	15.00	25.00	60.00	—
1936	23,817,000	0.15	0.25	1.00	4.00	—
1937	30,940,000	0.15	0.25	1.00	3.00	—
1938	66,165,000	0.15	0.25	1.00	2.50	—
1939	48,434,000	0.15	0.25	1.00	3.00	—
1940	25,525,000	0.15	0.25	1.00	3.50	—
1941	34,705,000	0.15	0.25	1.00	3.00	—

KM# 885a.1 FRANC **Composition:** Aluminum **Note:** Thick and thin planchets exist.

Date	Mintage	F	VF	XF	Unc	BU
1941	60,877,000	0.10	0.20	1.00	4.00	—
1943	4,400	1,200	1,500	2,250	4,000	—
1944	22,608,000	0.10	0.20	1.50	5.00	—
1945	61,780,000	0.10	0.15	0.50	2.00	—
1946	52,516,000	0.10	0.15	0.25	2.00	—
1947	110,448,000	0.10	0.15	0.25	2.00	—
1948	96,092,000	0.10	0.15	0.25	2.00	—
1949	41,090,000	0.10	0.15	0.25	2.00	—
1950	27,882,000	0.10	0.15	0.50	2.50	—
1957	16,497,000	0.10	0.15	0.75	3.00	—
1958	21,197,000	0.10	0.15	0.75	3.00	—
1959	41,985,000	0.10	0.15	0.25	1.25	—

KM# 902.1 FRANC **Composition:** Aluminum **Note:** Without mint mark. Vichy French State Issues. Struck at Paris Mint. Thick and thin planchets exist.

Date	Mintage	F	VF	XF	Unc	BU
1942	152,144,000	0.25	0.50	1.50	4.00	—
1942 Without LB	Inc. above	—	—	—	—	—
1943	205,564,000	0.10	0.25	1.00	2.50	—
1943 Thin flan	Inc. above	0.10	0.25	1.00	2.50	—
1944	50,605,000	0.50	1.25	2.00	10.00	—

KM# 902.2 FRANC **Composition:** Aluminum

Date	Mintage	F	VF	XF	Unc	BU
1943B	68,082,000	5.00	9.00	28.00	80.00	—
1944B	13,622,000	1.50	3.00	12.00	25.00	—

KM# 885b FRANC **Composition:** Zinc **Note:** Struck for colonial use in Africa.

Date	F	VF	XF	Unc	BU
1943A	750	1,100	1,700	3,200	—

KM# 885a.3 FRANC **Composition:** Aluminum

Date	Mintage	F	VF	XF	Unc	BU
1944C	33,600,000	0.50	1.50	3.50	12.00	—
1945C	5,220,000	1.50	3.50	9.00	25.00	—

KM# 885a.2 FRANC **Composition:** Aluminum

Date	Mintage	F	VF	XF	Unc	BU
1945B	4,251,000	1.00	3.50	9.00	28.00	—
1946B	26,493,000	0.10	0.20	1.50	5.00	—
1947B	51,562,000	0.10	0.20	1.00	4.00	—
1948B	45,481,000	0.10	0.20	1.00	3.50	—
1949B	35,840,000	0.10	0.20	1.00	4.00	—
1950B	18,800,000	1.00	2.00	3.50	15.00	—
1957B	63,976,000	0.10	0.20	1.00	4.00	—
1958B	13,412,000	0.25	0.75	2.00	5.50	—

KM# 845.1 2 FRANCS **Weight:** 10.0000 g. **Composition:** 0.8250 Silver .2684 oz. ASW **Note:** Without mint mark. Struck at Paris Mint.

Date	Mintage	F	VF	XF	Unc	BU
1898	5,000,000	3.00	5.00	20.00	45.00	—
1898 Proof	—	Value: 425				
1899	3,500,000	4.00	7.00	25.00	50.00	—
1900	500,000	30.00	80.00	200	450	—
1900 Proof	—	Value: 400				
1901	1,860,000	6.50	18.00	50.00	150	—
1902	2,000,000	6.50	18.00	50.00	125	—
1904	1,500,000	7.50	18.00	40.00	175	—
1905	2,000,000	6.50	18.00	50.00	150	—
1908	2,502,000	3.50	6.00	20.00	75.00	—
1909	1,000,000	8.00	18.00	40.00	175	—
1910	2,190,000	3.50	6.00	20.00	75.00	—
1912	1,000,000	7.00	18.00	40.00	125	—
1913	500,000	15.00	25.00	50.00	150	—
1914	5,719,000	1.50	2.50	7.00	25.00	—
1915	13,963,000	BV	1.50	4.00	18.00	—
1916	17,887,000	BV	1.50	4.00	18.00	—
1917	16,555,000	BV	1.50	4.00	18.00	—
1918	12,026,000	BV	1.50	4.00	18.00	—
1919	9,261,000	1.50	2.50	4.50	15.00	—
1920	3,014,000	2.00	4.00	7.00	25.00	—

KM# 845.2 2 FRANCS **Weight:** 10.0000 g. **Composition:** 0.8352 Silver .2684 oz. ASW

Date	Mintage	F	VF	XF	Unc	BU
1914C	462,000	7.50	15.00	30.00	50.00	—
1914C Matte Proof	—	Value: 625				

KM# 877 2 FRANCS **Composition:** Aluminum-Bronze **Subject:** French Chamber of Commerce **Reverse:** Seated allegorical chamber of commerce figure **Note:** Without mint mark. Struck at Paris Mint.

Date	Mintage	F	VF	XF	Unc	BU
1920	14,363,000	6.00	15.00	40.00	90.00	—
1921	Inc. above	0.75	1.50	3.00	12.50	—
1922	29,463,000	0.50	1.00	2.00	7.50	—
1923	43,960,000	0.50	1.00	2.00	7.50	—
1924	—	—	—	—	—	—
1924 Open 4	29,631,000	0.50	1.00	2.00	7.50	—
1924	—	—	—	—	—	—
1924 Closed 4	Inc. above	0.65	1.50	3.00	10.00	—
1925/3	31,607,000	0.75	1.75	4.00	12.50	—
1925	Inc. above	0.50	1.00	2.00	8.00	—
1926	2,962,000	7.00	18.00	50.00	100	—
1927	1,678,000	100	150	300	700	—

KM# 886 2 FRANCS **Composition:** Aluminum-Bronze

Date	Mintage	F	VF	XF	Unc	BU
1931	1,717,000	3.00	6.00	12.00	35.00	—
1932	8,943,000	0.75	1.50	3.00	10.00	—
1933	8,413,000	0.75	1.50	3.00	10.00	—
1934	6,896,000	1.25	2.50	6.00	12.00	—
1935	298,000	12.00	20.00	40.00	90.00	—
1936	12,394,000	0.25	1.00	2.00	6.00	—
1937	11,055,000	0.25	1.00	2.00	6.00	—
1938	28,072,000	0.20	0.50	1.00	5.00	—
1939	25,403,000	0.20	0.50	1.00	5.00	—
1940	9,716,000	1.00	2.00	3.50	10.00	—
1941	16,684,000	0.25	1.00	2.00	6.00	—

KM# 886a.1 2 FRANCS **Composition:** Aluminum

Date	Mintage	F	VF	XF	Unc	BU
1941	Inc. above	0.25	0.50	1.00	3.00	—
1944	7,224,000	0.75	1.50	4.00	12.00	—
1945	16,636,000	0.50	1.00	2.50	7.00	—
1946	34,930,000	0.20	0.50	1.00	3.50	—
1947	78,984,000	0.20	0.30	1.00	2.50	—
1948	32,354,000	0.20	0.50	1.00	3.50	—
1949	13,683,000	0.25	0.50	1.00	2.50	—
1950	12,191,000	0.25	0.50	1.00	2.50	—
1958	9,906,000	0.20	0.50	1.00	3.50	—
1959	17,774,000	0.20	0.50	1.00	3.50	—

KM# 904.2 2 FRANCS **Composition:** Aluminum

Date	Mintage	F	VF	XF	Unc	BU
1943B	34,131,000	3.50	7.00	18.00	30.00	—
1944B	10,298,000	1.50	3.00	6.00	18.00	—

KM# 904.1 2 FRANCS **Composition:** Aluminum **Note:** Without mint mark. Issued for Vichy French State. Struck at Paris Mint.

Date	Mintage	F	VF	XF	Unc	BU
1943	106,997,000	0.20	0.50	1.00	6.00	—
1944	25,546,000	0.75	1.50	3.50	8.00	—

KM# 904.3 2 FRANCS **Composition:** Aluminum

Date	Mintage	F	VF	XF	Unc	BU
1944C	19,470,000	1.25	2.50	5.00	18.00	—

KM# 905 2 FRANCS **Composition:** Brass **Note:** Without mint mark. Issued during Allied Occupation.

Date	Mintage	F	VF	XF	Unc	BU
1944	50,000,000	1.00	2.00	5.00	25.00	—

KM# 886a.2 2 FRANCS **Composition:** Aluminum

Date	Mintage	F	VF	XF	Unc	BU
1944B	170,000	—	—	—	—	—
1945B	1,726,000	3.00	7.00	15.00	40.00	—
1946B	6,018,000	2.00	4.00	8.00	25.00	—
1947B	26,220,000	0.20	0.50	1.00	3.50	—
1948B	39,090,000	0.20	0.50	1.00	3.00	—

Date	Mintage	F	VF	XF	Unc	BU
1949B	23,955,000	0.20	0.50	1.00	3.50	—
1950B	18,185,000	0.50	1.00	3.00	5.00	—

KM# 886a.3 2 FRANCS **Composition:** Aluminum

Date	Mintage	F	VF	XF	Unc	BU
1945C	1,165,000	5.00	10.00	25.00	65.00	—

KM# 887 5 FRANCS **Composition:** Nickel **Note:** Without mint mark. Struck at Paris Mint.

Date	Mintage	F	VF	XF	Unc	BU
1933 (a)	160,078,000	0.75	1.50	3.50	9.00	—

KM# 888 5 FRANCS **Composition:** Nickel **Note:** Without mint mark. Struck at Paris Mint.

Date	Mintage	F	VF	XF	Unc	BU
1933 (a)	56,686,000	0.25	0.75	2.50	8.00	—
1935 (a)	54,164,000	0.25	0.75	2.50	8.00	—
1936 (a)	117,000	400	700	1,200	1,850	—
1937 (a)	157,000	35.00	60.00	120	225	—
1938 (a)	4,977,000	12.00	25.00	50.00	120	—
1939 (a)	—	700	1,200	2,000	4,000	—

KM# 888a.1 5 FRANCS **Composition:** Aluminum-Bronze **Note:** Struck for colonial use in Algeria

Date	Mintage	F	VF	XF	Unc	BU
1938 (a)	10,144,000	6.00	10.00	18.00	85.00	—
1939 (a)	Inc. above	2.50	5.00	12.00	30.00	—
1940 (a)	38,758,000	1.00	2.00	3.50	10.00	—

KM# 901 5 FRANCS **Composition:** Copper-Nickel **Note:** Without mint mark. Struck at Paris Mint.

Date	Mintage	F	VF	XF	Unc	BU
1941 (a)	13,782,000	65.00	100	150	250	—

Note: Never released for circulation

KM# 888b.1 5 FRANCS **Composition:** Aluminum **Note:** Without mint mark. Struck at Paris Mint.

Date	Mintage	F	VF	XF	Unc	BU
1945 (a) Open 9	95,399,000	0.20	0.35	1.50	6.00	—
1946 (a) Open 9	61,332,000	0.20	0.35	1.50	6.00	—
1947 (a) Open & closed 9	46,576,000	0.20	0.35	1.50	6.00	—
1948 (a) Open 9	104,473,000	1.00	3.00	6.00	12.50	—
1948 (a) closed 9	Inc. above	1.00	3.00	6.00	12.50	—
1949 (a) closed 9	203,252	0.20	0.35	0.75	3.00	—
1950 (a) closed 9	128,372	0.20	0.35	0.75	3.00	—
1952 (a) closed 9	4,000,000	20.00	40.00	100	225	—

KM# 888a.3 5 FRANCS **Composition:** Aluminum-Bronze

Date		F	VF	XF	Unc	BU
1945C Open 9		3.00	7.00	15.00	30.00	—
1946C Open 9		5.00	15.00	30.00	60.00	—

KM# 888b.2 5 FRANCS **Composition:** Aluminum

Date	Mintage	F	VF	XF	Unc	BU
1945B Open 9	6,043,000	1.50	3.00	5.00	15.00	—
1946B Open 9	13,360,000	0.75	1.50	3.00	12.00	—
1947B Open & closed 9	30,839,000	0.50	1.00	2.50	8.00	—
1948B Open & closed 9	28,047,000	20.00	40.00	100	175	—
1949B Closed 9	48,414,000	0.50	1.00	2.50	8.00	—
1950B Closed 9	28,952,000	0.75	1.50	3.50	9.00	—

KM# 888b.3 5 FRANCS **Composition:** Aluminum

Date	Mintage	F	VF	XF	Unc	BU
1945C Open 9	2,208,000	7.00	15.00	28.00	60.00	—
1946C Open 9	1,269,000	8.00	18.00	38.00	75.00	—

KM# 888a.2 5 FRANCS **Composition:** Aluminum-Bronze **Note:** Struck for colonial use in Africa.

Date	Mintage	F	VF	XF	Unc	BU
1945 (a) Open 9	13,044,000	1.00	2.00	4.00	11.00	—
1946 (a) Open 9	21,790,000	1.00	2.00	4.00	11.00	—
1947 (a)	2,662,000	150	350	550	1,000	—

Note: Date exists with both open and closed 9's

KM#846 10 FRANCS **Weight:** 3.2258 g. **Composition:** 0.9000 Gold .0933 oz. AGW **Note:** Without mint mark. Struck at Paris Mint.

Date	Mintage	F	VF	XF	Unc	BU
1901	2,100,000	BV	42.00	52.00	75.00	—
1901	2,100,000	BV	42.00	52.00	75.00	—
1905	1,426,000	BV	42.00	52.00	75.00	—
1905	1,426,000	BV	42.00	52.00	75.00	—
1906	3,665,000	BV	42.00	52.00	75.00	—
1907	3,364,000	BV	42.00	52.00	75.00	—
1908	1,650,000	BV	42.00	52.00	75.00	—
1909	599,000	BV	50.00	65.00	110	—
1910	2,110,000	BV	42.00	52.00	75.00	—
1911	1,881,000	BV	42.00	52.00	75.00	—
1912	1,756,000	BV	42.00	52.00	75.00	—
1914	3,041,000	BV	42.00	52.00	75.00	—

KM# 878 10 FRANCS **Weight:** 10.0000 g. **Composition:** 0.6800 Silver .2186 oz. ASW **Note:** Without mint mark. Struck at Paris Mint.

Date	Mintage	F	VF	XF	Unc	BU
1929	16,292,000	BV	2.25	5.50	12.00	—
1930	36,986,000	BV	1.75	4.25	9.00	—
1931	35,468,000	BV	1.75	4.25	9.00	—
1932	40,288,000	BV	1.75	3.00	7.00	—
1933	31,146,000	BV	1.75	3.00	7.00	—
1934	52,001,000	BV	1.75	3.00	7.00	—
1936	—	—	—	—	—	—
1937	52,000	65.00	125	250	360	—
1938	14,090,000	BV	2.00	6.00	12.50	—
1939	8,298,999	2.50	3.50	8.00	17.50	—

KM# 908.1 10 FRANCS **Composition:** Copper-Nickel **Obverse:** Long leaves and short leaves

Date	Mintage	F	VF	XF	Unc	BU
1945 (ll)	6,557,000	0.25	0.75	2.00	6.00	—
1945 (sl)	Inc. above	15.00	30.00	50.00	90.00	—
1946 (ll)	24,409,000	185	300	400	—	—
1946 (sl)	Inc. above	0.25	0.50	2.00	5.00	—
1947	41,627,000	0.25	0.50	1.00	3.00	—

KM# 908.2 10 FRANCS **Composition:** Copper-Nickel

Date	Mintage	F	VF	XF	Unc	BU
1946B (ll)	8,452,000	20.00	35.00	50.00	85.00	—
1946B (sl)	Inc. above	0.25	0.75	2.00	6.00	—
1947B	17,188,000	0.25	0.50	2.00	5.00	—

KM# 909.2 10 FRANCS **Composition:** Copper-Nickel **Obverse:** Large head.

Date	Mintage	F	VF	XF	Unc	BU
1947B	Inc. above	1.00	2.50	6.00	17.00	—
1948B	40,500,000	0.35	0.75	2.00	4.00	—
1949B	29,518,000	0.35	0.75	2.00	4.00	—

KM# 909.1 10 FRANCS **Composition:** Copper-Nickel **Obverse:** Small head **Note:** Without mint mark. Struck at Paris Mint.

Date	Mintage	F	VF	XF	Unc	BU
1947	Inc. above	0.30	0.75	1.50	3.50	—
1948	155,945,000	0.20	0.35	0.75	2.00	—
1949	118,149,000	0.20	0.35	0.75	2.00	—

KM# 915.1 10 FRANCS **Composition:** Aluminum-Bronze **Note:** Without mint mark. Struck at Paris Mint.

Date	Mintage	F	VF	XF	Unc	BU
1950	13,534,000	0.35	0.65	1.50	5.00	—
1951	153,689,000	0.20	0.35	0.75	2.00	—
1952	76,810,000	0.20	0.35	0.75	2.00	—
1953	46,272,000	0.25	0.50	0.75	2.50	—
1954	2,207,000	5.00	15.00	30.00	50.00	—
1955	47,466,000	0.20	0.35	0.75	2.50	—
1956 Reported, not confirmed	2,570,000	—	—	—	—	—
1957	26,351,000	0.50	1.00	2.00	4.50	—
1958 (w)	27,213,000	0.50	1.00	2.00	4.50	—
1959 Reported, not confirmed	125,000	—	—	—	—	—

KM# 915.2 10 FRANCS **Composition:** Aluminum-Bronze

Date	Mintage	F	VF	XF	Unc	BU
1950B	4,808,000	1.00	3.00	6.00	17.50	—
1951B	106,866,000	0.20	0.35	0.75	2.00	—
1952B	72,346,000	0.20	0.35	0.75	2.00	—
1953B	36,466,000	0.25	0.50	1.00	3.00	—
1954B	21,634,000	0.75	1.50	3.50	7.00	—
1958B Reported, not confirmed	1,500,000	—	—	—	—	—

KM# 847 20 FRANCS **Weight:** 6.4516 g. **Composition:** 0.9000 Gold .1867 oz. AGW **Edge Lettering:** DIEU PROTEGE LA FRANCE

Date	Mintage	F	VF	XF	Unc	BU
1901	2,643,000	BV	70.00	80.00	125	—
1901	2,643,000	BV	70.00	80.00	125	—
1902	2,394,000	BV	70.00	80.00	125	—
1902	2,394,000	BV	70.00	80.00	125	—
1903	4,405,000	BV	70.00	80.00	125	—
1904	7,706,000	BV	70.00	80.00	125	—
1905	9,158,000	BV	70.00	80.00	125	—
1906	14,613,000	BV	70.00	80.00	125	—

KM# 857 20 FRANCS **Weight:** 6.4516 g. **Composition:** 0.9000 Gold .1867 oz. AGW **Edge Lettering:** LIBERTE EGALITE FRATERNITE **Note:** ALl dates from 1907-1914 have been officially restruck.

Date	Mintage	F	VF	XF	Unc	BU
1906	—	BV	65.00	75.00	115	—
1907	17,716,000	BV	65.00	75.00	115	—
1908	6,721,000	BV	65.00	75.00	115	—
1909	9,637,000	BV	65.00	75.00	115	—
1910	5,779,000	BV	65.00	75.00	115	—
1911	5,346,000	BV	65.00	75.00	115	—
1912	10,332,000	BV	65.00	75.00	115	—
1913	12,163,000	BV	65.00	75.00	115	—
1914	6,518,000	BV	65.00	75.00	115	—

KM# 879 20 FRANCS **Weight:** 20.0000 g. **Composition:** 0.6800 Silver .4372 oz. ASW **Reverse:** Long Leaves & Short Leaves **Note:** Without mint mark. Struck at Paris Mint.

Date	Mintage	F	VF	XF	Unc	BU
1929 (ll)	3,234,000	BV	6.00	9.00	35.00	—
1933 (sl)	—	BV	4.50	5.50	18.00	—

Note: Counterfeits exist in bronze-aluminum with thin silver sheath

Date	Mintage	F	VF	XF	Unc	BU
1933 (ll)	Inc. above	BV	4.50	5.50	18.00	—
1934 (sl)	11,785,000	BV	4.50	10.00	30.00	—
1936 (sl)	48,000	200	300	450	—	—
1937 (sl)	1,189,000	10.00	15.00	25.00	50.00	—
1938 (sl)	10,910,000	BV	4.50	7.00	20.00	—
1939 (sl)	3,918	1,000	2,000	2,750	4,500	—

KM# 917.1 20 FRANCS Composition: Aluminum-Bronze **Obverse:** G. GUIRAUD behind head **Note:** Without mint mark. Struck at Paris Mint.

Date	Mintage	F	VF	XF	Unc	BU
1950 (3 plumes)	120,656,000	2.00	6.00	12.00	40.00	—
1950 (4 plumes)	Inc. above	0.25	0.40	1.00	2.50	—
1951 (4 plumes)	97,922,000	0.25	0.40	1.00	2.50	—
1952 (4 plumes)	130,281,000	0.25	0.40	1.00	2.50	—
1953 (4 plumes)	60,158,000	0.30	0.50	1.00	2.50	—

KM# 916.1 20 FRANCS Composition: Aluminum-Bronze **Obverse:** GEORGES GUIRAUD behind head

Date	Mintage	F	VF	XF	Unc	BU
1950 (3 plumes)	5,779,000	0.50	1.00	2.50	7.00	—
1950 (4 plumes)	—	125	200	350	700	—

KM# 916.2 20 FRANCS Composition: Aluminum-Bronze

Date	F	VF	XF	Unc	BU
1950B (3 plumes)	1.50	3.00	7.00	20.00	—
1950B (4 plumes)	40.00	85.00	150	225	—

KM# 917.2 20 FRANCS Composition: Aluminum-Bronze

Date	Mintage	F	VF	XF	Unc	BU
1950B (3 plumes)	43,355,000	25.00	35.00	50.00	135	—
1950B (4 plumes)	Inc. above	0.50	1.00	3.00	6.50	—
1951B (4 plumes)	46,815,000	0.30	0.50	1.75	3.50	—
1952B (4 plumes)	54,381,000	0.30	0.50	1.75	3.50	—
1953B (4 plumes)	42,410,000	0.30	0.50	1.75	3.50	—
1954B (4 plumes)	1,573,000	125	200	350	900	—

KM# 831 50 FRANCS Weight: 16.1290 g. **Composition:** 0.9000 Gold .4467 oz. AGW

Date	Mintage	F	VF	XF	Unc	BU
1904A	20,000	300	550	900	1,600	—
1904A	20,000	300	550	900	1,600	—

KM# 918.1 50 FRANCS Composition: Aluminum-Bronze **Note:** Without mint mark. Struck at Paris Mint.

Date	Mintage	F	VF	XF	Unc	BU
1950	600,000	75.00	150	350	625	—
1951	68,630,000	0.50	1.00	2.25	5.50	—
1952	74,212,000	0.50	1.00	2.25	5.50	—
1953	63,172,000	0.50	1.00	2.25	5.50	—
1954	997,000	15.00	35.00	65.00	110	—
1958 (w)	501,000	25.00	60.00	110	240	—

KM# 918.2 50 FRANCS Composition: Aluminum-Bronze

Date	Mintage	F	VF	XF	Unc	BU
1951B	11,829,000	0.75	1.50	3.00	9.00	—
1952B	13,432,000	1.00	2.00	5.00	15.00	—
1953B	23,376,000	0.65	1.25	2.50	8.00	—
1954B	6,531,000	3.00	5.50	11.50	30.00	—

KM# 832 100 FRANCS Weight: 32.2581 g. **Composition:** 0.9000 Gold .9335 oz. AGW **Edge Lettering:** DIEU PROTEGE LA FRANCE

Date	Mintage	F	VF	XF	Unc	BU
1900A	20,000	450	475	525	675	—
1900A Proof	—	Value: 5,000				
1901A	10,000	450	475	525	675	—
1901A	10,000	450	475	525	675	—
1902A	10,000	450	475	525	675	—
1902A	10,000	450	475	525	675	—
1903A	10,000	450	475	525	675	—
1904A	20,000	450	475	525	675	—
1905A	10,000	450	475	525	675	—
1906A	30,000	450	475	525	675	—

KM# 858 100 FRANCS Weight: 32.2581 g. **Composition:** 0.9000 Gold .9335 oz. AGW **Edge Lettering:** LIBERTE EGALITE FRATERNITE

Date	Mintage	F	VF	XF	Unc	BU
1907	20,000	350	375	400	550	—
1908	23,000	350	375	400	550	—
1909	20,000	350	375	400	550	—
1910	20,000	350	375	400	550	—
1911	30,000	350	375	400	550	—
1912	20,000	350	375	400	550	—
1913	30,000	350	375	400	550	—
1914 Rare	1,281	—	—	—	—	—

KM# 880 100 FRANCS Weight: 6.5500 g. **Composition:** 0.9000 Gold .1895 oz. AGW **Note:** Without mint mark. Struck at Paris Mint.

Date	F	VF	XF	Unc	BU
1929	—	—	2,500	4,000	—
1932	—	—	3,100	4,600	—
1933	—	—	1,650	2,250	—
1934 Rare	—	—	—	—	—
1935	—	—	500	800	—
1936	—	—	500	800	—

KM# 919.1 100 FRANCS Composition: Copper-Nickel

Date	Mintage	F	VF	XF	Unc	BU
1954	97,285,000	0.50	1.00	2.50	7.00	—
1955	152,517,000	0.25	0.75	1.50	4.50	—
1956	7,578,000	3.50	7.50	15.00	40.00	—
1957	11,312,000	1.50	3.00	6.00	18.00	—
1958 (w)	3,256,000	2.50	5.50	12.50	35.00	—
1958 (o)	Inc. above	20.00	40.00	90.00	175	—

KM# 919.2 100 FRANCS Composition: Copper-Nickel

Date	Mintage	F	VF	XF	Unc	BU
1954B	86,261,000	0.50	1.25	2.50	5.00	—
1955B	136,585,000	0.25	0.75	1.50	3.50	—
1956B	19,154,000	1.00	2.00	4.50	10.00	—
1957B	25,702,000	1.00	2.00	4.50	12.50	—
1958B	54,072,000	1.00	2.00	4.50	11.50	—

REFORM COINAGE

(Commencing 1960)

1 Old Franc = 1 New Centime; 100 New Centimes = 1 New Franc

KM# 928 CENTIME Composition: Chrome-Steel **Note:** 1991-1993 dated coins, non-Proof, exist in both coin and medal alignment. Values given here are for medal alignment examples. Pieces struck in coin alignment have been traded for as much as $50.00. Struck at Paris Mint.

Date	Mintage	F	VF	XF	Unc	BU
1962	34,200,000	—	—	0.10	0.25	—
1963	16,811,000	—	0.10	0.15	0.35	—
1964	22,654,000	—	—	0.10	0.25	—
1965	47,799,000	—	—	0.10	0.25	—
1966	19,688,000	—	—	0.10	0.25	—
1967	52,308,000	—	—	0.10	0.25	—
1968	40,890,000	—	—	0.10	0.25	—
1969	35,430,000	—	—	0.10	0.25	—
1970	29,600,000	—	—	0.10	0.25	—
1971	3,082,000	—	—	0.10	0.25	—
1972	1,014,999	—	0.10	0.15	0.35	—
1973	1,806,000	—	0.10	0.15	0.35	—
1974	7,949,000	—	—	0.10	0.25	—
1975	771,000	—	0.10	0.25	1.00	—
1976	4,482,000	—	—	0.10	0.25	—
1977	6,425,000	—	—	0.10	0.25	—
1978	1,236,000	—	0.10	0.15	0.35	—
1979	2,213,000	—	—	0.10	0.25	—
1980	60,000	—	—	—	1.00	—
1981	50,000	—	—	—	1.00	—
1982	69,000	—	—	—	1.00	—
1983	101,000	—	—	—	1.00	—
1984	50,000	—	—	—	1.00	—
1985 In sets only	20,000	—	—	—	1.00	—
1986 In sets only	48,000	—	—	—	1.00	—
1987	100,000	—	—	—	1.00	—
1988	100,000	—	—	—	1.00	—
1989	83,000	—	—	—	1.00	—
1990	15,000	—	—	—	1.00	—
1991	5,000	—	—	—	1.00	—
1991 Proof	10,000	Value: 2.00				
1992	85,000	—	—	—	1.00	—
1992 Proof	15,000	Value: 2.00				
1993	40,000	—	—	—	1.00	—
1993 Proof	10,000	Value: 2.00				
1994 (bee)	20,000	—	—	—	—	—
1994 (fish)	10,000	—	—	—	—	—
1995	25,000	—	—	—	1.00	—
1995 Proof	10,000	Value: 2.00				
1996	17,000	—	—	—	1.00	—
1996 Proof	8,000	Value: 2.00				
1997	15,000	—	—	—	1.00	—
1997 Proof	10,000	Value: 2.00				
1998	—	—	—	—	1.00	—
1998 Proof	—	Value: 2.00				
1999	—	—	—	—	1.00	—
1999 Proof	—	Value: 2.00				
2000	—	—	—	—	1.00	—
2000 Proof	—	Value: 2.00				
2001	—	—	—	—	1.00	—
2001 Proof	—	Value: 2.00				

KM# 928a CENTIME Weight: 2.5000 g. **Composition:** 0.7500 Gold .0603 oz. AGW **Obverse:** Medallic alignment **Reverse:** Medallic alignment **Edge:** Plain **Note:** Last Centime. Struck at Paris Mint.

Date	F	VF	XF	Unc	BU
2000	—	—	—	50.00	—
2001	—	—	—	70.00	—

KM# 927 5 CENTIMES Composition: Chrome-Steel **Note:** Struck at Paris Mint.

Date	Mintage	F	VF	XF	Unc	BU
1961	39,000,000	0.10	0.20	0.50	2.00	—
1962	166,360,000	0.10	0.15	0.20	0.75	—
1963	71,900,000	0.10	0.20	0.40	1.00	—
1964	126,480,000	0.10	0.15	0.30	0.75	—

KM# 933 5 CENTIMES **Composition:** Aluminum-Bronze **Note:** 1991-1993 dated coins, non-Proof exist in both coin and medal alignment.

Date	Mintage	F	VF	XF	Unc	BU
1966	502,512,000	—	—	—	0.10	—
1967	11,747,000	—	—	0.10	0.25	—
1968	110,395,000	—	—	—	0.10	—
1969	94,955,000	—	—	—	0.10	—
1970	58,900,000	—	—	—	0.10	—
1971	93,190,000	—	—	—	0.10	—
1972	100,515,000	—	—	—	0.10	—
1973	100,344,000	—	—	—	0.10	—
1974	103,890,000	—	—	—	0.10	—
1975	95,835,000	—	—	—	0.10	—
1976	148,395,000	—	—	—	0.10	—
1977	115,285,000	—	—	—	0.10	—
1978	189,804,000	—	—	—	0.10	—
1979	180,000,000	—	—	—	0.10	—
1980	180,010,000	—	—	—	0.10	—
1981	50,000	—	—	—	0.50	—
1982	138,000,000	—	—	—	0.10	—
1983	132,000,000	—	—	—	0.10	—
1984	150,000,000	—	—	—	0.10	—
1985	170,000,000	—	—	—	0.10	—
1986	280,000,000	—	—	—	0.10	—
1987	310,000,000	—	—	—	0.10	—
1988	200,000,000	—	—	—	0.10	—
1989	72,000	—	—	—	0.20	—
1990	79,992,000	—	—	—	0.20	—
1991	49,994,000	—	—	—	0.20	—
1991 Proof	10,000	Value: 1.00				
1992	179,996,000	—	—	—	0.20	—
1992 Proof	15,000	Value: 1.00				
1993	154,988,000	—	—	—	0.20	—
1993 Proof	10,000	Value: 1.00				
1994	—	—	—	—	0.20	—
1994 (Fish)	60,000,000	—	—	—	0.20	—
1994 (Fish) Proof	10,000	—	—	—	—	—
1994 (Bee)	59,996,000	—	—	—	0.20	—
1995	129,991,999	—	—	—	0.20	—
1995 Proof	10,000	Value: 1.00				
1996	139,990,000	—	—	—	0.20	—
1996 Proof	8,000	Value: 1.00				
1997	199,995,000	—	—	—	0.20	—
1997 Proof	10,000	Value: 1.00				
1998	—	—	—	—	0.20	—
1998 Proof	—	Value: 1.00				
1999	—	—	—	—	0.20	—
1999 Proof	—	Value: 1.00				
2000	—	—	—	—	0.20	—
2000 Proof	—	Value: 1.00				
2001	—	—	—	—	0.20	—
2001 Proof	—	Value: 1.00				

KM# 929 10 CENTIMES **Composition:** Aluminum-Bronze **Note:** Without mint mark. Struck at Paris Mint. 1991-1993 dated coins, non-Proof, exist in both coin and medal alignment.

Date	Mintage	F	VF	XF	Unc	BU
1962	29,100,000	—	—	0.10	0.40	—
1963	217,601,000	—	—	—	0.10	—
1964	93,409,000	—	—	0.10	0.20	—
1965	41,220,000	—	—	0.10	0.30	—
1966	16,428,999	—	0.10	0.15	0.40	—
1967	196,728,000	—	—	—	0.10	—
1968	111,700,000	—	—	—	0.10	—
1969	129,530,000	—	—	—	0.10	—
1970	77,020,000	—	—	—	0.10	—
1971	26,280,000	—	—	—	0.10	—
1972	45,700,000	—	—	—	0.10	—
1973	58,000,000	—	—	—	0.10	—
1974	91,990,000	—	—	—	0.10	—
1975	74,450,000	—	—	—	0.10	—
1976	137,320,000	—	—	—	0.10	—
1977	140,110,000	—	—	—	0.10	—
1978	154,360,000	—	—	—	0.10	—
1979	140,000,000	—	—	—	0.10	—
1980	140,010,000	—	—	—	0.10	—
1981	135,000,000	—	—	—	0.10	—
1982	110,000,000	—	—	—	0.10	—
1983	150,000,000	—	—	—	0.10	—
1984	200,000,000	—	—	—	0.10	—
1985	170,000,000	—	—	—	0.10	—
1986	150,000,000	—	—	—	0.10	—
1987	150,000,000	—	—	—	0.10	—
1988	145,000,000	—	—	—	0.10	—
1989	179,984,000	—	—	—	0.10	—
1990	179,992,000	—	—	—	0.10	—

Date	Mintage	F	VF	XF	Unc	BU
1991	179,986,000	—	—	—	0.10	—
1991 Proof	10,000	Value: 1.00				
1992	179,996,000	—	—	—	0.10	—
1992 Proof	15,000	Value: 1.00				
1993	154,988,000	—	—	—	0.10	—
1993 Proof	10,000	Value: 1.00				
1994	—	—	—	—	0.10	—
1994 (Fish)	103,000,000	—	—	—	0.10	—
1994 (Fish) Proof	10,000	Value: 1.00				
1994 (Bee)	76,988,000	—	—	—	0.10	—
1995	169,996,000	—	—	—	0.10	—
1995 Proof	10,000	Value: 1.00				
1996	179,981,000	—	—	—	0.10	—
1996 Proof	8,000	Value: 1.00				
1997	551,991,000	—	—	—	0.10	—
1997 Proof	10,000	Value: 1.00				
1998	—	—	—	—	0.10	—
1998 Proof	—	Value: 1.00				
1999	—	—	—	—	0.10	—
1999 Proof	—	Value: 1.00				
2000	—	—	—	—	0.10	—
2000 Proof	—	Value: 1.00				
2001	—	—	—	—	0.10	—
2001 Proof	—	Value: 1.00				

KM# 930 20 CENTIMES **Composition:** Aluminum-Bronze **Note:** Without mint mark. Struck at Paris Mint. 1991-1993 dated coins, non-Proof, exist in both coin and medal alignment.

Date	Mintage	F	VF	XF	Unc	BU
1962	48,200,000	—	—	0.10	0.40	—
1963	190,330,000	—	—	0.10	0.30	—
1964	127,521,000	—	—	0.10	0.30	—
1965	27,024,000	—	0.10	0.20	0.40	—
1966	21,762,000	—	0.10	0.20	0.40	—
1967	138,780,000	—	—	0.10	0.15	—
1968	77,408,000	—	—	0.10	0.20	—
1969	50,570,000	—	—	0.10	0.20	—
1970	70,040,000	—	—	0.10	0.15	—
1971	31,080,000	—	—	0.10	0.15	—
1972	39,740,000	—	—	0.10	0.15	—
1973	45,240,000	—	—	0.10	0.15	—
1974	54,250,000	—	—	0.10	0.15	—
1975	40,570,000	—	—	0.10	0.15	—
1976	117,610,000	—	—	—	0.10	—
1977	100,340,000	—	—	—	0.10	—
1978	125,015,000	—	—	—	0.10	—
1979	70,000,000	—	—	—	0.10	—
1980	20,010,000	—	—	0.10	0.15	—
1981	125,000,000	—	—	—	0.10	—
1982	150,000,000	—	—	—	0.10	—
1983	110,000,000	—	—	—	0.10	—
1984	200,000,000	—	—	—	0.10	—
1985	150,000,000	—	—	—	0.10	—
1986	40,000,000	—	—	—	0.10	—
1987	60,000,000	—	—	—	0.10	—
1988	220,000,000	—	—	—	0.10	—
1989	139,985,000	—	—	—	0.10	—
1990	49,990,000	—	—	—	0.10	—
1991	39,992,000	—	—	—	0.10	—
1991 1 Proof	10,000	Value: 1.00				
1992	89,985,000	—	—	—	0.10	—
1992 1 Proof	15,000	Value: 1.00				
1993	10,990,000	—	—	—	0.10	—
1993 1 Proof	10,000	Value: 1.00				
1994	—	—	—	—	0.10	—
1994 (Fish)	60,000,000	—	—	—	0.10	—
1994 (Fish) Proof	10,000	Value: 1.00				
1994 (Bee)	79,900,000	—	—	—	0.10	—
1995	109,995,000	—	—	—	0.10	—
1995 Proof	10,000	Value: 1.00				
1996	139,987,000	—	—	—	0.10	—
1996 Proof	8,000	Value: 1.00				
1997	435,990,000	—	—	—	0.10	—
1997 Proof	10,000	Value: 1.00				
1998	—	—	—	—	0.10	—
1998 Proof	—	Value: 1.00				
1999	—	—	—	—	0.10	—
1999 Proof	—	Value: 1.00				
2000	—	—	—	—	0.10	—
2000 Proof	—	Value: 1.00				
2001	—	—	—	—	0.10	—
2001 Proof	—	Value: 1.00				

KM# 939.1 50 CENTIMES **Composition:** Aluminum-Bronze **Obverse:** 3 folds in collar

Date	Mintage	F	VF	XF	Unc	BU
1962	37,560,000	0.30	0.60	1.50	3.00	—
1963	62,482,000	0.20	0.40	1.00	2.00	—

KM# 939.2 50 CENTIMES **Composition:** Aluminum-Bronze **Obverse:** 4 folds in collar

Date	Mintage	F	VF	XF	Unc	BU
1962	Inc. above	30.00	70.00	120	160	—
1963	Inc. above	0.20	0.40	1.00	2.00	—
1964	41,471,000	0.45	0.90	2.00	6.00	—

KM# 931.1 1/2 FRANC **Composition:** Nickel **Note:** Without mint mark. Struck at Paris Mint.

Date	Mintage	F	VF	XF	Unc	BU
1965 Small legends	184,834,000	—	—	0.15	0.30	—
1965 Large legends	Inc. above	—	—	0.15	0.30	—
1966 Without O. ROTY	88,890,000	—	—	0.15	0.30	—
1967	28,394,000	—	—	0.15	0.40	—
1968 Without O. ROTY	57,548,000	—	—	0.15	0.30	—
1969	47,144,000	—	—	0.15	0.30	—
1970	42,298,000	—	—	0.15	0.30	—
1971	36,068,000	—	—	0.15	0.30	—
1972	42,302,000	—	—	0.15	0.30	—
1972 Without O. ROTY	Inc. above	25.00	50.00	100	150	—
1973 Without O. ROTY	48,372,000	—	—	0.15	0.30	—
1974	37,072,000	—	—	0.15	0.30	—
1975	22,803,000	—	—	0.15	0.40	—
1976	115,314,000	—	—	0.15	0.30	—
1977	131,644,000	—	—	0.15	0.30	—
1978	63,360,000	—	—	0.15	0.30	—
1979	51,000	—	—	—	0.50	—
1980 In sets only	60,000	—	—	—	0.50	—
1981	50,000	—	—	—	0.50	—
1982	78,000	—	—	—	0.50	—
1983	50,000,000	—	—	0.15	0.30	—
1984	80,000,000	—	—	0.15	0.30	—
1985	50,000,000	—	—	—	1.50	—
1986	110,000,000	—	—	—	1.50	—
1987	50,000,000	—	—	—	0.30	—
1988	100,000	—	—	—	0.40	—
1989	83,000	—	—	—	0.40	—
1990	15,000	—	—	—	0.40	—
1991	—	—	—	—	0.40	—
Note: Exists in both coin and medal alignment						
1992	—	—	—	—	0.40	—
Note: Exists in both coin and medal alignment						
1993	—	—	—	—	0.40	—
1994	—	—	—	—	0.40	—
1995	—	—	—	—	0.40	—
1996	—	—	—	—	0.40	—
1997	—	—	—	—	0.40	—
1998	—	—	—	—	0.40	—
1999	—	—	—	—	0.40	—

KM# 931.2 1/2 FRANC **Composition:** Nickel **Obverse:** Modified sower, engraver's signature. O. ROTY preceded by D'AP **Edge:** Plain

Date	Mintage	F	VF	XF	Unc	BU
1991	49,990,000	—	—	—	0.40	—
1991 Proof	10,000	Value: 1.50				
1992	29,988,000	—	—	—	0.40	—
1992 Proof	15,000	Value: 1.50				
1993	24,992,000	—	—	—	0.40	—
1993 Proof	10,000	Value: 1.50				
1994 (Fish)	10,000,000	—	—	—	0.40	—
1994 (Fish) Proof	10,000	Value: 1.50				
1994 (Bee)	29,992,000	—	—	—	0.40	—
1995	29,996,000	—	—	—	0.40	—
1995 Proof	10,000	Value: 1.50				
1996	55,983,000	—	—	—	0.40	—
1996 Proof	8,000	Value: 1.50				
1997	99,991,000	—	—	—	0.40	—
1997 Proof	10,000	Value: 1.50				
1998 Proof	—	Value: 1.50				
1999 Proof	—	Value: 1.50				
2000	—	—	—	—	0.40	—
2000 Proof	—	Value: 1.50				

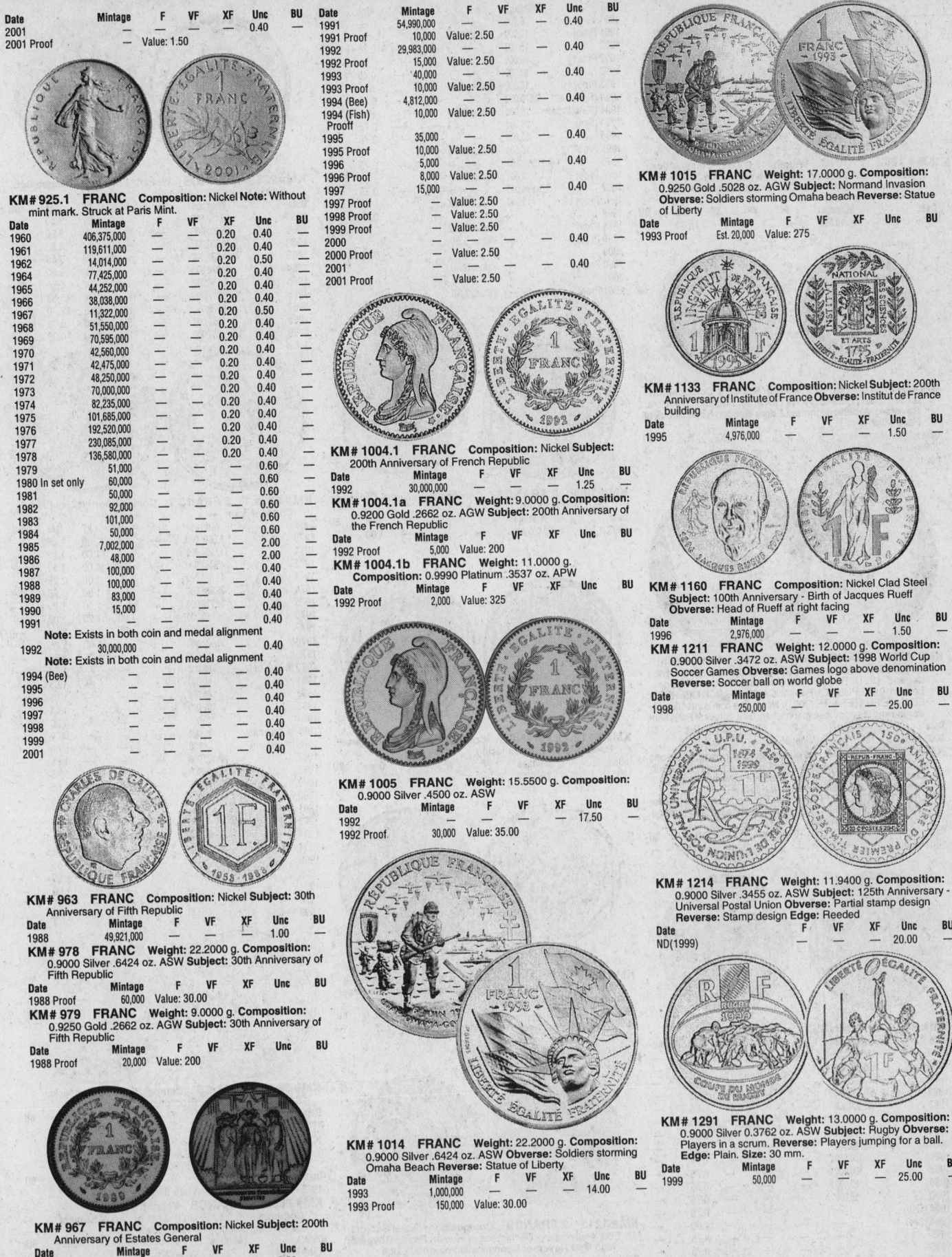

Date	Mintage	F	VF	XF	Unc	BU
2001	—	—	—	—	0.40	—
2001 Proof	—	Value: 1.50				

KM# 925.1 FRANC Composition: Nickel **Note:** Without mint mark. Struck at Paris Mint.

Date	Mintage	F	VF	XF	Unc	BU
1960	406,375,000	—	—	0.20	0.40	—
1961	119,611,000	—	—	0.20	0.40	—
1962	14,014,000	—	—	0.20	0.50	—
1964	77,425,000	—	—	0.20	0.40	—
1965	44,252,000	—	—	0.20	0.40	—
1966	38,038,000	—	—	0.20	0.40	—
1967	11,322,000	—	—	0.20	0.50	—
1968	51,550,000	—	—	0.20	0.40	—
1969	70,595,000	—	—	0.20	0.40	—
1970	42,560,000	—	—	0.20	0.40	—
1971	42,475,000	—	—	0.20	0.40	—
1972	48,250,000	—	—	0.20	0.40	—
1973	70,000,000	—	—	0.20	0.40	—
1974	82,235,000	—	—	0.20	0.40	—
1975	101,685,000	—	—	0.20	0.40	—
1976	192,520,000	—	—	0.20	0.40	—
1977	230,085,000	—	—	0.20	0.40	—
1978	136,580,000	—	—	0.20	0.40	—
1979	51,000	—	—	—	0.60	—
1980 In set only	60,000	—	—	—	0.60	—
1981	50,000	—	—	—	0.60	—
1982	92,000	—	—	—	0.60	—
1983	101,000	—	—	—	0.60	—
1984	50,000	—	—	—	0.60	—
1985	7,002,000	—	—	—	2.00	—
1986	48,000	—	—	—	2.00	—
1987	100,000	—	—	—	0.40	—
1988	100,000	—	—	—	0.40	—
1989	83,000	—	—	—	0.40	—
1990	15,000	—	—	—	0.40	—
1991	—	—	—	—	0.40	—
Note: Exists in both coin and medal alignment						
1992	30,000,000	—	—	—	0.40	—
Note: Exists in both coin and medal alignment						
1994 (Bee)	—	—	—	—	0.40	—
1995	—	—	—	—	0.40	—
1996	—	—	—	—	0.40	—
1997	—	—	—	—	0.40	—
1998	—	—	—	—	0.40	—
1999	—	—	—	—	0.40	—
2001	—	—	—	—	0.40	—

KM# 963 FRANC Composition: Nickel **Subject:** 30th Anniversary of Fifth Republic

Date	Mintage	F	VF	XF	Unc	BU
1988	49,921,000	—	—	—	1.00	—

KM# 978 FRANC Weight: 22.2000 g. **Composition:** 0.9000 Silver .6424 oz. ASW **Subject:** 30th Anniversary of Fifth Republic

Date	Mintage	F	VF	XF	Unc	BU
1988 Proof	60,000	Value: 30.00				

KM# 979 FRANC Weight: 9.0000 g. **Composition:** 0.9250 Gold .2662 oz. AGW **Subject:** 30th Anniversary of Fifth Republic

Date	Mintage	F	VF	XF	Unc	BU
1988 Proof	20,000	Value: 200				

KM# 967 FRANC Composition: Nickel **Subject:** 200th Anniversary of Estates General

Date	Mintage	F	VF	XF	Unc	BU
1989	5,010,000	—	—	—	2.50	—

KM# 925.2 FRANC Composition: Nickel **Obverse:** Modified sower, engraver's signature: O. ROTY, preceded by D'AP **Edge:** Plain

Date	Mintage	F	VF	XF	Unc	BU
1991	54,990,000	—	—	—	0.40	—
1991 Proof	10,000	Value: 2.50				
1992	29,983,000	—	—	—	0.40	—
1992 Proof	15,000	Value: 2.50				
1993	40,000	—	—	—	0.40	—
1993 Proof	10,000	Value: 2.50				
1994 (Bee)	4,812,000	—	—	—	0.40	—
1994 (Fish) Prooff	10,000	Value: 2.50				
1995	35,000	—	—	—	0.40	—
1995 Proof	10,000	Value: 2.50				
1996	5,000	—	—	—	0.40	—
1996 Proof	8,000	Value: 2.50				
1997	15,000	—	—	—	0.40	—
1997 Proof	—	Value: 2.50				
1998 Proof	—	Value: 2.50				
1999 Proof	—	Value: 2.50				
2000	—	—	—	—	0.40	—
2000 Proof	—	Value: 2.50				
2001	—	—	—	—	0.40	—
2001 Proof	—	Value: 2.50				

KM# 1004.1 FRANC Composition: Nickel **Subject:** 200th Anniversary of French Republic

Date	Mintage	F	VF	XF	Unc	BU
1992	30,000,000	—	—	—	1.25	—

KM# 1004.1a FRANC Weight: 9.0000 g. **Composition:** 0.9200 Gold .2662 oz. AGW **Subject:** 200th Anniversary of the French Republic

Date	Mintage	F	VF	XF	Unc	BU
1992 Proof	5,000	Value: 200				

KM# 1004.1b FRANC Weight: 11.0000 g. **Composition:** 0.9990 Platinum .3537 oz. APW

Date	Mintage	F	VF	XF	Unc	BU
1992 Proof	2,000	Value: 325				

KM# 1005 FRANC Weight: 15.5500 g. **Composition:** 0.9000 Silver .4500 oz. ASW

Date	Mintage	F	VF	XF	Unc	BU
1992	—	—	—	—	17.50	—
1992 Proof	30,000	Value: 35.00				

KM# 1014 FRANC Weight: 22.2000 g. **Composition:** 0.9000 Silver .6424 oz. ASW **Obverse:** Soldiers storming Omaha Beach **Reverse:** Statue of Liberty

Date	Mintage	F	VF	XF	Unc	BU
1993	1,000,000	—	—	—	14.00	—
1993 Proof	150,000	Value: 30.00				

KM# 1015 FRANC Weight: 17.0000 g. **Composition:** 0.9250 Gold .5028 oz. AGW **Subject:** Normand Invasion **Obverse:** Soldiers storming Omaha beach **Reverse:** Statue of Liberty

Date	Mintage	F	VF	XF	Unc	BU
1993 Proof	Est. 20,000	Value: 275				

KM# 1133 FRANC Composition: Nickel **Subject:** 200th Anniversary of Institute of France **Obverse:** Institut de France building

Date	Mintage	F	VF	XF	Unc	BU
1995	4,976,000	—	—	—	1.50	—

KM# 1160 FRANC Composition: Nickel Clad Steel **Subject:** 100th Anniversary - Birth of Jacques Rueff **Obverse:** Head of Rueff at right facing

Date	Mintage	F	VF	XF	Unc	BU
1996	2,976,000	—	—	—	1.50	—

KM# 1211 FRANC Weight: 12.0000 g. **Composition:** 0.9000 Silver .3472 oz. ASW **Subject:** 1998 World Cup Soccer Games **Obverse:** Games logo above denomination **Reverse:** Soccer ball on world globe

Date	Mintage	F	VF	XF	Unc	BU
1998	250,000	—	—	—	25.00	—

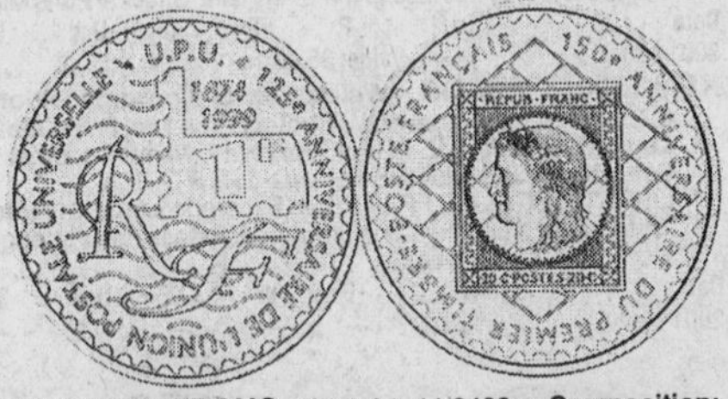

KM# 1214 FRANC Weight: 11.9400 g. **Composition:** 0.9000 Silver .3455 oz. ASW **Subject:** 125th Anniversary - Universal Postal Union **Obverse:** Partial stamp design **Reverse:** Stamp design **Edge:** Reeded

Date	F	VF	XF	Unc	BU
ND(1999)	—	—	—	20.00	—

KM# 1291 FRANC Weight: 13.0000 g. **Composition:** 0.9000 Silver 0.3762 oz. ASW **Subject:** Rugby **Obverse:** Players in a scrum. **Reverse:** Players jumping for a ball. **Edge:** Plain. **Size:** 30 mm.

Date	Mintage	F	VF	XF	Unc	BU
1999	50,000	—	—	—	25.00	—

KM# 1262 FRANC **Weight:** 13.0000 g. **Composition:** 0.9000 Silver .3762 oz. ASW **Subject:** World Soccer Championship **Obverse:** Soccer ball design **Reverse:** Soccer player **Edge:** Reeded

Date	Mintage	F	VF	XF	Unc	BU
2000	10,000	—	—	—	25.00	—

KM# 925.1a FRANC **Weight:** 8.0000 g. **Composition:** 0.7500 Gold .1929 oz. AGW **Obverse:** Medallic alignment **Reverse:** Medallic alignment **Edge:** Reeded **Note:** Struck at Paris Mint.

Date	F	VF	XF	Unc	BU
2000	—	—	—	100	—
2001	—	—	—	135	—

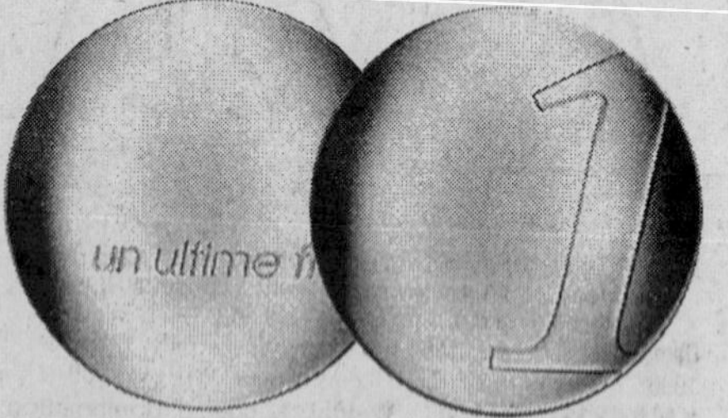

KM# 1290 FRANC **Weight:** 17.7700 g. **Composition:** 0.9800 Silver .5599 oz. ASW **Subject:** The Last Franc **Obv. Legend:** UN ULTIME FRANC **Reverse:** Number "1" **Edge Lettering:** REPUBLIQUE FRANCAISE STARCK LIBERTE EGALITE FRATERNITE (2001). **Note:** The coin is intentionally warped and the edge inscription is very faint. Struck at Paris Mint.

Date	F	VF	XF	Unc	BU
2001 Matte	—	Value: 35.00			

KM# 1290a FRANC **Weight:** 26.1000 g. **Composition:** 0.7500 Gold .6294 oz. AGW **Subject:** The Last Franc **Obv. Legend:** UN ULTIME FRANC **Reverse:** Number 1 **Edge Lettering:** REPUBLIQUE FRANCAISE.STARCK. LIBERTE. EGALITE.FRATERNITE (cornucopia) 2001 **Note:** This coin has an intentionally warped surface and the edge inscription is very weak.

Date	Mintage	F	VF	XF	Unc	BU
2001 Matte	5,000	—	—	—	450	—

KM# 942.1 2 FRANCS **Composition:** Nickel

Date	Mintage	F	VF	XF	Unc	BU
1979	130,000,000	—	—	0.40	0.65	—
1980	100,010,000	—	—	0.40	0.65	—
1981	120,000,000	—	—	0.40	0.65	—
1982	90,000,000	—	—	0.40	0.65	—
1983	90,000,000	—	—	0.40	0.65	—
1984	50,000	—	—	—	0.75	—
1985	20,000	—	—	—	2.00	—
1986	48,000	—	—	—	2.00	—
1987	100,000	—	—	—	0.75	—
1988	100,000	—	—	—	0.75	—
1989	83,000	—	—	—	0.75	—
1990	15,000	—	—	—	0.75	—
1994 (Fish)	—	—	—	—	0.75	—
1994 (Bee)	—	—	—	—	14.00	—
1995	—	—	—	—	0.75	—
1996	—	—	—	—	0.75	—
1997	—	—	—	—	0.75	—
1998	—	—	—	—	0.75	—
1999	—	—	—	—	0.75	—

KM# 942.2 2 FRANCS **Composition:** Nickel **Edge:** Plain

Date	Mintage	F	VF	XF	Unc	BU
1991	5,000	—	—	—	—	—
1991 Proof	10,000	Value: 3.50				
1992	15,000	—	—	—	0.75	—
1992 Proof	85,000	Value: 3.50				
1993	40,000	—	—	—	0.75	—
1993 Proof	10,000	Value: 3.50				
1994 (Fish)	9,870,000	—	—	—	0.75	—
1994 (Fish) Proof	10,000	Value: 3.50				
1994 (Bee)	20,000	—	—	—	0.75	—
1995	20,000	—	—	—	0.75	—
1995 Proof	10,000	Value: 3.50				
1996	11,980,000	—	—	—	0.75	—
1996 Proof	8,000	Value: 3.50				
1997	9,990,000	—	—	—	0.75	—
1997 Proof	10,000	Value: 3.50				
1998	—	—	—	—	0.75	—
1998 Proof	—	Value: 3.50				
1999 Proof	—	Value: 3.50				
2000	—	—	—	—	0.75	—
2000 Proof	—	Value: 3.50				
2001	—	—	—	—	0.75	—
2001 Proof	—	Value: 3.50				

KM# 1062 2 FRANCS **Composition:** Nickel **Obverse:** Jean Moulin facing

Date	Mintage	F	VF	XF	Unc	BU
1993	30,000,000	—	—	—	1.00	—

KM# 1119 2 FRANCS **Composition:** Nickel **Obverse:** Head of Louis Pasteur facing

Date	Mintage	F	VF	XF	Unc	BU
1995	9,975,000	—	—	—	2.00	—

KM# 1187 2 FRANCS **Composition:** Nickel **Obverse:** Georges Guynemer, WWI fighter pilot ace facing **Reverse:** Guynemer's stork emblem

Date	F	VF	XF	Unc	BU
1997	—	—	—	2.25	—

KM# 1213 2 FRANCS **Composition:** Nickel **Subject:** 50th Anniversary- Declaration of Human Rights **Obverse:** Head right **Reverse:** Denomination on world globe

Date	F	VF	XF	Unc	BU
1998	—	—	—	2.25	—

KM# 926 5 FRANCS **Weight:** 12.0000 g. **Composition:** 0.8350 Silver .3221 oz. ASW

Date	Mintage	F	VF	XF	Unc	BU
1960	55,182,000	—	—	BV	3.50	—
1961	15,630,000	—	—	BV	3.50	—
1962	42,500,000	—	—	BV	3.50	—
1963	37,936,000	—	—	BV	3.50	—
1964	32,378,000	—	—	BV	3.50	—
1965	5,156,000	—	—	BV	5.50	—
1966	5,017,000	—	—	BV	5.50	—
1967	502,000	—	BV	4.00	12.00	—
1968	557,000	—	BV	3.00	10.00	—
1969	504,000	—	BV	3.00	10.00	—

KM# 926a.1 5 FRANCS **Composition:** Nickel Clad Copper-Nickel

Date	Mintage	F	VF	XF	Unc	BU
1970	57,890,000	—	—	1.00	1.25	—
1971	142,204,000	—	—	1.00	1.25	—
1972	45,492,000	—	—	1.00	1.50	—
1973	45,079,000	—	—	1.00	1.25	—
1974	26,888,000	—	—	1.00	1.25	—
1975	16,712,000	—	—	1.00	1.25	—
1976	1,662,000	—	1.00	1.25	2.00	—
1977	485,000	—	1.00	1.50	2.25	—
1978	30,022,000	—	—	1.00	1.25	—
1979	51,000	—	—	1.75	3.50	—
1980 In sets only	60,000	—	—	—	1.65	—
1981	50,000	—	—	—	1.65	—
1982	60,000	—	—	—	1.65	—
1983	101,000	—	—	—	1.65	—
1984	49,000	—	—	—	4.50	—
1985 In sets only	20,000	—	—	—	6.00	—
1986 In sets only	48,000	—	—	—	5.00	—
1987	20,000,000	—	—	—	1.65	—
1988	100,000	—	—	—	1.65	—
1989	83,000	—	—	—	1.65	—
1990	15,000	—	—	—	1.65	—
1991	—	—	—	—	1.65	—
1993	—	—	—	—	1.65	—
1994 (Bee)	—	—	—	—	1.65	—
1994 (Fish)	—	—	—	—	1.65	—
1995	—	—	—	—	1.65	—
1996	—	—	—	—	1.65	—
1997	—	—	—	—	1.65	—
1998	—	—	—	—	1.65	—
1999	—	—	—	—	1.65	—

KM# 968 5 FRANCS **Composition:** Copper-Nickel **Subject:** Centennial - Erection of Eiffel Tower

Date	Mintage	F	VF	XF	Unc	BU
1989	9,910,000	—	—	—	6.00	—

KM# 968a 5 FRANCS **Weight:** 12.0000 g. **Composition:** 0.9000 Silver .3473 oz. ASW **Subject:** Centennial - Erection of Eiffel Tower

Date	Mintage	F	VF	XF	Unc	BU
1989 Proof	80,000	Value: 28.00				

KM# 968b 5 FRANCS **Weight:** 14.0000 g. **Composition:** 0.9250 Gold .4141 oz. AGW **Subject:** Centennial - Erection of Eiffel Tower

Date	Mintage	F	VF	XF	Unc	BU
1989 Proof	30,000	Value: 225				

KM# 968c 5 FRANCS **Weight:** 16.0000 g. **Composition:** 0.9990 Platinum .5145 oz. APW **Subject:** Centennial - Erection of Eiffel Tower

Date	Mintage	F	VF	XF	Unc	BU
1989 Proof	Est. 3,000	Value: 350				

Note: 1,800 pieces were melted by MTB Banking

KM# 926a.2 5 FRANCS Composition: Nickel Clad Copper-Nickel **Obverse:** Modified sower, engraver's signature: O. ROTY preceded by D'AP **Edge:** Plain

Date	Mintage	F	VF	XF	Unc	BU
1991	7,490,000	—	—	—	1.65	—
1991 Proof	10,000	Value: 6.50				
1992	9,986,000	—	—	—	1.65	—
1992 Proof	15,000	Value: 6.50				
1992	—	—	—	—	1.65	—
1993	14,990,000	—	—	—	1.65	—
1993 Proof	10,000	Value: 6.50				
1994 (Fish)	6,000,000	—	—	—	1.65	—
1994 (Fish) Proof	10,000	Value: 6.50				
1994 (Bee)	3,990,000	—	—	—	1.65	—
1995	20,006,000	—	—	—	6.50	—
1995 Proof	—	Value: 1.65				
1996	17,000	—	—	—	1.65	—
1996 Proof	8,000	Value: 6.50				
1997	15,000	—	—	—	1.65	—
1997 Proof	—	Value: 6.50				
1998 Proof	—	Value: 6.50				
1999 Proof	—	Value: 6.50				
2000	—	—	—	—	1.65	—
2000 Proof	—	Value: 6.50				
2001	—	—	—	—	1.65	—
2001 Proof	—	Value: 6.50				

KM# 1006 5 FRANCS Composition: Copper-Nickel **Reverse:** Bust of Pierre Mendes facing

Date	Mintage	F	VF	XF	Unc	BU
1992	10,000,000	—	—	—	4.00	—

KM# 1006a 5 FRANCS Weight: 12.0000 g. **Composition:** 0.9000 Silver .3473 oz. ASW **Reverse:** Bust of Pierre Mendes facing

Date	Mintage	F	VF	XF	Unc	BU
1992 Proof	10,000	Value: 30.00				

KM# 1006b 5 FRANCS Weight: 14.0000 g. **Composition:** 0.9200 Gold .4141 oz. AGW **Reverse:** Bust of Pierre Mendes facing

Date	Mintage	F	VF	XF	Unc	BU
1992 Proof	1,000	Value: 265				

KM# 1007 5 FRANCS Weight: 12.0000 g. **Composition:** 0.9000 Silver .3473 oz. ASW **Subject:** French Antarctic Territories **Reverse:** 3 Albatross in flight

Date	Mintage	F	VF	XF	Unc	BU
1992 Proof	15,000	Value: 45.00				

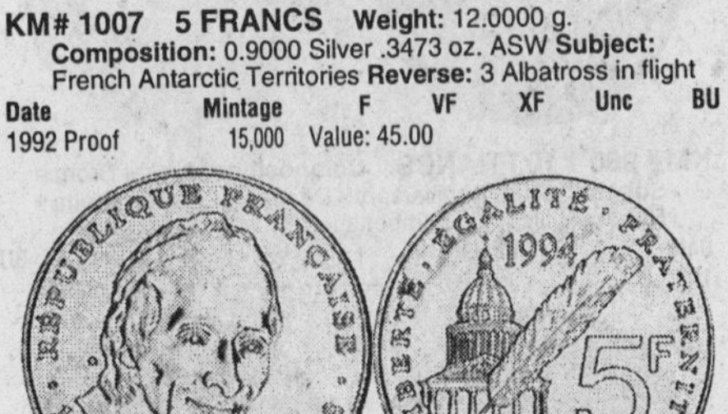

KM# 1063 5 FRANCS Composition: Nickel Clad Copper-Nickel **Obverse:** Head of Voltaire, the poet 1/2 right

Date	Mintage	F	VF	XF	Unc	BU
1994	15,000,000	—	—	—	4.00	—

KM# 1118 5 FRANCS Weight: 12.0000 g. **Composition:** 0.9000 Silver .3473 oz. ASW **Subject:** 50th Anniversary - United Nations

Date	Mintage	F	VF	XF	Unc	BU
1995 Proof	250,000	Value: 26.50				

KM# 1118a 5 FRANCS Weight: 14.0000 g. **Composition:** 0.9200 Gold .4141 oz. AGW

Date	Mintage	F	VF	XF	Unc	BU
1995 Proof	125,000	Value: 26.50				

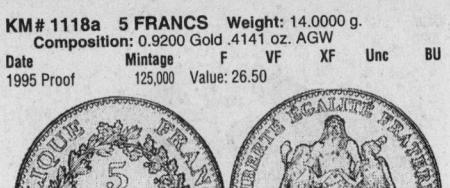

KM# 1155 5 FRANCS Composition: Nickel Clad Steel **Reverse:** Hercules group design

Date	Mintage	F	VF	XF	Unc	BU
1996	4,976,000	—	—	—	4.50	—

KM# 1212 5 FRANCS Weight: 12.0000 g. **Composition:** 0.9000 Silver .3472 oz. ASW **Subject:** 1998 World Cup Soccer Games: French Victory **Obverse:** Game logo above denomination **Reverse:** Hand held trophy with stadium in background

Date	Mintage	F	VF	XF	Unc	BU
1998 Proof	Est. 100,000	Value: 45.00				

KM# 1215 5 FRANCS Weight: 12.0000 g. **Composition:** 0.9000 Silver .3472 oz. ASW **Subject:** Yves St. Laurent **Obverse:** RF monogram **Reverse:** Fashion show scene **Note:** Struck at Paris Mint.

Date	F	VF	XF	Unc	BU
2000	—	—	—	30.00	—

KM# 1222 5 FRANCS Weight: 10.0000 g. **Composition:** Copper-Nickel Plated Nickel **Subject:** 2000 Years of French Coinage **Obverse:** Denomination in wreath **Reverse:** 1st century B.C. Celtic Parisii Stater coin design **Edge:** Reeded **Note:** Struck at Paris Mint.

Date	Mintage	F	VF	XF	Unc	BU
2000	50,000	—	—	—	9.50	—

KM# 1223 5 FRANCS Weight: 10.0000 g. **Composition:** Copper-Nickel Plated Nickel **Subject:** 2000 Years of French Coinage **Obverse:** Denomination in wreath **Reverse:** Charlemagne Denar coin design **Edge:** Reeded **Note:** Struck at Paris Mint.

Date	Mintage	F	VF	XF	Unc	BU
2000	50,000	—	—	—	9.50	—

KM# 1224 5 FRANCS Weight: 10.0000 g. **Composition:** Copper-Nickel Plated Nickel **Subject:** 2000 Years of French Coinage **Obverse:** Denomination in wreath **Reverse:** Louis IX Gold Ecu design **Edge:** Reeded **Note:** Struck at Paris Mint.

Date	Mintage	F	VF	XF	Unc	BU
2000	50,000	—	—	—	9.50	—

KM# 1255 6.55957 FRANCS Weight: 22.2000 g. **Composition:** 0.9000 Silver .6424 oz. ASW **Obverse:** Europa allegorical portrait **Reverse:** Country names and euro-currency equivalents around RF and denomination in center plus French coin designs **Edge:** Plain

Date	Mintage	F	VF	XF	Unc	BU
1999 Proof	25,000	Value: 40.00				

KM# 1254 6.55957 FRANCS Weight: 13.0000 g. **Composition:** 0.9000 Silver .3762 oz. ASW **Subject:** Euro Conversion Series **Obverse:** Europa allegorical portrait **Reverse:** Country names and euro-currency equivalents around RF and denomination in center **Edge:** Plain **Note:** Struck at Paris Mint.

Date	Mintage	F	VF	XF	Unc	BU
1999	200,000	—	—	—	30.00	—

KM# 1226 6.55957 FRANCS Weight: 22.2000 g. **Composition:** 0.9000 Silver .6424 oz. ASW **Series:** European Art Styles - Renaissance Classic and Baroque **Note:** Struck at Paris Mint.

Date	Mintage	F	VF	XF	Unc	BU
2000 Proof	15,000	Value: 35.00				

KM# 1227 6.55957 FRANCS Weight: 22.2000 g. **Composition:** 0.9000 Silver .6424 oz. ASW **Series:** European Art Styles Renaissance - Art Nouveau **Note:** Struck at Paris Mint.

Date	Mintage	F	VF	XF	Unc	BU
2000 Proof	15,000	Value: 35.00				

KM# 1228 6.55957 FRANCS Weight: 22.2000 g. **Composition:** 0.9000 Silver .6424 oz. ASW **Series:** European Art Styles Renaissance - Modern **Note:** Struck at Paris Mint.

Date	Mintage	F	VF	XF	Unc	BU
2000 Proof	15,000	Value: 35.00				

KM# 1244 6.55957 FRANCS **Weight:** 22.2000 g. **Composition:** 0.9000 Silver .6424 oz. ASW **Series:** European Art Styles Renaissance - Greek and Roman **Note:** Struck at Paris Mint.

Date	Mintage	F	VF	XF	Unc	BU
2000 Proof	15,000	Value: 35.00				

KM# 1245 6.55957 FRANCS **Weight:** 22.2000 g. **Composition:** 0.9000 Silver .6424 oz. ASW **Series:** European Art Styles Renaissance - Roman Art and Structures **Note:** Struck at Paris Mint.

Date	Mintage	F	VF	XF	Unc	BU
2000 Proof	15,000	Value: 35.00				

KM# 1246 6.55957 FRANCS **Weight:** 22.2000 g. **Composition:** 0.9000 Silver .6424 oz. ASW **Series:** European Art Styles Renaissance - Gothic **Note:** Struck at Paris Mint.

Date	Mintage	F	VF	XF	Unc	BU
2000 Proof	15,000	Value: 35.00				

KM# 1225 6.55957 FRANCS **Weight:** 22.2000 g. **Composition:** 0.9000 Silver .6424 oz. ASW **Subject:** European Art Styles Renaissance **Obverse:** Denomination and partial portrait **Reverse:** Renaissance style buildings **Edge Lettering:** Europa repeated four times

Date	Mintage	F	VF	XF	Unc	BU
2000 Proof	15,000	Value: 35.00				

KM# 1258 6.55957 FRANCS **Weight:** 13.0000 g. **Composition:** 0.9000 Silver .3762 oz. ASW **Obverse:** Country names and euro-currency equivalents around RF and denomination **Reverse:** Europa allegorical portrait **Edge:** Plain

Date	Mintage	F	VF	XF	Unc	BU
2000	200,000	—	—	—	30.00	—

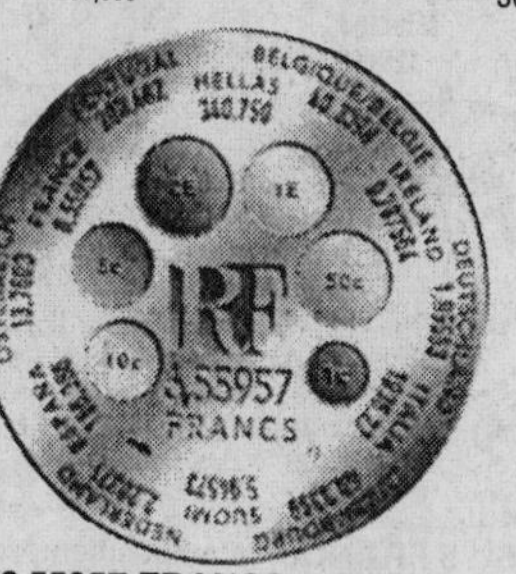

KM# 1259 6.55957 FRANCS **Weight:** 13.0000 g. **Composition:** 0.9000 Silver .3762 oz. ASW **Obverse:** Country names and euro-currency equivalents around RF, denomination and French euro coin designs **Edge:** Plain

Date	Mintage	F	VF	XF	Unc	BU
2000 Proof	10,000	Value: 40.00				

KM# 1265.1 (KM1265) 6.55957 FRANCS **Weight:** 13.0000 g. **Composition:** 0.9000 Silver .3762 oz. ASW **Subject:** Last Year of the French Franc **Obverse:** French and other European euro currency equivalents **Reverse:** Similar to KM#1258 but with addition of "last year of the franc" logo after the date **Edge:** Reeded

Date	F	VF	XF	Unc	BU
2001	—	—	—	18.00	—
2001	—	—	—	18.00	—

KM# 1265.2 (KM1265.1) 6.55957 FRANCS **Weight:** 22.2000 g. **Composition:** 0.9000 Silver .6424 oz. ASW **Edge:** Plain

Date	Mintage	F	VF	XF	Unc	BU
2001 Proof only	Est. 10,000	Value: 35.00				
2001 Proof only	Est. 10,000	Value: 35.00				

KM# 1276 6.55957 FRANCS **Weight:** 22.2000 g. **Composition:** 0.9000 Silver .6424 oz. ASW **Subject:** Mottos **Obverse:** Denomination **Reverse:** FRATERNITE in red letters **Edge:** Reeded

Date	Mintage	F	VF	XF	Unc	BU
2001 Proof	20,000	Value: 38.50				

KM# 1277 6.55957 FRANCS **Weight:** 22.2000 g. **Composition:** 0.9000 Silver .6424 oz. ASW **Subject:** Mottos **Reverse:** EGALITE in white letters

Date	Mintage	F	VF	XF	Unc	BU
2001 Proof	20,000	Value: 38.50				

KM# 1278 6.55957 FRANCS **Weight:** 22.2000 g. **Composition:** 0.9000 Silver .6424 oz. ASW **Subject:** Mottos **Reverse:** LIBERTE in white letters

Date	Mintage	F	VF	XF	Unc	BU
2001 Proof	20,000	Value: 38.50				

KM# 932 10 FRANCS **Weight:** 25.0000 g. **Composition:** 0.9000 Silver .7234 oz. ASW **Note:** Without mint mark. Struck at Paris Mint.

Date	Mintage	F	VF	XF	Unc	BU
1965	8,051,000	—	BV	6.00	10.00	—
1966	9,800,000	—	BV	6.00	10.00	—
1967	10,100,000	—	BV	6.00	10.00	—
1968	3,887,000	—	BV	8.00	12.00	—
1969	761,000	—	BV	10.00	15.00	—
1970	5,013,000	—	BV	6.00	10.00	—
1971	513,000	—	BV	10.00	17.50	—
1972	915,000	—	BV	8.00	12.00	—
1973	207,000	—	BV	10.00	20.00	—

KM# 940 10 FRANCS **Composition:** Nickel-Brass

Date	F	VF	XF	Unc	BU
1974	—	—	2.00	2.50	—
1975	—	—	2.00	2.50	—
1976	—	—	2.00	2.50	—
1977	—	—	2.00	2.50	—
1978	—	—	2.00	2.50	—
1979	—	—	2.00	2.50	—
1980	—	—	2.00	2.50	—
1981	—	—	—	2.75	—
1982	—	—	—	2.75	—
1983	—	—	—	2.75	—
1984	—	—	2.00	2.50	—
1985	—	—	2.00	2.50	—
1987	—	—	—	2.50	—

KM# 950 10 FRANCS **Composition:** Nickel-Bronze **Subject:** 100th Anniversary - Death of Leon Gambetta **Reverse:** Head of Gambetta left

Date	Mintage	F	VF	XF	Unc	BU
1982	3,045,000	—	—	2.50	4.00	—

KM# 952 10 FRANCS **Composition:** Nickel-Bronze **Subject:** 200th Anniversary - Montgolfier Balloon **Reverse:** Balloon

Date	Mintage	F	VF	XF	Unc	BU
1983	3,001,000	—	—	2.50	4.00	—

Date	Mintage	F	VF	XF	Unc	BU
2001 Proof	20,000	Value: 38.50				

KM# 953 10 FRANCS Composition: Nickel-Bronze **Subject:** 200th Anniversary - Birth of Stendhal **Obverse:** Head of Stendhal facing

Date	Mintage	F	VF	XF	Unc	BU
1983	2,951,000	—	—	2.50	4.00	—

KM# 954 10 FRANCS Composition: Nickel-Bronze **Subject:** 200th Anniversary - Birth of Francois Rude **Obverse:** Head of Francois Rude 1/2 right

Date	Mintage	F	VF	XF	Unc	BU
1984	10,000,000	—	—	2.50	3.50	—

KM# 956 10 FRANCS Composition: Nickel-Bronze **Subject:** Centennial - Death of Victor Hugo **Reverse:** Head of Hugo facing

Date	Mintage	F	VF	XF	Unc	BU
1985	10,000,000	—	—	2.50	3.50	—

KM# 956a 10 FRANCS Weight: 12.0000 g. **Composition:** 0.9000 Silver .3472 oz. ASW **Subject:** Centennial - Death of Victor Hugo **Reverse:** Head of Hugo facing

Date	Mintage	F	VF	XF	Unc	BU
1985	20,000	—	—	—	20.00	—

KM# 956b 10 FRANCS Weight: 12.0000 g. **Composition:** 0.9990 Silver .3854 oz. ASW **Subject:** Centennial - Death of Victor Hugo **Reverse:** Head of Hugo facing

Date	Mintage	F	VF	XF	Unc	BU
1985 Proof	8,000	Value: 40.00				

KM# 959 10 FRANCS Composition: Nickel **Reverse:** Madam Republic

Date	Mintage	F	VF	XF	Unc	BU
1986	110,015,000	—	—	3.00	10.00	—

Note: Recalled and melted, no longer legal tender

KM# 958 10 FRANCS Composition: Nickel **Subject:** 100th Anniversary - Birth of Robert Schuman **Obverse:** Rooster at left, denomination right **Reverse:** Half head of Schuman right

Date	Mintage	F	VF	XF	Unc	BU
1986	9,961,000	—	—	3.00	6.50	—

KM# 958a 10 FRANCS Weight: 7.0000 g. **Composition:** 0.9000 Silver .2025 oz. ASW **Obverse:** Rooster at left, denomination right **Reverse:** Half head of Schuman right

Date	Mintage	F	VF	XF	Unc	BU
1986	20,000	—	—	—	18.50	—

KM# 958b 10 FRANCS Weight: 7.0000 g. **Composition:** 0.9500 Silver .2138 oz. ASW **Obverse:** Rooster at left, denomination right **Reverse:** Half head of Schuman right

Date	Mintage	F	VF	XF	Unc	BU
1986 Proof	6,000	Value: 45.00				

KM# 958c 10 FRANCS Weight: 7.0000 g. **Composition:** 0.9200 Gold .2071 oz. AGW **Subject:** 100th Anniversary - Birth of Robert Schuman **Obverse:** Rooster at left, denomination right **Reverse:** Half head of Schuman right

Date	Mintage	F	VF	XF	Unc	BU
1986 Proof	5,000	Value: 150				

KM# 961 10 FRANCS Weight: 12.0000 g. **Composition:** 0.9000 Silver .3473 oz. ASW **Subject:** Millennium of King Capet and France

Date	Mintage	F	VF	XF	Unc	BU
1987	20,000	—	—	—	18.50	—

KM# 961a 10 FRANCS Weight: 12.0000 g. **Composition:** 0.9500 Silver .3665 oz. ASW **Subject:** Millennium of King Capet and France

Date	Mintage	F	VF	XF	Unc	BU
1987 Proof	10,000	Value: 40.00				

KM# 961b 10 FRANCS Weight: 12.0000 g. **Composition:** 0.9200 Gold .3549 oz. AGW **Subject:** Millennium of King Capet and France

Date	Mintage	F	VF	XF	Unc	BU
1987 Proof	6,000	Value: 200				

KM# 961c 10 FRANCS Weight: 14.0000 g. **Composition:** 0.9990 Platinum .4497 oz. APW **Subject:** Millennium of King Capet and France

Date	Mintage	F	VF	XF	Unc	BU
1987 Proof	1,000	Value: 340				

KM# 961d 10 FRANCS Composition: Nickel-Bronze **Subject:** Millennium of King Capet and France

Date	Mintage	F	VF	XF	Unc	BU
1987	70,000,000	—	—	3.00	6.50	—

KM# 964.1 10 FRANCS Ring Composition: Aluminum-Bronze **Center Composition:** Steel **Subject:** Spirit of Bastille

Date	Mintage	F	VF	XF	Unc	BU
1988	100,000,000	—	—	2.50	6.00	—
1989	249,980,000	—	—	2.50	6.00	—
1990	250,000,000	—	—	2.50	6.00	—
1991	—	—	—	2.50	6.50	—

Note: Exist in both medal and coin alignment

Date	Mintage	F	VF	XF	Unc	BU
1992	—	—	—	2.50	6.50	—

Note: Exists in both medal and coin alignment

KM# 964.1a 10 FRANCS Ring Composition: 0.9200 Gold **Center Composition:** Gold With Palladium And Silver Alloys **Subject:** Spirit of Bastille

Date	Mintage	F	VF	XF	Unc	BU
1988 Proof	5,000	Value: 350				

KM# 965 10 FRANCS Composition: Aluminum-Bronze **Subject:** 100th Anniversary - Birth of Roland Garros

Date	Mintage	F	VF	XF	Unc	BU
1988	30,000,000	—	—	2.50	4.00	—

KM# 965a 10 FRANCS Weight: 12.0000 g. **Composition:** 0.9000 Silver .3472 oz. ASW

Date	Mintage	F	VF	XF	Unc	BU
1988	10,000	—	—	—	18.50	—

KM# 965b 10 FRANCS Weight: 12.0000 g. **Composition:** 0.9500 Silver .3665 oz. ASW

Date	Mintage	F	VF	XF	Unc	BU
1988 Proof	10,000	Value: 35.00				

KM# 965c 10 FRANCS Weight: 12.0000 g. **Composition:** 0.9200 Gold .3550 oz. AGW **Subject:** 100th Anniversary - Birth of Roland Garros

Date	Mintage	F	VF	XF	Unc	BU
1988 Proof	3,000	Value: 210				

KM# 969 10 FRANCS Ring Composition: Aluminum-Bronze **Center Composition:** Steel **Subject:** 300th Anniversary - Birth of Montesquieu **Obverse:** Bust of Montesquieu right

Date	Mintage	F	VF	XF	Unc	BU
1989	15,000	—	—	6.50	17.50	—

KM# 969a 10 FRANCS Ring Composition: 0.9200 Gold **Center Composition:** Gold With Palladium And Silver Alloys **Subject:** 300th Anniversary - Birth of Montesquieu **Obverse:** Bust of Montesquieu right

Date	Mintage	F	VF	XF	Unc	BU
1989 Proof	5,000	Value: 325				

KM# 964.2 10 FRANCS Composition: Aluminum-Bronze **Edge:** Plain

Date	Mintage	F	VF	XF	Unc	BU
1991	249,989,000	—	—	—	—	—

Note: Exist in both medal and coin alignment

Date	Mintage	F	VF	XF	Unc	BU
1991 Proof	10,000	Value: 15.00				
1992	99,986,000	—	—	—	6.00	—

Note: Exist in both medal and coin alignment

Date	Mintage	F	VF	XF	Unc	BU
1992 Proof	15,000	Value: 15.00				
1993	20,000	—	—	—	6.00	—
1993 Proof	10,000	Value: 15.00				
1994 (Bee)	20,000	—	—	—	6.00	—
1994 (Fish) Proof	10,000	Value: 15.00				
1995	25,000	—	—	—	6.00	—
1995 Proof	10,000	Value: 15.00				
1996	17,000	—	—	—	6.00	—
1996 Proof	8,000	Value: 15.00				
1997	15,000	—	—	—	6.00	—
1997 Proof	10,000	Value: 15.00				
1998	—	—	—	—	6.00	—
1998 Proof	—	Value: 15.00				
1999	—	—	—	—	6.00	—
1999 Proof	—	Value: 15.00				
2000	—	—	—	—	6.00	—
2000 Proof	—	Value: 15.00				
2001	—	—	—	—	6.00	—
2001 Proof	—	Value: 15.00				

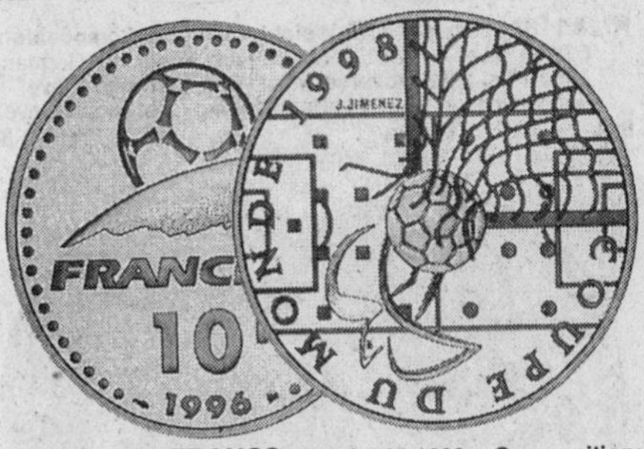

KM# 1144 10 FRANCS Weight: 21.1600 g. **Composition:** 0.9000 Silver .6412 oz. ASW **Subject:** World Cup - Coupe du Monde 1998 **Obverse:** World Cup 1998 logo above denomination **Reverse:** Soccer ball breaking net, stylized dove

Date	Mintage	F	VF	XF	Unc	BU
1996 Proof	Est. 40,000	Value: 40.00				

KM# 1166 10 FRANCS Weight: 21.1600 g. **Composition:** 0.9000 Silver .6412 oz. ASW **Subject:** World Cup - Uruguay 1930 1958 **Obverse:** World Cup 1998 logo above denoomination **Reverse:** Stylized gaucho and soccer player

Date	Mintage	F	VF	XF	Unc	BU
1996 Proof	100,000	Value: 35.00				

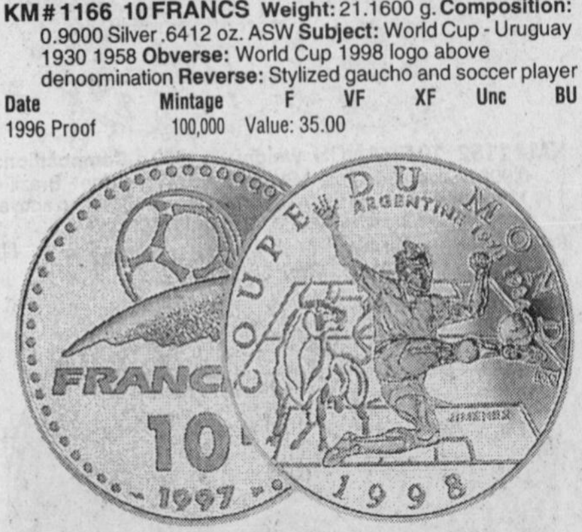

KM# 1161 10 FRANCS Weight: 21.1600 g. **Composition:** 0.9000 Silver .6412 oz. ASW **Subject:** World Cup - Argentina 1978 1986 **Obverse:** World Cup 1998 logo above denoomination **Reverse:** Stylized bull and soccer player

Date	Mintage	F	VF	XF	Unc	BU
1997 Proof	100,000	Value: 35.00				

KM# 1163 10 FRANCS **Weight:** 21.1600 g. **Composition:** 0.9000 Silver .6412 oz. ASW **Subject:** World Cup - England 1966 **Obverse:** World Cup 1998 logo above denoomination **Reverse:** Big Ben and soccer player

Date	Mintage	F	VF	XF	Unc	BU
1997 Proof	100,000	Value: 35.00				

KM# 1164 10 FRANCS **Weight:** 21.1600 g. **Composition:** 0.9000 Silver .6412 oz. ASW **Subject:** World Cup - Germany 1954 1974 1990 **Obverse:** World Cup 1998 logo above denoomination **Reverse:** Brandenburg gate, soccer player

Date	Mintage	F	VF	XF	Unc	BU
1997 Proof	100,000	Value: 35.00				

KM# 1165 10 FRANCS **Weight:** 21.1600 g. **Composition:** 0.9000 Silver .6412 oz. ASW **Subject:** World Cup - Italy 1934 1938 1982 **Obverse:** World Cup 1998 logo above denoomination **Reverse:** Colosseum and soccer player

Date	Mintage	F	VF	XF	Unc	BU
1997 Proof	100,000	Value: 35.00				

KM# 1162 10 FRANCS **Weight:** 21.1600 g. **Composition:** 0.9000 Silver .6412 oz. ASW **Subject:** World Cup - Brazil 1958 1968 1970 1994 **Obverse:** World Cup 1998 logo above denoomination **Reverse:** Pavilion and soccer player

Date	Mintage	F	VF	XF	Unc	BU
1998 Proof	100,000	Value: 35.00				

KM# 1167 10 FRANCS **Weight:** 21.1600 g. **Composition:** 0.9000 Silver .6412 oz. ASW **Subject:** World Cup - Coupe du Monte **Obverse:** World Cup 1998 logo above denoomination **Reverse:** World Cup trophy and 11 French city arms

Date	Mintage	F	VF	XF	Unc	BU
1998 Proof	100,000	Value: 35.00				

KM# 1205 10 FRANCS **Weight:** 22.2000 g. **Composition:** 0.9000 Silver .6424 oz. ASW **Series:** Treasures of the Nile - J.F. Champollion **Obverse:** Portrait and obelisk **Reverse:** Sphinx and pyramids

Date	Mintage	F	VF	XF	Unc	BU
1998 Proof	15,000	Value: 38.50				

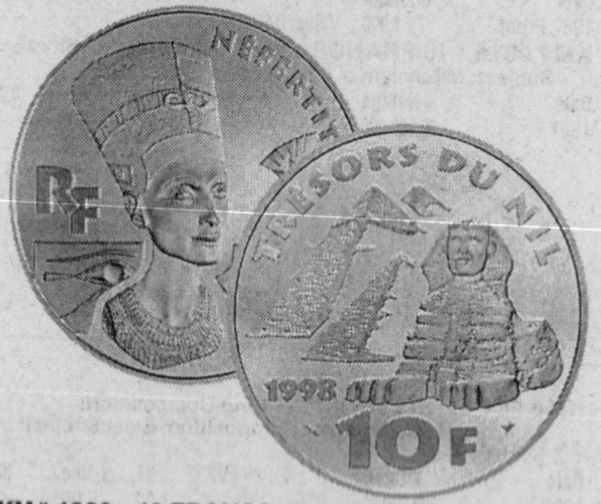

KM# 1206 10 FRANCS **Weight:** 22.2000 g. **Composition:** 0.9000 Silver .6424 oz. ASW **Series:** Treasures of the Nile - Nefertiti **Obverse:** Crowned bust **Reverse:** Sphinx and pyramids

Date	Mintage	F	VF	XF	Unc	BU
1998 Proof	15,000	Value: 38.50				

KM# 1207 10 FRANCS **Weight:** 22.2000 g. **Composition:** 0.9000 Silver .6424 oz. ASW **Series:** Treasures of the Nile - Ramses II **Obverse:** Seated figure **Reverse:** Sphinx and pyramids

Date	Mintage	F	VF	XF	Unc	BU
1998 Proof	15,000	Value: 38.50				

KM# 1294 10 FRANCS **Weight:** 22.2300 g. **Composition:** 0.9000 Silver 0.6432 oz. ASW **Subject:** Rugby **Obverse:** Players in a "scrum" **Reverse:** Players jumping for a ball **Edge:** Plain **Size:** 36.9 mm.

Date	Mintage	F	VF	XF	Unc	BU
1999A Proof	10,000	Value: 35.00				

KM# 1216 10 FRANCS **Weight:** 22.2300 g. **Composition:** 0.9000 Silver .6432 oz. ASW **Series:** XXth Century - Biology and Medicine **Obverse:** Double X design **Reverse:** Parents, fetus, hands **Edge:** Plain **Note:** Struck at Paris Mint.

Date	Mintage	F	VF	XF	Unc	BU
2000 Proof	10,000	Value: 40.00				

KM# 1217 10 FRANCS **Weight:** 22.2300 g. **Composition:** 0.9000 Silver .6432 oz. ASW **Series:** XXth Century - Physical Sciences **Obverse:** Einstein's portrait, atom and planets **Note:** Struck at Paris Mint.

Date	Mintage	F	VF	XF	Unc	BU
2000 Proof	10,000	Value: 40.00				

KM# 1218 10 FRANCS **Weight:** 22.2300 g. **Composition:** 0.9000 Silver .6432 oz. ASW **Series:** XXth Century - Communications **Obverse:** World, satellites and keyboard **Note:** Struck at Paris Mint.

Date	Mintage	F	VF	XF	Unc	BU
2000 Proof	10,000	Value: 40.00				

KM# 1219 10 FRANCS **Weight:** 22.2300 g. **Composition:** 0.9000 Silver .6432 oz. ASW **Series:** XXth Century - The Automobile **Obverse:** Race cars above horse **Note:** Struck at Paris Mint.

Date	Mintage	F	VF	XF	Unc	BU
2000 Proof	10,000	Value: 40.00				

KM# 1220 10 FRANCS **Weight:** 22.2300 g. **Composition:** 0.9000 Silver .6432 oz. ASW **Series:** XXth Century - Flight **Obverse:** Icarus in flight above Bleriot monoplane **Note:** Struck at Paris Mint.

Date	Mintage	F	VF	XF	Unc	BU
2000 Proof	10,000	Value: 40.00				

KM# 1221 10 FRANCS **Weight:** 22.2300 g. **Composition:** 0.9000 Silver .6432 oz. ASW **Series:** XXth Century - Space Travel **Reverse:** Astronaut weightless in space amidst planets **Note:** Struck at Paris Mint.

Date	Mintage	F	VF	XF	Unc	BU
2000 Proof	10,000	Value: 40.00				

KM# 1229 10 FRANCS **Weight:** 22.2000 g. **Composition:** 0.9000 Silver .6424 oz. ASW **Subject:** 2000 Years - French Coinage **Obverse:** Denomination **Reverse:** 1st century B.C. Celtic Parisii Stater coin design **Edge:** Plain **Note:** Struck at Paris Mint.

Date	Mintage	F	VF	XF	Unc	BU
2000 Proof	10,000	Value: 37.50				

KM# 1230 10 FRANCS **Weight:** 22.2000 g. **Composition:** 0.9000 Silver .6424 oz. ASW **Reverse:** Charlemagne Denar coin design **Note:** Struck at Paris Mint.

Date	Mintage	F	VF	XF	Unc	BU
2000 Proof	10,000	Value: 37.50				

KM# 1231 10 FRANCS **Weight:** 22.2000 g. **Composition:** 0.9000 Silver .6424 oz. ASW **Subject:** 2000 Years of French Coinage **Obverse:** Denomination **Reverse:** Louis IX gold ecu coin design **Edge:** Plain **Note:** Struck at Paris Mint.

Date	Mintage	F	VF	XF	Unc	BU
2000 Proof	10,000	Value: 37.50				

KM# 1235 10 FRANCS **Weight:** 22.2000 g. **Composition:** 0.9000 Silver .6424 oz. ASW **Subject:** Yves St. Laurent **Obverse:** RF monogram **Reverse:** Fashion show scene **Note:** Struck at Paris Mint.

Date	Mintage	F	VF	XF	Unc	BU
2000 Proof	30,000	Value: 37.50				

KM# 1263 10 FRANCS **Weight:** 22.2000 g. **Composition:** 0.9000 Silver .6424 oz. ASW **Subject:** Antoine de St. Exupery **Obverse:** RF Monogram, portrait and bi-plane **Reverse:** Multicolor "Little Prince" character and denomination **Note:** Struck at Paris Mint.

Date	Mintage	F	VF	XF	Unc	BU
2000 Proof	10,000	Value: 47.50				

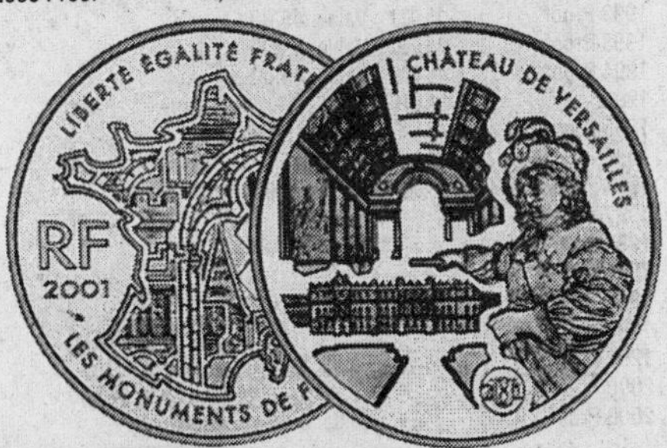

KM# 1268 10 FRANCS **Weight:** 22.2000 g. **Composition:** 0.9000 Silver .6424 oz. ASW **Subject:** Palace of Versailles **Obverse:** Stylized French map **Reverse:** Louis XIV with internal and external palace views **Edge:** Plain

Date	Mintage	F	VF	XF	Unc	BU
2001 Proof	Est. 20,000	Value: 35.00				

KM# 1270 10 FRANCS **Weight:** 22.2000 g. **Composition:** 0.9000 Silver .6424 oz. ASW **Obverse:** Champs-Elysees **Reverse:** Arch of Triumph partial close up and aerial views

Date	Mintage	F	VF	XF	Unc	BU
2001 Proof	Est. 20,000	Value: 35.00				

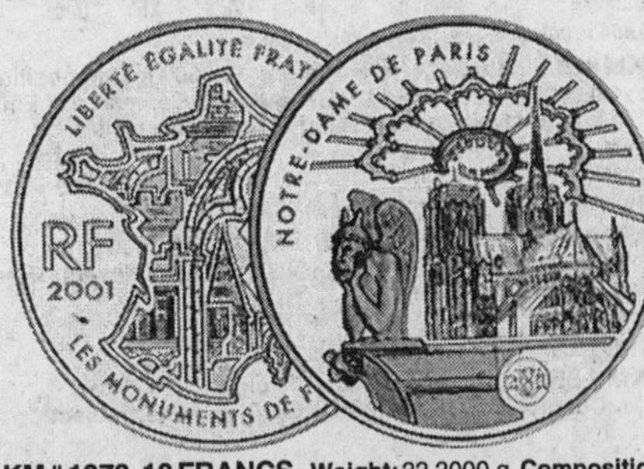

KM# 1272 10 FRANCS **Weight:** 22.2000 g. **Composition:** 0.9000 Silver .6424 oz. ASW **Obverse:** Notre-Dame Cathedral **Reverse:** Gargoyle and cathedral views

Date	Mintage	F	VF	XF	Unc	BU
2001 Proof	Est. 20,000	Value: 35.00				

KM# 1274 10 FRANCS **Weight:** 22.2000 g. **Composition:** 0.9000 Silver .6424 oz. ASW **Obverse:** Eiffel Tower **Reverse:** Two tower views

Date	Mintage	F	VF	XF	Unc	BU
2001 Proof	Est. 20,000	Value: 35.00				

KM# 1008.2b 20 FRANCS **Note:** .920 Gold center plug, .750 Gold inner ring, .920 Gold outer ring.

Date	Mintage	F	VF	XF	Unc	BU
1992 Proof	5,000	Value: 375				

KM# 1008.2a 20 FRANCS **Obverse:** Mont St. Michel; 5 bands of stripes in outer ring **Note:** 12.6600 g, .720 Gold center plug, .950 Silver inner ring, .750 Gold outer ring.

Date	Mintage	F	VF	XF	Unc	BU
1992 Proof	15,000	Value: 200				

KM# 1008.1 20 FRANCS **Obverse:** Mont St. Michel **Edge:** 4 milled bands **Note:** Copper-Aluminum-Nickel center plug, Nickel inner ring, Copper-Aluminum-Nickel outer ring.

Date	Mintage	F	VF	XF	Unc	BU
1992 closed V in outer ring	60,000,000	—	—	—	15.00	—
1992 open V in outer ring	Inc. above	—	—	—	15.00	—

KM# 1008.2 20 FRANCS **Edge:** 5 milled bands **Note:** Copper-Aluminum-Nickel center plug, Nickel inner ring, Copper-Aluminum-Nickel outer ring.

Date	Mintage	F	VF	XF	Unc	BU
1992 closed V in outer ring	59,986,000	—	—	—	6.50	—
1992 open V in outer ring	Inc. above	—	—	—	6.50	—
1992 Proof	15,000	Value: 25.00				

Note: Non-Proof, exist in both coin and medal alignment

Date	Mintage	F	VF	XF	Unc	BU
1993	54,990,000	—	—	—	7.00	—

Note: Non-Proof, exist in both coin and medal alignment

Date	Mintage	F	VF	XF	Unc	BU
1993 Proof	10,000	Value: 25.00				

Note: Non-Proof, exist in both coin and medal alignment

Date	Mintage	F	VF	XF	Unc	BU
1994	—	—	—	—	8.00	—
1994 Proof	—	Value: 25.00				
1994 (Fish)	5,000,000	—	—	—	10.00	—
1994 (Fish) Proof	10,000	Value: 25.00				
1994 (Bee)	9,990,000	—	—	—	9.00	—
1995	9,996,000	—	—	—	9.00	—
1995 Proof	10,000	Value: 25.00				
1996	17,000	—	—	—	6.50	—
1996 Proof	8,000	Value: 25.00				
1997	15,000	—	—	—	8.00	—
1997 Proof	10,000	Value: 25.00				
1998	—	—	—	—	8.00	—
1998 Proof	—	Value: 25.00				
1999	—	—	—	—	8.00	—
1999 Proof	—	Value: 25.00				
2000	—	—	—	—	8.00	—
2000 Proof	—	Value: 25.00				
2001	—	—	—	—	8.00	—
2001 Proof	—	Value: 25.00				

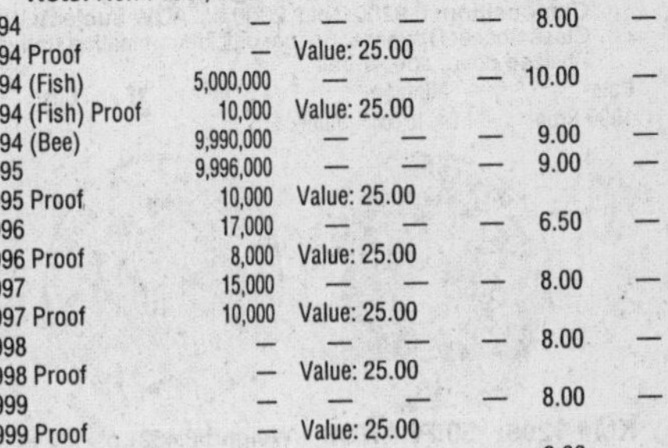

KM# 1016 20 FRANCS **Subject:** Mediterranean Games **Note:** Aluminum-Bronze center plug, Nickel inner ring, Copper-Aluminum-Nickel outer ring.

Date	Mintage	F	VF	XF	Unc	BU
1993	5,001,000	—	—	—	10.00	—

KM# 1036 20 FRANCS **Subject:** Founder of Modern Day Olympics - Pierre de Coubertin **Obverse:** Head of Coubertin left **Note:** Aluminum-Bronze center plug, Nickel inner ring, Copper-Aluminum-Nickel outer ring.

Date	Mintage	F	VF	XF	Unc	BU
1994	15,000,000	—	—	—	10.00	—

KM# 941.2 50 FRANCS **Weight:** 30.0000 g. **Composition:** 0.9000 Silver .8682 oz. ASW **Reverse:** Legend begins at the level of the beltline of the boddess of Hercules' left

Date	F	VF	XF	Unc	BU
1974	15.00	25.00	40.00	65.00	—

KM# 941.1 50 FRANCS **Weight:** 30.0000 g. **Composition:** 0.9000 Silver .8682 oz. ASW **Note:** Without mint mark. Struck at Paris Mint.

Date	Mintage	F	VF	XF	Unc	BU
1974	4,299,000	—	—	—	10.00	—
1975	4,551,000	—	—	—	12.50	—
1976	7,739,000	—	—	—	11.50	—
1977	7,884,000	—	—	—	10.00	—
1978	12,028,000	—	—	—	10.00	—
1979	12,041,000	—	—	—	10.00	—
1980 In sets only	60,000	—	—	—	50.00	—

KM# 1145 50 FRANCS **Weight:** 8.4521 g. **Composition:** 0.9200 Gold .2500 oz. AGW **Subject:** World Class Soccer **Obverse:** Soccer ball, denomination **Reverse:** Stylized dove, soccer ball

Date	Mintage	F	VF	XF	Unc	BU
1996 Proof	Est. 10,000	Value: 175				

KM# 1208 50 FRANCS **Weight:** 8.4521 g. **Composition:** 0.9200 Gold .2500 oz. AGW **Subject:** Treasures of the Nile **Obverse:** Portrait and obelisk **Reverse:** Sphinx and pyramids

Date	Mintage	F	VF	XF	Unc	BU
1998 Proof	3,000	Value: 260				

KM# 1236 50 FRANCS **Weight:** 8.4521 g. **Composition:** 0.9200 Gold .2500 oz. AGW **Subject:** Yves St. Laurent **Obverse:** RF monogram, denomination **Reverse:** Fashion show scene **Edge:** Plain

Date	Mintage	F	VF	XF	Unc	BU
2000 Proof	2,000	Value: 250				

KM# 1256 65.5997 FRANCS **Weight:** 8.4500 g. **Composition:** 0.9250 Gold .2499 oz. AGW **Series:** Euro Conversion Series **Obverse:** Country names with euro currency equivalents around RF, denomination and French coin designs **Reverse:** Europa allegorical portrait **Edge:** Plain

Date	Mintage	F	VF	XF	Unc	BU
1999 Proof	10,000	Value: 250				

KM# 1260 65.5997 FRANCS **Weight:** 8.4500 g **Composition:** 0.9250 Gold .2499 oz. AGW **Obverse.** Country names with euro-currency equivalents around RF, denomination and French euro coin designs

Date	Mintage	F	VF	XF	Unc	BU
2000 Proof	3,000	Value: 265				

KM# 1266 65.5997 FRANCS **Weight:** 8.4500 g. **Composition:** 0.9200 Gold .2499 oz. AGW **Subject:** Last Year of the French Franc **Obverse:** French and other European euro currency equivalents **Reverse:** Similar to KM#1258 but with addition of "last year of the franc" logo after the date **Edge:** Reeded

Date	Mintage	F	VF	XF	Unc	BU
2001 Proof	3,000	Value: 195				

KM# 951.1 100 FRANCS **Weight:** 15.0000 g. **Composition:** 0.9000 Silver .4340 oz. ASW **Obverse:** Pantheon **Note:** Without mint mark. Struck at Paris Mint.

Date	Mintage	F	VF	XF	Unc	BU
1982	3,030,000	—	—	—	27.50	—
1982 Proof	25,000	Value: 45.00				
1983	5,001,000	—	—	—	27.50	—
1983 Proof	17,000	Value: 45.00				
1984	5,000,000	—	—	—	27.50	—
1985	999,000	—	—	—	30.00	—
1985 Proof	13,000	Value: 45.00				
1986	519,000	—	—	—	30.00	—
1987	100,000	—	—	—	30.00	—
1988	100,000	—	—	—	30.00	—
1989	83,000	—	—	—	30.00	—
1990	15,000	—	—	—	35.00	—
1991	5,000	—	—	—	35.00	—
1991 Proof	10,000	Value: 55.00				
1992 Proof	15,000	Value: 45.00				
1993 Proof	15,000	Value: 45.00				
1994 Proof	15,000	Value: 45.00				
1995	4,011	—	—	—	32.00	—
1995 Proof	10,000	Value: 45.00				
1996	2,013	—	—	—	40.00	—
1996 Proof	8,000	Value: 50.00				
1997	—	—	—	—	40.00	—
1997 Proof	—	Value: 50.00				
1998	—	—	—	—	40.00	—
1998 Proof	—	Value: 50.00				
1999	—	—	—	—	40.00	—
1999 Proof	—	Value: 50.00				
2000	—	—	—	—	40.00	—
2000 Proof	—	Value: 50.00				

KM# 955 100 FRANCS **Weight:** 15.0000 g. **Composition:** 0.9000 Silver .4340 oz. ASW **Subject:** 50th Anniversary - Death of Marie Curie **Reverse:** Head of Marie Curie right

Date	Mintage	F	VF	XF	Unc	BU
1984	3,964,000	—	—	—	25.00	—

KM# 955a 100 FRANCS **Weight:** 15.0000 g. **Composition:** 0.9500 Silver .4582 oz. ASW **Reverse:** Head of Marie Curie right

Date	Mintage	F	VF	XF	Unc	BU
1984 Proof	1,000	Value: 200				

KM# 955b 100 FRANCS **Weight:** 17.0000 g. **Composition:** 0.9200 Gold .5028 oz. AGW **Subject:** 50th Anniversary - Death of Marie Curie **Reverse:** Head of Marie Curie right

Date	Mintage	F	VF	XF	Unc	BU
1984 Proof	5,000	Value: 400				

KM# 957 100 FRANCS **Weight:** 15.0000 g. **Composition:** 0.9000 Silver .4340 oz. ASW **Subject:** Centennial of Emile Zola's Novel **Reverse:** Head of Emile Zola right

Date	Mintage	F	VF	XF	Unc	BU
1985	3,980,000	—	—	—	28.00	—
1985 Proof	13,000	Value: 55.00				

KM# 957a 100 FRANCS **Weight:** 15.0000 g. **Composition:** 0.9500 Silver .4582 oz. ASW **Reverse:** Head of Emile Zola right

Date	Mintage	F	VF	XF	Unc	BU
1985 Proof	5,000	Value: 115				

KM# 957b 100 FRANCS **Weight:** 17.0000 g. **Composition:** 0.9200 Gold .5028 oz. AGW **Subject:** Centennial of Emile Zola's Novel **Reverse:** Head of Emile Zola right

Date	Mintage	F	VF	XF	Unc	BU
1985 Proof	5,000	Value: 400				

KM# 960 100 FRANCS **Weight:** 15.0000 g. **Composition:** 0.9000 Silver .4340 oz. ASW **Subject:** Centennial - Statue of Liberty **Obverse:** Statue of Liberty

Date	Mintage	F	VF	XF	Unc	BU
1986	4,427,000	—	—	—	11.50	—

KM# 960a 100 FRANCS **Weight:** 15.0000 g. **Composition:** 0.9500 Silver .4582 oz. ASW **Obverse:** Statue of Liberty

Date	Mintage	F	VF	XF	Unc	BU
1986 Proof	18,000	Value: 45.00				

KM# 960b 100 FRANCS **Weight:** 17.0000 g. **Composition:** 0.9200 Gold .5028 oz. AGW **Subject:** Centennial - Statue of Liberty **Obverse:** Statue of Liberty

Date	Mintage	F	VF	XF	Unc	BU
1986	13,000	—	—	—	200	—
1986 Proof	17,000	Value: 225				

KM# 960c 100 FRANCS **Weight:** 20.0000 g. **Composition:** 0.9990 Platinum .6430 oz. APW **Obverse:** Statue of Liberty

Date	Mintage	F	VF	XF	Unc	BU
1986 Proof	9,500	Value: 435				

KM# 960d 100 FRANCS **Weight:** 17.0000 g. **Composition:** 0.9000 Palladium .4920 oz. **Obverse:** Statue of Liberty

Date	Mintage	F	VF	XF	Unc	BU
1986 Proof	1,250	Value: 585				

KM# 962 100 FRANCS **Weight:** 15.0000 g. **Composition:** 0.9000 Silver .4340 oz. ASW **Subject:** 230th Anniversary - BIrth of General Lafayette **Obverse:** Bust of Lafayette left

Date	Mintage	F	VF	XF	Unc	BU
1987	4,801,000	—	—	—	20.00	—

KM# 962a 100 FRANCS **Weight:** 15.0000 g. **Composition:** 0.9500 Silver .4582 oz. ASW **Obverse:** Bust of Lafayette left

Date	Mintage	F	VF	XF	Unc	BU
1987 Proof	30,000	Value: 30.00				

KM# 962b 100 FRANCS **Weight:** 17.0000 g. **Composition:** 0.9200 Gold .5028 oz. AGW **Subject:** 230th Anniversary - Birth of General Lafayette **Obverse:** Bust of Lafayette left

Date	Mintage	F	VF	XF	Unc	BU
1987	10,000	—	—	—	200	—
1987 Proof	20,000	Value: 215				

KM# 962c 100 FRANCS **Weight:** 20.0000 g. **Composition:** 0.9990 Platinum .6430 oz. APW **Obverse:** Bust of Lafayette left

Date	Mintage	F	VF	XF	Unc	BU
1987 Proof	8,500	Value: 450				

KM# 962d 100 FRANCS **Weight:** 17.0000 g. **Composition:** 0.9000 Palladium .4920 oz. **Obverse:** Bust of Lafayette left

Date	Mintage	F	VF	XF	Unc	BU
1987 Proof	7,000	Value: 595				

KM# 966 100 FRANCS **Weight:** 15.0000 g. **Composition:** 0.9000 Silver .4340 oz. ASW **Subject:** Fraternity

Date	Mintage	F	VF	XF	Unc	BU
1988	4,853,000	—	—	—	26.50	—

KM# 966a 100 FRANCS **Weight:** 15.0000 g. **Composition:** 0.9500 Silver .4582 oz. ASW **Subject:** Fraternity

Date	Mintage	F	VF	XF	Unc	BU
1988 Proof	20,000	Value: 37.50				

KM# 966b 100 FRANCS Weight: 17.0000 g. **Composition:** 0.9200 Gold .5028 oz. AGW **Subject:** Fraternity

Date	Mintage	F	VF	XF	Unc	BU
1988	3,000	—	—	—	450	—
1988 Proof	12,000	Value: 300				

KM# 966c 100 FRANCS Weight: 20.0000 g. **Composition:** 0.9990 Platinum .6430 oz. AP\: **Subject:** Fraternity

Date	Mintage	F	VF	XF	Unc	BU
1988 Proof	5,000	Value: 550				

KM# 966d 100 FRANCS Weight: 17.0000 g. **Composition:** 0.9000 Palladium .4920 oz. **Subject:** Fraternity

Date	Mintage	F	VF	XF	Unc	BU
1988 Proof	7,000	Value: 575				

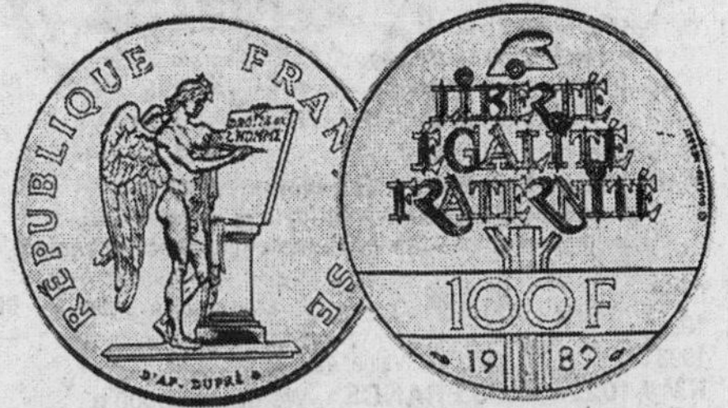

KM# 970 100 FRANCS Weight: 15.0000 g. **Composition:** 0.9000 Silver .4340 oz. ASW **Subject:** Human Rights

Date	Mintage	F	VF	XF	Unc	BU
1989	4,823,000	—	—	—	32.50	—

KM# 970a 100 FRANCS Weight: 15.0000 g. **Composition:** 0.9500 Silver .4582 oz. ASW **Subject:** Human Rights

Date	Mintage	F	VF	XF	Unc	BU
1989 Proof	40,000	Value: 47.50				

KM# 970b 100 FRANCS Weight: 17.0000 g. **Composition:** 0.9200 Gold .5028 oz. AGW **Subject:** Human Rights

Date	Mintage	F	VF	XF	Unc	BU
1989	1,000	—	—	—	600	—
1989 Proof	20,000	Value: 300				

KM# 970c 100 FRANCS Weight: 20.0000 g. **Composition:** 0.9990 Platinum .6430 oz. APW **Subject:** Human Rights

Date	Mintage	F	VF	XF	Unc	BU
1989 Proof	1,000	Value: 800				

KM# 970d 100 FRANCS Weight: 17.0000 g. **Composition:** 0.9000 Palladium .4920 oz. **Subject:** Human Rights

Date	Mintage	F	VF	XF	Unc	BU
1989 Proof	1,250	Value: 595				

KM# 971 100 FRANCS Weight: 22.2000 g. **Composition:** 0.9000 Silver .6424 oz. ASW **Subject:** 1992 Olympics **Note:** Similar to 500 Francs, KM#973.

Date	Mintage	F	VF	XF	Unc	BU
1989 Proof	136,000	Value: 30.00				

KM# 972 100 FRANCS Weight: 22.2000 g. **Composition:** 0.9000 Silver .6424 oz. ASW **Subject:** 1992 Olympics **Obverse:** Ice Skating Couple **Note:** Similar to 500 Francs, KM#974.

Date	Mintage	F	VF	XF	Unc	BU
1989 Proof	179,000	Value: 27.50				

KM# 980 100 FRANCS Weight: 22.2000 g. **Composition:** 0.9000 Silver .6424 oz. ASW **Series:** 1992 Olympics **Obverse:** Speed skaters

Date	Mintage	F	VF	XF	Unc	BU
1990 Proof	137,000	Value: 30.00				

KM# 981 100 FRANCS Weight: 22.2000 g. **Composition:** 0.9000 Silver .6424 oz. ASW **Series:** 1992 Olympics **Obverse:** Bobsledding **Reverse:** Games logo, value and legend

Date	Mintage	F	VF	XF	Unc	BU
1990 Proof	127,000	Value: 30.00				

KM# 982 100 FRANCS Weight: 15.0100 g. **Composition:** 0.9000 Silver .4340 oz. ASW **Subject:** Charlemagne

Date	Mintage	F	VF	XF	Unc	BU
1990	4,950,000	—	—	—	37.50	—

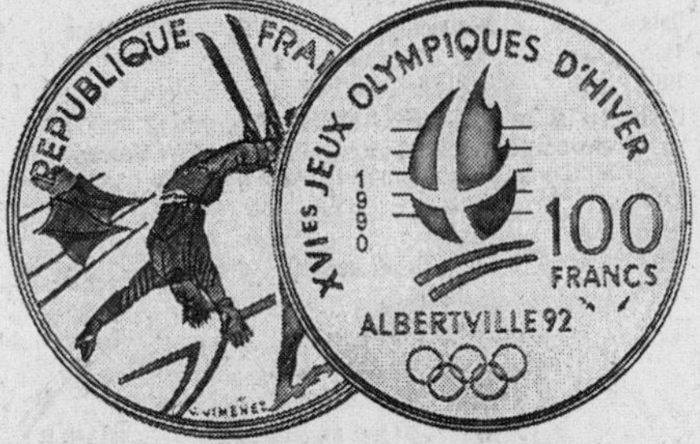

KM# 983 100 FRANCS Weight: 22.2000 g. **Composition:** 0.9000 Silver .6423 oz. ASW **Series:** 1992 Olympics **Obverse:** Free Style Skier

Date	Mintage	F	VF	XF	Unc	BU
1990 Proof	110,000	Value: 32.50				

KM# 984 100 FRANCS Weight: 22.2000 g. **Composition:** 0.9000 Silver .6423 oz. ASW **Subject:** 1992 Olympics **Obverse:** Slalom Skiers

Date	Mintage	F	VF	XF	Unc	BU
1990 Proof	110,000	Value: 30.00				

KM# 991 100 FRANCS Weight: 22.2000 g. **Composition:** 0.9000 Silver .6423 oz. ASW **Subject:** 100th Anniversary of Basketball **Obverse:** 2 players

Date	Mintage	F	VF	XF	Unc	BU
1991 Proof	13,000	Value: 65.00				

KM# 992 100 FRANCS Weight: 22.2000 g. **Composition:** 0.9000 Silver .6423 oz. ASW **Subject:** 100th Anniversary of Basketball **Obverse:** 1 player

Date	Mintage	F	VF	XF	Unc	BU
1991 Proof	13,000	Value: 65.00				

KM# 993 100 FRANCS Weight: 22.2000 g. **Composition:** 0.9000 Silver .6423 oz. ASW **Series:** 1992 Olympics **Obverse:** Hockey Players

Date	Mintage	F	VF	XF	Unc	BU
1991 Proof	93,000	Value: 37.50				

KM# 994 100 FRANCS Weight: 22.2000 g. **Composition:** 0.9000 Silver .6423 oz. ASW **Series:** 1992 Olympics **Obverse:** Cross Country Skier

Date	Mintage	F	VF	XF	Unc	BU
1991 Proof	93,000	Value: 35.00				

KM# 995 100 FRANCS Weight: 22.2000 g. **Composition:** 0.9000 Silver .6423 oz. ASW **Series:** 1992 Olympics **Obverse:** Ski Jumpers

Date	Mintage	F	VF	XF	Unc	BU
1991 Proof	90,000	Value: 37.50				

KM# 996 100 FRANCS Weight: 15.0100 g. **Composition:** 0.9000 Silver .4340 oz. ASW **Reverse:** Head of Descartes 1/2 right

Date	Mintage	F	VF	XF	Unc	BU
1991	3,985,000	—	—	—	32.50	—

KM# 1009 100 FRANCS Weight: 22.2000 g. **Composition:** 0.9000 Silver .6423 oz. ASW **Subject:** Paralympics **Obverse:** Segmented Flying Birds

Date	Mintage	F	VF	XF	Unc	BU
1992 Proof	5,000	Value: 95.00				

KM# 1010 100 FRANCS Weight: 22.2000 g. **Composition:** 0.9000 Silver .6423 oz. ASW **Subject:** French Antarctic Territories - Sea Lions

Date	Mintage	F	VF	XF	Unc	BU
1992 Proof	15,000	Value: 70.00				

KM# 1011 100 FRANCS Weight: 22.2000 g. **Composition:** 0.9000 Silver .6423 oz. ASW **Subject:** French Antarctic Territories - Penguins

Date	Mintage	F	VF	XF	Unc	BU
1992 Proof	15,000	Value: 70.00				

KM# 1120 100 FRANCS Weight: 15.0100 g. **Composition:** 0.9000 Silver .4340 oz. ASW **Subject:** Jean Monet

Date	Mintage	F	VF	XF	Unc	BU
1992	3,925,000	—	—	—	35.00	—

KM# 1017 100 FRANCS Weight: 22.2000 g. **Composition:** 0.9000 Silver .6423 oz. ASW **Series:** Bicentennial of the Louvre **Obverse:** Mona Lisa

Date	Mintage	F	VF	XF	Unc	BU
1993	—	—	—	—	—	—
1993 Proof	200,000	Value: 40.00				

KM# 1018.1 100 FRANCS Weight: 15.0000 g. **Composition:** 0.9000 Silver .4340 oz. ASW **Series:** Bicentennial of the Louvre **Obverse:** Liberty **Size:** 31 mm.

Date	F	VF	XF	Unc	BU
1993	—	—	—	35.00	—

KM# 1018.2 100 FRANCS Weight: 22.2000 g. **Composition:** 0.9000 Silver .6423 oz. ASW **Series:** Bicentennial of the Louvre **Obverse:** Liberty

Date	Mintage	F	VF	XF	Unc	BU
1993	—	—	—	—	—	—
1993 Proof	20,000	Value: 37.50				

KM# 1018.2a 100 FRANCS Weight: 17.0000 g. **Composition:** 0.9200 Gold .5028 oz. AGW **Series:** Bicentennial of the Louvre **Obverse:** Liberty

Date	Mintage	F	VF	XF	Unc	BU
1993	—	—	—	—	—	—
1993 Proof	5,000	Value: 400				

KM# 1019 100 FRANCS Weight: 22.2000 g. **Composition:** 0.9000 Silver .6420 oz. ASW **Series:** Bicentennial of the Louvre **Obverse:** Victory

Date	Mintage	F	VF	XF	Unc	BU
1993	—	—	—	—	—	—
1993 Proof	20,000	Value: 37.50				

KM# 1019a 100 FRANCS Weight: 17.0000 g. **Composition:** 0.9200 Gold .5028 oz. AGW **Series:** Bicentennial of the Louvre **Obverse:** Victory

Date	Mintage	F	VF	XF	Unc	BU
1993	—	—	—	—	—	—
1993 Proof	5,000	Value: 400				

KM# 1020 100 FRANCS Weight: 22.2600 g. **Composition:** 0.9000 Silver .6420 oz. ASW **Series:** Bicentennial of the Louvre **Obverse:** Venus de Milo

Date	Mintage	F	VF	XF	Unc	BU
1993	—	—	—	—	—	—
1993 Proof	20,000	Value: 40.00				

KM# 1021 100 FRANCS Weight: 22.2600 g. **Composition:** 0.9000 Silver .6420 oz. ASW **Series:** Bicentennial of the Louvre **Obverse:** Marie-Marguerite

Date	Mintage	F	VF	XF	Unc	BU
1993	—	—	—	—	—	—
1993 Proof	20,000	Value: 35.00				

KM# 1021a 100 FRANCS Weight: 17.0000 g. **Composition:** 0.9200 Gold .5028 oz. AGW **Series:** Bicentennial of the Louvre **Obverse:** Marie-Marguerite

Date	Mintage	F	VF	XF	Unc	BU
1993	—	—	—	—	—	—
1993 Proof	5,000	Value: 400				

KM# 1022 100 FRANCS Weight: 22.2600 g. **Composition:** 0.9000 Silver .6420 oz. ASW **Series:** Bicentennial of the Louvre **Obverse:** Napoleon crowning Josephine

Date	Mintage	F	VF	XF	Unc	BU
1993	—	—	—	—	—	—
1993 Proof	20,000	Value: 42.50				

KM# 1022a 100 FRANCS Weight: 17.0000 g. **Composition:** 0.9200 Gold .5028 oz. AGW **Series:** Bicentennial of the Louvre **Obverse:** Napoleon Crowning Josephine

Date	Mintage	F	VF	XF	Unc	BU
1993	—	—	—	—	—	—
1993 Proof	5,000	Value: 400				

KM# 1023 100 FRANCS Weight: 22.2000 g. **Composition:** 0.9000 Silver .6424 oz. ASW **Obverse:** Head of Jean Moulin facing

Date	Mintage	F	VF	XF	Unc	BU
1993	100,000	—	—	—	25.00	—
1993 Proof	50,000	Value: 40.00				

KM# 1037 100 FRANCS Weight: 22.2000 g. **Composition:** 0.9000 Silver .6424 oz. ASW **Subject:** Winston Churchill

Date	Mintage	F	VF	XF	Unc	BU
1994 Proof	Est. 30,000	Value: 42.50				

KM# 1038 100 FRANCS Weight: 22.2000 g. **Composition:** 0.9000 Silver .6424 oz. ASW **Obverse:** Bust of General de Gaulle right **Reverse:** Map of France, inscription overlay

Date	Mintage	F	VF	XF	Unc	BU
1994 Proof	Est. 30,000	Value: 42.50				

KM# 1039 100 FRANCS **Weight:** 22.2000 g. **Composition:** 0.9000 Silver .6424 oz. ASW **Obverse:** Bust of General Leclerc facing **Reverse:** Flag, inscription, fort, denomination

Date	Mintage	F	VF	XF	Unc	BU
1994 Proof	Est. 30,000	Value: 42.50				

KM# 1040 100 FRANCS **Weight:** 22.2000 g. **Composition:** 0.9000 Silver .6424 oz. ASW **Obverse:** Bust of General Marie Pierre Koenig facing 1/2 left **Reverse:** Battle scene

Date	Mintage	F	VF	XF	Unc	BU
1994 Proof	Est. 30,000	Value: 42.50				

KM# 1041 100 FRANCS **Weight:** 22.2000 g. **Composition:** 0.9000 Silver .6424 oz. ASW **Obverse:** Profile bust of General Juin right, map of Italy at right. Mountaintop building

Date	Mintage	F	VF	XF	Unc	BU
1994 Proof	Est. 30,000	Value: 42.50				

KM# 1042 100 FRANCS **Weight:** 22.2000 g. **Composition:** 0.9000 Silver .6424 oz. ASW **Obverse:** Bust of General Dwight David Eisenhower facing 1/2 left **Reverse:** Flags representing allied countries under Supreme Commander Eisenhower

Date	Mintage	F	VF	XF	Unc	BU
1994 Proof	Est. 30,000	Value: 42.50				

KM# 1043 100 FRANCS **Weight:** 22.2000 g. **Composition:** 0.9000 Silver .6424 oz. ASW **Subject:** Sainte - Mere - Eglise **Obverse:** Church, parachute behind

Date	Mintage	F	VF	XF	Unc	BU
1994 Proof	Est. 30,000	Value: 42.50				

KM# 1044 100 FRANCS **Weight:** 22.2000 g. **Composition:** 0.9000 Silver .6424 oz. ASW **Obverse:** Face in profile of General de Lattre de Tassigny right **Reverse:** Waving flags below denomination

Date	Mintage	F	VF	XF	Unc	BU
1994 Proof	Est. 30,000	Value: 42.50				

KM# 1045.2 100 FRANCS **Weight:** 22.2000 g. **Composition:** 0.9000 Silver .6424 oz. ASW

Date	Mintage	F	VF	XF	Unc	BU
1994	—	—	—	—	30.00	—
1994 Proof	Est. 30,000	Value: 42.50				

KM# 1046 100 FRANCS **Weight:** 22.2000 g. **Composition:** 0.9000 Silver .6424 oz. ASW **Obverse:** Facing busts of de Gaulle and Adenauer **Reverse:** Two hands joined in handshake

Date	Mintage	F	VF	XF	Unc	BU
1994 Proof	Est. 30,000	Value: 42.50				

KM# 1047 100 FRANCS **Weight:** 33.6300 g. **Composition:** 0.9250 Silver 1.0000 oz. ASW **Series:** 1996 Olympics **Reverse:** Discus thrower

Date	Mintage	F	VF	XF	Unc	BU
1994 Proof	250,000	Value: 32.50				

KM# 1048 100 FRANCS **Weight:** 33.6300 g. **Composition:** 0.9250 Silver 1.0000 oz. ASW **Subject:** 1996 Olympics **Reverse:** Javelin Thrower

Date	Mintage	F	VF	XF	Unc	BU
1994 Proof	250,000	Value: 32.50				

KM# 1072 100 FRANCS **Weight:** 22.2000 g. **Composition:** 0.9000 Silver .6424 oz. ASW **Series:** Centennial of Cinema **Obverse:** Antique movie camera **Reverse:** Conjoined busts of the Lumiere Brothers right

Date	Mintage	F	VF	XF	Unc	BU
1994 Proof	15,000	Value: 32.50				

KM# 1073 100 FRANCS **Weight:** 17.0000 g. **Composition:** 0.9200 Gold .5028 oz. AGW **Series:** Centennial of Cinema **Obverse:** Antique movie camera **Reverse:** Conjoined busts of the Lumiere Brothers right

Date	Mintage	F	VF	XF	Unc	BU
1994 Proof	5,000	Value: 400				

KM# 1076 100 FRANCS **Weight:** 22.2000 g. **Composition:** 0.9000 Silver .6424 oz. ASW **Series:** Centennial of Cinema **Reverse:** Head of Charlie Chaplin facing

Date	Mintage	F	VF	XF	Unc	BU
1994 Proof	15,000	Value: 42.00				

KM# 1077 100 FRANCS **Weight:** 17.0000 g. **Composition:** 0.9200 Gold .5028 oz. AGW **Series:** Centennial of Cinema **Reverse:** Head of Charlie Chaplin facing

Date	Mintage	F	VF	XF	Unc	BU
1994 Proof	5,000	Value: 425				

KM# 1182 100 FRANCS **Weight:** 22.2000 g. **Composition:** 0.9000 Silver .6424 oz. ASW **Reverse:** Voltaire

Date	Mintage	F	VF	XF	Unc	BU
1994 Proof	3,000	Value: 50.00				

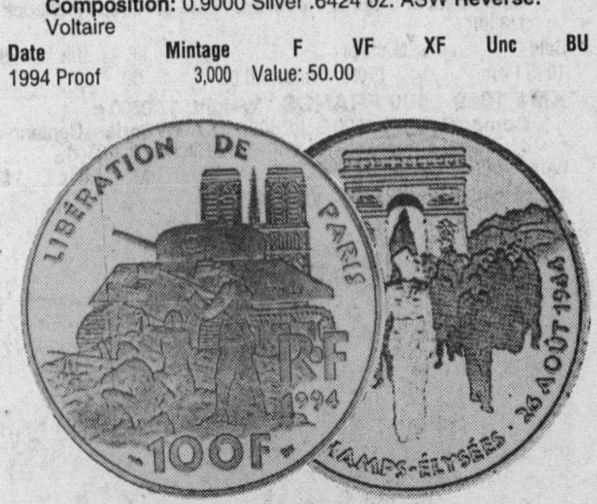

KM# 1045.1 100 FRANCS **Weight:** 15.0000 g. **Composition:** 0.9000 Silver .4340 oz. ASW **Subject:** Liberation of Paris **Obverse:** Battle scene **Reverse:** Triumphant troops marching down Champs Elysees **Size:** 31 mm. **Note:** Smaller size.

Date	Mintage	F	VF	XF	Unc	BU
1994	1,598,000	—	—	—	35.00	—

KM# 1116.1 100 FRANCS **Weight:** 15.0000 g. **Composition:** 0.9000 Silver .4340 oz. ASW **Subject:** V.E. Day **Obverse:** Victory in Europe date, May 8, 1945 **Size:** 31 mm. **Note:** Smaller size.

Date	Mintage	F	VF	XF	Unc	BU
1995	1,990,000	—	—	—	40.00	—

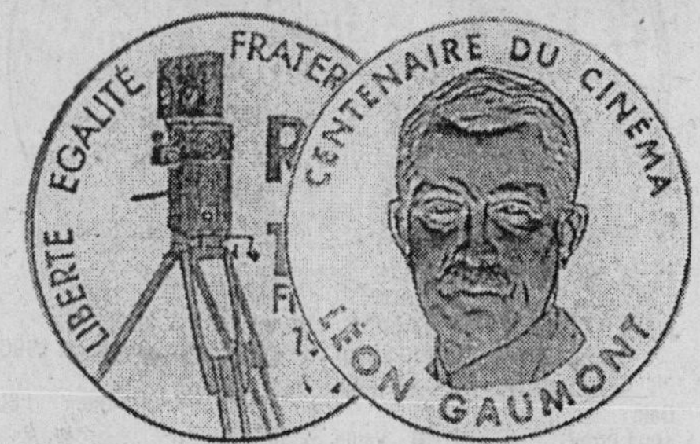

KM# 1080 100 FRANCS **Weight:** 22.2000 g. **Composition:** 0.9000 Silver .6424 oz. ASW **Series:** Centennial of Cinema **Reverse:** Head of Leon Gaumont facing

Date	Mintage	F	VF	XF	Unc	BU
1995 Proof	15,000	Value: 40.00				

KM# 1081 100 FRANCS **Weight:** 17.0000 g. **Composition:** 0.9200 Gold .5028 oz. AGW **Series:** Centennial of Cinema **Reverse:** Head of Leon Gaumont facing

Date	Mintage	F	VF	XF	Unc	BU
1995 Proof	5,000	Value: 425				

KM# 1084 100 FRANCS **Weight:** 22.2000 g. **Composition:** 0.9000 Silver .6424 oz. ASW **Series:** Centennial of Cinema **Reverse:** Head of Jean Renoir right

Date	Mintage	F	VF	XF	Unc	BU
1995 Proof	15,000	Value: 30.00				

KM# 1085 100 FRANCS **Weight:** 17.0000 g. **Composition:** 0.9200 Gold .5028 oz. AGW **Series:** Centennial of Cinema **Reverse:** Head of Jean Renoir right

Date	Mintage	F	VF	XF	Unc	BU
1995 Proof	5,000	Value: 400				

KM# 1088 100 FRANCS **Weight:** 22.2000 g. **Composition:** 0.9000 Silver .6424 oz. ASW **Series:** Centennial of Cinema **Reverse:** Head of Alfred Hitchcock 1/2 left

Date	Mintage	F	VF	XF	Unc	BU
1995 Proof	15,000	Value: 40.00				

KM# 1089 100 FRANCS **Weight:** 17.0000 g. **Composition:** 0.9200 Gold .5028 oz. AGW **Series:** Centennial of Cinema **Reverse:** Head of Alfred Hitchcock 1/2 left

Date	Mintage	F	VF	XF	Unc	BU
1995 Proof	5,000	Value: 475				

KM# 1092 100 FRANCS **Weight:** 22.2000 g. **Composition:** 0.9000 Silver .6424 oz. ASW **Series:** Centennial of Cinema **Obverse:** Antique movie camera **Reverse:** Head of Greta Garbo in profile right

Date	Mintage	F	VF	XF	Unc	BU
1995 Proof	15,000	Value: 37.50				

KM# 1093 100 FRANCS **Weight:** 17.0000 g. **Composition:** 0.9200 Gold .5028 oz. AGW **Series:** Centennial of Cinema **Obverse:** Antique movie camera **Reverse:** Head of Greta Garbo in profile right

Date	Mintage	F	VF	XF	Unc	BU
1995 Proof	5,000	Value: 475				

KM# 1096 100 FRANCS **Weight:** 22.2000 g. **Composition:** 0.9000 Silver .6424 oz. ASW **Series:** Centennial of Cinema **Obverse:** Antique movie camera **Reverse:** Head of Audrey Hepburn 1/2 left

Date	Mintage	F	VF	XF	Unc	BU
1995 Proof	15,000	Value: 37.50				

KM# 1097 100 FRANCS **Weight:** 17.0000 g. **Composition:** 0.9200 Gold .5028 oz. AGW **Series:** Centennial of Cinema **Obverse:** Antique movie camera **Reverse:** Head of Audrey Hepburn 1/2 left

Date	Mintage	F	VF	XF	Unc	BU
1995 Proof	5,000	Value: 400				

KM# 1100 100 FRANCS **Weight:** 22.2000 g. **Composition:** 0.9000 Silver .6424 oz. ASW **Series:** Centennial of Cinema **Obverse:** Antique movie camera **Reverse:** Bust of Federico Fellini 1/2 right

Date	Mintage	F	VF	XF	Unc	BU
1995 Proof	15,000	Value: 30.00				

KM# 1101 100 FRANCS **Weight:** 17.0000 g. **Composition:** 0.9200 Gold .5028 oz. AGW **Series:** Centennial of Cinema **Obverse:** Antique movie camera **Reverse:** Bust of Federico Fellini 1/2 right

Date	Mintage	F	VF	XF	Unc	BU
1995 Proof	5,000	Value: 450				

KM# 1104 100 FRANCS **Weight:** 22.2000 g. **Composition:** 0.9000 Silver .6424 oz. ASW **Series:** Centennial of Cinema **Obverse:** Antique movie camera **Reverse:** Bust of Yves Montand facing

Date	Mintage	F	VF	XF	Unc	BU
1995 Proof	15,000	Value: 30.00				

KM# 1105 100 FRANCS **Weight:** 17.0000 g. **Composition:** 0.9200 Gold .5028 oz. AGW **Series:** Centennial of Cinema **Obverse:** Antique movie camera **Reverse:** Bust of Yves Montand facing

Date	Mintage	F	VF	XF	Unc	BU
1995 Proof	5,000	Value: 450				

KM# 1108 100 FRANCS **Weight:** 22.2000 g. **Composition:** 0.9000 Silver .6424 oz. ASW **Series:** Centennial of Cinema **Obverse:** Antique movie camera **Reverse:** Bust of Romy Schneider 1/2 left

Date	Mintage	F	VF	XF	Unc	BU
1995 Proof	15,000	Value: 30.00				

KM# 1109 100 FRANCS **Weight:** 17.0000 g. **Composition:** 0.9200 Gold .5028 oz. AGW **Series:** Centennial of Cinema **Obverse:** Antique movie camera **Reverse:** Bust of Romy Schneider 1/2 left

Date	Mintage	F	VF	XF	Unc	BU
1995 Proof	5,000	Value: 400				

KM# 1116.2 100 FRANCS **Weight:** 22.2000 g. **Composition:** 0.9000 Silver .6424 oz. ASW

Date	Mintage	F	VF	XF	Unc	BU
1995 Proof	30,000	Value: 45.00				

KM# 1134 100 FRANCS **Weight:** 22.2000 g. **Composition:** 0.9000 Silver .6424 oz. ASW **Obverse:** Bust of Louis Pasteur facing **Reverse:** Lab bottles, denomination

Date	Mintage	F	VF	XF	Unc	BU
1995 Proof	10,000	Value: 45.00				

KM# 1136 100 FRANCS **Weight:** 22.2000 g. **Composition:** 0.9000 Silver .6424 oz. ASW **Obverse:** Bust of Jean de la Fontaine 1/2 left

Date	Mintage	F	VF	XF	Unc	BU
1995 Proof	10,000	Value: 45.00				

KM# 1138 100 FRANCS **Weight:** 22.2000 g. **Composition:** 0.9000 Silver .6424 oz. ASW **Obverse:** Bust of Madame de Sevigne 1/2 left

Date	Mintage	F	VF	XF	Unc	BU
1996 Proof	5,000	Value: 65.00				

KM# 1180 100 FRANCS **Weight:** 15.0500 g. **Composition:** 0.9000 Silver .4340 oz. ASW **Obverse:** Bust of King Clovis I facing **Reverse:** Baptism scene

Date	Mintage	F	VF	XF	Unc	BU
1996	2,000,000	—	—	—	32.50	—
1996 Proof	—	Value: 60.00				

KM# 1172 100 FRANCS **Weight:** 17.0000 g. **Composition:** 0.9200 Gold .5028 oz. AGW **Subject:** Coupe du Monde 1998 - France **Obverse:** World Cup 1998 logo above denomination **Reverse:** Segment of Eiffel tower, soccer player

Date	Mintage	F	VF	XF	Unc	BU
1996 Proof	25,000	Value: 375				

KM# 1168 100 FRANCS **Weight:** 17.0000 g. **Composition:** 0.9200 Gold .5028 oz. AGW **Subject:** Coupe du Monde 1998 - Africa **Reverse:** Soccer player and map of Africa

Date	Mintage	F	VF	XF	Unc	BU
1997 Proof	25,000	Value: 400				

KM# 1169 100 FRANCS **Weight:** 17.0000 g. **Composition:** 0.9200 Gold .5028 oz. AGW **Subject:** Coupe du Monde 1998 - America **Reverse:** Soccer player and map of North & South America

Date	Mintage	F	VF	XF	Unc	BU
1997 Proof	25,000	Value: 400				

KM# 1170 100 FRANCS **Weight:** 17.0000 g. **Composition:** 0.9200 Gold .5028 oz. AGW **Subject:** Coupe du Monde 1998 - Asia **Reverse:** Soccer player and map of Asia

Date	Mintage	F	VF	XF	Unc	BU
1997 Proof	25,000	Value: 400				

KM# 1173 100 FRANCS **Weight:** 17.0000 g. **Composition:** 0.9200 Gold .5028 oz. AGW **Subject:** Coupe du Monde 1998 - Oceania **Reverse:** Soccer player and map of the Pacific, with Australia highlighted in a box

Date	Mintage	F	VF	XF	Unc	BU
1997 Proof	25,000	Value: 400				

KM# 1188 100 FRANCS **Weight:** 15.1500 g. **Composition:** 0.9000 Silver .4384 oz. ASW **Obverse:** Head of Andre Malraux facing **Reverse:** Two cats flank denomination

Date	Mintage	F	VF	XF	Unc	BU
1997 Proof	3,000	Value: 50.00				
1997	3,000	—	—	—	32.50	—

KM# 1195 100 FRANCS **Weight:** 8.4500 g. **Composition:** 0.9200 Gold .2499 oz. AGW **Obverse:** Pantheon **Reverse:** Denomination and tree design

Date	Mintage	F	VF	XF	Unc	BU
1997 Proof	500	Value: 350				

KM# 1196 100 FRANCS **Weight:** 22.2000 g. **Composition:** 0.9000 Silver .6424 oz. ASW **Obverse:** Bust of Georges Guynemer 1/2 left **Reverse:** Guynemer's stork and denomination

Date	Mintage	F	VF	XF	Unc	BU
1997 Proof	3,000	Value: 50.00				

KM# 1198 100 FRANCS **Weight:** 22.2000 g. **Composition:** 0.9000 Silver .6424 oz. ASW **Obverse:** Conjoined busts of Pierre and Marie Curie left **Reverse:** Denomination

Date	Mintage	F	VF	XF	Unc	BU
1997 Proof	3,000	Value: 50.00				

KM# 1171 100 FRANCS **Weight:** 17.0000 g. **Composition:** 0.9200 Gold .5028 oz. AGW **Subject:** Coupe du Monte 1998 - Europe **Reverse:** Soccer player and map of Europe

Date	Mintage	F	VF	XF	Unc	BU
1998 Proof	25,000	Value: 400				

KM# 1201 100 FRANCS **Weight:** 22.2000 g. **Composition:** 0.9000 Silver .6424 oz. ASW **Obverse:** Bust of Marie Caritat Marquis de Condorcet 1/2 right **Reverse:** Denomination

Date	Mintage	F	VF	XF	Unc	BU
1998 Proof	3,000	Value: 50.00				

KM# 1203 100 FRANCS **Weight:** 22.2000 g. **Composition:** 0.9000 Silver .6424 oz. ASW **Obverse:** 3/4 bust of Gaspard Monge right **Reverse:** Denomination

Date	Mintage	F	VF	XF	Unc	BU
1998 Proof	3,000	Value: 50.00				

KM# 1209 100 FRANCS **Weight:** 17.0000 g. **Composition:** 0.9200 Gold .5028 oz. AGW **Subject:** Treasures of the Nile - King Tutankhamon **Obverse:** Burial mask and dog **Reverse:** Sphinx and pyramids

Date	Mintage	F	VF	XF	Unc	BU
1998 Proof	2,000	Value: 475				

KM# 1210 100 FRANCS **Weight:** 17.0000 g. **Composition:** 0.9200 Gold .5028 oz. AGW **Subject:** Treasures of the Nile - The Scribe Accroupi **Obverse:** Seated scribe **Reverse:** Denomination

Date	Mintage	F	VF	XF	Unc	BU
1998 Proof	2,000	Value: 475				

KM# 1295 100 FRANCS **Weight:** 22.3000 g. **Composition:** 0.9000 Silver 0.6453 oz. ASW **Subject:** Louis Braille **Obverse:** Portrait, dots and fingers **Reverse:** Braille text, tools and fingers **Edge:** Plain **Size:** 36.7 mm.

Date	Mintage	F	VF	XF	Unc	BU
1999 Proof	3,000	Value: 50.00				

KM# 1296 100 FRANCS **Weight:** 22.3000 g. **Composition:** 0.9000 Silver 0.6453 oz. ASW **Subject:** Jean Jaures **Obverse:** Bearded portrait **Reverse:** Floor plan and dome **Edge:** Plain **Size:** 36.7 mm.

Date	Mintage	F	VF	XF	Unc	BU
1999 Proof	3,000	Value: 50.00				

KM# 1232 100 FRANCS **Weight:** 17.0000 g. **Composition:** 0.9200 Gold .5028 oz. AGW **Subject:** 2000 Years - French Coinage **Obverse:** Denomination **Reverse:** 1st century B.C. Celtic Parisii Stater coin design **Edge:** Plain **Note:** Struck at Paris Mint.

Date	Mintage	F	VF	XF	Unc	BU
2000 Prof	1,000	Value: 485				

KM# 1233 100 FRANCS **Weight:** 17.0000 g. **Composition:** 0.9200 Gold .5028 oz. AGW **Subject:** 2000 Years - French Coinage **Reverse:** Charlemagne Denar coin design **Note:** Struck at Paris Mint.

Date	Mintage	F	VF	XF	Unc	BU
2000 Proof	1,000	Value: 485				

KM# 1234 100 FRANCS **Weight:** 17.0000 g. **Composition:** 0.9200 Gold .5028 oz. AGW **Subject:** 2000 Years - French Coinage **Reverse:** Louis IX gold Ecu coin design **Note:** Struck at Paris Mint.

Date	Mintage	F	VF	XF	Unc	BU
2000 Proof	1,000	Value: 485				

KM# 1238 100 FRANCS **Weight:** 17.0000 g. **Composition:** 0.9200 Gold .5028 oz. AGW **Series:** XXth Century **Subject:** Biology and Medicine **Obverse:** Double X design **Reverse:** Parents, fetus, hands **Note:** Struck at Paris Mint.

Date	Mintage	F	VF	XF	Unc	BU
2000 Proof	1,000	Value: 475				

KM# 1239 100 FRANCS **Weight:** 17.0000 g. **Composition:** 0.9200 Gold .5028 oz. AGW **Series:** XXth Century **Subject:** Physics **Reverse:** Einstein's portrait, atom and formula **Note:** Struck at Paris Mint.

Date	Mintage	F	VF	XF	Unc	BU
2000 Proof	1,000	Value: 475				

KM# 1240 100 FRANCS **Weight:** 17.0000 g. **Composition:** 0.9200 Gold .5028 oz. AGW **Series:** XXth Century **Subject:** Communications **Reverse:** World, satellites, keyboard **Note:** Struck at Paris Mint.

Date	Mintage	F	VF	XF	Unc	BU
2000 Proof	1,000	Value: 475				

KM# 1241 100 FRANCS **Weight:** 17.0000 g. **Composition:** 0.9200 Gold .5028 oz. AGW **Series:** XXth Century **Subject:** Automobile **Reverse:** Race cars above horse **Note:** Struck at Paris Mint.

Date	Mintage	F	VF	XF	Unc	BU
2000 Proof	1,000	Value: 475				

KM# 1242 100 FRANCS **Weight:** 17.0000 g. **Composition:** 0.9200 Gold .5028 oz. AGW **Series:** XXth Century **Subject:** Flight **Reverse:** Icarus in flight above Bleriot monoplane **Note:** Struck at Paris Mint.

Date	Mintage	F	VF	XF	Unc	BU
2000 Proof	1,000	Value: 475				

KM# 1243 100 FRANCS **Weight:** 17.0000 g. **Composition:** 0.9200 Gold .5028 oz. AGW **Series:** XXth Century **Subject:** Space Travel **Reverse:** Astronaut, footprint on moon, planets **Note:** Struck at Paris Mint.

Date	Mintage	F	VF	XF	Unc	BU
2000 Proof	1,000	Value: 475				

KM# 1264 100 FRANCS **Weight:** 17.0000 g. **Composition:** 0.9200 Gold .5028 oz. AGW **Subject:** Antoine de St. Exupery **Obverse:** Portrait, bi-plane **Reverse:** The "Little Prince" standing on a small planet **Note:** Struck at Paris Mint.

Date	Mintage	F	VF	XF	Unc	BU
2000 Proof	1,000	Value: 450				

KM# 1269 100 FRANCS **Weight:** 17.0000 g. **Composition:** 0.9200 Gold .5028 oz. AGW **Subject:** Palace of Versailles **Obverse:** Stylized French map **Reverse:** Louis XIV with internal and exteral palace views **Edge:** Plain

Date	Mintage	F	VF	XF	Unc	BU
2001 Proof	2,000	Value: 365				

KM# 1271 100 FRANCS **Weight:** 17.0000 g. **Composition:** 0.9200 Gold .5028 oz. AGW **Obverse:** Champs-Elysees **Reverse:** Arch of Triumph partial close up and aerial views

Date	Mintage	F	VF	XF	Unc	BU
2001 Proof	2,000	—	—	—	—	—

KM# 1273 100 FRANCS **Weight:** 17.0000 g. **Composition:** 0.9200 Gold .5028 oz. AGW **Obverse:** Notre-Dame Cathedral **Reverse:** Gargoyle and cathedral views

Date	Mintage	F	VF	XF	Unc	BU
2001 Proof	2,000	Value: 365				

KM# 1275 100 FRANCS **Weight:** 17.0000 g. **Composition:** 0.9200 Gold .5028 oz. AGW **Obverse:** Eiffel Tower **Reverse:** Two tower views

Date	Mintage	F	VF	XF	Unc	BU
2001 Proof	2,000	Value: 365				

KM# 974 500 FRANCS **Weight:** 17.0000 g. **Composition:** 0.9200 Gold .5029 oz. AGW **Series:** 1992 Olympics **Obverse:** Ice Skating Couple **Note:** Struck at Paris Mint.

Date	Mintage	F	VF	XF	Unc	BU
1989 Proof	Est. 17,000	Value: 210				

KM# 973 500 FRANCS **Weight:** 17.0000 g. **Composition:** 0.9200 Gold .5029 oz. AGW **Series:** 1992 Olympics **Obverse:** Alpine Skiing **Note:** Without mint mark. Struck at Paris Mint.

Date	Mintage	F	VF	XF	Unc	BU
1989 Proof	19,000	Value: 210				

KM# 988 500 FRANCS **Weight:** 17.0000 g. **Composition:** 0.9200 Gold .5029 oz. AGW **Series:** 1992 Olympics **Obverse:** Modern and old style slalom skiers **Note:** Struck at Paris Mint. Similar to 100 Francs, KM#284.

Date	Mintage	F	VF	XF	Unc	BU
1990 Proof	8,000	Value: 235				

KM# 985 500 FRANCS **Weight:** 17.0000 g. **Composition:** 0.9200 Gold .5029 oz. AGW **Series:** 1992 Olympics **Obverse:** Speed Skating **Note:** Struck at Paris Mint. Similar to 100 Francs, KM#980.

Date	Mintage	F	VF	XF	Unc	BU
1990 Proof	13,000	Value: 210				

KM# 986 500 FRANCS **Weight:** 17.0000 g. **Composition:** 0.9200 Gold .5029 oz. AGW **Series:** 1992 Olympics **Obverse:** Bobsledding **Note:** Struck at Paris Mint. Similar to 100 Francs, KM#981.

Date	Mintage	F	VF	XF	Unc	BU
1990 Proof	13,000	Value: 210				

KM# 987 500 FRANCS **Weight:** 17.0000 g. **Composition:** 0.9200 Gold .5029 oz. AGW **Series:** 1992 Olympics **Obverse:** Free style skier watched by chamois **Reverse:** Similar to KM#1000 obverse **Note:** Struck at Paris Mint. Similar to 100 Francs, KM#983.

Date	Mintage	F	VF	XF	Unc	BU
1990 Proof	8,000	Value: 235				

KM# 977 500 FRANCS **Weight:** 17.0000 g. **Composition:** 0.9200 Gold .5029 oz. AGW **Subject:** 100th Anniversary of Basketball **Obverse:** Player jumping for lay up shot, hoop behind **Note:** Struck at Paris Mint.

Date	Mintage	F	VF	XF	Unc	BU
1991 Proof	5,000	Value: 325				

KM# 997 500 FRANCS **Weight:** 17.0000 g. **Composition:** 0.9200 Gold .5029 oz. AGW **Series:** 1992 Olympics **Obverse:** 2 Hockey players and large Ibex ram **Note:** Struck at Paris Mint.

Date	Mintage	F	VF	XF	Unc	BU
1991 Proof	8,000	Value: 235				

KM# 998 500 FRANCS **Weight:** 17.0000 g. **Composition:** 0.9200 Gold .5029 oz. AGW **Note:** Struck at Paris Mint.

Date	Mintage	F	VF	XF	Unc	BU
1991 Proof	8,000	Value: 275				

KM# 999 500 FRANCS **Weight:** 17.0000 g. **Composition:** 0.9200 Gold .5029 oz. AGW **Series:** 1992 Olympics **Obverse:** Old style and modern ski jumpers **Note:** Struck at Paris Mint.

Date	Mintage	F	VF	XF	Unc	BU
1991 Proof	8,000	Value: 275				

KM# 1000 500 FRANCS **Weight:** 17.0000 g. **Composition:** 0.9200 Gold .5029 oz. AGW **Series:** 1992 Olympics **Obverse:** Head of Pierre de Coubertin facing **Note:** Struck at Paris Mint.

Date	Mintage	F	VF	XF	Unc	BU
1991 Proof	28,000	Value: 275				

KM# 1001 500 FRANCS **Weight:** 17.0000 g. **Composition:** 0.9200 Gold .5029 oz. AGW **Reverse:** Mozart in Paris at piano **Note:** Struck at Paris Mint.

Date	Mintage	F	VF	XF	Unc	BU
1991 Proof	Est. 5,000	Value: 300				

KM# 1024 500 FRANCS **Weight:** 31.1040 g. **Composition:** 0.9990 Gold 1.0000 oz. AGW **Series:** Bicentennial of the Louvre **Obverse:** Mona Lisa **Note:** Struck at Paris Mint.

Date	Mintage	F	VF	XF	Unc	BU
1993	—	—	—	—	—	—
1993 Proof	5,000	Value: 750				
1994 Proof	5,000	Value: 800				

KM# 1026 500 FRANCS **Weight:** 155.5175 g. **Composition:** 0.9990 Gold 5.0000 oz. AGW **Series:** Bicentennial of the Louvre **Obverse:** Liberty **Note:** Struck at Paris Mint.

Date	Mintage	F	VF	XF	Unc	BU
1993 Proof	99	Value: 3,100				
1994 Proof	99	Value: 3,500				

KM# 1027 500 FRANCS **Weight:** 155.5175 g. **Composition:** 0.9990 Gold 5.0000 oz. AGW **Series:** Bicentennial of the Louvre **Obverse:** Mona Lisa **Note:** Struck at Paris Mint.

Date	Mintage	F	VF	XF	Unc	BU
1993 Proof	99	Value: 3,100				
1994 Proof	99	Value: 3,500				

KM# 1028 500 FRANCS **Weight:** 17.0000 g. **Composition:** 0.9200 Gold .5028 oz. AGW **Obverse:** Head of Jean Moulin facing **Note:** Struck at Paris Mint.

Date	Mintage	F	VF	XF	Unc	BU
1993 Proof	5,000	Value: 325				

KM# 1183 500 FRANCS **Weight:** 155.5175 g. **Composition:** 0.9990 Gold 5.0000 oz. AGW **Series:** Bicentennial of the Louvre **Obverse:** Victory **Note:** Struck at Paris Mint.

Date	Mintage	F	VF	XF	Unc	BU
1993 Proof	99	Value: 4,200				
1994 Proof	99	Value: 4,300				

KM# 1184 500 FRANCS **Weight:** 155.5175 g. **Composition:** 0.9990 Gold 5.0000 oz. AGW **Series:** Bicentennial of the Louvre **Obverse:** Napoleon and Josephine **Note:** Struck at Paris Mint.

Date	Mintage	F	VF	XF	Unc	BU
1993 Proof	99	Value: 3,750				
1994 Proof	99	Value: 3,800				

KM# 1185 500 FRANCS **Weight:** 155.5175 g. **Composition:** 0.9990 Gold 5.0000 oz. AGW **Series:** Bicentennial of the Louvre **Obverse:** Marie Marguerite **Note:** Struck at Paris Mint.

Date	Mintage	F	VF	XF	Unc	BU
1993 Proof	99	Value: 3,750				
1994 Proof	99	Value: 3,800				

KM# 1025 500 FRANCS **Weight:** 31.1040 g. **Composition:** 0.9990 Gold 1.0000 oz. AGW **Series:** Bicentennial of the Louvre **Obverse:** Venus de Milo **Note:** Struck at Paris Mint. Similar to 100 Francs, KM#1020.

Date	Mintage	F	VF	XF	Unc	BU
1993	—	—	—	—	—	—
1993 Proof	5,000	Value: 750				

KM# 1049 500 FRANCS **Weight:** 17.0000 g. **Composition:** 0.9200 Gold .5028 oz. AGW **Obverse:** Bust of Winston Churchill right **Note:** Struck at Paris Mint.

Date	Mintage	F	VF	XF	Unc	BU
1994 Proof	Est. 2,000	Value: 325				

KM# 1051 500 FRANCS **Weight:** 17.0000 g. **Composition:** 0.9200 Gold .5028 oz. AGW **Obverse:** Bust of General Leclerc facing **Note:** Struck at Paris Mint.

Date	Mintage	F	VF	XF	Unc	BU
1994 Proof	Est. 2,000	Value: 325				

KM# 1050 500 FRANCS **Weight:** 17.0000 g. **Composition:** 0.9200 Gold .5028 oz. AGW **Obverse:** 3/4 bust of General de Gaulle in front of microphone **Note:** Struck at Paris Mint.

Date	Mintage	F	VF	XF	Unc	BU
1994 Proof	Est. 5,000	Value: 325				

KM# 1052 500 FRANCS **Weight:** 17.0000 g. **Composition:** 0.9200 Gold .5028 oz. AGW **Obverse:** Bust of General Marie Pierre Koenig 1/2 left **Note:** Struck at Paris Mint.

Date	Mintage	F	VF	XF	Unc	BU
1994 Proof	Est. 2,000	Value: 325				

KM# 1053 500 FRANCS **Weight:** 17.0000 g. **Composition:** 0.9200 Gold .5028 oz. AGW **Obverse:** Bust of General Juin right, map of Italy at right **Note:** Struck at Paris Mint.

Date	Mintage	F	VF	XF	Unc	BU
1994 Proof	Est. 2,000	Value: 325				

KM# 1054 500 FRANCS **Weight:** 17.0000 g. **Composition:** 0.9200 Gold .5028 oz. AGW **Obverse:** Bust of General Dwight David Eisenhower left **Note:** Struck at Paris Mint.

Date	Mintage	F	VF	XF	Unc	BU
1994 Proof	Est. 2,000	Value: 325				

KM# 1055 500 FRANCS **Weight:** 17.0000 g. **Composition:** 0.9200 Gold .5028 oz. AGW **Obverse:** Church of Sainte - Mere - Eglise, parachute behind **Note:** Struck at Paris Mint.

Date	Mintage	F	VF	XF	Unc	BU
1994 Proof	Est. 2,000	Value: 325				

KM# 1056 500 FRANCS **Weight:** 17.0000 g. **Composition:** 0.9200 Gold .5028 oz. AGW **Obverse:** Head of General de Lattre de Tassigny right **Note:** Struck at Paris Mint.

Date	Mintage	F	VF	XF	Unc	BU
1994 Proof	Est. 2,000	Value: 325				

KM# 1057 500 FRANCS **Weight:** 17.0000 g. **Composition:** 0.9200 Gold .5028 oz. AGW **Subject:** Liberation of Paris **Obverse:** Triumphant troops marching down Champs Elysees **Note:** Struck at Paris Mint.

Date	Mintage	F	VF	XF	Unc	BU
1994 Proof	Est. 5,000	Value: 325				

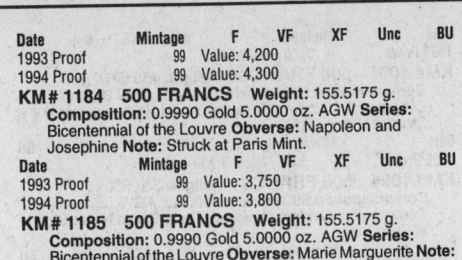

KM# 1058 500 FRANCS **Weight:** 17.0000 g. **Composition:** 0.9200 Gold .5028 oz. AGW **Obverse:** Heads of de Gaulle and Adenauer facing the center **Note:** Struck at Paris Mint.

Date	Mintage	F	VF	XF	Unc	BU
1994 Proof	Est. 2,000	Value: 320				

KM# 1059 500 FRANCS **Weight:** 16.9700 g. **Composition:** 0.9170 Gold .5000 oz. AGW **Subject:** 1996 Olympics **Reverse:** Archer in front of Eiffel Tower **Note:** Struck at Paris Mint.

Date	Mintage	F	VF	XF	Unc	BU
1994 Proof	60,000	Value: 265				

KM# 1074 500 FRANCS **Weight:** 31.0350 g. **Composition:** 0.9990 Gold 1.0000 oz. AGW **Series:** Centennial of Cinema **Obverse:** Antique camera **Reverse:** Conjoined busts of the Lumiere Brothers right **Note:** Struck at Paris Mint.

Date	Mintage	F	VF	XF	Unc	BU
1994 Proof	3,000	Value: 900				

KM# 1078 500 FRANCS **Weight:** 31.0350 g. **Composition:** 0.9990 Gold 1.0000 oz. AGW **Series:** Centennial of Cinema **Reverse:** Head of Charlie Chaplin facing **Note:** Struck at Paris Mint.

Date	Mintage	F	VF	XF	Unc	BU
1994 Proof	3,000	Value: 900				

KM# 1079 500 FRANCS **Weight:** 155.5175 g. **Composition:** 0.9990 Gold 5.0000 oz. AGW **Series:** Centennial of Cinema **Reverse:** Head of Charlie Chaplin facing **Note:** Struck at Paris Mint.

Date	Mintage	F	VF	XF	Unc	BU
1994 Proof	99	Value: 3,500				

KM# 1186 500 FRANCS **Weight:** 17.0000 g. **Composition:** 0.9200 Gold .5028 oz. AGW **Series:** Centennial of Cinema **Reverse:** Voltaire **Note:** Struck at Paris Mint.

Date	Mintage	F	VF	XF	Unc	BU
1994 Proof	350	Value: 350				

KM# 1082 500 FRANCS **Weight:** 31.0350 g. **Composition:** 0.9990 Gold 1.0000 oz. AGW **Series:** Centennial of Cinema **Reverse:** Leon Gaumont **Note:** Struck at Paris Mint.

Date	Mintage	F	VF	XF	Unc	BU
1995 Proof	3,000	Value: 900				

KM# 1083 500 FRANCS **Weight:** 155.5175 g. **Composition:** 0.9990 Gold 5.0000 oz. AGW **Series:** Centennial of Cinema **Reverse:** Leon Gaumont **Note:** Struck at Paris Mint.

Date	Mintage	F	VF	XF	Unc	BU
1995 Proof	99	Value: 3,200				

KM# 1086 500 FRANCS **Weight:** 31.0350 g. **Composition:** 0.9990 Gold 1.0000 oz. AGW **Series:** Centennial of Cinema **Reverse:** Jean Renoir **Note:** Struck at Paris Mint.

Date	Mintage	F	VF	XF	Unc	BU
1995 Proof	3,000	Value: 900				

KM# 1087 500 FRANCS **Weight:** 155.5175 g. **Composition:** 0.9990 Gold 5.0000 oz. AGW **Series:** Centennial of Cinema **Reverse:** Jean Renoir **Note:** Struck at Paris Mint.

Date	Mintage	F	VF	XF	Unc	BU
1995 Proof	99	Value: 3,700				

KM# 1090 500 FRANCS **Weight:** 31.0350 g. **Composition:** 0.9990 Gold 1.0000 oz. AGW **Series:** Centennial of Cinema **Reverse:** Alfred Hitchcock **Note:** Struck at Paris Mint.

Date	Mintage	F	VF	XF	Unc	BU
1995 Proof	3,000	Value: 900				

KM# 1091 500 FRANCS **Weight:** 155.5175 g. **Composition:** 0.9990 Gold 5.0000 oz. AGW **Series:** Centennial of Cinema **Reverse:** Alfred Hitchcock **Note:** Struck at Paris Mint.

Date	Mintage	F	VF	XF	Unc	BU
1995 Proof	99	Value: 3,200				

KM# 1094 500 FRANCS **Weight:** 31.0350 g. **Composition:** 0.9990 Gold 1.0000 oz. AGW **Series:** Centennial of Cinema **Reverse:** Greta Garbo **Note:** Struck at Paris Mint.

Date	Mintage	F	VF	XF	Unc	BU
1995 Proof	3,000	Value: 900				

KM# 1095 500 FRANCS **Weight:** 155.5175 g. **Composition:** 0.9990 Gold 5.0000 oz. AGW **Series:** Centennial of Cinema **Reverse:** Greta Garbo **Note:** Struck at Paris Mint.

Date	Mintage	F	VF	XF	Unc	BU
1995 Proof	99	Value: 3,200				

KM# 1098 500 FRANCS **Weight:** 31.0350 g. **Composition:** 0.9990 Gold 1.0000 oz. AGW **Series:** Centennial of Cinema **Reverse:** Audrey Hepburn **Note:** Struck at Paris Mint.

Date	Mintage	F	VF	XF	Unc	BU
1995 Proof	3,000	Value: 900				

KM# 1099 500 FRANCS **Weight:** 155.5175 g. **Composition:** 0.9990 Gold 5.0000 oz. AGW **Series:** Centennial of Cinema **Reverse:** Audrey Hepburn **Note:** Struck at Paris Mint.

Date	Mintage	F	VF	XF	Unc	BU
1995 Proof	99	Value: 3,200				

KM# 1102 500 FRANCS **Weight:** 31.0350 g. **Composition:** 0.9990 Gold 1.0000 oz. AGW **Series:** Centennial of Cinema **Reverse:** Federico Fellini **Note:** Struck at Paris Mint.

Date	Mintage	F	VF	XF	Unc	BU
1995 Proof	3,000	Value: 900				

KM# 1103 500 FRANCS **Weight:** 155.5175 g. **Composition:** 0.9990 Gold 5.0000 oz. AGW **Series:** Centennial of Cinema **Reverse:** Federico Fellini **Note:** Struck at Paris Mint.

Date	Mintage	F	VF	XF	Unc	BU
1995 Proof	99	Value: 3,200				

KM# 1106 500 FRANCS **Weight:** 31.0350 g. **Composition:** 0.9990 Gold 1.0000 oz. AGW **Series:** Centennial of Cinema **Reverse:** Yves Montand **Note:** Struck at Paris Mint.

Date	Mintage	F	VF	XF	Unc	BU
1995 Proof	3,000	Value: 900				

KM# 1107 500 FRANCS **Weight:** 155.5175 g. **Composition:** 0.9990 Gold 5.0000 oz. AGW **Series:** Centennial of Cinema **Reverse:** Yves Montand **Note:** Struck at Paris Mint.

Date	Mintage	F	VF	XF	Unc	BU
1995 Proof	99	Value: 3,200				

KM# 1110 500 FRANCS **Weight:** 31.0350 g. **Composition:** 0.9990 Gold 1.0000 oz. AGW **Series:** Centennial of Cinema **Reverse:** Romy Schneider **Note:** Struck at Paris Mint.

Date	Mintage	F	VF	XF	Unc	BU
1995 Proof	3,000	Value: 900				

KM# 1111 500 FRANCS **Weight:** 155.5175 g. **Composition:** 0.9990 Gold 5.0000 oz. AGW **Series:** Centennial of Cinema **Reverse:** Romy Schneider **Note:** Struck at Paris Mint.

Date	Mintage	F	VF	XF	Unc	BU
1995 Proof	99	Value: 3,200				

KM# 1117 500 FRANCS **Weight:** 17.0000 g. **Composition:** 0.9200 Gold .5028 oz. AGW **Subject:** V.E. Day **Obverse:** Victory in Europe date, May 8, 1945 **Note:** Struck at Paris Mint.

Date	Mintage	F	VF	XF	Unc	BU
1995 Proof	5,000	Value: 350				

KM# 1135 500 FRANCS **Weight:** 17.0000 g. **Composition:** 0.9200 Gold .5028 oz. AGW **Obverse:** Louis Pasteur **Note:** Struck at Paris Mint.

Date	Mintage	F	VF	XF	Unc	BU
1995 Proof	1,000	Value: 365				

KM# 1137 500 FRANCS **Weight:** 17.0000 g. **Composition:** 0.9200 Gold .5028 oz. AGW **Obverse:** Jean de la Fountain **Note:** Struck at Paris Mint.

Date	Mintage	F	VF	XF	Unc	BU
1995 Proof	1,000	Value: 365				

KM# 1139 500 FRANCS **Weight:** 17.0000 g. **Composition:** 0.9200 Gold .5028 oz. AGW **Obverse:** Madame de Sevigne **Note:** Struck at Paris Mint.

Date	Mintage	F	VF	XF	Unc	BU
1996 Proof	500	Value: 675				

KM# 1181 500 FRANCS **Weight:** 17.0000 g. **Composition:** 0.9200 Gold .5028 oz. AGW **Obverse:** King Clovis I **Note:** Struck at Paris Mint.

Date	Mintage	F	VF	XF	Unc	BU
1996 Proof	250	Value: 700				

KM# 1197 500 FRANCS **Weight:** 17.0000 g. **Composition:** 0.9200 Gold .5028 oz. AGW **Obverse:** Bust of Georges Guynemer facing, dates **Reverse:** Stork emblem and denomination **Note:** Struck at Paris Mint.

Date	Mintage	F	VF	XF	Unc	BU
1997 Proof	300	Value: 700				

KM# 1199 500 FRANCS **Weight:** 17.0000 g. **Composition:** 0.9200 Gold .5028 oz. AGW **Obverse:** Conjoined busts of Pierre and Marie Curie **Reverse:** Denomination **Note:** Struck at Paris Mint.

Date	Mintage	F	VF	XF	Unc	BU
1997 Proof	300	Value: 700				

KM# 1200 500 FRANCS **Weight:** 17.0000 g. **Composition:** 0.9200 Gold .5028 oz. AGW **Obverse:** Head of Andre Malraux facing **Reverse:** Cats flanking denomination **Note:** Struck at Paris Mint.

Date	Mintage	F	VF	XF	Unc	BU
1997 Proof	300	Value: 700				

KM# 1202 500 FRANCS **Weight:** 17.0000 g. **Composition:** 0.9200 Gold .5028 oz. AGW **Obverse:** Head of Marquis de Condorcet right **Reverse:** Denomination **Note:** Struck at Paris Mint.

Date	Mintage	F	VF	XF	Unc	BU
1998 Proof	300	Value: 700				

KM# 1204 500 FRANCS **Weight:** 17.0000 g. **Composition:** 0.9200 Gold .5028 oz. AGW **Obverse:** Head of Gaspard Monge 1/2 right **Reverse:** Denomination **Note:** Struck at Paris Mint.

Date	Mintage	F	VF	XF	Unc	BU
1998 Proof	300	Value: 700				

KM# 1237 500 FRANCS **Weight:** 31.1040 g. **Composition:** 0.9990 Gold .9990 oz. AGW **Subject:** Yves St. Laurent **Obverse:** RF monogram, denomination **Reverse:** Fashion show scene **Edge:** Plain **Note:** Struck at Paris Mint.

Date	Mintage	F	VF	XF	Unc	BU
2000 Proof	1,000	Value: 850				

KM# 1257 655.957 FRANCS **Weight:** 31.1040 g. **Composition:** 0.9990 Gold .9990 oz. AGW **Obverse:** Country names with euro-currency equivalents around RF, denomination and French coin designs **Reverse:** Europa allegorical portrait **Edge:** Plain **Note:** Euro Conversion Series. Struck at Paris Mint.

Date	Mintage	F	VF	XF	Unc	BU
1999 Proof	2,000	Value: 750				

KM# 1261 655.957 FRANCS **Weight:** 31.1040 g. **Composition:** 0.9990 Gold .9990 oz. AGW **Obverse:** Country names with euro-currency equivalents around RF, denomination and French euro coin design **Note:** Struck at Paris Mint.

Date	Mintage	F	VF	XF	Unc	BU
2000 Proof	2,000	Value: 750				

KM# 1247 655.957 FRANCS **Weight:** 15.5520 g. **Composition:** 0.9990 Gold .4995 oz. AGW **Series:** European Art Styles - Renaissance **Obverse:** Europe allegorical portrait **Reverse:** Greek and Roman style buildings **Note:** Struck at Paris Mint.

Date	Mintage	F	VF	XF	Unc	BU
2000 Proof	2,000	Value: 485				

KM# 1248 655.957 FRANCS **Weight:** 15.5520 g. **Composition:** 0.9990 Gold .4995 oz. AGW **Series:** European Art Styles - Roman **Reverse:** Roman sculpture and ancient buildings **Note:** Struck at Paris Mint.

Date	Mintage	F	VF	XF	Unc	BU
2000 Proof	2,000	Value: 485				

KM# 1249 655.957 FRANCS **Weight:** 15.5520 g. **Composition:** 0.9990 Gold .4995 oz. AGW **Series:** European Art Styles - Gothic **Reverse:** Gothic sculpture and buildings **Note:** Struck at Paris Mint.

Date	Mintage	F	VF	XF	Unc	BU
2000 Proof	2,000	Value: 485				

KM# 1250 655.957 FRANCS **Weight:** 15.5520 g. **Composition:** 0.9990 Gold .4995 oz. AGW **Series:** European Art Styles - Renaissance **Reverse:** Renaissance buildings **Note:** Struck at Paris Mint.

Date	Mintage	F	VF	XF	Unc	BU
2000 Proof	2,000	Value: 485				

KM# 1251 655.957 FRANCS **Weight:** 15.5520 g. **Composition:** 0.9990 Gold .4995 oz. AGW **Series:** European Art Styles - Classic and Baroque **Note:** Struck at Paris Mint.

Date	Mintage	F	VF	XF	Unc	BU
2000 Proof	2,000	Value: 485				

KM# 1252 655.957 FRANCS **Weight:** 15.5520 g. **Composition:** 0.9990 Gold .4995 oz. AGW **Series:** European Art Styles - Art Nouveau **Reverse:** Arches and scrollwork **Note:** Struck at Paris Mint.

Date	Mintage	F	VF	XF	Unc	BU
2000 Proof	2,000	Value: 485				

KM# 1253 655.957 FRANCS **Weight:** 15.5520 g. **Composition:** 0.9990 Gold .4995 oz. AGW **Series:** European Art Styles - Modern **Reverse:** Similar to 5 Francs, KM#1228 **Note:** Struck at Paris Mint.

Date	Mintage	F	VF	XF	Unc	BU
2000 Proof	2,000	Value: 485				

KM# 1267 655.957 FRANCS **Weight:** 31.1035 g. **Composition:** 0.9990 Gold 1.0000 oz. AGW **Subject:** Last Year of the French Franc **Obverse:** French and other European euro currency equivalents **Reverse:** Similar to KM#1258 but with addition of "last year of the franc" logo after the date **Edge:** Plain

Date	Mintage	F	VF	XF	Unc	BU
2001 Proof	2,000	Value: 635				

KM# 1267.1 655.957 FRANCS **Weight:** 155.5175 g. **Composition:** 0.9990 Gold 5.0000 oz. AGW **Edge:** Plain

Date	Mintage	F	VF	XF	Unc	BU
2001 Proof	99	Value: 4,000				

KM# 1279 655.957 FRANCS **Weight:** 17.0000 g. **Composition:** 0.9200 Gold .5028 oz. AGW **Subject:** Motto Series **Obverse:** Denomination **Reverse:** FRATERNITE **Edge:** Reeded

Date	Mintage	F	VF	XF	Unc	BU
2001 Proof	2,000	Value: 365				

KM# 1280 655.957 FRANCS **Weight:** 17.0000 g. **Composition:** 0.9200 Gold .5028 oz. AGW **Subject:** Motto Series **Obverse:** Denomination **Reverse:** EGALITE

Date	Mintage	F	VF	XF	Unc	BU
2001 Proof	2,000	Value: 365				

KM# 1281 655.957 FRANCS **Weight:** 17.0000 g. **Composition:** 0.9200 Gold .5028 oz. AGW **Subject:** Motto Series **Obverse:** Denomination **Reverse:** LIBERTE

Date	Mintage	F	VF	XF	Unc	BU
2001 Proof	2,000	Value: 365				

ECU / FRANCS COINAGE

European Currency Units

KM# 989 100 FRANCS - 15 ECUS **Weight:** 22.2000 g. **Composition:** 0.9000 Silver .6424 oz. ASW **Reverse:** Charlemagne

Date	Mintage	F	VF	XF	Unc	BU
1990 Proof	30,000	Value: 95.00				

KM# 1002 100 FRANCS - 15 ECUS **Weight:** 22.2000 g. **Composition:** 0.9000 Silver .6424 oz. ASW **Reverse:** Descartes

Date	Mintage	F	VF	XF	Unc	BU
1991 Proof	20,000	Value: 65.00				

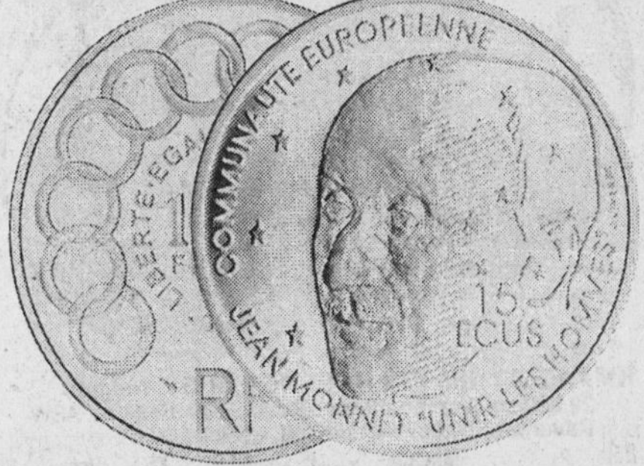

KM# 1012 100 FRANCS - 15 ECUS **Weight:** 22.2000 g. **Composition:** 0.9000 Silver .6424 oz. ASW **Obverse:** Denomination in center within legend and chain above RF **Reverse:** Jean Monet

Date	Mintage	F	VF	XF	Unc	BU
1992 Proof	30,000	Value: 55.00				

KM# 1029 100 FRANCS - 15 ECUS Weight: 22.2000 g. **Composition:** 0.9000 Silver .6424 oz. ASW **Subject:** Mediterranean Games **Reverse:** Swimming

Date	Mintage	F	VF	XF	Unc	BU
1993 Proof	15,000	Value: 47.50				

KM# 1030 100 FRANCS - 15 ECUS Weight: 22.2000 g. **Composition:** 0.9000 Silver .6424 oz. ASW **Subject:** Mediterranean Games **Reverse:** Soccer

Date	Mintage	F	VF	XF	Unc	BU
1993 Proof	15,000	Value: 47.50				

KM# 1031 100 FRANCS - 15 ECUS Weight: 22.2000 g. **Composition:** 0.9000 Silver .6424 oz. ASW **Reverse:** Arc de Triumph

Date	Mintage	F	VF	XF	Unc	BU
1993 Proof	20,000	Value: 42.50				

KM# 1032 100 FRANCS - 15 ECUS Weight: 22.2000 g. **Composition:** 0.9000 Silver .6424 oz. ASW **Reverse:** Brandenburg Gate

Date	Mintage	F	VF	XF	Unc	BU
1993 Proof	20,000	Value: 42.50				

KM# 1060 100 FRANCS - 15 ECUS Weight: 22.2000 g. **Composition:** 0.9000 Silver .6424 oz. ASW **Reverse:** Stylized Tunnel View - Map

Date	Mintage	F	VF	XF	Unc	BU
1994 Proof	20,000	Value: 30.00				

KM# 1068 100 FRANCS - 15 ECUS Weight: 22.2000 g. **Composition:** 0.9000 Silver .6424 oz. ASW **Reverse:** St. Mark's Cathedral, Venice

Date	Mintage	F	VF	XF	Unc	BU
1994 Proof	20,000	Value: 32.50				

KM# 1070 100 FRANCS - 15 ECUS Weight: 22.2000 g. **Composition:** 0.9000 Silver .6424 oz. ASW **Reverse:** Big Ben, London

Date	Mintage	F	VF	XF	Unc	BU
1994 Proof	20,000	Value: 32.50				

KM# 1112 100 FRANCS - 15 ECUS Weight: 22.2000 g. **Composition:** 0.9000 Silver .6424 oz. ASW **Reverse:** The Alhambra, Granada

Date	Mintage	F	VF	XF	Unc	BU
1995 Proof	20,000	Value: 35.00				

KM# 1114 100 FRANCS - 15 ECUS Weight: 22.2000 g. **Composition:** 0.9000 Silver .6424 oz. ASW **Reverse:** The Parthenon, Greece

Date	Mintage	F	VF	XF	Unc	BU
1995 Proof	20,000	Value: 35.00				

KM# 990 500 FRANCS - 70 ECUS Weight: 17.0000 g. **Composition:** 0.9200 Gold .5029 oz. AGW **Reverse:** Charlemagne

Date	Mintage	F	VF	XF	Unc	BU
1990 Proof	5,000	Value: 350				

KM# 990a 500 FRANCS - 70 ECUS Weight: 20.0000 g. **Composition:** 0.9990 Platinum .6431 oz. APW

Date	Mintage	F	VF	XF	Unc	BU
1990 Proof	2,000	Value: 450				

KM# 1003 500 FRANCS - 70 ECUS Weight: 17.0000 g. **Composition:** 0.9200 Gold .5029 oz. AGW **Reverse:** Descartes

Date	Mintage	F	VF	XF	Unc	BU
1991 Proof	3,000	Value: 425				

KM# 1003a 500 FRANCS - 70 ECUS Weight: 20.0000 g. **Composition:** 0.9990 Platinum .6431 oz. APW

Date	Mintage	F	VF	XF	Unc	BU
1991 Proof	1,000	Value: 500				

KM# 1013 500 FRANCS - 70 ECUS Weight: 17.0000 g. **Composition:** 0.9200 Gold .5029 oz. AGW **Reverse:** Jean Monet

Date	Mintage	F	VF	XF	Unc	BU
1992 Proof	5,000	Value: 400				

KM# 1013a 500 FRANCS - 70 ECUS Weight: 20.0000 g. **Composition:** 0.9990 Platinum .6431 oz. APW

Date	Mintage	F	VF	XF	Unc	BU
1992 Proof	2,000	Value: 450				

KM# 1033 500 FRANCS - 70 ECUS Weight: 17.0000 g. **Composition:** 0.9200 Gold .5029 oz. AGW **Subject:** Mediterranean Games

Date	Mintage	F	VF	XF	Unc	BU
1993 Proof	3,000	Value: 400				

KM# 1034 500 FRANCS - 70 ECUS Weight: 17.0000 g. **Composition:** 0.9200 Gold .5029 oz. AGW **Reverse:** Arc de Triumph

Date	Mintage	F	VF	XF	Unc	BU
1993 Proof	5,000	Value: 375				

KM# 1034a 500 FRANCS - 70 ECUS Weight: 19.8000 g. **Composition:** 0.9900 Platinum .6303 oz. APW **Reverse:** Arc de Triumph

Date	Mintage	F	VF	XF	Unc	BU
1993 Proof	2,000	Value: 425				

KM# 1035 500 FRANCS - 70 ECUS Weight: 17.0000 g. **Composition:** 0.9200 Gold .5029 oz. AGW **Reverse:** Brandenburg Gate

Date	Mintage	F	VF	XF	Unc	BU
1993 Proof	5,000	Value: 375				

KM# 1035a 500 FRANCS - 70 ECUS Weight: 19.8000 g. **Composition:** 0.9900 Platinum .6303 oz. APW **Reverse:** Brandenburg Gate

Date	Mintage	F	VF	XF	Unc	BU
1993 Proof	2,000	Value: 450				

KM# 1061 500 FRANCS - 70 ECUS Weight: 17.0000 g. **Composition:** 0.9200 Gold .5029 oz. AGW **Reverse:** Channel Tunnel

Date	Mintage	F	VF	XF	Unc	BU
1994 Proof	5,000	Value: 335				

KM# 1069 500 FRANCS - 70 ECUS Weight: 17.0000 g. **Composition:** 0.9200 Gold .5028 oz. AGW **Reverse:** St. Mark's Cathedral, Venice

Date	Mintage	F	VF	XF	Unc	BU
1994 Proof	5,000	Value: 375				

KM# 1069a 500 FRANCS - 70 ECUS Weight: 20.0000 g. **Composition:** 0.9990 Platinum .6431 oz. APW **Reverse:** St. Mark's Cathedral, Venice

Date	Mintage	F	VF	XF	Unc	BU
1994 Proof	2,000	Value: 425				

KM# 1071 500 FRANCS - 70 ECUS Weight: 17.0000 g. **Composition:** 0.9200 Gold .5028 oz. AGW **Reverse:** Big Ben, London

Date	Mintage	F	VF	XF	Unc	BU
1994 Proof	5,000	Value: 375				

KM# 1071a 500 FRANCS - 70 ECUS Weight: 20.0000 g. **Composition:** 0.9990 Platinum .6431 oz. APW **Reverse:** Big Ben, London

Date	Mintage	F	VF	XF	Unc	BU
1994 Proof	2,000	Value: 425				

KM# 1113 500 FRANCS - 70 ECUS Weight: 17.0000 g. **Composition:** 0.9200 Gold .5028 oz. AGW **Reverse:** The Alhambra, Granada

Date	Mintage	F	VF	XF	Unc	BU
1995 Proof	5,000	Value: 375				

KM# 1113a 500 FRANCS - 70 ECUS Weight: 20.0000 g. **Composition:** 0.9990 Platinum .6431 oz. APW **Reverse:** The Alhambra, Granada

Date	Mintage	F	VF	XF	Unc	BU
1995 Proof	2,000	Value: 425				

KM# 1115 500 FRANCS - 70 ECUS Weight: 17.0000 g. **Composition:** 0.9200 Gold .5028 oz. AGW **Reverse:** The Parthenon, Athens

Date	Mintage	F	VF	XF	Unc	BU
1995 Proof	5,000	Value: 375				

KM# 1115a 500 FRANCS - 70 ECUS Weight: 20.0000 g. **Composition:** 0.9990 Platinum .6431 oz. APW **Reverse:** The Parthenon, Athens

Date	Mintage	F	VF	XF	Unc	BU
1995 Proof	2,000	Value: 425				

EURO / FRANCS COINAGE

KM# 1121 10 FRANCS - 1.5 EURO Weight: 22.2000 g. **Composition:** 0.9000 Silver .6424 oz. ASW **Series:** Museum Treasures **Obverse:** La Source

Date	Mintage	F	VF	XF	Unc	BU
1996 Proof	15,000	Value: 35.00				

KM# 1122 10 FRANCS - 1.5 EURO Weight: 22.2000 g. **Composition:** 0.9000 Silver .6424 oz. ASW **Series:** Museum Treasures **Obverse:** Fife Player

Date	Mintage	F	VF	XF	Unc	BU
1996 Proof	15,000	Value: 35.00				

KM# 1123 10 FRANCS - 1.5 EURO Weight: 22.2000 g. **Composition:** 0.9000 Silver .6424 oz. ASW **Series:** Museum Treasures **Obverse:** Shang Dynasty Elephant

Date	Mintage	F	VF	XF	Unc	BU
1996 Proof	15,000	Value: 35.00				

KM# 1146 10 FRANCS - 1.5 EURO Weight: 22.2000 g. **Composition:** 0.9000 Silver .6424 oz. ASW **Series:** Museum Treasures **Obverse:** David

Date	Mintage	F	VF	XF	Unc	BU
1996 Proof	15,000	Value: 32.50				

KM# 1147 10 FRANCS - 1.5 EURO Weight: 22.2000 g. **Composition:** 0.9000 Silver .6424 oz. ASW **Series:** Museum Treasures **Obverse:** Van Gogh

Date	Mintage	F	VF	XF	Unc	BU
1996 Proof	15,000	Value: 35.00				

KM# 1148 10 FRANCS - 1.5 EURO Weight: 22.2000 g. **Composition:** 0.9000 Silver .6424 oz. ASW **Series:** Museum Treasures **Obverse:** Clothed Maya

Date	Mintage	F	VF	XF	Unc	BU
1996 Proof	15,000	Value: 32.50				

KM# 1158 10 FRANCS - 1.5 EURO Weight: 22.2000 g. **Composition:** 0.9000 Silver .6424 oz. ASW **Series:** Museum Treasures **Obverse:** Chinese Horseman

Date	Mintage	F	VF	XF	Unc	BU
1996 Proof	15,000	Value: 32.50				

KM# 1124 10 FRANCS - 1.5 EURO Weight: 22.2000 g. **Composition:** 0.9000 Silver .6424 oz. ASW **Series:** Museum Treasures **Obverse:** The Thinker **Note:** Silver coins sold as a set only.

Date	Mintage	F	VF	XF	Unc	BU
1996 Proof	15,000	Value: 35.00				

KM# 1292 10 FRANCS - 1.5 EURO Weight: 22.2200 g. **Composition:** 0.9000 Silver 0.643 oz. ASW **Subject:** Museum Treasures **Obverse:** The Little Dancer. **Reverse:** Denominations. **Edge:** Plain. **Size:** 36.9 mm.

Date	Mintage	F	VF	XF	Unc	BU
1997 Proof	15,000	Value: 35.00				

KM# 1297 10 FRANCS - 1.5 EURO Weight: 22.2200 g. **Composition:** 0.9000 Silver 0.643 oz. ASW **Obverse:** Woman carrying box.

Date	Mintage	F	VF	XF	Unc	BU
1997 Proof	15,000	Value: 30.00				

KM# 1298 10 FRANCS - 1.5 EURO Weight: 22.2200 g. **Composition:** 0.9000 Silver 0.643 oz. ASW **Obverse:** Durer's self portrait.

Date	Mintage	F	VF	XF	Unc	BU
1997 Proof	15,000	Value: 30.00				

KM# 1299 10 FRANCS - 1.5 EURO Weight: 22.2200 g. **Composition:** 0.9000 Silver 0.643 oz. ASW **Subject:** Klimt's "The Kiss".

Date	Mintage	F	VF	XF	Unc	BU
1997 Proof	15,000	Value: 30.00				

KM# 1140 100 FRANCS - 15 EURO Weight: 22.2000 g. **Composition:** 0.9000 Silver .6424 oz. ASW **Reverse:** St. Stephen's Cathedral, Vienna

Date	Mintage	F	VF	XF	Unc	BU
1996 Proof	20,000	Value: 50.00				

KM# 1142 100 FRANCS - 15 EURO Weight: 22.2000 g. **Composition:** 0.9000 Silver .6424 oz. ASW **Reverse:** Grand Place, Bruxelles

Date	Mintage	F	VF	XF	Unc	BU
1996 Proof	20,000	Value: 37.50				

KM# 1149 100 FRANCS - 15 EURO Weight: 17.0000 g. **Composition:** 0.9200 Gold .5028 oz. AGW **Series:** Museum Treasures **Obverse:** Van Gogh

Date	Mintage	F	VF	XF	Unc	BU
1996 Proof	5,000	Value: 375				

KM# 1150 100 FRANCS - 15 EURO Weight: 17.0000 g. **Composition:** 0.9200 Gold .5028 oz. AGW **Series:** Museum Treasures **Obverse:** Clothed Maya

Date	Mintage	F	VF	XF	Unc	BU
1996 Proof	5,000	Value: 375				

KM# 1156 100 FRANCS - 15 EURO Weight: 22.2000 g. **Composition:** 0.9000 Silver .6424 oz. ASW **Subject:** Amsterdam - Magere Brug **Reverse:** Bridge

Date	Mintage	F	VF	XF	Unc	BU
1996 Proof	20,000	Value: 37.50				

KM# 1159 100 FRANCS - 15 EURO Weight: 17.0000 g. **Composition:** 0.9200 Gold .5028 oz. AGW **Series:** Museum Treasures **Reverse:** Chinese Horseman **Note:** Similar to 10 Francs / 1-1/2 Euro, KM#1158.

Date	Mintage	F	VF	XF	Unc	BU
1996 Proof	5,000	Value: 375				

KM# 1125 100 FRANCS - 15 EURO Weight: 17.0000 g. **Composition:** 0.9200 Gold .5028 oz. AGW **Series:** Museum Treasures **Obverse:** La Source **Note:** Similar to 10 Francs / 1.5 Euro, KM#1121.

Date	Mintage	F	VF	XF	Unc	BU
1996 Proof	5,000	Value: 375				

KM# 1126 100 FRANCS - 15 EURO Weight: 17.0000 g. **Composition:** 0.9200 Gold .5028 oz. AGW **Series:** Museum Treasures **Obverse:** Fife Player **Note:** Similar to 10 Francs / 1.5 Euro, KM#1122.

Date	Mintage	F	VF	XF	Unc	BU
1996 Proof	5,000	Value: 375				

KM# 1127 100 FRANCS - 15 EURO Weight: 17.0000 g. **Composition:** 0.9200 Gold .5028 oz. AGW **Series:** Museum Treasures **Obverse:** Shang Dynasty Elephant **Note:** Similar to 10 Francs / 1.5 Euro, KM#1123.

Date	Mintage	F	VF	XF	Unc	BU
1996 Proof	5,000	Value: 375				

KM# 1174 100 FRANCS - 15 EURO Weight: 22.2000 g. **Composition:** 0.9000 Silver .6424 oz. ASW **Subject:** Lisbon **Obverse:** Denominations **Reverse:** Castle-like building Tour de Belem

Date	Mintage	F	VF	XF	Unc	BU
1997 Proof	20,000	Value: 50.00				

KM# 1176 100 FRANCS - 15 EURO Weight: 22.2000 g. **Composition:** 0.9000 Silver .6424 oz. ASW **Subject:** Helsinki **Obverse:** Denominations **Reverse:** Cathedral, Cathedrale Saint - Nicolas

Date	Mintage	F	VF	XF	Unc	BU
1997 Proof	20,000	Value: 50.00				

KM# 1178 100 FRANCS - 15 EURO Weight: 22.2000 g. **Composition:** 0.9000 Silver .6424 oz. ASW **Subject:** Copenhagen **Obverse:** Denominations **Reverse:** Statue of the Copenhagen mermaid, Petite Sirene

Date	Mintage	F	VF	XF	Unc	BU
1997 Proof	20,000	Value: 50.00				

KM# 1189 100 FRANCS - 15 EURO Weight: 22.2000 g. **Composition:** 0.9000 Silver .6424 oz. ASW **Subject:** Irlande - Rock of Cashel **Obverse:** Denomination **Reverse:** Celtic cross and castle

Date	Mintage	F	VF	XF	Unc	BU
1997 Proof	20,000	Value: 50.00				

KM# 1191 100 FRANCS - 15 EURO Weight: 22.2000 g. **Composition:** 0.9000 Silver .6424 oz. ASW **Subject:** Luxembourg - Wenceslaus Wall **Obverse:** Denomination **Reverse:** Walled palace

Date	Mintage	F	VF	XF	Unc	BU
1997 Proof	20,000	Value: 50.00				

KM# 1193 100 FRANCS - 15 EURO Weight: 22.2000 g. **Composition:** 0.9000 Silver .6424 oz. ASW **Subject:** Stockholm - Hotel de Ville **Obverse:** Denomination **Reverse:** Tower and building

Date	Mintage	F	VF	XF	Unc	BU
1997 Proof	20,000	Value: 50.00				

KM# 1128 500 FRANCS - 75 EURO Weight: 31.1035 g. **Composition:** 0.9990 Gold 1.0000 oz. AGW **Series:** Museum Treasures **Obverse:** The Thinker

Date	Mintage	F	VF	XF	Unc	BU
1996 Proof	5,000	Value: 575				

KM# 1129 500 FRANCS - 75 EURO Weight: 155.5175 g. **Composition:** 0.9990 Gold 5.0000 oz. AGW **Series:** Museum Treasures **Obverse:** La Source

Date	Mintage	F	VF	XF	Unc	BU
1996 Prof	99	Value: 3,250				

KM# 1130 500 FRANCS - 75 EURO Weight: 155.5175 g. **Composition:** 0.9990 Gold 5.0000 oz. AGW **Series:** Museum Treasures **Obverse:** Fife Player

Date	Mintage	F	VF	XF	Unc	BU
1996 Proof	99	Value: 3,250				

KM# 1131 500 FRANCS - 75 EURO Weight: 155.5175 g. **Composition:** 0.9990 Gold 5.0000 oz. AGW **Series:** Museum Treasures **Obverse:** Shang Dynasty Elephant

Date	Mintage	F	VF	XF	Unc	BU
1996 Proof	99	Value: 3,500				

KM# 1141 500 FRANCS - 75 EURO Weight: 17.0000 g. **Composition:** 0.9200 Gold .5028 oz. AGW **Subject:** St. Stephen's Cathedral, Vienna

Date	Mintage	F	VF	XF	Unc	BU
1996 Proof	5,000	Value: 375				

KM# 1141a 500 FRANCS - 75 EURO Weight: 20.0000 g. **Composition:** 0.9990 Platinum .6431 oz. APW **Subject:** St. Stephen's Cathedral, Vienna

Date	Mintage	F	VF	XF	Unc	BU
1996 Prof	2,000	Value: 450				

KM# 1143 500 FRANCS - 75 EURO Weight: 17.0000 g. **Composition:** 0.9200 Gold .5028 oz. AGW **Subject:** Grand Place, Bruxelles

Date	Mintage	F	VF	XF	Unc	BU
1996 Proof	5,000	Value: 375				

KM# 1143a 500 FRANCS - 75 EURO Weight: 20.0000 g. **Composition:** 0.9990 Platinum .6431 oz. APW **Subject:** Grand Place, Bruxelles

Date	Mintage	F	VF	XF	Unc	BU
1996 Proof	2,000	Value: 450				

KM# 1151 500 FRANCS - 75 EURO Weight: 31.1035 g. **Composition:** 0.9990 Gold 1.0000 oz. AGW **Series:** Museum Treasures **Obverse:** David

Date	Mintage	F	VF	XF	Unc	BU
1996 Proof	5,000	Value: 575				

KM# 1153 500 FRANCS - 75 EURO **Weight:** 155.5175 g. **Composition:** 0.9990 Gold 5.0000 oz. AGW **Series:** Museum Treasures **Obverse:** Van Gogh **Reverse:** Similar to KM#1151

Date	Mintage	F	VF	XF	Unc	BU
1996 Proof	99	Value: 3,250				

KM# 1154 500 FRANCS - 75 EURO **Weight:** 155.5175 g. **Composition:** 0.9990 Gold 5.0000 oz. AGW **Series:** Museum Treasures **Obverse:** Clothed Maya **Reverse:** Similar to KM#1151

Date	Mintage	F	VF	XF	Unc	BU
1996 Proof	99	Value: 3,250				

KM# 1157 500 FRANCS - 75 EURO **Weight:** 17.0000 g. **Composition:** 0.9200 Gold .5028 oz. AGW **Subject:** Amsterdam Magere Brug

Date	Mintage	F	VF	XF	Unc	BU
1996 Proof	5,000	Value: 375				

KM# 1157a 500 FRANCS - 75 EURO **Weight:** 20.0000 g. **Composition:** 0.9990 Platinum .6431 oz. APW **Subject:** Amsterdam Magere Brug

Date	Mintage	F	VF	XF	Unc	BU
1996 Proof	2,000	Value: 500				

KM# 1152 500 FRANCS - 75 EURO **Weight:** 155.5175 g. **Composition:** 0.9990 Gold 5.0000 oz. AGW **Series:** Museum Treasures **Obverse:** David **Note:** Similar to KM#1151.

Date	Mintage	F	VF	XF	Unc	BU
1996 Proof	99	Value: 3,250				

KM# 1179 500 FRANCS - 75 EURO **Weight:** 17.0000 g. **Composition:** 0.9200 Gold .5028 oz. AGW **Subject:** Copenhagen **Obverse:** Denominations **Reverse:** Statue of Copenhagen's Little Mermaid, Petite Siren

Date	Mintage	F	VF	XF	Unc	BU
1997 Proof	5,000	Value: 500				

KM# 1179a 500 FRANCS - 75 EURO **Weight:** 20.0000 g. **Composition:** 0.9990 Platinum .6431 oz. APW **Subject:** Copenhagen **Obverse:** Denominations **Reverse:** Statue of Copenhagen's Little Mermaid, Petite Siren

Date	Mintage	F	VF	XF	Unc	BU
1997 Proof	2,000	Value: 600				

KM# 1190 500 FRANCS - 75 EURO **Weight:** 17.0000 g. **Composition:** 0.9200 Gold .5028 oz. AGW **Subject:** Ireland - Rock of Cashel **Obverse:** Denomination **Reverse:** Celtic cross and castle

Date	Mintage	F	VF	XF	Unc	BU
1997 Proof	5,000	Value: 450				

KM# 1190a 500 FRANCS - 75 EURO **Weight:** 20.0000 g. **Composition:** 0.9990 Platinum .6431 oz. APW **Subject:** Ireland - Rock of Cashel **Obverse:** Denomination **Reverse:** Celtic cross and castle

Date	Mintage	F	VF	XF	Unc	BU
1997 Proof	2,000	Value: 500				

KM# 1192 500 FRANCS - 75 EURO **Weight:** 17.0000 g. **Composition:** 0.9200 Gold .5028 oz. AGW **Subject:** Luxembourg - Wenceslas Wall **Obverse:** Denomination **Reverse:** Walled palace

Date	Mintage	F	VF	XF	Unc	BU
1997 Proof	5,000	Value: 450				

KM# 1192a 500 FRANCS - 75 EURO **Weight:** 20.0000 g. **Composition:** 0.9990 Platinum .6431 oz. APW

Date	Mintage	F	VF	XF	Unc	BU
1997 Proof	2,000	Value: 500				

KM# 1175 500 FRANCS - 75 EURO **Weight:** 17.0000 g. **Composition:** 0.9200 Gold .5028 oz. AGW **Subject:** Lisbon **Obverse:** Denominations **Reverse:** Castle-like building Tour de Belem

Date	Mintage	F	VF	XF	Unc	BU
1997 Proof	5,000	Value: 385				

KM# 1175a 500 FRANCS - 75 EURO **Weight:** 20.0000 g. **Composition:** 0.9990 Platinum .6431 oz. APW **Subject:** Lisbon **Obverse:** Denominations **Reverse:** Castle-like building Tour de Belem

Date	Mintage	F	VF	XF	Unc	BU
1997 Proof	2,000	Value: 485				

KM# 1177 500 FRANCS - 75 EURO **Weight:** 17.0000 g. **Composition:** 0.9200 Gold .5028 oz. AGW **Subject:** Helsinki **Obverse:** Denominations **Reverse:** Cathedrale Saint Nicholas

Date	Mintage	F	VF	XF	Unc	BU
1997 Proof	5,000	Value: 385				

KM# 1194 500 FRANCS - 75 EURO **Weight:** 17.0000 g. **Composition:** 0.9990 Gold .5028 oz. AGW **Subject:** Stockholm - Hotel de Ville **Obverse:** Denomination **Reverse:** Tower and building

Date	Mintage	F	VF	XF	Unc	BU
1997 Proof	5,000	Value: 450				

KM# 1194a 500 FRANCS - 75 EURO **Weight:** 20.0000 g. **Composition:** 0.9990 Platinum .5028 oz. APW **Subject:** Stockholm - Hotel de Ville **Obverse:** Denomination **Reverse:** Tower and building

Date	Mintage	F	VF	XF	Unc	BU
1997 Proof	2,000	Value: 500				

KM# 1177a 500 FRANCS - 75 EURO **Weight:** 20.0000 g. **Composition:** 0.9990 Platinum .6431 oz. APW **Subject:** Helsinki **Obverse:** Denominations **Reverse:** Cathedral, Cathedrale Saint Nicholas

Date	Mintage	F	VF	XF	Unc	BU
1997 Proof	2,000	Value: 485				

EURO COINAGE

European Economic Community Issues

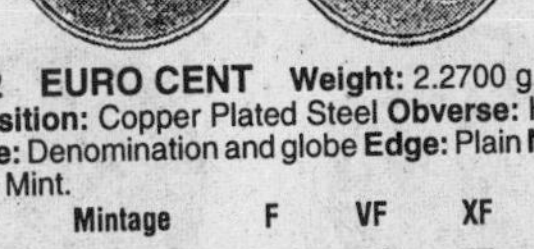

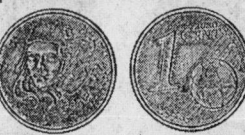

KM# 1282 EURO CENT **Weight:** 2.2700 g. **Composition:** Copper Plated Steel **Obverse:** Human face **Reverse:** Denomination and globe **Edge:** Plain **Note:** Struck at Paris Mint.

Date	Mintage	F	VF	XF	Unc	BU
1999	—	—	—	—	0.35	—
1999 Proof	—	Value: 10.00				
2000	—	—	—	—	0.35	—
2000 Proof	Est. 15,000	Value: 10.00				
2001	—	—	—	—	0.35	—
2001 Proof	Est. 15,000	Value: 10.00				
2002	—	—	—	—	5.00	—
2002 Proof	Est. 40,000	Value: 8.00				

KM# 1283 2 EURO CENTS **Weight:** 3.0300 g. **Composition:** Copper-Plated-Steel **Obverse:** Human face **Reverse:** Denomination and globe **Edge:** Grooved **Note:** Struck at Paris Mint.

Date	Mintage	F	VF	XF	Unc	BU
1999	—	—	—	—	0.50	—
1999 Proof	Est. 15,000	Value: 10.00				
2000	—	—	—	—	0.50	—
2000 Proof	Est. 15,000	Value: 10.00				
2001	—	—	—	—	0.50	—
2001 Proof	Est. 15,000	Value: 10.00				
2002	—	—	—	—	10.00	—
2002 Proof	Est. 40,000	Value: 8.00				

KM# 1284 5 EURO CENTS **Weight:** 3.8600 g. **Composition:** Copper-Plated-Steel **Note:** Struck at Paris Mint.

Date	Mintage	F	VF	XF	Unc	BU
1999	—	—	—	—	0.75	—
1999 Proof	Est. 15,000	Value: 12.00				
2000	—	—	—	—	0.75	—
2000 Proof	Est. 15,000	Value: 12.00				
2001	—	—	—	—	0.75	—
2001 Proof	Est. 15,000	Value: 12.00				
2002	—	—	—	—	0.75	—
2002 Proof	Est. 40,000	Value: 10.00				

KM# 1285 10 EURO CENTS **Weight:** 4.0700 g. **Composition:** Brass **Obverse:** Woman sowing seeds **Reverse:** Denomination and map **Edge:** Reeded **Note:** Struck at Paris Mint.

Date	Mintage	F	VF	XF	Unc	BU
1999	—	—	—	—	0.75	—
1999 Proof	Est. 15,000	Value: 12.00				
2000	—	—	—	—	0.75	—
2000 Proof	Est. 15,000	Value: 12.00				
2001	—	—	—	—	1.00	—
2001 Proof	Est. 15,000	Value: 12.00				
2002	—	—	—	—	0.75	—
2002 Proof	Est. 40,000	Value: 10.00				

KM# 1286 20 EURO CENTS **Weight:** 5.7300 g. **Composition:** Brass **Edge:** Notched **Note:** Struck at Paris Mint.

Date	Mintage	F	VF	XF	Unc	BU
1999	—	—	—	—	1.00	—
1999 Proof	Est. 15,000	Value: 14.00				
2000	—	—	—	—	1.25	—
2000 Proof	Est. 15,000	Value: 14.00				
2001	—	—	—	—	1.00	—
2001 Proof	Est. 15,000	Value: 14.00				
2002	—	—	—	—	1.00	—
2002 Proof	Est. 40,000	Value: 12.00				

KM# 1287 50 EURO CENTS **Weight:** 7.8100 g. **Composition:** Brass **Edge:** Reeded **Note:** Struck at Paris Mint.

Date	Mintage	F	VF	XF	Unc	BU
1999	—	—	—	—	1.50	—
1999 Proof	Est. 15,000	Value: 15.00				
2000	—	—	—	—	1.25	—
2000 Proof	Est. 15,000	Value: 15.00				

Date	Mintage	F	VF	XF	Unc	BU
2001		—	—	—	1.25	—
2001 Proof	Est. 15,000	Value: 15.00				
2002		—	—	—	1.25	—
2002 Proof	Est. 40,000	Value: 14.00				

KM# 1293 1/4 EURO Composition: Brass **Subject:** Childrens Design **Obverse:** Euro globe with children. **Reverse:** Denomination and stars. **Edge:** Plain. **Size:** 30 mm.

Date	F	VF	XF	Unc	BU
2002	—	—	—	18.00	—

KM# 1288 EURO Ring Composition: Brass**Center Weight:** 7.5000 g. **Center Composition:** Copper-Nickel **Obverse:** Stylized tree **Reverse:** Denomination and map **Edge:** Reeded and plain sections **Note:** Struck at Paris Mint.

Date	Mintage	F	VF	XF	Unc	BU
1999		—	—	—	2.50	—
1999 Proof	Est. 15,000	Value: 18.00				
2000		—	—	—	2.50	—
2000 Proof	Est. 15,000	Value: 18.00				
2001		—	—	—	2.75	—
2001 Proof	Est. 15,000	Value: 18.00				
2002		—	—	—	2.50	—
2002 Proof	Est. 40,000	Value: 16.00				

KM# 1289 2 EUROS Ring Composition: Copper-Nickel**Center Weight:** 8.5200 g. **Center Composition:** Brass **Edge:** Reeding with 2's and stars

Date	Mintage	F	VF	XF	Unc	BU
1999		—	—	—	4.00	—
1999 Proof	Est. 15,000	Value: 20.00				
2000		—	—	—	3.75	—
2000 Proof	Est. 15,000	Value: 20.00				
2001		—	—	—	3.75	—
2001 Proof	Est. 15,000	Value: 20.00				
2002		—	—	—	3.75	—
2002 Proof	Est. 40,000	Value: 18.00				

ESSAIS

Standard metals unless otherwise noted

KM#	Date	Mintage	Identification	Mkt Val

KM#	Date	Mintage	Identification	Mkt Val
E38	1903 (a)	—	25 Centimes. Nickel. KM#855.	140

KM#	Date	Mintage	Identification	Mkt Val
E-A39	1904 (a)	—	25 Centimes. Nickel. Without square around denomination, 22 sided flan.	150

KM#	Date	Mintage	Identification	Mkt Val
E39	1904 (a)	—	25 Centimes. Nickel. KM#856.	140

KM#	Date	Mintage	Identification	Mkt Val
E-A40	1904 (a)	—	25 Centimes. Nickel. 22 sided flan, KM#856.	140

KM#	Date	Mintage	Identification	Mkt Val
E-B40	1904 (a)	—	25 Centimes. Nickel. 18 sided flan, KM#856.	140
E40	1908 (a)	—	10 Centimes. Aluminum. KM#843.	140

KM#	Date	Mintage	Identification	Mkt Val
E-C40	1908 (a)	—	5 Centimes. KM#842.	—
E41	1910 (a)	—	5 Centimes. KM#842.	150
E42	1913 (a)	—	25 Centimes. KM#867.	100
E43	1914 (a)	104	5 Centimes. KM#865.	525
E44	1914 (a)	—	25 Centimes. KM#867.	100

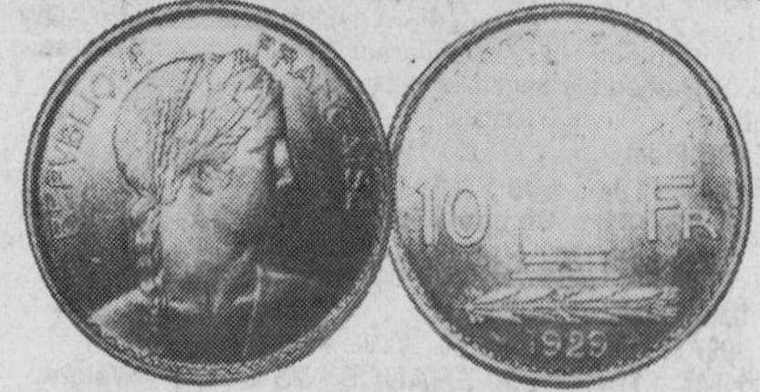

KM#	Date	Mintage	Identification	Mkt Val
E45	1929 (a)	—	10 Francs. Silver. Delannoy.	650
E46	1929 (a)	—	10 Francs. Aluminum-Bronze.	50.00
E47	1929 (a)	—	10 Francs. Aluminum-Bronze.	60.00
E48	1929 (a)	—	10 Francs. KM#878.	60.00
E49	1929 (a)	—	20 Francs. Silver. KM#879.	900
E50	1929 (a)	—	20 Francs. Aluminum-Bronze. KM#879.	110

KM#	Date	Mintage	Identification	Mkt Val
E51	1929 (a)	15	100 Francs. Gold.	3,700

KM#	Date	Mintage	Identification	Mkt Val
E52	1929	15	100 Francs. Gold.	3,700

KM#	Date	Mintage	Identification	Mkt Val
E53	1929 (a)	15	100 Francs. Gold.	3,700

KM#	Date	Mintage	Identification	Mkt Val
E54	1929 (a)	15	100 Francs. Gold.	3,700

KM#	Date	Mintage	Identification	Mkt Val
E55	1929 (a)	15	100 Francs. Gold.	3,700

KM#	Date	Mintage	Identification	Mkt Val
E56	1929 (a)	15	100 Francs. Gold.	3,700

KM#	Date	Mintage	Identification	Mkt Val
E57	1929 (a)	15	100 Francs. Gold.	3,700
E58	1929 (a)	15	100 Francs. Gold.	3,700

KM#	Date	Mintage	Identification	Mkt Val
E59	1929 (a)	15	100 Francs. Gold.	3,700

KM#	Date	Mintage	Identification	Mkt Val
E60	1929 (a)	15	100 Francs. Gold.	3,700
E62	1929 (a)	15	100 Francs. With Essai, KM#880.	3,900
E-A64	1931	—	50 Centimes. Aluminum-Bronze. KM#894.1, Morlon.	40.00
E-B64	1931	—	Franc. Aluminum-Bronze. KM#885, Morlon.	60.00
E64	1931	—	2 Francs. KM#886.	80.00
E-A65	1933	—	5 Francs. Nickel. KM#887, Bazor.	180

KM#	Date	Mintage	Identification	Mkt Val
E65	1933	—	5 Francs. KM#888.	95.00
E-A67	1933	—	5 Francs. Silver. Turin.	750

KM#	Date	Mintage	Identification	Mkt Val
E66	1933	—	5 Francs. Seated Liberty, date below. 5 FRANCS at center, legend and wheat spears around.	—
E67	1934 (a)	—	5 Francs. KM#888.	—
E68	1938 (a)	—	25 Centimes. KM#867b.	140
E69	1938 (a)	—	10 Francs. Nickel. KM#908.	300
E70	1938 (a)	—	20 Francs. Nickel. KM#879.	300
E71	1938 (a)	—	20 Francs. Aluminum. KM#879.	260
E72	1939 (a)	—	20 Francs. Copper-Nickel. KM#879.	240
E73	1940 (a)	—	25 Centimes. Zinc. KM#867b.	120
E74	1941 (a)	—	10 Centimes. KM#898.	110
E75	1941 (a)	—	20 Centimes. KM#899.	125
E76	1941 (a)	—	20 Centimes. KM#900.	125
E-A77	1941	—	2 Francs. Iron. KM#886, Morlon.	280

KM#	Date	Mintage	Identification	Mkt Val
E77	1941	—	5 Francs. Copper-Nickel. Bazor.	210

KM#	Date	Mintage	Identification	Mkt Val
E78	1941	—	10 Francs. Aluminum. Delannoy.	325

KM#	Date	Mintage	Identification	Mkt Val
E79	1941	—	10 Francs. Nickel.	500

KM#	Date	Mintage	Identification	Mkt Val
E-A80	1941	—	10 Francs. Aluminum. Simon.	310

KM#	Date	Mintage	Identification	Mkt Val
E80	1941 (a)	—	10 Francs. Nickel.	500

KM#	Date	Mintage	Identification	Mkt Val
E81	1941	—	10 Francs. Copper-Nickel. Galle.	350

KM#	Date	Mintage	Identification	Mkt Val
E82	1941	—	20 Francs. Aluminum. Cochet.	270

KM#	Date	Mintage	Identification	Mkt Val
E-A92	1941	—	20 Francs. Aluminum. Bouchard.	350
E83	1942	—	Franc. Aluminum. KM#902.1.	150
E84	1943 (a)	300	10 Centimes. KM#903.	140
E85	1943 (a)	300	2 Francs. KM#904.	200

KM#	Date	Mintage	Identification	Mkt Val
E86	1943	—	10 Francs. Copper-Nickel. Bazor.	250
E86a	1943	—	10 Francs. Aluminum. Bazor.	300
E87	1944 (a)	300	10 Centimes. KM#906.	150
E88	1945 (a)	40	20 Centimes. KM#907.	310
E89	1945 (a)	1,100	5 Francs. KM#888b.	100
E90	1945 (a)	1,100	10 Francs. KM#909.	80.00
E91	1950 (g)	1,700	10 Francs. KM#915.	30.00
E92	1950 (a)	25	20 Francs. Georges Guiraud, KM#916.	500
E93	1950 (a)	1,700	20 Francs. G. Guiraud, KM#971.	30.00
E94	1950 (a)	1,700	50 Francs. KM#918.	90.00

KM#	Date	Mintage	Identification	Mkt Val
E95	1950 (a)	50	100 Francs.	220
E-A96	1950	—	100 Francs. Copper-Nickel. KM#919.1.	4,000
E96	1951 (a)	28	20 Francs. KM#917.	600
E97	1954 (a)	1,200	100 Francs. KM#919.	75.00
E98	1959 (a)	4,000	Franc. KM#925.	60.00
E99	1959 (a)	4,000	Franc. KM#925.	40.00

KM#	Date	Mintage	Identification	Mkt Val
E100	1959	—	2 Francs. Silver. KM#845.1.	900

KM#	Date	Mintage	Identification	Mkt Val
E101	1959 (a)	4,000	5 Francs. KM#926.	50.00
E102	1959 (a)	I.A.	5 Francs. Small 5 in date, KM#926.	60.00
E103	1961 (a)	3,500	Centime. KM#928.	20.00
E104	1961 (a)	3,500	5 Centimes. KM#927.	20.00

KM#	Date	Mintage	Identification	Mkt Val
E105	1961	—	20 Centimes. KM#930.	30.00

KM#	Date	Mintage	Identification	Mkt Val
E106	1961	—	20 Centimes. Laureate bust with short hair.	30.00

KM#	Date	Mintage	Identification	Mkt Val
E107	1961	—	20 Centimes. Laureate bust with long hair.	—
E108	1962 (a)	3,500	10 Centimes. KM#929.	20.00
E109	1962 (a)	3,500	20 Centimes. KM#930.	20.00
E110	1962 (a)	3,500	50 Centimes. KM#939.	20.00
E111	1964 (a)	3,500	10 Francs. KM#932.	125
E112	1965 (a)	4,700	1/2 Franc. KM#931.	30.00
E113	1966 (a)	4,128	5 Centimes. KM#933.	25.00
E114	1970 (a)	5,000	5 Francs. KM#926a.	35.00
E115	1974	7,300	10 Francs. Nickel-Brass. KM#940.	40.00
E116	1974	9	10 Francs. Gold. KM#940.	2,500
E117	1974	13,800	50 Francs. Silver. KM#941.	65.00
E118	1974	5	50 Francs. Gold. KM#941.	2,700
E119	1978	6,000	2 Francs. Nickel. KM#942.	40.00
E120	1978	22	2 Francs. Silver. KM#942.	400
E121	1978	12	2 Francs. Gold. KM#942.	1,250
E122	1982	—	10 Francs. Copper-Nickel. Gambetta, KM#950.	55.00
E123	1982	—	100 Francs. Silver. KM#951.	85.00
E124	1983	4,000	10 Francs. Nickel-Bronze. Baloon, KM#952.	40.00
E125	1983	9	10 Francs. Gold. Baloon, KM#952.	1,700
E126	1983	4,000	10 Francs. Nickel-Bronze. Standhal, KM#953.	40.00
E127	1983	9	10 Francs. Gold. Standhal, KM#953.	1,700
E128	1984	—	10 Francs. Nickel-Bronze. Rude, KM#954.	40.00
E129	1984	—	100 Francs. Silver. Curie, KM#955.	60.00
E130	1985	1,700	10 Francs. Nickel-Bronze. Hugo, KM#956.	40.00
E131	1985	1,700	100 Francs. Silver. Zola, KM#957.	50.00
E132	1986	1,750	10 Francs. Nickel. KM#959.	40.00
E133	1986	9	10 Francs. Gold. KM#959.	1,700
E134	1986	1,750	10 Francs. Nickel. Schuman, KM#958d.	40.00
E135	1986	1,750	100 Francs. Silver. Liberty, KM#960.	70.00
E136	1987	1,850	10 Francs. Nickel-Bronze. Capet, KM#916d.	45.00
E137	1987	1,850	100 Francs. Silver. Lafayette, KM#962.	95.00
E138	1988	1,850	Franc. Nickel. KM#963.	70.00
E139	1988	1,850	10 Francs. Aluminum-Bronze. Garros, KM#965.	30.00
E140	1988	1,850	10 Francs. Steel center. Aluminum-Bronze ring. Bastille, KM#964.	40.00
E141	1988	1,850	100 Francs. Silver. Fraternity, KM#966.	40.00
E142	1989	—	Franc. Nickel. KM#967.	40.00
E143	1989	—	5 Francs. Nickel. Eiffel TOwer, KM#968.	45.00
E144	1989	—	10 Francs. Steel center. Aluminum-Bronze ring. Montesquieu, KM#969.	40.00
E145	1989	—	100 Francs. Silver. Human Rights, KM#970.	50.00

KM#	Date	Mintage	Identification	Mkt Val
E146	1994	—	20 Francs. Aluminum-Bronze center. Nickel inner ring, Copper-Aluminum-Nickel outer ring, KM#1036.	60.00

PATTERNS

Including off metal strikes

KM#	Date	Mintage	Identification	Mkt Val
Pn102	1929	—	100 Francs. Aluminum-Bronze. Bust left. Date. CENT FRANCS.	120
Pn103	1933	—	5 Francs. Liberty bust left. Legend above, date below. CENT FRANCS.	200
Pn104	1939	—	20 Francs. Copper-Nickel. Y#87.	750
Pn105	1941	—	10 Francs. Copper-Nickel. Petain bust left, legend in front. People working at sides. TRAVAIL/FAMILLE/PATRIE/10/FRANCS/1941	400
Pn106	1941	—	20 Francs. Copper-Nickel. Petain bust left. Sheaves of wheat bent outward, legend above, 20-FRS below.	400
Pn107	1941	—	20 Francs. Copper-Nickel. Petain bust left. Family group above FAMILLE divide 20-FR.	400
Pn108	1941	—	20 Francs. Nickel. Petain bust left. 3 figures, 2 standing, 1 sitting.	400
Pn109	1942	—	5 Francs. Copper-Nickel. Petain bust left. TRAVAIL/FAMILLE/PATRIE/5/FRANCS/1942	400
Pn110	1943	—	10 Francs. Copper-Nickel. Petain bust left. 3 figures, 2 standing, 1 sitting.	360
Pn111	1950	—	20 Francs. Liberty left. 20-FR divided by symbol.	70.00
Pn112	1950	—	20 Francs. Liberty left. Inscription above 20 dividing flowers, FRANCS and date below.	70.00
Pn113	1950	—	20 Francs. Liberty bust left. 20 over branch at left, FRANCS in center at right, date below.	70.00
Pn114	1950	—	20 Francs. Liberty bust left. 20 in small circle of branches, 4 branches to edge of coin.	70.00
Pn115	1950	—	100 Francs. Copper-Nickel.	300
Pn116	1964	131	10 Francs. Silver. KM#756. KM#932.	200
Pn117	1964	3,500	10 Francs. Silver. KM#932.	125
Pn118	1977	253	2 Francs. Nickel. KM#942.	75.00

PIEFORTS

Standard metals unless otherwise noted

KM#	Date	Mintage	Identification	Mkt Val
P251	1903	—	25 Centimes. Copper-Nickel-Zinc.	125
P270	1914	—	10 Centimes. KM#866.	100
P272	1914	—	25 Centimes. KM#867.	150
P280	1920	—	5 Centimes. KM#875.	125
P-A297	1920	—	2 Francs. Aluminum-Bronze. KM#877.	120
P297	1928	—	2 Francs. KM#845.	300
P300	1929	—	100 Francs. KM#880.	3,500
P305	1941	—	10 Centimes. KM#895.	200
P341	1962	500	Centime. KM#928.	21.00
P342	1962	50	Centime. Silver. KM#928.	60.00
P343	1962	20	Centime. Gold. KM#928.	250
P344	1962	500	10 Centimes. KM#929.	15.00
P345	1962	50	10 Centimes. Silver. KM#929.	80.00
P346	1962	20	10 Centimes. Gold. KM#929.	325
P347	1962	500	20 Centimes. KM#930.	20.00
P348	1962	50	20 Centimes. Silver. KM#930.	100
P349	1962	20	20 Centimes. Gold. KM#930.	350
P350	1962	500	50 Centimes. KM#939.	20.00
P351	1962	50	50 Centimes. Silver. KM#939.	110
P352	1962	20	50 Centimes. Gold. KM#939.	450
P353	1965	500	1/2 Franc. KM#931.	25.00
P354	1965	50	1/2 Franc. Silver. KM#931.	70.00
P355	1965	20	1/2 Franc. Gold. KM#931.	350
P356	1965	500	10 Francs. KM#932.	70.00
P357	1965	50	10 Francs. Gold. KM#932.	1,250
P358	1966	500	5 Centimes. KM#933.	15.00
P359	1966	50	5 Centimes. Silver. KM#933.	75.00
P360	1966	20	5 Centimes. Gold. KM#933.	300
P361	1967	500	Centime. KM#928.	15.00
P362	1967	50	Centime. Silver. KM#928.	30.00
P363	1967	20	Centime. Gold. KM#928.	250
P364	1967	500	5 Centimes. KM#933.	15.00
P365	1967	50	5 Centimes. Silver. KM#933.	45.00
P366	1967	20	5 Centimes. Gold. KM#933.	300
P367	1967	500	10 Centimes. KM#929.	15.00
P368	1967	50	10 Centimes. Silver. KM#929.	60.00
P369	1967	20	10 Centimes. Gold. KM#929.	300
P370	1967	500	20 Centimes. KM#930.	15.00
P371	1967	50	20 Centimes. Silver. KM#930.	120
P372	1967	20	20 Centimes. Gold. KM#930.	300
P373	1967	500	25 Centimes. KM#939.	15.00
P374	1967	50	50 Centimes. Silver. KM#939.	120
P375	1967	20	50 Centimes. Gold. KM#939.	375
P376	1967	500	1/2 Franc. KM#931.	20.00
P377	1967	50	1/2 Franc. Silver. KM#931.	75.00
P378	1967	20	1/2 Franc. Gold. KM#931.	400
P379	1967	500	Franc. KM#925.	20.00
P380	1967	50	Franc. Silver. KM#925.	75.00
P381	1967	20	Franc. Gold. KM#925.	450
P382	1967	500	5 Francs. KM#926.	30.00
P383	1967	50	5 Francs. Gold. KM#926.	650
P384	1967	500	10 Francs. KM#932.	45.00
P385	1967	50	10 Francs. Gold. KM#932.	1,000
P386	1968	500	Centime. KM#928.	30.00
P387	1968	50	Centime. Silver. KM#928.	50.00
P388	1968	20	Centime. Gold. KM#928.	150
P389	1968	500	5 Centimes. KM#933.	30.00
P390	1968	50	5 Centimes. Silver. KM#933.	50.00
P391	1968	20	5 Centimes. Gold. KM#933.	175
P392	1968	500	10 Centimes. KM#929.	30.00
P393	1968	50	10 Centimes. Silver. KM#929.	50.00
P394	1968	20	10 Centimes. Gold. KM#929.	200
P395	1968	500	20 Centimes. KM#930.	30.00
P396	1968	50	20 Centimes. Silver. KM#930.	50.00
P397	1968	20	20 Centimes. Gold. KM#930.	275
P398	1968	500	1/2 Franc. KM#931.	30.00
P399	1968	50	1/2 Franc. Silver. KM#931.	60.00
P400	1968	20	1/2 Franc. Gold. KM#931.	300
P401	1968	500	Franc. KM#925.	30.00
P402	1968	50	Franc. Silver. KM#925.	60.00
P403	1968	20	Franc. Gold. KM#925.	350
P404	1968	500	5 Francs. KM#926.	30.00
P405	1968	50	5 Francs. Gold. KM#926.	400
P406	1968	500	10 Francs. KM#932.	40.00
P407	1968	50	10 Francs. Gold. KM#932.	750
P408	1970	500	5 Francs. KM#926a.	40.00
P409	1970	200	5 Francs. Silver. KM#926a.	60.00
P410	1970	100	5 Francs. Gold. KM#926a.	500
P411	1970	100	5 Francs. Platinum. KM#926a.	900
P412	1971	500	Centime. KM#928.	20.00
P413	1971	250	Centime. Silver. KM#928.	30.00
P414	1971	100	Centime. Gold. KM#928.	125
P415	1971	500	5 Centimes. KM#933.	20.00
P416	1971	250	5 Centimes. Silver. KM#933.	30.00
P417	1971	100	5 Centimes. Gold. KM#933.	150
P418	1971	500	10 Centimes. KM#929.	20.00
P419	1971	250	10 Centimes. Silver. KM#929.	35.00
P420	1971	100	10 Centimes. Gold. KM#929.	175
P421	1971	500	20 Centimes. KM#930.	20.00
P422	1971	250	20 Centimes. Silver. KM#930.	35.00
P423	1971	100	20 Centimes. Gold. KM#930.	200
P424	1971	500	1/2 Franc. KM#931.	20.00
P425	1971	250	1/2 Franc. Silver. KM#931.	35.00
P426	1971	100	1/2 Franc. Gold. KM#931.	250
P427	1971	500	Franc. KM#925.	25.00
P428	1971	250	Franc. Silver. KM#925.	35.00
P429	1971	100	Franc. Gold. KM#925.	300
P430	1971	1,000	5 Francs. KM#926a.	20.00
P431	1971	500	5 Francs. Silver. KM#926a.	30.00
P432	1971	250	5 Francs. Gold. KM#926a.	525
P433	1971	100	5 Francs. Platinum. KM#926a.	1,000
P435	1971	500	10 Francs. KM#932.	50.00
P436	1971	250	10 Francs. Gold. KM#932.	800
P437	1972	250	Centime. KM#928.	20.00
P438	1972	150	Centime. Silver. KM#928.	25.00
P439	1972	75	Centime. Gold. KM#928.	125
P440	1972	250	5 Centimes. KM#933.	20.00
P441	1972	150	5 Centimes. Silver. KM#933.	25.00
P442	1972	75	5 Centimes. Gold. KM#933.	135
P443	1972	250	10 Centimes. KM#929.	20.00
P444	1972	150	10 Centimes. Silver. KM#929.	25.00
P445	1972	75	10 Centimes. Gold. KM#929.	150
P446	1972	250	20 Centimes. KM#930.	25.00
P447	1972	150	20 Centimes. Silver. KM#930.	35.00
P448	1972	75	20 Centimes. Gold. KM#930.	200
P449	1972	250	1/2 Franc. KM#931.	25.00
P450	1972	150	1/2 Franc. Silver. KM#931.	35.00
P451	1972	75	1/2 Franc. Gold. KM#931.	250
P452	1972	250	Franc. KM#925.	25.00
P453	1972	150	Franc. Silver. KM#925.	40.00
P454	1972	75	Franc. Gold. KM#925.	320
P455	1972	500	5 Francs. KM#926a.	25.00
P456	1972	250	5 Francs. Silver. KM#926a.	35.00
P457	1972	200	5 Francs. Gold. KM#926a.	425
P458	1972	500	10 Francs. KM#932.	70.00
P459	1972	200	10 Francs. Gold. KM#932.	800
P460	1972	20	10 Francs. Platinum. KM#932.	1,000
P461	1973	250	Centime. KM#928.	20.00
P462	1973	150	Centime. Silver. KM#928.	25.00
P463	1973	75	Centime. Gold. KM#928.	120
P464	1973	250	5 Centimes. KM#933.	20.00
P465	1973	150	5 Centimes. Silver. KM#933.	25.00
P466	1973	75	5 Centimes. Gold. KM#933.	120
P467	1973	250	10 Centimes. KM#929.	20.00
P468	1973	150	10 Centimes. Silver. KM#929.	25.00
P469	1973	75	10 Centimes. Gold. KM#929.	145
P470	1973	250	20 Centimes. KM#930.	20.00
P471	1973	150	20 Centimes. Silver. KM#930.	25.00
P472	1973	75	20 Centimes. Gold. KM#930.	160
P473	1973	250	1/2 Franc. KM#931.	20.00
P474	1973	150	1/2 Franc. Silver. KM#931.	25.00
P475	1973	75	1/2 Franc. Gold. KM#931.	175
P476	1973	250	Franc. KM#925.	20.00
P477	1973	150	Franc. Silver. KM#925.	25.00
P478	1973	75	Franc. Gold. KM#925.	250
P479	1973	500	5 Francs. KM#926a.	20.00
P480	1973	250	5 Francs. Silver. KM#926a.	35.00
P481	1973	200	5 Francs. Gold. KM#926a.	470
P482	1973	500	10 Francs. KM#932.	25.00
P483	1973	200	10 Francs. Gold. KM#932.	800
P484	1973	20	10 Francs. Platinum. KM#932.	1,000
P485	1974	127	Centime. KM#928.	30.00
P486	1974	242	Centime. Silver. KM#928.	35.00
P487	1974	96	Centime. Gold. KM#928.	110
P488	1974	98	5 Centimes. KM#933.	30.00
P489	1974	247	5 Centimes. Silver. KM#933.	35.00
P490	1974	96	5 Centimes. Gold. KM#933.	125
P491	1974	97	10 Centimes. KM#929.	30.00
P492	1974	246	10 Centimes. Silver. KM#929.	35.00
P493	1974	94	10 Centimes. Gold. KM#929.	150
P494	1974	101	20 Centimes. KM#930.	30.00
P495	1974	247	20 Centimes. Silver. KM#930.	35.00
P496	1974	98	20 Centimes. Gold. KM#930.	200
P497	1974	102	1/2 Franc. KM#931.	30.00
P498	1974	241	1/2 Franc. Silver. KM#931.	35.00
P499	1974	91	1/2 Franc. Gold. KM#931.	225
P500	1974	118	Franc. KM#925.	35.00
P501	1974	246	Franc. Silver. KM#925.	40.00
P502	1974	95	Franc. Gold. KM#925.	260
P503	1974	162	5 Francs. KM#926a.	35.00
P504	1974	245	5 Francs. Silver. KM#926a.	40.00
P505	1974	107	5 Francs. Gold. KM#926a.	400
P506	1974	493	10 Francs. KM#940.	35.00
P507	1974	491	10 Francs. Silver. KM#940.	40.00
P508	1974	172	10 Francs. Gold. KM#940.	450
P509	1974	982	50 Francs. KM#941.	85.00
P510	1974	241	50 Francs. Gold. KM#941.	1,200
P511	1974	18	50 Francs. Platinum. KM#941.	3,700
P512	1975	147	Centime. KM#928.	20.00
P513	1975	228	Centime. Silver. KM#928.	25.00
P514	1975	67	Centime. Gold. KM#928.	125
P515	1975	129	5 Centimes. KM#933.	20.00
P516	1975	203	5 Centimes. Silver. KM#933.	25.00
P517	1975	44	5 Centimes. Gold. KM#933.	140
P518	1975	127	10 Centimes. KM#929.	20.00
P519	1975	198	10 Centimes. Silver. KM#929.	25.00
P520	1975	39	10 Centimes. Gold. KM#929.	160
P521	1975	133	20 Centimes. KM#930.	20.00
P522	1975	212	20 Centimes. Silver. KM#930.	25.00
P523	1975	42	20 Centimes. Gold. KM#930.	170
P524	1975	131	1/2 Franc. KM#931.	20.00
P525	1975	213	1/2 Franc. Silver. KM#931.	25.00
P526	1975	40	1/2 Franc. Gold. KM#931.	220
P527	1975	145	Franc. KM#925.	20.00
P528	1975	250	Franc. Silver. KM#925.	25.00
P529	1975	51	Franc. Gold. KM#925.	300
P530	1975	202	5 Francs. KM#926a.	20.00
P531	1975	250	5 Francs. Silver. KM#926a.	30.00
P532	1975	60	5 Francs. Gold. KM#926a.	465
P533	1975	356	10 Francs. KM#940.	25.00
P534	1975	500	10 Francs. Silver. KM#940.	35.00
P535	1975	62	10 Francs. Gold. KM#940.	500
P536	1975	955	50 Francs. KM#941.	80.00
P537	1975	74	50 Francs. Gold. KM#941.	1,200
P538	1975	10	50 Francs. Platinum. KM#941.	3,500
P539	1976	200	Centime. KM#928.	20.00
P540	1976	300	Centime. Silver. KM#928.	25.00
P541	1976	100	Centime. Gold. KM#928.	100
P542	1976	200	5 Centimes. KM#933.	20.00
P543	1976	300	5 Centimes. Silver. KM#933.	25.00
P544	1976	100	5 Centimes. Gold. KM#933.	115
P545	1976	200	10 Centimes. KM#929.	20.00
P546	1976	300	10 Centimes. Silver. KM#929.	25.00
P547	1976	100	10 Centimes. Gold. KM#929.	125
P548	1976	200	20 Centimes. KM#930.	20.00
P549	1976	300	20 Centimes. Silver. KM#930.	25.00
P550	1976	100	20 Centimes. Gold. KM#930.	135
P551	1976	200	1/2 Franc. KM#931.	20.00
P552	1976	250	1/2 Franc. Silver. KM#931.	25.00
P553	1976	100	1/2 Franc. Gold. KM#931.	145
P554	1976	126	Franc. KM#925.	30.00
P555	1976	88	Franc. Silver. KM#925.	35.00
P556	1976	38	Franc. Gold. KM#925.	165
P557	1976	178	5 Francs. KM#926a.	30.00
P558	1976	104	5 Francs. Silver. KM#926a.	37.50
P559	1976	26	5 Francs. Gold. KM#926a.	500
P560	1976	175	10 Francs. KM#940.	30.00
P561	1976	121	10 Francs. Silver. KM#940.	40.00
P562	1976	36	10 Francs. Gold. KM#940.	535
P563	1976	213	50 Francs. KM#941.	150
P564	1976	54	50 Francs. Gold. KM#941.	1,300
P565	1976	6	50 Francs. Platinum. KM#941.	6,200
P566	1977	118	Centime. KM#928.	25.00

KM#	Date	Mintage	Identification	Mkt Val
P567	1977	247	Centime. Silver. KM#928.	30.00
P568	1977	53	Centime. Gold. KM#928.	100
P569	1977	89	5 Centimes. KM#933.	25.00
P570	1977	232	5 Centimes. Silver. KM#933.	30.00
P571	1977	41	5 Centimes. Gold. KM#933.	125
P572	1977	85	10 Centimes. KM#929.	25.00
P573	1977	231	10 Centimes. Silver. KM#929.	30.00
P574	1977	32	10 Centimes. Gold. KM#929.	175
P575	1977	88	20 Centimes. KM#930.	30.00
P576	1977	243	20 Centimes. Silver. KM#930.	35.00
P577	1977	32	20 Centimes. Gold. KM#930.	200
P578	1977	89	1/2 Franc. KM#931.	30.00
P579	1977	234	1/2 Franc. Silver. KM#931.	35.00
P580	1977	32	1/2 Franc. Gold. KM#931.	250
P581	1977	100	Franc. KM#925.	30.00
P582	1977	259	Franc. Silver. KM#925.	35.00
P583	1977	42	Franc. Gold. KM#925.	300
P584	1977	139	5 Francs. KM#926a.	30.00
P585	1977	282	5 Francs. Silver. KM#926a.	35.00
P586	1977	35	5 Francs. Gold. KM#926a.	450
P587	1977	146	10 Francs. KM#940.	30.00
P588	1977	296	10 Francs. Silver. KM#940.	40.00
P589	1977	43	10 Francs. Gold. KM#940.	500
P590	1977	465	50 Francs. KM#941.	125
P591	1977	50	50 Francs. Gold. KM#941.	1,250
P592	1977	19	50 Francs. Platinum. KM#941.	3,750
P593	1978	150	Centime. KM#928.	20.00
P594	1978	294	Centime. Silver. KM#928.	25.00
P595	1978	144	Centime. Gold. KM#928.	100
P596	1978	148	5 Centimes. KM#933.	20.00
P597	1978	295	5 Centimes. Silver. KM#933.	25.00
P598	1978	144	5 Centimes. Gold. KM#933.	125
P599	1978	147	10 Centimes. KM#929.	20.00
P600	1978	290	10 Centimes. Silver. KM#929.	25.00
P601	1978	139	10 Centimes. Gold. KM#929.	150
P602	1978	148	20 Centimes. KM#930.	20.00
P603	1978	296	20 Centimes. Silver. KM#930.	25.00
P604	1978	141	20 Centimes. Gold. KM#930.	175
P605	1978	149	1/2 Franc. KM#931.	20.00
P606	1978	296	1/2 Franc. Silver. KM#931.	25.00
P607	1978	141	1/2 Franc. Gold. KM#931.	200
P608	1978	149	Franc. KM#925.	20.00
P609	1978	297	Franc. Silver. KM#925.	25.00
P610	1978	142	Franc. Gold. KM#925.	300
P611	1978	350	2 Francs. Silver. KM#942.	30.00
P612	1978	—	2 Francs. Nickel. KM#942.	100
P613	1978	150	5 Francs. KM#926a.	20.00
P614	1978	306	5 Francs. Silver. KM#926a.	25.00
P615	1978	143	5 Francs. Gold. KM#926a.	450
P616	1978	174	10 Francs. KM#940.	25.00
P617	1978	345	10 Francs. Silver. KM#940.	35.00
P618	1978	144	10 Francs. Gold. KM#940.	525
P619	1978	599	50 Francs. KM#941.	110
P620	1978	149	50 Francs. Gold. KM#941.	1,700
P621	1978	25	50 Francs. Platinum. KM#941.	3,750
P622	1979	300	Centime. KM#928.	15.00
P623	1979	600	Centime. Silver. KM#928.	20.00
P624	1979	300	Centime. Gold. KM#928.	90.00
P625	1979	299	5 Centimes. KM#935.	15.00
P626	1979	600	5 Centimes. Silver. KM#933.	20.00
P627	1979	300	5 Centimes. Gold. KM#933.	100
P628	1979	300	10 Centimes. KM#929.	15.00
P629	1979	600	10 Centimes. Silver. KM#929.	20.00
P630	1979	300	10 Centimes. Gold. KM#929.	110
P631	1979	300	20 Centimes. KM#930.	15.00
P632	1979	600	20 Centimes. Silver. KM#930.	20.00
P633	1979	300	20 Centimes. Gold. KM#930.	120
P634	1979	300	1/2 Franc. KM#931.	15.00
P635	1979	600	1/2 Franc. Silver. KM#931.	20.00
P636	1979	300	1/2 Franc. Gold. KM#931.	200
P637	1979	500	Franc. KM#925.	20.00
P638	1979	1,250	Franc. Silver. KM#925.	25.00
P639	1979	600	Franc. Gold. KM#925.	250
P640	1979	500	2 Francs. KM#942.	20.00
P641	1979	1,250	2 Francs. Silver. KM#942.	30.00
P642	1979	600	2 Francs. Gold. KM#942.	350
P643	1979	40	2 Francs. Platinum. KM#942.	900
P644	1979	300	5 Francs. KM#926a.	20.00
P645	1979	600	5 Francs. Silver. KM#926a.	30.00
P646	1979	300	5 Francs. Gold. KM#926a.	450
P647	1979	349	10 Francs. KM#940.	25.00
P648	1979	700	10 Francs. Silver. KM#940.	35.00
P649	1979	300	10 Francs. Gold. KM#940.	500
P650	1979	2,250	50 Francs. KM#941.	100
P651	1979	400	50 Francs. Gold. KM#941.	1,400
P652	1979	30	50 Francs. Platinum. KM#941.	3,600
P653	1980	155	Centime. KM#928.	15.00
P654	1980	570	Centime. Silver. KM#928.	20.00
P655	1980	176	Centime. Gold. KM#928.	90.00
P656	1980	142	5 Centimes. KM#933.	15.00
P657	1980	547	5 Centimes. Silver. KM#933.	20.00
P658	1980	137	5 Centimes. Gold. KM#933.	100
P659	1980	148	10 Centimes. KM#929.	15.00
P660	1980	528	10 Centimes. Silver. KM#929.	20.00
P661	1980	127	10 Centimes. Gold. KM#929.	110
P662	1980	140	20 Centimes. KM#930.	15.00
P663	1980	569	20 Centimes. Silver. KM#930.	20.00
P664	1980	136	20 Centimes. Gold. KM#930.	120
P665	1980	156	1/2 Franc. KM#931.	15.00
P666	1980	537	1/2 Franc. Silver. KM#931.	20.00
P667	1980	118	1/2 Franc. Gold. KM#931.	220
P668	1980	132	Franc. KM#925.	15.00
P669	1980	563	Franc. Silver. KM#925.	20.00
P670	1980	193	Franc. Gold. KM#925.	310
P671	1980	194	2 Francs. KM#942.	15.00
P672	1980	772	2 Francs. Silver. KM#942.	20.00
P673	1980	130	2 Francs. Gold. KM#942.	500
P674	1980	271	5 Francs. KM#926a.	15.00
P675	1980	580	5 Francs. Silver. KM#926a.	20.00
P676	1980	213	5 Francs. Gold. KM#926a.	600
P677	1980	148	10 Francs. KM#940.	15.00
P678	1980	730	10 Francs. Silver. KM#940.	20.00
P679	1980	157	10 Francs. Gold. KM#940.	500
P680	1980	2,500	50 Francs. KM#941.	100
P681	1980	500	50 Francs. Gold. KM#941.	1,700
P682	1980	34	50 Francs. Platinum. KM#941.	3,700
P683	1981	150	Centime. KM#928.	15.00
P684	1981	362	Centime. Silver. KM#928.	20.00
P685	1981	69	Centime. Gold. KM#928.	110
P686	1981	105	5 Centimes. KM#933.	15.00
P687	1981	358	5 Centimes. Silver. KM#933.	20.00
P688	1981	42	5 Centimes. Gold. KM#933.	130
P689	1981	104	10 Centimes. KM#929.	15.00
P690	1981	357	10 Centimes. Silver. KM#929.	20.00
P691	1981	32	10 Centimes. Gold. KM#929.	235
P692	1981	106	20 Centimes. KM#930.	15.00
P693	1981	359	20 Centimes. Silver. KM#930.	20.00
P694	1981	30	20 Centimes. Gold. KM#930.	245
P695	1981	110	1/2 Franc. KM#931.	15.00
P696	1981	358	1/2 Franc. Silver. KM#931.	20.00
P697	1981	33	1/2 Franc. Gold. KM#931.	275
P698	1981	16	1/2 Franc. Platinum. KM#931.	1,000
P699	1981	122	Franc. KM#925.	15.00
P700	1981	358	Franc. Silver. KM#925.	20.00
P701	1981	42	Franc. Gold. KM#925.	400
P702	1981	16	Franc. Platinum. KM#925.	1,300
P703	1981	131	2 Francs. KM#942.	15.00
P704	1981	359	2 Francs. Silver. KM#942.	20.00
P705	1981	37	2 Francs. Gold. KM#942.	500
P706	1981	16	2 Francs. Platinum. KM#942.	1,500
P707	1981	150	5 Francs. KM#926a.	15.00
P708	1981	261	5 Francs. Silver. KM#926a.	20.00
P709	1981	52	5 Francs. Gold. KM#926a.	650
P710	1981	16	5 Francs. Platinum. KM#926a.	1,750
P711	1981	150	10 Francs. KM#940.	15.00
P712	1981	365	10 Francs. Silver. KM#940.	20.00
P713	1981	52	10 Francs. Gold. KM#940.	700
P714	1981	17	10 Francs. Platinum. KM#940.	1,850
P715	1982	70	Centime. Steel. KM#928.	20.00
P716	1982	195	Centime. Silver. KM#928.	25.00
P717	1982	36	Centime. Gold. KM#928.	200
P718	1982	53	5 Centimes. KM#933.	25.00
P719	1982	164	5 Centimes. Silver. KM#933.	25.00
P720	1982	26	5 Centimes. Gold. KM#933.	225
P721	1982	53	10 Centimes. KM#929.	25.00
P722	1982	163	10 Centimes. Silver. KM#929.	25.00
P723	1982	29	10 Centimes. Gold. KM#929.	250
P724	1982	53	20 Centimes. KM#930.	25.00
P725	1982	171	20 Centimes. Silver. KM#930.	25.00
P726	1982	26	20 Centimes. Gold. KM#930.	350
P727	1982	54	1/2 Franc. KM#931.	25.00
P728	1982	165	1/2 Franc. Silver. KM#931.	25.00
P729	1982	26	1/2 Franc. Gold. KM#931.	350
P730	1982	4	1/2 Franc. Platinum. KM#931.	2,500
P731	1982	57	Franc. KM#925.	25.00
P732	1982	252	Franc. Silver. KM#925.	25.00
P733	1982	29	Franc. Gold. KM#925.	400
P734	1982	6	Franc. Platinum. KM#925.	1,400
P735	1982	62	2 Francs. KM#942.	25.00
P736	1982	203	2 Francs. Silver. KM#942.	25.00
P737	1982	27	2 Francs. Gold. KM#942.	800
P738	1982	4	2 Francs. Platinum. KM#942.	2,750
P739	1982	69	5 Francs. KM#926a.	25.00
P740	1982	188	5 Francs. Silver. KM#926a.	25.00
P741	1982	27	5 Francs. Gold. KM#926a.	860
P742	1982	4	5 Francs. Platinum. KM#926a.	3,200
P743	1982	80	10 Francs. KM#940.	25.00
P744	1982	239	10 Francs. Silver. KM#940.	30.00
P745	1982	33	10 Francs. Gold. KM#940.	700
P746	1982	4	10 Francs. Platinum. KM#940.	3,250
P747	1982	326	10 Francs. KM#950.	20.00
P748	1982	812	10 Francs. Silver. KM#950.	30.00
P749	1982	87	10 Francs. Gold. KM#950.	700
P750	1982	14	10 Francs. Platinum. KM#950.	1,350
P751	1982	999	100 Francs. Silver. KM#951.	60.00
P752	1982	93	100 Francs. Gold. KM#951.	1,000
P753	1982	16	100 Francs. Platinum. KM#951.	1,650
P754	1983	50	Centime. Steel. KM#928.	20.00
P755	1983	98	Centime. Silver. KM#928.	25.00
P756	1983	17	Centime. Gold. KM#928.	200
P757	1983	42	Centime. KM#933.	20.00
P758	1983	90	5 Centimes. Silver. KM#933.	25.00
P759	1983	7	5 Centimes. Gold. KM#933.	725
P760	1983	42	10 Centimes. KM#929.	25.00
P761	1983	90	10 Centimes. Silver. KM#929.	30.00
P762	1983	6	10 Centimes. Gold. KM#929.	625
P763	1983	44	20 Centimes. KM#930.	25.00
P764	1983	95	20 Centimes. Silver. KM#930.	30.00
P765	1983	5	20 Centimes. Gold. KM#930.	650
P766	1983	43	1/2 Franc. KM#931.	25.00
P767	1983	89	1/2 Franc. Silver. KM#931.	35.00
P768	1983	5	1/2 Franc. Gold. KM#931.	600
P769	1983	3	1/2 Franc. Platinum. KM#931.	6,500
P770	1983	46	Franc. KM#925.	25.00
P771	1983	98	Franc. Silver. KM#925.	35.00
P772	1983	11	Franc. Gold. KM#925.	450
P773	1983	3	Franc. Platinum. KM#925.	6,500
P774	1983	51	2 Francs. KM#942.	25.00
P775	1983	121	2 Francs. Silver. KM#942.	35.00
P776	1983	9	2 Francs. Gold. KM#942.	600
P777	1983	3	2 Francs. Platinum. KM#942.	6,500
P778	1983	58	5 Francs. KM#926a.	25.00
P779	1983	97	5 Francs. Silver. KM#926a.	35.00
P780	1983	8	5 Francs. Gold. KM#926a.	750
P781	1983	3	5 Francs. Platinum. KM#926a.	6,750
P782	1983	286	10 Francs. KM#952.	20.00
P783	1983	454	10 Francs. Silver. KM#952.	40.00
P784	1983	34	10 Francs. Gold. KM#952.	760
P785	1983	13	10 Francs. Platinum. KM#952.	1,950
P786	1983	74	10 Francs. KM#940.	25.00
P787	1983	118	10 Francs. Silver. KM#940.	45.00
P788	1983	12	10 Francs. Gold. KM#940.	725
P789	1983	5	10 Francs. Platinum. KM#940.	2,500
P790	1983	206	10 Francs. KM#953.	20.00
P791	1983	314	10 Francs. Silver. KM#953.	50.00
P792	1983	29	10 Francs. Gold. KM#953.	720
P793	1983	5	10 Francs. Platinum. KM#953.	2,500
P794	1983	242	100 Francs. Silver. KM#951.	60.00
P795	1983	14	100 Francs. Gold. KM#951.	1,100
P796	1983	7	100 Francs. Platinum. KM#951.	2,350
P797	1984	56	Centime. Steel. KM#928.	25.00
P798	1984	64	Centime. Silver. KM#928.	25.00
P799	1984	10	Centime. Gold. KM#928.	200
P800	1984	36	5 Centimes. Copper-Nickel. KM#933.	30.00
P801	1984	49	5 Centimes. Silver. KM#933.	25.00
P802	1984	6	5 Centimes. Gold. KM#933.	450
P803	1984	34	10 Centimes. Copper-Nickel. KM#929.	30.00
P804	1984	54	10 Centimes. Silver. KM#929.	25.00
P805	1984	4	10 Centimes. Gold. KM#929.	650
P806	1984	34	20 Centimes. Copper-Nickel. KM#930.	30.00
P807	1984	60	20 Centimes. Silver. KM#930.	25.00
P808	1984	4	20 Centimes. Gold. KM#930.	1,000
P809	1984	34	1/2 Franc. Nickel. KM#931.	30.00
P900	1984	59	1/2 Franc. Silver. KM#931.	25.00
P901	1984	8	1/2 Franc. Gold. KM#931.	500
P902	1984	5	1/2 Franc. Platinum. KM#931.	1,400
P903	1984	40	Franc. Nickel. KM#925.	30.00
P904	1984	69	Franc. Silver. KM#925.	25.00
P905	1984	6	Franc. Gold. KM#925.	650
P906	1984	5	Franc. Platinum. KM#925.	2,500
P907	1984	42	2 Francs. Nickel. KM#942.	30.00
P908	1984	79	2 Francs. Silver. KM#942.	25.00
P909	1984	9	2 Francs. Gold. KM#942.	575
P910	1984	5	2 Francs. Platinum. KM#942.	1,750
P911	1984	55	5 Francs. Nickel Clad Copper-Nickel. KM#926a.	30.00
P912	1984	59	5 Francs. Silver. KM#926a.	30.00
P913	1984	4	5 Francs. Gold. KM#926a.	1,500
P914	1984	5	5 Francs. Platinum. KM#926a.	2,400
P915	1984	50	10 Francs. Copper-Nickel-Aluminum. KM#940.	30.00
P916	1984	79	10 Francs. Silver. KM#940.	30.00
P917	1984	6	10 Francs. Gold. KM#940.	750
P918	1984	5	10 Francs. Platinum. KM#940.	2,000
P919	1984	184	10 Francs. Copper-Nickel-Aluminum. KM#954.	25.00
P920	1984	244	10 Francs. Silver. KM#954.	30.00
P921	1984	18	10 Francs. Gold. KM#954.	725
P922	1984	5	10 Francs. Platinum. KM#954.	2,000
P923	1984	500	100 Francs. Silver. KM#955.	55.00
P924	1984	34	100 Francs. Gold. KM#955.	1,150
P925	1984	9	100 Francs. Platinum. KM#955.	1,900
P926	1984	100	100 Francs. Silver. KM#951.	75.00
P927	1984	10	100 Francs. Gold. KM#951.	1,150
P928	1984	5	100 Francs. Platinum. KM#951.	2,800
P929	1985	100	Centime. 0.9250 Silver. KM#928.	20.00
P930	1985	18	Centime. 0.9200 Gold. KM#928.	200
P931	1985	60	5 Centimes. 0.9250 Silver. KM#933.	30.00
P932	1985	6	5 Centimes. 0.9200 Gold. KM#933.	450
P933	1985	65	10 Centimes. 0.9250 Silver. KM#929.	32.00
P934	1985	4	10 Centimes. 0.9200 Gold. KM#929.	700
P935	1985	85	20 Centimes. 0.9250 Silver. KM#930.	35.00
P936	1985	4	20 Centimes. 0.9200 Gold. KM#930.	750
P937	1985	80	1/2 Franc. 0.9250 Silver. KM#931.	35.00
P938	1985	16	1/2 Franc. 0.9200 Gold. KM#931.	425
P939	1985	5	1/2 Franc. Platinum. KM#931.	2,000
P940	1985	90	Franc. 0.9250 Silver. KM#925.	35.00
P941	1985	5	Franc. 0.9200 Gold. KM#925.	575
P942	1985	5	Franc. Platinum. KM#925.	1,500
P943	1985	90	2 Francs. 0.9250 Silver. KM#942.	35.00
P944	1985	17	2 Francs. 0.9200 Gold. KM#942.	585
P945	1985	5	2 Francs. Platinum. KM#942.	1,500
P946	1985	70	5 Francs. 0.9250 Silver. KM#926a.	55.00
P947	1985	4	5 Francs. 0.9200 Gold. KM#926a.	1,000
P948	1985	5	5 Francs. Platinum. KM#926a.	2,150
P949	1985	120	10 Francs. 0.9250 Silver. KM#940.	50.00
P950	1985	12	10 Francs. 0.9200 Gold. KM#940.	720
P951	1985	5	10 Francs. Platinum. KM#940.	2,150
P952	1985	8	10 Francs. 0.9200 Gold. KM#952.	725
P953	1985	8	10 Francs. 0.9200 Gold. KM#953.	725

KM#	Date	Mintage	Identification	Mkt Val
P954	1985	45	10 Francs. 0.9250 Silver. KM#954.	60.00
P955	1985	8	10 Francs. 0.9200 Gold. KM#954.	725
P956	1985	215	10 Francs. 0.9250 Silver. KM#956.	50.00
P957	1985	17	10 Francs. 0.9200 Gold. KM#956.	720
P958	1985	15	10 Francs. Platinum. KM#956.	900
P959	1985	100	100 Francs. 0.9250 Silver. KM#951.	65.00
P960	1985	18	100 Francs. 0.9200 Gold. KM#951.	1,200
P961	1985	10	100 Francs. Platinum. KM#951.	2,850
P962	1985	200	100 Francs. 0.9250 Silver. KM#955a.	60.00
P963	1985	8	100 Francs. 0.9200 Gold. KM#955b.	1,400
P964	1985	440	100 Francs. 0.9250 Silver. KM#957.	50.00
P965	1985	30	100 Francs. 0.9200 Gold. KM#957.	1,100
P966	1985	15	100 Francs. Platinum. KM#957.	1,250
P967	1986	10	10 Francs. Platinum. KM#958.	1,400
P968	1986	200	10 Francs. 0.9500 Silver. KM#959.	55.00
P969	1986	5	10 Francs. Platinum. KM#959.	2,150
P970	1986	5	100 Francs. Platinum. KM#951.	3,000
P971	1986	250	100 Francs. Silver. KM#951.	55.00
P972	1986	5,000	100 Francs. 0.9000 Silver. KM#960.	15.00
P973	1986	15	100 Francs. Platinum. KM#960.	2,150
P973b	1986	50	100 Francs. Gold. KM#960b.	1,250
P974	1987	50	Centime. 0.9500 Silver. KM#928.	40.00
P975	1987	50	5 Centimes. 0.9500 Silver. KM#933.	50.00
P976	1987	50	10 Centimes. 0.9500 Silver. KM#929.	50.00
P977	1987	50	20 Centimes. 0.9500 Silver. KM#930.	50.00
P978	1987	50	1/2 Franc. 0.9500 Silver. KM#931.	50.00
P979	1987	50	Franc. 0.9500 Silver. KM#925.	40.00
P980	1987	50	2 Francs. 0.9500 Silver. KM#942.	50.00
P981	1987	50	5 Francs. 0.9500 Silver. KM#926a.	65.00
P982	1987	50	10 Francs. 0.9500 Silver. KM#940.	65.00
P983	1987	15	10 Francs. 0.9200 Gold. KM#940.	765
P984	1987	5	10 Francs. 0.9990 Platinum. KM#940.	2,000
P985	1987	1,000	10 Francs. 0.9500 Silver. KM#961.	50.00
P986	1987	25	10 Francs. 0.9200 Gold. KM#961.	765
P987	1987	10	10 Francs. 0.9990 Platinum. KM#961.	1,650
P988	1987	30	100 Francs. 0.9000 Silver. KM#951.	65.00
P989	1987	15	100 Francs. 0.9200 Gold. KM#951.	1,100
P990	1987	5	100 Francs. 0.9990 Platinum. KM#951.	2,850
P991	1987	51,000	100 Francs. 0.9500 Silver. KM#962, Proof.	20.00
P991a	1987	100,000	100 Francs. 0.9000 Silver. KM#962, Unc.	12.50
P992	1987	50	100 Francs. 0.9200 Gold. KM#962.	1,150
P993	1987	15	100 Francs. 0.9990 Platinum. KM#962.	2,150
P994	1988	5	Centime. Platinum. KM#928.	400
P995	1988	—	10 Francs. 0.9000 Silver. KM#965a, Proof.	100
P996	1988	—	10 Francs. Gold. KM#965c, Proof.	1,150
P997	1988	10	10 Francs. Platinum. KM#965.	1,150
P998	1988	5	100 Francs. Platinum. KM#951.	2,100
PSA999	1988	—	100 Francs. 0.9000 Silver. KM#966, Proof.	2,200
P999	1988	20,000	100 Francs. 0.9000 Silver. KM#966, Unc.	14.00
P1000	1988	10	100 Francs. Platinum. KM#966.	2,150
P1001	1989	5	Centime. Platinum. KM#928.	350
P1002	1989	10	Franc. Platinum. KM#925.	1,250
P1003	1989	300	Franc. Silver. KM#967.	35.00
P1004	1989	25	Franc. Gold. KM#967.	720
P1005	1989	10	Franc. Platinum. KM#967.	1,250
P1006	1989	10	5 Francs. Platinum. KM#968.	1,850
P1007	1989	5	100 Francs. Platinum. KM#951.	2,150
PA1008	1989	—	100 Francs. 0.9000 Silver. KM#970, Proof.	25.00
P1008	1989	10,000	100 Francs. 0.9000 Silver. KM#970, Unc.	16.00
P1009	1989	10	100 Francs. Platinum. KM#970.	2,150
P1011	1990	10	Centime. Gold. KM#928.	400
P1012	1990	5	Centime. Platinum. KM#928.	520
P1013	1990	50	5 Centimes. Silver. KM#933.	40.00
P1014	1990	50	10 Centimes. Silver. KM#929.	40.00
P1015	1990	50	20 Centimes. Silver. KM#930.	40.00
P1016	1990	5	20 Centimes. Gold. KM#930.	550
P1017	1990	50	1/2 Franc. Silver. KM#931.	40.00
P1018	1990	50	Franc. Silver. KM#925.	40.00
P1019	1990	50	2 Francs. Silver. KM#942.	40.00
P1020	1990	5	2 Francs. Gold. KM#942.	575
P1021	1990	50	5 Francs. Silver. KM#926a.	40.00
P1022	1990	10	10 Francs. Gold. Gold Alloy Spirit of Bastille.	600
P1023	1990	50	100 Francs. Silver. KM#951.	65.00
P1024	1990	10	100 Francs. Gold. KM#951.	750
P1025	1990	5	100 Francs. Platinum. KM#951.	1,000
P1026	1990	100	100 Francs. Silver. KM#982.	65.00
P1027	1990	10	100 Francs. Gold. KM#982.	750
P1028	1990	5	100 Francs. Platinum. KM#982.	1,000
P1010	1990	50	Centime. Silver. KM#928.	—
P1029	1991	—	100 Francs. Silver. KM#951.	65.00
P1030	1991	—	100 Francs. Silver. KM#996.	65.00

PIEFORTS WITH ESSAI

Double thickness; standard metals unless otherwise noted

KM#	Date	Mintage	Identification	Mkt Val
PE271	1914	—	10 Centimes. Nickel. KM#866.	550
PE272	1914	—	25 Centimes. KM#867.	500
PE-A281	1920	—	5 Centimes. Copper-Nickel. KM#875.	100
PE281	1920	—	50 Centimes. Aluminum-Bronze. KM#875.	100

KM#	Date	Mintage	Identification	Mkt Val
PE282	1920	—	Franc. Bronze-Aluminum.	100

KM#	Date	Mintage	Identification	Mkt Val
PE298	1929	—	10 Francs. KM#878.	300
PE299	1929	—	20 Francs. KM#879.	375
PE301	1931	—	50 Centimes. KM#894.1.	—
PE302	1931	—	Franc. KM#885.	—
PE303	1931	—	2 Francs. KM#886.	—
PE304	1941	—	20 Centimes. KM#899.	—
PE306	1941	—	10 Centimes. KM#898.	100
PE307	1941	—	20 Centimes. KM#900.	100

KM#	Date	Mintage	Identification	Mkt Val
PE308	1941	—	5 Francs. KM#901.	400
PE309	1943	—	2 Francs. KM#904.	120
PE310	1945	104	20 Centimes. KM#907.	140

KM#	Date	Mintage	Identification	Mkt Val
PE311	1945	104	5 Francs. KM#888.	100
PE312	1945	104	20 Francs. Copper-Nickel. KM#879.	175
PE313	1946	104	50 Centimes. KM#894.1a.	75.00
PE314	1946	104	Franc. KM#885a.	75.00
PE315	1946	104	2 Francs. KM#886a.	100

KM#	Date	Mintage	Identification	Mkt Val
PE316	1946	104	10 Francs. KM#909.	160
PE317	1950	—	10 Francs. KM#915.	60.00
PE318	1950	—	20 Francs. KM#916.	75.00
PE319	1950	—	50 Francs. KM#918.	120

KM#	Date	Mintage	Identification	Mkt Val
PE320	1952	104	10 Francs. KM#915.	60.00
PE321	1952	104	20 Francs. KM#917.	75.00
PE322	1952	104	50 Francs. KM#918.	100
PE323	1954	104	100 Francs. KM#919.	100
PE324	1958	65	100 Francs. Silver. KM#919.	500
PE325	1959	104	Franc. KM#925.	75.00
PE326	1959	104	5 Francs. KM#926.	120
PE327	1959	104	5 Francs. Silver. KM#926.	350
PE328	1960	50	Franc. Silver. KM#925.	145
PE329	1960	20	Franc. Gold. KM#925.	500
PE330	1960	500	Franc. KM#925.	35.00
PE331	1960	500	5 Francs. Silver. KM#926.	100
PE332	1960	50	5 Francs. Gold. KM#926.	725
PE333	1961	104	Centime. KM#928.	55.00
PE334	1961	104	5 Centimes. KM#927.	55.00
PE335	1961	500	5 Centimes. KM#927.	20.00
PE336	1961	50	5 Centimes. Silver. KM#927.	100
PE337	1961	20	5 Centimes. Gold. KM#927.	320
PE338	1962	104	10 Centimes. KM#929.	40.00
PE339	1962	104	20 Centimes. KM#930.	40.00
PE340	1962	104	50 Centimes. KM#939.	75.00
PE434	1971	100	5 Francs. Platinum. KM#926a.	1,250

MINT SETS

KM#	Date	Mintage	Identification	Issue Price	Mkt Val
MS1	1986 (10)	20,000	KM#925.1, 926a, 928-931, 933, 942, 951.1, 959	—	140
MS2	1987 (10)	4,000	KM#925.1, 926a, 928-931, 933, 940, 942, 961d	—	60.00
MS3	1988 (10)	2,000	KM#925.1, 926a, 928-931, 933, 942, 964-965	—	65.00
MS4	1989 (10)	2,000	KM#925.1, 926a, 928-931, 933, 942, 964, 969	—	65.00
MS6	1991 (9)	2,500	KM#925.1, 926a.1, 928-930, 931.1, 933, 942.1, 964.1, medal rotation	50.00	40.00
MS7	1992 (10)	20,000	KM#925.1, 926a.1, 928-930, 931.1, 933, 942.1, 964.1, 1008.2, medal rotation	—	45.00
MS8	1993 (10)	20,000	KM#925.1, 926a.1, 928-930, 931.1, 933, 942.1, 964.1, 1008.2, medal rotation	—	40.00
MS9	1994 (10)	20,000	KM#925.1, 926a.1, 928-930, 931.1, 933, 942.1, 964.2, 1008.2 bee privy mark	—	50.00
MS10	1995 (10)	20,000	KM#925.1, 926a.1, 928, 930, 931.1, 933, 942.1, 964.2, 1008.2	—	50.00
MS11	1996 (10)	5,000	KM#925.1, 926a.1, 928-930, 931.1, 933, 942.1, 964.2, 1008.2	—	60.00
MS12	1996 (3)	2,500	KM#1155, 1160, 1180	—	35.00
MS13	1997 (10)	15,000	KM#925.1, 926a.1, 928-930, 931.1, 933, 942.1, 964.2, 1008.2	—	50.00
MS14	1998 (10)	—	KM#925.1, 926a.1, 928-930, 931.1, 933, 942.1, 964.2, 1008.2	—	50.00
MS15	1999 (10)	—	KM#925.1, 926a.1, 928-930, 931.1, 933, 942.1, 964.2, 1008.2	—	50.00
MS18	1999 (8)	35,000	KM#1282-1289	20.25	50.00
MS16	2000 (3)	—	KM#1222-1224	—	30.00
MS17	2000 (10)	50,000	KM#925, 926a, 928-931, 933, 942, 964.2, 1008.2	—	50.00
MS19	2000 (8)	35,000	KM#1282-1289	20.25	50.00
MS20	2001 (2)	10,000	KM#925.1a, 928a	—	190
MS21	2001 (8)	35,000	KM#1282-1289	20.25	50.00
MS22	2002 (8)	35,000	KM#1282-1289	20.25	40.00

PROOF SETS

KM#	Date	Mintage	Identification	Issue Price	Mkt Val
PS6	1990-91 (9)	—	KM#971-972, 980-981, 983-984, 993-995	—	500
PS7	1991 (10)	10,000	KM#925.2, 926a.2, 928-930, 931.2, 933, 942.2, 951.2, 964.2	160	145
PS8	1991 (3)	15,000	KM#977, 991-992	—	500
PS10	1992 (3)	2,000	KM#1007, 1010-1011	—	200
PS9	1992 (11)	15,000	KM#925.2, 926a.2, 928-930, 931-2, 933, 942.2, 951.1, 964.2, 1008.2	—	125
PS11	1993 (11)	10,000	KM#925.1, 926a.1, 928-930, 931.2, 933, 942.1, 964.1, 961.1, 1008.2	—	135
PS12	1994 (11)	10,000	KM#925.2, 926a.2, 928-930, 931.2, 933, 942.2, 951.1, 964.2, 1008.2, fish privy mark	—	135
PS13	1995 (11)	10,000	KM#925.2, 926a.2, 928-930, 931.2, 933, 942.2, 951.1, 964.2, 1008.2	—	135
PS14	1996 (11)	8,000	KM#925.2, 926a.2, 928-930, 931.2, 933, 942.2, 951.1, 964.2, 1008.2	—	140
PS15	1997 (11)	10,000	KM#925.2, 926a.2, 928, 930, 931.2, 933, 942.2, 951.1, 964.2, 1008.2	—	135
PS16	1998 (11)	—	KM#925.2, 926a.2, 928, 930, 931.2, 933, 942.2, 951.1, 964.2, 1008.2	—	135
PS17	1999 (11)	—	KM#925.2, 926a.2, 928, 930, 941.2, 933, 942.2, 951.1, 964.2, 1008.2	—	135
PS19	1999 (8)	15,000	KM#1282-1289	59.00	110
PS18	2000 (11)	—	KM#925.2, 926a.2, 928, 930, 931.2, 933, 942.2, 951.1, 964.2, 1008.2	—	135
PS20	2000 (8)	15,000	KM#1282-1289	59.00	110
PS21	2001 (8)	15,000	KM#1282-1289	59.00	110

KM#	Date	Mintage	Identification	Issue Price	Mkt Val
PS22	2002 (8)	40,000	KM#1282-1289	59.00	95.00

SPECIMEN FDC SETS (FLEUR DE COIN)

KM#	Date	Mintage	Identification	Issue Price	Mkt Val
SS1	1964 (7)	25,600	KM#925-930, 939	4.00	7.00
SS2	1965 (7)	35,000	KM#925-926, 928-932	7.60	12.00
SS3	1966 (8)	7,171	KM#925-926, 928-933	9.00	45.00
SS4	1967 (8)	2,305	KM#925-926, 928-933	10.00	150
SS5	1968 (8)	3,000	With box KM#925-926, 928-933	10.00	350
SS5A	1968 (8)	I.A.	KM#925-926, 928-933 without box	—	75.00
SS6	1969 (8)	6,050	KM#925-926, 928-933	10.00	75.00
SS7	1970 (8)	10,000	KM#925, 926a, 928-933	9.00	20.00
SS8	1971 (8)	12,000	KM#925, 926a, 928-933	9.00	20.00
SS9	1972 (8)	15,000	KM#925, 926a, 928-933	9.00	20.00
SS10	1973 (8)	79,000	KM#925, 926a, 928-933	12.00	17.00
SS11	1974 (9)	98,800	KM#925, 926a, 928-931, 933, 940-941	31.00	15.00
SS12	1975 (9)	52,000	KM#925, 926a, 928-931, 933, 940-941	35.00	20.00
SS13	1976 (9)	35,700	KM#925, 926a, 928-931, 933, 940-941	35.00	20.00
SS14	1977 (9)	25,000	KM#925, 926a, 928-931, 933, 940-941	36.00	25.00
SS15	1978 (9)	24,000	KM#925, 926a, 928-931, 933, 940-941	39.00	30.00
SS16	1979 (10)	40,500	KM#925, 926a, 928-931, 933, 940--942	55.00	45.00
SS17	1980 (10)	60,000	KM#925, 926a, 928-931, 933, 940-942	90.00	40.00
SS18	1981 (9)	26,000	KM#925, 926a, 928-931, 933, 940, 942	—	35.00
SS19	1982 (11)	27,500	KM#925, 926a, 928-931, 933, 940, 942, 950-951	—	60.00
SS20	1983 (12)	16,561	KM#925, 926a, 928-931, 933, 940, 942, 951-953	—	75.00
SS21	1984 (12)	13,388	KM#825, 926a, 928-931, 933, 940, 942, 951, 954, 955	—	125
SS22	1985 (12)	12,224	KM#925, 926a, 928-931, 933, 940, 942, 951, 956-957	—	100
SS23	1986 (12)	13,000	KM#925.1, 926a.1, 928-931.1, 933, 942.1, 951, 958, 959, 960	—	110
SS24	1987 (12)	15,000	KM#925.1, 926a.1, 928-931.1, 933, 940, 942.1, 951, 961, 962	68.00	110
SS25	1987 (2)	—	KMP991-991a, Proof and BU	120	35.00
SS26	1988 (13)	13,000	KM#925.1, 926a.1, 928-931.1, 933, 941.1, 951, 963-966	—	120
SS27	1989 (14)	10,000	KM#925.1, 926a.1, 928-931.1, 933, 942.1, 951, 964, 967-970	—	130
SS28	1990 (13)	10,000	KM#925.1, 926a.1, 928-931.1, 933, 942.1, 951, 964, 980-982	—	120
SS29	1990 (11)	10,000	KM#925.1, 926a.1, 928-931.1, 933, 942.1, 951, 964, 982	—	110

FRENCH AFARS & ISSAS

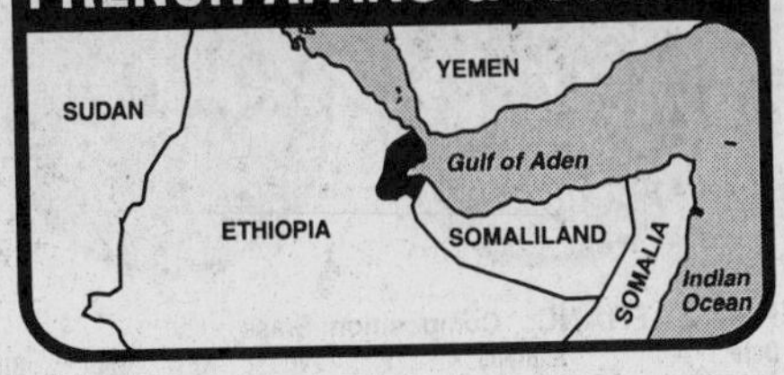

MINT MARKS
- Paris (privy marks only)

MONETARY SYSTEM
100 Centimes = 1 Franc

Note
For later coinage, see Djibouti
For earlier coinage, see French Somaliland

FRENCH COLONY

DECIMAL COINAGE

KM# 16 FRANC **Composition:** Aluminum

Date	Mintage	F	VF	XF	Unc	BU
1969(a)	100,000	1.00	2.00	3.50	6.00	—
1971(a)	100,000	1.00	2.00	3.50	6.00	—
1975(a)	300,000	0.75	1.25	2.00	3.00	—

KM# 13 2 FRANCS **Composition:** Aluminum

Date	Mintage	F	VF	XF	Unc	BU
1968	100,000	1.00	2.00	3.50	6.00	—
1975	180,000	0.75	1.50	2.50	5.00	—

KM# 14 5 FRANCS **Composition:** Aluminum

Date	Mintage	F	VF	XF	Unc	BU
1968(a)	100,000	1.00	2.00	3.50	6.00	—
1975(a)	300,000	0.75	1.25	2.00	4.00	—

KM# 17 10 FRANCS **Composition:** Aluminum-Bronze

Date	Mintage	F	VF	XF	Unc	BU
1969(a)	100,000	1.50	3.00	6.00	9.00	—
1970(a)	300,000	1.00	2.00	4.00	7.00	—
1975(a)	360,000	0.75	1.50	3.00	5.00	—

KM# 15 20 FRANCS **Composition:** Aluminum-Bronze

Date	Mintage	F	VF	XF	Unc	BU
1968(a)	300,000	1.50	2.50	4.50	8.00	—
1975(a)	300,000	1.25	2.00	4.00	7.00	—

KM# 18 50 FRANCS **Composition:** Copper Nickel
Reverse: Pair of dromedary camels, denomination

Date	Mintage	F	VF	XF	Unc	BU
1970(a)	300,000	1.50	3.00	6.00	10.00	—
1975(a)	180,000	1.50	3.00	6.00	10.00	—

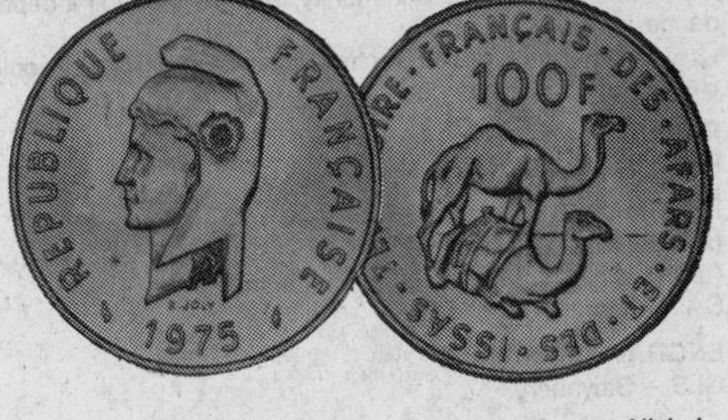

KM# 19 100 FRANCS **Composition:** Copper-Nickel
Reverse: Pair of dromedary camels, denomination

Date	Mintage	F	VF	XF	Unc	BU
1970(a)	600,000	2.50	4.00	7.00	11.50	—
1975(a)	400,000	2.50	4.50	7.50	12.50	—

ESSAIS

Standard metals unless otherwise noted

KM#	Date	Mintage	Identification	Issue Price	Mkt Val
E1	1968(a)	1,700	2 Francs. KM13.	—	15.00
E2	1968(a)	1,700	5 Francs. KM14.	—	20.00
E3	1968(a)	1,700	20 Francs. KM15.	—	25.00
E4	1969(a)	1,700	Franc. KM16.	—	20.00
E5	1969(a)	1,700	10 Francs. KM17.	—	25.00
E6	1970(a)	1,700	50 Francs. KM18.	—	30.00
E7	1970(a)	1,700	100 Francs. KM19.	—	35.00

FRENCH EQUATORIAL AFRICA

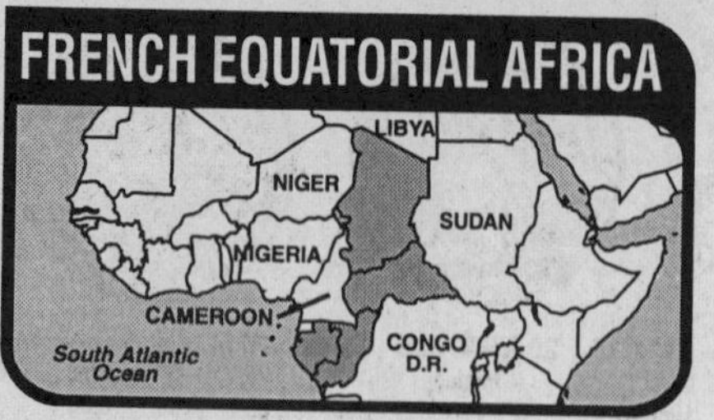

French Equatorial Africa, an area consisting of four self governing dependencies (Middle Congo, Ubangi-Shari, Chad and Gabon) in West-Central Africa, had an area of 969,111 sq. mi. (2,509,987 sq. km.). Capital: Brazzaville. The area, rich in natural resources, exported cotton, timber, coffee, cacao, diamonds and gold.

Little is known of the history of these parts of Africa prior to French occupation - which began with no thought of territorial acquisition. France's initial intent was simply to establish a few supply stations along the west coast of Africa to service the warships assigned to combat the slave trade in the early part of the 19th century. French settlement began in 1839. Gabon (then Gabun) and the Middle Congo were secured between 1885 and 1891; Chad and Ubangi-Shari between 1894 and 1897. The four colonies were joined to form French Equatorial Africa in 1910. The dependencies were changed from colonies to territories within the French Union in 1946, and all the inhabitants were made French citizens. In 1958 they voted to become autonomous republics within the new French Community, and attained full independence in 1960.

For later coinage see Central African States, Congo Peoples Republic, Gabon and Chad.

RULERS
French, until 1960

MINT MARKS
(a) - Paris, privy marks only
(t) - Poissy, privy marks only, thunderbolt
SA - Pretoria (1942-1943)

ENGRAVERS INITIALS
GLS – Steynberg

MONETARY SYSTEM
100 Centimes = 1 Franc

FRENCH COLONY

DECIMAL COINAGE

KM# 3 5 CENTIMES **Composition:** Aluminum-Bronze
Note: Similar to 10 Centimes, KM#4.

Date	F	VF	XF	Unc	BU
1943	90.00	150	325	650	—

Note: Not released for circulation

KM# 4 10 CENTIMES **Composition:** Aluminum-Bronze

Date	F	VF	XF	Unc	BU
1943	75.00	100	160	375	—

Note: Not released for circulation

KM# 5 25 CENTIMES **Composition:** Aluminum-Bronze
Note: Similar to 10 Centimes, KM#4.

Date	F	VF	XF	Unc	BU
1943	175	300	500	825	—

Note: Not released for circulation

KM# 1 50 CENTIMES **Composition:** Brass

Date	Mintage	F	VF	XF	Unc	BU
1942SA	8,000,000	1.50	3.00	8.00	20.00	25.00

KM# 1a 50 CENTIMES **Composition:** Bronze

Date	Mintage	F	VF	XF	Unc	BU
1943SA	16,000,000	1.25	2.50	7.00	18.00	25.00

KM# 2 FRANC **Composition:** Brass

Date	Mintage	F	VF	XF	Unc	BU
1942SA	3,000,000	2.00	3.50	10.00	22.50	30.00

KM# 2a FRANC **Composition:** Bronze

Date	Mintage	F	VF	XF	Unc	BU
1943SA	6,000,000	1.75	2.75	9.00	20.00	30.00

KM# 6 FRANC **Composition:** Aluminum

Date	Mintage	F	VF	XF	Unc	BU
1948(a)	15,000,000	0.15	0.25	0.50	2.00	—

KM# 7 2 FRANCS **Composition:** Aluminum

Date	Mintage	F	VF	XF	Unc	BU
1948(a)	5,040,000	0.25	0.50	1.50	4.00	—

TOKEN COINAGE

Middle Congo

KM# Tn1 NON-DENOMINATED **Composition:** Aluminum **Reverse:** Elephant walking left

Date	F	VF	XF	Unc	BU
1925(t)	35.00	65.00	115	300	—

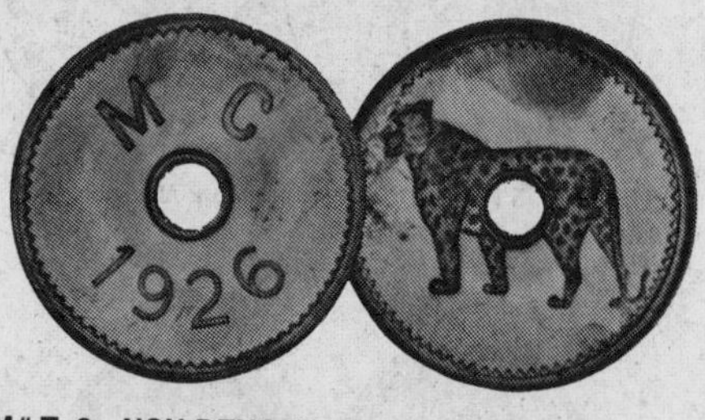

KM# Tn2 NON-DENOMINATED **Composition:** Aluminum **Reverse:** Leopard walking left

Date	F	VF	XF	Unc	BU
1926	40.00	75.00	150	325	—

ESSAIS

Standard metals unless otherwise noted

KM#	Date	Mintage	Identification	Mkt Val
E1	1948(a)	2,000	Franc. Copper-Nickel. KM#7	30.00
E2	1948(a)	2,000	2 Francs. Copper-Nickel. KM#7	35.00

PIEFORTS WITH ESSAI

Standard metals unless otherwise noted

KM#	Date	Mintage	Identification	Mkt Val
PE1	1948(a)	104	Franc. KM#6	65.00
PE2	1948(a)	104	2 Francs. KM#7	80.00

FRENCH INDO-CHINA

French Indo-China, made up of the protectorates of Annam, Tonkin, Cambodia and Laos and the colony of Cochin-China was located on the Indo-Chinese peninsula of Southeast Asia. The colony had an area of 286,194 sq. mi. (741,242 sq. km.). and a population of 30 million. Principal cities: Saigon, Haiphong, Vientiane, Pnom-Penh and Hanoi.

The forebears of the modern Indo-Chinese people originated in the Yellow River Valley of Northern China. From there, they were driven into the Indo-Chinese peninsula by the Han Chinese. The Chinese followed southward in the second century B.C., conquering the peninsula and ruling it until 938, leaving a lingering heritage of Chinese learning and culture. Indo-Chinese independence was basically maintained until the arrival of the French in the mid-19th century who established control over all of Vietnam, Laos and Cambodia. Activities directed toward obtaining self-determination accelerated during the Japanese occupation of World War II. The dependencies were changed from colonies to territories within the French Union in 1946, and all the inhabitants were made French citizens.

In Aug. of 1945, an uprising erupted involving the French and Vietnamese Nationalists, culminated in the French military disaster at Dien Bien Phu (May, 1954) and the subsequent Geneva Conference that brought an end to French colonial rule in Indo-China.

For later coinage see Kampuchea, Laos and Vietnam.

RULERS
French, until 1954

MINT MARKS
A - Paris
(a) - Paris, privy marks only
B - Beaumont-le-Roger
C - Castlesarrasin
H - Heaton, Birmingham
(p) - Thunderbolt - Poissy
S - San Francisco, U.S.A.
None - Osaka, Japan
None - Hanoi, Tonkin

MONETARY SYSTEM
5 Sapeques = 1 Cent
100 Cents = 1 Piastre

FRENCH COLONY

STANDARD COINAGE

KM# 6 SAPEQUE **Composition:** Bronze

Date	Mintage	F	VF	XF	Unc	BU
1901A	4,843,000	2.50	7.50	15.00	70.00	—
1902A	2,500,000	7.50	20.00	40.00	125	—

KM# 25 1/4 CENT **Composition:** Zinc **Note:** Lead counterfeits dated 1941 and 1942 are known.

Date	Mintage	F	VF	XF	Unc	BU
1942	221,800,000	8.00	15.00	35.00	75.00	—
1943	279,450,000	15.00	35.00	55.00	125	—
1944	46,122,000	150	250	325	1,000	—

KM# 20 1/2 CENT **Composition:** Bronze

Date	Mintage	F	VF	XF	Unc	BU
1935(a)	26,365,000	0.25	0.50	2.00	10.00	—
1936(a)	23,635,000	0.25	0.50	2.00	10.00	—
1937(a)	10,244,000	0.50	1.50	5.00	15.00	—
1938(a)	16,665,000	0.25	0.75	2.50	12.00	—

Date	Mintage	F	VF	XF	Unc	BU
1939(a)	17,305,000	0.25	0.75	2.50	12.00	—
1940(a)	11,218,000	4.00	8.00	20.00	40.00	—

KM# 20a 1/2 CENT **Composition:** Zinc

Date	Mintage	F	VF	XF	Unc	BU
1939(a)	185,000	100	200	300	600	—
1940(a)	—	200	300	400	725	—

KM# 8 CENT **Composition:** Bronze

Date	Mintage	F	VF	XF	Unc	BU
1901	9,750,000	2.00	3.00	7.50	25.00	—
1902	5,050,000	3.00	5.00	10.00	40.00	—
1903	8,000,000	2.50	4.00	8.00	30.00	—
1906	2,000,000	5.00	8.00	25.00	85.00	—

KM# 12.1 CENT **Composition:** Bronze

Date	Mintage	F	VF	XF	Unc	BU
1908	3,000,000	10.00	20.00	55.00	235	—
1909	5,000,000	20.00	40.00	80.00	275	—
1910	7,703,000	1.00	4.00	10.00	25.00	—
1911	15,234,000	0.75	3.00	10.00	20.00	—
1912	17,027,000	0.75	3.00	10.00	20.00	—
1913	3,945,000	2.00	7.00	18.00	45.00	—
1914	11,027,000	0.75	3.00	15.00	30.00	—
1916	1,312,000	8.00	15.00	28.00	50.00	—
1917	9,762,000	1.00	4.00	10.00	20.00	—
1918	2,372,000	6.00	12.50	25.00	50.00	—
1919	9,148,000	1.00	4.00	7.50	20.00	—
1920	18,305,000	0.75	3.00	5.00	12.50	—
1921	14,722,000	0.75	2.00	3.00	10.00	—
1922	8,850,000	1.00	3.00	5.00	20.00	—
1923	1,079,000	20.00	40.00	65.00	175	—
1926	11,672,000	0.75	2.00	4.00	10.00	—
1927	3,328,000	5.00	10.00	25.00	50.00	—
1930	4,682,000	1.25	2.75	5.00	10.00	—
1931 Torch privy mark	5,318,000	20.00	35.00	100	350	—
1931 Wing privy mark	Inc. above	30.00	60.00	150	450	—
1937	8,902,000	0.25	0.50	1.50	8.00	—
1938	15,499,000	0.25	0.50	1.00	6.00	—
1939	15,599,000	0.25	0.50	1.00	6.00	—

KM# 12.2 CENT **Composition:** Bronze **Note:** Without mint mark.

Date	Mintage	F	VF	XF	Unc	BU
1920	13,290,000	1.00	2.50	5.00	17.50	—
1921	1,610,000	35.00	70.00	225	450	—

KM# 12.3 CENT **Composition:** Bronze

Date	Mintage	F	VF	XF	Unc	BU
1922(p)	9,476,000	1.00	1.75	5.00	12.00	—
1923(p)	27,891,000	0.50	0.75	1.50	7.50	—

KM# 24.3 CENT **Composition:** Zinc **Note:** Vichy Government issue. Type 2: Rosette on Phrygian cap. Variety 2: 11 petals.

Date	F	VF	XF	Unc	BU
1940	5.00	12.00	25.00	60.00	—
1941	2.00	5.00	12.00	40.00	—

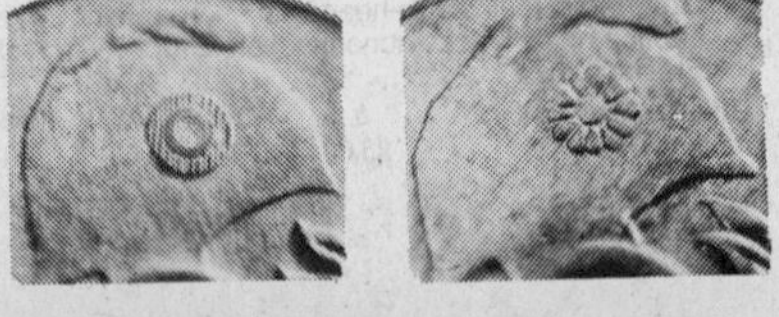

KM# 24.1 CENT **Composition:** Zinc **Note:** Vichy Government issue, circles and rosette. Type 1: Circles on Phrygian cap.

Date	Mintage	F	VF	XF	Unc	BU
1940	1,990,000	5.00	8.00	20.00	45.00	—

KM# 24.2 CENT **Composition:** Zinc **Note:** Vichy Government issue. Type 2: Rosette on Phrygian cap with 12 petals. Variety 2 with 11 petals.

Date	F	VF	XF	Unc	BU
1940	5.00	8.00	20.00	50.00	—

KM# 26 CENT **Composition:** Aluminum **Note:** Edge varieties exist - plain, grooved and partially grooved.

Date	F	VF	XF	Unc	BU
1943	0.25	0.50	1.00	3.00	—

KM# 18 (KM18.1) 5 CENTS **Weight:** 5.0000 g. **Composition:** Copper-Nickel **Note:** 1.6 milimeters thick.

Date	Mintage	F	VF	XF	Unc	BU
1923(a)	1,611,000	3.00	5.00	15.00	40.00	—
1923(a)	1,611,000	3.00	5.00	15.00	40.00	—
1924(a)	3,389,000	1.00	3.00	12.00	35.00	—
1924(a)	3,389,000	1.00	3.00	12.00	35.00	—
1925(a)	6,000,000	1.00	1.75	7.00	20.00	—
1925(a)	6,000,000	1.00	1.75	7.00	20.00	—
1930(a)	4,000,000	1.00	2.00	8.00	25.00	—
1930(a)	4,000,000	1.00	2.00	8.00	25.00	—
1937(a)	10,000,000	0.50	1.00	4.00	15.00	—
1937(a)	10,000,000	0.50	1.00	4.00	15.00	—
1938(a)	—	10.00	25.00	75.00	160	—
1938(a)	—	10.00	25.00	75.00	160	—
1938(a) Proof	—	Value: 275				
1938(a) Proof	—	Value: 275				

KM# 18.1a 5 CENTS **Weight:** 4.0000 g. **Composition:** Nickel-Brass **Note:** 1.3 milimeters thick.

Date	Mintage	F	VF	XF	Unc	BU
1938(a)	50,569,000	0.25	0.50	1.00	5.00	—
1939(a)	38,501,000	0.25	0.50	1.00	5.00	—

KM# 27 5 CENTS **Composition:** Aluminum **Note:** Vichy Government issue. Edge varieties exist: reeded - rare, plain, grooved, and partially grooved.

Date	F	VF	XF	Unc	BU
1943A	0.25	0.50	1.50	4.00	—

KM# 30.1 5 CENTS **Composition:** Aluminum

Date	Mintage	F	VF	XF	Unc	BU
1946(a)	28,000,000	0.25	0.60	1.00	5.00	—

KM# 30.2 5 CENTS **Composition:** Aluminum

Date	Mintage	F	VF	XF	Unc	BU
1946B	22,000,000	0.25	0.60	1.00	5.00	—

KM# 9 10 CENTS **Weight:** 2.7000 g. **Composition:** 0.8350 Silver .0725 oz. ASW **Rev. Legend:** TITRE 0.835. POIDS 2 GR. 7

Date	Mintage	F	VF	XF	Unc	BU
1901	2,950,000	7.00	25.00	60.00	200	—
1902	7,050,000	4.00	12.00	30.00	125	—
1903	1,300,000	12.00	30.00	80.00	325	—
1908	1,000,000	50.00	100	200	575	—
1909	1,000,000	30.00	75.00	130	425	—

Date	Mintage	F	VF	XF	Unc	BU
1910	2,689,000	25.00	60.00	100	350	—
1911	2,311,000	25.00	40.00	80.00	325	—
1912	2,500,000	25.00	35.00	70.00	275	—
1913	4,847,000	7.50	12.50	30.00	125	—
1914	2,667,000	10.00	30.00	60.00	175	—
1916	2,000,000	10.00	30.00	60.00	185	—
1917	1,500,000	25.00	50.00	100	300	—
1919	1,500,000	30.00	60.00	125	350	—

KM# 14 10 CENTS **Weight:** 3.0000 g. **Composition:** 0.4000 Silver .0386 oz. ASW **Reverse:** Without fineness indicated **Note:** Without mint mark.

Date	Mintage	F	VF	XF	Unc	BU
1920	10,000,000	10.00	15.00	40.00	100	—

KM# 16.1 10 CENTS **Weight:** 2.7000 g. **Composition:** 0.6800 Silver .0590 oz. ASW **Rev. Legend:** TITRE 0.680 POIDS 2 GR. 7

Date	Mintage	F	VF	XF	Unc	BU
1921A	12,516,000	1.50	3.00	9.00	25.00	—
1922A	22,381,000	1.50	3.00	9.00	25.00	—
1923A	21,755,000	1.50	3.00	9.00	25.00	—
1924A	2,816,000	2.00	5.00	16.50	45.00	—
1925A	4,909,000	1.75	3.50	15.00	35.00	—
1927A	6,471,000	2.50	7.00	17.50	40.00	—
1928A	1,593,000	25.00	70.00	150	460	—
1929A	5,831,000	1.50	3.00	10.00	30.00	—
1930A	6,608,000	1.50	3.00	10.00	30.00	—
1931A Proof	100	Value: 325				

KM# 16.2 10 CENTS **Weight:** 2.7000 g. **Composition:** 0.6800 Silver .0590 oz. ASW **Rev. Legend:** TITRE 0.680 POIDS 2 GR. 7

Date	Mintage	F	VF	XF	Unc	BU
1937(a)	25,000,000	1.00	1.50	3.00	8.00	—

KM# 21.1 10 CENTS **Composition:** Nickel **Note:** These coins have no dots left and right of date and are magnetic.

Date	Mintage	F	VF	XF	Unc	BU
1939(a)	16,841,000	0.25	0.50	1.00	5.00	—
1940(a)	25,505,000	0.25	0.50	1.00	5.00	—

KM# 21.1a 10 CENTS **Composition:** Copper-Nickel **Obverse:** Date without dots

Date	Mintage	F	VF	XF	Unc	BU
1941S	50,000,000	0.20	0.40	0.75	5.00	—

KM# 21.2 10 CENTS **Composition:** Copper-Nickel **Obverse:** Date between two dots

Date	Mintage	F	VF	XF	Unc	BU
.1939.(a)	2,237,000	8.00	15.00	30.00	75.00	—

KM# 28.1 10 CENTS **Composition:** Aluminum

Date	Mintage	F	VF	XF	Unc	BU
1945(a)	40,170,000	0.25	0.50	1.00	4.50	—

KM# 28.2 10 CENTS **Composition:** Aluminum

Date	Mintage	F	VF	XF	Unc	BU
1945B	9,830,000	0.50	1.50	3.00	12.50	—

KM# 10 20 CENTS **Weight:** 5.4000 g. **Composition:** 0.8350 Silver .1450 oz. ASW

Date	Mintage	F	VF	XF	Unc	BU
1901	1,375,000	20.00	50.00	100	300	—
1902	3,525,000	7.50	15.00	40.00	175	—
1903	675,000	50.00	100	150	600	—
1908	500,000	100	250	400	850	—
1909	200,000	100	200	350	850	—
1911	2,340,000	7.50	15.00	35.00	120	—
1912	160,000	100	200	400	1,000	—
1913	1,252,000	50.00	100	150	400	—
1914	2,500,000	7.50	15.00	25.00	120	—
1916	1,000,000	12.50	35.00	100	225	—

KM# 13 20 CENTS **Composition:** 0.8350 Silver **Obverse:** KM#10 **Reverse:** KM#3a **Note:** Mule.

Date	F	VF	XF	Unc	BU
1909	100	250	650	1,200	—

KM# 15 20 CENTS **Weight:** 6.0000 g. **Composition:** 0.4000 Silver .0772 oz. ASW **Reverse:** Without fineness indicated **Note:** Without mint mark.

Date	Mintage	F	VF	XF	Unc	BU
1920	4,000,000	12.50	25.00	50.00	125	—

KM# 17.1 20 CENTS **Weight:** 5.4000 g. **Composition:** 0.6800 Silver .1181 oz. ASW **Rev. Legend:** TITRE O.680 POIDS 5 GR. 4

Date	Mintage	F	VF	XF	Unc	BU
1921A	3,663,000	2.00	4.00	10.00	30.00	—
1922A	5,812,000	2.00	4.00	8.00	30.00	—
1923A	7,109,000	2.00	4.00	8.00	30.00	—
1924A	1,400,000	6.00	12.50	28.50	75.00	—
1925A	2,556,000	4.00	10.00	22.50	60.00	—
1927A	3,245,000	3.00	7.50	15.00	30.00	—
1928A	794,000	10.00	20.00	60.00	200	—
1929A	644,000	15.00	30.00	80.00	225	—
1930A	5,576,000	1.50	3.00	5.00	15.00	—

KM# 17.2 20 CENTS **Weight:** 5.4000 g. **Composition:** 0.6800 Silver .1181 oz. ASW **Rev. Legend:** TITRE O.680 POIDS 5 GR. 4

Date	Mintage	F	VF	XF	Unc	BU
1937(a)	17,500,000	1.00	1.50	3.00	10.00	—

KM# 23 20 CENTS **Composition:** Nickel **Note:** Security edge.

Date	Mintage	F	VF	XF	Unc	BU
1939(a)	318,000	15.00	30.00	70.00	125	—

KM# 23a.1 20 CENTS **Composition:** Copper-Nickel **Edge:** Reeded

Date	Mintage	F	VF	XF	Unc	BU
1939(a) Date between dots	14,676,000	0.25	0.50	1.00	6.00	—

KM# 23a.2 20 CENTS **Composition:** Copper-Nickel **Edge:** Reeded

Date	Mintage	F	VF	XF	Unc	BU
1941S Date between dots	25,000,000	0.25	0.50	1.00	5.00	—

KM# 29.1 20 CENTS **Composition:** Aluminum

Date	Mintage	F	VF	XF	Unc	BU
1945(a)	15,412,000	0.50	1.00	2.50	10.00	—

KM# 29.2 20 CENTS **Composition:** Aluminum

Date	Mintage	F	VF	XF	Unc	BU
1945B	6,665,000	2.00	4.00	8.00	25.00	—

KM# 29.3 20 CENTS **Composition:** Aluminum

Date	Mintage	F	VF	XF	Unc	BU
1945C	22,423,000	0.50	1.00	3.00	15.00	—

KM# 4a.2 50 CENTS **Weight:** 13.5000 g. **Composition:** 0.9000 Silver .3906 oz. ASW **Rev. Legend:** TITRE 0.900. POIDS 13 GR. 5

Date	Mintage	F	VF	XF	Unc	BU
1936(a)	4,000,000	3.00	4.00	8.00	20.00	—

KM# 31 50 CENTS **Composition:** Copper-Nickel **Rev. Legend:** BRONZE DE NICKEL

Date	Mintage	F	VF	XF	Unc	BU
1946(a)	32,292,000	2.00	4.00	9.00	25.00	—

KM# 5a.1 PIASTRE **Weight:** 27.0000 g. **Composition:** 0.9000 Silver .7812 oz. ASW **Rev. Legend:** TITRE 0.900 POIDS 27 GR.

Date	Mintage	F	VF	XF	Unc	BU
1901A	3,150,000	10.00	15.00	25.00	150	—
1902A	3,327,000	10.00	15.00	25.00	150	—
1903A	10,077,000	10.00	12.50	20.00	110	—
1904A	5,751,000	10.00	15.00	20.00	130	—
1905A	3,561,000	10.00	15.00	20.00	130	—
1906A	10,194,000	10.00	12.50	20.00	100	—
1907A	14,062,000	10.00	12.50	20.00	100	—
1908A	13,986,000	10.00	12.50	20.00	100	—
1909A	9,201,000	10.00	12.50	20.00	95.00	—
1910A	761,000	25.00	55.00	120	320	—
1913A	3,244,000	10.00	15.00	22.50	125	—
1924A	2,831,000	10.00	12.50	22.50	150	—
1925A	2,882,000	10.00	12.50	22.50	150	—
1926A	6,383,000	10.00	12.50	20.00	100	—
1927A	8,183,999	10.00	12.50	20.00	100	—
1928A	5,290,000	10.00	12.50	20.00	100	—

KM# 5a.2 PIASTRE **Weight:** 27.0000 g. **Composition:** 0.9000 Silver .7812 oz. ASW **Note:** Without mint mark

Date	Mintage	F	VF	XF	Unc	BU
1921	4,850,000	10.00	12.50	25.00	150	—
1922	1,150,000	12.50	20.00	40.00	200	—

KM# 5a.3 PIASTRE **Weight:** 27.0000 g. **Composition:** 0.9000 Silver .7812 oz. ASW

Date	Mintage	F	VF	XF	Unc	BU
1921H	8,430,000	10.00	12.50	20.00	100	—
1922H	8,570,000	10.00	12.50	20.00	100	—

KM# 19 PIASTRE **Weight:** 20.0000 g. **Composition:** 0.9000 Silver .5787 oz. ASW

Date	Mintage	F	VF	XF	Unc	BU
1931(a)	16,000,000	9.00	12.00	17.50	47.50	—

BULLION COINAGE WWII

Previously listed under Laos and China-Yunnan-Burma. KM#1-2 were originally struck in Hanoi under official direction of the Colonial Vichy Finance Department for payments in the flourishing opium trade in Laos and Tonkin. The origins of KM#3-4 still remain speculative.

KM# A1.1 (KM1.1) 1/2 TAEL (Liang) **Weight:** 19.2000 g. **Composition:** Silver **Obverse:** Chinese character "Fu" (wealth) **Reverse:** Laotian and Chinese denomination **Edge:** Milled

Date	F	VF	XF	Unc	BU
ND(1943-4)	—	—	400	600	—
ND(1943-4)	—	—	400	600	—

KM# A1.2 (KM1.2) 1/2 TAEL (Liang) **Composition:** Silver **Note:** Weight varies: 18.75-18.86 grams.

Date	F	VF	XF	Unc	BU
ND(1943-44)	15.00	30.00	50.00	100	—
ND(1943-44)	15.00	30.00	50.00	100	—

KM# A2 TAEL **Weight:** 34.0000 g. **Composition:** Silver **Edge:** Milled **Note:** Previous KM#2.

Date	F	VF	XF	Unc	BU
ND(1943-4)	20.00	40.00	60.00	125	—

KM# A2a TAEL **Weight:** 38.2000 g. **Composition:** Silver **Edge:** Milled **Note:** Previous KM#2a.

Date	F	VF	XF	Unc	BU
ND(1943-4)	20.00	40.00	60.00	125	—

KM# A3 TAEL **Weight:** 38.2000 g. **Composition:** Silver **Obverse:** Small stag's head with short antlers **Reverse:** Laotian and Chinese denomination **Edge:** Plain **Note:** Previous KM#3.

Date	F	VF	XF	Unc	BU
ND(1943-4)	25.00	45.00	85.00	150	—

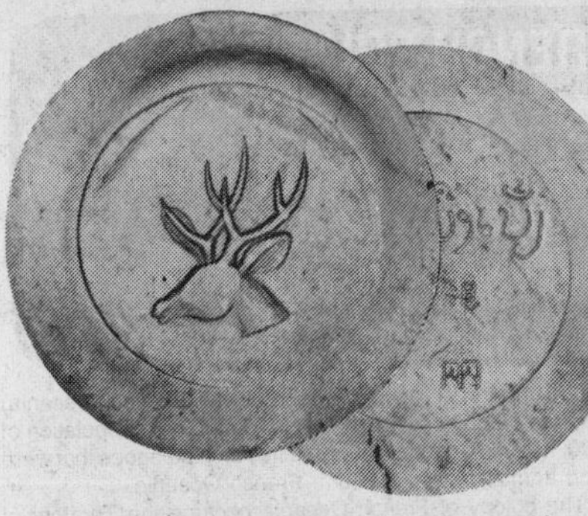

KM# A4 TAEL **Weight:** 38.2000 g. **Composition:** Silver **Obverse:** Larger stag's head with longer antlers **Reverse:** Smaller Chinese denomination **Edge:** Plain **Note:** Previous KM#4.

Date	F	VF	XF	Unc	BU
ND(1943-4)	—	—	650	900	—

FEDERATED STATES

French Union

STANDARD COINAGE

KM#32.1 PIASTRE **Composition:** Copper-Nickel **Note:** Security edge.

Date	Mintage	F	VF	XF	Unc	BU
1946(a)	2,520,000	7.50	12.50	20.00	85.00	—
1947(a)	261,000	10.00	17.50	35.00	135	—

KM# 32.2 PIASTRE **Composition:** Copper-Nickel **Edge:** Reeded **Note:** Similar coins dated 1946 with reverse legend: INDOCHINE - FRANCAISE are Essais.

Date	Mintage	F	VF	XF	Unc	BU
1947(a)	41,958,000	1.00	3.00	7.50	15.00	—

ESSAIS

Standard metals unless otherwise noted

KM#	Date	Mintage	Identification	Mkt Val
E7	1910	—	Cent. Copper-Nickel. ESSAI. KM#12.1	160
E8	1919	—	10 Cents. Fineness 0.700/0.835 incuse plus 0.700 incuse on field on reverse; KM#9.	250
E9	ND	—	20 Cents. Mule. Two reverses. KM#3.	—
E10	1923(p)	—	Cent. ESSAI in field; KM#12.1.	160
E11	1923(p)	—	Cent. ESSAI at rim; KM#12.1.	160

KM#	Date	Mintage	Identification	Mkt Val
E12	1923(a)	—	5 Cents. KM#18.1	120
E13	1928	—	20 Cents. Brass. Plain edge. KM#17.1	175
E14	1928(a)	—	20 Cents. Bronze. KM#17.1	185
E17	1930(a)	—	Piastre. Silver. Uniface.	4,650
E15	19(30a)	—	Cent. Silver. KM#12.1	625
E16	19(30a)	—	Cent. Aluminum-Bronze. KM#12.1	125
E19	19(31a)	—	10 Cents. Silver-Bronze. KM#16.1	325
E20	19(31)	—	20 Cents. Silver-Bronze.	1,100
E21	19(31a)	—	20 Cents. Silver-Bronze. KM#17.1	350

KM#	Date	Mintage	Identification	Mkt Val
E23	1(931a)	—	50 Cents. Silver-Bronze.	400

KM#	Date	Mintage	Identification	Mkt Val
E24	19(31a)	—	Piastre. Silver. KM#19	9,000
E25	19(31a)	—	Piastre. Silver-Bronze. KM#19	350
E18	19(31)	—	10 Cents. Medallic alignment.	—
E22	1(931)	—	50 Cents. Medallic alignment.	—

KM#	Date	Mintage	Identification	Mkt Val
E26	1931(a)	—	Piastre. Silver. KM#19	325
E27	1935(a)	—	1/2 Cent. KM#20	75.00
E28	1936(a)	—	50 Cents. Aluminum. KM#4a.2.	200
E29	1937(a)	—	10 Cents. Nickel. KM#16.2	125
E30	1937(a)	—	20 Cents. Silver. KM#17.2	300
E31	1937(a)	—	20 Cents. Nickel. KM#17.2	250
E32	1939(a)	—	10 Cents. KM#21	60.00
E33	1939(a)	—	20 Cents. Plain edge. KM#23	225
E34	1939(a)	—	20 Cents. Security edge; KM#23	150
E35	1939(a)	—	20 Cents. Reeded edge. KM#23a.1	130
E36	1940(a)	—	Cent. Zinc. KM#24.1	110
E37	1940(a)	—	Cent. Aluminum-Bronze. KM#24.1	60.00
E45	ND(1943)	—	Tael. Silver. KM#2.	—
E46	ND(1943)	—	1/2 Tael. Silver. KM#1	675

KM#	Date	Mintage	Identification	Mkt Val
E38	1945(a)	1,100	10 Cents. KM#28.1	20.00
E39	1945(a)	1,100	20 Cents. KM#29	25.00
E40	1946(a)	1,100	5 Cents. KM#30.1	30.00

KM#	Date	Mintage	Identification	Mkt Val
E41	1946(a)	1,100	50 Cents. KM#31	65.00

KM#	Date	Mintage	Identification	Mkt Val
E42	1946(a)	1,100	Piastre. Federation.	175

KM#	Date	Mintage	Identification	Mkt Val
E43	1946(a)	1,100	Piastre. Indochina. KM#32.1.	215

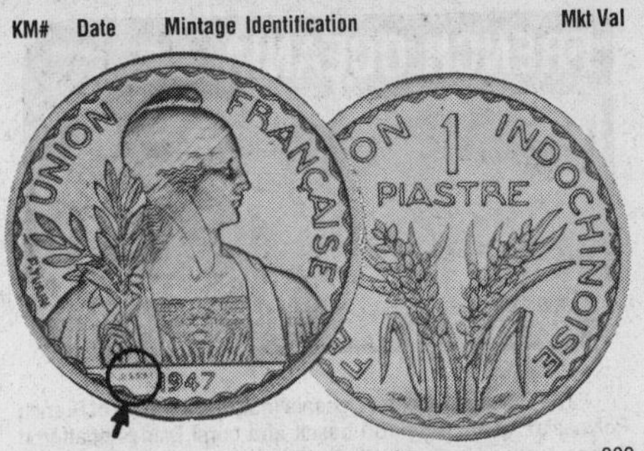

KM#	Date	Mintage	Identification	Mkt Val
E44	1947(a)	104	Piastre. Federation.	200

PIEFORTS

KM#	Date	Mintage	Identification	Mkt Val
P2	1908	—	Cent. Bronze. KM#12.1	250
P3	1920	—	20 Cents. Brass. Reeded edge. Medallic alignment. KM#15.	—
P4	1923	—	Cent. Filled center hole. KM#12.1.	—
P5	19(30)	—	Cent. Bronze. France Y#81. Filled center hole; KM#12.1.	—
P6	19(30)	—	Cent. Aluminum-Bronze. France Y#81. Filled center hole; KM#12.1.	—
P7	19(31)	—	20 Cents. Medallic alignment.	—
P8	1939	—	1/2 Cent. Zinc. KM#20a.	325

PIEFORTS WITH ESSAI

Double thickness - Standard metals unless otherwise noted

KM#	Date	Mintage	Identification	Mkt Val
PE1	1908	—	Cent. KM#12.1.	235
PE2	1923	—	5 Cents. KM#18.1.	175

KM#	Date	Mintage	Identification	Mkt Val
PE3	1931(a)	—	Piastre. KM#19.	2,000
PE4	1945(a)	104	10 Cents. KM#28.1.	100
PE5	1945(a)	104	20 Cents. KM#29.1.	140
PE6	1946(a)	104	5 Cents. KM#30.1.	100
PE7	1946(a)	104	50 Cents. KM#31.	150
PE8	1947(a)	104	Piastre. KM#32.	200

TRIAL STRIKES

KM#	Date	Mintage	Identification	Mkt Val
TS1	1921	—	Piastre. 0.9000 Silver. Without collar.	—
TS2	ND(1931)	—	Piastre. Uniface.	900

KM#	Date	Mintage	Identification	Mkt Val
TS3	1931	—	Piastre. Uniface.	750

FRENCH OCEANIA

The Colony of French Oceania (now the Territory of French Polynesia), comprising 130 basalt and coral islands scattered among five archipelagoes in the South Pacific, had an area of 1,544 sq. mi. (3,999 sq. km.). Capital: Papeete. The colony produced phosphates, copra and vanilla.

Tahiti of the Society Islands, the hub of French Oceania, was visited by Capt. Cook in 1769 and by Capt. Bligh in the Bounty 1788-89. The Society Islands were claimed by France in 1768, and in 1903 grouped with the Marquesas Islands, the Tuamotu Archipelago, the Gambier Islands and the Austral Islands under a single administrative head located at Papeete, Tahiti, to form the colony of French Oceania.

RULERS
French

MINT MARKS
- Paris, privy marks only

MONETARY SYSTEM
100 Centimes = 1 Franc

FRENCH COLONY

DECIMAL COINAGE

KM# 1 50 CENTIMES Composition: Aluminum

Date	Mintage	F	VF	XF	Unc	BU
1949(a)	795,000	0.50	0.75	1.50	3.50	—

KM# 2 FRANC Composition: Aluminum

Date	Mintage	F	VF	XF	Unc	BU
1949(a)	2,000,000	0.20	0.35	1.00	2.50	—

KM# 3 2 FRANCS Composition: Aluminum

Date	Mintage	F	VF	XF	Unc	BU
1949(a)	1,000,000	0.40	0.60	1.50	3.50	—

KM# 4 5 FRANCS Composition: Aluminum

Date	Mintage	F	VF	XF	Unc	BU
1952	2,000,000	0.50	0.75	1.50	4.50	—

ESSAIS

Standard metals unless otherwise noted

KM#	Date	Mintage	Identification	Issue Price	Mkt Val
E1	1948	1,100	50 Centimes.	—	20.00
E2	1948	1,100	50 Centimes.	—	20.00
E3	1948	1,100	Franc.	—	25.00
E4	1948	1,100	Franc.	—	25.00

KM#	Date	Mintage	Identification	Issue Price	Mkt Val
E5	1948	1,100	2 Francs.	—	30.00
E6	1948	1,100	2 Francs.	—	30.00
E7	1949(a)	2,000	50 Centimes. Copper-Nickel. KM1	—	20.00
E8	1949(a)	2,000	Franc. Copper-Nickel. KM2	—	25.00
E9	1949(a)	2,000	2 Francs. Copper-Nickel. KM3	—	30.00
E10	1952(a)	1,200	5 Francs. Copper-Nickel. KM4.	—	35.00

PIEFORTS WITH ESSAI

Double thickness - Standard metals unless otherwise noted

KM#	Date	Mintage	Identification	Issue Price	Mkt Val
PE1	1949(a)	104	50 Centimes.	—	50.00
PE2	1949(a)	104	Franc.	—	60.00
PE3	1949(a)	104	2 Francs.	—	75.00
PE4	1952(a)	104	5 Francs.	—	85.00

FRENCH POLYNESIA

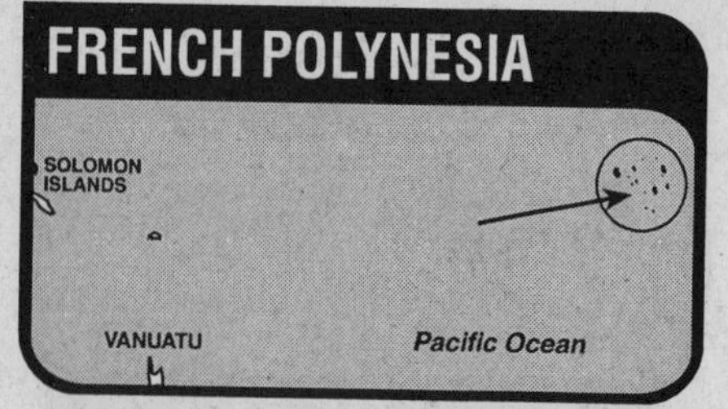

The Territory of French Polynesia (formerly French Oceania) has an area of 1,544 sq. mi. (3,941 sq. km.) and a population of 220,000. It is comprised of the same five archipelagoes that were grouped administratively to form French Oceania.

The colony of French Oceania became the Territory of French Polynesia by act of the French National Assembly in March, 1957. In Sept. of 1958 it voted in favor of the new constitution of the Fifth Republic, thereby electing to remain within the new French Community.

Picturesque, mountainous Tahiti, the setting of many tales of adventure and romance, is one of the most inspiringly beautiful islands in the world. Robert Louis Stevenson called it 'God's sweetest works'. It was there that Paul Gaugin, one of the pioneers of the Impressionist movement, painted the brilliant, exotic pictures that later made him famous. The arid coral atolls of Tuamotu comprise the most economically valuable area of French Polynesia. Pearl oysters thrive in the warm, limpid lagoons, and extensive portions of the atolls are valuable phosphate rock.

RULERS
French

MINT MARKS
- Paris, privy marks only

MONETARY SYSTEM
100 Centimes = 1 Franc

FRENCH COLONY

DECIMAL COINAGE

KM# 1 50 CENTIMES Composition: Aluminum

Date	Mintage	F	VF	XF	Unc	BU
1965(a)	895,000	0.10	0.25	0.50	1.50	—

KM# 2 FRANC Composition: Aluminum

Date	Mintage	F	VF	XF	Unc	BU
1965(a)	5,300,000	—	0.10	0.20	0.75	—

KM#11 FRANC Composition: Aluminum **Obv. Legend:** I. E. O. M. added flanking figure's feet

Date	Mintage	F	VF	XF	Unc	BU
1975(a)	2,000,000	—	0.10	0.15	0.45	—
1977(a)	1,000,000	—	0.10	0.15	0.45	—
1979(a)	1,500,000	—	0.10	0.15	0.45	—
1981(a)	1,000,000	—	0.10	0.15	0.45	—
1982(a)	2,000,000	—	0.10	0.15	0.45	—
1983(a)	2,200,000	—	0.10	0.15	0.45	—
1984(a)	1,500,000	—	0.10	0.15	0.45	—
1985(a)	2,000,000	—	0.10	0.15	0.45	—
1986(a)	2,000,000	—	0.10	0.15	0.45	—
1987(a)	2,000,000	—	0.10	0.15	0.45	—
1989(a)	1,000,000	—	0.10	0.15	0.45	—
1990(a)	—	—	0.10	0.15	0.45	—
1991(a)	—	—	0.10	0.15	0.35	—
1992(a)	—	—	0.10	0.15	0.35	—
1993(a)	—	—	0.10	0.15	0.35	—
1994(a)	—	—	0.10	0.15	0.25	—
1995(a)	—	—	0.10	0.15	0.25	—
1996(a)	—	—	0.10	0.15	0.25	—

Date	Mintage	F	VF	XF	Unc	BU
1997(a)	—	—	0.10	0.15	0.25	—
1999(a)	—	—	0.10	0.15	0.25	—

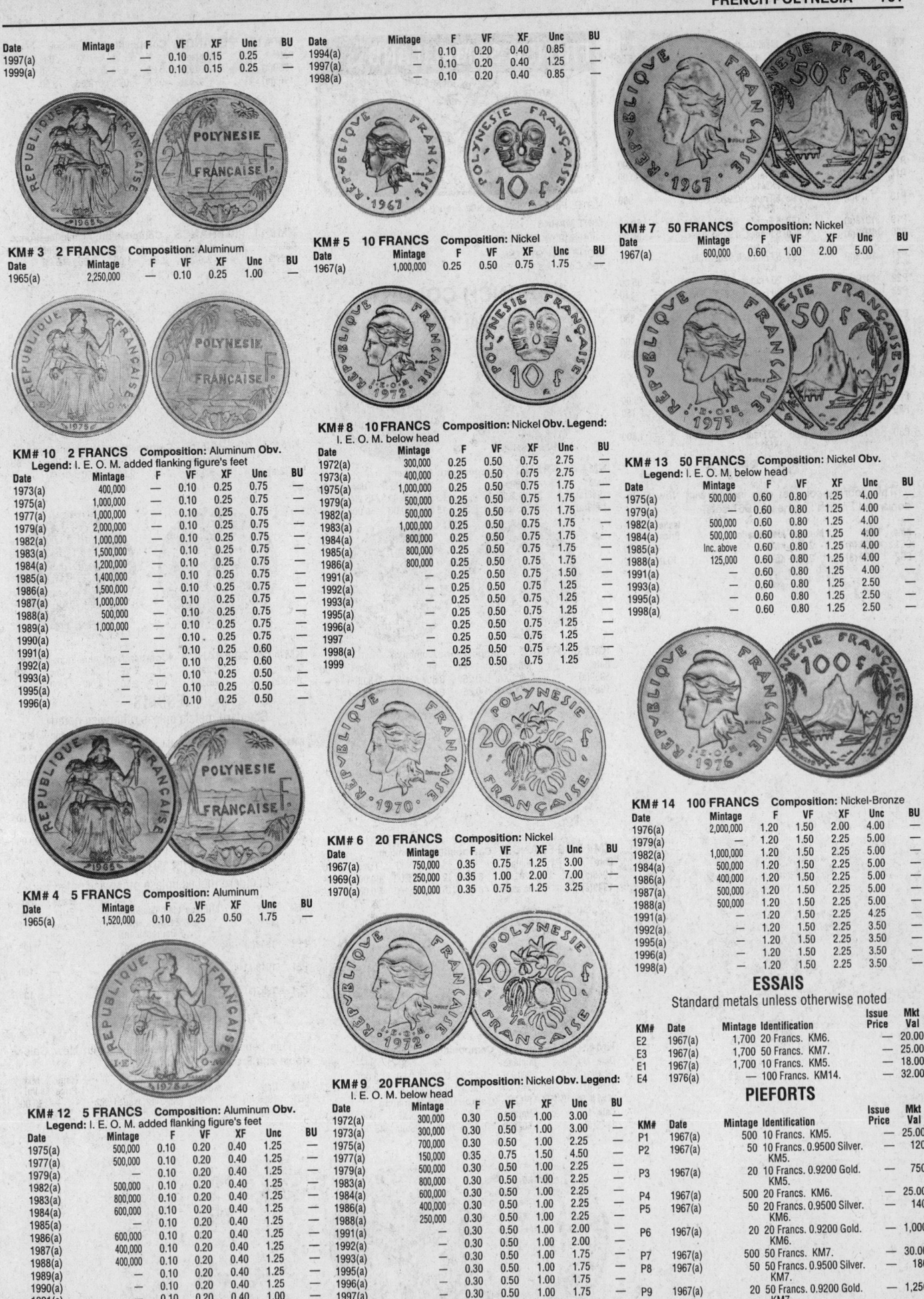

KM# 3 2 FRANCS **Composition:** Aluminum

Date	Mintage	F	VF	XF	Unc	BU
1965(a)	2,250,000	—	0.10	0.25	1.00	—

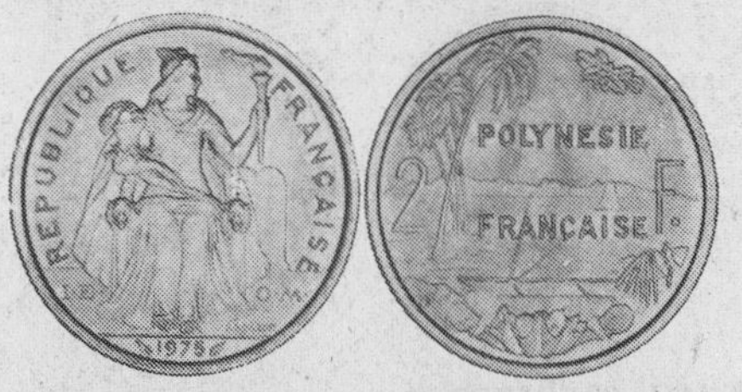

KM# 10 2 FRANCS **Composition:** Aluminum **Obv. Legend:** I. E. O. M. added flanking figure's feet

Date	Mintage	F	VF	XF	Unc	BU
1973(a)	400,000	—	0.10	0.25	0.75	—
1975(a)	1,000,000	—	0.10	0.25	0.75	—
1977(a)	1,000,000	—	0.10	0.25	0.75	—
1979(a)	2,000,000	—	0.10	0.25	0.75	—
1982(a)	1,000,000	—	0.10	0.25	0.75	—
1983(a)	1,500,000	—	0.10	0.25	0.75	—
1984(a)	1,200,000	—	0.10	0.25	0.75	—
1985(a)	1,400,000	—	0.10	0.25	0.75	—
1986(a)	1,500,000	—	0.10	0.25	0.75	—
1987(a)	1,000,000	—	0.10	0.25	0.75	—
1988(a)	500,000	—	0.10	0.25	0.75	—
1989(a)	1,000,000	—	0.10	0.25	0.75	—
1990(a)	—	—	0.10	0.25	0.75	—
1991(a)	—	—	0.10	0.25	0.60	—
1992(a)	—	—	0.10	0.25	0.60	—
1993(a)	—	—	0.10	0.25	0.50	—
1995(a)	—	—	0.10	0.25	0.50	—
1996(a)	—	—	0.10	0.25	0.50	—

KM# 4 5 FRANCS **Composition:** Aluminum

Date	Mintage	F	VF	XF	Unc	BU
1965(a)	1,520,000	0.10	0.25	0.50	1.75	—

KM# 12 5 FRANCS **Composition:** Aluminum **Obv. Legend:** I. E. O. M. added flanking figure's feet

Date	Mintage	F	VF	XF	Unc	BU
1975(a)	500,000	0.10	0.20	0.40	1.25	—
1977(a)	500,000	0.10	0.20	0.40	1.25	—
1979(a)	—	0.10	0.20	0.40	1.25	—
1982(a)	500,000	0.10	0.20	0.40	1.25	—
1983(a)	800,000	0.10	0.20	0.40	1.25	—
1984(a)	600,000	0.10	0.20	0.40	1.25	—
1985(a)	—	0.10	0.20	0.40	1.25	—
1986(a)	600,000	0.10	0.20	0.40	1.25	—
1987(a)	400,000	0.10	0.20	0.40	1.25	—
1988(a)	400,000	0.10	0.20	0.40	1.25	—
1989(a)	—	0.10	0.20	0.40	1.25	—
1990(a)	—	0.10	0.20	0.40	1.25	—
1991(a)	—	0.10	0.20	0.40	1.00	—
1992(a)	—	0.10	0.20	0.40	1.00	—
1993(a)	—	0.10	0.20	0.40	0.85	

Date	Mintage	F	VF	XF	Unc	BU
1994(a)	—	0.10	0.20	0.40	0.85	—
1997(a)	—	0.10	0.20	0.40	1.25	—
1998(a)	—	0.10	0.20	0.40	0.85	—

KM# 5 10 FRANCS **Composition:** Nickel

Date	Mintage	F	VF	XF	Unc	BU
1967(a)	1,000,000	0.25	0.50	0.75	1.75	—

KM# 8 10 FRANCS **Composition:** Nickel **Obv. Legend:** I. E. O. M. below head

Date	Mintage	F	VF	XF	Unc	BU
1972(a)	300,000	0.25	0.50	0.75	2.75	—
1973(a)	400,000	0.25	0.50	0.75	2.75	—
1975(a)	1,000,000	0.25	0.50	0.75	1.75	—
1979(a)	500,000	0.25	0.50	0.75	1.75	—
1982(a)	500,000	0.25	0.50	0.75	1.75	—
1983(a)	1,000,000	0.25	0.50	0.75	1.75	—
1984(a)	800,000	0.25	0.50	0.75	1.75	—
1985(a)	800,000	0.25	0.50	0.75	1.75	—
1986(a)	800,000	0.25	0.50	0.75	1.75	—
1991(a)	—	0.25	0.50	0.75	1.50	—
1992(a)	—	0.25	0.50	0.75	1.25	—
1993(a)	—	0.25	0.50	0.75	1.25	—
1995(a)	—	0.25	0.50	0.75	1.25	—
1996(a)	—	0.25	0.50	0.75	1.25	—
1997	—	0.25	0.50	0.75	1.25	—
1998(a)	—	0.25	0.50	0.75	1.25	—
1999	—	0.25	0.50	0.75	1.25	—

KM# 6 20 FRANCS **Composition:** Nickel

Date	Mintage	F	VF	XF	Unc	BU
1967(a)	750,000	0.35	0.75	1.25	3.00	—
1969(a)	250,000	0.35	1.00	2.00	7.00	—
1970(a)	500,000	0.35	0.75	1.25	3.25	—

KM# 9 20 FRANCS **Composition:** Nickel **Obv. Legend:** I. E. O. M. below head

Date	Mintage	F	VF	XF	Unc	BU
1972(a)	300,000	0.30	0.50	1.00	3.00	—
1973(a)	300,000	0.30	0.50	1.00	3.00	—
1975(a)	700,000	0.30	0.50	1.00	2.25	—
1977(a)	150,000	0.35	0.75	1.50	4.50	—
1979(a)	500,000	0.30	0.50	1.00	2.25	—
1983(a)	800,000	0.30	0.50	1.00	2.25	—
1984(a)	600,000	0.30	0.50	1.00	2.25	—
1986(a)	400,000	0.30	0.50	1.00	2.25	—
1988(a)	250,000	0.30	0.50	1.00	2.25	—
1991(a)	—	0.30	0.50	1.00	2.00	—
1992(a)	—	0.30	0.50	1.00	2.00	—
1993(a)	—	0.30	0.50	1.00	1.75	—
1995(a)	—	0.30	0.50	1.00	1.75	—
1996(a)	—	0.30	0.50	1.00	1.75	—
1997(a)	—	0.30	0.50	1.00	1.75	—
1998(a)	—	0.30	0.50	1.00	1.75	—

KM# 7 50 FRANCS **Composition:** Nickel

Date	Mintage	F	VF	XF	Unc	BU
1967(a)	600,000	0.60	1.00	2.00	5.00	—

KM# 13 50 FRANCS **Composition:** Nickel **Obv. Legend:** I. E. O. M. below head

Date	Mintage	F	VF	XF	Unc	BU
1975(a)	500,000	0.60	0.80	1.25	4.00	—
1979(a)	—	0.60	0.80	1.25	4.00	—
1982(a)	500,000	0.60	0.80	1.25	4.00	—
1984(a)	500,000	0.60	0.80	1.25	4.00	—
1985(a)	Inc. above	0.60	0.80	1.25	4.00	—
1988(a)	125,000	0.60	0.80	1.25	4.00	—
1991(a)	—	0.60	0.80	1.25	4.00	—
1993(a)	—	0.60	0.80	1.25	2.50	—
1995(a)	—	0.60	0.80	1.25	2.50	—
1998(a)	—	0.60	0.80	1.25	2.50	—

KM# 14 100 FRANCS **Composition:** Nickel-Bronze

Date	Mintage	F	VF	XF	Unc	BU
1976(a)	2,000,000	1.20	1.50	2.00	4.00	—
1979(a)	—	1.20	1.50	2.25	5.00	—
1982(a)	1,000,000	1.20	1.50	2.25	5.00	—
1984(a)	500,000	1.20	1.50	2.25	5.00	—
1986(a)	400,000	1.20	1.50	2.25	5.00	—
1987(a)	500,000	1.20	1.50	2.25	5.00	—
1988(a)	500,000	1.20	1.50	2.25	5.00	—
1991(a)	—	1.20	1.50	2.25	4.25	—
1992(a)	—	1.20	1.50	2.25	3.50	—
1995(a)	—	1.20	1.50	2.25	3.50	—
1996(a)	—	1.20	1.50	2.25	3.50	—
1998(a)	—	1.20	1.50	2.25	3.50	—

ESSAIS

Standard metals unless otherwise noted

KM#	Date	Mintage	Identification	Issue Price	Mkt Val
E2	1967(a)	1,700	20 Francs. KM6.	—	20.00
E3	1967(a)	1,700	50 Francs. KM7.	—	25.00
E1	1967(a)	1,700	10 Francs. KM5.	—	18.00
E4	1976(a)	—	100 Francs. KM14.	—	32.00

PIEFORTS

KM#	Date	Mintage	Identification	Issue Price	Mkt Val
P1	1967(a)	500	10 Francs. KM5.	—	25.00
P2	1967(a)	50	10 Francs. 0.9500 Silver. KM5.	—	120
P3	1967(a)	20	10 Francs. 0.9200 Gold. KM5.	—	750
P4	1967(a)	500	20 Francs. KM6.	—	25.00
P5	1967(a)	50	20 Francs. 0.9500 Silver. KM6.	—	140
P6	1967(a)	20	20 Francs. 0.9200 Gold. KM6.	—	1,000
P7	1967(a)	500	50 Francs. KM7.	—	30.00
P8	1967(a)	50	50 Francs. 0.9500 Silver. KM7.	—	180
P9	1967(a)	20	50 Francs. 0.9200 Gold. KM7.	—	1,250
P10	1979(a)	150	50 Centimes. KM11.	—	20.00

KM#	Date	Mintage	Identification	Issue Price	Mkt Val
P11	1979(a)	250	50 Centimes. 0.9250 Silver. KM11.	—	75.00
P12	1979(a)	93	50 Centimes. 0.9200 Gold. KM11.	—	425
P13	1979(a)	150	2 Francs. KM10.	—	30.00
P14	1979(a)	250	2 Francs. 0.9250 Silver. KM10.	—	85.00
P15	1979(a)	94	2 Francs. 0.9200 Gold. KM10.	—	650
P16	1979(a)	150	5 Francs. KM12.	—	40.00
P17	1979(a)	250	5 Francs. 0.9250 Silver. KM12.	—	90.00
P18	1979(a)	95	5 Francs. 0.9200 Gold. KM12.	—	900
P19	1979(a)	150	5 Francs. KM8.	—	50.00
P20	1979(a)	250	5 Francs. 0.9250 Silver. KM8.	—	90.00
P21	1979(a)	94	5 Francs. 0.9200 Gold. KM8.	—	675
P22	1979(a)	150	20 Francs. KM9.	—	55.00
P23	1979(a)	250	20 Francs. 0.9250 Silver. KM9.	—	110
P24	1979(a)	93	20 Francs. 0.9200 Gold. KM9.	—	850
P25	1979(a)	150	50 Francs. KM13.	—	60.00
P26	1979(a)	250	50 Francs. 0.9250 Silver. KM13.	—	130
P27	1979(a)	94	50 Francs. 0.9200 Gold. KM13.	—	925
P28	1979(a)	150	100 Francs. KM14.	—	75.00
P29	1979(a)	350	100 Francs. 0.9250 Silver. KM14.	—	150
P30	1979(a)	98	100 Francs. 0.9200 Gold. KM14.	—	1,300

"FDC" SETS

This fleur-de-coin set was issued with New Caledonia and French Polynesia 1967 sets.

KM#	Date	Mintage	Identification	Issue Price	Mkt Val
SS1	1965 (4)	2,200	KM1-4	—	7.00
SS2	1967 (3)	2,200	K5-7	10.00	17.00

FRENCH SOMALILAND

NOTE: For later coinage see French Afars & Issas.

MINT MARKS

- Paris (privy marks only)

MONETARY SYSTEM

100 Centimes = 1 Franc

FRENCH COLONY

DECIMAL COINAGE

KM# 4 FRANC Composition: Aluminum

Date	Mintage	F	VF	XF	Unc	BU
1948(a)	200,000	6.50	12.50	25.00	45.00	—
1949(a)	Inc. above	8.00	15.00	30.00	60.00	—

KM# 8 FRANC Composition: Aluminum

Date	Mintage	F	VF	XF	Unc	BU
1959(a)	500,000	0.25	0.50	1.50	3.00	—
1965(a)	200,000	0.35	0.60	2.00	4.00	—

KM# 5 2 FRANCS Composition: Aluminum

Date	Mintage	F	VF	XF	Unc	BU
1948(a)	200,000	6.50	12.50	25.00	60.00	—
1949(a)	Inc. above	8.00	15.00	30.00	70.00	—

KM# 9 2 FRANCS Composition: Aluminum

Date	Mintage	F	VF	XF	Unc	BU
1959(a)	200,000	0.25	0.75	2.50	5.00	—
1965(a)	240,000	0.25	0.75	2.50	5.00	—

KM# 6 5 FRANCS Composition: Aluminum

Date	Mintage	F	VF	XF	Unc	BU
1948(a)	500,000	5.00	10.00	25.00	45.00	—

KM# 10 5 FRANCS Composition: Aluminum

Date	Mintage	F	VF	XF	Unc	BU
1959(a)	500,000	0.25	0.75	2.50	5.50	—
1965(a)	200,000	0.25	0.75	3.00	6.50	—

KM# 11 10 FRANCS Composition: Aluminum-Bronze

Date	Mintage	F	VF	XF	Unc	BU
1965(a)	250,000	0.50	1.00	3.00	6.00	—

KM# 7 20 FRANCS Composition: Aluminum-Bronze

Date	Mintage	F	VF	XF	Unc	BU
1952(a)	500,000	1.25	2.50	4.50	10.00	—

KM# 12 20 FRANCS Composition: Aluminum-Bronze

Date	Mintage	F	VF	XF	Unc	BU
1965(a)	200,000	1.00	2.00	4.00	8.00	—

ESSAIS

Standard metals unless otherwise noted

KM#	Date	Mintage	Identification	Issue Price	Mkt Val
E2	1948(a)	2,000	2 Francs. Copper-Nickel. KM5.	—	15.00
E3	1948(a)	2,000	5 Francs. Copper-Nickel. KM6	—	18.00
E1	1948(a)	2,000	Franc. Copper-Nickel. KM4.	—	12.00
E4	1952(a)	1,200	20 Francs. (No Composition). KM7	—	22.00
E5	1965(a)	2,000	10 Francs. (No Composition). KM11	—	20.00

PIEFORTS WITH ESSAI

Standard metals unless otherwise noted

KM#	Date	Mintage	Identification	Issue Price	Mkt Val
PE2	1948(a)	104	2 Francs. (No Composition).	—	100
PE3	1948(a)	104	5 Francs. (No Composition).	—	125
PE1	1948(a)	104	Franc. (No Composition).	—	100
PE4	1952(a)	104	20 Francs. (No Composition).	—	125

"FDC" SETS

This fleur-de-coin set was issued with New Caledonia and French Polynesia 1967 sets.

KM#	Date	Mintage	Identification	Issue Price	Mkt Val
SS1	1965 (5)	1,898	KM#8-12; Issued with French Polynesia	—	30.00

FRENCH WEST AFRICA

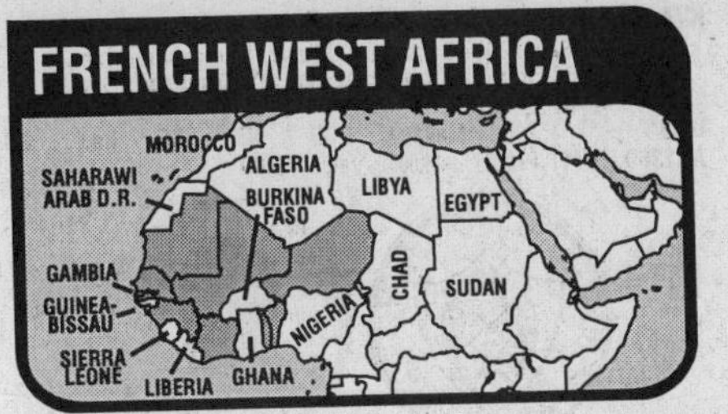

French West Africa (Afrique Occidentale Francaise), a former federation of French colonial territories on the northwest coast of Africa, had an area of 1,831,079 sq. mi. (4,742,495 sq. km.) and a population of about 17.4 million. Capital: Dakar. The constituent territories were Mauritania, Senegal, Dahomey, French Sudan, Ivory Coast, Upper Volta, Niger, French Guinea, and later on the mandated area of Togo. Peanuts, palm kernels, cacao, coffee and bananas were exported.

Prior to the mid-19th century, France, as the other European states, maintained establishments on the west coast of Africa for the purpose of trading in slaves and gum, but made no serious attempt at colonization. From 1854 onward, the coastal settlements were gradually extended into the interior until by the opening of the 20th century, acquisition ended and organization and development began. French West Africa was formed in 1895 by grouping the several colonies under one administration (at Dakar) while retaining a large measure of autonomy to each of the constituent territories. The inhabitants of French West Africa were made French citizens in 1946. With the exception of French Guinea, all of the colonies voted in 1958 to become autonomous members of the new French Community. French Guinea voted to become the fully independent Republic of Guinea. The present-day independent states are members of the "Union Monetaire Ouest-Africaine".<For later coinage see West African States.

RULERS
French

MINT MARKS
(a) - Paris, privy marks only
(L) - London

MONETARY SYSTEM
100 Centimes = 1 Franc
5 Francs = 1 Unit

FRENCH COLONY

COLONIAL COINAGE

KM# 1 50 CENTIMES **Composition:** Aluminum-Bronze

Date	Mintage	F	VF	XF	Unc	BU
1944(L)	10,000,000	2.00	4.00	10.00	28.00	—
1944(L) Proof	—	Value: 175				

KM# 2 FRANC **Composition:** Aluminum-Bronze

Date	Mintage	F	VF	XF	Unc	BU
1944(L)	15,000,000	1.00	2.00	5.00	20.00	—
1944(L) Proof	—	Value: 200				

KM# 3 FRANC **Composition:** Aluminum **Reverse:** Rhim gazelle facing

Date	Mintage	F	VF	XF	Unc	BU
1948(a)	30,110,000	0.15	0.20	0.35	1.00	—
1955(a)	5,200,000	0.20	0.35	0.50	1.50	—

KM# 4 2 FRANCS **Composition:** Aluminum **Reverse:** Rhim gazelle facing

Date	Mintage	F	VF	XF	Unc	BU
1948(a)	12,665,000	0.20	0.30	0.50	1.75	—
1955(a)	1,400,000	0.25	0.40	0.75	2.00	—

KM# 5 5 FRANCS **Composition:** Aluminum-Bronze **Reverse:** Rhim gazelle facing

Date	Mintage	F	VF	XF	Unc	BU
1956(a)	85,000,000	0.35	0.50	1.00	2.50	—

KM# 6 10 FRANCS **Composition:** Aluminum-Bronze **Reverse:** Rhim gazelle facing

Date	Mintage	F	VF	XF	Unc	BU
1956(a)	64,133,000	0.50	1.00	1.50	3.50	—

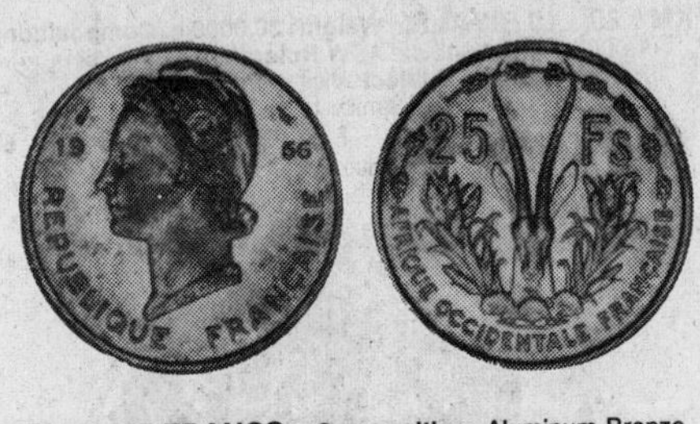

KM# 7 25 FRANCS **Composition:** Aluminum-Bronze **Reverse:** Rhim gazelle facing

Date	Mintage	F	VF	XF	Unc	BU
1956(a)	37,877,000	0.50	1.00	2.00	5.50	—

KM# 9 25 FRANCS **Composition:** Aluminum-Bronze **Reverse:** Rhim gazelle facing

Date	Mintage	F	VF	XF	Unc	BU
1957(a)	30,000	0.50	1.00	2.00	5.00	—

Note: Issued for circulation in French West Africa, including Togo

ESSAIS

Standard metals unless otherwise noted

KM#	Date	Mintage	Identification	Issue Price	Mkt Val
E1	1948(a)	2,000	Franc. Copper-Nickel. KM3.	—	25.00
E2	1948	2,000	2 Francs. Copper-Nickel. KM4.	—	30.00
E3	1956(a)	2,300	5 Francs. KM5	—	16.00
E4	1956(a)	2,300	10 Francs. KM6.	—	20.00
E5	1956(a)	2,300	25 Francs. KM7	—	22.00
e6	1957(a)	—	10 Francs. Aluminum-Bronze. KM8	—	20.00
e7	1957(a)	—	25 Francs. Aluminum-Bronze. KM9	—	22.00

PIEFORTS WITH ESSAI

Double thickness - Standard metals unless otherwise noted

KM#	Date	Mintage	Identification	Issue Price	Mkt Val
PE1	1948(a)	104	Franc. KM3	—	65.00
PE2	1948(a)	104	2 Francs. KM4.	—	75.00

AL FUJAIRAH

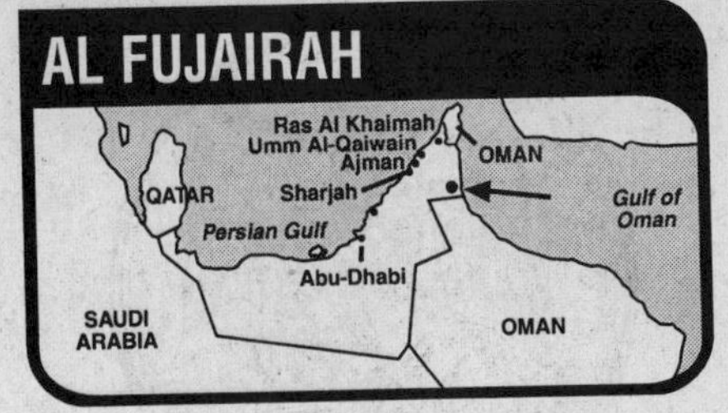

An original member of the United Arab Emirates, al-Fujairah is the only emirate that does not have territory on the Persian Gulf. It is on the eastern side of the "horn" of Oman. It has an estimated area of 450 sq. mi. (1200 sq. km.) and a population of 27,000. Al-Fujairah has been, historically a frequent rival of Sharjah. As recently as 1952 Great Britain recognized al-Fujairah as an autonomous state.

TITLES
al Fujaira(t) الفجيرة

RULERS
Muhammad bin Hamad al-Sharqi, 1952-74
Hamad bin Muhammad al-Sharqi, 1974--

EMIRATE

NON-CIRCULATING LEGAL TENDER COINAGE

KM# 1 RIYAL **Weight:** 3.0000 g. **Composition:** 1.0000 Silver .0964 oz. ASW **Ruler:** Muhammad bin Hamad al-Sharqi **Subject:** Desert Fort **Obverse:** Similar to KM#2

Date	Mintage	F	VF	XF	Unc	BU
AH1388 (1969) Proof	4,050	Value: 22.50				
AH1389 (1970) Proof	Inc. above	Value: 22.50				

KM# 2 2 RIYALS **Weight:** 6.0000 g. **Composition:** 1.0000 Silver .1928 oz. ASW **Ruler:** Muhammad bin Hamad al-Sharqi **Subject:** President Richard Nixon

Date	Mintage	F	VF	XF	Unc	BU
AH1388 (1969) Proof	6,250	Value: 28.50				
AH1389 (1970) Proof	Inc. above	Value: 28.50				

KM# 3 5 RIYALS **Weight:** 15.0000 g. **Composition:** 1.0000 Silver .4823 oz. ASW **Ruler:** Muhammad bin Hamad al-Sharqi **Series:** 1972 Munich Olympics

Date	Mintage	F	VF	XF	Unc	BU
AH1388 (1969) Proof	3,550	Value: 50.00				
AH1389 (1970) Proof	1,300	Value: 52.50				

KM# 5 10 RIYALS **Weight:** 30.0000 g. **Composition:** 1.0000 Silver .9645 oz. ASW **Ruler:** Muhammad bin Hamad al-Sharqi **Subject:** Apollo XII

Date	Mintage	F	VF	XF	Unc	BU
AH1388 (1969) Proof	15,000	Value: 47.50				
AH1389 (1970) Proof	15,000	Value: 47.50				

KM# 4.1 10 RIYALS **Weight:** 30.0000 g. **Composition:** 1.0000 Silver .9645 oz. ASW **Ruler:** Muhammad bin Hamad al-Sharqi **Subject:** Apollo XI **Obverse:** Fineness in oval at lower left, mintage figure at lower right

Date	Mintage	F	VF	XF	Unc	BU
AH1388 (1969) Proof	14,000	Value: 55.00				

KM# 4.2 10 RIYALS **Weight:** 30.0000 g. **Composition:** 1.0000 Silver .9645 oz. ASW **Ruler:** Muhammad bin Hamad al-Sharqi **Obverse:** Mintage figure stamped at lower left, fineness in oval at lower right

Date	F	VF	XF	Unc	BU
AH1389 (1970) Proof	—	Value: 55.00			

KM# 19 10 RIYALS **Weight:** 30.0000 g. **Composition:** 1.0000 Silver .9645 oz. ASW **Ruler:** Muhammad bin Hamad al-Sharqi **Subject:** Apollo XIII

Date	Mintage	F	VF	XF	Unc	BU
AH1389 (1970) Proof	15,000	Value: 50.00				

KM# 20 10 RIYALS **Weight:** 30.0000 g. **Composition:** 1.0000 Silver .9645 oz. ASW **Ruler:** Muhammad bin Hamad al-Sharqi **Subject:** Visit of Pope Paul VI to Philippines **Obverse:** Similar to 10 Riyals, KM#4.1

Date	Mintage	F	VF	XF	Unc	BU
AH1389 (1970) Proof	300	Value: 85.00				

KM# 21 10 RIYALS **Weight:** 30.0000 g. **Composition:** 1.0000 Silver .9645 oz. ASW **Ruler:** Muhammad bin Hamad al-Sharqi **Subject:** Visit of Pope Paul VI to Australia **Obverse:** Similar to 10 Riyals, KM#4.1

Date	Mintage	F	VF	XF	Unc	BU
AH1389 (1970) Proof	12,000	Value: 85.00				

KM# 22 10 RIYALS **Weight:** 30.0000 g. **Composition:** 1.0000 Silver .9645 oz. ASW **Ruler:** Muhammad bin Hamad al-Sharqi **Subject:** Apollo XIV **Obverse:** Similar to 10 Riyals, KM#4.1

Date	Mintage	F	VF	XF	Unc	BU
AH1389 (1971) Proof	14,000	Value: 75.00				

KM# 7 25 RIYALS **Weight:** 5.1800 g. **Composition:** 0.9000 Gold .1499 oz. AGW **Ruler:** Muhammad bin Hamad al-Sharqi **Subject:** U.S. President Richard Nixon **Obverse:** Similar to 10 Riyals, KM#4.1 **Note:** The 1969 issue has the fineness incuse, the 1970 issue has the fineness both raised and incuse.

Date	Mintage	F	VF	XF	Unc	BU
AH1388 (1969) Proof	3,280	Value: 125				
AH1389 (1970) Proof	Inc. above	Value: 125				

KM# 8 50 RIYALS **Weight:** 10.3600 g. **Composition:** 0.9000 Gold .2998 oz. AGW **Ruler:** Muhammad bin Hamad al-Sharqi **Series:** 1972 Munich Olympics

Date	Mintage	F	VF	XF	Unc	BU
AH1388 (1969) Proof	1,230	Value: 235				
AH1389 (1970) Proof	400	Value: 250				

KM# 9 100 RIYALS **Weight:** 20.7300 g. **Composition:** 0.9000 Gold .5999 oz. AGW **Ruler:** Muhammad bin Hamad al-Sharqi **Subject:** Apollo X **Obverse:** Similar to KM#24

Date	Mintage	F	VF	XF	Unc	BU
AH1388 (1969) Proof	2,140	Value: 385				

KM# 10 100 RIYALS **Weight:** 20.7300 g. **Composition:** 0.9000 Gold .5999 oz. AGW **Ruler:** Muhammad bin Hamad al-Sharqi **Subject:** Apollo XII **Obverse:** Similar to KM#24

Date	Mintage	F	VF	XF	Unc	BU
AH1388 (1969) Proof	3,040	Value: 375				
AH1389 (1970) Proof	—	Value: 375				

KM# 23 100 RIYALS **Weight:** 20.7300 g. **Composition:** 0.9000 Gold .5999 oz. AGW **Ruler:** Muhammad bin Hamad al-Sharqi **Subject:** Apollo XIII **Obverse:** Similar to KM#24 **Reverse:** Similar to 10 Riyals, KM#19

Date	Mintage	F	VF	XF	Unc	BU
AH1389 (1970) Proof	600	Value: 400				

KM# 24 100 RIYALS **Weight:** 20.7300 g. **Composition:** 0.9000 Gold .5999 oz. AGW **Ruler:** Muhammad bin Hamad al-Sharqi **Subject:** Visit of Pope Paul VI to Philippines

Date	Mintage	F	VF	XF	Unc	BU
AH1389 (1970) Proof	290	Value: 500				

KM# 26 100 RIYALS **Weight:** 20.7300 g. **Composition:** 0.9000 Gold .5999 oz. AGW **Ruler:** Muhammad bin Hamad al-Sharqi **Subject:** Visit of Pope Paul VI to Australia **Obverse:** Similar to KM#24 **Reverse:** Pope facing right, map of Australia **Note:** Similar to 10 Riyals, KM#21.

Date	Mintage	F	VF	XF	Unc	BU
AH1389 (1970) Proof	250	Value: 500				

KM# 25 100 RIYALS **Weight:** 20.7300 g. **Composition:** 0.9000 Gold .5999 oz. AGW **Ruler:** Muhammad bin Hamad al-Sharqi **Subject:** Apollo XIV **Obverse:** Similar to KM#24

Date	Mintage	F	VF	XF	Unc	BU
AH1389 (1971) Proof	550	Value: 375				

KM# 11 200 RIYALS **Weight:** 41.4600 g. **Composition:** 0.9000 Gold 1.1998 oz. AGW **Ruler:** Muhammad bin Hamad al-Sharqi **Subject:** Mohamad bin Hamad al-Sharqi **Obverse:** Arms

Date	Mintage	F	VF	XF	Unc	BU
AH1388 (1969) Proof	680	Value: 700				

Note: Serially numbered on the obverse

PATTERNS

KM#	Date	Mintage	Identification	Mkt Val
Pn1	1968	15	250 Fils. Silver.	400
Pn5	1968	1	Dinar. Silver. Matte proof.	1,100
Pn2	1968	15	500 Fils. Silver.	450
Pn3	1968	15	750 Fils. Silver.	550
Pn4	1968	50	Dinar. Silver.	650

TRIAL STRIKES

KM#	Date	Mintage	Identification	Mkt Val
TS4	1968	1	Dinar. Silver. Uniface.	400
TS2	1968	1	750 Fils. Silver. Uniface.	350
TS1	1968	1	500 Fils. Silver. Uniface.	350
TS3	1968	1	Dinar. Silver. Uniface.	400

PROOF SETS

KM#	Date	Mintage	Identification	Issue Price	Mkt Val
PS3	Mixed 1969-71 (8)	—	KM#4.2, 5, 19, 22, 9, 10, 23, 25	—	1,700
PS4	1969 (8)	—	KM#1-4.2, 7-9, 11	—	1,600
PS5	1969 (5)	2,550	KM#1-4.2, 5	40.00	220
PS6	1969 (5)	5,000	KM#7-11	280	1,750
PS7	1969 (4)	—	KM#1-4.2	—	170
PS2	Mixed 1969-71 (9)	—	KM#1-4.2, 5, 19-22	—	475
PS8	1970 (5)	200	KM#1-4.2, 5	40.00	220

GABON

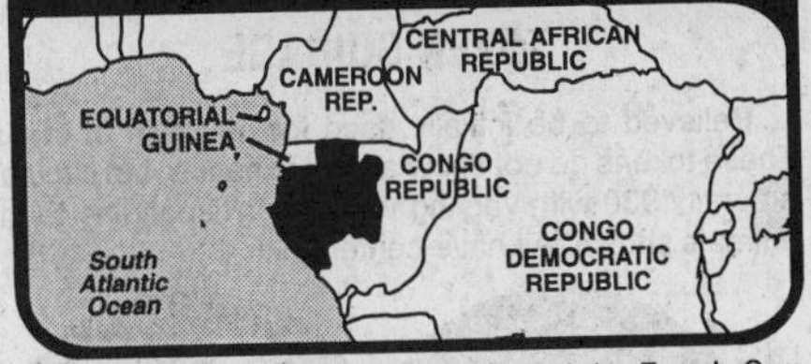

The Gabonese Republic, a member of the French Community, straddles the equator on the west coast of Africa. The hot and humid rain forest country has an area of 103,347 sq. mi. (267,670 sq. km.) and a population of 1.2 million, almost all of Bantu origin. Capital: Libreville. Extravagantly rich in resources, Gabon exports crude oil, manganese ore, gold and timbers.

Gabon was first visited by Portuguese navigator Diego Cam in the 15th century. Dutch, French and British traders, lured by the rich stands of hard woods and oil palms, quickly followed. The French founded their first settlement on the left bank of the Gabon River in 1839 and established their presence by signing treaties with the tribal chiefs. After gradually extending their influence into the interior during the last half of the 19th century, France occupied Gabon in 1885 and, in 1910, organized it as one of the four territories of French Equatorial Africa. It became an autonomous republic within the French Union in 1946, and on Aug. 17, 1960, became a completely independent republic within the new French Community.

For earlier coinage see French Equatorial Africa, Central African States and the Equatorial African States.

MINT MARKS

(a) - Paris, privy marks only
(t) - Poissy, privy marks only, thunderbolt

REPUBLIC

DECIMAL COINAGE

KM# 1 10 FRANCS **Weight:** 4.2000 g. **Composition:** 0.9000 Gold .1215 oz. AGW **Subject:** Independence **Obverse:** President Mba

Date	Mintage	F	VF	XF	Unc	BU
1960 Proof	500	Value: 100				

KM# 2 25 FRANCS **Weight:** 8.0000 g. **Composition:** 0.9000 Gold .2315 oz. AGW **Subject:** Independence **Obverse:** President Mba

Date	Mintage	F	VF	XF	Unc	BU
1960	10,000	—	—	—	125	—
1960 Proof	500	Value: 150				

KM# 3 50 FRANCS **Weight:** 16.0000 g. **Composition:** 0.9000 Gold .4630 oz. AGW **Subject:** Independence **Obverse:** President Mba

Date	Mintage	F	VF	XF	Unc	BU
1960 Proof	500	Value: 225				

KM# 4 100 FRANCS **Weight:** 32.0000 g. **Composition:** 0.9000 Gold .9260 oz. AGW **Subject:** Independence **Obverse:** President Mba

Date	Mintage	F	VF	XF	Unc	BU
1960 Proof	500	Value: 425				

KM# 12 100 FRANCS **Composition:** Nickel

Date	Mintage	F	VF	XF	Unc	BU
1971(a)	1,300,000	4.50	9.00	17.50	25.00	—
1972(a)	2,000,000	4.50	9.00	17.50	25.00	—

KM# 13 100 FRANCS **Composition:** Nickel

Date	F	VF	XF	Unc	BU
1975(a)	2.00	4.00	7.50	15.00	—
1977(a)	3.00	6.50	12.50	24.00	—
1978(a)	2.50	4.50	9.00	18.50	—
1982(a)	1.75	3.50	6.50	10.00	—
1983(a)	1.75	3.50	6.50	10.00	—
1984(a)	1.75	3.50	6.50	10.00	—
1985(a)	1.75	3.50	6.50	10.00	—

KM# 14 500 FRANCS **Composition:** Copper-Nickel

Date	F	VF	XF	Unc	BU
1985(a)	4.00	7.00	12.00	20.00	—

KM# 6 1000 FRANCS **Weight:** 3.5000 g. **Composition:** 0.9000 Gold .1012 oz. AGW **Obverse:** Albert Bernard Bongo **Reverse:** Stump of okume tree

Date	Mintage	F	VF	XF	Unc	BU
1969 Proof	4,000	Value: 75.00				

KM# 7 3000 FRANCS **Weight:** 10.5000 g. **Composition:** 0.9000 Gold .3038 oz. AGW **Obverse:** Albert Bernard Bongo **Reverse:** Arms

Date	Mintage	F	VF	XF	Unc	BU
1969 Proof	4,000	Value: 175				

KM# 8 5000 FRANCS **Weight:** 17.5000 g. **Composition:** 0.9000 Gold .5064 oz. AGW **Obverse:** Albert Bernard Bongo **Reverse:** Reliquary figure of Bakota

Date	Mintage	F	VF	XF	Unc	BU
1969 Proof	4,000	Value: 275				

KM# 11 5000 FRANCS **Weight:** 17.5000 g. **Composition:** 0.9000 Gold .5064 oz. AGW **Subject:** Visit of French President Georges Pompidou

Date	F	VF	XF	Unc	BU
1971 Proof	—	Value: 500			

KM# 9 10000 FRANCS **Weight:** 35.0000 g. **Composition:** 0.9000 Gold 1.0128 oz. AGW **Subject:** 1st Moon landing **Obverse:** Albert Bernard Bongo **Reverse:** Lunar module

Date	Mintage	F	VF	XF	Unc	BU
1969 Proof	4,000	Value: 485				

KM# 10 20000 FRANCS **Weight:** 70.0000 g. **Composition:** 0.9000 Gold 2.0257 oz. AGW **Subject:** 1st Moon landing - Cape Kennedy **Obverse:** Albert Bernard Bongo **Reverse:** Apollo XI at launching pad

Date	Mintage	F	VF	XF	Unc	BU
1969 Proof	4,000	Value: 975				

FRENCH EQUATORIAL AFRICAN TERRITORY

TOKEN COINAGE

Believed to be initially used for payment of taxes. These tokens do not show a denomination, but circulated until 1930 with varying values corresponding to the animals shown. All have center hole.

KM# Tn1 NON-DENOMINATED **Composition:** Aluminum **Reverse:** Elephant walking left

Date	F	VF	XF	Unc	BU
1925(t)	55.00	100	180	350	—

KM# Tn2 NON-DENOMINATED **Composition:** Aluminum **Reverse:** Leopard walking left

Date	F	VF	XF	Unc	BU
1926	100	175	325	550	—

KM# Tn3 NON-DENOMINATED **Composition:** Aluminum **Reverse:** Ox head facing

Date	F	VF	XF	Unc	BU
1927(t)	75.00	150	250	450	—

KM# Tn4 NON-DENOMINATED **Composition:** Aluminum **Reverse:** Pelican facing right

Date	F	VF	XF	Unc	BU
1928	125	200	350	550	—

KM# Tn5 NON-DENOMINATED **Composition:** Aluminum **Obverse:** "Gabon" above center hole, date below **Reverse:** Rhinoceros walking left

Date	F	VF	XF	Unc	BU
1929	85.00	175	300	500	—

ESSAIS

Standard metals unless otherwise noted

KM#	Date	Mintage	Identification	Issue Price	Mkt Val
E1	1960	10	25 Francs. KM2.	—	500
E2	1960	—	25 Francs. Silver. KM2.	—	250
E3	1971(a)	1,450	100 Francs. KM12.	—	20.00
E4	1971(a)	4	100 Francs. Gold. KM12.	—	1,600
E5	1971(a)	—	5000 Francs. Copper-Aluminum-Nickel. KM11.	—	175

KM#	Date	Mintage	Identification	Issue Price	Mkt Val

KM#	Date	Mintage	Identification	Issue Price	Mkt Val
E6	1975(a)	1,700	100 Francs. KM13.	—	20.00

KM#	Date	Mintage	Identification	Issue Price	Mkt Val
E7	1985(a)	1,700	500 Francs. KM14.	—	30.00

PROOF SETS

KM#	Date	Mintage	Identification	Issue Price	Mkt Val
PS1	1960 (4)	500	KM1-4	—	900
PS2	1969 (5)	4,000	KM6-10	—	2,000

GAMBIA

The Republic of The Gambia, occupies a strip of land 7 miles (11km.) to 20 miles (32 km.) wide and 200 miles (322 km.) long encompassing both sides of West Africa's Gambia River, and completely surrounded by Senegal. The republic, one of Africa's smallest countries, has an area of 4,127 sq. mi. (11,300 sq. km.) and a population of 989,273. Capital: Banjul. Agriculture and tourism are the principal industries. Peanuts constitute 95 per cent of export earnings.

The Gambia was once part of the great empires of Ghana and Songhay. When Portuguese gold seekers and slave traders visited The Gambia in the 15th century, it was part of the Kingdom of Mali. In 1588 the territory became, through purchase, the first British colony in Africa. English slavers established Fort James, the first settlement, on a small island a dozen miles up the Gambia River in 1664. After alternate periods of union with Sierra Leone and existence as a separate colony The Gambia became a British colony in 1888. On Feb. 18, 1965, The Gambia achieved independence as a constitutional monarchy within the Commonwealth of Nations, with Elizabeth II as Head of State as Queen of The Gambia. It became a republic on April 24, 1970, remaining a member of the Common- wealth, but with the president as Chief of State and Head of Government.

Together with Senegal, The Gambia formed a confederation on February 1, 1982. This confederation was officially dissolved on September 21, 1989. In July, 1994 a military junta took control of The Gambia and disbanded its elected government.

Gambia's 8 Shillings coin is a unique denomination in world coinage.

For earlier coinage see British West Africa.

RULERS
British until 1970

MONETARY SYSTEM
12 Pence = 1 Shilling
20 Shillings = 1 Pound

BRITISH COMMONWEALTH

STERLING COINAGE

KM# 1 PENNY **Composition:** Bronze **Reverse:** Sailing vessel

Date	Mintage	F	VF	XF	Unc	BU
1966	3,600,000	—	0.20	0.40	1.00	—
1966 Proof	6,600	Value: 1.00				

KM# 2 3 PENCE **Composition:** Nickel-Brass **Reverse:** Double-spurred francolin

Date	Mintage	F	VF	XF	Unc	BU
1966	2,000,000	—	0.30	0.50	1.50	—
1966 Proof	6,600	Value: 1.50				

KM# 3 6 PENCE **Composition:** Copper-Nickel **Reverse:** Peanuts

Date	Mintage	F	VF	XF	Unc	BU
1966	1,500,000	—	0.30	0.50	1.75	—
1966 Proof	6,600	Value: 1.75				

KM# 4 SHILLING **Composition:** Copper-Nickel **Reverse:** Oil palm

Date	Mintage	F	VF	XF	Unc	BU
1966	2,500,000	—	0.50	0.80	2.00	—
1966 Proof	6,600	Value: 2.00				

KM# 6 4 SHILLINGS **Composition:** Copper-Nickel **Reverse:** Slender-snouted crocodile

Date	Mintage	F	VF	XF	Unc	BU
1966	800,000	—	1.50	2.50	5.50	—
1966 Proof	6,600	Value: 7.50				

KM# 7 8 SHILLINGS **Composition:** Copper-Nickel **Reverse:** Hippopotamus

Date	Mintage	F	VF	XF	Unc	BU
1970	25,000	—	2.00	4.00	10.00	—

KM# 7a 8 SHILLINGS **Weight:** 32.4000 g. **Composition:** 0.9250 Silver .9635 oz. ASW **Reverse:** Hippopotamus

Date	Mintage	F	VF	XF	Unc	BU
1970 Proof	4,500	Value: 28.50				

Note: VIP issued proofs have a frosted relief, value: $175.00.

REPUBLIC

DECIMAL COINAGE

100 Bututs = 1 Dalasi

KM# 8 BUTUT **Composition:** Bronze **Reverse:** Peanuts

Date	Mintage	F	VF	XF	Unc	BU
1971	12,449,000	—	—	0.10	0.20	—
1971 Proof	32,000	Value: 0.50				
1973	3,000,000	—	—	0.10	0.25	—
1974	—	—	0.25	0.50	1.50	—
1975	—	—	—	0.10	0.25	—

KM# 14 BUTUT **Composition:** Bronze **Series:** F.A.O.

Date	Mintage	F	VF	XF	Unc	BU
1974	26,062,000	—	—	0.10	0.20	—
1985	4,500,000	—	—	0.15	0.25	—

KM# 54 BUTUT **Composition:** Copper Plated Steel **Obverse:** National arms **Reverse:** Peanuts

Date	F	VF	XF	Unc	BU
1998	—	—	—	0.20	—

KM# 9 5 BUTUTS **Composition:** Bronze **Reverse:** Sailing vessel

Date	Mintage	F	VF	XF	Unc	BU
1971	5,400,000	—	—	0.10	0.35	—
1971 Proof	32,000	Value: 0.50				
1977	1,506,000	—	—	0.10	0.35	—

KM# 55 5 BUTUTS **Composition:** Bronze **Obverse:** National arms **Reverse:** Sailboat

Date	F	VF	XF	Unc	BU
1998	—	—	—	0.35	—

KM# 10 10 BUTUTS **Composition:** Nickel-Brass **Reverse:** Double-spurred francolin

Date	Mintage	F	VF	XF	Unc	BU
1971	3,000,000	—	0.15	0.35	1.50	—
1971 Proof	32,000	Value: 2.00				
1977	750,000	—	0.15	0.35	1.50	—

KM# 56 10 BUTUTS **Composition:** Brass Plated Steel **Obverse:** National arms **Reverse:** Double-spurred francolin

Date	F	VF	XF	Unc	BU
1998	—	—	—	1.00	—

KM# 11 25 BUTUTS **Composition:** Copper-Nickel **Reverse:** Oil palm

Date	Mintage	F	VF	XF	Unc	BU
1971	3,040,000	—	0.15	0.30	0.75	—
1971 Proof	32,000	Value: 1.25				

KM# 57 25 BUTUTS **Composition:** Copper-Nickel **Obverse:** National arms **Reverse:** Oil palm

Date	F	VF	XF	Unc	BU
1998	—	—	—	1.00	—

KM# 12 50 BUTUTS **Composition:** Copper-Nickel **Reverse:** African domestic ox

Date	Mintage	F	VF	XF	Unc	BU
1971	1,700,000	—	0.35	0.65	1.50	—
1971 Proof	32,000	Value: 1.75				

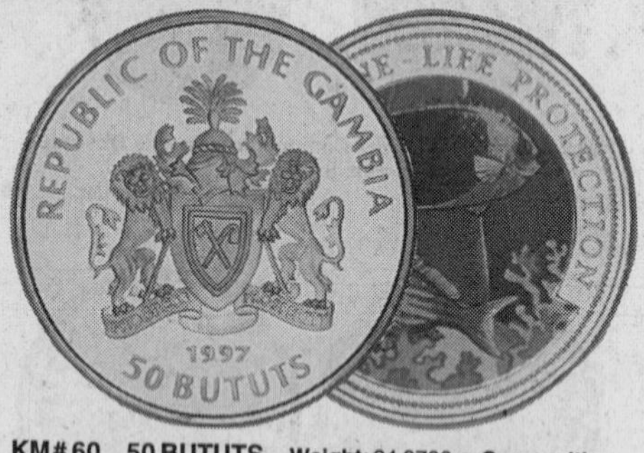

KM# 60 50 BUTUTS **Weight:** 24.9700 g. **Composition:** 0.9800 Silver .7867 oz. ASW **Subject:** Marine life protection **Obverse:** National arms **Reverse:** Pair of multicolored fish

Date	F	VF	XF	Unc	BU
1997 Proof	—	Value: 40.00			

KM# 58 50 BUTUTS **Composition:** Copper-Nickel **Obverse:** National arms **Reverse:** African domestic ox

Date	F	VF	XF	Unc	BU
1998	—	—	—	1.50	—

KM# 62 2000 BUTUTS **Weight:** 0.9250 g. **Composition:** Silver **Subject:** Millennium **Obverse:** National arms **Reverse:** Gambian map on radiant sun **Edge:** Reeded **Shape:** 10-sided **Size:** 37.5 mm. **Note:** Struck at British Royal Mint.

Date	F	VF	XF	Unc	BU
ND(1999) Proof	30,000	Value: 55.00			

KM# 13 DALASI **Composition:** Copper-Nickel **Reverse:** Slender-snouted crocodile

Date	Mintage	F	VF	XF	Unc	BU
1971	1,300,000	—	2.00	3.50	7.50	—
1971 Proof	32,000	Value: 5.00				

KM# 29 DALASI **Composition:** Copper-Nickel **Shape:** 7-sided

Date	F	VF	XF	Unc	BU
1987	—	1.75	2.75	5.50	—

KM# 59 DALASI **Composition:** Copper Nickel **Obverse:** National arms **Reverse:** Slender-snouted crocodile **Shape:** 7-sided

Date	F	VF	XF	Unc	BU
1998	—	1.75	2.75	5.50	—

KM# 46 2 DALASIS **Weight:** 9.9200 g. **Composition:** 0.5000 Silver .1595 oz. ASW **Subject:** Olympic Games 1996 **Obverse:** National arms **Reverse:** Two runners crossing a finish line

Date	Mintage	F	VF	XF	Unc	BU
1996 Proof	Est. 10,000	Value: 15.00				

KM# 49 2 DALASIS **Composition:** Copper-Nickel **Subject:** 70th birthday of Queen Elizabeth II **Obverse:** National arms

Date	Mintage	F	VF	XF	Unc	BU
1996	5,000	—	—	—	10.00	—

KM# 16 10 DALASIS **Weight:** 28.2800 g. **Composition:** 0.5000 Silver .4546 oz. ASW **Subject:** 10th anniversary of independence

Date	Mintage	F	VF	XF	Unc	BU
1975	50,000	—	—	—	8.00	—

KM# 16a 10 DALASIS **Weight:** 28.2800 g. **Composition:** 0.9250 Silver .8411 oz. ASW **Subject:** 10th anniversary of independence

Date	Mintage	F	VF	XF	Unc	BU
1975 Proof	20,000	Value: 15.00				

KM# 23 10 DALASIS **Weight:** 28.2800 g. **Composition:** 0.5000 Silver .4546 oz. ASW **Subject:** Commonwealth Games **Reverse:** Hurdlers

Date	F	VF	XF	Unc	BU
1986	—	—	—	12.50	—

KM# 23a 10 DALASIS **Weight:** 28.2800 g. **Composition:** 0.9250 Silver .8411 oz. ASW **Subject:** Commonwealth Games **Reverse:** Hurdlers

Date	Mintage	F	VF	XF	Unc	BU
1986 Proof	Est. 20,000	Value: 22.50				

KM# 28 10 DALASIS **Weight:** 28.2800 g. **Composition:** 0.9250 Silver .8411 oz. ASW **Subject:** Silver jubilee of independence

Date	Mintage	F	VF	XF	Unc	BU
1990 Proof	2,000	Value: 42.50				

KM# 30 10 DALASIS **Composition:** Copper-Nickel **Subject:** Papal visit

Date	F	VF	XF	Unc	BU
1992	—	—	—	6.50	—

KM# 30a 10 DALASIS **Weight:** 28.2800 g. **Composition:** 0.9250 Silver .8411 oz. ASW **Subject:** Papal visit

Date	Mintage	F	VF	XF	Unc	BU
1992 Proof	5,000	Value: 55.00				

KM# 50 10 DALASIS **Composition:** Copper Nickel **Subject:** 70th birthday of H.M. Queen Elizabeth II

Date	F	VF	XF	Unc	BU
1996	—	—	—	8.00	—

KM# 50a 10 DALASIS **Weight:** 28.2800 g. **Composition:** 0.9250 Silver .8411 oz. ASW **Subject:** 70th birthday of H.M. Queen Elizabeth II

Date	Mintage	F	VF	XF	Unc	BU
1996 Proof	70,000	Value: 40.00				

KM# 17 20 DALASIS **Weight:** 28.6300 g. **Composition:** 0.9250 Silver .8514 oz. ASW **Subject:** Conservation **Reverse:** Spur-winged goose

Date	Mintage	F	VF	XF	Unc	BU
1977	4,302	—	—	—	17.50	—

KM# 17a 20 DALASIS **Weight:** 28.2800 g. **Composition:** 0.9250 Silver .8411 oz. ASW **Subject:** Conservation **Reverse:** Spur-winged goose

Date	Mintage	F	VF	XF	Unc	BU
1977 Proof	4,404	Value: 22.50				

KM# 20 20 DALASIS **Weight:** 28.2800 g. **Composition:** 0.9250 Silver .8411 oz. ASW **Subject:** World Food Day **Obverse:** Similar to KM#17

Date	Mintage	F	VF	XF	Unc	BU
1981	10,000	—	—	—	25.00	—
1981 Proof	5,000	Value: 45.00				

KM# 21 20 DALASIS **Weight:** 28.2800 g. **Composition:** 0.9250 Silver .8411 oz. ASW **Subject:** Year of the Scout

Date	Mintage	F	VF	XF	Unc	BU
1983	—	—	—	—	25.00	—
1983 Proof	Inc. above	Value: 40.00				

KM# 24 20 DALASIS **Weight:** 28.2800 g. **Composition:** 0.9250 Silver .8411 oz. ASW **Subject:** World Wildlife Fund **Reverse:** Temminck's colobus monkey

Date	Mintage	F	VF	XF	Unc	BU
1987 Proof	Est. 25,000	Value: 27.50				

KM# 26 20 DALASIS **Weight:** 28.2800 g. **Composition:** 0.9250 Silver .8411 oz. ASW **Subject:** Save the Children Fund **Obverse:** Bust of President Alhaji Sir Dawda Dairaba Jawara **Reverse:** Girls playing "akara" (rythmic clapping and dancing game)

Date	Mintage	F	VF	XF	Unc	BU
1989	Est. 20,000	Value: 25.00				

KM# 32 20 DALASIS **Weight:** 31.4700 g. **Composition:** 0.9250 Silver .9359 oz. ASW **Subject:** 40th Anniversary - Coronation of Queen Elizabeth II

Date	Mintage	F	VF	XF	Unc	BU
1993 Proof	Est. 10,000	Value: 45.00				

KM# 33 20 DALASIS **Weight:** 31.2600 g. **Composition:** 0.9250 Silver .9296 oz. ASW **Series:** Olympics **Reverse:** Wrestling

Date	Mintage	F	VF	XF	Unc	BU
1993 Proof	Est. 40,000	Value: 22.50				

KM# 34 20 DALASIS **Weight:** 31.4700 g. **Composition:** 0.9250 Silver .9359 oz. ASW **Subject:** Prince Henry the Navigator

Date	Mintage	F	VF	XF	Unc	BU
1993 Proof	Est. 15,000	Value: 22.50				

KM# 36 20 DALASIS **Weight:** 31.4700 g. **Composition:** 0.9250 Silver .9359 oz. ASW **Subject:** Rendezvous in Space

Date	Mintage	F	VF	XF	Unc	BU
1993 Proof	Est. 10,000	Value: 30.00				

KM# 35 20 DALASIS **Weight:** 31.4700 g. **Composition:** 0.9250 Silver .9359 oz. ASW **Subject:** Soccer - World Cup 1994

Date	Mintage	F	VF	XF	Unc	BU
1994 Proof	Est. 15,000	Value: 30.00				

KM# 40 20 DALASIS **Weight:** 31.4700 g. **Composition:** 0.9250 Silver .9359 oz. ASW **Subject:** Elizabeth, the Queen Mother

Date	Mintage	F	VF	XF	Unc	BU
1994 Proof	Est. 30,000	Value: 37.50				

KM# 38 20 DALASIS **Weight:** 31.4700 g. **Composition:** 0.9250 Silver .9359 oz. ASW **Subject:** Endangered wildlife **Reverse:** Chimpanzee

Date	Mintage	F	VF	XF	Unc	BU
1994 Proof	Est. 15,000	Value: 32.50				

KM# 39 20 DALASIS **Weight:** 31.4700 g. **Composition:** 0.9250 Silver .9359 oz. ASW **Subject:** Mungo Park

Date	Mintage	F	VF	XF	Unc	BU
1994 Proof	Est. 10,000	Value: 32.50				

KM# 47 20 DALASIS **Weight:** 31.4700 g. **Composition:** 0.9250 Silver .9359 oz. ASW **Subject:** Olympic Games 1996 **Obverse:** National arms **Reverse:** Two runners crossing a finish line

Date	F	VF	XF	Unc	BU
1994 Proof	—	Value: 22.50			

KM# 37 20 DALASIS **Composition:** Copper-Nickel **Subject:** 50th Anniversary - United Nations

Date	F	VF	XF	Unc	BU
1995	—	—	—	8.00	—

KM# 37a 20 DALASIS **Weight:** 28.2800 g. **Composition:** 0.9250 Silver .8411 oz. ASW **Subject:** 50th Anniversary - United Nations

Date	F	VF	XF	Unc	BU
1995 Proof	—	Value: 32.50			

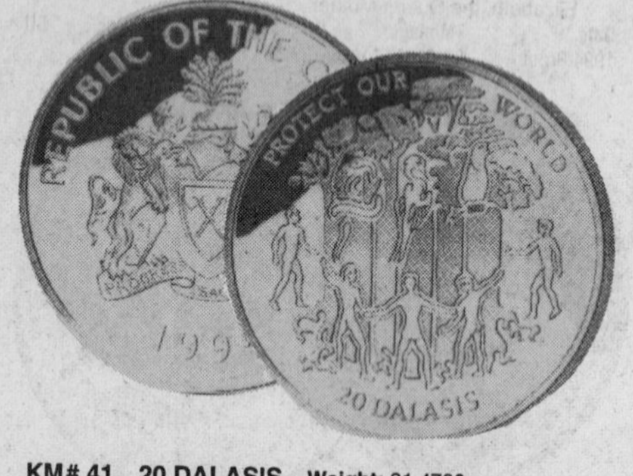

KM# 41 20 DALASIS **Weight:** 31.4700 g. **Composition:** 0.9250 Silver .9359 oz. ASW **Subject:** Protect Our World

Date	Mintage	F	VF	XF	Unc	BU
1995 Proof	Est. 10,000	Value: 40.00				

KM# 42 20 DALASIS **Weight:** 7.7760 g. **Composition:** 0.5833 Gold .1458 oz. AGW **Subject:** Endangered wildife **Reverse:** Black rhinoceros

Date	F	VF	XF	Unc	BU
1995	—	—	—	100	—

KM# 43 20 DALASIS **Weight:** 7.7760 g. **Composition:** 0.5833 Gold .1458 oz. AGW **Subject:** Endangered wildife **Reverse:** African elephant

Date	F	VF	XF	Unc	BU
1995	—	—	—	100	—

KM# 44 20 DALASIS **Weight:** 31.4700 g. **Composition:** 0.9250 Silver .9359 oz. ASW **Subject:** Victorian Age **Reverse:** Queen Victoria with first steam locomotive in background

Date	F	VF	XF	Unc	BU
1996	—	—	—	42.50	—

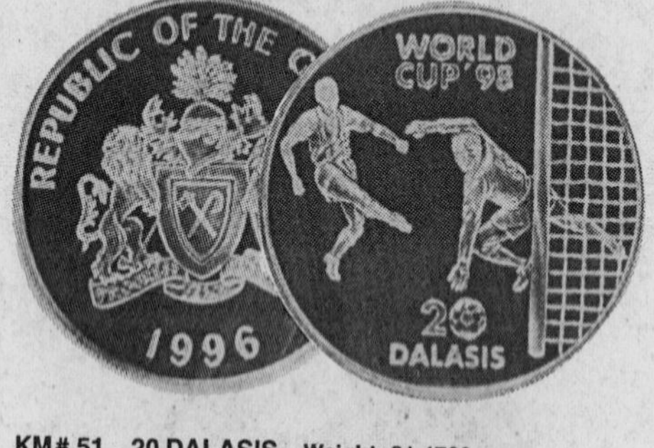

KM# 51 20 DALASIS **Weight:** 31.4700 g. **Composition:** 0.9990 Silver 1.0108 oz. ASW **Subject:** World Cup 1998 **Obverse:** National arms **Reverse:** Two soccer players

Date	Mintage	F	VF	XF	Unc	BU
1996 Proof	10,000	Value: 40.00				

KM# 18 40 DALASIS **Weight:** 35.2900 g. **Composition:** 0.9250 Silver 1.0495 oz. ASW **Subject:** Conservation **Reverse:** Aardvark

Date	Mintage	F	VF	XF	Unc	BU
1977	4,304	—	—	—	22.50	—

KM# 18a 40 DALASIS **Weight:** 35.0000 g. **Composition:** 0.9250 Silver 1.0409 oz. ASW **Subject:** Conservation **Reverse:** Aardvark

Date	Mintage	F	VF	XF	Unc	BU
1977 Proof	4,183	Value: 32.50				

KM# 52 50 DALASIS **Weight:** 1.2441 g. **Composition:** 0.9990 Gold .0400 oz. AGW **Subject:** Kankan Manga Musa **Obverse:** National arms **Reverse:** Seated king and supplicant

Date	F	VF	XF	Unc	BU
1997 Proof	—	Value: 40.00			

KM# 45 100 DALASIS **Weight:** 1000.0000 g. **Composition:** 0.9990 Silver 32.1186 oz. ASW **Subject:** Endangered Wildlife **Obverse:** National arms **Reverse:** Lion family **Size:** 100 mm. **Note:** Illustration reduced.

Date	Mintage	F	VF	XF	Unc	BU
1996 Proof	1,000	Value: 500				

KM# 53 100 DALASIS **Weight:** 3.1100 g. **Composition:** 0.5833 Gold .0583 oz. AGW **Series:** Olympic Games 2000 **Obverse:** National arms **Reverse:** Silhouette of three runners

Date	Mintage	F	VF	XF	Unc	BU
1997 Proof	5,000	Value: 50.00				

KM# 61 150 DALASIS **Weight:** 7.7760 g. **Composition:** 0.5830 Gold .1458 oz. AGW **Subject:** British Year of 3 kings and Queen Mother **Obverse:** National arms **Reverse:** Busts of Edward VIII, George V and George VI facing within circles

Date	F	VF	XF	Unc	BU
1996 Proof	—	Value: 145			

KM# 48 200 DALASIS **Weight:** 31.1035 g. **Composition:** 0.9990 Gold 1 oz. AGW **Subject:** Endangered Wildlife **Reverse:** Lion

Date	Mintage	F	VF	XF	Unc	BU
1996 Proof	1,000	Value: 500				

KM# 22 250 DALASIS **Weight:** 15.9800 g. **Composition:** 0.9170 Gold .4712 oz. AGW **Subject:** Year of the Scout

Date	Mintage	F	VF	XF	Unc	BU
1983	2,000	—	—	—	250	—
1983 Proof	2,000	Value: 325				

KM# 31 250 DALASIS **Weight:** 47.5400 g. **Composition:** 0.9170 Gold 1.4011 oz. AGW **Subject:** Papal visit **Obverse:** National coat of arms **Reverse:** Pope John Paul II giving a blessing

Date	Mintage	F	VF	XF	Unc	BU
1992 Proof	100	Value: 1,200				

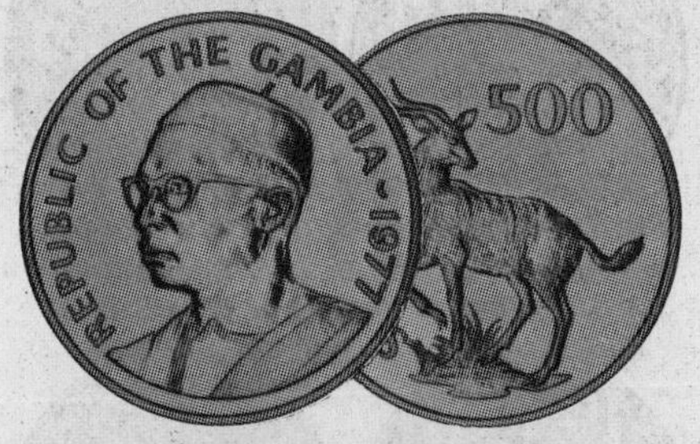

KM# 19 500 DALASIS **Weight:** 33.4370 g. **Composition:** 0.9000 Gold .9676 oz. AGW **Subject:** Conservation **Reverse:** Sitatunga

Date	Mintage	F	VF	XF	Unc	BU
1977	699	—	—	—	500	—
1977 Proof	285	Value: 750				

KM# 25 1000 DALASIS **Weight:** 10.0000 g. **Composition:** 0.9170 Gold .2948 oz. AGW **Subject:** World Wildlife Fund **Reverse:** Gambian puffback bird

Date	Mintage	F	VF	XF	Unc	BU
1987 Proof	Est. 5,000	Value: 185				

KM# 27 1000 DALASIS **Weight:** 10.0000 g. **Composition:** 0.9170 Gold .2948 oz. AGW **Subject:** Save the Children Fund

Date	Mintage	F	VF	XF	Unc	BU
1989 Proof	Est. 3,000	Value: 225				

PROOF SETS

KM#	Date	Mintage	Identification	Issue Price	Mkt Val
PS1	1966 (6)	5,100	KM1-6	13.00	16.50
PS2	1966 and 1970 (7)	1,500	KM1-6, 7a	25.00	42.50
PS3	1971 (6)	26,249	KM8-13	—	9.00
PS4	1977 (2)	—	KM17a, 18a	60.00	55.00

GEORGIA

Georgia (formerly the Georgian Social Democratic Republic under the U.S.S.R.), is bounded by the Black Sea to the west and by Turkey, Armenia and Azerbaijan. It occupies the western part of Transcaucasia covering an area of 26,900 sq. mi. (69,700 sq. km.) and a population of 5.7 million. Capitol: Tbilisi. Hydro-electricity, minerals, forestry and agriculture are the chief industries.

After the Russian Revolution the Georgians, Armenians, and Azerbaijanis formed the short-lived Transcaucasian Federal Republic on Sept. 20, 1917, which broke up into three independent republics on May 26, 1918. A Germano-- Georgian treaty was signed on May 28, 1918, followed by a Turko-Georgian peace treaty on June 4. The end of WW I and the collapse of the central powers allowed free elections.

On May 20, 1920, Soviet Russia concluded a peace treaty, recognizing its independence, but later invaded on Feb. 11, 1921 and a soviet republic was proclaimed. On March 12, 1922 Stalin included Georgia in a newly formed Transcaucasian Soviet Federated Socialist Republic. On Dec. 5, 1936 the T.S.F.S.R. was dissolved and Georgia became a direct member of the U.S.S.R. The collapse of the U.S.S.R. allowed full transition to independence and on April 9, 1991 a unanimous vote declared the republic an independent state based on its original treaty of independence of May 1918.

INDEPENDENT STATE (C.I.S.)

100 Thetri = 1 Lari

STANDARD COINAGE

KM# 76 THETRI **Composition:** Stainless Steel

Date	F	VF	XF	Unc	BU
1993	—	—	—	0.25	—

KM# 77 2 THETRI **Composition:** Stainless Steel **Reverse:** Stylized eagle

Date	F	VF	XF	Unc	BU
1993	—	—	—	0.35	—

KM# 78 5 THETRI **Composition:** Stainless Steel **Reverse:** Stylized lion

Date	F	VF	XF	Unc	BU
1993	—	—	—	0.80	—

KM# 79 10 THETRI **Composition:** Stainless Steel **Reverse:** St. Mamas riing lion right

Date	F	VF	XF	Unc	BU
1993	—	—	—	1.25	—

KM# 80 20 THETRI **Composition:** Stainless Steel **Reverse:** Elk

Date	F	VF	XF	Unc	BU
1993	—	—	—	1.50	—

KM# 81 50 THETRI **Composition:** Brass **Reverse:** Stylized griffin

Date	F	VF	XF	Unc	BU
1993	—	—	—	2.00	—

KM# 83 10 LARI **Weight:** 28.2800 g. **Composition:** 0.9250 Silver .8410 oz. ASW **Subject:** State System 3,000 Years **Obverse:** Denomination **Reverse:** Eagle and lion **Edge:** Reeded **Size:** 38.6 mm.

Date	Mintage	F	VF	XF	Unc	BU
2000 Proof	1,000	Value: 55.00				

KM# 84 10 LARI **Weight:** 28.2800 g. **Composition:** 0.9250 Silver .8410 oz. ASW **Subject:** Birth of Jesus 2,000th Anniversary **Obverse:** Denomination **Reverse:** Holy robe in center of arms

Date	Mintage	F	VF	XF	Unc	BU
2000 Proof	1,000	Value: 55.00				

KM# 82 500 LARI **Weight:** 17.0000 g. **Composition:** 0.9170 Gold .5010 oz. AGW **Subject:** 50th Anniversary - Defeat of Fascism **Reverse:** Profiles of Stalin, Roosevelt, Churchill and de Gaulle

Date	Mintage	F	VF	XF	Unc	BU
1995 Proof	2,000	Value: 500				

MINT SETS

KM#	Date	Mintage	Identification	Issue Price	Mkt Val
MS1	1993 (6)	—	KM76-81	—	7.50

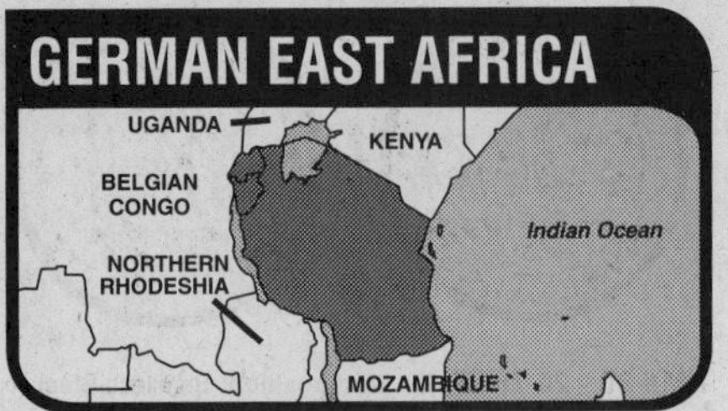

German East Africa (Tanganyika), located on the coast of east-central Africa between British East Africa (now Kenya) and Portuguese East Africa (now Mozambique), had an area of 362,284 sq. mi. (938,216 sq. km.) and a population of about 6 million. Capital: Dar es Salaam. Chief products prior to German control were ivory and slaves; after German control, sisal, coffee, and rubber. Germany acquired control of the area by treaties with coastal chiefs in 1884, established it as a protectorate in 1891, and proclaimed it the Colony of German East Africa in 1897. After World War I, Tanganyika was entrusted to Great Britain as a League of Nations mandate, and after World War II as a United Nations trust territory. Tanganyika became an independent nation within the British Commonwealth on Dec. 9, 1961. Coins dated up until 1901 were issued by the German East Africa Company. From 1904 onwards, coins were issued by the government.

NOTE: For later coinage see East Africa.

TITLES

شراكتة المانيا

Sharaka(t) Almania

RULERS

Wilhelm II, 1888-1918

MINT MARKS

A - Berlin
J - Hamburg
T - Tabora

MONETARY SYSTEM

Until 1904
64 Pesa = 1 Rupie
Commencing 1904
100 Heller = 1 Rupie

COLONIAL

STANDARD COINAGE

64 Pesa = 1 Rupee until 1904; 100 Heller = 1 Rupie commencing 1904

KM# 6 1/2 HELLER Composition: Bronze **Ruler:** Wihelm II

Date	Mintage	F	VF	XF	Unc	BU
1904A	1,201,000	1.25	3.50	6.50	28.00	40.00
1905A	7,192,000	2.25	5.25	9.00	32.50	45.00
1905J	4,000,000	2.25	5.25	9.00	32.50	45.00
1906J	6,000,000	1.25	3.50	6.50	28.00	40.00
1906J Proof	—	Value: 250				

KM# 7 HELLER Composition: Bronze **Ruler:** Wihelm II

Date	Mintage	F	VF	XF	Unc	BU
1904A	10,256,000	0.75	2.25	4.00	20.00	30.00
1904A Proof	—	Value: 125				
1904J	2,500,000	0.75	2.25	7.00	25.00	35.00
1905A	3,760,000	0.75	2.25	7.00	25.00	35.00
1905A Proof	—	Value: 125				
1905J	7,556,000	0.75	2.25	4.00	25.00	35.00
1906A	3,004,000	0.75	2.25	7.00	25.00	40.00
1906A Proof	—	Value: 200				
1906J	1,962,000	0.75	2.25	7.00	30.00	50.00
1907J	17,790,000	0.75	1.50	4.00	20.00	25.00
1908J	12,205,000	0.75	1.50	4.00	20.00	25.00
1908J Proof	—	Value: 135				
1909J	1,698,000	2.50	7.50	15.00	35.00	50.00
1909J Proof	—	Value: 135				
1910J	5,096,000	0.75	1.50	4.00	20.00	25.00
1910J Proof	—	Value: 135				
1911J	6,420,000	0.75	1.50	4.00	20.00	25.00
1911J Proof	—	Value: 135				
1912J	7,012,000	0.75	1.50	4.00	25.00	40.00
1912J Proof	—	Value: 135				
1913A	—	0.75	1.50	4.00	20.00	30.00

Date	Mintage	F	VF	XF	Unc	BU
1913A Proof	—	Value: 135				
1913J	5,186,000	0.75	1.50	4.00	20.00	30.00
1913J Proof	—	Value: 150				

KM# 11 5 HELLER Composition: Bronze **Ruler:** Wihelm II

Date	Mintage	F	VF	XF	Unc	BU
1908J	600,000	15.00	30.00	70.00	550	650
1908J Proof	—	Value: 975				
1909J	756,000	15.00	30.00	70.00	550	650
1909J Proof	60	Value: 975				

KM# 13 5 HELLER Composition: Copper-Nickel **Ruler:** Wihelm II

Date	Mintage	F	VF	XF	Unc	BU
1913A	1,000,000	6.00	15.00	25.00	55.00	100
1913A Proof	—	Value: 250				
1913J	1,000,000	6.00	15.00	25.00	50.00	100
1913J Proof	—	Value: 250				
1914J	1,000,000	5.00	12.00	22.00	50.00	100
1914J Proof	—	Value: 250				

KM# 14.1 5 HELLER Composition: Brass **Ruler:** Wihelm II **Obverse:** Oval base on crown **Note:** 1-1/2 - 2 millimeters thick.

Date	Mintage	F	VF	XF	Unc	BU
1916T	30,000	10.00	20.00	40.00	80.00	150

KM# 14.2 5 HELLER Composition: Brass **Ruler:** Wihelm II **Obverse:** Flat base on crown **Note:** 1 millimeter or less thick.

Date	F	VF	XF	Unc	BU
1916T	4.00	12.00	30.00	60.00	100

KM# 12 10 HELLER Composition: Copper-Nickel **Ruler:** Wihelm II

Date	Mintage	F	VF	XF	Unc	BU
1908J	—	5.00	15.00	30.00	90.00	125
1908J Proof	—	Value: 350				
1909J	1,990,000	3.00	10.00	20.00	80.00	125
1909J Proof	—	Value: 275				
1910J	500,000	3.00	10.00	20.00	80.00	150
1910J Proof	—	Value: 275				
1911A	500,000	5.00	15.00	35.00	100	150
1911A Proof	—	Value: 300				
1914J	200,000	10.00	30.00	60.00	125	200
1914 Proof	—	Value: 285				

Obverse A
Large Crown

Obverse B
Small Crown

Reverse A
Curled Tip On Second L

Reverse B
Pointed Tips On L's

Reverse C
Curled Tips On L's

KM# 15 20 HELLER Composition: Copper **Ruler:** Wihelm II **Note:** Obverse A and reverse A.

Date	Mintage	F	VF	XF	Unc	BU
1916T	300,000	6.00	10.00	20.00	85.00	100
Note: Obverse A and reverse A						
1916T	Inc. above	125	200	350	—	—
Note: Obverse A and reverse B						
1916T	Inc. above	60.00	85.00	140	—	—
Note: Obverse B and reverse A						
1916T	Inc. above	6.00	10.00	20.00	60.00	80.00
Note: Obverse B and reverse B						
1916T Rare	Inc. above	—	—	—	—	—
Note: Obverse A and reverse C						
1916T Rare	Inc. above	—	—	—	—	—
Note: Obverse B and reverse C						

KM# 15a 20 HELLER Composition: Brass **Ruler:** Wihelm II

Date	Mintage	F	VF	XF	Unc	BU
1916T	1,600,000	6.00	10.00	20.00	75.00	90.00
Note: Obverse A and reverse A						
1916T	Inc. above	7.00	12.50	25.00	85.00	100
Note: Obverse A and reverse B						
1916T	Inc. above	7.00	12.50	25.00	85.00	100
Note: Obverse B and reverse A						
1916T	Inc. above	6.00	10.00	20.00	65.00	80.00
Note: Obverse B and reverse B						
1916T	Inc. above	10.00	30.00	45.00	125	150
Note: Obverse A and reverse C						
1916T	Inc. above	12.00	35.00	50.00	135	150
Note: Obverse B and reverse C						

KM# 3 1/4 RUPIE Weight: 2.9160 g. **Composition:** 0.9170 Silver .0859 oz. ASW **Ruler:** Wihelm II

Date	Mintage	F	VF	XF	Unc	BU
1901	350,000	6.00	18.00	45.00	140	160

KM# 8 1/4 RUPIE Weight: 2.9160 g. **Composition:** 0.9170 Silver .0859 oz. ASW **Ruler:** Wihelm II

Date	Mintage	F	VF	XF	Unc	BU
1904A	300,000	5.00	12.00	37.50	110	150
1904A Proof	—	Value: 300				
1906A	300,000	5.00	12.00	37.50	110	150
1906A Proof	—	Value: 300				
1906J	100,000	10.00	35.00	75.00	250	300

Date	Mintage	F	VF	XF	Unc	BU
1907J	200,000	7.00	18.00	50.00	150	175
1907J Proof	—	Value: 375				
1909A	300,000	6.00	13.50	40.00	140	170
1910J	600,000	5.00	12.00	37.50	110	140
1910J Proof	—	Value: 350				
1912J	400,000	6.00	13.50	40.00	120	175
1912J Proof	—	Value: 350				
1913A	200,000	6.50	14.50	42.50	135	225
1913A Proof	—	Value: 350				
1913J	400,000	5.00	12.00	37.50	110	140
1913J Proof	—	Value: 300				
1914J	200,000	6.50	14.50	42.50	125	200
1914J Proof	—	Value: 300				

KM# 4 1/2 RUPIE Weight: 5.8319 g. **Composition:** 0.9170 Silver .1719 oz. ASW **Ruler:** Wihelm II

Date	Mintage	F	VF	XF	Unc	BU
1901	215,000	15.00	40.00	100	200	250

KM# 9 1/2 RUPIE Weight: 5.8319 g. **Composition:** 0.9170 Silver .1719 oz. ASW **Ruler:** Wihelm II

Date	Mintage	F	VF	XF	Unc	BU
1904A	400,000	15.00	40.00	95.00	275	300
1904A Proof	—	Value: 450				
1906A	50,000	75.00	150	350	750	1,000
1906A Proof	—	Value: 1,000				
1906J	50,000	75.00	150	350	750	1,000
1907J	140,000	20.00	50.00	125	300	350
1907J Proof	—	Value: 550				
1909A	100,000	30.00	65.00	150	350	400
1910J	300,000	20.00	40.00	100	250	275
1910J Proof	—	Value: 450				
1912J	200,000	15.00	40.00	95.00	250	300
1913A	100,000	20.00	45.00	110	300	400
1913J	200,000	15.00	40.00	95.00	200	250
1914J	100,000	20.00	45.00	100	285	350

KM# 2 RUPIE Weight: 11.6638 g. **Composition:** 0.9170 Silver .3437 oz. ASW **Ruler:** Wihelm II

Date	Mintage	F	VF	XF	Unc	BU
1901	319,000	12.50	25.00	75.00	175	225
1902	151,000	20.00	40.00	125	250	275

KM# 10 RUPIE Weight: 11.6638 g. **Composition:** 0.9170 Silver .3437 oz. ASW **Ruler:** Wihelm II

Date	Mintage	F	VF	XF	Unc	BU
1904A	1,000,000	11.50	22.50	45.00	130	150
1904A Proof	—	Value: 425				
1905A	300,000	15.00	27.50	60.00	185	250
1905A Proof	—	Value: 450				
1905J	1,000,000	11.50	22.50	45.00	130	160
1905J Proof	—	Value: 400				
1906A	950,000	11.50	22.50	45.00	130	160
1906J	700,000	15.00	27.50	65.00	175	200
1907J	880,000	9.00	15.00	35.00	180	200
1908J	500,000	12.50	25.00	50.00	190	225
1908J Proof	—	Value: 450				

Date	Mintage	F	VF	XF	Unc	BU
1909A	200,000	15.00	27.50	60.00	275	350
1910J	270,000	9.00	15.00	35.00	200	275
1911A	300,000	12.50	25.00	50.00	175	250
1911A Proof	—	Value: 450				
1911J	1,400,000	9.00	15.00	35.00	150	175
1911J Proof	—	Value: 400				
1912J	300,000	12.50	25.00	50.00	165	250
1912J Proof	—	Value: 450				
1913A	400,000	12.50	25.00	50.00	160	225
1913J	1,400,000	9.00	15.00	35.00	150	175
1913J Proof	—	Value: 400				
1914J	500,000	11.50	22.50	45.00	175	250

KM# 16.1 15 RUPIEN Weight: 7.1680 g. **Composition:** 0.7500 Gold .1728 oz. AGW **Ruler:** Wihelm II **Obverse:** Right arabesque ends below T of OSTAFRIKA

Date	Mintage	F	VF	XF	Unc	BU
1916T	9,803	600	900	1,200	1,800	2,250

KM# 16.2 15 RUPIEN Weight: 7.1680 g. **Composition:** 0.7500 Gold .1728 oz. AGW **Ruler:** Wihelm II **Obverse:** Right arabesque ends below first A of OSTAFRIKA

Date	Mintage	F	VF	XF	Unc	BU
1916T	6,395	600	900	1,250	1,800	2,250

PATTERNS

Including off metal strikes

KM#	Date	Mintage	Identification	Mkt Val
Pn1	1908	—	5 Heller. Bronze.	1,000
Pn2	1908	—	10 Heller. Nickel. Without sprigs	275
Pn2a	1908/1908	—	10 Heller. Nickel. Two obverses.	300
Pn3	1908J	—	25 Pfennig. Nickel. With sprigs.	200
Pn4	1908J	—	25 Pfennig. Nickel. With sprigs.	—
Pn5	ND	—	5 Rupien. White Metal. Uniface.	350
pn6	1913A	—	Rupie. Aluminum.	—

GERMAN STATES

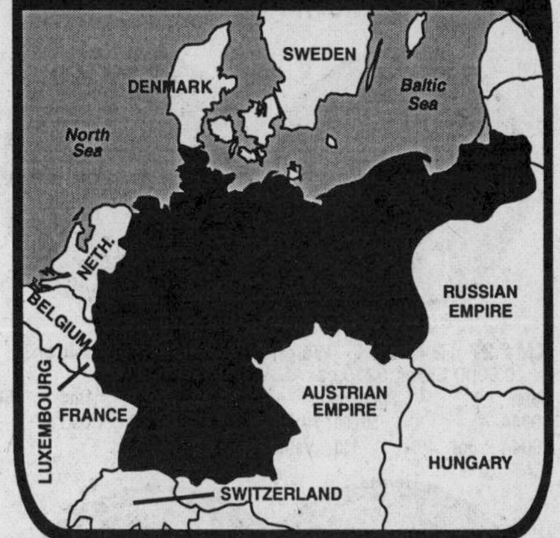

Although the origin of the German Empire can be traced to the Treaty of Verdun that ceded Charlemagne's lands east of the Rhine to German Prince Louis, it was for centuries little more than a geographic expression, con- sisting of hundreds of effectively autonomous big and little states. Nominally the states owed their allegiance to the Holy Roman Emperor, who was also a German king, but as the Emperors exhibited less and less concern for Germany the actual power devolved on the lords of the individual states. The fragmentation of the empire climaxed with the tragic denouement of the Thirty Years War, 1618-48, which devastated much of Germany, destroyed its agriculture and medieval commercial eminence and ended the attempt of the Hapsburgs to unify Germany. Deprived of administrative capacity by a lack of resources, the imperial authority became utterly powerless. At this time Germany contained an estimated 1,800 individual states, some with a population of as little as 300. The German Empire of recent history (the creation of Bis- marck) was formed on April 14, 1871, when the king of Prussia became German Emperor William I. The new empire comprised 4 kingdoms, 6 grand duchies, 12 duchies and principalities, 3 free cities and the nonautonomous province of Alsace-Lorraine. The states had the right to issue gold and silver coins of higher value than 1 Mark; coins of 1 Mark and under were general issues of the empire.

MINT MARKS

A - Berlin, 1750-date
D - Munich (Germany), 1872-date
E - Muldenhutten (Germany), 1887-1953
F - Stuttgart (Germany) 1872-date
G - Karlsruhe (Germany) 1872-date
J - Hamburg (Germany) 1873-date

MONETARY SYSTEM

After the German unification in 1871 when the old Thaler system was abandoned in favor of the Mark system (100 Pfennig = 1 Mark) the Vereinsthaler continued to circulate as a legal tender 3 Mark coin, and the double Thaler as a 6 Mark coin until 1908. In 1908 the Vereinsthalers were officially demonetized and the Thaler coinage was replaced by the new 3 Mark coin which had the same specifications as the old Vereinsthaler. The double Thaler coinage was not replaced as there was no great demand for a 6 Mark coin. Until the 1930's the German public continued to refer to the 3 Mark piece as a "Thaler".<

Commencing 1871

100 Pfennig = 1 Mark

VERRECHNUNGS & GUTSCHRIFTS TOKENS

These were metallic indebtedness receipts used for commercial and banking purposes due to the lack of available subsidiary coinage. These tokens could be redeemed in sufficient quantities.

ANHALT-DESSAU

Anhalt-Dessau was part of the 1252 division that included Zerbst and Köthen. In 1396, Anhalt-Zerbst was divided into Anhalt-Zerbst and Anhalt-Dessau. In 1508, Anhalt-Zerbst was absorbed into Anhalt-Dessau. The latter was given to the eldest son of Joachim Ernst in the division of 1603. As other lines became extinct, they fell to Anhalt-Dessau, which united all territories of the dynasty in 1863. The last ruler was forced to give up power at the end of World War I.

RULERS

Friedrich I, 1871-1904
Friedrich II, 1904-1918

MINT MARK

A – Berlin Mint, 1839-1914

DUCHY

REFORM COINAGE

KM# 27 2 MARK Weight: 11.1110 g. **Composition:** 0.9000 Silver .3215 oz. ASW **Ruler:** Friedrich II

Date	Mintage	F	VF	XF	Unc	BU
1904A	50,000	150	300	500	1,000	—
1904A Proof	150	Value: 1,100				

KM# 29 3 MARK Weight: 16.6670 g. **Composition:** 0.9000 Silver .4823 oz. ASW **Ruler:** Friedrich II

Date	Mintage	F	VF	XF	Unc	BU
1909A	100,000	35.00	75.00	150	285	—
1911A	100,000	35.00	75.00	150	285	—
Common date Proof	—	Value: 400				
Common date Proof	—	Value: 400				

KM# 30 3 MARK Weight: 16.6670 g. **Composition:** 0.9000 Silver .4823 oz. ASW **Ruler:** Friedrich II **Subject:** Silver wedding anniversary

Date	Mintage	F	VF	XF	Unc	BU
1914A	200,000	25.00	50.00	85.00	165	—
1914A Proof	1,000	Value: 275				

KM# 31 5 MARK Weight: 27.7770 g. **Composition:** 0.9000 Silver .8038 oz. ASW **Ruler:** Friedrich II **Subject:** Silver wedding anniversary

Date	Mintage	F	VF	XF	Unc	BU
1914A	30,000	65.00	180	285	450	—
1914A Proof	1,000	Value: 600				

KM# 25 10 MARK Weight: 3.9820 g. **Composition:** 0.9000 Gold .1152 oz. AGW **Ruler:** Friedrich I **Obverse:** Bust right

Date	Mintage	F	VF	XF	Unc	BU
1901A	20,000	400	800	1,100	1,500	—
1901A Proof	200	Value: 2,000				

KM# 26 20 MARK Weight: 7.9650 g. **Composition:** 0.9000 Gold .2304 oz. AGW **Ruler:** Friedrich I **Obverse:** Bust right

Date	Mintage	F	VF	XF	Unc	BU
1901A	15,000	425	800	1,100	1,600	—
1901A Proof	200	Value: 2,200				

KM# 28 20 MARK Weight: 7.9650 g. **Composition:** 0.9000 Gold .2304 oz. AGW **Ruler:** Friedrich II **Obverse:** Bust left

Date	Mintage	F	VF	XF	Unc	BU
1904A	25,000	400	700	1,000	1,700	—
1904A Proof	200	Value: 2,250				

PATTERNS

Including off metal strikes

KM#	Date	Mintage	Identification	Mkt Val
Pn1	1901A	—	2 Mark. Silver. KM23.	—
Pn2	1901A	—	5 Mark. Silver. KM24.	—
Pn3	1914	—	3 Mark. Silver. Wreath around rim. KM30.	—
Pn4	1914	—	3 Mark. Brass.	—
Pn5	1914	—	5 Mark. Silver. Pn6. KM31.	—
Pn6	1914	—	5 Mark. Silver. Lettered edge.	—
Pn7	1914	—	5 Mark. Silver. Plain edge.	—

BADEN

The earliest rulers of Baden, in the southwestern part of Germany along the Rhine, descended from the dukes of Zähringen in the late 11th century. The first division of the territory occurred in 1190, when separate lines of margraves were established in Baden and in Hachberg. Immediately prior to its extinction in 1418, Hachberg was sold back to Baden, which underwent several minor divisions itself during the next century. Baden acquired most of the countship of Sponheim from Electoral Pfalz near the end of the 15th century. In 1515, the most significant division of the patrimony took place, in which the Baden-Baden and Baden-(Pforzheim) Durlach lines were established.

Although Baden-Durlach was founded upon the division of Baden in 1515, the youngest son of Christoph I did not begin ruling in his own right until the demise of his father. This part of Baden was called Pforzheim until 1565, when the margrave moved his seat from the former to Durlach, located to the west and nearer the Rhine. After the male line of Baden-Baden failed in 1771 and the two parts of Baden were reunited, the fortunes of the margraviate continued to grow. Karlsruhe, near Durlach, was developed into a well-planned capital city. The ruler was given the rank of elector in 1803, only to be raised to grand duke three years later. The monarchy came to an end in 1918, but had by this time become one of the largest states in Germany.

RULERS
Friedrich I, Prince Regent 1852-1856,
Grand Duke 1856-1907
Friedrich II, 1907-1918

BADEN-DURLACH LINE

Grand Duchy

REFORM COINAGE

KM# 269 2 MARK Weight: 11.1110 g. **Composition:** 0.9000 Silver .3215 oz. ASW **Ruler:** Friedrich I as Grand Duke **Obverse:** Head left

Date	Mintage	F	VF	XF	Unc	BU
1901G	451,000	25.00	75.00	250	750	—
1901G Proof	—	Value: 2,500				
1902G	5,368	250	750	1,400	3,000	—
1902G Proof	—	Value: 3,500				

KM# 271 2 MARK Weight: 11.1110 g. **Composition:** 0.9000 Silver .3215 oz. ASW **Ruler:** Friedrich I as Grand Duke **Subject:** 50th year of reign

Date	Mintage	F	VF	XF	Unc	BU
1902	375,000	12.00	22.00	32.00	60.00	—

KM# 272 2 MARK Weight: 11.1110 g. **Composition:** 0.9000 Silver .3215 oz. ASW **Ruler:** Friedrich I as Grand Duke

Date	Mintage	F	VF	XF	Unc	BU
1902G	198,000	25.00	60.00	120	300	—
1903G	494,000	20.00	45.00	110	200	—
1904G	1,122,000	20.00	40.00	70.00	200	—
1905G	610,000	20.00	45.00	60.00	200	—
1906G	108,000	45.00	90.00	180	500	—
1907G	913,000	20.00	40.00	55.00	200	—

KM# 276 2 MARK Weight: 11.1110 g. **Composition:** 0.9000 Silver .3215 oz. ASW **Ruler:** Friedrich I as Grand Duke **Subject:** Golden Wedding Anniversary

Date	Mintage	F	VF	XF	Unc	BU
1906	350,000	15.00	30.00	40.00	65.00	—
1906 Matte proof	—	—	—	—	—	—

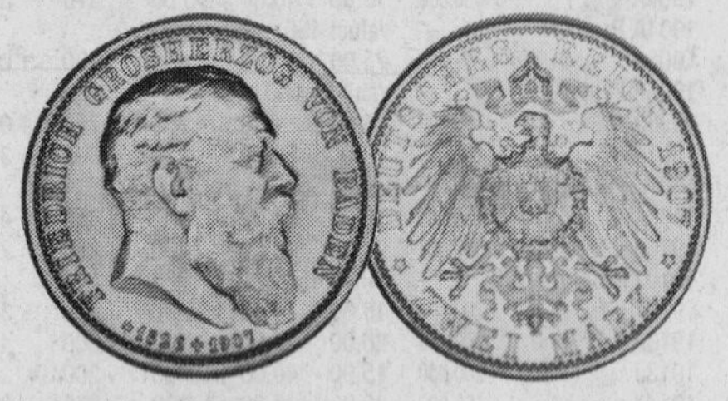

KM# 278 2 MARK Weight: 11.1110 g. **Composition:** 0.9000 Silver .3215 oz. ASW **Ruler:** Friedrich I as Grand Duke **Subject:** Death of Friedrich

Date	Mintage	F	VF	XF	Unc	BU
1907	350,000	20.00	40.00	50.00	80.00	—
1907 Proof	—	Value: 150				

KM# 283 2 MARK Weight: 11.1110 g. **Composition:** 0.9000 Silver .3215 oz. ASW **Ruler:** Friedrich II **Obverse:** Head left

Date	Mintage	F	VF	XF	Unc	BU
1911G	80,000	125	300	425	850	—
1913G	140,000	100	225	375	750	—
(1911-1913) Proof	—	Value: 1,200				

KM# 280 3 MARK Weight: 16.6670 g. **Composition:** 0.9000 Silver .4823 oz. ASW **Ruler:** Friedrich II **Obverse:** Head left

Date	Mintage	F	VF	XF	Unc	BU
1908G	300,000	10.00	22.00	35.00	75.00	—
1909G	760,000	10.00	22.00	35.00	75.00	—

Date	Mintage	F	VF	XF	Unc	BU
1910G	670,000	10.00	22.00	35.00	75.00	—
1911G	380,000	10.00	22.00	35.00	75.00	—
1912G	840,000	10.00	22.00	35.00	75.00	—
1914G	410,000	10.00	22.00	30.00	70.00	—
1915G	170,000	20.00	60.00	90.00	200	—
(1908-1915) G Proof	—	Value: 225				

KM# 268 5 MARK **Weight:** 27.7770 g. **Composition:** 0.9000 Silver .8038 oz. ASW **Ruler:** Friedrich I as Grand Duke

Date	Mintage	F	VF	XF	Unc	BU
1901G	128,000	25.00	70.00	275	1,500	—
1902G	43,000	35.00	85.00	250	2,000	—
(1891-1902)G Proof; common date	—	Value: 2,500				

KM# 273 5 MARK **Weight:** 27.7770 g. **Composition:** 0.9000 Silver .8038 oz. ASW **Ruler:** Friedrich I as Grand Duke **Subject:** 50th year of reign

Date	Mintage	F	VF	XF	Unc	BU
1902	50,000	35.00	75.00	135	185	—
1902 Proof	—	Value: 625				

KM# 274 5 MARK **Weight:** 27.7770 g. **Composition:** 0.9000 Silver .8038 oz. ASW **Ruler:** Friedrich I as Grand Duke

Date	Mintage	F	VF	XF	Unc	BU
1902G	128,000	35.00	65.00	225	600	—
1903G	439,000	20.00	45.00	165	585	—
1904G	238,000	20.00	45.00	165	585	—
1907G	244,000	20.00	45.00	165	585	—
(1902-1907G Proof	—	Value: 800				

KM# 277 5 MARK **Weight:** 27.7770 g. **Composition:** 0.9000 Silver .8038 oz. ASW **Ruler:** Friedrich I as Grand Duke **Subject:** Golden Wedding Anniversary

Date	Mintage	F	VF	XF	Unc	BU
1906	60,000	35.00	75.00	125	175	—
1906 Proof	—	Value: 275				

KM# 279 5 MARK **Weight:** 27.7770 g. **Composition:** 0.9000 Silver .8038 oz. ASW **Ruler:** Friedrich I as Grand Duke **Subject:** Death of Friedrich

Date	Mintage	F	VF	XF	Unc	BU
1907	60,000	55.00	110	145	200	—
1907 Proof	—	Value: 275				

KM# 281 5 MARK **Weight:** 27.7770 g. **Composition:** 0.9000 Silver .8038 oz. ASW **Ruler:** Friedrich II **Obverse:** Head left

Date	Mintage	F	VF	XF	Unc	BU
1908G	180,000	40.00	60.00	175	700	—
1913G	240,000	30.00	50.00	165	500	—
(1908-1913G Proof	—	Value: 1,000				

KM# 267 10 MARK **Weight:** 3.9820 g. **Composition:** 0.9000 Gold .1152 oz. AGW **Ruler:** Friedrich I as Grand Duke **Obverse:** Head left

Date	Mintage	F	VF	XF	Unc	BU
1901G	91,000	175	250	375	750	—
1901G Proof	—	Value: 1,700				

KM# 275 10 MARK **Weight:** 3.9820 g. **Composition:** 0.9000 Gold .1152 oz. AGW **Ruler:** Friedrich I as Grand Duke

Date	Mintage	F	VF	XF	Unc	BU
1902G	30,000	175	300	450	750	—
1903G	110,000	125	200	250	400	—
1904G	150,000	110	150	225	400	—
1905G	96,000	125	200	250	400	—
1906G	120,000	125	150	225	400	—
1907G	120,000	110	150	225	400	—
(1902-1907) G Proof	—	Value: 1,600				

KM# 282 10 MARK **Weight:** 3.9820 g. **Composition:** 0.9000 Gold .1152 oz. AGW **Ruler:** Friedrich II **Obverse:** Head right

Date	Mintage	F	VF	XF	Unc	BU
1909G	86,000	225	500	650	950	—
1910G	61,000	225	500	650	950	—
1911G	29,000	2,000	4,000	5,000	6,750	—
1912G	26,000	700	1,200	2,000	2,750	—
1913G	42,000	500	800	1,150	2,000	—
(1909-1913)G Proof	—	Value: 2,000				

KM# 284 20 MARK **Weight:** 7.9650 g. **Composition:** 0.9000 Gold .2304 oz. AGW **Ruler:** Friedrich II **Obverse:** Head left

Date	Mintage	F	VF	XF	Unc	BU
1911G	190,000	125	150	200	300	—
1912G	310,000	125	140	200	300	—
1913G	85,000	125	150	200	350	—
1914G	280,000	125	150	200	300	—
(1911-1914) G Proof	—	Value: 1,200				

BAVARIA

(Bayern)

Located in south Germany. In 1180 the Duchy of Bavaria was given to the Count of Wittelsbach by the emperor. He is the ancestor of all who ruled in Bavaria until 1918. Primogeniture was proclaimed in 1506 and in 1623 the dukes of Bavaria were given the electoral right. Bavaria, which had been divided for the various heirs, was reunited in 1799. The title of king was granted to Bavaria in 1805.

RULERS

Otto, 1886-1913, Prince Regent Luitpold, 1886-1912
Ludwig III, 1913-1918

MINT MARKS

D - Munich

KINGDOM

REFORM COINAGE

KM# 511.1 2 MARK **Weight:** 11.1110 g. **Composition:** 0.9000 Silver .3215 oz. ASW **Ruler:** Otto Prince Regent Luitpold **Obverse:** Closed curl

Date	Mintage	F	VF	XF	Unc	BU
1901D	809,000	12.00	25.00	55.00	135	—
1902D	1,321,000	10.00	22.00	45.00	120	—
1903D	1,406,000	10.00	22.00	45.00	110	—
1904D	2,320,000	8.00	20.00	35.00	100	—
1905D	1,406,000	10.00	22.00	45.00	95.00	—
1906D	1,055,000	10.00	22.00	55.00	120	—
1907D	2,106,000	8.00	20.00	35.00	85.00	—
1908D	633,000	10.00	22.00	45.00	95.00	—
1912D	214,000	10.00	22.00	45.00	110	—
1913D	98,000	40.00	80.00	160	250	—

KM# 516 2 MARK **Weight:** 11.1110 g. **Composition:** 0.9000 Silver .3215 oz. ASW **Ruler:** Otto Prince Regent Luitpold **Subject:** 90th Birthday of Prince Regent Luitpold

Date	Mintage	F	VF	XF	Unc	BU
1911D	640,000	12.00	20.00	30.00	50.00	—
1911D Proof	—	Value: 100				

KM# 519 2 MARK **Weight:** 11.1110 g. **Composition:** 0.9000 Silver .3215 oz. ASW **Ruler:** Ludwig III **Obverse:** Head left

Date	Mintage	F	VF	XF	Unc	BU
1914D	574,000	30.00	60.00	100	185	—

KM# 515 3 MARK **Weight:** 16.6670 g. **Composition:** 0.9000 Silver .4823 oz. ASW **Ruler:** Otto Prince Regent Luitpold **Obverse:** Head left

Date	Mintage	F	VF	XF	Unc	BU
1908D	681,000	12.00	20.00	35.00	70.00	—
1909D	1,827,000	10.00	18.00	30.00	65.00	—
1910D	1,496,000	10.00	18.00	30.00	65.00	—
1911D	843,000	12.00	20.00	35.00	70.00	—
1912D	1,014,000	12.00	20.00	35.00	70.00	—
1913D	731,000	12.00	20.00	35.00	70.00	—
1913D Proof	—	Value: 100				

KM# 517 3 MARK **Weight:** 16.6670 g. **Composition:** 0.9000 Silver .4823 oz. ASW **Ruler:** Otto Prince Regent Luitpold **Subject:** 90th Birthday of Prince Regent Luitpold

Date	Mintage	F	VF	XF	Unc	BU
1911D	640,000	12.00	20.00	32.00	65.00	—
1911D Proof	—	Value: 100				

KM# 520 3 MARK **Weight:** 16.6670 g. **Composition:** 0.9000 Silver .4823 oz. ASW **Ruler:** Ludwig III **Obverse:** Head left

Date	Mintage	F	VF	XF	Unc	BU
1914D	717,000	17.50	32.50	50.00	90.00	—
1914D Proof	—	Value: 150				

KM# 523 3 MARK **Weight:** 16.6670 g. **Composition:** 0.9000 Silver .4823 oz. ASW **Ruler:** Ludwig III **Subject:** Golden wedding anniversary

Date	Mintage	F	VF	XF	Unc	BU
1918D	130	—	15,000	28,000	40,000	—

KM# 512.1 5 MARK **Weight:** 27.7770 g. **Composition:** 0.9000 Silver .8038 oz. ASW **Ruler:** Otto **Obverse:** Closed curl

Date	Mintage	F	VF	XF	Unc	BU
1891D	98,000	17.50	35.00	100	400	—
1893D	98,000	25.00	50.00	120	400	—
1894D	141,000	17.50	35.00	120	400	—
1895D	141,000	22.50	45.00	110	400	—
1896D	28,000	55.00	125	600	1,250	—
1898D	303,000	15.00	30.00	65.00	250	—
1899D	141,000	25.00	50.00	90.00	325	—
1900D	295,000	15.00	30.00	80.00	300	—
(1891-1900)D Proof	—	Value: 1,000				
1901D	275,000	12.00	25.00	80.00	300	—
1902D	486,000	12.00	25.00	60.00	250	—
1903D	1,012,000	12.00	25.00	60.00	250	—
1904D	548,000	15.00	30.00	70.00	250	—
1906D	70,000	35.00	75.00	200	1,000	—
1907D	753,000	12.00	20.00	45.00	200	—
1908D	537,000	12.00	20.00	45.00	200	—
1913D	420,000	12.00	20.00	35.00	120	—
(1901-1913)D Proof	—	Value: 650				

KM# 512.2 5 MARK **Weight:** 27.7770 g. **Composition:** 0.9000 Silver .8038 oz. ASW **Ruler:** Otto **Obverse:** Open curl

Date	F	VF	XF	Unc	BU
1898D	12.00	25.00	70.00	300	—
1901D	12.00	25.00	70.00	300	—
1902D	12.00	25.00	70.00	300	—
1906D	35.00	75.00	200	800	—
1907D	12.00	20.00	45.00	200	—
1908D	12.00	20.00	45.00	200	—
1913D	12.00	20.00	35.00	120	—

KM# 512.3 5 MARK **Weight:** 27.7770 g. **Composition:** 0.9000 Silver .8038 oz. ASW **Ruler:** Otto **Obverse:** Many locks of hair above ear, closed curl

Date	F	VF	XF	Unc	BU
1891D	17.50	25.00	100	400	—
1893D	25.00	50.00	120	400	—
1894D	17.50	35.00	120	400	—
1898D	15.00	30.00	60.00	250	—
1899D	25.00	50.00	90.00	325	—
1913D	15.00	25.00	45.00	120	—

KM# 512.4 5 MARK **Weight:** 27.7770 g. **Composition:** 0.9000 Silver .8038 oz. ASW **Ruler:** Otto **Obverse:** Large lock of hair above ear, closed curl

Date	F	VF	XF	Unc	BU
1895D	22.50	45.00	110	400	—
1896D	55.00	125	600	1,250	—

Date	F	VF	XF	Unc	BU
1898D	12.00	20.00	60.00	250	—
1899D	25.00	50.00	90.00	325	—
1900D	15.00	30.00	80.00	300	—
1901D	15.00	30.00	80.00	300	—
1902D	12.00	28.00	65.00	300	—
1903D	12.00	28.00	65.00	300	—
1904D	15.00	30.00	70.00	300	—
1906D	35.00	75.00	200	800	—
1907D	12.00	20.00	45.00	200	—
1908D	12.00	20.00	45.00	200	—
1913D	12.00	20.00	35.00	120	—

KM# 518 5 MARK **Weight:** 27.7770 g. **Composition:** 0.9000 Silver .8038 oz. ASW **Ruler:** Otto Prince Regent Luitpold **Subject:** 90th Birthday of Prince Regent Luitpold

Date	Mintage	F	VF	XF	Unc	BU
1911D	160,000	25.00	60.00	85.00	160	—
1911D Proof	—	Value: 200				

KM# 521 5 MARK **Weight:** 27.7770 g. **Composition:** 0.9000 Silver .8038 oz. ASW **Ruler:** Ludwig III **Obverse:** Head left

Date	Mintage	F	VF	XF	Unc	BU
1914D	142,000	40.00	75.00	125	190	—

KM# 514 10 MARK **Weight:** 3.9820 g. **Composition:** 0.9000 Gold .1152 oz. AGW **Ruler:** Otto **Obv. Legend:** ... V. BAYERN

Date	Mintage	F	VF	XF	Unc	BU
1900D	Inc. above	65.00	140	225	325	—
1900D Proof	—	Value: 800				
1901D	141,000	65.00	125	200	300	—
1902D	68,000	65.00	125	200	300	—
1903D	534,000	65.00	120	180	250	—
1904D	211,000	65.00	120	180	250	—
1905D	281,000	65.00	120	180	250	—
1906D	141,000	65.00	125	190	250	—
1907D	211,000	65.00	120	190	250	—
1909D	209,000	65.00	120	190	250	—
1910D	141,000	65.00	120	190	250	—
1911D	72,000	65.00	125	200	300	—
1912D	141,000	65.00	125	190	250	—
(1901-1912)D Proof	—	Value: 1,000				

KM# 513 20 MARK **Weight:** 7.9650 g. **Composition:** 0.9000 Gold .2304 oz. AGW **Ruler:** Otto **Obverse:** Head left **Reverse:** Type III

Date	Mintage	F	VF	XF	Unc	BU
1895D	501,000	125	140	160	250	—
1895D Proof	—	Value: 800				
1900D	501,000	125	140	160	250	—
1905D	501,000	125	140	160	250	—
1905D Proof	—	Value: 1,250				

Date	Mintage	F	VF	XF	Unc	BU
1913D	311,000	—	17,500	22,500	25,000	—
1913D Proof	—	Value: 35,000				

KM# 522 20 MARK **Weight:** 7.9650 g. **Composition:** 0.9000 Gold .2304 oz. AGW **Ruler:** Ludwig III **Obverse:** Head left **Note:** Never officially released.

Date	Mintage	F	VF	XF	Unc	BU
1914D	533,000	—	2,000	2,500	3,000	—
1914D Proof	—	Value: 3,650				

PATTERNS

Including off metal strikes

KM#	Date	Mintage	Identification	Mkt Val
Pn14	1904	—	5 Mark. Silver. Eagle in ring. Reeded edge.	—
Pn15	1904D	—	5 Mark. Silver. Eagle in ring. Lettered edge.	—
Pn16	1904D	—	5 Mark. Silver. Without inner circle.	—
Pn17	1905D	—	5 Mark. Copper. Pn6. KM512.	—
Pn18	1911	—	3 Mark. Silver.	—
Pn19	1911D	—	3 Mark. Copper.	—
Pn25	1913D	—	3 Mark. Silver. Plain edge.	—
Pn35	1914D	—	3 Mark. Silver. Bust faces right.	—
Pn38	1914D	—	20 Mark. Gold. Lettered edge.	—
Pn36	1914D	—	5 Mark. Silver. Larger lettering, KM521.	—
Pn44	1914D	—	20 Mark. Silver Gilt. 18-millimeter bust. KM522. Hallmarked, plain edge.	—
Pn39	1914D	—	20 Mark. Silver Gilt. Hallmarked, plain edge.	150
Pn37	1914D	—	5 Mark. Silver. Plain edge. KM521.	—
Pn40	1914D	—	20 Mark. Silver Gilt. Hallmarked, plain edge. KM522.	—
Pn41	1914D	—	20 Mark. Gold. Denticled rim. KM522. Plain edge.	—
Pn42	1914D	—	20 Mark. Silver Gilt. Denticled rim. KM522. Hallmarked, plain edge.	—
Pn43	1914D	—	20 Mark. Gold. 18-millimeter bust. KM522. Lettered edge.	8,000
Pn45	1914D	—	20 Mark. Gold. Plain rim. KM522. Plain edge.	—
Pn46	1914D	—	20 Mark. Gold. Plain rim. KM522. Lettered edge.	—
Pn47	1914D	—	20 Mark. Gold. Round "O" in KOENIG. Lettered edge.	—
Pn48	1914D	—	20 Mark. Silver Gilt. Round "O" in KOENIG. KM522. Hallmarked, plain edge.	—
Pn49	ND J	—	Gulden. Gold. Bust of Ludwig III in uniform. Main bridge of Wurzburger.	—

BREMEN

Established at about the same time as the bishopric in 787, Bremen was under the control of the bishops and archbishops until joining the Hanseatic League in 1276. Archbishop Albrecht II granted the mint right to the city in 1369, but this was not formalized by imperial decree until 1541. In 1646, Bremen was raised to free imperial status and continued to strike its own coins into the early 20th century. The city lost its free imperial status in 1803 and was controlled by France from 1806 until 1813. Regaining it independence in 1815, Bremen joined the North German Confederation in 1867 and the German Empire in 1871. Since 1369, there was practically continuous coinage until 1907.

FREE CITY

REGULAR COINAGE

KM# 250 2 MARK **Weight:** 11.1110 g. **Composition:** 0.9000 Silver .3215 oz. ASW

Date	Mintage	F	VF	XF	Unc	BU
1904 J	100,000	20.00	40.00	80.00	175	—
1904 J Proof	200	Value: 400				

KM# 251 5 MARK **Weight:** 27.7770 g. **Composition:** 0.9000 Silver .8038 oz. ASW

Date	Mintage	F	VF	XF	Unc	BU
1906 J	41,000	75.00	185	285	450	—
1906 J Proof	600	Value: 750				

KM# 253 10 MARK **Weight:** 3.9820 g. **Composition:** 0.9000 Gold .1152 oz. AGW

Date	Mintage	F	VF	XF	Unc	BU
1907 J	20,000	400	675	1,000	1,600	—
1907 J Proof	—	Value: 2,000				

KM# 252 20 MARK **Weight:** 7.9650 g. **Composition:** 0.9000 Gold .2304 oz. AGW

Date	Mintage	F	VF	XF	Unc	BU
1906 J	20,000	400	675	1,000	1,650	—
1906 J Proof	—	Value: 2,500				

TOKEN COINAGE

Reckoning Tokens

These vouchers, issued March 18, 1924, were based on the American dollar. Issued in conjunction with Bremens issue of treasury. Due to monies being held to purchase Bremens 5% Dollar Bond, they rarely circulated. The tokens were withdrawn September 30 of that same year.

KM# Tn1 2 VERRECHNUNGS-PFENNIG
Composition: Brass **Obverse:** State arms **Reverse:** Denomination **Note:** Struck at Numberg.

Date	Mintage	F	VF	XF	Unc	BU
ND(1924)	501,000	10.00	25.00	45.00	85.00	—

KM# Tn2 5 VERRECHNUNGS-PFENNIG
Composition: Aluminum **Obverse:** State arms **Reverse:** Denomination **Note:** Struck at Numberg.

Date	Mintage	F	VF	XF	Unc	BU
ND(1924)	669,000	9.00	18.00	30.00	70.00	—

KM# Tn3 10 VERRECHNUNGS-PFENNIG
Composition: Aluminum **Obverse:** State arms **Reverse:** Denomination **Note:** Struck at Numberg.

Date	Mintage	F	VF	XF	Unc	BU
ND(1924)	695,000	10.00	20.00	35.00	75.00	—

KM# Tn4 20 VERRECHNUNGS-PFENNIG
Composition: Aluminum **Obverse:** State arms **Reverse:** Denomination **Note:** Struck at Numberg.

Date	Mintage	F	VF	XF	Unc	BU
ND(1924)	382,000	17.00	35.00	60.00	120	—

KM# Tn5 50 VERRECHNUNGS-PFENNIG
Composition: Aluminum **Obverse:** Lions supporting crowned arms **Reverse:** Denomination **Note:** Struck at Hamburg.

Date	Mintage	F	VF	XF	Unc	BU
ND(1924)	483,000	30.00	55.00	100	200	—

KM# Tn6 VERRECHNUNGSMARK **Composition:** Aluminum **Obverse:** Lions support crowned arms on pedestal **Reverse:** Denomination **Note:** Struck at Menden. This coin is listed in Jaeger & Funck as struck in aluminum. Kunker has listed it as having an iron core but doesn't indicate what metal clads or plates the piece.

Date	Mintage	F	VF	XF	Unc	BU
ND(1924)	382,000	75.00	150	275	500	—

PATTERNS

Including off metal strikes

KM#	Date	Mintage	Identification	Mkt Val
Pn40	1904 J	—	5 Mark. KM251.	—
Pn41	1905 J	—	2 Mark. KM250.	—
Pn42	1905 J	—	5 Mark. Silver. Larger lettering without beaded rim. KM251.	15,000
Pn43	1905 J	—	5 Mark. Tin.	—
Pn44	1906	—	5 Mark. Bronze.	—
Pn45	1906	—	5 Mark. Silver.	—
Pn46	1906	—	5 Mark. Tin.	—
Pn47	ND	—	S.M.. Copper.	—

BRUNSWICK-WOLFENBUTTEL

(Braunschweig-Wolfenbüttel)

Located in north-central Germany. Wolfenbüttel was annexed to Brunswick in 1257. One of the five surviving sons of Albrecht II founded the first line in Wolfenbüttel in 1318. A further division in Wolfenbüttel and Lüneburg was undertaken in 1373. Another division occurred in 1495, but the Wolfenbüttel duchy survived in the younger line. Heinrich IX was forced out of his territory during the religious wars of the mid-sixteenth century by Duke Johann Friedrich I of Saxony and Landgrave Philipp of Hessen in 1542, but was restored to his possessions in 1547. Duke Friedrich Ulrich was forced to cede the Grubenhagen lands, which had been acquired by Wolfenbüttel in 1596, to Lüneburg in 1617. When the succession died out in 1634, the lands and titles fell to the cadet line in Dannenberg. The line became extinct once again and passed to Brunswick-Bevern in 1735 from which a new succession of Wolfenbüttel dukes descended. The ducal family was beset by continual personal and political tragedy during the nineteenth century. Two of the dukes were killed in battles with Napoleon, the territories were occupied by the French and became part of the Kingdom of Westphalia, another duke was forced out by a revolt in 1823. From 1884 until 1913, Brunswick-Wolfenbüttel was governed by Prussia and then turned over to a younger prince of Brunswick who married a daughter of Kaiser Wilhelm II. His reign was short, however, as he was forced to abdicate at the end of World War I.

RULERS

Prussian rule, 1884-1913
Ernst August, 1913-1918

DUCHY

REFORM COINAGE

KM# 1161 3 MARK **Weight:** 16.6670 g. **Composition:** 0.9000 Silver .4823 oz. ASW **Ruler:** Ernst August **Subject:** Ernst August wedding and accession

Date	Mintage	F	VF	XF	Unc	BU
1915A	1,700	600	1,150	1,850	2,900	—
1915A Proof	—	Value: 3,200				

KM# 1162 3 MARK **Weight:** 16.6670 g. **Composition:** 0.9000 Silver .4823 oz. ASW **Ruler:** Ernst August **Subject:** Ernst August wedding and accession **Obv. Legend:** U LUNEB added

Date	Mintage	F	VF	XF	Unc	BU
1915A	32,000	50.00	110	175	300	—
1915A Proof	—	Value: 400				

KM# 1163 5 MARK **Weight:** 27.7770 g. **Composition:** 0.9000 Silver .8038 oz. ASW **Ruler:** Ernst August **Subject:** Ernst August wedding and accession

Date	Mintage	F	VF	XF	Unc	BU
1915A	1,400	700	1,350	2,250	3,500	—
1915A Proof	—	Value: 4,000				

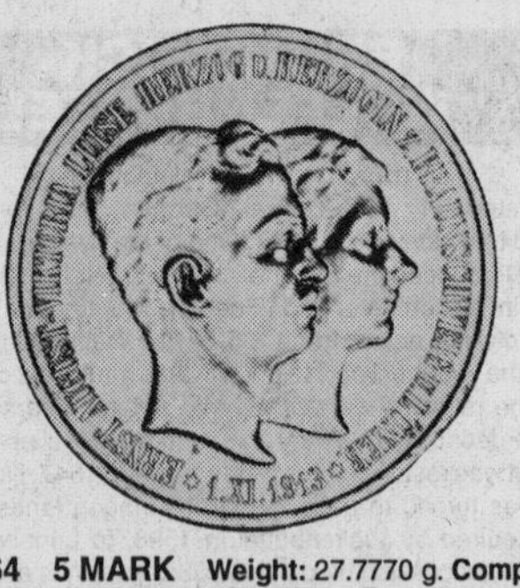

KM# 1164 5 MARK **Weight:** 27.7770 g. **Composition:** 0.9000 Silver .8038 oz. ASW **Ruler:** Ernst August **Subject:** Ernst August wedding and accession **Obv. Legend:** U. LUNEB added **Reverse:** Similar to KM#1163

Date	Mintage	F	VF	XF	Unc	BU
1915A	8,600	165	350	600	950	—
1915A Proof	—	Value: 1,000				

PATTERNS

Including off metal strikes

KM#	Date	Mintage	Identification	Mkt Val
Pn54	1913	—	3 Mark. Silver.	—
Pn55	1913	—	5 Mark. Silver.	—
Pn56	1915A	—	3 Mark. Silver. Plain edge. KM1161.	—
Pn57	1915A	—	3 Mark. Silver. Beaded rim. Weak 5 in date. Plain edge. KM1162.	—
Pn58	191x	—	5 Mark. Silver. Beaded rim, wedding portraits facing left. Partial date. Plain edge.	—

HAMBURG

The city of Hamburg is located on the Elbe River about 75 miles (125 kilometers) from the North Sea. Tradition states that it was founded by Charlemagne in the early 9th century. At first, the town was controlled by the archbishopric of Bremen and Hamburg (see Bremen). In 1110, Hamburg and the territory of Holstein came under the rule of Count Adolf I of Schauenburg (Schaumburg, ruled 1106-1128), which inaugurated a period stretching for four centuries in which the Holstein dynasty exercised authority over the city. Hamburg joined with Lübeck in 1241 to form the first partnership in what was to become the Hanseatic League. Count Adolf VI of Schauenburg (1290-1315) gave civic autonomy to Hamburg in 1292 and leased the mint right to the citizens the next year. Local *hohlpfennige* had already been struck fifty years previous. From this early time, the city struck an almost continuous series of coins throughout the centuries up to World War I. In 1510, Hamburg was granted the status of a Free City of the Empire, although it had actually been free for about 250 years. It was occupied by the French during the period of the Napoleonic Wars. In 1866, Hamburg joined the North German Confederation and became a part of the German Empire in 1871.

FREE CITY

REFORM COINAGE

KM# 294 2 MARK **Weight:** 11.1110 g. **Composition:** 0.9000 Silver .3215 oz. ASW

Date	Mintage	F	VF	XF	Unc	BU
Common date Proof	—	Value: 350				
1901J	482,000	12.50	20.00	50.00	200	—
1902J	779,000	12.50	20.00	50.00	200	—
1903J	817,000	12.50	20.00	40.00	200	—
1904J	1,248,000	12.50	20.00	40.00	200	—
1905J	204,000	25.00	40.00	75.00	450	—
1906J	1,225,000	12.50	20.00	40.00	200	—
1907J	1,226,000	12.50	20.00	40.00	200	—
1908J	368,000	12.50	25.00	45.00	200	—
1911J	204,000	12.50	25.00	45.00	200	—
1912J	79,000	15.00	40.00	95.00	400	—
1913J	105,000	12.50	25.00	55.00	200	—
1914J	328,000	10.00	20.00	40.00	150	—
Common date Proof	—	Value: 350				

KM# 296 3 MARK **Weight:** 16.6670 g. **Composition:** 0.9000 Silver .4823 oz. ASW

Date	Mintage	F	VF	XF	Unc	BU
1908J	408,000	12.50	25.00	40.00	80.00	—
1909J	1,389,000	12.50	25.00	40.00	80.00	—
1910J	526,000	12.50	25.00	40.00	80.00	—
1911J	922,000	12.50	25.00	40.00	80.00	—
1912J	491,000	12.50	25.00	40.00	80.00	—
1913J	344,000	12.50	25.00	40.00	80.00	—
1914J	575,000	12.50	25.00	40.00	80.00	—
Common dateJ Proof	—	Value: 250				

KM# 293 5 MARK **Weight:** 27.7770 g. **Composition:** 0.9000 Silver .8038 oz. ASW

Date	Mintage	F	VF	XF	Unc	BU
Common dateJ Proof	—	Value: 1,500				
1901J	172,000	17.50	40.00	100	500	—
1902J	294,000	17.50	35.00	80.00	400	—
1903J	588,000	17.50	35.00	75.00	275	—
1904J	319,000	15.00	32.00	75.00	275	—
1907J	326,000	15.00	32.00	75.00	275	—
1908J	458,000	15.00	32.00	75.00	220	—
1913J	327,000	15.00	32.00	60.00	165	—
Common dateJ Proof	—	Value: 1,500				

KM# 292 10 MARK **Weight:** 3.9820 g. **Composition:** 0.9000 Gold .1152 oz. AGW **Reverse:** Type II

Date	Mintage	F	VF	XF	Unc	BU
1901J	82,000	70.00	110	160	285	—
1902J	41,000	100	200	250	550	—
1903J	310,000	65.00	110	160	240	—
1905J	164,000	65.00	110	160	240	—
1906J	164,000	65.00	110	160	240	—
1907J	111,000	65.00	110	160	240	—
1908J	32,000	100	200	275	600	—
1909J	122,000	65.00	110	160	240	—
1909J Proof	—	Value: 850				
1910J	41,000	100	200	300	500	—
1910J	—	Value: 1,200				
1911J	75,000	70.00	130	200	325	—
1911J Proof	—	Value: 8,000				
1912J	48,000	150	200	300	475	—
1912J Proof	—	Value: 1,000				
1913J	41,000	150	200	300	400	—
1913J Proof	—	Value: 1,000				

KM# 295 20 MARK **Weight:** 7.9650 g. **Composition:** 0.9000 Gold .2304 oz/AGW **Reverse:** Type III

Date	Mintage	F	VF	XF	Unc	BU
1900J	501,000	115	135	160	225	—
1908J Rare	14	—	—	—	—	—
1913J	491,000	100	120	140	180	—
1913J Proof	—	Value: 1,000				

TOKEN COINAGE

Reckoning Tokens

KM# Tn1 1/100 VERRECHNUNGSMARKE **Composition:** Aluminum **Issuer:** Hamburg Bank **Obverse:** City arms **Reverse:** Denomination **Size:** 20.5 mm.

Date	Mintage	F	VF	XF	Unc	BU
1923	9,128,000	3.00	6.00	12.50	25.00	—

KM# Tn2 5/100 VERRECHNUNGSMARKE
Composition: Aluminum **Issuer:** Hamburg Bank **Obverse:** City arms **Reverse:** Denomination **Size:** 23 mm.

Date	Mintage	F	VF	XF	Unc	BU
1923	8,100,000	2.75	4.50	9.00	18.00	—

KM# Tn3 1/10 VERRECHNUNGSMARKE
Composition: Aluminum **Issuer:** Hamburg Bank **Obverse:** City arms **Reverse:** Denomination **Size:** 26.5 mm.

Date	Mintage	F	VF	XF	Unc	BU
1923	8,600,000	2.75	4.50	10.00	20.00	—

PATTERNS
Including off metal strikes

KM#	Date	Mintage	Identification	Mkt Val
Pn20	1906J	—	5 Mark. Copper. Plain edge. KM293.	—
Pn21	1913	—	5 Mark. Plain edge. KM293.	1,100
Pn22	1913J	—	5 Mark. Plain edge. KM293.	—
Pn23	1914J	—	3 Mark. Silver. Plain edge. KM296.	—
Pn24	1922J	—	1/2 Mark. Aluminum. Plain edge.	—
Pn38	1922J	—	5 Mark. Nickel Plated Iron. Plain edge.	—
Pn32	1922J	—	2 Mark. Nickel. Plain edge.	—
Pn28	1922J	—	Mark. Aluminum. Plain edge.	—
Pn35	1922J	—	3 Mark. Iron. Plain edge. Copper-nickel plated.	—
Pn25	1922J	—	1/2 Mark. Iron. Plain edge.	—
Pn33	1922J	—	2 Mark. Aluminum. Plain edge.	—
Pn36	1922J	—	3 Mark. Aluminum. Plain edge.	—
Pn39	1922J	—	5 Mark. Aluminum. Plain edge.	—
Pn29	1922J	—	Mark. Copper. Plain edge.	—
Pn30	1922J	—	Mark. Nickel. Plain edge.	—
Pn37	1922J	—	3 Mark. Nickel. Plain edge.	—
Pn40	1922J	—	5 Mark. Nickel. Plain edge.	—
Pn26	1922J	—	1/2 Mark. Nickel. Plain edge.	—
Pn34	1922J	—	2 Mark. Zinc. Plain edge.	—
Pn27	1922J	—	1/2 Mark. Copper. Plain edge.	225
Pn41	1922J	—	5 Mark. Zinc. Plain edge.	—
Pn31	1922J	—	Mark. Iron. Plain edge.	—

HESSE-DARMSTADT

(Hessen-Darmstadt)

Founded by the youngest of Philipp I's four sons upon the death of their father in 1567, Hesse-Darmstadt was one of the two main branches of the family which survived past the beginning of the 17th century. The Countship of Hanau-Lichtenberg was through marriage when the male line failed in 1736. Ludwig X was forced to cede that territory to France in 1801. In 1803, Darmstadt acquired part of the Palatinate, the city of Friedberg, part of the city of Mainz, and the Duchy of Westphalia in a general settlement with France. The Landgrave was elevated to the status of Grand Duke in 1806 and reacquired Hesse-Homburg. In 1815 the Congress of Vienna awarded Hesse-Darmstadt the city of Worms and all of Mainz. These were relinquished, along with Hesse-Homburg, to Prussia in 1866 and Hesse-Darmstadt was called just Hesse from 1867 onwards. Hesse became part of the German Empire in 1871, but ceased to exist as a semi-sovereign state at the end of World War I.

RULERS
Ernst Ludwig, 1892-1918

GRAND DUCHY

REFORM COINAGE

KM# 372 2 MARK Weight: 11.1110 g. **Composition:** 0.9000 Silver .3215 oz. ASW **Subject:** 40th birthday of Philipp the Magnanimous

Date	Mintage	F	VF	XF	Unc	BU
1904	100,000	20.00	40.00	65.00	90.00	—
1904 Proof	2,250	Value: 135				

Note: Obverse matte, reverse polished.

KM# 375 3 MARK Weight: 16.6670 g. **Composition:** 0.9000 Silver .4823 oz. ASW **Ruler:** Ernst Ludwig

Date	Mintage	F	VF	XF	Unc	BU
1910A	200,000	30.00	60.00	95.00	165	—
1910A Proof	—	Value: 325				

KM# 376 3 MARK Weight: 16.6670 g. **Composition:** 0.9000 Silver .4823 oz. ASW **Ruler:** Ernst Ludwig **Subject:** 25-Year Jubilee

Date	Mintage	F	VF	XF	Unc	BU
1917A	1,333	—	1,750	2,750	4,000	—
1917A Proof	Inc. above	Value: 6,000				

KM# 373 5 MARK Weight: 27.7770 g. **Composition:** 0.9000 Silver .8038 oz. ASW **Ruler:** Ernst Ludwig **Subject:** 400th birthday of Philipp the Magnanimous

Date	Mintage	F	VF	XF	Unc	BU
1904	40,000	45.00	95.00	145	265	—
1904 Proof	700	Value: 550				

Note: Obverse matte, reverse polished.

KM# 371 20 MARK Weight: 7.9650 g. **Composition:** 0.9000 Gold .2304 oz. AGW **Ruler:** Ernst Ludwig

Date	Mintage	F	VF	XF	Unc	BU
1901A	80,000	125	175	325	600	—
1901A Proof	600	Value: 1,750				
1903A	40,000	125	175	350	700	—
1903A Proof	100	Value: 1,750				

KM# 374 20 MARK Weight: 7.9650 g. **Composition:** 0.9000 Gold .2304 oz. AGW **Ruler:** Ernst Ludwig

Date	Mintage	F	VF	XF	Unc	BU
1905A	45,000	125	200	275	500	—
1905A Proof	200	Value: 1,750				
1906A	85,000	125	175	250	425	—
1906A Proof	199	Value: 1,750				
1908A	40,000	125	175	250	450	—
1908A Proof	—	Value: 1,750				
1911A Proof	—	Value: 1,500				
1911A	150,000	125	175	250	500	—

PATTERNS
Including off metal strikes

KM#	Date	Mintage	Identification	Mkt Val
Pn31	1910A	—	3 Mark. Silver.	—
Pn32	1917	—	3 Mark. Silver.	—
Pn33	1917A	—	3 Mark. Silver. Plain edge. Y82.	—

LIPPE-DETMOLD

After the division of 1613, the Counts of Lippe-Detmold, as the senior branch of the family, ruled over the largest portion of Lippe (see), a small patrimony in northwestern Germany. In 1620, Lippe-Sternberg became extinct and its lands and titles reverted to Lippe-Detmold. The younger brother of Hermann Adolf founded the line of Lippe-Sternberg-Schwalenberg (Biesterfeld) in 1652, which lasted into the 20th century. In 1720, the count was raised to the rank of prince, but did not use the title until 1789. Lippe joined the North German Confederation in 1866 and became part of the German Empire in 1871. Prince Alexander was declared insane and placed under a regency during his entire reign. There ensued a ten-year testamentary dispute between the Lippe-Biesterfeld and the Schaumburg-Lippe lines over the succession to the childless Alexander - a Wilhelmine cause célèbre. Leopold (V) of the Biesterfeld line gained the principality in 1905, but was forced to abdicate in 1918, at the end of World War I. In 1947, Lippe was absorbed by the German state of North Rhine-Westphalia.

RULERS
Alexander, 1895-1905
Leopold IV, 1905-1918

MINT MARKS
A - Berlin mint, 1843-1918

PRINCIPALITY

REFORM COINAGE

KM# 270 2 MARK Weight: 11.1110 g. **Composition:** 0.9000 Silver .3215 oz. ASW **Ruler:** Leopold IV

Date	Mintage	F	VF	XF	Unc	BU
1906A	20,000	100	200	300	475	—
1906A Proof	1,100	Value: 525				

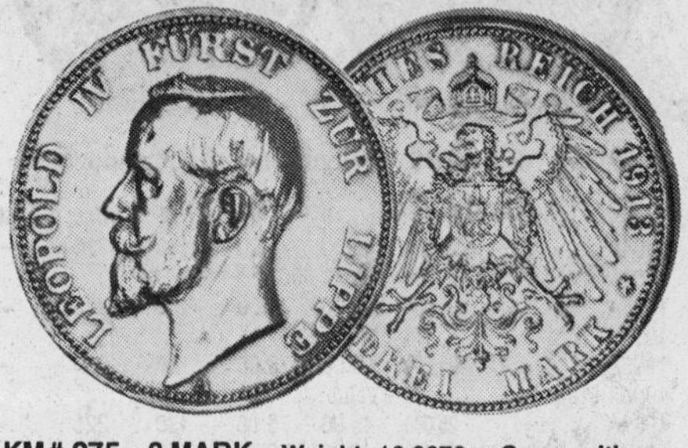

KM# 275 3 MARK Weight: 16.6670 g. **Composition:** 0.9000 Silver .4823 oz. ASW **Ruler:** Leopold IV

Date	Mintage	F	VF	XF	Unc	BU
1913A	15,000	125	250	335	500	—
1913A Proof	100	Value: 675				

LUBECK

The original settlement was called Liubice, the capital of a Slavic principality. It was located at the confluence of the Schwartau with the Trave Rivers and contained a castle with a merchant town on a harbor. The town was burned down in 1138 and Count Adolf II of Holstein (1128-64) refounded the city four miles (6.5 kilometers) up the Trave in 1143. Duke Heinirich III the Lion of Saxony (1153-80) forced Adolf II to relinquish Lübeck to him as his feudal overlord. Heinrich III no sooner had the city in his possession when a fire destroyed it. Heinrich III began rebuilding it in 1159 and this is now considered the traditional date of it founding. As the city and its trade on the Baltic grew in importance, special rights and privileges were granted to it in 1188 by Emperor Friedrich I Barbarossa. In 1226, Friedrich II raised Lübeck to the status of a free imperial city and a long period of self-government began. From about 1190 and into the 13th century, an imperial mint operated in the town. Although Lübeck was granted the mint right in 1188, reiterated in 1226 and 1340, its earliest civic coinage only began about 1350. The commercial importance of the city became even greater when it joined with Hamburg in 1241 to form the nucleus of what was to become the Hanseatic League. In 1358, the member cities of the League, which had grown very powerful during the preceding century, elected Lübeck as the administrative capital. By the beginning of the 15th century, the city was second only to Cologne as the largest in northern Germany.

The Protestant Reformation swept through Lübeck in 1529-30 (see Bishopric) and changes came rapidly as the governing city council was removed from office, only to be replaced by a revolutionary *burgomeister*, Jürgen Wullenwever. An unsuccessful war ensued against Denmark, Sweden and the Netherlands and caused the city to lose its powerful position in northern Europe. This began the dismemberment of the Hanseatic League and even a victorious war against Sweden during 1563-1570 was not enough to prevent the decline of Lübeck's fortunes. The demise of the League in 1630, during the Thirty Years' War, may have actually been beneficial to the city as it was able to remain neutral during the long years of struggle throughout Germany. The city was able to regain much of its lost economic power during the 18th century, partly due to increased trade with Russia through its new Baltic port of St. Petersburg. Lübeck's economy was completely ruined, however, during the Napoleonic Wars (1792-1815). Occupied by the French from 1811 to 1813, it was restored as a free city in the latter year. After 1815, the city was a member of the German Confederation and joined the North German Confederation in 1866. It remained a free city as part of the German Empire from 1871 until the end of World War I in 1918. However, its status as a self-governing entity, which had begun in 1226, did not end until 1937, when it was made a part of the province of Schleswig-Holstein.

FREE CITY

REFORM COINAGE

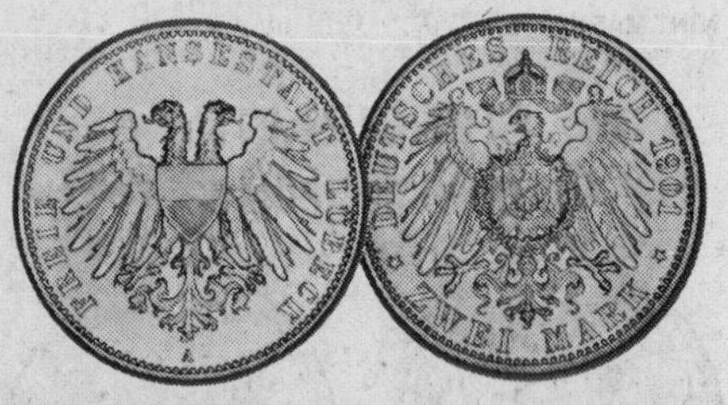

KM# 210 2 MARK **Weight:** 11.1110 g. **Composition:** 0.9000 Silver .3215 oz. ASW

Date	Mintage	F	VF	XF	Unc	BU
1901A	25,000	100	175	225	400	—
1901A Proof	—	Value: 450				

KM# 212 2 MARK **Weight:** 11.1110 g. **Composition:** 0.9000 Silver .3215 oz. ASW

Date	Mintage	F	VF	XF	Unc	BU
1904A	25,000	45.00	75.00	130	220	—
1904A Proof	200	Value: 300				
1905A	25,000	45.00	75.00	130	225	—
1905A Proof	178	Value: 300				
1906A	25,000	45.00	75.00	130	225	—
1906A Proof	200	Value: 300				
1907A	25,000	45.00	75.00	130	225	—
1911A	25,000	45.00	75.00	130	225	—
1911A Proof	—	Value: 350				
1912A	25,000	45.00	75.00	130	225	—
1912A Proof	—	Value: 350				

KM# 215 3 MARK **Weight:** 16.6670 g. **Composition:** 0.9000 Silver .4823 oz. ASW

Date	Mintage	F	VF	XF	Unc	BU
1908	33,000	25.00	65.00	110	185	—
1909A	33,000	25.00	65.00	110	185	—
1910A	33,000	25.00	65.00	110	185	—
1911A	33,000	25.00	65.00	110	185	—
1912A	34,000	25.00	65.00	110	185	—
1913A	30,000	25.00	65.00	110	185	—
1914A	10,000	35.00	85.00	150	250	—
Common dateA Proof	—	Value: 275				

KM# 213 5 MARK **Weight:** 27.7770 g. **Composition:** 0.9000 Silver .8038 oz. ASW

Date	Mintage	F	VF	XF	Unc	BU
1904A	10,000	100	250	375	500	—
1904A Proof	200	Value: 850				
1907A	10,000	100	250	375	550	—
1908A	10,000	100	275	400	600	—
1913A	6,000	100	275	425	650	—

KM# 211 10 MARK **Weight:** 3.9820 g. **Composition:** 0.9000 Gold .1152 oz. AGW

Date	Mintage	F	VF	XF	Unc	BU
1901A	10,000	375	675	1,000	1,500	—
1901A Proof	200	Value: 2,250				
1904A	10,000	375	675	1,000	1,500	—
1904A Proof	130	Value: 2,250				

KM# 214 10 MARK **Weight:** 3.9820 g. **Composition:** 0.9000 Gold .1152 oz. AGW

Date	Mintage	F	VF	XF	Unc	BU
1905A	10,000	300	500	1,000	1,300	—
1905A Proof	247	Value: 2,750				
1906A	10,000	300	500	1,000	1,300	—
1906A Proof	216	Value: 2,750				
1909A	10,000	300	500	1,000	1,300	—
1909A Proof	—	Value: 2,750				
1910A Proof	—	Value: 3,000				
1910A	10,000	300	500	1,000	1,300	—

PATTERNS

Including off metal strikes

KM#	Date	Mintage	Identification	Mkt Val
Pn38	1915A	—	3 Mark. Copper. Aluminum plated.	—
Pn39	1915A	—	3 Mark. Zinc. Aluminum-plated.	—
Pn40	1915A	—	3 Mark. Silver.	—

MECKLENBURG-SCHWERIN

The Duchy of Mecklenburg was divided in 1592 to form the branches of Mecklenburg-Schwerin and Mecklenburg-Güstrow. During the Thirty Years' War, the several dukes of the Mecklenburg states sided with the Protestant forces against the emperor. Albrecht von Wallenstein, Duke of Friedland and imperial general, ousted the Mecklenburg dukes from their territories in 1628. The rightful rulers were each restored to their lands in 1632. In 1658, Mecklenburg-Schwerin was divided by the four sons of Adolf Friedrich into the lines of Mecklenburg-Schwerin, Mecklenburg-Grabow, Mecklenburg-Mirow (extinct in 1675) and Mecklenburg-Strelitz (see). Mecklenburg-Schwerin and Mecklenburg-Güstrow fell extinct in the male line in 1692 and 1695 respectively, becoming a source of dispute between Mecklenburg-Grabow and Mecklenburg-Strelitz. Both parties finally agreed to a settlement in 1701 which awarded about eighty percent of all Mecklenburg territory to Grabow, which became the main Schwerin line, and the rest to Strelitz. No coinage was produced for Mecklenburg-Schwerin from 1708 until 1750. In 1815, the Congress of Vienna elevated the ruler to the rank of Grand Duke. Mecklenburg-Schwerin became a part of the German Empire in 1871. The last grand duke abdicated at the end of World War I in 1918.

RULERS

Friedrich Franz IV, 1897-1918

MINT MARKS

A - Berlin mint, 1852-1915

GRAND DUCHY

REFORM COINAGE

KM# 330 2 MARK **Weight:** 11.1110 g. **Composition:** 0.9000 Silver .3215 oz. ASW **Ruler:** Friedrich Franz IV **Subject:** Grand duke coming of age

Date	Mintage	F	VF	XF	Unc	BU
1901A	50,000	125	300	465	1,100	—
1901A Proof	1,000	Value: 1,200				

KM# 333 2 MARK **Weight:** 11.1110 g. **Composition:** 0.9000 Silver .3215 oz. ASW **Ruler:** Friedrich Franz IV **Subject:** Friedrich Franz IV wedding

Date	Mintage	F	VF	XF	Unc	BU
1904A	100,000	15.00	35.00	65.00	100	—
1904A Proof	6,000	Value: 175				

KM# 340 3 MARK **Weight:** 16.6670 g. **Composition:** 0.9000 Silver .4823 oz. ASW **Ruler:** Friedrich Franz IV **Subject:** 100 years as Grand Duchy

Date	Mintage	F	VF	XF	Unc	BU
1915A	33,000	40.00	85.00	150	235	—
1915A Proof	—	Value: 450				

KM# 334 5 MARK **Weight:** 27.7770 g. **Composition:** 0.9000 Silver .8038 oz. ASW **Ruler:** Friedrich Franz IV **Subject:** Friedrich Franz IV wedding

Date	Mintage	F	VF	XF	Unc	BU
1904A	40,000	40.00	100	175	250	—
1904A Proof	2,500	Value: 500				

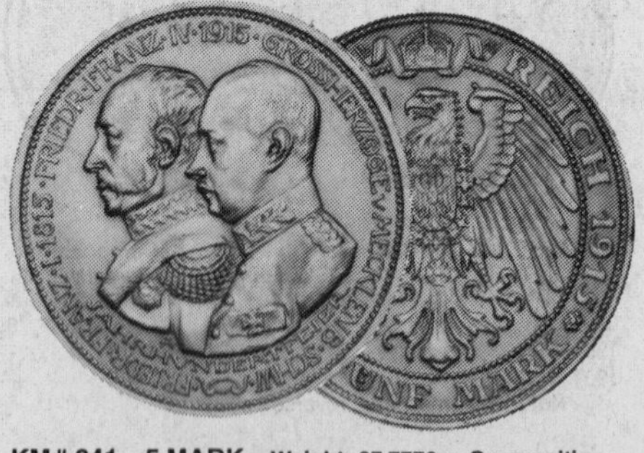

KM# 341 5 MARK **Weight:** 27.7770 g. **Composition:** 0.9000 Silver .8038 oz. ASW **Ruler:** Friedrich Franz IV **Subject:** 100 years as Grand Duchy

Date	Mintage	F	VF	XF	Unc	BU
1915A	10,000	125	265	500	850	—
1915A Proof	—	Value: 1,000				

KM# 331 10 MARK Weight: 3.9820 g. **Composition:** 0.9000 Gold .1152 oz. AGW **Ruler:** Friedrich Franz IV **Subject:** Grand duke coming of age **Reverse:** Type III

Date	Mintage	F	VF	XF	Unc	BU
1901A	10,000	750	1,200	1,750	2,800	—
1901A Proof	200	Value: 3,750				

KM# 332 20 MARK Weight: 7.9650 g. **Composition:** 0.9000 Gold .2304 oz. AGW **Ruler:** Friedrich Franz IV **Subject:** Grand duke coming of age **Reverse:** Type III

Date	Mintage	F	VF	XF	Unc	BU
1901A	5,000	1,000	1,750	3,000	4,250	—
1901A Proof	200	Value: 5,500				

PATTERNS

Including off metal strikes

KM#	Date	Mintage	Identification	Mkt Val
Pn26	1915A	—	3 Mark. Silver. Plain edge. KM340.	—
Pn27	1915A	—	3 Mark. Silver.	—
Pn28	1915A	—	5 Mark. Silver. KM341.	—

MECKLENBURG-STRELITZ

The Duchy of Mecklenburg-Strelitz was the youngest branch of the dynasty established when Mecklenburg-Schwerin was divided in 1658. Like its parent senior line, Mecklenburg-Strelitz became a grand duchy in 1815 as enacted by the Congress of Vienna. It became a constituent part of the German Empire in 1871, but all sovereignty ended with the conclusion of World War I in 1918.

RULERS

Friedrich Wilhelm, 1860-1904
Adolf Friedrich V, 1904-1914
Adolf Friedrich VI, 1914-1918

GRAND DUCHY

REFORM COINAGE

KM# 115 2 MARK Weight: 11.1110 g. **Composition:** 0.9000 Silver .3215 oz. ASW **Ruler:** Adolph Friedrich V

Date	Mintage	F	VF	XF	Unc	BU
1905A	10,000	135	300	575	775	—
1905A Proof	2,500	Value: 800				

KM# 120 3 MARK Weight: 16.6670 g. **Composition:** 0.9000 Silver .4823 oz. ASW **Ruler:** Adolph Friedrich V

Date	Mintage	F	VF	XF	Unc	BU
1913A	7,000	250	450	900	1,650	—
1913A Proof	—	Value: 1,850				

KM# 116 10 MARK Weight: 3.9820 g. **Composition:** 0.9000 Gold .1152 oz. AGW **Ruler:** Adolph Friedrich V

Date	Mintage	F	VF	XF	Unc	BU
1905A	1,000	1,500	2,250	3,250	4,800	—
1905A Proof	150	Value: 5,250				

KM# 117 20 MARK Weight: 7.9650 g. **Composition:** 0.9000 Gold .2304 oz. AGW **Ruler:** Adolph Friedrich V **Reverse:** Type III

Date	Mintage	F	VF	XF	Unc	BU
1905A	1,000	2,000	3,500	4,750	7,000	—
1905A Proof	160	Value: 8,000				

PATTERNS

Including off metal strikes

KM#	Date	Mintage	Identification	Mkt Val
Pn41	1913	—	3 Mark. Silver. KM120.	—

OLDENBURG

The county of Oldenburg was situated on the North Seacoast, to the east of the principality of East Friesland. It was originally part of the old duchy of Saxony and the first recorded lord ruled from the beginning of the 11th century. The first count was named in 1091 and had already acquired the county of Delmenhorst prior to that time. The first identifiable Oldenburg coinage was struck in the first half of the 13th century. Oldenburg was divided into Oldenburg and Delmenhorst in 1270, but the two lines were reunited by marriage five generations later. Through another marriage to the heiress of the duchy of Schleswig and county of Holstein, the royal house of Denmark descended through the Oldenburg line beginning in 1448, while a junior branch continued as counts of Oldenburg. The lordship of Jever was added to the county's domains in 1575. In 1667, the last count died without a direct heir and Oldenburg reverted to Denmark until 1773. In the following year, Oldenburg was given to the bishop of Lübeck, of the Holstein-Gottorp line, and raised to the status of a duchy. Oldenburg was occupied several times during the Napoleonic Wars and became a grand duchy in 1829. In 1817, Oldenburg acquired the principality of Birkenfeld from Prussia and struck coins in denominations used there. World War I spelled the end of temporal power for the Grand Duke in 1918, but the title has continued up to the present time. Grand Duke Anton Günther was born in 1923.

RULERS

Friedrich August, 1900-1918

MINT MARKS

A - Berlin mint, 1891-1901

GRAND DUCHY

REFORM COINAGE

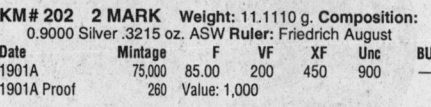

KM# 202 2 MARK Weight: 11.1110 g. **Composition:** 0.9000 Silver .3215 oz. ASW **Ruler:** Friedrich August

Date	Mintage	F	VF	XF	Unc	BU
1901A	75,000	85.00	200	450	900	—
1901A Proof	260	Value: 1,000				

KM# 203 5 MARK Weight: 27.7770 g. **Composition:** 0.9000 Silver .8038 oz. ASW **Ruler:** Friedrich August

Date	Mintage	F	VF	XF	Unc	BU
1901A	10,000	350	800	1,600	3,250	—
1901A	10,000	350	800	1,600	3,750	—
1901A Proof	170	Value: 4,500				
1901A Proof	170	Value: 4,000				

PRUSSIA

(Preussen)

Elector Friedrich III of Brandenburg-Prussia (1688-1713) was accorded the title of "King in Prussia" in 1701 as a reward for his support of Austria during the War of the Spanish Succession. Under successive strong leaders, Prussia gained increasing importance and added to its territories to become one of the leading countries of Europe in the course of the 18th century. As part of the reforms instituted by Friedrich II, the system of single letter mintmarks representing specific mints replaced the traditional incorporation of mint officials' symbols and/or initials as part of coin designs. Some of these very same mintmarks are still in use on modern German coins up to the present day. During the Napoleonic Wars (1792-1815), Prussia was allied with Saxony and they were soundly defeated at Jena in 1806. Prussia was forced to cede large portions of its territory at the time, but played a large part in the final defeat of Napoleon. The Congress of Vienna awarded Prussia part of Pomerania, the northern half of Saxony, much of Westphalia and the Rhineland, thus making it the largest state in Germany and a major power in European affairs. After defeating Denmark in 1864 and Austria in 1866, Prussia acquired Schleswig-Holstein, Hannover, Hesse-Cassel, Nassau and Frankfurt am Main. By this time, Prussia encompassed a large part of German territory and its population included two-thirds of all the German people. By winning the Franco-Prussian War (1870-71), Prussia became the pivotal state in the unification of Germany in 1871. King Wilhelm I was proclaimed Kaiser (Emperor) of all Germany, but World War I brought an end to both the Empire and the Kingdom of Prussia in 1918.

NOTE:

For coins of Neuchatel previously listed here, see Switzerland.

RULERS

Wilhelm II, 1888-1918

MINT MARKS

A - Berlin = Prussia, East Friesland, East Prussia, Posen

KINGDOM

REFORM COINAGE

KM# 522 2 MARK Weight: 11.1110 g. **Composition:** 0.9000 Silver .2215 oz. ASW **Ruler:** Wilhelm II

Date	Mintage	F	VF	XF	Unc	BU
1901	398,000	25.00	50.00	125	800	—
1901 Proof	—	Value: 2,500				
1902	3,948,000	7.00	13.50	40.00	125	—
1903	4,079,000	7.00	13.50	40.00	125	—
1904A	9,981,000	7.00	13.50	40.00	125	—
1905A	6,493,000	7.00	13.50	35.00	95.00	—
1905A Proof	620	Value: 300				
1906A	4,019,000	7.00	13.50	30.00	85.00	—
1906A Proof	85	Value: 300				
1907A	8,110,000	7.00	13.50	25.00	75.00	—
1908A	2,389,000	7.00	13.50	30.00	100	—
1911A	1,181,000	8.00	16.50	30.00	110	—
1912A	733,000	8.00	16.50	30.00	110	—

KM# 525 2 MARK **Weight:** 11.1110 g. **Composition:** 0.9000 Silver .3215 oz. ASW **Ruler:** Wilhelm II **Subject:** 200 Years - Kingdom of Prussia

Date	Mintage	F	VF	XF	Unc	BU
1901A	2,600,000	4.50	8.50	13.50	27.50	—
1901A Proof	—	Value: 70.00				

KM# 532 2 MARK **Weight:** 11.1110 g. **Composition:** 0.9000 Silver .3215 oz. ASW **Ruler:** Wilhelm II **Subject:** 100 Years - defeat of Napoleon

Date	Mintage	F	VF	XF	Unc	BU
1913A	1,500,000	8.00	12.00	18.50	32.00	—
1913A Proof	—	Value: 70.00				

KM# 533 2 MARK **Weight:** 11.1110 g. **Composition:** 0.9000 Silver .3215 oz. ASW **Ruler:** Wilhelm II **Subject:** 25th year of reign

Date	Mintage	F	VF	XF	Unc	BU
1913A	1,500,000	8.00	12.00	17.50	30.00	—
1913A Proof	5,000	Value: 75.00				

KM# 527 3 MARK **Weight:** 16.6670 g. **Composition:** 0.9000 Silver .4823 oz. ASW **Ruler:** Wilhelm II

Date	Mintage	F	VF	XF	Unc	BU
1908A	2,859,000	6.50	12.00	18.50	45.00	—
1909A	6,344,000	6.50	12.00	18.50	45.00	—
1910A	5,591,000	6.50	12.00	18.50	45.00	—
1911A	3,242,000	6.50	12.00	18.50	45.00	—
1912A	4,626,000	6.50	12.00	18.50	45.00	—
(1908-1912)A Proof	—	Value: 175				

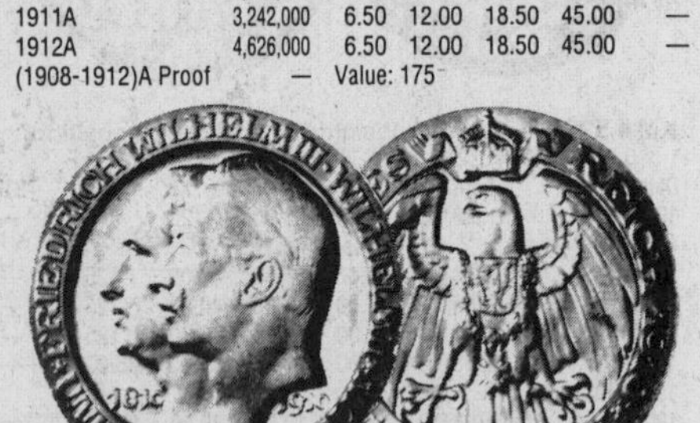

KM# 530 3 MARK **Weight:** 16.6670 g. **Composition:** 0.9000 Silver .4823 oz. ASW **Ruler:** Wilhelm II **Subject:** Berlin University

Date	Mintage	F	VF	XF	Unc	BU
1910A	200,000	15.00	30.00	55.00	85.00	—
1910A Proof	2,000	Value: 300				

KM# 531 3 MARK **Weight:** 16.6670 g. **Composition:** 0.9000 Silver .4823 oz. ASW **Ruler:** Wilhelm II **Subject:** Breslau University

Date	Mintage	F	VF	XF	Unc	BU
1911A	400,000	12.50	25.00	45.00	70.00	—
1911A Proof	—	Value: 235				

KM# 534 3 MARK **Weight:** 16.6670 g. **Composition:** 0.9000 Silver .4823 oz. ASW **Ruler:** Wilhelm II **Subject:** 100 Years - Defeat of Napoleon

Date	Mintage	F	VF	XF	Unc	BU
1913A	2,000,000	8.00	13.00	20.00	35.00	—
1913A Proof	—	Value: 100				

KM# 535 3 MARK **Weight:** 16.6670 g. **Composition:** 0.9000 Silver .4823 oz. ASW **Ruler:** Wilhelm II **Subject:** 25th Year of Reign

Date	Mintage	F	VF	XF	Unc	BU
1913A	2,000,000	8.00	13.00	20.00	35.00	—
1913A Proof	6,000	Value: 90.00				

KM# 538 3 MARK **Weight:** 16.6670 g. **Composition:** 0.9000 Silver .4823 oz. ASW **Ruler:** Wilhelm II

Date	Mintage	F	VF	XF	Unc	BU
1914A	2,564,000	8.00	13.00	20.00	32.50	—
1914A Proof	—	Value: 75.00				

KM# 539 3 MARK **Weight:** 16.6670 g. **Composition:** 0.9000 Silver .4823 oz. ASW **Ruler:** Wilhelm II **Subject:** Centenary - Absorption of Mansfeld

Date	Mintage	F	VF	XF	Unc	BU
1915A	30,000	100	400	600	750	—
1915A Proof	—	Value: 800				

KM# 523 5 MARK **Weight:** 27.7770 g. **Composition:** 0.9000 Silver .8038 oz. ASW **Ruler:** Wilhelm II **Reverse:** Type III

Date	Mintage	F	VF	XF	Unc	BU
1898A	1,134,000	15.00	30.00	100	450	—
1901A	668,000	15.00	30.00	80.00	325	—
1902A	1,951,000	15.00	25.00	70.00	275	—
1903A	3,856,000	15.00	22.50	65.00	275	—
1904A	2,060,000	15.00	22.50	65.00	275	—
1906A	231,000	20.00	35.00	90.00	400	—
1907A	2,902,000	15.00	22.50	50.00	250	—
1908A	2,231,000	15.00	22.50	50.00	250	—
(1891-1908)A	—	Value: 900				

KM# 526 5 MARK **Weight:** 27.7770 g. **Composition:** 0.9000 Silver .8038 oz. ASW **Ruler:** Wilhelm II **Subject:** 200 Years - Kingdom of Prussia

Date	Mintage	F	VF	XF	Unc	BU
1901A	460,000	22.50	37.50	65.00	100	—
1901A Proof	—	Value: 175				

KM# 536 5 MARK **Weight:** 27.7770 g. **Composition:** 0.9000 Silver .8038 oz. ASW **Ruler:** Wilhelm II

Date	Mintage	F	VF	XF	Unc	BU
1913A	1,962,000	14.00	22.00	32.00	70.00	—
1914A	1,587,000	16.00	24.00	35.00	85.00	—
(1913-1914)A Proof	—	Value: 600				

KM# 520 10 MARK **Weight:** 3.9820 g. **Composition:** 0.9000 Gold .1152 oz. AGW **Ruler:** Wilhelm II **Reverse:** Type III

Date	Mintage	F	VF	XF	Unc	BU
1901A	702,000	50.00	80.00	100	220	—
1901A Proof	—	Value: 900				
1902A	271,000	50.00	80.00	100	220	—
1902A Proof	—	Value: 900				
1903A	1,685,000	50.00	80.00	100	220	—
1903A Proof	—	Value: 900				
1904A	1,178,000	50.00	80.00	100	220	—
1905A	1,063,000	50.00	80.00	100	220	—
1905A Proof	117	Value: 900				
1906A	542,000	50.00	80.00	100	220	—
1906A Proof	150	Value: 900				
1907A	813,000	50.00	80.00	100	220	—
1907A Proof	—	Value: 900				
1909A	532,000	50.00	80.00	100	220	—
1909A Proof	—	Value: 900				

Date	Mintage	F	VF	XF	Unc	BU
1910A	803,000	50.00	80.00	100	220	—
1911A	271,000	50.00	80.00	100	220	—
1911A Proof	—	Value: 1,000				
1912A	542,000	50.00	80.00	100	220	—
1912A Proof	—	Value: 900				

KM# 521 20 MARK **Weight:** 7.9650 g. **Composition:** 0.9000 Gold .2304 oz. AGW **Ruler:** Wilhelm II **Reverse:** Type III

Date	Mintage	F	VF	XF	Unc	BU
1901A	5,188,000	BV	BV+3%	BV+10%	175	—
1901A Proof	—	Value: 600				
1902A	4,138,000	BV	BV+3%	BV+10%	175	—
1902A Proof	—	Value: 600				
1903A Proof	—	Value: 600				
1903A	2,870,000	BV	BV+3%	BV+10%	175	—
1904A	3,453,000	BV	BV+3%	BV+10%	175	—
1904A Proof	—	Value: 600				
1905A	4,176,000	BV	BV+3%	BV+10%	175	—
1905A Proof	287	Value: 600				
1905J	921,000	BV	100	150	225	—
1906A	7,788,000	BV	BV+3%	BV+10%	175	—
1906A Proof	124	Value: 600				
1906J	82,000	125	200	300	500	—
1907A	2,576,000	BV	BV+3%	BV+10%	175	—
1907A Proof	—	Value: 600				
1908A Proof	—	Value: 600				
1908A	3,274,000	BV	BV+3%	BV+10%	175	—
1909A	5,213,000	BV	BV+3%	BV+10%	175	—
1909A Proof	—	Value: 600				
1909J	350,000	115	150	175	200	—
1909J Proof	—	Value: 800				
1910A	8,646,000	BV	BV+3%	BV+10%	175	—
1910J	753,000	BV	BV+3%	150+10%	200	—
1911A	4,746,000	BV	BV+3%	BV+10%	175	—
1912A	5,569,000	BV	BV+3%	BV+10%	175	—
1912J	503,000	BV	100	150	200	—
1913A	6,102,000	BV	BV+3%	BV+10%	175	—
1913A Proof	—	Value: 600				

KM# 537 20 MARK **Weight:** 7.9650 g. **Composition:** 0.9000 Gold .2304 oz. AGW **Ruler:** Wilhelm II

Date	Mintage	F	VF	XF	Unc	BU
1913A	—	BV	115	135	175	—
1913A Proof	—	Value: 1,200				
1914A	2,137,000	BV	115	135	175	—
1914A Proof	—	Value: 1,200				
1915A	1,271,000	550	900	1,100	1,500	—

PATTERNS

Including off metal strikes

KM#	Date	Mintage	Identification	Mkt Val
Pn28	1901	—	5 Mark. Silver. Larger design. KM526.	—
PnA30	1901A	—	20 Mark. Silver. Plain edge.	—
Pn29	1901A	—	5 Mark. Silver. Larger design. KM526.	—
Pn30	1904A	—	2 Mark. Silver. Plain edge. Broader rim. KM522.	—
Pn31	1904A	—	5 Mark. Silver.	—
Pn32	1904A	—	5 Mark. Copper. "N.A." countermarked.	—
Pn33	1904A	—	5 Mark. Silver. Reeded edge. Without beaded rims. KM523.	—
Pn34	1904A	—	5 Mark. Silver. Smaller lettering. KM523.	—
Pn35	1904A	—	5 Mark. Silver. Eagle in ornamental in inner border.	—
Pn36	1905A	—	3 Mark. Silver.	—
Pn37	1905A	—	3 Mark. Silver. Legend in different position.	—
Pn39	1905A	—	3 Mark. Silver. KM527.	—
Pn38	1905A	—	3 Mark. Copper.	—
PnA40	1907A	—	20 Mark. Copper. 4.1100 g.	—
Pn40	1908A	—	5 Mark. Silver.	—
Pn42	1908J	—	20 Mark. Gold. KM521.2	—
Pn41	1908A	—	5 Mark. Brass.	—
Pn43	1909A	—	2 Mark. Nickel. KM522.	—
Pn44	1910	—	3 Mark. Silver.	—
Pn45	1910	—	3 Mark. Copper.	—
Pn46	1911	—	3 Mark. Silver. KM531.	—
Pn47	1911	—	3 Mark. Silver.	—
Pn48	1911A	—	3 Mark. Silver. KM531.	400
Pn49	1912A	—	2 Mark. Silver. KM533.	—
Pn52	1912A	—	3 Mark. Silver.	—
Pn50	1912	—	3 Mark. Silver.	—
Pn51	1912	—	3 Mark. Bronze.	—
Pn53	1912A	—	3 Mark. Bronze.	—
Pn61	1913A	—	5 Mark. Silver. Extra sharp design. KM536.	—
Pn54	1913A	—	2 Mark. Silver. Dots above "O" in KONIG. KM533.	—
Pn55	1913	—	3 Mark. Silver.	—
Pn56	1913	—	3 Mark. Bronze.	—
Pn57	1913A	—	3 Mark. Silver.	—
Pn58	1913A	—	3 Mark. Bronze.	—
Pn59	1913A	—	3 Mark. Silver. Dots above O in KONIG. KM535.	—
Pn60	1913A	—	3 Mark. Copper.	—
Pn62	1914A	—	3 Mark. Silver. Extra sharp design. KM538.	—
Pn63	1915	—	3 Mark. Silver. Gothic script. KM539.	—
Pn64	1915	—	3 Mark. White Metal.	—
Pn65	1915	—	3 Mark. Tin-iron.	—

RUESS

The Reuss family, whose lands were located in Thuringia, was founded c. 1035. By the end of the 12th century, the custom of naming all males in the ruling house Heinrich had been established. The Elder Line modified this strange practice in the late 17th century to numbering all males from 1 to 100, then beginning over again. The Younger Line, meanwhile, decided to start the numbering of Heinrichs with the first male born in each century. Greiz was founded in1303. Upper and Lower Greiz lines were founded in 1535 and the territories were divided until 1768. In 1778 the ruler was made a prince of the Holy Roman Empire. The principality endured until 1918.

MINT MARKS

A - Berlin
B - Hannover

REUSS-OBERGREIZ

The other branch of the division of 1635, Obergreiz went through a number of consolidations and further divisions. Upon the extinction of the Ruess-Untergreiz linein 1768, the latter passed to Reuss-Obergreiz and this line continued on into the 20th century, obtaining the rank of count back in 1673 and that of prince in 1778.

RULERS

Heinrich XXII, 1859-1902
Heinrich XXIV, 1902-1918

PRINCIPALITY

REFORM COINAGE

KM# 128 2 MARK **Weight:** 11.1110 g. **Composition:** 0.9000 Silver .3215 oz. ASW **Ruler:** Heinrich XXII

Date	Mintage	F	VF	XF	Unc	BU
1899A	10,000	100	200	400	650	—
1899A Proof	120	Value: 800				
1901A	10,000	100	200	400	650	—
1901A Proof	—	Value: 800				

KM# 130 3 MARK **Weight:** 16.6670 g. **Composition:** 0.9000 Silver .4823 oz. ASW **Ruler:** Heinrich XXIV

Date	Mintage	F	VF	XF	Unc	BU
1909A	10,000	120	275	450	800	—
1909A Proof	400	Value: 1,250				

PATTERNS

Including off metal strikes

KM#	Date	Mintage	Identification	Mkt Val
Pn4	1909A	—	3 Mark. Silver. Head faces left. KM130	—

SAXE-ALTENBURG

(Sachsen-Neu-Altenburg)

A new line was established at Altenburg when the Duke of Saxe-Hildburghausen exchanged Hildburghausen for Altenburg in 1826. This line lasted until the end of World War I, when the last duke was forced to abdicate.

RULERS

Ernst I, 1853-1908
Ernst II, 1908-1918

MINT MARKS

A – Berlin Mint, 1886-1918

DUCHY

REFORM COINAGE

KM# 144 2 MARK **Weight:** 11.1110 g. **Composition:** 0.9000 Silver .3215 oz. ASW **Ruler:** Ernst I **Subject:** Ernst 75th birthday

Date	Mintage	F	VF	XF	Unc	BU
1901A		100	200	400	650	—
1901A Proof	500	Value: 800				

KM# 145 5 MARK **Weight:** 27.7770 g. **Composition:** 0.9000 Silver .8038 oz. ASW **Ruler:** Ernst I **Subject:** Ernst 75th birthday

Date	Mintage	F	VF	XF	Unc	BU
1901A		200	425	800	1,400	—
1901A Proof	500	Value: 1,750				

KM# 147 5 MARK **Weight:** 27.7770 g. **Composition:** 0.9000 Silver .8038 oz. ASW **Ruler:** Ernst I **Subject:** Ernst's 50th Year of Reign

Date	Mintage	F	VF	XF	Unc	BU
1903		100	200	300	425	—
1903A Proof	300	Value: 500				

SAXE-COBURG-GOTHA

(Sachsen-Coburg-Gotha)

Upon the extinction of the ducal line in Saxe-Gotha-Altenburg in 1826, Gotha was assigned to Saxe-Coburg-Saalfeld and Saxe-Meiningen received Saalfeld. The resulting duchy became called Saxe-Coburg-Gotha. Albert, the son of Ernst I and younger brother of Ernst II, married Queen Victoria of Great Britain and the British royal dynastic name was that of Saxe-Coburg-Gotha. Their son, Alfred was made the Duke of Edinburgh and succeeded his uncle, Ernst II, as Duke of Saxe-Coburg-Gotha. Alfred's oldler brother, Eduard Albert, followed their mother as King Edward VII

(1901-1910). The last duke of Saxe-Coburg-Gotha was Alfred's son, Karl Eduard, forced to abdicate in 1918 as a result of World War I, which was fought in part against his cousin, King George V.

RULERS
Karl Eduard, 1900-1918

MINT MARKS
A – Berlin Mint, 1886-1911

DUCHY

REFORM COINAGE

KM# 152 2 MARK Weight: 11.1110 g. **Composition:** 0.9000 Silver .3215 oz. ASW **Ruler:** Karl Eduard

Date	Mintage	F	VF	XF	Unc	BU
1905A		125	275	600	1,100	—
1905A Proof	2,000	Value: 1,100				
1911A Proof	100	Value: 12,500				

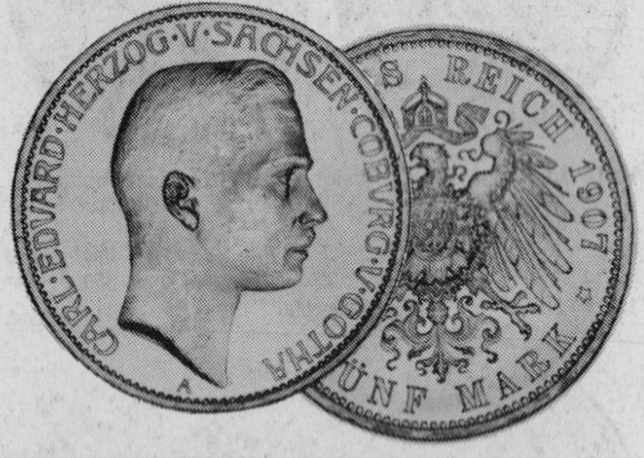

KM# 153 5 MARK Weight: 27.7770 g. **Composition:** 0.9000 Silver .8038 oz. ASW **Ruler:** Karl Eduard

Date	Mintage	F	VF	XF	Unc	BU
1907A	10,000	300	600	1,000	1,500	—
1907A Proof	—	Value: 2,250				

KM# 154 10 MARK Weight: 3.9820 g. **Composition:** 0.9000 Gold .1152 oz. AGW **Ruler:** Karl Eduard

Date	Mintage	F	VF	XF	Unc	BU
1905A		600	900	1,300	1,800	—
1905A Proof	489	Value: 3,500				

KM# 155 20 MARK Weight: 7.9650 g. **Composition:** 0.9000 Gold .2304 oz. AGW **Ruler:** Karl Eduard **Reverse:** Type I

Date	Mintage	F	VF	XF	Unc	BU
1905A		600	1,000	1,400	2,000	—
1905A Proof	484	Value: 3,750				

SAXE-MEININGEN

(Sachsen-Meiningen)

The duchy of Saxe-Meiningen was located in Thuringia (Thüringen), sandwiched between Saxe-Weimar-Eisenach on the west and north and the enclave of Schmalkalden belonging to Hesse-Cassel on the east. It was founded upon the division of the Ernestine line in Saxe-Gotha in 1680. In 1735, due to an exchange of some territory, the duchy became known as Saxe-Coburg-Meiningen. In 1826, Saxe-Coburg-Gotha assigned Saalfeld to Saxe-Meiningen. The duchy came under the strong influence of Prussia from 1866, when Bernhard II was forced to abdicate because of his support of Austria. The last duke was forced to give up his sovereign power at the end of World War I in 1918.

RULERS
Georg II, 1866-1914
Bernhard III, 1914-1918

DUCHY

REFORM COINAGE

KM# 196 2 MARK Weight: 11.1110 g. **Composition:** 0.9000 Silver .3215 oz. ASW **Ruler:** Georg II **Subject:** Duke's 75th birthday

Date	Mintage	F	VF	XF	Unc	BU
1901D	20,000	100	250	400	750	—
1901D Proof	—	Value: 1,000				

KM# 198 2 MARK Weight: 11.1110 g. **Composition:** 0.9000 Silver .3215 oz. ASW **Ruler:** Georg II **Obverse:** Long beard

Date	Mintage	F	VF	XF	Unc	BU
1902D	20,000	225	750	1,200	2,000	—

KM# 199 2 MARK Weight: 11.1110 g. **Composition:** 0.9000 Silver .3215 oz. ASW **Ruler:** Georg II **Obverse:** Short beard

Date	Mintage	F	VF	XF	Unc	BU
1902D	Inc. above	100	200	350	750	—
1913D	5,000	150	250	450	1,250	—

KM# 206 2 MARK Weight: 11.1110 g. **Composition:** 0.9000 Silver .3215 oz. ASW **Ruler:** Bernhard III **Subject:** Death of Georg II

Date	Mintage	F	VF	XF	Unc	BU
1915	30,000	35.00	60.00	140	200	—

KM# 203 3 MARK Weight: 16.6670 g. **Composition:** 0.9000 Silver .4823 oz. ASW **Ruler:** Georg II

Date	Mintage	F	VF	XF	Unc	BU
1908D	35,000	35.00	100	140	200	—
1908D Proof	—	Value: 430				
1913D	20,000	35.00	100	140	200	—

KM# 207 3 MARK Weight: 16.6670 g. **Composition:** 0.9000 Silver .4823 oz. ASW **Ruler:** Bernhard III **Subject:** Death of Georg II

Date	Mintage	F	VF	XF	Unc	BU
1915	30,000	30.00	65.00	135	200	—
1915 Proof	—	Value: 225				

KM# 197 5 MARK Weight: 27.7770 g. **Composition:** 0.9000 Silver .8038 oz. ASW **Ruler:** Georg II **Subject:** Duke's 75th birthday

Date	Mintage	F	VF	XF	Unc	BU
1901D	20,000	85.00	225	425	1,000	—
1901D Proof	—	Value: 1,500				

KM# 200 5 MARK Weight: 27.7770 g. **Composition:** 0.9000 Silver .8038 oz. ASW **Ruler:** Georg II **Obverse:** Long beard

Date	Mintage	F	VF	XF	Unc	BU
1902D	20,000	60.00	175	325	1,000	—

KM# 201 5 MARK Weight: 27.7770 g. **Composition:** 0.9000 Silver .8038 oz. ASW **Ruler:** Georg II **Obverse:** Short beard

Date	Mintage	F	VF	XF	Unc	BU
1902D	Inc. above	60.00	150	325	1,000	—
1908D	60,000	50.00	150	275	850	—

KM# 202 10 MARK Weight: 3.9820 g. **Composition:** 0.9000 Gold .1152 oz. AGW **Ruler:** Georg II

Date	Mintage	F	VF	XF	Unc	BU
1902D	2,000	900	1,600	2,500	3,500	—
1902D Proof	—	Value: 4,250				
1909D	2,000	900	1,800	2,500	3,500	—
1909D Proof	—	Value: 4,250				
1914D	1,002	900	1,700	2,500	3,500	—
1914D Proof	—	Value: 4,250				

KM# 195 20 MARK Weight: 7.9650 g. **Composition:** 0.9000 Gold .2304 oz. AGW **Ruler:** Georg II **Reverse:** Type III

Date	Mintage	F	VF	XF	Unc	BU
1900D	1,005	2,000	3,000	3,500	8,500	—
1900D Proof	—	Value: 11,000				
1905D	1,000	2,000	3,000	3,500	8,500	—
1905D Proof	—	Value: 11,000				

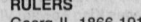

KM# 205 20 MARK Weight: 7.9650 g. **Composition:** 0.9000 Gold .2304 oz. AGW **Ruler:** Georg II

Date	Mintage	F	VF	XF	Unc	BU
1910D	1,004	1,500	3,000	4,000	5,500	—
1910D Proof	—	Value: 7,000				
1914D	1,000	1,500	3,000	4,000	5,500	—
1914D Proof	—	Value: 7,000				

PATTERNS

Including off metal strikes

KM#	Date	Mintage	Identification	Mkt Val
Pn16	1901D	—	10 Mark. Gold. With neck and beard variety. KM202.	—
Pn17	1901D	—	10 Mark. Gold. KM202.	—
Pn19	1915D	—	3 Mark. KM207.	—
Pn18	1915D	—	2 Mark. KM206.	—

SAXE-WEIMAR-EISENACH

(Sachsen-Weimar-Eisenach)

When the death of the duke of Saxe-Eisenach in 1741 heralded the extinction of that line, its possessions reverted to Saxe-Weimar, which henceforth was known as Saxe-Weimar-Eisenach. Because of the strong role played by the duke during the Napoleonic Wars, Saxe-Weimar-Eisenach was raised to the rank of a grand duchy in 1814 and granted the territory of Neustadt, taken from Saxony. The last grand duke abdicated at the end of World War I.

RULERS

Karl Alexander, 1853-1901
Wilhelm Ernst, 1901-1918

MINT MARKS

A – Berlin Mint, 1840-1915

GRAND DUCHY

REFORM COINAGE

Y# 170 2 MARK Weight: 11.1110 g. **Composition:** 0.9000 Silver .3215 oz. ASW **Ruler:** Wilhelm Ernst

Date	Mintage	F	VF	XF	Unc	BU
1901A	100,000	100	300	425	850	—
1901A Proof	—	Value: 1,200				

Y# 172 2 MARK Weight: 11.1110 g. **Composition:** 0.9000 Silver .3215 oz. ASW **Ruler:** Wilhelm Ernst **Subject:** Grand Duke's First Marriage

Date	Mintage	F	VF	XF	Unc	BU
1903A		35.00	60.00	100	140	—
1903A Proof	Est. 1,000	Value: 180				

Y# 174 2 MARK Weight: 11.1110 g. **Composition:** 0.9000 Silver .3215 oz. ASW **Ruler:** Wilhelm Ernst **Subject:** Jena University 350th Anniversary

Date	Mintage	F	VF	XF	Unc	BU
1908	50,000	25.00	50.00	100	125	—

Y# 176 3 MARK Weight: 16.6670 g. **Composition:** 0.9000 Silver .4823 oz. ASW **Ruler:** Wilhelm Ernst **Subject:** Grand Duke's Second Marriage

Date	Mintage	F	VF	XF	Unc	BU
1910	133,000	15.00	35.00	70.00	85.00	—
1910A Proof	—	Value: 125				

Y# 177 3 MARK Weight: 16.6670 g. **Composition:** 0.9000 Silver .4823 oz. ASW **Ruler:** Wilhelm Ernst **Subject:** Centenary of Grand Duchy

Date	Mintage	F	VF	XF	Unc	BU
1915A		25.00	75.00	125	175	—
1915A Proof	200	Value: 400				

Y# 173 5 MARK Weight: 27.7770 g. **Composition:** 0.9000 Silver .8038 oz. ASW **Ruler:** Wilhelm Ernst **Subject:** Grand Dule's First Marriage

Date	Mintage	F	VF	XF	Unc	BU
1903A		50.00	100	225	300	—
1903A Proof	Est. 1,000	Value: 425				

Y# 175 5 MARK Weight: 27.7770 g. **Composition:** 0.9000 Silver .8038 oz. ASW **Ruler:** Wilhelm Ernst **Subject:** Jena University 350th Anniversary

Date	Mintage	F	VF	XF	Unc	BU
1908A	40,000	60.00	100	180	220	—
1908A Proof	—	Value: 625				

Y# 171 20 MARK Weight: 7.9650 g. **Composition:** 0.9000 Gold .2304 oz. AGW **Ruler:** Wilhelm Ernst **Subject:** Golden Wedding of Carl Alexander

Date	Mintage	F	VF	XF	Unc	BU
1901A	5,000	1,000	1,800	2,250	3,750	—
1901A Proof	—	Value: 5,500				

PATTERNS

Including off metal strikes

KM#	Date	Mintage	Identification	Mkt Val
Pn1	1908	—	5 Mark. Silver. Figure smaller. Y#175.	—
Pn2	1910	—	3 Mark. Silver.	—
Pn3	1910	—	3 Mark. Brass.	—

SAXONY

Saxony, located in southeast Germany was founded in 850. The first coinage was struck c. 990. It was divided into two lines in 1464. The electoral right was obtained by the elder line in 1547. During the time of the Reformation, Saxony was one of the more powerful states in central Europe. It became a kingdom in 1806. At the Congress of Vienna in 1815, they were forced to cede half its territories to Prussia.

RULERS

Albert, 1873-1902
Georg, 1902-1904
Friedrich August III, 1904-1918

MINT MARKS

L - Leipzig

KINGDOM

REFORM COINAGE

KM# 1245 2 MARK Weight: 11.1110 g. **Composition:** 0.9000 Silver .3215 oz. ASW **Ruler:** Albert **Note:** Similar to KM#185.

Date	Mintage	F	VF	XF	Unc	BU
1901E	440,000	12.50	55.00	100	275	—
1902E	543,000	10.00	55.00	100	200	—

KM# 1255 2 MARK Weight: 11.1110 g. **Composition:** 0.9000 Silver .3215 oz. ASW **Ruler:** Georg **Subject:** Death of Albert

Date	Mintage	F	VF	XF	Unc	BU
1902E	168,000	15.00	40.00	65.00	100	—
1902E Proof	250	Value: 200				

KM# 1257 2 MARK Weight: 11.1110 g. **Composition:** 0.9000 Silver .3215 oz. ASW **Ruler:** Georg

Date	Mintage	F	VF	XF	Unc	BU
1903E	746,000	30.00	60.00	140	350	—
1903E Proof	50	Value: 600				
1904E	1,266,000	17.50	50.00	100	250	—

KM# 1261 2 MARK Weight: 11.1110 g. **Composition:** 0.9000 Silver .3215 oz. ASW **Ruler:** Friedrich August III **Subject:** Death of Georg

Date	Mintage	F	VF	XF	Unc	BU
1904E	150,000	15.00	35.00	60.00	95.00	—
1904E Proof	55	Value: 225				

KM# 1263 2 MARK **Weight:** 11.1110 g. **Composition:** 0.9000 Silver .3215 oz. ASW **Ruler:** Friedrich August III

Date	Mintage	F	VF	XF	Unc	BU
1905E	559,000	20.00	35.00	60.00	155	—
1905E Proof	100	Value: 300				
1906E	559,000	20.00	35.00	60.00	155	—
1907E	1,118,000	20.00	35.00	60.00	155	—
1908E	336,000	20.00	35.00	55.00	150	—
1911E	186,000	20.00	35.00	55.00	150	—
1912E	168,000	20.00	35.00	55.00	150	—
1914E	298,000	20.00	35.00	55.00	150	—
(1905-1914)E Proof	—	Value: 300				

KM# 1268 2 MARK **Weight:** 11.1110 g. **Composition:** 0.9000 Silver .3215 oz. ASW **Ruler:** Friedrich August III **Subject:** 500th anniversary - Leipzig University

Date	Mintage	F	VF	XF	Unc	BU
1909	125,000	15.00	30.00	65.00	90.00	—
1909 Proof	300	Value: 200				

KM# 1267 3 MARK **Weight:** 16.6670 g. **Composition:** 0.9000 Silver .4823 oz. ASW **Ruler:** Friedrich August III

Date	Mintage	F	VF	XF	Unc	BU
1908E	276,000	10.00	20.00	40.00	65.00	—
1909E	1,197,000	10.00	18.00	28.00	60.00	—
1910E	745,000	10.00	18.00	28.00	60.00	—
1911E	581,000	10.00	18.00	28.00	60.00	—
1912E	379,000	10.00	18.00	28.00	60.00	—
1913E	307,000	10.00	18.00	28.00	60.00	—
(1908-1913)E Proof	—	Value: 225				

KM# 1275 3 MARK **Weight:** 16.6670 g. **Composition:** 0.9000 Silver .4823 oz. ASW **Ruler:** Friedrich August III **Subject:** Battle of Leipzig centennial

Date	Mintage	F	VF	XF	Unc	BU
1913E	1,000,000	12.00	18.00	28.00	45.00	—
1913E Proof	17,000	Value: 100				

KM# 1276 3 MARK **Weight:** 16.6670 g. **Composition:** 0.9000 Silver .4823 oz. ASW **Ruler:** Friedrich August III **Subject:** Jubilee of Reformation

Date	Mintage	F	VF	XF	Unc	BU
1917E Proof	100	Value: 60,000				

KM# 1246 5 MARK **Weight:** 27.7770 g. **Composition:** 0.9000 Silver .8038 oz. ASW **Ruler:** Albert **Note:** Similar to KM#1256.

Date	Mintage	F	VF	XF	Unc	BU
1901E	156,000	25.00	55.00	300	700	—
1902E	168,000	20.00	40.00	250	500	—
1902E Proof	—	Value: 2,400				

KM# 1256 5 MARK **Weight:** 27.7770 g. **Composition:** 0.9000 Silver .8038 oz. ASW **Ruler:** Georg **Subject:** Death of Albert

Date	Mintage	F	VF	XF	Unc	BU
1902E	100,000	30.00	60.00	125	175	—
1902E Proof	250	Value: 425				

KM# 1258 5 MARK **Weight:** 27.7770 g. **Composition:** 0.9000 Silver .8038 oz. ASW **Ruler:** Georg

Date	Mintage	F	VF	XF	Unc	BU
1903E	536,000	20.00	40.00	125	650	—
1903E Proof	50	Value: 1,000				
1904E	291,000	25.00	50.00	160	750	—
1904E Proof	—	Value: 1,100				

KM# 1262 5 MARK **Weight:** 27.7770 g. **Composition:** 0.9000 Silver .8038 oz. ASW **Ruler:** Friedrich August III **Subject:** Death of Georg

Date	Mintage	F	VF	XF	Unc	BU
1904E	37,000	40.00	125	225	300	—
1904E Proof	70	Value: 500				

KM# 1266 5 MARK **Weight:** 27.7770 g. **Composition:** 0.9000 Silver .8038 oz. ASW **Ruler:** Friedrich August III

Date	Mintage	F	VF	XF	Unc	BU
1907E	398,000	20.00	40.00	85.00	300	—
1908E	317,000	20.00	40.00	85.00	250	—
1914E	298,000	17.50	35.00	80.00	200	—
1914E Proof	—	Value: 1,100				

KM# 1269 5 MARK **Weight:** 27.7770 g. **Composition:** 0.9000 Silver .8038 oz. ASW **Ruler:** Friedrich August III **Subject:** 500th anniversary - Leipzig University

Date	Mintage	F	VF	XF	Unc	BU
1909	50,000	40.00	90.00	165	235	—
1909 Proof	300	Value: 525				

KM# 1247 10 MARK **Weight:** 3.9820 g. **Composition:** 0.9000 Gold .1152 oz. AGW **Ruler:** Albert **Reverse:** Type III

Date	Mintage	F	VF	XF	Unc	BU
1901E	75,000	80.00	125	175	450	—
1902E	37,000	80.00	125	175	475	—
1902E Proof	—	Value: 1,500				

KM# 1259 10 MARK **Weight:** 3.9820 g. **Composition:** 0.9000 Gold .1152 oz. AGW **Ruler:** Georg

Date	Mintage	F	VF	XF	Unc	BU
1903E	284,000	100	200	300	600	—
1903E Proof	100	Value: 1,600				
1904E	149,000	100	200	300	600	—

KM# 1264 10 MARK **Weight:** 3.9820 g. **Composition:** 0.9000 Gold .1152 oz. AGW **Ruler:** Friedrich August III

Date	Mintage	F	VF	XF	Unc	BU
1905E	112,000	120	225	275	450	—
1905E Proof	100	Value: 1,400				
1906E	75,000	120	225	275	450	—
1906E Proof	—	Value: 1,500				
1907E Proof	—	Value: 1,500				
1907E	112,000	120	225	275	450	—
1909E	112,000	120	225	275	450	—
1910E	75,000	120	225	275	450	—
1910E Proof	—	Value: 1,400				
1911E	38,000	120	225	275	450	—
1912E	75,000	120	225	275	450	—

KM# 1260 20 MARK Weight: 7.9650 g. **Composition:** 0.9000 Gold .2304 oz. AGW **Ruler:** Georg **Reverse:** Type III

Date	Mintage	F	VF	XF	Unc	BU
1903E	250,000	120	165	250	450	—
1903E Proof	—	Value: 1,800				

KM# 1265 20 MARK Weight: 7.9650 g. **Composition:** 0.9000 Gold .2304 oz. AGW **Ruler:** Friedrich August III

Date	Mintage	VG	F	VF	XF	Unc
1905E	500,000	—	115	125	150	275
1905E Proof	86	Value: 1,500				
1913E	121,000	—	120	140	200	325
1914E	325,000	—	120	165	225	425
1914E Proof	—	Value: 1,750				

PATTERNS

Including off metal strikes

KM#	Date	Mintage	Identification	Mkt Val
Pn78	1902 E	—	5 Mark. Silver. KM1258.	—
PnA78	1905E	—	20 Mark. Copper. 4.0600 g.	—
PnB78	1905E	—	20 Mark. Copper. 4.8900 g. Bust in uniform.	—
Pn79	1913	—	3 Mark. Silver.	—
Pn80	1917 E	—	3 Mark. Aluminum. KM1267.	—

SCHAUMBURG-LIPPE

The tiny countship of Schaumburg-Lippe, with an area of only 131 square miles (218 square kilometers) in northwest Germany, was surrounded by the larger states of Brunswick-Lüneburg-Calenberg, an enclave of Hesse-Cassel, and the bishopric of Minden (part of Brandenburg-Prussia from 1648). It was founded in 1640 when Schaumburg-Gehmen was divided between Hesse-Cassel and Lippe-Alverdissen. The two became known as Schaumburg-Hessen and Schaumburg-Lippe. Philipp II, the youngest son of Count Simon VI of Lippe came into the possession of Alverdissen and Lipperode upon his father's death in 1613. In 1640, he also inherited half of Schaumburg-Bückeburg, becoming the first Count of Schaumburg-Lippe. A separate line of Schaumburg-Alverdissen was established in 1681 and, upon the extinction of the elder line in 1777, the lands and titles devolved onto Alverdissen, becoming the ruling line in the countship. In 1806, the count was raised to the rank of prince and Schaumburg-Lippe was incorporated into the Rhine Confederation. It became a part of the German Confederation in 1815 and joined the North German Confederation in 1866. The principality became a member state in the German Empire in 1871. The last sovereign prince resigned as a result of World War I.

RULERS

Albrecht Georg, 1893-1911
Adolf II Bernhard, 1911-1918

MINT MARKS

A - Berlin mint, 1858-1911

PRINCIPALITY

REFORM COINAGE

Y# 203 2 MARK Weight: 11.1110 g. **Composition:** 0.9000 Silver 0.3215 oz. ASW **Ruler:** Albrecht Georg **Subject:** Death of Prince George

Date	F	VF	XF	Unc	BU
1904A	200	400	700	1,250	—
1904A Proof	—	—	—	1,600	—

Y# 206 3 MARK Weight: 16.6670 g. **Composition:** 0.9000 Silver 0.4823 oz. ASW **Ruler:** Albrecht Georg **Subject:** Death of Prince George

Date	Mintage	F	VF	XF	Unc	BU
1911A	50,000	30.00	60.00	90.00	175	—
1911A Proof	—	—	—	—	300	—

Y# 204 5 MARK Weight: 27.7770 g. **Composition:** 0.9000 Silver 0.8038 oz. ASW **Ruler:** Albrecht Georg **Subject:** Death of Prince George

Date	F	VF	XF	Unc	BU
1904A	350	775	1,200	2,450	—
1904A Proof	—	—	—	3,500	—

Y# 205 20 MARK Weight: 7.9650 g. **Composition:** 0.9000 Gold 0.2304 oz. AGW **Ruler:** Albrecht Georg **Subject:** Death of Prince George

Date	F	VF	XF	Unc	BU
1904A	850	1,200	2,000	3,000	—
1904A Proof	—	—	—	4,500	—

SCHLESWIG-HOLSTEIN

Schleswig-Holstein is located along the border area between Denmark and Germany. The Duchy of Schleswig was predominantly Danish while the Duchy of Holstein was mostly German. Holstein-Gottorp was the ruling line in most of the territory from 1533 and lost Schleswig to Denmark permanently in 1721. Holstein-Gottorp was transferred by the 1773 Treaty of Zarskoje Selo to Denmark in exchange for Oldenburg. There was a great deal of trouble in the area during the 19th century and as a result of a war with Denmark, Prussia annexed the territory in 1864. After World War I, a plebiscite was held and the area was divided in 1920. North Slesvig went to Denmark while South Schleswig and Holstein became a permanent part of Germany.

STATE

GUTSCHRIFTSMARKE

KM# Tn1 5/100 GUTSCHRIFTSMARKE
Composition: Aluminum **Obverse:** Provincial arms **Reverse:** Denomination **Size:** 23 mm.

Date	Mintage	F	VF	XF	Unc	BU
1923	3,330,000	3.00	7.00	14.00	22.50	—

KM# Tn2 10/100 GUTSCHRIFTSMARKE
Composition: Aluminum **Obverse:** Provincial arms **Reverse:** Denomination **Size:** 27 mm.

Date	Mintage	F	VF	XF	Unc	BU
1923	4,500,000	4.00	8.00	16.00	25.00	—

SCHWARZBURG-RUDOLSTADT

The Countship of Schwarzburg-Rudolstadt came into being as the younger line upon the division of Schwarzburg-Blankenburg in 1552. Its territory of about 360 square miles (600 square kilometers) is located in the center of Thuringia (Thüringen), surrounded by several of the Saxon duchies and Reuss-Obergreiz. The count attained the rank of prince in 1711 and the small state was able to weather the political perils of the Napoleonic Wars (1792-1815). Schwarzburg-Rudolstadt joined the German Confederation at the end of hostilities and subsequently became a member of the North German Confederation in 1867, then the German Empire in 1871. The last prince obtained Schwarzburg-Sondershausen upon the latter's extinction in 1909, then was forced to abdicate in 1918.

RULERS

Günther Viktor, 1890-1918

MINT MARKS

A - Berlin mint, 1841-1901

PATTERNS

Including off metal strikes

KM#	Date	Mintage	Identification	Mkt Val
Pn3	1901 A	—	2 Mark. Y207.	—

SCHWARZBURG-SONDERSHAUSEN

The Countship of Schwarzburg-Sondershausen was established as the elder line of the family upon the division of Schwarzburg-Blankenburg in 1552. It contains territory of about 330 square miles (550 square kilometers) and is located just north of Thuringia (Thüringen), surrounded by the Prussian province of Saxony, between the ducal enclaves of Gotha and Weimar. The count was raised to the rank of prince in 1697 and underwent several minor divisions during the 18th century. Schwarzburg-Sondershausen joined the German Confederation in 1815 and became a member of the North German Confederation in 1867, as well as the German Empire in 1871. When Karl Günther died without an heir in 1909, his lands and titles went to Schwarzburg-Rudolstadt (see).

RULERS

Karl Günther, 1880-1909

MINT MARKS

A - Berlin mint, 1846-1909

PRINCIPALITY

REFORM COINAGE

Y# 211 2 MARK Weight: 11.1110 g. **Composition:** 0.9000 Silver .3215 oz. ASW **Ruler:** Karl Gunther **Subject:** 25th anniversary of reign **Note:** Thick rim.

Date	Mintage	F	VF	XF	Unc	BU
1905		40.00	75.00	145	220	—
1905 Proof	5,000	Value: 250				

Y# 211a 2 MARK Weight: 11.1110 g. **Composition:** 0.9000 Silver .3215 oz. ASW **Ruler:** Karl Gunther **Subject:** 25th anniversary of reign **Note:** Thin rim.

Date	Mintage	F	VF	XF	Unc	BU
1905 Proof	5,000	Value: 150				
1905		25.00	40.00	90.00	125	—

Y# 212 3 MARK Weight: 16.6670 g. **Composition:** 0.9000 Silver .4823 oz. ASW **Ruler:** Karl Gunther **Subject:** Death of Karl Gunther

Date	Mintage	F	VF	XF	Unc	BU
1909A		30.00	60.00	100	185	—
1909A Proof	100	Value: 350				

PATTERNS

Including off metal strikes

KM#	Date	Mintage	Identification	Mkt Val
Pn1	1901A	—	2 Mark. Y209.	—
Pn2	1901A	—	2 Mark. Y211.	—
Pn3	1909A	—	3 Mark. Silver.	—

WALDECK-PYRMONT

The Count of Waldeck-Eisenberg inherited the Countship of Pyrmont, located between Lippe and Hannover, in 1625, thus creating an entity which encompassed about 672 square miles (1120 square kilometers). Waldeck and Pyrmont were permanently united in 1668, thus continuing the Eisenberg line as Waldeck-Pyrmont from that date. The count was raised to the rank of prince in 1712 and the unification of the two territories was confirmed in 1812. Waldeck-Pyrmont joined the German Confederation in 1815 and the North German Confederation in 1867. The prince renounced his sovereignty on 1 October of that year and Waldeck-Pyrmont was incorporated into Prussia. However, coinage was struck into the early 20th century for Waldeck-Pyrmont as a member of the German Empire. The hereditary territorial titles were lost along with the war in 1918. Some coins were struck for issue in Pyrmont only in the 18th through 20th centuries and those are listed separately under that name.

RULERS
Friedrich, 1893-1918 (d.1946)

MINT OFFICIALS
AW - Albert Welle, mintmaster in Arolsen 1827-1840
FW, F*w, W, .W. – Friedrich Welle

MINT MARKS
A - Berlin mint, 1842-1903
B - Hannover mint, 1867

PRINCIPALITY

REFORM COINAGE

Y# 213 5 MARK **Weight:** 27.7770 g. **Composition:** 0.9000 Silver .8038 oz. ASW **Ruler:** Friedrich

Date	Mintage	F	VF	XF	Unc	BU
1903A		700	1,500	3,000	5,000	—
1903A Proof	300	Value: 5,500				

Y# 214 20 MARK **Weight:** 7.9650 g. **Composition:** 0.9000 Gold .2304 oz. AGW **Ruler:** Friedrich

Date	Mintage	F	VF	XF	Unc	BU
1903A		1,500	2,750	4,000	7,000	—
1903A Proof	150	Value: 9,000				

WURTTEMBERG

Located in South Germany, between Baden and Bavaria, Württemberg takes its name from the ancestral castle of the ruling dynasty. The early countship was located in the old duchy of Swabia, most of which was given to Count Ulrich II (1265-79) in 1268 by Conradin von Hohenstaufen. Ulrich's son, Eberhard II (1279-1325) moved the seat of his rule to Stuttgart. Württemberg obtained the mint right in 1374 and joined the Swabian monetary union two years later. The countship was divided into the lines of Württemberg-Urach and Württemberg-Stuttgart in 1441 and the elder Urach branch was raised to the rank of duke in 1495. It became extinct in the following year and the younger line in Württemberg-Stuttgart inherited the lands and ducal title. A cadet line of the family had been established in Mömpelgard in 1473 and, when the Württemberg-Stuttgart line fell extinct in 1593, the primacy of the dynasty fell to Württemberg-Mömpelgard. The latter took the Stuttgart title and spun off several cadet branches in Neustadt, Neuenburg and Weiltingen-Brenz. Meanwhile, the duke in Stuttgart succumbed to the French advances under Napoleon. Land west of the Rhine was exchanged with France for territories in and around Reutlingen, Heilbronn and seven other towns in 1802. More territories were added in Swabia at the expense of Austria in 1805. Napoleon elevated the duke to the status of elector in 1803 and then to king in 1806. Even more land was given to Württemberg that year, doubling the kingdom's size, and it joined the Confederation of the Rhine. At the close of the Napoleonic Wars (1792-1815), Württemberg joined the German Confederation, but sided with Austria in its war with Prussia in 1866. It sided with Prussia against France in 1870 and became a member of the German Empire in 1871. King Wilhelm II was forced to abdicate at the end of World War I in 1918.

RULERS
Wilhelm II, 1891-1918

MINT MARKS
C, CT - Christophstal Mint
F - Freudenstadt Mint
S - Stuttgart Mint
T - Tübingen Mint

KINGDOM

REFORM COINAGE

KM# 631 2 MARK **Weight:** 11.1110 g. **Composition:** 0.9000 Silver .3215 oz. ASW **Ruler:** Wilhelm II

Date	Mintage	F	VF	XF	Unc	BU
1901F	592,000	9.00	19.00	40.00	125	—
1902F	816,000	8.00	17.00	45.00	125	—
1903F	811,000	9.00	19.00	40.00	125	—
1904F	1,988,000	8.00	15.00	30.00	100	—
1905F	250,000	9.00	20.00	35.00	100	—
1906F	1,505,000	9.00	20.00	35.00	100	—
1907F	1,504,000	8.00	15.00	30.00	100	—
1908F	451,000	8.00	22.00	40.00	125	—
1912F	251,000	8.00	15.00	30.00	100	—
1913F	226,000	8.00	17.00	40.00	125	—
1914F	318,000	8.00	17.00	45.00	125	—
(1901-1914) Proof	—	Value: 175				

KM# 635 3 MARK **Weight:** 16.6670 g. **Composition:** 0.9000 Silver .4823 oz. ASW **Ruler:** Wilhelm II

Date	Mintage	F	VF	XF	Unc	BU
1908F	300,000	10.00	20.00	30.00	65.00	—
1909F	1,907,000	10.00	20.00	30.00	60.00	—
1910F	837,000	10.00	20.00	30.00	60.00	—
1911F	425,000	10.00	20.00	30.00	60.00	—
1912F	849,000	10.00	17.50	25.00	50.00	—
1913F	267,000	10.00	20.00	30.00	70.00	—
1914F	733,000	10.00	17.50	25.00	50.00	—
(1908-1914)F Proof	—	Value: 250				

KM# 636 3 MARK **Weight:** 16.6670 g. **Composition:** 0.9000 Silver .4823 oz. ASW **Ruler:** Wilhelm II **Subject:** Silver wedding anniversary **Obverse:** Normal bar in H of CHARLOTTE

Date	Mintage	F	VF	XF	Unc	BU
1911F	493,000	11.50	17.50	35.00	60.00	—
1911F Proof	—	Value: 125				

KM# 637 3 MARK **Weight:** 16.6670 g. **Composition:** 0.9000 Silver .4823 oz. ASW **Ruler:** Wilhelm II **Subject:** Silver wedding anniversary **Obverse:** High bar in H of CHARLOTTE

Date	Mintage	F	VF	XF	Unc	BU
1911F	7,000	100	250	450	600	—
1911F Proof	—	Value: 1,100				

KM# 638 3 MARK **Weight:** 16.6670 g. **Composition:** 0.9000 Silver .4823 oz. ASW **Ruler:** Wilhelm II **Subject:** 25th year of reign **Note:** 5,650 were melted.

Date	Mintage	F	VF	XF	Unc	BU
1916F Proof	1,000	Value: 6,500				

KM# 632 5 MARK **Weight:** 27.7770 g. **Composition:** 0.9000 Silver .8038 oz. ASW **Ruler:** Wilhelm II

Date	Mintage	F	VF	XF	Unc	BU
1901F	211,000	15.00	30.00	80.00	400	—
1902F	361,000	15.00	30.00	80.00	400	—
1903F	722,000	15.00	30.00	65.00	375	—
1904F	391,000	15.00	30.00	65.00	375	—
1906F	64,000	25.00	60.00	185	600	—
1906F Proof	50	Value: 1,500				
1907F	417,000	15.00	30.00	65.00	250	—
1908F	532,000	15.00	30.00	55.00	250	—
1913F	401,000	15.00	30.00	50.00	250	—
(1901-1913)F Proof	—	Value: 700				

KM# 633 10 MARK **Weight:** 3.9820 g. **Composition:** 0.9000 Gold .1152 oz. AGW **Ruler:** Wilhelm II

Date	Mintage	F	VF	XF	Unc	BU
1901F	110,000	65.00	120	160	300	—
1902F	50,000	125	150	200	375	—
1903F	180,000	65.00	100	160	300	—
1903F Proof	—	Value: 1,200				
1904F	350,000	65.00	100	150	300	—
1904F Proof	—	Value: 1,200				
1905F	200,000	65.00	100	150	300	—
1905F Proof	—	Value: 1,200				
1906F	100,000	65.00	100	160	300	—
1906F Proof	50	Value: 1,200				
1907F	150,000	65.00	100	150	300	—
1907F Proof	—	Value: 1,200				
1909F	100,000	65.00	120	160	300	—
1909F Proof	—	Value: 1,200				
1910F	150,000	65.00	120	160	300	—
1910F Proof	—	Value: 1,200				
1911F	50,000	140	275	425	650	—
1911F Proof	—	Value: 1,200				
1912F	49,000	140	275	375	650	—
1912F Proof	—	Value: 1,500				
1913F	50,000	140	275	375	600	—
1913F Proof	—	Value: 1,500				

KM# 634 20 MARK **Weight:** 7.9650 g. **Composition:** 0.9000 Gold .2304 oz. AGW **Ruler:** Wilhelm II

Date	Mintage	F	VF	XF	Unc	BU
1905F	506,000	100	120	145	250	—
1905F Proof	—	Value: 1,000				
1913F	43,000	4,000	11,000	25,000	35,000	—
1913F Proof	—	Value: 50,000				

Date	Mintage	F	VF	XF	Unc	BU
1914F	558,000	1,750	3,000	4,000	6,000	—
1914F Proof	—	Value: 10,000				

PATTERNS

Including off metal strikes

KM#	Date	Mintage	Identification	Mkt Val
Pn42	19xxF	—	5 Mark. Copper. Lettered edge.	—
Pn43	1904	—	5 Mark. Silver.	—
Pn44	1904F	—	5 Mark. Copper. Y222. Eagle within irregular inner circle, countermarked "N.A.".	—
Pn45	1905	—	5 Mark. Silver.	—
Pn46	1905	—	5 Mark. Silver. Beaded rim.	—
Pn47	1905F	—	5 Mark. Silver. Lettered edge.	—
Pn48	1905F	—	5 Mark. Silver. Reeded edge.	—
Pn49	1910F	—	3 Mark. Silver. Irregular "LH" under neck. Y225a.	—
Pn50	1911	—	3 Mark. Silver.	—
Pn51	1911	—	3 Mark. Silver. Busts divide date.	—
Pn52	1911F	—	3 Mark. Aluminum.	—
PnA53	1911F	—	3 Mark. Iron. Aluminum-plated.	—
Pn54	1911F	—	3 Mark. Silver.	—
Pn55	1911F	—	3 Mark. Copper.	—
Pn56	1911F	—	3 Mark. Silver.	—
Pn57	1911F	—	3 Mark. Copper.	—
Pn58	1911F	—	3 Mark. Silver.	—
Pn59	1911F	—	3 Mark. Copper.	—
Pn60	1913F	—	2 Mark. Aluminum.	—
Pn61	1913	—	5 Mark. Nickel.	—
Pn62	1916F	—	3 Mark. Aluminum.	—
Pn63	1916F	—	3 Mark. Silver.	—

TRIAL STRIKES

KM#	Date	Mintage	Identification	Mkt Val
TS3	1905	—	3 Mark. Silver. Uniface.	—
TS4	19xx	—	5 Mark. Silver. Uniface.	200

GERMANY

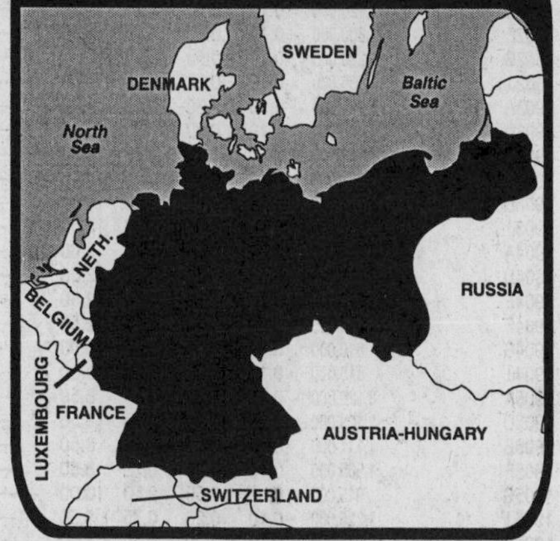

1871-1918

Germany, a nation of north-central Europe which from1871 to 1945 was, successively, an empire, a republic and a totalitarian state, attained its territorial peak as an empire when it comprised a 208,780 sq. mi. (540,740 sq. km.) homeland and an overseas colonial empire.

As the power of the Roman Empire waned, several war-like tribes residing in northern Germany moved south and west, invading France, Belgium, England, Italy and Spain. In 800 A.D. the Frankish king Charlemagne, who ruled most of France and Germany, was crowned Emperor of the Holy Roman Empire, a loose federation of an estimated 1,800 German States that lasted until 1806. Modern Germany was formed from the eastern part of Charlemagne's empire.

After 1812, the German States were reduced to a federation of 32, of which Prussia was the strongest. In 1871, Prussian chancellor Otto von Bismarck united the German States into an empire ruled by William I, the Prussian king. The empire initiated a colonial endeavor and became one of the world's greatest powers. Germany disintegrated as a result of World War I.

It was reestablished as the Weimar Republic. The humiliation of defeat, economic depression, poverty and discontent gave rise to Adolf Hitler, 1933, who reconstituted Germany as the Third Reich and after initial diplomatic and military triumphs, expanded his goals beyond Europe into Africa and USSR which led it into final disaster in World War II, ending on VE Day, May 7, 1945.

RULERS

Wilhelm II, 1888-1918

MINT MARKS

A - Berlin
D - Munich
E - Muldenhutten (1887-1953)
F - Stuttgart
G - Karlsruhe
J - Hamburg

MONETARY SYSTEM

(Until 1923)
100 Pfennig = 1 Mark

(Commencing 1945)
100 Pfennig = 1 Mark

EMPIRE

STANDARD COINAGE

KM# 10 PFENNIG Composition: Copper

Date	Mintage	F	VF	XF	Unc	BU
1901A	21,045,000	0.10	0.25	1.50	9.00	—
1901D	5,337,000	0.25	1.00	3.50	9.00	—
1901E	1,397,000	1.00	6.00	14.00	35.00	—
1901F	2,925,000	0.25	2.50	5.00	12.00	—
1901G	1,977,000	2.50	6.50	20.00	75.00	—
1901J	2,011,000	3.00	12.50	75.00	125	—
1902A	7,474,000	0.50	1.00	5.00	10.00	—
1902D	2,811,000	1.00	5.00	20.00	50.00	—
1902E	1,183,000	2.50	5.00	20.00	35.00	—
1902F	1,250,000	2.50	5.00	20.00	35.00	—
1902G	881,000	5.00	20.00	45.00	100	—
1902J	150	375	1,000	1,500	4,000	—
1903A	12,690,000	0.10	0.50	1.50	10.00	—
1903D	3,140,000	1.00	2.00	5.00	20.00	—
1903E	1,956,000	2.00	4.00	10.00	30.00	—
1903F	2,945,000	1.00	5.00	30.00	45.00	—
1903G	1,377,000	5.00	10.00	50.00	125	—
1903J	2,832,000	2.50	10.00	25.00	60.00	—
1904A	28,625,000	0.10	0.25	1.50	10.00	—
1904D	4,118,000	1.00	2.00	9.00	25.00	—
1904E	2,778,000	1.00	2.00	9.00	20.00	—
1904F	4,520,000	2.00	4.00	9.00	20.00	—
1904G	3,232,000	2.00	9.00	20.00	45.00	—
1904J	4,467,000	1.00	2.00	9.00	15.00	—
1905A	19,631,000	0.10	0.25	1.50	5.00	—
1905D	6,084,000	0.10	0.25	4.00	20.00	—
1905E	3,564,000	0.10	0.50	4.00	15.00	—
1905E Cross under denomination	Inc. above	—	—	2,500	—	—
1905F	4,153,000	0.10	0.20	1.50	20.00	—
1905G	3,051,000	0.20	1.00	3.00	15.00	—
1905J	4,085,000	0.10	0.20	1.50	30.00	—
1906A	46,921,000	0.10	0.50	1.50	6.00	—
1906D	5,633,000	0.10	0.50	1.50	20.00	—
1906E	7,278,000	0.10	0.50	1.50	10.00	—
1906F	7,173,000	0.10	0.50	1.50	12.50	—
1906G	5,194,000	0.10	0.50	1.50	25.00	—
1906J	3,622,000	0.10	0.50	1.50	25.00	—
1907A	33,711,000	0.10	0.50	1.50	6.00	—
1907D	14,691,000	0.10	0.50	1.50	12.50	—
1907E	3,719,000	0.10	0.50	1.50	17.50	—
1907F	7,026,000	0.10	0.20	1.50	12.50	—
1907G	3,052,000	0.10	0.50	1.50	22.50	—
1907J	6,722,000	0.10	0.50	1.50	17.50	—
1908A	21,922,000	0.10	0.50	1.50	9.00	—
1908D	10,629,000	0.10	0.50	1.50	12.50	—
1908E	3,400,000	0.10	0.50	1.50	17.50	—
1908F	6,112,000	0.10	0.20	1.50	17.50	—
1908G	3,663,000	0.10	0.50	1.50	12.50	—
1908J	5,581,000	0.10	0.50	1.50	12.50	—
1909A	21,430,000	0.10	0.25	1.00	3.50	—
1909D	2,814,000	0.20	1.00	2.50	8.50	—
1909E	2,562,000	1.50	4.00	6.00	12.00	—
1909F	2,425,000	1.50	4.00	6.00	12.00	—
1909G	1,220,000	1.50	4.00	7.50	17.50	—
1909J	1,634,000	1.50	4.00	6.50	15.00	—
1910A	10,761,000	0.10	0.50	1.50	6.00	—
1910D	4,221,000	0.10	0.25	1.00	4.00	—
1910E	1,600,000	0.25	1.50	5.00	12.00	—
1910F	3,009,000	0.20	1.50	5.00	8.50	—
1910G	1,834,000	0.25	4.00	6.00	12.00	—
1910J	2,450,000	0.25	5.00	7.50	17.50	—
1911A	38,172,000	0.10	0.50	1.50	5.00	—
1911D	8,657,000	0.10	0.50	1.50	5.50	—
1911E	5,236,000	0.10	0.50	1.50	6.00	—
1911F	5,780,000	0.10	0.50	1.50	6.00	—
1911G	2,075,000	0.10	0.50	1.50	6.00	—
1911J	5,594,000	0.10	0.50	1.50	6.00	—
1912A	42,693,000	0.10	0.50	1.50	5.00	—
1912D	10,173,000	0.10	0.50	1.50	5.50	—
1912E	5,689,000	0.10	0.50	1.50	6.00	—
1912F	7,441,000	0.10	0.50	1.50	6.00	—
1912G	5,526,000	0.10	0.50	1.50	6.00	—
1912J	5,615,000	0.10	0.50	1.50	6.00	—
1913A	32,671,000	0.10	0.50	1.50	5.00	—
1913D	8,161,000	0.10	0.50	1.50	5.50	—
1913E	2,258,000	1.50	4.00	7.50	17.50	—
1913F	6,620,000	0.10	0.20	1.00	4.00	—
1913G	3,209,000	0.10	0.50	1.50	6.00	—
1913J	1,456,000	0.50	5.00	10.00	25.00	—
1914A	9,976,000	0.10	0.50	1.50	5.50	—
1914D	1,842,000	0.10	0.50	1.50	6.00	—
1914E	2,926,000	0.20	1.00	2.00	7.00	—
1914F	3,316,000	0.10	0.50	1.50	6.00	—
1914G	2,100,000	0.20	1.00	2.00	7.00	—
1914J	4,368,000	0.10	0.50	1.50	5.50	—
1915A	14,738,000	0.10	0.50	1.50	5.50	—
1915D	1,771,000	0.10	0.25	2.50	7.00	—
1915E	2,779,000	0.20	1.50	3.50	8.50	—
1915F	1,411,000	0.20	1.50	3.50	11.50	—
1915G	2,041,000	0.20	1.50	4.00	10.00	—
1915J	2,981,000	0.20	1.50	3.50	8.50	—
1916A	5,960,000	0.10	0.50	1.50	5.50	—
1916D	5,401,000	0.20	1.00	3.00	8.00	—
1916E	818,000	1.00	5.00	7.50	12.00	—
1916F	1,104,000	0.50	2.00	5.00	10.00	—
1916G	671,000	1.50	7.50	10.00	18.50	—
1916J	898,000	1.50	6.00	9.00	15.00	—
1901-16 Common date proof	—	Value: 75.00				

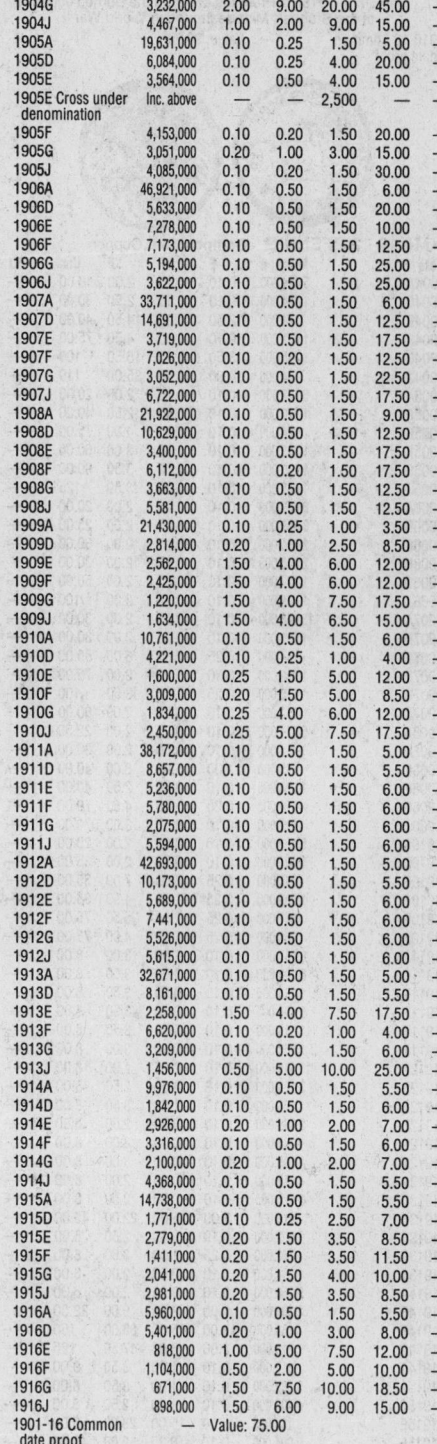

KM# 24 PFENNIG Composition: Aluminum

Date	Mintage	F	VF	XF	Unc	BU
1916G	—	125	225	350	600	—
1917A	27,159,000	0.15	0.50	2.00	5.00	—
1917A Proof	—	Value: 40.00				
1917D	6,940,000	0.15	0.50	2.00	6.00	—
1917E	3,862,000	0.50	2.00	4.50	8.00	—
1917E Proof	—	Value: 40.00				
1917F	5,125,000	0.25	2.00	4.00	7.00	—
1917G	3,139,000	0.25	2.00	4.50	8.00	—
1917G Proof	—	Value: 40.00				
1917J	4,182,000	0.25	2.00	4.00	8.00	—
1917J Proof	—	Value: 40.00				
1918A	—	300	500	3,500	6,000	—
1918D	318,000	10.00	20.00	27.50	40.00	—

Date	Mintage	F	VF	XF	Unc	BU
1918F	—	500	1,000	1,500	2,500	—

Note: The 1918F 1 Pfennigs are from the burned out ruins of the Stuttgart Mint destroyed in World War II

Date	Mintage	F	VF	XF	Unc	BU
1916-18 Common date proof	—	Value: 90.00				

KM# 16 2 PFENNIG Composition: Copper

Date	Mintage	F	VF	XF	Unc	BU
1904A	5,414,000	0.10	0.25	2.00	10.00	—
1904D	1,404,000	0.10	0.50	2.50	30.00	—
1904E	744,000	2.50	7.00	14.50	40.00	—
1904F	1,002,000	0.10	1.00	4.50	75.00	—
1904G	495,000	3.50	8.00	16.50	100	—
1904J	44,000	4.00	10.00	35.00	110	—
1905A	5,172,000	0.10	0.25	2.00	20.00	—
1905D	1,570,000	0.10	0.50	2.50	40.00	—
1905E	924,000	0.10	1.00	4.00	75.00	—
1905F	1,115,000	0.10	1.00	3.00	60.00	—
1905G	1,030,000	0.10	1.00	3.50	90.00	—
1905J	1,609,000	0.10	1.00	3.50	125	—
1906A	8,459,000	0.10	0.25	2.00	20.00	—
1906D	3,539,000	0.10	0.25	2.00	25.00	—
1906E	2,055,000	0.10	0.25	2.00	60.00	—
1906F	2,840,000	0.10	0.25	2.00	30.00	—
1906G	1,527,000	0.10	0.25	2.00	50.00	—
1906J	1,908,000	0.10	0.25	2.00	100	—
1907A	13,468,000	0.10	0.25	2.00	30.00	—
1907D	1,921,000	0.10	0.25	2.00	30.00	—
1907E	744,000	0.25	2.00	6.00	50.00	—
1907F	1,059,000	0.10	0.50	2.00	75.00	—
1907G	610,000	0.25	1.00	3.50	100	—
1907J	952,000	0.10	0.50	2.00	60.00	—
1908A	5,421,000	0.10	0.25	2.00	22.50	—
1908D	1,407,000	0.10	0.50	2.00	30.00	—
1908E	745,000	1.00	5.00	8.00	40.00	—
1908F	1,003,000	0.10	0.50	2.50	40.00	—
1908G	610,000	0.25	1.00	4.50	70.00	—
1908J	817,000	0.10	0.50	3.00	70.00	—
1910A	5,421,000	0.10	0.25	2.00	20.00	—
1910D	1,407,000	0.10	0.50	2.00	35.00	—
1910E	745,000	0.25	4.00	7.00	35.00	—
1910F	1,003,000	0.25	1.50	4.50	35.00	—
1910G	517,000	0.25	1.50	5.50	75.00	—
1910J	568,000	0.25	1.00	4.00	75.00	—
1911A	8,187,000	0.10	1.00	3.00	8.00	—
1911D	2,100,000	0.10	0.50	3.00	8.00	—
1911E	1,133,000	0.10	0.50	3.50	8.00	—
1911F	1,490,000	0.10	0.50	3.50	8.00	—
1911G	1,313,000	0.10	0.50	3.50	8.00	—
1911J	1,883,000	0.10	0.50	3.00	8.00	—
1912A	13,580,000	0.10	0.25	2.00	8.00	—
1912D	3,109,000	0.10	0.50	2.50	8.00	—
1912E	1,808,000	0.10	1.00	3.50	8.00	—
1912F	2,366,000	0.10	0.50	2.50	8.00	—
1912G	1,395,000	0.10	0.50	3.00	8.00	—
1912J	1,605,000	0.10	0.50	3.00	8.00	—
1913A	4,212,000	0.10	0.25	2.00	8.00	—
1913D	2,525,000	0.10	0.50	2.00	8.00	—
1913E	413,000	3.00	15.00	22.00	40.00	—
1913F	1,602,000	0.10	0.50	2.50	8.00	—
1913G	741,000	0.25	1.00	3.50	8.00	—
1913J	1,254,000	0.10	0.50	2.00	8.00	—
1914A	5,350,000	0.10	0.25	2.00	8.00	—
1914E	1,201,000	1.00	3.50	9.00	22.00	—
1914F	158,000	12.00	45.00	85.00	150	—
1914G	610,000	2.00	6.00	17.50	125	—
1914J	817,000	0.10	1.00	3.50	9.00	—
1915A	3,897,000	0.10	1.00	3.50	8.00	—
1915D	1,407,000	0.10	1.00	2.50	8.00	—
1915E	288,000	5.00	15.00	28.00	55.00	—
1915F	904,000	0.10	0.25	2.00	40.00	—
1916A	3,524,000	0.10	1.00	3.50	8.00	—
1916D	915,000	0.25	1.00	2.50	8.00	—
1916E	484,000	0.25	1.00	4.50	9.00	—
1916F	651,000	0.25	1.00	4.50	20.00	—
1916G	397,000	0.50	2.50	6.50	50.00	—
1916J	531,000	0.50	2.50	6.50	30.00	—
1904-16 Common date proof	—	Value: 150				

KM# 11 5 PFENNIG Composition: Copper-Nickel

Date	Mintage	F	VF	XF	Unc	BU
1901A	8,155,000	0.10	0.30	2.00	9.00	—
1901D	2,779,000	0.10	0.30	2.25	11.50	—
1901E	1,492,000	0.10	0.50	2.25	12.50	—
1901F	1,810,000	0.10	0.30	2.00	11.50	—
1901G	915,000	0.10	0.50	15.00	50.00	—
1901J	1,226,000	0.10	0.30	20.00	100	—
1902A	8,949,000	0.10	0.30	2.00	9.00	—
1902D	2,812,000	0.10	0.30	2.00	12.50	—
1902E	1,120,000	0.10	0.50	2.75	14.50	—
1902F	1,800,000	0.10	0.50	2.75	14.50	—
1902G	1,220,000	0.10	0.50	3.50	17.50	—
1902J	1,636,000	0.10	0.25	2.25	12.50	—
1903A	5,932,000	0.10	0.30	2.00	9.00	—
1903D	1,406,000	0.10	0.50	2.75	10.00	—
1903E	1,114,000	0.10	1.00	4.00	12.50	—
1903F	1,209,000	0.10	0.50	4.00	12.50	—
1903G	610,000	0.10	1.50	5.00	15.00	—
1903J	817,000	0.10	1.00	4.00	12.50	—
1904A	6,791,000	0.10	0.30	2.00	9.00	—
1904D	1,408,000	0.10	0.50	2.25	12.50	—
1904E	746,000	0.10	1.50	4.00	12.50	—
1904F	1,006,000	0.10	0.50	2.75	12.50	—
1904G	610,000	0.10	1.00	3.00	14.00	—
1904J	818,000	0.10	0.50	2.75	14.00	—
1905A	8,129,000	0.10	0.20	0.75	8.50	—
1905D	2,109,000	0.10	0.20	0.75	8.50	—
1905E	1,117,000	0.10	0.20	0.75	8.50	—
1905F	1,505,000	0.10	0.20	0.75	8.50	—
1905G	915,000	0.10	0.50	2.50	10.00	—
1905J	1,226,000	0.10	0.20	0.75	8.50	—
1906A	18,970,000	0.10	0.20	0.50	7.00	—
1906D	4,922,000	0.10	0.20	0.50	7.50	—
1906E	2,605,000	0.10	0.20	0.50	7.50	—
1906F	3,512,000	0.10	0.20	0.50	7.50	—
1906G	2,136,000	0.10	0.25	1.00	9.00	—
1906J	2,859,000	0.10	0.20	0.50	7.50	—
1907A	11,930,000	0.10	0.20	0.50	7.00	—
1907D	2,113,000	0.10	0.20	0.50	7.50	—
1907E	1,517,000	0.10	0.25	1.00	9.00	—
1907F	1,845,000	0.10	0.20	0.50	7.50	—
1907G	915,000	0.10	0.50	1.00	9.00	—
1907J	1,636,000	0.10	0.20	0.50	7.50	—
1908A	22,114,000	0.10	0.20	0.50	6.50	—
1908D	4,991,000	0.10	0.20	0.50	7.00	—
1908E	2,919,000	0.10	0.20	0.50	8.00	—
1908/7F	5,124,000	30.00	60.00	80.00	150	—
1908F	Inc. above	0.10	0.20	0.50	7.50	—
1908/10G	3,357,000	—	—	—	—	—
1908G	Inc. above	0.10	0.15	0.50	7.00	—
1908J	3,264,000	0.10	0.20	0.50	6.00	—
1909A	5,797,000	0.10	0.30	2.00	8.00	—
1909D	2,753,000	0.10	0.50	2.50	9.00	—
1909E	984,000	0.25	2.50	5.00	15.00	—
1909F	252,000	2.00	5.00	7.50	20.00	—
1909/8J	1,632,000	1.00	5.00	15.00	45.00	—
1909J	Inc. above	0.10	2.50	5.00	15.00	—
1910A	7,344,000	0.10	0.20	1.00	6.50	—
1910D	2,814,000	0.10	0.20	0.50	8.50	—
1910E	1,290,000	0.10	0.50	2.00	12.00	—
1910F	1,721,000	0.10	0.20	0.50	8.50	—
1910G	1,222,000	0.10	0.20	0.50	8.50	—
1910J	152,000	30.00	42.50	70.00	125	—
1911A	15,660,000	0.10	0.15	0.50	6.50	—
1911D	2,221,000	0.10	0.20	0.50	7.00	—
1911E	1,770,000	0.10	0.20	0.50	7.00	—
1911F	2,714,000	0.10	0.20	0.50	7.00	—
1911G	1,833,000	0.10	0.20	1.00	7.00	—
1911J	3,116,000	0.10	0.15	0.50	7.00	—
1912A	19,320,000	0.10	0.15	0.50	6.50	—
1912D	4,015,000	0.10	0.20	0.50	7.00	—
1912E	2,568,000	0.10	0.20	0.50	7.00	—
1912F	3,679,000	0.10	0.15	0.50	7.00	—
1912G	2,440,000	0.10	0.20	0.50	7.00	—
1912J	3,020,000	0.10	0.15	0.50	7.00	—
1913A	15,506,000	0.10	0.15	0.50	6.50	—
1913D	5,519,000	0.10	0.20	0.50	7.00	—
1913E	2,373,000	0.10	0.20	0.50	9.00	—
1913F	2,054,000	0.10	0.20	0.50	6.00	—
1913G	1,221,000	0.10	0.20	0.50	6.00	—
1913J	253,000	15.00	25.00	40.00	60.00	—
1914A	23,605,000	0.10	0.15	0.50	6.00	—
1914D	3,014,000	0.10	0.20	0.50	6.00	—
1914E	1,710,000	0.10	0.20	0.50	6.00	—
1914F	2,206,000	0.10	0.20	0.50	6.00	—
1914G	1,218,000	0.10	0.20	0.50	6.00	—
1914J	3,235,000	0.10	0.15	0.50	6.00	—
1915D	3,516,000	0.10	0.50	2.00	7.00	—
1915E	834,000	1.00	6.00	8.00	15.00	—
1915F	1,894,000	0.10	0.50	2.00	6.00	—
1915G	894,000	0.50	5.00	6.50	10.00	—
1915J	1,669,000	0.10	0.50	3.50	10.00	—
1901-15 Common date proof	—	Value: 100				

KM# 19 5 PFENNIG Composition: Iron

Date	Mintage	F	VF	XF	Unc	BU
1915A	34,631,000	0.10	0.25	2.00	9.00	—
1915D	2,021,000	0.50	6.50	10.00	17.50	—
1915E	4,670,000	0.50	4.00	7.50	15.00	—
1915F	3,500,000	0.25	2.50	5.00	7.50	—
1915G	3,676,000	0.25	2.00	5.00	7.50	—
1915J	2,100,000	0.25	2.00	5.00	7.50	—
1916A	51,003,000	0.10	0.25	1.50	6.00	—
1916D	19,590,000	0.10	0.50	1.50	6.00	—
1916E	2,271,000	1.00	10.00	30.00	40.00	—
1916F	10,479,000	0.15	1.00	2.00	6.00	—
1916G	5,599,000	0.25	1.50	3.50	20.00	—
1916J	10,253,000	0.25	3.00	7.50	15.00	—
1917A	87,315,000	0.10	0.50	1.00	9.00	—
1917D	19,581,000	0.10	0.50	1.00	9.00	—
1917E	11,092,000	0.50	5.00	7.50	12.00	—
1917F	10,930,000	0.10	0.50	2.00	10.00	—
1917F	—	—	—	—	—	—

Note: Mule with Polish reverse of Y#5, see Poland

Date	Mintage	F	VF	XF	Unc	BU
1917G	6,720,000	0.25	3.00	6.00	12.00	—
1917J	11,686,000	0.25	2.00	5.00	12.00	—
1918A	223,516,000	0.10	0.50	1.00	8.00	—
1918D	29,130,000	0.10	0.50	1.00	8.00	—
1918E	23,600,000	0.25	1.00	6.00	15.00	—
1918F	24,598,000	0.10	0.25	1.00	8.00	—
1918G	12,697,000	0.10	0.50	1.00	8.00	—
1918J	20,240,000	0.10	0.50	1.00	8.00	—
1919A	112,102,000	0.10	0.20	0.50	7.00	—
1919D	41,163,000	0.10	0.25	1.00	8.00	—
1919E	20,608,000	0.25	3.00	6.00	15.00	—
1919F	32,700,000	0.10	0.25	1.00	8.00	—
1919G	13,925,000	0.10	0.50	2.50	12.00	—
1919J	16,249,000	0.15	1.00	2.00	9.00	—
1920A	80,300,000	0.10	0.20	0.50	7.00	—
1920D	25,502,000	0.10	0.50	1.00	8.00	—
1920E	11,646,000	0.25	2.50	8.00	25.00	—
1920F	24,300,000	0.10	0.25	1.00	8.00	—
1920G	10,244,000	0.20	2.00	3.50	15.00	—
1920J	16,857,000	0.10	0.20	1.00	8.00	—
1921A	143,418,000	0.10	0.20	0.50	7.00	—
1921D	38,133,000	0.10	0.25	1.00	8.00	—
1921E	21,104,000	2.50	5.00	10.00	20.00	—
1921F	24,800,000	0.10	0.25	1.00	8.00	—
1921G	21,289,000	0.10	0.25	1.00	8.00	—
1921J	28,928,000	0.15	1.00	3.00	12.00	—
1922A Rare	89,062,000	—	—	—	—	—
1922D	31,240,000	0.10	0.25	1.00	8.00	—
1922E	19,156,000	2.50	5.00	10.00	20.00	—
1922F	16,436,000	0.10	0.25	1.00	8.00	—
1922G	19,708,000	0.10	0.25	1.00	8.00	—
1922J	16,820,000	0.25	2.50	6.00	15.00	—
1915-22 Common date proof	—	Value: 90.00				

KM# 12 10 PFENNIG Composition: Copper-Nickel

Date	Mintage	F	VF	XF	Unc	BU
1901A	10,200,000	0.10	0.25	1.00	7.00	—
1901D	3,259,000	0.10	0.25	1.00	12.00	—
1901E	1,863,000	0.10	0.30	1.00	12.00	—
1901F	2,594,000	0.10	0.25	1.00	12.00	—
1901G	1,527,000	0.10	0.25	1.00	12.00	—
1901J	1,225,000	0.10	0.25	1.00	12.00	—
1902A	5,878,000	0.10	0.25	1.00	6.00	—
1902D	1,406,000	0.10	0.25	1.00	12.00	—
1902E	502,000	0.25	3.00	6.00	15.00	—
1902F	1,003,000	0.10	0.25	1.00	14.00	—
1902G	610,000	0.25	1.50	3.50	14.00	—
1902J	815,000	0.25	1.50	3.00	14.00	—
1903A	5,131,000	0.10	0.25	1.00	7.00	—
1903D	1,406,000	0.10	0.30	1.50	12.00	—
1903E	988,000	0.15	0.30	1.00	12.00	—
1903F	1,003,000	0.10	0.25	1.00	12.00	—
1903G	610,000	0.25	0.50	1.50	14.00	—
1903J	816,000	0.20	0.40	1.50	14.00	—
1904A	5,189,000	0.10	0.25	1.00	6.00	—
1904D	1,056,000	0.10	0.30	1.00	12.00	—
1904E	559,000	0.25	1.00	2.50	12.00	—
1904F	753,000	0.10	0.25	1.00	12.00	—
1904G	457,000	1.00	5.00	7.50	16.00	—
1904J	612,000	0.25	1.50	3.50	16.00	—
1905A	8,650,000	0.10	0.25	1.00	6.00	—
1905A Proof	250	Value: 100				
1905D	1,846,000	0.10	0.25	1.00	7.50	—
1905E	980,000	0.15	0.30	1.00	7.50	—
1905F	1,310,000	0.10	0.25	1.00	7.50	—
1905G	642,000	0.25	1.00	2.00	10.00	—
1905J	1,430,000	0.10	0.25	1.00	7.50	—
1906A	14,470,000	0.10	0.25	1.00	7.50	—
1906D	4,132,000	0.10	0.25	1.00	7.50	—
1906E	2,189,000	0.10	0.25	1.00	7.50	—
1906F	2,953,000	0.10	0.25	1.00	7.50	—
1906G	1,952,000	0.10	0.25	1.00	7.50	—
1906J	2,042,000	0.10	0.25	1.00	7.50	—
1907A	17,971,000	0.10	0.25	1.00	6.50	—
1907D	2,813,000	0.10	0.25	1.00	7.50	—
1907E	2,291,000	0.10	0.25	1.00	7.50	—
1907F	3,206,000	0.10	0.25	1.00	7.50	—
1907G	1,889,000	0.10	0.25	1.00	7.50	—
1907J	2,750,000	0.10	0.25	1.00	7.50	—
1908A	20,410,000	0.10	0.25	1.00	6.50	—

Date	Mintage	F	VF	XF	Unc	BU
1908D	6,773,000	0.10	0.25	1.00	7.50	—
1908E	2,490,000	0.10	0.25	1.00	7.50	—
1908F	3,535,000	0.10	0.25	1.00	7.50	—
1908G	1,708,000	0.10	0.25	1.00	7.50	—
1908J	2,649,000	0.10	0.25	1.00	7.50	—
1909A	2,270,000	0.25	1.00	7.50	20.00	—
1909D	966,000	0.25	1.50	9.00	40.00	—
1909E	806,000	2.00	10.00	22.50	40.00	—
1909F	780,000	2.00	10.00	22.50	60.00	—
1909G	980,000	2.00	10.00	30.00	75.00	—
1909J	725,000	2.00	10.00	30.00	75.00	—
1910A	3,734,000	0.10	0.20	0.50	6.00	—
1910D	1,406,000	0.25	0.50	1.00	7.50	—
1910E	300,000	3.50	8.50	17.50	60.00	—
1910F	1,003,000	0.25	0.50	1.00	7.50	—
1910G	610,000	4.00	8.50	17.50	70.00	—
1911A	13,554,000	0.10	0.15	0.50	6.00	—
1911D	2,508,000	0.10	0.15	0.50	7.00	—
1911E	2,246,000	0.10	0.15	0.50	7.00	—
1911F	2,235,000	0.10	0.15	0.50	7.00	—
1911G	1,678,000	0.10	0.15	0.50	7.00	—
1911J	3,062,000	0.10	0.15	0.50	7.00	—
1912A	21,312,000	0.10	0.15	0.50	6.00	—
1912D	6,988,000	0.10	0.15	0.50	7.00	—
1912E	2,649,000	0.10	0.15	0.50	7.00	—
1912F	3,787,000	0.10	0.15	0.50	7.00	—
1912G	2,441,000	0.10	0.15	0.50	7.00	—
1912J	2,730,000	0.10	0.15	0.50	7.00	—
1913A	13,466,000	0.10	0.15	0.50	6.00	—
1913D	3,164,000	0.10	0.15	0.50	7.00	—
1913E	1,478,000	0.10	0.15	0.50	7.00	—
1913F	1,991,000	0.10	0.15	0.50	7.00	—
1913G	1,373,000	0.10	0.15	0.50	7.00	—
1913J	1,550,000	0.10	0.15	0.50	7.00	—
1914A	18,570,000	0.10	0.15	0.50	6.00	—
1914D	2,301,000	0.10	0.15	0.50	7.00	—
1914E	3,478,000	0.10	0.15	0.50	7.00	—
1914F	4,515,000	0.10	0.15	0.50	7.00	—
1914G	2,689,000	0.10	0.15	0.50	7.00	—
1914J	1,589,000	0.10	0.15	0.50	7.00	—
1915A	10,639,000	0.10	0.15	0.50	7.00	—
1915D	2,277,000	0.10	0.15	0.50	7.00	—
1915E	1,027,000	0.25	2.50	5.00	15.00	—
1915F	1,508,000	0.10	0.15	0.50	7.00	—
1915G	363,000	35.00	100	140	200	—
1915J	2,677,000	0.20	1.00	2.50	7.50	—
1916D	1,128,000	0.15	1.00	2.50	10.00	—
1901-16 Common date proof	—	Value: 80.00				

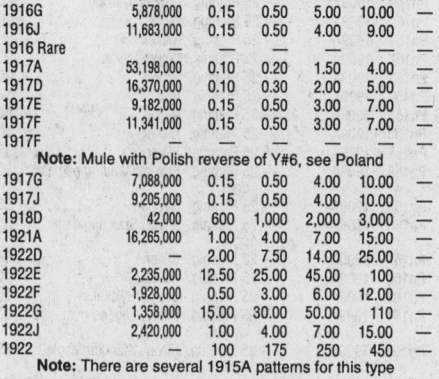

KM# 20 10 PFENNIG **Composition:** Iron

Date	Mintage	F	VF	XF	Unc	BU
1916A	69,143,000	0.10	0.35	2.00	8.00	—
1916D	11,609,000	0.10	0.30	2.00	9.00	—
1916E	8,280,000	0.15	0.50	5.00	10.00	—
1916F	7,473,000	0.15	0.50	5.00	10.00	—
1916G	5,878,000	0.15	0.50	5.00	10.00	—
1916J	11,683,000	0.15	0.50	4.00	9.00	—
1916 Rare	—	—	—	—	—	—
1917A	53,198,000	0.10	0.20	1.50	4.00	—
1917D	16,370,000	0.10	0.30	2.00	5.00	—
1917E	9,182,000	0.15	0.50	3.00	7.00	—
1917F	11,341,000	0.15	0.50	3.00	7.00	—
1917F	—	—	—	—	—	—

Note: Mule with Polish reverse of Y#6, see Poland

Date	Mintage	F	VF	XF	Unc	BU
1917G	7,088,000	0.15	0.50	4.00	10.00	—
1917J	9,205,000	0.15	0.50	4.00	10.00	—
1918D	42,000	600	1,000	2,000	3,000	—
1921A	16,265,000	1.00	4.00	7.00	15.00	—
1922D	—	2.00	7.50	14.00	25.00	—
1922E	2,235,000	12.50	25.00	45.00	100	—
1922F	1,928,000	0.50	3.00	6.00	12.00	—
1922G	1,358,000	15.00	30.00	50.00	110	—
1922J	2,420,000	1.00	4.00	7.00	15.00	—
1922	—	100	175	250	450	—

Note: There are several 1915A patterns for this type

Date	Mintage	F	VF	XF	Unc	BU
1916-22 Common date proof	—	Value: 95.00				

KM# 26 10 PFENNIG **Composition:** Zinc **Note:** Weight varies: 3.10-3.60 grams. Without mint mark. Variations in planchet thickness exist.

Date	Mintage	F	VF	XF	Unc	BU
1917	75,073,000	0.10	0.20	1.00	4.50	—
1918	202,008,000	0.10	0.20	1.00	4.50	—
1918 Proof	28	Value: 300				
1919	147,800,000	0.10	0.20	1.00	4.50	—
1919 Proof	50	Value: 100				
1920	223,019,000	0.10	0.20	1.00	4.50	—
1920 Proof	40	Value: 100				
1921	319,334,000	0.10	0.20	1.00	4.50	—
1921 Proof	24	Value: 300				
1922	274,499,000	0.10	0.20	1.00	4.50	—
1922 Proof	12	Value: 400				

KM# 25 10 PFENNIG **Composition:** Zinc **Note:** Eagle and beaded border similar to KM#20.

Date	F	VF	XF	Unc	BU
1917	100	200	250	350	—

KM# 18 25 PFENNIG **Composition:** Nickel

Date	Mintage	F	VF	XF	Unc	BU
1909A	962,000	2.50	7.00	11.50	25.00	—
1909D	1,406,000	2.50	7.00	11.50	25.00	—
1909E	250,000	15.00	27.50	40.00	90.00	—
1909F	400,000	4.00	10.00	20.00	40.00	—
1909G	610,000	4.00	10.00	20.00	40.00	—
1909J	10,000	500	750	1,200	1,500	—
1910A	9,522,000	2.50	7.00	11.50	22.50	—
1910D	1,408,000	2.50	7.00	11.50	22.50	—
1910E	1,242,000	2.50	7.00	11.50	22.50	—
1910F	1,605,000	2.50	7.00	15.00	25.00	—
1910G	330,000	3.00	8.00	18.50	35.00	—
1910J	1,561,000	2.50	7.00	15.00	25.00	—
1911A	3,179,000	2.50	7.00	11.50	20.00	—
1911D	506,000	3.00	8.00	18.50	40.00	—
1911E	747,000	3.00	8.00	18.50	40.00	—
1911G	892,000	3.00	8.00	18.50	40.00	—
1911J	516,000	3.00	8.00	18.50	40.00	—
1912A	2,590,000	2.50	7.00	11.50	—	—
1912D	900,000	3.00	8.00	17.50	32.50	—
1912F	1,003,000	3.00	8.00	18.50	35.00	—
1912J	362,000	12.50	25.00	35.00	80.00	—
1909-12 Common date proof	—	Value: 150				

KM# 15 50 PFENNIG **Weight:** 2.7770 g. **Composition:** 0.9000 Silver .0803 oz. ASW

Date	Mintage	F	VF	XF	Unc	BU
1896A	389,000	100	220	325	475	—
1898A	387,000	100	220	325	475	—
1900J	192,000	100	235	375	550	—
1900J Proof	—	Value: 650				
1896-1900 Common date proof	—	Value: 525				
1901A	194,000	150	250	300	400	—
1902F	95,000	250	300	475	1,150	—
1902F Proof	—	Value: 800				
1903A	384,000	125	200	250	325	—
1901-03 Common date proof	—	Value: 500				

KM# 17 1/2 MARK **Weight:** 2.7770 g. **Composition:** 0.9000 Silver .0803 oz. ASW

Date	Mintage	F	VF	XF	Unc	BU
1905A	37,766,000	0.75	1.00	4.50	12.00	—
1905D	7,636,000	0.75	1.50	4.50	12.00	—
1905E	4,908,000	0.75	1.50	4.50	12.00	—
1905F	6,310,000	0.75	1.50	4.50	12.00	—
1905G	3,886,000	0.75	1.50	4.50	15.00	—
1905J	6,316,000	0.75	1.50	4.50	12.00	—
1906A	29,754,000	0.75	1.50	4.50	12.00	—
1906D	11,977,000	0.75	1.50	4.50	12.00	—
1906E	5,821,000	0.75	1.50	4.50	15.00	—
1906F	8,036,000	0.75	1.50	4.50	12.00	—
1906G	4,273,000	0.75	1.50	4.50	18.00	—
1906J	2,179,000	0.75	2.50	7.50	60.00	—
1907A	14,168,000	0.75	1.50	4.50	12.00	—
1907D	2,884,000	0.75	1.50	4.50	12.00	—
1907E	600,000	2.50	9.00	20.00	60.00	—
1907F	1,202,000	0.75	1.50	4.50	12.00	—
1907G	927,000	3.00	10.00	20.00	60.00	—
1907J	3,268,000	0.75	1.50	20.00	45.00	—
1908A	5,018,000	0.75	1.50	4.50	12.00	—
1908D	400,000	7.50	17.50	32.50	70.00	—
1908E	591,000	2.50	10.00	25.00	60.00	—
1908F	1,000	2,000	5,000	7,000	9,000	—
1908G	675,000	1.25	30.00	60.00	200	—
1808/7J	1,309,000	1.25	30.00	60.00	200	—
1908J	Inc. above	1.25	10.00	80.00	200	—
1909A	5,404,000	0.75	1.50	4.50	12.00	—
1909/5D	1,001,000	0.75	1.50	4.50	12.00	—
1909D	Inc. above	0.75	1.50	4.50	12.00	—
1909E	745,000	1.25	5.00	10.00	28.00	—
1909F	999,000	0.75	2.50	7.50	15.00	—
1909G	607,000	1.25	5.00	10.00	75.00	—
1909J	816,000	1.25	5.00	10.00	20.00	—
1911A	2,710,000	1.25	5.00	7.50	22.00	—
1911/05D	703,000	1.25	5.00	7.50	22.00	—
1911D	Inc. above	1.25	5.00	7.50	22.00	—
1911E	376,000	5.00	17.50	25.00	70.00	—
1911F	502,000	2.50	7.50	17.50	50.00	—
1911G	610,000	2.50	7.50	17.50	50.00	—
1911J	418,000	5.00	17.50	27.50	85.00	—
1912A	2,709,000	1.25	5.00	7.50	25.00	—
1912/5D	703,000	1.50	10.00	15.00	30.00	—
1912D	Inc. above	1.50	10.00	15.00	30.00	—
1912E	369,000	5.00	17.50	25.00	65.00	—
1912F	501,000	2.50	7.50	12.50	65.00	—
1912J	399,000	6.00	20.00	50.00	120	—
1913A	5,419,000	0.75	1.50	4.50	12.00	—
1913/05D	1,406,000	0.75	1.50	4.50	12.00	—
1913D	Inc. above	0.75	1.50	4.50	12.00	—
1913E	745,000	2.50	5.00	10.00	22.00	—
1913F	1,003,000	0.75	1.50	5.00	12.00	—
1913G	610,000	1.25	5.00	10.00	22.00	—
1913J	817,000	1.25	5.00	10.00	28.00	—
1914A	13,525,000	0.75	1.50	3.50	10.00	—
1914/05D	328,000	2.50	10.00	15.00	35.00	—
1914D	Inc. above	2.50	10.00	15.00	35.00	—
1914J	2,292,000	0.75	3.00	5.00	12.00	—
1915A	13,015,000	0.75	1.50	3.50	10.00	—
1915/05D	5,117,000	0.75	1.50	3.00	10.00	—
1915D	Inc. above	0.75	1.50	3.00	10.00	—
1915E	3,308,000	0.75	1.50	3.00	10.00	—
1915F	5,309,000	0.75	1.50	3.00	10.00	—
1915G	2,730,000	0.75	1.50	3.00	10.00	—
1915J	2,285,000	0.75	1.50	3.00	10.00	—
1916A	9,750,000	0.75	1.50	3.00	10.00	—
1916/616D	4,397,000	0.75	1.50	3.00	10.00	—
1916/05D	Inc. above	0.75	1.50	3.00	10.00	—
1916/5D	Inc. above	0.75	1.50	3.00	10.00	—
1916D	Inc. above	0.75	1.50	3.00	10.00	—
1916E	1,640,000	0.75	1.50	3.00	10.00	—
1916F	2,410,000	0.75	1.50	3.00	10.00	—
1916G	1,779,000	0.75	1.50	3.00	10.00	—
1916J	1,464,000	0.75	1.50	3.00	10.00	—
1917A	14,692,000	0.75	1.50	3.00	10.00	—
1917/05D	979,000	0.75	1.50	3.00	10.00	—
1917D	Inc. above	0.75	1.50	3.00	10.00	—
1917E	1,561,000	0.75	1.50	3.00	10.00	—
1917F	450,000	2.50	10.00	15.00	50.00	—
1917G	619,000	2.50	10.00	15.00	50.00	—
1917J	1,039,000	1.50	4.00	6.00	15.00	—
1918A	14,622,000	0.75	1.50	3.00	10.00	—

Note: Some were issued with a black finish to prevent hoarding

Date	Mintage	F	VF	XF	Unc	BU
1918/05D	3,670,000	0.75	1.50	3.00	10.00	—
1918D	Inc. above	0.75	1.50	3.00	10.00	—

Note: Some were issued with a black finish to prevent hoarding

Date	Mintage	F	VF	XF	Unc	BU
1918E	2,807,000	1.50	6.00	10.00	20.00	—

Note: Some were issued with a black finish to prevent hoarding

Date	Mintage	F	VF	XF	Unc	BU
1918E Proof	19	—	—	—	—	—
1918F	4,010,000	0.75	1.50	3.50	10.00	—

Note: Some were issued with a black finish to prevent hoarding

Date	Mintage	F	VF	XF	Unc	BU
1918G	1,032,000	1.50	6.00	10.00	15.00	—

Note: Some were issued with a black finish to prevent hoarding

Date	Mintage	F	VF	XF	Unc	BU
1918J	3,452,000	0.75	1.50	4.00	12.00	—

Note: Some were issued with a black finish to prevent hoarding

Date	Mintage	F	VF	XF	Unc	BU
1919A	9,124,000	0.75	1.50	4.00	12.00	—

Note: Some were issued with a black finish to prevent hoarding

Date	Mintage	F	VF	XF	Unc	BU
1919/1619D	2,195,000	0.75	1.50	5.00	15.00	—
1919/05D	Inc. above	0.75	1.50	5.00	15.00	—
1919D	Inc. above	0.75	1.50	5.00	15.00	—

Note: Some were issued with a black finish to prevent hoarding

Date	Mintage	F	VF	XF	Unc	BU
1919E	1,767,000	2.50	7.50	12.50	20.00	—

Note: Some were issued with a black finish to prevent hoarding

Date	Mintage	F	VF	XF	Unc	BU
1919F	1,559,000	2.00	6.00	12.00	25.00	—

Note: Some were issued with a black finish to prevent hoarding

Date	Mintage	F	VF	XF	Unc	BU
1919J	1,875,000	1.00	3.00	5.00	15.00	—

Note: Some were issued with a black finish to prevent hoarding

Date	Mintage	F	VF	XF	Unc	BU
1905-19 Common date proof	—	Value: 115				

KM# 14 MARK **Weight:** 5.5500 g. **Composition:** 0.9000 Silver .1606 oz. ASW

Date	Mintage	F	VF	XF	Unc	BU
1901A	3,821,000	2.50	5.00	12.00	35.00	—
1901/800D	Inc. above	2.50	5.00	12.00	35.00	—
1901/801D	Inc. above	2.50	5.00	12.00	35.00	—
1901D	Inc. above	2.50	5.00	15.00	40.00	—
1901E	484,000	2.50	6.00	20.00	70.00	—
1901F	802,000	2.50	5.00	12.00	60.00	—
1901G	579,000	3.00	7.50	35.00	150	—
1901J	531,000	2.50	5.00	30.00	100	—
1902A	5,222,000	1.50	4.00	10.00	30.00	—
1902D	1,546,000	1.50	4.00	10.00	30.00	—
1902E	819,000	1.50	4.00	12.00	80.00	—
1902F	953,000	1.50	4.00	10.00	75.00	—
1902G	270,000	6.00	25.00	45.00	135	—
1902J	898,000	3.50	7.50	25.00	145	—
1903A	3,965,000	1.25	2.00	5.50	28.00	—
1903/803D	914,000	1.25	2.50	6.50	30.00	—
1903D	Inc. above	1.25	2.50	6.50	30.00	—
1903E	485,000	5.00	12.00	22.00	75.00	—
1903F	652,000	5.00	7.50	20.00	110	—
1903G	614,000	2.50	5.00	15.00	70.00	—
1903J	531,000	5.00	12.00	28.00	200	—
1904A	3,243,000	1.25	2.00	5.50	28.00	—
1904D	1,761,000	1.25	2.00	6.50	35.00	—
1904E	931,000	2.50	4.00	10.00	40.00	—
1904F	1,255,000	2.00	3.50	9.00	35.00	—
1904G	664,000	2.50	5.00	20.00	50.00	—
1904J	1,021,000	2.50	5.00	25.00	200	—
1905A	10,303,000	1.25	2.00	5.00	20.00	—
1905D	1,759,000	1.25	2.00	6.50	28.00	—
1905E	931,000	2.50	4.00	10.00	40.00	—
1905F	Inc. above	2,000	2,800	4,500	6,000	—
1905G	860,000	2.50	4.00	12.50	50.00	—
1905J	1,021,000	1.50	5.00	25.00	125	—
1906A	5,414,000	1.25	2.50	5.50	28.00	—
1906D	1,412,000	1.25	2.50	7.50	28.00	—
1906E	745,000	1.50	5.00	12.00	40.00	—
1906F	2,257,000	1.25	2.50	5.50	35.00	—
1906G	609,000	2.50	10.00	40.00	100	—
1906G Proof	—	—	—	—	—	—
1906J	372,000	5.00	12.00	35.00	200	—
1907A	9,201,000	1.25	2.50	5.00	20.00	—
1907D	2,387,000	1.25	2.50	5.00	20.00	—
1907E	1,265,000	1.25	2.50	6.50	25.00	—
1907F	1,704,000	1.25	2.50	6.50	20.00	—
1907G	1,035,000	1.25	2.50	12.00	30.00	—
1907J	1,833,000	1.25	2.50	12.00	90.00	—
1908A	4,338,000	1.25	2.50	5.00	15.00	—
1908D	1,126,000	1.25	2.50	5.50	20.00	—
1908E	596,000	2.50	5.00	12.50	45.00	—
1908F	802,000	1.25	2.50	6.50	40.00	—
1908G	488,000	2.50	5.00	12.00	45.00	—
1908J	653,000	2.50	5.00	12.00	75.00	—
1909A	4,151,000	1.25	2.50	5.00	25.00	—
1909D	1,968,000	1.25	2.50	5.50	15.00	—
1909E	Inc. below	35.00	90.00	150	245	—
1909G	854,000	4.00	12.00	22.00	35.00	—
1909J	53,000	85.00	175	285	650	—
1910A	5,870,000	1.25	1.50	5.00	17.50	—
1910D	1,406,000	1.25	2.50	5.50	20.00	—
1910E	1,050,000	2.50	4.50	7.00	25.00	—
1910F	1,631,000	2.50	4.50	7.00	20.00	—
1910G	610,000	2.50	5.00	12.00	55.00	—
1910J	1,094,000	2.50	5.00	12.00	75.00	—
1911A	5,693,000	1.25	2.50	5.50	15.00	—
1911D	126,000	10.00	20.00	40.00	100	—
1911E	738,000	4.00	6.00	15.00	50.00	—
1911F	773,000	2.50	6.00	45.00	200	—
1911G	305,000	4.00	6.00	15.00	50.00	—
1911J	812,000	4.00	6.00	40.00	175	—
1912A	2,439,000	1.25	2.50	5.50	15.00	—
1912D	632,000	1.25	2.50	5.50	20.00	—
1912E	708,000	2.50	5.00	10.00	20.00	—
1912F	502,000	2.50	5.00	12.00	40.00	—
1912J	409,000	5.00	10.00	20.00	125	—
1913F	450,000	15.00	25.00	40.00	60.00	—
1913G	275,000	20.00	30.00	45.00	65.00	—
1913J	368,000	20.00	30.00	45.00	70.00	—
1914A	11,304,000	1.25	1.50	3.50	15.00	—
1914/9D	3,515,000	1.25	1.50	3.00	14.00	—
1914D	Inc. above	1.25	1.50	3.50	15.00	—
1914E	2,235,000	1.25	1.50	3.50	15.00	—
1914F	2,300,000	1.25	1.50	3.50	15.00	—
1914G	1,911,000	1.25	1.50	3.50	15.00	—
1914J	2,978,000	1.25	1.50	3.50	15.00	—
1915A	13,817,000	1.25	1.50	3.50	15.00	—
1915D	4,218,000	1.25	1.50	3.50	15.00	—
1915E	2,235,000	1.25	1.50	3.50	15.00	—
1915F	2,911,000	1.25	1.50	3.50	15.00	—
1915G	1,749,000	1.25	1.50	3.50	15.00	—
1915J	1,634,000	1.25	1.50	3.50	15.00	—
1916F	306,000	12.00	22.00	35.00	75.00	—
1901-16 Common date proof	—	Value: 150				

MILITARY COINAGE - WWI

Issued under the authority of the German Military Commander of the East for use in Estonia, Latvia, Lithuania, Poland, and Northwest Russia.

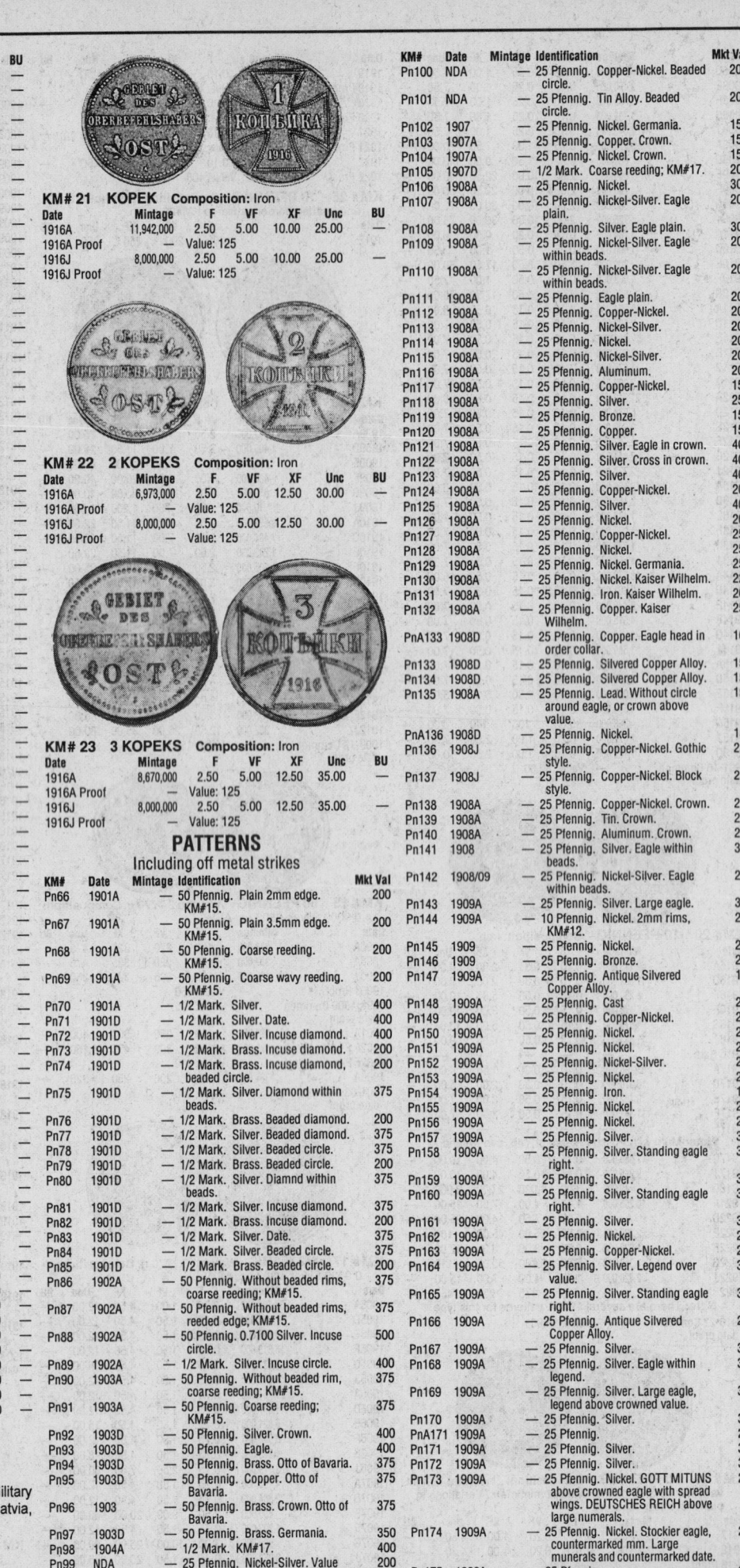

KM# 21 KOPEK Composition: Iron

Date	Mintage	F	VF	XF	Unc	BU
1916A	11,942,000	2.50	5.00	10.00	25.00	—
1916A Proof	—	Value: 125				
1916J	8,000,000	2.50	5.00	10.00	25.00	—
1916J Proof	—	Value: 125				

KM# 22 2 KOPEKS Composition: Iron

Date	Mintage	F	VF	XF	Unc	BU
1916A	6,973,000	2.50	5.00	12.50	30.00	—
1916A Proof	—	Value: 125				
1916J	8,000,000	2.50	5.00	12.50	30.00	—
1916J Proof	—	Value: 125				

KM# 23 3 KOPEKS Composition: Iron

Date	Mintage	F	VF	XF	Unc	BU
1916A	8,670,000	2.50	5.00	12.50	35.00	—
1916A Proof	—	Value: 125				
1916J	8,000,000	2.50	5.00	12.50	35.00	—
1916J Proof	—	Value: 125				

PATTERNS

Including off metal strikes

KM#	Date	Mintage	Identification	Mkt Val
Pn66	1901A	—	50 Pfennig. Plain 2mm edge. KM#15.	200
Pn67	1901A	—	50 Pfennig. Plain 3.5mm edge. KM#15.	200
Pn68	1901A	—	50 Pfennig. Coarse reeding. KM#15.	200
Pn69	1901A	—	50 Pfennig. Coarse wavy reeding. KM#15.	200
Pn70	1901A	—	1/2 Mark. Silver.	400
Pn71	1901D	—	1/2 Mark. Silver. Date.	400
Pn72	1901D	—	1/2 Mark. Silver. Incuse diamond.	400
Pn73	1901D	—	1/2 Mark. Brass. Incuse diamond.	200
Pn74	1901D	—	1/2 Mark. Brass. Incuse diamond, beaded circle.	200
Pn75	1901D	—	1/2 Mark. Silver. Diamond within beads.	375
Pn76	1901D	—	1/2 Mark. Brass. Beaded diamond.	200
Pn77	1901D	—	1/2 Mark. Silver. Beaded diamond.	375
Pn78	1901D	—	1/2 Mark. Silver. Beaded circle.	375
Pn79	1901D	—	1/2 Mark. Brass. Beaded circle.	200
Pn80	1901D	—	1/2 Mark. Silver. Diamnd within beads.	375
Pn81	1901D	—	1/2 Mark. Silver. Incuse diamond.	375
Pn82	1901D	—	1/2 Mark. Brass. Incuse diamond.	200
Pn83	1901D	—	1/2 Mark. Silver. Date.	375
Pn84	1901D	—	1/2 Mark. Silver. Beaded circle.	375
Pn85	1901D	—	1/2 Mark. Brass. Beaded circle.	200
Pn86	1902A	—	50 Pfennig. Without beaded rims, coarse reeding; KM#15.	375
Pn87	1902A	—	50 Pfennig. Without beaded rims, reeded edge; KM#15.	375
Pn88	1902A	—	50 Pfennig. 0.7100 Silver. Incuse circle.	500
Pn89	1902A	—	1/2 Mark. Silver. Incuse circle.	400
Pn90	1903A	—	50 Pfennig. Without beaded rim, coarse reeding; KM#15.	375
Pn91	1903A	—	50 Pfennig. Coarse reeding; KM#15.	375
Pn92	1903D	—	50 Pfennig. Silver. Crown.	400
Pn93	1903D	—	50 Pfennig. Eagle.	400
Pn94	1903D	—	50 Pfennig. Brass. Otto of Bavaria.	375
Pn95	1903D	—	50 Pfennig. Copper. Otto of Bavaria.	375
Pn96	1903	—	50 Pfennig. Brass. Crown. Otto of Bavaria.	375
Pn97	1903D	—	50 Pfennig. Brass. Germania.	350
Pn98	1904A	—	1/2 Mark. KM#17.	400
Pn99	NDA	—	25 Pfennig. Nickel-Silver. Value within beaded circle.	200
Pn100	NDA	—	25 Pfennig. Copper-Nickel. Beaded circle.	200
Pn101	NDA	—	25 Pfennig. Tin Alloy. Beaded circle.	200
Pn102	1907	—	25 Pfennig. Nickel. Germania.	150
Pn103	1907A	—	25 Pfennig. Copper. Crown.	150
Pn104	1907A	—	25 Pfennig. Nickel. Crown.	150
Pn105	1907D	—	1/2 Mark. Coarse reeding; KM#17.	200
Pn106	1908A	—	25 Pfennig. Nickel.	300
Pn107	1908A	—	25 Pfennig. Nickel-Silver. Eagle plain.	200
Pn108	1908A	—	25 Pfennig. Silver. Eagle plain.	300
Pn109	1908A	—	25 Pfennig. Nickel-Silver. Eagle within beads.	200
Pn110	1908A	—	25 Pfennig. Nickel-Silver. Eagle within beads.	200
Pn111	1908A	—	25 Pfennig. Eagle plain.	200
Pn112	1908A	—	25 Pfennig. Copper-Nickel.	200
Pn113	1908A	—	25 Pfennig. Nickel-Silver.	200
Pn114	1908A	—	25 Pfennig. Nickel.	200
Pn115	1908A	—	25 Pfennig. Nickel-Silver.	200
Pn116	1908A	—	25 Pfennig. Aluminum.	200
Pn117	1908A	—	25 Pfennig. Copper-Nickel.	150
Pn118	1908A	—	25 Pfennig. Silver.	250
Pn119	1908A	—	25 Pfennig. Bronze.	150
Pn120	1908A	—	25 Pfennig. Copper.	150
Pn121	1908A	—	25 Pfennig. Silver. Eagle in crown.	400
Pn122	1908A	—	25 Pfennig. Silver. Cross in crown.	400
Pn123	1908A	—	25 Pfennig. Silver.	400
Pn124	1908A	—	25 Pfennig. Copper-Nickel.	200
Pn125	1908A	—	25 Pfennig. Silver.	400
Pn126	1908A	—	25 Pfennig. Nickel.	200
Pn127	1908A	—	25 Pfennig. Copper-Nickel.	250
Pn128	1908A	—	25 Pfennig. Nickel.	250
Pn129	1908A	—	25 Pfennig. Nickel. Germania.	250
Pn130	1908A	—	25 Pfennig. Nickel. Kaiser Wilhelm.	225
Pn131	1908A	—	25 Pfennig. Iron. Kaiser Wilhelm.	200
Pn132	1908A	—	25 Pfennig. Copper. Kaiser Wilhelm.	250
PnA133	1908D	—	25 Pfennig. Copper. Eagle head in order collar.	100
Pn133	1908D	—	25 Pfennig. Silvered Copper Alloy.	150
Pn134	1908D	—	25 Pfennig. Silvered Copper Alloy.	150
Pn135	1908A	—	25 Pfennig. Lead. Without circle around eagle, or crown above value.	150
PnA136	1908D	—	25 Pfennig. Nickel.	150
Pn136	1908J	—	25 Pfennig. Copper-Nickel. Gothic style.	250
Pn137	1908J	—	25 Pfennig. Copper-Nickel. Block style.	250
Pn138	1908A	—	25 Pfennig. Copper-Nickel. Crown.	250
Pn139	1908A	—	25 Pfennig. Tin. Crown.	200
Pn140	1908A	—	25 Pfennig. Aluminum. Crown.	200
Pn141	1908	—	25 Pfennig. Silver. Eagle within beads.	350
Pn142	1908/09	—	25 Pfennig. Nickel-Silver. Eagle within beads.	250
Pn143	1909A	—	25 Pfennig. Silver. Large eagle.	300
Pn144	1909A	—	10 Pfennig. Nickel. 2mm rims, KM#12.	250
Pn145	1909	—	25 Pfennig. Nickel.	200
Pn146	1909	—	25 Pfennig. Bronze.	200
Pn147	1909A	—	25 Pfennig. Antique Silvered Copper Alloy.	175
Pn148	1909A	—	25 Pfennig. Cast	200
Pn149	1909A	—	25 Pfennig. Copper-Nickel.	200
Pn150	1909A	—	25 Pfennig. Nickel.	200
Pn151	1909A	—	25 Pfennig. Nickel.	200
Pn152	1909A	—	25 Pfennig. Nickel-Silver.	200
Pn153	1909A	—	25 Pfennig. Nickel.	200
Pn154	1909A	—	25 Pfennig. Iron.	175
Pn155	1909A	—	25 Pfennig. Nickel.	200
Pn156	1909A	—	25 Pfennig. Nickel.	200
Pn157	1909A	—	25 Pfennig. Silver.	350
Pn158	1909A	—	25 Pfennig. Silver. Standing eagle right.	350
Pn159	1909A	—	25 Pfennig. Silver.	350
Pn160	1909A	—	25 Pfennig. Silver. Standing eagle right.	350
Pn161	1909A	—	25 Pfennig. Silver.	300
Pn162	1909A	—	25 Pfennig. Nickel.	200
Pn163	1909A	—	25 Pfennig. Copper-Nickel.	200
Pn164	1909A	—	25 Pfennig. Silver. Legend over value.	300
Pn165	1909A	—	25 Pfennig. Silver. Standing eagle right.	350
Pn166	1909A	—	25 Pfennig. Antique Silvered Copper Alloy.	200
Pn167	1909A	—	25 Pfennig. Silver.	300
Pn168	1909A	—	25 Pfennig. Silver. Eagle within legend.	300
Pn169	1909A	—	25 Pfennig. Silver. Large eagle, legend above crowned value.	300
Pn170	1909A	—	25 Pfennig. Silver.	350
PnA171	1909A	—	25 Pfennig.	250
Pn171	1909A	—	25 Pfennig. Silver.	300
Pn172	1909A	—	25 Pfennig. Silver.	300
Pn173	1909A	—	25 Pfennig. Nickel. GOTT MITUNS above crowned eagle with spread wings. DEUTSCHES REICH above large numerals.	250
Pn174	1909A	—	25 Pfennig. Nickel. Stockier eagle, countermarked mm. Large munerals and countermarked date.	250
Pn175	1909A	—	25 Pfennig.	250

KM#	Date	Mintage	Identification	Mkt Val
Pn176	1909E	—	25 Pfennig. Silver Or Copper-Nickel.	300
Pn177	1909A	—	25 Pfennig. Antique Silvered Copper Alloy.	250
Pn178	NDA	—	25 Pfennig. Silver. Large eagle.	350
Pn179	1910E	—	25 Pfennig. Silver. Eagle within legend.	250
Pn180	1910A	—	1/2 Mark. Silver. KM#17.	350
Pn181	1910	—	Mark. Silver. Without mint mark, KM#7.	—
PnD182	1910A	—	3 Mark. Ernst Ludwig	—
PnA182	1911D	—	Mark. Aluminum Clad Zinc.	—
PnB182	1911D	—	2 Mark. Aluminum Clad Zinc. Bavaria	—
PnC182	1912D	—	3 Mark. Aluminum Clad Zinc. Bavaria	—
PnE182	1913	—	3 Mark. Silver. Without mint mark, Kaiser on horseback.	—
PnF182	1913	—	3 Mark. Copper.	—
Pn182	1914A	—	5 Pfennig. Reeded edge. KM#11	—
PnA183	1915	—	Non-Denominated. Gilt Bronze.	—
Pn183	1915A	—	Pfennig. Zinc. Reeded edge. KM#10	—
Pn184	1915A	—	Pfennig. Iron. Date below value, KM#24.	—
Pn185	1915A	—	Pfennig. Aluminum.	—
Pn186	1915	—	5 Pfennig. Without mint mark, KM#11.	—
Pn187	1915A	—	10 Pfennig. Brass. KM#17. KM#12.	—
Pn188	1915A	—	10 Pfennig. Brass. Broad rims, KM#12.	—
Pn189	1915A	—	10 Pfennig. Nickel. Broad rims.	—
Pn190	1915A	—	10 Pfennig. Copper-Nickel. Broad rims.	—
Pn191	1915A	—	10 Pfennig. Rusted Iron. Broad rims.	100
Pn192	1915A	—	10 Pfennig. Brass. Date above value.	—
Pn193	1915A	—	10 Pfennig. Nickel. Date above value.	—
Pn194	1915A	—	10 Pfennig. Iron. Date above value.	—
Pn195	1915A	—	10 Pfennig. Small "10".	—
Pn196	1915A	—	10 Pfennig. Large "10".	—
Pn197	1915A	—	10 Pfennig. Brass. Small "10", KM#20.	—
Pn198	1915A	—	10 Pfennig. Nickel. Small "10", KM#20.	—
Pn199	1915A	—	10 Pfennig. Iron. 67 beads on rim.	—
Pn200	1915A	—	10 Pfennig. Nickel. 67 beads on rim.	—
Pn201	1915A	—	10 Pfennig. Copper-Nickel. KM#20.	—
Pn202	1915A	—	10 Pfennig. Iron. KM#20.	500
Pn203	1915A	—	1/2 Mark. Silver. Large eagle.	—
Pn204	1915A	—	Mark. Aluminum. GOTT MIT UNS on rim, KM#14.	—
PnA205	ND	—	Pfenning. Copper. KM#24.	—
Pn205	1916A	—	Pfennig. Aluminum. KM#24.	—
Pn206	1916F	—	Pfennig. Aluminum. KM#24.	—
Pn207	1917	—	Pfennig. Aluminum. Without mint mark, KM#24.	—
Pn208	1917	—	10 Pfennig. Without mint mark, KM#20.	—
Pn209	1917A	—	10 Pfennig. Mint mark, KM#26.	—

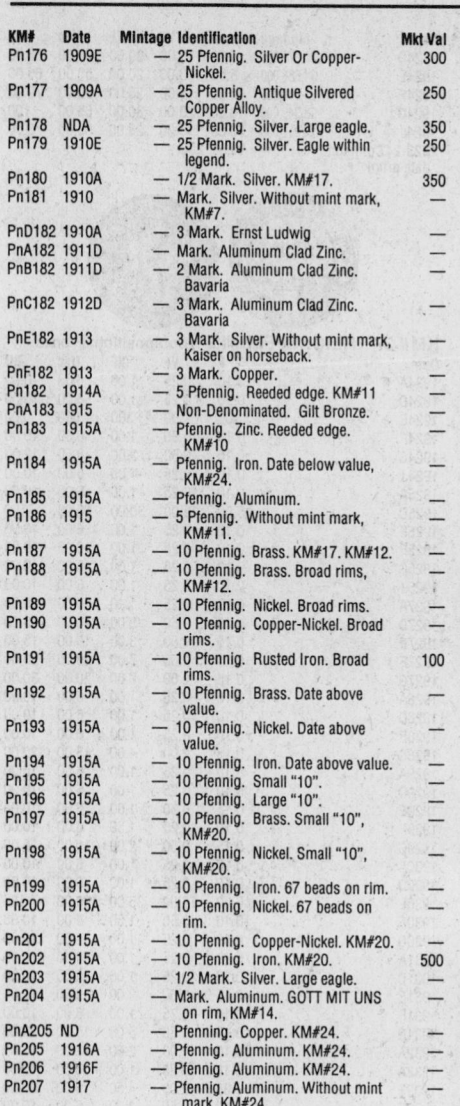

WEIMAR REPUBLIC

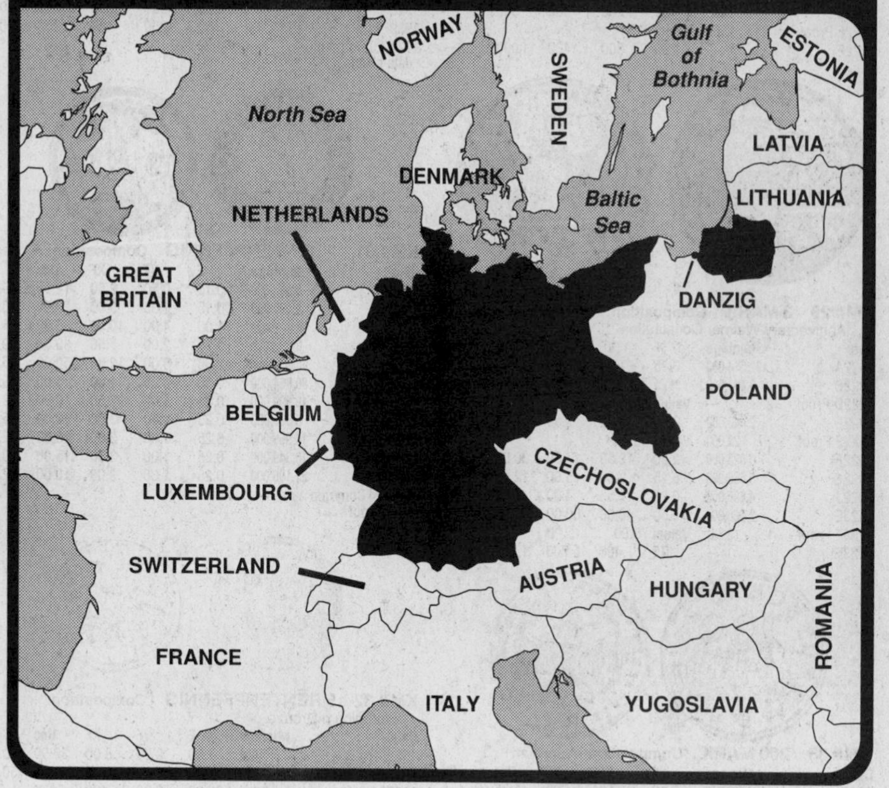

1919-1933

The Imperial German government disintegrated in a flurry of royal abdications as World War I ended. Desperate German parliamentarians, fearful of impending anarchy and civil war, hastily declared a German Republic. The new National Assembly, which was convened Feb. 6, 1919 in Weimar had to establish a legal government, draft a constitution, and then conclude a peace treaty with the Allies. Friedrich Ebert was elected as Reichs President. The harsh terms of the peace treaty imposed on Germany were economically and psychologically unacceptable to the German population regardless of political persuasion and the problem of German treaty compliance was to plague the Republic until the worldwide Great Depression of 1929. The new constitution paid less attention to fundamental individual rights and concentrated more power in the President and Central Government to insure a more stable social and economic order. The German bureaucracy survived the transition intact and had a stifling effect on the democratic process. The army started training large numbers of reservists in conjunction with the U.S.S.R. thereby circumventing treaty limitations on the size of the German military.

New anti-democratic ideologies were forming. Communism and Fascism were spreading. The National Socialist German Workers Party, under Hitler's leadership, incorporated the ever-present anti-Semitism into a new virulent Nazi Catechism.

In spite of the historic German inflation, the French occupation of the Rhineland, and the loss of vast territories and resources, the republic survived. By 1929 the German economy had been restored to its pre-war level. Much of the economic gains however were dependent on the extensive assistance provided by the U.S.A. and collapsed along with the world economy in 1929. Even during the good times, the Republic was never able to muster any loyal public support or patriotism. By 1930, Nationalists, Nazis, and Communists held nearly half of the Reichstag seats and the government was forced to rely more and more on presidential decrees as the only means to effectuate policy. In 1932, the Nazis won 230 Reichstag seats. As head of the largest party, Hitler claimed the right to form the next government. President Hindenburg's opposition forced a second election in which the Nazis lost 34 seats. Von Papen, however, convinced Hindenburg to name Hitler Chancellor by arguing that Hitler could be controlled! Hitler formed his cabinet and immediately began consolidating his power and laying the groundwork for the Third Reich.

MONETARY SYSTEM

(During 1918-1923)
100 Pfennig = 1 Mrk

(During 1923-1924)
100 Rentenpfennig = 1 Rentenmark

(Commencing 1924)
100 Reichspfennig = 1 Reichsmark

WEIMAR REPUBLIC

STANDARD COINAGE

KM# 27 50 PFENNIG Composition: Aluminum

Date	Mintage	F	VF	XF	Unc	BU
1919A	7,173,000	0.25	1.50	4.00	15.00	20.00
1919D	791,000	5.00	10.00	18.00	35.00	50.00
1919E	930,000	2.00	5.00	12.50	35.00	50.00
1919E Proof	35	Value: 250				
1919F	160,000	10.00	17.50	35.00	65.00	100
1919G	660,000	1.00	4.00	10.00	25.00	35.00
1919J	800,000	5.00	10.00	20.00	50.00	65.00
1920A	119,793,000	0.10	0.15	1.00	3.00	5.00
1920D	28,306,000	0.10	0.15	1.00	5.00	8.00
1920E	14,400,000	0.25	1.00	2.00	7.00	10.00
1920E Proof	226	Value: 100				
1920F	10,932,000	0.25	1.00	2.00	7.00	10.00
1920G	5,040,000	0.25	1.50	2.50	14.00	20.00
1920J	15,423,000	0.25	1.50	2.50	8.00	12.50
1921A	184,468,000	0.10	0.15	0.25	2.00	4.00
1921D	48,729,000	0.10	0.15	0.50	3.00	5.00
1921E	31,210,000	0.15	1.50	2.50	7.00	10.00
1921E Proof	332	Value: 100				
1921F	46,950,000	0.10	0.15	1.00	4.00	7.00
1921G	19,107,000	0.10	0.25	0.75	4.00	6.00
1921J	28,013,000	0.10	0.25	0.75	4.00	6.00
1922A	145,215,000	0.10	0.25	0.75	3.00	5.00
1922D	58,019,000	0.10	0.25	0.75	4.00	6.00
1922E	33,930,000	0.15	1.00	2.00	6.00	10.00
1922E Proof	333	Value: 100				
1922F	33,000,000	0.10	0.25	0.75	4.00	6.00
1922G	36,745,000	0.10	0.25	0.75	4.00	6.00
1922J	36,202,000	0.10	0.25	0.75	4.00	6.00

KM# 28 3 MARK Composition: Aluminum **Edge:** Reeded

Date	Mintage	F	VF	XF	Unc	BU
1922A	15,497,000	0.25	2.50	5.00	10.00	—
1922A Proof	—	Value: 75.00				
1922E	2,000	125	200	300	500	—
1922E Proof	1,000	Value: 325				
1922F	—	200	300	400	1,000	—

KM# 29 3 MARK Composition: Aluminum **Subject:** 3rd Anniversary Weimar Constitution

Date	Mintage	F	VF	XF	Unc	BU
1922A	32,514,000	0.25	1.00	1.50	2.50	—
1922D	8,441,000	175	250	400	550	—
1922D Proof	—	Value: 600				
1922E	2,440,000	0.50	5.00	7.50	15.00	—
1922E Proof	22,000	Value: 30.00				
1922F	6,023,000	2.50	12.50	17.50	30.00	—
1922G	3,655,000	0.25	2.50	5.00	12.50	—
1922J	4,896,000	0.25	1.50	4.00	7.50	—
1923E	2,060,000	17.50	40.00	60.00	85.00	—
1923E Proof	2,291	Value: 75.00				
1923F	—	175	400	700	1,500	—

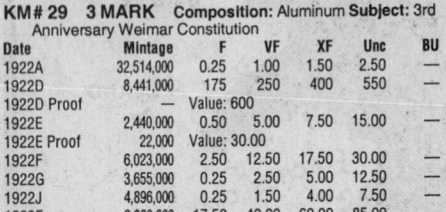

KM# 35 200 MARK Composition: Aluminum

Date	Mintage	F	VF	XF	Unc	BU
1923A	174,900,000	0.15	0.50	1.00	1.75	—
1923A Proof	—	Value: 50.00				
1923D	35,189,000	0.20	0.60	1.00	1.75	—
1923D Proof	—	Value: 50.00				
1923E	11,250,000	0.20	1.00	2.50	5.00	—
1923E Proof	4,095	Value: 50.00				
1923F	20,090,000	0.25	1.00	2.00	4.00	—
1923F Proof	—	Value: 50.00				
1923G	24,923,000	0.25	1.00	2.00	4.00	—
1923G Proof	—	Value: 50.00				
1923J	16,258,000	0.20	1.00	2.50	5.00	—
1923J Proof	—	Value: 50.00				

KM# 36 500 MARK Composition: Aluminum

Date	Mintage	F	VF	XF	Unc	BU
1923A	59,278,000	0.20	1.00	1.50	2.50	—
1923A Proof	—	Value: 75.00				
1923D	13,683,000	0.25	1.00	1.50	3.00	—
1923D Proof	—	Value: 75.00				
1923E	2,128,000	1.00	7.50	12.50	15.00	—
1923E Proof	2,053	Value: 75.00				
1923F	7,963,000	0.25	1.50	2.00	5.00	—
1923F Proof	—	Value: 75.00				
1923G	4,404,000	0.25	2.50	5.00	7.50	—
1923G Proof	—	Value: 75.00				
1923J	1,008,000	10.00	18.00	35.00	65.00	—
1923J Proof	—	Value: 250				

KM# 30 RENTENPFENNIG Composition: Bronze

Date	F	VF	XF	Unc	BU
1923A	0.15	0.50	1.50	5.00	10.00
1923D	0.25	2.00	5.00	22.00	27.00
1923E	1.50	4.00	8.00	22.00	27.00
1923F	1.50	4.00	12.00	40.00	60.00
1923G	0.25	1.50	6.00	22.00	27.00
1923J	2.00	5.00	13.00	50.00	70.00
1924A	0.15	0.50	2.50	7.50	9.00
1924D	0.20	1.50	4.00	10.00	13.00
1924E	1.00	2.00	6.00	15.00	20.00
1924F	1.00	2.00	6.00	15.00	20.00
1924G	1.00	2.00	8.00	20.00	30.00
1924J	1.00	2.00	6.00	15.00	20.00
1925A	750	1,250	2,000	2,500	3,000
1929F	150	250	400	750	1,000
1923-29 Common date proof	—	Value: 120			

KM# 31 2 RENTENPFENNIG Composition: Bronze

Date	Mintage	F	VF	XF	Unc	BU
1923A	8,587,000	0.15	0.50	2.50	12.50	16.00
1923D	1,490,000	0.15	1.00	5.00	20.00	30.00
1923F	Inc. above	1.00	4.00	10.00	35.00	45.00
1923G	Inc. above	0.75	2.00	7.50	30.00	40.00
1923J	Inc. above	2.00	5.00	12.50	50.00	65.00
1924A	80,864,000	0.10	0.25	1.00	6.00	10.00
1924D	19,899,000	0.25	1.00	2.50	10.00	12.50
1924E	6,595,000	0.25	1.00	3.00	12.00	15.00
1924F	14,969,000	0.25	1.00	3.00	10.00	12.50
1924G	10,349,000	0.25	1.00	3.00	15.00	20.00
1924J	21,196,000	0.25	1.00	3.00	10.00	12.50
1923-24 Common date proof	—	Value: 140				

KM# 32 5 RENTENPFENNIG Composition: Aluminum-Bronze

Date	Mintage	F	VF	XF	Unc	BU
1923A	3,083,000	1.00	2.50	8.00	30.00	40.00
1923D	Inc. below	1.00	3.00	10.00	40.00	50.00
1923F	Inc. below	35.00	65.00	100	175	225
1923G	Inc. below	10.00	20.00	50.00	150	180
1924A	171,966,000	0.25	1.00	3.00	10.00	15.00
1924D	31,163,000	0.25	1.00	5.00	15.00	20.00
1924E	12,206,000	0.25	1.00	5.00	20.00	25.00
1924F	29,032,000	0.25	1.00	5.00	15.00	20.00
1924G	19,217,000	0.25	1.00	5.00	20.00	25.00
1924J	32,332,000	0.25	1.00	5.00	15.00	20.00
1925F 1 known	—	—	4,800	—	—	—
1923-25 Common date proof	—	Value: 150				

KM# 33 10 RENTENPFENNIG Composition: Aluminum-Bronze

Date	Mintage	F	VF	XF	Unc	BU
1923A	Inc. below	0.25	2.50	6.00	17.50	22.50
1923D	Inc. below	0.50	5.00	10.00	25.00	35.00
1923F	Inc. below	70.00	110	160	250	300
1923G	Inc. below	2.50	12.50	25.00	75.00	100
1924A	169,956,000	0.25	1.00	2.50	8.00	12.50
1924D	33,894,000	0.25	1.00	2.00	10.00	15.00
1924E	18,679,000	0.25	1.00	3.00	15.00	20.00
1924F	42,237,000	0.25	1.00	3.00	15.00	20.00
1924F Proof	—	Value: 95.00				
1924G	18,758,000	0.25	1.00	3.00	15.00	20.00
1924J	33,928,000	0.25	1.00	3.00	15.00	20.00
1925F	13,000	750	1,100	1,600	2,500	3,000
1923-1925 Common date proof	—	Value: 150				

KM# 34 50 RENTENPFENNIG Composition: Aluminum-Bronze

Date	Mintage	F	VF	XF	Unc	BU
1923A	451,000	10.00	20.00	30.00	55.00	70.00
1923D	192,000	15.00	30.00	50.00	100	140
1923F	120,000	30.00	75.00	100	120	200
1923G	120,000	15.00	30.00	45.00	110	175
1923J	4,000	600	1,000	1,400	2,200	2,500
1924A	117,365,000	5.00	10.00	17.50	35.00	50.00
1924D	30,971,000	5.00	10.00	20.00	50.00	65.00
1924E	14,668,000	5.00	10.00	20.00	50.00	65.00
1924F	21,968,000	10.00	15.00	25.00	55.00	70.00
1924G	13,349,000	10.00	20.00	30.00	65.00	100
1924J	17,252,000	10.00	15.00	25.00	55.00	75.00
1923-24 Common date proof	—	Value: 200				

KM# 37 REICHSPFENNIG Composition: Bronze

Date	F	VF	XF	Unc	BU
1924A	0.10	0.25	1.00	6.00	10.00
1924D	0.10	0.25	1.00	6.00	10.00
1924E	100	200	300	600	700
1924F	0.15	0.30	1.00	6.00	10.00
1924G	0.15	0.50	2.00	8.50	12.00
1924J	0.10	0.25	1.00	6.00	10.00
1925A	0.10	0.25	1.00	5.00	10.00
1925D	5.00	15.00	30.00	60.00	100
1925E	0.10	0.25	1.00	6.00	10.00
1925F	0.10	0.25	1.00	6.00	10.00
1925G	0.10	0.25	1.00	6.00	10.00
1925J	0.10	0.25	1.00	6.00	10.00
1927A	0.10	0.25	1.00	10.00	15.00
1927D	0.15	0.50	2.00	10.00	15.00
1927E	0.15	1.00	3.00	10.00	15.00
1927F	0.25	2.00	7.00	20.00	30.00
1927G	0.15	2.00	7.00	20.00	30.00
1928A	0.10	0.25	1.00	6.00	10.00
1928D	0.10	0.25	1.00	6.00	10.00
1928F	0.10	0.25	1.00	6.00	10.00
1928G	0.15	2.00	4.00	15.00	20.00
1929A	0.10	0.25	1.00	6.00	10.00
1929D	0.10	0.25	1.00	6.00	10.00
1929E	0.15	0.30	1.00	6.00	10.00
1929F	0.10	0.25	1.50	6.00	10.00
1929G	0.15	0.50	2.00	10.00	15.00
1930A	0.10	0.25	1.00	6.00	10.00
1930D	0.10	0.25	1.00	6.00	10.00
1930E	6.00	15.00	35.00	90.00	120
1930F	0.10	0.50	1.50	6.00	10.00
1930G	0.10	0.25	1.00	6.00	10.00
1931A	0.10	0.25	1.00	6.00	10.00
1931D	0.10	0.25	1.00	6.00	10.00
1931E	0.15	0.50	2.00	6.00	10.00
1931F	0.10	0.25	1.00	6.00	10.00
1931G	0.15	0.50	5.00	15.00	25.00
1932A	0.10	1.00	2.00	12.00	15.00
1933A	0.10	0.25	1.00	6.00	10.00
1933E	0.35	2.00	4.50	15.00	25.00
1933F	0.10	0.50	1.00	6.00	10.00
1934A	0.10	0.25	1.00	5.00	7.00
1934D	0.10	0.25	1.00	6.00	10.00
1934E	0.50	3.50	7.50	20.00	30.00
1934F	0.10	0.25	1.00	5.00	10.00
1934G	0.15	0.30	1.00	5.00	10.00
1934J	0.15	0.50	3.00	8.50	12.00
1935A	0.10	0.25	1.00	5.00	8.00
1935D	0.10	0.25	1.00	5.00	8.00
1935E	0.15	0.50	2.00	7.50	10.00
1935F	0.10	0.25	1.00	5.00	8.00
1935G	0.10	0.25	1.00	6.00	10.00
1935J	0.10	0.25	1.00	6.00	10.00
1936A	0.10	0.25	1.00	5.00	8.00
1936D	0.10	0.25	1.00	6.00	10.00
1936E	0.50	3.00	7.00	20.00	25.00
1936F	0.10	0.25	1.00	6.00	10.00
1936G	0.15	0.30	1.00	6.00	10.00
1936J	0.15	0.50	1.00	6.00	10.00
1924-36 Common date proof	—	Value: 85.00			

KM# 38 2 REICHSPFENNIG Composition: Bronze

Date	Mintage	F	VF	XF	Unc	BU
1923F Proof	—	Value: 4,500				
1924A	19,620,000	0.10	0.25	1.00	6.00	10.00
1924D	3,482,000	0.10	0.30	1.50	12.00	15.00
1924E	4,253,000	0.15	1.50	7.50	15.00	20.00
1924F	4,567,000	0.10	0.20	1.00	10.00	15.00
1924G	7,560,000	0.10	0.20	1.00	10.00	15.00
1924J	7,489,000	0.10	0.25	1.00	10.00	15.00
1925A	22,433,000	0.10	0.25	1.00	6.00	10.00
1925D	2,412,000	0.15	0.60	2.50	15.00	20.00
1925E	5,414,000	0.10	0.30	1.50	10.00	15.00
1925F	4,851,000	0.10	0.30	1.50	10.00	15.00
1925G	2,456,000	1.00	5.00	12.00	35.00	50.00
1936A	3,220,000	0.25	2.00	7.50	17.50	20.00
1936D	6,525,000	0.10	0.30	1.50	6.00	10.00

Date	Mintage	F	VF	XF	Unc	BU
1936E	573,000	5.00	12.00	20.00	55.00	70.00
1936F	3,100,000	0.15	1.00	4.00	15.00	20.00
1923-36 Common date proof	—	Value: 90.00				

KM# 75 4 REICHSPFENNIG **Composition:** Bronze

Date	Mintage	F	VF	XF	Unc	BU
1932A	27,101,000	2.50	7.00	12.00	22.00	30.00
1932A Proof	—	Value: 150				
1932D	7,055,000	2.50	6.00	14.00	25.00	35.00
1932D Proof	—	Value: 150				
1932E	3,729,000	2.50	9.00	16.50	40.00	50.00
1932E Proof	—	Value: 150				
1932F	5,022,000	2.50	9.00	16.50	30.00	40.00
1932F Proof	—	Value: 150				
1932G	3,050,000	3.00	12.00	20.00	55.00	65.00
1932G Proof	—	Value: 150				
1932J	4,094,000	2.50	9.00	16.50	40.00	50.00
1932J Proof	—	Value: 150				

KM# 39 5 REICHSPFENNIG **Composition:** Aluminum-Bronze

Date	Mintage	F	VF	XF	Unc	BU
1924A	14,469,000	0.20	0.50	2.50	10.00	15.00
1924D	8,139,000	0.20	0.50	2.50	10.00	15.00
1924E	5,976,000	0.20	1.00	5.00	15.00	20.00
1924F	3,134,000	0.20	1.00	5.00	15.00	20.00
1924G	4,790,000	0.20	1.00	5.00	17.50	25.00
1924J	2,200,000	0.25	1.00	8.00	30.00	40.00
1925A	85,239,000	0.15	0.40	2.00	7.00	12.00
1925D	39,750,000	0.15	0.35	2.00	7.00	12.00
1925E	17,554,000	0.20	1.00	5.00	12.00	15.00
1925F Large 5	20,990,000	5.00	10.00	25.00	80.00	100
1925F Small 5	Inc. above	0.15	0.35	2.50	15.00	20.00
1925G	10,232,000	0.20	1.00	5.00	17.50	22.00
1925J	10,950,000	0.20	1.00	5.00	20.00	30.00
1926A	22,377,000	0.15	0.40	2.00	15.00	20.00
1926E	5,990,000	10.00	20.00	40.00	125	200
1926F	2,871,000	5.00	12.50	25.00	100	150
1930A	7,418,000	0.20	0.50	3.00	15.00	20.00
1935A	19,178,000	0.15	0.25	0.50	6.00	10.00
1935D	5,480,000	0.15	0.35	1.00	8.00	12.00
1935E	2,384,000	0.20	0.50	3.00	12.00	15.00
1935F	4,585,000	0.15	0.40	1.50	8.00	10.00
1935G	2,652,000	0.20	0.50	3.00	12.00	20.00
1935J	2,614,000	0.20	0.50	3.00	12.00	20.00
1936A	36,992,000	0.15	0.25	0.50	6.00	10.00
1936D	8,108,000	0.15	0.35	1.00	8.00	12.00
1936E	2,981,000	0.20	0.50	3.00	12.00	15.00
1936F	6,643,000	0.15	0.30	1.00	7.00	10.00
1936G	2,274,000	0.20	0.35	1.00	8.00	10.00
1936J	4,470,000	0.20	0.50	3.00	12.00	15.00
1924-36 Common date proof	—	Value: 100				

KM# 40 10 REICHSPFENNIG **Composition:** Aluminum-Bronze

Date	Mintage	F	VF	XF	Unc	BU
1924A	20,883,000	0.15	1.00	5.00	20.00	30.00
1924D	9,639,000	0.15	1.00	8.00	30.00	45.00
1924E	5,185,000	0.20	1.00	5.00	20.00	30.00
1924F	2,758,000	1.00	7.50	20.00	100	150
1924G	4,363,000	0.20	2.00	10.00	50.00	65.00
1924J	3,993,000	0.15	2.00	10.00	50.00	65.00
1925A	102,319,000	0.10	0.15	0.50	6.00	10.00
1925D	36,853,000	0.10	0.15	0.50	15.00	20.00
1925E	18,700,000	0.15	0.50	1.00	20.00	30.00
1925F	12,516,000	0.10	2.00	15.00	40.00	50.00
1925G	10,360,000	0.10	2.00	15.00	40.00	50.00
1925J	8,755,000	2.00	5.00	15.00	60.00	75.00
1926A	14,390,000	0.20	2.00	10.00	40.00	50.00
1926G	1,481,000	2.50	10.00	25.00	100	130
1928A	2,308,000	2.00	6.00	9.00	45.00	60.00
1928G	Inc. below	40.00	90.00	160	350	450
1929A	25,712,000	0.15	0.50	1.50	12.50	20.00
1929D	7,049,000	0.15	0.50	1.50	17.50	25.00
1929E	3,138,000	0.20	1.00	10.00	45.00	60.00

Date	Mintage	F	VF	XF	Unc	BU
1929F	3,740,000	0.20	1.00	10.00	45.00	60.00
1929G	2,729,000	0.30	3.50	15.00	70.00	85.00
1929J	4,086,000	0.20	2.50	10.00	50.00	65.00
1930A	7,540,000	0.20	2.00	2.50	12.50	20.00
1930D	2,148,000	0.25	3.50	5.00	20.00	30.00
1930E	2,090,000	1.00	5.00	12.00	55.00	70.00
1930F	2,006,000	1.00	5.00	10.00	40.00	50.00
1930G	1,542,000	2.00	5.00	20.00	70.00	90.00
1930J	1,637,000	2.50	5.00	10.00	60.00	80.00
1931A	9,661,000	0.20	2.50	5.00	15.00	20.00
1931D	664,000	15.00	35.00	65.00	100	140
1931F	1,482,000	7.50	15.00	35.00	100	130
1931G	38,000	150	225	400	800	1,100
1932A	4,528,000	0.25	3.50	6.00	15.00	20.00
1932D	2,812,000	0.50	5.00	7.50	15.00	20.00
1932E	1,491,000	4.00	8.00	12.00	50.00	65.00
1932F	1,806,000	4.00	8.00	12.00	50.00	70.00
1932G	137,000	350	750	1,150	1,500	2,000
1933A	1,349,000	15.00	25.00	50.00	100	150
1933/2G	1,046,000	6.00	12.50	27.50	65.00	85.00
1933G	Inc. above	5.00	10.00	25.00	60.00	80.00
1933J	1,634,000	1.00	8.50	15.00	35.00	50.00
1934A	3,200,000	0.20	1.00	6.00	17.50	25.00
1934D	1,252,000	1.00	7.50	10.00	60.00	80.00
1934E	Inc. below	20.00	35.00	50.00	125	175
1934F	100,000	15.00	30.00	50.00	100	150
1934G	150,000	15.00	30.00	60.00	200	250
1935A	35,890,000	0.10	0.15	1.00	8.50	12.00
1935D	8,960,000	0.10	0.25	1.50	12.50	15.00
1935E	5,966,000	0.15	0.35	2.00	15.00	20.00
1935F	7,944,000	0.10	0.30	1.50	12.50	15.00
1935G	4,847,000	0.10	0.50	3.00	15.00	20.00
1935J	8,995,000	0.10	0.30	1.50	12.50	15.00
1936A	24,527,000	0.10	0.15	0.50	7.50	12.00
1936D	8,092,000	0.10	0.20	1.00	12.50	15.00
1936E	2,441,000	0.20	0.50	2.50	15.00	20.00
1936F	4,889,000	0.10	0.30	1.50	12.50	15.00
1936G	1,715,000	0.15	2.00	10.00	30.00	40.00
1936J	1,632,000	0.25	3.00	15.00	45.00	60.00
1924-36 Common date proof	—	Value: 100				

KM# 41 50 REICHSPFENNIG **Composition:** Aluminum-Bronze

Date	Mintage	F	VF	XF	Unc	BU
1924A	801,000	500	900	1,200	1,500	1,750
1924A	—	Value: 1,750				
1924E	Inc. below	1,200	2,000	3,000	3,500	4,500
1924F	55,000	2,000	5,000	6,000	7,500	10,000
1924F Proof	—	Value: 10,500				

Note: Peus Auction #324 4-89 proof realized $10,360

Date	Mintage	F	VF	XF	Unc	BU
1924G	11,000	5,000	10,000	15,000	17,500	25,000
1924G Proof	—	—	—	—	—	—
1925E	1,805,000	500	750	1,000	2,000	2,500
1925E	196	Value: 3,000				
1925F	—	5,000	9,000	12,500	20,000	25,000
1925F Proof	—	Value: 25,000				

Note: Peus Auction #324 4-89 proof realized $23,830. Kurpfalische Munzhandlung Mannheim 6-91 proof realized $37,600

KM# 49 50 REICHSPFENNIG **Composition:** Nickel

Date	Mintage	F	VF	XF	Unc	BU
1927A	16,309,000	2.00	3.50	5.00	10.00	—
1927D	2,228,000	2.50	5.00	7.50	12.50	—
1927E	1,070,000	5.00	10.00	15.00	20.00	—
1927F	1,940,000	2.50	5.00	7.50	12.50	—
1927G	1,756,000	4.00	7.50	10.00	17.50	—
1927J	4,056,000	2.50	5.00	7.50	12.50	—
1928A	43,864,000	0.25	1.50	3.50	7.50	—
1928D	14,088,000	0.50	2.50	5.00	10.00	—
1928E	8,618,000	0.50	3.50	6.00	12.50	—
1928F	9,954,000	0.50	2.50	5.00	10.00	—
1928G	6,177,000	0.50	4.50	7.50	15.00	—
1928J	6,565,000	0.50	2.50	5.00	10.00	—
1929A	10,298,000	0.50	2.00	4.00	7.50	—
1929D	1,965,000	0.50	3.50	6.00	12.50	—
1929F	1,162,000	5.00	12.50	20.00	32.50	—
1930A	4,128,000	0.50	4.50	7.50	12.50	—
1930D	1,406,000	2.00	12.00	17.50	30.00	—
1930E	745,000	15.00	40.00	50.00	100	—
1930F	320,000	40.00	100	130	200	—
1930G	610,000	15.00	40.00	80.00	125	—
1930J	526,000	15.00	25.00	40.00	75.00	—

Date	Mintage	F	VF	XF	Unc	BU
1931A	5,624,000	0.50	4.00	7.50	10.00	—
1931D	1,125,000	1.50	12.50	17.50	30.00	—
1931F	1,484,000	1.50	12.00	16.00	25.00	—
1931G	60,000	175	300	450	675	—
1931J	291,000	30.00	90.00	150	200	—
1932E	598,000	30.00	80.00	150	225	—
1932G	96,000	800	1,200	1,500	2,250	—
1933G	333,000	40.00	85.00	135	200	—
1933J	654,000	35.00	75.00	120	175	—
1935A	6,390,000	0.50	4.00	6.00	8.50	—
1935D	2,812,000	2.50	7.50	15.00	20.00	—
1935E	745,000	7.50	30.00	40.00	50.00	—
1935F	2,006,000	2.50	7.50	10.00	15.00	—
1935G	650,000	12.50	37.50	50.00	70.00	—
1935J	1,635,000	2.00	15.00	20.00	27.50	—
1935	—	1.00	6.00	12.50	25.00	—
1936A	7,696,000	2.50	5.00	7.50	12.50	—
1936D	844,000	4.00	20.00	35.00	70.00	—
1936E	1,190,000	5.00	15.00	30.00	60.00	—
1936F	602,000	7.50	17.50	35.00	75.00	—
1936G	936,000	5.00	15.00	30.00	40.00	—
1936J	490,000	25.00	75.00	110	150	—
1937A	10,842,000	0.25	2.50	5.00	7.50	—
1937D	2,814,000	0.50	4.00	7.50	10.00	—
1937F	1,700,000	0.50	2.50	10.00	12.50	—
1937J	300,000	60.00	120	200	275	—
1938E	1,200,000	7.50	12.50	22.50	30.00	—
1938G	1,299,000	7.50	12.50	25.00	35.00	—
1938J	1,333,000	7.50	15.00	25.00	35.00	—
1927-38 Common date proof	—	Value: 150				

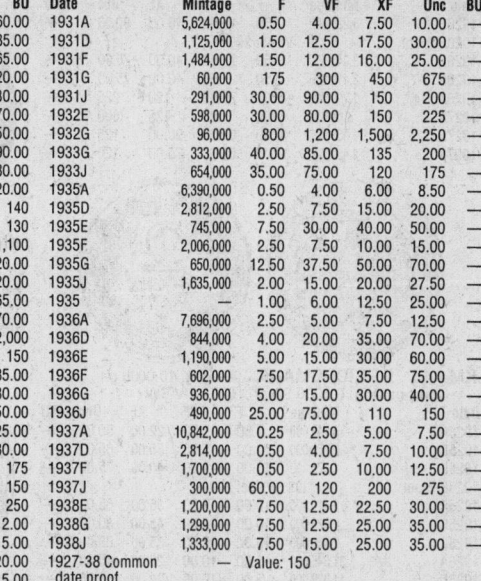

KM# 42 MARK **Weight:** 5.0000 g. **Composition:** 0.5000 Silver .0803 oz. ASW

Date	Mintage	F	VF	XF	Unc	BU
1924A	75,536,000	4.00	9.00	16.50	38.00	—
1924D	17,099,000	5.00	10.00	22.50	45.00	—
1924E	12,293,000	5.00	10.00	22.50	45.00	—
1924E Proof	115	Value: 275				
1924F	16,550,000	5.00	10.00	18.00	40.00	—
1924G	10,065,000	6.00	12.00	25.00	65.00	—
1924J	13,481,000	5.00	10.00	20.00	45.00	—
1925A	13,878,000	6.00	12.00	35.00	100	—
1925D	6,100,000	8.00	15.00	35.00	80.00	—
1924-25 Common date proof	—	Value: 250				

KM# 43 3 MARK **Weight:** 15.0000 g. **Composition:** 0.5000 Silver .2411 oz. ASW

Date	Mintage	F	VF	XF	Unc	BU
1924A	24,386,000	11.50	30.00	45.00	90.00	—
1924D	3,769,000	12.50	35.00	55.00	120	—
1924E	3,353,000	20.00	35.00	55.00	120	—
1924E Proof	115	Value: 350				
1924F	4,518,000	20.00	32.00	50.00	110	—
1924G	2,745,000	20.00	35.00	60.00	130	—
1924J	3,677,000	20.00	35.00	55.00	120	—
1925D	2,558,000	35.00	75.00	110	175	—
1924-25 Common date proof	—	Value: 280				

KM# 44 REICHSMARK **Weight:** 5.0000 g. **Composition:** 0.5000 Silver .0803 oz. ASW

Date	Mintage	F	VF	XF	Unc	BU
1925A	34,527,000	3.00	10.00	20.00	40.00	—
1925A Proof	600	Value: 200				
1925D	13,854,000	3.00	12.50	22.50	50.00	—
1925E	6,460,000	7.50	20.00	32.00	60.00	—
1925F	8,035,000	7.50	15.00	27.50	55.00	—
1925G	4,520,000	7.50	15.00	30.00	55.00	—
1925J	6,800,000	7.50	15.00	25.00	55.00	—
1926A	35,555,000	6.50	10.00	22.50	45.00	—
1926D	4,424,000	7.50	15.00	27.50	60.00	—

Date	Mintage	F	VF	XF	Unc	BU
1926E	3,225,000	7.50	15.00	45.00	90.00	—
1926E Proof	31	Value: 200				
1926F	3,045,000	7.50	27.50	40.00	75.00	—
1926G	3,410,000	7.50	27.50	40.00	75.00	—
1926J	1,290,000	25.00	75.00	120	225	—
1927A	364,000	200	300	425	600	—
1927F	1,959,000	40.00	60.00	90.00	125	—
1927J	2,451,000	35.00	55.00	75.00	120	—

KM# 45 2 REICHSMARK **Weight:** 10.0000 g. **Composition:** 0.5000 Silver .1608 oz. ASW

Date	Mintage	F	VF	XF	Unc	BU
1925A	16,145,000	7.50	12.50	22.00	55.00	—
1925D	2,272,000	10.00	15.00	35.00	65.00	—
1925E	1,971,000	10.00	17.50	40.00	75.00	—
1925E Proof	101	Value: 200				
1925F	2,414,000	10.00	17.50	35.00	65.00	—
1925G	929,000	10.00	20.00	45.00	80.00	—
1925J	2,326,000	10.00	17.50	35.00	65.00	—
1926A	31,645,000	5.00	10.00	20.00	45.00	—
1926D	11,322,000	5.00	10.00	22.00	55.00	—
1926E	5,107,000	7.50	12.50	30.00	60.00	—
1926E Proof	30	—	—	—	—	—
1926F	7,115,000	7.50	12.50	30.00	55.00	—
1926G	5,171,000	7.50	12.50	30.00	65.00	—
1926J	5,305,000	7.50	12.50	30.00	65.00	—
1927A	6,399,000	7.50	12.50	30.00	60.00	—
1927D	466,000	750	1,100	1,500	2,000	—
1927E	373,000	200	325	650	1,200	—
1927E Proof	53	Value: 2,150				
1927F	502,000	35.00	125	160	300	—
1927J	540,000	35.00	75.00	125	200	—
1931D	2,109,000	20.00	35.00	60.00	115	—
1931E	1,118,000	22.50	45.00	85.00	140	—
1931F	1,505,000	22.50	45.00	75.00	125	—
1931G	915,000	40.00	75.00	120	200	—
1931J	1,226,000	22.50	40.00	70.00	140	—
1925-31 Common date proof	—	Value: 160				

KM# 46 3 REICHSMARK **Weight:** 15.0000 g. **Composition:** 0.5000 Silver .2411 oz. ASW **Subject:** 1000th Year of the Rhineland

Date	Mintage	F	VF	XF	Unc	BU
1925A	3,052,000	17.50	30.00	40.00	50.00	—
1925A Proof	—	Value: 150				
1925D	1,123,000	22.50	35.00	45.00	70.00	—
1925D Proof	—	Value: 165				
1925E	441,000	22.50	40.00	60.00	75.00	—
1925E Proof	229	Value: 175				
1925F	173,000	30.00	45.00	60.00	100	—
1925F Proof	—	Value: 250				
1925G	300,000	22.50	40.00	55.00	75.00	—
1925G Proof	—	Value: 150				
1925J	492,000	22.50	40.00	55.00	75.00	—
1925J Proof	—	Value: 185				

KM# 48 3 REICHSMARK **Weight:** 15.0000 g. **Composition:** 0.5000 Silver .2411 oz. ASW **Subject:** 700 Years of Freedom for Lubeck

Date	Mintage	F	VF	XF	Unc	BU
1926A	200,000	50.00	80.00	110	175	—
1926A Proof	—	Value: 265				

KM# 50 3 REICHSMARK **Weight:** 15.0000 g. **Composition:** 0.5000 Silver .2411 oz. ASW **Subject:** 100th Anniversary of Bremerhaven

Date	Mintage	F	VF	XF	Unc	BU
1927A	150,000	60.00	100	130	200	—
1927A Proof	—	Value: 330				

KM# 52 3 REICHSMARK **Weight:** 15.0000 g. **Composition:** 0.5000 Silver .2411 oz. ASW **Subject:** 1000th Anniversary - Founding of Nordhausen

Date	Mintage	F	VF	XF	Unc	BU
1927A	100,000	50.00	80.00	130	200	—
1927A Proof	—	Value: 350				

KM# 53 3 REICHSMARK **Weight:** 15.0000 g. **Composition:** 0.5000 Silver .2411 oz. ASW **Subject:** 400th Anniversary - Philipps University in Marburg

Date	Mintage	F	VF	XF	Unc	BU
1927A	130,000	50.00	80.00	115	175	—
1927A Proof	—	Value: 250				

KM# 54 3 REICHSMARK **Weight:** 15.0000 g. **Composition:** 0.5000 Silver .2411 oz. ASW **Subject:** 450th Anniversary - Tubingen University

Date	Mintage	F	VF	XF	Unc	BU
1927F	50,000	150	225	325	450	—
1927F Proof	—	Value: 625				

KM# 57 3 REICHSMARK **Weight:** 15.0000 g. **Composition:** 0.5000 Silver .2411 oz. ASW **Subject:** 900th Anniversary - Founding of Naumburg

Date	Mintage	F	VF	XF	Unc	BU
1928A	100,000	60.00	100	145	200	—
1928A Matte proof	—	Value: 500				

KM# 58 3 REICHSMARK **Weight:** 15.0000 g. **Composition:** 0.5000 Silver .2411 oz. ASW **Subject:** 400th Anniversary - Death of Albrecht Durer

Date	Mintage	F	VF	XF	Unc	BU
1928D	50,000	125	225	325	450	—
1928D Matte proof	—	Value: 1,600				

KM# 59 3 REICHSMARK **Weight:** 15.0000 g. **Composition:** 0.5000 Silver .2411 oz. ASW **Subject:** 1000th Anniversary - Founding of Dinkelsbuhl

Date	Mintage	F	VF	XF	Unc	BU
1928D	40,000	225	400	600	800	—
1928D Proof	—	Value: 2,000				

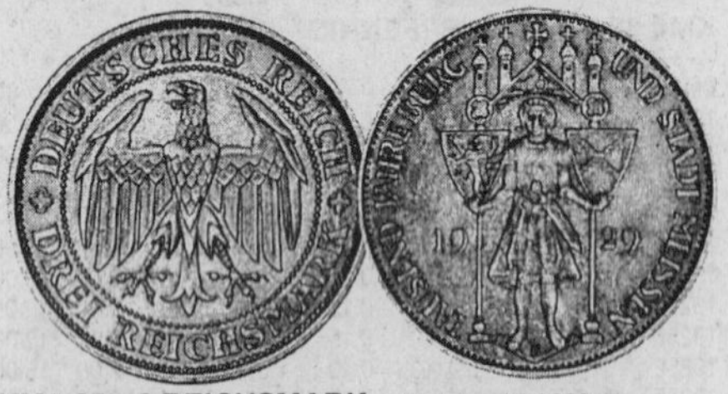

KM# 65 3 REICHSMARK **Weight:** 15.0000 g. **Composition:** 0.5000 Silver .2411 oz. ASW **Subject:** 1000th Anniversary - Meissen

Date	Mintage	F	VF	XF	Unc	BU
1929E	200,000	25.00	45.00	65.00	100	—
1929E Proof	—	Value: 320				

KM# 62 3 REICHSMARK **Weight:** 15.0000 g. **Composition:** 0.5000 Silver .2411 oz. ASW **Subject:** Waldeck-Prussia Union

Date	Mintage	F	VF	XF	Unc	BU
1929A	170,000	50.00	95.00	125	200	—
1929A Proof	—	Value: 250				

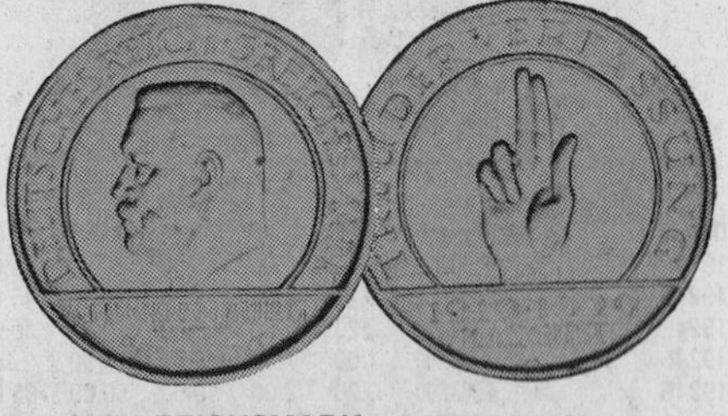

KM# 63 3 REICHSMARK **Weight:** 15.0000 g. **Composition:** 0.5000 Silver .2411 oz. ASW **Subject:** 10th Anniversary - Weimar Constitution

Date	Mintage	F	VF	XF	Unc	BU
1929A	1,421,000	17.50	35.00	50.00	65.00	—
1929A Proof	—	Value: 225				
1929A Matte proof	—	—	—	—	—	—
1929D	499,000	17.50	35.00	55.00	70.00	—
1929D Proof	—	Value: 225				
1929E	122,000	22.50	45.00	55.00	80.00	—
1929E Proof	—	Value: 300				
1929F	370,000	17.50	35.00	55.00	70.00	—
1929F Proof	—	Value: 250				

Date	Mintage	F	VF	XF	Unc	BU
1929G	256,000	22.50	45.00	60.00	80.00	—
1929G Proof	—	Value: 250				
1929J	342,000	17.50	35.00	55.00	70.00	—
1929J Proof	—	Value: 250				

KM# 60 3 REICHSMARK **Weight:** 15.0000 g. **Composition:** 0.5000 Silver .2411 oz. ASW **Subject:** 200th Anniversary - Birth of Gotthold Lessing

Date	Mintage	F	VF	XF	Unc	BU
1929A	217,000	17.50	30.00	60.00	90.00	—
1929A Proof	—	Value: 175				
1929D	56,000	20.00	35.00	65.00	100	—
1929D Proof	—	Value: 250				
1929E	30,000	20.00	35.00	70.00	110	—
1929E Proof	—	Value: 275				
1929F	40,000	20.00	35.00	65.00	100	—
1929F Proof	—	Value: 250				
1929G	24,000	20.00	35.00	80.00	110	—
1929G Proof	—	Value: 300				
1929J	33,000	20.00	35.00	80.00	100	—
1929J Proof	—	Value: 300				

KM# 67 3 REICHSMARK **Weight:** 15.0000 g. **Composition:** 0.5000 Silver .2411 oz. ASW **Subject:** Graf Zeppelin Flight

Date	Mintage	F	VF	XF	Unc	BU
1930A	542,000	40.00	60.00	85.00	110	—
1930A Proof	—	Value: 350				
1930D	141,000	35.00	60.00	90.00	125	—
1930D Proof	—	Value: 250				
1930E	75,000	35.00	60.00	90.00	140	—
1930E Proof	—	Value: 335				
1930F	100,000	35.00	60.00	90.00	125	—
1930F Proof	—	Value: 275				
1930G	61,000	40.00	65.00	95.00	150	—
1930G Proof	—	Value: 335				
1930J	82,000	40.00	65.00	95.00	130	—
1930J Proof	—	Value: 325				

KM# 69 3 REICHSMARK **Weight:** 15.0000 g. **Composition:** 0.5000 Silver .2411 oz. ASW **Subject:** 700th Anniversary - Death of Von Der Vogelweide

Date	Mintage	F	VF	XF	Unc	BU
1930A	163,000	35.00	55.00	85.00	125	—
1930A Proof	—	Value: 200				
1930A Matte proof	—	—	—	—	—	—
1930D	42,000	35.00	55.00	85.00	125	—
1930D Proof	—	Value: 225				
1930E	22,000	37.50	75.00	100	150	—
1930E Proof	—	Value: 225				
1930F	30,000	37.50	75.00	100	125	—
1930F Proof	—	Value: 325				
1930G	18,000	45.00	85.00	120	150	—
1930G Proof	—	Value: 225				
1930J	25,000	35.00	55.00	85.00	130	—
1930J Proof	—	Value: 225				

KM# 70 3 REICHSMARK **Weight:** 15.0000 g. **Composition:** 0.5000 Silver .2411 oz. ASW **Subject:** Liberation of Rhineland

Date	Mintage	F	VF	XF	Unc	BU
1930A	1,734,000	22.50	35.00	60.00	85.00	—
1930A Proof	—	Value: 150				
1930A Matte proof	—	—	—	—	—	—
1930D	450,000	22.50	35.00	60.00	85.00	—
1930D Proof	—	Value: 200				
1930E	38,000	65.00	125	175	250	—
1930E Proof	—	Value: 200				
1930F	321,000	22.50	35.00	60.00	85.00	—
1930F Proof	—	Value: 160				
1930G	195,000	22.50	35.00	65.00	85.00	—
1930G Proof	—	Value: 200				
1930J	261,000	22.50	35.00	65.00	85.00	—
1930J Proof	—	Value: 200				

KM# 72 3 REICHSMARK **Weight:** 15.0000 g. **Composition:** 0.5000 Silver .2411 oz. ASW **Subject:** 300th Anniversary - Magdeburg Rebuilding

Date	Mintage	F	VF	XF	Unc	BU
1931A	100,000	80.00	150	200	275	—
1931A Proof	—	Value: 450				

KM# 73 3 REICHSMARK **Weight:** 15.0000 g. **Composition:** 0.5000 Silver .2411 oz. ASW **Subject:** Centenary - Death of vom Stein

Date	Mintage	F	VF	XF	Unc	BU
1931A	150,000	40.00	90.00	150	200	—
1931A Proof	—	Value: 300				

KM# 74 3 REICHSMARK **Weight:** 15.0000 g. **Composition:** 0.5000 Silver .2411 oz. ASW

Date	Mintage	F	VF	XF	Unc	BU
1931A	13,324,000	100	200	275	400	—
1931D	2,232,000	125	225	350	450	—
1931E	2,235,000	140	275	350	550	—
1931F	2,357,000	125	225	350	450	—
1931G	1,468,000	145	275	375	600	—
1931J	1,115,000	145	275	375	600	—
1932A	2,933,000	125	200	275	400	—
1932D	1,986,000	145	250	375	500	—
1932F	653,000	300	500	800	1,150	—
1932G	210,000	550	800	1,400	3,000	—
1932J	1,336,000	145	225	375	500	—
1933G	152,000	800	1,300	2,200	4,000	—

Note: Less than 10 percent of issue was released

1931-33 Common date proof	—	Value: 1,250				

KM# 76 3 REICHSMARK **Weight:** 15.0000 g. **Composition:** 0.5000 Silver .2411 oz. ASW **Subject:** Centenary - Death of Goethe

Date	Mintage	F	VF	XF	Unc	BU
1932A	217,000	30.00	60.00	100	130	—
1932A Proof	—	Value: 250				
1932D	56,000	30.00	60.00	100	130	—
1932D Proof	—	Value: 250				
1932E	30,000	40.00	70.00	100	160	—
1932E Proof	—	Value: 300				
1932F	40,000	25.00	50.00	85.00	145	—
1932F Proof	—	Value: 250				
1932F Matte proof	—	—	—	—	—	—
1932G	24,000	45.00	80.00	110	160	—
1932G	—	Value: 300				
1932J	33,000	45.00	80.00	110	160	—
1932J	—	Value: 265				

KM# 47 5 REICHSMARK **Weight:** 25.0000 g. **Composition:** 0.5000 Silver .4019 oz. ASW **Subject:** 1000th Year of the Rhineland

Date	Mintage	F	VF	XF	Unc	BU
1925A	684,000	35.00	60.00	100	130	—
1925A Proof	—	Value: 325				
1925D	452,000	35.00	60.00	100	140	—
1925D Proof	—	Value: 400				
1925E	204,000	50.00	75.00	110	150	—
1925E Proof	226	Value: 400				
1925F	212,000	40.00	65.00	100	140	—
1925F Proof	—	Value: 425				
1925G	89,000	45.00	70.00	110	150	—
1925G Proof	—	Value: 475				
1925J	43,000	70.00	140	200	275	—
1925J Proof	—	Value: 550				

KM# 51 5 REICHSMARK **Weight:** 25.0000 g. **Composition:** 0.5000 Silver .4019 oz. ASW **Subject:** 100th Anniversary - Bremerhaven

Date	Mintage	F	VF	XF	Unc	BU
1927A	50,000	175	300	500	700	—
1927A Proof	—	Value: 1,000				

KM# 55 5 REICHSMARK **Weight:** 25.0000 g. **Composition:** 0.5000 Silver .4019 oz. ASW **Subject:** 450th Anniversary - University of Tubingen

Date	Mintage	F	VF	XF	Unc	BU
1927F	40,000	175	250	375	500	—
1927F Proof	—	Value: 800				

KM# 56 5 REICHSMARK **Weight:** 25.0000 g. **Composition:** 0.5000 Silver .4019 oz. ASW

Date	Mintage	F	VF	XF	Unc	BU
1927A	7,926,000	27.00	70.00	110	180	—
1927D	1,471,000	32.00	80.00	120	200	—
1927E	1,100,000	35.00	110	160	250	—
1927F	700,000	27.00	100	150	225	—
1927G	759,000	50.00	130	220	400	—
1927J	1,006,000	32.00	80.00	110	225	—
1928A	15,466,000	27.00	70.00	125	175	—
1928D	4,613,000	27.00	75.00	135	200	—
1928E	2,310,000	35.00	100	150	225	—
1928F	3,771,000	30.00	70.00	130	200	—
1928G	1,923,000	35.00	110	150	250	—
1928J	2,450,000	35.00	100	150	225	—
1929A	6,730,000	30.00	70.00	125	175	—
1929D	2,020,000	35.00	100	145	250	—
1929E	860,000	150	400	600	900	—
1929F	814,000	60.00	165	255	400	—
1929G	950,000	80.00	175	300	450	—
1929J	779,000	80.00	175	300	425	—
1930A	3,790,000	50.00	120	180	300	—
1930D	606,000	125	325	575	800	—
1930E	354,000	400	1,100	1,750	2,250	—
1930F	630,000	125	325	575	800	—
1930G	367,000	400	700	1,400	2,000	—
1930J	740,000	125	325	600	1,000	—
1931A	14,651,000	27.00	70.00	120	175	—
1931D	3,254,000	32.00	80.00	130	200	—
1931E	2,245,000	35.00	100	150	225	—
1931F	4,152,000	32.00	80.00	130	180	—
1931G	1,620,000	35.00	110	200	400	—
1931J	3,092,000	40.00	110	150	225	—
1932A	32,303,000	32.00	70.00	125	175	—
1932D	8,556,000	32.00	70.00	135	180	—
1932E	4,013,000	45.00	100	150	225	—
1932F	5,019,000	32.00	80.00	130	175	—
1932G	3,504,000	32.00	100	150	225	—
1932J	3,752,000	40.00	100	160	260	—
1933J	423,000	600	1,100	2,200	3,250	—
1933J Proof	—	Value: 4,250				
1927-33 Common date proof	—	Value: 700				

KM# 66 5 REICHSMARK **Weight:** 25.0000 g. **Composition:** 0.5000 Silver .4019 oz. ASW **Subject:** 1000th Anniversary - Meissen

Date	Mintage	F	VF	XF	Unc	BU
1929E	120,000	140	225	375	550	—
1929E Proof	—	Value: 1,000				

KM# 61 5 REICHSMARK **Weight:** 25.0000 g. **Composition:** 0.5000 Silver .4019 oz. ASW **Subject:** 200th Anniversasry - Birth of Gotthold Lessing

Date	Mintage	F	VF	XF	Unc	BU
1929A	87,000	50.00	100	135	200	—
1929A Proof	—	Value: 350				
1929D	22,000	50.00	100	150	225	—
1929D Proof	—	Value: 350				
1929E	12,000	60.00	120	165	250	—
1929E Proof	—	Value: 425				
1929F	16,000	50.00	100	150	225	—
1929F Proof	—	Value: 375				
1929G	9,760	60.00	120	165	250	—
1929G Proof	—	Value: 425				
1929J	13,000	55.00	110	150	225	—
1929J Proof	—	Value: 400				

KM# 64 5 REICHSMARK **Weight:** 25.0000 g. **Composition:** 0.5000 Silver .4019 oz. ASW **Subject:** 10th Anniversary - Weimar Constitution

Date	Mintage	F	VF	XF	Unc	BU
1929A	325,000	45.00	65.00	125	200	—
1929A Proof	—	Value: 450				
1929D	84,000	50.00	90.00	135	200	—
1929D Proof	—	Value: 400				
1929E	45,000	50.00	90.00	135	225	—
1929E Proof	—	Value: 625				
1929F	60,000	60.00	100	150	200	—
1929F Proof	—	Value: 400				
1929G	37,000	60.00	100	160	225	—
1929G Proof	—	Value: 500				

Date	Mintage	F	VF	XF	Unc	BU
1929J	49,000	50.00	90.00	160	225	—
1929J Proof	—	Value: 650				

KM# 68 5 REICHSMARK **Weight:** 25.0000 g. **Composition:** 0.5000 Silver .4019 oz. ASW **Subject:** Graf Zeppelin Flight

Date	Mintage	F	VF	XF	Unc	BU
1930A	217,000	60.00	100	165	250	—
1930A Proof	—	Value: 450				
1930A Matte proof	—	—	—	—	—	—
1930D	56,000	70.00	110	170	250	—
1930D Proof	—	Value: 650				
1930E	30,000	70.00	110	200	300	—
1930E Proof	—	Value: 700				
1930F	40,000	70.00	110	170	250	—
1930F Proof	—	Value: 600				
1930G	24,000	75.00	115	175	300	—
1930G Proof	—	Value: 700				
1930J	33,000	70.00	110	175	300	—
1930J Proof	—	Value: 700				

KM# 71 5 REICHSMARK **Weight:** 25.0000 g. **Composition:** 0.5000 Silver .4019 oz. ASW **Subject:** Liberation of Rhineland

Date	Mintage	F	VF	XF	Unc	BU
1930A	325,000	60.00	100	160	225	—
1930A Proof	—	Value: 425				
1930D	84,000	60.00	100	170	225	—
1930D Proof	—	Value: 575				
1930E	45,000	70.00	125	180	250	—
1930E Proof	—	Value: 500				
1930F	60,000	60.00	100	165	225	—
1930F Proof	—	Value: 475				
1930G	37,000	85.00	165	190	250	—
1930G Proof	—	Value: 575				
1930J	49,000	75.00	135	190	250	—
1930J Proof	—	Value: 550				

KM# 77 5 REICHSMARK **Weight:** 25.0000 g. **Composition:** 0.5000 Silver .4019 oz. ASW **Subject:** Centenary - Death of Goethe

Date	Mintage	F	VF	XF	Unc	BU
1932A	11,000	500	1,500	2,100	2,800	—
1932A Proof	—	Value: 4,500				
1932D	2,812	600	1,600	2,200	2,900	—
1932D Proof	—	Value: 4,000				
1932E	1,490	700	1,600	2,400	3,000	—
1932E Proof	—	Value: 4,500				
1932F	2,006	600	1,600	2,200	2,900	—
1932F Proof	—	Value: 5,500				
1932G	1,220	700	1,600	2,400	3,000	—
1932G Proof	—	Value: 5,000				
1932J	1,634	700	1,600	2,400	3,000	—
1932J Proof	—	Value: 5,000				

PATTERNS

Including off metal strikes

KM#	Date	Mintage	Identification	Mkt Val
PnA331	1927	—	3 Mark. Silver. Justus Von Liebig; never issued.	—

Note: An XF-AU example brought $15,957 at the Emporium Hamburg 1987 sale.

KM#	Date	Mintage	Identification	Mkt Val
Pn212	1919A	—	50 Pfennig. Brass.	200
Pn213	1919A	—	50 Pfennig. Silver.	300
Pn214	1919A	—	50 Pfennig. Nickel.	150
Pn215	1919A	—	50 Pfennig. Aluminum.	150
Pn216	1919A	—	50 Pfennig. Zinc.	150
Pn217	1919A	—	50 Pfennig. Zinc. Reeded edge.	—
Pn218	1919A	—	50 Pfennig. Aluminum. Reeded edge.	110
Pn219	1919A	—	50 Pfennig. Aluminum. Plain edge.	—
Pn220	1919A	—	50 Pfennig. Aluminum. Ornamental edge.	—
Pn221	1919A	—	50 Pfennig. Zinc. Ornamental edge.	—
Pn222	1919G	—	1/2 Mark. KM#17.	—
Pn223	1919G	—	Mark. Copper. KM#14.	—
Pn224	19xxA	—	Mark. Aluminum.	—
Pn225	1921A	—	Mark. Brass Plated Aluminum.	—
Pn226	1921A	—	Mark. Zinc.	—
Pn227	1921A	—	Mark.	—
Pn228	1921A	—	Mark. Aluminum Plated Steel.	—
Pn230	1921A	—	Mark. Silver.	—
Pn231	1921A	—	Mark. Iron.	—
Pn232	1921A	—	Mark. Copper Strips Inlaid On Silver Or Copper-Nickel.	—
Pn233	1921A	—	Mark. Copper Strips Inlaid On Aluminum.	—
Pn229	1921A	—	Mark. Nickel.	125
PnA234	1922A	—	10 Pfennig. Iron.	200
Pn234	1922A	—	50 Pfennig. Iron. Plain with 6 ridges edge. KM#27.	—
Pn235	1922F	—	3 Mark. KM#28; GOTT MIT UNS.	750

Note: Most 1922F lettered-edge 3 Marks were recovered from the burned out ruins of the Stuttgart Mint destroyed in World War II; the above value is for the one known perfect example, blackened VF examples are valued between $175 and $350

KM#	Date	Mintage	Identification	Mkt Val
Pn236	1922F	—	3 Mark. Reeded edge. KM#28.	—
Pn237	1922F	—	3 Mark. Plain edge. KM#28.	—
Pn238	1922G	—	3 Mark. Reeded edge. KM#28.	—
Pn239	1922A	—	5 Mark. Aluminum.	100
Pn239a	1922A	—	5 Mark. Aluminum Plated Copper.	700
Pn240	1922A	—	5 Mark. Roman lettering.	—
Pn241	1923	—	2 Pfennig. Without mintmark; KM#31.	—
Pn242	1923	—	50 Pfennig. Without mintmark; KM#34.	—
Pn243	1923F	—	3 Mark. KM#29.4.	225

Note: All pattern 1923F 3 Marks were recovered from the burned out ruins of the Stuttgart Mint destroyed in World War II; blackened VF examples range in value from $225 to $400

KM#	Date	Mintage	Identification	Mkt Val
Pn244	1923A	—	20 Mark. Aluminum.	—
Pn245	1923A	—	100 Mark. Aluminum.	—
Pn246	1923F	—	200 Mark. Doubled reeding; KM#35.	—
Pn247	1923F	—	1000 Mark. Aluminum. Reeded edge.	300
Pn248	1923F	—	1000 Mark. Silver. Reeded edge.	—
Pn249	1923F	—	1000 Mark. Aluminum. Plain edge.	—
Pn250	1924E	—	2 Pfennig. Copper. Eagle head left.	—
PnA250	1924	—	2 Pfennig. Brass. KM#31.	125
Pn251	1924E	—	10 Pfennig. Copper.	—
Pn252	1924E	—	10 Pfennig. Aluminum.	—
Pn253	1924E	—	10 Pfennig. Copper. Full eagle	—
Pn254	1924E	—	10 Pfennig. Aluminum. Full eagle	—
Pn255	1924E	—	10 Pfennig. Nickel. Full eagle.	—
Pn256	1924D	—	50 Pfennig. Lead. KM#41.	—
Pn257	1924A	—	Mark. Silver. Reeded, lettered edge.	—
Pn258	1924A	—	3 Mark. 0.5000 Silver. Ornamental edge.	—
Pn259	1924E	—	5 Mark. Silver.	—
Pn260	1925E	—	Pfennig. Copper.	—
Pn261	1925E	—	2 Pfennig. Copper.	—
Pn262	1925E	—	5 Pfennig. Copper-Nickel.	—
Pn263	1925E	—	5 Pfennig. Copper-Nickel. Larger eagle head.	—
Pn264	1925E	—	10 Pfennig. Copper-Nickel.	—
Pn265	1925	6	50 Pfennig. KM#41.	16,500

Note: An XF-AU example brought $15,957, Emporium Hamburg 1987 sale

KM#	Date	Mintage	Identification	Mkt Val
Pn266	1925F	—	50 Pfennig. Brass. Bundle.	100
Pn267	1925F	—	50 Pfennig. Bronze. Bundle.	100
Pn268	1925F	—	50 Pfennig. Copper-Nickel. Bundle.	100
Pn269	1925F	—	50 Pfennig. Nickel. Bundle.	100
Pn270	1925F	—	50 Pfennig. Nickel-Silver. Mercury	125
Pn271	1925F	—	50 Pfennig. Nickel. Mercury	125
Pn272	1925F	—	50 Pfennig. Brass. Mercury	—
Pn273	1925E	—	Mark. Silver. Thick wreath.	—
Pn274	1925E	—	Mark. Nickel. Thick wreath.	—
Pn275	1925E	—	Mark. 0.4500 Silver. Thin wreath.	—
Pn276	1925E	—	2 Mark. 0.5000 Silver. Thick wreath.	150
PnA276	1925F	—	3 Mark. Brass.	—
PnA277	1925	—	3 Mark. Brass. Woman's head.	—
Pn277	1925J	—	3 Mark. Iron. KM#46.	—
Pn278	1925E	—	3 Mark. Silver.	400
Pn279	1925E	—	5 Mark. Silver.	750
Pn280	1925E	—	5 Mark. Silver.	750
Pn281	1925F	—	5 Mark. Silver.	1,750
Pn281a	1925F	—	5 Mark. Silvered-Bronze.	150
Pn282	1925E	—	5 Mark. Silver.	1,400
Pn283	1925E	—	20 Mark. Gold.	7,500
Pn284	1925E	—	20 Mark. Brass.	—
Pn285	1926E	—	50 Pfennig. Copper-Nickel.	—
Pn286	1926	—	50 Pfennig.	—
Pn287	1926E	—	50 Pfennig. Copper-Nickel. Leaves through value	125
Pn288	1926A	—	50 Pfennig. Leaves below value	—
Pn289	1926E	—	50 Pfennig. Copper-Nickel. Leaves below value	—
Pn290	1926	—	50 Pfennig. Leaves below value.	—
Pn291	1926E	—	50 Pfennig. Copper-Nickel. Cornucopia.	125
Pn292	1926E	—	50 Pfennig. Copper-Nickel. Two leaves.	—
Pn293	1926E	—	50 Pfennig. Copper-Nickel. Wreath.	—
Pn294	1926E	—	50 Pfennig. Copper-Nickel. Wheat.	—
Pn295	1926E	—	50 Pfennig. Copper-Nickel. Eagle.	—
Pn296	1926E	—	50 Pfennig. Copper-Nickel. Two leaves.	—
Pn297	1926E	—	50 Pfennig. Copper-Nickel. Eagle.	—
Pn298	1926E	—	50 Pfennig. Copper-Nickel. Wheat.	—
Pn299	1926E	—	50 Pfennig. Copper-Nickel. Two leaves.	—
Pn300	1926E	—	50 Pfennig. Copper-Nickel. Eagle.	—
Pn301	1926E	—	50 Pfennig. Copper-Nickel. "Reichspfennig"	—
Pn302	1926E	—	50 Pfennig. Copper-Nickel.	—
Pn303	1926A	—	50 Pfennig. Nickel.	—
Pn304	1926E	—	50 Pfennig. Copper-Nickel.	—
Pn305	1926J	—	50 Pfennig. Nickel.	100
Pn306	1926J	—	50 Pfennig. Nickel. Smaller eagle.	—
Pn307	1926A	—	Mark. Brass.	100
Pn307a	1926A	—	Mark. Silver.	—
PnA308	1926	—	3 Mark.	—
Pn308	1926A	—	5 Mark. Silver.	—
Pn309	1926	—	5 Mark. Silver. Wreath aaround eagle.	—
Pn310	1926A	—	5 Mark. Silver.	750
Pn311	1926A	—	5 Mark. Silver.	750
Pn312	1926A	—	5 Mark. Silver.	1,000
Pn312a	1926D	—	5 Mark. Silver. Ship sailing right.	500
Pn313	1926E	—	5 Mark. Silver. Large eagle, small mint mark.	500
Pn314	1926	—	5 Mark. Silver. Small eagle, large mint mark.	500
Pn315	1926E	—	5 Mark. Silver.	800
Pn316	1926E	—	5 Mark. Silver.	800
Pn317	1926F	—	5 Mark. Silver. "PROBE"; with motto.	—
Pn318	1926F	—	5 Mark. Silver. With motto.	650
Pn319	1926F	—	5 Mark. Silver. "PROBE" without motto.	—
Pn320	1926F	—	5 Mark. Silver. Without motto..	800
Pn321	1927A	—	50 Pfennig. Deeper relief, KM#49.	—
Pn322	1927E	—	50 Pfennig. Silver.	—
Pn323	1927F	—	50 Pfennig. Copper-Nickel.	150
Pn324	1927	—	Mark. Pn307.	—
Pn325	1927F	—	Mark. 0.5000 Silver. Ornamental edge.	175
Pn326	1927F	—	Mark. 0.9930 Silver. Plain edge.	225
Pn327	1927A	—	3 Mark. 0.9930 Silver.	—
Pn327a	1927A	—	3 Mark. Copper-Nickel.	1,000
Pn328	1927F	—	3 Mark. Silver. Lettered edge. "PROBE"	—
Pn329	1927F	—	3 Mark. Silver. Lettered edge.	—
Pn330	1927F	—	3 Mark. Plain edge.	825
PnA331	1927F	—	3 Mark. Silver. Justus Von Liebig; never issued.	—
Pn331	1927A	—	5 Mark. Silver. Large eagle.	—
Pn332	NDA	—	5 Mark. Silvered Tin. Small eagle.	—
Pn334	1927A	—	5 Mark. 50 stars; KM#56.	—
Pn335	1927A	—	5 Mark. 47 stars; KM#56.	—
Pn336	1927A	—	5 Mark. 73 stars; KM#56.	—
Pn337	1929A	—	3 Mark. Script on edge; KM#60.	825
Pn338	1929A	—	3 Mark. Silver. "PROBE"; KM#62.	—
Pn339	1929A	—	5 Mark. Silver. Plain rims; "PROBE".	—
Pn340	1929A	—	5 Mark. Silver. Star rims; "PROBE".	—
Pn341	1929A	—	5 Mark. Silver. "PROBE".	1,850
Pn342	1929A	—	5 Mark. Pn346.	—
PnA343	1929E	—	3 Mark. PROBE	—
Pn343	1930	—	3 Mark. Silver. "PROBE"; KM#70.	—
Pn344	1930	—	3 Mark. Silver. "PROBE"	850
Pn345	1930A	—	3 Mark. Silver. "PROBE"; KM#69.	850
Pn346	1930A	—	5 Mark. Silver. "PROBE"; KM#68.	—
Pn347	1930	—	5 Mark. Silver.	—
PnA347	1931G	—	Pfennig. Brass.	75.00
Pn348	1931A	—	3 Mark.	—
Pn349	1931	—	5 Mark.	—
Pn350	1932A	—	4 Pfennig. Silvered Copper. "PROBE"	—
PnA351	1932	—	3 Mark. Silver.	—
Pn351	1932D	—	3 Mark. 0.7500 Silver. KM#74.	700
Pn352	1932F	—	3 Mark. Silver. Reeded edge. "PROBE"; KM#74.	—
Pn353	1932F	—	3 Mark. Silver. Reeded edge. Without "PROBE"; KM#74.	—
Pn353a	1932A	—	5 Mark. Nickel. "PROBE". KM#76.	350

THIRD REICH

1933-1945

A wide range of factors, such as humiliation of defeat, economic depression, poverty, and a pervasive feeling of discontent aided Hitler in his climb to power. After the unsuccessful Putsch (uprising against the Bavarian Government) in 1923, Hitler was imprisoned in Landsberg Fortress. While imprisoned Hitler dictated his book *"Mein Kampf"* which became the cornerstone of Nazism espousing Hitler's irrational ideology and the manipulation of power without moral constraint as the basis of strategy.

Master propagandist Josef Goebbels tried to attract the sympathetic attention of the German public. The usual tactic was to have Hitler promise all things to all people provided that they in turn would pledge to him their complete faith and obedience.

Once in power, coercion was used to elicit the appearance of unanimous endorsement. Public works and military rearmament helped overcome the depression. It took the Nazis only about two years to consolidate their system politically. The combined terrorism of the storm troops and the police forces, including the Gestapo, stifled potential opposition. By 1935, Nazi affiliated organizations controlled all German cultural, professional, and economic fields, assuring strict compliance with the party line.

With the passage of the Numberg Laws in 1935, the more ominous aspects of Nazi anti-Semitism came to light. Jews were deprived of their citizenship and forbidden to marry non-Jews. This was followed by confiscation of property and the required wearing of the Star of David for identification purposes, eventually culminating in the mass deportation to concentration and death camps.

By 1936, unemployment was virtually eliminated and economic production was up to 1929 levels. All sources of information were under the control of Josef Goebbels, while all police power was in the hands of Heinrich Himmler. Germans who were not convinced by Goebbel's propaganda machine would be silenced by Himmler's Gestapo. Usually the implied threat was enough. The majority of Germans did not suffer any ill effects at first and national pride stirred once again.

Hitler's audacity in foreign affairs met with success due to the trend of appeasement by the western powers. First, Germany withdrew from the League of Nations and the World Disarmament Council. In 1935, the Saar voted to return to Germany and Hitler renounced the reviled 1921 peace treaty and related pacts. In 1936, German forces reoccupied the Rhineland. In 1938, Austria was annexed and at the Munich Conference, which excluded Czechoslovakia, Great Britain and France agreed that the Sudatenland was to become German territory. In 1939, Slovakia became an independent Nazi Puppet State and the "Protectorate" of Bohemia and Moravia was established. Next came the German-Soviet non-aggression pact which secretly divided up Poland between the two totalitarian powers. Great Britain and France finally declared war when Poland was invaded. The years of 1939-1942 were a period of impressive victories for Germany's well-trained and equipped forces. However, when Hitler expanded his war beyond Western Europe by invading Africa and Russia and declaring war on the U.S.A., it started the chain of events which would culminate in the total and final German defeat on May 7, 1945, VE Day, ending the European theater of the Second World War and The Third Reich.

MINT MARKS
A - Berlin
B - Vienna, 1938-1944
D - Munich
E - Muldenhutten
F - Stuttgart
G - Karlsruhe
J - Hamburg

MONETARY SYSTEMS
(During 1923-1924)
100 Rentenpfennig = 1 Rentenmark

(Commencing 1924)
100 Reichspfennig = 1 Reichsmark

THIRD REICH

STANDARD COINAGE

KM# 89 REICHSPFENNIG **Composition:** Bronze

Date	Mintage	F	VF	XF	Unc	BU
1936A	—	1.50	5.00	7.50	30.00	75.00
Note: Mintage included with KM#37						
1936E	150,000	25.00	50.00	100	150	250
1936F	4,600,000	22.50	45.00	85.00	145	225
1936G	—	15.00	25.00	50.00	100	200
Note: Mintage included with KM#37						
1936J	—	10.00	25.00	40.00	85.00	100
Note: Mintage included with KM#37						
1937A	67,180,000	0.10	0.25	1.00	2.50	5.00
1937D	14,060,000	0.10	0.25	1.00	5.00	10.00
1937E	10,700,000	0.15	0.35	1.00	5.00	10.00
1937F	11,058,000	0.15	0.35	1.00	5.00	10.00
1937G	4,250,000	0.15	0.35	2.00	5.00	10.00
1937J	6,714,000	0.15	0.35	1.00	5.00	10.00
1938A	75,707,000	0.10	0.25	0.50	5.00	10.00
1938B	2,378,000	0.50	5.00	7.00	12.50	25.00
1938D	13,930,000	0.10	0.25	0.50	5.00	10.00
1938E	14,503,000	0.10	0.25	0.50	5.00	10.00
1938F	11,714,000	0.10	0.25	0.50	5.00	10.00
1938G	8,390,000	0.10	0.25	1.00	5.00	10.00
1938J	15,458,000	0.10	0.25	0.50	6.00	10.00
1939A	97,541,000	0.10	0.25	0.50	5.00	10.00
1939B	22,732,000	0.15	0.35	1.00	7.50	12.00
1939D	20,760,000	0.10	0.25	0.50	5.00	10.00
1939E	12,478,000	0.10	0.25	0.50	7.50	12.00
1939F	12,482,000	0.10	0.25	0.50	5.00	10.00
1939G	12,250,000	0.10	0.25	0.50	5.00	10.00
1939J	8,368,000	0.10	0.25	0.50	7.50	12.00
1940A	27,094,000	0.10	0.25	0.50	6.00	10.00
1940F	7,850,000	0.15	0.35	1.00	6.00	10.00
1940G	3,875,000	1.00	4.00	10.00	15.00	30.00
1940J	7,450,000	0.50	3.00	5.00	8.00	20.00
1936-1940 Common date proof	—	Value: 75.00				

KM# 97 REICHSPFENNIG **Composition:** Zinc

Date	Mintage	F	VF	XF	Unc	BU
1940A	223,948,000	0.10	0.20	1.00	5.00	6.00
1940B	62,198,000	0.10	0.20	1.00	5.00	7.00
1940D	43,951,000	0.10	0.20	1.00	5.00	7.00
1940E	20,749,000	0.20	1.00	5.00	10.00	15.00
1940F	33,854,000	0.10	0.20	1.00	5.00	10.00
1940G	20,165,000	0.10	0.20	1.00	5.00	12.00
1940J	24,459,000	0.10	0.20	1.00	5.00	10.00
1941A	281,618,000	0.10	0.15	0.50	4.00	6.00
1941B	62,285,000	0.20	1.00	1.50	5.00	6.00
1941D	73,745,000	0.10	0.15	0.50	5.00	7.00
1941E	49,041,000	0.10	0.50	1.50	7.50	15.00
1941F	51,017,000	0.10	0.15	0.50	5.00	7.00
1941G	44,810,000	0.10	0.50	1.00	7.50	12.00
1941J	57,625,000	0.10	0.15	0.50	5.00	10.00
1942A	558,877,000	0.10	0.15	0.50	5.00	7.00
1942B	124,740,000	0.10	0.20	1.00	6.00	7.00
1942D	134,145,000	0.10	0.15	0.50	6.00	7.00
1942E	84,674,000	0.15	1.50	2.50	8.50	12.00
1942F	90,788,000	0.10	0.15	0.50	6.00	7.00
1942G	59,858,000	0.10	0.15	0.50	6.00	10.00
1942J	122,934,000	0.10	0.50	1.00	6.00	7.00
1943A	372,401,000	0.10	0.15	0.50	6.00	7.00
1943B	79,315,000	0.10	0.50	1.00	6.00	7.00
1943D	91,629,000	0.10	0.15	0.50	6.00	7.00
1943E	34,191,000	0.50	2.50	7.50	12.00	20.00
1943F	70,269,000	0.10	0.50	1.00	6.00	7.00
1943G	24,688,000	0.15	1.50	2.50	7.50	12.00
1943J	37,695,000	0.15	1.50	2.50	6.00	7.00
1944A	124,421,000	0.10	0.50	2.00	5.00	7.00
1944B	87,850,000	0.20	1.00	2.00	5.00	9.00
1944D	56,755,000	0.20	1.00	2.50	7.00	12.00
1944E	41,729,000	0.20	2.00	5.00	10.00	20.00
1944F	15,580,000	0.50	4.00	6.00	15.00	25.00
1944G	34,967,000	0.10	0.50	1.00	4.00	10.00
1945A	17,145,000	0.25	2.50	7.50	20.00	25.00
1945E	6,800,000	45.00	60.00	90.00	150	250
1940-1945 Common date proof	—	Value: 100				

KM# 90 2 REICHSPFENNIG **Composition:** Bronze

Date	Mintage	F	VF	XF	Unc	BU
1936A	Inc. below	0.50	3.00	9.00	35.00	50.00
1936D	Inc. below	0.50	3.00	8.00	25.00	35.00
1936F	3,100,000	5.00	15.00	40.00	90.00	160
1937A	34,404,000	0.10	0.50	1.50	7.00	12.00
1937D	9,016,000	0.10	0.50	1.50	7.00	12.00
1937E	Inc. below	15.00	20.00	35.00	60.00	100
1937F	7,487,000	0.10	0.50	1.50	7.00	12.00
1937G	490,000	2.00	8.50	15.00	35.00	50.00
1937J	450,000	2.00	8.50	15.00	25.00	35.00
1938A	27,264,000	0.10	0.15	0.50	6.00	10.00
1938B	2,714,000	1.50	4.00	8.00	25.00	40.00
1938D	8,770,000	0.10	0.25	1.00	6.00	10.00
1938E	5,450,000	0.25	1.00	2.00	6.00	10.00
1938F	10,090,000	0.10	0.25	1.00	6.00	10.00
1938G	3,685,000	0.10	0.25	5.00	12.00	20.00
1938J	7,243,000	0.10	0.25	1.00	6.00	12.00
1939A	37,348,000	0.10	0.25	1.00	6.00	10.00
1939B	9,361,000	0.10	0.25	1.00	6.00	10.00
1939D	7,555,000	0.10	0.25	1.00	6.00	10.00
1939E	6,650,000	0.25	1.00	2.00	8.00	12.00
1939F	7,019,000	0.10	0.25	1.00	6.00	10.00
1939G	4,885,000	0.10	0.25	1.00	8.00	15.00
1939J	6,996,000	0.10	0.25	1.00	6.00	10.00
1940A	22,681,000	0.10	0.25	1.00	7.00	12.00
1940D	3,855,000	0.50	3.00	6.50	15.00	25.00
1940E	3,412,000	2.50	10.00	15.00	20.00	30.00
1940G	1,161,000	40.00	70.00	110	200	300
1940J	2,357,000	1.50	7.50	12.50	30.00	50.00
1936-1940 Common date proof	—	Value: 100				

KM# 91 5 REICHSPFENNIG Composition: Aluminum-Bronze

Date	Mintage	F	VF	XF	Unc	BU
1936A	Inc. below	25.00	60.00	80.00	120	160
1936D	Inc. below	25.00	60.00	80.00	120	150
1936G	Inc. below	45.00	80.00	120	200	300
1937A	29,700,000	0.10	0.20	1.00	6.00	10.00
1937D	4,992,000	0.10	0.20	1.00	10.00	20.00
1937E	4,474,000	0.20	1.00	3.00	15.00	30.00
1937F	2,092,000	0.10	0.20	5.00	15.00	40.00
1937G	2,749,000	2.50	7.50	15.00	30.00	50.00
1937J	6,991,000	0.25	2.50	5.00	20.00	30.00
1938A	54,012,000	0.25	2.50	5.00	10.00	15.00
1938B	3,447,000	0.25	1.50	5.00	10.00	20.00
1938D	17,708,000	0.10	0.25	1.50	7.00	10.00
1938E	8,602,000	0.10	0.40	4.00	9.00	20.00
1938F	8,147,000	0.10	0.25	1.50	8.00	20.00
1938G	7,323,000	0.10	0.25	1.50	8.00	20.00
1938J	7,646,000	0.10	0.25	1.50	8.00	20.00
1939A	35,337,000	0.10	0.25	1.50	7.00	10.00
1939B	8,313,000	0.10	0.20	1.00	7.50	11.00
1939D	8,304,000	0.20	1.00	2.00	7.50	12.00
1939E	5,138,000	0.20	1.00	2.00	7.50	12.00
1939F	10,339,000	0.10	0.20	1.00	6.00	10.00
1939G	4,266,000	0.25	2.50	7.50	12.50	20.00
1939J	4,177,000	0.20	2.00	7.50	10.00	20.00
1936-1939 Common date proof	—	Value: 100				

KM# 100 5 REICHSPFENNIG Composition: Zinc

Date	Mintage	F	VF	XF	Unc	BU
1940A	174,684,000	0.10	0.20	1.00	5.00	8.00
1940B	63,469,000	0.20	1.00	1.50	6.00	8.00
1940D	44,364,000	0.20	1.00	1.50	6.00	8.00
1940E	25,800,000	0.30	1.00	3.00	6.00	10.00
1940F	31,381,000	0.20	1.00	2.00	6.00	10.00
1940G	24,148,000	0.20	1.00	2.50	7.00	15.00
1940J	30,518,000	0.20	1.00	2.00	6.00	10.00
1941A	246,216,000	0.10	0.20	1.00	5.00	8.00
1941B	60,297,000	0.10	0.30	2.00	7.50	12.00
1941D	51,100,000	0.10	0.30	2.00	7.50	12.00
1941E	26,354,000	0.10	0.30	2.00	7.50	12.00
1941F	36,725,000	0.10	0.30	2.00	7.50	12.00
1941G	21,276,000	0.10	0.30	2.00	7.50	12.00
1941J	52,872,000	0.10	0.30	2.00	7.50	12.00
1942A	161,042,000	0.10	0.20	1.00	6.00	10.00
1942B	12,405,000	0.25	1.50	5.00	9.00	15.00
1942D	15,486,000	0.10	0.35	2.50	7.00	12.00
1942E	8,800,000	7.50	17.50	22.50	35.00	50.00
1942F	24,662,000	0.10	0.25	1.50	7.00	12.00
1942G	12,749,000	0.10	0.35	2.50	9.00	15.00
1943A	46,830,000	0.15	0.50	2.00	7.00	12.00
1943B	833,000	30.00	50.00	75.00	140	200
1943D	13,650,000	0.15	0.50	4.00	9.00	15.00
1943E	16,581,000	2.50	7.50	12.50	17.50	25.00
1943F	9,891,000	0.20	1.00	2.50	7.00	12.00
1943G	7,237,000	0.15	0.50	2.00	8.00	15.00
1944A	23,699,000	3.50	15.00	27.50	37.50	50.00
1944D	26,340,000	0.25	1.50	3.00	6.00	10.00
1944E	19,720,000	0.50	3.00	6.00	9.00	15.00
1944F	6,853,000	0.25	1.50	3.00	7.50	12.00
1944G	3,540,000	90.00	175	250	350	500
1940-1944 Common date proof	—	Value: 200				

KM# 92 10 REICHSPFENNIG Composition: Aluminum-Bronze

Date	Mintage	F	VF	XF	Unc	BU
1936A	Inc. below	17.50	35.00	50.00	90.00	110
1936E	245,000	80.00	135	175	275	350
1936G	129,000	175	225	300	400	650
1937A	36,830,000	0.10	0.50	2.00	10.00	20.00
1937D	6,882,000	0.25	1.50	3.00	10.00	20.00
1937E	3,786,000	2.00	10.00	18.00	40.00	60.00
1937F	5,934,000	0.50	2.50	5.00	20.00	40.00
1937G	2,131,000	1.00	5.00	7.50	25.00	50.00
1937J	4,439,000	0.50	2.50	5.00	15.00	30.00
1938A	70,068,000	0.10	0.20	1.00	6.00	10.00
1938B	7,852,000	0.50	2.50	5.00	12.50	20.00
1938D	16,990,000	0.10	0.50	2.00	8.00	15.00
1938E	10,739,000	0.20	1.00	2.50	9.00	15.00
1938F	12,307,000	0.20	1.00	2.50	10.00	20.00
1938G	8,584,000	0.20	1.00	2.50	10.00	20.00
1938J	10,389,000	0.20	1.00	2.50	10.00	20.00
1939A	40,171,000	0.20	1.00	2.00	8.00	15.00
1939B	7,814,000	0.20	1.00	2.00	9.00	15.00
1939D	11,307,000	0.20	1.00	2.00	10.00	20.00
1939E	5,079,000	0.50	2.50	7.50	14.00	20.00
1939F	6,993,000	0.25	1.50	3.00	10.00	20.00
1939G	5,532,000	0.50	5.00	10.00	15.00	20.00
1939J	5,557,000	0.20	1.00	2.00	10.00	20.00
1936-1939 Common date proof	—	Value: 95.00				

KM# 101 10 REICHSPFENNIG Composition: Zinc

Date	Mintage	F	VF	XF	Unc	BU
1940A	212,948,000	0.10	0.35	1.50	6.00	15.00
1940B	76,274,000	0.15	0.50	2.50	10.00	20.00
1940D	45,434,000	0.15	0.50	2.00	10.00	20.00
1940E	34,350,000	0.15	0.50	2.00	10.00	25.00
1940F	27,603,000	0.15	1.00	5.00	15.00	40.00
1940G	27,308,000	0.15	1.00	7.00	20.00	50.00
1940J	41,678,000	0.15	1.00	2.00	10.00	25.00
1941A	240,284,000	0.10	0.35	1.50	6.00	15.00
1941B	70,747,000	0.15	0.50	3.00	7.50	15.00
1941D	77,560,000	0.15	0.50	3.00	10.00	20.00
1941E	36,548,000	0.15	0.50	3.00	10.00	20.00
1941F	42,834,000	0.15	0.50	3.00	10.00	20.00
1941G	28,765,000	0.15	2.00	8.00	20.00	40.00
1941J	30,525,000	0.15	0.50	2.00	10.00	25.00
1942A	184,545,000	0.10	0.20	0.50	7.50	15.00
1942B	16,329,000	0.25	2.50	12.00	25.00	50.00
1942D	40,852,000	0.20	1.00	3.00	10.00	25.00
1942E	18,334,000	0.25	1.50	12.00	25.00	50.00
1942F	32,690,000	0.10	0.35	3.00	10.00	25.00
1942G	20,295,000	0.25	1.50	12.00	30.00	60.00
1942J	29,957,000	0.25	1.50	3.00	10.00	25.00
1943A	157,357,000	0.15	1.50	2.50	7.50	15.00
1943B	11,940,000	2.50	7.50	14.00	30.00	60.00
1943D	17,304,000	0.25	2.00	4.00	15.00	25.00
1943E	10,445,000	2.50	7.50	14.00	30.00	60.00
1943F	24,804,000	0.25	2.50	5.00	20.00	25.00
1943G	3,618,000	2.00	12.00	35.00	70.00	160
1943J	1,821,000	20.00	45.00	80.00	175	300
1944A	84,164,000	0.15	1.00	2.50	10.00	15.00
1944B	40,781,000	0.50	1.50	2.50	10.00	20.00
1944D	30,369,000	0.35	1.50	2.50	10.00	20.00
1944E	29,963,000	0.50	2.00	4.00	10.00	20.00
1944F	19,639,000	0.50	2.50	5.00	12.00	25.00
1944G	13,023,000	0.50	3.00	10.00	25.00	50.00
1945A	7,112,000	5.00	12.50	30.00	75.00	150
1945E	4,897,000	12.50	35.00	70.00	120	200
1940-1945 Common date proof	—	Value: 225				

KM# 87 50 REICHSPFENNIG Composition: Aluminum

Date	Mintage	F	VF	XF	Unc	BU
1935A	75,912,000	1.00	2.50	8.00	30.00	80.00
1935A Proof	—	Value: 200				
1935D	19,688,000	1.00	2.00	10.00	50.00	100
1935D Proof	—	Value: 75.00				
1935E	10,418,000	1.00	4.00	10.00	50.00	100
1935E Proof	—	Value: 200				
1935F	14,061,000	1.00	2.00	10.00	50.00	100
1935F Proof	—	Value: 200				
1935G	8,540,000	1.50	4.00	12.00	55.00	110
1935G Proof	—	Value: 200				
1935J	11,438,000	1.50	4.00	12.00	55.00	110
1935J Proof	—	Value: 200				

KM# 95 50 REICHSPFENNIG Composition: Nickel

Date	Mintage	F	VF	XF	Unc	BU
1938A	5,051,000	15.00	30.00	40.00	50.00	70.00
1938B	1,124,000	20.00	40.00	50.00	75.00	100
1938D	1,260,000	20.00	40.00	60.00	75.00	100
1938E	949,000	20.00	40.00	60.00	90.00	125
1938F	1,210,000	12.50	28.00	50.00	80.00	125
1938G	460,000	25.00	70.00	90.00	150	200
1938J	730,000	20.00	90.00	110	200	300
1939A	15,037,000	17.50	30.00	40.00	50.00	60.00
1939B	2,826,000	17.50	30.00	40.00	60.00	80.00
1939D	3,648,000	15.00	30.00	40.00	60.00	80.00
1939E	1,924,000	15.00	32.00	50.00	85.00	100
1939F	2,602,000	15.00	32.00	50.00	70.00	90.00
1939G	1,565,000	15.00	32.00	70.00	125	150
1939J	2,114,000	15.00	32.00	60.00	90.00	120
1938-1939 Common date proof	—	Value: 245				

KM# 96 50 REICHSPFENNIG Composition: Aluminum

Date	Mintage	F	VF	XF	Unc	BU
1939A	5,000,000	2.00	5.00	20.00	60.00	100
1939B	5,482,000	2.00	5.00	20.00	60.00	100
1939D	600,000	5.00	15.00	30.00	110	170
1939E	2,000,000	2.00	5.00	20.00	60.00	100
1939F	3,600,000	2.00	10.00	30.00	60.00	120
1939G	560,000	10.00	20.00	60.00	140	200
1939J	1,000,000	10.00	20.00	50.00	140	200
1940A	56,128,000	2.00	4.00	10.00	30.00	50.00
1940B	10,016,000	5.00	10.00	25.00	60.00	100
1940D	13,800,000	8.00	15.00	30.00	90.00	150
1940E	5,618,000	8.00	15.00	30.00	90.00	150
1940F	6,663,000	5.00	10.00	25.00	60.00	100
1940G	5,616,000	15.00	30.00	60.00	120	200
1940J	7,335,000	8.00	15.00	30.00	90.00	150
1941A	31,263,000	5.00	10.00	20.00	60.00	100
1941B	4,291,000	3.00	10.00	25.00	75.00	125
1941D	7,200,000	2.00	10.00	25.00	75.00	125
1941E	3,806,000	5.00	15.00	25.00	75.00	125
1941F	5,128,000	2.00	10.00	25.00	60.00	100
1941G	3,091,000	10.00	20.00	35.00	100	150
1941J	4,165,000	10.00	20.00	35.00	100	150
1942A	11,580,000	2.00	5.00	10.00	25.00	50.00
1942B	2,876,000	5.00	12.00	25.00	60.00	100
1942D	2,247,000	2.00	20.00	35.00	70.00	120
1942E	3,810,000	5.00	20.00	40.00	100	150
1942F	5,133,000	2.00	15.00	30.00	70.00	120
1942G	1,400,000	10.00	25.00	70.00	110	200
1943A	29,325,000	2.00	5.00	10.00	25.00	40.00
1943B	8,229,000	2.00	5.00	10.00	20.00	40.00
1943D	5,315,000	2.00	6.00	15.00	45.00	75.00
1943G	2,892,000	10.00	20.00	50.00	100	180
1943J	4,166,000	5.00	10.00	15.00	30.00	45.00
1944B	5,622,000	2.00	7.50	10.00	45.00	70.00
1944D	4,886,000	7.50	15.00	40.00	100	130
1944F	3,739,000	5.00	10.00	20.00	70.00	100
1944G	1,190,000	55.00	90.00	150	300	500
1940-1944 Common date proof	—	Value: 250				

KM# 78 REICHSMARK Composition: Nickel

Date	Mintage	F	VF	XF	Unc	BU
1933A	6,030,000	0.75	2.50	7.50	30.00	40.00
1933D	4,562,000	1.00	3.00	9.00	30.00	40.00
1933E	3,500,000	2.50	7.50	10.00	20.00	30.00
1933F	1,400,000	4.00	8.50	15.00	40.00	60.00
1933G	2,000,000	2.50	10.00	20.00	80.00	120
1934A	52,345,000	1.00	1.50	2.50	10.00	15.00
1934D	30,597,000	1.00	1.50	5.00	15.00	20.00
1934E	15,135,000	1.00	3.00	7.00	15.00	20.00
1934F	23,672,000	1.00	2.50	5.00	15.00	20.00
1934G	13,252,000	1.50	5.00	10.00	18.00	25.00

Date	Mintage	F	VF	XF	Unc	BU
1934J	16,820,000	1.00	3.50	7.50	15.00	20.00
1935A	57,896,000	1.00	2.50	5.00	12.50	15.00
1935J	3,621,000	10.00	15.00	30.00	100	150
1936A	20,287,000	1.25	4.00	7.00	18.00	25.00
1936D	4,940,000	2.50	7.50	15.00	35.00	50.00
1936E	3,200,000	10.00	15.00	30.00	100	150
1936F	2,075,000	20.00	30.00	50.00	100	150
1936G	620,000	30.00	75.00	150	225	275
1936J	2,975,000	7.50	15.00	30.00	100	150
1937A	49,976,000	1.00	1.50	2.50	8.00	12.50
1937D	10,529,000	2.00	5.00	10.00	20.00	30.00
1937E	2,926,000	3.00	10.00	20.00	50.00	70.00
1937F	6,221,000	3.00	10.00	20.00	70.00	100
1937G	2,143,000	2.50	8.00	15.00	40.00	60.00
1937J	4,721,000	2.50	8.00	15.00	60.00	80.00
1938A	9,829,000	1.25	4.00	10.00	30.00	40.00
1938E	2,073,000	4.00	17.50	30.00	80.00	120
1938F	2,739,000	5.00	17.50	22.50	70.00	100
1938G	4,381,000	10.00	30.00	60.00	130	200
1938J	1,269,000	27.50	60.00	90.00	150	225
1939A	52,150,000	5.00	12.50	15.00	35.00	50.00
1939B	9,836,000	50.00	110	160	250	325
1939D	12,522,000	9.00	22.50	37.50	75.00	100
1939E	6,570,000	20.00	35.00	70.00	120	150
1939F	10,033,000	10.00	20.00	40.00	100	140
1939G	5,475,000	60.00	130	200	350	400
1939J	8,478,000	15.00	35.00	60.00	110	150
1933-1939 Common date proof	—	Value: 225				

KM# 79 2 REICHSMARK **Weight:** 8.0000 g. **Composition:** 0.6250 Silver .1607 oz. ASW **Subject:** 450th Anniversary - Birth of Martin Luther

Date	Mintage	F	VF	XF	Unc	BU
1933A	542,000	9.00	22.50	30.00	50.00	60.00
1933A Proof	—	Value: 200				
1933D	141,000	10.00	25.00	32.00	60.00	75.00
1933D Proof	—	Value: 200				
1933E	75,000	12.50	30.00	40.00	60.00	75.00
1933E Proof	—	Value: 250				
1933F	100,000	10.00	25.00	35.00	60.00	75.00
1933F Proof	—	Value: 250				
1933G	61,000	14.00	30.00	42.00	75.00	90.00
1933G Proof	—	Value: 250				
1933J	82,000	10.00	25.00	40.00	60.00	75.00
1933J Proof	—	Value: 235				

KM# 81 2 REICHSMARK **Weight:** 8.0000 g. **Composition:** 0.6250 Silver .1607 oz. ASW **Subject:** 1st Anniversary - Nazi Rule **Reverse:** Potsdam Garrison Church

Date	Mintage	F	VF	XF	Unc	BU
1934A	2,710,000	4.50	10.00	22.00	50.00	75.00
1934A Proof	—	Value: 200				
1934D	703,000	5.50	12.00	30.00	70.00	100
1934D Proof	—	Value: 200				
1934E	373,000	7.50	16.50	40.00	90.00	120
1934E Proof	—	Value: 200				
1934F	502,000	6.00	12.00	32.50	75.00	100
1934F Proof	—	Value: 200				
1934G	305,000	7.00	15.00	50.00	100	125
1934G Proof	—	Value: 200				
1934J	409,000	7.00	15.00	40.00	90.00	125
1934J Proof	—	Value: 200				

KM# 84 2 REICHSMARK **Weight:** 8.0000 g. **Composition:** 0.6250 Silver .1607 oz. ASW **Subject:** 175th anniversary - birth of Schiller

Date	Mintage	F	VF	XF	Unc	BU
1934F	300,000	40.00	70.00	90.00	120	140
1934F Proof	—	Value: 225				

KM# 93 2 REICHSMARK **Weight:** 8.0000 g. **Composition:** 0.6250 Silver .1607 oz. ASW **Subject:** Swastika-Hindenburg issue

Date	Mintage	F	VF	XF	Unc	BU
1936D	840,000	3.00	6.00	20.00	50.00	80.00
1936E	Inc. below	8.00	30.00	50.00	100	160
1936G	Inc. below	6.00	20.00	30.00	70.00	120
1936J	Inc. below	20.00	60.00	150	350	500
1937A	23,425,000	2.50	3.50	5.00	10.00	15.00
1937D	6,190,000	2.50	3.50	5.00	15.00	20.00
1937E	3,725,000	2.50	3.50	5.00	20.00	30.00
1937F	5,015,000	2.50	3.50	5.00	15.00	20.00
1937G	1,913,000	2.50	5.00	10.00	30.00	40.00
1937J	2,756,000	2.50	3.50	5.00	20.00	30.00
1938A	13,201,000	2.50	3.50	5.00	10.00	15.00
1938B	13,163,000	2.50	3.50	5.00	15.00	20.00
1938D	3,711,000	2.50	3.50	5.00	15.00	25.00
1938E	4,731,000	2.50	3.50	5.00	15.00	25.00
1938F	1,882,000	3.00	4.00	6.00	20.00	30.00
1938G	2,313,000	2.50	3.50	5.00	15.00	25.00
1938J	2,306,000	3.00	4.00	5.00	15.00	25.00
1939A	26,855,000	2.50	3.50	5.00	10.00	15.00
1939B	3,522,000	2.50	3.50	5.00	12.00	20.00
1939D	5,357,000	2.50	3.50	5.00	12.00	20.00
1939E	251,000	12.50	30.00	40.00	100	125
1939F	3,180,000	2.50	3.50	5.00	12.00	20.00
1939G	2,305,000	2.50	3.50	7.50	20.00	30.00
1939J	3,414,000	2.50	3.50	7.50	15.00	25.00
1936-1939 Common date proof	—	Value: 185				

KM# 80 5 REICHSMARK **Weight:** 13.8800 g. **Composition:** 0.9000 Silver .4016 oz. ASW **Subject:** 450th Anniversary - Birth of Martin Luther

Date	Mintage	F	VF	XF	Unc	BU
1933A	108,000	50.00	100	150	200	250
1933A Proof	—	Value: 350				
1933D	28,000	60.00	125	175	200	250
1933D Proof	—	Value: 400				
1933E	12,000	70.00	145	180	200	250
1933E Proof	—	Value: 400				
1933F	20,000	60.00	125	160	200	250
1933F Proof	—	Value: 475				
1933G	12,000	100	175	250	300	350
1933G Proof	—	Value: 500				
1933J	16,000	75.00	145	180	250	300
1933J Proof	—	Value: 500				

KM# 82 5 REICHSMARK **Weight:** 13.8800 g. **Composition:** 0.9000 Silver .4016 oz. ASW **Subject:** 1st Anniversary - Nazi Rule **Reverse:** Potsdam Garrison Church

Date	Mintage	F	VF	XF	Unc	BU
1934A	2,168,000	10.00	12.00	40.00	100	120
1934D	562,000	10.00	15.00	50.00	110	130
1934E	298,000	10.00	18.00	50.00	140	170
1934F	401,000	10.00	14.00	45.00	110	130
1934G	244,000	10.00	18.00	50.00	150	180
1934J	327,000	10.00	18.00	50.00	150	180
1934 Proof	—	Value: 275				

Note: Impaired proofs are common and valued around $200

KM# 83 5 REICHSMARK **Weight:** 13.8800 g. **Composition:** 0.9000 Silver .4016 oz. ASW **Subject:** 1st Anniversary - Nazi Rule **Reverse:** Potsdam Garrison Church, date 21 MARZ 1933 dropped

Date	Mintage	F	VF	XF	Unc	BU
1934A	14,526,000	4.00	6.00	12.00	35.00	—
1934D	6,303,000	4.00	6.00	15.00	50.00	—
1934E	2,739,000	5.00	7.50	17.50	65.00	—
1934F	4,844,000	4.00	6.00	15.00	50.00	—
1934G	2,304,000	5.00	7.50	17.50	65.00	—
1934J	4,294,000	4.00	6.00	15.00	50.00	—
1935A	23,407,000	3.00	5.00	10.00	30.00	—
1935D	3,539,000	4.00	6.00	15.00	50.00	—
1935E	2,476,000	5.00	7.50	17.50	65.00	—
1935F	2,177,000	5.00	7.50	17.50	75.00	—
1935G	1,966,000	5.00	7.50	17.50	75.00	—
1935J	1,425,000	6.00	10.00	25.00	110	—
1934-1935 Common date proof	—	Value: 250				

KM# 85 5 REICHSMARK **Weight:** 13.8800 g. **Composition:** 0.9000 Silver .4016 oz. ASW **Subject:** 175th Anniversary - Birth of Schiller

Date	Mintage	F	VF	XF	Unc	BU
1934F	100,000	150	200	280	400	450
1934F Proof	—	Value: 650				

KM# 86 5 REICHSMARK **Weight:** 13.8800 g. **Composition:** 0.9000 Silver .4016 oz. ASW **Subject:** Hindenburg issue

Date	Mintage	F	VF	XF	Unc	BU
1935A	19,325,000	3.00	6.00	10.00	15.00	20.00
1935D	6,596,000	3.00	6.00	10.00	20.00	25.00
1935E	3,260,000	4.00	6.50	12.50	25.00	30.00
1935F	4,372,000	3.00	6.00	10.00	25.00	30.00
1935G	2,371,000	3.00	6.00	12.50	32.50	40.00
1935J	2,830,000	3.00	6.00	12.50	40.00	50.00
1936A	30,611,000	3.00	6.00	10.00	16.00	20.00
1936D	7,032,000	3.00	6.00	10.00	18.00	25.00
1936E	3,320,000	3.00	6.00	12.50	25.00	30.00
1936F	4,926,000	3.00	6.00	12.50	25.00	30.00
1936G	2,734,000	3.00	6.00	15.00	45.00	60.00
1936J	3,706,000	3.00	6.00	15.00	35.00	50.00
1935-1936 Common date proof	—	Value: 200				

KM# 94 5 REICHSMARK **Weight:** 13.8800 g. **Composition:** 0.9000 Silver .4016 oz. ASW **Subject:** Swastika-Hindenburg issue

Date	Mintage	F	VF	XF	Unc	BU
1936A	8,430,000	3.00	6.00	10.00	17.50	25.00
1936D	1,872,000	3.00	7.00	15.00	27.50	35.00
1936E	870,000	5.00	8.00	17.50	35.00	45.00
1936F	1,732,000	3.00	7.00	15.00	40.00	50.00
1936G	743,000	5.00	8.50	20.00	65.00	80.00
1936J	640,000	8.00	20.00	30.00	75.00	100
1937A	6,662,000	3.00	6.00	10.00	20.00	25.00
1937D	2,173,000	3.00	6.00	10.00	20.00	30.00
1937E	1,490,000	5.00	8.00	15.00	30.00	40.00
1937F	1,578,000	4.00	7.50	15.00	30.00	40.00
1937G	1,472,000	5.00	8.00	15.00	30.00	40.00
1937J	2,191,000	3.00	6.00	12.50	30.00	40.00
1938A	6,789,000	3.00	6.00	10.00	20.00	25.00
1938D	1,304,000	3.00	6.00	12.50	25.00	35.00
1938E	425,000	5.00	8.00	15.00	40.00	50.00
1938F	740,000	3.50	6.50	12.50	40.00	50.00
1938G	861,000	4.00	7.50	15.00	40.00	50.00
1938J	1,302,000	3.50	6.50	12.50	30.00	40.00
1939A	3,428,000	4.00	7.50	12.50	20.00	30.00
1939B	1,942,000	5.00	8.00	15.00	25.00	35.00
1939D	1,216,000	7.50	12.50	20.00	40.00	50.00
1939E	1,320,000	15.00	20.00	40.00	80.00	100
1939F	1,060,000	7.50	12.50	25.00	70.00	90.00
1939G	567,000	12.50	18.00	35.00	100	125
1939J	1,710,000	5.00	10.00	20.00	60.00	75.00
1936-1939 Common date proof	—	Value: 200				

MILITARY COINAGE

WWII

KM# 98 5 REICHSPFENNIG **Composition:** Zinc **Note:** Circulated only in occupied territories.

Date	Mintage	F	VF	XF	Unc	BU
1940A	—	15.00	20.00	25.00	60.00	80.00
1940B	3,020,000	100	150	300	400	600
1940D	—	25.00	45.00	60.00	100	150
1940E	2,445,000	100	175	275	400	600
1940F	—	150	250	350	500	800
1940G	—	5,000	10,000	—	—	—
1940J	—	100	200	275	450	600
1941A	—	200	400	700	1,200	2,500
1941F	—	5,000	11,000	—	—	—
1940-1941 Common date proof	—	Value: 750				

KM# 99 10 REICHSPFENNIG **Composition:** Zinc **Note:** Circulated only in occupied territories.

Date	Mintage	F	VF	XF	Unc	BU
1940A	—	10.00	15.00	22.50	45.00	60.00
1940B	840,000	90.00	250	600	900	—
1940D	—	5,000	6,000	10,000	15,000	—
1940E	5,100,000	3,000	4,500	6,000	10,000	—
1940F	—	200	400	1,500	2,000	2,500
1940G	150,000	75.00	100	225	350	450
1940J	—	350	1,000	1,300	2,000	3,000
1941A	—	500	900	2,000	3,000	4,000
1941F 2 known	—	—	10,000	—	14,500	—
1940-1941 Proof	—	Value: 1,000				

ALLIED OCCUPATION

POST WW II COINAGE

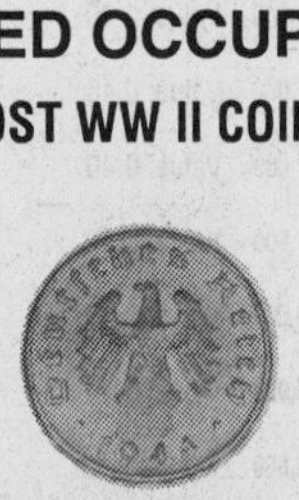

KM# A102 REICHSPFENNIG **Composition:** Zinc **Obverse:** Modified design, swastika and wreath removed **Reverse:** Eagle missing tail feathers

Date	F	VF	XF	Unc	BU
1944D	—	—	10,000	—	—

Note: Possibly a pattern

KM# A103 REICHSPFENNIG **Composition:** Zinc

Date	Mintage	F	VF	XF	Unc	BU
1945F	2,984,000	5.00	10.00	18.00	35.00	50.00
1946F	1,633,000	15.00	35.00	70.00	130	160
1946G	1,500,000	35.00	65.00	110	165	200
1945-1946 Common date proof	—	Value: 200				

KM# A105 5 REICHSPFENNIG **Composition:** Zinc

Date	Mintage	F	VF	XF	Unc	BU
1947A	—	2.50	7.50	15.00	40.00	50.00
1947D	16,528,000	2.50	4.50	6.50	20.00	30.00
1948A	—	5.00	15.00	20.00	40.00	55.00
1948E	7,666,000	150	300	400	700	800
1947-1948 Proof	—	Value: 200				

KM# A104 10 REICHSPFENNIG **Composition:** Zinc

Date	Mintage	F	VF	XF	Unc	BU
1945F	5,942,000	4.50	7.50	15.00	30.00	40.00
1946F	3,738,000	10.00	20.00	30.00	85.00	100
1946G	1,600,000	35.00	65.00	100	180	280
1947A	—	4.50	10.00	20.00	30.00	45.00
1947E	2,612,000	200	300	575	775	875
1947F	1,269,000	1.50	3.50	8.00	17.50	25.00
1948A	—	5.00	20.00	25.00	35.00	45.00
1948F	19,579,000	1.50	3.50	8.00	28.00	35.00
1946-1948 Common date proof	—	Value: 200				

PATTERNS

Including off metal strikes

KM#	Date	Mintage	Identification	Mkt Val
Pn354	1933	—	Mark. Nickel. Legend above eagle. PROBE.	250
Pn355	1933A	—	Mark. Nickel. "PROBE."	250
Pn356	1933A	—	Mark. Nickel. Rays above eagle.	250
Pn357	1933A	—	Mark. Nickel. Plain above eagle.	250
Pn358	1933A	—	Mark. Nickel. Large 1 with rays. "PROBE."	250
Pn359	1933A	—	Mark. Nickel. "PROBE."	250
Pn360	1933J	—	Mark. Nickel. KM78.	250
PnA361	1933/6	—	5 Mark. Copper-Nickel. Martin Luther. Eagle. KM94.	—
Pn361	1934	—	2 Mark. KM79. KM81.	—
Pn362	1934A	—	2 Mark. Silver. KM84.	—
Pn363	NDD	—	5 Mark. Similar to Pn351 edge. KM80.	—
Pn364	1934A	—	5 Mark. Silver. KM85. "PROBE".	—
Pn365	1934A	—	5 Pfennig. Brass. KM91.	—
Pn366	1934A	—	5 Pfennig. Aluminum-Bronze. KM91.1. "PROBE."	—
Pn367	1935A	—	50 Pfennig. Aluminum.	—
Pn370	1935A	—	5 Mark. Silver. "PROBE."	—
Pn368	1935A	—	50 Pfennig. Oak leaves next to date. "PROBE". Wavy edge.	—
Pn371	1935A	—	5 Mark. Silver. "PROBE."	—
Pn369	1935E	—	Mark. KM78.	—
Pn372	1935A	—	5 Mark. Silver. Masses entering. "PROBE."	—
Pn373	1935A	—	5 Mark. 0.9000 Silver. Family entering. "PROBE."	—
Pn374	1935A	—	5 Mark. Electrotype.	—
Pn375	1936D	—	Pfennig. Copper Plated Iron. KM89.	—
PnA375	1936D	—	Reichspfennig. Copper Plated Iron. KM30.	—
Pn376	1937	—	5 Pfennig. Iron. KM91. Hindenburg.	—
Pn377	1937A	—	50 Pfennig. Nickel. KM95. "PROBE."	—
Pn378	1939A	—	5 Pfennig. KM100.	—
Pn379	1939A	—	Mark. Nickel. "PROBE" on rim.	—
Pn380	1939A	—	Mark. Pn379. Pn381.	—
Pn381	1939A	—	Mark.	225
Pn382	1939A	—	Mark. Aluminum. KM78. Pn381.	—
Pn383	1939/1940	—	Mark. Iron. "PROBE." Copper-nickel plated.	200
Pn384	1940	—	Mark. Silver.	400
Pn385	1942A	—	5 Mark. Silvered Copper. Eagle.	—
Pn386	1942	—	5 Reichspfennig. Copper. Klippe.	—
Pn388	1942A	—	5 Mark. Silvered Copper. Steel helmet in laurel wreath.	—
Pn387	1942	—	5 Reichsmark. Silver. Klippe.	6,500
PnA389	1946G	—	Pfennig. Aluminum.	—
PnB390	1946G	—	10 Pfennig. Brass.	900
Pn390	1947J	—	50 Pfennig. Aluminum.	—
Pn391	1947D	—	5 Pfennig. Aluminum.	—
Pn394	1947D	—	10 Pfennig. Aluminum.	—
PnB389	1947J	—	5 Pfennig. Zinc. without swastika. KM100.	3,350
PnC389	1947D	—	5 Pfennig. Aluminum. Reeded edge.	—
PnD389	1947A	—	10 Pfennig. Zinc. with slavic 7. KM104	6,000
PnC390	1947A	—	10 Pfennig. Dur-Aluminum.	—
Pn389	1947J	—	10 Pfennig. Zinc. Without swastika. KM101.	3,350
Pn392	1947	—	5 Pfennig. Brass Plated Aluminum.	—
Pn395	1947D	—	10 Pfennig. Iron. Copper-nickel plated.	—
PnA390	1947D	—	10 Pfennig. Aluminum. Plain edge.	—
Pn393	1947D	—	5 Pfennig. Copper-Nickel Plated Iron. Copper-nickel plated.	—
Pn396	1948F	—	10 Pfennig. Zinc.	—

GERMANY-FEDERAL REPUBLIC

1949-

The Federal Republic of Germany, located in north-central Europe, has an area of 137,744 sq. mi. (356,910sq. km.) and a population of 81.1 million. Capital: Berlin. The economy centers about one of the world's foremost industrial establishments. Machinery, motor vehicles, iron, steel, yarns and fabrics are exported.

During the post-Normandy phase of World War II, Allied troops occupied the western German provinces of Schleswig-Holstein, Hamburg, Lower Saxony, Bremen, North Rhine-Westphalia, Hesse, Rhineland-Palatinate, Baden-Wurttemberg, Bavaria and Saarland. The conquered provinces were divided into American, British and French occupation zones. Five eastern German provinces were occupied and administered by the forces of the Soviet Union.

The post-World War II division of Germany was ended Oct. 3, 1990, when the German Democratic Republic (East Germany) ceased to exist and its five constituent provinces were formally admitted to the Federal Republic of Germany. An election Dec. 2, 1990, chose representatives to the united federal parliament (Bundestag), which then conducted its opening session in Berlin in the old Reichstag building. Though Berlin technically is the capital of a united Germany, the actual seat of government remains for the time being in Bonn.

MINT MARKS

A - Berlin
D - Munich
F - Stuttgart
G - Karlsruhe
J - Hamburg

MONETARY SYSTEM

100 Pfennig = 1 Deutsche Mark (DM)

FEDERAL REPUBLIC

STANDARD COINAGE

KM# A101 PFENNIG Composition: Bronze-Clad Steel
Note: Currency reform.

Date	Mintage	F	VF	XF	Unc	BU
1948D	46,325,000	—	0.50	15.00	40.00	—
1948F	68,203,000	—	0.50	8.00	32.50	—
1948F Proof	250	Value: 150				
1948G	45,604,000	—	0.50	15.00	60.00	—
1948J	79,304,000	—	0.50	15.00	50.00	—
1949D	99,863,000	—	0.50	6.00	27.50	—
1949D Proof	—	Value: 100				
1949F	70,900,000	—	0.50	6.00	22.50	—
1949F Proof	250	Value: 60.00				
1949G	50,500,000	—	0.50	10.00	40.00	—
1949J	101,932,000	—	0.50	6.00	27.50	—
1949J Proof	—	Value: 85.00				

KM# 105 PFENNIG Composition: Copper Plated Steel
Note: Federal Republic.

Date	Mintage	F	VF	XF	Unc	BU
1950D	—	—	—	0.10	1.00	—
1950F	—	—	—	0.10	1.00	—
1950F Proof	620	Value: 27.50				
1950G	—	—	—	0.10	1.00	—
1950G Proof	1,800	Value: 5.00				
1950J	—	—	—	0.10	1.00	—
1950J Proof	—	Value: 12.00				
1966D	—	—	—	0.10	2.00	—
1966F	—	—	—	0.10	2.00	—
1966F Proof	100	Value: 35.00				
1966G	—	—	—	0.10	2.00	—
1966G Proof	3,070	Value: 4.00				
1966J	—	—	—	0.10	3.00	—
1966J Proof	1,000	Value: 8.00				
1967D	—	—	—	0.10	3.00	—
1967F	—	—	—	0.10	3.00	—
1967F Proof	1,500	Value: 6.00				
1967G	—	—	—	0.10	3.00	—
1967G Proof	4,500	Value: 3.50				
1967J	—	—	—	0.10	4.00	—
1967J Proof	1,500	Value: 8.00				
1968D	—	—	—	0.10	1.00	—
1968F	—	—	—	0.10	1.00	—
1968F Proof	3,000	Value: 5.00				
1968G	—	—	—	0.10	1.00	—
1968G Proof	6,023	Value: 4.00				
1968J	—	—	—	0.25	1.00	—
1968J Proof	2,000	Value: 6.50				
1969D	—	—	—	0.10	0.50	—
1969F	—	—	—	0.10	0.50	—
1969F Proof	5,100	Value: 1.50				
1969G	—	—	—	0.10	0.50	—
1969G Proof	8,700	Value: 1.25				
1969J	—	—	—	0.10	0.50	—
1969J Proof	5,000	Value: 1.50				
1970D	—	—	—	0.10	0.25	—
1970F	—	—	—	0.10	0.25	—
1970F Proof	5,240	Value: 1.50				
1970G	—	—	—	0.10	0.25	—
1970G Proof	10,200	Value: 1.00				
1970 Small J	—	—	—	0.10	0.25	—
1970 Large J	—	—	—	0.10	0.25	—
1970J Proof	5,000	Value: 1.50				
1971D	—	—	—	0.10	0.25	—
1971D Proof	8,000	Value: 1.00				
1971F	—	—	—	0.10	0.25	—
1971F Proof	8,000	Value: 1.00				
1971G	—	—	—	0.10	0.25	—
1971G Proof	10,200	Value: 1.00				
1971J	—	—	—	0.10	0.25	—
1971J Proof	8,000	Value: 1.00				
1972D	—	—	—	0.10	0.25	—
1972D Proof	8,000	Value: 1.00				
1972F	—	—	—	0.10	0.25	—
1972F Proof	8,000	Value: 1.00				
1972G	—	—	—	0.10	0.25	—
1972G Proof	10,000	Value: 1.00				
1972J	—	—	—	0.10	0.25	—
1972J Proof	8,000	Value: 1.00				
1973D	—	—	—	0.10	0.25	—
1973D Proof	9,000	Value: 1.00				
1973F	—	—	—	0.10	0.25	—
1973F Proof	9,000	Value: 1.00				
1973G	—	—	—	0.10	0.25	—
1973G Proof	9,000	Value: 1.00				
1973J	—	—	—	0.10	0.25	—
1973J Proof	9,000	Value: 1.00				
1974D	—	—	—	0.10	0.25	—
1974D Proof	35,000	Value: 0.40				
1974F	—	—	—	0.10	0.25	—
1974F Proof	35,000	Value: 0.40				
1974G	—	—	—	0.10	0.25	—
1974G Proof	35,000	Value: 0.40				
1974J	—	—	—	0.10	0.25	—
1974J Proof	35,000	Value: 0.40				
1975D	—	—	—	0.10	0.25	—
1975D Proof	43,000	Value: 0.40				
1975F	—	—	—	0.10	0.25	—
1975F Proof	43,000	Value: 0.40				
1975G	—	—	—	0.10	0.25	—
1975G Proof	43,000	Value: 0.40				
1975J	—	—	—	0.10	0.25	—
1975J Proof	43,000	Value: 0.40				
1976D	—	—	—	0.10	0.25	—
1976D Proof	43,000	Value: 0.40				
1976F	—	—	—	0.10	0.25	—
1976F Proof	43,000	Value: 0.40				
1976G	—	—	—	0.10	0.25	—
1976G Proof	43,000	Value: 0.40				
1976J	—	—	—	0.10	0.25	—
1976J Proof	43,000	Value: 0.40				
1977D	—	—	—	0.10	0.25	—
1977D Proof	52,000	Value: 0.40				
1977F	—	—	—	0.10	0.25	—
1977F Proof	51,000	Value: 0.40				
1977G	—	—	—	0.10	0.25	—
1977G Proof	51,000	Value: 0.40				
1977J	—	—	—	0.10	0.25	—
1977J Proof	51,000	Value: 0.40				
1978D	—	—	—	0.10	0.25	—
1978D Proof	54,000	Value: 0.40				
1978F	—	—	—	0.10	0.25	—
1978F Proof	54,000	Value: 0.40				
1978G	—	—	—	0.10	0.25	—
1978G Proof	54,000	Value: 0.40				
1978J	—	—	—	0.10	0.25	—
1978J Proof	54,000	Value: 0.40				
1979D	—	—	—	0.10	0.25	—
1979D Proof	89,000	Value: 0.40				
1979F	—	—	—	0.10	0.25	—
1979F Proof	89,000	Value: 0.40				
1979G	—	—	—	0.10	0.25	—
1979G Proof	89,000	Value: 0.40				
1979J	—	—	—	0.10	0.25	—
1979J Proof	89,000	Value: 0.40				
1980D	—	—	—	0.10	0.25	—
1980D Proof	110,000	Value: 0.40				
1980F	—	—	—	0.10	0.25	—
1980F Proof	110,000	Value: 0.40				
1980G	—	—	—	0.10	0.25	—
1980G Proof	110,000	Value: 0.40				
1980J	—	—	—	0.10	0.25	—
1980J Proof	110,000	Value: 0.40				
1981D	—	—	—	0.10	0.25	—
1981D Proof	91,000	Value: 0.40				
1981F	—	—	—	0.10	0.25	—
1981F Proof	91,000	Value: 0.40				
1981G	—	—	—	0.10	0.25	—
1981G Proof	91,000	Value: 0.40				
1981J	—	—	—	0.10	0.25	—
1981J Proof	91,000	Value: 0.40				
1982D	—	—	—	0.10	0.20	—
1982D Proof	78,000	Value: 0.40				
1982F	—	—	—	0.10	0.20	—
1982F Proof	78,000	Value: 0.40				
1982G	—	—	—	0.10	0.20	—
1982G Proof	78,000	Value: 0.40				
1982J	—	—	—	0.10	0.20	—
1982J Proof	78,000	Value: 0.40				
1983D	—	—	—	0.10	0.20	—
1983D Proof	75,000	Value: 0.40				
1983F	—	—	—	0.10	0.20	—

Date	Mintage	F	VF	XF	Unc	BU
1983F Proof	75,000	Value: 0.40				
1983G		—	—	0.10	0.20	—
1983G Proof	75,000	Value: 0.40				
1983J		—	—	0.10	0.20	—
1983J Proof	75,000	Value: 0.40				
1984D		—	—	0.10	0.20	—
1984D Proof	64,000	Value: 0.40				
1984F		—	—	0.10	0.20	—
1984F Proof	64,000	Value: 0.40				
1984G		—	—	0.10	0.20	—
1984G Proof	64,000	Value: 0.40				
1984J		—	—	0.10	0.20	—
1984J Proof	64,000	Value: 0.40				
1985D		—	—	0.10	0.20	—
1985D Proof	56,000	Value: 0.40				
1985F		—	—	0.10	0.20	—
1985F Proof	54,000	Value: 0.40				
1985G		—	—	—	0.10	—
1985G Proof	55,000	Value: 0.40				
1985J		—	—	—	0.10	—
1985J Proof	54,000	Value: 0.40				
1986D		—	—	—	0.10	—
1986D Proof	44,000	Value: 0.40				
1986F		—	—	—	0.10	—
1986F Proof	44,000	Value: 0.40				
1986G		—	—	—	0.10	—
1986G Proof	44,000	Value: 0.40				
1986J		—	—	—	0.10	—
1986J Proof	44,000	Value: 0.40				
1987D		—	—	—	0.10	—
1987D Proof	45,000	Value: 0.40				
1987F		—	—	—	0.10	—
1987F Proof	45,000	Value: 0.40				
1987G		—	—	—	0.10	—
1987G Proof	45,000	Value: 0.40				
1987J		—	—	—	0.10	—
1987J Proof	45,000	Value: 0.40				
1988D		—	—	—	0.10	—
1988D Proof	45,000	Value: 0.40				
1988F		—	—	—	0.10	—
1988F Proof	45,000	Value: 0.40				
1988G		—	—	—	0.10	—
1988G Proof	45,000	Value: 0.40				
1988J		—	—	—	0.10	—
1988J Proof	45,000	Value: 0.40				
1989D		—	—	—	0.10	—
1989D Proof	45,000	Value: 0.40				
1989F		—	—	—	0.10	—
1989F Proof	45,000	Value: 0.40				
1989G		—	—	—	0.10	—
1989G Proof	45,000	Value: 0.40				
1989J		—	—	—	0.10	—
1989J Proof	45,000	Value: 0.40				
1990D		—	—	—	0.10	—
1990D Proof	45,000	Value: 0.40				
1990F		—	—	—	0.10	—
1990F Proof	45,000	Value: 0.40				
1990G		—	—	—	0.10	—
1990G Proof	45,000	Value: 0.40				
1990J		—	—	—	0.10	—
1990J Proof	45,000	Value: 0.40				
1991A		—	—	—	0.10	—
1991A Proof	45,000	Value: 0.40				
1991D		—	—	—	0.10	—
1991D Proof	45,000	Value: 0.40				
1991F		—	—	—	0.10	—
1991F Proof	45,000	Value: 0.40				
1991G		—	—	—	0.10	—
1991G Proof	45,000	Value: 0.40				
1991J		—	—	—	0.10	—
1991J Proof	45,000	Value: 0.40				
1992A		—	—	—	0.10	—
1992A Proof	45,000	Value: 0.40				
1992D		—	—	—	0.10	—
1992D Proof	45,000	Value: 0.40				
1992F		—	—	—	0.10	—
1992F Proof	45,000	Value: 0.40				
1992G		—	—	—	0.10	—
1992G Proof	45,000	Value: 0.40				
1992J		—	—	—	0.10	—
1992J Proof	45,000	Value: 0.40				
1993A		—	—	—	0.10	—
1993A Proof	45,000	Value: 0.40				
1993D		—	—	—	0.10	—
1993D Proof	45,000	Value: 0.40				
1993F		—	—	—	0.10	—
1993F Proof	45,000	Value: 0.40				
1993G		—	—	—	0.10	—
1993G Proof	45,000	Value: 0.40				
1993J		—	—	—	0.10	—
1993J Proof	45,000	Value: 0.40				
1994A		—	—	—	0.10	—
1994A Proof	45,000	Value: 0.40				
1994D		—	—	—	0.10	—
1994D Proof	45,000	Value: 0.40				
1994F		—	—	—	0.10	—
1994F Proof	45,000	Value: 0.40				
1994G		—	—	—	0.10	—
1994G Proof	45,000	Value: 0.40				
1994J		—	—	—	0.10	—
1994J Proof	45,000	Value: 0.40				
1995A		—	—	—	0.15	—
1995A Proof	45,000	Value: 0.45				
1995D		—	—	—	0.15	—
1995D Proof	45,000	Value: 0.45				
1995F		—	—	—	0.15	—
1995F Proof	45,000	Value: 0.45				
1995G		—	—	—	0.15	—
1995G Proof	45,000	Value: 0.45				
1995J		—	—	—	0.15	—
1995J Proof	45,000	Value: 0.45				
1996A		—	—	—	0.20	—
1996A Proof	45,000	Value: 0.50				
1996D		—	—	—	0.20	—
1996D Proof	45,000	Value: 0.50				
1996F		—	—	—	0.20	—
1996F Proof	45,000	Value: 0.50				
1996G		—	—	—	0.20	—
1996G Proof	45,000	Value: 0.50				
1996J		—	—	—	0.20	—
1996J Proof	45,000	Value: 0.50				
1997A In sets only		—	—	—	1.75	—
1997A Proof	45,000	Value: 2.00				
1997D In sets only		—	—	—	1.75	—
1997D Proof	45,000	Value: 2.00				
1997F In sets only		—	—	—	1.75	—
1997F Proof	45,000	Value: 2.00				
1997G In sets only		—	—	—	1.75	—
1997G Proof	45,000	Value: 2.00				
1997J In sets only		—	—	—	1.75	—
1997J Proof	45,000	Value: 2.00				
1998A In sets only		—	—	—	1.75	—
1998A Proof	45,000	Value: 2.00				
1998D In sets only		—	—	—	1.75	—
1998D Proof	45,000	Value: 2.00				
1998F In sets only		—	—	—	1.75	—
1998F Proof	45,000	Value: 2.00				
1998G In sets only		—	—	—	1.75	—
1998G Proof	45,000	Value: 2.00				
1998J In sets only		—	—	—	1.75	—
1998J Proof	45,000	Value: 2.00				
1999A In sets only		—	—	—	1.75	—
1999A Proof	45,000	Value: 2.00				
1999D In sets only		—	—	—	1.75	—
1999D Proof	45,000	Value: 2.00				
1999F In sets only		—	—	—	1.75	—
1999F Proof	45,000	Value: 2.00				
1999G In sets only		—	—	—	1.75	—
1999G Proof	45,000	Value: 2.00				
1999J In sets only		—	—	—	1.75	—
1999J Proof	45,000	Value: 2.00				
2000A In sets only		—	—	—	1.75	—
2000A Proof	45,000	Value: 2.00				
2000D In sets only		—	—	—	1.75	—
2000D Proof	45,000	Value: 2.00				
2000F In sets only		—	—	—	1.75	—
2000F Proof	45,000	Value: 2.00				
2000G In sets only		—	—	—	1.75	—
2000G Proof	45,000	Value: 2.00				
2000J In sets only		—	—	—	1.75	—
2000J Proof	45,000	Value: 2.00				
2001A In sets only		—	—	—	5.00	—
2001A Proof	78,000	Value: 5.00				
2001D In sets only		—	—	—	5.00	—
2001D Proof	78,000	Value: 5.00				
2001F In sets only		—	—	—	5.00	—
2001F Proof	78,000	Value: 5.00				
2001G In sets only		—	—	—	5.00	—
2001G Proof	78,000	Value: 5.00				
2001J In sets only		—	—	—	5.00	—
2001J Proof	78,000	Value: 5.00				

KM# 106 2 PFENNIG Composition: Bronze **Note:** Federal Republic.

Date	Mintage	F	VF	XF	Unc	BU
1950D		—	0.10	1.00	10.00	—
1950D Proof	—	Value: 50.00				
1950F		—	0.10	1.00	10.00	—
1950F Proof		—	—	—	—	—
1950G		—	0.10	50.00	75.00	—
1950G Proof	—	Value: 90.00				
1950J		—	0.10	1.00	10.00	—
1950J Proof	—	Value: 40.00				
1958D		—	0.10	1.00	10.00	—
1958F		—	0.10	1.00	10.00	—
1958F Proof		—	—	—	—	—
1958G		—	0.10	1.00	10.00	—
1958J		—	0.10	1.00	10.00	—
1959D		—	—	0.25	10.00	—
1959F		—	—	0.25	10.00	—
1959F Proof		—	—	—	—	—
1959G		—	—	0.25	10.00	—
1959J		—	—	0.25	10.00	—
1960D		—	—	0.25	6.00	—
1960F		—	—	0.25	6.00	—
1960F Proof		—	—	—	—	—
1960G		—	0.10	0.25	6.00	—
1960J		—	—	0.25	6.00	—
1961D		—	—	0.25	6.00	—
1961F		—	—	0.25	6.00	—
1961G		—	—	0.25	6.00	—
1961J		—	—	0.25	6.00	—
1962D		—	—	0.25	6.00	—
1962F		—	—	0.25	4.00	—
1962G		—	—	0.25	4.00	—
1962J		—	—	0.25	4.00	—
1963D		—	—	0.25	7.00	—
1963F		—	—	0.25	2.00	—
1963G		—	—	0.25	2.00	—
1963G Proof		—	—	—	—	—
1963J		—	—	0.25	2.00	—
1964D		—	—	0.25	3.00	—
1964F		—	—	0.10	1.00	—
1964G		—	—	0.10	1.00	—
1964G Proof	Est. 600	Value: 12.00				
1964J		—	—	0.10	1.00	—
1965D		—	—	0.10	1.00	—
1965F		—	—	0.10	1.00	—
1965F Proof	Est. 80	Value: 70.00				
1965G		—	—	0.10	1.00	—
1965G Proof	1,200	Value: 5.00				
1965J		—	—	0.10	1.00	—
1966D		—	—	0.10	0.25	—
1966F		—	—	0.10	0.25	—
1966F Proof	100	Value: 80.00				
1966G		—	—	0.10	0.25	—
1966G Proof	3,070	Value: 5.50				
1966J		—	—	0.10	0.25	—
1966J Proof	1,000	Value: 40.00				
1967D		—	—	0.10	2.00	—
1967F		—	—	0.10	1.00	—
1967F Proof	1,500	Value: 7.00				
1967G		—	—	1.00	3.00	—
1967G Proof	4,500	Value: 4.50				
1967J		—	—	0.10	1.00	—
1967J Proof	1,500	Value: 10.00				
1968D		—	—	1.00	3.00	—
1968G		—	—	0.10	1.00	—
1968G Proof	3,651	Value: 4.00				
1968J		—	150	225	350	—

Note: A 1968J error of 1963J exists with coin alignment

Date	Mintage	F	VF	XF	Unc	BU
1969J		—	150	225	350	—

KM# 106a 2 PFENNIG Composition: Bronze Clad Steel

Date	Mintage	F	VF	XF	Unc	BU
1967G Proof	520	Value: 720				
1968D	19,523,000	—	—	0.10	0.25	—
1968F	30,000,000	—	—	0.10	0.25	—
1968F Proof	3,000	Value: 6.00				
1968G	13,004,000	—	—	0.10	0.25	—
1968G Proof	2,372	Value: 4.00				
1968J	20,026,000	—	—	0.10	0.25	—
1968J Proof	2,000	Value: 7.50				
1969D	39,012,000	—	—	0.10	0.25	—
1969D Proof		Value: 1.25				
1969F	45,029,000	—	—	0.10	0.25	—
1969F Proof	5,100	Value: 1.25				
1969G	32,156,999	—	—	0.10	0.25	—
1969G Proof	8,700	Value: 1.25				
1969J	40,102,000	—	—	0.10	0.25	—
1969J Proof	5,000	Value: 2.50				
1970D	45,525,000	—	—	0.10	0.25	—
1970F	73,851,000	—	—	0.10	0.25	—
1970F Proof	5,140	Value: 1.25				
1970G	30,330,000	—	—	0.10	0.25	—
1970G Proof	10,200	Value: 1.25				
1970 Small J	46,730,000	—	—	0.10	0.25	—
1970 Large J	Inc. above	—	—	0.10	0.25	—
1970J Proof	5,000	Value: 1.75				
1971D	71,755,000	—	—	0.10	0.25	—
1971D Proof	8,000	Value: 1.25				
1971F	82,765,000	—	—	0.10	0.25	—
1971F Proof	8,000	Value: 1.25				
1971G	47,850,000	—	—	0.10	0.25	—
1971G Proof	10,000	Value: 1.25				
1971J	73,641,000	—	—	0.10	0.25	—
1971J Proof	8,000	Value: 1.25				
1972D	52,403,000	—	—	0.10	0.25	—
1972D Proof	8,000	Value: 1.00				
1972F	60,272,000	—	—	0.10	0.25	—
1972F Proof	8,000	Value: 1.00				
1972G	34,864,000	—	—	0.10	0.25	—
1972G Proof	10,000	Value: 1.00				
1972J	53,673,000	—	—	0.10	0.25	—
1972J Proof	8,000	Value: 1.00				
1973D	26,190,000	—	—	0.10	0.25	—
1973D Proof	9,000	Value: 1.00				
1973F	30,160,000	—	—	0.10	0.25	—
1973F Proof	9,000	Value: 1.00				

Date	Mintage	F	VF	XF	Unc	BU
1973G	17,379,000	—	—	0.10	0.25	—
1973G Proof	9,000	Value: 1.00				
1973J	26,830,000	—	—	0.10	0.25	—
1973J Proof	9,000	Value: 1.00				
1974D	58,667,000	—	—	0.10	0.25	—
1974D Proof	35,000	Value: 0.50				
1974F	67,596,000	—	—	0.10	0.25	—
1974F Proof	35,000	Value: 0.50				
1974G	39,007,000	—	—	0.10	0.25	—
1974G Proof	35,000	Value: 0.50				
1974J	60,195,000	—	—	0.10	0.25	—
1974J Proof	35,000	Value: 0.50				
1975D	58,634,000	—	—	0.10	0.25	—
1975D Proof	43,000	Value: 0.50				
1975F	67,685,000	—	—	0.10	0.25	—
1975F Proof	43,000	Value: 0.50				
1975G	39,391,000	—	—	0.10	0.25	—
1975G Proof	43,000	Value: 0.50				
1975J	60,207,000	—	—	0.10	0.25	—
1975J Proof	43,000	Value: 0.50				
1976D	78,074,000	—	—	0.10	0.25	—
1976D Proof	43,000	Value: 0.50				
1976F	90,130,000	—	—	0.10	0.25	—
1976F Proof	43,000	Value: 0.50				
1976G	51,988,000	—	—	0.10	0.25	—
1976G Proof	43,000	Value: 0.50				
1976J	80,145,000	—	—	0.10	0.25	—
1976J Proof	43,000	Value: 0.50				
1977D	84,516,000	—	—	0.10	0.20	—
1977D Proof	51,000	Value: 0.40				
1977F	97,504,000	—	—	0.10	0.20	—
1977F Proof	51,000	Value: 0.40				
1977G	56,276,000	—	—	0.10	0.20	—
1977G Proof	51,000	Value: 0.40				
1977J	86,888,000	—	—	0.10	0.20	—
1977J Proof	51,000	Value: 0.40				
1978D	84,500,000	—	—	0.10	0.20	—
1978D Proof	54,000	Value: 0.40				
1978F	97,500,000	—	—	0.10	0.20	—
1978F Proof	54,000	Value: 0.40				
1978G	56,225,000	—	—	0.10	0.20	—
1978G Proof	54,000	Value: 0.40				
1978J	86,775,000	—	—	0.10	0.20	—
1978J Proof	54,000	Value: 0.40				
1979D	91,000,000	—	—	0.10	0.20	—
1979D Proof	89,000	Value: 0.40				
1979F	105,000,000	—	—	0.10	0.20	—
1979F Proof	89,000	Value: 0.40				
1979G	60,550,000	—	—	0.10	0.20	—
1979G Proof	89,000	Value: 0.40				
1979J	93,480,000	—	—	0.10	0.20	—
1979J Proof	89,000	Value: 0.40				
1980D	93,360,000	—	—	0.10	0.20	—
1980D Proof	110,000	Value: 0.40				
1980F	120,360,000	—	—	0.10	0.20	—
1980F Proof	110,000	Value: 0.40				
1980G	50,830,000	—	—	0.10	0.20	—
1980G Proof	110,000	Value: 0.40				
1980J	102,260,000	—	—	0.10	0.20	—
1980J Proof	110,000	Value: 0.40				
1981D	93,910,000	—	—	0.10	0.20	—
1981D Proof	91,000	Value: 0.40				
1981F	83,710,000	—	—	0.10	0.20	—
1981F Proof	91,000	Value: 0.40				
1981G	89,850,000	—	—	0.10	0.20	—
1981G Proof	91,000	Value: 0.40				
1981J	87,250,000	—	—	0.10	0.20	—
1981J Proof	91,000	Value: 0.40				
1982D	64,390,000	—	—	0.10	0.20	—
1982D Proof	78,000	Value: 0.40				
1982F	36,870,000	—	—	0.10	0.20	—
1982F Proof	78,000	Value: 0.40				
1982G	58,590,000	—	—	0.10	0.20	—
1982G Proof	78,000	Value: 0.40				
1982J	57,690,000	—	—	0.10	0.20	—
1982J Proof	78,000	Value: 0.40				
1983D	71,500,000	—	—	0.10	0.20	—
1983D Proof	75,000	Value: 0.40				
1983F	82,500,000	—	—	0.10	0.20	—
1983F Proof	75,000	Value: 0.40				
1983G	47,575,000	—	—	0.10	0.20	—
1983G Proof	75,000	Value: 0.40				
1983J	73,425,000	—	—	0.10	0.20	—
1983J Proof	75,000	Value: 0.40				
1984D	58,500,000	—	—	0.10	0.20	—
1984D Proof	64,000	Value: 0.40				
1984F	67,500,000	—	—	0.10	0.20	—
1984F Proof	64,000	Value: 0.40				
1984G	38,900,000	—	—	0.10	0.20	—
1984G Proof	64,000	Value: 0.40				
1984J	60,100,000	—	—	0.10	0.20	—
1984J Proof	64,000	Value: 0.40				
1985D	19,500,000	—	—	—	0.10	—
1985D Proof	56,000	Value: 0.40				
1985F	22,500,000	—	—	—	0.10	—
1985F Proof	54,000	Value: 0.40				
1985G	13,000,000	—	—	—	0.10	—
1985G Proof	55,000	Value: 0.40				
1985J	20,000,000	—	—	—	0.10	—
1985J Proof	54,000	Value: 0.40				
1986D	39,000,000	—	—	—	0.10	—
1986D Proof	44,000	Value: 0.40				
1986F	45,000,000	—	—	—	0.10	—
1986F Proof	44,000	Value: 0.40				
1986G	25,900,000	—	—	—	0.10	—
1986G Proof	44,000	Value: 0.40				
1986J	40,100,000	—	—	—	0.10	—
1986J Proof	44,000	Value: 0.40				
1987D	6,500,000	—	1.00	2.50	5.00	—
1987D Proof	45,000	Value: 0.40				
1987F	7,500,000	—	1.00	2.50	5.00	—
1987F Proof	45,000	Value: 0.40				
1987G	4,330,000	—	1.00	2.50	5.00	—
1987G Proof	45,000	Value: 0.40				
1987J	6,680,000	—	1.00	2.50	5.00	—
1987J Proof	45,000	Value: 0.40				
1988D	52,000,000	—	—	—	0.10	—
1988D Proof	45,000	Value: 0.40				
1988F	60,000,000	—	—	—	0.10	—
1988F Proof	45,000	Value: 0.40				
1988G	34,600,000	—	—	—	0.10	—
1988G Proof	45,000	Value: 0.40				
1988J	53,400,000	—	—	—	0.10	—
1988J Proof	45,000	Value: 0.40				
1989D	52,000,000	—	—	—	0.10	—
1989D Proof	45,000	Value: 0.40				
1989F	60,000,000	—	—	—	0.10	—
1989F Proof	45,000	Value: 0.40				
1989G	34,600,000	—	—	—	0.10	—
1989G Proof	45,000	Value: 0.40				
1989J	53,400,000	—	—	—	0.10	—
1989J Proof	45,000	Value: 0.40				
1990D	71,500,000	—	—	—	0.10	—
1990D Proof	45,000	Value: 0.40				
1990F	82,500,000	—	—	—	0.10	—
1990F Proof	45,000	Value: 0.40				
1990G	47,570,000	—	—	—	0.10	—
1990G Proof	45,000	Value: 0.40				
1990J	73,420,000	—	—	—	0.10	—
1990J Proof	45,000	Value: 0.40				
1991A	115,000,000	—	—	—	0.10	—
1991A Proof	45,000	Value: 0.40				
1991D	120,750,000	—	—	—	0.10	—
1991D Proof	45,000	Value: 0.40				
1991F	138,000,000	—	—	—	0.10	—
1991F Proof	45,000	Value: 0.40				
1991G	80,500,000	—	—	—	0.10	—
1991G Proof	45,000	Value: 0.40				
1991J	120,750,000	—	—	—	0.10	—
1991J Proof	45,000	Value: 0.40				
1992A	60,000,000	—	—	—	0.10	—
1992A Proof	45,000	Value: 0.40				
1992D	63,000,000	—	—	—	0.10	—
1992D Proof	45,000	Value: 0.40				
1992F	72,000,000	—	—	—	0.10	—
1992F Proof	45,000	Value: 0.40				
1992G	42,000,000	—	—	—	0.10	—
1992G Proof	45,000	Value: 0.40				
1992J	63,000,000	—	—	—	0.10	—
1992J Proof	45,000	Value: 0.40				
1993A	10,000,000	—	—	—	0.10	—
1993A Proof	45,000	Value: 0.40				
1993D	10,500,000	—	—	—	0.10	—
1993D Proof	45,000	Value: 0.40				
1993F	12,000,000	—	—	—	0.10	—
1993F Proof	45,000	Value: 0.40				
1993G	7,000,000	—	—	—	0.10	—
1993G Proof	45,000	Value: 0.40				
1993J	10,000,000	—	—	—	0.10	—
1993J Proof	45,000	Value: 0.40				
1994A	55,000,000	—	—	—	0.10	—
1994A Proof	45,000	Value: 0.40				
1994D	57,750,000	—	—	—	0.10	—
1994D Proof	45,000	Value: 0.40				
1994F	66,000,000	—	—	—	0.10	—
1994F Proof	45,000	Value: 0.40				
1994G	38,500,000	—	—	—	0.10	—
1994G Proof	45,000	Value: 0.40				
1994J	57,750,000	—	—	—	0.10	—
1994J Proof	45,000	Value: 0.40				
1995A	1,000,000,000	—	—	—	0.15	—
1995A Proof	45,000	Value: 0.45				
1995D	105,000,000	—	—	—	0.15	—
1995D Proof	45,000	Value: 0.45				
1995F	120,000,000	—	—	—	0.15	—
1995F Proof	45,000	Value: 0.45				
1995G	70,000,000	—	—	—	0.15	—
1995G Proof	45,000	Value: 0.45				
1995J	105,000,000	—	—	—	0.15	—
1995J Proof	45,000	Value: 0.45				
1996A	40,000,000	—	—	—	0.20	—
1996A Proof	45,000	Value: 0.50				
1996D	42,000,000	—	—	—	0.20	—
1996D Proof	45,000	Value: 0.50				
1996F	48,000,000	—	—	—	0.20	—
1996F Proof	45,000	Value: 0.50				
1996G	28,000,000	—	—	—	0.20	—
1996G Proof	45,000	Value: 0.50				
1996J	42,000,000	—	—	—	0.20	—
1996J Proof	45,000	Value: 0.50				
1997A In sets only	70,000	—	—	—	1.75	—
1997A Proof	45,000	Value: 2.00				
1997D In sets only	70,000	—	—	—	1.75	—
1997D Proof	45,000	Value: 2.00				
1997F In sets only	70,000	—	—	—	1.75	—
1997F Proof	45,000	Value: 2.00				
1997G In sets only	70,000	—	—	—	1.75	—
1997G Proof	45,000	Value: 2.00				
1997J In sets only	70,000	—	—	—	1.75	—
1997J Proof	45,000	Value: 2.00				
1998A In sets only	70,000	—	—	—	1.75	—
1998A Proof	45,000	Value: 2.00				
1998D In sets only	70,000	—	—	—	1.75	—
1998D Proof	45,000	Value: 2.00				
1998F In sets only	70,000	—	—	—	1.75	—
1998F Proof	45,000	Value: 2.00				
1998G In sets only	70,000	—	—	—	1.75	—
1998G Proof	45,000	Value: 2.00				
1998J In sets only	70,000	—	—	—	1.75	—
1998J Proof	45,000	Value: 2.00				
1999A In sets only	70,000	—	—	—	1.75	—
1999A Proof	45,000	Value: 2.00				
1999D In sets only	70,000	—	—	—	1.75	—
1999D Proof	45,000	Value: 2.00				
1999F In sets only	70,000	—	—	—	1.75	—
1999F Proof	45,000	Value: 2.00				
1999G In sets only	70,000	—	—	—	1.75	—
1999G Proof	45,000	Value: 2.00				
1999J In sets only	70,000	—	—	—	1.75	—
1999J Proof	45,000	Value: 2.00				
2000A In sets only	70,000	—	—	—	1.75	—
2000A Proof	45,000	Value: 2.00				
2000D In sets only	70,000	—	—	—	1.75	—
2000D Proof	45,000	Value: 2.00				
2000F In sets only	70,000	—	—	—	1.75	—
2000F Proof	45,000	Value: 2.00				
2000G In sets only	70,000	—	—	—	1.75	—
2000G Proof	45,000	Value: 2.00				
2000J In sets only	70,000	—	—	—	1.75	—
2000J Proof	45,000	Value: 2.00				
2001A In sets only	130,000	—	—	—	5.00	—
2001A Proof	78,000	Value: 5.00				
2001D In sets only	130,000	—	—	—	5.00	—
2001D Proof	78,000	Value: 5.00				
2001F In sets only	130,000	—	—	—	5.00	—
2001F Proof	78,000	Value: 5.00				
2001G In sets only	130,000	—	—	—	5.00	—
2001G Proof	78,000	Value: 5.00				
2001J In sets only	130,000	—	—	—	5.00	—
2001J Proof	78,000	Value: 5.00				

KM# 102 5 PFENNIG **Composition:** Bronze-Clad Steel **Note:** Currency Reform.

Date	Mintage	F	VF	XF	Unc	BU
1949D	60,026,000	—	0.20	7.50	45.00	—
1949D Proof	—	Value: 150				
1949F	66,081,999	—	0.20	7.50	35.00	—
1949F Proof	250	Value: 80.00				
1949G	57,356,000	—	0.20	7.50	50.00	—
1949J	68,977,000	—	0.20	7.50	40.00	—
1949J Proof	—	Value: 80.00				

KM# 107 5 PFENNIG **Composition:** Brass Plated Steel

Date	Mintage	F	VF	XF	Unc	BU
1950D	271,962,000	—	—	1.50	5.00	—
1950F	362,880,000	—	—	1.50	5.00	—
1950F Proof	500	Value: 65.00				
1950G	180,492,000	—	—	1.50	5.00	—
1950G	1,800	—	—	1.50	4.00	—
1950J Large J	285,283,000	—	—	1.50	5.00	—
1950J Small J	Inc. above	—	—	1.50	5.00	—
1966D	26,036,000	—	—	1.50	8.50	—
1966F	30,047,000	—	—	1.50	8.50	—
1966F Proof	100	—	—	—	60.00	—
1966G	17,333,000	—	—	1.50	8.50	—
1966G Proof	3,070	—	—	—	7.50	—
1966J	26,741,000	—	—	1.50	8.50	—
1966J Proof	1,000	—	—	1.50	17.50	—
1967D	10,418,000	—	—	1.50	8.50	—
1967F	12,012,000	—	—	1.50	8.50	—
1967F Proof	1,500	Value: 15.00				
1967G	1,736,000	—	2.00	4.00	25.00	—
1967G Proof	4,500	Value: 7.50				
1967J	10,706,000	—	—	1.50	8.50	—
1967J Proof	1,500	Value: 15.00				
1968D	13,047,000	—	—	0.25	5.00	—
1968F	15,026,000	—	—	0.25	5.00	—
1968F Proof	3,000	Value: 9.00				
1968G	13,855,000	—	—	0.25	5.00	—
1968G Proof	6,023	Value: 6.00				

Date	Mintage	F	VF	XF	Unc	BU
1968J	13,362,000	—	—	0.25	5.00	—
1968J Proof	2,000	Value: 15.00				
1969D	23,488,000	—	—	0.10	1.50	—
1969F	27,046,000	—	—	0.10	1.50	—
1969F Proof	5,000	Value: 3.00				
1969G	15,631,000	—	—	0.10	1.50	—
1969G Proof	8,700	Value: 2.50				
1969J	24,120,000	—	—	0.10	1.50	—
1969J Proof	5,000	Value: 2.00				
1970D	39,940,000	—	—	0.10	0.25	—
1970F	45,517,000	—	—	0.10	0.25	—
1970F Proof	5,140	Value: 2.50				
1970G	27,638,000	—	—	0.10	0.25	—
1970G Proof	10,200	Value: 1.50				
1970J	40,873,000	—	—	0.10	0.25	—
1970J Proof	5,000	Value: 2.50				
1971D	57,345,000	—	—	0.10	0.25	—
1971D Proof	8,000	Value: 1.50				
1971F	66,426,000	—	—	0.10	0.25	—
1971F Proof	8,000	Value: 1.50				
1971G	38,284,000	—	—	0.10	0.25	—
1971G Proof	10,000	Value: 1.50				
1971J	58,566,000	—	—	0.10	0.25	—
1971J Proof	8,000	Value: 1.50				
1972D	52,325,000	—	—	0.10	0.25	—
1972D Proof	8,000	Value: 1.50				
1972F	60,292,000	—	—	0.10	0.25	—
1972F Proof	8,000	Value: 1.50				
1972G	34,719,000	—	—	0.10	0.25	—
1972G Proof	10,000	Value: 1.50				
1972J	54,218,000	—	—	0.10	0.25	—
1972J Proof	8,000	Value: 1.50				
1973D	15,596,000	—	—	0.10	0.25	—
1973D Proof	9,000	Value: 1.50				
1973F	18,039,000	—	—	0.10	0.25	—
1973F Proof	9,000	Value: 1.50				
1973G	10,391,000	—	—	0.10	0.25	—
1973G Proof	9,000	Value: 1.50				
1973J	16,035,000	—	—	0.10	0.25	—
1973J Proof	9,000	Value: 1.50				
1974D	15,769,000	—	—	0.10	0.25	—
1974D Proof	35,000	Value: 0.50				
1974F	18,143,000	—	—	0.10	0.25	—
1974F Proof	35,000	Value: 0.50				
1974G	10,508,000	—	—	0.10	0.25	—
1974G Proof	35,000	Value: 0.50				
1974J	16,055,000	—	—	0.10	0.25	—
1974J Proof	35,000	Value: 0.50				
1975D	15,715,000	—	—	0.10	0.25	—
1975D Proof	43,000	Value: 0.50				
1975F	18,013,000	—	—	0.10	0.25	—
1975F Proof	43,000	Value: 0.50				
1975G	10,466,000	—	—	0.10	0.25	—
1975G Proof	43,000	Value: 0.50				
1975J	16,201,000	—	—	0.10	0.25	—
1975J Proof	43,000	Value: 0.50				
1976D	47,091,000	—	—	0.10	0.25	—
1976D Proof	43,000	Value: 0.50				
1976F	54,370,000	—	—	0.10	0.25	—
1976F Proof	43,000	Value: 0.50				
1976G	31,367,000	—	—	0.10	0.25	—
1976G Proof	43,000	Value: 0.50				
1976J	48,321,000	—	—	0.10	0.25	—
1976J Proof	43,000	Value: 0.50				
1977D	52,159,000	—	—	0.10	0.20	—
1977D Proof	51,000	Value: 0.40				
1977F	60,124,000	—	—	0.10	0.20	—
1977F Proof	51,000	Value: 0.40				
1977G	34,600,000	—	—	0.10	0.20	—
1977G Proof	51,000	Value: 0.40				
1977J	53,481,000	—	—	0.10	0.20	—
1977J Proof	51,000	Value: 0.40				
1978D	41,600,000	—	—	0.10	0.20	—
1978D Proof	54,000	Value: 0.40				
1978F	48,000,000	—	—	0.10	0.20	—
1978F Proof	54,000	Value: 0.40				
1978G	27,680,000	—	—	0.10	0.20	—
1978G Proof	54,000	Value: 0.40				
1978J	42,720,000	—	—	0.10	0.20	—
1978J Proof	54,000	Value: 0.40				
1979D	41,600,000	—	—	0.10	0.20	—
1979D Proof	89,000	Value: 0.40				
1979F	48,000,000	—	—	0.10	0.20	—
1979F Proof	89,000	Value: 0.40				
1979G	27,680,000	—	—	0.10	0.20	—
1979G Proof	89,000	Value: 0.40				
1979J	42,711,000	—	—	0.10	0.20	—
1979J Proof	89,000	Value: 0.40				
1980D	39,880,000	—	—	0.10	0.20	—
1980D Proof	110,000	Value: 0.40				
1980F	53,270,000	—	—	0.10	0.20	—
1980F Proof	110,000	Value: 0.40				
1980G	43,070,000	—	—	0.10	0.20	—
1980G Proof	110,000	Value: 0.40				
1980J	59,130,000	—	—	0.10	0.20	—
1980J Proof	110,000	Value: 0.40				
1981D	82,250,000	—	—	0.10	0.20	—
1981D Proof	91,000	Value: 0.40				
1981F	84,910,000	—	—	0.10	0.20	—
1981F Proof	91,000	Value: 0.40				
1981G	41,910,000	—	—	0.10	0.20	—
1981G Proof	91,000	Value: 0.40				

Date	Mintage	F	VF	XF	Unc	BU
1981J	49,290,000	—	—	0.10	0.20	—
1981J Proof	91,000	Value: 0.40				
1982D	57,500,000	—	—	0.10	0.20	—
1982D Proof	78,000	Value: 0.40				
1982F	53,290,000	—	—	0.10	0.20	—
1982F Proof	78,000	Value: 0.40				
1982G	23,750,000	—	—	0.10	0.20	—
1982G Proof	78,000	Value: 0.40				
1982J	62,000,000	—	—	0.10	0.20	—
1982J Proof	78,000	Value: 0.40				
1983D	46,800,000	—	—	0.10	0.20	—
1983D Proof	75,000	Value: 0.40				
1983F	54,000,000	—	—	0.10	0.20	—
1983F Proof	75,000	Value: 0.40				
1983G	31,140,000	—	—	0.10	0.20	—
1983G Proof	75,000	Value: 0.40				
1983J	48,060,000	—	—	0.10	0.20	—
1983J Proof	75,000	Value: 0.40				
1984D	36,400,000	—	—	0.10	0.20	—
1984D Proof	64,000	Value: 0.40				
1984F	42,000,000	—	—	0.10	0.20	—
1984F Proof	64,000	Value: 0.40				
1984G	24,200,000	—	—	0.10	0.20	—
1984G Proof	64,000	Value: 0.40				
1984J	37,400,000	—	—	0.10	0.20	—
1984J Proof	64,000	Value: 0.40				
1985D	15,600,000	—	—	—	0.10	—
1985D Proof	56,000	Value: 0.40				
1985F	18,000,000	—	—	—	0.10	—
1985F Proof	54,000	Value: 0.40				
1985G	10,400,000	—	—	—	0.10	—
1985G Proof	55,000	Value: 0.40				
1985J	16,000,000	—	—	—	0.10	—
1985J Proof	54,000	Value: 0.40				
1986D	36,400,000	—	—	—	0.10	—
1986D Proof	44,000	Value: 0.40				
1986F	42,000,000	—	—	—	0.10	—
1986F Proof	44,000	Value: 0.40				
1986G	24,200,000	—	—	—	0.10	—
1986G Proof	44,000	Value: 0.40				
1986J	37,400,000	—	—	—	0.10	—
1986J Proof	44,000	Value: 0.40				
1987D	52,000,000	—	—	—	0.10	—
1987D Proof	45,000	Value: 0.40				
1987F	60,000,000	—	—	—	0.10	—
1987F Proof	45,000	Value: 0.40				
1987G	34,600,000	—	—	—	0.10	—
1987G Proof	45,000	Value: 0.40				
1987J	53,400,000	—	—	—	0.10	—
1987J Proof	45,000	Value: 0.40				
1988D	52,400,000	—	—	—	0.10	—
1988D Proof	45,000	Value: 0.40				
1988F	72,000,000	—	—	—	0.10	—
1988F Proof	45,000	Value: 0.40				
1988G	41,500,000	—	—	—	0.10	—
1988G Proof	45,000	Value: 0.40				
1988J	64,099,999	—	—	—	0.10	—
1988J Proof	45,000	Value: 0.40				
1989D	93,600,000	—	—	—	0.10	—
1989D Proof	45,000	Value: 0.40				
1989F	108,000,000	—	—	—	0.10	—
1989F Proof	45,000	Value: 0.40				
1989G	62,280,000	—	—	—	0.10	—
1989G Proof	45,000	Value: 0.40				
1989J	96,120,000	—	—	—	0.10	—
1989J Proof	45,000	Value: 0.40				
1990A	70,000,000	—	—	—	0.10	—
1990D	93,600,000	—	—	—	0.10	—
1990D Proof	45,000	Value: 0.40				
1990F	108,000,000	—	—	—	0.10	—
1990F Proof	45,000	Value: 0.40				
1990G	62,280,000	—	—	—	0.10	—
1990G Proof	45,000	Value: 0.40				
1990J	96,120,000	—	—	—	0.10	—
1990J Proof	45,000	Value: 0.40				
1991A	128,000,000	—	—	—	0.10	—
1991A Proof	45,000	Value: 0.40				
1991D	134,400,000	—	—	—	0.10	—
1991D Proof	45,000	Value: 0.40				
1991F	153,600,000	—	—	—	0.10	—
1991F Proof	45,000	Value: 0.40				
1991G	89,600,000	—	—	—	0.10	—
1991G Proof	45,000	Value: 0.40				
1991J	134,400,000	—	—	—	0.10	—
1991J Proof	45,000	Value: 0.40				
1992A	28,000,000	—	—	—	0.10	—
1992A Proof	45,000	Value: 0.40				
1992D	29,400,000	—	—	—	0.10	—
1992D Proof	45,000	Value: 0.40				
1992F	33,600,000	—	—	—	0.10	—
1992F Proof	45,000	Value: 0.40				
1992G	19,600,000	—	—	—	0.10	—
1992G Proof	45,000	Value: 0.40				
1992J	29,400,000	—	—	—	0.10	—
1992J Proof	45,000	Value: 0.40				
1993A	36,000,000	—	—	—	0.10	—
1993A Proof	45,000	Value: 0.40				
1993D	37,800,000	—	—	—	0.10	—
1993D Proof	45,000	Value: 0.40				
1993F	43,200,000	—	—	—	0.10	—
1993F Proof	45,000	Value: 0.40				
1993G	25,200,000	—	—	—	0.10	—

Date	Mintage	F	VF	XF	Unc	BU
1993G Proof	45,000	Value: 0.40				
1993J	37,800,000	—	—	—	0.10	—
1993J Proof	45,000	Value: 0.40				
1994A	38,000,000	—	—	—	0.10	—
1994A Proof	45,000	Value: 0.40				
1994D	39,900,000	—	—	—	0.10	—
1994D Proof	45,000	Value: 0.40				
1994F	45,600,000	—	—	—	0.10	—
1994F Proof	45,000	Value: 0.40				
1994G	26,600,000	—	—	—	0.10	—
1994G Proof	45,000	Value: 0.40				
1994J	39,900,000	—	—	—	0.10	—
1994J Proof	45,000	Value: 0.40				
1995A	48,000,000	—	—	—	0.15	—
1995A Proof	45,000	Value: 0.45				
1995D	50,400,000	—	—	—	0.15	—
1995D Proof	45,000	Value: 0.45				
1995F	57,600,000	—	—	—	0.15	—
1995F Proof	45,000	Value: 0.45				
1995G	33,600,000	—	—	—	0.15	—
1995G Proof	45,000	Value: 0.45				
1995J	50,400,000	—	—	—	0.15	—
1995J Proof	45,000	Value: 0.45				
1996A	48,000,000	—	—	—	0.20	—
1996A Proof	45,000	Value: 0.50				
1996D	50,400,000	—	—	—	0.20	—
1996D Proof	45,000	Value: 0.50				
1996F	57,600,000	—	—	—	0.20	—
1996F Proof	45,000	Value: 0.50				
1996G	33,600,000	—	—	—	0.20	—
1996G Proof	45,000	Value: 0.50				
1996J	50,400,000	—	—	—	0.20	—
1996J Proof	45,000	Value: 0.50				
1997A In sets only	70,000	—	—	—	1.75	—
1997A Proof	45,000	Value: 2.00				
1997D In sets only	70,000	—	—	—	1.75	—
1997D Proof	45,000	Value: 2.00				
1997F In sets only	70,000	—	—	—	1.75	—
1997F Proof	45,000	Value: 2.00				
1997G In sets only	70,000	—	—	—	1.75	—
1997G Proof	45,000	Value: 2.00				
1997J In sets only	70,000	—	—	—	1.75	—
1997J Proof	45,000	Value: 2.00				
1998A In sets only	70,000	—	—	—	1.75	—
1998A Proof	45,000	Value: 2.00				
1998D In sets only	70,000	—	—	—	1.75	—
1998D Proof	45,000	Value: 2.00				
1998F In sets only	70,000	—	—	—	1.75	—
1998F Proof	45,000	Value: 2.00				
1998G In sets only	70,000	—	—	—	1.75	—
1998G Proof	45,000	Value: 2.00				
1998J In sets only	70,000	—	—	—	1.75	—
1998J Proof	45,000	Value: 2.00				
1999A In sets only	70,000	—	—	—	1.75	—
1999A Proof	45,000	Value: 2.00				
1999D In sets only	70,000	—	—	—	1.75	—
1999D Proof	45,000	Value: 2.00				
1999F In sets only	70,000	—	—	—	1.75	—
1999F Proof	45,000	Value: 2.00				
1999G In sets only	70,000	—	—	—	1.75	—
1999G Proof	45,000	Value: 2.00				
1999J In sets only	70,000	—	—	—	1.75	—
1999J Proof	45,000	Value: 2.00				
2000A In sets only	45,000	—	—	—	1.75	—
2000A Proof	70,000	Value: 2.00				
2000D In sets only	45,000	—	—	—	1.75	—
2000D Proof	70,000	Value: 2.00				
2000F In sets only	45,000	—	—	—	1.75	—
2000F Proof	70,000	Value: 2.00				
2000G In sets only	45,000	—	—	—	1.75	—
2000G Proof	70,000	Value: 2.00				
2000J In sets only	45,000	—	—	—	1.75	—
2000J Proof	70,000	Value: 2.00				
2001A In sets only	130,000	—	—	—	5.00	—
2001A Proof	78,000	Value: 5.00				
2001D In sets only	130,000	—	—	—	5.00	—
2001D Proof	78,000	Value: 5.00				
2001F In sets only	130,000	—	—	—	5.00	—
2001F Proof	78,000	Value: 5.00				
2001G In sets only	130,000	—	—	—	5.00	—
2001G Proof	78,000	Value: 5.00				
2001J In sets only	130,000	—	—	—	5.00	—
2001J Proof	78,000	Value: 5.00				

KM# 103 10 PFENNIG **Composition:** Brass Clad Steel
Note: Currency Reform.

Date	Mintage	F	VF	XF	Unc	BU
1949D	140,558,000	—	0.50	7.50	30.00	—
1949D Proof	—	Value: 150				
1949F	120,932,000	—	0.50	7.50	30.00	—
1949F Proof	250	Value: 140				
1949G	82,933,000	—	1.00	7.50	40.00	—
1949J Large J	154,095,000	—	0.50	7.50	30.00	—

Date	Mintage	F	VF	XF	Unc	BU
1949J Proof	—	Value: 60.00				
1949J Small J	Inc. above	—	0.50	7.50	30.00	—
1949J Proof	—	Value: 60.00				

KM# 108 10 PFENNIG **Composition:** Brass Plated Steel **Note:** Federal Republic.

Date	Mintage	F	VF	XF	Unc	BU
1950D	393,209,000	—	—	0.20	4.00	—
1950F	584,340,000	—	—	0.20	4.00	—
1950F Proof	500	Value: 45.00				
1950G	309,045,000	—	—	0.20	4.00	—
1950G Proof	1,800	Value: 5.00				
1950J	402,452,000	—	—	0.20	4.00	—
1950J Proof	—	Value: 20.00				
1966D	31,220,000	—	—	0.20	4.00	—
1966F	36,097,000	—	—	0.20	4.00	—
1966F Proof	100	Value: 75.00				
1966G	25,338,000	—	—	0.20	4.00	—
1966G Proof	3,070	Value: 7.50				
1966J	32,116,000	—	—	0.20	4.00	—
1966J Proof	1,000	Value: 12.50				
1967D	15,632,000	—	—	0.20	5.00	—
1967F	18,049,000	—	—	0.20	5.00	—
1967F Proof	1,500	Value: 15.00				
1967G	1,518,000	—	2.00	6.00	20.00	—
1967G Proof	4,500	Value: 7.50				
1967J	16,050,999	—	—	0.20	5.00	—
1967J Proof	1,500	Value: 12.50				
1968D	5,207,000	—	—	0.20	3.50	—
1968F	6,010,000	—	—	0.20	3.50	—
1968F Proof	3,000	Value: 10.00				
1968G	12,384,000	—	0.15	0.50	3.50	—
Note: Error exists without reeding						
1968G Proof	6,023	Value: 5.00				
1968J	5,422,000	—	—	0.20	4.00	—
1968J Proof	2,000	Value: 10.00				
1969D	41,693,000	—	—	0.15	2.50	—
1969F	48,084,000	—	—	0.15	0.25	—
1969F Proof	5,000	Value: 3.00				
1969G	48,760,000	—	—	0.15	0.25	—
1969G Proof	8,700	Value: 2.50				
1969J	42,756,000	—	—	0.15	0.25	—
1969J Proof	5,000	Value: 2.50				
1970D	54,085,000	—	—	0.15	0.25	—
1970F	60,086,000	—	—	0.15	0.25	—
1970F Proof	5,140	Value: 3.00				
1970G	35,900,000	—	—	0.15	0.25	—
1970G Proof	10,200	Value: 2.00				
1970J	40,115,000	—	—	0.15	0.25	—
1970J Proof	5,000	Value: 2.50				
1971D	54,022,000	—	—	0.15	0.25	—
1971D Proof	8,000	Value: 2.50				
1971F	92,534,000	—	—	0.15	0.25	—
1971F Proof	8,000	Value: 2.50				
1971G	88,614,000	—	—	0.15	0.25	—
1971G Proof	10,000	Value: 2.00				
1971 Small J	65,622,000	—	—	0.15	0.25	—
1971 Large J	Inc. above	—	—	0.15	0.25	—
1971J Proof	8,000	Value: 1.50				
1972D	104,345,000	—	—	0.15	0.25	—
1972D Proof	8,000	Value: 1.50				
1972F	110,177,000	—	—	0.15	0.25	—
1972F Proof	8,000	Value: 1.50				
1972G	71,766,000	—	—	0.15	0.25	—
1972G Proof	10,000	Value: 1.50				
1972J	96,991,000	—	—	0.15	0.25	—
1972J Proof	8,000	Value: 1.50				
1973D	26,052,000	—	—	0.15	0.25	—
1973D Proof	9,000	Value: 1.50				
1973F	30,070,000	—	—	0.15	0.25	—
1973F Proof	9,000	Value: 1.50				
1973G	17,294,000	—	—	0.15	0.25	—
1973G Proof	9,000	Value: 1.50				
1973J	26,774,000	—	—	0.15	0.25	—
1973J Proof	9,000	Value: 1.50				
1974D	15,707,000	—	—	0.15	0.25	—
1974D Proof	35,000	Value: 0.75				
1974F	18,135,000	—	—	0.15	0.25	—
1974F Proof	35,000	Value: 0.75				
1974G	10,450,000	—	—	0.15	0.25	—
1974G Proof	35,000	Value: 0.75				
1974J	16,056,000	—	—	0.15	0.25	—
1974J Proof	35,000	Value: 0.75				
1975D	15,654,000	—	—	0.15	0.25	—
1975D Proof	43,000	Value: 0.75				
1975F	18,043,000	—	—	0.15	0.25	—
1975F Proof	43,000	Value: 0.75				
1975G	10,403,000	—	—	0.15	0.25	—
1975G Proof	43,000	Value: 0.75				
1975J	16,111,000	—	—	0.15	0.25	—
1975J Proof	43,000	Value: 0.75				
1976D	65,200,000	—	—	0.15	0.25	—
1976D Proof	43,000	Value: 0.75				
1976F	75,282,000	—	—	0.15	0.25	—
1976F Proof	43,000	Value: 0.75				
1976G	43,372,000	—	—	0.15	0.25	—
1976G Proof	43,000	Value: 0.75				
1976J	66,930,000	—	—	0.15	0.25	—
1976J Proof	43,000	Value: 0.75				
1977D	64,989,000	—	—	0.10	0.20	—
1977D Proof	51,000	Value: 0.50				
1977F	75,052,000	—	—	0.10	0.20	—
1977F Proof	51,000	Value: 0.50				
1977G	43,300,000	—	—	0.10	0.20	—
1977G Proof	51,000	Value: 0.50				
1977J	66,800,000	—	—	0.10	0.20	—
1977J Proof	51,000	Value: 0.50				
1978D	91,000,000	—	—	0.10	0.20	—
1978D Proof	54,000	Value: 0.50				
1978F	105,000,000	—	—	0.10	0.20	—
1978F Proof	54,000	Value: 0.50				
1978G	60,590,000	—	—	0.10	0.20	—
1978G Proof	54,000	Value: 0.50				
1978J	93,490,000	—	—	0.10	0.20	—
1978J Proof	54,000	Value: 0.50				
1979D	104,000,000	—	—	0.10	0.20	—
1979D Proof	89,000	Value: 0.50				
1979F	120,000,000	—	—	0.10	0.20	—
1979F Proof	89,000	Value: 0.50				
1979G	69,200,000	—	—	0.10	0.20	—
1979G Proof	89,000	Value: 0.50				
1979J	106,800,000	—	—	0.10	0.20	—
1979J Proof	89,000	Value: 0.50				
1980D	65,450,000	—	—	0.10	0.20	—
1980D Proof	110,000	Value: 0.50				
1980F	122,780,000	—	—	0.10	0.20	—
1980F Proof	110,000	Value: 0.50				
1980G	75,410,000	—	—	0.10	0.20	—
1980G Proof	110,000	Value: 0.50				
1980J	70,960,000	—	—	0.10	0.20	—
1980J Proof	110,000	Value: 0.50				
1981D	135,200,000	—	—	0.10	0.20	—
1981D Proof	91,000	Value: 0.50				
1981F	117,410,000	—	—	0.10	0.20	—
1981F Proof	91,000	Value: 0.50				
1981G	69,440,000	—	—	0.10	0.20	—
1981G Proof	91,000	Value: 0.50				
1981J	138,360,000	—	—	0.10	0.20	—
1981J Proof	91,000	Value: 0.50				
1982D	74,690,000	—	—	0.10	0.20	—
1982D Proof	78,000	Value: 0.50				
1982F	85,140,000	—	—	0.10	0.20	—
1982F Proof	78,000	Value: 0.50				
1982G	50,840,000	—	—	0.10	0.20	—
1982G Proof	78,000	Value: 0.50				
1982J	80,620,000	—	—	0.10	0.20	—
1982J Proof	78,000	Value: 0.50				
1983D	33,800,000	—	—	0.10	0.20	—
1983D Proof	75,000	Value: 0.50				
1983F	39,000,000	—	—	0.10	0.20	—
1983F Proof	75,000	Value: 0.50				
1983G	22,490,000	—	—	0.10	0.20	—
1983G Proof	75,000	Value: 0.50				
1983J	34,710,000	—	—	0.10	0.20	—
1983J Proof	75,000	Value: 0.50				
1984D	52,000,000	—	—	0.10	0.20	—
1984D Proof	64,000	Value: 0.50				
1984F	60,000,000	—	—	0.10	0.20	—
1984G Proof	64,000	Value: 0.50				
1984G	34,600,000	—	—	0.10	0.20	—
1984G Proof	64,000	Value: 0.50				
1984J	53,400,000	—	—	0.10	0.20	—
1984J Proof	64,000	Value: 0.50				
1985D	78,000,000	—	—	—	0.15	—
1985D Proof	56,000	Value: 0.50				
1985F	90,000,000	—	—	—	0.15	—
1985F Proof	54,000	Value: 0.50				
1985G	51,900,000	—	—	—	0.15	—
1985G Proof	55,000	Value: 0.50				
1985J	80,100,000	—	—	—	0.15	—
1985J Proof	54,000	Value: 0.50				
1986D	41,600,000	—	—	—	0.15	—
1986D Proof	44,000	Value: 0.50				
1986F	48,000,000	—	—	—	0.15	—
1986F Proof	44,000	Value: 0.50				
1986G	27,700,000	—	—	—	0.15	—
1986G Proof	44,000	Value: 0.50				
1986J	42,700,000	—	—	—	0.15	—
1986J Proof	44,000	Value: 0.15				
1987D	58,500,000	—	—	—	0.10	—
1987D Proof	45,000	Value: 0.15				
1987F	67,500,000	—	—	—	0.10	—
1987F Proof	45,000	Value: 0.15				
1987G	38,900,000	—	—	—	0.10	—
1987G Proof	45,000	Value: 0.50				
1987J	60,100,000	—	—	—	0.15	—
1987J Proof	45,000	Value: 0.50				
1988D	109,200,000	—	—	—	0.15	—
1988D Proof	45,000	Value: 0.50				
1988F	126,000,000	—	—	—	0.15	—
1988F Proof	45,000	Value: 0.50				
1988G	72,700,000	—	—	—	0.15	—
1988G Proof	45,000	Value: 0.50				
1988J	112,100,000	—	—	—	0.15	—
1988J Proof	45,000	Value: 0.50				
1989D	119,600,000	—	—	—	0.15	—
1989D Proof	45,000	Value: 0.50				
1989F	138,000,000	—	—	—	0.15	—
1989F Proof	45,000	Value: 0.50				
1989G	79,580,000	—	—	—	0.15	—
1989G Proof	45,000	Value: 0.50				
1989J	122,820,000	—	—	—	0.15	—
1989J Proof	45,000	Value: 0.50				
1990A	100,000,000	—	—	—	0.15	—
1990D	156,000,000	—	—	—	0.15	—
1990D Proof	45,000	Value: 0.50				
1990F	180,000,000	—	—	—	0.15	—
1990F Proof	45,000	Value: 0.50				
1990G	103,800,000	—	—	—	0.15	—
1990G Proof	45,000	Value: 0.50				
1990J	160,200,000	—	—	—	0.15	—
1990J Proof	45,000	Value: 0.50				
1991A	170,000,000	—	—	—	0.15	—
1991A Proof	45,000	Value: 0.40				
1991D	178,550,000	—	—	—	0.15	—
1991D Proof	45,000	Value: 0.40				
1991F	204,000,000	—	—	—	0.15	—
1991F Proof	45,000	Value: 0.40				
1991G	119,000,000	—	—	—	0.15	—
1991G Proof	45,000	Value: 0.40				
1991J	178,500,000	—	—	—	0.15	—
1991J Proof	45,000	Value: 0.40				
1992A	80,000,000	—	—	—	0.10	—
1992A Proof	45,000	Value: 0.40				
1992D	84,000,000	—	—	—	0.10	—
1992D Proof	45,000	Value: 0.40				
1992F	96,000,000	—	—	—	0.10	—
1992F Proof	45,000	Value: 0.40				
1992G	56,000,000	—	—	—	0.10	—
1992G Proof	45,000	Value: 0.40				
1992J	84,000,000	—	—	—	0.10	—
1992J Proof	45,000	Value: 0.40				
1993A	80,000,000	—	—	—	0.10	—
1993A Proof	45,000	Value: 0.40				
1993D	84,000,000	—	—	—	0.10	—
1993D Proof	45,000	Value: 0.40				
1993F	96,000,000	—	—	—	0.10	—
1993F Proof	45,000	Value: 0.40				
1993G	56,000,000	—	—	—	0.10	—
1993G Proof	45,000	Value: 0.40				
1993J	84,000,000	—	—	—	0.10	—
1993J Proof	45,000	Value: 0.40				
1994A	100,000,000	—	—	—	0.10	—
1994A Proof	45,000	Value: 0.40				
1994D	105,000,000	—	—	—	0.10	—
1994D Proof	45,000	Value: 0.40				
1994F	120,000,000	—	—	—	0.10	—
1994F Proof	45,000	Value: 0.40				
1994G	70,000,000	—	—	—	0.10	—
1994G Proof	45,000	Value: 0.40				
1994J	105,000,000	—	—	—	0.10	—
1994J Proof	45,000	Value: 0.40				
1995A	110,000,000	—	—	—	0.15	—
1995A Proof	45,000	Value: 0.45				
1995D	115,000,000	—	—	—	0.15	—
1995D Proof	45,000	Value: 0.45				
1995F	132,000,000	—	—	—	0.15	—
1995F Proof	45,000	Value: 0.45				
1995G	77,000,000	—	—	—	0.15	—
1995G Proof	45,000	Value: 0.45				
1995J	115,500,000	—	—	—	0.15	—
1995J Proof	45,000	Value: 0.45				
1996A	90,000,000	—	—	—	0.20	—
1996A Proof	45,000	Value: 0.50				
1996D	94,500,000	—	—	—	0.20	—
1996D Proof	45,000	Value: 0.50				
1996F	108,000,000	—	—	—	0.20	—
1996F Proof	45,000	Value: 0.50				
1996G	63,000,000	—	—	—	0.20	—
1996G Proof	45,000	Value: 0.50				
1996J	94,500,000	—	—	—	0.20	—
1996J Proof	45,000	Value: 0.50				
1997A In sets only	70,000	—	—	—	1.75	—
1997A Proof	45,000	Value: 2.00				
1997D In sets only	70,000	—	—	—	1.75	—
1997D Proof	45,000	Value: 2.00				
1997F In sets only	70,000	—	—	—	1.75	—
1997F Proof	45,000	Value: 2.00				
1997G In sets only	70,000	—	—	—	1.75	—
1997G Proof	45,000	Value: 2.00				
1997J In sets only	70,000	—	—	—	1.75	—
1997J Proof	45,000	Value: 2.00				
1998A	—	—	—	—	1.75	—
1998A Proof	—	Value: 2.00				
1998D	—	—	—	—	1.75	—
1998D Proof	—	Value: 2.00				
1998F In sets only	70,000	—	—	—	1.75	—
1998F Proof	45,000	Value: 2.00				
1998G	—	—	—	—	1.75	—
1998G Proof	—	Value: 2.00				
1998J	—	—	—	—	1.75	—
1998J Proof	—	Value: 2.00				
1999A	—	—	—	—	1.75	—
1999A Proof	—	Value: 2.00				
1999D	—	—	—	—	1.75	—
1999D Proof	—	Value: 2.00				
1999F In sets only	70,000	—	—	—	1.75	—

Date	Mintage	F	VF	XF	Unc	BU
1999F Proof	45,000	Value: 2.00				
1999G	—	—	—	—	1.75	—
1999G Proof	—	Value: 2.00				
1999J	—	—	—	—	1.75	—
1999J Proof	—	Value: 2.00				
2000A In sets only	70,000	—	—	—	1.75	—
2000A Proof	45,000	Value: 2.00				
2000D In sets only	70,000	—	—	—	1.75	—
2000D Proof	45,000	Value: 2.00				
2000F In sets only	70,000	—	—	—	1.75	—
2000F Proof	45,000	Value: 2.00				
2000G In sets only	70,000	—	—	—	1.75	—
2000G Proof	45,000	Value: 2.00				
2000J In sets only	70,000	—	—	—	1.75	—
2000J Proof	45,000	Value: 2.00				
2001A In sets only	130,000	—	—	—	5.00	—
2001A Proof	78,000	Value: 5.00				
2001D In sets only	130,000	—	—	—	5.00	—
2001D Proof	78,000	Value: 5.00				
2001F In sets only	130,000	—	—	—	5.00	—
2001F Proof	78,000	Value: 5.00				
2001G In sets only	130,000	—	—	—	5.00	—
2001G Proof	78,000	Value: 5.00				
2001J In sets only	130,000	—	—	—	5.00	—
2001J Proof	78,000	Value: 5.00				

KM# 104 50 PFENNIG **Composition:** Copper-Nickel
Note: Currency Reform.

Date	Mintage	F	VF	XF	Unc	BU
1949D	39,108,000	—	0.75	4.50	45.00	—
1949F	45,118,000	—	0.75	4.50	45.00	—
1949F Proof	200	Value: 125				
1949G	25,924,000	—	0.75	5.00	55.00	—
1949J	42,303,000	—	0.75	4.50	55.00	—
1949J Proof	—	Value: 135				
1950G	30,000	—	250	400	700	—

Note: The 1950G dated coin was restruck without authorization by a mint official using genuine dies - quantity unknown

KM# 109.1 50 PFENNIG **Composition:** Copper-Nickel
Edge: Reeded **Note:** Federal Republic

Date	Mintage	F	VF	XF	Unc	BU
1950D	100,735,000	—	0.50	0.75	9.00	—
1950F	143,510,000	—	0.50	0.75	9.00	—
1950F Proof	450	Value: 85.00				
1950G	66,421,000	—	0.50	0.75	10.00	—
1950G Proof	1,800	Value: 5.00				
1950J	102,736,000	—	0.50	0.75	9.00	—
1950J Proof	—	Value: 25.00				
1966D	8,327,999	—	0.50	0.75	15.00	—
1966F	9,605,000	—	0.50	0.75	15.00	—
1966F Proof	100	Value: 125				
1966G	5,543,000	—	0.50	0.65	15.00	—
1966G Proof	3,070	Value: 10.00				
1966J	8,569,000	—	0.50	0.65	15.00	—
1966J Proof	1,000	Value: 20.00				
1967D	5,207,000	—	0.50	0.65	15.00	—
1967F	6,005,000	—	0.50	0.65	15.00	—
1967F Proof	1,500	Value: 18.00				
1967G	1,843,000	—	0.50	1.00	18.00	—
1967G Proof	4,500	Value: 15.00				
1967J	10,684,000	—	0.50	0.65	15.00	—
1967J Proof	1,500	Value: 18.00				
1968D	7,809,000	—	0.50	0.60	12.00	—
1968F	3,000,000	—	0.50	0.60	12.00	—
1968F Proof	3,000	Value: 15.00				
1968G	6,818,000	—	0.50	0.60	12.00	—
1968G Proof	6,023	Value: 8.00				
1968J	2,672,000	—	0.50	0.65	17.50	—
1968J Proof	2,000	Value: 15.00				
1969D	14,561,000	—	0.45	0.55	2.50	—
1969F	16,804,000	—	0.45	0.55	2.50	—
1969F Proof	5,000	Value: 4.00				
1969G	9,704,000	—	0.45	0.55	2.50	—
1969G Proof	8,700	Value: 3.50				
1969J	14,969,000	—	0.45	0.55	2.50	—
1969J Proof	5,000	Value: 10.00				
1970D	25,294,000	—	0.45	0.55	1.00	—
1970F	26,455,000	—	0.45	0.55	1.00	—
1970F Proof	5,140	Value: 3.50				
1970G	11,955,000	—	0.45	0.55	1.00	—
1970G Proof	10,200	Value: 3.00				
1970J	10,683,000	—	0.45	0.55	1.00	—
1970J Proof	5,000	Value: 3.50				
1971D	23,393,000	—	0.45	0.55	0.75	—
1971D Proof	8,000	Value: 3.00				
1971F	29,746,000	—	0.45	0.55	0.75	—
1971F Proof	8,000	Value: 3.00				
1971G	15,556,000	—	0.45	0.55	0.75	—
1971G Proof	10,000	Value: 3.00				
1971 Large J	24,044,000	—	0.45	0.55	0.75	—
1971 Small J	Inc. above	—	0.45	0.55	0.75	—
1971J Proof	8,000	Value: 3.00				

KM# 109.2 50 PFENNIG **Composition:** Copper-Nickel
Edge: Plain **Note:** Counterfeits of 1972 dated coins with reeded edges exisit.

Date	Mintage	F	VF	XF	Unc	BU
1972D	—	—	—	0.45	0.60	—
1972D Proof	8,000	Value: 2.00				
1972F	—	—	—	0.45	0.60	—
1972F Proof	8,000	Value: 2.00				
1972G	—	—	—	0.45	0.60	—
1972G Proof	10,000	Value: 2.00				
1972J	—	—	—	0.45	0.60	—
1972J Proof	8,000	Value: 2.00				
1973D	—	—	—	0.45	1.00	—
1973D Proof	9,000	Value: 2.00				
1973F	—	—	—	0.45	0.60	—
1973F Proof	9,000	Value: 2.00				
1973G	—	—	—	0.45	0.60	—
1973G Proof	9,000	Value: 2.00				
1973J	—	—	—	0.45	0.60	—
1973J Proof	9,000	Value: 2.00				
1974D	—	—	—	0.45	1.00	—
1974D Proof	35,000	Value: 1.00				
1974 Large F	—	—	—	0.45	0.60	—
1974 Small F	—	—	—	0.45	1.00	—
1974F Proof	35,000	Value: 1.00				
1974G	—	—	—	0.45	0.60	—
1974G Proof	35,000	Value: 1.00				
1974J	—	—	—	0.45	0.60	—
1974J Proof	35,000	Value: 1.00				
1975D	—	—	—	0.45	1.00	—
1975D Proof	43,000	Value: 1.00				
1975F	—	—	—	0.45	0.60	—
1975F Proof	43,000	Value: 1.00				
1975G	—	—	—	0.45	0.60	—
1975G Proof	43,000	Value: 1.00				
1975J	—	—	—	0.45	0.60	—
1975J Proof	43,000	Value: 1.00				
1976D	—	—	—	0.45	1.00	—
1976D Proof	43,000	Value: 1.00				
1976F	—	—	—	0.45	0.60	—
1976F Proof	43,000	Value: 1.00				
1976G	—	—	—	0.45	0.60	—
1976G Proof	43,000	Value: 1.00				
1976J	—	—	—	0.45	0.60	—
1976J Proof	43,000	Value: 1.00				
1977D	—	—	—	0.45	1.00	—
1977D Proof	51,000	Value: 0.75				
1977F	—	—	—	0.45	0.60	—
1977F Proof	51,000	Value: 0.75				
1977G	—	—	—	0.45	0.60	—
1977G Proof	51,000	Value: 0.75				
1977J	—	—	—	0.45	0.60	—
1977J Proof	51,000	Value: 0.75				
1978D	—	—	—	0.45	0.60	—
1978D Proof	54,000	Value: 0.75				
1978F	—	—	—	0.45	0.60	—
1978F Proof	54,000	Value: 0.75				
1978G	—	—	—	0.45	0.60	—
1978G Proof	54,000	Value: 0.75				
1978J	—	—	—	0.45	0.60	—
1978J Proof	54,000	Value: 0.75				
1979D	—	—	—	0.45	0.60	—
1979D Proof	89,000	Value: 0.75				
1979F	—	—	—	0.45	0.60	—
1979F Proof	89,000	Value: 0.75				
1979G	—	—	—	0.45	0.60	—
1979G Proof	89,000	Value: 0.75				
1979J	—	—	—	0.45	0.60	—
1979J Proof	89,000	Value: 0.75				
1980D	—	—	—	0.45	0.60	—
1980D Proof	110,000	Value: 0.75				
1980F	—	—	—	0.45	0.60	—
1980F Proof	110,000	Value: 0.75				
1980G	—	—	—	0.45	0.60	—
1980G Proof	110,000	Value: 0.75				
1980J	—	—	—	0.45	0.60	—
1980J Proof	110,000	Value: 0.75				
1981D	—	—	—	0.45	0.60	—
1981D Proof	91,000	Value: 0.75				
1981F	—	—	—	0.45	0.60	—
1981F Proof	91,000	Value: 0.75				
1981G	—	—	—	0.45	0.60	—
1981G Proof	91,000	Value: 0.75				
1981J	—	—	—	0.45	0.60	—
1981J Proof	91,000	Value: 0.75				
1982D	—	—	—	0.45	0.60	—
1982D Proof	78,000	Value: 0.75				
1982F	—	—	—	0.45	0.60	—
1982F Proof	78,000	Value: 0.75				
1982G	—	—	—	0.45	0.60	—
1982G Proof	78,000	Value: 0.75				
1982J	—	—	—	0.45	0.60	—
1982J Proof	78,000	Value: 0.75				
1983D	—	—	—	0.45	0.60	—
1983D Proof	75,000	Value: 0.75				
1983F	—	—	—	0.45	0.60	—
1983F Proof	75,000	Value: 0.75				
1983G	—	—	—	0.45	0.60	—
1983G Proof	75,000	Value: 0.75				
1983J	—	—	—	0.45	0.60	—
1983J Proof	75,000	Value: 0.75				
1984D	—	—	—	0.45	0.60	—
1984D Proof	64,000	Value: 0.75				
1984F	—	—	—	0.45	0.60	—
1984F Proof	64,000	Value: 0.75				
1984G	—	—	—	0.45	0.60	—
1984G Proof	64,000	Value: 0.75				
1984J	—	—	—	0.45	0.60	—
1984J Proof	64,000	Value: 0.75				
1985D	—	—	—	—	0.50	—
1985D Proof	56,000	Value: 0.75				
1985F	—	—	—	—	0.50	—
1985F Proof	54,000	Value: 0.75				
1985G	—	—	—	—	0.50	—
1985G Proof	55,000	Value: 0.75				
1985J	—	—	—	—	0.50	—
1985J Proof	54,000	Value: 0.75				
1986D	—	—	—	—	0.50	—
1986D Proof	44,000	Value: 0.75				
1986F	—	—	—	—	0.50	—
1986F Proof	44,000	Value: 0.75				
1986G	—	—	—	—	0.50	—
1986G Proof	44,000	Value: 0.75				
1986J	—	—	—	—	0.50	—
1986J Proof	44,000	Value: 0.75				
1987D	—	—	2.50	6.50	13.50	—
1987D Proof	45,000	Value: 0.75				
1987F	—	—	2.50	5.00	10.00	—
1987F Proof	45,000	Value: 0.75				
1987G	—	—	4.50	13.50	28.00	—
1987G Proof	45,000	Value: 0.75				
1987J	—	—	2.50	5.00	10.00	—
1987J Proof	45,000	Value: 0.75				
1988D	—	—	—	—	0.50	—
1988D Proof	45,000	Value: 0.75				
1988F	—	—	—	—	0.50	—
1988F Proof	45,000	Value: 0.75				
1988G	—	—	—	—	0.50	—
1988G Proof	45,000	Value: 0.75				
1988J	—	—	—	—	0.50	—
1988J Proof	45,000	Value: 0.75				
1989D	—	—	—	—	0.50	—
1989D Proof	45,000	Value: 0.75				
1989F	—	—	—	—	0.50	—
1989F Proof	45,000	Value: 0.75				
1989G	—	—	—	—	0.50	—
1989G Proof	45,000	Value: 0.75				
1989J	—	—	—	—	0.50	—
1989J Proof	45,000	Value: 0.75				
1990A	—	—	—	—	1.00	—
1990D	—	—	—	—	0.50	—
1990D Proof	45,000	Value: 0.75				
1990F	—	—	—	—	0.50	—
1990F Proof	45,000	Value: 0.75				
1990G	—	—	—	—	0.50	—
1990G Proof	45,000	Value: 0.75				
1990J	—	—	—	—	0.50	—
1990J Proof	45,000	Value: 0.75				
1991A	—	—	—	—	0.50	—
1991A Proof	45,000	Value: 0.75				
1991D	—	—	—	—	0.50	—
1991D Proof	45,000	Value: 0.75				
1991F	—	—	—	—	0.50	—
1991F Proof	45,000	Value: 0.75				
1991G	—	—	—	—	0.50	—
1991G Proof	45,000	Value: 0.75				
1991J	—	—	—	—	0.50	—
1991J Proof	45,000	Value: 0.75				
1992A	—	—	—	—	0.50	—
1992A Proof	45,000	Value: 0.75				
1992D	—	—	—	—	0.50	—
1992D Proof	45,000	Value: 0.75				
1992F	—	—	—	—	0.50	—
1992F Proof	45,000	Value: 0.75				
1992G	—	—	—	—	0.50	—
1992G Proof	45,000	Value: 0.75				
1992J	—	—	—	—	0.50	—
1992J Proof	45,000	Value: 0.75				
1993A	—	—	—	—	0.50	—
1993A Proof	45,000	Value: 0.75				
1993D	—	—	—	—	0.50	—
1993D Proof	45,000	Value: 0.75				
1993F	—	—	—	—	0.50	—
1993F Proof	45,000	Value: 0.75				
1993G	—	—	—	—	0.50	—
1993G Proof	45,000	Value: 0.75				
1993J	—	—	—	—	0.50	—
1993J Proof	45,000	Value: 0.75				

Date	Mintage	F	VF	XF	Unc	BU
1994A		—	—	—	0.50	—
1994A Proof	45,000	Value: 0.75				
1994D		—	—	—	2.00	—
1994D Proof	45,000	Value: 0.75				
1994F		—	—	—	0.50	—
1994F Proof	45,000	Value: 0.75				
1994G		—	—	—	0.50	—
1994G Proof	45,000	Value: 0.75				
1994J		—	—	—	0.50	—
1994J Proof	45,000	Value: 0.75				
1995A		—	—	—	2.25	—
1995A Proof	45,000	Value: 6.00				
1995D		—	—	—	2.25	—
1995D Proof	45,000	Value: 6.00				
1995F		—	—	—	90.00	—
1995F Proof	45,000	Value: 12.00				
1995G		—	—	—	100	—
1995G Proof	45,000	Value: 12.00				
1995J		—	—	—	12.00	—
1995J Proof	45,000	Value: 12.00				
1996A In sets only		—	—	—	12.00	—
1996A Proof	45,000	Value: 13.50				
1996D In sets only		—	—	—	12.00	—
1996D Proof	45,000	Value: 13.50				
1996F In sets only		—	—	—	12.00	—
1996F Proof	45,000	Value: 13.50				
1996G In sets only		—	—	—	12.00	—
1996G Proof	45,000	Value: 13.50				
1996J In sets only		—	—	—	12.00	—
1996J Proof	45,000	Value: 13.50				
1997A In sets only		—	—	—	4.75	—
1997A Proof	45,000	Value: 5.00				
1997D In sets only		—	—	—	4.75	—
1997D Proof	45,000	Value: 5.00				
1997F In sets only		—	—	—	4.75	—
1997F Proof	45,000	Value: 5.00				
1997G In sets only		—	—	—	4.75	—
1997G Proof	45,000	Value: 5.00				
1997J In sets only		—	—	—	4.75	—
1997J Proof	45,000	Value: 5.00				
1998A In sets only		—	—	—	4.75	—
1998A Proof	45,000	Value: 5.00				
1998D In sets only		—	—	—	4.75	—
1998D Proof	45,000	Value: 5.00				
1998F In sets only		—	—	—	4.75	—
1998F Proof	45,000	Value: 5.00				
1998G In sets only		—	—	—	4.75	—
1998G Proof	45,000	Value: 5.00				
1998J In sets only		—	—	—	4.75	—
1998J Proof	45,000	Value: 5.00				
1999A In sets only		—	—	—	4.75	—
1999A Proof	45,000	Value: 5.00				
1999D In sets only		—	—	—	4.75	—
1999D Proof	45,000	Value: 5.00				
1999F In sets only		—	—	—	4.75	—
1999F Proof	45,000	Value: 5.00				
1999G In sets only		—	—	—	4.75	—
1999G Proof	45,000	Value: 5.00				
1999J In sets only		—	—	—	4.75	—
1999J Proof	45,000	Value: 5.00				
2000A In sets only		—	—	—	5.00	—
2000A Proof	45,000	Value: 5.00				
2000D In sets only		—	—	—	5.00	—
2000D Proof	45,000	Value: 5.00				
2000F In sets only		—	—	—	5.00	—
2000F Proof	45,000	Value: 5.00				
2000G In sets only		—	—	—	5.00	—
2000G Proof	45,000	Value: 5.00				
2000J In sets only		—	—	—	5.00	—
2000J Proof	45,000	Value: 5.00				
2001A In sets only		—	—	—	10.00	—
2001A Proof	78,000	Value: 10.00				
2001D In sets only		—	—	—	10.00	—
2001D Proof	78,000	Value: 10.00				
2001F In sets only		—	—	—	10.00	—
2001F Proof	78,000	Value: 10.00				
2001G In sets only		—	—	—	10.00	—
2001G Proof	78,000	Value: 10.00				
2001J In sets only		—	—	—	10.00	—
2001J Proof	78,000	Value: 10.00				

KM# 110 MARK **Composition:** Copper-Nickel **Note:** Federal Republic.

Date	Mintage	F	VF	XF	Unc	BU
1950D		—	0.75	4.00	55.00	—
1950D Proof	—	Value: 200				
1950F		—	0.75	5.00	65.00	—
1950F Proof	150	Value: 450				
1950G		—	0.75	5.00	100	—
1950G Proof	Est. 200	Value: 375				
1950J		—	0.75	4.00	60.00	—
1950J Proof	—	Value: 200				
1954D		—	1.00	15.00	385	—
1954D Proof	—	Value: 925				
1954F		—	1.00	15.00	450	—
1954F Proof	175	Value: 800				
1954G		—	20.00	450	1,750	—
1954G Proof	15	Value: 2,250				
1954J		—	1.00	15.00	385	—
1954J Proof	—	Value: 1,000				
1955D		—	1.00	15.00	325	—
1955D Proof	—	Value: 1,000				
1955F		—	1.00	15.00	300	—
1955F Proof	Est. 20	Value: 900				
1955G		—	8.00	100	1,500	—
1955G Proof	—	Value: 2,750				
1955J		—	1.00	10.00	200	—
1955J Proof	—	Value: 450				
1956D		—	1.00	8.50	215	—
1956D Proof	—	Value: 525				
1956F		—	1.00	12.50	325	—
1956F Proof	100	Value: 475				
1956G		—	1.00	6.50	165	—
1956G Proof	—	Value: 325				
1956J		—	1.00	9.00	185	—
1956J Proof	—	Value: 1,000				
1957D		—	1.00	9.00	175	—
1957D Proof	100	Value: 450				
1957F		—	1.00	9.00	180	—
1957F Proof	100	Value: 475				
1957G		—	1.00	15.00	600	—
1957G Proof	27	Value: 1,650				
1957J		—	1.00	9.00	170	—
1957J Proof	200	Value: 325				
1958D		—	1.00	6.50	160	—
1958D Proof	200	Value: 350				
1958F		—	1.00	7.50	210	—
1958F Proof	100	Value: 575				
1958G		—	1.00	8.50	300	—
1958G Proof	20	Value: 2,100				
1958J		—	1.00	7.00	185	—
1958J Proof	37	Value: 1,150				
1959D		—	0.85	6.00	140	—
1959D Proof	40	Value: 850				
1959F		—	0.85	5.00	125	—
1959F Proof	100	Value: 525				
1959G		—	0.85	5.00	225	—
1959G Proof	20	Value: 2,100				
1959J		—	0.85	5.00	250	—
1959J Proof	25	Value: 1,800				
1960D		—	0.85	5.00	150	—
1960D Proof	100	Value: 475				
1960F		—	0.85	5.00	125	—
1960F Proof	100	Value: 475				
1960G		—	0.85	6.00	250	—
1960G Proof	100	Value: 500				
1960J		—	0.85	5.00	175	—
1960J Proof	36	Value: 1,150				
1961D		—	0.85	5.00	100	—
1961D Proof	60	Value: 650				
1961F		—	0.85	5.00	100	—
1961F Proof	50	Value: 700				
1961G		—	0.85	6.50	400	—
1961G Proof	70	Value: 600				
1961J		—	0.85	6.00	325	—
1961J Proof	28	Value: 1,200				
1962D		—	0.85	4.00	65.00	—
1962D Proof	40	Value: 600				
1962F		—	0.85	4.00	75.00	—
Note: Errors exist without reeding						
1962F Proof	45	Value: 550				
1962G		—	0.85	5.50	200	—
1962G Proof	100	Value: 450				
1962J		—	0.85	4.00	125	—
Note: Errors exist without reeding						
1962J Proof	28	Value: 1,200				
1963D		—	0.85	4.00	80.00	—
1963D Proof	40	Value: 600				
1963F		—	0.85	4.00	90.00	—
1963F Proof	45	Value: 550				
1963G		—	0.85	4.00	80.00	—
Note: Errors exist without reeding						
1963G Proof	200	Value: 300				
1963J		—	0.85	4.00	80.00	—
1963J Proof	28	Value: 1,200				
1964D		—	0.85	4.00	100	—
1964D Proof	30	Value: 1,000				
1964F		—	0.85	4.00	90.00	—
1964F Proof	25	Value: 1,900				
1964G		—	0.85	4.00	120	—
1964G Proof	368	Value: 145				
1964J		—	0.85	4.00	75.00	—
1964J Proof	33	Value: 900				
1965D		—	0.75	3.00	37.50	—
1965F		—	0.75	3.00	40.00	—
1965F Proof	Est. 80	Value: 175				
1965G		—	0.75	3.00	47.50	—
1965G Proof	1,200	Value: 65.00				
1965J		—	0.75	3.00	55.00	—
1966D		—	0.75	3.00	42.50	—
1966F		—	0.75	3.00	42.50	—
1966F Proof	100	Value: 150				
1966G		—	0.75	3.00	55.00	—
1966G Proof	3,070	Value: 35.00				
1966J		—	0.75	3.00	42.50	—
1966J Proof	1,000	Value: 65.00				
1967D		—	0.75	3.00	32.50	—
1967F		—	0.75	5.00	100	—
1967F Proof	1,500	Value: 65.00				
1967G		—	0.75	3.00	55.00	—
1967G Proof	4,500	Value: 50.00				
1967J		—	0.75	3.00	40.00	—
1967J Proof	1,500	Value: 65.00				
1968D		—	0.75	4.00	55.00	—
1968F		—	0.75	4.00	40.00	—
1968F Proof	3,000	Value: 35.00				
1968G		—	0.75	4.00	55.00	—
1968G Proof	6,023	Value: 15.00				
1968J		—	0.75	5.50	165	—
1968J Proof	2,000	Value: 75.00				
1969D		—	0.75	1.50	20.00	—
1969F		—	0.75	1.50	20.00	—
1969F Proof	5,000	Value: 15.00				
1969G		—	0.75	1.50	32.50	—
1969G Proof	8,700	Value: 12.50				
1969J		—	0.75	1.50	25.00	—
1969J Proof	5,000	Value: 15.00				
1970D		—	0.75	1.00	20.00	—
1970F		—	0.75	1.00	25.00	—
1970F Proof	5,140	Value: 15.00				
1970G		—	0.75	1.00	32.50	—
1970G Proof	10,200	Value: 9.00				
1970J		—	0.75	1.00	20.00	—
1970J Proof	5,000	Value: 15.00				
1971D		—	0.75	1.00	10.00	—
1971D Proof	8,000	Value: 8.00				
1971F		—	0.75	1.00	10.00	—
1971F Proof	8,000	Value: 8.00				
1971G		—	0.75	1.00	12.50	—
1971G Proof	10,000	Value: 8.00				
1971J		—	0.75	1.00	10.00	—
1971J Proof	8,000	Value: 8.00				
1972D		—	0.75	1.00	10.00	—
Note: Errors exist without reeding						
1972D Proof	8,000	Value: 7.00				
1972F		—	0.75	1.00	10.00	—
1972F Proof	8,000	Value: 7.00				
1972G		—	0.75	1.00	10.00	—
1972G Proof	10,000	Value: 7.00				
1972J		—	0.75	1.00	10.00	—
1972J Proof	8,000	Value: 7.00				
1973D		—	0.75	1.00	6.00	—
1973D Proof	9,000	Value: 5.00				
1973F		—	0.75	1.00	6.00	—
1973F Proof	9,000	Value: 5.00				
1973G		—	0.75	1.00	6.00	—
1973G Proof	9,000	Value: 5.00				
1973J		—	0.75	1.00	6.00	—
1973J Proof	9,000	Value: 5.00				
1974D		—	0.75	1.00	6.00	—
1974D Proof	35,000	Value: 4.00				
1974F		—	0.75	1.00	6.00	—
1974F Proof	35,000	Value: 4.00				
1974G		—	0.75	1.00	6.00	—
1974G Proof	35,000	Value: 4.00				
1974J		—	0.75	1.00	6.00	—
1974J Proof	35,000	Value: 4.00				
1975D		—	0.75	1.00	6.00	—
1975D Proof	43,000	Value: 4.00				
1975F		—	0.75	1.00	6.00	—
1975F Proof	43,000	Value: 4.00				
1975G		—	0.75	1.00	6.50	—
1975G Proof	43,000	Value: 4.00				
1975J		—	0.75	1.00	6.00	—
1975J Proof	43,000	Value: 4.00				
1976D		—	0.75	1.00	6.00	—
1976D Proof	43,000	Value: 4.00				
1976F		—	0.75	1.00	6.00	—
1976F Proof	43,000	Value: 4.00				
1976G		—	0.75	1.00	6.00	—
1976G Proof	43,000	Value: 4.00				
1976J		—	0.75	1.00	6.00	—
1976J Proof	43,000	Value: 4.00				
1977D		—	0.75	0.85	3.00	—
1977D Proof	51,000	Value: 2.00				
1977F		—	0.75	0.85	3.00	—
1977F Proof	51,000	Value: 2.00				
1977G		—	0.75	0.85	3.00	—
1977G Proof	51,000	Value: 2.00				
1977J		—	0.75	0.85	3.00	—
1977J Proof	51,000	Value: 2.00				
1978D		—	0.75	0.85	2.00	—
1978D Proof	54,000	Value: 1.25				
1978F		—	0.75	0.85	2.00	—
1978F Proof	54,000	Value: 1.25				
1978G		—	0.75	0.85	2.00	—
1978G Proof	54,000	Value: 1.25				
1978J		—	0.75	0.85	2.00	—
Note: Error with coin alignment exists						
1978J Proof	54,000	Value: 1.25				
1979D		—	0.75	0.85	2.00	—
1979D Proof	89,000	Value: 1.25				
1979F		—	0.75	0.85	2.00	—
1979F Proof	89,000	Value: 1.25				
1979G		—	0.75	0.85	2.00	—
1979G Proof	89,000	Value: 1.25				
1979J		—	0.75	0.85	2.00	—

Date	Mintage	F	VF	XF	Unc	BU
1979J Proof	89,000	Value: 1.25				
1980D		—	—	0.75	0.90	—
1980D Proof	110,000	Value: 1.00				
1980F		—	—	0.75	0.90	—
1980F Proof	110,000	Value: 1.00				
1980G		—	—	0.75	0.90	—
1980G Proof	110,000	Value: 1.00				
1980J		—	—	0.75	0.90	—
1980J Proof	110,000	Value: 1.00				
1981D		—	—	0.75	0.90	—
1981D Proof	91,000	Value: 1.00				
1981F		—	—	0.75	0.90	—
1981F Proof	91,000	Value: 1.00				
1981G		—	—	0.75	0.90	—
1981G Proof	91,000	Value: 1.00				
1981J		—	—	0.75	0.90	—
1981J Proof	91,000	Value: 1.00				
1982D		—	—	0.75	0.90	—
1982D Proof	78,000	Value: 1.00				
1982F		—	—	0.75	0.90	—
1982F Proof	78,000	Value: 1.00				
1982G		—	—	0.75	0.90	—
1982G Proof	78,000	Value: 1.00				
1982J		—	—	0.75	0.90	—
1982J Proof	78,000	Value: 1.00				
1983D		—	—	0.75	0.90	—
1983D Proof	75,000	Value: 1.00				
1983F		—	—	0.75	0.90	—
1983F Proof	75,000	Value: 1.00				
1983G		—	—	0.75	0.90	—
1983G Proof	75,000	Value: 1.00				
1983J		—	—	0.75	0.90	—
1983J Proof	75,000	Value: 1.00				
1984D		—	—	0.75	0.90	—
1984D Proof	64,000	Value: 1.50				
1984F		—	—	0.75	0.90	—
1984F Proof	64,000	Value: 1.50				
1984G		—	—	0.75	0.90	—
1984G Proof	64,000	Value: 1.50				
1984J		—	—	0.75	0.90	—
1984J Proof	64,000	Value: 1.50				
1985D		—	—	—	0.85	—
1985D Proof	56,000	Value: 1.50				
1985F		—	—	—	0.85	—
1985F Proof	54,000	Value: 1.50				
1985G		—	—	—	0.85	—
1985G Proof	55,000	Value: 1.50				
1985J		—	—	—	0.85	—
1985J Proof	54,000	Value: 1.50				
1986D		—	—	—	0.85	—
1986D Proof	44,000	Value: 1.50				
1986F		—	—	—	0.85	—
1986F Proof	44,000	Value: 1.50				
1986G		—	—	—	0.85	—
1986G Proof	44,000	Value: 1.50				
1986J		—	—	—	0.85	—
1986J Proof	44,000	Value: 1.50				
1987D		—	3.50	7.50	15.00	—
1987D Proof	45,000	Value: 1.50				
1987F		—	3.50	7.50	15.00	—
1987F Proof	45,000	Value: 1.50				
1987G		—	3.50	7.50	15.00	—
1987G Proof	45,000	Value: 1.50				
1987J		—	3.50	7.50	15.00	—
1987J Proof	45,000	Value: 1.50				
1988D		—	—	—	0.85	—
1988D Proof	45,000	Value: 1.50				
1988F		—	—	—	0.85	—
1988F Proof	45,000	Value: 1.50				
1988G		—	—	—	0.85	—
1988G Proof	45,000	Value: 1.50				
1988J		—	—	—	0.85	—
1988J Proof	45,000	Value: 1.50				
1989D		—	—	—	0.85	—
1989D Proof	45,000	Value: 1.50				
1989F		—	—	—	0.85	—
1989F Proof	45,000	Value: 1.50				
1989G		—	—	—	0.85	—
1989G Proof	45,000	Value: 1.50				
1989J		—	—	—	0.85	—
1989J Proof	45,000	Value: 1.50				
1990A		—	—	—	2.00	—
1990D		—	—	—	0.85	—
1990D Proof	45,000	Value: 1.50				
1990F		—	—	—	0.85	—
1990F Proof	45,000	Value: 1.50				
1990G		—	—	—	0.85	—
1990G Proof	45,000	Value: 1.50				
1990J		—	—	—	0.85	—
1990J Proof	45,000	Value: 1.50				
1991A		—	—	—	0.85	—
1991A Proof	45,000	Value: 1.50				
1991D		—	—	—	0.85	—
1991D Proof	45,000	Value: 1.50				
1991F		—	—	—	0.85	—
1991F Proof	45,000	Value: 1.50				
1991G		—	—	—	0.85	—
1991G Proof	45,000	Value: 1.50				
1991J		—	—	—	0.85	—
1991J Proof	45,000	Value: 1.50				
1992A		—	—	—	0.85	—
1992A Proof	45,000	Value: 1.50				

Date	Mintage	F	VF	XF	Unc	BU
1992D		—	—	—	0.85	—
1992D Proof	45,000	Value: 1.50				
1992F		—	—	—	0.85	—
1992F Proof	45,000	Value: 1.50				
1992G		—	—	—	0.85	—
1992G Proof	45,000	Value: 1.50				
1992J		—	—	—	0.85	—
1992J Proof	45,000	Value: 1.50				
1993A		—	—	—	0.85	—
1993A Proof	45,000	Value: 1.50				
1993D		—	—	—	0.85	—
1993D Proof	45,000	Value: 1.50				
1993F		—	—	—	0.85	—
1993F Proof	45,000	Value: 1.50				
1993G		—	—	—	0.85	—
1993G Proof	45,000	Value: 1.50				
1993J		—	—	—	0.85	—
1993J Proof	45,000	Value: 1.50				
1994A		—	—	—	0.85	—
1994A Proof	45,000	Value: 1.50				
1994D		—	—	—	0.85	—
1994D Proof	45,000	Value: 1.50				
1994F		—	—	—	0.85	—
1994F Proof	45,000	Value: 1.50				
1994G		—	—	—	0.85	—
1994G Proof	45,000	Value: 1.50				
1994J		—	—	—	0.85	—
1994J Proof	45,000	Value: 1.50				
1995A In sets only		—	—	—	70.00	—
1995A Proof	45,000	Value: 20.00				
1995D In sets only		—	—	—	70.00	—
1995D Proof	45,000	Value: 20.00				
1995F In sets only		—	—	—	70.00	—
1995F Proof	45,000	Value: 20.00				
1995G In sets only		—	—	—	70.00	—
1995G Proof	45,000	Value: 20.00				
1995J		—	—	—	18.00	—
1995J Proof	45,000	Value: 20.00				
1996A In sets only		—	—	—	12.50	—
1996A Proof	45,000	Value: 14.00				
1996D In sets only		—	—	—	12.50	—
1996D Proof	45,000	Value: 14.00				
1996F In sets only		—	—	—	12.50	—
1996F Proof	45,000	Value: 14.00				
1996G In sets only		—	—	—	12.50	—
1996G Proof	45,000	Value: 14.00				
1996J In sets only		—	—	—	12.50	—
1996J Proof	45,000	Value: 14.00				
1997A In sets only		—	—	—	4.75	—
1997A Proof	45,000	Value: 5.00				
1997D In sets only		—	—	—	4.75	—
1997D Proof	45,000	Value: 5.00				
1997F In sets only		—	—	—	4.75	—
1997F Proof	45,000	Value: 5.00				
1997G In sets only		—	—	—	4.75	—
1997G Proof	45,000	Value: 5.00				
1997J In sets only		—	—	—	4.75	—
1997J Proof	45,000	Value: 5.00				
1998A In sets only		—	—	—	4.75	—
1998A Proof	45,000	Value: 5.00				
1998D In sets only		—	—	—	4.75	—
1998D Proof	45,000	Value: 5.00				
1998F In sets only		—	—	—	4.75	—
1998F Proof	45,000	Value: 5.00				
1998G In sets only		—	—	—	4.75	—
1998G Proof	45,000	Value: 5.00				
1998J In sets only		—	—	—	4.75	—
1998J Proof	45,000	Value: 5.00				
1999A In sets only		—	—	—	4.75	—
1999A Proof	45,000	Value: 5.00				
1999D In sets only		—	—	—	4.75	—
1999D Proof	45,000	Value: 5.00				
1999F In sets only		—	—	—	4.75	—
1999F Proof	45,000	Value: 5.00				
1999G In sets only		—	—	—	4.75	—
1999G Proof	45,000	Value: 5.00				
1999J In sets only		—	—	—	4.75	—
1999J Proof	45,000	Value: 5.00				
2000A In sets only		—	—	—	5.00	—
2000A Proof	45,000	Value: 5.00				
2000D In sets only		—	—	—	5.00	—
2000D Proof	45,000	Value: 5.00				
2000F In sets only		—	—	—	5.00	—
2000F Proof	45,000	Value: 5.00				
2000G In sets only		—	—	—	5.00	—
2000G Proof	45,000	Value: 5.00				
2000J In sets only		—	—	—	5.00	—
2000J Proof	45,000	Value: 5.00				
2001A In sets only		—	—	—	15.00	—
2001A Proof	78,000	Value: 15.00				
2001D In sets only		—	—	—	15.00	—
2001D Proof	78,000	Value: 15.00				
2001F In sets only		—	—	—	15.00	—
2001F Proof	78,000	Value: 15.00				
2001G In sets only		—	—	—	15.00	—
2001G Proof	78,000	Value: 15.00				
2001J In sets only		—	—	—	15.00	—
2001J Proof	78,000	Value: 15.00				

KM# 203 MARK **Weight:** 11.8500 g. **Composition:** 0.9990 Gold .3806 oz. AGW **Subject:** Retirement of the mark currency **Obverse:** Eagle **Reverse:** Denomination **Edge:** Lettered **Size:** 23.5 mm.

Date	Mintage	F	VF	XF	Unc	BU
2001A Proof	200,000	Value: 335				
2001D Proof	200,000	Value: 335				
2001G Proof	200,000	Value: 335				
2001J Proof	200,000	Value: 335				
2001F Proof	200,000	Value: 335				

KM# 111 2 MARK **Composition:** Copper-Nickel **Note:** Federal Republic.

Date	Mintage	F	VF	XF	Unc	BU
1951D		—	30.00	55.00	150	—
1951D Proof	200	Value: 450				
1951F		—	20.00	45.00	110	—
1951F Proof	150	Value: 500				
1951G		—	40.00	100	210	—

Note: The 1951G dated coin was restruck without authorization by a mint official using genuine dies - quantity unknown

Date	Mintage	F	VF	XF	Unc	BU
1951G Proof	33	Value: 1,200				

Note: The 1951G dated coin was restruck without authorization by a mint official using genuine dies - quantity unknown

Date	Mintage	F	VF	XF	Unc	BU
1951J		—	28.00	45.00	110	—
1951J Proof	180	Value: 450				

KM# 116 2 MARK **Composition:** Copper-Nickel **Reverse:** Head of Max Planck facing left

Date	Mintage	F	VF	XF	Unc	BU
1957D	7,452,000	—	2.00	6.00	65.00	—
1957D Proof	350	Value: 235				
1957F	6,337,000	—	2.00	6.00	65.00	—
1957F Proof	100	Value: 325				
1957G	2,598,000	—	3.00	7.50	135	—
1957G Proof	56	Value: 600				
1957J	11,210,000	—	2.00	6.00	60.00	—
1957J Proof	370	Value: 175				
1958D	12,623,000	—	1.50	5.00	50.00	—
1958D Proof	1,240	Value: 85.00				
1958F	16,825,000	—	1.50	4.00	45.00	—
1958F Proof	300	Value: 200				
1958G	10,744,000	—	1.50	4.00	45.00	—
1958G Proof	45	Value: 700				
1958J	9,408,000	—	1.50	4.00	45.00	—
1958J Proof	100	Value: 400				
1959D	1,020,000	—	4.00	10.00	220	—
1959D Proof	38	Value: 800				
1959F	203,000	—	15.00	60.00	365	—
1959F Proof	24	Value: 900				
1960D	3,535,000	—	1.50	4.00	35.00	—
1960D Proof	100	Value: 325				
1960F	3,692,000	—	1.50	4.00	35.00	—
1960F Proof	50	Value: 600				
1960G	2,695,000	—	2.00	4.00	35.00	—
1960G Proof	130	Value: 300				
1960J	4,676,000	—	1.50	4.00	35.00	—
1960J Proof	36	Value: 800				
1961D	3,918,000	—	1.50	4.00	35.00	—
1961D Proof	50	Value: 600				
1961F	3,872,000	—	1.50	4.00	35.00	—
1961F Proof	46	Value: 650				
1961G	2,776,000	—	2.00	4.00	35.00	—
1961G Proof	100	Value: 325				
1961J	2,940,000	—	1.50	4.00	35.00	—
1961J Proof	28	Value: 750				
1962D	4,105,000	—	2.00	6.00	35.00	—
1962D Proof	50	Value: 600				
1962F	3,344,000	—	2.00	6.00	35.00	—
1962F Proof	42	Value: 625				
1962G	1,800,000	—	2.00	6.00	35.00	—

Date	Mintage	F	VF	XF	Unc	BU
1962G Proof	130	Value: 300				
1962J	3,609,000	—	2.00	6.00	25.00	—
1962J Proof	28	Value: 750				
1963D	4,411,000	—	1.50	4.00	25.00	—
1963D Proof	40	Value: 650				
1963F	3,752,000	—	1.50	4.00	25.00	—
1963F Proof	47	Value: 600				
1963G	3,448,000	—	1.50	4.00	25.00	—
1963G Proof	200	Value: 250				
1963J	7,348,000	—	1.50	4.00	25.00	—
1963J Proof	32	Value: 700				
1964D	5,205,000	—	1.50	4.00	20.00	—
1964D Proof	40	Value: 650				
1964F	4,834,000	—	1.50	4.00	20.00	—
1964F Proof	36	Value: 800				
1964G	3,044,000	—	1.50	4.00	20.00	—
1964G Proof	368	Value: 150				
1964J	2,681,000	—	1.50	4.00	20.00	—
1964J Proof	43	Value: 600				
1965D	3,903,000	—	1.50	2.50	15.00	—
1965D Proof	35	Value: 800				
1965F	4,045,000	—	1.50	2.50	15.00	—
1965F Proof	300	Value: 250				
1965G	2,599,000	—	1.50	2.50	15.00	—
1965G Proof	8,233	Value: 5.00				
1965J	4,006,999	—	1.50	2.50	15.00	—
Note: Error exists without edge inscription						
1965J Proof	36	Value: 750				
1966D	5,855,000	—	1.50	2.50	12.00	—
1966D Proof	20	Value: 900				
1966F	3,750,000	—	1.50	2.50	12.00	—
1966F Proof	450	Value: 250				
1966G	3,895,000	—	1.50	2.50	12.00	—
1966G Proof	3,070	Value: 20.00				
1966J	6,014,000	—	1.50	2.50	12.00	—
1966J Proof	1,000	Value: 35.00				
1967D	3,254,000	—	1.50	2.50	12.00	—
1967D Proof	20	Value: 900				
1967F	3,758,000	—	1.50	2.50	12.00	—
1967F Proof	1,600	Value: 32.00				
1967G	1,878,000	—	1.50	4.00	16.50	—
1967G Proof	5,363	Value: 28.00				
1967J	6,684,000	—	1.25	2.50	12.00	—
1967J Proof	1,500	Value: 32.00				
1968D	4,166,000	—	1.50	2.50	15.00	—
1968D Proof	30	Value: 850				
1968F	1,050,000	—	2.00	5.00	20.00	—
1968F Proof	3,100	Value: 22.00				
1968G	3,060,000	—	2.00	2.50	12.00	—
1968G Proof	6,023	Value: 15.00				
1968J	939,000	—	2.00	4.00	20.00	—
1968J Proof	2,000	Value: 28.00				
1969D	2,602,000	—	2.00	2.50	15.00	—
1969F	3,005,000	—	2.00	2.50	15.00	—
1969F Proof	5,100	Value: 6.00				
1969G	1,754,000	—	2.00	2.50	16.50	—
1969G Proof	8,700	Value: 6.00				
1969J	2,680,000	—	2.00	2.50	10.00	—
1969J Proof	5,000	Value: 6.00				
1970D	5,203,000	—	1.50	2.00	4.00	—
1970F	6,018,000	—	1.50	2.00	4.00	—
1970F Proof	5,140	Value: 7.50				
1970G	3,461,000	—	1.50	2.00	4.00	—
1970G Proof	10,000	Value: 5.00				
1970J	5,691,000	—	1.50	2.00	4.00	—
1970J Proof	5,000	Value: 6.00				
1971D	8,451,000	—	1.00	1.25	3.00	—
1971D Proof	8,000	Value: 5.00				
1971F	10,017,000	—	1.00	1.25	3.00	—
1971F Proof	8,000	Value: 5.00				
1971G	5,631,000	—	1.00	1.25	3.00	—
1971G Proof	10,000	Value: 5.00				
1971J	8,786,000	—	1.00	1.25	3.00	—
1971J Proof	8,000	Value: 6.00				

KM# 124 2 MARK Composition: Copper-Nickel Clad Nickel **Reverse:** Head of Konrad Adenauer facing left

Date	Mintage	F	VF	XF	Unc	BU
1969D	7,001,000	—	—	1.50	3.00	—
1969F	7,006,000	—	—	1.50	3.00	—
1969G	7,010,000	—	—	1.50	3.00	—
1969J	7,000,000	—	—	1.50	3.00	—
1970D	7,318,000	—	—	1.50	3.00	—
1970F	8,422,000	—	—	1.50	3.00	—
1970G	4,844,000	—	—	1.50	3.00	—
1970J	7,476,000	—	—	1.50	3.00	—
1971D	7,287,000	—	—	1.50	3.00	—
1971F	8,400,000	—	—	1.50	3.00	—
1971G	4,848,000	—	—	1.50	3.00	—
1971J	7,476,000	—	—	1.50	3.00	—
1972D	7,286,000	—	—	1.50	3.00	—
1972D Proof	8,000	Value: 4.50				
1972F	8,392,000	—	—	1.50	3.00	—
1972F Proof	8,000	Value: 4.50				
1972G	4,848,000	—	—	1.50	3.00	—
1972G Proof	10,000	Value: 4.50				
1972J	7,476,000	—	—	1.50	3.00	—
1972J Proof	8,000	Value: 4.50				
1973D	10,393,000	—	—	1.50	3.00	—
1973D Proof	9,000	Value: 4.50				
1973F	11,015,000	—	—	1.50	3.00	—
Note: Errors exist without edge inscription						
1973F Proof	9,000	Value: 4.50				
1973G	9,022,000	—	—	1.50	3.00	—
1973G Proof	9,000	Value: 4.50				
1973J	12,272,000	—	—	1.50	3.00	—
Note: Errors with coin alignment exist						
1973J Proof	9,000	Value: 4.50				
1974D	5,151,000	—	—	1.50	3.00	—
1974D Proof	35,000	Value: 2.25				
1974F	5,894,000	—	—	1.50	3.00	—
1974F Proof	35,000	Value: 2.25				
1974G	3,790,000	—	—	1.50	3.00	—
1974G Proof	35,000	Value: 2.25				
1974J	5,282,000	—	—	1.50	3.00	—
1974J Proof	35,000	Value: 2.25				
1975D	4,553,000	—	—	1.50	2.50	—
1975D Proof	43,000	Value: 2.25				
1975F	5,270,000	—	—	1.50	2.50	—
1975F Proof	43,000	Value: 2.25				
1975G	3,035,000	—	—	1.50	2.50	—
1975G Proof	43,000	Value: 2.25				
1975J	4,673,000	—	—	1.50	2.50	—
1975J Proof	43,000	Value: 2.25				
1976D	4,576,000	—	—	1.50	2.50	—
1976D Proof	43,000	Value: 2.25				
1976F	5,257,000	—	—	1.50	2.50	—
1976F Proof	43,000	Value: 2.25				
1976G	3,028,000	—	—	1.50	2.50	—
1976G Proof	43,000	Value: 2.25				
1976J	4,673,000	—	—	1.50	2.50	—
1976J Proof	43,000	Value: 2.25				
1977D	5,906,000	—	—	1.50	2.50	—
1977D Proof	51,000	Value: 2.00				
1977F	6,765,000	—	—	1.50	2.50	—
1977F Proof	51,000	Value: 2.00				
1977G	3,892,000	—	—	1.50	2.50	—
1977G Proof	51,000	Value: 2.00				
1977J	6,007,000	—	—	1.50	2.50	—
1977J Proof	51,000	Value: 2.00				
1978D	3,304,000	—	—	1.50	2.50	—
1978D Proof	54,000	Value: 2.00				
1978F	3,804	—	—	1.50	2.50	—
1978F Proof	54,000	Value: 2.00				
1978G	2,217,000	—	—	1.50	2.50	—
1978G Proof	54,000	Value: 2.00				
1978J	3,392,000	—	—	1.50	2.50	—
1978J Proof	54,000	Value: 2.00				
1979D	3,209,000	—	—	1.50	2.50	—
1979D Proof	89,000	Value: 2.00				
1979F	3,689,000	—	—	1.50	2.50	—
1979F Proof	89,000	Value: 2.00				
1979G	2,165,000	—	—	1.50	2.50	—
1979G Proof	89,000	Value: 2.00				
1979J	3,293,000	—	—	1.50	2.50	—
1979J Proof	89,000	Value: 2.00				
1980D	10,810,000	—	—	1.50	2.00	—
1980D Proof	110,000	Value: 2.00				
1980F	8,910,000	—	—	1.50	2.00	—
1980F Proof	110,000	Value: 2.00				
1980G	1,170,000	—	—	1.50	2.00	—
1980G Proof	110,000	Value: 2.00				
1980J	4,670,000	—	—	1.50	2.00	—
1980J Proof	110,000	Value: 2.00				
1981D	8,180,000	—	—	1.50	2.00	—
1981D Proof	91,000	Value: 2.00				
1981F	7,690,000	—	—	1.50	2.00	—
1981F Proof	91,000	Value: 2.00				
1981G	7,070,000	—	—	1.50	2.00	—
1981G Proof	91,000	Value: 2.00				
1981J	8,289,999	—	—	1.50	2.00	—
1981J Proof	91,000	Value: 2.00				
1982D	9,220,000	—	—	1.50	2.00	—
1982D Proof	78,000	Value: 2.00				
1982F	11,260,000	—	—	1.50	2.00	—
1982F Proof	78,000	Value: 2.00				
1982G	6,640,000	—	—	1.50	2.00	—
1982G Proof	78,000	Value: 2.00				
1982J	9,790,000	—	—	1.50	2.00	—
1982J Proof	78,000	Value: 2.00				
1983D	1,560,000	—	—	1.50	2.00	—
1983D Proof	75,000	Value: 2.00				
1983F	1,800,000	—	—	1.50	2.00	—
1983F Proof	75,000	Value: 2.00				
1983G	1,030,000	—	—	1.50	2.00	—
1983G Proof	75,000	Value: 2.00				
1983J	1,600,000	—	—	1.50	2.00	—
1983J Proof	75,000	Value: 2.00				
1984D	52,000	—	2.00	4.50	8.50	—
1984D Proof	64,000	Value: 2.00				
1984F	60,000	—	2.00	4.50	8.50	—
1984F Proof	64,000	Value: 2.00				
1984G	35,000	—	3.00	6.00	11.50	—
1984G Proof	64,000	Value: 2.00				
1984J	53,000	—	2.00	4.50	8.50	—
1984J Proof	64,000	Value: 2.00				
1985D	2,600,000	—	—	—	2.00	—
1985D Proof	56,000	Value: 2.25				
1985F	3,000,000	—	—	—	1.75	—
1985F Proof	54,000	Value: 2.25				
1985G	1,730,000	—	—	—	1.75	—
1985G Proof	55,000	Value: 2.25				
1985J	2,670,000	—	—	—	1.75	—
1985J Proof	54,000	Value: 2.25				
1986D	2,600,000	—	—	—	1.75	—
1986D Proof	44,000	Value: 2.25				
1986F	3,000,000	—	—	—	1.75	—
1986F Proof	44,000	Value: 2.25				
1986G	1,730,000	—	—	—	1.75	—
1986G Proof	44,000	Value: 2.25				
1986J	2,670,000	—	—	—	1.75	—
1986J Proof	44,000	Value: 2.25				
1987D	4,420,000	—	—	—	1.75	—
1987D Proof	45,000	Value: 2.25				
1987F	5,100,000	—	—	—	1.75	—
1987F Proof	45,000	Value: 2.25				
1987G	2,940,000	—	—	—	1.75	—
1987G Proof	45,000	Value: 2.25				
1987J	4,540,000	—	—	—	1.75	—
1987J Proof	45,000	Value: 2.25				

KM# A127 2 MARK Composition: Copper-Nickel Clad Nickel **Reverse:** Head of Theodor Heuss facing left

Date	Mintage	F	VF	XF	Unc	BU
1970D	7,317,000	—	—	1.50	3.00	—
1970F	8,426,000	—	—	1.50	3.00	—
1970G	4,844,000	—	—	1.50	3.00	—
1970J	7,476,000	—	—	1.50	3.00	—
1971D	7,280,000	—	—	1.50	3.00	—
1971F	8,403,000	—	—	1.50	3.00	—
1971G	4,841,000	—	—	1.50	3.00	—
1971J	7,476,000	—	—	1.50	3.00	—
1972D	7,288,000	—	—	1.50	3.00	—
1972D Proof	8,000	Value: 4.50				
1972F	8,401,000	—	—	1.50	3.00	—
1972F Proof	8,000	Value: 4.50				
1972G	4,859,000	—	—	1.50	3.00	—
1972G Proof	10,000	Value: 4.50				
1972J	7,476,000	—	—	1.50	3.00	—
1972J Proof	8,000	Value: 4.50				
1973D	10,379,000	—	—	1.50	3.00	—
1973D Proof	9,000	Value: 4.50				
1973F	11,018,000	—	—	1.50	3.00	—
1973F Proof	9,000	Value: 4.50				
1973G	8,975,000	—	—	1.50	3.00	—
1973G Proof	9,000	Value: 4.50				
1973J	12,360,000	—	—	1.50	3.00	—
1973J Proof	9,000	Value: 4.50				
1974D	5,147,000	—	—	1.50	3.00	—
1974D Proof	35,000	Value: 2.00				
1974F	5,899,000	—	—	1.50	3.00	—
1974F Proof	35,000	Value: 2.00				
1974G	3,820,000	—	—	1.50	3.00	—
1974G Proof	35,000	Value: 2.00				
1974J	5,280,000	—	—	1.50	3.00	—
1974J Proof	35,000	Value: 2.00				
1975D	4,623,000	—	—	1.50	2.00	—
1975D Proof	43,000	Value: 2.00				
1975F	5,251,000	—	—	1.50	2.00	—
1975F Proof	43,000	Value: 2.00				
1975G	3,034,000	—	—	1.50	2.00	—
1975G Proof	43,000	Value: 2.00				
1975J	4,675,000	—	—	1.50	2.00	—
1975J Proof	43,000	Value: 2.00				
1976D	4,546,000	—	—	1.50	2.00	—
1976D Proof	43,000	Value: 2.00				
1976F	5,259,000	—	—	1.50	2.00	—
1976F Proof	43,000	Value: 2.00				
1976G	3,028,000	—	—	1.50	2.00	—
1976G Proof	43,000	Value: 2.00				
1976J	4,681,000	—	—	1.50	2.00	—
1976J Proof	43,000	Value: 2.00				
1977D	5,857,000	—	—	1.50	2.00	—
1977D Proof	51,000	Value: 1.75				
1977F	6,752,000	—	—	1.50	2.00	—
1977F Proof	51,000	Value: 1.75				
1977G	3,892,000	—	—	1.50	2.00	—
1977G Proof	51,000	Value: 1.75				
1977J	6,009,000	—	—	1.50	2.00	—
1977J Proof	51,000	Value: 1.75				
1978D	3,804,000	—	—	1.50	2.00	—
Note: Errors without edge inscription exist						
1978D Proof	54,000	Value: 1.75				
1978F	3,804,000	—	—	1.50	2.00	—

Date	Mintage	F	VF	XF	Unc	BU
1978F Proof	54,000	Value: 1.75				
1978G	2,217,000	—	—	1.50	2.00	—
1978G Proof	54,000	Value: 1.75				
1978J	3,392,000	—	—	1.50	2.00	—
1978J Proof	54,000	Value: 1.75				
1979D	3,209,000	—	—	1.50	2.00	—
1979D Proof	89,000	Value: 1.75				
1979F	3,689,000	—	—	1.50	2.00	—
1979F Proof	89,000	Value: 1.75				
1979G	2,165,000	—	—	1.50	2.00	—
1979G Proof	89,000	Value: 1.75				
1979J	3,293,000	—	—	1.50	2.00	—
1979J Proof	89,000	Value: 1.75				
1980D	2,000,000	—	—	1.50	1.75	—
1980D Proof	110,000	Value: 1.75				
1980F	2,300,000	—	—	1.50	1.75	—
1980F Proof	110,000	Value: 1.75				
1980G	1,300,000	—	—	1.50	1.75	—
1980G Proof	110,000	Value: 1.75				
1980J	2,000,000	—	—	1.50	1.75	—
1980J Proof	110,000	Value: 1.75				
1981D	2,000,000	—	—	1.50	1.75	—
1981D Proof	91,000	Value: 1.75				
1981F	2,300,000	—	—	1.50	1.75	—
1981F Proof	91,000	Value: 1.75				
1981G	1,300,000	—	—	1.50	1.75	—
1981G Proof	91,000	Value: 1.75				
1981J	2,000,000	—	—	1.50	1.75	—
1981J Proof	91,000	Value: 1.75				
1982D	3,100,000	—	—	1.50	1.75	—
1982D Proof	78,000	Value: 1.75				
1982F	3,600,000	—	—	1.50	1.75	—
1982F Proof	78,000	Value: 1.75				
1982G	2,100,000	—	—	1.50	1.75	—
1982G Proof	78,000	Value: 1.75				
1982J	3,200,000	—	—	1.50	1.75	—
1982J Proof	78,000	Value: 1.75				
1983D	1,560,000	—	—	1.50	1.75	—
1983D Proof	75,000	Value: 1.75				
1983F	1,800,000	—	—	1.50	1.75	—
1983F Proof	75,000	Value: 1.75				
1983G	1,030,000	—	—	1.50	1.75	—
1983G Proof	75,000	Value: 1.75				
1983J	1,600,000	—	—	1.50	1.75	—
1983J Proof	75,000	Value: 1.75				
1984D	52,000	—	2.00	4.50	8.50	—
1984D Proof	64,000	Value: 2.00				
1984F	60,000	—	2.00	4.50	8.50	—
1984F Proof	64,000	Value: 2.00				
1984G	35,000	—	3.00	6.00	11.50	—
1984G Proof	64,000	Value: 2.00				
1984J	53,000	—	2.00	4.50	8.50	—
1984J Proof	64,000	Value: 2.00				
1985D	2,600,000	—	—	—	1.75	—
1985D Proof	56,000	Value: 2.25				
1985F	3,000,000	—	—	—	1.75	—
1985F Proof	54,000	Value: 2.25				
1985G	1,730,000	—	—	—	1.75	—
1985G Proof	55,000	Value: 2.25				
1985J	2,670,000	—	—	—	1.75	—
1985J Proof	54,000	Value: 2.25				
1986D	2,600,000	—	—	—	1.75	—
1986D Proof	44,000	Value: 2.25				
1986F	3,000,000	—	—	—	1.75	—
1986F Proof	44,000	Value: 2.25				
1986G	1,730,000	—	—	—	1.75	—
1986G Proof	44,000	Value: 2.25				
1986J	2,670,000	—	—	—	1.75	—
1986J Proof	44,000	Value: 2.25				
1987D	4,420,000	—	—	—	1.75	—
1987D Proof	45,000	Value: 2.25				
1987F	5,100,000	—	—	—	1.75	—
1987F Proof	45,000	Value: 2.25				
1987G	2,940,000	—	—	—	1.75	—
1987G Proof	45,000	Value: 2.25				
1987J	4,540,000	—	—	—	1.75	—
1987J Proof	45,000	Value: 2.25				

KM# 149 2 MARK Composition: Copper-Nickel Clad Nickel **Reverse:** Head of Dr. Kurt Schumacher facing forward

Date	Mintage	F	VF	XF	Unc	BU
1979D	3,209,000	—	—	1.50	2.00	—
1979D Proof	89,000	Value: 1.75				
1979F	3,689,000	—	—	1.50	2.00	—
1979F Proof	89,000	Value: 1.75				
1979G	2,165,000	—	—	1.50	2.00	—
1979G Proof	89,000	Value: 1.75				
1979J	3,293,000	—	—	1.50	2.00	—
1979J Proof	89,000	Value: 1.75				
1980D	2,000,000	—	—	1.50	2.00	—
1980D Proof	110,000	Value: 1.75				
1980F	2,300,000	—	—	1.50	2.00	—
1980F Proof	110,000	Value: 1.75				
1980G	1,300,000	—	—	1.50	2.00	—
1980G Proof	110,000	Value: 1.75				
1980J	2,000,000	—	—	1.50	2.00	—
1980J Proof	110,000	Value: 1.75				
1981D	2,000,000	—	—	1.50	2.00	—
1981D Proof	91,000	Value: 1.75				
1981F	2,000,000	—	—	1.50	2.00	—

Note: Errors without edge inscription exist

Date	Mintage	F	VF	XF	Unc	BU
1981F Proof	91,000	Value: 1.75				
1981G	1,300,000	—	—	1.50	2.00	—
1981G Proof	91,000	Value: 1.75				
1981J	2,000,000	—	—	1.50	2.00	—
1981J Proof	91,000	Value: 1.75				
1982D	3,100,000	—	—	1.50	2.00	—
1982D Proof	78,000	Value: 1.75				
1982F	3,600,000	—	—	1.50	2.00	—
1982F Proof	78,000	Value: 1.75				
1982G	2,100,000	—	—	1.50	2.00	—
1982G Proof	78,000	Value: 1.75				
1982J	3,200,000	—	—	1.50	2.00	—
1982J Proof	78,000	Value: 1.75				
1983D	1,560,000	—	—	1.50	2.00	—
1983D Proof	75,000	Value: 1.75				
1983F	1,800,000	—	—	1.50	2.00	—
1983F Proof	75,000	Value: 1.75				
1983G	1,030,000	—	—	1.50	2.00	—
1983G Proof	75,000	Value: 1.75				
1983J	1,600,000	—	—	1.50	2.00	—
1983J Proof	75,000	Value: 1.75				
1984D	52,000	—	2.00	4.50	8.50	—
1984D Proof	64,000	Value: 1.75				
1984F	60,000	—	2.00	4.50	8.50	—
1984F Proof	64,000	Value: 1.75				
1984G	35,000	—	3.00	6.00	11.50	—
1984G Proof	64,000	Value: 1.75				
1984J	53,000	—	2.00	4.50	8.50	—
1984J Proof	64,000	Value: 1.75				
1985D	2,600,000	—	—	—	1.75	—
1985D Proof	56,000	Value: 2.25				
1985F	3,000,000	—	—	—	1.75	—
1985F Proof	54,000	Value: 2.25				
1985G	1,730,000	—	—	—	1.75	—
1985G Proof	55,000	Value: 2.25				
1985J	2,670,000	—	—	—	1.75	—
1985J Proof	54,000	Value: 2.25				
1986D	2,600,000	—	—	—	1.75	—
1986D Proof	44,000	Value: 2.25				
1986F	3,000,000	—	—	—	1.75	—
1986F Proof	44,000	Value: 2.25				
1986G	1,730,000	—	—	—	1.75	—
1986G Proof	44,000	Value: 2.25				
1986J	2,670,000	—	—	—	1.75	—
1986J Proof	44,000	Value: 2.25				
1987D	4,420,000	—	—	—	1.75	—
1987D Proof	45,000	Value: 2.25				
1987F	5,100,000	—	—	—	1.75	—
1987F Proof	45,000	Value: 2.25				
1987G	2,940,000	—	—	—	1.75	—
1987G Proof	45,000	Value: 2.25				
1987J	4,540,000	—	—	—	1.75	—
1987J Proof	45,000	Value: 2.25				
1988D	5,850,000	—	—	—	1.75	—
1988D Proof	45,000	Value: 2.25				
1988F	6,750,000	—	—	—	1.75	—
1988F Proof	45,000	Value: 2.25				
1988G	3,890,000	—	—	—	1.75	—
1988G Proof	45,000	Value: 2.25				
1988J	6,010,000	—	—	—	1.75	—
1988J Proof	45,000	Value: 2.25				
1989D	10,400,000	—	—	—	1.75	—
1989D Proof	45,000	Value: 2.25				
1989F	12,000,000	—	—	—	1.75	—
1989F Proof	45,000	Value: 2.25				
1989G	6,920,000	—	—	—	1.75	—
1989G Proof	45,000	Value: 2.25				
1989J	10,680,000	—	—	—	1.75	—
1989J Proof	45,000	Value: 2.25				
1990D	18,370,000	—	—	—	1.75	—
1990D Proof	45,000	Value: 2.25				
1990F	21,200,000	—	—	—	1.75	—
1990F Proof	45,000	Value: 2.25				
1990G	12,220,000	—	—	—	1.75	—
1990G Proof	45,000	Value: 2.25				
1990J	18,870,000	—	—	—	1.75	—
1990J Proof	45,000	Value: 2.25				
1991A	4,000,000	—	—	—	1.75	—
1991A Proof	45,000	Value: 2.25				
1991D	4,200,000	—	—	—	1.75	—
1991D Proof	45,000	Value: 2.25				
1991F	4,800,000	—	—	—	1.75	—
1991F Proof	45,000	Value: 2.25				
1991G	2,800,000	—	—	—	1.75	—
1991G Proof	45,000	Value: 2.25				
1991J	4,200,000	—	—	—	1.75	—
1991J Proof	45,000	Value: 2.25				
1992A	7,330,000	—	—	—	1.75	—
1992A Proof	45,000	Value: 2.25				
1992D	7,700,000	—	—	—	1.75	—
1992D Proof	45,000	Value: 2.25				
1992F	8,800,000	—	—	—	1.75	—
1992F Proof	45,000	Value: 2.25				
1992G	5,130,000	—	—	—	1.75	—
1992G Proof	45,000	Value: 2.25				
1992J	7,700,000	—	—	—	1.75	—
1992J Proof	45,000	Value: 2.25				
1993A	600,000	—	—	3.00	7.00	—
1993A Proof	45,000	Value: 2.25				
1993D	630,000	—	—	3.00	7.00	—
1993D Proof	45,000	Value: 2.25				
1993F	720,000	—	—	3.00	7.00	—
1993F Proof	45,000	Value: 2.25				
1993G	420,000	—	—	4.00	10.00	—
1993G Proof	45,000	Value: 2.25				
1993J	630,000	—	—	3.00	7.00	—
1993J Proof	45,000	Value: 2.25				

KM# 170 2 MARK Composition: Copper-Nickel Clad Nickel **Reverse:** Head of Ludwig Erhard facing forward

Date	Mintage	F	VF	XF	Unc	BU
1988D	5,850,000	—	—	—	1.65	—
1988D Proof	45,000	Value: 2.00				
1988F	6,750,000	—	—	—	1.65	—
1988F Proof	45,000	Value: 2.00				
1988G	3,890,000	—	—	—	1.65	—
1988G Proof	45,000	Value: 2.00				
1988J	6,010,000	—	—	—	1.65	—
1988J Proof	45,000	Value: 2.00				
1989D	10,400,000	—	—	—	1.65	—
1989D Proof	45,000	Value: 2.00				
1989F	12,000,000	—	—	—	1.65	—
1989F Proof	45,000	Value: 2.00				
1989G	6,920,000	—	—	—	1.65	—
1989G Proof	45,000	Value: 2.00				
1989J	10,680,000	—	—	—	1.65	—
1989J Proof	45,000	Value: 2.00				
1990D	18,370,000	—	—	—	1.65	—
1990D Proof	45,000	Value: 2.00				
1990F	21,200,000	—	—	—	1.65	—
1990F Proof	45,000	Value: 2.00				
1990G	12,220,000	—	—	—	1.65	—
1990G Proof	45,000	Value: 2.00				
1990J	18,870,000	—	—	—	1.65	—
1990J Proof	45,000	Value: 2.00				
1991A	4,000,000	—	—	—	1.65	—
1991A Proof	45,000	Value: 2.00				
1991D	4,200,000	—	—	—	1.65	—
1991D Proof	45,000	Value: 2.00				
1991F	4,800,000	—	—	—	1.65	—
1991F Proof	45,000	Value: 2.00				
1991G	2,800,000	—	—	—	1.65	—

Note: Errors without edge inscription exist

Date	Mintage	F	VF	XF	Unc	BU
1991G Proof	45,000	Value: 2.00				
1991J	4,200,000	—	—	—	1.65	—
1991J Proof	45,000	Value: 2.00				
1992A	7,330,000	—	—	—	1.75	—
1992A Proof	45,000	Value: 2.25				
1992D	7,700,000	—	—	—	1.75	—
1992D Proof	45,000	Value: 2.25				
1992F	8,800,000	—	—	—	1.75	—
1992F Proof	45,000	Value: 2.25				
1992G	5,130,000	—	—	—	1.75	—
1992G Proof	45,000	Value: 2.25				
1992J	7,700,000	—	—	—	1.75	—
1992J Proof	45,000	Value: 2.25				
1993A	600,000	—	—	3.00	7.00	—
1993A Proof	45,000	Value: 2.25				
1993D	630,000	—	—	3.00	7.00	—
1993D Proof	45,000	Value: 2.25				
1993F	720,000	—	—	3.00	7.00	—
1993F Proof	45,000	Value: 2.25				
1993G	420,000	—	—	4.00	10.00	—
1993G Proof	45,000	Value: 2.25				
1993J	630,000	—	—	3.00	7.00	—
1993J Proof	45,000	Value: 2.25				
1994A	5,000,000	—	—	—	1.75	—
1994A Proof	45,000	Value: 2.25				
1994D	5,250,000	—	—	—	1.75	—
1994D Proof	45,000	Value: 2.25				
1994F	6,000,000	—	—	—	1.75	—
1994F Proof	45,000	Value: 2.25				
1994G	3,500,000	—	—	—	1.75	—
1994G Proof	45,000	Value: 2.25				
1994J	5,250,000	—	—	—	1.75	—
1994J Proof	45,000	Value: 2.25				
1995A	1,595,000	—	—	—	3.50	—
1995A Proof	45,000	Value: 17.50				
1995D In sets only	20,000	—	—	—	60.00	—
1995D Proof	45,000	Value: 17.50				
1995F In sets only	20,000	—	—	—	60.00	—
1995F Proof	45,000	Value: 17.50				
1995G	920,000	—	—	—	6.00	—

Date	Mintage	F	VF	XF	Unc	BU
1995G Proof	45,000	Value: 17.50				
1995J In sets only	20,000	—	—	—	60.00	—
1995J Proof	45,000	Value: 17.50				
1996A	—	—	—	—	5.00	—
1996A Proof	45,000	Value: 6.00				
1996D	—	—	—	—	5.00	—
1996D Proof	45,000	Value: 6.00				
1996F	—	—	—	—	5.00	—
1996F Proof	45,000	Value: 6.00				
1996G	—	—	—	—	5.00	—
1996G Proof	45,000	Value: 6.00				
1996J	—	—	—	—	5.00	—
1996J Proof	45,000	Value: 6.00				
1997A In sets only	70,000	—	—	—	4.25	—
1997A Proof	45,000	Value: 5.00				
1997D In sets only	70,000	—	—	—	4.25	—
1997D Proof	45,000	Value: 5.00				
1997F In sets only	70,000	—	—	—	4.25	—
1997F Proof	45,000	Value: 5.00				
1997G In sets only	70,000	—	—	—	4.25	—
1997G Proof	45,000	Value: 5.00				
1997J In sets only	70,000	—	—	—	4.25	—
1997J Proof	45,000	Value: 5.00				
1998A In sets only	70,000	—	—	—	4.25	—
1998A Proof	45,000	Value: 5.00				
1998D In sets only	70,000	—	—	—	4.25	—
1998D Proof	45,000	Value: 5.00				
1998F In sets only	70,000	—	—	—	4.25	—
1998F Proof	45,000	Value: 5.00				
1998G In sets only	70,000	—	—	—	4.25	—
1998G Proof	45,000	Value: 5.00				
1998J In sets only	70,000	—	—	—	4.25	—
1998J Proof	45,000	Value: 5.00				
1999A In sets only	70,000	—	—	—	4.25	—
1999A Proof	45,000	Value: 5.00				
1999D In sets only	70,000	—	—	—	4.25	—
1999D Proof	45,000	Value: 5.00				
1999F In sets only	70,000	—	—	—	4.25	—
1999F Proof	45,000	Value: 5.00				
1999G In sets only	70,000	—	—	—	4.75	—
1999G Proof	45,000	Value: 5.00				
1999J In sets only	70,000	—	—	—	4.75	—
1999J Proof	45,000	Value: 5.00				
2000A In sets only	70,000	—	—	—	5.00	—
2000A Proof	45,000	Value: 5.00				
2000D In sets only	70,000	—	—	—	5.00	—
2000D Proof	45,000	Value: 5.00				
2000F In sets only	70,000	—	—	—	5.00	—
2000F Proof	45,000	Value: 5.00				
2000G In sets only	70,000	—	—	—	5.00	—
2000G Proof	45,000	Value: 5.00				
2000J In sets only	70,000	—	—	—	5.00	—
2000J Proof	45,000	Value: 5.00				
2001A In sets only	130,000	—	—	—	10.00	—
2001A Proof	78,000	Value: 10.00				
2001D In sets only	130,000	—	—	—	10.00	—
2001D Proof	78,000	Value: 10.00				
2001F In sets only	130,000	—	—	—	10.00	—
2001F Proof	78,000	Value: 10.00				
2001G In sets only	130,000	—	—	—	10.00	—
2001G Proof	78,000	Value: 10.00				
2001J In sets only	130,000	—	—	—	10.00	—
2001J Proof	78,000	Value: 10.00				

KM# 175 2 MARK Composition: Copper-Nickel Clad Nickel **Reverse:** Head of Franz Joseph Strauss facing left

Date	Mintage	F	VF	XF	Unc	BU
1990D	18,370,000	—	—	—	1.75	—
1990D Proof	45,000	Value: 2.25				
1990F	21,200,000	—	—	—	1.75	—
1990F Proof	45,000	Value: 2.25				
1990G	12,220,000	—	—	—	1.75	—
1990G Proof	45,000	Value: 2.25				
1990J	18,870,000	—	—	—	1.75	—
1990J Proof	45,000	Value: 2.25				
1991A	4,000,000	—	—	—	1.75	—
1991A Proof	45,000	Value: 2.25				
1991D	4,200,000	—	—	—	1.75	—
1991D Proof	45,000	Value: 2.25				
1991F	4,800,000	—	—	—	1.75	—
1991F Proof	45,000	Value: 2.25				
1991G	2,800,000	—	—	—	1.75	—
1991G Proof	45,000	Value: 2.25				
1991J	4,200,000	—	—	—	1.75	—
1991J Proof	45,000	Value: 2.25				
1992A	7,330,000	—	—	—	1.75	—
1992A Proof	45,000	Value: 2.25				
1992D	7,700,000	—	—	—	1.75	—
1992D Proof	45,000	Value: 2.25				
1992F	8,800,000	—	—	—	1.75	—
1992F Proof	45,000	Value: 2.25				
1992G	5,130,000	—	—	—	1.75	—
1992G Proof	45,000	Value: 2.25				
1992J	7,700,000	—	—	—	1.75	—
1992J Proof	45,000	Value: 2.25				
1993A	600,000	—	—	3.00	7.00	—
1993A Proof	45,000	Value: 2.25				
1993D	630,000	—	—	3.00	7.00	—
1993D Proof	45,000	Value: 2.25				
1993F	720,000	—	—	3.00	7.00	—
1993F Proof	45,000	Value: 2.25				
1993G	420,000	—	—	4.00	10.00	—
1993G Proof	45,000	Value: 2.25				
1993J	630,000	—	—	3.00	7.00	—
1993J Proof	45,000	Value: 2.25				
1994A	5,000,000	—	—	—	1.75	—
1994A Proof	45,000	Value: 2.25				
1994D	5,250,000	—	—	—	1.75	—
1994D Proof	45,000	Value: 2.25				
1994F	6,000,000	—	—	—	1.75	—
1994F Proof	45,000	Value: 2.25				
1994G	3,500,000	—	—	—	1.75	—
1994G Proof	45,000	Value: 2.25				
1994J	5,250,000	—	—	—	1.75	—
1994J Proof	45,000	Value: 2.25				
1995A	1,595,000	—	—	—	3.50	—
1995A Proof	45,000	Value: 17.50				
1995D In sets only	20,000	—	—	—	60.00	—
1995D Proof	45,000	Value: 17.50				
1995F In sets only	20,000	—	—	—	60.00	—
1995F Proof	45,000	Value: 17.50				
1995G	620,000	—	—	—	7.00	—
1995G Proof	45,000	Value: 17.50				
1995J In sets only	20,000	—	—	—	60.00	—
1995J Proof	45,000	Value: 17.50				
1996A	—	—	—	—	5.00	—
1996A Proof	45,000	Value: 6.00				
1996D	—	—	—	—	5.00	—
1996D Proof	45,000	Value: 6.00				
1996F	—	—	—	—	5.00	—
1996F Proof	45,000	Value: 6.00				
1996G	—	—	—	—	5.00	—
1996G Proof	45,000	Value: 6.00				
1996J	—	—	—	—	5.00	—
1996J Proof	45,000	Value: 6.00				
1997A In sets only	70,000	—	—	—	4.25	—
1997A Proof	45,000	Value: 5.00				
1997D In sets only	70,000	—	—	—	4.25	—
1997D Proof	45,000	Value: 5.00				
1997F In sets only	70,000	—	—	—	4.25	—
1997F Proof	45,000	Value: 5.00				
1997G In sets only	70,000	—	—	—	4.25	—
1997G Proof	45,000	Value: 5.00				
1997J In sets only	70,000	—	—	—	4.25	—
1997J Proof	45,000	Value: 5.00				
1998A In sets only	70,000	—	—	—	4.25	—
1998A Proof	45,000	Value: 5.00				
1998D In sets only	70,000	—	—	—	4.25	—
1998D Proof	45,000	Value: 5.00				
1998F In sets only	70,000	—	—	—	4.25	—
1998F Proof	45,000	Value: 5.00				
1998G In sets only	70,000	—	—	—	4.25	—
1998G Proof	45,000	Value: 5.00				
1998J In sets only	70,000	—	—	—	4.25	—
1998J Proof	45,000	Value: 5.00				
1999A In sets only	70,000	—	—	—	4.25	—
1999A Proof	45,000	Value: 5.00				
1999D In sets only	70,000	—	—	—	4.25	—
1999D Proof	45,000	Value: 5.00				
1999F In sets only	70,000	—	—	—	4.25	—
1999F Proof	45,000	Value: 5.00				
1999G In sets only	70,000	—	—	—	4.25	—
1999G Proof	45,000	Value: 5.00				
1999J In sets only	70,000	—	—	—	4.25	—
1999J Proof	45,000	Value: 5.00				
2000A In sets only	70,000	—	—	—	5.00	—
2000A Proof	45,000	Value: 5.00				
2000D In sets only	70,000	—	—	—	5.00	—
2000D Proof	45,000	Value: 5.00				
2000F In sets only	70,000	—	—	—	5.00	—
2000F Proof	45,000	Value: 5.00				
2000G In sets only	70,000	—	—	—	5.00	—
2000G Proof	45,000	Value: 5.00				
2000J In sets only	70,000	—	—	—	5.00	—
2000J Proof	45,000	Value: 5.00				
2001A In sets only	130,000	—	—	—	10.00	—
2001A Proof	78,000	Value: 10.00				
2001D In sets only	130,000	—	—	—	10.00	—
2001D Proof	78,000	Value: 10.00				
2001F In sets only	130,000	—	—	—	10.00	—
2001F Proof	78,000	Value: 10.00				
2001G In sets only	130,000	—	—	—	10.00	—
2001G Proof	78,000	Value: 10.00				
2001J In sets only	130,000	—	—	—	10.00	—
2001J Proof	78,000	Value: 10.00				

KM# 183 2 MARK Composition: Copper-Nickel Clad Nickel **Reverse:** Head of Willy Brandt facing forward

Date	Mintage	F	VF	XF	Unc	BU
1994A	5,000,000	—	—	—	2.00	—
1994A Proof	45,000	Value: 2.50				
1994D	5,250,000	—	—	—	2.00	—
1994D Proof	45,000	Value: 2.50				
1994F	6,000,000	—	—	—	2.00	—
1994F Proof	45,000	Value: 2.50				
1994G	3,600,000	—	—	—	2.00	—
1994G Proof	45,000	Value: 2.50				
1994J	5,250,000	—	—	—	2.00	—
1994J Proof	45,000	Value: 2.50				
1995A	1,595,000	—	—	—	3.50	—
1995A Proof	45,000	Value: 17.50				
1995D In sets only	20,000	—	—	—	65.00	—
1995D Proof	45,000	Value: 17.50				
1995F In sets only	20,000	—	—	—	65.00	—
1995F Proof	45,000	Value: 17.50				
1995G	1,220,000	—	—	—	4.50	—
1995G Proof	45,000	Value: 17.50				
1995J	75,000	—	—	—	30.00	—
1995J Proof	45,000	Value: 17.50				
1996A	—	—	—	—	5.50	—
1996A Proof	45,000	Value: 6.50				
1996D	—	—	—	—	5.50	—
1996D Proof	45,000	Value: 6.50				
1996F	—	—	—	—	5.50	—
1996F Proof	45,000	Value: 6.50				
1996G	—	—	—	—	5.50	—
1996G Proof	45,000	Value: 6.50				
1996J	—	—	—	—	5.50	—
1996J Proof	45,000	Value: 6.50				
1997A In sets only	70,000	—	—	—	4.25	—
1997A Proof	45,000	Value: 5.00				
1997D In sets only	70,000	—	—	—	4.25	—
1997D Proof	45,000	Value: 5.00				
1997F In sets only	70,000	—	—	—	4.25	—
1997F Proof	45,000	Value: 5.00				
1997G In sets only	70,000	—	—	—	4.25	—
1997G Proof	45,000	Value: 5.00				
1997J In sets only	70,000	—	—	—	4.25	—
1997J Proof	45,000	Value: 5.00				
1998A In sets only	70,000	—	—	—	4.25	—
1998A Proof	45,000	Value: 5.00				
1998D In sets only	70,000	—	—	—	4.25	—
1998D Proof	45,000	Value: 5.00				
1998F In sets only	70,000	—	—	—	4.25	—
1998F Proof	45,000	Value: 5.00				
1998G In sets only	70,000	—	—	—	4.25	—
1998G Proof	45,000	Value: 5.00				
1998J In sets only	70,000	—	—	—	4.25	—
1998J Proof	45,000	Value: 5.00				
1999A In sets only	70,000	—	—	—	4.25	—
1999A Proof	45,000	Value: 5.00				
1999D In sets only	70,000	—	—	—	4.25	—
1999D Proof	45,000	Value: 5.00				
1999F In sets only	70,000	—	—	—	4.25	—
1999F Proof	45,000	Value: 5.00				
1999G In sets only	70,000	—	—	—	4.25	—
1999G Proof	45,000	Value: 5.00				
1999J In sets only	70,000	—	—	—	4.25	—
1999J Proof	45,000	Value: 5.00				
2000A In sets only	70,000	—	—	—	5.00	—
2000A Proof	45,000	Value: 5.00				
2000D In sets only	70,000	—	—	—	5.00	—
2000D Proof	45,000	Value: 5.00				
2000F In sets only	70,000	—	—	—	5.00	—
2000F Proof	45,000	Value: 5.00				
2000G In sets only	70,000	—	—	—	5.00	—
2000G Proof	45,000	Value: 5.00				
2000J In sets only	70,000	—	—	—	5.00	—
2000J Proof	45,000	Value: 5.00				
2001A In sets only	130,000	—	—	—	10.00	—
2001A Proof	78,000	Value: 10.00				
2001D In sets only	130,000	—	—	—	10.00	—
2001D Proof	78,000	Value: 10.00				
2001F In sets only	130,000	—	—	—	10.00	—
2001F Proof	78,000	Value: 10.00				
2001G In sets only	130,000	—	—	—	10.00	—
2001G Proof	78,000	Value: 10.00				
2001J In sets only	130,000	—	—	—	10.00	—
2001J Proof	78,000	Value: 10.00				

KM# 112.1 5 MARK **Weight:** 11.2000 g. **Composition:** 0.6250 Silver .2250 oz. ASW **Note:** Federal Republic.

Date	F	VF	XF	Unc	BU
1951D	—	4.00	15.00	65.00	—
1951D Proof	—	Value: 250			
1951F	—	4.00	15.00	75.00	—
1951F Proof	280	Value: 250			
1951G	—	4.00	15.00	75.00	—
1951G Proof	—	Value: 450			
1951J	—	4.00	15.00	60.00	—
1951J Proof	—	Value: 225			
1956D	—	15.00	60.00	225	—
1956D Proof	—	Value: 450			
1956F	—	10.00	75.00	375	—
1956F Proof	23	Value: 1,000			
1956J	—	10.00	60.00	225	—
1956J Proof	—	Value: 450			
1957D	—	10.00	85.00	400	—
1957D Proof	—	Value: 475			
1957F	—	7.50	50.00	300	—
1957F Proof	—	Value: 500			
1957G	—	10.00	65.00	350	—
1957G Proof	—	Value: 400			
1957J	—	7.50	30.00	150	—
1957J Proof	—	Value: 250			
1958D	—	7.50	30.00	150	—
1958D Proof	—	Value: 300			
1958F	—	20.00	125	600	—
1958F Proof	100	Value: 800			
1958G	—	7.50	28.00	130	—
1958G Proof	—	Value: 400			
1958J	—	1,100	2,500	3,750	—
1958J Proof	—	Value: 4,000			
1959D	—	10.00	45.00	245	—
1959D Proof	—	Value: 400			
1959G	—	15.00	55.00	235	—
1959G Proof	—	Value: 500			
1959J	—	8.00	40.00	225	—
1959J Proof	—	Value: 375			
1960D	—	7.00	20.00	110	—
1960D Proof	—	Value: 300			
1960F	—	7.00	20.00	110	—
1960F Proof	50	Value: 700			
1960G	—	7.00	22.00	125	—
1960G Proof	—	Value: 250			
1960J	—	7.00	18.00	90.00	—
1960J Proof	—	Value: 400			
1961D	—	4.50	15.00	80.00	—
1961D Proof	—	Value: 225			
1961F	—	4.50	22.00	125	—
1961F Proof	—	Value: 450			
1961J	—	6.00	28.00	135	—
1961J Proof	—	Value: 550			
1963D	—	4.50	15.00	60.00	—
1963D Proof	—	Value: 350			
1963F	—	4.50	18.00	70.00	—
1963F Proof	—	Value: 350			
1963G	—	7.50	20.00	100	—
1963G Proof	Est. 100	Value: 400			
1963J	—	4.50	15.00	60.00	—
1963J Proof	—	Value: 350			
1964D	—	15.00	50.00	175	—
1964D Proof	—	Value: 375			
1964F	—	4.50	15.00	60.00	—
1964F Proof	—	Value: 350			
1964G	—	4.50	15.00	45.00	—
1964G Proof	Est. 600	Value: 80.00			
1964J	—	4.00	15.00	45.00	—
1964J Proof	—	Value: 200			
1965D	—	4.00	12.50	30.00	—
1965D Proof	—	Value: 175			
1965F	—	4.00	8.00	30.00	—
1965F Proof	Est. 80	Value: 385			
1965G	—	4.00	7.00	25.00	—
1965G Proof	8,233	Value: 42.00			
1965J	—	4.00	7.00	25.00	—
1965J Proof	—	Value: 250			
1966D	—	4.00	7.00	22.50	—
1966D Proof	—	Value: 250			
1966F	—	4.00	7.00	22.50	—
1966F Proof	100	Value: 385			
1966G	—	4.00	7.00	22.50	—
1966G Proof	3,070	Value: 45.00			
1966J	—	4.00	7.00	22.50	—
1966J Proof	1,000	Value: 110			
1967D	—	4.00	7.00	22.50	—
1967D Proof	—	Value: 200			
1967F	—	4.00	7.00	22.50	—
1967F Proof	1,500	Value: 75.00			
1967G	—	4.00	7.00	25.00	—
1967G Proof	4,500	Value: 35.00			

Date	F	VF	XF	Unc	BU
1967J	—	4.00	7.00	22.50	—
Note: Errors exist with coin alignment					
1967J Proof	1,500	Value: 90.00			
1968D	—	4.00	10.00	35.00	—
1968D Proof	—	Value: 60.00			
1968F	—	4.00	10.00	35.00	—
1968F Proof	3,000	Value: 75.00			
1968G	—	4.00	10.00	35.00	—
1968G Proof	6,023	Value: 35.00			
1968J	—	4.00	10.00	35.00	—
1968J Proof	2,000	Value: 65.00			
1969D	—	4.00	7.00	20.00	—
1969D Proof	—	Value: 25.00			
1969F	—	4.00	7.00	20.00	—
1969F Proof	5,000	Value: 25.00			
1969G	—	4.00	7.00	20.00	—
1969G Proof	8,700	Value: 20.00			
1969J	—	4.00	7.00	20.00	—
1969J Proof	5,000	Value: 25.00			
1970D	—	4.00	7.00	20.00	—
1970D Proof	—	Value: 20.00			
1970F	—	4.00	7.00	20.00	—
1970F Proof	5,140	Value: 25.00			
1970G	—	3.50	4.50	8.50	—
1970G Proof	10,200	Value: 18.00			
1970J	—	3.50	4.50	8.50	—
1970J Proof	5,000	Value: 25.00			
1971D	—	3.50	4.50	8.50	—
1971D Proof	8,000	Value: 20.00			
1971F	—	3.50	4.50	8.50	—
1971F Proof	8,000	Value: 20.00			
1971G	—	3.50	4.50	8.50	—
1971G Proof	10,000	Value: 18.00			
1971J	—	3.50	4.50	8.50	—
1971J Proof	8,000	Value: 20.00			
1972D	—	3.50	4.50	8.50	—
1972D Proof	8,000	Value: 20.00			
1972F	—	3.50	4.50	8.50	—
1972F Proof	8,100	Value: 20.00			
1972G	—	3.50	4.50	8.50	—
1972G Proof	10,000	Value: 18.00			
1972J	—	3.50	4.50	7.50	—
1972J Proof	8,000	Value: 20.00			
1973D	—	3.50	4.50	7.50	—
1973D Proof	9,000	Value: 18.00			
1973F	—	3.50	4.50	7.50	—
1973F Proof	9,100	Value: 18.00			
1973G	—	3.50	4.50	7.50	—
1973G Proof	9,000	Value: 18.00			
1973J	—	3.50	4.50	7.50	—
1973J Proof	9,000	Value: 18.00			
1974D	—	3.50	4.50	7.50	—
1974D Proof	35,000	Value: 15.00			
1974F	—	3.50	4.50	7.50	—
1974F Proof	35,000	Value: 15.00			
1974G	—	3.50	4.50	7.50	—
1974G Proof	35,000	Value: 15.00			
1974J	—	3.50	4.50	7.50	—
1974J Proof	35,000	Value: 15.00			

KM# 112.3 5 MARK **Weight:** 11.2000 g. **Composition:** 0.6250 Silver .2250 oz. ASW **Note:** Error. With edge lettering. GRUSS DICH DEUTSCHLAND AUS HERZENSGRUND.

Date	F	VF	XF	Unc	BU
1957J	—	1,250	1,650	2,400	—

KM# 112.2 5 MARK **Weight:** 11.2000 g. **Composition:** 0.6250 Silver .2250 oz. ASW **Note:** Uninscribed plain edge errors.

Date	F	VF	XF	Unc	BU
1959D	—	60.00	120	175	—
1959J	—	60.00	120	175	—
1963J	—	60.00	120	175	—
1964F	—	60.00	120	175	—
1964G	—	—	—	—	—
1965J	—	—	—	—	—
1965F	—	60.00	120	175	—
1965G	—	60.00	120	175	—
1966F	—	125	250	345	—
1966G	—	60.00	120	175	—
Note: Errors without edge inscription exist with coin alignment					
1967D	—	125	250	345	—
1967G	—	60.00	120	175	—
1969F	—	—	—	—	—
1970F	—	—	—	—	—
1970G	—	—	—	—	—
1971F	—	—	—	—	—
1972F	—	—	—	—	—
1973F	—	—	—	—	—
1974F	—	—	—	—	—

KM# 112.4 5 MARK **Weight:** 11.2000 g. **Composition:** 0.6250 Silver .2250 oz. ASW **Note:** Error. With edge lettering. ALLE MENSCHEN WERDEN BRUDER.

Date	F	VF	XF	Unc	BU
1970F	—	1,250	1,650	2,400	—

KM# 140.1 5 MARK **Weight:** 10.0000 g. **Composition:** Copper-Nickel Clad Nickel

Date	Mintage	F	VF	XF	Unc	BU
1975D	65,663,000	—	—	3.50	4.50	—
Note: Error strikes exist without edge inscription						
1975D Proof	43,000	Value: 7.00				
1975F	75,002,000	—	—	3.50	4.50	—
Note: Error strikes exist without edge inscription						
1975F Proof	43,000	Value: 7.00				
1975G	43,297,000	—	—	3.50	4.50	—
1975G Proof	43,000	Value: 7.00				
1975J	67,372,000	—	—	3.50	4.50	—
1975J Proof	43,000	Value: 7.00				
1976D	7,821,000	—	—	3.50	5.00	—
1976D Proof	43,000	Value: 7.00				
1976F	9,072,000	—	—	3.50	5.00	—
1976F Proof	43,000	Value: 7.00				
1976G	5,784,000	—	—	3.50	5.00	—
1976G Proof	43,000	Value: 7.00				
1976J	8,068,000	—	—	3.50	5.00	—
1976J Proof	43,000	Value: 7.00				
1977D	8,321,000	—	—	3.50	5.00	—
1977D Proof	51,000	Value: 6.00				
1977F	9,612,000	—	—	3.50	5.00	—
1977F Proof	51,000	Value: 6.00				
1977G	5,746,000	—	—	3.50	5.00	—
1977G Proof	51,000	Value: 6.00				
1977J	8,577,000	—	—	3.50	5.00	—
1977J Proof	51,000	Value: 6.00				
1978D	7,854,000	—	—	3.50	5.00	—
1978D Proof	54,000	Value: 6.00				
1978F	9,054,000	—	—	3.50	5.00	—
1978F Proof	54,000	Value: 6.00				
1978G	5,244,000	—	—	3.50	5.00	—
1978G Proof	54,000	Value: 6.00				
1978J	8,064,000	—	—	3.50	5.00	—
1978J Proof	54,000	Value: 6.00				
1979D	7,889,000	—	—	3.50	5.00	—
1979D Proof	89,000	Value: 6.00				
1979F	9,089,000	—	—	3.50	5.00	—
1979F Proof	89,000	Value: 6.00				
1979G	5,279,000	—	—	3.50	5.00	—
1979G Proof	89,000	Value: 6.00				
1979J	8,099,000	—	—	3.50	5.00	—
1979J Proof	89,000	Value: 6.00				
1980D	8,300,000	—	—	3.50	5.00	—
1980D Proof	110,000	Value: 6.00				
1980F	9,640,000	—	—	3.50	5.00	—
1980F Proof	110,000	Value: 6.00				
1980G	5,500,000	—	—	3.50	5.00	—
1980G Proof	110,000	Value: 6.00				
1980J	8,500,000	—	—	3.50	5.00	—
1980J Proof	110,000	Value: 6.00				
1981D	8,300,000	—	—	3.50	5.00	—
1981D Proof	91,000	Value: 6.00				
1981F	9,600,000	—	—	3.50	5.00	—
1981F Proof	91,000	Value: 6.00				
1981G	5,500,000	—	—	3.50	5.00	—
1981G Proof	91,000	Value: 6.00				
1981J	8,500,000	—	—	3.50	5.00	—
1981J Proof	91,000	Value: 6.00				
1982D	8,900,000	—	—	3.50	5.00	—
1982D Proof	78,000	Value: 6.00				
1982F	10,300,000	—	—	3.50	5.00	—
1982F Proof	78,000	Value: 6.00				
1982G	5,990,000	—	—	3.50	5.00	—
1982G Proof	78,000	Value: 6.00				
1982J	9,100,000	—	—	3.50	5.00	—
1982J Proof	78,000	Value: 6.00				
1983D	6,240,000	—	—	3.50	5.00	—
1983D Proof	75,000	Value: 6.00				
1983F	7,200,000	—	—	3.50	5.00	—
1983F Proof	75,000	Value: 6.00				
1983G	4,152,000	—	—	3.50	5.00	—
1983G Proof	75,000	Value: 6.00				
1983J	6,408,000	—	—	3.50	5.00	—
1983J Proof	75,000	Value: 6.00				
1984D	6,000,000	—	—	3.50	5.00	—
1984D Proof	64,000	Value: 6.00				
1984F	6,900,000	—	—	3.50	5.00	—
1984F Proof	64,000	Value: 6.00				
1984G	4,000,000	—	—	3.50	5.00	—
1984G Proof	64,000	Value: 6.00				
1984J	6,100,000	—	—	3.50	5.00	—
1984J Proof	64,000	Value: 6.00				
1985D	4,900,000	—	—	3.50	5.00	—
1985D Proof	56,000	Value: 6.00				
1985F	5,700,000	—	—	3.50	5.00	—
1985F Proof	54,000	Value: 6.00				
1985G	3,300,000	—	—	3.50	5.00	—
1985G Proof	55,000	Value: 6.00				

Date	Mintage	F	VF	XF	Unc	BU
1985J	5,100,000	—	—	3.50	5.00	—
1985J Proof	54,000	Value: 6.00				
1986D	4,900,000	—	—	3.50	5.00	—
1986D Proof	44,000	Value: 6.00				
1986F	5,700,000	—	—	3.50	5.00	—
1986F Proof	44,000	Value: 6.00				
1986G	3,300,000	—	—	3.50	5.00	—
1986G Proof	44,000	Value: 6.00				
1986J	5,100,000	—	—	3.50	5.00	—
1986J Proof	44,000	Value: 6.00				
1987D	6,760,000	—	—	3.50	5.00	—
1987D Proof	45,000	Value: 6.00				
1987F	7,800,000	—	—	3.50	5.00	—
1987F Proof	45,000	Value: 6.00				
1987G	4,500,000	—	—	3.50	5.00	—
1987G Proof	45,000	Value: 6.00				
1987J	6,940,000	—	—	3.50	5.00	—
1987J Proof	45,000	Value: 6.00				
1988D	11,960,000	—	—	—	4.00	—
1988D Proof	45,000	Value: 5.00				
1988F	13,800,000	—	—	—	4.00	—
1988F Proof	45,000	Value: 5.00				
1988G	7,960,000	—	—	—	4.00	—
1988G Proof	45,000	Value: 5.00				
1988J	12,280,000	—	—	—	4.00	—
1988J Proof	45,000	Value: 5.00				
1989D	17,160,000	—	—	—	4.00	—
1989D Proof	45,000	Value: 5.00				
1989F	19,800,000	—	—	—	4.00	—
1989F Proof	45,000	Value: 5.00				
1989G	11,420,000	—	—	—	4.00	—
1989G Proof	45,000	Value: 5.00				
1989J	17,620,000	—	—	—	4.00	—
1989J Proof	45,000	Value: 5.00				
1990D	20,900,000	—	—	—	4.00	—
1990D Proof	45,000	Value: 5.00				
1990F	24,120,000	—	—	—	4.00	—
1990F Proof	45,000	Value: 5.00				
1990G	13,910,000	—	—	—	4.00	—
1990G Proof	45,000	Value: 5.00				
1990J	21,470,000	—	—	—	4.00	—
1990J Proof	45,000	Value: 5.00				
1991A	18,000,000	—	—	—	4.00	—
1991A Proof	45,000	Value: 5.00				
1991D	18,900,000	—	—	—	4.00	—
1991D Proof	45,000	Value: 5.00				
1991F	21,600,000	—	—	—	4.00	—
1991F Proof	45,000	Value: 5.00				
1991G	12,600,000	—	—	—	4.00	—
1991G Proof	45,000	Value: 5.00				
1991J	18,900,000	—	—	—	4.00	—
1991J Proof	45,000	Value: 5.00				
1992A	16,000,000	—	—	—	4.00	—
1992A Proof	45,000	Value: 5.00				
1992D	16,800,000	—	—	—	4.00	—
1992D Proof	45,000	Value: 5.00				
1992F	19,200,000	—	—	—	4.00	—
1992F Proof	45,000	Value: 5.00				
1992G	11,200,000	—	—	—	4.00	—
1992G Proof	45,000	Value: 5.00				
1992J	16,800,000	—	—	—	4.00	—
1992J Proof	45,000	Value: 5.00				
1993A	3,200,000	—	—	—	4.00	—
1993A Proof	45,000	Value: 5.00				
1993D	3,380,000	—	—	—	4.00	—
1993D Proof	45,000	Value: 5.00				
1993F	3,840,000	—	—	—	4.00	—
1993F Proof	45,000	Value: 5.00				
1993G	2,240,000	—	—	—	4.00	—
1993G Proof	45,000	Value: 5.00				
1993J	3,360,000	—	—	—	4.00	—
1993J Proof	45,000	Value: 5.00				
1994A	4,000,000	—	—	—	4.00	—
1994A Proof	45,000	Value: 5.00				
1994D	4,200,000	—	—	—	4.00	—
1994D Proof	45,000	Value: 5.00				
1994F	4,800,000	—	—	—	4.00	—
1994F Proof	45,000	Value: 5.00				
1994G	2,800,000	—	—	—	4.00	—
1994G Proof	45,000	Value: 5.00				
1994J	4,200,000	—	—	—	4.00	—
1994J Proof	45,000	Value: 5.00				
1995A In sets only	20,000	—	—	—	80.00	—
1995A Proof	45,000	Value: 30.00				
1995D In sets only	20,000	—	—	—	80.00	—
1995D Proof	45,000	Value: 30.00				
1995F In sets only	20,000	—	—	—	80.00	—
1995F Proof	45,000	Value: 30.00				
1995G In sets only	20,000	—	—	—	80.00	—
1995G Proof	45,000	Value: 30.00				
1995J In sets only	20,000	—	—	—	80.00	—
1995J Proof	45,000	Value: 30.00				
1996A In sets only	50,000	—	—	—	15.00	—
1996A Proof	45,000	Value: 17.50				
1996D In sets only	50,000	—	—	—	15.00	—
1996D Proof	45,000	Value: 17.50				
1996F In sets only	50,000	—	—	—	15.00	—
1996F Proof	45,000	Value: 17.50				
1996G In sets only	50,000	—	—	—	15.00	—
1996G Proof	45,000	Value: 17.50				
1996J In sets only	50,000	—	—	—	15.00	—
1996J Proof	45,000	Value: 17.50				

Date	Mintage	F	VF	XF	Unc	BU
1997A In sets only	70,000	—	—	—	6.00	—
1997A Proof	45,000	Value: 7.00				
1997D In sets only	70,000	—	—	—	6.00	—
1997D Proof	45,000	Value: 7.00				
1997F In sets only	70,000	—	—	—	6.00	—
1997F Proof	45,000	Value: 7.00				
1997G In sets only	70,000	—	—	—	6.00	—
1997G Proof	45,000	Value: 7.00				
1997J In sets only	70,000	—	—	—	6.00	—
1997J Proof	45,000	Value: 7.00				
1998A In sets only	70,000	—	—	—	6.00	—
1998A Proof	45,000	Value: 7.00				
1998D In sets only	70,000	—	—	—	6.00	—
1998D Proof	45,000	Value: 7.00				
1998F In sets only	70,000	—	—	—	6.00	—
1998F Proof	45,000	Value: 7.00				
1998G In sets only	70,000	—	—	—	6.00	—
1998G Proof	45,000	Value: 7.00				
1998J In sets only	70,000	—	—	—	6.00	—
1998J Proof	45,000	Value: 7.00				
1999A In sets only	70,000	—	—	—	6.00	—
1999A Proof	45,000	Value: 7.00				
1999D In sets only	70,000	—	—	—	6.00	—
1999D Proof	45,000	Value: 7.00				
1999F In sets only	70,000	—	—	—	6.00	—
1999F Proof	45,000	Value: 7.00				
1999G In sets only	70,000	—	—	—	6.00	—
1999G Proof	45,000	Value: 7.00				
1999J In sets only	70,000	—	—	—	6.00	—
1999J Proof	45,000	Value: 7.00				
2000A In sets only	70,000	—	—	—	15.00	—
2000A Proof	45,000	Value: 15.00				
2000D In sets only	70,000	—	—	—	15.00	—
2000D Proof	45,000	Value: 15.00				
2000F In sets only	70,000	—	—	—	15.00	—
2000F Proof	45,000	Value: 15.00				
2000G In sets only	70,000	—	—	—	15.00	—
2000G Proof	45,000	Value: 15.00				
2000J In sets only	70,000	—	—	—	15.00	—
2000J Proof	45,000	Value: 15.00				
2001A In sets only	130,000	—	—	—	30.00	—
2001A Proof	78,000	Value: 30.00				
2001D In sets only	130,000	—	—	—	30.00	—
2001D Proof	78,000	Value: 30.00				
2001F In sets only	130,000	—	—	—	30.00	—
2001F Proof	78,000	Value: 30.00				
2001G In sets only	130,000	—	—	—	30.00	—
2001G Proof	78,000	Value: 30.00				
2001J In sets only	130,000	—	—	—	30.00	—
2001J Proof	78,000	Value: 30.00				

KM# 140.2 5 MARK **Weight:** 5.4400 g. **Composition:** Copper-Nickel Clad Nickel **Note:** Thin variety.

Date	F	VF	XF	Unc	BU
1975J	—	—	90.00	150	—

Note: Illegally produced by a German Mint official

COMMEMORATIVE COINAGE

KM# 113 5 MARK **Weight:** 11.2000 g. **Composition:** 0.6250 Silver .2250 oz. ASW **Subject:** Centenary - Nurnberg Museum

Date	Mintage	F	VF	XF	Unc	BU
1952D	199,000	—	450	750	1,150	—
1952D Proof	1,345	Value: 3,250				

KM# 114 5 MARK **Weight:** 11.2000 g. **Composition:** 0.6250 Silver .2250 oz. ASW **Subject:** 150th Anniversary - Death of Friedrich von Schiller

Date	Mintage	F	VF	XF	Unc	BU
1955F	199,000	—	200	450	650	—
1955F Proof	1,217	Value: 1,650				

KM# 115 5 MARK **Weight:** 11.2000 g. **Composition:** 0.6250 Silver .2250 oz. ASW **Subject:** 300th Anniversary - Birth of Ludwig von Baden

Date	Mintage	F	VF	XF	Unc	BU
1955G	—	—	200	325	550	—
1955G Proof	Est. 2,000	Value: 1,550				

Note: This coin was restruck without authorization by a mint official using genuine dies - quantity unknown

KM# 117 5 MARK **Weight:** 11.2000 g. **Composition:** 0.6250 Silver .2250 oz. ASW **Subject:** Centenary - Death of Joseph Freiherr von Eichendorff

Date	Mintage	F	VF	XF	Unc	BU
1957J	198,000	—	200	325	575	—
1957J Proof	2,000	Value: 1,600				

KM# 118.1 5 MARK **Weight:** 11.2000 g. **Composition:** 0.6250 Silver .2250 oz. ASW **Subject:** 150th Anniversary - Death of Johann Gottlieb Fichte

Date	Mintage	F	VF	XF	Unc	BU
1964J	495,000	—	50.00	95.00	185	—
1964J Proof	5,000	Value: 700				

KM# 118.2 5 MARK **Weight:** 11.2000 g. **Composition:** 0.6250 Silver .2250 oz. ASW **Note:** Error. Plain edge.

Date	F	VF	XF	Unc	BU
1964J	—	250	500	900	—

KM# 119.1 5 MARK **Weight:** 11.2000 g. **Composition:** 0.6250 Silver .2250 oz. ASW **Subject:** 250th Anniversary - Death of Gottfried Wilhelm Leibniz

Date	Mintage	F	VF	XF	Unc	BU
1966D	1,940,000	—	10.00	20.00	35.00	—
1966D Proof	60,000	Value: 95.00				

KM# 119.2 5 MARK **Weight:** 11.2000 g. **Composition:** 0.6250 Silver .2250 oz. ASW **Note:** Error. Plain edge.

Date	F	VF	XF	Unc	BU
1966D	—	225	425	700	—

KM# 120.2 5 MARK **Weight:** 11.2000 g. **Composition:** 0.6250 Silver .2250 oz. ASW **Note:** Error. Plain edge.

Date	F	VF	XF	Unc	BU
1967F	—	225	425	700	—

KM# 120.1 5 MARK **Weight:** 11.2000 g. **Composition:** 0.6250 Silver .2250 oz. ASW **Subject:** Wilhelm and Alexander von Humboldt

Date	Mintage	F	VF	XF	Unc	BU
1967F	2,000,000	—	12.00	20.00	40.00	—
1967F Proof	60,000	Value: 110				

KM# 121 5 MARK **Weight:** 11.2000 g. **Composition:** 0.6250 Silver .2250 oz. ASW **Subject:** 150th Anniversary - Birth of Friedrich Raiffeisen

Date	Mintage	F	VF	XF	Unc	BU
1968J	3,860,000	—	3.50	5.00	9.00	—
1968J Proof	140,000	Value: 32.00				

KM# 122 5 MARK **Weight:** 11.2000 g. **Composition:** 0.6250 Silver .2250 oz. ASW **Subject:** 500th Anniversary - Death of Johannes Gutenberg

Date	Mintage	F	VF	XF	Unc	BU
1968G	2,900,000	—	4.00	9.00	15.00	—
1968G Proof	100,000	Value: 45.00				

KM# 123.1 5 MARK **Weight:** 11.2000 g. **Composition:** 0.6250 Silver .2250 oz. ASW **Subject:** 150th Anniversary - Birth of Max von Pettenkofer

Date	Mintage	F	VF	XF	Unc	BU
1968D	2,900,000	—	4.00	8.50	13.50	—
1968D Proof	100,000	Value: 37.50				

KM# 123.2 5 MARK **Weight:** 11.2000 g. **Composition:** 0.6250 Silver .2250 oz. ASW **Note:** Polished devices.

Date	F	VF	XF	Unc	BU
1968D Proof	—	Value: 300			

KM# 125.1 5 MARK **Weight:** 11.2000 g. **Composition:** 0.6250 Silver .2250 oz. ASW **Subject:** 150th Anniversary - Birth of Theodor Fontane

Date	Mintage	F	VF	XF	Unc	BU
1969G	2,830,000	—	4.00	8.50	14.50	—
1969G Proof	170,000	Value: 27.50				

KM# 126.1 5 MARK **Weight:** 11.2000 g. **Composition:** 0.6250 Silver .2250 oz. ASW **Subject:** 375th Anniversary - Death of Gerhard Mercator

Date	Mintage	F	VF	XF	Unc	BU
1969F	5,004,000	—	—	—	5.50	—
1969F Proof	200,000	Value: 15.00				

KM# 126.2 5 MARK **Weight:** 11.2000 g. **Composition:** 0.6250 Silver .2250 oz. ASW **Note:** Error. Plain edge.

Date	F	VF	XF	Unc	BU
1969F	—	250	450	750	—

KM# 125.2 5 MARK **Weight:** 11.2000 g. **Composition:** 0.6250 Silver .2250 oz. ASW **Note:** Error. Incomplete nose and hair.

Date	F	VF	XF	Unc	BU
1969G Proof	—	Value: 140			

KM# 126.3 5 MARK **Weight:** 11.2000 g. **Composition:** 0.6250 Silver .2250 oz. ASW **Note:** Error. With edge lettering; Einigkeit und Recht und Freiheit.

Date	F	VF	XF	Unc	BU
1969F	—	600	1,000	1,600	—

KM# 126.4 5 MARK **Weight:** 11.2000 g. **Composition:** 0.6250 Silver .2250 oz. ASW **Note:** Error. With long R.

Date	F	VF	XF	Unc	BU
1969F	—	25.00	55.00	100	—

KM# 127 5 MARK **Weight:** 11.2000 g. **Composition:** 0.6250 Silver .2250 oz. ASW **Subject:** 200th Anniversary - Birth of Ludwig van Beethoven

Date	Mintage	F	VF	XF	Unc	BU
1970F	5,000,000	—	—	4.00	7.50	—
1970F Proof	200,000	Value: 15.00				

KM# 129 5 MARK **Weight:** 11.2000 g. **Composition:** 0.6250 Silver .2250 oz. ASW **Subject:** 500th Anniversary - Birth of Albrecht Durer

Date	Mintage	F	VF	XF	Unc	BU
1971D	8,000,000	—	—	—	5.00	—
1971D Proof	200,000	Value: 20.00				

KM# 128.1 5 MARK **Weight:** 11.2000 g. **Composition:** 0.6250 Silver .2250 oz. ASW **Subject:** German Unification

Date	Mintage	F	VF	XF	Unc	BU
1971G	5,000,000	—	4.00	5.50	10.00	—
1971G Proof	200,000	Value: 20.00				

KM# 128.2 5 MARK **Weight:** 11.2000 g. **Composition:** 0.6250 Silver .2250 oz. ASW **Note:** Error. With weak window details.

Date	F	VF	XF	Unc	BU
1971F Proof	—	Value: 100			

KM# 136 5 MARK **Weight:** 11.2000 g. **Composition:** 0.6250 Silver .2250 oz. ASW **Subject:** 500th Anniversary - Birth of Nicholas Copernicus

Date	Mintage	F	VF	XF	Unc	BU
1973J	8,000,000	—	—	—	5.00	—
1973J Proof	250,000	Value: 12.00				

KM# 137 5 MARK **Weight:** 11.2000 g. **Composition:** 0.6250 Silver .2250 oz. ASW **Subject:** 125th Anniversary - Frankfurt Parliament

Date	Mintage	F	VF	XF	Unc	BU
1973G	8,000,000	—	—	—	5.00	—
1973G Proof	250,000	Value: 12.00				

KM# 138 5 MARK **Weight:** 11.2000 g. **Composition:** 0.6250 Silver .2250 oz. ASW **Subject:** 25th Anniversary - Constitutional Law

Date	Mintage	F	VF	XF	Unc	BU
1974F	8,000,000	—	—	—	5.00	—
1974F Proof	250,000	Value: 12.00				

KM# 139 5 MARK **Weight:** 11.2000 g. **Composition:** 0.6250 Silver .2250 oz. ASW **Subject:** 250th Anniversary - Birth of Immanuel Kant

Date	Mintage	F	VF	XF	Unc	BU
1974D	8,000,000	—	—	—	5.00	—
1974D Proof	250,000	Value: 14.00				

KM# 143 5 MARK **Weight:** 5.3000 g. **Composition:** 0.6250 Silver .2250 oz. ASW **Subject:** Centenary - Birth of Albert Schweitzer

Date	Mintage	F	VF	XF	Unc	BU
1975G	8,000,000	—	—	—	5.00	—
1975G Proof	250,000	Value: 14.00				

KM# 141 5 MARK **Weight:** 11.2000 g. **Composition:** 0.6250 Silver .2250 oz. ASW **Subject:** 50th Anniversary - Death of Friedrich Ebert

Date	Mintage	F	VF	XF	Unc	BU
1975J	8,000,000	—	—	—	5.00	—
1975J Proof	250,000	Value: 14.00				

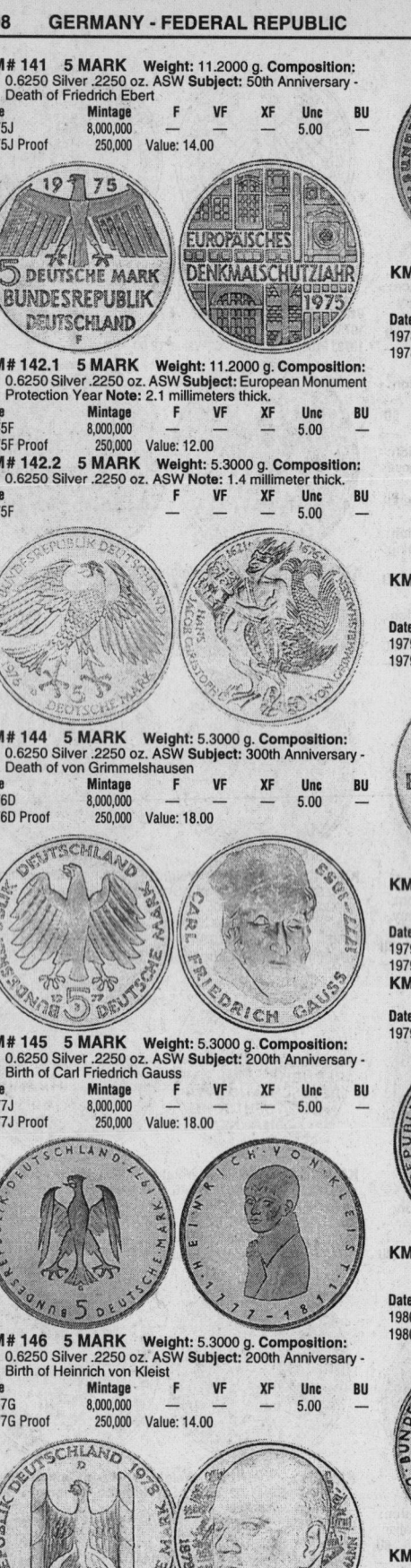

KM# 142.1 5 MARK **Weight:** 11.2000 g. **Composition:** 0.6250 Silver .2250 oz. ASW **Subject:** European Monument Protection Year **Note:** 2.1 millimeters thick.

Date	Mintage	F	VF	XF	Unc	BU
1975F	8,000,000	—	—	—	5.00	—
1975F Proof	250,000	Value: 12.00				

KM# 142.2 5 MARK **Weight:** 5.3000 g. **Composition:** 0.6250 Silver .2250 oz. ASW **Note:** 1.4 millimeter thick.

Date	F	VF	XF	Unc	BU
1975F	—	—	—	5.00	—

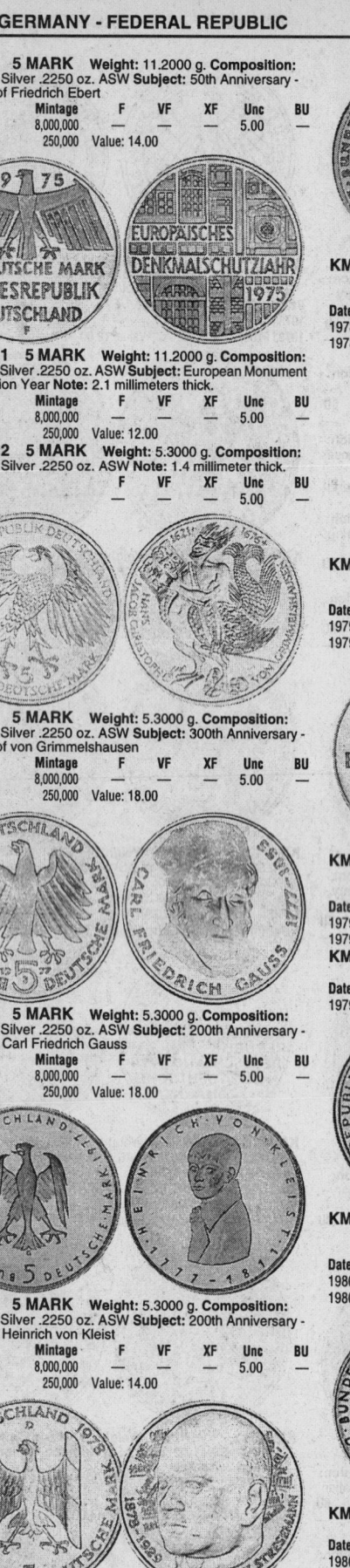

KM# 144 5 MARK **Weight:** 5.3000 g. **Composition:** 0.6250 Silver .2250 oz. ASW **Subject:** 300th Anniversary - Death of von Grimmelshausen

Date	Mintage	F	VF	XF	Unc	BU
1976D	8,000,000	—	—	—	5.00	—
1976D Proof	250,000	Value: 18.00				

KM# 145 5 MARK **Weight:** 5.3000 g. **Composition:** 0.6250 Silver .2250 oz. ASW **Subject:** 200th Anniversary - Birth of Carl Friedrich Gauss

Date	Mintage	F	VF	XF	Unc	BU
1977J	8,000,000	—	—	—	5.00	—
1977J Proof	250,000	Value: 18.00				

KM# 146 5 MARK **Weight:** 5.3000 g. **Composition:** 0.6250 Silver .2250 oz. ASW **Subject:** 200th Anniversary - Birth of Heinrich von Kleist

Date	Mintage	F	VF	XF	Unc	BU
1977G	8,000,000	—	—	—	5.00	—
1977G Proof	250,000	Value: 14.00				

KM# 147 5 MARK **Weight:** 5.3000 g. **Composition:** 0.6250 Silver .2250 oz. ASW **Subject:** 100th Anniversary - Birth of Gustav Stresemann

Date	Mintage	F	VF	XF	Unc	BU
1978D	8,000,000	—	—	—	5.00	—
1978D Proof	250,000	Value: 14.00				

KM# 148 5 MARK **Weight:** 5.3000 g. **Composition:** 0.6250 Silver .2250 oz. ASW **Subject:** 225th Anniversary - Death of Balthasar Neumann

Date	Mintage	F	VF	XF	Unc	BU
1978F	8,000,000	—	—	—	5.00	—
1978F Proof	259,000	Value: 12.00				

KM# 150 5 MARK **Weight:** 5.3000 g. **Composition:** 0.6250 Silver .2250 oz. ASW **Subject:** 150th Anniversary - German Archaeological Institute

Date	Mintage	F	VF	XF	Unc	BU
1979J	8,000,000	—	—	—	5.00	—
1979J Proof	250,000	Value: 14.00				

KM# 151 5 MARK **Weight:** 10.0000 g. **Composition:** Copper-Nickel Clad Nickel **Subject:** 100th Anniversary - Birth of Otto Hahn

Date	Mintage	F	VF	XF	Unc	BU
1979G	5,000,000	—	—	4.00	7.00	—
1979G Proof	350,000	Value: 10.00				

KM# 151a 5 MARK **Weight:** 11.2000 g. **Composition:** 0.6250 Silver .2250 oz. ASW

Date	Mintage	F	VF	XF	Unc	BU
1979G	18	—	—	—	22,500	—

KM# 152 5 MARK **Composition:** Copper-Nickel Clad Nickel **Subject:** 750th Anniversary - Death of von der Vogelweide

Date	Mintage	F	VF	XF	Unc	BU
1980D	5,000,000	—	—	4.00	7.00	—
1980D Proof	350,000	Value: 11.50				

KM# 153 5 MARK **Composition:** Copper-Nickel Clad Nickel **Subject:** 100th Anniversary - Cologne Cathedral

Date	Mintage	F	VF	XF	Unc	BU
1980F	5,000,000	—	—	4.50	8.50	—
1980F Proof	350,000	Value: 13.50				

KM# 154 5 MARK **Composition:** Copper-Nickel Clad Nickel **Subject:** 200th Anniversary - Death of Gotthold Ephraim Lessing

Date	Mintage	F	VF	XF	Unc	BU
1981J	6,500,000	—	—	—	4.50	—
1981J Proof	350,000	Value: 10.00				

KM# 155 5 MARK **Composition:** Copper-Nickel Clad Nickel **Subject:** 150th Anniversary - Death of Carl vom Stein

Date	Mintage	F	VF	XF	Unc	BU
1981G	6,500,000	—	—	—	4.50	—
1981G Proof	350,000	Value: 10.00				

KM# 156 5 MARK **Composition:** Copper-Nickel Clad Nickel **Subject:** 150th Anniversary - Death of Johann Wolfgang von Goethe

Date	Mintage	F	VF	XF	Unc	BU
1982D	8,000,000	—	—	—	4.50	—
1982D Proof	350,000	Value: 11.50				

KM# 157 5 MARK **Composition:** Copper-Nickel Clad Nickel **Subject:** 10th Anniversary - U.N. Environmental Conference

Date	Mintage	F	VF	XF	Unc	BU
1982F	8,000,000	—	—	—	4.50	—
1982F Proof	350,000	Value: 10.00				

KM# 158 5 MARK **Composition:** Copper-Nickel Clad Nickel **Subject:** 100th Anniversary - Death of Karl Marx

Date	Mintage	F	VF	XF	Unc	BU
1983J	8,000,000	—	—	—	4.50	—
1983J Proof	350,000	Value: 10.00				

KM# 159 5 MARK Composition: Copper-Nickel Clad Nickel **Subject:** 500th Anniversary - Birth of Martin Luther

Date	Mintage	F	VF	XF	Unc	BU
1983G	8,000,000	—	—	—	4.50	—
1983G Proof	350,000	Value: 13.50				

KM# 160 5 MARK Composition: Copper-Nickel Clad Nickel **Subject:** 150th Anniversary - German Customs Union

Date	Mintage	F	VF	XF	Unc	BU
1984D	8,000,000	—	—	—	4.50	—
1984D Proof	350,000	Value: 11.50				

KM# 161 5 MARK Composition: Copper-Nickel Clad Nickel **Subject:** 175th Anniversary - Birth of Felix Bartholdy

Date	Mintage	F	VF	XF	Unc	BU
1984J	8,000,000	—	—	—	4.50	—
1984J Proof	350,000	Value: 12.50				

KM# 162 5 MARK Composition: Copper-Nickel Clad Nickel **Subject:** European Year of Music

Date	Mintage	F	VF	XF	Unc	BU
1985F	8,000,000	—	—	—	4.50	—
1985F Proof	350,000	Value: 11.50				

KM# 163 5 MARK Composition: Copper-Nickel Clad Nickel **Subject:** 150th Anniversary - German Railroad

Date	Mintage	F	VF	XF	Unc	BU
1985G	8,000,000	—	—	—	4.50	—
1985G Proof	350,000	Value: 10.00				

KM# 164 5 MARK Composition: Copper-Nickel Clad Nickel **Subject:** 600th Anniversary - Heidelberg University

Date	Mintage	F	VF	XF	Unc	BU
1986D	8,000,000	—	—	—	4.50	—
1986D Proof	350,000	Value: 10.00				

KM# 165 5 MARK Composition: Copper-Nickel Clad Nickel **Subject:** 200th Anniversary - Death of Frederick the Great

Date	Mintage	F	VF	XF	Unc	BU
1986F	8,000,000	—	—	—	4.50	—
1986F Proof	350,000	Value: 12.50				

KM# 130 10 MARK Weight: 15.5000 g. **Composition:** 0.6250 Silver .3115 oz. ASW **Series:** Munich Olympics **Reverse:** "In Deutschland" with spiraling symbol

Date	Mintage	F	VF	XF	Unc	BU
1972D	2,500,000	—	—	—	9.50	—
1972D Proof	125,000	Value: 32.00				
1972F	2,375,000	—	—	—	9.50	—
1972F Proof	125,000	Value: 32.00				
1972G	2,500,000	—	—	—	9.50	—
1972G Proof	125,000	Value: 32.00				
1972J	2,500,000	—	—	—	9.50	—
1972J Proof	125,000	Value: 32.00				

KM# 131 10 MARK Weight: 15.5000 g. **Composition:** 0.6250 Silver .3115 oz. ASW **Series:** Munich Olympics **Reverse:** Schleife (knot)

Date	Mintage	F	VF	XF	Unc	BU
1972D	5,000,000	—	—	—	9.50	—
1972D Proof	125,000	Value: 25.00				
1972F	4,875,000	—	—	—	9.50	—
1972F Proof	125,000	Value: 25.00				
1972G	5,000,000	—	—	—	9.50	—
1972G Proof	125,000	Value: 25.00				
1972J	5,000,000	—	—	—	9.50	—
1972J Proof	125,000	Value: 25.00				

KM# 132 10 MARK Weight: 15.5000 g. **Composition:** 0.6250 Silver .3115 oz. ASW **Series:** Munich Olympics **Reverse:** Athletes kneeling

Date	Mintage	F	VF	XF	Unc	BU
1972D	5,000,000	—	—	—	8.50	—
1972D Proof	150,000	Value: 20.00				
1972F	4,850,000	—	—	—	8.50	—
1972F Proof	150,000	Value: 20.00				
1972G	5,000,000	—	—	—	8.50	—
1972G Proof	150,000	Value: 20.00				
1972J	5,000,000	—	—	—	8.50	—
1972J Proof	150,000	Value: 20.00				

KM# 133 10 MARK Weight: 15.5000 g. **Composition:** 0.6250 Silver .3115 oz. ASW **Series:** Munich Olympics **Reverse:** Stadium - aerial view

Date	Mintage	F	VF	XF	Unc	BU
1972D	5,000,000	—	—	—	8.50	—
1972D Proof	150,000	Value: 20.00				
1972F	4,850,000	—	—	—	8.50	—
1972F Proof	150,000	Value: 20.00				
1972G	5,000,000	—	—	—	8.50	—
1972G Proof	150,000	Value: 20.00				
1972J	5,000,000	—	—	—	8.50	—
1972J Proof	150,000	Value: 20.00				

KM# 134.1 10 MARK Weight: 15.5000 g. **Composition:** 0.6250 Silver .3115 oz. ASW **Series:** Munich Olympics **Reverse:** "In Munchen" - with spiral symbol **Edge:** Lettering separated by periods

Date	Mintage	F	VF	XF	Unc	BU
1972D	2,500,000	—	—	—	9.50	—
1972D Proof	150,000	Value: 25.00				
1972F	2,350,000	—	—	—	9.50	—
1972F Proof	150,000	Value: 25.00				
1972G	2,500,000	—	—	—	9.50	—
1972G Proof	150,000	Value: 25.00				
1972J	2,500,000	—	—	—	9.50	—
1972J Proof	150,000	Value: 25.00				

KM# 135 10 MARK Weight: 15.5000 g. **Composition:** 0.6250 Silver .3115 oz. ASW **Series:** Munich Olympics **Reverse:** Olympic Flame - Rings and spiral symbol

Date	Mintage	F	VF	XF	Unc	BU
1972D	5,000,000	—	—	—	8.50	—
1972D Proof	150,000	Value: 20.00				
1972F	4,850,000	—	—	—	8.50	—
1972F Proof	150,000	Value: 20.00				
1972G	5,000,000	—	—	—	8.50	—
1972G Proof	150,000	Value: 20.00				
1972J	5,000,000	—	—	—	8.50	—
1972J Proof	150,000	Value: 20.00				

KM# 134.2 10 MARK Weight: 15.5000 g. **Composition:** 0.6250 Silver .3115 oz. ASW **Edge:** Lettering separated by arabesques **Note:** Error.

Date	Mintage	F	VF	XF	Unc	BU
1972D	—	—	—	—	2,760	—
1972F	—	—	—	—	2,760	—
1972G	—	—	—	—	2,760	—
1972J	600	—	200	300	550	—

KM# 166 10 MARK Weight: 15.5000 g. **Composition:** 0.6250 Silver .3115 oz. ASW **Subject:** 750th Anniversary - Berlin

Date	Mintage	F	VF	XF	Unc	BU
1987J	8,000,000	—	—	—	10.00	—
1987J Proof	350,000	Value: 85.00				

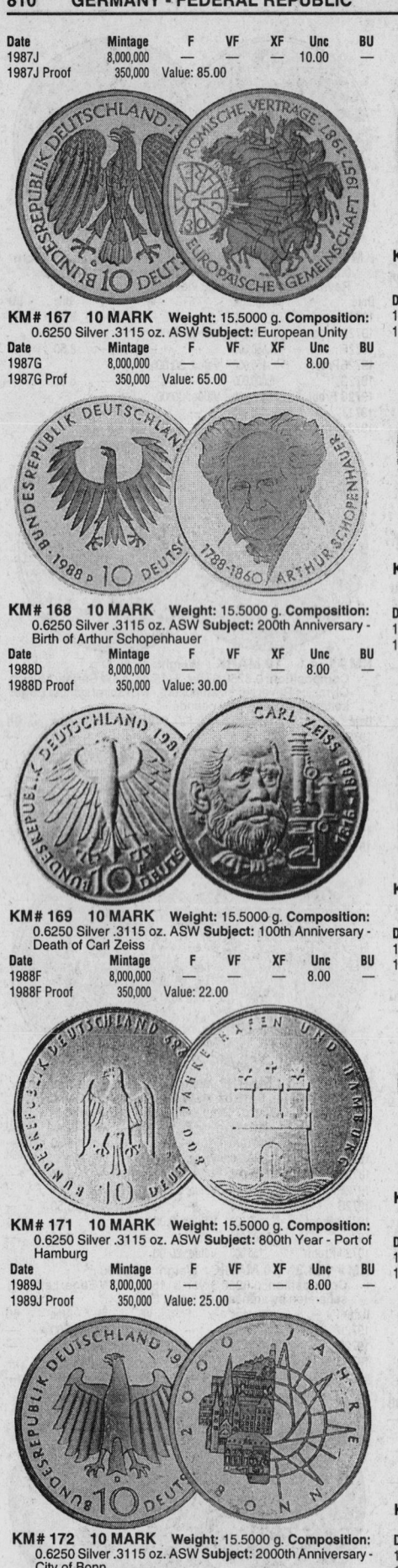

KM# 167 10 MARK Weight: 15.5000 g. **Composition:** 0.6250 Silver .3115 oz. ASW **Subject:** European Unity

Date	Mintage	F	VF	XF	Unc	BU
1987G	8,000,000	—	—	—	8.00	—
1987G Prof	350,000	Value: 65.00				

KM# 168 10 MARK Weight: 15.5000 g. **Composition:** 0.6250 Silver .3115 oz. ASW **Subject:** 200th Anniversary - Birth of Arthur Schopenhauer

Date	Mintage	F	VF	XF	Unc	BU
1988D	8,000,000	—	—	—	8.00	—
1988D Proof	350,000	Value: 30.00				

KM# 169 10 MARK Weight: 15.5000 g. **Composition:** 0.6250 Silver .3115 oz. ASW **Subject:** 100th Anniversary - Death of Carl Zeiss

Date	Mintage	F	VF	XF	Unc	BU
1988F	8,000,000	—	—	—	8.00	—
1988F Proof	350,000	Value: 22.00				

KM# 171 10 MARK Weight: 15.5000 g. **Composition:** 0.6250 Silver .3115 oz. ASW **Subject:** 800th Year - Port of Hamburg

Date	Mintage	F	VF	XF	Unc	BU
1989J	8,000,000	—	—	—	8.00	—
1989J Proof	350,000	Value: 25.00				

KM# 172 10 MARK Weight: 15.5000 g. **Composition:** 0.6250 Silver .3115 oz. ASW **Subject:** 2000th Anniversary - City of Bonn

Date	Mintage	F	VF	XF	Unc	BU
1989D	8,000,000	—	—	—	8.00	—
1989D Proof	350,000	Value: 25.00				

KM# 173 10 MARK Weight: 15.5000 g. **Composition:** 0.6250 Silver .3115 oz. ASW **Subject:** 40th Anniversary - Republic

Date	Mintage	F	VF	XF	Unc	BU
1989G	8,000,000	—	—	—	8.00	—
1989G Proof	350,000	Value: 25.00				

KM# 174 10 MARK Weight: 15.5000 g. **Composition:** 0.6250 Silver .3115 oz. ASW **Subject:** Death of Kaiser Friedrich Barbarossa

Date	Mintage	F	VF	XF	Unc	BU
1990F	7,850,000	—	—	—	8.00	—
1990F Proof	400,000	Value: 20.00				

KM# 176 10 MARK Weight: 15.5000 g. **Composition:** 0.6250 Silver .3115 oz. ASW **Subject:** 800th Anniversary - The Teutonic Order

Date	Mintage	F	VF	XF	Unc	BU
1990J	8,850,000	—	—	—	8.00	—
1990J Proof	450,000	Value: 12.50				

KM# 177 10 MARK Weight: 15.5000 g. **Composition:** 0.6250 Silver .3115 oz. ASW **Subject:** German Unity - Brandenburg Gate

Date	Mintage	F	VF	XF	Unc	BU
1991A	8,850,000	—	—	—	8.00	—
1991A Proof	450,000	Value: 13.50				

KM# 178 10 MARK Weight: 15.5000 g. **Composition:** 0.6250 Silver .3115 oz. ASW **Subject:** Kathe Kollwitz - Artist

Date	Mintage	F	VF	XF	Unc	BU
1992G	8,450,000	—	—	—	8.00	—
1992G Proof	450,000	Value: 11.50				

KM# 179 10 MARK Weight: 15.5000 g. **Composition:** 0.6250 Silver .3115 oz. ASW **Subject:** Civil Pour-le-Merite Order

Date	Mintage	F	VF	XF	Unc	BU
1992D	8,450,000	—	—	—	8.00	—
1992D Proof	450,000	Value: 11.50				

KM# 180 10 MARK Weight: 15.5000 g. **Composition:** 0.6250 Silver .3115 oz. ASW **Subject:** 1000th Anniversary - Potsdam

Date	Mintage	F	VF	XF	Unc	BU
1993F	7,950,000	—	—	—	8.00	—
1993F Proof	450,000	Value: 11.50				

KM# 181 10 MARK Weight: 15.5000 g. **Composition:** 0.6250 Silver .3115 oz. ASW **Reverse:** Head of Robert Koch facing forward

Date	Mintage	F	VF	XF	Unc	BU
1993J	7,450,000	—	—	—	8.00	—
1993J Proof	450,000	Value: 11.50				

KM# 182 10 MARK Weight: 15.5000 g. **Composition:** 0.6250 Silver .3115 oz. ASW **Subject:** Attempt on Hitler's Life, July 20, 1944

Date	Mintage	F	VF	XF	Unc	BU
1994A	7,450,000	—	—	—	8.00	—
1994A Proof	450,000	Value: 11.50				

KM# 184 10 MARK Weight: 15.5000 g. **Composition:** 0.6250 Silver .3115 oz. ASW **Reverse:** Head of Johann Gottfried Herder facing right

Date	Mintage	F	VF	XF	Unc	BU
1994G	7,450,000	—	—	—	8.00	—
1994G Proof	450,000	Value: 11.50				

KM# 185 10 MARK Weight: 15.5000 g. **Composition:** 0.6250 Silver .3115 oz. ASW **Subject:** 50th Anniversary of Peace and Reconciliation **Edge Lettering:** STEINERNE GLOCKE SYMBOL FUER TOLERANZ

Date	Mintage	F	VF	XF	Unc	BU
1995J	7,450,000	—	—	—	8.00	—
1995J Proof	450,000	Value: 11.50				

KM# 186 10 MARK Weight: 15.5000 g. **Composition:** 0.6250 Silver .3115 oz. ASW **Subject:** Henry the Lion **Edge Lettering:** HEINRICH DER LOEWE AUS KAISERLICHEM STAMM

Date	Mintage	F	VF	XF	Unc	BU
1995F	7,450,000	—	—	—	8.00	—
1995F Proof	450,000	Value: 11.50				

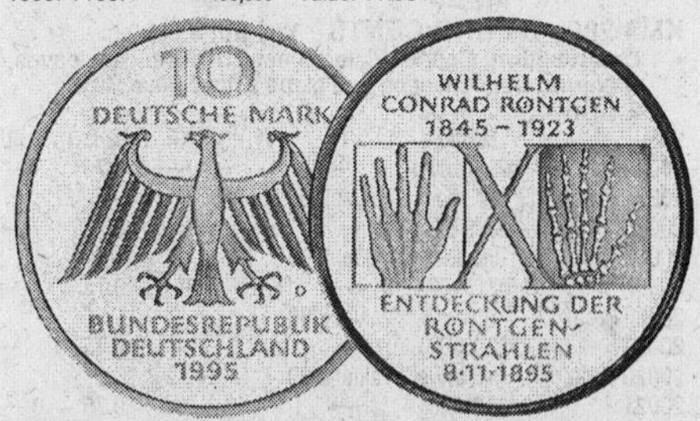

KM# 187 10 MARK Weight: 15.5000 g. **Composition:** 0.6250 Silver .3115 oz. ASW **Subject:** Wilhelm Conrad Rontgen **Reverse:** Hand and X-rayed hand **Edge Lettering:** ERSTER NOBEL PREIS FUER PHYSIK

Date	Mintage	F	VF	XF	Unc	BU
1995D	6,900,000	—	—	—	8.00	—
1995D Proof	450,000	Value: 11.50				

KM# 188 10 MARK Weight: 15.5000 g. **Composition:** 0.6250 Silver .3115 oz. ASW **Subject:** Kolpingwerk **Edge Lettering:** TAETIGE LIEBE HEILT ALLE WUNDEN

Date	Mintage	F	VF	XF	Unc	BU
1996A	5,600,000	—	—	—	8.00	—
1996A Proof	400,000	Value: 11.50				

KM# 189.1 10 MARK Weight: 15.5000 g. **Composition:** 0.6250 Silver .3115 oz. ASW **Subject:** Philipp Melanchthon **Obverse:** Stylized eagle **Reverse:** Portrait, dates

Date	Mintage	F	VF	XF	Unc	BU
1997A Proof	150,000	Value: 22.50				
1997D Proof	150,000	Value: 22.50				
1997F Proof	150,000	Value: 22.50				
1997G Proof	150,000	Value: 22.50				
1997J	3,000,000	—	—	—	10.00	—
1997J Proof	150,000	Value: 22.50				

KM# 189.2 10 MARK Weight: 15.5000 g. **Composition:** 0.6250 Silver .3115 oz. ASW **Reverse:** Different forelock on portrait

Date	F	VF	XF	Unc	BU
1997J	—	—	—	10.00	—
1997J Proof	—	Value: 28.00			

KM# 190 10 MARK Weight: 15.5000 g. **Composition:** 0.6250 Silver .3115 oz. ASW **Subject:** Heinrich Heine **Obverse:** Stylized eagle **Reverse:** Portrait with handwritten text in background

Date	Mintage	F	VF	XF	Unc	BU
1997A Proof	150,000	Value: 22.50				
1997D	3,000,000	—	—	—	10.00	—
1997D Proof	750,000	Value: 22.50				
1997F Proof	150,000	Value: 22.50				
1997G Proof	150,000	Value: 22.50				
1997J Proof	150,000	Value: 22.50				

KM# 192 10 MARK Weight: 15.5000 g. **Composition:** 0.6250 Silver .3115 oz. ASW **Subject:** Diesel Engine Centennial **Obverse:** Stylized eagle **Reverse:** First diesel engine

Date	Mintage	F	VF	XF	Unc	BU
1997A Proof	150,000	Value: 22.50				
1997D Proof	150,000	Value: 22.50				
1997F	3,000,000	—	—	—	10.00	—
1997F Proof	150,000	Value: 22.50				
1997G Proof	150,000	Value: 22.50				
1997J Proof	150,000	Value: 22.50				

KM# 191 10 MARK Weight: 15.5000 g. **Composition:** 0.9250 Silver .4610 oz. ASW **Subject:** 300th Anniversary - Peace of Westphalia **Obverse:** Stylized eagle **Reverse:** Clasped hands, dove and quill

Date	Mintage	F	VF	XF	Unc	BU
1998A Proof	200,000	Value: 22.50				
1998D Proof	200,000	Value: 22.50				
1998F Proof	200,000	Value: 22.50				
1998G Proof	200,000	Value: 22.50				
1998J	3,500,000	—	—	—	10.00	—
1998J Proof	200,000	Value: 22.50				

Note: A 1997 strike of this coin does not exist

KM# 193 10 MARK Composition: 0.9250 Silver **Subject:** 900th Birthday of Hildegard von Bingen **Obverse:** Stylized eagle **Reverse:** Seated nun writing **Edge Lettering:** WISSE DIE WEGE DES HERRN

Date	Mintage	F	VF	XF	Unc	BU
1998A Proof	200,000	Value: 22.50				
1998D Proof	200,000	Value: 22.50				
1998F Proof	200,000	Value: 22.50				
1998G	3,500,000	—	—	—	10.00	—
1998G Proof	200,000	Value: 22.50				
1998J Proof	200,000	Value: 22.50				

KM# 194 10 MARK Weight: 15.5000 g. **Composition:** 0.9000 Silver .5345 oz. ASW **Subject:** 300th Anniversary Franckesche Charitable Endowment

Date	F	VF	XF	Unc	BU
1998A	—	—	—	10.00	—
1998A Proof	—	Value: 22.50			
1998D Proof	—	Value: 22.50			
1998F Proof	—	Value: 22.50			
1998G Proof	—	Value: 22.50			
1998J Proof	—	Value: 22.50			

KM# 195 10 MARK Weight: 15.5000 g. **Composition:** 0.9250 Silver .4610 oz. ASW **Subject:** 50 Years of German Deutsch Mark **Obverse:** Denomination above eagle **Reverse:** Seven coin designs **Edge Lettering:** EINIGKEIT UND RECHT UND FREIHEIT

Date	F	VF	XF	Unc	BU
1998A Proof	—	Value: 21.50			
1998D Proof	—	Value: 21.50			
1998F	—	—	—	10.00	—
1998F Proof	—	Value: 21.50			
1998G Proof	—	Value: 21.50			
1998J Proof	—	Value: 21.50			

KM# 196 10 MARK Weight: 15.5000 g. **Composition:** 0.9250 Silver .4610 oz. ASW **Subject:** 50th Anniversary - Bundes Republic **Obverse:** Denomination below eagle **Reverse:** German constitution **Edge Lettering:** FUR DAS GESAMTE DEUTSCH VOLK

Date	F	VF	XF	Unc	BU
1999A Proof	—	Value: 20.00			
1999D	—	—	—	10.00	—
1999D Proof	—	Value: 20.00			
1999F Proof	—	Value: 20.00			
1999G Proof	—	Value: 20.00			
1999J Proof	—	Value: 20.00			

KM# 197 10 MARK Weight: 15.5000 g. **Composition:** 0.9250 Silver .4610 oz. ASW **Subject:** 250th Anniversary - Birth of J.W. von Goethe **Obverse:** Denomination below eagle **Reverse:** Portrait of von Goethe facing inscribed field **Edge Lettering:** WIRKE GUT SO WIRKST DU LANGER

Date	F	VF	XF	Unc	BU
1999A Proof	—	Value: 20.00			
1999D Proof	—	Value: 20.00			
1999F	—	—	—	10.00	—
1999F Proof	—	Value: 20.00			
1999G Proof	—	Value: 20.00			
1999J Proof	—	Value: 20.00			

KM# 198 10 MARK **Weight:** 15.5000 g. **Composition:** 0.9250 Silver .4610 oz. ASW **Subject:** SOS Kinderdorfs **Obverse:** Denomination below eagle **Reverse:** Stylized globe, children playing **Edge Lettering:** SOS - KINDERDORFS - EINE IDEE FUR DIE WELT

Date		F	VF	XF	Unc	BU
1999A Proof	—	Value: 20.00				
1999D Proof	—	Value: 20.00				
1999F Proof	—	Value: 20.00				
1999G Proof	—	Value: 20.00				
1999J		—	—	—	10.00	—
1999J Proof	—	Value: 20.00				

Note: NOTE: A 1997 strike of this coin does not exist.

KM# 199 10 MARK **Weight:** 15.5000 g. **Composition:** 0.9250 Silver .4610 oz. ASW **Subject:** Expo 2000 **Obverse:** Stylized eagle **Reverse:** Childlike drawing of human balance scale **Edge Lettering:** WELTAUSSTELLUNG EXPO 2000 HANNOVER

Date	Mintage	F	VF	XF	Unc	BU
2000A	3,000,000	—	—	—	10.00	—
2000A Proof	160,000	Value: 20.00				
2000D Proof	160,000	Value: 20.00				
2000F Proof	160,000	Value: 20.00				
2000G Proof	160,000	Value: 20.00				
2000J Proof	160,000	Value: 20.00				

KM# 200 10 MARK **Weight:** 15.5000 g. **Composition:** 0.9250 Silver .4610 oz. ASW **Subject:** Charlemagne **Obverse:** Stylized eagle **Reverse:** Charlemagne handing church model to Madonna and child **Edge Lettering:** URBS AQUENSIS - URBS REGALIS

Date	Mintage	F	VF	XF	Unc	BU
2000A Proof	160,000	Value: 20.00				
2000D Proof	160,000	Value: 20.00				
2000F Proof	160,000	Value: 20.00				
2000G	3,000,000	—	—	—	10.00	—
2000G Proof	160,000	Value: 20.00				
2000J Proof	160,000	Value: 20.00				

KM# 201 10 MARK **Weight:** 15.5000 g. **Composition:** 0.9250 Silver .4610 oz. ASW **Subject:** 10th Anniversary of Reunification **Obverse:** Eagle and denomination **Reverse:** Parliament building **Edge Lettering:** "WIR SIND DAS VOLK WIR SIND EIN VOLK" **Size:** 32.5 mm.

Date		F	VF	XF	Unc	BU
2000A Proof	—	Value: 22.50				
2000D		—	—	—	10.00	—
2000D Proof	—	Value: 22.50				
2000F Proof	—	Value: 22.50				
2000G Proof	—	Value: 22.50				
2000J Proof	—	Value: 22.50				

KM# 202 10 MARK **Weight:** 15.5000 g. **Composition:** 0.9250 Silver .4610 oz. ASW **Obverse:** Eagle and denomination **Reverse:** Portrait **Edge Lettering:** "JOHANN SEBASTIAN BACH 250 TODESTAG" **Size:** 32.5 mm.

Date		F	VF	XF	Unc	BU
2000A Proof	—	Value: 22.50				
2000D Proof	—	Value: 22.50				
2000F Proof	—	Value: 10.00				
2000F Proof	—	Value: 22.50				
2000G Proof	—	Value: 22.50				
2000J Proof	—	Value: 22.50				

KM# 204 10 MARK **Weight:** 15.5000 g. **Composition:** 0.9250 Silver .4610 oz. ASW **Edge Lettering:** "OHNE WASSER KEIN LEBEN" **Size:** 32.5 mm.

Date	Mintage	F	VF	XF	Unc	BU
2001A	2,500,000	—	—	—	10.00	—
2001A Proof	160,000	Value: 22.50				
2001D Proof	160,000	Value: 22.50				
2001F Proof	160,000	Value: 22.50				
2001G Proof	160,000	Value: 22.50				
2001J Proof	160,000	Value: 22.50				

KM# 205 10 MARK **Weight:** 15.5000 g. **Composition:** 0.9250 Silver .4610 oz. ASW **Subject:** Albert Gustav Lortzing **Obverse:** Stylized eagle **Reverse:** Portrait and music **Edge Lettering:** "WILDSCHUETZ*UNDINE"ZAR UND ZIMMER MANN" **Size:** 32.5 mm.

Date	Mintage	F	VF	XF	Unc	BU
2001A Proof	160,000	Value: 22.50				
2001D Proof	160,000	Value: 22.50				
2001F Proof	160,000	Value: 22.50				
2001G Proof	160,000	Value: 22.50				
2001J	2,500,000	—	—	—	10.00	—
2001J Proof	160,000	Value: 22.50				

KM# 206 10 MARK **Weight:** 15.5000 g. **Composition:** 0.9250 Silver .4610 oz. ASW **Subject:** Federal Constitution: 50th Anniversary **Obverse:** Stylized eagle **Reverse:** Justice holding books and scale **Edge:** Lettered **Size:** 32.5 mm.

Date	Mintage	F	VF	XF	Unc	BU
2001A Proof	160,000	Value: 22.50				
2001D Proof	160,000	Value: 22.50				
2001F Proof	160,000	Value: 22.50				
2001G	2,500,000	—	—	—	10.00	—
2001G Proof	160,000	Value: 22.50				
2001J Proof	160,000	Value: 22.50				

EURO COINAGE

European Economic Community Issues

KM# 207 EURO CENT **Weight:** 2.2700 g. **Composition:** Copper Plated Steel **Obverse:** Oak leaves **Reverse:** Denomination and globe **Edge:** Plain **Size:** 16.3 mm.

Date	Mintage	F	VF	XF	Unc	BU
2002A	740,000,000	—	—	—	0.35	—
2002A Proof	Inc. above	Value: 1.00				
2002D	777,000,000	—	—	—	0.35	—
2002D Proof	Inc. above	Value: 1.00				
2002F	888,000,000	—	—	—	0.35	—
2002F Proof	Inc. above	Value: 1.00				
2002G	518,000,000	—	—	—	0.35	—
2002G Proof	Inc. above	Value: 1.00				
2002J	777,000,000	—	—	—	0.35	—
2002J Proof	Inc. above	Value: 1.00				

KM# 208 2 EURO CENTS **Weight:** 3.0000 g. **Composition:** Copper Plated Steel **Obverse:** Oak leaves **Reverse:** Denomination and globe **Edge:** Grooved **Size:** 18.7 mm.

Date	Mintage	F	VF	XF	Unc	BU
2002A	360,000,000	—	—	—	0.50	—
2002A Proof	Inc. above	Value: 1.50				
2002D	378,000,000	—	—	—	0.50	—
2002D Proof	Inc. above	Value: 1.50				
2002F	432,000,000	—	—	—	0.50	—
2002F Proof	Inc. above	Value: 1.50				
2002G	252,000,000	—	—	—	0.50	—
2002G Proof	Inc. above	Value: 1.50				
2002J	378,000,000	—	—	—	0.50	—
2002J Proof	Inc. above	Value: 1.50				

KM# 209 5 EURO CENTS **Weight:** 3.8600 g. **Composition:** Copper Plated Steel **Obverse:** Oak leaves **Reverse:** Denomination and globe **Edge:** Plain **Size:** 21.2 mm.

Date	Mintage	F	VF	XF	Unc	BU
2002A	460,000,000	—	—	—	0.75	—
2002A Proof	Inc. above	Value: 2.00				
2002D	483,000,000	—	—	—	0.75	—
2002D Proof	Inc. above	Value: 2.00				
2002F	552,000,000	—	—	—	0.75	—
2002F Proof	Inc. above	Value: 2.00				
2002G	322,000,000	—	—	—	0.75	—
2002G Proof	Inc. above	Value: 2.00				
2002J	483,000,000	—	—	—	0.75	—
2002J Proof	Inc. above	Value: 2.00				

KM# 210 10 EURO CENTS **Weight:** 4.0000 g. **Composition:** Brass **Obverse:** Brandenburg Gate **Reverse:** Denomination and map **Edge:** Reeded **Size:** 19.7 mm.

Date	Mintage	F	VF	XF	Unc	BU
2002A	660,000,000	—	—	—	0.75	—
2002A Proof	Inc. above	Value: 2.00				
2002D	693,000,000	—	—	—	0.75	—
2002D Proof	Inc. above	Value: 2.00				
2002F	792,000,000	—	—	—	0.75	—
2002F Proof	Inc. above	Value: 2.00				
2002G	462,000,000	—	—	—	0.75	—
2002G Proof	Inc. above	Value: 2.00				
2002J	693,000,000	—	—	—	0.75	—
2002J Proof	Inc. above	Value: 2.00				

KM# 211 20 EURO CENTS **Weight:** 5.7300 g. **Composition:** Brass **Obverse:** Brandenburg Gate **Reverse:** Denomination and map **Edge:** Notched **Size:** 22.2 mm.

Date	Mintage	F	VF	XF	Unc	BU
2002A	320,000,000	—	—	—	1.00	—
2002A Proof	Inc. above	Value: 3.00				
2002D	336,000,000	—	—	—	1.00	—
2002D Proof	Inc. above	Value: 3.00				
2002F	384,000,000	—	—	—	1.00	—
2002F Proof	Inc. above	Value: 3.00				
2002G	224,000,000	—	—	—	1.00	—
2002G Proof	Inc. above	Value: 3.00				
2002J	336,000,000	—	—	—	1.00	—
2002J Proof	Inc. above	Value: 3.00				

KM# 212 50 EURO CENTS **Weight:** 7.8100 g. **Composition:** Brass **Obverse:** Brandenburg Gate **Reverse:** Denomination and map **Edge:** Reeded **Size:** 24.2 mm.

Date	Mintage	F	VF	XF	Unc	BU
2002A	320,000,000	—	—	—	1.75	—
2002A Proof	Inc. above	Value: 4.00				
2002D	336,000,000	—	—	—	1.75	—
2002D Proof	Inc. above	Value: 4.00				
2002F	384,000,000	—	—	—	1.75	—
2002F Proof	Inc. above	Value: 4.00				
2002G	224,000,000	—	—	—	1.75	—
2002G Proof	Inc. above	Value: 4.00				
2002J	336,000,000	—	—	—	1.75	—
2002J Proof	Inc. above	Value: 4.00				

KM# 213 EURO **Ring Composition:** Brass **Center Weight:** 7.5000 g. **Center Composition:** Copper Nickel **Subject:** Currency Reform **Obverse:** Stylized eagle **Reverse:** Denomination over map **Edge:** Three normally reeded and three very finely reeded sections **Size:** 23.3 mm.

Date	Mintage	F	VF	XF	Unc	BU
2002A	340,000,000	—	—	—	2.50	—
2002A Proof	Inc. above	Value: 6.50				
2002D	357,000,000	—	—	—	2.50	—
2002D Proof	Inc. above	Value: 6.50				
2002F	408,000,000	—	—	—	2.50	—
2002F Proof	Inc. above	Value: 6.50				
2002G	238,000,000	—	—	—	2.50	—
2002G Proof	Inc. above	Value: 6.50				
2002J	357,000,000	—	—	—	2.50	—
2002J Proof	Inc. above	Value: 6.50				

KM# 214 2 EUROS **Ring Composition:** Copper Nickel **Center Weight:** 8.5200 g. **Center Composition:** Brass **Obverse:** Stylized eagle **Reverse:** Denomination and map **Edge:** Reeded and "EINIGKEIT UND RECHT UND FREIHEIT" **Size:** 25.6 mm.

Date	Mintage	F	VF	XF	Unc	BU
2002A	200,000,000	—	—	—	4.50	—
2002A Proof	Inc. above	Value: 12.50				
2002D	210,000,000	—	—	—	4.50	—
2002D Proof	Inc. above	Value: 12.50				
2002F	240,000,000	—	—	—	4.50	—
2002F Proof	Inc. above	Value: 12.50				
2002G	140,000,000	—	—	—	4.50	—
2002G Proof	Inc. above	Value: 12.50				
2002J	210,000,000	—	—	—	4.50	—
2002J Proof	Inc. above	Value: 12.50				

KM# 215 10 EURO **Weight:** 18.0000 g. **Composition:** 0.9250 Silver 0.5353 oz. ASW **Subject:** Introduction of the Euro Currency **Obverse:** Stylized round eagle **Reverse:** Euro symbol and map **Edge Lettering:** IM ZEICHEN DER EINIGUNG EUROPAS **Size:** 32.5 mm.

Date	Mintage	F	VF	XF	Unc	BU
2002F	2,000,000	—	—	—	20.00	—
2002F Proof	400,000	Value: 25.00				

KM# 216 10 EURO **Weight:** 18.0000 g. **Composition:** 0.9250 Silver 0.5353 oz. ASW **Subject:** Berlin Subway Centennial **Obverse:** Stylized squarish eagle **Reverse:** Elevated and subterranean train views **Edge Lettering:** HISTORISCH UND **Size:** 32.5 mm.

Date	Mintage	F	VF	XF	Unc	BU
2002D	2,000,000	—	—	—	18.50	—
2002D Proof	400,000	Value: 22.50				

KM# 217 10 EURO **Weight:** 18.0000 g. **Composition:** 0.9250 Silver 0.5353 oz. ASW **Subject:** "Documenta Kassel" Art Exposition **Obverse:** Stylized eagle above inscription **Reverse:** Exposition logo **Edge Lettering:** ART (in nine languages) **Size:** 32.5 mm.

Date	Mintage	F	VF	XF	Unc	BU
2002J	2,000,000	—	—	—	18.50	—
2002J Proof	400,000	Value: 22.50				

KM# 218 10 EURO **Weight:** 18.0000 g. **Composition:** 0.9250 Silver 0.5353 oz. ASW **Subject:** Museum Island, Berlin **Obverse:** Stylized eagle **Reverse:** Aerial view of museum complex **Edge:** Lettered **Size:** 32.5 mm.

Date	Mintage	F	VF	XF	Unc	BU
2002A	2,000,000	—	—	—	18.50	—
2002A Proof	400,000	Value: 22.50				

KM# 219 10 EURO **Weight:** 18.0000 g. **Composition:** 0.9250 Silver 0.5353 oz. ASW **Subject:** 50 Years - German Television **Obverse:** Stylized eagle silhouette **Reverse:** Television screen silhouette **Edge Lettering:** BILDUNG UNTERHALTUNG INFORMATION **Size:** 32.5 mm. **Note:** This coin has not been issued yet.

Date	Mintage	F	VF	XF	Unc	BU
2002G	2,000,000	—	—	—	18.50	—
2002G Proof	400,000	Value: 22.50				

KM# 220 100 EURO **Weight:** 15.5500 g. **Composition:** 0.9990 Gold 0.4994 oz. AGW **Subject:** Introduction of the Euro Currency **Obverse:** Stylized round eagle **Reverse:** Euro symbol and arches **Edge:** Reeded **Size:** 28 mm.

Date	Mintage	F	VF	XF	Unc	BU
2002A Proof	100,000	Value: 375				
2002D Proof	100,000	Value: 375				
2002F Proof	100,000	Value: 375				
2002G Proof	100,000	Value: 375				
2002J Proof	100,000	Value: 375				

KM# 221 200 EURO **Weight:** 31.1000 g. **Composition:** 0.9990 Gold 0.9989 oz. AGW **Subject:** Introduction of the Euro Currency **Obverse:** Stylized round eagle **Reverse:** Euro symbol and arches **Edge Lettering:** IM...ZEICHEN...DER...EINIGUNG...EUROPAS **Size:** 32.5 mm.

Date	Mintage	F	VF	XF	Unc	BU
2002A Proof	20,000	Value: 1,275				
2002D Proof	20,000	Value: 1,275				
2002F Proof	20,000	Value: 1,275				
2002G Proof	20,000	Value: 1,275				
2002J Proof	20,000	Value: 1,275				

PATTERNS

Including off metal strikes

KM#	Date	Mintage	Identification	Mkt Val
Pn397	1950D	—	2 Mark. Copper-Nickel. With Hole, PN#400.	—
Pn399	1951F	—	2 Mark. Copper-Nickel. Max Planck.	—
Pn398	1951D	—	2 Mark. Copper-Nickel. Max Planck.	—
Pn400	1955J	—	2 Mark.	—
Pn401	1959F	—	2 Pfennig. Brass.	—
Pn402	1960F	—	2 Pfennig. Zinc.	—

TRIAL STRIKES

KM#	Date	Mintage	Identification	Mkt Val
TS1	NDJ	—	10 Pfennig. KM#4. Uniface.	—
TS2	NDJ	—	2 Mark. Silver. Pn400. Uniface.	—
TS3	1950J	—	2 Mark. Silver. Pn400. Uniface.	—
TS4	NDJ	—	2 Mark. Lead. Pn400. Uniface.	—
TS5	1950J	—	2 Mark. Lead. Pn400. Uniface.	—
TS6	1951F	—	2 Mark. Lead. Max Planck. Uniface.	—
TS7	NDF	—	2 Mark. Lead. Max Planck. Uniface.	—
TS8	1951J	—	2 Mark. Iron. Max Planck. Uniface.	—
TS9	NDJ	—	2 Mark. Iron. Max Planck. Uniface.	—
TS10	1951J	—	2 Mark. Lead. Max Planck. Uniface.	—
TS11	NDJ	—	2 Mark. Lead. Max Planck. Uniface.	—

MINT SETS

KM#	Date	Mintage	Identification	Issue Price	Mkt Val
MS1	1974D (9)	20,000	KM#105, 106a, 107-108, 109.2, 110, 112.1, 124, A127	—	45.00
MS2	1974F (9)	20,000	KM#105, 106a, 107-108, 109.2, 110, 112.1, 124, A127	—	45.00
MS3	1974G (9)	20,000	KM#105, 106a, 107-108, 109.2, 110, 112.1, 124, A127	—	45.00
MS4	1974J (9)	20,000	KM#105, 106a, 107-108, 109.2, 110, 112.1, 124, A127	—	45.00
MS5	1975D (9)	26,000	KM#105, 106a, 107-108, 109.2, 110, 124, A127, 140.1	—	28.00
MS6	1975F (9)	26,000	KM#105, 106a, 107-108, 109.2, 110, 124, A127, 140.1	—	28.00
MS7	1975G (9)	26,000	KM#105, 106a, 107-108, 109.2, 110, 124, A127, 140.1	—	28.00
MS8	1975J (9)	26,000	KM#105, 106a, 107-108, 109.2, 110, 124, A127, 140.1	—	28.00
MS9	1976D (9)	26,000	KM#105, 106a, 107-108, 109.2, 110, 124, A127, 140.1	—	28.00
MS10	1976F (9)	26,000	KM#105, 106a, 107-108, 1092., 110, 124, A127, 140.1	—	28.00
MS11	1976G (9)	26,000	KM#105, 106a, 107-108, 109.2, 110, 124, A127, 140.1	—	28.00
MS12	1976J (9)	26,000	KM#105, 106a, 107-108, 109.2, 110, 124, A127, 140.1	—	28.00
MS13	1977D (9)	29,000	KM#105, 106a, 107-108, 109.2, 110, 124, A127, 140.1	—	20.00
MS14	1977F (9)	29,000	KM#105, 106a, 107-108, 109.2, 110, 124, A127, 140.1	—	20.00

KM#	Date	Mintage	Identification	Issue Price	Mkt Val
MS15	1977G (9)	29,000	KM#105, 106a, 107-108, 109.2, 110, 124, A127, 140.1	—	20.00
MS16	1977J (9)	29,000	KM#105, 106a, 107-108, 109.2, 110, 124, A127, 140.1	—	20.00
MS17	1978D (9)	30,000	KM#105, 106a, 107-108, 109.2, 110, 124, A127, 140.1	—	17.50
MS18	1978F (9)	30,000	KM#105, 106a, 107-108, 109.2, 110, 124, A127, 140.1	—	17.50
MS19	1978g (9)	30,000	KM#105, 106a, 107-108, 109.2, 110, 124, A127, 140.1	—	17.50
MS20	1978J (9)	30,000	KM#105, 106a, 107-108, 109.2, 110, 124, A127, 140.1	—	17.50
MS21	1979D (10)	34,000	KM105, 106a, 107-108, 109.2, 110, 124, A127, 140.1, 149	11.00	17.50
MS22	1979F (10)	34,000	KM105, 106a, 107-108, 109.2, 110, 124, A127, 140.1, 149	11.00	17.50
MS23	1979G (10)	34,000	KM105, 106a, 107-108, 109.2, 110, 124, A127, 140.1, 149	11.00	17.50
MS24	1979J (10)	34,000	KM105, 106a, 107-108, 109.2, 110, 124, A127, 140.1, 149	11.00	17.50
MS25	1980D (10)	36,000	KM105, 106a, 107-108, 109.2, 110, 124, A127, 140.1, 149	11.00	17.50
MS26	1980F (10)	36,000	KM105, 106a, 107-108, 109.2, 110, 124, A127, 140.1, 149	11.00	17.50
MS27	1980G (10)	36,000	KM105, 106a, 107-108, 109.2, 110, 124, A127, 140.1, 149	11.00	17.50
MS28	1980J (10)	36,000	KM105, 106a, 107-108, 109.2, 110, 124, A127, 140.1, 149	11.00	17.50
MS29	1981D (10)	38,000	KM105, 106a, 107-108, 109.2, 110, 124, A127, 140.1, 149	11.00	17.50
MS30	1981F (10)	38,000	KM105, 106a, 107-108, 109.2, 110, 124, A127, 140.1, 149	11.00	17.50
MS31	1981G (10)	38,000	KM105, 106a, 107-108, 109.2, 110, 124, A127, 140.1, 149	11.00	17.50
MS32	1981J (10)	38,000	KM105, 106a, 107-108, 109.2, 110, 124, A127, 140.1, 149	11.00	17.50
MS33	1982D (10)	33,000	KM105, 106a, 107-108, 109.2, 110, 124, A127, 140.1, 149	11.00	17.50
MS34	1982F (10)	33,000	KM105, 106a, 107-108, 109.2, 110, 124, A127, 140.1, 149	11.00	17.50
MS35	1982G (10)	33,000	KM105, 106a, 107-108, 109.2, 110, 124, A127, 140.1, 149	11.00	17.50
MS36	1982J (10)	33,000	KM105, 106a, 107-108, 109.2, 110, 124, A127, 140.1, 149	11.00	17.50
MS37	1983D (10)	31,000	KM105, 106a, 107-108, 109.2, 110, 124, A127, 140.1, 149	11.00	17.50
MS38	1983F (10)	31,000	KM105, 106a, 107-108, 109.2, 110, 124, A127, 140.1, 149	11.00	17.50
MS39	1983G (10)	31,000	KM105, 106a, 107-108, 109.2, 110, 124, A127, 140.1, 149	11.00	17.50
MS40	1983J (10)	31,000	KM105, 106a, 107-108, 109.2, 110, 124, A127, 140.1, 149	11.00	17.50
MS41	1984D (10)	25,000	KM105, 106a, 107-108, 109.2, 110, 124, A127, 140.1, 149	11.00	35.00
MS42	1984F (10)	25,000	KM105, 106a, 107-108, 109.2, 110, 124, A127, 140.1, 149	11.00	35.00
MS43	1984G (10)	25,000	KM105, 106a, 107-108, 109.2, 110, 124, A127, 140.1, 149	11.00	40.00
MS44	1984J (10)	25,000	KM105, 106a, 107-108, 109.2, 110, 124, A127, 140.1, 149	11.00	35.00
MS45	1985D (10)	23,000	KM105, 106a, 107-108, 109.2, 110, 124, A127, 140.1, 149	11.00	27.50
MS46	1985F (10)	23,000	KM105, 106a, 107-108, 109.2, 110, 124, A127, 140.1, 149	11.00	27.50
MS47	1985G (10)	23,000	KM105, 106a, 107-108, 109.2, 110, 124, A127, 140.1, 149	11.00	27.50
MS48	1985J (10)	23,000	KM105, 106a, 107-108, 109.2, 110, 124, A127, 140.1, 149	11.00	27.50
MS49	1986D (10)	15,000	KM105, 106a, 107-108, 109.2, 110, 124, A127, 140.1, 149	11.00	50.00
MS50	1986F (10)	15,000	KM105, 106a, 107-108, 109.2, 110, 124, A127, 140.1, 149	11.00	50.00
MS51	1986G (10)	15,000	KM105, 106a, 107-108, 109.2, 110, 124, A127, 140.1, 149	11.00	50.00

KM#	Date	Mintage	Identification	Issue Price	Mkt Val
MS52	1986J (10)	15,000	KM105, 106a, 107-108, 109.2, 110, 124, A127, 140.1, 149	11.00	50.00
MS53	1987D (10)	18,000	KM105, 106a, 107-108, 109.2, 110, 124, A127, 140.1, 149	11.00	35.00
MS54	1987F (10)	18,000	KM105, 106a, 107-108, 109.2, 110, 124, A127, 140.1, 149	11.00	35.00
MS55	1987G (10)	18,000	KM105, 106a, 107-108, 109.2, 110, 124, A127, 140.1, 149	11.00	45.00
MS56	1987J (10)	18,000	KM105, 106a, 107-108, 109.2, 110, 124, A127, 140.1, 149	11.00	35.00
MS57	1988D (9)	18,000	KM105, 106a, 107-108, 109.2, 110, 140.1, 149, 170	—	27.50
MS58	1988F (9)	18,000	KM105, 106a, 107-108, 109.2, 110, 140.1, 149, 170	—	27.50
MS59	1988G (9)	18,000	KM105, 106a, 107-108, 109.2, 110, 140.1, 149, 170	—	27.50
MS60	1988J (9)	18,000	KM105, 106a, 107-108, 109.2, 110, 140.1, 149, 170	—	27.50
MS61	1989D (9)	18,000	KM105, 106a, 107-108, 109.2, 110, 140.1, 149, 170	—	27.50
MS62	1989F (9)	18,000	KM105, 106a, 107-108, 109.2, 110, 140.1, 149, 170	—	27.50
MS63	1989G (9)	18,000	KM105, 106a, 107-108, 109.2, 110, 140.1, 149, 170	—	27.50
MS64	1989J (9)	18,000	KM105, 106a, 107-108, 109.2, 110, 140.1, 149, 170	—	27.50
MS65	1990D (10)	20,000	KM105, 106a, 107-108, 109.2, 110, 140.1, 149, 170, 175	—	25.00
MS66	1990F (10)	20,000	KM105, 106a, 107-108, 109.2, 110, 140.1, 149, 170, 175	—	25.00
MS67	1990G (10)	20,000	KM105, 106a, 107-108, 109.2, 110, 140.1, 149, 170, 175	—	25.00
MS68	1990J (10)	20,000	KM105, 106a, 107-108, 109.2, 110, 140.1, 149, 170, 175	—	25.00
MS69	1991A (10)	20,000	KM105, 106a, 107-108, 109.2, 110, 140.1, 149, 170, 175	—	22.50
MS70	1991D (10)	20,000	KM105, 106a, 107-108, 109.2, 110, 140.1, 149, 170, 175	—	22.50
MS71	1991F (10)	20,000	KM105, 106a, 107-108, 109.2, 110, 140.1, 149, 170, 175	—	22.50
MS72	1991G (10)	20,000	KM105, 106a, 107-108, 109.2, 110, 140.1, 149, 170, 175	—	22.50
MS73	1991J (10)	20,000	KM105, 106a, 107-108, 109.2, 110, 140.1, 149, 170, 175	—	22.50
MS74	1992A (10)	20,000	KM105, 106a, 107-108, 109.2, 110, 140.1, 149, 170, 175	—	22.50
MS75	1992D (10)	20,000	KM105, 106a, 107-108, 109.2, 110, 140.1, 149, 170, 175	—	22.50
MS76	1992F (10)	20,000	KM105, 106a, 107-108, 109.2, 110, 140.1, 149, 170, 175	—	22.50
MS77	1992G (10)	20,000	KM105, 106a, 107-108, 109.2, 110, 140.1, 149, 170, 175	—	22.50
MS78	1992J (10)	20,000	KM105, 106a, 107-108, 109.2, 110, 140.1, 149, 170, 175	—	22.50
MS79	1993A (10)	20,000	KM105, 106a, 107-108, 109.2, 110, 140.1, 149, 170, 175	—	40.00
MS80	1993D (10)	20,000	KM105, 106a, 107-108, 109.2, 110, 140.1, 149, 170, 175	—	40.00
MS81	1993F (10)	20,000	KM105, 106a, 107-108, 109.2, 110, 140.1, 149, 170, 175	—	40.00
MS82	1993G (10)	20,000	KM105, 106a, 107-108, 109.2, 110, 140.1, 149, 170, 175	—	40.00
MS83	1993J (10)	20,000	KM105, 106a, 107-108, 109.2, 110, 140.1, 149, 170, 175	—	40.00
MS84	1994A (10)	10,000	KM105, 106A, 107-108, 109.2, 110, 140.1, 170, 175, 183	—	37.50
MS85	1994D (10)	20,000	KM105, 106a, 107-108, 109.2, 110, 140.1, 170, 175, 183	—	37.50
MS86	1994F (10)	20,000	KM105, 106a, 107-108, 109.2, 110, 140.1, 170, 175, 183	—	37.50
MS87	1994G (10)	20,000	KM105, 106a, 107-108, 109.2, 110, 140.1, 170, 175, 183	—	37.50
MS88	1994J (10)	20,000	KM105, 106a, 107-108, 109.2, 110, 140.1, 170, 175, 183	—	37.50

KM#	Date	Mintage	Identification	Issue Price	Mkt Val
MS89	1995A (10)	20,000	KM105, 106a, 107-108, 109.2, 110, 140.1, 170, 175, 183	—	175
MS90	1995D (10)	20,000	KM105, 106a, 107-108, 109.2, 110, 140.1, 170, 175, 183	—	335
MS91	1995F (10)	20,000	KM105, 106a, 107-108, 109.2, 110, 140.1, 170, 175, 183	—	425
MS92	1995G (10)	20,000	KM105, 106a, 107-108, 109.2, 110, 140.1, 170, 175, 183	—	265
MS93	1995J (10)	20,000	KM105, 106A, 107-108, 109.2, 110, 140.1, 170, 175, 183	—	260
MS94	1996A (10)	50,000	KM105, 106a, 107-108, 109.2, 110, 140.1, 170, 175, 183	—	55.00
MS95	1996D (10)	50,000	KM105, 106a, 107-108, 109.2, 110, 140.1, 170, 175, 183	—	55.00
MS96	1996F (10)	50,000	KM105, 106a, 107-108, 109.2, 110, 140.1, 170, 175, 183	—	55.00
MS97	1996G (10)	50,000	KM105, 106a, 107-108, 109.2, 110, 140.1, 170, 175, 183	—	55.00
MS98	1996J (10)	50,000	KM105, 106a, 107-108, 109.2, 110, 140.1, 170, 175, 183	—	55.00
MS99	1997A (9)	70,000	KM105, 106a, 108, 109.2, 110, 140.1, 170, 175, 183	—	35.00
MS100	1997D (10)	70,000	KM105, 106a, 107-108, 109.2, 110, 140.1, 170, 175, 183	—	35.00
MS101	1997F (10)	70,000	KM105, 106a, 107-108, 109.2, 110, 140.1, 170, 175, 183	—	35.00
MS102	1997G (10)	70,000	KM105, 106a, 107-108, 109.2, 110, 140.1, 170, 175, 183	—	35.00
MS103	1997J (10)	70,000	KM105, 106a, 107-108, 109.2, 110, 140.1, 170, 175, 183	—	35.00
MS104	1998A (10)	70,000	KM105, 106a, 107-108, 109.2, 110, 140.1, 170, 175, 183	—	35.00
MS105	1998D (10)	70,000	KM105, 106a, 107-108, 109.2, 110, 140.1, 170, 175, 183	—	35.00
MS107	1998G (10)	70,000	KM105, 106a, 107-108, 109.2, 110, 140.1, 170, 175, 183	—	35.00
MS108	1998J (10)	70,000	KM105, 106a, 107-108, 109.2, 110, 140.1, 170, 175, 183	—	35.00
MS109	1999A (10)	70,000	KM105, 106a, 107-108, 109.2, 110, 140.1, 170, 175, 183	—	35.00
MS110	1999D (10)	70,000	km105, 106A, 107-108, 109.2, 110, 140.1, 170, 175, 183	—	35.00
MS112	1999G (10)	70,000	KM105, 106a, 107-108, 109.2, 110, 140.1, 170, 175, 183	—	35.00
MS114	1999J (10)	70,000	KM105, 106a, 107-108, 109.2, 110, 140.1, 170, 175, 183	—	35.00
MS115	2000D (10)	20,000	KM105, 106a, 107-108, 109.2, 110, 140.1, 170, 175, 183	—	40.00
MS116	2000F (10)	20,000	KM105, 160a, 107-108, 109.2, 110, 140.1, 170, 175, 183	—	40.00
MS117	2000G (10)	20,000	KM105, 106a, 107-108, 109.2, 110, 140.1, 170, 175, 183	—	40.00
MS118	2000J (10)	20,000	KM105, 106a, 107-108, 109.2, 110, 140.1, 170, 175, 183	—	40.00
MS119	2001A (10)	130,000	KM105,106a,107-108,109.2,110,140.1,170,175,183	—	30.00
MS120	2001D (10)	130,000	KM105,106a,107-108,109.2,110,140.1,170,175,183	—	30.00
MS121	2001F (10)	130,000	KM105,106a,107-108,109.2,110,140.1,170,175,183	—	30.00
MS122	2001G (10)	130,000	KM105,106a,107-108,109.2,110,140.1,170,175,183	—	30.00
MS123	2001J (10)	130,000	KM105,106a,107-108,109.2,110,140.1,170,175,183	—	30.00
MS124	2002A (8)	—	KM#207-214	—	27.50
MS125	2002D (8)	—	KM#207-214	—	27.50
MS126	2002F (8)	—	KM#207-214	—	27.50
MS127	2002G (8)	—	KM#207-214	—	27.50
MS128	2002J (8)	—	KM#207-214	—	27.50

PROOF SETS

KM#	Date	Mintage	Identification	Issue Price	Mkt Val
PS4	1966F (8)	450	KM105-108, 109.1, 110, 112.1, 116	—	2,000
PS5	1966G (8)	3,070	KM105-108, 109.1, 110, 112.1, 116	—	175
PS6	1966J (8)	1,000	KM105-108, 109.1, 110, 112.1, 116	—	450

KM#	Date	Mintage	Identification	Issue Price	Mkt Val
PS9	1967G (8)	520	KM105, 106a*, 107-108, 109.1, 110, 112.1, 116	—	1,600
PS7	1967F (8)	1,600	KM105-108, 109.1, 110, 112.1, 116	—	350
PS8	1967G (8)	3,630	KM105-108, 109.1, 110, 112.1, 116	—	175
PS10	1967J (8)	1,500	KM105, 106a, 107-108, 109.1, 110, 112.1, 116	—	450
PS11	1968F (8)	3,000	KM105, 106a, 107-108, 109.1, 110, 112.1, 116	—	350
PS12	1968G (8)	3,651	KM105, 106, 107-108, 109.1, 110, 112.1, 116	—	175
PS12a	1968G (8)	2,372	KM105, 106a, 107-108, 109.1, 110, 112.1, 116	—	225
PS13	1968J (8)	2,000	KM105, 106a, 107-108, 109.1, 110, 112.1, 116	—	375
PS14	1969F (8)	5,000	KM105, 106a, 107-108, 109.1, 110, 112.1, 116	—	100
PS15	1969G (8)	8,700	KM105, 106a, 107-108, 109.1, 110, 112.1, 116	—	85.00
PS16	1969J (8)	5,000	KM105, 106a, 107-108, 109.1, 110, 112.1, 116	—	100
PS17	1970F (8)	5,140	KM105, 106a, 107-108, 109.1, 110, 112.1, 116	—	100
PS18	1970G (8)	10,200	KM105, 106a, 107-108, 109.1, 110, 112.1, 116	—	80.00
PS19	1970J (8)	5,000	KM105, 106a, 107-108, 109.1, 110, 112.1, 116	—	90.00
PS20	1971D (8)	8,000	KM105, 106a, 107-108, 109.1, 110, 112.1, 116	—	95.00
PS21	1971F (8)	8,000	KM105, 106a, 107-108, 109.1, 110, 112.1, 116	—	90.00
PS22	1971G (8)	10,200	KM105, 106a, 107-108, 109.1, 110, 112.1, 116	—	90.00
PS23	1971J (8)	8,000	KM105, 106a, 107-108, 109.1, 110, 112.1, 116	—	95.00
PS24	1972D (9)	8,000	KM105, 106a, 107-108, 109.2, 110, 112.1, 124, A127	—	95.00
PS25	1972F (9)	8,000	KM105, 106a, 107-108, 109.2, 110, 112.1, 124, A127	—	95.00
PS26	1972G (9)	10,000	KM105, 106a, 107-108, 109.2, 110, 112.1, 124, A127	—	85.00
PS27	1972J (9)	8,000	KM105, 106a, 107-108, 109.2, 110, 112.1, 124, A127	—	85.00
PS28	1973D (9)	9,000	KM105, 106a, 107-108, 109.2, 110, 112.1, 124, A127	—	85.00
PS29	1973F (9)	9,000	KM105, 106a, 107-108, 109.2, 110, 112.1, 124, A127	—	85.00
PS30	1973G (9)	9,000	KM105, 106a, 107-108, 109.2, 110, 112.1, 124, A127	—	85.00
PS31	1973J (9)	9,000	KM105, 106a, 107-108, 109.2, 110, 112.1, 124, A127	—	85.00
PS32	1974D (9)	35,000	KM105, 106a, 107-108, 109.2, 110,112.1, 124, A127	10.00	30.00
PS33	1974F (9)	35,000	KM105, 106a, 107-108, 109.2, 110, 112.1, 124, A127	10.00	30.00
PS34	1974G (9)	35,000	KM105, 106a, 107-108, 109.2, 110, 112.1, 124, A127	10.00	30.00
PS35	1974J (9)	35,000	KM105, 106a, 107-108, 109.2, 110, 112.1, 124, A127	10.00	30.00
PS36	1975D (9)	43,120	KM105, 106a, 107-108, 109.2, 110, 124, A127, 140.1	10.00	20.00
PS37	1975F (9)	43,100	KM105, 106a, 107-108, 109.2, 110, 124, A127, 140.1	10.00	20.00
PS38	1975G (9)	43,100	KM105, 106a, 107-108, 109.2, 110, 124, A127, 140.1	10.00	20.00
PS39	1975J (9)	43,120	KM105, 106a, 107-108, 109.2, 110, 124, A127, 140.1	10.00	20.00
PS40	1976D (9)	43,120	KM105, 106a, 107-108, 109.2, 110, 124, A127,140.1	10.00	20.00
PS41	1976F (9)	43,100	KM105, 106a, 107-108, 109.2, 110, 124, A127, 140.1	10.00	20.00
PS42	1976G (9)	43,100	KM105, 106a, 107-108, 109.2, 110, 124, A127, 140.1	10.00	20.00
PS43	1976J (9)	43,120	KM105, 106a, 107-108, 109.2, 110, 124, A127, 140.1	10.00	20.00
PS44	1977D (9)	50,620	KM105, 106a, 107-108, 109.2, 110, 124, A127, 140.1	12.50	17.50
PS45	1977F (9)	50,600	KM105, 106a, 107-108, 109.2, 110, 124, A127, 140.1	12.50	17.50
PS46	1977G (9)	50,600	KM105, 106a, 107-108, 109.2, 110, 124, A127, 140.1	12.50	17.50
PS47	1977J (9)	50,620	KM105, 106a, 107-108, 109.2, 110, 124, A127, 140.1	12.50	17.50
PS48	1978D (9)	54,000	KM105, 106A, 107-108, 109.2, 110, 124, A127, 140.1	13.00	17.50
PS49	1978F (9)	54,000	KM105, 106a, 107-108, 109.2, 110, 124, A127, 140.1	13.00	17.50
PS50	1978G (9)	54,000	KM105, 106a, 107-108, 109.2, 110, 124, A127, 140.1	13.00	17.50
PS51	1978J (9)	54,000	KM105, 106a, 107-108, 109.2, 110, 124, A127, 140.1	13.00	17.50
PS52	1979D (10)	89,000	KM105, 106a, 107-108, 109.2, 110, 124, A127, 140.1, 149	15.00	17.50
PS53	1979F (10)	89,000	KM105, 106a, 107-108, 109.2, 110, 124, A127, 140.1, 149	15.00	17.50
PS54	1979G (10)	89,000	KM105, 106a, 107-108, 109.2, 110, 124, A127, 140.1, 149	15.00	17.50
PS55	1979J (10)	89,000	KM105, 106a, 107-108, 109.2, 110, 124, A127, 140.1, 149	15.00	17.50
PS56	1980D (10)	60,000	KM105, 106a, 107-108, 109.2, 110, 124, A127, 140.1, 149	15.00	17.50
PS57	1980F (10)	60,000	KM105, 106a, 107-108, 109.2, 110, 124, A127, 140.1, 149	15.00	17.50
PS58	1980G (10)	60,000	KM105, 106a, 107-108, 109.2, 110, 124, A127, 140.1, 149	15.00	17.50
PS59	1980J (10)	60,000	KM105, 106a, 107-108, 109.2, 110, 124, A127, 140.1, 149	15.00	17.50
PS60	1981D (10)	60,000	KM105, 106a, 107-108, 109.2, 110, 124, A127, 140.1, 149	15.00	17.50
PS61	1981F (10)	91,000	KM105, 106a, 107-108, 109.2, 110, 124, A127, 140.1, 149	15.00	17.50
PS62	1981G (10)	91,000	KM105, 106a, 107-108, 109.2, 110, 124, A127, 140.1, 149	15.00	17.50
PS63	1981J (10)	78,000	KM105, 106a, 107-108, 109.2, 110, 124, A127, 140.1, 149	15.00	17.50
PS64	1982D (10)	78,000	KM105, 106a, 107-108, 109.2, 110, 124, A127, 140.1, 149	15.00	17.50
PS65	1982F (10)	78,000	KM105, 106a,107-108, 109.2, 110, 124, A127, 140.1, 149	15.00	17.50
PS66	1982G (10)	78,000	KM105, 106a, 107-108, 109.2, 110, 124, A127, 140.1, 149	15.00	17.50
PS67	1982J (10)	78,000	KM105, 106a, 107-108, 109.2, 110, 124, A127, 140.1, 149	15.00	17.50
PS68	1983D (10)	75,000	KM105, 106a, 107-108, 109.2, 110, 124, A127, 140.1, 149	15.00	17.50
PS69	1983F (10)	75,000	KM105, 106a, 107-108, 109.2, 110, 124, A127, 140.1, 149	15.00	17.50
PS70	1983G (10)	75,000	KM105, 106a, 107-108, 109.2, 110, 124, A127, 140.1, 149	15.00	17.50
PS71	1983J (10)	75,000	KM105, 106a, 107-108, 109.2, 110, 124, A127, 140.1, 149	15.00	17.50
PS72	1984D (10)	64,000	KM105, 106a, 107-108, 109.2, 110, 124, A127, 140.1, 149	15.00	26.50
PS73	1984F (10)	64,000	KM105, 106a, 107-108, 109.2, 110, 124, A127, 140.1, 149	15.00	26.50
PS74	1984G (10)	64,000	KM105, 106a, 107-108, 109.2, 110, 124, A127, 140.1, 149	15.00	26.50
PS75	1985D (10)	56,000	KM105, 106a, 107-108, 109.2, 110, 124, A127, 140.1, 149	15.00	26.50
PS77	1985F (10)	54,000	KM105, 106a, 107-108, 109.2, 110, 124, A127, 140.1, 149	15.00	25.00
PS78	1985G (10)	55,000	KM105, 106a, 107-108, 109.2, 110, 124, A127, 140.1, 149	15.00	25.00
PS79	1985J (10)	54,000	KM105, 106a, 107-108, 109.2, 110, 124, A127, 140.1, 149	15.00	25.00
PS80	1986D (10)	44,000	KM105, 106a, 107-108, 109.2, 110, 124, A127, 140.1, 149	15.00	27.50
PS81	1986F (10)	44,000	KM105, 106a, 107-108, 109.2, 110, 124, A127, 140.1, 149	15.00	27.50
PS82	1986G (10)	44,000	KM105, 106a, 107-108, 109.2, 110, 124, A127, 140.1, 149	15.00	27.50
PS83	1986J (10)	44,000	KM105, 106a, 107-108, 109.2, 110, 124, A127, 140.1, 149	15.00	27.50
PS84	1987D (10)	45,000	KM105, 106a, 107-108, 109.2, 110, 124, A127, 140.1, 149	15.00	25.00
PS85	1987F (10)	45,000	KM105, 106a, 107-108, 109.2, 110, 124, A127, 140.1, 149	15.00	25.00
PS86	1987G (10)	45,000	KM105, 106a, 107-108, 109.2, 110, 124, A127, 140.1, 149	15.00	25.00
PS87	1987J (10)	45,000	KM105, 106a, 107-108, 109.2, 110, 124, A127, 140.1, 149	15.00	25.00
PS88	1988D (9)	45,000	KM105, 106a, 107-108, 109.2, 110, 140.1, 149, 170	—	25.00
PS89	1988F (9)	45,000	KM105, 106a, 107-108, 109.2, 110, 140.1, 149, 170	—	25.00
PS90	1988G (9)	45,000	KM105, 106a, 107-108, 109.2, 110, 140.1, 149, 170	—	25.00
PS91	1988J (9)	45,000	KM105, 106a, 107-108, 109.2, 110, 140.1, 149, 170	—	25.00
PS92	1989D (9)	45,000	KM105, 106a, 107-108, 109.2, 110, 140.1, 149, 170	—	25.00
PS93	1989F (9)	45,000	KM105, 106a, 107-108, 109.2, 110, 140.1, 149, 170	—	25.00
PS94	1989G (9)	45,000	KM105-106a, 107-108, 109.2, 110, 140.1, 149, 170	—	25.00
PS95	1989J (9)	45,000	KM105-106a, 107-108, 109.2, 110, 140.1, 149, 170	—	25.00
PS96	1990D (10)	45,000	KM105, 106a, 107-108, 109.2, 110, 140.1, 149, 170, 175	—	25.00
PS97	1990F (10)	45,000	KM105, 106a, 107-108, 109.2, 110, 140.1, 149, 170, 175	—	25.00
PS98	1990G (10)	45,000	KM105,106a,107-180,109.2,110,140.1,149,170,175	—	25.00
PS99	1990J (10)	45,000	KM105,106a,107-108,109.2,110,140.1,149,170,175	—	25.00
PS100	1991A (10)	45,000	KM105,106a,107-108,109.2,110,140.1,149,170,175	—	27.50
PS101	1991D (10)	45,000	KM105,106a,107-108,109.2,110,140.1,149,170,175	—	27.50
PS102	1991F (10)	45,000	KM105,106a,107-108,109.2,110,140.1,149,170,175	—	27.50
PS103	1991G (10)	45,000	KM105,106a,107-108,109.2,110,140.1,149,170,175	—	27.50
PS104	1991J (10)	45,000	KM105,106a,107-108,109.2,110,140.1,149,170,175	—	27.50
PS105	1992A (10)	45,000	KM105,106a,107-108,109.2,110,140.1,149,170,175	—	27.50
PS106	1992D (10)	45,000	KM105,106a,107-108,109.2,110,140.1,149,170,175	—	27.50
PS107	1992F (10)	45,000	KM105,106a,107-108,109.2,110,140.1,149,170,175	—	27.50
PS108	1992G (10)	45,000	KM105,106a,107,108,109.2,110,140.1,149,170,175	—	27.50
PS109	1992J (10)	45,000	KM105,106a,107-108,109.2,110,140.1,149,170,175	—	27.50
PS110	1993A (10)	45,000	KM105,106a,107-108,109.2,110,140.1,149,170,175	—	35.00
PS111	1993D (10)	45,000	KM105,106a,107-108,109.2,110,140.1,149,170,175	—	35.00
PS112	1993F (10)	45,000	KM105,106a,107-108,109.2,110,140.1,149,170,175	—	35.00
PS113	1993J (10)	45,000	KM105,106a,107-108,109.2,110,140.1,149,170,175	—	35.00
PS114	1993J	45,000	KM105,106a,107-108,109.2,110,140.1,149,170,175	—	35.00
PS115	1994A (10)	45,000	KM105,106a,107-108,109.2,110,140.1,170,175,183	—	35.00
PS116	1994D (10)	45,000	KM105,106a,107-108,109.2,110,140.1,170,175,183	—	35.00
PS117	1994F (10)	45,000	KM105,106a,107-108,109.2,110,140.1,170,175,183	—	35.00
PS118	1994G (10)	45,000	KM105,106a,107-108,109.2,110,140.1,170,175,183	—	35.00
PS119	1994J (10)	45,000	KM105,106a,107-108,109.2,110,140.1,170,175,183	—	35.00
PS120	1995A (10)	45,000	KM105,106a,107-108,109.2,110,140.1,170,175,183	—	115
PS121	1995D (10)	45,000	KM105,106a,107-108,109.2,110,140.1,170,175,183	—	115
PS123	1995G (10)	45,000	KM105,106a,107-108,109.2,110,140.1,170,175,183	—	115
PS122	1995F (10)	45,000	KM105,106a,107-108,109.2,110,140.1,170,175,183	—	115

KM#	Date	Mintage	Identification	Issue Price	Mkt Val
PS124	1995J (10)	45,000	KM105,106a,107-108,109.2,110,140.1,170,175,183	—	115
PS125	1996A (10)	45,000	KM105,106a,107-108,109.2,110,140.1,170,175,183	—	60.00
PS126	1996D (10)	45,000	KM105,106a,107-108,109.2,110,140.1,170,175,183	—	60.00
PS127	1996F (10)	45,000	KM105,106a,107-108,109.2,110,140.1,170,175,183	—	60.00
PS128	1996G (10)	45,000	KM105,106a,107-108,109.2,110,140.1,170,175,183	—	60.00
PS129	1996J (10)	45,000	KM105,106a,107-108,109.2,110,140.1,170,175,183	—	60.00
PS130	1997A (10)	45,000	KM105,106a,107-108,109.2,110,140.1,170,175,183	—	37.50
PS131	1997D (10)	45,000	KM105,106a,107-108,109.2,110,140.1,170,175,183	—	37.50
PS132	1997F (10)	45,000	KM105,106a,107-108,109.2,11o,140.1,170,175,183	—	37.50
PS133	1997G (10)	45,000	KM105,106a,107-108,109.2,110,140.1,170,175,183	—	37.50
PS134	1997J (10)	45,000	KM105,106a,107-108,109.2,110,140.1,170,175,183	—	37.50
PS135	1998A (10)	45,000	KM105,106a,107-108,109.2,110,140.1,170,175,183	—	37.50
PS136	1998D (10)	45,000	KM105,106a,107-108,109.2,110,140.1,170,175,183	—	37.50
PS137	1998F (10)	45,000	KM105,106a,107-108,109.2,110,140.1,170,175,183	—	37.50
PS142	1999F (10)	45,000	KM105,106a,107-108,109.2,110,140.1,170,175,183	—	37.50
PS138	1998G (10)	45,000	KM105,106a,107-108,109.2,110,140.1,170,175,183	—	37.50
PS139	1998J (10)	45,000	KM105,106a,107-108,109.2,110,140.1,170,175,183	—	37.50
PS144	1999J (10)	45,000	KM105,106a,107-108,109.2,110,140.1,170,175,183	—	50.00
PS140	1999A (10)	45,000	KM105,106a,107-108,109.2,110,140.1,170,175,183	—	37.50
PS141	1999D (10)	45,000	KM105,106a,107-108,109.2,110,140.1,170,175,183	—	37.50
PS143	1999G (10)	45,000	KM105,106a,107-108,109.2,110,140.1,170,175,183	—	37.50
PS145	2000A (10)	45,000	KM105,106a,107-108,109.2,110,140.1,170,175,183	—	50.00
PS146	2000D (10)	45,000	KM105,106a,107-108,109.2,110,140.1,170,175,183	—	50.00
PS147	2000F (10)	45,000	KM105,106a,107,108,109.2,110,140.1,170,175,183	—	50.00
PS148	2000G (10)	45,000	KM105,106a,107-108,109.2,110,140.1,170,175,183	—	50.00
PS149	2000J (10)	45,000	KM105,106a,107-108,109.2,110,140.1,170,175,183	—	50.00
PS150	2001A (10)	78,000	KM105,106a,107-108,109.2,110,140.1,170,175,183	—	65.00
PS151	2001D (10)	78,000	KM105,106a,107-108,109.2,110,140.1,170,175,183	—	65.00
PS152	2001F (10)	78,000	KM105,106a,107-108,110,140.1,170,175,183	—	65.00
PS153	2001G (10)	78,000	KM105,106a,107-108,109.2,110,140.1,170,175,183	—	65.00
PS154	2001J (10)	78,000	KM105,106a,107-108,109.2,110,140.1,170,175,183	—	65.00
PS155	2002A (8)	—	KM#207-214	—	32.50
PS156	2002D (8)	—	KM#207-214	—	32.50
PS157	2002F (8)	—	KM#207-214	—	32.50
PS158	2002G (8)	—	KM#207-214	—	32.50
PS159	2002J (8)	—	KM#207-214	—	32.50

1949-1990

The German Democratic Republic, formerly East Germany, was located on the great north European plain, had an area of 41,768 sq. mi. (108,330 sq. km.) and a population of 16.6 million. The figures included East Berlin, which had been incorporated into the G.D.R. Capital: East Berlin. The economy was highly industrialized. Machinery, transport equipment chemicals, and lignite were exported.

During the closing days of World War II in Europe, Soviet troops advancing into Germany from the east occupied the German provinces of Mecklenburg, Brandenburg, Lusatia, Saxony and Thuringia. These five provinces comprised the occupation zone administered by the Soviet Union after the cessation of hostilities. The other three zones were administered by the U.S., Great Britain and France. Under the Potsdam agreement, questions affecting Germany as a whole were to be settled by the commanders of the occupation zones acting jointly and by unanimous decision. When Soviet intransigence rendered the quadripartite commission inoperable, the three western zones were united to form the Federal Republic of Germany, May 23, 1949. Thereupon the Soviet Union dissolved its occupation zone and established it as the Democratic Republic of Germany, Oct. 7, 1949.

The post-WW II division of Germany was ended Oct. 3,1990, when the German Democratic Republic (East Germany) ceased to exist and its five constituent provinces were formally admitted to the Federal Republic of Germany. An election Dec. 2, 1990, chose representatives to the united federal parliament (Bundestag), which then conducted its opening session in Berlin in the old Reichstag building. Although Berlin technically is the capital of the reunited Germany, the actual seat of government remains for the time being in Bonn.

MINT MARKS

A - Berlin
E - Muldenhutten

MONETARY SYSTEM

100 Pfennig = 1 Mark

DEMOCRATIC REPUBLIC

STANDARD COINAGE

KM# 1 PFENNIG Composition: Aluminum

Date	Mintage	F	VF	XF	Unc	BU
1948A	243,000,000	—	1.00	8.00	35.00	—
1949A	Inc. above	—	1.00	8.00	35.00	—
1949E	55,200,000	—	11.50	45.00	300	—
1950A	—	—	1.00	8.00	35.00	—
1950E	—	—	7.50	20.00	100	—

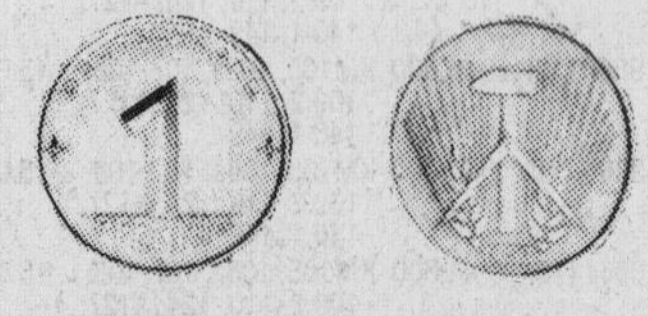

KM# 5 PFENNIG Composition: Aluminum

Date	Mintage	F	VF	XF	Unc	BU
1952A	297,213,000	—	0.50	1.75	6.00	—
1952E	49,296,000	—	5.00	12.00	55.00	—
1953A	114,002,000	—	0.50	1.75	6.00	—
1953E	50,876,000	—	5.00	15.00	60.00	—

KM# 8.1 PFENNIG Composition: Aluminum

Date	Mintage	F	VF	XF	Unc	BU
1960A	101,808,000	—	0.25	0.75	3.50	—
1961A	101,776,000	—	0.25	0.75	3.50	—
1962A	81,459,000	—	0.25	0.75	3.50	—
1963A	101,402,000	—	0.25	0.75	3.50	—
1964A	98,967,000	—	0.25	0.75	3.50	—
1965A	38,585,000	—	3.00	15.00	35.00	—
1968A	813,680,000	—	0.25	0.75	2.50	—
1972A	4,801,000	—	2.00	10.00	25.00	—
1973A	5,518,000	—	1.50	8.00	22.50	—
1975A	202,752,000	—	0.25	0.75	2.50	—

KM# 8.2 PFENNIG Composition: Aluminum **Obverse:** Smaller design features **Reverse:** Smaller design features

Date	Mintage	F	VF	XF	Unc	BU
1977A	61,560,000	—	0.10	0.25	2.00	—
1978A	200,050,000	—	0.10	0.20	0.50	—
1979A	100,640,000	—	0.10	0.20	0.50	—
1979A Proof	—	Value: 45.00				
1980A	153,000,000	—	0.10	0.20	0.50	—
1980A Proof	—	Value: 45.00				
1981A	200,436,000	—	0.10	0.20	0.50	—
1981A Proof	40	—	—	—	—	—
1982A	99,200,000	—	0.10	0.20	0.50	—
1982A Proof	2,500	Value: 10.00				
1983A	150,000,000	—	0.10	0.20	0.50	—
1983A Proof	2,550	Value: 18.00				
1984A	137,600,000	—	0.10	0.20	0.50	—
1984A Proof	3,015	Value: 4.50				
1985A	125,060,000	—	0.10	0.20	0.50	—
1985A Proof	2,816	Value: 4.50				
1986A	73,900,000	—	0.10	0.20	0.50	—
1986A Proof	2,800	Value: 4.50				
1987A	50,015,000	—	0.10	0.20	0.50	—
1987A Proof	2,345	Value: 4.50				
1988A	75,450,000	—	0.10	0.20	0.50	—
1988A Proof	2,300	Value: 4.50				
1989A	84,410,000	—	0.10	0.20	0.50	—
1989A Proof	2,300	Value: 4.50				
1990A	15,670,000	—	0.10	0.20	2.00	—

KM# 2 5 PFENNIG Composition: Aluminum

Date	Mintage	F	VF	XF	Unc	BU
1948A	205,072,000	—	2.50	5.50	50.00	—
1949A	Inc. above	—	2.50	5.50	45.00	—
1950A	Inc. above	—	2.50	5.50	35.00	—

KM# 6 5 PFENNIG Composition: Aluminum

Date	Mintage	F	VF	XF	Unc	BU
1952A	113,397,000	—	2.00	5.00	12.50	—
1952E	24,024,000	—	3.50	8.00	35.00	—
1953A	40,994,000	—	2.00	5.00	17.50	—
1953E	28,665,000	—	5.00	17.50	90.00	—

KM# 9.1 5 PFENNIG Composition: Aluminum

Date	Mintage	F	VF	XF	Unc	BU
1968A	282,303,000	—	0.50	1.00	2.00	—
1972A	51,462,000	—	0.50	1.00	3.50	—
1975A	84,710,000	—	0.50	1.00	2.00	—

KM# 9.2 5 PFENNIG Composition: Aluminum **Obverse:** Smaller design features **Reverse:** Smaller design features **Note:** Varieties exist.

Date	Mintage	F	VF	XF	Unc	BU
1976A 2 known		—	—	—	—	—
1978A		—	0.15	0.25	0.60	—
1979A		—	0.15	0.25	0.60	—
1979A Proof	—	Value: 45.00				
1980A		—	0.15	0.25	0.60	—
1980A Proof	—	Value: 45.00				
1981A		—	0.15	0.25	0.60	—
1981A Proof		—	—	—	—	—
1982A		—	1.75	7.50	22.50	—
1982A Proof	2,500	Value: 10.00				
1983A		—	0.15	0.25	0.60	—
1983A Proof	2,550	Value: 18.00				
1984A		—	—	—	30.00	—
1984A Proof	3,015	Value: 4.50				
1985A		—	1.50	6.50	18.50	—
1985A Proof	2,816	Value: 4.50				
1986A		—	1.50	6.50	18.50	—
1986A Proof	2,800	Value: 4.50				
1987A		—	—	—	12.50	—
1987A Proof	2,345	Value: 4.50				
1988A		—	0.15	0.25	0.60	—
1988A Proof	2,300	Value: 4.50				
1989A		—	0.15	0.25	0.60	—
1989A Proof	2,300	Value: 4.50				
1990A		—	0.15	0.25	0.60	—

KM# 3 10 PFENNIG Composition: Aluminum **Note:** Also exists with medallic die rotation (1950E).

Date	Mintage	F	VF	XF	Unc	BU
1948A	216,537,000	—	2.50	17.50	75.00	—
1949A	Inc. above	—	2.50	17.50	70.00	—
1950A	Inc. above	—	2.50	8.50	70.00	—
1950E	16,000,000	—	17.50	175	1,000	—

KM# 7 10 PFENNIG Composition: Aluminum

Date	Mintage	F	VF	XF	Unc	BU
1952A	70,427,000	—	1.50	11.50	55.00	—
1952E	21,498,000	—	15.00	40.00	280	—
1953A	18,611,000	—	3.50	17.50	75.00	—
1953E	11,500,000	—	15.00	70.00	650	—

KM# 10 10 PFENNIG Composition: Aluminum

Date	Mintage	F	VF	XF	Unc	BU
1963A		—	6.00	30.00	85.00	—
1965A		—	0.15	0.25	2.50	—
1967A		—	0.15	0.25	2.50	—
1968A		—	0.15	0.25	0.75	—
1970A		—	0.15	0.25	1.00	—
1971A		—	0.15	0.25	0.75	—
1972A		—	0.50	3.00	12.00	—
1973A		—	0.15	0.25	1.50	—
1978A		—	0.15	0.25	1.50	—
1979A		—	0.15	0.25	0.60	—
1979A Proof	—	Value: 45.00				
1980A		—	0.15	0.25	0.60	—
1980A Proof	—	Value: 45.00				
1981A		—	0.15	0.25	0.60	—
1981A Proof		—	—	—	—	—
1982A		—	0.15	0.25	1.50	—
1982A Proof	2,500	Value: 10.00				
1983A		—	0.15	0.25	0.60	—
1983A Proof	2,550	Value: 20.00				
1984A		—	—	—	25.00	—

Note: Issued in sets only, remainder unaccountable

Date	Mintage	F	VF	XF	Unc	BU
1984A Proof	3,015	Value: 4.50				
1985A		—	0.35	4.50	17.50	—
1985A Proof	2,816	Value: 4.50				
1986A		—	0.35	4.50	17.50	—
1986A Proof	2,800	Value: 4.50				
1987A		—	—	—	12.00	—

Note: Issued in sets only, remainder unaccountable

Date	Mintage	F	VF	XF	Unc	BU
1987A Proof	2,345	Value: 4.50				
1988A		—	0.15	0.25	0.75	—
1988A Proof	2,300	Value: 4.50				
1989A		—	0.15	0.25	0.60	—
1989A Proof	2,300	Value: 4.50				
1990A		—	—	—	15.00	—

Note: Issued in sets only, remainder unaccountable

KM# 11 20 PFENNIG Composition: Brass **Note:** Ribbon width varieties exist.

Date	Mintage	F	VF	XF	Unc	BU
1969		—	0.25	1.50	4.00	—
1971		—	0.25	2.50	6.00	—
1972A		—	0.25	2.50	10.00	—
1973A		—	0.25	4.50	20.00	—
1974A		—	0.25	2.50	10.00	—
1979A		—	0.25	1.50	7.50	—
1979A Proof	—	Value: 50.00				
1980A		—	0.20	0.50	5.00	—
1980A Proof	—	Value: 50.00				
1981A		—	0.20	0.75	7.50	—
1981A Proof		—	—	—	—	—
1982A		—	0.20	2.50	8.50	—
1982A Proof	2,500	Value: 12.50				
1983A		—	0.20	0.50	3.00	—
1983A Proof	2,550	Value: 25.00				
1984A		—	0.20	0.50	3.00	—
1984A Proof	3,015	Value: 5.50				
1985A		—	0.20	0.50	4.00	—
1985A Proof	2,816	Value: 5.50				
1986A		—	0.20	0.50	4.00	—
1986A Proof	2,800	Value: 5.50				
1987A		—	—	—	8.00	—

Note: Issued in sets only, remainder unaccountable

Date	Mintage	F	VF	XF	Unc	BU
1987A Proof	2,345	Value: 5.50				
1988A		—	—	—	10.00	—

Note: Issued in sets only, remainder unaccountable

Date	Mintage	F	VF	XF	Unc	BU
1988A Proof	2,300	Value: 5.50				
1989A		—	0.20	0.50	2.00	—
1989A Proof	2,300	Value: 5.50				
1990A		—	—	—	15.00	—

Note: Issued in sets only, remainder unaccountable

KM# 4 50 PFENNIG Composition: Aluminum-Bronze

Date	Mintage	F	VF	XF	Unc	BU
1949A	Inc. below	—	—	7,500	—	—
1950A	67,703,000	—	3.50	8.50	32.50	—

Note: Some authorities believe the 1949 dated piece is a pattern

KM# 12.1 50 PFENNIG Composition: Aluminum **Obverse:** Small coat of arms

Date	Mintage	F	VF	XF	Unc	BU
1958A	101,606,000	—	0.35	2.50	10.00	—

KM# 12.2 50 PFENNIG Composition: Aluminum **Obverse:** Larger coat of arms **Note:** Inscription varieties exist.

Date	Mintage	F	VF	XF	Unc	BU
1968A		—	0.35	0.75	5.00	—
1971A		—	0.35	0.75	3.00	—
1972A		—	0.35	0.75	4.50	—
1973A		—	0.35	0.75	7.50	—
1979A		—	0.35	0.75	7.50	—
1979A Proof		—	—	—	—	—
1980A		—	0.35	0.75	8.00	—
1980A Proof		—	—	—	—	—
1981A		—	0.35	0.75	2.50	—
1981A Proof		—	—	—	—	—
1982A		—	0.35	0.75	2.50	—
1982A Proof	2,500	Value: 12.50				
1983A		—	0.35	0.75	7.50	—
1983A Proof	2,550	Value: 25.00				
1984A		—	—	—	30.00	—
1984A Proof	3,015	Value: 5.50				
1985A		—	0.35	0.75	7.50	—
1985A Proof	2,816	Value: 5.50				
1986A		—	0.35	0.75	7.50	—
1986A Proof	2,800	Value: 5.50				
1987A		—	—	—	12.00	—

Note: Issued in sets only, remainder unaccountable

Date	Mintage	F	VF	XF	Unc	BU
1987A Proof	2,345	Value: 5.50				
1988A		—	—	—	14.00	—

Note: Issued in sets only, remainder unaccountable

Date	Mintage	F	VF	XF	Unc	BU
1988A Proof	2,300	Value: 5.50				
1989A		—	0.35	0.75	7.50	—
1989A Proof	2,300	Value: 5.50				
1990A		—	—	—	15.00	—

Note: Issued in sets only, remainder unaccountable

KM# 13 MARK Composition: Aluminum

Date	Mintage	F	VF	XF	Unc	BU
1956A	112,108,000	—	0.50	1.00	9.00	—
1962A	45,920,000	—	0.50	2.00	10.00	—
1963A	31,910,000	—	0.50	2.50	12.00	—

KM# 35.1 MARK Composition: Aluminum **Reverse:** Large 1

Date	Mintage	F	VF	XF	Unc	BU
1972A	30,288,000	—	0.50	2.50	5.00	—

KM# 35.2 MARK Composition: Aluminum **Reverse:** Small 1

Date	Mintage	F	VF	XF	Unc	BU
1973A		—	0.50	2.00	10.00	—
1975A		—	0.50	1.00	6.50	—
1977A		—	0.50	1.00	2.00	—
1978A		—	0.50	1.00	2.50	—
1979A		—	0.50	1.25	7.50	—
1979A Proof		—	—	—	—	—
1980A		—	0.50	1.25	7.50	—
1980A Proof		—	—	—	—	—
1981A		—	0.50	1.25	7.50	—
1981A Proof		—	—	—	—	—
1982A		—	0.50	1.00	2.00	—
1982A Proof	2,500	Value: 25.00				
1983A		—	0.50	1.25	7.50	—
1983A Proof	2,550	Value: 30.00				
1984A		—	—	—	65.00	—
1984A Proof	3,015	Value: 7.50				
1985A		—	—	1.25	7.50	—
1985A Proof	2,816	Value: 7.50				
1986A		—	0.50	1.25	7.50	—
1986A Proof	2,800	Value: 7.50				
1987A		—	—	—	5.50	—

Note: Issued in sets only, reminader unaccountable

Date	Mintage	F	VF	XF	Unc	BU
1987A Proof	2,345	Value: 7.50				
1988A		—	—	—	7.50	—

Note: Issued in sets only, remainder unaccountable

Date	Mintage	F	VF	XF	Unc	BU
1988A Proof	2,300	Value: 7.50				
1989A		—	0.50	1.00	5.00	—
1989A Proof	2,300	Value: 7.50				
1990A		—	—	—	20.00	—

Note: Issued in sets only, remainder unaccountable

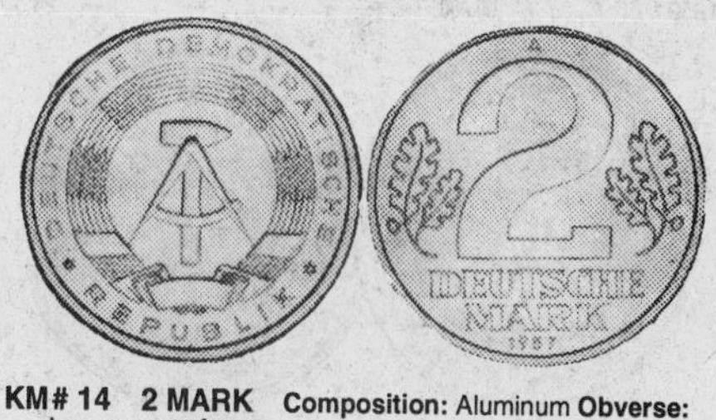

KM# 14 2 MARK Composition: Aluminum **Obverse:** Larger coat of arms

Date	Mintage	F	VF	XF	Unc	BU
1957A	77,961,000	—	1.00	3.00	10.00	—

KM# 48 2 MARK Composition: Aluminum **Obverse:** Smaller coat of arms

Date	Mintage	F	VF	XF	Unc	BU
1972A 3 pieces known		—	—	—	—	—
1974A		—	1.00	3.50	12.00	—
1975A		—	0.90	2.00	10.00	—
1977A		—	0.90	2.00	10.00	—
1978A		—	0.90	2.00	10.00	—
1979A		—	0.90	1.75	7.50	—
1979A Proof		—	—	—	—	—
1980A		—	0.90	1.75	7.50	—
1980A Proof		—	—	—	—	—
1981A		—	0.90	1.75	7.50	—
1981A Proof		—	—	—	—	—
1982A		—	0.80	1.00	2.00	—
1982A Proof	2,500	Value: 55.00				
1983A		—	0.90	1.25	5.00	—
1983A Proof	2,550	Value: 75.00				
1984A		—	—	—	30.00	—
1984A Proof	3,015	Value: 20.00				
1985A		—	0.90	1.25	5.00	—
1985A Proof	2,816	Value: 20.00				
1986A		—	0.90	1.25	6.00	—
1986A Proof	2,800	Value: 20.00				
1987A		—	—	—	6.00	—

Note: Issued in sets only, remainder unaccountable

Date	Mintage	F	VF	XF	Unc	BU
1987A Proof	2,345	Value: 20.00				
1988A		—	—	—	6.50	—

Note: Issued in sets only, remainder unaccountable

Date	Mintage	F	VF	XF	Unc	BU
1988A Proof	2,300	Value: 20.00				
1989A		—	0.90	1.25	6.50	—
1989A Proof	2,300	Value: 20.00				
1990A		—	—	—	20.00	—

Note: Issued in sets only, remainder unaccountable

KM# 19.1 5 MARK Composition: Copper-Nickel **Subject:** 125th Anniversary of Birth of Robert Koch

Date	Mintage	F	VF	XF	Unc	BU
1968	100,000	—	—	—	—	30.00

KM# 19.2 5 MARK Composition: Copper-Nickel **Note:** Error: plain edge.

Date	F	VF	XF	Unc	BU
1968	—	—	—	—	450

KM# 23 5 MARK Composition: Copper-Nickel **Subject:** Heinrich Hertz

Date	Mintage	F	VF	XF	Unc	BU
1969	100,000	—	—	—	—	24.50

KM# 22.1 5 MARK Composition: Nickel-Bronze **Subject:** 20th Anniversary D.D.R

Date	Mintage	F	VF	XF	Unc	BU
1969	50,222,000	—	—	3.00	4.50	7.50

Note: 10% nickel and 90% copper

KM# 22.1a 5 MARK Composition: Copper-Nickel

Date	Mintage	F	VF	XF	Unc	BU
1969	12,741	—	50.00	75.00	—	—

Note: 25% nickel and 75% copper

KM# 22.2 5 MARK Composition: Nickel-Bronze **Note:** Error: plain edge.

Date	F	VF	XF	Unc	BU
1969	—	—	—	—	150

KM# 22.3 5 MARK Composition: Nickel-Bronze **Note:** Error: Mongolian inscription and dates on edge.

Date	F	VF	XF	Unc	BU
1969	—	—	—	—	—

KM# 26 5 MARK Composition: Copper-Nickel **Subject:** Wilhelm Conrad Rontgen

Date	Mintage	F	VF	XF	Unc	BU
1970	100,000	—	—	—	—	24.50

KM# 29 5 MARK Composition: Copper-Nickel **Subject:** Brandenburg Gate

Date	Mintage	F	VF	XF	Unc	BU
1971A	4,000,000	—	—	—	—	10.00
1979A	32,000	—	—	—	—	35.00
1979A Proof	2,500	—	—	—	—	—
1980A	30,000	—	—	—	—	32.00
1980A Proof	2,500	—	—	—	—	—
1981A	30,000	—	—	—	—	28.00
1981A Proof	2,500	—	—	—	—	—
1982A	28,000	—	—	—	—	26.50
1982A Proof	2,500	Value: 195				
1983A	3,000	—	—	—	—	1,100
1984A	28,000	—	—	—	—	95.00
1984A Proof	3,015	Value: 135				
1985A	3,000	—	—	—	—	1,100
1986A	28,000	—	—	—	—	125
1986A Proof	2,800	Value: 140				
1987A	220,000	—	—	—	—	20.00
1987A Proof	6,424	Value: 75.00				
1988A	28,000	—	—	—	—	40.00
1988A Proof	2,300	Value: 115				
1989A	28,000	—	—	—	—	40.00
1989A Proof	2,405	Value: 115				
1990A	50,000	—	—	—	—	50.00

KM# 30 5 MARK Composition: Copper-Nickel **Subject:** Johannes Kepler

Date	Mintage	F	VF	XF	Unc	BU
1971	100,000	—	—	—	—	24.50

KM# 37 5 MARK Composition: Copper-Nickel **Subject:** City of Meissen

Date	Mintage	F	VF	XF	Unc	BU
1972A	3,500,000	—	—	—	4.00	8.50
1981A Proof	40	Value: 2,750				

Date	Mintage	F	VF	XF	Unc	BU
1983A	28,000	—	—	—	—	180
1983A Proof	2,550	Value: 300				

KM# 36.1 5 MARK Composition: Copper-Nickel **Subject:** 75th Anniversary - Death of Johannes Brahms **Reverse:** Name, musical score, dates

Date	Mintage	F	VF	XF	Unc	BU
1972	55,000	—	—	—	—	26.50

KM# 36.2 5 MARK Composition: Copper-Nickel **Note:** Error: Double edge inscription.

Date	F	VF	XF	Unc	BU
1972	—	—	—	—	575

KM# 43 5 MARK Composition: Copper-Nickel **Subject:** 125th Anniversary - Birth of Otto Lilienthal **Obverse:** Plane divides dates

Date	Mintage	F	VF	XF	Unc	BU
1973	100,000	—	—	—	—	38.00

KM# 49 5 MARK Composition: Copper-Nickel **Subject:** Centenary - Death of Philipp Reis

Date	Mintage	F	VF	XF	Unc	BU
1974	100,000	—	—	—	—	24.50

KM# 54 5 MARK Composition: Copper-Nickel **Subject:** 100th Anniversary - Birth of Thomas Mann **Reverse:** Bust left

Date	Mintage	F	VF	XF	Unc	BU
1975	100,000	—	—	—	—	18.50

KM# 55 5 MARK Composition: Copper-Nickel **Subject:** International Women's Year **Reverse:** Profiles of three women right

Date	Mintage	F	VF	XF	Unc	BU
1975	250,000	—	—	—	—	20.00

KM# 60 5 MARK Composition: Copper-Nickel **Subject:** 200th Anniversary - Birth of Ferdinand von Schill **Reverse:** Hat divides dates above sword and name

Date	Mintage	F	VF	XF	Unc	BU
1976	100,000	—	—	—	—	30.00

KM# 64 5 MARK Composition: Copper-Nickel **Subject:** 125th Anniversary - Death of Friedrich Ludwig Jahn **Reverse:** Bust of Jahn half right

Date	Mintage	F	VF	XF	Unc	BU
1977	90,000	—	—	—	—	42.00
1977 Proof	10,000	Value: 48.00				

KM# 67 5 MARK Composition: Copper-Nickel **Subject:** 175th Anniversary - Death of Friedrich Klopstock **Reverse:** Bust left

Date	Mintage	F	VF	XF	Unc	BU
1978	96,000	—	—	—	—	38.00
1978 Proof	4,500	Value: 65.00				

KM# 68 5 MARK Composition: Copper-Nickel **Subject:** Anti-Apartheid Year **Reverse:** Raised clenched fist

Date	Mintage	F	VF	XF	Unc	BU
1978A	196,000	—	—	—	—	24.50
1978A Proof	4,000	Value: 70.00				

KM# 72 5 MARK Composition: Copper-Nickel **Subject:** 100th Anniversary - Birth of Albert Einstein **Reverse:** Head of Einstein half right

Date	Mintage	F	VF	XF	Unc	BU
1979	56,000	—	—	—	—	65.00
1979 Proof	4,500	Value: 85.00				

KM# 76 5 MARK Composition: Copper-Nickel **Subject:** 75th Anniversary - Death of Adolph von Menzel **Reverse:** Bust left

Date	Mintage	F	VF	XF	Unc	BU
1980	55,000	—	—	—	—	37.50
1980 Proof	5,500	Value: 60.00				

KM# 79 5 MARK Composition: Copper-Nickel **Subject:** 450th Anniversary - Death of Tilman Riemenschneider **Reverse:** Bust half left

Date	Mintage	F	VF	XF	Unc	BU
1981	55,000	—	—	—	—	65.00
1981 Proof	5,500	Value: 85.00				

KM# 84 5 MARK Composition: Copper-Nickel **Subject:** 200th Anniversary - Birth of Friedrich Frobel **Reverse:** Three children with building blocks

Date	Mintage	F	VF	XF	Unc	BU
1982	55,000	—	—	—	—	60.00
1982 Proof	5,500	Value: 75.00				

KM# 85 5 MARK Composition: Copper-Nickel-Zinc **Subject:** Goethe's Weimar Cottage

Date	Mintage	F	VF	XF	Unc	BU
1982A	245,000	—	—	—	—	35.00
1982A Proof	5,500	Value: 75.00				
1982A Matte	210	Value: 3,000				

KM# 86 5 MARK Composition: Copper-Nickel-Zinc **Subject:** Wartburg Castle

Date	Mintage	F	VF	XF	Unc	BU
1982A	245,000	—	—	—	—	32.50
1982A Proof	5,500	Value: 70.00				
1983A	10,000	—	—	—	—	375

KM# 89 5 MARK Composition: Copper-Nickel **Subject:** Wittenberg Church

Date	Mintage	F	VF	XF	Unc	BU
1983A	245,000	—	—	—	—	30.00
1983A Proof	5,500	Value: 70.00				

KM# 90 5 MARK Composition: Copper-Nickel **Subject:** Martin Luther's Birthplace

Date	Mintage	F	VF	XF	Unc	BU
1983A	245,000	—	—	—	—	35.00
1983A Proof	5,500	Value: 65.00				

KM# 91 5 MARK Composition: Copper-Nickel-Zinc **Subject:** 125th Anniversary - Birth of Max Planck **Reverse:** Head right

Date	Mintage	F	VF	XF	Unc	BU
1983	56,000	—	—	—	—	38.00
1983 Proof	4,200	Value: 70.00				

KM# 96 5 MARK Composition: Copper-Nickel **Subject:** Leipzig Old City Hall

Date	Mintage	F	VF	XF	Unc	BU
1984A	245,000	—	—	—	—	30.00
1984A Proof	5,500	Value: 60.00				

KM# 97 5 MARK Composition: Copper-Nickel **Subject:** Thomas Church of Leipzig

Date	Mintage	F	VF	XF	Unc	BU
1984A	245,000	—	—	—	—	30.00
1984A Proof	5,500	Value: 60.00				

KM# 98 5 MARK Composition: Copper-Nickel **Subject:** 150th Anniversary - Death of Adolf Freiherr von Lutzow

Date	Mintage	F	VF	XF	Unc	BU
1984A	55,000	—	—	—	—	58.00
1984A Proof	5,000	Value: 90.00				

KM# 102 5 MARK Composition: Copper-Nickel **Subject:** Restoration of Dresden Women's Church

Date	Mintage	F	VF	XF	Unc	BU
1985A	245,000	—	—	—	—	32.00
1985A Proof	8,476	Value: 60.00				

KM# 103 5 MARK Composition: Copper-Nickel
Subject: Restoration of Dresden Zwinger

Date	Mintage	F	VF	XF	Unc	BU
1985A	245,000	—	—	—	—	32.00
1985A Proof	5,500	Value: 60.00				

KM# 104 5 MARK Composition: Copper-Nickel
Subject: 225th Anniversary - Death of Caroline Neuber

Date	Mintage	F	VF	XF	Unc	BU
1985A	56,000	—	—	—	—	70.00
1985A Proof	4,000	Value: 90.00				

KM# 110 5 MARK Composition: Copper-Nickel
Subject: Potsdam - Sanssouci Palace

Date	Mintage	F	VF	XF	Unc	BU
1986A	296,000	—	—	—	—	12.50
1986A Proof	4,200	Value: 65.00				

KM# 111 5 MARK Composition: Copper-Nickel
Subject: Potsdam - New Palace

Date	Mintage	F	VF	XF	Unc	BU
1986A	296,000	—	—	—	—	12.50
1986A Proof	4,200	Value: 65.00				

KM# 112 5 MARK Composition: Copper-Nickel
Subject: 175th Anniversary - Death of Heinrich von Kleist
Reverse: Bust of von Kleist left

Date	Mintage	F	VF	XF	Unc	BU
1986A	56,000	—	—	—	—	125
1986A Proof	4,000	Value: 135				

KM# 114 5 MARK Composition: Copper-Zinc-Nickel
Subject: Berlin - Nikolai Quarter

Date	Mintage	F	VF	XF	Unc	BU
1987A	496,000	—	—	—	—	11.50
1987A Proof	4,200	Value: 52.50				

KM# 115 5 MARK Composition: Copper-Zinc-Nickel
Subject: Berlin - Red City Hall

Date	Mintage	F	VF	XF	Unc	BU
1987A	496,000	—	—	—	—	11.50
1987A Proof	4,200	Value: 52.50				

KM# 116 5 MARK Composition: Copper-Zinc-Nickel
Subject: Berlin - Universal Time Clock

Date	Mintage	F	VF	XF	Unc	BU
1987A	496,000	—	—	—	—	11.50
1987A Proof	4,200	Value: 52.50				

KM# 120 5 MARK Composition: Copper-Nickel
Subject: Germany's First Railroad

Date	Mintage	F	VF	XF	Unc	BU
1988A	496,000	—	—	—	—	12.50
1988A Proof	4,200	Value: 100				

KM# 121 5 MARK Composition: Copper-Nickel
Subject: Port City of Rostock

Date	Mintage	F	VF	XF	Unc	BU
1988A	496,000	—	—	—	—	12.50
1988A Proof	4,200	Value: 72.50				

KM# 122 5 MARK Composition: Copper-Nickel
Subject: 50th Anniversary - Death of Ernst Barlach **Reverse:** Full-length figure of Barlach playing horn

Date	Mintage	F	VF	XF	Unc	BU
1988A	56,000	—	—	—	—	55.00
1988A Proof	4,000	Value: 100				

KM# 129 5 MARK Composition: Copper-Zinc-Nickel
Subject: Katharinen Kirche in Zwickau

Date	Mintage	F	VF	XF	Unc	BU
1989A	496,000	—	—	—	—	9.50
1989A Proof	4,200	Value: 67.50				

KM# 130 5 MARK Composition: Copper-Zinc-Nickel
Subject: Marien Kirche in Muhlhausen

Date	Mintage	F	VF	XF	Unc	BU
1989A	496,000	—	—	—	—	9.50
1989A Proof	4,200	Value: 67.50				

KM# 131 5 MARK Composition: Copper-Zinc-Nickel
Subject: 100th Anniversary - Birth of Carl von Ossietzky
Reverse: Bust of Ossietzky left

Date	Mintage	F	VF	XF	Unc	BU
1989A	56,000	—	—	—	—	72.50
1989A Proof	4,000	Value: 90.00				

KM# 133 5 MARK Composition: Copper-Zinc-Nickel
Subject: 100th Anniversary - Birth of Kurt Tucholsky
Reverse: Head of Tucholsky facing

Date	Mintage	F	VF	XF	Unc	BU
1990A	51,000	—	—	—	—	42.50
1990A Proof	4,000	Value: 72.50				

KM# 134 5 MARK Composition: Copper-Zinc-Nickel
Subject: 500 Years of Postal Service

Date	Mintage	F	VF	XF	Unc	BU
1990A	496,000	—	—	—	—	9.50
1990A Proof	4,200	Value: 55.00				

KM# 135 5 MARK Composition: Copper-Zinc-Nickel **Subject:** Zeughaus Museum

Date	Mintage	F	VF	XF	Unc	BU
1990A	496,000	—	—	—	—	7.50
1990A Proof	4,200	Value: 50.00				

KM# 15.1 10 MARK Weight: 17.0000 g. **Composition:** 0.8000 Silver .4373 oz. ASW **Subject:** 125th Anniversary - Death of Karl Friedrich Schinkel **Edge Lettering:** 10 MARK DER DEUTSCHEN NOTEN BANK

Date	Mintage	F	VF	XF	Unc	BU
1966	50,000	—	—	—	—	345

KM# 15.2 10 MARK Weight: 17.0000 g. **Composition:** 0.8000 Silver .4373 oz. ASW **Note:** Error: Plain edge.

Date	F	VF	XF	Unc	BU
1966	—	—	—	—	—

KM# 17.1 10 MARK Weight: 17.0000 g. **Composition:** 0.8000 Silver .4373 oz. ASW **Subject:** 100th Anniversary - Birth of Kathe Kollwitz

Date	Mintage	F	VF	XF	Unc	BU
1967	97,000	—	—	—	—	70.00

KM# 17.2 10 MARK Weight: 17.0000 g. **Composition:** 0.8000 Silver .4373 oz. ASW **Subject:** 100th Anniversary - Birth of Kathe Kollwitz **Note:** Error, edge: 10 MARK*10 MARK*10 MARK*

Date	Mintage	F	VF	XF	Unc	BU
1967	3,000	—	—	—	—	225

KM# 20.1 10 MARK Weight: 17.0000 g. **Composition:** 0.6250 Silver .3416 oz. ASW **Subject:** 500th Anniversary - Death of Johann Gutenberg

Date	Mintage	F	VF	XF	Unc	BU
1968	100,000	—	—	—	—	55.00

KM# 20.2 10 MARK Weight: 17.0000 g. **Composition:** 0.6250 Silver .3416 oz. ASW **Subject:** 500th Anniversary - Death of Johann Gutenberg **Note:** Error: Plain edge.

Date	F	VF	XF	Unc	BU
1968	—	—	—	—	700

KM# 24 10 MARK Weight: 17.0000 g. **Composition:** 0.6250 Silver .3416 oz. ASW **Subject:** 250th Anniversary - Death of Johann Friedrich Bottger

Date	Mintage	F	VF	XF	Unc	BU
1969	100,000	—	—	—	—	55.00

KM# 27.1 10 MARK Weight: 17.0000 g. **Composition:** 0.6250 Silver .3416 oz. ASW **Subject:** Ludwig Van Beethoven **Reverse:** Head left

Date	Mintage	F	VF	XF	Unc	BU
1970	100,000	—	—	—	—	55.00

KM# 27.2 10 MARK Weight: 17.0000 g. **Composition:** 0.6250 Silver .3416 oz. ASW **Reverse:** Head left **Note:** Error: Plain edge.

Date	F	VF	XF	Unc	BU
1970	—	—	—	—	575

KM# 31 10 MARK Weight: 17.0000 g. **Composition:** 0.6250 Silver .3416 oz. ASW **Subject:** Albrecht Durer

Date	Mintage	F	VF	XF	Unc	BU
1971	100,000	—	—	—	—	57.50

KM# 38 10 MARK Composition: Copper-Nickel **Subject:** Buchenwald Memorial

Date	Mintage	F	VF	XF	Unc	BU
1972A	2,500,000	—	—	—	5.00	7.50

KM# 39 10 MARK Weight: 17.0000 g. **Composition:** 0.6250 Silver .3416 oz. ASW **Subject:** 175th Anniversary - Birth of Heinrich Heine **Reverse:** Bust of Heine half left between dates, name below

Date	Mintage	F	VF	XF	Unc	BU
1972	100,000	—	—	—	—	60.00

KM# 44 10 MARK Composition: Copper-Nickel **Subject:** 10th Youth Festival Games

Date	Mintage	F	VF	XF	Unc	BU
1973A	1,500,000	—	—	—	5.50	8.00

KM# 45 10 MARK Weight: 17.0000 g. **Composition:** 0.6250 Silver .3416 oz. ASW **Subject:** 75th Anniversary - Birth of Bertolt Brecht

Date	Mintage	F	VF	XF	Unc	BU
1973	100,000	—	—	—	—	58.00

KM# 50 10 MARK Composition: Copper-Nickel **Subject:** 25th Anniversary, with state motto

Date	Mintage	F	VF	XF	Unc	BU
1974A	3,000,000	—	—	—	5.50	8.50

KM# 51 10 MARK Weight: 17.0000 g. **Composition:** 0.6250 Silver .3416 oz. ASW **Subject:** 25th Anniversary D.D.R

Date	Mintage	F	VF	XF	Unc	BU
1974	70,000	—	—	—	—	58.00
1974 Proof	200	Value: 2,500				

KM# 52 10 MARK Weight: 17.0000 g. **Composition:** 0.6250 Silver .3416 oz. ASW **Subject:** 200th Anniversary - Birth of Caspar David Friedrich **Reverse:** Bust of Friedrich right within inner circle

Date	Mintage	F	VF	XF	Unc	BU
1974	75,000	—	—	—	—	57.50

KM# 56 10 MARK **Weight:** 17.0000 g. **Composition:** 0.6250 Silver .3416 oz. ASW **Subject:** Centenary - Birth of Albert Schweitzer **Reverse:** Head of Schweitzer left

Date	Mintage	F	VF	XF	Unc	BU
1975	99,000	—	—	—	—	57.50
1975 Proof	1,040	Value: 1,450				

KM# 57 10 MARK **Weight:** 17.0000 g. **Composition:** 0.5000 Silver .2733 oz. ASW **Subject:** Mule **Obverse:** KM#58 **Reverse:** KM#56 **Edge:** Plain

Date	Mintage	F	VF	XF	Unc	BU
1975A	6,700	—	—	—	—	150

KM# 58 10 MARK **Composition:** Copper-Nickel **Subject:** 20th Anniversary - Warsaw Pact

Date	Mintage	F	VF	XF	Unc	BU
1975A	2,500,000	—	—	—	5.50	8.50

KM# 61 10 MARK **Composition:** Copper-Nickel **Subject:** 20th Anniversary - National People's Army **Reverse:** Bust of soldier half left

Date	Mintage	F	VF	XF	Unc	BU
1976A	750,000	—	—	—	—	9.00

KM# 62 10 MARK **Weight:** 17.0000 g. **Composition:** 0.5000 Silver .2733 oz. ASW **Subject:** 150th Anniversary - Death of Carl Maria von Weber **Reverse:** Bust of Weber right

Date	Mintage	F	VF	XF	Unc	BU
1976	94,000	—	—	—	—	70.00
1976 Proof	6,037	Value: 90.00				

KM# 65 10 MARK **Weight:** 17.0000 g. **Composition:** 0.5000 Silver .2733 oz. ASW **Subject:** 375th Anniversary - Birth of Otto von Guericke

Date	Mintage	F	VF	XF	Unc	BU
1977	69,000	—	—	—	—	82.50
1977 Proof	6,000	Value: 97.50				

KM# 69 10 MARK **Weight:** 17.0000 g. **Composition:** 0.5000 Silver .2733 oz. ASW **Subject:** 175th Anniversary - Birth of Justus von Liebig **Reverse:** Bust of Liebig right

Date	Mintage	F	VF	XF	Unc	BU
1978	71,000	—	—	—	—	77.50
1978 Proof	4,500	Value: 92.50				

KM# 70 10 MARK **Composition:** Copper-Nickel **Subject:** Joint USSR-DDR Orbital Flight

Date	Mintage	F	VF	XF	Unc	BU
1978A	748,000	—	—	—	—	25.00
1978A Proof	2,200	Value: 520				

KM# 73 10 MARK **Weight:** 17.0000 g. **Composition:** 0.5000 Silver .2733 oz. ASW **Subject:** 175th Anniversary - Birth of Ludwig Feuerbach

Date	Mintage	F	VF	XF	Unc	BU
1979	51,000	—	—	—	—	85.00
1979 Proof	4,500	Value: 100				

KM# 77 10 MARK **Weight:** 17.0000 g. **Composition:** 0.5000 Silver .2733 oz. ASW **Subject:** 225th Anniversary - Birth of Gerhard von Scharnhorst **Reverse:** Bust left

Date	Mintage	F	VF	XF	Unc	BU
1980	55,000	—	—	—	—	52.50
1980 Proof	5,500	Value: 75.00				

KM# 80 10 MARK **Composition:** Copper-Nickel **Subject:** 25th Anniversary - National People's Army **Reverse:** Plane above, ship at center, tank below, dates at sides

Date	Mintage	F	VF	XF	Unc	BU
1981A	745,000	—	—	—	—	15.00
1981A Proof	5,500	Value: 60.00				

KM# 81 10 MARK **Weight:** 17.0000 g. **Composition:** 0.5000 Silver .2733 oz. ASW **Subject:** 150th Anniversary - Death of Georg Hegel **Reverse:** Head of Hegel right

Date	Mintage	F	VF	XF	Unc	BU
1981	50,000	—	—	—	—	52.50
1981 Proof	5,500	Value: 80.00				

KM# 82 10 MARK **Composition:** Copper-Nickel **Subject:** 700th Anniversary - Berlin Mint

Date	Mintage	F	VF	XF	Unc	BU
1981	55,000	—	—	—	—	48.00
1981 Proof	5,500	Value: 82.00				

KM# 87 10 MARK **Weight:** 17.0000 g. **Composition:** 0.5000 Silver .2733 oz. ASW **Subject:** Leipzig Gewandhaus

Date	Mintage	F	VF	XF	Unc	BU
1982	50,000	—	—	—	—	52.50
1982 Proof	5,500	Value: 85.00				

KM# 92 10 MARK **Weight:** 17.1100 g. **Composition:** 0.5000 Silver .2751 oz. ASW **Subject:** 100th Anniversary - Death of Richard Wagner

Date	Mintage	F	VF	XF	Unc	BU
1983	44,000	—	—	—	—	52.50
1983 Proof	5,500	Value: 85.00				

KM# 93 10 MARK Composition: Copper-Nickel-Zinc **Subject:** 30th Anniversary - Worker's Militia **Reverse:** Two soldiers facing left

Date	Mintage	F	VF	XF	Unc	BU
1983A	495,000	—	—	—	—	17.50
1983A Proof	5,000	Value: 55.00				

KM# 99 10 MARK Weight: 17.0000 g. **Composition:** 0.5000 Silver .2733 oz. ASW **Subject:** 100th Anniversary - Death of Alfred Brehm

Date	Mintage	F	VF	XF	Unc	BU
1984A	50,000	—	—	—	—	80.00
1984A Proof	5,000	Value: 95.00				

KM# 101 10 MARK Weight: 17.0000 g. **Composition:** 0.5000 Silver .2733 oz. ASW **Subject:** Restoration of Semper Opera in Dresden

Date	Mintage	F	VF	XF	Unc	BU
1985A	50,000	—	—	—	—	62.50
1985A Proof	5,000	Value: 97.50				

KM# 106 10 MARK Composition: Copper-Nickel-Zinc **Subject:** 40th Anniversary - Liberation from Fascism

Date	Mintage	F	VF	XF	Unc	BU
1985A	745,000	—	—	—	—	14.50
1985A Proof	5,500	Value: 65.00				

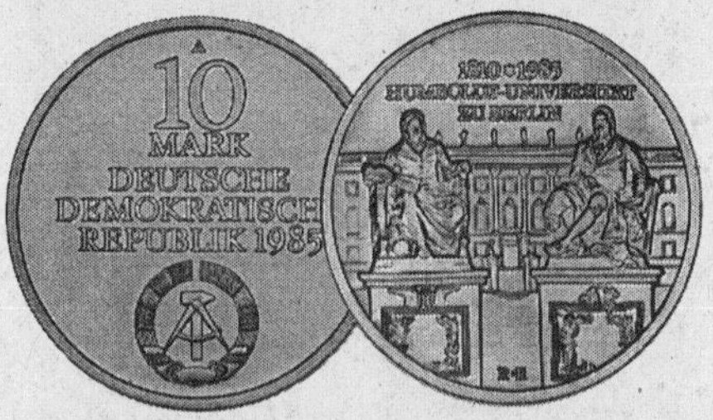

KM# 107 10 MARK Composition: Copper-Nickel-Zinc **Subject:** 175th Anniversary - Humboldt University

Date	Mintage	F	VF	XF	Unc	BU
1985A	51,000	—	—	—	—	77.50
1985A Proof	4,000	Value: 97.50				

KM# 109 10 MARK Composition: Copper-Nickel **Subject:** 100th Anniversary - Birth of Ernst Thalmann

Date	Mintage	F	VF	XF	Unc	BU
1986A	746,000	—	—	—	—	12.50
1986A Proof	4,000	Value: 65.00				

KM# 113 10 MARK Weight: 17.0000 g. **Composition:** 0.5000 Silver .2733 oz. ASW **Subject:** Charite - Berlin

Date	Mintage	F	VF	XF	Unc	BU
1986A	51,000	—	—	—	—	60.00
1986A Proof	4,000	Value: 90.00				

KM# 118 10 MARK Weight: 17.0000 g. **Composition:** 0.5000 Silver .2733 oz. ASW **Subject:** Berlin - Theater

Date	Mintage	F	VF	XF	Unc	BU
1987A	51,000	—	—	—	—	60.00
1987A Proof	4,000	Value: 92.50				

KM# 123 10 MARK Weight: 17.0000 g. **Composition:** 0.5000 Silver .2733 oz. ASW **Subject:** 500th Anniversary - Birth of Ulrich von Hutten

Date	Mintage	F	VF	XF	Unc	BU
1988A	52,000	—	—	—	—	85.00
1988A Proof	3,500	Value: 200				

KM# 125 10 MARK Composition: Copper-Nickel **Subject:** East German Sports **Reverse:** Three women running left

Date	Mintage	F	VF	XF	Unc	BU
1988A	747,000	—	—	—	—	12.50
1988A Proof	3,200	Value: 120				

KM# 126 10 MARK Composition: Copper-Nickel **Subject:** Council of Mutual Economic Aid

Date	Mintage	F	VF	XF	Unc	BU
1989A	—	—	—	—	—	40.00
1989A Proof	3,000	Value: 185				

KM# 128 10 MARK Weight: 17.0000 g. **Composition:** 0.5000 Silver .2733 oz. ASW **Subject:** 225th Anniversary - Birth of Johann Gottfried Schadow

Date	Mintage	F	VF	XF	Unc	BU
1989A	51,000	—	—	—	—	115
1989A Proof	4,000	Value: 245				

KM# 132 10 MARK Composition: Copper-Nickel-Zinc **Subject:** 40th Anniversary - East German Government

Date	Mintage	F	VF	XF	Unc	BU
1989A	746,000	—	—	—	—	14.50
1989A Proof	3,080	Value: 175				

KM# 136 10 MARK Composition: Copper-Nickel-Zinc **Subject:** International Labor Day

Date	Mintage	F	VF	XF	Unc	BU
1990A	747,000	—	—	—	—	9.00
1990A Proof	4,367	Value: 60.00				

KM# 137 10 MARK Weight: 17.0000 g. **Composition:** 0.5000 Silver .2733 oz. ASW **Reverse:** Johann Gottlieb Fichte at lectern facing left

Date	Mintage	F	VF	XF	Unc	BU
1990A	37,000	—	—	—	—	85.00
1990A Proof	4,900	Value: 135				

KM# 16.1 20 MARK **Weight:** 20.9000 g. **Composition:** 0.8000 Silver .5376 oz. ASW **Subject:** 250th Anniversary - Death of Gottfried Wilhelm Leibniz **Edge Lettering:** 20 MARK DER DEUTSCHEN NOTEN BANK

Date	Mintage	F	VF	XF	Unc	BU
1966	50,000	—	—	—	—	210

KM# 16.2 20 MARK **Weight:** 20.9000 g. **Composition:** 0.8000 Silver .5376 oz. ASW **Edge:** Error: In inscription **Edge Lettering:** 10 MARK DER DEUTSCHEN NOTEN BANK

Date	F	VF	XF	Unc	BU
1966	—	—	—	—	—

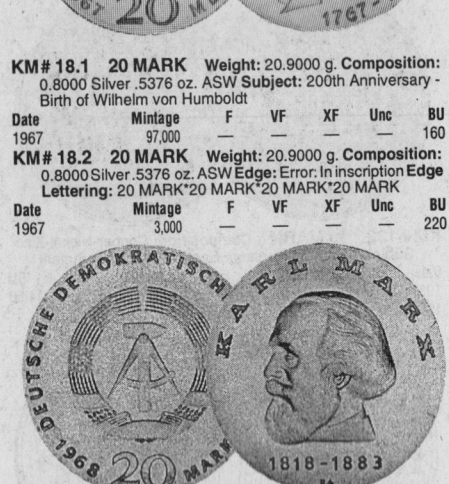

KM# 18.1 20 MARK **Weight:** 20.9000 g. **Composition:** 0.8000 Silver .5376 oz. ASW **Subject:** 200th Anniversary - Birth of Wilhelm von Humboldt

Date	Mintage	F	VF	XF	Unc	BU
1967	97,000	—	—	—	—	160

KM# 18.2 20 MARK **Weight:** 20.9000 g. **Composition:** 0.8000 Silver .5376 oz. ASW **Edge:** Error: In inscription **Edge Lettering:** 20 MARK*20 MARK*20 MARK*20 MARK

Date	Mintage	F	VF	XF	Unc	BU
1967	3,000	—	—	—	—	220

KM# 21 20 MARK **Weight:** 20.9000 g. **Composition:** 0.8000 Silver .5376 oz. ASW **Subject:** 150th Anniversary - Birth of Karl Marx **Reverse:** Head of Marx left

Date	Mintage	F	VF	XF	Unc	BU
1968	100,000	—	—	—	—	90.00

KM# 25 20 MARK **Weight:** 20.9000 g. **Composition:** 0.6250 Silver .4200 oz. ASW **Reverse:** Head of Johann Wolfgang von Goethe left

Date	Mintage	F	VF	XF	Unc	BU
1969	100,000	—	—	—	—	135
1969 Proof; Rare	—	—	—	—	—	—

KM# 28 20 MARK **Weight:** 20.9000 g. **Composition:** 0.6250 Silver .4200 oz. ASW **Subject:** 150th Anniversary - Birth of Friedrich Engels **Reverse:** Head of Engels left

Date	Mintage	F	VF	XF	Unc	BU
1970	100,000	—	—	—	—	100
1970 Proof; Rare	—	—	—	—	—	—

KM# 32 20 MARK **Weight:** 20.9000 g. **Composition:** 0.6250 Silver .4200 oz. ASW **Subject:** Karl Kiebknecht - Rosa Luxemburg **Reverse:** Conjoined busts left

Date	Mintage	F	VF	XF	Unc	BU
1971	100,000	—	—	—	—	75.00

KM# 33 20 MARK **Composition:** Copper-Nickel **Subject:** 100th Anniversary - Birth of Heinrich Mann **Reverse:** Head of Mann left

Date	Mintage	F	VF	XF	Unc	BU
1971	2,000,000	—	—	4.00	5.00	9.00

KM# 34 20 MARK **Composition:** Copper-Nickel **Subject:** 85th Birthday of Ernst Thalmann **Reverse:** Head of Thalmann left **Note:** Edge varieties exist.

Date	Mintage	F	VF	XF	Unc	BU
1971A	2,500,000	—	—	4.00	5.00	9.00

KM# 40 20 MARK **Composition:** Copper-Nickel **Reverse:** Head of Friedrich von Schiller right

Date	Mintage	F	VF	XF	Unc	BU
1972A	3,000,000	—	—	4.00	5.00	9.00

KM# 41 20 MARK **Weight:** 20.9000 g. **Composition:** 0.6250 Silver .4200 oz. ASW **Subject:** 500th Anniversary - Birth of Lucas Cranach

Date	Mintage	F	VF	XF	Unc	BU
1972	100,000	—	—	—	—	82.00

KM# 42 20 MARK **Composition:** Copper-Nickel **Reverse:** Head of Wilhelm Pieck left

Date	Mintage	F	VF	XF	Unc	BU
1972A	2,500,000	—	—	4.00	5.00	9.00

KM# 46 20 MARK **Weight:** 20.9000 g. **Composition:** 0.6250 Silver .4200 oz. ASW **Subject:** 60th Anniversary - Death of August Bebel **Reverse:** Bust of Bebel half facing

Date	Mintage	F	VF	XF	Unc	BU
1973	100,000	—	—	—	—	70.00

KM# 47 20 MARK **Composition:** Copper-Nickel **Reverse:** Head of Otto Grotewohl left

Date	Mintage	F	VF	XF	Unc	BU
1973A	2,500,000	—	—	5.00	6.00	10.00

KM# 53 20 MARK **Weight:** 20.9000 g. **Composition:** 0.6250 Silver .4200 oz. ASW **Subject:** 250th Anniversary - Death of Immanuel Kant **Reverse:** Bust of Kant half left

Date	Mintage	F	VF	XF	Unc	BU
1974	96,000	—	—	—	—	72.00
1974 Proof	4,221	Value: 140				

KM# 59 20 MARK **Weight:** 20.9000 g. **Composition:** 0.6250 Silver .4200 oz. ASW **Subject:** 225th Anniversary - Death of Johann Sebastian Bach **Reverse:** Musical score

Date	Mintage	F	VF	XF	Unc	BU
1975	100,000	—	—	—	—	100
1975 Proof	Inc. above	Value: 3,500				

KM# 63 20 MARK **Weight:** 20.9000 g. **Composition:** 0.6250 Silver .4200 oz. ASW **Subject:** 150th Anniversary - Birth of Wilhelm Liebknecht **Reverse:** Bust of Liebknecht half left

Date	Mintage	F	VF	XF	Unc	BU
1976	96,000	—	—	—	—	75.00
1976 Proof	4,000	Value: 150				

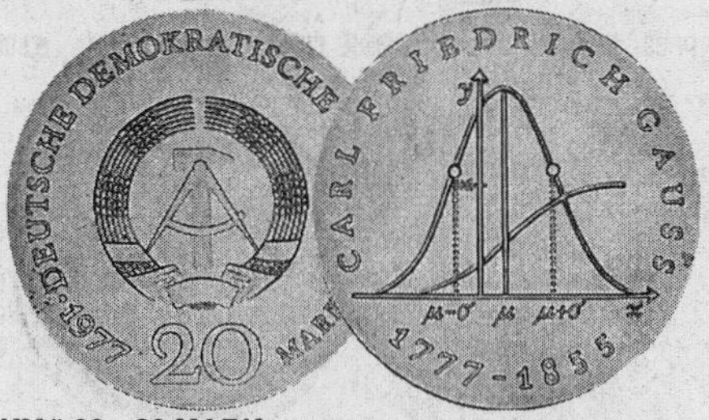

KM# 66 20 MARK **Weight:** 20.9000 g. **Composition:** 0.5000 Silver .3360 oz. ASW **Subject:** 200th Anniversary - Birth of Carl Friedrich Gauss

Date	Mintage	F	VF	XF	Unc	BU
1977	55,000	—	—	—	—	90.00

KM# 71 20 MARK **Weight:** 20.9000 g. **Composition:** 0.5000 Silver .3360 oz. ASW **Subject:** 175th Anniversary - Death of Johann von Herder **Reverse:** Head of Herder half left

Date	Mintage	F	VF	XF	Unc	BU
1978	51,000	—	—	—	—	87.50
1978 Proof	4,500	Value: 120				

KM# 74 20 MARK **Weight:** 20.9000 g. **Composition:** 0.5000 Silver .3360 oz. ASW **Subject:** 250th Anniversary - Birth of Gotthold Ephraim Lessing

Date	Mintage	F	VF	XF	Unc	BU
1979	41,000	—	—	—	—	100
1979 Proof	4,500	Value: 150				

KM# 75 20 MARK **Composition:** Copper-Nickel **Subject:** 30th Anniversary - East German Regime

Date	Mintage	F	VF	XF	Unc	BU
1979A	1,000,000	—	—	—	—	14.50

KM# 78 20 MARK **Weight:** 20.9200 g. **Composition:** 0.5000 Silver .3360 oz. ASW **Subject:** 75th Anniversary - Death of Ernst Abbe

Date	Mintage	F	VF	XF	Unc	BU
1980	40,000	—	—	—	—	70.00
1980 Proof	5,500	Value: 120				

KM# 83 20 MARK **Weight:** 20.9200 g. **Composition:** 0.5000 Silver .3360 oz. ASW **Subject:** 150th Anniversary - Death of vom Stein **Reverse:** Small bust half left below name

Date	Mintage	F	VF	XF	Unc	BU
1981	40,000	—	—	—	—	60.00
1981 Proof	5,500	Value: 100				

KM# 88 20 MARK **Weight:** 20.9200 g. **Composition:** 0.5000 Silver .3360 oz. ASW **Subject:** 125th Anniversary - Birth of Clara Zetkin **Reverse:** Bust of Zetkin half left

Date	Mintage	F	VF	XF	Unc	BU
1982	40,000	—	—	—	—	60.00
1982 Proof	5,500	Value: 90.00				

KM# 94 20 MARK **Weight:** 20.9200 g. **Composition:** 0.5000 Silver .3360 oz. ASW **Subject:** 500th Anniversary - Birth of Martin Luther **Reverse:** Bust of Luther holding bible half left

Date	Mintage	F	VF	XF	Unc	BU
1983	45,000	—	—	—	—	540
1983 Proof	5,000	Value: 550				

KM# 95 20 MARK **Composition:** Copper-Nickel **Subject:** 100th Anniversary - Death of Karl Marx

Date	Mintage	F	VF	XF	Unc	BU
1983A	995,000	—	—	—	—	14.50
1983A Proof	5,000	Value: 65.00				

KM# 100 20 MARK **Weight:** 20.9200 g. **Composition:** 0.5000 Silver .3360 oz. ASW **Subject:** 225th Anniversary - Death of Georg Friedrich Handel **Reverse:** Bust of Handel half right

Date	Mintage	F	VF	XF	Unc	BU
1984A	41,000	—	—	—	—	165
1984A Proof	4,500	Value: 195				

KM# 105 20 MARK **Weight:** 20.9200 g. **Composition:** 0.5000 Silver .3360 oz. ASW **Subject:** 125th Anniversary - Death of Ernst Moritz Arndt **Reverse:** Bust of Arndt half right

Date	Mintage	F	VF	XF	Unc	BU
1985A	41,000	—	—	—	—	95.00
1985A Proof	4,000	Value: 115				

KM# 108 20 MARK **Weight:** 20.9000 g. **Composition:** 0.6250 Silver .4200 oz. ASW **Subject:** 200th Anniversary - Birth of Jacob and Wilhelm Grimm **Reverse:** "Puss 'n Boots"

Date	Mintage	F	VF	XF	Unc	BU
1986A	37,000	—	—	—	—	220
1986A Proof	3,500	Value: 285				

KM# 119.1 20 MARK **Weight:** 20.9000 g. **Composition:** 0.6250 Silver .4200 oz. ASW **Subject:** Berlin - City Seal

Date	Mintage	F	VF	XF	Unc	BU
1987A	42,000	—	—	—	—	450
1987A Proof	2,100	Value: 1,650				

Note: Seal on reverse totally frosted on proof coins

KM# 119.2 20 MARK **Weight:** 20.9000 g. **Composition:** 0.6250 Silver .4200 oz. ASW **Reverse:** Fields in seal polished

Date	Mintage	F	VF	XF	Unc	BU
1987A Proof	2,100	Value: 1,650				

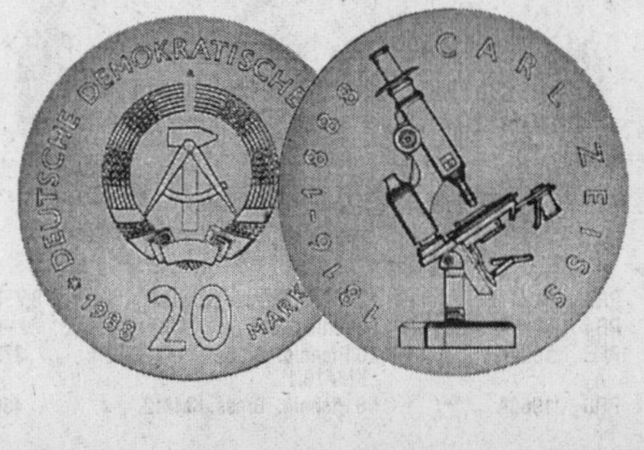

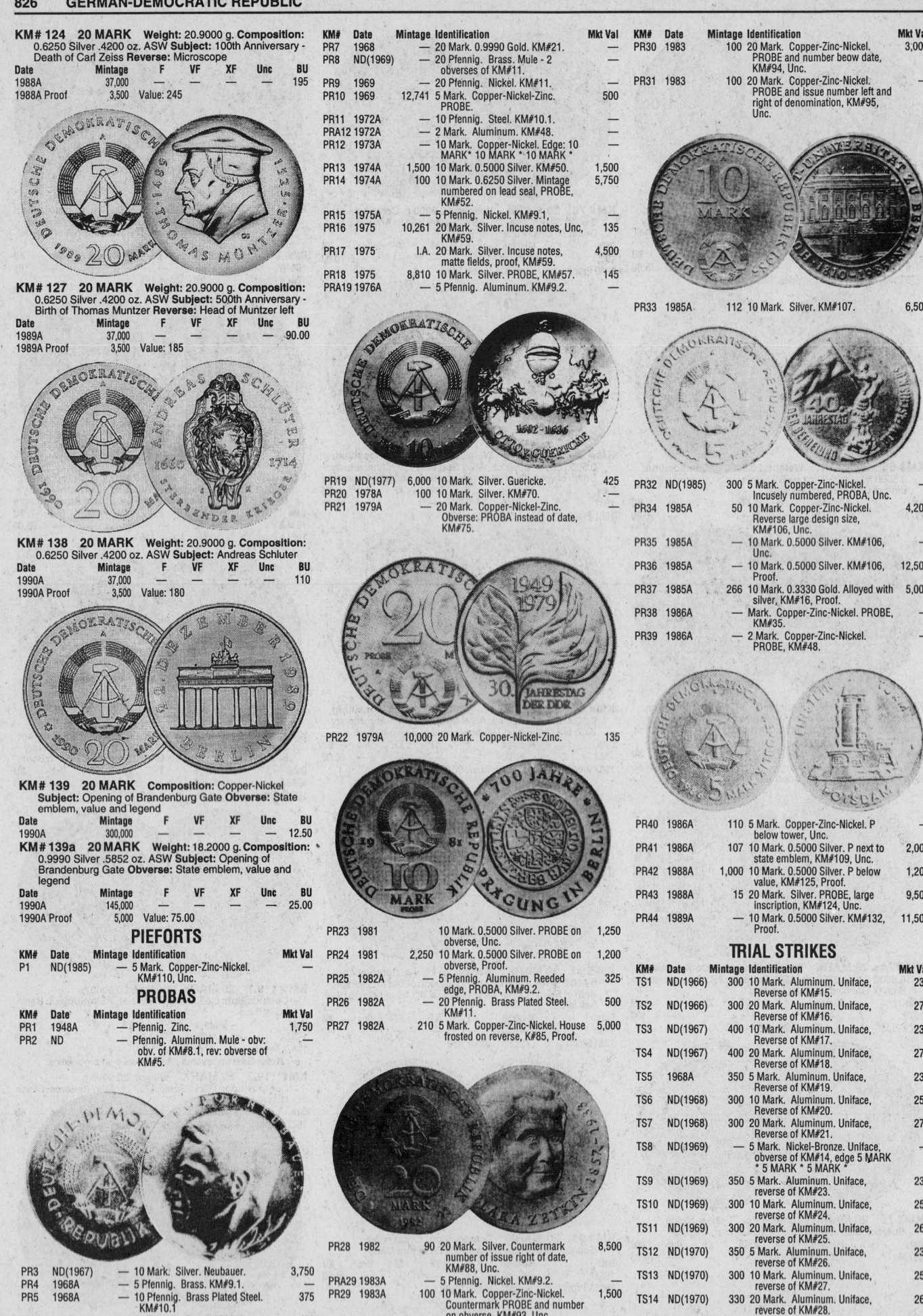

KM# 124 20 MARK **Weight:** 20.9000 g. **Composition:** 0.6250 Silver .4200 oz. ASW **Subject:** 100th Anniversary - Death of Carl Zeiss **Reverse:** Microscope

Date	Mintage	F	VF	XF	Unc	BU
1988A	37,000	—	—	—	—	195
1988A Proof	3,500	Value: 245				

KM# 127 20 MARK **Weight:** 20.9000 g. **Composition:** 0.6250 Silver .4200 oz. ASW **Subject:** 500th Anniversary - Birth of Thomas Muntzer **Reverse:** Head of Muntzer left

Date	Mintage	F	VF	XF	Unc	BU
1989A	37,000	—	—	—	—	90.00
1989A Proof	3,500	Value: 185				

KM# 138 20 MARK **Weight:** 20.9000 g. **Composition:** 0.6250 Silver .4200 oz. ASW **Subject:** Andreas Schluter

Date	Mintage	F	VF	XF	Unc	BU
1990A	37,000	—	—	—	—	110
1990A Proof	3,500	Value: 180				

KM# 139 20 MARK **Composition:** Copper-Nickel **Subject:** Opening of Brandenburg Gate **Obverse:** State emblem, value and legend

Date	Mintage	F	VF	XF	Unc	BU
1990A	300,000	—	—	—	—	12.50

KM# 139a 20 MARK **Weight:** 18.2000 g. **Composition:** 0.9990 Silver .5852 oz. ASW **Subject:** Opening of Brandenburg Gate **Obverse:** State emblem, value and legend

Date	Mintage	F	VF	XF	Unc	BU
1990A	145,000	—	—	—	—	25.00
1990A Proof	5,000	Value: 75.00				

PIEFORTS

KM#	Date	Mintage	Identification	Mkt Val
P1	ND(1985)	—	5 Mark. Copper-Zinc-Nickel. KM#110, Unc.	—

PROBAS

KM#	Date	Mintage	Identification	Mkt Val
PR1	1948A	—	Pfennig. Zinc.	1,750
PR2	ND	—	Pfennig. Aluminum. Mule - obv: obv. of KM#8.1, rev: obverse of KM#5.	—

KM#	Date	Mintage	Identification	Mkt Val
PR3	ND(1967)	—	10 Mark. Silver. Neubauer.	3,750
PR4	1968A	—	5 Pfennig. Brass. KM#9.1.	—
PR5	1968A	—	10 Pfennig. Brass Plated Steel. KM#10.1	375
PR6	1968A	—	50 Pfennig. Brass. KM#12.	450
PR7	1968	—	20 Mark. 0.9990 Gold. KM#21.	—
PR8	ND(1969)	—	20 Pfennig. Brass. Mule - 2 obverses of KM#11.	—
PR9	1969	—	20 Pfennig. Nickel. KM#11.	—
PR10	1969	12,741	5 Mark. Copper-Nickel-Zinc. PROBE.	500
PR11	1972A	—	10 Pfennig. Steel. KM#10.1.	—
PRA12	1972A	—	2 Mark. Aluminum. KM#48.	—
PR12	1973A	—	10 Mark. Copper-Nickel. Edge: 10 MARK* 10 MARK * 10 MARK *	—
PR13	1974A	1,500	10 Mark. 0.5000 Silver. KM#50.	1,500
PR14	1974A	100	10 Mark. 0.6250 Silver. Mintage numbered on lead seal, PROBE, KM#52.	5,750
PR15	1975A	—	5 Pfennig. Nickel. KM#9.1,	—
PR16	1975	10,261	20 Mark. Silver. Incuse notes, Unc, KM#59.	135
PR17	1975	I.A.	20 Mark. Silver. Incuse notes, matte fields, proof, KM#59.	4,500
PR18	1975	8,810	10 Mark. Silver. PROBE, KM#57.	145
PRA19	1976A	—	5 Pfennig. Aluminum. KM#9.2.	—

KM#	Date	Mintage	Identification	Mkt Val
PR19	ND(1977)	6,000	10 Mark. Silver. Guericke.	425
PR20	1978A	100	10 Mark. Silver. KM#70.	—
PR21	1979A	—	20 Mark. Copper-Nickel-Zinc. Obverse: PROBA instead of date, KM#75.	—

KM#	Date	Mintage	Identification	Mkt Val
PR22	1979A	10,000	20 Mark. Copper-Nickel-Zinc.	135

KM#	Date	Mintage	Identification	Mkt Val
PR23	1981		10 Mark. 0.5000 Silver. PROBE on obverse, Unc.	1,250
PR24	1981	2,250	10 Mark. 0.5000 Silver. PROBE on obverse, Proof.	1,200
PR25	1982A	—	5 Pfennig. Aluminum. Reeded edge, PROBA, KM#9.2.	325
PR26	1982A	—	20 Pfennig. Brass Plated Steel. KM#11.	500
PR27	1982A	210	5 Mark. Copper-Zinc-Nickel. House frosted on reverse, K#85, Proof.	5,000

KM#	Date	Mintage	Identification	Mkt Val
PR28	1982	90	20 Mark. Silver. Countermark number of issue right of date, KM#88, Unc.	8,500
PRA29	1983A	—	5 Pfennig. Nickel. KM#9.2.	—
PR29	1983A	100	10 Mark. Copper-Nickel-Zinc. Countermark PROBE and number on obverse, KM#93, Unc.	1,500
PR30	1983	100	20 Mark. Copper-Zinc-Nickel. PROBE and number beow date, KM#94, Unc.	3,000
PR31	1983	100	20 Mark. Copper-Zinc-Nickel. PROBE and issue number left and right of denomination, KM#95, Unc.	—

KM#	Date	Mintage	Identification	Mkt Val
PR33	1985A	112	10 Mark. Silver. KM#107.	6,500

KM#	Date	Mintage	Identification	Mkt Val
PR32	ND(1985)	300	5 Mark. Copper-Zinc-Nickel. Incusely numbered, PROBA, Unc.	—
PR34	1985A	50	10 Mark. Copper-Zinc-Nickel. Reverse large design size, KM#106, Unc.	4,200
PR35	1985A	—	10 Mark. 0.5000 Silver. KM#106, Unc.	—
PR36	1985A	—	10 Mark. 0.5000 Silver. KM#106, Proof.	12,500
PR37	1985A	266	10 Mark. 0.3330 Gold. Alloyed with silver, KM#16, Proof.	5,000
PR38	1986A	—	Mark. Copper-Zinc-Nickel. PROBE, KM#35.	—
PR39	1986A	—	2 Mark. Copper-Zinc-Nickel. PROBE, KM#48.	—

KM#	Date	Mintage	Identification	Mkt Val
PR40	1986A	110	5 Mark. Copper-Zinc-Nickel. P below tower, Unc.	—
PR41	1986A	107	10 Mark. 0.5000 Silver. P next to state emblem, KM#109, Unc.	2,000
PR42	1988A	1,000	10 Mark. 0.5000 Silver. P below value, KM#125, Proof.	1,200
PR43	1988A	15	20 Mark. Silver. PROBE, large inscription, KM#124, Unc.	9,500
PR44	1989A	—	10 Mark. 0.5000 Silver. KM#132, Proof.	11,500

TRIAL STRIKES

KM#	Date	Mintage	Identification	Mkt Val
TS1	ND(1966)	300	10 Mark. Aluminum. Uniface, Reverse of KM#15.	230
TS2	ND(1966)	300	20 Mark. Aluminum. Uniface, Reverse of KM#16.	270
TS3	ND(1967)	400	10 Mark. Aluminum. Uniface, Reverse of KM#17.	230
TS4	ND(1967)	400	20 Mark. Aluminum. Uniface, Reverse of KM#18.	270
TS5	1968A	350	5 Mark. Aluminum. Uniface, Reverse of KM#19.	235
TS6	ND(1968)	300	10 Mark. Aluminum. Uniface, Reverse of KM#20.	250
TS7	ND(1968)	300	20 Mark. Aluminum. Uniface, Reverse of KM#21.	270
TS8	ND(1969)	—	5 Mark. Nickel-Bronze. Uniface, obverse of KM#14, edge 5 MARK * 5 MARK * 5 MARK *	—
TS9	ND(1969)	350	5 Mark. Aluminum. Uniface, reverse of KM#23.	235
TS10	ND(1969)	300	10 Mark. Aluminum. Uniface, reverse of KM#24.	250
TS11	ND(1969)	300	20 Mark. Aluminum. Uniface, reverse of KM#25.	260
TS12	ND(1970)	350	5 Mark. Aluminum. Uniface, reverse of KM#26.	235
TS13	ND(1970)	300	10 Mark. Aluminum. Uniface, reverse of KM#27.	250
TS14	ND(1970)	330	20 Mark. Aluminum. Uniface, reverse of KM#28.	260

KM#	Date	Mintage	Identification	Mkt Val
TS15	ND(1971)	450	5 Mark. Aluminum. Uniface, reverse of KM#30.	235
TS16	ND(1971)	300	10 Mark. Aluminum. Uniface, reverse of KM#31.	250
TS17	ND(1971)	410	20 Mark. Aluminum. Uniface, reverse of KM#32.	250
TS18	ND(1972)	300	5 Mark. Aluminum. Uniface, reverse of KM#36.	235
TS19	ND(1972)	300	10 Mark. Aluminum. Uniface, reverse of KM#39.	250
TS20	ND(1972)	300	20 Mark. Aluminum. Uniface, reverse of KM#41.	260
TS21	ND(1973)	300	5 Mark. Aluminum. Uniface, reverse of KM#43.	235
TS22	ND(1973)	—	20 Mark. Copper-Zinc-Nickel. Uniface, reverse of KM#47.	—
TS23	ND(1973)	—	20 Mark. Copper-Zinc-Nickel. Uniface, reverse with portrait within circular legend, KM#47.	—
TS24	ND(1975)	306	10 Mark. Aluminum. Uniface, reverse of KM#56.	220
TS25	1979	—	20 Mark. Copper-Zinc-Nickel. Uniface, reverse of PR22.	—

MINT SETS

KM#	Date	Mintage	Identification	Issue Price	Mkt Val
MS1	1979A (8)	26,000	KM#8.2-10, 11-12.2, 29, 35.2, 48	—	50.00
MS2	1980A (8)	25,000	KM#8.2-10, 11-12.2, 35.2, 48	—	75.00
MS3	1981 (8)	25,000	KM#8.2-10, 11-12.2, 29, 35.2, 48	—	55.00
MS4	1982 (8)	21,000	KM#8.2-10, 11-12.2, 29, 35.2, 48	—	80.00
MS5	1982 (7)	4,500	KM#8.2-10, 11-12.2, 35.2, 48	—	90.00
MS6	1983 (8)	19,000	KM#8.2-10, 11-12.2, 35.2, 37, 48	—	200
MS7	1983 (7)	4,500	KM#8.2-10, 11-12.2, 35.2, 48	—	140
MS8	1984 (8)	19,000	KM#8.2-10, 11-12.2, 29, 35.2, 48	—	135
MS9	1984 (7)	4,500	KM#8.2-10, 11-12.2, 35.2, 48	—	110
MS10	1985 (8)	6,000	KM#8.2-10, 11-12.2, 35.2, 48, 102	—	60.00
MS11	1985 (7)	4,500	KM#8.2-10, 11-12.2, 35.2, 48	—	55.00
MS12	1986 (8)	7,000	KM#8.2-10, 11-12, 29, 35.2, 48	—	110
MS13	1986 (7)	4,500	KM#8.2-10, 11-12.2, 35.2, 48	—	65.00
MS14	1987 (8)	8,000	KM#8.2-10, 11-12.2, 29, 35.2, 48	—	50.00
MS15	1987 (7)	4,500	KM#8.2-10, 11-12.2, 35.2, 48	—	60.00
MS16	1988 (8)	11,000	KM#8.2-10, 11-12.2, 29, 35.2, 48	—	60.00
MS17	1988 (7)	4,500	KM#8.2-10, 11-12.2, 35.2, 48	—	60.00
MS18	1989 (8)	11,000	KM8.2-10, 11-12.2, 29, 35.2, 48	—	55.00
MS19	1989 (7)	4,500	KM#8.2-10, 11-12.2, 35.2,48	—	60.00
MS20	1990 (8)	11,000	KM#8.2-10, 11-12.2, 29, 35.2, 48	—	135
MS21	1990 (7)	4,500	KM#8.2-10, 11-12.2, 35.2, 48	—	100

PROOF SETS

KM#	Date	Mintage	Identification	Issue Price	Mkt Val
PS1	1981 (8)	20	KM#8.2-10, 11-12.2, 35.2, 48, 79	—	—
PS2	1981 (8)	20	KM#8.2-10, 11-12.2, 35.2, 37, 48	—	—
PS3	1982 (8)	2,500	KM#8.2-10, 11-12.2, 29, 35.2, 48	—	410
PS4	1983 (8)	2,550	KM#8.2-10, 11-12.2, 35.2, 37, 48	—	300
PS5	1984 (8)	3,015	KM#8.2-10, 11-12.2, 29, 35.2, 48	—	120
PS6	1985 (8)	2,816	KM#8.2-10, 11-12.2, 35.2, 48, 102	—	95.00
PS7	1986 (8)	2,800	KM#8.2-10, 11-12.2, 29, 35.2, 48	—	120
PS8	1987 (8)	2,345	KM#8.2-10, 11-12.2, 29, 35.2, 48	—	115
PS9	1988 (8)	2,300	KM#8.2-10, 11-12.2, 28, 35.2, 48	—	120
PS10	1989 (8)	2,300	KM#8.2-10, 11-12.2, 28, 35.2, 48	—	130

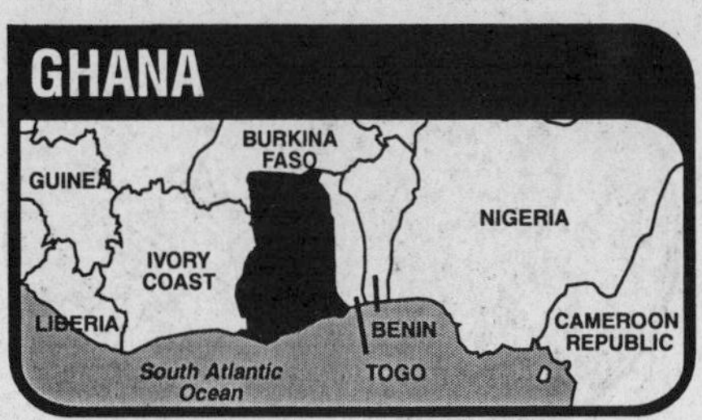

The Republic of Ghana, a member of the Commonwealth of Nations situated on the West Coast of Africa between Ivory Coast and Togo, has an area of 92,100 sq. mi. (238,540 sq. km.) and a population of 14 million, almost entirely African. Capital: Accra. Cocoa (the major crop), coconuts, palm kernels and coffee are exported. Mining, second in importance to agriculture, is concentrated on gold, manganese and industrial diamonds.

The state of Ghana, comprising the Gold Coast and British Togoland, obtained independence on March 6, 1957, becoming the first Negro African colony to do so. On July l, 1960, Ghana adopted a republican constitution, changing from a ministerial to a presidential form of government. The government was overthrown, the constitution suspended and the National Assembly dissolved by the Ghanaian army and police on Feb. 24, 1966. The government was returned to civilian authority in Oct. 1969, but was again seized by military officers in a bloodless coup on Jan. 13, 1972, but 3 further coups occurred in 1978, 1979 and 1981. The latter 2 coups were followed by suspension of the constitution and banning of political parties. A new constitution, which allowed multiparty politics, was approved in April 1992.

Ghana's monetary denomination of Cedi' is derived from the word 'sedie' meaning cowrie, a shell money commonly employed by coastal tribes.

MONETARY SYSTEM
12 Pence = 1 Shilling

REPUBLIC

STANDARD COINAGE

KM# 1 1/2 PENNY Composition: Bronze **Obverse:** Dr. Kwame Nkrumah bust right

Date	Mintage	F	VF	XF	Unc	BU
1958	32,200,000	—	0.10	0.25	0.50	—
1958 Proof	20,000	Value: 0.75				

KM# 2 PENNY Composition: Bronze **Obverse:** Dr. Kwame Nkrumah bust right

Date	Mintage	F	VF	XF	Unc	BU
1958	60,000,000	—	0.15	0.35	0.75	—
1958 Proof	20,000	Value: 1.00				

KM# 3 3 PENCE Composition: Copper Nickel **Obverse:** Dr. Kwame Nkrumah bust right

Date	Mintage	F	VF	XF	Unc	BU
1958	25,200,000	—	0.20	0.45	1.00	—
1958 Proof	20,000	Value: 1.50				

KM# 4 6 PENCE Composition: Copper Nickel **Obverse:** Dr. Kwame Nkrumah bust right

Date	Mintage	F	VF	XF	Unc	BU
1958	15,200,000	—	0.20	0.45	1.00	—
1958 Proof	—	Value: 1.50				

KM# 5 SHILLING Composition: Copper Nickel **Obverse:** Dr. Kwame Nkrumah bust right

Date	Mintage	F	VF	XF	Unc	BU
1958	34,400,000	—	0.25	0.50	1.75	—
1958 Proof	20,000	Value: 2.50				

KM# 6 2 SHILLING Composition: Copper Nickel **Obverse:** Dr. Kwame Nkrumah bust right

Date	Mintage	F	VF	XF	Unc	BU
1958	72,700,000	—	0.35	0.75	2.25	—
1958 Proof	20,000	Value: 3.50				

KM# 7 10 SHILLING Weight: 28.2800 g. **Composition:** 0.9250 Silver .8411 oz. ASW **Obverse:** Dr. Kwame Nkrumah bust right

Date	Mintage	F	VF	XF	Unc	BU
1958 Proof	11,000	Value: 12.50				

DECIMAL COINAGE

KM# 12 1/2 PESEWA Composition: Bronze **Obverse:** Brush drums

Date	Mintage	F	VF	XF	Unc	BU
1967	30,000,000	—	0.10	0.20	0.50	—
1967 Proof	2,000	Value: 1.00				

KM# 13 PESEWA Composition: Bronze **Obverse:** Brush drums

Date	Mintage	F	VF	XF	Unc	BU
1967	30,000,000	—	0.15	0.25	0.60	—
1967 Proof	2,000	Value: 1.25				
1975	50,250,000	—	0.10	0.20	0.50	—
1979	50,000,000	—	0.10	0.20	0.50	—

KM# 14 2-1/2 PESEWAS Composition: Copper-Nickel **Obverse:** Cocoa beans

Date	Mintage	F	VF	XF	Unc	BU
1967	6,000,000	—	0.10	0.20	0.75	—
1967 Proof	2,000	Value: 1.50				

KM# 8 5 PESEWAS **Composition:** Copper-Nickel **Obverse:** Dr. Kwame Nkrumah bust right

Date	Mintage	F	VF	XF	Unc	BU
1965	30,000,000	—	0.20	0.35	1.25	—

KM# 15 5 PESEWAS **Composition:** Copper-Nickel **Obverse:** Cocoa beans

Date	Mintage	F	VF	XF	Unc	BU
1967	30,000,000	—	0.15	0.25	0.75	—
1967 Proof	2,000	Value: 2.00				
1973	8,000,000	—	0.15	0.25	0.75	—
1975	20,000,000	—	0.15	0.25	0.75	—

KM# 9 10 PESEWAS **Composition:** Copper-Nickel **Obverse:** Dr. Kwame Nkrumah bust right

Date	Mintage	F	VF	XF	Unc	BU
1965	50,000,000	—	0.25	0.50	1.25	—

KM# 16 10 PESEWAS **Composition:** Copper-Nickel **Obverse:** Cocoa beans

Date	Mintage	F	VF	XF	Unc	BU
1967	13,200,000	—	0.20	0.40	1.50	—
1967 Proof	2,000	Value: 2.50				
1975	20,000,000	—	0.20	0.40	1.25	—
1979	5,500,000	—	0.20	0.40	1.25	—

KM# 17 20 PESEWAS **Composition:** Copper-Nickel **Obverse:** Cocoa beans

Date	Mintage	F	VF	XF	Unc	BU
1967	25,800,000	—	0.25	0.50	1.75	—
1967 Proof	2,000	Value: 3.00				
1975	—	—	0.25	0.50	1.75	—
1979	5,000,000	—	0.25	0.50	1.75	—

KM# 10 25 PESEWAS **Composition:** Copper-Nickel **Obverse:** Dr. Kwame Nkrumah bust right

Date	Mintage	F	VF	XF	Unc	BU
1965	60,100,000	—	0.35	0.75	2.00	—

KM# 11 50 PESEWAS **Composition:** Copper-Nickel **Obverse:** Dr. Kwame Nkrumah bust right

Date	Mintage	F	VF	XF	Unc	BU
1965	18,200,000	—	0.75	1.50	3.50	—

KM# 18 50 PESEWAS **Composition:** Brass **Series:** F.A.O. **Obverse:** Cocoa beans

Date	Mintage	F	VF	XF	Unc	BU
1979	60,000,000	—	0.45	0.75	2.25	—

KM# 24 50 PESEWAS **Composition:** Brass **Obverse:** Cocoa beans

Date	Mintage	F	VF	XF	Unc	BU
1984	10,000,000	—	0.10	0.25	0.60	—

KM# 19 CEDI **Composition:** Brass **Series:** F.A.O. **Obverse:** Cauri

Date	Mintage	F	VF	XF	Unc	BU
1979	160,000,000	—	0.35	0.85	3.00	—

KM# 25 CEDI **Composition:** Brass **Obverse:** Cauri

Date	Mintage	F	VF	XF	Unc	BU
1984	40,000,000	—	0.10	0.25	1.00	—

KM# 26 5 CEDIS **Composition:** Brass **Obverse:** Bush drums

Date	Mintage	F	VF	XF	Unc	BU
1984	88,920,000	—	0.10	0.20	0.50	—

KM# 33 5 CEDIS **Composition:** Brass Plated Steel **Obverse:** Bush drums

Date	F	VF	XF	Unc	BU
1991	—	0.10	0.20	0.50	—

KM# 29 10 CEDIS **Composition:** Nickel Clad Steel

Date	F	VF	XF	Unc	BU
1991	—	—	0.25	0.75	—

KM# 30 20 CEDIS **Composition:** Nickel Clad Steel

Date	F	VF	XF	Unc	BU
1991	—	—	0.35	1.00	—
1995	—	—	0.35	1.00	—

KM# 20 50 CEDIS **Weight:** 28.2800 g. **Composition:** 0.9250 Silver .8411 oz. ASW **Subject:** International Year of Disabled Persons

Date	Mintage	F	VF	XF	Unc	BU
1981	10,000	—	—	—	25.00	—
1981 Proof	10,000	Value: 35.00				

KM# 21 50 CEDIS **Composition:** Copper Nickel **Series:** F.A.O. **Subject:** World Fisheries Conference

Date	Mintage	F	VF	XF	Unc	BU
ND(1984)	100,000	—	—	—	6.50	—

KM# 21a 50 CEDIS **Weight:** 28.2800 g. **Composition:** 0.9250 Silver .8411 oz. ASW **Series:** F.A.O. **Subject:** World Fisheries Conference

Date	Mintage	F	VF	XF	Unc	BU
ND(1984) Proof	21,000	Value: 55.00				

KM# 21b 50 CEDIS **Weight:** 47.5400 g. **Composition:** 0.9170 Gold 1.4017 oz. AGW **Series:** F.A.O. **Subject:** World Fisheries Conference

Date	Mintage	F	VF	XF	Unc	BU
ND(1984) Proof	105	Value: 2,000				

KM# 22 50 CEDIS **Weight:** 28.2800 g. **Composition:** 0.9250 Silver .8411 oz. ASW **Subject:** Year of the Scout

Date	Mintage	F	VF	XF	Unc	BU
ND(1984)	10,000	—	—	—	40.00	—
ND(1984) Proof	Inc. above	Value: 50.00				

KM# 31a (KM31) 50 CEDIS **Composition:** Nickel Plated Steel

Date	F	VF	XF	Unc	BU
1995	—	—	1.00	2.25	—
1995	—	—	1.00	2.25	—
1997	—	—	1.00	2.25	—
1997	—	—	1.00	2.25	—
1999	—	—	1.00	2.25	—
1999	—	—	1.00	2.25	—

KM# 31 50 CEDIS **Composition:** Copper-Nickel

Date	F	VF	XF	Unc	BU
1991	—	—	1.00	2.25	—

KM# 31b 50 CEDIS **Composition:** Copper-Nickel

Date	F	VF	XF	Unc	BU
1991	—	—	1.00	2.25	—

KM# 27 100 CEDIS **Weight:** 28.2800 g. **Composition:** 0.5000 Silver .4546 oz. ASW **Subject:** Commonwealth Games

Date	Mintage	F	VF	XF	Unc	BU
1986	50,000	—	—	—	17.50	—

KM# 27a 100 CEDIS **Weight:** 28.2800 g. **Composition:** 0.9250 Silver .8411 oz. ASW **Subject:** Commonwealth Games

Date	Mintage	F	VF	XF	Unc	BU
1986 Proof	20,000	Value: 27.50				

KM# 32 100 CEDIS **Ring Composition:** Copper-Nickel **Center Composition:** Brass **Obverse:** Cocoa beans

Date	F	VF	XF	Unc	BU
1991	—	—	1.75	3.75	—
1997	—	—	1.50	3.25	—
1998	—	—	1.50	3.25	—

KM# 35 200 CEDIS **Composition:** Nickel Plated Steel **Obverse:** Cowrie shell **Reverse:** National arms, denomination

Date	F	VF	XF	Unc	BU
1996	—	—	—	3.75	—
1998	—	—	—	3.25	—

Note: Center design frosted

KM# 28 500 CEDIS **Weight:** 15.9800 g. **Composition:** 0.9170 Gold .4711 oz. AGW **Subject:** International Year of Disabled Persons

Date	F	VF	XF	Unc	BU
1981	—	—	—	325	—
1981 Proof	—	Value: 400			

KM# 23 500 CEDIS **Weight:** 15.9800 g. **Composition:** 0.9170 Gold .4711 oz. AGW **Subject:** Year of the Scout

Date	Mintage	F	VF	XF	Unc	BU
ND(1984)	2,000	—	—	—	300	—
ND(1984) Proof	2,000	Value: 375				

KM# 34 500 CEDIS **Composition:** Nickel-Brass **Obverse:** Drums **Reverse:** National arms, denomination

Date	F	VF	XF	Unc	BU
1996	—	—	—	4.75	—
1998	—	—	—	4.75	—

KM# 40 500 SIKA **Weight:** 31.1035 g. **Composition:** 0.9990 Silver 0.999 oz. ASW **Subject:** 2004 Olympics **Obverse:** National arms **Reverse:** High relief chariot **Edge:** Reeded **Size:** 40 mm.

Date	Mintage	F	VF	XF	Unc	BU
2001 Antique Finish	15,000	—	—	—	50.00	—

KM# 41 500 SIKA **Weight:** 26.0000 g. **Composition:** 0.9990 Gold Plated Silver 0.8351 oz. ASW AGW **Subject:** Japanese Royal Baby **Obverse:** Queen Elizabeth's portrait above national arms **Reverse:** Red heart shaped crystal in hollowed out surface **Edge:** Plain **Size:** 22 mm.

Date	Mintage	F	VF	XF	Unc	BU
2001	2,000	—	—	—	140	—

KM# 38 500 SIKA **Weight:** 24.9300 g. **Composition:** 0.9000 Silver 0.7214 oz. ASW **Subject:** Ancient Navigator's **Obverse:** National arms below Queen Elizabeth's head right **Reverse:** Ancient Egyptian boat with rowers **Edge:** Reeded **Size:** 38.6 mm.

Date	F	VF	XF	Unc	BU
2002 Proof	—	Value: 50.00			

KM# 39 500 SIKA **Weight:** 24.9300 g. **Composition:** 0.9000 Silver 0.7214 oz. ASW **Subject:** Ancient Navigators **Obverse:** National arms below Queen Elizabeth's head right **Reverse:** Ancient Phoenician ship **Edge:** Reeded **Size:** 38.6 mm.

Date	F	VF	XF	Unc	BU
2002 Proof	—	Value: 50.00			

KM# 37 500 SIKA **Weight:** 4.9500 g. **Composition:** 0.3750 Gold 0.0597 oz. AGW **Subject:** Queen Elizabeth's Golden Jubilee **Obverse:** St. George **Reverse:** Young multicolor portrait of the Queen **Edge:** Reeded **Size:** 22 mm.

Date	Mintage	F	VF	XF	Unc	BU
2002 Proof	10,000	Value: 85.00				

PIEFORTS

KM#	Date	Mintage	Identification	Issue Price	Mkt Val
P1	1981	1,050	50 Cedis. Silver. KM20.	—	65.00
P2	1981	—	500 Cedis. Gold. KM28.	—	1,200
P3	ND(1984)	520	50 Cedis. Silver. KM21a.	—	80.00

PROOF SETS

KM#	Date	Mintage	Identification	Issue Price	Mkt Val
PS1	1958 (7)	6,431	KM1-7	—	23.50
PS2	1967 (6)	100	KM12-17	8.53	11.50

GIBRALTAR

The British Colony of Gibraltar, located at the southernmost point of the Iberian Peninsula, has an area of 2.25sq. mi. (6.5 sq. km.) and a population of 29,651. Capital (and only town): Gibraltar. Aside from its strategic importance as guardian of the western entrance to the Mediterranean Sea, Gibraltar is also a free port and a British naval base.

Gibraltar, rooted in Greek mythology as one of the Pillars of Hercules, has long been a coveted stronghold. Moslems took it from Spain and fortified it in 711. Spain retook it in 1309, lost it again to the Moors in 1333 and retook it in 1462. After 1540 Spain strengthened its defenses and held it until the War of the Spanish Succession when it was captured by a combined British and Dutch force in 1704. Britain held it against the Franco-Spanish attacks of 1704-05 and through the historic Great Siege of 1779-83.Recently Spain has attempted to discourage British occupancy by harassment and economic devices. In 1967, Gibraltar's inhabitants voted 12,138 to 44 to remain under British rule.

Gibraltar's celebrated Barbary Ape, the last monkey to be found in a wild state in Europe, is featured on the colony's first decimal crown, released in 1972.

RULERS
British

MINT MARKS
PM - Pobjoy Mint

MINT PRIVY MARKS
U - Unc finish

DIE MARKS
1988: AA-AE
1989: AA-AF
1990: AA-AB
1991: AA
1992: AA-BB
1993: AA-BB
1994-1999: AA

MONETARY SYSTEM
4 Farthings = 1 Penny
12 Pence = 1 Shilling
2 Shillings = 1 Crown
5 Shillings = 1 Crown
20 Shillings = 1 Pound

BRITISH COLONY

CROWN COINAGE

KM# 4 CROWN **Composition:** Copper-Nickel

Date	Mintage	F	VF	XF	Unc	BU
1967	125,000	—	0.50	1.00	2.50	—
1968	40,000	—	0.65	1.25	3.00	—
1969	40,000	—	0.65	1.25	3.00	—
1970	45,000	—	0.65	1.25	3.00	—

KM# 4a CROWN **Weight:** 28.2800 g. **Composition:** 0.5000 Silver .4546 oz. ASW

Date	Mintage	F	VF	XF	Unc	BU
1967 Proof	10,000	Value: 12.50				
1967 Frosted Proof	50	Value: 200				

DECIMAL COINAGE

KM# 20 PENNY **Composition:** Bronze **Reverse:** Barbary partridge

Date	F	VF	XF	Unc	BU
1988 AA	—	—	—	0.25	—
1988 AB	—	—	—	0.25	—
1988 AC	—	—	—	0.25	—
1988 AD	—	—	—	0.25	—
1988 AE	—	—	—	0.25	—
1989 AA	—	—	—	0.25	—
1989 AB	—	—	—	0.25	—
1989 AC	—	—	—	0.25	—
1989 AD	—	—	—	0.25	—
1989 AE	—	—	—	0.25	—
1989 AF	—	—	—	0.25	—
1990 AA	—	—	—	0.25	—
1990 AB	—	—	—	0.25	—
1991 AA	—	—	—	0.25	—
1992 AA	—	—	—	0.25	—
1992 BB	—	—	—	0.25	—
1993 AA	—	—	—	0.25	—
1993 BB	—	—	—	0.25	—
1994 AA	—	—	—	0.25	—
1995 AA	—	—	—	0.25	—
1995 AB	—	—	—	0.25	—

KM# 20a PENNY **Composition:** Bronze Plated Steel

Date	F	VF	XF	Unc	BU
1995 AA	—	—	—	0.25	—
1995PM AB	—	—	—	0.25	—
1996 AA	—	—	—	0.25	—
1997 AA	—	—	—	0.25	—

KM# 773 PENNY **Composition:** Bronze Plated Steel **Obverse:** Portrait of Queen Elizabeth II **Obv. Designer:** Rank-Broadley **Reverse:** Barbary partridge

Date	F	VF	XF	Unc	BU
1998 AA	—	—	—	0.25	—
1999 AA	—	—	—	0.25	—
2000 AA	—	—	—	0.25	—
2001	—	—	—	0.25	—

KM# 21 2 PENCE **Composition:** Bronze **Reverse:** Lighthouse on Europa Point

Date	F	VF	XF	Unc	BU
1988 AA	—	—	—	0.50	—
1988 AB	—	—	—	0.50	—
1988 AC	—	—	—	0.50	—
1988 AD	—	—	—	0.50	—
1988 AE	—	—	—	0.50	—
1989 AA	—	—	—	0.50	—
1989 AB	—	—	—	0.50	—
1989 AC	—	—	—	0.50	—
1989 AD	—	—	—	0.50	—
1989 AE	—	—	—	0.50	—
1989 AF	—	—	—	0.50	—
1990 AA	—	—	—	0.50	—
1990 AB	—	—	—	0.50	—
1991 AA	—	—	—	0.50	—
1991 AB	—	—	—	0.50	—
1992 AA	—	—	—	0.50	—
1992 BB	—	—	—	0.50	—
1993 AA	—	—	—	0.50	—
1993 BB	—	—	—	0.50	—
1994 AA	—	—	—	0.50	—
1995 AB	—	—	—	0.50	—

KM# 21a 2 PENCE **Composition:** Bronze Plated Steel

Date	F	VF	XF	Unc	BU
1995 AA	—	—	—	0.50	—
1996 AA	—	—	—	0.50	—
1997 AA	—	—	—	0.50	—

KM# 774 2 PENCE **Composition:** Bronze Plated Steel **Obverse:** Portrait of Queen Elizabeth II **Obv. Designer:** Rank-Broadley

Date	F	VF	XF	Unc	BU
1998 AA	—	—	—	0.50	—
1999 AA	—	—	—	0.50	—
2000	—	—	—	0.50	—
2001	—	—	—	0.50	—

KM# 22 5 PENCE **Composition:** Copper-Nickel **Obverse:** Queen's portrait **Reverse:** Barbary Ape

Date	F	VF	XF	Unc	BU
1988 AA	—	—	—	0.75	—
1989 AA	—	—	—	0.75	—
1989 AB	—	—	—	0.75	—
1990 AA	—	—	—	0.75	—
1990 AB	—	—	—	0.75	—

KM# 22a 5 PENCE **Composition:** Copper-Nickel **Obverse:** Queen's portrait **Reverse:** Barbary Ape **Note:** Reduced size: 18 millimeters.

Date	F	VF	XF	Unc	BU
1990 AA	—	—	—	0.50	—
1991 AA	—	—	—	0.50	—
1992 AA	—	—	—	0.50	—
1992 AB	—	—	—	0.50	—
1993 AB	—	—	—	0.50	—
1993 AA	—	—	—	0.50	—
1994 AA	—	—	—	0.50	—
1995 AA	—	—	—	0.50	—
1996 AA	—	—	—	0.50	—
1997 AA	—	—	—	0.50	—

KM# 22b 5 PENCE **Weight:** 3.2500 g. **Composition:** 0.9250 Silver .0966 oz. ASW **Obverse:** Queen's portrait **Reverse:** Barbary Ape

Date	Mintage	F	VF	XF	Unc	BU
1990 Proof	5,000	Value: 25.00				

KM# 22c 5 PENCE **Weight:** 3.2500 g. **Composition:** 0.9170 Gold .0958 oz. AGW **Obverse:** Queen's portrait **Reverse:** Barbary Ape

Date	Mintage	F	VF	XF	Unc	BU
1990 Proof	1,000	Value: 125				

KM# 775 5 PENCE **Composition:** Copper-Nickel **Obverse:** Portrait of Queen Elizabeth II **Obv. Designer:** Rank-Broadley

Date	F	VF	XF	Unc	BU
1998 AA	—	—	—	0.50	—
1999 AA	—	—	—	0.50	—
2000	—	—	—	0.50	—
2001	—	—	—	0.50	—

KM# 23 10 PENCE **Composition:** Copper-Nickel **Reverse:** Moorish castle

Date	F	VF	XF	Unc	BU
1988 AA	—	—	—	1.00	—
1988 AB	—	—	—	1.00	—
1989 AA	—	—	—	1.00	—
1990 AA	—	—	—	1.00	—
1990 AB	—	—	—	1.00	—
1990 AC	—	—	—	1.00	—
1991 AA	—	—	—	1.00	—
1991 AB	—	—	—	1.00	—

KM# 112 10 PENCE **Composition:** Copper-Nickel **Reverse:** Europort

Date	F	VF	XF	Unc	BU
1992 AA	—	—	—	0.75	—
1993 AA	—	—	—	0.75	—
1995 AA	—	—	—	0.75	—
1996 AA	—	—	—	0.75	—
1997 AA	—	—	—	0.75	—

KM# 112a 10 PENCE **Weight:** 6.5000 g. **Composition:** 0.9250 Silver .1933 oz. ASW **Reverse:** Europort

Date	Mintage	F	VF	XF	Unc	BU
1992 Proof	25,000	Value: 25.00				

KM# 112b 10 PENCE **Weight:** 6.5000 g. **Composition:** 0.9170 Gold .1916 oz. AGW **Reverse:** Europort

Date	Mintage	F	VF	XF	Unc	BU
1992 Proof	3,500	—	—	—	—	—

KM# 112c 10 PENCE **Weight:** 6.5000 g. **Composition:** 0.9500 Platinum .1985 oz. APW **Reverse:** Europort

Date	Mintage	F	VF	XF	Unc	BU
1992 Proof	3,500	—	—	—	—	—

KM# 23a 10 PENCE **Composition:** Copper-Nickel

Date	F	VF	XF	Unc	BU
1994	—	—	—	1.00	—

KM# 776 10 PENCE **Composition:** Copper-Nickel **Obverse:** Portrait of Queen Elizabeth II **Obv. Designer:** Rank-Broadley

Date	F	VF	XF	Unc	BU
1998 AA	—	—	—	1.00	—
1999 AA	—	—	—	1.00	—
2000	—	—	—	1.00	—
2001	—	—	—	1.00	—

KM# 16 20 PENCE **Composition:** Copper-Nickel **Reverse:** Our Lady of Europe

Date	F	VF	XF	Unc	BU
1988 AA	—	—	—	1.50	—
1988 AB	—	—	—	1.50	—
1988 AC	—	—	—	1.50	—
1988 AA Proof	—	—	—	—	—
1989 AA	—	—	—	1.50	—
1990 AA	—	—	—	1.50	—
1991 AA	—	—	—	1.50	—
1992 AA	—	—	—	1.50	—
1993 AA	—	—	—	1.50	—
1994 AA	—	—	—	1.50	—
1995 AA	—	—	—	1.50	—
1995 AA Proof	—	—	—	—	—
1996 AA	—	—	—	1.50	—
1997 AA	—	—	—	1.50	—

KM# 777 20 PENCE **Composition:** Copper-Nickel **Obverse:** Portrait of Queen Elizabeth II **Obv. Designer:** Rank-Broadley

Date	F	VF	XF	Unc	BU
1998 AA	—	—	—	1.50	—
1999 AA	—	—	—	1.50	—
2000	—	—	—	1.50	—
2001	—	—	—	1.50	—

KM# 5 25 NEW PENCE **Composition:** Copper-Nickel **Reverse:** Barbary Ape

Date	Mintage	F	VF	XF	Unc	BU
1971	75,000	—	—	2.00	6.00	7.50

KM# 5a 25 NEW PENCE **Weight:** 28.2800 g. **Composition:** 0.5000 Silver .4546 oz. ASW **Reverse:** Barbary Ape

Date	Mintage	F	VF	XF	Unc	BU
1971 Proof	20,000	Value: 10.00				
1971 Frosted Proof	50	Value: 200				

KM# 6 25 NEW PENCE **Composition:** Copper-Nickel **Subject:** 25th Wedding Anniversary **Reverse:** Arms of Queen Elizabeth II and Prince Philip

Date	Mintage	F	VF	XF	Unc	BU
1972	70,000	—	—	1.50	3.50	—

KM# 6a 25 NEW PENCE **Weight:** 28.2800 g. **Composition:** 0.9250 Silver .8411 oz. ASW **Subject:** 25th Wedding Anniversary **Obverse:** Arms of Queen Elizabeth II and Prince Philip

Date	Mintage	F	VF	XF	Unc	BU
1972 Proof	15,000	Value: 12.50				

KM# 10 25 NEW PENCE **Composition:** Silver **Subject:** Queen's Silver Jubilee **Reverse:** Shield within wreath of apes and laurel

Date	Mintage	F	VF	XF	Unc	BU
1977	65,000	—	—	1.50	3.50	—

KM# 10a 25 NEW PENCE **Weight:** 28.2800 g. **Composition:** 0.9250 Silver .8411 oz. ASW **Subject:** Queen's Silver Jubilee **Obverse:** Shield within wreath of apes and laurel

Date	Mintage	F	VF	XF	Unc	BU
1977 Proof	24,000	Value: 12.50				

KM# 17 50 PENCE **Composition:** Copper-Nickel **Reverse:** Denomination in wreath of Candytuft flowers **Shape:** 7-sided

Date	Mintage	F	VF	XF	Unc	BU
1988 AA	30,000	—	—	—	2.00	—
1988 AB	—	—	—	—	2.00	—
1989 AA	—	—	—	—	2.00	—
1989 AB	—	—	—	—	2.00	—

KM# 19 50 PENCE **Composition:** Copper-Nickel **Subject:** Christmas **Reverse:** The Three Wise Men

Date	Mintage	F	VF	XF	Unc	BU
1988	—	—	—	—	4.00	—
1988 Proof	Est. 30,000	Value: 15.00				

KM# 19a 50 PENCE **Weight:** 15.5000 g. **Composition:** 0.9250 Silver .4610 oz. ASW **Subject:** Christmas **Reverse:** The Three Wise Men

Date	Mintage	F	VF	XF	Unc	BU
1988 Proof	Est. 5,000	Value: 15.00				

KM# 19b 50 PENCE **Weight:** 26.0000 g. **Composition:** 0.9170 Gold .7665 oz. AGW **Subject:** Christmas **Reverse:** The Three Wise Men

Date	Mintage	F	VF	XF	Unc	BU
1988 Proof	250	Value: 450				

KM# 19c 50 PENCE **Weight:** 30.4000 g. **Composition:** 0.9950 Platinum .9725 oz. APW **Subject:** Christmas **Reverse:** The Three Wise Men

Date	Mintage	F	VF	XF	Unc	BU
1988 Proof	50	Value: 700				

KM# 31 50 PENCE **Composition:** Copper-Nickel **Subject:** Christmas **Reverse:** Choir Boy **Shape:** 7-sided

Date	Mintage	F	VF	XF	Unc	BU
1989 AA	—	—	—	—	4.00	—
1989 AA Proof	Est. 30,000	Value: 6.50				

KM# 31a 50 PENCE **Weight:** 15.5000 g. **Composition:** 0.9250 Silver .4610 oz. ASW **Subject:** Christmas **Reverse:** Choir Boy

Date	Mintage	F	VF	XF	Unc	BU
1989 Proof	Est. 5,000	Value: 45.00				

KM# 31b 50 PENCE **Weight:** 26.0000 g. **Composition:** 0.9170 Gold .7665 oz. AGW **Subject:** Christmas **Reverse:** Choir Boy

Date	Mintage	F	VF	XF	Unc	BU
1989 Proof	Est. 250	Value: 750				

KM# 31c 50 PENCE **Weight:** 30.4000 g. **Composition:** 0.9950 Platinum .9628 oz. APW **Subject:** Christmas **Reverse:** Choir Boy

Date	Mintage	F	VF	XF	Unc	BU
1989 Proof	Est. 50	Value: 1,000				

KM# 39 50 PENCE **Composition:** Copper-Nickel **Reverse:** Dolphins **Shape:** 7-sided

Date	F	VF	XF	Unc	BU
1990 AA	—	—	—	4.50	—
1991 AA	—	—	—	4.50	—
1992 AA	—	—	—	4.50	—
1993 AA	—	—	—	4.50	—
1994 AA	—	—	—	4.50	—
1995 AA	—	—	—	4.50	—
1996 AA	—	—	—	4.50	—
1997	—	—	—	4.00	—

KM# 39a 50 PENCE **Weight:** 15.5000 g. **Composition:** 0.9250 Silver .4610 oz. ASW **Reverse:** Dolphins

Date	Mintage	F	VF	XF	Unc	BU
1990 Proof	2,500	Value: 47.50				
1993 Proof	—	Value: 50.00				

KM# 39b 50 PENCE **Weight:** 26.0000 g. **Composition:** 0.9170 Gold .7665 oz. AGW **Reverse:** Dolphins

Date	Mintage	F	VF	XF	Unc	BU
1990 Proof	250	Value: 800				

KM# 47 50 PENCE **Composition:** Copper-Nickel **Subject:** Christmas **Reverse:** Two women with child **Shape:** 7-sided

Date	Mintage	F	VF	XF	Unc	BU
1990 Proof	Est. 30,000	Value: 8.00				

KM# 47a 50 PENCE **Weight:** 15.5000 g. **Composition:** 0.9250 Silver .4610 oz. ASW **Subject:** Christmas **Reverse:** Two women with child **Shape:** 7-sided

Date	Mintage	F	VF	XF	Unc	BU
1990 Proof	5,000	Value: 45.00				

KM# 47b 50 PENCE **Weight:** 26.0000 g. **Composition:** 0.9170 Gold .7665 oz. AGW **Subject:** Christmas **Reverse:** Two women with child **Shape:** 7-sided

Date	Mintage	F	VF	XF	Unc	BU
1990 Proof	250	Value: 700				

KM# 47c 50 PENCE **Weight:** 30.4000 g. **Composition:** 0.9950 Platinum .9723 oz. APW **Subject:** Christmas **Reverse:** Two women with child **Shape:** 7-sided

Date	Mintage	F	VF	XF	Unc	BU
1990 Proof	50	Value: 1,000				

KM# 83 50 PENCE **Composition:** Copper-Nickel **Subject:** Christmas **Reverse:** Family caroling **Shape:** 7-sided

Date	Mintage	F	VF	XF	Unc	BU
1991 AA	—	—	—	—	4.00	—
1991 AA Proof	Est. 30,000	Value: 6.50				

KM# 83a 50 PENCE **Weight:** 15.5000 g. **Composition:** 0.9250 Silver .4610 oz. ASW **Subject:** Christmas **Reverse:** Family caroling **Shape:** 7-sided

Date	Mintage	F	VF	XF	Unc	BU
1991 Proof	Est. 5,000	Value: 40.00				

KM# 83b 50 PENCE **Weight:** 26.0000 g. **Composition:** 0.9170 Gold .7665 oz. AGW **Subject:** Christmas **Reverse:** Family caroling **Shape:** 7-sided

Date	Mintage	F	VF	XF	Unc	BU
1991 Proof	250	Value: 685				

KM# 83c 50 PENCE **Weight:** 30.4000 g. **Composition:** 0.9500 Platinum .9286 oz. APW **Subject:** Christmas **Reverse:** Family caroling **Shape:** 7-sided

Date	Mintage	F	VF	XF	Unc	BU
1991 Proof	50	Value: 860				

KM# 108 50 PENCE **Composition:** Copper-Nickel **Subject:** Christmas **Reverse:** Bust of Santa **Shape:** 7-sided

Date	F	VF	XF	Unc	BU
1992 AA	—	—	—	3.50	—
1992 AA Proof	— Value: 6.50				

KM# 108a 50 PENCE **Weight:** 15.5000 g. **Composition:** 0.9250 Silver .4610 oz. ASW **Subject:** Christmas **Reverse:** Bust of Santa **Shape:** 7-sided

Date	Mintage	F	VF	XF	Unc	BU
1992 Proof	Est. 5,000	Value: 40.00				

KM# 108b 50 PENCE **Weight:** 26.0000 g. **Composition:** 0.9170 Gold .7665 oz. AGW **Subject:** Christmas **Reverse:** Bust of Santa **Shape:** 7-sided

Date	Mintage	F	VF	XF	Unc	BU
1992 Proof	250	Value: 685				

KM# 108c 50 PENCE **Weight:** 30.4000 g. **Composition:** 0.9950 Platinum .9725 oz. APW **Subject:** Christmas **Reverse:** Bust of Santa **Shape:** 7-sided

Date	Mintage	F	VF	XF	Unc	BU
1992 Proof	50	Value: 860				

KM# 190 50 PENCE **Composition:** Copper-Nickel **Subject:** Christmas **Reverse:** Santa in automobile **Shape:** 7-sided

Date	Mintage	F	VF	XF	Unc	BU
1993 AA	30,000	—	—	—	3.50	—

KM# 190a 50 PENCE **Weight:** 15.5000 g. **Composition:** 0.9250 Silver .4610 oz. ASW **Subject:** Christmas **Reverse:** Santa in automobile **Shape:** 7-sided

Date	Mintage	F	VF	XF	Unc	BU
1993 Proof	Est. 5,000	Value: 40.00				

KM# 190b 50 PENCE **Weight:** 26.0000 g. **Composition:** 0.9170 Gold .7665 oz. AGW **Subject:** Christmas **Reverse:** Santa in automobile **Shape:** 7-sided

Date	Mintage	F	VF	XF	Unc	BU
1993 Proof	Est. 250	Value: 685				

KM# 190c 50 PENCE **Weight:** 30.4000 g. **Composition:** 0.9500 Platinum .9286 oz. APW **Subject:** Christmas **Reverse:** Santa in automobile **Shape:** 7-sided

Date	Mintage	F	VF	XF	Unc	BU
1993 Proof	Est. 50	Value: 860				

KM# 294 50 PENCE **Composition:** Copper-Nickel **Subject:** Christmas **Reverse:** Santa, balloon and sack **Shape:** 7-sided

Date	Mintage	F	VF	XF	Unc	BU
1994 AA	30,000	—	—	—	3.50	—

KM# 294a 50 PENCE **Weight:** 15.5000 g. **Composition:** 0.9250 Silver .4610 oz. ASW **Subject:** Christmas **Reverse:** Santa, baloon and sack **Shape:** 7-sided

Date	Mintage	F	VF	XF	Unc	BU
1994 Proof	Est. 5,000	Value: 40.00				

KM# 294b 50 PENCE **Weight:** 26.0000 g. **Composition:** 0.9170 Gold .7665 oz. AGW **Subject:** Christmas **Reverse:** Santa, balloon and sack **Shape:** 7-sided

Date	Mintage	F	VF	XF	Unc	BU
1994 Proof	Est. 250	Value: 700				

KM# 294c 50 PENCE **Weight:** 30.4000 g. **Composition:** 0.9500 Platinum .9286 oz. APW **Subject:** Christmas **Reverse:** Santa, baloon and sack **Shape:** 7-sided

Date	Mintage	F	VF	XF	Unc	BU
1994 Proof	Est. 50	Value: 875				

KM# 336 50 PENCE **Composition:** Copper-Nickel **Subject:** Christmas **Reverse:** Penguins parading **Shape:** 7-sided

Date	F	VF	XF	Unc	BU
1995 AA	—	—	—	4.00	—

KM# 336a 50 PENCE **Weight:** 15.5000 g. **Composition:** 0.9250 Silver .4610 oz. ASW **Subject:** Christmas **Reverse:** Penguins parading **Shape:** 7-sided

Date	Mintage	F	VF	XF	Unc	BU
1995 Proof	Est. 5,000	Value: 40.00				

KM# 336b 50 PENCE **Weight:** 26.0000 g. **Composition:** 0.9170 Gold .7665 oz. AGW **Subject:** Christmas **Reverse:** Penguins parading **Shape:** 7-sided

Date	Mintage	F	VF	XF	Unc	BU
1995 Proof	Est. 250	Value: 700				

KM# 336c 50 PENCE **Weight:** 30.4000 g. **Composition:** 0.9950 Platinum .9769 oz. APW **Subject:** Christmas **Reverse:** Penguins parading **Shape:** 7-sided

Date	Mintage	F	VF	XF	Unc	BU
1995 Proof	50	Value: 875				

KM# 453 50 PENCE **Composition:** Copper-Nickel **Subject:** Christmas **Reverse:** Santa Claus and biplane **Shape:** 7-sided

Date	F	VF	XF	Unc	BU
1996	—	—	—	4.00	—

KM# 453a 50 PENCE **Weight:** 15.0000 g. **Composition:** 0.9250 Silver .4610 oz. ASW **Subject:** Christmas **Reverse:** Santa Claus and biplane **Shape:** 7-sided

Date	Mintage	F	VF	XF	Unc	BU
1996 Proof	Est. 5,000	Value: 35.00				

KM# 453b 50 PENCE **Weight:** 26.0000 g. **Composition:** 0.9170 Gold .7665 oz. AGW **Subject:** Christmas **Reverse:** Santa Claus and biplane **Shape:** 7-sided

Date	Mintage	F	VF	XF	Unc	BU
1996 Proof	Est. 250	Value: 645				

KM# 606 50 PENCE **Composition:** Copper-Nickel **Subject:** Christmas **Obverse:** Queen's portrait **Reverse:** Santa Claus in sleigh **Shape:** 7-sided

Date	F	VF	XF	Unc	BU
1997	—	—	—	4.00	—

KM# 606a 50 PENCE **Weight:** 8.0000 g. **Composition:** 0.9250 Silver .2379 oz. ASW **Subject:** Christmas **Reverse:** Santa Claus in sleigh **Shape:** 7-sided

Date	Mintage	F	VF	XF	Unc	BU
1997 Proof	Est. 5,000	Value: 35.00				

KM# 606b 50 PENCE **Weight:** 8.0000 g. **Composition:** 0.9170 Gold .2359 oz. AGW **Subject:** Christmas **Obverse:** Queen's portrait **Reverse:** Santa in sleigh **Shape:** 7-sided

Date	Mintage	F	VF	XF	Unc	BU
1997 Proof	Est. 250	Value: 645				

KM# 39.1 50 PENCE **Weight:** 8.0000 g. **Composition:** Copper-Nickel 27.30 oz. **Obverse:** Queen's portrait **Reverse:** Configuration of five dolphins and denomination **Shape:** 7-sided

Date	F	VF	XF	Unc	BU
1997 AA	—	—	—	4.25	—

KM# 39.1a 50 PENCE **Weight:** 8.0000 g. **Composition:** 0.9250 Silver .2379 oz. ASW **Obverse:** Queen's portrait **Reverse:** Configuration of five dolphins and denomination **Shape:** 7-sided

Date	Mintage	F	VF	XF	Unc	BU
1997 Proof	Est. 5,000	Value: 35.00				

KM# 39.1b 50 PENCE **Weight:** 8.0000 g. **Composition:** 0.9999 Gold .2569 oz. AGW **Obverse:** Queen's portrait **Reverse:** Configuration of five dolphins and denomination **Shape:** 7-sided

Date	Mintage	F	VF	XF	Unc	BU
1997 Proof	Est. 250	Value: 400				

KM# 778 50 PENCE **Weight:** 8.0000 g. **Composition:** Copper-Nickel **Obverse:** Portrait of Queen Elizabeth II **Obv. Designer:** Rank-Broadley **Reverse:** Dolphins **Edge:** Plain **Shape:** 7-sided **Size:** 27.3 mm.

Date	F	VF	XF	Unc	BU
1998PM AA	—	—	—	4.00	—
1999PM AA	—	—	—	4.00	—
2001 AA	—	—	—	4.00	—
2001 AB	—	—	—	4.00	—

KM# 769 50 PENCE **Composition:** Copper-Nickel **Obverse:** Queen's portrait **Reverse:** Santa Claus in chimney **Shape:** 7-sided

Date	F	VF	XF	Unc	BU
1998	—	—	—	4.00	—

KM# 769a 50 PENCE **Weight:** 8.0000 g. **Composition:** 0.9250 Silver .2379 oz. ASW **Obverse:** Queen's portrait **Reverse:** Santa Claus in Chimney **Shape:** 7-sided

Date	Mintage	F	VF	XF	Unc	BU
1998 Proof	Est. 5,000	Value: 35.00				

KM# 769b 50 PENCE **Weight:** 8.0000 g. **Composition:** 0.9170 Gold .2359 oz. AGW **Obverse:** Queen's portrait **Reverse:** Santa Claus in chimney **Shape:** 7-sided

Date	Mintage	F	VF	XF	Unc	BU
1998 Proof	Est. 250	Value: 645				

KM# 866 50 PENCE Composition: Copper-Nickel **Obverse:** Portrait of Queen Elizabeth II **Obv. Designer:** Rank-Broadley **Reverse:** Santa with pair of monkeys **Shape:** 7-sided

Date	F	VF	XF	Unc	BU
1999 BB	—	—	—	4.00	—
1999 BB Prooflike	—	—	—	4.00	—

KM# 866a 50 PENCE Weight: 8.0000 g. **Composition:** 0.9250 Silver .2379 oz. ASW **Obverse:** Portrait of Queen Elizabeth II **Reverse:** Santa with pair of monkeys **Shape:** 7-sided

Date	Mintage	F	VF	XF	Unc	BU
1999 Proof	Est. 5,000	Value: 35.00				

KM# 866b 50 PENCE Weight: 8.0000 g. **Composition:** 0.9170 Gold .2359 oz. AGW **Obverse:** Portrait of Queen Elizabeth II **Reverse:** Santa with pair of monkeys **Shape:** 7-sided

Date	Mintage	F	VF	XF	Unc	BU
1999 Proof	Est. 250	Value: 645				

KM# 887 50 PENCE Weight: 8.0000 g. **Composition:** Copper-Nickel **Subject:** Christmas **Obverse:** Bust Queen right **Reverse:** Madonna and child with angels **Edge:** Plain **Shape:** 7-sided

Date	Mintage	F	VF	XF	Unc	BU
2000	30,000	—	—	—	4.00	—

KM# 887a 50 PENCE Weight: 8.0000 g. **Composition:** 0.9250 Silver .2379 oz. ASW **Subject:** Christmas **Reverse:** Madonna and child with angels **Shape:** 7-sided

Date	Mintage	F	VF	XF	Unc	BU
2000 Proof	5,000	Value: 35.00				

KM# 887b 50 PENCE Weight: 8.0000 g. **Composition:** 0.9160 Gold .2356 oz. AGW **Subject:** Christmas **Reverse:** Madonna and child with angels **Shape:** 7-sided **Note:** KM#310-317 previously listed here do not exist and have been removed.

Date	Mintage	F	VF	XF	Unc	BU
2000 Proof	250	Value: 645				

KM# 971 50 PENCE Weight: 8.0000 g. **Composition:** Copper-Nickel **Subject:** Christmas **Obverse:** Queen's portrait **Reverse:** Three wise men **Edge:** Plain **Shape:** 7-sided **Size:** 27.3 mm.

Date	Mintage	F	VF	XF	Unc	BU
2001	30,000	—	—	—	10.00	—

KM# 971a 50 PENCE Weight: 8.0000 g. **Composition:** 0.9250 Silver .2379 oz. ASW **Edge:** Plain **Shape:** 7-sided **Size:** 27.3 mm.

Date	Mintage	F	VF	XF	Unc	BU
2001 Proof	5,000	Value: 34.00				

KM# 971b 50 PENCE Weight: 8.0000 g. **Composition:** 0.9167 Gold .2358 oz. AGW **Edge:** Plain **Shape:** 7-sided **Size:** 27.3 mm.

Date	Mintage	F	VF	XF	Unc	BU
2001 Proof	250	Value: 645				

KM# 1026 50 PENCE Weight: 8.0000 g. **Composition:** Copper-Nickel **Subject:** Christmas **Obverse:** Queen's portrait **Reverse:** Shepherds **Edge:** Plain, seven sided **Size:** 27.3 mm.

Date	Mintage	F	VF	XF	Unc	BU
2002PM	30,000	—	—	—	10.00	—

KM# 1026a 50 PENCE Weight: 8.0000 g. **Composition:** 0.9250 Silver 0.2379 oz. ASW **Subject:** Christmas **Obverse:** Queen's portrait **Reverse:** Two Shepherds **Edge:** Plain, seven sided **Size:** 27.3 mm.

Date	Mintage	F	VF	XF	Unc	BU
2002PM Proof	2,002	Value: 34.00				

KM# 124 1/25 CROWN Weight: 1.2440 g. **Composition:** 0.9999 Gold .0400 oz. AGW **Reverse:** Japanese Royal Wedding

Date	Mintage	F	VF	XF	Unc	BU
1993 Proof	Est. 25,000	Value: 50.00				

KM# 206 1/25 CROWN Weight: 1.2440 g. **Composition:** 0.9999 Gold .0400 oz. AGW **Series:** Peter Rabbit Centennial **Subject:** Tiggy-Winkel **Reverse:** Mrs. Tiggy-Winkel ironing **Note:** Similar to 1 Crown, KM#205.

Date	Mintage	F	VF	XF	Unc	BU
1993 Proof	Est. 25,000	Value: 40.00				

KM# 210 1/25 CROWN Weight: 1.2440 g. **Composition:** 0.9999 Gold .0400 oz. AGW **Series:** Peter Rabbit Centennial **Subject:** Jeremy Fisher **Reverse:** Jeremy Fisher fishing **Note:** Similar to 1 Crown, KM#209.

Date	Mintage	F	VF	XF	Unc	BU
1993 Proof	Est. 25,000	Value: 40.00				

KM# 214 1/25 CROWN Weight: 1.2440 g. **Composition:** 0.9999 Gold .0400 oz. AGW **Series:** Peter Rabbit Centennial **Subject:** Tom Kitten **Reverse:** Tom Kitten with mother cat **Note:** Similar to 1 Crown, KM#213.

Date	Mintage	F	VF	XF	Unc	BU
1993 Proof	Est. 25,000	Value: 40.00				

KM# 218 1/25 CROWN Weight: 1.2440 g. **Composition:** 0.9999 Gold .0400 oz. AGW **Series:** Peter Rabbit Centennial **Subject:** Benjamin Bunny **Reverse:** Benjamin Bunny wearing hat and holding coat **Note:** Similar to 1 Crown, KM#217.

Date	Mintage	F	VF	XF	Unc	BU
1993 Proof	Est. 25,000	Value: 40.00				

KM# 222 1/25 CROWN Weight: 1.2440 g. **Composition:** 0.9999 Gold .0400 oz. AGW **Series:** Peter Rabbit Centennial **Subject:** Jemima Puddle-Duck **Reverse:** Jemima Puddle Duck talking with fox **Note:** Similar to 1 Crown, KM#221.

Date	Mintage	F	VF	XF	Unc	BU
1993 Proof	Est. 25,000	Value: 40.00				

KM# 202 1/25 CROWN Weight: 1.2440 g. **Composition:** 0.9999 Gold .0400 oz. AGW **Series:** Peter Rabbit Centennial **Subject:** Peter Rabbit **Obverse:** Portrait of Queen Elizabeth II **Reverse:** Peter Rabbit eating carrots **Note:** Similar to 1 Crown, KM#201.

Date	Mintage	F	VF	XF	Unc	BU
1993 Proof	Est. 25,000	Value: 40.00				

KM# 202a 1/25 CROWN Weight: 1.2440 g. **Composition:** 0.9950 Platinum .0400 oz. APW **Series:** Peter Rabbit Centennial **Subject:** Peter Rabbit **Obverse:** Portrait of Queen Elizabeth II **Reverse:** Peter Rabbit eating carrots

Date	Mintage	F	VF	XF	Unc	BU
1993 Proof	7,500	Value: 55.00				

KM# 437 1/25 CROWN Weight: 1.2440 g. **Composition:** 0.9999 Gold .0400 oz. AGW **Series:** Peter Rabbit Centennial **Subject:** Mother and Bunnies **Note:** Similar to 1 Crown, KM#444.

Date	Mintage	F	VF	XF	Unc	BU
1994 Proof	25,000	Value: 45.00				

KM# 437a 1/25 CROWN Weight: 1.2440 g. **Composition:** 0.9950 Platinum .0400 oz. APW **Series:** Peter Rabbit Centennial **Subject:** Mother and Bunnies **Note:** Similar to 1 Crown, KM#444.

Date	Mintage	F	VF	XF	Unc	BU
1994 Proof	Est. 7,500	Value: 55.00				

KM# 454 1/25 CROWN Weight: 1.2441 g. **Composition:** 0.9999 Gold .0400 oz. AGW **Series:** Centenary of the Cinema **Subject:** Wizard of Oz **Note:** Similar to 1 Crown, KM#457.

Date	Mintage	F	VF	XF	Unc	BU
1996 Proof	Est. 25,000	Value: 45.00				

KM# 458 1/25 CROWN Weight: 1.2441 g. **Composition:** 0.9999 Gold .0400 oz. AGW **Series:** Centenary of the Cinema **Subject:** Marx Brothers **Note:** Similar to 1 Crown, KM#461.

Date	Mintage	F	VF	XF	Unc	BU
1996 Proof	Est. 25,000	Value: 45.00				

KM# 462 1/25 CROWN Weight: 1.2441 g. **Composition:** 0.9999 Gold .0400 oz. AGW **Series:** Centenary of the Cinema **Subject:** Elvis Presley **Note:** Similar to 1 Crown, KM#465.

Date	Mintage	F	VF	XF	Unc	BU
1996 Proof	Est. 25,000	Value: 45.00				

KM# 466 1/25 CROWN Weight: 1.2441 g. **Composition:** 0.9999 Gold .0400 oz. AGW **Series:** Centenary of the Cinema **Subject:** Casablanca **Note:** Similar to 1 Crown, KM#469.

Date	Mintage	F	VF	XF	Unc	BU
1996 Proof	Est. 25,000	Value: 45.00				

KM# 470 1/25 CROWN Weight: 1.2441 g. **Composition:** 0.9999 Gold .0400 oz. AGW **Series:** Centenary of the Cinema **Subject:** E.T. **Note:** Similar to 1 Crown, KM#473.

Date	Mintage	F	VF	XF	Unc	BU
1996 Proof	Est. 25,000	Value: 45.00				

KM# 474 1/25 CROWN Weight: 1.2441 g. **Composition:** 0.9999 Gold .0400 oz. AGW **Series:** Centenary of the Cinema **Subject:** Alfred Hitchcock **Note:** Similar to 1 Crown, KM#477.

Date	Mintage	F	VF	XF	Unc	BU
1996 Proof	Est. 25,000	Value: 45.00				

KM# 410 1/25 CROWN Weight: 1.2441 g. **Composition:** 0.9999 Gold .0400 oz. AGW **Series:** Centenary of the Cinema **Subject:** Bruce Lee **Note:** Similar to 1 Crown, KM#413.

Date	Mintage	F	VF	XF	Unc	BU
1996 Proof	Est. 25,000	Value: 55.00				

KM# 415 1/25 CROWN Weight: 1.2441 g. **Composition:** 0.9999 Gold .0400 oz. AGW **Series:** Centenary of the Cinema **Subject:** Charlie Chaplin **Note:** Similar to 1 Crown, KM#418.

Date	Mintage	F	VF	XF	Unc	BU
1996 Proof	Est. 25,000	Value: 55.00				

KM# 420 1/25 CROWN Weight: 1.2441 g. **Composition:** 0.9999 Gold .0400 oz. AGW **Series:** Centenary of the Cinema **Subject:** Gone With The Wind **Note:** Similar to 1 Crown, KM#423.

Date	Mintage	F	VF	XF	Unc	BU
1996 Proof	Est. 25,000	Value: 55.00				

KM# 425 1/25 CROWN Weight: 1.2441 g. **Composition:** 0.9999 Gold .0400 oz. AGW **Series:** Centenary of the Cinema **Subject:** The Flintstones **Note:** Similar to 1 Crown, KM#428.

Date	Mintage	F	VF	XF	Unc	BU
1996 Proof	Est. 25,000	Value: 55.00				

KM# 375 1/25 CROWN Weight: 1.2441 g. **Composition:** 0.9999 Gold .0400 oz. AGW **Series:** Peter Rabbit Centennial **Subject:** Rabbit Escaping

Date	Mintage	F	VF	XF	Unc	BU
1996 Proof	Est. 25,000	Value: 45.00				

KM# 375a 1/25 CROWN Weight: 1.2500 g. **Composition:** 0.9950 Platinum .0400 oz. APW **Series:** Peter Rabbit Centennial **Subject:** Rabbit Escaping

Date	Mintage	F	VF	XF	Unc	BU
1996 Proof	Est. 7,500	Value: 55.00				

KM# 368 1/25 CROWN Weight: 1.2441 g. **Composition:** 0.9999 Gold .0400 oz. AGW **Reverse:** Roses **Note:** Similar to 1 Crown, KM#373.

Date	Mintage	F	VF	XF	Unc	BU
1996 Proof	Est. 25,000	Value: 45.00				

KM# 390 1/25 CROWN Weight: 1.2441 g. **Composition:** 0.9999 Gold .0400 oz. AGW **Series:** Centenary of the Cinema **Subject:** Grace Kelly **Note:** Similar to 1 Crown, KM#393.

Date	Mintage	F	VF	XF	Unc	BU
1996 Proof	Est. 25,000	Value: 45.00				

KM# 395 1/25 CROWN Weight: 1.2441 g. **Composition:** 0.9999 Gold .0400 oz. AGW **Series:** Centenary of the Cinema **Subject:** James Dean **Note:** Similar to 1 Crown, KM#398.

Date	Mintage	F	VF	XF	Unc	BU
1996 Proof	Est. 25,000	Value: 45.00				

KM# 400 1/25 CROWN Weight: 1.2441 g. **Composition:** 0.9999 Gold .0400 oz. AGW **Series:** Centenary of the Cinema **Subject:** Marilyn Monroe **Note:** Similar to 1 Crown, KM#403.

Date	Mintage	F	VF	XF	Unc	BU
1996 Proof	Est. 25,000	Value: 45.00				

KM# 452 1/25 CROWN Weight: 1.2441 g. **Composition:** 0.9999 Gold .0400 oz. AGW **Series:** Centenary of the Cinema **Subject:** James Dean **Note:** Similar to 1/10 Crown, KM#453.

Date	Mintage	F	VF	XF	Unc	BU
1996 Proof	Est. 25,000	Value: 60.00				

KM# 405 1/25 CROWN Weight: 1.2441 g. **Composition:** 0.9999 Gold .0400 oz. AGW **Series:** Centenary of the Cinema **Subject:** Audrey Hepburn **Note:** Similar to 1 Crown, KM#408.

Date	Mintage	F	VF	XF	Unc	BU
1996 Proof	25,000	Value: 45.00				

KM# 405a 1/25 CROWN Weight: 1.2500 g. **Composition:** 0.9950 Platinum .0400 oz. APW **Series:** Centenary of the Cinema **Subject:** Audrey Hepburn

Date	Mintage	F	VF	XF	Unc	BU
1996 Proof	Est. 1,000	Value: 65.00				

KM# 537 1/25 CROWN Weight: 1.2440 g. **Composition:** 0.9999 Gold .0400 oz. AGW **Subject:** Peonies **Note:** Similar to 1 Crown, KM#540.

Date	Mintage	F	VF	XF	Unc	BU
1997 Proof	Est. 25,000	Value: 45.00				

KM# 541 1/25 CROWN Weight: 1.2440 g. **Composition:** 0.9999 Gold .0400 oz. AGW **Subject:** Nefertiti **Note:** Similar to 1 Crown, KM#544.

Date	Mintage	F	VF	XF	Unc	BU
1997 Proof	Est. 10,000	Value: 45.00				

KM# 545 1/25 CROWN Weight: 1.2440 g. **Composition:** 0.9999 Gold .0400 oz. AGW **Subject:** Cleopatra **Note:** Similar to 1 Crown, KM#548.

Date	Mintage	F	VF	XF	Unc	BU
1997 Proof	Est. 10,000	Value: 45.00				

KM# 549 1/25 CROWN Weight: 1.2440 g. **Composition:** 0.9999 Gold .0400 oz. AGW **Subject:** Europa **Note:** Similar to 1 Crown, KM#552.

Date	Mintage	F	VF	XF	Unc	BU
1997 Proof	Est. 10,000	Value: 45.00				

KM# 553 1/25 CROWN Weight: 1.2440 g. **Composition:** 0.9999 Gold .0400 oz. AGW **Subject:** Liberty **Note:** Similar to 1 Crown, KM#556.

Date	Mintage	F	VF	XF	Unc	BU
1997 Proof	Est. 10,000	Value: 45.00				

KM# 581 1/25 CROWN **Weight:** 1.2440 g. **Composition:** 0.9999 Gold .0400 oz. AGW **Series:** Evolution of Mankind **Subject:** Egypt **Note:** Similar to 1 Crown, KM#582.

Date	Mintage	F	VF	XF	Unc	BU
1997 Proof	Est. 15,000	Value: 40.00				

KM# 583 1/25 CROWN **Weight:** 1.2440 g. **Composition:** 0.9999 Gold .0400 oz. AGW **Series:** Evolution of Mankind **Subject:** Israel **Note:** Similar to 1 Crown, KM#584.

Date	Mintage	F	VF	XF	Unc	BU
1997 Proof	Est. 15,000	Value: 40.00				

KM# 585 1/25 CROWN **Weight:** 1.2440 g. **Composition:** 0.9999 Gold .0400 oz. AGW **Series:** Evolution of Mankind **Subject:** China **Note:** Similar to 1 Crown, KM#586.

Date	Mintage	F	VF	XF	Unc	BU
1997 Proof	Est. 15,000	Value: 40.00				

KM# 587 1/25 CROWN **Weight:** 1.2440 g. **Composition:** 0.9999 Gold .0400 oz. AGW **Series:** Evolution of Mankind **Subject:** Greece **Note:** Similar to 1 Crown, KM#588.

Date	Mintage	F	VF	XF	Unc	BU
1997 Proof	Est. 15,000	Value: 40.00				

KM# 589 1/25 CROWN **Weight:** 1.2440 g. **Composition:** 0.9999 Gold .0400 oz. AGW **Series:** Evolution of Mankind **Subject:** Rome **Note:** Similar to 1 Crown, KM#590.

Date	Mintage	F	VF	XF	Unc	BU
1997 Proof	Est. 15,000	Value: 40.00				

KM# 591 1/25 CROWN **Weight:** 1.2440 g. **Composition:** 0.9999 Gold .0400 oz. AGW **Series:** Evolution of Mankind **Subject:** India **Note:** Similar to 1 Crown, KM#592.

Date	Mintage	F	VF	XF	Unc	BU
1997 Proof	Est. 15,000	Value: 40.00				

KM# 593 1/25 CROWN **Weight:** 1.2440 g. **Composition:** 0.9999 Gold .0400 oz. AGW **Series:** Evolution of Mankind **Subject:** Holy Roman Empire **Note:** Similar to 1 Crown, KM#594.

Date	Mintage	F	VF	XF	Unc	BU
1997 Proof	Est. 15,000	Value: 40.00				

KM# 595 1/25 CROWN **Weight:** 1.2440 g. **Composition:** 0.9999 Gold .0400 oz. AGW **Series:** Evolution of Mankind **Subject:** Macedonia **Note:** Similar to 1 Crown, KM#596.

Date	Mintage	F	VF	XF	Unc	BU
1997 Proof	Est. 15,000	Value: 40.00				

KM# 597 1/25 CROWN **Weight:** 1.2440 g. **Composition:** 0.9999 Gold .0400 oz. AGW **Series:** Evolution of Mankind **Subject:** Native America **Note:** Similar to 1 Crown, KM#598.

Date	Mintage	F	VF	XF	Unc	BU
1997 Proof	Est. 15,000	Value: 40.00				

KM# 599 1/25 CROWN **Weight:** 1.2440 g. **Composition:** 0.9999 Gold .0400 oz. AGW **Series:** Evolution of Mankind **Subject:** Asia **Note:** Similar to 1 Crown, KM#600.

Date	Mintage	F	VF	XF	Unc	BU
1997 Proof	Est. 15,000	Value: 40.00				

KM# 601 1/25 CROWN **Weight:** 1.2440 g. **Composition:** 0.9999 Gold .0400 oz. AGW **Series:** Evolution of Mankind **Subject:** Inca Empire **Note:** Similar to 1 Crown, KM#602.

Date	Mintage	F	VF	XF	Unc	BU
1997 Proof	Est. 15,000	Value: 40.00				

KM# 603 1/25 CROWN **Weight:** 1.2440 g. **Composition:** 0.9999 Gold .0400 oz. AGW **Series:** Evolution of Mankind **Subject:** Islamic Civilization **Note:** Similar to 1 Crown, KM#604.

Date	Mintage	F	VF	XF	Unc	BU
1997 Proof	Est. 15,000	Value: 40.00				

KM# 608 1/25 CROWN **Weight:** 1.2440 g. **Composition:** 0.9999 Gold .0400 oz. AGW **Series:** Traders of the World **Subject:** Sir Francis Drake **Obverse:** Queen's portrait **Reverse:** Sir Francis Drake, ship and beach **Note:** Similar to 1 Crown, KM#609.

Date	Mintage	F	VF	XF	Unc	BU
1997 Proof	Est. 15,000	Value: 45.00				

KM# 610 1/25 CROWN **Weight:** 1.2440 g. **Composition:** 0.9999 Gold .0400 oz. AGW **Series:** Traders of the World **Subject:** Romans **Obverse:** Queen's portrait **Reverse:** Lion, lioness, ship, map **Note:** Similar to 1 Crown, KM#611.

Date	Mintage	F	VF	XF	Unc	BU
1997 Proof	Est. 15,000	Value: 45.00				

KM# 612 1/25 CROWN **Weight:** 1.2440 g. **Composition:** 0.9999 Gold .0400 oz. AGW **Series:** Traders of the World **Subject:** Venetians **Obverse:** Queen's portrait **Reverse:** Pair of oysters with pearls, Venetian canal scene **Note:** Similar to 1 Crown, KM#613.

Date	Mintage	F	VF	XF	Unc	BU
1997 Proof	Est. 15,000	Value: 45.00				

KM# 614 1/25 CROWN **Weight:** 1.2440 g. **Composition:** 0.9999 Gold .0400 oz. AGW **Series:** Traders of the World **Subject:** Portuguese **Obverse:** Queen's portrait **Reverse:** Gold ingots and Portuguese ship **Note:** Similar to 1 Crown, KM#615.

Date	Mintage	F	VF	XF	Unc	BU
1997 Proof	Est. 15,000	Value: 45.00				

KM# 616 1/25 CROWN **Weight:** 1.2440 g. **Composition:** 0.9999 Gold .0400 oz. AGW **Series:** Traders of the World **Subject:** Spanish **Obverse:** Queen's portrait **Reverse:** Tobacco leaves, ship, map and gems **Note:** Similar to 1 Crown, KM#617.

Date	Mintage	F	VF	XF	Unc	BU
1997 Proof	Est. 15,000	Value: 45.00				

KM# 618 1/25 CROWN **Weight:** 1.2440 g. **Composition:** 0.9999 Gold .0400 oz. AGW **Series:** Traders of the World **Subject:** English **Obverse:** Queen's portrait **Reverse:** Profile of Queen above fighting ships **Note:** Similar to 1 Crown, KM#619.

Date	Mintage	F	VF	XF	Unc	BU
1997 Proof	Est. 15,000	Value: 45.00				

KM# 620 1/25 CROWN **Weight:** 1.2440 g. **Composition:** 0.9999 Gold .0400 oz. AGW **Series:** Traders of the World **Subject:** Captain Bligh **Obverse:** Queen's portrait **Reverse:** Captain Bligh on beach, ship **Note:** Similar to 1 Crown, KM#621.

Date	Mintage	F	VF	XF	Unc	BU
1997 Proof	Est. 15,000	Value: 45.00				

KM# 622 1/25 CROWN **Weight:** 1.2440 g. **Composition:** 0.9999 Gold .0400 oz. AGW **Series:** Traders of the World **Subject:** Captain Cook **Obverse:** Queen's portrait **Reverse:** Beaver on rock, ship, Captain Cook **Note:** Similar to 1 Crown, KM#623.

Date	Mintage	F	VF	XF	Unc	BU
1997 Proof	Est. 15,000	Value: 45.00				

KM# 518 1/25 CROWN **Weight:** 1.2441 g. **Composition:** 0.9999 Gold .0400 oz. AGW **Subject:** The Tale of Peter Rabbit **Note:** Similar to 1 Crown, KM#525.

Date	Mintage	F	VF	XF	Unc	BU
1997 Proof	Est. 25,000	Value: 45.00				

KM# 518a 1/25 CROWN **Weight:** 1.2504 g. **Composition:** 0.9950 Platinum .0400 oz. APW **Subject:** The Tale of Peter Rabbit

Date	Mintage	F	VF	XF	Unc	BU
1997 Proof	Est. 7,500	Value: 55.00				

KM# 691 1/25 CROWN **Weight:** 1.2440 g. **Composition:** 0.9999 Gold .0400 oz. AGW **Subject:** Traders of the World **Obverse:** Queen's portrait **Reverse:** Phoenician Galley (200 BC-600AD), shells below **Note:** Similar to 1 Crown, KM#692.

Date	Mintage	F	VF	XF	Unc	BU
1998 Proof	Est. 10,000	Value: 45.00				

KM# 693 1/25 CROWN **Weight:** 1.2440 g. **Composition:** 0.9999 Gold .0400 oz. AGW **Subject:** Traders of the World **Obverse:** Queen's portrait **Reverse:** Viking ship (900 AD), pair of fish **Note:** Similar to 1 Crown, KM#694.

Date	Mintage	F	VF	XF	Unc	BU
1998 Proof	Est. 10,000	Value: 45.00				

KM# 695 1/25 CROWN **Weight:** 1.2440 g. **Composition:** 0.9999 Gold .0400 oz. AGW **Subject:** Traders of the World **Obverse:** Queen's portrait **Reverse:** Marco Polo with ship (1254-1324) **Note:** Similar to 1 Crown, KM#696.

Date	Mintage	F	VF	XF	Unc	BU
1998 Proof	Est. 10,000	Value: 45.00				

KM# 697 1/25 CROWN **Weight:** 1.2440 g. **Composition:** 0.9999 Gold .0400 oz. AGW **Subject:** Traders of the World **Obverse:** Queen's portrait **Reverse:** Hanseatic Kogge (circa 1350), coins **Note:** Similar to 1 Crown, KM#698.

Date	Mintage	F	VF	XF	Unc	BU
1998 Proof	Est. 10,000	Value: 45.00				

KM# 699 1/25 CROWN **Weight:** 1.2440 g. **Composition:** 0.9999 Gold .0400 oz. AGW **Subject:** Traders of the World **Obverse:** Queen's portrait **Reverse:** Chinese Junk (1400s) **Note:** Similar to 1 Crown, KM#700.

Date	Mintage	F	VF	XF	Unc	BU
1998 Proof	Est. 10,000	Value: 45.00				

KM# 701 1/25 CROWN **Weight:** 1.2440 g. **Composition:** 0.9999 Gold .0400 oz. AGW **Subject:** Traders of the World **Obverse:** Queen's portrait **Reverse:** Christopher Columbus (1451-1506) and ship **Note:** Similar to 1 Crown, KM#702.

Date	Mintage	F	VF	XF	Unc	BU
1998 Proof	Est. 10,000	Value: 45.00				

KM# 703 1/25 CROWN **Weight:** 1.2440 g. **Composition:** 0.9999 Gold .0400 oz. AGW **Subject:** Traders of the World **Obverse:** Queen's portrait **Reverse:** Sir Walter Raleigh (1552-1618) **Note:** Similar to 1 Crown, KM#704.

Date	Mintage	F	VF	XF	Unc	BU
1998 Proof	Est. 10,000	Value: 45.00				

KM# 705 1/25 CROWN **Weight:** 1.2440 g. **Composition:** 0.9999 Gold .0400 oz. AGW **Subject:** Traders of the World **Obverse:** Queen's portrait **Reverse:** Sinking ships at the Boston Tea Party (1773), tea leaf **Note:** Similar to 1 Crown, KM#706.

Date	Mintage	F	VF	XF	Unc	BU
1998 Proof	Est. 10,000	Value: 45.00				

KM# 709 1/25 CROWN **Weight:** 1.2440 g. **Composition:** 0.9999 Gold .0400 oz. AGW **Subject:** Evolution of Mankind **Obverse:** Queen's portrait **Reverse:** Homo-Habilis, using tools **Note:** Similar to 1 Crown, KM#710.

Date	Mintage	F	VF	XF	Unc	BU
1998 Proof	Est. 15,000	Value: 45.00				

KM# 711 1/25 CROWN **Weight:** 1.2440 g. **Composition:** 0.9999 Gold .0400 oz. AGW **Subject:** Evolution of Mankind **Obverse:** Queen's portrait **Reverse:** Homo Erectus - using fire **Note:** Similar to 1 Crown, KM#712.

Date	Mintage	F	VF	XF	Unc	BU
1998 Proof	Est. 15,000	Value: 45.00				

KM# 713 1/25 CROWN **Weight:** 1.2440 g. **Composition:** 0.9999 Gold .0400 oz. AGW **Subject:** Evolution of Mankind **Obverse:** Queen's portrait **Reverse:** Gibraltar skull, man and "The Rock" **Note:** Similar to 1 Crown, KM#714.

Date	Mintage	F	VF	XF	Unc	BU
1998 Proof	Est. 15,000	Value: 45.00				

KM# 715 1/25 CROWN **Weight:** 1.2440 g. **Composition:** 0.9999 Gold .0400 oz. AGW **Subject:** Evolution of Mankind **Obverse:** Queen's portrait **Reverse:** Neanderthal Man, burial scene **Note:** Similar to 1 Crown, KM#716.

Date	Mintage	F	VF	XF	Unc	BU
1998 Proof	Est. 15,000	Value: 45.00				

KM# 717 1/25 CROWN **Weight:** 1.2440 g. **Composition:** 0.9999 Gold .0400 oz. AGW **Subject:** Evolution of Mankind **Obverse:** Queen's portrait **Reverse:** Homo Sapiens and cave painting **Note:** Similar to 1 Crown, KM#718.

Date	Mintage	F	VF	XF	Unc	BU
1998 Proof	Est. 15,000	Value: 45.00				

KM# 719 1/25 CROWN **Weight:** 1.2440 g. **Composition:** 0.9999 Gold .0400 oz. AGW **Subject:** Evolution of Mankind **Obverse:** Queen's portrait **Reverse:** Homo Sapiens killing mammoth **Note:** Similar to 1 Crown, KM#720.

Date	Mintage	F	VF	XF	Unc	BU
1998 Proof	Est. 15,000	Value: 45.00				

KM# 722 1/25 CROWN **Weight:** 1.2440 g. **Composition:** 0.9999 Gold .0400 oz. AGW **Subject:** Evolution of Mankind **Obverse:** Queen's portrait **Reverse:** Illustrated theory of evolution **Note:** Similar to 1 Crown, KM#722.

Date	Mintage	F	VF	XF	Unc	BU
1998 Proof	Est. 15,000	Value: 45.00				

KM# 723 1/25 CROWN **Weight:** 1.2440 g. **Composition:** 0.9999 Gold .0400 oz. AGW **Subject:** Evolution of Mankind **Obverse:** Queen's portrait **Reverse:** Human and primate mothers with young **Note:** Similar to 1 Crown, KM#724.

Date	Mintage	F	VF	XF	Unc	BU
1998 Proof	Est. 15,000	Value: 45.00				

KM# 725 1/25 CROWN **Weight:** 1.2440 g. **Composition:** 0.9999 Gold .0400 oz. AGW **Subject:** Evolution of Mankind **Obverse:** Queen's portrait **Reverse:** Charles Darwin **Note:** Similar to 1 Crown, KM#726.

Date	Mintage	F	VF	XF	Unc	BU
1998 Proof	Est. 15,000	Value: 45.00				

KM# 727 1/25 CROWN **Weight:** 1.2440 g. **Composition:** 0.9999 Gold .0400 oz. AGW **Subject:** Evolution of Mankind **Obverse:** Queen's portrait **Reverse:** Raymond Dart with skull **Note:** Similar to 1 Crown, KM#728.

Date	Mintage	F	VF	XF	Unc	BU
1998 Proof	Est. 15,000	Value: 45.00				

KM# 729 1/25 CROWN **Weight:** 1.2440 g. **Composition:** 0.9999 Gold .0400 oz. AGW **Subject:** Evolution of Mankind **Obverse:** Queen's portrait **Reverse:** 20th century Homo Sapiens **Note:** Similar to 1 Crown, KM#730.

Date	Mintage	F	VF	XF	Unc	BU
1998 Proof	Est. 15,000	Value: 45.00				

KM# 707 1/25 CROWN **Weight:** 1.2440 g. **Composition:** 0.9999 Gold .0400 oz. AGW **Subject:** Evolution of Mankind **Obverse:** Queen's portrait **Reverse:** Australopithecus - Lucy **Note:** Similar to 1 Crwn, KM#708.

Date	Mintage	F	VF	XF	Unc	BU
1998 Proof	Est. 15,000	Value: 45.00				

KM# 657 1/25 CROWN **Weight:** 1.2441 g. **Composition:** 0.9999 Gold .0400 oz. AGW **Subject:** Chrysanthemum **Obverse:** Queen's portrait **Reverse:** Three blossoms **Note:** Similar to 1 Crown, KM#661.

Date	Mintage	F	VF	XF	Unc	BU
1998 Proof	Est. 25,000	Value: 45.00				

KM# 662 1/25 CROWN **Weight:** 1.2441 g. **Composition:** 0.9999 Gold .0400 oz. AGW **Subject:** Brittania **Obverse:** Queen's portrait **Reverse:** Profile of helmeted Brittania **Note:** Similar to 1 Crown, KM#674.

Date	Mintage	F	VF	XF	Unc	BU
1998 Proof	Est. 10,000	Value: 45.00				

KM# 663 1/25 CROWN **Weight:** 1.2441 g. **Composition:** 0.9999 Gold .0400 oz. AGW **Subject:** Juno **Obverse:** Queen's portrait **Reverse:** Facing portrait **Note:** Similar to 1 Crown, KM#675.

Date	Mintage	F	VF	XF	Unc	BU
1998 Proof	Est. 10,000	Value: 45.00				

KM# 664 1/25 CROWN **Weight:** 1.2441 g. **Composition:** 0.9999 Gold .0400 oz. AGW **Subject:** Athena **Obverse:** Queen's portrait **Reverse:** Profile of helmeted Athena **Note:** Similar to 1 Crown, KM#676.

Date	Mintage	F	VF	XF	Unc	BU
1998 Proof	Est. 10,000	Value: 45.00				

KM# 665 1/25 CROWN **Weight:** 1.2441 g. **Composition:** 0.9999 Gold .0400 oz. AGW **Subject:** Arethusa **Obverse:** Queen's portrait **Reverse:** Profile with dolphins **Note:** Similar to 1 Crown, KM#677.

Date	Mintage	F	VF	XF	Unc	BU
1998 Proof	Est. 10,000	Value: 45.00				

KM# 678 1/25 CROWN **Weight:** 1.2441 g. **Composition:** 0.9999 Gold .0400 oz. AGW **Subject:** Paddington Bear **Obverse:** Queen's portrait **Reverse:** Paddington with suitcase **Note:** Similar to 1 Crown, KM#682.

Date	Mintage	F	VF	XF	Unc	BU
1998 Proof	Est. 7,500	Value: 45.00				

KM# 649 1/25 CROWN **Weight:** 1.2440 g. **Composition:** 0.9999 Gold .0400 oz. AGW **Subject:** The Tale of Peter Rabbit **Obverse:** Queen's portrait **Reverse:** Peter Rabbit **Note:** Similar to 1 Crown, KM#656.

Date	Mintage	F	VF	XF	Unc	BU
1998 Proof	Est. 25,000	Value: 45.00				

KM# 649a 1/25 CROWN **Weight:** 1.2441 g. **Composition:** 0.9950 Platinum .0398 oz. APW **Subject:** The Tale of Peter Rabbit **Obverse:** Queen's portrait **Reverse:** Peter Rabbit

Date	Mintage	F	VF	XF	Unc	BU
1998 Proof	Est. 7,500	Value: 55.00				

KM# 678a 1/25 CROWN **Weight:** 1.2440 g. **Composition:** 0.9950 Platinum .0400 oz. APW **Subject:** Paddington Bear **Obverse:** Queen's portrait **Reverse:** Paddington with suitcase

Date	Mintage	F	VF	XF	Unc	BU
1998 Proof	Est. 5,000	Value: 55.00				

KM# 779.2 1/25 CROWN **Weight:** 1.2440 g. **Composition:** 0.9999 Gold .0400 oz. AGW **Reverse:** Rabbit reading, sparrow; without Chinese characters

Date	Mintage	F	VF	XF	Unc	BU
1999 Proof	Inc. above	Value: 45.00				

KM# 779.1 1/25 CROWN **Weight:** 1.2440 g. **Composition:** 0.9999 Gold .0400 oz. AGW **Subject:** 1999 The Year of the Rabbit **Obverse:** Queen's portrait **Reverse:** Sparrow, Peter Rabbit reading, Chinese characters **Note:** Similar to 1 Crown, KM#783.1.

Date	Mintage	F	VF	XF	Unc	BU
1999 Proof	Est. 5,000	Value: 45.00				

KM# 779.1a 1/25 CROWN **Weight:** 1.2400 g. **Composition:** 0.9950 Platinum .0400 oz. APW **Subject:** 1999 The Year of the Rabbit **Obverse:** Queen's portrait **Reverse:** Sparrow, Peter Rabbit reading, Chinese characters

Date	Mintage	F	VF	XF	Unc	BU
1999 Proof	Est. 3,000	Value: 55.00				

KM# 779.2a 1/25 CROWN **Weight:** 1.2400 g. **Composition:** 0.9950 Platinum .0400 oz. APW **Reverse:** Rabbit reading, sparrow; without Chinese characters

Date	Mintage	F	VF	XF	Unc	BU
1999 Proof	Inc. above	Value: 55.00				

KM# 1016 1/25 CROWN **Weight:** 1.2441 g. **Composition:** 0.9999 Gold 0.04 oz. AGW **Subject:** Peter Pan **Obverse:** Bust of Queen Elizabeth Ii right. **Reverse:** Peter Pan and Tinkerbell flying above city. **Edge:** Reeded. **Size:** 13.92 mm.

Date	Mintage	F	VF	XF	Unc	BU
2002 Proof	10,000	Value: 49.50				

KM# 988 1/25 CROWN **Weight:** 1.2240 g. **Composition:** 0.9990 Gold 0.0393 oz. AGW **Subject:** Peter Rabbit Centennial **Obverse:** Bust of Queen Elizabeth II right **Reverse:** Peter Rabbit **Edge:** Reeded **Size:** 13.92 mm.

Date	Mintage	F	VF	XF	Unc	BU
2002 Proof	5,000	Value: 49.50				

KM# 988a 1/25 CROWN **Weight:** 1.2240 g. **Composition:** 0.9990 Platinum 0.0393 oz. APW **Subject:** Peter Rabbit Centennial **Obverse:** Bust of Queen Elizabeth II right **Reverse:** Peter Rabbit **Edge:** Reeded **Size:** 13.92 mm.

Date	Mintage	F	VF	XF	Unc	BU
2002 Proof	3,000	Value: 58.00				

KM# 51 1/10 CROWN **Weight:** 3.1100 g. **Composition:** 0.9999 Gold .1000 oz. AGW **Series:** Barcelona Olympics **Subject:** Chariot Racing **Note:** Similar to 1 Crown, KM#67.

Date	Mintage	F	VF	XF	Unc	BU
1991 Proof	Est. 20,000	Value: 75.00				
1992 Proof	Est. 20,000	Value: 90.00				

KM# 50 1/10 CROWN **Weight:** 3.1100 g. **Composition:** 0.9999 Gold .1000 oz. AGW **Series:** Barcelona Olympics **Subject:** Discus Thrower **Note:** Similar to 1 Crown, KM#66.

Date	Mintage	F	VF	XF	Unc	BU
1991 Proof	Est. 20,000	Value: 75.00				
1992 Proof	Est. 20,000	Value: 90.00				

KM# 52 1/10 CROWN **Weight:** 3.1100 g. **Composition:** 0.9999 Gold .1000 oz. AGW **Series:** Barcelona Olympics **Subject:** Runners **Note:** Similar to 1 Crown, KM#68.

Date	Mintage	F	VF	XF	Unc	BU
1991 Proof	Est. 20,000	Value: 75.00				
1992 Proof	Est. 20,000	Value: 90.00				

KM# 53 1/10 CROWN **Weight:** 3.1100 g. **Composition:** 0.9999 Gold .1000 oz. AGW **Series:** Barcelona Olympics **Subject:** Javelin Thrower **Note:** Similar to 1 Crown, KM#69.

Date	Mintage	F	VF	XF	Unc	BU
1991 Proof	Est. 20,000	Value: 75.00				
1992 Proof	Est. 20,000	Value: 90.00				

KM# 54 1/10 CROWN **Weight:** 3.1100 g. **Composition:** 0.9999 Gold .1000 oz. AGW **Series:** Barcelona Olympics **Subject:** Wrestlers **Note:** Similar to 1 Crown, KM#70.

Date	Mintage	F	VF	XF	Unc	BU
1991 Proof	Est. 20,000	Value: 75.00				
1992 Proof	Est. 20,000	Value: 90.00				

KM# 55 1/10 CROWN **Weight:** 3.1100 g. **Composition:** 0.9999 Gold .1000 oz. AGW **Series:** Barcelona Olympics **Subject:** Boxers **Note:** Similar to 1 Crown, KM#71.

Date	Mintage	F	VF	XF	Unc	BU
1991 Proof	Est. 20,000	Value: 75.00				
1992 Proof	Est. 20,000	Value: 90.00				

KM# 56 1/10 CROWN **Weight:** 3.1100 g. **Composition:** 0.9999 Gold .1000 oz. AGW **Series:** Barcelona Olympics **Subject:** Long Jumper **Note:** Similar to 1 Crown, KM#72.

Date	Mintage	F	VF	XF	Unc	BU
1991 Proof	Est. 20,000	Value: 75.00				
1992 Proof	Est. 20,000	Value: 90.00				

KM# 57 1/10 CROWN **Weight:** 3.1100 g. **Composition:** 0.9999 Gold .1000 oz. AGW **Series:** Barcelona Olympics **Subject:** Olympic Victor **Note:** Similar to 1 Crown, KM#73.

Date	Mintage	F	VF	XF	Unc	BU
1991 Proof	Est. 20,000	Value: 75.00				
1992 Proof	Est. 20,000	Value: 90.00				

KM# 125 1/10 CROWN **Weight:** 3.1100 g. **Composition:** 0.9999 Gold .1000 oz. AGW **Subject:** Japanese Royal Wedding

Date	Mintage	F	VF	XF	Unc	BU
1993 Proof	Est. 10,000	Value: 95.00				

KM# 207 1/10 CROWN **Weight:** 3.1100 g. **Composition:** 0.9990 Platinum .1000 oz. APW **Series:** Peter Rabbit Centennial **Subject:** Tiggy-Winkel **Reverse:** Mrs. Tiggy-Winkel ironing **Note:** Similar to 1 Crown, KM#205.

Date	Mintage	F	VF	XF	Unc	BU
1993 Proof	Est. 20,000	Value: 80.00				

KM# 211 1/10 CROWN **Weight:** 3.1100 g. **Composition:** 0.9990 Platinum .1000 oz. APW **Series:** Peter Rabbit Centennial **Subject:** Jeremy Fisher **Reverse:** Jeremy Fisher fishing **Note:** Similar to 1 Crown, KM#209.

Date	Mintage	F	VF	XF	Unc	BU
1993 Proof	Est. 20,000	Value: 80.00				

KM# 215 1/10 CROWN **Weight:** 3.1100 g. **Composition:** 0.9990 Platinum .1000 oz. APW **Series:** Peter Rabbit Centennial **Subject:** Tom Kitten **Reverse:** Tom Kitten with mother cat **Note:** Similar to 1 Crown, KM#213.

Date	Mintage	F	VF	XF	Unc	BU
1993 Proof	Est. 20,000	Value: 80.00				

KM# 219 1/10 CROWN **Weight:** 3.1100 g. **Composition:** 0.9990 Platinum .1000 oz. APW **Series:** Peter Rabbit Centennial **Subject:** Benjamin Bunny **Reverse:** Benjamin Bunny wearing hat and holding coat **Note:** Similar to 1 Crown, KM#217.

Date	Mintage	F	VF	XF	Unc	BU
1993 Proof	Est. 20,000	Value: 80.00				

KM# 223 1/10 CROWN **Weight:** 3.1100 g. **Composition:** 0.9990 Platinum .1000 oz. APW **Series:** Peter Rabbit Centennial **Subject:** Jemima Puddle-Duck **Reverse:** Jemima Puddle Duck talking with fox **Note:** Similar to 1 Crown, KM#221.

Date	Mintage	F	VF	XF	Unc	BU
1993 Proof	Est. 20,000	Value: 80.00				

KM# 203 1/10 CROWN **Weight:** 3.1100 g. **Composition:** 0.9999 Gold .1000 oz. AGW **Series:** Peter Rabbit Centennial **Subject:** Peter Rabbit **Obverse:** Queen's portrait **Reverse:** Peter Rabbit eating carrots **Note:** Similar to 1 Crown, KM#201.

Date	Mintage	F	VF	XF	Unc	BU
1993 Proof	Est. 20,000	Value: 80.00				

KM# 203a 1/10 CROWN **Weight:** 3.1100 g. **Composition:** 0.9990 Platinum .1000 oz. APW **Series:** Peter Rabbit Centennial **Subject:** Peter Rabbit **Obverse:** Queen's portrait **Reverse:** Peter Rabbit eating carrots

Date	Mintage	F	VF	XF	Unc	BU
1993 Proof	Est. 5,000	Value: 120				

KM# 439 1/10 CROWN **Weight:** 3.1100 g. **Composition:** 0.9990 Platinum .1000 oz. APW **Series:** Peter Rabbit Centennial **Subject:** Mother and Bunnies **Note:** Similar to 1 Crown, KM#444.

Date	Mintage	F	VF	XF	Unc	BU
1994 Proof	Est. 20,000	Value: 95.00				

KM# 439a 1/10 CROWN **Weight:** 3.1103 g. **Composition:** 0.9950 Platinum .1000 oz. APW **Series:** Peter Rabbit Centennial **Subject:** Mother and Bunnies **Note:** Similar to 1 Crown, KM#444.

Date	Mintage	F	VF	XF	Unc	BU
1994 Proof	Est. 5,000	Value: 120				

KM# 446 1/10 CROWN **Weight:** 3.1103 g. **Composition:** 0.9999 Gold .1000 oz. AGW **Subject:** Lord Buddha **Note:** Similar to 1 Crown, KM#449.

Date	Mintage	F	VF	XF	Unc	BU
1996 Proof	Est. 10,000	Value: 95.00				

KM# 455 1/10 CROWN **Weight:** 3.1103 g. **Composition:** 0.9999 Gold .1000 oz. AGW **Series:** Centenary of the Cinema **Subject:** Wizard of Oz **Note:** Similar to 1 Crown, KM#457.

Date	Mintage	F	VF	XF	Unc	BU
1996 Proof	Est. 20,000	Value: 80.00				

KM# 459 1/10 CROWN **Weight:** 3.1103 g. **Composition:** 0.9999 Gold .1000 oz. AGW **Series:** Centenary of the Cinema **Subject:** Marx Brothers **Note:** Similar to 1 Crown, KM#461.

Date	Mintage	F	VF	XF	Unc	BU
1996 Proof	Est. 20,000	Value: 80.00				

KM# 463 1/10 CROWN **Weight:** 3.1103 g. **Composition:** 0.9999 Gold .1000 oz. AGW **Series:** Centenary of the Cinema **Subject:** Elvis Presley **Note:** Similar to 1 Crown, KM#465.

Date	Mintage	F	VF	XF	Unc	BU
1996 Proof	Est. 20,000	Value: 80.00				

KM# 467 1/10 CROWN **Weight:** 3.1103 g. **Composition:** 0.9999 Gold .1000 oz. AGW **Series:** Centenary of the Cinema **Subject:** Casablanca **Note:** Similar to 1 Crown, KM#469.

Date	Mintage	F	VF	XF	Unc	BU
1996 Proof	Est. 20,000	Value: 80.00				

KM# 471 1/10 CROWN **Weight:** 3.1103 g. **Composition:** 0.9999 Gold .1000 oz. AGW **Series:** Centenary of the Cinema **Subject:** E.T. **Note:** Similar to 1 Crown, KM#473.

Date	Mintage	F	VF	XF	Unc	BU
1996 Proof	Est. 20,000	Value: 80.00				

KM# 475 1/10 CROWN **Weight:** 3.1103 g. **Composition:** 0.9999 Gold .1000 oz. AGW **Series:** Centenary of the Cinema **Subject:** Alfred Hitchcock **Note:** Similar to 1 Crown, KM#477.

Date	Mintage	F	VF	XF	Unc	BU
1996 Proof	Est. 20,000	Value: 80.00				

KM# 391 1/10 CROWN **Weight:** 3.1103 g. **Composition:** 0.9999 Gold .1000 oz. AGW **Series:** Centenary of the Cinema **Subject:** Grace Kelly **Note:** Similar to 1 Crown, KM#393.

Date	Mintage	F	VF	XF	Unc	BU
1996 Proof	Est. 20,000	Value: 80.00				

KM# 396 1/10 CROWN **Weight:** 3.1103 g. **Composition:** 0.9999 Gold .1000 oz. AGW **Series:** Centenary of the Cinema **Subject:** James Dean **Note:** Similar to 1 Crown, KM#398.

Date	Mintage	F	VF	XF	Unc	BU
1996 Proof	Est. 20,000	Value: 80.00				

KM# 401 1/10 CROWN **Weight:** 3.1103 g. **Composition:** 0.9999 Gold .1000 oz. AGW **Series:** Centenary of the Cinema **Subject:** Marilyn Monroe **Note:** Similar to 1 Crown, KM#403.

Date	Mintage	F	VF	XF	Unc	BU
1996 Proof	Est. 20,000	Value: 80.00				

KM# 411 1/10 CROWN **Weight:** 3.1103 g. **Composition:** 0.9999 Gold .1000 oz. AGW **Series:** Centenary of the Cinema **Subject:** Bruce Lee **Note:** Similar to 1 Crown, KM#413.

Date	Mintage	F	VF	XF	Unc	BU
1996 Proof	Est. 20,000	Value: 80.00				

KM# 416 1/10 CROWN **Weight:** 3.1103 g. **Composition:** 0.9999 Gold .1000 oz. AGW **Series:** Centenary of the Cinema **Subject:** Charlie Chaplin **Note:** Similar to 1 Crown, KM#418.

Date	Mintage	F	VF	XF	Unc	BU
1996 Proof	Est. 20,000	Value: 80.00				

KM# 421 1/10 CROWN **Weight:** 3.1103 g. **Composition:** 0.9999 Gold .1000 oz. AGW **Series:** Centenary of the Cinema **Subject:** Gone With The Wind **Note:** Similar to 1 Crown, KM#423.

Date	Mintage	F	VF	XF	Unc	BU
1996 Proof	Est. 20,000	Value: 80.00				

KM# 426 1/10 CROWN **Weight:** 3.1103 g. **Composition:** 0.9999 Gold .1000 oz. AGW **Series:** Centenary of the Cinema **Subject:** The Flintstones **Note:** Similar to 1 Crown, KM#428.

Date	Mintage	F	VF	XF	Unc	BU
1996 Proof	Est. 20,000	Value: 80.00				

KM# A453 1/10 CROWN **Weight:** 3.1103 g. **Composition:** 0.9999 Gold .1000 oz. AGW **Series:** Centenary of the Cinema **Subject:** James Dean

Date	Mintage	F	VF	XF	Unc	BU
1996 Proof	20,000	Value: 95.00				

KM# 369 1/10 CROWN **Weight:** 3.1103 g. **Composition:** 0.9999 Gold .1000 oz. AGW **Subject:** Roses **Note:** Similar to 1 Crown, KM#373.

Date	Mintage	F	VF	XF	Unc	BU
1996 Proof	Est. 20,000	Value: 80.00				

KM# 377 1/10 CROWN **Weight:** 3.1103 g. **Composition:** 0.9999 Gold .1000 oz. AGW **Series:** Peter Rabbit Centennial **Subject:** Rabbit Escaping

Date	Mintage	F	VF	XF	Unc	BU
1996 Proof	Est. 20,000	Value: 80.00				

KM# 406 1/10 CROWN **Weight:** 3.1103 g. **Composition:** 0.9999 Gold .1000 oz. AGW **Series:** Centenary of the Cinema **Subject:** Audrey Hepburn **Note:** Similar to 1 Crown, KM#408.

Date	Mintage	F	VF	XF	Unc	BU
1996 Proof	Est. 20,000	Value: 80.00				

KM# 406a 1/10 CROWN **Weight:** 3.1103 g. **Composition:** 0.9950 Platinum .1000 oz. APW **Series:** Centenary of the Cinema **Subject:** Audrey Hepburn

Date	Mintage	F	VF	XF	Unc	BU
1996 Proof	Est. 1,000	Value: 135				

KM# 377a 1/10 CROWN **Weight:** 3.1259 g. **Composition:** 0.9950 Platinum .1000 oz. APW **Series:** Peter Rabbit Centennial **Subject:** Rabbit Escaping **Note:** Similar to 1 Crown, KM#382.

Date	Mintage	F	VF	XF	Unc	BU
1996 Proof	Est. 10,000	Value: 95.00				

KM# 538 1/10 CROWN **Weight:** 3.1100 g. **Composition:** 0.9999 Gold .1000 oz. AGW **Subject:** Peonies **Note:** Similar to 1 Crown, KM#540.

Date	Mintage	F	VF	XF	Unc	BU
1997 Proof	Est. 20,000	Value: 75.00				

KM# 542 1/10 CROWN **Weight:** 3.1100 g. **Composition:** 0.9999 Gold .1000 oz. AGW **Subject:** Nefertiti **Note:** Similar to 1 Crown, KM#544.

Date	Mintage	F	VF	XF	Unc	BU
1997 Proof	Est. 7,500	Value: 75.00				

KM# 546 1/10 CROWN **Weight:** 3.1100 g. **Composition:** 0.9999 Gold .1000 oz. AGW **Subject:** Cleopatra **Note:** Similar to 1 Crown, KM#548.

Date	Mintage	F	VF	XF	Unc	BU
1997 Proof	Est. 7,500	Value: 75.00				

KM# 550 1/10 CROWN **Weight:** 3.1100 g. **Composition:** 0.9999 Gold .1000 oz. AGW **Subject:** Europa **Note:** Similar to 1 Crown, KM#552.

Date	Mintage	F	VF	XF	Unc	BU
1997 Proof	Est. 7,500	Value: 75.00				

KM# 554 1/10 CROWN **Weight:** 3.1100 g. **Composition:** 0.9999 Gold .1000 oz. AGW **Subject:** Liberty **Note:** Similar to 1 Crown, KM#556.

Date	Mintage	F	VF	XF	Unc	BU
1997 Proof	Est. 7,500	Value: 75.00				

KM# 520 1/10 CROWN **Weight:** 3.1103 g. **Composition:** 0.9999 Gold .1000 oz. AGW **Subject:** Tale of Peter Rabbit **Note:** Similar to 1 Crown, KM#525.

Date	Mintage	F	VF	XF	Unc	BU
1997 Proof	Est. 20,000	Value: 80.00				

KM# 520a 1/10 CROWN **Weight:** 3.1259 g. **Composition:** 0.9950 Platinum .1000 oz. APW **Subject:** Tale of Peter Rabbit

Date	Mintage	F	VF	XF	Unc	BU
1997 Proof	Est. 5,000	Value: 120				

KM# 666 1/10 CROWN **Weight:** 3.1100 g. **Composition:** 0.9999 Gold .1000 oz. AGW **Subject:** Brittania **Obverse:** Queen's portrait **Reverse:** Helmeted Brittania **Note:** Similar to 1 Crown, KM#674.

Date	Mintage	F	VF	XF	Unc	BU
1998 Proof	Est. 7,500	Value: 90.00				

KM# 667 1/10 CROWN **Weight:** 3.1100 g. **Composition:** 0.9999 Gold .1000 oz. AGW **Subject:** Juno **Obverse:** Queen's portrait **Reverse:** Facing portrait of Juno **Note:** Similar to 1 Crown, KM#675.

Date	Mintage	F	VF	XF	Unc	BU
1998 Proof	Est. 7,500	Value: 90.00				

KM# 668 1/10 CROWN **Weight:** 3.1100 g. **Composition:** 0.9999 Gold .1000 oz. AGW **Subject:** Athena **Obverse:** Queen's portrait **Reverse:** Helmeted Athena **Note:** Similar to 1 Crown, KM#676.

Date	Mintage	F	VF	XF	Unc	BU
1998 Proof	Est. 7,500	Value: 90.00				

KM# 669 1/10 CROWN **Weight:** 3.1100 g. **Composition:** 0.9999 Gold .1000 oz. AGW **Subject:** Arethusa **Obverse:** Queen's portrait **Reverse:** Portrait with dolphins **Note:** Similar to 1 Crown, KM#677.

Date	Mintage	F	VF	XF	Unc	BU
1998 Proof	Est. 7,500	Value: 90.00				

KM# 658 1/10 CROWN **Weight:** 3.1100 g. **Composition:** 0.9999 Gold .1000 oz. AGW **Subject:** Chrysanthemum **Obverse:** Queen's portrait **Reverse:** Three blossoms **Note:** Similar to 1 Crown, KM#661.

Date	Mintage	F	VF	XF	Unc	BU
1998 Proof	Est. 20,000	Value: 90.00				

KM# 679 1/10 CROWN **Weight:** 3.1100 g. **Composition:** 0.9999 Gold .1000 oz. AGW **Subject:** Paddington Bear **Obverse:** Queen's portrait **Reverse:** Bear with suitcase **Note:** Similar to 1 Crown, KM#682.

Date	Mintage	F	VF	XF	Unc	BU
1998 Proof	Est. 7,500	Value: 90.00				

KM# 651 1/10 CROWN **Weight:** 3.1100 g. **Composition:** 0.9999 Gold .1000 oz. AGW **Subject:** Tale of Peter Rabbit **Obverse:** Queen's portrait **Reverse:** Peter Rabbit **Note:** Similar to 1 Crown, KM#656.

Date	Mintage	F	VF	XF	Unc	BU
1998 Proof	Est. 20,000	Value: 90.00				

KM# 651a 1/10 CROWN **Weight:** 3.1103 g. **Composition:** 0.9950 Platinum .1000 oz. APW **Subject:** Tale of Peter Rabbit **Obverse:** Queen's portrait **Reverse:** Peter Rabbit

Date	Mintage	F	VF	XF	Unc	BU
1998 Proof	Est. 5,000	Value: 120				

KM# 679a 1/10 CROWN **Weight:** 3.1103 g. **Composition:** 0.9950 Platinum .1000 oz. APW **Subject:** Paddington Bear **Obverse:** Queen's portrait **Reverse:** Bear with suitcase

Date	Mintage	F	VF	XF	Unc	BU
1998 Proof	Est. 5,000	Value: 120				

KM# 1017 1/10 CROWN **Weight:** 3.1104 g. **Composition:** 0.9999 Gold 0.1 oz. AGW **Subject:** Peter Pan **Obverse:** Bust of Queen Elizabeth II right. **Reverse:** Peter Pan and Tinkerbell flying above city. **Edge:** Reeded. **Size:** 17.95 mm.

Date	Mintage	F	VF	XF	Unc	BU
2002 Proof	7,500	Value: 95.00				

KM# 989 1/10 CROWN **Weight:** 3.1100 g. **Composition:** 0.9990 Gold 0.0999 oz. AGW **Subject:** Peter Rabbit Centennial **Obverse:** Bust of Queen Elizabeth II right **Reverse:** Peter Rabbit **Edge:** Reeded **Size:** 17.95 mm.

Date	Mintage	F	VF	XF	Unc	BU
2002 Proof	5,000	Value: 95.00				

KM# 989a 1/10 CROWN **Weight:** 3.1100 g. **Composition:** 0.9990 Platinum 0.0999 oz. APW **Subject:** Peter Rabbit Centennial **Obverse:** Bust of Queen Elizabeth II right **Reverse:** Peter Rabbit **Edge:** Reeded **Size:** 17395 mm.

Date	Mintage	F	VF	XF	Unc	BU
2002 Proof	2,000	Value: 95.00				

KM# 48 1/5 CROWN **Weight:** 6.2200 g. **Composition:** 0.9990 Gold .2000 oz. AGW **Subject:** Penny Black Stamp **Note:** Similar to 1 Crown, KM#49.

Date	Mintage	F	VF	XF	Unc	BU
1990 Proof	Est. 5,000	Value: 215				

KM# 77 1/5 CROWN **Weight:** 6.2200 g. **Composition:** 0.9999 Gold .2000 oz. AGW **Series:** World Cup Soccer **Reverse:** Map of Italy **Note:** Similar to 1 Crown, KM#34.

Date	Mintage	F	VF	XF	Unc	BU
1990 Proof	Est. 5,000	Value: 215				

KM# 76a 1/5 CROWN **Weight:** 6.2200 g. **Composition:** 0.9950 Platinum .2000 oz. APW **Series:** World Cup Soccer **Reverse:** Italian Flag

Date	Mintage	F	VF	XF	Unc	BU
1990 Proof	Est. 1,000	Value: 325				

KM# 76 1/5 CROWN **Weight:** 6.2200 g. **Composition:** 0.9990 Gold .2000 oz. AGW **Series:** World Cup Soccer **Reverse:** Italian Flag **Note:** Similar to 1 Crown, KM#33.

Date	Mintage	F	VF	XF	Unc	BU
1990 Proof	Est. 5,000	Value: 215				

KM# 77a 1/5 CROWN **Weight:** 6.2200 g. **Composition:** 0.9950 Platinum .2000 oz. APW **Series:** World Cup Soccer **Reverse:** Map of Italy

Date	Mintage	F	VF	XF	Unc	BU
1990 Proof	Est. 1,000	Value: 325				

KM# 78 1/5 CROWN **Weight:** 6.2200 g. **Composition:** 0.9999 Gold .2000 oz. AGW **Series:** World Cup Soccer **Reverse:** Goalie catching ball **Note:** Similar to 1 Crown, KM#35.

Date	Mintage	F	VF	XF	Unc	BU
1990 Proof	Est. 5,000	Value: 215				

KM# 78a 1/5 CROWN **Weight:** 6.2200 g. **Composition:** 0.9950 Platinum .2000 oz. APW **Series:** World Cup Soccer **Reverse:** Goalie catching ball

Date	Mintage	F	VF	XF	Unc	BU
1990 Proof	Est. 1,000	Value: 325				

KM# 79 1/5 CROWN **Weight:** 6.2200 g. **Composition:** 0.9999 Gold .2000 oz. AGW **Series:** World Cup Soccer **Reverse:** One player **Note:** Similar to 1 Crown, KM#36.

Date	Mintage	F	VF	XF	Unc	BU
1990 Proof	Est. 5,000	Value: 215				

KM# 79a 1/5 CROWN **Weight:** 6.2200 g. **Composition:** 0.9950 Platinum .2000 oz. APW **Series:** World Cup Soccer **Reverse:** One player

Date	Mintage	F	VF	XF	Unc	BU
1990 Proof	Est. 1,000	Value: 325				

KM# 80 1/5 CROWN **Weight:** 6.2200 g. **Composition:** 0.9999 Gold .2000 oz. AGW **Series:** World Cup Soccer **Reverse:** Two players **Note:** Similar to 1 Crown, KM#37.

Date	Mintage	F	VF	XF	Unc	BU
1990 Proof	Est. 5,000	Value: 215				

KM# 80a 1/5 CROWN **Weight:** 6.2200 g. **Composition:** 0.9950 Platinum .2000 oz. APW **Series:** World Cup Soccer **Reverse:** Two players

Date	Mintage	F	VF	XF	Unc	BU
1990 Proof	Est. 1,000	Value: 325				

KM# 81 1/5 CROWN **Weight:** 6.2200 g. **Composition:** 0.9999 Gold .2000 oz. AGW **Series:** World Cup Soccer **Reverse:** Three players **Note:** Similar to 1 Crown, KM#38.

Date	Mintage	F	VF	XF	Unc	BU
1990 Proof	Est. 5,000	Value: 215				

KM# 81a 1/5 CROWN **Weight:** 6.2200 g. **Composition:** 0.9950 Platinum .2000 oz. APW **Series:** World Cup Soccer **Reverse:** Three players

Date	Mintage	F	VF	XF	Unc	BU
1990 Proof	Est. 1,000	Value: 325				

KM# 58 1/5 CROWN **Weight:** 6.2200 g. **Composition:** 0.9999 Gold .2000 oz. AGW **Series:** Barcelona Olympics **Reverse:** Discus thrower **Note:** Similar to 1 Crown, KM#66.

Date	Mintage	F	VF	XF	Unc	BU
1991 Proof	Est. 5,000	Value: 150				
1992 Proof	Est. 5,000	Value: 150				

KM# 59 1/5 CROWN **Weight:** 6.2200 g. **Composition:** 0.9999 Gold .2000 oz. AGW **Series:** Barcelona Olympics **Reverse:** Chariot racing **Note:** Similar to 1 Crown, KM#67.

Date	Mintage	F	VF	XF	Unc	BU
1991 Proof	Est. 5,000	Value: 150				
1992 Proof	Est. 5,000	Value: 150				

KM# 62 1/5 CROWN **Weight:** 6.2200 g. **Composition:** 0.9999 Gold .2000 oz. AGW **Series:** Barcelona Olympics **Reverse:** Wrestlers **Note:** Similar to 1 Crown, KM#70.

Date	Mintage	F	VF	XF	Unc	BU
1991 Proof	Est. 5,000	Value: 150				
1992 Proof	Est. 5,000	Value: 150				

KM# 63 1/5 CROWN **Weight:** 6.2200 g. **Composition:** 0.9999 Gold .2000 oz. AGW **Series:** Barcelona Olympics **Reverse:** Boxers **Note:** Similar to 1 Crown, KM#71.

Date	Mintage	F	VF	XF	Unc	BU
1991 Proof	Est. 5,000	Value: 150				
1992 Proof	Est. 5,000	Value: 150				

KM# 64 1/5 CROWN **Weight:** 6.2200 g. **Composition:** 0.9999 Gold .2000 oz. AGW **Series:** Barcelona Olympics **Reverse:** Long jumper **Note:** Similar to 1 Crown, KM#72.

Date	Mintage	F	VF	XF	Unc	BU
1991 Proof	Est. 5,000	Value: 150				
1992 Proof	Est. 5,000	Value: 150				

KM# 65 1/5 CROWN **Weight:** 6.2200 g. **Composition:** 0.9999 Gold .2000 oz. AGW **Series:** Barcelona Olympics **Reverse:** Olympic victor **Note:** Similar to 1 Crown, KM#73.

Date	Mintage	F	VF	XF	Unc	BU
1991 Proof	Est. 5,000	Value: 150				
1992 Proof	—	Value: 150				

KM# 60 1/5 CROWN **Weight:** 6.2200 g. **Composition:** 0.9999 Gold .2000 oz. AGW **Series:** Barcelona Olympics **Reverse:** Runners **Note:** Similar to 1 Crown, KM#68.

Date	Mintage	F	VF	XF	Unc	BU
1991 Proof	Est. 5,000	Value: 150				
1992 Proof	Est. 5,000	Value: 150				

KM# 61 1/5 CROWN **Weight:** 6.2200 g. **Composition:** 0.9999 Gold .2000 oz. AGW **Series:** Barcelona Olympics **Reverse:** Javelin thrower **Note:** Similar to 1 Crown, KM#69.

Date	Mintage	F	VF	XF	Unc	BU
1991 Proof	Est. 5,000	Value: 150				
1992 Proof	Est. 5,000	Value: 150				

KM# 58a 1/5 CROWN **Weight:** 6.2200 g. **Composition:** 0.9950 Platinum .2000 oz. APW **Series:** Barcelona Olympics **Reverse:** Discus thrower

Date	Mintage	F	VF	XF	Unc	BU
1991 Proof	Est. 1,000	Value: 275				

KM# 59a 1/5 CROWN **Weight:** 6.2200 g. **Composition:** 0.9950 Platinum .2000 oz. APW **Series:** Barcelona Olympics **Reverse:** Chariot racing

Date	Mintage	F	VF	XF	Unc	BU
1991 Proof	Est. 1,000	Value: 275				

KM# 60a 1/5 CROWN **Weight:** 6.2200 g. **Composition:** 0.9950 Platinum .2000 oz. APW **Series:** Barcelona Olympics **Reverse:** Runners

Date	Mintage	F	VF	XF	Unc	BU
1991 Proof	Est. 1,000	Value: 275				

KM# 61a 1/5 CROWN **Weight:** 6.2200 g. **Composition:** 0.9950 Platinum .2000 oz. APW **Series:** Barcelona Olympics **Reverse:** Javelin thrower

Date	Mintage	F	VF	XF	Unc	BU
1991 Proof	Est. 1,000	Value: 275				

KM# 62a 1/5 CROWN **Weight:** 6.2200 g. **Composition:** 0.9950 Platinum .2000 oz. APW **Series:** Barcelona Olympics **Reverse:** Wrestlers

Date	Mintage	F	VF	XF	Unc	BU
1991 Proof	Est. 1,000	Value: 275				

KM# 63a 1/5 CROWN **Weight:** 6.2200 g. **Composition:** 0.9950 Platinum .2000 oz. APW **Series:** Barcelona Olympics **Reverse:** Boxers

Date	Mintage	F	VF	XF	Unc	BU
1991 Proof	Est. 1,000	Value: 275				

KM# 64a 1/5 CROWN **Weight:** 6.2200 g. **Composition:** 0.9950 Platinum .2000 oz. APW **Series:** Barcelona Olympics **Reverse:** Long jumper

Date	Mintage	F	VF	XF	Unc	BU
1991 Proof	Est. 1,000	Value: 275				

KM# 65a 1/5 CROWN **Weight:** 6.2200 g. **Composition:** 0.9950 Platinum .2000 oz. APW **Series:** Barcelona Olympics **Reverse:** Olympic victor

Date	Mintage	F	VF	XF	Unc	BU
1991 Proof	Est. 1,000	Value: 275				

KM# 150 1/5 CROWN **Weight:** 6.2200 g. **Composition:** 0.9999 Gold .2000 oz. AGW **Series:** Preserve Planet Earth **Subject:** Cetiosaurus **Obverse:** Queen's portrait **Reverse:** Long-necked dinosaur

Date	Mintage	F	VF	XF	Unc	BU
1993 Proof	Est. 5,000	Value: 125				

KM# 152 1/5 CROWN **Weight:** 6.2200 g. **Composition:** 0.9999 Gold .2000 oz. AGW **Series:** Preserve Planet Earth **Subject:** Stegosaurus **Obverse:** Queen's portrait **Reverse:** Dinosaur with pointed plates along spine

Date	Mintage	F	VF	XF	Unc	BU
1993 Proof	Est. 5,000	Value: 135				

KM# 153 1/5 CROWN **Weight:** 6.2200 g. **Composition:** 0.9999 Gold .2000 oz. AGW **Series:** WWII Warships **Reverse:** USS Philadelphia

Date	Mintage	F	VF	XF	Unc	BU
1993 Proof	Est. 5,000	Value: 165				

KM# 154 1/5 CROWN **Weight:** 6.2200 g. **Composition:** 0.9999 Gold .2000 oz. AGW **Series:** WWII Warships **Reverse:** USS McLanahan

Date	Mintage	F	VF	XF	Unc	BU
1993 Proof	Est. 5,000	Value: 165				

KM# 155 1/5 CROWN **Weight:** 6.2200 g. **Composition:** 0.9999 Gold .2000 oz. AGW **Series:** WWII Warships **Reverse:** HNLMS Isaac Sweers

Date	Mintage	F	VF	XF	Unc	BU
1993 Proof	Est. 5,000	Value: 165				

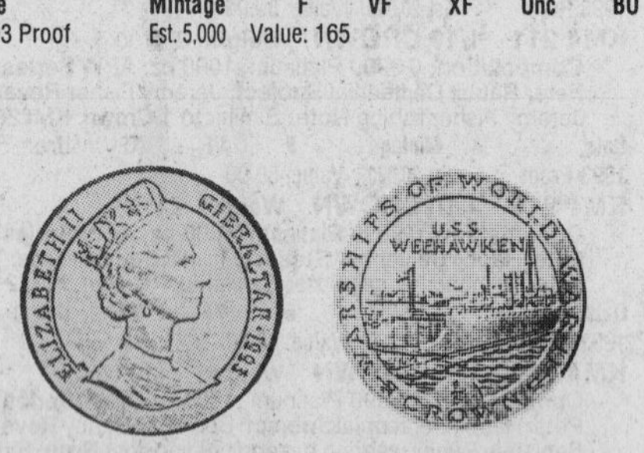

KM# 156 1/5 CROWN **Weight:** 6.2200 g. **Composition:** 0.9999 Gold .2000 oz. AGW **Series:** WWII Warships **Reverse:** USS Weehawken

Date	Mintage	F	VF	XF	Unc	BU
1993 Proof	Est. 5,000	Value: 165				

Circle of athletes with female discus thrower **Note:** Similar to 1 Crown, KM#329.

Date	Mintage	F	VF	XF	Unc	BU
1995 Proof	Est. 5,000	Value: 160				

KM# 330 1/5 CROWN Weight: 6.2200 g. **Composition:** 0.9999 Gold .2000 oz. AGW **Series:** Island Games **Reverse:** Circle of athletes with high jumper **Note:** Similar to 1 Crown, KM#331.

Date	Mintage	F	VF	XF	Unc	BU
1995 Proof	Est. 5,000	Value: 160				

KM# 342 1/5 CROWN Weight: 6.2200 g. **Composition:** 0.9999 Gold .2000 oz. AGW **Series:** Olympics **Obverse:** Queen's portrait **Reverse:** Tennis player **Note:** Similar to 1 Crown, KM#348.

Date	Mintage	F	VF	XF	Unc	BU
1996 Proof	Est. 5,000	Value: 165				

KM# 343 1/5 CROWN Weight: 6.2200 g. **Composition:** 0.9999 Gold .2000 oz. AGW **Series:** Olympics **Reverse:** Wrestlers **Note:** Similar to 1 Crown, KM#349.

Date	Mintage	F	VF	XF	Unc	BU
1996 Proof	Est. 5,000	Value: 165				

KM# 344 1/5 CROWN Weight: 6.2200 g. **Composition:** 0.9999 Gold .2000 oz. AGW **Series:** Olympics **Reverse:** Baseball players **Note:** Similar to 1 Crown, KM#350.

Date	Mintage	F	VF	XF	Unc	BU
1996 Proof	Est. 5,000	Value: 165				

KM# 345 1/5 CROWN Weight: 6.2200 g. **Composition:** 0.9999 Gold .2000 oz. AGW **Series:** Olympics **Reverse:** Flame **Note:** Similar to 1 Crown, KM#351.

Date	Mintage	F	VF	XF	Unc	BU
1996 Proof	Est. 5,000	Value: 165				

KM# 346 1/5 CROWN Weight: 6.2200 g. **Composition:** 0.9999 Gold .2000 oz. AGW **Series:** Olympics **Reverse:** Volleyball game **Note:** Similar to 1 Crown, KM#352.

Date	Mintage	F	VF	XF	Unc	BU
1996 Proof	Est. 5,000	Value: 165				

KM# 347 1/5 CROWN Weight: 6.2200 g. **Composition:** 0.9999 Gold .2000 oz. AGW **Series:** Olympics **Reverse:** Basketball game **Note:** Similar to 1 Crown, KM#353.

Date	Mintage	F	VF	XF	Unc	BU
1996 Proof	Est. 5,000	Value: 165				

KM# 357 1/5 CROWN Weight: 6.2200 g. **Composition:** 0.9999 Gold .2000 oz. AGW **Subject:** Nefusat Yehuda Synagogue Renovation **Obverse:** Queen's portrait **Reverse:** Hebrew symbol, rock, arms and building **Note:** Similar to 1 Crown, KM#358.

Date	Mintage	F	VF	XF	Unc	BU
1996 Proof	Est. 5,000	Value: 165				

KM# 379 1/5 CROWN Weight: 6.2207 g. **Composition:** 0.9999 Gold .2000 oz. AGW **Series:** Peter Rabbit Centennial **Reverse:** Peter Rabbit escaping **Note:** Similar to 1 Crown, KM#382.

Date	Mintage	F	VF	XF	Unc	BU
1996 Proof	Est. 7,500	Value: 165				

KM# 384 1/5 CROWN Weight: 6.2207 g. **Composition:** 0.9999 Gold .2000 oz. AGW **Series:** Preserve Planet Earth **Reverse:** Shag Birds **Note:** Similar to 1 Crown, KM#386.

Date	Mintage	F	VF	XF	Unc	BU
1996 Proof	Est. 5,000	Value: 165				

KM# 385 1/5 CROWN Weight: 6.2207 g. **Composition:** 0.9999 Gold .2000 oz. AGW **Series:** Preserve Planet Earth **Reverse:** Puffins **Note:** Similar to 1 Crown, KM#387.

Date	Mintage	F	VF	XF	Unc	BU
1996 Proof	Est. 5,000	Value: 165				

KM# 392 1/5 CROWN Weight: 6.2207 g. **Composition:** 0.9999 Gold .2000 oz. AGW **Series:** Cinema Centennial **Reverse:** Grace Kelly **Note:** Similar to 1 Crown, KM#393.

Date	Mintage	F	VF	XF	Unc	BU
1996 Proof	Est. 5,000	Value: 165				

KM# 397 1/5 CROWN Weight: 6.2207 g. **Composition:** 0.9999 Gold .2000 oz. AGW **Series:** Centenary of the Cinema **Reverse:** James Dean **Note:** Similar to 1 Crown, KM#398.

Date	Mintage	F	VF	XF	Unc	BU
1996 Proof	Est. 5,000	Value: 165				

KM# 402 1/5 CROWN Weight: 6.2207 g. **Composition:** 0.9999 Gold .2000 oz. AGW **Series:** Centenary of the Cinema **Reverse:** Marilyn Monroe **Note:** Similar to 1 Crown, KM#403.

Date	Mintage	F	VF	XF	Unc	BU
1996 Proof	Est. 5,000	Value: 165				

KM# 407 1/5 CROWN Weight: 6.2207 g. **Composition:** 0.9999 Gold .2000 oz. AGW **Series:** Centenary of the Cinema **Reverse:** Audrey Hepburn **Note:** Similar to 1 Crown, KM#408.

Date	Mintage	F	VF	XF	Unc	BU
1996 Proof	Est. 5,000	Value: 165				

KM# 412 1/5 CROWN Weight: 6.2207 g. **Composition:** 0.9999 Gold .2000 oz. AGW **Series:** Centenary of the Cinema **Reverse:** Bruce Lee **Note:** Similar to 1 Crown, KM#413.

Date	Mintage	F	VF	XF	Unc	BU
1996 Proof	Est. 5,000	Value: 165				

KM# 417 1/5 CROWN Weight: 6.2207 g. **Composition:** 0.9999 Gold .2000 oz. AGW **Series:** Centenary of the Cinema **Reverse:** Charlie Chaplin **Note:** Similar to 1 Crown, KM#418.

Date	Mintage	F	VF	XF	Unc	BU
1996 Proof	Est. 5,000	Value: 165				

KM# 422 1/5 CROWN Weight: 6.2207 g. **Composition:** 0.9999 Gold .2000 oz. AGW **Series:** Centenary of the Cinema **Reverse:** Gone With The Wind scene **Note:** Similar to 1 Crown, KM#423.

Date	Mintage	F	VF	XF	Unc	BU
1996 Proof	Est. 5,000	Value: 165				

KM# 427 1/5 CROWN Weight: 6.2207 g. **Composition:** 0.9999 Gold .2000 oz. AGW **Series:** Centenary of the Cinema **Reverse:** The Flintstones **Note:** Similar to 1 Crown, KM#428.

Date	Mintage	F	VF	XF	Unc	BU
1996 Proof	Est. 5,000	Value: 165				

KM# 431 1/5 CROWN Weight: 6.2207 g. **Composition:** 0.9999 Gold .2000 oz. AGW **Series:** Duke of Edinburgh Awards Scheme **Reverse:** 7 events **Note:** Similar to 1 Crown, KM#432.

Date	Mintage	F	VF	XF	Unc	BU
1996 Proof	Est. 5,000	Value: 165				

KM# 434 1/5 CROWN Weight: 6.2207 g. **Composition:** 0.9999 Gold .2000 oz. AGW **Series:** Duke of Edinburgh Awards Scheme **Reverse:** Cameo - horses **Note:** Similar to 1 Crown, KM#435.

Date	Mintage	F	VF	XF	Unc	BU
1996 Proof	Est. 5,000	Value: 165				

KM# 360 1/5 CROWN Weight: 6.2200 g. **Composition:** 0.9999 Gold .2000 oz. AGW **Series:** Euro 96 **Reverse:** England

Date	Mintage	F	VF	XF	Unc	BU
1996 Proof	Est. 5,000	Value: 175				

KM# 370a 1/5 CROWN Weight: 6.2518 g. **Composition:** 0.9950 Platinum .2000 oz. APW **Reverse:** Roses

Date	Mintage	F	VF	XF	Unc	BU
1996 Proof	Est. 1,000	Value: 220				

KM# 379a 1/5 CROWN Weight: 6.2200 g. **Composition:** 0.9950 Platinum .2000 oz. APW **Series:** Peter Rabbit Centennial **Reverse:** Peter Rabbit escaping

Date	Mintage	F	VF	XF	Unc	BU
1996 Proof	Est. 5,000	Value: 210				

KM# 392a 1/5 CROWN Weight: 6.2200 g. **Composition:** 0.9950 Platinum .2000 oz. APW **Series:** Cinema Centennial **Reverse:** Grace Kelly

Date	Mintage	F	VF	XF	Unc	BU
1996 Proof	Est. 1,000	Value: 220				

KM# 397a 1/5 CROWN Weight: 6.2200 g. **Composition:** 0.9950 Platinum .2000 oz. APW **Series:** Centenary of the Cinema **Reverse:** James Dean

Date	Mintage	F	VF	XF	Unc	BU
1996 Proof	Est. 1,000	Value: 220				

KM# 402a 1/5 CROWN Weight: 6.2200 g. **Composition:** 0.9950 Platinum .2000 oz. APW **Series:** Centenary of the Cinema **Reverse:** Marilyn Monroe

Date	Mintage	F	VF	XF	Unc	BU
1996 Proof	Est. 1,000	Value: 220				

KM# 407a 1/5 CROWN Weight: 6.2200 g. **Composition:** 0.9950 Platinum .2000 oz. APW **Series:** Centenary of the Cinema **Reverse:** Audrey Hepburn

Date	Mintage	F	VF	XF	Unc	BU
1996 Proof	Est. 1,000	Value: 220				

KM# 447 1/5 CROWN Weight: 6.2207 g. **Composition:** 0.9999 Gold .2000 oz. AGW **Subject:** Lord Buddha **Note:** Similar to 1 Crown, KM#449.

Date	Mintage	F	VF	XF	Unc	BU
1996 Proof	Est. 8,000	Value: 185				

KM# 456 1/5 CROWN Weight: 6.2207 g. **Composition:** 0.9999 Gold .2000 oz. AGW **Series:** Centenary of the Cinema **Subject:** Wizard of Oz **Note:** Similar to 1 Crown, KM#457.

Date	Mintage	F	VF	XF	Unc	BU
1996 Proof	Est. 5,000	Value: 165				

KM# 460 1/5 CROWN Weight: 6.2207 g. **Composition:** 0.9999 Gold .2000 oz. AGW **Series:** Centenary of the Cinema **Reverse:** Marx Brothers **Note:** Similar to 1 Crown, KM#461.

Date	Mintage	F	VF	XF	Unc	BU
1996 Proof	Est. 5,000	Value: 165				

KM# 464 1/5 CROWN Weight: 6.2207 g. **Composition:** 0.9999 Gold .2000 oz. AGW **Series:** Centenary of the Cinema **Reverse:** Elvis Presley **Note:** Similar to 1 Crown, KM#465.

Date	Mintage	F	VF	XF	Unc	BU
1996 Proof	Est. 5,000	Value: 165				

KM# 468 1/5 CROWN Weight: 6.2207 g. **Composition:** 0.9999 Gold .2000 oz. AGW **Series:** Centenary of the Cinema - Casablanca **Reverse:** Bogart and Bergman **Note:** Similar to 1 Crown, KM#469.

Date	Mintage	F	VF	XF	Unc	BU
1996 Proof	Est. 5,000	Value: 165				

KM# 472 1/5 CROWN Weight: 6.2207 g. **Composition:** 0.9999 Gold .2000 oz. AGW **Series:** Centenary of the Cinema **Reverse:** E.T. **Note:** Similar to 1 Crown, KM#473.

Date	Mintage	F	VF	XF	Unc	BU
1996 Proof	Est. 5,000	Value: 165				

KM# 476 1/5 CROWN Weight: 6.2207 g. **Composition:** 0.9999 Gold .2000 oz. AGW **Series:** Centenary of the Cinema **Reverse:** Alfred Hitchcock **Note:** Similar to 1 Crown, KM#477.

Date	Mintage	F	VF	XF	Unc	BU
1996 Proof	Est. 5,000	Value: 165				

KM# 370 1/5 CROWN Weight: 6.2200 g. **Composition:** 0.9999 Gold .2000 oz. AGW **Reverse:** Roses **Note:** Similar to 1 Crown, KM#373.

Date	Mintage	F	VF	XF	Unc	BU
1996 Proof	Est. 5,000	Value: 165				

KM# 513 1/5 CROWN Weight: 6.2207 g. **Composition:** 0.9999 Gold .2000 oz. AGW **Reverse:** Peacock **Note:** Similar to 1 Crown, KM#514.

Date	Mintage	F	VF	XF	Unc	BU
1997 Proof	Est. 5,000	Value: 185				

KM# 522 1/5 CROWN Weight: 6.2207 g. **Composition:** 0.9999 Gold .2000 oz. AGW **Subject:** The Tale of Peter Rabbit **Note:** Similar to 1 Crown, KM#525.

Date	Mintage	F	VF	XF	Unc	BU
1997 Proof	Est. 10,000	Value: 165				

KM# 529 1/5 CROWN Weight: 6.2207 g. **Composition:** 0.9999 Gold .2000 oz. AGW **Series:** Golden Wedding Anniversary **Reverse:** Queen Elizabeth and Prince Philip **Note:** Similar to 1 Crown, KM#530.

Date	Mintage	F	VF	XF	Unc	BU
1997 Proof	Est. 3,500	Value: 150				

KM# 531 1/5 CROWN Weight: 6.2207 g. **Composition:** 0.9999 Gold .2000 oz. AGW **Series:** Golden Wedding Anniversary **Reverse:** Queen Elizabeth and Prince Philip **Note:** Similar to 1 Crown, KM#532.

Date	Mintage	F	VF	XF	Unc	BU
1997 Proof	Est. 3,500	Value: 150				

KM# 533 1/5 CROWN Weight: 6.2207 g. **Composition:** 0.9999 Gold .2000 oz. AGW **Series:** Golden Wedding Anniversary **Reverse:** Queen Elizabeth and Prince Philip **Note:** Similar to 1 Crown, KM#534.

Date	Mintage	F	VF	XF	Unc	BU
1997 Proof	Est. 3,500	Value: 150				

KM# 535 1/5 CROWN Weight: 6.2207 g. **Composition:** 0.9999 Gold .2000 oz. AGW **Series:** Golden Wedding Anniversary **Reverse:** Queen Elizabeth and Prince Philip **Note:** Similar to 1 Crown, KM#536.

Date	Mintage	F	VF	XF	Unc	BU
1997 Proof	Est. 3,500	Value: 150				

KM# 539 1/5 CROWN Weight: 6.2207 g. **Composition:** 0.9999 Gold .2000 oz. AGW **Reverse:** Peonies **Note:** Similar to 1 Crown, KM#540.

Date	Mintage	F	VF	XF	Unc	BU
1997 Proof	Est. 5,000	Value: 150				

KM# 543 1/5 CROWN Weight: 6.2200 g. **Composition:** 0.9999 Gold .2000 oz. AGW **Reverse:** Nefertiti **Note:** Similar to 1 Crown, KM#544.

Date	Mintage	F	VF	XF	Unc	BU
1997 Proof	Est. 5,000	Value: 150				

KM# 547 1/5 CROWN Weight: 6.2200 g. **Composition:** 0.9999 Gold .2000 oz. AGW **Reverse:** Cleopatra **Note:** Similar to 1 Crown, KM#548.

Date	Mintage	F	VF	XF	Unc	BU
1997 Proof	Est. 5,000	Value: 150				

KM# 551 1/5 CROWN Weight: 6.2200 g. **Composition:** 0.9999 Gold .2000 oz. AGW **Reverse:** Europa **Note:** Similar to 1 Crown, KM#552.

Date	Mintage	F	VF	XF	Unc	BU
1997 Proof	Est. 5,000	Value: 150				

KM# 555 1/5 CROWN Weight: 6.2200 g. **Composition:** 0.9999 Gold .2000 oz. AGW **Reverse:** Liberty **Note:** Similar to 1 Crown, KM#556.

Date	Mintage	F	VF	XF	Unc	BU
1997 Proof	Est. 5,000	Value: 150				

KM# 562 1/5 CROWN Weight: 6.2200 g. **Composition:** 0.9999 Gold .2000 oz. AGW **Series:** Queen's Birthday **Reverse:** Queen mounted on horse to left **Note:** Similar to 1 Crown, KM#566.

Date	Mintage	F	VF	XF	Unc	BU
1997 Proof	Est. 5,000	Value: 165				

KM# 563 1/5 CROWN Weight: 6.2200 g. **Composition:** 0.9999 Gold .2000 oz. AGW **Series:** Queen's Birthday **Note:** Similar to 1 Crown, KM#567.

Date	Mintage	F	VF	XF	Unc	BU
1997 Proof	Est. 5,000	Value: 165				

KM# 564 1/5 CROWN Weight: 6.2200 g. **Composition:** 0.9999 Gold .2000 oz. AGW **Series:** Queen's Birthday **Note:** Similar to 1 Crown, KM#568.

Date	Mintage	F	VF	XF	Unc	BU
1997 Proof	Est. 5,000	Value: 165				

KM# 565 1/5 CROWN Weight: 6.2200 g. **Composition:** 0.9999 Gold .2000 oz. AGW **Series:** Queen's Birthday **Note:** Similar to 1 Crown, KM#569.

Date	Mintage	F	VF	XF	Unc	BU
1997 Proof	Est. 5,000	Value: 165				

KM# 570 1/5 CROWN Weight: 6.2200 g. **Composition:** 0.9999 Gold .2000 oz. AGW **Subject:** The New Mosque **Note:** Similar to 1 Crown, KM#571.

Date	Mintage	F	VF	XF	Unc	BU
1997 Proof	Est. 5,000	Value: 165				

KM# 522a 1/5 CROWN Weight: 6.2518 g. **Composition:** 0.9950 Platinum .2000 oz. APW **Subject:** The Tale of Peter Rabbit

Date	Mintage	F	VF	XF	Unc	BU
1997 Proof	Est. 2,500	Value: 210				

KM# 539a 1/5 CROWN Weight: 6.2200 g. **Composition:** 0.9950 Platinum .1990 oz. APW **Reverse:** Peonies

Date	Mintage	F	VF	XF	Unc	BU
1997 Proof	Est. 1,000	Value: 200				

KM# 543a 1/5 CROWN Weight: 6.2200 g. **Composition:** 0.9950 Platinum .1990 oz. APW **Reverse:** Nefertiti

Date	Mintage	F	VF	XF	Unc	BU
1997 Proof	Est. 1,000	Value: 200				

KM# 547a 1/5 CROWN Weight: 6.2200 g. **Composition:** 0.9950 Platinum .1990 oz. APW **Reverse:** Cleopatra

Date	Mintage	F	VF	XF	Unc	BU
1997 Proof	Est. 1,000	Value: 200				

KM# 551a 1/5 CROWN Weight: 6.2200 g. **Composition:** 0.9950 Platinum .1990 oz. APW **Reverse:** Europa

Date	Mintage	F	VF	XF	Unc	BU
1997 Proof	Est. 1,000	Value: 200				

KM# 555a 1/5 CROWN Weight: 6.2200 g. **Composition:** 0.9950 Platinum .1990 oz. APW **Reverse:** Liberty

Date	Mintage	F	VF	XF	Unc	BU
1997 Proof	Est. 1,000	Value: 200				

KM#653a 1/5 CROWN **Weight:** 6.2200 g. **Composition:** 0.9950 Platinum .2000 oz. APW **Subject:** Peter Rabbit **Obverse:** Queen's portrait **Reverse:** Peter Rabbit

Date	Mintage	F	VF	XF	Unc	BU
1998 Proof	Est. 2,500	Value: 200				

KM#659a 1/5 CROWN **Weight:** 6.2200 g. **Composition:** 0.9950 Platinum .2000 oz. APW **Reverse:** Chrysanthemum

Date	Mintage	F	VF	XF	Unc	BU
1998 Proof	Est. 1,000	Value: 200				

KM# 671a 1/5 CROWN **Weight:** 6.2200 g. **Composition:** 0.9950 Platinum .2000 oz. APW **Obverse:** Queen's portrait **Reverse:** Facing portrait of Juno

Date	Mintage	F	VF	XF	Unc	BU
1998 Proof	Est. 1,000	Value: 200				

KM# 672a 1/5 CROWN **Weight:** 6.2200 g. **Composition:** 0.9950 Platinum .2000 oz. APW **Obverse:** Queen's portrait **Reverse:** Helmeted portrait of Athena

Date	Mintage	F	VF	XF	Unc	BU
1998 Proof	Est. 1,000	Value: 200				

KM# 673a 1/5 CROWN **Weight:** 6.2200 g. **Composition:** 0.9950 Platinum .2000 oz. APW **Obverse:** Queen's portrait **Reverse:** Portrait of Arethusa with dolphins

Date	Mintage	F	VF	XF	Unc	BU
1998 Proof	Est. 1,000	Value: 200				

KM# 680a 1/5 CROWN **Weight:** 6.2200 g. **Composition:** 0.9950 Platinum .2000 oz. APW **Subject:** Paddington Bear **Obverse:** Queen's portrait **Reverse:** Bear with suitcase

Date	Mintage	F	VF	XF	Unc	BU
1998 Proof	Est. 2,000	Value: 200				

KM#741 1/5 CROWN **Weight:** 6.2200 g. **Composition:** 0.9999 Gold .2000 oz. AGW **Subject:** Year of the Ocean **Obverse:** Queen's portrait **Reverse:** Polar bear and walrus

Date	Mintage	F	VF	XF	Unc	BU
1998 Proof	Est. 5,000	Value: 165				

KM#742 1/5 CROWN **Weight:** 6.2200 g. **Composition:** 0.9999 Gold .2000 oz. AGW **Subject:** Year of the Ocean **Obverse:** Queen's portrait **Reverse:** Seals and penguins

Date	Mintage	F	VF	XF	Unc	BU
1998 Proof	Est. 5,000	Value: 165				

KM#743 1/5 CROWN **Weight:** 6.2200 g. **Composition:** 0.9999 Gold .2000 oz. AGW **Subject:** Year of the Ocean **Obverse:** Queen's portrait **Reverse:** Sea cow with calf

Date	Mintage	F	VF	XF	Unc	BU
1998 Proof	Est. 5,000	Value: 165				

KM#744 1/5 CROWN **Weight:** 6.2200 g. **Composition:** 0.9999 Gold .2000 oz. AGW **Subject:** Year of the Ocean **Obverse:** Queen's portrait **Reverse:** Surfer

Date	Mintage	F	VF	XF	Unc	BU
1998 Proof	Est. 5,000	Value: 165				

KM#635 1/5 CROWN **Weight:** 6.2200 g. **Composition:** 0.9999 Gold .2000 oz. AGW **Subject:** Winter Olympics Japan **Obverse:** Queen's portrait **Reverse:** Speed skater and "Bullet Train" **Note:** Similar to 1 Crown, KM#636.

Date	Mintage	F	VF	XF	Unc	BU
1998 Proof	Est. 5,000	Value: 165				

KM#637 1/5 CROWN **Weight:** 6.2200 g. **Composition:** 0.9999 Gold .2000 oz. AGW **Series:** Winter Olympics Japan **Obverse:** Queen's portrait **Reverse:** Ski jumper and Buddha **Note:** Similar to 1 Crown, KM#638.

Date	Mintage	F	VF	XF	Unc	BU
1998 Proof	Est. 5,000	Value: 165				

KM#639 1/5 CROWN **Weight:** 6.2200 g. **Composition:** 0.9999 Gold .2000 oz. AGW **Series:** Winter Olympics Japan **Obverse:** Queen's portrait **Reverse:** Cross country skiers **Note:** Similar to 1 Crown, KM#640.

Date	Mintage	F	VF	XF	Unc	BU
1998 Proof	Est. 5,000	Value: 165				

KM#641 1/5 CROWN **Weight:** 6.2200 g. **Composition:** 0.9999 Gold .2000 oz. AGW **Series:** Winter Olympics Japan **Obverse:** Queen's portrait **Reverse:** Slalom skier and Zenkoji temple **Note:** Similar to 1 Crown, KM#642.

Date	Mintage	F	VF	XF	Unc	BU
1998 Proof	Est. 5,000	Value: 165				

KM#653 1/5 CROWN **Weight:** 6.2200 g. **Composition:** 0.9999 Gold .2000 oz. AGW **Obverse:** Queen's portrait **Reverse:** Peter Rabbit **Note:** Similar to 1 Crown, KM#656.

Date	Mintage	F	VF	XF	Unc	BU
1998 Proof	Est. 10,000	Value: 165				

KM#659 1/5 CROWN **Weight:** 6.2200 g. **Composition:** 0.9999 Gold .2000 oz. AGW **Reverse:** Chrysanthemum **Note:** Similar to 1 Crown, KM#661.

Date	Mintage	F	VF	XF	Unc	BU
1998 Proof	Est. 5,000	Value: 165				

KM#671 1/5 CROWN **Weight:** 6.2200 g. **Composition:** 0.9999 Gold .2000 oz. AGW **Obverse:** Queen's portrait **Reverse:** Facing portrait of Juno **Note:** Similar to 1 Crown, KM#675.

Date	Mintage	F	VF	XF	Unc	BU
1998 Proof	Est. 5,000	Value: 165				

KM#672 1/5 CROWN **Weight:** 6.2200 g. **Composition:** 0.9999 Gold .2000 oz. AGW **Obverse:** Queen's portrait **Reverse:** Helmeted portrait of Athena **Note:** Similar to 1 Crown, KM#676.

Date	Mintage	F	VF	XF	Unc	BU
1998 Proof	Est. 5,000	Value: 165				

KM#673 1/5 CROWN **Weight:** 6.2200 g. **Composition:** 0.9999 Gold .2000 oz. AGW **Obverse:** Queen's portrait **Reverse:** Portrait of Arethusa with dolphins **Note:** Similar to 1 Crown, KM#677.

Date	Mintage	F	VF	XF	Unc	BU
1998 Proof	Est. 5,000	Value: 165				

KM#731 1/5 CROWN **Weight:** 6.2200 g. **Composition:** 0.9999 Gold .2000 oz. AGW **Obverse:** Queen's portrait **Reverse:** Cupid with hologram heart **Note:** Similar to 1/2 Crown, KM#647.

Date	Mintage	F	VF	XF	Unc	BU
1998 Proof	Est. 5,000	Value: 165				

KM#686 1/5 CROWN **Weight:** 6.2200 g. **Composition:** 0.9999 Gold .2000 oz. AGW **Subject:** World Cup France 1998 **Obverse:** Queen's portrait **Reverse:** Two players, map of Europe **Note:** Similar to 1 Crown, KM#690.

Date	Mintage	F	VF	XF	Unc	BU
1998 Proof	Est. 5,000	Value: 165				

KM#680 1/5 CROWN **Weight:** 6.2200 g. **Composition:** 0.9999 Gold .2000 oz. AGW **Subject:** Paddington Bear **Obverse:** Queen's portrait **Reverse:** Bear with suitcase **Note:** Similar to 1 Crown, KM#682.

Date	Mintage	F	VF	XF	Unc	BU
1998 Proof	Est. 5,000	Value: 165				

KM#683 1/5 CROWN **Weight:** 6.2200 g. **Composition:** 0.9999 Gold .2000 oz. AGW **Subject:** World Cup France 1998 **Obverse:** Queen's portrait **Reverse:** Goalie, map of Europe **Note:** Similar to 1 Crown, KM#687.

Date	Mintage	F	VF	XF	Unc	BU
1998 Proof	Est. 5,000	Value: 165				

KM#684 1/5 CROWN **Weight:** 6.2200 g. **Composition:** 0.9999 Gold .2000 oz. AGW **Subject:** World Cup France 1998 **Obverse:** Queen's portrait **Reverse:** Player kicking to left **Note:** Similar to 1 Crown, KM#688.

Date	Mintage	F	VF	XF	Unc	BU
1998 Proof	Est. 5,000	Value: 165				

KM#685 1/5 CROWN **Weight:** 6.2200 g. **Composition:** 0.9999 Gold .2000 oz. AGW **Subject:** World Cup France 1998 **Obverse:** Queen's portrait **Reverse:** Player dribbling **Note:** Similar to 1 Crown, KM#689.

Date	Mintage	F	VF	XF	Unc	BU
1998 Proof	Est. 5,000	Value: 165				

KM#767 1/5 CROWN **Weight:** 6.2200 g. **Composition:** 0.9999 Gold .2000 oz. AGW **Subject:** Gibraltar Regiment New Colours **Obverse:** Queen's portrait **Reverse:** Soldiers presenting keys **Note:** Similar to 1 Crown, KM#758.

Date	Mintage	F	VF	XF	Unc	BU
1998 Proof	Est. 5,000	Value: 165				

KM#798 1/5 CROWN **Weight:** 6.2200 g. **Composition:** 0.9999 Gold .2000 oz. AGW **Obverse:** Queen's portrait **Reverse:** Portrait of Dwight D. Eisenhower, North African invasion scene **Note:** Similar to 1 Crown, KM#799.

Date	Mintage	F	VF	XF	Unc	BU
1998 Proof	Est. 5,000	Value: 165				

KM#800 1/5 CROWN **Weight:** 6.2200 g. **Composition:** 0.9999 Gold .2000 oz. AGW **Obverse:** Queen's portrait **Reverse:** Alfred the Great, dates **Note:** Similar to 1 Crown, KM#801.

Date	Mintage	F	VF	XF	Unc	BU
1999 Proof	Est. 5,000	Value: 165				

KM#802 1/5 CROWN **Weight:** 6.2200 g. **Composition:** 0.9999 Gold .2000 oz. AGW **Obverse:** Queen's portrait **Reverse:** King Canute, dates **Note:** Similar to 1 Crown, KM#803.

Date	Mintage	F	VF	XF	Unc	BU
1999 Proof	Est. 5,000	Value: 165				

KM#804 1/5 CROWN **Weight:** 6.2200 g. **Composition:** 0.9999 Gold .2000 oz. AGW **Obverse:** Queen's portrait **Reverse:** Edward the Confessor, dates **Note:** Similar to 1 Crown, KM#805.

Date	Mintage	F	VF	XF	Unc	BU
1999 Proof	Est. 5,000	Value: 165				

KM#806 1/5 CROWN **Weight:** 6.2200 g. **Composition:** 0.9999 Gold .2000 oz. AGW **Series:** House of Normandy **Obverse:** Queen's portrait **Reverse:** King William I, dates **Note:** Similar to 1 Crown, KM#807.

Date	Mintage	F	VF	XF	Unc	BU
1999 Proof	Est. 5,000	Value: 165				

KM#808 1/5 CROWN **Weight:** 6.2200 g. **Composition:** 0.9999 Gold .2000 oz. AGW **Series:** House of Plantagenet **Obverse:** Queen's portrait **Reverse:** King Richard I, dates **Note:** Similar to 1 Crown, KM#809.

Date	Mintage	F	VF	XF	Unc	BU
1999 Proof	Est. 5,000	Value: 165				

KM#810 1/5 CROWN **Weight:** 6.2200 g. **Composition:** 0.9999 Gold .2000 oz. AGW **Series:** House of Plantagenet **Obverse:** Queen's portrait **Reverse:** King John, dates **Note:** Similar to 1 Crown, KM#811.

Date	Mintage	F	VF	XF	Unc	BU
1999 Proof	Est. 5,000	Value: 165				

KM#812 1/5 CROWN **Weight:** 6.2200 g. **Composition:** 0.9999 Gold .2000 oz. AGW **Series:** House of Lancaster **Obverse:** Queen's portrait **Reverse:** King Henry V, dates **Note:** Similar to 1 Crown, KM#813.

Date	Mintage	F	VF	XF	Unc	BU
1999 Proof	Est. 5,000	Value: 165				

KM#814 1/5 CROWN **Weight:** 6.2200 g. **Composition:** 0.9999 Gold .2000 oz. AGW **Series:** House of York **Obverse:** Queen's portrait **Reverse:** King Richard III, dates **Note:** Similar to 1 Crown, KM#815.

Date	Mintage	F	VF	XF	Unc	BU
1999 Proof	Est. 5,000	Value: 165				

KM#816 1/5 CROWN **Weight:** 6.2200 g. **Composition:** 0.9999 Gold .2000 oz. AGW **Series:** House of Tudor **Obverse:** Queen's portrait **Reverse:** King Henry VIII, dates **Note:** Similar to 1 Crown, KM#817.

Date	Mintage	F	VF	XF	Unc	BU
1999 Proof	Est. 5,000	Value: 165				

KM#818 1/5 CROWN **Weight:** 6.2200 g. **Composition:** 0.9999 Gold .2000 oz. AGW **Series:** House of Tudor **Obverse:** Queen's portrait **Reverse:** Queen Elizabeth I, dates **Note:** Similar to 1 Crown, KM#819.

Date	Mintage	F	VF	XF	Unc	BU
1999 Proof	Est. 5,000	Value: 165				

KM#820 1/5 CROWN **Weight:** 6.2200 g. **Composition:** 0.9999 Gold .2000 oz. AGW **Series:** House of Stuart **Obverse:** Queen's portrait **Reverse:** King Charles I, dates **Note:** Similar to 1 Crown, KM#821.

Date	Mintage	F	VF	XF	Unc	BU
1999 Proof	Est. 5,000	Value: 165				

KM#822 1/5 CROWN **Weight:** 6.2200 g. **Composition:** 0.9999 Gold .2000 oz. AGW **Series:** House of Stuart **Obverse:** Queen's portrait **Reverse:** King Charles II, dates **Note:** Similar to 1 Crown, KM#823.

Date	Mintage	F	VF	XF	Unc	BU
1999 Proof	Est. 5,000	Value: 165				

KM#824 1/5 CROWN **Weight:** 6.2200 g. **Composition:** 0.9999 Gold .2000 oz. AGW **Subject:** The Wedding of Prince Edward and Miss Sophie Rhys-Jones **Obverse:** Queen's portrait **Reverse:** Prince and bride **Note:** Similar to 1 Crown, KM#826.

Date	Mintage	F	VF	XF	Unc	BU
1999 Proof	Est. 5,000	Value: 165				

KM#826 1/5 CROWN **Weight:** 6.2200 g. **Composition:** 0.9999 Gold .2000 oz. AGW **Subject:** The Wedding of Prince Edward and Miss Sophie Rhys-Jones **Obverse:** Queen's portrait **Reverse:** St. George's Chapel **Note:** Similar to 1 Crown, KM#827.

Date	Mintage	F	VF	XF	Unc	BU
1999 Proof	Est. 5,000	Value: 165				

KM#834 1/5 CROWN **Weight:** 6.2200 g. **Composition:** 0.9999 Gold .2000 oz. AGW **Subject:** The Life of Queen Elizabeth **Obverse:** Queen's portrait **Reverse:** 1905 portrait of Queen Mother as a girl **Note:** Similar to 1 Crown, KM#835.

Date	Mintage	F	VF	XF	Unc	BU
1999 Proof	Est. 5,000	Value: 165				

KM#836 1/5 CROWN **Weight:** 6.2200 g. **Composition:** 0.9999 Gold .2000 oz. AGW **Subject:** The Life of Queen Elizabeth **Obverse:** Queen's portrait **Reverse:** 1918 portrait of Queen Mother with wounded veteran **Note:** Similar to 1 Crown, KM#837.

Date	Mintage	F	VF	XF	Unc	BU
1999 Proof	Est. 5,000	Value: 165				

KM#838 1/5 CROWN **Weight:** 6.2200 g. **Composition:** 0.9999 Gold .2000 oz. AGW **Subject:** The Life of Queen Elizabeth **Obverse:** Queen's portrait **Reverse:** 1923 wedding portrait **Note:** Similar to 1 Crown, KM#839.

Date	Mintage	F	VF	XF	Unc	BU
1999 Proof	Est. 5,000	Value: 165				

KM#840 1/5 CROWN **Weight:** 6.2200 g. **Composition:** 0.9999 Gold .2000 oz. AGW **Subject:** The Life of Queen Elizabeth **Obverse:** Queen's portrait **Reverse:** 1936 family portrait **Note:** Similar to 1 Crown, KM#841.

Date	Mintage	F	VF	XF	Unc	BU
1999 Proof	Est. 5,000	Value: 165				

KM#843 1/5 CROWN **Weight:** 6.2200 g. **Composition:** 0.9999 Gold .2000 oz. AGW **Subject:** The World of War **Obverse:** Queen's portrait **Reverse:** Franklin D. Roosevelt and Zero fighter **Note:** Similar to 1 Crown, KM#843.1.

Date	Mintage	F	VF	XF	Unc	BU
1999 Proof	—	Value: 165				

KM#844 1/5 CROWN **Weight:** 6.2200 g. **Composition:** 0.9999 Gold .2000 oz. AGW **Subject:** The World At War **Obverse:** Queen's portrait **Reverse:** Operation Manna, bomber dropping food packets **Note:** Similar to 1 Crown, KM#845.

Date	Mintage	F	VF	XF	Unc	BU
1999 Proof	Est. 5,000	Value: 165				

KM#847 1/5 CROWN **Weight:** 6.2200 g. **Composition:** 0.9999 Gold .2000 oz. AGW **Subject:** The World At War **Obverse:** Queen's portrait **Reverse:** Robert Oppenheimer, B-29 and mushroom cloud **Note:** Similar to 1 Crown, KM#847.

Date	Mintage	F	VF	XF	Unc	BU
1999 Proof	Est. 5,000	Value: 165				

KM#848 1/5 CROWN **Weight:** 6.2200 g. **Composition:** 0.9999 Gold .2000 oz. AGW **Subject:** The World At War **Obverse:** Queen's portrait **Reverse:** Barnes Wallis portrait, bomber above dam **Note:** Similar to 1 Crown, KM#849.

Date	Mintage	F	VF	XF	Unc	BU
1999 Proof	Est. 5,000	Value: 165				

KM# 850 1/5 CROWN **Weight:** 6.2200 g. **Composition:** 0.9999 Gold .2000 oz. AGW **Subject:** The World At War **Obverse:** Queen's portrait **Reverse:** Douglas Bader portrait, planes in combat **Note:** Similar to 1 Crown, KM#851.

Date	Mintage	F	VF	XF	Unc	BU
1999 Proof	Est. 5,000	Value: 165				

KM# 852 1/5 CROWN **Weight:** 6.2200 g. **Composition:** 0.9999 Gold .2000 oz. AGW **Subject:** The World At War **Obverse:** Queen's portrait **Reverse:** Winston Churchill, crowd **Note:** Similar to 1 Crown, KM#853.

Date	Mintage	F	VF	XF	Unc	BU
1999 Proof	Est. 5,000	Value: 165				

KM# 854 1/5 CROWN **Weight:** 6.2200 g. **Composition:** 0.9999 Gold .2000 oz. AGW **Subject:** The World At War **Obverse:** Queen's portrait **Reverse:** Tirpitz, battleship and sailor **Note:** Similar to 1 Crown, KM#855.

Date	Mintage	F	VF	XF	Unc	BU
1999 Proof	Est. 5,000	Value: 165				

KM# 856 1/5 CROWN **Weight:** 6.2200 g. **Composition:** 0.9999 Gold .2000 oz. AGW **Subject:** The World At War **Obverse:** Queen's portrait **Reverse:** Soldier kissing child goodbye **Note:** Similar to 1 Crown, KM#857.

Date	Mintage	F	VF	XF	Unc	BU
1999 Proof	Est. 5,000	Value: 165				

KM# 858 1/5 CROWN **Weight:** 6.2200 g. **Composition:** 0.9999 Gold .2000 oz. AGW **Subject:** The World At War **Obverse:** Queen's portrait **Reverse:** 2 firemen in action after air raid **Note:** Similar to 1 Crown, KM#859.

Date	Mintage	F	VF	XF	Unc	BU
1999 Proof	Est. 5,000	Value: 165				

KM# 860 1/5 CROWN **Weight:** 6.2200 g. **Composition:** 0.9999 Gold .2000 oz. AGW **Subject:** The World At War **Obverse:** Queen's portrait **Reverse:** D-Day landing scene **Note:** Similar to 1 Crown, KM#861.

Date	Mintage	F	VF	XF	Unc	BU
1999 Proof	Est. 5,000	Value: 165				

KM# 862 1/5 CROWN **Weight:** 6.2200 g. **Composition:** 0.9999 Gold .2000 oz. AGW **Subject:** The World At War **Obverse:** Queen's portrait **Reverse:** Operation Heavywater military skier **Note:** Similar to 1 Crown, KM#863.

Date	Mintage	F	VF	XF	Unc	BU
1999 Proof	Est. 5,000	Value: 165				

KM# 864 1/5 CROWN **Weight:** 6.2200 g. **Composition:** 0.9999 Gold .2000 oz. AGW **Subject:** The World At War **Obverse:** Queen's portrait **Reverse:** German tanks in Russia **Note:** Similar to 1 Crown, KM#865.

Date	Mintage	F	VF	XF	Unc	BU
1999 Proof	Est. 5,000	Value: 165				

KM# 786 1/5 CROWN **Weight:** 6.2200 g. **Composition:** 0.9999 Gold .2000 oz. AGW **Series:** Summer Olympics - Sydney **Obverse:** Queen's portrait **Reverse:** Sailboats and platypus **Note:** Similar to 1 Crown, KM#787.

Date	Mintage	F	VF	XF	Unc	BU
1999 Proof	Est. 5,000	Value: 165				

KM# 788 1/5 CROWN **Weight:** 6.2200 g. **Composition:** 0.9999 Gold .2000 oz. AGW **Series:** Summer Olympics - Sydney **Obverse:** Queen's portrait **Reverse:** Swimmer and koala bear **Note:** Similar to 1 Crown, KM#789.

Date	Mintage	F	VF	XF	Unc	BU
1999 Proof	Est. 5,000	Value: 165				

KM# 792 1/5 CROWN **Weight:** 6.2200 g. **Composition:** 0.9999 Gold .2000 oz. AGW **Series:** Summer Olympics - Sydney **Obverse:** Queen's portrait **Reverse:** Man with torch and dog **Note:** Similar to 1 Crown, KM#793.

Date	Mintage	F	VF	XF	Unc	BU
1999 Proof	Est. 5,000	Value: 165				

KM# 796 1/5 CROWN **Weight:** 6.2200 g. **Composition:** 0.9999 Gold .2000 oz. AGW **Subject:** Millennium 2000 **Obverse:** Queen's portrait **Reverse:** Sundial, digital clock face, candle and traditional clock face **Note:** Similar to 5 Pounds, KM#797.

Date	Mintage	F	VF	XF	Unc	BU
1999 Proof	Est. 5,000	Value: 165				

KM# 781.1 1/5 CROWN **Weight:** 6.2200 g. **Composition:** 0.9999 Gold .2000 oz. AGW **Subject:** 1999 Year of the Rabbit **Obverse:** Queen's portrait **Reverse:** Rabbit reading, sparrow, Chinese characters

Date	Mintage	F	VF	XF	Unc	BU
1999 Proof	Est. 3,500	Value: 165				

KM# 781.2 1/5 CROWN **Weight:** 6.2200 g. **Composition:** 0.9999 Gold .2000 oz. AGW **Reverse:** Rabbit reading, sparrow. Without Chinese characters

Date	Mintage	F	VF	XF	Unc	BU
1999 Proof	Inc. above	Value: 165				

KM# 781.1a 1/5 CROWN **Weight:** 6.2200 g. **Composition:** 0.9950 Platinum .2000 oz. APW **Subject:** 1999 Year of the Rabbit **Obverse:** Queen's portrait **Reverse:** Rabbit reading, sparrow, Chinese characters

Date	Mintage	F	VF	XF	Unc	BU
1999 Proof	Est. 1,500	Value: 200				

KM# 781.2a 1/5 CROWN **Weight:** 6.2200 g. **Composition:** 0.9950 Platinum .2000 oz. APW **Reverse:** Rabbit reading, sparrow; without Chinese characters

Date	Mintage	F	VF	XF	Unc	BU
1999 Proof	Inc. above	Value: 200				

KM# 784 1/5 CROWN **Weight:** 6.2200 g. **Composition:** 0.9999 Gold .2000 oz. AGW **Series:** Summer Olympics - Sydney **Obverse:** Queen's portrait **Reverse:** Broad Jumper with kangaroo

Date	Mintage	F	VF	XF	Unc	BU
1999 Proof	Est. 5,000	Value: 165				

KM# 790 1/5 CROWN **Weight:** 6.2200 g. **Composition:** 0.9999 Gold .2000 oz. AGW **Series:** Summer Olympics - Sydney **Obverse:** Queen's portrait **Reverse:** Two oarsmen and cockatoos

Date	Mintage	F	VF	XF	Unc	BU
1999 Proof	Est. 5,000	Value: 165				

KM# 794 1/5 CROWN **Weight:** 6.2200 g. **Composition:** 0.9999 Gold .2000 oz. AGW **Series:** Summer Olympics - Sydney **Obverse:** Queen's portrait **Reverse:** Torch runner, portrait of Aboriginal and Ayers Rock

Date	Mintage	F	VF	XF	Unc	BU
1999 Proof	Est. 5,000	Value: 165				

KM# 870 1/5 CROWN **Weight:** 6.2200 g. **Composition:** 0.9999 Gold .2000 oz. AGW **Series:** Queen Mother **Obverse:** Bust Queen right **Reverse:** 1937 Coronation scene

Date	Mintage	F	VF	XF	Unc	BU
2000 Proof	5,000	Value: 175				

KM# 872 1/5 CROWN **Weight:** 6.2200 g. **Composition:** 0.9999 Gold .2000 oz. AGW **Series:** Queen Mother **Obverse:** Bust Queen right **Reverse:** 1938 Visit to France

Date	Mintage	F	VF	XF	Unc	BU
2000 Proof	5,000	Value: 175				

KM# 874 1/5 CROWN **Weight:** 6.2200 g. **Composition:** 0.9999 Gold .2000 oz. AGW **Series:** Queen Mother **Obverse:** Bust Queen right **Reverse:** 1940 Bomb damage

Date	Mintage	F	VF	XF	Unc	BU
2000 Proof	5,000	Value: 175				

KM# 876 1/5 CROWN **Weight:** 6.2200 g. **Composition:** 0.9999 Gold .2000 oz. AGW **Series:** Queen Mother **Obverse:** Bust Queen right

Date	Mintage	F	VF	XF	Unc	BU
2000 Proof	5,000	Value: 175				

KM# 879 1/5 CROWN **Weight:** 6.2200 g. **Composition:** 0.9999 Gold .2000 oz. AGW **Subject:** 18th Birthday of Prince William **Obverse:** Bust Queen right **Reverse:** Bust Prince William facing **Edge:** Reeded

Date	Mintage	F	VF	XF	Unc	BU
2000 Proof	5,000	Value: 175				

KM# 881 1/5 CROWN **Weight:** 6.2200 g. **Composition:** 0.9999 Gold .2000 oz. AGW **Series:** 100th Birthday of the Queen Mother **Obverse:** Bust Queen right **Reverse:** Queen Mother's portrait facing **Note:** Queen Mother's portrait has a real diamond chip (.015) set in her crown.

Date	Mintage	F	VF	XF	Unc	BU
2000 Proof	2,000	Value: 175				

KM# 902 1/5 CROWN **Weight:** 6.2200 g. **Composition:** 0.9999 Gold .2000 oz. AGW **Subject:** Queen Mother **Obverse:** Queen's portrait **Reverse:** 1953 Coronation scene **Edge:** Reeded **Size:** 22 mm.

Date	Mintage	F	VF	XF	Unc	BU
2001 Proof	5,000	Value: 175				

KM# 903 1/5 CROWN **Weight:** 6.2200 g. **Composition:** 0.9999 Gold .2000 oz. AGW **Obverse:** Queen's portrait **Reverse:** Queen Mother and Prince Charles in 1954

Date	Mintage	F	VF	XF	Unc	BU
2001 Proof	5,000	Value: 175				

KM# 909 1/5 CROWN **Weight:** 6.2200 g. **Composition:** 0.9999 Gold .2000 oz. AGW **Series:** Victorian Era **Subject:** Victoria's Coronation 1838 **Obverse:** Queen's portrait **Reverse:** 1838 Coronation scene **Edge:** Reeded **Size:** 22 mm.

Date	Mintage	F	VF	XF	Unc	BU
2001 Proof	5,000	Value: 175				

KM# 909.1 1/5 CROWN **Weight:** 6.2200 g. **Composition:** 0.9999 Gold Clad Silver .2000 oz. **Series:** Victorian Era **Reverse:** 1838 Coronation scene with a tiny emerald set in the field below the 1838 date **Edge:** Reeded **Size:** 22 mm.

Date	Mintage	F	VF	XF	Unc	BU
2001 Proof	2,001	Value: 200				

KM# 911.1 1/5 CROWN **Weight:** 6.2200 g. **Composition:** 0.9999 Gold .2000 oz. AGW **Series:** Victorian Era **Subject:** Empress of India 1876 **Obverse:** Queen's portrait **Reverse:** Crowned portrait of Victoria and two elephants **Edge:** Reeded **Size:** 22 mm.

Date	Mintage	F	VF	XF	Unc	BU
2001 Proof	5,000	Value: 175				

KM# 911.2 1/5 CROWN **Weight:** 6.2200 g. **Composition:** 0.9999 Gold .2000 oz. AGW **Series:** Victorian Era **Reverse:** Same but with a tiny ruby set in the field behind Victoria's head **Edge:** Reeded **Size:** 22 mm.

Date	Mintage	F	VF	XF	Unc	BU
2001 Proof	2,001	Value: 200				

KM# 913.1 1/5 CROWN **Weight:** 6.2200 g. **Composition:** 0.9999 Gold .2000 oz. AGW **Series:** Victorian Era **Subject:** Diamond Jubilee 1897 **Obverse:** Queen's portrait **Reverse:** Victoria's cameo portrait above naval ships **Edge:** Reeded **Size:** 22 mm.

Date	Mintage	F	VF	XF	Unc	BU
2001 Proof	5,000	Value: 175				

KM# 913.2 1/5 CROWN **Weight:** 6.2200 g. **Composition:** 0.9999 Gold .2000 oz. AGW **Series:** Victorian Era **Reverse:** Same but with a tiny diamond set at the top of the fourth mast **Edge:** Reeded **Size:** 22 mm.

Date	Mintage	F	VF	XF	Unc	BU
2001 Proof	2,001	Value: 200				

KM# 915.1 1/5 CROWN **Weight:** 6.2200 g. **Composition:** 0.9999 Gold .2000 oz. AGW **Series:** Victorian Era **Subject:** Victoria's Death 1901 **Obverse:** Queen's portrait **Reverse:** Victoria's cameo portrait and Osborne Manor **Edge:** Reeded **Size:** 22 mm.

Date	Mintage	F	VF	XF	Unc	BU
2001 Proof	5,000	Value: 175				

KM# 915.2 1/5 CROWN **Weight:** 6.2200 g. **Composition:** 0.9999 Gold .2000 oz. AGW **Series:** Victorian Era **Reverse:** Same but with a tiny sapphire set in the field between the towers **Edge:** Reeded **Size:** 22 mm.

Date	Mintage	F	VF	XF	Unc	BU
2001 Proof	2,001	Value: 200				

KM# 921 1/5 CROWN **Weight:** 6.2200 g. **Composition:** 0.9999 Gold .2000 oz. AGW **Series:** Victorian Era **Subject:** Charles Dickens **Obverse:** Queen's portrait **Reverse:** Portrait and scene from "Oliver Twist" **Edge:** Reeded **Size:** 22 mm.

Date	Mintage	F	VF	XF	Unc	BU
2001 Proof	5,000	Value: 175				

KM# 917 1/5 CROWN **Weight:** 6.2200 g. **Composition:** 0.9999 Gold .2000 oz. AGW **Series:** Victorian Era **Subject:** Prince Albert and the Great Exhibition 1851 **Obverse:** Queen's portrait **Reverse:** Albert's cameo portrait and the exhibit hall **Edge:** Reeded **Size:** 22 mm.

Date	Mintage	F	VF	XF	Unc	BU
2001 Proof	5,000	Value: 175				

KM# 919 1/5 CROWN **Weight:** 6.2200 g. **Composition:** 0.9999 Gold .2000 oz. AGW **Series:** Victorian Era **Subject:** Isambard K. Brunel **Obverse:** Queen's portrait **Reverse:** Portrait in top hat and railroad bridge **Edge:** Reeded **Size:** 22 mm.

Date	Mintage	F	VF	XF	Unc	BU
2001 Proof	5,000	Value: 175				

KM# 923 1/5 CROWN **Weight:** 6.2200 g. **Composition:** 0.9999 Gold .2000 oz. AGW **Series:** Victorian Era **Subject:** Charles Darwin **Obverse:** Queen's portrait **Reverse:** Portrait, ship and a squatting aboriginal figure **Edge:** Reeded **Size:** 22 mm.

Date	Mintage	F	VF	XF	Unc	BU
2001 Proof	5,000	Value: 175				

KM# 925 1/5 CROWN **Weight:** 6.2200 g. **Composition:** 0.9999 Gold .2000 oz. AGW **Series:** Mythology of the Solar System **Obverse:** Queen's portrait **Reverse:** Standing goddess with snake basket **Edge:** Reeded **Size:** 22 mm.

Date	Mintage	F	VF	XF	Unc	BU
2001 Proof	5,000	Value: 175				

KM# 926 1/5 CROWN **Ring Weight:** 12.1100 g. **Ring Composition:** 0.9999 Gold .3893 oz. AGW **Center Weight:** 5.7900 g. **Center Composition:** 0.9250 Silver .1722 oz. ASW **Series:** Mythology of the Solar System **Subject:** Solar System **Obverse:** Queen's portrait **Reverse:** Standing goddess with snake basket **Edge:** Reeded **Size:** 32.25 mm.

Date	Mintage	F	VF	XF	Unc	BU
2001 In Proof sets only	999	Value: 350				

KM# 929.1 1/5 CROWN **Weight:** 6.2200 g. **Composition:** 0.9999 Gold .2000 oz. AGW **Series:** Mythology of the Solar System **Subject:** Sun **Obverse:** Queen's portrait **Reverse:** Helios in chariot and the sun **Edge:** Reeded **Size:** 22 mm.

Date	Mintage	F	VF	XF	Unc	BU
2001 Proof	5,000	Value: 175				

KM# 929.2 1/5 CROWN **Weight:** 6.2200 g. **Composition:** 0.9999 Gold .2000 oz. AGW **Series:** Mythology of the Solar System **Reverse:** Similar but with a fiery hologram in the sun **Edge:** Reeded **Size:** 22 mm.

Date	Mintage	F	VF	XF	Unc	BU
2001 In Proof sets only	999	Value: 350				

KM# 931.1 1/5 CROWN **Weight:** 6.2200 g. **Composition:** 0.9999 Gold .2000 oz. AGW **Series:** Mythology of the Solar System **Subject:** Moon **Obverse:** Queen's portrait **Reverse:** Goddess Diana and the moon **Edge:** Reeded **Size:** 22 mm.

Date	Mintage	F	VF	XF	Unc	BU
2001 Proof	5,000	Value: 175				

KM# 931.2 1/5 CROWN Weight: 6.2200 g. **Composition:** 0.9999 Gold .2000 oz. AGW **Series:** Mythology of the Solar System **Reverse:** Similar but with a small pearl set in the moon **Edge:** Reeded **Size:** 22 mm.

Date	Mintage	F	VF	XF	Unc	BU
2001 In Proof sets only	999	Value: 350				

KM# 933.1 1/5 CROWN Weight: 6.2200 g. **Composition:** 0.9999 Gold .2000 oz. AGW **Series:** Mythology of the Solar System **Subject:** Earth **Obverse:** Queen's portrait **Reverse:** Atlas carrying the earth **Edge:** Reeded **Size:** 22 mm.

Date	Mintage	F	VF	XF	Unc	BU
2001 Proof	5,000	Value: 175				

KM# 933.2 1/5 CROWN Weight: 6.2200 g. **Composition:** 0.9999 Gold .2000 oz. AGW **Series:** Mythology of the Solar System **Reverse:** Similar but with a tiny diamond set in the earth **Edge:** Reeded **Size:** 22 mm.

Date	Mintage	F	VF	XF	Unc	BU
2001 In Proof sets only	999	Value: 350				

KM# 935 1/5 CROWN Weight: 6.2200 g. **Composition:** 0.9999 Gold .2000 oz. AGW **Series:** Mythology of the Solar System **Subject:** Neptune **Obverse:** Queen's portrait **Reverse:** Seated god with trident and ringed planet **Edge:** Reeded **Size:** 22 mm.

Date	Mintage	F	VF	XF	Unc	BU
2001 Proof	5,000	Value: 175				

KM# 937 1/5 CROWN Weight: 6.2200 g. **Composition:** 0.9999 Gold .2000 oz. AGW **Series:** Mythology of the Solar System **Subject:** Jupiter **Obverse:** Queen's portrait **Reverse:** Seated god with lightening bolts and a planet **Edge:** Reeded **Size:** 22 mm.

Date	Mintage	F	VF	XF	Unc	BU
2001 Proof	5,000	Value: 175				

KM# 939 1/5 CROWN Weight: 6.2200 g. **Composition:** 0.9999 Gold .2000 oz. AGW **Series:** Mythology of the Solar System **Subject:** Mars **Obverse:** Queen's portrait **Reverse:** Standing Roman solider and a planet **Edge:** Reeded **Size:** 22 mm.

Date	Mintage	F	VF	XF	Unc	BU
2001 Proof	5,000	Value: 175				

KM# 941 1/5 CROWN Weight: 6.2200 g. **Composition:** 0.9999 Gold .2000 oz. AGW **Series:** Mythology of the Solar System **Subject:** Mercury **Obverse:** Queen's portrait **Reverse:** Seated god with cadceus and a planet **Edge:** Reeded **Size:** 22 mm.

Date	Mintage	F	VF	XF	Unc	BU
2001 Proof	5,000	Value: 175				

KM# 943 1/5 CROWN Weight: 6.2200 g. **Composition:** 0.9999 Gold .2000 oz. AGW **Series:** Mythology of the Solar System **Subject:** Uranus **Obverse:** Queen's portrait **Reverse:** Seated god with scepter **Edge:** Reeded **Size:** 22 mm.

Date	Mintage	F	VF	XF	Unc	BU
2001 Proof	5,000	Value: 175				

KM# 945 1/5 CROWN Weight: 6.2200 g. **Composition:** 0.9999 Gold .2000 oz. AGW **Series:** Mythology of the Solar System **Subject:** Saturn **Obverse:** Queen's portrait **Reverse:** Seated god with long handled sickle and a ringed planet **Edge:** Reeded **Size:** 22 mm.

Date	Mintage	F	VF	XF	Unc	BU
2001 Proof	5,000	Value: 175				

KM# 947 1/5 CROWN Weight: 6.2200 g. **Composition:** 0.9999 Gold .2000 oz. AGW **Series:** Mythology of the Solar System **Subject:** Pluto **Obverse:** Queen's portrait **Reverse:** Seated god with dogs and a planet **Edge:** Reeded **Size:** 22 mm.

Date	Mintage	F	VF	XF	Unc	BU
2001 Proof	5,000	Value: 175				

KM# 949 1/5 CROWN Weight: 6.2200 g. **Composition:** 0.9999 Gold .2000 oz. AGW **Series:** Mythology of the Solar System **Subject:** Venus **Obverse:** Queen's portrait **Reverse:** Goddess seated on a half shell **Edge:** Reeded **Size:** 22 mm.

Date	Mintage	F	VF	XF	Unc	BU
2001 Proof	5,000	Value: 175				

KM# 951 1/5 CROWN Weight: 6.2200 g. **Composition:** 0.9999 Gold .2000 oz. AGW **Subject:** Queen's 76th Birthday **Obverse:** Queen's portrait **Reverse:** Queen in Order of the Garter robes with a tiny inset diamond **Edge:** Reeded **Size:** 22 mm.

Date	Mintage	F	VF	XF	Unc	BU
2001 Proof	2,001	Value: 200				

KM# 954 1/5 CROWN Weight: 6.2200 g. **Composition:** 0.9999 Gold .2000 oz. AGW **Series:** Victorian Age Part II **Subject:** Victoria's Accession to the Throne **Obverse:** Queen's portrait **Reverse:** Victoria learning of her accession **Edge:** Reeded **Size:** 22 mm.

Date	Mintage	F	VF	XF	Unc	BU
2001 Proof	5,000	Value: 175				

KM# 956 1/5 CROWN Weight: 6.2200 g. **Composition:** 0.9999 Gold .2000 oz. AGW **Series:** Victorian Age Part II **Subject:** Royal Family **Reverse:** Victoria and Albert seated with children **Edge:** Reeded **Size:** 22 mm.

Date	Mintage	F	VF	XF	Unc	BU
2001 Proof	5,000	Value: 175				

KM# 958 1/5 CROWN Weight: 6.2200 g. **Composition:** 0.9999 Gold .2000 oz. AGW **Series:** Victorian Age Part II **Subject:** Victoria in Scotland **Reverse:** Victoria on horse and servant **Edge:** Reeded **Size:** 22 mm.

Date	Mintage	F	VF	XF	Unc	BU
2001 Proof	5,000	Value: 175				

KM# 960 1/5 CROWN Weight: 6.2200 g. **Composition:** 0.9999 Gold .2000 oz. AGW **Series:** Victorian Age Part II **Reverse:** Portraits of Gladstone and Disaraeli **Edge:** Reeded **Size:** 22 mm.

Date	Mintage	F	VF	XF	Unc	BU
2001 Proof	5,000	Value: 175				

KM# 962 1/5 CROWN Weight: 6.2200 g. **Composition:** 0.9999 Gold .2000 oz. AGW **Series:** Victorian Age Part II **Reverse:** Florence Nightingale holding lantern **Edge:** Reeded **Size:** 22 mm.

Date	Mintage	F	VF	XF	Unc	BU
2001 Proof	5,000	Value: 175				

KM# 964 1/5 CROWN Weight: 6.2200 g. **Composition:** 0.9999 Gold .2000 oz. AGW **Series:** Victorian Age Part II **Reverse:** Lord Tennyson with the Light Brigade in background **Edge:** Reeded **Size:** 22 mm.

Date	Mintage	F	VF	XF	Unc	BU
2001 Proof	5,000	Value: 175				

KM# 966 1/5 CROWN Weight: 6.2200 g. **Composition:** 0.9999 Gold .2000 oz. AGW **Series:** Victorian Age Part II **Reverse:** Stanley meeting Dr. Livingstone **Edge:** Reeded **Size:** 22 mm.

Date	Mintage	F	VF	XF	Unc	BU
2001 Proof	5,000	Value: 175				

KM# 968 1/5 CROWN Weight: 6.2200 g. **Composition:** 0.9999 Gold .2000 oz. AGW **Series:** Victorian Age Part II **Reverse:** Bronte sisters **Edge:** Reeded **Size:** 22 mm.

Date	Mintage	F	VF	XF	Unc	BU
2001 Proof	5,000	Value: 175				

KM# 978 1/5 CROWN Weight: 6.2200 g. **Composition:** 0.9990 Gold 0.1998 oz. AGW **Subject:** Queen Mother's Life **Obverse:** Bust of Queen Elizabeth II right **Reverse:** Prince William's christening scene **Edge:** Reeded **Size:** 22 mm.

Date	Mintage	F	VF	XF	Unc	BU
2002 Proof	5,000	Value: 175				

KM# 990 1/5 CROWN Weight: 6.2200 g. **Composition:** 0.9990 Gold 0.1998 oz. AGW **Subject:** Peter Rabbit Centennial **Obverse:** Bust of Queen Elizabeth II right **Reverse:** Peter Rabbit **Edge:** Reeded **Size:** 22 mm.

Date	Mintage	F	VF	XF	Unc	BU
2002 Proof	3,500	Value: 175				

KM# 990a 1/5 CROWN Weight: 6.2200 g. **Composition:** 0.9990 Platinum 0.1998 oz. APW **Subject:** Peter Rabbit Centennial **Obverse:** Bust of Queen Elizabeth II right **Reverse:** Peter Rabbit **Edge:** Reeded **Size:** 22 mm.

Date	Mintage	F	VF	XF	Unc	BU
2002 Proof	1,500	Value: 205				

KM# 980 1/5 CROWN Weight: 6.2200 g. **Composition:** 0.9999 Gold 0.2 oz. AGW **Subject:** World Cup Soccer **Obverse:** Bust of Queen Elizabeth II right **Reverse:** Two players about to collide **Edge:** Reeded **Size:** 22 mm.

Date	Mintage	F	VF	XF	Unc	BU
2002 Proof	5,000	Value: 175				

KM# 982 1/5 CROWN Weight: 6.2200 g. **Composition:** 0.9999 Gold 0.2 oz. AGW **Subject:** World Cup Soccer **Obverse:** Bust of Queen Elizabeth II right **Reverse:** Two players facing viewer **Edge:** Reeded **Size:** 22 mm.

Date	Mintage	F	VF	XF	Unc	BU
2002 Proof	5,000	Value: 175				

KM# 984 1/5 CROWN Weight: 6.2200 g. **Composition:** 0.9999 Gold 0.2 oz. AGW **Subject:** World Cup Soccer **Obverse:** Bust of Queen Elizabeth II right **Reverse:** Two horizontal players **Edge:** Reeded **Size:** 22 mm.

Date	Mintage	F	VF	XF	Unc	BU
2002 Proof	5,000	Value: 175				

KM# 986 1/5 CROWN Weight: 6.2200 g. **Composition:** 0.9999 Gold 0.2 oz. AGW **Subject:** World Cup Soccer **Obverse:** Bust of Queen Elizabeth II right **Reverse:** Two players moving to the left **Edge:** Reeded **Size:** 22 mm.

Date	Mintage	F	VF	XF	Unc	BU
2002 Proof	5,000	Value: 175				

KM# 993 1/5 CROWN Weight: 6.2200 g. **Composition:** 0.3750 Gold 0.075 oz. AGW **Subject:** Queen's Golden Jubilee **Obverse:** Bust of Queen Elizabeth II right **Reverse:** Royal couple and tree house **Edge:** Reeded **Size:** 22 mm.

Date	Mintage	F	VF	XF	Unc	BU
2002 Proof	5,000	Value: 70.00				

KM# 993a 1/5 CROWN Weight: 6.2200 g. **Composition:** 0.9999 Gold 0.2 oz. AGW **Subject:** Queen's Golden Jubilee **Obverse:** Bust of Queen Elizabeth II right **Reverse:** Royal couple and tree house **Edge:** Reeded **Size:** 22 mm.

Date	Mintage	F	VF	XF	Unc	BU
2002 Proof	2,002	Value: 175				

KM# 995 1/5 CROWN Weight: 6.2200 g. **Composition:** 0.3750 Gold 0.075 oz. AGW **Subject:** Queen's Golden Jubilee **Obverse:** Bust of Queen Elizabeth II right **Reverse:** Royal coach **Edge:** Reeded **Size:** 22 mm.

Date	Mintage	F	VF	XF	Unc	BU
2002 Proof	5,000	Value: 70.00				

KM# 995a 1/5 CROWN Weight: 6.2200 g. **Composition:** 0.9999 Gold 0.2 oz. AGW **Subject:** Queen's Golden Jubilee **Obverse:** Bust of Queen Elizabeth II right **Reverse:** Royal coach **Edge:** Reeded **Size:** 22 mm.

Date	Mintage	F	VF	XF	Unc	BU
2002 Proof	2,002	Value: 175				

KM# 997 1/5 CROWN Weight: 6.2200 g. **Composition:** 0.3750 Gold 0.075 oz. AGW **Subject:** Queen's Golden Jubilee **Obverse:** Bust of Queen Elizabeth II right **Reverse:** Queen holding baby **Edge:** Reeded **Size:** 22 mm.

Date	Mintage	F	VF	XF	Unc	BU
2002 Proof	5,000	Value: 70.00				

KM# 997a 1/5 CROWN Weight: 6.2200 g. **Composition:** 0.9999 Gold 0.2 oz. AGW **Subject:** Queen's Golden Jubilee **Obverse:** Bust of Queen Elizabeth II right **Reverse:** Queen holding baby **Edge:** Reeded **Size:** 22 mm.

Date	Mintage	F	VF	XF	Unc	BU
2002 Proof	2,002	Value: 175				

KM# 999 1/5 CROWN Weight: 6.2200 g. **Composition:** 0.3750 Gold 0.075 oz. AGW **Subject:** Queen's Golden Jubilee **Obverse:** Bust of Queen Elizabeth II right **Reverse:** Yacht under Tower bridge **Edge:** Reeded **Size:** 22 mm.

Date	Mintage	F	VF	XF	Unc	BU
2002 Proof	5,000	Value: 70.00				

KM# 999a 1/5 CROWN Weight: 6.2200 g. **Composition:** 0.9999 Gold 0.2 oz. AGW **Subject:** Queen's Golden Jubilee **Obverse:** Bust of Queen Elizabeth II right **Reverse:** Yacht under Tower bridge **Edge:** Reeded **Size:** 22 mm.

Date	Mintage	F	VF	XF	Unc	BU
2002 Proof	2,002	Value: 175				

KM# 1001 1/5 CROWN Weight: 6.2200 g. **Composition:** 0.9999 Gold 0.2 oz. AGW **Subject:** Queen's Golden Jubilee **Obverse:** Bust of Queen Elizabeth II right **Reverse:** Crown jewels inset with a tiny diamond, ruby, sapphire and emerald **Edge:** Reeded **Size:** 22 mm.

Date	Mintage	F	VF	XF	Unc	BU
2002 Proof	2,002	Value: 175				

KM# 1003 1/5 CROWN Weight: 3.1100 g. **Composition:** 0.9990 Gold-Silver 0.0999 oz. **Series:** Electrum **Obverse:** Bust of Queen Elizabeth II right **Reverse:** Athena **Edge:** Reeded **Size:** 22 mm.

Date	Mintage	F	VF	XF	Unc	BU
2002 Proof	3,500	Value: 95.00				

KM# 1005 1/5 CROWN Weight: 3.1100 g. **Composition:** 0.9990 Gold-Silver 0.0999 oz. **Series:** Electrum **Obverse:** Bust of Queen Elizabeth II right **Reverse:** Hercules **Edge:** Reeded **Size:** 22 mm.

Date	Mintage	F	VF	XF	Unc	BU
2002 Proof	3,500	Value: 95.00				

KM# 1007 1/5 CROWN Weight: 3.1100 g. **Composition:** 0.9990 Gold-Silver 0.0999 oz. **Series:** Electrum **Obverse:** Bust of Queen Elizabeth II right **Reverse:** Pegasus **Edge:** Reeded **Size:** 22 mm.

Date	Mintage	F	VF	XF	Unc	BU
2002 Proof	3,500	Value: 95.00				

KM# 1009 1/5 CROWN Weight: 3.1100 g. **Composition:** 0.9990 Gold-Silver 0.0999 oz. **Series:** Electrum **Obverse:** Bust of Queen Elizabeth II right **Reverse:** Lion and bull **Edge:** Reeded **Size:** 22 mm.

Date	Mintage	F	VF	XF	Unc	BU
2002 Proof	3,500	Value: 95.00				

KM# 1012 1/5 CROWN Weight: 6.2200 g. **Composition:** 0.9999 Gold 0.2 oz. AGW **Subject:** Queen Mother **Obverse:** Bust of Queen Elizabeth II right **Reverse:** Queen Mother trout fishing **Edge:** Reeded **Size:** 22 mm.

Date	Mintage	F	VF	XF	Unc	BU
2002 Proof	5,000	Value: 175				

KM# 1014 1/5 CROWN Weight: 6.2200 g. **Composition:** 0.9999 Gold 0.2 oz. AGW **Subject:** Princess Diana **Obverse:** Bust of Queen Elizabeth II right **Reverse:** Diana's portrait **Edge:** Reeded **Size:** 22 mm.

Date	Mintage	F	VF	XF	Unc	BU
2002 Proof	5,000	Value: 175				

KM# 1018 1/5 CROWN Weight: 6.2200 g. **Composition:** 0.9999 Gold 0.2 oz. AGW **Subject:** Peter Pan **Obverse:** Bust of Queen Elizabeth II right **Reverse:** Peter Pan and Tinkerbell flying above city **Edge:** Reeded **Size:** 22 mm.

Date	Mintage	F	VF	XF	Unc	BU
2002 Proof	5,000	Value: 175				

KM# 1020 1/5 CROWN Weight: 6.2200 g. **Composition:** 0.9999 Gold 0.2 oz. AGW **Subject:** Grand Masonic Lodge **Obverse:** Bust of Queen Elizabeth II right **Reverse:** Masonic seal above Gibraltar **Edge:** Reeded **Size:** 22 mm.

Date	Mintage	F	VF	XF	Unc	BU
2002 Proof	5,000	Value: 175				

KM# 868.2 1/4 CROWN Weight: 7.7800 g. **Composition:** 0.9250 Silver .2314 oz. ASW **Reverse:** Rabbit reading, sparrow; without Chinese characters

Date	Mintage	F	VF	XF	Unc	BU
1999 Proof	Inc. above	Value: 35.00				

KM# 868.1 1/4 CROWN Weight: 7.7800 g. **Composition:** 0.9250 Silver .2314 oz. ASW **Subject:** 1999 The Year of the Rabbit **Obverse:** Queen's portrait **Reverse:** Peter Rabbit reading, sparrow, Chinese characters **Note:** Similar to 1 Crown, KM#783.1.

Date	Mintage	F	VF	XF	Unc	BU
1999 Proof	Est. 25,000	Value: 35.00				

KM# 886 1/2 CROWN Weight: 15.5500 g. **Composition:** 0.9999 Gold .5000 oz. AGW **Subject:** Rotary Club of Gibraltar

Date	Mintage	F	VF	XF	Unc	BU
1991 Proof	5,000	Value: 500				

KM# 127 1/2 CROWN Weight: 15.5500 g. **Composition:** 0.9999 Gold .5000 oz. AGW **Subject:** Japanese Royal Wedding

Date	Mintage	F	VF	XF	Unc	BU
1993 Proof	5,000	Value: 260				

KM# 177 1/2 CROWN Weight: 15.5500 g. **Composition:** 0.9990 Silver .5000 oz. ASW **Series:** WWII Warships **Reverse:** HMS Hood

Date	F	VF	XF	Unc	BU
1993	—	—	—	35.00	—

KM# 198 1/2 CROWN Weight: 15.5500 g. **Composition:** 0.9990 Silver .5000 oz. ASW **Reverse:** Edward VIII

Date	Mintage	F	VF	XF	Unc	BU
1993 Proof	Est. 30,000	Value: 27.50				

KM# 572 1/2 CROWN Weight: 15.5500 g. **Composition:** 0.9990 Silver .5000 oz. ASW **Obverse:** Queen's portrait **Reverse:** Sherlock Holmes smoking pipe

Date	Mintage	F	VF	XF	Unc	BU
1994 Proof	Est. 30,000	Value: 20.00				

KM# 443 1/2 CROWN Weight: 15.5500 g. **Composition:** 0.9999 Gold .5000 oz. AGW **Series:** Peter Rabbit Centennial **Reverse:** Mother and bunnies **Note:** Similar to 1 Crown, KM#444.

Date	Mintage	F	VF	XF	Unc	BU
1994 Proof	Est. 5,000	Value: 350				

KM# 448 1/2 CROWN Weight: 15.5500 g. **Composition:** 0.9999 Gold .5000 oz. AGW **Subject:** Lord Buddha **Note:** Similar to 1 Crown, KM#449.

Date	Mintage	F	VF	XF	Unc	BU
1996 Proof	Est. 5,000	Value: 350				

KM# 381 1/2 CROWN Weight: 15.5500 g. **Composition:** 0.9999 Gold .5000 oz. AGW **Series:** Peter Rabbit Centennial **Reverse:** Peter Rabbit escaping

Date	Mintage	F	VF	XF	Unc	BU
1996 Proof	Est. 5,000	Value: 350				

KM# 372 1/2 CROWN Weight: 15.5500 g. **Composition:** 0.9999 Gold .5000 oz. AGW **Reverse:** Roses **Note:** Similar to 1 Crown, KM#373.

Date	Mintage	F	VF	XF	Unc	BU
1996 Proof	Est. 3,000	Value: 350				

KM# 524 1/2 CROWN Weight: 15.5500 g. **Composition:** 0.9999 Gold .5000 oz. AGW **Subject:** The Tale of Peter Rabbit **Note:** Similar to 1 Crown, KM#525.

Date	Mintage	F	VF	XF	Unc	BU
1997 Proof	Est. 2,500	Value: 350				

KM# 655 1/2 CROWN Weight: 15.5500 g. **Composition:** 0.9999 Gold .5000 oz. AGW **Obverse:** Queen's portrait **Reverse:** Peter Rabbit **Note:** Similar to 1 Crown, KM#656.

Date	Mintage	F	VF	XF	Unc	BU
1998 Proof	Est. 2,500	Value: 325				

KM# 681 1/2 CROWN Weight: 15.5500 g. **Composition:** 0.9999 Gold .5000 oz. AGW **Subject:** Paddington Bear **Obverse:** Queen's portrait **Reverse:** Bear with suitcase **Note:** Similar to 1 Crown, KM#682.

Date	Mintage	F	VF	XF	Unc	BU
1998 Proof	Est. 2,500	Value: 325				

KM# 647 1/2 CROWN Weight: 15.5500 g. **Composition:** 0.9999 Gold .5000 oz. AGW **Obverse:** Queen's portrait **Reverse:** Cupid with hologram heart

Date	Mintage	F	VF	XF	Unc	BU
1998 Proof	Est. 3,500	Value: 325				

KM# 732 1/2 CROWN Weight: 15.5500 g. **Composition:** 0.9999 Gold .5000 oz. AGW **Subject:** Peacocks **Obverse:** Queen's portrait **Reverse:** Pair of peacocks, one with full display in hologram

Date	Mintage	F	VF	XF	Unc	BU
1998 Proof	Est. 3,500	Value: 325				

KM# 895 1/2 CROWN Weight: 15.7800 g. **Composition:** 0.9990 Silver .5068 oz. ASW **Subject:** Cupid **Obverse:** Queen's portrait **Reverse:** Cupid with multicolor holographic heart similar to 1/2 crown KM#-647 but without the metal content statement **Edge:** Reeded **Size:** 32.25 mm.

Date	Mintage	F	VF	XF	Unc	BU
1998 Proof	10,000	Value: 50.00				

KM# 782.2 1/2 CROWN Weight: 15.5500 g. **Composition:** 0.9999 Gold .5000 oz. AGW **Reverse:** Rabbit reading, sparrow. Without Chinese characters

Date		F	VF	XF	Unc	BU
1999		—	—	—	325	—

KM# 782.1 1/2 CROWN Weight: 15.5500 g. **Composition:** 0.9999 Gold .5000 oz. AGW **Subject:** 1999 The Year of the Rabbit **Obverse:** Queen's portrait **Reverse:** Rabbit reading, sparrow, Chinese characters **Note:** Similar to 1 Crown, KM#783.1.

Date	Mintage	F	VF	XF	Unc	BU
1999 Proof	Est. 1,000	Value: 325				

KM# 894 1/2 CROWN Weight: 15.5517 g. **Composition:** 0.9990 Gold .5000 oz. AGW **Edge:** Reeded **Note:** Similar to 1/2 Crown, KM#883.

Date	Mintage	F	VF	XF	Unc	BU
2000 Proof	999	Value: 325				

KM# 883 1/2 CROWN Ring Weight: 9.0000 g. **Ring Composition:** 0.9990 Gold .2893 oz. AGW **Center Composition:** Titanium **Series:** 160th Anniversary **Subject:** Uniform Penny Post **Obverse:** Bust Queen right **Reverse:** Postage stamp design **Edge:** Reeded

Date	Mintage	F	VF	XF	Unc	BU
2000 Proof	5,000	Value: 175				

KM# 991 1/2 CROWN Weight: 15.5500 g. **Composition:** 0.9990 Gold 0.4994 oz. AGW **Subject:** Peter Rabbit Centennial **Obverse:** Bust of Queen Elizabeth II right **Reverse:** Peter Rabbit **Edge:** Reeded **Size:** 30 mm.

Date	Mintage	F	VF	XF	Unc	BU
2002 Proof	1,000	Value: 340				

KM# 1002 1/2 CROWN Weight: 15.5500 g. **Composition:** 0.9999 Gold 0.4999 oz. AGW **Subject:** Queen's Golden Jubilee **Obverse:** Bust of Queen Elizabeth II right **Reverse:** Crown jewels inset with a tiny diamond, ruby, sapphire and emerald **Edge:** Reeded **Size:** 30 mm.

Date	Mintage	F	VF	XF	Unc	BU
2002 Proof	999	Value: 350				

KM# 1004 1/2 CROWN Weight: 7.7750 g. **Composition:** 0.9990 Gold-Silver 0.2497 oz. **Series:** Electrum **Obverse:** Bust of Queen Elizabeth II right **Reverse:** Head of Athena left **Edge:** Reeded **Size:** 32.2 mm.

Date	Mintage	F	VF	XF	Unc	BU
2002 Proof	2,000	Value: 205				

KM# 1006 1/2 CROWN Weight: 7.7750 g. **Composition:** 0.9990 Gold-Silver 0.2497 oz. **Series:** Electrum **Obverse:** Bust of Queen Elizabeth II right **Reverse:** Head of Hercules right **Edge:** Reeded **Size:** 32.2 mm.

Date	Mintage	F	VF	XF	Unc	BU
2002 Proof	2,000	Value: 205				

KM# 1008 1/2 CROWN Weight: 7.7750 g. **Composition:** 0.9990 Gold-Silver 0.2497 oz. **Series:** Electrum **Obverse:** Bust of Queen Elizabeth II right **Reverse:** Pegasus **Edge:** Reeded **Size:** 32.2 mm.

Date	Mintage	F	VF	XF	Unc	BU
2002 Proof	2,000	Value: 205				

KM# 1010 1/2 CROWN Weight: 7.7750 g. **Composition:** 0.9990 Gold-Silver 0.2497 oz. **Series:** Electrum. **Obverse:** Bust of Queen Elizabeth II right **Reverse:** Lion and bull **Edge:** Reeded **Size:** 32.2 mm.

Date	Mintage	F	VF	XF	Unc	BU
2002 Proof	2,000	Value: 205				

KM# 11 CROWN **Composition:** Copper-Nickel **Subject:** 80th Birthday of Queen Mother

Date	F	VF	XF	Unc	BU
1980	—	—	1.50	3.00	—

KM# 11a CROWN **Weight:** 28.2800 g. **Composition:** 0.9250 Silver .8411 oz. ASW **Subject:** 80th Birthday of Queen Mother

Date	Mintage	F	VF	XF	Unc	BU
1980 Proof	Est. 25,000	Value: 12.50				

KM# 12 CROWN **Composition:** Copper-Nickel **Subject:** 175th Anniversary - Death of Nelson

Date	F	VF	XF	Unc	BU
1980	—	—	1.00	2.00	—

KM# 12a CROWN **Weight:** 28.2800 g. **Composition:** 0.9250 Silver .8411 oz. ASW **Subject:** 175th Anniversary - Death of Nelson

Date	Mintage	F	VF	XF	Unc	BU
1980 Proof	Est. 15,000	Value: 20.00				

KM# 14 CROWN **Composition:** Copper-Nickel **Reverse:** Wedding of Prince Charles and Lady Diana

Date	F	VF	XF	Unc	BU
1981	—	—	1.00	2.50	—

KM# 14a CROWN **Weight:** 28.2800 g. **Composition:** 0.9250 Silver .8411 oz. ASW

Date	Mintage	F	VF	XF	Unc	BU
1981 Proof	Est. 30,000	Value: 11.50				

KM# 33 CROWN **Composition:** Copper-Nickel **Series:** World Cup Soccer **Reverse:** Italian flag

Date	F	VF	XF	Unc	BU
1990	—	—	—	3.50	—

KM# 33a CROWN **Weight:** 28.2800 g. **Composition:** 0.9250 Silver .8411 oz. ASW

Date	Mintage	F	VF	XF	Unc	BU
1990 Proof	Est. 30,000	Value: 32.50				

KM# 34 CROWN **Composition:** Copper-Nickel **Series:** World Cup Soccer **Obverse:** Similar to KM#33 **Reverse:** Map of Italy

Date	F	VF	XF	Unc	BU
1990	—	—	—	3.50	—

KM# 34a CROWN **Weight:** 28.2800 g. **Composition:** 0.9250 Silver .8411 oz. ASW

Date	Mintage	F	VF	XF	Unc	BU
1990 Proof	Est. 30,000	Value: 32.50				

KM# 35 CROWN **Composition:** Copper-Nickel **Series:** World Cup Soccer **Obverse:** Similar to KM#33 **Reverse:** Goalie catching ball

Date	F	VF	XF	Unc	BU
1990	—	—	—	3.50	—

KM# 35a CROWN **Weight:** 28.2800 g. **Composition:** 0.9250 Silver .8411 oz. ASW

Date	Mintage	F	VF	XF	Unc	BU
1990 Proof	Est. 30,000	Value: 32.50				

KM# 36 CROWN **Composition:** Copper-Nickel **Series:** World Cup Soccer **Obverse:** Similar to KM#33 **Reverse:** Ball at head

Date	F	VF	XF	Unc	BU
1990	—	—	—	3.50	—

KM# 36a CROWN **Weight:** 28.2800 g. **Composition:** 0.9250 Silver .8411 oz. ASW

Date	Mintage	F	VF	XF	Unc	BU
1990 Proof	Est. 30,000	Value: 32.50				

KM# 37 CROWN **Composition:** Copper-Nickel **Series:** World Cup Soccer **Obverse:** Similar to KM#33 **Reverse:** Ball at feet

Date	F	VF	XF	Unc	BU
1990	—	—	—	3.50	—

KM# 37a CROWN **Weight:** 28.2800 g. **Composition:** 0.9250 Silver .8411 oz. ASW

Date	Mintage	F	VF	XF	Unc	BU
1990 Proof	Est. 30,000	Value: 32.50				

KM# 38 CROWN **Composition:** Copper-Nickel **Series:** World Cup Soccer **Obverse:** Similar to KM#33 **Reverse:** Three players

Date	F	VF	XF	Unc	BU
1990	—	—	—	3.50	—

KM# 38a CROWN **Weight:** 28.2800 g. **Composition:** 0.9250 Silver .8411 oz. ASW

Date	Mintage	F	VF	XF	Unc	BU
1990 Proof	Est. 30,000	Value: 32.50				

KM# 40 CROWN **Composition:** Copper-Nickel **Subject:** 21st Anniversary - Constitution **Obverse:** Similar to KM#33

Date	F	VF	XF	Unc	BU
1990	—	—	—	6.50	—

KM# 40a CROWN **Weight:** 28.2800 g. **Composition:** 0.9250 Silver .8411 oz. ASW

Date	Mintage	F	VF	XF	Unc	BU
1990 Proof	Est. 30,000	Value: 50.00				

KM# 46 CROWN **Composition:** Copper-Nickel **Obverse:** Similar to KM#33. **Reverse:** Queen Mother

Date	F	VF	XF	Unc	BU
1990	—	—	—	4.50	—

KM# 46a CROWN **Weight:** 28.2800 g. **Composition:** 0.9250 Silver .8411 oz. ASW **Reverse:** Queen Mother

Date	Mintage	F	VF	XF	Unc	BU
1990 Proof	Est. 30,000	Value: 17.50				

KM# 46b CROWN **Weight:** 6.2200 g. **Composition:** 0.9999 Gold .2000 oz. AGW **Subject:** Queen Mother

Date	Mintage	F	VF	XF	Unc	BU
1990 Proof	Est. 5,000	Value: 175				

KM# 46c CROWN **Weight:** 6.2200 g. **Composition:** 0.9950 Platinum .2000 oz. APW **Reverse:** Queen Mother

Date	Mintage	F	VF	XF	Unc	BU
1990 Proof	Est. 1,000	Value: 200				

KM# 49 CROWN **Composition:** Copper-Nickel **Reverse:** Penny Black Stamp

Date	Mintage	F	VF	XF	Unc	BU
1990	—	—	—	—	7.50	—
1990 Proof	Est. 50,000	Value: 18.00				

KM# 49a CROWN Weight: 28.2800 g. Composition: 0.9250 Silver .8411 oz. ASW

Date	Mintage	F	VF	XF	Unc	BU
1990 Proof	Est. 30,000	Value: 45.00				

KM# 49b CROWN Weight: 31.1000 g. Composition: 0.9999 Gold .9999 oz. AGW Reverse: Penny Black Stamp

Date	Mintage	F	VF	XF	Unc	BU
1990 Proof	Est. 1,000	Value: 1,100				

KM# 49c CROWN Weight: 15.5500 g. Composition: 0.9999 Gold .4999 oz. AGW

Date	Mintage	F	VF	XF	Unc	BU
1990 Proof	Est. 2,500	Value: 500				

KM# 66 CROWN Composition: Copper-Nickel Series: Barcelona Olympics Reverse: Discus thrower

Date	Mintage	F	VF	XF	Unc	BU
1991 Proof	Est. 8,000	Value: 22.50				
1991	—	—	—	—	4.50	—
1992	—	—	—	—	5.00	—

KM# 66a CROWN Weight: 28.2800 g. Composition: 0.9250 Silver .8411 oz. ASW

Date	Mintage	F	VF	XF	Unc	BU
1991 Proof	Est. 30,000	Value: 27.50				
1992 Proof	—	Value: 100				

KM# 67 CROWN Composition: Copper-Nickel Series: Barcelona Olympics Obverse: Similar to KM#66 Reverse: Chariot racing

Date	Mintage	F	VF	XF	Unc	BU
1991 Proof	Est. 8,000	Value: 22.50				
1991	—	—	—	—	5.00	—
1992	—	—	—	—	5.00	—

KM# 68 CROWN Composition: Copper-Nickel Series: Barcelona Olympics Obverse: Similar to KM#66 Reverse: Runners

Date	Mintage	F	VF	XF	Unc	BU
1991 Proof	Est. 8,000	Value: 22.50				
1991	—	—	—	—	4.50	—
1992	—	—	—	—	5.00	—

KM# 69 CROWN Composition: Copper-Nickel Series: Barcelona Olympics Obverse: Similar to KM#66. Reverse: Javelin thrower

Date	Mintage	F	VF	XF	Unc	BU
1991 Proof	Est. 8,000	Value: 22.50				
1991	—	—	—	—	4.50	—
1992	—	—	—	—	5.00	—

KM# 69a CROWN Weight: 28.2800 g. Composition: 0.9250 Silver .8411 oz. ASW

Date	Mintage	F	VF	XF	Unc	BU
1991 Proof	Est. 30,000	Value: 27.50				
1992 Proof	—	Value: 65.00				

KM# 70 CROWN Composition: Copper-Nickel Series: Barcelona Olympics Obverse: Similar to KM#66 Reverse: Wrestlers

Date	Mintage	F	VF	XF	Unc	BU
1991 Proof	Est. 8,000	Value: 22.50				
1991	—	—	—	—	4.50	—
1992	—	—	—	—	5.00	—

KM# 71 CROWN Composition: Copper-Nickel Series: Barcelona Olympics Obverse: Similar to KM#66 Reverse: Boxers

Date	Mintage	F	VF	XF	Unc	BU
1991 Proof	Est. 8,000	Value: 22.50				
1991	—	—	—	—	4.50	—
1992	—	—	—	—	5.00	—

KM# 72 CROWN Composition: Copper-Nickel Series: Barcelona Olympics Obverse: Similar to KM#66 Reverse: Long jumper

Date	Mintage	F	VF	XF	Unc	BU
1991 Proof	Est. 8,000	Value: 22.50				
1991	—	—	—	—	4.50	—
1992	—	—	—	—	5.00	—

KM# 73 CROWN Composition: Copper-Nickel Series: Barcelona Olympics Obverse: Similar to KM#66 Reverse: Olympic victor

Date	Mintage	F	VF	XF	Unc	BU
1991 Proof	Est. 8,000	Value: 22.50				
1991	—	—	—	—	4.50	—
1992	—	—	—	—	5.00	—

KM# 84 CROWN Composition: Copper-Nickel Subject: 10th Wedding Anniversary Reverse: Prince Charles

Date	F	VF	XF	Unc	BU
1991	—	—	—	4.00	—

KM# 84a CROWN Weight: 28.2800 g. Composition: 0.9250 Silver .8411 oz. ASW Subject: 10th Wedding Anniversary Reverse: Prince Charles

Date	Mintage	F	VF	XF	Unc	BU
1991 Proof	Est. 30,000	Value: 35.00				

KM# 84b CROWN Weight: 6.2200 g. Composition: 0.9999 Gold .2000 oz. AGW Reverse: Prince Charles

Date	Mintage	F	VF	XF	Unc	BU
1991 Proof	Est. 5,000	Value: 185				

KM# 85 CROWN Composition: Copper-Nickel Subject: 10th Wedding Anniversary Reverse: Princess Diana

Date	F	VF	XF	Unc	BU
1991	—	—	—	4.00	—

KM# 85a CROWN Weight: 28.2800 g. Composition: 0.9250 Silver .8411 oz. ASW Subject: 10th Wedding Anniversary Reverse: Princess Diana

Date	F	VF	XF	Unc	BU
1991 Proof	—	Value: 37.50			

KM# 85b CROWN Weight: 6.2200 g. Composition: 0.9999 Gold .2000 oz. AGW Reverse: Princess Diana

Date	F	VF	XF	Unc	BU
1991 Proof	—	Value: 185			

KM# 86 CROWN **Composition:** Copper-Nickel **Subject:** 10th Wedding Anniversary **Reverse:** Royal Yacht "Britannia"

Date	F	VF	XF	Unc	BU
1991	—	—	—	4.00	—

KM# 86a CROWN **Weight:** 28.2800 g. **Composition:** 0.9250 Silver .8411 oz. ASW **Subject:** 10th Wedding Anniversary **Reverse:** Royal Yacht "Britannia"

Date	Mintage	F	VF	XF	Unc	BU
1991 Proof	Est. 30,000	Value: 35.00				

KM# 86b CROWN **Weight:** 6.2200 g. **Composition:** 0.9999 Gold .2000 oz. AGW **Subject:** 10th Wedding Anniversary **Reverse:** Royal Yacht "Britannia"

Date	Mintage	F	VF	XF	Unc	BU
1991 Proof	Est. 5,000	Value: 185				

KM# 95 CROWN **Composition:** Copper-Nickel **Reverse:** Corgi Dog

Date	F	VF	XF	Unc	BU
1991	—	—	—	12.00	—

KM# 95a CROWN **Weight:** 31.1030 g. **Composition:** 0.9990 Silver 1.0000 oz. ASW

Date	Mintage	F	VF	XF	Unc	BU
1991 Proof	Est. 50,000	Value: 30.00				

KM# 67a CROWN **Weight:** 28.2800 g. **Composition:** 0.9250 Silver .8411 oz. ASW

Date	Mintage	F	VF	XF	Unc	BU
1991 Proof	Est. 30,000	Value: 27.50				

KM# 68a CROWN **Weight:** 28.2800 g. **Composition:** 0.9250 Silver .8411 oz. ASW

Date	Mintage	F	VF	XF	Unc	BU
1991 Proof	Est. 30,000	Value: 27.50				

KM# 70a CROWN **Weight:** 28.2800 g. **Composition:** 0.9250 Silver .8411 oz. ASW

Date	Mintage	F	VF	XF	Unc	BU
1991 Proof	Est. 30,000	Value: 27.50				

KM# 71a CROWN **Weight:** 28.2800 g. **Composition:** 0.9250 Silver .8411 oz. ASW

Date	Mintage	F	VF	XF	Unc	BU
1991 Proof	Est. 30,000	Value: 27.50				

KM# 72a CROWN **Weight:** 28.2800 g. **Composition:** 0.9250 Silver .8411 oz. ASW

Date	Mintage	F	VF	XF	Unc	BU
1991 Proof	Est. 30,000	Value: 27.50				

KM# 73a CROWN **Weight:** 28.2800 g. **Composition:** 0.9250 Silver .8411 oz. ASW

Date	Mintage	F	VF	XF	Unc	BU
1991 Proof	Est. 30,000	Value: 27.50				

KM# 74 CROWN **Composition:** Copper-Nickel **Reverse:** Rotary Club of Gibraltar

Date	F	VF	XF	Unc	BU
1991	—	—	—	4.50	—

KM# 74b CROWN **Weight:** 15.5500 g. **Composition:** 0.9990 Gold 0.4994 oz. AGW **Subject:** Rotary Club of Gibraltar
Size: 32.25 mm.

Date	Mintage	F	VF	XF	Unc	BU
1991 Proof	5,000	Value: 650				

KM# 74a CROWN **Weight:** 28.2800 g. **Composition:** 0.9250 Silver .8411 oz. ASW **Reverse:** Rotary Club of Gibraltar

Date	Mintage	F	VF	XF	Unc	BU
1991 Proof	Est. 30,000	Value: 22.50				

KM# 103 CROWN **Composition:** Copper-Nickel **Obverse:** Similar to KM#95 **Reverse:** Cocker Spaniel

Date	F	VF	XF	Unc	BU
1992	—	—	—	9.00	—

KM# 103a CROWN **Weight:** 28.2800 g. **Composition:** 0.9250 Silver .8411 oz. ASW

Date	F	VF	XF	Unc	BU
1992	—	—	—	26.50	—

KM# 178 CROWN **Composition:** Copper-Nickel **Reverse:** Gibraltar City Charter

Date	F	VF	XF	Unc	BU
1992	—	—	—	5.00	—

KM# 178a CROWN **Weight:** 28.2800 g. **Composition:** 0.9250 Silver .8411 oz. ASW

Date	Mintage	F	VF	XF	Unc	BU
1992 Proof	Est. 30,000	Value: 35.00				

KM# 113 CROWN **Composition:** Copper-Nickel **Series:** WWII Warships **Reverse:** USS Philadelphia

Date	F	VF	XF	Unc	BU
1993	—	—	—	4.00	—

KM# 113a CROWN **Weight:** 28.2800 g. **Composition:** 0.9250 Silver .8411 oz. ASW

Date	Mintage	F	VF	XF	Unc	BU
1993 Proof	Est. 30,000	Value: 26.50				

KM# 114 CROWN **Composition:** Copper-Nickel **Series:** WWII Warships **Reverse:** USS McLanahan

Date	F	VF	XF	Unc	BU
1993	—	—	—	4.00	—

KM# 114a CROWN **Weight:** 28.2800 g. **Composition:** 0.9250 Silver .8411 oz. ASW

Date	Mintage	F	VF	XF	Unc	BU
1993 Proof	Est. 30,000	Value: 26.50				

KM# 115 CROWN **Composition:** Copper-Nickel **Series:** WWII Warships **Reverse:** HNLMS Isaac Sweers

Date	F	VF	XF	Unc	BU
1993	—	—	—	4.00	—

KM# 115a CROWN **Weight:** 28.2800 g. **Composition:** 0.9250 Silver .8411 oz. ASW

Date	Mintage	F	VF	XF	Unc	BU
1993 Proof	Est. 30,000	Value: 26.50				

KM# 116 CROWN **Composition:** Copper-Nickel **Series:** WWII Warships **Reverse:** USS Weehawken

Date	F	VF	XF	Unc	BU
1993	—	—	—	4.00	—

KM# 116a CROWN **Weight:** 28.2800 g. **Composition:** 0.9250 Silver .8411 oz. ASW

Date	Mintage	F	VF	XF	Unc	BU
1993 Proof	Est. 30,000	Value: 26.50				

KM# 117 CROWN **Composition:** Copper-Nickel **Series:** WWII Warships **Reverse:** HMS Warspite

Date	F	VF	XF	Unc	BU
1993	—	—	—	4.00	—

KM# 117a CROWN **Weight:** 28.2800 g. **Composition:** 0.9250 Silver .8411 oz. ASW

Date	Mintage	F	VF	XF	Unc	BU
1993 Proof	Est. 30,000	Value: 26.50				

KM# 118 CROWN **Composition:** Copper-Nickel **Series:** WWII Warships **Reverse:** HMS Hood

Date	F	VF	XF	Unc	BU
1993	—	—	—	4.00	—

KM# 118a CROWN **Weight:** 28.2800 g. **Composition:** 0.9250 Silver .8411 oz. ASW

Date	Mintage	F	VF	XF	Unc	BU
1993 Proof	Est. 30,000	Value: 26.50				

KM# 119 CROWN **Composition:** Copper-Nickel **Series:** WWII Warships **Reverse:** HMS Penelope

Date	F	VF	XF	Unc	BU
1993	—	—	—	4.00	—

KM# 119a CROWN **Weight:** 28.2800 g. **Composition:** 0.9250 Silver .8411 oz. ASW

Date	Mintage	F	VF	XF	Unc	BU
1993 Proof	Est. 30,000	Value: 26.50				

KM# 120 CROWN **Composition:** Copper-Nickel **Series:** WWII Warships **Reverse:** HMCS Prescott

Date	F	VF	XF	Unc	BU
1993	—	—	—	4.00	—

KM# 120a CROWN **Weight:** 28.2800 g. **Composition:** 0.9250 Silver .8411 oz. ASW

Date	Mintage	F	VF	XF	Unc	BU
1993 Proof	Est. 30,000	Value: 26.50				

KM# 121 CROWN **Composition:** Copper-Nickel **Series:** WWII Warships **Reverse:** HMS Ark Royal

Date	F	VF	XF	Unc	BU
1993	—	—	—	4.00	—

KM# 121a CROWN **Weight:** 28.2800 g. **Composition:** 0.9250 Silver .8411 oz. ASW

Date	Mintage	F	VF	XF	Unc	BU
1993 Proof	Est. 30,000	Value: 26.50				

KM# 122 CROWN **Composition:** Copper-Nickel **Series:** WWII Warships **Reverse:** USS Gleaves

Date	F	VF	XF	Unc	BU
1993	—	—	—	4.00	—

KM# 122a CROWN **Weight:** 28.2800 g. **Composition:** 0.9250 Silver .8411 oz. ASW

Date	Mintage	F	VF	XF	Unc	BU
1993 Proof	Est. 30,000	Value: 26.50				

KM# 123 CROWN **Composition:** Copper-Nickel **Series:** WWII Warships **Reverse:** HMAS Waterhen

Date	F	VF	XF	Unc	BU
1993	—	—	—	4.00	—

KM# 123a CROWN **Weight:** 28.2800 g. **Composition:** 0.9250 Silver .8411 oz. ASW

Date	Mintage	F	VF	XF	Unc	BU
1993 Proof	Est. 30,000	Value: 26.50				

KM# 132 CROWN **Composition:** Copper-Nickel **Reverse:** Queen Anne - 1702-1714

Date	F	VF	XF	Unc	BU
1993 Prooflike	—	—	—	4.00	—

KM# 132a CROWN **Weight:** 28.2800 g. **Composition:** 0.9250 Silver .8411 oz. ASW

Date	Mintage	F	VF	XF	Unc	BU
1993 Proof	Est. 30,000	Value: 35.00				

KM# 133 CROWN **Composition:** Copper-Nickel **Reverse:** King George I - 1714-1727

Date	F	VF	XF	Unc	BU
1993 Prooflike	—	—	—	4.00	—

KM# 133a CROWN **Weight:** 28.2800 g. **Composition:** 0.9250 Silver .8411 oz. ASW

Date	Mintage	F	VF	XF	Unc	BU
1993 Proof	Est. 30,000	Value: 35.00				

KM# 134 CROWN **Composition:** Copper-Nickel **Reverse:** King George II - 1727-1760

Date	F	VF	XF	Unc	BU
1993 Prooflike	—	—	—	4.00	—

KM# 134a CROWN **Weight:** 28.2800 g. **Composition:** 0.9250 Silver .8411 oz. ASW

Date	Mintage	F	VF	XF	Unc	BU
1993 Proof	Est. 30,000	Value: 32.50				

KM# 135 CROWN **Composition:** Copper-Nickel **Reverse:** King George III - 1760-1820

Date	F	VF	XF	Unc	BU
1993 Prooflike	—	—	—	4.00	—

KM# 135a CROWN **Weight:** 28.2800 g. **Composition:** 0.9250 Silver .8411 oz. ASW

Date	Mintage	F	VF	XF	Unc	BU
1993 Proof	Est. 30,000	Value: 32.50				

KM# 136 CROWN **Composition:** Copper-Nickel **Reverse:** King George IV - 1820-1830

Date	F	VF	XF	Unc	BU
1993 Prooflike	—	—	—	4.00	—

KM# 136a CROWN **Weight:** 28.2800 g. **Composition:** 0.9250 Silver .8411 oz. ASW

Date	Mintage	F	VF	XF	Unc	BU
1993 Proof	Est. 30,000	Value: 35.00				

KM# 137 CROWN **Composition:** Copper-Nickel **Reverse:** King William IV - 1830-1837

Date	F	VF	XF	Unc	BU
1993 Prooflike	—	—	—	4.00	—

KM# 137a CROWN **Weight:** 28.2800 g. **Composition:** 0.9250 Silver .8411 oz. ASW

Date	Mintage	F	VF	XF	Unc	BU
1993 Proof	Est. 30,000	Value: 35.00				

KM# 138 CROWN **Composition:** Copper-Nickel **Reverse:** Queen Victoria - 1837-1901

Date	F	VF	XF	Unc	BU
1993 Prooflike	—	—	—	4.00	—

KM# 138a CROWN **Weight:** 28.2800 g. **Composition:** 0.9250 Silver .8411 oz. ASW

Date	Mintage	F	VF	XF	Unc	BU
1993 Proof	Est. 30,000	Value: 35.00				

KM# 139 CROWN **Composition:** Copper-Nickel **Reverse:** King Edward VII - 1901-1910

Date	F	VF	XF	Unc	BU
1993 Prooflike	—	—	—	4.00	—

KM# 139a CROWN **Weight:** 28.2800 g. **Composition:** 0.9250 Silver .8411 oz. ASW

Date	Mintage	F	VF	XF	Unc	BU
1993 Proof	Est. 30,000	Value: 37.50				

KM# 140 CROWN **Composition:** Copper-Nickel **Reverse:** King George V - 1910-1936

Date	F	VF	XF	Unc	BU
1993 Prooflike	—	—	—	4.00	—

KM# 140a CROWN **Weight:** 28.2800 g. **Composition:** 0.9250 Silver .8411 oz. ASW

Date	Mintage	F	VF	XF	Unc	BU
1993 Proof	Est. 30,000	Value: 35.00				

KM# 141 CROWN **Composition:** Copper-Nickel **Reverse:** King Edward VIII - 1936

Date	F	VF	XF	Unc	BU
1993 Prooflike	—	—	—	4.00	—

KM# 141a CROWN **Weight:** 28.2800 g. **Composition:** 0.9250 Silver .8411 oz. ASW

Date	Mintage	F	VF	XF	Unc	BU
1993 Proof	Est. 30,000	Value: 35.00				

KM# 142 CROWN **Composition:** Copper-Nickel **Reverse:** King George VI - 1936-1952

Date	F	VF	XF	Unc	BU
1993 Prooflike	—	—	—	4.00	—

KM# 142a CROWN **Weight:** 28.2800 g. **Composition:** 0.9250 Silver .8411 oz. ASW

Date	Mintage	F	VF	XF	Unc	BU
1993 Proof	Est. 30,000	Value: 35.00				

KM# 143 CROWN **Composition:** Copper-Nickel **Reverse:** Coronation of Queen Elizabeth II

Date	F	VF	XF	Unc	BU
1993	—	—	—	4.00	—

KM# 143a CROWN **Weight:** 28.2800 g. **Composition:** 0.9250 Silver .8411 oz. ASW

Date	Mintage	F	VF	XF	Unc	BU
1993 Proof	Est. 30,000	Value: 35.00				

KM# 144 CROWN **Composition:** Copper-Nickel **Reverse:** WWII Warships - FSS Savorgnan de Brazza

Date	F	VF	XF	Unc	BU
1993	—	—	—	4.00	—

KM# 144a CROWN **Weight:** 28.2800 g. **Composition:** 0.9250 Silver .8411 oz. ASW

Date	Mintage	F	VF	XF	Unc	BU
1993 Proof	Est. 30,000	Value: 26.50				

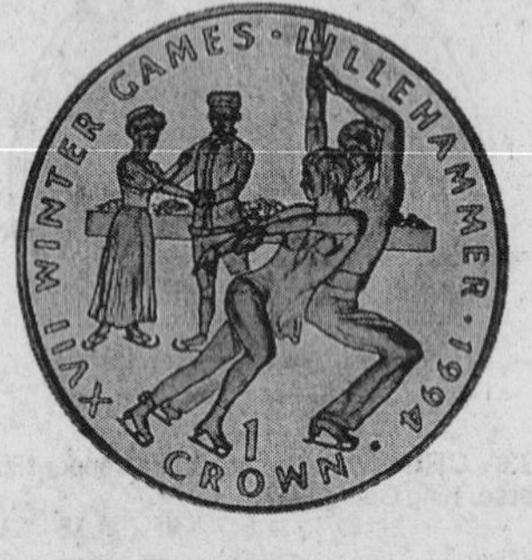

KM# 145 CROWN **Composition:** Copper-Nickel **Series:** XVII Winter Olympics **Reverse:** Skaters

Date	F	VF	XF	Unc	BU
1993 Proof	—	Value: 4.00			

KM# 145a CROWN **Weight:** 28.2800 g. **Composition:** 0.9250 Silver .8411 oz. ASW **Series:** XVII Winter Olympics

Date	Mintage	F	VF	XF	Unc	BU
1993 Proof	Est. 30,000	Value: 35.00				

KM# 145b CROWN **Weight:** 6.2200 g. **Composition:** 0.9999 Gold .2000 oz. AGW **Series:** XVII Winter Olympics **Reverse:** Skaters

Date	Mintage	F	VF	XF	Unc	BU
1993 Proof	Est. 5,000	Value: 200				

KM# 146 CROWN **Composition:** Copper-Nickel **Series:** XVII Winter Olympics **Reverse:** Ice hockey

Date	F	VF	XF	Unc	BU
1993 Proof	—	Value: 4.00			

KM# 146a CROWN **Weight:** 28.2800 g. **Composition:** 0.9250 Silver .8411 oz. ASW **Series:** XVII Winter Olympics

Date	Mintage	F	VF	XF	Unc	BU
1993 Proof	Est. 30,000	Value: 35.00				

KM# 146b CROWN **Weight:** 6.2200 g. **Composition:** 0.9999 Gold .2000 oz. AGW **Series:** XVII Winter Olympics **Reverse:** Ice hockey

Date	Mintage	F	VF	XF	Unc	BU
1993 Proof	Est. 5,000	Value: 200				

KM# 147 CROWN **Composition:** Copper-Nickel **Series:** XVII Winter Olympics **Reverse:** Bobsledding

Date	F	VF	XF	Unc	BU
1993 Proof	—	Value: 4.00			

KM# 147a CROWN **Weight:** 28.2800 g. **Composition:** 0.9250 Silver .8411 oz. ASW **Series:** XVII Winter Olympics

Date	Mintage	F	VF	XF	Unc	BU
1993 Proof	Est. 30,000	Value: 35.00				

KM# 147b CROWN **Weight:** 6.2200 g. **Composition:** 0.9999 Gold .2000 oz. AGW **Series:** XVII Winter Olympics **Reverse:** Bobsledding

Date	Mintage	F	VF	XF	Unc	BU
1993 Proof	Est. 5,000	Value: 200				

KM# 148 CROWN **Composition:** Copper-Nickel **Series:** XVII Winter Olympics **Reverse:** Skiers

Date	F	VF	XF	Unc	BU
1993 Proof	—	Value: 4.00			

KM# 148a CROWN **Weight:** 28.2800 g. **Composition:** 0.9250 Silver .8411 oz. ASW **Series:** XVII Winter Olympics

Date	Mintage	F	VF	XF	Unc	BU
1993 Proof	Est. 30,000	Value: 35.00				

KM# 148b CROWN **Weight:** 6.2200 g. **Composition:** 0.9999 Gold .2000 oz. AGW **Reverse:** XVII Winter Olympics

Date	Mintage	F	VF	XF	Unc	BU
1993 Proof	Est. 5,000	Value: 200				

KM# 149 CROWN **Composition:** Copper-Nickel **Series:** Preserve Planet Earth **Reverse:** Cetiosaurus

Date	F	VF	XF	Unc	BU
1993	—	—	—	8.50	—

KM# 149a CROWN **Weight:** 28.2800 g. **Composition:** 0.9250 Silver .8411 oz. ASW **Series:** Preserve Planet Earth

Date	Mintage	F	VF	XF	Unc	BU
1993 Proof	Est. 30,000	Value: 32.50				

KM# 151 CROWN Composition: Copper-Nickel **Series:** Preserve Planet Earth **Reverse:** Stegosaurus

Date	F	VF	XF	Unc	BU
1993	—	—	—	8.50	—

KM# 151a CROWN Weight: 28.2800 g. **Composition:** 0.9250 Silver .8411 oz. ASW **Series:** Preserve Planet Earth

Date	Mintage	F	VF	XF	Unc	BU
1993 Proof	Est. 30,000	Value: 32.50				

KM# 180 CROWN Composition: Copper-Nickel **Series:** International Friendship **Obverse:** Similar to KM#178 **Reverse:** Stylized panda

Date	F	VF	XF	Unc	BU
1993	—	—	—	6.50	—

KM# 180a CROWN Weight: 28.2800 g. **Composition:** 0.9250 Silver .8411 oz. ASW **Series:** International Friendship

Date	F	VF	XF	Unc	BU
1993 Proof	Est. 30,000	Value: 35.00			

KM# 184 CROWN Composition: Copper-Nickel **Series:** International Friendship **Reverse:** Natural panda

Date	F	VF	XF	Unc	BU
1993	—	—	—	8.50	—

KM# 184a CROWN Weight: 28.2800 g. **Composition:** 0.9250 Silver .8411 oz. ASW **Series:** International Friendship

Date	Mintage	F	VF	XF	Unc	BU
1993 Proof	Est. 30,000	Value: 35.00				

KM# 188 CROWN Composition: Copper-Nickel **Series:** International Friendship **Reverse:** General Sikorski

Date	F	VF	XF	Unc	BU
1993	—	—	—	5.00	—

KM# 188a CROWN Weight: 28.2800 g. **Composition:** 0.9250 Silver .8411 oz. ASW **Series:** International Friendship

Date	Mintage	F	VF	XF	Unc	BU
1993 Proof	Est. 30,000	Value: 35.00				

KM# 192.1 CROWN Composition: Copper-Nickel **Reverse:** Long-haired Dachshund

Date	F	VF	XF	Unc	BU
1993	—	—	—	9.00	—

KM# 192.1a CROWN Weight: 31.1030 g. **Composition:** 0.9250 Silver 1.0000 oz. ASW

Date	Mintage	F	VF	XF	Unc	BU
1993 Proof	Est. 50,000	Value: 30.00				

KM# 192.2 CROWN Composition: Copper-Nickel **Reverse:** Mint mark left of dog

Date	F	VF	XF	Unc	BU
1993(c)	—	—	—	8.00	—

KM# 192.2a CROWN Weight: 28.2800 g. **Composition:** 0.9250 Silver .8411 oz. ASW **Reverse:** Mint mark left of dog

Date	F	VF	XF	Unc	BU
1993	—	—	—	27.50	—

KM# 200 CROWN Composition: Copper-Nickel **Reverse:** Dependent Territories Conference

Date	F	VF	XF	Unc	BU
1993	—	—	—	5.50	—

KM# 200a CROWN Weight: 28.2800 g. **Composition:** 0.9250 Silver .8411 oz. ASW

Date	Mintage	F	VF	XF	Unc	BU
1993 Proof	Est. 30,000	Value: 35.00				

KM# 201 CROWN Composition: Copper-Nickel **Series:** Peter Rabbit Centennial **Reverse:** Peter Rabbit

Date	F	VF	XF	Unc	BU
1993	—	—	—	7.50	—

KM# 201a CROWN Weight: 28.2800 g. **Composition:** 0.9250 Silver .8411 oz. ASW

Date	Mintage	F	VF	XF	Unc	BU
1993 Proof	Est. 30,000	Value: 37.50				

KM# 205 CROWN Composition: Copper-Nickel **Series:** Peter Rabbit Centennial **Reverse:** Tiggy-Winkel

Date	F	VF	XF	Unc	BU
1993	—	—	—	7.50	—

KM# 205a CROWN Weight: 28.2800 g. **Composition:** 0.9250 Silver .8411 oz. ASW

Date	Mintage	F	VF	XF	Unc	BU
1993 Proof	Est. 30,000	Value: 25.00				

KM# 209 CROWN Composition: Copper-Nickel **Series:** Peter Rabbit Centennial **Reverse:** Jeremy Fisher

Date	F	VF	XF	Unc	BU
1993	—	—	—	7.50	—

KM# 209a CROWN Weight: 28.2800 g. **Composition:** 0.9250 Silver .8411 oz. ASW

Date	Mintage	F	VF	XF	Unc	BU
1993 Proof	Est. 30,000	Value: 25.00				

KM# 213 CROWN Composition: Copper-Nickel **Series:** Peter Rabbit Centennial **Reverse:** Tom Kitten

Date	F	VF	XF	Unc	BU
1993	—	—	—	7.50	—

KM# 213a CROWN Weight: 28.2800 g. **Composition:** 0.9250 Silver .8411 oz. ASW

Date	Mintage	F	VF	XF	Unc	BU
1993 Proof	Est. 30,000	Value: 25.00				

KM# 217 CROWN Composition: Copper-Nickel **Series:** Peter Rabbit Centennial **Reverse:** Benjamin Bunny

Date	F	VF	XF	Unc	BU
1993	—	—	—	7.50	—

KM# 217a CROWN Weight: 28.2800 g. **Composition:** 0.9250 Silver .8411 oz. ASW

Date	Mintage				
1993 Proof	Est. 30,000	Value: 25.00			

KM# 221 CROWN Composition: Copper-Nickel **Series:** Peter Rabbit Centennial **Reverse:** Jemima Puddle-Duck

Date	F	VF	XF	Unc	BU
1993	—	—	—	7.50	—

KM# 221a CROWN Weight: 28.2800 g. **Composition:** 0.9250 Silver .8411 oz. ASW

Date	Mintage				
1993 Proof	Est. 30,000	Value: 25.00			

KM# 342C CROWN Composition: Copper-Nickel **Subject:** Year of the Cockerel **Obverse:** Queen's portrait **Reverse:** Cockerel (rooster)

Date	F	VF	XF	Unc	BU
1993	—	—	—	8.00	—

KM# 225 CROWN Composition: Copper-Nickel **Subject:** World Cup Soccer **Reverse:** 3 Players

Date	F	VF	XF	Unc	BU
1994	—	—	—	4.75	—

KM# 225a CROWN Weight: 28.2800 g. **Composition:** 0.9250 Silver .8411 oz. ASW

Date	Mintage	F	VF	XF	Unc	BU
1994 Proof	Est. 30,000	Value: 30.00				

KM# 227 CROWN Composition: Copper-Nickel **Subject:** World Cup Soccer **Reverse:** 2 Players Facing

Date	F	VF	XF	Unc	BU
1994	—	—	—	4.75	—

KM# 227a CROWN Weight: 28.2800 g. **Composition:** 0.9250 Silver .8411 oz. ASW

Date	Mintage	F	VF	XF	Unc	BU
1994 Proof	Est. 30,000	Value: 30.00				

KM# 229 CROWN Composition: Copper-Nickel **Subject:** World Cup Soccer **Reverse:** Goalie and Scorer

Date	F	VF	XF	Unc	BU
1994	—	—	—	4.75	—

KM# 229a CROWN Weight: 28.2800 g. **Composition:** 0.9250 Silver .8411 oz. ASW

Date	Mintage	F	VF	XF	Unc	BU
1994 Proof	Est. 30,000	Value: 30.00				

KM# 231 CROWN Composition: Copper-Nickel **Subject:** World Cup Soccer **Reverse:** 1 Player

Date	F	VF	XF	Unc	BU
1994	—	—	—	4.75	—

KM# 231a CROWN Weight: 28.2800 g. **Composition:** 0.9250 Silver .8411 oz. ASW

Date	Mintage	F	VF	XF	Unc	BU
1994	Est. 30,000	Value: 30.00				

KM# 233 CROWN Composition: Copper-Nickel **Reverse:** World Cup Soccer - 2 Players, 1 Kicking

Date	F	VF	XF	Unc	BU
1994	—	—	—	4.75	—

KM# 233a CROWN Weight: 28.2800 g. **Composition:** 0.9250 Silver .8411 oz. ASW

Date	Mintage	F	VF	XF	Unc	BU
1994 Proof	Est. 30,000	Value: 30.00				

KM# 235 CROWN Composition: Copper-Nickel **Subject:** World Cup Soccer **Reverse:** 2 Players Sideways

Date	F	VF	XF	Unc	BU
1994	—	—	—	4.75	—

KM# 235a CROWN Weight: 28.2800 g. **Composition:** 0.9250 Silver .8411 oz. ASW

Date	Mintage	F	VF	XF	Unc	BU
1994 Proof	Est. 30,000	Value: 30.00				

KM# 239a CROWN Weight: 28.2800 g. **Composition:** 0.9250 Silver .8411 oz. ASW

Date	Mintage	F	VF	XF	Unc	BU
1994 Proof	Est. 30,000	Value: 35.00				

KM# 241 CROWN Composition: Copper-Nickel **Series:** Preserve Planet Earth **Reverse:** Spanish Imperial Eagle

Date	F	VF	XF	Unc	BU
1994	—	—	—	7.00	—

KM# 241a CROWN Weight: 28.2800 g. **Composition:** 0.9250 Silver .8411 oz. ASW

Date	Mintage	F	VF	XF	Unc	BU
1994 Proof	Est. 30,000	Value: 37.50				

KM# 243 CROWN Composition: Copper-Nickel **Series:** Preserve Planet Earth **Reverse:** Striped Dolphins

Date	F	VF	XF	Unc	BU
1994	—	—	—	6.00	—

KM# 243a CROWN Weight: 28.2800 g. **Composition:** 0.9250 Silver .8411 oz. ASW

Date	Mintage	F	VF	XF	Unc	BU
1994 Proof	Est. 30,000	Value: 37.50				

KM# 245 CROWN Composition: Copper-Nickel **Series:** Preserve Planet Earth **Reverse:** African Elephants

Date	F	VF	XF	Unc	BU
1994	—	—	—	8.50	—

KM# 245a CROWN Weight: 28.2800 g. **Composition:** 0.9250 Silver .8411 oz. ASW

Date	Mintage	F	VF	XF	Unc	BU
1994 Proof	Est. 30,000	Value: 37.50				

KM# 246 CROWN **Composition:** Copper-Nickel **Reverse:** Pekingese Dog

Date	F	VF	XF	Unc	BU
1994	—	—	—	7.00	—

KM# 259 CROWN **Composition:** Copper-Nickel **Series:** World War II **Reverse:** Maltese convoy

Date	F	VF	XF	Unc	BU
1994	—	—	—	6.00	—

KM# 259a CROWN **Weight:** 28.2800 g. **Composition:** 0.9250 Silver .8411 oz. ASW

Date	Mintage	F	VF	XF	Unc	BU
1994 Proof	Est. 30,000	Value: 32.50				

KM# 260 CROWN **Composition:** Copper-Nickel **Series:** World War II **Reverse:** Squadron 202 in Gibraltar

Date	F	VF	XF	Unc	BU
1994	—	—	—	6.00	—

KM# 260a CROWN **Weight:** 28.2800 g. **Composition:** 0.9250 Silver .8411 oz. ASW

Date	Mintage	F	VF	XF	Unc	BU
1994 Proof	Est. 30,000	Value: 32.50				

KM# 261 CROWN **Composition:** Copper-Nickel **Series:** World War II **Reverse:** Admiral Somerville

Date	F	VF	XF	Unc	BU
1994	—	—	—	6.00	—

KM# 261a CROWN **Weight:** 28.2800 g. **Composition:** 0.9250 Silver .8411 oz. ASW

Date	Mintage	F	VF	XF	Unc	BU
1994 Proof	Est. 30,000	Value: 32.50				

KM# 262 CROWN **Composition:** Copper-Nickel **Series:** World War II **Reverse:** Glen Miller

Date	F	VF	XF	Unc	BU
1994	—	—	—	6.00	—

KM# 262a CROWN **Weight:** 28.2800 g. **Composition:** 0.9250 Silver .8411 oz. ASW

Date	Mintage	F	VF	XF	Unc	BU
1994 Proof	Est. 30,000	Value: 30.00				

KM# 263 CROWN **Composition:** Copper-Nickel **Series:** World War II **Reverse:** King George VI and pilots

Date	F	VF	XF	Unc	BU
1994	—	—	—	6.00	—

KM# 263a CROWN **Weight:** 28.2800 g. **Composition:** 0.9250 Silver .8411 oz. ASW

Date	Mintage	F	VF	XF	Unc	BU
1994 Proof	Est. 30,000	Value: 35.00				

KM# 264 CROWN **Composition:** Copper-Nickel **Series:** World War II **Reverse:** General Eisenhower

Date	F	VF	XF	Unc	BU
1994	—	—	—	6.00	—

KM# 264a CROWN **Weight:** 28.2800 g. **Composition:** 0.9250 Silver .8411 oz. ASW

Date		F	VF	XF	Unc	BU
1994 Proof	—	Value: 35.00				

KM# 271 CROWN **Composition:** Copper-Nickel **Series:** First Man on Moon **Reverse:** Dr. Wernher von Braun

Date	F	VF	XF	Unc	BU
1994	—	—	—	5.75	—

KM# 271a CROWN **Weight:** 28.2800 g. **Composition:** 0.9250 Silver .8411 oz. ASW

Date	Mintage	F	VF	XF	Unc	BU
1994 Proof	Est. 30,000	Value: 28.00				

KM# 272 CROWN **Composition:** Copper-Nickel **Series:** First Man on Moon **Reverse:** Rocket launching

Date	F	VF	XF	Unc	BU
1994	—	—	—	5.75	—

KM# 272a CROWN **Weight:** 28.2800 g. **Composition:** 0.9250 Silver .8411 oz. ASW

Date	Mintage	F	VF	XF	Unc	BU
1994 Proof	Est. 30,000	Value: 28.00				

KM# 273 CROWN **Composition:** Copper-Nickel **Series:** First Man on Moon **Reverse:** Space capsule recovery

Date	F	VF	XF	Unc	BU
1994	—	—	—	5.75	—

KM# 273a CROWN **Weight:** 28.2800 g. **Composition:** 0.9250 Silver .8411 oz. ASW

Date	Mintage	F	VF	XF	Unc	BU
1994 Proof	Est. 30,000	Value: 25.00				

KM# 274 CROWN **Composition:** Copper-Nickel **Series:** First Man on Moon **Reverse:** First manned lunar landing

Date	F	VF	XF	Unc	BU
1994	—	—	—	5.75	—

KM# 274a CROWN **Weight:** 28.2800 g. **Composition:** 0.9250 Silver .8411 oz. ASW

Date	Mintage	F	VF	XF	Unc	BU
1994 Proof	Est. 30,000	Value: 28.00				

KM# 275 CROWN **Composition:** Copper-Nickel **Series:** First Man on Moon **Reverse:** First step on moon

Date	F	VF	XF	Unc	BU
1994	—	—	—	5.75	—

KM# 275a CROWN **Weight:** 28.2800 g. **Composition:** 0.9250 Silver .8411 oz. ASW

Date	Mintage	F	VF	XF	Unc	BU
1994 Proof	Est. 30,000	Value: 25.00				

KM# 276 CROWN **Composition:** Copper-Nickel **Series:** First Man on Moon **Reverse:** First flag planted on moon

Date	F	VF	XF	Unc	BU
1994	—	—	—	5.75	—

KM# 276a CROWN **Weight:** 28.2800 g. **Composition:** 0.9250 Silver .8411 oz. ASW

Date	Mintage	F	VF	XF	Unc	BU
1994 Proof	Est. 30,000	Value: 25.00				

KM# 285 CROWN **Composition:** Copper-Nickel **Reverse:** Sherlock Holmes holding pipe

Date	F	VF	XF	Unc	BU
1994	—	—	—	6.00	—

KM# 285a CROWN **Weight:** 28.2800 g. **Composition:** 0.9250 Silver .8411 oz. ASW

Date	Mintage	F	VF	XF	Unc	BU
1994 Proof	Est. 30,000	Value: 27.50				

KM# 286 CROWN **Composition:** Copper-Nickel **Reverse:** Sherlock Holmes playing violin for Dr. Watson

Date	F	VF	XF	Unc	BU
1994	—	—	—	6.00	—

KM# 286a CROWN **Weight:** 28.2800 g. **Composition:** 0.9250 Silver .8411 oz. ASW

Date	Mintage	F	VF	XF	Unc	BU
1994 Proof	Est. 30,000	Value: 27.50				

KM# 287 CROWN **Composition:** Copper-Nickel **Reverse:** Sherlock Holmes at 221 B Baker Street

Date	F	VF	XF	Unc	BU
1994	—	—	—	6.00	—

KM# 287a CROWN **Weight:** 28.2800 g. **Composition:** 0.9250 Silver .8411 oz. ASW

Date	Mintage	F	VF	XF	Unc	BU
1994 Proof	Est. 30,000	Value: 22.50				

KM# 288 CROWN **Composition:** Copper-Nickel **Reverse:** Sherlock Holmes, The Empty House

Date	F	VF	XF	Unc	BU
1994	—	—	—	6.00	—

KM# 288a CROWN **Weight:** 28.2800 g. **Composition:** 0.9250 Silver .8411 oz. ASW

Date	Mintage	F	VF	XF	Unc	BU
1994 Proof	Est. 30,000	Value: 22.50				

KM# 289 CROWN **Composition:** Copper-Nickel **Reverse:** Sherlock Holmes, The Mary Celeste

Date	F	VF	XF	Unc	BU
1994	—	—	—	6.00	—

KM# 289a CROWN **Weight:** 28.2800 g. **Composition:** 0.9250 Silver .8411 oz. ASW

Date	Mintage	F	VF	XF	Unc	BU
1994 Proof	Est. 30,000	Value: 37.50				

KM# 290 CROWN **Composition:** Copper-Nickel **Reverse:** Sherlock Holmes, The Hound of the Baskervilles

Date	F	VF	XF	Unc	BU
1994	—	—	—	6.00	—

KM# 290a CROWN **Weight:** 28.2800 g. **Composition:** 0.9250 Silver .8411 oz. ASW

Date	Mintage	F	VF	XF	Unc	BU
1994 Proof	Est. 30,000	Value: 35.00				

KM# 291 CROWN **Composition:** Copper-Nickel **Reverse:** Sherlock Holmes, The Three Garriders

Date	F	VF	XF	Unc	BU
1994	—	—	—	6.00	—

KM# 291a CROWN **Weight:** 28.2800 g. **Composition:** 0.9250 Silver .8411 oz. ASW

Date	Mintage	F	VF	XF	Unc	BU
1994 Proof	Est. 30,000	Value: 20.00				

KM# 292 CROWN **Composition:** Copper-Nickel **Reverse:** Sherlock Holmes, The Final Problem

Date	F	VF	XF	Unc	BU
1994	—	—	—	6.00	—

KM# 292a CROWN **Weight:** 28.2800 g. **Composition:** 0.9250 Silver .8411 oz. ASW

Date	Mintage	F	VF	XF	Unc	BU
1994 Proof	Est. 30,000	Value: 20.00				

KM# 444 CROWN **Composition:** Copper-Nickel **Subject:** The Tale of Peter Rabbit

Date	F	VF	XF	Unc	BU
1994	—	—	—	7.50	—

KM# 444a CROWN **Weight:** 28.2800 g. **Composition:** 0.9250 Silver .8411 oz. ASW

Date	Mintage	F	VF	XF	Unc	BU
1994 Proof	Est. 30,000	Value: 40.00				

KM# 239 CROWN **Composition:** Copper-Nickel **Series:** Preserve Planet Earth **Obverse:** Similar to KM#241 **Reverse:** Sabre Tooth Tiger **Note:** Similar to 1/5 Crown, KM#238.

Date	F	VF	XF	Unc	BU
1994	—	—	—	7.00	—

KM# 327 CROWN **Composition:** Copper-Nickel **Reverse:** Peter Rabbit **Note:** Similar to 1/5 Crown, KM#326.

Date	F	VF	XF	Unc	BU
1995	—	—	—	6.50	—

KM# 299 CROWN **Composition:** Copper-Nickel **Series:** Atlanta Olympics **Reverse:** Long jumper

Date	F	VF	XF	Unc	BU
1995 Proof	—	Value: 5.50			

KM# 299a CROWN **Weight:** 28.2800 g. **Composition:** 0.9250 Silver .8411 oz. ASW

Date	Mintage	F	VF	XF	Unc	BU
1995 Proof	Est. 30,000	Value: 27.50				

KM# 300 CROWN **Composition:** Copper-Nickel **Series:** Atlanta Olympics **Reverse:** Discus thrower

Date	F	VF	XF	Unc	BU
1995	—	—	—	5.50	—

KM# 300a CROWN **Weight:** 28.2800 g. **Composition:** 0.9250 Silver .8411 oz. ASW

Date	Mintage	F	VF	XF	Unc	BU
1995 Proof	Est. 30,000	Value: 27.50				

KM# 301 CROWN **Composition:** Copper-Nickel **Reverse:** Relay runners

Date	F	VF	XF	Unc	BU
1995	—	—	—	5.50	—

KM# 301a CROWN **Weight:** 28.2800 g. **Composition:** 0.9250 Silver .8411 oz. ASW

Date	Mintage	F	VF	XF	Unc	BU
1995 Proof	Est. 30,000	Value: 27.50				

KM# 302 CROWN **Composition:** Copper-Nickel **Series:** Atlanta Olympics **Reverse:** Javelin throwers

Date	F	VF	XF	Unc	BU
1995	—	—	—	5.50	—

KM# 302a CROWN **Weight:** 28.2800 g. **Composition:** 0.9250 Silver .8411 oz. ASW

Date	Mintage	F	VF	XF	Unc	BU
1995 Proof	Est. 30,000	Value: 27.50				

KM# 304 CROWN **Composition:** Copper-Nickel **Reverse:** Sun rising over Rock of Gibraltar

Date	F	VF	XF	Unc	BU
1995	—	—	—	6.50	—

KM# 304a CROWN **Weight:** 28.2800 g. **Composition:** 0.9250 Silver .8411 oz. ASW

Date	Mintage	F	VF	XF	Unc	BU
1995 Proof	Est. 30,000	Value: 40.00				

KM# 306 CROWN **Composition:** Copper-Nickel **Series:** Preserve Planet Earth **Reverse:** Monkeys

Date	F	VF	XF	Unc	BU
1995	—	—	—	8.50	—

KM# 306a CROWN **Weight:** 28.2800 g. **Composition:** 0.9250 Silver .8411 oz. ASW

Date	Mintage	F	VF	XF	Unc	BU
1995 Proof	Est. 30,000	Value: 42.50				

KM# 308 CROWN **Composition:** Copper-Nickel **Series:** Preserve Planet Earth **Reverse:** Sperm Whale

Date	F	VF	XF	Unc	BU
1995	—	—	—	8.50	—

KM# 308a CROWN **Weight:** 28.2800 g. **Composition:** 0.9250 Silver .8411 oz. ASW

Date	Mintage	F	VF	XF	Unc	BU
1995 Proof	Est. 30,000	Value: 42.50				

KM# 327a CROWN **Weight:** 28.2800 g. **Composition:** 0.9250 Silver .8411 oz. ASW

Date	Mintage	F	VF	XF	Unc	BU
1995 Proof	Est. 30,000	Value: 37.50				

KM# 329 CROWN **Composition:** Copper-Nickel **Series:** Island Games **Reverse:** Numerous athletes

Date	F	VF	XF	Unc	BU
1995	—	—	—	6.00	—

KM# 329a CROWN **Weight:** 28.2800 g. **Composition:** 0.9250 Silver .8411 oz. ASW

Date	Mintage	F	VF	XF	Unc	BU
1995 Proof	Est. 30,000	Value: 35.00				

KM# 331 CROWN **Composition:** Copper-Nickel **Series:** Island Games **Reverse:** High jumpers

Date	F	VF	XF	Unc	BU
1995	—	—	—	6.00	—

KM# 331a CROWN **Weight:** 28.2800 g. **Composition:** 0.9250 Silver .8411 oz. ASW

Date	Mintage	F	VF	XF	Unc	BU
1995 Proof	Est. 30,000	Value: 35.00				

KM# 348 CROWN **Composition:** Copper-Nickel **Series:** 1996 Atlanta Olympics **Reverse:** Tennis player

Date	F	VF	XF	Unc	BU
1996	—	—	—	6.00	—

KM# 348a CROWN **Weight:** 28.2800 g. **Composition:** 0.9250 Silver .8411 oz. ASW

Date	Mintage	F	VF	XF	Unc	BU
1996 Proof	Est. 30,000	Value: 42.50				

KM# 349 CROWN **Weight:** 28.2800 g. **Composition:** 0.9250 Silver .8411 oz. ASW **Series:** 1996 Atlanta Olympics **Reverse:** Wrestlers

Date	F	VF	XF	Unc	BU
1996	—	—	—	6.00	—

KM# 349a CROWN **Weight:** 28.2800 g. **Composition:** 0.9250 Silver .8411 oz. ASW

Date	Mintage	F	VF	XF	Unc	BU
1996 Proof	Est. 30,000	Value: 42.50				

KM# 350 CROWN **Composition:** Copper-Nickel **Series:** 1996 Atlanta Olympics **Reverse:** Baseball

Date	F	VF	XF	Unc	BU
1996	—	—	—	6.00	—

KM# 350a CROWN **Weight:** 28.2800 g. **Composition:** 0.9250 Silver .8411 oz. ASW

Date	Mintage	F	VF	XF	Unc	BU
1996 Proof	Est. 30,000	Value: 42.50				

KM# 351 CROWN **Composition:** Copper-Nickel **Series:** 1996 Atlanta Olympics **Reverse:** Flame

Date	F	VF	XF	Unc	BU
1996	—	—	—	6.00	—

KM# 351a CROWN **Weight:** 28.2800 g. **Composition:** 0.9250 Silver .8411 oz. ASW

Date	Mintage	F	VF	XF	Unc	BU
1996 Proof	Est. 30,000	Value: 42.50				

KM# 352 CROWN **Composition:** Copper-Nickel **Series:** 1996 Atlanta Olympics **Reverse:** Volleyball game

Date	F	VF	XF	Unc	BU
1996	—	—	—	6.00	—

KM# 352a CROWN **Weight:** 28.2800 g. **Composition:** 0.9250 Silver .8411 oz. ASW

Date	Mintage	F	VF	XF	Unc	BU
1996 Proof	Est. 30,000	Value: 42.50				

KM# 353 CROWN **Composition:** Copper-Nickel **Series:** 1996 Atlanta Olympics **Reverse:** Basketball game

Date	F	VF	XF	Unc	BU
1996	—	—	—	6.00	—

KM# 353a CROWN **Weight:** 28.2800 g. **Composition:** 0.9250 Silver .8411 oz. ASW

Date	Mintage	F	VF	XF	Unc	BU
1996 Proof	Est. 30,000	Value: 42.50				

KM# 358 CROWN **Composition:** Copper-Nickel **Reverse:** Mefusot Yehuda Synagogue Renovation

Date	F	VF	XF	Unc	BU
1996	—	—	—	7.00	—

KM# 358a CROWN **Weight:** 28.2800 g. **Composition:** 0.9250 Silver .8411 oz. ASW

Date	Mintage	F	VF	XF	Unc	BU
1996 Proof	Est. 30,000	Value: 40.00				

KM# 359 CROWN **Composition:** Copper-Nickel **Reverse:** Euro Soccer 96

Date	F	VF	XF	Unc	BU
1996	—	—	—	8.00	—

KM# 359a CROWN **Weight:** 28.2800 g. **Composition:** 0.9250 Silver .8411 oz. ASW

Date	Mintage	F	VF	XF	Unc	BU
1996 Proof	Est. 30,000	Value: 45.00				

KM# 373 CROWN **Composition:** Copper-Nickel **Reverse:** Roses

Date	F	VF	XF	Unc	BU
1996	—	—	—	8.00	—

KM# 373a CROWN **Weight:** 28.2800 g. **Composition:** 0.9250 Silver .8411 oz. ASW

Date	Mintage	F	VF	XF	Unc	BU
1996 Proof	Est. 30,000	Value: 40.00				

KM# 382 CROWN **Composition:** Copper-Nickel **Series:** Peter Rabbit Centennial **Reverse:** Peter Rabbit escaping

Date	F	VF	XF	Unc	BU
1996	—	—	—	6.50	—

KM# 382a CROWN **Weight:** 28.2800 g. **Composition:** 0.9250 Silver .8411 oz. ASW

Date	Mintage	F	VF	XF	Unc	BU
1996 Proof	Est. 30,000	Value: 40.00				

KM# 386 CROWN **Composition:** Copper-Nickel **Series:** Preserve Planet Earth **Reverse:** Shag Birds

Date	F	VF	XF	Unc	BU
1996	—	—	—	8.50	—

KM# 386a CROWN **Weight:** 28.2800 g. **Composition:** 0.9250 Silver .8411 oz. ASW

Date	Mintage	F	VF	XF	Unc	BU
1996 Proof	Est. 30,000	Value: 40.00				

KM# 387 CROWN **Composition:** Copper-Nickel **Series:** Preserve Planet Earth **Reverse:** Atlantic Puffins

Date	F	VF	XF	Unc	BU
1996	—	—	—	8.50	—

KM# 387a CROWN **Weight:** 28.2800 g. **Composition:** 0.9250 Silver .8411 oz. ASW

Date	Mintage	F	VF	XF	Unc	BU
1996 Proof	Est. 30,000	Value: 40.00				

KM# 393 CROWN **Composition:** Copper-Nickel **Series:** Centenary of the Cinema **Reverse:** Grace Kelly

Date	F	VF	XF	Unc	BU
1996	—	—	—	8.00	—

KM# 393a CROWN **Weight:** 28.2800 g. **Composition:** 0.9250 Silver .8411 oz. ASW

Date	Mintage	F	VF	XF	Unc	BU
1996 Proof	Est. 30,000	Value: 37.50				

KM# 398 CROWN **Composition:** Copper-Nickel **Series:** Centenary of the Cinema **Reverse:** James Dean

Date	F	VF	XF	Unc	BU
1996	—	—	—	8.00	—

KM# 398a CROWN **Weight:** 28.2800 g. **Composition:** 0.9250 Silver .8411 oz. ASW

Date	Mintage	F	VF	XF	Unc	BU
1996 Proof	Est. 30,000	Value: 40.00				

KM# 403 CROWN **Composition:** Copper-Nickel **Series:** Centenary of the Cinema **Reverse:** Marilyn Monroe

Date	F	VF	XF	Unc	BU
1996	—	—	—	8.00	—

KM# 403a CROWN **Weight:** 28.2800 g. **Composition:** 0.9250 Silver .8411 oz. ASW

Date	F	VF	XF	Unc	BU
1996	—	—	—	40.00	—

KM# 408 CROWN **Composition:** Copper-Nickel **Series:** Centenary of the Cinema **Reverse:** Audrey Hepburn

Date	F	VF	XF	Unc	BU
1996	—	—	—	8.00	—

KM# 408a CROWN **Weight:** 28.2800 g. **Composition:** 0.9250 Silver .8411 oz. ASW

Date	Mintage	F	VF	XF	Unc	BU
1996 Proof	Est. 30,000	Value: 37.50				

KM# 413 CROWN **Composition:** Copper-Nickel **Series:** Centenary of the Cinema **Reverse:** Bruce Lee

Date	F	VF	XF	Unc	BU
1996	—	—	—	8.00	—

KM# 413a CROWN **Weight:** 28.2800 g. **Composition:** 0.9250 Silver .8411 oz. ASW

Date	Mintage	F	VF	XF	Unc	BU
1996 Proof	Est. 30,000	Value: 40.00				

KM# 418 CROWN **Composition:** Copper-Nickel **Series:** Centenary of the Cinema **Reverse:** Charlie Chaplin

Date	F	VF	XF	Unc	BU
1996	—	—	—	8.00	—

KM# 418a CROWN **Weight:** 28.2800 g. **Composition:** 0.9250 Silver .8411 oz. ASW

Date	Mintage	F	VF	XF	Unc	BU
1996 Proof	Est. 30,000	Value: 37.50				

KM# 423 CROWN Composition: Copper-Nickel **Series:** Centenary of the Cinema **Reverse:** Gone WIth The Wind

Date	F	VF	XF	Unc	BU
1996	—	—	—	8.00	—

KM# 423a CROWN Weight: 28.2800 g. **Composition:** - 0.9250 Silver .8411 oz. ASW

Date	Mintage	F	VF	XF	Unc	BU
1996 Proof	Est. 30,000	Value: 40.00				

KM# 428 CROWN Composition: Copper-Nickel **Series:** Centenary of the Cinema **Reverse:** The Flintstones

Date	F	VF	XF	Unc	BU
1996	—	—	—	8.00	—

KM# 428a CROWN Weight: 28.2800 g. **Composition:** 0.9250 Silver .8411 oz. ASW

Date	Mintage	F	VF	XF	Unc	BU
1996 Proof	Est. 30,000	Value: 40.00				

KM# 430 CROWN Weight: 28.2800 g. **Composition:** 0.9250 Silver .8411 oz. ASW **Reverse:** European Football Championship - Goliath

Date	Mintage	F	VF	XF	Unc	BU
1996 Proof	Est. 10,000	Value: 32.50				

KM# 432 CROWN Composition: Copper-Nickel **Reverse:** Duke of Edinburgh Awards Scheme - 7 Scenes

Date	F	VF	XF	Unc	BU
1996	—	—	—	8.00	—

KM# 432a CROWN Weight: 28.2800 g. **Composition:** 0.9250 Silver .8411 oz. ASW

Date	Mintage	F	VF	XF	Unc	BU
1996 Proof	Est. 30,000	Value: 40.00				

KM# 435 CROWN Composition: Copper-Nickel **Reverse:** Duke of Edinburgh Awards Scheme - Cameo/Horses

Date	F	VF	XF	Unc	BU
1996	—	—	—	8.00	—

KM# 435a CROWN Weight: 28.2800 g. **Composition:** 0.9250 Silver .8411 oz. ASW

Date	Mintage	F	VF	XF	Unc	BU
1996 Proof	Est. 30,000	Value: 40.00				

KM# 449 CROWN Composition: Copper-Nickel **Reverse:** Lord Buddha

Date	F	VF	XF	Unc	BU
1996	—	—	—	7.50	—

KM# 449a CROWN Weight: 28.2800 g. **Composition:** 0.9250 Silver .8411 oz. ASW

Date	Mintage	F	VF	XF	Unc	BU
1996 Proof	Est. 15,000	Value: 25.00				

KM# 457 CROWN Composition: Copper-Nickel **Series:** Centenary of the Cinema **Reverse:** Wizard of Oz characters

Date	F	VF	XF	Unc	BU
1996	—	—	—	7.75	—

KM# 457a CROWN Weight: 28.2800 g. **Composition:** 0.9250 Silver .8411 oz. ASW

Date	Mintage	F	VF	XF	Unc	BU
1996 Proof	Est. 30,000	Value: 40.00				

KM# 461 CROWN Composition: Copper-Nickel **Series:** Centenary of the Cinema **Reverse:** Marx Brothers

Date	F	VF	XF	Unc	BU
1996	—	—	—	7.75	—

KM# 461a CROWN Weight: 28.2800 g. **Composition:** 0.9250 Silver .8411 oz. ASW

Date	Mintage	F	VF	XF	Unc	BU
1996 Proof	Est. 30,000	Value: 37.50				

KM# 465 CROWN Composition: Copper-Nickel **Series:** Centenary of the Cinema **Reverse:** Elvis Presley

Date	F	VF	XF	Unc	BU
1996	—	—	—	7.75	—

KM# 465a CROWN Weight: 28.0000 g. **Composition:** 0.9250 Silver .8411 oz. ASW

Date	Mintage	F	VF	XF	Unc	BU
1996 Proof	Est. 30,000	Value: 40.00				

KM# 469 CROWN Composition: Copper-Nickel **Series:** Centenary of the Cinema **Reverse:** Casablanca, Bogart and Bergman

Date	F	VF	XF	Unc	BU
1996	—	—	—	7.75	—

KM# 469a CROWN Weight: 28.0000 g. **Composition:** 0.9250 Silver .8411 oz. ASW

Date	Mintage	F	VF	XF	Unc	BU
1996 Proof	Est. 30,000	Value: 37.50				

KM# 473 CROWN Composition: Copper-Nickel **Series:** Centenary of the Cinema **Reverse:** E.T.

Date	F	VF	XF	Unc	BU
1996	—	—	—	7.75	—

KM# 473a CROWN Weight: 28.0000 g. **Composition:** 0.9250 Silver .8411 oz. ASW

Date	Mintage	F	VF	XF	Unc	BU
1996 Proof	Est. 30,000	Value: 37.50				

KM# 477 CROWN Composition: Copper-Nickel **Series:** Centenary of the Cinema **Reverse:** Alfred Hitchcock

Date	F	VF	XF	Unc	BU
1996	—	—	—	7.75	—

KM# 477a CROWN Weight: 28.0000 g. **Composition:** 0.9250 Silver .8411 oz. ASW

Date	Mintage	F	VF	XF	Unc	BU
1996 Proof	Est. 30,000	Value: 37.50				

KM# 514 CROWN **Composition:** Copper-Nickel **Reverse:** Two peacocks

Date	F	VF	XF	Unc	BU
1997	—	—	—	9.00	—

KM# 514a CROWN **Weight:** 28.2800 g. **Composition:** 0.9250 Silver .8411 oz. ASW

Date	Mintage	F	VF	XF	Unc	BU
1997	Est. 30,000	Value: 40.00				

KM# 525 CROWN **Composition:** Copper-Nickel **Series:** The Tale of Peter Rabbit **Reverse:** Peter Rabbit standing

Date	F	VF	XF	Unc	BU
1997	—	—	—	8.50	—

KM# 526 CROWN **Weight:** 28.2800 g. **Composition:** 0.9250 Silver .8411 oz. ASW

Date	Mintage	F	VF	XF	Unc	BU
1997 Proof	Est. 30,000	Value: 40.00				

KM# 530 CROWN **Composition:** Copper-Nickel **Subject:** Queen Elizabeth and Prince Phillip **Obverse:** Queen's portrait **Reverse:** Engagement portrait of Queen and Prince

Date	F	VF	XF	Unc	BU
1997	—	—	—	7.50	—

KM# 530a CROWN **Weight:** 28.2800 g. **Composition:** 0.9250 Gold Clad Silver .8411 oz.

Date	Mintage	F	VF	XF	Unc	BU
1997 Proof	Est. 10,000	Value: 45.00				

KM# 532 CROWN **Composition:** Copper-Nickel **Subject:** Golden Wedding Anniversary - Queen Elizabeth and Prince Philip **Obverse:** Queen's portrait **Reverse:** The Queen with her first-born, Prince Charles

Date	F	VF	XF	Unc	BU
1997	—	—	—	7.50	—

KM# 532a CROWN **Weight:** 28.2800 g. **Composition:** 0.9250 Gold Clad Silver .8411 oz.

Date	Mintage	F	VF	XF	Unc	BU
1997 Proof	Est. 10,000	Value: 45.00				

KM# 534 CROWN **Composition:** Copper-Nickel **Subject:** Golden Wedding Anniversary - Queen Elizabeth and Prince Philip **Obverse:** Queen's portrait **Reverse:** The Queen, two children and a monkey

Date	F	VF	XF	Unc	BU
1997	—	—	—	7.50	—

KM# 534a CROWN **Weight:** 28.2800 g. **Composition:** 0.9250 Gold Clad Silver .8411 oz.

Date	Mintage	F	VF	XF	Unc	BU
1997 Proof	Est. 10,000	Value: 45.00				

KM# 536 CROWN **Composition:** Copper-Nickel **Subject:** Golden Wedding Anniversary - Queen Elizabeth and Prince Philip **Obverse:** Queen's portrait **Reverse:** The Queen and adoring crowd

Date	F	VF	XF	Unc	BU
1997	—	—	—	7.50	—

KM# 536a CROWN **Weight:** 28.2800 g. **Composition:** 0.9250 Gold Clad Silver .8411 oz.

Date	Mintage	F	VF	XF	Unc	BU
1997 Proof	Est. 10,000	Value: 45.00				

KM# 540 CROWN **Composition:** Copper-Nickel **Obverse:** Queen's portrait **Reverse:** Peonies

Date	F	VF	XF	Unc	BU
1997	—	—	—	8.00	—

KM# 540a CROWN **Weight:** 28.2800 g. **Composition:** 0.9250 Silver .8411 oz. ASW

Date	Mintage	F	VF	XF	Unc	BU
1997 Proof	Est. 30,000	Value: 40.00				

KM# 544 CROWN **Weight:** 28.2800 g. **Composition:** 0.9250 Silver .8411 oz. ASW **Obverse:** Queen's portrait **Reverse:** Head of Nefertiti right

Date	Mintage	F	VF	XF	Unc	BU
1997 Proof	Est. 10,000	Value: 40.00				

KM# 548 CROWN **Weight:** 28.2800 g. **Composition:** 0.9250 Silver .8411 oz. ASW **Obverse:** Queen's portrait **Reverse:** Facing head of Cleopatra

Date	Mintage	F	VF	XF	Unc	BU
1997 Proof	Est. 10,000	Value: 40.00				

KM# 552 CROWN **Weight:** 28.2800 g. **Composition:** 0.9250 Silver .8411 oz. ASW **Obverse:** Queen's portrait **Reverse:** Europa portrait

Date	Mintage	F	VF	XF	Unc	BU
1997 Proof	Est. 10,000	Value: 40.00				

KM# 556 CROWN **Weight:** 28.2800 g. **Composition:** 0.9250 Silver .8411 oz. ASW **Obverse:** Queen's portrait **Reverse:** Head of Liberty, right

Date	Mintage	F	VF	XF	Unc	BU
1997 Proof	Est. 10,000	Value: 40.00				

KM# 566 CROWN **Composition:** Copper-Nickel **Series:** Queen's Birthday **Obverse:** Queen's portrait **Reverse:** Queen on horse, Rock of Gibraltar in background

Date	F	VF	XF	Unc	BU
1997	—	—	—	8.50	—

KM# 566a CROWN **Weight:** 28.2800 g. **Composition:** 0.9250 Silver .8411 oz. ASW

Date	Mintage	F	VF	XF	Unc	BU
1997 Proof	Est. 30,000	Value: 40.00				

KM# 567 CROWN **Composition:** Copper-Nickel **Series:** Queen's Birthday **Obverse:** Queen's portrait **Reverse:** Queen on horseback returning salute

Date	F	VF	XF	Unc	BU
1997	—	—	—	8.50	—

KM# 567a CROWN **Weight:** 28.2800 g. **Composition:** 0.9250 Silver .8411 oz. ASW

Date	Mintage	F	VF	XF	Unc	BU
1997 Proof	Est. 30,000	Value: 40.00				

KM# 568 CROWN **Composition:** Copper-Nickel **Series:** Queen's Birthday **Obverse:** Queen's portrait **Reverse:** Trooping the Clors scene, portrait of Queen

Date	F	VF	XF	Unc	BU
1997	—	—	—	8.50	—

KM# 568a CROWN **Weight:** 28.2800 g. **Composition:** 0.9250 Silver .8411 oz. ASW

Date	Mintage	F	VF	XF	Unc	BU
1997 Proof	Est. 30,000	Value: 40.00				

KM# 569 CROWN **Composition:** Copper-Nickel **Series:** Queen's Birthday **Obverse:** Queen's portrait **Reverse:** Gurkha troops with dragons

Date	F	VF	XF	Unc	BU
1997	—	—	—	8.50	—

KM# 569a CROWN **Weight:** 28.2800 g. **Composition:** 0.9250 Silver ,8411 oz. ASW

Date	F	VF	XF	Unc	BU
1997	—	—	—	40.00	—

KM# 571 CROWN **Composition:** Copper-Nickel **Subject:** The New Mosque **Obverse:** Queen's portrait **Reverse:** Two Moorish calvary riders with mosque in background

Date	F	VF	XF	Unc	BU
1997	—	—	—	8.00	—

KM# 571a CROWN **Weight:** 28.2800 g. **Composition:** 0.9250 Silver .8411 oz. ASW

Date	Mintage	F	VF	XF	Unc	BU
1997 Proof	Est. 30,000	Value: 40.00				

KM# 573 CROWN **Weight:** 28.2800 g. **Composition:** 0.9250 Silver .8411 oz. ASW **Series:** Wonders of the World **Subject:** Mausoleum at Halicarnassus **Obverse:** Queen's portrait **Reverse:** Gold coin design inset on mausoleum

Date	Mintage	F	VF	XF	Unc	BU
1997 Proof	Est. 7,500	Value: 50.00				

KM# 574 CROWN **Weight:** 28.2800 g. **Composition:** 0.9250 Silver .8411 oz. ASW **Series:** Wonders of the World **Subject:** Statue of Zeus at Olympia **Obverse:** Queen's portrait **Reverse:** Gold coin design inset on statue of Zeus

Date	Mintage	F	VF	XF	Unc	BU
1997 Proof	Est. 7,500	Value: 50.00				

KM# 575 CROWN **Weight:** 28.2800 g. **Composition:** 0.9250 Silver .8411 oz. ASW **Series:** Wonders of the World **Subject:** The Pharos of Alexandria **Obverse:** Queen's portrait **Reverse:** Gold coin design inset on lighthouse

Date	Mintage	F	VF	XF	Unc	BU
1997 Proof	Est. 7,500	Value: 50.00				

KM# 576 CROWN **Weight:** 28.2800 g. **Composition:** 0.9250 Silver .8411 oz. ASW **Series:** Wonders of the World **Subject:** The Pillars of Hercules **Obverse:** Queen's portrait **Reverse:** Gold coin design inset on the Rock of Gibraltar

Date	Mintage	F	VF	XF	Unc	BU
1997 Proof	Est. 7,500	Value: 50.00				

KM# 577 CROWN **Weight:** 28.2800 g. **Composition:** 0.9250 Silver .8411 oz. ASW **Series:** Wonders of the World **Subject:** The Colossus of Rhodes **Obverse:** Queen's portrait **Reverse:** Gold coin design inset on large statue

Date	Mintage	F	VF	XF	Unc	BU
1997 Proof	Est. 7,500	Value: 50.00				

KM# 578 CROWN **Weight:** 28.2800 g. **Composition:** 0.9250 Silver .8411 oz. ASW **Series:** Wonders of the World **Subject:** The Pyramids of Egypt **Obverse:** Queen's portrait **Reverse:** Gold coin design inset on pyramids

Date	Mintage	F	VF	XF	Unc	BU
1997 Proof	Est. 7,500	Value: 50.00				

KM# 579 CROWN **Weight:** 28.2800 g. **Composition:** 0.9250 Silver .8411 oz. ASW **Series:** Wonders of the World **Subject:** The Hanging Gardens of Babylon **Obverse:** Queen's portrait **Reverse:** Gold coin design inset on an overgrown building

Date	Mintage	F	VF	XF	Unc	BU
1997 Proof	Est. 7,500	Value: 50.00				

KM# 580 CROWN **Weight:** 28.2800 g. **Composition:** 0.9250 Silver .8411 oz. ASW **Series:** Wonders of the World **Subject:** The Temple of Artemis at Ephesus **Obverse:** Queen's portrait **Reverse:** Gold coin design inset on classic Greek building

Date	Mintage	F	VF	XF	Unc	BU
1997	Est. 7,500	Value: 50.00				

KM# 582 CROWN **Weight:** 28.2800 g. **Composition:** 0.9250 Silver .8411 oz. ASW **Series:** Evolution of Mankind **Subject:** Egypt **Obverse:** Queen's portrait **Reverse:** Three ancient Egyptians, pyramids, hieroglyphics

Date	Mintage	F	VF	XF	Unc	BU
1997 Proof	Est. 10,000	Value: 40.00				

KM# 584 CROWN **Weight:** 28.2800 g. **Composition:** 0.9250 Silver .8411 oz. ASW **Series:** Evolution of Mankind **Subject:** Israel **Obverse:** Queen's portrait **Reverse:** Star of David, Moses and Temple of Solomon

Date	Mintage	F	VF	XF	Unc	BU
1997 Proof	Est. 10,000	Value: 40.00				

KM# 586 CROWN **Weight:** 28.2800 g. **Composition:** 0.9250 Silver .8411 oz. ASW **Series:** Evolution of Mankind **Subject:** China **Obverse:** Queen's portrait **Reverse:** Emperor and the Great Wall

Date	Mintage	F	VF	XF	Unc	BU
1997 Proof	Est. 10,000	Value: 40.00				

KM# 588 CROWN **Weight:** 28.2800 g. **Composition:** 0.9250 Silver .8411 oz. ASW **Series:** Evolution of Mankind **Subject:** Greece **Obverse:** Queen's portrait **Reverse:** Aristotle, classic Greek building

Date	Mintage	F	VF	XF	Unc	BU
1997 Proof	Est. 10,000	Value: 40.00				

KM# 590 CROWN **Weight:** 28.2800 g. **Composition:** 0.9250 Silver .8411 oz. ASW **Series:** Evolution of Mankind **Subject:** Rome **Obverse:** Queen's portrait **Reverse:** Julius Caesar and Stonehenge

Date	Mintage	F	VF	XF	Unc	BU
1997 Proof	Est. 10,000	Value: 40.00				

KM# 592 CROWN **Weight:** 28.2800 g. **Composition:** 0.9250 Silver .8411 oz. ASW **Series:** Evolution of Mankind **Subject:** India **Obverse:** Queen's portrait **Reverse:** Krishna playing flute by a temple

Date	Mintage	F	VF	XF	Unc	BU
1997 Proof	Est. 10,000	Value: 40.00				

KM# 594 CROWN **Weight:** 28.2800 g. **Composition:** 0.9250 Silver .8411 oz. ASW **Series:** Evolution of Mankind **Subject:** Holy Roman Empire **Obverse:** Queen's portrait **Reverse:** Charlemagne and soldiers on horseback

Date	Mintage	F	VF	XF	Unc	BU
1997 Proof	Est. 10,000	Value: 40.00				

KM# 596 CROWN **Weight:** 28.2800 g. **Composition:** 0.9250 Silver .8411 oz. ASW **Series:** Evolution of Mankind **Subject:** Macedonia **Obverse:** Queen's portrait **Reverse:** Alexander the Great on horseback

Date	Mintage	F	VF	XF	Unc	BU
1997 Proof	Est. 10,000	Value: 40.00				

KM# 598 CROWN **Weight:** 28.2800 g. **Composition:** 0.9250 Silver .8411 oz. ASW **Series:** Evolution of Mankind **Subject:** Native America **Obverse:** Queen's portrait **Reverse:** North American native on horseback and totem pole

Date	Mintage	F	VF	XF	Unc	BU
1997 Proof	Est. 10,000	Value: 40.00				

KM# 600 CROWN **Weight:** 28.2800 g. **Composition:** 0.9250 Silver .8411 oz. ASW **Series:** Evolution of Mankind **Subject:** Asia **Obverse:** Queen's portrait **Reverse:** Buddha and temple

Date	Mintage	F	VF	XF	Unc	BU
1997 Proof	Est. 10,000	Value: 40.00				

KM# 602 CROWN **Weight:** 28.2800 g. **Composition:** 0.9250 Silver .8411 oz. ASW **Series:** Evolution of Mankind **Subject:** Inca Empire **Obverse:** Queen's portrait **Reverse:** Incan Emperor and Machu Picchu

Date	Mintage	F	VF	XF	Unc	BU
1997 Proof	Est. 10,000	Value: 40.00				

KM# 604 CROWN **Weight:** 28.2800 g. **Composition:** 0.9250 Silver .8411 oz. ASW **Series:** Evolution of Mankind **Subject:** Islamic Civilization **Obverse:** Queen's portrait **Reverse:** General Tariq Ibn Ziyad and building

Date	Mintage	F	VF	XF	Unc	BU
1997 Proof	Est. 10,000	Value: 40.00				

KM# 609 CROWN **Weight:** 28.2800 g. **Composition:** 0.9250 Silver .8410 oz. ASW **Series:** Traders of the World **Subject:** Sir Francis Drake **Obverse:** Queen's portrait **Reverse:** Sir Francis Drake, ship and beach

Date	Mintage	F	VF	XF	Unc	BU
1997 Proof	Est. 10,000	Value: 45.00				

KM# 611 CROWN **Weight:** 28.2800 g. **Composition:** 0.9250 Silver .8410 oz. ASW **Series:** Traders of the World **Subject:** Romans **Obverse:** Queen's portrait **Reverse:** Lion, lioness, ship, map

Date	Mintage	F	VF	XF	Unc	BU
1997 Proof	Est. 10,000	Value: 45.00				

KM# 613 CROWN **Weight:** 28.2800 g. **Composition:** 0.9250 Silver .8410 oz. ASW **Series:** Traders of the World **Subject:** Venetians **Obverse:** Queen's portrait **Reverse:** Pair of oysters with pearls, Venetian canal scene

Date	Mintage	F	VF	XF	Unc	BU
1997 Proof	Est. 10,000	Value: 45.00				

KM# 615 CROWN **Weight:** 28.2800 g. **Composition:** 0.9250 Silver .8410 oz. ASW **Series:** Traders of the World **Subject:** Portuguese **Obverse:** Queen's portrait **Reverse:** Gold ingots and Portuguese ship

Date	Mintage	F	VF	XF	Unc	BU
1997 Proof	Est. 10,000	Value: 45.00				

KM# 617 CROWN **Weight:** 28.2800 g. **Composition:** 0.9250 Silver .8410 oz. ASW **Series:** Traders of the World **Subject:** Spanish **Obverse:** Queen's portrait **Reverse:** Tobacco leaves, ship, map, gems

Date	Mintage	F	VF	XF	Unc	BU
1997 Proof	Est. 10,000	Value: 45.00				

KM# 619 CROWN **Weight:** 28.2800 g. **Composition:** 0.9250 Silver .8410 oz. ASW **Series:** Traders of the World **Subject:** English **Obverse:** Queen's portrait **Reverse:** Profile of Queen Elizabeth I above fighting ships

Date	Mintage	F	VF	XF	Unc	BU
1997 Proof	Est. 10,000	Value: 45.00				

KM# 621 CROWN **Weight:** 28.2800 g. **Composition:** 0.9250 Silver .8410 oz. ASW **Series:** Traders of the World **Subject:** Captain Bligh **Obverse:** Queen's portrait **Reverse:** Captain Bligh on beach, ship

Date	Mintage	F	VF	XF	Unc	BU
1997 Proof	Est. 10,000	Value: 45.00				

KM# 623 CROWN **Weight:** 28.2800 g. **Composition:** 0.9250 Silver .8410 oz. ASW **Series:** Traders of the World **Subject:** Captain Cook **Obverse:** Queen's portrait **Reverse:** Beaver on rock, ship, Captain Cook

Date	Mintage	F	VF	XF	Unc	BU
1997 Proof	Est. 10,000	Value: 45.00				

KM# 561 CROWN **Composition:** Copper-Nickel **Subject:** Yorkshire Terrier **Note:** Similar to 1 Royal, KM#561a.

Date	F	VF	XF	Unc	BU
1997	—	—	—	9.00	—

KM# 636 CROWN **Composition:** Copper-Nickel **Series:** Winter Olympics - Japan **Obverse:** Queen's portrait **Reverse:** Speed skater and Bullet Train

Date	F	VF	XF	Unc	BU
1998	—	—	—	8.00	—

KM# 636a CROWN **Weight:** 28.2800 g. **Composition:** 0.9250 Silver .8410 oz. ASW

Date	Mintage	F	VF	XF	Unc	BU
1998 Proof	Est. 30,000	Value: 45.00				

KM# 638 CROWN **Composition:** Copper-Nickel **Series:** Winter Olympics - Japan **Obverse:** Queen's portrait **Reverse:** Ski jumper and Buddha

Date	F	VF	XF	Unc	BU
1998	—	—	—	8.00	—

KM# 638a CROWN **Weight:** 28.2800 g. **Composition:** 0.9250 Silver .8410 oz. ASW

Date	Mintage	F	VF	XF	Unc	BU
1998 Proof	Est. 30,000	Value: 45.00				

KM# 640 CROWN **Composition:** Copper-Nickel **Series:** Winter Olympics - Japan **Obverse:** Queen's portrait **Reverse:** Cross country skiers

Date	F	VF	XF	Unc	BU
1998	—	—	—	8.00	—

KM# 640a CROWN **Weight:** 28.2800 g. **Composition:** 0.9250 Silver .8410 oz. ASW

Date	Mintage	F	VF	XF	Unc	BU
1998 Proof	Est. 30,000	Value: 45.00				

KM# 642 CROWN **Composition:** Copper-Nickel **Series:** Winter Olympics - Japan **Obverse:** Queen's portrait **Reverse:** Slalom skier, Zenkoji temple

Date	F	VF	XF	Unc	BU
1998	—	—	—	8.00	—

KM# 642a CROWN **Weight:** 28.2800 g. **Composition:** 0.9250 Silver .8410 oz. ASW

Date	Mintage	F	VF	XF	Unc	BU
1998 Proof	Est. 30,000	Value: 45.00				

KM# 656 CROWN **Composition:** Copper-Nickel **Series:** The Tale of Peter Rabbit **Obverse:** Queen's portrait **Reverse:** Peter Rabbit

Date	F	VF	XF	Unc	BU
1998	—	—	—	8.00	—

KM# 656a CROWN **Weight:** 28.2800 g. **Composition:** 0.9250 Silver .8411 oz. ASW

Date	Mintage	F	VF	XF	Unc	BU
1998 Proof	Est. 30,000	Value: 50.00				

KM# 661 CROWN **Composition:** Copper-Nickel **Subject:** Chrysanthemum **Obverse:** Queen's portrait **Reverse:** Three blossoms

Date	F	VF	XF	Unc	BU
1998	—	—	—	10.00	—

KM# 661a CROWN **Weight:** 28.2800 g. **Composition:** 0.9250 Silver .8411 oz. ASW

Date	Mintage	F	VF	XF	Unc	BU
1998 Proof	Est. 30,000	Value: 50.00				

KM# 674 CROWN **Weight:** 28.2800 g. **Composition:** 0.9250 Silver .8411 oz. ASW **Subject:** Brittania **Obverse:** Queen's portrait **Reverse:** Helmeted portrait of Brittania

Date	Mintage	F	VF	XF	Unc	BU
1998 Proof	Est. 10,000	Value: 50.00				

KM# 675 CROWN **Weight:** 28.2800 g. **Composition:** 0.9250 Silver .8411 oz. ASW **Subject:** Juno **Obverse:** Queen's portrait **Reverse:** Frontal portrait of Juno

Date	Mintage	F	VF	XF	Unc	BU
1998 Proof	Est. 10,000	Value: 50.00				

KM# 676 CROWN **Weight:** 28.2800 g. **Composition:** 0.9250 Silver .8411 oz. ASW **Subject:** Athena **Obverse:** Queen's portrait **Reverse:** Helmeted portrait of Athena

Date	Mintage	F	VF	XF	Unc	BU
1998 Proof	Est. 10,000	Value: 50.00				

KM# 677 CROWN **Weight:** 28.2800 g. **Composition:** 0.9250 Silver .8411 oz. ASW **Subject:** Arethusa **Obverse:** Queen's portrait **Reverse:** Portrait of Arethusa with dolphins

Date	Mintage	F	VF	XF	Unc	BU
1998 Proof	Est. 10,000	Value: 50.00				

KM# 682 CROWN **Composition:** Copper-Nickel **Subject:** Paddington Bear **Obverse:** Queen's portrait **Reverse:** Bear with suitcase

Date	F	VF	XF	Unc	BU
1998	—	—	—	10.00	—

KM# 682a CROWN **Weight:** 28.2800 g. **Composition:** 0.9250 Silver .8410 oz. ASW

Date	Mintage	F	VF	XF	Unc	BU
1998 Proof	Est. 30,000	Value: 50.00				

KM# 687 CROWN **Composition:** Copper-Nickel **Series:** World Cup France 1998 **Obverse:** Queen's portrait **Reverse:** Goalie

Date	F	VF	XF	Unc	BU
1998	—	—	—	8.00	—

KM# 687a CROWN **Weight:** 28.2800 g. **Composition:** 0.9250 Silver .8410 oz. ASW

Date	Mintage	F	VF	XF	Unc	BU
1998 Proof	Est. 30,000	Value: 50.00				

KM# 688 CROWN **Composition:** Copper-Nickel **Series:** World Cup France 1998 **Obverse:** Queen's portrait **Reverse:** Player kicking to the left

Date	F	VF	XF	Unc	BU
1998	—	—	—	8.00	—

KM# 688a CROWN **Weight:** 28.2800 g. **Composition:** 0.9250 Silver .8410 oz. ASW

Date	F	VF	XF	Unc	BU
1998	—	—	—	50.00	—

KM# 689 CROWN **Composition:** Copper-Nickel **Series:** World Cup France 1998 **Obverse:** Queen's portrait **Reverse:** Player advancing ball

Date	F	VF	XF	Unc	BU
1998	—	—	—	8.00	—

KM# 689a CROWN **Weight:** 28.2800 g. **Composition:** 0.9250 Silver .8410 oz. ASW

Date	Mintage	F	VF	XF	Unc	BU
1998 Proof	Est. 30,000	Value: 50.00				

KM# 690 CROWN **Composition:** Copper-Nickel **Series:** World Cup France 1998 **Obverse:** Queen's portrait **Reverse:** Two players

Date	F	VF	XF	Unc	BU
1998	—	—	—	8.00	—

KM# 690a CROWN **Weight:** 28.2800 g. **Composition:** 0.9250 Silver .8410 oz. ASW

Date	Mintage	F	VF	XF	Unc	BU
1998 Proof	Est. 30,000	Value: 50.00				

KM# 692 CROWN **Weight:** 28.2800 g. **Composition:** 0.9250 Silver .8410 oz. ASW **Series:** Traders of the World **Obverse:** Queen's portrait **Reverse:** Phoenecian Galley (200BC-600AD), shells below

Date	Mintage	F	VF	XF	Unc	BU
1998 Proof	Est. 10,000	Value: 50.00				

KM# 694 CROWN **Weight:** 28.2800 g. **Composition:** 0.9250 Silver .8410 oz. ASW **Series:** Traders of the World **Obverse:** Queen's portrait **Reverse:** Viking ship (900AD), pair of fish and elephant tusks

Date	Mintage	F	VF	XF	Unc	BU
1998 Proof	Est. 10,000	Value: 50.00				

KM# 696 CROWN **Weight:** 28.2800 g. **Composition:** 0.9250 Silver .8410 oz. ASW **Series:** Traders of the World **Obverse:** Queen's portrait **Reverse:** Marco Polo (1254-1324), ship, chop sticks with noodles below

Date	Mintage	F	VF	XF	Unc	BU
1998 Proof	Est. 10,000	Value: 50.00				

KM# 698 CROWN **Weight:** 28.2800 g. **Composition:** 0.9250 Silver .8410 oz. ASW **Series:** Traders of the World **Obverse:** Queen's portrait **Reverse:** Hanseatic Kogge (circa 1350) coins of the Hanseatic League nations above, map

Date	Mintage	F	VF	XF	Unc	BU
1998 Proof	Est. 10,000	Value: 50.00				

KM# 700 CROWN **Weight:** 28.2800 g. **Composition:** 0.9250 Silver .8410 oz. ASW **Series:** Traders of the World **Obverse:** Queen's portrait **Reverse:** Chinese Junk (1400s), silk worm, pottery

Date	Mintage	F	VF	XF	Unc	BU
1998 Proof	Est. 10,000	Value: 50.00				

KM# 702 CROWN **Weight:** 28.2800 g. **Composition:** 0.9250 Silver .8410 oz. ASW **Series:** Traders of the World **Obverse:** Queen's portrait **Reverse:** Christopher Columbus (1451-1506) and ship

Date	Mintage	F	VF	XF	Unc	BU
1998 Proof	Est. 10,000	Value: 50.00				

KM# 704 CROWN **Composition:** Copper-Nickel **Series:** Traders of the World **Obverse:** Queen's portrait **Reverse:** Sir Walter Raleigh (1552-1618)

Date	F	VF	XF	Unc	BU
1998	—	—	—	10.00	—

KM# 704a CROWN **Weight:** 28.2800 g. **Composition:** 0.9250 Silver .8410 oz. ASW

Date	Mintage	F	VF	XF	Unc	BU
1998 Proof	Est. 10,000	Value: 50.00				

KM# 706 CROWN **Weight:** 28.2800 g. **Composition:** 0.9250 Silver .8410 oz. ASW **Series:** Traders of the World **Obverse:** Queen's portrait **Reverse:** Boston Tea Party (1773) scene, tea leaf above

Date	Mintage	F	VF	XF	Unc	BU
1998 Proof	Est. 10,000	Value: 50.00				

KM# 708 CROWN **Composition:** Copper-Nickel **Series:** Evolution of Mankind **Obverse:** Queen's portrait **Reverse:** Australopithecus, Lucy

Date	F	VF	XF	Unc	BU
1998	—	—	—	10.00	—

KM# 708a CROWN **Weight:** 28.2800 g. **Composition:** 0.9250 Silver .8410 oz. ASW

Date	Mintage	F	VF	XF	Unc	BU
1998 Proof	Est. 10,000	Value: 50.00				

KM# 710 CROWN **Composition:** Copper-Nickel **Series:** Evolution of Mankind **Obverse:** Queen's portrait **Reverse:** Homo Habilis, use of tools

Date	F	VF	XF	Unc	BU
1998	—	—	—	10.00	—

KM# 710a CROWN **Weight:** 28.2800 g. **Composition:** 0.9250 Silver .8410 oz. ASW

Date	Mintage	F	VF	XF	Unc	BU
1998 Proof	Est. 10,000	Value: 50.00				

KM# 712 CROWN **Composition:** Copper-Nickel **Series:** Evolution of Mankind **Obverse:** Queen's portrait **Reverse:** Homo Erectus, use of fire

Date	F	VF	XF	Unc	BU
1998	—	—	—	10.00	—

KM# 712a CROWN **Weight:** 28.2800 g. **Composition:** 0.9250 Silver .8410 oz. ASW

Date	Mintage	F	VF	XF	Unc	BU
1998 Proof	Est. 10,000	Value: 50.00				

KM# 714 CROWN **Composition:** Copper-Nickel **Series:** Evolution of Mankind **Obverse:** Queen's portrait **Reverse:** Skull, 1848, Rock of Gibraltar

Date	F	VF	XF	Unc	BU
1998	—	—	—	10.00	—

KM# 714a CROWN **Weight:** 28.2800 g. **Composition:** 0.9250 Silver .8410 oz. ASW

Date	Mintage	F	VF	XF	Unc	BU
1998 Proof	Est. 10,000	Value: 50.00				

KM# 716 CROWN **Composition:** Copper-Nickel **Series:** Evolution of Mankind **Obverse:** Queen's portrait **Reverse:** Neanderthal Man, burial scene

Date	F	VF	XF	Unc	BU
1998	—	—	—	10.00	—

KM# 716a CROWN **Weight:** 28.2800 g. **Composition:** 0.9250 Silver .8410 oz. ASW

Date	Mintage	F	VF	XF	Unc	BU
1998 Proof	Est. 10,000	Value: 50.00				

KM# 718 CROWN **Composition:** Copper-Nickel **Series:** Evolution of Mankind **Obverse:** Queen's portrait **Reverse:** Homo Sapiens, cave painting

Date	F	VF	XF	Unc	BU
1998	—	—	—	10.00	—

KM# 718a CROWN **Weight:** 28.2800 g. **Composition:** 0.9250 Silver .8410 oz. ASW

Date	Mintage	F	VF	XF	Unc	BU
1998 Proof	Est. 10,000	Value: 50.00				

KM# 720 CROWN **Composition:** Copper-Nickel **Series:** Evolution of Mankind **Obverse:** Queen's portrait **Reverse:** Homo Sapiens hunting mammoth

Date	F	VF	XF	Unc	BU
1998	—	—	—	10.00	—

KM# 720a CROWN **Weight:** 28.2800 g. **Composition:** 0.9250 Silver .8410 oz. ASW

Date	Mintage	F	VF	XF	Unc	BU
1998 Proof	Est. 10,000	Value: 50.00				

KM# 722a CROWN **Weight:** 28.2800 g. **Composition:** 0.9250 Silver .8410 oz. ASW

Date	Mintage	F	VF	XF	Unc	BU
1998 Proof	Est. 10,000	Value: 50.00				

KM# 724 CROWN **Composition:** Copper-Nickel **Series:** Evolution of Mankind **Obverse:** Queen's portrait **Reverse:** Human and primate mothers with young, "The Common Ancentry of Ape and Man"

Date	F	VF	XF	Unc	BU
1998	—	—	—	10.00	—

KM# 724a CROWN **Weight:** 28.2800 g. **Composition:** 0.9250 Silver .8410 oz. ASW

Date	Mintage	F	VF	XF	Unc	BU
1998 Proof	Est. 10,000	Value: 50.00				

KM# 726 CROWN **Composition:** Copper-Nickel **Series:** Evolution of Mankind **Obverse:** Queen's portrait **Reverse:** Charles Darwin, dates

Date	F	VF	XF	Unc	BU
1998	—	—	—	10.00	—

KM# 726a CROWN **Weight:** 28.2800 g. **Composition:** 0.9250 Silver .8410 oz. ASW

Date	Mintage	F	VF	XF	Unc	BU
1998 Proof	Est. 10,000	Value: 50.00				

KM# 728 CROWN **Composition:** Copper-Nickel **Series:** Evolution of Mankind **Obverse:** Queen's portrait **Reverse:** Raymond Dart, dates, the Tuang Skull

Date	F	VF	XF	Unc	BU
1998	—	—	—	10.00	—

KM# 722.1 CROWN **Composition:** Copper-Nickel **Series:** Evolution of Mankind **Obverse:** Queen's portrait **Reverse:** Pictorial representation of theory of evolution

Date	F	VF	XF	Unc	BU
1998	—	—	—	10.00	—

KM# 728a CROWN **Weight:** 28.2800 g. **Composition:** 0.9250 Silver .8410 oz. ASW

Date	Mintage	F	VF	XF	Unc	BU
1998 Proof	Est. 10,000	Value: 50.00				

KM# 730 CROWN **Composition:** Copper-Nickel **Series:** Evolution of Mankind **Obverse:** Queen's portrait **Reverse:** Four people of different races

Date	F	VF	XF	Unc	BU
1998	—	—	—	10.00	—

KM# 730a CROWN **Weight:** 28.2800 g. **Composition:** 0.9250 Silver .8410 oz. ASW

Date	Mintage	F	VF	XF	Unc	BU
1998 Proof	Est. 10,000	Value: 50.00				

KM# 733 CROWN **Weight:** 28.2800 g. **Composition:** 0.9250 Silver .8410 oz. ASW **Series:** Wonders of the World **Obverse:** Queen's portrait **Reverse:** Guilin Hills, China with Chinese coin design inlay

Date	Mintage	F	VF	XF	Unc	BU
1998 Proof	Est. 7,500	Value: 60.00				

KM# 734 CROWN **Weight:** 28.2800 g. **Composition:** 0.9250 Silver .8410 oz. ASW **Series:** Wonders of the World **Obverse:** Queen's portrait **Reverse:** Victoria Falls, Africa, with African coin design inlay

Date	Mintage	F	VF	XF	Unc	BU
1998 Proof	Est. 7,500	Value: 60.00				

KM# 735 CROWN **Weight:** 28.2800 g. **Composition:** 0.9250 Silver .8410 oz. ASW **Series:** Wonders of the World **Obverse:** Queen's portrait **Reverse:** The Matterhorn, Switzerland, Italy with Swiss coin design inlay

Date	Mintage	F	VF	XF	Unc	BU
1998 Proof	Est. 7,500	Value: 60.00				

KM# 736 CROWN **Weight:** 28.2800 g. **Composition:** 0.9250 Silver .8410 oz. ASW **Series:** Wonders of the World **Obverse:** Queen's portrait **Reverse:** Taroko Gorge, Taiwan, with Taiwanese coin design inlay

Date	Mintage	F	VF	XF	Unc	BU
1998 Proof	Est. 7,500	Value: 60.00				

KM# 737 CROWN **Weight:** 28.2800 g. **Composition:** 0.9250 Silver .8410 oz. ASW **Series:** Wonders of the World **Obverse:** Queen's portrait **Reverse:** Niagara Falls, Canada, USA, with American coin design inlay

Date	Mintage	F	VF	XF	Unc	BU
1998 Proof	Est. 7,500	Value: 60.00				

KM# 738 CROWN Weight: 28.2800 g. **Composition:** 0.9250 Silver .8410 oz. ASW **Series:** Wonders of the World **Obverse:** Queen's portrait **Reverse:** Mount Fuji, Japan, with Japanese coin design inlay

Date	Mintage	F	VF	XF	Unc	BU
1998 Proof	Est. 7,500	Value: 60.00				

KM# 739 CROWN Weight: 28.2800 g. **Composition:** 0.9250 Silver .8410 oz. ASW **Series:** Wonders of the World **Obverse:** Queen's portrait **Reverse:** Ulura, Australia with Australian coin design inlay

Date	Mintage	F	VF	XF	Unc	BU
1998 Proof	Est. 7,500	Value: 60.00				

KM# 745 CROWN Composition: Copper-Nickel **Series:** Year of the Ocean **Obverse:** Queen's portrait **Reverse:** Mermaid and dolphin

Date	F	VF	XF	Unc	BU
1998	—	—	—	9.00	—

KM# 745a CROWN Weight: 28.2800 g. **Composition:** 0.9250 Silver .8410 oz. ASW

Date	Mintage	F	VF	XF	Unc	BU
1998 Proof	Est. 30,000	Value: 50.00				

KM# 746 CROWN Composition: Copper-Nickel **Series:** Year of the Ocean **Obverse:** Queen's portrait **Reverse:** Octopus, fish and coral

Date	F	VF	XF	Unc	BU
1998	—	—	—	8.50	—

KM# 746a CROWN Weight: 28.2800 g. **Composition:** 0.9250 Silver .8410 oz. ASW

Date	Mintage	F	VF	XF	Unc	BU
1998 Proof	Est. 30,000	Value: 50.00				

KM# 747 CROWN Composition: Copper-Nickel **Series:** Year of the Ocean **Obverse:** Queen's portrait **Reverse:** Jelly fish, stingray, fish

Date	F	VF	XF	Unc	BU
1998	—	—	—	8.50	—

KM# 747a CROWN Weight: 28.2800 g. **Composition:** 0.9250 Silver .8410 oz. ASW

Date	Mintage	F	VF	XF	Unc	BU
1998 Proof	Est. 30,000	Value: 60.00				

KM# 748 CROWN Composition: Copper-Nickel **Series:** Year of the Ocean **Obverse:** Queen's portrait **Reverse:** Two wind surfers

Date	F	VF	XF	Unc	BU
1998	—	—	—	9.00	—

KM# 748a CROWN Weight: 28.2800 g. **Composition:** 0.9250 Silver .8410 oz. ASW

Date	Mintage	F	VF	XF	Unc	BU
1998 Proof	Est. 30,000	Value: 60.00				

KM# 768 CROWN Composition: Copper-Nickel **Subject:** The Gibraltar Regiment New Colors **Obverse:** Queen's portrait **Reverse:** Soldier presenting keys

Date	F	VF	XF	Unc	BU
1998	—	—	—	10.00	—

KM# 768a CROWN Weight: 28.2800 g. **Composition:** 0.9250 Silver .8410 oz. ASW

Date	Mintage	F	VF	XF	Unc	BU
1998 Proof	Est. 30,000	Value: 50.00				

KM# 799 CROWN Composition: Copper-Nickel **Obverse:** Queen's portrait **Reverse:** Portrait of Eisenhower and North African invasion scene

Date	F	VF	XF	Unc	BU
1998	—	—	—	8.00	—

KM# 799a CROWN Weight: 28.2800 g. **Composition:** 0.9250 Silver .8410 oz. ASW

Date	Mintage	F	VF	XF	Unc	BU
1998 Proof	Est. 10,000	Value: 50.00				

KM# 783.1 CROWN Composition: Copper-Nickel **Subject:** 1999 The Year of the Rabbit **Obverse:** Queen's portrait **Reverse:** Rabbit reading, sparrow, Chinese characters

Date	F	VF	XF	Unc	BU
1999	—	—	—	10.00	—

KM# 783.2 CROWN Composition: Copper-Nickel **Reverse:** Rabbit reading, sparrow. Without Chinese characters

Date	F	VF	XF	Unc	BU
1999	—	—	—	10.00	—

KM# 783.1a CROWN Weight: 28.2800 g. **Composition:** 0.9250 Silver .8410 oz. ASW

Date	Mintage	F	VF	XF	Unc	BU
1999 Proof	Est. 10,000	Value: 50.00				

KM# 783.2a CROWN Weight: 28.2800 g. **Composition:** 0.9250 Silver .8410 oz. ASW **Reverse:** Rabbit reading, sparrow. Without Chinese characters

Date	Mintage	F	VF	XF	Unc	BU
1999 Proof	Inc. above	Value: 50.00				

KM# 785 CROWN Composition: Copper-Nickel **Series:** Summer Olympics - Sydney **Obverse:** Queen's portrait **Reverse:** Broad jumper and kangaroo

Date	F	VF	XF	Unc	BU
1999	—	—	—	8.00	—

KM# 785a CROWN Weight: 28.2800 g. **Composition:** 0.9250 Silver .8410 oz. ASW

Date	Mintage	F	VF	XF	Unc	BU
1999 Proof	Est. 30,000	Value: 50.00				

KM# 787 CROWN Composition: Copper-Nickel **Series:** Summer Olympics - Sydney **Obverse:** Queen's portrait **Reverse:** Sailboats and platypus

Date	F	VF	XF	Unc	BU
1999	—	—	—	8.00	—

KM# 787a CROWN Weight: 28.2800 g. **Composition:** 0.9250 Silver .8410 oz. ASW

Date	Mintage	F	VF	XF	Unc	BU
1999 Proof	Est. 30,000	Value: 50.00				

KM# 789 CROWN **Composition:** Copper-Nickel **Series:** Summer Olympics - Sydney **Obverse:** Queen's portrait **Reverse:** Swimmer and koala bear

Date	F	VF	XF	Unc	BU
1999	—	—	—	8.00	—

KM# 789a CROWN **Weight:** 28.2800 g. **Composition:** 0.9250 Silver .8410 oz. ASW

Date	Mintage	F	VF	XF	Unc	BU
1999 Proof	Est. 30,000	Value: 50.00				

KM# 791 CROWN **Weight:** 28.2800 g. **Composition:** 0.9250 Silver .8410 oz. ASW

Date	Mintage	F	VF	XF	Unc	BU
1999 Proof	Est. 30,000	Value: 50.00				

KM# 793 CROWN **Composition:** Copper-Nickel **Obverse:** Queen's portrait **Reverse:** Man with torch and dog

Date	F	VF	XF	Unc	BU
1999	—	—	—	8.00	—

KM# 793a CROWN **Weight:** 28.2800 g. **Composition:** 0.9250 Silver .8410 oz. ASW

Date	Mintage	F	VF	XF	Unc	BU
1999 Proof	Est. 30,000	Value: 50.00				

KM# 795 CROWN **Composition:** Copper-Nickel **Obverse:** Queen's portrait **Reverse:** Runner with torch, Aboriginal portrait and Ayer's Rock

Date	F	VF	XF	Unc	BU
1999	—	—	—	8.00	—

KM# 795a CROWN **Weight:** 28.2800 g. **Composition:** 0.9250 Silver .8410 oz. ASW

Date	Mintage	F	VF	XF	Unc	BU
1999 Proof	Est. 30,000	Value: 50.00				

KM# 801 CROWN **Composition:** Copper-Nickel **Subject:** King Alfred the Great **Obverse:** Queen's portrait **Reverse:** Alfred the Great, date

Date	F	VF	XF	Unc	BU
1999	—	—	—	7.50	—

KM# 801a CROWN **Weight:** 28.2800 g. **Composition:** 0.9250 Silver .8410 oz. ASW

Date	Mintage	F	VF	XF	Unc	BU
1999 Proof	Est. 10,000	Value: 45.00				

KM# 791.1 CROWN **Composition:** Copper-Nickel **Series:** Summer Olympics - Sydney **Obverse:** Queen's portrait **Reverse:** Two oarsmen below cockatoos

Date	F	VF	XF	Unc	BU
1999	—	—	—	8.00	—

KM# 803 CROWN **Composition:** Copper-Nickel **Obverse:** Queen's portrait **Reverse:** King Canute, dates

Date	F	VF	XF	Unc	BU
1999	—	—	—	7.50	—

KM# 803a CROWN **Weight:** 28.2800 g. **Composition:** 0.9250 Silver .8410 oz. ASW

Date	Mintage	F	VF	XF	Unc	BU
1999 Proof	Est. 10,000	Value: 45.00				

KM# 805 CROWN **Composition:** Copper-Nickel **Obverse:** Queen's portrait **Reverse:** King Edward the Confessor, dates

Date	F	VF	XF	Unc	BU
1999	—	—	—	7.50	—

KM# 805a CROWN **Weight:** 28.2800 g. **Composition:** 0.9250 Silver .8410 oz. ASW

Date	Mintage	F	VF	XF	Unc	BU
1999 Proof	Est. 10,000	Value: 45.00				

KM# 807 CROWN **Composition:** Copper-Nickel **Obverse:** Queen's portrait **Reverse:** King William I, dates

Date	F	VF	XF	Unc	BU
1999	—	—	—	7.50	—

KM# 807a CROWN **Weight:** 28.2800 g. **Composition:** 0.9250 Silver .8410 oz. ASW

Date	Mintage	F	VF	XF	Unc	BU
1999 Proof	Est. 10,000	Value: 45.00				

KM# 809 CROWN **Composition:** Copper-Nickel **Obverse:** Queen's portrait **Reverse:** King Richard I, dates

Date	F	VF	XF	Unc	BU
1999	—	—	—	7.50	—

KM# 809a CROWN **Weight:** 28.2800 g. **Composition:** 0.9250 Silver .8410 oz. ASW

Date	Mintage	F	VF	XF	Unc	BU
1999 Proof	Est. 10,000	Value: 50.00				

KM# 811 CROWN **Composition:** Copper-Nickel **Obverse:** Queen's portrait **Reverse:** King John, dates

Date	F	VF	XF	Unc	BU
1999	—	—	—	7.50	—

KM# 811a CROWN **Weight:** 28.2800 g. **Composition:** 0.9250 Silver .8410 oz. ASW

Date	Mintage	F	VF	XF	Unc	BU
1999 Proof	Est. 10,000	Value: 45.00				

KM# 813 CROWN **Composition:** Copper-Nickel **Obverse:** Queen's portrait **Reverse:** King Henry V, dates

Date	F	VF	XF	Unc	BU
1999	—	—	—	7.50	—

KM# 813a CROWN **Weight:** 28.2800 g. **Composition:** 0.9250 Silver .8410 oz. ASW

Date	Mintage	F	VF	XF	Unc	BU
1999 Proof	Est. 10,000	Value: 45.00				

KM# 815 CROWN **Composition:** Copper-Nickel **Obverse:** Queen's portrait **Reverse:** King Richard III, dates

Date	F	VF	XF	Unc	BU
1999	—	—	—	7.50	—

KM# 815a CROWN **Weight:** 28.2800 g. **Composition:** 0.9250 Silver .8410 oz. ASW

Date	Mintage	F	VF	XF	Unc	BU
1999 Proof	Est. 10,000	Value: 45.00				

KM# 817 CROWN Composition: Copper-Nickel **Obverse:** Queen's portrait **Reverse:** King Henry VIII, dates

Date	F	VF	XF	Unc	BU
1999	—	—	—	7.50	—

KM# 817a CROWN Weight: 28.2800 g. **Composition:** 0.9250 Silver .8410 oz. ASW

Date	Mintage	F	VF	XF	Unc	BU
1999 Proof	Est. 10,000	Value: 45.00				

KM# 819 CROWN Composition: Copper-Nickel **Obverse:** Queen's portrait **Reverse:** Queen Elizabeth I, dates

Date	F	VF	XF	Unc	BU
1999	—	—	—	7.50	—

KM# 819a CROWN Weight: 28.2800 g. **Composition:** 0.9250 Silver .8410 oz. ASW

Date	Mintage	F	VF	XF	Unc	BU
1999 Proof	Est. 10,000	Value: 45.00				

KM# 821 CROWN Composition: Copper-Nickel **Obverse:** Queen's portrait **Reverse:** King Charles I, dates

Date	F	VF	XF	Unc	BU
1999	—	—	—	7.50	—

KM# 821a CROWN Weight: 28.2800 g. **Composition:** 0.9250 Silver .8410 oz. ASW

Date	Mintage	F	VF	XF	Unc	BU
1999 Proof	Est. 10,000	Value: 45.00				

KM# 823 CROWN Composition: Copper-Nickel **Obverse:** Queen's portrait **Reverse:** King Charles II, dates

Date	F	VF	XF	Unc	BU
1999	—	—	—	7.50	—

KM# 823a CROWN Weight: 28.2800 g. **Composition:** 0.9250 Silver .8410 oz. ASW

Date	Mintage	F	VF	XF	Unc	BU
1999 Proof	Est. 10,000	Value: 45.00				

KM# 826a CROWN Weight: 28.2800 g. **Composition:** 0.9250 Silver .8410 oz. ASW

Date	Mintage	F	VF	XF	Unc	BU
1999 Proof	10,000	Value: 50.00				

KM# 827 CROWN Weight: 28.2800 g. **Composition:** 0.9250 Silver .8410 oz. ASW **Subject:** The Wedding of Prince Edward and Miss Sophie Rhys-Jones **Obverse:** Queen's portrait **Reverse:** St. George's Chapel

Date	F	VF	XF	Unc	BU
1999	—	—	—	8.00	—

KM# 827a CROWN Weight: 28.2800 g. **Composition:** 0.9250 Silver .8410 oz. ASW

Date	Mintage	F	VF	XF	Unc	BU
1999 Proof	Est. 10,000	Value: 50.00				

KM# 835 CROWN Composition: Copper-Nickel **Subject:** The Life of Queen Elizabeth **Obverse:** Queen's portrait **Reverse:** 1903 portrait of Queen Mother as a girl

Date	F	VF	XF	Unc	BU
1999	—	—	—	8.00	—

KM# 835a CROWN Weight: 28.2800 g. **Composition:** 0.9250 Silver .8410 oz. ASW

Date	Mintage	F	VF	XF	Unc	BU
1999 Proof	Est. 10,000	Value: 50.00				

KM# 837 CROWN Composition: Copper-Nickel **Subject:** The Life of Queen Elizabeth **Obverse:** Queen's portrait **Reverse:** 1918 portrait with wounded soldier

Date	F	VF	XF	Unc	BU
1999	—	—	—	8.00	—

KM# 826.1 CROWN Composition: Copper-Nickel **Subject:** The Wedding of Prince Edward and Miss Sophie Rhys-Jones **Obverse:** Queen's portrait **Reverse:** Prince and bride

Date	F	VF	XF	Unc	BU
1999	—	—	—	8.00	—

KM# 837a CROWN Weight: 28.2800 g. **Composition:** 0.9250 Silver .8410 oz. ASW

Date	Mintage	F	VF	XF	Unc	BU
1999 Proof	Est. 10,000	Value: 50.00				

KM# 839 CROWN Composition: Copper-Nickel **Subject:** The Life of Queen Elizabeth **Obverse:** Queen's portrait **Reverse:** 1923 wedding portrait

Date	F	VF	XF	Unc	BU
1999	—	—	—	8.00	—

KM# 839a CROWN Weight: 28.2800 g. **Composition:** 0.9250 Silver .8410 oz. ASW

Date	Mintage	F	VF	XF	Unc	BU
1999 Proof	Est. 10,000	Value: 50.00				

KM# 841 CROWN Composition: Copper-Nickel **Subject:** The Life of Queen Elizabeth **Obverse:** Queen's portrait **Reverse:** 1936 family protrait

Date	F	VF	XF	Unc	BU
1999	—	—	—	8.00	—

KM# 841a CROWN Weight: 28.2800 g. **Composition:** 0.9250 Silver .8410 oz. ASW

Date	Mintage	F	VF	XF	Unc	BU
1999 Proof	Est. 10,000	Value: 50.00				

KM# 843a CROWN Weight: 28.2800 g. **Composition:** 0.9250 Silver .8410 oz. ASW

Date	Mintage	F	VF	XF	Unc	BU
1999 Proof	Est. 10,000	Value: 50.00				

KM# 845 CROWN Composition: Copper-Nickel **Subject:** The World at War **Obverse:** Queen's portrait **Reverse:** Operation Manna, bomber dropping food packets

Date	F	VF	XF	Unc	BU
1999	—	—	—	10.00	—

KM# 845a CROWN Weight: 28.2800 g. **Composition:** 0.9250 Silver .8410 oz. ASW

Date	Mintage	F	VF	XF	Unc	BU
1999 Proof	Est. 10,000	Value: 50.00				

KM# 843.1 CROWN Weight: 28.2800 g. **Composition:** 0.9250 Silver .8410 oz. ASW **Subject:** The World at War **Obverse:** Queen's portrait **Reverse:** Franklin Roosevelt and Zero fighter

Date	F	VF	XF	Unc	BU
1999	—	—	—	10.00	—

KM# 847.1 CROWN **Composition:** Copper-Nickel **Subject:** The World at War **Obverse:** Queen's portrait **Reverse:** Robert Oppenheimer, B-29 and mushroom cloud

Date	F	VF	XF	Unc	BU
1999	—	—	—	10.00	—

KM# 847a CROWN **Weight:** 28.2800 g. **Composition:** 0.9250 Silver .8410 oz. ASW

Date	Mintage	F	VF	XF	Unc	BU
1999 Proof	Est. 10,000	Value: 50.00				

KM# 849 CROWN **Composition:** Copper-Nickel **Subject:** The World at War **Obverse:** Queen's portrait **Reverse:** Barnes Wallis portrait, bomber above dam

Date	F	VF	XF	Unc	BU
1999	—	—	—	10.00	—

KM# 849a CROWN **Weight:** 28.2800 g. **Composition:** 0.9250 Silver .8410 oz. ASW

Date	Mintage	F	VF	XF	Unc	BU
1999 Proof	Est. 10,000	Value: 50.00				

KM# 851 CROWN **Composition:** Copper-Nickel **Subject:** The World at War **Obverse:** Queen's portrait **Reverse:** Douglas Bader portrait, planes in combat

Date	F	VF	XF	Unc	BU
1999	—	—	—	10.00	—

KM# 851a CROWN **Weight:** 28.2800 g. **Composition:** 0.9250 Silver .8410 oz. ASW

Date	Mintage	F	VF	XF	Unc	BU
1999 Proof	Est. 10,000	Value: 50.00				

KM# 853 CROWN **Composition:** Copper-Nickel **Subject:** The World at War **Obverse:** Queen's portrait **Reverse:** Winston Churchill and crowd

Date	F	VF	XF	Unc	BU
1999	—	—	—	10.00	—

KM# 853a CROWN **Weight:** 28.2800 g. **Composition:** 0.9250 Silver .8410 oz. ASW

Date	Mintage	F	VF	XF	Unc	BU
1999 Proof	Est. 10,000	Value: 50.00				

KM# 855 CROWN **Composition:** Copper-Nickel **Subject:** The World at War **Obverse:** Queen's portrait **Reverse:** Tirpitz, battleship and sailor

Date	F	VF	XF	Unc	BU
1999	—	—	—	10.00	—

KM# 855a CROWN **Weight:** 28.2800 g. **Composition:** 0.9250 Silver .8410 oz. ASW

Date	Mintage	F	VF	XF	Unc	BU
1999 Proof	Est. 10,000	Value: 50.00				

KM# 857 CROWN **Composition:** Copper-Nickel **Subject:** The World at War **Obverse:** Queen's portrait **Reverse:** Soldier kissing child goodbye

Date	F	VF	XF	Unc	BU
1999	—	—	—	10.00	—

KM# 857a CROWN **Weight:** 28.2800 g. **Composition:** 0.9250 Silver .8410 oz. ASW

Date	Mintage	F	VF	XF	Unc	BU
1999 Proof	Est. 10,000	Value: 50.00				

KM# 859 CROWN **Composition:** Copper-Nickel **Subject:** The World at War **Obverse:** Queen's portrait **Reverse:** Fire fighters in action after air raid

Date	F	VF	XF	Unc	BU
1999	—	—	—	10.00	—

KM# 859a CROWN **Weight:** 28.2800 g. **Composition:** 0.9250 Silver .8410 oz. ASW

Date	Mintage	F	VF	XF	Unc	BU
1999 Proof	Est. 10,000	Value: 50.00				

KM# 861 CROWN **Composition:** Copper-Nickel **Subject:** The World at War **Obverse:** Queen's portrait **Reverse:** D-Day landing scene

Date	F	VF	XF	Unc	BU
1999	—	—	—	10.00	—

KM# 861a CROWN **Weight:** 28.2800 g. **Composition:** 0.9250 Silver .8410 oz. ASW

Date	Mintage	F	VF	XF	Unc	BU
1999 Proof	Est. 10,000	Value: 50.00				

KM# 863 CROWN **Composition:** Copper-Nickel **Subject:** The World at War **Obverse:** Queen's portrait **Reverse:** Operation Heavywater military skier

Date	F	VF	XF	Unc	BU
1999	—	—	—	10.00	—

KM# 863a CROWN **Weight:** 28.2800 g. **Composition:** 0.9250 Silver .8410 oz. ASW

Date	Mintage	F	VF	XF	Unc	BU
1999 Proof	Est. 10,000	Value: 50.00				

KM# 865 CROWN **Composition:** Copper-Nickel **Subject:** The World at War **Obverse:** Queen's portrait **Reverse:** German tanks in Russia

Date	F	VF	XF	Unc	BU
1999	—	—	—	10.00	—

KM# 865a CROWN **Weight:** 28.2800 g. **Composition:** 0.9250 Silver .8410 oz. ASW

Date	Mintage	F	VF	XF	Unc	BU
1999 Proof	Est. 10,000	Value: 50.00				

KM# 796.1 CROWN **Weight:** 6.2200 g. **Composition:** 0.9999 Gold .2000 oz. AGW **Subject:** Millenium 2000 **Obverse:** Rank-Broadley portrait of Queen Elizabeth II **Reverse:** Sundial, digital clock face, candle and traditional clock face **Note:** Similar to 5 Pounds, KM#796.

Date	Mintage	F	VF	XF	Unc	BU
1999 Proof	5,000	Value: 175				

KM# 871 CROWN **Weight:** 28.2800 g. **Composition:** Copper-Nickel **Subject:** The Life of Queen Elizabeth - The Queen Mother **Obverse:** Queen's head right **Reverse:** 1937 coronation scene

Date	F	VF	XF	Unc	BU
2000	—	—	—	10.00	—

KM# 871a CROWN **Weight:** 28.2800 g. **Composition:** 0.9250 Silver .8410 oz. ASW

Date	Mintage	F	VF	XF	Unc	BU
2000 Proof	10,000	Value: 50.00				

KM# 873 CROWN **Composition:** Copper-Nickel **Subject:** The Life of Queen Elizabeth - The Queen Mother **Reverse:** 1938 visit to France

Date	F	VF	XF	Unc	BU
2000	—	—	—	10.00	—

KM# 873a CROWN **Weight:** 28.2800 g. **Composition:** 0.9250 Silver .8410 oz. ASW

Date	Mintage	F	VF	XF	Unc	BU
2000 Proof	10,000	Value: 50.00				

KM# 875 CROWN **Composition:** Copper-Nickel **Subject:** The Life of Queen Elizabeth - The Queen Mother **Reverse:** 1940 bomb damage

Date	F	VF	XF	Unc	BU
2000	—	—	—	10.00	—

KM# 875a CROWN **Weight:** 28.2800 g. **Composition:** 0.9250 Silver .8410 oz. ASW

Date	Mintage	F	VF	XF	Unc	BU
2000 Proof	10,000	Value: 50.00				

KM# 877 CROWN **Composition:** Copper-Nickel **Subject:** The Life of Queen Elizabeth - The Queen Mother **Reverse:** 1945 victory

Date	F	VF	XF	Unc	BU
2000	—	—	—	10.00	—

KM# 877a CROWN **Weight:** 28.2800 g. **Composition:** 0.9250 Silver .8410 oz. ASW

Date	Mintage	F	VF	XF	Unc	BU
2000 Proof	10,000	Value: 50.00				

KM# 880 CROWN **Weight:** 28.2800 g. **Composition:** Copper-Nickel **Subject:** 18th Birthday - H.R.H. The Prince William **Obverse:** Queen's head right **Reverse:** Prince William's head right

Date	F	VF	XF	Unc	BU
2000	—	—	—	10.00	—

KM# 880a CROWN **Weight:** 28.2800 g. **Composition:** 0.9250 Silver .8410 oz. ASW

Date	Mintage	F	VF	XF	Unc	BU
2000 Proof	10,000	Value: 50.00				

KM# 882 CROWN **Composition:** Copper-Nickel **Subject:** Queen Mother **Obverse:** Queen's portrait **Reverse:** Queen Mother's portrait

Date	F	VF	XF	Unc	BU
2000	—	—	—	10.00	—

KM# 884 CROWN **Ring Weight:** 26.3000 g. **Ring Composition:** 0.9990 Gold .8455 oz. AGW **Center Composition:** Titanium **Subject:** 160th Anniversary - Uniform Penny Post **Reverse:** Postage stamp design **Edge:** Reeded

Date	Mintage	F	VF	XF	Unc	BU
2000 Proof	999	Value: 600				

KM# 904 CROWN **Weight:** 28.2800 g. **Composition:** Copper-Nickel **Subject:** Queen Mother **Obverse:** Queen's portrait **Reverse:** 1953 Coronation scene **Edge:** Reeded **Size:** 38.6 mm.

Date	F	VF	XF	Unc	BU
2001	—	—	—	10.00	—

KM# 904a CROWN **Weight:** 28.2800 g. **Composition:** 0.9250 Silver .8410 oz. ASW

Date	Mintage	F	VF	XF	Unc	BU
2001 Proof	10,000	Value: 47.50				

KM# 905 CROWN **Weight:** 28.2800 g. **Composition:** Copper-Nickel **Subject:** Queen Mother **Obverse:** Queen's portrait **Reverse:** Queen Mother with Prince Charles in 1954 **Edge:** Reeded **Size:** 38.6 mm.

Date	F	VF	XF	Unc	BU
2001	—	—	—	10.00	—

KM# 905a CROWN **Weight:** 28.2800 g. **Composition:** 0.9250 Silver .8410 oz. ASW

Date	Mintage	F	VF	XF	Unc	BU
2001 Proof	10,000	Value: 47.50				

KM# 906 CROWN **Weight:** 28.2800 g. **Composition:** Copper-Nickel **Subject:** 21st Century **Obverse:** Queen's portrait **Reverse:** Celtic cross, Viking ship and modern technological items **Edge:** Reeded **Size:** 38.6 mm.

Date	F	VF	XF	Unc	BU
2001	—	—	—	10.00	—

KM# 906b CROWN **Ring Weight:** 14.2000 g. **Ring Composition:** 0.9999 Silver .4565 oz. ASW **Center Weight:** 5.2000 g. **Center Composition:** 0.9995 Platinum .1671 oz. APW

Date	Mintage	F	VF	XF	Unc	BU
2001 Proof	999	Value: 400				

KM# 910 CROWN **Weight:** 28.2800 g. **Composition:** Copper-Nickel **Series:** Victorian Era **Obverse:** Queen's portrait **Reverse:** 1838 Coronation scene **Edge:** Reeded **Size:** 38.6 mm.

Date	F	VF	XF	Unc	BU
2001	—	—	—	10.00	—

KM# 910a CROWN **Weight:** 28.2800 g. **Composition:** 0.9250 Silver .8410 oz. ASW **Series:** Victorian Era

Date	Mintage	F	VF	XF	Unc	BU
2001 Proof	10,000	Value: 47.50				

KM# 912 CROWN **Composition:** Copper-Nickel **Series:** Victorian Era **Subject:** Empress of India 1876 **Obverse:** Queen's portrait **Reverse:** Crowned portrait of Victoria and two elephants

Date	F	VF	XF	Unc	BU
2001	—	—	—	10.00	—

KM# 912a CROWN **Weight:** 28.2800 g. **Composition:** 0.9250 Silver .8410 oz. ASW **Series:** Victorian Era

Date	Mintage	F	VF	XF	Unc	BU
2001 Proof	10,000	Value: 47.50				

KM# 914 CROWN **Composition:** Copper-Nickel **Series:** Victorian Era **Subject:** Diamond Jubilee 1897 **Obverse:** Queen's portrait **Reverse:** Victoria's cameo portrait above naval ships

Date	F	VF	XF	Unc	BU
2001	—	—	—	10.00	—

KM# 914a CROWN **Weight:** 28.2800 g. **Composition:** 0.9250 Silver .8410 oz. ASW **Series:** Victorian Era

Date	Mintage	F	VF	XF	Unc	BU
2001 Proof	10,000	Value: 47.50				

KM# 916 CROWN **Composition:** Copper-Nickel **Series:** Victorian Era **Subject:** Victoria's Death 1901 **Obverse:** Queen's portrait **Reverse:** Victoria's cameo portrait and Osborne Manor

Date	F	VF	XF	Unc	BU
2001	—	—	—	10.00	—

KM# 916a CROWN **Weight:** 28.2800 g. **Composition:** 0.9250 Silver .8410 oz. ASW **Series:** Victorian Era

Date	Mintage	F	VF	XF	Unc	BU
2001 Proof	10,000	Value: 47.50				

KM# 918 CROWN **Composition:** Copper-Nickel **Series:** Victorian Era **Subject:** Prince Albert and the Great Exhibition 1851 **Obverse:** Queen's portrait **Reverse:** Albert's cameo portrait and the exhibit hall

Date	Mintage	F	VF	XF	Unc	BU
2001 Proof	5,000	Value: 175				

KM# 918a CROWN **Weight:** 28.2800 g. **Composition:** 0.9250 Silver .8410 oz. ASW **Series:** Victorian Era

Date	Mintage	F	VF	XF	Unc	BU
2001 Proof	10,000	Value: 47.50				

KM# 920 CROWN **Composition:** Copper-Nickel **Series:** Victorian Era **Subject:** Isambard K. Brunel **Obverse:** Queen's portrait **Reverse:** Portrait in top hat and railroad bridge

Date	F	VF	XF	Unc	BU
2001	—	—	—	10.00	—

KM# 920a CROWN **Weight:** 28.2800 g. **Composition:** 0.9250 Silver .8410 oz. ASW **Series:** Victorian Era

Date	Mintage	F	VF	XF	Unc	BU
2001 Proof	10,000	Value: 47.50				

KM# 922 CROWN **Composition:** Copper-Nickel **Series:** Victorian Era **Subject:** Charles Dickens **Obverse:** Queen's portrait **Reverse:** Portrait and scene from "Oliver Twist"

Date	F	VF	XF	Unc	BU
2001	—	—	—	10.00	—

KM# 922a CROWN **Weight:** 28.2800 g. **Composition:** 0.9250 Silver .8410 oz. ASW **Series:** Victorian Era

Date	Mintage	F	VF	XF	Unc	BU
2001 Proof	10,000	Value: 47.50				

KM# 924 CROWN **Composition:** Copper-Nickel **Series:** Victorian Era **Subject:** Charles Darwin **Obverse:** Queen's portrait **Reverse:** Portrait, ship and a squatting aboriginal figure

Date	F	VF	XF	Unc	BU
2001	—	—	—	10.00	—

KM# 924a CROWN **Weight:** 28.2800 g. **Composition:** 0.9250 Silver .8410 oz. ASW **Series:** Victorian Era

Date	Mintage	F	VF	XF	Unc	BU
2001 Proof	10,000	Value: 47.50				

KM# 927 CROWN **Weight:** 28.2800 g. **Composition:** Copper-Nickel **Series:** Mythology of the Solar System **Obverse:** Queen's portrait **Reverse:** Standing goddess with snake basket **Edge:** Reeded **Size:** 38.6 mm.

Date	F	VF	XF	Unc	BU
2001	—	—	—	10.00	—

KM# 927a CROWN **Weight:** 28.2800 g. **Composition:** 0.9250 Silver .8410 oz. ASW **Series:** Mythology of the Solar System **Edge:** Reeded **Size:** 38.6 mm.

Date	Mintage	F	VF	XF	Unc	BU
2001 Proof	10,000	Value: 47.50				

KM# 928 CROWN **Ring Weight:** 12.9900 g. **Ring Composition:** 0.9250 Silver .3863 oz. ASW **Center Weight:** 5.0000 g. **Center Composition:** Titanium **Series:** Mythology of the Solar System **Obverse:** Queen's portrait **Reverse:** Standing goddess with snake basket **Edge:** Reeded **Size:** 32.25 mm.

Date	Mintage	F	VF	XF	Unc	BU
2001 In Proof sets only	2,001	Value: 87.50				

KM# 930 CROWN **Composition:** Copper-Nickel **Series:** Mythology of the Solar System **Obverse:** Queen's portrait **Reverse:** Helios in chariot and the sun

Date	F	VF	XF	Unc	BU
2001	—	—	—	10.00	—

KM# 930a CROWN **Weight:** 28.2800 g. **Composition:** 0.9250 Silver .8410 oz. ASW **Series:** Mythology of the Solar System

Date	Mintage	F	VF	XF	Unc	BU
2001 Proof	10,000	Value: 47.50				

KM# 930a.1 CROWN **Weight:** 28.2800 g. **Composition:** 0.9250 Silver .8410 oz. ASW **Series:** Mythology of the Solar System **Reverse:** Similar but with a fiery hologram in the sun

Date	Mintage	F	VF	XF	Unc	BU
2001 In Proof sets only	2,001	Value: 87.50				

KM# 932 CROWN **Composition:** Copper-Nickel **Series:** Mythology of the Solar System **Subject:** Moon **Obverse:** Queen's portrait **Reverse:** Goddess Diana and the moon

Date	Mintage	F	VF	XF	Unc	BU
2001 Proof	5,000	Value: 175				

KM# 932a CROWN **Weight:** 28.2800 g. **Composition:** 0.9250 Silver .8410 oz. ASW **Series:** Mythology of the Solar System

Date	Mintage	F	VF	XF	Unc	BU
2001 Proof	10,000	Value: 47.50				

KM# 932a.1 CROWN **Weight:** 28.2800 g. **Composition:** 0.9250 Silver .8410 oz. ASW **Series:** Mythology of the Solar System **Reverse:** Similar but with a small pearl set in the moon

Date	Mintage	F	VF	XF	Unc	BU
2001 In Proof sets only	2,001	Value: 87.50				

KM# 934 CROWN **Composition:** Copper-Nickel **Series:** Mythology of the Solar System **Obverse:** Queen's portrait **Reverse:** Atlas carrying the earth

Date	F	VF	XF	Unc	BU
2001	—	—	—	10.00	—

KM# 934a CROWN **Weight:** 28.2800 g. **Composition:** 0.9250 Silver .8410 oz. ASW **Series:** Mythology of the Solar System

Date	Mintage	F	VF	XF	Unc	BU
2001 Proof	10,000	Value: 47.50				

KM# 934a.1 CROWN **Weight:** 28.2800 g. **Composition:** 0.9250 Silver .8410 oz. ASW **Series:** Mythology of the Solar System **Reverse:** Similar but with a fancy diamond set in the earth

Date	Mintage	F	VF	XF	Unc	BU
2001 In Proof sets only	2,001	Value: 87.50				

KM# 936 CROWN **Composition:** Copper-Nickel **Series:** Mythology of the Solar System **Obverse:** Queen's portrait **Reverse:** Seated Neptune with trident and ringed planet

Date	F	VF	XF	Unc	BU
2001	—	—	—	10.00	—

KM# 936a CROWN **Weight:** 28.2800 g. **Composition:** 0.9250 Silver .8410 oz. ASW **Series:** Mythology of the Solar System

Date	Mintage	F	VF	XF	Unc	BU
2001 Proof	10,000	Value: 47.50				

KM# 938 CROWN **Composition:** Copper-Nickel **Series:** Mythology of the Solar System **Obverse:** Queen's portrait **Reverse:** Seated Jupiter with lightening bolts and a planet

Date	F	VF	XF	Unc	BU
2001	—	—	—	10.00	—

KM# 938a CROWN **Weight:** 28.2800 g. **Composition:** 0.9250 Silver .8410 oz. ASW **Series:** Mythology of the Solar System

Date	Mintage	F	VF	XF	Unc	BU
2001 Proof	10,000	Value: 47.50				

KM# 940 CROWN **Composition:** Copper-Nickel **Series:** Mythology of the Solar System **Subject:** Mars **Obverse:**

Queen's portrait **Reverse:** Standing Roman soldier and a planet

Date	F	VF	XF	Unc	BU
2001	—	Value: 10.00			

KM# 940a CROWN **Weight:** 28.2800 g. **Composition:** 0.9250 Silver .8410 oz. ASW **Series:** Mythology of the Solar System

Date	Mintage	F	VF	XF	Unc	BU
2001 Proof	10,000	Value: 47.50				

KM# 942 CROWN **Composition:** Copper-Nickel **Series:** Mythology of the Solar System **Obverse:** Queen's portrait **Reverse:** Seated Mercury with caduceus and a planet

Date	F	VF	XF	Unc	BU
2001	—	—	—	10.00	—

KM# 942a CROWN **Weight:** 28.2800 g. **Composition:** 0.9250 Silver .8410 oz. ASW **Series:** Mythology of the Solar System

Date	Mintage	F	VF	XF	Unc	BU
2001 Proof	10,000	Value: 47.50				

KM# 944 CROWN **Composition:** Copper-Nickel **Series:** Mythology of the Solar System **Obverse:** Queen's portrait **Reverse:** Seated Uranus with scepter

Date	F	VF	XF	Unc	BU
2001	—	—	—	10.00	—

KM# 944a CROWN **Weight:** 28.2800 g. **Composition:** 0.9250 Silver .8410 oz. ASW **Series:** Mythology of the Solar System

Date	Mintage	F	VF	XF	Unc	BU
2001 Proof	10,000	Value: 47.50				

KM# 946 CROWN **Composition:** Copper-Nickel **Series:** Mythology of the Solar System **Obverse:** Queen's portrait **Reverse:** Seated Saturn with long handled sickle and a ringed planet

Date	F	VF	XF	Unc	BU
2001	—	—	—	10.00	—

KM# 946a CROWN **Weight:** 28.2800 g. **Composition:** 0.9250 Silver .8410 oz. ASW **Series:** Mythology of the Solar System

Date	Mintage	F	VF	XF	Unc	BU
2001 Proof	10,000	Value: 47.50				

KM# 948 CROWN **Composition:** Copper-Nickel **Series:** Mythology of the Solar System **Obverse:** Queen's portrait **Reverse:** Seated Pluto with dogs and planet

Date	F	VF	XF	Unc	BU
2001	—	—	—	10.00	—

KM# 948a CROWN **Weight:** 28.2800 g. **Composition:** 0.9250 Silver .8410 oz. ASW **Series:** Mythology of the Solar System

Date	Mintage	F	VF	XF	Unc	BU
2001 Proof	10,000	Value: 47.50				

KM# 950 CROWN **Composition:** Copper-Nickel **Series:** Mythology of the Solar System **Obverse:** Queen's portrait **Reverse:** Venus seated on a half shell

Date	F	VF	XF	Unc	BU
2001	—	—	—	10.00	—

KM# 950a CROWN **Weight:** 28.2800 g. **Composition:** 0.9250 Silver .8410 oz. ASW **Series:** Mythology of the Solar System

Date	Mintage	F	VF	XF	Unc	BU
2001 Proof	10,000	Value: 47.50				

KM# 952 CROWN **Weight:** 28.2800 g. **Composition:** Copper-Nickel **Subject:** Queen's 75th Birthday **Obverse:** Queen's portrait **Reverse:** Queen in Order of Garter robes **Edge:** Reeded **Size:** 38.6 mm.

Date	F	VF	XF	Unc	BU
2001	—	—	—	10.00	—

KM# 952a CROWN **Weight:** 28.2800 g. **Composition:** 0.9250 Silver .8410 oz. ASW

Date	Mintage	F	VF	XF	Unc	BU
2001 Proof	10,000	Value: 47.50				

KM# 955 CROWN **Weight:** 28.2800 g. **Composition:** Copper-Nickel **Series:** Victorian Age Part II **Obverse:** Queen's portrait **Reverse:** Victoria learning of her accession **Edge:** Reeded **Size:** 38.6 mm.

Date	F	VF	XF	Unc	BU
2001	—	—	—	10.00	—

KM# 955a CROWN **Weight:** 28.2800 g. **Composition:** 0.9250 Silver .8410 oz. ASW **Series:** Victorian Age Part II **Edge:** Reeded **Size:** 38.6 mm.

Date	Mintage	F	VF	XF	Unc	BU
2001 Proof	10,000	Value: 47.50				

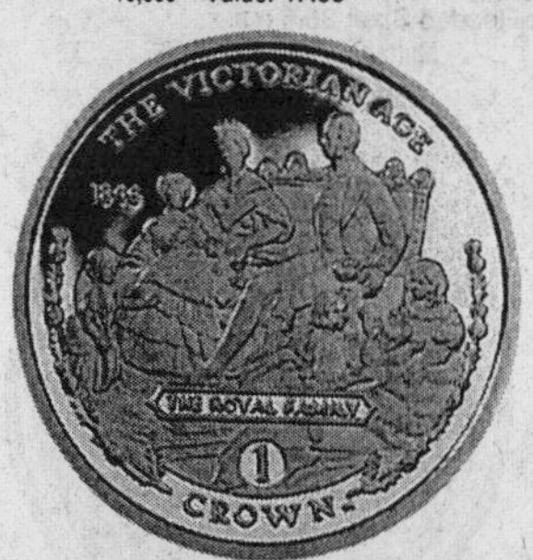

KM# 957 CROWN **Composition:** Copper-Nickel **Series:** Victorian Age Part II **Subject:** Royal Family **Reverse:** Victoria and Albert seated with children **Edge:** Reeded **Size:** 38.6 mm.

Date	F	VF	XF	Unc	BU
2001	—	—	—	10.00	—

KM# 957a CROWN **Weight:** 28.2800 g. **Composition:** 0.9250 Silver .8410 oz. ASW **Series:** Victorian Age Part II **Edge:** Reeded **Size:** 38.6 mm.

Date	Mintage	F	VF	XF	Unc	BU
2001 Proof	10,000	Value: 47.50				

KM# 959 CROWN **Composition:** Copper-Nickel **Series:** Victorian Age Part II **Subject:** Victoria in Scotland **Reverse:** Victoria on horse with servant **Edge:** Reeded **Size:** 38.6 mm.

Date	Mintage	F	VF	XF	Unc	BU
2001	2,001	—	—	—	10.00	—

KM# 959a CROWN **Weight:** 28.2800 g. **Composition:** 0.9250 Silver .8410 oz. ASW **Series:** Victorian Age Part II **Edge:** Reeded **Size:** 38.6 mm.

Date	Mintage	F	VF	XF	Unc	BU
2001 Proof	10,000	Value: 47.50				

KM# 961 CROWN **Composition:** Copper-Nickel **Series:** Victorian Age Part II **Subject:** Gladstone and Disraeli **Reverse:** Portraits of both politicians **Edge:** Reeded **Size:** 38.6 mm.

Date	F	VF	XF	Unc	BU
2001	—	—	—	10.00	—

KM# 961a CROWN **Weight:** 28.2800 g. **Composition:** 0.9250 Silver .8410 oz. ASW **Series:** Victorian Age Part II **Edge:** Reeded **Size:** 38.6 mm.

Date	Mintage	F	VF	XF	Unc	BU
2001 Proof	10,000	Value: 47.50				

KM# 963 CROWN **Composition:** Copper-Nickel **Series:** Victorian Age Part II **Reverse:** Florence Nightingale holding lantern **Edge:** Reeded **Size:** 38.6 mm.

Date	F	VF	XF	Unc	BU
2001	—	—	—	10.00	—

KM# 963a CROWN **Weight:** 28.2800 g. **Composition:** 0.9250 Silver .8410 oz. ASW **Series:** Victorian Age Part II **Edge:** Reeded **Size:** 38.6 mm.

Date	Mintage	F	VF	XF	Unc	BU
2001 Proof	10,000	Value: 47.50				

KM# 965 CROWN **Composition:** Copper-Nickel **Series:** Victorian Age Part II **Reverse:** Lord Tennyson with the Light Brigade in background **Edge:** Reeded **Size:** 38.6 mm.

Date	F	VF	XF	Unc	BU
2001	—	—	—	10.00	—

KM# 965a CROWN **Weight:** 28.2800 g. **Composition:** 0.9250 Silver .8410 oz. ASW **Series:** Victorian Age Part II **Edge:** Reeded **Size:** 38.6 mm.

Date	Mintage	F	VF	XF	Unc	BU
2001 Proof	10,000	Value: 47.50				

KM# 967 CROWN **Composition:** Copper-Nickel **Series:** Victorian Age Part II **Reverse:** Stanley meeting Dr. Livingstone **Edge:** Reeded **Size:** 38.6 mm.

Date	F	VF	XF	Unc	BU
2001	—	—	—	10.00	—

KM# 967a CROWN **Weight:** 28.2800 g. **Composition:** 0.9250 Silver .8410 oz. ASW **Series:** Victorian Age Part II **Edge:** Reeded **Size:** 38.6 mm.

Date	Mintage	F	VF	XF	Unc	BU
2001 Proof	10,000	Value: 47.50				

KM# 969 CROWN **Composition:** Copper-Nickel **Series:** Victorian Age Part II **Reverse:** Bronte sisters **Edge:** Reeded **Size:** 38.6 mm.

Date	F	VF	XF	Unc	BU
2001	—	—	—	10.00	—

KM# 969a CROWN **Weight:** 28.2800 g. **Composition:** 0.9250 Silver .8410 oz. ASW **Edge:** Reeded **Size:** 38.6 mm.

Date	Mintage	F	VF	XF	Unc	BU
2001 Proof	10,000	Value: 47.50				

KM# 906a CROWN **Weight:** 31.1035 g. **Composition:** 0.9990 Silver 1.0000 oz. ASW **Note:** 31.1035 .999 Silver, 1.0000 ASW with a gold plated inner ring and a blackened outer ring.

Date	Mintage	F	VF	XF	Unc	BU
2001 Proof	2,001	Value: 47.50				

KM# 1025 CROWN **Weight:** 28.2800 g. **Composition:** Copper Nickel **Subject:** Calpe Conference **Obverse:** Queen's portrait **Reverse:** Crossed flags and arms **Edge:** Reeded **Size:** 38.6 mm.

Date	F	VF	XF	Unc	BU
2002PM	—	—	—	10.00	—

KM# 1025a CROWN **Weight:** 28.2800 g. **Composition:** 0.9250 Silver 0.841 oz. ASW **Subject:** Calpe Conference **Obverse:** Queen's portrait **Reverse:** Crossed flags and arms **Edge:** Reeded **Size:** 38.6 mm.

Date	Mintage	F	VF	XF	Unc	BU
2002PM	10,000	Value: 47.50				

Note: Proof

KM# 979 CROWN **Weight:** 28.2800 g. **Composition:** Copper-Nickel **Subject:** Queen Mother's Life **Obverse:** Bust of Queen Elizabeth II right **Reverse:** Christening of Prince William **Edge:** Reeded **Size:** 38.6 mm.

Date	F	VF	XF	Unc	BU
2002	—	—	—	10.00	—

KM# 979a CROWN **Weight:** 28.2800 g. **Composition:** 0.9250 Silver 0.841 oz. ASW **Subject:** Queen Mother's Life **Obverse:** Bust of Queen Elizabeth II right **Reverse:** Prince William's christening scene **Edge:** Reeded **Size:** 38.6 mm.

Date	Mintage	F	VF	XF	Unc	BU
2002 Proof	10,000	Value: 47.50				

KM# 992 CROWN **Weight:** 28.2800 g. **Composition:** Copper-Nickel **Subject:** Peter Rabbit Centennial **Obverse:** Bust of Queen Elizabeth II right. **Reverse:** Peter Rabbit. **Edge:** Reeded. **Size:** 38.6 mm.

Date	F	VF	XF	Unc	BU
2002	—	—	—	10.00	—

KM# 992a CROWN **Weight:** 28.2800 g. **Composition:** 0.9250 Silver 0.841 oz. ASW **Subject:** Peter Rabbit Centennial **Obverse:** Bust of Queen Elizabeth II right. **Reverse:** Peter Rabbit. **Edge:** Reeded. **Size:** 38.6 mm.

Date	Mintage	F	VF	XF	Unc	BU
2002 Proof	10,000	Value: 47.50				

KM# 981 CROWN **Weight:** 28.2800 g. **Composition:** Copper-Nickel **Subject:** World Cup Soccer **Obverse:** Bust of Queen Elizabeth II right **Reverse:** Two players about to collide **Edge:** Reeded **Size:** 38.6 mm.

Date	F	VF	XF	Unc	BU
2002	—	—	—	10.00	—

KM# 981a CROWN **Weight:** 28.2800 g. **Composition:** 0.9250 Silver 0.841 oz. ASW **Subject:** World Cup Soccer **Obverse:** Bust of Queen Elizabeth II right **Reverse:** Two players above to collide **Edge:** Reeded **Size:** 38.6 mm.

Date	Mintage	F	VF	XF	Unc	BU
2002 Proof	10,000	Value: 47.50				

KM# 983 CROWN **Weight:** 28.2800 g. **Composition:** Copper-Nickel **Subject:** World Cup Soccer **Obverse:** Bust of Queen Elizabeth II right **Reverse:** Two players facing viewer **Edge:** Reeded **Size:** 38.6 mm.

Date	F	VF	XF	Unc	BU
2002	—	—	—	10.00	—

KM# 983a CROWN **Weight:** 28.2800 g. **Composition:** 0.9250 Silver 0.841 oz. ASW **Subject:** World Cup Soccer **Obverse:** Bust of Queen Elizabeth II right **Reverse:** Two players facing viewer **Edge:** Reeded **Size:** 38.6 mm.

Date	Mintage	F	VF	XF	Unc	BU
2002 Proof	10,000	Value: 47.50				

KM# 985 CROWN **Weight:** 28.2800 g. **Composition:** Copper-Nickel **Subject:** World Cup Soccer **Obverse:** Bust of Queen Elizabeth II right **Reverse:** Two horizontal players **Edge:** Reeded **Size:** 38.6 mm.

Date	F	VF	XF	Unc	BU
2002	—	—	—	10.00	—

KM# 985a CROWN **Weight:** 28.2800 g. **Composition:** 0.9250 Silver 0.841 oz. ASW **Subject:** World Cup Soccer **Obverse:** Bust of Queen Elizabeth II right **Reverse:** Two horizontal players **Edge:** Reeded **Size:** 38.6 mm.

Date	Mintage	F	VF	XF	Unc	BU
2002 Proof	10,000	Value: 47.50				

KM# 987 CROWN **Weight:** 28.2800 g. **Composition:** Copper-Nickel **Subject:** World Cup Soccer **Obverse:** Bust of Queen Elizabeth II right **Reverse:** Two players moving to left **Edge:** Reeded **Size:** 38.6 mm.

Date	F	VF	XF	Unc	BU
2002	—	—	—	10.00	—

KM# 987a CROWN **Weight:** 28.2800 g. **Composition:** 0.9250 Silver 0.841 oz. ASW **Subject:** World Cup Soccer **Obverse:** Bust of Queen Elizabeth II right **Reverse:** Two players moving to left **Edge:** Reeded **Size:** 38.6 mm.

Date	Mintage	F	VF	XF	Unc	BU
2002 Proof	10,000	Value: 47.50				

KM# 994 CROWN **Weight:** 28.2800 g. **Composition:** Copper-Nickel **Subject:** Queen's Golden Jubilee **Obverse:** Bust of Queen Elizabeth II right **Reverse:** Royal couple and tree house **Edge:** Reeded **Size:** 38.6 mm.

Date	F	VF	XF	Unc	BU
2002	—	—	—	10.00	—

KM# 994a CROWN **Composition:** Yellow Brass **Subject:** Queen's Golden Jubilee **Obverse:** Bust of Queen Elizabeth II right **Reverse:** Royal couple and tree house **Edge:** Reeded

Date	Mintage	F	VF	XF	Unc	BU
2002 Proof	15,000	Value: 20.00				

KM# 994b CROWN **Weight:** 28.2800 g. **Composition:** 0.9250 Gold Clad Silver 0.841 oz. **Subject:** Queen's Golden Jubilee **Obverse:** Bust of Queen Elizabeth II right **Reverse:** Royal couple and tree house **Edge:** Reeded **Size:** 38.6 mm.

Date	Mintage	F	VF	XF	Unc	BU
2002 Proof	10,000	Value: 50.00				

KM# 996 CROWN **Weight:** 28.2800 g. **Composition:** Copper-Nickel **Subject:** Queen's Golden Jubilee **Obverse:** Bust of Queen Elizabeth II right **Reverse:** Royal coach **Edge:** Reeded **Size:** 38.6 mm.

Date	F	VF	XF	Unc	BU
2002	—	—	—	10.00	—

KM# 996a CROWN **Composition:** Yellow Brass **Subject:** Queen's Golden Jubilee **Obverse:** Bust of Queen Elizabeth II right **Reverse:** Royal coach **Edge:** Reeded

Date	Mintage	F	VF	XF	Unc	BU
2002 Proof	15,000	Value: 20.00				

KM# 996b CROWN **Weight:** 28.2800 g. **Composition:** 0.9250 Gold Clad Silver 0.841 oz. **Subject:** Queen's Golden Jubilee **Obverse:** Bust of Queen Elizabeth II right **Reverse:** Royal coach **Edge:** Reeded **Size:** 38.6 mm.

Date	F	VF	XF	Unc	BU
2002 Proof	—	—	—	50.00	—

KM# 998 CROWN **Weight:** 28.2800 g. **Composition:** Copper-Nickel **Subject:** Queen's Golden Jubilee **Obverse:** Bust of Queen Elizabeth II right **Reverse:** Royal couple with baby **Edge:** Reeded **Size:** 38.6 mm.

Date	F	VF	XF	Unc	BU
2002	—	—	—	10.00	—

KM# 998a CROWN **Composition:** Yellow Brass **Subject:** Queen's Golden Jubilee **Obverse:** Bust of Queen Elizabeth II right **Reverse:** Royal couple with baby **Edge:** Reeded

Date	Mintage	F	VF	XF	Unc	BU
2002 Proof	15,000	Value: 20.00				

KM# 998b CROWN **Weight:** 28.2800 g. **Composition:** 0.9250 Gold Clad Silver 0.841 oz. **Subject:** Queen's Golden Jubilee **Obverse:** Bust of Queen Elizabeth II right **Reverse:** Royal couple with baby **Edge:** Reeded **Size:** 38.6 mm.

Date	Mintage	F	VF	XF	Unc	BU
2002 Proof	1,000	Value: 50.00				

KM# 1000 CROWN **Weight:** 28.2800 g. **Composition:** Copper-Nickel **Subject:** Queen's Golden Jubilee **Obverse:** Bust of Queen Elizabeth II right **Reverse:** Royal yacht under Tower bridge **Edge:** Reeded **Size:** 38.6 mm.

Date	F	VF	XF	Unc	BU
2002	—	—	—	10.00	—

KM# 1000a CROWN **Composition:** Yellow Brass **Subject:** Queen's Golden Jubilee **Obverse:** Bust of Queen Elizabeth II right **Reverse:** Royal yacht under Tower bridge **Edge:** Reeded

Date	Mintage	F	VF	XF	Unc	BU
2002 Proof	15,000	Value: 20.00				

KM# 1000b CROWN **Weight:** 28.2800 g. **Composition:** 0.9250 Gold Clad Silver 0.841 oz. **Subject:** Queen's Golden Jubilee **Obverse:** Bust of Queen Elizabeth II right **Reverse:** Royal yacht under Tower bridge **Edge:** Reeded **Size:** 38.6 mm.

Date	Mintage	F	VF	XF	Unc	BU
2002 Proof	10,000	Value: 50.00				

KM# 1013 CROWN **Weight:** 28.2800 g. **Composition:** Blackened Copper-Nickel **Subject:** Queen Mother **Obverse:** Bust of Queen Elizabeth II right **Reverse:** Queen Mother trout fishing **Edge:** Reeded **Size:** 38.6 mm.

Date	F	VF	XF	Unc	BU
2002	—	—	—	1.00	—

KM# 1015 CROWN **Weight:** 28.2800 g. **Composition:** Copper-Nickel **Subject:** Princess Diana **Obverse:** Bust of Queen Elizabeth II right **Reverse:** Diana's portrait **Edge:** Reeded **Size:** 38.6 mm.

Date	F	VF	XF	Unc	BU
2002	—	—	—	10.00	—

KM# 1015a CROWN **Weight:** 28.2800 g. **Composition:** 0.9250 Silver 0.841 oz. ASW **Subject:** Princess Diana **Obverse:** Bust of Queen Elizabeth II right **Reverse:** Diana's portrait **Edge:** Reeded **Size:** 38.6 mm.

Date	Mintage	F	VF	XF	Unc	BU
2002 Proof	10,000	Value: 47.50				

KM# 1019 CROWN **Weight:** 28.2800 g. **Composition:** Copper-Nickel **Subject:** Peter Pan **Obverse:** Bust of Queen Elizabeth II right. **Reverse:** Peter Pan and Tinkerbell flying above city **Edge:** Reeded **Size:** 38.6 mm.

Date	F	VF	XF	Unc	BU
2002	—	—	—	10.00	—

KM# 1019a CROWN **Weight:** 28.2800 g. **Composition:** 0.9250 Silver 0.841 oz. ASW **Subject:** Peter Pan **Obverse:** Bust of Queen Elizabeth II right **Reverse:** Peter Pan and Tinkerbell flying above city **Edge:** Reeded **Size:** 38.6 mm.

Date	Mintage	F	VF	XF	Unc	BU
2002 Proof	10,000	Value: 47.50				

KM# 1021 CROWN **Weight:** 28.2800 g. **Composition:** Copper-Nickel **Subject:** Grand Masonic Lodge **Obverse:** Bust of Queen Elizabeth II right **Reverse:** Masonic seal above Gibraltar **Edge:** Reeded **Size:** 38.6 mm.

Date	Mintage	F	VF	XF	Unc	BU
2002 Proof	5,000	Value: 10.00				

KM# 1021a CROWN **Weight:** 28.2800 g. **Composition:** 0.9250 Silver 0.841 oz. ASW **Subject:** Grand Masonic Lodge **Obverse:** Bust of Queen Elizabeth II right **Reverse:** Masonic seal above Gibraltar **Edge:** Reeded **Size:** 38.6 mm.

Date	Mintage	F	VF	XF	Unc	BU
2002 Proof	10,000	Value: 47.50				

KM# 128 2 CROWN **Weight:** 62.2070 g. **Composition:** 0.9990 Silver 2.0000 oz. ASW **Subject:** Japanese Royal Wedding **Obverse:** Queen's portrait **Reverse:** Pair of peacocks at ease

Date	Mintage	F	VF	XF	Unc	BU
1993 Proof	Est. 20,000	Value: 65.00				

KM# 128a 2 CROWN **Weight:** 62.2070 g. **Composition:** 0.9999 Gold 2.0000 oz. AGW **Subject:** Japanese Royal Wedding **Obverse:** Queen's portrait **Reverse:** Pair of peacocks at ease

Date	Mintage	F	VF	XF	Unc	BU
1993 Proof	Est. 2,500	Value: 1,000				

KM# 129 2 CROWN **Weight:** 62.2070 g. **Composition:** 0.9990 Silver 2.0000 oz. ASW **Subject:** Japanese Royal Wedding **Obverse:** Queen's portrait **Reverse:** Two peacocks, one in full display

Date	Mintage	F	VF	XF	Unc	BU
1993 Proof	Est. 20,000	Value: 37.50				

KM# 129a 2 CROWN **Weight:** 62.2070 g. **Composition:** 0.9999 Gold 2.0000 oz. AGW **Subject:** Japanese Royal Wedding **Obverse:** Queen's portrait **Reverse:** Two peacocks, one in full display

Date	Mintage	F	VF	XF	Unc	BU
1993 Proof	Est. 2,500	Value: 900				

KM# 1034 2 CROWN **Weight:** 41.5000 g. **Composition:** Bi-Metallic **Subject:** Euro's First Anniversary **Obverse:** Queen's portrait **Reverse:** Europa riding a bull **Edge:** Reeded **Size:** 50 mm.

Date	Mintage	F	VF	XF	Unc	BU
2003PM Proof	3,500	Value: 100				

KM# 1034a 2 CROWN **Weight:** 50.0000 g. **Composition:** Bi-Metallic **Subject:** Euro's First Anniversary **Obverse:** Queen's portrait **Reverse:** Europa riding the bull **Edge:** Reeded **Size:** 50 mm.

Date	Mintage	F	VF	XF	Unc	BU
2003PM Proof	2,003	Value: 775				

KM# 1034b 2 CROWN **Weight:** 56.3000 g. **Composition:** Bi-Metallic **Subject:** Euro's First Anniversary **Obverse:** Queen's portrait **Reverse:** Europa riding the bull **Edge:** Reeded **Size:** 50 mm.

Date	Mintage	F	VF	XF	Unc	BU
2003PM Proof	2,003	Value: 800				

KM#106 5 CROWN **Weight:** 155.9230 g. **Composition:** 0.9990 Silver 5.0000 oz. ASW **Series:** Olympics - Barcelona **Obverse:** Queen's portrait **Reverse:** Discus thrower **Note:** Illustration reduced. Actual size 65 millimeters.

Date	Mintage	F	VF	XF	Unc	BU
1991 Proof	Est. 1,000	Value: 225				

KM#451 5 CROWN **Weight:** 155.5175 g. **Composition:** 0.9999 Gold 5.0000 oz. AGW **Subject:** Lord Buddha **Note:** Similar to 1 Crown, KM#449.

Date	F	VF	XF	Unc	BU
1996 Proof	—	—	—	—	—

KM# 907 5 CROWN **Ring Weight:** 73.4100 g. **Ring Composition:** 0.9999 Silver 2.3599 oz. ASW **Center Weight:** 26.9000 g. **Center Composition:** 0.9995 Platinum .8644 oz. APW **Subject:** 21st Century **Obverse:** Like Crown KM#906 **Reverse:** Like Crown KM#906 **Edge:** Reeded **Size:** 50 mm.

Date	Mintage	F	VF	XF	Unc	BU
2001 Proof	199	Value: 1,740				

KM# 107 10 CROWN **Weight:** 311.8460 g. **Composition:** 0.9990 Silver 10.0000 oz. ASW **Series:** Olympics - Barcelona **Obverse:** Queen's portrait **Reverse:** Ancient runners **Size:** 73 mm. **Note:** Illustration reudced.

Date	Mintage	F	VF	XF	Unc	BU
1991 Proof	Est. 1,000	Value: 300				

KM# 130 10 CROWN **Weight:** 311.8460 g. **Composition:** 0.9990 Silver 10.0000 oz. ASW **Subject:** Japanese Royal Wedding **Note:** Similar to 2 Crown, KM#128.

Date	Mintage	F	VF	XF	Unc	BU
1993 Proof	Est. 5,000	Value: 285				

KM# 131 10 CROWN **Weight:** 311.8460 g. **Composition:** 0.9990 Silver 10.0000 oz. ASW **Subject:** Japanese Royal Wedding **Note:** Similar to 2 Crown, KM#129.

Date	Mintage	F	VF	XF	Unc	BU
1993 Proof	Est. 5,000	Value: 285				

KM# 333 40 CROWN **Weight:** 1244.1400 g. **Composition:** 0.9990 Silver 40.0000 oz. ASW **Reverse:** Rock of Gibraltar and the rising sun **Size:** 100 mm. **Note:** Illustration reduced.

Date	Mintage	F	VF	XF	Unc	BU
1994 Proof	Est. 1,500	Value: 550				

KM# 18 POUND **Composition:** Nickel-Brass **Reverse:** Gibraltar castle and key

Date	F	VF	XF	Unc	BU
1988 AA	—	—	—	3.50	—
1990 AA	—	—	—	3.50	—
1991 AA	—	—	—	3.50	—
1991 AC	—	—	—	3.50	—
1992 AA	—	—	—	3.50	—
1993 AA	—	—	—	3.50	—
1996 AA	—	—	—	3.50	—
1997 AA	—	—	—	3.50	—

KM# 18a POUND **Weight:** 9.5000 g. **Composition:** 0.9250 Silver .2825 oz. ASW

Date	F	VF	XF	Unc	BU
1988 Proof	—	Value: 15.00			

KM# 18b POUND **Weight:** 9.5000 g. **Composition:** 0.9170 Gold .2801 oz. AGW

Date	F	VF	XF	Unc	BU
1988 Proof	—	Value: 350			

KM# 32 POUND **Composition:** Nickel-Brass **Subject:** 150th Anniversary of Gibraltar Coinage **Reverse:** Gibraltar castle and key

Date	F	VF	XF	Unc	BU
1989	—	—	—	4.00	—

KM# 32a POUND **Weight:** 9.5000 g. **Composition:** 0.9250 Silver .2826 oz. ASW

Date	Mintage	F	VF	XF	Unc	BU
1989 Proof	Est. 2,500	Value: 35.00				

KM# 32b POUND **Weight:** 9.5000 g. **Composition:** 0.9170 Gold .2801 oz. AGW **Subject:** 150th Anniversary of Gibraltar Coinage

Date	Mintage	F	VF	XF	Unc	BU
1989 Proof	150	Value: 350				

KM# 32c POUND **Weight:** 9.0000 g. **Composition:** 0.9500 Platinum .2749 oz. APW

Date	Mintage	F	VF	XF	Unc	BU
1989 Proof	100	Value: 375				

KM# 191 POUND **Composition:** Nickel-Brass **Subject:** Referendum of 1967 **Obverse:** Queen's portrait right **Reverse:** Gibraltar arms above Rock of Gibraltar with Union Jack background

Date	F	VF	XF	Unc	BU
1993	—	—	—	4.50	—

KM# 191a POUND **Weight:** 9.5000 g. **Composition:** 0.9250 Silver .2825 oz. ASW

Date	Mintage	F	VF	XF	Unc	BU
1993 Proof	Est. 5,000	Value: 35.00				

KM# 191b POUND **Weight:** 9.5000 g. **Composition:** 0.9170 Gold .2801 oz. AGW **Subject:** Referendum of 1967 **Obverse:** Queen's portrait right **Reverse:** Gibraltar arms above Rock of Gibraltar with Union Jack background

Date	Mintage	F	VF	XF	Unc	BU
1993 Proof	Est. 3,500	Value: 350				

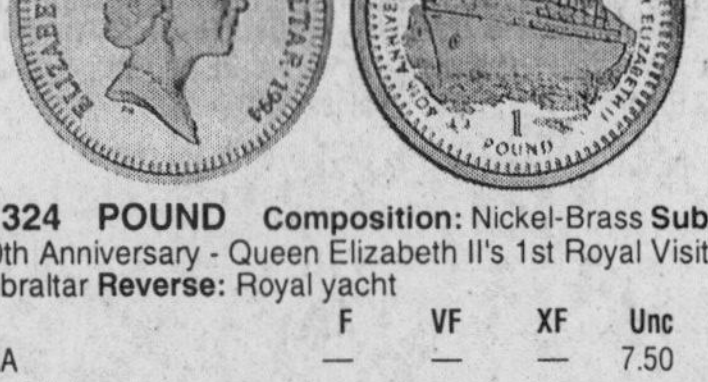

KM# 324 POUND **Composition:** Nickel-Brass **Subject:** 40th Anniversary - Queen Elizabeth II's 1st Royal Visit to Gibraltar **Reverse:** Royal yacht

Date	F	VF	XF	Unc	BU
1994 AA	—	—	—	7.50	—

KM# 340 POUND **Composition:** Nickel-Brass **Subject:** National Day **Reverse:** Rock of Gibraltar

Date	F	VF	XF	Unc	BU
1995 AA	—	—	—	3.50	—

KM# 340a POUND **Weight:** 9.5000 g. **Composition:** 0.9250 Silver .2825 oz. ASW

Date	Mintage	F	VF	XF	Unc	BU
1995 Proof	3,500	Value: 35.00				

KM#869 POUND **Composition:** Nickel-Brass **Obverse:** Portrait of Queen Elizabeth II **Obv. Designer:** Rank-Broadley **Reverse:** Gibraltar castle and key

Date	F	VF	XF	Unc	BU
1998 AA	—	—	—	3.50	—
1999 AA	—	—	—	3.50	—
2001 AA	—	—	—	3.50	—

KM# 24 2 POUNDS **Composition:** Virenium **Reverse:** Cannon in tunnel of fortress

Date	F	VF	XF	Unc	BU
1988 AA	—	—	—	7.50	—
1989 AA	—	—	—	7.50	—
1990 AA	—	—	—	7.50	—
1991 AA	—	—	—	7.50	—
1993 AA	—	—	—	7.50	—
1995 AA	—	—	—	7.50	—
1995 AB	—	—	—	7.50	—
1995 AC	—	—	—	7.50	—
1996 AA	—	—	—	7.50	—

KM# 98 2 POUNDS **Composition:** Virenium **Reverse:** Columbus and ship

Date	F	VF	XF	Unc	BU
1992 AA	—	—	—	6.50	—

KM# 98a 2 POUNDS **Weight:** 9.3000 g. **Composition:** 0.9250 Silver .2766 oz. ASW

Date	Mintage	F	VF	XF	Unc	BU
1992 Proof	Est. 5,000	Value: 40.00				

KM#98b 2 POUNDS **Weight:** 15.9400 g. **Composition:** 0.9170 Gold .4700 oz. AGW **Reverse:** Columbus and ship

Date	F	VF	XF	Unc	BU
1992 Proof	—	—	—	—	—

KM#98c 2 POUNDS **Weight:** 18.0000 g. **Composition:** 0.9500 Platinum .5498 oz. APW

Date	F	VF	XF	Unc	BU
1992 Proof	—	—	—	—	—

KM# 325 2 POUNDS **Composition:** Virenium **Subject:** 40th Anniversary - Queen Elizabeth II's 1st Royal Visit to Gibraltar **Reverse:** Royal yacht

Date	F	VF	XF	Unc	BU
1994 AA	—	—	—	6.50	—

KM# 755a 2 POUNDS **Weight:** 12.0000 g. **Composition:** 0.9990 Gold Plated Silver .999 oz. ASW AGW

Date	Mintage	F	VF	XF	Unc	BU
1997 Proof	Est. 7,500	Value: 60.00				

KM# 758a 2 POUNDS **Composition:** 0.9990 Gold Plated Silver .999 oz. ASW AGW

Date	Mintage	F	VF	XF	Unc	BU
1997 Proof	7,500	Value: 60.00				

KM# 756a 2 POUNDS **Weight:** 12.0000 g. **Composition:** 0.9990 Gold Plated Silver .999 oz. ASW AGW

Date		F	VF	XF	Unc	BU
1997 Proof	Est. 7,500	Value: 60.00				

KM# 757a 2 POUNDS **Weight:** 12.0000 g. **Composition:** 0.9990 Gold Plated Silver .999 oz. ASW AGW

Date		F	VF	XF	Unc	BU
1997 Proof	Est. 7,500	Value: 60.00				

KM# 755 2 POUNDS **Ring Composition:** Brass **Center Composition:** Copper-Nickel **Subject:** The Labours of Hercules **Obverse:** Queen's portrait **Obv. Designer:** Maklouf **Reverse:** Hercules wrestling the Nimean Lion **Note:** Varieties exist with and without die letters exist.

Date	F	VF	XF	Unc	BU
1997	—	—	—	7.50	—

KM# 758 2 POUNDS **Ring Composition:** Brass **Center Composition:** Copper-Nickel **Subject:** The Labours of Hercules **Obverse:** Queen's portrait **Reverse:** Hercules wrestles the Erymanthian Boar

Date	F	VF	XF	Unc	BU
1998 AA	—	—	—	7.50	—

KM# 757 2 POUNDS **Ring Composition:** Brass **Center Composition:** Copper-Nickel **Subject:** The Labours of Hercules **Obverse:** Queen's portrait **Reverse:** Hercules and the Ceryneian Hind

Date	F	VF	XF	Unc	BU
1998 AA	—	—	—	7.50	—

KM# 756 2 POUNDS **Ring Composition:** Brass **Center Composition:** Copper-Nickel **Subject:** The Labours of Hercules **Obverse:** Portrait of Queen Elizabeth II **Obv. Designer:** Rank-Broadley **Reverse:** Hercules fighting the Hydra

Date	F	VF	XF	Unc	BU
1998 AA	—	—	—	7.50	—

KM# 759 2 POUNDS **Composition:** 0.9990 Gold Plated Silver .999 oz. ASW AGW **Subject:** The Labours of Hercules **Obverse:** Queen's portrait **Reverse:** Hercules and the Augean Stables

Date	F	VF	XF	Unc	BU
1999 AA	—	—	—	7.50	—

KM# 759a 2 POUNDS **Weight:** 10.0000 g. **Composition:** 0.9990 Gold Plated Silver .999 oz. ASW AGW

Date	Mintage	F	VF	XF	Unc	BU
1999 Proof	Est. 25,000	Value: 60.00				

KM# 760 2 POUNDS **Center Composition:** Copper-Nickel **Subject:** The Labours of Hercules **Obverse:** Queen's portrait **Reverse:** Hercules and the Cretan Bull

Date	F	VF	XF	Unc	BU
1999 AA	—	—	—	7.50	—

KM# 760a 2 POUNDS **Weight:** 10.0000 g. **Composition:** 0.9990 Gold Plated Silver .999 oz. ASW AGW

Date	Mintage	F	VF	XF	Unc	BU
1999 Proof	Est. 25,000	Value: 60.00				

KM# 761 2 POUNDS **Ring Composition:** Brass **Center Composition:** Copper-Nickel **Subject:** The Labours of Hercules **Obverse:** Queen's portrait **Reverse:** Hercules and the Stymphalian Birds

Date	F	VF	XF	Unc	BU
1999 AA	—	—	—	7.50	—

KM# 761a 2 POUNDS **Weight:** 10.0000 g. **Composition:** 0.9990 Gold Plated Silver .999 oz. ASW AGW

Date	Mintage	F	VF	XF	Unc	BU
1999 Proof	Est. 25,000	Value: 60.00				

KM# 762 2 POUNDS **Ring Composition:** Brass **Center Composition:** Copper-Nickel **Subject:** The Labours of Hercules **Obverse:** Queen's portrait **Reverse:** Hercules and the Mares of Diomedes

Date	F	VF	XF	Unc	BU
1999 AA	—	—	—	7.50	—

KM# 762a 2 POUNDS **Weight:** 10.0000 g. **Composition:** 0.9990 Gold Plated Silver .999 oz. ASW AGW

Date	Mintage	F	VF	XF	Unc	BU
1999 Proof	Est. 25,000	Value: 60.00				

KM# 763 2 POUNDS **Ring Composition:** Brass **Center Composition:** Copper-Nickel **Subject:** The Labours of Hercules **Obverse:** Queen's portrait **Reverse:** Hercules and Hippolyta's Girdle **Edge:** Reeded

Date	F	VF	XF	Unc	BU
2000 AA	—	—	—	7.50	—

KM# 764 2 POUNDS **Ring Composition:** Brass **Center Weight:** 12.0000 g. **Center Composition:** Copper-Nickel **Subject:** The Labours of Hercules - Geryon's Cattle **Obverse:** Queen's portrait **Reverse:** Hercules with cow and three devils shot by one arrow **Edge:** Reeded

Date	F	VF	XF	Unc	BU
2000 AA	—	—	—	7.50	—

KM# 765 2 POUNDS **Ring Composition:** Brass **Center Composition:** Copper-Nickel **Subject:** The Labours of Hercules **Obverse:** Queen's portrait **Reverse:** Hercules carrying the world while facing a man with a bushel of apples **Edge:** Reeded

Date	F	VF	XF	Unc	BU
2000 AA	—	—	—	7.50	—

KM# 766 2 POUNDS **Ring Composition:** Brass **Center Composition:** Copper-Nickel **Subject:** The Labours of Hercules **Obverse:** Queen's portrait **Reverse:** Hercules chaining Cerberus

Date	F	VF	XF	Unc	BU
2000 AA	—	—	—	7.50	—

KM# 763a 2 POUNDS **Weight:** 12.0000 g. **Composition:** 0.9990 Silver .3854 oz. ASW **Subject:** The Labours of Hercules **Note:** Partially gold plated.

Date	Mintage	F	VF	XF	Unc	BU
2000 Proof	7,500	Value: 60.00				

KM# 764a 2 POUNDS **Weight:** 12.0000 g. **Composition:** 0.9990 Silver .3854 oz. ASW **Subject:** The Labours of Hercules **Note:** Partially gold plated.

Date	Mintage	F	VF	XF	Unc	BU
2000 Proof	7,500	Value: 60.00				

KM# 765a 2 POUNDS **Weight:** 12.0000 g. **Composition:** 0.9990 Silver .3854 oz. ASW **Subject:** The Labours of Hercules **Note:** Partially gold plated.

Date	Mintage	F	VF	XF	Unc	BU
2000 Proof	7,500	Value: 60.00				

KM# 766a 2 POUNDS **Weight:** 12.0000 g. **Composition:** 0.9990 Silver .3854 oz. ASW **Subject:** The Labours of Hercules **Note:** Partially gold plated.

Date	Mintage	F	VF	XF	Unc	BU
2000 Proof	7,500	Value: 60.00				

KM# 970 2 POUNDS **Ring Weight:** 12.0000 g. **Ring Composition:** Brass **Center Composition:** Steel Copper-Nickel **Subject:** Bicentennial of the Union Jack **Obverse:** Queen's portrait **Reverse:** Standing Britannia wearing flag as a cape **Edge:** Reeded **Size:** 28.4 mm.

Date	F	VF	XF	Unc	BU
2001	—	—	—	10.00	—

KM# 970a 2 POUNDS **Ring Composition:** 0.9990 Gold Plated Silver .3854 oz. ASW AGW **Center Weight:** 12.0000 g. **Center Composition:** 0.9990 Silver **Edge:** Reeded **Size:** 28.4 mm.

Date	Mintage	F	VF	XF	Unc	BU
2001	7,500	—	—	—	30.00	—

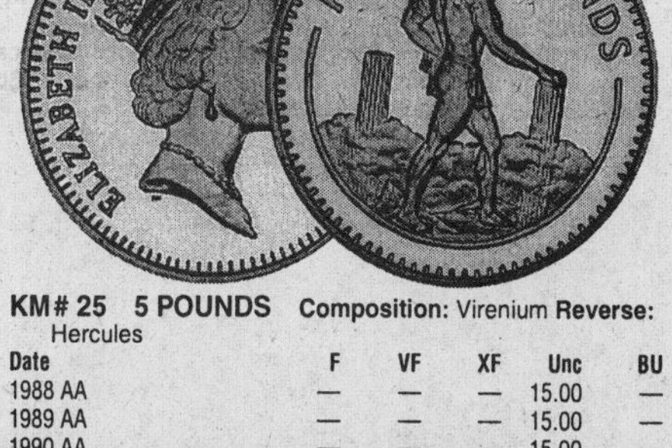

KM# 25 5 POUNDS **Composition:** Virenium **Reverse:** Hercules

Date	F	VF	XF	Unc	BU
1988 AA	—	—	—	15.00	—
1989 AA	—	—	—	15.00	—
1990 AA	—	—	—	15.00	—
1991 AA	—	—	—	15.00	—

Date	F	VF	XF	Unc	BU
1992 AA	—	—	—	15.00	—
1993 AA	—	—	—	15.00	—

KM# 309 5 POUNDS **Composition:** Virenium **Reverse:** D-Day - Solider, sailor and pilot

Date	Mintage	F	VF	XF	Unc	BU
1994		—	—	—	16.50	—
1994 Proof	Est. 5,000	Value: 20.00				

KM# 309a 5 POUNDS **Weight:** 23.5000 g. **Composition:** 0.9250 Silver .6989 oz. ASW

Date	Mintage	F	VF	XF	Unc	BU
1994 Proof	Est. 5,000	Value: 40.00				

KM# 309b 5 POUNDS **Weight:** 39.8300 g. **Composition:** 0.9170 Gold 1.1743 oz. AGW **Reverse:** D-Day - Soldier, sailor and pilot

Date	F	VF	XF	Unc	BU
1994 Proof	—	—	—	—	—

KM# 332 5 POUNDS **Composition:** Virenium **Reverse:** 50th Anniversary - VE Day

Date	Mintage	F	VF	XF	Unc	BU
1995		—	—	—	16.50	—
1995 Proof	Est. 5,000	Value: 20.00				

KM# 332a 5 POUNDS **Weight:** 23.5000 g. **Composition:** 0.9250 Silver .6989 oz. ASW

Date	Mintage	F	VF	XF	Unc	BU
1995 Proof	Est. 5,000	Value: 40.00				

KM# 332b 5 POUNDS **Weight:** 39.8300 g. **Composition:** 0.9170 Gold 1.1743 oz. AGW **Reverse:** 50th Anniversary - VE Day

Date	Mintage	F	VF	XF	Unc	BU
1995 Proof	Est. 850	Value: 850				

KM# 334 5 POUNDS **Composition:** Virenium **Reverse:** Queen Mother viewing bomb damaged Buckingham Palace

Date	F	VF	XF	Unc	BU
1995	—	—	—	15.00	—

KM# 334a 5 POUNDS **Weight:** 25.5000 g. **Composition:** 0.9250 Silver .6980 oz. ASW

Date	Mintage	F	VF	XF	Unc	BU
1995 Proof	Est. 5,000	Value: 40.00				

KM# 334b 5 POUNDS **Weight:** 39.8300 g. **Composition:** 0.9170 Gold 1.1743 oz. AGW **Reverse:** Queen Mother viewing bomb damaged Buckingham Palace

Date	Mintage	F	VF	XF	Unc	BU
1995 Proof	Est. 850	Value: 750				

KM# 335 5 POUNDS **Composition:** Virenium **Reverse:** VJ Day - Flag Raising

Date	Mintage	F	VF	XF	Unc	BU
1995		—	—	—	16.50	—
1995 Proof	Est. 5,000	Value: 20.00				

KM# 335a 5 POUNDS **Weight:** 23.5000 g. **Composition:** 0.9250 Silver .6989 oz. ASW

Date	Mintage	F	VF	XF	Unc	BU
1995 Proof	Est. 5,000	Value: 40.00				

KM# 335b 5 POUNDS **Weight:** 39.8300 g. **Composition:** 0.9170 Gold 1.1743 oz. AGW **Reverse:** VJ Day - Flag Raising

Date	Mintage	F	VF	XF	Unc	BU
1995 Proof	Est. 850	Value: 850				

KM# 341 5 POUNDS **Composition:** Virenium **Reverse:** 190th Anniversary - Death of Admiral Nelson

Date	F	VF	XF	Unc	BU
1995	—	—	—	15.00	—

KM# 341a 5 POUNDS **Weight:** 23.5000 g. **Composition:** 0.9250 Silver .6989 oz. ASW

Date	Mintage	F	VF	XF	Unc	BU
1995 Proof	Est. 5,000	Value: 40.00				

KM# 341b 5 POUNDS **Weight:** 39.0830 g. **Composition:** 0.9170 Gold 1.1743 oz. AGW **Reverse:** 190th Anniversary - Death of Admiral Nelson

Date	Mintage	F	VF	XF	Unc	BU
1995 Proof	Est. 850	Value: 900				

KM# 354 5 POUNDS **Composition:** Virenium **Reverse:** 70th Birthday of Queen Elizabeth II

Date	F	VF	XF	Unc	BU
1996	—	—	—	16.50	—

KM# 354a 5 POUNDS **Weight:** 23.5000 g. **Composition:** 0.9250 Silver .6989 oz. ASW

Date	Mintage	F	VF	XF	Unc	BU
1996 Proof	Est. 5,000	Value: 40.00				

KM# 354b 5 POUNDS **Weight:** 39.8300 g. **Composition:** 0.9170 Gold 1.1743 oz. AGW **Reverse:** 70th Birthday of Queen Elizabeth II

Date	Mintage	F	VF	XF	Unc	BU
1996 Proof	Est. 850	Value: 650				

KM# 355 5 POUNDS **Composition:** Virenium **Reverse:** Olympics - Zeus on Throne

Date	F	VF	XF	Unc	BU
1996	—	—	—	16.50	—

KM# 355a 5 POUNDS **Weight:** 23.5000 g. **Composition:** 0.9250 Silver .3989 oz. ASW

Date	Mintage	F	VF	XF	Unc	BU
1996 Proof	Est. 5,000	Value: 40.00				

KM# 355b 5 POUNDS **Weight:** 39.8300 g. **Composition:** 0.9170 Gold 1.1743 oz. AGW **Reverse:** Olympics - Zeus on Throne

Date	Mintage	F	VF	XF	Unc	BU
1996 Proof	850	Value: 750				

KM# 527 5 POUNDS **Composition:** Virenium **Subject:** Queen Elizabeth II's Golden Wedding Anniversary **Obverse:** Queen's portrait **Reverse:** Two hands

Date	F	VF	XF	Unc	BU
1997	—	—	—	17.50	—

KM# 527a 5 POUNDS **Weight:** 25.5000 g. **Composition:** 0.9250 Silver .6989 oz. ASW

Date	Mintage	F	VF	XF	Unc	BU
1997 Proof	Est. 10,000	Value: 40.00				

KM# 527b 5 POUNDS **Weight:** 39.8300 g. **Composition:** 0.9170 Gold 1.1743 oz. AGW **Subject:** Queen Elizabeth II's Golden Wedding Anniversary **Obverse:** Queen's portrait **Reverse:** Two hands

Date	Mintage	F	VF	XF	Unc	BU
1997 Proof	Est. 850	Value: 750				

KM# 605 5 POUNDS **Composition:** Virenium **Subject:** Bicentennial - Arrival of Commodore Nelson **Obverse:** Queen's portrait **Reverse:** Cameo portrait of Nelson above left of his ship

Date	F	VF	XF	Unc	BU
1997 AA	—	—	—	16.50	—

KM# 605a 5 POUNDS **Weight:** 23.5000 g. **Composition:** 0.9250 Silver .6989 oz. ASW

Date	Mintage	F	VF	XF	Unc	BU
1997 Proof	Est. 10,000	Value: 40.00				

KM# 605b 5 POUNDS **Weight:** 39.8300 g. **Composition:** 0.9170 Gold 1.1743 oz. AGW **Subject:** Bicentennial - Arrival of Commodore Nelson **Obverse:** Queen's portrait **Reverse:** Cameo portrait of Nelson above left of his ship

Date	Mintage	F	VF	XF	Unc	BU
1997 Proof	Est. 850	Value: 850				

KM# 607 5 POUNDS **Composition:** Virenium **Subject:** Last Voyage of Britannia **Obverse:** Queen's portrait **Reverse:** Ship sailing past Gibraltar

Date	F	VF	XF	Unc	BU
1997 AA	—	—	—	16.50	—

KM# 607a 5 POUNDS **Weight:** 23.5000 g. **Composition:** 0.9250 Silver .6989 oz. ASW

Date	Mintage	F	VF	XF	Unc	BU
1997 Proof	Est. 5,000	Value: 50.00				

KM# 607b 5 POUNDS **Weight:** 39.8300 g. **Composition:** 0.9170 Gold 1.1743 oz. AGW **Subject:** Last Voyage of Britannia **Obverse:** Queen's portrait **Reverse:** Ship sailing past Gibraltar

Date	Mintage	F	VF	XF	Unc	BU
1997 Proof	Est. 850	Value: 850				

KM# 740 5 POUNDS **Composition:** Virenium **Subject:** 40th Anniversary of Radio Gibraltar **Obverse:** Queen's portrait **Reverse:** Radio broadcaster on the job

Date	F	VF	XF	Unc	BU
1998	—	—	—	16.00	—

KM# 740a 5 POUNDS **Weight:** 23.5000 g. **Composition:** 0.9250 Silver .6989 oz. ASW

Date	Mintage	F	VF	XF	Unc	BU
1998 Proof	Est. 5,000	Value: 40.00				

KM# 740b 5 POUNDS **Weight:** 39.8300 g. **Composition:** 0.9170 Gold 1.1743 oz. AGW **Subject:** 40th Anniversary of Radio Gibraltar **Obverse:** Queen's portrait **Reverse:** Radio broadcaster on the job

Date	Mintage	F	VF	XF	Unc	BU
1998 Proof	Est. 850	Value: 850				

KM# 770 5 POUNDS **Composition:** Virenium **Subject:** 80th Anniversary of the RAF **Obverse:** Queen's portrait **Reverse:** Eurofighter over map

Date	F	VF	XF	Unc	BU
1998	—	—	—	16.00	—

KM# 770a 5 POUNDS **Weight:** 23.5000 g. **Composition:** 0.9250 Silver .6989 oz. ASW

Date	Mintage	F	VF	XF	Unc	BU
1998 Proof	Est. 5,000	Value: 50.00				

KM# 770b 5 POUNDS **Weight:** 39.8300 g. **Composition:** 0.9170 Gold 1.1743 oz. AGW **Subject:** 80th Anniversary of the RAF **Obverse:** Queen's portrait

Date	Mintage	F	VF	XF	Unc	BU
1998 Proof	Est. 850	Value: 850				

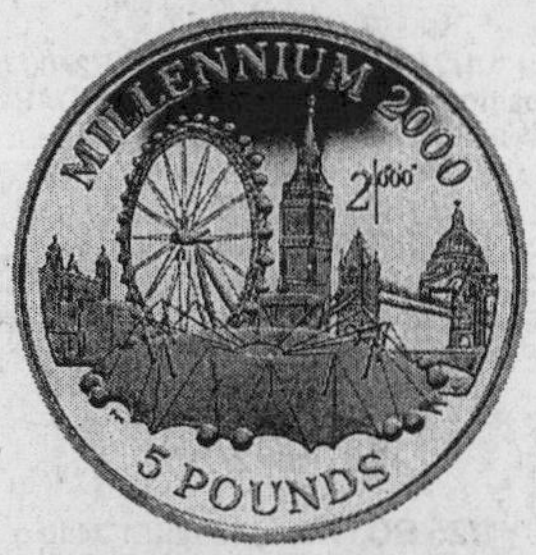

KM# 771 5 POUNDS **Composition:** Virenium **Subject:** Millennium 2000 **Obverse:** Queen's portrait **Reverse:** Landmarks of London

Date	F	VF	XF	Unc	BU
1998	—	—	—	16.00	—

KM# 771a 5 POUNDS **Weight:** 23.5000 g. **Composition:** 0.9250 Silver .6989 oz. ASW

Date	Mintage	F	VF	XF	Unc	BU
1998 Proof	Est. 5,000	Value: 50.00				

KM# 771b 5 POUNDS **Weight:** 39.8300 g. **Composition:** 0.9170 Gold 1.1743 oz. AGW **Reverse:** Millennium 2000

Date	Mintage	F	VF	XF	Unc	BU
1998 Proof	850	Value: 875				

KM# 772 5 POUNDS **Composition:** Virenium **Subject:** 50th Birthday of Prince Charles **Obverse:** Queen's portrait **Reverse:** Heads of Prince Charles and sons William and Harry

Date	F	VF	XF	Unc	BU
1998 AA	—	—	—	16.00	—

KM# 772a 5 POUNDS **Weight:** 23.5000 g. **Composition:** 0.9250 Silver .6989 oz. ASW

Date	Mintage	F	VF	XF	Unc	BU
1998 Proof	5,000	Value: 50.00				

KM# 772b 5 POUNDS **Weight:** 39.8300 g. **Composition:** 0.9170 Gold 1.1743 oz. AGW

Date	Mintage	F	VF	XF	Unc	BU
1998 Proof	850	Value: 875				

KM# 797 5 POUNDS **Composition:** Virenium **Subject:** Millennium 2000 **Obverse:** Portrait of Queen Elizabeth II **Obv. Designer:** Rank-Broadley **Reverse:** Sundial, digital clock face, candle and traditional clock face

Date	F	VF	XF	Unc	BU
1999	—	—	—	16.00	—

KM# 797a 5 POUNDS **Composition:** Titanium

Date	F	VF	XF	Unc	BU
1999	—	—	—	35.00	—

KM# 797b 5 POUNDS **Weight:** 28.2800 g. **Composition:** 0.9250 Silver .8410 oz. ASW

Date	Mintage	F	VF	XF	Unc	BU
1999 Proof	Est. 5,000	Value: 65.00				

KM# 867 5 POUNDS **Composition:** Virenium **Subject:** Mediterranean Rowing Club **Obverse:** Portrait of Queen Elizabeth II **Obv. Designer:** Rank-Broadley **Reverse:** A one-man and a four-man row boat

Date	F	VF	XF	Unc	BU
1999	—	—	—	16.00	—

KM# 867a 5 POUNDS **Weight:** 23.5000 g. **Composition:** 0.8250 Silver .6989 oz. ASW

Date	Mintage	F	VF	XF	Unc	BU
1999 Proof	Est. 5,000	Value: 65.00				

KM# 867b 5 POUNDS **Weight:** 39.8300 g. **Composition:** 0.9170 Gold 1.1743 oz. AGW

Date	Mintage	F	VF	XF	Unc	BU
1999 Proof	Est. 850	Value: 885				

KM# 878 5 POUNDS **Composition:** Virenium **Subject:** Battle of Britain **Obverse:** Queen's portrait **Reverse:** Spitfire in flight

Date	F	VF	XF	Unc	BU
2000	—	—	—	15.00	—

KM# 878a 5 POUNDS **Weight:** 23.5000 g. **Composition:** 0.9250 Silver 69.89 oz. ASW

Date	Mintage	F	VF	XF	Unc	BU
2000 Proof	Est. 10,000	Value: 50.00				

KM# 878b 5 POUNDS **Weight:** 39.8300 g. **Composition:** 0.9160 Gold 1.1738 oz. AGW **Subject:** Battle of Britain **Obverse:** Queen's portrait **Reverse:** Spitfire in flight

Date	Mintage	F	VF	XF	Unc	BU
2000 Proof	Est. 850	Value: 885				

KM# 885 5 POUNDS **Weight:** 10.0000 g. **Composition:** Titanium **Subject:** 160th Anniversary - Uniform Penny Post **Obverse:** Bust Queen right **Reverse:** Postage stamp design **Edge:** Reeded

Date	Mintage	F	VF	XF	Unc	BU
2000 Proof	15,000	Value: 35.00				

KM# 953 5 POUNDS **Weight:** 20.0000 g. **Composition:** Virenium **Subject:** Gibraltar Chronicle 200 Years **Obverse:** Queen's portrait **Reverse:** Naval battle scene with newspaper in background **Edge:** Reeded **Size:** 36.1 mm.

Date	F	VF	XF	Unc	BU
2001	—	—	—	15.00	—

KM# 953a 5 POUNDS **Weight:** 23.5000 g. **Composition:** 0.9250 Silver .6989 oz. ASW **Edge:** Reeded **Size:** 36.1 mm.

Date	Mintage	F	VF	XF	Unc	BU
2001 Proof	10,000	Value: 50.00				

KM# 953b 5 POUNDS **Weight:** 39.8300 g. **Composition:** 0.9167 Gold 1.1739 oz. AGW **Edge:** Reeded **Size:** 36.1 mm.

Date	Mintage	F	VF	XF	Unc	BU
2001 Proof	850	Value: 885				

KM# 1011 5 POUNDS **Weight:** 20.0000 g. **Composition:** Virenium **Subject:** Queen's Golden Jubilee **Obverse:** Bust of Queen Elizabeth II right **Reverse:** Coronation scene **Edge:** Reeded **Size:** 36.1 mm.

Date	F	VF	XF	Unc	BU
2002	—	—	—	15.00	—

KM# 1011a 5 POUNDS **Weight:** 23.5000 g. **Composition:** 0.9250 Silver 0.6989 oz. ASW **Subject:** Queen's Golden Jubilee **Obverse:** Bust of Queen Elizabeth II right **Reverse:** Coronation scene **Edge:** Reeded **Size:** 36.1 mm.

Date	Mintage	F	VF	XF	Unc	BU
2002 Proof	10,000	Value: 50.00				

KM# 1011b 5 POUNDS **Weight:** 39.8300 g. **Composition:** 0.9166 Gold 1.1738 oz. AGW **Subject:** Queen's Golden Jubilee **Obverse:** Bust of Queen Elizabeth II right **Reverse:** Coronation scene **Edge:** Reeded **Size:** 36.1 mm.

Date	Mintage	F	VF	XF	Unc	BU
2002 Proof	850	Value: 885				

KM# 7 25 POUNDS **Weight:** 7.7700 g. **Composition:** 0.9170 Gold .2291 oz. AGW **Subject:** 250th Anniversary - Introduction of British Sterling

Date	Mintage	F	VF	XF	Unc	BU
1975	2,395	—	—	—	120	—
1975 Proof	750	Value: 180				

KM# 8 50 POUNDS **Weight:** 15.5500 g. **Composition:** 0.9170 Gold .4585 oz. AGW **Subject:** 250th Anniversary - Introduction of British Sterling **Obverse:** Similar to 25 Pounds, KM#7

Date	Mintage	F	VF	XF	Unc	BU
1975	1,625	—	—	—	220	—
1975 Proof	750	Value: 320				

KM# 13 50 POUNDS **Weight:** 15.9760 g. **Composition:** 0.9170 Gold .4711 oz. AGW **Reverse:** 175th Anniversary - Death of Admiral Nelson

Date	Mintage	F	VF	XF	Unc	BU
1980	—	—	—	—	200	—
1980 Proof	Est. 5,000	Value: 225				

KM# 15 50 POUNDS **Weight:** 15.9760 g. **Composition:** 0.9170 Gold .4711 oz. AGW **Reverse:** Wedding of Prince Charles and Lady Diana

Date	Mintage	F	VF	XF	Unc	BU
1981	—	—	—	—	210	—
1981 Proof	Est. 2,500	Value: 235				

KM# 9 100 POUNDS **Weight:** 31.1000 g. **Composition:** 0.9170 Gold .9170 oz. AGW **Subject:** 250th Anniversary - Introduction of British Sterling **Obverse:** Similar to 25 Pounds, KM#7

Date	Mintage	F	VF	XF	Unc	BU
1975	1,625	—	—	—	420	—
1975 Proof	750	Value: 500				

SOVEREIGN COINAGE

KM# 26 1/4 SOVEREIGN **Weight:** 1.9900 g. **Composition:** 0.9170 Gold .0587 oz. AGW **Subject:** 150th Anniversary of Regal Coinage **Reverse:** Una and the Lion **Note:** Similar to 5 Sovereigns, KM#30.

Date	Mintage	F	VF	XF	Unc	BU
1989 U	—	—	—	—	—	—
1989 Proof	Est. 1,989	Value: 70.00				

KM# 41 1/4 SOVEREIGN **Weight:** 1.9900 g. **Composition:** 0.9170 Gold .0587 oz. AGW **Subject:** 21st Anniversary - Constitution **Obverse:** Similar to 5 Sovereigns, KM#30.1 **Reverse:** Similar to 5 Sovereigns, KM#45

Date	Mintage	F	VF	XF	Unc	BU
1990 Proof	Est. 1,000	Value: 65.00				

KM# 515 1/4 SOVEREIGN **Weight:** 1.2241 g. **Composition:** 0.9999 Gold .0400 oz. AGW **Subject:** Una and the Lion **Note:** Similar to 1 Sovereign, KM#517.

Date		F	VF	XF	Unc	BU
1997 Proof	—	Value: 50.00				

KM# 27 1/2 SOVEREIGN **Weight:** 3.9800 g. **Composition:** 0.9170 Gold .1173 oz. AGW **Subject:** 150th Anniversary of Regal Coinage **Reverse:** Una and the Lion **Note:** Similar to 5 Sovereigns, KM#30.2.

Date	Mintage	F	VF	XF	Unc	BU
1989 U	—	—	—	—	—	—
1989 Proof	Est. 1,989	Value: 135				

KM# 42 1/2 SOVEREIGN **Weight:** 3.9800 g. **Composition:** 0.9170 Gold .1173 oz. AGW **Subject:** 21st Anniversary - Constitution **Obverse:** Similar to 5 Sovereigns, KM#30.1 **Reverse:** Similar to 5 Sovereigns, KM#45

Date	Mintage	F	VF	XF	Unc	BU
1990 Proof	1,000	Value: 125				

KM# 516 1/2 SOVEREIGN **Weight:** 3.1103 g. **Composition:** 0.9999 Gold .10000 oz. AGW **Subject:** Una and the Lion **Note:** Similar to 1 Sovereign, KM#517.

Date		F	VF	XF	Unc	BU
1997 Proof	—	Value: 85.00				

KM# 28 SOVEREIGN **Weight:** 7.9600 g. **Composition:** 0.9170 Gold .2347 oz. AGW **Subject:** 150th Anniversary of Regal Coinage **Note:** Similar to 5 Sovereigns, KM#30.2.

Date	Mintage	F	VF	XF	Unc	BU
1989 U	—	—	—	—	—	—
1989 Proof	Est. 1,989	Value: 265				

KM# 43 SOVEREIGN **Weight:** 7.9600 g. **Composition:** 0.9170 Gold .2347 oz. AGW **Subject:** 21st Anniversary - Constitution **Obverse:** Similar to 5 Sovereigns, KM#30.1 **Reverse:** Similar to 5 Sovereigns, KM#45

Date	Mintage	F	VF	XF	Unc	BU
1990 Proof	Est. 1,000	Value: 250				

KM# 517 SOVEREIGN **Weight:** 6.2207 g. **Composition:** 0.9999 Gold .2000 oz. AGW **Obverse:** Queen's portrait **Reverse:** Una in toga with scepter and lion

Date		F	VF	XF	Unc	BU
1997 Proof	—	Value: 175				

KM# 29 2 SOVEREIGNS **Weight:** 15.9400 g. **Composition:** 0.9170 Gold .4700 oz. AGW **Subject:** 150th Anniversary of Regal Coinage **Reverse:** Una and the Lion **Note:** Similar to 5 Sovereigns, KM#30.

Date	Mintage	F	VF	XF	Unc	BU
1989 Proof	1,989	Value: 550				

KM# 44 2 SOVEREIGNS **Weight:** 15.9400 g. **Composition:** 0.9170 Gold .4700 oz. AGW **Subject:** 21st Anniversary - Constitution **Obverse:** Similar to 5 Sovereigns, KM#30.1 **Reverse:** Similar to 5 Sovereigns, KM#45

Date	Mintage	F	VF	XF	Unc	BU
1990 Proof	1,000	Value: 500				

KM# 30 5 SOVEREIGNS **Weight:** 39.8300 g. **Composition:** 0.9170 Gold 1.1743 oz. AGW **Subject:** 150th Anniversary of Regal Coinage **Reverse:** Una and the Lion

Date	Mintage	F	VF	XF	Unc	BU
1989 Proof	1,989	Value: 1,100				

KM# 45 5 SOVEREIGNS **Weight:** 39.8300 g. **Composition:** 0.9170 Gold 1.1743 oz. AGW **Subject:** 21st Anniversary - Constitution **Obverse:** Similar to KM#30

Date	Mintage	F	VF	XF	Unc	BU
1990 Proof	Est. 1,000	Value: 950				

ROYAL COINAGE

KM# 91 1/25 ROYAL **Weight:** 1.2400 g. **Composition:** 0.9999 Gold .0400 oz. AGW **Reverse:** Corgi **Note:** Similar to 1 Royal, KM#97.

Date	Mintage	F	VF	XF	Unc	BU
1991	—	—	—	—	75.00	—
1991 Proof	Est. 1,000	Value: 76.50				

KM# 99 1/25 ROYAL **Weight:** 1.2400 g. **Composition:** 0.9999 Gold .0400 oz. AGW **Reverse:** Cocker Spaniel **Note:** Similar to 1 Royal, KM#105.

Date	Mintage	F	VF	XF	Unc	BU
1992	—	—	—	—	35.00	—
1992 Proof	Est. 1,000	Value: 36.50				

KM# 193 1/25 ROYAL **Weight:** 1.2400 g. **Composition:** 0.9999 Gold .0400 oz. AGW **Reverse:** Long-haired Dachshund **Note:** Similar to 1 Royal, KM#197.

Date	Mintage	F	VF	XF	Unc	BU
1993	—	—	—	—	35.00	—
1993 Proof	Est. 1,000	Value: 36.50				

KM# 248 1/25 ROYAL **Weight:** 1.2400 g. **Composition:** 0.9999 Gold .0400 oz. AGW **Reverse:** Pekingese **Note:** Similar to 1/5 Royal, KM#250.

Date	Mintage	F	VF	XF	Unc	BU
1994	—	—	—	—	35.00	—
1994 Proof	Est. 1,000	Value: 36.50				

KM# 319 1/25 ROYAL **Weight:** 1.2400 g. **Composition:** 0.9999 Gold .0400 oz. AGW **Reverse:** Collie **Note:** Similar to 1 Royal, KM#323.

Date	Mintage	F	VF	XF	Unc	BU
1995	—	—	—	—	35.00	—
1995 Proof	Est. 1,000	Value: 36.50				

KM# 361 1/25 ROYAL **Weight:** 1.2400 g. **Composition:** 0.9999 Gold .0400 oz. AGW **Reverse:** Bulldog **Note:** Similar to 1 Royal, KM#365b.

Date	Mintage	F	VF	XF	Unc	BU
1996	—	—	—	—	35.00	—
1996 Proof	Est. 1,000	Value: 36.50				

KM# 557 1/25 ROYAL **Weight:** 1.2400 g. **Composition:** 0.9999 Gold .0400 oz. AGW **Reverse:** Yorkshire Terrier **Note:** Similar to 1 Royal, KM#561b.

Date	Mintage	F	VF	XF	Unc	BU
1997	—	—	—	—	50.00	—
1997 Proof	Est. 1,000	Value: 52.00				

KM# 749 1/25 ROYAL **Weight:** 1.2400 g. **Composition:** 0.9999 Gold .0400 oz. AGW **Obverse:** Queen's portrait **Reverse:** Kissing cherubs **Note:** Similar to 1 Royal, KM#754.

Date	Mintage	F	VF	XF	Unc	BU
1998	—	—	—	—	50.00	—
1998 Proof	Est. 1,000	Value: 52.00				

KM# 749a 1/25 ROYAL **Weight:** 1.2400 g. **Composition:** 0.9950 Platinum .0400 oz. APW **Reverse:** Kissing cherubs

Date		F	VF	XF	Unc	BU
1998 Proof	—	Value: 75.00				

KM# 828 1/25 ROYAL **Weight:** 1.2400 g. **Composition:** 0.9990 Gold .0400 oz. AGW **Obverse:** Queen's portrait **Reverse:** Cherub

Date	Mintage	F	VF	XF	Unc	BU
1999 U	—	—	—	—	35.00	—
1999 U Y2K	—	—	—	—	35.00	—
1999 Proof	Est. 1,000	Value: 36.50				

KM# 828a 1/25 ROYAL **Weight:** 1.2400 g. **Composition:** 0.9950 Platinum .0400 oz. APW **Obverse:** Queen's portrait **Reverse:** One cherub

Date	Mintage	F	VF	XF	Unc	BU
1999 Proof	Est. 1,000	Value: 75.00				

KM# 896 1/25 ROYAL **Weight:** 1.2441 g. **Composition:** 0.9999 Gold .0400 oz. AGW **Subject:** Bullion **Obverse:** Queen's portrait **Reverse:** Two cherubs **Edge:** Reeded **Size:** 13.92 mm.

Date	Mintage	F	VF	XF	Unc	BU
2001	—	—	—	—	32.00	—
2001 In Proof sets only	1,000	Value: 50.00				

KM# 972 1/25 ROYAL **Weight:** 1.2440 g. **Composition:** 0.9990 Gold 0.04 oz. AGW **Subject:** Cherubs **Obverse:** Queen Elizabeth II's bust right **Reverse:** Two cherubs shooting arrrows **Edge:** Reeded **Size:** 13.92 mm.

Date	Mintage	F	VF	XF	Unc	BU
2002	—	—	—	—	32.00	—
2002 Proof	1,000	Value: 49.50				

KM# 1027 1/25 ROYAL **Weight:** 1.2440 g. **Composition:** 0.9999 Gold 0.04 oz. AGW **Subject:** Cherub **Obverse:** Queen's portrait **Reverse:** Cherub with crossed arms **Edge:** Reeded **Size:** 13.92 mm.

Date		F	VF	XF	Unc	BU
2003PM		—	—	—	32.00	—
2003PM Proof	—	Value: 49.50				

KM# 92 1/10 ROYAL **Weight:** 3.1100 g. **Composition:** 0.9999 Gold .1000 oz. AGW **Reverse:** Corgi **Note:** Similar to 1 Royal, KM#97.

Date	Mintage	F	VF	XF	Unc	BU
1991	—	—	—	—	75.00	—
1991 Proof	Est. 1,000	Value: 76.50				

KM# 100 1/10 ROYAL **Weight:** 3.1100 g. **Composition:** 0.9999 Gold .1000 oz. AGW **Reverse:** Cocker Spaniel **Note:** Similar to 1 Royal, KM#105.

Date	Mintage	F	VF	XF	Unc	BU
1992	—	—	—	—	75.00	—
1992 Proof	Est. 1,000	Value: 76.50				

KM# 194 1/10 ROYAL Weight: 3.1100 g. **Composition:** 0.9999 Gold .1000 oz. AGW **Reverse:** Long-haired Dachshund

Date	Mintage	F	VF	XF	Unc	BU
1993		—	—	—	60.00	—
1993 Proof	Est. 1,000	Value: 62.00				

KM# 249 1/10 ROYAL Weight: 3.1100 g. **Composition:** 0.9999 Gold .1000 oz. AGW **Reverse:** Pekingese **Note:** Similar to 1/5 Royal, KM#250.

Date	Mintage	F	VF	XF	Unc	BU
1994		—	—	—	60.00	—
1994 Proof	Est. 1,000	Value: 62.00				

KM# 320 1/10 ROYAL Weight: 3.1100 g. **Composition:** 0.9999 Gold .1000 oz. AGW **Reverse:** Collie **Note:** Similar to 1 Royal, KM#323.

Date	Mintage	F	VF	XF	Unc	BU
1995		—	—	—	60.00	—
1995 Proof	Est. 1,000	Value: 62.00				

KM# 362 1/10 ROYAL Weight: 3.1100 g. **Composition:** 0.9999 Gold .1000 oz. AGW **Reverse:** Bulldog **Note:** Similar to 1 Royal, KM#365b.

Date	Mintage	F	VF	XF	Unc	BU
1996		—	—	—	60.00	—
1996 Proof	Est. 1,000	Value: 62.00				

KM# 558 1/10 ROYAL Weight: 3.1100 g. **Composition:** 0.9999 Gold .1000 oz. AGW **Reverse:** Yorkshire Terrier **Note:** Similar to 1 Royal, KM#561b.

Date	Mintage	F	VF	XF	Unc	BU
1997		—	—	—	75.00	—
1997 Proof	Est. 1,000	Value: 76.50				

KM# 750 1/10 ROYAL Weight: 3.1100 g. **Composition:** 0.9999 Gold .1000 oz. AGW **Subject:** Kissing Cherubs **Obverse:** Queen's portrait **Reverse:** Kissing cherubs **Note:** Similar to 1 Royal, KM#754.

Date	Mintage	F	VF	XF	Unc	BU
1998		—	—	—	75.00	—
1998 Proof	Est. 1,000	Value: 76.50				

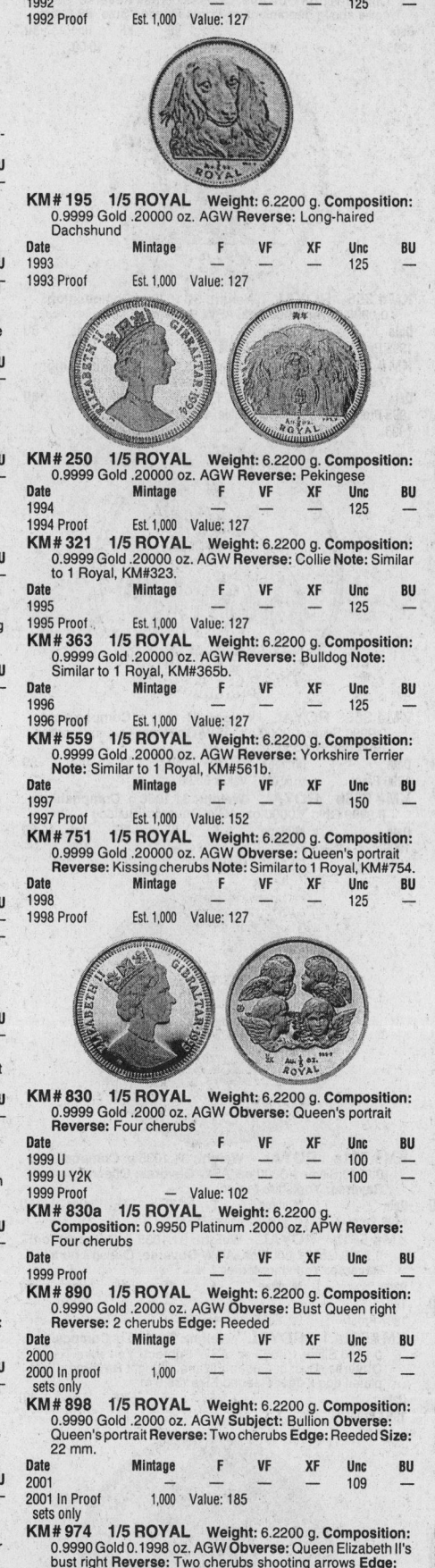

KM# 829 1/10 ROYAL Weight: 3.1100 g. **Composition:** 0.9999 Gold .1000 oz. AGW **Obverse:** Queen's portrait **Reverse:** Cherub

Date		F	VF	XF	Unc	BU
1999 U		—	—	—	50.00	—
1999 U Y2K		—	—	—	50.00	—
1999 Proof	—	Value: 52.00				

KM# 829a 1/10 ROYAL Weight: 3.1100 g. **Composition:** 0.9950 Platinum .0999 oz. APW **Reverse:** Cherub

Date	Mintage	F	VF	XF	Unc	BU
1999 Proof		—	—	—	—	—

KM# 889 1/10 ROYAL Weight: 3.1100 g. **Composition:** 0.9990 Gold .1000 oz. AGW **Obverse:** Bust Queen right **Reverse:** Two cherubs **Edge:** Reeded

Date	Mintage	F	VF	XF	Unc	BU
2000	—	—	—	—	75.00	—
2000 In mint sets only	1,000	Value: 76.50				

KM# 897 1/10 ROYAL Weight: 3.1100 g. **Composition:** 0.9999 Gold .1000 oz. AGW **Subject:** Bullion **Obverse:** Queen's portrait **Reverse:** Two cherubs **Edge:** Reeded **Size:** 18 mm.

Date	Mintage	F	VF	XF	Unc	BU
2001	—	—	—	—	70.00	—
2001 In Proof sets only	1,000	Value: 100				

KM# 973 1/10 ROYAL Weight: 3.1100 g. **Composition:** 0.9990 Gold 0.0999 oz. AGW **Subject:** Cherubs **Obverse:** Queen Elizabeth II's bust right **Reverse:** Two cherubs shooting arrows **Edge:** Reeded **Size:** 17.95 mm.

Date	Mintage	F	VF	XF	Unc	BU
2002	—	—	—	—	70.00	—
2002 Proof	1,000	Value: 95.00				

KM# 1028 1/10 ROYAL Weight: 3.1100 g. **Composition:** 0.9999 Gold 0.1 oz. AGW **Subject:** Cherub **Obverse:** Queen's portrait **Reverse:** Cherub with crossed arms **Edge:** Reeded **Size:** 17.95 mm.

Date		F	VF	XF	Unc	BU
2003PM		—	—	—	70.00	—
2003PM Proof	—	Value: 95.00				

KM# 93 1/5 ROYAL Weight: 6.2200 g. **Composition:** 0.9999 Gold .20000 oz. AGW **Reverse:** Corgi **Note:** Similar to 1 Royal, KM#97.

Date	Mintage	F	VF	XF	Unc	BU
1991		—	—	—	175	—
1991 Proof	Est. 1,000	Value: 177				

KM# 101 1/5 ROYAL Weight: 6.2200 g. **Composition:** 0.9999 Gold .20000 oz. AGW **Reverse:** Cocker Spaniel **Note:** Similar to 1 Royal, KM#105.

Date	Mintage	F	VF	XF	Unc	BU
1992		—	—	—	125	—
1992 Proof	Est. 1,000	Value: 127				

KM# 195 1/5 ROYAL Weight: 6.2200 g. **Composition:** 0.9999 Gold .20000 oz. AGW **Reverse:** Long-haired Dachshund

Date	Mintage	F	VF	XF	Unc	BU
1993		—	—	—	125	—
1993 Proof	Est. 1,000	Value: 127				

KM# 250 1/5 ROYAL Weight: 6.2200 g. **Composition:** 0.9999 Gold .20000 oz. AGW **Reverse:** Pekingese

Date	Mintage	F	VF	XF	Unc	BU
1994		—	—	—	125	—
1994 Proof	Est. 1,000	Value: 127				

KM# 321 1/5 ROYAL Weight: 6.2200 g. **Composition:** 0.9999 Gold .20000 oz. AGW **Reverse:** Collie **Note:** Similar to 1 Royal, KM#323.

Date	Mintage	F	VF	XF	Unc	BU
1995		—	—	—	125	—
1995 Proof	Est. 1,000	Value: 127				

KM# 363 1/5 ROYAL Weight: 6.2200 g. **Composition:** 0.9999 Gold .20000 oz. AGW **Reverse:** Bulldog **Note:** Similar to 1 Royal, KM#365b.

Date	Mintage	F	VF	XF	Unc	BU
1996		—	—	—	125	—
1996 Proof	Est. 1,000	Value: 127				

KM# 559 1/5 ROYAL Weight: 6.2200 g. **Composition:** 0.9999 Gold .20000 oz. AGW **Reverse:** Yorkshire Terrier **Note:** Similar to 1 Royal, KM#561b.

Date	Mintage	F	VF	XF	Unc	BU
1997		—	—	—	150	—
1997 Proof	Est. 1,000	Value: 152				

KM# 751 1/5 ROYAL Weight: 6.2200 g. **Composition:** 0.9999 Gold .20000 oz. AGW **Obverse:** Queen's portrait **Reverse:** Kissing cherubs **Note:** Similar to 1 Royal, KM#754.

Date	Mintage	F	VF	XF	Unc	BU
1998		—	—	—	125	—
1998 Proof	Est. 1,000	Value: 127				

KM# 830 1/5 ROYAL Weight: 6.2200 g. **Composition:** 0.9999 Gold .2000 oz. AGW **Obverse:** Queen's portrait **Reverse:** Four cherubs

Date		F	VF	XF	Unc	BU
1999 U		—	—	—	100	—
1999 U Y2K		—	—	—	100	—
1999 Proof	—	Value: 102				

KM# 830a 1/5 ROYAL Weight: 6.2200 g. **Composition:** 0.9950 Platinum .2000 oz. APW **Reverse:** Four cherubs

Date		F	VF	XF	Unc	BU
1999 Proof		—	—	—	—	—

KM# 890 1/5 ROYAL Weight: 6.2200 g. **Composition:** 0.9990 Gold .2000 oz. AGW **Obverse:** Bust Queen right **Reverse:** 2 cherubs **Edge:** Reeded

Date	Mintage	F	VF	XF	Unc	BU
2000	—	—	—	—	125	—
2000 In proof sets only	1,000	—	—	—	—	—

KM# 898 1/5 ROYAL Weight: 6.2200 g. **Composition:** 0.9990 Gold .2000 oz. AGW **Subject:** Bullion **Obverse:** Queen's portrait **Reverse:** Two cherubs **Edge:** Reeded **Size:** 22 mm.

Date	Mintage	F	VF	XF	Unc	BU
2001	—	—	—	—	109	—
2001 In Proof sets only	1,000	Value: 185				

KM# 974 1/5 ROYAL Weight: 6.2200 g. **Composition:** 0.9990 Gold 0.1998 oz. AGW **Obverse:** Queen Elizabeth II's bust right **Reverse:** Two cherubs shooting arrows **Edge:** Reeded **Size:** 22 mm.

Date	Mintage	F	VF	XF	Unc	BU
2002	—	—	—	—	110	—
2002 Proof	1,000	Value: 175				

KM# 1029 1/5 ROYAL Weight: 6.2200 g. **Composition:** 0.9999 Gold 0.2 oz. AGW **Subject:** Cherub **Obverse:** Queen's portrait **Reverse:** Cherub with crossed arms **Edge:** Reeded **Size:** 22 mm.

Date		F	VF	XF	Unc	BU
2003PM		—	—	—	109	—
2003PM Proof	—	Value: 205				

KM# 94 1/2 ROYAL Weight: 15.5500 g. **Composition:** 0.9999 Gold .5000 oz. AGW **Reverse:** Corgi **Note:** Similar to 1 Royal, KM#97.

Date	Mintage	F	VF	XF	Unc	BU
1991		—	—	—	375	—
1991 Proof	Est. 1,000	Value: 377				

KM# 102 1/2 ROYAL Weight: 15.5500 g. **Composition:** 0.9999 Gold .5000 oz. AGW **Reverse:** Cocker Spaniel **Note:** Simuler to 1 Royal, KM#105.

Date	Mintage	F	VF	XF	Unc	BU
1992		—	—	—	300	—
1992 Proof	Est. 1,000	Value: 302				

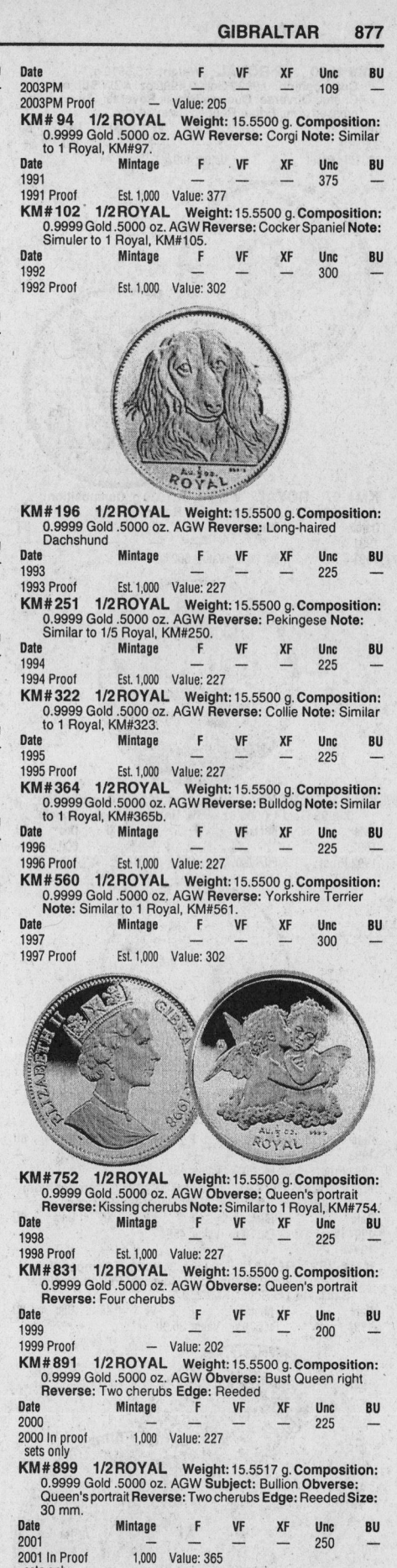

KM# 196 1/2 ROYAL Weight: 15.5500 g. **Composition:** 0.9999 Gold .5000 oz. AGW **Reverse:** Long-haired Dachshund

Date	Mintage	F	VF	XF	Unc	BU
1993		—	—	—	225	—
1993 Proof	Est. 1,000	Value: 227				

KM# 251 1/2 ROYAL Weight: 15.5500 g. **Composition:** 0.9999 Gold .5000 oz. AGW **Reverse:** Pekingese **Note:** Similar to 1/5 Royal, KM#250.

Date	Mintage	F	VF	XF	Unc	BU
1994		—	—	—	225	—
1994 Proof	Est. 1,000	Value: 227				

KM# 322 1/2 ROYAL Weight: 15.5500 g. **Composition:** 0.9999 Gold .5000 oz. AGW **Reverse:** Collie **Note:** Similar to 1 Royal, KM#323.

Date	Mintage	F	VF	XF	Unc	BU
1995		—	—	—	225	—
1995 Proof	Est. 1,000	Value: 227				

KM# 364 1/2 ROYAL Weight: 15.5500 g. **Composition:** 0.9999 Gold .5000 oz. AGW **Reverse:** Bulldog **Note:** Similar to 1 Royal, KM#365b.

Date	Mintage	F	VF	XF	Unc	BU
1996		—	—	—	225	—
1996 Proof	Est. 1,000	Value: 227				

KM# 560 1/2 ROYAL Weight: 15.5500 g. **Composition:** 0.9999 Gold .5000 oz. AGW **Reverse:** Yorkshire Terrier **Note:** Similar to 1 Royal, KM#561.

Date	Mintage	F	VF	XF	Unc	BU
1997		—	—	—	300	—
1997 Proof	Est. 1,000	Value: 302				

KM# 752 1/2 ROYAL Weight: 15.5500 g. **Composition:** 0.9999 Gold .5000 oz. AGW **Reverse:** Kissing cherubs **Note:** Similar to 1 Royal, KM#754.

Date	Mintage	F	VF	XF	Unc	BU
1998		—	—	—	225	—
1998 Proof	Est. 1,000	Value: 227				

KM# 831 1/2 ROYAL Weight: 15.5500 g. **Composition:** 0.9999 Gold .5000 oz. AGW **Obverse:** Queen's portrait **Reverse:** Four cherubs

Date		F	VF	XF	Unc	BU
1999		—	—	—	200	—
1999 Proof	—	Value: 202				

KM# 891 1/2 ROYAL Weight: 15.5500 g. **Composition:** 0.9999 Gold .5000 oz. AGW **Obverse:** Bust Queen right **Reverse:** Two cherubs **Edge:** Reeded

Date	Mintage	F	VF	XF	Unc	BU
2000	—	—	—	—	225	—
2000 In proof sets only	1,000	Value: 227				

KM# 899 1/2 ROYAL Weight: 15.5517 g. **Composition:** 0.9999 Gold .5000 oz. AGW **Subject:** Bullion **Obverse:** Queen's portrait **Reverse:** Two cherubs **Edge:** Reeded **Size:** 30 mm.

Date	Mintage	F	VF	XF	Unc	BU
2001	—	—	—	—	250	—
2001 In Proof sets only	1,000	Value: 365				

KM# 975 1/2 ROYAL Weight: 15.5510 g. **Composition:** 0.9990 Gold 0.4995 oz. AGW **Obverse:** Queen Elizabeth II's bust right **Reverse:** Two cherubs shooting arrows **Edge:** Reeded **Size:** 30 mm.

Date	Mintage	F	VF	XF	Unc	BU
2002	—	—	—	—	250	—
2002 Proof	1,000	Value: 340				

KM# 1030 1/2 ROYAL **Weight:** 15.5510 g. **Composition:** 0.9999 Gold 0.4999 oz. AGW **Subject:** Cherub **Obverse:** Queen's portrait **Reverse:** Cherub with crossed arms **Edge:** Reeded **Size:** 30 mm.

Date	F	VF	XF	Unc	BU
2003PM	—	—	—	250	—
2003PM Proof	— Value: 400				

KM# 97 ROYAL **Weight:** 31.1030 g. **Composition:** 0.9999 Gold 1.0000 oz. AGW **Reverse:** Corgi

Date	Mintage	F	VF	XF	Unc	BU
1991	—	—	—	—	600	—
1991	Est. 1,000	Value: 602				

KM# 105 ROYAL **Weight:** 31.1030 g. **Composition:** 0.9999 Gold 1.0000 oz. AGW **Reverse:** Cocker Spaniel

Date	Mintage	F	VF	XF	Unc	BU
1992	—	—	—	—	600	—
1992 Proof	Est. 1,000	Value: 602				

KM# 197 ROYAL **Weight:** 31.1030 g. **Composition:** 0.9999 Gold 1.0000 oz. AGW **Reverse:** Long-haired Dachshund

Date	Mintage	F	VF	XF	Unc	BU
1993	—	—	—	—	450	—
1993 Proof	Est. 1,000	Value: 452				

KM# 252a ROYAL **Weight:** 31.1030 g. **Composition:** 0.9999 Gold 1.0000 oz. AGW **Reverse:** Pekingese

Date	Mintage	F	VF	XF	Unc	BU
1994 Proof	Est. 1,000	Value: 452				
1994	—	—	—	—	450	—

KM# 252 ROYAL **Weight:** 31.1000 g. **Composition:** 0.9990 Silver .9989 oz. ASW **Reverse:** Pekingese **Note:** Similar to 1/5 Royal, KM#250.

Date	Mintage	F	VF	XF	Unc	BU
1994 Proof	Est. 50,000	Value: 35.00				

KM# 318 ROYAL **Weight:** 28.6200 g. **Composition:** Copper-Nickel **Obverse:** Queen's portrait **Reverse:** Seated collie above denomination **Edge:** Reeded **Size:** 38.8 mm.

Date	F	VF	XF	Unc	BU
1995	—	—	—	10.00	—

KM# 356 ROYAL **Weight:** 31.1030 g. **Composition:** 0.9990 Silver 1.0000 oz. ASW **Reverse:** Collie

Date	Mintage	F	VF	XF	Unc	BU
1995 Proof	Est. 50,000	Value: 35.00				

KM# 356a ROYAL **Weight:** 31.1030 g. **Composition:** 0.9999 Gold 1.0000 oz. AGW **Reverse:** Collie

Date	Mintage	F	VF	XF	Unc	BU
1995 Proof	Est. 1,000	Value: 452				
1995	—	—	—	—	450	—

KM# 365 ROYAL **Weight:** 31.1030 g. **Composition:** 0.9990 Silver 1.0000 oz. ASW **Obverse:** Queen's portrait **Reverse:** Bulldog

Date	Mintage	F	VF	XF	Unc	BU
1996 Proof	Est. 50,000	Value: 35.00				

KM# 365b ROYAL **Weight:** 31.1030 g. **Composition:** 0.9999 Gold 1.0000 oz. AGW **Reverse:** Bulldog

Date	Mintage	F	VF	XF	Unc	BU
1996	—	—	—	—	500	—
1996 Proof	Est. 1,000	Value: 502				

KM# 561a ROYAL **Weight:** 31.1035 g. **Composition:** 0.9990 Silver 1.0000 oz. ASW **Obverse:** Queen's portrait **Reverse:** Yorkshire terrier

Date	Mintage	F	VF	XF	Unc	BU
1997 Proof	Est. 50,000	Value: 35.00				

KM# 561b ROYAL **Weight:** 31.1035 g. **Composition:** 0.9999 Gold 1.0000 oz. AGW **Obverse:** Queen's portrait **Reverse:** Yorkshire terrier

Date	Mintage	F	VF	XF	Unc	BU
1997	—	—	—	—	500	—
1997 Proof	Est. 1,000	Value: 502				

KM# 561a.1 ROYAL **Weight:** 31.3000 g. **Composition:** 0.9990 Silver 1.0053 oz. ASW **Subject:** Yorkshire Terrier **Obverse:** Bust of Queen Elizabeth II right **Reverse:** Gold-plated dog **Edge:** Reeded **Size:** 38.5 mm.

Date	F	VF	XF	Unc	BU
1997 Proof	—	—	—	50.00	—

KM# 753 ROYAL **Composition:** Copper-Nickel **Obverse:** Queen's portrait **Reverse:** Kissing cherubs

Date	F	VF	XF	Unc	BU
1998	—	—	—	10.00	—

KM# 753a ROYAL **Weight:** 28.2800 g. **Composition:** 0.9990 Silver 1.0000 oz. ASW

Date	Mintage	F	VF	XF	Unc	BU
1998 Proof	Est. 20,000	Value: 45.00				

KM# 754 ROYAL **Weight:** 31.1030 g. **Composition:** 0.9999 Gold 1.0000 oz. AGW **Obverse:** Queen's portrait **Reverse:** Kissing cherubs

Date	Mintage	F	VF	XF	Unc	BU
1998	—	—	—	—	400	—
1998 Proof	Est. 1,000	Value: 402				

KM# 832 ROYAL **Composition:** Copper-Nickel **Obverse:** Queen's portrait **Reverse:** Four cherubs

Date	F	VF	XF	Unc	BU
1999	—	—	—	10.00	—

KM# 832a ROYAL **Weight:** 31.1035 g. **Composition:** 0.9990 Silver 1.0000 oz. ASW

Date	Mintage	F	VF	XF	Unc	BU
1999 Proof	Est. 50,000	Value: 50.00				

KM# 833 ROYAL **Weight:** 31.1030 g. **Composition:** 0.9999 Gold 1.0000 oz. AGW **Obverse:** Queen's portrait **Reverse:** Four cherubs

Date	F	VF	XF	Unc	BU
1999 U	—	—	—	350	—
1999 Proof	— Value: 352				

KM# 892 ROYAL **Weight:** 28.2800 g. **Composition:** Copper-Nickel **Obverse:** Bust Queen right **Reverse:** 2 cherubs **Edge:** Reeded

Date	F	VF	XF	Unc	BU
2000	—	—	—	10.00	—

KM# 892a ROYAL Weight: 31.1035 g. **Composition:** 0.9990 Silver 1.0000 oz. ASW

Date	Mintage	F	VF	XF	Unc	BU
2000 Proof	10,000	Value: 50.00				

KM# 893 ROYAL Weight: 31.1035 g. **Composition:** 0.9990 Gold 1.0000 oz. AGW **Obverse:** Bust Queen right **Reverse:** Two cherubs **Edge:** Reeded

Date	Mintage	F	VF	XF	Unc	BU
2000	—	—	—	—	400	—
2000 In proof sets only	1,000	Value: 402				

KM# 900 ROYAL Weight: 28.2800 g. **Composition:** Copper-Nickel **Obverse:** Queen's portrait **Reverse:** Two cherubs **Edge:** Reeded **Size:** 38.6 mm.

Date	F	VF	XF	Unc	BU
2001	—	—	—	10.00	—

KM# 900a ROYAL Weight: 31.1035 g. **Composition:** 0.9990 Silver 1.0000 oz. ASW

Date	Mintage	F	VF	XF	Unc	BU
2001 Proof	10,000	Value: 47.50				

KM# 901 ROYAL Weight: 31.1035 g. **Composition:** 0.9999 Gold 1.0000 oz. AGW **Subject:** Bullion **Obverse:** Queen's portrait **Reverse:** Two cherubs **Edge:** Reeded **Size:** 32.7 mm.

Date	Mintage	F	VF	XF	Unc	BU
2001	—	—	—	—	470	—
2001 In Proof sets only	1,000	Value: 650				

KM# 977 ROYAL Weight: 31.1035 g. **Composition:** 0.9990 Gold 0.999 oz. AGW **Obverse:** Queen Elizabeth II's bust right **Reverse:** Two cherubs shooting arrows **Edge:** Reeded **Size:** 32.7 mm.

Date	Mintage	F	VF	XF	Unc	BU
2002	—	—	—	—	470	—
2002 Proof	1,000	Value: 650				

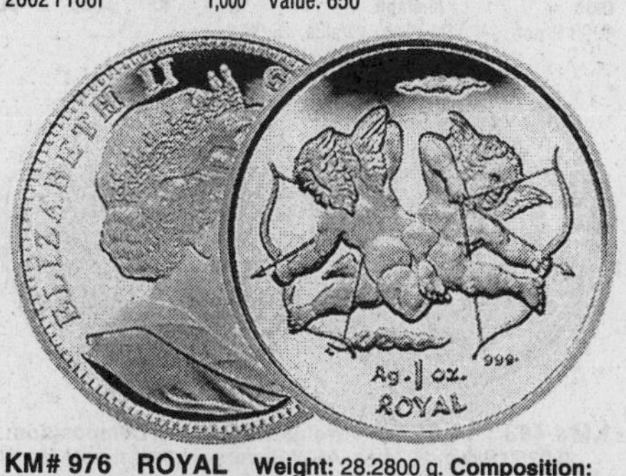

KM# 976 ROYAL Weight: 28.2800 g. **Composition:** Copper-Nickel **Obverse:** Queen Elizabeth II's bust right **Reverse:** Two cherubs shooting arrows **Edge:** Reeded **Size:** 38.6 mm.

Date	F	VF	XF	Unc	BU
2002	—	—	—	10.00	—

KM# 976a ROYAL Weight: 31.1035 g. **Composition:** 0.9990 Silver 0.999 oz. ASW **Obverse:** Bust of Queen Elizabeth II right **Reverse:** Two cherubs shooting arrows **Edge:** Reeded

Date	Mintage	F	VF	XF	Unc	BU
2002 Proof	1,000	Value: 47.50				

KM# 1031 ROYAL Weight: 28.2800 g. **Composition:** Copper-Nickel **Subject:** Cherub **Obverse:** Queen's portrait **Reverse:** Cherub with crossed arms **Edge:** Reeded **Size:** 38.6 mm.

Date	F	VF	XF	Unc	BU
2003PM	—	—	—	10.00	—

EUROPEAN CURRENCY UNITS - DUAL DENOMINATION COINAGE

KM# 293 2.8 ECUS - 2 Pounds Composition: Copper-Nickel **Reverse:** Mounted rider left

Date	F	VF	XF	Unc	BU
1992	—	—	—	12.50	—

KM# 87 14 ECUS - 10 Pounds Weight: 10.0000 g. **Composition:** 0.9250 Silver .2974 oz. ASW **Subject:** European Currency Unit **Obverse:** Uncouped portrait **Reverse:** Mounted rider left

Date	Mintage	F	VF	XF	Unc	BU
1991 Proof	Est. 10,000	Value: 20.00				
1992 Proof	Est. 5,000	Value: 30.00				
1993		—	—	—	75.00	—
1994		—	—	—	75.00	—

KM# 109 14 ECUS - 10 Pounds Weight: 10.0000 g. **Composition:** 0.9250 Silver .2974 oz. ASW **Obverse:** Couped portrait **Reverse:** Mounted rider left

Date	Mintage	F	VF	XF	Unc	BU
1992		—	—	—	15.00	—
1992 Proof		—	—	—	—	—
1993 Proof	—	Value: 35.00				

KM# 624 14 ECUS - 10 Pounds Weight: 10.0000 g. **Composition:** 0.9250 Silver .2974 oz. ASW **Obverse:** Queen's portrait **Reverse:** Knight on horseback jumping left, shield

Date	Mintage	F	VF	XF	Unc	BU
1992 Proof	Est. 2,500	Value: 25.00				

KM# 89 14 ECUS - 10 Pounds Weight: 10.0000 g. **Composition:** 0.9250 Silver .2974 oz. ASW **Obverse:** Couped portrait **Reverse:** Knight on horse jumping right

Date	F	VF	XF	Unc	BU
1992A Matte	—	—	—	20.00	—

KM# 337 14 ECUS - 10 Pounds Weight: 10.0000 g. **Composition:** 0.9250 Silver .2974 oz. ASW **Reverse:** Torch shield

Date	Mintage	F	VF	XF	Unc	BU
1992 Proof	2,500	Value: 25.00				

KM# 627 14 ECUS - 10 Pounds Weight: 10.0000 g. **Composition:** 0.9250 Silver .2974 oz. ASW **Obverse:** Queen's portrait **Reverse:** Knight on horseback jumping right, three lions on shield

Date	Mintage	F	VF	XF	Unc	BU
1993 Proof	Est. 2,500	Value: 25.00				

KM# 88 35 ECUS - 25 Pounds Weight: 28.2800 g. **Composition:** 0.9250 Silver .8411 oz. ASW **Obverse:** Uncouped portrait **Reverse:** Knight left **Note:** Similar to 14 Ecus - 10 Pounds, KM#87.

Date	Mintage	F	VF	XF	Unc	BU
1991 Proof	Est. 10,000	Value: 60.00				
1992		—	—	—	40.00	—
1992 Proof	Est. 15,000	Value: 60.00				

KM# 110 35 ECUS - 25 Pounds Weight: 28.2800 g. **Composition:** 0.9250 Silver .8411 oz. ASW **Obverse:** Uncouped portrait **Reverse:** Knight right

Date	Mintage	F	VF	XF	Unc	BU
1992 Proof	Est. 15,000	Value: 50.00				
1993 Proof	—	Value: 70.00				

KM# 338 35 ECUS - 25 Pounds Weight: 28.2800 g. **Composition:** 0.9250 Silver .8411 oz. ASW **Reverse:** Knight on horseback jumping left, torch shield

Date	Mintage	F	VF	XF	Unc	BU
1992 Proof	Est. 2,000	Value: 85.00				

KM# 625 35 ECUS - 25 Pounds Weight: 28.2800 g. **Composition:** 0.9250 Silver .8411 oz. ASW **Obverse:** Queen's portrait **Reverse:** Knight on horseback jumping left, small horse on shield

Date	Mintage	F	VF	XF	Unc	BU
1992 Proof	Est. 2,000	Value: 100				

KM# 628 35 ECUS - 25 Pounds **Weight:** 28.2800 g. **Composition:** 0.9250 Silver .8411 oz. ASW **Obverse:** Queen's portrait **Reverse:** Knight on horseback jumping right, three lions on shield

Date	Mintage	F	VF	XF	Unc	BU
1993 Proof	Est. 2,000	Value: 75.00				

KM# 75 70 ECUS - 50 Pounds **Weight:** 6.1200 g. **Composition:** 0.5000 Gold .1000 oz. AGW **Obverse:** Couped portrait

Date	Mintage	F	VF	XF	Unc	BU
1991 Proof	Est. 5,000	Value: 200				
1991		—	—	—	85.00	—
1992		—	—	—	85.00	—
1992 Proof	Est. 2,000	Value: 225				
1994		—	—	—	250	—

KM# 111 70 ECUS - 50 Pounds **Weight:** 6.1200 g. **Composition:** 0.5000 Gold .1000 oz. AGW **Reverse:** Knight charging right

Date	Mintage	F	VF	XF	Unc	BU
1992 Proof	Est. 2,000	Value: 175				
1993 Proof	Est. 1,000	Value: 200				

KM# 339 70 ECUS - 50 Pounds **Weight:** 6.1200 g. **Composition:** 0.5000 Gold .1000 oz. AGW **Reverse:** Knight on horseback jumping left, torch shield

Date	Mintage	F	VF	XF	Unc	BU
1992 Proof	Est. 1,000	Value: 200				

KM# 626 70 ECUS - 50 Pounds **Weight:** 6.1200 g. **Composition:** 0.5000 Gold .1000 oz. AGW **Obverse:** Queen's portrait **Reverse:** Knight on horseback jumping left, small horse on shield

Date	Mintage	F	VF	XF	Unc	BU
1992 Proof	Est. 1,000	Value: 200				

KM# 629 70 ECUS - 50 Pounds **Weight:** 6.1200 g. **Composition:** 0.5000 Gold .1000 oz. AGW **Obverse:** Queen's portrait **Reverse:** Knight on horseback jumping right, three lions on shield

Date	Mintage	F	VF	XF	Unc	BU
1993 Proof	Est. 1,000	Value: 150				

STERLING ECU

KM# 478 2.8 ECUS **Composition:** Copper-Nickel **Subject:** Euro Tunnel **Reverse:** Train exiting tunnel

Date	F	VF	XF	Unc	BU
1993	—	—	—	9.50	—

KM# 630 2.8 ECUS **Composition:** Copper-Nickel **Subject:** A'riane - European Space Programme **Obverse:** Queen's portrait **Reverse:** Rocket orbitting Earth **Note:** Similar to 70 Ecus, KM#634.

Date	F	VF	XF	Unc	BU
1993	—	—	—	7.50	—

KM# 1022 2.8 ECUS **Composition:** Copper Nickel **Obverse:** Europa sowing seeds

Date	F	VF	XF	Unc	BU
1994	—	—	—	9.00	—

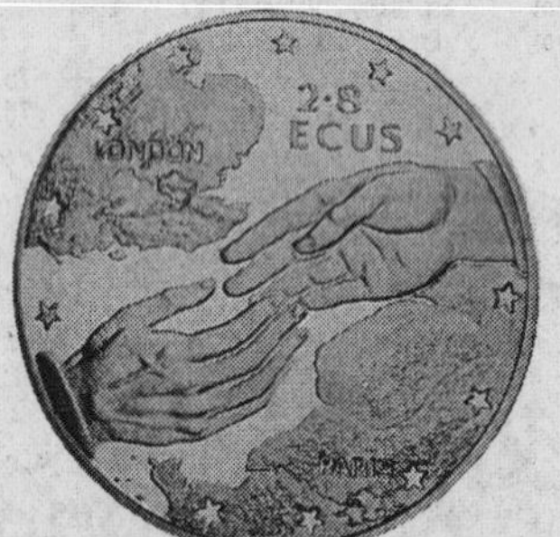

KM# 484 2.8 ECUS **Composition:** Copper-Nickel **Subject:** Euro Tunnel **Reverse:** Clasping hands

Date	F	VF	XF	Unc	BU
1994	—	—	—	9.00	—

KM# 489 2.8 ECUS **Composition:** Copper-Nickel **Subject:** Mythology **Reverse:** Winged Victory above chariot

Date	F	VF	XF	Unc	BU
1994	—	—	—	8.50	—

KM# 494 2.8 ECUS **Composition:** Copper-Nickel **Subject:** 190th Anniversary of Admiral Nelson's Death **Reverse:** Admiral Nelson and ship

Date	F	VF	XF	Unc	BU
1995	—	—	—	8.50	—

KM# 508 2.8 ECUS **Composition:** Copper-Nickel **Reverse:** Austrian Knight **Note:** Similar to 70 Ecus, KM#512.

Date	F	VF	XF	Unc	BU
1996	—	—	—	8.50	—

KM# 1033 4.2 ECUS **Ring Weight:** 7.5000 g. **Ring Composition:** Copper-Nickel **Center Composition:** Brass **Reverse:** Mounted rider left **Size:** 26 mm. **Note:** Similar to KM#87.

Date	Mintage	F	VF	XF	Unc	BU
1994 Prooflike	10,000	—	—	—	11.50	—

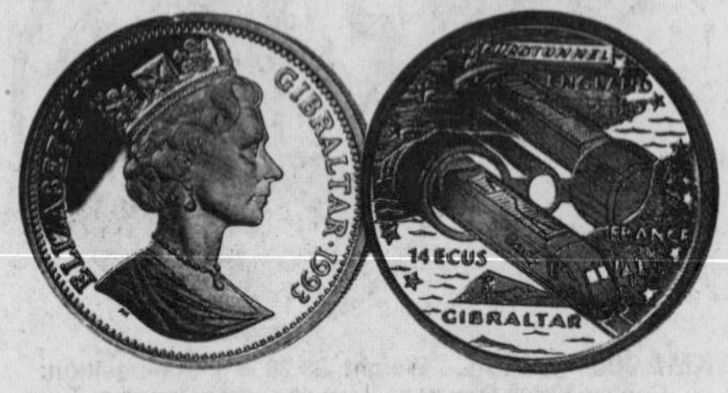

KM# 479 14 ECUS **Weight:** 10.0000 g. **Composition:** 0.9250 Silver .2974 oz. ASW **Subject:** Euro Tunnel **Reverse:** Train exiting tunnel

Date	Mintage	F	VF	XF	Unc	BU
1993 Proof	30,000	Value: 13.50				

KM# 631 14 ECUS **Weight:** 10.0000 g. **Composition:** 0.9250 Silver .2974 oz. ASW **Subject:** Sir Winston Churchill **Obverse:** Queen's portrait **Reverse:** Churchill in uniform

Date	Mintage	F	VF	XF	Unc	BU
1993 Proof	Est. 20,000	Value: 15.00				

KM# 483 14 ECUS **Weight:** 10.0000 g. **Composition:** 0.9250 Silver .2974 oz. ASW **Reverse:** International Aid for Europe

Date	Mintage	F	VF	XF	Unc	BU
1994 Proof	Est. 30,000	Value: 18.50				

KM# 485 14 ECUS **Weight:** 10.0000 g. **Composition:** 0.9250 Silver .2974 oz. ASW **Subject:** Euro Tunnel **Reverse:** Train exiting tunnel

Date		F	VF	XF	Unc	BU
1994 Proof	Est. 30,000	Value: 20.00				

KM# 490 14 ECUS **Weight:** 10.0000 g. **Composition:** 0.9250 Silver .2974 oz. ASW **Reverse:** Parthenon and Brandenburg Gate

Date	Mintage	F	VF	XF	Unc	BU
1994 Proof	Est. 30,000	Value: 14.50				

KM# 495 14 ECUS **Weight:** 10.0000 g. **Composition:** 0.9250 Silver .2974 oz. ASW **Reverse:** L'Arc de Triumph - Ceres

Date	Mintage	F	VF	XF	Unc	BU
1995 Proof	Est. 30,000	Value: 17.50				

KM# 496 14 ECUS **Weight:** 10.0000 g. **Composition:** 0.9250 Silver .2974 oz. ASW **Reverse:** Richard the Lionheart

Date	Mintage	F	VF	XF	Unc	BU
1995 Proof	Est. 30,000	Value: 17.50				

KM# 509 14 ECUS **Weight:** 10.0000 g. **Composition:** 0.9250 Silver .2974 oz. ASW **Reverse:** Napoleon Above European Battle Site

Date	Mintage	F	VF	XF	Unc	BU
1996 Proof	Est. 30,000	Value: 16.50				

KM# 510 14 ECUS **Weight:** 10.0000 g. **Composition:** 0.9250 Silver .2974 oz. ASW **Reverse:** Leaning Tower of Pisa, Irish Harp

Date	Mintage	F	VF	XF	Unc	BU
1996 Proof	Est. 30,000	Value: 16.50				

KM# 497 15 ECUS **Weight:** 1.2400 g. **Composition:** 0.9999 Gold .0399 oz. AGW **Reverse:** Knight with shield and banner

Date	Mintage	F	VF	XF	Unc	BU
1995 Proof	15,000	Value: 30.00				

KM# 504 15 ECUS **Weight:** 1.2400 g. **Composition:** 0.9999 Gold .0399 oz. AGW **Reverse:** Sir Francis Drake's ship "Golden Hind"

Date	Mintage	F	VF	XF	Unc	BU
1996 Proof	Est. 1,500	Value: 40.00				

KM# 480 21 ECUS **Weight:** 19.2000 g. **Composition:** 0.9250 Silver .5710 oz. ASW **Subject:** Euro Tunnel **Reverse:** Trains exiting tunnel

Date	Mintage	F	VF	XF	Unc	BU
1993 Proof	Est. 15,000	Value: 32.50				

KM# 482 21 ECUS **Weight:** 19.2000 g. **Composition:** 0.9250 Silver .5710 oz. ASW **Subject:** Euro Tunnel **Reverse:** Tunnel view and Napoleon

Date	Mintage	F	VF	XF	Unc	BU
1993 Proof	Est. 15,000	Value: 22.50				

KM# 632 21 ECUS **Weight:** 19.2000 g. **Composition:** 0.9250 Silver .5710 oz. ASW **Subject:** European Economic Community **Obverse:** Queen's portrait **Reverse:** European coins

Date	Mintage	F	VF	XF	Unc	BU
1993 Proof	Est. 15,000	Value: 27.50				

KM# 486 21 ECUS **Weight:** 19.2000 g. **Composition:** 0.9250 Silver .5710 oz. ASW **Subject:** Euro Tunnel **Reverse:** Two trains and motor vehicle

Date	Mintage	F	VF	XF	Unc	BU
1994 Proof	Est. 15,000	Value: 27.50				

KM# 491 21 ECUS **Weight:** 19.2000 g. **Composition:** 0.9250 Silver .5710 oz. ASW **Reverse:** 21 Years - European Community Membership

Date	Mintage	F	VF	XF	Unc	BU
1994 Proof	Est. 15,000	Value: 30.00				

KM# 498 21 ECUS **Weight:** 19.2000 g. **Composition:** 0.9250 Silver .5710 oz. ASW **Reverse:** Europa with Shields of Austria, Sweden and Finland

Date	Mintage	F	VF	XF	Unc	BU
1995 Proof	Est. 15,000	Value: 35.00				

KM# 499 21 ECUS **Weight:** 19.2000 g. **Composition:** 0.9250 Silver .5710 oz. ASW **Subject:** Agreement of Cooperation between Russia and the European Union

Date	Mintage	F	VF	XF	Unc	BU
1995 Proof	Est. 15,000	Value: 35.00				

KM# 505 35 ECUS **Weight:** 3.1100 g. **Composition:** 0.9999 Gold .1000 oz. AGW **Reverse:** Ship "Hanseatic Kogge"

Date	Mintage	F	VF	XF	Unc	BU
1996 Proof	Est. 1,500	Value: 75.00				

KM# 634 70 ECUS **Weight:** 6.2200 g. **Composition:** 0.9999 Gold .2000 oz. AGW **Subject:** Ariane - European Space Programme **Obverse:** Queen's portrait **Reverse:** Rocket orbitting Earth

Date	Mintage	F	VF	XF	Unc	BU
1993 Proof	Est. 2,000	Value: 165				
1994 Proof	Est. 1,000	Value: 170				

KM# 1023 70 ECUS **Weight:** 155.5175 g. **Composition:** 0.9990 Silver 4.995 oz. ASW **Obverse:** European coins

Date	Mintage	F	VF	XF	Unc	BU
1993 Proof	Est. 2,000	Value: 125				

KM# 633 70 ECUS **Weight:** 155.5175 g. **Composition:** 0.9990 Silver 5.0000 oz. ASW **Subject:** Ariane - European Space Programme **Obverse:** Queen's portrait **Reverse:** Rocket orbitting Earth **Note:** Similar to 70 Ecus, KM#634.

Date	Mintage	F	VF	XF	Unc	BU
1993 Proof	Est. 2,000	Value: 165				

KM# 1024 70 ECUS Weight: 155.5175 g. **Composition:** 0.9990 Silver 4.995 oz. ASW **Obverse:** Train exiting tunnel

Date	F	VF	XF	Unc	BU
1994 Proof	—	Value: 165			

KM# 487 70 ECUS Weight: 155.5175 g. **Composition:** 0.9990 Silver 5.0000 oz. ASW **Subject:** Euro Tunnel **Obverse:** Portrait of Queen **Reverse:** Tunnel view and Napoleon **Shape:** 65 **Note:** Illustration reduced.

Date	Mintage	F	VF	XF	Unc	BU
1994 Proof	Est. 2,000	Value: 135				

KM# 492 70 ECUS Weight: 155.5175 g. **Composition:** 0.9990 Silver 5.0000 oz. ASW **Subject:** European Unity **Reverse:** Goddesses with quadrigia **Size:** 65 mm. **Note:** Illustration reduced.

Date	Mintage	F	VF	XF	Unc	BU
1994 Proof	Est. 2,000	Value: 135				

KM# 488 70 ECUS Weight: 6.2200 g. **Composition:** 0.9999 Gold .2000 oz. AGW **Subject:** Euro Tunnel **Reverse:** Outreached hands above English Channel

Date	Mintage	F	VF	XF	Unc	BU
1994 Proof	Est. 2,000	Value: 125				

KM# 493 70 ECUS Weight: 6.2200 g. **Composition:** 0.9999 Gold .2000 oz. AGW **Subject:** Mythology **Reverse:** Europa sowing seeds

Date	Mintage	F	VF	XF	Unc	BU
1994 Proof	Est. 2,000	Value: 125				

KM# 501 70 ECUS Weight: 155.9200 g. **Composition:** 0.9990 Silver 5.0079 oz. ASW **Reverse:** Liberty and Brittania seated above Euro Tunnel

Date	Mintage	F	VF	XF	Unc	BU
1995 Proof	Est. 2,000	Value: 165				

KM# 502 70 ECUS Weight: 6.2200 g. **Composition:** 0.9999 Gold .2000 oz. AGW **Reverse:** Mercury above ship

Date	Mintage	F	VF	XF	Unc	BU
1995 Proof	Est. 2,000	Value: 160				

KM# 503 70 ECUS Weight: 6.2200 g. **Composition:** 0.9999 Gold .2000 oz. AGW **Reverse:** Richard the Lionheart

Date	Mintage	F	VF	XF	Unc	BU
1995 Proof	Est. 2,000	Value: 160				

KM# 500 70 ECUS Weight: 155.9200 g. **Composition:** 0.9990 Silver 5.0079 oz. ASW **Subject:** 190th Anniversary of Admiral Nelson's Death **Reverse:** Admiral Nelson and HMS Victory **Size:** 65 mm. **Note:** Illustration reduced.

Date	Mintage	F	VF	XF	Unc	BU
1995 Proof	2,000	Value: 165				

KM# 512 70 ECUS Weight: 6.2200 g. **Composition:** 0.9999 Gold .2000 oz. AGW **Note:** Similar to 2.8 Ecus, KM#508.

Date	Mintage	F	VF	XF	Unc	BU
1996 Proof	2,000	Value: 160				

KM# 506 70 ECUS Weight: 6.2200 g. **Composition:** 0.9999 Gold .2000 oz. AGW **Reverse:** HMS Victory

Date	Mintage	F	VF	XF	Unc	BU
1996 Proof	Est. 1,500	Value: 165				

KM# 511 70 ECUS Weight: 155.5175 g. **Composition:** 0.9990 Silver 5.000 oz. ASW **Reverse:** Sir Francis Drake and "Golden Hind"

Date	Mintage	F	VF	XF	Unc	BU
1996 Proof	Est. 2,000	Value: 165				

KM# 528 75 ECUS Ring Weight: 3.8880 g. **Ring Composition:** 0.9999 Gold .1250 oz. AGW **Center Weight:** 3.8880 g. **Center Composition:** 0.9995 Platinum .1250 oz. APW **Subject:** Austrian Centennial **Obverse:** Queen's portrait **Reverse:** Standing allegorical figure with shield and trident

Date	Mintage	F	VF	XF	Unc	BU
1996 Proof	1,500	Value: 250				

KM# 507 140 ECUS Center Weight: 15.5500 g. **Center Composition:** 0.9999 Gold .4999 oz. AGW **Reverse:** Viking Longship

Date	F	VF	XF	Unc	BU
1996 In Proof sets only	—	—	—	350	—

PATTERNS

Including off metal strikes

KM#	Date	Mintage	Identification	Mkt Val
Pn5	1989	—	1/2 Sovereign. Gold. Similar to Pn8.	—
Pn4	1989	—	1/4 Sovereign. Gold. Similar to Pn8.	—
Pn7	1989	—	2 Sovereigns. Gold. Similar to Pn8.	—
Pn8	1989	—	5 Sovereigns. Gold. Una and the lion with the Rock of Gibraltar in background.	—
Pn6	1989	—	Sovereign. Gold. Similar to Pn8.	—

PIEFORTS

KM#	Date	Mintage	Identification	Mkt Val
P1	1990	5,000	5 Pence. 0.9250 Silver. 6.0000 g. KM#22b.	65.00

KM#	Date	Mintage	Identification	Mkt Val
P2	1990	1,000	5 Pence. 0.9160 Gold. 6.0000 g. KM#22c.	—
P3	1993	5,000	14 Ecus. 0.9250 Silver. KM#631.	50.00

MINT SETS

KM#	Date	Mintage	Identification	Issue Price	Mkt Val
MS1	1975 (3)	1,625	KM#7-9	—	750
MS2	1988 (9)	—	KM#16-18, 20-25	21.00	32.00
MS3	1989 (9)	—	KM#16-17, 20-25, 32	—	35.00
MS4	1990 (9)	—	km#16, 18, 20-21, 22A, 23-25, 39	25.00	35.00
MS5	1991 (9)	—	KM#16, 18, 20-21, 22a, 23-25, 39	25.00	35.00
MS7	1995 (9)	—	KM#16, 20-21, 22A, 24, 39, 112, 334, 340	—	35.00
MS6	1996-1998 (6)	5,000	KM#201, 327, 382,444, 525, 656	—	45.00
MS8	1996 (9)	—	KM#16, 18, 20-21, 22, 24, 39, 112, 355	—	35.00
MS9	1997 (9)	—	KM#16, 18, 20-21, 22a, 24, 39, 113, 355	—	35.00

PROOF SETS

KM#	Date	Mintage	Identification	Issue Price	Mkt Val
PS1	1975 (3)	750	KM#7-9	875	1,000
PS2	1989 (5)	—	KM#26-30	—	2,130
PS3	1989 (2)	—	KM#29-30	—	1,650
PS6	1990 (5)	1,000	KM#41-45	1,800	1,900
PS4	1990 (6)	500	KM#76-81	—	1,500
PS5	1990 (6)	250	KM#76a-81a	—	2,100
PS11	1991 (5)	1,000	KM#91-94, 97	—	1,310
PS7	1991 (8)	20,000	KM#50-57	—	640
PS10	1991 (8)	50	KM#66-73	120	120
PS8	1991 (8)	5,000	KM#58-65	—	1,280
PS9	1991 (8)	1,000	KM#58a-65a	—	2,200
PS12	1992 (5)	1,000	KM#99-102, 105	—	1,150
PS14	1993 (5)	300	KM#124-128	—	625
PS13	1993 (5)	1,000	KM#193-197	—	910
PS16	1994-95 (3)	5,000	KM#309, 332, 335	—	60.00
PS17	1994-95 (3)	3,000	KM#309a, 332a, 335a	—	120
PS18	1994-95 (3)	3,000	KM#309, 332, 335	—	120
PS15	1994 (5)	1,000	KM#248-251, 252a	—	910
PS19	1995 (5)	1,000	KM#319-323	—	910
PS22	1996 (4)	1,500	KM#504-507	—	650
PS21	1996 (5)	1,000	KM#361-364, 365b	—	960
PS23	1997 (5)	1,000	KM#557-560, 561b	—	1,100
PS24	1998 (5)	1,000	KM#749-752, 754	1,309	890
PS25	1999 (5)	1,000	KM#828-831, 833	1,310	750
PS26	2000 (5)	1,000	KM#888-891, 893	—	875
PS29	2001 (5)	1,000	KM#896-899, 901	—	1,350
PS30	2003 (5)	1,000	KM#1027-30, 1032	—	1,400

PROOF-LIKE SETS (PL)

KM#	Date	Mintage	Identification	Issue Price	Mkt Val
PL1	1992 (8)	—	KM#66-73	—	100

GREAT BRITAIN

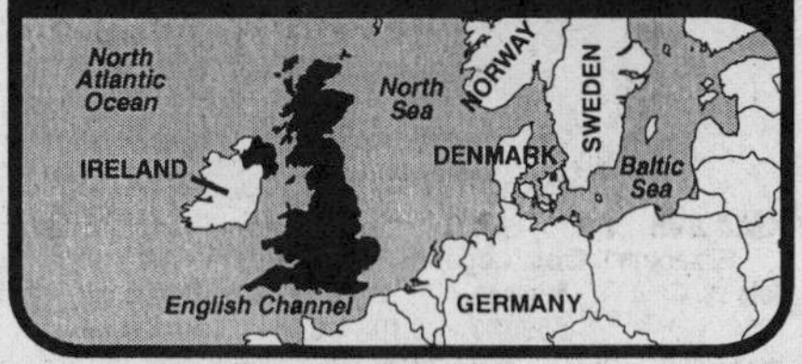

The United Kingdom of Great Britain and Northern Ireland, located off the northwest coast of the European continent, has an area of 94,227sq. mi. (244,820 sq. km.) and a population of 54 million. Capital: London. The economy is based on industrial activity and trading. Machinery, motor vehicles, chemicals, and textile yarns and fabrics are exported.

After the departure of the Romans, who brought Britain into a more active relationship with Europe, it fell prey to invaders from Scandinavia and the Low Countries who drove the original Britons into Scotland and Wales, and established a profusion of kingdoms that finally united in the 11th century under the Danish King Canute. Norman rule, following the conquest of 1066, stimulated the development of those institutions, which have since distinguished British life. Henry VIII (1509-47) turned Britain from continental adventuring and faced it to the sea - a decision that made Britain a world power during the reign of Elizabeth I (1558-1603). Strengthened by the Industrial Revolution and the defeat of Napoleon, 19thcentury Britain turned to the remote parts of the world and established a colonial empire of such extent and prosperity that the world has never seen its like. World Wars I and II sealed the fate of the Empire and relegated Britain to a lesser role in world affairs by draining her resources and inaugurating a worldwide movement toward national self-determination in her former colonies.

By the mid-20th century, most of the territories formerly comprising the British Empire had gained independence, and the empire had evolved into the Commonwealth of Nations, an association of equal and autonomous states, which enjoy special trade interests. The Commonwealth is presently composed of 54 member nations, including the United Kingdom. All recognize the British monarch as head of the Commonwealth. Fifteen continue to recognize the British monarch as Head of State. They are: United Kingdom, Antigua and Barbuda, Australia, Bahamas, Barbados, Belize, Canada, Grenada, Jamaica, New Zealand, Papua New Guinea, St. Christopher & Nevis, Saint Lucia, Saint Vincent and the Grenadines, Solomon Islands, and Tuvalu. Elizabeth II is personally, and separately, the Queen of the sovereign, independent countries just mentioned. There is no other British connection between the several individual, national sovereignties, except that High Commissioners represent them each instead of ambassadors in each others countries.

RULERS

Victoria, 1837-1901
Edward VII, 1901-1910
George V, 1910-1936
Edward VIII, 1936
George VI, 1936-1952
Elizabeth II, 1952--

Mint Marks

H - Heaton
KN - King's Norton

MONETARY SYSTEM

(Until 1970)

4 Farthings = 1 Penny
12 Pence = 1 Shilling
2 Shillings = 1 Florin
5 Shillings = 1 Crown
20 Shillings = 1 Pound (Sovereign)
21 Shillings = 1 Guinea

NOTE: Proofs exist for many dates of British coins in the 19th and early 20th centuries and for virtually all coins between 1926 and 1964. Those not specifically listed here are extremely rare.

KINGDOM

Resumed

POUND COINAGE

KM# 791 1/3 FARTHING **Weight:** 0.9500 g. **Composition:** Bronze **Ruler:** Edward VII **Obverse:** Bust of Edward VII right **Note:** Homeland style struck for Malta.

Date	Mintage	F	VF	XF	Unc	BU
1902	288,000	2.50	5.00	8.00	25.00	—

KM# 823 1/3 FARTHING **Weight:** 0.9500 g. **Composition:** Bronze **Ruler:** George V **Obverse:** Bust of George V left **Note:** Homeland style struck for Malta.

Date	Mintage	F	VF	XF	Unc	BU
1913	288,000	2.50	5.00	8.00	24.00	—

KM# 788.2 FARTHING **Weight:** 2.8000 g. **Composition:** Bronze **Ruler:** Victoria **Note:** Blackened finish.

Date	Mintage	F	VF	XF	Unc	BU
1901	8,016,000	0.30	0.50	2.00	8.00	—

KM# 792 FARTHING **Composition:** Bronze **Ruler:** Edward VII

Date	Mintage	F	VF	XF	Unc	BU
1902	5,125,000	0.50	1.50	4.00	15.00	—
1903	5,331,000	0.75	1.75	6.00	22.50	—
1903 Shield heraldically colored; Proof	—	Value: 800				
1904	3,629,000	1.50	3.00	8.00	22.50	—
1905	4,077,000	0.50	1.50	6.00	22.50	—
1906	5,340,000	0.50	1.50	6.00	22.50	—
1907	4,399,000	0.50	1.50	6.00	22.50	—
1908	4,265,000	0.75	1.50	6.00	22.50	—
1909	8,852,000	0.75	1.50	6.00	22.50	—
1910	2,598,000	1.00	4.00	8.00	25.00	—

KM# 808.1 FARTHING **Composition:** Bronze **Ruler:** George V

Date	Mintage	F	VF	XF	Unc	BU
1911	5,197,000	0.60	1.00	3.00	10.00	—
1912	7,670,000	0.35	0.75	2.50	8.00	—
1913	4,184,000	0.50	0.75	2.50	8.00	—
1914	6,127,000	0.35	0.75	2.50	9.00	—
1915	7,129,000	0.50	0.75	5.00	14.00	—
1916	10,993,000	0.35	0.75	1.75	8.00	—
1917	21,435,000	0.15	0.35	1.50	8.00	—
1918	19,363,000	0.75	1.50	10.00	27.00	—

KM# 808.2 FARTHING **Composition:** Bronze **Ruler:** George V **Note:** Bright finish.

Date	Mintage	F	VF	XF	Unc	BU
1918	Inc. above	0.20	0.40	1.00	7.50	—
1919	15,089,000	0.20	0.40	1.00	7.50	—
1920	11,481,000	0.20	0.40	1.00	7.50	—
1921	9,469,000	0.20	0.40	1.00	8.00	—
1922	9,957,000	0.20	0.40	1.00	8.00	—
1923	8,034,000	0.20	0.40	1.00	8.00	—
1924	8,733,000	0.20	0.40	1.00	8.00	—
1925	12,635,000	0.20	0.40	1.00	6.50	—

KM# 825 FARTHING **Composition:** Bronze **Ruler:** George V **Obverse:** Modified effigy

Date	Mintage	F	VF	XF	Unc	BU
1926	9,792,000	0.15	0.40	1.00	6.50	—
1926 Proof	—	Value: 275				
1927	7,868,000	0.15	0.40	1.00	6.00	—
1927 Proof	—	Value: 250				
1928	11,626,000	0.15	0.35	1.00	5.00	—
1928 Proof	—	Value: 200				
1929	8,419,000	0.15	0.35	1.00	5.00	—
1929 Proof	—	Value: 200				
1930	4,195,000	0.25	0.50	1.00	6.00	—
1930 Proof	—	Value: 200				
1931	6,595,000	0.15	0.35	1.00	5.00	—
1931 Proof	—	Value: 200				

Date	Mintage	F	VF	XF	Unc	BU
1932	9,293,000	0.15	0.35	1.00	5.00	—
1932 Proof	—	Value: 200				
1933	4,560,000	0.15	0.35	1.00	4.00	—
1933 Proof	—	Value: 200				
1934	3,053,000	0.35	0.75	1.75	7.00	—
1934 Proof	—	Value: 200				
1935	2,227,000	1.00	2.00	3.50	10.00	—
1935 Proof	—	Value: 200				
1936	9,734,000	0.15	0.35	1.00	5.00	—
1936 Proof	—	Value: 200				

KM# 843 FARTHING **Composition:** Bronze **Ruler:** George VI

Date	Mintage	F	VF	XF	Unc	BU
1937	8,131,000	0.15	0.25	0.50	3.50	—
1937 Matte Proof; Rare	—	—	—	—	—	—

Note: There are reportedly 3-4 pieces known of this variety struck specifically for use in photographs.

Date	Mintage	F	VF	XF	Unc	BU
1937 Proof	26,000	Value: 5.00				
1938	7,450,000	0.15	0.30	0.60	5.00	—
1938 Proof	—	Value: 175				
1939	31,440,000	0.10	0.25	0.50	3.00	—
1939 Proof	—	Value: 175				
1940	18,360,000	0.10	0.25	0.50	3.00	—
1940 Proof	—	Value: 175				
1941	27,312,000	0.10	0.25	0.50	2.50	—
1941 Proof	—	Value: 175				
1942	28,858,000	0.10	0.20	0.50	2.50	—
1942 Proof	—	Value: 175				
1943	33,345,999	0.10	0.15	0.50	2.50	—
1943 Proof	—	Value: 175				
1944	25,138,000	0.10	0.15	0.50	2.50	—
1944 Proof	—	Value: 175				
1945	23,736,000	0.10	0.20	0.50	2.50	—
1945 Proof	—	Value: 175				
1946	24,365,000	0.10	0.20	0.50	2.50	—
1946 Proof	—	Value: 175				
1947	14,746,000	0.10	0.20	0.50	2.50	—
1947 Proof	—	Value: 175				
1948	16,622,000	0.10	0.20	0.50	2.50	—
1948 Proof	—	Value: 175				

KM# 867 FARTHING **Composition:** Bronze **Ruler:** George VI **Obv. Legend:** Without IND IMP

Date	Mintage	F	VF	XF	Unc	BU
1949	8,424,000	0.10	0.20	0.50	4.00	—
1949 Proof	—	Value: 175				
1950	10,325,000	0.10	0.20	0.50	4.00	—
1950 Matte Proof; Rare	—	Value: 3.50				

Note: There are reportedly 3-4 known of this variety, struck specifically for use in photographs

Date	Mintage	F	VF	XF	Unc	BU
1950 Proof	18,000	Value: 8.00				
1951	14,016,000	0.10	0.20	0.50	3.50	—
1951 Matte Proof; Rare	—	—	—	—	—	—

Note: There are reportedly 3-4 known of this variety, struck specifically for use in photographs

Date	Mintage	F	VF	XF	Unc	BU
1951 Proof	20,000	Value: 9.00				
1952	5,251,000	0.10	0.20	0.50	3.50	—
1952 Proof	—	Value: 175				

KM# 881 FARTHING **Composition:** Bronze **Ruler:** Elizabeth II

Date	Mintage	F	VF	XF	Unc	BU
1953	6,131,000	0.15	0.25	0.50	3.00	—
1953 Proof	40,000	Value: 8.00				
1953 Matte Proof; Rare	—	—	—	—	—	—

Note: There are reportedly 1-2 known of this variety, struck specifically for use in photographs

KM# 895 FARTHING **Composition:** Bronze **Ruler:** Elizabeth II **Obv. Legend:** Without BRITT OMN

Date	Mintage	F	VF	XF	Unc	BU
1954	6,566,000	0.10	0.15	0.50	3.00	—
1954 Proof	—	Value: 175				
1955	5,779,000	0.10	0.15	0.50	3.00	—
1955 Proof	—	Value: 175				
1956	1,997,000	0.25	0.50	1.50	5.00	—
1956 Proof	—	Value: 175				

KM# 789 1/2 PENNY **Weight:** 5.7000 g. **Composition:** Bronze **Ruler:** Victoria

Date	Mintage	F	VF	XF	Unc	BU
1901	11,127,000	0.40	0.75	5.00	12.50	—
1901 Proof	—	Value: 500				

KM# 793.1 1/2 PENNY **Composition:** Bronze **Ruler:** Edward VII **Reverse:** Low horizon

Date	Mintage	F	VF	XF	Unc	BU
1902	13,673,000	8.00	25.00	50.00	125	—

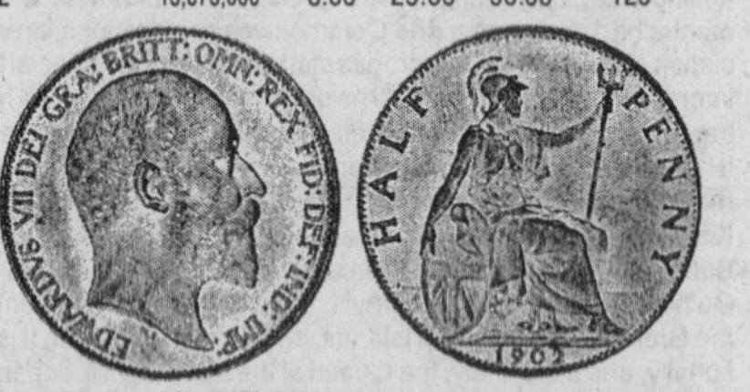

KM# 793.2 1/2 PENNY **Composition:** Bronze **Ruler:** Edward VII **Reverse:** High horizon

Date	Mintage	F	VF	XF	Unc	BU
1902	Inc. above	0.50	1.50	5.00	18.00	—
1903	11,451,000	0.75	2.50	8.00	35.00	—
1904	8,131,000	1.50	3.50	12.00	40.00	—
1905	10,125,000	1.00	3.00	8.00	35.00	—
1906	11,101,000	0.75	2.00	6.00	30.00	—
1907	16,849,000	0.75	2.00	6.00	25.00	—
1908	16,620,999	0.75	2.00	6.00	25.00	—
1909	8,279,000	1.00	3.00	8.00	35.00	—
1910	10,770,000	1.00	3.00	8.00	30.00	—

KM# 809 1/2 PENNY **Composition:** Bronze **Ruler:** George V

Date	Mintage	F	VF	XF	Unc	BU
1911	12,571,000	0.75	1.50	4.50	25.00	—
1912	21,186,000	0.50	1.25	4.00	30.00	—
1913	17,476,000	0.75	2.25	8.00	30.00	—
1914	20,289,000	0.75	1.50	5.00	30.00	—
1915	21,563,000	0.75	1.50	5.00	30.00	—
1916	39,386,000	0.75	1.50	5.00	30.00	—
1917	38,245,000	0.75	1.50	5.00	30.00	—
1918	22,321,000	0.75	1.50	5.00	30.00	—
1919	28,104,000	0.50	1.50	5.00	27.50	—
1920	35,147,000	0.50	1.50	5.00	27.50	—
1921	28,027,000	0.75	1.50	3.00	22.00	—
1922	10,735,000	1.00	2.00	6.00	35.00	—
1923	12,266,000	0.50	1.50	5.00	22.00	—
1924	13,971,000	0.75	2.00	5.00	22.00	—
1925	12,216,000	1.00	2.00	5.00	22.00	—

KM# 824 1/2 PENNY **Composition:** Bronze **Ruler:** George V **Obverse:** Modified effigy

Date	Mintage	F	VF	XF	Unc	BU
1925	Inc. above	1.50	4.00	8.00	38.00	—
1926	6,712,000	1.50	3.00	6.00	27.50	—
1926 Proof	—	Value: 325				
1927	15,590,000	0.75	1.50	5.00	25.00	—
1927 Proof	—	Value: 325				

KM# 837 1/2 PENNY **Composition:** Bronze **Ruler:** George V **Obverse:** Smaller head

Date	Mintage	F	VF	XF	Unc	BU
1928	20,935,000	0.25	0.50	2.50	17.50	—
1928 Proof	—	Value: 325				
1929	25,680,000	0.25	0.50	2.50	17.50	—
1929 Proof	—	Value: 325				
1930	12,533,000	0.25	0.50	2.50	17.50	—
1930 Proof	—	Value: 325				
1931	16,138,000	0.25	0.50	2.50	17.50	—
1931 Proof	—	Value: 325				
1932	14,448,000	0.25	0.50	2.50	20.00	—
1932 Proof	—	Value: 325				
1933	10,560,000	0.25	0.50	2.50	17.50	—
1933 Proof	—	Value: 325				
1934	7,704,000	0.50	0.50	3.50	25.00	—
1934 Proof	—	Value: 350				
1935	12,180,000	0.25	0.50	2.00	16.50	—
1935 Proof	—	Value: 300				
1936	23,009,000	0.25	0.50	1.50	12.50	—
1936 Proof	—	Value: 300				

KM# 844 1/2 PENNY **Composition:** Bronze **Ruler:** George VI

Date	Mintage	F	VF	XF	Unc	BU
1937		0.25	0.35	0.50	4.00	—
1937 Proof	26,000	Value: 5.00				
1937 Matte Proof; Rare	—	—	—	—	—	—
1938		0.25	0.50	1.25	6.00	—
1938 Proof	—	Value: 300				
1939		0.25	0.50	1.25	7.00	—
1939 Proof	—	Value: 300				
1940		0.25	0.50	2.00	8.00	—
1940 Proof	—	Value: 300				
1941		0.20	0.50	1.50	4.50	—
1941 Proof	—	Value: 300				
1942		0.10	0.20	0.60	4.50	—
1942 Proof	—	Value: 300				
1943		0.10	0.25	1.00	4.50	—
1943 Proof	—	Value: 300				
1944		0.10	0.25	1.00	4.50	—
1944 Proof	—	Value: 300				
1945		0.10	0.25	0.90	4.50	—
1945 Proof	—	Value: 300				
1946		0.20	0.50	2.75	7.00	—
1946 Proof	—	Value: 300				
1947		0.10	0.25	2.00	5.50	—
1947 Proof	—	Value: 300				
1948		0.10	0.25	0.90	4.50	—
1948 Proof	—	Value: 300				

KM# 868 1/2 PENNY **Composition:** Bronze **Ruler:** George VI **Obv. Legend:** Without IND IMP

Date	Mintage	F	VF	XF	Unc	BU
1949	24,744,000	0.10	0.25	1.00	9.00	—
1949 Proof	—	Value: 250				
1950	24,154,000	0.10	0.25	0.75	7.00	—
1950 Proof	18,000	Value: 7.00				
1950 Matte Proof; Rare	—	—	—	—	—	—

Note: There are reportedly 1-2 known of this variety, struck specifically for use in photographs

Date	Mintage	F	VF	XF	Unc	BU
1951	14,868,000	0.25	0.50	1.50	12.50	—
1951 Proof	20,000	Value: 9.00				
1951 Matte Proof; Rare	—	—	—	—	—	—

Date	Mintage	F	VF	XF	Unc	BU
Note: There are reportedly 1-2 known of this variety, struck specifically for use in photographs						
1952	33,278,000	0.10	0.25	0.50	6.00	—
1952 Proof	—	Value: 275				

KM# 882 1/2 PENNY Composition: Bronze **Ruler:** Elizabeth II

Date	Mintage	F	VF	XF	Unc	BU
1953	8,926,000	0.20	0.40	1.00	5.00	—
1953 Proof	40,000	Value: 8.00				
1953 Matte Proof; Rare	—	—	—	—	—	—

Note: There are reportedly 1-2 known of this variety, struck specifically for use in photographs.

KM# 896 1/2 PENNY Composition: Bronze **Ruler:** Elizabeth II **Obv. Legend:** Without BRITT OMN

Date	Mintage	F	VF	XF	Unc	BU
1954	19,375,000	0.10	0.25	1.50	4.00	—
1954 Proof	—	Value: 250				
1955	18,799,000	0.10	0.25	1.50	3.00	—
1955 Proof	—	Value: 250				
1956	21,799,000	0.15	0.50	1.50	3.00	—
1956 Proof	—	Value: 250				
1957	43,684,000	0.10	0.25	0.50	2.00	—
1957 Proof	—	Value: 250				
1958	62,318,000	—	0.10	0.20	1.00	—
1958 Proof	—	Value: 250				
1959	79,176,000	—	0.10	0.15	0.75	—
1959 Proof	—	Value: 250				
1960	41,340,000	—	0.10	0.15	0.50	—
1960 Proof	—	Value: 250				
1962	41,779,000	—	—	0.10	0.45	—
1962 Proof	—	Value: 250				
1963	45,036,000	—	—	0.10	0.45	—
1963 Proof	—	Value: 250				
1964	78,583,000	—	—	0.10	0.35	—
1964 Proof	—	Value: 250				
1965	98,083,000	—	—	—	0.25	—
1965 Proof	—	—	—	—	—	—
1966	95,289,000	—	—	—	0.20	—
1966 Proof	—	—	—	—	—	—
1967	146,491,000	—	—	—	0.20	—
1967 Proof	—	—	—	—	—	—
1970 Proof	750,000	Value: 2.00				

KM# 775 PENNY Weight: 0.4713 g. **Composition:** 0.9250 Silver .0140 oz. ASW **Ruler:** Victoria

Date	Mintage	F	VF	XF	Unc	BU
1901 Prooflike	18,000	—	—	—	12.50	—

KM# 790 PENNY Weight: 9.4500 g. **Composition:** Bronze **Ruler:** Victoria

Date	Mintage	F	VF	XF	Unc	BU
1901	22,206,000	0.30	1.00	5.00	15.50	—
1901 Proof	—	—	—	—	—	—

KM# 794.1 PENNY Weight: 9.4500 g. **Composition:** Bronze **Ruler:** Edward VII **Reverse:** Low sea level

Date	Mintage	F	VF	XF	Unc	BU
1902	26,977,000	4.00	9.00	22.50	90.00	—

KM# 794.2 PENNY Composition: Bronze **Ruler:** Edward VII **Reverse:** High sea level

Date	Mintage	F	VF	XF	Unc	BU
1902	Inc. above	0.50	2.00	4.00	30.00	—
1903	21,415,000	0.50	2.50	9.00	40.00	—
1904	12,913,000	1.00	3.00	15.00	60.00	—
1905	17,784,000	0.50	2.50	12.00	45.00	—
1906	37,990,000	0.50	2.00	10.00	45.00	—
1907	47,322,000	0.50	2.00	10.00	45.00	—
1908	31,506,000	0.50	2.00	10.00	45.00	—
1908 Matte Proof; Rare	3	—	—	—	—	—
1909	19,617,000	0.50	2.00	10.00	45.00	—
1910	29,549,000	0.35	1.50	8.00	35.00	—

KM# 795 PENNY Weight: 0.4713 g. **Composition:** 0.9250 Silver .0140 oz. ASW **Ruler:** Edward VII

Date	Mintage	F	VF	XF	Unc	BU
1902 Prooflike	21,000	—	—	—	12.50	—
1903 Prooflike	17,000	—	—	—	12.50	—
1904 Prooflike	19,000	—	—	—	12.50	—
1905 Prooflike	18,000	—	—	—	12.50	—
1906 Prooflike	19,000	—	—	—	12.50	—
1907 Prooflike	18,000	—	—	—	12.50	—
1908 Prooflike	18,000	—	—	—	12.50	—
1909 Prooflike	2,948	—	—	—	15.00	—
1910 Prooflike	3,392	—	—	—	20.00	—

KM# 810 PENNY Weight: 9.4500 g. **Composition:** Bronze **Ruler:** George V

Date	Mintage	F	VF	XF	Unc	BU
1911	23,079,000	0.40	1.25	7.00	25.00	—
1912	48,306,000	0.35	1.00	8.00	27.50	—
1912H	16,800,000	1.00	8.00	50.00	145	—
1913	65,497,000	0.40	2.00	15.00	35.00	—
1914	50,821,000	0.35	1.00	7.00	27.50	—
1915	47,311,000	0.50	1.25	8.00	32.50	—
1916	86,411,000	0.35	1.00	6.50	27.50	—
1917	107,905,000	0.35	1.00	6.50	27.50	—
1918	84,227,000	0.35	1.00	6.50	27.50	—
1918H	2,573,000	2.00	15.00	150	350	—
1918KN	Inc. above	3.50	27.50	200	550	—
1919	113,761,000	0.50	1.00	6.50	27.50	—
1919H	4,526,000	1.25	15.00	120	375	—
1919KN	Inc. above	5.00	30.00	225	600	—
1920	124,693,000	0.50	1.50	6.50	27.50	—
1921	129,717,999	0.30	0.75	5.50	27.50	—
1922	16,347,000	0.75	3.50	15.00	50.00	—
1926	4,499,000	2.50	8.00	20.00	75.00	—
1926 Proof	—	Value: 850				

KM# 811 PENNY Weight: 0.4713 g. **Composition:** 0.9250 Silver .0140 oz. ASW **Ruler:** George V

Date	Mintage	F	VF	XF	Unc	BU
1911 Prooflike	1,913	—	—	—	15.00	—
1912 Prooflike	1,616	—	—	—	15.00	—
1913 Prooflike	1,590	—	—	—	15.00	—
1914 Prooflike	1,818	—	—	—	15.00	—
1915 Prooflike	2,072	—	—	—	15.00	—
1916 Prooflike	1,647	—	—	—	15.00	—
1917 Prooflike	1,820	—	—	—	15.00	—
1918 Prooflike	1,911	—	—	—	15.00	—
1919 Prooflike	1,699	—	—	—	15.00	—
1920 Prooflike	1,715	—	—	—	15.00	—

KM# 811a PENNY Weight: 0.4713 g. **Composition:** 0.5000 Silver .0076 oz. ASW **Ruler:** George V

Date	Mintage	F	VF	XF	Unc	BU
1921 Prooflike	1,847	—	—	—	15.00	—
1922 Prooflike	1,758	—	—	—	15.00	—
1923 Prooflike	1,840	—	—	—	15.00	—
1924 Prooflike	1,619	—	—	—	15.00	—
1925 Prooflike	1,890	—	—	—	15.00	—
1926 Prooflike	2,180	—	—	—	15.00	—
1927 Prooflike	1,647	—	—	—	15.00	—

KM# 826 PENNY Composition: Bronze **Ruler:** George V **Obverse:** Modified head

Date	Mintage	F	VF	XF	Unc	BU
1926	—	20.00	90.00	750	2,500	—
1926 Proof	—	—	—	—	—	—
1927	60,990,000	0.35	0.75	7.00	20.00	—
1927 Proof	—	Value: 750				

KM# 838 PENNY Composition: Bronze **Ruler:** George V **Obverse:** Smaller head

Date	Mintage	F	VF	XF	Unc	BU
1928	50,178,000	0.25	0.50	6.00	17.50	—
1928 Proof	—	Value: 500				
1929	49,133,000	0.25	0.50	6.00	17.50	—
1929 Proof	—	Value: 400				
1930	29,098,000	0.25	1.00	8.00	25.00	—
1930 Proof	—	Value: 400				
1931	19,843,000	0.25	1.00	8.00	30.00	—
1931 Proof	—	Value: 400				
1932	8,278,000	1.00	4.50	17.50	60.00	—
1932 Proof	—	Value: 500				
1933 Rare	—	—	—	—	—	—
1933 Proof	—	—	—	—	—	—
1934	13,966,000	0.50	4.00	16.00	50.00	—
1934 Proof	—	Value: 500				
1935	56,070,000	0.25	0.50	3.50	16.00	—
1935 Proof	—	Value: 375				
1936	154,296,000	0.25	0.40	3.00	14.00	—
1936 Proof	—	Value: 375				

KM# 839 PENNY Weight: 0.4713 g. **Composition:** 0.5000 Silver .0076 oz. ASW **Ruler:** George V **Obverse:** Modified effigy

Date	Mintage	F	VF	XF	Unc	BU
1928 Prooflike	1,846	—	—	—	15.00	—
1929 Prooflike	1,837	—	—	—	20.00	—
1930 Prooflike	1,724	—	—	—	15.00	—
1931 Prooflike	1,759	—	—	—	15.00	—
1932 Prooflike	1,835	—	—	—	15.00	—
1933 Prooflike	1,872	—	—	—	15.00	—
1934 Prooflike	1,919	—	—	—	15.00	—
1935 Prooflike	1,975	—	—	—	15.00	—
1936 Prooflike	1,329	—	—	—	15.00	—

KM# 845 PENNY **Weight:** 9.4500 g. **Composition:** Bronze **Ruler:** George VI

Date	Mintage	F	VF	XF	Unc	BU
1937		0.20	0.35	1.25	5.00	—
1937 Proof	26,000	Value: 12.50				
1937 Matte Proof; Rare		—	—	—	—	—
1938		0.20	0.35	1.25	6.50	—
1938 Proof	—	Value: 350				
1939		0.25	0.50	1.50	10.00	—
1939 Proof	—	Value: 350				
1940		0.25	0.50	2.00	12.00	—
1940 Proof	—	Value: 350				
1944		0.25	0.50	2.25	14.00	—
1944 Proof		—	—	—	—	—
1945		0.20	0.35	1.50	12.00	—
1945 Proof		—	—	—	—	—
1946		0.20	0.35	1.00	12.00	—
1946 Proof		—	—	—	—	—
1947		0.15	0.25	0.75	5.00	—
1947 Proof		—	—	—	—	—
1948		0.15	0.25	0.75	5.00	—
1948 Proof		—	—	—	—	—

KM# 846 PENNY **Weight:** 0.4713 g. **Composition:** 0.5000 Silver .0076 oz. ASW **Ruler:** George VI

Date	Mintage	F	VF	XF	Unc	BU
1937 Prooflike	1,329	—	—	—	15.00	—
1938 Prooflike	1,275	—	—	—	15.00	—
1939 Prooflike	1,253	—	—	—	15.00	—
1940 Prooflike	1,375	—	—	—	15.00	—
1941 Prooflike	1,255	—	—	—	15.00	—
1942 Prooflike	1,243	—	—	—	15.00	—
1943 Prooflike	1,347	—	—	—	15.00	—
1944 Prooflike	1,259	—	—	—	15.00	—
1945 Prooflike	1,367	—	—	—	15.00	—
1946 Prooflike	1,479	—	—	—	15.00	—

KM# 846a PENNY **Weight:** 0.4713 g. **Composition:** 0.9250 Silver .0140 oz. ASW **Ruler:** George VI

Date	Mintage	F	VF	XF	Unc	BU
1947 Prooflike	1,387	—	—	—	15.00	—
1948 Prooflike	1,397	—	—	—	15.00	—

KM# 869 PENNY **Composition:** Bronze **Ruler:** George VI **Obv. Legend:** Without IND IMP

Date	Mintage	F	VF	XF	Unc	BU
1949	14,324,000	0.20	0.35	1.00	5.00	—
1949 Proof		—	—	—	—	—
1950	240,000	2.00	6.00	21.00	37.00	—
1950 Matte Proof; Rare		—	—	—	—	—

Note: There are reportedly 1-2 known of this variety, struck specifically for use in photography

Date	Mintage	F	VF	XF	Unc	BU
1950 Proof	18,000	Value: 30.00				
1951	120,000	3.00	10.00	30.00	50.00	—
1951 Matte Proof; Rare		—	—	—	—	—

Note: There are reportedly 1-2 known of this variety, struck specifically for use in photography

Date	Mintage	F	VF	XF	Unc	BU
1951 Proof	20,000	Value: 40.00				
1952 Unique		—	—	—	—	—

KM# 870 PENNY **Weight:** 0.4713 g. **Composition:** 0.9250 Silver .0140 oz. ASW **Ruler:** George VI **Obv. Legend:** Without IND IMP

Date	Mintage	F	VF	XF	Unc	BU
1949 Prooflike	1,407	—	—	—	15.00	—
1950 Prooflike	1,527	—	—	—	15.00	—

Date	Mintage	F	VF	XF	Unc	BU
1951 Prooflike	1,480	—	—	—	15.00	—
1952 Prooflike	1,024	—	—	—	15.00	—

KM# 883 PENNY **Composition:** Bronze **Ruler:** Elizabeth II

Date	Mintage	F	VF	XF	Unc	BU
1953	1,308,000	0.75	1.50	3.50	9.00	—
1953 Proof	40,000	Value: 15.00				
1953 Matte Proof; Rare		—	—	—	—	—

Note: There are reportedly 1-2 known of this variety, struck specifically for use in photography

KM# 884 PENNY **Weight:** 0.4713 g. **Composition:** 0.9250 Silver .0140 oz. ASW **Ruler:** Elizabeth II

Date	Mintage	F	VF	XF	Unc	BU
1953 Prooflike	1,050	—	—	—	150	—

KM# 897 PENNY **Composition:** Bronze **Ruler:** Elizabeth II **Obv. Legend:** Without BRITT OMN

Date	Mintage	F	VF	XF	Unc	BU
1954 1 Known		—	—	—	—	—
1961	48,313,000	—	0.10	0.15	1.00	—
1961 Proof		—	—	—	—	—
1962	143,309,000	—	—	0.10	0.45	—
1962 Proof		—	—	—	—	—
1963	125,236,000	—	—	0.10	0.45	—
1963 Proof		—	—	—	—	—
1964	153,294,000	—	—	—	0.25	—
1964 Proof		—	—	—	—	—
1965	121,310,000	—	—	—	0.25	—
1966	165,739,000	—	—	—	0.25	—
1967	654,564,000	—	—	—	0.20	—
1970 Proof	750,000	Value: 5.00				

KM# 898 PENNY **Weight:** 0.4713 g. **Composition:** 0.9250 Silver .0140 oz. ASW **Ruler:** Elizabeth II

Date	Mintage	F	VF	XF	Unc	BU
1954 Prooflike	1,088	—	—	—	15.00	—
1955 Prooflike	1,036	—	—	—	15.00	—
1956 Prooflike	1,100	—	—	—	15.00	—
1957 Prooflike	1,168	—	—	—	15.00	—
1958 Prooflike	1,112	—	—	—	15.00	—
1959 Prooflike	1,118	—	—	—	15.00	—
1960 Prooflike	1,124	—	—	—	15.00	—
1961 Prooflike	1,200	—	—	—	15.00	—
1962 Prooflike	1,127	—	—	—	15.00	—
1963 Prooflike	1,133	—	—	—	15.00	—
1964 Prooflike	1,215	—	—	—	15.00	—
1965 Prooflike	1,143	—	—	—	15.00	—
1966 Prooflike	1,206	—	—	—	15.00	—
1967 Prooflike	1,068	—	—	—	15.00	—
1968 Prooflike	964	—	—	—	15.00	—
1969 Prooflike	1,002	—	—	—	15.00	—
1970 Prooflike	980	—	—	—	15.00	—
1971 Prooflike	1,108	—	—	—	15.00	—
1972 Prooflike	1,026	—	—	—	15.00	—
1973 Prooflike	1,004	—	—	—	15.00	—
1974 Prooflike	1,138	—	—	—	15.00	—
1975 Prooflike	1,050	—	—	—	15.00	—
1976 Prooflike	1,158	—	—	—	15.00	—
1977 Prooflike	1,240	—	—	—	17.50	—
1978 Prooflike	1,178	—	—	—	17.50	—
1979 Prooflike	1,188	—	—	—	17.50	—
1980 Prooflike	1,198	—	—	—	17.50	—
1981 Prooflike	1,288	—	—	—	17.50	—
1982 Prooflike	1,218	—	—	—	17.50	—
1983 Prooflike	1,228	—	—	—	17.50	—
1984 Prooflike	1,354	—	—	—	17.50	—
1985 Prooflike	1,248	—	—	—	17.50	—
1986 Prooflike	1,378	—	—	—	17.50	—
1987 Prooflike	1,512	—	—	—	17.50	—
1988 Prooflike	1,402	—	—	—	17.50	—
1989 Prooflike	1,353	—	—	—	17.50	—
1990 Prooflike	1,523	—	—	—	17.50	—

Date	Mintage	F	VF	XF	Unc	BU
1991 Prooflike	1,514	—	—	—	17.50	—
1992 Prooflike	1,556	—	—	—	17.50	—
1993 Prooflike	1,440	—	—	—	17.50	—
1994 Prooflike	1,443	—	—	—	17.50	—
1995 Prooflike	1,466	—	—	—	17.50	—
1996 Prooflike	1,629	—	—	—	17.50	—
1997 Prooflike	1,786	—	—	—	17.50	—
1998 Prooflike	—	—	—	—	17.50	—
1999 Prooflike	—	—	—	—	17.50	—
2000 Prooflike	—	—	—	—	17.50	—

KM# 776 2 PENCE **Weight:** 0.9426 g. **Composition:** 0.9250 Silver .0280 oz. ASW **Ruler:** Victoria

Date	Mintage	F	VF	XF	Unc	BU
1901 Prooflike	14,000	—	—	—	12.50	—

KM# 796 2 PENCE **Weight:** 0.9426 g. **Composition:** 0.9250 Silver .0280 oz. ASW **Ruler:** Edward VII

Date	Mintage	F	VF	XF	Unc	BU
1902 Prooflike	14,000	—	—	—	12.50	—
1903 Prooflike	13,000	—	—	—	12.50	—
1904 Prooflike	14,000	—	—	—	12.50	—
1905 Prooflike	11,000	—	—	—	12.50	—
1906 Prooflike	11,000	—	—	—	12.50	—
1907 Prooflike	8,760	—	—	—	12.50	—
1908 Prooflike	15,000	—	—	—	12.50	—
1909 Prooflike	2,695	—	—	—	15.00	—
1910 Prooflike	2,998	—	—	—	20.00	—

KM# 812 2 PENCE **Weight:** 0.9426 g. **Composition:** 0.9250 Silver .0280 oz. ASW **Ruler:** George V

Date	Mintage	F	VF	XF	Unc	BU
1911 Prooflike	1,635	—	—	—	17.50	—
1912 Prooflike	1,678	—	—	—	17.50	—
1913 Prooflike	1,880	—	—	—	17.50	—
1914 Prooflike	1,659	—	—	—	17.50	—
1915 Prooflike	1,465	—	—	—	17.50	—
1916 Prooflike	1,509	—	—	—	17.50	—
1917 Prooflike	1,506	—	—	—	17.50	—
1918 Prooflike	1,547	—	—	—	17.50	—
1919 Prooflike	1,567	—	—	—	17.50	—
1920 Prooflike	1,630	—	—	—	17.50	—

KM# 812a 2 PENCE **Weight:** 0.9426 g. **Composition:** 0.5000 Silver .0152 oz. ASW **Ruler:** George V

Date	Mintage	F	VF	XF	Unc	BU
1921 Prooflike	1,794	—	—	—	20.00	—
1922 Prooflike	3,074	—	—	—	20.00	—
1923 Prooflike	1,527	—	—	—	20.00	—
1924 Prooflike	1,602	—	—	—	20.00	—
1925 Prooflike	1,670	—	—	—	20.00	—
1926 Prooflike	1,902	—	—	—	20.00	—
1927 Prooflike	1,766	—	—	—	20.00	—

KM# 840 2 PENCE **Weight:** 0.9426 g. **Composition:** 0.5000 Silver .0152 oz. ASW **Ruler:** George V **Obverse:** Modified effigy

Date	Mintage	F	VF	XF	Unc	BU
1928 Prooflike	1,706	—	—	—	17.50	—
1929 Prooflike	1,862	—	—	—	17.50	—
1930 Prooflike	1,901	—	—	—	17.50	—
1931 Prooflike	1,897	—	—	—	17.50	—
1932 Prooflike	1,960	—	—	—	17.50	—
1933 Prooflike	2,066	—	—	—	17.50	—
1934 Prooflike	1,927	—	—	—	17.50	—
1935 Prooflike	1,928	—	—	—	17.50	—
1936 Prooflike	1,365	—	—	—	20.00	—

KM# 847 2 PENCE **Weight:** 0.9426 g. **Composition:** 0.5000 Silver .0152 oz. ASW **Ruler:** George VI

Date	Mintage	F	VF	XF	Unc	BU
1937 Prooflike	1,472	—	—	—	17.50	—
1938 Prooflike	1,374	—	—	—	17.50	—
1939 Prooflike	1,436	—	—	—	17.50	—
1940 Prooflike	1,277	—	—	—	17.50	—
1941 Prooflike	1,345	—	—	—	17.50	—
1942 Prooflike	1,231	—	—	—	17.50	—
1943 Prooflike	1,239	—	—	—	17.50	—
1944 Prooflike	1,345	—	—	—	17.50	—
1945 Prooflike	1,355	—	—	—	17.50	—
1946 Prooflike	1,365	—	—	—	17.50	—

KM# 847a 2 PENCE **Weight:** 0.9426 g. **Composition:** 0.9250 Silver .0280 oz. ASW **Ruler:** George VI

Date	Mintage	F	VF	XF	Unc	BU
1947 Prooflike	1,479	—	—	—	17.50	—
1948 Prooflike	1,385	—	—	—	17.50	—

KM# 871 2 PENCE **Weight:** 0.9426 g. **Composition:** 0.9250 Silver .0280 oz. ASW **Ruler:** George VI **Obv. Legend:** Without IND IMP

Date	Mintage	F	VF	XF	Unc	BU
1949 Prooflike	1,395	—	—	—	17.50	—
1950 Prooflike	1,405	—	—	—	17.50	—
1951 Prooflike	1,580	—	—	—	17.50	—
1952 Prooflike	1,064	—	—	—	17.50	—

KM# 885 2 PENCE **Weight:** 0.9426 g. **Composition:** 0.9250 Silver .0280 oz. ASW **Ruler:** Elizabeth II

Date	Mintage	F	VF	XF	Unc	BU
1953 Prooflike	1,025	—	—	—	85.00	—

KM# 899 2 PENCE **Weight:** 0.9426 g. **Composition:** 0.9250 Silver .0280 oz. ASW **Ruler:** Elizabeth II **Obv. Legend:** Without BRITT OMN

Date	Mintage	F	VF	XF	Unc	BU
1954 Prooflike	1,020	—	—	—	20.00	—
1955 Prooflike	1,082	—	—	—	20.00	—
1956 Prooflike	1,088	—	—	—	20.00	—
1957 Prooflike	1,094	—	—	—	20.00	—
1958 Prooflike	1,164	—	—	—	20.00	—
1959 Prooflike	1,106	—	—	—	20.00	—
1960 Prooflike	1,112	—	—	—	20.00	—
1961 Prooflike	1,118	—	—	—	20.00	—
1962 Prooflike	1,197	—	—	—	20.00	—
1963 Prooflike	1,131	—	—	—	20.00	—
1964 Prooflike	1,137	—	—	—	20.00	—
1965 Prooflike	1,221	—	—	—	20.00	—
1966 Prooflike	1,206	—	—	—	20.00	—
1967 Prooflike	986	—	—	—	20.00	—
1968 Prooflike	1,048	—	—	—	20.00	—
1969 Prooflike	1,002	—	—	—	20.00	—
1970 Prooflike	980	—	—	—	20.00	—
1971 Prooflike	1,018	—	—	—	20.00	—
1972 Prooflike	1,026	—	—	—	20.00	—
1973 Prooflike	1,004	—	—	—	20.00	—
1974 Prooflike	1,042	—	—	—	20.00	—
1975 Prooflike	1,148	—	—	—	20.00	—
1976 Prooflike	1,158	—	—	—	20.00	—
1977 Prooflike	1,138	—	—	—	22.00	—
1978 Prooflike	1,282	—	—	—	22.00	—
1979 Prooflike	1,188	—	—	—	22.00	—
1980 Prooflike	1,198	—	—	—	22.00	—
1981 Prooflike	1,178	—	—	—	22.00	—
1982 Prooflike	1,330	—	—	—	22.00	—
1983 Prooflike	1,228	—	—	—	22.00	—
1984 Prooflike	1,238	—	—	—	22.00	—
1985 Prooflike	1,366	—	—	—	22.00	—
1986 Prooflike	1,378	—	—	—	22.00	—
1987 Prooflike	1,390	—	—	—	22.00	—
1988 Prooflike	1,526	—	—	—	22.00	—
1989 Prooflike	1,353	—	—	—	22.00	—
1990 Prooflike	1,523	—	—	—	22.00	—
1991 Prooflike	1,384	—	—	—	22.00	—
1992 Prooflike	1,424	—	—	—	22.00	—
1993 Prooflike	1,440	—	—	—	22.00	—
1994 Prooflike	1,443	—	—	—	22.00	—
1995 Prooflike	1,466	—	—	—	22.00	—
1996 Prooflike	1,629	—	—	—	22.00	—
1997 Prooflike	1,786	—	—	—	22.00	—
1998 Prooflike	—	—	—	—	22.00	—
1999 Prooflike	—	—	—	—	22.00	—
2000 Prooflike	—	—	—	—	22.00	—

KM# 777 3 PENCE **Weight:** 1.4138 g. **Composition:** 0.9250 Silver .0420 oz. ASW **Ruler:** Victoria

Date	Mintage	F	VF	XF	Unc	BU
1901	6,100,000	1.00	2.00	6.50	20.00	—
1901 Prooflike	8,976	—	—	—	30.00	—

KM# 797.1 3 PENCE **Weight:** 1.4138 g. **Composition:** 0.9250 Silver .0420 oz. ASW **Ruler:** Edward VII **Note:** The prooflike coins come with a mirror or satin finish.

Date	Mintage	F	VF	XF	Unc	BU
1902	8,287,000	0.50	2.50	7.50	15.00	—
1902 Prooflike	8,976	—	—	—	18.00	—
1902 Matte Proof	15,000	Value: 22.50				
1903	5,235,000	2.50	6.50	25.00	50.00	—
1903 Prooflike	8,976	—	—	—	18.00	—
1904	3,630,000	5.00	12.00	32.00	90.00	—
1904 Prooflike	8,876	—	—	—	25.00	—

KM# 797.2 3 PENCE **Weight:** 1.4138 g. **Composition:** 0.9250 Silver .0420 oz. ASW **Ruler:** Edward VII **Note:** The below Prooflike listings can be of mirror or satin-like finish, which are more difficult to separate from the currency strikes, especially for the years 1903-1906.

Date	Mintage	F	VF	XF	Unc	BU
1904	Inc. above	4.50	10.00	30.00	70.00	—
1905	3,563,000	3.00	8.00	22.50	65.00	—
1905 Prooflike	8,976	—	—	—	22.50	—
1906	3,174,000	4.00	10.00	30.00	100	—
1906 Prooflike	8,800	—	—	—	22.50	—
1907	4,841,000	2.00	4.00	20.00	50.00	—
1907 Prooflike	11,000	—	—	—	22.50	—
1908	8,176,000	2.00	4.00	15.00	35.00	—
1908 Prooflike	8,760	—	—	—	22.50	—
1909	4,054,999	2.00	4.00	20.00	45.00	—
1909 Prooflike	1,983	—	—	—	30.00	—
1910	4,565,000	1.00	2.00	10.00	30.00	—
1910 Prooflike	1,140	—	—	—	30.00	—

KM# 813 3 PENCE **Weight:** 1.4138 g. **Composition:** 0.9250 Silver .0420 oz. ASW **Ruler:** George V

Date	Mintage	F	VF	XF	Unc	BU
1911	5,843,000	0.50	1.00	4.50	15.00	—
1911 Prooflike	1,991	—	—	—	22.50	—
1911 Proof	6,007	Value: 35.00				
1912	8,934,000	0.50	1.00	4.50	15.00	—
1912 Prooflike	1,246	—	—	—	22.50	—
1913	7,144,000	0.50	1.00	4.50	15.00	—
1913 Prooflike	1,228	—	—	—	30.00	—
1914	6,735,000	0.50	1.00	4.50	15.00	—
1914 Prooflike	982	—	—	—	32.50	—
1915	5,452,000	0.50	1.00	4.00	15.00	—
1915 Prooflike	1,293	—	—	—	25.00	—
1916	18,556,000	0.40	0.85	3.00	12.50	—
1916 Prooflike	1,128	—	—	—	22.50	—
1917	21,664,000	0.40	0.85	3.00	12.50	—
1917 Prooflike	1,237	—	—	—	22.50	—
1918	20,632,000	0.40	0.85	3.00	12.50	—
1918 Prooflike	1,375	—	—	—	22.50	—
1919	16,846,000	0.40	0.85	3.00	12.50	—
1919 Prooflike	1,258	—	—	—	22.50	—
1920	16,704,999	0.40	0.85	3.00	18.00	—
1920 Prooflike	1,399	—	—	—	25.00	—

KM# 813a 3 PENCE **Weight:** 1.4138 g. **Composition:** 0.5000 Silver .0227 oz. ASW **Ruler:** George V

Date	Mintage	F	VF	XF	Unc	BU
1920	Inc. above	—	BV	2.50	16.00	—
1921	8,751,000	—	BV	3.00	16.50	—
1921 Prooflike	1,386	—	—	—	20.00	—
1922	7,981,000	—	BV	7.00	22.50	—
1922 Prooflike	1,373	—	—	—	20.00	—
1923 Prooflike	1,430	—	—	—	25.00	—
1924 Prooflike	1,515	—	—	—	25.00	—
1925	3,733,000	0.50	2.00	12.50	32.50	—
1925 Prooflike	1,438	—	—	—	25.00	—
1926	4,109,000	1.50	5.00	17.50	50.00	—
1926 Prooflike	1,504	—	—	—	25.00	—
1927 Prooflike	1,690	—	—	—	25.00	—

KM# 827 3 PENCE **Weight:** 1.4138 g. **Composition:** 0.5000 Silver .0227 oz. ASW **Ruler:** George V **Obverse:** Modified effigy

Date	Mintage	F	VF	XF	Unc	BU
1926	Inc. above	1.00	2.50	8.00	40.00	—
1928 Prooflike	1,835	—	—	—	22.50	—
1929 Prooflike	1,761	—	—	—	22.50	—
1930 Prooflike	1,948	—	—	—	22.50	—
1931 Prooflike	1,818	—	—	—	22.50	—
1932 Prooflike	2,042	—	—	—	22.50	—
1933 Prooflike	1,920	—	—	—	22.50	—
1934 Prooflike	1,887	—	—	—	22.50	—
1935 Prooflike	2,007	—	—	—	22.50	—
1936 Prooflike	1,307	—	—	—	25.00	—

KM# 831 3 PENCE **Weight:** 1.4138 g. **Composition:** 0.5000 Silver .0227 oz. ASW **Ruler:** George V

Date	Mintage	F	VF	XF	Unc	BU
1927 Proof	15,000	Value: 50.00				
1928	1,302,000	2.50	4.00	15.00	35.00	—
1928 Proof	—	Value: 275				
1930	1,319,000	2.00	3.50	12.50	35.00	—
1930 Proof	—	Value: 250				
1931	6,252,000	BV	0.50	1.50	6.50	—
1931 Proof	—	Value: 225				
1932	5,887,000	BV	0.50	2.50	7.00	—
1932 Proof	—	Value: 225				
1933	5,579,000	BV	0.50	2.50	7.00	—
1933 Proof	—	Value: 225				
1934	7,406,000	BV	0.50	1.50	6.50	—
1934 Proof	—	Value: 225				
1935	7,028,000	BV	0.50	1.50	6.50	—
1935 Proof	—	Value: 225				
1936	3,239,000	BV	0.50	1.50	8.00	—
1936 Proof	—	Value: 225				

KM# 848 3 PENCE **Weight:** 1.4138 g. **Composition:** 0.5000 Silver .0227 oz. ASW **Ruler:** George VI

Date	Mintage	F	VF	XF	Unc	BU
1937	8,148,000	BV	0.50	1.50	6.50	—
1937 Proof	26,000	Value: 9.00				
1937 Matte Proof; Rare	—	—	—	—	—	—

Note: There are reportedly 2-4 known of this variety, struck specifically for use in photography

Date	Mintage	F	VF	XF	Unc	BU
1938	6,402,000	BV	0.50	1.50	6.00	—
1938 Proof	—	Value: 200				
1939	1,356,000	BV	0.75	5.00	15.00	—
1939 Proof	—	Value: 225				
1940	7,914,000	BV	0.50	1.00	8.00	—
1940 Proof	—	Value: 200				
1941	7,979,000	BV	0.50	1.50	10.00	—
1941 Proof	—	Value: 200				
1942	4,144,000	BV	2.50	7.50	30.00	—
1942 Proof	—	Value: 200				
1943	1,379,000	BV	2.50	10.00	40.00	—
1943 Proof	—	Value: 225				
1944	2,005,999	1.00	8.00	20.00	50.00	—
1944 Proof	—	Value: 300				
1945 Rare	320,000	—	—	—	—	—

Note: Issue melted, only one known

KM# 849 3 PENCE **Composition:** Nickel-Brass **Ruler:** George VI

Date	Mintage	F	VF	XF	Unc	BU
1937	45,708,000	0.25	0.40	1.00	6.50	—
1937 Proof	26,000	Value: 8.50				
1937 Matte Proof ; Rare	—	—	—	—	—	—

Note: There are reportedly 2-4 known of this variety, struck specifically for use in photography

Date	Mintage	F	VF	XF	Unc	BU
1938	14,532,000	0.40	0.80	3.50	17.50	—
1938 Proof	—	Value: 250				
1939	5,603,000	0.40	1.50	6.00	32.50	—
1939 Proof	—	Value: 250				
1940	12,636,000	0.25	0.50	2.50	12.00	—
1940 Proof	—	Value: 250				
1941	60,239,000	0.25	0.40	1.00	7.50	—
1941 Proof	—	Value: 250				
1942	103,214,000	0.25	0.40	1.00	6.50	—
1942 Proof	—	—	—	—	—	—
1943	101,702,000	0.25	0.40	1.00	6.50	—
1943 Proof	—	—	—	—	—	—
1944	69,760,000	0.25	0.40	1.00	7.00	—
1944 Proof	—	—	—	—	—	—
1945	33,942,000	0.25	0.50	1.50	10.00	—
1945 Proof	—	—	—	—	—	—
1946	621,000	2.50	8.00	45.00	250	—
1946 Proof	—	Value: 500				
1948	4,230,000	0.60	1.50	5.50	30.00	—
1948 Proof	—	—	—	—	—	—

KM# 850 3 PENCE **Weight:** 1.4138 g. **Composition:** 0.5000 Silver .0227 oz. ASW **Ruler:** George VI

Date	Mintage	F	VF	XF	Unc	BU
1937 Prooflike	1,351	—	—	—	20.00	—
1938 Prooflike	1,350	—	—	—	20.00	—
1939 Prooflike	1,234	—	—	—	20.00	—
1940 Prooflike	1,290	—	—	—	20.00	—
1941 Prooflike	1,253	—	—	—	20.00	—
1942 Prooflike	1,325	—	—	—	20.00	—
1943 Prooflike	1,335	—	—	—	20.00	—
1944 Prooflike	1,345	—	—	—	20.00	—
1945 Prooflike	1,355	—	—	—	20.00	—
1946 Prooflike	1,365	—	—	—	20.00	—

KM# 850a 3 PENCE **Weight:** 1.4138 g. **Composition:** 0.9250 Silver .0420 oz. ASW **Ruler:** George VI

Date	Mintage	F	VF	XF	Unc	BU
1947 Prooflike	1,375	—	—	—	20.00	—
1948 Prooflike	1,491	—	—	—	20.00	—

KM# 872 3 PENCE **Weight:** 1.4138 g. **Composition:** 0.9250 Silver .0420 oz. ASW **Ruler:** George VI **Obv. Legend:** Without IND IMP

Date	Mintage	F	VF	XF	Unc	BU
1949 Prooflike	1,395	—	—	—	20.00	—
1950 Prooflike	1,405	—	—	—	20.00	—
1951 Prooflike	1,468	—	—	—	20.00	—
1952 Prooflike	1,012	—	—	—	22.50	—

KM# 873 3 PENCE **Composition:** Nickel-Brass **Ruler:** George VI **Obv. Legend:** Without IND IMP

Date	Mintage	F	VF	XF	Unc	BU
1949	464,000	5.00	20.00	80.00	300	—
1949 Proof	—	Value: 600				
1950	1,600,000	1.00	3.00	15.00	50.00	—
1950 Proof	18,000	Value: 35.00				
1950 Matte Proof; Rare	—	—	—	—	—	—

Note: There are reportedly 2-4 known of this variety, struck specifically for use in photography

Date	Mintage	F	VF	XF	Unc	BU
1951	1,184,000	1.00	3.00	20.00	60.00	—
1951 Proof	20,000	Value: 40.00				
1951 Matte Proof; Rare	—	—	—	—	—	—

Note: There are reportedly 2-4 known of this variety, struck specifically for use in photography

Date	Mintage	F	VF	XF	Unc	BU
1952	25,494,000	0.25	0.50	2.00	12.00	—
1952 Proof	—	Value: 450				

KM# 886 3 PENCE **Composition:** Nickel-Brass **Ruler:** Elizabeth II

Date	Mintage	F	VF	XF	Unc	BU
1953	30,618,000	0.25	0.50	1.00	3.00	—
1953 Proof	40,000	Value: 7.50				
1953 Matte Proof; Rare	—	—	—	—	—	—

Note: There are reportedly 2-4 known of this variety, struck specifically for use in photography

KM# 887 3 PENCE **Weight:** 1.4138 g. **Composition:** 0.9250 Silver .0420 oz. ASW **Ruler:** Elizabeth II

Date	Mintage	F	VF	XF	Unc	BU
1953 Prooflike	1,078	—	—	—	85.00	—

KM# 900 3 PENCE **Composition:** Nickel-Brass **Ruler:** Elizabeth II **Obv. Legend:** Without BRITT OMN

Date	Mintage	F	VF	XF	Unc	BU
1954	41,720,000	—	0.25	0.50	6.00	—
1954 Proof	—	Value: 200				
1955	41,075,000	—	—	0.75	6.50	—
1955 Proof	—	Value: 200				
1956	36,902,000	—	—	1.00	7.00	—
1956 Proof	—	Value: 200				
1957	24,294,000	—	—	0.50	5.00	—
1957 Proof	—	Value: 200				
1958	20,504,000	—	0.25	0.50	8.00	—
1958 Proof	—	Value: 250				
1959	28,499,000	—	—	0.50	4.50	—
1959 Proof	—	Value: 200				
1960	83,078,000	—	—	0.40	4.50	—
1960 Proof	—	Value: 200				
1961	41,102,000	—	—	0.25	1.50	—
1961 Proof	—	Value: 200				
1962	47,242,000	—	—	0.25	1.00	—
1962 Proof	—	Value: 200				
1963	35,280,000	—	—	0.25	0.50	—
1963 Proof	—	Value: 200				
1964	47,440,000	—	—	0.25	0.50	—
1964 Proof	—	Value: 200				
1965	23,907,000	—	—	0.25	0.50	—
1965 Proof	—	Value: 250				
1966	55,320,000	—	—	0.25	0.50	—
1966 Proof	—	Value: 250				
1967	49,000,000	—	0.15	0.25	0.50	—
1967 Proof	—	—	—	—	—	—
1970 Proof	750,000	Value: 2.50				

KM# 901 3 PENCE **Weight:** 1.4138 g. **Composition:** 0.9250 Silver .0420 oz. ASW **Ruler:** Elizabeth II **Obv. Legend:** Without BRITT OMN

Date	Mintage	F	VF	XF	Unc	BU
1954 Prooflike	1,076	—	—	—	20.00	—
1955 Prooflike	1,082	—	—	—	20.00	—
1956 Prooflike	1,088	—	—	—	20.00	—
1957 Prooflike	1,094	—	—	—	20.00	—
1958 Prooflike	1,100	—	—	—	20.00	—
1959 Prooflike	1,172	—	—	—	20.00	—
1960 Prooflike	1,112	—	—	—	20.00	—
1961 Prooflike	1,118	—	—	—	20.00	—
1962 Prooflike	1,125	—	—	—	20.00	—
1963 Prooflike	1,205	—	—	—	20.00	—
1964 Prooflike	1,213	—	—	—	20.00	—
1965 Prooflike	1,221	—	—	—	20.00	—
1966 Prooflike	1,206	—	—	—	20.00	—
1967 Prooflike	986	—	—	—	20.00	—
1968 Prooflike	964	—	—	—	20.00	—
1969 Prooflike	1,088	—	—	—	20.00	—
1970 Prooflike	980	—	—	—	20.00	—
1971 Prooflike	1,018	—	—	—	20.00	—
1972 Prooflike	1,026	—	—	—	20.00	—
1973 Prooflike	1,098	—	—	—	20.00	—
1974 Prooflike	1,138	—	—	—	20.00	—
1975 Prooflike	1,148	—	—	—	20.00	—
1976 Prooflike	1,158	—	—	—	20.00	—
1977 Prooflike	1,138	—	—	—	22.00	—
1978 Prooflike	1,178	—	—	—	22.00	—
1979 Prooflike	1,294	—	—	—	22.00	—
1980 Prooflike	1,198	—	—	—	22.00	—
1981 Prooflike	1,178	—	—	—	22.00	—
1982 Prooflike	1,218	—	—	—	22.00	—
1983 Prooflike	1,342	—	—	—	22.00	—
1984 Prooflike	1,354	—	—	—	22.00	—
1985 Prooflike	1,366	—	—	—	22.00	—
1986 Prooflike	1,378	—	—	—	22.00	—
1987 Prooflike	1,390	—	—	—	22.00	—
1988 Prooflike	1,528	—	—	—	22.00	—
1989 Prooflike	1,353	—	—	—	22.00	—
1990 Prooflike	1,523	—	—	—	22.00	—
1991 Prooflike	1,384	—	—	—	22.00	—
1992 Prooflike	1,424	—	—	—	22.00	—
1993 Prooflike	1,440	—	—	—	22.00	—
1994 Prooflike	1,433	—	—	—	22.00	—
1995 Prooflike	1,466	—	—	—	22.00	—
1996 Prooflike	1,629	—	—	—	22.00	—
1997 Prooflike	1,786	—	—	—	22.00	—
1998 Prooflike	—	—	—	—	22.00	—
1999 Prooflike	—	—	—	—	22.00	—
2000 Prooflike	—	—	—	—	22.00	—

KM# 778 4 PENCE (Groat) **Weight:** 1.8851 g. **Composition:** 0.9250 Silver .0561 oz. ASW **Ruler:** Victoria

Date	Mintage	F	VF	XF	Unc	BU
1901 Prooflike	12,000	—	—	—	15.00	—

KM# 798 4 PENCE (Groat) **Weight:** 1.8851 g. **Composition:** 0.9250 Silver .0561 oz. ASW **Ruler:** Edward VII

Date	Mintage	F	VF	XF	Unc	BU
1902 Prooflike	10,000	—	—	—	15.00	—
1903 Prooflike	9,729	—	—	—	15.00	—
1904 Prooflike	12,000	—	—	—	15.00	—
1905 Prooflike	11,000	—	—	—	15.00	—
1906 Prooflike	11,000	—	—	—	15.00	—
1907 Prooflike	11,000	—	—	—	15.00	—
1908 Prooflike	9,929	—	—	—	15.00	—
1909 Prooflike	2,428	—	—	—	20.00	—
1910 Prooflike	2,755	—	—	—	22.50	—

KM# 814 4 PENCE (Groat) **Weight:** 1.8851 g. **Composition:** 0.9250 Silver .0561 oz. ASW **Ruler:** George V

Date	Mintage	F	VF	XF	Unc	BU
1911 Prooflike	1,768	—	—	—	17.50	—
1912 Prooflike	1,700	—	—	—	17.50	—
1913 Prooflike	1,798	—	—	—	17.50	—
1914 Prooflike	1,651	—	—	—	17.50	—
1915 Prooflike	1,441	—	—	—	17.50	—
1916 Prooflike	1,499	—	—	—	17.50	—
1917 Prooflike	1,478	—	—	—	17.50	—
1918 Prooflike	1,479	—	—	—	17.50	—
1919 Prooflike	1,524	—	—	—	17.50	—
1920 Prooflike	1,460	—	—	—	17.50	—

KM# 814a 4 PENCE (Groat) **Weight:** 1.8851 g. **Composition:** 0.5000 Silver .0303 oz. ASW **Ruler:** George V

Date	Mintage	F	VF	XF	Unc	BU
1921 Prooflike	1,542	—	—	—	17.50	—
1922 Prooflike	1,609	—	—	—	17.50	—
1923 Prooflike	1,635	—	—	—	17.50	—
1924 Prooflike	1,665	—	—	—	17.50	—
1925 Prooflike	1,786	—	—	—	17.50	—
1926 Prooflike	1,762	—	—	—	17.50	—
1927 Prooflike	1,681	—	—	—	17.50	—

KM# 841 4 PENCE (Groat) **Weight:** 1.8851 g. **Composition:** 0.5000 Silver .0303 oz. ASW **Ruler:** George V **Obverse:** Modified effigy

Date	Mintage	F	VF	XF	Unc	BU
1928 Prooflike	1,642	—	—	—	20.00	—
1929 Prooflike	1,969	—	—	—	20.00	—
1930 Prooflike	1,744	—	—	—	20.00	—
1931 Prooflike	1,915	—	—	—	20.00	—
1932 Prooflike	1,937	—	—	—	20.00	—
1933 Prooflike	1,931	—	—	—	20.00	—
1934 Prooflike	1,893	—	—	—	20.00	—
1935 Prooflike	1,995	—	—	—	20.00	—
1936 Prooflike	1,323	—	—	—	22.50	—

KM# 851 4 PENCE (Groat) **Weight:** 1.8851 g. **Composition:** 0.5000 Silver .0303 oz. ASW **Ruler:** George VI

Date	Mintage	F	VF	XF	Unc	BU
1937 Prooflike	1,325	—	—	—	20.00	—
1938 Prooflike	1,424	—	—	—	20.00	—
1939 Prooflike	1,332	—	—	—	20.00	—
1940 Prooflike	1,367	—	—	—	20.00	—
1941 Prooflike	1,345	—	—	—	20.00	—
1942 Prooflike	1,325	—	—	—	20.00	—
1943 Prooflike	1,335	—	—	—	20.00	—
1944 Prooflike	1,345	—	—	—	20.00	—
1945 Prooflike	1,355	—	—	—	20.00	—
1946 Prooflike	1,365	—	—	—	20.00	—

KM# 851a 4 PENCE (Groat) **Weight:** 1.8851 g. **Composition:** 0.9250 Silver .0561 oz. ASW **Ruler:** George VI

Date	Mintage	F	VF	XF	Unc	BU
1947 Prooflike	1,375	—	—	—	20.00	—
1948 Prooflike	1,385	—	—	—	20.00	—

KM# 874 4 PENCE (Groat) **Weight:** 1.8851 g. **Composition:** 0.9250 Silver .0561 oz. ASW **Ruler:** George VI **Obv. Legend:** Without IND IMP

Date	Mintage	F	VF	XF	Unc	BU
1949 Prooflike	1,503	—	—	—	20.00	—
1950 Prooflike	1,515	—	—	—	20.00	—
1951 Prooflike	1,580	—	—	—	20.00	—
1952 Prooflike	1,064	—	—	—	22.50	—

KM# 888 4 PENCE (Groat) **Weight:** 1.8851 g. **Composition:** 0.9250 Silver .0561 oz. ASW **Ruler:** Elizabeth II

Date	Mintage	F	VF	XF	Unc	BU
1953 Prooflike	1,078	—	—	—	85.00	—

KM# 902 4 PENCE (Groat) **Weight:** 1.8851 g. **Composition:** 0.9250 Silver .0561 oz. ASW **Ruler:** Elizabeth II **Obv. Legend:** Without BRITT OMN

Date	Mintage	F	VF	XF	Unc	BU
1954 Prooflike	1,076	—	—	—	20.00	—
1955 Prooflike	1,082	—	—	—	20.00	—
1956 Prooflike	1,088	—	—	—	20.00	—
1957 Prooflike	1,094	—	—	—	20.00	—
1958 Prooflike	1,100	—	—	—	20.00	—
1959 Prooflike	1,106	—	—	—	20.00	—
1960 Prooflike	1,180	—	—	—	20.00	—
1961 Prooflike	1,118	—	—	—	20.00	—
1962 Prooflike	1,197	—	—	—	20.00	—
1963 Prooflike	1,205	—	—	—	20.00	—
1964 Prooflike	1,213	—	—	—	20.00	—
1965 Prooflike	1,221	—	—	—	20.00	—
1966 Prooflike	1,206	—	—	—	20.00	—
1967 Prooflike	986	—	—	—	20.00	—
1968 Prooflike	964	—	—	—	20.00	—
1969 Prooflike	1,002	—	—	—	20.00	—
1970 Prooflike	1,068	—	—	—	20.00	—
1971 Prooflike	1,108	—	—	—	20.00	—
1972 Prooflike	1,118	—	—	—	20.00	—
1973 Prooflike	1,098	—	—	—	20.00	—
1974 Prooflike	1,138	—	—	—	20.00	—
1975 Prooflike	1,148	—	—	—	20.00	—
1976 Prooflike	1,158	—	—	—	20.00	—
1977 Prooflike	1,138	—	—	—	22.00	—
1978 Prooflike	1,178	—	—	—	22.00	—
1979 Prooflike	1,188	—	—	—	22.00	—
1980 Prooflike	1,306	—	—	—	22.00	—
1981 Prooflike	1,288	—	—	—	22.00	—
1982 Prooflike	1,330	—	—	—	22.00	—
1983 Prooflike	1,342	—	—	—	22.00	—
1984 Prooflike	1,354	—	—	—	22.00	—
1985 Prooflike	1,366	—	—	—	22.00	—
1986 Prooflike	1,378	—	—	—	22.00	—
1987 Prooflike	1,390	—	—	—	22.00	—
1988 Prooflike	1,402	—	—	—	22.00	—
1989 Prooflike	1,353	—	—	—	22.00	—
1990 Prooflike	1,523	—	—	—	22.00	—
1991 Prooflike	1,514	—	—	—	22.00	—
1992 Prooflike	1,556	—	—	—	22.00	—
1993 Prooflike	1,440	—	—	—	22.00	—
1994 Prooflike	1,433	—	—	—	22.00	—
1995 Prooflike	1,466	—	—	—	22.00	—
1996 Prooflike	1,629	—	—	—	22.00	—
1997 Prooflike	1,786	—	—	—	22.00	—
1998 Prooflike	—	—	—	—	22.00	—
1999 Prooflike	—	—	—	—	22.00	—
2000 Prooflike	—	—	—	—	22.00	—

KM# 779 6 PENCE **Weight:** 3.0100 g. **Composition:** 0.9250 Silver .0895 oz. ASW **Ruler:** Victoria

Date	Mintage	F	VF	XF	Unc	BU
1901	5,109,000	2.50	5.50	14.00	35.00	—

KM# 799 6 PENCE **Weight:** 3.0100 g. **Composition:** 0.9250 Silver .0895 oz. ASW **Ruler:** Edward VII

Date	Mintage	F	VF	XF	Unc	BU
1902	6,356,000	3.50	7.50	25.00	50.00	—
1902 Matte Proof	15,000	Value: 50.00				
1903	5,411,000	3.50	10.00	30.00	75.00	—
1904	4,487,000	5.00	15.00	45.00	130	—
1905	4,236,000	4.00	12.00	35.00	90.00	—
1906	7,641,000	2.50	7.50	25.00	55.00	—
1907	8,734,000	3.50	7.50	30.00	80.00	—
1908	6,739,000	4.00	12.00	40.00	100	—
1909	6,584,000	3.50	10.00	35.00	90.00	—
1910	12,491,000	2.50	5.50	20.00	45.00	—

KM# 815 6 PENCE **Weight:** 3.0100 g. **Composition:** 0.9250 Silver .0895 oz. ASW **Ruler:** George V

Date	Mintage	F	VF	XF	Unc	BU
1911	9,165,000	1.50	4.50	12.00	30.00	—
1911 Proof	6,007	Value: 50.00				
1912	10,984,000	2.50	6.00	20.00	50.00	—
1913	7,500,000	3.00	7.50	30.00	65.00	—
1914	22,715,000	1.50	4.50	12.00	35.00	—
1915	15,695,000	1.50	4.50	12.00	35.00	—
1916	22,207,000	1.50	4.50	12.00	35.00	—
1917	7,725,000	2.50	6.50	25.00	60.00	—
1918	27,559,000	1.50	4.50	12.00	35.00	—
1919	13,375,000	2.00	5.50	18.00	42.50	—
1920	14,136,000	2.00	5.50	18.00	45.00	—

KM# 815a.1 6 PENCE **Weight:** 2.8276 g. **Composition:** 0.5000 Silver .0455 oz. ASW **Ruler:** George V **Note:** Narrow rim.

Date	Mintage	F	VF	XF	Unc	BU
1920	Inc. above	1.00	2.50	10.00	32.00	—
1921	30,340,000	1.00	2.50	10.00	32.00	—
1922	16,879,000	1.00	3.50	12.00	38.00	—
1923	6,383,000	2.00	5.00	18.00	50.00	—
1924	17,444,000	1.00	2.50	10.00	30.00	—
1925	12,721,000	1.50	3.50	12.00	35.00	—

KM# 815a.2 6 PENCE **Weight:** 2.8276 g. **Composition:** 0.5000 Silver .0455 oz. ASW **Ruler:** George V **Note:** Wide rim.

Date	Mintage	F	VF	XF	Unc	BU
1925	Inc. above	1.00	2.50	10.00	35.00	—
1926	21,810,000	1.50	3.50	12.00	35.00	—

KM# 828 6 PENCE **Weight:** 2.8276 g. **Composition:** 0.5000 Silver .0455 oz. ASW **Ruler:** George V **Obverse:** Modified effigy, slightly smaller bust

Date	Mintage	F	VF	XF	Unc	BU
1926	Inc. above	BV	1.50	6.50	22.50	—
1927	8,925,000	1.50	2.50	10.00	25.00	—
1927 Proof	—	Value: 800				

KM# 832 6 PENCE **Weight:** 2.8276 g. **Composition:** 0.5000 Silver .0455 oz. ASW **Ruler:** George V **Reverse:** Oak sprigs with acorns **Note:** Varieties in edge milling exist.

Date	Mintage	F	VF	XF	Unc	BU
1927 Proof	15,000	Value: 35.00				
1927 Matte Proof; Rare	—	—	—	—	—	—

Note: There are reportedly 3-4 known of this variety, struck specifically for use in photographs

Date	Mintage	F	VF	XF	Unc	BU
1928	23,123,000	BV	1.50	4.00	20.00	—
1928 Proof	—	Value: 325				
1929	28,319,000	BV	1.50	4.00	22.00	—
1929 Proof	—	Value: 350				
1930	16,990,000	BV	1.50	4.00	18.00	—
1930 Proof	—	Value: 325				
1931	16,873,000	1.50	2.50	8.00	25.00	—
1931 Proof	—	Value: 325				
1932	9,406,000	1.50	4.00	15.00	35.00	—
1932 Proof	—	Value: 350				
1933	22,185,000	1.50	2.50	7.00	20.00	—
1933 Proof	—	Value: 325				
1934	9,304,000	1.50	2.50	9.00	30.00	—
1934 Proof	—	Value: 325				
1935	13,996,000	BV	1.50	3.50	18.00	—
1935 Proof	—	Value: 325				
1936	24,380,000	BV	1.50	2.50	15.00	—
1936 Proof	—	Value: 325				

KM# 852 6 PENCE **Weight:** 2.8276 g. **Composition:** 0.5000 Silver .0455 oz. ASW **Ruler:** George VI

Date	Mintage	F	VF	XF	Unc	BU
1937	22,303,000	—	BV	1.00	6.00	—
1937 Proof	26,000	Value: 9.00				
1937 Matte Proof; Rare	—	—	—	—	—	—

Note: There are reportedly 3-4 known of this variety, struck specifically for use in photographs

Date	Mintage	F	VF	XF	Unc	BU
1938	13,403,000	BV	1.50	3.50	20.00	—
1938 Proof	—	Value: 250				
1939	28,670,000	—	BV	1.00	10.00	—
1939 Proof	—	Value: 235				
1940	20,875,000	—	BV	1.00	10.00	—
1940 Proof	—	Value: 250				
1941	23,087,000	—	BV	1.00	10.00	—
1941 Proof	—	Value: 235				
1942	44,943,000	—	BV	1.00	7.00	—
1942 Proof	—	Value: 235				
1943	46,927,000	—	BV	1.00	7.00	—
1943 Proof	—	Value: 235				
1944	36,953,000	—	BV	1.00	6.00	—
1944 Proof	—	Value: 250				
1945	39,939,000	—	BV	1.00	6.00	—
1945 Proof	—	Value: 250				
1946	43,466,000	—	BV	1.00	6.00	—
1946 Proof	—	Value: 250				

KM# 862 6 PENCE **Composition:** Copper-Nickel **Ruler:** George VI

Date	Mintage	F	VF	XF	Unc	BU
1947	29,993,000	—	0.20	0.50	6.00	—
1947 Proof	—	Value: 250				
1948	88,324,000	—	0.20	0.50	5.00	—
1948 Proof	—	Value: 275				

KM# 875 6 PENCE **Composition:** Copper-Nickel **Ruler:** George VI **Rev. Legend:** Without IND IMP

Date	Mintage	F	VF	XF	Unc	BU
1949	41,336,000	—	0.20	0.50	7.00	—
1949 Proof	—	Value: 275				
1950	32,741,999	—	0.20	0.50	7.00	—
1950 Proof	18,000	Value: 10.00				
1950 Matte Proof; Rare	—	—	—	—	—	—

Note: There are reportedly 3-4 known of this variety, struck specifically for use in photographs

Date	Mintage	F	VF	XF	Unc	BU
1951	40,399,000	—	0.20	0.50	12.00	—
1951 Proof	20,000	Value: 11.00				
1951 Matte Proof; Rare	—	—	—	—	—	—

Note: There are reportedly 3-4 known of this variety, struck specifically for use in photographs

Date	Mintage	F	VF	XF	Unc	BU
1952	1,012,999	1.25	2.50	16.00	50.00	—
1952 Proof	—	Value: 800				

KM# 889 6 PENCE **Composition:** Copper-Nickel **Ruler:** Elizabeth II

Date	Mintage	F	VF	XF	Unc	BU
1953	70,324,000	—	0.15	0.50	3.00	—
1953 Proof	40,000	Value: 4.50				
1953 Matte Proof; Rare	—	—	—	—	—	—

Note: There are reportedly 3-4 known of this variety, struck specifically for use in photographs

KM# 903 6 PENCE **Composition:** Copper-Nickel **Ruler:** Elizabeth II **Obv. Legend:** Without BRITT OMN

Date	Mintage	F	VF	XF	Unc	BU
1954	105,241,000	—	0.15	0.50	6.00	—
1954 Proof	—	Value: 200				
1955	109,930,000	—	0.15	0.35	4.00	—
1955 Proof	—	Value: 200				
1956	109,842,000	—	0.15	0.35	4.00	—
1956 Proof	—	Value: 200				
1957	105,654,000	—	0.15	0.35	3.50	—
1957 Proof	—	Value: 200				
1958	123,519,000	—	0.15	0.35	3.00	—
1958 Proof	—	Value: 200				
1959	93,089,000	—	0.15	0.35	1.50	—
1959 Proof	—	Value: 200				
1960	103,283,000	—	0.15	0.35	3.00	—
1960 Proof	—	Value: 200				
1961	115,052,000	—	0.15	0.35	2.00	—
1961 Proof	—	Value: 200				
1962	166,484,000	—	0.15	0.35	1.00	—
1962 Proof	—	Value: 200				
1963	120,056,000	—	0.15	0.30	0.75	—
1963 Proof	—	Value: 200				
1964	152,336,000	—	0.15	0.25	0.75	—
1964 Proof	—	Value: 200				
1965	129,644,000	—	0.10	0.20	0.50	—
1965 Proof	—	Value: 250				
1966	175,676,000	—	0.10	0.20	0.50	—
1966 Proof	—	Value: 250				
1967 Proof	—	Value: 250				
1967	240,788,000	—	0.10	0.20	0.50	—
1970 Proof	750,000	Value: 2.00				

KM# 780 SHILLING **Weight:** 5.6552 g. **Composition:** 0.9250 Silver .1682 oz. ASW **Ruler:** Victoria

Date	Mintage	F	VF	XF	Unc	BU
1901	3,426,000	3.00	6.50	20.00	50.00	—

KM# 800 SHILLING **Weight:** 5.6552 g. **Composition:** 0.9250 Silver .1682 oz. ASW **Ruler:** Edward VII

Date	Mintage	F	VF	XF	Unc	BU
1902	7,890,000	4.00	12.50	32.50	80.00	—
1902 Matte Proof	15,000	Value: 60.00				
1903	2,061,999	6.00	20.00	85.00	250	—
1904	2,040,000	5.00	15.00	70.00	230	—
1905	488,000	40.00	100	400	1,250	—
1906	10,791,000	4.50	12.00	40.00	100	—
1907	14,083,000	4.50	12.00	45.00	135	—
1908	3,807,000	8.00	22.00	90.00	300	—
1909	5,665,000	8.00	22.00	90.00	300	—
1910	26,547,000	3.00	10.00	35.00	90.00	—

KM# 816 SHILLING **Weight:** 5.6552 g. **Composition:** 0.9250 Silver .1682 oz. ASW **Ruler:** George V

Date	Mintage	F	VF	XF	Unc	BU
1911	20,066,000	2.00	4.50	17.50	50.00	—
1911 Proof	6,007	Value: 70.00				
1912	15,594,000	3.00	6.00	22.50	70.00	—
1913	9,002,000	4.00	8.00	32.50	85.00	—
1914	23,416,000	2.50	4.00	20.00	45.00	—
1915	39,279,000	2.00	3.50	18.00	45.00	—
1916	35,862,000	2.00	3.50	15.00	40.00	—
1917	22,203,000	2.00	4.00	20.00	50.00	—
1918	34,916,000	2.00	3.50	15.00	40.00	—
1919	10,824,000	3.00	6.00	22.50	65.00	—

KM# 816a SHILLING **Weight:** 5.6552 g. **Composition:** 0.5000 Silver .0909 oz. ASW **Ruler:** George V

Date	Mintage	F	VF	XF	Unc	BU
1920	22,825,000	2.00	4.00	20.00	50.00	—
1921	22,649,000	2.50	6.00	27.50	70.00	—
1922	27,216,000	2.00	4.00	20.00	60.00	—
1923	14,575,000	2.00	3.50	18.00	50.00	—
1924	9,250,000	2.00	5.00	30.00	70.00	—
1925	5,419,000	4.00	8.00	45.00	90.00	—
1926	22,516,000	2.00	5.00	22.00	50.00	—

KM# 829 SHILLING **Weight:** 5.6552 g. **Composition:** 0.5000 Silver .0909 oz. ASW **Ruler:** George V **Obverse:** Modified effigy, slightly smaller bust

Date	Mintage	F	VF	XF	Unc	BU
1926	Inc. above	1.50	3.50	15.00	45.00	—
1927	9,262,000	1.50	4.00	18.00	45.00	—

KM# 833 SHILLING **Weight:** 5.6552 g. **Composition:** 0.5000 Silver .0909 oz. ASW **Ruler:** George V

Date	Mintage	F	VF	XF	Unc	BU
1927	Inc. above	1.50	3.00	15.00	40.00	—
1927 Proof	15,000	Value: 45.00				
1927 Matte Proof; Rare	—	—	—	—	—	—

Note: There are reportedly 1-2 of this variety, struck specifically for use in photographs

Date	Mintage	F	VF	XF	Unc	BU
1928	18,137,000	BV	2.00	12.00	25.00	—
1928 Proof	—	Value: 425				
1929	19,343,000	BV	2.00	10.00	24.00	—
1929 Proof	—	Value: 500				
1930	3,137,000	2.50	6.00	25.00	60.00	—
1930 Proof	—	Value: 500				
1931	6,994,000	2.00	3.50	12.00	25.00	—
1931 Proof	—	Value: 425				
1932	12,168,000	2.00	3.50	12.00	25.00	—
1932 Proof	—	Value: 425				
1933	11,512,000	1.50	3.00	9.00	25.00	—
1933 Proof	—	Value: 425				
1934	6,138,000	2.00	6.00	20.00	45.00	—
1934 Proof	—	Value: 450				
1935	9,183,000	1.50	3.00	9.00	25.00	—
1935 Proof	—	Value: 425				
1936	11,911,000	1.50	2.50	8.00	25.00	—
1936 Proof	—	Value: 425				

KM# 853 SHILLING **Weight:** 5.6552 g. **Composition:** 0.5000 Silver .0909 oz. ASW **Ruler:** George VI **Reverse:** English crest

Date	Mintage	F	VF	XF	Unc	BU
1937	8,359,000	BV	1.00	3.00	8.00	—
1937 Proof	26,000	Value: 15.00				
1937 Matte Proof; Rare	—	—	—	—	—	—

Note: There are reportedly 1-2 known of this variety, struck specifically for use in photographs

Date	Mintage	F	VF	XF	Unc	BU
1938	4,833,000	BV	1.00	5.00	30.00	—
1938 Proof	—	Value: 450				
1939	11,053,000	BV	1.00	3.00	17.50	—
1939 Proof	—	Value: 400				
1940	11,099,000	—	BV	2.50	12.00	—
1940 Proof	—	Value: 400				
1941	11,392,000	—	BV	2.00	12.00	—
1941 Proof	—	Value: 400				
1942	17,454,000	—	BV	2.00	8.50	—
1942 Proof	—	Value: 400				
1943	11,404,000	—	BV	2.00	8.50	—
1943 Proof	—	Value: 350				
1944	11,587,000	—	BV	2.00	8.50	—
1944 Proof	—	Value: 350				
1945	15,143,000	—	BV	2.00	8.50	—
1945 Proof	—	Value: 400				
1946	18,664,000	—	BV	1.50	8.00	—
1946 Proof	—	Value: 400				

KM# 854 SHILLING **Weight:** 5.6552 g. **Composition:** 0.5000 Silver .0909 oz. ASW **Ruler:** George VI **Reverse:** Scottish crest

Date	Mintage	F	VF	XF	Unc	BU
1937	6,749,000	—	BV	2.50	8.00	—
1937 Proof	26,000	Value: 15.00				
1937 Matte Proof; Rare	—	—	—	—	—	—

Note: There are reportedly 1-2 known of this variety, struck specifically for use in photographs

Date	Mintage	F	VF	XF	Unc	BU
1938	4,798,000	—	BV	4.00	30.00	—
1938 Proof	—	Value: 400				
1939	10,264,000	—	BV	3.00	17.00	—
1939 Proof	—	Value: 400				
1940	9,913,000	—	BV	2.50	12.50	—
1940 Proof	—	Value: 400				
1941	8,086,000	—	BV	2.00	12.00	—
1941 Proof	—	Value: 400				
1942	13,677,000	—	BV	2.00	9.00	—
1942 Proof	—	Value: 375				
1943 Proof	—	Value: 350				
1943	9,824,000	—	BV	2.00	9.00	—
1944	10,990,000	—	BV	2.00	8.00	—
1944 Proof	—	Value: 350				
1945	15,106,000	—	BV	2.00	8.00	—
1945 Proof	—	Value: 400				
1946	16,382,000	—	BV	2.00	8.00	—
1946 Proof	—	—	—	—	—	—

KM# 863 SHILLING **Composition:** Copper-Nickel **Ruler:** George VI **Reverse:** English crest

Date	Mintage	F	VF	XF	Unc	BU
1947	12,121,000	0.10	0.25	1.00	7.00	—
1947 Proof	—	Value: 325				
1948	45,577,000	0.10	0.20	1.00	6.00	—
1948 Proof	—	Value: 350				

KM# 864 SHILLING **Composition:** Copper-Nickel **Ruler:** George VI **Reverse:** Scottish crest

Date	Mintage	F	VF	XF	Unc	BU
1947	12,283,000	0.10	0.25	1.00	7.00	—
1947 Proof	—	Value: 325				
1948	45,352,000	0.10	0.20	1.00	6.00	—
1948 Proof	—	Value: 350				

KM# 876 SHILLING **Composition:** Copper-Nickel **Ruler:** George VI **Reverse:** English crest **Rev. Legend:** Without IND IMP

Date	Mintage	F	VF	XF	Unc	BU
1949	19,328,000	0.10	0.25	1.50	10.00	—
1949 Proof	—	Value: 400				
1950	19,244,000	0.10	0.25	1.50	12.50	—
1950 Proof	18,000	Value: 15.00				
1950 Matte Proof; Rare	—	—	—	—	—	—

Note: There are reportedly 1-2 known of this variety, struck specifically for use in photographs

Date	Mintage	F	VF	XF	Unc	BU
1951	9,957,000	0.10	0.25	3.50	15.00	—
1951 Proof	20,000	Value: 18.00				
1951 Matte Proof; Rare	—	—	—	—	—	—

Note: There are reportedly 1-2 known of this variety, struck specifically for use in photographs

Date	Mintage	F	VF	XF	Unc	BU
1952 Matte Proof; Rare	—	—	—	—	—	—

Note: There are reportedly 1-2 known of this variety, struck specifically for use in photographs

KM# 877 SHILLING Composition: Copper-Nickel **Ruler:** George VI **Reverse:** Scottish crest

Date	Mintage	F	VF	XF	Unc	BU
1949	21,243,000	0.10	0.25	1.50	11.50	—
1949 Proof	—	Value: 400				
1950	14,300,000	0.10	0.25	1.50	12.50	—
1950 Proof	18,000	Value: 15.00				
1950 Matte Proof; Rare	—	—	—	—	—	—

Note: There are reportedly 1-2 known of this variety, struck specifically for use in photographs

Date	Mintage	F	VF	XF	Unc	BU
1951	10,961,000	0.10	0.25	1.50	15.00	—
1951 Proof	20,000	Value: 18.00				
1951 Matte Proof; Rare	—	—	—	—	—	—

Note: There are reportedly 1-2 known of this variety, struck specifically for use in photographs

KM# 890 SHILLING Composition: Copper-Nickel **Ruler:** Elizabeth II **Reverse:** English arms

Date	Mintage	F	VF	XF	Unc	BU
1953	41,943,000	—	0.15	0.50	5.00	—
1953 Proof	40,000	Value: 8.00				
1953 Matte Proof; Rare	—	—	—	—	—	—

Note: There are reportedly 1-2 known of this variety, struck specifically for use in photographs

KM# 891 SHILLING Composition: Copper-Nickel **Ruler:** Elizabeth II **Reverse:** Scottish arms

Date	Mintage	F	VF	XF	Unc	BU
1953	20,664,000	—	0.15	0.50	6.00	—
1953 Proof	40,000	Value: 8.00				
1953 Matte Proof; Rare	—	—	—	—	—	—

Note: There are reportedly 1-2 known of this variety, struck specifically for use in photographs

KM# 904 SHILLING Composition: Copper-Nickel **Ruler:** Elizabeth II **Obv. Legend:** Without BRITT OMN **Reverse:** English arms

Date	Mintage	F	VF	XF	Unc	BU
1954	30,162,000	—	0.15	0.50	4.00	—
1954 Proof	—	Value: 300				
1955	45,260,000	—	0.15	0.50	4.00	—
1955 Proof	—	Value: 300				
1956	44,970,000	—	0.15	0.50	10.00	—
1956 Proof	—	Value: 300				
1957	42,774,000	—	0.15	0.50	3.50	—
1957 Proof	—	Value: 300				
1958	14,392,000	0.25	0.50	3.50	22.50	—
1958 Proof	—	Value: 325				
1959	19,443,000	—	0.15	0.40	4.00	—
1959 Proof	—	Value: 300				
1960	27,028,000	—	0.15	0.35	4.00	—
1960 Proof	—	Value: 300				
1961	39,817,000	—	0.15	0.35	2.50	—
1961 Proof	—	Value: 275				
1962	36,704,000	—	0.15	0.25	1.75	—
1962 Proof	—	Value: 275				
1963	49,434,000	—	—	0.25	0.75	—
1963 Proof	—	Value: 275				
1964	8,591,000	—	—	0.25	0.75	—
1964 Proof	—	Value: 300				
1965	9,216,000	—	—	0.25	0.75	—
1965 Proof	—	Value: 300				
1966	15,002,000	—	—	0.25	0.75	—
1966 Proof	—	Value: 300				
1970 Proof	750,000	Value: 4.00				

KM# 905 SHILLING Composition: Copper-Nickel **Ruler:** Elizabeth II **Reverse:** Scottish arms

Date		F	VF	XF	Unc	BU
1954		—	0.15	0.25	4.25	—
1954 Proof	—	Value: 300				
1954 Matte Proof; Rare		—	—	—	—	—
1955		—	0.15	0.35	5.50	—
1955 Proof	—	Value: 300				
1956		—	0.15	1.00	12.00	—
1956 Proof	—	Value: 300				
1957		—	0.25	4.50	25.00	—
1957 Proof	—	Value: 325				
1958		—	0.15	0.50	3.25	—
1958 Proof	—	Value: 300				
1959		1.00	2.00	5.00	25.00	—
1959 Proof	—	Value: 325				
1960		—	0.15	0.50	3.25	—
1960 Proof	—	Value: 300				
1961		0.25	0.20	1.25	8.00	—
1961 Proof	—	Value: 300				
1962		—	0.15	0.25	4.50	—
1962 Proof	—	Value: 275				
1963		—	0.15	0.25	0.75	—
1963 Proof	—	Value: 275				
1964		—	0.15	0.25	2.00	—
1964 Proof	—	Value: 300				
1965		—	0.15	0.25	2.50	—
1965 Proof	—	Value: 325				
1966		—	0.15	0.25	0.85	—
1966 Proof	—	Value: 325				
1970 Proof	750,000	Value: 4.00				

KM# 781 FLORIN (Two Shillings) Weight: 11.3104 g. **Composition:** 0.9250 Silver .3364 oz. ASW **Ruler:** Victoria

Date	Mintage	F	VF	XF	Unc	BU
1901	2,649,000	6.00	12.50	30.00	70.00	—

KM# 801 FLORIN (Two Shillings) Weight: 11.3104 g. **Composition:** 0.9250 Silver .3364 oz. ASW **Ruler:** Edward VII

Date	Mintage	F	VF	XF	Unc	BU
1902	2,190,000	7.50	20.00	45.00	100	—
1902 Matte Proof	15,000	Value: 100				
1903	995,000	10.00	30.00	85.00	275	—
1904	2,770,000	10.00	40.00	90.00	300	—
1905	1,188,000	40.00	90.00	300	1,000	—
1906	6,910,000	9.00	22.50	70.00	300	—
1907	5,948,000	9.00	22.50	80.00	350	—
1908	3,280,000	12.50	35.00	175	475	—
1909	3,483,000	12.50	35.00	150	375	—
1910	5,651,000	9.00	20.00	55.00	165	—

KM# 817 FLORIN (Two Shillings) Weight: 11.3104 g. **Composition:** 0.9250 Silver .3364 oz. ASW **Ruler:** George V

Date	Mintage	F	VF	XF	Unc	BU
1911	5,951,000	5.00	10.00	30.00	90.00	—
1911 Proof	6,007	Value: 110				
1912	8,572,000	5.00	12.00	40.00	100	—
1913	4,545,000	6.50	15.00	55.00	140	—
1914	21,253,000	3.00	6.00	25.00	60.00	—
1915	12,358,000	4.00	8.00	30.00	85.00	—
1916	21,064,000	3.00	6.00	20.00	70.00	—
1917	11,182,000	4.00	7.00	25.00	75.00	—
1918	29,212,000	3.00	6.00	20.00	65.00	—
1919	9,469,000	5.00	12.00	30.00	85.00	—

KM# 817a FLORIN (Two Shillings) Weight: 11.3104 g. **Composition:** 0.5000 Silver .1818 oz. ASW **Ruler:** George V

Date	Mintage	F	VF	XF	Unc	BU
1920	15,388,000	2.50	6.00	25.00	70.00	—
1921	34,864,000	2.50	5.50	22.50	55.00	—
1922	23,861,000	2.50	4.50	20.00	55.00	—
1923	21,547,000	2.00	3.50	18.00	45.00	—
1924	4,582,000	3.50	7.00	30.00	85.00	—
1925	1,404,000	18.00	35.00	120	250	—
1926	5,125,000	3.50	8.50	40.00	100	—

KM# 834 FLORIN (Two Shillings) Weight: 11.3104 g. **Composition:** 0.5000 Silver .1818 oz. ASW **Ruler:** George V

Date	Mintage	F	VF	XF	Unc	BU
1927 Proof	15,000	Value: 75.00				
1928	11,088,000	1.50	3.00	8.00	25.00	—
1928 Proof	—	Value: 500				
1929	16,397,000	1.50	3.00	8.00	25.00	—
1929 Proof	—	Value: 600				
1930	5,734,000	2.00	5.00	15.00	37.50	—
1930 Proof	—	Value: 500				
1931	6,556,000	2.00	5.00	12.00	35.00	—
1931 Proof	—	Value: 500				
1932	717,000	20.00	40.00	120	280	—
1932 Proof	—	Value: 1,200				
1933	8,685,000	1.50	2.50	10.00	30.00	—
1933 Proof	—	Value: 500				
1935	7,541,000	1.50	2.50	8.00	22.50	—
1935 Proof	—	Value: 500				
1936	9,897,000	1.50	2.50	8.00	22.50	—
1936 Proof	—	Value: 500				

KM# 855 FLORIN (Two Shillings) Weight: 11.3104 g. **Composition:** 0.5000 Silver .1818 oz. ASW **Ruler:** George VI

Date	Mintage	F	VF	XF	Unc	BU
1937	13,007,000	—	BV	3.00	8.00	—
1937 Proof	26,000	Value: 18.00				
1937 Matte Proof; Rare	—	—	—	—	—	—

Note: There are reportedly 1-2 known of this variety, struck specifically for use in photographs

Date	Mintage	F	VF	XF	Unc	BU
1938	7,909,000	BV	2.50	7.50	30.00	—
1938 Proof	—	Value: 450				
1939	20,851,000	—	BV	3.50	12.00	—
1939 Proof	—	Value: 400				
1940	18,700,000	—	BV	3.00	12.00	—
1940 Proof	—	Value: 400				
1941	24,451,000	—	BV	3.00	12.00	—
1941 Proof	—	Value: 400				
1942	39,895,000	—	BV	3.00	10.00	—
1942 Proof	—	Value: 400				
1943	26,712,000	—	BV	3.00	10.00	—

Date	Mintage	F	VF	XF	Unc	BU
1943 Proof	—	Value: 400				
1944	27,560,000	—	BV	3.00	10.00	—
1944 Proof	—	Value: 400				
1945	25,858,000	—	BV	3.00	10.00	—
1945 Proof	—	Value: 600				
1946	22,300,000	—	BV	3.00	10.00	—
1946 Proof	—	Value: 600				

KM# 865 FLORIN (Two Shillings) Composition: Copper-Nickel **Ruler:** George VI

Date	Mintage	F	VF	XF	Unc	BU
1947	22,910,000	0.20	0.35	1.00	7.00	—
1947 Proof	—	Value: 325				
1948	67,554,000	0.20	0.35	1.00	6.50	—
1948 Proof	—	Value: 325				

KM# 878 FLORIN (Two Shillings) Composition: Copper-Nickel **Ruler:** George VI **Rev. Legend:** Without IND IMP

Date	Mintage	F	VF	XF	Unc	BU
1949	28,615,000	0.20	0.35	1.00	8.00	—
1949 Proof	—	Value: 325				
1950	24,357,000	0.20	0.35	1.00	12.00	—
1950 Proof	18,000	Value: 15.00				
1950 Matte Proof; Rare	—	—	—	—	—	—

Note: There are reportedly 1-2 known of this variety, struck specifically for use in photographs

Date	Mintage	F	VF	XF	Unc	BU
1951	27,412,000	0.20	0.35	1.00	14.00	—
1951 Proof	20,000	Value: 20.00				
1951 Matte Proof; Rare	—	—	—	—	—	—

Note: There are reportedly 1-2 known of this variety, struck specifically for use in photographs

KM# 892 FLORIN (Two Shillings) Composition: Copper-Nickel **Ruler:** Elizabeth II

Date	Mintage	F	VF	XF	Unc	BU
1953	11,959,000	0.25	0.50	1.00	7.00	—
1953 Proof	40,000	Value: 10.00				
1953 Matte Proof; Rare	—	—	—	—	—	—

Note: There are reportedly 1-2 known of this variety, struck specifically for use in photographs

KM# 906 FLORIN (Two Shillings) Composition: Copper-Nickel **Ruler:** Elizabeth II **Obverse:** Without BRITT OMN

Date	Mintage	F	VF	XF	Unc	BU
1954	13,085,000	0.20	0.50	6.00	45.00	—
1954 Proof	—	Value: 325				
1955	25,887,000	0.20	0.50	2.00	6.00	—
1955 Proof	—	Value: 300				
1956	47,824,000	0.20	0.30	1.00	6.00	—
1956 Proof	—	Value: 300				
1957	33,070,999	0.20	0.40	5.00	45.00	—
1957 Proof	—	Value: 300				
1958	9,565,000	0.25	1.50	6.00	25.00	—
1958 Proof	—	Value: 350				
1959	14,080,000	0.25	0.50	5.00	40.00	—
1959 Proof	—	Value: 300				
1960	13,832,000	—	0.20	1.50	6.00	—
1960 Proof	—	Value: 300				
1961	37,735,000	—	0.20	1.00	5.00	—
1961 Proof	—	Value: 300				
1962	35,148,000	—	0.20	0.75	3.50	—
1962 Proof	—	Value: 300				
1963	26,471,000	—	0.20	0.75	3.00	—
1963 Proof	—	Value: 300				
1964	16,539,000	—	0.20	0.50	3.00	—
1965	48,163,000	—	0.20	0.50	2.50	—
1966	83,999,000	—	0.20	0.30	2.50	—
1967	39,718,000	—	0.20	0.30	2.00	—
1970 Proof	750,000	Value: 4.00				

KM# 782 1/2 CROWN Weight: 14.1380 g. **Composition:** 0.9250 Silver .4205 oz. ASW **Ruler:** Victoria

Date	Mintage	F	VF	XF	Unc	BU
1901	1,577,000	7.50	13.50	35.00	85.00	—

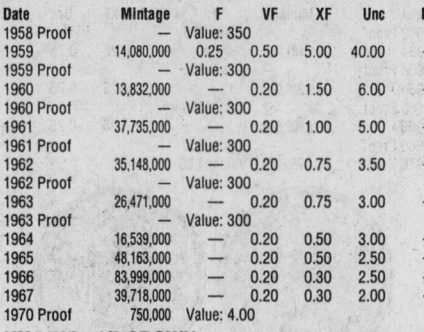

KM# 802 1/2 CROWN Weight: 14.1380 g. **Composition:** 0.9250 Silver .4205 oz. ASW **Ruler:** Edward VII

Date	Mintage	F	VF	XF	Unc	BU
1902	1,316,000	15.00	30.00	60.00	125	—
1902 Matte Proof	15,000	Value: 125				
1903	275,000	55.00	200	800	2,000	—
1904	710,000	35.00	125	450	1,250	—
1905	166,000	125	400	1,200	2,500	—
1906	2,886,000	20.00	40.00	145	350	—
1907	3,694,000	20.00	40.00	145	400	—
1908	1,759,000	25.00	50.00	200	600	—
1909	3,052,000	20.00	40.00	145	400	—
1910	2,558,000	12.00	25.00	85.00	275	—

KM# 818.1 1/2 CROWN Weight: 14.1380 g. **Composition:** 0.9250 Silver .4205 oz. ASW **Ruler:** George V

Date	Mintage	F	VF	XF	Unc	BU
1911	2,915,000	5.00	12.00	40.00	125	—
1911 Proof	6,007	Value: 125				
1912	4,701,000	5.00	15.00	50.00	150	—
1913	4,090,000	6.00	18.00	55.00	150	—
1914	18,333,000	4.00	7.00	20.00	65.00	—
1915	32,433,000	4.00	7.00	20.00	60.00	—
1916	29,530,000	4.00	7.00	20.00	60.00	—
1917	11,172,000	5.00	12.00	35.00	85.00	—
1918	29,080,000	4.00	7.00	20.00	60.00	—
1919	10,267,000	5.00	12.00	35.00	85.00	—

KM# 818.1a 1/2 CROWN Weight: 14.1380 g. **Composition:** 0.5000 Silver .2273 oz. ASW **Ruler:** George V **Reverse:** Crown touches shield

Date	Mintage	F	VF	XF	Unc	BU
1920	17,983,000	3.50	6.00	25.00	75.00	—
1921	23,678,000	3.50	10.00	30.00	85.00	—
1922	16,396,999	3.50	7.00	35.00	95.00	—

KM# 818.2 1/2 CROWN Weight: 14.1380 g. **Composition:** 0.5000 Silver .2273 oz. ASW **Ruler:** George V **Reverse:** Groove between crown and shield

Date	Mintage	F	VF	XF	Unc	BU
1922	Inc. above	3.50	6.00	25.00	95.00	—
1923	26,309,000	2.50	5.00	15.00	45.00	—
1924	5,866,000	4.00	9.00	35.00	80.00	—
1925	1,413,000	18.50	40.00	165	350	—
1926	4,474,000	5.00	10.00	40.00	125	—

KM# 830 1/2 CROWN Weight: 14.1380 g. **Composition:** 0.5000 Silver .2273 oz. ASW **Ruler:** George V **Obverse:** Modified effigy, larger beads

Date	Mintage	F	VF	XF	Unc	BU
1926	Inc. above	5.00	10.00	50.00	135	—
1927	6,838,000	3.00	7.00	20.00	60.00	—

KM# 835 1/2 CROWN Weight: 14.1380 g. **Composition:** 0.5000 Silver .2273 oz. ASW **Ruler:** George V

Date	Mintage	F	VF	XF	Unc	BU
1927 Proof	15,000	Value: 60.00				
1927 Matte Proof; Rare	—	—	—	—	—	—

Note: There are reportedly 1-2 known of this variety, struck specifically for use in photographs

Date	Mintage	F	VF	XF	Unc	BU
1928	18,763,000	2.00	4.50	12.00	30.00	—
1928 Proof	—	Value: 600				
1929	17,633,000	2.00	4.50	12.00	30.00	—
1929 Proof	—	Value: 600				
1930	810,000	10.00	25.00	110	300	—
1930 Proof	—	Value: 1,000				
1931	11,264,000	2.00	4.50	12.00	30.00	—
1931 Proof	—	Value: 600				
1932	4,794,000	4.00	8.00	18.00	60.00	—
1932 Proof	—	Value: 700				
1933	10,311,000	2.00	4.50	12.00	30.00	—
1933 Proof	—	Value: 600				
1934	2,422,000	3.50	10.00	25.00	85.00	—
1934 Proof	—	Value: 750				
1935	7,022,000	2.00	4.50	12.00	28.00	—
1935 Proof	—	Value: 600				
1936	7,039,000	2.00	3.00	7.00	25.00	—
1936 Proof	—	Value: 600				

KM# 856 1/2 CROWN Weight: 14.1380 g. **Composition:** 0.5000 Silver .2273 oz. ASW **Ruler:** George VI

Date	Mintage	F	VF	XF	Unc	BU
1937	9,106,000	—	BV	3.50	12.00	—
1937 Proof	26,000	Value: 20.00				
1937 Matte Proof; Rare	—	—	—	—	—	—

Note: There are reportedly 1-2 known of this variety, struck specifically for use in photographs

Date	Mintage	F	VF	XF	Unc	BU
1938	6,426,000	BV	2.50	7.50	30.00	—
1938 Proof	—	Value: 750				
1939	15,479,000	BV	2.00	3.50	12.00	—
1939 Proof	—	Value: 500				
1940	17,948,000	BV	2.00	3.00	12.00	—
1940 Proof	—	Value: 500				
1941	15,774,000	BV	1.75	3.00	12.00	—
1941 Proof	—	Value: 500				
1942	31,220,000	BV	1.75	3.00	10.00	—
1942 Proof	—	Value: 400				
1943	15,463,000	BV	1.75	3.00	12.00	—
1943 Proof	—	Value: 400				
1944	15,255,000	BV	1.75	3.00	10.00	—
1944 Proof	—	Value: 400				
1945	19,849,000	BV	1.75	3.00	10.00	—
1945 Proof	—	Value: 500				
1946	22,725,000	BV	1.50	3.00	10.00	—
1946 Proof	—	Value: 500				

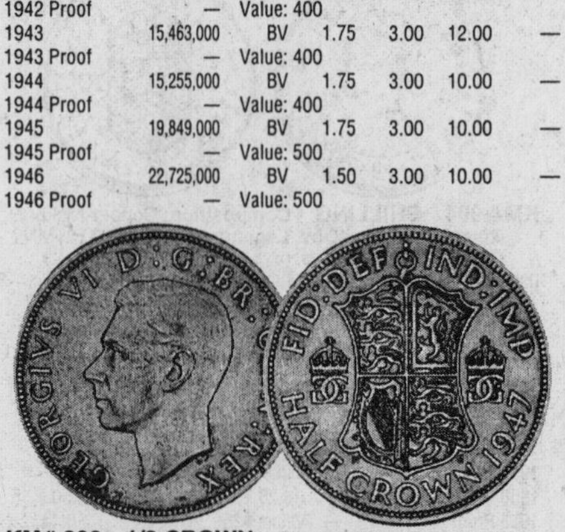

KM# 866 1/2 CROWN Composition: Copper-Nickel **Ruler:** George VI

Date	Mintage	F	VF	XF	Unc	BU
1947	21,910,000	0.25	0.50	1.25	6.00	—
1947 Proof	—	Value: 400				
1948	71,165,000	0.25	0.50	1.25	6.00	—
1948 Proof	—	Value: 350				

KM# 879 1/2 CROWN **Composition:** Copper-Nickel **Ruler:** George VI **Rev. Legend:** Without IND IMP

Date	Mintage	F	VF	XF	Unc	BU
1949		0.25	0.50	1.25	10.00	—
1949 Proof	—	Value: 400				
1950		0.25	0.50	1.25	12.00	—
1950 Proof	18,000	Value: 18.00				
1950 Matte Proof; Rare		—	—	—	—	—

Note: There are reportedly 1-2 known of this variety, struck specifically for use in photographs

Date	Mintage	F	VF	XF	Unc	BU
1951		0.50	0.75	1.50	16.00	—
1951 Proof	20,000	Value: 22.00				
1951 Matte Proof; Rare		—	—	—	—	—

Note: There are reportedly 1-2 known of this variety, struck specifically for use in photographs

Date	Mintage	F	VF	XF	Unc	BU
1952		—	12,000	—	—	—
1952 Proof	Est. 1	Value: 40,000				

KM# 893 1/2 CROWN **Composition:** Copper-Nickel **Ruler:** Elizabeth II

Date	Mintage	F	VF	XF	Unc	BU
1953	4,333,000	0.50	0.75	1.75	12.00	—
1953 Proof	40,000	Value: 15.00				
1953 Matte Proof; Rare	—	—	—	—	—	—

Note: There are reportedly 1-2 known of this variety, struck specifically for use in photographs

KM# 907 1/2 CROWN **Composition:** Copper-Nickel **Ruler:** Elizabeth II **Obv. Legend:** Without BRITT OMN

Date	Mintage	F	VF	XF	Unc	BU
1954	11,615,000	0.50	1.00	5.00	25.00	—
1954 Proof	—	Value: 400				
1955	23,629,000	0.25	0.50	1.00	7.00	—
1955 Proof	—	—	—	—	—	—
1956	33,935,000	0.25	0.50	1.00	9.00	—
1956 Proof	—	—	—	—	—	—
1957	34,201,000	0.25	0.50	0.75	5.50	—
1957 Proof	—	—	—	—	—	—
1958	15,746,000	0.25	0.75	4.00	20.00	—
1958 Proof	—	—	—	—	—	—
1959	9,029,000	1.00	1.50	6.50	35.00	—
1959 Proof	—	—	—	—	—	—
1960	19,929,000	0.25	0.50	0.75	7.00	—
1960 Proof	—	—	—	—	—	—
1961	25,888,000	0.25	0.50	0.75	3.50	—
1961 Prooflike	—	—	—	—	15.00	—
1961 Proof	—	—	—	—	—	—
1962	24,013,000	0.25	0.50	0.75	3.50	—
1962 Proof	—	—	—	—	—	—
1963	17,625,000	0.25	0.50	0.75	3.50	—
1963 Proof	—	—	—	—	—	—
1964	5,974,000	0.25	0.50	0.75	5.50	—
1965	9,778,000	0.20	0.30	0.50	3.00	—
1966	13,375,000	0.20	0.30	0.50	1.50	—
1967	33,058,000	0.20	0.30	0.50	1.50	—
1970 Proof	750,000	Value: 4.00				

KM# 803 CROWN **Weight:** 28.2759 g. **Composition:** 0.9250 Silver .8409 oz. ASW **Ruler:** Edward VII **Reverse:** St. George slaying the dragon

Date	Mintage	F	VF	XF	Unc	BU
1902	256,000	35.00	65.00	100	185	—
1902 Matte Proof	15,000	Value: 185				

KM# 836 CROWN **Weight:** 28.2759 g. **Composition:** 0.5000 Silver .4546 oz. ASW **Ruler:** George V

Date	Mintage	F	VF	XF	Unc	BU
1927 Proof	15,000	Value: 200				
1928	9,034	50.00	80.00	125	225	—
1928 Proof	—	Value: 1,800				
1929	4,994	60.00	80.00	125	285	—
1929 Proof	—	Value: 2,000				
1930	4,847	70.00	100	150	300	—
1930 Proof	—	Value: 2,000				
1931	4,056	70.00	100	150	350	—
1931 Proof	—	Value: 2,000				
1932	2,395	100	200	325	500	—
1932 Proof	—	Value: 2,500				
1933	7,132	60.00	80.00	125	285	—
1933 Proof	—	Value: 2,000				
1934	932	450	750	1,200	1,800	—
1934 Proof	—	Value: 3,500				
1936	2,473	100	200	325	500	—
1936 Proof	—	Value: 2,500				

KM# 842 CROWN **Weight:** 28.2759 g. **Composition:** 0.5000 Silver .4546 oz. ASW **Ruler:** George V **Subject:** Silver Jubilee **Obverse:** Bust of George V left **Reverse:** St. George slaying the dragon

Date	Mintage	F	VF	XF	Unc	BU
1935 Incused edge lettering	715,000	10.00	15.00	18.00	45.00	—
1935 Proof	—	Value: 2,000				
1935 Specimen in box of issue	—	—	—	—	75.00	—
1935	Inc. above	—	250	500	1,000	—

Note: (Error) Edge lettering: MEN.ANNO-REGNIXXV

KM# 842a CROWN **Composition:** 0.9250 Silver **Ruler:** George V **Subject:** Silver Jubilee

Date	Mintage	F	VF	XF	Unc	BU
1935 Raised edge lettering	2,500	Value: 400				
1935 Proof	—	Value: 1,250				

Note: (Error) Edge lettering: DECUS ANNO REGNI TUTAMEN•XXV•

KM# 857 CROWN **Composition:** 0.5000 Silver **Ruler:** George VI

Date	Mintage	F	VF	XF	Unc	BU
1937	419,000	8.00	12.00	18.00	45.00	—
1937 Proof	26,000	Value: 60.00				
1937 Frosted cameo relief; V.I.P. Proof	—	Value: 500				
1937 Matte Proof; Rare; 1-2 pieces	—	—	—	—	—	—

KM# 880 CROWN **Composition:** Copper-Nickel **Ruler:** George VI **Subject:** Festival of Britain

Date	Mintage	F	VF	XF	Unc	BU
1951 Prooflike	2,004,000	—	—	—	20.00	—
1951 Proof	—	Value: 25.00				
1951 30-50 pieces; Frosted cameo relief; V.I.P. Proof	—	Value: 450				
1951 Matte Proof; Rare; 1-2 pieces	—	—	—	—	—	—

KM# 894 CROWN **Composition:** Copper-Nickel **Ruler:** Elizabeth II **Subject:** Coronation of Queen Elizabeth II

Date	Mintage	F	VF	XF	Unc	BU
1953	5,963,000	—	—	5.00	15.00	—
1953 Proof	40,000	Value: 25.00				
1953 20-30 pieces; V.I.P. Proof	—	Value: 450				
1953 Matte Proof; Rare; 1-2 pieces	—	—	—	—	—	—

KM# 909 CROWN **Composition:** Copper-Nickel **Ruler:** Elizabeth II **Subject:** British Exhibition in New York

Date	Mintage	F	VF	XF	Unc	BU
1960	1,024,000	—	—	6.50	9.50	—
1960 Prooflike	70,000	—	—	—	22.00	—
1960 V.I.P. Proof; 30-50 pieces	—	Value: 450				

KM# 910 CROWN **Composition:** Copper-Nickel **Ruler:** Elizabeth II **Reverse:** Head of Winston Churchill right **Note:** The Specimen is struck with satin-finish.

Date	Mintage	F	VF	XF	Unc	BU
1965	9,640,000	—	—	0.65	1.00	—
1965 Specimen	—	—	—	—	600	—

SOVEREIGN COINAGE

KM# 784 1/2 SOVEREIGN **Weight:** 3.9940 g. **Composition:** 0.9170 Gold .1177 oz. AGW **Ruler:** Victoria

Date	Mintage	F	VF	XF	Unc	BU
1901	2,037,999	BV	50.00	70.00	125	—

KM# 804 1/2 SOVEREIGN **Weight:** 3.9940 g. **Composition:** 0.9170 Gold .1177 oz. AGW **Ruler:** Edward VII **Reverse:** St. George slaying the dragon

Date	Mintage	F	VF	XF	Unc	BU
1902	4,244,000	BV	60.00	70.00	100	—
1902 Proof	15,000	Value: 175				
1903	2,522,000	BV	60.00	70.00	100	—
1904	1,717,000	BV	60.00	70.00	100	—
1905	3,024,000	BV	60.00	70.00	100	—
1906	4,245,000	BV	60.00	70.00	100	—
1907	4,233,000	BV	60.00	70.00	100	—
1908	3,997,000	BV	60.00	70.00	100	—
1909	4,011,000	BV	60.00	70.00	100	—
1910	5,024,000	BV	60.00	70.00	100	—

KM# 819 1/2 SOVEREIGN **Weight:** 3.9940 g. **Composition:** 0.9170 Gold .1177 oz. AGW **Ruler:** George V **Reverse:** St. George slaying the dragon

Date	Mintage	F	VF	XF	Unc	BU
1911	6,104,000	BV	60.00	70.00	100	—
1911 Proof	3,764	Value: 325				
1912	6,224,000	BV	60.00	70.00	100	—
1913	6,094,000	BV	60.00	70.00	100	—
1914	7,251,000	BV	60.00	70.00	100	—
1915	2,043,000	BV	60.00	70.00	100	—

KM# 858 1/2 SOVEREIGN **Weight:** 3.9940 g. **Composition:** 0.9170 Gold .1177 oz. AGW **Ruler:** George VI **Reverse:** St. George slaying the dragon

Date	Mintage	F	VF	XF	Unc	BU
1937 Proof	5,500	Value: 300				
1937 Matte Proof; Unique	—	—	—	—	—	—

KM# 922 1/2 SOVEREIGN **Weight:** 3.9900 g. **Composition:** 0.9170 Gold .1176 oz. AGW **Ruler:** Elizabeth II **Reverse:** St. George slaying the dragon

Date	Mintage	F	VF	XF	Unc	BU
1980 Proof	10,000	Value: 60.00				
1982	2,500,000	—	—	—	50.00	—
1982 Proof	23,000	Value: 60.00				
1983 Proof	22,000	Value: 60.00				
1984 Proof	22,000	Value: 60.00				

KM# 942 1/2 SOVEREIGN **Weight:** 3.9900 g. **Composition:** 0.9170 Gold .1176 oz. AGW **Ruler:** Elizabeth II **Obverse:** New portrait of Elizabeth II **Reverse:** St. George slaying the dragon

Date	Mintage	F	VF	XF	Unc	BU
1985 Proof	25,000	Value: 60.00				
1986 Proof	25,000	Value: 60.00				
1987 Proof	23,000	Value: 60.00				
1988 Proof	Est. 23,000	Value: 60.00				
1990 Proof	Est. 20,000	Value: 85.00				
1991 Proof	Est. 9,000	Value: 100				
1992 Proof	7,500	Value: 100				
1993 Proof	7,500	Value: 100				
1994 Proof	Est. 7,500	Value: 100				
1995 Proof	4,900	Value: 100				
1996 Proof	5,730	Value: 125				
1997 Proof	7,500	Value: 125				

KM# 955 1/2 SOVEREIGN **Weight:** 3.9900 g. **Composition:** 0.9170 Gold .1176 oz. AGW **Ruler:** Elizabeth II **Subject:** 500th Anniversary of the Gold Sovereign

Date	Mintage	F	VF	XF	Unc	BU
ND(1989) Proof	Est. 25,000	Value: 85.00				

KM# 1001 1/2 SOVEREIGN **Weight:** 3.9900 g. **Composition:** 0.9170 Gold .1176 oz. AGW **Ruler:** Elizabeth II **Obverse:** Portrait of Queen Elizabeth II **Obv. Designer:** Rank-Broadley **Reverse:** St. George slaying the dragon

Date	Mintage	F	VF	XF	Unc	BU
1998 Proof	6,144	Value: 125				
1999 Proof	7,500	Value: 125				
2000 Proof	7,500	Value: 125				
2001	—	—	—	—	77.50	—
2001 Proof	10,000	Value: 145				

KM# 1025 1/2 SOVEREIGN **Weight:** 3.9900 g. **Composition:** 0.9167 Gold 0.1176 oz. AGW **Ruler:** Elizabeth II **Subject:** Queen Elizabeth II's Golden Jubilee **Obverse:** Queen's head right **Reverse:** Crowned arms **Edge:** Reeded **Size:** 19.3 mm.

Date	Mintage	F	VF	XF	Unc	BU
2002 Proof	18,000	Value: 145				

KM# 785 SOVEREIGN **Weight:** 7.9881 g. **Composition:** 0.9170 Gold .2354 oz. AGW **Ruler:** Victoria

Date	Mintage	F	VF	XF	Unc	BU
1901	1,579,000	—	—	BV	115	—

KM# 805 SOVEREIGN **Weight:** 7.9881 g. **Composition:** 0.9170 Gold .2354 oz. AGW **Ruler:** Edward VII **Reverse:** St. George slaying the dragon

Date	Mintage	F	VF	XF	Unc	BU
1902	4,738,000	—	—	BV	110	—
1902 Proof	15,000	Value: 275				
1903	8,889,000	—	—	BV	110	—
1904	10,041,000	—	—	BV	110	—
1905	5,910,000	—	—	BV	110	—
1906	10,467,000	—	—	BV	110	—
1907	18,459,000	—	—	BV	110	—
1908	11,729,000	—	—	BV	110	—
1909	12,157,000	—	—	BV	110	—
1910	22,380,000	—	—	BV	110	—

KM# 820 SOVEREIGN **Weight:** 7.9881 g. **Composition:** 0.9170 Gold .2354 oz. AGW **Ruler:** George V **Reverse:** St. George slaying the dragon

Date	Mintage	F	VF	XF	Unc	BU
1911	30,044,000	—	—	BV	110	—
1911 Proof	3,764	Value: 500				
1912	30,318,000	—	—	BV	110	—
1913	24,540,000	—	—	BV	110	—
1914	11,501,000	—	—	BV	110	—
1915	20,295,000	—	—	BV	110	—
1916	1,554,000	—	—	BV	115	—
1917	1,014,999	2,850	3,175	5,500	10,000	—
1925	4,406,000	—	—	BV	110	—

KM# 859 SOVEREIGN **Weight:** 7.9881 g. **Composition:** 0.9170 Gold .2354 oz. AGW **Ruler:** George VI **Reverse:** St. George slaying the dragon

Date	Mintage	F	VF	XF	Unc	BU
1937 Proof	5,500	Value: 550				
1937 Matte Proof; Unique	—	—	—	—	—	—

KM# 908 SOVEREIGN **Weight:** 7.9881 g. **Composition:** 0.9170 Gold .2354 oz. AGW **Ruler:** Elizabeth II **Reverse:** St. George slaying the dragon

Date	Mintage	F	VF	XF	Unc	BU
1957	2,072,000	—	—	BV	95.00	—
1957 Proof	—	—	—	—	—	—
1958	8,700,000	—	—	BV	90.00	—
1958 Proof	—	—	—	—	—	—
1959	1,358,000	—	—	BV	115	—
1959 Proof	—	—	—	—	—	—
1962	3,000,000	—	—	BV	90.00	—
1962 Proof	—	—	—	—	—	—
1963	7,400,000	—	—	BV	90.00	—
1963 Proof	—	—	—	—	—	—
1964	3,000,000	—	—	BV	90.00	—
1965	3,800,000	—	—	BV	90.00	—
1966	7,050,000	—	—	BV	90.00	—
1967	5,000,000	—	—	BV	90.00	—
1968	4,203,000	—	—	BV	90.00	—

KM# 919 SOVEREIGN **Weight:** 7.9881 g. **Composition:** 0.9170 Gold .2354 oz. AGW **Ruler:** Elizabeth II **Reverse:** St. George slaying the dragon

Date	Mintage	F	VF	XF	Unc	BU
1974	5,003,000	—	—	BV	90.00	—
1976	4,150,000	—	—	BV	90.00	—
1978	6,350,000	—	—	BV	90.00	—
1979	9,100,000	—	—	BV	90.00	—
1979 Proof	50,000	Value: 110				
1980	5,100,000	—	—	BV	90.00	—
1980 Proof	91,000	Value: 110				
1981	5,000,000	—	—	BV	90.00	—
1981 Proof	33,000	Value: 110				
1982	2,950,000	—	—	BV	90.00	—
1982 Proof	23,000	Value: 110				
1983 Proof	21,000	Value: 110				
1984 Proof	20,000	Value: 110				

KM# 943 SOVEREIGN **Weight:** 7.9881 g. **Composition:** 0.9170 Gold .2354 oz. AGW **Ruler:** Elizabeth II **Obverse:** New portrait of Elizabeth II **Reverse:** St. George slaying the dragon

Date	Mintage	F	VF	XF	Unc	BU
1985 Proof	17,000	Value: 135				
1986 Proof	25,000	Value: 135				
1987 Proof	22,000	Value: 135				
1988 Proof	Est. 25,000	Value: 135				
1990 Proof	Est. 20,000	Value: 150				
1991 Proof	Est. 9,000	Value: 150				
1992 Proof	7,500	Value: 175				
1993 Proof	7,500	Value: 175				
1994 Proof	Est. 7,500	Value: 175				
1995 Proof	7,500	Value: 175				
1996 Proof	7,500	Value: 175				
1997 Proof	7,500	Value: 175				

KM# 956 SOVEREIGN **Weight:** 7.9881 g. **Composition:** 0.9170 Gold .2354 oz. AGW **Ruler:** Elizabeth II **Subject:** 500th Anniversary of the Gold Sovereign

Date		F	VF	XF	Unc	BU
ND(1989) Proof	Est. 28,000	Value: 225				

KM# 1002 SOVEREIGN **Weight:** 7.9881 g. **Composition:** 0.9170 Gold .2354 oz. AGW **Ruler:** Elizabeth II **Obverse:** Portrait of Queen Elizabeth II **Obv. Designer:** Rank-Broadley **Reverse:** St. George slaying the dragon

Date	Mintage	F	VF	XF	Unc	BU
1998 Proof	10,000	Value: 175				
1999 Proof	10,000	Value: 225				
2000 Proof	10,000	Value: 175				
2001	—	—	—	—	135	—
2001 Proof	15,000	Value: 215				

KM# 1026 SOVEREIGN **Weight:** 7.9800 g. **Composition:** 0.9167 Gold 0.2352 oz. AGW **Ruler:** Elizabeth II **Subject:** Queen Elizabeth II's Golden Jubilee **Obverse:** Queen's head right **Reverse:** Crowned arms **Edge:** Reeded **Size:** 22 mm.

Date	Mintage	F	VF	XF	Unc	BU
2002 Proof	20,500	Value: 215				

KM# 1005a POUND **Weight:** 9.5000 g. **Composition:** 0.9250 Silver 0.2825 oz. ASW **Ruler:** George VI **Subject:** Wales **Obverse:** Queen's head right **Reverse:** Welsh dragon **Edge:** Reeded **Edge Lettering:** PLEIDIOL WYF I'M GWLAD **Size:** 22.5 mm.

Date	Mintage	F	VF	XF	Unc	BU
2000 Proof	15,865	Value: 40.00				

KM# 806 2 POUNDS **Weight:** 15.9761 g. **Composition:** 0.9170 Gold .4708 oz. AGW **Ruler:** Edward VII **Reverse:** St. George slaying the dragon

Date	Mintage	F	VF	XF	Unc	BU
1902	46,000	250	300	450	550	—
1902 Proof	8,066	Value: 650				

Note: Proof issues with mint mark S below right rear hoof of horse were struck at Sydney, refer to Australia listings

KM# 821 2 POUNDS **Weight:** 15.9761 g. **Composition:** 0.9170 Gold .4708 oz. AGW **Ruler:** George V **Reverse:** St. George slaying the dragon

Date	Mintage	F	VF	XF	Unc	BU
1911 Proof	2,812	Value: 1,200				

KM# 860 2 POUNDS **Weight:** 15.9761 g. **Composition:** 0.9170 Gold .4708 oz. AGW **Ruler:** George VI **Reverse:** St. George slaying the dragon

Date	Mintage	F	VF	XF	Unc	BU
1937 Proof	5,500	Value: 600				
1937 Matte Proof; Unique	—	—	—	—	—	—

KM# 923 2 POUNDS **Weight:** 15.9200 g. **Composition:** 0.9170 Gold .4694 oz. AGW **Ruler:** Elizabeth II

Date	Mintage	F	VF	XF	Unc	BU
1980 Proof	10,000	Value: 225				
1982 Proof	2,500	Value: 250				
1983 Proof	13,000	Value: 225				

KM# 944 2 POUNDS **Weight:** 15.9200 g. **Composition:** 0.9170 Gold .4694 oz. AGW **Ruler:** Elizabeth II **Obverse:** New portrait of Elizabeth II **Reverse:** St. George slaying the dragon

Date	Mintage	F	VF	XF	Unc	BU
1985 Proof	5,849	Value: 275				
1987 Proof	14,000	Value: 275				
1988 Proof	15,000	Value: 275				
1990 Proof	Est. 12,000	Value: 275				
1991 Proof	Est. 5,000	Value: 300				
1992 Proof	3,000	Value: 300				
1993 Proof	3,000	Value: 300				
1999 Proof	—	Value: 400				

KM# 957 2 POUNDS **Weight:** 15.9800 g. **Composition:** 0.9170 Gold .4708 oz. AGW **Ruler:** Elizabeth II **Subject:** 500th Anniversary of the Gold Sovereign

Date	Mintage	F	VF	XF	Unc	BU
ND(1989) Proof	Est. 17,000	Value: 350				

KM# 1027 2 POUNDS **Weight:** 15.9700 g. **Composition:** 0.9167 Gold 0.4707 oz. AGW **Ruler:** Elizabeth II **Subject:** Queen Elizabeth II's Golden Jubilee **Obverse:** Queen's head right **Reverse:** Crowned arms **Edge:** Reeded **Size:** 28.4 mm. **Note:** In proof sets only.

Date	Mintage	F	VF	XF	Unc	BU
2002	8,000	Value: 435				

KM# 807 5 POUNDS **Weight:** 39.9403 g. **Composition:** 0.9170 Gold 1.1773 oz. AGW **Ruler:** Edward VII

Date	Mintage	F	VF	XF	Unc	BU
1902	—	600	650	750	1,000	—

Note: 27,000 pieces were remelted

Date	Mintage	F	VF	XF	Unc	BU
1902 Proof	8,066	Value: 1,250				

Note: Proof issues with mint mark S below right rear hoof of horse were struck at Sydney, refer to Australia listings

KM# 822 5 POUNDS **Weight:** 39.9403 g. **Composition:** 0.9170 Gold 1.1773 oz. AGW **Ruler:** George V

Date	Mintage	F	VF	XF	Unc	BU
1911 Proof	2,812	Value: 2,000				

KM# 861 5 POUNDS **Weight:** 39.9403 g. **Composition:** 0.9170 Gold 1.1773 oz. AGW **Ruler:** George V

Date	Mintage	F	VF	XF	Unc	BU
1937 Proof	5,500	Value: 1,000				

Note: Impaired and blemished proofs of the 1937 issue are common and trade at much lower values. The value listed here is for blemish free examples

Date	Mintage	F	VF	XF	Unc	BU
1937 Matte Proof; Unique	—	—	—	—	—	—

KM# 924 5 POUNDS **Weight:** 39.9400 g. **Composition:** 0.9170 Gold 1.1775 oz. AGW **Ruler:** Elizabeth II

Date	Mintage	F	VF	XF	Unc	BU
1980 Proof	10,000	Value: 550				
1981 Proof	5,400	Value: 650				
1982 Proof	2,500	Value: 650				
1984	25,000	—	—	—	550	—
1984 Proof	8,000	Value: 650				

KM# 945 5 POUNDS **Weight:** 39.9400 g. **Composition:** 0.9170 Gold 1.1775 oz. AGW **Ruler:** Elizabeth II **Obverse:** New portrait of Elizabeth II

Date	Mintage	F	VF	XF	Unc	BU
1985		—	—	—	550	—
1985 Proof	13,000	Value: 650				
1986		—	—	—	550	—
1990		—	—	—	550	—
1990 Proof	Est. 2,500	Value: 650				
1991		—	—	—	575	—
1991 Proof	Est. 1,500	Value: 675				
1992 Proof	1,250	Value: 675				
1992		—	—	—	575	—
1993		—	—	—	575	—
1994 Proof	Est. 1,250	Value: 675				
1995 Proof	Est. 1,000	Value: 675				
1995 Proof	Est. 1,250	Value: 675				
1996		—	—	—	575	—
1997		—	—	—	575	—

KM# 949 5 POUNDS **Weight:** 39.9400 g. **Composition:** 0.9170 Gold 1.1775 oz. AGW **Ruler:** Elizabeth II **Obverse:** Draped bust

Date		F	VF	XF	Unc	BU
1987		—	—	—	550	—
1988		—	—	—	550	—

KM# 958 5 POUNDS **Weight:** 39.9400 g. **Composition:** 0.9170 Gold 1.1775 oz. AGW **Ruler:** Elizabeth II **Subject:** 500th Anniversary of the Gold Sovereign

Date	Mintage	F	VF	XF	Unc	BU
1989		—	—	—	600	—
1989 Proof	Est. 5,000	Value: 650				

KM# 1003 5 POUNDS **Weight:** 39.9400 g. **Composition:** 0.9170 Gold 1.1775 oz. AGW **Ruler:** Elizabeth II **Obverse:** Portrait of Queen Elizabeth II **Obv. Designer:** Rank-Broadley **Reverse:** St. George slaying dragon **Edge:** Reeded **Size:** 36 mm.

Date	Mintage	F	VF	XF	Unc	BU
1999 Proof	—	Value: 925				
2000		—	—	—	525	—
2001 Proof	1,000	Value: 835				

KM# 1028 5 POUNDS **Weight:** 39.9400 g. **Composition:** 0.9167 Gold 1.1771 oz. AGW **Ruler:** Elizabeth II **Subject:** Queen Elizabeth II's Golden Jubilee **Obverse:** Queen's head right **Reverse:** Crowned arms **Edge:** Reeded **Size:** 36 mm.

Date	Mintage	F	VF	XF	Unc	BU
2002	3,000	Value: 850				

DECIMAL COINAGE

1971-1981, 100 New Pence = 1 Pound; 1982, 100 Pence = 1 Pound

KM# 914 1/2 NEW PENNY **Composition:** Bronze **Ruler:** Elizabeth II

Date	Mintage	F	VF	XF	Unc	BU
1971	1,394,188,000	—	—	0.10	0.20	—
1971 Proof	350,000	Value: 1.00				
1972 Proof	150,000	Value: 3.00				
1973	365,680,000	—	—	0.15	0.40	—
1973 Proof	100,000	Value: 1.00				
1974	365,448,000	—	—	0.15	0.35	—
1974 Proof	100,000	Value: 1.00				
1975	197,600,000	—	—	0.15	0.45	—
1975 Proof	100,000	Value: 1.00				
1976	412,172,000	—	—	0.15	0.35	—
1976 Proof	100,000	Value: 1.00				
1977	66,367,999	—	—	0.15	0.25	—
1977 Proof	194,000	Value: 1.00				
1978	59,532,000	—	—	0.15	0.25	—
1978 Proof	88,000	Value: 1.00				
1979	219,132,000	—	—	0.15	0.25	—
1979 Proof	81,000	Value: 1.00				
1980	202,788,000	—	—	0.15	0.25	—
1980 Proof	143,000	Value: 1.00				
1981	32,484,000	—	—	0.15	0.45	—
1981 Proof	100,000	Value: 1.00				

KM# 926 1/2 PENNY **Composition:** Bronze **Ruler:** Elizabeth II **Reverse:** HALF PENNY above crown and fraction **Note:** Denomination now demonetized.

Date	Mintage	F	VF	XF	Unc	BU
1982		—	—	0.15	0.25	—
1982 Proof	107,000	Value: 1.00				
1983		—	—	0.25	0.60	—
1983 Proof	108,000	Value: 1.50				
1984 In sets only		—	—	—	2.00	—
1984 Proof	107,000	Value: 2.50				

KM# 915 NEW PENNY **Composition:** Bronze **Ruler:** Elizabeth II

Date	Mintage	F	VF	XF	Unc	BU
1971	1,521,666,000	—	—	0.15	0.25	—
1971 Proof	350,000	Value: 1.25				
1972 Proof	150,000	Value: 3.00				
1973	280,196,000	—	—	0.15	0.45	—
1973 Proof	100,000	Value: 1.25				
1974	330,892,000	—	—	0.15	0.45	—
1974 Proof	100,000	Value: 1.25				
1975	221,604,000	—	—	0.15	0.60	—
1975 Proof	100,000	Value: 1.25				
1976	241,800,000	—	—	0.15	0.30	—
1976 Proof	100,000	Value: 1.25				
1977	285,430,000	—	—	0.15	0.25	—
1977 Proof	194,000	Value: 1.25				
1978	292,770,000	—	—	0.15	0.50	—
1978 Proof	88,000	Value: 1.25				
1979	459,000,000	—	—	0.15	0.25	—
1979 Proof	81,000	Value: 1.25				
1980	416,304,000	—	—	0.15	0.25	—
1980 Proof	143,000	Value: 1.25				
1981	301,800,000	—	—	0.15	0.25	—
1981 Proof	100,000	Value: 1.25				

KM# 927 PENNY **Composition:** Bronze **Ruler:** Elizabeth II

Date	Mintage	F	VF	XF	Unc	BU
1982	121,429,000	—	—	0.15	0.25	—
1982 Proof	107,000	Value: 1.25				
1983	243,002,000	—	—	0.15	0.40	—
1983 Proof	108,000	Value: 1.25				
1984	154,760,000	—	—	0.20	1.25	—
1984 Proof	107,000	Value: 1.25				

KM# 935 PENNY **Composition:** Bronze **Ruler:** Elizabeth II **Note:** Reduced size.

Date	Mintage	F	VF	XF	Unc	BU
1985	200,605,000	—	—	0.15	0.35	—
1985 Proof	102,000	Value: 1.25				
1986	369,989,000	—	—	0.15	0.35	—
1986 Proof	125,000	Value: 1.25				
1987	499,946,000	—	—	0.15	0.25	—
1987 Proof	89,000	Value: 1.25				
1988	793,492,000	—	—	0.15	0.25	—
1988 Proof	125,000	Value: 1.25				
1989	658,142,000	—	—	0.15	0.25	—
1989 Proof	100,000	Value: 1.25				
1990	529,048,000	—	—	0.15	0.25	—
1990 Proof	100,000	Value: 1.25				
1991	206,458,000	—	—	0.15	0.25	—
1991 Proof	—	Value: 1.25				
1992	—	—	—	—	0.50	—
1992 Proof	—	Value: 1.75				

Note: in sets only

KM# 935a PENNY **Composition:** Copper Plated Steel **Ruler:** Elizabeth II

Date	Mintage	F	VF	XF	Unc	BU
1992	253,867,000	—	—	0.15	0.25	—
1993	602,590,000	—	—	0.15	0.25	—
1993 Proof	—	Value: 1.25				
1994	843,834,000	—	—	0.15	0.25	—
1994 Proof	—	Value: 1.25				
1995	303,314,000	—	—	0.15	0.25	—
1995 Proof	—	Value: 1.25				
1996	723,840,000	—	—	—	0.25	—
1996 Proof	—	Value: 1.25				
1997	396,874,000	—	—	—	0.25	—
1997 Proof	—	Value: 1.25				

KM# 935b PENNY **Composition:** 0.9250 Silver **Ruler:** Elizabeth II

Date		F	VF	XF	Unc	BU
1996 Proof	—	Value: 16.50				

KM# 986 PENNY **Composition:** Copper Plated Steel **Ruler:** Elizabeth II **Obverse:** Effigy of Queen Elizabeth II **Obv. Designer:** Rank-Broadley **Reverse:** Crowned portcullis

Date	Mintage	F	VF	XF	Unc	BU
1998		—	—	—	0.20	—
1998 Proof	Est. 100,000	Value: 3.25				
1999		—	—	—	0.20	—
1999 Proof	—	Value: 3.25				
2000		—	—	—	0.20	—
2001		—	—	—	0.20	—
2002		—	—	—	0.20	—
2003 Proof	—	Value: 3.25				

KM# 986a PENNY **Composition:** Bronze **Ruler:** Elizabeth II

Date	Mintage	F	VF	XF	Unc	BU
1999		—	—	—	0.20	—
1999 Proof	79,401	Value: 2.50				
2000		—	—	—	0.20	—
2000 Proof	100,000	Value: 2.50				
2001		—	—	—	0.20	—
2001 Proof	100,000	Value: 2.50				

KM# 986b PENNY **Weight:** 3.5600 g. **Composition:** 0.9250 Silver 0.1059 oz. ASW **Ruler:** Elizabeth II **Obverse:** Queen Elizabeth II **Reverse:** Portcullis **Edge:** Plain **Size:** 20.3 mm.

Date	Mintage	F	VF	XF	Unc	BU
2000 Proof	15	Value: 16.50				

KM# 916 2 NEW PENCE **Composition:** Bronze **Ruler:** Elizabeth II

Date	Mintage	F	VF	XF	Unc	BU
1971	1,454,856,000	—	—	0.10	0.20	—
1971 Proof	350,000	Value: 1.50				
1972 Proof	150,000	Value: 3.50				
1973 Proof	100,000	Value: 3.50				
1974 Proof	100,000	Value: 3.50				
1975	145,545,000	—	—	0.15	0.40	—
1975 Proof	100,000	Value: 1.50				
1976	181,379,000	—	—	0.15	0.30	—
1976 Proof	100,000	Value: 1.50				
1977	109,281,000	—	—	0.15	0.25	—
1977 Proof	194,000	Value: 1.50				
1978	189,658,000	—	—	0.15	0.40	—
1978 Proof	88,000	Value: 1.50				
1979	268,300,000	—	—	0.15	0.25	—
1979 Proof	81,000	Value: 1.50				
1980	408,527,000	—	—	0.15	0.25	—
1980 Proof	143,000	Value: 1.50				
1981	353,191,000	—	—	0.15	0.25	—
1981 Proof	100,000	Value: 1.50				

KM# 928 2 PENCE **Composition:** Bronze **Ruler:** Elizabeth II

Date	Mintage	F	VF	XF	Unc	BU
1982 In sets only	205,000	—	—	—	1.00	—
1982 Proof	107,000	Value: 1.50				
1983 In sets only	631,000	—	—	—	1.00	—
1983 Proof	108,000	Value: 1.50				
1984 In sets only	159,000	—	—	—	1.50	—
1984 Proof	107,000	Value: 1.50				

KM# 936 2 PENCE **Composition:** Bronze **Ruler:** Elizabeth II

Date	Mintage	F	VF	XF	Unc	BU
1985	107,113,000	—	—	0.15	0.25	—
1985 Proof	102,000	Value: 1.50				
1986	168,968,000	—	—	0.15	0.50	—
1986 Proof	125,000	Value: 1.50				
1987	218,101,000	—	—	0.15	0.25	—
1987 Proof	89,000	Value: 1.50				
1988	419,889,000	—	—	0.15	0.25	—
1988 Proof	125,000	Value: 1.50				
1989	359,226,000	—	—	0.15	0.25	—
1989 Proof	100,000	Value: 1.50				
1990	204,500,000	—	—	0.15	0.25	—
1990 Proof	100,000	Value: 1.50				
1991	86,625,000	—	—	0.15	0.25	—
1991 Proof	—	Value: 1.50				
1992	96,000,000	—	—	—	0.50	—

KM# 936a 2 PENCE **Composition:** Copper Plated Steel **Ruler:** Elizabeth II

Date	Mintage	F	VF	XF	Unc	BU
1992	102,247,000	—	—	0.15	0.25	—
1993	235,674,000	—	—	0.15	0.25	—
1993 Proof	—	Value: 1.50				
1994	531,628,000	—	—	0.10	0.25	—
1994 Proof	—	Value: 1.50				
1995	124,482,000	—	—	0.10	0.25	—
1995 Proof	—	Value: 1.50				
1996	296,278,000	—	—	0.10	0.25	—
1996 Proof	—	Value: 1.50				
1997	439,975,000	—	—	0.10	0.25	—
1997 Proof	—	Value: 1.50				

KM# 936b 2 PENCE **Composition:** 0.9250 Silver **Ruler:** Elizabeth II

Date		F	VF	XF	Unc	BU
1996 Proof	—	Value: 17.50				

KM# 987 2 PENCE **Composition:** Copper Plated Steel **Ruler:** Elizabeth II **Obverse:** Effigy of Queen Elizabeth II **Obv. Designer:** Rank-Broadley **Reverse:** Prince of Wales badge

Date	Mintage	F	VF	XF	Unc	BU
1998		—	—	—	0.25	—
1998 Proof	Est. 100,000	Value: 3.25				
1999		—	—	—	0.25	—
1999 Proof	—	Value: 3.25				
2000		—	—	—	0.25	—
2001		—	—	—	0.25	—
2002		—	—	—	0.25	—
2003 Proof	—	Value: 3.25				

KM# 987a 2 PENCE **Composition:** Bronze **Ruler:** Elizabeth II

Date	Mintage	F	VF	XF	Unc	BU
1999		—	—	—	0.25	—
1999 Proof	79,401	Value: 2.50				
2000		—	—	—	0.25	—
2000 Proof	Est. 100,000	Value: 2.50				
2001		—	—	—	0.25	—
2001 Proof	Est. 100,000	Value: 2.50				
2002		—	—	—	0.25	—

KM# 987b 2 PENCE **Weight:** 7.1200 g. **Composition:** 0.9250 Silver 0.2117 oz. ASW **Ruler:** Elizabeth II **Obverse:** Queen Elizabeth II **Reverse:** Prince of Wales badge **Edge:** Plain **Size:** 25.9 mm.

Date	Mintage	F	VF	XF	Unc	BU
2000 Proof	15,000	Value: 17.50				

KM# 911 5 NEW PENCE **Composition:** Copper-Nickel **Ruler:** Elizabeth II

Date	Mintage	F	VF	XF	Unc	BU
1968	98,868,000	—	—	0.15	0.30	—
1969	119,270,000	—	—	0.15	0.40	—
1970	225,948,000	—	—	0.15	0.40	—
1971	81,783,000	—	—	0.15	0.50	—
1971 Proof	350,000	Value: 1.75				
1972 Proof	150,000	Value: 3.50				
1973 Proof	100,000	Value: 3.50				
1974 Proof	100,000	Value: 3.50				
1975	116,906,000	—	—	0.15	0.30	—
1975 Proof	100,000	Value: 1.50				
1976 Proof	100,000	Value: 3.50				
1977	24,308,000	—	—	0.15	0.35	—
1977 Proof	194,000	Value: 1.50				
1978	61,094,000	—	—	0.15	0.55	—
1978 Proof	88,000	Value: 1.50				
1979	155,456,000	—	—	0.15	0.30	—
1979 Proof	81,000	Value: 1.50				
1980	203,020,000	—	—	0.15	0.30	—
1980 Proof	143,000	Value: 1.50				
1981 Proof	100,000	Value: 1.75				

KM# 929 5 PENCE **Composition:** Copper-Nickel **Ruler:** Elizabeth II

Date	Mintage	F	VF	XF	Unc	BU
1982 In sets only	205,000	—	—	—	2.25	—
1982 Proof	107,000	Value: 1.75				
1983 In sets only	637,000	—	—	—	1.75	—
1983 Proof	108,000	Value: 1.75				
1984 In sets only	159,000	—	—	—	1.75	—
1984 Proof	107,000	Value: 1.50				

KM# 937 5 PENCE **Composition:** Copper-Nickel **Ruler:** Elizabeth II

Date	Mintage	F	VF	XF	Unc	BU
1985 In sets only	178,000	—	—	—	2.00	—
1985 Proof	102,000	Value: 1.50				
1986 In sets only	167,000	—	—	—	1.00	—
1986 Proof	125,000	Value: 1.50				
1987	48,220,000	—	—	0.15	0.30	—
1987 Proof	89,000	Value: 1.75				
1988	120,775,000	—	—	0.15	0.30	—
1988 Proof	125,000	Value: 1.75				
1989	101,406,000	—	—	0.15	0.30	—
1989 Proof	100,000	Value: 1.75				
1990 In sets only		—	—	—	2.50	—
1990 Proof	—	Value: 2.75				

KM# 937a 5 PENCE **Weight:** 5.6000 g. **Composition:** 0.9250 Silver .1683 oz. ASW **Ruler:** Elizabeth II

Date	Mintage	F	VF	XF	Unc	BU
1990 Proof	35,000	Value: 22.00				

KM# 937c 5 PENCE **Weight:** 3.2500 g. **Composition:** 0.9250 Silver .0967 oz. ASW **Ruler:** Elizabeth II

Date	Mintage	F	VF	XF	Unc	BU
1990 Proof	35,000	Value: 20.00				
1996 Proof	—	Value: 20.00				

KM# 937d 5 PENCE **Weight:** 6.5000 g. **Composition:** 0.9250 Silver .1933 oz. ASW **Ruler:** Elizabeth II

Date	Mintage	F	VF	XF	Unc	BU
1990 Proof	20,000	Value: 25.00				

KM# 937b 5 PENCE **Composition:** Copper-Nickel **Ruler:** Elizabeth II **Note:** Reduced size. Varieties in thickness and edge milling exist.

Date	Mintage	F	VF	XF	Unc	BU
1990	1,634,840,000	—	—	—	0.35	—
1990 Proof	—	Value: 2.00				
1991	724,979,000	—	—	—	0.35	—
1991 Proof	—	Value: 2.00				
1992	453,174,000	—	—	—	0.35	—
1992 Proof	—	Value: 2.00				
1993 In sets only	56,945	—	—	—	1.25	—
1993 Proof	—	Value: 2.00				
1994	93,602,000	—	—	—	0.35	—
1994 Proof	—	Value: 2.00				
1995	183,384,000	—	—	—	0.35	—
1995 Proof	—	Value: 2.00				
1996	302,902,000	—	—	—	0.35	—
1996 Proof	—	Value: 2.00				
1997	736,596,000	—	—	—	0.35	—
1997 Proof	—	Value: 2.00				

KM# 988 5 PENCE **Composition:** Copper-Nickel **Ruler:** Elizabeth II **Obverse:** Effigy of Queen Elizabeth II **Obv. Designer:** Rank-Broadley **Reverse:** Crowned Scottish thistle

Date		F	VF	XF	Unc	BU
1998		—	—	—	0.30	—
1998 Proof	Est. 100,000	Value: 3.25				
1999		—	—	—	0.30	—
1999 Proof	79,401	Value: 3.00				
2000		—	—	—	0.30	—
2000 Proof	Est. 100,000	Value: 3.00				
2001		—	—	—	0.30	—
2001 Proof	Est. 100,000	Value: 3.00				
2002		—	—	—	0.30	—
2003 Proof	—	Value: 3.00				

KM# 988a 5 PENCE **Weight:** 3.2500 g. **Composition:** 0.9250 Silver 0.0967 oz. ASW **Ruler:** Elizabeth II **Obverse:** Queen Elizabeth II **Reverse:** Scottish Thistle **Edge:** Reeded **Size:** 18 mm.

Date	Mintage	F	VF	XF	Unc	BU
2000 Proof	15,000	Value: 20.00				

KM# 912 10 NEW PENCE **Composition:** Copper-Nickel **Ruler:** Elizabeth II

Date	Mintage	F	VF	XF	Unc	BU
1968	336,143,000	—	—	0.25	0.50	—
1969	314,008,000	—	—	0.25	0.60	—
1970	133,571,000	—	—	0.25	0.75	—
1971	63,205,000	—	—	0.25	1.00	—
1971 Proof	350,000	Value: 1.75				
1972 Proof	150,000	Value: 3.75				
1973	152,174,000	—	—	0.25	0.50	—
1973 Proof	100,000	Value: 1.75				
1974	92,741,000	—	—	0.25	0.50	—
1974 Proof	100,000	Value: 1.75				
1975	181,559,000	—	—	0.25	0.50	—
1975 Proof	100,000	Value: 1.75				
1976	228,220,000	—	—	0.25	0.50	—
1976 Proof	100,000	Value: 1.75				
1977	59,323,000	—	—	0.25	0.60	—
1977 Proof	194,000	Value: 1.75				
1978 Proof	88,000	Value: 5.25				
1979	115,457,000	—	—	0.25	0.60	—
1979 Proof	81,000	Value: 1.75				
1980	88,650,000	—	—	0.25	0.65	—
1980 Proof	143,000	Value: 1.75				
1981	3,433,000	—	0.25	0.50	2.00	—
1981 Proof	100,000	Value: 1.75				

KM# 930 10 PENCE **Composition:** Copper-Nickel **Ruler:** Elizabeth II

Date	Mintage	F	VF	XF	Unc	BU
1982 In sets only	205,000	—	—	—	2.75	—
1982 Proof	107,000	Value: 1.75				
1983 In sets only	637,000	—	—	—	2.75	—
1983 Proof	108,000	Value: 1.75				
1984 In sets only	159,000	—	—	—	2.00	—
1984 Proof	107,000	Value: 1.75				

KM# 938 10 PENCE **Composition:** Copper-Nickel **Ruler:** Elizabeth II

Date	Mintage	F	VF	XF	Unc	BU
1985 In sets only	178,000	—	—	—	2.75	—
1985 Proof	102,000	Value: 1.75				
1986 In sets only	167,000	—	—	—	1.75	—
1986 Proof	125,000	Value: 1.75				
1987 In sets only	172,000	—	—	—	2.75	—
1987 Proof	89,000	Value: 2.75				
1988 In sets only	134,000	—	—	—	2.75	—
1988 Proof	125,000	Value: 2.75				
1989 In sets only	78,000	—	—	—	3.50	—
1989 Proof	100,000	Value: 2.75				
1990	—	—	—	—	3.50	—
1990 Proof	100,000	Value: 2.75				
1991 In sets only	—	—	—	—	3.50	—
1991 Proof	—	Value: 2.75				
1992 In sets only	—	—	—	—	2.75	—
1992 Proof	—	Value: 3.50				

KM# 938c 10 PENCE **Weight:** 6.5000 g. **Composition:** 0.9250 Silver .1933 oz. ASW **Ruler:** Elizabeth II

Date	Mintage	F	VF	XF	Unc	BU
1992 Proof	35,000	Value: 17.50				
1996 Proof	—	Value: 17.50				

KM# 938a 10 PENCE **Weight:** 11.3100 g. **Composition:** 0.9250 Silver .3363 oz. ASW **Ruler:** Elizabeth II **Note:** Date varieties exist.

Date	Mintage	F	VF	XF	Unc	BU
1992 Proof	35,000	Value: 25.00				

KM# 938b 10 PENCE **Composition:** Copper-Nickel **Ruler:** Elizabeth II **Note:** Reduced size. Varieties in thickness and edge milling exist.

Date	Mintage	F	VF	XF	Unc	BU
1992	1,395,497,000	—	—	0.25	0.50	—
1992 Proof	—	Value: 2.75				
1993 In sets only	—	—	—	—	1.00	—
1993 Proof	—	Value: 1.75				
1994 In sets only	—	—	—	—	1.00	—
1994 Proof	—	Value: 1.75				
1995	43,259,000	—	—	—	1.00	—
1995 Proof	—	Value: 1.75				
1996	118,738,000	—	—	—	1.00	—
1996 Proof	—	Value: 1.75				
1997	99,196,000	—	—	—	1.00	—
1997 Proof	—	Value: 1.75				

KM# 989 10 PENCE **Composition:** Copper-Nickel **Ruler:** Elizabeth II **Obverse:** Effigy of Queen Elizabeth II **Obv. Designer:** Rank-Broadley **Reverse:** Crowned lion

Date	Mintage	F	VF	XF	Unc	BU
1998 Proof, in proof & mint sets only	—	Value: 4.50				
1998		—	—	—	1.25	—
1999 In sets only		—	—	—	1.25	—
1999 Proof, in sets only	79,401	Value: 3.25				
2000		—	—	—	0.40	—
2000 Proof	Est. 100,000	Value: 3.25				
2001		—	—	—	0.40	—
2001 Proof	Est. 100,000	Value: 3.25				
2002		—	—	—	0.40	—
2003 Proof	—	Value: 3.25				

KM# 989a 10 PENCE **Weight:** 6.5000 g. **Composition:** 0.9250 Silver 0.1933 oz. ASW **Ruler:** Elizabeth II **Obverse:** Queen Elizabeth II **Obv. Designer:** Rank-Broadley **Reverse:** Crowned Lion **Edge:** Reeded **Size:** 24.5 mm.

Date	Mintage	F	VF	XF	Unc	BU
2000 Proof	15,000	Value: 17.50				

KM# 931 20 PENCE **Composition:** Copper-Nickel **Ruler:** Elizabeth II **Reverse:** Crowned rose

Date	Mintage	F	VF	XF	Unc	BU
1982	740,815,000	—	—	0.45	0.65	—
1982 Proof	107,000	Value: 5.00				
1983	158,463,000	—	—	0.45	0.65	—
1983 Proof	108,000	Value: 2.50				
1984	65,351,000	—	—	0.45	0.65	—
1984 Proof	107,000	Value: 2.50				

KM# 939 20 PENCE **Composition:** Copper-Nickel **Ruler:** Elizabeth II **Reverse:** Crowned rose **Shape:** 7-sided

Date	Mintage	F	VF	XF	Unc	BU
1985	74,274,000	—	—	0.45	0.75	—
1985 Proof	102,000	Value: 5.00				
1986 In sets only	167,000	—	—	—	1.00	—
1986 Proof	125,000	Value: 5.00				
1987	137,450,000	—	—	0.45	0.75	—
1987 Proof	89,000	Value: 5.00				
1988	38,038,000	—	—	0.45	0.75	—
1988 Proof	125,000	Value: 5.00				
1989	132,014,000	—	—	0.45	0.75	—
1989 Proof	100,000	Value: 5.00				
1990	88,098,000	—	—	0.45	0.75	—
1990 Proof	100,000	Value: 5.00				
1991	35,901,000	—	—	0.45	1.00	—
1991 Proof	—	Value: 5.00				
1992	31,205,000	—	—	0.45	1.00	—
1992 Proof	—	Value: 5.00				
1993	123,124,000	—	—	0.45	0.75	—
1993 Proof	—	Value: 5.00				
1994	67,131,000	—	—	0.45	1.00	—
1994 Proof	—	Value: 5.00				
1995	102,005,000	—	—	0.45	0.75	—
1995 Proof	—	Value: 5.00				
1996	83,164,000	—	—	0.45	0.75	—
1996 Proof	—	Value: 5.00				
1997	89,519,000	—	—	0.45	0.75	—
Note: Variations in portrait exist						
1997 Proof	—	Value: 5.00				

KM# 939a 20 PENCE **Composition:** 0.9250 Silver **Ruler:** Elizabeth II

Date		F	VF	XF	Unc	BU
1996 Proof	—	Value: 18.50				

KM# 978 20 PENCE **Weight:** 3.2400 g. **Composition:** 0.9580 Silver .0998 oz. ASW **Ruler:** Elizabeth II **Obverse:** Queen's portrait **Reverse:** Britannia in chariot **Note:** Similar to 2 Pounds, KM#981.

Date	Mintage	F	VF	XF	Unc	BU
1997 Proof	8,686	Value: 25.00				

KM# 990 20 PENCE **Composition:** Copper-Nickel **Ruler:** Elizabeth II **Obverse:** Effigy of Queen Elizabeth II **Obv. Designer:** Rank-Broadley **Reverse:** Crowned rose

Date		F	VF	XF	Unc	BU
1998		—	—	—	0.60	—
1998 Proof	Est. 100,000	Value: 3.50				
Note: In sets only						
1999		—	—	—	0.60	—
1999 Proof	79,401	Value: 3.00				
2000		—	—	—	0.60	—
2000 Proof	Est. 100,000	Value: 3.25				
2001		—	—	—	0.60	—
2001 Proof	Est. 100,000	Value: 3.25				
2002		—	—	—	0.60	—
2003 Proof	—	Value: 3.25				

KM# 990a 20 PENCE **Weight:** 5.0000 g. **Composition:** 0.9250 Silver 0.1487 oz. ASW **Ruler:** Elizabeth II **Obverse:** Queen Elizabeth II **Reverse:** Crowned rose **Edge:** Plain **Shape:** 7-sided **Size:** 21.4 mm.

Date	Mintage	F	VF	XF	Unc	BU
2000 Proof	15,000	Value: 18.50				

KM# 1016 20 PENCE **Weight:** 3.2400 g. **Composition:** 0.9584 Silver .0998 oz. ASW **Ruler:** Elizabeth II **Subject:** Britannia Bullion **Obverse:** Queen's portrait **Reverse:** Stylized "Una and the Lion" **Edge:** Reeded **Size:** 16.5 mm.

Date	Mintage	F	VF	XF	Unc	BU
2001 Proof	15,000	Value: 25.00				

KM# 917 25 NEW PENCE **Composition:** Copper-Nickel **Ruler:** Elizabeth II **Subject:** Royal Silver Wedding Anniversary

Date	Mintage	F	VF	XF	Unc	BU
ND(1972)	7,452,000	—	—	0.65	1.75	—
ND(1972) Proof	150,000	Value: 7.50				

KM# 917a 25 NEW PENCE **Weight:** 28.2759 g. **Composition:** 0.9250 Silver .8409 oz. ASW **Ruler:** Elizabeth II

Date	Mintage	F	VF	XF	Unc	BU
ND(1972) Proof	100,000	Value: 25.00				

KM# 920 25 NEW PENCE **Composition:** Copper-Nickel **Ruler:** Elizabeth II **Subject:** Silver Jubilee of Reign

Date	Mintage	F	VF	XF	Unc	BU
1977	36,989,000	—	—	0.65	1.50	—
1977 Proof	194,000	Value: 6.00				
1977 (RMF)	—	—	—	—	4.00	—
Note: Seated in Royal Mint Folder and First Day Covers						
1981 (RMF)	—	—	—	—	—	—
Note: Reported, not confirmed						

KM# 920a 25 NEW PENCE **Weight:** 28.2759 g. **Composition:** 0.9250 Silver .8409 oz. ASW **Ruler:** Elizabeth II

Date	Mintage	F	VF	XF	Unc	BU
1977 Proof	377,000	Value: 20.00				

KM# 921 25 NEW PENCE **Composition:** Copper-Nickel **Ruler:** Elizabeth II **Subject:** 80th Birthday of Queen Mother

Date	Mintage	F	VF	XF	Unc	BU
ND(1980)	9,478,000	—	—	0.65	1.75	—

KM# 921a 25 NEW PENCE **Weight:** 28.2759 g. **Composition:** 0.9250 Silver .8409 oz. ASW **Ruler:** Elizabeth II

Date	Mintage	F	VF	XF	Unc	BU
ND(1980) Proof	84,000	Value: 55.00				

KM# 925 25 NEW PENCE **Composition:** Copper-Nickel **Ruler:** Elizabeth II **Subject:** Wedding of Prince Charles and Lady Diana

Date	Mintage	F	VF	XF	Unc	BU
1981	27,360,000	—	—	0.65	1.75	—

KM# 925a 25 NEW PENCE **Weight:** 28.2759 g. **Composition:** 0.9250 Silver .8409 oz. ASW **Ruler:** Elizabeth II

Date	Mintage	F	VF	XF	Unc	BU
1981 Proof	218,000	Value: 27.50				

KM# 913 50 NEW PENCE **Composition:** Copper-Nickel **Ruler:** Elizabeth II **Shape:** 7-sided

Date	Mintage	F	VF	XF	Unc	BU
1969	188,400,000	—	—	1.25	2.50	—
1970	19,461,000	—	—	1.25	3.50	—
1971 Proof	350,000	Value: 3.50				
1972 Proof	150,000	Value: 6.50				

Date	Mintage	F	VF	XF	Unc	BU
1974 Proof	100,000	Value: 3.00				
1975 Proof	100,000	Value: 3.00				
1976	43,747,000	—	—	1.75	3.50	—
1976 Proof	100,000	Value: 2.50				
1977	49,536,000	—	—	1.75	3.50	—
1977 Proof	194,000	Value: 2.50				
1978	72,005,000	—	—	1.75	3.50	—
1978 Proof	88,000	Value: 2.75				
1979	58,680,000	—	—	1.75	2.25	—
1979 Proof	81,000	Value: 2.75				
1980	89,086,000	—	—	1.75	2.25	—
1980 Proof	143,000	Value: 2.50				
1981	74,003,000	—	—	1.75	2.25	—
1981 Proof	100,000	Value: 2.50				

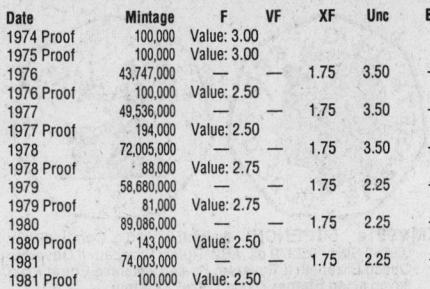

KM# 918 50 PENCE **Composition:** Copper-Nickel **Ruler:** Elizabeth II **Subject:** Entry Into E.E.C **Shape:** 7-sided

Date	Mintage	F	VF	XF	Unc	BU
1973	89,775,000	—	—	1.25	2.00	—
1973 Proof	357,000	Value: 6.00				

KM# 932 50 PENCE **Composition:** Copper-Nickel **Ruler:** Elizabeth II **Shape:** 7-sided

Date	F	VF	XF	Unc	BU
1982	—	—	1.25	1.75	—
1982 Proof 107,000	Value: 2.50				
1983	—	—	1.25	2.00	—
1983 Proof 125,000	Value: 2.50				
1984 In sets only	—	—	—	2.75	—
1984 Proof 125,000	Value: 2.50				

KM# 940.1 50 PENCE **Composition:** Copper-Nickel **Ruler:** Elizabeth II **Shape:** 7-sided

Date	Mintage	F	VF	XF	Unc	BU
1985	680,000	—	—	1.25	5.50	—
1985 Proof	102,000	Value: 2.75				
1986 In sets only	167,000	—	—	—	2.75	—
1986 Proof	125,000	Value: 2.75				
1987 In sets only	172,000	—	—	—	2.75	—
1987 Proof	89,000	Value: 2.75				
1988 In sets only	134,000	—	—	—	2.75	—
1988 Proof	125,000	Value: 3.50				
1989 In sets only	78,000	—	—	—	3.50	—
1989 Proof	100,000	Value: 2.75				
1990 In sets only	—	—	—	—	3.50	—
1990 Proof	100,000	Value: 6.00				
1991 In sets only	—	—	—	—	3.50	—
1991 Proof	—	Value: 6.50				
1992 In sets only	—	—	—	—	3.50	—
1992 Proof	—	Value: 6.50				
1993 In sets only	—	—	—	—	3.50	—
1993 Proof	—	Value: 3.50				
1995	—	—	—	—	2.75	—
1995 Proof	—	Value: 3.50				
1996	—	—	—	—	2.75	—
1996 Proof	—	Value: 3.50				
1997 In sets only	—	—	—	—	2.75	—
1997 Proof	—	Value: 3.50				

KM# 963 50 PENCE **Composition:** Copper-Nickel **Ruler:** Elizabeth II **Subject:** British Presidency of European Council of Ministers **Shape:** 7-sided

Date	Mintage	F	VF	XF	Unc	BU
ND(1992)	—	—	—	—	5.75	—
ND(1992) Proof	Est. 100,000	Value: 13.50				

KM# 963a 50 PENCE **Weight:** 13.5000 g. **Composition:** 0.9250 Silver .4014 oz. ASW **Ruler:** Elizabeth II

Date	Mintage	F	VF	XF	Unc	BU
ND(1992) Proof	Est. 35,000	Value: 30.00				

KM# 963b 50 PENCE **Weight:** 26.3200 g. **Composition:** 0.9170 Gold .7757 oz. AGW **Ruler:** Elizabeth II **Subject:** British Presidency of European Council of Ministers

Date	Mintage	F	VF	XF	Unc	BU
ND(1992) Proof	Est. 2,500	Value: 350				

KM# 966 50 PENCE **Composition:** Copper-Nickel **Ruler:** Elizabeth II **Subject:** 50th Anniversary of Normandy Invasion **Shape:** 7-sided

Date	Mintage	F	VF	XF	Unc	BU
1994	6,673,000	—	—	—	2.50	—
1994 Proof	—	Value: 13.50				

KM# 966a 50 PENCE **Weight:** 13.5000 g. **Composition:** 0.9250 Silver .4014 oz. ASW **Ruler:** Elizabeth II

Date	F	VF	XF	Unc	BU
1994 Proof —	Value: 45.00				

KM# 966b 50 PENCE **Weight:** 27.0000 g. **Composition:** 0.9250 Silver .8028 oz. ASW **Ruler:** Elizabeth II

Date	Mintage	F	VF	XF	Unc	BU
1994 Proof	10,000	Value: 85.00				

KM# 966c 50 PENCE **Weight:** 26.3200 g. **Composition:** 0.9170 Gold .7757 oz. AGW **Ruler:** Elizabeth II

Date	F	VF	XF	Unc	BU
1994 Proof —	Value: 500				

KM# 940.1a 50 PENCE **Composition:** Silver **Ruler:** Elizabeth II

Date	F	VF	XF	Unc	BU
1996 In Proof sets only —	Value: 30.00				

KM# 940.2 50 PENCE **Composition:** Copper-Nickel **Ruler:** Elizabeth II **Shape:** 7-sided **Note:** Reduced size.

Date	Mintage	F	VF	XF	Unc	BU
1997	456,364,000	—	—	—	2.75	—
1997 Proof	—	Value: 3.50				

KM# 979 50 PENCE **Weight:** 8.1100 g. **Composition:** 0.9580 Silver .2498 oz. ASW **Ruler:** Elizabeth II **Obverse:** Queen's portrait **Reverse:** Britannia in chariot **Note:** Similar to 2 Pounds, KM#981.

Date	Mintage	F	VF	XF	Unc	BU
1997 In proof sets only	Est. 15,000	Value: 25.00				

KM# 991 50 PENCE **Composition:** Copper-Nickel **Ruler:** Elizabeth II **Obverse:** Portrait of Queen Elizabeth II **Obv. Designer:** Rank-Broadley **Reverse:** Seated Brittania **Shape:** 7-sided

Date	Mintage	F	VF	XF	Unc	BU
1998		—	—	—	1.75	—
1998 Proof	Est. 100,000	Value: 2.50				
1999		—	—	—	1.75	—
1999 Proof	79,401	Value: 2.50				
2000		—	—	—	1.75	—
2000 Proof	Est. 100,000	Value: 2.50				
2001		—	—	—	1.75	—
2001 Proof	Est. 100,000	Value: 2.50				
2002		—	—	—	1.75	—
2003 Proof	—	Value: 2.50				

KM# 992 50 PENCE **Composition:** Copper-Nickel **Ruler:** Elizabeth II **Subject:** 25th Anniversary - Britain in the Common Market **Obverse:** Portrait of Queen Elizabeth II **Obv. Designer:** Rank-Broadley **Reverse:** Bouquet of stars **Shape:** 7-sided

Date	Mintage	F	VF	XF	Unc	BU
1998		—	—	—	2.75	—
1998 Proof	Est. 100,000	Value: 10.00				

KM# 992a 50 PENCE **Weight:** 8.0000 g. **Composition:** 0.9250 Silver .2379 oz. ASW **Ruler:** Elizabeth II

Date	Mintage	F	VF	XF	Unc	BU
1998 Proof	—	Value: 45.00				

KM# 996 50 PENCE **Composition:** Copper-Nickel **Ruler:** Elizabeth II **Subject:** National Health Service **Obverse:** Portrait of Queen Elizabeth II **Obv. Designer:** Rank-Broadley **Reverse:** Radiant hands **Shape:** 7-sided

Date	Mintage	F	VF	XF	Unc	BU
1998	5,001,000	—	—	—	2.75	—
1998 BU with folder	—	—	—	—	8.50	—
1998 Proof	—	Value: 14.00				

KM# 996a 50 PENCE **Weight:** 8.0000 g. **Composition:** 0.9250 Silver .2379 oz. ASW **Ruler:** Elizabeth II

Date	Mintage	F	VF	XF	Unc	BU
1998 Proof	Est. 25,000	Value: 45.00				

KM# 996b 50 PENCE **Weight:** 15.5000 g. **Composition:** 0.9167 Gold .4568 oz. AGW **Ruler:** Elizabeth II **Subject:** National Health Service **Obverse:** Portrait of Queen Elizabeth II **Obv. Designer:** Rank-Broadley **Reverse:** Radiant hands

Date	Mintage	F	VF	XF	Unc	BU
1998 Proof	Est. 1,500	Value: 475				

KM# 1004 50 PENCE **Composition:** Copper-Nickel **Ruler:** Elizabeth II **Subject:** Public Library **Obverse:** Bust Queen right **Reverse:** Open book above building and CD's **Edge:** Plain edge **Shape:** 7-sided

Date	Mintage	F	VF	XF	Unc	BU
2000		—	—	—	2.75	—
2000 Proof	100,000	Value: 15.00				

KM# 991a 50 PENCE **Weight:** 8.0000 g. **Composition:** 0.9250 Silver 0.2379 oz. ASW **Ruler:** Elizabeth II **Obverse:** Queen Elizabeth II **Reverse:** Seated Britannia **Edge:** Plain seven sided **Shape:** 7-sided **Size:** 27.3 mm.

Date	Mintage	F	VF	XF	Unc	BU
2000 Proof	15,000	Value: 25.00				

KM# 1017 50 PENCE **Weight:** 8.1100 g. **Composition:** 0.9584 Silver .2499 oz. ASW **Ruler:** Elizabeth II **Subject:** Britannia Bullion **Obverse:** Queen's portrait **Reverse:** Stylized "Una and the Lion" **Edge:** Reeded **Size:** 22 mm.

Date	Mintage	F	VF	XF	Unc	BU
2001 Proof	5,000	Value: 25.00				

KM# 1036 50 PENCE **Weight:** 8.0000 g. **Composition:** Copper Nickel **Ruler:** Elizabeth II **Subject:** Woman's Suffrage **Obverse:** Queen's portrait **Reverse:** Standing woman with banner **Edge:** Plain **Shape:** 7-sided **Size:** 27.3 mm.

Date		F	VF	XF	Unc	BU
2003		—	—	—	2.50	—
2003 Proof	—	Value: 10.00				

KM# 933 POUND **Composition:** Nickel-Brass **Ruler:** Elizabeth II **Edge Lettering:** DECUS ET TUTAMEN

Date	Mintage	F	VF	XF	Unc	BU
1983	443,054,000	—	—	2.25	4.00	5.50
1983 Proof	108,000	Value: 6.00				

KM# 933a POUND **Weight:** 9.5000 g. **Composition:** 0.9250 Silver .2825 oz. ASW **Ruler:** Elizabeth II

Date	Mintage	F	VF	XF	Unc	BU
1983 Proof	50,000	Value: 27.50				

KM# 934 POUND **Composition:** Nickel-Brass **Ruler:** Elizabeth II **Reverse:** Scottish thistle **Edge Lettering:** NEMO ME IMPUNE LACESSIT

Date	Mintage	F	VF	XF	Unc	BU
1984	146,257,000	—	—	2.25	4.00	5.50
1984 Proof	107,000	Value: 6.00				

KM# 934a POUND **Weight:** 9.5000 g. **Composition:** 0.9250 Silver .2825 oz. ASW **Ruler:** Elizabeth II

Date	Mintage	F	VF	XF	Unc	BU
1984 Proof	45,000	Value: 27.50				

KM# 941 POUND **Composition:** Nickel-Brass **Ruler:** Elizabeth II **Reverse:** Welsh leek **Edge Lettering:** PLEIDIOL WYF I'M GWLAD

Date	Mintage	F	VF	XF	Unc	BU
1985	228,431,000	—	—	2.00	3.50	5.00
1985 Proof	102,000	Value: 6.00				
1990	97,269,000	—	—	2.00	4.00	5.50
1990 Proof	100,000	Value: 6.00				

KM# 941a POUND **Weight:** 9.5000 g. **Composition:** 0.9250 Silver .2825 oz. ASW **Ruler:** Elizabeth II

Date	Mintage	F	VF	XF	Unc	BU
1985 Proof	50,000	Value: 27.50				
1990 Proof	Est. 25,000	Value: 36.50				

KM# 946 POUND **Composition:** Nickel-Brass **Ruler:** Elizabeth II **Reverse:** Northern Ireland - Blooming Flax

Date	Mintage	F	VF	XF	Unc	BU
1986	10,410,000	—	—	2.00	4.00	5.50
1986 Proof	125,000	Value: 6.00				
1991	38,444,000	—	—	2.00	4.00	5.50
1991 Proof	—	Value: 6.00				

KM# 946a POUND **Weight:** 9.5000 g. **Composition:** 0.9250 Silver .2825 oz. ASW **Ruler:** Elizabeth II

Date	Mintage	F	VF	XF	Unc	BU
1986 Proof	50,000	Value: 27.50				
1991 Proof	Est. 25,000	Value: 35.00				

KM# 948 POUND **Composition:** Nickel-Brass **Ruler:** Elizabeth II **Reverse:** Oak tree **Edge Lettering:** DECUS ET TUTAMEN

Date	Mintage	F	VF	XF	Unc	BU
1987	39,299,000	—	—	—	3.50	5.00
1987 Proof	125,000	Value: 6.00				
1992	36,320,000	—	—	—	4.00	5.50
1992 Proof	—	Value: 6.00				

KM# 948a POUND **Weight:** 9.5000 g. **Composition:** 0.9250 Silver .2825 oz. ASW **Ruler:** Elizabeth II

Date	Mintage	F	VF	XF	Unc	BU
1987 Proof	50,000	Value: 27.50				
1992 Proof	Est. 25,000	Value: 36.50				

KM# 954 POUND **Composition:** Nickel-Brass **Ruler:** Elizabeth II **Edge Lettering:** DECUS ET TUTAMEN

Date	Mintage	F	VF	XF	Unc	BU
1988		—	—	—	4.00	5.50
1988 Proof	Est. 125,000	Value: 7.00				

KM# 954a POUND **Weight:** 9.5000 g. **Composition:** 0.9250 Silver .2825 oz. ASW **Ruler:** Elizabeth II

Date	Mintage	F	VF	XF	Unc	BU
1988 Proof	Est. 50,000	Value: 40.00				

KM# 959 POUND **Composition:** Nickel-Brass **Ruler:** Elizabeth II **Obverse:** Queen's portrait **Reverse:** Scottish thistle **Edge Lettering:** NEMO ME IMPUNE LACESSIT

Date	Mintage	F	VF	XF	Unc	BU
1989	70,581,000	—	—	—	4.00	5.50
1989 Proof	100,000	Value: 6.00				

KM# 959a POUND **Weight:** 9.5000 g. **Composition:** 0.9250 Silver .2825 oz. ASW **Ruler:** Elizabeth II

Date	Mintage	F	VF	XF	Unc	BU
1989 Proof	Est. 25,000	Value: 32.50				

KM# 964 POUND **Composition:** Nickel-Brass **Ruler:** Elizabeth II **Reverse:** Royal coat of arms **Edge Lettering:** DECUS ET TUTAMEN

Date	Mintage	F	VF	XF	Unc	BU
1993	114,745,000	—	—	—	4.00	5.50
1993 Proof	—	Value: 6.00				

Date	Mintage	F	VF	XF	Unc	BU
1999 Proof	Est. 3,000	Value: 55.00				

KM# 779.2a 1/25 CROWN **Weight:** 1.2400 g. **Composition:** 0.9950 Platinum .0400 oz. APW **Reverse:** Rabbit reading, sparrow; without Chinese characters

Date	Mintage	F	VF	XF	Unc	BU
1999 Proof	Inc. above	Value: 55.00				

KM# 1016 1/25 CROWN **Weight:** 1.2441 g. **Composition:** 0.9999 Gold 0.04 oz. AGW **Subject:** Peter Pan **Obverse:** Bust of Queen Elizabeth Ii right. **Reverse:** Peter Pan and Tinkerbell flying above city. **Edge:** Reeded. **Size:** 13.92 mm.

Date	Mintage	F	VF	XF	Unc	BU
2002 Proof	10,000	Value: 49.50				

KM# 988 1/25 CROWN **Weight:** 1.2240 g. **Composition:** 0.9990 Gold 0.0393 oz. AGW **Subject:** Peter Rabbit Centennial **Obverse:** Bust of Queen Elizabeth II right **Reverse:** Peter Rabbit **Edge:** Reeded **Size:** 13.92 mm.

Date	Mintage	F	VF	XF	Unc	BU
2002 Proof	5,000	Value: 49.50				

KM# 988a 1/25 CROWN **Weight:** 1.2240 g. **Composition:** 0.9990 Platinum 0.0393 oz. APW **Subject:** Peter Rabbit Centennial **Obverse:** Bust of Queen Elizabeth II right **Reverse:** Peter Rabbit **Edge:** Reeded **Size:** 13.92 mm.

Date	Mintage	F	VF	XF	Unc	BU
2002 Proof	3,000	Value: 58.00				

KM# 51 1/10 CROWN **Weight:** 3.1100 g. **Composition:** 0.9999 Gold .1000 oz. AGW **Series:** Barcelona Olympics **Subject:** Chariot Racing **Note:** Similar to 1 Crown, KM#67.

Date	Mintage	F	VF	XF	Unc	BU
1991 Proof	Est. 20,000	Value: 75.00				
1992 Proof	Est. 20,000	Value: 90.00				

KM# 50 1/10 CROWN **Weight:** 3.1100 g. **Composition:** 0.9999 Gold .1000 oz. AGW **Series:** Barcelona Olympics **Subject:** Discus Thrower **Note:** Similar to 1 Crown, KM#66.

Date	Mintage	F	VF	XF	Unc	BU
1991 Proof	Est. 20,000	Value: 75.00				
1992 Proof	Est. 20,000	Value: 90.00				

KM# 52 1/10 CROWN **Weight:** 3.1100 g. **Composition:** 0.9999 Gold .1000 oz. AGW **Series:** Barcelona Olympics **Subject:** Runners **Note:** Similar to 1 Crown, KM#68.

Date	Mintage	F	VF	XF	Unc	BU
1991 Proof	Est. 20,000	Value: 75.00				
1992 Proof	Est. 20,000	Value: 90.00				

KM# 53 1/10 CROWN **Weight:** 3.1100 g. **Composition:** 0.9999 Gold .1000 oz. AGW **Series:** Barcelona Olympics **Subject:** Javelin Thrower **Note:** Similar to 1 Crown, KM#69.

Date	Mintage	F	VF	XF	Unc	BU
1991 Proof	Est. 20,000	Value: 75.00				
1992 Proof	Est. 20,000	Value: 90.00				

KM# 54 1/10 CROWN **Weight:** 3.1100 g. **Composition:** 0.9999 Gold .1000 oz. AGW **Series:** Barcelona Olympics **Subject:** Wrestlers **Note:** Similar to 1 Crown, KM#70.

Date	Mintage	F	VF	XF	Unc	BU
1991 Proof	Est. 20,000	Value: 75.00				
1992 Proof	Est. 20,000	Value: 90.00				

KM# 55 1/10 CROWN **Weight:** 3.1100 g. **Composition:** 0.9999 Gold .1000 oz. AGW **Series:** Barcelona Olympics **Subject:** Boxers **Note:** Similar to 1 Crown, KM#71.

Date	Mintage	F	VF	XF	Unc	BU
1991 Proof	Est. 20,000	Value: 75.00				
1992 Proof	Est. 20,000	Value: 90.00				

KM# 56 1/10 CROWN **Weight:** 3.1100 g. **Composition:** 0.9999 Gold .1000 oz. AGW **Series:** Barcelona Olympics **Subject:** Long Jumper **Note:** Similar to 1 Crown, KM#72.

Date	Mintage	F	VF	XF	Unc	BU
1991 Proof	Est. 20,000	Value: 75.00				
1992 Proof	Est. 20,000	Value: 90.00				

KM# 57 1/10 CROWN **Weight:** 3.1100 g. **Composition:** 0.9999 Gold .1000 oz. AGW **Series:** Barcelona Olympics **Subject:** Olympic Victor **Note:** Similar to 1 Crown, KM#73.

Date	Mintage	F	VF	XF	Unc	BU
1991 Proof	Est. 20,000	Value: 75.00				
1992 Proof	Est. 20,000	Value: 90.00				

KM# 125 1/10 CROWN **Weight:** 3.1100 g. **Composition:** 0.9999 Gold .1000 oz. AGW **Subject:** Japanese Royal Wedding

Date	Mintage	F	VF	XF	Unc	BU
1993 Proof	Est. 10,000	Value: 95.00				

KM# 207 1/10 CROWN **Weight:** 3.1100 g. **Composition:** 0.9990 Platinum .1000 oz. APW **Series:** Peter Rabbit Centennial **Subject:** Tiggy-Winkel **Reverse:** Mrs. Tiggy-Winkel ironing **Note:** Similar to 1 Crown, KM#205.

Date	Mintage	F	VF	XF	Unc	BU
1993 Proof	Est. 20,000	Value: 80.00				

KM# 211 1/10 CROWN **Weight:** 3.1100 g. **Composition:** 0.9990 Platinum .1000 oz. APW **Series:** Peter Rabbit Centennial **Subject:** Jeremy Fisher **Reverse:** Jeremy Fisher fishing **Note:** Similar to 1 Crown, KM#209.

Date	Mintage	F	VF	XF	Unc	BU
1993 Proof	Est. 20,000	Value: 80.00				

KM# 215 1/10 CROWN **Weight:** 3.1100 g. **Composition:** 0.9990 Platinum .1000 oz. APW **Series:** Peter Rabbit Centennial **Subject:** Tom Kitten **Reverse:** Tom Kitten with mother cat **Note:** Similar to 1 Crown, KM#213.

Date	Mintage	F	VF	XF	Unc	BU
1993 Proof	Est. 20,000	Value: 80.00				

KM# 219 1/10 CROWN **Weight:** 3.1100 g. **Composition:** 0.9990 Platinum .1000 oz. APW **Series:** Peter Rabbit Centennial **Subject:** Benjamin Bunny **Reverse:** Benjamin Bunny wearing hat and holding coat **Note:** Similar to 1 Crown, KM#217.

Date	Mintage	F	VF	XF	Unc	BU
1993 Proof	Est. 20,000	Value: 80.00				

KM# 223 1/10 CROWN **Weight:** 3.1100 g. **Composition:** 0.9990 Platinum .1000 oz. APW **Series:** Peter Rabbit Centennial **Subject:** Jemima Puddle-Duck **Reverse:** Jemima Puddle Duck talking with fox **Note:** Similar to 1 Crown, KM#221.

Date	Mintage	F	VF	XF	Unc	BU
1993 Proof	Est. 20,000	Value: 80.00				

KM# 203 1/10 CROWN **Weight:** 3.1100 g. **Composition:** 0.9999 Gold .1000 oz. AGW **Series:** Peter Rabbit Centennial **Subject:** Peter Rabbit **Obverse:** Queen's portrait **Reverse:** Peter Rabbit eating carrots **Note:** Similar to 1 Crown, KM#201.

Date	Mintage	F	VF	XF	Unc	BU
1993 Proof	Est. 20,000	Value: 80.00				

KM# 203a 1/10 CROWN **Weight:** 3.1100 g. **Composition:** 0.9990 Platinum .1000 oz. APW **Series:** Peter Rabbit Centennial **Subject:** Peter Rabbit **Obverse:** Queen's portrait **Reverse:** Peter Rabbit eating carrots

Date	Mintage	F	VF	XF	Unc	BU
1993 Proof	Est. 5,000	Value: 120				

KM# 439 1/10 CROWN **Weight:** 3.1100 g. **Composition:** 0.9990 Platinum .1000 oz. APW **Series:** Peter Rabbit Centennial **Subject:** Mother and Bunnies **Note:** Similar to 1 Crown, KM#444.

Date	Mintage	F	VF	XF	Unc	BU
1994 Proof	Est. 20,000	Value: 95.00				

KM# 439a 1/10 CROWN **Weight:** 3.1103 g. **Composition:** 0.9950 Platinum .1000 oz. APW **Series:** Peter Rabbit Centennial **Subject:** Mother and Bunnies **Note:** Similar to 1 Crown, KM#444.

Date	Mintage	F	VF	XF	Unc	BU
1994 Proof	Est. 5,000	Value: 120				

KM# 446 1/10 CROWN **Weight:** 3.1103 g. **Composition:** 0.9999 Gold .1000 oz. AGW **Subject:** Lord Buddha **Note:** Similar to 1 Crown, KM#449.

Date	Mintage	F	VF	XF	Unc	BU
1996 Proof	Est. 10,000	Value: 95.00				

KM# 455 1/10 CROWN **Weight:** 3.1103 g. **Composition:** 0.9999 Gold .1000 oz. AGW **Series:** Centenary of the Cinema **Subject:** Wizard of Oz **Note:** Similar to 1 Crown, KM#457.

Date	Mintage	F	VF	XF	Unc	BU
1996 Proof	Est. 20,000	Value: 80.00				

KM# 459 1/10 CROWN **Weight:** 3.1103 g. **Composition:** 0.9999 Gold .1000 oz. AGW **Series:** Centenary of the Cinema **Subject:** Marx Brothers **Note:** Similar to 1 Crown, KM#461.

Date	Mintage	F	VF	XF	Unc	BU
1996 Proof	Est. 20,000	Value: 80.00				

KM# 463 1/10 CROWN **Weight:** 3.1103 g. **Composition:** 0.9999 Gold .1000 oz. AGW **Series:** Centenary of the Cinema **Subject:** Elvis Presley **Note:** Similar to 1 Crown, KM#465.

Date	Mintage	F	VF	XF	Unc	BU
1996 Proof	Est. 20,000	Value: 80.00				

KM# 467 1/10 CROWN **Weight:** 3.1103 g. **Composition:** 0.9999 Gold .1000 oz. AGW **Series:** Centenary of the Cinema **Subject:** Casablanca **Note:** Similar to 1 Crown, KM#469.

Date	Mintage	F	VF	XF	Unc	BU
1996 Proof	Est. 20,000	Value: 80.00				

KM# 471 1/10 CROWN **Weight:** 3.1103 g. **Composition:** 0.9999 Gold .1000 oz. AGW **Series:** Centenary of the Cinema **Subject:** E.T. **Note:** Similar to 1 Crown, KM#473.

Date	Mintage	F	VF	XF	Unc	BU
1996 Proof	Est. 20,000	Value: 80.00				

KM# 475 1/10 CROWN **Weight:** 3.1103 g. **Composition:** 0.9999 Gold .1000 oz. AGW **Series:** Centenary of the Cinema **Subject:** Alfred Hitchcock **Note:** Similar to 1 Crown, KM#477.

Date	Mintage	F	VF	XF	Unc	BU
1996 Proof	Est. 20,000	Value: 80.00				

KM# 391 1/10 CROWN **Weight:** 3.1103 g. **Composition:** 0.9999 Gold .1000 oz. AGW **Series:** Centenary of the Cinema **Subject:** Grace Kelly **Note:** Similar to 1 Crown, KM#393.

Date	Mintage	F	VF	XF	Unc	BU
1996 Proof	Est. 20,000	Value: 80.00				

KM# 396 1/10 CROWN **Weight:** 3.1103 g. **Composition:** 0.9999 Gold .1000 oz. AGW **Series:** Centenary of the Cinema **Subject:** James Dean **Note:** Similar to 1 Crown, KM#398.

Date	Mintage	F	VF	XF	Unc	BU
1996 Proof	Est. 20,000	Value: 80.00				

KM# 401 1/10 CROWN **Weight:** 3.1103 g. **Composition:** 0.9999 Gold .1000 oz. AGW **Series:** Centenary of the Cinema **Subject:** Marilyn Monroe **Note:** Similar to 1 Crown, KM#403.

Date	Mintage	F	VF	XF	Unc	BU
1996 Proof	Est. 20,000	Value: 80.00				

KM# 411 1/10 CROWN **Weight:** 3.1103 g. **Composition:** 0.9999 Gold .1000 oz. AGW **Series:** Centenary of the Cinema **Subject:** Bruce Lee **Note:** Similar to 1 Crown, KM#413.

Date	Mintage	F	VF	XF	Unc	BU
1996 Proof	Est. 20,000	Value: 80.00				

KM# 416 1/10 CROWN **Weight:** 3.1103 g. **Composition:** 0.9999 Gold .1000 oz. AGW **Series:** Centenary of the Cinema **Subject:** Charlie Chaplin **Note:** Similar to 1 Crown, KM#418.

Date	Mintage	F	VF	XF	Unc	BU
1996 Proof	Est. 20,000	Value: 80.00				

KM# 421 1/10 CROWN **Weight:** 3.1103 g. **Composition:** 0.9999 Gold .1000 oz. AGW **Series:** Centenary of the Cinema **Subject:** Gone With The Wind **Note:** Similar to 1 Crown, KM#423.

Date	Mintage	F	VF	XF	Unc	BU
1996 Proof	Est. 20,000	Value: 80.00				

KM# 426 1/10 CROWN **Weight:** 3.1103 g. **Composition:** 0.9999 Gold .1000 oz. AGW **Series:** Centenary of the Cinema **Subject:** The Flintstones **Note:** Similar to 1 Crown, KM#428.

Date	Mintage	F	VF	XF	Unc	BU
1996 Proof	Est. 20,000	Value: 80.00				

KM# A453 1/10 CROWN **Weight:** 3.1103 g. **Composition:** 0.9999 Gold .1000 oz. AGW **Series:** Centenary of the Cinema **Subject:** James Dean

Date	Mintage	F	VF	XF	Unc	BU
1996 Proof	20,000	Value: 95.00				

KM# 369 1/10 CROWN **Weight:** 3.1103 g. **Composition:** 0.9999 Gold .1000 oz. AGW **Subject:** Roses **Note:** Similar to 1 Crown, KM#373.

Date	Mintage	F	VF	XF	Unc	BU
1996 Proof	Est. 20,000	Value: 80.00				

KM# 377 1/10 CROWN **Weight:** 3.1103 g. **Composition:** 0.9999 Gold .1000 oz. AGW **Series:** Peter Rabbit Centennial **Subject:** Rabbit Escaping

Date	Mintage	F	VF	XF	Unc	BU
1996 Proof	Est. 20,000	Value: 80.00				

KM# 406 1/10 CROWN **Weight:** 3.1103 g. **Composition:** 0.9999 Gold .1000 oz. AGW **Series:** Centenary of the Cinema **Subject:** Audrey Hepburn **Note:** Similar to 1 Crown, KM#408.

Date	Mintage	F	VF	XF	Unc	BU
1996 Proof	Est. 20,000	Value: 80.00				

KM# 406a 1/10 CROWN **Weight:** 3.1103 g. **Composition:** 0.9950 Platinum .1000 oz. APW **Series:** Centenary of the Cinema **Subject:** Audrey Hepburn

Date	Mintage	F	VF	XF	Unc	BU
1996 Proof	Est. 1,000	Value: 135				

KM# 377a 1/10 CROWN **Weight:** 3.1259 g. **Composition:** 0.9950 Platinum .1000 oz. APW **Series:** Peter Rabbit Centennial **Subject:** Rabbit Escaping **Note:** Similar to 1 Crown, KM#382.

Date	Mintage	F	VF	XF	Unc	BU
1996 Proof	Est. 10,000	Value: 95.00				

KM# 538 1/10 CROWN **Weight:** 3.1100 g. **Composition:** 0.9999 Gold .1000 oz. AGW **Subject:** Peonies **Note:** Similar to 1 Crown, KM#540.

Date	Mintage	F	VF	XF	Unc	BU
1997 Proof	Est. 20,000	Value: 75.00				

KM# 542 1/10 CROWN **Weight:** 3.1100 g. **Composition:** 0.9999 Gold .1000 oz. AGW **Subject:** Nefertiti **Note:** Similar to 1 Crown, KM#544.

Date	Mintage	F	VF	XF	Unc	BU
1997 Proof	Est. 7,500	Value: 75.00				

KM# 546 1/10 CROWN **Weight:** 3.1100 g. **Composition:** 0.9999 Gold .1000 oz. AGW **Subject:** Cleopatra **Note:** Similar to 1 Crown, KM#548.

Date	Mintage	F	VF	XF	Unc	BU
1997 Proof	Est. 7,500	Value: 75.00				

KM# 550 1/10 CROWN **Weight:** 3.1100 g. **Composition:** 0.9999 Gold .1000 oz. AGW **Subject:** Europa **Note:** Similar to 1 Crown, KM#552.

Date	Mintage	F	VF	XF	Unc	BU
1997 Proof	Est. 7,500	Value: 75.00				

KM# 554 1/10 CROWN **Weight:** 3.1100 g. **Composition:** 0.9999 Gold .1000 oz. AGW **Subject:** Liberty **Note:** Similar to 1 Crown, KM#556.

Date	Mintage	F	VF	XF	Unc	BU
1997 Proof	Est. 7,500	Value: 75.00				

KM# 520 1/10 CROWN **Weight:** 3.1103 g. **Composition:** 0.9999 Gold .1000 oz. AGW **Subject:** Tale of Peter Rabbit **Note:** Similar to 1 Crown, KM#525.

Date	Mintage	F	VF	XF	Unc	BU
1997 Proof	Est. 20,000	Value: 80.00				

KM# 520a 1/10 CROWN **Weight:** 3.1259 g. **Composition:** 0.9950 Platinum .1000 oz. APW **Subject:** Tale of Peter Rabbit

Date	Mintage	F	VF	XF	Unc	BU
1997 Proof	Est. 5,000	Value: 120				

KM# 666 1/10 CROWN **Weight:** 3.1100 g. **Composition:** 0.9999 Gold .1000 oz. AGW **Subject:** Brittania **Obverse:** Queen's portrait **Reverse:** Helmeted Brittania **Note:** Similar to 1 Crown, KM#674.

Date	Mintage	F	VF	XF	Unc	BU
1998 Proof	Est. 7,500	Value: 90.00				

KM# 667 1/10 CROWN **Weight:** 3.1100 g. **Composition:** 0.9999 Gold .1000 oz. AGW **Subject:** Juno **Obverse:** Queen's portrait **Reverse:** Facing portrait of Juno **Note:** Similar to 1 Crown, KM#675.

Date	Mintage	F	VF	XF	Unc	BU
1998 Proof	Est. 7,500	Value: 90.00				

KM# 668 1/10 CROWN **Weight:** 3.1100 g. **Composition:** 0.9999 Gold .1000 oz. AGW **Subject:** Athena **Obverse:** Queen's portrait **Reverse:** Helmeted Athena **Note:** Similar to 1 Crown, KM#676.

Date	Mintage	F	VF	XF	Unc	BU
1998 Proof	Est. 7,500	Value: 90.00				

KM# 669 1/10 CROWN **Weight:** 3.1100 g. **Composition:** 0.9999 Gold .1000 oz. AGW **Subject:** Arethusa **Obverse:** Queen's portrait **Reverse:** Portrait with dolphins **Note:** Similar to 1 Crown, KM#677.

Date	Mintage	F	VF	XF	Unc	BU
1998 Proof	Est. 7,500	Value: 90.00				

KM# 658 1/10 CROWN **Weight:** 3.1100 g. **Composition:** 0.9999 Gold .1000 oz. AGW **Subject:** Chrysanthemum **Obverse:** Queen's portrait **Reverse:** Three blossoms **Note:** Similar to 1 Crown, KM#661.

Date	Mintage	F	VF	XF	Unc	BU
1998 Proof	Est. 20,000	Value: 90.00				

KM# 679 1/10 CROWN **Weight:** 3.1100 g. **Composition:** 0.9999 Gold .1000 oz. AGW **Subject:** Paddington Bear **Obverse:** Queen's portrait **Reverse:** Bear with suitcase **Note:** Similar to 1 Crown, KM#682.

Date	Mintage	F	VF	XF	Unc	BU
1998 Proof	Est. 7,500	Value: 90.00				

KM# 651 1/10 CROWN **Weight:** 3.1100 g. **Composition:** 0.9999 Gold .1000 oz. AGW **Subject:** Tale of Peter Rabbit **Obverse:** Queen's portrait **Reverse:** Peter Rabbit **Note:** Similar to 1 Crown, KM#656.

Date	Mintage	F	VF	XF	Unc	BU
1998 Proof	Est. 20,000	Value: 90.00				

KM#651a 1/10 CROWN **Weight:** 3.1103 g. **Composition:** 0.9950 Platinum .1000 oz. APW **Subject:** Tale of Peter Rabbit **Obverse:** Queen's portrait **Reverse:** Peter Rabbit

Date	Mintage	F	VF	XF	Unc	BU
1998 Proof	Est. 5,000	Value: 120				

KM#679a 1/10 CROWN **Weight:** 3.1103 g. **Composition:** 0.9950 Platinum .1000 oz. APW **Subject:** Paddington Bear **Obverse:** Queen's portrait **Reverse:** Bear with suitcase

Date	Mintage	F	VF	XF	Unc	BU
1998 Proof	Est. 5,000	Value: 120				

KM#1017 1/10 CROWN **Weight:** 3.1104 g. **Composition:** 0.9999 Gold 0.1 oz. AGW **Subject:** Peter Pan **Obverse:** Bust of Queen Elizabeth II right. **Reverse:** Peter Pan and Tinkerbell flying above city. **Edge:** Reeded. **Size:** 17.95 mm.

Date	Mintage	F	VF	XF	Unc	BU
2002 Proof	7,500	Value: 95.00				

KM# 989 1/10 CROWN **Weight:** 3.1100 g. **Composition:** 0.9990 Gold 0.0999 oz. AGW **Subject:** Peter Rabbit Centennial **Obverse:** Bust of Queen Elizabeth II right **Reverse:** Peter Rabbit **Edge:** Reeded **Size:** 17.95 mm.

Date	Mintage	F	VF	XF	Unc	BU
2002 Proof	5,000	Value: 95.00				

KM#989a 1/10 CROWN **Weight:** 3.1100 g. **Composition:** 0.9990 Platinum 0.0999 oz. APW **Subject:** Peter Rabbit Centennial **Obverse:** Bust of Queen Elizabeth II right **Reverse:** Peter Rabbit **Edge:** Reeded **Size:** 17395 mm.

Date	Mintage	F	VF	XF	Unc	BU
2002 Proof	2,000	Value: 95.00				

KM# 48 1/5 CROWN **Weight:** 6.2200 g. **Composition:** 0.9990 Gold .2000 oz. AGW **Subject:** Penny Black Stamp **Note:** Similar to 1 Crown, KM#49.

Date	Mintage	F	VF	XF	Unc	BU
1990 Proof	Est. 5,000	Value: 215				

KM# 77 1/5 CROWN **Weight:** 6.2200 g. **Composition:** 0.9999 Gold .2000 oz. AGW **Series:** World Cup Soccer **Reverse:** Map of Italy **Note:** Similar to 1 Crown, KM#34.

Date	Mintage	F	VF	XF	Unc	BU
1990 Proof	Est. 5,000	Value: 215				

KM#76a 1/5 CROWN **Weight:** 6.2200 g. **Composition:** 0.9950 Platinum .2000 oz. APW **Series:** World Cup Soccer **Reverse:** Italian Flag

Date	Mintage	F	VF	XF	Unc	BU
1990 Proof	Est. 1,000	Value: 325				

KM# 76 1/5 CROWN **Weight:** 6.2200 g. **Composition:** 0.9990 Gold .2000 oz. AGW **Series:** World Cup Soccer **Reverse:** Italian Flag **Note:** Similar to 1 Crown, KM#33.

Date	Mintage	F	VF	XF	Unc	BU
1990 Proof	Est. 5,000	Value: 215				

KM#77a 1/5 CROWN **Weight:** 6.2200 g. **Composition:** 0.9950 Platinum .2000 oz. APW **Series:** World Cup Soccer **Reverse:** Map of Italy

Date	Mintage	F	VF	XF	Unc	BU
1990 Proof	Est. 1,000	Value: 325				

KM# 78 1/5 CROWN **Weight:** 6.2200 g. **Composition:** 0.9999 Gold .2000 oz. AGW **Series:** World Cup Soccer **Reverse:** Goalie catching ball **Note:** Similar to 1 Crown, KM#35.

Date	Mintage	F	VF	XF	Unc	BU
1990 Proof	Est. 5,000	Value: 215				

KM#78a 1/5 CROWN **Weight:** 6.2200 g. **Composition:** 0.9950 Platinum .2000 oz. APW **Series:** World Cup Soccer **Reverse:** Goalie catching ball

Date	Mintage	F	VF	XF	Unc	BU
1990 Proof	Est. 1,000	Value: 325				

KM# 79 1/5 CROWN **Weight:** 6.2200 g. **Composition:** 0.9999 Gold .2000 oz. AGW **Series:** World Cup Soccer **Reverse:** One player **Note:** Similar to 1 Crown, KM#36.

Date	Mintage	F	VF	XF	Unc	BU
1990 Proof	Est. 5,000	Value: 215				

KM#79a 1/5 CROWN **Weight:** 6.2200 g. **Composition:** 0.9950 Platinum .2000 oz. APW **Series:** World Cup Soccer **Reverse:** One player

Date	Mintage	F	VF	XF	Unc	BU
1990 Proof	Est. 1,000	Value: 325				

KM# 80 1/5 CROWN **Weight:** 6.2200 g. **Composition:** 0.9999 Gold .2000 oz. AGW **Series:** World Cup Soccer **Reverse:** Two players **Note:** Similar to 1 Crown, KM#37.

Date	Mintage	F	VF	XF	Unc	BU
1990 Proof	Est. 5,000	Value: 215				

KM#80a 1/5 CROWN **Weight:** 6.2200 g. **Composition:** 0.9950 Platinum .2000 oz. APW **Series:** World Cup Soccer **Reverse:** Two players

Date	Mintage	F	VF	XF	Unc	BU
1990 Proof	Est. 1,000	Value: 325				

KM# 81 1/5 CROWN **Weight:** 6.2200 g. **Composition:** 0.9999 Gold .2000 oz. AGW **Series:** World Cup Soccer **Reverse:** Three players **Note:** Similar to 1 Crown, KM#38.

Date	Mintage	F	VF	XF	Unc	BU
1990 Proof	Est. 5,000	Value: 215				

KM#81a 1/5 CROWN **Weight:** 6.2200 g. **Composition:** 0.9950 Platinum .2000 oz. APW **Series:** World Cup Soccer **Reverse:** Three players

Date	Mintage	F	VF	XF	Unc	BU
1990 Proof	Est. 1,000	Value: 325				

KM# 58 1/5 CROWN **Weight:** 6.2200 g. **Composition:** 0.9999 Gold .2000 oz. AGW **Series:** Barcelona Olympics **Reverse:** Discus thrower **Note:** Similar to 1 Crown, KM#66.

Date	Mintage	F	VF	XF	Unc	BU
1991 Proof	Est. 5,000	Value: 150				
1992 Proof	Est. 5,000	Value: 150				

KM# 59 1/5 CROWN **Weight:** 6.2200 g. **Composition:** 0.9999 Gold .2000 oz. AGW **Series:** Barcelona Olympics **Reverse:** Chariot racing **Note:** Similar to 1 Crown, KM#67.

Date	Mintage	F	VF	XF	Unc	BU
1991 Proof	Est. 5,000	Value: 150				
1992 Proof	Est. 5,000	Value: 150				

KM# 62 1/5 CROWN **Weight:** 6.2200 g. **Composition:** 0.9999 Gold .2000 oz. AGW **Series:** Barcelona Olympics **Reverse:** Wrestlers **Note:** Similar to 1 Crown, KM#70.

Date	Mintage	F	VF	XF	Unc	BU
1991 Proof	Est. 5,000	Value: 150				
1992 Proof	Est. 5,000	Value: 150				

KM# 63 1/5 CROWN **Weight:** 6.2200 g. **Composition:** 0.9999 Gold .2000 oz. AGW **Series:** Barcelona Olympics **Reverse:** Boxers **Note:** Similar to 1 Crown, KM#71.

Date	Mintage	F	VF	XF	Unc	BU
1991 Proof	Est. 5,000	Value: 150				
1992 Proof	Est. 5,000	Value: 150				

KM# 64 1/5 CROWN **Weight:** 6.2200 g. **Composition:** 0.9999 Gold .2000 oz. AGW **Series:** Barcelona Olympics **Reverse:** Long jumper **Note:** Similar to 1 Crown, KM#72.

Date	Mintage	F	VF	XF	Unc	BU
1991 Proof	Est. 5,000	Value: 150				
1992 Proof	Est. 5,000	Value: 150				

KM# 65 1/5 CROWN **Weight:** 6.2200 g. **Composition:** 0.9999 Gold .2000 oz. AGW **Series:** Barcelona Olympics **Reverse:** Olympic victor **Note:** Similar to 1 Crown, KM#73.

Date	Mintage	F	VF	XF	Unc	BU
1991 Proof	Est. 5,000	Value: 150				
1992 Proof	—	Value: 150				

KM# 60 1/5 CROWN **Weight:** 6.2200 g. **Composition:** 0.9999 Gold .2000 oz. AGW **Series:** Barcelona Olympics **Reverse:** Runners **Note:** Similar to 1 Crown, KM#68.

Date	Mintage	F	VF	XF	Unc	BU
1991 Proof	Est. 5,000	Value: 150				
1992 Proof	Est. 5,000	Value: 150				

KM# 61 1/5 CROWN **Weight:** 6.2200 g. **Composition:** 0.9999 Gold .2000 oz. AGW **Series:** Barcelona Olympics **Reverse:** Javelin thrower **Note:** Similar to 1 Crown, KM#69.

Date	Mintage	F	VF	XF	Unc	BU
1991 Proof	Est. 5,000	Value: 150				
1992 Proof	Est. 5,000	Value: 150				

KM#58a 1/5 CROWN **Weight:** 6.2200 g. **Composition:** 0.9950 Platinum .2000 oz. APW **Series:** Barcelona Olympics **Reverse:** Discus thrower

Date	Mintage	F	VF	XF	Unc	BU
1991 Proof	Est. 1,000	Value: 275				

KM#59a 1/5 CROWN **Weight:** 6.2200 g. **Composition:** 0.9950 Platinum .2000 oz. APW **Series:** Barcelona Olympics **Reverse:** Chariot racing

Date	Mintage	F	VF	XF	Unc	BU
1991 Proof	Est. 1,000	Value: 275				

KM#60a 1/5 CROWN **Weight:** 6.2200 g. **Composition:** 0.9950 Platinum .2000 oz. APW **Series:** Barcelona Olympics **Reverse:** Runners

Date	Mintage	F	VF	XF	Unc	BU
1991 Proof	Est. 1,000	Value: 275				

KM#61a 1/5 CROWN **Weight:** 6.2200 g. **Composition:** 0.9950 Platinum .2000 oz. APW **Series:** Barcelona Olympics **Reverse:** Javelin thrower

Date	Mintage	F	VF	XF	Unc	BU
1991 Proof	Est. 1,000	Value: 275				

KM#62a 1/5 CROWN **Weight:** 6.2200 g. **Composition:** 0.9950 Platinum .2000 oz. APW **Series:** Barcelona Olympics **Reverse:** Wrestlers

Date	Mintage	F	VF	XF	Unc	BU
1991 Proof	Est. 1,000	Value: 275				

KM#63a 1/5 CROWN **Weight:** 6.2200 g. **Composition:** 0.9950 Platinum .2000 oz. APW **Series:** Barcelona Olympics **Reverse:** Boxers

Date	Mintage	F	VF	XF	Unc	BU
1991 Proof	Est. 1,000	Value: 275				

KM#64a 1/5 CROWN **Weight:** 6.2200 g. **Composition:** 0.9950 Platinum .2000 oz. APW **Series:** Barcelona Olympics **Reverse:** Long jumper

Date	Mintage	F	VF	XF	Unc	BU
1991 Proof	Est. 1,000	Value: 275				

KM#65a 1/5 CROWN **Weight:** 6.2200 g. **Composition:** 0.9950 Platinum .2000 oz. APW **Series:** Barcelona Olympics **Reverse:** Olympic victor

Date	Mintage	F	VF	XF	Unc	BU
1991 Proof	Est. 1,000	Value: 275				

KM#150 1/5 CROWN **Weight:** 6.2200 g. **Composition:** 0.9999 Gold .2000 oz. AGW **Series:** Preserve Planet Earth **Subject:** Cetiosaurus **Obverse:** Queen's portrait **Reverse:** Long-necked dinosaur

Date	Mintage	F	VF	XF	Unc	BU
1993 Proof	Est. 5,000	Value: 125				

KM#152 1/5 CROWN **Weight:** 6.2200 g. **Composition:** 0.9999 Gold .2000 oz. AGW **Series:** Preserve Planet Earth **Subject:** Stegosaurus **Obverse:** Queen's portrait **Reverse:** Dinosaur with pointed plates along spine

Date	Mintage	F	VF	XF	Unc	BU
1993 Proof	Est. 5,000	Value: 135				

KM#153 1/5 CROWN **Weight:** 6.2200 g. **Composition:** 0.9999 Gold .2000 oz. AGW **Series:** WWII Warships **Reverse:** USS Philadelphia

Date	Mintage	F	VF	XF	Unc	BU
1993 Proof	Est. 5,000	Value: 165				

KM#154 1/5 CROWN **Weight:** 6.2200 g. **Composition:** 0.9999 Gold .2000 oz. AGW **Series:** WWII Warships **Reverse:** USS McLanahan

Date	Mintage	F	VF	XF	Unc	BU
1993 Proof	Est. 5,000	Value: 165				

KM#155 1/5 CROWN **Weight:** 6.2200 g. **Composition:** 0.9999 Gold .2000 oz. AGW **Series:** WWII Warships **Reverse:** HNLMS Isaac Sweers

Date	Mintage	F	VF	XF	Unc	BU
1993 Proof	Est. 5,000	Value: 165				

KM#156 1/5 CROWN **Weight:** 6.2200 g. **Composition:** 0.9999 Gold .2000 oz. AGW **Series:** WWII Warships **Reverse:** USS Weehawken

Date	Mintage	F	VF	XF	Unc	BU
1993 Proof	Est. 5,000	Value: 165				

KM# 964a POUND **Weight:** 9.5000 g. **Composition:** 0.9250 Silver .2825 oz. ASW **Ruler:** Elizabeth II

Date	Mintage	F	VF	XF	Unc	BU
1993 Proof	Est. 25,000	Value: 40.00				

KM# 967 POUND **Composition:** Nickel-Brass **Ruler:** Elizabeth II **Reverse:** Scotland arms **Edge Lettering:** NEMO ME IMPUNE LACESSIT

Date	Mintage	F	VF	XF	Unc	BU
1994	29,753,000	—	—	—	3.50	5.00
1994 Proof	—	Value: 6.00				

KM# 967a POUND **Weight:** 9.5000 g. **Composition:** 0.9250 Silver .2825 oz. ASW **Ruler:** Elizabeth II

Date	Mintage	F	VF	XF	Unc	BU
1994 Proof	Est. 25,000	Value: 60.00				

KM# 969 POUND **Composition:** Nickel-Brass **Ruler:** Elizabeth II **Reverse:** Wales - Welsh Dragon **Edge Lettering:** PLEIDIOL WYF I'M GWLAD

Date	Mintage	F	VF	XF	Unc	BU
1995	34,504,000	—	—	—	3.50	5.00
1995 Proof	100,000	Value: 6.00				

KM# 969a POUND **Weight:** 9.5000 g. **Composition:** 0.9250 Silver .2825 oz. ASW **Ruler:** Elizabeth II

Date	Mintage	F	VF	XF	Unc	BU
1995 Proof	27,000	Value: 37.50				

KM# 972 POUND **Composition:** Nickel-Brass **Ruler:** Elizabeth II **Reverse:** Northern Ireland - Celtic Collar on Cross **Edge Lettering:** DECUS ET TUTAMEN

Date	Mintage	F	VF	XF	Unc	BU
1996	—	—	—	—	3.50	5.00
1996 Proof	Est. 100,000	Value: 6.00				

KM# 972a POUND **Weight:** 9.5000 g. **Composition:** 0.9250 Silver .2825 oz. ASW **Ruler:** Elizabeth II

Date	Mintage	F	VF	XF	Unc	BU
1996 Proof	40,000	Value: 37.50				

KM# 975 POUND **Composition:** Nickel-Brass **Ruler:** Elizabeth II **Obverse:** Queen's portrait **Reverse:** Plantagenet lions **Edge Lettering:** DECUS ET TUTAMEN

Date	Mintage	F	VF	XF	Unc	BU
1997	—	—	—	—	3.50	5.00
1997 Proof	Est. 100,000	Value: 6.00				

KM# 975a POUND **Weight:** 9.5000 g. **Composition:** 0.9250 Silver .2825 oz. ASW **Ruler:** Elizabeth II **Edge Lettering:** DECUS ET TUTAMEN

Date	Mintage	F	VF	XF	Unc	BU
1997 Proof	30,000	Value: 40.00				

KM# 980 POUND **Weight:** 16.2200 g. **Composition:** 0.9580 Silver .4996 oz. ASW **Ruler:** Elizabeth II **Obverse:** Queen's portrait **Reverse:** Britannia in chariot **Note:** Similar to 2 Pounds, KM#981.

Date	Mintage	F	VF	XF	Unc	BU
1997 Proof	Est. 15,000	Value: 40.00				

KM# 993 POUND **Composition:** Nickel-Brass **Ruler:** Elizabeth II **Obverse:** Portrait of Queen Elizabeth II **Obv. Designer:** Rank-Broadley **Reverse:** British Royal Arms **Edge Lettering:** DECUS ET TUTAMEN

Date	F	VF	XF	Unc	BU
1998	—	—	—	8.50	10.00
2003 Proof	—	—	—	4.50	6.00

KM# 993a POUND **Weight:** 9.5000 g. **Composition:** 0.9250 Silver .2825 oz. ASW **Ruler:** Elizabeth II

Date	Mintage	F	VF	XF	Unc	BU
1998	13,863	—	—	—	40.00	—

KM# 998 POUND **Composition:** Nickel-Brass **Ruler:** Elizabeth II **Obverse:** Portrait of Queen Elizabeth II **Obv. Designer:** Rank-Broadley **Reverse:** Scottish lion

Date	Mintage	F	VF	XF	Unc	BU
1999 In mint sets only		—	—	—	3.50	5.00
1999 Proof	Est. 100,000	Value: 6.00				

KM# 998a POUND **Weight:** 9.5000 g. **Composition:** 0.9250 Silver .2825 oz. ASW **Ruler:** Elizabeth II

Date	Mintage	F	VF	XF	Unc	BU
1999 Proof	23,000	Value: 40.00				
1999 frosted reverse		—	—	—	—	—

KM# 1005 POUND **Composition:** Nickel-Brass **Ruler:** Elizabeth II **Obverse:** Bust Queen right **Reverse:** Welsh dragon **Edge:** Reeded and lettered **Edge Lettering:** PLEIDIOL WYF I'M GWLAD

Date	Mintage	F	VF	XF	Unc	BU
2000 Proof	Est. 100,000	Value: 6.00				
2000		—	—	—	3.50	5.00

KM# 1013 POUND **Weight:** 9.5000 g. **Composition:** Nickel-Brass **Ruler:** Elizabeth II **Subject:** Northern Ireland **Obverse:** Queen's new portrait **Reverse:** Celtic style cross **Edge:** Reeding **Edge Lettering:** "DEBUS ET TUTAMEN" **Size:** 22.5 mm.

Date	Mintage	F	VF	XF	Unc	BU
2001	81,000,000	—	—	—	3.50	5.00
2001 Proof	—	Value: 6.00				

KM# 1018 POUND **Weight:** 16.2200 g. **Composition:** 0.9584 Silver .4998 oz. ASW **Ruler:** Elizabeth II **Subject:** Britannia Bullion **Obverse:** Queen's portrait **Reverse:** Stylized "Una and the Lion" **Edge:** Reeded **Size:** 27 mm.

Date	Mintage	F	VF	XF	Unc	BU
2001 Proof	5,000	Value: 40.00				

KM# 1013a POUND **Weight:** 9.5000 g. **Composition:** 0.9250 Silver 0.2825 oz. ASW **Ruler:** Elizabeth II **Subject:** Northern Ireland **Obverse:** Queen's new portrait **Obv. Designer:** Rank-Broadley **Reverse:** Celtic cross design **Edge:** Reeded **Edge Lettering:** DECUS ET TUTAMEN **Size:** 22.5 mm.

Date	Mintage	F	VF	XF	Unc	BU
2001 Proof	25,000	—	—	—	39.00	—

KM# 1030 POUND **Weight:** 9.5000 g. **Composition:** Nickel-Brass **Ruler:** Elizabeth II **Obverse:** Queen's new portrait **Obv. Designer:** Rank-Broadley **Reverse:** Three lions. **Edge:** Reeded **Edge Lettering:** Over "DECUS ET TUTANIEM" **Size:** 22.5 mm.

Date	Mintage	F	VF	XF	Unc	BU
2002	—	—	—	—	3.50	—
2002 Proof	100,000	Value: 6.00				

KM# 1030a POUND **Weight:** 9.5000 g. **Composition:** 0.9250 Silver 0.2825 oz. ASW **Ruler:** Elizabeth II **Obverse:** Queen's new portrait **Obv. Designer:** Rank-Broadley **Reverse:** Three lions **Edge:** Reeded **Edge Lettering:** Over "DECUS ET TUTANIEN"

Date	Mintage	F	VF	XF	Unc	BU
2002 Proof	—	Value: 40.00				

KM# 947 2 POUNDS **Composition:** Nickel-Brass **Ruler:** Elizabeth II **Subject:** Commonwealth Games **Edge Lettering:** XIII COMMONWEALTH GAMES SCOTLAND 1986

Date	Mintage	F	VF	XF	Unc	BU
1986	8,212,000	—	—	4.50	6.50	10.00
1986 Proof	125,000	Value: 12.00				

KM# 947a 2 POUNDS **Weight:** 15.9800 g. **Composition:** 0.5000 Silver .2569 oz. ASW **Ruler:** Elizabeth II **Subject:** Commonwealth Games

Date	Mintage	F	VF	XF	Unc	BU
1986	125,000	—	—	—	15.00	20.00

KM# 947b 2 POUNDS **Weight:** 15.9800 g. **Composition:** 0.9250 Silver .4752 oz. ASW **Ruler:** Elizabeth II **Subject:** Commonwealth Games

Date	Mintage	F	VF	XF	Unc	BU
1986 Proof	75,000	Value: 25.00				

KM# 947c 2 POUNDS **Weight:** 15.9800 g. **Composition:** 0.9170 Gold .4710 oz. AGW **Ruler:** Elizabeth II **Subject:** Commonwealth Games

Date	Mintage	F	VF	XF	Unc	BU
1986 Proof	18,000	Value: 200				

KM# 960 2 POUNDS **Composition:** Nickel-Brass **Ruler:** Elizabeth II **Subject:** Tercentenary - Bill of Rights

Date	Mintage	F	VF	XF	Unc	BU
ND(1989)	4,397,000	—	—	—	6.50	10.00
ND(1989) Proof	100,000	Value: 12.00				

KM# 960a 2 POUNDS **Weight:** 15.9800 g. **Composition:** 0.9250 Silver .4752 oz. ASW **Ruler:** Elizabeth II **Subject:** Tercentenary - Bill of Rights

Date	Mintage	F	VF	XF	Unc	BU
ND(1989) Proof	25,000	Value: 25.00				

KM# 961 2 POUNDS **Composition:** Nickel-Brass **Ruler:** Elizabeth II **Subject:** Tercentenary - Claim of Right

Date	Mintage	F	VF	XF	Unc	BU
ND(1989)	346,000	—	—	—	9.00	15.00
ND(1989) Proof	100,000	Value: 17.50				

KM# 961a 2 POUNDS **Weight:** 15.9800 g. **Composition:** 0.9250 Silver .4752 oz. ASW **Ruler:** Elizabeth II **Subject:** Tercentenary - Claim of Right

Date	Mintage	F	VF	XF	Unc	BU
ND(1989) Proof	25,000	Value: 25.00				

KM# 968 2 POUNDS **Composition:** Nickel-Brass **Ruler:** Elizabeth II **Subject:** 300th Anniversary - Bank of England **Edge Lettering:** SIC VOS NON VOBIS

Date	Mintage	F	VF	XF	Unc	BU
ND(1994)	1,441,000	—	—	—	5.50	9.00
ND(1994) Proof	—	Value: 10.00				

KM# 968a 2 POUNDS **Weight:** 15.9800 g. **Composition:** 0.9250 Silver .4752 oz. ASW **Ruler:** Elizabeth II **Subject:** 300th Anniversary - Bank of England

Date	Mintage	F	VF	XF	Unc	BU
ND(1994) Proof	Est. 40,000	Value: 40.00				

KM# 968c 2 POUNDS **Weight:** 15.9800 g. **Composition:** 0.9170 Gold .4710 oz. AGW **Ruler:** Elizabeth II **Subject:** 300th Anniversary - Bank of England

Date	Mintage	F	VF	XF	Unc	BU
ND(1994) Proof	Est. 3,500	Value: 470				

KM# 1012 2 POUNDS **Weight:** 15.9800 g. **Composition:** 0.9170 Gold .4710 oz. AGW **Ruler:** Elizabeth II **Obverse:** 2 Pounds, KM#944 **Reverse:** 2 Pounds, KM#968c **Note:** Muled die error.

Date	F	VF	XF	Unc	BU
ND(1994) Rare	—	—	—	—	—
2000	—	—	—	—	—
2002	—	—	—	—	—

KM# 970 2 POUNDS **Composition:** Nickel-Brass **Ruler:** Elizabeth II **Subject:** End of World War II - Dove **Edge Lettering:** 1945 IN PEACE GOODWILL 1995

Date	Mintage	F	VF	XF	Unc	BU
ND(1995)	6,033,000	—	—	—	6.00	9.00
ND(1995) Proof	100,000	Value: 10.00				

KM# 970a 2 POUNDS **Weight:** 15.9800 g. **Composition:** 0.9250 Silver .4752 oz. ASW **Ruler:** Elizabeth II

Date	Mintage	F	VF	XF	Unc	BU
ND(1995) Proof	50,000	Value: 40.00				

KM# 970c 2 POUNDS **Weight:** 15.9800 g. **Composition:** 0.9170 Gold .4710 oz. AGW **Ruler:** Elizabeth II **Subject:** End of World War II - Dove

Date	Mintage	F	VF	XF	Unc	BU
ND(1995) Proof	2,500	Value: 470				

KM# 971 2 POUNDS **Composition:** Nickel-Brass **Ruler:** Elizabeth II **Subject:** 50th Anniversary - United Nations **Note:** Mintage included with KM#970.

Date	F	VF	XF	Unc	BU
ND(1995)	—	—	—	6.00	9.00

KM# 971a 2 POUNDS **Weight:** 15.9760 g. **Composition:** 0.9250 Silver .4751 oz. ASW **Ruler:** Elizabeth II **Subject:** 50th Anniversary - United Nations

Date	Mintage	F	VF	XF	Unc	BU
ND(1995) Proof	Est. 175,000	Value: 40.00				

KM# 971c 2 POUNDS **Weight:** 15.9760 g. **Composition:** 0.9170 Gold .4708 oz. AGW **Ruler:** Elizabeth II **Subject:** 50th Anniversary - United Nations

Date	Mintage	F	VF	XF	Unc	BU
ND(1995) Proof	Est. 5,000	Value: 475				

KM# 973 2 POUNDS **Composition:** Nickel-Brass **Ruler:** Elizabeth II **Reverse:** Soccer ball **Edge Lettering:** TENTH EUROPEAN CHAMPIONSHIP

Date	Mintage	F	VF	XF	Unc	BU
1996	—	—	—	—	6.50	10.00
1996 Proof	Est. 100,000	Value: 12.00				

KM# 973a 2 POUNDS **Weight:** 15.9760 g. **Composition:** 0.9250 Silver .4751 oz. ASW **Ruler:** Elizabeth II

Date		F	VF	XF	Unc	BU
1996 Proof	—	Value: 40.00				

KM# 981 2 POUNDS **Weight:** 32.5400 g. **Composition:** 0.9580 Silver .9995 oz. ASW **Ruler:** Elizabeth II **Obverse:** Queen's portrait **Reverse:** Britannia in chariot

Date	Mintage	F	VF	XF	Unc	BU
1997 Proof	Est. 35,000	Value: 50.00				

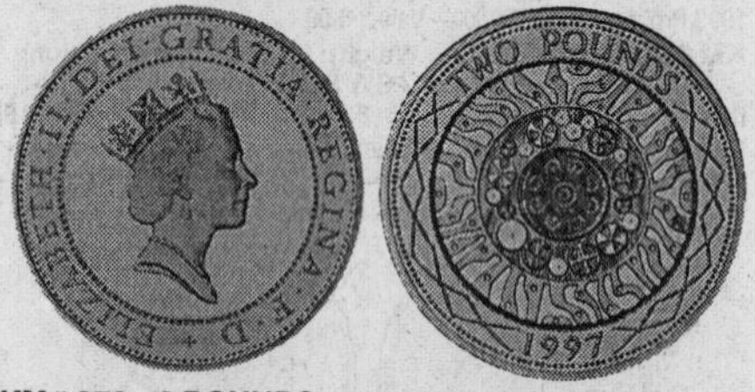

KM# 976 2 POUNDS **Ring Composition:** Nickel-Brass **Center Composition:** Copper-Nickel **Ruler:** Elizabeth II **Obverse:** Queen's new portrait **Reverse:** Celtic designs **Edge Lettering:** STANDING ON THE SHOULDERS OF GIANTS

Date	Mintage	F	VF	XF	Unc	BU
1997	—	—	—	—	7.50	12.50
1997 Proof	Est. 100,000	Value: 14.50				

KM# 976a 2 POUNDS **Weight:** 12.0000 g. **Composition:** 0.9250 Silver .3568 oz. ASW **Ruler:** Elizabeth II **Note:** Gold plated silver ring, silver center.

Date	Mintage	F	VF	XF	Unc	BU
1997 Proof	Est. 40,000	Value: 45.00				

KM# 976b 2 POUNDS **Weight:** 15.9800 g. **Composition:** 0.9170 Gold .4710 oz. AGW **Ruler:** Elizabeth II **Note:** Red gold ring, yellow gold center.

Date	Mintage	F	VF	XF	Unc	BU
1997 Proof	Est. 2,500	Value: 675				

KM# 994 2 POUNDS **Ring Composition:** Nickel-Brass **Center Composition:** Copper-Nickel **Ruler:** Elizabeth II **Obverse:** Portrait of Queen Elizabeth II **Reverse:** Celtic design **Obv. Designer:** Rank-Broadley **Edge Lettering:** STANDING ON THE SHOULDERS OF GIANTS **Size:** 28.35 mm.

Date	Mintage	F	VF	XF	Unc	BU
1998	—	—	—	—	6.00	8.50
1998 Proof	Est. 100,000	Value: 10.00				
1999	—	—	—	—	6.00	8.50
1999 Proof	—	Value: 10.00				
2000	—	—	—	—	6.00	8.50
2000 Proof	—	Value: 10.00				
2001	—	—	—	—	6.00	8.50
2001 Proof	—	Value: 10.00				
2002	—	—	—	—	6.00	8.50
2003 Proof	—	Value: 10.00				

KM# 994a 2 POUNDS **Weight:** 12.0000 g. **Composition:** 0.9250 Silver .3568 oz. ASW **Ruler:** Elizabeth II **Note:** Gold plated silver ring, silver center.

Date	Mintage	F	VF	XF	Unc	BU
1998 Proof	7,646	Value: 50.00				
2000 Proof	—	—	—	—	—	—

KM# 994b 2 POUNDS **Weight:** 12.0000 g. **Composition:** 0.9250 Silver .3568 oz. ASW **Ruler:** Elizabeth II **Note:** Without gold plating.

Date	Mintage	F	VF	XF	Unc	BU
1998 Proof	19,978	Value: 40.00				

KM# 1029 2 POUNDS **Weight:** 32.5400 g. **Composition:** 0.9580 Silver .9995 oz. ASW **Subject:** Britannia Bullion **Obverse:** Queen's new portrait **Reverse:** Standing Britannia **Edge:** Reeded **Size:** 40 mm.

Date	F	VF	XF	Unc	BU
1998	—	—	—	20.00	—

KM# 1000 2 POUNDS **Weight:** 32.5400 g. **Composition:** 0.9580 Silver .9995 oz. ASW **Ruler:** Elizabeth II **Obverse:** Portrait of Queen Elizabeth II **Obv. Designer:** Rank-Broadley **Reverse:** Britannia in chariot

Date	Mintage	F	VF	XF	Unc	BU
1999 Proof	Est. 100,000	Value: 45.00				

KM# 999 2 POUNDS **Ring Composition:** Nickel-Brass **Center Composition:** Copper-Nickel **Ruler:** Elizabeth II **Subject:** Rugby World Cup **Obverse:** Portrait of Queen Elizabeth II **Reverse:** 2-tone rugby design **Obv. Designer:** Rank-Broadley **Note:** Varieties exist.

Date	Mintage	F	VF	XF	Unc	BU
1999	—	—	—	—	7.00	9.00
1999 Proof	Est. 100,000	Value: 12.00				

KM# 999a 2 POUNDS **Weight:** 12.0000 g. **Composition:** 0.9250 Silver .3569 oz. ASW **Ruler:** Elizabeth II **Edge:** Reeded, lettered edge **Note:** Gold plated ring.

Date	Mintage	F	VF	XF	Unc	BU
1999 Proof	Est. 25,000	Value: 47.50				

KM# 999b 2 POUNDS **Weight:** 15.9800 g. **Composition:** 0.9170 Gold .4710 oz. AGW **Ruler:** Elizabeth II

Date	Mintage	F	VF	XF	Unc	BU
1999 Proof	4,250	Value: 525				

KM# 999c 2 POUNDS **Weight:** 24.0000 g. **Composition:** 0.9250 Silver .7137 oz. ASW **Ruler:** Elizabeth II **Obverse:** Queen's portrait within gold-plated ring **Reverse:** Multicolor hologram center within gold-plated ring **Edge:** Reeded, lettered edge

Date	Mintage	F	VF	XF	Unc	BU
1999 Proof	10,000	Value: 80.00				

KM# 1014 2 POUNDS **Ring Weight:** 11.9700 g. **Ring Composition:** Nickel-Brass **Center Composition:** Copper-Nickel **Ruler:** Elizabeth II **Subject:** First Transatlantic Radio Transmission **Obverse:** Queen's new portrait **Reverse:** Symbolic design **Edge:** Reeded and inscribed **Size:** 28.4 mm.

Date	Mintage	F	VF	XF	Unc	BU
2001	20,500,000	—	—	—	5.00	—
2001 Proof	—	Value: 10.00				

KM# 1014a 2 POUNDS **Weight:** 24.0000 g. **Composition:** 0.9250 Silver .7137 oz. ASW **Ring Composition:** Gold Plated **Ruler:** Elizabeth II **Edge:** Reeded and inscribed **Edge Lettering:** "WIRELESS BRIDGES THE ATLANTIC...MARCONI 1901..." **Size:** 28.4 mm.

Date	Mintage	F	VF	XF	Unc	BU
2001 Proof	25,000	Value: 33.50				

KM# 1014b 2 POUNDS **Weight:** 15.9700 g. **Composition:** 0.9166 Gold .4706 oz. AGW **Ring Composition:** Red Gold **Center Composition:** Yellow Gold Plated Red Gold **Ruler:** Elizabeth II **Size:** 28.4 mm.

Date	Mintage	F	VF	XF	Unc	BU
2001 Proof	1,500	Value: 445				

KM# 1019 2 POUNDS **Weight:** 32.4500 g. **Composition:** 0.9584 Silver .9999 oz. ASW **Ruler:** Elizabeth II **Subject:** Britannia Bullion **Obverse:** Queen's portrait **Reverse:** Stylized "Una and the Lion" **Edge:** Reeded **Size:** 40 mm.

Date	Mintage	F	VF	XF	Unc	BU
2001	100,000	—	—	—	15.75	—
2001 Proof	15,000	Value: 55.00				

KM# 1031 2 POUNDS **Ring Composition:** Copper-Nickel**Center Weight:** 12.0000 g. **Center Composition:** Nickel-Brass **Ruler:** Elizabeth II **Subject:** Commonwealth Games - England **Obverse:** Head of Queen Elizabeth II right **Reverse:** Runner breaking ribbon at finish line **Edge:** Reeded and lettered **Size:** 28.4 mm.

Date	F	VF	XF	Unc	BU
2002	—	—	—	5.00	—
2002 Proof	—	Value: 8.75			

KM# 1031a 2 POUNDS **Ring Composition:** Gold Plated Silver**Center Weight:** 12.0000 g. **Center Composition:** Silver **Ruler:** Elizabeth II **Subject:** Commonwealth Games - England **Obverse:** Head of Queen Elizabeth II right **Reverse:** Runner breaking ribbon at finish line **Edge:** Reeded and lettered **Size:** 28.4 mm.

Date	Mintage	F	VF	XF	Unc	BU
2002 Proof	10,000	—	—	—	30.00	—

KM# 1031b 2 POUNDS **Ring Composition:** Red Gold**Center Weight:** 15.9800 g. **Center Composition:** 0.9160 Yellow Gold 0.4706 oz. AGW **Ruler:** Elizabeth II **Subject:** Commonwealth Games - England **Obverse:** Head of Queen Elizabeth II right **Reverse:** Runner breaking ribbon at finish line **Edge:** Reeded and lettered **Size:** 28.4 mm.

Date	Mintage	F	VF	XF	Unc	BU
2002 Proof	500	Value: 418				

KM# 1032 2 POUNDS **Ring Composition:** Copper-Nickel**Center Weight:** 12.0000 g. **Center Composition:** Nickel-Brass **Ruler:** Elizabeth II **Subject:** Commonwealth Games - Scotland **Obverse:** Head of Queen Elizabeth II right **Reverse:** Runner breaking ribbon at finish line **Edge:** Reeded and lettered **Size:** 28.4 mm.

Date	F	VF	XF	Unc	BU
2002	—	—	—	5.00	—
2002 Proof	—	Value: 8.75			

KM# 1032a 2 POUNDS **Ring Composition:** Gold Plated Silver**Center Weight:** 12.0000 g. **Center Composition:** Silver **Ruler:** Elizabeth II **Subject:** Commonwealth Games - Scotland **Obverse:** Head of Queen Elizabeth II right **Reverse:** Runner breaking ribbon at finish line **Edge:** Reeded and lettered **Size:** 28.4 mm.

Date	Mintage	F	VF	XF	Unc	BU
2002 Proof	10,000	Value: 30.00				

KM# 1032b 2 POUNDS **Ring Composition:** Red Gold**Center Weight:** 15.9800 g. **Center Composition:** Yellow Gold **Ruler:** Elizabeth II **Subject:** Commonwealth Games - Scotland **Obverse:** Head of Queen Elizabeth II right **Reverse:** Runner breaking ribbon at finish line **Edge:** Reeded and lettered **Size:** 28.4 mm.

Date	Mintage	F	VF	XF	Unc	BU
2002 Proof	500	Value: 418				

KM# 1033 2 POUNDS **Ring Composition:** Copper-Nickel**Center Weight:** 12.0000 g. **Center Composition:** Nickel-Brass **Ruler:** Elizabeth II **Subject:** Commonwealth Games - Wales **Obverse:** Head of Queen Elizabeth II right **Reverse:** Runner breaking ribbon at finish line **Edge:** Reeded and lettered **Size:** 28.4 mm.

Date	F	VF	XF	Unc	BU
2002	—	—	—	5.00	—
2002 Proof	—	Value: 8.75			

KM# 1033a 2 POUNDS **Ring Composition:** Gold Plated Silver**Center Weight:** 12.0000 g. **Center Composition:** Silver **Ruler:** Elizabeth II **Subject:** Commonwealth Games - Wales **Obverse:** Head of Queen Elizabeth II right **Reverse:** Runner breaking ribbon at finish line **Edge:** Reeded and lettered **Size:** 28.4 mm.

Date	Mintage	F	VF	XF	Unc	BU
2002 Proof	10,000	Value: 30.00				

KM# 1033b 2 POUNDS **Ring Composition:** Red Gold**Center Weight:** 15.9800 g. **Center Composition:** Yellow Gold **Ruler:** Elizabeth II **Subject:** Commonwealth Games - Wales **Obverse:** Head of Queen Elizabeth II right **Reverse:** Runner breaking ribbon at finish line **Edge:** Reeded and lettered **Size:** 28.4 mm.

Date	Mintage	F	VF	XF	Unc	BU
2002 Proof	500	Value: 418				

KM# 1034 2 POUNDS **Ring Composition:** Copper-Nickel**Center Weight:** 12.0000 g. **Center Composition:** Nickel-Brass **Ruler:** Elizabeth II **Subject:** Commonwealth Games - Northern Ireland **Obverse:** Head of Queen Elizabeth II right **Reverse:** Runner breaking ribbon at finish line **Edge:** Reeded and lettered **Size:** 28.4 mm.

Date	F	VF	XF	Unc	BU
2002	—	—	—	5.00	—
2002 Proof	—	Value: 8.75			

KM# 1034a 2 POUNDS **Ring Composition:** Gold Plated Silver**Center Weight:** 12.0000 g. **Center Composition:** Silver **Ruler:** Elizabeth II **Subject:** Commonwealth Games - Northern Ireland **Obverse:** Head of Queen Elizabeth II right **Reverse:** Runner breaking ribbon at finish line **Edge:** Reeded and lettered **Size:** 28.4 mm.

Date	Mintage	F	VF	XF	Unc	BU
2002 Proof	10,000	Value: 30.00				

KM# 1034b 2 POUNDS **Ring Composition:** Red Gold**Center Weight:** 15.9800 g. **Center Composition:** Yellow Gold **Ruler:** Elizabeth II **Subject:** Commonwealth Games - Northern Ireland **Obverse:** Head of Queen Elizabeth II right **Reverse:** Runner breaking ribbon at finish line **Edge:** Reeded and lettered **Size:** 28.4 mm.

Date	Mintage	F	VF	XF	Unc	BU
2002 Proof	500	Value: 418				

KM# 1037 2 POUNDS **Weight:** 12.0000 g. **Composition:** Bi-Metallic **Ruler:** Elizabeth II **Subject:** D N A **Obverse:** Queen's portrait **Reverse:** DNA Double Helix **Edge:** Reeded and inscribed **Size:** 28.4 mm.

Date	F	VF	XF	Unc	BU
2003	—	—	—	5.00	—
2003 Proof	—	Value: 10.00			

KM# 962 5 POUNDS **Composition:** Copper-Nickel **Ruler:** Elizabeth II **Subject:** 90th Birthday of Queen Mother

Date	Mintage	F	VF	XF	Unc	BU
ND(1990)	2,755,000	—	—	—	15.00	—

KM# 962a 5 POUNDS **Weight:** 28.2800 g. **Composition:** 0.9250 Silver .8411 oz. ASW **Ruler:** Elizabeth II

Date	Mintage	F	VF	XF	Unc	BU
ND(1990) Proof	Est. 150,000	Value: 40.00				

KM# 962b 5 POUNDS **Weight:** 39.9400 g. **Composition:** 0.9170 Gold 1.1775 oz. AGW **Ruler:** Elizabeth II **Subject:** 90th Birthday of Queen Mother

Date	Mintage	F	VF	XF	Unc	BU
ND(1990) Proof	Est. 2,500	Value: 650				

KM# 965 5 POUNDS **Composition:** Copper-Nickel **Ruler:** Elizabeth II **Subject:** 40th Anniversary of Reign

Date	Mintage	F	VF	XF	Unc	BU
ND(1993)	—	—	—	—	14.00	—
ND(1993) Proof	Est. 100,000	Value: 20.00				

KM# 965a 5 POUNDS **Weight:** 28.2800 g. **Composition:** 0.9250 Silver .8411 oz. ASW **Ruler:** Elizabeth II

Date	Mintage	F	VF	XF	Unc	BU
ND(1993) Proof	Est. 100,000	Value: 45.00				

KM# 965b 5 POUNDS **Weight:** 39.9400 g. **Composition:** 0.9170 Gold 1.1775 oz. AGW **Ruler:** Elizabeth II **Subject:** 40th Anniversary of Reign

Date	Mintage	F	VF	XF	Unc	BU
ND(1993) Proof	Est. 2,500	Value: 950				

KM# 974 5 POUNDS **Composition:** Copper-Nickel **Ruler:** Elizabeth II **Subject:** 70th Birthday of Queen Elizabeth II

Date	Mintage	F	VF	XF	Unc	BU
ND(1996)	2,936,000	—	—	—	15.00	—
ND(1996) Proof	—	Value: 22.00				

KM# 974a 5 POUNDS **Weight:** 28.2800 g. **Composition:** 0.9250 Silver .8411 oz. ASW **Ruler:** Elizabeth II

Date	Mintage	F	VF	XF	Unc	BU
ND(1996) Proof	Est. 70,000	Value: 45.00				

KM# 974b 5 POUNDS **Weight:** 39.9400 g. **Composition:** 0.9170 Gold 1.1775 oz. AGW **Ruler:** Elizabeth II **Subject:** 70th Birthday of Queen Elizabeth II

Date	Mintage	F	VF	XF	Unc	BU
ND(1996) Proof	Est. 2,750	Value: 1,000				

KM# 977 5 POUNDS **Composition:** Copper-Nickel **Ruler:** Elizabeth II **Subject:** Queen Elizabeth II's Golden Wedding Anniversary **Obverse:** Portrait of Queen Elizabeth II and Prince Philip **Reverse:** Two coats of arms

Date	Mintage	F	VF	XF	Unc	BU
ND(1997)	1,733,000	—	—	—	16.50	—
ND(1997) Proof	—	Value: 22.00				

KM# 977a 5 POUNDS **Weight:** 28.2800 g. **Composition:** 0.9250 Silver .8411 oz. ASW **Ruler:** Elizabeth II

Date	Mintage	F	VF	XF	Unc	BU
ND(1997) Proof	Est. 70,000	Value: 50.00				

KM# 977b 5 POUNDS **Weight:** 39.9400 g. **Composition:** 0.9170 Gold 1.1775 oz. AGW **Ruler:** Elizabeth II

Date	Mintage	F	VF	XF	Unc	BU
ND(1997) Proof	Est. 2,750	Value: 995				

KM# 995 5 POUNDS **Composition:** Copper-Nickel **Ruler:** Elizabeth II **Subject:** 50th Birthday - Prince Charles **Obverse:** Rank-Broadley portrait of Queen Elizabeth II **Reverse:** Portrait of Prince Charles

Date	Mintage	F	VF	XF	Unc	BU
1998	—	—	—	—	16.50	—
1998 Proof	Est. 100,000	Value: 20.00				

KM# 995a 5 POUNDS **Weight:** 28.2800 g. **Composition:** 0.9250 Silver .8411 oz. ASW **Ruler:** Elizabeth II **Subject:** 50th Birthday - Prince Charles

Date	Mintage	F	VF	XF	Unc	BU
1998 Proof	13,379	Value: 50.00				

KM# 995b 5 POUNDS **Weight:** 39.9400 g. **Composition:** 0.9167 Gold 1.1771 oz. AGW **Ruler:** Elizabeth II **Subject:** 50th Birthday - Prince Charles

Date	Mintage	F	VF	XF	Unc	BU
1998 Proof	773	Value: 900				

KM# 997 5 POUNDS **Weight:** 28.2800 g. **Composition:** 0.9250 Silver .8411 oz. ASW **Ruler:** Elizabeth II **Obverse:** Portrait of Queen Elizabeth II **Obv. Designer:** Rank-Broadley **Reverse:** Portrait of Princess Diana, dates

Date	Mintage	F	VF	XF	Unc	BU
1999	—	—	—	—	16.50	—
1999 Proof	Est. 100,000	Value: 22.00				

KM# 997a 5 POUNDS **Weight:** 28.2800 g. **Composition:** 0.9250 Silver .8410 oz. ASW **Ruler:** Elizabeth II

Date	Mintage	F	VF	XF	Unc	BU
1999 Proof	Est. 49,545	Value: 50.00				

KM# 997b 5 POUNDS **Weight:** 39.9400 g. **Composition:** 0.9170 Gold 1.1775 oz. AGW **Ruler:** Elizabeth II

Date	Mintage	F	VF	XF	Unc	BU
1999 Proof	Est. 7,500	Value: 925				

KM# 1006 5 POUNDS **Composition:** Copper-Nickel **Ruler:** Elizabeth II **Obverse:** Bust Queen right **Reverse:** Map with Greenwich Meridian **Edge Lettering:** WHAT'S PAST IS PROLOGUE

Date	Mintage	F	VF	XF	Unc	BU
1999 Proof	—	Value: 20.00				
1999	—	—	—	—	15.00	—
2000	—	—	—	—	15.00	—
2000 Proof	Est. 100,000	Value: 20.00				

KM# 1006a 5 POUNDS **Weight:** 28.2800 g. **Composition:** 0.9250 Silver .8410 oz. ASW **Ruler:** Elizabeth II

Date	Mintage	F	VF	XF	Unc	BU
1999 Proof	75,000	Value: 55.00				
2000 Proof	50,000	Value: 55.00				

KM# 1006b 5 POUNDS **Weight:** 39.9400 g. **Composition:** 0.9170 Gold 1.1771 oz. AGW **Ruler:** Elizabeth II

Date	Mintage	F	VF	XF	Unc	BU
1999 Proof	2,500	Value: 995				
2000 Proof	2,500	Value: 895				

KM# 1006c 5 POUNDS **Weight:** 28.2800 g. **Composition:** 0.9990 Silver 0.9083 oz. ASW **Note:** With gold-plated British map.

Date	F	VF	XF	Unc	BU
2000 Proof	—	—	—	—	—

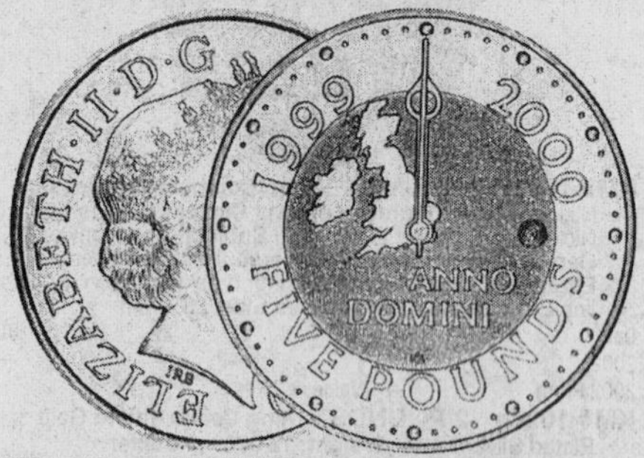

KM# 1006.1 5 POUNDS **Composition:** Copper-Nickel **Ruler:** Elizabeth II **Reverse:** Same as KM#1006 but with the addition of a world globe at 3 o'clock in inner circle

Date	F	VF	XF	Unc	BU
2000	—	—	—	20.00	—

KM# 1007 5 POUNDS **Composition:** Copper-Nickel **Ruler:** Elizabeth II **Subject:** 100th Birthday - Queen Elizabeth, The Queen Mother **Reverse:** Bust Queen Mother left with signature **Edge:** Reeded

Date	F	VF	XF	Unc	BU
2000	—	—	—	16.50	—

KM# 1007a 5 POUNDS **Weight:** 28.2800 g. **Composition:** 0.9250 Silver .8410 oz. ASW **Ruler:** Elizabeth II **Subject:** Queen Mother's Centennial **Obverse:** Queen's portrait **Reverse:** Queen Mother's portrait and signature **Edge:** Reeded

Date	Mintage	F	VF	XF	Unc	BU
2000 Proof	100,000	Value: 55.00				

KM# 1007b 5 POUNDS **Weight:** 39.9400 g. **Composition:** 0.9167 Gold 1.0003 oz. AGW **Ruler:** Elizabeth II

Date	Mintage	F	VF	XF	Unc	BU
2000 Proof	3,000	Value: 950				

KM# 1015 5 POUNDS **Weight:** 28.2800 g. **Composition:** Copper-Nickel **Ruler:** Elizabeth II **Subject:** Centennial of Queen Victoria **Obverse:** Queen Elizabeth's portrait **Reverse:** Queen Victoria's portrait **Edge:** Reeded **Size:** 38.6 mm.

Date	F	VF	XF	Unc	BU
2001 Proof	—	Value: 20.00			
2001	—	—	—	15.00	—

KM# 1015b 5 POUNDS **Weight:** 39.9400 g. **Composition:** 0.9167 Gold 1.1771 oz. AGW

Date	F	VF	XF	Unc	BU
2001 Proof	—	—	—	—	—

KM# 1035 5 POUNDS **Weight:** 28.2800 g. **Composition:** Copper Nickel **Ruler:** Elizabeth II **Subject:** Queen Mother **Obverse:** Bust of Queen Elizabeth II right. **Reverse:** Queen Mother's portrait in wreath. **Edge:** Reeded. **Size:** 38.6 mm.

Date	F	VF	XF	Unc	BU
ND(2002) Proof	—	Value: 20.00			

KM# 1035a 5 POUNDS **Weight:** 28.2800 g. **Composition:** Copper Nickel **Ruler:** Elizabeth II **Subject:** Queen Mother **Obverse:** Bust of Queen Elizabeth II right. **Reverse:** Queen Mother's portrait in wreath. **Edge:** Reeded. **Size:** 38.6 mm.

Date	Mintage	F	VF	XF	Unc	BU
ND(2002) Proof	25,000	Value: 50.00				

KM# 1035b 5 POUNDS **Weight:** 39.9400 g. **Composition:** 0.9167 Gold 1.1771 oz. AGW **Ruler:** Elizabeth II **Subject:** Queen Mother **Obverse:** Bust of Queen Elizabeth II right. **Reverse:** Queen Mother's portrait in wreath. **Edge:** Reeded. **Size:** 38.6 mm.

Date	Mintage	F	VF	XF	Unc	BU
ND(2002) Proof	3,000	Value: 950				

KM# 1024 5 POUNDS **Weight:** 28.2800 g. **Composition:** Copper-Nickel **Ruler:** Elizabeth II **Subject:** Queen's Golden Jubilee of Reign **Obverse:** Queen's portrait **Reverse:** Queen on horse **Edge:** Reeded **Size:** 38.6 mm.

Date	F	VF	XF	Unc	BU
2002	—	—	—	15.00	—
2002 Proof	—	Value: 20.00			

KM# 1024a 5 POUNDS **Weight:** 28.2800 g. **Composition:** 0.9250 Silver .8410 oz. ASW **Ruler:** Elizabeth II **Edge:** Reeded **Size:** 38.6 mm.

Date	F	VF	XF	Unc	BU
2002 Proof	—	Value: 50.00			

KM# 1024b 5 POUNDS **Weight:** 39.9400 g. **Composition:** 0.9167 Gold 1.0003 oz. AGW **Ruler:** Elizabeth II **Edge:** Reeded **Size:** 38.6 mm.

Date	F	VF	XF	Unc	BU
2002 Proof	—	Value: 950			

KM# 1038 5 POUNDS **Weight:** 28.2800 g. **Composition:** Copper Nickel **Ruler:** Elizabeth II **Subject:** Queen's Golden Jubilee **Obverse:** Queen's stylized portrait **Reverse:** Chil- like lettering **Edge:** Reeded **Size:** 38.6 mm.

Date	F	VF	XF	Unc	BU
2003	—	—	—	15.00	—
2003 Proof	—	Value: 20.00			

BULLION COINAGE

Until 1990, .917 Gold was commonly alloyed with copper by the British Royal Mint.

All proof issues have designers name as P. Nathan. The uncirculated issues use only Nathan.

KM# 950 10 POUNDS (1/10 Ounce - Britannia)
Weight: 3.4120 g. **Composition:** 0.9170 Gold .1000 oz. AGW **Ruler:** Elizabeth II **Note:** Copper alloy.

Date	Mintage	F	VF	XF	Unc	BU
1987		—	—	—	BV+16%	—
1987 Proof	26,000	Value: 60.00				
1988		—	—	—	BV+16%	—
1988 Proof	Est. 19,000	Value: 60.00				
1989		—	—	—	BV+16%	—
1989 Proof	Est. 6,500	Value: 60.00				

KM# 950a 10 POUNDS (1/10 Ounce - Britannia)
Weight: 3.4120 g. **Composition:** 0.9170 Gold .1000 oz. AGW **Ruler:** Elizabeth II **Note:** Silver alloy.

Date	Mintage	F	VF	XF	Unc	BU
1990 Proof	Est. 5,000	Value: 60.00				
1991 Proof	2,750	Value: 100				
1992 Proof	1,500	Value: 100				
1993 Proof	Est. 1,000	Value: 100				
1994 Proof	1,500	Value: 95.00				
1995 Proof	1,500	Value: 95.00				
1996 Proof	Est. 3,000	Value: 90.00				
1999 Proof	Est. 5,750	Value: 80.00				

KM# 982 10 POUNDS (1/10 Ounce - Britannia)
Weight: 3.4100 g. **Composition:** 0.9167 Gold .1005 oz. AGW **Ruler:** Elizabeth II **Obverse:** Queen's portrait **Reverse:** Britannia in chariot **Note:** Similar to 2 Pounds, KM#981.

Date	Mintage	F	VF	XF	Unc	BU
1997 Proof	Est. 6,500	Value: 120				

KM# 1008 10 POUNDS (1/10 Ounce - Britannia)
Weight: 3.4100 g. **Composition:** 0.9167 Gold .1005 oz. AGW **Ruler:** Elizabeth II **Reverse:** Britannia standing **Edge:** Reeded

Date	Mintage	F	VF	XF	Unc	BU
1999 Proof	1,058	Value: 115				
2000 Proof	3,250	Value: 100				
2002 Proof	2,500	Value: 115				

KM# 1020 10 POUNDS (1/10 Ounce - Britannia)
Weight: 3.4100 g. **Composition:** 0.9167 Gold .1005 oz. AGW **Ruler:** Elizabeth II **Subject:** Britannia Bullion **Obverse:** Queen's portrait **Reverse:** Stylized "Una and the Lion" **Edge:** Reeded **Size:** 16.5 mm.

Date	Mintage	F	VF	XF	Unc	BU
2001	25,000	—	—	—	BV+16%	—
2001 Proof	3,500	Value: 115				

KM# 951 25 POUNDS (1/4 Ounce - Britannia)
Weight: 8.5130 g. **Composition:** 0.9170 Gold .2500 oz. AGW **Ruler:** Elizabeth II **Note:** Copper alloy.

Date	Mintage	F	VF	XF	Unc	BU
1987		—	—	—	BV+8%	—
1987 Proof	26,000	Value: 125				
1988		—	—	—	BV+8%	—
1988 Proof	Est. 14,000	Value: 125				
1989		—	—	—	BV+8%	—
1989 Proof	Est. 4,000	Value: 125				

KM# 951a 25 POUNDS (1/4 Ounce - Britannia)
Weight: 8.5130 g. **Composition:** 0.9170 Gold .2500 oz. AGW **Ruler:** Elizabeth II **Note:** Silver alloy.

Date	Mintage	F	VF	XF	Unc	BU
1990 Proof	Est. 2,500	Value: 125				
1991 Proof	750	Value: 225				
1992 Proof	500	Value: 225				
1993 Proof	Est. 500	Value: 225				
1994 Proof	500	Value: 210				
1995 Proof	500	Value: 210				
1996 Proof	2,500	Value: 210				
1999 Proof	1,750	Value: 210				

KM# 983 25 POUNDS (1/4 Ounce - Britannia)
Weight: 8.5100 g. **Composition:** 0.9167 Gold .2508 oz. AGW **Ruler:** Elizabeth II **Obverse:** Queen's portrait **Reverse:** Britannia in chariot **Note:** Similar to 2 Pounds, KM#981.

Date	Mintage	F	VF	XF	Unc	BU
1997 Proof	Est. 4,000	Value: 215				

KM# 1009 25 POUNDS (1/4 Ounce - Britannia)
Weight: 8.5100 g. **Composition:** 0.9167 Gold .2508 oz. AGW **Ruler:** Elizabeth II **Reverse:** Britannia standing **Edge:** Reeded

Date	Mintage	F	VF	XF	Unc	BU
1999 Proof	1,000	Value: 220				
2000 Proof	Est. 500	Value: 200				
2002 Proof	1,750	Value: 225				

KM# 1021 25 POUNDS (1/4 Ounce - Britannia)
Weight: 8.5100 g. **Composition:** 0.9167 Gold .2508 oz. AGW **Ruler:** Elizabeth II **Subject:** Britannia Bullion **Obverse:** Queen's portrait **Reverse:** Stylized "Una and the Lion" **Edge:** Reeded **Size:** 22 mm.

Date	Mintage	F	VF	XF	Unc	BU
2001	25,000	—	—	—	BV+8%	—
2001 Proof	1,500	Value: 225				

KM# 952 50 POUNDS (1/2 Ounce - Britannia)
Weight: 17.0250 g. **Composition:** 0.9170 Gold .5000 oz. AGW **Ruler:** Elizabeth II **Note:** Copper alloy.

Date	Mintage	F	VF	XF	Unc	BU
1987		—	—	—	BV+6%	—
1987 Proof	13,000	Value: 245				
1988		—	—	—	BV+6%	—
1988 Proof	Est. 6,500	Value: 245				
1989		—	—	—	BV+6%	—
1989 Proof	Est. 2,500	Value: 250				

KM# 952a 50 POUNDS (1/2 Ounce - Britannia)
Weight: 17.0250 g. **Composition:** 0.9170 Gold .5000 oz. AGW **Ruler:** Elizabeth II **Note:** Silver alloy.

Date	Mintage	F	VF	XF	Unc	BU
1990 Proof	Est. 2,500	Value: 250				
1991 Proof	750	Value: 380				
1992 Proof	500	Value: 420				
1993 Proof	—	—	—	—	—	—
1994 Proof	500	Value: 420				
1995 Proof	500	Value: 420				
1996 Proof	Est. 2,500	Value: 395				
1999 Proof	Est. 750	Value: 440				

KM# 984 50 POUNDS (1/2 Ounce - Britannia)
Weight: 17.0300 g. **Composition:** 0.9167 Gold .5019 oz. AGW **Ruler:** Elizabeth II **Obverse:** Queen's portrait **Reverse:** Britannia in chariot **Note:** Similar to 2 Pounds, KM#281.

Date	Mintage	F	VF	XF	Unc	BU
1997 Proof	Est. 1,500	Value: 400				

KM# 1010 50 POUNDS (1/2 Ounce - Britannia)
Weight: 17.0300 g. **Composition:** 0.9167 Gold .5019 oz. AGW **Ruler:** Elizabeth II **Reverse:** Britannia standing **Edge:** Reeded

Date	Mintage	F	VF	XF	Unc	BU
1999 Proof	—	Value: 425				
2000 Proof	750	Value: 425				
2002 Proof	1,000	Value: 445				

KM# 1022 50 POUNDS (1/2 Ounce - Britannia)
Weight: 17.0200 g. **Composition:** 0.9167 Gold .5016 oz. AGW **Ruler:** Elizabeth II **Subject:** Britannia Bullion **Obverse:** Queen's portrait **Reverse:** Stylized "Una and the Lion" **Edge:** Reeded **Size:** 27 mm.

Date	Mintage	F	VF	XF	Unc	BU
2001	25,000	—	—	—	BV+6%	—
2001 Proof	1,000	Value: 432				

KM# 953 100 POUNDS (1 Ounce - Britannia)
Weight: 34.0500 g. **Composition:** 0.9170 Gold 1.0000 oz. AGW **Ruler:** Elizabeth II **Note:** Copper alloy.

Date	Mintage	F	VF	XF	Unc	BU
1987		—	—	—	BV+4%	—
1987 Proof	13,000	Value: 500				
1988		—	—	—	BV+4%	—
1988 Proof	Est. 8,500	Value: 500				
1989		—	—	—	BV+4%	—
1989 Proof	Est. 2,600	Value: 500				

KM# 953a 100 POUNDS (1 Ounce - Britannia)
Weight: 34.0500 g. **Composition:** 0.9170 Gold 1.0000 oz. AGW **Ruler:** Elizabeth II **Note:** Silver alloy.

Date	Mintage	F	VF	XF	Unc	BU
1990 Proof	3,500	Value: 500				
1991 Proof	1,250	Value: 750				
1992 Proof	500	Value: 785				
1993 Proof	Est. 500	Value: 785				
1994 Proof	Est. 500	Value: 760				
1995 Proof	Est. 500	Value: 800				
1996 Proof	2,500	Value: 550				
1999 Proof	Est. 750	Value: 835				

KM# 985 100 POUNDS (1 Ounce - Britannia)
Weight: 34.0500 g. **Composition:** 0.9167 Gold 1.0035 oz. AGW **Ruler:** Elizabeth II **Obverse:** Queen's portrait **Reverse:** Britannia in chariot

Date	Mintage	F	VF	XF	Unc	BU
1997 Proof	Est. 2,500	Value: 845				

KM# 1011 100 POUNDS (1 Ounce - Britannia)
Weight: 34.0500 g. **Composition:** 0.9167 Gold 1.0035 oz. AGW **Ruler:** Elizabeth II **Reverse:** Britannia standing **Edge:** Reeded

Date	Mintage	F	VF	XF	Unc	BU
1999 Proof	—	Value: 850				
2000 Proof	750	Value: 850				
2002 Proof	1,000	Value: 900				

KM# 1023 100 POUNDS (1 Ounce - Britannia)
Weight: 34.0500 g. **Composition:** 0.9167 Gold 1.0035 oz. AGW **Ruler:** Elizabeth II **Subject:** Britannia Bullion **Obverse:** Queen's portrait **Reverse:** Stylized "Una and the Lion" **Edge:** Reeded **Size:** 32.7 mm.

Date	Mintage	F	VF	XF	Unc	BU
2001	25,000	—	—	—	BV+4%	—
2001 Proof	1,000	Value: 865				

TRADE COINAGE

Britannia Series

Issued to facilitate British trade in the Orient, the reverse design incorporated the denomination in Chinese characters and Malay script.

This issue was struck at the Bombay (B) and Calcutta (C) Mints in India, except for 1925 and 1930 issues which were struck at London. Through error the mint marks did not appear on some early (1895-1900) issues as indicated.

KM# T5 DOLLAR Weight: 26.9568 g. Composition: 0.9000 Silver .7800 oz. ASW

Date	Mintage	F	VF	XF	Unc	BU
1901/OB	25,680,000	40.00	60.00	100	200	—
1901B	Inc. above	15.00	20.00	25.00	60.00	—
1901B Proof	Inc. above	Value: 800				
1901C	1,514,000	25.00	45.00	100	200	—
1902B	30,404,000	15.00	20.00	25.00	60.00	—
1902B Proof	Inc. above	Value: 800				
1902C	1,267,000	25.00	45.00	80.00	175	—
1902C Proof	Inc. above	Value: 800				
1903/2B	3,956,000	12.00	25.00	40.00	75.00	—
1903B	Inc. above	12.00	20.00	—	60.00	—
1903B Proof	Inc. above	Value: 800				
1904/898B	649,000	50.00	80.00	125	200	—
1904/3B	Inc. above	30.00	50.00	100	225	—
1904/0B	Inc. above	80.00	125	175	300	—
1904B	Inc. above	40.00	60.00	100	250	—
1904B Proof	Inc. above	Value: 700				
1907B	1,946,000	12.00	20.00	25.00	60.00	—
1908/3B	6,871,000	40.00	60.00	100	175	—
1908/7B	Inc. above	35.00	50.00	90.00	125	—
1908B	Inc. above	12.00	20.00	25.00	60.00	—
1908B Proof	Inc. above	Value: 700				
1909/8B	5,954,000	30.00	45.00	80.00	125	—
1909B	Inc. above	12.00	20.00	25.00	60.00	—
1910/00B	553,000	40.00	60.00	100	175	—
1910B	Inc. above	12.00	20.00	25.00	60.00	—
1911/00B	—	30.00	50.00	100	150	—
1911B	37,471,000	12.00	20.00	25.00	60.00	—
1912B	5,672,000	12.00	20.00	25.00	60.00	—
1912B Proof	Inc. above	Value: 800				
1913/2B	—	100	150	250	700	—
1913B	1,567,000	30.00	60.00	125	300	—
1913B Proof	Inc. above	Value: 800				
1921B	5	—	—	—	15,000	—
Note: Original mintage 50,211						
1921B Restrike; Proof	—	Value: 4,500				
1925	6,870,000	15.00	20.00	25.00	70.00	—
1929/1B	5,100,000	30.00	50.00	80.00	200	—
1929B	Inc. above	12.00	20.00	25.00	60.00	—
1929B Proof	Inc. above	Value: 800				
1930B	10,400,000	12.00	20.00	25.00	60.00	—
1930B Proof	Inc. above	Value: 800				
1930	666,000	12.00	20.00	25.00	60.00	—
1934B	17,335,000	75.00	150	200	500	—
1934B Proof	Inc. above	Value: 3,500				
1934B Restrike; Proof	20	Value: 3,000				
1935B	5	1,000	1,500	2,500	5,000	—
Note: Original mintage 6,811,995						
1935B Proof	20	Value: 7,500				
1935B Restrike; Proof	20	Value: 4,000				

KM# T5a DOLLAR Composition: Gold

Date		F	VF	XF	Unc	BU
1901B Restrike; Proof	—	Value: 7,500				
1902B Restrike; Proof	—	Value: 7,500				

PATTERNS

Including off metal strikes

KM#	Date	Mintage	Identification	Mkt Val
PnA121	1922	—	Florin. Gold. KM817a	15,000
PnB121	1923	—	3 Pence. Nickel. KM#813a.	1,250
	1923	—	3 Pence. Nickel. KM#813a.	1,250
PnC121	1923	—	Shilling. Nickel. KM816a	1,000
Pn121	1924	—	Shilling. Nickel. KM816a	1,000
PnD121	1924	1	3 Pence. Gold. KM813a	10,000
Pne121	1924	—	6 Pence. Gold. KM815.a1	10,000
PnF121	1924	—	Shilling. Nickel. 5.0000 g. KM816a	1,000
PnA122	1925	—	3 Pence. Nickel. Modified effigy. KM#831.	1,250
PnB122	1925	—	3 Pence. Silver. MODEL. Matte proof; KM#831.	1,500
PnC122	1925	—	6 Pence. Nickel. Modified effigy. KM#832.	1,500
PnD122	1925	—	6 Pence. Silver. MODEL. Matte proof; KM#832.	1,500
PnE122	1925	—	Shilling. Nickel. Modified effigy. KM#833.	2,500
PnF122	1925	—	Shilling. Silver. MODEL. Matte proof; KM#833.	2,000
PnG122	1926	—	1/2 Crown. Silver. MODEL. Matte proof; KM#835.	—
PnH122	1926	—	Crown. Silver. MODEL. Matte proof; KM#836.	—
PnI122	1927	—	6 Pence. Nickel. KM#828	1,200
PnJ122	1927	—	Florin. Silver. MODEL. Matte proof, KM#834.	—
	1927	—	Florin. Silver. MODEL. Matte proof, KM#834.	—
PnK122	1927	—	1/2 Crown. Nickel. Modified effigy. KM830	—
PnL122	1927	—	1/2 Crown. Gold. Modified Effigy. KM830	—
PnM122	1935	—	Crown. Gold. similar to KM842.	14,500
	1935	—	Crown. Gold. similar to KM842.	14,500
Pn122	1937	18,000	Farthing. Bronze. Edward VIII.	—
Pn123	1937	18,000	1/2 Penny. Bronze. Edward VIII.	—
Pn124	1937	25,000	Penny. Bronze. Edward VIII.	—
Pn125	1937	—	3 Pence. Nickel-Brass. Edward VIII.	—
Pn126	1937	—	3 Pence. Nickel-Brass. Inner circle. Edward VIII.	45,000
Pn127	1937	18,000	6 Pence. 0.5000 Silver. Edward VIII.	—
Pn128	1937	25,000	Shilling. 0.5000 Silver. Edward VIII.	37,000
Pn129	1937	35,000	Florin. 0.5000 Silver. Edward VIII.	—
Pn130	1937	60,000	1/2 Crown. 0.5000 Silver. Edward VIII.	—
Pn131	1937	120,000	Crown. 0.5000 Silver. Edward VIII.	—
Pn132	1937	6	Sovereign. 0.9160 Gold. Edward VIII.	120,000
Pn133	1946	—	6 Pence. Copper-Nickel.	—
PnA134	1950	—	4 Shilling. Copper-Nickel.	—
PnB134	1952	—	Shilling. Nickel. KM#876.	—
Pn134	1953	—	Penny. Bronze. Dentilated border.	—
PnA135	1953	—	Crown. Copper-Nickel. Matte, KM#894.	—
Pn135	1953	—	1/2 Sovereign. 0.9160 Gold.	
Pn136	1953	—	Sovereign. 0.9160 Gold. Y#137.	40,000
Pn137	1953	—	2 Pounds. 0.9160 Gold.	—
Pn138	1953	—	5 Pounds. 0.9160 Gold.	—
Pn139	1961	—	Cent. Bronze.	—
Pn140	1961	—	2 Cents. Bronze.	—
Pn141	1961	—	5 Cents. Copper-Nickel.	—
Pn142	1961	—	10 Cents. Copper-Nickel.	—
Pn143	1961	—	20 Cents. Copper-Nickel.	—
Pn144	1961	—	50 Cents. Silver.	—
Pn145	1963	—	1/2 Penny. Bronze. Decimal.	—
Pn146	1963	—	Penny. Bronze. Decimal.	—

PRIVATE PATTERNS

KM#	Date	Mintage	Identification	Mkt Val
PPn119	1902	—	Crown. Silver.	1,700
PPn120	1902	—	Crown. Gold.	5,000
PPn121	1902	—	1/2 Pound. Silver.	4,000
PPn122	1902	—	Pound. Silver.	3,250
PPn-A123	MDCDX	—	Crown. Gold. Plain edge.	—
PPn-B123	MDCDX	—	Crown. Gold. Milled edge.	—
PPn-C123	MDCDX	—	Crown. Silver. Plain edge.	3,500
PPn-D123	MDCDX	—	Crown. Silver. Milled edge.	3,500
PPn-E123	MDCDX	2	Crown. Silver Plated Copper. Matte.	8,000
PPn-F123	MDCDX	—	Crown. Copper. Matte.	—
PPn-G123	1910	—	Crown. Gold. Plain edge.	—
PPn-H123	1910	—	Crown. Gold. Milled edge.	—
PPn-I123	1910	10	Crown. Silver. Plain edge.	3,500
PPn-J123	1910	10	Crown. Silver. 32.6300 g. Milled edge.	3,500
PPn-K123	1910	—	Crown. Silver. Milled edge. Weight varies 27.54-28.38 grams; Matte.	—
PPn-L123	1910	—	Crown. Copper.	—
PPn123	1911	—	2 Florins. Silver. Plain edge.	900
PPn124	1911	—	2 Florins. Silver. Reeded edge.	900
PPn125	1911	—	2 Florins. Silver. REX 19 11 BRI. Plain edge.	1,000
PPn126	1913	—	Octorino. Silver. Reeded edge.	800
PPn127	1913	—	Octorino. Gold. Reeded edge.	3,000
PPn128	1913	—	Octorino. Platinum. Reeded edge.	2,850
PPn129	1913	—	Octorino. Copper. Reeded edge.	500
PPn130	1913	—	Octorino. Lead. Plain edge.	450
PPn-A130	1913	—	Octorino. Iron.	2,000
PPn131	1913	—	8 Pence. Silver. Reeded edge.	500
PPn132	1913	—	8 Pence. Gold. Reeded edge.	2,000
PPn133	1913	—	8 Pence. Platinum. Reeded edge.	2,000
PPn134	1913	—	8 Pence. Copper. Reeded edge.	350
PPn135	1913	—	8 Pence. Nickel. Reeded edge.	350
PPn136	1914	—	12 Groats. Silver. Plain edge.	750
PPn-A136	1914	—	12 Groats. Silver. Reeded edge.	750
PPn137	1914	—	12 Groats. Platinum. Plain edge.	3,000
PPn138	1914	—	12 Groats. Platinum. Reeded edge.	3,000
PPn139	1914	—	12 Groats. Gold. Reeded edge.	2,400
PPn140	1933	4	Penny. Bronze. Plain edge.	—

PIEFORTS

KM#	Date	Mintage	Identification	Mkt Val
P1	1973	—	50 Pence. 0.9250 Silver.	1,250
P2	1982	—	20 Pence. 0.9250 Silver.	50.00
P3	1983	10,000	Pound. 0.9250 Silver. KM#933.	125
P4	1984	15,000	Pound. 0.9250 Silver. KM#934.	50.00
P5	1985	15,000	Pound. 0.9250 Silver. KM#941.	40.00
P6	1986	15,000	Pound. 0.9250 Silver. KM#946.	40.00
P7	1987	15,000	Pound. 0.9250 Silver. KM#948.	40.00
P8	1988	15,000	Pound. 0.9250 Silver. KM#954.	40.00
P9	1989	15,000	Pound. 0.9250 Silver. KM#959.	40.00
P10	1989	25,000	2 Pounds. 0.9250 Silver. KM#960a.	45.00
P11	1989	10,000	2 Pounds. 0.9250 Silver. KM#961a.	45.00
P12	1990	20,000	5 Pence. 0.9250 Silver. KM#937c.	25.00
P13	1992	15,000	10 Pence. 0.9250 Silver. KM#938b.	50.00
P15	1992	—	50 Pence. 0.9250 Silver. KM#963a.	70.00
P16	1993	—	Pound. 0.9250 Silver. KM#964.	45.00
P17	1994	—	50 Pence. 0.9250 Silver. KM#966b.	65.00
P18	1994	—	Pound. 0.9250 Silver. KM#967.	70.00
P19	1994	—	2 Pounds. 0.9250 Silver. KM#968a.	80.00
P20	1995	8,458	Pound. 0.9250 Silver. KM#969.	65.00
P21	1995	—	2 Pounds. 0.9250 Silver. KM#970a.	70.00
P22	1995	—	2 Pounds. 0.9250 Silver. KM#971a.	70.00
P23	1996	10,000	Pound. 0.9250 Silver. KM#972.	60.00
P24	1997	—	50 Pence. 0.9250 Silver. KM#963.	70.00
P25	1997	—	Pound. 0.9250 Silver. KM#975.	70.00
P26	1998	—	Pound. 0.9250 Silver. KM#993a.	—
P27	1997	—	2 Pounds. 0.9250 Silver. KM#976a.	75.00
P28	1998	—	50 Pence. 0.9250 Silver. KM#992a.	70.00
P29	1998	—	50 Pence. 0.9250 Silver. KM#996a.	70.00
P30	1998	—	2 Pounds. 0.9250 Silver. KM#994a.	75.00
P31	1999	—	Pound. 0.9250 Silver. KM998a	—

TRIAL STRIKES

KM#	Date	Mintage	Identification	Mkt Val
TS5	1926	—	1/2 Crown. Silver. MODEL.	1,500

KM#	Date	Mintage	Identification	Mkt Val
TS2	1926	—	6 Pence. Silver. MODEL.	1,000

KM#	Date	Mintage	Identification	Mkt Val
TS3	1926	—	Shilling. Silver. MODEL.	1,250

KM#	Date	Mintage	Identification	Mkt Val
TS4	1926	—	2 Shilling. Silver. MODEL.	1,350
TSA6	1926	—	Crown. Silver. MODEL.	—

Note: A complete set of silver plated copper electro types officially prepared for the designer has been recorded. Market value $2,000

KM#	Date	Mintage	Identification	Mkt Val

TS6	1926	—	Crown. Silver. Blank.	—

TS1	1926	—	3 Pence. Silver. MODEL.	1,000

TS7	1963	—	1/4 New Penny. Aluminum. Uniface.	—

TS11	1963	—	5 New Pence. Silver. Uniface.	—

TS12	1963	—	10 New Pence. Silver. Uniface.	—

TS13	1963	—	20 New Pence. Silver. Uniface.	—

TS8	1963	—	1/2 New Penny. Bronze. Uniface.	—

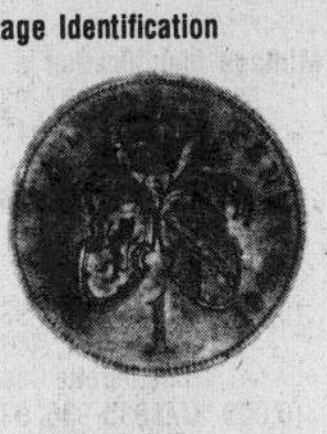

TS9	1963	—	New Penny. Bronze. Uniface.	—

TS10	1963	—	2 New Pence. Bronze. Uniface.	—

TS14	1963	—	20 New Pence. Silver. Uniface.	—

MAUNDY SETS

KM#	Date	Mintage	Identification	Issue Price	Mkt Val
MDS157	1901 (4)	8,976	KM#775-778	—	80.00
MDS158	1902 (4)	8,976	KM#795-796, 797.1-798	—	80.00
MDS159	1902 (4)	—	KM#795-796, 797.1-798 Proof	—	80.00
MDS160	1903 (4)	8,976	KM#795-796; 797.1-798	—	75.00
MDS161	1904 (4)	8,976	KM#795-796, 797.1-798	—	75.00
MDS162	1905 (4)	8,976	KM#795-796, 797.2-798	—	75.00
MDS163	1906 (4)	8,800	KM#795-796, 797.2-798	—	75.00
MDS164	1907 (4)	8,760	KM#795-796, 797.2-798	—	75.00
MDS165	1908 (4)	8,760	KM#795-796, 797.2-798	—	75.00
MDS166	1909 (4)	1,983	KM#795-796, 797.2-798	—	110
MDS167	1910 (4)	1,440	KM#795-796, 797.2-798	—	110
MDS168	1911 (4)	1,768	KM#811-814	—	95.00
MDS169	1911 (4)	6,007	KM#811-814 Proof	—	110
MDS170	1912 (4)	1,246	KM#811-814	—	95.00
MDS171	1913 (4)	1,228	KM#811-814	—	95.00
MDS172	1914 (4)	982	KM#811-814	—	95.00
MDS173	1915 (4)	1,293	KM#811-814	—	95.00
MDS174	1916 (4)	1,128	KM#811-814	—	95.00
MDS175	1917 (4)	1,237	KM#811-814	—	95.00
MDS176	1918 (4)	1,375	KM#811-814	—	95.00
MDS177	1919 (4)	1,258	KM#811-814	—	95.00
MDS178	1920 (4)	1,399	KM#811-814	—	110
MDS179	1921 (4)	1,386	KM#811a-814a	—	95.00
MDS180	1922 (4)	1,373	KM#811a-814a	—	95.00
MDS181	1923 (4)	1,430	KM#811a-814a	—	95.00
MDS182	1924 (4)	1,515	KM#811a-814a	—	95.00
MDS183	1925 (4)	1,438	KM#811a-814a	—	95.00
MDS184	1926 (4)	1,504	KM#811a-814a	—	95.00
MDS185	1927 (4)	1,647	KM#811a-814a	—	95.00
MDS186	1928 (4)	1,642	KM#827, 839-841	—	95.00
MDS187	1929 (4)	1,761	KM#827, 839-841	—	110
MDS188	1930 (4)	1,724	KM#827, 839-841	—	95.00
MDS189	1931 (4)	1,759	KM#827, 839-841	—	95.00
MDS190	1932 (4)	1,835	KM#827, 839-841	—	95.00
MDS191	1933 (4)	1,872	KM#827, 839-841	—	95.00
MDS192	1934 (4)	1,887	KM#827, 839-841	—	95.00
MDS193	1935 (4)	1,926	KM#827, 839-841	—	110
MDS194	1936 (4)	1,323	KM#827, 839-841	—	180
MDS195	1937 (4)	1,325	KM#846-847, 850-851	—	90.00
MDS196	1937 (4)	26,000	KM#846-847, 850-851 Proof	—	95.00
MDS197	1938 (4)	1,275	KM#846-847, 850-851	—	95.00
MDS198	1939 (4)	1,234	KM#846-847, 850-851	—	95.00
MDS199	1940 (4)	1,277	KM#846-847, 850-851	—	110
MDS200	1941 (4)	1,253	KM#846-847, 850-851	—	95.00
MDS201	1942 (4)	1,231	KM#846-847, 850-851	—	95.00
MDS202	1943 (4)	1,239	KM#846-847, 850-851	—	95.00
MDS203	1944 (4)	1,259	KM#846-847, 850-851	—	95.00
MDS204	1945 (4)	1,355	KM#846-847, 850-851	—	95.00
MDS205	1946 (4)	1,365	KM#846-847, 850-851	—	95.00
MDS206	1947 (4)	1,375	KM#846a-847a, 850a-851a	—	95.00
MDS207	1948 (4)	1,385	KM#846a-847a, 850a-851a	—	95.00
MDS208	1949 (4)	1,395	KM#870-872, 874	—	95.00
MDS209	1950 (4)	1,405	KM#870-872, 874	—	120
MDS210	1951 (4)	1,468	KM#870-872, 874	—	95.00
MDS211	1952 (4)	1,012	KM#870-872, 874	—	95.00
MDS212	1953 (4)	1,025	KM#884-885, 887-888	—	450
MDS213	1954 (4)	1,020	KM#898-899, 901-902	—	95.00
MDS214	1955 (4)	1,036	KM#898-899, 901-902	—	95.00
MDS215	1956 (4)	1,088	KM#898-899, 901-902	—	95.00
MDS216	1957 (4)	1,094	KM#898-899, 901-902	—	95.00
MDS217	1958 (4)	1,100	KM#898-899, 901-902	—	95.00
MDS218	1959 (4)	1,106	KM#898-899, 901-902	—	95.00
MDS219	1960 (4)	1,112	KM#898-899, 901-902	—	110
MDS220	1961 (4)	—	KM#898-899, 901-902	—	95.00
MDS221	1962 (4)	1,125	KM#898-899, 901-902	—	95.00
MDS222	1963 (4)	1,131	KM#898-899, 901-902	—	95.00
MDS223	1964 (4)	1,137	KM#898-899, 901-902	—	95.00
MDS224	1965 (4)	1,143	KM#898-899, 901-902	—	95.00
MDS225	1966 (4)	1,206	KM#898-899, 901-902	—	95.00
MDS226	1967 (4)	986	KM#898-899, 901-902	—	95.00
MDS227	1968 (4)	964	KM#898-899, 901-902	—	95.00
MDS228	1969 (4)	1,002	KM#898-899, 901-902	—	110
MDS229	1970 (4)	980	KM#898-899, 901-902	—	110
MDS230	1971 (4)	1,018	KM#898-899, 901-902	—	80.00
MDS231	1972 (4)	1,026	KM#898-899, 901-902	—	80.00
MDS232	1973 (4)	1,004	KM#898-899, 901-902	—	80.00
MDS233	1974 (4)	1,042	KM#898-899, 901-902	—	80.00
MDS234	1975 (4)	1,050	KM#898-899, 901-902	—	80.00
MDS235	1976 (4)	1,257	KM#898-899, 901-902	—	80.00
MDS236	1977 (4)	1,248	KM#898-899, 901-902	—	85.00
MDS237	1978 (4)	1,179	KM#898-899, 901-902	—	85.00
MDS238	1979 (4)	1,180	KM#898-899, 901-902	—	85.00
MDS239	1980 (4)	1,148	KM#898-899, 901-902	—	85.00
MDS240	1981 (4)	1,398	KM#898-899, 901-902	—	85.00
MDS241	1982 (4)	1,220	KM#898-899, 901-902	—	85.00
MDS242	1983 (4)	1,228	KM#898-899, 901-902	—	85.00
MDS243	1984 (4)	1,238	KM#898-899, 901-902	—	85.00
MDS244	1985 (4)	1,248	KM#898-899, 901-902	—	85.00
MDS245	1986 (4)	1,378	KM#898-899, 901-902	—	85.00
MDS246	1987 (4)	1,390	KM#898-899, 901-902	—	110
MDS247	1988 (4)	1,402	KM#898-899, 901-902	—	110
MDS248	1989 (4)	1,353	KM#898-899, 901-902	—	110
MDS249	1990 (4)	1,523	KM#898-899, 901-902	—	110
MDS250	1991 (4)	1,384	KM#898-899, 901-902	—	110
MDS251	1992 (4)	1,424	KM#898-899, 901-902	—	110
MDS252	1993 (4)	1,440	KM#898-899, 901-902	—	110
MDS253	1994 (4)	1,433	KM#898-899, 901-902	—	110
MDS254	1995 (4)	1,466	KM#898-899, 901-902	—	120
MDS255	1996 (4)	1,629	KM#898-899, 901-902	—	125
MDS256	1997 (4)	1,786	KM#898-899, 901-902	—	135
MDS257	1998 (4)	1,619	KM#898-899, 901-902	—	140
MDS258	1999 (4)	—	KM#898-899, 901-902	—	145

MINT SETS

KM#	Date	Mintage	Identification	Issue Price	Mkt Val
MS101	1953 (9)	—	KM#881-883, 886, 889-893	1.25	12.00
MS102	1968/71 (5)	—	KM#911-912 (1968), 914-916 (1971), blue wallet	0.50	2.00
MS103	1982 (7)	205,000	KM#926-932	6.00	12.50
MS104	1983 (8)	637,100	KM#926-933	8.75	22.00
MS105	1984 (8)	158,820	KM#926-932, 934	8.75	19.00
MS106	1985 (7)	178,375	KM#935-940.1, 941	8.75	15.00
MS107	1986 (8)	167,224	KM#935-940.1, 946-947	9.75	20.00
MS108	1987 (7)	172,425	KM#935-940.1, 948	9.00	21.50
MS109	1988 (7)	134,067	KM#935-940.1, 954	9.00	17.50
MS110	1989 (7)	77,569	KM#935-940.1, 959	10.00	26.00
MS111	1989 (2)	—	KM#960-961	11.00	17.00
MS112	1990 (8)	102,606	KM#935-936, 937, 936b, 938-940.1, 941	15.00	23.50
MS113	1991 (7)	74,975	KM#935-936, 937b, 938-940.1, 946	15.00	20.00
MS114	1991 (7)	—	KM#935-936, 937b, 938-940.1, 946 Baby Pack	18.50	22.50
MS115	1992 (9)	78,421	KM#935-936, 937b, 938, 938b, 939-940.1, 948, 963	17.50	20.00
MS116	1992 (9)	—	KM#935-936, 937b, 938, 938b, 939-940.1, 948, 963	22.50	20.00
MS117	1993 (8)	56,945	KM#935a-936a, 937b, 938b, 939-940.1, 963-964	22.50	22.50
MS118	1994 (8)	177,971	KM#935a-936a, 937b, 938b, 939, 966-968	22.50	20.00
MS119	1995 (8)	105,647	KM#935a-936a, 937b-938b, 939-940.1, 969-970	—	20.00
MS120	1996 (8)	86,501	KM#935a-936a, 937b-938b, 939-940.1, 972-973	18.50	20.00
MS121	1997 (9)	109,557	KM#935a, 936a, 937b, 938b, 939-940.1, 940.2, 975-976	—	20.00
MS122	1998 (9)	—	KM#986-994	25.00	15.00
MS124	1998 (2)	96,149	KM#991-992	15.00	9.50
MS125	1999 (8)	136,492	KM#986a-991, 998-999	20.00	18.00
MS126	2000 (9)	—	KM#986a-991, 994, 1004-1005 Wedding Collection	20.00	20.00
MS127	2000 (9)	—	KM#986a-991, 994, 1004-1005	25.00	25.00
MS128	2000 (9)	—	M#986a-991, 994, 1004-1005 Baby Gift Set	25.00	25.00

KM#	Date	Mintage	Identification	Issue Price	Mkt Val
MS129	2001 (9)	—	KM#986-991, 994, 1013-1015	22.50	—
MS130	2001 (9)	—	KM#986-991, 994, 1013-1014	27.50	—
MS131	2001 (9)	—	KM#986-991, 994, 1013-1014	27.50	—
MS132	2002 (8)	—	KM#986-991, 994, 1030	22.50	25.00
MS133	2002 (8)	—	KM#986-991, 994, 1030	27.50	28.00
MS134	2002 (8)	—	KM#986-991, 994, 1030	27.50	28.00
MS135	2003 (10)	—	KM#986-991, 993, 994, 1036-1037	22.50	—
MS136	2003 (10)	—	KM#986-991, 993, 994, 1036-1037	27.50	—
MS137	2003 (10)	—	KM#986-991, 993, 994, 1036-1037	27.50	—

PROOF SETS

KM#	Date	Mintage	Identification	Issue Price	Mkt Val
PS15	1902 (13)	8,066	KM#795-797.1, 798-807	—	2,000
PS16	1902 (11)	7,057	KM#795-797.1, 798-805	—	600
PS17	1911 (12)	2,812	KM#811-818.1, 819-822	—	3,500
PS18	1911 (10)	952	KM#811-818.1, 819-820	—	900
PS19	1911 (8)	2,241	KM#811-818.1	—	400
PS20	1927 (6)	15,030	KM#831-836	—	375
PSA20	1927 (6)	—	KM#831-836 Matte Proof; Rare	—	—
PS21	1937 (15)	26,402	KM#843-857	—	225
PSA21	1937 (15)	—	KM#843-857 Matte Proof; Rare	—	—
PS22	1937 (4)	5,500	KM#858-861	—	2,250
PSA22	1937 (4)	1	KM#858-861 Matte Proof; Unique	—	—
PS23	1950 (9)	17,513	KM#867-869, 873, 875-879	2.50	75.00
PSA23	1950 (9)	3	KM#867-869, 873, 875-879; Rare, matte proof	—	—
PS24	1951 (10)	20,000	KM#867-869, 873, 875-880	2.80	80.00
PSA24	1951 (10)	3	KM#867-869, 873, 875-880; Rare, matte proof	—	—
PS25	1953 (10)	40,000	KM#881-883, 886, 889-894	3.50	95.00
PSA25	1953 (10)	3	KM#881-883, 886, 889-894; Rare, matte proof	—	—
PS26	1970 (8)	750,000	KM#896-897, 900, 903-907 (Issued 1971)	8.75	20.00
PS27	1971 (6)	350,000	KM#911-916 (Issued 1973)	8.85	14.50
PS28	1972 (7)	150,000	KM#911-917 (Issued 1976)	13.00	19.00
PS29	1973 (6)	100,000	KM#911-912, 914-916, 918 (Issued 1976)	13.00	17.50
PS30	1974 (6)	100,000	KM#911-916 (Issued 1976)	13.00	13.50
PS31	1975 (6)	100,000	KM#911-916 (Issued 1976)	13.00	13.50
PS32	1976 (6)	100,000	KM#911-916	13.00	14.00
PS33	1977 (7)	193,800	KM#911-916, 920	17.00	17.50
PS34	1978 (6)	88,100	KM#911-916	15.00	19.50
PS35	1979 (6)	81,000	KM#911-916	15.00	16.00
PS37	1980 (4)	10,000	KM#919, 922-924	2,650	1,150
PS36	1980 (6)	143,400	KM#911-916	23.00	15.50
PS38	1981 (2)	2,500	KM#919, 925a	—	160
PS39	1981 (6)	—	KM#911-916	26.00	15.50
PS40	1981 (9)	5,000	KM#911-916, 919, 924, 925a	—	935
PS42	1982 (4)	2,500	KM#919, 922-924	—	1,350
PS41	1982 (7)	—	KM#926-932	21.60	16.00
PS44	1983 (3)	—	KM#919, 922-923	775	535
PS43	1983 (8)	125,000	KM#926-933	29.95	25.00
PS46	1984 (3)	—	KM#919, 922, 924	1,275	910
PS45	1984 (8)	125,000	KM#926-932, 934	29.95	23.50
PS48	1985 (4)	12,500	KM#942-945	1,395	1,175
PS47	1985 (7)	125,000	KM#935-940.1, 941	29.75	23.50
PS50	1986 (3)	12,500	KM#942-943, 947c	675	535
PS49	1986 (8)	125,000	KM#935-940.1, 946-947	29.75	28.50
PS53	1987 (3)	12,500	KM#942-944	675	535
PS51	1987 (7)	125,000	KM#935-940.1, 948	29.75	25.00
PS52	1987 (4)	10,000	KM#950-953	1,595	1,000
PS54	1987 (2)	12,500	KM#950-951	325	190
PS57	1988 (3)	—	KM#942-944	775	510
PS55	1988 (7)	125,000	KM#935-940.1, 954	29.75	27.50
PS56	1988 (4)	6,500	KM#950-953	1,595	1,000
PS58	1988 (2)	7,500	KM#950-951	340	190
PS61	1989 (4)	5,000	KM#955-958	1,595	1,600
PS62	1989 (3)	15,000	KM#955-957	775	675
PS64	1989 (2)	—	KM#960a-961a	—	55.00
PS59	1989 (9)	100,000	KM#935-940.1, 959-961	34.95	46.00
PS60	1989 (4)	2,500	KM#950-953	1,595	1,000
PS63	1989 (2)	1,500	KM#950-951	340	200
PS68	1990 (4)	2,500	KM#942-944, 949	1,595	1,400
PS69	1990 (4)	2,500	KM#950a-953a	1,595	1,000
PS70	1990 (3)	7,500	KM#942-944	775	570
PS71	1990 (2)	35,000	KM#937a-937c	47.50	39.00
PS66	1990 (8)	100,000	KM#935-937, 937b, 938-940.1, 941 Leatherette Case	35.00	36.00
PS67	1990 (8)	I.A.	KM#935-937, 937b, 938-940.1, 941 Leather Case	45.00	35.00
PS74	1991 (4)	1,500	KM#942-944, 949	1,750	1,500
PS75	1991 (4)	750	KM#950a-953a	1,750	1,500
PS76	1991 (3)	2,500	KM#942-944	895	665
PS72	1991 (7)	10,000	KM#935-936, 937b, 938-940.1, 946 Leatherette Case	38.50	22.50
PS73	1991 (7)	10,000	KM#935-936, 937b, 938-940.1, 946 Leather Case	48.50	27.50
PS79	1992 (4)	1,250	KM#942-945	1,750	1,450
PS80	1992 (4)	1,000	KM#938b, 938c, 948a, 963a	122	125
PS81	1992 (3)	1,250	KM#942-944	895	710
PS82	1992 (2)	—	KM#938a-938c	59.45	46.00
PS77	1992 (9)	100,000	KM#935-936, 937b, 938, 938b, 939-94.1, 948, 963 Leatherette Case	44.50	46.00
PS78	1992 (9)	100,000	KM#935-936, 937b, 938, 938b, 939-940.1, 948, 963 Leather Case	44.50	40.00
PS85	1993 (4)	500	KM#950a-953a	1,755	1,600
PS86	1993 (4)	1,250	KM#942-945	1,560	1,530
PS87	1993 (3)	1,250	KM#942-944	800	670
PS83	1993 (8)	100,000	KM#935a-936a, 937b, 938b, 939-940.1, 964-965 Standard Case	50.00	47.00
PS84	1993 (8)	I.A.	KM#935a-936a, 937b, 938b, 939-940.1, 964-965 Deluxe Case	60.00	55.00
PS90	1994 (4)	500	KM#950a-953a	1,499	1,500
PS91	1994 (4)	1,250	KM#942-943, 945, 968c	—	1,550
PS92	1994 (3)	1,250	KM#942-943, 968c	—	760
PS88	1994 (8)	100,000	KM#935a-936a, 937b, 938b, 939, 966-968 Standard Case	45.00	34.00
PS89	1994 (8)	I.A.	KM#935a-936a, 937b, 938b, 939, 966-968 Deluxe Case	55.00	50.00
PS93	1995 (8)	42,842	KM#935a-936a, 937b-938b, 939-940.1, 969-970	—	41.50
PS94	1995 (8)	17,797	KM#935a-936a, 937b-938b, 939-940.1, 969-970 Deluxe Case	—	60.00
PS95	1995 (4)	1,250	KM#942-943, 945, 971c	—	1,675
PS96	1995 (4)	500	KM#950a-953a	1,500	1,500
PS97	1995 (3)	1,250	KM#942-943, 945	—	860
PS100	1996 (4)	2,500,000	KM#950a-953a	1,600	1,500
PS101	1996 (7)	—	KM#935b, 936b, 937c, 938c, 939a, 940.1a, 972a	—	155
PS98	1996 (9)	100,000	KM#935a-936a, 937b-938b, 939-940.1, 972-973	44.75	42.50
PS99	1996 (9)	—	KM#935a-936a, 937b-938b, 939-940.1, 972-973 Deluxe Case	56.00	55.00
PS102	1997 (10)	70,000	KM#935a, 936a, 937b, 938b, 939, 940.1, 940.2, 975-976, 977a	—	50.00
PS103	1997 (4)	15,000	KM#978-981	145	135
PS104	1997 (4)	1,500	KM#982-985	1,600	1,650
PS105	1998 (10)	100,000	KM#986-995	55.00	50.00
PSA105	1998 (2)	10,000	Piefort versions of KM#992a, 996a	—	140
PS107	1999 (4)	1,000	KM#999a, 1001-1003	1,725	1,725
PS108	1999 (3)	1,250	KM#1001-1003	—	955
PS109	1999 (4)	750	KM#950a-953a	1,495	1,500
PS110	1999 (4)	—	KM#1008-1011	1,595	—
PS106	1999 (9)	100,000	KM#986a-987a, 988-991, 997-999	50.00	50.00
PS114	2000 (4)	750	KM#1008-1011	1,495	1,498
PS115	2000 (13)	15,000	KM#898, 899, 901, 902, 986b, 987a, 988a, 989a, 990a, 991a, 994a, 1005a, 1006a	—	375
PSA115	2000 (3)	1,250	KM#994b, 1001, 1002	—	—
PSB115	2000 (13)	15,000	KM#898, 899, 901, 902, 986b, 987b, 988a-991a, 994a, 1005a	—	—
PS111	2000 (10)	90,000	KM#986a-991, 994, 1004-1006 Standard Set	50.00	50.00
PS112	2000 (10)	10,000	KM#986a-991, 994, 1004-1006 Deluxe Set	65.00	65.00
PS113	2000 (10)	15,000	KM#986-991, 994, 1004-1006 Executive Set	115	115
PS116	2001 (3)	1,500	KM#1001-1002, 1014a	795	—
PS117	2001 (4)	1,000	KM#1001-1003,1014a	1,645	—
PS118	2001 (4)	5,000	KM#1016-1019	—	140
PS127	2001 (10)	10,000	KM#986-991, 994, 1013-1015	115	—
PS128	2001 (10)	30,000	KM#986-991, 994, 1013-1015	72.50	—
PS129	2001 (10)	60,000	KM#986-991, 994, 1013-1015	50.00	—
PS130	2001 (10)	I.A.	KM#986-991, 994, 1013-1015	65.00	—
PSA119	2001 (3)	1,500	KM#1001, 1002, 1014b	—	—
PSB119	2001 (4)	1,000	KM#1001, 1002, 1014b, 1015b	—	—
PS120	2002 (3)	5,000	KM#1025-1027	795	—
PS121	2002 (4)	3,000	KM#1025-1028	1,645	—
PS122	2002 (4)	—	KM#1031-1034; Standard Set	34.95	—
PS123	2002 (4)	—	KM#1031-1034; Display Set	44.95	—
PS124	2002 (4)	10,000	KM#1031a-1034a; Display Set	120	—
PS125	2002 (4)	500	KM#1031b-1034b; Display Set	1,675	—
PS126	2002 (4)	1,000	KM#1008-1011	1,600	1,625
PS131	2002 (9)	5,000	KM#986-991, 994, 1024, 1030	100	100
PS132	2002 (9)	30,000	KM#986-991, 994, 1024, 1030	70.00	75.00
PS133	2002 (9)	65,000	KM#986-991, 994, 1024, 1030	48.00	50.00
PS134	2002 (9)	I.A.	KM#986-991, 994, 1024, 1030	62.40	65.00
PS135	2003 (11)	—	KM#986-991, 993, 994, 1036-1038	100	—
PS136	2003 (11)	—	KM#986-991, 993, 994, 1036-1038	72.00	—
PS137	2003 (11)	—	KM#986-991, 993, 994, 1036-1038	50.00	—

GREECE

The Hellenic (Greek) Republic is situated in southeastern Europe on the southern tip of the Balkan Peninsula. The republic includes many islands, the most important of which are Crete and the Ionian Islands. Greece (including islands) has an area of 50,944 sq. mi. (131,940 sq. km.) and a population of 10.3 million. Capital: Athens. Greece is still largely agricultural. Tobacco, cotton, fruit and wool are exported.

Greece, the Mother of Western civilization, attained the peak of its culture in the 5th century B.C., when it contributed more to government, drama, art and architecture than any other people to this time. Greece fell under Roman domination in the 2nd and 1st centuries B.C., becoming part of the Byzantine Empire until Constantinople fell to the Crusaders in 1202. With the fall of Constantinople to the Turks in 1453, Greece became part of the Ottoman Empire. Independence from Turkey was won with the revolution of 1821-27. In 1833, Greece was established as a monarchy, with sovereignty guaranteed by Britain, France and Russia. After a lengthy power struggle between the monarchist forces and democratic factions, Greece was proclaimed a republic in 1925. The monarchy was restored in 1935 and reconfirmed by a plebiscite in 1946. The Italians invaded Greece via Albania on Oct. 28, 1940 but were driven back well within the Albanian border. Germany began their invasion in April 1941 and quickly overran the entire country and drove off a British Expeditionary force by the end of April. King George II and his new government went into exile. The German--Italian occupation of Greece lasted until Oct. 1944 after which only German troops remained until the end of the occupation. On April 21, 1967, a military junta took control of the government and suspended the constitution. King Constantine II made an unsuccessful attempt against the junta in the fall of 1968 and consequently fled to Italy. The monarchy was formally abolished by plebiscite, Dec. 8, 1974, and Greece was established as the Hellenic Republic, the third republic in Greek history.

RULERS

George I, 1863-1913
Constantine I, 1913-1917, 1920-1922
Alexander I, 1917-1920
George II, 1922-1923, 1935-1947
Paul I, 1947-1964
Constantine II, 1964-1973

MINT MARKS

(a) - Paris, privy marks only
A - Paris
B - Vienna
BB - Strassburg
H - Heaton, Birmingham
K - Bordeaux
KN - King's Norton
(p) - Poissy - Thunderbolt

MONETARY SYSTEM

Commencing 1831
100 Lepta = 1 Drachma

KINGDOM

DECIMAL COINAGE

KM# 62 5 LEPTA Composition: Nickel **Reverse:** Owl on amphora

Date	Mintage	F	VF	XF	Unc	BU
1912(a)	25,053,000	0.75	1.50	5.00	30.00	—

KM# 63 10 LEPTA Composition: Nickel **Reverse:** Owl on amphora

Date	Mintage	F	VF	XF	Unc	BU
1912(a)	28,973,000	0.75	1.50	5.00	30.00	—

KM# 66.1 10 LEPTA Weight: 1.5200 g. **Composition:** Aluminum **Note:** 1.77mm thick.

Date	Mintage	F	VF	XF	Unc	BU
1922(p)	120,000,000	1.00	2.00	6.50	30.00	—

KM# 66.2 10 LEPTA Weight: 1.6500 g. **Composition:** Aluminum **Note:** 2.2mm thick.

Date	F	VF	XF	Unc	BU
1922(p)	—	—	—	—	—

KM# 64 20 LEPTA Composition: Nickel **Rev. Legend:** Goddess Athena

Date	Mintage	F	VF	XF	Unc	BU
1912(a)	10,145,000	0.75	2.00	6.50	50.00	—

KM# 65 50 LEPTA Composition: Copper-Nickel **Note:** Most of these were melted and only 30 - 40 of each piece are known to exist.

Date	Mintage	F	VF	XF	Unc	BU
1921H	1,000,000	300	600	1,200	2,500	—
1921KN	1,524,000	500	1,000	2,000	3,750	—

KM# 60 DRACHMA Weight: 5.0000 g. **Composition:** 0.8350 Silver .1342 oz. ASW **Obverse:** George I **Reverse:** Mythological figure Thetis with shield of Achilles, seated on sea-horse

Date	Mintage	F	VF	XF	Unc	BU
1910(a)	4,570,000	7.50	15.00	30.00	100	—
1911(a)	1,881,000	9.00	20.00	40.00	125	—

KM# 61 2 DRACHMAI Weight: 10.0000 g. **Composition:** 0.8350 Silver .2684 oz. ASW **Obverse:** George I **Reverse:** Mythological figure Thetis with shield of Achilles seated on sea-horse

Date	Mintage	F	VF	XF	Unc	BU
1911(a)	1,500,000	10.00	30.00	60.00	200	—

REPUBLIC

DECIMAL COINAGE

KM# 67 20 LEPTA Composition: Copper-Nickel **Reverse:** Helmeted goddess Athena

Date	Mintage	F	VF	XF	Unc	BU
1926	20,000,000	0.75	1.50	4.50	12.50	—

KM# 68 50 LEPTA Composition: Copper-Nickel

Date	Mintage	F	VF	XF	Unc	BU
1926	20,000,000	0.45	1.00	3.50	12.50	—
1926B (1930)	20,000,000	0.45	1.00	3.50	12.50	—

KM# 69 DRACHMA Composition: Copper-Nickel

Date	Mintage	F	VF	XF	Unc	BU
1926	15,000,000	0.45	1.00	3.50	20.00	—
1926B (193	20,000,000	0.45	1.00	3.50	20.00	—

KM# 70 2 DRACHMAI Composition: Copper-Nickel

Date	Mintage	F	VF	XF	Unc	BU
1926	22,000,000	1.00	2.00	5.00	25.00	—

KM# 71.1 5 DRACHMAI Composition: Nickel **Obverse:** Phoenix **Note:** LONDON MINT: In second set of berries on left only 1 berry will have a dot on it.

Date	Mintage	F	VF	XF	Unc	BU
1930	23,500,000	0.75	1.50	5.50	30.00	—
1930 Proof	—	Value: 400				

KM# 71.2 5 DRACHMAI Composition: Nickel **Note:** BRUSSELLS MINT: 2 berries will have dots.

Date	Mintage	F	VF	XF	Unc	BU
1930	1,500,000	1.50	3.50	10.00	50.00	—

KM# 72 10 DRACHMAI Weight: 7.0000 g. **Composition:** 0.5000 Silver .1125 oz. ASW

Date	Mintage	F	VF	XF	Unc	BU
1930	7,500,000	5.00	10.00	20.00	100	—
1930 Proof	—	Value: 500				

KM# 73 20 DRACHMAI **Weight:** 11.3100 g. **Composition:** 0.5000 Silver .1818 oz. ASW **Obverse:** Prow of ancient ship **Reverse:** Neptune

Date	Mintage	F	VF	XF	Unc	BU
1930	11,500,000	6.00	12.50	25.00	150	—
1930 Proof	—	Value: 600				

KINGDOM

DECIMAL COINAGE

KM# 77 5 LEPTA **Composition:** Aluminum

Date	Mintage	F	VF	XF	Unc	BU
1954	15,000,000	—	0.20	0.50	2.00	—
1971	1,002,000	0.20	0.50	1.00	5.00	—

Note: 1971 dated coins have smaller hole at center

KM# 78 10 LEPTA **Composition:** Aluminum

Date	Mintage	F	VF	XF	Unc	BU
1954	48,000,000	—	0.15	0.45	3.00	—
1959	20,000,000	—	0.15	0.45	3.00	—
1964	12,000,000	—	0.15	0.45	3.00	—
1965 In sets only	—	—	—	—	3.50	—
1965 In proof sets only	4,987	Value: 5.00				
1966	20,000,000	—	0.15	0.45	3.00	—
1969	20,000,000	—	0.15	0.45	3.00	—
1971 Small center hole	5,922,000	—	0.35	1.00	5.00	—

KM# 102 10 LEPTA **Composition:** Aluminum **Obverse:** Soldier and Phoenix

Date	Mintage	F	VF	XF	Unc	BU
1973	2,742,000	—	0.20	1.00	5.00	—

KM# 79 20 LEPTA **Composition:** Aluminum

Date	Mintage	F	VF	XF	Unc	BU
1954	24,000,000	—	0.15	0.50	2.00	—
1959	20,000,000	—	0.15	0.50	2.00	—
1964	8,000,000	—	0.15	0.50	2.00	—
1966	15,000,000	—	0.15	0.50	2.00	—
1969	20,000,000	—	0.15	0.50	2.00	—
1971 Small center hole	4,108,000	—	0.35	1.00	2.50	—

KM# 104 20 LEPTA **Composition:** Aluminum **Obverse:** Soldier in front of phoenix, anniverary date below **Reverse:** Olive branch, denomination

Date	Mintage	F	VF	XF	Unc	BU
1973	2,718,000	—	0.20	0.60	5.00	—

KM# 80 50 LEPTA **Composition:** Copper-Nickel

Date	Mintage	F	VF	XF	Unc	BU
1954	37,228,000	0.15	0.25	1.00	5.50	—
1957	5,108,000	0.25	1.00	10.00	30.00	—
1957 Proof	—	Value: 175				
1959	10,160,000	0.15	0.25	1.00	5.50	—
1962 Plain edge	20,500,000	0.15	0.25	0.75	4.50	—
1962 Serrated edge	Inc. above	0.15	0.25	0.75	4.50	—
1964	20,000,000	0.15	0.25	0.75	4.50	—
1965 In sets only	—	—	—	—	6.00	—
1965 In proof sets only	4,987	Value: 7.50				

KM# 88 50 LEPTA **Composition:** Copper-Nickel

Date	Mintage	F	VF	XF	Unc	BU
1966	30,000,000	0.20	0.50	1.00	4.50	—
1970	10,160,000	0.30	0.60	1.50	5.00	—

KM# 97.1 50 LEPTA **Composition:** Copper-Nickel **Obverse:** Small head

Date	Mintage	F	VF	XF	Unc	BU
1971	10,999,000	—	0.10	0.15	3.00	—
1973	9,342,000	—	0.20	0.50	4.00	—

KM# 97.2 50 LEPTA **Composition:** Copper-Nickel **Obverse:** Large head

Date	F	VF	XF	Unc	BU
1973	—	0.20	0.50	4.00	—

KM# 81 DRACHMA **Composition:** Copper-Nickel

Date	Mintage	F	VF	XF	Unc	BU
1954	24,091,000	0.15	0.25	0.75	5.50	—
1957	8,151,000	0.15	0.25	2.00	30.00	—
1957 Proof	—	Value: 225				
1959	10,180,000	0.15	0.25	2.00	10.00	—
1962	20,060,000	0.15	0.25	0.75	5.50	—
1965 In sets only	—	—	—	—	6.00	—
1965 In proof sets only	4,987	Value: 7.50				

KM# 89 DRACHMA **Composition:** Copper-Nickel

Date	Mintage	F	VF	XF	Unc	BU
1966	20,000,000	—	0.15	0.45	3.50	—
1967	20,000,000	—	0.15	0.45	3.50	—
1970	7,001,000	—	0.50	1.00	6.00	—

KM# 98 DRACHMA **Composition:** Copper-Nickel

Date	Mintage	F	VF	XF	Unc	BU
1971	11,985,000	—	0.20	0.75	3.50	—
1973	8,196,000	—	0.25	1.00	4.50	—

KM# 82 2 DRACHMAI **Composition:** Copper-Nickel

Date	Mintage	F	VF	XF	Unc	BU
1954	12,609,000	0.50	0.75	1.50	6.00	—
1957	10,171,000	0.50	0.75	2.50	30.00	—
1957 Proof	—	Value: 300				
1959	5,000,000	0.50	0.75	2.50	10.00	—
1962	10,096,000	0.50	0.75	1.50	6.00	—
1965 In sets only	—	—	—	—	5.00	—
1965 In proof sets only	4,987	Value: 7.50				

KM# 90 2 DRACHMAI **Composition:** Copper-Nickel

Date	Mintage	F	VF	XF	Unc	BU
1966	10,000,000	0.15	0.25	0.50	3.50	—
1967	10,000,000	0.15	0.25	0.50	3.50	—
1970	7,000,000	0.50	1.00	2.00	7.00	—

KM# 99 2 DRACHMAI **Composition:** Copper-Nickel

Date	Mintage	F	VF	XF	Unc	BU
1971	9,998,000	0.15	0.25	0.75	3.50	—
1973	7,972,000	0.20	0.50	1.50	4.50	—

KM# 83 5 DRACHMAI **Composition:** Copper-Nickel

Date	Mintage	F	VF	XF	Unc	BU
1954	21,000,000	0.25	0.50	1.00	6.00	—
1965 In sets only	—	—	—	—	5.50	—
1965 In proof sets only	4,987	Value: 10.00				

KM# 91 5 DRACHMAI **Composition:** Copper-Nickel

Date	Mintage	F	VF	XF	Unc	BU
1966	12,000,000	0.15	0.25	1.00	5.00	—
1970	5,000,000	0.50	1.00	3.00	9.00	—

KM# 100 5 DRACHMAI Composition: Copper-Nickel

Date	Mintage	F	VF	XF	Unc	BU
1971	4,014,000	0.25	0.50	2.00	5.00	—
1973	3,166,000	0.25	0.50	1.50	4.50	—

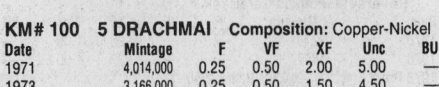

KM# 84 10 DRACHMAI Composition: Nickel

Date	Mintage	F	VF	XF	Unc	BU
1959	20,000,000	0.30	0.50	1.50	6.00	—
1959 Proof	—	Value: 225				
1965 In sets only	—	—	—	—	5.50	—
1965 In proof sets only	4,987	Value: 10.00				

KM# 84a 10 DRACHMAI Composition: Silver

Date	F	VF	XF	Unc	BU
1959 Proof	—	Value: 600			

KM# 96 10 DRACHMAI Composition: Copper-Nickel

Date	Mintage	F	VF	XF	Unc	BU
1968	40,000,000	0.25	0.50	0.75	4.50	—

KM# 101 10 DRACHMAI Composition: Copper-Nickel **Reverse:** Phoenix

Date	Mintage	F	VF	XF	Unc	BU
1971	502,000	0.25	0.50	1.00	6.50	—
1973	541,000	0.50	1.00	2.50	7.00	—

KM# 74 20 DRACHMAI Weight: 6.4516 g. **Composition:** 0.9000 Gold .1867 oz. AGW **Subject:** 5th Anniversary - Restoration of Monarchy

Date	Mintage	F	VF	XF	Unc	BU
ND Proof	200	Value: 6,500				

KM# 85 20 DRACHMAI Weight: 7.5000 g. **Composition:** 0.8350 Silver .2013 oz. ASW

Date	Mintage	F	VF	XF	Unc	BU
1960	20,000,000	—	—	BV	6.00	—
1960 Proof	—	Value: 350				
1965	—	—	—	—	7.00	—
1965 In proof sets only	4,987	Value: 12.50				

KM# 92 20 DRACHMAI Weight: 6.4516 g. **Composition:** 0.9000 Gold .1867 oz. AGW

Date	Mintage	F	VF	XF	Unc	BU
ND (1970)	20,000	—	—	—	225	—

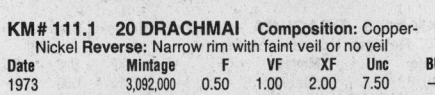

KM# 111.1 20 DRACHMAI Composition: Copper-Nickel **Reverse:** Narrow rim with faint veil or no veil

Date	Mintage	F	VF	XF	Unc	BU
1973	3,092,000	0.50	1.00	2.00	7.50	—

KM# 111.2 20 DRACHMAI Composition: Copper-Nickel **Reverse:** Wide rim with heavy veil and broken wave design at rear hoof

Date	F	VF	XF	Unc	BU
1973	1.00	2.00	4.00	12.00	—

KM# 111.3 20 DRACHMAI Composition: Copper-Nickel **Reverse:** Wide rim with continuous wave design at rear hoof

Date	F	VF	XF	Unc	BU
1973	0.50	1.00	2.00	7.50	—

KM# 93 30 DRACHMAI Weight: 12.5000 g. **Composition:** 0.8350 Silver .3355 oz. ASW **Subject:** 1967 Revolution

Date	Mintage	F	VF	XF	Unc	BU
1967(1970)	100,000	—	—	25.00	30.00	—

KM# 86 30 DRACHMAI Weight: 18.0000 g. **Composition:** 0.8350 Silver .4832 oz. ASW **Subject:** Centennial - Royal Greek Dynasty

Date	Mintage	F	VF	XF	Unc	BU
ND (1963)	3,000,000	—	BV	6.50	10.00	—

KM# 87 30 DRACHMAI Weight: 12.0000 g. **Composition:** 0.8350 Silver .3221 oz. ASW **Subject:** Constantine and Anne-Marie Wedding

Date	Mintage	F	VF	XF	Unc	BU
1964 Berne: small edge lettering	1,000	—	BV	4.50	9.00	—
1964 Kongsberg: large edge lettering	1,000	—	BV	4.50	8.00	—

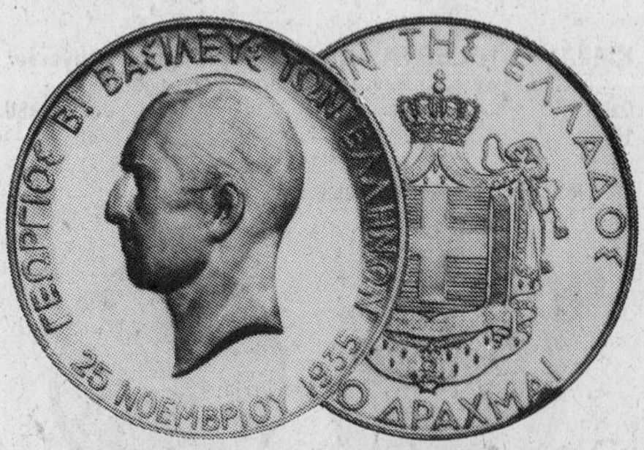

KM# 75 100 DRACHMAI Weight: 25.0000 g. **Composition:** 0.9000 Silver .7235 oz. ASW **Subject:** 5th Anniversary - Restoration of Monarchy **Obverse:** George I **Reverse:** Crowned and mantled arms

Date	Mintage	F	VF	XF	Unc	BU
ND (1940) Proof	500	Value: 1,200				

KM# 76 100 DRACHMAI Weight: 32.2580 g. **Composition:** 0.9000 Gold .9335 oz. AGW

Date	Mintage	F	VF	XF	Unc	BU
ND (1940) Proof	140	Value: 11,000				

KM# 94 100 DRACHMAI **Weight:** 25.0000 g. **Composition:** 0.8350 Silver .6712 oz. ASW **Subject:** 1967 Revolution

Date	Mintage	F	VF	XF	Unc	BU
ND (1970)	30,000	—	—	35.00	60.00	—

KM# 95 100 DRACHMAI **Weight:** 32.2580 g. **Composition:** 0.9000 Gold .9335 oz. AGW **Subject:** 1967 Revolution

Date	Mintage	F	VF	XF	Unc	BU
ND (1970)	10,000	—	—	—	700	—
ND (1970)	10,000	—	—	—	700	—

REPUBLIC

DECIMAL COINAGE

KM# 103 10 LEPTA **Composition:** Aluminum **Obverse:** Modified design; soldier replaced with phoenix **Reverse:** Pair of dolphins flank trident

Date	Mintage	F	VF	XF	Unc	BU
1973	15,134,472	—	0.10	0.50	2.00	—

KM# 113 10 LEPTA **Composition:** Aluminum **Obverse:** Shield in wereath **Reverse:** Charging bull, right

Date	Mintage	F	VF	XF	Unc	BU
1976	2,043,000	—	0.10	0.30	2.00	—
1978	791,000	0.50	1.00	2.50	5.00	—
1978 Proof	20,000	Value: 5.00				

KM# 105 20 LEPTA **Composition:** Aluminum **Obverse:** Modified design; soldier replaced with phoenix

Date	Mintage	F	VF	XF	Unc	BU
1973	15,265,797	—	0.20	0.50	2.50	—

KM# 114 20 LEPTA **Composition:** Aluminum **Obverse:** Shield in wreath **Reverse:** Bust of stallion, left

Date	Mintage	F	VF	XF	Unc	BU
1976	2,506,000	—	0.15	0.40	2.50	—
1978	803,000	0.45	1.00	2.50	5.00	—
1978 Proof	20,000	Value: 5.00				

KM# 106 50 LEPTA **Composition:** Nickel-Brass

Date	Mintage	F	VF	XF	Unc	BU
1973	55,231,898	—	—	0.15	1.00	—

KM# 115 50 LEPTA **Composition:** Nickel-Brass **Reverse:** Markos Botsaris

Date	Mintage	F	VF	XF	Unc	BU
1976	51,016,000	—	—	0.15	1.00	—
1978	12,010,000	—	—	0.15	1.00	—
1978 Proof	20,000	Value: 3.00				
1980	6,682,000	—	—	0.15	1.25	—
1982	3,365,000	—	—	0.15	1.25	—
1984	1,208,000	—	—	0.15	1.25	—
1986	—	—	—	0.15	1.25	—

KM# 107 DRACHMA **Composition:** Nickel-Brass

Date	Mintage	F	VF	XF	Unc	BU
1973	45,218,431	—	0.25	0.75	2.75	—

KM# 116 DRACHMA **Composition:** Nickel-Brass **Reverse:** Konstantinos Kanaris

Date	Mintage	F	VF	XF	Unc	BU
1976	102,060,000	—	—	0.15	1.00	—
Note: Varieties exist						
1978	21,200,000	—	—	0.15	1.00	—
1978 Proof	20,000	Value: 2.50				
1980	52,503,000	—	—	0.15	1.00	—
1982	54,186,000	—	—	0.15	1.00	—
1984	33,665,000	—	—	0.15	1.00	—
1986	17,901,000	—	—	0.15	1.00	—

KM# 150 DRACHMA **Composition:** Copper **Obverse:** Sailing ship **Reverse:** Bouboulina - Heroine

Date	Mintage	F	VF	XF	Unc	BU
1988	36,707,000	—	—	—	0.50	—
1990	—	—	—	—	0.50	—
1992	—	—	—	—	0.50	—
1993	—	—	—	—	0.50	—
1993 Proof	—	Value: 3.50				
1994	—	—	—	—	0.50	—
1998	—	—	—	—	0.50	—
2000	—	—	—	—	0.50	—

KM# 189 DRACHMA **Weight:** 8.5000 g. **Composition:** 0.9167 Gold 0.2505 oz. AGW **Obverse:** Sailing ship **Reverse:** Bouboulina - Heroine

Date	F	VF	XF	Unc	BU
2000 Proof	—	Value: 400			

KM# 108 2 DRACHMAI **Composition:** Nickel-Brass

Date	Mintage	F	VF	XF	Unc	BU
1973	51,163,812	—	0.50	1.25	3.50	—

KM# 117 2 DRACHMAI **Composition:** Nickel-Brass **Reverse:** Georgios Karaiskakis

Date	Mintage	F	VF	XF	Unc	BU
1976	92,401,000	—	—	0.25	1.00	—
1978	16,772,000	—	—	0.25	1.00	—
1978 Proof	20,000	Value: 2.50				
1980	45,955,000	—	—	0.25	1.00	—

KM# 130 2 DRACHMES **Composition:** Nickel-Brass **Reverse:** Georgios Karaiskakis

Date	Mintage	F	VF	XF	Unc	BU
1982	64,414,000	—	—	0.20	1.00	—
1984	37,861,000	—	—	0.20	1.00	—
1986	21,019,000	—	—	0.20	1.00	—

KM# 151 2 DRACHMES **Composition:** Copper **Reverse:** Manto Mavrogenous

Date	Mintage	F	VF	XF	Unc	BU
1988	36,707,000	—	—	—	0.50	—
1990	—	—	—	—	0.50	—
1992	—	—	—	—	0.50	—
1993	—	—	—	—	0.50	—
1993 Proof	—	Value: 4.50				
1994	—	—	—	—	0.50	—
1998	—	—	—	—	0.50	—
2000	—	—	—	—	0.50	—

KM# 109.1 5 DRACHMAI **Composition:** Copper-Nickel **Note:** Denomination spelling ends with I.

Date	Mintage	F	VF	XF	Unc	BU
1973	33,957,473	0.75	1.25	2.00	3.50	—

KM# 109.2 5 DRACHMAI **Composition:** Copper-Nickel **Note:** Denomination spelling ends with A.

Date	F	VF	XF	Unc	BU
1973	1.00	2.00	4.00	10.00	—

KM# 118 5 DRACHMAI **Composition:** Copper-Nickel **Reverse:** Aristotle

Date	Mintage	F	VF	XF	Unc	BU
1976	85,187,000	—	0.20	0.35	1.00	—
1978	17,404,000	—	0.20	0.35	1.00	—
1978 Proof	20,000	Value: 2.00				
1980	33,701,000	—	0.20	0.35	1.00	—

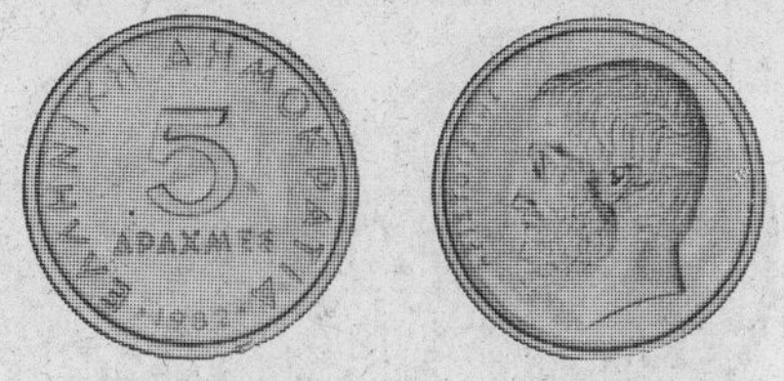

KM# 131 5 DRACHMES **Composition:** Copper-Nickel

Date	Mintage	F	VF	XF	Unc	BU
1982	42,647,000	—	0.20	0.35	1.00	—
1984	29,778,000	—	0.20	0.35	1.00	—
1986	16,730,000	—	0.20	0.35	1.00	—
1988	30,273,000	—	—	0.30	0.75	—
1990	—	—	—	0.30	0.75	—
1992	—	—	—	0.30	0.75	—
1993	—	—	—	0.30	0.75	—
1993 Proof	—	Value: 4.50				
1994	—	—	—	—	0.75	—
1998	—	—	—	—	0.75	—
1999	—	—	—	—	0.75	—
2000	—	—	—	—	0.75	—

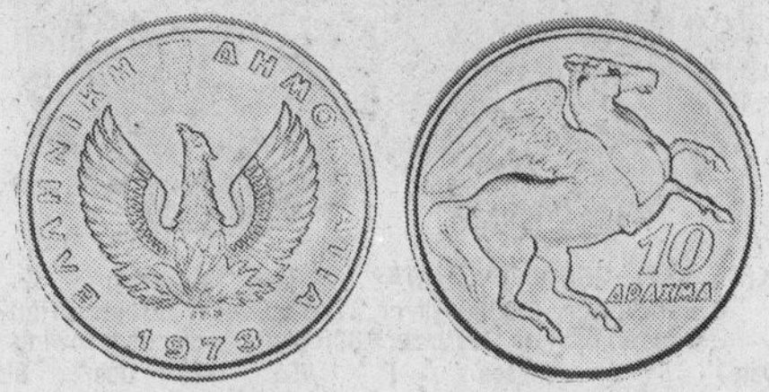

KM# 110 10 DRACHMAI **Composition:** Copper-Nickel

Date	Mintage	F	VF	XF	Unc	BU
1973	22,599,848	1.00	1.50	2.50	4.50	—

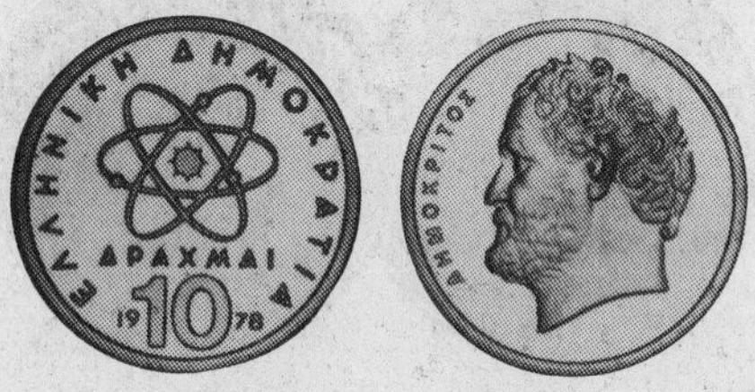

KM# 119 10 DRACHMAI **Composition:** Copper-Nickel
Reverse: Democritus

Date	Mintage	F	VF	XF	Unc	BU
1976	76,816,000	—	0.25	0.50	1.00	—
1978	14,637,000	—	0.25	0.50	1.00	—
1978 Proof	20,000	Value: 2.50				
1980	28,733,000	—	0.25	0.50	1.00	—

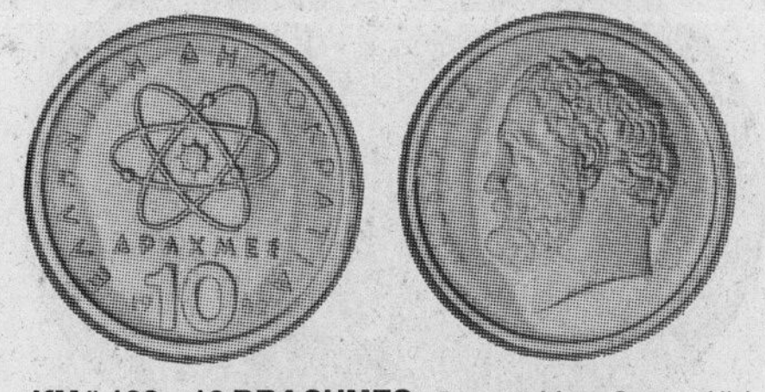

KM# 132 10 DRACHMES **Composition:** Copper-Nickel

Date	Mintage	F	VF	XF	Unc	BU
1982	35,539,000	—	0.25	0.50	1.00	—
1984	23,802,000	—	0.25	0.50	1.00	—
1986	24,441,000	—	0.25	0.50	1.00	—
1988	16,869,000	—	0.20	0.45	1.00	—
1990	—	—	0.20	0.45	1.00	—
1992	—	—	0.20	0.45	1.00	—
1993	—	—	0.20	0.45	1.00	—
1993 Proof	—	Value: 5.00				
1994	—	—	0.20	0.45	1.00	—
1998	—	—	0.20	0.45	1.00	—
2000	—	—	—	—	1.00	—
2002	—	—	0.20	0.45	1.00	—

KM# 112 20 DRACHMAI **Composition:** Copper-Nickel

Date	Mintage	F	VF	XF	Unc	BU
1973	20,650,087	0.35	0.50	1.00	2.00	—

KM# 120 20 DRACHMAI **Composition:** Copper-Nickel
Reverse: Pericles

Date	Mintage	F	VF	XF	Unc	BU
1976	53,167,500	—	0.30	0.50	1.25	—
1978	65,353,000	—	0.30	0.50	1.50	—
1978 Proof	20,000	Value: 3.00				
1980	17,562,000	—	0.30	0.50	1.25	—

KM# 133 20 DRACHMES **Composition:** Copper-Nickel

Date	Mintage	F	VF	XF	Unc	BU
1982	24,299,000	—	0.30	0.50	1.00	—
1984	13,412,000	—	0.30	0.50	1.25	—
1986	10,553,000	—	0.30	0.50	1.00	—
1988	16,196,000	—	—	0.50	1.00	—

KM# 154 20 DRACHMES **Composition:** Nickel-Bronze
Reverse: Dionysious Solomos, composer of National Anthem

Date	F	VF	XF	Unc	BU
1990	—	—	—	1.25	—
1992	—	—	—	1.25	—
1993	—	—	—	1.25	—
1993 Proof	—	Value: 6.50			
1994	—	—	—	1.25	—
1998	—	—	—	1.25	—
2000	—	—	—	1.25	—

KM# 124 50 DRACHMAI **Composition:** Copper-Nickel
Reverse: Solon the Archon of Athens

Date	Mintage	F	VF	XF	Unc	BU
1980	32,250,999	0.50	0.75	1.50	3.50	—

KM# 134 50 DRACHMES **Composition:** Copper-Nickel **Obverse:** Denomination in modern Greek

Date	Mintage	F	VF	XF	Unc	BU
1982	18,899,000	0.40	0.60	1.00	1.50	—
1984	11,411,000	0.40	0.60	1.00	1.50	—

KM# 147 50 DRACHMES **Composition:** Nickel-Brass
Obverse: Ancient sailing boat

Date	Mintage	F	VF	XF	Unc	BU
1986	12,078,000	—	0.50	1.00	2.50	—
1988	23,589,000	—	—	0.75	1.50	—
1990	—	—	—	0.75	1.75	—
1992	—	—	—	0.75	1.75	—
1993	—	—	—	0.75	1.75	—
1993 Proof	—	Value: 7.50				
1994	—	—	—	0.75	1.75	—
1998	—	—	—	—	1.75	—
2000	—	—	—	—	1.75	—

KM# 164 50 DRACHMES **Composition:** Brass
Subject: 150th Anniversary of the Constitution **Obverse:** Portrait of Dimitrios Kallergis

Date	Mintage	F	VF	XF	Unc	BU
ND (1994)	7,500,000	—	—	—	3.00	—

KM# 168 50 DRACHMES **Composition:** Brass
Subject: 150th Anniversary of the Constitution **Obverse:** Portrait of Makrygiannis **Reverse:** Center of Parliament Building

Date	Mintage	F	VF	XF	Unc	BU
ND (1994)	7,500,000	—	—	—	3.00	—

KM# 171 50 DRACHMES **Composition:** Brass
Obverse: National arms **Reverse:** Portrait of Rhigas Feriaou, dates flanking

Date	F	VF	XF	Unc	BU
ND (1998)	—	—	—	3.50	—

KM# 172 50 DRACHMES **Composition:** Brass
Obverse: National arms **Reverse:** Portrait of Dionysious Solomos, date flanking

Date	F	VF	XF	Unc	BU
ND (1998)	—	—	—	3.50	—

KM# 121 100 DRACHMAI **Weight:** 13.0000 g. **Composition:** 0.6500 Silver .2717 oz. ASW **Subject:** 50th Anniversary - Bank of Greece

Date	Mintage	F	VF	XF	Unc	BU
1978 Proof	25,000	Value: 45.00				

KM# 125 100 DRACHMAI **Weight:** 5.7800 g. **Composition:** 0.9000 Silver .1672 oz. ASW **Subject:** Pan-European Games **Reverse:** Ancient olympic broad jump

Date	Mintage	F	VF	XF	Unc	BU
1981	150,000	—	—	—	8.00	—
1981 Proof	150,000	Value: 15.00				

KM# 135 100 DRACHMAI **Weight:** 5.7800 g. **Composition:** 0.9000 Silver .1672 oz. ASW **Subject:** Pan-European Games **Reverse:** Olympic high jump

Date	Mintage	F	VF	XF	Unc	BU
1982	150,000	—	—	—	8.00	—
1982 Proof	Inc. above	Value: 15.00				

KM# 136 100 DRACHMAI **Weight:** 5.7800 g. **Composition:** 0.9000 Silver .1672 oz. ASW **Subject:** Pan-European Games **Reverse:** Pole vault

Date	Mintage	F	VF	XF	Unc	BU
1982	150,000	—	—	—	8.00	—
1982 Proof	Inc. above	Value: 15.00				

KM# 152 100 DRACHMES **Composition:** Copper-Nickel **Subject:** 28th Chess Olympics

Date	Mintage	F	VF	XF	Unc	BU
1988	30,000	—	—	—	12.00	—

KM# 159 100 DRACHMES **Composition:** Brass **Subject:** Macedonia - Alexander the Great

Date	F	VF	XF	Unc	BU
1990	—	—	—	2.35	—
1992	—	—	—	2.35	—
1993	—	—	—	2.35	—
1993 Proof	—	Value: 8.50			
1994	—	—	—	2.35	—
1998	—	—	—	2.35	—
2000	—	—	—	2.35	—

KM# 169 100 DRACHMES **Composition:** Brass **Subject:** VI Universal Track Championship Games **Obverse:** Ancient city view and track above denomination **Reverse:** Runner

Date	Mintage	F	VF	XF	Unc	BU
1997	5,000,000	—	—	—	2.75	—

KM# 170 100 DRACHMES **Composition:** Brass **Subject:** 13th World Basketball Championships **Obverse:** Cup in ball design above denomination **Reverse:** Four basketball players in action

Date	F	VF	XF	Unc	BU
1998	—	—	—	4.50	—

KM# 173 100 DRACHMES **Weight:** 10.0000 g. **Composition:** Brass **Obverse:** Ancient wrestlers **Reverse:** Modern wrestlers **Edge:** Reeded and plain sectioned edge

Date	F	VF	XF	Unc	BU
1999	—	—	—	3.50	—

KM# 174 100 DRACHMES **Weight:** 10.0000 g. **Composition:** Brass **Obverse:** Statue of Atlas **Reverse:** Weight lifter **Edge:** Reeded and plain sectioned edge

Date	F	VF	XF	Unc	BU
1999	—	—	—	3.50	—

KM# 126 250 DRACHMAI **Weight:** 14.4400 g. **Composition:** 0.9000 Silver .4178 oz. ASW **Subject:** Pan-European Games **Reverse:** Ancient olympic javelin throwing

Date	Mintage	F	VF	XF	Unc	BU
1981	150,000	—	—	—	12.50	—
1981 Proof	150,000	Value: 20.00				

KM# 137 250 DRACHMAI **Weight:** 14.4400 g. **Composition:** 0.9000 Silver .4178 oz. ASW **Subject:** Pan-European Games **Reverse:** 1896 olympic discus throwing

Date	Mintage	F	VF	XF	Unc	BU
1982	150,000	—	—	—	12.50	—
1982 Proof	Inc. above	Value: 20.00				

KM# 138 250 DRACHMAI **Weight:** 14.4400 g. **Composition:** 0.9000 Silver .4178 oz. ASW **Subject:** Pan-European Games **Reverse:** Shot put

Date	Mintage	F	VF	XF	Unc	BU
1982	150,000	—	—	—	12.50	—
1982 Proof	Inc. above	Value: 20.00				

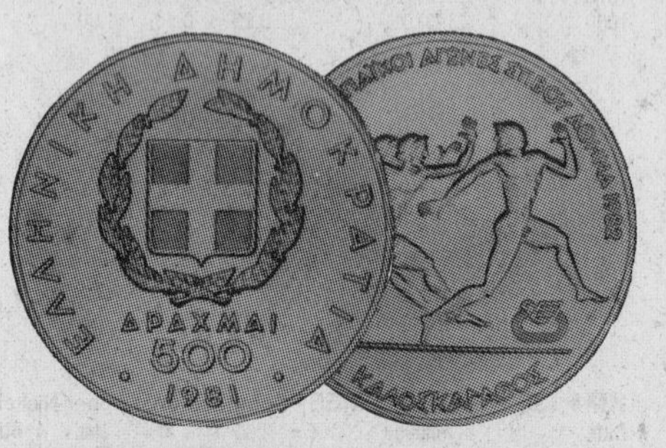

KM# 127 500 DRACHMAI **Weight:** 28.8800 g. **Composition:** 0.9000 Silver .8357 oz. ASW **Subject:** Pan-European Games **Reverse:** Ancient olympic relay race

Date	Mintage	F	VF	XF	Unc	BU
1981	150,000	—	—	—	20.00	—
1981 Proof	150,000	Value: 27.50				

KM# 139 500 DRACHMAI **Weight:** 28.8800 g. **Composition:** 0.9000 Silver .8357 oz. ASW **Subject:** Pan-

European Games **Reverse:** 1896 olympic racers at starting blocks

Date	Mintage	F	VF	XF	Unc	BU
1982	150,000	—	—	—	20.00	—
1982 Proof	Inc. above	Value: 27.50				

KM# 140 500 DRACHMAI **Weight:** 28.8800 g. **Composition:** 0.9000 Silver .8357 oz. ASW **Subject:** Pan-European Games **Reverse:** Racers

Date	Mintage	F	VF	XF	Unc	BU
1982	150,000	—	—	—	20.00	—
1982 Proof	Inc. above	Value: 27.50				

KM# 122 500 DRACHMES **Weight:** 13.0000 g. **Composition:** 0.9000 Silver .3762 oz. ASW **Subject:** Common Market Membership

Date	Mintage	F	VF	XF	Unc	BU
ND (1979)	—	—	—	—	—	—
ND (1979) Proof	18,000	Value: 200				

KM# 145 500 DRACHMES **Weight:** 18.0000 g. **Composition:** 0.9000 Silver .5209 oz. ASW **Subject:** Olympics **Obverse:** Torch

Date	Mintage	F	VF	XF	Unc	BU
1984	25,000	—	—	—	75.00	—
1984 Proof	25,000	Value: 100				

KM# 153 500 DRACHMES **Weight:** 18.1100 g. **Composition:** 0.9000 Silver .5240 oz. ASW **Subject:** 28rh Chess Olympics

Date	Mintage	F	VF	XF	Unc	BU
1988 Proof	3,000	Value: 125				

KM# 157 500 DRACHMES **Weight:** 18.0000 g. **Composition:** 0.9000 Silver .5208 oz. ASW **Subject:** XI Mediterranean Games

Date	Mintage	F	VF	XF	Unc	BU
1991 Proof	10,000	Value: 45.00				

KM# 160 500 DRACHMES **Weight:** 17.0000 g. **Composition:** 0.9250 Silver .5056 oz. ASW **Subject:** 2500th Anniversary of Democracy

Date	Mintage	F	VF	XF	Unc	BU
1993 Proof	Est. 30,000	Value: 45.00				

KM# 162 500 DRACHMES **Weight:** 17.0000 g. **Composition:** 0.9250 Silver .5056 oz. ASW **Subject:** Volleyball Centennial

Date	Mintage	F	VF	XF	Unc	BU
1994 Proof	1,750	Value: 75.00				

KM# 175 500 DRACHMES **Weight:** 9.5400 g. **Composition:** Copper-Nickel **Subject:** 2004 Olympics **Obverse:** Laurel wreath, games logo **Reverse:** Arched entry to ancient Olympic stadium **Edge:** Plain

Date	F	VF	XF	Unc	BU
2000	—	—	—	4.50	—

KM# 176 500 DRACHMES **Weight:** 9.5400 g. **Composition:** Copper-Nickel **Reverse:** Runner receiving Olympic torch **Edge:** Plain

Date	F	VF	XF	Unc	BU
2000	—	—	—	4.50	—

KM# 177 500 DRACHMES **Weight:** 9.5400 g. **Composition:** Copper-Nickel **Reverse:** Ancient winner Diagoras being carried **Edge:** Plain

Date	F	VF	XF	Unc	BU
2000	—	—	—	4.50	—

KM# 178 500 DRACHMES **Weight:** 9.5400 g. **Composition:** Copper-Nickel **Reverse:** Conjoined busts of President Vikelas and Baron Couberten **Edge:** Plain

Date	F	VF	XF	Unc	BU
2000	—	—	—	4.50	—

KM# 179 500 DRACHMES **Weight:** 9.5400 g. **Composition:** Copper-Nickel **Reverse:** Standing Spyros Louis, 1896 marathon winner **Edge:** Plain

Date	F	VF	XF	Unc	BU
2000	—	—	—	4.50	—

KM# 180 500 DRACHMES **Weight:** 9.5400 g. **Composition:** Copper-Nickel **Reverse:** 1896 Olympic gold medal design **Edge:** Plain

Date	F	VF	XF	Unc	BU
2000	—	—	—	4.50	—

KM# 148 1000 DRACHMES **Weight:** 23.3300 g. **Composition:** 0.9250 Silver .6939 oz. ASW **Subject:** Decade For Women

Date	Mintage	F	VF	XF	Unc	BU
1985 Proof	3,660	Value: 65.00				

KM# 155 1000 DRACHMES Weight: 18.0000 g. **Composition:** 0.9000 Silver .5208 oz. ASW **Subject:** 50th Anniversary - Italian Invasion of Greece

Date	Mintage	F	VF	XF	Unc	BU
1990 Proof	7,000	Value: 75.00				

KM# 165 1000 DRACHMES Weight: 33.6300 g. **Composition:** 0.9250 Silver 1.001 oz. ASW **Subject:** Olympics **Reverse:** 4 ancient runners

Date	Mintage	F	VF	XF	Unc	BU
1996 Proof	100,000	Value: 45.00				

KM# 166 1000 DRACHMES Weight: 33.6300 g. **Composition:** 0.9250 Silver 1.001 oz. ASW **Subject:** Olympics **Reverse:** 2 ancient wrestlers

Date	Mintage	F	VF	XF	Unc	BU
1996 Proof	100,000	Value: 45.00				

KM# 128 2500 DRACHMAI Weight: 6.4500 g. **Composition:** 0.9000 Gold .1866 oz. AGW **Subject:** Pan-European Games - Ancient Olympics

Date	Mintage	F	VF	XF	Unc	BU
1981 Proof	75,000	Value: 100				

KM# 141 2500 DRACHMAI Weight: 6.4500 g. **Composition:** 0.9000 Gold .1866 oz. AGW **Subject:** Pan-European Games - 1896 Olympics

Date	Mintage	F	VF	XF	Unc	BU
1982 Proof	50,000	Value: 100				

KM# 142 2500 DRACHMAI Weight: 6.4500 g. **Composition:** 0.9000 Gold .1866 oz. AGW **Subject:** Pan-European Games

Date	Mintage	F	VF	XF	Unc	BU
1982 Proof	50,000	Value: 100				

KM# 129 5000 DRACHMAI Weight: 12.5000 g. **Composition:** 0.9000 Gold .3617 oz. AGW **Subject:** Pan-European Games - Ancient Olympics

Date	Mintage	F	VF	XF	Unc	BU
1981 Proof	75,000	Value: 220				

KM# 143 5000 DRACHMAI Weight: 12.5000 g. **Composition:** 0.9000 Gold .3617 oz. AGW **Subject:** Pan-European Games - 1896 Olympics

Date	Mintage	F	VF	XF	Unc	BU
1982 Proof	50,000	Value: 185				

KM# 144 5000 DRACHMAI Weight: 12.5000 g. **Composition:** 0.9000 Gold .3617 oz. AGW **Subject:** Pan-European Games

Date	Mintage	F	VF	XF	Unc	BU
1982 Proof	50,000	Value: 185				

KM# 146 5000 DRACHMAI Weight: 8.0000 g. **Composition:** 0.9000 Gold .2315 oz. AGW **Subject:** Olympics **Obverse:** Arms at left, torch at right, similar to 500 Drachmai, KM#145 **Reverse:** Apollo

Date	Mintage	F	VF	XF	Unc	BU
1984 Proof	15,000	Value: 400				

KM# 123 10000 DRACHMES Weight: 20.0000 g. **Composition:** 0.9000 Gold .5787 oz. AGW **Subject:** Common Market Membership

Date	F	VF	XF	Unc	BU
ND (1979)	—	—	—	400	—

KM# 149 10000 DRACHMES Weight: 7.1300 g. **Composition:** 0.9000 Gold .2063 oz. AGW **Subject:** Decade For Women

Date	Mintage	F	VF	XF	Unc	BU
1985 Proof	2,835	Value: 375				

KM# 158 10000 DRACHMES Weight: 8.0000 g. **Composition:** 0.9000 Gold .2315 oz. AGW **Subject:** XI Mediterranean Games

Date	Mintage	F	VF	XF	Unc	BU
1991 Proof	2,000	Value: 400				

KM# 161 10000 DRACHMES Weight: 8.5000 g. **Composition:** 0.9170 Gold .2506 oz. AGW **Subject:** 2500th Anniversary of Democracy

Date	Mintage	F	VF	XF	Unc	BU
1993 Proof	Est. 10,000	Value: 350				

KM# 163 10000 DRACHMES Weight: 8.5000 g. **Composition:** 0.9170 Gold .2506 oz. AGW **Subject:** Volleyball Centennial

Date	Mintage	F	VF	XF	Unc	BU
1994 Proof	500	Value: 600				

KM# 156 20000 DRACHMES Weight: 8.0000 g. **Composition:** 0.9000 Gold .2315 oz. AGW **Subject:** 50th Anniversary - Italian Invasion of Greece

Date	Mintage	F	VF	XF	Unc	BU
1990 Proof	1,000	Value: 1,350				

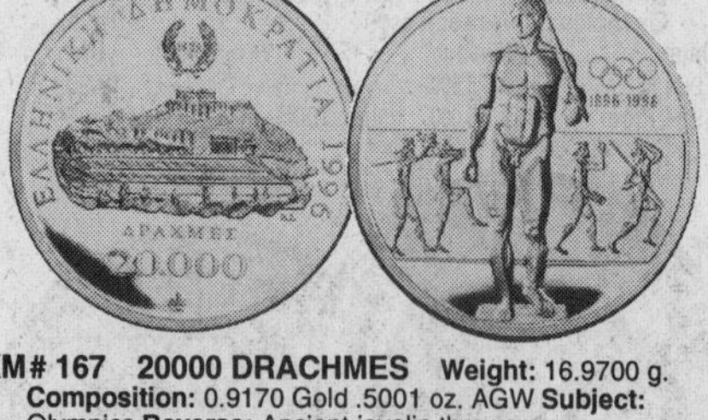

KM# 167 20000 DRACHMES Weight: 16.9700 g. **Composition:** 0.9170 Gold .5001 oz. AGW **Subject:** Olympics **Reverse:** Ancient javelin throwers

Date	Mintage	F	VF	XF	Unc	BU
1996 Proof	60,000	Value: 350				

EURO COINAGE

European Economic Community Issues

KM# 181 EURO CENT Weight: 2.2700 g. **Composition:** Copper Plated Steel **Subject:** Euro Coinage **Obverse:** Ancient ship. **Reverse:** Denomination and globe. **Edge:** Plain. **Size:** 16.2 mm.

Date	F	VF	XF	Unc	BU
2002	—	—	—	0.35	—
2002 F in star	—	—	—	1.25	—

KM# 182 2 EURO CENTS **Weight:** 3.0300 g. **Composition:** Copper Plated Steel **Subject:** Euro Coinage **Obverse:** Sailing ship. **Reverse:** Denomination and globe. **Edge:** Grooved. **Size:** 18.7 mm.

Date	F	VF	XF	Unc	BU
2002	—	—	—	0.50	—
2002 F in star	—	—	—	1.00	—

KM# 183 5 EURO CENTS **Weight:** 3.8600 g. **Composition:** Copper Plated Steel **Subject:** Euro Coinage **Obverse:** Freighter. **Reverse:** Denominaton and globe. **Edge:** Plain. **Size:** 21.2 mm.

Date	F	VF	XF	Unc	BU
2002	—	—	—	1.00	—
2002 F in star	—	—	—	1.25	—

KM# 184 10 EURO CENTS **Weight:** 4.0700 g. **Composition:** Brass **Subject:** Euro Coinage **Obverse:** Rhgas Feriaou's portrait **Reverse:** Denominaton and map **Edge:** Reeded **Size:** 19.7 mm.

Date	Mintage	F	VF	XF	Unc	BU
2002	233,000,000	—	—	—	1.25	—
2002 F in star	24,000,000	—	—	—	2.00	—

KM# 185 20 EURO CENTS **Weight:** 5.7300 g. **Composition:** Brass **Subject:** Euro Coinage **Obverse:** John Kapodistrias' portrait **Reverse:** Denomination and map **Edge:** Notched **Size:** 22.1 mm.

Date	Mintage	F	VF	XF	Unc	BU
2002	370,000,000	—	—	—	1.25	—
2002 E in star	21,000,000	—	—	—	2.25	—

KM# 186 50 EURO CENTS **Weight:** 7.8100 g. **Composition:** Brass **Subject:** Euro Coinage **Obverse:** El. Benizelos' portrait **Reverse:** Denomination and map **Edge:** Reeded **Size:** 24.2 mm.

Date	Mintage	F	VF	XF	Unc	BU
2002	127,000,000	—	—	—	1.50	—
2002 F in star	18,000,000	—	—	—	2.50	—

KM# 187 EURO **Ring Composition:** Brass**Center Weight:** 7.5000 g. **Center Composition:** Copper Nickel **Subject:** Euro Coinage **Obverse:** Ancient coin design **Reverse:** Denomination and map **Edge:** Reeded and plain sections **Size:** 23.2 mm.

Date	Mintage	F	VF	XF	Unc	BU
2002	118,000,000	—	—	—	3.00	—
2002 S in star	15,000,000	—	—	—	4.50	—

KM# 188 2 EUROS **Ring Composition:** Copper Nickel**Center Weight:** 8.5200 g. **Center Composition:** Brass **Subject:** Euro Coinage **Obverse:** Europa seated on a bull **Reverse:** Denomination and map **Edge:** Reeded with 2's and stars **Size:** 25.7 mm.

Date	Mintage	F	VF	XF	Unc	BU
2002	162,000,000	—	—	—	4.00	—
2002 S in star	6,000,000	—	—	—	6.50	—

ESSAIS

KM#	Date	Mintage	Identification	Mkt Val

KM#	Date	Mintage	Identification	Mkt Val
E23	1911	4	2 Drachmai. Silver. 1868 2 Drachmai. ESSAI to right of denomination.	8,500

KM#	Date	Mintage	Identification	Mkt Val
EA23	1911	2	2 Drachmai. Silver. Without mintmark, ESSAI to right of sea-horse.	10,000

KM#	Date	Mintage	Identification	Mkt Val
E24	1912	—	5 Lepta. Nickel. ESSAI, plain edge, without mintmark	1,200
E25	1912	—	5 Lepta. Zinc. ESSAI	1,500

KM#	Date	Mintage	Identification	Mkt Val
E26	1912	—	10 Lepta. Nickel. ESSAI, plain edge, without mintmark.	1,200
E27	1912	—	10 Lepta. Zinc. ESSAI.	1,500

KM#	Date	Mintage	Identification	Mkt Val
E28	1912	—	10 Lepta. Nickel. ESSAI, with mintmark	1,400

KM#	Date	Mintage	Identification	Mkt Val
E29	1912	—	20 Lepta. Nickel. ESSAI.	1,200
E30	1912	—	20 Lepta. Zinc. ESSAI.	1,500

KM#	Date	Mintage	Identification	Mkt Val
E31	1913	—	Drachma. Silver. ESSAI.	—

KM#	Date	Mintage	Identification	Mkt Val
E34	1915	—	Drachma. Gold. 9.2000 g. ESSAI.	—

KM#	Date	Mintage	Identification	Mkt Val
E35	1915	—	2 Drachmai. Silver. ESSAI.	—

KM#	Date	Mintage	Identification	Mkt Val
E32	1915	—	Drachma. Copper-Nickel. ESSAI.	—

KM#	Date	Mintage	Identification	Mkt Val
E36	1915	—	2 Drachmai. Gold. 15.9000 g. ESSAI.	—

KM#	Date	Mintage	Identification	Mkt Val
E33	1915	—	Drachma. Silver. ESSAI.	—

KM#	Date	Mintage	Identification	Mkt Val
E37	1922	—	10 Lepta. Aluminum. ESSAI.	2,500

PATTERNS

Including off metal strikes

KM#	Date	Mintage	Identification	Mkt Val
Pn40	1910	—	Drachma. Silver. Value in lower case letters.	4,500
Pn41	1910	—	Drachma. Silver. Without mintmark.	4,500
Pn42	1911	—	2 Drachmai. Silver. Sea-horse. Without mintmark.	—
PnA44	1922	3	10 Lepta. Nickel. With (IAKOBIAHS) engravers name.	5,000
Pn44	1926	—	Drachma. Nickel. Large letters.	700

KM#	Date	Mintage	Identification	Mkt Val
Pn54	1926	—	2 Drachmai. Nickel. Large letters.	1,000
Pn55	1930	—	5 Drachmai. Nickel. With "MODEL" edge.	1,000
Pn59	ND	—	20 Drachmai. Copper. 21mm, KM74.	3,500
PnA59	ND	—	20 Drachmai. Copper. 22mm, KM74.	3,500
Pn60	ND	—	20 Drachmai. Gold. Without "20", KM74.	25,000
Pn61	ND	—	100 Drachmai. Copper. KM75.	5,000
Pn62	ND	—	100 Drachmai. Copper. KM76.	5,000
PnA63	ND(1950)	—	1000 Drachmai. Silver. Head of Hermes right. Denominatin above branch.	1,250
PnB63	ND(1950)	—	1000 Drachmai. Aluminum. Head of Hermes right. Denomination above branch.	550
Pn63	1954	50	50 Lepta. Copper-Nickel. "ANAMNKETIKON" above date.	500
Pn64	1954	10	50 Lepta. Gold.	6,000
Pn65	1954	—	50 Lepta. Copper-Nickel. "hollow cheek".	400
Pn66	1954	50	Drachma. Copper Nickel. "ANAMNHETIKON" above date.	2,000
Pn67	1954	10	Drachma. Gold.	6,000
Pn70	1954	10	2 Drachmai. Gold.	6,000
Pn73	1954	10	5 Drachmai. Gold.	6,000
Pn68	1954	—	Drachma. Copper-Nickel. "hollow cheek".	500
Pn71	1954	—	2 Drachmai. Copper-Nickel. "hollow cheek".	600
Pn69	1954	50	2 Drachmai. Copper-Nickel. "ANAMNHETIKON" above date.	2,000
Pn72	1954	50	5 Drachmai. Copper-Nickel. "ANAMNHETIKON" above date.	2,000
Pn74	1954	—	5 Drachmai. Copper-Nickel. "hollow cheek".	—
Pn75	1959	10	10 Drachmai. Gold.	6,000
Pn78	1963	—	30 Drachmai. Silver. With "ANAMNHETIKON".	5,000
Pn79	1964	—	30 Drachmai. Gold.	6,000
Pn80	1966	—	50 Lepta. Gold.	—
Pn82	1966	—	Drachma. Gold.	—
Pn84	1966	—	2 Drachmai. Gold.	—
Pn86	1966	—	5 Drachmai. Gold.	—
Pn81	1966	—	50 Lepta. Platinum.	6,500
Pn83	1966	—	Drachma. Platinum.	6,500
Pn85	1966	—	2 Drachmai. Platinum.	6,500
Pn87	1966	—	5 Drachmai. Platinum.	6,500
Pn88	1973	—	20 Drachmai. Bronze-Nickel. Low relief and date, without veil.	75.00
Pn89	1976	—	Drachma. Nickel. 4 sails and 2 waves.	1,000
Pn90	1986	4	Drachma. Aluminum.	1,500
Pn91	1986	4	2 Drachmai. Aluminum.	1,500
pn92	1987	—	Drachma. Copper.	—
pn93	1987	—	2 Drachmes. Nickel-Brass.	—

PIEFORTS

KM#	Date	Mintage	Identification	Mkt Val
P1	1922	—	10 Lepta. Copper. With ESSAI.	500
P3	ND	2	20 Drachmai. Lead. KM74.	2,200

TRIAL STRIKES

KM#	Date	Mintage	Identification	Mkt Val
TS19	1921	—	5 Lepta. Aluminum. Uniface.	—
TS20	1921	—	5 Lepta. Aluminum. Uniface.	—
TS21	1921	—	50 Lepta. Aluminum. Uniface.	500
TS22	1926	—	2 Drachmai. Copper. With E.	50.00
TS23	1930	—	5 Drachmai. Copper. Uniface. With E.	50.00
TS24	1930	—	20 Drachmai. Brass. Test marks.	50.00
TS25	1960	—	20 Drachmai. Copper.	100

MINT SETS

KM#	Date	Mintage	Identification	Issue Price	Mkt Val
MS1	1965 (7)	—	KM78, 80-85	—	25.00
MS3	1982 (7)	—	KM115-116, 130-134	—	20.00

PROOF SETS

KM#	Date	Mintage	Identification	Issue Price	Mkt Val
PS1	1965 (7)	4,987	KM78, 80-85	10.25	55.00
PS2	1978 (8)	20,000	KM113-120	—	45.00
PS3	1993 (8)	—	KM131-132, 147, 150-151, 154, 159-160	—	150
PS4	1994 (2)	—	KM162-163	—	700

GREENLAND

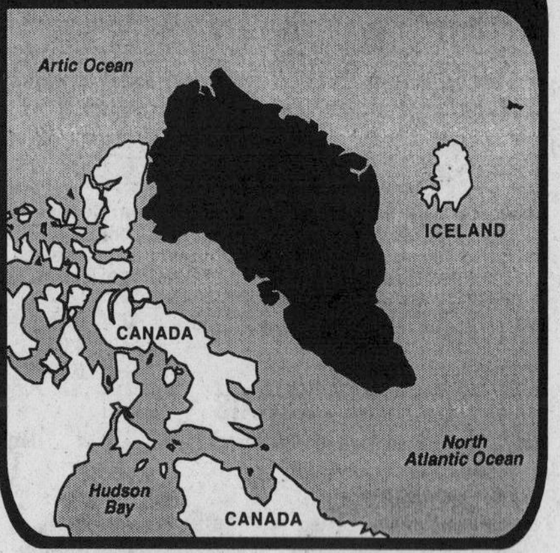

Greenland, an integral part of the Danish realm is situated between the North Atlantic Ocean and the Polar Sea, almost entirely within the Arctic Circle. An island nation, it has an area of 840,000 sq. mi. (2,175,600 sq. km.) and a population of 57,000 Capital: Nuuk (formerly Godthaab). Greenland is the world's only source of natural cryolite, a fluoride of sodium and aluminum important in making aluminum. Fish products and minerals are exported.

Eric the Red discovered Greenland in 982 and established the first settlement in 986. Greenland was a republic until 1261, when the sovereignty of Norway was extended to the island. The original colony was abandoned about 1400 when increasing cold interfered with the breeding of cattle. Successful recolonization was undertaken by Denmark in 1721. In 1921 Denmark extended its claim to include the entire island, and made it a colony of the crown in 1924. The island's colonial status was abolished by amendment to the Danish constitution on June 5, 1953, and Greenland became an integral part of the Kingdom of Denmark. It has been an autonomous state since May 1, 1979.

RULERS
Danish

MINT MARKS
Heart (h) Copenhagen (Kobenhavn)

MINTMASTERS INITIALS
HCN - Hans Christian Nielsen, 1919-1927
C - Alfred Kristian Frederik Christiansen, 1956-1971
GJ - Knud Gunnar Jensen, 1901-1933
S - Harald Salomon, 1933-1968

MONETARY SYSTEM
100 Øre = 1 Krone

DANISH COLONY
1921-1953
MILLED COINAGE

KM# 6 25 ORE **Composition:** Copper-Nickel **Note:** Center hole added to KM#5.

Date	Mintage	F	VF	XF	Unc	BU
1926(h) HCN, GJ	60,000	20.00	40.00	—	—	—

Note: The hole was added to avoid confusion with the 1 Krone coins of Denmark.

KM# 5 25 ORE **Composition:** Copper-Nickel **Obverse:** Crowned arms of Denmark **Obv. Legend:** GRONLANDS STYRELSE **Reverse:** Value over polar bear walking left, date below **Note:** Struck in Philadelphia.

Date	Mintage	F	VF	XF	Unc	BU
1926(h) HCN, GJ	310,000	4.00	7.00	12.50	25.00	—

Note: Was withdrawn from circulation during 1940-42 and sent to the United States for alteration.

KM# 7 50 ORE **Composition:** Aluminum-Bronze **Obverse:** Crowned arms of Denmark **Obv. Legend:** GRONLANDS STYRELSE **Reverse:** Value over polar bear walking left, date below.

Date	Mintage	F	VF	XF	Unc	BU
1926(h) HCN, CJ	196,000	5.50	9.00	15.00	30.00	—

KM# 8 KRONE **Composition:** Aluminum-Bronze **Obverse:** Crowned arms of Denmark **Obv. Legend:** GRONLANDS STYRELSE **Reverse:** Value over polar bear walking left, date below.

Date	Mintage	F	VF	XF	Unc	BU
1926(h) HCN, CJ	287,000	4.50	8.50	18.00	45.00	—

KM# 9 5 KRONER **Composition:** Brass **Obverse:** Crowned arms of Denmark **Obv. Legend:** GRONLANDS STYRELSE **Reverse:** Value over polar bear walking left, date below.

Date	Mintage	F	VF	XF	Unc	BU
1944	100,000	30.00	45.00	65.00	100	—

TOKEN COINAGE

KM# Tn1 10 ORE **Composition:** Nickel Plated Zinc **Issuer:** Greenland Mining Ltd; Josvas Copper Mines **Obv. Legend:** GRONLANDSK MINEDRIFTS-ARTIESELSKAB **Reverse:** Crossed hammers over "10"

Date	Mintage	VG	F	VF	XF	Unc
1911	5,000	3.00	8.00	12.00	25.00	—

KM# Tn2 25 ORE **Composition:** Nickel Plated Zinc **Issuer:** Greenland Mining Ltd; Josvas Copper Mines **Obv. Legend:** GRONLANDSK MINEDRIFTS-ARTIESELSKAB **Reverse:** Crossed hammers over "25"

Date	Mintage	VG	F	VF	XF	Unc
1911	5,000	3.00	8.00	12.00	25.00	—

KM# Tn3 100 ORE **Composition:** Nickel Plated Zinc **Issuer:** Greenland Mining Ltd; Josvas Copper Mines **Obv. Legend:** GRONLANDSK MINEDRIFTS-ARTIESELSKAB **Reverse:** Crossed hammers over "100"

Date	Mintage	VG	F	VF	XF	Unc
1911	5,000	3.00	8.00	12.00	25.00	—

Note: Struck at L. Chr. Lauer, Nurnberg, Germany

TOKEN COINAGE
Series IV, 1922

KM# Tn46 10 ORE Composition: Copper-Nickel **Issuer:** Ivigtut Cryolite Mining & Trading Co. **Obverse:** Seated polar bear on frame **Obv. Legend:** IVIGTUT KRYOLITHBRUD **Rev. Legend:** KRYOLITH MINE HANDELS SELSKABET

Date	Mintage	F	VF	XF	Unc	BU
1922	10,018,000	10.00	15.00	30.00	—	—

KM# Tn47 50 ORE Composition: Copper-Nickel **Issuer:** Ivigtut Cryolite Mining & Trading Co. **Obverse:** Seated polar bear on frame **Obv. Legend:** IVIGTUT KRYOLITHBRUD **Rev. Legend:** KRYOLITH MINE HANDELS SELSKABET

Date	Mintage	VG	F	VF	XF	Unc
1922	4,018,000	16.00	40.00	65.00	90.00	—

KM# Tn48 2 KRONER Composition: Copper-Nickel **Issuer:** Ivigtut Cryolite Mining & Trading Co. **Obverse:** Seated polar bear on frame **Obv. Legend:** IVIGTUT KRYOLITHBRUD **Rev. Legend:** KRYOLITH MINE HANDELS SELSKABET

Date	Mintage	VG	F	VF	XF	Unc
1922	4,018,000	15.00	35.00	60.00	85.00	—

KM# Tn49 10 KRONER Composition: Copper-Nickel **Issuer:** Ivigtut Cryolite Mining & Trading Co. **Obverse:** Seated polar bear on frame **Obv. Legend:** IVIGTUT KRYOLITHBRUD **Rev. Legend:** KRYOLITH MINE HANDELS SELSKABET

Date	Mintage	VG	F	VF	XF	Unc
1922	10,706,000	20.00	50.00	80.00	110	—

Note: Was struck in 1926 using 1922 dies

KM# Tn49a 10 KRONER Composition: Aluminum **Issuer:** Ivigtut Cryolite Mining & Trading Co.

Date	Mintage	VG	F	VF	XF	Unc
1922	7,018,000	—	—	750	900	—

Note: This token was removed from circulation because it had the same size and weight of Denmark's 2 Kroner, issued in 1924. These tokens were used until 1957

DANISH STATE
1953-1979

MILLED COINAGE

KM# 10 KRONE Composition: Aluminum-Bronze **Issuer:** Royal Greenland Trade Company **Obverse:** Crowned arms of Denmark and Greenland **Obv. Legend:** DEN KONGELIGE GRONLANDSKE HANDEL **Reverse:** Value in sprays

Date	Mintage	F	VF	XF	Unc	BU
1957(h) C, S	100,000	6.00	10.00	20.00	45.00	—

KM# 10a KRONE Composition: Copper-Nickel **Issuer:** Royal Greenland Trade Company

Date	Mintage	F	VF	XF	Unc	BU
1960(h) C, S	109,000	3.00	6.00	10.00	18.50	—
1964(h) C, S	110,000	4.00	8.00	12.50	20.00	—

THULE-KAP YORK

The Thule (Gaanaaq)-Cape York Artic trading station located in northwestern Greenland on the coast of the Hayes Peninsula north of Cap York was established in 1910 by polar explorer Knud Rasmussen. U.S. military bases are currently there.

THULE KAP YORK

TOKEN COINAGE

KM# Tn5.1 5 ORE Composition: Aluminum **Obv. Legend:** THULE *KAP YORK* **Reverse:** "5" above date, with hole in center

Date	Mintage	F	VF	XF	Unc	BU
1910	5,000	2.00	4.50	8.00	15.00	—

Note: Struck in 1913

KM# Tn5.2 5 ORE Composition: Aluminum **Note:** Error - struck without center hole.

Date	F	VF	XF	Unc	BU
1910 Rare	—	—	—	—	—

Note: Struck in 1913

KM# Tn6 25 ORE Composition: Aluminum **Obv. Legend:** THULE *KAP YORK* **Reverse:** "25" above date, with hole in center

Date	Mintage	F	VF	XF	Unc	BU
1910	5,000	2.00	3.50	6.00	12.00	—

KM# Tn7 100 ORE Composition: Aluminum **Obv. Legend:** THULE *KAP YORK* **Reverse:** "100" above date, with hole in center

Date	Mintage	F	VF	XF	Unc	BU
1910	2,000	4.00	10.00	16.00	30.00	—

KM# Tn8 500 ORE Composition: Aluminum **Obv. Legend:** THULE *KAP YORK* **Reverse:** "500" above date, with hole in center

Date	Mintage	F	VF	XF	Unc	BU
1910	2,000	6.00	15.00	22.00	40.00	—

Note: Tn5-8 were struck at L. Chr. Lauer, Nurnberg, Germany

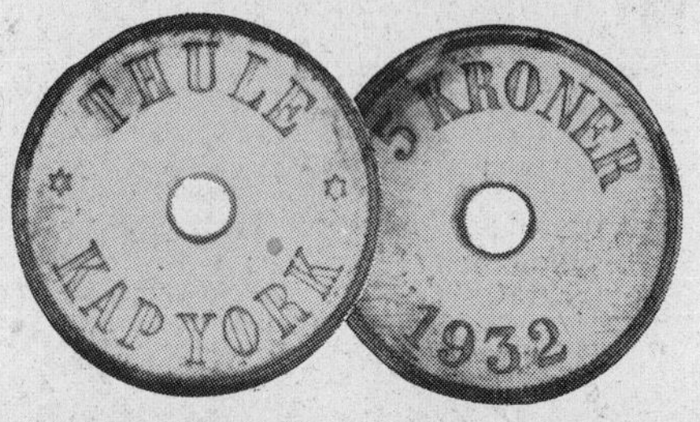

KM# Tn9 5 KRONER Composition: Aluminum **Obv. Legend:** THULE *KAP YORK* **Reverse:** "5" above date, with hole in center

Date	Mintage	F	VF	XF	Unc	BU
1932	500	15.00	30.00	50.00	90.00	—

KM# Tn10 10 KRONER Composition: Aluminum **Obv. Legend:** THULE *KAP YORK* **Reverse:** "10" above date, with hole in center

Date	Mintage	F	VF	XF	Unc	BU
1932	500	40.00	85.00	140	200	—

Note: Tn9-10 were struck at a private mint in Copenhagen

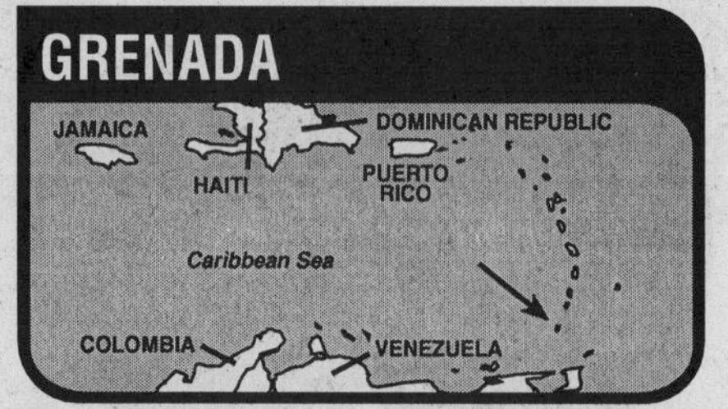

The State of Grenada, located in the Windward Islands of the Caribbean Sea 90 miles (145 km.) north of Trinidad, has(with Carriacou and Petit Martinique) an area of 133 sq. mi. (344 sq. km.) and a population of 94,000. Capital: St.George's. Grenada is the smallest independent nation in the Western Hemisphere. The economy is based on agriculture and tourism. Sugar, coconuts, nutmeg, cocoa and bananas are exported.

Columbus discovered Grenada in 1498 during his third voyage to the Americas. Spain failed to colonize the island, and in 1627 granted it to the British who sold it to the French who colonized it in 1650. Grenada was captured by the British in 1763, retaken by the French in 1779, and finally ceded to the British in 1783. In 1958 Grenada joined the Federation of the West Indies, which was dissolved in 1962. In 1967 it became an internally self-governing British associated state. Full independence was attained on Feb. 4, 1974. Grenada is a member of the Commonwealth of Nations. The prime minister is the Head of Government. Elizabeth II is Head of State as Queen of Grenada.

The early coinage of Grenada consists of cut and countermarked pieces of Spanish or Spanish Colonial Reales, which were valued at 11 Bits. In 1787 8 Reales coins were cut into 11 triangular pieces and countermarked with an incuse G. Later in 1814 large denomination cut pieces were issued being 1/2, 1/3 or 1/6 cuts and countermarked with a TR, incuse G and a number 6, 4,2, or 1 indicating the value in bitts.

RULERS
British

INDEPENDENT STATE

Commonwealth of Nations

MODERN COINAGE

KM# 15 4 DOLLARS Composition: Copper-Nickel **Series:** F.A.O.

Date	Mintage	F	VF	XF	Unc	BU
1970	13,000	—	4.50	7.50	13.50	—
1970 Proof	2,000	Value: 32.50				

KM# 16 10 DOLLARS Composition: Copper-Nickel **Subject:** Royal Visit

Date	F	VF	XF	Unc	BU
1985	—	—	4.50	9.00	—

KM# 16a 10 DOLLARS Weight: 28.2800 g. **Composition:** 0.9250 Silver .8411 oz. ASW **Subject:** Royal Visit

Date	Mintage	F	VF	XF	Unc	BU
1985 Proof	Est. 5,000	Value: 55.00				

KM# 16b 10 DOLLARS Weight: 47.5400 g. **Composition:** 0.9170 Gold 1.4013 oz. AGW **Subject:** Royal Visit

Date	Mintage	F	VF	XF	Unc	BU
1985 Proof	Est. 250	Value: 1,200				

KM# 17 100 DOLLARS Weight: 129.5900 g. **Composition:** 0.9250 Silver 3.8543 oz. ASW **Subject:** Tropical Birds - Grenada Dove **Obverse:** Arms in circle, country name above, date below **Size:** 63 mm. **Note:** Illustration reduced.

Date	Mintage	F	VF	XF	Unc	BU
1988 Proof	Est. 10,000	Value: 125				

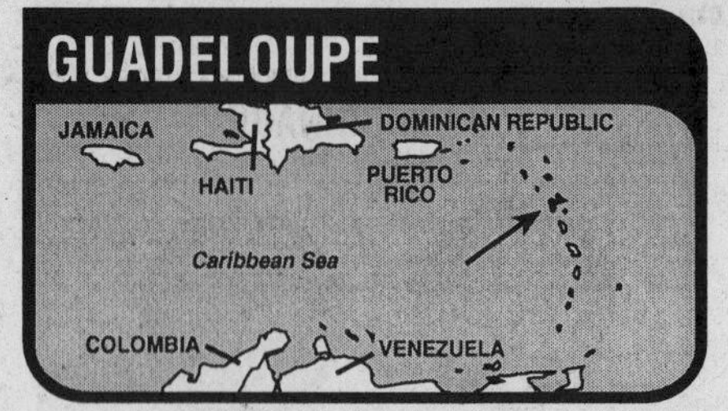

The French Overseas Department of Guadeloupe, located in the Leeward Islands of the West Indies about300 miles (493 km.) southeast of Puerto Rico, has an area of 687 sq. mi. (1,780 sq. km.) and a population of 306,000. Actually it is two islands separated by a narrow saltwater stream: volcanic Basse-Terre to the west and the flatter limestone formation of Grande-Terre to the east. Capital: Basse-Terre, on the island of that name. The principal industries are agriculture, the distillation of liquors, and tourism. Sugar, bananas, and rum are exported.

Guadeloupe was discovered by Columbus in 1493 and settled in 1635 by two Frenchmen, L'Olive and Duplessis, who took possession in the name of the French Company of the Islands of America. When repeated efforts by private companies to colonize the island failed, it was relinquished to the French crown in 1674, and established as a dependency of Martinique. The British occupied the island on two occasions, 1759-63 and 1810-16, before it passed permanently to France. A colony until 1946 Guadeloupe was then made an overseas territory of the FrenchUnion. In 1958 it voted to become an Overseas Department within the new French Community.

The well-known R.F. in garland oval countermark of the French Government is only legitimate if on a French Colonies 12 deniers 1767 C#4. Two other similar but incuse RF countermarks are on cut pieces in the values of 1 and 4 escalins. Contemporary and modern counterfeits are known of both these types.

RULERS
French 1816-

MONETARY SYSTEM
100 Centimes = 1 Franc

FRENCH COLONY

MODERN COINAGE

KM# 45 50 CENTIMES Composition: Copper-Nickel

Date	Mintage	F	VF	XF	Unc	BU
1903	600,000	16.00	35.00	85.00	240	—
1921	600,000	12.00	30.00	75.00	185	—

KM# 46 FRANC Composition: Copper-Nickel

Date	Mintage	F	VF	XF	Unc	BU
1903	700,000	20.00	40.00	90.00	250	—
1921	700,000	15.00	30.00	80.00	200	—

ESSAIS

KM#	Date	Mintage	Identification	Mkt Val
E1	1903	—	50 Centimes. Copper-Nickel.	180
E2	1903	—	50 Centimes. Silver.	350
E3	1903	—	Franc. Copper-Nickel.	250
E4	1903	—	Franc. Silver.	540
E5	19(21)	—	Franc. Bronze.	160

PIEFORTS

KM#	Date	Mintage	Identification	Mkt Val
P1	1903	—	50 Centimes. Copper-Nickel.	400

KM#	Date	Mintage	Identification	Mkt Val

KM#	Date	Mintage	Identification	Mkt Val
P2	1903	—	Franc. Copper-Nickel.	500

GUATEMALA

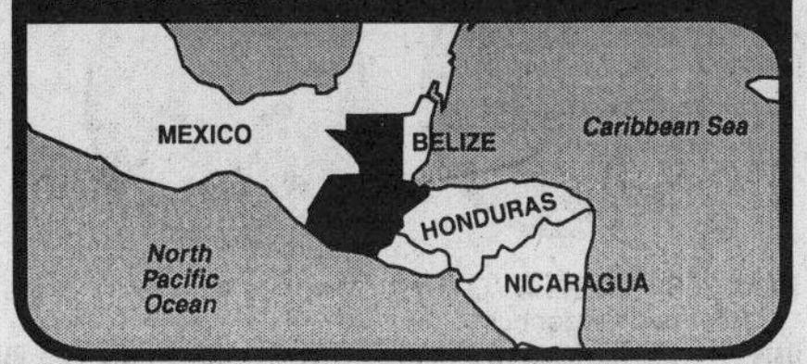

The Republic of Guatemala, the northernmost of the five Central American republics, has an area of 42,042 sq. mi. (108,890 sq. km.) and a population of 10.7 million. Capital: Guatemala City. The economy of Guatemala is heavily dependent on agriculture, however, the country is rich in nickel resources which are being developed. Coffee, cotton and bananas are exported.

Guatemala, once the site of an ancient Mayan civilization, was conquered by Pedro de Alvarado, the resourceful lieutenant of Cortes who undertook the conquest from Mexico. Cruel but strategically skillful, he progressed rapidly along the Pacific coastal lowlands to the highland plain of Quetzaltenango where the decisive battle for Guatemala was fought. After routing the Indian forces, he established the city of Guatemala in 1524. The Spanish Captaincy-General of Guatemala included all Central America but Panama. Guatemala declared its independence of Spain in 1821 and was absorbed into the Mexican empire of Augustin Iturbide (1822-23). From1823 to 1839 Guatemala was a constituent state of the Central American Republic. Upon dissolution of that confederation, Guatemala proclaimed itself an independent republic. Like El Salvador, Guatemala suffered from internal strife between right-wing, US-backed military government and leftist indigenous peoples from ca. 1954 to ca. 1997.

MINT MARKS

H - Heaton, Birmingham
(KN) – Birmingham, King's Norton Mint
(L) – London, Royal Mint
(P) – Philadelphia, USA
NG - ??? 1992
(S) – San Francisco, USA

REPUBLIC

REAL COINAGE

8 Reales = 1 Peso

KM# 175 1/4 REAL Composition: Copper-Nickel

Date	Mintage	F	VF	XF	Unc	BU
1901H	5,056,000	0.15	0.35	0.75	2.00	—

KM# 176 1/2 REAL (Medio) Composition: Copper-Nickel

Date	Mintage	F	VF	XF	Unc	BU
1901(H)	6,652,000	0.35	0.65	1.00	2.50	—

KM# 177 REAL Composition: Copper-Nickel

Date	Mintage	F	VF	XF	Unc	BU
1901(H)	7,388,000	—	0.30	0.85	1.50	—
1910H	4,000,000	—	0.35	0.85	1.75	—
1911(H)	2,000,000	—	0.40	1.25	2.50	—
1912(H)	8,000,000	—	0.30	0.85	1.50	—

PROVISIONAL COINAGE

1915-1923

KM# 230 12-1/2 CENTAVOS Composition: Copper

Date	Mintage	F	VF	XF	Unc	BU
1915	6,000,000	0.75	1.25	3.50	10.00	—

KM# 231 25 CENTAVOS Composition: Copper

Date	Mintage	F	VF	XF	Unc	BU
1915	4,000,000	0.75	1.25	4.75	12.00	—

KM# 232.1 50 CENTAVOS Composition: Aluminum-Bronze Note: Thin numerals in denomination.

Date	Mintage	F	VF	XF	Unc	BU
1922	3,803,000	0.80	1.50	3.50	12.00	—

KM# 232.2 50 CENTAVOS Composition: Aluminum-Bronze Note: Thick numerals in denomination.

Date	F	VF	XF	Unc	BU
1922	0.80	1.50	3.50	12.00	—

KM# 233 PESO Composition: Aluminum-Bronze

Date	Mintage	F	VF	XF	Unc	BU
1923	1,477,000	1.50	2.50	6.50	22.50	—

KM# 234 5 PESOS Composition: Aluminum-Bronze

Date	Mintage	F	VF	XF	Unc	BU
1923	440,000	1.75	3.85	8.75	32.50	—

KM# 234a 5 PESOS Composition: Copper

Date	F	VF	XF	Unc	BU
1923	1.75	3.85	8.75	32.50	—

REFORM COINAGE

100 Centavos = 1 Quetzol

KM# 248 1/2 CENTAVO (Medio) Composition: Brass

Date	Mintage	F	VF	XF	Unc	BU
1932(L)	6,000,000	0.15	0.50	1.00	3.00	—
1932(L) Proof	—	Value: 150				
1946	640,000	0.75	1.75	3.75	15.00	—

KM# 237 CENTAVO (Un) **Composition:** Copper
Obverse: Incuse legend on scroll

Date	Mintage	F	VF	XF	Unc	BU
1925	357,000	4.50	7.50	16.50	37.50	—

KM# 237a CENTAVO (Un) **Composition:** Bronze

Date	F	VF	XF	Unc	BU
1925	5.00	8.00	15.00	40.00	—

KM# 247 CENTAVO (Un) **Composition:** Copper

Date	Mintage	F	VF	XF	Unc	BU
1929(L)	500,000	2.00	3.00	6.00	22.50	—
1929(L) Proof	—	—	—	—	—	—

KM# 249 CENTAVO (Un) **Composition:** Brass

Date	Mintage	F	VF	XF	Unc	BU
1932(L)	3,000,000	0.40	1.00	3.00	10.00	—
1932(L) Proof	—	—	—	—	—	—
1933(L)	1,500,000	0.60	1.50	4.50	12.00	—
1933(L) Proof	—	—	—	—	—	—
1934(L)	1,000,000	0.50	1.25	4.50	12.00	—
1934(L) Proof	—	—	—	—	—	—
1936(L)	1,500,000	0.40	1.00	4.50	12.00	—
1936(L) Proof	—	—	—	—	—	—
1938/7(L)	1,000,000	0.40	1.00	5.00	12.50	—
1938(L)	Inc. above	0.40	1.00	4.50	12.00	—
1938(L) Proof	—	—	—	—	—	—
1939(L)	1,500,000	0.50	1.25	4.50	9.50	—
1939(L) Proof	—	—	—	—	—	—
1946	539,000	—	0.15	0.65	4.50	—
1947	1,121,000	—	0.15	0.35	2.50	—
1948	1,651,000	—	0.15	0.35	3.50	—
1949	1,022,000	—	0.15	0.45	3.50	—

KM# 251 CENTAVO (Un) **Weight:** 3.0000 g.
Composition: Brass

Date	Mintage	F	VF	XF	Unc	BU
1943(P)	450,000	3.00	6.00	10.00	30.00	—
1944(S)	2,049,999	0.50	1.25	2.50	8.00	—

KM# 254 CENTAVO (Un) **Composition:** Brass
Reverse: Fray Bartolome de las Casas

Date	Mintage	F	VF	XF	Unc	BU
1949	1,091,000	—	0.15	0.35	5.00	—
1950	3,663,000	—	0.15	0.25	1.75	—
1951	3,586,000	—	0.15	0.50	15.00	—
1952	1,445,000	—	0.15	0.30	5.00	—
1953	2,214,000	—	0.15	0.25	1.00	—
1954	1,455,000	—	0.15	0.30	2.25	—

KM# 259 CENTAVO (Un) **Composition:** Nickel-Brass
Reverse: Larger bust

Date	Mintage	F	VF	XF	Unc	BU
1954(KN)	10,000,000	—	—	0.15	1.50	—
1957(KN)	1,600,000	—	0.15	0.25	0.75	—
1958(KN)	2,000,000	—	0.15	0.25	1.00	—

KM# 260 CENTAVO (Un) **Composition:** Brass
Obverse: Larger legend

Date	Mintage	F	VF	XF	Unc	BU
1958	10,001,000	—	—	0.15	0.50	—
1961	1,826,000	—	—	0.15	0.30	—
1963	4,926,000	—	—	0.15	0.30	—
1964	4,280,000	—	—	0.15	0.30	—

KM# 265 CENTAVO (Un) **Composition:** Brass **Size:** 19 mm. **Note:** Size reduced. Varieties in size and style of date exist.

Date	Mintage	F	VF	XF	Unc	BU
1965	3,845,000	—	—	0.15	0.75	—
1966	6,100,000	—	—	0.15	0.25	—
1967	6,400,000	—	—	0.15	0.25	—
1968	2,590,000	—	—	0.15	0.25	—
1969	13,780,000	—	—	0.15	0.25	—
1970	10,511,000	—	—	0.15	0.25	—

KM# 273 CENTAVO (Un) **Composition:** Brass
Obverse: Smaller legend and date

Date	Mintage	F	VF	XF	Unc	BU
1972	11,500,000	—	—	0.15	0.25	—
1973	12,000,000	—	—	0.15	0.25	—

KM# 275.1 CENTAVO (Un) **Composition:** Brass
Obverse: Larger legend and date **Reverse:** Large head

Date	Mintage	F	VF	XF	Unc	BU
1974	10,000,000	—	—	0.15	0.25	—
1975	15,000,000	—	—	0.15	0.25	—
1976	15,230,000	—	—	0.15	0.25	—
1977	30,000,000	—	—	0.15	0.25	—
1978	30,000,000	—	—	0.15	0.25	—
1979	30,000,000	—	—	0.15	0.25	—

KM# 275.2 CENTAVO (Un) **Composition:** Brass
Reverse: Smaller head, legend and date **Note:** Varieties exist.

Date	Mintage	F	VF	XF	Unc	BU
1979	Inc. above	—	—	0.15	0.25	—
1980	20,000,000	—	—	0.15	0.25	—
1984	20,000,000	—	—	0.15	0.25	—
1985	—	—	—	0.15	0.25	—
1986	—	—	—	0.15	0.25	—
1987	50,000,000	—	—	0.15	0.25	—
1988	51,400,000	—	—	0.15	0.25	—
1989	—	—	—	0.15	0.25	—
1990	—	—	—	0.15	0.25	—
1991	—	—	—	0.15	0.25	—
1992	—	—	—	0.15	0.25	—

KM# 275.4 CENTAVO (Un) **Composition:** Brass
Obverse: Legend on scroll in relief **Note:** Varieties exist.

Date	Mintage	F	VF	XF	Unc	BU
1981	30,000,000	—	—	0.15	0.25	—
1982	30,000,000	—	—	0.15	0.25	—

KM# 275.5 CENTAVO (Un) **Composition:** Brass
Reverse: Modified portrait of Fray de las Casas

Date	F	VF	XF	Unc	BU
1993	—	—	0.15	0.25	—
1994	—	—	0.15	0.25	—
1995	—	—	0.15	0.25	—

KM# 282 CENTAVO (Un) **Weight:** 0.8000 g.
Composition: Aluminum **Obverse:** National arms **Reverse:** Bust of Las Casas left **Edge:** Plain

Date	F	VF	XF	Unc	BU
1999	—	—	0.15	0.25	—

KM# 250 2 CENTAVOS (Dos) **Composition:** Brass

Date	Mintage	F	VF	XF	Unc	BU
1932(L)	3,000,000	0.50	1.25	3.50	17.50	—
1932(L) Proof	—	—	—	—	—	—

KM# 252 2 CENTAVOS (Dos) **Weight:** 6.0000 g.
Composition: Brass

Date	Mintage	F	VF	XF	Unc	BU
1943(P)	150,000	3.00	7.50	12.00	32.00	—
1944(S)	1,100,000	0.60	2.00	3.75	10.00	—

KM# 238.1 5 CENTAVOS **Weight:** 1.6667 g.
Composition: 0.7200 Silver .0386 oz. ASW **Obverse:** Long-tailed quetzal **Reverse:** Engraver's initials, JAC, below "Centavos"

Date	Mintage	F	VF	XF	Unc	BU
1925	573,000	3.00	5.75	11.50	25.00	—
1944	1,026,000	BV	1.25	2.50	12.00	—
1945	4,026,000	BV	0.75	2.00	9.00	—
1947	1,834,000	BV	1.00	2.00	7.50	—
1948	1,103,000	BV	1.00	2.00	10.00	—
1949	551,000	0.50	1.50	3.00	20.00	—

KM# 238.1a 5 CENTAVOS **Weight:** 2.5000 g.
Composition: 0.9000 Gold .0723 oz. AGW

Date	Mintage	F	VF	XF	Unc	BU
1925	8	—	—	750	950	—

KM# 238.2 5 CENTAVOS Weight: 1.6667 g. **Composition:** 0.7200 Silver .0386 oz. ASW **Obverse:** Short-tailed quetzal **Reverse:** Without engraver's initials

Date	Mintage	F	VF	XF	Unc	BU
1928(L)	1,000,000	BV	1.00	2.00	28.00	—
1928(L) Proof	—	Value: 400				
1929(L)	1,000,000	BV	1.00	2.00	7.50	—
1929(L) Proof	—	—	—	—	—	—
1932(L)	2,000,000	BV	1.00	1.50	6.50	—
1932(L) Proof	—	—	—	—	—	—
1933(L)	600,000	BV	1.00	2.50	9.00	—
1933(L) Proof	—	—	—	—	—	—
1934(L)	1,200,000	BV	1.00	2.00	7.50	—
1934(L) Proof	—	—	—	—	—	—
1937(L)	400,000	BV	1.00	1.50	7.50	—
1937(L) Proof	—	—	—	—	—	—
1938(L)	300,000	0.50	1.50	2.50	14.00	—
1938(L) Proof	—	—	—	—	—	—
1943(P)	900,000	BV	0.75	1.50	7.00	—

KM# 255 5 CENTAVOS Weight: 1.6667 g. **Composition:** 0.7200 Silver .0386 oz. ASW **Note:** Varieties exist with and without dashes.

Date	Mintage	F	VF	XF	Unc	BU
1949	305,000	0.50	1.50	3.50	22.00	—

KM# 257.1 5 CENTAVOS Weight: 1.6667 g. **Composition:** 0.7200 Silver .0386 oz. ASW

Date	Mintage	F	VF	XF	Unc	BU
1950	453,000	BV	1.00	2.00	9.00	—
1951	1,032,000	BV	1.00	1.50	5.00	—
1952	913,000	BV	1.00	1.50	4.00	—
1953	447,000	BV	1.00	2.50	4.00	—
1954	520,000	BV	1.00	1.50	8.00	—
1955	2,061,999	BV	1.00	1.50	3.00	—
1956	1,301,000	BV	1.00	1.50	3.00	—
1957	2,941,000	BV	1.00	1.50	2.50	—

KM# 257.1a 5 CENTAVOS Weight: 2.7300 g. **Composition:** 0.6200 Gold .0544 oz. AGW **Note:** Distributed among delegates.

Date	Mintage	F	VF	XF	Unc	BU
1953	25	—	—	—	550	—

KM# 257.2 5 CENTAVOS Weight: 1.6670 g. **Composition:** 0.7200 Silver .0386 oz. ASW **Obverse:** Long-tailed quetzal **Note:** Small crude date and large crude dates.

Date	Mintage	F	VF	XF	Unc	BU
1958 Small date	3,025,000	BV	0.75	1.00	2.50	—
1958 Large date	Inc. above	BV	1.00	1.75	3.50	—
1959	232,000	BV	1.00	1.50	2.00	—

KM# 257.3 5 CENTAVOS Weight: 1.6670 g. **Composition:** 0.7200 Silver .0386 oz. ASW **Obverse:** Short-tailed quetzal

Date	F	VF	XF	Unc	BU
1958 Small date	BV	1.00	1.75	3.50	—

KM# 261 5 CENTAVOS Weight: 1.6670 g. **Composition:** 0.7200 Silver .0386 oz. ASW **Reverse:** Level ground at tree

Date	Mintage	F	VF	XF	Unc	BU
1960	4,770,000	—	BV	0.50	1.00	—
1961	6,756,000	—	BV	0.50	1.00	—
1964	1,529,000	—	BV	0.50	1.00	—

KM# 266 5 CENTAVOS Composition: Copper-Nickel **Note:** Date size varieties exist.

Date	Mintage	F	VF	XF	Unc	BU
1965	1,642,000	—	0.15	0.50	4.00	—
1966	3,600,000	—	—	0.15	0.35	—
1967	2,800,000	—	—	0.15	0.35	—
1968	4,030,000	—	—	0.15	0.35	—
1969	7,210,000	—	—	0.15	0.35	—
1970	8,121,000	—	—	0.15	0.35	—

KM# 270 5 CENTAVOS Composition: Copper-Nickel **Obverse:** Legend on scroll incuse. Small shield and quetzal

Date	Mintage	F	VF	XF	Unc	BU
1971	8,270,000	—	—	0.15	0.35	—
1974	10,575,000	—	—	0.15	0.35	—
1975	10,000,000	—	—	0.15	0.35	—
1976	6,000,000	—	—	0.15	0.35	—
1977	20,000,000	—	—	0.15	0.35	—

KM# 276.1 5 CENTAVOS Composition: Copper-Nickel **Obverse:** Large shield and quetzal

Date	Mintage	F	VF	XF	Unc	BU
1977	Inc. above	—	—	0.15	0.35	—
1978	15,000,000	—	—	0.15	0.30	—
1979	12,000,000	—	—	0.15	0.30	—

KM# 276.2 5 CENTAVOS Composition: Copper-Nickel **Obverse:** Legend on scroll in relief

Date	Mintage	F	VF	XF	Unc	BU
1980	8,000,000	—	—	0.15	0.30	—

KM# 276.3 5 CENTAVOS Composition: Copper-Nickel **Reverse:** Different tree

Date	Mintage	F	VF	XF	Unc	BU
1981	8,000,000	—	—	0.15	0.30	—
1985	—	—	—	0.15	0.30	—

KM# 276.4 5 CENTAVOS Composition: Copper-Nickel **Obverse:** Legend on scroll incuse **Reverse:** Smaller tree, less ground below **Note:** Varieties exist.

Date	Mintage	F	VF	XF	Unc	BU
1985	—	—	—	0.15	0.30	—
1986 Large date	—	—	—	0.15	0.30	—
1986 Small date	—	—	—	—	—	—
1987	25,000,000	—	—	0.15	0.30	—
1988	21,800,000	—	—	0.15	0.30	—
1989	—	—	—	0.15	0.30	—
1990	—	—	—	0.15	0.30	—
1991	—	—	—	0.15	0.30	—
1992	—	—	—	0.15	0.30	—
1993	—	—	—	0.15	0.30	—
1994	—	—	—	0.15	0.30	—
1996	—	—	—	0.15	0.30	—
1998	—	—	—	0.15	0.30	—

KM#276.5 5 CENTAVOS Composition: Copper-Nickel **Obverse:** Smaller letters, REPUBLICA DE GUATEMALA

Date	F	VF	XF	Unc	BU
1995	—	—	0.15	0.30	—

KM# 276.6 5 CENTAVOS Composition: Copper-Nickel **Obverse:** Smaller sized emblem **Note:** Varieties exist.

Date	F	VF	XF	Unc	BU
1997	—	—	0.15	0.30	—
1998	—	—	0.15	0.30	—

KM# 239.1a 10 CENTAVOS Weight: 5.0000 g. **Composition:** 0.9000 Gold .1446 oz. AGW

Date	Mintage	F	VF	XF	Unc	BU
1925 Rare	8	—	—	—	—	—

KM# 239.1 10 CENTAVOS Weight: 3.3333 g. **Composition:** 0.7200 Silver .0772 oz. ASW **Obverse:** Long-tailed quetzal **Reverse:** Engraver's initials below "CENTAVOS" **Note:** Varieties exist.

Date	Mintage	F	VF	XF	Unc	BU
1925	573,000	3.50	6.50	15.00	32.50	—
1944	155,000	1.25	3.50	7.00	16.50	—
1945	1,499,000	BV	1.25	2.00	4.00	—
1947	471,000	BV	1.50	2.50	8.00	—
1948	324,000	BV	1.50	2.50	5.50	—
1949	145,000	BV	2.00	4.50	10.00	—

KM# 239.2 10 CENTAVOS Weight: 3.3333 g. **Composition:** 0.7200 Silver .0772 oz. ASW **Obverse:** Short-tailed quetzal **Reverse:** Without engraver's initials

Date	Mintage	F	VF	XF	Unc	BU
1928(L)	500,000	BV	2.50	5.00	25.00	—
1928(L) Proof	—	Value: 250				
1929(L)	500,000	BV	2.00	3.50	22.50	—
1929(L) Proof	—	—	—	—	—	—
1932(L)	500,000	BV	2.00	3.50	12.00	—
1932(L) Proof	—	—	—	—	—	—
1933(L)	650,000	BV	1.75	3.00	15.00	—
1933(L) Proof	—	—	—	—	—	—
1934(L)	300,000	BV	1.75	3.00	15.00	—
1934(L) Proof	—	—	—	—	—	—
1936(L)	200,000	BV	2.50	4.50	17.50	—
1936(L) Proof	—	—	—	—	—	—
1938(L)	150,000	1.00	3.00	5.00	12.50	—
1938(L) Proof	—	—	—	—	—	—
1943(P)	600,000	BV	1.25	2.50	7.50	—

KM# 239.3 10 CENTAVOS Weight: 3.3333 g. **Composition:** 0.7200 Silver .0772 oz. ASW **Reverse:** With engraver's initials **Note:** Mintage included above, in KM#239.1. Varieties exist.

Date	F	VF	XF	Unc	BU
1947	BV	3.00	4.00	8.50	—

KM# 256.1 10 CENTAVOS Weight: 3.3333 g. **Composition:** 0.7200 Silver .0772 oz. ASW **Reverse:** Small monolith

Date	Mintage	F	VF	XF	Unc	BU
1949	281,000	BV	2.50	3.50	10.00	—
1950	550,000	BV	1.50	2.50	5.00	—
1951	263,000	BV	2.50	4.50	12.50	—
1952	307,000	BV	1.50	2.50	5.00	—
1953	388,000	BV	1.50	2.50	5.00	—
1955	896,000	BV	1.50	2.50	5.00	—
1956	501,000	BV	1.50	2.50	12.50	—
1958	1,528,000	BV	1.50	2.50	6.00	—

KM# 256.2 10 CENTAVOS Weight: 3.3333 g. **Composition:** 0.7200 Silver .0772 oz. ASW **Reverse:** Larger monolith

Date	Mintage	F	VF	XF	Unc	BU
1957	1,123,000	BV	1.25	2.00	3.00	—

Date	Mintage	F	VF	XF	Unc	BU
1958	Inc. above	BV	1.50	2.50	5.00	—
1958 Medallic die alignment	Inc. above	6.00	12.00	22.50	40.00	—

KM# 256.3 10 CENTAVOS Weight: 3.3333 g. **Composition:** 0.7200 Silver .0772 oz. ASW **Obverse:** Long-tailed quetzal **Reverse:** Small monolith

Date	Mintage	F	VF	XF	Unc	BU
1958	Inc. above	BV	1.25	2.00	3.00	—
1959	461,000	BV	1.25	2.00	3.00	—
1959 Medallic die alignment	Inc. above	6.00	12.00	22.50	37.50	—

KM# 262 10 CENTAVOS Weight: 3.3333 g. **Composition:** 0.7200 Silver .0772 oz. ASW

Date	Mintage	F	VF	XF	Unc	BU
1960	1,743,000	BV	1.50	2.00	2.50	—
1961	2,647,000	BV	1.50	2.00	2.50	—
1964	965,000	BV	1.50	2.00	2.50	—

KM# 267 10 CENTAVOS Composition: Copper-Nickel **Note:** Varieties of 9 in date exist.

Date	Mintage	F	VF	XF	Unc	BU
1965	2,227,000	—	0.15	0.25	0.75	—
1966	1,550,000	—	0.15	0.35	0.85	—
1967	3,120,000	—	0.15	0.25	0.75	—
1968	3,220,000	—	0.15	0.25	0.75	—
1969	3,530,000	—	0.15	0.25	0.75	—
1970	4,153,000	—	0.15	0.25	0.75	—

KM# 271.1 10 CENTAVOS Composition: Copper-Nickel **Obverse:** Small wreath

Date	Mintage	F	VF	XF	Unc	BU
1971	4,580,000	—	0.15	0.25	0.75	—

KM# 271.2 10 CENTAVOS Composition: Copper-Nickel **Obverse:** Large wreath

Date	F	VF	XF	Unc	BU
1971	—	0.15	0.25	0.75	—
1973	—	0.15	0.25	0.75	—

KM# 274 10 CENTAVOS Composition: Copper-Nickel

Date	Mintage	F	VF	XF	Unc	BU
1974	3,500,000	—	0.15	0.25	0.75	—
1975 Dots flank date	6,000,000	—	0.15	0.25	0.75	—

KM# 277.1 10 CENTAVOS Composition: Copper-Nickel **Note:** Wide rim toothed border.

Date	Mintage	F	VF	XF	Unc	BU
1976	2,000,000	—	0.15	0.25	0.75	—
1977	5,000,000	—	0.15	0.25	0.75	—

KM# 277.2 10 CENTAVOS Composition: Copper-Nickel **Note:** Round beads instead of toothed border.

Date	Mintage	F	VF	XF	Unc	BU
1978	8,500,000	—	0.15	0.25	0.75	—
1979	11,000,000	—	0.15	0.25	0.75	—

KM# 277.3 10 CENTAVOS Composition: Copper-Nickel **Obverse:** Legend on scroll in relief, quetzal in silhouette **Reverse:** Different design

Date	Mintage	F	VF	XF	Unc	BU
1980	5,000,000	—	0.15	0.25	0.75	—
1981	4,000,000	—	0.15	0.25	0.75	—

KM# 277.4 10 CENTAVOS Composition: Copper-Nickel **Obverse:** Quetzal is solid, larger monolith

Date	Mintage	F	VF	XF	Unc	BU
1983	20,000,000	—	0.15	0.25	0.75	—
1986	—	—	0.15	0.25	0.75	—

KM# 277.5 10 CENTAVOS Composition: Copper-Nickel **Reverse:** Larger 10 **Note:** Varieties exist.

Date	Mintage	F	VF	XF	Unc	BU
1986	—	—	0.15	0.25	0.75	—
1987	17,000,000	—	0.15	0.25	0.75	—
1988	13,250,000	—	0.15	0.25	0.75	—
1989	—	—	0.15	0.25	0.75	—
1990	—	—	0.15	0.25	0.75	—
1991	—	—	0.15	0.25	0.75	—
1992	—	—	0.15	0.25	0.75	—
1993	—	—	0.15	0.25	0.75	—
1994	—	—	0.15	0.25	0.75	—

KM# 277.6 10 CENTAVOS Composition: Copper-Nickel **Obverse:** Smaller letters in REPUBLICA DE GUATEMALA **Note:** Varieties exist.

Date	F	VF	XF	Unc	BU
1995	—	0.15	0.25	0.75	—
1996	—	0.15	0.25	0.75	—
1997	—	0.15	0.25	0.75	—
1998	—	0.15	0.25	0.75	—

KM# 240.1 1/4 QUETZAL Weight: 8.3333 g. **Composition:** 0.7200 Silver .1929 oz. ASW **Edge:** Lettered

Date	Mintage	F	VF	XF	Unc	BU
1925(P)	1,160,000	3.75	8.00	25.00	50.00	—

KM# 240.2 1/4 QUETZAL Weight: 8.3333 g. **Composition:** 0.7200 Silver .1929 oz. ASW **Obverse:** Without NOBLES below scroll

Date	F	VF	XF	Unc	BU
1925 (P)	37.50	75.00	175	400	—

KM# 240a 1/4 QUETZAL Composition: 0.9000 Gold

Date	Mintage	F	VF	XF	Unc	BU
1925 (P) Rare	8	—	—	—	—	—

KM# 243.1 1/4 QUETZAL Weight: 8.3333 g. **Composition:** 0.7200 Silver .1929 oz. ASW **Reverse:** Larger design

Date	Mintage	F	VF	XF	Unc	BU
1926(L)	2,000,000	2.00	3.50	10.00	55.00	—
1926(L) Proof	—	—	—	—	—	—
1928(L)	400,000	2.50	4.00	10.00	55.00	—
1928(L) Proof	—	—	—	—	—	—
1929(L)	400,000	2.50	4.50	12.50	45.00	—
1929(L) Proof	—	—	—	—	—	—

KM# 243.2 1/4 QUETZAL Weight: 8.3333 g. **Composition:** 0.7200 Silver .1929 oz. ASW **Edge:** Reeded

Date	Mintage	F	VF	XF	Unc	BU
1946	203,000	3.00	6.50	13.50	22.00	—
1947	134,000	3.75	8.00	12.50	20.00	—
1948	129,000	3.75	7.50	12.00	20.00	—
1949/8	25,000	5.25	10.00	16.50	30.00	—
1949	Inc. above	12.50	27.50	55.00	100	—

KM# 253 25 CENTAVOS Weight: 8.3333 g. **Composition:** 0.7200 Silver .1929 oz. ASW

Date	Mintage	F	VF	XF	Unc	BU
1943(P)	900,000	2.50	5.50	10.00	40.00	—

Note: 150,000 of total mintage struck in 1943, remainder struck in 1944

KM# 258 25 CENTAVOS Weight: 8.3333 g. **Composition:** 0.7200 Silver .1929 oz. ASW **Note:** Denticulated rims.

Date	Mintage	F	VF	XF	Unc	BU
1950	81,000	2.25	4.00	8.00	30.00	—
1951	11,000	8.50	17.50	27.50	70.00	—
1952	112,000	BV	2.75	6.00	15.00	—
1954	246,000	BV	2.75	5.00	10.00	—
1955	409,000	BV	2.75	5.00	10.00	—
1956	342,000	BV	2.75	5.00	10.00	—
1957	257,000	BV	2.75	5.00	9.00	—
1958	394,000	BV	2.75	5.00	9.00	—
1959/8	277,000	BV	2.75	5.00	9.00	—
1959	Inc. above	BV	2.75	6.00	12.50	—

KM# 263 25 CENTAVOS **Weight:** 8.3333 g. **Composition:** 0.7200 Silver .1929 oz. ASW **Note:** Scalloped rims.

Date	Mintage	F	VF	XF	Unc	BU
1960	560,000	BV	2.25	3.25	6.00	—
1960 Medallic die alignment	Inc. above	20.00	50.00	100	175	—

Note: Planchet size and weight vary in 1960 type as well as density of reeding

Date	Mintage	F	VF	XF	Unc	BU
1961	750,000	BV	2.25	3.25	6.00	—
1962	—	BV	2.25	3.25	6.00	—
1963	1,100,000	BV	2.00	3.00	5.50	—
1964	299,000	BV	2.25	3.25	6.00	—

KM# 268 25 CENTAVOS **Composition:** Copper-Nickel

Date	Mintage	F	VF	XF	Unc	BU
1965	1,178,000	0.15	0.25	0.60	1.75	—
1966	910,000	0.15	0.25	0.60	1.75	—

KM# 269 25 CENTAVOS **Composition:** Copper-Nickel **Reverse:** Modified design

Date	Mintage	F	VF	XF	Unc	BU
1967	1,140,000	0.15	0.25	0.60	1.75	—
1968	1,540,000	0.15	0.25	0.60	1.50	—
1969 Large date	2,069,000	0.15	0.25	0.60	1.50	—
1970	2,501,000	0.15	0.25	0.60	1.50	—

KM# 272 25 CENTAVOS **Composition:** Copper-Nickel **Obverse:** Smaller arms, legend on scroll incuse

Date	Mintage	F	VF	XF	Unc	BU
1971	2,850,000	0.15	0.25	0.50	1.00	—
1975	1,592,000	0.15	0.25	0.50	1.00	—
1976	2,000,000	0.15	0.25	0.50	1.00	—

KM# 278.1 25 CENTAVOS **Composition:** Copper-Nickel **Reverse:** Large head

Date	Mintage	F	VF	XF	Unc	BU
1977	2,000,000	0.15	0.25	0.50	1.00	—
1978	4,400,000	0.15	0.25	0.35	0.85	—
1979	5,400,000	0.15	0.25	0.35	0.85	—

KM# 278.2 25 CENTAVOS **Composition:** Copper-Nickel **Obverse:** Legend on scroll in relief **Reverse:** Small head **Note:** Wide rim

Date	Mintage	F	VF	XF	Unc	BU
1981	1,600,000	0.15	0.25	0.50	1.00	—

KM# 278.4 25 CENTAVOS **Composition:** Copper-Nickel **Obverse:** Quetzal is solid **Note:** Narrow rim.

Date	Mintage	F	VF	XF	Unc	BU
1982	2,000,000	0.15	0.25	0.50	1.00	—

KM# 278.3 25 CENTAVOS **Composition:** Copper-Nickel **Obverse:** Legend on scroll incuse **Reverse:** Small head and denomination

Date	Mintage	F	VF	XF	Unc	BU
1984	2,000,000	0.15	0.25	0.50	1.00	—

KM# 278.5 25 CENTAVOS **Composition:** Copper-Nickel **Reverse:** Large head and denomination **Note:** Varieties exist in number of wing feathers and details on head.

Date	Mintage	F	VF	XF	Unc	BU
1985	—	0.15	0.25	0.35	0.85	—
1986	—	0.15	0.25	0.35	0.85	—
1987	13,316,000	0.15	0.25	0.35	0.85	—
1988	6,600,000	0.15	0.25	0.35	0.85	—
1989	—	0.15	0.25	0.35	0.85	—
1990	—	0.15	0.25	0.35	0.85	—
1991	—	0.15	0.25	0.35	0.85	—
1992	—	0.15	0.25	0.35	0.85	—
1993	—	0.15	0.25	0.35	0.85	—
1994	—	0.15	0.25	0.35	0.85	—
1995	—	0.15	0.25	0.35	0.85	—

KM# 278.6 25 CENTAVOS **Composition:** Copper-Nickel **Obverse:** Smaller design with wider rims **Reverse:** Smaller design with wider rims **Edge Lettering:** REPUBLICA DE GUATEMALA CA **Note:** Varieties exist.

Date	F	VF	XF	Unc	BU
1996	0.15	0.25	0.35	0.85	—
1997	0.15	0.25	0.35	0.85	—
1998	0.15	0.25	0.35	0.85	—

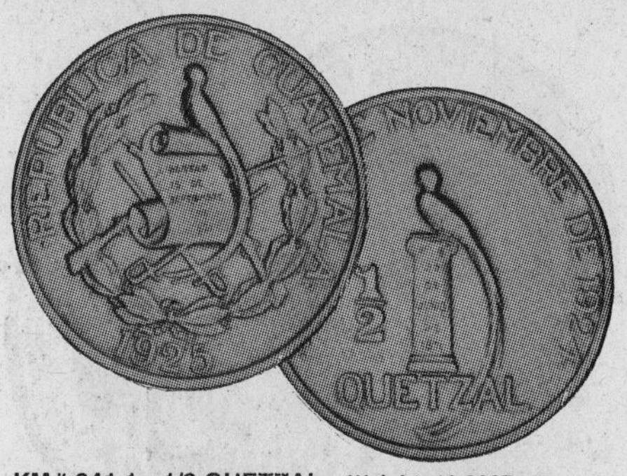

KM# 241.1 1/2 QUETZAL **Weight:** 16.6667 g. **Composition:** 0.7200 Silver .3858 oz. ASW

Date	Mintage	F	VF	XF	Unc	BU
1925(P)	400,000	16.50	27.50	58.00	220	—

KM# 241.2 1/2 QUETZAL **Weight:** 16.6667 g. **Composition:** 0.7200 Silver .3858 oz. ASW **Obverse:** Without NOBLES below scroll

Date	F	VF	XF	Unc	BU
1925 (P)	70.00	100	200	550	—

KM# 264 50 CENTAVOS **Weight:** 12.0000 g. **Composition:** 0.7200 Silver .2777 oz. ASW

Date	Mintage	F	VF	XF	Unc	BU
1962	1,983,000	—	BV	2.50	5.00	—
1963/2	350,000	3.50	7.50	12.50	20.00	—
1963	Inc. above	—	—	2.50	5.00	—

KM# 283 50 CENTAVOS **Weight:** 5.5400 g. **Composition:** Brass **Obverse:** National arms **Reverse:** National flower "MONJA BLANCA" **Edge:** Reeded **Size:** 24.2 mm.

Date	F	VF	XF	Unc	BU
1998	—	—	0.50	1.25	—

KM# 242 QUETZAL **Weight:** 33.3333 g. **Composition:** 0.7200 Silver .7716 oz. ASW

Date	F	VF	XF	Unc	BU
1925(P)	475	650	950	2,000	—

Note: 7,000 pieces were withdrawn and remelted in 1927 and 1928. Of those remaining, an addiitonal unknown quantity was melted in 1932, leaving somewhat less than 3000 survivors of this type.

KM# 279 QUETZAL **Weight:** 27.0000 g. **Composition:** 0.9250 Silver .8030 oz. ASW **Note:** Carlos Merida

Date	F	VF	XF	Unc	BU
1992NG Proof	—	Value: 50.00			

KM# 280 QUETZAL **Weight:** 27.0000 g. **Composition:** 0.9250 Silver .8030 oz. ASW **Subject:** Environmental Protection **Reverse:** Horned Guan

Date	Mintage	F	VF	XF	Unc	BU
1994 Proof	20,000	Value: 45.00				

KM# 281 QUETZAL **Weight:** 27.0000 g. **Composition:** 0.9250 Silver .8030 oz. ASW **Subject:** 50th Anniversary - National Bank of Guatemala **Obverse:** Coin designs around national emblem **Reverse:** Pre-Columbian artisans

Date	F	VF	XF	Unc	BU
1996 Proof	—	Value: 45.00			

KM# 284 QUETZAL **Weight:** 11.1000 g. **Composition:** Brass **Obverse:** National arms **Reverse:** Signature **Edge:** Reeded

Date	F	VF	XF	Unc	BU
1999	—	—	1.00	2.50	—

KM# 286 QUETZAL **Weight:** 27.0000 g. **Composition:** 0.9250 Silver 0.803 oz. ASW **Subject:** Ibero-America Series **Obverse:** National arms in circle of arms **Reverse:** Horse pulling a walk-behind plow **Edge:** Reeded **Size:** 40 mm.

Date	F	VF	XF	Unc	BU
2000	—	Value: 100			

Note: Proof

KM# 244 5 QUETZALES **Weight:** 8.3592 g. **Composition:** 0.9000 Gold .2419 oz. AGW

Date	Mintage	F	VF	XF	Unc	BU
1926(P)	48,000	125	185	250	325	—

KM# 245 10 QUETZALES **Weight:** 16.7185 g. **Composition:** 0.9000 Gold .4838 oz. AGW

Date	Mintage	F	VF	XF	Unc	BU
1926(P)	18,000	250	325	425	700	—

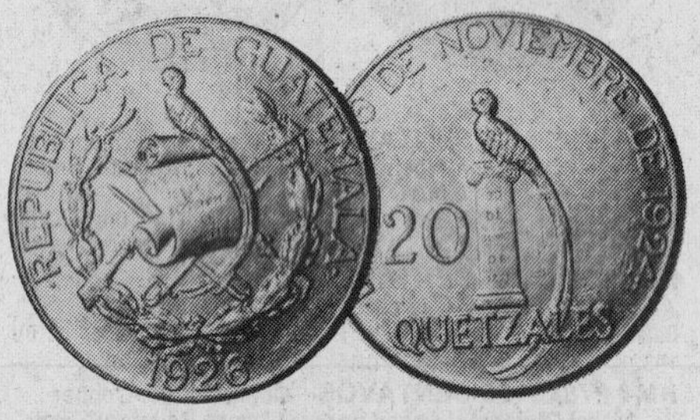

KM# 246 20 QUETZALES **Weight:** 33.4370 g. **Composition:** 0.9000 Gold .9676 oz. AGW

Date	Mintage	F	VF	XF	Unc	BU
1926(P)	49,000	350	450	600	900	—

PATTERNS

Including off metal strikes

KM#	Date	Mintage	Identification	Mkt Val
Pn18	1921	—	Peso. Copper-Nickel. 5.1000 g. 25 mm. Plain edge. MONEDA NACIONAL NIQUEL.	—
Pn19	1922	—	5 Pesos. Silver. 3/4 facing bust of Barrios.	—
Pn20	1922	—	5 Pesos. Aluminum-Brass. 3/4 facing bust of Barrios.	—
Pn21	1923	—	5 Pesos. Gold. KM234	—
Pn22	1949	20	Centavo. Brass. large bust.	450
Pn23	1949	20	5 Centavos. 0.7200 Silver.	475
Pn24	1949	20	10 Centavos. 0.7200 Silver.	525
Pn25	1949	20	25 Centavos. 0.7200 Silver.	575
Pn26	1960	—	25 Centavos. Aluminum. Plain edge. KM#263.	—
Pn27	1995	100	Quetzal. Brass center. Silver ring. 22.4300 g. 38 mm. National arms. Humming bird flying above lake. Reeded edge. Brass center in Silver ring within Brass ring.	100
Pn28	1995	100	Quetzal. Brass center. Silver ring. 22.2400 g. 38 mm. National arms. Parrot on branch, buildings in back. Reeded edge. Brass center in Silver ring within Brass ring.	100

GUERNSEY

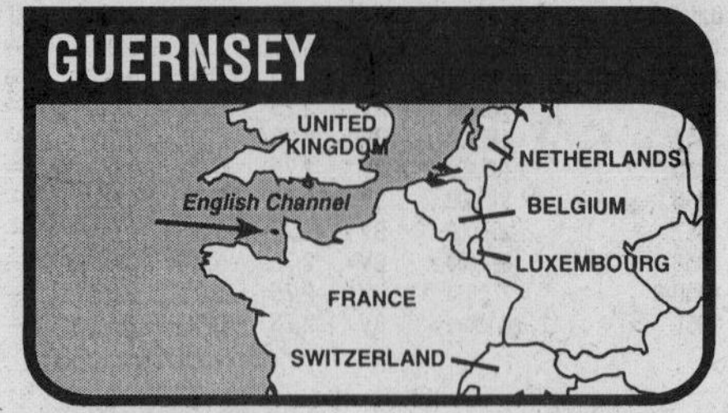

The Bailiwick of Guernsey, a British crown dependency located in the English Channel 30 miles (48 km.) west of Normandy, France, has an area of 30 sq. mi. (194 sq. km.)(including the isles of Alderney, Jethou, Herm, Brechou, and Sark), and a population of 54,000. Capital: St. Peter Port. Agriculture and cattle breeding are the main occupations.

Militant monks from the duchy of Normandy established the first permanent settlements on Guernsey prior to the Norman invasion of England, but the prevalence of prehistoric monuments suggests an earlier occupancy. The island, the only part of the duchy of Normandy belonging to the British crown, has been a possession of Britain since the Norman Conquest of 1066. During the Anglo-French wars, the harbors of Guernsey were employed in the building and out-fitting of ships for the English privateers preying on French shipping. Guernsey is administered by its own laws and customs. Unless the island is mentioned specifically, acts passed by the British Parliament are not applicable to Guernsey. During World War II, German troops occupied the island from June 30, 1940 till May 9,1945.

RULERS
British

MINT MARKS
H - Heaton, Birmingham

MONETARY SYSTEM
8 Doubles = 1 Penny
12 Pence = 1 Shilling
5 Shillings = 1 Crown
20 Shillings = 1 Pound

1 Stem

3 Stems

BRITISH DEPENDENCY

STANDARD COINAGE

KM# 10 DOUBLE **Composition:** Bronze

Date	Mintage	F	VF	XF	Unc	BU
1902H	84,000	0.20	0.60	2.25	4.00	—
1902H Proof	—	Value: 250				
1903H	112,000	0.15	0.30	1.25	2.50	—
1911H	45,000	0.50	1.50	4.00	12.00	—

KM# 11 DOUBLE **Composition:** Bronze

Date	Mintage	F	VF	XF	Unc	BU
1911H	90,000	0.30	1.20	3.00	6.00	—
1914H	45,000	1.50	3.00	6.00	12.00	—
1929H	79,000	0.30	0.85	2.50	5.50	—
1933H	96,000	0.30	0.85	2.50	5.50	—
1938H	96,000	0.30	0.85	2.50	5.50	—

KM# 9 2 DOUBLES **Composition:** Bronze **Obverse:** Leaves with 3 stems above shield

Date	Mintage	F	VF	XF	Unc	BU
1902H	18,000	4.50	9.00	18.00	30.00	—
1902H Proof	—	Value: 250				
1903H	18,000	6.00	12.50	22.00	35.00	—
1906H	18,000	6.00	12.50	22.00	35.00	—
1908H	18,000	6.00	12.50	22.00	35.00	—
1911H	29,000	4.50	9.00	15.00	27.50	—

KM# 12 2 DOUBLES Composition: Bronzed Copper

Date	Mintage	F	VF	XF	Unc	BU
1914H	29,000	4.50	9.00	18.50	27.50	—
1914H Proof	—	Value: 125				
1917H	15,000	20.00	35.00	70.00	155	—
1918H	57,000	1.25	2.50	9.00	15.00	—
1920H	57,000	1.25	2.50	9.00	15.00	—
1929H	79,000	0.35	1.25	6.00	10.00	—

KM# 5 4 DOUBLES Composition: Bronze **Obverse:** Leaves with 3 stems above shield **Note:** Varieties exist.

Date	Mintage	F	VF	XF	Unc	BU
1874	69,000	1.50	3.00	11.50	22.50	—
1902H	105,000	0.85	1.75	3.00	7.50	—
1902H Proof	—	Value: 250				
1903H	52,000	1.50	3.00	9.00	25.00	—
1906H	52,000	1.50	3.00	9.00	25.00	—
1908H	26,000	3.00	7.50	15.00	30.00	—
1910H	52,000	1.50	3.00	9.00	25.00	—
1910H Proof	—	Value: 250				
1911H	52,000	2.25	4.50	13.50	27.50	—

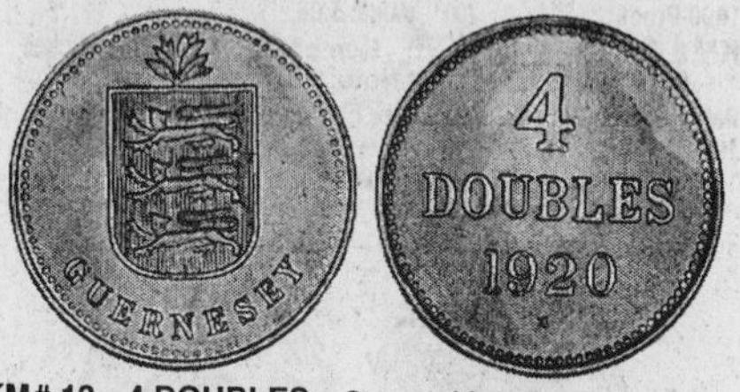

KM# 13 4 DOUBLES Composition: Bronze

Date	Mintage	F	VF	XF	Unc	BU
1914H	209,000	0.75	1.50	4.50	12.50	—
1918H	157,000	0.75	1.50	6.00	17.50	—
1920H	157,000	0.45	1.25	4.50	10.00	—
1945H	96,000	0.45	1.25	4.50	10.00	—
1949H	19,000	1.50	3.00	12.00	20.00	—

KM# 15 4 DOUBLES Composition: Bronze **Note:** Guernsey Lily

Date	Mintage	F	VF	XF	Unc	BU
1956	240,000	0.25	0.45	0.75	2.00	—
1956 Proof	2,100	Value: 4.00				
1966 Proof	10,000	Value: 1.75				

KM# 7 8 DOUBLES Composition: Bronze

Date	Mintage	F	VF	XF	Unc	BU
1902H	235,000	1.25	2.25	6.00	12.50	—
1902H Proof	—	Value: 250				
1903H	118,000	0.50	1.75	4.50	10.00	—

Date	Mintage	F	VF	XF	Unc	BU
1910H	91,000	1.25	2.50	12.50	25.00	—
1910H Proof	—	Value: 250				
1911H	78,000	3.00	8.50	15.00	30.00	—

KM# 14 8 DOUBLES Composition: Bronze

Date	Mintage	F	VF	XF	Unc	BU
1914H	157,000	0.65	1.75	4.50	10.00	—
1914H Proof	—	Value: 150				
1918H	157,000	0.65	1.75	4.50	10.00	—
1920H	157,000	0.50	1.50	4.00	9.00	—
1920H Proof	—	Value: 150				
1934H	124,000	0.50	1.50	4.00	9.00	—
1934H Proof	500	Value: 175				
1938H	120,000	0.50	1.50	4.00	9.00	—
1938H Proof	—	Value: 250				
1945H	192,000	0.40	0.85	2.00	5.50	—
1947H	240,000	0.30	0.60	2.25	5.00	—
1949H	230,000	0.30	0.60	2.25	5.00	—

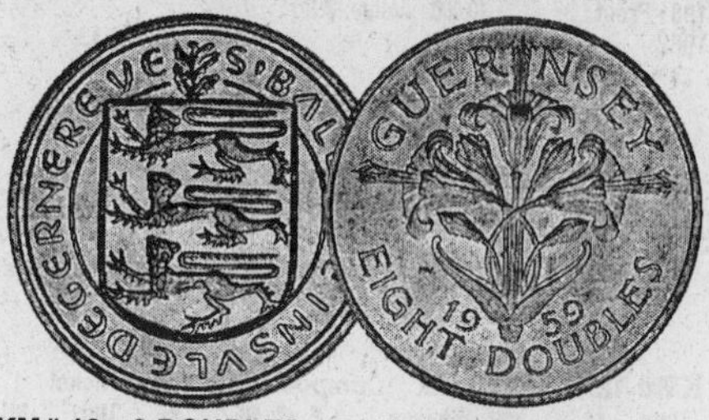

KM# 16 8 DOUBLES Composition: Bronze **Obverse:** Three-flowered lily

Date	Mintage	F	VF	XF	Unc	BU
1956	500,000	0.10	0.20	0.50	1.25	—
1956 Proof	2,100	Value: 4.00				
1959	500,000	0.10	0.20	0.50	1.25	—
1959 Proof	—	—	—	—	—	—
1966 Proof	10,000	Value: 1.75				

KM# 17 3 PENCE Composition: Copper Nickel **Obverse:** Guernsey cow **Shape:** Scalloped **Note:** Thin flan.

Date	Mintage	F	VF	XF	Unc	BU
1956	500,000	0.10	0.20	0.50	1.25	—
1956 Proof	2,100	Value: 4.00				

KM# 18 3 PENCE Composition: Copper Nickel **Obverse:** Guernsey cow **Shape:** Scalloped **Note:** Thick flan.

Date	Mintage	F	VF	XF	Unc	BU
1959	500,000	0.10	0.20	0.50	1.00	—
1959 Proof	—	Value: 150				
1966 Proof	10,000	Value: 1.75				

KM# 19 10 SHILLING Composition: Copper Nickel **Subject:** 900th Anniversary - Norman Conquest **Reverse:** William I portrait left **Shape:** Square

Date	Mintage	F	VF	XF	Unc	BU
1966	300,000	—	1.00	1.25	1.75	—
1966 Proof	10,000	Value: 3.00				

DECIMAL COINAGE

100 Pence = 1 Pound

KM# 20 1/2 NEW PENNY Composition: Bronze

Date	Mintage	F	VF	XF	Unc	BU
1971	2,066,000	—	—	0.15	0.30	—
1971 Proof	10,000	Value: 1.00				

KM# 33 1/2 PENNY Composition: Bronze

Date	Mintage	F	VF	XF	Unc	BU
1979 Proof	20,000	Value: 1.00				

KM# 21 NEW PENNY Composition: Bronze **Reverse:** Gannet

Date	Mintage	F	VF	XF	Unc	BU
1971	1,922,000	—	—	0.15	0.25	—
1971 Proof	10,000	Value: 1.00				

KM# 27 PENNY Composition: Bronze **Reverse:** Gannet

Date	Mintage	F	VF	XF	Unc	BU
1977	640,000	—	—	0.15	0.25	—
1979	2,400,000	—	—	0.15	0.25	—
1979 Proof	20,000	Value: 1.00				
1981 Proof	10,000	Value: 2.00				

KM# 40 PENNY Composition: Bronze **Reverse:** Chancre crab

Date	Mintage	F	VF	XF	Unc	BU
1985		—	—	0.15	0.35	—
1985 Proof	2,500	Value: 2.00				
1986		—	—	0.15	0.35	—
1986 Proof	2,500	Value: 2.00				
1987		—	—	0.15	0.35	—
1987 In proof sets only	2,500	Value: 2.00				
1988		—	—	0.15	0.35	—
1988 Proof	2,500	Value: 2.00				
1989		—	—	0.15	0.35	—
1989 In proof sets only	2,500	Value: 2.00				
1990		—	—	0.15	0.35	—
1990 Proof	700	Value: 4.00				

KM# 40a PENNY Composition: Copper Plated Steel **Reverse:** Chancre crab

Date	Mintage	F	VF	XF	Unc	BU
1992 In sets only	—	—	—	—	0.35	—
1992 In proof sets only	—	Value: 5.00				
1994	750,000	—	—	—	0.35	—
1997	2,000,000	—	—	—	0.35	—

KM# 89 PENNY Composition: Copper Plated Steel **Obverse:** Rank-Broadley portrait of Queen Elizabeth II **Reverse:** Chancre crab

Date	F	VF	XF	Unc	BU
1998	—	—	—	0.35	—

KM# 22 2 NEW PENCE **Composition:** Bronze **Reverse:** Windmill from Sark

Date	Mintage	F	VF	XF	Unc	BU
1971	1,680,000	—	—	0.15	0.35	—
1971 Proof	10,000	Value: 1.00				

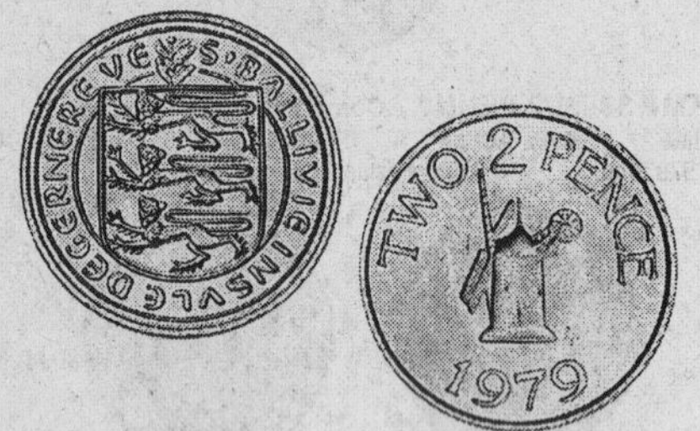

KM# 28 2 PENCE **Composition:** Bronze **Reverse:** Windmill from Sark

Date	Mintage	F	VF	XF	Unc	BU
1977	700,000	—	—	0.15	0.25	—
1979	2,400,000	—	—	0.15	0.25	—
1979 Proof	20,000	Value: 1.00				
1981 Proof	10,000	Value: 2.00				

KM# 41 2 PENCE **Composition:** Bronze **Reverse:** Guernsey cow

Date	Mintage	F	VF	XF	Unc	BU
1985	60,000	—	—	0.20	0.60	—
1985 Proof	2,500	Value: 2.00				
1986	510,000	—	—	0.20	0.60	—
1986 Proof	2,500	Value: 2.00				
1987	5,000	—	—	0.20	0.60	—
1987 In proof sets only	2,500	Value: 2.00				
1988	500,000	—	—	0.20	0.60	—
1988 Proof	2,500	Value: 2.00				
1989	500,000	—	—	0.20	0.60	—
1989 In proof sets only	2,500	Value: 2.00				
1990	380,000	—	—	0.20	0.60	—
1990 Proof	700	Value: 4.00				

KM# 41a 2 PENCE **Weight:** 7.2000 g. **Composition:** Copper Plated Steel **Reverse:** Guernsey cow **Edge:** Plain **Size:** 25.9 mm. **Note:** British Royal Mint.

Date	Mintage	F	VF	XF	Unc	BU
1992 In sets only	—	—	—	—	0.30	—
1992 In proof sets only	—	Value: 5.00				
1996	500,000	—	—	—	0.30	—
1997	—	—	—	—	0.30	—

KM# 96 2 PENCE **Weight:** 7.2000 g. **Composition:** Copper Plated Steel **Obverse:** Queen's new portrait **Reverse:** Guernsey cow **Edge:** Plain

Date	Mintage	F	VF	XF	Unc	BU
1999	600,000	—	—	—	0.25	—

KM# 23 5 NEW PENCE **Composition:** Copper-Nickel **Reverse:** Guernsey lilly

Date	Mintage	F	VF	XF	Unc	BU
1968	800,000	—	0.15	0.25	0.40	—
1971 Proof	10,000	Value: 1.50				

KM# 29 5 PENCE **Composition:** Copper-Nickel **Reverse:** Guernsey lilly

Date	Mintage	F	VF	XF	Unc	BU
1977	250,000	—	—	0.20	0.45	—
1979	200,000	—	—	0.20	0.45	—
1979 Proof	20,000	Value: 2.00				
1981 Proof	10,000	Value: 3.00				
1982	200,000	—	—	0.20	0.45	—

KM# 42.1 5 PENCE **Composition:** Copper-Nickel

Date	Mintage	F	VF	XF	Unc	BU
1985		—	—	0.20	0.45	—
1985 Proof	2,500	Value: 2.50				
1986		—	—	0.20	0.45	—
1986 Proof	2,500	Value: 2.50				
1987		—	—	0.20	0.45	—
1987 In proof sets only	Est. 2,5002,500	Value: 2.50				
1988		—	—	0.20	0.45	—
1988 Proof	2,500	Value: 2.50				
1989		—	—	0.20	0.50	—
1989 In proof sets only	2,500	Value: 2.50				
1990 In sets only		—	—	—	0.60	—
1990 Proof	700	Value: 5.00				

KM# 42.2 5 PENCE **Weight:** 3.2600 g. **Composition:** Copper-Nickel **Size:** 18 mm. **Note:** Reduced size. British Royal Mint.

Date	Mintage	F	VF	XF	Unc	BU
1990	2,400,000	—	—	0.20	0.45	—
1990 Proof	700	Value: 5.00				
1992	1,300,000	—	—	—	0.50	—
1997	—	—	—	—	0.50	—

KM# 97 5 PENCE **Weight:** 3.2600 g. **Composition:** Copper-Nickel **Obverse:** Queen's new portrait **Reverse:** Sail boats **Edge:** Reeded

Date	Mintage	F	VF	XF	Unc	BU
1999	1,700,000	—	—	—	0.45	—

KM# 24 10 NEW PENCE **Composition:** Copper-Nickel **Reverse:** Guernsey cow

Date	Mintage	F	VF	XF	Unc	BU
1968	600,000	—	0.20	0.40	1.00	—
1970	300,000	—	0.20	0.40	1.00	—
1971 Proof	10,000	Value: 2.00				

KM# 30 10 PENCE **Composition:** Copper-Nickel **Reverse:** Guernsey cow

Date	Mintage	F	VF	XF	Unc	BU
1977	480,000	—	—	0.25	0.85	—
1979	659,000	—	—	0.25	0.85	—
1979 Proof	20,000	Value: 2.00				
1981 Proof	10,000	Value: 3.00				
1982	200,000	—	—	0.25	1.00	—
1984	400,000	—	—	0.25	0.85	—

KM# 43.1 10 PENCE **Composition:** Copper-Nickel **Reverse:** Tomato plant

Date	Mintage	F	VF	XF	Unc	BU
1985		—	—	0.25	0.60	—
1985 Proof	2,500	Value: 2.50				
1986		—	—	0.25	0.60	—
1986 Proof	2,500	Value: 6.00				
1987		—	—	0.25	0.60	—
1987 In proof sets only	2,500	Value: 2.50				
1988		—	—	0.25	0.60	—
1988 Proof	2,500	Value: 2.50				
1989		—	—	0.25	0.60	—
1989 In proof sets only	2,500	Value: 2.50				
1990		—	—	0.25	0.60	—
1990 Proof	700	Value: 5.00				

KM# 43.2 10 PENCE **Composition:** Copper-Nickel **Reverse:** Tomato plant **Note:** Reduced size.

Date	Mintage	F	VF	XF	Unc	BU
1992	3,500,000	—	—	—	0.60	—
1992	—	Value: 6.00				
Note: In proof sets only						
1997	—	—	—	—	0.60	—

KM# 38 20 PENCE **Composition:** Copper-Nickel **Reverse:** Guernsey milk can **Shape:** 7-sided.

Date	Mintage	F	VF	XF	Unc	BU
1982	500,000	—	—	0.45	0.90	—
1983	500,000	—	—	0.45	0.90	—

KM# 44 20 PENCE **Composition:** Copper-Nickel **Shape:** 7-sided.

Date	Mintage	F	VF	XF	Unc	BU
1985		—	—	0.45	0.85	—
1985 Proof	2,500	Value: 3.00				
1986		—	—	0.45	0.85	—
1986 Proof	2,500	Value: 3.00				
1987		—	—	0.45	0.85	—
1987 Proof	2,500	Value: 3.00				
1988		—	—	0.45	0.85	—
1988 Proof	2,500	Value: 3.00				
1989		—	—	0.45	0.85	—
1989 Proof	Est. 2,5002,500	Value: 3.00				
1990		—	—	0.45	0.85	—
1990 Proof	700	Value: 6.00				
1992		—	—	—	1.00	—
1992 Proof	—	Value: 7.00				
1997		—	—	—	1.00	—

KM# 90 20 PENCE **Composition:** Copper-Nickel **Obverse:** Rank-Broadley portrait of Queen Elizabeth II

Date	Mintage	F	VF	XF	Unc	BU
1999	800,000	—	—	—	0.90	—
1999 Proof	—	Value: 3.00				

KM# 26 25 PENCE **Composition:** Copper-Nickel **Subject:** 25th Wedding Anniversary - Elizabeth and Philip

Date	Mintage	F	VF	XF	Unc	BU
1972	56,000	—	—	2.50	5.50	—

KM# 26a 25 PENCE **Weight:** 28.2759 g. **Composition:** 0.9250 Silver .8410 oz. ASW **Subject:** 25th Wedding Anniversary - Elizabeth and Philip

Date	Mintage	F	VF	XF	Unc	BU
1972 Proof	15,000	Value: 12.50				

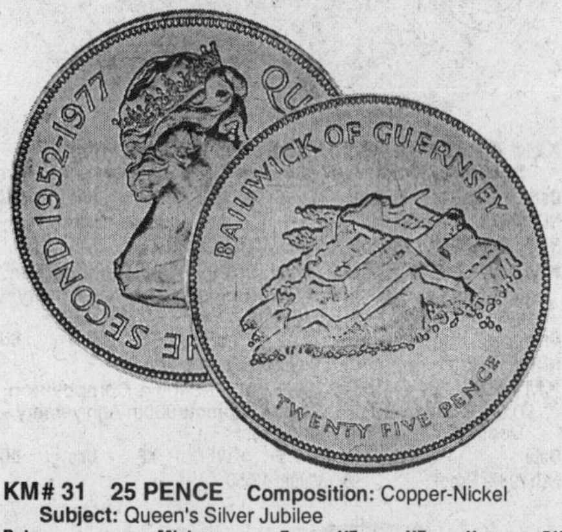

KM# 31 25 PENCE **Composition:** Copper-Nickel **Subject:** Queen's Silver Jubilee

Date	Mintage	F	VF	XF	Unc	BU
ND(1977)	207,000	—	—	1.25	2.25	—

KM# 31a 25 PENCE **Weight:** 28.2759 g. **Composition:** 0.9250 Silver .8410 oz. ASW **Subject:** Queen's Silver Jubilee

Date	Mintage	F	VF	XF	Unc	BU
ND(1977) Proof	25,000	Value: 11.50				

KM# 32 25 PENCE **Composition:** Copper-Nickel **Subject:** Royal Visit

Date	Mintage	F	VF	XF	Unc	BU
1978	105,000	—	—	1.25	2.50	—

KM# 32a 25 PENCE **Weight:** 28.2759 g. **Composition:** 0.9250 Silver .8410 oz. ASW **Subject:** Royal Visit

Date	Mintage	F	VF	XF	Unc	BU
1978 Proof	25,000	Value: 12.50				

KM# 35 25 PENCE **Composition:** Copper-Nickel **Subject:** Queen Mother's 80th Birthday

Date	Mintage	F	VF	XF	Unc	BU
ND(1980)	150,000	—	—	1.25	2.50	—

KM# 35a 25 PENCE **Weight:** 28.2759 g. **Composition:** 0.9250 Silver .8410 oz. ASW **Subject:** Queen Mother's 80th Birthday

Date	Mintage	F	VF	XF	Unc	BU
ND(1980) Proof	25,000	Value: 14.50				

KM# 36 25 PENCE **Composition:** Copper-Nickel **Subject:** Wedding of Prince Charles and Lady Diana **Obverse:** Similar to 25 New Pence, KM#35

Date	Mintage	F	VF	XF	Unc	BU
1981	114,000	—	—	1.50	3.00	—

KM# 36a 25 PENCE **Weight:** 28.2759 g. **Composition:** 0.9250 Silver .8410 oz. ASW **Subject:** Wedding of Prince Charles and Lady Diana **Obverse:** Similar to 25 New Pence, KM#35

Date	Mintage	F	VF	XF	Unc	BU
1981 Proof	12,000	Value: 16.50				

KM# 25 50 NEW PENCE **Composition:** Copper-Nickel **Reverse:** Ducal cap of the Duke of Normandy **Shape:** 7-sided.

Date	Mintage	F	VF	XF	Unc	BU
1969	200,000	—	1.00	1.50	2.50	—
1970	200,000	—	1.00	1.50	2.50	—
1971 Proof	10,000	Value: 3.00				

KM# 34 50 PENCE **Composition:** Copper-Nickel **Reverse:** Ducal cap of the Duke of Normandy **Shape:** 7-sided.

Date	Mintage	F	VF	XF	Unc	BU
1979 Proof	20,000	Value: 4.50				
1981	200,000	—	—	0.90	1.45	—
1981 Proof	10,000	Value: 5.50				
1982	150,000	—	—	0.90	1.45	—
1983	200,000	—	—	0.90	1.45	—
1984	200,000	—	—	0.90	1.45	—

KM# 45.1 50 PENCE **Composition:** Copper-Nickel **Shape:** 7-sided.

Date	Mintage	F	VF	XF	Unc	BU
1985		—	—	0.90	1.45	—
1985 Proof	2,500	Value: 4.00				
1986		—	—	0.90	1.45	—
1986 Proof	2,500	Value: 4.00				
1987		—	—	0.90	1.45	—
1987 In proof sets only	2,500	Value: 4.50				
1988		—	—	0.90	1.45	—
1988 Proof	2,500	Value: 4.50				
1989		—	—	0.90	1.45	—
1989 In proof sets only	2,500	Value: 4.50				
1990		—	—	0.90	1.45	—
1990 Proof	700	Value: 7.50				
1992		—	—	—	2.00	—
1997 In proof sets only	—	Value: 7.50				

KM# 45.2 50 PENCE **Composition:** Copper-Nickel **Obverse:** Queen's portrait **Reverse:** Crossed flowers **Shape:** 7-sided. **Size:** 27.3 mm.

Date	Mintage	F	VF	XF	Unc	BU
1997	1,000,000	—	—	—	1.75	—

KM# 105 50 PENCE **Weight:** 7.9700 g. **Composition:** Copper-Nickel **Subject:** Battle of Britain **Obverse:** Queen's portrait **Reverse:** Pilot and fighter plane **Edge:** Plain **Shape:** 7-sided. **Size:** 27.3 mm.

Date	Mintage	F	VF	XF	Unc	BU
2000	10,000	—	—	—	1.50	—

KM# 105a 50 PENCE **Weight:** 8.1000 g. **Composition:** 0.9250 Silver .2409 oz. ASW **Shape:** 7-sided.

Date	Mintage	F	VF	XF	Unc	BU
2000 Proof	15,000	Value: 25.00				

KM# 105b 50 PENCE **Weight:** 15.5000 g. **Composition:** 0.9170 Gold .4570 oz. AGW **Edge:** Plain **Shape:** 7-sided. **Size:** 27.3 mm.

Date	Mintage	F	VF	XF	Unc	BU
2000 Proof	1,500	Value: 300				

KM# 37 POUND **Composition:** Nickel-Brass **Reverse:** Guernsey lily

Date	Mintage	F	VF	XF	Unc	BU
1981	200,000	—	1.80	2.00	3.50	—
1981 Proof	10,000	Value: 4.50				

KM# 37a POUND **Weight:** 8.0000 g. **Composition:** 0.9170 Gold .2358 oz. AGW **Reverse:** Guernsey lily

Date	Mintage	F	VF	XF	Unc	BU
1981 Proof	4,500	Value: 125				

KM# 39 POUND **Composition:** Nickel-Brass **Reverse:** H.M.S. Crescent

Date	Mintage	F	VF	XF	Unc	BU
1983	269,000	—	1.80	2.00	3.50	—

KM# 46 POUND **Composition:** Nickel-Brass

Date	Mintage	F	VF	XF	Unc	BU
1985		—	—	1.75	2.50	—
1985 Proof	2,500	Value: 6.50				
1986		—	—	1.75	2.50	—
1986 Proof	2,500	Value: 6.50				
1987		—	—	1.75	2.50	—
1987 In proof sets only	2,500	Value: 6.50				
1988		—	—	1.75	2.50	—
1988 Proof	2,500	Value: 6.50				
1989		—	—	1.75	2.50	—
1989 In proof sets only	2,500	Value: 6.50				
1990		—	—	1.75	2.50	—
1990 Proof	700	Value: 10.00				
1992 Proof		—	—	—	12.50	—
1997 Proof		—	—	—	3.50	—

KM# 77 POUND **Weight:** 9.5000 g. **Composition:** 0.9250 Silver .2825 oz. ASW **Subject:** Queen Elizabeth the Queen Mother **Note:** Similar to 5 Pounds, KM#66

Date		F	VF	XF	Unc	BU
1995 Proof	—	Value: 27.50				

KM# 78 POUND **Weight:** 9.5000 g. **Composition:** 0.9250 Silver .2825 oz. ASW **Subject:** 70th Birthday of Queen Elizabeth II

Date		F	VF	XF	Unc	BU
1996 Proof	—	Value: 20.00				

KM# 70 POUND **Weight:** 9.5000 g. **Composition:** 0.9250 Silver .2825 oz. ASW **Subject:** Golden Wedding Anniversary **Obverse:** Queen's portrait **Reverse:** Queen Elizabeth II and Prince Philip, monogrammed shield, Westminster Abbey.

Date	Mintage	F	VF	XF	Unc	BU
1997 Proof	Est. 50,000	Value: 20.00				

KM# 73 POUND **Weight:** 9.5000 g. **Composition:** 0.9250 Silver .2825 oz. ASW **Series:** Castle **Subject:** Tower of London

Date	Mintage	F	VF	XF	Unc	BU
1997 Proof	15,000	Value: 32.50				

KM# 84 POUND **Weight:** 9.5000 g. **Composition:** 0.9250 Silver .2825 oz. ASW **Subject:** 80th Anniversary - Royal Air Force **Obverse:** Rank-Broadley portrait of Queen Elizabeth II **Reverse:** Three Spitfires and RAF Benevolent Fund Crest

Date	Mintage	F	VF	XF	Unc	BU
1998 Proof	Est. 30,000	Value: 45.00				

KM# 120 POUND **Weight:** 9.5000 g. **Composition:** 0.9250 Silver 0.2825 oz. ASW **Subject:** Queen Mother **Obverse:** Queen Elizabeth's head right. **Reverse:** Bust of Queen Mother 1/2 right. **Edge:** Reeded. **Size:** 22.4 mm.

Date		F	VF	XF	Unc	BU
1999 Proof	—	Value: 35.00				

KM# 109 POUND **Weight:** 9.5000 g. **Composition:** 0.9250 Silver .2825 oz. ASW **Subject:** Winston Churchill **Obverse:** Queen's portrait **Reverse:** Churchill's portrait **Edge:** Reeded **Size:** 22.5 mm.

Date		F	VF	XF	Unc	BU
1999 Proof	—	Value: 22.50				

KM# 95 POUND **Weight:** 9.5000 g. **Composition:** 0.9250 Silver .2825 oz. ASW **Subject:** Prince Edward's Wedding **Obverse:** Queen's portrait **Reverse:** Portraits of Edward and Sophie **Edge:** Reeded **Size:** 22.5 mm. **Note:** British Royal Mint.

Date	Mintage	F	VF	XF	Unc	BU
1999 Proof	50,000	Value: 30.00				

KM# 87 POUND **Weight:** 9.5000 g. **Composition:** 0.9250 Gold Plated Silver .2825 oz. ASW AGW **Subject:** Year 2000 **Obverse:** Queen's portrait **Reverse:** Handheld planet Earth **Note:** Millennium insert for 5 pounds, KM#86.

Date	F	VF	XF	Unc	BU
2000	—	—	—	—	—

KM# 99 POUND **Weight:** 9.5000 g. **Composition:** 0.9250 Silver .2825 oz. ASW **Subject:** Queen Mother's 100th Birthday **Obverse:** Queen's portrait **Reverse:** Queen Mother's portrait **Edge:** Reeded **Size:** 22.5 mm.

Date	Mintage	F	VF	XF	Unc	BU
2000 Proof	30,000	Value: 25.00				

KM# 110 POUND **Weight:** 9.5000 g. **Composition:** Copper-Nickel-Zinc **Subject:** Circulation Type **Obverse:** Queen's new portrait **Reverse:** Denomination **Edge:** Reeded **Size:** 22.5 mm.

Date	F	VF	XF	Unc	BU
2001	—	—	—	2.50	—

KM# 111 POUND **Weight:** 9.5000 g. **Composition:** 0.9250 Silver .2825 oz. ASW **Subject:** Queen's 75th Birthday **Obverse:** Queen's portrait **Reverse:** Queen's portrait in wreath **Edge:** Reeded **Size:** 22.5 mm.

Date		F	VF	XF	Unc	BU
2001 Proof	—	Value: 25.00				

KM# 47 2 POUNDS **Composition:** Copper-Nickel **Subject:** 40th Anniversary - Liberation from Germany

Date	Mintage	F	VF	XF	Unc	BU
ND(1985)	75,000	—	—	3.50	6.00	—
ND(1985) Proof	2,500	Value: 8.00				

KM# 47a 2 POUNDS **Weight:** 28.2800 g. **Composition:** 0.9250 Silver .8411 oz. ASW **Subject:** 40th Anniversary - Liberation from Germany

Date	Mintage	F	VF	XF	Unc	BU
ND (1985) Proof	2,500	Value: 30.00				

KM# 48 2 POUNDS **Composition:** Copper-Nickel **Subject:** Commonwealth Games

Date	Mintage	F	VF	XF	Unc	BU
1986		—	—	—	6.00	—
1986 In proof sets only	Est. 2,500	Value: 10.00				

KM# 48a 2 POUNDS **Weight:** 28.2800 g. **Composition:** 0.5000 Silver .4547 oz. ASW **Subject:** Commonwealth Games

Date	F	VF	XF	Unc	BU
1986	—	—	—	13.50	—

KM# 48b 2 POUNDS **Weight:** 28.2800 g. **Composition:** 0.9250 Silver .8411 oz. ASW **Subject:** Commonwealth Games

Date	Mintage	F	VF	XF	Unc	BU
1986 Proof	Est. 20,000	Value: 22.50				

KM# 49 2 POUNDS **Composition:** Copper-Nickel **Subject:** 900th Anniversary - Death of William the Conqueror

Date	Mintage	F	VF	XF	Unc	BU
ND(1987)		—	—	—	6.50	—
ND(1987) Proof	Est. 2,500	Value: 10.00				

KM# 49a 2 POUNDS **Weight:** 28.2800 g. **Composition:** 0.9250 Silver .8411 oz. ASW **Subject:** 900th Anniversary - Death of William the Conqueror

Date	Mintage	F	VF	XF	Unc	BU
ND(1987) Proof	2,500	Value: 30.00				

KM# 49b 2 POUNDS **Weight:** 47.5400 g. **Composition:** 0.9170 Gold 1.4012 oz. AGW **Subject:** 900th Anniversary - Death of William the Conqueror

Date	Mintage	F	VF	XF	Unc	BU
ND(1987) Proof	90	Value: 1,550				

KM# 50 2 POUNDS **Composition:** Copper-Nickel **Reverse:** William II

Date	Mintage	F	VF	XF	Unc	BU
1988	7,500	—	—	—	6.50	—
1988 Proof	2,500	Value: 10.00				

KM# 50a 2 POUNDS **Weight:** 28.2800 g. **Composition:** 0.9250 Silver .8411 oz. ASW **Reverse:** William II

Date	Mintage	F	VF	XF	Unc	BU
1988 Proof	2,500	Value: 28.00				

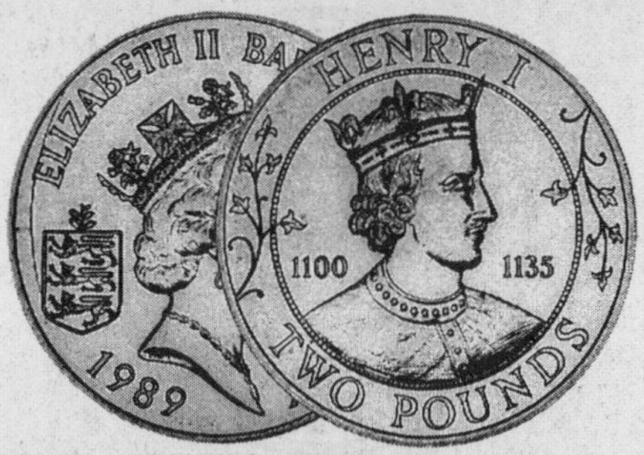

KM# 51 2 POUNDS Composition: Copper-Nickel **Reverse:** Henry I

Date	Mintage	F	VF	XF	Unc	BU
1989	—	—	—	—	7.00	—
1989 Proof	Est. 2,500	Value: 10.00				

KM# 51a 2 POUNDS Weight: 28.2800 g. **Composition:** 0.9250 Silver .8411 oz. ASW **Reverse:** Henry I

Date	Mintage	F	VF	XF	Unc	BU
1989 Proof	Est. 2,500	Value: 28.00				

KM# 52 2 POUNDS Composition: Copper-Nickel **Subject:** Royal Visit

Date	Mintage	F	VF	XF	Unc	BU
1989	5,000	—	—	—	8.00	—

KM# 52a 2 POUNDS Weight: 28.2800 g. **Composition:** 0.9250 Silver .8411 oz. ASW **Subject:** Royal Visit

Date	Mintage	F	VF	XF	Unc	BU
1989 Proof	5,000	Value: 35.00				

KM# 53 2 POUNDS Composition: Copper-Nickel **Subject:** 90th Birthday of Queen Mother

Date	Mintage	F	VF	XF	Unc	BU
ND(1990)	9,000	—	—	—	7.00	—

KM# 53a 2 POUNDS Weight: 28.2800 g. **Composition:** 0.9250 Silver .8411 oz. ASW **Subject:** 90th Birthday of Queen Mother

Date	Mintage	F	VF	XF	Unc	BU
ND(1990) Proof	1,302	Value: 50.00				

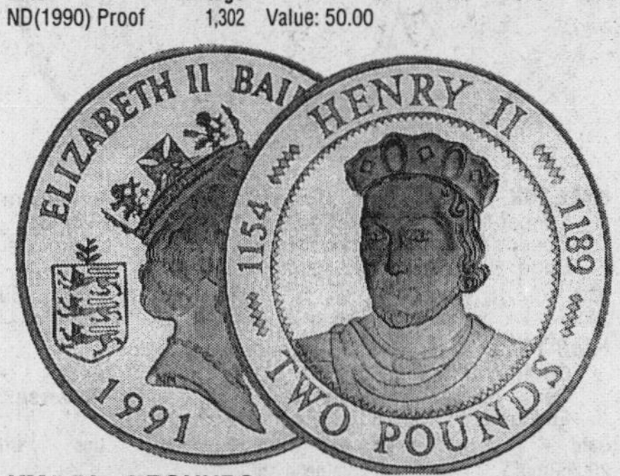

KM# 54 2 POUNDS Composition: Copper-Nickel **Reverse:** Henry II

Date	Mintage	F	VF	XF	Unc	BU
1991	1,200	—	—	—	7.00	—

KM# 54a 2 POUNDS Weight: 28.2800 g. **Composition:** 0.9250 Silver .8411 oz. ASW **Reverse:** Henry II

Date	Mintage	F	VF	XF	Unc	BU
1991 Proof	Est. 2,500	Value: 50.00				

KM# 55 2 POUNDS Composition: Copper-Nickel **Subject:** 40th Anniversary of Coronation

Date	Mintage	F	VF	XF	Unc	BU
ND(1993)	13,000	—	—	—	6.50	—

KM# 55a 2 POUNDS Weight: 28.2800 g. **Composition:** 0.9250 Silver .8411 oz. ASW **Subject:** 40th Anniversary of Coronation

Date	Mintage	F	VF	XF	Unc	BU
ND(1993) Proof	Est. 10,000	Value: 45.00				

KM# 56 2 POUNDS Composition: Copper-Nickel **Subject:** 50th Anniversary - Normandy Landing

Date	Mintage	F	VF	XF	Unc	BU
ND(1994)	49,000	—	—	—	7.50	—

KM# 56a 2 POUNDS Weight: 28.2800 g. **Composition:** 0.9250 Silver .8411 oz. ASW **Subject:** 50th Anniversary - Normandy Landing

Date	Mintage	F	VF	XF	Unc	BU
ND(1994) Proof	Est. 10,000	Value: 35.00				

KM# 61 2 POUNDS Composition: Copper-Nickel **Subject:** 50th Anniversary of Liberation

Date	Mintage	F	VF	XF	Unc	BU
ND(1995)	42,000	—	—	—	7.50	—

KM# 61a 2 POUNDS Weight: 28.2800 g. **Composition:** 0.9250 Silver .8411 oz. ASW **Subject:** 50th Anniversary of Liberation

Date	Mintage	F	VF	XF	Unc	BU
ND(1995) Proof	7,000	Value: 35.00				

KM# 61b 2 POUNDS Weight: 56.5600 g. **Composition:** 0.9250 Silver .16822 oz. ASW **Subject:** 50th Anniversary of Liberation

Date	Mintage	F	VF	XF	Unc	BU
ND(1995) Proof	800	Value: 60.00				

KM# 80 2 POUNDS Composition: Copper-Nickel **Subject:** WWF Conserving Nature **Obverse:** Queen's portrait **Reverse:** Emperor Moth

Date	F	VF	XF	Unc	BU
1997	—	—	—	8.50	—

KM# 80a 2 POUNDS Weight: 28.2800 g. **Composition:** 0.9250 Silver .841 oz. ASW **Subject:** WWF Conserving Nature **Obverse:** Queen's portrait **Reverse:** Emperor moth

Date	Mintage	F	VF	XF	Unc	BU
1997 Proof	Est. 15,000	Value: 50.00				

KM# 88 2 POUNDS Ring Composition: Nickel-Brass **Center Composition:** Copper Nickel **Obverse:** Queen's portrait by Maklouf **Reverse:** Arms on cross design

Date	F	VF	XF	Unc	BU
1997	—	—	—	8.50	—

Note: In mint sets only

Date	Mintage	F	VF	XF	Unc	BU
1997 Proof	—	Value: 12.00				

Note: In proof sets only

KM# 83 2 POUNDS Ring Composition: Nickel-Brass **Center Composition:** Copper Nickel **Obverse:** Rank-Broadley portrait of Queen Elizabeth II **Reverse:** Latent image arms on cross **Edge:** Bailiwick of Guernsey

Date	F	VF	XF	Unc	BU
1998	—	—	—	8.50	—
2002	—	—	—	8.50	—

KM# 81 2 POUNDS Composition: Copper-Nickel **Subject:** WWF Conserving Nature **Obverse:** Queen's portrait **Reverse:** Brimstone butterfly

Date	F	VF	XF	Unc	BU
1998	—	—	—	8.50	—

KM# 66 5 POUNDS Composition: Copper-Nickel **Reverse:** Queen Mother

Date	Mintage	F	VF	XF	Unc	BU
1995	56,000	—	—	—	15.00	—

KM# 66a 5 POUNDS Weight: 28.2800 g. **Composition:** 0.9250 Silver .8411 oz. ASW **Reverse:** Queen Mother

Date	Mintage	F	VF	XF	Unc	BU
1995 Proof	Est. 40,000	Value: 50.00				

KM# 67 5 POUNDS Weight: 7.8100 g. **Composition:** 0.9990 Gold .2508 oz. AGW **Reverse:** Queen Mother

Date	Mintage	F	VF	XF	Unc	BU
1995 Proof	Est. 2,500	Value: 210				

KM# 68 5 POUNDS Composition: Copper-Nickel **Subject:** European Football **Reverse:** Soccer ball and European map

Date	F	VF	XF	Unc	BU
1996	—	—	—	15.00	—

KM# 68a 5 POUNDS **Weight:** 28.2800 g. **Composition:** 0.9250 Silver .8411 oz. ASW **Subject:** European Football **Reverse:** Soccer ball and European map

Date	Mintage	F	VF	XF	Unc	BU
1996 Proof	Est. 20,000	Value: 65.00				

KM# 79 5 POUNDS **Composition:** Copper-Nickel **Subject:** 70th Birthday of Queen Elizabeth II

Date	F	VF	XF	Unc	BU
1996	—	—	—	15.00	—

KM# 79a 5 POUNDS **Weight:** 28.2800 g. **Composition:** 0.9250 Silver .8411 oz. ASW **Subject:** 70th Birthday of Queen Elizabeth II

Date	F	VF	XF	Unc	BU
1996 Proof	—	Value: 45.00			

KM# 71 5 POUNDS **Composition:** Copper-Nickel **Subject:** Queen Elizabeth II's Golden Wedding Anniversary **Note:** Similar to Pound, KM#70.

Date	Mintage	F	VF	XF	Unc	BU
1997	22,000	—	—	—	12.50	—

KM# 71a 5 POUNDS **Weight:** 28.2800 g. **Composition:** 0.9250 Silver .8411 oz. ASW **Subject:** Queen Elizabeth II's Golden Wedding Anniversary **Note:** Similar to Pound, KM#70.

Date	Mintage	F	VF	XF	Unc	BU
1997 Proof	Est. 20,000	Value: 65.00				

KM# 74 5 POUNDS **Composition:** Copper-Nickel **Subject:** Castle Cornet **Obverse:** Queen's portrait **Reverse:** Castle

Date	F	VF	XF	Unc	BU
1997	—	—	—	10.00	—

KM# 74a 5 POUNDS **Weight:** 28.2800 g. **Composition:** 0.9250 Silver .8411 oz. ASW **Subject:** Castle Cornet **Obverse:** Queen's portrait **Reverse:** Castle

Date	Mintage	F	VF	XF	Unc	BU
1997 Proof	Est. 10,000	Value: 60.00				

KM# 75 5 POUNDS **Weight:** 28.2800 g. **Composition:** 0.9250 Silver .8411 oz. ASW **Subject:** Castle Caernarfon **Obverse:** Queen's portrait **Reverse:** Caernarfon castle

Date	Mintage	F	VF	XF	Unc	BU
1997 Proof	Est. 10,000	Value: 60.00				

KM# 76 5 POUNDS **Weight:** 28.2800 g. **Composition:** 0.9250 Silver .8411 oz. ASW **Subject:** Castle Leeds **Obverse:** Queen's portrait **Reverse:** Leeds castle

Date	Mintage	F	VF	XF	Unc	BU
1997 Proof	Est. 10,000	Value: 60.00				

KM# 98 5 POUNDS **Weight:** 1.2000 g. **Composition:** 0.9167 Gold .0354 oz. AGW **Subject:** Queen's 50th Wedding Anniversary **Reverse:** Royal couple, shield and church **Edge:** Reeded **Size:** 9 mm. **Note:** Struck at the British Royal Mint.

Date	F	VF	XF	Unc	BU
1997 Proof	—	Value: 35.00			

KM# 82 5 POUNDS **Composition:** Copper-Nickel **Subject:** 80th Anniversary of the Royal Air Force **Obverse:** Rank-Broadley portrait of Queen Elizabeth II **Reverse:** Three Spitfires and an oval crest

Date	F	VF	XF	Unc	BU
1998	—	—	—	12.50	—

KM# 82a 5 POUNDS **Weight:** 28.2800 g. **Composition:** 0.9250 Silver .8410 oz. ASW **Subject:** 80th Anniversary of the Royal Air Force **Obverse:** Rank-Broadley portrait of Queen Elizabeth II **Reverse:** Three Spitfires and an oval crest

Date	Mintage	F	VF	XF	Unc	BU
1998 Proof	15,000	Value: 55.00				

KM# 86 5 POUNDS **Weight:** 28.2800 g. **Composition:** 0.9250 Silver .8410 oz. ASW **Subject:** Millennium 2000 **Obverse:** Queen's portrait and legend **Reverse:** Rising sun design, denomination, date

Date	Mintage	F	VF	XF	Unc	BU
1999 Proof	Est. 50,000	Value: 40.00				

KM# 91 5 POUNDS **Ring Composition:** Copper-Nickel **Center Composition:** Brass **Subject:** Millennium 2000 **Obverse:** Queen's portrait in center and below **Reverse:** Hands holding planet earth in center, rising sun design around

Date	Mintage	F	VF	XF	Unc	BU
1999	22,000	—	—	—	18.00	—

KM# 92 5 POUNDS **Weight:** 27.7100 g. **Composition:** Copper Nickel **Subject:** Prince Edward's Marriage **Obverse:** Queen's portrait **Reverse:** Portraits of Edward and Sophie **Edge:** Reeded **Size:** 38.6 mm.

Date	Mintage	F	VF	XF	Unc	BU
1999	19,000	—	—	—	15.00	—

KM# 92a 5 POUNDS **Weight:** 28.2800 g. **Composition:** 0.9250 Silver .8410 oz. ASW **Subject:** Prince Edward's Marriage **Obverse:** Queen's portrait **Reverse:** Portrait's of Edward and Sophie

Date	F	VF	XF	Unc	BU
1999 Proof	—	Value: 37.50			

KM# 93 5 POUNDS **Weight:** 27.7100 g. **Composition:** Copper-Nickel **Subject:** Queen Mother **Obverse:** Queen's portrait **Reverse:** Queen Mother's portrait

Date	Mintage	F	VF	XF	Unc	BU
1999	5,000	—	—	—	16.50	—

KM# 94 5 POUNDS **Weight:** 27.7100 g. **Composition:** Copper-Nickel **Subject:** Winston Churchill **Obverse:** Queen's portrait **Reverse:** Churchill's portrait **Edge:** Reeded.

Date	Mintage	F	VF	XF	Unc	BU
1999	5,000	—	—	—	16.50	—

KM# 94a 5 POUNDS **Weight:** 47.5400 g. **Composition:** 0.9166 Gold 1.4011 oz. AGW **Subject:** Winston Churchill **Obverse:** Queen's portrait **Reverse:** Churchill's portrait **Edge:** Reeded **Note:** British Royal Mint

Date	Mintage	F	VF	XF	Unc	BU
1999 Proof	125,000	Value: 865				

KM# 100 5 POUNDS **Weight:** 28.2800 g. **Composition:** Copper-Nickel **Obverse:** Queen's portrait **Reverse:** Queen Mother's portrait **Edge:** Reeded **Size:** 38.6 mm.

Date	F	VF	XF	Unc	BU
2000	—	—	—	7.50	—

KM# 100a 5 POUNDS **Weight:** 28.2800 g. **Composition:** 0.9250 Silver .8410 oz. ASW **Subject:** Queen Mother's 100th Birthday **Obverse:** Queen Mother's portrait with gold plated "100" **Edge:** Reeded **Size:** 38.6 mm.

Date	Mintage	F	VF	XF	Unc	BU
2000 Proof	20,000	Value: 47.50				

KM# 101 5 POUNDS **Weight:** 1.1300 g. **Composition:** 0.9170 Gold .0333 oz. AGW **Subject:** Queen Mother's 100th Birthday **Obverse:** Queen's portrait **Reverse:** Queen Mother's portrait **Edge:** Reeded **Size:** 13.9 mm.

Date	Mintage	F	VF	XF	Unc	BU
2000 Proof	20,000	Value: 57.50				

KM# 102 5 POUNDS **Weight:** 27.9500 g. **Composition:** Copper-Nickel **Subject:** Century of Monarchy **Obverse:** Queen's portrait **Reverse:** Portraits of past five sovereigns **Edge:** Reeded **Size:** 38.4 mm.

Date	F	VF	XF	Unc	BU
2000	—	—	—	11.00	—

KM# 102a 5 POUNDS **Weight:** 28.2800 g. **Composition:** 0.9250 Silver .8410 oz. ASW **Subject:** Century of Monarchy **Obverse:** Queen's portrait **Reverse:** Five royal portraits **Edge:** Reeded **Size:** 38.6 mm.

Date	Mintage	F	VF	XF	Unc	BU
2000 Proof	20,000	Value: 47.50				

KM# 113 5 POUNDS **Weight:** 1.1300 g. **Composition:** 0.9170 Gold .0333 oz. AGW **Subject:** 20th Century Monarchy **Obverse:** Queen's portrait **Reverse:** Five portraits **Edge:** Reeded **Size:** 13.9 mm.

Date	F	VF	XF	Unc	BU
2000 Proof	—	Value: 57.50			

KM# 106 5 POUNDS **Weight:** 28.2800 g. **Composition:** Copper-Nickel **Subject:** Queen Victoria Centennial **Obverse:** Queen Elizabeth's portrait **Reverse:** Queen Victoria's portrait **Edge:** Reeded **Size:** 38.6 mm.

Date	Mintage	F	VF	XF	Unc	BU
2001	—	—	—	—	7.50	—
2001 Proof	30,000	Value: 20.00				

KM# 106a 5 POUNDS **Weight:** 28.2800 g. **Composition:** 0.9250 Silver .8410 oz. ASW **Subject:** Queen Victoria 1837-1901 **Obverse:** Queen's portrait **Reverse:** Queen Victoria's portrait **Edge:** Reeded **Size:** 38.6 mm.

Date	Mintage	F	VF	XF	Unc	BU
2001 Proof	10,000	Value: 47.50				

KM# 108 5 POUNDS **Weight:** 28.0000 g. **Composition:** Copper-Nickel **Subject:** Queen Elizabeth's 75th Birthday **Obverse:** Queen Elizabeth's portrait **Reverse:** Queen's portrait in wreath **Edge:** Reeded **Size:** 38.6 mm.

Date	F	VF	XF	Unc	BU
2001	—	—	—	6.00	—

KM# 108a 5 POUNDS **Weight:** 28.2800 g. **Composition:** 0.9250 Silver .8410 oz. ASW **Subject:** Queen's 75th Birthday **Obverse:** Queen's portrait **Reverse:** Queen's portrait in wreath **Edge:** Reeded **Size:** 38.6 mm.

Date	F	VF	XF	Unc	BU
2001 Proof	—	Value: 55.00			

KM# 114 5 POUNDS **Weight:** 28.2800 g. **Composition:** Copper-Nickel **Subject:** 19th Century Monarchy **Obverse:** Queen's portrait **Reverse:** Four portraits **Edge:** Reeded **Size:** 38.6 mm.

Date	F	VF	XF	Unc	BU
2001	—	—	—	11.50	—

KM# 114a 5 POUNDS **Weight:** 28.2800 g. **Composition:** 0.9250 Silver .8410 oz. ASW **Edge:** Reeded **Size:** 38.6 mm.

Date	F	VF	XF	Unc	BU
2001 Proof	—	Value: 55.00			

KM# 115 5 POUNDS **Weight:** 1.1300 g. **Composition:** 0.9170 Gold .0333 oz. AGW **Subject:** 19th Century Monarchy **Obverse:** Queen's portrait **Reverse:** Four portraits **Edge:** Reeded **Size:** 13.9 mm.

Date	F	VF	XF	Unc	BU
2001 Proof	—	Value: 57.50			

KM# 117 5 POUNDS **Weight:** 1.1300 g. **Composition:** 0.9170 Gold .0333 oz. AGW **Subject:** Queen Victoria 1837-1901 **Obverse:** Queen's portrait **Reverse:** Queen Victoria's portrait **Edge:** Reeded **Size:** 13.9 mm.

Date	F	VF	XF	Unc	BU
2001 Proof	—	Value: 55.00			

KM# 118 5 POUNDS **Weight:** 1.1300 g. **Composition:** 0.9170 Gold .0333 oz. AGW **Subject:** Queen's 75th Birthday **Obverse:** Queen's portrait **Reverse:** Queen's portrait in wreath **Edge:** Reeded **Size:** 13.9 mm.

Date	F	VF	XF	Unc	BU
2001 Proof	—	Value: 57.50			

KM# 119 5 POUNDS **Weight:** 27.7100 g. **Composition:** Copper-Nickel 0.8018 oz. **Subject:** The Golden Jubilee **Obverse:** Bust of Queen Elizabeth II right. **Reverse:** The queen in her coach. **Edge:** Reeded. **Size:** 38.6 mm.

Date	F	VF	XF	Unc	BU
2002	—	—	—	17.50	—

KM# 119a 5 POUNDS **Weight:** 28.2800 g. **Composition:** 0.9250 Silver 0.841 oz. ASW **Subject:** Queen's Golden Jubilee **Obverse:** Bust of Queen Elizabeth II right. **Reverse:** Queen in her coach. **Edge:** Reeded. **Size:** 38.6 mm.

Date	Mintage	F	VF	XF	Unc	BU
2002 Proof	15,000	Value: 50.00				

KM# 121 5 POUNDS **Weight:** 27.7100 g. **Composition:** Copper Nickel **Subject:** Queen's Golden Jubilee **Obverse:** Bust of Queen Elizabeth II right. **Reverse:** Trooping the Colors scene. **Edge:** Reeded. **Size:** 38.6 mm.

Date	F	VF	XF	Unc	BU
2002	—	—	—	17.50	—

KM# 121a 5 POUNDS **Weight:** 28.2800 g. **Composition:** 0.9250 Silver 0.841 oz. ASW **Subject:** Queen's Golden Jubilee **Obverse:** Bust of Queen Elizabeth II right. **Reverse:** Trooping the Colors scene. **Edge:** Reeded. **Size:** 38.6 mm.

Date	Mintage	F	VF	XF	Unc	BU
2002 Proof	15,000	Value: 50.00				

KM# 122 5 POUNDS **Weight:** 28.2800 g. **Composition:** Copper Nickel **Subject:** Princess Diana **Obverse:** Queen's portrait **Reverse:** World and children behind cameo portrait of Diana **Edge:** Reeded **Size:** 38.6 mm.

Date	F	VF	XF	Unc	BU
2002	—	—	—	13.50	—

KM# 122a 5 POUNDS **Subject:** Princess Diana **Obverse:** Queen's portrait **Reverse:** world and children behind diana's cameo portrait **Edge:** Reeded

Date	Mintage	F	VF	XF	Unc	BU
2002 Proof	20,000	Value: 45.00				

KM# 122b 5 POUNDS **Weight:** 39.9400 g. **Composition:** 0.9167 Gold 1.1771 oz. AGW **Subject:** Princess Diana **Obverse:** Queen's portrait **Reverse:** World and children behind Diana's cameo portrait **Edge:** Reeded **Size:** 1.1771 mm.

Date	Mintage	F	VF	XF	Unc	BU
2002 Proof	100	Value: 800				

KM# 124 5 POUNDS **Weight:** 28.2800 g. **Composition:** Copper Nickel **Subject:** British Monarchy 18th Century **Obverse:** Queen's portrait **Reverse:** Five royal portraits **Edge:** Reeded **Size:** 38.6 mm.

Date	F	VF	XF	Unc	BU
2002	—	—	—	15.00	—

KM# 124a 5 POUNDS **Weight:** 28.2800 g. **Composition:** 0.9250 Silver 0.841 oz. ASW **Subject:** British Monarchy 18th Century **Obverse:** Queen's portrait **Reverse:** Five royal portraits **Edge:** Reeded **Size:** 38.6 mm.

Date	F	VF	XF	Unc	BU
2002 Proof	—	Value: 50.00			

KM# 125 (KM124b) 5 POUNDS **Weight:** 1.1300 g. **Composition:** 0.9166 Gold 0.0333 oz. AGW **Subject:** British Monarchy 18th Century **Obverse:** Queen's portrait **Reverse:** Five royal portraits **Edge:** Reeded **Size:** 13.9 mm.

Date	Mintage	F	VF	XF	Unc	BU
2002 Proof	55	Value: 55.00				

KM# 127 5 POUNDS **Weight:** 28.2800 g. **Composition:** Copper-Nickel **Subject:** Queen Mother **Obverse:** Queen's portrait **Reverse:** The late Queen Mother's portrait **Edge:** Reeded **Size:** 38.6 mm.

Date	F	VF	XF	Unc	BU
2002	—	—	—	15.00	—
2002 Proof	—	Value: 20.00			

KM# 127a 5 POUNDS **Weight:** 28.2800 g. **Composition:** 0.9250 Silver 0.841 oz. ASW **Subject:** Queen Mother **Obverse:** Queen's portrait **Reverse:** The late Queen Mother's portrait **Edge:** Reeded **Size:** 38.6 mm.

Date	F	VF	XF	Unc	BU
2002 Proof	—	Value: 50.00			

KM# 128 5 POUNDS **Weight:** 1.1300 g. **Composition:** 0.9166 Gold 0.0333 oz. AGW **Subject:** Queen Mother **Obverse:** Queen's portrait **Reverse:** The late Queen Mother's portrait **Edge:** Reeded **Size:** 13.9 mm.

Date	F	VF	XF	Unc	BU
2002 Proof	—	Value: 55.00			

KM# 129 5 POUNDS **Weight:** 28.2800 g. **Composition:** Copper-Nickel **Subject:** The Duke of Wellington **Obverse:** Queen's portrait **Reverse:** Portrait with mounted dragoons in background **Edge:** Reeded **Size:** 38.6 mm.

Date	F	VF	XF	Unc	BU
2002	—	—	—	17.50	—

KM# 129a 5 POUNDS **Weight:** 28.2800 g. **Composition:** 0.9250 Silver 0.841 oz. ASW **Subject:** The Duke of Wellington **Obverse:** Queen's portrait **Reverse:** Portrait with multicolor mounted dragoons in background **Edge:** Reeded **Size:** 38.6 mm.

Date	F	VF	XF	Unc	BU
2002 Proof	—	Value: 50.00			

KM# 57 10 POUNDS **Weight:** 3.1300 g. **Composition:** 0.9990 Gold .1005 oz. AGW **Subject:** 50th Anniversary - Normandy Invasion

Date	Mintage	F	VF	XF	Unc	BU
ND(1994)	Est. 500	Value: 75.00				

Note: Sold only in sets

KM# 62 10 POUNDS **Weight:** 3.1300 g. **Composition:** 0.9990 Gold .1005 oz. AGW **Subject:** 50th Anniversary of Liberation

Date	Mintage	F	VF	XF	Unc	BU
ND(1995) Proof	Est. 500	Value: 75.00				

Note: Sold only in sets

KM# 104 10 POUNDS **Weight:** 141.7500 g. **Composition:** 0.9990 Silver 4.5528 oz. ASW **Subject:** Century of Monarchy **Obverse:** Queen's portrait **Reverse:** Five royal portraits **Edge:** Reeded **Size:** 65 mm.

Date	Mintage	F	VF	XF	Unc	BU
2000 Proof	950	Value: 200				

KM# 116 10 POUNDS **Weight:** 141.7500 g. **Composition:** 0.9990 Silver 4.5528 oz. ASW **Subject:** 19th Century Monarchy **Obverse:** Queen's portrait **Reverse:** Four portraits **Edge:** Reeded **Size:** 65 mm.

Date	F	VF	XF	Unc	BU
2001 Proof	—	Value: 200			

KM# 126 10 POUNDS **Weight:** 155.5175 g. **Composition:** 0.9990 Silver 4.995 oz. ASW **Subject:** British

Monarchy 18th Century **Obverse:** Queen's portrait **Reverse:** Five royal portraits **Edge:** Reeded **Size:** 65 mm.

Date		F	VF	XF	Unc	BU
2002 Proof	—	Value: 200				

KM# 58 25 POUNDS **Weight:** 7.8100 g. **Composition:** 0.9990 Gold .2509 oz. AGW **Subject:** 50th Anniversary - Normandy Invasion

Date	Mintage	F	VF	XF	Unc	BU
ND(1994)	—	—	—	—	200	—
ND(1994) Proof	Est. 500	Value: 185				

Note: Sold only in sets

KM# 63 25 POUNDS **Weight:** 7.8100 g. **Composition:** 0.9990 Gold .2509 oz. AGW **Subject:** 50th Anniversary of Liberation

Date	Mintage	F	VF	XF	Unc	BU
ND(1995) In proof sets only	Est. 500	Value: 185				

KM# 69 25 POUNDS **Weight:** 7.8100 g. **Composition:** 0.9990 Gold .2509 oz. AGW **Subject:** European Football **Reverse:** Soccer ball and European map **Note:** Similar to 5 Pounds, KM#68.

Date	Mintage	F	VF	XF	Unc	BU
1996 Proof	1,500	Value: 175				

KM# 72 25 POUNDS **Weight:** 7.8100 g. **Composition:** 0.9990 Gold .2509 oz. AGW **Subject:** Queen Elizabeth II's Golden Wedding Anniversary **Note:** Similar to Pound, KM#70.

Date	Mintage	F	VF	XF	Unc	BU
1997 Proof	Est. 5,000	Value: 275				

KM# 85 25 POUNDS **Weight:** 7.8100 g. **Composition:** 0.9990 Gold .2509 oz. AGW **Subject:** 80th Anniversary - Royal Air Force **Obverse:** Rank-Broadley portrait of Queen Elizabeth II **Reverse:** Three Spitfires and RAF Benevolent Fund Crest

Date	Mintage	F	VF	XF	Unc	BU
1998 Proof	Est. 2,500	Value: 175				

KM# 103 25 POUNDS **Weight:** 7.8100 g. **Composition:** 0.9170 Gold .2303 oz. AGW **Subject:** Queen Mother's 100th Birthday **Obverse:** Queen's portrait **Reverse:** Queen Mother's portrait **Edge:** Reeded **Size:** 22 mm.

Date	Mintage	F	VF	XF	Unc	BU
2000 Proof	5,000	Value: 230				

KM# 107 25 POUNDS **Weight:** 7.8100 g. **Composition:** 0.9170 Gold .2303 oz. AGW **Subject:** Queen Victoria Centennial **Obverse:** Queen Elizabeth's portrait **Reverse:** Queen Victoria's portrait **Edge:** Reeded **Size:** 22 mm.

Date	Mintage	F	VF	XF	Unc	BU
2001 Proof	2,500	Value: 267				

KM# 112 25 POUNDS **Weight:** 7.8100 g. **Composition:** 0.9170 Gold .2303 oz. AGW **Subject:** Queen's 75th Birthday **Obverse:** Queen's portrait **Reverse:** Queen's portrait in wreath **Edge:** Reeded **Size:** 22 mm.

Date		F	VF	XF	Unc	BU
2001 Proof	—	Value: 230				

KM# 123 25 POUNDS **Weight:** 7.9800 g. **Composition:** 0.9167 Gold 0.2352 oz. AGW **Subject:** Princess Diana **Obverse:** Queen's portrait **Reverse:** Diana's cameo portrait in wreath **Edge:** Reeded **Size:** 22.05 mm.

Date	Mintage	F	VF	XF	Unc	BU
2002	2,500	Value: 290				

Note: Proof

KM# 131 25 POUNDS **Weight:** 7.8100 g. **Composition:** 0.9166 Gold 0.2302 oz. AGW **Subject:** The Duke of Wellington **Obverse:** Queen's portrait **Reverse:** Portrait with mounted dragoons in the background **Edge:** Reeded **Size:** 22 mm.

Date		F	VF	XF	Unc	BU
2002 Proof	—	Value: 230				

KM# 59 50 POUNDS **Weight:** 15.6100 g. **Composition:** 0.9990 Gold .5014 oz. AGW **Subject:** 50th Anniversary - Normandy Invasion

Date	Mintage	F	VF	XF	Unc	BU
ND(1994) In proof sets only	Est. 500	Value: 365				

KM# 64 50 POUNDS **Weight:** 15.6100 g. **Composition:** 0.9990 Gold .5014 oz. AGW **Subject:** 50th Anniversary of Liberation

Date	Mintage	F	VF	XF	Unc	BU
ND(1995) In proof sets only	Est. 500	Value: 365				

KM# 60 100 POUNDS **Weight:** 31.2100 g. **Composition:** 0.9990 Gold 1.0025 oz. AGW **Subject:** 50th Anniversary - Normandy Invasion

Date	Mintage	F	VF	XF	Unc	BU
ND(1994) In proof sets only	Est. 500	Value: 725				

KM# 65 100 POUNDS **Weight:** 31.2100 g. **Composition:** 0.9990 Gold 1.0025 oz. AGW **Subject:** 50th Anniversary of Liberation

Date	Mintage	F	VF	XF	Unc	BU
ND(1995) In proof sets only	Est. 500	Value: 725				

PIEFORTS

KM#	Date	Mintage	Identification	Mkt Val
P1	1981	500	Pound. 16.0000 g. KM#37a.	265
P2	2000	10,000	50 Pence. 0.9250 Silver. 16.2000 g. KM#105a.	55.00

MINT SETS

KM#	Date	Mintage	Identification	Issue Price	Mkt Val
MS1	1985 (8)	10,000	KM40-41, 42.1, 43-47	8.75	12.50
MS2	1985 (7)	—	KM40-41, 42.1, 43-46	—	—
MS3	1986 (7)	5,000	KM40-46	8.75	6.50
MS4	1987 (7)	7,500	KM40-46	11.00	6.50
MS5	1988 (7)	5,000	KM40-46	13.00	15.00
MS6	1989 (7)	5,000	KM40-46	17.00	16.50
MS7	1990 (8)	2,520	KM40-41, 42.1-42.2, 43-46	16.00	20.00
MS8	1992 (7)	1,500	KM40-41, 42.2, 43-46	22.50	25.00
MS9	1997 (8)	—	KM40a, 41a, 42.2, 43.2, 44, 45.2, 46, 88	—	25.00

PROOF SETS

KM#	Date	Mintage	Identification	Issue Price	Mkt Val
PS3	1902H (4)	—	KM5, 7-8, 10	—	1,000
PS4	1910H (2)	—	KM5, 7	—	500
PS5	1956 (6)	1,050	KM15-17 double set	—	22.50
PS6	1966 (4)	10,000	KM15-16, 18, 19	—	8.50
PS7	1971 (6)	10,000	KM20-25	16.00	9.50
PS8	1979 (6)	4,963	KM27-30, 33-34	25.00	11.50
PS9	1981 (6)	10,000	KM27-30, 34, 37	29.00	20.00
PS10	1985 (8)	2,500	KM40-47	29.75	30.00
PS11	1986 (8)	2,500	KM40-46, 48	35.00	32.00
PS12	1987 (8)	2,500	KM40-46, 49	33.00	32.00
PS13	1988 (8)	2,500	KM40-46, 50	45.00	32.00
PS14	1989 (8)	2,500	KM40-46, 51	45.00	32.00
PS15	1990 (9)	700	KM40-41, 42.1-42.2, 43-46	46.00	46.00
PS16	1992 (7)	500	KM40-41, 42.2, 43.2, 44-46	52.50	55.00
PS17	1994 (4)	500	KM57-60	1,595	1,350
PS18	ND (1995) (4)	500	KM62-65	1,600	1,350
PS19	1996 (2)	1,500	KM68a, 69	—	275
PS20	1997 (3)	—	KM70, 71a, 72	—	420
PS21	1997 (4)	—	KM73, 74a, 75-76	181	215

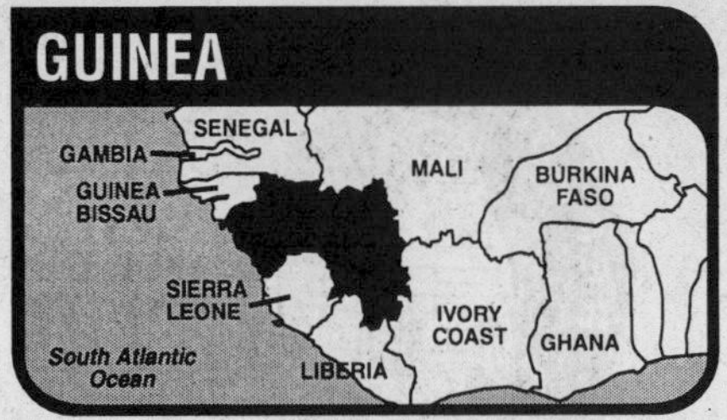

The Republic of Guinea, situated on the Atlantic Coast of Africa between Sierra Leone and Guinea-Bissau, has an area of 94,964 sq. mi. (245,860 sq. km.) and a population of 6.4 million. Capital: Conakry. Although Guinea contains one-third of the world's reserves of bauxite and significant deposits of iron ore, gold and diamonds, the economy is still dependent on agriculture, aluminum, bananas, copra and coffee are exported.

The coast of Guinea was known to Portuguese navigators of the 15th century but was seldom visited by European traders of the 16th-18th centuries because of its dangerous coastal waters. French penetration of the area began in the mid-19th century with the entering into of protectorate treaties with several of the coastal chiefs. After a long struggle with Guinea's native leader Samory Toure, France secured the area and until 1890 administered it as a part of Senegal. In 1895 the colony (Guinee Francais) became an autonomous part of the federation of French West Africa. The inhabitants were extended French citizenship in 1946 when the colony became an overseas territory of the French Union. Guinea became an independent republic on Oct. 2, 1958, when it declined to enter the new French Community.

MONETARY SYSTEM
100 Centimes = 1 Franc

REPUBLIC

DECIMAL COINAGE

KM# 4 FRANC Composition: Copper-Nickel **Obverse:** Ahmed Sekou Toure

Date	F	VF	XF	Unc	BU
1962	1.25	2.00	3.50	7.00	—
1962 Proof	—	Value: 50.00			

KM# 1 5 FRANCS Composition: Aluminum-Bronze **Obverse:** Ahmed Sekou Toure

Date	F	VF	XF	Unc	BU
1959	2.75	4.75	9.00	22.50	—

KM# 5 5 FRANCS Composition: Copper-Nickel **Note:** Mule with two obverses exists.

Date	F	VF	XF	Unc	BU
1962	1.25	2.00	3.00	6.50	—
1962 Proof	—	Value: 70.00			

KM# 2 10 FRANCS Composition: Aluminum-Bronze **Obverse:** Ahmed Sekou Toure

Date	F	VF	XF	Unc	BU
1959	5.00	10.00	20.00	45.00	—

KM# 6 10 FRANCS Composition: Copper-Nickel **Obverse:** Ahmed Sekou Toure

Date	F	VF	XF	Unc	BU
1962	1.75	2.75	6.00	12.00	—
1962 Proof	—	Value: 85.00			

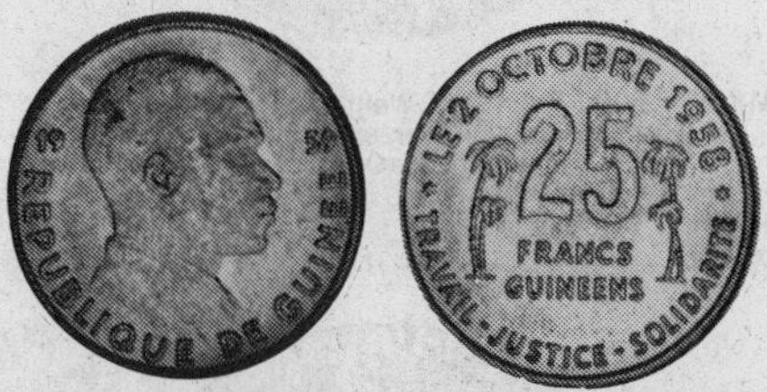

KM# 3 25 FRANCS Composition: Aluminum-Bronze **Obverse:** Ahmed Sekou Toure

Date	F	VF	XF	Unc	BU
1959	9.00	16.00	30.00	90.00	—

KM# 7 25 FRANCS Composition: Copper-Nickel **Obverse:** Ahmed Sekou Toure

Date	F	VF	XF	Unc	BU
1962	2.50	4.00	7.50	15.00	—
1962 Proof	—	Value: 120			

KM# 8 50 FRANCS Composition: Copper-Nickel **Obverse:** Ahmed Sekou Toure **Note:** Not released into circulation.

Date	Mintage	F	VF	XF	Unc	BU
1969	4,000,000	—	—	35.00	55.00	—

KM# 9 100 FRANCS Weight: 5.6500 g. **Composition:** 0.9990 Silver .1816 oz. ASW **Subject:** 10th Anniversary of Independence **Obverse:** Dr. Martin Luther King

Date	Mintage	F	VF	XF	Unc	BU
1969 Proof	9,700	Value: 7.00				
1970 Proof	Inc. above	Value: 7.00				

KM# 41 100 FRANCS Composition: Copper-Nickel **Obverse:** Ahmed Sekou Toure **Note:** Not released into circulation.

Date	Mintage	F	VF	XF	Unc	BU
1971	2,585,000	—	—	22.50	45.00	—

KM# 10 200 FRANCS Weight: 11.7000 g. **Composition:** 0.9990 Silver .3761 oz. ASW **Subject:** 10th Anniversary of Independence **Obverse:** John and Robert Kennedy

Date	Mintage	F	VF	XF	Unc	BU
1969 Proof	10,000	Value: 10.00				
1970 Proof	Inc. above	Value: 10.00				

KM# 11 200 FRANCS Weight: 11.7000 g. **Composition:** 0.9990 Silver .3761 oz. ASW **Subject:** 10th Anniversary of Independence **Obverse:** Almamy Toure

Date	Mintage	F	VF	XF	Unc	BU
1969 Proof	6,100	Value: 10.00				
1970 Proof	Inc. above	Value: 10.00				

KM# 12 250 FRANCS Weight: 14.5300 g. **Composition:** 0.9990 Silver .4671 oz. ASW **Subject:** 10th Anniversary of Independence **Obverse:** Lunar landing

Date	Mintage	F	VF	XF	Unc	BU
1969 Proof	26,000	Value: 12.50				
1970 Proof	Inc. above	Value: 12.50				

KM# 13 250 FRANCS Weight: 14.5300 g. **Composition:** 0.9990 Silver .4671 oz. ASW **Subject:** 10th Anniversary of Independence **Obverse:** Alpha Yaya Diallo

Date	Mintage	F	VF	XF	Unc	BU
1969 Proof	6,100	Value: 12.50				
1970 Proof	Inc. above	Value: 12.50				

KM# 14 250 FRANCS Weight: 14.5300 g. **Composition:** 0.9990 Silver .4671 oz. ASW **Subject:** 10th Anniversary of Independence **Obverse:** Apollo XIII

Date	Mintage	F	VF	XF	Unc	BU
1969 Proof	4,450	Value: 20.00				
1970 Proof	Inc. above	Value: 20.00				

KM# 21 250 FRANCS **Weight:** 14.5300 g. **Composition:** 0.9990 Silver .4671 oz. ASW **Subject:** 10th Anniversary of Independence **Obverse:** Spacecraft Soyuz

Date	Mintage	F	VF	XF	Unc	BU
1970 Proof	3,500	Value: 20.00				

KM# 15 500 FRANCS **Weight:** 29.0800 g. **Composition:** 0.9990 Silver .9349 oz. ASW **Subject:** 10th Anniversary of Independence **Obverse:** Munich Olympics

Date	Mintage	F	VF	XF	Unc	BU
1969 Proof	7,200	Value: 32.50				
1970 Proof	1,900	Value: 42.50				

KM# 16 500 FRANCS **Weight:** 29.0800 g. **Composition:** 0.9990 Silver .9349 oz. ASW **Subject:** 10th Anniversary of Independence **Obverse:** Oiseaux Dancers **Reverse:** Similar to KM#15

Date	Mintage	F	VF	XF	Unc	BU
1969 Proof	7,150	Value: 35.00				
1970 Proof	—	Value: 45.00				

KM# 22 500 FRANCS **Weight:** 29.0800 g. **Composition:** 0.9990 Silver .9349 oz. ASW **Subject:** 10th Anniversary of Independence **Obverse:** Ikhnaton **Reverse:** Similar to KM#15

Date	Mintage	F	VF	XF	Unc	BU
1970 Proof	4,180	Value: 28.00				

KM# 23 500 FRANCS **Weight:** 29.0800 g. **Composition:** 0.9990 Silver .9349 oz. ASW **Subject:** 10th Anniversary of Independence **Obverse:** Chephren **Reverse:** Similar to KM#15

Date	Mintage	F	VF	XF	Unc	BU
1970 Proof	4,150	Value: 31.50				

KM# 24 500 FRANCS **Weight:** 29.0800 g. **Composition:** 0.9990 Silver .9349 oz. ASW **Subject:** 10th Anniversary of Independence **Obverse:** Cleopatra **Reverse:** Similar to KM#15

Date	Mintage	F	VF	XF	Unc	BU
1970 Proof	5,250	Value: 32.50				

KM# 25 500 FRANCS **Weight:** 29.0800 g. **Composition:** 0.9990 Silver .9349 oz. ASW **Subject:** 10th Anniversary of Independence **Obverse:** Queen Nefertiti **Reverse:** Similar to KM#15

Date	Mintage	F	VF	XF	Unc	BU
1970 Proof	4,610	Value: 35.00				

KM# 26 500 FRANCS **Weight:** 29.0800 g. **Composition:** 0.9990 Silver .9349 oz. ASW **Subject:** 10th Anniversary of Independence **Obverse:** Ramses III **Reverse:** Similar to KM#15

Date	Mintage	F	VF	XF	Unc	BU
1970 Proof	4,330	Value: 30.00				

KM# 27 500 FRANCS **Weight:** 29.0800 g. **Composition:** 0.9990 Silver .9349 oz. ASW **Subject:** 10th Anniversary of Independence **Obverse:** Tutankhamen **Reverse:** Similar to KM#15

Date	Mintage	F	VF	XF	Unc	BU
1970 Proof	4,280	Value: 40.00				

KM# 28 500 FRANCS **Weight:** 29.0800 g. **Composition:** 0.9990 Silver .9349 oz. ASW **Subject:** 10th Anniversary of Independence **Obverse:** Queen Teyi **Reverse:** Similar to KM#15

Date	Mintage	F	VF	XF	Unc	BU
1970 Proof	4,120	Value: 28.00				

KM# 29 500 FRANCS **Weight:** 29.0800 g. **Composition:** 0.9990 Silver .9349 oz. ASW **Subject:** 10th Anniversary of Independence **Obverse:** Gamal Abdel Nasser **Reverse:** Similar to KM#15

Date	Mintage	F	VF	XF	Unc	BU
1970 Proof	950	Value: 55.00				

KM# 17 1000 FRANCS **Weight:** 4.0000 g. **Composition:** 0.9000 Gold .1157 oz. AGW **Subject:** 10th Anniversary of Independence **Obverse:** John and Robert Kennedy

Date	Mintage	F	VF	XF	Unc	BU
1969 Proof	6,600	Value: 75.00				
1970 Proof	Inc. above	Value: 75.00				

KM# 18 2000 FRANCS **Weight:** 8.0000 g. **Composition:** 0.9000 Gold .2315 oz. AGW **Subject:** 10th Anniversary of Independence **Obverse:** Lunar landing

Date	Mintage	F	VF	XF	Unc	BU
1969 Proof	15,000	Value: 125				

KM# 30 2000 FRANCS **Weight:** 8.0000 g. **Composition:** 0.9000 Gold .2315 oz. AGW **Subject:** 10th Anniversary of Independence **Obverse:** Apollo XIII

Date	Mintage	F	VF	XF	Unc	BU
1970 Proof	1,775	Value: 165				

KM# 31 2000 FRANCS **Weight:** 8.0000 g. **Composition:** 0.9000 Gold .2315 oz. AGW **Subject:** 10th Anniversary of Independence **Obverse:** Spacecraft Soyuz, similar to 250 Francs, KM#21

Date	Mintage	F	VF	XF	Unc	BU
1970 Proof	2,840	Value: 150				

KM# 32 5000 FRANCS **Weight:** 20.0000 g. **Composition:** 0.9000 Gold .5787 oz. AGW **Subject:** 10th Anniversary of Independence **Obverse:** Munich Olympics

Date	Mintage	F	VF	XF	Unc	BU
1969 Proof	2,740	Value: 250				
1970 Proof	500	Value: 350				

KM# 19 5000 FRANCS **Weight:** 20.0000 g. **Composition:** 0.9000 Gold .5787 oz. AGW **Subject:** 10th Anniversary of Independence **Obverse:** Gamal Abedel Nasser

Date	Mintage	F	VF	XF	Unc	BU
1970 Proof	4,000	Value: 325				

KM# 33 5000 FRANCS **Weight:** 20.0000 g. **Composition:** 0.9000 Gold .5787 oz. AGW **Subject:** 10th Anniversary of Independence **Obverse:** Ikhnaton, similar to 500 Francs, KM#22

Date	Mintage	F	VF	XF	Unc	BU
1970 Proof	685	Value: 475				

KM# 34 5000 FRANCS **Weight:** 20.0000 g. **Composition:** 0.9000 Gold .5787 oz. AGW **Subject:** 10th Anniversary of Independence **Obverse:** Chephren, similar to 500 Francs, KM#23

Date	Mintage	F	VF	XF	Unc	BU
1970 Proof	675	Value: 475				

KM# 35 5000 FRANCS **Weight:** 20.0000 g. **Composition:** 0.9000 Gold .5787 oz. AGW **Subject:** 10th Anniversary of Independence **Obverse:** Cleopatra, similar to 500 Francs, KM#24

Date	Mintage	F	VF	XF	Unc	BU
1970 Proof	789	Value: 475				

KM# 36 5000 FRANCS **Weight:** 20.0000 g. **Composition:** 0.9000 Gold .5787 oz. AGW **Subject:** 10th Anniversary of Independence **Obverse:** Queen Nefertiti, similar to 500 Francs, KM#25

Date	Mintage	F	VF	XF	Unc	BU
1970 Proof	774	Value: 475				

KM# 37 5000 FRANCS **Weight:** 20.0000 g. **Composition:** 0.9000 Gold .5787 oz. AGW **Subject:** 10th Anniversary of Independence **Obverse:** Ramses III, similar to 500 Francs, KM#26

Date	Mintage	F	VF	XF	Unc	BU
1970 Proof	695	Value: 475				

KM# 39 5000 FRANCS **Weight:** 20.0000 g. **Composition:** 0.9000 Gold .5787 oz. AGW **Subject:** 10th Anniversary of Independence **Obverse:** Queen Teyi, similar to 500 Francs, KM#28

Date	Mintage	F	VF	XF	Unc	BU
1970 Proof	685	Value: 475				

KM# 40 5000 FRANCS **Weight:** 20.0000 g. **Composition:** 0.9000 Gold .5787 oz. AGW **Subject:** 10th Anniversary of Independence **Obverse:** Gamal Abdel Nasser, similar to 500 Francs, KM#29

Date	Mintage	F	VF	XF	Unc	BU
1970 Proof	185	Value: 600				

KM# 20 10000 FRANCS **Weight:** 40.0000 g. **Composition:** 0.9000 Gold 1.1575 oz. AGW **Subject:** 10th Anniversary of Independence **Obverse:** Ahmed Sekou Toure **Reverse:** Similar to 5000 Francs, KM#19

Date	Mintage	F	VF	XF	Unc	BU
1969 Proof	2,300	Value: 750				
1970 Proof	—	Value: 950				

KM# 64 20000 FRANCS **Weight:** 31.4700 g. **Composition:** 0.9250 Silver .9359 oz. ASW **Subject:** 35th Anniversary of Guinea Franc **Reverse:** Woman planting palm tree

Date	F	VF	XF	Unc	BU
ND(1995)	—	—	—	40.00	—

DECIMAL COINAGE

100 Cauris = 1 Syli

KM# 42 50 CAURIS **Composition:** Aluminum **Note:** Nkrumah

Date	F	VF	XF	Unc	BU
1971	1.00	2.00	3.50	6.00	—

KM# 43 SYLI **Composition:** Aluminum

Date	F	VF	XF	Unc	BU
1971	2.00	3.00	5.50	12.50	—

KM# 44 2 SYLIS **Composition:** Aluminum

Date	F	VF	XF	Unc	BU
1971	1.00	2.00	4.00	8.00	—

KM# 45 5 SYLIS **Composition:** Aluminum

Date	F	VF	XF	Unc	BU
1971	1.25	2.25	4.50	9.00	—

KM# 46 500 SYLI **Weight:** 40.0000 g. **Composition:** 0.9250 Silver 1.1897 oz. ASW **Obverse:** Miriam Makeba

Date	Mintage	F	VF	XF	Unc	BU
1977	500	—	—	—	100	—
1977 Proof	500	Value: 125				

KM# 47 500 SYLI **Weight:** 40.0000 g. **Composition:** 0.9250 Silver 1.1897 oz. ASW **Obverse:** Patrice Lumumba **Reverse:** Similar to KM#46

Date	Mintage	F	VF	XF	Unc	BU
1977	250	—	—	—	150	—
1977 Proof	150	Value: 200				

KM# 48 1000 SYLI **Weight:** 2.9300 g. **Composition:** 0.9000 Gold .0847 oz. AGW **Obverse:** Miriam Makeba **Reverse:** Similar to 2000 Sylis, KM#50

Date	Mintage	F	VF	XF	Unc	BU
1977	300	—	—	—	80.00	—
1977 Proof	250	Value: 90.00				

KM# 49 1000 SYLI **Weight:** 2.9300 g. **Composition:** 0.9000 Gold .0847 oz. AGW **Obverse:** Nkrumah **Reverse:** Similar to 2000 Sylis, KM#50

Date	Mintage	F	VF	XF	Unc	BU
1977	150	—	—	—	100	—
1977 Proof	150	Value: 115				

KM# 50 2000 SYLI **Weight:** 5.8700 g. **Composition:** 0.9000 Gold .1698 oz. AGW **Obverse:** Mao Tse Tung

Date	Mintage	F	VF	XF	Unc	BU
1977	200	—	—	—	200	—
1977 Proof	200	Value: 250				

KM# 51 2000 SYLI **Weight:** 5.8700 g. **Composition:** 0.9000 Gold .1698 oz. AGW **Obverse:** Sekou Toure

Date	Mintage	F	VF	XF	Unc	BU
1977	100	—	—	—	200	—
1977 Proof	50	Value: 275				

REFORM COINAGE

KM# 56 FRANC **Composition:** Brass Clad Steel

Date	F	VF	XF	Unc	BU
1985	0.10	0.20	0.40	1.00	—

KM# 53 5 FRANCS **Composition:** Brass Clad Steel

Date	F	VF	XF	Unc	BU
1985	0.10	0.20	0.40	1.00	—

KM# 52 10 FRANCS **Composition:** Brass Clad Steel

Date	F	VF	XF	Unc	BU
1985	0.20	0.40	0.80	1.25	—

KM# 60 25 FRANCS **Composition:** Brass

Date	F	VF	XF	Unc	BU
1987	0.20	0.40	0.85	1.75	—

KM# 63 50 FRANCS **Composition:** Copper-Nickel

Date	F	VF	XF	Unc	BU
1994	0.30	0.60	1.25	2.75	—

KM# 57 100 FRANCS **Weight:** 16.0000 g. **Composition:** 0.9990 Silver .5144 oz. ASW **Subject:** 1992 Olympics **Reverse:** Discus thrower

Date	F	VF	XF	Unc	BU
1988 Matte	—	—	—	45.00	—

KM# 58 200 FRANCS **Weight:** 16.0000 g. **Composition:** 0.9990 Silver .5144 oz. ASW **Subject:** 1992 Olympics **Reverse:** Basketball players

Date	F	VF	XF	Unc	BU
1988 Matte	—	—	—	45.00	—

KM# 59 300 FRANCS **Weight:** 16.0000 g. **Composition:** 0.9990 Silver .5144 oz. ASW **Subject:** 1992 Olympics **Reverse:** Stadium

Date	F	VF	XF	Unc	BU
1988	—	—	—	65.00	—

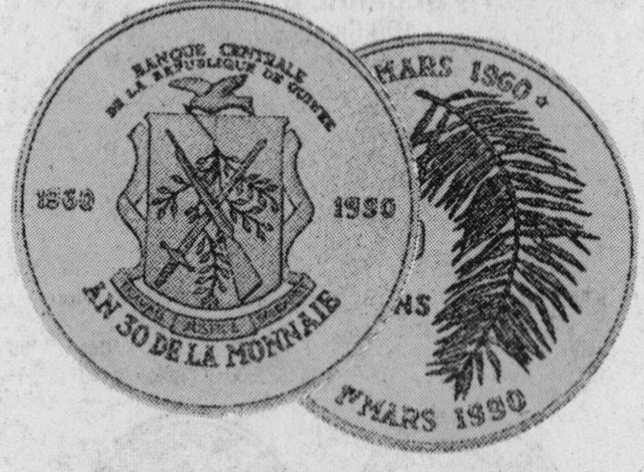

KM# 61 10000 FRANCS **Weight:** 25.0000 g. **Composition:** 0.9990 Silver .8038 oz. ASW **Subject:** 30th Anniversary of Currency **Reverse:** Palm branches and denomination

Date	Mintage	F	VF	XF	Unc	BU
ND(1990) Proof	1,000	Value: 75.00				

KM# 62 10000 FRANCS **Weight:** 15.9760 g. **Composition:** 0.9170 Gold .4708 oz. AGW **Subject:** 30th Anniversary of Currency **Obverse:** Arms with dates on each side **Reverse:** Palm branches and denomination

Date	F	VF	XF	Unc	BU
1990 Proof	—	—	—	—	—

TRIAL STRIKES

KM#	Date	Mintage	Identification	Mkt Val
TS1	ND(1969)	—	100 Francs. KM#9.	30.00
TS2	ND(1969)	—	200 Francs. KM#11.	30.00
TS3	ND(1969)	—	250 Francs. KM#13.	35.00
TS4	ND(1969)	—	500 Francs. KM#16.	55.00

KM#	Date	Mintage	Identification	Mkt Val
TS5	ND(1969)	—	1000 Francs. Goldine. KM#17.	65.00

KM#	Date	Mintage	Identification	Mkt Val
TS6	ND(1984)	—	200 Syli. Lead. M1.	35.00

MINT SETS

KM#	Date	Mintage	Identification	Issue Price	Mkt Val
MS1	1977 (6)	—	KM46-51	—	830
MS2	1988 (3)	5,000	KM57-59	150	170

PROOF SETS

KM#	Date	Mintage	Identification	Issue Price	Mkt Val
PS1	1962 (4)	—	KM4-7	—	325
PS2	1969 (7)	—	KM9-13,15-16	62.50	120
PS3	1969 (4)	—	KM17-20	236	1,275
PS4	1970 (7)	—		62.50	140
PS5	1970 (7)	—	KM22-28	85.00	265
PS7	1970 (3)	—	KM12, 14, 21	29.95	50.00
PS6	1970 (7)	—	KM33-39	440	3,325
PS8	1977 (6)	—	KM46-51. Coins were issued in sets made per order containing from 1 to 11 different coins	—	1,050

GUINEA-BISSAU

The Republic of Guinea-Bissau, formerly Portuguese Guinea, an overseas province on the west coast of Africa between Senegal and Guinea, has an area of 13,948 sq. mi. (36,120sq. km.) and a population of 1.1 million. Capital: Bissau. The country has undeveloped deposits of oil and bauxite. Peanuts, oil-palm kernels and hides are exported.

Portuguese Guinea was discovered by Portuguese navigator, Nuno Tristao, in 1446. Trading rights in the area were granted to Cape Verde islanders but few prominent posts were established before 1851, and they were principally coastal installations. The chief export of this colony's early period was slaves for South America, a practice that adversely affected trade with the native people and retarded subjection of the interior. Territorial disputes with France delayed final demarcation of the colony's frontiers until 1905.

The African Party for the Independence of Guinea-Bissau was founded in 1956, and several years later began a guerrilla warfare that grew in effectiveness until 1974, when the rebels controlled most of the colony. Portugal's costly overseas wars in her African territories resulted in a military coup in Portugal in April 1974, which appreciably brightened the prospects for freedom for Guinea-Bissau. In August 1974, the Lisbon government signed an agreement granting independence to Portuguese Guinea effective Sept. 10, 1974. The new republic took the name of Guinea-Bissau.

RULERS
Portuguese until 1974

PORTUGUESE GUINEA

DECIMAL COINAGE

KM# 1 5 CENTAVOS Composition: Bronze

Date	Mintage	F	VF	XF	Unc	BU
1933	100,000	30.00	60.00	90.00	165	—

KM# 2 10 CENTAVOS Composition: Bronze

Date	Mintage	F	VF	XF	Unc	BU
1933	250,000	28.00	85.00	500	1,000	—

KM# 12 10 CENTAVOS Composition: Aluminum

Date	Mintage	F	VF	XF	Unc	BU
1973	100,000	4.00	8.00	15.00	30.00	—

KM# 3 20 CENTAVOS Composition: Bronze

Date	Mintage	F	VF	XF	Unc	BU
1933	350,000	4.00	8.50	35.00	65.00	—

KM# 13 20 CENTAVOS Composition: Bronze

Date	Mintage	F	VF	XF	Unc	BU
1973	100,000	3.00	6.00	15.00	30.00	—

KM# 4 50 CENTAVOS Composition: Nickel-Bronze

Date	Mintage	F	VF	XF	Unc	BU
1933	600,000	15.00	50.00	200	450	—

KM# 6 50 CENTAVOS Composition: Bronze **Subject:** 500th Anniversary of Discovery

Date	Mintage	F	VF	XF	Unc	BU
ND(1946)	2,000,000	1.00	3.00	15.00	30.00	—

KM# 8 50 CENTAVOS Composition: Bronze

Date	Mintage	F	VF	XF	Unc	BU
1952	10,000,000	0.35	0.75	2.00	5.00	—

KM# 5 ESCUDO Composition: Nickel-Bronze

Date	Mintage	F	VF	XF	Unc	BU
1933	800,000	7.50	22.50	200	450	—

KM# 7 ESCUDO Composition: Bronze **Subject:** 500th Anniversary of Discovery

Date	Mintage	F	VF	XF	Unc	BU
ND(1946)	2,000,000	0.75	2.00	6.00	18.00	—

KM# 14 ESCUDO Composition: Bronze

Date	Mintage	F	VF	XF	Unc	BU
1973	250,000	6.50	12.50	22.50	40.00	—

KM# 9 2-1/2 ESCUDOS Composition: Copper-Nickel

Date	Mintage	F	VF	XF	Unc	BU
1952	3,010,000	0.50	1.50	3.00	7.00	—

KM# 15 5 ESCUDOS Composition: Copper-Nickel

Date	Mintage	F	VF	XF	Unc	BU
1973	800,000	2.50	5.00	10.00	20.00	—

KM# 10 10 ESCUDOS Weight: 5.0000 g. **Composition:** 0.7200 Silver .1157 oz. ASW

Date	Mintage	F	VF	XF	Unc	BU
1952	1,200,000	3.50	18.00	70.00	140	—

KM# 16 10 ESCUDOS Composition: Copper-Nickel

Date	Mintage	F	VF	XF	Unc	BU
1973	1,700,000	2.50	10.00	20.00	40.00	—

KM# 11 20 ESCUDOS Weight: 10.0000 g. **Composition:** 0.7200 Silver .2315 oz. ASW

Date	Mintage	F	VF	XF	Unc	BU
1952	750,000	5.00	15.00	45.00	90.00	—

GUINEA-BISSAU

DECIMAL COINAGE

KM# 17 50 CENTAVOS Composition: Aluminum **Series:** F.A.O.

Date	Mintage	F	VF	XF	Unc	BU
1977	6,000,000	2.00	3.00	4.50	8.00	—

KM# 18 PESO **Composition:** Aluminum-Bronze **Series:** F.A.O.

Date	Mintage	F	VF	XF	Unc	BU
1977	7,000,000	2.25	3.50	5.50	9.00	—

KM# 19 2-1/2 PESOS **Composition:** Aluminum-Bronze **Series:** F.A.O.

Date	Mintage	F	VF	XF	Unc	BU
1977	4,000,000	2.25	4.50	6.50	10.00	—

KM# 20 5 PESOS **Composition:** Copper-Nickel **Series:** F.A.O.

Date	Mintage	F	VF	XF	Unc	BU
1977	6,000,000	2.50	5.00	7.00	11.50	—

KM# 21 20 PESOS **Composition:** Copper-Nickel **Series:** F.A.O.

Date	Mintage	F	VF	XF	Unc	BU
1977	2,500,000	4.00	6.50	11.50	18.00	—

KM# 28 2000 PESOS **Composition:** Nickel Plated Steel **Reverse:** Olympics - Handball Player

Date	Mintage	F	VF	XF	Unc	BU
1991	5,000	—	—	—	17.50	—

KM# 38 2000 PESOS **Composition:** Nickel Plated Steel **Subject:** 50th Anniversary - FAO **Obverse:** National emblem **Reverse:** Pineapple harvest

Date	F	VF	XF	Unc	BU
ND(1995)	—	—	—	17.50	—

KM# 27 10000 PESOS **Weight:** 16.0000 g. **Composition:** 0.9990 Silver .5144 oz. ASW **Reverse:** Nuno Tristad - Discovery of Guinea-Bissau

Date	F	VF	XF	Unc	BU
1991 Proof	—	Value: 30.00			

KM# 29 10000 PESOS **Weight:** 11.9700 g. **Composition:** 0.9990 Silver .3848 oz. ASW **Reverse:** Soccer Player

Date	F	VF	XF	Unc	BU
1991	—	—	—	32.00	—

KM# 30 10000 PESOS **Weight:** 19.6700 g. **Composition:** 0.9990 Silver .6324 oz. ASW **Reverse:** XXV Olympics - Floor Exercise

Date	Mintage	F	VF	XF	Unc	BU
1992 Proof	Est. 10,000	Value: 25.00				

KM# 39 10000 PESOS **Weight:** 20.0000 g. **Composition:** 0.9990 Silver 0.6424 oz. ASW

Date	F	VF	XF	Unc	BU
1992 Proof	—	Value: 27.50			

KM# 31 10000 PESOS **Weight:** 15.0000 g. **Composition:** 0.9990 Silver .4823 oz. ASW **Reverse:** Elephant Standing on Africa

Date	F	VF	XF	Unc	BU
1993 Proof	—	Value: 28.00			

KM# 32 10000 PESOS **Weight:** 15.0000 g. **Composition:** 0.9990 Silver .4823 oz. ASW **Reverse:** Prehistoric Life - Stegosaurus

Date	F	VF	XF	Unc	BU
1993 Proof	—	Value: 27.50			

KM# 35 10000 PESOS **Weight:** 16.1000 g. **Composition:** 0.9990 Silver .5177 oz. ASW **Reverse:** Prehistoric Life - Vulcanodon

Date	F	VF	XF	Unc	BU
1994 Proof	—	Value: 45.00			

KM# 25 20000 NUEVO PESOS **Weight:** 25.0000 g. **Composition:** 0.9990 Silver .8039 oz. ASW **Reverse:** II Extraordinary Congress

Date	Mintage	F	VF	XF	Unc	BU
ND(1990)	2,000	—	—	—	42.50	—

KM# 26 20000 NUEVO PESOS **Weight:** 25.0000 g. **Composition:** 0.9990 Silver .8039 oz. ASW **Reverse:** 10th Anniversary - L. Cabral Deposed

Date	Mintage	F	VF	XF	Unc	BU
1990 Proof	Est. 2,500	Value: 47.50				

KM# 33 20000 NUEVO PESOS **Weight:** 20.0000 g. **Composition:** 0.9990 Silver .6430 oz. ASW **Reverse:** Defense of Nature - Elephant

Date	F	VF	XF	Unc	BU
1993 Proof	—	Value: 37.50			

KM# 34 20000 NUEVO PESOS **Weight:** 20.1000 g. **Composition:** 0.9990 Silver .6456 oz. ASW **Reverse:** Sailing Ship - Passat

Date	Mintage	F	VF	XF	Unc	BU
1993	100	—	—	—	275	—
1993 Proof	—	Value: 37.50				

KM# 36 50000 PESOS **Weight:** 31.4700 g. **Composition:** 0.9250 Silver .9359 oz. ASW **Reverse:** Hippopotamus Female and Calf

Date	Mintage	F	VF	XF	Unc	BU
1996 Proof	Est. 15,000	Value: 55.00				

KM# 37 50000 PESOS **Weight:** 31.4700 g. **Composition:** 0.9250 Silver .9359 oz. ASW **Reverse:** Alvise Da Cadamosto - Sailing Ship

Date	Mintage	F	VF	XF	Unc	BU
1996 Proof	Est. 10,000	Value: 50.00				

PROVAS

Standard metals; stamped

KM#	Date	Mintage	Identification	Issue Price	Mkt Val
Pr1	1933	—	5 Centavos. KM#1.	—	30.00
Pr2	1933	—	10 Centavos. KM#2.	—	30.00
Pr3	1933	—	20 Centavos. KM#3.	—	30.00
Pr4	1933	—	50 Centavos. KM#4.	—	40.00
Pr5	1933	—	Escudo. KM#5.	—	45.00
Pr6	1946	—	50 Centavos. KM#6.	—	15.00
Pr7	1946	—	Escudo. KM#7.	—	15.00
Pr8	1952	—	50 Centavos. KM#8.	—	15.00
Pr9	1952	—	2-1/2 Escudos. KM#9.	—	20.00
Pr10	1952	—	10 Escudos. KM#10.	—	45.00
Pr11	1952	—	20 Escudos. KM#11.	—	50.00
Pr12	1973	—	Escudo. KM#14.	—	20.00
Pr13	1973	—	10 Escudos. KM#16.	—	25.00

TRIAL STRIKES

KM#	Date	Mintage	Identification	Mkt Val
TS1	1984	—	250 Pesos. Lead. KM-M1.	35.00

GUYANA (British Guiana)

The Cooperative Republic of Guyana, is situated on the northeast coast of South America, has an area of 83,000sq. mi. (214,970 sq. km.) and a population of 729,000. Capital: Georgetown. The economy is basically agrarian. Sugar, rice and bauxite are exported.

The original area of Essequibo and Demerary, which included present-day Suriname, French Guiana, and parts of Brazil and Venezuela was sighted by Columbus in 1498.The first European settlement was made late in the 16th century by the Dutch, however, the region was claimed for the British by Sir Walter Raleigh during the reign of Elizabeth I. For the next 150 years, possession alternated between the Dutch and the British, with a short interval of French control. The British exercised de facto control after 1796, although the area, which included the Dutch colonies of Essequibo, Demerary and Berbice, was not ceded to them by the Dutch until 1814. From 1803 to1831, Essequibo and Demerary were administered separately from Berbice. The three colonies were united in the British Crown Colony of British Guiana in 1831. British Guiana won internal self-government in 1952 and full independence, under the traditional name of Guyana, on May 26,1966. Guyana became a republic on Feb. 23, 1970. It is a member of the Commonwealth of Nations. The president is the Chief of State. The prime minister is the Head of Government. Guyana is a member of the Caribbean Community and Common Market (CARIÇOM).

RULERS

British, until 1966

***NOTE:** From 1975-1985 the Franklin Mint produced coinage in up to 3 different qualities. Qualities of issue are designated in ( ) after each date and are defined as follows:

(M) MATTE - Normal circulation strike or a dull finish produced by sandblasting special uncirculated (polish finish) or proof quality dies.

(U) SPECIAL UNCIRCULATED - Polished or proof-like in appearance without any frosted features.

(P) PROOF - The highest quality obtainable having mirror-like fields and frosted features.

BRITISH GUIANA AND WEST INDIES

STERLING COINAGE

KM# 26 4 PENCE **Weight:** 1.8851 g. **Composition:** 0.9250 Silver .0560 oz. ASW

Date	Mintage	F	VF	XF	Unc	BU
1901	60,000	3.00	7.50	17.50	55.00	—

KM# 27 4 PENCE **Weight:** 1.8851 g. **Composition:** 0.9250 Silver .0560 oz. ASW

Date	Mintage	F	VF	XF	Unc	BU
1903	60,000	3.00	7.50	17.50	55.00	—
1903 Matte proof	—	Value: 450				
1908	30,000	5.00	12.50	25.00	90.00	—
1909	36,000	5.00	12.50	25.00	90.00	—
1910	66,000	3.00	10.00	22.50	85.00	—

KM# 28 4 PENCE **Weight:** 1.8851 g. **Composition:** 0.9250 Silver .0560 oz. ASW

Date	Mintage	F	VF	XF	Unc	BU
1911	30,000	6.00	14.50	35.00	115	—
1913	30,000	6.00	14.50	35.00	115	—
1916	30,000	6.00	14.50	35.00	115	—

BRITISH GUIANA

STERLING COINAGE

KM# 29 4 PENCE **Weight:** 1.8851 g. **Composition:** 0.9250 Silver .0560 oz. ASW

Date	Mintage	F	VF	XF	Unc	BU
1917	72,000	3.00	7.50	22.50	90.00	—
1917 Matte proof	—	Value: 450				
1918	210,000	1.25	3.50	15.00	55.00	—
1921	90,000	3.00	7.50	17.50	70.00	—
1923	12,000	20.00	45.00	85.00	160	—
1925	30,000	3.50	8.50	32.50	100	—
1926	30,000	3.50	8.50	25.00	65.00	—
1931	15,000	10.00	25.00	60.00	120	—
1931 Proof	—	Value: 175				
1935	36,000	3.00	7.50	20.00	175	—
1935 Proof	—	Value: 175				
1936	63,000	1.75	2.50	10.00	30.00	—
1936 Proof	—	Value: 225				

KM# 30 4 PENCE **Weight:** 1.8851 g. **Composition:** 0.9250 Silver .0560 oz. ASW

Date	Mintage	F	VF	XF	Unc	BU
1938	30,000	1.75	2.50	10.00	25.00	—
1938 Proof	—	Value: 175				
1939	48,000	1.75	2.50	7.50	20.00	—
1939 Proof	—	Value: 175				
1940	90,000	1.25	2.00	3.50	18.50	—
1940 Proof	—	Value: 175				
1941	120,000	1.25	1.75	3.00	12.50	—
1941 Proof	—	Value: 175				
1942	180,000	1.25	1.75	3.00	12.50	—
1942 Proof	—	Value: 175				
1943	—	1.25	1.75	2.50	8.00	—
1943 Proof	—	Value: 400				

KM# 30a 4 PENCE **Weight:** 1.8851 g. **Composition:** 0.5000 Silver .0303 oz. ASW

Date	Mintage	F	VF	XF	Unc	BU
1944	90,000	0.75	1.25	2.50	8.00	—
1945	120,000	0.50	1.00	2.00	7.00	—
1945 Proof	—	Value: 200				

REPUBLIC OF GUYANA

DECIMAL COINAGE

KM# 31 CENT **Composition:** Nickel-Brass **Reverse:** Stylized lotus flower

Date	Mintage	F	VF	XF	Unc	BU
1967	6,000,000	—	—	0.10	0.25	—
1967 Proof	5,100	Value: 2.00				
1969	4,000,000	—	—	0.10	0.25	—
1970	6,000,000	—	—	0.10	0.25	—
1971	4,000,000	—	—	0.10	0.25	—
1972	4,000,000	—	—	0.10	0.25	—
1973	4,000,000	—	—	0.10	0.25	—
1974	11,000,000	—	—	0.10	0.20	—
1975	—	—	—	0.10	0.25	—
1976	—	—	—	0.10	0.25	—
1977	16,000,000	—	—	0.10	0.20	—
1978	10,450,000	—	—	0.10	0.20	—
1979	—	—	—	0.10	0.20	—
1980	12,000,000	—	—	0.10	0.20	—
1981	10,000,000	—	—	0.10	0.20	—
1982	8,000,000	—	—	0.10	0.20	—
1983	12,000,000	—	—	0.10	0.20	—
1985	8,000,000	—	—	0.10	0.20	—
1987	6,000,000	—	—	0.10	0.20	—
1988	80,000	—	—	0.10	0.20	—
1989	—	—	—	0.10	0.20	—
1991	—	—	—	0.10	0.20	—
1992	—	—	—	0.10	0.20	—

KM# 37 CENT **Composition:** Nickel-Brass **Subject:** 10th Anniversary of Independence **Reverse:** Manatee

Date	Mintage	F	VF	XF	Unc	BU
1976FM (M)	15,000	—	—	0.15	1.00	1.50
1976FM (U)	50	—	—	—	—	—
1976FM (P)	28,000	Value: 1.50				
1977FM (M)	—	—	—	—	3.00	—
1977FM (U)	15,000	—	—	0.20	1.00	1.50
1977FM (P)	7,215	Value: 1.50				
1978FM (M)	—	—	—	—	3.00	—
1978FM (U)	15,000	—	—	0.20	1.00	1.50
1978FM (P)	5,044	Value: 1.50				
1979FM (U)	15,000	—	—	0.20	1.00	1.50
1979FM (P)	3,547	Value: 1.50				
1980FM (U)	30,000	—	—	0.20	1.00	1.50
1980FM (P)	2,763	Value: 1.75				

KM# 32 5 CENTS **Composition:** Nickel-Brass **Reverse:** Stylized lotus flower **Note:** Varieties exist.

Date	Mintage	F	VF	XF	Unc	BU
1967	4,600,000	—	—	0.10	0.25	—
1967 Proof	5,100	Value: 2.00				
1972	1,200,000	—	—	0.10	0.30	—
1974	3,000,000	—	—	0.10	0.30	—
1975	—	—	—	0.10	0.30	—
1976	—	—	—	0.10	0.30	—
1977	1,500,000	—	—	0.10	0.30	—
1978	2,000	—	—	0.50	4.00	—
1979	—	—	—	—	—	—
1980	1,000,000	—	—	0.10	0.30	—
1981	1,000,000	—	—	0.10	0.30	—
1982	2,000,000	—	—	0.10	0.30	—
1985	3,000,000	—	—	0.10	0.30	—
1986	4,000,000	—	—	0.10	0.30	—
1987	3,000,000	—	—	0.10	0.30	—
1988	2,000,000	—	—	0.10	0.30	—
1989	—	—	—	0.10	0.30	—
1990	—	—	—	0.10	0.30	—
1991	—	—	—	0.10	0.30	—
1992	—	—	—	0.10	0.30	—

KM# 38 5 CENTS **Composition:** Nickel-Brass **Subject:** 10th Anniversary of Independence **Reverse:** Jaguar

Date	Mintage	F	VF	XF	Unc	BU
1976FM (M)	15,000	—	—	0.20	1.50	—
1976FM (U)	50	—	—	—	—	—
1976FM (P)	28,000	Value: 1.75				
1977FM (M)	—	—	—	—	5.00	—
1977FM (U)	15,000	—	—	0.20	1.50	—
1977FM (P)	7,215	Value: 2.00				
1978FM (M)	—	—	—	—	5.00	—
1978FM (U)	15,000	—	—	0.20	1.50	—
1978FM (P)	5,044	Value: 2.00				
1979FM (U)	15,000	—	—	0.20	1.50	—
1979FM (P)	3,547	Value: 2.00				
1980FM (U)	30,000	—	—	0.20	1.50	—
1980FM (P)	2,763	Value: 2.25				

KM# 33 10 CENTS **Composition:** Copper-Nickel

Date	Mintage	F	VF	XF	Unc	BU
1967	4,000,000	—	0.10	0.20	0.35	—
1967 Proof	5,100	Value: 2.50				
1973	1,500,000	—	0.10	0.20	0.35	—
1974	1,700,000	—	0.10	0.20	0.35	—
1976	—	—	0.10	0.20	0.35	—
1977	4,000,000	—	0.10	0.20	0.35	—
1978	2,010,000	—	0.10	0.20	0.35	—
1979	—	—	0.10	0.20	0.35	—
1980	1,000,000	—	0.10	0.20	0.35	—
1981	1,000,000	—	0.10	0.20	0.35	—
1982	2,000,000	—	0.10	0.20	0.35	—
1985	3,000,000	—	0.10	0.20	0.35	—
1986	4,000,000	—	0.10	0.20	0.35	—
1987	3,000,000	—	0.10	0.20	0.35	—
1988	2,000,000	—	0.10	0.20	0.35	—
1989	—	—	0.10	0.20	0.35	—
1990	—	—	0.10	0.20	0.35	—
1991	—	—	0.10	0.20	0.35	—
1992	—	—	0.10	0.20	0.35	—

KM# 39 10 CENTS **Composition:** Copper-Nickel **Subject:** 10th Anniversary of Independence **Reverse:** Squirrel Monkey

Date	Mintage	F	VF	XF	Unc	BU
1976	2,006,000	—	—	0.25	1.50	—
1976FM (M)	10,000	—	—	0.25	1.50	—
1976FM (U)	50	—	—	—	—	—
1976FM (P)	28,000	Value: 3.00				
1977	1,500,000	—	—	0.25	1.50	—
1977FM (M)	—	—	—	—	8.00	—
1977FM (U)	10,000	—	—	0.25	1.50	—
1977FM (P)	7,215	Value: 3.00				
1978FM (M)	—	—	—	—	8.00	—
1978FM (U)	10,000	—	—	0.25	1.50	—
1978FM (P)	5,044	Value: 3.00				
1979FM (U)	10,000	—	—	0.25	1.50	—
1979FM (P)	3,547	Value: 3.00				
1980FM (U)	20,000	—	—	0.25	1.50	—
1980FM (P)	2,763	Value: 4.00				

KM# 34 25 CENTS **Composition:** Copper-Nickel

Date	Mintage	F	VF	XF	Unc	BU
1967	3,500,000	—	0.15	0.25	0.65	—
1967 Proof	5,100	Value: 2.50				
1972	1,000,000	—	0.15	0.25	0.65	—
1974	4,000,000	—	0.15	0.25	0.65	—
1975	—	—	0.15	0.25	0.65	—
1976	—	—	0.15	0.25	0.65	—
1977	4,000,000	—	0.15	0.25	0.65	—
1978	2,006,000	—	0.15	0.25	0.65	—
1981	1,000,000	—	0.15	0.25	0.65	—
1982	1,500,000	—	0.15	0.25	0.65	—
1984	1,000,000	—	0.15	0.25	0.65	—
1985	2,000,000	—	0.15	0.25	0.65	—
1986	4,000,000	—	0.15	0.25	0.65	—
1987	3,000,000	—	0.15	0.25	0.65	—
1988	4,000,000	—	0.15	0.25	0.65	—
1989	—	—	0.15	0.25	0.65	—
1990	—	—	0.15	0.25	0.65	—
1991	—	—	0.15	0.25	0.65	—
1992	—	—	0.15	0.25	0.65	—

KM# 40 25 CENTS **Composition:** Copper-Nickel **Subject:** 10th Anniversary of Independence **Reverse:** Harpy Eagle

Date	Mintage	F	VF	XF	Unc	BU
1976FM (M)	4,000	—	—	0.30	2.50	—
1976FM (U)	50	—	—	—	—	—
1976FM (P)	28,000	Value: 3.00				
1977	2,000,000	—	0.15	0.25	2.00	—
1977FM (M)	—	—	—	—	10.00	—
1977FM (U)	4,000	—	—	0.30	4.00	—
1977FM (P)	7,215	Value: 3.00				
1978FM (M)	—	—	—	—	10.00	—
1978FM (U)	4,000	—	—	0.30	4.00	—
1978FM (P)	5,044	Value: 3.00				
1979FM (U)	4,000	—	—	0.30	4.00	—
1979FM (P)	3,547	Value: 3.00				
1980FM (U)	8,437	—	—	0.30	4.00	—
1980FM (P)	2,763	Value: 4.00				

KM# 35 50 CENTS **Composition:** Copper-Nickel

Date	Mintage	F	VF	XF	Unc	BU
1967	1,000,000	—	0.25	0.35	0.75	—
1967 Proof	5,100	Value: 3.50				

KM# 41 50 CENTS **Composition:** Copper-Nickel **Subject:** 10th Anniversary of Independence **Reverse:** Hoatzin

Date	Mintage	F	VF	XF	Unc	BU
1976FM (M)	2,000	—	—	0.40	5.00	—
1976FM (U)	50	—	—	—	—	—
1976FM (P)	28,000	Value: 4.00				
1977FM (M)	—	—	—	—	20.00	—
1977FM (U)	2,000	—	—	0.40	5.00	—
1977FM (P)	7,215	Value: 4.00				
1978FM (M)	—	—	—	—	20.00	—
1978FM (U)	2,000	—	—	0.40	5.00	—
1978FM (P)	5,044	Value: 4.00				
1979FM (U)	2,000	—	—	0.40	5.00	—
1979FM (P)	3,547	Value: 4.00				
1980FM (U)	4,437	—	—	0.40	3.50	—
1980FM (P)	2,763	Value: 5.00				

KM# 36 DOLLAR **Composition:** Copper-Nickel **Series:** F.A.O.

Date	Mintage	F	VF	XF	Unc	BU
1970	500,000	—	0.50	1.50	3.50	—
1970 Proof	5,000	Value: 5.00				

KM# 42 DOLLAR **Composition:** Copper-Nickel **Series:** F.A.O. **Subject:** 10th Anniversary of Independence **Reverse:** Common Caiman

Date	Mintage	F	VF	XF	Unc	BU
1976FM (M)	600	—	—	0.50	6.00	—
1976FM (U)	50	—	—	—	—	—
1976FM (P)	28,000	Value: 5.00				
1977FM (M)	—	—	—	—	30.00	—
1977FM (U)	500	—	—	0.50	6.00	—
1977FM (P)	7,215	Value: 7.00				
1978FM (M)	—	—	—	—	30.00	—
1978FM (U)	500	—	—	0.50	6.00	—
1978FM (P)	5,044	Value: 7.00				
1979FM (U)	500	—	—	0.50	6.00	—
1979FM (P)	3,547	Value: 7.00				
1980FM (U)	1,437	—	—	0.50	6.00	—
1980FM (P)	2,763	Value: 8.00				

KM# 50 DOLLAR **Composition:** Copper Plated Steel **Reverse:** Hand gathering rice

Date	F	VF	XF	Unc	BU
1996	—	—	—	0.50	—

KM# 43 5 DOLLARS **Composition:** Copper-Nickel **Subject:** 10th Anniversary of Independence **Obverse:** Similar to 1 Dollar, KM#42.

Date	Mintage	F	VF	XF	Unc	BU
1976FM (M)	400	—	—	—	15.00	—
1976FM (U)	150	—	—	—	17.50	—
1977FM (M)	—	—	—	—	45.00	—
1977FM (U)	100	—	—	—	25.00	—
1978FM (M)	—	—	—	—	45.00	—
1978FM (U)	100	—	—	—	25.00	—
1979FM (U)	100	—	—	—	25.00	—
1980FM (U)	200	—	—	—	15.00	—

KM# 43a 5 DOLLARS **Weight:** 37.3000 g. **Composition:** 0.5000 Silver .5996 oz. ASW

Date	Mintage	F	VF	XF	Unc	BU
1976FM (P)	18,000	Value: 8.50				
1977FM (P)	5,685	Value: 10.00				
1978FM (P)	3,825	Value: 12.00				
1979FM (P)	2,665	Value: 15.00				
1980FM (P)	2,763	Value: 15.00				

KM# 51 5 DOLLARS **Composition:** Copper Plated Steel **Reverse:** Sugar cane

Date	F	VF	XF	Unc	BU
1996	—	—	—	0.75	—

KM# 44 10 DOLLARS **Composition:** Copper-Nickel **Subject:** 10th Anniversary of Independence **Obverse:** Similar to 1 Dollar, KM#42

Date	Mintage	F	VF	XF	Unc	BU
1976FM (M)	300	—	—	—	30.00	—
1976FM (U)	300	—	—	—	30.00	—
1977FM (M)	—	—	—	—	80.00	—
1977FM (U)	100	—	—	—	50.00	—
1978FM (M)	—	—	—	—	80.00	—
1978FM (U)	100	—	—	—	50.00	—
1979FM (U)	100	—	—	—	50.00	—
1980FM (U)	200	—	—	—	40.00	—

KM# 44a 10 DOLLARS **Weight:** 43.2300 g. **Composition:** 0.9250 Silver 1.2856 oz. ASW

Date	Mintage	F	VF	XF	Unc	BU
1976FM (P)	18,000	Value: 12.50				
1977FM (P)	5,685	Value: 15.00				
1978FM (P)	3,825	Value: 18.00				
1979FM (P)	2,665	Value: 20.00				
1980FM (P)	2,763	Value: 20.00				

KM# 52 10 DOLLARS **Composition:** Nickel Plated Steel **Reverse:** Gold mining scene **Edge:** Plain **Shape:** 7-sided

Date	F	VF	XF	Unc	BU
1996	—	—	—	1.25	—

KM# 45 50 DOLLARS **Weight:** 48.3000 g. **Composition:** 0.9250 Silver 1.4365 oz. ASW **Subject:** 10th Anniversary of Independence **Note:** Enmore Martyrs

Date	Mintage	F	VF	XF	Unc	BU
1976FM (U)	100	—	—	—	100	—
1976FM (P)	1,001	Value: 70.00				

KM# 48 50 DOLLARS **Weight:** 28.2800 g. **Composition:** 0.9250 Silver .8411 oz. ASW **Subject:** Royal Visit **Note:** Similar to 500 Dollars, KM#49.

Date	Mintage	F	VF	XF	Unc	BU
1994 Proof	—	Value: 50.00				

KM# 46 100 DOLLARS **Weight:** 5.7400 g. **Composition:** 0.5000 Gold .0923 oz. AGW **Subject:** 10th Anniversary of Independence **Reverse:** Arawak Indian

Date	Mintage	F	VF	XF	Unc	BU
1976FM (U)	100	—	—	—	80.00	—
1976FM (P)	21,000	Value: 60.00				

KM# 47 100 DOLLARS **Weight:** 5.5800 g. **Composition:** 0.5000 Gold .0897 oz. AGW **Reverse:** Legendary Golden Man

Date	Mintage	F	VF	XF	Unc	BU
1977FM (U)	100	—	—	—	85.00	—
1977FM (P)	7,635	Value: 65.00				

KM# 49 500 DOLLARS **Weight:** 47.5400 g. **Composition:** 0.9170 Gold 1.4017 oz. AGW **Subject:** Royal Visit

Date	Mintage	F	VF	XF	Unc	BU
1994 Proof	100	Value: 1,000				

KM# 53 2000 DOLLARS **Composition:** 0.9250 Silver **Subject:** Millennium **Obverse:** National arms **Reverse:** World globe and radiant sun **Edge:** Plain **Shape:** 12-sided

Date	Mintage	F	VF	XF	Unc	BU
ND(1999) Proof	Est. 30,000	Value: 45.00				

PATTERNS

Including off metal strikes

KM#	Date	Mintage	Identification	Mkt Val
Pn1	1967	—	5 Cents. Silver. KM#32.	—

MINT SETS

KM#	Date	Mintage	Identification	Issue Price	Mkt Val
MS1	1977 (8)	—	KM#37-44	—	150
MS2	1978 (8)	—	KM#37-44	—	150

PROOF SETS

KM#	Date	Mintage	Identification	Issue Price	Mkt Val
PS1	1967 (5)	5,100	KM#31-35	10.50	9.00
PS2	1976 (8)	17,536	KM#37-42, 43a, 44a	45.00	37.50
PS3	1976 (6)	10,302	KM#37-42	15.00	17.00
PS4	1977 (8)	5,685	KM#37-42, 43a, 44a	45.00	42.00
PS5	1977 (6)	1,530	KM#37-42	15.00	20.00
PS6	1978 (8)	3,825	KM#37-42, 43a, 44a	47.50	47.50
PS7	1978 (6)	1,219	KM#37-42	16.00	20.00
PS8	1979 (8)	2,665	KM#37-42, 43a, 44a	47.50	52.00
PS9	1979 (6)	882	KM#37-42	16.00	20.00
PS10	1980 (8)	1,900	KM#37-42, 43a, 44a	100	58.00
PS11	1980 (6)	863	KM#37-42	19.00	22.50

HAITI

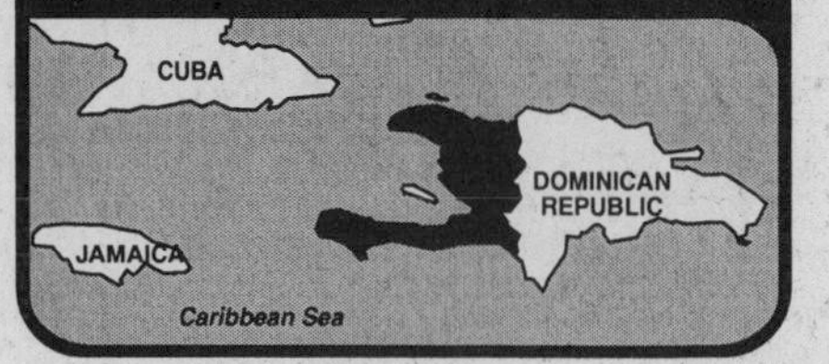

The Republic of Haiti, which occupies the western one-third of the island of Hispaniola in the Caribbean Sea between Puerto Rico and Cuba, has an area of 10,714 sq. mi. (27,750 sq. km.) and a population of 6.5 million. Capital: Port-au-Prince. The economy is based on agriculture; but light manufacturing and tourism are increasingly important. Coffee, bauxite, sugar, essential oils and handicrafts are exported.

Columbus discovered Hispaniola in 1492. Spain colonized the island, making Santo Domingo the base for exploration of the Western Hemisphere. The area that is now Haiti was ceded to France by Spain in 1697. Slaves brought from Africa to work the coffee and sugar cane plantations made it one of the richest colonies of the French Empire. A slave revolt in the 1790's led to the establishment of the Republic of Haiti in1804, making it the oldest Black republic in the world and the second oldest republic (after the United States) in the Western Hemisphere.

The French language is used on Haitian coins although it is spoken by only about 10% of the populace. A form of Creole is the language of the Haitians.

MINT MARKS

A - Paris
(a) - Paris, privy marks only
HEATON - Birmingham
R - Rome
(w) = Waterbury (Connecticut, USA) (Scoville Mfg. Co.)
(p) – Philadelphia (U.S.A. mint)

MONETARY SYSTEM

100 Centimes = 1 Gourde

THIRD REPUBLIC

DECIMAL COINAGE

100 Centimes = 1 Gourde

KM# 53 5 CENTIMES (0.05 Gourdes) Composition: Copper-Nickel **Obverse:** President Nord Alexis

Date	Mintage	F	VF	XF	Unc	BU
1904(w)	2,000,000	1.00	3.00	7.00	20.00	—
1904(w) Proof	—	Value: 90.00				
1905(w)	20,000,000	0.75	2.00	5.00	20.00	—
1905(w) Proof	—	Value: 100				
1906(w)	10,000,000	—	—	—	—	—

Note: Reported, not confirmed

KM# 52 5 CENTIMES (0.05 Gourdes) Composition: Copper-Nickel **Note:** Struck at the Scovill Mfg. Co., Waterbury, Connecticut; design incorporates Paris privy and mint director's marks.

Date	F	VF	XF	Unc	BU
1904(w)	3.00	7.00	15.00	45.00	—
1904(w) Proof	Value: 120				

KM# 57 5 CENTIMES (0.05 Gourdes) Composition: Copper-Nickel **Obverse:** President Dumarsais Estime

Date	Mintage	F	VF	XF	Unc	BU
1949(p)	10,000,000	0.25	0.50	1.00	4.00	—

KM# 59 5 CENTIMES (0.05 Gourdes) Composition: Nickel-Silver **Obverse:** President Paul E. Magloire

Date	Mintage	F	VF	XF	Unc	BU
1953(p)	3,000,000	0.15	0.25	0.50	1.50	—

KM# 62 5 CENTIMES (0.05 Gourdes) Composition: Copper-Nickel **Obverse:** President Francois Duvalier

Date	Mintage	F	VF	XF	Unc	BU
1958(p)	15,000,000	—	—	0.10	0.25	—
1970	5,000,000	—	—	0.10	0.20	—

KM# 119 5 CENTIMES (0.05 Gourdes) Composition: Copper-Nickel **Series:** F.A.O **Obverse:** President Jean-Claude Duvalier

Date	Mintage	F	VF	XF	Unc	BU
1975	16,000,000	—	—	0.10	0.20	—

KM# 145 5 CENTIMES (0.05 Gourdes) Composition: Copper-Nickel **Series:** F.A.O.

Date	Mintage	F	VF	XF	Unc	BU
1981	15,000	—	0.10	0.25	0.65	—

KM# 154 5 CENTIMES (0.05 Gourdes) Composition: Nickel-Plated Steel **Obverse:** Portrait of national hero, Charlemagne Peralte **Reverse:** National emblem

Date	F	VF	XF	Unc	BU
1995	—	—	—	0.25	—

KM# 154a 5 CENTIMES (0.05 Gourdes) Composition: Nickel Plated Steel

Date	F	VF	XF	Unc	BU
1995	—	—	—	0.35	—
1997	—	—	—	0.35	—

KM# 54 10 CENTIMES (0.10 Gourdes) Composition: Copper-Nickel **Obverse:** President Nord Alexis

Date	Mintage	F	VF	XF	Unc	BU
1906(w)	10,000,000	1.00	3.00	7.00	20.00	—
1906(w) Proof	—	Value: 100				

KM# 58 10 CENTIMES (0.10 Gourdes) Composition: Copper-Nickel **Obverse:** President Dumarsais Estime

Date	Mintage	F	VF	XF	Unc	BU
1949(p)	5,000,000	0.50	1.00	4.00	10.00	—

KM# 60 10 CENTIMES (0.10 Gourdes) Composition: Nickel-Silver **Obverse:** President Paul E. Magloire

Date	Mintage	F	VF	XF	Unc	BU
1953(p)	1,500,000	—	0.10	0.25	1.25	—

KM# 63 10 CENTIMES (0.10 Gourdes) Composition: Copper-Nickel **Obverse:** President Francois Duvalier

Date	Mintage	F	VF	XF	Unc	BU
1958(p)	7,500,000	—	0.10	0.15	0.35	—
1970	2,500,000	—	—	0.10	0.20	—

KM# 120 10 CENTIMES (0.10 Gourdes)
Composition: Copper-Nickel **Series:** F.A.O. **Obverse:** President Jean-Claude Duvalier

Date	Mintage	F	VF	XF	Unc	BU
1975	12,000,000	—	—	0.10	0.20	—
1983	2,000,000	—	—	0.10	0.30	—

KM# 146 10 CENTIMES (0.10 Gourdes)
Composition: Copper-Nickel **Series:** F.A.O.

Date	Mintage	F	VF	XF	Unc	BU
1981R	15,000	—	0.10	0.25	0.85	—

KM# 55 20 CENTIMES Composition: Copper-Nickel **Obverse:** President Nord Alexis

Date	Mintage	F	VF	XF	Unc	BU
1907(w)	5,000,000	2.00	4.00	10.00	30.00	—
1907(w) Proof	—	Value: 125				
1908(w)	—	—	—	—	—	—

Note: Reported, not confirmed

KM# 61 20 CENTIMES Composition: Nickel-Silver **Obverse:** President Paul E. Magliore

Date	Mintage	F	VF	XF	Unc	BU
1956(p)	2,500,000	0.50	1.00	2.00	5.00	—

KM# 77 20 CENTIMES Composition: Nickel-Silver **Obverse:** President Francios Duvalier

Date	Mintage	F	VF	XF	Unc	BU
1970	1,000,000	—	0.10	0.20	0.80	—

KM# 100 20 CENTIMES Composition: Copper-Nickel **Series:** F.A.O. **Obverse:** President Jean-Claude Duvalier

Date	Mintage	F	VF	XF	Unc	BU
1972	1,500,000	—	0.10	0.25	1.00	—
1975	4,000,000	—	0.10	0.20	0.80	—
1983	1,500,000	—	0.10	0.20	0.80	—

KM# 147 20 CENTIMES Composition: Copper-Nickel **Series:** F.A.O.

Date	Mintage	F	VF	XF	Unc	BU
1981R	15,000	—	0.10	0.25	1.00	—

KM# 152 20 CENTIMES Composition: Copper-Nickel **Obverse:** Portrait of national hero, Charlemagne Perlalte **Reverse:** National emblem

Date	Mintage	F	VF	XF	Unc	BU
1986	2,500,000	—	0.10	0.20	0.60	—
1989	—	—	0.10	0.20	0.60	—
1991	—	—	0.10	0.20	0.60	—

KM# 152a 20 CENTIMES Composition: Nickel Plated Steel

Date	F	VF	XF	Unc	BU
1995	—	—	—	0.75	—

KM# 56 50 CENTIMES (0.50 Gourdes) Composition: Copper-Nickel **Obverse:** President Nord Alexis

Date	Mintage	F	VF	XF	Unc	BU
1907(w)	2,000,000	1.00	3.50	9.00	32.50	—
1907(w) Proof	—	Value: 175				
1908(w)	800,000	1.25	4.00	10.00	35.00	—
1908(w) Proof	—	Value: 200				

KM# 101 50 CENTIMES (0.50 Gourdes)
Composition: Copper-Nickel **Series:** F.A.O. **Obverse:** President Jean-Claude Duvalier

Date	Mintage	F	VF	XF	Unc	BU
1972	600,000	—	0.10	0.25	1.50	—

KM# 101a 50 CENTIMES (0.50 Gourdes)
Composition: Copper-Nickel-Zinc **Note:** Varieties exist.

Date	Mintage	F	VF	XF	Unc	BU
1975	1,200,000	—	0.10	0.20	1.00	—
1979	2,000,000	—	0.10	0.20	1.00	—
1983	1,000,000	—	0.10	0.20	1.00	—
1985	—	—	—	—	0.75	—

KM# 148 50 CENTIMES (0.50 Gourdes)
Composition: Copper-Nickel **Series:** F.A.O.

Date	Mintage	F	VF	XF	Unc	BU
1981R	15,000	—	0.10	0.50	1.50	—

KM# 153 50 CENTIMES (0.50 Gourdes)
Composition: Copper-Nickel **Obverse:** Portrait of national hero, Charlemagne Peralte **Reverse:** National emblem

Date	Mintage	F	VF	XF	Unc	BU
1986	2,000,000	—	0.10	0.25	1.00	—
1989	—	—	0.10	0.25	1.00	—
1991	—	—	0.10	0.25	1.00	—

KM# 153a 50 CENTIMES (0.50 Gourdes)
Composition: Nickel Plated Steel

Date	F	VF	XF	Unc	BU
1995	—	0.10	0.25	1.25	—

KM# 155 GOURDE Composition: Brass Plated Steel **Obverse:** Hilltop ediface **Reverse:** National emblem **Shape:** 7-sided

Date	F	VF	XF	Unc	BU
1995	—	—	—	1.75	—

KM# 64.1 5 GOURDES Weight: 23.5200 g. **Composition:** 0.9990 Silver .7555 oz. ASW **Series:** 10th Anniversary of Revolution **Subject:** Columbus Discovers America

Date	Mintage	F	VF	XF	Unc	BU
1967 IC Proof	4,650	Value: 11.50				
1968 IC Proof	5,750	Value: 11.50				
1969 IC Proof	1,175	Value: 20.00				
1970 IC Proof	2,060	Value: 18.00				

KM# 64.2 5 GOURDES Weight: 23.5200 g. **Composition:** 0.9990 Silver .7555 oz. ASW **Reverse:** Additional "1 AR" countermark at 8 o'clock

Date	F	VF	XF	Unc	BU
1970 Proof	—	Value: 25.00			

KM# 78 5 GOURDES Weight: 23.5200 g. **Composition:** 0.9990 Silver .7555 oz. ASW **Reverse:** Haitienne Paradise

Date	Mintage	F	VF	XF	Unc	BU
1971 IC Proof	1,585	Value: 60.00				

KM# 156 5 GOURDES Composition: Brass Plated Steel **Obverse:** Four cameos in circle of Haitian statesmen **Reverse:** National emblem **Shape:** 7-sided

Date	F	VF	XF	Unc	BU
1995	—	—	—	2.75	—

KM# 65.1 10 GOURDES Weight: 47.0500 g. **Composition:** 0.9990 Silver 1.5113 oz. ASW **Series:** 10th Anniversary of Revolution **Obverse:** General Louverture

Date	Mintage	F	VF	XF	Unc	BU
1967 IC Proof	6,750	Value: 22.00				
1968 IC Proof	5,725	Value: 22.00				
1969 IC Proof	1,100	Value: 30.00				
1970 IC Proof	1,500	Value: 30.00				

KM# 65.2 10 GOURDES Weight: 47.0500 g. **Composition:** 0.9990 Silver 1.5113 oz. ASW **Reverse:** Additional "1 AR" countermark left of the initials "IC"

Date	F	VF	XF	Unc	BU
1970 IC Proof	—	Value: 65.50			

KM# 79 10 GOURDES Weight: 47.0500 g. **Composition:** 0.9990 Silver 1.5113 oz. ASW **Obverse:** Seminole Chief - Osceola **Reverse:** Similar to KM#65

Date	Mintage	F	VF	XF	Unc	BU
1971 IC Proof	3,535	Value: 35.00				

KM# 80 10 GOURDES Weight: 47.0500 g. **Composition:** 0.9990 Silver 1.5113 oz. ASW **Obverse:** Sioux Chief - Sitting Bull **Reverse:** Similar to KM#65

Date	Mintage	F	VF	XF	Unc	BU
1971 IC Proof	3,185	Value: 35.00				

KM# 81 10 GOURDES Weight: 47.0500 g. **Composition:** 0.9990 Silver 1.5113 oz. ASW **Obverse:** Fox Chief - Playing Fox **Reverse:** Similar to KM#65

Date	Mintage	F	VF	XF	Unc	BU
1971 IC Proof	3,035	Value: 35.00				

KM# 82 10 GOURDES Weight: 47.0500 g. **Composition:** 0.9990 Silver 1.5113 oz. ASW **Obverse:** Chiricahua Chief - Geronimo **Reverse:** Similar to KM#65

Date	Mintage	F	VF	XF	Unc	BU
1971 IC Proof	3,285	Value: 35.00				

KM# 83 10 GOURDES Weight: 47.0500 g. **Composition:** 0.9990 Silver 1.5113 oz. ASW **Obverse:** Seminole Chief - Billy Bowlegs **Reverse:** Similar to KM#65

Date	Mintage	F	VF	XF	Unc	BU
1971 IC Proof	3,735	Value: 35.00				

KM# 84 10 GOURDES Weight: 47.0500 g. **Composition:** 0.9990 Silver 1.5113 oz. ASW **Obverse:** Nez Perce Chief - Joseph **Reverse:** Similar to KM#65

Date	Mintage	F	VF	XF	Unc	BU
1971 IC Proof	3,235	Value: 35.00				

KM# 85 10 GOURDES **Weight:** 47.0500 g. **Composition:** 0.9990 Silver 1.5113 oz. ASW **Obverse:** Yankton Sioux Chief - War Eagle **Reverse:** Similar to KM#65

Date	Mintage	F	VF	XF	Unc	BU
1971 IC Proof	3,135	Value: 35.00				

KM# 86 10 GOURDES **Weight:** 47.0500 g. **Composition:** 0.9990 Silver 1.5113 oz. ASW **Obverse:** Oglala Sioux Chief - Red Cloud **Reverse:** Similar to KM#65

Date	Mintage	F	VF	XF	Unc	BU
1971 IC Proof	3,235	Value: 35.00				

KM# 87 10 GOURDES **Weight:** 47.0500 g. **Composition:** 0.9990 Silver 1.5113 oz. ASW **Obverse:** Cherokee Chief - Stalking Turkey **Reverse:** Similar to KM#65

Date	Mintage	F	VF	XF	Unc	BU
1971 IC Proof	3,185	Value: 35.00				

KM# 66 20 GOURDES **Weight:** 3.9500 g. **Composition:** 0.9000 Gold .1143 oz. AGW **Series:** 10th Anniversary of Revolution **Note:** Mackandal

Date	Mintage	F	VF	XF	Unc	BU
1967 IC Proof	10,351	Value: 50.00				
1968 IC Proof	—	Value: 50.00				
1969 IC Proof	—	Value: 60.00				
1970 IC Proof	—	Value: 65.00				

KM# 67.1 25 GOURDES **Weight:** 117.6000 g. **Composition:** 0.9990 Silver 3.7809 oz. ASW **Subject:** 10th Anniversary of Revolution **Obverse:** Art objects **Reverse:** Similar to 5 Gourdes, KM#64 **Size:** 60 mm.

Date	Mintage	F	VF	XF	Unc	BU
1967 IC Proof	4,650	Value: 45.00				
1968 IC Proof	5,810	Value: 45.00				
1969 IC Proof	1,115	Value: 65.00				
1970 IC Proof	1,000	Value: 65.00				

KM# 67.2 25 GOURDES **Weight:** 117.6000 g. **Composition:** 0.9990 Silver 3.7809 oz. ASW **Reverse:** Additional "1 AR" countermark at 8 o'clock **Size:** 60 mm.

Date	F	VF	XF	Unc	BU
1970 Proof	—	Value: 160			

KM# 88 25 GOURDES **Weight:** 117.6000 g. **Composition:** 0.9990 Silver 3.7809 oz. ASW **Obverse:** International airport **Reverse:** Similar to KM#67; similar to 5 Gourdes KM#64 **Size:** 60 mm.

Date	Mintage	F	VF	XF	Unc	BU
1971 IC Proof	1,935	Value: 75.00				

KM# 102 25 GOURDES **Weight:** 10.0000 g. **Composition:** 0.9250 Silver .2973 oz. ASW

Date	Mintage	F	VF	XF	Unc	BU
1973	6,100	—	—	—	6.00	—
1973 Proof	5,470	Value: 7.00				
1974 Proof	—	Value: 30.00				

KM# 103 25 GOURDES **Weight:** 10.0000 g. **Composition:** 0.9250 Silver .2973 oz. ASW **Subject:** World Soccer Championship Games

Date	Mintage	F	VF	XF	Unc	BU
1973	57,000	—	—	—	5.50	—
1973 Proof	6,430	Value: 7.00				
1974 Proof	—	Value: 30.00				

KM# 112.1 25 GOURDES **Weight:** 8.3750 g. **Composition:** 0.9250 Silver .2491 oz. ASW **Series:** United States Bicentennial

Date	Mintage	F	VF	XF	Unc	BU
1974	25,000	—	—	—	6.00	—
1974 Proof	600	Value: 20.00				
1975 Proof	—	Value: 35.00				
1976 Proof	10,000	Value: 12.50				

KM# 112.2 25 GOURDES **Weight:** 8.3750 g. **Composition:** 0.9250 Silver .2491 oz. ASW **Obverse:** Error; without country name at top

Date	Mintage	F	VF	XF	Unc	BU
1974	25,000	—	—	—	40.00	—

KM# 121 25 GOURDES **Weight:** 8.3750 g. **Composition:** 0.9250 Silver .2491 oz. ASW **Series:** International Women's Year **Reverse:** Similar to KM#67

Date	Mintage	F	VF	XF	Unc	BU
1975	7,180	—	—	—	16.50	—
1975 Proof	1,440	Value: 35.00				

KM# 72 30 GOURDES **Weight:** 9.1100 g. **Composition:** 0.8580 Gold .1713 oz. AGW **Series:** 10th Anniversary of Revolution **Obverse:** Citadel of Saint Christopher

Date	Mintage	F	VF	XF	Unc	BU
1969 IC Proof	1,185	Value: 125				
1970 IC Proof	Inc. above	Value: 150				

KM# 73 40 GOURDES **Weight:** 12.1500 g. **Composition:** 0.5850 Gold .2285 oz. AGW **Series:** 10th Anniversary of Revolution **Obverse:** J. J. Dessalines

Date	Mintage	F	VF	XF	Unc	BU
1969 Proof	1,005	Value: 200				
1970 Proof	Inc. above	Value: 220				

KM# 68 50 GOURDES **Weight:** 9.8700 g. **Composition:** 0.9000 Gold .2856 oz. AGW **Series:** 10th Anniversary of Revolution **Obverse:** Dancer

Date	Mintage	F	VF	XF	Unc	BU
1967 IC Proof	8,681	Value: 130				
1968 IC Proof	—	Value: 180				
1969 IC Proof	—	Value: 210				
1970 IC Proof	—	Value: 235				

KM# 89 50 GOURDES **Weight:** 9.8700 g. **Composition:** 0.9000 Gold .2856 oz. AGW **Series:** 10th Anniversary of Revolution **Reverse:** Similar to KM#68 **Note:** Heros de Vertieres

Date	Mintage	F	VF	XF	Unc	BU
1971 IC Proof	485	Value: 300				

KM# 104 50 GOURDES **Weight:** 20.0000 g. **Composition:** 0.9250 Silver .5949 oz. ASW **Obverse:** Woman on the beach

Date	Mintage	F	VF	XF	Unc	BU
1973	8,685	—	—	—	16.50	—
1973 Proof	5,973	Value: 20.00				
1974 Proof	—	Value: 45.00				

KM# 105 50 GOURDES **Weight:** 20.0000 g. **Composition:** 0.9250 Silver .5949 oz. ASW **Obverse:** Woman and child

Date	Mintage	F	VF	XF	Unc	BU
1973	7,300	—	—	—	13.50	—
1973 Proof	5,853	Value: 16.50				
1974	—	—	—	—	37.50	—
1974 Proof	—	Value: 45.00				

KM# 106 50 GOURDES **Weight:** 16.7500 g. **Composition:** 0.9250 Silver .4982 oz. ASW **Series:** World Soccer Championship Games

Date	Mintage	F	VF	XF	Unc	BU
1973 Proof	12,000	Value: 15.00				

KM# 113 50 GOURDES **Weight:** 16.7500 g. **Composition:** 0.9250 Silver .4982 oz. ASW **Series:** 1976 Montreal Olympiad

Date	Mintage	F	VF	XF	Unc	BU
1974	21,000	—	—	—	15.00	—
1974 Proof	2,358	Value: 22.00				
1975 Proof	—	Value: 27.50				
1976	—	—	—	—	—	—
1976 Thin 6; Proof	8,000	Value: 25.00				
1976 Thick 6; Proof	Inc. above	Value: 30.00				

KM# 114 50 GOURDES **Weight:** 16.7500 g. **Composition:** 0.9250 Silver .4982 oz. ASW **Reverse:** Smaller 4 in date

Date	F	VF	XF	Unc	BU
1974	—	—	—	20.00	—
1974 Proof	— Value: 30.00				

KM# 123 50 GOURDES **Weight:** 16.7500 g. **Composition:** 0.9250 Silver .4982 oz. ASW **Subject:** Holy Year

Date	Mintage	F	VF	XF	Unc	BU
1974	—	—	—	—	12.50	—
1974 Proof	960	Value: 25.00				
1975	—	—	—	—	35.00	—
1976 Proof	6,000	Value: 25.00				

KM# 127 50 GOURDES **Weight:** 21.3000 g. **Composition:** 0.9250 Silver .6334 oz. ASW **Series:** World Soccer Championsip Games **Reverse:** Similar to KM#104

Date	Mintage	F	VF	XF	Unc	BU
1977	11,000	—	—	—	20.00	—
1977 Proof	9,000	Value: 25.00				

KM# 128 50 GOURDES **Weight:** 21.3000 g. **Composition:** 0.9250 Silver .6334 oz. ASW **Subject:** Human Rights **Reverse:** Similar to KM#104

Date	Mintage	F	VF	XF	Unc	BU
1977	800	—	—	—	27.50	—
1977 Proof	545	Value: 35.00				

KM# 129 50 GOURDES **Weight:** 21.3000 g. **Composition:** 0.9250 Silver .6334 oz. ASW **Series:** 1980 Moscow Olympics

Date	Mintage	F	VF	XF	Unc	BU
1977	—	—	—	—	22.50	—
1977 Proof	3,720	Value: 27.50				
1978 Proof	Est. 350	Value: 225				

KM# 130.1 50 GOURDES **Weight:** 21.3000 g. **Composition:** 0.9250 Silver .6334 oz. ASW **Series:** 20th Anniversary of European Market

Date	Mintage	F	VF	XF	Unc	BU
1977	421	—	—	—	65.00	—
1977 Proof	364	Value: 80.00				
1978	—	—	—	—	65.00	—

KM# 130.2 50 GOURDES **Weight:** 21.3000 g. **Composition:** 0.9250 Silver .6334 oz. ASW **Obverse:** Entire area within circle frosted **Reverse:** Date added below arms

Date	F	VF	XF	Unc	BU
1978	—	—	—	75.00	—
1978 Proof	—	Value: 90.00			

KM# 131 50 GOURDES **Weight:** 21.3000 g. **Composition:** 0.9250 Silver .6334 oz. ASW **Obverse:** Queen of the sugar **Reverse:** Similar to KM#104

Date	Mintage	F	VF	XF	Unc	BU
1977	321	—	—	—	30.00	—
1977 Proof	602	Value: 37.50				

KM# 149 50 GOURDES **Weight:** 20.0000 g. **Composition:** 0.9250 Silver .5948 oz. ASW **Series:** F.A.O.

Date	F	VF	XF	Unc	BU
1981R	—	—	—	30.00	—
1981R Proof	—	Value: 55.00			

KM# 150 50 GOURDES **Weight:** 20.0000 g. **Composition:** 0.9250 Silver .5948 oz. ASW **Subject:** Holy Year

Date	Mintage	F	VF	XF	Unc	BU
1983R Proof	1,000	Value: 85.00				

KM# 74 60 GOURDES **Weight:** 18.2200 g. **Composition:** 0.5850 Gold .3427 oz. AGW **Series:** 10th Anniversary of the Revolution **Obverse:** Alexandre Petion

Date	Mintage	F	VF	XF	Unc	BU
1969 IC Proof	935	Value: 225				
1970 IC Proof	Inc. above	Value: 375				

KM# 69 100 GOURDES **Weight:** 19.7500 g. **Composition:** 0.9000 Gold .5715 oz. AGW **Series:** 10th Anniversary of the Revolution **Obverse:** Marie Jeanne

Date	Mintage	F	VF	XF	Unc	BU
1967 IC Proof	Est. 8,682	Value: 285				
1968 IC Proof	—	Value: 325				
1969 IC Proof	—	Value: 325				
1970 IC Proof	—	Value: 350				

KM# 90 100 GOURDES **Weight:** 19.7500 g. **Composition:** 0.9000 Gold .5715 oz. AGW **Obverse:** Seminole Tribal Chief - Osceola **Reverse:** Similar to KM#69

Date	Mintage	F	VF	XF	Unc	BU
1971 IC Proof	435	Value: 375				

KM# 91 100 GOURDES **Weight:** 19.7500 g. **Composition:** 0.9000 Gold .5715 oz. AGW **Obverse:** Sioux Chief - Sitting Bull **Reverse:** Similar to KM#69

Date	Mintage	F	VF	XF	Unc	BU
1971 IC Proof	475	Value: 375				

KM# 92 100 GOURDES **Weight:** 19.7500 g. **Composition:** 0.9000 Gold .5715 oz. AGW **Obverse:** Fox Chief - Playing Fox **Reverse:** Similar to KM#69

Date	Mintage	F	VF	XF	Unc	BU
1971 IC Proof	425	Value: 375				

KM# 93 100 GOURDES **Weight:** 19.7500 g. **Composition:** 0.9000 Gold .5715 oz. AGW **Obverse:** Chiricahua Chief - Geronimo **Reverse:** Similar to KM#69

Date	Mintage	F	VF	XF	Unc	BU
1971 IC Proof	520	Value: 375				

KM# 94 100 GOURDES **Weight:** 19.7500 g. **Composition:** 0.9000 Gold .5715 oz. AGW **Obverse:** Seminole Chiel - Billy Bowlegs **Reverse:** Similar to KM#69

Date	Mintage	F	VF	XF	Unc	BU
1971 IC Proof	425	Value: 375				

KM# 95 100 GOURDES **Weight:** 19.7500 g. **Composition:** 0.9000 Gold .5715 oz. AGW **Obverse:** Nez Perce Chief - Joseph **Reverse:** Similar to KM#69

Date	Mintage	F	VF	XF	Unc	BU
1971 IC Proof	455	Value: 375				

KM# 96 100 GOURDES **Weight:** 19.7500 g. **Composition:** 0.9000 Gold .5715 oz. AGW **Obverse:** Yankton Sioux Chief - War Eagle **Reverse:** Similar to KM#69

Date	Mintage	F	VF	XF	Unc	BU
1971 IC Proof	455	Value: 375				

KM# 97 100 GOURDES **Weight:** 19.7500 g. **Composition:** 0.9000 Gold .5715 oz. AGW **Obverse:** Oglala Sioux Chief - War Eagle **Reverse:** Similar to KM#69

Date	Mintage	F	VF	XF	Unc	BU
1971 IC Proof	455	Value: 375				

KM# 98 100 GOURDES **Weight:** 19.7500 g. **Composition:** 0.9000 Gold .5715 oz. AGW **Obverse:** Cherokee Chief - Stalking Turkey **Reverse:** Similar to KM#69

Date	Mintage	F	VF	XF	Unc	BU
1971 IC Proof	425	Value: 375				

KM# 107 100 GOURDES **Weight:** 1.4500 g. **Composition:** 0.9000 Gold .0419 oz. AGW **Obverse:** Christopher Columbus

Date	Mintage	F	VF	XF	Unc	BU
1973	3,233	—	—	—	32.00	—
1973 Proof	915	Value: 55.00				

KM# 132 100 GOURDES **Weight:** 43.0000 g. **Composition:** 0.9250 Silver 1.2789 oz. ASW **Obverse:** Presidents Sadat and Begin profiles facing each other, dove of peace above **Reverse:** Similar to KM#69

Date	Mintage	F	VF	XF	Unc	BU
1977	550	—	—	—	55.00	—
1977 Proof	500	Value: 80.00				

KM# 133 100 GOURDES **Weight:** 43.0000 g. **Composition:** 0.9250 Silver 1.2789 oz. ASW **Subject:** 20th Anniversary of European Market **Reverse:** Similar to KM#69; similar to KM#132

Date	Mintage	F	VF	XF	Unc	BU
1977	321	—	—	—	85.00	—
1977 Proof	214	Value: 100				

KM# 134 100 GOURDES **Weight:** 43.0000 g. **Composition:** 0.9250 Silver 1.2789 oz. ASW **Subject:** 50th Anniversary of Lindbergh's New York to Paris Flight **Reverse:** Similar to KM#69; similar to KM#132

Date	Mintage	F	VF	XF	Unc	BU
1977	321	—	—	—	80.00	—
1977 Proof	214	Value: 125				

KM# 135 100 GOURDES **Weight:** 43.0000 g. **Composition:** 0.9250 Silver 1.2789 oz. ASW **Obverse:** Statue of Liberty **Reverse:** Similar to KM#69; similar to KM#132

Date	Mintage	F	VF	XF	Unc	BU
1977	321	—	—	—	80.00	—
1977 Proof	214	Value: 125				

KM# 158 100 GOURDES **Weight:** 40.0000 g. **Composition:** 0.9250 Silver 1.1896 oz. ASW **Subject:** 10th Anniversary of the Presidency of Jean Claude Duvalier **Obverse:** Similar to 50 Centimes KM#148 but without FAO **Reverse:** Nurse and child

Date	F	VF	XF	Unc	BU
1981R Proof	—	Value: 150			

KM# 159 100 GOURDES **Weight:** 40.0000 g. **Composition:** 0.9250 Silver 1.1896 oz. ASW **Subject:** 10th Anniversary of the Presidency of Jean Claude Duvalier **Obverse:** Similar to 50 Centimes KM#148 but without FAO **Reverse:** Infants on open book

Date	F	VF	XF	Unc	BU
1981R Proof	—	Value: 150			

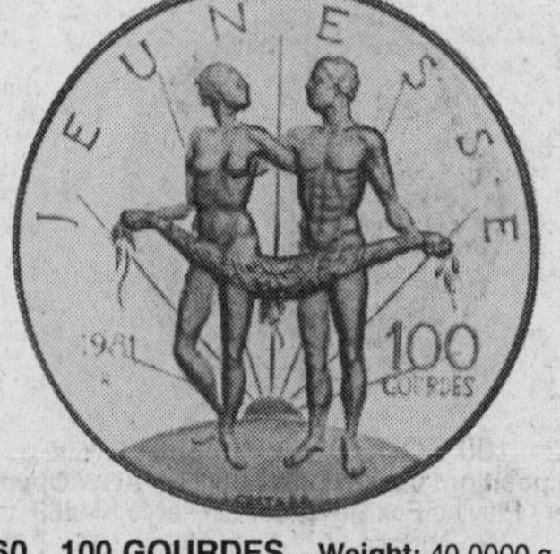

KM# 160 100 GOURDES **Weight:** 40.0000 g. **Composition:** 0.9250 Silver 1.1896 oz. ASW **Subject:** 10th Anniversary of the Presidency of Jean Claude Duvalier **Obverse:** Similar to 50 Centimes KM#148 but without FAO **Reverse:** Nude woman and man

Date	F	VF	XF	Unc	BU
1981R Proof	—	Value: 175			

KM# 70 200 GOURDES **Weight:** 39.4900 g. **Composition:** 0.9000 Gold 1.1427 oz. AGW **Series:** 10th Anniversary of Revolution **Subject:** Revolt of Santo Domingo

Date	Mintage	F	VF	XF	Unc	BU
1967 IC Proof	Est. 4,199	Value: 485				
1968 IC Proof	—	Value: 500				
1969 IC Proof	—	Value: 500				
1970 IC Proof	—	Value: 550				

KM# 99 200 GOURDES **Weight:** 39.4900 g. **Composition:** 0.9000 Gold 1.1427 oz. AGW **Reverse:** Similar to 100 Gourdes, KM#69 **Note:** Revolutionist from Saint Dominique

Date	Mintage	F	VF	XF	Unc	BU
1971 IC Proof	235	Value: 800				

KM# 108 200 GOURDES **Weight:** 2.9100 g. **Composition:** 0.9000 Gold .0842 oz. AGW **Series:** World Soccer Championship Games

Date	Mintage	F	VF	XF	Unc	BU
1973	5,167	—	—	—	55.00	—
1973 Proof	915	Value: 80.00				

KM# 115 200 GOURDES **Weight:** 2.9100 g. **Composition:** 0.9000 Gold .0842 oz. AGW **Subject:** Holy Year **Reverse:** Fineness stamped on hexagonal mound, spears with spearheads

Date	Mintage	F	VF	XF	Unc	BU
1974	4,965	—	—	—	55.00	—
1974 Proof	660	Value: 75.00				

KM# 124 200 GOURDES **Weight:** 2.9100 g. **Composition:** 0.9000 Gold .0842 oz. AGW **Subject:** Holy Year **Reverse:** Finess stamped on oval mound, spears with arrowheads

Date	F	VF	XF	Unc	BU
1975 Proof	—	Value: 85.00			

KM# 125 200 GOURDES **Weight:** 2.9100 g. **Composition:** 0.9000 Gold .0842 oz. AGW **Series:** International Women's Year **Reverse:** Similar to KM#124

Date	Mintage	F	VF	XF	Unc	BU
1975	2,260	—	—	—	65.00	—
1975 Proof	840	Value: 125				

KM# 75 250 GOURDES **Weight:** 75.9500 g. **Composition:** 0.5850 Gold 1.4286 oz. AGW **Series:** 10th Anniversary of Revolution **Obverse:** King H. Christophe **Reverse:** Similar to KM#136

Date	Mintage	F	VF	XF	Unc	BU
1969 IC Proof	470	Value: 700				
1970 IC Proof	—	Value: 1,000				

KM# 136 250 GOURDES **Weight:** 4.2500 g. **Composition:** 0.9000 Gold .1229 oz. AGW **Subject:** Human Rights

Date	Mintage	F	VF	XF	Unc	BU
1977	282	—	—	—	100	—
1977 Proof	288	Value: 115				

KM# 137 250 GOURDES **Weight:** 4.2500 g. **Composition:** 0.9000 Gold .1229 oz. AGW **Obverse:** Presidents Sadat and Begin

Date	Mintage	F	VF	XF	Unc	BU
1977	270	—	—	—	100	—
1977 Proof	520	Value: 95.00				

KM# 138 250 GOURDES **Weight:** 4.2500 g. **Composition:** 0.9000 Gold .1229 oz. AGW **Subject:** 20th Anniversary of European Market

Date	Mintage	F	VF	XF	Unc	BU
1977	107	—	—	—	165	—
1977 Proof	107	Value: 185				

KM# 139 250 GOURDES **Weight:** 4.2500 g. **Composition:** 0.9000 Gold .1229 oz. AGW **Subject:** 50th Anniversary of Lindbergh's New York to Paris Flight **Obverse:** Portrait of Lindbergh in flier's cap above "Spirit of St. Louis" **Reverse:** Similar to KM#137

Date	Mintage	F	VF	XF	Unc	BU
1977	107	—	—	—	215	—
1977 Proof	107	Value: 225				

KM# 76 500 GOURDES **Weight:** 151.9000 g. **Composition:** 0.5850 Gold 2.8572 oz. AGW **Series:** 10th Anniversary of Revolution **Obverse:** Haitian native art **Reverse:** Similar to KM#141 **Size:** 68 mm. **Note:** Illustration reduced.

Date	Mintage	F	VF	XF	Unc	BU
1969 IC Proof	435	Value: 2,000				
1970 IC Proof	—	Value: 2,500				

KM# 109 500 GOURDES **Weight:** 7.2800 g. **Composition:** 0.9000 Gold .2106 oz. AGW

Date	Mintage	F	VF	XF	Unc	BU
1973	2,380	—	—	—	135	—
1973 Proof	915	Value: 160				

KM# 110 500 GOURDES **Weight:** 7.2800 g. **Composition:** 0.9000 Gold .2106 oz. AGW

Date	Mintage	F	VF	XF	Unc	BU
1973	2,265	—	—	—	115	—
1973 Proof	915	Value: 130				

KM# 116 500 GOURDES **Weight:** 6.5000 g. **Composition:** 0.9000 Gold .1881 oz. AGW **Obverse:** Same as 1000 Gourdes, KM#118 **Reverse:** Similar to KM#141

Date		F	VF	XF	Unc	BU
1974 Proof	—	Value: 135				

KM# 117 500 GOURDES **Weight:** 6.5000 g. **Composition:** 0.9000 Gold .1881 oz. AGW **Series:** 1976 Montreal Olympics **Reverse:** Fineness stamped on hexagonal mound, spears with spearheads

Date	Mintage	F	VF	XF	Unc	BU
1974	3,489	—	—	—	100	—
1974 Proof	1,140	Value: 125				

KM# 126 500 GOURDES **Weight:** 6.5000 g. **Composition:** 0.9000 Gold .1881 oz. AGW **Series:** 1976 Montreal Olympics **Reverse:** Fineness stamped on hexagonal mound, spears with arrowheads

Date	Mintage	F	VF	XF	Unc	BU
1975	120	—	—	—	450	—

KM# 140 500 GOURDES **Weight:** 8.5000 g. **Composition:** 0.9000 Gold .2459 oz. AGW **Series:** World Soccer Championship Games

Date	Mintage	F	VF	XF	Unc	BU
1977	450	—	—	—	175	—
1977 Proof	200	Value: 250				

KM# 141 500 GOURDES **Weight:** 8.5000 g. **Composition:** 0.9000 Gold .2459 oz. AGW **Series:** 1980 Moscow Olympics

Date	Mintage	F	VF	XF	Unc	BU
1977	—	—	—	—	165	—
1977 Proof	504	Value: 195				
1978 Proof	Est. 350	Value: 350				

KM# 142 500 GOURDES **Weight:** 8.5000 g. **Composition:** 0.9000 Gold .2459 oz. AGW **Subject:** 20th Anniversary of European Common Market **Obverse:** Map of Europe **Reverse:** Similar to KM#141

Date	Mintage	F	VF	XF	Unc	BU
1977	—	—	—	—	225	—
1977 Proof	257	Value: 265				
1978	—	—	—	—	300	—
1978 Proof	150	Value: 400				

KM# 143 500 GOURDES **Weight:** 8.5000 g. **Composition:** 0.9000 Gold .2459 oz. AGW **Subject:** Economic Connections

Date	Mintage	F	VF	XF	Unc	BU
1977	107	—	—	—	225	—
1977 Proof	107	Value: 300				

KM# 144 500 GOURDES **Weight:** 8.5000 g. **Composition:** 0.9000 Gold .2459 oz. AGW **Obverse:** Jean-Claude Duvalier

Date	Mintage	F	VF	XF	Unc	BU
1977	107	—	—	—	225	—
1977 Proof	328	Value: 200				

KM# 161 500 GOURDES **Weight:** 7.0000 g. **Composition:** 0.9000 Gold .2025 oz. AGW **Subject:** 10th Anniversary of the Presidency of Jean Claude Duvalier **Obverse:** Similar to 10 Centimes KM#146 without FAO **Reverse:** Similar to 10 Centimes, KM#146

Date		F	VF	XF	Unc	BU
1981R Proof	—	Value: 650				

KM# 162 500 GOURDES **Weight:** 7.0000 g. **Composition:** 0.9000 Gold .2025 oz. AGW **Subject:** 10th Anniversary of the Presidency of Jean Claude Duvalier **Obverse:** Similar to 20 Centimes KM#147 but without FAO **Reverse:** Similar to 20 Centimes, KM#147

Date	F	VF	XF	Unc	BU
1981R Proof	—	Value: 650			

KM# 163 500 GOURDES **Weight:** 7.0000 g. **Composition:** 0.9000 Gold .2025 oz. AGW **Subject:** 10th Anniversary of the Presidency of Jean Claude Duvalier **Obverse:** Similar to 50 Centimes KM#148 but without FAO **Reverse:** Similar to 50 Centimes, KM#148

Date	F	VF	XF	Unc	BU
1981R Proof	—	Value: 650			

KM# 151 500 GOURDES **Weight:** 10.5000 g. **Composition:** 0.9000 Gold .3038 oz. AGW **Subject:** Papal Visit

Date	Mintage	F	VF	XF	Unc	BU
1983R Proof	1,000	Value: 185				

KM# 165 500 GOURDES **Weight:** 28.2300 g. **Composition:** 0.9250 Silver 0.8395 oz. ASW **Subject:** Millennium **Obverse:** Multicolor and gold-plated national arms **Reverse:** Dove and partially gold-plated sun rays **Edge:** Reeded **Size:** 38.5 mm.

Date	F	VF	XF	Unc	BU
ND(1999) Proof	—	Value: 100			

KM# 71 1000 GOURDES **Weight:** 197.4800 g. **Composition:** 0.9000 Gold 5.7148 oz. AGW **Series:** 10th Anniversary of Revolution **Obverse:** Dr. Francios Duvalier **Reverse:** Similar to KM#118

Date	Mintage	F	VF	XF	Unc	BU
1967 IC Proof	Est. 2,950	Value: 2,400				
1968 IC Proof	—	Value: 2,600				
1969 IC Proof	—	Value: 2,850				
1970 IC Proof	—	Value: 3,100				

KM# 111 1000 GOURDES **Weight:** 14.5600 g. **Composition:** 0.9000 Gold .4213 oz. AGW **Obverse:** President Jean Claude Duvalier

Date	Mintage	F	VF	XF	Unc	BU
1973	—	—	—	—	200	—
1973 Proof	915	Value: 250				

KM# 118.1 1000 GOURDES **Weight:** 13.0000 g. **Composition:** 0.9000 Gold .3762 oz. AGW **Series:** United States Bicentennial

Date	Mintage	F	VF	XF	Unc	BU
1974	3,040	—	—	—	190	—
1974 Proof	480	Value: 275				
1975 Proof	—	Value: 600				

KM# 118.2 1000 GOURDES **Weight:** 13.0000 g. **Composition:** 0.9000 Gold .3762 oz. AGW **Obverse:** Error; without country name at top

Date	F	VF	XF	Unc	BU
1974	—	—	—	750	—

KM# 164 1000 GOURDES **Weight:** 14.0000 g. **Composition:** 0.9000 Gold .4051 oz. AGW **Subject:** 10th Anniversary of the Presidency of Jean Claude Duvalier **Obverse:** Similar to 50 Centimes KM#148 but without FAO **Reverse:** Three nudes and flag

Date	F	VF	XF	Unc	BU
1981R Proof	—	Value: 1,150			

PATTERNS

Including off metal strikes

KM#	Date	Mintage	Identification	Mkt Val
Pn87	1974	—	25 Gourdes. 0.9250 Silver. KM#112	—

TRIAL STRIKES

KM#	Date	Mintage	Identification	Mkt Val
TS1	ND(1971)	—	100 Gourdes. Gilt Bronze. KM#93	85.00

MINT SETS

KM#	Date	Mintage	Identification	Issue Price	Mkt Val
MS1	1973 (8)	8,000	KM#102, 104-105, 107-111,	490	580
MS2	1973 (8)	—	KM#102, 104, 105, 107-111	60.00	37.50
MS3	1974 (2)	—	KM#115, 123	—	70.00
MS4	1975 (2)	—	KM#121, 125	50.25	65.00
MS5	1976 (2)	—	KM#113, 117	—	—
MS6	1995 (5)	—	KM#152a-156a	—	10.00

PROOF SETS

KM#	Date	Mintage	Identification	Issue Price	Mkt Val
PS1	1967 (5)	2,525	KM#66, 68-71	722	3,250
PS2	1967 (3)	4,650	KM#64.1, 65.1, 67.1	47.00	85.00
PS3	1968 (5)	475	KM#66, 68-71	823	3,875
PS5	1969 (5)	435	KM#72-76	475	3,250
PS6	1969 (5)	140	KM#66, 68-71	823	4,150
PS8	1970 (5)	—	KM#66, 68-71	823	4,500
PS9	1970 (3)	—	KM#64.2, 65.2, 67.2	—	260
PSA10	1970-71 (5)	—	KM#64.1, 65.1, 67.1, 78, 88	265	—
PS10	1971 (9)	—	KM#79-87	135	320
PS11	1971 (9)	—	KM#90-98	—	3,375
PSA11	1971 (18)	—	KM#79-87, 90-98	—	3,700
PS12	1973 (8)	1,250	KM#102-105, 107-109, 111	830	575
PS13	1973 (4)	3,500	KM#102-105	60.00	50.00
PS14	1974 (4)	—	KM#102-105	—	140
PS15	1975 (2)	—	KM#121, 125	67.25	150
PS18	1978 (2)	350	KM#129, 141	—	475
PS19	1978 (2)	—	KM#130.2, 142	—	450
PS20	1981R (7)	10	KM#158-164	—	3,450

Hejaz, a province of Saudi Arabia and a former vilayet of the Ottoman Empire, occupies an 800-mile long (1,287km.) coastal strip between Nejd and the Red Sea. The province was a Turkish dependency until freed in World War I. Husain Ibn Ali, Amir of Mecca, opposed the Turkish control and, with the aid of Lawrence of Arabia, wrested much of Hejaz from the Turks and in 1916 assumed the title of King of Hejaz. Abd Al-Aziz Bin Sa'ud, of Nejd conquered Hejaz in 1925, and in 1926 combined it and Nejd into a single kingdom.

TITLES

al-Hejaz الحجاز

RULERS

al Husain Ibn Ali, AH1334-42/1916-24AD
Abd Al-Aziz Bin Sa'ud, AH1343-1373/1925-1953AD

MONETARY SYSTEM

40 Para = 1 Piastre (Ghirsh)
20 Piastres = 1 Riyal
100 Piastres = 1 Dinar

KINGDOM

COUNTERMARKED COINAGE

Minor Coins

Following the defeat of the Ottomans in 1916, Turkish 20 and 40 Para coins of Muhammed V and Muhammed VI were countermarked al-Hejaz in Arabic. The countermark was applied to the obverse side effacing the Ottoman Sultan's toughra, and thus refuting Turkish rule in Hejaz.

Countermarks on the reverse are rare errors. The 10 Para of Muhammed V and 10 and 20 Para (billon) of Abdul Mejid exist with a smaller, 6-milimeter countermark. These are probably unofficial and not contemporary. Other host coins are considered spurious.

KM# 2 10 PARA **Composition:** Nickel **Countermark:** "Hejaz" **Obverse:** Reshat **Note:** Large countermark on Turkey 10 Para, KM#760. Accession date: 1327.

CM Date	Host Date	Good	VG	F	VF	XF
AH(AH1327)	AH1327//7 Rare	—	—	—	—	—
AH(1327)	AH1327//2-7 Rare	—	—	—	—	—

KM# 3 20 PARA **Composition:** Nickel **Countermark:** "Hejaz" **Note:** Countermark on Turkey 20 Para, KM#761. Accession date: 1327.

CM Date	Host Date	Good	VG	F	VF	XF
AH(1327)	AH1327//2	5.00	9.00	18.00	35.00	—
AH(1327)	AH1327//3	4.00	7.00	15.00	30.00	—
AH(1327)	AH1327//4	3.00	6.00	12.00	25.00	—
AH(1327)	AH1327//5	3.00	6.00	12.00	25.00	—
AH(1327)	AH1327//6	3.00	6.00	12.00	25.00	—
AH(1327)	AH1327//7	3.00	6.00	12.00	25.00	—
AH(1327)	AH1327//x p.y. obliterated	2.00	5.00	10.00	20.00	—

KM# 4 40 PARA **Composition:** Nickel **Countermark:** "Hejaz" **Obverse:** El Ghazi **Note:** Countermark on Turkey 40 Para, KM#766. Accession date: 1327.

CM Date	Host Date	Good	VG	F	VF	XF
AH(1327)	AH1327//3	6.00	10.00	20.00	40.00	—
AH(1327)	AH1327//4	3.00	6.00	12.00	25.00	—
AH(1327)	AH1327//5	3.00	6.00	12.00	25.00	—
AH(1327)	AH1327//x p.y. obliterated	2.00	5.00	10.00	20.00	—

KM# 5 40 PARA **Composition:** Copper-Nickel **Countermark:** "Hejaz" **Note:** Countermark on Turkey 40 Para, KM#779. Accession date: 1327.

CM Date	Host Date	Good	VG	F	VF	XF
AH(1327)	AH1327//8	4.00	6.00	12.00	25.00	—
AH(1327)	AH1327//9	9.00	18.00	35.00	75.00	—
AH(1327)	AH1327//x p.y. obliterated	3.00	6.00	10.00	20.00	—

KM# 6 40 PARA **Composition:** Copper-Nickel **Countermark:** "Hejaz" **Note:** Countermark on Turkey 40 Para, KM#828. Accession date: 1336.

CM Date	Host Date	Good	VG	F	VF	XF
AH(1326)	AH1336//4	15.00	30.00	60.00	100	—
AH(1326)	AH1336//x	10.00	20.00	40.00	75.00	—

COUNTERMARKED COINAGE

Silver Coins

Silver coins of various sizes were also countermarked al-Hejaz. The most common host coins include the Maria Theresa Thaler of Austria, and 5, 10, and 20 Kurush or Qirsh of Turkey and Egypt. The countermark occurs in various sizes and styles of script. These countermarks may have been applied by local silversmiths to discourage re-exportation of the badly needed hard currency and silver of known fineness.

Some crown-sized examples exist with both the al-Hejaz and Nejd countermarks. The authenticity of the silver countermarked coins has long been discussed, and it is likely that most were privately produced. Other host coins are considered spurious.

KM# 10 5 PIASTRES **Composition:** Silver **Countermark:** "Hejaz" **Note:** Countermark on Turkey 5 Kurush, KM#750. Accession date: 1327.

CM Date	Host Date	Good	VG	F	VF	XF
ND(1916-20)	ND(AH1327//1-7)	20.00	40.00	75.00	150	—

KM# 11 5 PIASTRES **Composition:** Silver **Countermark:** "Hejaz" **Note:** Countermark on Turkey 5 Kurush, KM#771. Accession date: 1327.

CM Date	Host Date	Good	VG	F	VF	XF
ND(1916-20)	ND(AH1327//7-9)	20.00	40.00	75.00	150	—

KM# 12 5 PIASTRES **Composition:** Silver **Countermark:** "Hejaz" **Note:** Countermark on Egypt 5 Qirsh, KM#308. Accession date: 1327.

CM Date	Host Date	Good	VG	F	VF	XF
ND(1916-20)	ND(AH1327// 2H-4H, 6H)	20.00	40.00	75.00	150	—

KM# 13 10 PIASTRES **Composition:** Silver **Countermark:** "Hejaz" **Note:** Countermark on Turkey 10 Kurush, KM#751. Accession date: 1327.

CM Date	Host Date	Good	VG	F	VF	XF
ND(1916-20)	ND(AH1327//1-7)	25.00	45.00	80.00	160	—

KM# 14 10 PIASTRES **Composition:** Silver **Countermark:** "Hejaz" **Note:** Countermark on Turkey 10 Kurush, KM#772. Accession date: 1327.

CM Date	Host Date	Good	VG	F	VF	XF
ND(1916-20)	ND(AH1327//7-10)	25.00	45.00	80.00	160	—

KM# 15 10 PIASTRES **Composition:** Silver **Countermark:** "Hejaz" **Note:** Countermark on Egypt 10 Qirsh, KM#309. Accession date: 1327.

CM Date	Host Date	Good	VG	F	VF	XF
ND(1916-20)	ND(AH1327// 2H-4H, 6H)	25.00	45.00	80.00	160	—

KM# 16 20 PIASTRES **Composition:** Silver **Countermark:** "Hejaz" **Note:** Countermark on Egypt 20 Qirsh, KM#310. Accession date: 1327.

CM Date	Host Date	Good	VG	F	VF	XF
ND(1916-20)	ND(AH1327// 2H-4H, 6H)	35.00	60.00	100	150	—

KM# 17 20 PIASTRES **Composition:** Silver **Countermark:** "Hejaz" **Note:** Countermark on Turkey 20 Kurush, KM#780. Accession date: 1327.

CM Date	Host Date	Good	VG	F	VF	XF
ND(1916-20)	ND(AH1327//8-10)	35.00	60.00	100	150	—

KM# 18 20 PIASTRES **Composition:** Silver **Countermark:** "Hejaz" **Note:** Countermark on Austria Maria Theresa Thaler, KM#T1. Accession date: 1327.

CM Date	Host Date	Good	VG	F	VF	XF
(1916-20)	1780	15.00	30.00	60.00	125	—

REGULAR COINAGE

All the regular coins of Hejaz bear the accessional date AH1334 of Al-Husain Ibn Ali, plus the regnal year. Many of the bronze coins occur with a light silver wash mostly on thicker specimens. A variety of planchet thicknesses exist.

KM# 21 1/8 PIASTRE **Composition:** Bronze **Note:** Reeded and plain edge varieties exist.

Date	Good	VG	F	VF	XF
AH1334//5	—	25.00	50.00	100	200

KM# 22 1/4 PIASTRE **Weight:** 1.1400 g. **Composition:** Bronze **Note:** Reeded and plain edge varieties exist.

Date	Good	VG	F	VF	XF
AH1334//5	—	4.00	10.00	20.00	35.00
AH1334//6/5	—	75.00	300	600	1,200
AH1334//6	—	400	750	1,500	—
AH1334//8/5	—	—	—	—	—

KM# 25 1/4 PIASTRE **Composition:** Bronze **Edge:** Plain

Date	Good	VG	F	VF	XF
AH1334//8	—	5.00	10.00	20.00	35.00

KM# 23 1/2 PIASTRE **Composition:** Bronze **Note:** Reeded and plain edge varieties exist.

Date	Good	VG	F	VF	XF
AH1334//5	—	3.00	10.00	20.00	35.00

KM# 26 1/2 PIASTRE **Composition:** Bronze **Note:** Similar to 1/4 Piatre, KM#25. All known specimens were overstruck as "Nejd" KM#1.

Date	Good	VG	F	VF	XF
AH1334//8 Rare	—	—	—	—	—

KM# 24 PIASTRE **Composition:** Bronze **Edge:** Reeded

Date	Good	VG	F	VF	XF
AH1334//5	—	6.00	10.00	20.00	35.00
AH1334//6/5	—	100	200	400	600

KM# 27 PIASTRE **Composition:** Bronze **Edge:** Plain

Date	Good	VG	F	VF	XF
AH1334//8	—	10.00	20.00	35.00	60.00

KM# 28 5 PIASTRES **Weight:** 6.1000 g. **Composition:** 0.9170 Silver .1798 oz. ASW

Date	Good	VG	F	VF	XF
AH1334//8	—	15.00	40.00	75.00	150

KM# 29 10 PIASTRES **Weight:** 12.0500 g. **Composition:** 0.9170 Silver .3552 oz. ASW

Date	Good	VG	F	VF	XF
AH1334//8	—	100	200	400	800

KM# 30 20 PIASTRES (1 Riyal) **Weight:** 24.1000 g. **Composition:** 0.9170 Silver .7105 oz. ASW

Date	Good	VG	F	VF	XF
AH1334//8	—	20.00	45.00	90.00	120
AH1334//9	—	30.00	62.50	125	200

KM# 31 DINAR HASHIMI **Composition:** Gold

Date	Good	VG	F	VF	XF
AH1334//8	—	—	125	250	350

MECCA

KINGDOM

TRANSITIONAL COINAGE

Struck at Hejaz Mint during occupied Mecca by Abd Al-Aziz Bin Sa'ud while establishing his kingdom.

KM# 1 1/4 GHIRSH **Composition:** Copper Or Bronze
Note: Several varieties exist, including reeded and plain edges. Some specimens struck over bronze Hejaz 1/4 and 1/2 Piastres (KM#23 and KM#26), and some occur with a light silver wash.

Date	Good	VG	F	VF	XF
AH1343	—	15.00	25.00	50.00	75.00

KM# 2.1 1/2 GHIRSH **Composition:** Copper Or Bronze
Obverse: Legend right of toughra **Obv. Legend:** "al-Faisal al Saud"

Date	Good	VG	F	VF	XF
AH1343	—	10.00	20.00	40.00	75.00

KM# 2.2 1/2 GHIRSH **Composition:** Copper Or Bronze
Obverse: Legend right of toughra **Obv. Legend:** "al-Faisal"

Date	Good	VG	F	VF	XF
AH1343	—	18.00	35.00	75.00	150

KM# A3 1/2 GHIRSH **Composition:** Bronze

Date	VG	F	VF	XF	Unc
AH1344//2	4.00	10.00	25.00	45.00	—

REGULAR COINAGE

KM# 4 1/4 GHIRSH **Composition:** Copper-Nickel

Date	Good	VG	F	VF	XF
AH1344	—	1.25	2.00	6.00	15.00
AH1344 Proof	—	—	—	—	—

KM# 5 1/2 GHIRSH **Composition:** Copper-Nickel

Date	Good	VG	F	VF	XF
AH1344	—	2.50	4.00	12.00	18.00
AH1344 Proof	—	—	—	—	—

KM# 6 GHIRSH **Composition:** Copper-Nickel

Date	Good	VG	F	VF	XF
AH1344	—	2.00	3.00	7.00	15.00
AH1344 Proof	—	—	—	—	—

HEJAZ & NEJD

KINGDOM

REGULAR COINAGE

KM# 7 1/4 GHIRSH **Composition:** Copper-Nickel

Date	Mintage	VG	F	VF	XF	Unc
AH1346	3,000,000	3.00	5.00	8.00	20.00	—

KM# 13 1/4 GHIRSH **Composition:** Copper-Nickel

Date	VG	F	VF	XF	Unc
AH1348	3.00	5.00	8.00	20.00	—
AH1348 Proof	—	—	—	—	—

KM# 3 1/2 GHIRSH **Composition:** Bronze

Date	VG	F	VF	XF	Unc
AH1344	4.00	10.00	25.00	45.00	—

KM# 8 1/2 GHIRSH **Composition:** Copper-Nickel

Date	Mintage	VG	F	VF	XF	Unc
AH1346	3,000,000	3.00	5.00	8.00	20.00	—

KM# 14 1/2 GHIRSH **Composition:** Copper-Nickel

Date	VG	F	VF	XF	Unc
AH1348	3.00	5.00	8.00	25.00	—
AH1348 Proof	—	—	—	—	—

KM# 9 GHIRSH **Composition:** Copper-Nickel

Date	Mintage	VG	F	VF	XF	Unc
AH1346	3,000,000	3.00	5.00	10.00	35.00	—

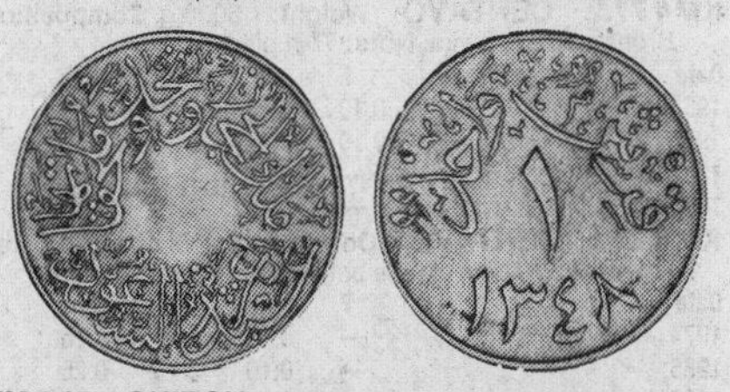

KM# 15 GHIRSH **Composition:** Copper-Nickel

Date	VG	F	VF	XF	Unc
AH1348	3.00	5.00	8.50	25.00	—
AH1348 Proof	—	—	—	—	—

KM# 10 1/4 RIYAL **Weight:** 6.0500 g. **Composition:** 0.9170 Silver .1783 oz. ASW

Date	Mintage	VG	F	VF	XF	Unc
AH1346	400,000	12.50	20.00	45.00	75.00	—
AH1346 Proof	—	—	—	—	—	—
AH1348	200,000	17.50	30.00	60.00	100	—
AH1348 Proof	—	—	—	—	—	—

KM# 11 1/2 RIYAL **Weight:** 12.1000 g. **Composition:** 0.9170 Silver .3567 oz. ASW

Date	Mintage	VG	F	VF	XF	Unc
AH1346	200,000	55.00	100	165	300	—
AH1346 Proof	—	Value: 200				
AH1348	100,000	55.00	100	165	300	—
AH1348 Proof	—	—	—	—	—	—

KM# 12 RIYAL **Weight:** 24.1000 g. **Composition:** 0.9170 Silver .7105 oz. ASW

Date	Mintage	VG	F	VF	XF	Unc
AH1346	800,000	15.00	25.00	50.00	80.00	—
AH1346 Proof	—	Value: 350				
AH1348	400,000	20.00	30.00	85.00	120	—
AH1348 Proof	—	—	—	—	—	—

HONDURAS

The Republic of Honduras, situated in Central America alongside El Salvador, between Nicaragua and Guatemala, has an area of 43,277sq. mi. (112,090 sq. km.) and a population of 5.6 million. Capital: Tegucigalpa. Agriculture, mining (gold and silver), and logging are the major economic activities, with increasing tourism and emerging petroleum resource discoveries. Precious metals, bananas, timber and coffee are exported.

The eastern part of Honduras was part of the ancient Mayan Empire; however, the largest Indian community in Honduras was the not too well known Lencas. Honduras was claimed for Spain by Columbus in 1502, during his last voyage to the Americas. The first settlement was made by Cristobal de Olid under orders from Hernando Cortes, then in Mexico. The area, regarded as one of the most promising sources of gold and silver in the New World, was a part of the Captaincy General of Guatemala throughout the colonial period. After declaring its independence from Spain on September 15, 1821, Honduras fell under the Mexican empire of Augustin de Iturbide, and then joined the Central American Republic (1823-39). Upon the effective dissolution of that federation (ca. 1840), Honduras reclaimed its independence as a self-standing republic. Honduras forces played a major part in permanently ending the threat of William Walker to establish a slave holding empire in Central America based on his self engineered elections to the Presidency of Nicaragua. Thrice expelled from Central America, Walker was shot by a Honduran firing squad in 1860. 1876 to 1933 saw a period of instability and for some months U.S. Marine Corp military occupation. From 1933 to 1940 General Tiburcio Carias Andino was dictator president of the Republic. Since 1990 democratic practices have become more consistent.

Mint Marks

(P) – Philadelphia, U.S.A.

REPUBLIC

DECIMAL COINAGE

100 Centavos = 1 Peso

KM# 46 CENTAVO **Composition:** Bronze **Edge:** Plain, reeded, and plain and reeded **Note:** Varieties exist.

Date	Mintage	VG	F	VF	XF	Unc
1901/0	98,000	5.00	12.50	26.50	45.00	—
1901	Inc. above	5.00	12.50	26.50	45.00	—
1902 large 0	—	3.50	8.00	18.00	40.00	—
1902 small 0	—	3.50	8.00	18.00	40.00	—
1903/2/0	—	5.50	15.00	30.00	55.00	—
1903/2/1 5 known	—	—	—	—	—	—
1904	—	4.50	15.00	30.00	55.00	—
1907/4	234,000	7.50	18.50	32.50	57.50	—
1907	Inc. above	6.50	16.50	30.00	55.00	—

KM# 59 CENTAVO **Composition:** Bronze **Obverse:** KM#46 **Reverse:** Altered KM#49 **Note:** Varieties exist.

Date	Mintage	VG	F	VF	XF	Unc
1907 large UN	—	0.50	1.50	3.25	7.50	15.00
Note: Mintage included in KM#46						
1907 small UN	—	0.50	1.50	3.25	7.50	15.00
Note: Mintage included in KM#46						
1908/7	263,000	7.00	13.50	27.50	60.00	—
1908	—	7.00	13.50	27.50	60.00	—

KM# 61 CENTAVO **Composition:** Bronze **Obverse:** KM#49 **Reverse:** Altered KM#49 **Note:** The 1890, 1891 and

1908 dates are found with a die-cutting error or broken die that reads REPLBLICA. Other varieties exist.

Date	VG	F	VF	XF	Unc
1908	6.00	12.50	22.50	47.50	—

KM# 65 CENTAVO **Composition:** Bronze **Obverse:** KM#45 **Reverse:** Altered KM#45 **Note:** Varieties exist.

Date	Mintage	VG	F	VF	XF	Unc
1910/5	410,000	10.00	22.00	35.00	60.00	—
1910 large 0	410,000	8.50	20.00	32.50	50.00	—
1911/811	62,000	10.00	22.00	35.00	60.00	—
1911/885	Inc. above	10.00	22.00	35.00	60.00	—
1911/886	Inc. above	10.00	22.00	35.00	60.00	—
1911 CENTAVO	Inc. above	6.00	15.00	25.00	40.00	—
1911 CENTAVOS; rare	Inc. above	—	—	—	—	—

KM# 66 CENTAVO **Composition:** Bronze **Obverse:** KM#48 **Reverse:** Altered KM#45

Date	VG	F	VF	XF	Unc
1910	9.00	25.00	40.00	85.00	—
1610 error, inverted 9	50.00	100	175	350	—
1910 error, second 1 inverted	15.00	30.00	55.00	100	—

KM# 67 CENTAVO **Composition:** Bronze **Obverse:** KM#48 **Reverse:** Altered KM#48

Date	VG	F	VF	XF	Unc
1910	4.50	9.00	18.00	42.50	—

KM# 68 CENTAVO **Composition:** Bronze **Obverse:** KM#45 **Reverse:** Altered KM#48

Date	VG	F	VF	XF	Unc
1910	20.00	45.00	85.00	170	—

KM# 70 CENTAVO **Composition:** Bronze **Note:** Similar to KM#65, CENTAVO omitted.

Date	Mintage	VG	F	VF	XF	Unc
1919	168,000	1.75	3.50	7.50	30.00	—
1920	30,000	3.00	6.00	15.00	40.00	—

KM# 64 2 CENTAVOS **Composition:** Bronze **Obverse:** KM#46 **Reverse:** Altered KM#49

Date	VG	F	VF	XF	Unc
1907 Rare	—	—	—	—	—
1908	40.00	80.00	150	300	—

KM# 69 2 CENTAVOS **Composition:** Bronze **Obverse:** KM#46 **Reverse:** Altered KM#46 **Note:** Reverse dies often very crudely recut, especially 1910 and 1911. Some coins of 1910 appear to be struck over earlier 1 or 2 Centavos, probably 1907 or 1908.

Date	Mintage	VG	F	VF	XF	Unc
1910	435,000	1.25	3.50	7.50	16.50	32.50
1911	68,000	4.50	12.00	30.00	60.00	—
1912 CENTAVOS	88,000	1.00	2.50	5.50	17.50	—
1912 CENTAVO	Inc. above	3.00	6.00	14.50	30.00	—
1913	258,000	0.75	2.50	6.00	18.00	—

KM# 71 2 CENTAVOS **Composition:** Bronze **Reverse:** CENTAVOS omitted **Note:** Varieties exist.

Date	Mintage	VG	F	VF	XF	Unc
1919	117,000	1.50	3.25	9.00	25.00	—
1920	283,000	0.65	1.25	3.30	15.00	—
1920 Dot divides date	Inc. above	1.00	2.00	5.00	20.00	—

KM# 48 5 CENTAVOS **Weight:** 1.2500 g. **Composition:** 0.8350 Silver .0336 oz. ASW

Date	VG	F	VF	XF	Unc
1902	25.00	65.00	150	350	—

KM# 50a 25 CENTAVOS **Weight:** 6.2500 g. **Composition:** 0.8350 Silver .1678 oz. ASW **Note:** Varieties exist.

Date	Mintage	VG	F	VF	XF	Unc
1901/801	—	4.00	6.50	13.50	30.00	—
1901/11	—	6.00	12.50	30.00	60.00	—
1901 large first 1	54,000	3.00	5.00	9.00	20.00	—
1902/801	—	8.50	17.50	25.00	50.00	—
1902/802	—	8.50	17.50	25.00	50.00	—
1902/812	—	8.50	17.50	25.00	50.00	—
1902/891	—	8.50	17.50	25.00	50.00	—
1902/1 F	—	4.00	6.00	10.00	20.00	—
1902 F	—	4.00	7.50	13.50	25.00	—
1904	—	15.00	30.00	50.00	90.00	—
1907/4	14,000	6.00	10.00	17.50	30.00	—
1907	Inc. above	6.50	11.50	20.00	32.00	—
1913/0	52,000	—	—	—	—	—
1913/2	Inc. above	—	—	—	—	—
1913	Inc. above	10.00	18.50	30.00	55.00	—

KM# 51a 50 CENTAVOS **Weight:** 12.5000 g. **Composition:** Silver .3355 oz. ASW **Note:** Fineness can be .8350 or .9000.

Date	Mintage	VG	F	VF	XF	Unc
1908/897	447	40.00	85.00	150	245	—
1908	Inc. above	27.50	57.50	90.00	200	—

KM# 51 50 CENTAVOS **Weight:** 12.5000 g. **Composition:** 0.9000 Silver .3617 oz. ASW

Date	Mintage	VG	F	VF	XF	Unc
1910	602	500	900	—	—	—

KM# 56 PESO **Weight:** 1.6120 g. **Composition:** 0.9000 Gold .0467 oz. AGW

Date	F	VF	XF	Unc	BU
1901	150	300	600	1,150	—
1902	140	300	500	1,000	—
1907	140	250	450	900	—
1914/882	275	450	600	1,150	—
1914/03	275	450	600	1,150	—
1919	150	300	550	1,100	—
1920	150	300	550	1,100	—
1922	140	250	450	900	—
ND	—	—	—	—	—

KM# 52 PESO **Weight:** 25.0000 g. **Composition:** 0.9000 Silver .7234 oz. ASW **Reverse:** Large CENTRO-AMERICA **Note:** Overdates and recut dies are prevalent.

Date	Mintage	VG	F	VF	XF	Unc
1902	—	27.50	50.00	80.00	130	—
1903 flat-top 3	—	27.50	45.00	70.00	120	—
1903 round-top 3	—	30.00	55.00	90.00	160	—
1904	20,000	30.00	55.00	90.00	160	—
1914	—	200	500	900	1,500	—

KM# 53 5 PESOS **Weight:** 8.0645 g. **Composition:** 0.9000 Gold .2333 oz. AGW

Date	Mintage	F	VF	XF	Unc	BU
1902	—	450	650	1,000	2,500	—
1908/888	—	450	650	1,000	2,500	—
1913	1,200	450	650	1,000	2,500	—

KM# 57 20 PESOS **Weight:** 32.2580 g. **Composition:** 0.9000 Gold .9335 oz. AGW

Date	F	VF	XF	Unc	BU
1908/888	9,000	12,000	17,500	—	—
1908/897 Rare	—	—	—	—	—

Note: Stack's Hammel sale 9-82 VF 1908/897 realized $12,000. Ponterio & Associates NYINC. sale 12-86 choice XF realized $30,800. Superior Casterline sale 5-89 choice XF realized $28,600.

Date	F	VF	XF	Unc	BU
1908	9,000	12,000	17,500	—	—

REFORM COINAGE

100 Centavos = 1 Lempira

KM# 77.1 CENTAVO **Weight:** 2.0000 g. **Composition:** Bronze **Size:** 15 mm. **Note:** Thick planchet.

Date	Mintage	F	VF	XF	Unc	BU
1935(P)	2,000,000	0.25	0.75	2.50	10.00	—
1939(P)	2,000,000	0.25	0.50	2.00	8.00	—
1949(P)	4,000,000	0.10	0.30	1.00	3.00	—

KM# 77.2 CENTAVO **Weight:** 1.5000 g. **Composition:** Bronze **Size:** 15 mm. **Note:** Thin planchet.

Date	Mintage	F	VF	XF	Unc	BU
1954	3,500,000	0.10	0.15	0.25	1.00	—
1956	2,000,000	0.10	0.15	0.25	0.50	—
1957/6	28,000,000	—	—	—	—	—
1957	Inc. above	—	0.10	0.15	0.30	—

KM# 77a CENTAVO **Composition:** Copper Clad Steel **Obverse:** Without clouds behind pyramids

Date	F	VF	XF	Unc	BU
1974	—	0.10	0.15	0.25	—
1985	—	0.10	0.15	0.25	—
1992	—	0.10	0.15	0.25	—
1998	—	0.10	0.15	0.25	—

KM# 77b CENTAVO **Composition:** Copper Plated Steel **Obverse:** Clouds behind pyramids

Date	Mintage	F	VF	XF	Unc	BU
1988	50,000,000	—	0.10	0.15	0.25	—

KM# 78 2 CENTAVOS **Weight:** 3.0000 g. **Composition:** Bronze

Date	Mintage	F	VF	XF	Unc	BU
1939(P)	2,000,000	0.25	0.50	2.50	8.00	—
1949(P)	3,000,000	0.10	0.25	1.50	5.00	—
1954	2,000,000	0.10	0.25	1.00	3.00	—
1956	20,000,000	—	0.10	0.25	1.00	—

KM# 78a 2 CENTAVOS **Composition:** Bronze Clad Steel

Date	F	VF	XF	Unc	BU
1974	—	0.10	0.15	0.25	—

KM# 72.1 5 CENTAVOS **Weight:** 5.0000 g. **Composition:** Copper-Nickel **Note:** Dentilated border.

Date	Mintage	F	VF	XF	Unc	BU
1931(P)	2,000,000	0.50	1.50	3.50	18.00	—
1932(P)	1,000,000	0.35	0.75	2.50	12.00	—
1949(P)	2,000,000	0.20	0.50	1.50	7.00	—
1956(P)	10,070,000	—	0.15	0.25	0.60	—
1972	5,000,000	—	0.10	0.15	0.35	—

KM# 72.2 5 CENTAVOS **Composition:** Copper-Nickel **Note:** Beaded border.

Date	Mintage	F	VF	XF	Unc	BU
1954	1,400,000	0.15	0.25	0.60	2.50	—
1980	20,000,000	—	0.10	0.15	0.35	—

KM# 72.2a 5 CENTAVOS **Composition:** Brass **Obverse:** Large letters and coat of arms, without clouds behind pyramids

Date	Mintage	F	VF	XF	Unc	BU
1975	20,000,000	—	0.10	0.15	0.35	—
1989	—	—	0.10	0.15	0.35	—

KM# 72.3 5 CENTAVOS **Composition:** Brass **Obverse:** Small letters and coat of arms, with clouds behind pyramids

Date	F	VF	XF	Unc	BU
1993	—	0.10	0.15	0.35	—
1994	—	0.10	0.15	0.35	—

KM# 72.4 5 CENTAVOS **Composition:** Brass **Obverse:** Without clouds behind pyramids

Date	F	VF	XF	Unc	BU
1995	—	0.10	0.15	0.35	—
1999	—	0.10	0.15	0.35	—

KM# 76.1 10 CENTAVOS **Weight:** 7.0000 g. **Composition:** Copper-Nickel **Note:** Dentilated border.

Date	Mintage	F	VF	XF	Unc	BU
1932(P)	1,500,000	1.00	2.50	6.50	30.00	—
1951(P)	1,000,000	0.50	1.00	2.50	8.00	—
1956(P)	7,560,000	0.10	0.25	0.50	1.00	—

KM# 76.2 10 CENTAVOS **Composition:** Copper-Nickel **Note:** Beaded border.

Date	Mintage	F	VF	XF	Unc	BU
1954	1,200,000	0.10	0.25	0.75	5.00	—
1967	—	0.10	0.25	0.50	2.00	—
1980	15,000,000	0.10	0.25	0.50	2.00	—
1993	—	0.10	0.25	0.50	2.00	—

KM# 76.1a 10 CENTAVOS **Composition:** Brass **Obverse:** Large letters and coat of arms **Note:** Dentilated border.

Date	F	VF	XF	Unc	BU
1976	0.10	0.15	0.25	0.60	—
1989	0.10	0.15	0.25	0.60	—

KM# 76.2a 10 CENTAVOS **Composition:** Brass **Obverse:** Small letters and coat of arms, without clouds behind pyramids **Note:** Beaded border.

Date	F	VF	XF	Unc	BU
1993	—	0.10	0.20	0.45	—
1994	—	0.10	0.20	0.45	—

KM# 76.3 10 CENTAVOS **Composition:** Brass **Obverse:** Small letters and coat of arms, with clouds

Date	F	VF	XF	Unc	BU
1995	—	0.10	0.20	0.45	—
1999	—	0.10	0.20	0.45	—

KM# 73 20 CENTAVOS **Weight:** 2.5000 g. **Composition:** 0.9000 Silver .0723 oz. ASW **Reverse:** Chief of the Lempira

Date	Mintage	F	VF	XF	Unc	BU
1931(P)	1,000,000	1.25	3.50	9.00	30.00	—
1932(P)	750,000	1.25	3.50	8.00	22.50	—
1951(P)	1,500,000	BV	1.25	3.00	8.00	—
1952	2,500,000	BV	1.25	2.50	7.00	—
1958	2,000,000	BV	1.25	2.00	6.00	—

KM# 79 20 CENTAVOS **Composition:** Copper-Nickel

Date	Mintage	F	VF	XF	Unc	BU
1967	12,000,000	—	0.10	0.35	1.00	—

KM# 81 20 CENTAVOS **Composition:** Copper-Nickel **Note:** Different style lettering.

Date	Mintage	F	VF	XF	Unc	BU
1973	15,000,000	—	0.10	0.20	0.60	—

KM# 83.1 20 CENTAVOS **Composition:** Copper-Nickel **Obverse:** National arms **Reverse:** Lempira brave

Date	Mintage	F	VF	XF	Unc	BU
1978	30,000,000	—	0.10	0.20	0.60	—
1990	—	—	0.10	0.20	0.60	—

KM# 83.1a 20 CENTAVOS **Composition:** Nickel Plated Steel **Obverse:** Small arms and legend, with clouds behind pyramids

Date	F	VF	XF	Unc	BU
1991	—	0.10	0.20	0.60	—
1993	—	0.10	0.20	0.60	—
1994	—	0.10	0.20	0.60	—

KM# 83.2a 20 CENTAVOS **Composition:** Nickel Plated Steel **Obverse:** Without clouds

Date	F	VF	XF	Unc	BU
1995	—	0.10	0.20	0.60	—
1996	—	0.10	0.20	0.60	—
1999	—	0.10	0.20	0.60	—

KM# 74 50 CENTAVOS **Weight:** 6.2500 g. **Composition:** 0.9000 Silver .1808 oz. ASW **Reverse:** Chief of the Lempira

Date	Mintage	F	VF	XF	Unc	BU
1931(P)	500,000	1.50	4.50	10.00	35.00	—
1932(P)	1,100,000	1.00	3.00	7.00	30.00	—
1937(P)	1,000,000	1.00	3.00	7.00	30.00	—
1951(P)	500,000	1.00	2.50	5.00	25.00	—

KM# 80 50 CENTAVOS **Composition:** Copper-Nickel

Date	Mintage	F	VF	XF	Unc	BU
1967	4,800,000	—	0.25	0.35	1.25	—

KM# 82 50 CENTAVOS **Composition:** Copper-Nickel **Series:** F.A.O. **Obverse:** National arms **Reverse:** Lempira brave

Date	Mintage	F	VF	XF	Unc	BU
1973	4,400,000	—	0.25	0.35	1.25	—

KM# 84 50 CENTAVOS **Composition:** Copper-Nickel **Obverse:** With clouds behind pyramids

Date	Mintage	F	VF	XF	Unc	BU
1978	12,000,000	—	0.25	0.35	1.00	—
1990	—	—	0.25	0.35	1.00	—

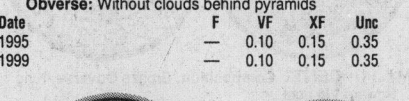

KM# 84.a1 50 CENTAVOS **Composition:** Nickel Plated Steel

Date	F	VF	XF	Unc	BU
1991	—	0.25	0.35	1.00	—
1994	—	0.25	0.35	1.00	—

KM# 88 50 CENTAVOS **Composition:** Nickel-Plated Steel **Subject:** 50th Anniversary F.A.O. **Obverse:** National arms **Reverse:** Lempira brave

Date	Mintage	F	VF	XF	Unc	BU
1994	2,000,000	—	—	—	1.50	—

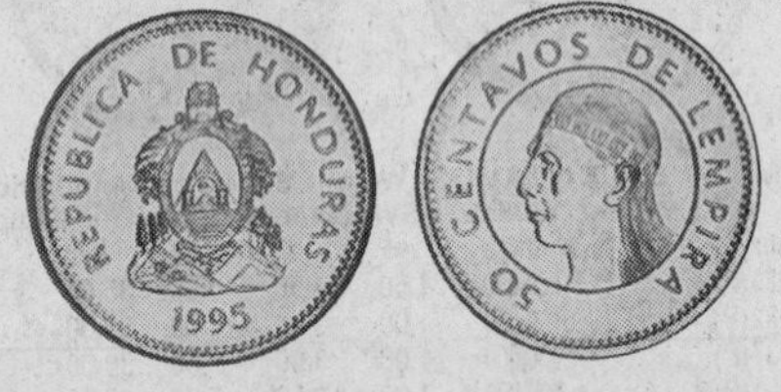

KM# 84.a2 50 CENTAVOS **Composition:** Nickel Plated Steel **Obverse:** No clouds behind pyramid in arms

Date	F	VF	XF	Unc	BU
1995	—	0.25	0.35	1.00	—
1996	—	0.25	0.35	1.00	—

KM# 75 LEMPIRA **Weight:** 12.5000 g. **Composition:** 0.9000 Silver .3617 oz. ASW **Reverse:** Chief of the Lempira

Date	Mintage	F	VF	XF	Unc	BU
1931(P)	550,000	2.50	7.50	15.00	65.00	—
1932(P)	1,000,000	2.00	6.00	12.50	55.00	—
1933(P)	400,000	BV	4.00	8.00	35.00	—
1934(P)	600,000	BV	4.00	8.00	30.00	—
1935(P)	1,000,000	—	BV	7.00	30.00	—
1937(P)	4,000,000	—	BV	6.00	22.50	—

KM# 89 LEMPIRA **Weight:** 33.6250 g. **Composition:** 0.9250 Silver 1.0000 oz. ASW **Subject:** Central Bank's 50th Anniversary **Obverse:** National arms **Reverse:** Bank building **Edge:** Plain **Size:** 38 mm.

Date	Mintage	F	VF	XF	Unc	BU
ND(2000) Proof	3,000	Value: 25.00				

KM# 90 LEMPIRA **Weight:** 7.7750 g. **Composition:** 0.9990 Gold .2497 oz. AGW **Subject:** Central Bank's 50th Anniversary **Obverse:** National arms **Reverse:** Bank building **Edge:** Reeded **Size:** 24 mm.

Date	Mintage	F	VF	XF	Unc	BU
ND(2000) Proof	1,200	Value: 150				

KM# 85 100 LEMPIRAS **Weight:** 27.0000 g. **Composition:** 0.9250 Silver .8030 oz. ASW **Subject:** 500th Anniversary - Discovery of America **Reverse:** Ship approaching curved wall

Date	Mintage	F	VF	XF	Unc	BU
1992 Proof	5,000,000	Value: 60.00				

KM# 86 200 LEMPIRAS **Weight:** 6.5000 g. **Composition:** 0.9000 Gold .1881 oz. AGW **Subject:** Bicentenary of Birth - Gen. Francisco Morazan

Date	Mintage	F	VF	XF	Unc	BU
1992 Proof	1,500,000	Value: 150				

KM# 87 500 LEMPIRAS **Weight:** 12.5000 g. **Composition:** 0.9000 Gold .3617 oz. AGW **Subject:** Bicentenary of Birth - Gen. Francisco Morazan

Date	Mintage	F	VF	XF	Unc	BU
1992	1,500,000	Value: 240				

PATTERNS

Including off metal strikes

Rosettes separate legends on Pn1-Pn5a.

KM#	Date	Mintage	Identification	Mkt Val
Pn22	1909	—	Centavo. Copper.	150
Pn23	1919	—	Peso. Copper. KM#56.	100

HONG KONG

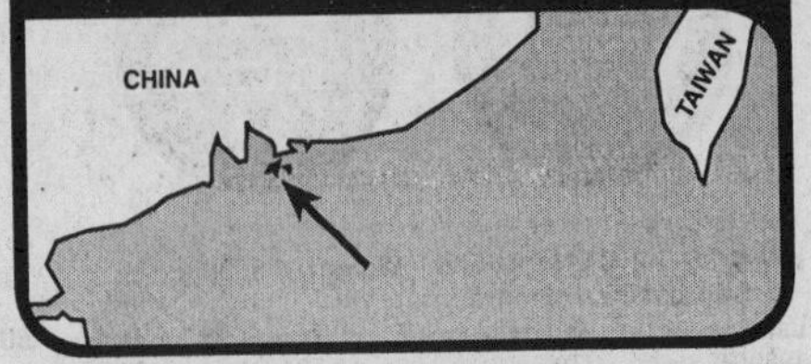

Hong Kong, a former British colony, reverted to control of the People's Republic of China on July 1, 1997 as a Special Administrative Region. It is situated at the mouth of the Canton or Pearl River 90 miles (145 km.) southeast of Canton, has an area of 403 sq. mi. (1,040 sq. km.) and an estimated population of 6.3 million. Capital: Victoria. The free port of Hong Kong, the commercial center of the Far East, is a trans-shipment point for goods destined for China and the countries of the Pacific Rim. Light manufacturing and tourism are important components of the economy.

Long a haven for fishermen-pirates and opium smugglers, the island of Hong Kong was ceded to Britain at the conclusion of the first Opium War, 1839-1842. At the time, the acquisition of a 'barren rock' was ridiculed by both London and English merchants operating in the Far East. The Kowloon Peninsula and Stonecutter's Island were ceded in 1860, and the so-called New Territories, comprising most of the mainland of the colony, were leased to Britain for 99 years in 1898.

The legends on Hong Kong coinage are bilingual: English and Chinese. The rare 1941 cent was dispatched to Hong Kong in several shipments. One fell into Japanese hands, while another was melted down by the British and a third was sunk during enemy action.

RULERS

British 1842-1997

MINT MARKS

H - Heaton

KN - King's Norton

MONETARY SYSTEM

10 Mils (Wen, Ch'ien) = 1 Cent (Hsien)

10 Cents = 1 Chiao

100 Cents = 10 Chiao = 1 Dollar (Yuan)

BRITISH COLONY

DECIMAL COINAGE

KM# 4.3 CENT **Composition:** Bronze **Obverse:** Five pearls in center of crown

Date	Mintage	F	VF	XF	Unc	BU
1901	5,000,000	2.50	5.50	16.00	70.00	—
1901H	10,000,000	2.50	5.50	16.00	60.00	—

KM# 11 CENT **Composition:** Bronze **Obverse:** King Edward VIII right

Date	Mintage	F	VF	XF	Unc	BU
1902	5,000,000	2.50	4.50	15.00	40.00	—
1903	5,000,000	2.50	4.50	15.00	40.00	—
1904H	10,000,000	1.75	3.50	12.00	32.00	—
1905	2,500,000	3.75	7.50	20.00	55.00	—
1905H	12,500,000	2.50	4.50	15.00	40.00	—

KM# 16 CENT **Composition:** Bronze **Obverse:** King George V left

Date	Mintage	F	VF	XF	Unc	BU
1919	2,500,000	2.00	4.00	14.00	40.00	—
1923	2,500,000	1.50	3.00	10.00	28.00	—
1924	5,000,000	1.25	2.50	5.50	20.00	—
1925	2,500,000	1.25	2.50	5.50	20.00	—
1926	2,500,000	1.25	2.50	5.50	20.00	—
1926 Proof	—	Value: 350				

KM# 17 CENT **Composition:** Bronze **Obverse:** King George V left

Date	Mintage	F	VF	XF	Unc	BU
1931	5,000,000	0.75	1.00	2.00	5.50	—
1931 Proof	—	Value: 250				
1933	6,500,000	0.75	1.00	2.00	5.50	—
1933 Proof	—	Value: 250				
1934	5,000,000	0.75	1.00	2.00	5.50	—
1934 Proof	—	Value: 250				

KM# 24 CENT **Composition:** Bronze **Obverse:** King George VI left

Date	Mintage	F	VF	XF	Unc	BU
1941	5,000,000	750	1,500	3,250	5,750	—
1941 Proof	—	Value: 8,500				

KM# 5 5 CENTS **Weight:** 1.3577 g. **Composition:** 0.8000 Silver .0349 oz. ASW **Obverse:** Queen Victoria left **Note:** Coins dated 1866-1868 struck at the Hong Kong Mint; coins dated 1872-1901 struck at the British Royal Mint.

Date	Mintage	F	VF	XF	Unc	BU
1901	10,000,000	1.00	2.50	5.00	15.00	—

KM# 12 5 CENTS **Weight:** 1.3577 g. **Composition:** 0.8000 Silver .0349 oz. ASW **Obverse:** King Edward VII right

Date	Mintage	F	VF	XF	Unc	BU
1903	6,000,000	1.00	2.00	4.00	12.50	—
1903 Proof	—	Value: 225				
1904	8,000,000	1.00	2.00	4.00	12.50	—
1904 Proof	—	Value: 200				
1905	1,000,000	1.25	3.00	6.50	17.50	—
1905H	7,000,000	1.00	2.00	4.00	12.50	—

KM# 18 5 CENTS **Weight:** 1.3577 g. **Composition:** 0.8000 Silver .0349 oz. ASW **Obverse:** King George V left

Date	Mintage	F	VF	XF	Unc	BU
1932	3,000,000	1.00	1.50	2.50	6.50	—
1932 Proof	—	Value: 165				
1933	2,000,000	1.00	1.50	2.75	7.50	—
1933 Proof	—	Value: 165				

KM# 18a 5 CENTS **Composition:** Copper-Nickel **Obverse:** King George V left

Date	Mintage	F	VF	XF	Unc	BU
1935	1,000,000	1.00	2.00	4.50	16.50	—
1935 Proof	—	Value: 115				

KM# 20 5 CENTS **Composition:** Nickel

Date	Mintage	F	VF	XF	Unc	BU
1937	3,000,000	0.75	1.25	2.25	7.50	—
1937 Proof	—	Value: 85.00				

KM# 22 5 CENTS **Composition:** Nickel **Obverse:** King George VI left

Date	Mintage	F	VF	XF	Unc	BU
1938	3,000,000	0.50	1.00	2.00	6.50	—
1938 Proof	—	Value: 125				
1939H	3,090,000	0.50	1.00	2.00	6.50	—
1939H Proof	—	Value: 125				
1939KN	4,710,000	0.50	1.00	2.00	6.50	—
1941H	777,000	350	750	1,400	2,850	—
1941KN	1,075,000	100	175	350	700	—

KM# 26 5 CENTS **Composition:** Nickel-Brass **Obverse:** King George left

Date	Mintage	F	VF	XF	Unc	BU
1949	15,000,000	0.25	0.50	1.25	7.50	—
1949 Proof	—	Value: 125				
1950	20,400,000	0.25	0.50	1.25	7.50	—
1950 Proof	—	Value: 125				

KM# 29.1 5 CENTS **Composition:** Nickel-Brass **Obverse:** Queen Elizabeth II right **Edge:** Reeded and security

Date	Mintage	F	VF	XF	Unc	BU
1958H	5,000,000	—	0.25	0.75	4.50	—
1960	5,000,000	—	0.15	0.50	3.50	—
1960 Proof	—	Value: 65.00				
1963	7,000,000	—	0.15	0.50	3.50	—
1963 Proof	—	Value: 65.00				
1964	—	16.00	35.00	90.00	225	—
1965	18,000,000	—	0.10	0.40	2.00	—
1965H	6,000,000	—	0.10	0.40	2.00	—
1967	10,000,000	—	0.10	0.40	2.00	—

KM# 29.2 5 CENTS **Composition:** Nickel-Brass **Obverse:** Queen Elizabeth II right **Edge:** Reeded without security **Note:** Error.

Date		F	VF	XF	Unc	BU
1958H		2.50	5.00	9.00	20.00	—
1960		2.50	5.00	9.00	20.00	—

KM# 29.3 5 CENTS **Composition:** Nickel-Brass **Obverse:** Queen Elizabeth II right **Edge:** Reeded

Date	Mintage	F	VF	XF	Unc	BU
1971KN	14,000,000	—	—	0.25	0.50	—
1971H	6,000,000	—	—	0.25	0.50	—
1972H	14,000,000	—	—	0.25	0.50	—
1977	6,000,000	—	—	0.25	0.50	—
1978	10,000,000	—	—	0.25	0.50	—
1979	4,000,000	—	—	0.25	0.50	—

KM# 61 5 CENTS **Composition:** Nickel-Brass **Obverse:** Queen Elizabeth II right **Reverse:** Legend around inscription

Date	Mintage	F	VF	XF	Unc	BU
1988	50,000	—	—	—	4.00	—
1988 Proof	25,000	Value: 5.00				

KM# 6.3 10 CENTS **Weight:** 2.7154 g. **Composition:** 0.8000 Silver .0698 oz. ASW **Obverse:** Queen Victoria left **Note:** Coins dated 1866-1868 struck at the Hong Kong Mint; coins dated 1869-1901 struck at the British Royal Mint.

Date	Mintage	F	VF	XF	Unc	BU
1901	25,000,000	1.00	2.00	4.00	18.50	—

KM# 13 10 CENTS **Weight:** 2.7154 g. **Composition:** 0.8000 Silver .0698 oz. ASW **Obverse:** King Edward right

Date	Mintage	F	VF	XF	Unc	BU
1902	18,000,000	1.00	2.00	4.00	16.50	—
1902 Proof	—	Value: 200				
1903	25,000,000	1.00	2.00	4.00	16.50	—
1903 Proof	—	Value: 200				
1904	30,000,000	1.00	2.00	4.00	16.50	—
1904 Proof	—	Value: 165				
1905	33,487,000	225	400	650	1,500	—
1905 Proof	—	Value: 1,750				

KM# 19 10 CENTS **Composition:** Copper-Nickel **Obverse:** King George V left

Date	Mintage	F	VF	XF	Unc	BU
1935	10,000,000	0.50	1.00	3.50	15.00	—
1935 Proof	—	Value: 75.00				
1936	5,000,000	0.50	1.00	3.50	15.00	—
1936 Proof	—	Value: 75.00				

KM# 21 10 CENTS **Composition:** Nickel **Obverse:** King George left

Date	Mintage	F	VF	XF	Unc	BU
1937	17,500,000	0.50	0.80	1.50	6.50	—
1937 Proof	—	Value: 85.00				

KM# 23 10 CENTS **Composition:** Nickel **Obverse:** King George VI left

Date	Mintage	F	VF	XF	Unc	BU
1938	7,500,000	0.65	1.00	2.25	7.50	—
1938 Proof	—	Value: 85.00				
1939H	5,000,000	0.65	1.00	2.25	7.50	—
1939KN	5,000,000	0.65	1.00	2.25	7.50	—
1939KN Proof	—	Value: 85.00				

KM# 25 10 CENTS **Composition:** Nickel-Brass **Obverse:** King George left **Edge:** Reeded and security

Date	Mintage	F	VF	XF	Unc	BU
1948	30,000,000	0.25	0.50	1.25	6.50	—
1948 Proof	—	Value: 65.00				
1949	35,000,000	0.25	0.50	1.25	6.50	—
1949 Proof	—	Value: 65.00				
1950	20,000,000	0.25	0.50	1.25	6.50	—
1950 Proof	—	Value: 65.00				
1951	5,000,000	0.50	1.00	3.00	22.50	—
1951 Proof	—	Value: 85.00				

KM# 25a 10 CENTS **Composition:** Nickel-Brass **Edge:** Reeded without security **Note:** Error.

Date		F	VF	XF	Unc	BU
1950		3.50	6.50	12.50	25.00	—

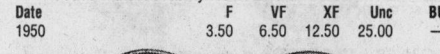

KM# 28.1 10 CENTS **Composition:** Nickel-Brass **Obverse:** Queen Elizabeth II right **Edge:** Reeded with security

Date	Mintage	F	VF	XF	Unc	BU
1955	10,000,000	0.15	0.25	0.50	5.50	—
1955 Proof	—	Value: 50.00				
1956	3,110,000	0.25	0.50	1.25	15.00	—
1956 Proof	—	Value: 50.00				
1956H	4,488,000	0.15	0.25	1.00	10.00	—
1956KN	2,500,000	0.25	0.50	2.00	16.50	—
1957H	5,250,000	0.15	0.25	0.50	10.00	—
1957KN	2,800,000	0.15	0.25	1.00	15.00	—
1958KN	10,000,000	0.15	0.25	0.50	10.00	—
1959H	20,000,000	0.10	0.15	0.25	6.00	—
1960	12,500,000	0.10	0.15	0.25	6.00	—
1960 Proof	—	Value: 50.00				
1960H	10,000,000	0.10	0.15	0.25	6.00	—
1961	20,000,000	0.10	0.15	0.25	4.00	—
1961 Proof	—	Value: 50.00				
1961H	5,000,000	0.15	0.25	0.50	5.00	—
1961KN	5,000,000	0.15	0.25	0.50	5.00	—
1963	27,000,000	0.10	0.15	0.25	4.00	—
1963 Proof	—	Value: 50.00				
1963H	3,000,000	0.20	0.30	0.50	4.00	—
1963KN	Inc. above	0.10	0.15	0.25	3.50	—
1964	9,000,000	0.10	0.15	0.25	2.00	—
1964H	21,000,000	0.10	0.15	0.25	2.00	—
1965	40,000,000	0.10	0.15	0.25	2.00	—
1965H	8,000,000	0.10	0.15	0.25	2.50	—
1965KN	Inc. above	0.10	0.15	0.25	2.50	—
1967	10,000,000	0.10	0.15	0.25	2.00	—
1968H	15,000,000	0.10	0.15	0.25	2.00	—

KM# 28.2 10 CENTS Composition: Nickel-Brass **Edge:** Reeded without security **Note:** Error.

Date	F	VF	XF	Unc	BU
1956	2.25	4.50	8.50	25.00	—
1963	2.25	4.50	8.50	25.00	—

KM# 28.3 10 CENTS Composition: Nickel-Brass **Edge:** Reeded

Date	Mintage	F	VF	XF	Unc	BU
1971H	22,000,000	—	0.10	0.15	0.65	—
1972KN	20,000,000	—	0.10	0.15	0.65	—
1973	2,250,000	0.15	0.25	0.65	3.50	—
1974	4,600,000	—	0.10	0.15	0.65	—
1975	44,840,000	—	0.10	0.15	0.65	—
1978	57,500,000	—	0.10	0.15	0.65	—
1979	101,500,000	—	0.10	0.15	0.65	—
1980	24,000,000	—	7.00	15.00	35.00	—

Note: Few pieces were released for circulation in 1980, but large numbers have found their way onto the market in subsequent years. About 3,500 are known to exist.

KM# 49 10 CENTS Composition: Nickel-Brass

Date	Mintage	F	VF	XF	Unc	BU
1982	—	—	0.10	0.15	0.25	—
1983	110,016,000	—	0.10	0.15	0.25	—
1984	30,016,000	—	0.10	0.15	0.25	—

KM# 55 10 CENTS Composition: Nickel-Brass

Date	Mintage	F	VF	XF	Unc	BU
1985	34,016,000	—	0.10	0.15	0.25	—
1986	40,000,000	—	0.10	0.15	0.25	—
1987	—	—	0.10	0.15	0.25	—
1988	30,000,000	—	0.10	0.15	0.25	—
1988 Proof	20,000	Value: 5.00				
1989	40,000,000	—	0.10	0.15	0.25	—
1990	—	—	0.10	0.15	0.25	—
1991	—	—	0.10	0.15	0.25	—
1992	24,000,000	—	0.10	0.15	0.25	—

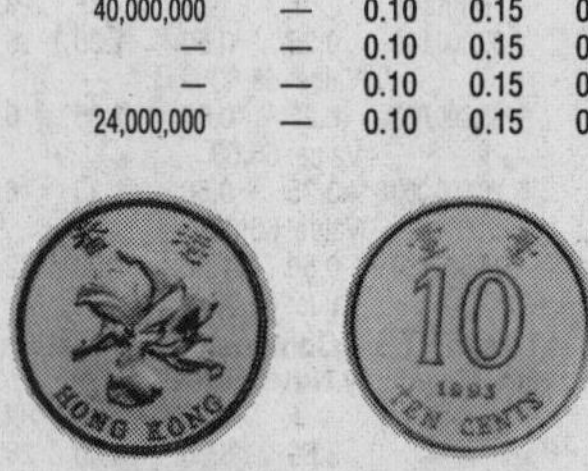

KM# 66 10 CENTS Composition: Brass Plated Steel **Obverse:** Bauhinia flower

Date	F	VF	XF	Unc	BU
1993	—	0.10	0.15	0.30	—
1993 Proof	— Value: 2.50				
1994	—	0.10	0.15	0.30	—
1995	—	0.10	0.15	0.30	—
1996	—	0.10	0.15	0.30	—
1997	—	0.10	0.15	0.30	—
1998	—	0.10	0.15	0.30	—

KM# 14 20 CENTS Weight: 5.4308 g. **Composition:** 0.8000 Silver .1397 oz. ASW

Date	Mintage	F	VF	XF	Unc	BU
1902	250,000	20.00	40.00	90.00	250	—
1902 Proof	—	Value: 1,200				
1904	250,000	20.00	40.00	90.00	250	—
1905	750,000	300	600	1,200	1,850	—
1905 Proof	—	Value: 3,000				

KM# 36 20 CENTS Composition: Nickel-Brass **Shape:** Scalloped

Date	Mintage	F	VF	XF	Unc	BU
1975	71,000,000	—	0.10	0.20	0.35	—
1976	42,000,000	—	0.10	0.20	0.35	—
1977	Inc. above	—	0.10	0.20	0.35	—
1978	86,000,000	—	0.10	0.20	0.35	—
1979	94,500,000	—	0.10	0.20	0.35	—
1980	65,000,000	—	0.10	0.20	0.35	—
1982	30,000,000	—	0.10	0.20	0.35	—
1983	15,000,000	—	0.10	0.20	0.35	—

KM# 59 20 CENTS Composition: Brass **Obverse:** Mature queen's portrait **Shape:** Scalloped

Date	Mintage	F	VF	XF	Unc	BU
1985		—	0.10	0.20	0.35	—
1988		—	0.10	0.20	0.35	—
1988 Proof	Est. 20,000	Value: 5.00				
1989		—	0.10	0.20	0.35	—
1990		—	0.10	0.20	0.35	—
1991		—	0.10	0.20	0.35	—
1992		—	0.10	0.20	0.35	—

KM# 67 20 CENTS Composition: Nickel-Brass **Obverse:** Bauhinia flower **Shape:** Scalloped

Date	F	VF	XF	Unc	BU
1993	—	0.10	0.20	0.40	—
1993 Proof	— Value: 2.50				
1994	—	0.10	0.20	0.40	—
1995	—	0.10	0.20	0.40	—
1997	—	0.10	0.20	0.40	—
1998	—	0.10	0.20	0.40	—

KM# 15 50 CENTS Weight: 13.5769 g. **Composition:** 0.8000 Silver .3492 oz. ASW

Date	Mintage	F	VF	XF	Unc	BU
1902	100,000	25.00	35.00	50.00	135	—
1902 Proof	—	Value: 650				
1904	100,000	25.00	35.00	60.00	125	—
1904 Proof	—	Value: 650				
1905	300,000	20.00	25.00	50.00	110	—
1905 Proof	—	Value: 650				

KM# 27.1 50 CENTS Composition: Copper-Nickel **Edge:** Reeded and security

Date	Mintage	F	VF	XF	Unc	BU
1951	15,000,000	1.00	2.00	3.50	12.00	—
1951 Proof	—	Value: 250				

KM# 27.2 50 CENTS Composition: Copper-Nickel **Edge:** Reeded without security **Note:** Error.

Date	F	VF	XF	Unc	BU
1951	3.00	5.00	10.00	22.00	—

KM# 30.1 50 CENTS Composition: Copper-Nickel **Edge:** Reeded and security

Date	Mintage	F	VF	XF	Unc	BU
1958H	4,000,000	—	0.50	1.25	4.50	—
1960	4,000,000	—	0.40	1.00	4.00	—
1960 Proof	—	Value: 100				
1961	6,000,000	—	0.40	1.00	3.50	—
1961 Proof	—	Value: 100				
1963H	10,000,000	—	0.40	1.00	3.50	—
1964	5,000,000	—	0.40	1.00	3.50	—
1965KN	8,000,000	—	0.40	1.00	3.50	—
1966	5,000,000	—	0.40	1.00	3.50	—
1967	12,000,000	—	0.40	1.00	3.00	—
1968H	12,000,000	—	0.40	1.00	3.00	—
1970H	4,600,000	—	0.40	1.00	3.00	—

KM# 30.2 50 CENTS Composition: Copper-Nickel **Edge:** Reeded without security **Note:** Error.

Date	F	VF	XF	Unc	BU
1958H	2.00	4.00	8.00	20.00	—

KM# 34 50 CENTS Composition: Copper-Nickel **Edge:** Reeded

Date	Mintage	F	VF	XF	Unc	BU
1971KN	—	—	0.20	0.40	1.50	—
1972	30,000,000	—	0.20	0.40	1.50	—
1973	36,800,000	—	0.20	0.40	1.50	—
1974	6,000,000	—	0.20	0.40	1.50	—
1975	8,000,000	—	0.20	0.40	1.50	—

KM# 41 50 CENTS Composition: Nickel-Brass

Date	Mintage	F	VF	XF	Unc	BU
1977	60,001,000	—	0.20	0.30	0.80	—
1978	70,000,000	—	0.20	0.30	0.80	—
1979	60,640,000	—	0.20	0.30	0.80	—
1980	120,000,000	—	0.20	0.30	0.80	—

KM# 62 50 CENTS Composition: Nickel-Brass **Obverse:** Mature queen's portrait

Date	Mintage	F	VF	XF	Unc	BU
1988	50,000	—	—	—	8.00	—
1988 Proof	25,000	Value: 10.00				
1990	27,000	—	0.20	0.30	0.80	—

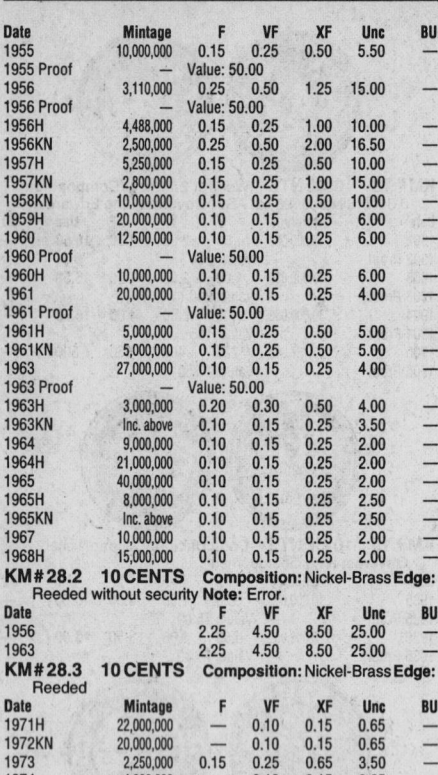

KM# 68 50 CENTS **Composition:** Brass Plated Steel **Obverse:** Bauhinia flower

Date	F	VF	XF	Unc	BU
1993	—	0.20	0.30	0.80	—
1993 Proof	—	Value: 5.50			
1994	—	0.20	0.30	0.80	—
1995	—	0.20	0.30	0.80	—
1997	—	0.20	0.30	0.80	—

KM# 31.1 DOLLAR **Composition:** Copper-Nickel **Reverse:** Mint mark is below "LL" of "DOLLAR"

Date	Mintage	F	VF	XF	Unc	BU
1960H	40,000,000	—	0.60	1.75	5.50	—
1960H Proof	—	Value: 3,350				
1960KN	40,000,000	—	0.60	1.75	5.50	—
1970H	15,000,000	—	0.60	1.25	4.50	—

KM# 31.2 DOLLAR **Composition:** Copper-Nickel **Reverse:** Mint mark is below "LL" of "DOLLAR" **Edge:** Reeded without security **Note:** Error.

Date	F	VF	XF	Unc	BU
1960H	4.00	7.00	15.00	30.00	—

KM# 35 DOLLAR **Composition:** Copper-Nickel **Edge:** Reeded

Date	Mintage	F	VF	XF	Unc	BU
1971H	8,000,000	—	0.60	1.25	4.50	—
1972	20,000,000	—	0.60	1.25	3.50	—
1973	8,125,000	—	0.60	1.25	4.50	—
1974	26,000,000	—	0.60	1.25	3.50	—
1975	22,500,000	—	0.60	1.25	3.50	—

KM# 43 DOLLAR **Composition:** Copper-Nickel

Date	Mintage	F	VF	XF	Unc	BU
1978	120,000,000	—	0.40	0.70	1.50	—
1979	104,908,000	—	0.40	0.70	1.50	—
1980	100,000,000	—	0.40	0.70	1.50	—

KM# 63 DOLLAR **Composition:** Copper-Nickel **Obverse:** Mature queen's portrait **Reverse:** Lion within legend

Date	Mintage	F	VF	XF	Unc	BU
1987	—	—	0.30	0.50	1.00	—
1988	20,000,000	—	0.30	0.50	1.00	—
1988 Proof	20,000	Value: 20.00				
1989	20,000,000	—	0.30	0.50	1.00	—
1990	—	—	0.30	0.50	1.00	—
1991	—	—	0.30	0.50	1.00	—
1992	25,000,000	—	0.30	0.50	1.00	—

KM# 69 DOLLAR **Composition:** Nickel Plated Steel **Obverse:** Bauhinia flower

Date	F	VF	XF	Unc	BU
1993	—	0.30	0.50	1.00	—
1993 Proof	—	Value: 10.00			

KM# 69a DOLLAR **Composition:** Copper-Nickel **Obverse:** Bauhinia flower

Date	F	VF	XF	Unc	BU
1994	—	0.30	0.50	1.00	—
1995	—	0.30	0.50	1.00	—
1996	—	0.30	0.50	1.00	—
1997	—	0.30	0.50	1.00	—
1998	—	0.30	0.50	1.00	—

KM# 37 2 DOLLARS **Composition:** Copper-Nickel **Shape:** Scalloped

Date	Mintage	F	VF	XF	Unc	BU
1975	60,000,000	—	0.45	0.85	1.75	—
1978	504,000	—	0.45	1.00	10.00	—
1979	9,032,000	—	0.45	0.85	1.75	—
1980	30,000,000	—	0.45	0.85	1.75	—
1981	30,000,000	—	0.45	0.85	1.75	—
1982	30,000,000	—	0.45	0.85	1.75	—
1983	7,002,000	—	0.45	0.85	1.75	—
1984	22,002,000	—	0.45	0.85	1.75	—

KM# 60 2 DOLLARS **Composition:** Copper-Nickel **Obverse:** Mature queen's portrait **Shape:** Scalloped

Date	Mintage	F	VF	XF	Unc	BU
1985	10,002,000	—	0.45	0.65	1.25	—
1986	15,000,000	—	0.45	0.65	1.25	—
1987	—	—	0.45	0.65	1.25	—
1988	5,000,000	—	0.45	0.65	1.25	—
1988 Proof	20,000	Value: 35.00				
1989	33,000,000	—	0.45	0.65	1.25	—
1990	—	—	0.45	0.65	1.25	—
1991	—	—	0.45	0.65	1.25	—
1992	4,370,000	—	0.45	0.65	1.25	—

KM# 64 2 DOLLARS **Composition:** Copper-Nickel **Obverse:** Bauhinia flower **Shape:** Scalloped

Date	F	VF	XF	Unc	BU
1993	—	0.45	0.65	1.25	—
1993 Proof	—	Value: 12.50			
1994	—	0.45	0.65	1.25	—
1995	—	0.45	0.65	1.25	—
1997	—	0.45	0.65	1.25	—

KM# 39 5 DOLLARS **Composition:** Copper-Nickel **Shape:** 10-sided

Date	Mintage	F	VF	XF	Unc	BU
1976	30,000,000	—	1.00	1.50	2.50	—
1978	10,000,000	—	1.00	1.50	3.00	—
1979	12,000,000	—	1.00	1.50	2.50	—

KM# 46 5 DOLLARS **Composition:** Copper-Nickel

Date	Mintage	F	VF	XF	Unc	BU
1980	40,000,000	—	1.00	1.50	2.50	—
1981	20,000,000	—	1.00	1.50	2.50	—
1982	10,000,000	—	1.00	1.50	2.50	—
1983	4,000,000	—	1.00	1.50	2.50	—
1984	4,500,000	—	1.00	1.50	2.50	—

KM# 56 5 DOLLARS **Composition:** Copper-Nickel

Date	Mintage	F	VF	XF	Unc	BU
1985	6,000,000	—	0.75	1.25	2.25	—
1986	8,000,000	—	0.75	1.25	2.25	—
1987	—	—	0.75	1.25	2.25	—
1988	16,000,000	—	0.75	1.25	2.25	—
1988 Proof	25,000	Value: 45.00				
1989	37,000,000	—	0.75	1.25	2.25	—
1991	—	—	0.75	1.25	2.25	—

KM# 65 5 DOLLARS **Composition:** Copper-Nickel **Obverse:** Bauhinia flower

Date	F	VF	XF	Unc	BU
1993	—	0.75	1.25	2.25	—
1993 Proof	—	Value: 20.00			
1994	—	0.75	1.25	2.25	—
1995	—	0.75	1.25	2.25	—
1997	—	0.75	1.25	2.25	—

KM# 70 10 DOLLARS **Ring Composition:** Copper Nickel **Center Composition:** Nickel-Brass **Obverse:** Bauhinia flower **Reverse:** Shou character

Date	Mintage	F	VF	XF	Unc	BU
1993	—	—	2.50	4.50	10.00	—
1993 Proof	Est. 30,000	Value: 20.00				
1994	—	—	1.50	2.50	5.00	—
1995	—	—	1.50	2.50	5.00	—

KM# 70a 10 DOLLARS **Ring Composition:** 0.3750 Gold **Center Weight:** 18.3000 g. **Center Composition:** 0.9170 Gold .3826 oz. AGW **Obverse:** Bauhinia flower **Reverse:** Shou character

Date	Mintage	F	VF	XF	Unc	BU
1994 Proof	20,000	Value: 200				

KM# 38 1000 DOLLARS **Weight:** 15.9700 g. **Composition:** 0.9170 Gold .4708 oz. AGW **Subject:** Visit of Queen Elizabeth

Date	Mintage	F	VF	XF	Unc	BU
1975	15,000	—	—	—	275	325
1975 Proof	5,005	Value: 1,150				

KM# 40 1000 DOLLARS **Weight:** 15.9700 g. **Composition:** 0.9170 Gold .4708 oz. AGW **Subject:** Year of the Dragon

Date	Mintage	F	VF	XF	Unc	BU
1976	20,000	—	—	—	465	500
1976 Proof	6,911	Value: 1,000				

KM# 42 1000 DOLLARS **Weight:** 15.9700 g. **Composition:** 0.9170 Gold .4708 oz. AGW **Subject:** Year of the Snake

Date	Mintage	F	VF	XF	Unc	BU
1977	20,000	—	—	—	285	365
1977 Proof	10,000	Value: 500				

KM# 44 1000 DOLLARS **Weight:** 15.9700 g. **Composition:** 0.9170 Gold .4708 oz. AGW **Subject:** Year of the Horse

Date	Mintage	F	VF	XF	Unc	BU
1978	20,000	—	—	—	250	300
1978 Proof	10,000	Value: 450				

KM# 45 1000 DOLLARS **Weight:** 15.9700 g. **Composition:** 0.9170 Gold .4708 oz. AGW **Subject:** Year of the Goat

Date	Mintage	F	VF	XF	Unc	BU
1979	30,000	—	—	—	225	275
1979 Proof	15,000	Value: 320				

KM# 47 1000 DOLLARS **Weight:** 15.9700 g. **Composition:** 0.9170 Gold .4708 oz. AGW **Subject:** Year of the Monkey

Date	Mintage	F	VF	XF	Unc	BU
1980	31,000	—	—	—	220	275
1980 Proof	18,000	Value: 300				

KM# 48 1000 DOLLARS **Weight:** 15.9700 g. **Composition:** 0.9170 Gold .4708 oz. AGW **Subject:** Year of the Cockerel

Date	Mintage	F	VF	XF	Unc	BU
1981	33,000	—	—	—	220	275
1981 Proof	22,000	Value: 300				

KM# 50 1000 DOLLARS **Weight:** 15.9700 g. **Composition:** 0.9170 Gold .4708 oz. AGW **Subject:** Year of the Dog

Date	Mintage	F	VF	XF	Unc	BU
1982	33,000	—	—	—	215	265
1982 Proof	22,000	Value: 320				

KM# 51 1000 DOLLARS **Weight:** 15.9700 g. **Composition:** 0.9170 Gold .4708 oz. AGW **Subject:** Year of the Pig

Date	Mintage	F	VF	XF	Unc	BU
1983	33,000	—	—	—	400	475
1983 Proof	22,000	Value: 675				

KM# 52 1000 DOLLARS **Weight:** 15.9700 g. **Composition:** 0.9170 Gold .4708 oz. AGW **Subject:** Year of the Rat

Date	Mintage	F	VF	XF	Unc	BU
1984	20,000	—	—	—	325	400
1984 Proof	10,000	Value: 550				

KM# 53 1000 DOLLARS **Weight:** 15.9700 g. **Composition:** 0.9170 Gold .4708 oz. AGW **Subject:** Year of the Ox

Date	Mintage	F	VF	XF	Unc	BU
1985	30,000	—	—	—	325	400
1985 Proof	10,000	Value: 550				

KM# 54 1000 DOLLARS **Weight:** 15.9700 g. **Composition:** 0.9170 Gold .4708 oz. AGW **Subject:** Year of the Tiger

Date	Mintage	F	VF	XF	Unc	BU
1986	20,000	—	—	—	275	325
1986 Proof	10,000	Value: 500				

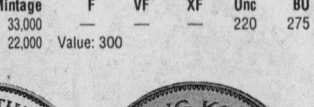

KM# 57 1000 DOLLARS **Weight:** 15.9700 g. **Composition:** 0.9170 Gold .4708 oz. AGW **Subject:** Royal visit of Queen Elizabeth II

Date	Mintage	F	VF	XF	Unc	BU
1986	20,000	—	—	—	235	285
1986 Proof	12,000	Value: 350				

KM# 58 1000 DOLLARS **Weight:** 15.9700 g. **Composition:** 0.9170 Gold .4708 oz. AGW **Subject:** Year of the Rabbit

Date	Mintage	F	VF	XF	Unc	BU
1987	20,000	—	—	—	235	285
1987 Proof	12,000	Value: 350				

HONG KONG S.A.R.

DECIMAL COINAGE

KM# 72 10 CENTS **Composition:** Brass Plated Steel **Obverse:** Bauhinia flower **Reverse:** Sailing junk

Date	Mintage	F	VF	XF	Unc	BU
1997	—	0.15	0.15	0.30	—	
1997 Proof	Est. 97,000	Value: 1.50				

KM# 73 20 CENTS **Composition:** Nickel-Brass **Obverse:** Bauhinia flower **Reverse:** Butterfly kites

Date	F	VF	XF	Unc	BU
1997	—	0.10	0.20	0.40	—
1997 Proof	—	Value: 1.50			
1998	—	0.10	0.20	0.40	—

KM# 74 50 CENTS Composition: Brass Plated Steel **Obverse:** Bauhinia flower **Reverse:** Ox

Date	Mintage	F	VF	XF	Unc	BU
1997		—	0.20	0.30	0.80	—
1997 Proof	Est. 97,000	Value: 2.50				
1998		—	0.20	0.30	0.80	—

KM# 75 DOLLAR Composition: Copper-Nickel **Obverse:** Bauhinia flower **Reverse:** Chinese unicorn

Date	F	VF	XF	Unc	BU
1997	—	0.30	0.50	1.00	—
1997 Proof	—	Value: 5.50			

KM# 76 2 DOLLARS Composition: Copper-Nickel **Obverse:** Bauhinia flower **Reverse:** Ho Ho brothers

Date	Mintage	F	VF	XF	Unc	BU
1997		—	0.45	0.65	1.25	—
1997 Proof	Est. 97,000	Value: 8.00				

KM# 77 5 DOLLARS Composition: Copper-Nickel **Obverse:** Bauhinia flower **Reverse:** Shou character

Date	Mintage	F	VF	XF	Unc	BU
1997		—	0.75	1.25	2.25	—
1997 Proof	Est. 97,000	Value: 12.50				

KM# 78 10 DOLLARS Ring Composition: Copper Nickel **Center Composition:** Nickel-Brass **Obverse:** Bauhinia flower **Reverse:** Suspension bridge

Date	Mintage	F	VF	XF	Unc	BU
1997		—	1.75	3.50	6.50	—
1997 Proof	Est. 97,000	Value: 13.50				

KM# 71 1000 DOLLARS Weight: 15.9700 g. **Composition:** 0.9170 Gold .4708 oz. AGW **Subject:** Return of Hong Kong to China

Date	Mintage	F	VF	XF	Unc	BU
1997 Proof	97,000	Value: 300				

KM# 79 1000 DOLLARS Weight: 15.9700 g. **Composition:** 0.9170 Gold .4708 oz. AGW **Subject:** Hong Kong International Airport

Date	Mintage	F	VF	XF	Unc	BU
1998 Proof	15,000	Value: 450				

MINT SETS

KM#	Date	Mintage	Identification	Issue Price	Mkt Val
MS1	1988 (7)	50,000	KM55-56, 59-63	13.00	65.00
MS2	1993 (7)	—	KM64-70	20.00	32.50
MS3	1997 (7)	—	KM72-78	30.00	12.50

PROOF SETS

KM#	Date	Mintage	Identification	Issue Price	Mkt Val
PS4	1988 (7)	25,000	KM55-56, 59-63	39.75	125
PS5	1993 (7)	30,000	KM64-70	50.00	72.50
PS6	1997 (7)	97,000	KM72-78	—	45.00

HUNGARY

The Republic of Hungary, located in central Europe, has an area of 35,929 sq. mi. (93,030 sq. km.) and a population of 10.7 million. Capital: Budapest. The economy is based on agriculture, bauxite and a rapidly expanding industrial sector. Machinery, chemicals, iron and steel, and fruits and vegetables are exported.

The ancient kingdom of Hungary, founded by the Magyars in the 9th century, achieved its greatest extension in the mid-14th century when its dominions touched the Baltic, Black and Mediterranean Seas. After suffering repeated Turkish invasions, Hungary accepted Habsburg rule to escape Turkish occupation, regaining independence in 1867 with the Emperor of Austria as king of a dual Austro-Hungarian monarchy.

After World War I, Hungary lost 2/3 of its territory and 1/2 of its population and underwent a period of drastic political revision. The short-lived republic of 1918 was followed by a chaotic interval of communist rule, 1919, and the restoration of the monarchy in 1920 with Admiral Horthy as regent of the kingdom. Although a German ally in World War II, Hungary was occupied by German troops who imposed a pro-Nazi dictatorship, 1944. Soviet armies drove out the Germans in 1945 and assisted the communist minority in seizing power. A revised constitution published on Aug. 20, 1949, established Hungary as a People's Republic' of the Soviet type. On October 23, 1989, Hungary was pro-claimed the Republic of Hungary.

RULERS

Franz Joseph I, 1848-1916
Karl I, 1916-1918

MINT MARKS

B, K, KB - Kremnitz (Kormoczbanya)
BP - Budapest

MONETARY SYSTEM

1892-1925

100 Filler = 1 Korona

1926-1945

100 Filler = 1 Pengo

Commencing 1946

100 Filler = 1 Forint

NOTE: Many coins of Hungary through 1948, especially1925-1945, have been restruck in recent times. These may be identified by a rosette in the vicinity of the mintmark. Restrike mintages for KM#440-449, 451-458, 468-469,475-477, 480-483, 494, 496-498 are usually about 1000 pieces, later date mintages are not known.

KINGDOM

REFORM COINAGE

100 Filler = 1 Korona

KM# 480 FILLER Composition: Bronze

Date	Mintage	F	VF	XF	Unc	BU
1901KB	5,994,000	4.00	8.00	17.00	32.50	—
1902KB	16,299,000	0.20	0.50	1.25	4.00	—
1903KB	2,291,000	12.00	25.00	65.00	110	—
1906KB	61,000	65.00	120	180	275	—
1914KB	—	65.00	90.00	135	210	—
1914KB Proof	—	Value: 350				

KM# 481 2 FILLER Composition: Bronze

Date	Mintage	F	VF	XF	Unc	BU
1901KB	25,805,000	0.50	1.00	2.50	5.00	—
1902KB	6,937,000	5.50	8.50	13.50	20.00	—
1903KB	4,052,000	12.00	20.00	35.00	50.00	—
1904KB	4,203,000	6.00	12.00	25.00	40.00	—
1905KB	9,335,000	0.70	1.75	3.00	6.00	—
1906KB	3,140,000	1.75	2.50	5.00	7.50	—
1907KB	9,943,000	5.50	9.00	12.00	17.50	—
1908KB	16,486,000	0.50	1.00	2.50	5.00	—
1909KB	19,075,000	0.50	1.00	2.50	5.00	—
1910KB	5,338,000	4.50	7.50	10.00	15.00	—
1910KB Proof, restrike with rosette	—	Value: 10.00				

Date	Mintage	F	VF	XF	Unc	BU
1914KB	4,106,000	0.50	1.00	2.50	5.00	—
1915KB	1,294,000	1.50	2.00	4.00	7.00	—

KM# 497 2 FILLER **Composition:** Iron **Note:** Varieties in planchet thickness exist for 1917.

Date	F	VF	XF	Unc	BU
1916	6.00	10.00	15.00	25.00	—
1917	1.00	2.50	6.00	12.00	—
1918	2.00	4.50	9.00	15.00	—

KM# 482 10 FILLER **Composition:** Nickel **Note:** Edge varieties exist.

Date	Mintage	F	VF	XF	Unc	BU
1906KB	56,000	75.00	175	250	325	—
1908KB	6,819,000	0.25	0.50	1.50	4.00	—
1909KB	17,204,000	0.30	0.60	2.00	4.00	—
1914KB	—	175	275	550	900	—

KM# 494 10 FILLER **Composition:** Copper-Nickel-Zinc **Note:** Varieties exist.

Date	Mintage	F	VF	XF	Unc	BU
1914	4,400,000	200	300	500	900	—
1915	Inc. above	0.30	0.60	1.50	4.00	—
1915 Proof, restrike with rosette	Inc. above	Value: 4.00				
1916	Inc. above	0.50	1.25	2.50	5.00	—

KM# 496 10 FILLER **Composition:** Iron **Note:** Varieties exist.

Date	Mintage	F	VF	XF	Unc	BU
1915	11,500,000	9.00	20.00	32.50	55.00	—
1916 Rare	Inc. above	—	—	—	—	—
1918	Inc. above	15.00	30.00	55.00	85.00	—
1918 Proof, restrike	—	Value: 18.00				
1920	3,275,000	4.50	9.00	15.00	25.00	—
1920 Proof, restrike	—	Value: 18.00				

KM# 483 20 FILLER **Composition:** Nickel **Note:** Edge varieties exist.

Date	Mintage	F	VF	XF	Unc	BU
1906KB	67,000	275	400	600	1,250	—
1907KB	1,248,000	3.00	6.00	12.00	24.00	—
1908KB	10,770,000	0.75	1.75	3.75	7.50	—
1914KB	5,387,000	3.75	6.50	10.00	15.00	—
1914KB Restrike; proof	—	Value: 12.50				

KM# 498 20 FILLER **Composition:** Iron **Note:** Edge varieties exist.

Date	Mintage	F	VF	XF	Unc	BU
1914	18,826,000	18.00	32.50	45.00	70.00	—
1916	Inc. above	0.50	1.25	2.50	7.00	—
1917	Inc. above	0.75	1.75	3.50	8.00	—
1918	Inc. above	0.75	1.75	3.50	8.00	—
1918 Proof, restrike	—	Value: 6.00				
1920	12,000,000	2.50	5.00	9.00	18.00	—
1921	Inc. above	18.00	32.50	45.00	70.00	—
1921 Proof, restrike	—	Value: 12.00				
1922 Rare	—	—	—	—	—	—
1922 Proof, restrike	—	Value: 12.00				

KM# 498a 20 FILLER **Composition:** Brass

Date	Mintage	F	VF	XF	Unc	BU
1922	400	—	—	—	—	—
1922 Proof, restrike	—	Value: 30.00				

KM# 484 KORONA **Weight:** 5.0000 g. **Composition:** 0.8350 Silver .1342 oz. ASW **Note:** Obverse varieties exist.

Date	Mintage	F	VF	XF	Unc	BU
1906KB	24,000	150	200	300	425	—

KM# 492 KORONA **Weight:** 5.0000 g. **Composition:** 0.8350 Silver .1342 oz. ASW

Date	Mintage	F	VF	XF	Unc	BU
1912	4,004,000	2.50	5.00	10.00	15.00	—
1913	5,214	50.00	80.00	140	200	—
1914	5,886,000	BV	3.75	6.50	10.00	—
1915	3,934,000	BV	3.00	4.50	6.00	—
1916	—	BV	3.50	6.00	8.00	—

KM# 493 2 KORONA **Weight:** 10.0000 g. **Composition:** 0.8350 Silver .2685 oz. ASW

Date	Mintage	F	VF	XF	Unc	BU
1912KB	4,000,000	BV	4.50	6.50	13.50	—
1913KB	3,000,000	BV	4.50	6.50	13.50	—
1914KB	500,000	20.00	30.00	50.00	80.00	—

KM# 488 5 KORONA **Weight:** 24.0000 g. **Composition:** 0.9000 Silver .6944 oz. ASW

Date	Mintage	F	VF	XF	Unc	BU
1906KB	1,263	1,000	1,500	2,000	2,500	—
1907KB	500,000	12.00	20.00	40.00	85.00	—
1908KB	1,742,000	10.00	18.00	40.00	75.00	—
1909KB	1,299,000	10.00	18.00	40.00	90.00	—
1909KB U.P. Proof, restrike	—	Value: 35.00				

KM# 489 5 KORONA **Weight:** 24.0000 g. **Composition:** 0.9000 Silver .6944 oz. ASW **Subject:** 40th Anniversary - Coronation of Franz Josef

Date	Mintage	F	VF	XF	Unc	BU
1907	300,000	15.00	22.00	35.00	55.00	—
1907 Proof, restrike	—	Value: 30.00				
1907 U.P. Proof, restrike	—	Value: 30.00				

KM# 485 10 KORONA **Weight:** 3.3875 g. **Composition:** 0.9000 Gold .0980 oz. AGW

Date	Mintage	F	VF	XF	Unc	BU
1901KB	230,000	BV	45.00	55.00	85.00	—
1902KB	243,000	BV	45.00	55.00	85.00	—
1903KB	228,000	BV	45.00	55.00	85.00	—
1904KB	1,531,000	BV	45.00	55.00	85.00	—
1905KB	869,000	BV	45.00	55.00	85.00	—
1906KB	748,000	BV	45.00	55.00	85.00	—
1907KB	752,000	BV	45.00	55.00	85.00	—
1908KB	509,000	BV	45.00	55.00	85.00	—
1909KB	574,000	BV	45.00	55.00	85.00	—
1910KB	1,362,000	BV	45.00	55.00	85.00	—
1911KB	1,828,000	BV	45.00	55.00	85.00	—
1912KB	739,000	50.00	60.00	70.00	100	—
1913KB	137,000	50.00	75.00	100	130	—
1914KB	115,000	50.00	80.00	135	165	—
1915KB	54,000	1,000	2,000	3,000	4,000	—

KM# 486 20 KORONA **Weight:** 6.7750 g. **Composition:** 0.9000 Gold .1960 oz. AGW

Date	Mintage	F	VF	XF	Unc	BU
1901KB	510,000	BV	80.00	90.00	135	—
1901KB	510,000	BV	80.00	90.00	135	—
1902KB	523,000	BV	80.00	90.00	135	—
1903KB	505,000	BV	80.00	90.00	135	—
1904KB	572,000	BV	80.00	90.00	135	—
1905KB	526,000	BV	80.00	90.00	135	—
1906KB	353,000	BV	80.00	90.00	135	—
1907KB	194,000	100	150	175	200	—
1908KB	138,000	BV	80.00	90.00	135	—
1909KB	459,000	BV	80.00	90.00	135	—
1910KB	85,000	125	175	250	300	—
1911KB	63,000	BV	80.00	90.00	135	—
1912KB	211,000	BV	80.00	90.00	135	—
1913KB	320,000	110	140	165	200	—
1914KB	176,000	BV	80.00	90.00	135	—
1915KB	690,000	110	140	165	200	—

KM# 495 20 KORONA **Weight:** 6.7750 g. **Composition:** 0.9000 Gold .1960 oz. AGW **Reverse:** Bosnian arms added

Date	F	VF	XF	Unc	BU
1914	BV	90.00	100	145	—
1915	—	—	—	—	—
1916	125	175	275	400	—

KM# 500 20 KORONA **Weight:** 6.7750 g. **Composition:** 0.9000 Gold .1960 oz. AGW **Obv. Legend:** KAROLY...

Date	F	VF	XF	Unc	BU
1918 Rare	—	—	—	—	—

KM# 490 100 KORONA **Weight:** 33.8753 g. **Composition:** 0.9000 Gold .9802 oz. AGW **Subject:** 40th Anniversary - Coronation of Franz Josef

Date	Mintage	F	VF	XF	Unc	BU
1907KB	11,000	500	650	900	1,350	—
1907KB U.P. Restrike	—	—	—	—	800	—

KM# 491 100 KORONA **Weight:** 33.8753 g. **Composition:** 0.9000 Gold .9802 oz. AGW

Date	Mintage	F	VF	XF	Unc	BU
1907	1,088	600	1,100	1,450	1,900	—
1907 U.P. Restrike	—	—	—	—	350	—
1908	4,038	550	850	1,250	1,800	—
1908 U.P Restrike	—	—	—	—	350	—

REGENCY COINAGE

1926 - 1945

KM# 505 FILLER **Composition:** Bronze

Date	Mintage	F	VF	XF	Unc	BU
1926BP	6,471,000	0.50	1.00	2.00	4.00	—
1927BP	16,529,000	0.10	0.20	0.50	3.00	—
1928BP	7,000,000	0.25	0.50	1.00	3.75	—
1929BP	418,000	5.00	10.00	20.00	35.00	—
1930BP	3,734,000	0.30	0.60	1.50	5.00	—
1931BP	10,849,000	0.10	0.20	0.60	3.00	—
1932BP	5,000,000	0.25	0.50	1.00	4.00	—
1932BP Proof, restrike	—	Value: 3.75				
1933BP	5,000,000	0.25	0.50	1.00	4.00	—
1934BP	3,111,000	0.30	0.60	1.20	4.50	—
1935BP	6,889,000	0.25	0.50	1.00	4.00	—
1936BP	10,000,000	0.10	0.20	0.60	2.50	—
1938BP	10,575,000	0.10	0.20	0.60	2.50	—
1939BP	10,425,000	0.10	0.20	0.60	2.50	—

KM# 506 2 FILLER **Composition:** Bronze

Date	Mintage	F	VF	XF	Unc	BU
1926BP	17,777,000	0.10	0.20	0.40	2.00	—
1927BP	44,836,000	0.10	0.20	0.40	2.00	—
1928BP	11,448,000	0.10	0.20	0.40	2.00	—
1929BP	8,995,000	0.10	0.25	0.50	2.50	—
1930BP	6,943,000	0.10	0.25	0.50	2.50	—
1931BP	826,000	0.40	0.90	2.50	6.50	—
1932BP	4,174,000	4.00	8.00	15.00	25.00	—
1933BP	501,000	3.00	6.00	10.00	18.00	—
1934BP	9,499,000	0.10	0.20	0.40	2.00	—
1935BP	10,000,000	0.10	0.20	0.40	2.00	—
1936BP	2,049,000	0.15	0.30	0.75	4.00	—
1937BP	7,951,000	0.10	0.25	0.50	2.00	—
1938BP	14,125,000	0.10	0.20	0.40	1.50	—
1939BP	16,875,000	0.10	0.20	0.40	1.50	—
1940BP	7,000,000	0.10	0.25	0.50	1.50	—

KM# 518.1 2 FILLER **Composition:** Steel

Date	Mintage	F	VF	XF	Unc	BU
1940	64,500,000	1.00	2.00	5.00	10.00	—

KM# 518.2 2 FILLER **Composition:** Steel

Date	Mintage	F	VF	XF	Unc	BU
1940	78,000,000	0.50	1.00	2.00	4.50	—
1941	12,000,000	30.00	65.00	125	200	—
1942	13,000,000	0.50	1.00	2.00	4.50	—
1942 Proof, restrike	—	Value: 6.50				

KM# 519 2 FILLER **Composition:** Zinc **Note:** Variations in planchets exist.

Date	Mintage	F	VF	XF	Unc	BU
1943	37,000,000	0.10	0.20	0.70	3.00	—
1943 Proof, restrike	—	Value: 6.50				
1944	55,159,000	0.10	0.20	0.70	2.50	—

KM# 507 10 FILLER **Composition:** Copper-Nickel

Date	Mintage	F	VF	XF	Unc	BU
1926BP	20,001,000	0.50	1.50	3.00	10.00	—
1927BP	12,255,000	0.50	1.50	3.00	7.00	—
1935BP	4,740,000	0.50	1.50	3.00	4.50	—
1936BP	3,005,000	0.50	1.50	3.00	4.50	—
1938BP	6,700,000	0.50	1.50	3.00	4.50	—
1939BP	4,460,000	3.00	5.00	10.00	20.00	—
1940BP	960,000	15.00	30.00	50.00	75.00	—

KM# 507a 10 FILLER **Composition:** Steel

Date	Mintage	F	VF	XF	Unc	BU
1940	45,927,000	0.10	0.20	0.80	3.50	—
1941	24,963,000	0.10	0.20	0.80	3.50	—
1942	44,110,000	0.10	0.20	0.80	3.50	—

KM# 508 20 FILLER **Composition:** Copper-Nickel

Date	Mintage	F	VF	XF	Unc	BU
1926BP	25,000,000	1.50	3.50	10.00	15.00	—
1927BP	830,000	10.00	30.00	60.00	100	—
1938BP	20,150,000	0.10	0.25	1.00	2.50	—
1939BP	2,020,000	6.50	10.00	20.00	35.00	—
1940BP	2,470,000	4.00	7.50	18.00	30.00	—

KM# 520 20 FILLER **Composition:** Steel

Date	Mintage	F	VF	XF	Unc	BU
1941	75,007,000	0.10	0.20	0.90	4.00	—
1943	7,500,000	0.10	0.20	0.90	4.00	—
1944	25,000,000	0.10	0.20	0.90	4.00	—
1944 Proof, restrike	—	Value: 7.00				

KM# 509 50 FILLER **Composition:** Copper-Nickel

Date	Mintage	F	VF	XF	Unc	BU
1926BP	14,921,000	0.75	2.00	3.50	6.00	—
1938BP	20,079,000	0.20	0.40	1.00	3.00	—
1939BP	2,770,000	6.50	15.00	30.00	50.00	—
1939BP Proof, restrike	—	Value: 20.00				
1940BP	6,230,000	4.00	7.50	18.00	30.00	—

KM# 510 PENGO **Weight:** 5.0000 g. **Composition:** 0.6400 Silver .1029 oz. ASW

Date	Mintage	F	VF	XF	Unc	BU
1926BP	15,000,000	BV	2.50	6.50	20.00	—
1927BP	18,000,000	BV	1.50	4.50	12.00	—
1937BP	4,000,000	BV	1.50	2.50	6.00	—
1938BP	5,000,000	BV	1.50	2.50	6.00	—
1939BP	13,000,000	BV	1.00	2.00	5.00	—

KM# 521 PENGO **Composition:** Aluminum

Date	Mintage	F	VF	XF	Unc	BU
1941	80,000,000	0.10	0.20	0.50	1.00	—
1942	19,000,000	0.10	0.20	0.50	1.00	—
1943	2,000,000	1.00	4.00	8.00	15.00	—
1944	16,000,000	0.10	0.20	0.50	1.00	—

KM# 511 2 PENGO **Weight:** 10.0000 g. **Composition:** 0.6400 Silver .2058 oz. ASW

Date	Mintage	F	VF	XF	Unc	BU
1929BP	5,000,000	1.25	3.00	6.50	12.50	—
1931BP	110,000	10.00	25.00	45.00	90.00	—
1932BP	602,000	1.50	4.00	8.00	15.00	—
1933BP	1,051,000	1.25	3.00	6.00	12.50	—
1935BP	50,000	25.00	65.00	120	250	—
1936BP	711,000	2.00	5.00	10.00	20.00	—
1937BP	1,500,000	1.25	3.00	4.75	8.50	—
1938BP	6,417,000	1.25	3.00	4.75	8.50	—
1939BP	2,103,000	1.25	3.00	4.75	8.50	—

KM# 513 2 PENGO **Weight:** 10.0000 g. **Composition:** 0.6400 Silver .2058 oz. ASW **Subject:** Tercentenary - Founding of Pazmany University

Date	Mintage	F	VF	XF	Unc	BU
1935	50,000	3.00	6.00	10.00	20.00	—
1935 Proof, restrike not marked	—	Value: 22.50				

KM# 514 2 PENGO **Weight:** 10.0000 g. **Composition:** 0.6400 Silver .2058 oz. ASW **Subject:** Bicentennial - Death of Rakoczi

Date	Mintage	F	VF	XF	Unc	BU
1935	100,000	2.00	4.00	6.00	10.00	—
1935 Proof, restrike not marked	—	Value: 22.50				

KM# 515 2 PENGO **Weight:** 10.0000 g. **Composition:** 0.6400 Silver .2058 oz. ASW **Subject:** 50th Anniversary - Death of Liszt

Date	Mintage	F	VF	XF	Unc	BU
1936	200,000	1.50	2.50	4.50	8.00	—
1936 Proof, restrike not marked	—	Value: 18.00				

KM# 522.1 2 PENGO **Composition:** Aluminum

Date	Mintage	F	VF	XF	Unc	BU
1941	24,000,000	0.15	0.30	0.50	0.80	—
1942	8,000,000	0.15	0.30	0.50	0.80	—
1943	10,000,000	0.15	0.30	0.50	0.80	—

KM# 522.2 2 PENGO **Composition:** Aluminum **Reverse:** Base of 2 is wavy

Date	Mintage	F	VF	XF	Unc	BU
1941	40,000	10.00	20.00	35.00	65.00	—
1941 Restrike, rose	—	—	—	—	—	—

KM# 512.2 5 PENGO **Weight:** 25.3300 g. **Composition:** 0.6400 Silver .5145 oz. ASW

Date	F	VF	XF	Unc	BU
1930 Proof, restrike	—	Value: 18.50			

KM# 512.1 5 PENGO **Weight:** 25.0000 g. **Composition:** 0.6400 Silver .5213 oz. ASW **Subject:** 10th Anniversary - Regency of Admiral Horthy **Edge:** Raised, sharp reeding

Date	Mintage	F	VF	XF	Unc	BU
1930BP	3,650,000	4.50	7.00	12.00	17.50	—

KM# 516 5 PENGO **Weight:** 25.0000 g. **Composition:** 0.6400 Silver .5145 oz. ASW **Subject:** 900th Anniversary - Death of St. Stephan

Date	Mintage	F	VF	XF	Unc	BU
1938	600,000	4.50	7.50	12.50	25.00	—
1938 Proof, restrike not marked	—	Value: 28.50				

KM# 517 5 PENGO **Weight:** 25.0000 g. **Composition:** 0.6400 Silver .5145 oz. ASW **Subject:** Admiral Miklos Horthy **Edge:** Smooth, ornamented

Date	Mintage	F	VF	XF	Unc	BU
1938	60	—	—	—	800	—
1939	408,000	4.50	7.50	12.50	25.00	—

KM# 523 5 PENGO **Composition:** Aluminum **Subject:** 75th Birthday of Admiral Horthy

Date	Mintage	F	VF	XF	Unc	BU
1943	2,000,000	0.50	1.00	2.00	4.00	—
1943 Proof, restrike	—	Value: 6.00				

PROVISIONAL GOVERNMENT

1944-1946

STANDARD COINAGE

KM# 525 5 PENGO **Composition:** Aluminum

Date	Mintage	F	VF	XF	Unc	BU
1945BP	5,002,000	0.50	1.00	3.00	6.50	—
1945BP PROBAVERET Proof, restrike	—	Value: 17.50				

1ST REPUBLIC

1946-1949

DECIMAL COINAGE

KM# 529 2 FILLER **Weight:** 3.0000 g. **Composition:** Bronze **Obverse:** Arms of the Republic **Reverse:** Value

Date	Mintage	F	VF	XF	Unc	BU
1946BP	13,665,000	0.25	0.50	1.00	2.00	—
1947BP	23,865,000	0.25	0.50	1.00	2.50	—
1947BP Proof, restrike	—	Value: 6.50				

KM# 535 5 FILLER **Weight:** 6.0000 g. **Composition:** Aluminum **Obverse:** Young girl's head **Reverse:** Value

Date	Mintage	F	VF	XF	Unc	BU
1948BP	24,000,000	0.40	1.00	2.00	5.00	—
1951BP	15,000,000	0.40	0.75	1.75	5.00	—

KM# 530 10 FILLER **Weight:** 3.0000 g. **Composition:** Aluminum-Bronze **Obverse:** Dove **Reverse:** Value

Date	Mintage	F	VF	XF	Unc	BU
1946BP	23,565,000	0.15	0.30	0.70	2.00	—
1947BP	29,580,000	0.15	0.30	0.70	2.00	—
1947BP Proof, restrike	—	Value: 7.50				
1948BP	4,885,000	2.00	3.00	4.00	8.00	—
1950BP	8,000,000	1.00	2.00	3.50	7.50	—

KM# 530a 10 FILLER **Weight:** 1.0000 g. **Composition:** Aluminum **Obverse:** Dove **Reverse:** Value

Date	F	VF	XF	Unc	BU
1950	20.00	30.00	40.00	60.00	—

KM# 531 20 FILLER **Weight:** 4.0000 g. **Composition:** Aluminum-Bronze **Obverse:** Three wheat ears **Reverse:** Value

Date	Mintage	F	VF	XF	Unc	BU
1946BP	16,560,000	0.40	0.80	1.50	3.00	—
1946BP Proof, restrike	—	Value: 8.00				
1947BP	18,260,000	0.50	1.00	2.00	4.00	—
1948BP	5,180,000	2.00	4.00	8.00	12.00	—
1950BP	6,000,000	1.00	2.00	4.00	10.00	—

KM# 536 50 FILLER **Weight:** 1.4000 g. **Composition:** Aluminum **Obverse:** Man sitting on anvil **Reverse:** Value

Date	Mintage	F	VF	XF	Unc	BU
1948BP	15,000,000	50.00	70.00	120	—	—
1948BP Proof, restrike	—	—	—	—	—	—

KM# 532 FORINT **Weight:** 1.5000 g. **Composition:** Aluminum **Obverse:** Arms of the Republic **Reverse:** Value

Date	Mintage	F	VF	XF	Unc	BU
1946BP	38,900,000	1.00	2.00	4.00	10.00	—
1947BP	2,600,000	4.00	8.00	15.00	25.00	—
1949BP	17,000,000	2.50	5.00	10.00	20.00	—

KM# 533 2 FORINT **Weight:** 2.8000 g. **Composition:** Aluminum **Obverse:** Arms of the Republic **Reverse:** Value

Date	Mintage	F	VF	XF	Unc	BU
1946BP	10,000,000	2.00	5.00	10.00	20.00	—
1947BP	3,500,000	3.00	7.50	15.00	30.00	—

KM# 534b 5 FORINT **Weight:** 13.0000 g. **Composition:** 0.8350 Silver .3490 oz. ASW **Obverse:** Arms of the Republic **Reverse:** Lajos Kossuth

Date	Mintage	F	VF	XF	Unc	BU
1966 Proof, restrike	5,006	Value: 22.50				
1967 Proof, restrike	5,015	Value: 22.50				

KM# 534a 5 FORINT Weight: 12.0000 g. **Composition:** 0.5000 Silver .1929 oz. ASW **Obverse:** Arms of the Republic **Reverse:** Lajos Kossuth **Note:** 1.7 millimeter thin planchet.

Date	Mintage	F	VF	XF	Unc	BU
1947	10,004,252	BV	1.75	3.00	5.00	—
1947 Proof, restrike	—	Value: 12.00				

KM# 534 5 FORINT Weight: 20.0000 g. **Composition:** 0.8350 Silver .5369 oz. ASW **Obverse:** Arms of the Republic **Reverse:** Lajos Kossuth **Note:** Thick planchet.

Date	Mintage	F	VF	XF	Unc	BU
1946BP	39,802	5.00	10.00	15.00	30.00	—

KM# 537 5 FORINT Weight: 12.0000 g. **Composition:** 0.5000 Silver .1929 oz. ASW **Subject:** Centenary of 1848 Revolution **Obverse:** Value **Reverse:** Sandor Petofi

Date	Mintage	F	VF	XF	Unc	BU
1948	100,000	1.25	2.50	6.00	10.00	—
1948 Proof, restrike	—	Value: 15.00				

KM# 538 10 FORINT Weight: 20.0000 g. **Composition:** 0.5000 Silver .3215 oz. ASW **Subject:** Centenary of 1848 Revolution **Obverse:** Value **Reverse:** Istvan Szechenyi

Date	Mintage	F	VF	XF	Unc	BU
1948BP	100,000	2.50	3.50	7.00	15.00	—
1948BP Proof, restrike	—	Value: 22.50				

KM# 539 20 FORINT Weight: 28.0000 g. **Composition:** 0.5000 Silver .4501 oz. ASW **Subject:** Centenary of 1848 Revolution **Obverse:** Arms of the Republic, value below **Reverse:** Mihaly Tancsics

Date	Mintage	F	VF	XF	Unc	BU
1948BP	50,000	5.00	9.00	17.50	30.00	—
1948BP Proof, restrike	—	Value: 40.00				

PEOPLES REPUBLIC
1949-1989

DECIMAL COINAGE

KM# 546 2 FILLER Composition: Aluminum

Date	Mintage	F	VF	XF	Unc	BU
1950BP	24,990,000	—	0.10	0.20	0.50	—
1952BP	5,600,000	—	0.10	0.30	1.00	—
1953BP	9,400,000	—	0.10	0.20	0.50	—
1954BP	10,000,000	—	0.10	0.20	0.50	—
1955BP	6,029,000	—	0.10	0.25	0.75	—
1956BP	4,000,000	—	0.15	0.30	1.00	—
1957BP	5,000,000	—	0.10	0.25	0.50	—
1960BP	3,000,000	0.10	0.15	0.30	0.60	—
1961BP	2,000,000	0.20	0.40	0.60	1.00	—
1962BP	3,000,000	0.10	0.15	0.30	0.60	—
1963BP	2,082,000	0.10	0.20	0.35	0.70	—
1965BP	540,000	—	4.00	8.00	16.00	—
1971BP	1,041,000	0.10	0.15	0.30	0.60	—
1972BP	1,000,000	0.10	0.15	0.30	0.60	—
1973BP	2,820,000	0.10	0.15	0.30	0.60	—
1974BP	50,000	—	0.40	0.80	1.50	—
1975BP	50,000	—	0.40	0.80	1.50	—
1976BP	50,000	—	0.40	0.80	1.50	—
1977BP	60,000	—	0.40	0.80	1.50	—
1978BP	50,000	—	0.40	0.80	1.50	—
1979BP	30,000	—	0.75	1.25	2.50	—
1980BP	30,000	—	0.75	1.25	2.50	—
1981BP	30,000	—	0.75	1.25	2.50	—
1982BP	30,000	—	0.75	1.25	2.50	—
1983BP	30,000	—	0.75	1.25	2.50	—
1984BP	30,000	—	0.75	1.25	2.50	—
1985BP	30,000	—	0.75	1.25	2.50	—
1986BP	30,000	—	0.75	1.25	2.50	—
1987BP	30,000	—	0.75	1.25	2.50	—
1988BP	30,000	—	0.75	1.25	2.50	—
1989BP	30,000	—	0.75	1.25	2.50	—

KM# 546a 2 FILLER Composition: Copper-Nickel

Date	Mintage	F	VF	XF	Unc	BU
1966 Proof	5,000	Value: 4.00				
1967 Proof	5,000	Value: 4.00				

KM# 549 5 FILLER Composition: Aluminum

Date	Mintage	F	VF	XF	Unc	BU
1953BP	10,000,000	0.10	0.15	0.30	0.50	—
1955BP	6,005,000	0.15	0.20	0.50	1.00	—
1956BP	6,012,000	0.15	0.20	0.50	1.00	—
1957BP	5,000,000	0.20	0.30	0.60	1.20	—
1959BP	8,000,000	0.15	0.20	0.50	1.00	—
1960BP	7,000,000	0.15	0.20	0.50	1.00	—
1961BP	4,410,000	0.20	0.30	0.60	1.20	—
1962BP	5,590,000	0.20	0.30	0.60	1.20	—
1963BP	4,020,000	0.20	0.30	0.60	1.20	—
1964BP	3,600,000	0.20	0.30	0.60	1.20	—
1965BP	6,000,000	0.20	0.30	0.60	1.20	—
1970BP	3,900,000	—	2.50	5.00	10.00	—
1971BP	100,000	—	0.25	0.50	1.00	—
1972BP	50,000	—	0.25	0.50	1.00	—
1973BP	105,000	—	0.25	0.50	1.00	—
1974BP	60,000	—	0.25	0.50	1.00	—
1975BP	60,000	—	0.25	0.50	1.00	—
1976BP	50,000	—	0.25	0.50	1.00	—
1977BP	60,000	—	0.25	0.50	1.00	—
1978BP	50,000	—	0.25	0.50	1.00	—
1979BP	30,000	—	0.50	1.00	2.00	—
1980BP	30,000	—	0.50	1.00	2.00	—
1981BP	30,000	—	0.50	1.00	2.00	—
1982BP	30,000	—	0.50	1.00	2.00	—
1983BP	30,000	—	0.50	1.00	2.00	—
1984BP	30,000	—	0.50	1.00	2.00	—
1985BP	30,000	—	0.50	1.00	2.00	—
1986BP	30,000	—	0.50	1.00	2.00	—
1987BP	30,000	—	0.50	1.00	2.00	—
1988BP	30,000	—	0.50	1.00	2.00	—
1989BP	30,000	—	0.50	1.00	2.00	—

KM# 549a 5 FILLER Composition: Copper-Nickel

Date	Mintage	F	VF	XF	Unc	BU
1966 Proof	5,000	Value: 5.00				
1967 Proof	5,000	Value: 5.00				

KM# 547 10 FILLER Composition: Aluminum

Date	Mintage	F	VF	XF	Unc	BU
1950BP	5,040,000	10.00	20.00	30.00	50.00	—
1951BP	80,950,000	1.50	3.00	5.00	10.00	—
1955BP	10,019,000	2.00	4.00	7.00	15.00	—
1957BP	13,000,000	2.00	4.00	7.00	15.00	—
1958BP	12,015,000	2.00	4.00	7.00	15.00	—
1959BP	15,000,000	2.00	4.00	7.00	15.00	—
1960BP	5,000,000	2.50	5.00	8.00	17.00	—
1961BP	13,000,000	2.00	4.00	7.00	15.00	—
1962BP	4,000,000	2.50	5.00	9.00	18.00	—
1963BP	8,000,000	2.50	5.00	8.00	17.00	—
1964BP	17,008,000	2.00	4.00	7.00	15.00	—
1965BP	21,880,000	2.00	4.00	7.00	15.00	—
1966BP	8,120,000	2.50	5.00	8.00	17.00	—

KM# 547a 10 FILLER Composition: Copper-Nickel

Date	Mintage	F	VF	XF	Unc	BU
1966 Proof	5,000	Value: 6.00				
1967 Proof	5,000	Value: 6.00				

KM# 572 10 FILLER Composition: Aluminum **Note:** Reduced size.

Date	Mintage	F	VF	XF	Unc	BU
1967	5,000	5.00	10.00	20.00	45.00	—
1968	16,000,000	0.50	1.00	2.50	5.00	—
1969	50,760,000	0.50	1.00	2.50	5.00	—
1970	28,470,000	0.50	1.00	2.50	5.00	—
1971	28,800,000	—	0.50	1.25	2.50	—
1972	17,220,000	—	0.50	1.25	2.50	—
1973	33,720,000	—	0.50	1.25	2.50	—
1974	24,930,000	—	0.50	1.25	2.50	—
1975	30,000,000	—	0.50	1.25	2.50	—
1976	20,025,000	—	0.50	1.25	2.50	—
1977	30,075,000	—	0.50	1.25	2.50	—
1978	36,005,000	—	0.40	1.00	2.00	—
1979	36,060,000	—	0.40	1.00	2.00	—
1980	36,010,000	—	0.40	1.00	2.00	—
1981	36,000,000	—	0.40	1.00	2.00	—
1982	45,015,000	—	0.30	0.75	1.50	—
1983	45,030,000	—	0.30	0.75	1.50	—
1984	42,075,000	—	0.30	0.75	1.50	—
1985	40,035,000	—	0.30	0.75	1.50	—
1986	48,075,000	—	0.30	0.75	1.50	—
1987	45,000,000	—	0.30	0.75	1.50	—
1988	48,015,000	—	0.30	0.75	1.50	—
1989	55,515,000	—	—	0.10	0.50	—

KM# 550 20 FILLER Composition: Aluminum

Date	Mintage	F	VF	XF	Unc	BU
1953BP	45,000,000	1.00	2.00	4.00	8.00	—
1955BP	10,023,000	1.25	2.50	5.00	10.00	—
1957BP	5,000,000	1.75	3.50	7.00	15.00	—
1958BP	10,000,000	1.25	2.50	5.00	10.00	—
1959BP	13,000,000	1.25	2.50	5.00	10.00	—
1961BP	9,000,000	1.25	2.50	5.00	10.00	—
1963BP	7,000,000	1.50	3.00	6.00	12.00	—
1964BP	10,400,000	1.25	2.50	5.00	10.00	—
1965BP	15,000,000	1.25	2.50	5.00	10.00	—
1966BP	5,000,000	1.50	3.00	6.50	12.50	—

KM# 550a 20 FILLER Composition: Copper-Nickel

Date	Mintage	F	VF	XF	Unc	BU
1966 Proof	5,000	Value: 8.00				
1967 Proof	5,000	Value: 8.00				

KM# 573 20 FILLER Composition: Aluminum Note: Reduced size.

Date	Mintage	F	VF	XF	Unc	BU
1967	10,000,000	0.25	0.75	2.50	6.00	—
1968	56,500,000	0.10	0.40	1.25	3.00	—
1969	28,550,000	0.15	0.45	1.50	4.00	—
1970	19,960,000	0.20	0.60	2.00	5.00	—
1971	31,090,000	0.10	0.20	0.75	2.00	—
7971 Error	11,000	3.50	7.50	15.00	30.00	—
1972	21,070,000	0.15	0.30	0.75	1.50	—
1973	22,970,000	0.15	0.30	0.75	1.50	—
1974	35,010,000	0.15	0.30	0.75	1.50	—
1975	30,010,000	0.15	0.30	0.75	1.50	—
1976	30,010,000	0.15	0.30	0.75	1.50	—
1977	30,050,000	0.15	0.30	0.75	1.50	—
1978	30,140,000	0.15	0.30	0.75	1.50	—
1979	32,010,000	0.15	0.30	0.75	1.50	—
1980	45,010,000	0.10	0.20	0.50	1.00	—
1981	34,030,000	0.10	0.20	0.50	1.00	—
1982	35,010,000	0.10	0.20	0.50	1.00	—
1983	43,210,000	0.10	0.20	0.50	1.00	—
1984	42,270,000	0.10	0.20	0.50	1.00	—
1985	40,440,000	0.10	0.20	0.50	1.00	—
1986	48,000,000	0.10	0.20	0.50	1.00	—
1987	55,000,000	0.10	0.20	0.50	1.00	—
1988	48,010,000	0.10	0.20	0.50	1.00	—
1989	64,660,000	—	—	0.10	0.50	—

KM# 627 20 FILLER Composition: Aluminum Series: F.A.O.

Date	Mintage	F	VF	XF	Unc	BU
1983	50,000	—	0.50	1.00	2.50	—

KM# 551 50 FILLER Composition: Aluminum

Date	Mintage	F	VF	XF	Unc	BU
1953BP	10,017,000	1.50	3.00	6.00	12.00	—
1965BP	3,005,000	1.25	2.50	5.00	10.00	—
1966BP	1,500,000	1.75	3.50	7.00	15.00	—

KM# 551a 50 FILLER Composition: Copper-Nickel

Date	Mintage	F	VF	XF	Unc	BU
1966 Proof	5,000	Value: 10.00				
1967 Proof	5,000	Value: 10.00				

KM# 574 50 FILLER Composition: Aluminum

Date	Mintage	F	VF	XF	Unc	BU
1967	20,000,000	0.50	1.00	2.00	4.00	—
1968	13,861,000	0.60	1.25	2.50	5.00	—
1969	10,085,000	0.60	1.25	2.50	5.00	—
1971	50,000	0.30	0.60	1.25	2.50	—
1972	470,000	0.20	0.50	1.00	2.00	—
1973	7,600,000	0.20	0.50	1.00	2.00	—
1974	5,000,000	0.20	0.50	1.00	2.00	—
1975	10,160,000	0.10	0.30	0.75	1.50	—
1976	15,130,000	0.10	0.30	0.75	1.50	—
1977	10,050,000	0.10	0.30	0.75	1.50	—
1978	10,110,000	0.10	0.30	0.75	1.50	—
1979	10,070,000	0.10	0.30	0.75	1.50	—
1980	15,000,000	0.10	0.30	0.75	1.50	—
1981	10,030,000	0.10	0.30	0.75	1.50	—
1982	10,000,000	0.10	0.30	0.75	1.50	—
1983	10,070,000	0.10	0.30	0.75	1.50	—
1984	14,060,000	0.10	0.30	0.75	1.50	—
1985	12,020,000	0.10	0.30	0.75	1.50	—
1986	17,140,000	0.10	0.30	0.75	1.50	—
1987	23,000,000	—	0.10	0.50	1.00	—

Date	Mintage	F	VF	XF	Unc	BU
1988	18,050,000	—	0.10	0.50	1.00	—
1989	18,200,000	—	0.10	0.50	1.00	—

KM# 545 FORINT Composition: Aluminum

Date	Mintage	F	VF	XF	Unc	BU
1949BP	19,440,000	1.50	3.00	6.00	12.00	—
1950BP	39,060,000	2.25	4.50	9.00	18.00	—
1952BP	63,018,000	2.00	4.00	8.00	16.00	—

KM# 555 FORINT Composition: Aluminum

Date	Mintage	F	VF	XF	Unc	BU
1957	7,500,000	2.00	4.00	8.00	16.00	—
1958	5,070,000	1.50	3.00	6.00	12.00	—
1960	5,000,000	1.25	2.50	5.00	10.00	—
1961	5,000,000	1.25	2.50	5.00	10.00	—
1963	3,000,000	1.50	3.00	6.50	12.50	—
1964	6,080,000	1.00	2.00	4.00	8.00	—
1965	9,810,000	1.00	2.00	4.00	8.00	—
1966	5,680,000	1.75	3.50	7.50	15.00	—

KM# 555a FORINT Weight: 5.8500 g. Composition: 0.8350 Silver .0570 oz. ASW

Date	Mintage	F	VF	XF	Unc	BU
1966 Proof	5,000	Value: 12.00				
1967 Proof	5,000	Value: 12.00				

KM# 575 FORINT Composition: Aluminum

Date	Mintage	F	VF	XF	Unc	BU
1967	60,000,000	0.65	1.25	2.50	5.00	—
1968	53,230,000	0.65	1.25	2.50	6.00	—
1969	27,664,000	1.00	2.00	4.00	8.00	—
1970	11,290,000	1.00	2.00	4.00	10.00	—
1971	100,000	0.10	0.20	0.50	1.00	—
1972	110,000	0.25	0.50	1.00	2.00	—
1973	1,990,000	0.10	0.20	0.50	1.00	—
1974	4,990,000	0.10	0.20	0.50	1.00	—
1975	10,000,000	0.10	0.20	0.40	0.80	—
1976	15,000,000	0.10	0.20	0.40	0.80	—
1977	10,050,000	0.10	0.20	0.40	0.80	—
1978	50,000	0.20	0.40	0.85	1.75	—
1979	10,070,000	0.10	0.20	0.35	0.70	—
1980	20,040,000	0.10	0.20	0.35	0.70	—
1981	25,040,000	0.10	0.20	0.35	0.70	—
1982	10,000,000	0.10	0.20	0.35	0.70	—
1983	20,140,000	0.10	0.20	0.35	0.70	—
1984	6,010,000	0.15	0.30	0.60	1.20	—
1985	30,000	0.25	0.50	1.00	2.00	—
1986	30,000	0.25	0.50	1.00	2.00	—
1987	13,000,000	0.10	0.20	0.50	1.00	—
1988	20,080,000	0.10	0.20	0.35	0.75	—
1989	115,920,000	—	0.15	0.30	0.60	—

KM# 548 2 FORINT Composition: Copper-Nickel

Date	Mintage	F	VF	XF	Unc	BU
1950BP	18,500,000	1.75	3.50	7.00	15.00	—
1951BP	4,000,000	2.00	4.00	8.00	16.00	—
1952BP	4,530,000	2.00	4.00	8.00	16.00	—

KM# 556 2 FORINT Composition: Copper-Nickel

Date	Mintage	F	VF	XF	Unc	BU
1957	5,000,000	1.50	3.00	6.00	12.50	—
1958	1,033,000	1.75	3.50	7.00	15.00	—
1960	4,000,000	1.50	3.00	6.00	12.50	—
1961	690,000	2.00	4.00	8.00	16.00	—
1962	1,190,000	1.50	3.00	6.00	12.50	—

KM# 556a 2 FORINT Composition: Copper-Nickel-Zinc

Date	Mintage	F	VF	XF	Unc	BU
1962	1,210,000	1.25	2.50	5.00	10.00	—
1963	3,100,000	1.25	2.50	5.00	10.00	—
1964	3,250,000	1.25	2.50	5.00	10.00	—
1965	4,395,000	1.25	2.50	5.00	10.00	—
1966	6,630,000	1.25	2.50	5.00	10.00	—

KM# 556b 2 FORINT Weight: 6.1200 g. Composition: 0.8350 Silver .1643 oz. ASW

Date	Mintage	F	VF	XF	Unc	BU
1966 Proof	5,000	Value: 14.00				
1967 Proof	5,000	Value: 14.00				

KM# 591 2 FORINT Composition: Brass

Date	Mintage	F	VF	XF	Unc	BU
1970	49,195,000	0.50	1.00	2.00	4.00	—
1971	10,830,000	0.10	0.50	1.00	2.00	—
1972	10,015,000	0.10	0.50	1.00	2.00	—
1973	820,000	1.00	2.00	4.00	8.00	—
1974	10,000,000	0.25	0.75	1.50	3.00	—
1975	20,030,000	0.25	0.75	1.50	3.00	—
1976	15,000,000	0.25	0.75	1.50	3.00	—
1977	10,115,000	0.25	0.75	1.50	3.00	—
1978	12,000,000	0.25	0.75	1.50	3.00	—
1979	10,127,000	0.25	0.75	1.50	3.00	—
1980	12,005,000	0.25	0.75	1.50	3.00	—
1981	10,010,000	0.25	0.75	1.50	3.00	—
1982	10,005,000	0.25	0.75	1.50	3.00	—
1983	20,160,000	0.25	0.75	1.50	3.00	—
1984	5,000,000	0.75	1.50	3.00	6.00	—
1985	10,675,000	0.25	0.75	1.50	3.00	—
1986	30,000	1.50	3.00	6.00	12.00	—
1987	5,030,000	0.50	1.00	2.00	4.00	—
1988	5,035,000	0.50	1.00	2.00	4.00	—
1989	79,223,000	0.10	0.25	0.50	1.00	—

KM# 576 5 FORINT Composition: Copper-Nickel Note: Lajos Kossuth.

Date	Mintage	F	VF	XF	Unc	BU
1967BP	20,000,000	0.50	1.00	2.50	5.00	—
1968BP	29,000	5.00	10.00	20.00	35.00	—

KM# 594 5 FORINT Composition: Nickel

Date	Mintage	F	VF	XF	Unc	BU
1971	20,004,000	0.20	0.35	0.75	1.50	—
1972	5,000,000	0.25	0.50	1.00	2.00	—
1973	100,000	0.35	0.75	1.50	3.00	—
1974	50,000	0.35	0.75	1.50	3.00	—
1975	50,000	0.35	0.75	1.50	3.00	—
1976	5,090,000	0.25	0.50	1.00	2.00	—
1977	50,000	0.35	0.75	1.50	3.00	—
1978	6,000,000	0.25	0.50	1.00	2.00	—
1979	10,000,000	0.25	0.50	1.00	2.00	—
1980	6,002,000	0.25	0.50	1.00	2.00	—
1981	5,002,000	0.25	0.50	1.00	2.00	—
1982	936,000	0.30	0.60	1.25	2.50	—

KM# 628 5 FORINT Composition: Nickel **Series:** F.A.O.

Date	Mintage	F	VF	XF	Unc	BU
1983	50,000	—	1.00	2.00	3.50	—

KM# 635 5 FORINT Composition: Copper-Nickel
Obverse: Head of Lajos Kossuth right

Date	Mintage	F	VF	XF	Unc	BU
1983	15,240,000	0.15	0.25	0.50	1.00	—
1984	25,018,000	0.15	0.25	0.50	1.00	—
1985	25,286,000	0.15	0.25	0.50	1.00	—
1986	1,030,000	0.20	0.35	0.75	1.50	—
1987	30,000	0.30	0.60	1.25	2.50	—
1988	4,050,000	0.20	0.35	0.75	1.50	—
1989	39,014,000	0.15	0.25	0.50	1.00	—

KM# 552 10 FORINT Weight: 12.5000 g. **Composition:** 0.8000 Silver .3215 oz. ASW **Subject:** 10th Anniversary of Forint

Date	Mintage	F	VF	XF	Unc	BU
1956BP	22,000	3.00	5.00	8.00	16.00	—

KM# 595 10 FORINT Composition: Nickel

Date	Mintage	F	VF	XF	Unc	BU
1971	24,998,000	0.35	0.75	1.50	3.00	—
1972	25,078,000	0.35	0.75	1.50	3.00	—
1973	78,000	0.60	1.25	2.50	5.00	—
1974	50,000	0.60	1.25	2.50	5.00	—
1975	50,000	0.60	1.25	2.50	5.00	—
1976	3,568,000	0.50	1.00	2.00	4.00	—
1977	4,618,000	0.50	1.00	2.00	4.00	—
1978	50,000	0.60	1.25	2.50	5.00	—
1979	5,000,000	0.50	1.00	2.00	4.00	—
1980	2,550,000	0.50	1.00	2.00	4.00	—
1982	30,000	0.60	1.25	2.50	5.00	—

KM# 620 10 FORINT Composition: Nickel **Series:** F.A.O.

Date	Mintage	F	VF	XF	Unc	BU
1981	60,000	—	—	2.50	5.00	—

KM# 629 10 FORINT Composition: Nickel **Series:** F.A.O.

Date	Mintage	F	VF	XF	Unc	BU
1983	50,000	—	—	2.50	5.00	—

KM# 636 10 FORINT Composition: Aluminum-Bronze
Note: Circulation coinage.

Date	Mintage	F	VF	XF	Unc	BU
1983	11,004,000	0.25	0.50	1.00	2.00	—
1984	7,578,000	0.25	0.50	1.00	2.00	—
1985	27,648,000	0.25	0.50	1.00	2.00	—
1986	15,006,000	0.25	0.50	1.00	2.00	—
1987	10,000,000	0.25	0.50	1.00	2.00	—
1988	5,000,000	0.25	0.50	1.00	2.00	—
1989	37,094,000	0.25	0.50	1.00	2.00	—

KM# 553 20 FORINT Weight: 17.5000 g. **Composition:** 0.8000 Silver .4501 oz. ASW **Subject:** 10th Anniversary of Forint

Date	Mintage	F	VF	XF	Unc	BU
1956BP	22,000	4.50	8.00	12.00	20.00	—

KM# 630 20 FORINT Composition: Copper-Nickel
Obverse: Dozsa

Date	Mintage	F	VF	XF	Unc	BU
1982	13,404,000	0.25	0.50	0.80	1.60	—
1983	18,006,000	0.25	0.50	0.80	1.60	—
1984	31,016,000	0.25	0.50	0.80	1.60	—
1985	20,122,000	0.25	0.50	0.80	1.60	—
1986	6,000,000	0.35	0.65	1.25	2.25	—
1987	30,000	0.40	0.75	1.50	3.00	—
1988	30,000	0.40	0.75	1.50	3.00	—
1989	31,890,000	0.25	0.50	0.80	1.60	—

KM# 637 20 FORINT Composition: Copper-Nickel
Subject: Forestry for Development

Date	Mintage	F	VF	XF	Unc	BU
1984	15,000	—	—	—	3.00	—
1984 Proof	5,000	Value: 7.00				

KM# 653 20 FORINT Composition: Copper-Nickel
Series: F.A.O.

Date	Mintage	F	VF	XF	Unc	BU
1985	25,000	—	—	—	3.00	—
1985 Proof	—	Value: 6.50				

KM# 554 25 FORINT (Huszonot) Weight: 20.0000 g. **Composition:** 0.8000 Silver .5144 oz. ASW **Subject:** 10th Anniversary Forint

Date	Mintage	F	VF	XF	Unc	BU
1956BP	22,000	5.00	10.00	15.00	20.00	—

KM# 557 25 FORINT (Huszonot) Weight: 17.5000 g. **Composition:** 0.7500 Silver .4220 oz. ASW **Subject:** 150th Anniversary - Birth of Liszt

Date	Mintage	F	VF	XF	Unc	BU
1961 Proof	15,000	Value: 15.50				

KM# 558 25 FORINT (Huszonot) Weight: 17.5000 g. **Composition:** 0.7500 Silver .4220 oz. ASW **Subject:** 80th Anniversary - Birth of Bartok

Date	Mintage	F	VF	XF	Unc	BU
1961 Proof	15,000	Value: 16.50				

KM# 567 25 FORINT (Huszonot) Weight: 12.0000 g. **Composition:** 0.6400 Silver .2469 oz. ASW **Subject:** 40th Anniversary - Death of Zrinyi

Date	Mintage	F	VF	XF	Unc	BU
1966 Proof	11,000	Value: 20.00				

KM# 577 25 FORINT (Huszonot) **Weight:** 12.0000 g. **Composition:** 0.7500 Silver .2893 oz. ASW **Subject:** 85th Birthday of Kodaly

Date	Mintage	F	VF	XF	Unc	BU
1967	15,000	—	—	—	10.00	—
1967 Proof	—	Value: 12.50				

KM# 559 50 FORINT (Otven) **Weight:** 20.0000 g. **Composition:** 0.7500 Silver .4922 oz. ASW **Subject:** 150th Anniversary - Birth of Liszt

Date	Mintage	F	VF	XF	Unc	BU
1961BP Proof	15,000	Value: 20.00				

KM# 560 50 FORINT (Otven) **Weight:** 3.8380 g. **Composition:** 0.9860 Gold .1217 oz. AGW **Subject:** 150th Anniversary - Birth of Liszt

Date	Mintage	F	VF	XF	Unc	BU
1961 Proof	2,503	Value: 85.00				

KM# 561 50 FORINT (Otven) **Weight:** 20.0000 g. **Composition:** 0.7500 Silver .4822 oz. ASW **Subject:** 80th Anniversary - Birth of Bartok

Date	Mintage	F	VF	XF	Unc	BU
1961 Proof	15,000	Value: 20.00				

KM# 562 50 FORINT (Otven) **Weight:** 3.8380 g. **Composition:** 0.9860 Gold .1217 oz. AGW **Subject:** 80th Anniversary - Birth of Bartok

Date	Mintage	F	VF	XF	Unc	BU
1961 Proof	2,503	Value: 90.00				

KM# 568 50 FORINT (Otven) **Weight:** 20.0000 g. **Composition:** 0.6400 Silver .4115 oz. ASW **Subject:** 400th Anniversary - Death of Zrinyi

Date	Mintage	F	VF	XF	Unc	BU
1966BP Proof	11,000	Value: 25.00				

KM# 578 50 FORINT (Otven) **Weight:** 20.0000 g. **Composition:** 0.7500 Silver .4822 oz. ASW **Subject:** 85th Birthday of Kodaly

Date	Mintage	F	VF	XF	Unc	BU
1967	15,000	—	—	—	10.00	—
1967 Proof	—	Value: 12.50				

KM# 582 50 FORINT (Otven) **Weight:** 20.0000 g. **Composition:** 0.6400 Silver .4115 oz. ASW **Subject:** 150th Anniversary - Birth of Semmelweis

Date	Mintage	F	VF	XF	Unc	BU
1968	20,000	—	—	—	10.00	—
1968 Proof	4,750	Value: 12.50				

KM# 583 50 FORINT (Otven) **Weight:** 4.2050 g. **Composition:** 0.9000 Gold .1217 oz. AGW **Subject:** 150th Anniversary - Birth of Semmelweis

Date	Mintage	F	VF	XF	Unc	BU
1968 Proof	25,000	Value: 75.00				

KM# 589 50 FORINT (Otven) **Weight:** 16.0000 g. **Composition:** 0.6400 Silver .3292 oz. ASW **Subject:** 50th Anniversary - Republic of Councils

Date	Mintage	F	VF	XF	Unc	BU
1969	12,000	—	—	—	8.00	—
1969 Proof	3,000	Value: 15.00				

KM# 592 50 FORINT (Otven) **Weight:** 16.0000 g. **Composition:** 0.6400 Silver .3292 oz. ASW **Subject:** 25th Anniversary of Liberation

Date	Mintage	F	VF	XF	Unc	BU
1970	20,000	—	—	—	7.00	—
1970 Proof	5,000	Value: 12.50				

KM# 596 50 FORINT (Otven) **Weight:** 16.0000 g. **Composition:** 0.6400 Silver .3292 oz. ASW **Subject:** 1000th Anniversary - Birth of St. Stephen

Date	Mintage	F	VF	XF	Unc	BU
1972	24,000	—	—	—	10.00	—
1972 Proof	6,000	Value: 15.00				

KM# 599 50 FORINT (Otven) **Weight:** 16.0000 g. **Composition:** 0.6400 Silver .3292 oz. ASW **Subject:** 150th Anniversary - Birth of Sandor Petofi

Date	Mintage	F	VF	XF	Unc	BU
1973	24,000	—	—	—	8.00	—
1973 Proof	6,000	Value: 12.00				

KM# 601 50 FORINT (Otven) **Weight:** 16.0000 g. **Composition:** 0.6400 Silver .3292 oz. ASW **Subject:** 50th Anniversary of National Bank

Date	Mintage	F	VF	XF	Unc	BU
1974	24,000	—	—	—	7.00	—
1974 Proof	6,000	Value: 9.00				

KM# 663 50 FORINT (Otven) **Composition:** Copper-Nickel **Subject:** 25th Anniversary of World Wildlife Foundation **Reverse:** Red-footed Falcon

Date	Mintage	F	VF	XF	Unc	BU
1988	45,000	—	—	—	6.50	—

KM# 563 100 FORINT (Szaz) **Weight:** 7.6760 g. **Composition:** 0.9860 Gold .2431 oz. AGW **Subject:** 150th Anniversary - Birth of Liszt

Date	Mintage	F	VF	XF	Unc	BU
1961BP Proof	2,500	Value: 155				

KM# 564 100 FORINT (Szaz) **Weight:** 7.6760 g. **Composition:** 0.9860 Gold .2431 oz. AGW **Subject:** 80th Anniversary - Birth of Bartok

Date	Mintage	F	VF	XF	Unc	BU
1961 Proof	2,500	Value: 155				

KM# 569 100 FORINT (Szaz) **Weight:** 8.4100 g. **Composition:** 0.9000 Gold .2433 oz. AGW **Subject:** 400th Anniversary - Death of Zrinyi

Date	Mintage	F	VF	XF	Unc	BU
1966 Proof	3,300	Value: 155				

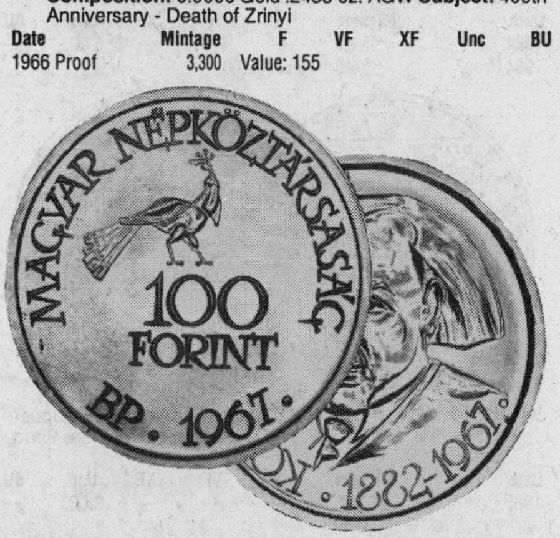

KM# 579 100 FORINT (Szaz) **Weight:** 28.0000 g. **Composition:** 0.7500 Silver .6752 oz. ASW **Subject:** 85th Birthday of Kodaly

Date	Mintage	F	VF	XF	Unc	BU
1967BP	10,000	—	—	—	25.00	—
1967BP Proof	—	Value: 40.00				

KM# 584 100 FORINT (Szaz) **Weight:** 28.0000 g. **Composition:** 0.6400 Silver .5762 oz. ASW **Subject:** 150th Anniversary - Birth of Semmelweis

Date	Mintage	F	VF	XF	Unc	BU
1968	20,000	—	—	—	9.00	—
1968 Proof	4,750	Value: 17.50				

KM# 585 100 FORINT (Szaz) **Weight:** 8.4100 g. **Composition:** 0.9000 Gold .2433 oz. AGW **Subject:** 150th Anniversary - Birth of Semmelweis

Date	Mintage	F	VF	XF	Unc	BU
1968 Proof	23,000	Value: 145				

KM# 590 100 FORINT (Szaz) **Weight:** 22.0000 g. **Composition:** 0.6400 Silver .4527 oz. ASW **Subject:** 50th Anniversary - Republic of Councils

Date	Mintage	F	VF	XF	Unc	BU
1969	12,000	—	—	—	10.00	—
1969 Proof	3,000	Value: 15.00				

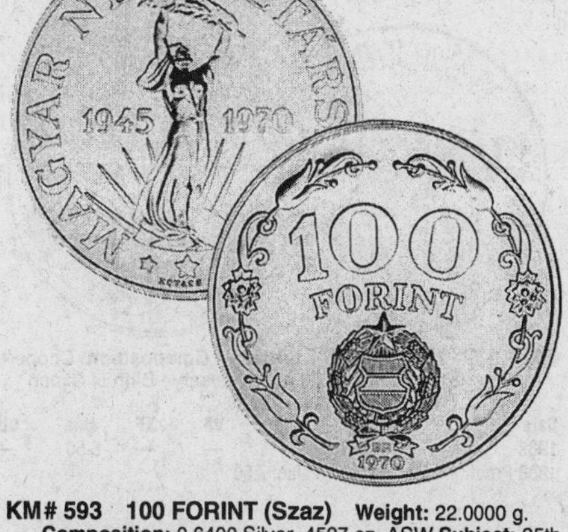

KM# 593 100 FORINT (Szaz) **Weight:** 22.0000 g. **Composition:** 0.6400 Silver .4527 oz. ASW **Subject:** 25th Anniversary of Liberation

Date	Mintage	F	VF	XF	Unc	BU
1970	20,000	—	—	—	9.00	—
1970 Proof	5,000	Value: 12.00				

KM# 597 100 FORINT (Szaz) **Weight:** 22.0000 g. **Composition:** 0.6400 Silver .4527 oz. ASW **Subject:** 1000th Anniversary - Birth of St. Stephen

Date	Mintage	F	VF	XF	Unc	BU
1972	24,000	—	—	—	10.00	—
1972 Proof	6,000	Value: 15.00				

KM# 598 100 FORINT (Szaz) **Weight:** 22.0000 g. **Composition:** 0.6400 Silver .4527 oz. ASW **Subject:** Buda and Pest Union Centennial

Date	Mintage	F	VF	XF	Unc	BU
1972	25,000	—	—	—	10.00	—
1972 Proof	6,000	Value: 15.00				

KM# 600 100 FORINT (Szaz) **Weight:** 22.0000 g. **Composition:** 0.6400 Silver .4527 oz. ASW **Subject:** 150th Anniversary - Birth of Sandor Petofi

Date	Mintage	F	VF	XF	Unc	BU
1973	24,000	—	—	—	8.50	—
1973 Proof	6,000	Value: 12.50				

KM# 602 100 FORINT (Szaz) **Weight:** 22.0000 g. **Composition:** 0.6400 Silver .4527 oz. ASW **Subject:** 25th Anniversary of KGST

Date	Mintage	F	VF	XF	Unc	BU
1974	20,000	—	—	—	8.50	—
1974 Proof	5,000	Value: 10.00				

KM# 603 100 FORINT (Szaz) **Weight:** 22.0000 g. **Composition:** 0.6400 Silver .4527 oz. ASW **Subject:** 50th Anniversary of National Bank

Date	Mintage	F	VF	XF	Unc	BU
1974	24,000	—	—	—	7.50	—
1974 Proof	6,000	Value: 10.00				

KM# 617 100 FORINT (Szaz) **Composition:** Nickel **Subject:** 1st Soviet-Hungarian Space Flight

Date	Mintage	F	VF	XF	Unc	BU
1980	180,000	—	—	—	4.00	—
1980 Proof	20,000	Value: 8.00				

KM# 621 100 FORINT (Szaz) **Composition:** Nickel **Subject:** World Food Day

Date	Mintage	F	VF	XF	Unc	BU
1981	80,000	—	—	—	5.00	—
1981	20,000	Value: 10.00				

KM# 622 100 FORINT (Szaz) **Composition:** Copper-Nickel-Zinc **Subject:** 1300th Anniversary of Bulgarian Statehood

Date	Mintage	F	VF	XF	Unc	BU
1981 Proof	50,000	Value: 8.00				

KM# 626 100 FORINT (Szaz) **Composition:** Copper-Nickel **Subject:** World Football Championship

Date	Mintage	F	VF	XF	Unc	BU
1982	150,000	—	—	—	2.50	—

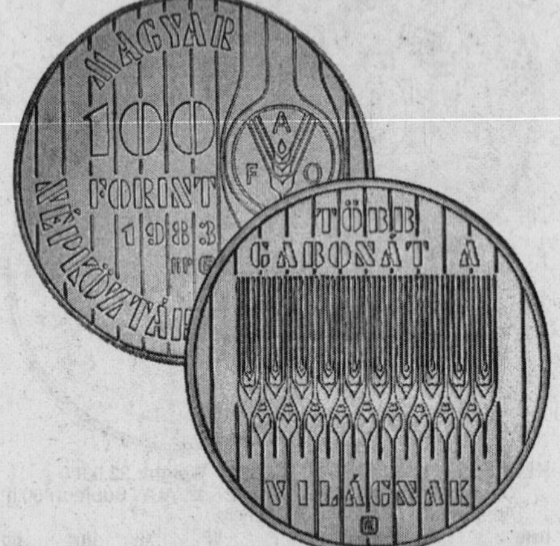

KM# 631 100 FORINT (Szaz) **Composition:** Copper-Nickel **Series:** F.A.O.

Date	Mintage	F	VF	XF	Unc	BU
1983	50,000	—	—	—	3.50	—
1983 Proof	10,000	Value: 5.50				

KM# 632 100 FORINT (Szaz) **Composition:** Copper-Nickel-Zinc **Subject:** 200th Anniversary - Birth of Simon Bolivar **Reverse:** Andean Condor

Date	Mintage	F	VF	XF	Unc	BU
1983	20,000	—	—	—	6.50	—
1983 Proof	10,000	Value: 7.50				

KM# 633 100 FORINT (Szaz) **Composition:** Copper-Nickel-Zinc **Reverse:** Count Szechenyi Istvan

Date	Mintage	F	VF	XF	Unc	BU
1983	30,000	—	—	—	6.00	—
1983 Proof	20,000	Value: 9.00				

KM# 634 100 FORINT (Szaz) **Composition:** Copper-Nickel-Zinc **Subject:** 100th Anniversary - Birth of Czobel Bela - Painter

Date	Mintage	F	VF	XF	Unc	BU
1983	20,000	—	—	—	6.00	—
1983 Proof	10,000	Value: 10.00				

KM# 638 100 FORINT (Szaz) **Composition:** Copper-Nickel-Zinc **Subject:** 200th Anniversary - Birth of Korosi Csoma Sandor

Date	Mintage	F	VF	XF	Unc	BU
1984	20,000	—	—	—	6.00	—
1984 Proof	10,000	Value: 10.00				

KM# 639 100 FORINT (Szaz) **Composition:** Copper-Nickel-Zinc **Subject:** Forestry for Development

Date	Mintage	F	VF	XF	Unc	BU
1984	15,000	—	—	—	6.00	—
1984 Proof	5,000	Value: 10.00				

KM# 644 100 FORINT (Szaz) **Composition:** Copper-Nickel-Zinc **Subject:** Wildlife Preservation **Reverse:** Pond Turtle

Date	Mintage	F	VF	XF	Unc	BU
1985	20,000	—	—	—	9.00	—

KM# 645 100 FORINT (Szaz) **Composition:** Copper-Nickel-Zinc **Subject:** Wildlife Preservation **Reverse:** European Otter

Date	Mintage	F	VF	XF	Unc	BU
1985	20,000	—	—	—	9.00	—

KM# 646 100 FORINT (Szaz) **Composition:** Copper-Nickel-Zinc **Subject:** Wildlife Preservation **Reverse:** Wildcat

Date	Mintage	F	VF	XF	Unc	BU
1985	20,000	—	—	—	9.00	—

KM# 647 100 FORINT (Szaz) **Composition:** Copper-Nickel-Zinc **Subject:** World Football **Reverse:** Map of Mexico

Date	Mintage	F	VF	XF	Unc	BU
1985	30,000	—	—	—	7.50	—

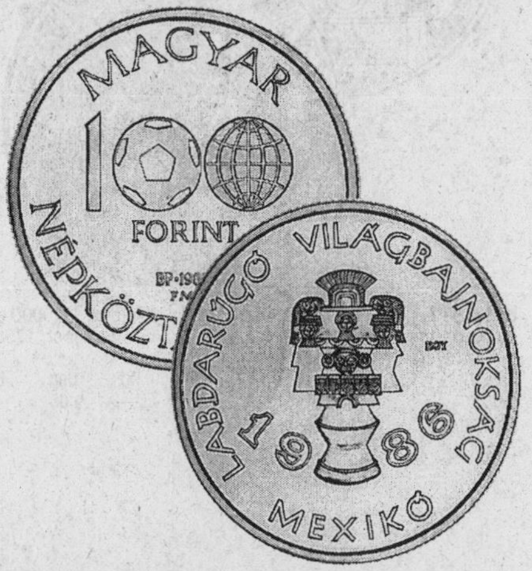

KM# 648 100 FORINT (Szaz) **Composition:** Copper-Nickel-Zinc **Subject:** World Football **Reverse:** Native Mexican artifacts

Date	Mintage	F	VF	XF	Unc	BU
1985	30,000	—	—	—	7.50	—

KM# 651 100 FORINT (Szaz) **Composition:** Copper-Nickel-Zinc **Subject:** Budapest Cultural Forum

Date	Mintage	F	VF	XF	Unc	BU
1985	40,000	—	—	—	5.00	—
1985 Proof	—	Value: 8.00				

KM# 654 100 FORINT (Szaz) **Composition:** Copper-Nickel-Zinc **Series:** F.A.O.

Date	Mintage	F	VF	XF	Unc	BU
1985	20,000	—	—	—	5.00	—
1985 Proof	5,000	Value: 8.00				

KM# 655 100 FORINT (Szaz) **Composition:** Copper-Nickel-Zinc **Subject:** 200th Anniversary - Birth of Andras Fay

Date	Mintage	F	VF	XF	Unc	BU
1986	42,000	—	—	—	5.00	—
1986 Proof	8,000	Value: 8.00				

KM# 664 100 FORINT (Szaz) **Composition:** Copper-Nickel **Subject:** 1990 World Cup Soccer

Date	Mintage	F	VF	XF	Unc	BU
1988	23,000	—	—	—	9.00	—

KM# 665 100 FORINT (Szaz) **Composition:** Copper-Nickel-Zinc **Subject:** Europe Football Championship

Date	Mintage	F	VF	XF	Unc	BU
1988	20,000	—	—	—	9.00	—

KM# 668 100 FORINT (Szaz) **Composition:** Copper-Nickel **Subject:** 1990 World Cup Soccer

Date	Mintage	F	VF	XF	Unc	BU
1989	23,000	—	—	—	9.00	—

KM# 586 200 FORINT (Ketszaz) **Weight:** 16.8210 g. **Composition:** 0.9000 Gold .4867 oz. AGW **Subject:** 150th Anniversary - Birth of Ignac Semmelweis

Date	Mintage	F	VF	XF	Unc	BU
1968BP Proof	14,000	Value: 275				

KM# 604 200 FORINT (Ketszaz) **Weight:** 28.0000 g. **Composition:** 0.6400 Silver .5762 oz. ASW **Subject:** 30th Anniversary of Liberation

Date	Mintage	F	VF	XF	Unc	BU
1975BP	20,000	—	—	—	10.00	—
1975BP Proof	10,000	Value: 12.50				

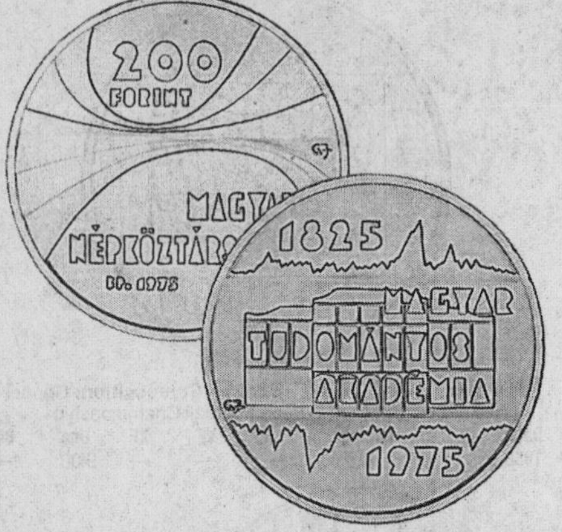

KM# 605 200 FORINT (Ketszaz) **Weight:** 28.0000 g. **Composition:** 0.6400 Silver .5762 oz. ASW **Subject:** 150th Anniversary - Academy of Science

Date	Mintage	F	VF	XF	Unc	BU
1975	20,000	—	—	—	10.00	—
1975 Proof	10,000	Value: 12.50				

KM# 608 200 FORINT (Ketszaz) **Weight:** 28.0000 g. **Composition:** 0.6400 Silver .5762 oz. ASW **Reverse:** Pal Szinyei Merse

Date	Mintage	F	VF	XF	Unc	BU
1976	25,000	—	—	—	9.00	—
1976 Proof	5,000	Value: 12.50				

KM# 611 200 FORINT (Ketszaz) **Weight:** 28.0000 g. **Composition:** 0.6400 Silver .5762 oz. ASW **Reverse:** Tivadar CS. Kosztka

Date	Mintage	F	VF	XF	Unc	BU
1977	25,000	—	—	—	9.00	—
1977 Proof	5,000	Value: 12.50				

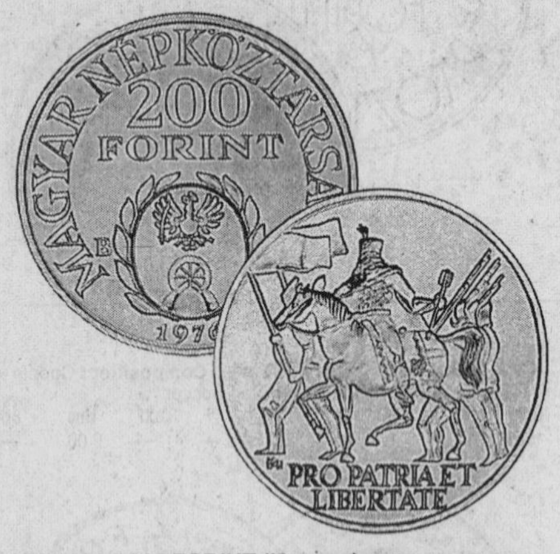

KM# 606 200 FORINT (Ketszaz) **Weight:** 28.0000 g. **Composition:** 0.6400 Silver .5762 oz. ASW **Subject:** 300th Anniversary - Birth of Ferencz Rakoczi II

Date	Mintage	F	VF	XF	Unc	BU
1976	25,000	—	—	—	10.00	—
1976 Proof	5,000	Value: 13.50				

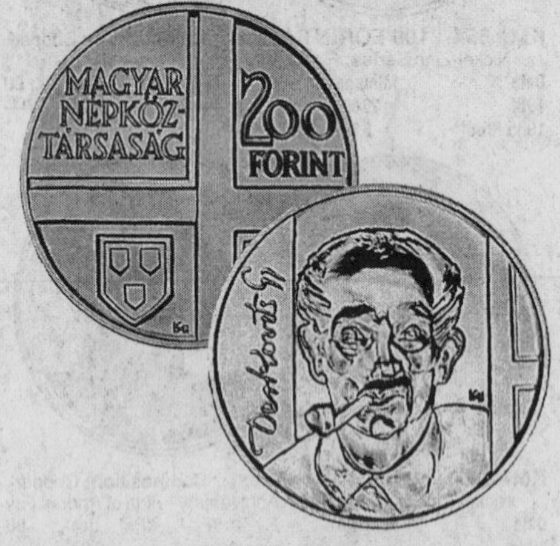

KM# 609 200 FORINT (Ketszaz) **Weight:** 28.0000 g. **Composition:** 0.6400 Silver .5762 oz. ASW **Reverse:** Gyula Derkovits

Date	Mintage	F	VF	XF	Unc	BU
1976	25,000	—	—	—	9.00	—
1976 Proof	5,000	Value: 12.50				

KM# 612 200 FORINT (Ketszaz) **Weight:** 28.0000 g. **Composition:** 0.6400 Silver .5762 oz. ASW **Reverse:** Jozsef Rippl-Ronai

Date	Mintage	F	VF	XF	Unc	BU
1977	25,000	—	—	—	9.00	—
1977 Proof	5,000	Value: 12.50				

KM# 607 200 FORINT (Ketszaz) **Weight:** 28.0000 g. **Composition:** 0.6400 Silver .5762 oz. ASW **Reverse:** Mihaly Munkacsy

Date	Mintage	F	VF	XF	Unc	BU
1976	25,000	—	—	—	9.00	—
1976 Proof	5,000	Value: 12.50				

KM# 610 200 FORINT (Ketszaz) **Weight:** 28.0000 g. **Composition:** 0.6400 Silver .5762 oz. ASW **Reverse:** Adam Manyoki

Date	Mintage	F	VF	XF	Unc	BU
1977	25,000	—	—	—	9.00	—
1977 Proof	5,000	Value: 12.50				

KM# 613 200 FORINT (Ketszaz) **Weight:** 28.0000 g. **Composition:** 0.6400 Silver .5762 oz. ASW **Subject:** 175th Anniversary of National Museum

Date	Mintage	F	VF	XF	Unc	BU
1977	25,000	—	—	—	9.00	—
1977 Proof	5,000	Value: 15.00				

KM# 614 200 FORINT (Ketszaz) **Weight:** 28.0000 g. **Composition:** 0.6400 Silver .5762 oz. ASW **Subject:** First Hungarian Gold Forint

Date	Mintage	F	VF	XF	Unc	BU
1978	25,000	—	—	—	9.00	—
1978 Proof	5,000	Value: 15.00				

KM# 615 200 FORINT (Ketszaz) **Weight:** 28.0000 g. **Composition:** 0.6400 Silver .5762 oz. ASW **Subject:** International Year of the Child

Date	Mintage	F	VF	XF	Unc	BU
1979	9,000	—	—	—	10.00	—
1979 Proof	21,000	Value: 14.00				

KM# 616 200 FORINT (Ketszaz) **Weight:** 22.0000 g. **Composition:** 0.6400 Silver .4527 oz. ASW **Subject:** 350th Anniversary - Death of Gabor Bethlen

Date	Mintage	F	VF	XF	Unc	BU
1979	15,000	—	—	—	13.50	—
1979 Proof	5,000	Value: 18.50				

KM# 618 200 FORINT (Ketszaz) **Weight:** 16.0000 g. **Composition:** 0.6400 Silver .3292 oz. ASW **Series:** XIII Winter Olympics - Lake Placid **Reverse:** Two figure skaters

Date	Mintage	F	VF	XF	Unc	BU
1980 Proof	15,000	Value: 10.00				

KM# 643 200 FORINT (Ketszaz) **Weight:** 16.0000 g. **Composition:** 0.6400 Silver .3292 oz. ASW **Subject:** Wildlife Preservation **Reverse:** Otter

Date	Mintage	F	VF	XF	Unc	BU
1985	13,000	—	—	—	12.00	—
1985 Proof	2,000	Value: 13.50				

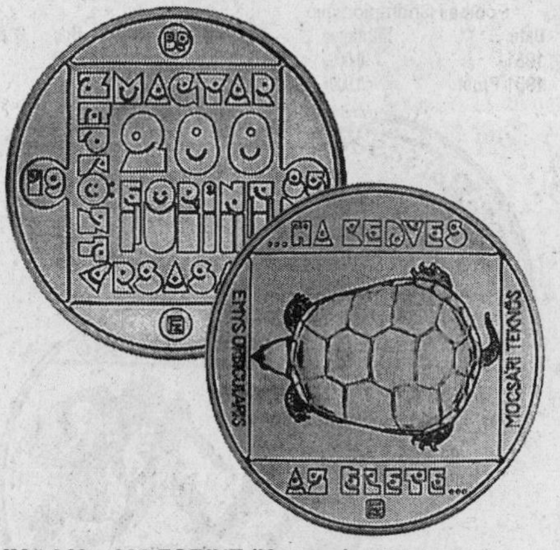

KM# 649 200 FORINT (Ketszaz) **Weight:** 16.0000 g. **Composition:** 0.6400 Silver .3292 oz. ASW **Subject:** Wildlife Preservation **Reverse:** Pond Turtle

Date	Mintage	F	VF	XF	Unc	BU
1985	13,000	—	—	—	14.00	—
1985 Proof	2,000	Value: 15.00				

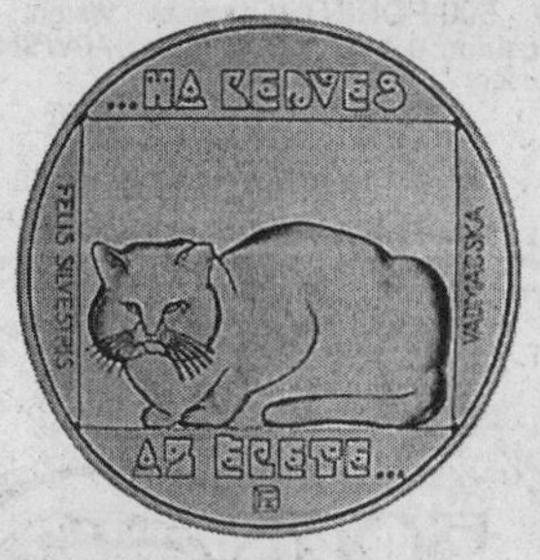

KM# 650 200 FORINT (Ketszaz) **Weight:** 16.0000 g. **Composition:** 0.6400 Silver .3292 oz. ASW **Subject:** Wildlife Preservation **Reverse:** Wildcat

Date	Mintage	F	VF	XF	Unc	BU
1985	13,000	—	—	—	12.00	—
1985 Proof	2,000	Value: 13.50				

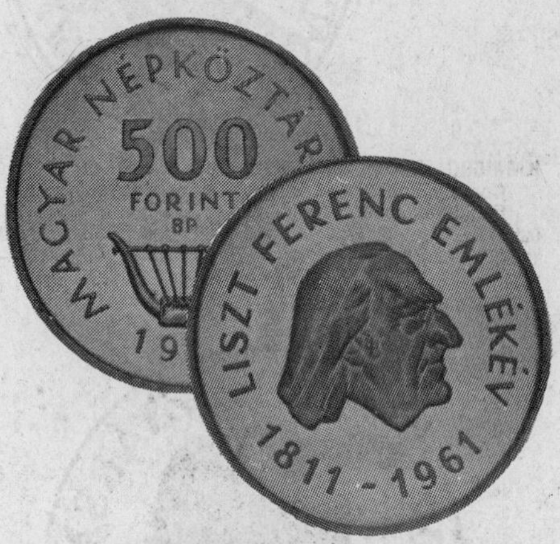

KM# 565 500 FORINT (Otszaz) **Weight:** 38.3800 g. **Composition:** 0.9860 Gold 1.2168 oz. AGW **Subject:** 150th Anniversary - Birth of Ferenc Liszt

Date	Mintage	F	VF	XF	Unc	BU
1961BP	2,503	Value: 700				

KM# 566 500 FORINT (Otszaz) **Weight:** 38.3800 g. **Composition:** 0.9860 Gold 1.2168 oz. AGW **Subject:** 80th Anniversary - Birth of Bela Bartok

Date	Mintage	F	VF	XF	Unc	BU
1961	2,503	Value: 700				

KM# 570 500 FORINT (Otszaz) **Weight:** 42.0522 g. **Composition:** 0.9000 Gold 1.2169 oz. AGW **Subject:** 400th Anniversary - Death of Miklos Zrinyl

Date	Mintage	F	VF	XF	Unc	BU
1966 Proof	1,100	Value: 750				

KM# 580 500 FORINT (Otszaz) **Weight:** 42.0522 g. **Composition:** 0.9000 Gold 1.2169 oz. AGW **Subject:** 85th Birthday of Zoltan Kodaly

Date	Mintage	F	VF	XF	Unc	BU
1967	—	—	—	—	650	—
1967 Proof	1,000	Value: 800				

KM# 587 500 FORINT (Otszaz) **Weight:** 42.0522 g. **Composition:** 0.9000 Gold 1.2169 oz. AGW **Subject:** 150th Anniversary - Birth of Ignacz Semmelweis **Reverse:** Similar to 50 Forint, KM#583

Date	Mintage	F	VF	XF	Unc	BU
1968 Proof	9,000	Value: 650				

KM# 619 500 FORINT (Otszaz) **Weight:** 39.0000 g. **Composition:** 0.6400 Silver .8025 oz. ASW **Series:** XIII Winter Olympics - Lake Placid **Reverse:** Two figure skaters

Date	Mintage	F	VF	XF	Unc	BU
1980BP Proof	13,000	Value: 55.00				

KM# 623 500 FORINT (Otszaz) **Weight:** 25.0000 g. **Composition:** 0.6400 Silver .5144 oz. ASW **Subject:** Centennial - Birth of Bela Bartok

Date	Mintage	F	VF	XF	Unc	BU
1981	13,000	—	—	—	17.50	—
1981 Proof	13,000	Value: 20.00				

KM# 624 500 FORINT (Otszaz) **Weight:** 28.0000 g. **Composition:** 0.6400 Silver .5762 oz. ASW **Subject:** World Football Championship

Date	Mintage	F	VF	XF	Unc	BU
1981	6,000	—	—	—	20.00	—
1981 Proof	40,000	Value: 16.50				

KM# 625 500 FORINT (Otszaz) **Weight:** 28.0000 g. **Composition:** 0.6400 Silver .5762 oz. ASW **Subject:** World Football Championship

Date	Mintage	F	VF	XF	Unc	BU
1981	6,000	—	—	—	20.00	—
1981 Proof	40,000	Value: 16.50				

KM# 640 500 FORINT (Otszaz) **Weight:** 28.0000 g. **Composition:** 0.6400 Silver .5762 oz. ASW **Subject:** Decade for Women

Date	Mintage	F	VF	XF	Unc	BU
1984	8,000	—	—	—	18.50	—
1984 Proof	20,000	Value: 22.50				

KM# 641 500 FORINT (Otszaz) **Weight:** 28.0000 g. **Composition:** 0.6400 Silver .5762 oz. ASW **Series:** Winter Olympics - Sarajevo **Reverse:** Cross country skiers

Date	Mintage	F	VF	XF	Unc	BU
1984	8,000	—	—	—	11.50	—
1984 Proof	12,000	Value: 12.50				

KM# 642 500 FORINT (Otszaz) **Weight:** 28.0000 g. **Composition:** 0.6400 Silver .5762 oz. ASW **Subject:** Los Angeles Olympics **Reverse:** Gymnast

Date	Mintage	F	VF	XF	Unc	BU
1984	8,000	—	—	—	11.50	—
1984 Proof	12,000	Value: 12.50				

KM# 652 500 FORINT (Otszaz) **Weight:** 28.0000 g. **Composition:** 0.6400 Silver .5762 oz. ASW **Subject:** Budapest Cultural Forum

Date	Mintage	F	VF	XF	Unc	BU
1985	15,000	—	—	—	11.50	—
1985 Proof	10,000	Value: 17.50				

KM# 658 500 FORINT (Otszaz) **Weight:** 28.0000 g. **Composition:** 0.9000 Silver .8102 oz. ASW **Subject:** 300th Anniversary - Repossession of Buda from the Turks

Date	Mintage	F	VF	XF	Unc	BU
1986	20,000	—	—	—	20.00	—
1986 Proof	10,000	Value: 25.00				

KM# 661 500 FORINT (Otszaz) **Weight:** 28.0000 g. **Composition:** 0.9000 Silver .8102 oz. ASW **Subject:** World Wildlife Fund **Reverse:** Montagu's Harrier

Date	Mintage	F	VF	XF	Unc	BU
1988	10,000	—	—	—	21.50	—
1988 Proof	25,000	Value: 25.00				

KM# 656 500 FORINT (Otszaz) **Weight:** 28.0000 g. **Composition:** 0.6400 Silver .5762 oz. ASW **Subject:** World Football Championship **Reverse:** Football players

Date	Mintage	F	VF	XF	Unc	BU
1986	8,000	—	—	—	14.00	—
1986 Proof	17,000	Value: 12.50				

KM# 659 500 FORINT (Otszaz) **Weight:** 28.0000 g. **Composition:** 0.9000 Silver .8102 oz. ASW **Series:** Winter Olympics - Calgary 1988 **Reverse:** Speed skater

Date	Mintage	F	VF	XF	Unc	BU
1986	15,000	—	—	—	12.50	—
1986 Proof	15,000	Value: 15.00				

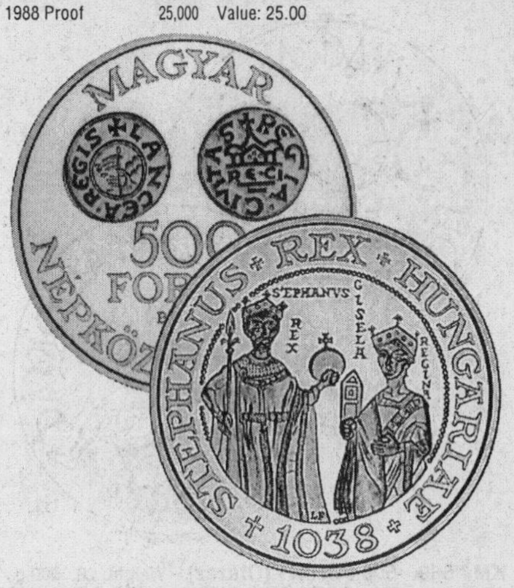

KM# 662 500 FORINT (Otszaz) **Weight:** 28.0000 g. **Composition:** 0.9000 Silver .8102 oz. ASW **Subject:** 950th Anniversary - Death of St. Stephan

Date	Mintage	F	VF	XF	Unc	BU
1988	5,000	—	—	—	38.00	—
1988 Proof	15,000	Value: 25.00				

KM# 657 500 FORINT (Otszaz) **Weight:** 28.0000 g. **Composition:** 0.6400 Silver .5762 oz. ASW **Subject:** World Football Championship **Reverse:** Stadium

Date	Mintage	F	VF	XF	Unc	BU
1986	8,000	—	—	—	14.00	—
1986 Proof	17,000	Value: 12.50				

KM# 660 500 FORINT (Otszaz) **Weight:** 28.0000 g. **Composition:** 0.9000 Silver .8102 oz. ASW **Subject:** Seoul Olympics **Reverse:** Wrestlers

Date	Mintage	F	VF	XF	Unc	BU
1987	15,000	—	—	—	14.50	—
1987 Proof	15,000	Value: 22.50				

KM# 666 500 FORINT (Otszaz) **Weight:** 28.0000 g. **Composition:** 0.9000 Silver .8102 oz. ASW **Subject:** Europe Football Championship

Date	Mintage	F	VF	XF	Unc	BU
1988	8,000	—	—	—	17.50	—
1988 Proof	12,000	Value: 16.50				

KM# 667 500 FORINT (Otszaz) **Weight:** 28.0000 g. **Composition:** 0.9000 Silver .8102 oz. ASW **Subject:** World Football Championship

Date	Mintage	F	VF	XF	Unc	BU
1988	7,000	—	—	—	18.50	—
1988 Proof	15,000	Value: 17.50				

KM# 669 500 FORINT (Otszaz) **Weight:** 28.0000 g. **Composition:** 0.9000 Silver .8102 oz. ASW **Subject:** World Football Championship **Reverse:** Two players

Date	Mintage	F	VF	XF	Unc	BU
1989	7,000	—	—	—	18.50	—
1989 Proof	15,000	Value: 17.50				

KM# 670 500 FORINT (Otszaz) **Weight:** 28.0000 g. **Composition:** 0.9000 Silver .8102 oz. ASW **Subject:** Save the Children Fund

Date	Mintage	F	VF	XF	Unc	BU
1989	10,000	—	—	—	22.50	—
1989 Proof	20,000	Value: 22.50				

KM# 671 500 FORINT (Otszaz) **Weight:** 28.0000 g. **Composition:** 0.9000 Silver .8102 oz. ASW **Series:** 1992 Barcelona Olympics **Reverse:** Torch bearer lighting the flame

Date	Mintage	F	VF	XF	Unc	BU
1989	15,000	—	—	—	22.50	—
1989 Proof	15,000	Value: 27.50				

KM# 571 1000 FORINT (Ezer) **Weight:** 84.1040 g. **Composition:** 0.9000 Gold 2.4339 oz. AGW **Subject:** 400th Anniversary - Death of Miklos Zrinyi **Obverse:** Similar to 500 Forint, KM#570

Date	Mintage	F	VF	XF	Unc	BU
1966 Proof	330	Value: 1,750				

KM# 581 1000 FORINT (Ezer) **Weight:** 84.1040 g. **Composition:** 0.9000 Gold 2.4339 oz. AGW **Subject:** 85th Birthday of Zoltan Kodaly **Obverse:** Similar to 500 Forint, KM#580

Date	Mintage	F	VF	XF	Unc	BU
1967 Proof	500	Value: 1,450				

KM# 588 1000 FORINT (Ezer) **Weight:** 84.1040 g. **Composition:** 0.9000 Gold 2.4339 oz. AGW **Subject:** 150th Anniversary - Birth of Ignacz Semmelweis **Reverse:** Similar to 500 forint, KM#587

Date	Mintage	F	VF	XF	Unc	BU
1968	7,000	Value: 1,250				

TRANSITIONAL COINAGE

KM# 736 FORINT **Composition:** Aluminum **Note:** Similar to Forint, KM#575. Communist design type with New Republic legends.

Date	Mintage	F	VF	XF	Unc	BU
1990	10,000	—	—	—	10.00	—

KM# 737 2 FORINT **Composition:** Brass **Note:** Similar to 2 Forint, KM#591. Communist design type with New Republic legends.

Date	Mintage	F	VF	XF	Unc	BU
1990	10,000	—	—	—	15.00	—

KM# 738 5 FORINT **Composition:** Copper-Nickel **Note:** Similar to 5 Forint, KM#635. Communist design with New Republic legends.

Date	Mintage	F	VF	XF	Unc	BU
1990	10,000	—	—	—	20.00	—

KM# 739 10 FORINT **Composition:** Aluminum-Bronze **Note:** Similar to 10 Forint, KM#636.

Date	Mintage	F	VF	XF	Unc	BU
1990	10,000	—	—	—	25.00	—

KM# 740 20 FORINT **Composition:** Copper-Nickel **Note:** Similar to 20 Forint, KM#630.

Date	Mintage	F	VF	XF	Unc	BU
1990	10,000	—	—	—	30.00	—

2ND REPUBLIC

1989-present

DECIMAL COINAGE

KM# 673 2 FILLER **Weight:** 6.5000 g. **Composition:** Aluminum **Obverse:** Wreath **Reverse:** Value

Date	Mintage	F	VF	XF	Unc	BU
1990BP	10,000	—	—	—	2.00	—
1991BP	10,000	—	—	—	3.00	—
1992BP	30,000	—	—	—	3.00	—

KM# 674 5 FILLER **Weight:** 6.0000 g. **Composition:** Aluminum **Obverse:** Young girl's head **Reverse:** Value

Date	Mintage	F	VF	XF	Unc	BU
1990BP	10,000	—	—	—	2.00	—
1991BP	10,000	—	—	—	3.00	—
1992BP	30,000	—	—	—	3.00	—

KM# 675 10 FILLER **Weight:** 6.0000 g. **Composition:** Aluminum **Obverse:** Dove **Reverse:** Value

Date	Mintage	F	VF	XF	Unc	BU
1990BP	46,515,000	0.10	0.15	0.20	0.35	—
1991BP	2,370,000	0.25	0.40	0.55	0.75	—
1992BP	15,828,000	0.15	0.25	0.35	0.50	—
1993BP	30,000	—	—	—	1.00	—
1994BP	30,000	—	—	—	1.00	—

Date	Mintage	F	VF	XF	Unc	BU
1995BP	30,000	—	—	—	1.00	—
1996BP	20,000	—	—	—	1.20	—

KM# 676 20 FILLER **Weight:** 0.9000 g. **Composition:** Aluminum **Obverse:** Three wheat ears **Reverse:** Value

Date	Mintage	F	VF	XF	Unc	BU
1990BP	59,360,000	0.10	0.15	0.20	0.35	—
1991BP	20,210,000	0.20	0.35	0.50	0.75	—
1992BP	30,000	—	—	—	1.00	—
1993BP	30,000	—	—	—	1.00	—
1994BP	30,000	—	—	—	1.00	—
1995BP	30,000	—	—	—	1.00	—
1996BP	20,000	—	—	—	1.25	—

KM# 677 50 FILLER **Weight:** 1.2000 g. **Composition:** Aluminum **Obverse:** Erzsebet Bridge **Reverse:** Value

Date	Mintage	F	VF	XF	Unc	BU
1990BP	20,550,000	—	0.10	0.20	0.30	—
1991BP	31,250,000	—	—	0.10	0.25	—
1992BP	440,000	—	—	—	0.85	—
1993BP	30,000	—	—	—	1.20	—
1994BP	30,000	—	—	—	1.20	—
1995BP	30,000	—	—	—	1.20	—
1996BP	20,000	—	—	—	1.60	—
1997BP	10,000	—	—	—	2.50	—
1998BP	10,000	—	—	—	2.50	—
1999BP	10,000	—	—	—	2.50	—

KM# 692 FORINT **Weight:** 2.0500 g. **Composition:** Brass **Obverse:** Arms of the Republic **Reverse:** Value

Date	Mintage	F	VF	XF	Unc	BU
1992		—	0.10	0.25	0.35	—
1992 Proof	1,000	Value: 6.00				
1993		—	—	0.10	0.25	—
1993 Proof	30,000	Value: 1.00				
1994		—	—	0.10	0.25	—
1994 Proof	15,000	Value: 1.20				
1995		—	—	0.10	0.25	—
1995 Proof	15,000	Value: 1.20				
1996		—	—	0.10	0.25	—
1996 Proof	10,000	Value: 1.40				
1997		—	—	0.10	0.25	—
1997 Proof	3,000	Value: 3.75				
1998		—	—	0.10	0.25	—
1998 Proof	3,000	Value: 3.75				
1999		—	—	0.10	0.25	—
1999 Proof	3,000	Value: 3.75				
2000		—	—	0.10	0.25	—
2000 Proof	3,000	Value: 3.75				
2001		—	—	—	0.25	—
2001	3,000	Value: 3.75				
2002		—	—	—	0.25	—

KM# 693 2 FORINT **Weight:** 3.1000 g. **Composition:** Copper-Nickel **Obverse:** Native flower: Colchicum Hungaricum **Reverse:** Value

Date	Mintage	F	VF	XF	Unc	BU
1992		0.10	0.25	0.35	0.50	—
1992 Proof	1,000	Value: 6.00				
1993		—	0.10	0.25	0.35	—
1993 Proof	30,000	Value: 1.50				
1994		—	0.10	0.25	0.35	—
1994 Proof	15,000	Value: 1.75				
1995		—	0.10	0.25	0.35	—
1995 Proof	15,000	Value: 1.75				
1996		—	0.10	0.25	0.35	—
1996 Proof	10,000	Value: 1.95				
1997		—	0.10	0.20	0.35	—
1997 Proof	3,000	Value: 4.25				
1998		—	—	—	0.35	—
1998 Proof	3,000	Value: 4.25				

Date	Mintage	F	VF	XF	Unc	BU
1999		—	—	—	0.35	—
1999 Proof	3,000	Value: 4.25				
2000		—	—	—	0.35	—
2000 Proof	3,000	Value: 4.25				
2001		—	—	—	0.35	—
2001 Proof	3,000	Value: 4.25				

KM# 694 5 FORINT **Weight:** 4.2000 g. **Composition:** Brass **Obverse:** Great White Egret

Date	Mintage	F	VF	XF	Unc	BU
1992		0.15	0.30	0.60	1.00	—
1992 Proof	1,000	Value: 7.00				
1993		0.10	0.25	0.45	0.75	—
1993 Proof	30,000	Value: 2.00				
1994		0.10	0.20	0.30	0.65	—
1994 Proof	15,000	Value: 2.50				
1995		0.15	0.30	0.40	0.75	—
1995 Proof	15,000	Value: 2.50				
1996		0.25	0.50	0.65	0.80	—
1996 Proof	10,000	Value: 3.00				
1997		0.15	0.30	0.40	0.75	—
1997 Proof	3,000	Value: 5.00				
1998		—	—	—	3.00	—
1998 Proof	3,000	Value: 5.00				
1999		0.15	0.30	0.40	0.75	—
1999 Proof	3,000	Value: 5.00				
2000		0.10	0.25	0.35	0.75	—
2000 Proof	3,000	Value: 5.00				
2001		—	—	—	0.75	—
2001 Proof	3,000	Value: 5.00				

KM# 695 10 FORINT **Weight:** 6.1000 g. **Composition:** Copper-Nickel Clad Brass **Obverse:** Arms of the Republic **Reverse:** Value

Date	Mintage	F	VF	XF	Unc	BU
1992		—	—	—	6.00	—
1992 Proof	1,000	Value: 8.00				
1993		0.10	0.25	0.45	1.00	—
1993 Proof	30,000	Value: 2.50				
1994		—	0.15	0.35	0.85	—
1994 Proof	15,000	Value: 3.00				
1995		0.10	0.25	0.45	1.00	—
1995 Proof	15,000	Value: 3.00				
1996		0.15	0.30	0.50	1.00	—
1996 Proof	10,000	Value: 3.50				
1997		0.20	0.35	0.55	1.00	—
1997 Proof	3,000	Value: 5.50				
1998		—	—	—	2.50	—
1998 Proof	3,000	Value: 5.50				
1999		—	—	—	2.50	—
1999 Proof	3,000	Value: 5.50				
2000		—	—	—	2.50	—
2000 Proof	3,000	Value: 5.50				
2001		—	—	—	2.50	—
2001 Proof	3,000	Value: 5.50				

KM# 696 20 FORINT **Weight:** 6.9000 g. **Composition:** Nickel-Brass **Obverse:** Hungarian Iris **Reverse:** Value

Date	Mintage	F	VF	XF	Unc	BU
1992		—	—	—	7.00	—
1992 Proof	1,000	Value: 9.00				
1993		0.20	0.30	0.60	1.50	—
1993 Proof	30,000	Value: 3.50				
1994		0.15	0.25	0.50	1.25	—
1994 Proof	15,000	Value: 4.00				
1995		0.15	0.25	0.50	1.25	—
1995 Proof	15,000	Value: 4.00				
1996		0.20	0.35	0.70	1.50	—
1996 Proof	10,000	Value: 4.00				
1997		—	—	—	5.00	—
1997 Proof	3,000	Value: 6.00				
1998		—	—	—	3.50	—
1998 Proof	3,000	Value: 6.00				
1999		—	—	—	3.50	—

Date	Mintage	F	VF	XF	Unc	BU
1999 Proof	3,000	Value: 6.00				
2000		—	—	—	3.50	—
2000 Proof	3,000	Value: 6.00				
2001		—	—	—	1.50	—
2001 Proof	3,000	Value: 4.00				

KM# 697 50 FORINT **Weight:** 7.7000 g. **Composition:** Copper-Nickel Clad Brass **Obverse:** Saker falcon **Reverse:** Value

Date	Mintage	F	VF	XF	Unc	BU
1992		—	—	—	10.00	—
1992 Proof	1,000	Value: 12.00				
1993		0.50	0.65	1.25	3.00	—
1993 Proof	30,000	Value: 5.00				
1994		0.25	0.45	0.85	3.00	—
1994 Proof	15,000	Value: 5.00				
1995		—	0.25	0.50	2.50	—
1995 Proof	15,000	Value: 5.00				
1996		0.30	0.50	1.00	3.00	—
1996 Proof	10,000	Value: 5.00				
1997		—	—	—	3.00	—
1997 Proof	3,000	Value: 6.50				
1998		—	—	—	5.50	—
1998 Proof	3,000	Value: 6.50				
1999		—	—	—	5.50	—
1999 Proof	3,000	Value: 6.50				
2000		—	—	—	5.50	—
2000 Proof	3,000	Value: 6.50				
2001		—	—	—	3.00	—
2001 Proof	3,000	Value: 5.00				

KM# 734 75 FORINT **Weight:** 31.4600 g. **Composition:** 0.9250 Silver .9356 oz. ASW **Subject:** 75th Anniversary - Hungarian National Bank **Obverse:** National arms above denomination **Reverse:** Goddess Juno

Date	Mintage	F	VF	XF	Unc	BU
1999		—	—	—	32.50	—
1999 Proof	Est. 4,500	Value: 40.00				

KM# 678 100 FORINT (Szaz) **Weight:** 12.0000 g. **Composition:** Copper-Nickel-Zinc **Obverse:** Value **Reverse:** Adreas Fay

Date	Mintage	F	VF	XF	Unc	BU
1990BP	20,000	—	—	—	5.00	—
1990BP Proof	10,000	Value: 7.00				

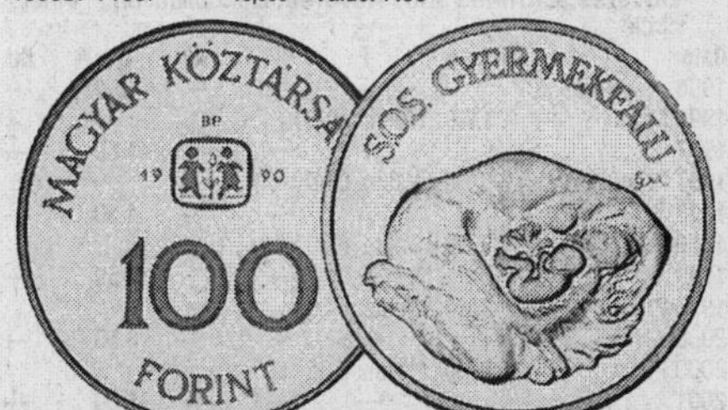

KM# 700 100 FORINT (Szaz) **Weight:** 12.0000 g. **Composition:** Copper-Nickel **Subject:** S.O.S. Gyermekfalu, Children's Village **Obverse:** Value **Reverse:** Mother protecting child

Date	Mintage	F	VF	XF	Unc	BU
1990 Proof	50,000	Value: 12.00				

KM# 701 100 FORINT (Szaz) Weight: 12.0000 g. **Composition:** Copper-Nickel **Subject:** Hungarian Theatre **Obverse:** Value **Reverse:** Theatre scene

Date	Mintage	F	VF	XF	Unc	BU
1990	5,000	—	—	—	10.00	—
1990 Proof	5,000	Value: 12.00				

KM# 682 100 FORINT (Szaz) Weight: 12.0000 g. **Composition:** Copper-Nickel-Zinc **Subject:** Papal Visit **Obverse:** Arms of the Republic **Reverse:** Pope John Paul II

Date	Mintage	F	VF	XF	Unc	BU
1991	30,000	—	—	—	3.00	—
1991 Proof	30,000	Value: 6.00				

KM# 698 100 FORINT (Szaz) Weight: 9.4000 g. **Composition:** Brass **Obverse:** Arms of the Republic **Reverse:** Value

Date	Mintage	F	VF	XF	Unc	BU
1992	—	—	—	—	12.00	—
1992 Proof	1,000	Value: 15.00				
1993	—	—	—	—	3.00	—
1993 Proof	30,000	Value: 6.00				
1994	—	—	—	—	2.50	—
1994 Proof	15,000	Value: 6.00				
1995	—	—	—	—	2.50	—
1995 Proof	15,000	Value: 6.00				
1996	—	—	—	—	2.50	—
1996 Proof	10,000	Value: 6.00				
1997	—	—	—	—	6.00	—
1997 Proof	3,000	Value: 8.00				
1998	—	—	—	—	6.00	—
1998 Proof	3,000	Value: 8.00				

KM# 721 100 FORINT (Szaz) Ring Composition: Stainless Steel **Center Composition:** Brass Plated Steel **Obverse:** Crowned arms **Reverse:** Denomination in inner circle

Date	Mintage	F	VF	XF	Unc	BU
1996	—	—	—	—	4.50	—
1996 Proof	1,000	Value: 12.00				
1997	—	—	—	—	4.50	—
1997 Proof	3,000	Value: 8.00				
1998	—	—	—	—	4.50	—
1998 Proof	3,000	Value: 8.00				
1999	—	—	—	—	6.50	—
1999 Proof	3,000	Value: 8.00				
2000	—	—	—	—	6.50	—
2000 Proof	3,000	Value: 8.00				
2001	—	—	—	—	5.00	—
2001 Proof	3,000	Value: 8.00				
2002	—	—	—	—	5.00	—
2002 Proof	3,000	Value: 8.00				

KM# 726 100 FORINT (Szaz) Weight: 9.4000 g. **Composition:** Bronze **Subject:** Revolution of 1848 **Obverse:** Hungarian Order of Military Merit (1848-1849) II Class **Reverse:** Revolutionary ribbon badge above poetry verse

Date	Mintage	F	VF	XF	Unc	BU
1998	15,000	—	—	—	7.00	—
1998 Proof	15,000	Value: 9.00				

KM# 760 100 FORINT Ring Composition: Stainless SteelCenter **Weight:** 8.0000 g. **Center Composition:** Brass Plated Steel **Obverse:** Head of Kossuth right in inner circle **Reverse:** Value **Edge:** Reeded **Size:** 23.7 mm.

Date	Mintage	F	VF	XF	Unc	BU
2002	—	—	—	—	2.00	—
2002 Proof	10,000	Value: 5.00				

KM# 688 200 FORINT Weight: 10.0000 g. **Composition:** 0.5000 Silver .1608 oz. ASW **Reverse:** White storks

Date	Mintage	F	VF	XF	Unc	BU
1992BP	20,000	—	—	—	8.00	—
1992BP Proof	80,000	Value: 10.00				

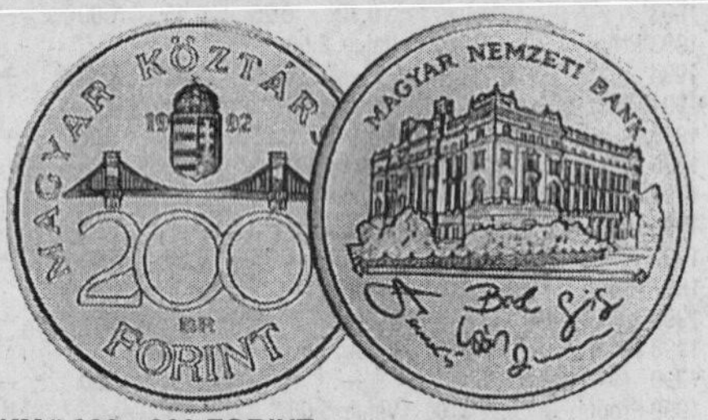

KM# 689 200 FORINT Weight: 12.0000 g. **Composition:** 0.5000 Silver .1929 oz. ASW **Obverse:** Erzsebet Bridge **Reverse:** National Bank

Date	Mintage	F	VF	XF	Unc	BU
1992	3,514,023	—	—	—	6.00	—
1992 Proof	29,998	Value: 9.00				
1993	2,540,993	—	—	—	6.00	—
1993 Proof	30,000	Value: 9.00				

KM# 707 200 FORINT Weight: 12.0000 g. **Composition:** 0.5000 Silver .1929 oz. ASW **Obverse:** Erzsebet Bridge **Reverse:** Ferenc Deak

Date	Mintage	F	VF	XF	Unc	BU
1994	—	—	—	—	6.50	—
1994 Proof	15,000	Value: 10.00				
1995	—	—	—	—	7.50	—
1995 Proof	15,000	Value: 10.00				
1997	—	—	—	—	10.00	—
1997 Proof	3,000	Value: 12.00				

Date	Mintage	F	VF	XF	Unc	BU
1998	—	—	—	—	10.00	—
1998 Proof	3,000	Value: 12.00				

KM# 745 200 FORINT Weight: 9.5600 g. **Composition:** Brass **Subject:** Millennium **Obverse:** Crowned arms above denomination **Reverse:** Rodin's "The Thinker" statue and solar system **Edge:** Plain **Note:** Similar to 2000 Forint, KM#743.

Date	Mintage	F	VF	XF	Unc	BU
2000	—	—	—	—	4.50	—
2000 Proof	10,000	Value: 6.00				

KM# 754 200 FORINT Weight: 9.4000 g. **Composition:** Brass **Subject:** Childrens Literature: Ludas Matyi **Obverse:** Denomination **Reverse:** Man holding a goose **Edge:** Plain **Size:** 29.2 mm.

Date	Mintage	F	VF	XF	Unc	BU
2001	12,000	—	—	—	6.50	—
2001 Proof	5,000	Value: 12.50				

KM# 755 200 FORINT Composition: Brass **Subject:** Childrens Literature: Janos Vitez **Obverse:** Denomination **Reverse:** Soldier riding a flying bird **Edge:** Plain **Size:** 29.2 mm.

Date	Mintage	F	VF	XF	Unc	BU
2001	12,000	—	—	—	6.50	—
2001 Proof	5,000	Value: 12.50				

KM# 756 200 FORINT Composition: Brass **Subject:** Childrens Literature: Toldi **Obverse:** Denomination **Reverse:** Knight kicking a boat off the shore **Edge:** Plain **Size:** 29.2 mm.

Date	Mintage	F	VF	XF	Unc	BU
2001	12,000	—	—	—	6.50	—
2001 Proof	5,000	Value: 12.50				

KM# 757 200 FORINT Composition: Brass **Subject:** Childrens Literature: A Pal Utcai Fiuk **Obverse:** Denomination **Reverse:** Two men and cord wood **Edge:** Plain **Size:** 29.2 mm.

Date	Mintage	F	VF	XF	Unc	BU
2001	12,000	—	—	—	6.50	—
2001 Proof	5,000	Value: 12.50				

KM# 672 500 FORINT (Otszaz) **Weight:** 28.0000 g. **Composition:** 0.9000 Silver .8102 oz. ASW **Series:** Albertville Olympics 1992 **Obverse:** Denominatin

Date	Mintage	F	VF	XF	Unc	BU
1989BP	15,000	—	—	—	27.50	—
1989BP Proof	15,000	Value: 30.00				

KM# 699 500 FORINT (Otszaz) **Weight:** 28.0000 g. **Composition:** 0.9000 Silver .8102 oz. ASW **Subject:** 200th Anniversary - Birth of Ferenc Kolcsey **Obverse:** Crowned arms and denomination **Reverse:** Kölcsey Ferenc

Date	Mintage	F	VF	XF	Unc	BU
1990BP	10,000	—	—	—	40.00	—
1990BP Proof	5,000	Value: 50.00				

KM# 686 500 FORINT (Otszaz) **Weight:** 28.0000 g. **Composition:** 0.9000 Silver .8102 oz. ASW **Obverse:** Value **Reverse:** Anjou Liliom **Rev. Legend:** Karoly Robert Emlekere

Date	Mintage	F	VF	XF	Unc	BU
1992BP	10,000	—	—	—	25.00	—
1992BP Proof	20,000	Value: 30.00				

KM# 679 500 FORINT (Otszaz) **Weight:** 28.0000 g. **Composition:** 0.9000 Silver .8102 oz. ASW **Obverse:** King Mathias on horse facing left **Reverse:** King Mathias and Queen Beatrix

Date	Mintage	F	VF	XF	Unc	BU
1990BP	15,000	—	—	—	32.50	—
1990BP Proof	15,000	Value: 37.50				

KM# 683 500 FORINT (Otszaz) **Weight:** 28.0000 g. **Composition:** 0.9000 Silver .8102 oz. ASW **Subject:** Papal Visit **Obverse:** Arms of the Republic **Reverse:** Pope John Paul II

Date	Mintage	F	VF	XF	Unc	BU
1991BP	10,000	—	—	—	22.50	—
1991BP Proof	20,000	Value: 28.50				

KM# 687 500 FORINT (Otszaz) **Weight:** 28.0000 g. **Composition:** 0.9000 Silver .8102 oz. ASW **Subject:** Canonization of King Ladislaus **Obverse:** Ladislaus Denar (obv. and rev.) and value **Reverse:** King Ladislaus

Date	Mintage	F	VF	XF	Unc	BU
1992BP	10,000	—	—	—	25.00	—
1992BP Proof	20,000	Value: 32.50				

KM# 680 500 FORINT (Otszaz) **Weight:** 28.0000 g. **Composition:** 0.9000 Silver .8102 oz. ASW **Obverse:** Denomination **Reverse:** Two capital cities of King Mathias

Date	Mintage	F	VF	XF	Unc	BU
1990	15,000	—	—	—	32.50	—
1990 Proof	15,000	Value: 37.50				

KM# 685 500 FORINT (Otszaz) **Weight:** 28.0000 g. **Composition:** 0.9000 Silver .8102 oz. ASW **Subject:** 200th Anniversary - Birth of Count Szechenyi **Obverse:** Locomotive and value **Reverse:** Istvan Szechenyi

Date	Mintage	F	VF	XF	Unc	BU
1991BP	15,000	—	—	—	25.00	—
1991BP Proof	15,000	Value: 32.50				

KM# 690 500 FORINT (Otszaz) **Weight:** 31.4600 g. **Composition:** 0.9250 Silver .9356 oz. ASW **Obverse:** Crowned arms and denomination **Reverse:** Telstar I satelite

Date	Mintage	F	VF	XF	Unc	BU
1992BP	—	—	—	—	22.50	—
1992BP Proof	Est. 15,000	Value: 27.50				

KM# 702 500 FORINT (Otszaz) **Weight:** 31.4600 g. **Composition:** 0.9250 Silver .9356 oz. ASW **Obverse:** Denomination and crowned arms **Reverse:** Old Danube Ship "Arpad"

Date	Mintage	F	VF	XF	Unc	BU
1993BP	10,000	—	—	—	15.00	—
1993BP Proof	15,000	Value: 16.50				

KM# 708 500 FORINT (Otszaz) **Weight:** 31.4600 g. **Composition:** 0.9250 Silver .9357 oz. ASW **Reverse:** Old Danube Ship "Carolina"

Date	Mintage	F	VF	XF	Unc	BU
1994	10,000	—	—	—	18.00	—
1994 Proof	15,000	Value: 20.00				

KM# 764 500 FORINT **Weight:** 13.9000 g. **Composition:** Copper Nickel **Subject:** Farkas Kempelen's Chess Machine **Obverse:** Denomination **Reverse:** Robotic human form chess playing machine built in 1769 **Edge:** Plain **Shape:** Square **Size:** 28.5 mm.

Date	Mintage	F	VF	XF	Unc	BU
2002BP	5,000	—	—	—	7.50	—
2002BP Proof	5,000	Value: 8.00				

KM# 704 500 FORINT (Otszaz) **Weight:** 31.4600 g. **Composition:** 0.9250 Silver .9357 oz. ASW **Obverse:** Crowned arms and denomination **Reverse:** European Currency Union

Date	Mintage	F	VF	XF	Unc	BU
1993BP	10,000	—	—	—	18.50	—
1993BP Proof	30,000	Value: 21.50				

KM# 709 500 FORINT (Otszaz) **Weight:** 31.4600 g. **Composition:** 0.9250 Silver .9357 oz. ASW **Subject:** Death of Lajos Kossuth

Date	Mintage	F	VF	XF	Unc	BU
1994	10,000	—	—	—	23.50	—
1994 Proof	10,000	Value: 28.50				

KM# 765 500 FORINT **Weight:** 13.8000 g. **Composition:** Copper Nickel **Subject:** Rubik's Cube **Obverse:** Inscription on Rubik's Cube design **Reverse:** Rubik's Cube with inscription **Edge:** Plain **Shape:** Square **Size:** 28.5 mm.

Date	Mintage	F	VF	XF	Unc	BU
2002BP	5,000	—	—	—	7.50	—
2002BP Proof	5,000	Value: 8.00				

KM# 705 500 FORINT (Otszaz) **Weight:** 31.4600 g. **Composition:** 0.9250 Silver .9357 oz. ASW **Subject:** Expo '96

Date	Mintage	F	VF	XF	Unc	BU
1993	20,000	—	—	—	17.50	—
1993 Proof	80,000	Value: 20.00				

KM# 710 500 FORINT (Otszaz) **Weight:** 31.4600 g. **Composition:** 0.9250 Silver .9357 oz. ASW **Subject:** International European Union **Reverse:** St. Istvan and Halaszbastya

Date	Mintage	F	VF	XF	Unc	BU
1994	10,000	—	—	—	22.50	—
1994 Proof	30,000	Value: 27.50				

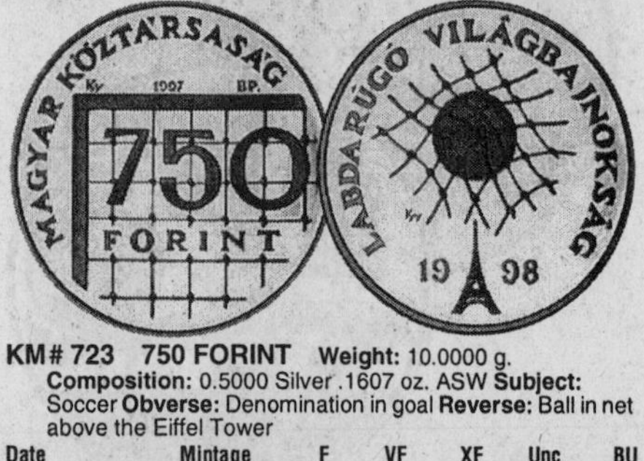

KM# 723 750 FORINT **Weight:** 10.0000 g. **Composition:** 0.5000 Silver .1607 oz. ASW **Subject:** Soccer **Obverse:** Denomination in goal **Reverse:** Ball in net above the Eiffel Tower

Date	Mintage	F	VF	XF	Unc	BU
1997	3,000	—	—	—	25.00	—
1997 Proof	17,000	Value: 20.00				

KM# 725 750 FORINT **Weight:** 10.0000 g. **Composition:** 0.5000 Silver .1607 oz. ASW **Subject:** 125th

Anniversary - Budapest **Obverse:** Lanc Bridge **Reverse:** City map and arms

Date	Mintage	F	VF	XF	Unc	BU
1998	3,000	—	—	—	30.00	—
1998 Proof	12,000	Value: 20.00				

KM# 706 1000 FORINT Weight: 31.4600 g. **Composition:** 0.9250 Silver .9357 oz. ASW **Subject:** World Cup Soccer **Reverse:** Goalie

Date	Mintage	F	VF	XF	Unc	BU
1993BP	10,000	—	—	—	23.50	—
1993BP Proof	15,000	Value: 27.50				

KM# 712 1000 FORINT Weight: 31.4600 g. **Composition:** 0.9250 Silver .9357 oz. ASW **Series:** Atlanta Olympics **Reverse:** Swimmers

Date	Mintage	F	VF	XF	Unc	BU
1994	10,000	—	—	—	21.50	—
1994 Proof	40,000	Value: 23.50				

KM# 713 1000 FORINT Weight: 31.4600 g. **Composition:** 0.9250 Silver .9357 oz. ASW **Subject:** Protect Our World **Reverse:** Globe in trunk

Date	Mintage	F	VF	XF	Unc	BU
1994	10,000	—	—	—	25.00	—
1994 Proof	10,000	Value: 30.00				

KM# 714 1000 FORINT Weight: 31.4600 g. **Composition:** 0.9250 Silver .9357 oz. ASW **Reverse:** Old Danube Ship "Hableany"

Date	Mintage	F	VF	XF	Unc	BU
1995	10,000	—	—	—	25.00	—
1995 Proof	20,000	Value: 27.50				

KM# 715 1000 FORINT Weight: 31.4600 g. **Composition:** 0.9250 Silver .9357 oz. ASW **Obverse:** Abbot's seal impression and value **Reverse:** Panndnhalma ruins

Date	Mintage	F	VF	XF	Unc	BU
1995	10,000	—	—	—	28.00	—
1995 Proof	10,000	Value: 32.50				

KM# 716 1000 FORINT Weight: 31.4600 g. **Composition:** 0.9250 Silver .9357 oz. ASW **Series:** Atlanta Olympics **Reverse:** Fencing match

Date	Mintage	F	VF	XF	Unc	BU
1995	5,000	—	—	—	30.00	—
1995 Proof	25,000	Value: 27.50				

KM# 720 1000 FORINT Weight: 31.4600 g. **Composition:** 0.9250 Silver .9357 oz. ASW **Subject:** European Union **Obverse:** Crowned arms divide date **Reverse:** Hungarian Parliament building, "ecu"

Date	Mintage	F	VF	XF	Unc	BU
1995	5,000	—	—	—	32.50	—
1995 Proof	18,000	Value: 30.00				

KM# 766 1000 FORINT Weight: 19.5000 g. **Composition:** Copper-Nickel **Obverse:** Denomination and satellite dish **Reverse:** Mercury

Date	Mintage	F	VF	XF	Unc	BU
2002BP	15,000	—	—	—	15.00	—

KM# 718 2000 FORINT Weight: 31.4600 g. **Composition:** 0.9250 Silver .9357 oz. ASW **Subject:** 1100th Anniversary of Hungarian Nartionhood **Reverse:** Three equestrian archers above old shield

Date	Mintage	F	VF	XF	Unc	BU
1996	10,000	—	—	—	35.00	—
1996 Proof	10,000	Value: 45.00				

KM# 717 2000 FORINT Weight: 31.4600 g. **Composition:** 0.9250 Silver .9357 oz. ASW **Subject:** 50th Anniversary Forint Rebirth **Reverse:** 13 coin designs

Date	Mintage	F	VF	XF	Unc	BU
1996	5,000	—	—	—	35.00	—
1996 Proof	5,000	Value: 45.00				

KM# 722 2000 FORINT **Weight:** 31.4600 g. **Composition:** 0.9250 Silver .9357 oz. ASW **Obverse:** Lake Balaton view above denomination **Reverse:** Steam ships "Helka" and "Kelen"

Date	Mintage	F	VF	XF	Unc	BU
1997	5,000	—	—	—	38.00	—
1997 Proof	15,000	Value: 35.00				

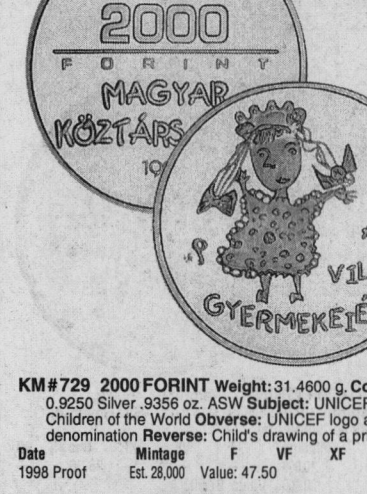

KM# 729 2000 FORINT **Weight:** 31.4600 g. **Composition:** 0.9250 Silver .9356 oz. ASW **Subject:** UNICEF - For the Children of the World **Obverse:** UNICEF logo above denomination **Reverse:** Child's drawing of a princess

Date	Mintage	F	VF	XF	Unc	BU
1998 Proof	Est. 28,000	Value: 47.50				

KM# 732 2000 FORINT **Weight:** 31.4600 g. **Composition:** 0.9250 Silver .9356 oz. ASW **Subject:** 150th Birthday - Lorand Eotvos **Obverse:** Denomination **Reverse:** Framed portrait and scientific instrument

Date	Mintage	F	VF	XF	Unc	BU
1998	3,000	—	—	—	40.00	—
1998 Proof	3,000	Value: 45.00				

KM# 724 2000 FORINT **Weight:** 31.1035 g. **Composition:** 0.9250 Silver .9250 oz. ASW **Subject:** European Union **Obverse:** Crowned arms divide date above denomination **Reverse:** Royal Palace of Budapest

Date	Mintage	F	VF	XF	Unc	BU
1997	3,000	—	—	—	37.50	—
1997 Proof	27,000	Value: 35.00				

KM# 730 2000 FORINT **Weight:** 31.4600 g. **Composition:** 0.9250 Silver .9356 oz. ASW **Subject:** World Wildlife Fund **Obverse:** World Wildlife Fund logo above Hungarian arms and denomination **Reverse:** Fork-tailed chimney swallows

Date	Mintage	F	VF	XF	Unc	BU
1998 Proof	Est. 18,000	Value: 55.00				

KM# 733 2000 FORINT **Weight:** 31.4600 g. **Composition:** 0.9250 Silver .9356 oz. ASW **Subject:** European Union **Obverse:** National arms **Reverse:** Monuments, Euro logo

Date	Mintage	F	VF	XF	Unc	BU
1998	—	—	—	—	40.00	—
1998 Proof	12,000	Value: 50.00				

KM# 727 2000 FORINT **Weight:** 31.4600 g. **Composition:** 0.9250 Silver .9356 oz. ASW **Subject:** Revolution of 1848 **Obverse:** Hungarian Order of Military Merit (1848-1849) I Class **Reverse:** Hungarian military flag over European map

Date	Mintage	F	VF	XF	Unc	BU
1998	5,000	—	—	—	37.50	—
1998 Proof	10,000	Value: 35.00				

KM# 731 2000 FORINT **Weight:** 31.4600 g. **Composition:** 0.9250 Silver .9356 oz. ASW **Obverse:** Sailboats on Lake Balaton above denomination **Reverse:** The "Phoenix" under full sail

Date	Mintage	F	VF	XF	Unc	BU
1998	—	—	—	—	37.50	—
1998 Proof	Est. 10,000	Value: 32.50				

KM# 743 2000 FORINT **Weight:** 20.0000 g. **Composition:** 0.9250 Silver .5948 oz. ASW **Subject:** Millennium **Obverse:** National arms **Reverse:** Rodin's "The Thinker" and solar system **Edge:** Plain **Shape:** 7-sided

Date	Mintage	F	VF	XF	Unc	BU
1999	—	—	—	—	30.00	—
1999 Proof	15,000	Value: 35.00				

KM# 744 2000 FORINT **Weight:** 20.0000 g. **Composition:** 0.9250 Silver .5948 oz. ASW **Subject:** Olympics **Obverse:** National arms **Reverse:** Hammer throw

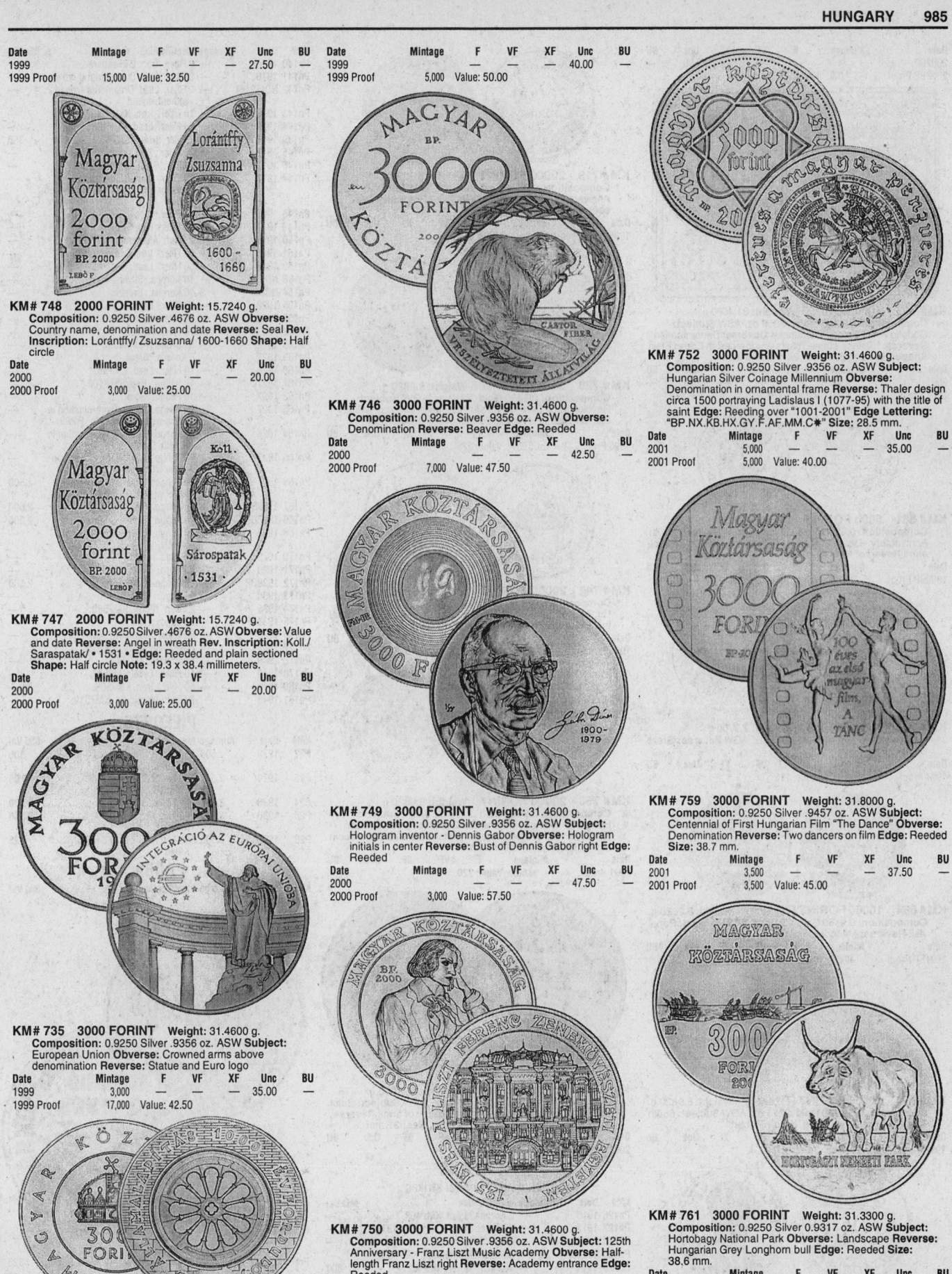

Date	Mintage	F	VF	XF	Unc	BU
1999	—	—	—	—	27.50	—
1999 Proof	15,000	Value: 32.50				

KM# 748 2000 FORINT Weight: 15.7240 g. **Composition:** 0.9250 Silver .4676 oz. ASW **Obverse:** Country name, denomination and date **Reverse:** Seal **Rev. Inscription:** Lorántffy/ Zsuzsanna/ 1600-1660 **Shape:** Half circle

Date	Mintage	F	VF	XF	Unc	BU
2000	—	—	—	—	20.00	—
2000 Proof	3,000	Value: 25.00				

KM# 747 2000 FORINT Weight: 15.7240 g. **Composition:** 0.9250 Silver .4676 oz. ASW **Obverse:** Value and date **Reverse:** Angel in wreath **Rev. Inscription:** Koll./ Saraspatak/ • 1531 • **Edge:** Reeded and plain sectioned **Shape:** Half circle **Note:** 19.3 x 38.4 millimeters.

Date	Mintage	F	VF	XF	Unc	BU
2000	—	—	—	—	20.00	—
2000 Proof	3,000	Value: 25.00				

KM# 735 3000 FORINT Weight: 31.4600 g. **Composition:** 0.9250 Silver .9356 oz. ASW **Subject:** European Union **Obverse:** Crowned arms above denomination **Reverse:** Statue and Euro logo

Date	Mintage	F	VF	XF	Unc	BU
1999	3,000	—	—	—	35.00	—
1999 Proof	17,000	Value: 42.50				

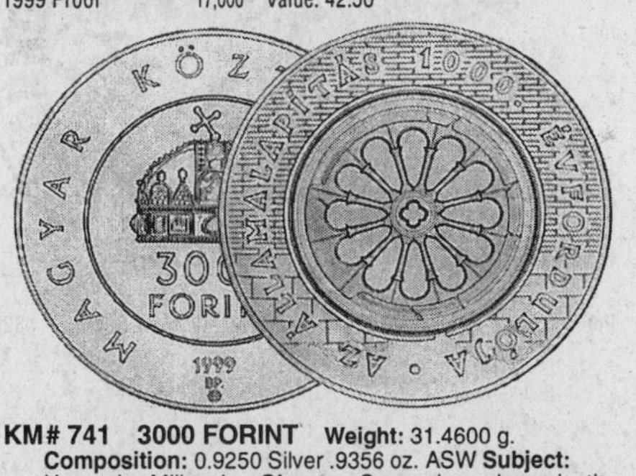

KM# 741 3000 FORINT Weight: 31.4600 g. **Composition:** 0.9250 Silver .9356 oz. ASW **Subject:** Hungarian Millennium **Obverse:** Crown above denomination **Reverse:** Round window design **Edge:** Plain **Note:** Gold-plated center.

Date	Mintage	F	VF	XF	Unc	BU
1999	—	—	—	—	40.00	—
1999 Proof	5,000	Value: 50.00				

KM# 746 3000 FORINT Weight: 31.4600 g. **Composition:** 0.9250 Silver .9356 oz. ASW **Obverse:** Denomination **Reverse:** Beaver **Edge:** Reeded

Date	Mintage	F	VF	XF	Unc	BU
2000	—	—	—	—	42.50	—
2000 Proof	7,000	Value: 47.50				

KM# 749 3000 FORINT Weight: 31.4600 g. **Composition:** 0.9250 Silver .9356 oz. ASW **Subject:** Hologram inventor - Dennis Gabor **Obverse:** Hologram initials in center **Reverse:** Bust of Dennis Gabor right **Edge:** Reeded

Date	Mintage	F	VF	XF	Unc	BU
2000	—	—	—	—	47.50	—
2000 Proof	3,000	Value: 57.50				

KM# 750 3000 FORINT Weight: 31.4600 g. **Composition:** 0.9250 Silver .9356 oz. ASW **Subject:** 125th Anniversary - Franz Liszt Music Academy **Obverse:** Half-length Franz Liszt right **Reverse:** Academy entrance **Edge:** Reeded

Date	Mintage	F	VF	XF	Unc	BU
2000	—	—	—	—	47.50	—
2000 Proof	3,000	Value: 57.50				

KM# 752 3000 FORINT Weight: 31.4600 g. **Composition:** 0.9250 Silver .9356 oz. ASW **Subject:** Hungarian Silver Coinage Millennium **Obverse:** Denomination in ornamental frame **Reverse:** Thaler design circa 1500 portraying Ladislaus I (1077-95) with the title of saint **Edge:** Reeding over "1001-2001" **Edge Lettering:** "BP.NX.KB.HX.GY.F.AF.MM.C✱" **Size:** 28.5 mm.

Date	Mintage	F	VF	XF	Unc	BU
2001	5,000	—	—	—	35.00	—
2001 Proof	5,000	Value: 40.00				

KM# 759 3000 FORINT Weight: 31.8000 g. **Composition:** 0.9250 Silver .9457 oz. ASW **Subject:** Centennial of First Hungarian Film "The Dance" **Obverse:** Denomination **Reverse:** Two dancers on film **Edge:** Reeded **Size:** 38.7 mm.

Date	Mintage	F	VF	XF	Unc	BU
2001	3,500	—	—	—	37.50	—
2001 Proof	3,500	Value: 45.00				

KM# 761 3000 FORINT Weight: 31.3300 g. **Composition:** 0.9250 Silver 0.9317 oz. ASW **Subject:** Hortobagy National Park **Obverse:** Landscape **Reverse:** Hungarian Grey Longhorn bull **Edge:** Reeded **Size:** 38.6 mm.

Date	Mintage	F	VF	XF	Unc	BU
2002	5,000	—	—	—	30.00	—
2002 Proof	5,000	Value: 35.00				

KM# 767 3000 FORINT Weight: 31.4600 g. **Composition:** 0.9250 Silver 0.9356 oz. ASW **Subject:** 100th Anniversary - Birth of Kovacs Margit (1902-1977) **Obverse:** Denomination **Reverse:** The "Trumpet of Judgement Day"

Date	Mintage	F	VF	XF	Unc	BU
2002BP		—	—	—	38.00	—
2002BP Proof	4,000	Value: 48.00				

KM# 751 4000 FORINT Weight: 31.4600 g. **Composition:** 0.9250 Silver .9356 oz. ASW **Subject:** Godollo Artist Colony Centennial **Obverse:** Denomination **Reverse:** "Sisters" stained glass window design **Edge:** Plain **Shape:** Rectangular **Size:** 26.4 x 39.6 mm.

Date	Mintage	F	VF	XF	Unc	BU
2001	4,000	—	—	—	40.00	—
2001 Proof	4,000	Value: 50.00				

KM# 681 5000 FORINT Weight: 6.9820 g. **Composition:** 0.9860 Gold .2213 oz. AGW **Subject:** 500th Anniversary - Death of Mathias I **Obverse:** Hunyadi coat-of-arms **Reverse:** King Mathias

Date	Mintage	F	VF	XF	Unc	BU
1990BP Proof	10,000	Value: 145				

KM# 711 5000 FORINT Weight: 7.7700 g. **Composition:** 0.5840 Gold .1459 oz. AGW **Reverse:** Great Bustard Bird

Date	Mintage	F	VF	XF	Unc	BU
1994 Proof	5,000	Value: 115				

KM# 684 10000 FORINT (Tizezer) Weight: 6.9820 g. **Composition:** 0.9860 Gold .2213 oz. AGW **Subject:** Papal visit **Reverse:** Madonna and child

Date	Mintage	F	VF	XF	Unc	BU
1991BP Proof	10,000	Value: 165				

KM# 691 10000 FORINT (Tizezer) Weight: 6.9820 g. **Composition:** 0.9860 Gold .2213 oz. AGW **Subject:** 650th Anniversary - Death of Kg. Karoly Robert

Date	Mintage	F	VF	XF	Unc	BU
1992 Proof	10,000	Value: 150				

KM# 703 10000 FORINT (Tizezer) Weight: 6.9820 g. **Composition:** 0.9860 Gold .2213 oz. AGW **Subject:** Centennial - Death of Ferenc Erkel

Date	Mintage	F	VF	XF	Unc	BU
1993 Proof	5,000	Value: 165				

KM# 719 20000 FORINT Weight: 6.9820 g. **Composition:** 0.9860 Gold .2213 oz. AGW **Subject:** 1100th Anniversary of Hungarian Nationhood **Reverse:** Two equestrian archers

Date	Mintage	F	VF	XF	Unc	BU
1996 Proof	5,000	Value: 225				

KM# 728 20000 FORINT Weight: 6.9820 g. **Composition:** 0.9860 Gold .2213 oz. AGW **Subject:** Revolution of 1848 **Obverse:** Hungarian Order of Military Merit III Class **Reverse:** Portrait of Lajos Batthyany

Date	Mintage	F	VF	XF	Unc	BU
1998 Proof	Est. 5,000	Value: 225				

KM# 742 20000 FORINT Weight: 6.9820 g. **Composition:** 0.9860 Gold .2213 oz. AGW **Subject:** Hungarian State Millennium **Obverse:** Portrait of St. Michael the Archangel **Reverse:** Crown **Edge:** Plain

Date	F	VF	XF	Unc	BU
1999 Proof	Est. 3,000	Value: 250			

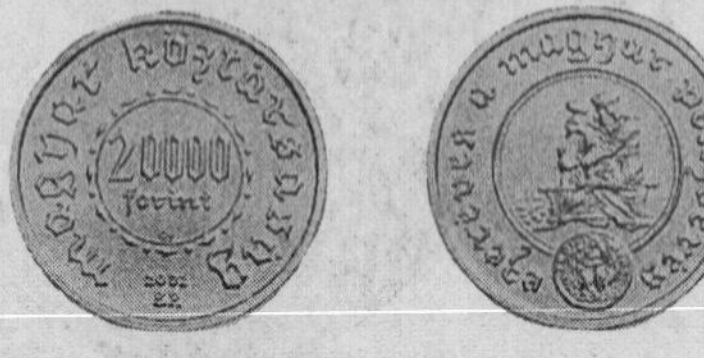

KM# 753 20000 FORINT Weight: 6.9820 g. **Composition:** 0.9860 Gold .2213 oz. AGW **Subject:** Hungarian Coinage Millennium **Obverse:** Denomination **Reverse:** Hammered coinage minting scene above old coin design **Edge:** Plain **Size:** 22 mm.

Date	Mintage	F	VF	XF	Unc	BU
2001 Proof	3,000	Value: 220				

KM# 758 100000 FORINT Weight: 31.1040 g. **Composition:** 0.9860 Gold .9860 oz. AGW **Subject:** Saint Stephen **Obverse:** Angels crowning coat of arms **Reverse:** King seated on throne **Edge:** Reeded **Size:** 37 mm.

Date	Mintage	F	VF	XF	Unc	BU
2001 Proof	3,000	Value: 650				

PATTERNS

Including off metal strikes

KM#	Date	Mintage	Identification	Mkt Val
Pn126	1910	—	2 Korona. Lead. KM#493.	—
Pn127	1913	—	2 Korona. Aluminum. KM#493.	—
Pn128	1914	—	Filler. Steel. KM#480.	—
Pn130	1914	—	2 Korona. Aluminum. KM#493.	—
Pn129	1914	—	10 Filler. Silver. KM#482.	800
Pn131	1915	—	2 Filler. New Silver. KM#481	130
Pn134	1915	—	20 Filler. Iron. KM#498.	250
Pn136	1915	—	20 Filler. Silver. KM#483.	1,000
Pn137	1915	—	1/2 Korona. Silver. Franz Joseph I bust right. Value in wreath.	1,000
Pn132	1915	—	10 Filler. Nickel. KM#494.	—
Pn133	1915	—	10 Filler. Nickel. KM#496.	—
Pn135	1915	—	20 Filler. Iron. Circle around crown.	—
Pn138	1916	—	2 Heller. Lead. One side.	—
Pn140	1916	—	2 Filler. Iron. 2 in square.	—
Pn141	1916	—	2 Filler. Iron. Circle around crown.	—
Pn142	ND(1916)	—	2 Filler. Lead. Ornaments around 2, without legend.	—
Pn143	1916KB	—	10 Filler. Iron. KM#496	—
Pn144	1916	—	20 Filler. Lead. KM#498.	—
Pn139	1916	—	2 Filler. Iron. KM#481	350
Pn145	1917	—	20 Filler. Zinc.	—
Pn146	1917	—	2 Filler. Steel. With rosette.	—
Pn147	1917	—	10 Filler. Iron. Crown above sceptor and wsord. Value between wheat.	—
Pn148	1917	—	10 Filler. Zinc.	—
Pn149	1917	—	10 Filler. New Silver.	—
Pn150	1918	—	2 Filler. Aluminum. KM#497	—
Pn151	1918	—	50 Filler. Iron. Large crown.	—
Pn152	1918	—	50 Filler. Lead.	—
Pn153	NDBP	—	10 Korona. Silver.	—
Pn154	NDBP	3	10 Korona. Bronze.	—
Pn155	1922	—	20 Filler. Bronze.	—
Pn156	1922	—	20 Filler. New Silver.	—
Pn157	1922	—	20 Filler. Nickel.	—
Pn158	1922	—	5 Korona. Aluminum.	—
Pn159	1922	—	5 Korona. Brass.	—
Pn160	1926	—	10 Filler. Lead. KM#507	—
Pn161	1927	—	10 Pengo. Brass. Fr#100	—
Pn162	1927	—	10 Pengo. Gold.	—
Pn163	1927	—	20 Pengo. Brass. Denomination in grape-wheat ear wreath. Fr#99.	—
Pn164	1927	—	20 Pengo. Brass. Denomination in wreath. Fr#99.	—
Pn165	1927	—	20 Pengo. Gold. Denomination in grape-wheat ear wreath.	—
Pn166	1927	—	20 Pengo. Gold. Denomination in laurel wreath.	2,500
Pn167	1928BP	—	10 Pengo. Gold. Fr#100	2,500
Pn169	1928BP	—	20 Pengo. Gold. Fr#99.	2,500
Pn168	1928	—	20 Pengo. Brass. Smaller arms. Fr#99a.	—
Pn170	1929	—	5 Pengo. Lead.	—
Pn171	1929	—	5 Pengo. Silver.	—
Pn172	1929BP	—	20 Pengo. Gold. Fr#99a.	2,500
Pn173	1930	—	5 Pengo. Y#44	—
Pn174	1935	—	2 Filler. Nickel. KM#506.	—
Pn175	1935BP	—	2 Pengo.	—
Pn176	1938	—	50 Filler. Aluminum. KM#509.	—
Pn177	1939	—	Filler. Aluminum. KM#505.	—
Pn178	1940	—	Filler. Iron. KM#505.	—
Pn179	1940	—	10 Filler. Lead. KM#507.	—
Pn180	1941	—	50 Filler. Iron. KM#509.	—
Pn181	1943	—	2 Filler. Aluminum. KM#519.	—

PIEFORTS

KM#	Date	Mintage	Identification	Mkt Val
P22	1979	2,500	200 Forint. Silver. 0.6400 g. KM#615	100
P23	1979	2,500	200 Forint. Silver. 0.6400 g. KM#616	40.00
P24	1980	3,000	100 Forint. KM#617	30.00
P25	1980	3,000	200 Forint. Silver. 0.6400 g. KM#618	27.50
P26	1980	1,500	500 Forint. Silver. 0.6400 g. KM#619	125

PROBA

KM#	Date	Mintage	Identification	Mkt Val
Pr1	1986	—	500 Forint. Silver. KM#656. Soccer players.	325

KM#	Date	Mintage	Identification	Mkt Val

KM#	Date	Mintage	Identification	Mkt Val
Pr2	1986	—	500 Forint. Silver. KM#657. Stadium.	325

KM#	Date	Mintage	Identification	Mkt Val
Pr3	1988	—	100 Forint. Copper-Nickel. KM#664. Soccer players.	—

KM#	Date	Mintage	Identification	Mkt Val
Pr4	1988	—	100 Forint. Copper-Nickel. KM#665. Soccer goalie in net.	—

KM#	Date	Mintage	Identification	Mkt Val
Pr5	1989	—	100 Forint. Copper-Nickel. KM#668. Soccer players shaking hands.	—

TRIAL STRIKES

KM#	Date	Mintage	Identification	Mkt Val
TS39	1907	—	100 Korona. Bronze. KM#491.	—
TS40	1907	—	100 Korona. Bronze. KM#490. Without legend.	—
TS41	1910	—	2 Korona. Lead. KM#493.	—
TS42	1913	—	2 Korona. Aluminum. KM#493.	—
TS43	1914KB	—	Filler. Iron. KM#480.	—
TS44	1914KB	—	2 Filler. Nickel. KM#481.	—
TS45	1914KB	—	10 Filler. Copper-Zinc. KM#482.	—
TS46	1914	—	10 Filler. Silver Plated Copper-Nickel-Zinc.	—
TS47	1914KB	—	10 Filler. Silver. KM#482.	—
TS48	1914KB	—	20 Filler. Iron. KM#483.	—
TS49	1914	—	2 Korona. Aluminum. KM#493.	—
TS50	1914	—	2 Korona. Bronze. KM#486.	—
TS51	1915KB	—	2 Filler. Iron. KM#481.	—
TS52	1915KB	—	10 Filler. Nickel. KM#496.	—
TS53	1915KB	—	20 Filler. Silver. KM#483.	1,200
TS55	1916KB	—	1/2 Korona. Silver.	1,200
TS54	1916	—	20 Filler. Lead. KM#498.	—
TS56	1917KB	—	10 Filler. Lead.	—
TS57	1917KB	—	10 Filler. Zinc.	—
TS58	1917KB	—	10 Filler. Copper-Nickel-Zinc.	—
TS59	1918KB	—	50 Filler. Lead.	—
TS60	1918	—	20 Korona. Lead. KM#486.	—
TS61	1920	—	10 Filler. Copper-Nickel-Zinc. KM#496.	—
TS62	1922	—	20 Filler. Nickel. KM#498.	—
TS63	1922	—	20 Filler. Bronze. KM#498.	—
TS64	1922	—	20 Filler. Brass. KM#498.	—
TS65	1922	—	20 Filler. Copper-Nickel-Zinc. KM#498.	—
TS66	1930	—	5 Pengo. Lead. Obverse only, KM#512.	—
TS67	1930	—	5 Pengo. Lead. Reverse only, KM#512.	—
TS68	1935	—	2 Filler. Nickel. KM#506	—
TS69	1935	—	2 Pengo. Lead. Reverse only, KM#514.	—
TS70	1936	—	2 Pengo. Lead. Obverse only, KM#515.	—
TS71	1938	—	5 Pengo. Copper-Zinc. KM#517.	—
TS72	1938	—	5 Pengo. Copper-Zinc. KM#516.	—
TS73	1938	—	5 Pengo. Lead. Obverse only, KM#516.	—
TS74	1938	—	5 Pengo. Lead. Reverse only, KM#516.	—
TS75	1939	—	Filler. Aluminum. KM#505.	—
TS76	1939	—	50 Filler. Aluminum. KM#509.	—
TS77	1941	—	50 Filler. Iron. KM#509.	—
TS78	1943	—	2 Filler. Aluminum. KM#519.	—
TS79	1943	—	5 Pengo. Copper-Zinc. KM#523.	—

MINT SETS

KM#	Date	Mintage	Identification	Issue Price	Mkt Val
MS-A1	1956 (3)	—	KM#552, 553, 554	—	55.00
MS1	1971 (9)	—	KM#546, 549, 572-575, 591, 594, 595	—	5.00
MS2	1972 (9)	—	KM#546, 549, 572-575, 591, 594, 595	—	5.00
MS3	1973 (9)	—	KM#546, 549, 572-575, 591, 594, 595	—	5.00
MS4	1974 (9)	—	KM#546, 549, 572-575, 591, 594, 595	—	5.00
MS5	1975 (9)	—	KM#546, 549, 572-575, 591, 594, 595	—	5.00
MS6	1976 (9)	—	KM#546, 549, 572-575, 591, 594, 595	—	5.00
MS7	1977 (9)	—	KM#546, 549, 572-575, 591, 594, 595	—	5.00
MSA7	1977 (3)	—	KM#610-612	—	35.00
MS8	1978 (9)	—	KM#546, 549, 572-575, 591, 594, 595	—	5.00
MS9	1979 (9)	—	KM#546, 549, 572-575, 591, 594, 595	—	5.00
MS10	1980 (9)	—	KM#546, 549, 572-575, 591, 594, 595	—	5.00
MS11	1981 (9)	—	KM#546, 549, 572-575, 591, 594, 620	—	5.00
MS12	1982 (9)	—	KM#546, 549, 572-575, 591, 594, 595	—	5.00
MS13	1983 (10)	—	KM#546, 549, 572-575, 591, 630, 635, 636	—	5.50
MSA13	1983 (3)	—	KM#627, 628, 629	—	10.00
MS14	1984 (10)	—	KM#546, 549, 572-575, 591, 630, 635, 636	—	5.50
MS15	1985 (10)	—	KM#546, 549, 572-575, 591, 630, 635, 636	—	5.50
MS16	1986 (10)	—	KM#546, 549, 572-575, 591, 630, 635, 636	—	5.50
MS17	1987 (10)	—	KM#546, 549, 572-575, 591, 630, 635, 636	—	5.50
MS18	1988 (10)	—	KM#546, 549, 572-575, 591, 630, 635, 636	—	5.50
MS19	1989 (10)	—	KM#546, 549, 572-575, 591, 630, 635, 636	—	5.50
MS20	1990 (5)	—	KM673-677	—	5.00
MS21	1991 (5)	—	KM673-677	—	7.00
MS22	1992 (8)	—	KM689, 692-698	—	30.00
MSA22	1992 (5)	—	KM673-677	—	9.00
MS23	1993 (11)	—	KM675-677, 689, 692-698	—	20.00
MS24	1994 (11)	—	KM675-677, 692-698, 707	—	18.00
MS25	1995 (10)	—	KM675-677, 692-698	—	10.00
MS26	1995 (11)	—	KM675-677, 692-698, 707	17.50	20.00
MS27	1996 (10)	—	KM675-677, 692-698	—	10.00
MS28	1997 (10)	7,000	KM677, 692-698, 707, 721	18.50	20.00
MS29	1998 (11)	—	KM677, 692-698, 707, 721, 726	22.50	30.00
MS30	1999 (8)	—	KM677, 692-697, 721	—	17.50
MS31	2000 (8)	—	KM692-697, 721, 745	—	16.50
MS32	2001 (7)	—	KM#692-697, 721	—	16.50

PROOF SETS

KM#	Date	Mintage	Identification	Issue Price	Mkt Val
PS3	1966 (8)	2,000	KM534b, 546a, 547a, 549a-551a, 555a, 556b	15.00	48.00
PSA1	1948 (3)	—	KM537-539	70.00	70.00
PS1	1961 (6)	2,500	KM560, 562-566	—	2,100
PS2	1961 (4)	—	KM557-559, 561	—	80.00
PS4	1966 (3)	330	KM569-571	430	2,675
PS5	1966 (2)	11,000	KM567-568	7.50	45.00
PS6	1967 (8)	5,000	KM534b, 546a, 547a, 549a-551a, 555a, 556b	15.00	55.00
PS7	1967 (2)	500	KM580, 581	—	2,250
PS8	1968 (5)	7,000	KM583, 585-588	—	2,850
PS9	1968 (2)	4,750	KM582, 584	35.00	30.00
PS10	1969 (2)	3,000	KM589, 590	35.00	30.00
PS11	1970 (2)	4,000	KM592, 593	25.00	25.00
PS12	1972 (2)	6,000	KM596, 597	25.00	32.50
PS13	1973 (2)	6,000	KM599, 600	—	27.50
PS14	1974 (2)	—	KM601, 603	—	25.00
PS15	1976 (3)	5,000	KM607-609	—	50.00
PS16	1977 (3)	—	KM610-612	—	50.00
PS17	1992 (8)	1,000	KM689, 692-698	—	80.00
PS18	1993 (8)	—	KM 689, 692-698	—	47.50
PSA19	1993/4 (2)	—	KM704, 710	—	52.50
PS19	1994 (8)	—	KM692-698, 707	—	47.50
PS20	1995 (8)	—	KM692-698, 707	24.50	47.50
PS21	1997 (8)	3,000	KM692-698, 707, 721	29.50	50.00
PS22	1998 (3)	5,000	KM726-728	267	270
PS24	1999 (2)	—	KM741, 742	239	265
PS23	1999 (7)	—	KM692-697, 721	—	32.50
PS25	2000 (8)	—	KM692-697, 721, 745	—	40.00
PS26	2001 (7)	—	KM#692-697, 721	35.00	37.50

SPECIMEN SETS (SS)

KM#	Date	Mintage	Identification	Issue Price	Mkt Val
SS1	1977 (9)	—	KM546, 549, 572-575, 591, 594-595	—	10.00
SS2	1978 (9)	—	KM546, 549, 572-575, 591, 594-595	—	10.00
SS3	1979 (9)	—	KM546, 549, 572-575, 591, 594-595	—	10.00
SS4	1981 (9)	—	KM546, 549, 572-575, 591, 594, 620	—	10.00
SS5	1989 (10)	—	KM546, 549, 572-575, 591, 630, 635, 636	—	9.00

ICELAND

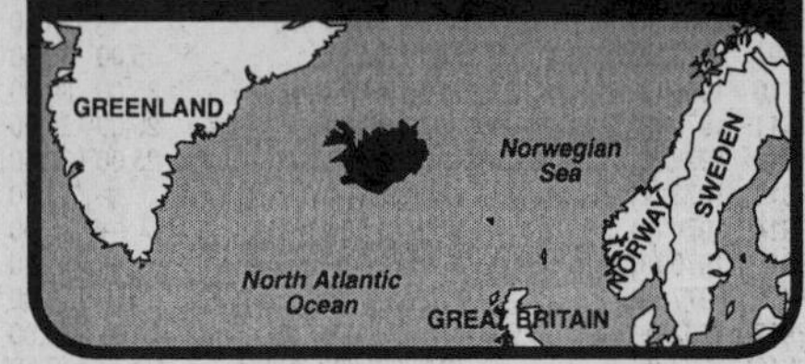

The Republic of Iceland, an island of recent volcanic origin in the North Atlantic east of Greenland and immediately south of the Arctic Circle, has an area of 39,768sq. mi. (103,000 sq. km.) and a population of 275,264. Capital: Reykjavik. Fishing is the chief industry and accounts for more than 70 percent of the exports.

Iceland was settled by Norwegians in the 9th century and established as an independent republic in 930. The Icelandic assembly called the Althingi', also established in 930, is the oldest parliament in the world. Iceland came under Norwegian sovereignty in 1262, and passed to Denmark when Norway and Denmark were united under the Danish crown in 1380. In 1918 it was established as a virtually independent kingdom in union with Denmark. On June 17, 1944, while Denmark was still under occupation by troops of the Third Reich, Iceland was established by plebiscite as an independent republic.

RULERS
Christian X, 1912-1944

MINT MARKS
Heart (h) - Copenhagen

MINTMASTERS INITIALS
HCN - Hans Christian Nielsen, 1919-1927
(for Iceland, 1922-1926)
N - Niels Peter Nielsen, 1927-1955
(for Iceland, 1929-1940)

MONEYERS INITIALS
GJ - Knud Gunnar Jensen, 1901-1933

MONETARY SYSTEM
100 Aurar = 1 Krona

KINGDOM

DECIMAL COINAGE

KM# 5.1 EYRIR Composition: Bronze

Date	Mintage	F	VF	XF	Unc	BU
1926(h) HCN-GJ	405,000	1.50	3.00	7.50	28.50	—
1931(h) N-GJ	462,000	1.00	2.50	6.00	26.00	—
1937(h) N-GJ Wide date	211,000	2.00	4.00	8.00	32.00	—
1938(h) N-GJ	279,000	1.00	2.00	4.00	13.50	—
1938(h) N-GJ Large 3 over small 3	—	1.00	2.00	3.50	12.50	—
1939(h) N-GJ Large 3	305,000	1.00	2.00	3.50	12.50	—
1939(h) N-GJ Small 3	Inc. above	1.00	2.00	3.50	12.50	—

KM# 5.2 EYRIR Composition: Bronze

Date	Mintage	F	VF	XF	Unc	BU
1940	1,000,000	0.25	0.50	1.00	2.50	—
1940 Proof	—	Value: 235				
1942	2,000,000	0.25	0.40	0.75	2.00	—

KM# 6.1 2 AURAR Composition: Bronze **Note:** Varieties exist in the appearance of the numeral 8 in 1938 dated coins. As the die slowly deteriorated, "globs" were added to the upper loop and later to the lower loop.

Date	Mintage	F	VF	XF	Unc	BU
1926(h) HCN-GJ	498,000	1.50	3.00	8.00	32.00	—
1931(h) N-GJ	446,000	1.00	2.50	7.00	26.50	—
1938(h) N-GJ	206,000	6.00	12.00	17.50	42.50	—
1940(h) N-GJ	257,000	5.00	10.00	15.00	33.50	—

KM# 6.2 2 AURAR Composition: Bronze

Date	Mintage	F	VF	XF	Unc	BU
1940	1,000,000	0.40	0.75	1.50	3.00	—
1940 Proof	—	Value: 275				
1942	2,000,000	0.20	0.50	1.00	2.00	—

KM# 7.1 5 AURAR Composition: Bronze

Date	Mintage	F	VF	XF	Unc	BU
1926(h) HCN-GJ	355,000	5.00	10.00	25.00	72.50	—
1931(h) N-GJ	311,000	5.00	10.00	25.00	72.50	—

KM# 7.2 5 AURAR Composition: Bronze

Date	Mintage	F	VF	XF	Unc	BU
1940	1,000,000	0.60	1.25	2.50	5.00	—
1940 Proof	—	Value: 295				
1942	2,000,000	0.35	0.85	1.50	3.00	—

KM# 1.1 10 AURAR Composition: Copper-Nickel

Date	Mintage	F	VF	XF	Unc	BU
1922(h) HCN GJ	300,000	2.00	3.50	7.00	36.50	—
1923(h) HCN GJ	302,000	3.00	4.50	9.00	40.00	—
1925(h) HCN GJ	321,000	15.00	25.00	40.00	90.00	—
1929(h) N-GJ	176,000	15.00	25.00	45.00	95.00	—
1933(h) N-GJ	157,000	10.00	20.00	30.00	75.00	—
1936(h)	213,000	3.00	6.00	10.00	35.00	—
1939/6(h) N-GJ	208,000	5.00	10.00	15.00	42.50	—
1939(h) N-GJ	Inc. above	4.00	8.00	12.00	32.50	—

KM# 1.2 10 AURAR Composition: Copper-Nickel

Date	Mintage	F	VF	XF	Unc	BU
1940	1,500,000	0.35	0.75	1.50	4.50	—
1940 Proof	—	Value: 235				

KM# 1a 10 AURAR Composition: Zinc

Date	Mintage	F	VF	XF	Unc	BU
1942	2,000,000	1.50	3.00	6.00	28.50	—
1942 Prooflike	—	—	—	—	—	—

KM# 2.1 25 AURAR Composition: Copper-Nickel

Date	Mintage	F	VF	XF	Unc	BU
1922(h) HCN GJ	300,000	1.00	2.50	4.00	32.50	—
1923(h) HCN GJ	304,000	1.00	2.50	4.00	32.50	—
1925(h) HCN GJ	207,000	2.50	4.50	10.00	42.50	—
1933(h) N-GJ	104,000	10.00	15.00	25.00	85.00	—
1937(h) N-GJ Near 7	201,000	3.00	5.00	9.00	40.00	—
1937(h) N-GJ Far 7	Inc. above	3.00	5.00	9.00	40.00	—

KM# 2.2 25 AURAR Composition: Copper-Nickel

Date	Mintage	F	VF	XF	Unc	BU
1940	1,500,000	0.25	0.50	1.00	2.50	—
1940 Proof	—	Value: 255				

KM# 2a 25 AURAR Composition: Zinc

Date	Mintage	F	VF	XF	Unc	BU
1942	2,000,000	1.00	2.50	5.00	26.50	—
1942 Prooflike	—	—	—	—	—	—

KM# 3.1 KRONA Composition: Aluminum-Bronze

Date	Mintage	F	VF	XF	Unc	BU
1925(h) HCN GJ	252,000	3.00	6.00	25.00	165	—
1929(h) N-GJ	154,000	5.00	10.00	32.00	190	—
1940(h) N-GJ	209,000	1.50	2.50	5.00	15.00	—

KM# 3.2 KRONA Composition: Aluminum-Bronze

Date	Mintage	F	VF	XF	Unc	BU
1940	715,000	1.00	2.00	4.00	10.00	—
1940 Proof; rare	—	—	—	—	—	—

KM# 4.1 2 KRONUR Composition: Aluminum-Bronze

Date	Mintage	F	VF	XF	Unc	BU
1925(h) HCN GJ	126,000	7.50	12.50	40.00	200	—
1929(h) N-GJ	77,000	10.00	20.00	65.00	300	—

KM# 4.2 2 KRONUR Composition: Aluminum-Bronze

Date	Mintage	F	VF	XF	Unc	BU
1940	546,000	0.75	1.50	3.50	10.00	—
1940 Proof; rare	—	—	—	—	—	—

TOKEN COINAGE

Under the Scandinavian Monetary Convention of 1873, the coinage of Denmark, Norway, and Sweden could circulate with validity in Iceland. Despite the various options for exchange, very few coins appear to have made their way to Iceland. As a result, Icelandic merchants resorted to manufacturing their own tokens. While some bare the crudeness of a homemade token, others had been elaborately struck by such well known manufacturers as L. Chr. Lauer of Nurnberg, who most likely had N. Chr. Hansen and Co., Copenhagen as an agent.

Merchants posting inflated token prices alongside legal coinage prices on goods for sale led to the 1901 law which prohibited the manufacture and usage of private coinage, ending the token era which started in the mid 1800s.

NOTE: There are at least four different types of tokens for this time period. Only Type I tokens are cataloged here.

TYPE I: Tokens with stated values; first in shillings, later in kronur and aurar.

TYPE II: Bread Tokens, used to barter for prearranged quantities of goods or labor.

TYPE III: Advertising or Address Tokens.

TYPE IV: Miscellaneous Tokens.

KM#Tn12 10 AURAR **Weight:** 1.7000 g. **Composition:** Brass **Issuer:** P.J. Thorsteinsson, Bildudal **Note:** Similar to 100 Aurar, KM#Tn21. Struck by L. Chr. Lauer of Nurnberg.

Date	VG	F	VF	XF	Unc
ND(1901)	12.00	25.00	50.00	110	—

KM#Tn15 25 AURAR **Weight:** 1.7000 g. **Composition:** Brass **Issuer:** P.J. Thorsteinsson, Bildudal **Note:** Similar to 100 Aurar, KM#Tn21. Struck by L. Chr. Lauer of Nurnberg.

Date	VG	F	VF	XF	Unc
ND(1901)	6.00	12.00	25.00	55.00	—

KM#Tn18 50 AURAR **Weight:** 2.2000 g. **Composition:** Brass **Issuer:** P.J. Thorsteinsson, Bildudal **Note:** Similar to 100 Aurar, KM#Tn21. Struck by L. Chr. Lauer of Nurnberg.

Date	VG	F	VF	XF	Unc
ND(1901)	6.00	12.00	25.00	55.00	—

KM# Tn21 100 AURAR **Weight:** 1.1000 g. **Composition:** Aluminum **Issuer:** P.J. Thorsteinsson, Bildudal **Note:** Struck by L. Chr. Lauer of Nurnberg.

Date	VG	F	VF	XF	Unc
ND(1901) Rare	—	—	—	—	—

KM# Tn22 500 AURAR **Weight:** 1.1000 g. **Composition:** Aluminum **Issuer:** P.J. Thorsteinsson, Bildudal **Note:** Similar to 100 Aurar, KM#Tn21. Struck by L. Chr. Lauer of Nurnberg.

Date	VG	F	VF	XF	Unc
ND(1901)	7.00	15.00	30.00	65.00	—

KM# Tn3 10 ORE **Composition:** Bronze **Issuer:** N. Chr. Gram., Thingeyri **Note:** Similar to 25 Ore, KM#Tn4.

Date	VG	F	VF	XF	Unc
ND(1902) Rare	—	—	—	—	—

KM# Tn4 25 ORE **Composition:** Bronze **Issuer:** N. Chr. Gram., Thingeyri

Date	VG	F	VF	XF	Unc
ND(1902) Rare	—	—	—	—	—

KM# Tn23 50 ORE **Composition:** Bronze **Issuer:** N. Chr. Gram., Thingeyri **Note:** Similar to 25 Ore, KM#Tn4.

Date	VG	F	VF	XF	Unc
ND(1902) Rare	—	—	—	—	—

REPUBLIC

DECIMAL COINAGE

KM#8 EYRIR **Composition:** Bronze **Note:** Values for the 1953-59 proof issues are for impaired proofs. Brilliant proofs may bring 3 to 4 times these figures.

Date	Mintage	F	VF	XF	Unc	BU
1946	4,000,000	0.10	0.15	0.50	1.00	—
1946 Proof	—	Value: 250				
1953	4,000,000	0.10	0.15	0.40	0.75	—
1953 Proof	—	Value: 65.00				
1956	2,000,000	0.10	0.15	0.40	0.75	—
1956 Proof	—	Value: 65.00				
1957	2,000,000	0.10	0.15	0.40	0.75	—
1957 Proof	—	Value: 65.00				
1958	2,000,000	0.10	0.15	0.40	0.75	—
1958 Proof	—	Value: 65.00				
1959	1,600,000	0.10	0.15	0.40	0.75	—
1959 Proof	—	Value: 65.00				
1966	1,000,000	0.10	0.15	0.40	0.75	—
1966 Proof	15,000	Value: 3.25				

KM# 9 5 AURAR **Composition:** Bronze **Note:** Values for the 1958-63 proof issues are for impaired proofs. Brilliant proofs may bring 3 to 4 times these figures.

Date	Mintage	F	VF	XF	Unc	BU
1946	4,000,000	0.10	0.25	0.50	1.25	—
1946 Proof	—	Value: 400				
1958	400,000	0.50	2.00	3.50	5.00	—
1958 Proof	—	Value: 100				
1959	600,000	0.50	2.00	3.00	4.50	—
1959 Proof	—	Value: 100				
1960	1,200,000	0.15	0.40	1.00	1.75	—
1960 Proof	—	Value: 100				
1961	1,200,000	0.15	0.40	1.00	1.75	—
1961 Proof	—	Value: 100				
1963	1,200,000	0.10	0.30	0.75	1.50	—
1963 Proof	—	Value: 100				
1965	800,000	0.10	0.20	0.50	1.00	—
1966	1,000,000	0.10	0.20	0.50	1.00	—
1966 Proof	15,000	Value: 3.25				

KM# 10 10 AURAR **Composition:** Copper-Nickel **Note:** Values for the 1953-63 proof issues are for impaired proofs. Brilliant proofs may bring 3 to 4 times these figures.

Date	Mintage	F	VF	XF	Unc	BU
1946	4,000,000	—	0.10	0.20	0.60	—
1946 Proof	—	Value: 400				
1953	4,000,000	—	0.10	0.20	0.50	—
1953 Proof	—	Value: 65.00				
1957	1,200,000	0.25	0.75	2.00	5.00	—
1957 Proof	—	Value: 65.00				
1958	500,000	0.20	0.50	1.00	2.00	—
1958 Proof	—	Value: 65.00				
1959	3,000,000	0.20	0.50	1.50	4.00	—
1959 Proof	—	Value: 65.00				
1960	1,000,000	0.10	0.20	0.40	1.00	—
1960 Proof	—	Value: 65.00				
1961	2,000,000	—	—	0.10	0.30	—
1961 Proof	—	Value: 65.00				
1962	3,000,000	—	—	0.10	0.20	—
1962 Proof	—	Value: 65.00				
1963	4,000,000	—	—	0.10	0.20	—
1963 Proof	—	Value: 65.00				
1965	2,000,000	—	—	0.10	0.20	—
1966	4,000,000	—	—	0.10	0.20	—
1967	2,000,000	—	—	0.10	0.20	—
1969 Coarse edge reeding	3,200,000	—	—	0.10	0.20	—
1969 Fine edge reeding	Inc. above	—	—	0.10	0.20	—

KM# 10a 10 AURAR **Composition:** Aluminum

Date	Mintage	F	VF	XF	Unc	BU
1970	4,800,000	—	—	0.10	0.20	—
1971	11,200,000	—	—	0.10	0.20	—
1973	4,800,000	—	—	0.10	0.20	—
1974	4,800,000	—	—	0.10	0.20	—
1974 Proof	15,000	Value: 3.25				

KM# 11 25 AURAR **Composition:** Copper-Nickel **Note:** Values for the 1951-63 proof issues are for impaired proofs. Brilliant proofs may bring 3 to 4 times these figures.

Date	Mintage	F	VF	XF	Unc	BU
1946	2,000,000	0.10	0.15	0.35	1.25	—
1946 Proof	—	Value: 400				
1951	2,000,000	0.10	0.15	0.35	0.75	—
1951 Proof	—	Value: 75.00				
1954	2,000,000	0.10	0.15	0.35	0.75	—
1954 Proof	—	Value: 75.00				
1957	1,000,000	0.20	0.50	1.50	3.50	—
1957 Proof	—	Value: 75.00				
1958	500,000	0.20	0.40	0.60	1.00	—
1958 Proof	—	Value: 75.00				
1959	2,000,000	0.20	0.50	1.50	3.00	—
1959 Proof	—	Value: 75.00				
1960	1,000,000	—	—	0.10	0.30	—
1960 Proof	—	Value: 75.00				
1961	1,200,000	—	—	0.10	0.30	—
1961 Proof	—	Value: 75.00				
1962	2,000,000	—	—	0.10	0.25	—
1962 Proof	—	Value: 75.00				
1963	3,000,000	—	—	0.10	0.25	—
1963 Proof	—	Value: 75.00				
1965	4,000,000	—	—	0.10	0.25	—
1966	2,000,000	—	—	0.10	0.25	—
1967	3,000,000	—	—	0.10	0.25	—
1967 Proof	15,000	Value: 3.25				

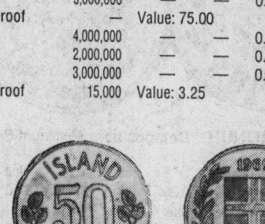

KM# 17 50 AURAR **Composition:** Nickel-Brass

Date	Mintage	F	VF	XF	Unc	BU
1969	2,000,000	—	—	0.10	0.30	—
1970	2,000,000	—	—	0.10	0.30	—
1971	2,000,000	—	—	0.10	0.30	—
1973	1,000,000	—	—	0.10	0.30	—
1974	2,000,000	—	—	0.10	0.30	—
1974 Proof	15,000	Value: 3.25				

KM# 12 KRONA **Composition:** Aluminum-Bronze

Date	Mintage	F	VF	XF	Unc	BU
1946	2,175,000	—	0.10	0.40	1.50	—
1946 Proof	—	Value: 400				

KM# 12a KRONA **Composition:** Nickel-Brass **Note:** Values for the 1957-63 proof issues are for impaired proofs. Brilliant proofs may bring 3 to 4 times these figures.

Date	Mintage	F	VF	XF	Unc	BU
1957	1,000,000	0.10	0.15	0.40	1.50	—
1957 Proof	—	Value: 85.00				
1959	500,000	0.10	0.20	0.75	2.00	—
1959 Proof	—	Value: 85.00				
1961	500,000	0.10	0.20	0.75	2.00	—
1961 Proof	—	Value: 85.00				
1962	1,000,000	0.10	0.15	0.20	0.60	—
1962 Proof	—	Value: 85.00				
1963	1,500,000	—	0.10	0.15	0.50	—
1963 Proof	—	Value: 85.00				
1965	2,000,000	—	—	0.10	0.50	—
1966	2,000,000	—	—	0.10	0.50	—
1969	2,000,000	—	—	0.10	0.25	—
1970	3,000,000	—	—	0.10	0.25	—
1971	2,500,000	—	—	0.10	0.25	—

Date	Mintage	F	VF	XF	Unc	BU
1973 Large round knob 3	2,500,000	—	—	0.10	0.50	—
1973 Thin, sharp end 3	3,500,000	—	—	0.10	0.25	—
1974	5,000,000	—	—	0.10	0.25	—
1975	10,500,000	—	—	0.10	0.25	—
1975 Proof	15,000	Value: 3.25				

KM# 23 KRONA Composition: Aluminum

Date	Mintage	F	VF	XF	Unc	BU
1976	10,000,000	—	—	0.10	0.20	—
1977	10,000,000	—	—	0.10	0.20	—
1978	13,000,000	—	—	0.10	0.20	—
1980	7,225,000	—	—	0.10	0.20	—
1980 Proof	15,000	Value: 3.25				

KM# 13 2 KRONUR Composition: Aluminum-Bronze
Note: Republic

Date	Mintage	F	VF	XF	Unc	BU
1946	1,086,000	0.20	0.40	0.80	3.50	—
1946 Proof	—	Value: 450				

KM# 13a.1 2 KRONUR Composition: Nickel-Brass
Note: Values for the 1958-63 proof issues are for impaired proofs. Brilliant proofs may bring 3 to 4 times these figures.

Date	Mintage	F	VF	XF	Unc	BU
1958	500,000	0.20	0.50	1.00	3.00	—
1958 Proof	—	Value: 115				
1962	500,000	0.20	0.50	1.00	3.00	—
1962 Proof	—	Value: 115				
1963	750,000	0.15	0.30	0.60	2.00	—
1963 Proof	—	Value: 115				
1966	1,000,000	0.10	0.20	0.40	1.50	—
1966 Proof	15,000	Value: 3.25				

KM# 13a.2 2 KRONUR Weight: 11.5000 g. **Composition:** Nickel-Brass **Note:** Thick planchet.

Date	Mintage	F	VF	XF	Unc	BU
1966	300	—	—	325	425	—

KM# 18 5 KRONUR Composition: Copper-Nickel

Date	Mintage	F	VF	XF	Unc	BU
1969	2,000,000	—	0.15	0.25	0.50	—
1970	1,000,000	—	0.15	0.25	0.50	—
1971	500,000	0.10	0.20	0.50	1.00	—
1973	1,100,000	—	0.10	0.20	0.40	—
1974	1,200,000	—	0.10	0.15	0.25	—
1975	1,500,000	—	0.10	0.15	0.25	—
1976	500,000	—	0.10	0.20	0.40	—
1977	1,000,000	—	0.10	0.15	0.25	—
1978	4,672,000	—	0.10	0.15	0.25	—
1980	2,400,000	—	0.10	0.15	0.25	—
1980 Proof	15,000	Value: 3.25				

KM# 15 10 KRONUR Composition: Copper-Nickel

Date	Mintage	F	VF	XF	Unc	BU
1967	1,000,000	0.15	0.25	0.50	1.50	—
1969	500,000	0.15	0.30	0.75	2.00	—
1970	1,500,000	—	0.15	0.30	0.75	—
1971	1,500,000	—	0.15	0.30	0.75	—
1973	1,500,000	—	0.15	0.30	0.75	—
1974	2,000,000	—	0.10	0.25	0.60	—
1975	2,500,000	—	0.10	0.25	0.60	—
1976	2,500,000	—	0.10	0.25	0.60	—
1977	2,000,000	—	0.10	0.25	0.60	—
1978	10,500,000	—	0.10	0.25	0.60	—
1980	4,600,000	—	0.10	0.25	0.60	—
1980 Proof	15,000	Value: 3.25				

KM# 16 50 KRONUR Composition: Nickel **Subject:** 50th Anniversary of Sovereignty

Date	Mintage	F	VF	XF	Unc	BU
1968	100,000	1.50	2.50	4.00	7.00	—

KM# 19 50 KRONUR Composition: Copper-Nickel
Reverse: Parliament building

Date	Mintage	F	VF	XF	Unc	BU
1970	800,000	0.25	0.50	1.00	2.00	—
1971	500,000	0.25	0.50	1.00	2.50	—
1973	50,000	1.00	1.50	2.50	4.00	—
1974	200,000	0.25	0.50	1.00	2.00	—
1975	500,000	0.20	0.35	0.75	1.50	—
1976	500,000	0.20	0.35	0.75	1.50	—
1977	200,000	0.20	0.35	0.75	1.50	—
1978	2,040,000	0.20	0.35	0.50	1.00	—
1980	1,500,000	0.20	0.35	0.50	1.00	—
1980 Proof	15,000	Value: 3.25				

KM# 14 500 KRONUR Weight: 8.9604 g. **Composition:** 0.9000 Gold .2593 oz. AGW **Subject:** Jon Sigurdsson Sesquicentennial

Date	Mintage	F	VF	XF	Unc	BU
ND(1961)	10,000	—	—	—	150	—
ND(1961) Proof	—	Value: 800				

KM# 20 500 KRONUR Weight: 20.0000 g. **Composition:** 0.9250 Silver .5968 oz. ASW **Subject:** 1100th Anniversary - 1st Settlement

Date	Mintage	F	VF	XF	Unc	BU
ND(1974)		—	—	—	10.00	—
ND(1974) Proof	Est. 58,000	Value: 12.50				

Note: 17,000 proof coins were remelted

KM# 21 1000 KRONUR Weight: 30.0000 g. **Composition:** 0.9250 Silver .8923 oz. ASW **Subject:** 1100th Anniversary - 1st Settlement

Date	Mintage	F	VF	XF	Unc	BU
ND(1974)		—	—	—	12.50	—
ND(1974) Proof	Est. 58,000	Value: 17.50				

Note: 17,000 proof coins were remelted

KM# 22 10000 KRONUR Weight: 15.5000 g. **Composition:** 0.9000 Gold .4485 oz. AGW **Subject:** 1100th Anniversary - 1st Settlement

Date	Mintage	F	VF	XF	Unc	BU
ND(1974)	12,000	—	—	—	200	—
ND(1974) Proof	8,000	Value: 260				

REFORM COINAGE

100 Old Kronur = 1 New Krona

KM# 24 5 AURAR Composition: Bronze **Reverse:** Skate

Date	Mintage	F	VF	XF	Unc	BU
1981	15,000,000	—	—	—	0.35	—
1981 Proof	15,000	Value: 3.50				

KM# 25 10 AURAR Composition: Bronze **Reverse:** Cuttle-fish

Date	Mintage	F	VF	XF	Unc	BU
1981	50,000,000	—	—	—	0.35	—
1981 Proof	15,000	Value: 5.00				

KM# 26 50 AURAR Composition: Bronze **Reverse:** Shrimp

Date	Mintage	F	VF	XF	Unc	BU
1981	10,000,000	—	—	0.10	0.50	—
1981 Proof	15,000	Value: 6.00				

KM# 26a 50 AURAR Composition: Bronze Coated Steel **Reverse:** Shrimp

Date	Mintage	F	VF	XF	Unc	BU
1986	2,144,000	—	—	—	0.50	—

KM# 27 KRONA **Composition:** Copper-Nickel **Reverse:** Cod

Date	Mintage	F	VF	XF	Unc	BU
1981	18,000,000	—	—	0.15	0.75	—
1981 Proof	15,000	Value: 8.00				
1984	7,000,000	—	—	0.15	0.75	—
1987	7,500,000	—	—	0.15	0.75	—

KM# 27a KRONA **Composition:** Nickel Coated Steel **Reverse:** Cod

Date	Mintage	F	VF	XF	Unc	BU
1989	5,000,000	—	—	—	0.75	—
1991	5,180,000	—	—	—	0.75	—
1992	5,000,000	—	—	—	0.75	—
1994	5,000,000	—	—	—	0.75	—
1996	6,000,000	—	—	—	0.75	—
1999	10,000,000	—	—	—	0.75	—
2000	10,000	—	—	—	1.50	—

KM# 28 5 KRONUR **Composition:** Copper-Nickel **Obverse:** Four national icons **Reverse:** Two dolphins, denomination

Date	Mintage	F	VF	XF	Unc	BU
1981	4,350,000	—	—	0.25	1.50	—
1981 Proof	15,000	Value: 10.00				
1984	1,000,000	—	—	0.25	1.50	—
1987	3,000,000	—	—	0.25	1.50	—
1992	2,000,000	—	—	0.25	1.50	—

KM# 28a 5 KRONUR **Composition:** Nickel Clad Steel **Obverse:** Four national icons **Reverse:** Two dolphins, denomination

Date	Mintage	F	VF	XF	Unc	BU
1996	1,500,000	—	—	—	1.50	—
1999	2,000,000	—	—	—	1.50	—
2000	10,000	—	—	—	2.00	—

KM# 29.1 10 KRONUR **Composition:** Copper-Nickel **Obverse:** Four national icons **Reverse:** Four capelins, denomination **Edge:** Reeded

Date	Mintage	F	VF	XF	Unc	BU
1984	10,000,000	—	—	0.35	1.75	—
1987	7,500,000	—	—	0.35	1.75	—
1994	2,500,000	—	—	0.35	1.75	—

KM# 29.2 10 KRONUR **Composition:** Nickel Clad Steel **Obverse:** Four national icons **Note:** Security edge. (Struck on flan of Indian Rupee in error.)

Date	F	VF	XF	Unc	BU
1984	—	—	65.00	100	—

KM# 29.1a 10 KRONUR **Composition:** Nickel Clad Steel **Obverse:** Four national icons **Reverse:** Four capelins, denomination

Date	Mintage	F	VF	XF	Unc	BU
1996	4,000,000	—	—	—	1.75	—
2000	10,000	—	—	—	2.50	—

KM# 31 50 KRONUR **Composition:** Nickel-Brass **Reverse:** Crab

Date	Mintage	F	VF	XF	Unc	BU
1987	4,000,000	—	—	—	3.25	—
1992	2,000,000	—	—	—	3.25	—
2000	10,000	—	—	—	4.00	—
2001	2,000,000	—	—	—	3.25	—

KM# 35 100 KRONUR **Composition:** Nickel-Brass **Reverse:** Lumpfish

Date	Mintage	F	VF	XF	Unc	BU
1995	6,000,000	—	—	—	6.00	—
2000	10,000	—	—	—	7.00	—
2001	2,140,000	—	—	—	6.00	—

KM# 30 500 KRONUR **Weight:** 20.0000 g. **Composition:** 0.5000 Silver .3215 oz. ASW **Subject:** 100th Anniversary of Icelandic Banknotes

Date	Mintage	F	VF	XF	Unc	BU
ND(1986)	15,000	—	—	—	45.00	—

KM# 30a 500 KRONUR **Weight:** 20.0000 g. **Composition:** 0.9250 Silver .5968 oz. ASW **Subject:** 100th Anniversary of Icelandic Banknotes

Date	Mintage	F	VF	XF	Unc	BU
ND(1986) Proof	5,000	Value: 65.00				

KM# 32 1000 KRONUR **Weight:** 30.0000 g. **Composition:** 0.9250 Silver .8922 oz. ASW **Subject:** 50th Anniversary of Icelandic Republic **Obverse:** Arms **Reverse:** Head of Sveinn Bjornsson left **Note:** In sets only.

Date	Mintage	F	VF	XF	Unc	BU
ND(1994)	6,000	—	—	—	55.00	—
ND(1994) Proof	3,000	Value: 85.00				

KM# 33 1000 KRONUR **Weight:** 30.0000 g. **Composition:** 0.9250 Silver .8922 oz. ASW **Obverse:** Arms **Reverse:** Head of Asgeir Asgeirsson left **Note:** In sets only.

Date	Mintage	F	VF	XF	Unc	BU
ND(1994)	6,000	—	—	—	55.00	—
ND(1994) Proof	3,000	Value: 85.00				

KM# 34 1000 KRONUR **Weight:** 30.0000 g. **Composition:** 0.9250 Silver .8922 oz. ASW **Obverse:** Arms **Reverse:** Head of Kristjan Eldjarn left **Note:** In sets only.

Date	Mintage	F	VF	XF	Unc	BU
ND(1994)	6,000	—	—	—	55.00	—
ND(1994) Proof	3,000	Value: 85.00				

KM# 37 1000 KRONUR **Weight:** 27.7300 g. **Composition:** 0.9000 Silver .7720 oz. ASW **Subject:** Leif Ericson Millennium

Date	Mintage	F	VF	XF	Unc	BU
2000 Proof	150,000	Value: 55.00				

KM# 36 10000 KRONUR **Weight:** 8.6500 g. **Composition:** 0.9000 Gold .2503 oz. AGW **Subject:** 1000 Years of Christianity **Obverse:** National arms **Reverse:** Old crosier top

Date	Mintage	F	VF	XF	Unc	BU
ND(2000) Proof	3,000	Value: 225				

MINT SETS

KM#	Date	Mintage	Identification	Issue Price	Mkt Val
MS2	1970 (6)	—	KM#10a, 12a, 15, 17-19	—	11.50
MS3	1971 (6)	—	KM#10a, 12a, 15, 17-19	—	10.00
MS4	1973 (6)	—	KM#10a, 12a (knob 3), 15, 17-19	3.25	9.00
MS5	1974 (6)	—	KM#10a, 12a, 15, 17-19	3.25	7.50
MS6	1974 (2)	70,000	KM#20-21	30.00	20.00
MS7	1975 (4)	—	KM#12a, 15, 18-19	—	5.50
MS8	1976 (4)	—	KM#15, 18-19, 23	—	5.50
MS9	1977 (4)	—	KM#15, 18-19, 23	—	5.50
MS10	1978 (4)	—	KM#15, 18-19, 23	—	5.50
MS11	1980 (4)	—	KM#15, 18-19, 23	—	5.50
MS12	1981 (5)	—	KM#24-28	—	5.50
MS13	1981-1996 (8)	—	1981: KM#24-25; 1986: KM#26a; 1992: KM#31; 1995: KM#35; 1996: KM#27a, 28a, 29.1a	—	12.50
MS14	1994 (3)	6,000	KM#32-34	110	165
MS15	2000 (5)	10,000	KM#27a, 28a, 29.1a, 31, 35	—	18.50

PROOF SETS

KM#	Date	Mintage	Identification	Issue Price	Mkt Val
PS3	1966-1980 (11)	15,000	1966: KM#8-9, 13a.1; 1967: KM#11; 1974: KM#10a, 17; 1975: KM#12a; 1980: KM#15, 18-19, 23	40.00	37.50
PS1	1974 (3)	8,000	KM#20-22	272	300
PS2	1974 (2)	58,000	KM#20-21	38.00	32.00
PS4	1981 (5)	15,000	KM#24-28	32.00	37.50
PS5	1994 (3)	3,000	KM#32-34	155	275
PS6	2000 (2)	150,000	KM#37 and US Ericson Dollar	68.00	85.00

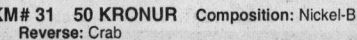

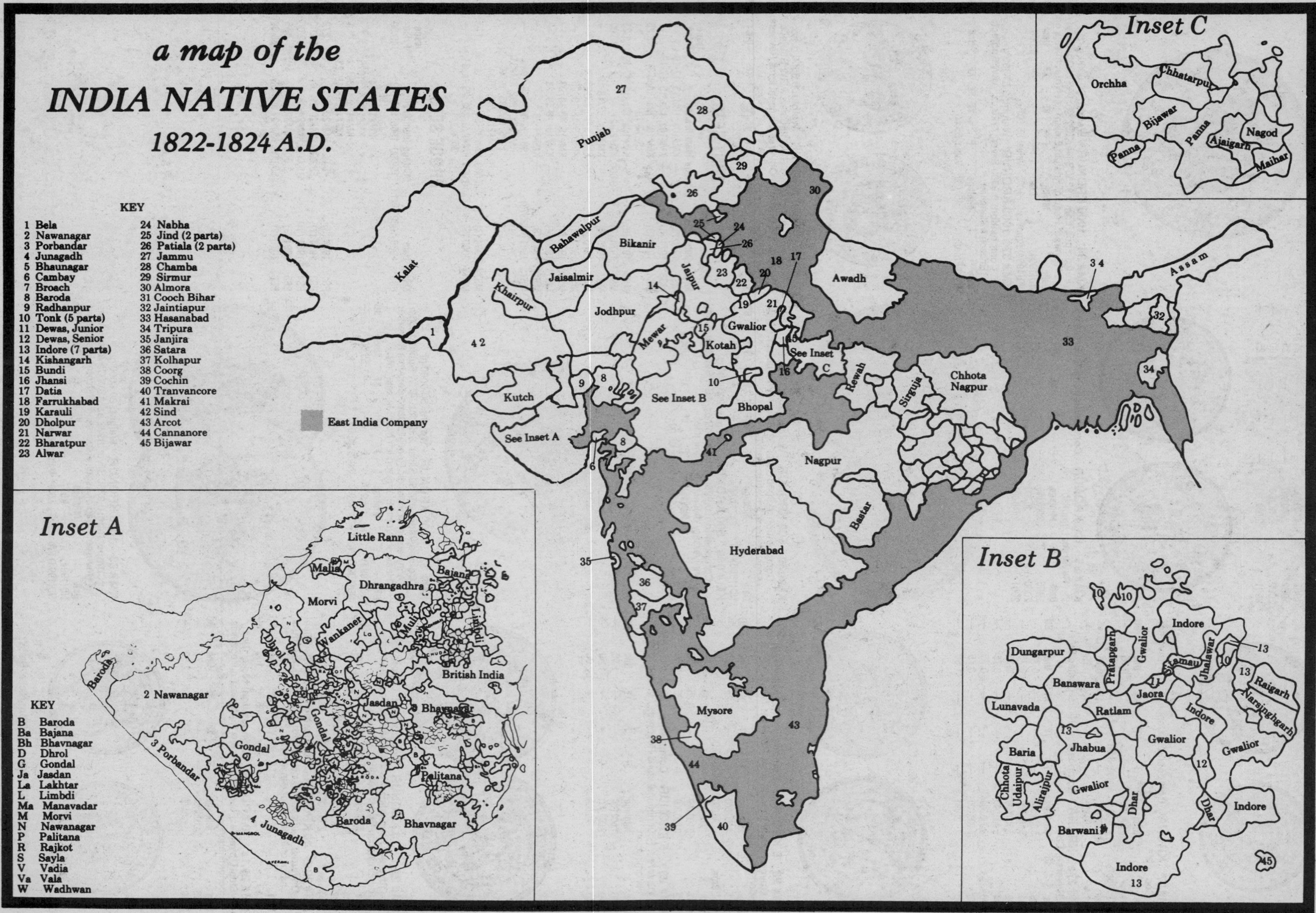
a map of the
INDIA NATIVE STATES
1822-1824 A.D.
KEY
1 Bela
2 Nawanagar
3 Porbandar
4 Junagadh
5 Bhaunagar
6 Cambay
7 Broach
8 Baroda
9 Radhanpur
10 Tonk (5 parts)
11 Dewas, Junior
12 Dewas, Senior
13 Indore (7 parts)
14 Kishangarh
15 Bundi
16 Jhansi
17 Datia
18 Farrukhabad
19 Karauli
20 Dholpur
21 Narwar
22 Bharatpur
23 Alwar
24 Nabha
25 Jind (2 parts)
26 Patiala (2 parts)
27 Jammu
28 Chamba
29 Sirmur
30 Almora
31 Cooch Bihar
32 Jaintiapur
33 Hasanabad
34 Tripura
35 Janjira
36 Satara
37 Kolhapur
38 Coorg
39 Cochin
40 Tranvancore
41 Makrai
42 Sind
43 Arcot
44 Cannanore
45 Bijawar
East India Company
Kalat
Punjab
Bahawalpur
Bikanir
Khairpur
Jaisalmir
Jodhpur
Jaipur
Mewar
Kutch
See Inset A
See Inset B
Gwalior
Kotah
Bhopal
Awadh
See Inset C
Rewah
Sirguja
Chhota Nagpur
Nagpur
Bastar
Hyderabad
Mysore
Assam
Inset C
Orchha
Chhatarpur
Bijawar
Panna
Ajaigarh
Nagod
Maihar
Inset A
Little Rann
Malia
Dhrangadhra
Bajana
Morvi
Wankaner
Muli
Limbdi
Dhrol
British India
Baroda
2 Nawanagar
Jasdan
Bhavnagar
Gondal
3 Porbandar
Palitana
4 Junagadh
Bhavnagar
KEY
B Baroda
Ba Bajana
Bh Bhavnagar
D Dhrol
G Gondal
Ja Jasdan
La Lakhtar
L Limbdi
Ma Manavadar
M Morvi
N Nawanagar
P Palitana
R Rajkot
S Sayla
V Vadia
Va Vala
W Wadhwan
Inset B
Dungarpur
Pratapgarh
Gwalior
Indore
Jhalawar
Banswara
Jaora
Raigarh
Narsinghgarh
Lunavada
Ratlam
Indore
Jhabua
Gwalior
Baria
Chhota Udaipur
Alirajpur
Gwalior
Dhar
Dhar
Indore
Barwani
Indore

INDIA - PRINCELY STATES

MONETARY SYSTEMS

In each state, local rates of exchange prevailed. There was no fixed rate between copper, silver or gold coin, but the rates varied in accordance with the values of the metal and by the edict of the local authority.

Within the subcontinent, different regions used distinctive coinage standards. In North India and the Deccan, the silver rupee (11.6 g) and gold mohur (11.0 g) predominated. In Gujarat, the silver kori (4.7 g) and gold kori (6.4 g) were the main currency. In South India the silver fanam (0.7-1.0 g) and gold hun or Pagoda (3.4 g) were current. Copper coins in all parts of India were produced to a myriad of local metrologies with seemingly endless varieties.

NAZARANA ISSUES

Throughout the Indian Princely States listings are Nazarana designations for special full flan strikings of copper, silver and some gold coinage. The purpose of these issues was for presentation to the local monarch to gain favor. For example if one had an audience with one's ruler he would exchange goods, currency notes or the cruder struck circulating coinage for Nazarana pieces which he would present to the ruler as a gift. The borderline between true Nazarana pieces and well struck regular issues is often indistinct. The Nazaranas sometimes circulated alongside the cruder "dump" issues.

PRICING

As the demand for Indian Princely coinage develops, and more dealers handle the material, sale records and price lists enable a firmer basis for pricing most series. For scarcer types adequate sale records are often not available, and prices must be regarded as tentative. Inasmuch as date collectors of Princely States series are few, dates known to be scarce are usually worth little more than common ones. Coins of a dated type, which do not show the full date on their flans should be valued at about 70 per cent of the prices indicated.

DATING

Coins are dated in several eras. Arabic and Devanagari numerals are used in conjunction with the Hejira era (AH), the Vikrama Samvat (VS), Saka Samvat (Saka), Fasli era(FE) Mauludi era (AM), and Malabar era (ME), as well as the Christian era (AD).

GRADING

Copper coins are rarely found in high grade, as they were the workhorse of coinage circulation, and were everywhere used for day-to-day transactions. Moreover, they were carelessly struck and even when 'new', can often only be distinguished from VF coins with difficulty, if at all.

Silver coins were often hoarded and not infrequently, turn up in nearly as-struck condition. The silver coins of Hyderabad (dump coins) are common in high grades, and the rupees of some states are scarcer 'used' than 'new'. Great caution must be exercised in determining the value or scarcity of high grade dump coins.

Dump gold was rarely circulated, and usually occurs in high grades, or is found made into jewelry.

BAHAWALPUR

The Amirs of Bahawalpur established their independence from Afghan control towards the close of the 18th century. In the 1830's the state's independence under British suzerainty became guaranteed by treaty. With the creation of Pakistan in 1947 Bahawalpur, with an area of almost 17,500 square miles, became its premier Princely State. Bahawalpur State, named after its capital, stretched for almost three hundred miles along the left bank of the Sutlej, Panjnad and Indus rivers.

For earlier issues in the names of the Durrani rulers, see Afghanistan.

RULERS

Amirs

Alhaj Muhammad Bahawal Khan V, AH1317-1325/1899-1907AD

Sir Sadiq Muhammad Khan V, AH1325-1365/1907-1947AD

Anonymous
(Alhaj Muhammad Bahawal Khan V)

ANONYMOUS HAMMERED 'DUMP' COINAGE

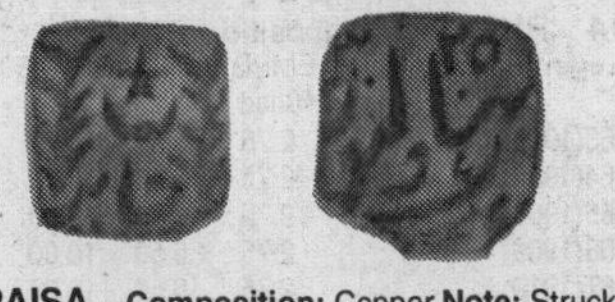

Y# 2.1 PAISA **Composition:** Copper **Note:** Struck at Bahawalpur Mint.

Date	Good	VG	F	VF	XF
AH1321(1903-04)	3.50	6.00	8.50	12.50	20.00
AH1325(1907-08)	3.50	6.00	8.50	12.50	20.00

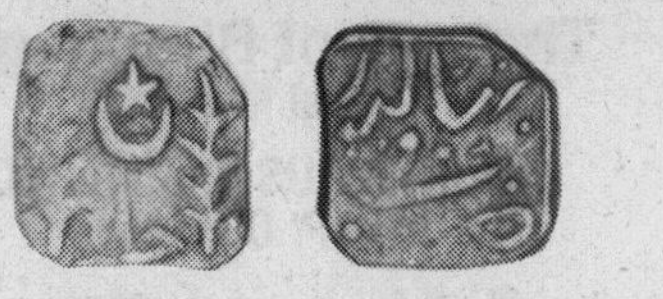

Y# 2.2 PAISA **Composition:** Copper **Note:** Struck at Bahawalpur Mint.

Date	Good	VG	F	VF	XF
ND(c. 1909)	4.00	7.50	12.00	20.00	32.50

Alhaj Muhammad Bahawal Khan V
AH1317-1325 / 1899-1907AD

HAMMERED 'DUMP' COINAGE

Y# 6 PAISA **Composition:** Copper **Obverse:** Legend in Persian **Obv. Legend:** Muhammad Bahawal ... **Note:** Struck at Bahawalpur Mint. For anonymous Paisas struck during the years of his reign, see Y#2.1, 2.2.

Date	Good	VG	F	VF	XF
AH1324(1906-07)	3.50	6.00	8.00	12.50	20.00
AH1325(1907-08)	3.50	6.00	8.00	12.50	20.00

Sir Sadiq Muhammad Khan V
AH1325-1365 / 1907-1947AD

HAMMERED 'DUMP' COINAGE

Y# 7.1 PAISA **Composition:** Copper **Obverse:** Legend in Persian **Obv. Legend:** Sadiq Muhammad ... **Note:** Struck at Bahawalpur Mint.

Date	Good	VG	F	VF	XF
AH1326(1908-09)	3.50	6.00	9.00	12.50	20.00
AH1327(1909-10)	3.50	6.00	9.00	12.50	20.00

Y# 7.2 PAISA **Composition:** Copper **Obverse:** Legend in Persian **Obv. Legend:** Sadiq Muhammad ... **Reverse:** Without date **Note:** Struck at Bahawalpur Mint.

Date	Good	VG	F	VF	XF
ND(c. 1910)	4.00	7.50	12.50	20.00	32.50

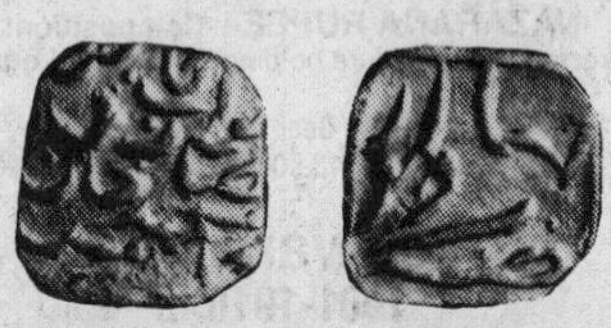

Y# 7.3 PAISA **Composition:** Copper **Obverse:** Legend in Persian **Obv. Legend:** Sadiq Muhammad ... **Reverse:** Without date or star **Note:** Struck at Bahawalpur Mint.

Date	Good	VG	F	VF	XF
ND(c. 1910)	5.50	9.00	13.50	20.00	32.50

Y# 8 PAISA **Composition:** Copper **Obverse:** Toughra **Note:** Struck at Bahawalpur Mint.

Date	Good	VG	F	VF	XF
AH1342(1923-24)	7.50	11.00	15.00	20.00	32.50
AH1343(1924-25)	7.50	11.00	15.00	20.00	32.50

MILLED COINAGE

Y# 12 1/2 PICE **Composition:** Copper **Obverse:** Bust of Muhammad Bahawal Khan V left **Reverse:** Toughra **Note:** Struck at Bahawalpur Mint.

Date	VG	F	VF	XF	Unc
AH1359(1940-41)	0.15	0.35	0.75	1.25	2.00
AH1359(1940-41) Proof	—	—	—	—	—

Y# 9 PAISA (1/4 Anna) **Composition:** Copper Or Bronze **Obverse:** Toughra **Reverse:** Three branches in square **Note:** Struck at Bahawalpur Mint.

Date	VG	F	VF	XF	Unc
AH1343(1924-25)	4.50	11.50	17.50	25.00	40.00

Y# 9a PAISA (1/4 Anna) **Composition:** Brass **Obverse:** Toughra **Reverse:** Three branches in square **Note:** Struck at Bahawalpur Mint.

Date	VG	F	VF	XF	Unc
AH1343(1924-25)	—	11.50	17.50	25.00	40.00

Y# 13 PAISA (1/4 Anna) **Composition:** Copper **Obverse:** Bust of Muhammad Bahawal Khan V left **Reverse:** Toughra **Note:** Struck at Bahawalpur Mint.

Date	VG	F	VF	XF	Unc
AH1359(1940-41)	0.30	0.75	1.25	2.00	3.00
AH1359(1940-41) Proof	—	—	—	—	—

Y# 14 RUPEE **Weight:** 6.5000 g. **Composition:** Silver **Obverse:** Toughra **Note:** Struck at Bahawalpur Mint. Possible pattern.

Date	VG	F	VF	XF	Unc
AH1343(1924-25)	16.50	40.00	55.00	75.00	100

Y# 10 NAZARANA RUPEE **Weight:** 12.3000 g. **Composition:** Silver **Obverse:** Bust of Muhammad Bahawal Khan V left **Reverse:** Ornate helmeted arms **Note:** Struck at Bahawalpur Mint. Design prepared for the nawab by Spink & Son Ltd., London.

Date	VG	F	VF	XF	Unc
AH1343(1924-25)	—	—	250	325	400

Y# 11 ASHRAFI **Weight:** 7.0000 g. **Composition:** Gold **Obverse:** Bust of Muhammad Bahawal Khan V left **Reverse:** Ornate helmeted arms **Size:** 22.5 mm. **Note:** Struck at Bahawalpur Mint. Design prepared for the nawab by Spink & Son Ltd., London.

Date	VG	F	VF	XF	Unc
AH1343(1924-25)	—	—	400	500	650

Y# 11a ASHRAFI **Weight:** 10.0000 g. **Composition:** Gold **Obverse:** Bust of Muhammad Bahawal Khan V left **Reverse:** Ornate helmeted arms **Note:** Struck at Bahawalpur Mint. Design prepared for the nawab by Spink & Son Ltd., London.

Date	VG	F	VF	XF	Unc
AH1343(1924-25) Proof	—	Value: 2,000			

BARODA

Maratha state located in western India. The ruling line was descended from Damaji, a Maratha soldier, who received the title of "Distinguished Swordsman" in 1721 (hence the scimitar on most Baroda coins). The Baroda title "Gaikwara" comes from "gaikwar" or cow herd, Damaji's father's occupation.

The Maratha rulers of Baroda, the Gaekwar family rose to prominence in the mid-18th century by carving out for themselves a dominion from territories, which were previously under the control of the Poona Marathas, and to a lesser extent, of the Raja of Jodhpur. Chronic internal disputes regarding the succession to the masnad culminated in the intervention of British troops in support of one candidate, Anand Rao Gaekwar, in 1800. Then, in 1802, an agreement with the East India Company released the Baroda princes from their fear of domination by the Maratha Peshwa of Poona but subordinated them to Company interests. Nevertheless, for almost the next century and a half Baroda maintained a good relationship with the British and continued as a major Princely State right up to 1947, when it acceded to the Indian Union.

RULERS

Gaekwars

Sayaji Rao III, AH1292-1357/VS1932-1995/1875-1938AD

Pratap Singh, VS1995-2008/1938-1951AD

Sayaji Rao II
AH1292-1357 / VS1932-1995 / 1875-1938AD

MILLED COINAGE

Y# 37 1/6 MOHUR **Composition:** Gold **Obverse:** Bust of Sayaji Rao III right **Size:** 14.5 mm. **Note:** 1.04-1.18 grams.

Date	VG	F	VF	XF	Unc
VS1951(1894)	—	165	225	275	350
VS1953(1896)	—	165	225	275	350
VS1959(1902)	—	165	225	275	350

Y# 38 1/3 MOHUR **Composition:** Gold **Obverse:** Bust of Sayaji Rao III right **Size:** 16 mm. **Note:** 2.07-2.39 grams.

Date	VG	F	VF	XF	Unc
VS1959(1902)	—	185	250	325	400

Y# 39 MOHUR **Composition:** Gold **Obverse:** Bust of Sayaji Rao III right **Size:** 21 mm. **Note:** 6.20-6.40 grams.

Date	VG	F	VF	XF	Unc
VS1959(1902)	—	250	325	450	650

Pratap Singh
VS1995-2008 / 1938-1951AD

MILLED COINAGE

Y# 40 1/3 MOHUR **Composition:** Gold **Obverse:** Bust of Pratap Singh right **Size:** 18 mm. **Note:** 2.07-2.13 grams.

Date	VG	F	VF	XF	Unc
VS1995(1938)	—	—	400	600	900

Y# 41 MOHUR **Composition:** Gold **Obverse:** Bust of Pratap Singh right **Size:** 21 mm. **Note:** 6.20-6.40 grams.

Date	VG	F	VF	XF	Unc
VS1995(1938)	—	—	400	600	900

BHAUNAGAR

State located in northwest India on the west shore of the Gulf of Cambay.

The Thakurs of Bhaunagar, as the rulers were titled, were Gohel Rajputs. They traced their control of the area back to the 13th century. Under the umbrella of British paramountcy, the Thakurs of Bhaunagar were regarded as relatively enlightened rulers. The State was absorbed into Saurashtra in February 1948.

Anonymous Types: Bearing the distinguishing Nagari legend *Bahadur* in addition to the Mughal legends.

MONETARY SYSTEM

2 Trambiyo = 1 Dokda

1-1/2 Dokda = 1 Dhingla

Thakurs of Bhaunagar
Gohel Rajputs

ANONYMOUS HAMMERED 'DUMP' COINAGE

KM# 1 DOKDA **Composition:** Copper

Date	Good	VG	F	VF	XF
VS2004(1947)	4.00	6.00	10.00	15.00	—

BUNDI

State in Rajputana in northwest India.

Bundi was founded in 1342 by a Chauhan Rajput, Rao Dewa (Deoraj). Until the Maratha defeat early in the 19th century, Bundi was greatly harassed by the forces of Holkar and Sindhia. In 1818 it came under British protection and control and remained so until 1947. In 1948 the State was absorbed into Rajasthan.

RULERS

Raghubir Singh VS1946-1984/1889-1927AD

Ishwari Singh VS1984-2004/1927-1947AD

MINT

	PERSO-ARABIC	DEVANAGARI
Bundi	بندي	बुन्दी

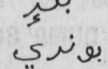

Mintname: Bundi بوندي

Victoria
1837-1901AD

REGAL COINAGE
(Hammered "Dump" Coinage)

Y# 10 NAZARANA RUPEE **Composition:** Silver **Obverse:** Seated figure holding katar **Obv. Legend:** VICTORIA QUEEN

Date	Good	VG	F	VF	XF
VS1958(1901)	18.50	37.50	55.00	90.00	140

Edward VII
1901-1910AD

REGAL COINAGE
(Hammered "Dump" Coinage)

Y# A12 1/2 PAISA **Composition:** Copper **Obverse:** Katar **Obv. Legend:** EDWARD VII EMPEROR **Note:** 4.70-5.10 grams.

Date	Good	VG	F	VF	XF
ND(VS1963-1976) Date off flan	3.00	4.50	6.50	8.50	—
VS1965(1908)	6.00	9.00	12.50	16.50	—
VS1973(1916)	6.00	9.00	12.50	16.50	—
VS1974(1917)	6.00	9.00	12.50	16.50	—
VS1976(1919)	6.00	9.00	12.50	16.50	—

Y# A2 1/2 PAISA **Composition:** Copper **Obverse:** Katar, inscription: VIC/TORIA/QUEEN **Obv. Legend:** EMPEROR EDWARD **Note:** 5.00-5.20 grams.

Date	Good	VG	F	VF	XF
VS1963(1906)	0.75	1.25	2.25	3.50	—
VS1965(1908)	0.75	1.25	2.25	3.50	—
VS1966(1909)	0.75	1.25	2.25	3.50	—
VS1967(1910)	0.75	1.25	2.25	3.50	—

Y# B11 1/4 RUPEE **Composition:** Silver **Obverse:** Seated figure holding katar **Obv. Legend:** EMPEROR-EDWARD VII **Note:** 2.65-2.70 grams.

Date	Good	VG	F	VF	XF
VS1958(1901)	5.50	13.50	21.50	30.00	40.00
VS1959(1902)	5.50	13.50	21.50	30.00	40.00
VS1961(1904)	5.50	13.50	21.50	30.00	40.00
VS1962(1905)	5.50	13.50	21.50	30.00	40.00

Y# 12 1/4 RUPEE **Composition:** Silver **Obverse:** Katar **Obv. Legend:** EDWARD VII EMPEROR **Note:** 2.65-2.70 grams.

Date	Good	VG	F	VF	XF
VS1963(1906)	1.50	4.00	6.00	9.00	13.50
VS1964(1907)	1.50	4.00	6.00	9.00	13.50
VS1965(1908)	1.50	4.00	6.00	9.00	13.50
VS1966(1909)	1.50	4.00	6.00	9.00	13.50

Y# A11 1/2 RUPEE **Composition:** Silver **Obverse:** Seated figure holding katar **Obv. Legend:** EMPEROR-EDWARD VII **Size:** 16-18 mm. **Note:** 5.30-5.40 grams.

Date	Good	VG	F	VF	XF
VS1958(1901)	6.00	15.00	21.50	30.00	40.00

Y# 13 1/2 RUPEE **Composition:** Silver **Obverse:** Katar **Obv. Legend:** EDWARD VII EMPEROR **Size:** 16-18 mm. **Note:** 5.30-5.40 grams.

Date	Good	VG	F	VF	XF
VS1963(1906)	2.25	5.50	8.00	12.50	18.50
VS1964(1907)	2.00	5.00	7.00	10.00	15.00
VS1965(1908)	2.00	5.00	7.00	10.00	15.00
VS1966(1909)	2.00	5.00	7.00	10.00	15.00

Y# 11 RUPEE **Composition:** Silver **Obverse:** Seated figure holding katar **Obv. Legend:** EMPEROR-EDWARD VII **Note:** 10.60-10.70 grams.

Date	Good	VG	F	VF	XF
VS1958(1901)	2.75	6.50	10.00	15.00	22.50
VS1959(1902)	2.75	6.50	10.00	15.00	22.50
VS1960(1903)	2.75	6.50	10.00	15.00	22.50
VS1961(1904)	2.75	6.50	10.00	15.00	22.50
VS1962(1905)	2.75	6.50	10.00	15.00	22.50
VS1963(1906)	2.75	6.50	10.00	15.00	22.50

Y# 14 RUPEE **Composition:** Silver **Obverse:** Katar **Obv. Legend:** EDWARD VII EMPEROR **Note:** 10.60-10.70 grams.

Date	Good	VG	F	VF	XF
VS1963(1906)	2.75	6.50	10.00	15.00	22.50
VS1964(1907)	2.75	6.50	10.00	15.00	22.50
VS1965(1908)	2.75	6.50	10.00	15.00	22.50
VS1966(1909)	2.75	6.50	10.00	15.00	22.50
VS1967(1910)	2.75	6.50	10.00	15.00	22.50
VS1968(1911)	2.75	6.50	10.00	15.00	22.50
VS1969(1912)	2.75	6.50	10.00	15.00	22.50

Y# 11a NAZARANA RUPEE **Composition:** Silver **Obverse:** Seated figure holding katar **Obv. Legend:** EMPEROR-EDWARD VII **Note:** 10.60-10.70 grams. Broad, square flan.

Date	Good	VG	F	VF	XF
VS1962(1905)	18.50	37.50	60.00	100	175

Y# 14a NAZARANA RUPEE **Composition:** Silver **Obverse:** Katar **Obv. Legend:** EDWARD VII EMPEROR **Note:** 10.60-10.70 grams.

Date	Good	VG	F	VF	XF
VS1965(1908)	17.50	35.00	55.00	90.00	150
VS1966(1909)	17.50	35.00	55.00	90.00	150
VS1967(1910)	17.50	35.00	55.00	90.00	150
VS1968(1911)	17.50	35.00	55.00	90.00	150
VS1969(1912)	17.50	35.00	55.00	90.00	150
VS1970(1913)	17.50	35.00	55.00	90.00	150

Y# 14b NAZARANA RUPEE **Composition:** Silver **Obverse:** Katar **Obv. Legend:** EDWARD VII EMPEROR **Note:** 10.60-10.70 grams. Round flan.

Date	Good	VG	F	VF	XF
VS1966(1909)	5.00	12.50	20.00	35.00	60.00
VS1967(1910)	5.00	12.50	20.00	35.00	60.00
VS1968(1911)	5.00	12.50	20.00	35.00	60.00
VS1969(1912)	6.00	15.00	21.50	30.00	40.00
VS1970(1913)	6.00	15.00	21.50	30.00	40.00

George V
1910-1936AD
REGAL COINAGE
(Hammered "Dump" Coinage)

Y# 15.1 1/2 PAISA **Composition:** Copper **Obverse:** Katar **Obv. Legend:** EMPEROR-GEORGE V **Note:** 5.00-5.35 grams.

Date	Good	VG	F	VF	XF
VS1973(1916)	1.50	2.25	3.00	4.00	—
VS1974(1917)	1.50	2.25	3.00	4.00	—
VS1976(1919)	1.50	2.25	3.00	4.00	—
VS1977(1920)	1.50	2.25	3.00	4.00	—

Y# 15.2 1/2 PAISA **Composition:** Copper **Obverse:** Katar **Obv. Legend:** GEORGE V EMPEROR **Note:** 5.00-5.35 grams. Size and weight vary.

Date	Good	VG	F	VF	XF
VS1980(1923)	1.50	2.25	3.00	4.00	—
VS1981(1924)	1.50	2.25	3.00	4.00	—
VS1982(1925)	1.50	2.25	3.00	4.00	—
VS1983(1926)	1.50	2.25	3.00	4.00	—
VS1984(1927)	1.50	2.25	3.00	4.00	—
VS1986(1929)	2.00	3.00	4.00	5.00	—
VS1987(1930)	2.00	3.00	4.00	5.00	—
VS1988(1931)	3.00	4.00	5.50	7.50	—
VS1990(1933)	3.00	4.00	5.50	7.50	—
VS1991(1934)	3.00	4.00	5.50	7.50	—
VS1992(1935)	3.00	4.00	5.50	7.50	—

Y# 16.1 1/4 RUPEE **Composition:** Silver **Obverse:** Katar **Obv. Legend:** EMPEROR-GEORGE V **Note:** 2.60-2.70 grams.

Date	Good	VG	F	VF	XF
VS1972(1915)	1.25	3.00	4.50	6.50	10.00
VS1973(1916)	1.25	3.00	4.50	6.50	10.00
VS1974(1917)	1.25	3.00	4.50	6.50	10.00

Y# 16.2 1/4 RUPEE **Composition:** Silver **Obverse:** Katar **Obv. Legend:** GEORGE V EMPEROR **Note:** 2.60-2.70 grams.

Date	Good	VG	F	VF	XF
VS1980(1923)	1.25	3.00	4.50	6.50	10.00
VS1981(1924)	1.25	3.00	4.50	6.50	10.00
VS1982(1925)	1.25	3.00	4.50	6.50	10.00

Y# A19 1/4 RUPEE **Composition:** Silver **Obverse:** Date 1925 at center **Obv. Legend:** EMPEROR GEORGE V **Size:** 13 mm. **Note:** 2.60-2.70 grams.

Date	Good	VG	F	VF	XF
VS1915(1925)	10.00	20.00	31.50	42.50	60.00

Y# 17.1 1/2 RUPEE **Composition:** Silver **Note:** 5.30-5.40 grams.

Date	Good	VG	F	VF	XF
VS1972(1915)	2.00	5.00	7.00	10.00	15.00
VS1973(1916)	2.00	5.00	7.00	10.00	15.00
VS1974(1917)	1.50	4.00	6.00	9.00	13.50
VS1979(1922)	1.50	4.00	6.00	9.00	13.50

Y# 17.2 1/2 RUPEE **Composition:** Silver **Obverse:** Legend arranged differently **Note:** 5.30-5.40 grams.

Date	Good	VG	F	VF	XF
VS1979(1922)	1.50	4.00	6.00	9.00	13.50
VS1980(1923)	1.50	4.00	6.00	9.00	13.50
VS1981(1924)	1.50	4.00	6.00	9.00	13.50
VS1982(1925)	1.50	4.00	6.00	9.00	13.50
VS1983(1926)	1.50	4.00	6.00	9.00	13.50
VS1984(1927)	1.50	4.00	6.00	9.00	13.50

Y# 19 1/2 RUPEE **Composition:** Silver **Obverse:** Date 1925 at center **Obv. Legend:** EMPEROR GEORGE V **Note:** 5.30-5.40 grams.

Date	Good	VG	F	VF	XF
VS1915(1925)	11.50	23.50	38.50	55.00	80.00

Y# 18.1 RUPEE **Composition:** Silver **Obverse:** Katar **Obv. Legend:** EMPEROR GEORGE V **Note:** 10.60-10.70 grams.

Date	Good	VG	F	VF	XF
VS1972(1915)	2.50	6.00	9.00	13.50	20.00
VS1973(1916)	2.50	6.00	9.00	13.50	20.00
VS1974(1917)	2.50	6.00	9.00	13.50	20.00
VS1975(1918)	2.50	6.00	9.00	13.50	20.00
VS1979(1922)	2.50	6.00	9.00	13.50	20.00

Y# 18.2 RUPEE **Composition:** Silver **Obverse:** Katar **Obv. Legend:** GEORGE V EMPEROR **Note:** 10.60-10.70 grams.

Date	Good	VG	F	VF	XF
VS1979(1922)	2.50	6.00	9.00	13.50	20.00
VS1980(1923)	2.50	6.00	9.00	13.50	20.00
VS1981(1924)	2.50	6.00	9.00	13.50	20.00
VS1982(1925)	2.50	6.00	9.00	13.50	20.00
VS1983(1926)	2.50	6.00	9.00	13.50	20.00
VS1984(1927)	2.50	6.00	9.00	13.50	20.00
VS1985(1928)	2.50	6.00	9.00	13.50	20.00
VS1987(1930)	2.50	6.00	9.00	13.50	20.00
VS1989(1932)	2.50	6.00	9.00	13.50	20.00
VS1979-1989 Date off flan	1.50	4.00	6.00	9.00	13.50

Y# 20 RUPEE **Composition:** Silver **Obverse:** Date 1925 at center **Obv. Legend:** EMPEROR GEORGE V **Note:** 10.60-10.70 grams.

Date	Good	VG	F	VF	XF
VS1915(1925)	—	45.00	70.00	100	140

Y# 18a.1 NAZARANA RUPEE **Composition:** Silver **Obverse:** Katar **Obv. Legend:** EMPEROR GEORGE V **Note:** 10.55-10.80 grams. Square.

Date	Good	VG	F	VF	XF
VS1965(1908)	13.50	27.50	45.00	75.00	125
VS1971(1914)	13.50	27.50	45.00	75.00	125
VS1974(1917)	13.50	27.50	45.00	75.00	125
VS1975(1918)	13.50	27.50	45.00	75.00	125
VS1977(1920)	13.50	27.50	45.00	75.00	125

Y# 18a.2 NAZARANA RUPEE **Composition:** Silver **Obverse:** Katar **Obv. Legend:** GEORGE V **Note:** 10.55-10.80 grams. Square.

Date	Good	VG	F	VF	XF
VS1979(1922)	13.50	27.50	45.00	75.00	125
VS1980(1923)	13.50	27.50	45.00	75.00	125
VS1981(1924)	13.50	27.50	45.00	75.00	125
VS1983(1926)	13.50	27.50	45.00	75.00	125
VS1984(1927)	13.50	27.50	45.00	75.00	125
VS1987(1930)	13.50	27.50	45.00	75.00	125

Y# 20a NAZARANA RUPEE **Composition:** Silver **Obverse:** Date 1925 at center **Obv. Legend:** EMPEROR GEORGE V **Note:** 10.55-10.80 grams.

Date	Good	VG	F	VF	XF
VS1915(1925)	22.50	45.00	75.00	110	150

CAMBAY

Khanbayat

Although of very ancient origins as a port, located at the head of the Gulf of Cambay in West India, Cambay did not come into existence as a separate state until about 1730 after the breakdown of Mughal authority in Delhi. The nawabs of Cambay traced their ancestry to Momin Khan II, the last of the Muslim governors of Gujerat. The State came under British control after two decades of Maratha rule.

RULERS

Ja'far Ali Khan, AH1297-1333/VS1937-1972/1880-1915AD

Mint: Khanbayat

Jafar Ali Khan
1937-1972AD
ANONYMOUS HAMMERED 'DUMP' COINAGE

Y# 5 1/2 PAISA **Composition:** Copper **Obverse:** Persian legend **Obv. Legend:** Cambay **Reverse:** Denomination in words **Note:** Varieties in countermark exist.

Date	Good	VG	F	VF	XF
VS1963(1906)	3.50	6.50	9.00	12.50	—
VS1964(1907)	3.50	6.50	9.00	12.50	—

Y# 5a 1/2 PAISA **Composition:** Copper **Obverse:** Persian legend **Obv. Legend:** Cambay **Reverse:** Denomination in numerals

Date	Good	VG	F	VF	XF
VS1964(1907)	3.00	5.00	7.50	10.00	—
VS1965(1908)	3.00	5.00	7.50	10.00	—
VS1966(1909)	3.00	5.00	7.50	10.00	—

Y# 6 PAISA **Composition:** Copper **Obverse:** Persian legend **Obv. Legend:** Cambay **Note:** Varieties exist.

Date	Good	VG	F	VF	XF
VS1962(1905)	1.00	1.50	2.00	3.50	—
VS1963(1906)	1.00	1.50	2.00	3.50	—
VS1964(1907)	1.25	1.75	2.50	4.25	—
VS1965(1908)	1.00	1.50	2.00	3.50	—
VS1966(1909)	1.00	1.50	2.00	3.50	—
VS1968(1911)	1.00	1.50	2.00	3.50	—
VS1970(1913)	1.65	2.50	4.00	5.00	—

Y# 10 RUPEE **Composition:** Silver **Obverse:** Persian legend **Obv. Legend:** Ja'afar Ali Khan **Reverse:** Mint name **Note:** Struck at Cambay. 10.70-11.60 grams.

Date	Good	VG	F	VF	XF
AH1319(1901-1902)	15.00	30.00	50.00	80.00	120

COUNTERMARKED 'DUMP' COINAGE

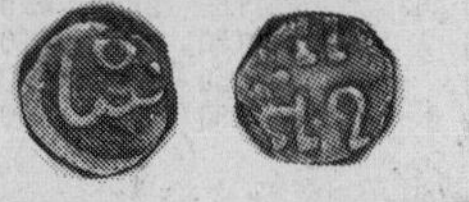

Y# 2 1/4 PAISA **Composition:** Copper **Countermark:** Persian "Shah" **Note:** Varieties in countermark exist.

Date	Good	VG	F	VF	XF
ND(c. 1905-1909)	3.00	5.50	7.50	10.00	—

Y# 3 1/2 PAISA **Composition:** Copper **Countermark:** Persian "Shah" **Note:** Round flan. Varieties in countermark exist.

Date	Good	VG	F	VF	XF
VS(19)62(1905)	3.00	5.50	7.50	10.00	—

Y# 4 PAISA **Composition:** Copper **Countermark:** Persian "Shah" **Note:** Round flan.

Date	Good	VG	F	VF	XF
VS194x	1.25	2.00	3.00	4.25	—

Y# 4a PAISA **Composition:** Copper **Countermark:** Persian "Shah" **Note:** Square flan.

Date	Good	VG	F	VF	XF
ND	1.50	2.25	3.25	4.50	—

CIS-SUTLEJ STATES

The name Cis-Sutlej States was applied to those states in the tract of land south of the Sutlej and to the north of the Delhi territory. Before 1846 the majority of these chieftains were substantially independent, subject only to the general oversight of an agent of the Governor-General. After the first Sikh war (1845-1846) this independence became somewhat circumscribed and in 1849 the Punjab was annexed and the Cis-Sutlej States were merged into the new province of British India. Perhaps surprisingly, most of these States distinguished themselves on the side of the British during the Great Revolt of 1857.

CIS-SUTLEJ STATES - MALER KOLTA

State located in the Punjab in northwest India, founded by the Maler Kotla family who were Sherwani Afghans who had travelled to India from Kabul in 1467 as officials of the Delhi emperors.

Coins are rupees of Ahmad Shah Durrani, and except for the last ruler, contain the chief's initial on the reverse. The chiefs were called Ra'is until 1821, Nawabs thereafter.

For similar issues see Jind, Nabha and Patiala.

RULERS:
Ibrahim Ali Khan, AH1288-1326/1871-1908AD
Ahmad ali Khan, AH1326-/1908-AD

Ibrahim Ali Khan
AH1288-1326/1871-1908AD

HAMMERED 'DUMP' COINAGE

Y# 4 1/4 RUPEE **Composition:** Silver **Note:** 2.68-2.90 grams.

Date	VG	F	VF	XF	Unc
ND (1871)	40.00	65.00	100	150	—

Ahmad Ali Khan
AH1326-/1908-AD

HAMMERED 'DUMP' COINAGE

Y# 7 1/2 PAISA **Composition:** Copper **Obverse:** Persian inscription: Ahmad Ali Khan ...

Date	Good	VG	F	VF	XF
ND (1908)	7.00	11.00	16.50	25.00	—

Y# 8 PAISA **Composition:** Copper **Obverse:** Persian inscription: Ahmad Ali Khan ...

Date	Good	VG	F	VF	XF
AH1326(1908-09)	17.50	25.00	—	35.00	50.00

Note: Error for 1326

Y# 9 RUPEE **Composition:** Silver **Obverse:** Persian inscription: Ahmad Ali Khan ... **Note:** 10.70-11.60 grams.

Date	Good	VG	F	VF	XF
ND(1908)	—	6.00	9.00	13.50	20.00

Y# 10 NAZARANA 2 RUPEE **Weight:** 22.0000 g. **Composition:** Silver **Obverse:** Persian inscription: Ahmad Ali Khan ...

Date	Good	VG	F	VF	XF
AH1326(1908-09) Rare	—	—	—	—	—

CIS-SUTLEJ STATES - PATIALA

State located in the Punjab in northwest India. In the mid-18th century the Raja was given his title and mint right by Ahmad Shah Durrani of Afghanistan, whose coin he copied.

The rulers became Maharajas in 1810AD. The maharaja of Patiala was also recognized as the leader of the Phulkean tribe. Unlike others, Patiala's Sikh rulers had never hesitated to seek British assistance at those times when they felt threatened by their co-religionist neighbors. In 1857, Patiala's forces were immediately made available on the side of the British.

RULERS:
Bhupindar Singh, VS1958-1994/1900-1937AD
Yadvindar Singh, VS1994-2005/1937-1948AD

UNCERTAIN COINAGE

KM# 1 RUPEE **Composition:** Silver **Note:** 10.70-11.60 grams, unknown date (ca.1900's).

Date	Good	VG	F	VF	XF
AHxxxx // 4 (1938)	—	12.50	18.50	25.00	35.00

Bhupindar Singh
VS1958-94/1900-37AD

HAMMERED 'DUMP' COINAGE

Y# A3 RUPEE **Composition:** Silver **Obverse:** Persian inscription: Guru Govind Singh **Note:** 11.10-11.20 grams.

Date	VG	F	VF	XF	Unc
VS1958 (1901)	—	—	—	—	—

Y# 14 1/6 MOHUR **Weight:** 1.7500 g. **Composition:** Gold **Obverse:** Persian inscription: Ahmad Shah Durrani **Reverse:** Dagger at left

Date	VG	F	VF	XF	Unc
VS(19)58 (1901)	—	85.00	100	125	175

KM# 15 1/3 MOHUR **Weight:** 3.5000 g. **Composition:** Gold **Obverse:** Persian inscription: Ahmad Shah Durrani

Date	VG	F	VF	XF	Unc
VS(19)58 (1901)	—	85.00	100	125	175

Y# 16 2/3 MOHUR **Weight:** 7.0000 g. **Composition:** Gold **Obverse:** Persian inscription: Ahmad Shah Durrani **Size:** 18 mm.

Date	VG	F	VF	XF	Unc
VS(19)58 (1901)	—	125	140	200	300

Y# 17 MOHUR **Weight:** 10.5000 g. **Composition:** Gold **Obverse:** Persian inscription: Ahmad Shah Durrani

Date	VG	F	VF	XF	Unc
VS(19)58 (1901)	—	150	200	275	400

Yadvindar Singh
VS1994-2005/1934-48AD

HAMMERED 'DUMP' COINAGE

Y# A1 RUPEE **Composition:** Silver **Obverse:** Persian inscription: Guru Govind Singh **Note:** 11.10-11.20 grams.

Date	VG	F	VF	XF	Unc
VS1994 (1937)	—	—	—	—	—

Y# 19 1/6 MOHUR **Weight:** 1.7500 g. **Composition:** Gold **Obverse:** Persian inscription: Ahmad Shah Durrani **Reverse:** Bayoneted rifle at left

Date	VG	F	VF	XF	Unc
VS(19)94 (1937)	—	75.00	100	125	175

KM# 20 1/3 MOHUR **Weight:** 3.5000 g. **Composition:** Gold **Obverse:** Persian inscription: Ahmad Shah Durrani

Date	VG	F	VF	XF	Unc
VS(19)94 (1937)	—	75.00	100	125	175

Y# 21 2/3 MOHUR **Weight:** 7.0000 g. **Composition:** Gold **Obverse:** Persian inscription: Ahmad Shah Durrani

Date	VG	F	VF	XF	Unc
VS(19)94 (1937)	—	150	185	225	275

COOCH BEHAR

Cooch Behar was relatively peaceful until there was a dispute over the succession in 1772. After a confusing period during which the Bhutanese installed their own nominated ruler and captured Dhairyendra Narandra, the Chief Minister appealed to the British for assistance. With an eye on the potentially lucrative Tibetan trade, which had increased somewhat in volume since Prithvi Narayan's rise to power in Nepal, the British agreed to support Darendra Narayan, so long as British suzerainty was acknowledged.

Over the following decades the British gradually increased their control over the state. After large numbers of debased silver half, or "Narainy" rupees had been struck, the British decided to close the mint, and after that a few coins only were struck at the coronation of each ruler, although it was only in 1866 that the local coins ceased to be legal tender.

RULERS
Nripendra Narayan, CB353-401/SE1785-1833/1863-1911AD
Raja Rajendra Narayan, CB401-403/SE1833-1835/1911-1913AD
Jitendra Narayan, CB403-412/SE1835-1844/1913-1922AD
Jagaddipendra Narayan, CB412-439/SE1844-1871/1922-1949AD

Raja Rajendra Narayan
CB401-403; SE1833-1835; 1911-1913AD

MILLED COINAGE

KM# 195 NAZARANA 1/2 RUPEE **Weight:** 4.7000 g. **Composition:** Silver **Obverse:** Arms

Date	Mintage	VG	F	VF	XF	Unc
CB402(1912)	1,001	—	—	50.00	70.00	100

KM# 200 NAZARANA MOHUR **Composition:** Gold **Obverse:** Arms **Note:** Weight varies 8.5 - 9.4 grams.

Date	Mintage	VG	F	VF	XF	Unc
CB402(1912)	100	—	—	—	1,200	1,800

Jitendra Narayan
CB403-412; SE1835-1844; 1913-1922AD

MILLED COINAGE

KM# 210 NAZARANA 1/2 RUPEE **Weight:** 4.7000 g. **Composition:** Silver **Obverse:** Arms

Date	Mintage	VG	F	VF	XF	Unc
CB404(1914)	1,004	—	—	50.00	70.00	100

KM# 215 NAZARANA MOHUR **Weight:** 8.0000 g. **Composition:** Gold **Obverse:** Arms

Date	Mintage	VG	F	VF	XF	Unc
CB404(1914)	100	—	—	—	1,200	1,800

Jagaddipendra Narayan
CB412-439; SE1844-1871; 1922-1949AD

MILLED COINAGE

KM# 225 NAZARANA 1/2 RUPEE **Weight:** 5.4000 g. **Composition:** Silver **Obverse:** Arms

Date	VG	F	VF	XF	Unc
CB413(1923)	—	—	35.00	50.00	70.00

STANDARD COINAGE

KM# 230 NAZARANA 1/2 RUPEE **Weight:** 8.7000 g. **Composition:** Gold **Obverse:** Arms

Date	F	VF	XF	Unc
CB413 (1923)	—	—	1,200	1,800

DATIA

State located in north-central India, governed by Maharajas. Datia was founded in 1735 by Bhagwan Das, son of Narsingh Dev of the Orchha royal house. In 1804 the State concluded its first treaty with the East India Company and thereafter came under British protection and control.

RULERS
Bhawani Singh, AH1274-1325/1857-1907AD
Govind Singh, AH1325-1368/1907-1948AD

MINT

دلیپ نگر

Dalipnagar

Gaja Shahi Series

Struck for more than 100 years, with the AH date on the obverse and the regnal year on the reverse bearing little relationship to each other. These are close copies of Orchha C#24-32 and can only be distinguished by the symbols, which are always different from those of Orchha, except for the Gaja (mace):

Gaja always on reverse 

On obverse (Datia Mint Symbol) 

On reverse 

Bhawani Singh
AH1274-1325/1857-1907AD

HAMMERED 'DUMP' COINAGE
Gaja Shahi Series

Struck for more than 100 years, with the AH date on the obverse and the regnal year on the reverse bearing little relationship to each other. These are close copies of Orchha C#24-32 and can only be distinguised by the symbols, which are different from those of Orchha, accept for the Gaja (mace).

C# 22 1/2 PAISA **Weight:** 6.0000 g. **Composition:** Copper

Date	Good	VG	F	VF	XF
AH1320(1902)	3.00	4.50	6.50	10.00	—

C# 23 PAISA **Composition:** Copper **Note:** Round or somewhat square shape, weight varies 12 - 13 grams.

Date	Good	VG	F	VF	XF
AH1246//24 (1830)	2.50	3.25	4.00	5.50	—
AH1248 (1832)	2.50	3.25	4.00	5.50	—
AH1258 (1842)	2.50	3.25	4.00	5.50	—
AH--//39 (1842)	2.50	3.25	4.00	5.50	—
AH--//40 (1842)	2.50	3.25	4.00	5.50	—
AH1274//45 (1857)	2.50	3.25	4.00	5.50	—
AH1275//41 (1858)	2.50	3.25	4.00	5.50	—
AH1278//45 (1861)	2.50	3.25	4.00	5.50	—
AH1282//4x (1865)	2.50	3.25	4.00	5.50	—
AH1283 (1866)	2.50	3.25	4.00	5.50	—
AH1320 / yr.46 (1902)	2.50	3.25	4.00	5.50	—

DEWAS

A Maratha state located in west-central India. The raja, the brother of the raja of Dewas Senior Branch had a palace in Dewas City. They descended from two brothers, Tukoji and Jiwaji who were given Dewas City in 1726 by Peshwa Baji Rao as a reward for army services.

Largely due to its geographical location Dewas suffered much at the hands of the armies of Holkar and Sindhia,and from Pindari incursions. In 1818 the State came under British protection.

LOCAL RULERS
Vikrama Simha Rao, 1937-1948AD

Senior Branch

Vikrama Simha Rao
VS1994-2005/1937-1948AD

MILLED COINAGE

KM# 13 PAISA **Composition:** Copper **Obverse:** Bust of Vikrama Simha Rao right **Reverse:** Arms

Date	VG	F	VF	XF	Unc
2000/1944	11.50	27.50	55.00	90.00	150
2001/1944	11.50	22.50	45.00	75.00	125

DUNGARPUR

A district in northwest India which became part of Rajasthan in 1948.

The maharawals of Dungarpur were descended from the Mewar chieftains of the 12th century. In 1527 the upper Mahi basin was bifurcated to form the Princely States of Dungarpur and Banswara. Thereafter Dungarpur came successively under Mughal and Maratha control until in 1818 it came under British protection.

RULERS
Bijey Singh, VS1955-1975/1898-1918AD
Lakshman Singh, VS1975-2005/1918-1948AD

Lakshman Singh
VS1975-2005/1918-1948AD

HAMMERED 'DUMP' COINAGE

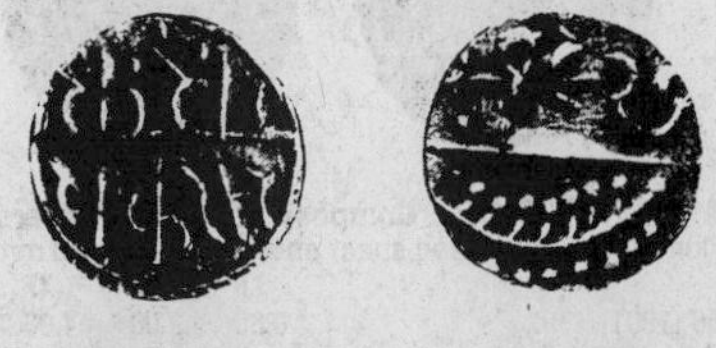

KM# 9 NAZARANA MOHUR **Weight:** 11.0000 g. **Composition:** Gold

Date	Good	VG	F	VF	XF
VS1996(1939) Rare	—	—	—	—	—
VS2001(1944) Rare	—	—	—	—	—

WW II EMERGENCY COINAGE

KM# 7 PAISA **Composition:** Copper **Reverse:** 2 bars above 'P' in "Paisa"

Date	VG	F	VF	XF	Unc
VS2001(1944)	18.50	30.00	50.00	75.00	—

KM# 8 PAISA **Composition:** Copper **Reverse:** One bar above 'P' in "Paisa"

Date	VG	F	VF	XF	Unc
VS2001(1944)	9.00	15.00	25.00	37.50	—

GWALIOR

Sindhia

State located in central India. Capital originally was Ujjain (= Daru-l-fath), but was later transferred to Gwalior in 1810. The Gwalior ruling family, the Sindhias, were descendants of the Maratha chief Ranoji Sindhia (d.1750). His youngest son, Mahadji Sindhia (d.1794) was anxious to establish his independence from the overlordship of the Peshwas of Poona. Unable to achieve this alone, it was the Peshwa's crushing defeat by Ahmad Shah Durrani at Panipat in 1761, which helped realize his ambitions. Largely in the interests of sustaining this autonomy, but partly as a result of a defeat at East India Company hands in 1781, Mahadji concluded an alliance with the British in 1782. In 1785, he reinstalled the fallen Mughal Emperor, Shah Alam, on the throne at Dehli. Very early in the 19th century, Gwalior's relationship with the British began to deteriorate, a situation which culminated in the Anglo-Maratha War of 1803. Gwalior's forces under Daulat Rao were defeated. In consequence, and by the terms of the peace treaty which followed, his territory was truncated. In 1818, Gwalior suffered a further loss of land at British hands. In the years that ensued, as the East India Company's possessions became transformed into empire and as the Pax Britannica swept across the subcontinent, the Sindhia family's relationship with their British overlords steadily improved.

RULERS
Madho Rao, VS1943-1982/1886-1925AD
Jivaji Rao, VS1982-2005/1925-1948AD

MINTS

Gwalior Fort گوالیار

Madho Rao
VS1943-82/1886-1925AD
MILLED COINAGE

KM# 164 1/2 PICE **Composition:** Copper **Obverse:** Plumes above crossed spear and trident **Size:** 20 mm.

Date	F	VF	XF	Unc
VS1958 (1901)	0.65	2.00	4.00	10.00

KM# 169 1/4 ANNA **Composition:** Copper **Obverse:** Plumes above crossed spear and trident

Date	F	VF	XF	Unc
VS1958 (1901)	0.75	2.25	4.50	11.00

KM# 170 1/4 ANNA **Weight:** 6.6000 g. **Composition:** Copper **Obverse:** Bust of Madho Rao right **Reverse:** Arms **Note:** Thick planchet (2.2 millimeters).

Date	F	VF	XF	Unc
VS1970 (1913)	0.25	0.75	1.50	3.00

KM# 171 1/4 ANNA **Weight:** 5.1000 g. **Composition:** Copper **Obverse:** Bust of Madho Rao right **Reverse:** Arms **Note:** Thin planchet (1.6 millimeters).

Date	F	VF	XF	Unc
VS1970 (1913)	1.25	3.50	5.00	7.00
VS1974 (1917)	0.25	0.75	1.50	3.00

KM# 172 1/4 ANNA **Composition:** Copper **Obverse:** Bust of Madho Rao right, continuous legend around portrait **Reverse:** Arms

Date	F	VF	XF	Unc
VS1974 (1917)	4.00	6.00	9.00	12.50

KM# 175 1/3 MOHUR **Weight:** 3.4500 g. **Composition:** Gold **Obverse:** Bust of Madho Rao right **Reverse:** Arms

Date	F	VF	XF	Unc
VS1959 (1902)	265	550	900	1,300

Jivaji Rao
VS1985-2005/1925-48AD
MILLED COINAGE

KM# 177 1/4 ANNA **Composition:** Copper **Obverse:** Crude style bust of Jivaji Rao left **Reverse:** Arms **Note:** Thin planchet. 3.00-3.15 grams.

Date	F	VF	XF	Unc
VS1986 (1929)	0.75	2.50	3.50	6.00
VS1999 (1942)	1.00	3.50	5.00	7.50

KM# 176.1 1/4 ANNA **Composition:** Copper **Obverse:** Fine style bust of Jivaji Rao left **Reverse:** Arms **Note:** Thick planchet. 4.65-5.15 grams.

Date	F	VF	XF	Unc
VS1986 (1929)	0.25	0.75	1.50	3.00

KM# 176.2 1/4 ANNA **Composition:** Copper **Obverse:** Crude style "pug-nose" bust of Jivaji Rao left **Reverse:** Arms

Date	F	VF	XF	Unc
VS1986 (1929)	0.25	0.75	1.50	3.00

KM# 178.1 1/4 ANNA **Composition:** Copper **Obverse:** Facing coiled cobras below bust of Jivaji Rao left **Reverse:** Arms, without inscription on side

Date	F	VF	XF	Unc
VS1999 (1942)	0.20	0.60	1.00	2.00

KM# 178.2 1/4 ANNA **Composition:** Copper **Obverse:** Without facing coiled cobras below bust of Jivaji Rao left **Reverse:** Arms

Date	F	VF	XF	Unc
VS1999 (1942)	0.20	0.60	1.00	2.00

KM# 179 1/2 ANNA **Composition:** Brass **Obverse:** Bust of Jivaji Rao left **Reverse:** Arms

Date	F	VF	XF	Unc
VS1999 (1942)	0.20	0.60	1.00	2.00
VS1999 (1942) Proof	—	Value: 50.00		

PATTERNS
Including off metal strikes

KM#	Date	Mintage	Identification	Mkt Val

KM#	Date	Mintage	Identification	Mkt Val
Pn1	VS1977(1920)	—	4 Anna. Silver.	—

HYDERABAD

Haidarabad

Hyderabad State, the largest Indian State and the last remnant of Mughal suzerainty in South or Central India, traced its foundation to Nizam-ul Mulk, the Mughal viceroy in the Deccan. From about 1724 the first nizam, as the rulers of Hyderabad came to be called, took advantage of Mughal decline in the North to assert an all but ceremonial independence of the emperor. The East India Company defeated Hyderabad's natural enemies, the Muslim rulers of Mysore and the Marathas, with the help of troops furnished under alliances between them and the Nizam. This formed the beginning of a relationship, which persisted for a century and a half until India's Independence. Hyderabad was the premier Princely State, with a population (in 1935) of fourteen and a half million. It was not absorbed into the Indian Union until 1948. Hyderabad City is located beside Golkonda, the citadel of the Qutb Shahi sultans until they were overthrown by Aurangzeb in 1687. A beautifully located city on the bank of the Musi river, the mint epithet was appropriately Farkhanda Bunyad, "of happy foundation".

Hyderabad exercised authority over a number of feudatories or samasthans. Some of these, such as Gadwal and Shorapur, paid tribute to both the Nizam and the Marathas. These feudatories were generally in the hands of local rajas whose ancestry predated the establishment of Hyderabad State. There were also many mints in the State, both private and government. There was little or no standardization of the purity of silver coinage until the 20th century. At least one banker, Pestonji Meherji by name, was distinguished by minting his own coins.

RULERS

Mir Mahbub Ali Khan II, AH1285-1329/1869-1911AD
Mir Usman Ali Khan, AH1329-1367/1911-1948AD

MINTS

فرخنده بنیاد حیدراباد

Haidarabad
Mintname: Farkhanda Bunyad Haidarabad

Mir Mahbub Ali Khan II
AH1285-1329/1869-1911AD
HAMMERED 'DUMP' COINAGE

Y# 13 1/16 RUPEE **Weight:** 0.6980 g. **Composition:** 0.8180 Silver .0183 oz. ASW **Obverse:** Inscription: Asaf Jah, Nizam al-Mulk, Founder of the Nizami line; Persian letter "M" for Mahbub above "k" of "Mulk"

Date	VG	F	VF	XF	Unc
AH1321/37(1903-04)	1.00	1.75	2.50	4.00	—

Y# 14 1/8 RUPEE **Weight:** 1.3970 g. **Composition:** 0.8180 Silver .0367 oz. ASW **Obverse:** Inscription: Asaf Jah, Nizam al-Mulk, Founder of the Nizami line; Persian letter "M" for Mahbub above "k" of "Mulk"

Date	VG	F	VF	XF	Unc
AH1321/37(1903-04)	1.75	2.25	3.00	4.50	—

Y# 15 1/4 RUPEE **Weight:** 2.7940 g. **Composition:** 0.8180 Silver .0735 oz. ASW **Obverse:** Inscription: Asaf Jah, Nizam al-Mulk, Founder of the Nizami line; Persian letter "M" for Mahbub above "k" of "Mulk"

Date	VG	F	VF	XF	Unc
AH1321/37(1903-04)	2.00	2.75	4.50	7.00	—

Y# 17 RUPEE **Weight:** 11.1780 g. **Composition:** 0.8180 Silver .2940 oz. ASW **Obverse:** Inscription: Asaf Jah, Nizam al-Mulk, Founder of the Nizami line; Persian letter "M" for Mahbub above "k" of "Mulk"

Date	VG	F	VF	XF	Unc
AH1318/34(1900-01)	4.50	5.50	7.00	14.00	—

Y# 18 1/16 ASHRAFI **Weight:** 0.6980 g. **Composition:** 0.9100 Gold **Obverse:** Inscription: Asaf Jah, Nizam al-Mulk, Founder of the Nizami line; Persian letter "M" for Mahbub above "k" of "Mulk"

Date	VG	F	VF	XF	Unc
AH1321/37(1903-04)	20.00	30.00	40.00	60.00	—

Y# 19 1/8 ASHRAFI **Weight:** 1.3970 g. **Composition:** 0.9100 Gold **Obverse:** Inscription: Asaf Jah, Nizam al-Mulk, Founder of the Nizami line; Persian letter "M" for Mahbub above "k" of "Mulk"

Date	VG	F	VF	XF	Unc
AH1293 (1876)	25.00	40.00	60.00	75.00	—
AH1302 (1884)	25.00	40.00	60.00	75.00	—
AH1306 (1888)	25.00	40.00	60.00	75.00	—
AH1309 (1891)	25.00	40.00	60.00	75.00	—
AH1313 (1895)	25.00	40.00	60.00	75.00	—
AH1316 (1898)	25.00	40.00	60.00	75.00	—
AH1317/33 (1899)	25.00	40.00	60.00	75.00	—
AH1318 (1900)	25.00	40.00	60.00	75.00	—
AH1320 (1902)	25.00	40.00	60.00	75.00	—
AH1321 (1903)	25.00	40.00	60.00	75.00	—

Y# 20 1/4 ASHRAFI **Weight:** 2.7940 g. **Composition:** 0.9100 Gold **Obverse:** Inscription: Asaf Jah, Nizam al-Mulk, Founder of the Nizami line; Persian letter "M" for Mahbub above "k" of "Mulk"

Date	VG	F	VF	XF	Unc
AH1301 (1883)	45.00	60.00	80.00	100	—
AH1304 (1886)	45.00	60.00	80.00	100	—
AH1306 (1888)	45.00	60.00	80.00	100	—
AH1309 (1891)	45.00	60.00	80.00	100	—
AH1314/30 (1896)	45.00	60.00	80.00	100	—
AH1315 (1897)	45.00	60.00	80.00	100	—
AH1316 (1898)	45.00	60.00	80.00	100	—
AH1318/35 (1901)	45.00	60.00	80.00	100	—
AH1319/35 (1901)	45.00	60.00	80.00	100	—

Y# 21 1/2 ASHRAFI **Weight:** 5.5890 g. **Composition:** 0.9100 Gold **Obverse:** Inscription: Asaf Jah, Nizam al-Mulk, Founder of the Nizami line; Persian letter "M" for Mahbub above "k" of "Mulk"

Date	VG	F	VF	XF	Unc
AH1301/17 (1883)	—	—	—	—	—
AH1316 (1898)	75.00	90.00	110	140	—
AH1317 (1899)	75.00	90.00	110	140	—
AH1320 (1902)	75.00	90.00	110	140	—
AH1321 (1903)	75.00	90.00	110	140	—

Y# 22 ASHRAFI **Weight:** 11.1780 g. **Composition:** 0.9100 Gold **Obverse:** Inscription: Asaf Jah, Nizam al-Mulk, Founder of the Nizami line; Persian letter "M" for Mahbub above "k" of "Mulk"

Date	VG	F	VF	XF	Unc
AH1319 (1901)	150	170	200	250	—
AH1320	150	170	200	250	—
AH1321	150	170	200	250	—

MILLED COINAGE
Provisional Series

Y# 29 2 ANNAS **Weight:** 1.3970 g. **Composition:** 0.8180 Silver **Obverse:** Inscription: Asaf Jah, Nizam al-Mulk, Founder of the Nizami line; Persian letter "M" for Mahbub above "k" of "Mulk"

Date	VG	F	VF	XF	Unc
AH1318/35(1901)	10.00	17.50	27.50	37.50	—

Y# 30 4 ANNAS **Weight:** 2.7940 g. **Composition:** 0.8180 Silver **Obverse:** Inscription: Asaf Jah, Nizam al-Mulk, Founder of the Nizami line; Persian letter "M" for Mahbub above "k" of "Mulk"

Date	VG	F	VF	XF	Unc
AH1318/34(1900-01)	8.50	16.50	25.00	33.50	—
AH1318/35(1901)	8.50	16.50	25.00	33.50	—

Y# 31 8 ANNAS **Weight:** 5.5890 g. **Composition:** 0.8180 Silver **Obverse:** Inscription: Asaf Jah, Nizam al-Mulk, Founder of the Nizami line; Persian letter "M" for Mahbub above "k" of "Mulk"

Date	VG	F	VF	XF	Unc
AH1318/34(1900-01)	10.00	20.00	30.00	40.00	—
AH1318/35(1901)	10.00	20.00	30.00	40.00	—

MILLED COINAGE
Standard Series

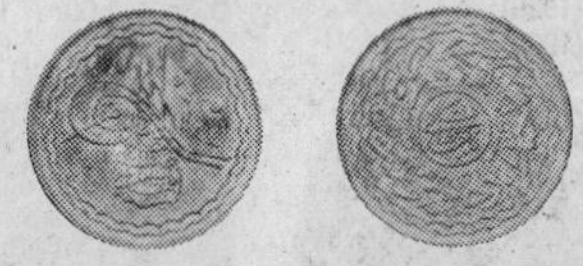

Y# 34 PAI **Composition:** Copper **Obverse:** Toughra

Date	F	VF	XF	Unc
AH1326/42 (1908)	4.00	6.00	9.00	15.00
AH1327/42 (1909)	4.00	6.00	9.00	15.00

Y# 35 2 PAI **Composition:** Copper **Obverse:** Toughra

Date	F	VF	XF	Unc
AH1322/37 (1904)	1.00	1.25	1.75	2.75
AH1322/38 (1904)	0.75	1.00	1.50	2.50
AH1322/39 (1905)	1.00	1.25	1.75	2.75
AH1323/38 (1905)	1.00	1.25	1.75	2.75
AH1323/39 (1905)	0.60	0.75	1.00	1.50
AH1323/40 (1906)	0.75	1.00	1.50	2.50
AH1323/41 (1906)	0.75	1.00	1.50	2.50
AH1324/39 (1906)	1.00	1.25	1.75	2.75
AH1324/40 (1906)	0.60	0.85	1.25	1.75
AH1324/41 (1907)	0.75	1.00	1.50	2.50
AH1325/40 (1907)	1.00	1.25	1.75	2.75
AH1325/41 (1907)	0.75	1.00	1.50	2.50
AH1329/43 (1911)	0.50	0.65	1.00	1.75
AH1329/44 (1911)	0.50	0.65	1.00	1.75
AH1329/45 (1911)	0.50	0.65	1.00	1.75

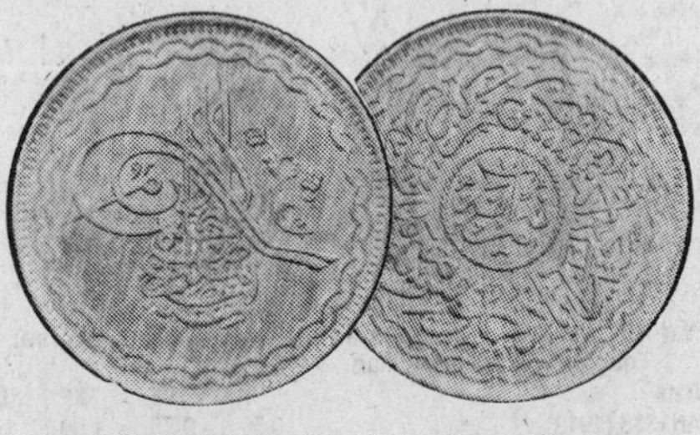

Y# 36 1/2 ANNA **Composition:** Copper **Obverse:** Toughra

Date	VG	F	VF	XF	Unc
AH1324/38(1906)	1.00	2.50	4.00	6.00	10.00
AH1324/40(1906-07)	0.60	1.50	2.25	3.00	4.00
AH1325/40(1907)	0.80	2.00	3.25	3.75	5.50
AH1325/41(1907)	0.80	2.00	3.25	3.75	5.50
AH1324/41(1907-08)	0.90	2.25	3.00	3.50	4.50
AH1326/41(1908)	1.00	2.50	3.75	4.50	7.00
AH1329/44(1911)	0.60	1.50	2.50	3.00	4.00

Y# 37 2 ANNAS **Weight:** 1.3900 g. **Composition:** 0.8180 Silver .0367 oz. ASW **Obverse:** Chahar Minar gateway

Date	VG	F	VF	XF	Unc
AH1323/34(1905)	0.60	1.50	2.50	5.00	8.00
Note: R.Y. '34' error for '39'					
AH1323/39(1905-06)	0.30	0.75	1.25	3.00	5.00

Y# 38.1 4 ANNAS **Weight:** 2.7940 g. **Composition:** 0.8180 Silver .0735 oz. ASW **Obverse:** Chahar Minar gateway, signature variety Type I between minarets

Date	VG	F	VF	XF	Unc
AH1323/39(1905-06)	1.50	4.00	4.75	5.50	9.00
AH1326/43(1909)	3.50	8.50	16.50	25.00	32.50

Y# 38.2 4 ANNAS **Weight:** 2.7940 g. **Composition:** 0.8180 Silver .0735 oz. ASW **Obverse:** Chahar Minar gateway, signature variety Type I between minarets **Note:** Struck with dies of 1/2 Ashrafi.

Date	VG	F	VF	XF	Unc
AH1324/40(1906-07)	—	—	—	—	—

Y# 38.3 4 ANNAS **Weight:** 2.7940 g. **Composition:** 0.8180 Silver .0735 oz. ASW **Obverse:** Chahar Minar gateway, signature variety Type II between minarets

Date	VG	F	VF	XF	Unc
AH1328/43(1910)	1.50	4.00	4.75	6.00	10.00
AH1329/44(1911)	1.50	4.00	4.75	5.50	9.00

Y# 39.1 8 ANNAS **Weight:** 5.5890 g. **Composition:** 0.8180 Silver .1470 oz. ASW **Obverse:** Chahar Minar gateway, signature variety Type I

Date	VG	F	VF	XF	Unc
AH1322/38(1904-05)	—	—	—	—	—

Y# 39.2 8 ANNAS **Weight:** 5.5890 g. **Composition:** 0.8180 Silver .1470 oz. ASW **Obverse:** Chahar Minar gateway, signature variety Type II between minarets

Date	VG	F	VF	XF	Unc
AH1328/43(1910)	2.75	6.50	7.50	9.00	15.00
AH1329/44(1911)	2.75	6.50	7.50	9.00	15.00

Y# 40.1 RUPEE **Weight:** 11.1780 g. **Composition:** 0.8180 Silver .2940 oz. ASW **Obverse:** Chahar Minar gateway, signature variety Type I between minarets

Date	VG	F	VF	XF	Unc
AH1319/35(1901-02)	4.75	11.50	13.50	16.50	27.50
AH1321/37(1903-04)	4.75	11.50	13.50	16.50	27.50
AH1322/38(1904)	4.75	11.50	13.50	15.00	25.00
AH1321/38(1904-05)	4.75	11.50	13.50	15.00	25.00
AH1323/39(1905-06)	4.75	11.50	13.50	15.00	25.00
AH1322/39(1905)	4.75	11.50	13.50	15.00	25.00
AH1324/40(1906-07)	4.75	11.50	13.50	15.00	25.00
AH1325/41(1907)	4.75	11.50	13.50	15.00	25.00
AH1326/41(1908)	4.75	11.50	13.50	15.00	25.00

Y# 40.2 RUPEE **Weight:** 11.1780 g. **Composition:** 0.8180 Silver .2940 oz. ASW **Obverse:** Chahar Minar gateway, signature variety Type II between minarets

Date	VG	F	VF	XF	Unc
AH1328/43(1910)	4.75	11.50	13.50	15.00	25.00
AH1329/44(1911)	4.75	11.50	13.50	15.00	25.00

Y# 41.1 1/8 ASHRAFI **Weight:** 1.3940 g. **Composition:** 0.9100 Gold **Obverse:** Chahar Minar gateway, signature variety Type I between minarets

Date	VG	F	VF	XF	Unc
AH1325/41(1907-08)	—	35.00	50.00	65.00	85.00

Y# 41.2 1/8 ASHRAFI **Weight:** 1.3940 g. **Composition:** 0.9100 Gold **Obverse:** Chahar Minar gateway, signature variety Type II between minarets

Date	VG	F	VF	XF	Unc
AH1329/44 (1911)	—	35.00	50.00	65.00	85.00

Y# 42.1 1/4 ASHRAFI **Weight:** 2.7940 g. **Composition:** 0.9100 Gold **Obverse:** Chahar Minar gateway, signature variety Type I between minarets

Date	VG	F	VF	XF	Unc
AH1325/41(1907-08)	—	50.00	65.00	85.00	125

Y# 42.2 1/4 ASHRAFI **Weight:** 2.7940 g. **Composition:** 0.9100 Gold **Obverse:** Chahar Minar gateway, signature variety Type II between minarets

Date	VG	F	VF	XF	Unc
AH1328/43 (1910)	—	50.00	65.00	85.00	125
AH1329/44 (1911)	—	50.00	65.00	85.00	125

Y# 43.1 1/2 ASHRAFI **Weight:** 5.5890 g. **Composition:** 0.9100 Gold **Obverse:** Chahar Minar gateway, signature variety Type I between minarets

Date	VG	F	VF	XF	Unc
AH1325/41 (1907)	—	80.00	110	150	250
AH1326/41 (1908)	—	80.00	110	150	250

Y# 43.2 1/2 ASHRAFI **Weight:** 5.5890 g. **Composition:** 0.9100 Gold **Obverse:** Chahar Minar gateway, signature variety Type II between minarets

Date	VG	F	VF	XF	Unc
AH1328/43 (1910)	—	80.00	110	150	250
AH1329/44 (1911)	—	80.00	110	150	250

Y# 44.1 ASHRAFI **Weight:** 11.1780 g. **Composition:** 0.9100 Gold **Obverse:** Chahar Minar gateway, signature variety Type I between minarets

Date	F	VF	XF	Unc
AH1325/41 (1907)	165	225	300	400

Y# 44.2 ASHRAFI **Weight:** 11.1780 g. **Composition:** 0.9100 Gold **Obverse:** Chahar Minar gateway, signature variety Type II between minarets

Date	F	VF	XF	Unc
AH1328/43 (1910)	165	225	300	400
AH1329/44 (1911)	165	225	300	400

Mir Usman Ali Khan
AH1329-67/1911-48AD

MILLED COINAGE
First Series

Y# 45 PAI **Composition:** Bronze **Obverse:** Toughra

Date	F	VF	XF	Unc
AH1338 (1919)	1.50	2.00	2.50	4.00
AH1344/15 (1925)	0.60	0.75	1.00	1.50
AH1349/20 (1930)	0.60	0.75	1.00	1.50
AH1352/23 (1933)	1.00	1.25	1.50	2.50
AH1352/24 (1934)	1.00	1.25	1.50	2.50
AH1353/23 (1934)	1.00	1.25	1.50	2.50
AH1353/24 (1934)	0.70	0.85	1.10	1.75

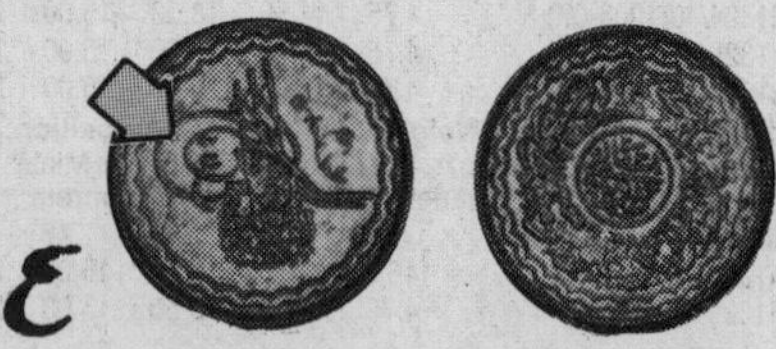

Y# 46a 2 PAI **Composition:** Bronze **Obverse:** Full "Ain" in toughra

Date	F	VF	XF	Unc
AH1330/1 (1911)	1.50	2.00	2.50	3.50
AH1331/2 (1912)	0.35	0.50	0.65	1.00
AH1330/2 (1912)	0.35	0.50	0.65	1.00
AH1332/3 (1913)	0.35	0.50	0.65	1.00
AH1331/3 (1913)	0.50	0.65	0.75	1.00
AH1333/3 (1914)	0.60	0.75	1.00	1.50
AH1332/4 (1914)	0.60	0.75	1.00	1.50
AH1333/4 (1914)	0.35	0.50	0.65	1.00
AH1334/3 (1915)	0.60	0.75	1.00	1.50

Date	F	VF	XF	Unc
AH1333/5 (1915)	0.75	1.00	1.25	2.00
AH1335/6 (1916)	0.35	0.50	0.65	1.00
AH1336/7 (1917)	0.35	0.50	0.65	1.00
AH1335/7 (1917)	0.35	0.50	0.65	1.00
AH1337/7 (1918)	0.75	1.00	1.25	2.00
AH1336/8 (1918)	0.50	0.65	0.80	1.25
AH1337/8 (1918)	0.60	0.75	1.00	1.50
AH1338/8 (1919)	0.75	1.00	1.25	2.00
AH1338/9 (1919)	0.35	0.50	0.65	1.00
AH1339/10 (1920)	0.75	1.00	1.25	2.00
AH1338/11 (1920)	0.50	0.75	1.00	1.50
AH1339/11 (1921)	0.75	1.00	1.25	2.00
AH1342/13 (1923)	0.60	0.75	1.00	1.50
AH1343/14 (1924)	0.35	0.50	0.65	1.00
AH1342/14 (1924)	0.35	0.50	0.65	1.00
AH1344/15 (1925)	0.50	0.65	0.80	1.25
AH1343/15 (1925)	0.40	0.60	0.75	1.25
AH1345/16 (1926)	0.35	0.50	0.65	1.00
AH1347/18 (1928)	0.75	1.00	1.25	2.00
AH1348/19 (1929)	0.35	0.50	0.65	1.00
AH1347/19 (1929)	0.75	1.00	1.25	2.00
AH1349/20 (1930)	0.35	0.50	0.65	1.00

Y# 46 2 PAI **Composition:** Bronze **Obverse:** Short "Ain" in toughra **Note:** See also 1 Rupee, Y#53 and Y#53a.

Date	F	VF	XF	Unc
AH1330/1 (1911)	8.00	12.50	20.00	32.50
AH1329/1 (1911)	10.00	15.00	22.50	35.00

Y# 47 1/2 ANNA **Composition:** Bronze **Obverse:** Toughra

Date	F	VF	XF	Unc
AH1332/2 (1913)	0.75	1.00	1.25	2.00
AH1332/3 (1913)	0.75	1.00	1.25	2.00
AH1334/4 (1915)	1.25	1.50	2.00	3.25
AH1344/15 (1925)	1.25	1.50	2.00	3.25
AH1348/20 (1930)	1.00	1.35	1.75	2.75

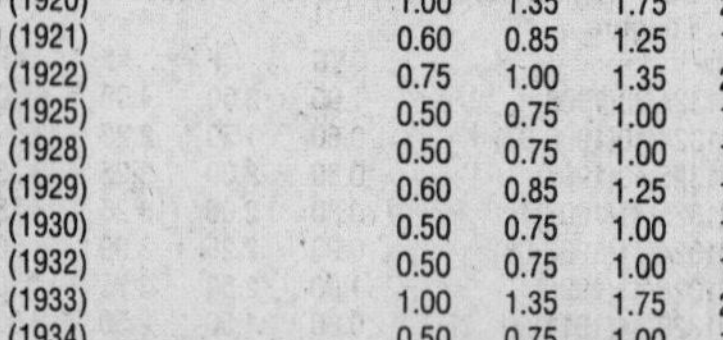

Y# 48 ANNA **Composition:** Copper-Nickel **Obverse:** Toughra **Note:** Round flan.

Date	F	VF	XF	Unc
AH1338 (1919)	0.50	0.75	1.00	1.50
AH1339 (1920)	1.00	1.35	1.75	2.75
AH1340 (1921)	0.60	0.85	1.25	1.75
AH1341 (1922)	0.75	1.00	1.35	2.00
AH1344 (1925)	0.50	0.75	1.00	1.50
AH1347 (1928)	0.50	0.75	1.00	1.50
AH1348 (1929)	0.60	0.85	1.25	1.75
AH1349 (1930)	0.50	0.75	1.00	1.50
AH1351 (1932)	0.50	0.75	1.00	1.50
AH1352 (1933)	1.00	1.35	1.75	2.75
AH1353 (1934)	0.50	0.75	1.00	1.50
AH1354 (1935)	0.50	0.75	1.00	1.50

Y# 49 ANNA **Composition:** Copper-Nickel **Obverse:** Toughra **Note:** Square flan.

Date	F	VF	XF	Unc
AH1356 (1937)	0.35	0.50	0.65	1.00
AH1357 (1938)	0.50	0.65	0.85	1.35
AH1358 (1939)	0.35	0.50	0.65	1.00
AH1359 (1940)	0.75	1.00	1.25	2.00

Date	F	VF	XF	Unc
AH1360 (1941)	0.75	1.00	1.25	2.00
AH1361 (1942)	0.75	1.00	1.25	2.00

Y# 50 2 ANNAS **Weight:** 1.3970 g. **Composition:** 0.8180 Silver .0367 oz. ASW **Obverse:** Chahar Minar gateway

Date	F	VF	XF	Unc
AH1335/6 (1916)	1.25	1.75	2.50	4.00
AH1337/9 (1919)	1.00	1.50	2.50	4.00
AH1338/10 (1920)	1.00	1.50	2.50	4.00
AH1340/11 (1921)	1.00	1.50	2.50	4.00
AH1341/13 (1923)	1.00	1.50	2.50	4.00
AH1342/13 (1923)	1.00	1.50	2.50	4.00
AH1341/14 (1923)	1.25	2.00	3.00	5.00
AH1343/14 (1924)	1.00	1.50	2.25	3.50
AH1343/15 (1925)	1.00	1.50	2.25	3.50
AH1347 (1928)	1.25	2.00	3.00	5.00
AH1348/19 (1929)	1.00	1.50	2.25	3.50
AH1351/22 (1932)	1.00	1.50	2.50	4.00
AH1355/26 (1936)	1.00	1.50	2.50	4.00

Y# 51 4 ANNAS **Weight:** 2.7940 g. **Composition:** 0.8180 Silver .0735 oz. ASW **Obverse:** Chahar Minar gateway

Date	F	VF	XF	Unc
AH1337/9 (1919)	1.75	3.00	4.50	7.00
AH1340/11 (1921)	1.75	3.00	4.50	7.00
AH1342/13 (1923)	1.75	3.00	4.50	7.00
AH1342/14 (1924)	1.75	3.00	4.50	7.00
AH1348/19 (1929)	1.75	3.00	4.50	7.00
AH1351/22 (1932)	1.75	3.00	4.50	7.00
AH1354/25 (1935)	1.75	3.00	4.50	7.00
AH1358/30 (1940)	1.75	3.00	4.50	7.00

Y# 52 8 ANNAS **Weight:** 5.5890 g. **Composition:** 0.8180 Silver .1470 oz. ASW **Obverse:** Chahar Minar gateway

Date	F	VF	XF	Unc
AH1337/9 (1919)	3.50	5.00	8.00	12.00
AH1342/13 (1923)	3.50	5.00	8.00	12.00
AH1343/13 (1924)	3.50	5.00	8.00	12.00
AH1354/25 (1935)	3.50	5.00	8.00	12.00

Y# 53 RUPEE **Weight:** 11.1780 g. **Composition:** 0.8180 Silver .2940 oz. ASW **Obverse:** Chahar Minar gateway with partial initials "Ain" in doorway

Date	F	VF	XF	Unc
AH1330/1 (1911)	5.50	9.00	15.00	25.00

Y# 53a RUPEE **Weight:** 11.1780 g. **Composition:** 0.8180 Silver .2940 oz. ASW **Obverse:** Chahar Minar gateway with full "Ain" in doorway

Date	F	VF	XF	Unc
AH1330/1 (1911)	5.50	9.00	15.00	25.00
AH1331/2 (1912)	4.50	7.50	12.50	20.00
AH1330/2 (1912)	5.50	9.00	15.00	25.00
AH1332/3 (1913)	4.50	7.50	12.50	20.00
AH1331/3 (1913)	4.50	7.50	12.50	20.00
AH1334/6 (1916)	4.50	7.50	12.50	20.00
AH1335/6 (1916)	4.50	7.50	12.50	20.00
AH1335/7 (1917)	4.50	7.50	12.50	20.00
AH1336/7 (1917)	4.50	7.50	12.50	20.00
AH1337/8 (1918)	4.50	7.50	12.50	20.00
AH1338/9 (1919)	4.50	7.50	12.50	20.00
AH1337/9 (1919)	7.50	12.50	20.00	35.00
AH1339/9 (1920)	4.50	7.50	12.50	20.00
AH1340/11 (1921)	4.50	7.50	12.50	20.00
AH1341/12 (1922)	4.50	7.50	12.50	20.00
AH1342/13 (1923)	4.50	7.50	12.50	20.00
AH1343/14 (1924)	4.50	7.50	12.50	20.00

Y# 54.1 1/8 ASHRAFI **Weight:** 1.3940 g. **Composition:** 0.9100 Gold **Obverse:** Chahar Minar gateway with partial "Ain" in doorway

Date	F	VF	XF	Unc
AH1329/1 (1911) Rare	—	—	—	—

Y# 54.2 1/8 ASHRAFI **Weight:** 1.3940 g. **Composition:** 0.9100 Gold **Obverse:** Chahar Minar gateway with full "Ain" in doorway

Date	F	VF	XF	Unc
AH1337/8 (1918)	30.00	37.50	50.00	70.00
AH1340/11 (1921)	30.00	37.50	50.00	70.00
AH1343 (1924)	30.00	37.50	50.00	70.00
AH1344/15 (1925)	30.00	37.50	50.00	70.00
AH1353 (1934)	30.00	37.50	50.00	70.00
AH1354/25 (1935)	30.00	37.50	50.00	70.00
AH1356/27 (1937)	30.00	37.50	50.00	70.00
AH1360 (1941)	30.00	37.50	50.00	70.00
AH1366/37 (1947)	30.00	37.50	50.00	70.00
AH1368/39 (1950)	30.00	37.50	50.00	70.00

Y# 55 1/4 ASHRAFI **Weight:** 2.7940 g. **Composition:** 0.9100 Gold **Obverse:** Chahar Minar gateway

Date	F	VF	XF	Unc
AH1337/8 (1918)	40.00	60.00	85.00	125
AH1342/13 (1923)	40.00	60.00	85.00	125
AH1342/14 (1924)	40.00	60.00	85.00	125
AH1349/20 (1930)	40.00	60.00	85.00	125
AH1353/23 (1934)	40.00	60.00	85.00	125
AH1354/25 (1935)	40.00	60.00	85.00	125
AH1357 (1938)	40.00	60.00	85.00	125
AH1360/31 (1941)	40.00	60.00	85.00	125
AH1367/38 (1948)	40.00	60.00	85.00	125

Y# 56.1 1/2 ASHRAFI **Weight:** 5.5890 g. **Composition:** 0.9100 Gold **Obverse:** Chahar Minar gateway with partial "Ain" in doorway

Date	F	VF	XF	Unc
AH1329/1 (1911)	85.00	125	175	250

Y# 56.2 1/2 ASHRAFI **Weight:** 5.5890 g. **Composition:** 0.9100 Gold **Obverse:** Chahar Minar gateway with full "Ain" in doorway

Date	F	VF	XF	Unc
AH1337/8 (1918)	75.00	100	140	200
AH1342/14 (1924)	75.00	100	140	200
AH1343/14 (1924)	75.00	100	140	200
AH1344/14 (1925)	75.00	100	140	200
AH1345/16 (1926)	75.00	100	140	200
AH1349/20 (1930)	75.00	100	140	200
AH1354/25 (1935)	75.00	100	140	200
AH1357/29 (1939)	75.00	100	140	200
AH1366/37 (1947)	75.00	100	140	200
AH1367/38 (1948)	75.00	100	140	200

Y# 57 ASHRAFI **Weight:** 11.1780 g. **Composition:** 0.9100 Gold **Obverse:** Chahar Minar gateway with partial initial "Ain" in doorway

Date	F	VF	XF	Unc
AH1329/1 (1911)	165	220	325	450
AH1330/1 (1911)	165	220	325	450

Y# 57a ASHRAFI **Weight:** 11.1780 g. **Composition:** 0.9100 Gold **Obverse:** Chahar Minar gateway with full initial "Ain" in doorway

Date	F	VF	XF	Unc
AH1331/3 (1913)	140	160	240	350
AH1333/4 (1914)	140	160	240	350
AH1337/8 (1918)	140	160	240	350
AH1337/9 (1919)	140	160	240	350
AH1338/9 (1919)	140	160	240	350
AH1340/11 (1921)	140	160	240	350
AH1342/14 (1924)	140	165	240	350
AH1343/14 (1924)	140	160	240	350
AH1344/15 (1925)	140	160	240	350
AH1348/19 (1929)	140	160	240	350
AH1349/20 (1930)	140	160	240	350
AH1354/25 (1935)	140	160	240	350
AH1358/30 (1940)	140	160	240	350
AH1360/31 (1941)	140	160	240	350
AH1362/34 (1943)	140	160	240	350

MILLED COINAGE

Second Series

Y# 58 2 PAI **Composition:** Bronze

Date	F	VF	XF	Unc
AH1362/33 (1943)	0.25	0.35	0.50	0.75
AH1363/34 (1944)	0.25	0.35	0.50	0.75
AH1363/35 (1944)	0.20	0.25	0.50	0.75
AH1364/35 (1945)	0.20	0.25	0.50	0.75
AH1365/36 (1946)	0.20	0.25	0.50	0.75
AH1366/37 (1947)	0.20	0.25	0.50	0.75
AH1368/39 (1950)	0.20	0.25	0.50	0.75

Y# 59 ANNA **Composition:** Bronze **Obverse:** Toughra **Note:** Square flan.

Date	F	VF	XF	Unc
AH1361 (1942)	0.40	0.50	0.75	1.50
AH1362 (1943)	0.40	0.50	0.75	1.50
AH1364 (1945)	0.40	0.50	0.75	1.50
AH1365 (1946)	0.40	0.50	0.75	1.50
AH1366 (1946)	0.40	0.50	0.75	1.50
AH1368 (1948)	0.40	0.50	0.75	1.50

Y# 60 2 ANNAS **Weight:** 1.3970 g. **Composition:** Silver .0367 oz. ASW

Date	F	VF	XF	Unc
AH1362/33 (1943)	0.40	0.60	1.00	2.00

Y# 64 2 ANNAS **Composition:** Nickel

Date	F	VF	XF	Unc
AH1366/37 (1947)	0.15	0.25	0.35	1.00
AH1368/39 (1950)	0.25	0.35	0.45	1.50

Y# 61 4 ANNAS **Weight:** 2.7940 g. **Composition:** Silver .0735 oz. ASW

Date	F	VF	XF	Unc
AH1362/33 (1943)	0.60	0.80	1.00	2.00
AH1362/34 (1944)	0.75	0.90	1.10	2.25
AH1364/33 (1945)	0.80	1.00	1.25	2.50
AH1364/35 (1945)	0.80	1.00	1.25	2.50
AH1364/36 (1946)	0.80	1.00	1.25	2.50
AH1365/36 (1946)	0.80	1.00	1.25	2.50

Y# 65 4 ANNAS **Composition:** Nickel

Date	F	VF	XF	Unc
AH1366/37 (1947)	0.40	0.50	0.75	1.50
AH1368/39 (1950)	0.40	0.50	0.75	1.50

Y# 62 8 ANNAS **Weight:** 5.5890 g. **Composition:** Silver .1470 oz. ASW

Date	F	VF	XF	Unc
AH1363/34 (1944)	3.50	6.00	10.00	17.50

Y# 66 8 ANNAS **Composition:** Nickel

Date	F	VF	XF	Unc
AH1366/37 (1947)	0.60	0.80	1.00	2.00

Y# 63 RUPEE **Weight:** 11.1780 g. **Composition:** Silver .2940 oz. ASW

Date	F	VF	XF	Unc
AH1361/31 (1942)	4.50	7.50	12.50	20.00
AH1361/32 (1942)	4.50	7.50	12.50	20.00
AH1362/34 (1944)	4.50	7.50	12.50	20.00
AH1364/35 (1945)	4.50	7.50	12.50	20.00
AH1364/36 (1946)	4.50	7.50	12.50	20.00
AH1365/36 (1946)	4.50	7.50	12.50	20.00

Y# 67 ASHRAFI **Weight:** 11.1780 g. **Composition:** Gold

Date	F	VF	XF	Unc
AH1368/39 (1950)	—	—	—	—

PATTERNS

Including off metal strikes

KM#	Date	Mintage	Identification	Mkt Val
Pn10	1319/35	—	Rupee. Silver. Y#53a.	—
Pn11	1324/40	—	1/2 Ashrafi. Silver. Y#43.	—
Pn12	1324/40	—	Ashrafi. Silver. Y#44.	—

INDORE

The Holkars were one of the three dominant Maratha powers (with the Peshwas and Sindhias), with major landholdings in Central India.

Indore State originated in 1728 with a grant of land north of the Narbada river by the Maratha Peshwa of Poona to Malhar Rao Holkar, a cavalry commander in his service. After Holkar's death (ca.1765) his daughter-in-law, Ahalya Bai, assumed the position of Queen Regent. Together with Tukoji Rao she effectively ruled the State until her death thirty years later. But it was left to Tukoji's son, Jaswant Rao, to challenge the dominance of the Poona Marathas in the Maratha Confederacy, eventually defeating the Peshwa's army in 1802. But at this point the fortunes of the Holkars suffered a serious reverse. Although Jaswant Rao had initially defeated a small British force under Col. William Monson, he was badly beaten by a contingent under Lord Lake. As a result Holkar was forced to cede a considerable portion of his territory and from this time until India's independence in 1947, the residual State of Indore was obliged to accept British protection.

For more detailed data on the Indore series, see *A Study of Holkar State Coinage*, by P.K.Sethi, S.K. Bhatt and R. Holkar (1976).

HOLKAR RULERS
Shivaji Rao, VS1943-1960/FE1296-1313/1886-1903AD
Tukoji Rao III, VS1960-1983/1903-1926AD
Yashwant Rao, VS1983-2005/1926-1948AD

HONORIFIC TITLE
Bahadur

MINTS
Indore اندور or इंदौर

INDORE MINT
Coins issued intermittently from 1772-1935AD.

Shivaji Rao
VS1943-1960/FE1296-1313/1886-1903AD

MILLED COINAGE

KM# 33.3 1/4 ANNA Composition: Copper **Obverse:** Continuous legend around reclining bull **Obv. Legend:** Shivaji Rao...Bahadur **Reverse:** "Indore" above denomination and date **Note:** Floral border varieties exist. Struck at the Indore Mint.

Date	VG	F	VF	XF	Unc
VS1958 (1901)	1.25	1.75	3.50	7.00	—
VS1959 (1902)	1.25	1.75	3.50	7.00	—

KM# 35.3 1/2 ANNA Composition: Copper **Obverse:** Continuous legend around reclining bull **Obv. Legend:** Shivaji Rao **Reverse:** "Indore" above denomination and date **Note:** Struck at the Indore Mint.

Date	VG	F	VF	XF	Unc
VS1958 (1901)	1.50	2.00	4.00	8.00	—
VS1959 (1902)	1.50	2.00	4.00	8.00	—

MILLED COINAGE
Third Series

This series was introduced in 1898 to counteract counterfeiting of the second series which had begun to proliferate as a result of a sharp fall in the price of silver. Idle minting machines were reactivated for this purpose, but the series was short-lived.

KM# 47.2 RUPEE Weight: 11.2000 g. **Composition:** Silver **Obverse:** Bust of Shivaji Rao facing; continuous legend **Reverse:** Arms **Note:** Struck at the Indore Mint.

Date	VG	F	VF	XF	Unc
VS1958 (1901)	70.00	140	200	275	400

Yashwant Rao
VS1983-2005/1926-1948AD

MILLED COINAGE
Fourth Series

KM#49 1/4 ANNA Composition: Copper **Obverse:** Bust of Yeshwant Rao facing 3/4 right **Note:** Struck at the Indore Mint.

Date	VG	F	VF	XF	Unc
VS1992 (1935)	0.40	1.00	2.00	3.50	6.00

KM#50 1/2 ANNA Composition: Copper **Obverse:** Bust of Yeshwant Rao facing **Note:** Struck at the Indore Mint.

Date	VG	F	VF	XF	Unc
VS1992 (1935)	0.50	1.25	2.50	4.00	7.00

JAIPUR

Tradition has it that the region of Jaipur, located in northwest India, once belonged to an ancient Kachwaha Rajput dynasty which claimed descent from Kush, one of the sons of Rama, King of Ayodhya. But the Princely State of Jaipur originated in the 12th century. Comparatively small in size, the State remained largely unnoticed until after the 16th century when the Jaipur royal house became famous for its military skills and thereafter supplied the Mughals with some of their more distinguished generals. The city of Jaipur was founded about 1728 by Maharaja Jai Singh II who was well known for his knowledge of mathematics and astronomy. The late 18th and early 19th centuries were difficult times for Jaipur. They were marked by internal rivalry, exacerbated by Maratha or Pindari incursions. In 1818 this culminated with a treaty whereby Jaipur came under British protection and oversight.

RULERS
Madho Singh II, 1880-1922AD
Man Singh II, 1922-1949AD

MINTNAMES
Coins were struck at two mints, which bear the following characteristic marks on the reverse:
Sawai Jaipur
Sawai Madhopur

JAIPUR MINT
In the names of Queen Victoria

گوین وکٹوریا

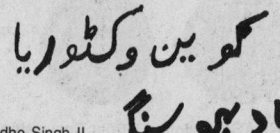

And Madho Singh II مادہو سنگہ

Years 1-43/1880-1922AD

NOTE: Queen Victoria's name was retained on Madho Singh II's coinage until 1922AD. No coins were struck with Edward VII's name by Madho Singh II.

Madho Singh
1880-1922AD

HAMMERED 'DUMP' COINAGE

KM# 130 PAISA Composition: Copper **Obverse:** Inscription: Queen Victoria... **Reverse:** Jhar; inscription: Madho Singh II.... **Note:** Weight varies 6.15-6.30g .

Date	VG	F	VF	XF	Unc
ND(1901)/22	0.65	1.35	2.00	—	—
ND(1902)/23	0.65	1.35	2.00	—	—
ND(1903)/24	0.65	1.35	2.00	—	—
ND(1904)/25	0.65	1.35	2.00	—	—
ND(1906)/27	0.65	1.35	2.00	—	—
ND(1907)/28	0.65	1.35	2.00	—	—
ND(1908)/29	0.65	1.35	2.00	—	—
ND(1916)/37	0.65	1.35	2.00	—	—
ND(1917)/38	0.65	1.35	2.00	—	—
ND(1918)/39	0.65	1.35	2.00	—	—
ND(1920)/41	0.65	1.35	2.00	—	—

KM# 135 1/16 RUPEE Composition: Silver **Obverse:** Inscription: Queen Victoria... **Reverse:** Jhar; inscription: Madho Singh II.... **Note:** Weight varies 0.67-0.72g.

Date	VG	F	VF	XF	Unc
ND(1912)/33	5.00	7.00	10.00	15.00	—

KM# 137 1/8 RUPEE Composition: Silver **Obverse:** Inscription: Queen Victoria... **Reverse:** Jhar; inscription: Madho Singh II.... **Note:** Weight varies 1.34-1.45g.

Date	VG	F	VF	XF	Unc
ND(1901)/22	2.50	3.50	5.00	8.00	—
ND(1902)/23	2.50	3.50	5.00	8.00	—
ND(1905)/26	2.50	3.50	5.00	8.00	—
ND(1906)/27	2.50	3.50	5.00	8.00	—
ND(1907)/28	2.50	3.50	5.00	8.00	—
ND(1908)/29	2.50	3.50	5.00	8.00	—
ND(1920)/41	2.50	3.50	5.00	8.00	—
ND(1921)/42	2.50	3.50	5.00	8.00	—
ND(1933)/4	2.50	3.50	5.00	8.00	—

KM# 139 1/4 RUPEE Composition: Silver **Obverse:** Inscription: Queen Victoria... **Reverse:** Jhar; inscription: Madho Singh II.... **Note:** Weight varies 2.68-2.90g.

Date	VG	F	VF	XF	Unc
ND(1901)/22	3.00	4.50	6.50	10.00	—
ND(1902)/23	3.00	4.50	6.50	10.00	—
ND(1903)/24	3.00	4.50	6.50	10.00	—
ND(1905)/26	3.00	4.50	6.50	10.00	—
ND(1906)/27	3.00	4.50	6.50	10.00	—
ND(1907)/28	3.00	4.50	6.50	10.00	—
ND(1908)/29	3.00	4.50	6.50	10.00	—
ND(1909)/30	3.00	4.50	6.50	10.00	—
ND(1913)/34	3.00	4.50	6.50	10.00	—
ND(1916)/37	3.00	4.50	6.50	10.00	—
ND(1917)/38	3.00	4.50	6.50	10.00	—
ND(1921)/42	3.00	4.50	6.50	10.00	—

KM# 142 1/2 RUPEE Composition: Silver **Obverse:** Inscription: Queen Victoria... **Reverse:** Jhar; inscription: Madho Singh II.... **Note:** Weight varies 5.35-5.80g.

Date	VG	F	VF	XF	Unc
ND(1901)/22	3.50	5.00	7.50	12.50	—
ND(1902)/23	3.50	5.00	7.50	12.50	—
ND(1904)/25	3.50	5.00	7.50	12.50	—
ND(1905)/26	3.50	5.00	7.50	12.50	—
ND(1906)/27	3.50	5.00	7.50	12.50	—
ND(1907)/28	3.50	5.00	7.50	12.50	—
ND(1908)/29	3.50	5.00	7.50	12.50	—
ND(1909)/30	3.50	5.00	7.50	12.50	—
ND(1913)/34	3.50	5.00	7.50	12.50	—
ND(1916)/37	3.50	5.00	7.50	12.50	—

KM# 145 RUPEE Composition: Silver **Obverse:** Inscription: Queen Victoria... **Reverse:** Jhar; inscription: Madho Singh II.... **Note:** Weight varies 10.70-11.60g.

Date	VG	F	VF	XF	Unc
ND(1902)/23	4.00	6.00	9.00	14.00	—
ND(1903)/24	4.00	6.00	9.00	14.00	—
ND(1904)/25	4.00	6.00	9.00	14.00	—
ND(1905)/26	4.00	6.00	9.00	14.00	—
ND(1906)/27	4.00	6.00	9.00	14.00	—
ND(1908)/29	4.00	6.00	9.00	14.00	—
ND(1909)/30	4.00	6.00	9.00	14.00	—
ND(1910)/31	4.00	6.00	9.00	14.00	—
ND(1912)/33	4.00	6.00	9.00	14.00	—
ND(1916)/37	4.00	6.00	9.00	14.00	—
191(8)/39	4.00	6.00	9.00	14.00	—
ND(1919)/40	4.00	6.00	9.00	14.00	—
ND(1921)/42	4.00	6.00	9.00	14.00	—
1922/43	4.00	6.00	9.00	14.00	—

KM# 150 MOHUR Composition: Gold **Obverse:** Inscription: Queen Victoria.... **Reverse:** Jhar; inscription: Madho Singh II.... **Note:** Weight varies 10.70-11.40 g.

Date	VG	F	VF	XF	Unc
ND(1904)/25	135	155	185	225	—
ND(1916)/37	135	155	185	225	—
ND(1916)/37	135	155	185	225	—
ND(1919)/40	135	155	185	225	—
ND(1920)/41	135	155	185	225	—

MILLED COINAGE

KM# 132 NAZARANA NEW PAISA Composition: Copper **Obverse:** Inscription: Queen Victoria... **Reverse:** Jhar; inscription: Madho Singh II.... **Note:** Well-centered issues on thin planchets may be restrikes.

Date	VG	F	VF	XF	Unc
1880/1	12.50	17.50	25.00	40.00	—
1901/22	12.50	17.50	25.00	40.00	—
1902/23	12.50	17.50	25.00	40.00	—
1903/24	12.50	17.50	25.00	40.00	—
1904/25	12.50	17.50	25.00	40.00	—
1905/26	12.50	17.50	25.00	40.00	—
1906/27	12.50	17.50	25.00	40.00	—
1907/28	12.50	17.50	25.00	40.00	—
1908/29	12.50	17.50	25.00	40.00	—
1909/30	12.50	17.50	25.00	40.00	—
1910/31	12.50	17.50	25.00	40.00	—
1911/32	12.50	17.50	25.00	40.00	—
1912/33	12.50	17.50	25.00	40.00	—
1913/34	12.50	17.50	25.00	40.00	—
1914/35	12.50	17.50	25.00	40.00	—
1915/36	12.50	17.50	25.00	40.00	—
1916/37	12.50	17.50	25.00	40.00	—
1917/38	12.50	17.50	25.00	40.00	—

KM# 147 NAZARANA RUPEE Composition: Silver **Obverse:** Inscription: Queen Victoria.... **Reverse:** Jhar; inscription: Madho Singh II.... **Note:** Size varies 36-37mm.

Date	VG	F	VF	XF	Unc
1901/22	27.50	40.00	52.50	75.00	—
1903/24	27.50	40.00	52.50	75.00	—
1904/25	27.50	40.00	52.50	75.00	—
1906/27	27.50	40.00	52.50	75.00	—
1908/29	27.50	40.00	52.50	75.00	—
1909/30	27.50	40.00	52.50	75.00	—
1910/31	27.50	40.00	52.50	75.00	—
1911/32	27.50	40.00	52.50	75.00	—
1912/33	27.50	40.00	52.50	75.00	—
1913/34	27.50	40.00	52.50	75.00	—
1916/37	27.50	40.00	52.50	75.00	—
1920/41	27.50	40.00	52.50	75.00	—
1921/42	27.50	40.00	52.50	75.00	—

Man Singh II
1922-1949AD

HAMMERED 'DUMP' COINAGE

KM# 175 1/2 PAISA Composition: Copper **Obverse:** Inscription: Edward VIII.... **Reverse:** Jhar; inscription: Singh II....

Date	VG	F	VF	XF	Unc
ND(1942)/21	1.00	1.75	2.50	4.50	—

KM# 158 RUPEE Weight: 10.7000 g. **Composition:** Silver **Obverse:** Inscription: George V.... **Reverse:** Jhar; inscription: Man Singh II....

Date	VG	F	VF	XF	Unc
1922/1	25.00	40.00	65.00	90.00	—

KM# 163 MOHUR Composition: Gold **Obverse:** Inscription: George V.... **Reverse:** Jhar; inscription: Man Singh II.... **Note:** Weight varies 10.70-11.40 g.

Date	VG	F	VF	XF	Unc
ND(1923)/2	150	200	300	425	—
1(924)/3	150	200	300	425	—
1925/4	150	200	300	425	—
19(28)/7	150	200	300	425	—

KM# 200 MOHUR Composition: Gold **Obverse:** Inscription: George VI.... **Reverse:** Madho Singh II.... **Note:** Weight varies 10.70-11.40 g.

Date	VG	F	VF	XF	Unc
ND(1941)/20	135	155	185	250	—
ND(1943)/22	135	155	185	250	—
ND(1947)/26	135	155	185	250	—
ND(1948)/27	135	155	185	250	—
1949	135	155	185	250	—

MILLED COINAGE

KM# 185 ANNA Composition: Brass **Obverse:** Jhar

Date	Good	VG	F	VF	XF
1943	—	0.20	0.40	0.60	1.00
1944/3	0.15	0.40	0.80	1.20	2.00
1944	—	0.20	0.40	0.60	1.00

KM# 186 ANNA Weight: 5.1700 g. **Composition:** Brass **Obverse:** Jhar **Note:** Brass, thick planchet.

Date	Good	VG	F	VF	XF
1943	0.10	0.25	0.50	0.80	1.50

KM# 187 ANNA Weight: 2.7800 g. **Composition:** Brass **Obverse:** Jhar **Note:** Brass, thin planchet.

Date	Good	VG	F	VF	XF
1943	—	0.20	0.40	0.60	1.00

KM# 188 ANNA Composition: Brass **Obverse:** Bust of Man Singh II right **Reverse:** Jhar

Date	Good	VG	F	VF	XF
1944	—	0.20	0.40	0.60	1.00
1944 Proof	—	—	—	—	—

KM# 190 2 ANNA Composition: Brass **Reverse:** Jhar **Note:** Square flan.

Date	Good	VG	F	VF	XF
1942/21	1.25	3.00	4.50	6.00	10.00

KM# 176 1/2 PAISA Composition: Copper **Obverse:** Inscription: Edward VIII.... **Reverse:** Jhar; inscription: Man Singh II.... **Note:** Crude struck in collar.

Date	Good	VG	F	VF	XF
ND(1943)/22	0.40	1.00	1.75	2.50	4.50
ND(1944)/23	0.40	1.00	1.75	2.50	4.50

KM# 155 NAZARANA PAISA Composition: Copper **Obverse:** Inscription: George V.... **Reverse:** Jhar; inscription: Man Singh II....

Date	Good	VG	F	VF	XF
1922/1	6.00	15.00	25.00	40.00	60.00
1923/2	6.00	15.00	25.00	40.00	60.00
1924/3	6.00	15.00	25.00	40.00	60.00
1924/4	6.00	15.00	25.00	40.00	60.00
1925/4	6.00	15.00	25.00	40.00	60.00
1926/5	6.00	15.00	25.00	40.00	60.00
1927/5	6.00	15.00	25.00	40.00	60.00
1927/6	6.00	15.00	25.00	40.00	60.00
1928/7	6.00	15.00	25.00	40.00	60.00
1930/9	6.00	15.00	25.00	40.00	60.00
19(30)/10	6.00	15.00	25.00	40.00	60.00
1931/10	6.00	15.00	25.00	40.00	60.00
1932/11	6.00	15.00	25.00	40.00	60.00
1933/12	6.00	15.00	25.00	40.00	60.00
1934/13	6.00	15.00	25.00	40.00	60.00
1935/14	6.00	15.00	25.00	40.00	60.00

KM# 157 NAZARANA PAISA Composition: Copper **Obverse:** Inscription: George V.... **Reverse:** Jhar; inscription: Man Singh II....

Date	Good	VG	F	VF	XF
1929/8	6.00	15.00	25.00	40.00	60.00

KM# 167 NAZARANA PAISA Weight: 6.4400 g. **Composition:** Copper **Obverse:** Inscription: Edward VIII.... **Reverse:** Jhar; inscription: Man Singh II....

Date	Good	VG	F	VF	XF
1936/15	125	250	275	325	400

KM# 180 NAZARANA PAISA Composition: Copper **Obverse:** Inscription: Edward VIII.... **Reverse:** Jhar; inscription: Man Singh II....

Date	Good	VG	F	VF	XF
1937/16	4.00	10.00	17.50	25.00	40.00
1938/17	4.00	10.00	17.50	25.00	40.00
1939/18	4.00	10.00	17.50	25.00	40.00
1940/19	4.00	10.00	17.50	25.00	40.00
1941/19	4.00	10.00	17.50	25.00	40.00
1941/20	4.00	10.00	17.50	25.00	40.00
1942/21	4.00	10.00	17.50	25.00	40.00
1943/22	4.00	10.00	17.50	25.00	40.00
19(44)/23	4.00	10.00	17.50	25.00	40.00
1945/24	4.00	10.00	17.50	25.00	40.00
1946/25	4.00	10.00	17.50	25.00	40.00
1947/26	4.00	10.00	17.50	25.00	40.00
1947/27	4.00	10.00	17.50	25.00	40.00
1948/27	4.00	10.00	17.50	25.00	40.00
1949/28	4.00	10.00	17.50	25.00	40.00

KM# 159 NAZARANA RUPEE Weight: 10.7000 g. **Composition:** Silver **Obverse:** Inscription: George V.... **Reverse:** Jhar; inscription: Man Singh II....

Date	VG	F	VF	XF	Unc
1924/3	40.00	62.50	85.00	120	—
1928/7	40.00	62.50	85.00	120	—
1932/11	40.00	62.50	85.00	120	—

KM# 170 NAZARANA RUPEE **Weight:** 10.7000 g. **Composition:** Silver **Obverse:** Inscription: Edward VIII.... **Reverse:** Jhar; inscription: Man Singh II....

Date	VG	F	VF	XF	Unc
1936/15 Rare	—	—	—	—	—

KM# 196 NAZARANA RUPEE **Composition:** Silver **Obverse:** Inscription: George VI.... **Reverse:** Madho Singh II.... **Note:** Similar rupees approximately 30mm in diameter are modern forgeries.

Date	VG	F	VF	XF	Unc
1938/20	—	—	70.00	100	—
1939/18	10.00	16.00	28.50	40.00	—
1941/20	10.00	16.00	28.50	40.00	—
1943/22	10.00	16.00	28.50	40.00	—
1945/24	10.00	16.00	28.50	40.00	—
1948/27	10.00	16.00	28.50	40.00	—
1949/28	10.00	16.00	28.50	40.00	—

KM# 195 NAZARANA RUPEE **Composition:** Silver **Obverse:** Mule; inscription: George VI.... **Reverse:** Madho Singh II.... **Note:** Weight varies 10.70-11.60 g.

Date	Good	VG	F	VF	XF
1949/3	12.50	25.00	32.50	55.00	80.00

KM# 201 NAZARANA MOHUR **Composition:** Gold **Obverse:** Inscription: George VI.... **Reverse:** Man Singh II....

Date	Good	VG	F	VF	XF
ND(1949)/28	—	—	—	—	—

JODHPUR

Jodhpur, also known as Marwar, located in northwest India, was the largest Princely State in the Rajputana Agency. Its population in 1941 exceeded two and a half million. The "Maharajadhirajas" ("Great Kings of Kings") of Jodhpur were Rathor Rajputs who claimed an extremely ancient ancestry from Rama, king of Ayodhya. With the collapse of the Rathor rulers of Kanauj in 1194 the family entered Marwar where they laid the foundation of the new state. The city of Jodhpur was built by Rao Jodha in 1459, and the city and the state were named after him. In 1561 the Mughal Emperor Akbar invaded Jodhpur, forcing its submission. In 1679 Emperor Aurangzeb sacked the city, an experience which stimulated the Rajput royal house to forge a new unity among themselves in order to extricate themselves from Mughal hegemony. Internal dissension once again asserted itself and Rajput unity, which had both benefited from and accelerated Mughal decline, fell apart before the Marathas. In 1818 Jodhpur came under British protection and control and after Indian independence in 1947 the State was merged into Rajasthan. Jodhpur is best known for its particular style of riding breeches (jodpurs) which became very popular in the West in the late 19th century.

RULERS

Sardar Singh, VS1952-1968/1895-1911AD
Sumer Singh, VS1968-1975/1911-1918AD
Umaid Singh, VS1975-2004/1918-1947AD
Hanwant Singh, as Titular Ruler, VS2004-2009/1947-1949AD

MINTS

Jodhpur جودھ پور

Jodpur جودپور

Dar-al-Mansur دارالمنصور

MINT MARKS

Before 1858AD

Sojat, always on reverse. (KM#226)
Sojat, sometimes on obverse. (KM#226)
Pali, (KM#227)
Pali, Sojat
Nagor, (on reverse of KM#177.2)
Usually on obverse.
Jodhpur, on obverse. (KM#47)

Issues of 1858-1873AD

After 1858AD, the mint marks vary, and are given for each listing, wherever there is a difference.

All gold coins struck at Jodhpur Mint. All mints except Jodhpur closed by or before 1893AD. All copper coins were probably struck at the Jodhpur Mint, but if struck elsewhere, they bear no distinguishing marks.

In addition to the mint marks indicating the mint cities, there are also the marks of the Darogas (mint overseers), which are very useful in identifying the mints, especially when the city marks are missing or off the flan. These are given by cat.# and mint: (Only one of the marks appears on any one coin, always on the obverse.)

Issues of Edward VII and George V and Sardar Singh and Sumer Singh

Jodhpur (KM#91-95, 98-100, 109, 113-115) म
Jodhpur (KM#120)

Issues of George V and Sumer Singh

Jodhpur (KM#111-112) द

Issues of George V and Umaid Singh

Jodhpur (KM#128 & 129) अँ

Jodhpur (KM#129) आ

Issues of Edward VIII and Umaid Singh

Jodhpur all रं

Issues of George VI and Umaid Singh

Jodhpur (KM#141-143) रं

Jodhpur (KM#144-147, 150-151) गो

Issues of George VI and Hanwant Singh

Jodhpur all गो

The Daroga's marks generally consist of a symbol or a single Nagari letter, sometimes inverted, and even lying on its side. Some letters are found on more than one series, so that the mark is not a positive identification, but taken together with the city mark and the style of the coin, will provide a correct attribution.

JODHPUR MINT

Operative between 1761AD (AH1175) and 1945AD (VS2002). There are a number of mules of late Jodhpur types struck in 1945 and later for collectors.

Sardar Singh

HAMMERED 'DUMP' COINAGE

KM# 91.1 1/4 ANNA **Weight:** 10.5000 g. **Composition:** Copper **Obverse:** Inscription: Edward (VII)... **Reverse:** Inscription: Sardar Singh...; date at top **Note:** Other blundered dates may exist. Cross reference Y#20. Struck at the Jodhpur Mint.

Date	Good	VG	F	VF	XF
1901	1.50	2.50	3.75	5.50	—
1902	1.50	2.50	3.75	5.50	—
1903	1.50	2.50	3.75	5.50	—
1904	1.50	2.50	3.75	5.50	—
1905	1.50	2.50	3.75	5.50	—
1906	0.50	1.00	1.75	2.50	—
1609	1.50	2.50	3.75	5.50	—
1907	1.00	2.00	3.25	4.50	—
1908	1.00	2.00	3.25	4.50	—
1909	1.00	2.00	3.25	4.50	—
1910	1.00	2.00	3.25	4.50	—
1290(1910) Error	1.25	2.25	3.00	4.00	—
1291(1910) Error	0.75	1.50	2.25	3.25	—
1292(1910) Error	—	—	—	—	—
1967(1910) Error	1.25	2.25	3.00	4.00	—
2091(1910) Error	1.25	2.25	3.00	4.00	—
5201(1910) Error	1.25	2.25	3.00	4.00	—
5291(1910) Error	—	—	—	—	—

KM# 91.2 1/4 ANNA **Weight:** 10.5000 g. **Composition:** Copper **Obverse:** Inscription: Edward (VII)... **Reverse:** Inscription: Sardar Singh...; date at bottom **Note:** Cross reference Y#20. Struck at the Jodhpur Mint.

Date	Good	VG	F	VF	XF
1906	—	—	—	—	—

KM# 92.1 1/2 ANNA **Composition:** Copper **Obverse:** Inscription: Edward (VII)... **Reverse:** Inscription: Sardar Singh... **Note:** 20.00-21.00 grams. Cross reference Y#21. Struck at the Jodhpur Mint.

Date	Good	VG	F	VF	XF
1906	3.50	5.00	7.50	11.50	—

KM# 92.2 1/2 ANNA **Composition:** Copper **Obverse:** Inscription: Edward (VII)... **Reverse:** Inscription: Sardar Singh...; legend without Bahadur **Note:** Cross reference Y#21. Struck at the Jodhpur Mint.

Date	Good	VG	F	VF	XF
1906	3.50	5.00	7.50	11.50	—
1908	3.50	5.00	7.50	11.50	—

KM# 93 1/8 RUPEE **Weight:** 1.4000 g. **Composition:** Silver **Obverse:** Inscription: Edward (VII)... **Reverse:** Inscription: Sardar Singh...

Date	VG	F	VF	XF	Unc
ND (1908)	17.50	25.00	35.00	50.00	—

KM# 94 1/4 RUPEE **Weight:** 2.8000 g. **Composition:** Silver **Obverse:** Inscription: Edward (VII)... **Reverse:** Inscription: Sardar Singh... **Note:** Cross reference Y#22.

Date	VG	F	VF	XF	Unc
VS1965	18.50	26.50	37.50	55.00	—

KM# 95 1/2 RUPEE **Weight:** 5.6000 g. **Composition:** Silver **Obverse:** Inscription: Edward (VII)... **Reverse:** Inscription: Sardar Singh... **Note:** Struck at the Jodhpur Mint.

Date	VG	F	VF	XF	Unc
ND	20.00	31.50	42.50	60.00	—

KM# 98 1/4 MOHUR Weight: 2.8000 g. **Composition:** Gold **Obverse:** Inscription: Edward (VII)... **Reverse:** Inscription: Sardar Singh... **Note:** Cross reference Y#23. Struck at the Jodhpur Mint.

Date	VG	F	VF	XF	Unc
ND(1906)	60.00	85.00	110	165	—

KM# 99 1/2 MOHUR Weight: 5.5000 g. **Composition:** Gold **Obverse:** Inscription: Edward (VII)... **Reverse:** Inscription: Sardar Singh... **Note:** Cross reference Y#24. Struck at the Jodhpur Mint.

Date	VG	F	VF	XF	Unc
ND(1906)	100	150	210	300	—

KM# 100.1 MOHUR Weight: 11.0000 g. **Composition:** Gold **Obverse:** Inscription: Edward (VII)...; "Ma." **Reverse:** Inscription: Sardar Singh... **Note:** Cross reference Y#25. Struck at the Jodhpur Mint.

Date	VG	F	VF	XF	Unc
1906	175	250	350	550	—

KM# 100.2 MOHUR Weight: 11.0000 g. **Composition:** Gold **Obverse:** Inscription: Edward (VII)...; "Sa." **Reverse:** Inscription: Sardar Singh... **Note:** Cross reference Y#25. Struck at the Jodhpur Mint.

Date	VG	F	VF	XF	Unc
1906	175	250	350	550	—

Sumar Singh

HAMMERED 'DUMP' COINAGE

KM# 110 1/4 ANNA Weight: 10.5000 g. **Composition:** Copper **Obverse:** Inscription: George V, "Emperor"... **Reverse:** Inscription: Sumar Singh... **Note:** Cross reference Y#27. Struck at the Jodhpur Mint.

Date	Good	VG	F	VF	XF
1914	6.50	9.00	12.50	17.50	—

KM# 111 1/4 ANNA Weight: 10.5000 g. **Composition:** Copper **Obverse:** Inscription: George V, "Shah"... **Reverse:** Inscription: Sumar Singh... **Note:** Cross reference Y#27. Struck at the Jodhpur Mint.

Date	Good	VG	F	VF	XF
1914	—	—	—	—	—

KM# 112.1 1/2 ANNA Weight: 21.0000 g. **Composition:** Copper **Obverse:** Inscription: George V, "Emperor"... **Reverse:** Inscription: Sumar Singh... **Note:** Cross reference Y#28. Struck at the Jodhpur Mint.

Date	Good	VG	F	VF	XF
1914	5.00	8.50	12.50	20.00	—

KM# 112.2 1/2 ANNA Weight: 21.0000 g. **Composition:** Copper **Obverse:** Inscription: George V, "Shah"... **Reverse:** Inscription: Sumar Singh... **Note:** Cross reference Y#28. Struck at the Jodhpur Mint.

Date	Good	VG	F	VF	XF
1914	5.00	8.50	12.50	20.00	—

KM# 113 1/8 RUPEE Weight: 1.4000 g. **Composition:** Silver **Obverse:** Inscription: George V, "Shah"... **Reverse:** Inscription: Sumar Singh... **Note:** Cross reference Y#29. Struck at the Jodhpur Mint.

Date	VG	F	VF	XF	Unc
ND(1911-18)	15.00	21.50	30.00	40.00	—

KM# 114 1/4 RUPEE Weight: 2.8000 g. **Composition:** Silver **Note:** Cross reference Y#30. Struck at the Jodhpur Mint.

Date	Good	VG	F	VF	XF
ND(1911-18)	15.00	21.50	30.00	40.00	—

KM# 115 1/2 RUPEE Weight: 5.6000 g. **Composition:** Silver **Note:** Cross reference Y#31. Struck at the Jodhpur Mint.

Date	Good	VG	F	VF	XF
ND(1911-18)	15.00	21.50	30.00	40.00	—

KM# 116 RUPEE Weight: 11.2000 g. **Composition:** Silver **Note:** Cross reference Y#32. Struck at the Jodhpur Mint.

Date	Good	VG	F	VF	XF
ND(1911-18)	18.50	26.50	37.50	55.00	—

KM# 119 1/2 MOHUR Weight: 5.5000 g. **Composition:** Gold **Note:** Cross reference Y#26. Struck at the Jodhpur Mint.

Date	VG	F	VF	XF	Unc
ND(1911-18)	87.50	125	175	250	—

KM# 120.1 MOHUR Weight: 11.0000 g. **Composition:** Gold **Obverse:** "Ma." **Note:** Cross reference Y#33. Struck at the Jodhpur Mint.

Date	VG	F	VF	XF	Unc
ND(1911-18)	175	250	350	550	—

KM# 120.2 MOHUR Weight: 11.0000 g. **Composition:** Gold **Obverse:** "Ha." **Note:** Cross reference Y#33. Struck at the Jodhpur Mint.

Date	VG	F	VF	XF	Unc
ND(1911-18)	200	300	400	600	—

Umaid Singh

HAMMERED 'DUMP' COINAGE

KM# 131 1/4 ANNA Weight: 10.5000 g. **Composition:** Copper **Obverse:** Inscription: Edward (VIII)...; without Persian "8" left of Daroga's mark **Reverse:** Inscription: Umaid Singh... **Note:** Cross reference Y#39. Struck at the Jodhpur Mint.

Date	Good	VG	F	VF	XF
1936	1.75	2.75	4.00	6.50	—

KM# 132 1/4 ANNA Weight: 10.5000 g. **Composition:** Copper **Obverse:** Inscription: Edward (VIII)...; large Persian "8" left of Daroga's mark **Reverse:** Inscription: Umaid Singh... **Note:** Struck at the Jodhpur Mint.

Date	Good	VG	F	VF	XF
1936	1.75	2.75	4.00	6.50	—

Note: Blundered legend varieties also exist

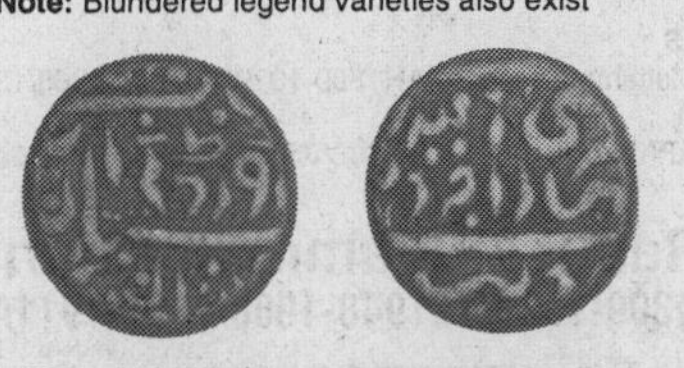

KM# 133 1/4 ANNA Weight: 10.5000 g. **Composition:** Copper **Obverse:** Inscription: Edward (VIII)...; small Persian "8" left of Daroga's mark **Reverse:** Inscription: Umaid Singh... **Note:** Struck at the Jodhpur Mint.

Date	Good	VG	F	VF	XF
1936	1.75	2.75	4.00	6.50	—

KM# 141 1/4 ANNA Composition: Copper **Obverse:** Inscription: George (VI)... **Reverse:** Inscription: Umaid Singh...; date at top **Note:** Thick, 10.50-10.70 grams. Cross reference Y#40. Struck at the Jodhpur Mint.

Date	Good	VG	F	VF	XF
1937	1.25	1.75	2.50	3.50	—
1938	1.25	1.75	2.50	3.50	—
1939	1.25	1.75	2.50	3.50	—

KM# 142 1/4 ANNA Composition: Copper **Obverse:** Inscription: George (VI)... **Reverse:** Inscription: Umaid Singh... **Note:** Struck at the Jodhpur Mint.

Date	Good	VG	F	VF	XF
VS1996	2.00	3.00	4.00	6.00	—

KM# 143 1/4 ANNA Composition: Copper **Obverse:** Inscription: George (VI)... **Reverse:** Inscription: Umaid Singh... **Note:** Struck at the Jodhpur Mint.

Date	Good	VG	F	VF	XF
ND	3.00	4.50	6.50	10.00	—

KM# 124 1/4 RUPEE Weight: 3.1000 g. **Composition:** Silver **Obverse:** Inscription: George (V)... **Reverse:** Inscription: Umaid Singh... **Note:** Cross reference Y#35. Struck at the Jodhpur Mint.

Date	VG	F	VF	XF	Unc
ND(1918-35)	18.50	26.50	37.50	55.00	—

KM# 125 1/2 RUPEE Composition: Silver **Obverse:** Inscription: George (V)... **Reverse:** Inscription: Umaid Singh... **Note:** Round. Struck at the Jodhpur Mint.

Date	VG	F	VF	XF	Unc
ND(1918-35)	—	—	—	—	—

KM# 125a 1/2 RUPEE Composition: Silver **Obverse:** Inscription: George (V)... **Reverse:** Inscription: Umaid Singh... **Note:** Square flan. Struck at the Jodhpur Mint.

Date	VG	F	VF	XF	Unc
ND(1918-35)	—	—	—	—	—

KM# 126 RUPEE Composition: Silver **Obverse:** Inscription: George (V)... **Reverse:** Inscription: Umaid Singh... **Note:** Struck at the Jodhpur Mint.

Date	VG	F	VF	XF	Unc
ND(1918-35)	—	—	—	—	—

KM# 127.1 1/4 MOHUR Weight: 2.7000 g. **Composition:** Gold **Obverse:** Inscription: George (V)...; "OM" or "AVM" **Reverse:** Inscription: Umaid Singh... **Note:** Cross reference Y#36. Struck at the Jodhpur Mint.

Date	VG	F	VF	XF	Unc
ND(1918-35)	60.00	90.00	120	175	—

KM# 127.2 1/4 MOHUR Weight: 2.7000 g. **Composition:** Gold **Obverse:** Inscription: George (V)...; "Shri." **Reverse:** Inscription: Umaid Singh... **Note:** Cross reference Y#36. Struck at the Jodhpur Mint.

Date	VG	F	VF	XF	Unc
ND(1918-35)	60.00	90.00	120	175	—

KM# 128 1/2 MOHUR Weight: 5.5000 g. **Composition:** Gold **Obverse:** Inscription: George (V)... **Reverse:** Inscription: Umaid Singh... **Note:** Cross reference Y#37. Struck at the Jodhpur Mint.

Date	VG	F	VF	XF	Unc
ND(1918-35)	100	150	210	300	—

KM# 129 MOHUR Weight: 11.0000 g. **Composition:** Gold **Obverse:** Inscription: George (V)...; "170m" **Reverse:** Inscription: Umaid Singh... **Note:** Cross reference Y#38. Struck at the Jodhpur Mint.

Date	VG	F	VF	XF	Unc
19x8	175	250	350	550	—

KM# 130 MOHUR Weight: 11.0000 g. **Composition:** Gold **Obverse:** Inscription: George (V)...; "Shri." **Reverse:** Inscription: Umaid Singh... **Note:** Cross reference Y#38. Struck at the Jodhpur Mint.

Date	VG	F	VF	XF	Unc
ND(1918-35)	165	210	300	450	—

KM# 140 MOHUR Weight: 11.0100 g. **Composition:** Gold **Note:** Struck at the Jodhpur Mint.

Date	VG	F	VF	XF	Unc
1936	—	—	—	—	—

KM# 150 MOHUR **Weight:** 11.0000 g. **Composition:** Gold **Obverse:** Inscription: George (VI)...; large legend, Persian "6" after "George" **Reverse:** Inscription: Umaid Singh...; large legend, Persian "6" after "George" **Note:** Cross reference Y#42. Struck at the Jodhpur Mint.

Date	VG	F	VF	XF	Unc
ND (1943)	165	225	350	650	—

KM# 151 MOHUR **Weight:** 11.0200 g. **Composition:** Gold **Obverse:** Inscription: George (VI)...; small legend, without Persian "6" **Reverse:** Inscription: Umaid Singh...; small legend, without Persian "6" **Note:** Struck at the Jodhpur Mint.

Date	VG	F	VF	XF	Unc
ND (1943)	165	225	350	650	—
VS2000 (1943)	165	225	350	650	—

MILLED COINAGE

KM# 144 1/4 ANNA **Weight:** 3.0000 g. **Composition:** Copper **Obverse:** Inscription: George (VI)...; without Persian "6" below Daroga's mark **Reverse:** Inscription: Umaid Singh... **Note:** Thin flan. Cross reference Y#41. Struck at the Jodhpur Mint.

Date	Good	VG	F	VF	XF
VS2000 (1943)	1.75	2.75	4.00	5.50	—
ND (1943) Date off flan	0.20	0.30	0.50	1.00	—

KM# 147 1/4 ANNA **Weight:** 2.6000 g. **Composition:** Copper **Obverse:** Inscription: George (VI)...; cock with wings raised facing left, legend around **Reverse:** Inscription: Umaid Singh...; date and "Rajya Marwar" **Note:** Struck at the Jodhpur Mint.

Date	Good	VG	F	VF	XF
VS2000 (1943) Rare	—	—	—	—	—

KM# 145 1/4 ANNA **Weight:** 2.6000 g. **Composition:** Copper **Obverse:** Inscription: George (VI)...; Persian "6" below Daroga's mark **Reverse:** Inscription: Umaid Singh... **Note:** Varieties exist. Struck at the Jodhpur Mint.

Date	Good	VG	F	VF	XF
VS2001 (1944)	1.75	2.75	4.00	5.50	—
VS2002 (1945)	1.75	2.75	4.00	5.50	—

KM# 146 1/4 ANNA **Weight:** 2.6000 g. **Composition:** Copper **Obverse:** Inscription: George (VI)...; Persian 2 (error for 6) below Daroga's mark **Reverse:** Inscription: Umaid Singh... **Note:** Struck at the Jodhpur Mint.

Date	Good	VG	F	VF	XF
VS (1945)	—	—	—	—	—

Hanwant Singh
as Titular Ruler

HAMMERED 'DUMP' COINAGE

KM# 152 1/4 ANNA **Weight:** 4.2000 g. **Composition:** Copper **Obverse:** Inscription: George (VI)... **Reverse:** Inscription: Hanwant Singh... **Note:** Cross reference Y#43. Struck at the Jodhpur Mint.

Date	Good	VG	F	VF	XF
VS(2004) (1947)	12.50	20.00	32.50	50.00	—

KM# 158 1/4 MOHUR **Weight:** 2.7000 g. **Composition:** Gold **Obverse:** Inscription: George (VI)... **Reverse:** Inscription: Hanwant Singh... **Note:** Struck at the Jodhpur Mint.

Date	VG	F	VF	XF	Unc
VS(2004) (1947) Rare	—	—	—	—	—

KM# 160 MOHUR **Weight:** 11.0000 g. **Composition:** Gold **Obverse:** Inscription: George (VI)... **Reverse:** Inscription: Hanwant Singh... **Note:** Struck at the Jodhpur Mint.

Date	VG	F	VF	XF	Unc
VS(2004) (1947)	250	350	500	650	—

JUNAGADH

A state located in the Kathiawar peninsula of Western India was originally a petty Rajput kingdom until conquered by the Sultan of Ahmadabad in 1472. It became a Mughal dependency under the Emperor Akbar, administered by the Ahmadabad Subah. In 1735, when the empire began to disintegrate, a Mughal officer and military adventurer, Sher Khan Babi, expelled the Mughal governor and asserted his independence. From that time until Indian independence his descendents ruled the state as nawabs. In 1947 the Nawab of Junagadh tried to acceed to the new nation of Pakistan but the Hindu majority in the state objected and Junagadh was absorbed by the Republic of India.

Junagadh first entered into treaty relations with the British in 1807 and maintained a close and friendly association with the Raj. In 1924 this relationship was formalized when Junagadh was placed under an Agent to the Governor General in the western India States. In 1935 the state comprised 3,337 square miles with a population of 545,152, four-fifths of whom were Hindus.

RULERS

Rasul Muhammad Khan, AH1309-1329/VS1948-1968/1891-1911AD

Mahabat Khan III, AH1329-1368/VS1968-2005/1911-1948AD

Rasul Muhammad Khan
AH1309-1329/VS1948-1968/1891-1911AD

MILLED COINAGE

KM# 44.1 DOKDO **Composition:** Copper **Obverse:** Inscription: Perso-Arabic Ek paisa Junagadh Riiyaasat (government) **Reverse:** Inscription: Devanagari-Shri Sorath Sarkaar; date without rosettes **Note:** Struck at Junagadh.

Date	Good	VG	F	VF	XF
VS1963(1906)	1.25	2.00	3.00	4.50	7.50
VS1964(1907)	—	—	—	—	—

KM# 43 DOKDO **Composition:** Copper **Obverse:** Inscription: Perso-Arabic "Ek paisa Junagadh Riiyaasat (government)" **Reverse:** Inscription: "Devanagari-Shri Sorath Sarkaar" **Note:** Struck at Junagadh.

Date	Good	VG	F	VF	XF
AH1325/VS1963	4.50	6.50	10.00	15.00	25.00

KM# 44.2 DOKDO **Composition:** Copper **Obverse:** Inscription: Perso-Arabic Ek paisa Junagadh Riiyaasat (government) **Reverse:** Inscription: Devanagari-Shri Sorath Sarkaar; date with annulets **Note:** Struck at Junagadh.

Date	Good	VG	F	VF	XF
VS1964(1907)	1.25	2.00	3.00	4.50	7.50

KM# 44.3 DOKDO **Composition:** Copper **Obverse:** Inscription: Perso-Arabic Ek paisa Junagadh Riiyaasat (government) **Reverse:** Inscription: Devanagari-Shri Sorath Sarkaar; date between solid stars **Note:** Struck at Junagadh.

Date	Good	VG	F	VF	XF
VS1964(1907)	1.25	2.00	3.00	4.50	7.50

KM# 44.3a DOKDO **Composition:** Copper **Obverse:** Inscription: Perso-Arabic Ek paisa Junagadh Riiyaasat (government) **Reverse:** Inscription: Devanagari-Shri Sorath Sarkaar; solid star only to left of date **Note:** Struck at Junagadh.

Date	Good	VG	F	VF	XF
VS1964(1907)	2.50	4.00	6.00	10.00	16.50

KM# 44.4 DOKDO **Composition:** Copper **Obverse:** Inscription: Perso-Arabic Ek paisa Junagadh Riiyaasat (government) **Reverse:** Inscription: Devanagari-Shri Sorath Sarkaar; date with outlined stars **Note:** Struck at Junagadh.

Date	Good	VG	F	VF	XF
VS1964(1907)	1.25	2.00	3.00	4.50	7.50

KM# 45.1 DOKDO **Composition:** Copper **Obverse:** Inscription: Perso-Arabic Ek paisa Junagadh Riiyaasat (government) **Reverse:** Inscription: Devanagari-Shri Sorath Sarkaar; date between rosettes **Note:** Struck at Junagadh.

Date	Good	VG	F	VF	XF
VS1964(1907)	0.50	0.85	1.25	1.75	3.00
VS1965(1908)	0.50	0.85	1.25	1.75	3.00
VS1966(1909)	0.50	0.85	1.25	1.75	3.00
VS1967(1910)	0.75	0.50	2.50	3.50	6.00

KM# 45.2 DOKDO **Composition:** Copper **Obverse:** Inscription: Perso-Arabic Ek paisa Junagadh Riiyaasat (government) **Reverse:** Inscription: Devanagari-Shri Sorath Sarkaar; date divided by space in legend **Note:** Struck at Junagadh.

Date	Good	VG	F	VF	XF
VS1966(1909)	0.75	1.50	2.50	3.50	6.00

KM# 45.3 DOKDO **Composition:** Copper **Obverse:** Inscription: Perso-Arabic Ek paisa Junagadh Riiyaasat (government) **Reverse:** Inscription: Devanagari-Shri Sorath Sarkaar; date at top in legend **Note:** Struck at Junagadh.

Date	Good	VG	F	VF	XF
VS1966(1909)	1.75	2.75	4.00	6.50	11.50

KM# 46.1 DOKDO Composition: Copper **Obverse:** Inscription: Perso-Arabic Ek paisa Junagadh Riiyaasat (government) **Reverse:** Inscription: Devanagari-Shri Sorath Sarkaar **Note:** Struck at Junagadh.

Date	Good	VG	F	VF	XF
ND	1.75	2.75	4.00	6.50	11.50

KM# 46.2 DOKDO Composition: Copper **Obverse:** Inscription: Perso-Arabic Ek paisa Junagadh Riiyaasat (government) **Reverse:** Inscription: Devanagari-Shri Sorath Sarkaar; stars between inscriptions **Note:** Struck at Junagadh.

Date	Good	VG	F	VF	XF
ND	1.75	2.75	4.00	6.50	11.50

KM# 48 2 DOKDA Composition: Copper **Obverse:** Inscription: Perso-Arabic Ek paisa Junagadh Riiyaasat (government) **Reverse:** Inscription: Devanagari-Shri Sorath Sarkaar **Note:** Struck at Junagadh.

Date	Good	VG	F	VF	XF
VS1964(1907)	7.50	12.50	20.00	30.00	50.00

KM# 52 KORI Weight: 4.6000 g. **Composition:** Silver

Date	VG	F	VF	XF	Unc
VS1966(1909)	17.50	25.00	35.00	50.00	—

KM# 58 GOLD KORI Composition: Gold **Obverse:** Inscription: Perso-Arabic Nawab Bahadur Muhammad Khanji **Reverse:** Date, mint name **Note:** 4.02-4.77 grams

Date	VG	F	VF	XF	Unc
AH1325/VS1963	—	—	500	850	1,250

KM# 60 MOHUR Weight: 11.5400 g. **Composition:** Gold **Obverse:** Inscription: Perso-Arabic Nawab Bahadur Muhammad Khanji **Reverse:** Date, mint name

Date	VG	F	VF	XF	Unc
AH1325/VS1963	—	—	—	2,000	2,800

Mahabat Khan III

AH1329-1368/VS1968-2005/1911-1948AD

MILLED COINAGE

KM# 61 DOKDO Weight: 11.5400 g. **Composition:** Gold **Obverse:** "Shri Divan" in Devanagari below

Date	Good	VG	F	VF	XF
AH1325(1907) Rare	—	—	—	—	—

KM# 63 DOKDO Composition: Copper

Date	VG	F	VF	XF	Unc
VS1985(1928)	16.50	25.00	40.00	65.00	—
VS1990(1933)	16.50	25.00	40.00	65.00	—

KISHANGARH

The maharajas of Kishangarh, a small state in northwest India, in the vicinity of Ajmer, belonged to the Rathor Rajputs. The town of Kishangarh, which gave its name to the state, was founded in 1611 and was itself named after Kishen Singh, the first ruler. The maharajas succeeded in reaching terms with Akbar in the late 16th century, and again in 1818 with the British. In 1949 the state was merged into Rajasthan.

RULERS

Sardul Singh, VS1936-1957/1879-1900AD
Madan Singh, VS1957-1983/1900-1926AD
Yaghyanarayan Singh, VS1983-1995/1926-1938AD
Sumer Singh, VS1995-2000/1938-1949AD

MINT

Kishangarh 

Mint mark: 

Symbol on reverse: Jhar

ANONYMOUS HAMMERED "DUMP" COINAGE

First Series

Y# 9 1/8 RUPEE Weight: 1.3500 g. **Composition:** Silver **Obverse:** Inscription: Nagari "Chadi" (silver) **Reverse:** Jhar

Date	VG	F	VF	XF	Unc
ND(ca.1902-38)	40.00	65.00	100	150	—

Y# 10 1/4 RUPEE Weight: 2.7000 g. **Composition:** Silver **Obverse:** Inscription: Nagari "Chadi" (silver) **Reverse:** Jhar

Date	VG	F	VF	XF	Unc
ND(ca.1902-38)	40.00	65.00	100	150	—

Y# 11 1/2 RUPEE Weight: 5.4000 g. **Composition:** Silver **Obverse:** Inscription: Nagari "Chadi" (silver) **Reverse:** Jhar

Date	VG	F	VF	XF	Unc
ND(ca.1902-38)	40.00	65.00	100	150	—
ND(ca. 1902-38)	40.00	65.00	100	150	—

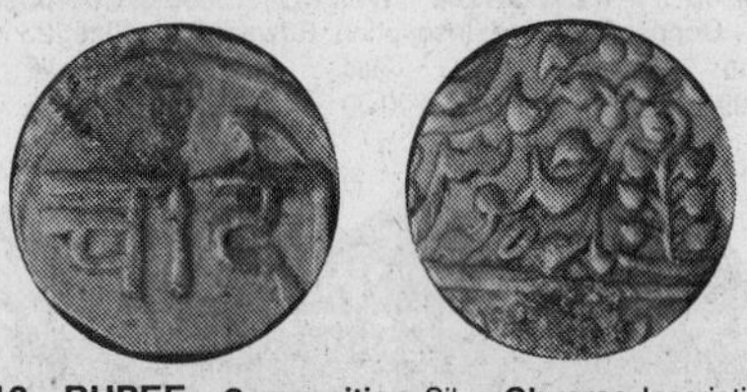

Y# 12 RUPEE Composition: Silver **Obverse:** Inscription: Nagari "Chadi" (silver) **Reverse:** Jhar **Note:** 10.85-11.05 grams

Date	VG	F	VF	XF	Unc
ND(ca.1902-38)	25.00	40.00	60.00	90.00	—

ANONYMOUS HAMMERED "DUMP" COINAGE

Second Series

Denominations in Nagari, Persian and "merchants numerals", in Annas on obverse.

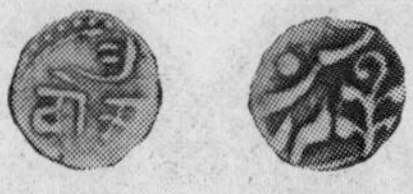

Y# 13 2 ANNAS Weight: 1.3200 g. **Composition:** Silver **Reverse:** Jhar

Date	VG	F	VF	XF	Unc
ND(ca.1902-38)	15.00	25.00	40.00	60.00	—

Y# 14 4 ANNAS Weight: 2.6200 g. **Composition:** Silver **Reverse:** Jhar

Date	VG	F	VF	XF	Unc
ND(ca.1902-38)	12.50	20.00	30.00	50.00	—

Y# 15 8 ANNAS Weight: 5.3500 g. **Composition:** Silver **Reverse:** Jhar

Date	VG	F	VF	XF	Unc
ND(ca.1902-38)	15.00	25.00	40.00	60.00	—

HAMMERED "DUMP" COINAGE

1900-1926AD

Y# B3 1/4 RUPEE Weight: 2.7000 g. **Composition:** Silver **Obverse:** Inscription: Edward (VII)... **Reverse:** Jhar; inscription: Madan Singh...

Date	VG	F	VF	XF	Unc
ND(1902)	12.50	20.00	28.50	40.00	—

Y# A3 1/2 RUPEE Weight: 5.4000 g. **Composition:** Silver **Obverse:** Inscription: Empress Victoria... **Reverse:** Jhar; inscription: Madan Singh...

Date	VG	F	VF	XF	Unc
ND(1900-01)	40.00	65.00	100	145	—

Y# 3 1/2 RUPEE Weight: 5.4000 g. **Composition:** Silver **Obverse:** Inscription: Edward (VII)... **Reverse:** Jhar; inscription: Madan Singh...

Date	VG	F	VF	XF	Unc
1902	12.50	20.00	28.00	40.00	—

Y# C3 RUPEE Weight: 10.8000 g. **Composition:** Silver **Obverse:** Inscription: Empress Victoria... **Reverse:** Jhar; inscription: Madan Singh...

Date	VG	F	VF	XF	Unc
ND(1900-01)	—	—	—	—	—

Y# D3 MOHUR Weight: 10.9000 g. **Composition:** Gold **Obverse:** Inscription: Empress Victoria... **Reverse:** Jhar; inscription: Madan Singh...

Date	VG	F	VF	XF	Unc
ND(1900-01)	200	300	550	900	—

HAMMERED "DUMP" COINAGE

1926-1938AD

Y# 4 1/4 RUPEE Weight: 2.7000 g. **Composition:** Silver **Obverse:** Inscription: George (V)... **Reverse:** Jhar; inscription: Yaghyanarayan...

Date	VG	F	VF	XF	Unc
ND(1926-38)	12.50	20.00	28.50	40.00	—

Y# 5 1/2 RUPEE Weight: 5.4000 g. **Composition:** Silver **Obverse:** Inscription: George (V)... **Reverse:** Jhar; inscription: Yaghyanarayan...

Date	VG	F	VF	XF	Unc
ND(1926-38)	12.50	20.00	28.50	40.00	—

Y# 6 RUPEE Weight: 10.8000 g. **Composition:** Silver **Obverse:** Inscription: George (V)... **Reverse:** Jhar; inscription: Yaghyanarayan...

Date	VG	F	VF	XF	Unc
ND(1926-38)	18.50	31.50	42.50	60.00	—

Y# 6a NAZARANA RUPEE Composition: Silver **Obverse:** Inscription: George (V)... **Reverse:** Jhar; inscription: Yaghyanarayan... **Note:** 10.70-10.80 grams

Date	VG	F	VF	XF	Unc
ND(1926-38)	60.00	100	140	200	—

Y# 7 1/2 MOHUR Composition: Gold **Obverse:** Inscription: George (V)... **Reverse:** Jhar; inscription: Yaghyanarayan... **Note:** Ca. 5.50 grams

Date	VG	F	VF	XF	Unc
ND(1926-38)	135	225	550	850	—

Y# 8 MOHUR **Composition:** Gold **Obverse:** Inscription: George (V)... **Reverse:** Jhar; inscription: Yaghyanarayan... **Note:** Ca. 11.00 grams

Date	VG	F	VF	XF	Unc
ND(1926-38)	185	300	500	800	—

KUTCH

State located in northwest India, consisting of a peninsula north of the Gulf of Kutch.

The rulers of Kutch were Jareja Rajputs who, coming from Tatta in Sind, conquered Kutch in the 14th or 15th centuries. The capital city of Bhuj is thought to date from the mid-16th century. In 1617, after Akbar's conquest of Gujerat and the fall of the Gujerat sultans, the Kutch ruler, Rao Bharmal I (1586-1632) visited Jahangir and established a relationship which was sufficiently warm as to leave Kutch virtually independent throughout the Mughal period. Early in the 19th century internal disorder and the existence of rival claimants to the throne resulted in British intrusion into the state's affairs. Rao Bharmalji II was deposed in favor of Rao Desalji II who proved much more amenable to the Government of India's wishes. He and his successors continued to rule in a manner considered by the British to be most enlightened and, as a result, Maharao Khengarji III was created a Knight Grand Commander of the Indian Empire. In view of its geographical isolation Kutch came under the direct control of the Central Government at India's independence.

First coinage was struck in 1617AD.

RULERS

Khengarji III, VS1932-1999/1875-1942AD

M(a)-ha-ra-o Sri Khen-ga-r-ji

मा हा रा उ खेंगारजी

Ma-ha-ra-o Khen-ga-r-ji

मा हाराजा।धिराज।मिरजा महाराओश्री

Ma-ha-ra-ja Dhi-ra-j Mi-r-ja M(a)-ha-ra-o Sri

खेंगारजी बहादरकछभुज

Khen-ga-r-ji B(a)-ha-du-r K(a)-chh-bhu-j

।मिरजामहाराओश्री खेंगारजी

Mi-r-jan M(a)-ha-ra-o Sri Khen-ga-r-ji

महाराओं श्री खेंगारजी

M(a)-ha-ra-o Sri Khen-ga-r-ji

महाराजा।धिराज।मिरजा महाराउ

M(a)-ha-ra-ja Dhi-ra-j Mi-r-jan M(a)-ha-ra-o

श्री खेंगारजीबहादर

Sri-Khen-ga-r-ji B(a)-ha-du-r

श्री खेंगारजीसवाई बहादर

Sri Khen-ga-r-ji Sa-va-i B(a)-ha-du-r

महाराउश्री खेंगारजी क छभुज

M(a)-ha-ra-o Sri Khen-ga-r-ji K(a)-chchh-bhu-j

Vijayarajji
VS1999-2004/1942-1947AD

।विजयराजजी

Vi-j(a)-y(a)-ra-j-ji

महाराओश्री ।विजय राजजी

M(a)-ha-ra-o Sri Vi-j(a)-y(a)-ra-j-ji K(a)-chchh 2000

Madanasinhji

मदन।सिंहजी

M(a)-d(a)-n(a)-sin-h-ji

Pragmalji III & Maharani Pritidevi, VS2048-/1991AD-

MINT

भुज or بهوج

Bhuj (Devanagari) (Persian)

KINGDOM

Khengarji III
VS1932-98/1875-1942AD

MILLED COINAGE
Regal Issues - Second Series

Y# 35.1 KORI **Weight:** 4.7000 g. **Composition:** 0.6100 Silver .0921 oz. ASW **Obverse:** Inscription: Victoria, Empress of India **Reverse:** Open crescent

Date	Good	VG	F	VF	XF
1901/VS1957	1.25	3.00	4.50	6.50	10.00

Y# 37.6 5 KORI **Weight:** 13.8700 g. **Composition:** 0.9370 Silver .4178 oz. ASW **Obverse:** Inscription: Victoria, Empress of India

Date	Good	VG	F	VF	XF
1899/VS1955	—	6.50	10.00	15.00	22.50
1899/VS1956	—	6.50	10.00	15.00	22.50
1901/VS1957	7.00	17.50	25.00	35.00	50.00

MILLED COINAGE
Regal Issues - Third Series

Y# 38 TRAMBIYO **Weight:** 4.0000 g. **Composition:** Copper **Obverse:** Inscription: Edward VII...

Date	Good	VG	F	VF	XF
1908/VS1965	0.60	1.50	2.50	3.50	4.50
1909/VS1965	0.25	0.60	1.00	1.50	2.50
1909/VS1966	0.25	0.60	1.00	1.50	2.00
1910/VS1966	0.85	1.65	2.75	4.25	6.00

Y# 39 DOKDO **Weight:** 8.0000 g. **Composition:** Copper **Obverse:** Inscription: Edward VII...

Date	Good	VG	F	VF	XF
1909/VS1965	0.30	0.75	1.25	1.50	2.00
1909/VS1966	0.30	0.75	1.25	1.50	2.00

Y# 40 1-1/2 DOKDA **Weight:** 12.0000 g. **Composition:** Copper **Obverse:** Inscription: Edward VII... **Size:** 23 mm.

Date	Good	VG	F	VF	XF
1909/VS1965	30.00	60.00	100	115	150

Y# 41 3 DOKDA **Weight:** 24.0000 g. **Composition:** Copper **Obverse:** Inscription: Edward VII...

Date	Good	VG	F	VF	XF
1909/VS1965	30.00	60.00	100	115	150

Y# 45 5 KORI **Weight:** 13.8700 g. **Composition:** 0.9370 Silver .4178 oz. ASW **Obverse:** Inscription: Edward VII...

Date	Good	VG	F	VF	XF
1902/VS1959	60.00	120	185	250	375
1903/VS1960	60.00	120	185	250	375
1904/VS1961	60.00	120	185	250	375
1905/VS1962	60.00	120	185	250	375
1906/VS1963	60.00	120	185	250	375
1907/VS1964	60.00	120	185	250	375
1908/VS1965	50.00	100	150	235	350
1909/VS1966	50.00	100	150	235	350

MILLED COINAGE
Regal Issues - Fourth Series

Y# 46 TRAMBIYO **Weight:** 4.0000 g. **Composition:** Copper **Obverse:** Inscription: George V...

Date	Good	VG	F	VF	XF
1919/VS1976	0.10	0.30	0.50	0.75	1.00
1920/VS1976	0.10	0.30	0.50	0.75	1.50
1920/VS1977	0.10	0.30	0.50	0.75	1.50

Y# 54 TRAMBIYO **Weight:** 4.0000 g. **Composition:** Copper **Obverse:** Inscription: George V...

Date	Good	VG	F	VF	XF
1928/VS1984	0.25	0.60	1.00	2.00	3.00
1928/VS1985	0.10	0.30	0.50	0.75	1.00

Y# 47 DOKDO **Weight:** 8.0000 g. **Composition:** Copper **Obverse:** Inscription: George V...

Date	Good	VG	F	VF	XF
1920/VS1976	0.25	0.60	1.00	1.25	2.00
1920/VS1977	0.25	0.60	1.00	1.25	2.00

Y# 55 DOKDO **Weight:** 8.0000 g. **Composition:** Copper **Obverse:** Inscription: George V...

Date	Good	VG	F	VF	XF
1922/VS1982 (sic)	0.50	1.25	1.75	2.50	3.50
1928/VS1984	0.25	0.60	1.00	1.25	1.50
1929/VS1985	0.25	0.60	1.00	1.25	1.50

Y# 48 1-1/2 DOKDA **Weight:** 12.0000 g. **Composition:** Copper **Obverse:** Inscription: George V...

Date	Good	VG	F	VF	XF
1926/VS1982	0.35	0.90	1.50	2.50	3.00

Y# 56 1-1/2 DOKDA **Weight:** 12.0000 g. **Composition:** Copper **Obverse:** Inscription: George V...

Date	Good	VG	F	VF	XF
1928/VS1985	0.20	0.50	0.75	1.00	1.50
1929/VS1985	0.20	0.50	0.75	1.00	1.50
1929/VS1986	0.20	0.50	0.75	1.00	1.50
1931/VS1987	0.20	0.50	0.75	1.00	1.50
1931/VS1988	0.20	0.50	0.75	1.00	1.50
1932/VS1988	0.40	1.00	1.50	2.50	4.00
1932/VS1989	0.20	0.50	0.75	1.00	1.50

Y# 49 3 DOKDA **Weight:** 24.0000 g. **Composition:** Copper **Obverse:** Inscription: George V...

Date	Good	VG	F	VF	XF
1926/VS1982	0.60	1.50	2.50	3.50	4.50

Y# 57 3 DOKDA **Weight:** 24.0000 g. **Composition:** Copper **Obverse:** Inscription: George V...

Date	Good	VG	F	VF	XF
1928/VS1985	0.25	0.60	1.00	1.50	2.25
1929/VS1985	0.25	0.60	1.00	1.50	2.25
1929/VS1986	0.25	0.60	1.00	1.50	2.25
1930/VS1987	0.25	0.60	1.00	1.50	2.25
1931/VS1987	0.25	0.60	1.00	1.50	2.25
1934/VS1990	0.25	0.60	1.00	1.50	2.25
1934/VS1991	0.25	0.60	1.00	1.50	2.25
1935/VS1992	0.25	0.60	1.00	1.50	2.25

Y# 58 1/2 KORI **Weight:** 2.3500 g. **Composition:** 0.6010 Silver .0460 oz. ASW **Obverse:** Inscription: George V...

Date	Good	VG	F	VF	XF
1928/VS1985	0.75	2.00	3.00	4.00	7.00

Y# 51 KORI **Weight:** 4.7000 g. **Composition:** 0.6010 Silver .0921 oz. ASW **Obverse:** Inscription: George V...

Date	VG	F	VF	XF	Unc
1913/VS1970	0.75	2.00	3.00	4.00	7.00
1923/VS1979	0.75	2.00	3.00	4.00	7.00
1923/VS1980	0.75	2.00	3.00	4.00	7.00
1927/VS1984	1.00	2.50	3.50	5.00	8.00

Y# 59 KORI **Weight:** 4.7000 g. **Composition:** 0.6010 Silver .0921 oz. ASW **Obverse:** Inscription: George V...

Date	VG	F	VF	XF	Unc
1928/VS1985	1.00	2.50	3.50	5.00	8.00
1929/VS1985	1.00	2.50	3.50	5.00	8.00
1931/VS1987	2.75	6.50	10.00	15.00	22.50
1931/VS1988	1.00	2.50	3.00	5.00	8.00
1932/VS1988	1.00	2.50	3.00	5.00	8.00
1932/VS1989	1.00	2.50	3.00	5.00	8.00
1933/VS1989	1.00	2.50	3.00	5.00	8.00
1933/VS1990	1.00	2.50	3.00	5.00	8.00
1934/VS1990	1.00	2.50	3.00	5.00	8.00
1934/VS1991	1.00	2.50	3.00	5.00	8.00
1935/VS1991	1.00	2.50	3.00	5.00	8.00
1935/VS1992	1.00	2.50	3.00	5.00	8.00
1936/VS1992	1.25	3.00	4.50	6.50	10.00

Y# 52 2-1/2 KORI **Weight:** 6.9350 g. **Composition:** 0.9370 Silver .2089 oz. ASW **Obverse:** Inscription: George V...

Date	VG	F	VF	XF	Unc
1916/VS1973	1.50	4.00	6.00	9.00	13.50
1917/VS1973	1.50	4.00	6.00	9.00	13.50
1917/VS1974	1.50	4.00	6.00	9.00	13.50
1918/VS1974	1.50	4.00	6.00	9.00	13.50
1919/VS1975	1.50	4.00	6.00	9.00	13.50
1922/VS1978	1.50	4.00	6.00	9.00	13.50
1922/VS1979	1.50	4.00	6.00	9.00	13.50
1924/VS1981	1.50	4.00	6.00	9.00	13.50
1926/VS1983	1.50	4.00	6.00	9.00	13.50

Y# 52a 2-1/2 KORI **Weight:** 6.9350 g. **Composition:** 0.9370 Silver .2089 oz. ASW **Obverse:** Inscription: George V... **Reverse:** Smaller legend

Date	VG	F	VF	XF	Unc
1927/VS1984	2.00	5.00	7.00	10.00	15.00
1928/VS1985	1.50	4.00	6.00	9.00	13.50
1930/VS1986	1.50	4.00	6.00	9.00	13.50
1930/VS1987	1.50	4.00	6.00	9.00	13.50
1932/VS1988	1.50	4.00	6.00	9.00	13.50
1932/VS1989	1.50	4.00	6.00	9.00	13.50
1933/VS1989	1.50	4.00	6.00	9.00	13.50
1933/VS1990	1.50	4.00	6.00	9.00	13.50
1934/VS1990	1.50	4.00	6.00	9.00	13.50
1934/VS1991	1.50	4.00	6.00	9.00	13.50
1935/VS1991	1.50	4.00	6.00	9.00	13.50
1935/VS1992	1.50	4.00	6.00	9.00	13.50

Y# 53 5 KORI **Weight:** 13.8700 g. **Composition:** 0.9370 Silver .4178 oz. ASW **Obverse:** Inscription: George V... **Note:** 5 Kori coins were issued with reeded edges until 1928AD, which is when the security edge was introduced. Due to counterfeiting the government recalled pieces and added lettering as s mark of authentication.

Date	VG	F	VF	XF	Unc
1913/VS1970	2.75	6.50	10.00	15.00	22.50
1915/VS1972	2.75	6.50	10.00	15.00	22.50
1916/VS1973	2.75	6.50	10.00	15.00	22.50
1916/VS1975 (Sic)	5.00	12.50	18.50	25.00	35.00
1917/VS1973	2.75	6.50	10.00	15.00	22.50
1917/VS1974	2.75	6.50	10.00	15.00	22.50
1918/VS1974	2.75	6.50	10.00	15.00	22.50
1918/VS1975	2.75	6.50	10.00	15.00	22.50
1919/VS1975	2.75	6.50	10.00	15.00	22.50
1919/VS1976	12.50	25.00	37.50	50.00	70.00
1920/VS1977	3.00	7.50	11.50	16.50	25.00
1921/VS1977	2.75	6.50	10.00	15.00	22.50
1921/VS1978	2.75	6.50	10.00	15.00	22.50
1922/VS1974 (Sic)	—	—	—	—	—
1922/VS1978	2.75	6.50	10.00	15.00	22.50
1922/VS1979	2.75	6.50	10.00	15.00	22.50
1922/VS1982 (Sic)	3.00	7.50	12.50	18.50	27.50
1923/VS1979	2.75	6.50	10.00	15.00	22.50
1924/VS1978 (Sic)	10.00	20.00	31.50	42.50	60.00
1924/VS1980	2.75	6.50	10.00	15.00	22.50
1924/VS1981	2.75	6.50	10.00	15.00	22.50
1925/VS1982	2.75	6.50	10.00	15.00	22.50
1926/VS1978 (Sic)	5.00	12.50	18.50	25.00	35.00
1926/VS1982	2.75	6.50	10.00	15.00	22.50
1926/VS1893	2.75	6.50	10.00	15.00	22.50
1927/VS1984	7.00	17.50	25.00	35.00	50.00
1927/VS1984 Proof	—	Value: 275			

Y# 53a 5 KORI **Weight:** 13.8700 g. **Composition:** 0.9370 Silver .4178 oz. ASW **Obverse:** Inscription: George V...; smaller legend **Reverse:** Smaller legend

Date	VG	F	VF	XF	Unc
1928/VS1985	6.00	15.00	21.50	30.00	40.00
1929/VS1986	2.75	6.50	10.00	15.00	22.50
1930/VS1986	2.75	6.50	10.00	15.00	22.50
1930/VS1987	2.75	6.50	10.00	15.00	22.50
1931/VS1987	2.75	6.50	10.00	15.00	22.50
1931/VS1988	2.75	6.50	10.00	15.00	22.50
1932/VS1988	2.75	6.50	10.00	15.00	22.50
1932/VS1989	2.75	6.50	10.00	15.00	22.50
1933/VS1989	2.75	6.50	10.00	15.00	22.50
1933/VS1990	2.75	6.50	10.00	15.00	22.50
1934/VS1990	2.75	6.50	10.00	15.00	22.50
1934/VS1991	2.75	6.50	10.00	15.00	22.50
1935/VS1991	2.75	6.50	10.00	15.00	22.50
1935/VS1992	2.75	6.50	10.00	15.00	22.50
1936/VS1992	2.75	6.50	10.00	15.00	22.50

MILLED COINAGE

Regal Issues - Fifth Series

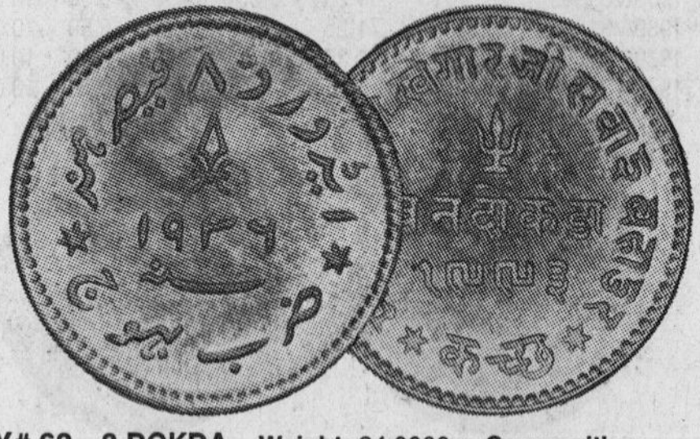

Y# 63 3 DOKDA **Weight:** 24.0000 g. **Composition:** Copper **Obverse:** Inscription: Edward VIII...

Date	Good	VG	F	VF	XF
1936/VS1993	1.25	3.00	5.00	7.50	10.00

Y# 65 KORI **Weight:** 4.7000 g. **Composition:** 0.6010 Silver .0921 oz. ASW **Obverse:** Inscription: Edward VIII...

Date	VG	F	VF	XF	Unc
1936/VS1992	1.25	3.00	4.50	6.50	10.00
1936/VS1993	1.25	3.00	4.50	6.50	10.00

Y# 66 2-1/2 KORI **Weight:** 6.9350 g. **Composition:** 0.9370 Silver .2089 oz. ASW **Obverse:** Inscription: Edward VIII...

Date	VG	F	VF	XF	Unc
1936/VS1992	5.00	11.50	17.50	23.50	32.50
1936/VS1993	5.00	11.50	17.50	23.50	32.50

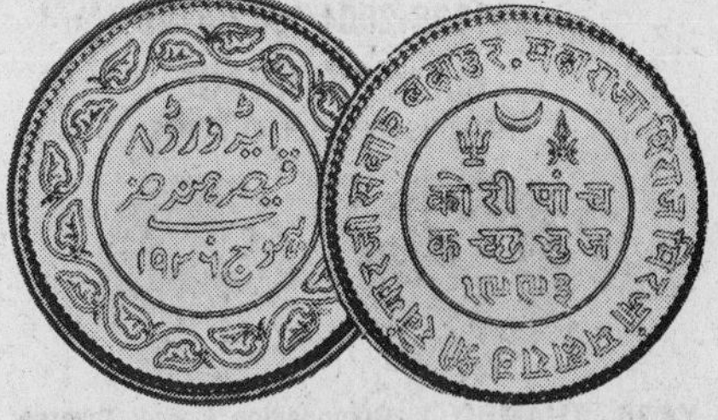

Y# 67 5 KORI **Weight:** 13.8700 g. **Composition:** 0.9370 Silver .4178 oz. ASW **Obverse:** Inscription: Edward VIII...

Date	VG	F	VF	XF	Unc
1936/VS1992	2.00	5.00	7.00	10.00	15.00
1936/VS1993	2.00	5.00	7.00	10.00	15.00

MILLED COINAGE

Regal Issues - Sixth Series

Y# 71 3 DOKDA **Weight:** 24.0000 g. **Composition:** Copper **Obverse:** Inscription: George VI

Date	Good	VG	F	VF	XF
1937/VS1993	0.35	0.90	1.50	2.00	3.00

Y# 73 KORI **Weight:** 4.7000 g. **Composition:** 0.6010 Silver .0921 oz. ASW **Obverse:** Inscription: George VI

Date	VG	F	VF	XF	Unc
1937/VS1993	1.25	3.00	4.50	6.50	10.00
1937/VS1994	1.25	3.00	4.50	6.50	10.00
1938/VS1995	1.25	3.00	4.50	6.50	10.00
1939/VS1995	1.25	3.00	4.50	6.50	10.00
1939/VS1996	1.25	3.00	4.50	6.50	10.00
1940/VS1996	1.25	3.00	4.50	6.50	10.00

Y# 74 2-1/2 KORI **Weight:** 6.9350 g. **Composition:** 0.9370 Silver .2089 oz. ASW **Obverse:** Inscription: George VI

Date	VG	F	VF	XF	Unc
1937/VS1993	2.00	5.00	7.00	10.00	15.00

Y# 75 5 KORI **Weight:** 13.8700 g. **Composition:** 0.9370 Silver .4178 oz. ASW **Obverse:** Inscription: George VI

Date	VG	F	VF	XF	Unc
1936/VS1993	3.00	7.50	11.50	16.50	25.00
1937/VS1993	2.75	6.50	10.00	15.00	22.50
1937/VS1994	2.75	6.50	10.00	15.00	22.50
1938/VS1994	2.75	6.50	10.00	15.00	22.50
1938/VS1995	2.75	6.50	10.00	15.00	22.50
1941/VS1997	4.00	10.00	15.00	21.50	30.00
1941/VS1998	2.75	6.50	10.00	15.00	22.50

Vijayarajji

VS1998-2004/1942-47AD

MILLED COINAGE

Regal Issues - Sixth Series

Y# 76 TRAMBIYO **Composition:** Copper **Obverse:** Inscription: George VI

Date	VG	F	VF	XF	Unc
1943/VS2000	0.10	0.25	0.50	1.00	1.50
1944/VS2000	0.10	0.25	0.50	1.00	1.50

Y# 78 DHABU (1/8 Kori = 3 Dokda) **Composition:** Copper **Obverse:** Inscription: George VI

Date	VG	F	VF	XF	Unc
1943/VS1999	0.10	0.25	0.40	0.65	1.00
1943/VS2000	0.10	0.25	0.40	0.65	1.00
1944/VS2000	0.10	0.25	0.40	0.65	1.00
1947/VS2004	0.10	0.25	0.40	0.65	1.00

Y# 77 DHINGLO (1/16 Kori = 1-1/2 Dokda) **Composition:** Copper **Obverse:** Inscription: George VI

Date	VG	F	VF	XF	Unc
1943/VS2000	0.10	0.25	0.40	0.65	1.00
1944/VS2000	0.10	0.25	0.40	0.65	1.00
1947/VS2004	0.10	0.25	0.40	0.65	1.00
1948/VS2004	0.20	0.50	1.00	2.00	3.50

Y# 79 PAYALO (1/4 Kori) **Composition:** Copper **Obverse:** Inscription: George VI

Date	VG	F	VF	XF	Unc
1943/VS1999	0.30	0.75	1.00	1.50	2.50
1943/VS2000	0.30	0.75	1.00	1.50	2.50
1944/VS2000	0.30	0.75	1.00	1.50	2.50
1944/VS2001	0.30	0.75	1.00	1.50	2.50
1945/VS2001	0.15	0.35	0.50	0.75	1.25
1945/VS2002	0.15	0.35	0.50	0.75	1.25
1946/VS2002	0.15	0.35	0.50	0.75	1.25
1946/VS2003	0.15	0.35	0.50	0.75	1.25
1947/VS2003	0.30	0.75	1.00	1.50	2.50

Y# 80 ADHIO (1/2 Kori) **Composition:** Copper **Obverse:** Inscription: George VI

Date	VG	F	VF	XF	Unc
1943/VS1999	0.60	1.50	1.75	2.00	3.50
1943/VS2000	0.60	1.50	1.75	2.00	3.50
1944/VS2001	0.60	1.25	1.50	1.75	3.00
1945/VS2001	0.60	1.50	1.75	2.00	3.50
1945/VS2002	0.60	1.50	1.75	2.00	3.50
1946/VS2002	0.60	1.50	1.75	2.00	3.50

Y# 81 KORI **Weight:** 4.7000 g. **Composition:** 0.6010 Silver .0921 oz. ASW **Obverse:** Inscription: George VI

Date	VG	F	VF	XF	Unc
1942/VS1999	1.00	2.50	3.50	5.00	8.00
1943/VS1999	1.00	2.50	3.50	5.00	8.00
1943/VS2000	1.00	2.50	3.50	5.00	8.00
1944/VS2000	1.00	2.50	3.50	5.00	8.00
1944/VS2001	1.00	2.50	3.50	5.00	8.00

Y# A81 KORI **Weight:** 4.6600 g. **Composition:** Silver **Obverse:** Inscription: George VI **Note:** Similar to Y#51.

Date	VG	F	VF	XF	Unc
1942/VS1998 Rare	—	—	—	—	—

Y# 82 5 KORI **Weight:** 13.8700 g. **Composition:** 0.9370 Silver .4178 oz. ASW **Obverse:** Inscription: George VI

Date	VG	F	VF	XF	Unc
1942/VS1998	2.75	6.50	10.00	15.00	22.50
1942/VS1999	2.75	6.50	10.00	15.00	22.50

Y# 82A 10 KORI **Weight:** 17.3900 g. **Composition:** Silver **Obverse:** Inscription: George VI

Date	VG	F	VF	XF	Unc
1943/VS1999 Rare	—	—	—	—	—

Madanasinghji

VS2004-05/1947-48AD

MILLED COINAGE

Regal Issues - Sixth Series

Y# 83 DHABU (1/8 Kori) **Composition:** Copper **Subject:** Victory for Indian Independence

Date	VG	F	VF	XF	Unc
VS2004/1947	0.30	0.75	1.25	1.75	3.00

Y# 84 KORI **Weight:** 4.7000 g. **Composition:** 0.6010 Silver .0921 oz. ASW **Subject:** Victory for Indian Independence

Date	VG	F	VF	XF	Unc
VS2004/1947	—	5.00	7.00	10.00	15.00

Y# 85 5 KORI **Weight:** 13.8700 g. **Composition:** 0.9370 Silver .4178 oz. ASW **Subject:** Victory for Indian Independence

Date	VG	F	VF	XF	Unc
VS2004/1947	—	80.00	125	170	240

LUNAVADA

This small state in the Panch Mahal district of western India was ruled by Solanki Rajputs who claimed descent from Sidraj Jaisingh, the ruler of Anhalwara Patan and Gujerat. The rulers, or maharanas, traced their sovereignty to the early decades of the 15th century. At different times the State was feudatory to either Baroda or Sindhia.

Wakhat Singhji
VS1924-1986/1867-1929AD

HAMMERED 'DUMP' COINAGE

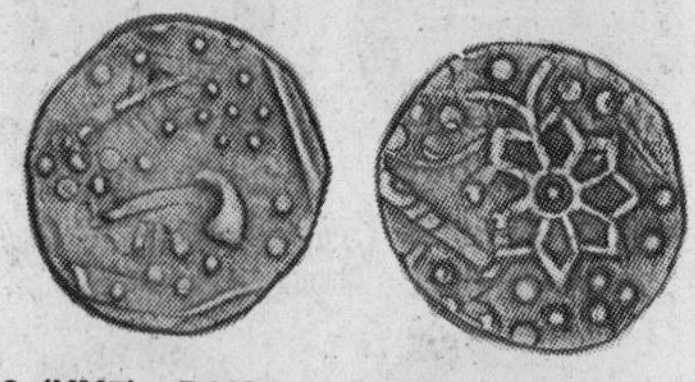

KM# 12 (KM7) PAISA Composition: Copper **Obverse:** Lotus Blossom **Reverse:** Persian legend **Note:** Round, weight varies 6.5-8.3 grams.

Date	Good	VG	F	VF	XF
ND(ca.1911)	2.50	4.00	5.50	8.50	—
ND(ca.1911)	2.50	4.00	5.50	8.50	—
VS1968(1911)	2.50	4.00	5.50	8.50	—
VS1968(1911)	2.50	4.00	5.50	8.50	—

MAKRAI

Raja Bharat Shah
1886-1920AD

HAMMERED 'DUMP' COINAGE

KM# 1 PAISA Composition: Copper **Obverse:** Katar **Reverse:** Hindi legend "Shri/Mak/Rai" **Note:** Weight varies 9-11 grams.

Date	Good	VG	F	VF	XF
ND(1886-1920)	2.50	4.00	6.00	9.00	—

KM# 2 PAISA Composition: Copper **Obverse:** Katar **Reverse:** Hindi legend "Shri/Mak/Rai" **Note:** Square, weight varies 9-11 grams.

Date	Good	VG	F	VF	XF
ND(1886-1920)	3.50	6.00	9.00	13.50	—

MEWAR

State located in Rajputana, northwest India. Capital:Udaipur.

The rulers of Mewar were universally regarded as the highest ranking Rajput house in India. The maharana of Mewar was looked upon as the representative of Rama, the ancient king of Ayodhya - and the family who were Sesodia Rajputs of the Gehlot clan, traced its descent through Rama to Kanak Sen who ruled in the 2nd century. The clan is believed to have migrated to Chitor from Gujarat sometime in the 8th century.

None of the indigenous rulers of India resisted the Muslim invasions into India with greater tenacity than the Rajputs of Mewar. It was their proud boast that they had never permitted a daughter to go into the Mughal harem. Three times the fortress and town of Chitor had fallen to Muslim invaders, to Alauddin Khilji (1303), to Bahadur Shah of Gujarat (1534) and to Akbar (1568). Each time Chitor gradually recovered but the last was the most traumatic experience of all. Rather than to submit to the Mughal onslaught, the women burned themselves on funeral pyres in a fearful rite called jauhar, and the men fell on the swords of the invaders.

After the sacking of Chitor the rana, Udai Singh, retired to the Aravali hills where he founded Udaipur, the capital after 1570. Udai Singh's son, Partab, refused to submit to the Mughal and recovered most of the territory lost in 1568. In the early 19th century Mewar suffered much at the hands of Marathas - Holkar, Sindhia and the Pindaris - until, in 1818, the State came under British supervision. In April 1948 Mewar was merged into Rajasthan and the maharana became governor Maharaj pramukh of the new province.

RULERS

Fatteh Singh, VS1941-1986/1884-1929AD
Bhupal Singh, VS1987-2005/1930-1948AD

MINTS

Bhilwara بھیلوارا

Chitor चितोड़

Chitarkot चित्रकूट

Udaipur उदयपुर

NOTE: All Mewar coinage is struck without ruler's name, and is largely undated. Certain types were generally struck over several reigns.

UDAIPUR MINT

Swarupshahi Series
Legend: Dosit Landhan "Friendship with London".

Struck at the Udaipur Mint between ca. 1858-1920AD. Many die varieties exist.

MILLED COINAGE

Y# 7.1 1/16 RUPEE Weight: 0.6500 g. **Composition:** Silver **Series:** Swarupshahi **Obverse:** Inscription: Chitarkot/Udaipur **Note:** Struck at Udaipor Mint. Round.

Date	VG	F	VF	XF	Unc
ND(1858-1920)	2.50	3.50	5.00	8.00	—

Y# 7.2 1/16 RUPEE Weight: 0.6500 g. **Composition:** Silver **Obverse:** Inscription: Chitarkot/Udaipur **Size:** 8-10 mm. **Note:** Struck at Udaipor Mint; Swarupshahi Series. Irregular shape.

Date	VG	F	VF	XF	Unc
ND(1858-1920)	3.00	4.50	6.50	10.00	—

Y# 8 1/8 RUPEE Weight: 1.3000 g. **Composition:** Silver **Series:** Swarupshahi **Obverse:** Inscription: Chitarkot/Udaipur **Size:** 11-12 mm. **Note:** Struck at Udaipor Mint.

Date	VG	F	VF	XF	Unc
ND(1858-1920)	3.00	4.50	6.50	10.00	—

Y# 9 1/4 RUPEE Weight: 2.6000 g. **Composition:** Silver **Series:** Swarupshahi **Obverse:** Inscription: Chitarkot/Udaipur **Note:** Struck at Udaipor Mint.

Date	VG	F	VF	XF	Unc
ND(1858-1920)	2.50	3.50	5.00	8.00	—

Y# 10 1/2 RUPEE Composition: Silver **Series:** Swarupshahi **Obverse:** Inscription: Chitarkot/Udaipur **Note:** Struck at Udaipor Mint; 5.20-5.40 grams.

Date	VG	F	VF	XF	Unc
ND(1858-1920)	3.00	4.50	6.50	10.00	—

Y# 11 RUPEE Composition: Silver **Series:** Swarupshahi **Obverse:** Inscription: Chitarkot/Udaipur **Note:** Struck at Udaipor Mint; 10.75-10.85 grams.

Date	VG	F	VF	XF	Unc
ND(1858-1920)	4.00	6.00	9.00	14.00	—

Y# B12 1/8 MOHUR Weight: 1.3500 g. **Composition:** Gold **Series:** Swarupshahi **Obverse:** Inscription: Chitarkot/Udaipur **Note:** Struck at Udaipur Mint.

Date	VG	F	VF	XF	Unc
ND(1858-1920)	—	150	225	400	600

Y# A12 1/4 MOHUR Composition: Gold **Series:** Swarupshahi **Obverse:** Inscription: Chitarkot/Udaipur **Note:** Struck at Udaipur Mint; 2.70-2.75 grams.

Date	VG	F	VF	XF	Unc
ND(1858-1920)	—	150	300	500	750

Y# C12 1/2 MOHUR Weight: 5.4000 g. **Composition:** Gold **Series:** Swarupshahi **Obverse:** Inscription: Chitarkot/Udaipur **Note:** Struck at Udaipor Mint.

Date	VG	F	VF	XF	Unc
ND(1858-1920)	—	150	300	500	750

Y# 12 MOHUR Weight: 10.9500 g. **Composition:** Gold **Series:** Swarupshahi **Obverse:** Inscription: Chitarkot/Udaipur **Note:** Struck at Udaipur Mint.

Date	VG	F	VF	XF	Unc
ND(1858-1920)	—	165	225	350	525

Fatteh Singh
VS1941-1986/1884-1929AD

MILLED COINAGE

VS1985 ie. 1928AD, but actually struck at the Alipore Mint in Calcutta between 1931-1932AD, the Y#22 rupee in 1931, the rest in 1932

Y# 13 PIE Weight: 2.5000 g. **Composition:** Copper **Obverse:** Inscription: Chitor, date **Reverse:** Inscription: Udaipur **Note:** Struck at Udaipur Mint.

Date	Good	VG	F	VF	XF
VS1975(1918)	7.50	12.50	18.50	27.50	—

Y# 14 PIE Weight: 2.1000 g. **Composition:** Copper **Obverse:** Inscription: Chitor, date **Reverse:** Inscription: Udaipur **Note:** Struck at Udaipur Mint.

Date	Good	VG	F	VF	XF
VS1978(1921)	6.00	10.00	15.00	22.50	—

Y# 18 1/16 RUPEE Weight: 0.9500 g. **Composition:** Silver **Obverse:** Inscription: Chitarkot/Udaipur **Reverse:** Inscription: Dosti Lundhun (Friendship with London)

Date	Mintage	VG	F	VF	XF	Unc
VS1985(1928)	3,262,000	0.75	2.00	3.00	4.00	7.00

Y# 19 1/8 RUPEE Weight: 1.3600 g. **Composition:** Silver **Obverse:** Inscription: Chitarkot/Udaipur **Reverse:** Inscription: Dosti Lundhun (Friendship with London)

Date	Mintage	VG	F	VF	XF	Unc
VS1985(1928)	800,000	1.00	2.50	3.50	5.00	8.00

Y# 20 1/4 RUPEE **Weight:** 2.7200 g. **Composition:** Silver **Obverse:** Inscription: Chitarkot/Udaipur **Reverse:** Inscription: Dosti Lundhun (Friendship with London)

Date	Mintage	VG	F	VF	XF	Unc
VS1985(1928)	839,000	1.25	3.00	4.00	6.50	10.00

Y# 21 1/2 RUPEE **Weight:** 5.4600 g. **Composition:** Silver **Obverse:** Inscription: Chitarkot/Udaipur **Reverse:** Inscription: Dosti Lundhun (Friendship with London)

Date	Mintage	VG	F	VF	XF	Unc
VS1985(1928)	648,000	1.65	4.00	6.00	9.00	14.00

Y# 21a 1/2 RUPEE **Composition:** Gold **Obverse:** Inscription: Chitarkot/Udaipur **Reverse:** Inscription: Dosti Lundhun (Friendship with London) **Note:** 5.35-5.70 grams.

Date		VG	F	VF	XF	Unc
VS1985(1928) Proof	—	Value: 1,000				

Y# 22.1 RUPEE **Weight:** 10.8600 g. **Composition:** Silver **Obverse:** Thin legends, inscription: Chitarkot/Udaipur **Reverse:** Inscription: Dosti Lundhun (Friendship with London)

Date	Mintage	VG	F	VF	XF	Unc
VS1985(1928)	14,906,000	2.00	5.00	7.00	10.00	15.00

Y# 22.2 RUPEE **Weight:** 10.8600 g. **Composition:** Silver **Obverse:** Thick legends, inscription: Chitarkot/Udaipur **Reverse:** Inscription: Dosti Lundhun (Friendship with London)

Date	VG	F	VF	XF	Unc
VS1985(1928)	6.00	15.00	20.00	30.00	45.00

Y# 22a RUPEE **Composition:** Gold **Obverse:** Inscription: Chitarkot/Udaipur **Reverse:** Inscription: Dosti Lundhun (Friendship with London)

Date		VG	F	VF	XF	Unc
VS1985(1928) Proof	—	Value: 1,500				

Bhupal Singh
VS1987-2005/1930-1948

MILLED COINAGE

Y# 15 1/4 ANNA **Weight:** 2.2000 g. **Composition:** Copper **Obverse:** Inscription: Chitarkot/Udaipur

Date	F	VF	XF	Unc
VS1999 (1942)	0.50	0.85	1.25	2.00

Y# 16.1 1/2 ANNA **Weight:** 3.5000 g. **Composition:** Copper **Obverse:** Large inscription: Chitarkot/Udaipur

Date	F	VF	XF	Unc
VS1999 (1942)	0.50	0.85	1.25	2.00

Y# 16.2 1/2 ANNA **Weight:** 3.5000 g. **Composition:** Copper **Obverse:** Small inscription: Chitarkot/Udaipur

Date	F	VF	XF	Unc
VS1999 (1942)	0.50	0.85	1.25	2.00

Y# 17 ANNA **Weight:** 4.3000 g. **Composition:** Copper **Obverse:** Inscription: Chitarkot/Udaipur **Note:** Variations with 3 or 4 brushes exist.

Date	F	VF	XF	Unc
VS2000 (1943)	0.60	1.00	1.25	2.50

LOCAL COINAGE
Umarda

Y# 24 1/2 PAISA **Composition:** Copper **Note:** Varieties exist.

Date	Good	VG	F	VF	XF
ND(1938-1941)	0.75	1.25	1.75	2.50	—

PATTERNS
Including off metal strikes

KM#	Date	Mintage	Identification	Mkt Val
Pn1	1985(1928)	—	1/16 Rupee. Silver. Inscription: Chitor, Udaipur	—
Pn2	1985(1928)	—	1/8 Rupee. Silver. Inscription: Chitor, Udaipur	—
Pn3	1985(1928)	—	1/4 Rupee. Gold. Inscription: Chitarkot, UdaipurKM20.	750
Pn4	1985(1928)	—	1/4 Rupee. Silver. Inscription: Chitor, Udaipur	—
Pn5	1985(1928)	—	1/2 Rupee. Silver. Inscription: Chitor, Udaipur	—
Pn6	1985(1928)	—	Rupee. Silver. Inscription: Chitor, Udaipur	—

RATLAM

State located northwest of Indore in Madhya Pradesh.

The rajas of Ratlam were Rathor Rajputs, descendants of the younger branch of the Jodhpur ruling family. Ratlam became the premier Rajput state in western Malwa. The founder, Ratan Singh, received the territory as a grant from Shah Jahan in 1631. Before Maratha collapse some 15% of the state's annual revenue went to Sindhia as tribute. Under British protection it was supervised by the Central India Agency and in 1948 Ratlam became a district of Madhya Bharat.

RULERS
Ranjit Singh, VS1921-1950/1864-1893AD

MINT
Ratlam

NOTE: For 1 Paisa previously listed here refer to Banswara-IPS.

Ranjit Singh
VS1921-1950/1864-1893AD

MILLED COINAGE
WW II Emergency Issues

KM# 25 PAISA **Composition:** Copper **Obverse:** Hannman walking left **Note:** Thin, crude restrike of KM#24.

Date	VG	F	VF	XF	Unc
VS1947(1890)	0.65	1.00	1.75	—	—

Note: Restruck ca.1942-1945AD

REWA

State located in eastern north-central India.

The rulers of Rewa were Baghela Rajputs of the Solanki clan who probably migrated from Anhilwara Patan in Gujarat about the 11th century. Arriving in Bundelkhand they carved out for themselves a substantial kingdom, which remained independent until 1597, when they were obliged to become Mughal tributaries under Akbar. With Mughal decline Rewa began to move once more towards independence, this time under the nominal suzerainty of the Peshwa. In 1812 the raja of Rewa, Jai Singh Deo was coerced into a treaty with the British and, failing to observe its conditions, was forced to yield to British control in 1813-1814. In 1948 Rewa was merged into Vindhya Pradesh.

RULERS
Venkat Raman Singh, VS1937-1975/1880-1918AD
Gulab Singh, VS1975-2003/1918-1946AD

Gulab Singh
VS1975-2003/1918-1946AD

MILLED COINAGE

KM# 29 1/2 RUPEE **Composition:** Silver **Note:** Accession; thin flan.

Date	VG	F	VF	XF	Unc
VS1975(1918)	18.50	31.50	42.50	60.00	—

KM# 31 RUPEE **Composition:** Silver **Obverse:** Arms **Note:** Accession; thick flan.

Date	VG	F	VF	XF	Unc
VS1975(1918)	20.00	35.00	55.00	90.00	—

KM# 33 1/2 MOHUR **Composition:** Gold **Obverse:** Arms **Note:** Accession; Weight varies 4.40-5.40 grams.

Date	VG	F	VF	XF	Unc
VS1975(1918)	200	300	425	600	—

KM# 35 MOHUR **Composition:** Gold **Obverse:** Arms **Note:** Accession; Weight varies 10.70-11.71 grams.

Date	VG	F	VF	XF	Unc
VS1975(1918)	165	225	425	600	—

KM# 36 MOHUR **Composition:** Gold **Obverse:** Arms **Note:** Weight varies 10.70-11.71 grams.

Date	VG	F	VF	XF	Unc
VS1975(1918)	165	225	425	600	—

KM# 38 MOHUR **Weight:** 11.3600 g. **Composition:** Gold **Obverse:** Arms with plain border banner below penant supporters **Note:** Weight varies 10.70-11.71 grams.

Date	VG	F	VF	XF	Unc
VS1976(1919)	225	385	550	800	—

KM# 40 MOHUR **Weight:** 8.8000 g. **Composition:** Gold **Obverse:** Arms **Note:** Reduced weight.

Date	VG	F	VF	XF	Unc
VS1977(1920)	175	265	385	650	—

SAILANA

This small state in west-central India, of slightly over one hundred square miles had once been part of Ratlam, but about 1709 it asserted its independence under the leadership of Pratab Singh, the second son of Chhatrasal. The town of Sailana was founded in 1730 by Jai Singh's successor, and from that date the state was named after it. Due to its small size and vulnerability, Sailana was obliged to become tributary to Sindhia to ensure its survival. In 1819 this payment was limited to one-third of the state's revenues. Later, under agreements of 1840 and 1860, the tribute went to the British for the support of British Indian troops in the region. Barmawal was feudatory to Sailana.

LOCAL RULERS

Jaswant Singh, 1895-1919AD
Dilip Singh Bahadur, 1919-1948

Jaswant Singh
1890-1919AD

MILLED COINAGE
Regal Issues

KM#15 1/4 ANNA **Composition:** Copper **Obverse:** Bust of King Edward VII right

Date	Mintage	VG	F	VF	XF	Unc
1908	224,000	5.00	12.50	25.00	50.00	100
1908 Proof	—	Value: 175				

KM#16 1/4 ANNA **Composition:** Copper **Obverse:** Bust of King George V left

Date	Mintage	VG	F	VF	XF	Unc
1912	224,000	1.25	3.50	6.50	12.50	25.00
1912 Proof	—	Value: 175				

TONK

Tunk

State located partially in Rajputana and in central India. Tonk was founded in 1806 by Amir Khan (d. 1834), the Pathan Pindari leader who received the territory from Holkar. Amir Khan caused great havoc in Central India by his lightning raids into neighboring states. In 1817 he was forced into submission by the East India Company and remained under British control until India's independence. In March 1948 Tonk was incorporated into Rajasthan.

RULERS

Muhammad Ibrahim Ali Khan, AH1284-1349/1868-1930AD
Muhammad Sa'adat Ali Khan, AH1349-1368/1930-1949AD

MINT MARKS

Sironj سرونج

Tonk تونک

Flower (on all) 

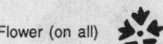

Leaf (several forms) 

Beginning with the reign of Muhammad Ibrahim Ali Khan, most coins have both AD and AH dates. Coins with both dates fully legible are worth about 20% more than listed prices. Coins with one date fully legible are worth prices shown. Coins with both dates off are of little value.

There are many minor and major variations of type, varying with location of date, orientation of leaf, arrangement of legend. Although these fall into easily distinguished patterns, they are strictly for the specialist and are omitted here.

The Tonk rupee was known as the "Chanwarshahi".

TONK MINT

NOTE: All coins with both AH and AD dates clearly readable command about a 50 percent premium.

Muhammad Ibrahim Ali Khan
AH1284-1349 / 1868-1930AD

HAMMERED "DUMP" COINAGE

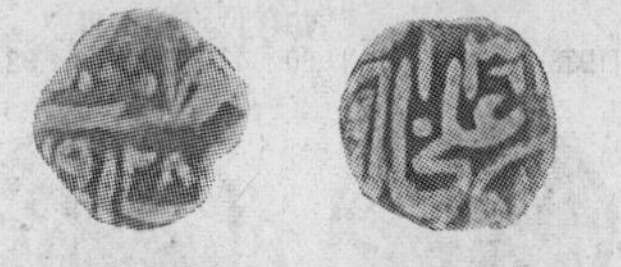

Y# A24 1/2 PAISA **Weight:** 5.4000 g. **Composition:** Copper **Obverse:** Inscription: George V... **Reverse:** Inscription: Muhammad Ibrahim Ali Khan... **Note:** Struck at Tonk Mint.

Date	Good	VG	F	VF	XF
AH13(46) (1928)	3.00	6.00	10.00	15.00	—

Y#24.1 PAISA **Weight:** 7.3000 g. **Composition:** Copper **Obverse:** Inscription: George V... **Reverse:** Inscription: Muhammad Ibrahim Ali Khan... **Note:** Struck at Tonk Mint.

Date	Good	VG	F	VF	XF
AH1329 (1911)	1.25	2.25	3.50	5.50	—
AH1329(sic) (1911)	1.25	2.25	3.50	5.50	—
1911(sic) (1911)	1.25	2.25	3.50	5.50	—
AH1329(sic) (1911)	1.25	2.25	3.50	5.50	—
AH1330 (1911)	1.25	2.25	3.50	5.50	—

Y#24.2 PAISA **Weight:** 5.0000 g. **Composition:** Copper **Obverse:** Inscription: George V... **Reverse:** Inscription: Muhammad Ibrahim Ali Khan... **Note:** Struck at Tonk Mint. Reduced weight.

Date	Good	VG	F	VF	XF
AH1335 (1917)	1.25	2.25	3.50	5.50	—
AH(13)38 (1924)	1.25	2.25	3.50	5.50	—
AH1342 (1924)	1.00	1.75	2.50	4.50	—
AH1344 (1925)	1.00	1.75	2.50	4.50	—
AH1344 (1925)	1.00	1.75	2.50	4.50	—
AH1345 (1926)	1.00	1.75	2.50	4.50	—
AH134x (1928)	1.00	1.75	2.50	4.50	—

Y# A25.1 1/4 ANNA **Weight:** 8.3000 g. **Composition:** Copper **Obverse:** Inscription: George V... **Reverse:** Inscription: Muhammad Ibrahim Ali Khan... **Note:** Struck at Tonk Mint.

Date	Good	VG	F	VF	XF
AH1335 (1917)	1.25	2.25	3.50	5.50	—
AH1336 (1917)	1.25	2.25	3.50	5.50	—

Y# A25.2 1/4 ANNA **Weight:** 5.4000 g. **Composition:** Copper **Obverse:** Inscription: George V... **Reverse:** Inscription: Muhammad Ibrahim Ali Khan... **Note:** Struck at Tonk Mint. Reduced weight.

Date	Good	VG	F	VF	XF
AH1336 (1917)	1.00	1.75	2.50	4.50	—

Y# 25 1/8 RUPEE **Composition:** Silver **Obverse:** Inscription: George V... **Reverse:** Inscription: Muhammad Ibrahim Ali Khan... **Note:** Struck at Tonk Mint. 1.34-1.45 grams.

Date	Good	VG	F	VF	XF
AH1340 (1922)	2.75	6.50	10.00	15.00	22.50
AH1346 (1928)	2.75	6.50	10.00	15.00	22.50

Y# 26 1/4 RUPEE **Composition:** Silver **Obverse:** Inscription: George V... **Reverse:** Inscription: Muhammad Ibrahim Ali Khan... **Note:** Struck at Tonk Mint. 2.68-2.90 grams.

Date	VG	F	VF	XF	Unc
AH1346 (1928)	6.50	10.00	15.00	22.50	—

Y# 27 1/2 RUPEE Composition: Silver **Obverse:** Inscription: George V... **Reverse:** Inscription: Muhammad Ibrahim Ali Khan... **Note:** Struck at Tonk Mint. 5.35-5.80 grams.

Date	VG	F	VF	XF	Unc
AH1346 (1928)	11.50	17.50	23.50	32.50	—

Y# 28 RUPEE Composition: Silver **Obverse:** Inscription: George V... **Reverse:** Inscription: Muhammad Ibrahim Ali Khan... **Note:** Struck at Tonk Mint. 10.70-11.60 grams.

Date	VG	F	VF	XF	Unc
AH1329 (1911)	5.50	8.50	13.50	20.00	—
AH1330 (1912)	5.50	8.50	13.50	20.00	—
AH1341 (1923)	5.50	8.50	13.50	20.00	—
AH1342 (1923)	5.50	8.50	13.50	20.00	—
AH1342 (1924)	5.50	8.50	13.50	20.00	—
AH1343 (1924)	5.50	8.50	13.50	20.00	—
AH1343 (1925)	5.50	8.50	13.50	20.00	—
AH1344 (1925)	5.50	8.50	13.50	20.00	—
AH1344 (1926)	5.50	8.50	13.50	20.00	—
AH1345 (1926)	5.50	8.50	13.50	20.00	—
AH1346 (1926)	5.50	8.50	13.50	20.00	—
AH1346 (1927)	5.50	8.50	13.50	20.00	—
AH1347 (1928)	5.50	8.50	13.50	20.00	—
AH1348 (1928)	5.50	8.50	13.50	20.00	—
AH1348 (1929)	5.50	8.50	13.50	20.00	—
AH134x (1930)	5.50	8.50	13.50	20.00	—

Muhammad Sa'adat Ali Khan

AH1349-1368 / 1930-1949AD

HAMMERED "DUMP" COINAGE

Y# 30 1/8 RUPEE Composition: Silver **Obverse:** Inscription: George V... **Reverse:** Inscription: Muhammad Sa'adat Ali Khan... **Note:** Struck at Tonk Mint. 1.34-1.45 grams.

Date	VG	F	VF	XF	Unc
AH1351 (1932)	4.00	6.50	10.00	15.00	—
AH1352 (1933)	4.00	6.50	10.00	15.00	—
AH1353 (1934)	4.00	6.50	10.00	15.00	—

MILLED COINAGE

KM# 29 PICE (Paisa) Composition: Copper **Obverse:** Arms **Reverse:** Leaf

Date	Mintage	VG	F	VF	XF	Unc
AH1350//1932	640,000	0.20	0.50	1.00	2.00	3.50

KM# 29a PICE (Paisa) Composition: Copper **Obverse:** Arms **Reverse:** Leaf

Date	Mintage	VG	F	VF	XF	Unc
AH1350//1932	640,000	—	0.25	0.50	1.00	1.75

TRAVANCORE

State located in extreme southwest India. A mint was established in ME965/1789-1790AD.

The region of Travancore had a lengthy history before being annexed by the Vijayanagar kingdom. With Vijayanagar's defeat at the battle of Talikota in 1565, Travancore passed under Muslim control until the late 18th century, when it merged as a state in its own right under Raja Martanda Varma. At this time the raja allied himself with British interests as a protection against the Muslim dynasty of Mysore. In 1795 the raja of Travancore officially accepted a subsidiary alliance with the East India Company, and remained within the orbit of British influence from then until India's independence.

RULERS

Rama Varma VI, ME1062-1101/1885-1924AD

Bala Rama Varma II, ME1101-1126/1924-1949AD

DATING

ME dates are of the Malabar Era. Add 824 or 825 to the ME date for the AD date. (i.e., ME1112 plus 824-825 = 1936-1937AD).

Rama Varma IV

ME1035-1055/1860-1880AD

HAMMERED "DUMP" COINAGE

KM# 21 CHUCKRAM Composition: Silver

Date	VG	F	VF	XF	Unc
ND(1860-1901)	0.85	1.40	2.00	3.00	—

Rama Varma VI

ME1062-1101 / 1885-1924AD

MILLED COINAGE

KM# 40 CASH Weight: 0.6500 g. **Composition:** Copper **Obv. Legend:** CASH 1

Date	VG	F	VF	XF	Unc
ND(1901)	—	9.00	15.00	22.50	35.00

KM# 46 CASH Weight: 0.6500 g. **Composition:** Copper **Obverse:** Sankha (conch shell) in 6-pointed star **Note:** Thick

Date	VG	F	VF	XF	Unc
ND(1901-10)	—	0.50	0.70	1.00	1.50

Note: Refer to Bala Rama Varma II listings for thin variety, KM#57

KM# 41 4 CASH Composition: Copper **Obverse:** RV monogram **Obv. Legend:** CASH FOUR **Reverse:** Sankha (conch shell) in sprays

Date	VG	F	VF	XF	Unc
ND(1901-10)	1.25	3.00	5.00	7.00	10.00

KM# 47 4 CASH Composition: Copper **Obverse:** RV monogram **Obv. Legend:** FOUR CASH **Reverse:** Malayalam "Oru Kasu" (One Cash)

Date	VG	F	VF	XF	Unc
ND(1906-35)	0.40	1.00	1.75	2.50	3.50
ND(1906-35) Proof	—	Value: 65.00			

KM# 42 8 CASH Composition: Copper **Obverse:** RV monogram **Obv. Legend:** CASH EIGHT **Reverse:** Sankha (conch shell) in sprays

Date	VG	F	VF	XF	Unc
ND(1901-10)	1.75	4.50	7.00	10.00	15.00

KM# 48 8 CASH Composition: Copper **Obverse:** RV monogram **Obv. Legend:** EIGHT CASH **Reverse:** Sankha (conch shell) in sprays

Date	VG	F	VF	XF	Unc
ND(1906-35)	0.50	1.35	2.25	3.00	5.00
ND(1906-35) Proof	—	Value: 75.00			

KM# 43 CHUCKRAM Composition: Copper **Obverse:** RV monogram **Obv. Legend:** CHUCKRAM ONE **Reverse:** Sankha (conch shell) in sprays

Date	VG	F	VF	XF	Unc
ND(1901-10)	1.75	4.50	7.00	10.00	15.00

KM# 49 CHUCKRAM Composition: Copper **Obverse:** RV monogram **Obv. Legend:** ONE CHUCKRAM **Reverse:** Sankha (conch shell) in sprays

Date	VG	F	VF	XF	Unc
ND(1906-35)	0.50	1.35	2.25	3.00	4.50

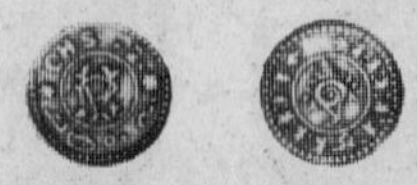

KM# 44 2 CHUCKRAMS Composition: Silver **Obverse:** RV monogram **Obv. Legend:** CHS. 2 **Reverse:** Sankha (conch shell) in sprays

Date	VG	F	VF	XF	Unc
ND(1901)	1.75	4.50	7.00	10.00	15.00

KM# 50 2 CHUCKRAMS Composition: Silver **Obverse:** RV monogram **Obv. Legend:** 2 CHS. **Reverse:** Sankha (conch shell) in sprays

Date	VG	F	VF	XF	Unc
ND(1906-28)	0.75	2.00	3.50	5.00	7.00

KM# 45 FANAM Composition: Silver **Obverse:** RV monogram **Obv. Legend:** FANAM ONE **Reverse:** Sankha (conch shell) in sprays **Edge:** Plain

Date	VG	F	VF	XF	Unc
ND(1901)	1.35	3.50	6.00	8.50	12.00

KM# 51 FANAM Composition: 0.9500 Silver **Reverse:** Sankha (conch shell) in sprays

Date	Mintage	VG	F	VF	XF	Unc
ME1086 (1909)	—	1.35	3.00	5.00	7.00	—
ME1087(1911)	1,100,000	1.25	3.00	5.00	7.00	10.00
ME1087 (1911)	1,100,000	1.35	3.00	5.00	7.00	10.00
ME1096 (1920)	350,000	1.35	3.50	6.00	8.50	12.00
ME1096(1911)	350,000	1.35	3.50	6.00	8.50	12.00
ME1099 (1923)	350,000	1.35	3.50	6.00	8.50	12.00
ME1100 (1924)	700,000	1.35	3.50	6.00	8.50	12.00
ME1103 (1927)	700,000	1.35	3.50	6.00	8.50	12.00

KM# 54 FANAM Composition: Silver **Obverse:** RV monogram **Obv. Legend:** ONE FANAM **Reverse:** Sankha (conch shell) in sprays **Edge:** Plain

Date	VG	F	VF	XF	Unc
ND(1911)	4.00	10.00	17.50	25.00	35.00

KM# 55 FANAM Composition: Silver **Obverse:** RV monogram **Obv. Legend:** FANAM ONE **Reverse:** Sankha (conch shell) in sprays **Edge:** Reeded

Date	VG	F	VF	XF	Unc
ND(1911)	1.25	3.00	5.00	7.00	10.00

KM# 52 1/4 RUPEE **Weight:** 2.7200 g. **Composition:** 0.9500 Silver .0831 oz. ASW **Obv. Legend:** RAMA VURMA-TRAVENCORE **Reverse:** Sankha (conch shell) in sprays

Date	Mintage	VG	F	VF	XF	Unc
ME1082 (1906)	—	2.50	6.00	10.00	14.00	20.00
ME1083 (1907)	—	2.50	6.00	10.00	14.00	20.00
ME1085 (1909)	—	2.50	6.00	10.00	14.00	20.00
ME1086 (1910)	—	2.50	6.00	10.00	14.00	20.00
ME1087 (1911)	400,000	1.75	4.50	7.00	10.00	15.00
ME1096 (1920)	—	1.25	3.00	5.00	7.00	10.00
ME1099 (1923)	—	1.25	3.00	5.00	7.00	10.00
ME1100 (1924)	—	1.25	3.00	5.00	7.00	10.00
ME1103 (1927)	200,000	1.25	3.00	5.00	7.00	10.00
ME1106 (1930)	200,000	1.25	3.00	5.00	7.00	10.00

KM# 53 1/2 RUPEE **Weight:** 5.4400 g. **Composition:** 0.9500 Silver .1662 oz. ASW **Reverse:** Legend shorter on bottom

Date	Mintage	VG	F	VF	XF	Unc
ME1084 (1908)	—	3.50	8.50	14.00	20.00	28.00
ME1085 (1909)	—	3.50	8.50	14.00	20.00	28.00
ME1086 (1910)	—	3.50	8.50	14.00	20.00	28.00
ME1087 (1911)	300,000	2.50	6.00	10.00	14.00	20.00
ME1103 (1927)	100,000	3.00	7.50	12.50	17.50	25.00
ME1086 (1929) Proof	—	—	—	—	—	—
ME1106 (1930)	100,000	3.00	7.50	12.50	17.50	25.00
ME1107 (1931)	800,000	2.50	6.00	10.00	14.00	20.00

Bala Rama Varma II
ME1101-1126 / 1924-1949AD

MILLED COINAGE

KM# 58 4 CASH **Composition:** Bronze **Obverse:** BRV monogram **Reverse:** Sankha (conch shell) in sprays

Date	VG	F	VF	XF	Unc
ND(1938-49)	0.25	0.60	1.00	1.50	2.25

KM# 59 8 CASH **Composition:** Bronze **Obverse:** BRV monogram **Reverse:** Sankha (conch shell) in sprays

Date	VG	F	VF	XF	Unc
ND(1938-49)	0.35	0.85	1.50	2.25	3.00

KM# 60 CHUCKRAM **Composition:** Bronze **Obverse:** Bust of Bala Rama Barma II right **Reverse:** Sankha (conch shell) in sprays

Date	VG	F	VF	XF	Unc
ME1114(1938)	0.50	1.25	2.25	3.50	5.00
ND(1939-49)	0.25	0.60	1.00	1.50	2.50

KM# 60a CHUCKRAM **Composition:** Bronze **Obverse:** Bust of Bala Rama Barma II right **Reverse:** Sankha (conch shell) in sprays

Date	VG	F	VF	XF	Unc
ND(1939-49) Prooflike; restrike	—	—	—	—	5,000

KM# 61 FANAM **Composition:** Silver **Obv. Legend:** BALA RAMA VARMA-TRAVENCORE **Reverse:** Sankha (conch shell) in sprays

Date	Mintage	VG	F	VF	XF	Unc
ME1112(1937)	350,000	1.25	3.00	5.00	7.00	10.00

KM# 65 FANAM **Composition:** 0.5000 Silver 1.51 oz. ASW **Obv. Legend:** BALA RAMA VARMA-TRAVENCORE **Reverse:** Sankha (conch shell) in sprays

Date	Mintage	VG	F	VF	XF	Unc
ME1116(1941)	2,096,000	0.35	0.90	1.50	2.00	3.00
ME1116(1941) Proof	—	Value: 50.00				
ME1118(1942)	4,157,000	0.35	0.90	1.50	2.00	3.00
ME1118(1942) Proof	—	Value: 50.00				
ME1119(1946)	1,925,000	0.50	1.25	2.25	3.50	5.00

KM# 62 1/4 RUPEE **Composition:** Silver **Obv. Legend:** BALA RAMA VARMA-TRAVENCORE

Date	Mintage	VG	F	VF	XF	Unc
ME1112(1936)	200,000	1.75	4.50	7.00	10.00	15.00

KM# 66 1/4 RUPEE **Composition:** 0.5000 Silver 2.66 oz. ASW **Obv. Legend:** BALA RAMA VARMA-TRAVENCORE

Date	Mintage	VG	F	VF	XF	Unc
ME1116(1941)	126,000	0.90	2.25	3.75	5.50	8.00
ME1116(1941) Proof	—	Value: 65.00				
ME1118(1942)	—	1.50	4.00	7.00	10.00	15.00

KM# 57 1/2 RUPEE **Weight:** 0.4800 g. **Composition:** Copper **Obverse:** Sankha (conch shell) in 6-pointed star **Reverse:** Malayalam "Oru Kasu" (one cash) **Note:** Thin

Date		VG	F	VF	XF	Unc
ND(1928-49)		—	0.15	0.25	0.35	0.50
ND(1928-49)	—	Value: 40.00				

Note: Refer to Rama Varma VI listings for thick variety, KM#46

KM# 63 1/2 RUPEE **Composition:** Silver **Obv. Legend:** BALA RAMA VARMA-TRAVENCORE

Date	Mintage	VG	F	VF	XF	Unc
ME1112(1937)	200,000	3.50	8.50	14.00	20.00	28.50

KM# 64 1/2 CHITRA RUPEE **Composition:** Silver **Obv. Legend:** BALA RAMA VARMA-TRAVENCORE **Edge:** Reeded

Date	VG	F	VF	XF	Unc
ME1114 (1938-39)	2.50	6.00	10.00	14.00	20.00

KM# 67 1/2 CHITRA RUPEE **Composition:** 0.5000 Silver 5.31 oz. ASW **Obv. Legend:** BALA RAMA VARMA-TRAVENCORE **Edge:** Security

Date	Mintage	VG	F	VF	XF	Unc
ME1116(1941)	1,600,000	1.25	3.00	5.00	7.00	10.00
ME1118/6(194	1,111,000	1.50	4.00	7.00	10.00	15.00
ME1118(1942)	Inc. above	1.25	3.00	5.00	7.00	10.00
ME1118(1942) Proof	—	Value: 75.00				
ME1121(1946)	200,000	1.25	3.00	5.00	7.00	10.00

PATTERNS
Including off metal strikes

KM#	Date	Mintage	Identification	Mkt Val
Pn3	1086(1909)	—	1/4 Rupee. Bronze. KM#52	75.00

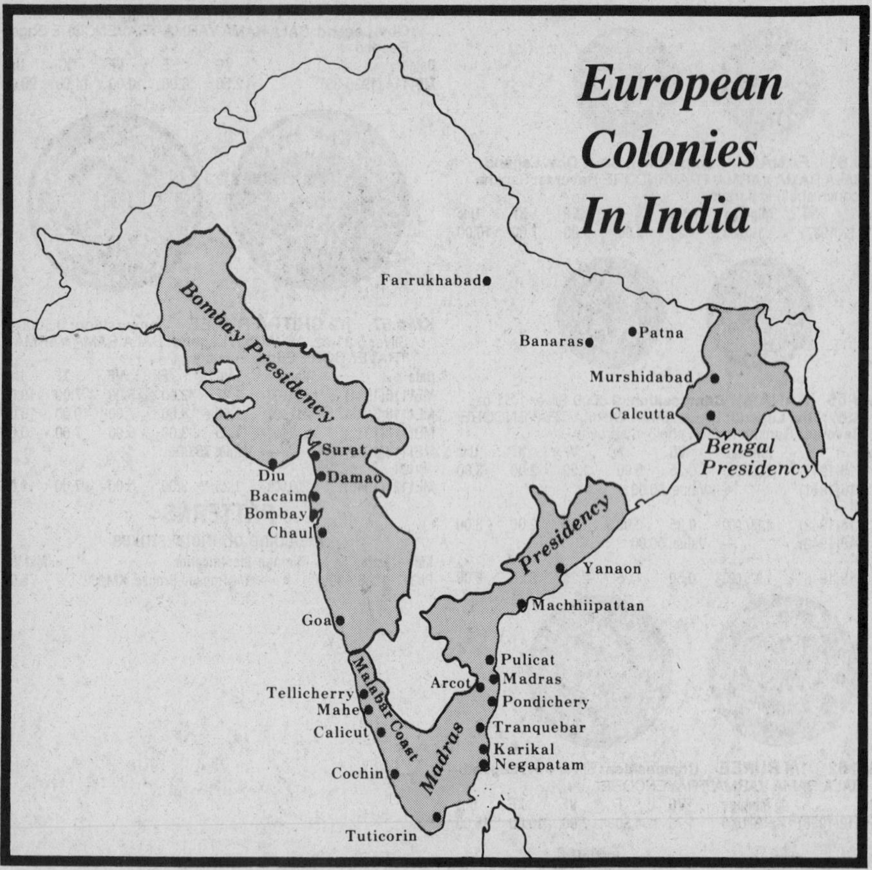

Vasco da Gama, the Portuguese explorer, first visited India in 1498. Portugal seized control of a number of islands and small enclaves on the west coast of India, and for the next hundred years enjoyed a monopoly on trade. With the arrival of powerful Dutch and English fleets in the first half of the 17th century, Portuguese power in the area declined until virtually all of India that remained under Portuguese control were the west coast enclaves of Goa, Damao and Diu. They were forcibly annexed by India in 1962.

RULERS
Portuguese, until 1961

DENOMINATION
The denomination of most copper coins appears in numerals on the reverse, though 30 Reis is often given as "1/2 T", and 60 Reis as "T" (T = Tanga). The silver coins have the denomination in words, usually on the obverse until 1850, then on the reverse.

MONETARY SYSTEM
960 Reis = 16 Tanga = 1 Rupia

PORTUGUESE COLONY
(Kingdom)
COLONIAL COINAGE

KM# 13 1/12 TANGA **Composition:** Bronze **Obverse:** Carlos I bust right **Note:** Roman numeral dating.

Date	Mintage	F	VF	XF	Unc	BU
1901	960,000	6.00	12.00	28.00	55.00	—
1901 Prooflike	—	—	—	—	—	—
1903	960,000	6.00	12.00	28.00	55.00	—

KM# 14 1/8 TANGA **Composition:** Bronze **Obverse:** Carlos I, Roman numeral dating

Date	Mintage	F	VF	XF	Unc	BU
1901	960,000	7.00	15.00	32.00	70.00	—
1901 Prooflike	—	—	—	—	—	—
1903	960,000	7.00	15.00	32.00	70.00	—

KM# 15 1/4 TANGA (15 Reis) **Composition:** Bronze **Obverse:** Carlos I **Note:** Roman numeral dating.

Date	Mintage	F	VF	XF	Unc	BU
1901	800,000	7.50	16.00	35.00	75.00	—
1901 Prooflike	—	—	—	—	200	—
1903	800,000	7.50	16.00	35.00	75.00	—

KM# 16 1/2 TANGA (30 Reis) **Composition:** Bronze **Obverse:** Carlos I **Note:** Roman numeral dating.

Date	Mintage	F	VF	XF	Unc	BU
1901	800,000	8.00	17.50	37.50	80.00	—
1901 Prooflike	—	—	—	—	225	—
1903	800,000	8.00	17.50	37.50	80.00	—

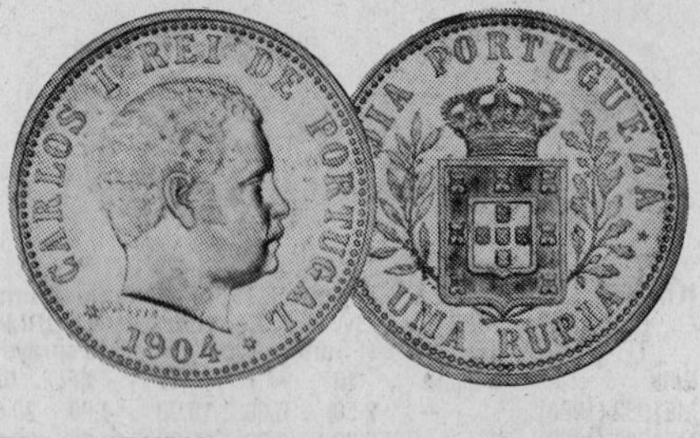

KM# 17 RUPIA **Weight:** 11.6600 g. **Composition:** 0.9170 Silver .3438 oz. ASW **Obverse:** Carlos I

Date	Mintage	F	VF	XF	Unc	BU
1903	200,000	8.00	16.00	32.00	65.00	—
1904	100,000	9.00	18.00	35.00	70.00	—

PORTUGUESE COLONY
(Republic)
COLONIAL COINAGE

KM# 28 TANGA **Composition:** Bronze

Date	Mintage	F	VF	XF	Unc	BU
1952	9,600,000	1.00	4.00	9.00	20.00	—

KM# 19 TANGA (60 Reis) **Composition:** Bronze

Date	Mintage	F	VF	XF	Unc	BU
1934	100,000	25.00	70.00	245	500	—

KM# 24 TANGA (60 Reis) **Composition:** Bronze **Obverse:** Denomination

Date	Mintage	F	VF	XF	Unc	BU
1947	1,000,000	2.00	7.00	15.00	30.00	—

KM# 20 2 TANGAS **Composition:** Copper-Nickel

Date	Mintage	F	VF	XF	Unc	BU
1934	150,000	10.00	20.00	185	400	—

KM# 21 4 TANGAS **Composition:** Copper-Nickel

Date	Mintage	F	VF	XF	Unc	BU
1934	100,000	20.00	60.00	210	450	—

KM# 25 1/4 RUPIA **Composition:** Copper-Nickel **Obverse:** Denomination

Date	Mintage	F	VF	XF	Unc	BU
1947	800,000	5.00	10.00	20.00	40.00	—
1952	4,000,000	2.00	4.00	12.00	25.00	—

KM# 23 1/2 RUPIA **Weight:** 6.0000 g. **Composition:** 0.8350 Silver .1610 oz. ASW

Date	Mintage	F	VF	XF	Unc	BU
1936	100,000	18.00	30.00	50.00	100	—

KM# 26 1/2 RUPIA **Composition:** Copper-Nickel **Obverse:** Denomination

Date	Mintage	F	VF	XF	Unc	BU
1947	600,000	7.00	15.00	30.00	60.00	—
1952	2,000,000	2.00	5.00	12.00	25.00	—

KM# 18 RUPIA **Weight:** 11.6600 g. **Composition:** 0.9170 Silver .3438 oz. ASW

Date	Mintage	F	VF	XF	Unc	BU
1912/1	300,000	75.00	150	285	500	—
1912/1 Proof	—	Value: 1,250				
1912	Inc. above	35.00	75.00	150	285	—

KM# 22 RUPIA **Weight:** 12.0000 g. **Composition:** 0.9170 Silver .3536 oz. ASW

Date	Mintage	F	VF	XF	Unc	BU
1935	300,000	7.50	15.00	30.00	55.00	—

KM# 27 RUPIA **Weight:** 12.0000 g. **Composition:** 0.5000 Silver .1929 oz. ASW

Date	Mintage	F	VF	XF	Unc	BU
1947	900,000	7.50	15.00	30.00	60.00	—

KM# 29 RUPIA **Composition:** Copper-Nickel

Date	Mintage	F	VF	XF	Unc	BU
1952	1,000,000	7.50	15.00	30.00	60.00	—

DECIMAL COINAGE

100 Centavos = 1 Escudo

KM# 30 10 CENTAVOS **Composition:** Bronze **Obverse:** Denomination

Date	Mintage	F	VF	XF	Unc	BU
1958	5,000,000	1.00	3.00	7.00	16.00	—
1959	Inc. above	1.00	3.00	7.00	16.00	—
1961	1,000,000	0.50	1.00	1.50	3.00	—

KM# 31 30 CENTAVOS **Composition:** Bronze **Obverse:** Denomination

Date	Mintage	F	VF	XF	Unc	BU
1958	5,000,000	0.75	2.50	7.00	16.00	—
1959	Inc. above	2.50	7.00	15.00	30.00	—

KM# 32 60 CENTAVOS **Composition:** Copper-Nickel

Date	Mintage	F	VF	XF	Unc	BU
1958	5,000,000	2.00	4.00	10.00	20.00	—
1959	Inc. above	1.25	2.50	6.50	13.50	—

KM# 33 ESCUDO **Composition:** Copper-Nickel

Date	Mintage	F	VF	XF	Unc	BU
1958	6,000,000	1.25	2.50	7.50	16.00	—
1959	Inc. above	1.25	2.50	6.50	13.50	—

KM# 34 3 ESCUDOS **Composition:** Copper-Nickel

Date	Mintage	F	VF	XF	Unc	BU
1958	5,000,000	2.50	5.00	12.00	22.00	—
1959	Inc. above	2.50	4.50	9.00	18.00	—

KM# 35 6 ESCUDOS **Composition:** Copper-Nickel

Date	Mintage	F	VF	XF	Unc	BU
1959	4,000,000	2.50	4.50	9.00	20.00	—

PATTERNS

Including off metal strikes

KM#	Date	Mintage	Identification	Mkt Val
Pn28	1901	—	1/2 Tanga. Aluminum. KM#13	145
Pn29	1901	—	1/8 Tanga. Aluminum. KM#14	145
Pn30	1901	—	1/4 Tanga. Aluminum. KM#15	145
Pn31	1911	—	Rupia. Silver. KM#18	—
Pn32	1911	—	Rupia. Copper. KM#18	700

PROVAS

Standard metals unless otherwise noted; stamped

KM#	Date	Mintage	Identification	Issue Price	Mkt Val
Pr1	1934	—	Tanga. KM#19	—	325
Pr2	1934	—	2 Tangas. KM#20	—	335
Pr3	1934	—	4 Tangas. KM#21	—	340
Pr4	1935	—	Rupia. KM#22	—	140
Pr5	1936	—	1/2 Rupia. KM#23	—	95.00
Pr7	1947	—	1/2 Rupia. KM#26	—	50.00
Pr6	1947	—	1/4 Rupia. KM#25	—	50.00
Pr8	1947	—	Tanga. KM#24	—	50.00
Pr9	1947	—	Rupia. KM#27	—	85.00
Pr10	1952	—	1/4 Rupia. KM#25	—	50.00
Pr11	1952	—	1/2 Rupia. KM#26	—	40.00
Pr12	1952	—	Tanga. KM#28	—	40.00
Pr13	1952	—	Rupia. KM#29	—	50.00
Pr14	1954	—	Rupia. KM#29	—	250
Pr15	1958	—	10 Centavos. KM#30	—	30.00
Pr16	1958	—	30 Centavos. KM#31	—	40.00
Pr17	1958	—	60 Centavos. KM#32	—	40.00
Pr18	1958	—	Escudo. KM#33	—	45.00
Pr19	1958	—	3 Escudos. KM#34	—	45.00
Pr25	1959	—	6 Escudos. KM#35	—	40.00
Pr20	1959	—	10 Centavos. KM#30	—	40.00
Pr21	1959	—	30 Centavos. KM#31	—	40.00
Pr22	1959	—	60 Centavos. KM#32	—	40.00
Pr23	1959	—	Escudo. KM#33	—	40.00
Pr24	1959	—	3 Escudos. KM#34	—	40.00
Pr27	1961	—	10 Centavos. Nickel-Brass. Incuse N; KM#30	—	45.00
Pr26	1961	—	10 Centavos. KM#30	—	35.00

INDIA-BRITISH

The civilization of India, which began about 2500 B.C., flourished under a succession of empires - notably those of the Mauryas, the Kushans, the Guptas, the Delhi Sultans and the Mughals – until undermined in the 18th and 19th centuries by European colonial powers.

The Portuguese were the first to arrive, off Calicut in May 1498. It wasn't until 1612, after the Portuguese and Spanish power had begun to wane, that the British East India Company established its initial settlement at Surat. Britain could not have chosen a more propitious time as the central girdle of petty states, and the southern Vijayanagar Empire were crumbling and ripe for foreign exploitation. By the end of the century, English traders were firmly established in Bombay, Madras, Calcutta and lesser places elsewhere, and Britain was implementing its announced policy to create such civil and military institutions as may be the foundation of secure English domination for all time'. By 1757, following the successful conclusion of a war of colonial rivalry with France during which the military victories of Robert Clive, a young officer with the British East India Company, made him a powerful man in India, the British were firmly settled in India not only as traders but as conquerors. During the next 60 years, the British East India Company acquired dominion over most of India by bribery and force, and governed it directly or through puppet princelings.

As a result of the Sepoy Mutiny of 1857-58, a large-scale mutiny among Indian soldiers of the Bengal army, control of the government of India was transferred from the East India Company to the British Crown. At this point in world history, India was the brightest jewel in the British imperial diadem, but even then a movement for greater Indian representation in government presaged the Indian Empire's twilight hour less than a century later- it would pass into history on Aug. 15, 1947.

COLONIAL COINAGE

This section lists the coins of British India from the reign of William IV (1835) to the reign of George VI (1947). The issues are divided into two main parts:

Coins struck under the authority of the East India Company (E.I.C.) from 1835 until the trading monopoly of the E.I.C. was abolished in 1853. From August 2, 1858 the property and powers of the Company were transferred to the British Crown. From November 1, 1858 to November 1, 1862 the coins continued to bear the design and inscription of the Company.

Coins struck under the authority of the Crown (Regal issues) from 1862 until 1947.

The first regal issues bear the date 1862 and were struck with the date 1862 unchanged until 1874. From then onward all coins bear the year date.

The copper coins dated 1862 have been tentatively attributed by their size to the mint of issue. The silver coins dated 1862 have been attributed to various years of issue by their characteristic marks according to mint records.

In 1877 Queen Victoria was proclaimed Empress of India and the title of the obverse legend was changed accordingly.

For a detailed account of the work of the various mints and the numerous die varieties the general collector and specialist should refer to *The Coins of the British Commonwealth of Nations*, to the end of the reign of King George VI – 1952, Part 4, India, Vol. 1 and 2, by F. Pridmore, Spink, 1980.

RULERS

British until 1947

MINT MARKS

The coins of British India were struck at the following mints, indicated in the catalogue by either capital letters after the date when the actual letter appears on the coins or small letters in () designating the mint of issue. Plain dates indicate Royal Mint strikes.

B – Bombay, 1835-1947
C or CM – Calcutta, 1835-1947
I – Bombay, 1918-1919
L – Lahore, 1943-1945
P – Pretoria, South Africa, 1943-1944

In 1947 British rule came to an end and India was divided into two self-governing countries, India and Pakistan. In 1971 Bangladash seceded from Pakistan. All are now independent republics and although they are still members of the British Commonwealth of Nations, their coinages do not belong to the British India series.

MONETARY SYSTEM

3 Pies = 1 Pice (Paisa)
4 Pice = 1 Anna
16 Annas = 1 Rupee
15 Rupees = 1 Mohur

The transition from the coins of the Moslem monetary system began with the silver pattern Rupees of William IV, 1834, issued by the East India Company, with the value on the reverse, given in English, Bengali, Persian and Nagari characters. This coinage was struck for several years, as dated, except for the currency, Rupee, which was struck from 1835-1840, all dated 1835.

The portrait coins issued by the East India Company for Victoria show two different head designs on the obverse, which are called Type I and Type II. The coins with Type I head have a continuous obverse legend and were struck from 1840 to 1851. The coins with the Type II head have a divided obverse legend and were struck from 1850 (Calcutta) until 1862. The date on the coins remained unchanged: The Rupee, 1/2 Rupee and 1/4 Rupee are dated 1840. Noticeable differences in the ribbon designs of the English vs. Indian obverses exist.

Type I coins have on the reverse a dot after the date those of Type II have no dot, except for some rare 1/4 Rupees and 2 Annas. The latter are mules, struck from reverse dies of the preceding issue.

KING GEORGE VI: First and Second Heads

While King George VI's First Head is engraved in somewhat higher relief than his second head on all denominations from the 1/12 Anna to the Rupee, an easier way of distinguishing between the two types is that on the First Head the two *fleurs de lis* on the royal crown are larger and extend upward to touch the beaded crest at the top of the crown, while the two *fleurs de lis* on the crown of the Second Head are smaller and extend upward to touch only the line on the crown below the beaded crest.

ENGRAVER INITIALS

The following initials appear on the obverse on the truncation:
S incuse (Type I).
WW raised or incuse (Type II).
WWS or SWW (Type II).
WWB raised (Type II).

Proof and Prooflike restrikes

Original proofs are similar to early English Specimen strikes with wire edges and matte finish busts, arms, etc. Restrikes of most of the coins minted from the period 1835 were regularly supplied until this practice was discontinued on July 1, 1970.

Early proof restrikes are found with slight hairlining from polishing of the old dies. Bust, field, arms, etc. are of even smoothness.

Modern proof-like (P/L) restrikes are usually heavily hairlined from excessive polishing of the old dies and have a glassy, varnished or proof-like appearance. Many are common while some are quite scarce including some unusual mulings. These listings are indicated by **P/L-R** after the date and mint mark, for example; "1907(s) P/L R".

BRITISH COLONIAL

MILLED COINAGE

KM# 484 1/2 PICE Composition: Copper **Obv. Legend:** VICTORIA EMPRESS

Date	Mintage	F	VF	XF	Unc	BU
1901(c)	16,057,000	1.00	1.75	3.50	8.50	—
1901(c) Proof	—	Value: 50.00				
1901(c) P/L-R	—	—	—	—	20.00	—

KM# 484b 1/2 PICE Composition: Silver

Date	F	VF	XF	Unc	BU
1901(c) P/L-R	—	—	—	75.00	—

KM# 484c 1/2 PICE Composition: Gold

Date	F	VF	XF	Unc	BU
1901(c) P/L-R	—	—	—	700	—

KM# 499 1/2 PICE Composition: Copper **Obv. Legend:** EDWARD VII KING & EMPEROR

Date	Mintage	F	VF	XF	Unc	BU
1903(c)	5,376,000	0.75	1.50	5.00	15.00	—
1903(c) Proof	—	Value: 45.00				
1903(c) P/L-R	—	—	—	—	20.00	—
1904(c)	8,464,000	0.75	1.50	5.00	15.00	—
1904(c) Proof	—	Value: 45.00				
1904(c) P/L-R	—	—	—	—	20.00	—
1905(c)	8,922,000	0.75	1.50	5.00	15.00	—
1905(c) P/L-R	—	—	—	—	20.00	—
1906(c)	6,346,000	0.75	1.50	5.00	15.00	—
1906(c) Proof	—	Value: 45.00				
1906(c) P/L-R	—	—	—	—	20.00	—

KM# 500 1/2 PICE Composition: Bronze **Obv. Legend:** EDWARD VII KING & EMPEROR **Note:** Thinner planchets.

Date	Mintage	F	VF	XF	Unc	BU
1904(c) Proof	—	Value: 45.00				
1906(c)	5,860,000	0.75	1.50	4.50	12.50	—
1906(c) Proof	—	Value: 45.00				
1907(c)	8,060,000	0.75	1.50	4.50	12.50	—
1907(c) Proof	—	Value: 45.00				
1907(c) P/L-R	—	—	—	—	20.00	—
1908(c)	10,035,000	0.75	1.50	4.50	12.50	—
1908(c) Proof	—	Value: 45.00				
1908(c) P/L-R	—	—	—	—	20.00	—
1909(c)	8,493,000	0.75	1.50	4.50	12.50	—
1909(c) P/L-R	—	—	—	—	20.00	—
1910(c)	17,408,000	0.75	1.50	4.50	12.50	—

KM# 500a 1/2 PICE Composition: Aluminum

Date	F	VF	XF	Unc	BU
1909(c) Proof	—	Value: 100			

KM# 500b 1/2 PICE Composition: Nickel

Date	F	VF	XF	Unc	BU
1904(c) Proof	—	Value: 100			

KM# 500c 1/2 PICE Composition: Silver

Date	F	VF	XF	Unc	BU
1903(c) P/L-R	—	—	—	75.00	—
1904(c) P/L-R	—	—	—	75.00	—
1905(c) P/L-R	—	—	—	75.00	—

KM# 510 1/2 PICE Composition: Bronze **Obv. Legend:** GEORGE V KING EMPEROR

Date	Mintage	F	VF	XF	Unc	BU
1912(c)	12,911,000	0.25	0.50	0.75	3.00	—
1912(c) Proof	—	Value: 40.00				
1912(c) P/L-R	—	—	—	—	20.00	—
1913(c)	10,897,000	0.25	0.50	0.75	3.00	—
1913(c) Proof	—	Value: 40.00				
1913(c) P/L-R	—	—	—	—	20.00	—
1914(c)	4,877,000	0.15	0.30	0.50	2.50	—
1914(c) Proof	—	Value: 40.00				
1914(c) P/L-R	—	—	—	—	20.00	—
1915(c)	9,830,000	0.15	0.30	0.50	2.50	—
1915(c) Proof	—	Value: 40.00				
1915(c) P/L-R	—	—	—	—	20.00	—
1916(c)	5,734,000	0.15	0.30	0.50	2.50	—
1916(c) Proof	—	Value: 40.00				
1916(c) P/L-R	—	—	—	—	20.00	—
1917(c)	15,296,000	0.15	0.30	0.50	2.50	—
1917(c) Proof	—	Value: 40.00				
1917(c) P/L-R	—	—	—	—	20.00	—
1918(c)	6,244,000	0.15	0.30	0.50	2.50	—
1918(c) Proof	—	Value: 40.00				
1918(c) P/L-R	—	—	—	—	20.00	—
1919(c)	11,162,000	0.15	0.30	0.50	2.50	—
1919(c) Proof	—	Value: 40.00				
1919(c) P/L-R	—	—	—	—	20.00	—
1920(c)	4,493,000	0.15	0.30	0.50	2.50	—
1920(c) Proof	—	Value: 40.00				
1920(c) P/L-R	—	—	—	—	20.00	—
1921(c)	6,234,000	0.15	0.30	0.50	2.50	—
1921(c) Proof	—	Value: 40.00				
1921(c) P/L-R	—	—	—	—	20.00	—
1922(c)	6,336,000	0.15	0.30	0.50	2.50	—
1922(c) Proof	—	Value: 40.00				
1922(c) P/L-R	—	—	—	—	20.00	—
1923(c)	7,411,000	0.15	0.30	0.50	2.50	—
1923(c) Proof	—	Value: 40.00				
1923(c) P/L-R	—	—	—	—	20.00	—
1924(c)	9,523,000	0.15	0.30	0.50	2.50	—
1924(c) Proof	—	Value: 40.00				
1924(c) P/L-R	—	—	—	—	20.00	—
1925(c)	3,981,000	0.50	0.75	1.50	4.50	—
1925(c) Proof	—	Value: 40.00				
1925(c) P/L-R	—	—	—	—	20.00	—
1926(c)	7,885,000	0.15	0.30	0.50	2.50	—
1926(c) Proof	—	Value: 40.00				
1926(c) P/L-R	—	—	—	—	20.00	—
1927(c)	5,888,000	0.15	0.30	0.50	2.50	—
1927(c) Proof	—	Value: 40.00				
1927(c) P/L-R	—	—	—	—	20.00	—
1928(c)	5,456,000	0.15	0.30	0.50	2.50	—
1928(c) Proof	—	Value: 40.00				
1928(c) P/L-R	—	—	—	—	20.00	—
1929(c)	7,654,000	0.15	0.30	0.50	2.50	—
1929(c) Proof	—	Value: 40.00				
1929(c) P/L-R	—	—	—	—	20.00	—
1930(c)	7,181,000	0.15	0.30	0.50	2.50	—
1930(c) Proof	—	Value: 40.00				
1930(c) P/L-R	—	—	—	—	20.00	—
1931(c)	8,794,000	0.15	0.30	0.50	2.50	—
1931(c) Proof	—	Value: 40.00				
1931(c) P/L-R	—	—	—	—	20.00	—
1932(c)	5,440,000	0.15	0.30	0.50	2.50	—
1932(c) Proof	—	Value: 40.00				
1932(c) P/L-R	—	—	—	—	20.00	—
1933(c)	9,242,000	0.15	0.30	0.50	2.50	—
1933(c) Proof	—	Value: 40.00				
1933(c) P/L-R	—	—	—	—	20.00	—
1934(c)	8,947,000	0.15	0.30	0.50	2.50	—
1934(c) Proof	—	Value: 40.00				
1934(c) P/L-R	—	—	—	—	20.00	—
1935(c)	15,501,000	0.15	0.30	0.50	2.50	—
1935(c) Proof	—	Value: 40.00				
1935(c) P/L-R	—	—	—	—	20.00	—
1936(c)	26,726,000	0.10	0.25	0.40	1.25	—
1936(c) P/L-R	—	—	—	—	20.00	—

KM# 528 1/2 PICE **Composition:** Bronze **Obverse:** First head; high relief **Obv. Legend:** GEORGE VI KING EMPEROR **Note:** Calcutta Mint issues have no mint mark. Mumbai (Bombay) Mint issues have a small dot below the date.

Date	Mintage	F	VF	XF	Unc	BU
1938(c) Proof	—	Value: 30.00				
1938(c) P/L-R	—	—	—	—	25.00	—

Note: Calcutta Mint reported 11,161,000 mintage for 1938 but only proof and modern prooflike restrikes are known

Date	Mintage	F	VF	XF	Unc	BU
1939(c)	17,357,000	0.15	0.40	0.60	1.75	—
1939(c) Proof	—	Value: 30.00				
1939(b)	9,343,000	0.20	0.45	0.85	3.50	—
1939(b) Proof	—	Value: 30.00				
1939(b) P/L-R	—	—	—	—	25.00	—
1940(c)	23,770,000	0.15	0.40	0.65	1.75	—
1940(c) Proof	—	Value: 30.00				
1940(c) P/L-R	—	—	—	—	25.00	—

KM# 529 1/2 PICE **Composition:** Bronze **Obverse:** Second head; low relief **Obv. Legend:** GEORGE VI KING EMPEROR

Date	F	VF	XF	Unc	BU
1942(b) Proof	—	Value: 50.00			
1942(b) P/L-R	—	—	—	35.00	—

KM# 483 1/12 ANNA (1 Pie) **Composition:** Copper **Obv. Legend:** VICTORIA EMPRESS

Date	Mintage	F	VF	XF	Unc	BU
1901(c)	21,345,000	0.35	0.75	1.75	4.00	—
1901(c) Proof	—	Value: 50.00				
1901(c) P/L-R	—	—	—	—	20.00	—

KM# 483b 1/12 ANNA (1 Pie) **Composition:** Silver

Date	F	VF	XF	Unc	BU
1901(c) P/L-R	—	—	—	75.00	—

KM# 483c 1/12 ANNA (1 Pie) **Composition:** Gold

Date	F	VF	XF	Unc	BU
1901(c) P/L-R	—	—	—	400	—

KM# 497 1/12 ANNA (1 Pie) **Composition:** Copper **Obv. Legend:** EDWARD VII KING & EMPEROR **Note:** Thick planchet.

Date	Mintage	F	VF	XF	Unc	BU
1903(c)	7,883,000	0.35	1.25	6.00	15.00	—
1903(c) Proof	—	Value: 60.00				
1903(c) P/L-R	—	—	—	—	20.00	—
1904(c)	16,506,000	0.25	1.00	4.00	12.00	—
1904(c) Proof	—	Value: 60.00				
1904(c) P/L-R	—	—	—	—	20.00	—
1905(c)	13,060,000	0.25	1.00	4.00	12.00	—
1905(c) P/L-R	—	—	—	—	20.00	—
1906(c)	9,072,000	0.25	1.00	4.00	12.00	—
1906(c) Proof	—	Value: 60.00				
1906(c) P/L-R	—	—	—	—	20.00	—

KM# 497a 1/12 ANNA (1 Pie) **Composition:** Silver

Date	F	VF	XF	Unc	BU
1904(c) P/L-R	—	—	—	75.00	—
1905(c) P/L-R	—	—	—	75.00	—

KM# 498 1/12 ANNA (1 Pie) **Composition:** Bronze **Obv. Legend:** EDWARD VII KING & EMPEROR **Note:** Thin planchet.

Date	Mintage	F	VF	XF	Unc	BU
1906(c)	2,184,000	0.35	0.75	5.00	15.00	—
1906(c) Proof	—	Value: 50.00				
1907(c)	20,985,000	0.25	0.50	3.00	9.00	—
1907(c) Proof	—	Value: 50.00				
1907(c) P/L-R	—	—	—	—	20.00	—
1908(c)	22,036,000	0.25	0.50	3.00	9.00	—
1908(c) Proof	—	Value: 50.00				
1908(c) P/L-R	—	—	—	—	20.00	—
1909(c)	12,316,000	0.25	0.50	3.00	9.00	—
1909(c) P/L-R	—	—	—	—	20.00	—
1910(c)	23,520,000	0.25	0.50	3.00	9.00	—
1910(c) P/L-R	—	—	—	—	20.00	—

KM# 498a 1/12 ANNA (1 Pie) **Composition:** Aluminum

Date	F	VF	XF	Unc	BU
1909(c) Proof	—	Value: 75.00			

KM# 509 1/12 ANNA (1 Pie) **Composition:** Bronze **Obv. Legend:** GEORGE V KING EMPEROR

Date	Mintage	F	VF	XF	Unc	BU
1912(c)	25,938,000	0.50	0.75	1.50	4.50	—
1912(c) Proof	—	Value: 50.00				
1912(c) P/L-R	—	—	—	—	20.00	—
1913(c)	16,149,000	0.25	0.50	1.00	3.00	—
1913(c) Proof	—	Value: 40.00				
1913(c) P/L-R Prooflike, restrike	—	—	—	—	20.00	—
1914(c)	19,814,000	0.25	0.50	0.75	2.00	—
1914(c) Proof	—	Value: 40.00				
1914(c) P/L-R	—	—	—	—	20.00	—
1915(c)	20,563,000	0.25	0.50	0.75	2.00	—
1915(c) Proof	—	Value: 40.00				
1915(c) P/L-R	—	—	—	—	20.00	—
1916(c)	14,438,000	0.25	0.50	0.75	2.00	—
1916(c) Proof	—	Value: 40.00				
1916(c) P/L-R	—	—	—	—	20.00	—
1917(c)	35,174,000	0.25	0.50	0.75	2.00	—
1917(c) Proof	—	Value: 40.00				
1917(c) P/L-R	—	—	—	—	20.00	—
1918(c)	24,192,000	0.25	0.50	0.75	2.00	—
1918(c) Proof	—	Value: 40.00				
1918(c) P/L-R	—	—	—	—	20.00	—
1919(c)	17,472,000	0.25	0.50	0.75	2.00	—
1919(c) Proof	—	Value: 40.00				
1919(c) P/L-R	—	—	—	—	20.00	—
1920(c)	39,878,000	0.25	0.50	0.75	2.00	—
1920(c) Proof	—	Value: 40.00				
1920(c) P/L-R	—	—	—	—	20.00	—
1921(c)	19,334,000	0.25	0.50	0.75	2.00	—
1921(c) Proof	—	Value: 40.00				
1921(c) P/L-R	—	—	—	—	20.00	—
1923(c)	8,429,000	0.25	0.50	0.75	2.00	—
1923(c) Proof	—	Value: 40.00				
1923(b)	8,717,000	0.25	0.50	0.75	2.00	—
1923(b) Proof	—	Value: 40.00				
1924(c)	7,200,000	0.50	0.75	1.50	4.50	—
1924(c) Proof	—	Value: 40.00				
1924(b)	9,869,000	0.25	0.50	0.75	2.00	—
1924(b) Proof	—	Value: 40.00				
1924(b) P/L-R	—	—	—	—	20.00	—
1925(c)	5,818,000	0.50	0.75	1.50	4.50	—
1925(c) Proof	—	Value: 40.00				
1925(b)	6,415,000	0.50	0.75	1.50	4.50	—
1925(b) Proof	—	Value: 40.00				
1925(b) P/L-R	—	—	—	—	20.00	—
1926(c)	4,147,000	0.50	0.75	1.50	4.50	—
1926(c) Proof	—	Value: 40.00				
1926(b)	15,464,000	0.25	0.50	0.75	2.00	—
1926(b) Proof	—	Value: 40.00				
1926(b) P/L-R	—	—	—	—	20.00	—
1927(c)	6,662,000	0.50	0.75	1.50	4.50	—
1927(c) Proof	—	Value: 40.00				
1927(b)	6,788,000	0.50	0.75	1.50	4.50	—
1927(b) Proof	—	Value: 40.00				
1927(b) P/L-R	—	—	—	—	20.00	—
1928(c)	8,064,000	0.25	0.50	0.75	2.00	—
1928(c) Proof	—	Value: 40.00				
1928(b)	6,135,000	0.50	0.75	1.50	4.50	—
1928(b) Proof	—	Value: 40.00				
1928(b) P/L-R	—	—	—	—	20.00	—
1929(c)	15,130,000	0.25	0.50	0.75	2.00	—
1929(c) Proof	—	Value: 40.00				
1929(c) P/L-R	—	—	—	—	20.00	—
1930(c)	13,498,000	0.25	0.50	0.75	2.00	—
1930(c) Proof	—	Value: 40.00				
1930(c) P/L-R	—	—	—	—	20.00	—
1931(c)	18,278,000	0.25	0.50	0.75	2.00	—
1931(c) Proof	—	Value: 40.00				
1931(c) P/L-R	—	—	—	—	20.00	—
1932(c)	23,213,000	0.25	0.50	0.75	2.00	—
1932(c) Proof	—	Value: 40.00				
1932(c) P/L-R	—	—	—	—	20.00	—
1933(c)	16,896,000	0.25	0.50	0.75	2.00	—
1933(c) Proof	—	Value: 40.00				
1933(c) P/L-R	—	—	—	—	20.00	—
1934(c)	17,146,000	0.25	0.50	0.75	2.00	—
1934(c) Proof	—	Value: 40.00				
1934(c) P/L-R	—	—	—	—	20.00	—
1935(c)	19,142,000	0.25	0.50	0.75	2.00	—
1935(c) Proof	—	Value: 40.00				
1935(c) P/L-R	—	—	—	—	20.00	—
1936(c)	23,213,000	0.25	0.50	0.75	2.00	—
1936(b)	12,887,000	0.25	0.50	0.75	2.00	—
1936(b) P/L-R	—	—	—	—	20.00	—

KM# 526 1/12 ANNA (1 Pie) **Composition:** Bronze **Obv. Legend:** GEORGE VI KING EMPEROR **Note:** First head.

Date	Mintage	F	VF	XF	Unc	BU
1938(c) Proof	—	Value: 35.00				
1939(c)	3,571,000	0.50	0.75	1.50	4.50	—
1939(b)	17,407,000	0.25	0.50	1.00	2.50	—

KM# 527 1/12 ANNA (1 Pie) **Composition:** Bronze **Obv. Legend:** GEORGE VI KING EMPEROR **Note:** Second head.

Date	Mintage	F	VF	XF	Unc	BU
1938(c) P/L-R	—	—	—	—	20.00	—
1939(c)	5,245,000	0.25	0.50	1.00	2.50	—
1939(c) Proof	—	Value: 35.00				
1939(b)	31,306,000	0.25	0.50	0.75	2.00	—
1939(b) Proof	—	Value: 35.00				
1939(b) P/L-R	—	—	—	—	20.00	—
1941(b)	6,137,000	0.25	0.50	0.75	2.00	—
1942(b)	6,124,000	0.50	0.75	1.50	4.50	—
1942(b) Proof	—	Value: 35.00				
1942(b) P/L-R	—	—	—	—	20.00	—

PICE

NOTE: There are three types of the crown, which is on the obverse at the top. These are shown below and are designated as (RC) Round Crown, (HC) High Crown, and (FC) Flat Crown. Calcutta Mint issues have no mint mark. The issues from the other mints have the mint mark below the date as following: Lahore, raised "L"; Pretoria, small round dot; Bombay, diamond dot or "large" round dot. On the Bombay issues dated 1944 the mint mark appears to be a large dot over a diamond.

Round Crown (RC)

High Crown (HC) Flat Crown (FC)

KM# 532 PICE **Composition:** Bronze **Obverse:** Small date, small legends

Date	Mintage	F	VF	XF	Unc	BU
1943(b) (RC) diamond	164,659	0.30	0.50	1.00	3.50	—

KM# 533 PICE **Composition:** Bronze **Obverse:** Large date, large legends

Date	Mintage	F	VF	XF	Unc	BU
1943(b) (HC) large dot	—	0.15	0.35	0.65	1.25	—
1943(p) (HC) small dot	98,997,000	0.15	0.35	0.65	1.25	—
1944(c) (HC)	—	0.15	0.35	0.65	1.25	—
1944(c) (HC) Proof	—	Value: 25.00				
1944(b) (HC) large dot	195,354,000	0.15	0.35	0.65	1.25	—
1944(b) (HC) diamond	—	0.20	0.40	0.75	2.00	—
1944(b) (FC) large dot	—	0.20	0.40	0.75	2.00	—
1944(b) P/L-R	—	—	—	—	20.00	—
1944(p) (HC) small dot	141,003,000	0.20	0.40	0.75	2.00	—
1944L (HC)	29,802,000	0.20	0.40	0.80	3.50	—
1945(c) (FC)	156,322,000	0.15	0.35	0.65	1.25	—
1945(b) (FC) diamond	237,197,000	0.15	0.35	0.65	1.25	—
1945(b) (FC) large dot	Inc. above	0.15	0.35	0.65	1.25	—
1945(b) P/L-R	—	—	—	—	20.00	—
1945L (FC)	238,825,000	0.15	0.35	0.65	1.25	—
1947(c) (HC)	153,702,000	0.15	0.35	0.65	1.25	—
1947(b) (HC) diamond	43,654,000	0.20	0.40	0.80	3.50	—
1947(b) Proof	—	Value: 25.00				
1947 P/L-R	—	—	—	—	20.00	—

KM# 486 1/4 ANNA **Composition:** Copper **Obv. Legend:** VICTORIA EMPRESS

Date	Mintage	F	VF	XF	Unc	BU
1901(c)	136,091,000	0.35	0.75	1.50	4.50	—
1901(c) Proof	—	Value: 65.00				
1901(c) Restrike; prooflike	—	—	—	—	25.00	—

KM# 486b 1/4 ANNA **Composition:** Silver

Date	F	VF	XF	Unc	BU
1901(c) P/L-R	—	—	—	75.00	—

KM# 486c 1/4 ANNA **Composition:** Gold

Date	F	VF	XF	Unc	BU
1901(c) P/L-R	—	—	—	750	—

KM# 501 1/4 ANNA **Composition:** Copper **Obv. Legend:** EDWARD VII KING & EMPEROR

Date	Mintage	F	VF	XF	Unc	BU
1903(c)	105,974,000	0.35	1.75	7.50	35.00	—
1903(c) Proof	—	Value: 50.00				
1903(c) P/L-R	—	—	—	—	25.00	—
1904(c)	104,595,000	0.35	1.75	7.50	35.00	—
1904(c) Proof	—	Value: 50.00				
1904(c) P/L-R	—	—	—	—	25.00	—
1905(c)	130,058,000	0.35	1.75	7.50	35.00	—
1905(c) Proof	—	Value: 50.00				
1905(c) P/L-R	—	—	—	—	25.00	—
1906(c)	47,229,000	0.35	1.75	7.50	35.00	—
1906(c) Proof	—	Value: 50.00				

KM# 501b 1/4 ANNA **Composition:** Silver

Date	F	VF	XF	Unc	BU
1903(c) P/L-R	—	—	—	100	—
1904(c) P/L-R	—	—	—	100	—
1905(c) P/L-R	—	—	—	100	—

KM# 501a 1/4 ANNA **Composition:** Nickel

Date	F	VF	XF	Unc	BU
1906(c) Proof	— Value: 150				

KM# 502 1/4 ANNA **Composition:** Bronze **Obv. Legend:** EDWARD VII KING & EMPEROR **Note:** Thinner planchet.

Date	Mintage	F	VF	XF	Unc	BU
1906(c)	115,786,000	0.35	1.25	6.50	30.00	—
1906(c) Proof	—	Value: 40.00				
1907(c)	234,682,000	0.35	1.25	6.50	30.00	—
1907(c) Proof	—	Value: 40.00				
1907(c) P/L-R	—	—	—	—	20.00	—
1908(c)	58,066,000	0.35	1.25	6.50	30.00	—
1908(c) Proof	—	Value: 40.00				
1908(c) P/L-R	—	—	—	—	20.00	—
1909(c)	29,966,000	0.35	1.25	6.50	30.00	—
1909(c) Proof	—	Value: 40.00				
1909(c) P/L-R	—	—	—	—	20.00	—
1910(c)	47,265,000	0.35	1.25	6.50	30.00	—
1910(c) P/L-R	—	—	—	—	20.00	—

KM# 502a 1/4 ANNA **Composition:** Aluminum

Date	VG	F	VF	XF	Unc
1908(c) Proof	—	Value: 150			

KM# 511 1/4 ANNA **Composition:** Bronze **Obverse:** Type I **Obv. Legend:** GEORGE V KING EMPEROR **Note:** Calcutta Mint issues have no mint mark. Mumbai (Bombay) Mint issues have a small dot below the date. The pieces dated 1911, like the other coins with that date, show the "Pig" elephant.

Date	Mintage	F	VF	XF	Unc	BU
1911(c)	55,918,000	0.75	2.00	5.00	20.00	—
1911(c) Proof	—	Value: 55.00				
1911(c) P/L-R	—	—	—	—	20.00	—

KM# 512 1/4 ANNA **Composition:** Bronze **Obverse:** Type II **Obv. Legend:** GEORGE V KING EMPEROR

Date	Mintage	F	VF	XF	Unc	BU
1912(c)	107,456,000	0.20	0.40	1.00	4.00	—
1912(c) Proof	—	Value: 35.00				
1912(c) P/L-R	—	—	—	—	20.00	—
1913(c)	82,061,000	0.25	0.50	1.25	4.50	—
1913(c) Proof	—	Value: 35.00				
1913(c) P/L-R	—	—	—	—	20.00	—
1914(c)	40,576,000	0.50	0.75	1.50	3.50	—
1914(c) Proof	—	Value: 35.00				
1914(c) P/L-R	—	—	—	—	20.00	—
1916(c)	1,632,000	3.50	7.00	12.00	25.00	—
1916(c) Proof	—	Value: 50.00				
1917(c)	69,370,000	0.20	0.40	0.80	3.50	—
1917(c) Proof	—	Value: 35.00				
1917(c) P/L-R	—	—	—	—	20.00	—
1918(c)	84,045,000	0.20	0.40	0.80	3.50	—
1918(c) Proof	—	Value: 35.00				
1918(c) P/L-R	—	—	—	—	20.00	—
1919(c)	212,467,000	0.20	0.40	0.80	3.50	—
1919(c) Proof	—	Value: 35.00				
1919(c) P/L-R	—	—	—	—	20.00	—
1920(c)	96,019,000	0.20	0.40	0.80	3.50	—
1920(c) Proof	—	Value: 35.00				
1920(c) P/L-R	—	—	—	—	20.00	—
1921(c) Proof	—	Value: 35.00				
1924(b)	16,322,000	0.20	0.40	0.80	3.50	—
1924(b) Proof	—	Value: 35.00				
1925(c)	14,598,000	0.20	0.40	0.80	3.50	—
1925(b)	14,588,000	0.20	0.40	0.80	3.50	—
1925(b) Proof	—	Value: 35.00				
1926(c)	17,389,000	0.20	0.40	0.80	3.50	—
1926(c) Proof	—	Value: 35.00				
1926(b)	16,073,000	0.20	0.40	0.80	3.50	—
1926(b) Proof	—	Value: 35.00				
1926(b) P/L-R	—	—	—	—	20.00	—
1927(c)	6,925,000	0.50	0.75	1.50	4.50	—
1927(c) Proof	—	Value: 35.00				
1927(b)	12,440,000	0.20	0.40	0.80	3.50	—
1927(b) Proof	—	Value: 35.00				
1927(b) P/L-R	—	—	—	—	20.00	—
1928(c)	257,779,000	0.20	0.40	0.80	3.50	—
1928(c) Proof	—	Value: 35.00				
1928(b)	10,057,000	0.20	0.40	0.80	3.50	—
1928(b) Proof	—	Value: 35.00				
1928(b) P/L-R	—	—	—	—	20.00	—
1929(c)	61,542,000	0.20	0.40	0.80	3.50	—
1929(c) Proof	—	Value: 35.00				
1929(c) P/L-R	—	—	—	—	20.00	—
1930(c)	40,698,000	0.20	0.40	0.80	3.50	—
1930(c) Proof	—	Value: 35.00				
1930(b)	9,646,000	0.50	0.75	1.50	4.50	—
1930(b) Proof	—	Value: 35.00				
1930(b) P/L-R	—	—	—	—	20.00	—
1931(c)	6,835,000	0.50	0.75	1.50	4.50	—
1931(c) Proof	—	Value: 35.00				
1931(c) P/L-R	—	—	—	—	20.00	—
1933(c)	40,230,000	0.20	0.40	0.80	3.50	—
1933(c) Proof	—	Value: 35.00				
1933(c) P/L-R	—	—	—	—	20.00	—
1934(c)	80,506,000	0.20	0.40	0.80	3.50	—
1934(c) Proof	—	Value: 35.00				
1934(c) P/L-R	—	—	—	—	20.00	—
1935(c)	92,595,000	0.20	0.40	0.80	3.50	—
1935(c) Proof	—	Value: 35.00				
1935(c) P/L-R	—	—	—	—	20.00	—
1936(c)	227,501,000	0.20	0.40	0.80	3.50	—
1936(b)	61,926,000	0.20	0.40	0.80	3.50	—
1936(b) Proof	—	Value: 35.00				
1936(b) P/L-R	—	—	—	—	20.00	—

KM# 530 1/4 ANNA **Composition:** Bronze **Obverse:** First head; high relief **Obv. Legend:** GEORGE VI KING EMPEROR

Date	Mintage	F	VF	XF	Unc	BU
1938(c)	33,792,000	0.25	0.40	0.75	2.00	—
1938(c) Proof	—	Value: 35.00				
1938(b)	16,796,000	0.50	0.75	1.50	4.50	—
1938(b) P/L-R	—	—	—	—	30.00	—
1939(c)	78,279,000	0.30	0.50	1.00	2.50	—
1939(c) Proof	—	Value: 35.00				
1939(b)	60,171,000	0.30	0.50	1.00	3.50	—
1939(b) Proof	—	Value: 35.00				
1939(b) P/L-R	—	—	—	—	30.00	—
1940(b)	116,721,000	0.35	0.75	1.50	3.50	—

KM# 531 1/4 ANNA **Composition:** Bronze **Obverse:** Second head; low relief **Obv. Legend:** GEORGE VI KING EMPEROR

Date	Mintage	F	VF	XF	Unc	BU
1940(c)	140,410,000	0.30	0.50	1.00	3.50	—
1940(c) Proof	—	Value: 35.00				
1940(b)	—	0.30	0.50	1.00	3.50	—
Note: Mintage included in KM#530						
1940(b) P/L-R	—	—	—	—	25.00	—
1941(c)	121,107,000	0.30	0.50	1.00	3.50	—
1941(c) P/L-R	—	—	—	—	25.00	—
1941(b)	1,446,000	0.40	0.90	2.00	6.00	—
1942(c)	34,298,000	0.30	0.50	1.00	3.50	—
1942(b)	8,768,000	0.30	0.50	1.00	3.50	—
1942(b) P/L-R	—	—	—	—	25.00	—

KM# 503 1/2 ANNA **Composition:** Copper **Obverse:** Head of Edward VII **Reverse:** Similar to KM#487

Date	F	VF	XF	Unc	BU
1904(c) Proof	— Value: 2,000				

KM# 534 1/2 ANNA **Composition:** Copper-Nickel **Obv. Legend:** GEORGE VI KING EMPERPOR **Rev. Legend:** • INDIA • **Shape:** 4-sided

Date	F	VF	XF	Unc	BU
1940(c) Proof	— Value: 325				
1940(c) P/L-R	—	—	—	50.00	—

KM# 534a 1/2 ANNA **Composition:** Gold

Date	F	VF	XF	Unc	BU
1940(c) P/L-R	—	—	—	250	—

KM# 534b.2 1/2 ANNA **Composition:** Nickel-Brass **Rev. Legend:** • INDIA •

Date	Mintage	F	VF	XF	Unc	BU
1942(c)	159,000,000	0.10	0.25	0.50	2.00	—
1942(c) Proof	—	Value: 30.00				
1943(c)	437,760,000	0.10	0.25	0.50	2.00	—
1943(c) Proof	—	Value: 40.00				
1944(c)	514,800,000	0.10	0.25	0.50	2.00	—

Date	Mintage	F	VF	XF	Unc	BU
1944(c) Proof	—	Value: 40.00				
1945(c)	215,732,000	0.10	0.25	0.50	2.00	—
1945(c) Proof	—	Value: 40.00				

KM# 534b.1 1/2 ANNA Composition: Nickel-Brass **Obverse:** Second head **Obv. Legend:** GEORGE VI KING EMPEROR **Rev. Legend:** INDIA (without dots) **Note:** Bombay Mint issues dated 1942-1945 are without a dot before and after India.

Date	Mintage	F	VF	XF	Unc	BU
1942(b)	7,945,000	0.30	0.50	1.00	3.50	—
1942(b) P/L-R	—	—	—	—	40.00	—
1943(b) P/L-R	—	—	—	—	40.00	—
1944(b) P/L-R	—	—	—	—	40.00	—
1945(b) P/L-R	—	—	—	—	25.00	—

The Calcutta Mint continued to issue this denomination with the dot before and after INDIA in 1946 and 1947. Bombay also struck in 1946 and 1947, the 1946 issue denoted by a small dot in the center of the dashes before and after the date on the reverse (as well as a dot before and after INDIA, like Calcutta); the characteristics of the 1947 Bombay issue have not been determined but are thought also to resemble the 1946 issue. This denomination is also reported to have been struck in a quantity of 50,829,000 pieces in 1946 at the new Lahore Mint but no way of distinguishing this issue has been found. The proof issue in 1946 was struck by Bombay, not Calcutta. Source: Pridmore.

KM# 535.1 1/2 ANNA Composition: Copper-Nickel **Shape:** Square

Date	Mintage	F	VF	XF	Unc	BU
1946(b)	48,744,000	0.10	0.25	0.50	2.00	—
1946(b) Proof	—	Value: 30.00				
1946(b) P/L-R	—	—	—	—	25.00	—
1947(b) P/L-R	—	—	—	—	50.00	—

KM# 535.2 1/2 ANNA Composition: Copper-Nickel **Shape:** Square

Date	Mintage	F	VF	XF	Unc	BU
1946(c)	75,159,000	0.15	0.30	0.50	2.50	—
1947(c)	126,392,000	0.10	0.20	0.45	1.25	—
1947(c) Proof	—	Value: 40.00				
1947(c) P/L-R	—	—	—	—	25.00	—

KM# 504 ANNA Composition: Copper-Nickel **Obv. Legend:** EDWARD VII KING & EMPEROR **Shape:** Scalloped **Note:** Struck only at the Mumbai (Bombay) Mint. Small incuse "B" mint mark in the space below the cross pattee of the crown on the obverse.

Date	Mintage	F	VF	XF	Unc	BU
1906B	200,000	20.00	50.00	125	300	—
1907B	37,256,000	0.50	1.25	2.00	5.00	—
1907B Proof	—	Value: 60.00				
1908B	22,536,000	0.50	1.25	2.00	5.00	—
1908B Proof	—	Value: 60.00				
1909B	24,800,000	0.50	1.25	2.00	5.00	—
1909B Proof	—	Value: 60.00				
1910B	40,200,000	0.50	1.25	2.00	5.00	—
1910B Proof	—	Value: 60.00				

KM# 513 ANNA Composition: Copper-Nickel **Obv. Legend:** GEORGE VI KING EMPEROR **Shape:** Scalloped **Note:** Until 1920, all were struck at the Mumbai (Bombay) Mint without mint mark. From 1923 on, the Mumbai (Bombay) Mint issues have a small, raised bead or dot below the date. Calcutta Mint issues have no mint mark.

Date	Mintage	F	VF	XF	Unc	BU
1912(b)	39,400,000	0.40	1.00	2.50	6.00	—
1912 Proof	—	Value: 50.00				
1913(b)	39,776,000	0.40	1.00	2.50	6.00	—
1913 Proof	—	Value: 50.00				
1914(b)	48,000,000	0.25	0.50	1.75	4.00	—
1914 Proof	—	Value: 50.00				
1915(b)	7,670,000	0.40	1.00	2.50	6.00	—
1915 Proof	—	Value: 50.00				
1916(b)	39,087,000	0.25	0.50	1.75	4.00	—
1917(b)	58,067,000	0.25	0.50	1.75	4.00	—
1917 Proof	—	Value: 50.00				
1918(b)	80,692,000	0.25	0.50	1.75	4.00	—
1918(b) Proof	—	Value: 50.00				
1919(b)	122,795,000	0.25	0.50	1.75	4.00	—
1919(b) Proof	—	Value: 50.00				
1919(c) Proof	—	Value: 50.00				
1920(b)	9,264,000	0.25	0.50	1.75	4.50	—
1920(b) Proof	—	Value: 50.00				
1923(b)	7,125,000	0.25	0.50	1.75	4.50	—
1923(b) Proof	—	Value: 50.00				
1924(c)	16,640,000	0.25	0.50	1.75	4.00	—
1924(c) Proof	—	Value: 50.00				
1924(b)	17,285,000	0.25	0.50	2.00	5.00	—
1924(b) Proof	—	Value: 50.00				
1924(b) P/L-R	—	—	—	—	20.00	—
1925(c)	22,388,000	0.25	0.50	2.00	5.00	—
1925(c) Proof	—	Value: 50.00				
1925(b)	11,763,000	0.25	0.50	2.00	5.00	—
1925(b) Proof	—	Value: 50.00				
1925(b) P/L-R	—	—	—	—	20.00	—
1926(c)	13,440,000	0.25	0.50	2.00	5.00	—
1926(c) Proof	—	Value: 50.00				
1926(b)	8,088,000	0.25	0.50	2.00	5.00	—
1926(b) Proof	—	Value: 50.00				
1926(b) P/L-R	—	—	—	—	20.00	—
1927(c)	6,296,000	0.40	1.00	2.50	6.00	—
1927(c) Proof	—	Value: 50.00				
1927(b)	12,953,000	0.25	0.50	2.00	5.00	—
1927(b) Proof	—	Value: 50.00				
1927(b) P/L-R	—	—	—	—	20.00	—
1928(c)	29,568,000	1.00	1.75	3.50	8.50	—
1928(c) Proof	—	Value: 50.00				
1928(b)	4,832,000	0.25	0.50	2.00	5.00	—
1928(b) Proof	—	Value: 50.00				
1928(b) P/L-R	—	—	—	—	20.00	—
1929(c)	42,200,000	0.25	0.50	2.00	5.00	—
1929(c) Proof	—	Value: 50.00				
1929(c) P/L-R	—	—	—	—	20.00	—
1930(c)	22,816,000	0.25	0.50	2.00	5.00	—
1930(c) Proof	—	Value: 50.00				
1930(c) P/L-R	—	—	—	—	20.00	—
1933(c)	17,432,000	0.25	0.50	2.00	5.00	—
1933(c) Proof	—	Value: 50.00				
1933(c) P/L-R	—	—	—	—	20.00	—
1934(c)	34,216,000	0.25	0.40	1.50	4.00	—
1934(c) Proof	—	Value: 50.00				
1934(c) P/L-R	—	—	—	—	20.00	—
1935(c)	12,952,000	0.25	0.40	1.50	4.00	—
1935(c) Proof	—	Value: 50.00				
1935(b)	41,112,000	0.25	0.40	1.50	4.00	—
1935(b) Proof	—	Value: 50.00				
1935(b) P/L-R	—	—	—	—	20.00	—
1936(c)	21,592,000	0.25	0.40	1.50	4.00	—
1936(b)	107,136,000	0.20	0.35	1.25	3.00	—
1936(b) Proof	—	Value: 50.00				

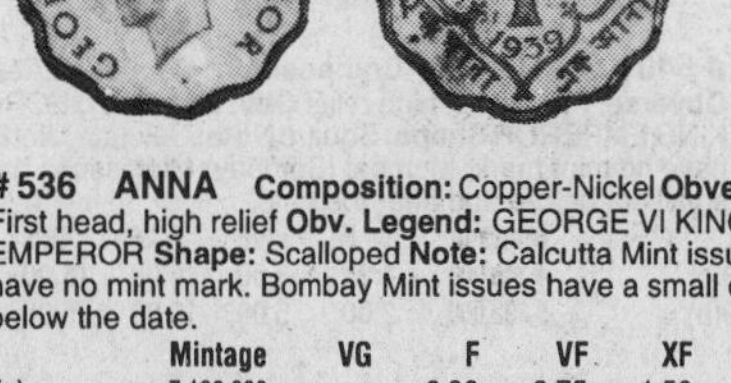

KM# 536 ANNA Composition: Copper-Nickel **Obverse:** First head, high relief **Obv. Legend:** GEORGE VI KING EMPEROR **Shape:** Scalloped **Note:** Calcutta Mint issues have no mint mark. Bombay Mint issues have a small dot below the date.

Date	Mintage	VG	F	VF	XF	Unc
1938(c)	7,128,000	—	0.30	0.75	1.50	5.00
1938(c) Proof	—	Value: 40.00				
1938(b)	3,126,000	—	0.40	1.00	2.00	5.00
1938(b) P/L-R	—	—	—	—	—	20.00
1939(c)	18,192,000	—	0.30	0.75	1.50	3.00
1939(b)	36,157,000	—	0.30	0.75	1.50	3.00
1939(b) P/L-R	—	—	—	—	—	20.00
1940(c)	60,945,000	—	0.30	0.75	1.50	3.00
1940(c) P/L-R	—	—	—	—	—	20.00
1940(b)	—	—	1.00	2.00	4.00	10.00

KM# 537 ANNA Composition: Copper-Nickel **Obverse:** Second head, low relief, large crown **Obv. Legend:** GEORGE VI KING EMPEROR **Reverse:** Large "I" **Shape:** Scalloped

Date	Mintage	VG	F	VF	XF	Unc
1940(c)	76,392,000	—	0.10	0.25	0.50	2.00
1940(c) P/L-R	—	—	—	—	—	25.00
1940(b)	144,712,000	—	0.10	0.25	0.50	2.00
1940(b) P/L-R	—	—	—	—	—	20.00
1941(c)	62,480,000	—	0.10	0.25	0.50	2.00
1941(b)	40,170,000	—	0.15	0.40	1.00	1.50
1941(b) P/L-R	—	—	—	—	—	25.00

KM# 537a ANNA Composition: Nickel-Brass **Obv. Legend:** GEORGE VI KING EMPEROR **Shape:** Scalloped

Date	Mintage	VG	F	VF	XF	Unc
1942(c)	194,056,000	—	0.10	0.25	0.50	2.00
1942(c) Proof	—	Value: 35.00				
1942(b)	103,240,000	—	0.15	0.40	1.00	2.50
1942(b) P/L-R	—	—	—	—	—	20.00
1943(c)	352,256,000	—	0.10	0.25	0.50	2.00
1943(c) Proof	—	Value: 35.00				
1943(b)	134,500,000	—	0.10	0.25	0.50	2.00
1943(b) P/L-R	—	—	—	—	—	20.00
1944(c)	457,608,000	—	0.10	0.25	0.50	2.00
1944(c) Proof	—	Value: 35.00				
1944(b)	175,208,000	—	0.10	0.25	0.50	2.00
1944(b) P/L-R	—	—	—	—	—	20.00
1945(c)	278,360,000	—	0.10	0.25	0.50	2.00
1945(b)	61,228,000	—	0.20	0.40	0.80	3.50

KM# 539 ANNA Composition: Copper-Nickel **Obverse:** Second head, low relief, small crown **Obv. Legend:** GEORGE VI KING EMPEROR **Reverse:** Small "I" **Shape:** Scalloped

Date	Mintage	VG	F	VF	XF	Unc
1945(c)	278,360,000	—	0.10	0.25	0.75	2.00
1945(c) Proof	—	Value: 35.00				
1945(b)	61,228,000	—	0.10	0.25	0.75	2.00
1945(b) P/L-R	—	—	—	—	—	25.00

KM# 538 ANNA Composition: Copper-Nickel **Obverse:** Second head, low relief, small crown **Obv. Legend:** GEORGE VI KING EMPEROR **Reverse:** Small "I" **Shape:** Scalloped

Date	Mintage	F	VF	XF	Unc	BU
1946(c)	100,820,000	0.10	0.15	0.35	1.50	—
1946(b)	82,052,000	0.10	0.15	0.35	1.50	—
1946(b) Proof	—	Value: 40.00				
1946(b) P/L-R	—	—	—	—	25.00	—
1947(c)	148,656,000	0.10	0.25	0.35	1.50	—
1947(c) Proof	—	Value: 40.00				
1947(b)	50,096,000	0.10	0.25	0.50	2.00	—
1947(b) Proof	—	Value: 40.00				

KM# 488 2 ANNAS Weight: 1.4600 g. **Composition:** 0.9170 Silver .0430 oz. ASW **Obv. Legend:** VICTORIA EMPRESS

Date	Mintage	F	VF	XF	Unc	BU
1901C B/II, "C" incuse	8,944,000	1.25	2.50	5.00	10.00	—
1901C Proof	Inc. above	Value: 35.00				
1901B B/I, "B" incuse	—	2.50	5.00	10.00	20.00	—
1901B B/II, "B" incuse	1,706,000	1.25	2.50	5.00	10.00	—
1901B Proof	—	Value: 100				
1901B P/L-R	—	—	—	—	30.00	—
1901B B/I, "B" raised	—	2.50	5.00	10.00	20.00	—
1901B B/II, "B" raised	Inc. above	1.25	2.50	5.00	10.00	—

KM# 505 2 ANNAS **Weight:** 1.4600 g. **Composition:** 0.9170 Silver .0430 oz. ASW **Obverse:** KM#469 **Obv. Legend:** EDWARD VII KING AND EMPEROR **Reverse:** KM#488 **Note:** Mule.

Date	Mintage	F	VF	XF	Unc	BU
1903(c)	4,434,000	1.75	3.50	7.00	14.00	—
1903(c) Proof	—	Value: 65.00				
1903(c) P/L-R	—	—	—	—	25.00	—
1904(c)	14,632,000	1.50	3.00	6.00	12.00	—
1904(c) Proof	—	Value: 65.00				
1904(c) P/L-R	—	—	—	—	25.00	—
1905(c)	19,303,000	1.50	3.00	6.00	12.00	—
1905(c) P/L-R	—	—	—	—	25.00	—
1906(c)	13,031,000	1.50	3.00	6.00	12.00	—
1906(c) P/L-R	—	—	—	—	25.00	—
1907(c)	22,145,000	1.50	3.00	6.00	12.00	—
1907(c) Proof	—	Value: 65.00				
1908(c)	21,600,000	1.50	3.00	6.00	12.00	—
1908(c) Proof	—	Value: 65.00				
1908(c) P/L-R	—	—	—	—	25.00	—
1909(c)	6,769,000	1.75	3.50	7.00	14.00	—
1909(c) Proof	—	Value: 65.00				
1909(c) P/L-R	—	—	—	—	25.00	—
1910(c)	1,604,000	1.75	3.50	7.00	14.00	—
1910(c) Proof	—	Value: 65.00				
1910(c) P/L-R	—	—	—	—	25.00	—

KM# 505a 2 ANNAS **Composition:** Gold **Obverse:** KM#469 **Obv. Legend:** EDWARD VII KING AND EMPEROR **Reverse:** KM#488

Date	F	VF	XF	Unc	BU
1904(c) P/L-R	—	—	—	600	—
1906(c) P/L-R	—	—	—	600	—
1910(c) P/L-R	—	—	—	600	—

KM# 514 2 ANNAS **Weight:** 1.4600 g. **Composition:** 0.9170 Silver .0430 oz. ASW **Obverse:** Type I **Obv. Legend:** GEORGE V KING EMPEROR

Date	Mintage	F	VF	XF	Unc	BU
1911(c)	16,760,000	1.50	3.00	6.00	12.00	—
1911(c) Proof	—	Value: 75.00				
1911(c) P/L-R	—	—	—	—	50.00	—

KM# 515 2 ANNAS **Weight:** 1.4600 g. **Composition:** 0.9170 Silver .0430 oz. ASW **Obverse:** Type II **Obv. Legend:** GEORGE V KING EMPEROR

Date	Mintage	F	VF	XF	Unc	BU
1912(c)	7,724,000	1.25	2.50	5.00	10.00	—
1912(c) Proof	—	Value: 50.00				
1912(b)	2,462,000	1.50	3.00	6.00	12.00	—
1912(b) Proof	—	Value: 50.00				
1912(b) P/L-R	—	—	—	—	25.00	—
1913(c)	13,959,000	1.25	2.50	5.00	10.00	—
1913(c) Proof	—	Value: 50.00				
1913(b)	5,461,000	1.25	2.50	5.00	10.00	—
1913(b) Proof	—	Value: 50.00				
1913(b) P/L-R	—	—	—	—	25.00	—
1914(c)	13,622,000	1.25	2.50	5.00	10.00	—
1914(c) Proof	—	Value: 50.00				
1914(b)	8,579,000	1.25	2.50	5.00	10.00	—
1914(b) P/L-R	—	—	—	—	25.00	—
1915(c)	5,892,000	1.25	2.50	5.00	10.00	—
1915(c) Proof	—	Value: 50.00				
1915(b)	5,943,000	1.25	2.50	5.00	10.00	—
1915(b) P/L-R	—	—	—	—	25.00	—
1916(c)	197,878,000	1.25	2.00	4.00	8.00	—
1916(c) Proof	—	Value: 50.00				
1916(c) P/L-R	—	—	—	—	25.00	—
1917(c)	25,560,000	1.25	2.00	4.00	8.00	—
1917(c) Proof	—	Value: 50.00				
1917(c) P/L-R	—	—	—	—	25.00	—

KM# 516 2 ANNAS **Composition:** Copper-Nickel **Obv. Legend:** GEORGE V KING EMPEROR **Shape:** Square **Note:** Calcutta Mint issues have no mint mark. Bombay Mint issues have a small raised dot on the reverse at the bottom near the rim.

Date	Mintage	F	VF	XF	Unc	BU
1918(c)	53,412,000	1.25	1.75	4.00	10.00	—
1918(c) Proof	—	Value: 50.00				
1918(b)	9,191,000	1.25	1.75	4.00	10.00	—
1918(b) Proof	—	Value: 50.00				
1918(b) P/L-R	—	—	—	—	20.00	—
1919(c)	89,040,000	1.25	1.75	4.00	10.00	—
1919(c) Proof	—	Value: 50.00				
1919(c) P/L-R	—	—	—	—	20.00	—
1920(b) Proof	—	Value: 125				
1920(c)	13,520,000	1.25	1.75	4.00	10.00	—
1920(c) Proof	—	Value: 50.00				
1921(c) P/L-R	—	1.25	1.75	4.00	10.00	—
1923(c)	7,656,000	1.25	1.75	4.00	10.00	—
1923(c) Proof	—	Value: 50.00				
1923(b)	6,431,000	1.25	1.75	4.00	10.00	—
1923(b) Proof	—	Value: 50.00				
1923(b) P/L-R	—	—	—	—	20.00	—
1924(c)	8,384,000	1.25	1.75	4.00	10.00	—
1924(c) Proof	—	Value: 50.00				
1924(b)	4,818,000	1.50	3.00	6.00	12.00	—
1924(b) Proof	—	Value: 50.00				
1924(b) P/L-R	—	—	—	—	20.00	—
1925(c)	10,848,000	1.25	1.75	4.00	10.00	—
1925(c) Proof	—	Value: 50.00				
1925(b)	8,348,000	1.25	1.75	4.00	10.00	—
1925(b) Proof	—	Value: 50.00				
1925(b) P/L-R	—	—	—	—	220	—
1926(c)	8,352,000	1.25	1.75	4.00	10.00	—
1926(c) Proof	—	Value: 50.00				
1926(b)	2,927,000	1.75	3.50	7.00	14.00	—
1926(b) Proof	—	Value: 50.00				
1926(b) P/L-R	—	—	—	—	20.00	—
1927(c)	6,424,000	1.25	1,375	4.00	10.00	—
1927(c) Proof	—	Value: 50.00				
1927(b)	4,835,000	1.50	3.00	6.00	12.00	—
1927(b) Proof	—	Value: 50.00				
1927(b) P/L-R	—	—	—	—	20.00	—
1928(c)	7,352,000	1.25	1.75	4.00	10.00	—
1928(c) Proof	—	Value: 50.00				
1928(b)	4,876,000	1.50	3.00	6.00	12.00	—
1928(b) Proof	—	Value: 50.00				
1928(b) P/L-R	—	—	—	—	20.00	—
1929(c)	13,408,000	1.25	1.75	4.00	10.00	—
1929(c) Proof	—	Value: 50.00				
1929(c) P/L-R	—	—	—	—	20.00	—
1930(c)	8,888,000	1.25	1.75	4.00	10.00	—
1930(c) Proof	—	Value: 50.00				
1930(c) P/L-R	—	—	—	—	20.00	—
1930(b)	—	1.25	1.75	4.00	10.00	—
1933(c)	4,300,000	1.50	3.00	6.00	12.00	—
1933(c) Proof	—	Value: 50.00				
1933(c) P/L-R	—	—	—	—	20.00	—
1934(c)	7,016,000	1.25	1.75	4.00	10.00	—
1934(c) Proof	—	Value: 50.00				
1934(c) P/L-R	—	—	—	—	20.00	—
1935(c)	12,344,000	1.25	1.75	4.00	10.00	—
1935(b)	21,017,000	1.00	1.50	3.00	8.00	—
1935(b) Proof	—	Value: 50.00				
1935(b) P/L-R	—	—	—	—	20.00	—
1936(b)	36,295,000	1.00	1.50	3.00	8.00	—
1936(b) Proof	—	Value: 50.00				

KM# 540 2 ANNAS **Composition:** Copper-Nickel **Obverse:** First head, high relief **Obv. Legend:** GEORGE VI KING EMPEROR **Shape:** Square **Note:** Calcutta Mint issues have no mint mark. Mumbai (Bombay) Mint issues have a small dot before and after the date.

Date	Mintage	F	VF	XF	Unc	BU
1939(c)	4,148,000	1.25	3.00	6.00	15.00	—
1939(b)	3,392,000	2.00	5.00	10.00	25.00	—

KM# 541 2 ANNAS **Composition:** Copper-Nickel **Obverse:** Second head, low relief, large crown **Obv. Legend:** GEORGE VI KING EMPEROR **Shape:** Square

Date	Mintage	F	VF	XF	Unc	BU
1939(c)	Inc. above	1.25	2.00	2.50	4.00	—
1939(c) Proof	—	Value: 40.00				
1939(b)	Inc. above	0.20	0.30	0.50	1.50	—
1939(b) Proof	—	Value: 40.00				
1939(b) P/L-R	—	—	—	—	25.00	—
1940(c)	37,636,000	0.20	0.30	0.50	2.00	—
1940(c) Proof	—	Value: 40.00				
1940(b)	50,599,000	0.20	0.30	0.50	2.00	—
1940(b) P/L-R	—	—	—	—	25.00	—
1941(c)	63,456,000	0.20	0.30	0.50	1.50	—
1941(b)	10,760,000	1.25	2.00	2.50	4.00	—
1941(b) Proof	—	Value: 40.00				
1941(b) P/L-R	—	—	—	—	25.00	—

KM# 541a 2 ANNAS **Composition:** Nickel-Brass **Obverse:** Second head, low relief, large crown **Obv. Legend:** GEORGE VI KING EMPEROR **Shape:** Square

Date	Mintage	F	VF	XF	Unc	BU
1942(b) Small 4	133,000,000	0.25	0.35	0.50	2.25	—
1942(b) Large 4	Inc. above	0.20	0.35	0.50	2.25	—
1943(b)	343,680,000	0.25	0.35	0.50	2.25	—
1944L	6,352,000	0.50	1.25	2.00	5.00	—

Note: On 1944 Lahore issues, a tiny L replaces the decorative stroke in the four quatrefoil angles.

Date	Mintage	F	VF	XF	Unc	BU
1944(b) Small 4	219,700,000	0.25	0.35	0.50	2.25	—
1944(b) Large 4	Inc. above	0.25	0.35	0.50	2.25	—

KM# 543 2 ANNAS **Composition:** Nickel-Brass **Obverse:** Second head, low relief, large crown **Obv. Legend:** GEORGE VI KING EMPEROR **Reverse:** Small "2" **Shape:** Square

Date	Mintage	F	VF	XF	Unc	BU
1945(c)	24,260,000	0.25	0.75	1.25	2.75	—
1945(c) Proof	—	Value: 40.00				
1945(b)	136,688,000	0.25	0.35	0.50	1.50	—
1945(b) P/L-R	—	—	—	—	25.00	—

KM# 542 2 ANNAS **Composition:** Copper-Nickel **Obverse:** Second head, low relief, small crown **Obv. Legend:** GEORGE VI KING EMPEROR **Reverse:** Small "2" **Shape:** Square

Date	Mintage	F	VF	XF	Unc	BU
1946(c)	67,267,000	0.20	0.30	0.50	2.25	—
1946(c)	52,500,000	0.20	0.30	0.50	2.25	—
1946(b) Proof	—	Value: 40.00				
1946(b) P/L-R	—	—	—	—	25.00	—
1946(l)	25,480,000	0.20	0.30	0.50	2.25	—

Note: Without "L" mintmark but with small diamond-shaped mark left of "I" on reverse

Date	Mintage	F	VF	XF	Unc	BU
1947(c)	57,428,000	0.20	0.30	0.50	2.25	—
1947(b)	38,908,000	0.20	0.30	0.50	2.25	—
1947(b) Proof	—	Value: 40.00				
1947(b) P/L-R	—	—	—	—	25.00	—

KM# 519 4 ANNAS **Composition:** Copper-Nickel **Obv. Legend:** GEORGE V KING EMPEROR • INDIA • **Shape:**

Scalloped **Note:** Calcutta Mint issues have no mint mark. Bombay Mint issues have a small raised dot on the reverse at the bottom near the rim.

Date	Mintage	F	VF	XF	Unc	BU
1919(c)	18,632	2.50	5.00	10.00	20.00	—
1919(c) Proof	—	Value: 150				
1919(b)	7,672,000	3.25	6.50	12.50	25.00	—
1919 P/L-R	—	—	—	—	25.00	—
1920(c)	18,191,000	2.50	5.00	10.00	20.00	—
1920(c) Proof	—	Value: 150				
1920(b)	1,666,000	3.25	6.50	12.50	25.00	—
1920(b) Proof	—	Value: 150				
1920(b) P/L-R	—	—	—	—	25.00	—
1921(c) Proof	—	Value: 150				
1921(c) P/L-R	—	—	—	—	25.00	—
1921(b)	1,219,000	3.75	7.50	15.00	30.00	—
1921(b) Proof	—	—	—	—	150	—

KM# 520 8 ANNAS **Composition:** Copper-Nickel **Obv. Legend:** GEORGE V KING EMPEROR **Note:** Calcutta Mint issues have no mint mark. Mumbai (Bombay) Mint issues have a small raised dot on the reverse at the bottom near the rim.

Date	Mintage	F	VF	XF	Unc	BU
1919(c)	2,980,000	3.75	7.50	15.00	30.00	—
1919(c) Proof	—	Value: 150				
1919(b)	1,400,000	4.00	8.50	17.50	35.00	—
1919(b) P/L-R	—	—	—	—	30.00	—
1920(c) Proof	—	Value: 150				
1920(c) P/L-R	—	—	—	—	75.00	—
1920(b)	1,000,000	12.50	25.00	50.00	100	—
1920(b) Proof	—	Value: 150				
1920(b) P/L-R	—	—	—	—	30.00	—

1/4 RUPEE

NOTE: The distinguishing features of the 3 busts and 2 reverses are as following:
BUST A - The front of dress has 4 panels w/flower at right on bottom panel.
BUST B - Front of dress has 3-3/4 panels w/flower at center on incomplete bottom panel.
BUST C - Front of dress has 3 panels w/flower at left on bottom panel.

REVERSE I - The 2 large petals above the base of the top flower are long and curved downward; long stroke between "1/4".
REVERSE II - The 2 large petals above the base of the top flower are short and horizontal; short stroke between "1/4".

KM# 490 1/4 RUPEE **Weight:** 2.9200 g. **Composition:** 0.9170 Silver .0860 oz. ASW **Obverse:** 5 Rupee, KM#476 **Obv. Legend:** VICTORIA EMPRRESS **Reverse:** 1/4 Rupee, KM#470

Date	Mintage	F	VF	XF	Unc	BU
1901C C/II, "C" incuse	4,476,000	2.00	3.00	6.00	15.00	—
1901C Proof	—	Value: 125				
1901C P/L-R	—	—	—	—	30.00	—

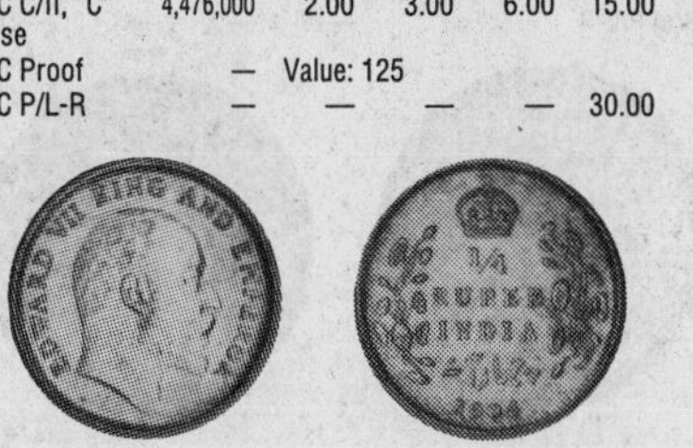

KM# 506 1/4 RUPEE **Weight:** 2.9200 g. **Composition:** 0.9170 Silver .0860 oz. ASW **Obv. Legend:** EDWARD VII KING AND EMPEROR

Date	Mintage	F	VF	XF	Unc	BU
1903(c)	7,060,000	1.50	3.00	8.00	20.00	—
1903(c) Proof	—	Value: 100				
1903(c) P/L-R	—	—	—	—	30.00	—
1904(c)	10,026,000	1.50	3.00	8.00	20.00	—
1904(c) Proof	—	Value: 100				
1904(c) P/L-R	—	—	—	—	30.00	—
1905(c)	6,300,000	1.50	3.00	8.00	20.00	—
1905(c) Proof	—	Value: 100				
1905(c) P/L-R	—	—	—	—	30.00	—
1906(c)	10,672,000	1.50	3.00	8.00	20.00	—
1906(c) P/L-R	—	—	—	—	30.00	—
1907(c)	11,464,000	1.50	3.00	8.00	20.00	—
1907(c) Proof	—	Value: 100				
1907(c) P/L-R	—	—	—	—	30.00	—
1908(c)	7,084,000	1.50	3.00	8.00	20.00	—
1908(c) Proof	—	Value: 100				
1908(c) P/L-R	—	—	—	—	30.00	—
1909(c) Proof	—	Value: 125				
1909(c) P/L-R	—	—	—	—	30.00	—
1910(c)	8,024,000	1.50	3.00	8.00	20.00	—
1910(c) Proof	—	Value: 100				
1910(c) P/L-R	—	—	—	—	30.00	—

KM# 506a 1/4 RUPEE **Composition:** Gold

Date	F	VF	XF	Unc	BU
1910(c) P/L-R	—	—	—	800	—

KM# 517 1/4 RUPEE **Weight:** 2.9200 g. **Composition:** 0.9170 Silver .0860 oz. ASW **Obverse:** Type I **Obv. Legend:** GEORGE V KING EMPEROR

Date	Mintage	F	VF	XF	Unc	BU
1911(c)	2,245,000	2.00	4.00	8.00	8.00	—
1911(c) Proof	—	Value: 90.00				
1911(c) P/L-R	—	—	—	—	60.00	—

KM# 518 1/4 RUPEE **Weight:** 2.9200 g. **Composition:** 0.9170 Silver .0860 oz. ASW **Obverse:** Type II **Obv. Legend:** GEORGE V KING EMPEROR

Date	Mintage	F	VF	XF	Unc	BU
1912(c)	9,587,000	2.00	2.75	5.00	12.00	—
1912(c) Proof	—	Value: 65.00				
1912(b)	2,200,000	2.00	2.75	5.00	12.00	—
1912(b) Proof	—	Value: 65.00				
1912(b) P/L-R	—	—	—	—	22.00	—
1913(c)	12,686,000	2.00	2.75	5.00	12.00	—
1913(c) Proof	—	Value: 65.00				
1913(b)	2,276,000	2.00	2.75	5.00	12.00	—
1913(b) Proof	—	Value: 65.00				
1913(b) P/L-R	—	—	—	—	22.00	—
1914(c)	1,423,000	2.00	2.75	5.00	12.00	—
1914(c) Proof	—	Value: 65.00				
1914(b)	7,949,000	2.00	2.75	5.00	10.00	—
1914(b) P/L-R	—	—	—	—	22.00	—
1915(c)	851,000	2.25	4.00	10.00	35.00	—
1915(c) Proof	—	Value: 65.00				
1915(b)	2,096,000	2.00	2.75	5.00	12.00	—
1915(c) P/L-R	—	—	—	—	—	—
1915(b) P/L-R	—	—	—	—	22.00	—
1916(c)	13,178,000	2.00	2.75	5.00	12.00	—
1916(c) Proof	—	Value: 65.00				
1916(c) P/L-R	—	—	—	—	22.00	—
1917(c)	21,072,000	2.00	2.75	5.00	12.00	—
1917(c) Proof	—	Value: 65.00				
1917(c) P/L-R	—	—	—	—	22.00	—
1918(c)	50,575,000	2.00	2.75	5.00	12.00	—
1918(c) Proof	—	Value: 65.00				
1919(b)	—	3.50	7.50	15.00	30.00	—
1919(c)	26,135,000	2.00	2.75	5.00	12.00	—
1919(c) Proof	—	Value: 65.00				
1920(b)	—	3.25	6.50	12.50	25.00	—
1925(b)	4,007,000	2.00	2.75	5.00	12.00	—
1925(b) Proof	—	Value: 65.00				
1925(b) P/L-R	—	—	—	—	22.00	—
1926(c)	8,169,000	2.00	2.75	5.00	12.00	—
1926(c) Proof	—	Value: 65.00				
1926(c) P/L-R	—	—	—	—	22.00	—
1928(b)	4,023,000	2.00	2.75	5.00	12.00	—
1928(b) Proof	—	Value: 65.00				
1929(c)	4,013,000	2.00	2.75	5.00	12.00	—
1929(c) Proof	—	Value: 65.00				
1929(c) P/L-R	—	—	—	—	22.00	—
1930(c)	3,222,000	2.00	2.75	5.00	12.00	—
1930(c) Proof	—	Value: 65.00				
1930(c) P/L-R	—	—	—	—	22.00	—
1934(c)	3,946,000	2.00	2.75	5.00	10.00	—
1936(c)	25,744,000	1.25	2.25	4.00	8.00	—
1936(b)	9,864,000	1.25	2.25	4.00	8.00	—
1936(b) P/L-R	—	—	—	—	22.00	—

First Head

Second Head (small) Second Head (large)

From 1942 to 1945 the reverse designs of the silver coins change slightly every year. However, a distinct reverse variety occurs on Rupees and 1/4 Rupees dated 1943-44 and on the half Rupee dated 1944, all struck at Bombay. This variety may be distinguished from the other coins by the design of the center bottom flower as illustrated, and is designated as Reverse B.

On the normal common varieties dated 1943-44 the three "scalloped circles" are not connected to each other and the bead in the center is not attached to the nearest circle.

Obv: First head, reeded edge.

NOTE: Calcutta Mint issues have no mint mark. Bombay coins have a small bead below the lotus flower at the bottom on the reverse, except those dated 1943-1944 with reverse B which have a diamond. Lahore Mint issues have a small "L" in the same position. The nickel coins have a diamond below the date on the reverse.

KM# 544 1/4 RUPEE **Weight:** 2.9200 g. **Composition:** 0.9170 Silver .0860 oz. ASW **Obv. Legend:** GEORGE VI KING EMPEROR

Date	Mintage	F	VF	XF	Unc	BU
1938(c) Proof	—	Value: 65.00				
1938(c) P/L-R	—	—	—	—	25.00	—
1939(c)	3,072,000	2.00	3.50	6.00	12.00	—
1939(c) Proof	—	Value: 65.00				
1939(b)	6,770,000	2.00	3.50	5.00	10.00	—
1939(b) P/L-R	—	—	—	—	25.00	—

KM# 544a 1/4 RUPEE **Weight:** 2.9200 g. **Composition:** 0.5000 Silver .0469 oz. ASW **Obv. Legend:** GEORGE VI KING EMPEROR

Date	Mintage	F	VF	XF	Unc	BU
1940(b)	24,635,000	2.00	3.50	5.00	10.00	—

KM# 545 1/4 RUPEE Weight: 2.9200 g. **Composition:** 0.5000 Silver .0469 oz. ASW **Obverse:** Large second head, small rim decoration **Obv. Legend:** GEORGE VI KING EMPEROR **Edge:** Reeded

Date	Mintage	VG	F	VF	XF	Unc
1940(c)	68,675,000	—	BV	1.50	2.50	6.00
1940(c) Proof	—	Value: 65.00				
1940(b)	28,947,000	—	BV	1.50	2.50	6.00

KM# 546 1/4 RUPEE Weight: 2.9200 g. **Composition:** 0.5000 Silver .0469 oz. ASW **Obverse:** Small second head, large rim decoration **Obv. Legend:** GEORGE VI KING EMPEROR **Edge:** Reeded

Date	Mintage	F	VF	XF	Unc	BU
1942(c)	88,096,000	BV	1.50	2.25	4.50	—
1943(c)	90,994,000	BV	1.50	2.25	4.50	—

KM# 547 1/4 RUPEE Weight: 2.9200 g. **Composition:** 0.5000 Silver .0469 oz. ASW **Obverse:** Small second head, large rim decoration **Obv. Legend:** GEORGE VI KING EMPEROR **Edge:** Security

Date	Mintage	F	VF	XF	Unc	BU
1943B	95,200,000	BV	1.50	2.25	4.50	—
1943B Proof	—	Value: 60.00				
1943B Reverse B	Inc. above	BV	1.50	2.25	4.50	—
1943L	23,700,000	BV	1.50	2.25	4.50	—
1944B	170,504,000	BV	1.50	2.25	4.50	—
1944B Reverse B	Inc. above	BV	1.50	2.25	4.50	—
1944L	86,400,000	BV	1.50	2.25	4.50	—
1945(b) Small 5	181,648,000	BV	1.50	2.25	4.50	—
1945(b) Large 5	Inc. above	10.00	15.00	25.00	40.00	—
1945L Small 5	29,751,000	BV	1.50	2.25	4.50	—
1945L Large 5	Inc. above	BV	1.00	2.00	5.00	—

KM# 548 1/4 RUPEE Composition: Nickel **Obv. Legend:** GEORGE VI KING EMPEROR **Reverse:** Indian tiger **Edge:** Reeded

Date	Mintage	F	VF	XF	Unc	BU
1946(b)	83,600,000	0.40	0.75	1.50	5.00	—
1947(b)	109,948,000	0.40	0.75	1.50	5.00	—
1947(b) Proof	—	Value: 50.00				

KM# 507 1/2 RUPEE Weight: 5.8300 g. **Composition:** 0.9170 Silver .1719 oz. ASW **Obv. Legend:** EDWARD VII KING AND EMPEROR **Note:** Calcutta Mint issues have no mint mark. Mumbai (Bombay) Mint issues have a small incuse "B" in the space below the cross pattee of the crown on the reverse.

Date	Mintage	F	VF	XF	Unc	BU
1904(c) Proof	—	Value: 175				
1904(c) P/L-R	—	—	—	—	40.00	—
1905(c)	823,000	3.50	10.00	25.00	50.00	—
1905(c) P/L-R	—	—	—	—	40.00	—
1906(c)	3,036,000	3.50	10.00	25.00	50.00	—
1906B	400,000	3.75	12.50	30.00	60.00	—
1906B P/L-R	—	—	—	—	40.00	—
1907(c)	2,786,000	3.50	10.00	25.00	50.00	—
1907(c) Proof	—	Value: 150				
1907B	1,856,000	3.50	10.00	25.00	50.00	—
1907B Proof	—	Value: 150				
1907B P/L-R	—	—	—	—	40.00	—
1908(c)	1,577,000	3.50	10.00	25.00	50.00	—
1908(c) Proof	—	Value: 150				
1908(c) P/L-R	—	—	—	—	40.00	—
1909(c)	1,569,000	3.50	10.00	25.00	50.00	—
1909(c) Proof	—	Value: 150				
1909(c) P/L-R	—	—	—	—	40.00	—
1909B Proof	—	Value: 450				
1909B P/L-R	—	—	—	—	90.00	—
1910(c)	3,413,000	3.50	10.00	25.00	50.00	—
1910(c) Proof	—	Value: 150				
1910B	809,000	3.50	10.00	25.00	50.00	—
1910B "B" raised	—	10.00	15.00	30.00	55.00	—
1910B Proof	—	Value: 150				
1910B P/L-R	—	—	—	—	40.00	—

KM# 521 1/2 RUPEE Weight: 5.8300 g. **Composition:** 0.9170 Silver .1719 oz. ASW **Obverse:** Type I **Obv. Legend:** GEORGE V KING EMPEROR **Note:** Calcutta Mint issues have no mint mark. Mumbai (Bombay) Mint issues have a small raised bead or dot in the space below the lotus flower at the bottom of the reverse. The half Rupee dated 1911 like the Rupee and all the other issues of that year has the "Pig" elephant. It was struck only at the Calcutta Mint.

Date	Mintage	F	VF	XF	Unc	BU
1911(c)	2,293,000	2.00	6.00	12.50	30.00	—
1911(c) Proof	—	Value: 175				
1911(c) P/L-R	—	—	—	—	75.00	—

KM# 522 1/2 RUPEE Weight: 5.8300 g. **Composition:** 0.9170 Silver .1719 oz. ASW **Obverse:** Type II **Obv. Legend:** GEORGE V KING EMPEROR

Date	Mintage	F	VF	XF	Unc	BU
1912(c)	3,390,000	2.00	6.00	12.00	28.00	—
1912(c) Proof	—	Value: 125				
1912(b)	1,505,000	2.00	6.00	12.00	28.00	—
1912(b) Proof	—	Value: 125				
1912(b) P/L-R	—	—	—	—	22.00	—
1913(c)	2,723,000	2.00	6.00	12.00	28.00	—
1913(c) Proof	—	Value: 125				
1913(b)	1,825,000	2.00	6.00	12.00	28.00	—
1913(b) Proof	—	Value: 125				
1913(b) P/L-R	—	—	—	—	22.00	—
1914(c)	1,400,000	2.00	6.00	12.00	28.00	—
1914(c) Proof	—	Value: 125				
1914(b)	903,000	2.00	6.00	12.50	30.00	—
1914(b) P/L-R	—	—	—	—	22.00	—
1915(c)	2,804,000	2.00	6.00	12.00	28.00	—
1915(c) Proof	—	Value: 125				
1915(c) P/L-R	—	2.00	6.00	12.00	28.00	—
1916(c)	3,644,000	2.00	6.00	12.00	28.00	—
1916(c) Proof	—	Value: 125				
1916(b)	5,880,000	2.00	6.00	12.00	28.00	—
1917(c) Proof	—	Value: 125				
1917(b)	8,822,000	2.00	6.00	12.00	28.00	—
1917(b) Proof	—	Value: 125				
1918(c) P/L-R	—	—	—	—	22.00	—
1918(b) P/L-R	—	—	—	—	22.00	—
1918(b)	10,325,000	2.00	6.00	12.00	28.00	—
1919(b)	8,958,000	2.00	6.00	12.00	28.00	—
1919(b) Proof	—	Value: 125				
1919(b) P/L-R	—	—	—	—	22.00	—
1919(c) P/L-R	—	—	—	—	22.00	—
1921(c)	5,804,000	2.00	6.00	12.00	28.00	—
1921(c) Proof	—	Value: 125				
1921(c) P/L-R	—	—	—	—	22.00	—
1922(c)	5,551,000	2.00	6.00	12.00	28.00	—
1922(c) Proof	—	Value: 125				
1922(b)	1,037,000	2.00	6.00	12.00	28.00	—
1922(b) Proof	—	Value: 125				
1922(b) P/L-R	—	—	—	—	22.00	—
1923(c)	3,925,000	2.00	6.00	12.00	28.00	—
1923(c) P/L-R	—	—	—	—	22.00	—
1923(b)	2,076,000	2.00	6.00	12.00	28.00	—
1923(b) Proof	—	Value: 125				
1923(b) P/L-R	—	—	—	—	22.00	—
1924(c)	4,007,000	2.00	6.00	12.00	28.00	—
1924(c) Proof	—	Value: 125				
1924(b)	2,664,000	2.00	6.00	12.00	28.00	—
1924(b) Proof	—	Value: 125				
1924(b) P/L-R	—	—	—	—	22.00	—
1925(c)	4,119,000	2.00	6.00	12.00	28.00	—
1925(c) Proof	—	Value: 125				
1925(b)	1,627,000	2.00	6.00	12.00	28.00	—
1925(b) Proof	—	Value: 125				
1925(b) P/L-R	—	—	—	—	22.00	—
1926(c)	4,027,000	2.00	6.00	12.00	28.00	—
1926(c) Proof	—	Value: 125				
1926(b)	2,011,000	2.00	6.00	12.00	28.00	—
1926(b) Proof	—	Value: 125				
1926(b) P/L-R	—	—	—	—	22.00	—
1927(c)	2,032,000	2.00	6.00	12.00	28.00	—
1927(c) Proof	—	Value: 125				
1927(c) P/L-R	—	—	—	—	22.00	—
1928(b)	2,466,000	2.00	6.00	12.00	28.00	—
1928(b) Proof	—	Value: 125				
1929(c)	4,050,000	2.00	6.00	12.00	28.00	—
1929(c) Proof	—	Value: 125				
1929(c) P/L-R	—	—	—	—	22.00	—
1930(c)	2,036,000	2.00	6.00	12.00	28.00	—
1930(c) Proof	—	Value: 125				
1930(c) P/L-R	—	—	—	—	22.00	—
1933/2(c)	4,056,000	5.00	10.00	25.00	50.00	—
1933(c)	Inc. above	2.00	6.00	12.00	28.00	—
1933(c) Proof	—	Value: 75.00				
1933(c) P/L-R	—	—	—	—	22.00	—
1934(c)	4,056,000	2.00	6.00	12.00	28.00	—
1934(c) Proof	—	Value: 125				
1934(c) P/L-R	—	—	—	—	22.00	—
1936(c)	16,919,000	2.00	6.00	12.00	28.00	—
1936(b)	6,693,000	2.00	6.00	12.00	28.00	—
1936(b) P/L-R	—	—	—	—	22.00	—

Obv: First head, reeded edge.

NOTE: Calcutta Mint issues have no mint mark. Bombay coins dated 1938-43 and 1945 have a bead below the lotus flower at the bottom of the reverse. Specimens dated 1944 with Reverse B have a diamond in the same position. Those dated 1944 with the normal common reverse have either a bead or a diamond. Lahore Mint issues have a small raised "L" in the same position as the Bombay coins. Bombay Mint 1943 coins have either large or small denticles on obverse. The nickel pieces of the last issue have a diamond below the date on the reverse.

KM# 549 1/2 RUPEE Weight: 5.8300 g. **Composition:** 0.9170 Silver .1719 oz. ASW **Obverse:** First head **Obv. Legend:** GEORGE VI KING EMPEROR **Edge:** Reeded

Date	Mintage	F	VF	XF	Unc	BU
1938(c) Proof	—	Value: 100				
1938(b)	2,200,000	BV	3.00	7.50	15.00	—
1938(b) P/L-R	—	—	—	—	25.00	—
1939(c)	3,300,000	BV	3.00	7.50	15.00	—
1939(c) Proof	—	Value: 75.00				
1939(b)	10,096,000	BV	3.00	7.50	15.00	—
1939(b) Proof	—	Value: 75.00				
1939(b) P/L-R	—	—	—	—	25.00	—

NOTE: Example of large 5 in date 1945.

KM# A553 1/2 RUPEE Composition: Copper-Nickel **Obverse:** KM#552 **Obv. Legend:** GEORGE VI KING EMPEROR **Reverse:** KM#549 **Note:** Mule.

Date	F	VF	XF	Unc	BU
1938(c) P/L-R	—	—	—	—	—

KM# 550 1/2 RUPEE Weight: 5.8300 g. **Composition:** 0.9170 Silver .1719 oz. ASW **Obverse:** Large second head, small rim decoration **Obv. Legend:** GEORGE VI KING EMPEROR **Edge:** Reeded

Date	VG	F	VF	XF	Unc
1939(c)	—	BV	3.00	6.50	15.00
1939(b)	—	BV	3.00	6.50	13.50

KM# 550a 1/2 RUPEE Weight: 5.8300 g. **Composition:** 0.5000 Silver .0937 oz. ASW **Obv. Legend:** GEORGE VI KING EMPEROR

Date	Mintage	F	VF	XF	Unc	BU
1940(c)	32,898,000	BV	3.00	6.00	12.00	—
1940(c) Proof	—	Value: 75.00				
1940(b)	17,811,000	BV	3.00	6.50	13.50	—
1940(b) P/L-R	—	—	—	—	25.00	—

KM# 551 1/2 RUPEE Weight: 5.8300 g. **Composition:** 0.5000 Silver .0937 oz. ASW **Obverse:** Large second head, small rim decoration **Obv. Legend:** GEORGE VI KING EMPEROR **Edge:** Security

Date	Mintage	VG	F	VF	XF	Unc
1941(b)	26,100,000	—	BV	2.00	5.00	12.50
1942(b)	61,600,000	—	BV	2.00	5.00	12.50

KM# 552 1/2 RUPEE **Weight:** 5.8300 g. **Composition:** 0.5000 Silver .0937 oz. ASW **Obverse:** Small second head, large rim decoration **Obv. Legend:** GEORGE VI KING EMPEROR **Reverse:** Denomination and inner circle smaller **Edge:** Security

Date	Mintage	F	VF	XF	Unc	BU
1942(b)	Inc. above	BV	2.00	4.50	9.00	—
1943(b) Dot	90,400,000	BV	2.00	4.50	9.00	—
1943(b) Proof	—	Value: 75.00				
1943(b) Diamond	—	BV	2.00	4.50	9.00	—
1943L	9,000,000	BV	2.00	4.50	9.00	—
1943L Proof	—	Value: 75.00				
1944(b) Dot	46,200,000	BV	2.00	4.50	9.00	—
1944(b) Diamond	Inc. above	BV	2.00	4.50	9.00	—
1944L	79,100,000	BV	2.00	4.50	9.00	—
1944L Proof	—	Value: 75.00				
1945(b) Small 5	32,722,000	BV	2.00	4.50	9.00	—
1945(b) Large 5	—	20.00	25.00	35.00	50.00	—
1945L Small dot	79,192,000	BV	2.00	4.50	9.00	—
1945L Proof	—	Value: 75.00				
1945L Large dot	Inc. above	2.50	5.00	10.00	20.00	—

KM# 553 1/2 RUPEE **Composition:** Nickel **Obv. Legend:** GEORGE VI KING EMPEROR **Reverse:** Indian tiger **Edge:** Reeded

Date	Mintage	F	VF	XF	Unc	BU
1946(b)	47,500,000	0.50	1.00	2.25	4.50	—
1947(b)	62,724,000	0.50	1.00	2.00	4.00	—
1947(b) Proof	—	Value: 65.00				

KM# 492 RUPEE **Weight:** 11.6600 g. **Composition:** 0.9170 Silver .3438 oz. ASW **Obv. Legend:** VICTORIA EMPRESS

Date	Mintage	F	VF	XF	Unc	BU
1901C C/I, "C" incuse	72,017,000	5.00	8.00	12.00	25.00	—
1901C Proof	Inc. above	Value: 175				
1901B A/I, "B" incuse	130,258,000	5.00	8.00	12.00	25.00	—
1901B Proof	—	Value: 175				
1901B P/L-R	—	—	—	—	35.00	—
1901B C/I, "B" incuse	Inc. above	5.00	8.00	12.00	25.00	—

KM# 508 RUPEE **Composition:** Gold **Obv. Legend:** EDWARD VII KING & EMPEROR **Note:** Calcutta Mint issues have no mint mark. Mumbai (Bombay) Mint issues have a small incuse "B" in the space below the cross pattee of the crown on the reverse.

Date	Mintage	F	VF	XF	Unc	BU
1903(c)	49,403,000	5.00	8.00	12.00	25.00	—
1903(c) Proof	—	Value: 350				
1903B In relief	52,969	5.00	8.00	12.00	25.00	—
1903B Proof	—	Value: 350				
1903B Incuse	Inc. above	5.00	8.00	12.00	25.00	—
1903B P/L-R	—	—	—	—	30.00	—
1904(c)	58,339,000	5.00	8.00	12.00	25.00	—
1904(c) Proof	—	Value: 350				
1904B	101,949,000	5.00	8.00	12.00	25.00	—
1904B Proof	—	Value: 350				
1904B P/L-R	—	—	—	—	30.00	—
1905(c)	51,258,000	5.00	8.00	12.00	25.00	—
1905(c) Proof	—	Value: 350				
1905B	76,202,000	5.00	8.00	12.00	25.00	—
1905B Proof	—	Value: 350				
1905B P/L-R	—	—	—	—	30.00	—
1906(c)	104,797,000	5.00	8.00	15.00	30.00	—
1906B	158,953,000	5.00	8.00	15.00	30.00	—
1906B Proof	—	Value: 350				
1906B P/L-R	—	—	—	—	30.00	—
1907(c)	81,338,000	5.00	8.00	15.00	30.00	—
1907(c) Proof	—	Value: 350				
1907B	170,912,000	5.00	8.00	15.00	30.00	—
1907B Proof	—	Value: 350				
1907B P/L-R	—	—	—	—	30.00	—
1908(c)	20,218,000	5.00	8.00	15.00	30.00	—
1908(c) Proof	—	Value: 350				
1908B	10,715,000	8.50	15.00	30.00	60.00	—
1908B Proof	—	Value: 350				
1908B P/L-R	—	—	—	—	30.00	—
1909(c)	12,759,000	5.00	8.00	15.00	30.00	—
1909(c) Proof	—	Value: 350				
1909B	9,539,000	8.50	15.00	30.00	60.00	—
1909B Proof	—	Value: 350				
1909B P/L-R	—	—	—	—	30.00	—
1910(c)	12,627,000	5.00	8.00	15.00	30.00	—
1910(c) Proof	—	Value: 350				
1910B	10,885,000	5.00	8.00	15.00	30.00	—
1910B Proof	—	Value: 350				
1910B P/L-R	—	—	—	—	30.00	—

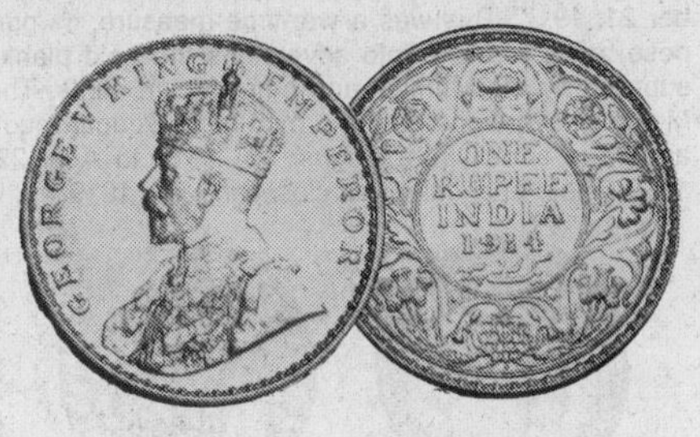

NOTE: Calcutta Mint issues have no mint mark. Bombay Mint issues have a small raised bead or dot in the space below the lotus flower at the bottom of the reverse.

Obverse Dies

Type I Type II

Type I - Obv. die w/elephant with pig-like feet and short tail. Nicknamed "pig rupee".

Type II - Obv. die w/redesigned elephant with outlined ear, heavy feet and long tail.

The Rupees dated 1911 were rejected by the public because the elephant, on the Order of the Indian Empire shown on the King's robe, was thought to resemble a pig, an animal considered unclean by most Indians. Out of a total of 9.4 million pieces struck at both mints, only 700,000 were issued, and many of these were withdrawn and melted with unissued pieces. The issues dated 1912 and later have a re-designed elephant.

KM# 523 RUPEE **Composition:** 0.9170 Silver **Obverse:** Type I **Obv. Legend:** GEORGE V KING EMPEROR

Date	Mintage	F	VF	XF	Unc	BU
1911(c)	4,300	10.00	20.00	40.00	100	—
1911(c) Proof	—	Value: 600				
1911(b)	5,143,000	10.00	20.00	40.00	100	—
1911(b) P/L-R	—	—	—	—	75.00	—

KM# 524 RUPEE **Composition:** 0.9170 Silver **Obverse:** Type II **Obv. Legend:** GEORGE V KING EMPEROR

Date	Mintage	F	VF	XF	Unc	BU
1912(c)	45,122,000	5.00	9.50	15.00	35.00	—
1912(c) Proof	—	Value: 500				
1912(b)	79,067,000	5.00	8.00	12.50	25.00	—
1912(b) Proof	—	Value: 500				
1912B P/L-R	—	—	—	—	30.00	—
1913(c)	75,800,000	5.00	8.00	12.50	25.00	—
1913(c) Proof	—	Value: 500				
1913(b)	87,466,000	5.00	8.00	12.50	25.00	—
1913(b) Proof	—	Value: 500				
1913(b) P/L-R	—	—	—	—	30.00	—
1914(c)	33,100,000	5.00	8.00	12.50	25.00	—
1914(c) Proof	—	Value: 500				
1914(b)	15,270,000	5.00	8.00	12.50	25.00	—
1914(b) Proof	—	Value: 500				
1914(b) P/L-R	—	—	—	—	30.00	—
1915(c)	9,900,000	8.50	15.00	30.00	60.00	—
1915(c) Proof	—	Value: 500				
1915(b)	5,372,000	10.00	20.00	40.00	80.00	—
1915(b) Proof	—	Value: 500				
1915(b) P/L-R	—	—	—	—	30.00	—
1916(c)	115,000,000	5.00	8.00	12.50	20.00	—
1916(c) Proof	—	Value: 500				
1916(b)	97,900,000	5.00	8.00	12.50	20.00	—
1916(b) Proof	—	—	—	—	—	—
1916(b) P/L-R	—	—	—	—	30.00	—
1917(c)	114,974,000	5.00	8.00	12.50	20.00	—
1917(c) Proof	—	Value: 500				
1917(b)	151,583,000	5.00	8.00	12.50	20.00	—
1917(b) Proof	—	Value: 500				
1917(b) P/L-R	—	—	—	—	30.00	—
1918(c)	205,420,000	5.00	8.00	12.50	20.00	—
1918(c) Proof	—	Value: 500				
1918(b)	210,550,000	5.00	8.00	12.50	20.00	—
1918(b) Proof	—	Value: 500				
1918(b) P/L-R	—	—	—	—	30.00	—
1919(c)	211,206,000	5.00	8.00	12.50	20.00	—
1919(c) Proof	—	Value: 500				
1919(c)	226,706,000	5.00	8.00	12.50	20.00	—
1919(b) Proof	—	Value: 500				
1919(b) P/L-R	—	—	—	—	30.00	—
1920(c)	50,500,000	5.00	8.00	12.50	20.00	—
1920(c) Proof	—	Value: 500				
1920(b)	55,937,000	5.00	8.00	12.50	20.00	—
1920(b) Proof	—	Value: 500				
1921(b)	5,115,000	12.00	22.00	45.00	125	—
1921(b) Proof	—	Value: 500				
1922(b)	2,051,000	12.00	22.00	45.00	125	—
1922(b) Proof	—	Value: 500				
1935(c) Proof	—	Value: 500				
1935(c) P/L-R	—	—	—	—	125	—
1936(c) Proof	—	Value: 500				

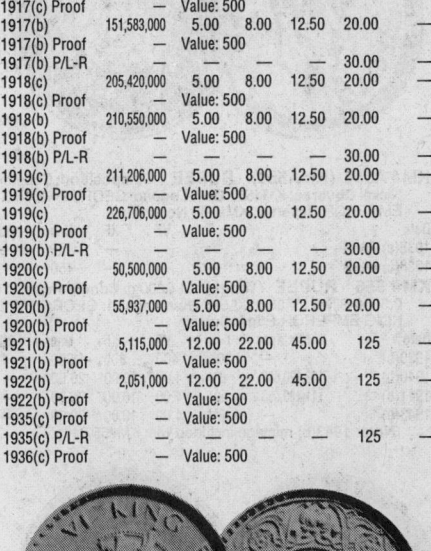

KM# 554 RUPEE **Composition:** 0.9170 Silver **Obverse:** First head **Obv. Legend:** GEORGE VI KING EMPEROR **Edge:** Reeded

Date		F	VF	XF	Unc	BU
1938(c) Proof	—	Value: 275				
1939(c) Proof	—	Value: 350				

NOTE: No rupees with the "First Head" were struck for circulation. Those dated 1938-39 were struck in 1940 before the fineness of the silver coins was reduced to .500.

The pieces struck at Calcutta have no mint mark. Bombay issues dated 1938-41 and 1944-45 have a bead below the lotus flower at the bottom of the reverse while those dated 1942-44 have a small diamond mark in the same position. On the specimens dated 1944 with Reverse B the mint mark appears to be a "bead over a diamond". Lahore Mint issues have a small raised "L" in the same position as the Bombay coins. The last issue nickel rupees struck at Bombay have a small diamond below the date on the reverse. The rupees dated 1943 occur with large and small "Second Head" and with

KM# 555 RUPEE **Composition:** 0.9170 Silver **Obverse:** Second head, small rim decoration **Obv. Legend:** GEORGE VI KING EMPEROR **Edge:** Reeded

Date	Mintage	F	VF	XF	Unc	BU
1938(b) Without dot	7,352,000	7.50	11.50	16.50	27.50	—
1938(b) Dot	Inc. above	7.50	11.50	16.50	27.50	—
1938(b) P/L-R	—	—	—	—	50.00	—
1939(b) Dot	2,450,000	150	300	600	1,200	—

KM# A556 (KMA559) RUPEE **Composition:** Copper-Nickel **Obverse:** KM#557 **Obv. Legend:** GEORGE VI KING EMPEROR **Reverse:** KM#555 **Note:** Mule.

Date	F	VF	XF	Unc	BU
1938(c) P/L-R	—	—	—	150	—
1938(c) P/L-R	—	—	—	150	—

KM# 556 RUPEE **Weight:** 11.6600 g. **Composition:** 0.5000 Silver .3438 oz. ASW **Obv. Legend:** GEORGE VI KING EMPEROR **Edge:** Security

Date	Mintage	F	VF	XF	Unc	BU
1939(b)	—	200	400	800	1,500	—
1940(b)	153,120,000	BV	4.00	10.00	20.00	—
1941(b)	111,480,000	BV	4.00	10.00	20.00	—
1943(b)	—	BV	4.00	10.00	20.00	—

Note: 1943(b) mintage included with KM#557.1.

KM# 557.1 RUPEE **Weight:** 11.6600 g. **Composition:** 0.5000 Silver .1874 oz. ASW **Obverse:** Small second head, large rim decoration **Obv. Legend:** GEORGE VI KING EMPEROR **Edge:** Security

Date	Mintage	F	VF	XF	Unc	BU
1942(b) Without dot	7,352,000	BV	4.00	10.00	20.00	—
1943(b)	65,995,000	BV	4.00	10.00	20.00	—
1943(b) Reverse B	Inc. above	BV	4.00	10.00	20.00	—
1944(b) Reverse B	146,206,000	BV	4.00	10.00	20.00	—
1944(b)	Inc. above	BV	4.00	10.00	20.00	—
1944L Small L	91,400,000	BV	4.00	10.00	20.00	—
1944L Large L	Inc. above	BV	4.00	10.00	20.00	—
1945(b) Small 5	142,666,000	BV	3.00	6.00	12.50	—
1945(b) Large 5	Inc. above	30.00	35.00	45.00	60.00	—
1945(b) Proof	—	—	—	—	—	—
1945L	118,126,000	BV	3.00	6.00	12.50	—

KM# 557a RUPEE **Composition:** Copper-Nickel **Obv. Legend:** GEORGE VI KING EMPEROR

Date	F	VF	XF	Unc	BU
1943(b) P/L-R	—	—	—	125	—

KM# 559 RUPEE **Composition:** Nickel **Reverse:** Indian tiger **Edge:** Security

Date	Mintage	F	VF	XF	Unc	BU
1947(b)	118,028,000	1.50	2.50	5.00	10.00	—
1947B Proof	—	Value: 75.00				

Note: Mumbai (Bombay) issue has diamond mark below date

Date	Mintage	F	VF	XF	Unc	BU
1947(l)	41,911,000	1.50	3.00	6.00	12.00	—

Note: Lahore without privy mark

KM# 525 15 RUPEES **Weight:** 7.9881 g. **Composition:** 0.9170 Gold .2354 oz. AGW **Obv. Legend:** GEORGE V KING EMPEROR **Note:** This issue is equal in weight and fineness to the British sovereign.

Date	Mintage	F	VF	XF	Unc	BU
1918(b)	—	200	275	350	475	—
1918(b) Proof	12	Value: 2,500				
1918(b) P/L-R		—	—	—	500	—

TRADE COINAGE

The Mansfield Commission of 1868 allowed for the admission of British and Australian sovereigns (see Australian section; sovereigns with shield reverse were struck for export to India) as payment for sums due.

The fifth branch of the Royal Mint was established in a section of the Mumbai (Bombay) Mint as of December 21, 1917. This was a war-time measure, its purpose being to strike into sovereigns the gold blanks supplied by the Mumbai and other Indian mints. The Mumbai sovereigns bear the mint mark "I" and were struck from August 15, 1918 to April 22, 1919. The branch mint was closed in May, 1919.

KM# 525A SOVEREIGN **Weight:** 7.9881 g. **Composition:** 0.9170 Gold .2354 oz. AGW

Date	Mintage	F	VF	XF	Unc	BU
1918I	1,295,000	110	125	155	200	—
1918I Proof	—	—	—	—	—	—
1918I P/L-R	—	—	—	—	575	—

BULLION COINAGE

KM# 496A TOLA **Weight:** 11.7000 g. **Composition:** 0.9960 Gold .3747 oz. AGW **Shape:** Scalloped

Date	VG	F	VF	XF	Unc
ND(1931)	—	—	BV	175	225

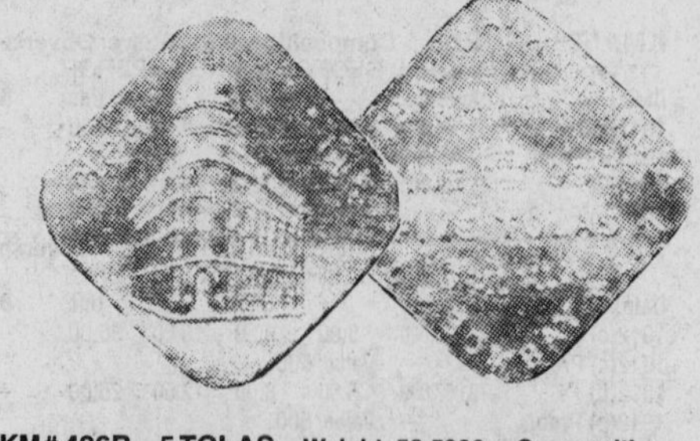

KM# 496B 5 TOLAS **Weight:** 58.5000 g. **Composition:** 0.9957 Gold 1.8727 oz. AGW **Shape:** Square

Date	VG	F	VF	XF	Unc
ND(1931)	—	—	BV	850	1,100

KM# 496C 10 TOLAS **Weight:** 117.0000 g. **Composition:** 0.9956 Gold 3.7451 oz. AGW **Shape:** Rectangular **Note:** Uniface.

Date	VG	F	VF	XF	Unc
ND(1921)	—	—	BV	1,800	2,100

KM# 496D 10 TOLAS **Composition:** 0.9957 Gold **Shape:** Rectangular

Date	VG	F	VF	XF	Unc
ND(1922)	—	—	BV	1,800	2,100

PATTERNS

Including off metal strikes

P# are in reference to The Coins of the British Commonwealth of Nation Part 4, India, Vol. 1 and 2 by F. Pridmore (Spink and Son Ltd., London 1980).

KM#	Date	Mintage	Identification	Mkt Val
Pn66	1901(c)	—	Rupee. Silver. P#1045	1,750
Pn67	1901(c)	—	Rupee. Silver. P#1046	1,750
Pn68	1903(c)	—	1/4 Rupee. Silver. With "718.93 " countermark. P#1074	—
Pn69	1903(c)	—	Anna. Nickel. P#1053	450
Pn70	1904(c)	—	1/4 Anna. Copper. P#1051	750
Pn71	1904(c)	—	Anna. Copper-Nickel. P#1054	300
Pn72	1904(c)	—	Anna. Tin. 22 mm. P#1055	450
Pn73	1904(c)	—	Anna. Copper-Nickel. 21 mm. P#1056	300
Pn74	1904(c)	—	Anna. Copper-Nickel. P#1058	300
Pn75	1904(c)	—	Anna. Copper-Nickel. P#1059	300
Pn76	1904(c)	—	Anna. Copper-Nickel. P#1060	300
Pn77	1904(c)	—	Anna. White Metal. P#1061	300
Pn78	1904(c)	—	Anna. Copper-Nickel. P#1062	300
Pn79	1904(c)	—	Anna. Copper-Nickel. P#1063	300
Pn80	1904(c)	—	1/4 Rupee. Nickel. P#1075	300
Pn81	1905(c)	—	Anna. Copper-Nickel. P#924	—
Pn82	1905(c)	—	Anna. White Metal. P#1057	300
Pn83	1905(c)	—	Anna.	30.00
Pn84	1905(c)	—	Anna. White Metal. Low relief bust; P#1066	300
Pn85	1905(c)	—	Anna. White Metal. High relief bust; P#1067	300
Pn86	1905(c)	—	Anna. Copper. High relief bust; P#1069	300
Pn87	1905(c)	—	Anna. Silver. High relief bust; P#1068	300
Pn88	1905(c)	—	Anna. White Metal. Without dot border. P#1070A	300
Pn89	1905	—	Anna. Copper-Nickel.	—
Pn90	1905(c)	—	Anna. Silver. Without dot border. P#1070B	300
Pn91	1906(c)	—	Anna. White Metal. Raised bar edge. P#1064	300
Pn92	1906(c)	—	Anna. White Metal. Double raised bar edge. P#1065	300
Pn93	1906(c)	—	Anna. Copper-Nickel. Scalloped planchet; P#1071	300
Pn94	1906(c)	—	Rupee. Copper-Nickel. "SPECIMEN" divided by crown. Lettered edge. P#1047	1,000
Pn95	1907(b)	—	Rupee. Silver. P#1048	—
Pn96	1908	—	1/2 Anna. Copper-Nickel.	300
Pn97	1908(c)	—	1/2 Anna. White Metal. P#1073	500
Pn98	1909	—	1/2 Pice. Aluminum.	175
Pn99	1910(c)	—	Rupee. Silver. P#1049	1,750
Pn100	1910(c)	—	Rupee. Gold. P#1050	—
Pn101	ND(c)	—	2 Annas. Tin. P#1052	—
Pn102	1917(c)	—	2 Annas. Copper-Nickel. Round; P#1078	—
Pn103	1917(c)	—	2 Annas. Copper-Nickel. Square; P#1079	—
Pn104	1918(c)	—	4 Annas. Copper-Nickel. Round with center hole; P#1076	—
Pn105	1919(c)	—	2 Annas. Copper-Nickel. Eight-lobed planchet; P#1087	—
Pn106	1919(c)	—	4 Annas. Copper-Nickel. Triangle; P#1077	—
Pn107	1921(c)	—	Anna. Copper-Nickel. P#1080	250
Pn108	1921(c)	—	Anna. Copper. P#1081	250
Pn109	1921(c)	—	Anna. Gold. P#1082	—
Pn110	1929(c)	—	Anna. Copper-Nickel. P#1083	400
Pn111	1929(c)	—	Anna. Copper-Nickel. Wide border; P#1084	400
Pn112	1937(c)	—	2 Annas. Copper-Nickel. P#1093	800
Pn113	1937(c)	—	2 Annas. Copper-Nickel. Serrated circular border. P#1094	800
Pn114	1938(b)	—	1/4 Anna. Bronze. Head of George V	—
Pn115	1938(c)	—	1/2 Anna. Nickel. P#1095	—
Pn116	1938(b)	—	Rupee. Silver. Head of George V	—
Pn117	1941(c)	—	Dollar. Silver. P#1088A	2,500
Pn118	1941(c)	—	Dollar. Silver. Fine milled edge.	750
Pn119	1941(b)	—	Dollar. Silver. "S" in "RUPEES" 1/2 to left of large "1"; P#1088B	—
Pn120	1941(c)	—	Dollar. Silver. P#1089	2,500

KM#	Date	Mintage	Identification	Mkt Val
Pn121	1943(c)	—	Pice. Bronze. P#1091	450
Pn122	1945(c)	—	Pie. Bronze. P#1092	—
Pn123	1946(c)	—	Pie. Bronze. Tiger left. P#1090	—

PROOF SETS

KM#	Date	Mintage	Identification	Issue Price	Mkt Val
PS3	1904 (5)	—	KM#497, 499, 503, Pn70(2)	—	3,000
PS4	1904 (3)	—	KM#497, 499, 501(bronze) with "1" countermark on reverse	—	3,000
PS5	1911(c) (4)	—	KM#514, 517, 521, 523	—	400
PS6	1919(c) (8)	—	KM#513, 516, 519-520 (2 each - V.I.P.)	—	1,500
PS7	1938(c) (6)	—	KM#527-528, 530, 536, 544, 555	—	350
PS8	1947(b) (7)	—	KM#533, 535, 538, 542, 548, 553, 559	—	300

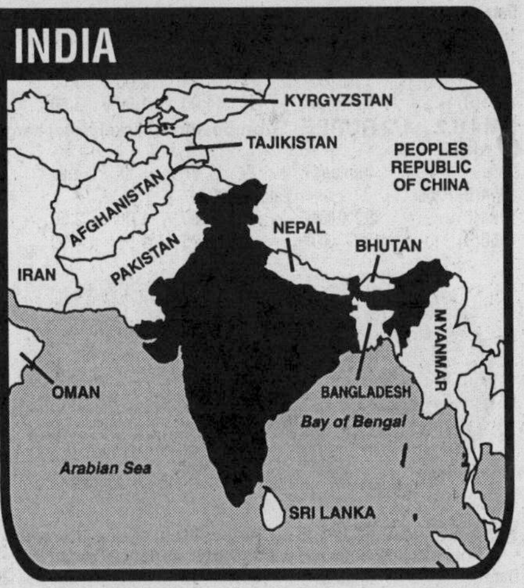

The Republic of India, a subcontinent jutting southward from the mainland of Asia, has an area of 1,269,346 sq. mi. (3,287,590 sq. km.) and a population of over 900 million, second only to that of the People's Republic of China. Capital: New Delhi. India's economy is based on agriculture and industrial activity. Engineering goods, cotton apparel and fabrics, handicrafts, tea, iron and steel are exported.

The people of India have had a continuous civilization since about 2,500 B.C., when an urban culture based on commerce and trade, and to a lesser extent, agriculture, was developed by the inhabitants of the Indus River Valley. The origins of this civilization are uncertain, but it declined about 1,500 B.C., when the region was conquered by the Aryans. Over the following 2,000 years, the Aryans developed a Brahmanic civilization and introduced the caste system. Several successive empires flourished in India over the following centuries, notably those of the Mauryans, Guptas, and Mughals. In the 8th century A.D., the Arabs expanded into western India, bringing with them the Islamic faith. A Muslim dynasty (the Mughal Empire) controlled virtually the entire subcontinent during the period preceding the arrival of the Europeans; an Indo-Islamic style of art and architecture evolved, of which the Taj Mahal is a splendid example.

The Portuguese were the first Europeans to arrive, off Calicut in May 1498. It wasn't until 1612, after Portuguese and Spanish power began to wane, that the British East India Company established its initial settlement at Surat. By the end of the century, English traders were firmly established in Bombay, Madras, and Calcutta, as well as in some parts of the interior, and Britain was implementing a policy to create the civil and military institutions that would insure British dominion over the country. By 1757, following the successful conclusion of a war of colonial rivalry with France, the British were firmly established in India as not only traders, but as conquerors. During the next 60 years, the British East India Company acquired dominion over most of India by intrigue and force, and ruled directly, or through puppet princelings.

The Indian Mutiny (called the first War of Independence by Indian Nationalists) of 1857-58, begun by Indian troops in the service of the British East India Company, revealed the intensity of the growing resentment against British domination. The widespread rebellion against British rule was unsuccessful, but resulted in the transfer of government from the company to the British crown, and was a source of inspiration, to later Indian nationalists. Agitation for representation in the government continued.

Following World War I, in which India sent six million troops to fight at the side of the Allies, Indian nationalism intensified under the banner of the Indian National Congress and the leadership of Mohandas Karamchand Gandhi, who called for non-violent revolt against British authority. The Government of India Act of 1935 proposed a federal status linking the British Indian provinces with the many princely states; in addition, provincial legislatures were to be created. The federal status was never implemented, but the legislatures were created after the election of 1937, with the National Congress winning majorities in most of the provinces.

When Britain declared war on Germany in Sept. 1939, the Viceroy declared India also to be at war with a common enemy. The Congress, however, demanded independence as a condition for cooperation; Britain refused. But as the Japanese advanced into Asia, Britain offered to transfer to Indians power over all but military affairs during the war, and set forth a plan for postwar independence. Congress was willing to accept the wartime transfer of power, but both Congress and the Muslim League rejected Britain's plan for independence; Congress because it did not sufficiently safeguard Indian unity, the Muslims (who wanted a separate Muslim state) because of fears of what would happen to Muslims within a united India.

Early in 1947, Prime Minister Clement Attlee announced that Britain would leave India "by a date not later than June 1948," even though the Hindus and Muslims could not agree among themselves on a plan for self-government. The National Congress, aware that the Muslim League would revolt rather than accept an all-India government, reluctantly agreed to the formation of a separate Muslim state. The Muslim-majority provinces of the North West Frontier. Sindh and West Punjab in the west, and East Bengal in the east were separated from India to form the Muslim state of Pakistan, which became independent on Aug. 14, 1947. India became independent on the following day. Because British India coins dated 1947 were struck until 1950, they can be considered the first coins of Independent India. India became a republic on Jan. 26, 1950.

The Republic of India is a member of the Common-wealth of Nations. The president is the Chief of State. The prime minister is the Head of Government.

MINT MARKS

(Mint marks usually appear directly below the date.)

B -- Mumbai (Bombay), proof issues only
(B) - Mumbai (Bombay), diamond
C - Ottawa
(1985 25 Paise; 1988 10, 25 & 50 Paise)
(C) - Calcutta, no mint mark
H - Birmingham (1985 Rupee only)
(H) - Hyderabad, star (1963--)
(Hd) - Hyderabad, diamond split vertically (1953-1960)
(Hy) - Hyderabad, incuse dot in diamond (1960-1968)
(K) - Kremnica, Slovakia, MK in circle
(L) - London, diamond below first date digit
M - Mumbai (Bombay), proof only after 1996
(M) - Mexico City, M beneath O
(N) - Noida, dot
(P) - Pretoria, M in oval
(R) – Moscow, MMD in oval
(T) - Taegu (Korea), star below first date digit

From 1950 through 1964 the Republic of India proof coins carry the regular diamond mint mark and can be distinguished from circulation issues only by their proof-like finish. From 1969 proofs carry the capital "B" mint mark. Some Bombay issues after1969 have a "proof-like" appearance although bearing the diamond mint mark of circulation issues. Beginning in 1972 proofs of the larger denominations - 10, 20 and 100 rupees -were partly frosted on their main features, including numerals. From 1975 all proofs were similarly frosted, from the 1 paisa to 100 rupees. Proof-like issues are often erroneously offered as proofs.

MONETARY SYSTEM

(Until 1957)

4 Pice = 1 Anna
16 Annas = 1 Rupee

REPUBLIC

STANDARD COINAGE

KM#1.1 PICE Composition: Bronze **Note:** Var. 1: 1.6mm thick, 0.3mm edge rim.

Date	Mintage	F	VF	XF	Unc	BU
1950(B)	32,080,000	—	1.00	2.00	3.00	—

KM#1.2 PICE Composition: Bronze **Note:** Var. 2: 1.6mm thick, 1.0mm edge rim.

Date	Mintage	F	VF	XF	Unc	BU
1950(B)	Inc. above	—	0.40	0.80	1.50	2.00
1950(B) Proof	—	Value: 2.50				
1950C	14,000,000	—	0.50	1.00	1.75	2.25

KM#1.3 PICE Composition: Bronze **Note:** Var. 3: 1.2mm thick, 0.8mm edge rim.

Date	Mintage	F	VF	XF	Unc	BU
1951(B)	104,626,000	—	0.20	0.40	0.75	1.50
1951(C)	127,300,000	—	0.20	0.40	0.75	1.50

KM# 1.4 PICE Composition: Bronze **Note:** Variety 4, Larger date, 2mm thick, .8mm edge rim.

Date	Mintage	F	VF	XF	Unc	BU
1952(B)	213,830,000	—	0.25	0.40	0.80	1.50
1953(B)	242,358,000	—	0.25	0.50	1.00	1.50
1953(C)	111,000,000	—	—	—	—	—
1953(Hd)	Inc. above	—	15.00	20.00	—	—
1954(B)	136,758,000	—	0.25	0.50	1.00	1.50
1954(B) Proof	Inc. above	Value: 5.00				
1954(C)	52,600,000	—	0.35	0.70	1.25	2.00
1954(Hd)	Inc. above	—	10.00	15.00	—	—
1955(B)	24,423,000	—	0.50	1.25	2.00	2.50
1955(Hd)	Inc. above	—	15.00	20.00	—	—

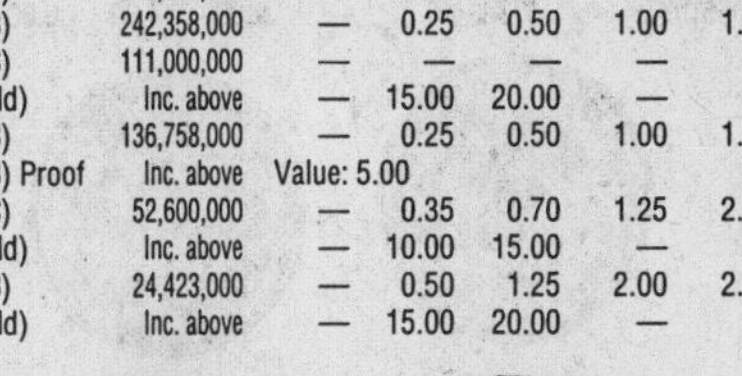

KM# 2.1 1/2 ANNA Composition: Copper-Nickel **Shape:** Square

Date	Mintage	F	VF	XF	Unc	BU
1950(B)	26,076,000	—	0.20	0.40	1.00	—
1950(B) Proof	—	Value: 3.00				
1950(C)	3,100,000	—	1.25	2.00	3.25	—

KM# 2.2 1/2 ANNA Composition: Copper-Nickel **Reverse:** Larger date **Shape:** Square

Date	Mintage	F	VF	XF	Unc	BU
1954(B)	14,000,000	—	0.40	0.65	1.25	—
1954(B) Proof	—	Value: 5.00				
1954(C)	20,800,000	—	0.30	0.50	1.00	—
1955(B)	22,488,000	—	0.40	0.65	1.25	—

KM# 3.1 ANNA **Composition:** Copper-Nickel **Shape:** Scalloped **Note:** A similar shaped Independence commemorative issued in 1947, bearing a map of India, circulated to some degree as an Anna coin.

Date	Mintage	F	VF	XF	Unc	BU
1950(B)	9,944,000	—	0.45	0.75	1.50	—
1950(B) Proof	—	Value: 4.00				

KM# 3.2 ANNA **Composition:** Copper-Nickel **Reverse:** Larger date, first Hindi letter varieties **Shape:** Scalloped

Date	Mintage	F	VF	XF	Unc	BU
1954(B)	20,388,000	—	0.35	0.60	1.25	—
1954(B) Proof	—	Value: 6.50				
1955(B)	—	—	15.00	20.00	30.00	—

KM# 4.1 2 ANNAS **Composition:** Copper-Nickel **Note:** A similar shaped Independence commemorative issued in 1947, bearing a map of India, circulated to some degree as a 2 Anna coin.

Date	Mintage	F	VF	XF	Unc	BU
1950(B)	7,536,000	—	0.75	1.50	2.50	—
1950(B) Proof	—	Value: 5.00				

KM# 4.2 2 ANNAS **Composition:** Copper-Nickel **Note:** Larger date.

Date	Mintage	F	VF	XF	Unc	BU
1954(B)	10,548,000	—	0.75	1.50	2.50	—
1954(B) Proof	—	Value: 8.00				
1955(B)	—	—	15.00	20.00	30.00	—

KM# 5.1 1/4 RUPEE **Composition:** Nickel **Note:** Var. 1: Large lion.

Date	Mintage	F	VF	XF	Unc	BU
1950(B)	7,650,000	—	0.60	1.50	2.50	—
1950(B) Proof	—	Value: 5.00				
1950(C)	7,800,000	—	0.60	1.50	2.50	—
1951(B)	41,439,000	—	0.45	1.00	2.00	—
1951(C)	13,500,000	—	0.55	1.00	2.00	—

KM# 5.2 1/4 RUPEE **Composition:** Nickel **Note:** Larger date.

Date	Mintage	F	VF	XF	Unc	BU
1954(B) Proof	Inc. above	Value: 6.00				
1954(C)	58,300,000	—	0.65	1.50	2.50	—
1955(B)	57,936,000	—	2.00	4.00	6.00	—

KM# 5.3 1/4 RUPEE **Composition:** Nickel **Note:** Variety 2: Small lion.

Date	Mintage	F	VF	XF	Unc	BU
1954(C)	Inc. above	—	0.40	1.00	1.75	—
1955(C)	28,900,000	—	0.40	1.00	1.75	—
1956(C)	22,000,000	—	0.70	1.25	2.00	—

KM# 6.1 1/2 RUPEE **Composition:** Nickel **Note:** Variety 1: Large lion.

Date	Mintage	F	VF	XF	Unc	BU
1950(B)	12,352,000	—	0.75	1.25	2.50	—
1950(B) Proof	—	Value: 5.50				
1950(C)	1,100,000	—	1.25	2.00	5.00	—
1951(B)	9,239,000	—	1.00	1.50	3.50	—

KM# 6.2 1/2 RUPEE **Composition:** Nickel **Note:** Larger date.

Date	Mintage	F	VF	XF	Unc	BU
1954(B) Proof	—	Value: 8.00				
1954(C)	36,300,000	—	0.50	1.00	2.50	—
1955(B)	18,977,000	—	0.75	1.50	4.50	—

KM# 6.3 1/2 RUPEE **Composition:** Nickel **Obverse:** Dots missing between words **Note:** Variety 2: Small lion.

Date	Mintage	F	VF	XF	Unc	BU
1956(C)	24,900,000	—	0.50	1.00	2.50	—

KM# 7.1 RUPEE **Composition:** Nickel

Date	Mintage	F	VF	XF	Unc	BU
1950(B)	19,412,000	—	1.50	2.50	4.50	—
1950(B) Proof	—	Value: 7.00				

KM# 7.2 RUPEE **Composition:** Nickel **Reverse:** First Hindi letter varieties

Date		F	VF	XF	Unc	BU
1954(B)		—	2.00	3.00	5.50	—
1954(B) Proof		—	Value: 10.00			

KM# 129.6 2 RUPEES **Composition:** Copper-Nickel **Note:** As KM#129.5, but with die damage below Ashoka column on obverse.

Date	F	VF	XF	Unc	BU
1996(B)	20.00	30.00	42.50	65.00	—

KM# 293 50 RUPEES **Composition:** Copper-Nickel **Subject:** Supreme Court - 50 Years **Note:** Similar to 2 Rupees KM#291.

Date	F	VF	XF	Unc	BU
2000(B)	—	—	—	15.00	—

DECIMAL COINAGE

100 Naye Paise = 1 Rupee (1957-63); 100 Paise = 1 Rupee (1964-)

NOTE: The Paisa was at first called Naya Paisa (= New Paisa), so that people would distinguish from the old non-decimal Paisa (or Pice, equal to 1/64 Rupee). After 7 years, the word new was dropped, and the coin was simply called a Paisa.

NOTE: Many of the Paisa standard types come with three obverse varieties.

1957-1989

TYPE I: Side lions toothless with 2 to 3 fur rows, dot in wheel center, short squat D in INDIA.

1967-1994

TYPE II: Asoka lion pedestal more imposing. Side lions with 3 or 4 fur rows, more elegant D in INDIA. The shape of the D in INDIA is the easiest way to distinguish this obverse.

1979-

TYPE III: Similar to obverse I but 2 teeth, 4 to 5 fur rows, bull fatter, without central wheel dot.

NOTE: Paisa standard pieces with mint mark B, 1969 to date, were struck only in proof.

NOTE: Indian mintage figures are not divided by mint, and often include dates other than the year in which struck. They should be regarded with reserve.

KM# 9 PAISA **Composition:** Nickel-Brass **Note:** Type I.

Date	Mintage	F	VF	XF	Unc	BU
1964(B)	539,068,000	—	0.20	0.35	0.60	—
1964(C)	Inc. above	—	0.20	0.35	0.60	—
1964(H)	Inc. above	—	0.20	0.35	0.60	—

KM# 9a PAISA **Composition:** Bronze **Note:** Included in mintage of KM#9.

Date	Mintage	F	VF	XF	Unc	BU
1964(H)	Inc. above	—	—	—	—	—

KM# 10.1 PAISA **Composition:** Aluminum **Shape:** Rounded-off square **Note:** Type I.

Date	Mintage	F	VF	XF	Unc	BU
1965(B)	223,480,000	—	0.40	0.65	1.00	—
1965(Hy)	Inc. above	—	0.40	0.65	1.00	—
1966(B)	404,200,000	—	0.20	0.30	0.50	—
1966(C)	Inc. above	—	0.30	0.50	1.00	—
1966(Hy)	Inc. above	—	0.20	0.30	0.50	—
1967(B)	450,433,000	—	0.20	0.30	0.50	—
1967(C)	Inc. above	—	0.20	0.30	0.50	—
1967(Hy)	Inc. above	—	0.20	0.30	0.50	—
1968(B)	302,720,000	—	0.20	0.30	0.50	—
1968(C)	Inc. above	—	0.20	0.30	0.50	—
1968(Hy)	Inc. above	—	0.20	0.30	0.50	—
1969(B)	125,930,000	—	1.50	2.25	3.00	—
1969B Proof	9,147	Value: 1.50				
1969(H)	Inc. above	—	3.00	4.00	5.00	—
1970(B)	15,800,000	—	2.00	2.50	5.00	—

Note: 1970(B) is found only in the uncirculated sets of that year. It has a mirrorlike surface

Date	Mintage	F	VF	XF	Unc	BU
1970B Proof	3,046	Value: 1.00				
1971B Proof	4,375	Value: 1.00				
1971(H)	112,100,000	—	0.20	0.30	0.50	—

Date	Mintage	F	VF	XF	Unc	BU
1972(B)	62,090,000	—	0.20	0.30	0.50	—
1972B Proof	7,895	Value: 1.00				
1972(H)	Inc. above	—	0.20	0.30	0.50	—
1973B Proof	7,562	Value: 1.00				
1974B Proof	—	Value: 1.00				
1975B Proof	—	Value: 1.00				
1976B Proof	—	Value: 1.00				
1977B Proof	—	Value: 1.00				
1978B Proof	—	Value: 1.00				
1979B Proof	—	Value: 1.00				
1980B Proof	—	Value: 1.00				
1981B Proof	—	Value: 1.00				

KM# 10.2 PAISA **Composition:** Aluminum **Note:** Type II.

Date	F	VF	XF	Unc	BU
1969(C)	—	2.50	3.00	4.00	—
1970(C)	—	0.40	0.65	1.00	—

KM# 8 NAYA PAISA **Composition:** Bronze

Date	Mintage	F	VF	XF	Unc	BU
1957(B)	618,630,000	—	0.30	0.50	0.85	—
1957(C)	Inc. above	—	0.30	0.50	0.85	—
1957(Hd)	Inc. above	—	0.30	0.50	0.85	—
1958(B)	468,630,000	—	0.45	0.75	1.50	—
1958(Hd)	Inc. above	—	0.45	0.75	1.50	—
1959(B)	351,120,000	—	0.30	0.50	0.85	—
1959(C)	Inc. above	—	0.30	0.50	0.85	—
1959(Hd)	Inc. above	—	0.30	0.50	0.85	—
1960(B)	357,940,000	—	0.30	0.50	0.85	—
1960(B) Proof	—	Value: 2.00				
1960(C)	Inc. above	—	2.25	3.50	5.00	—
1960(Hd)	Inc. above	—	3.25	4.00	5.00	—
1961(B)	573,170,000	—	0.30	0.50	0.85	—
1961(B) Proof	—	Value: 2.00				
1961(C)	Inc. above	—	0.30	0.50	0.85	—
1961(Hy)	Inc. above	—	0.50	0.75	1.25	—
1962(B)	—	—	—	—	—	—

Note: 1962(B) has only been found in some of the 1962 uncirculated mint sets; Varieties of the split diamond have been reported

KM# 8a NAYA PAISA **Composition:** Nickel-Brass

Date	Mintage	F	VF	XF	Unc	BU
1962(B)	235,103,000	—	0.20	0.35	0.70	—
1962(B) Proof	—	Value: 1.50				
1962(C)	Inc. above	—	0.20	0.35	0.70	—
1962(Hy)	Inc. above	—	0.50	0.75	1.25	—
1963(B)	343,313,000	—	0.20	0.35	0.70	—
1963(B) Proof	—	Value: 1.50				
1963(C)	Inc. above	—	0.25	0.50	1.00	—
1963(H)	Inc. above	—	0.25	0.40	0.80	—

KM# 11 2 NAYE PAISE **Composition:** Copper-Nickel

Date	Mintage	F	VF	XF	Unc	BU
1957(B)	406,230,000	—	0.15	0.40	0.80	—
1957(C)	Inc. above	—	0.15	0.40	0.80	—
1958(B)	245,660,000	—	0.15	0.40	0.80	—
1958(C)	Inc. above	—	0.15	0.40	0.80	—
1959(B)	171,445,000	—	0.15	0.40	0.80	—
1959(C)	Inc. above	—	0.15	0.40	0.80	—
1960(B)	121,820,000	—	0.15	0.40	0.80	—
1960(B) Proof	—	Value: 2.00				
1960(C)	Inc. above	—	0.20	0.40	0.80	—
1961(B)	190,610,000	—	0.20	0.40	0.80	—
1961(B) Proof	—	Value: 2.00				
1961(C)	Inc. above	—	0.20	0.40	0.80	—
1962(B)	318,181,000	—	0.20	0.40	0.80	—
1962(B) Proof	—	Value: 1.50				
1962(C)	Inc. above	—	0.20	0.40	0.80	—
1963(B)	372,380,000	—	0.20	0.40	0.80	—
1963(B) Proof	—	Value: 1.50				
1963(C)	Inc. above	—	0.20	0.40	0.80	—

KM# 12 2 PAISE **Composition:** Copper-Nickel **Note:** Type I.

Date	Mintage	F	VF	XF	Unc	BU
1964(B)	323,504,000	—	0.20	0.40	0.80	—
1964(C)	Inc. above	—	0.20	0.40	0.80	—

KM# 13.1 2 PAISE **Composition:** Aluminum **Reverse:** 10mm "2" **Note:** Type I. Obv. 1 INDIA starts farther from right lion.

Date	Mintage	F	VF	XF	Unc	BU
1965(B)	175,770,000	—	0.20	0.40	0.80	—
1965(C)	Inc. above	—	0.40	0.65	1.00	—
1966(B)	386,795,000	—	0.20	0.30	0.50	—
1966(C)	Inc. above	—	0.20	0.30	0.50	—
1967(B)	454,593,000	—	0.20	0.30	0.50	—

KM# 13.2 2 PAISE **Composition:** Aluminum **Reverse:** 10-1/2mm "2" **Note:** Type 1.

Date	F	VF	XF	Unc	BU
1967(C)	—	0.40	0.65	1.25	—

KM# 13.3 2 PAISE **Composition:** Aluminum **Reverse:** 10mm "2" **Note:** Type 2.

Date	F	VF	XF	Unc	BU
1967(B)	—	3.00	5.00	8.00	—

KM# 13.4 2 PAISE **Composition:** Aluminum **Reverse:** 11mm "2" **Note:** Type 1.

Date	F	VF	XF	Unc	BU
1968(C)	—	6.00	8.00	10.00	—
1977(B)	—	0.60	1.00	1.50	—
1978(B)	—	0.40	0.65	1.00	—

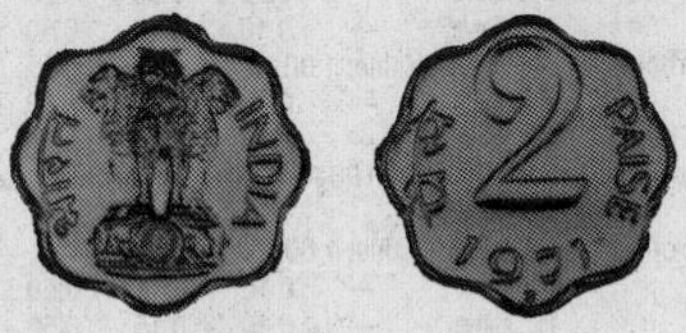

KM# 13.5 2 PAISE **Composition:** Aluminum **Reverse:** 11mm "2" **Note:** Type 2.

Date	Mintage	F	VF	XF	Unc	BU
1968(C)	Inc. above	—	0.20	0.30	0.50	—
1968(B)	305,205,000	—	0.10	0.25	0.50	—
1969(B)	5,335,000	—	2.00	3.00	5.00	—
1969B Proof	9,147	Value: 1.00				
1970(B)	—	—	—	—	5.00	—

Note: 1970(B) is found only in the uncirculated sets of that year. It has a mirrorlike surface

Date	Mintage	F	VF	XF	Unc	BU
1970B Proof	3,046	Value: 1.00				
1970(C)	79,100,000	—	0.20	0.30	0.50	—
1971B Proof	4,375	Value: 1.00				
1971(C)	207,900,000	—	0.20	0.30	0.50	—

KM# 13.6 2 PAISE **Composition:** Aluminum **Reverse:** Small date **Note:** Varieties of date size exist.

Date	Mintage	F	VF	XF	Unc	BU
1972B Proof	7,895	Value: 1.00				
1972(C)	261,270,000	—	0.20	0.30	0.50	—
1972(H)	Inc. above	—	0.20	0.30	0.50	—
1973B Proof	7,562	Value: 1.00				
1973(C)	—	—	0.15	0.25	0.50	—
1973(H)	—	—	0.15	0.25	0.50	—
1974B Proof	—	Value: 1.00				
1974(C)	—	—	0.15	0.25	0.50	—
1974(H)	—	—	0.15	0.25	0.50	—
1975B Proof	—	Value: 1.00				
1975(C)	184,500,000	—	0.40	0.65	1.00	—
1975(H)	Inc. above	—	0.15	0.25	0.50	—
1976(B)	68,140,000	—	0.15	0.25	0.50	—
1976B Proof	—	Value: 1.00				
1976(H)	—	—	1.50	2.25	3.00	—
1977(B)	251,955,000	—	0.25	0.40	0.70	—
1977B Proof	—	Value: 1.00				
1977(H)	Inc. above	—	0.15	0.25	0.50	—
1978B Proof	—	Value: 1.00				
1978(H)	144,010,000	—	0.15	0.25	0.50	—
1979B Proof	—	Value: 1.00				
1979(H)	—	—	0.65	1.00	1.50	—
1980B Proof	—	Value: 1.00				
1981B Proof	—	Value: 1.00				

KM# 14.1 3 PAISE **Composition:** Aluminum **Shape:** 6-sided **Note:** Type 1.

Date	Mintage	F	VF	XF	Unc	BU
1964(B)	138,890,000	—	0.20	0.40	0.70	—
1964(C)	Inc. above	—	0.20	0.40	0.70	—
1965(B)	459,825,000	—	0.20	0.30	0.60	—
1965(C)	Inc. above	—	0.20	0.30	0.60	—
1966(B)	390,440,000	—	0.20	0.30	0.60	—
1966(C)	Inc. above	—	0.20	0.30	0.60	—

Date	Mintage	F	VF	XF	Unc	BU
1966(Hy)	Inc. above	—	0.20	0.30	0.60	—
1967(B)	167,018,000	—	0.20	0.30	0.60	—
1967(C)	Inc. above	—	0.20	0.30	0.60	—
1967(H)	Inc. above	—	0.75	1.25	2.00	—
1968(B)	—	—	3.00	4.00	6.00	—
1968(H)	—	—	—	—	—	—

KM# 14.2 3 PAISE **Composition:** Aluminum **Shape:** 6-sided **Note:** Type 2.

Date	Mintage	F	VF	XF	Unc	BU
1967(C)	—	—	4.00	6.00	8.00	—
1967(H)	Inc. above	—	4.00	6.00	8.00	—
1968(B)	246,390,000	—	—	0.25	0.50	—
1968(C)	Inc. above	—	0.10	0.25	0.50	—
1968(H)	Inc. above	—	0.20	0.35	0.60	—
1969(B)	—	—	0.10	0.25	0.50	—
1969B Proof	9,147	Value: 1.00				
1969(C)	7,025,000	—	0.20	0.30	0.50	—
1969(H)	Inc. above	—	1.75	2.50	4.00	—
1970(B)	—	—	—	—	5.00	—

Note: (1970(B) is found only in the uncirculated sets of that year. It has a mirrorlike surface

Date	Mintage	F	VF	XF	Unc	BU
1970B Proof	3,046	Value: 1.00				
1970(C)	15,300,000	—	0.10	0.25	0.50	—
1971B Proof	4,375	Value: 1.00				
1971(C)	203,100,000	—	—	0.25	0.50	—
1971(H)	Inc. above	—	—	0.25	0.50	—

KM# 15 3 PAISE **Composition:** Aluminum **Shape:** 6-sided **Note:** Type 2.

Date	Mintage	F	VF	XF	Unc	BU
1972B Proof	7,895	Value: 1.00				
1973B Proof	7,562	Value: 1.00				
1974B Proof	—	Value: 1.00				
1975B Proof	—	Value: 1.00				
1976B Proof	—	Value: 1.00				
1977B Proof	—	Value: 1.00				
1978B Proof	—	Value: 1.00				
1979B Proof	—	Value: 1.00				
1980B Proof	—	Value: 1.00				
1981B	—	Value: 1.00				

KM# 16 5 NAYE PAISE **Composition:** Copper-Nickel **Shape:** Rounded-off square

Date	Mintage	F	VF	XF	Unc	BU
1957(B)	227,210,000	—	0.25	0.45	1.00	—
1957(C)	Inc. above	—	0.25	0.45	1.00	—
1958(B)	214,320,000	—	0.25	0.45	1.00	—
1958(C)	Inc. above	—	0.25	0.45	1.00	—
1959(B)	137,105,000	—	0.25	0.45	1.00	—
1959(C)	Inc. above	—	2.50	4.00	7.00	—
1960(B)	93,345,000		0.25	0.45	1.00	—
1960(B) Proof	—	Value: 2.00				
1960(C)	Inc. above	—	0.25	0.45	1.00	—
1960(Hy)	Inc. above	—	6.00	10.00	—	—
1961(B)	197,620,000		0.25	0.45	1.00	—
1961(B) Proof	—	Value: 2.00				
1961(C)	Inc. above	—	0.35	0.60	1.00	—
1961(Hy)	Inc. above	—	6.00	10.00	—	—
1962(B)	224,277,000	—	0.25	0.45	1.00	—
1962(B) Proof	—	Value: 1.50				
1962(C)	Inc. above	—	0.25	0.45	1.00	—
1962(Hy)	Inc. above	—	2.00	3.25	7.00	—
1963(B)	332,600,000	—	0.20	0.35	0.80	—
1963(B) Proof	—	Value: 1.50				
1963(C)	Inc. above	—	2.00	3.00	6.00	—
1963(H)	Inc. above	—	2.00	3.25	7.00	—

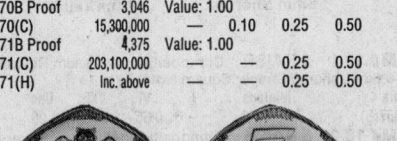

KM# 17 5 PAISE **Composition:** Copper-Nickel **Shape:** Rounded-off square **Note:** Type 1.

Date	Mintage	F	VF	XF	Unc	BU
1964(B)	156,000,000	—	0.40	0.60	1.00	—
1964(C)	Inc. above	—	0.40	0.60	1.00	—
1964(H)	Inc. above	—	6.00	10.00	—	—
1965(B)	203,855,000	—	0.25	0.45	0.75	—
1965(C)	Inc. above	—	0.40	0.60	1.00	—
1965(H)	Inc. above	—	6.00	10.00	—	—
1966(B)	101,395,000	—	0.75	1.25	2.00	—
1966(C)	Inc. above	—	0.40	0.60	1.00	—

6mm Short 5 7mm Tall 5

KM# 18.1 5 PAISE **Composition:** Aluminum **Reverse:** 6mm, short 5 **Shape:** Square **Note:** Type 1.

Date	Mintage	F	VF	XF	Unc	BU
1967(B)	608,533,000	—	0.35	0.60	1.00	—

KM# 18.2 5 PAISE **Composition:** Aluminum **Reverse:** 7mm, tall 5

Date	Mintage	F	VF	XF	Unc	BU
1967(C)	Inc. above	—	0.15	0.25	0.50	—
1967(H)	Inc. above	—	0.15	0.25	0.50	—
1967(B)	Inc. above	—	0.15	0.25	0.50	—
1968(B)	—	—	3.50	5.00	8.50	—
1968(C)	—	—	3.50	5.00	8.50	—
1968(H)	666,750,000	—	0.75	1.25	2.00	—
1971(H)	499,200,000	—	0.10	0.25	0.50	—

KM# 18.3 5 PAISE **Composition:** Aluminum **Note:** Type 2.

Date	Mintage	F	VF	XF	Unc	BU
1967(H)	—	—	4.50	7.00	10.00	—
1968(B)	—	—	0.15	0.25	0.50	—
Note: Mintage included in KM18.2						
1968(C)	—	—	0.15	0.25	0.50	—
Note: Mintage included in KM18.2						
1968(H)	—	—	0.40	0.60	1.00	—
Note: Mintage included in KM18.2						
1969(B)	3,740,000	—	2.00	3.50	5.00	—
1969B Proof	9,147	Value: 1.00				
1970(B)	39,900,000	—	1.25	2.00	3.50	—
1970B Proof	3,046	Value: 1.00				
1970(C)	Inc. above	—	0.25	0.35	0.60	—
1970(H)	Inc. above	—	0.25	0.40	0.75	—
1971(B)	—	—	0.10	0.15	0.50	—
Note: Included with 1971(H) of KM18.2						
1971B Proof	4,375	Value: 1.00				
1971(C)	Inc. above	—	0.10	0.15	0.50	—
1971(H)	—	—	0.25	0.45	0.75	—

KM# 18.4 5 PAISE **Composition:** Aluminum **Note:** Type 1, new reverse.

Date	Mintage	F	VF	XF	Unc	BU
1972(H)	512,430,000	—	0.35	0.60	1.00	—

KM# 18.5 5 PAISE **Composition:** Aluminum **Reverse:** Larger 5

Date	Mintage	F	VF	XF	Unc	BU
1973(H)		—	2.50	3.50	5.50	—
1977(B)		—	2.00	3.00	5.00	—
1978(B)		—	0.75	1.25	2.00	—

KM# 18.6 5 PAISE **Composition:** Aluminum **Note:** Type 2.

Date	Mintage	F	VF	XF	Unc	BU
1972(B)	—	—	0.10	0.15	0.50	—
Note: Mintage included in KM18.4						
1972B Proof	7,895	Value: 1.00				
1972(C)	—	—	0.10	0.15	0.50	—
Note: Mintage included in KM18.4						
1972(H)	—	—	3.50	5.00	7.00	—
1973(B)	—	—	0.10	0.15	0.50	—
1973B Proof	7,562	Value: 1.00				
1973(C)	—	—	0.20	0.30	0.60	—
1973(H)	—	—	0.10	0.15	0.50	—
1974B Proof	—	Value: 1.00				
1974(B)	—	—	0.10	0.15	0.50	—
1974(C)	—	—	0.10	0.15	0.50	—
1974(H)	—	—	0.10	0.15	0.50	—
1975(B)	—	—	0.10	0.15	0.50	—
1975B Proof	—	Value: 1.00				
1975(C)	289,080,000	—	0.20	0.30	0.60	—
1975(H)	Inc. above	—	0.10	0.15	0.50	—
1976(B)	53,205,000	—	0.10	0.15	0.50	—
1976(C)	—	—	—	0.10	0.20	—
1976(H)	—	—	0.10	0.15	0.50	—
1977(B)	257,899,999	—	0.10	0.15	0.50	—
1977(C)	Inc. above	—	0.10	0.15	0.50	—
1977(H)	Inc. above	—	0.10	0.15	0.50	—
1978(C)	—	—	0.10	0.15	0.50	—
1978(H)	—	—	0.10	0.15	0.50	—
1979(B)	—	—	0.10	0.15	0.50	—
1979(C)	—	—	0.20	0.35	0.80	—
1979(H)	—	—	0.10	0.15	0.50	—
1980(B)	21,440,000	—	0.10	0.15	0.50	—
1980B Proof	—	Value: 1.00				
1980(C)	Inc. above	—	0.20	0.30	0.60	—
1980(H)	Inc. above	—	0.10	0.15	0.50	—
1981B Proof	—	Value: 1.00				
1981(C)	4,365,000	—	0.10	0.15	0.50	—
1981(H)	Inc. above	—	0.10	0.15	0.50	—
Note: Due to faulty dies, 1981(H) often resembles the non-existent 1981(B).						
1982B Proof	3,499,000	Value: 1.00				
1982(C)	Inc. above	—	0.10	0.15	0.50	—
1982(H)	Inc. above	—	0.10	0.15	0.50	—
1983(C)	3,110,000	—	0.25	0.50	1.00	—
1983(H)	Inc. above	—	0.10	0.15	0.50	—
1984(C)	—	—	0.25	0.50	1.00	—
1984(H)	Inc. above	—	0.10	0.15	0.50	—
Note: Due to faulty dies, 1981(H) often resembles the non-existent 1981(B).						

KM# 19 5 PAISE **Composition:** Aluminum **Series:** F.A.O. **Subject:** Food and Work For All

Date	Mintage	F	VF	XF	Unc	BU
1976(B)	34,680,000	—	0.35	0.50	1.00	—
1976B Proof	—	Value: 1.00				
1976(C)	60,040,000	—	0.35	0.50	1.00	—
1976(H)	60,290,000	—	0.35	1.00	2.00	—

KM# 20 5 PAISE **Composition:** Aluminum **Series:** F.A.O. **Subject:** Save For Development **Shape:** Square

Date	Mintage	F	VF	XF	Unc	BU
1977(B)	20,100,000	—	0.30	0.50	1.00	—
1977B Proof	2,224	Value: 1.25				
1977(C)	40,470,000	—	0.30	0.50	1.00	—
1977(H)	20,380,000	—	2.25	3.50	5.00	—

KM# 21 5 PAISE **Composition:** Aluminum **Series:** F.A.O. **Subject:** Food and Shelter For All **Shape:** Square

Date	Mintage	F	VF	XF	Unc	BU
1978(B)	28,440,000	—	0.35	0.50	1.00	—
1978B Proof	—	Value: 1.25				
1978(C)	30,870,000	—	0.50	1.00	2.00	—
1978(H)	21,100,000	—	1.00	1.50	2.25	—

KM# 22 5 PAISE **Composition:** Aluminum **Series:** International Year of the Child **Shape:** Square

Date	Mintage	F	VF	XF	Unc	BU
1979(B)	39,860,000	—	0.35	0.50	1.00	—
1979B Proof	—	Value: 1.25				
1979(C)	80,370,000	—	0.35	0.50	1.00	—
1979(H)	1,100,000	—	1.50	2.00	2.50	—

KM# 23 5 PAISE **Composition:** Aluminum **Shape:** Square **Note:** Weight reduced.

Date	Mintage	F	VF	XF	Unc	BU
1984(C)	—	—	6.00	8.00	10.00	—
1985(B)	54,860,000	—	6.00	8.00	10.00	—
1985(C)	Inc. above	—	10.00	15.00	20.00	—
1985(H)	Inc. above	—	0.50	0.75	1.00	—
1986(C)	—	—	0.50	0.75	1.00	—
1986(H)	—	—	0.50	0.75	1.00	—
1987(C)	—	—	0.50	0.75	1.00	—
1987(H)	—	—	0.75	1.00	2.00	—
1988(C)	—	—	0.25	0.50	1.00	—
1988(H)	—	—	0.50	1.00	2.00	—
1989(C)	—	—	0.50	1.00	2.00	—
1989(H)	—	—	0.50	1.00	2.00	—
1990(C)	—	—	1.00	1.50	2.50	—
1990(H)	—	—	1.00	1.50	2.50	—
1991(C)	—	—	0.50	0.75	1.25	—
1991(H)	—	—	0.25	0.50	1.00	—
1992(B)	—	—	1.00	1.50	2.50	—
1992(H)	—	—	0.25	0.50	1.00	—
1993(C)	—	—	1.00	1.50	2.50	—
1993(H)	—	—	0.25	0.50	1.00	—
1994(H)	—	—	0.25	0.50	1.00	—

KM# 24.1 10 NAYE PAISE **Composition:** Copper-Nickel **Reverse:** 6.5mm "10" **Shape:** Scalloped

Date	Mintage	F	VF	XF	Unc	BU
1957(B)	139,655,000	—	0.25	0.50	1.00	—
1957(C)	Inc. above	—	0.25	0.50	1.00	—

KM# 24.2 10 NAYE PAISE **Composition:** Copper-Nickel **Reverse:** 7mm "10"

Date	Mintage	F	VF	XF	Unc	BU
1958(B)	123,160,000	—	0.25	0.50	1.00	—
1958(C)	Inc. above	—	0.25	0.50	1.00	—
1959(B)	148,570,000	—	0.25	0.50	1.00	—
1959(C)	Inc. above	—	0.25	0.50	1.00	—
1960(B)	52,335,000	—	0.35	0.75	2.00	—
1960(B) Proof	—	Value: 2.00				
1961(B)	172,545,000	—	0.25	0.50	1.00	—
1961(B) Proof	—	Value: 2.00				
1961(C)	Inc. above	—	0.25	0.50	1.00	—
1961(Hy)	Inc. above	—	3.50	6.50	11.50	—
1962(B)	172,777,000	—	0.25	0.50	1.00	—
1962(B) Proof	—	Value: 1.50				
1962(C)	Inc. above	—	0.25	0.50	1.00	—
1962(Hy)	Inc. above	—	3.25	5.00	9.00	—
1963(B)	182,834,000	—	0.25	0.50	1.00	—
1963(B) Proof	—	Value: 1.50				
1963(C)	Inc. above	—	0.25	0.50	1.00	—
1963(H)	Inc. above	—	1.00	2.50	5.00	—

KM# 25 10 PAISE **Composition:** Copper-Nickel **Reverse:** 6.5mm "10" **Shape:** Scalloped **Note:** Type 1.

Date	Mintage	F	VF	XF	Unc	BU
1964(B) Open 4	84,112,000	—	0.20	0.50	1.00	—
1964(B) Closed 4	Inc. above	—	5.00	7.00	10.00	—
1964(C)	Inc. above	—	0.20	0.50	1.00	—
1964(H)	Inc. above	—	3.00	5.00	7.00	—
1965(B)	253,430,000	—	0.20	0.50	1.00	—
1965(C)	Inc. above	—	0.20	0.50	1.00	—
1965(Hy)	Inc. above	—	4.00	6.00	8.00	—
1965(H)	Inc. above	—	3.00	5.00	7.00	—
1966(B)	326,990,000	—	0.20	0.50	1.00	—
1966(C)	Inc. above	—	0.20	1.00	1.00	—
1966(Hy)	Inc. above	—	0.40	0.75	1.25	—
1967(B)	59,443,000	—	0.40	0.75	1.25	—
1967(C)	Inc. above	—	0.40	0.75	1.25	—
1967(H)	Inc. above	—	3.00	5.00	7.00	—

KM# 26.1 10 PAISE **Composition:** Nickel-Brass
Note: Type 1.

Date	Mintage	F	VF	XF	Unc	BU
1968(H)	55,940,000	—	30.00	50.00	80.00	—

KM# 26.2 10 PAISE **Composition:** Nickel-Brass
Obverse: Obverse 2 **Reverse:** 6.5mm "10" **Shape:** Scalloped

Date	F	VF	XF	Unc	BU
1968(B)	—	0.20	0.50	1.00	—
Note: Mintage included in KM26.1					
1968(C)	—	0.20	0.50	1.00	—
Note: Mintage included in KM26.1					
1968(H)	—	0.20	0.50	1.00	—
Note: Mintage included in KM26.1					

KM# 26.3 10 PAISE **Composition:** Nickel-Brass
Reverse: 7mm "10" **Shape:** Scalloped **Note:** Type 2.

Date	Mintage	F	VF	XF	Unc	BU
1969(B)	65,405,000	—	0.20	0.50	1.00	—
1969B Proof	9,147	Value: 1.50				
1969(C)	Inc. above	—	0.20	0.50	1.00	—
1969(H)	Inc. above	—	0.20	0.50	1.00	—
1970(B)	48,400,000	—	0.20	0.50	1.00	—
1970B Proof	3,046	Value: 1.50				
1970(C)	Inc. above	—	0.20	0.50	1.00	—
1971(B)	88,800,000	—	0.20	0.50	1.00	—
1971B Proof	4,375	Value: 1.30				

KM# 27.1 10 PAISE **Composition:** Aluminum
Reverse: 9mm "10" **Shape:** Scalloped **Note:** Type 2.

Date	Mintage	F	VF	XF	Unc	BU
1971(B)	146,100,000	—	0.20	0.50	1.00	—
1971(C)	Inc. above	—	0.20	0.50	1.00	—
1971(H)	Inc. above	—	0.50	1.00	2.00	—
1972(B)	735,090,000	—	0.20	0.35	1.00	—
1972B Proof	7,895	Value: 1.30				
1972(C)	Inc. above	—	0.20	0.50	1.00	—
1973(B)	—	—	0.20	0.50	1.00	—
1973B Proof	7,567	Value: 1.30				
1973(C)	—	—	0.20	0.50	1.00	—
1973(H)	—	—	0.20	0.50	1.00	—
1974(B)	—	—	0.20	0.50	1.00	—
1974(C)	—	—	0.20	0.50	1.00	—
1974(H)	—	—	2.00	3.00	5.00	—
1975(B)	—	—	1.00	2.00	3.00	—
1975(C)	298,830,000	—	1.00	2.00	3.00	—
1976(C)	Inc. above	—	2.00	3.00	5.00	—
1977(B)	25,288,000	—	1.00	2.00	3.00	—
1977(C)	Inc. above	—	0.25	0.50	1.00	—
1978(B)	48,215,000	—	0.15	0.30	1.00	—
1978(C)	Inc. above	—	0.15	0.30	1.00	—
1978(H)	Inc. above	—	0.15	0.30	1.00	—

KM# 27.3 10 PAISE **Composition:** Aluminum **Note:** Type 3.

Date	F	VF	XF	Unc	BU
1980(B)	—	0.20	0.50	1.00	—
1980(C)	—	0.20	0.50	1.00	—
1980(H)	—	0.20	0.50	1.00	—
1981(B)	—	0.20	0.50	1.00	—
1981(C)	—	0.20	0.50	1.00	—
1982(C)	—	0.20	0.50	1.00	—
1982(H)	—	0.20	0.50	1.00	—

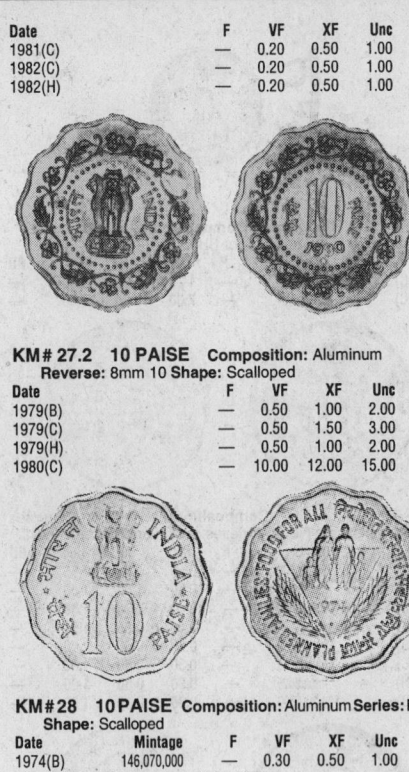

KM# 27.2 10 PAISE **Composition:** Aluminum
Reverse: 8mm 10 **Shape:** Scalloped

Date	F	VF	XF	Unc	BU
1979(B)	—	0.50	1.00	2.00	—
1979(C)	—	0.50	1.50	3.00	—
1979(H)	—	0.50	1.00	2.00	—
1980(C)	—	10.00	12.00	15.00	—

KM# 28 10 PAISE **Composition:** Aluminum **Series:** F.A.O.
Shape: Scalloped

Date	Mintage	F	VF	XF	Unc	BU
1974(B)	146,070,000	—	0.30	0.50	1.00	—
1974B Proof	—	Value: 1.00				
1974(C)	168,500,000	—	0.50	1.00	2.00	—
1974(H)	10,010,000	—	3.00	4.00	6.00	—

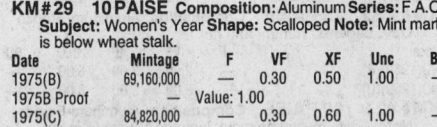

KM# 29 10 PAISE **Composition:** Aluminum **Series:** F.A.O.
Subject: Women's Year **Shape:** Scalloped **Note:** Mint mark is below wheat stalk.

Date	Mintage	F	VF	XF	Unc	BU
1975(B)	69,160,000	—	0.30	0.50	1.00	—
1975B Proof	—	Value: 1.00				
1975(C)	84,820,000	—	0.30	0.60	1.00	—

KM# 30 10 PAISE **Composition:** Aluminum **Series:** F.A.O.
Subject: Food and Work For All **Shape:** Scalloped

Date	Mintage	F	VF	XF	Unc	BU
1976(B)	36,040,000	—	1.00	1.50	2.00	—
1976B Proof	—	Value: 3.00				
1976(C)	26,180,000	—	2.00	3.00	5.00	—

KM# 31 10 PAISE **Composition:** Aluminum **Series:** F.A.O.
Subject: Save For Development **Shape:** Scalloped

Date	Mintage	F	VF	XF	Unc	BU
1977(B)	17,040,000	—	0.25	0.50	1.00	—
1977B Proof	2,224	Value: 1.00				
1977(C)	8,020,000	—	2.00	3.00	5.00	—

KM# 32 10 PAISE **Composition:** Aluminum **Series:** F.A.O.
Subject: Food and Shelter For All **Shape:** Scalloped

Date	Mintage	F	VF	XF	Unc	BU
1978(B)	24,470,000	—	0.25	0.50	1.00	—
1978B Proof	—	Value: 1.00				
1978(C)	26,160,000	—	1.00	1.50	2.00	—
1978(H)	12,100,000	—	1.00	1.50	2.00	—

KM# 33 10 PAISE **Composition:** Aluminum
Series: International Year of the Child **Shape:** Scalloped

Date	Mintage	F	VF	XF	Unc	BU
1979(B)	39,270,000	—	0.25	0.50	1.00	—
1979B Proof	—	Value: 1.00				
1979(C)	61,700,000	—	0.50	1.00	2.50	—
1979(H)	2,250,000	—	0.60	1.00	2.50	—

KM# 34 10 PAISE **Composition:** Aluminum
Obverse: KM#32 **Reverse:** KM#33 **Note:** Mule.

Date	F	VF	XF	Unc	BU
1979(B)	—	5.00	7.50	10.00	—

KM# 35 10 PAISE **Composition:** Aluminum **Subject:** Rural Women's Advancement **Shape:** Scalloped

Date	Mintage	F	VF	XF	Unc	BU
1980(B)	38,080,000	—	0.25	0.40	1.00	—
1980B Proof	—	Value: 1.00				
1980(C)	42,830,000	—	0.25	0.50	1.00	—
1980(H)	11,070,000	—	0.50	1.00	1.50	—

KM# 36 10 PAISE **Composition:** Aluminum **Subject:** World Food Day **Shape:** Scalloped

Date	Mintage	F	VF	XF	Unc	BU
1981(B)	83,280,000	—	0.25	0.40	1.00	—
1981B Proof	—	Value: 1.00				
1981(C)	33,930,000	—	0.25	0.50	1.00	—

KM# 37 10 PAISE **Composition:** Aluminum **Subject:** IX Asian Games **Shape:** Scalloped

Date	Mintage	F	VF	XF	Unc	BU
1982(B)	—	—	0.25	0.45	0.75	—
1982B Proof	—	Value: 1.00				
1982(C)	30,560,000	—	0.25	0.45	0.75	—
1982(H)	17,080,000	—	0.25	0.50	1.00	—

KM# 38 10 PAISE Composition: Aluminum **Subject:** World Food Day **Shape:** Scalloped

Date	Mintage	F	VF	XF	Unc	BU
1982(C)	2,970,000	—	2.50	3.50	5.00	—
1982(H)	11,690,000	—	0.50	1.00	2.00	—

KM# 39 10 PAISE Composition: Aluminum **Shape:** Scalloped

Date	Mintage	F	VF	XF	Unc	BU
1983(B)	—	—	0.10	0.25	0.50	—
1983(C)	—	—	0.10	0.25	0.50	—
1983(H)	—	—	0.10	0.25	0.50	—
1984(B)	112,050,000	—	0.10	0.25	0.50	—
1984(C)	Inc. above	—	0.25	0.50	1.00	—
1984(H)	Inc. above	—	0.10	0.25	0.50	—
1985(B)	184,655,000	—	0.20	0.30	0.50	—
1985(C)	Inc. above	—	0.20	0.30	0.50	—
1985(H)	Inc. above	—	0.20	0.30	0.50	—
1986(B)	298,525,000	—	0.10	0.15	0.30	—
1986(C)	Inc. above	—	0.20	0.30	0.50	—
1986(H)	Inc. above	—	0.50	1.00	1.50	—
1987(C)	299,460,000	—	0.15	0.25	0.45	—
1987(H)	Inc. above	—	0.15	0.25	0.45	—
1988(B)	264,510,000	—	0.10	0.15	0.30	—
1988(C)	Inc. above	—	0.10	0.15	0.30	—
1988(H)	Inc. above	—	1.00	1.50	2.00	—
1989(B)	—	—	0.15	0.25	0.45	—
1989(C)	—	—	0.15	0.25	0.45	—
1989(H)	—	—	0.15	0.25	0.45	—
1990(B)	—	—	0.50	0.75	1.25	—
1991(B)	—	—	0.15	0.25	0.45	—
1991(C)	—	—	0.15	0.25	0.45	—
1991(H)	—	—	0.15	0.25	0.45	—
1993(C)	—	—	0.15	0.30	0.60	—
1993(H)	—	—	0.30	0.50	0.75	—

KM# 40.1 10 PAISE Composition: Stainless Steel

Date	Mintage	F	VF	XF	Unc	BU
1988C	183,040,000	—	0.10	0.15	0.25	—
1988(B)	4,040,000	—	0.25	0.40	0.75	—
1988(C)	—	—	5.00	7.00	10.00	—
1988(H)	Inc. above	—	3.00	5.00	8.00	—
1988(N)	—	—	0.15	0.25	0.40	—
1989(B)	—	—	0.60	1.00	1.50	—
1989(C)	—	—	0.40	0.70	1.00	—
1989(H)	—	—	0.20	0.30	0.50	—
1989(N)	—	—	0.25	0.40	0.75	—
1990(B)	—	—	0.15	0.30	0.50	—
1990(C)	—	—	0.40	0.70	1.00	—
1990(H)	—	—	0.20	0.30	0.50	—
1990(N) Small mm	—	—	0.15	0.30	0.50	—
1990(N) Large mm	—	—	1.25	1.75	2.50	—
1991(C)	—	—	0.15	0.30	0.50	—
1991(H)	—	—	0.15	0.30	0.50	—
1991(N)	—	—	0.15	0.30	0.50	—
1992(N)	—	—	0.30	0.60	1.00	—
1992(B)	—	—	1.00	1.50	2.50	—
1993(H)	—	—	0.15	0.30	0.50	—
1996(C)	—	—	0.15	0.30	0.50	—
1996(N)	—	—	0.15	0.30	0.50	—
1997(C)	—	—	0.15	0.30	0.50	—
1997(H)	—	—	0.20	0.30	0.50	—
1998(B)	—	—	0.25	0.40	0.70	—
1998(C)	—	—	0.25	0.40	0.70	—

KM# 40.2 10 PAISE Composition: Stainless Steel **Obverse:** Error: MARAT for BHARAT

Date	Mintage	F	VF	XF	Unc	BU
1988(C)		—	1.25	2.00	3.00	—
1989(C)		—	7.00	10.00	15.00	—

KM# 41 20 PAISE Composition: Nickel-Brass **Reverse:** Lotus Blossom **Note:** Varieties of high and low date exist.

Date	Mintage	F	VF	XF	Unc	BU
1968(B)	10,585,000	—	0.50	1.00	1.50	—
1968(C)	Inc. above	—	0.50	1.00	1.50	—
1969(B)	197,940,000	—	0.40	0.85	1.50	—
1969(C)	—	—	0.40	0.85	1.50	—
1970(B)	Inc. above	—	0.30	0.60	1.00	—
1970(C)	Inc. above	—	0.30	0.60	1.00	—
1970(H)	Inc. above	—	0.30	0.60	1.00	—
1971(B)	124,200,000	—	0.30	0.60	1.00	—

KM# 42.1 20 PAISE Composition: Aluminum-Bronze **Subject:** Centennial - Birth of Mahatma Gandhi **Obv. Legend:** .7-.9 from rims

Date	Mintage	F	VF	XF	Unc	BU
ND(1969)(B)	45,010	—	0.40	0.65	1.00	—
ND(1969)B Proof	9,147	Value: 2.00				
ND(1969)(C)	45,070,000	—	0.50	0.80	1.50	—
ND(1969)(H)	3,000,000	—	0.75	1.50	2.50	—

KM# 42.2 20 PAISE Composition: Aluminum-Bronze **Obv. Legend:** 1.2mm from rim

Date	F	VF	XF	Unc	BU
ND(1969)(B)	—	2.00	3.00	5.00	—
ND(1969)(C)	—	3.00	5.00	8.00	—

KM# 42.3 20 PAISE Composition: Aluminum-Bronze **Note:** Eyes, mustache recut, legends 1.2mm from rim.

Date	F	VF	XF	Unc	BU
ND(1969)(B)	—	0.60	1.00	1.50	—

Note: Struck during 1969 and 1970

KM# 43.1 20 PAISE Composition: Aluminum-Bronze **Series:** F.A.O. **Subject:** Food For All **Note:** Wide rims.

Date	Mintage	F	VF	XF	Unc	BU
1970(B)	5,160,000	—	0.75	1.25	2.00	—
1970B Proof	3,046	Value: 2.00				
1970(C)	5,010,000	—	0.75	1.25	2.00	—

KM# 43.2 20 PAISE Composition: Aluminum-Bronze **Note:** Narrow rims, lions' fur recut.

Date	Mintage	F	VF	XF	Unc	BU
1971(B)	60,000	—	0.70	0.90	1.25	—
1971B Proof	4,375	Value: 2.00				

KM# 45 20 PAISE Composition: Aluminum **Series:** F.A.O. **Shape:** 6-sided **Note:** Similar to 10 Paise, KM#38.

Date	F	VF	XF	Unc	BU
1982(C)	—	2.00	3.25	5.00	—
1982(H)	—	1.00	1.50	2.50	—

KM# 44 20 PAISE Composition: Aluminum **Shape:** 6-sided

Date	Mintage	F	VF	XF	Unc	BU
1982(B)	—	—	0.25	0.40	1.00	—
1982(H)	—	—	0.25	0.40	1.00	—
1982(H) Without mm	—	—	0.25	0.40	1.00	—
1983(C)	28,505,000	—	0.25	0.40	1.00	—
1983(H)	Inc. above	—	0.25	0.40	1.00	—
1984(C)	Inc. above	—	0.25	0.40	1.00	—
1984(H)	Inc. above	—	0.25	0.40	1.00	—
1985(B)	84,495,000	—	0.25	0.40	1.00	—
1985(C)	Inc. above	—	0.25	0.40	1.00	—
1985(H)	Inc. above	—	0.25	0.40	1.00	—
1986(B)	155,610,000	—	0.25	0.40	0.75	—
1986(C)	Inc. above	—	0.15	0.30	0.75	—
1986(H)	Inc. above	—	0.15	0.30	0.75	—
1987(C)	—	—	0.15	0.30	0.75	—
1987(H)	153,073,000	—	0.15	0.30	0.75	—
1988(B)	125,048,000	—	0.15	0.30	0.75	—
1988(C)	Inc. above	—	0.15	0.30	0.75	—
1988(H)	Inc. above	—	0.35	0.60	1.00	—
1989(C)	—	—	0.35	0.60	1.00	—
1989(H)	—	—	0.15	0.25	0.75	—
1990(C)	—	—	0.35	0.60	1.00	—
1990(H)	—	—	0.15	0.25	0.75	—
1991(C)	—	—	0.15	0.25	0.75	—
1991(H)	—	—	0.15	0.25	0.75	—
1992(H)	—	—	0.15	0.25	0.75	—
1994(H)	—	—	0.15	0.25	0.75	—

KM# 46 20 PAISE Composition: Aluminum **Series:** F.A.O. **Subject:** Fisheries **Shape:** 6-sided

Date	F	VF	XF	Unc	BU
1983(C)	—	1.00	1.50	2.50	—

Note: Mintage included in KM44

Date	F	VF	XF	Unc	BU
1983(H)	—	1.00	1.50	2.50	—

Note: Mintage included in KM44

KM# 47.1 25 NAYE PAISE Composition: Nickel

Date	Mintage	F	VF	XF	Unc	BU
1957(B)	5,640,000	—	0.75	1.25	2.00	—
1957(C)	Inc. above	—	0.75	1.25	2.00	—
1959(B)	43,080,000	—	0.45	0.75	1.25	—
1959(C)	Inc. above	—	0.45	0.75	1.25	—
1960(B)	115,320,000	—	0.30	0.60	1.00	—
1960(B) Proof	—	Value: 2.00				
1960(C)	Inc. above	—	0.30	0.60	1.00	—

KM# 47.2 25 NAYE PAISE Composition: Nickel **Reverse:** Large 25

Date	Mintage	F	VF	XF	Unc	BU
1961(B)	109,008,000	—	0.30	0.60	1.00	—
1961(B) Proof	—	Value: 2.00				
1961(C)	Inc. above	—	0.30	0.60	1.00	—
1962(B)	79,242,000	—	0.30	0.60	1.00	—
1962(B) Proof	—	Value: 2.00				
1962(C)	Inc. above	—	0.30	0.60	1.00	—
1963(B)	101,565,000	—	0.30	0.60	1.00	—
1963(B) Proof	—	Value: 2.00				
1963(C)	Inc. above	—	0.30	0.60	1.00	—

KM# 48.1 25 PAISE Composition: Nickel **Note:** Type 1, Type 1.

Date	Mintage	F	VF	XF	Unc	BU
1964(B)	85,321,000	—	0.30	0.60	1.25	—
1964(C)	Inc. above	—	0.30	0.60	1.25	—

KM# 48.2 25 PAISE **Composition:** Nickel **Note:** Type 1, Reverse 2.

Date	Mintage	F	VF	XF	Unc	BU
1965(B)	143,662,000	—	0.30	0.60	1.00	—
1965(C)	Inc. above	—	0.30	0.60	1.00	—
1966(B)	59,040,000	—	0.30	0.60	1.00	—
1966(C)	Inc. above	—	0.30	0.60	1.00	—
1967(B)	30,027,000	—	4.50	6.00	8.00	—

KM# 48.3 25 PAISE **Composition:** Nickel **Note:** Type 2, Reverse 2.

Date	F	VF	XF	Unc	BU
1967(C)	—	0.30	0.70	1.50	—

Note: Mintage included in KM48.2

Date	F	VF	XF	Unc	BU
1968(C)	—	1.50	2.25	3.50	—

Note: Mintage included in KM48.2

KM# 49.1 25 PAISE **Composition:** Copper-Nickel **Note:** Type 1a, lion with whiskers, faces and wheel redesigned. 1984-86 have edges rounded (local blanks) or flat (Korean blanks).

Date	Mintage	F	VF	XF	Unc	BU
1972(B)	367,640,000	—	0.20	0.40	0.70	—
1972B Proof	7,895	Value: 1.00				
1972(H)	Inc. above	—	0.45	1.00	2.00	—
1973(B)	—	—	0.20	0.40	0.70	—
1973B Proof	7,567	Value: 1.00				
1973(H)	—	—	0.35	0.60	1.00	—
1974(B)	—	—	0.20	0.40	0.70	—
1974B Proof	—	Value: 1.00				
1974(H)	—	—	0.45	0.75	1.25	—
1975(B)	559,980,000	—	0.20	0.40	0.70	—
1975B Proof	—	Value: 1.00				
1975(H)	Inc. above	—	3.00	4.00	5.00	—
1976(B)	30,016,000	—	0.60	1.00	1.50	—
1976B Proof	Inc. above	Value: 1.00				
1976(H)	Inc. above	—	0.60	1.00	1.50	—
1977(B)	270,520,000	—	0.20	0.40	0.70	—
1977(C)	Inc. above	—	0.35	0.60	1.00	—
1977(H)	Inc. above	—	0.35	0.60	1.00	—
1978B Proof	—	Value: 1.00				
1978(C)	131,632,000	—	0.25	0.40	0.70	—
1978(H)	—	—	0.25	0.40	0.70	—
1979(C)	—	—	0.50	1.00	1.50	—
1979(H)	—	—	0.50	1.00	1.50	—
1980(C)	6,175,000	—	0.25	0.40	0.70	—
1980(H)	Inc. above	—	0.25	0.40	0.70	—
1981(B)	11,048,000	—	0.25	0.40	0.70	—
1981(C)	Inc. above	—	1.50	2.00	2.50	—
1981(H)	Inc. above	—	0.45	0.75	1.25	—
1982(C)	38,288,000	—	0.45	0.75	1.25	—
1983(C)	137,488,000	—	0.45	0.75	1.25	—
1984(B)	98,740,000	—	0.45	0.75	1.25	—
1984(C)	Inc. above	—	0.45	0.75	1.25	—
1985(B)	113,872,000	—	0.45	0.75	1.25	—
1985C	Inc. above	—	0.15	0.25	0.50	—
1985(C)	Inc. above	—	0.45	0.75	1.25	—
1985(H)	Inc. above	—	0.45	0.75	1.25	—
1986(B)	362,624,000	—	0.60	0.90	1.50	—
1986(C)	Inc. above	—	0.60	0.90	1.50	—
1986(H)	Inc. above	—	0.60	0.90	1.50	—
1987(C)	341,160,000	—	0.60	0.90	1.50	—
1987(H)	Inc. above	—	0.60	0.90	1.50	—
1988(H)	303,252,000	—	0.60	0.90	1.50	—

KM# 49.2 25 PAISE **Composition:** Copper-Nickel **Note:** Type 2, 9mm between lion nosetips, 15mm across field.

Date	F	VF	XF	Unc	BU
1972(C)	—	0.35	0.60	1.00	—
1977(B)	—	0.35	0.60	1.00	—

Note: Mintage included in KM49.1

Date	F	VF	XF	Unc	BU
1977B Proof	—	Value: 1.50			

Note: Mintage included in KM49.1

Date	F	VF	XF	Unc	BU
1978(B)	—	3.25	5.00	7.00	—

Note: Mintage included in KM49.1

Date	F	VF	XF	Unc	BU
1979B Proof	—	Value: 1.50			

KM# 49.3 25 PAISE **Composition:** Copper-Nickel **Note:** Type 2, 10mm between lion nosetips, 16-16.3mm across field. Bull has three legs.

Date	F	VF	XF	Unc	BU
1972(C)	—	2.50	3.50	5.00	—

Note: Mintage included in KM49.1

Date	F	VF	XF	Unc	BU
1973(C)	—	0.85	1.25	2.00	—
1974(C)	—	0.85	1.25	2.00	—

KM# 49.4 25 PAISE **Composition:** Copper-Nickel **Note:** Type 1b, central lion, bull and horse re-engraved.

Date	F	VF	XF	Unc	BU
1974(B)	—	2.00	5.00	6.50	—
1975(B)	—	5.00	7.00	12.00	—
1975(H)	—	1.00	3.00	5.00	—
1976(H)	—	6.00	8.00	15.00	—
1978(B)	—	2.00	3.00	5.00	—
1979(B)	—	2.50	5.00	7.00	—
1981(B)	—	4.00	6.00	8.00	—

KM# 49.5 25 PAISE **Composition:** Copper-Nickel **Note:** Type 3.

Date	F	VF	XF	Unc	BU
1986(B)	—	0.15	0.30	1.00	—
1986(C)	—	0.45	0.75	1.25	—
1986(H)	—	0.45	0.75	1.25	—
1987(B)	—	0.15	0.30	1.00	—
1987(C)	—	0.25	0.40	1.50	—
1987(C) Long 7	—	0.25	0.40	1.50	—
1988(B)	—	0.20	0.35	1.25	—
1988(C) 8's 1.3mm tall	—	0.45	0.75	2.00	—
1988(C) 8's 1.8mm tall	—	0.45	0.75	2.00	—
1988(H)	—	0.45	1.00	1.75	—
1989(B)	—	0.45	1.00	1.75	—
1989(C)	—	2.00	2.50	3.00	—
1990(B)	—	2.00	3.50	7.00	—

KM# 49.6 25 PAISE **Composition:** Copper-Nickel **Note:** 9-1/2mm between lion nosetips. Bull has four legs.

Date	F	VF	XF	Unc	BU
1974(C)	—	0.85	1.25	2.00	—
1975(C)	—	0.85	1.25	2.00	—
1976(C)	—	2.00	3.50	5.00	—

KM# 49.7 25 PAISE **Composition:** Nickel **Reverse:** Large 25 **Note:** Type 1, lion without whiskers.

Date	F	VF	XF	Unc	BU
1972(B)	—	8.00	12.00	18.00	—

KM# 50 25 PAISE **Composition:** Copper-Nickel **Subject:** Rural Women's Advancement

Date	Mintage	F	VF	XF	Unc	BU
1980(B)	15,050,000	—	0.30	0.50	1.00	—
1980B Proof	—	Value: 1.00				
1980(C)	8,520,000	—	0.50	1.00	1.50	—
1980(H)	10,380,000	—	1.00	1.50	2.00	—

KM# 51 25 PAISE **Composition:** Copper-Nickel **Subject:** World Food Day

Date	Mintage	F	VF	XF	Unc	BU
1981(B)	2,170,000	—	1.00	1.50	2.00	—
1981B Proof	—	Value: 2.00				
1981(C)	4,500,000	—	1.00	1.50	2.00	—
1981(H)	9,340,000	—	1.50	2.00	3.00	—

KM# 52 25 PAISE **Composition:** Copper-Nickel **Subject:** IX Asian Games

Date	Mintage	F	VF	XF	Unc	BU
1982(B)	12,000,000	—	0.30	0.50	1.00	—
1982B Proof	—	Value: 1.00				
1982(C)	12,000,000	—	0.30	0.50	1.00	—
1982(H)	330,000	—	2.50	3.50	5.00	—

KM# 53.1 25 PAISE **Composition:** Copper-Nickel **Subject:** Forestry **Edge:** Rounded

Date	F	VF	XF	Unc	BU
1985(B)	—	1.50	2.00	2.75	—

Note: Mintage included in KM49.1

Date	F	VF	XF	Unc	BU
1985(H)	—	5.00	7.00	10.00	—

Note: Mintage included in KM49.1

KM# 53.2 25 PAISE **Composition:** Copper-Nickel **Edge:** Flat

Date	F	VF	XF	Unc	BU
1985(B)	—	5.00	7.00	10.00	—
1985(C)	—	3.00	5.00	7.00	—

KM# 54 25 PAISE **Composition:** Stainless Steel **Note:** Varieties of date size exist.

Date	Mintage	F	VF	XF	Unc	BU
1988C	305,280,000	—	0.10	0.20	0.40	—
1988(B)	—	—	0.45	0.75	1.25	—
1988(C)	18,920,000	—	3.50	5.00	8.00	—
1988(H)	—	—	6.00	8.00	10.00	—
1988(N)	Inc. above	—	0.45	0.75	1.25	—
1989(B)	—	—	0.65	1.00	1.50	—
1989(C)	—	—	0.65	1.00	1.50	—
1989(H)	—	—	1.00	2.00	3.00	—
1989(N)	—	—	0.15	0.30	0.50	—
1990(B)	—	—	0.25	0.50	1.00	—
1990(C)	—	—	0.25	0.50	1.00	—
1990(H)	—	—	0.25	0.40	0.70	—
1990(N) Small mm	—	—	0.40	0.65	1.00	—
1991(B)	—	—	0.25	0.40	0.70	—
1991(C)	—	—	0.25	0.40	0.70	—
1991(H)	—	—	0.25	0.40	0.70	—
1991(N)	—	—	0.25	0.40	0.70	—
1992(B)	—	—	0.25	0.40	0.70	—
1992(C)	—	—	1.00	2.00	3.00	—
1992(H)	—	—	1.00	2.00	3.00	—
1992(N)	—	—	0.50	1.00	2.00	—
1993(B)	—	—	0.50	1.00	2.00	—
1993(C)	—	—	0.50	1.00	2.00	—
1993(H)	—	—	2.00	3.00	5.00	—
1993(N)	—	—	0.50	0.70	1.00	—
1994(B)	—	—	0.15	0.30	0.50	—
1994(C)	—	—	0.10	0.20	0.40	—
1994(H)	—	—	0.10	0.20	0.40	—
1994(N)	—	—	0.10	0.20	0.40	—
1995(B)	—	—	0.10	0.20	0.40	—
1995(C)	—	—	0.25	0.50	1.00	—
1995(H)	—	—	0.10	0.20	0.40	—
1995(N)	—	—	0.10	0.20	0.40	—
1996(B)	—	—	0.10	0.20	0.40	—
1996(C)	—	—	0.10	0.20	0.40	—
1996(H)	—	—	0.10	0.20	0.40	—
1996(N)	—	—	0.10	0.20	0.35	—
1997(B)	—	—	0.10	0.20	0.40	—
1997(C)	—	—	0.10	0.20	0.40	—
1997(H)	—	—	0.50	1.00	2.00	—
1997(N)	—	—	0.10	0.20	0.40	—
1998(B)	—	—	0.10	0.20	0.40	—
1998(C)	—	—	0.10	0.20	0.40	—
1998(H)	—	—	0.10	0.20	0.40	—
1998(N)	—	—	0.10	0.20	0.40	—
1999(B)	—	—	0.10	0.20	0.40	—
1999(C)	—	—	0.10	0.20	0.40	—
1999(H)	—	—	0.10	0.20	0.40	—
1999(N)	—	—	0.10	0.20	0.40	—
2000(B)	—	—	0.10	0.20	0.40	—
2000(C)	—	—	0.10	0.20	0.40	—
2000(H)	—	—	0.10	0.20	0.40	—
2000(N)	—	—	0.10	0.20	0.40	—
2001(B)	—	—	0.10	0.20	0.40	—
2001(C)	—	—	0.10	0.20	0.40	—
2001(H)	—	—	0.15	0.25	0.60	—
2002(B)	—	—	0.15	0.25	0.60	—
2002(C)	—	—	0.15	0.25	0.60	—
2002(H)	—	—	0.25	0.40	1.00	—

KM# 55 50 NAYE PAISE **Composition:** Nickel

Date	Mintage	F	VF	XF	Unc	BU
1960(B)	11,224,000	—	1.00	1.50	2.50	—
1960(B) Proof	—	Value: 3.00				
1960(C)	Inc. above	—	0.50	1.25	2.00	—
1961(B)	45,992,000	—	0.25	0.60	1.25	—
1961(B) Proof	—	Value: 3.00				
1961(C)	Inc. above	—	0.25	0.60	1.25	—
1962(B)	64,227,999	—	0.25	0.60	1.25	—
1962(B) Proof	—	Value: 3.00				

Date	Mintage	F	VF	XF	Unc	BU
1962(C)	Inc. above	—	0.25	0.60	1.25	—
1963(B)	58,168,000	—	0.25	0.60	1.25	—
1963(B) Proof	—	Value: 3.00				
1963(C)	Inc. above	—	1.00	1.50	2.50	—

KM# 56 50 PAISE **Composition:** Nickel **Subject:** Death of Jawaharlal Nehru **Rev. Legend:** English

Date	Mintage	F	VF	XF	Unc	BU
ND(1964)(B)	21,900,000	—	0.40	0.65	1.00	—
ND(1964)B Proof	—	Value: 2.50				
ND(1964)(C)	7,160,000	—	0.75	1.50	2.75	—

KM# 57 50 PAISE **Composition:** Nickel **Rev. Legend:** Hindi **Note:** Nehru commemorative issues were struck from 1964 until 1967.

Date	Mintage	F	VF	XF	Unc	BU
ND(1964)(B)	36,190,000	—	0.40	0.65	1.00	—
ND(1964)(C)	28,350,000	—	0.40	0.65	1.00	—

KM# 58.1 50 PAISE **Composition:** Nickel **Note:** Obverse 1, Reverse 1.

Date	Mintage	F	VF	XF	Unc	BU
1964(C)	23,361,000	—	0.50	1.00	1.75	—
1967(B)	19,267,000	—	0.50	1.00	1.75	—

Note: Varieties of 1967(B) reverse edges exist, half teeth and the scarce full teeth

KM# 58.2 50 PAISE **Composition:** Nickel **Note:** Obverse 2, Reverse 2.

Date	Mintage	F	VF	XF	Unc	BU
1967(C)	—	—	0.60	1.00	1.50	—
1968(B)	28,076,000	—	0.25	0.60	1.00	—
Note: A scarce 1968(b) variety exists with crude obverse, no whiskers, thick horsetail						
1968(C)	Inc. above	—	0.25	0.60	1.00	—
1969(B)	59,388,000	—	0.25	0.60	1.00	—
1969(C)	Inc. above	—	0.35	0.75	1.25	—
1970(B)	Inc. above	—	0.35	0.75	1.25	—
1970(C)	Inc. above	—	0.25	0.60	1.00	—
1971(C)	57,900,000	—	0.25	0.50	0.85	—

KM# 58.3 50 PAISE **Composition:** Nickel **Note:** Obverse 1, Reverse 2.

Date	Mintage	F	VF	XF	Unc	BU
1970(B)	—	—	1.00	2.00	3.00	—
Note: Included 1969						
1970B Proof	3,046	Value: 2.00				
1971B Proof	4,375	Value: 2.00				

KM# 59 50 PAISE **Composition:** Nickel **Subject:** Centennial - Birth of Mahatma Gandhi **Note:** Struck during 1969 and 1970.

Date	Mintage	F	VF	XF	Unc	BU
ND(1969)(B)	10,260,000	—	0.25	0.50	1.00	—
ND(1969)B Proof	9,147	Value: 2.00				
ND(1969)(C)	12,100,000	—	0.25	0.50	1.00	—

KM# 60 50 PAISE **Composition:** Copper-Nickel **Subject:** 25th Anniversary of Independence

Date	Mintage	F	VF	XF	Unc	BU
ND(1972)(B)	43,800,000	—	0.30	0.50	1.00	—
ND(1972)B Proof	7,895	Value: 2.00				
ND(1972)(C)	40,080,000	—	0.45	0.75	1.50	—

KM# 61 50 PAISE **Composition:** Copper-Nickel **Reverse:** Lettering spaced out **Note:** Type 2.

Date	F	VF	XF	Unc	BU
1972(C)	—	0.35	0.60	1.00	—
1972(B)	—	0.35	0.60	1.00	—
1973(B)	—	0.35	0.60	1.00	—
1973(C)	—	2.00	3.50	6.00	—

KM# 62 50 PAISE **Composition:** Copper-Nickel **Series:** F.A.O. **Subject:** Grow More Food

Date	Mintage	F	VF	XF	Unc	BU
1973(B)	28,720,000	—	0.30	0.50	1.00	—
1973B Proof	11,000	Value: 2.00				
1973(C)	40,100,000	—	0.30	0.50	1.00	—

KM# 63 50 PAISE **Composition:** Copper-Nickel **Reverse:** Lettering close **Note:** Type 2.

Date	Mintage	F	VF	XF	Unc	BU
1974(B)	—	—	0.25	0.50	1.00	—
1974B Proof	—	Value: 2.00				
1974(C)	—	—	0.35	0.75	1.50	—
1975(B)	225,880,000	—	0.25	0.50	1.00	—
1975B Proof	—	Value: 2.00				
1975(C)	Inc. above	—	0.25	0.50	1.00	—
1975(H)	—	—	0.75	1.25	2.00	—
1976(B)	99,564,000	—	0.25	0.50	1.00	—
1976B Proof	Inc. above	Value: 2.00				
1976(C)	Inc. above	—	0.35	0.75	1.50	—
1976(H)	Inc. above	—	0.75	1.25	2.00	—
1977(B)	97,272,000	—	0.25	0.50	1.00	—
1977B Proof	Inc. above	Value: 2.00				
1977(C)	Inc. above	—	0.40	0.75	1.50	—
1977(H)	Inc. above	—	0.40	0.75	1.50	—
1978B Proof	25,648,000	Value: 2.00				

Date	Mintage	F	VF	XF	Unc	BU
1978(C)	—	—	0.25	0.50	1.00	—
1979B Proof	—	Value: 2.00				
1980(B)	—	—	0.25	0.50	1.00	—
1980B Proof	—	Value: 2.00				
1980(C)	—	—	5.00	8.00	12.00	—
1981B Proof	—	Value: 2.00				
1983(C)	62,634,000	—	5.00	8.00	12.00	—

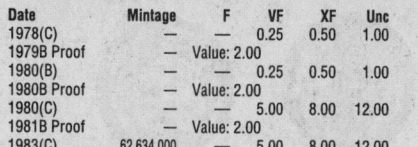

KM# 64 50 PAISE **Composition:** Copper-Nickel **Subject:** National Integration

Date	Mintage	F	VF	XF	Unc	BU
1982(B)	9,804,000	—	0.40	0.75	1.25	—
1982B Proof	—	Value: 3.00				
1982(C)	Inc. above	—	10.00	15.00	20.00	—

KM# 65 50 PAISE **Composition:** Copper-Nickel **Note:** Type 3.

Date	Mintage	F	VF	XF	Unc	BU
1984(B)	61,548,000	—	0.25	0.50	0.85	—
1984(C)	Inc. above	—	1.00	1.50	2.50	—
1984(H)	—	—	2.00	3.00	5.00	—
1985(B)	210,964,000	—	0.25	0.50	0.85	—
1985(C)	Inc. above	—	0.25	0.50	0.85	—
1985(H)	Inc. above	—	1.00	1.50	3.00	—
1985(T)	Inc. above	—	0.20	0.30	0.65	—
1986(C)	117,576,000	—	0.50	1.00	2.00	—
1987(B)	—	—	0.25	0.50	0.85	—
1987(C)	145,140,000	—	0.25	0.50	0.85	—
1987(H)	Inc. above	—	0.40	0.75	1.50	—
1988(B)	149,092,000	—	0.25	0.50	0.85	—
1988(C)	Inc. above	—	1.00	1.50	3.00	—
1988(H)	Inc. above	—	1.00	1.50	2.50	—
1989(B)	—	—	0.50	1.00	2.00	—
1989(C)	—	—	0.50	1.00	2.00	—
1990(B)	—	—	2.00	4.00	7.00	—

KM# 66 50 PAISE **Composition:** Copper-Nickel **Subject:** Golden Jubilee of Reserve Bank of India

Date	F	VF	XF	Unc	BU
ND(1985)(B)	—	0.50	1.00	2.50	—
Note: Mintage included in KM65					
ND(1985)B Proof	—	Value: 15.00			
Note: Mintage included in KM680					
ND(1985)(C)	—	2.00	3.00	5.00	—
ND(1985)(H)	—	0.75	1.25	2.75	—
Note: Mintage included in KM65					

KM# 67.1 50 PAISE **Composition:** Copper-Nickel **Subject:** Death of Indira Gandhi

Date	F	VF	XF	Unc	BU
ND(1985)(B)	—	0.20	0.40	1.00	—
Note: Mintage included in KM65					
ND(1985)B Proof	—	Value: 17.50			
Note: Mintage included in KM65					
ND(1985)(C)	—	0.20	0.40	1.00	—
Note: Mintage included in KM65					
ND(1985)(H)	—	0.65	1.00	1.50	—
Note: Mintage included in KM65					

KM# 67.2 50 PAISE Composition: Copper-Nickel **Obverse:** KM#68 **Reverse:** KM#67 **Note:** Mule.

Date	F	VF	XF	Unc	BU
ND(1985)(C)	—	35.00	50.00	80.00	—

KM# 68.1 50 PAISE Composition: Copper-Nickel **Series:** F.A.O. **Subject:** Fisheries

Date	F	VF	XF	Unc	BU
1986(B)	—	0.30	0.50	1.00	—
Note: Mintage included in KM65					
1986B Proof	—	Value: 15.00			
Note: Mintage included in KM65					
1986(C)	—	2.00	3.00	5.00	—
1986(H)	—	2.00	3.00	5.00	—
Note: Mintage included in KM65					

KM# 68.2 50 PAISE Composition: Copper-Nickel **Obverse:** KM#67 **Reverse:** KM#68 **Note:** Mule.

Date	F	VF	XF	Unc	BU
1986(C)	—	50.00	70.00	100	—

KM# 69 50 PAISE Composition: Stainless Steel **Subject:** Parliament Building in New Delhi

Date	Mintage	F	VF	XF	Unc	BU
1988C	272,160,000	—	0.20	0.30	0.50	—
1988(B)	—	—	0.20	0.40	0.75	—
1988(C)	2,195,000	—	6.00	9.00	14.00	—
1988(H)	Inc. above	—	6.00	9.00	14.00	—
1988(N)	—	—	0.20	0.40	0.75	—
1989(B)	—	—	0.20	0.40	0.75	—
1989(C)	—	—	1.50	3.00	5.00	—
1989(H)	—	—	0.50	1.00	2.00	—
1989(N)	—	—	0.15	0.50	1.00	—
1990(B)	—	—	0.15	0.50	1.00	—
1990(C)	—	—	0.50	1.00	2.00	—
1990(H)	—	—	0.15	0.50	1.00	—
1990(N) Small mm	—	—	0.15	0.50	1.00	—
1990(N) Large mm	—	—	0.15	0.50	1.00	—
1991(B)	—	—	0.15	0.50	1.00	—
1991(C)	—	—	0.15	0.50	1.00	—
1991(H)	—	—	0.15	0.25	0.50	—
1991(N)	—	—	0.10	0.35	0.60	—
1992(B)	—	—	0.10	0.35	0.60	—
1992(C)	—	—	0.50	1.00	2.00	—
1992(H)	—	—	0.10	0.35	0.60	—
1992(N)	—	—	0.10	0.35	0.60	—
1993(C)	—	—	0.50	1.00	2.00	—
1993(N)	—	—	0.10	0.35	0.60	—
1994(B)	—	—	0.10	0.35	0.60	—
1994(C)	—	—	0.50	1.00	2.00	—
1994(H)	—	—	0.10	0.35	0.60	—
1994(N)	—	—	0.10	0.35	0.60	—
1995(B)	—	—	0.10	0.20	0.35	—
1995(C)	—	—	0.50	1.00	2.00	—
1995(H)	—	—	0.20	0.30	0.50	—
1995(N)	—	—	0.10	0.20	0.35	—
1996(B)	—	—	0.10	0.20	0.35	—
1996(C)	—	—	0.10	0.20	0.35	—
1996(H)	—	—	0.10	0.20	0.35	—
1996(N)	—	—	0.10	0.20	0.35	—
1997(B)	—	—	0.10	0.20	0.35	—
1997(C)	—	—	0.10	0.20	0.35	—
1997(H)	—	—	2.00	3.00	5.00	—
1997(N)	—	—	0.10	0.20	0.35	—
1998(B)	—	—	0.10	0.20	0.35	—
1998(C)	—	—	0.10	0.20	0.35	—
1998(H)	—	—	1.00	1.50	3.00	—
1998(N)	—	—	0.10	0.20	0.35	—
1999(B)	—	—	0.15	0.25	0.50	—
1999(C)	—	—	0.15	0.25	0.50	—
1999(H)	—	—	0.15	0.25	0.50	—
1999(N)	—	—	0.15	0.25	0.50	—
2000(B)	—	—	0.15	0.25	0.50	—
2000(C)	—	—	0.15	0.25	0.50	—
2000(H)	—	—	0.15	0.25	0.50	—
2000(N)	—	—	0.15	0.25	0.50	—
2001(B)	—	—	0.15	0.25	0.50	—
2001(C)	—	—	0.15	0.25	0.50	—
2001(H)	—	—	0.20	0.40	0.75	—
2001(N)	—	—	0.15	0.25	0.50	—
2002(B)	—	—	0.15	0.25	0.50	—
2002(C)	—	—	0.15	0.25	0.50	—
2002(H)	—	—	0.15	0.25	0.50	—

KM# 70 50 PAISE Composition: Stainless Steel **Subject:** 50th Anniversary of Independence

Date	F	VF	XF	Unc	BU
1997(B)	—	0.25	0.40	0.75	—
1997(C)	—	0.25	0.40	0.75	—
1997(H)	—	0.25	0.40	0.75	—
1997(M) Proof	—	Value: 15.00			
1997(N)	—	0.25	0.40	0.75	—

KM# 75.1 RUPEE Weight: 10.0000 g. **Composition:** Nickel **Note:** Obverse 1.

Date	Mintage	F	VF	XF	Unc	BU
1962(B) Proof	—	—	—	—	—	—
1962(C)	3,689,000	—	1.00	2.00	3.00	—

KM# 75.2 RUPEE Weight: 10.0000 g. **Composition:** Nickel **Reverse:** Smaller date and denomination

Date	Mintage	F	VF	XF	Unc	BU
1970(B)	Inc. above	—	3.50	5.00	7.00	—
1970B Proof	3,046	Value: 3.00				
1971B Proof	4,375	Value: 3.00				
1972B Proof	7,895,000	Value: 2.50				
1973B Proof	7,567	Value: 2.50				
1974B Proof	—	Value: 2.50				

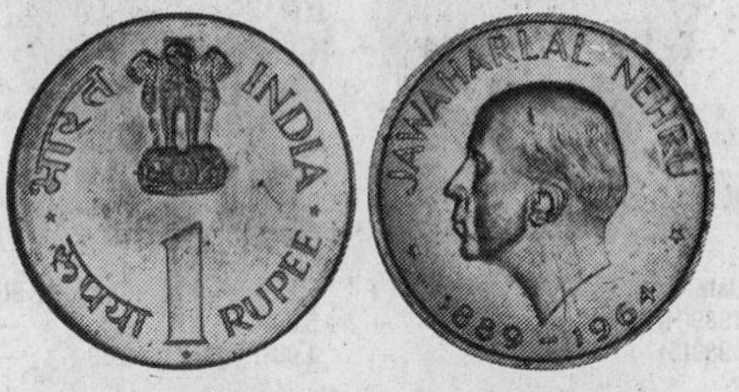

KM# 76 RUPEE Weight: 10.0000 g. **Composition:** Nickel **Subject:** Death of Jawaharlal Nehru **Note:** Nehru commemorative issues were struck until 1967.

Date	Mintage	F	VF	XF	Unc	BU
ND(1964)(B)	10,010,000	—	0.65	1.00	2.00	—
ND(1964)B Proof	—	Value: 5.00				
ND(1964)(C)	10,020,000	—	0.65	1.00	2.00	—

KM# 77 RUPEE Weight: 10.0000 g. **Composition:** Nickel **Subject:** Centennial - Birth of Mahatma Gandhi **Note:** Struck during 1969 and 1970.

Date	Mintage	F	VF	XF	Unc	BU
ND(1969)(B)	5,180,000	—	0.70	1.25	2.00	—
ND(1969)B Proof	9,147	Value: 3.00				
ND(1969)(C)	6,690,000	—	1.00	1.50	2.50	—

KM# 78.1 RUPEE Weight: 8.0000 g. **Composition:** Copper-Nickel

Date	Mintage	F	VF	XF	Unc	BU
1975(B)	98,850,000	—	0.40	0.85	1.50	—
1975B Proof	—	Value: 2.50				
1975(C)	—	—	6.50	8.00	10.00	—
1976(B)	161,895,000	—	0.35	0.75	1.50	—
1976B Proof	Inc. above	Value: 2.50				
1977(B)	177,105,000	—	0.35	0.75	1.50	—
1977B Proof	Inc. above	Value: 2.50				
1978(B)	127,348,000	—	0.40	0.80	1.50	—
1978B Proof	Inc. above	Value: 2.50				
1978(C)	Inc. above	—	0.50	1.00	1.75	—
1979(C)	—	—	8.00	11.00	15.00	—

KM# 78.2 RUPEE Weight: 8.0000 g. **Composition:** Copper-Nickel **Note:** Type 2.

Date	F	VF	XF	Unc	BU
1975(C)	—	0.40	0.85	1.50	—
Note: Mintage included in KM78.1					
1976(C)	—	0.50	1.25	2.25	—
Note: Mintage included in KM78.1					

KM# 78.3 RUPEE Weight: 8.0000 g. **Composition:** Copper-Nickel **Note:** Type 3. Border varieties of long vs. short teeth on 1981 reverse and 1982 obverse.

Date	Mintage	F	VF	XF	Unc	BU
1979(B)	—	—	0.35	0.60	1.00	—
1979B Proof	—	Value: 2.50				
1979(C)	—	—	0.40	0.75	1.50	—
1980(B)	84,768,000	—	0.35	0.60	1.00	—
1980B Proof	—	Value: 2.50				
1980(C)	Inc. above	—	0.40	0.75	1.25	—
1981(B)	82,458,000	—	0.35	0.60	1.00	—
1981B Proof	—	Value: 2.50				
1981(C)	Inc. above	—	0.40	0.75	1.25	—
1982(B)	116,811,000	—	0.40	0.75	1.25	—

KM# 79.1 RUPEE Weight: 6.0000 g. **Composition:** Copper-Nickel **Edge:** Security **Note:** Lions' hair and ears on 1984(B)-1989(B) issues vary from others.

Date	Mintage	F	VF	XF	Unc	BU
1983(B)	32,490,000	—	0.30	0.50	1.00	—
1983(C)	Inc. above	—	0.30	0.50	1.00	—
1984(B)	152,378,000	—	0.25	0.40	0.75	—
1984(C)	Inc. above	—	0.25	0.40	0.75	—
1984(H)	Inc. above	—	1.50	2.25	3.00	—
1985(B)	444,516,000	—	0.25	0.40	0.75	—
1985(C)	Inc. above	—	0.25	0.40	0.75	—
1985H	Inc. above	—	0.25	0.40	0.75	—
1985(L)	Inc. above	—	0.25	0.40	0.75	—
1986(B)	1,396,074,000	—	0.25	0.40	0.75	—
1986(C)	Inc. above	—	0.25	0.40	0.75	—
1986(H)	Inc. above	—	1.50	2.25	3.00	—
1987(B)	685,502,000	—	0.25	0.40	0.75	—
1987(C)	Inc. above	—	0.25	0.40	0.75	—
1987(H)	Inc. above	—	0.25	0.40	0.75	—
1988(B)	240,447,000	—	0.75	1.25	2.00	—
1988(C)	Inc. above	—	0.25	0.40	0.75	—
1988(H)	Inc. above	—	0.40	0.75	1.25	—
1989(B)	—	—	1.50	2.25	3.00	—
1989(C)	—	—	0.25	0.45	0.75	—
1989(H)	—	—	0.25	0.45	0.75	—
1990(C)	—	—	1.50	2.25	3.00	—
1990(H)	—	—	0.25	0.45	0.75	—

KM# 79.2 RUPEE Weight: 6.0000 g. **Composition:** Copper-Nickel **Obverse:** Horse in pedestal shorter, more detailed

Date	F	VF	XF	Unc	BU
1988(B)	—	1.00	1.50	2.50	—

Date	F	VF	XF	Unc	BU
1989(N)	—	1.00	1.50	2.50	—
1990(N)	—	1.00	1.50	2.50	—

KM# 79.3 RUPEE **Weight:** 6.0000 g. **Composition:** Copper-Nickel **Obverse:** Lions' chest hairs restyled

Date	F	VF	XF	Unc	BU
1988(B)	—	0.25	0.50	1.00	—
1989(B)	—	0.25	0.50	1.00	—
1990(B)	—	0.25	0.50	1.00	—

KM# 79.4 RUPEE **Weight:** 6.0000 g. **Composition:** Copper-Nickel **Obverse:** Similar to 79.1 **Edge:** Milled **Note:** Traces of security edge and/or mostly smooth edges are frequently encountered, especially for 1989. 1989-1991(c) is a variety with bulging eyes on side lions and irregular straight hair on central lion.

Date	F	VF	XF	Unc	BU
1989(B)	—	10.00	15.00	20.00	—
1989(C)	—	5.00	7.00	11.00	—
1989(H)	—	10.00	15.00	20.00	—
1990(C)	—	0.35	0.50	1.00	—
1990(H)	—	0.50	0.75	1.50	—
1991(C)	—	0.35	0.50	1.00	—

KM# 79.5 RUPEE **Weight:** 6.0000 g. **Composition:** Copper-Nickel **Obverse:** Lions similar to KM#79.3

Date	F	VF	XF	Unc	BU
1990(C)	—	0.50	1.00	2.00	—
1990(B)	—	0.35	0.60	1.00	—
1991(B)	—	0.20	0.35	0.85	—
1991(H)	—	0.35	0.60	1.00	—

KM# 80 RUPEE **Weight:** 6.0000 g. **Composition:** Copper-Nickel **Subject:** Youth Year **Edge:** Security

Date	F	VF	XF	Unc	BU
1985(B)	—	0.35	0.60	1.25	—
Note: Mintage included in KM79.1					
1985(C)	—	0.50	1.00	2.00	—
Note: Mintage included in KM79.1					
1985(C) Proof	—	Value: 10.00			
Note: Mintage included in KM79.1					
1985(H)	—	2.00	3.00	5.00	—

KM# 81 RUPEE **Weight:** 6.0000 g. **Composition:** Copper-Nickel **Series:** F.A.O. **Reverse:** Small Farmers

Date	Mintage	F	VF	XF	Unc	BU
1987(B)	234,223,000	—	0.35	0.60	1.25	—
1987B Proof	—	Value: 5.00				
1987(C)	Inc. above	—	0.50	1.00	2.00	—
1987(H)	191,120,000	—	1.50	3.00	4.00	—

KM# 82 RUPEE **Weight:** 6.0000 g. **Composition:** Copper-Nickel **Series:** F.A.O. **Reverse:** Rainfed Farming

Date	F	VF	XF	Unc	BU
1988(B)	—	1.00	1.50	3.00	—
Note: Mintage included in KM79.1					
1988(C)	—	1.00	2.00	4.00	—
1988(H)	—	3.00	5.00	8.00	—

KM# 83 RUPEE **Weight:** 6.0000 g. **Composition:** Copper-Nickel **Subject:** 100th Anniversary of Nehru's Birth

Date	F	VF	XF	Unc	BU
1989B Proof	—	Value: 5.00			
1989(C)	—	1.00	2.00	3.00	—
1989(B)	—	0.25	0.50	1.00	—
1989(H)	—	1.00	2.00	3.00	—

KM# 84 RUPEE **Weight:** 6.0000 g. **Composition:** Copper-Nickel **Series:** F.A.O. **Subject:** Food and Environment

Date	F	VF	XF	Unc	BU
1989(H)	—	5.00	8.00	10.00	—
1989(B)	—	1.00	2.00	3.50	—

KM# 87.1 RUPEE **Weight:** 6.0000 g. **Composition:** Copper-Nickel **Subject:** SAARC Year - Care for the Girl Child

Date	F	VF	XF	Unc	BU
1990(B)	—	0.40	0.80	2.00	—

KM# 87.2 RUPEE **Weight:** 6.0000 g. **Composition:** Copper-Nickel **Edge:** Milled **Note:** Edge varieties exist.

Date	F	VF	XF	Unc	BU
1990(B)	—	0.50	1.25	3.00	—
1990(H)	—	0.50	1.25	3.00	—

KM# 85 RUPEE **Weight:** 6.0000 g. **Composition:** Copper-Nickel **Subject:** Dr. Ambedkar

Date	F	VF	XF	Unc	BU
1990(B)	—	0.20	0.75	1.50	—
1990(H)	—	0.40	1.25	2.50	—

KM# 86 RUPEE **Weight:** 6.0000 g. **Composition:** Copper-Nickel **Subject:** 15th Anniversary of I.C.D.S.

Date	F	VF	XF	Unc	BU
ND(1990)(B)	—	0.20	0.75	1.50	—
ND(1990)(H)	—	0.40	1.25	2.50	—

KM# 88 RUPEE **Weight:** 6.0000 g. **Composition:** Copper-Nickel **Series:** F.A.O. **Reverse:** Farming Scene

Date	F	VF	XF	Unc	BU
1990(C)	—	3.00	5.00	8.00	—
Note: 1990(C) is seldom well struck					
1990(H)	—	5.00	7.00	10.00	—

KM# 89 RUPEE **Weight:** 6.0000 g. **Composition:** Copper-Nickel **Subject:** Rajiv Gandhi **Note:** Edge varieties exist.

Date	F	VF	XF	Unc	BU
ND(1991)(B)	—	0.35	0.75	1.50	—
Note: The Mumbai (Bombay) mint mark occasionally resembles the Noida mintmark					
ND(1991)(H)	—	0.40	1.00	2.00	—

KM# 90 RUPEE **Weight:** 6.0000 g. **Composition:** Copper-Nickel **Subject:** Commonwealth Parliamentary Conference

Date	F	VF	XF	Unc	BU
1991(B)	—	0.35	0.75	1.50	—
1991(B) Prooflike	—	—	—	3.00	—
1991B Proof	—	Value: 5.00			

KM# 91 RUPEE **Weight:** 6.0000 g. **Composition:** Copper-Nickel **Subject:** Tourism Year

Date	F	VF	XF	Unc	BU
1991(B)	—	0.35	0.75	1.50	—
1991(H)	—	0.60	1.25	2.50	—
1991(B) Prooflike	—	—	—	3.00	—
1991B Proof	—	Value: 5.00			

KM# 92.1 RUPEE **Composition:** Stainless Steel **Note:** Milled edge, sometimes faint.

Date	F	VF	XF	Unc	BU
1992(H)	—	0.20	0.30	0.60	—
1992(B)	—	0.20	0.30	0.60	—
1993(B)	—	0.20	0.30	0.60	—
Note: Two mintmark varieties exist for 1993(B) and 1994(B)					
1993(C)	—	0.20	0.30	0.60	—
1993(H)	—	0.20	0.30	0.60	—
1993(N)	—	0.20	0.30	0.60	—
1994(B)	—	0.15	0.25	0.50	—
Note: Two mintmark varieties exist for 1993(B) and 1994(B)					
1994(C)	—	0.15	0.25	0.50	—
1994(H)	—	0.15	0.25	0.50	—
1994(N)	—	0.15	0.25	0.50	—
1995(B)	—	0.15	0.25	0.50	—
1995(C)	—	0.15	0.25	0.50	—
1995(H)	—	0.15	0.25	0.50	—
1995(N)	—	0.15	0.25	0.50	—
1996(H)	—	1.00	1.50	2.50	—

KM# 92.2 RUPEE **Composition:** Stainless Steel
Edge: Plain starting in 1996

Date	F	VF	XF	Unc	BU
1995(B)	—	1.00	1.50	2.50	—
1995(H)	—	1.00	1.50	2.50	—
1995(N)	—	1.00	1.50	2.50	—
1996(B)	—	0.15	0.35	0.60	—
1996(C)	—	0.15	0.35	0.60	—
1996(H)	—	0.15	0.35	0.60	—
1996(N)	—	0.15	0.35	0.60	—
1997(B)	—	0.15	0.35	0.60	—
1997(C)	—	0.15	0.35	0.60	—
1997(H)	—	1.50	2.00	3.00	—
1997(M)	—	0.15	0.35	0.50	—
1997(N)	—	0.15	0.35	0.50	—
1998(B)	—	0.15	0.35	0.50	—
1998(C)	—	0.15	0.35	0.50	—
1998(H)	—	0.15	0.35	0.50	—
1998(K)	—	0.15	0.35	0.50	—
1998(N)	—	0.15	0.35	0.50	—
1999(B)	—	0.15	0.35	0.50	—
1999(K)	—	0.15	0.30	0.45	—
1999(N)	—	0.15	0.30	0.45	—
1999(C)	—	0.15	0.35	0.50	—
1999(H)	—	0.15	0.35	0.50	—
2000(B)	—	0.15	0.30	0.45	—
2000(K)	—	0.15	0.30	0.45	—
2000(C)	—	0.15	0.30	0.45	—
2000(H)	—	0.15	0.30	0.45	—
2000(N)	—	0.15	0.30	0.45	—
2001(B)	—	0.15	0.30	0.45	—
2001(C)	—	0.15	0.30	0.45	—
2001(H)	—	0.15	0.30	0.45	—
Note: Small and large mint mark exist, doubled left or right of wheat stalks					
2001(K)	—	0.15	0.30	0.45	—
2001(N)	—	0.15	0.30	0.45	—
2002(B)	—	0.15	0.30	0.45	—
2002(C)	—	0.15	0.30	0.45	—
2002(N)	—	0.15	0.30	0.45	—

KM# 93 RUPEE **Composition:** Copper-Nickel
Subject: Quit India **Edge:** Milled

Date	F	VF	XF	Unc	BU
ND(1992)(C)	—	1.00	3.00	6.00	—
ND(1992)(H)	—	2.00	3.50	8.00	—
ND(1992)(B)	—	0.50	1.00	2.00	—

KM# 94 RUPEE **Composition:** Copper-Nickel
Series: World Food Day

Date	F	VF	XF	Unc	BU
1992(C)	—	1.50	2.50	4.50	—

KM# 95 RUPEE **Composition:** Copper-Nickel
Subject: Inter Parliamentary Union Conference

Date	F	VF	XF	Unc	BU
1993(B)	—	0.50	1.25	3.00	—

KM# 96 RUPEE **Composition:** Stainless Steel
Subject: International Year of the Family

Date	F	VF	XF	Unc	BU
1994(B)	—	0.40	0.75	2.00	—
1994(N)	—	1.00	1.50	2.50	—

KM# 97.1 RUPEE **Composition:** Stainless Steel
Subject: Eighth World Tamil Conference **Obverse:** Asoka column **Reverse:** St. Thiruvalluvar

Date	F	VF	XF	Unc	BU
1995(B)	—	0.50	1.00	1.50	—
1995(H)	—	0.70	1.25	2.00	—
1995(N)	—	0.50	1.00	1.75	—

KM# 97.2 RUPEE **Composition:** Stainless Steel **Edge:** Plain

Date	F	VF	XF	Unc	BU
1995(H)	—	4.00	7.00	10.00	—
1995(N)	—	4.00	7.00	10.00	—

KM# 98 RUPEE **Composition:** Stainless Steel
Reverse: Port Blajr Jail **Note:** Variation exist.

Date	F	VF	XF	Unc	BU
1997(B)	—	0.30	0.50	0.80	—
1997(C)	—	0.30	0.50	0.80	—
1997(H)	—	0.30	0.50	0.80	—
1997(N)	—	0.40	0.60	1.00	—

KM# 295 RUPEE **Weight:** 10.0000 g. **Composition:** 0.9990 Gold .3215 oz. AGW **Subject:** St. Dnyaneshwar **Note:** Stainless steel.

Date	F	VF	XF	Unc	BU
1999(B)	—	0.40	0.60	1.00	—
1999(C)	—	0.60	0.90	1.50	—

2 RUPEES

2 Rupee Obverses

A. Asoka column 15mm tall. 5 fur rows on right lion. No lion whiskers, circle in central wheel.

B. Asoka column 14mm tall. 3 fur rows on right lion. 5 lion whiskers, no circle in central wheel.

C. Asoka column 13mm tall. 4 fur rows on right lion. No dot in central wheel.

D. Asoka column 13mm tall. 4 fur rows. Recut chest on central lion. Dot in central wheel.

E. Asoka column 13mm tall. No fur rows on right lion. 2 whiskers on central lion.

NOTE: Obverses C and D include both 4.5 x 5mm and 5 x 5.5mm numeral 2 varieties.

KM# 120 2 RUPEES **Composition:** Copper-Nickel
Subject: IX Asian Games

Date	Mintage	F	VF	XF	Unc	BU
1982(B)	12,720,000	—	0.35	0.50	1.25	—
1982B Proof	Inc. above	Value: 2.50				
1982(C)	Inc. above	—	0.35	0.50	1.25	—

KM# 121.1 2 RUPEES **Composition:** Copper-Nickel
Subject: National Integration **Obverse:** Asoka column 14mm tall **Reverse:** Small date

Date	F	VF	XF	Unc	BU
1982B Proof	—	Value: 3.50			
1982(C)	—	0.30	1.00	2.25	—
Note: Mintage included in KM120					
1982(B)	—	0.30	1.00	1.75	—
Note: Mintage included in KM120					

KM# 121.2 2 RUPEES **Composition:** Copper-Nickel
Obverse: Asoka column 15mm tall **Reverse:** Large date

Date	F	VF	XF	Unc	BU
1990(B)	—	0.40	1.00	2.25	—
1990(C)	—	0.40	1.00	2.25	—
1990(H)	—	0.80	3.00	5.00	—

KM# 121.3 2 RUPEES **Composition:** Copper-Nickel
Obverse: Asoka column 15mm tall **Size:** 26 mm.
Note: Reduced size.

Date	F	VF	XF	Unc	BU
1992(B)	—	2.50	4.00	7.00	—
1992(C)	—	0.30	0.50	1.00	—
1992(H)	—	0.40	1.00	1.50	—
1993(C)	—	0.40	1.25	2.00	—
1993(H)	—	0.35	0.60	1.25	—
1994(C)	—	0.40	1.25	2.00	—
1994(H)	—	0.35	0.80	1.50	—
1995(B)	—	2.50	4.00	7.00	—
1995(C)	—	0.30	0.50	1.00	—
1995(H)	—	0.30	0.50	1.00	—
1996(C)	—	0.30	0.50	1.00	—
1996(H)	—	0.30	0.50	1.00	—
1997(C)	—	0.30	0.50	1.00	—
1997(H)	—	0.30	0.50	1.00	—
1998(C)	—	0.30	0.50	1.00	—
1999(C)	—	0.30	0.50	1.00	—
2000(C)	—	0.30	0.50	1.00	—
2001(B)	—	0.30	0.50	1.00	—
2001(C)	—	0.30	0.50	1.00	—
2002(C)	—	0.30	0.50	1.00	—

KM# 121.4 2 RUPEES **Composition:** Copper-Nickel
Obverse: B

Date	F	VF	XF	Unc	BU
1992(B)	—	0.30	0.50	1.00	—
1993(B)	—	0.30	0.50	1.00	—
1994(B)	—	0.30	0.50	1.00	—
1994(H)	—	2.75	5.00	6.50	—
1994(N)	—	2.75	5.00	6.50	—
1995(B)	—	0.30	0.50	1.00	—
1995(H)	—	3.00	5.50	8.00	—
1995(N)	—	0.30	0.50	1.00	—
1996(B)	—	2.50	4.00	6.00	—
1996(B-H)	—	5.00	10.00	15.00	—
1996(N)	—	0.30	0.50	1.00	—
1997(B)	—	0.30	0.50	1.00	—
1998(N)	—	0.30	0.50	1.00	—

KM# 121.5 2 RUPEES **Composition:** Copper-Nickel
Obverse: C

Date	F	VF	XF	Unc	BU
1995(B)	—	2.50	4.00	6.00	—
1996(B)	—	0.30	0.50	1.00	—
1996(H)	—	0.30	0.50	1.00	—
1997(B)	—	0.30	0.50	1.00	—
1997(H)	—	0.30	0.50	1.00	—
1997(T)	—	0.30	0.50	1.00	—
1998(B)	—	0.30	0.50	1.00	—
1998(H)	—	0.30	0.50	1.00	—
1998(P)	—	0.30	0.50	1.00	—
1998(T)	—	0.30	0.50	1.00	—
1999(B)	—	0.30	0.50	1.00	—
1999(H)	—	0.30	0.50	1.00	—
1999(Ld)	—	0.30	0.50	1.00	—
1999(N)	—	0.30	0.50	1.00	—
1999(C)	—	0.30	0.50	1.00	—
2000(B)	—	0.30	0.50	1.00	—
2000(C)	—	0.30	0.50	1.00	—
2000(H)	—	0.30	0.50	1.00	—
2000(N)	—	0.30	0.50	1.00	—
2000(R)	—	0.30	0.50	1.00	—
2001(B)	—	0.30	0.50	1.00	—
2001(N)	—	0.30	0.50	1.00	—
2001(H)	—	0.30	0.50	1.00	—
2002(B)	—	0.30	0.50	1.00	—
2002(H)	—	0.30	0.50	1.00	—

KM# 121.6 2 RUPEES **Composition:** Copper-Nickel
Obverse: D

Date	F	VF	XF	Unc	BU
1998(B)	—	0.30	0.50	1.00	—
1998(H)	—	0.30	0.50	1.00	—
1999(B)	—	0.75	1.00	1.50	—
2000(B)	—	0.75	1.00	1.50	—

KM# 122 2 RUPEES **Composition:** Copper-Nickel
Subject: Golden Jubilee of Reserve Bank of India

Date	F	VF	XF	Unc	BU
ND(1985)(B) Proof	—	Value: 60.00			

KM# 123 2 RUPEES **Composition:** Copper-Nickel
Subject: Tourism **Note:** Similar to 1 Rupee, KM#91.

Date	F	VF	XF	Unc	BU
1991 Prooflike	—	—	—	6.00	—
1991 Proof	—	Value: 10.00			

KM# 124.1 2 RUPEES **Composition:** Copper-Nickel
Subject: Small Family Happy Family

Date	F	VF	XF	Unc	BU
1993(B)	—	0.50	0.90	1.50	—

KM# 124.2 2 RUPEES **Composition:** Copper-Nickel
Obverse: A

Date	F	VF	XF	Unc	BU
1993(H)	—	2.00	3.00	5.00	—

KM# 125.1 2 RUPEES **Composition:** Copper-Nickel
Series: World Food Day **Subject:** Bio Diversity

Date	F	VF	XF	Unc	BU
1993(B)	—	0.50	0.90	1.50	—

KM# 125.2 2 RUPEES **Composition:** Copper-Nickel
Obverse: A

Date	F	VF	XF	Unc	BU
1993(H)	—	2.00	3.00	5.00	—

KM# 126.1 2 RUPEES **Composition:** Copper-Nickel
Series: F.A.O. **Subject:** Water For Life

Date	F	VF	XF	Unc	BU
1994(B)	—	0.60	1.10	2.00	—
1994(C)	—	1.00	2.00	4.00	—
1994(H)	—	2.00	4.50	11.00	—

KM# 126.2 2 RUPEES **Composition:** Copper-Nickel
Obverse: B

Date	F	VF	XF	Unc	BU
1994(B)	—	—	—	—	—

KM# 127.1 2 RUPEES **Composition:** Copper-Nickel
Subject: Globalizing Indian Agriculture - Agriexpo 95
Obverse: A **Reverse:** Steerhead in wreath of two stalks of wheat

Date	F	VF	XF	Unc	BU
1995(B)	—	0.60	1.25	2.00	—
1995(C)	—	1.00	3.00	6.00	—

KM# 127.2 2 RUPEES **Composition:** Copper-Nickel
Obverse: B

Date	F	VF	XF	Unc	BU
1995(B)	—	3.00	5.00	10.00	—

KM# 127.3 2 RUPEES **Composition:** Copper-Nickel
Obverse: C

Date	F	VF	XF	Unc	BU
1995(B)	—	—	—	—	—

KM# 128 2 RUPEES **Composition:** Copper-Nickel
Subject: Eighth World Tamil Conference **Obverse:** Asoka column 13mm tall **Reverse:** St. Thiruvalluvar

Date	F	VF	XF	Unc	BU
1995(B)	—	0.60	1.00	1.75	—

KM# 129.1 2 RUPEES **Composition:** Copper-Nickel
Subject: Sardar Vallabhbhai Patel **Obverse:** A **Reverse:** Portrait of Patel

Date	F	VF	XF	Unc	BU
1995(B)	—	2.50	4.00	7.00	—
1996M Proof	—	Value: 8.00			

KM# 129.2 2 RUPEES **Composition:** Copper-Nickel
Obverse: B

Date	F	VF	XF	Unc	BU
1996(N)	—	1.00	1.50	3.00	—

KM# 129.3 2 RUPEES **Composition:** Copper-Nickel
Obverse: C

Date	F	VF	XF	Unc	BU
1996(B)	—	2.00	3.00	5.00	—
1996(H)	—	0.40	0.70	1.25	—

KM# 129.4 2 RUPEES **Composition:** Copper-Nickel
Obverse: D

Date	F	VF	XF	Unc	BU
1996(B)	—	0.40	0.70	1.25	—
1996(C)	—	0.30	0.60	1.00	—

KM# 129.5 2 RUPEES **Composition:** Copper-Nickel
Obverse: E

Date	F	VF	XF	Unc	BU
1996(B)	30.00	40.00	55.00	80.00	—

KM# 130.1 2 RUPEES **Composition:** Copper-Nickel
Obverse: C **Reverse:** Subhas Chandra Bose

Date	F	VF	XF	Unc	BU
1996(C)	—	10.00	12.00	15.00	—
1997(B)	—	0.60	0.90	1.25	—
1997(C)	—	0.60	0.90	1.25	—
1997(H)	—	1.50	2.50	4.00	—
1997(M) Proof	—	Value: 3.25			

KM# 130.2 2 RUPEES **Composition:** Copper-Nickel
Obverse: B

Date	F	VF	XF	Unc	BU
1997(N)	—	1.00	2.00	3.50	—
1997(H)	—	0.60	0.90	1.25	—

KM# 131.1 2 RUPEES **Composition:** Copper-Nickel **Obverse:** C **Reverse:** Sri Aurobindo

Date	F	VF	XF	Unc	BU
1998(B)	—	0.60	0.90	1.50	—
1998(N)	—	1.00	1.50	3.00	—
1998(C)	—	1.00	1.50	3.00	—
1998(M) Proof	—	Value: 3.50			

KM# 131.2 2 RUPEES **Composition:** Copper-Nickel **Obverse:** D

Date	F	VF	XF	Unc	BU
1998(B)	—	3.00	5.00	8.00	—

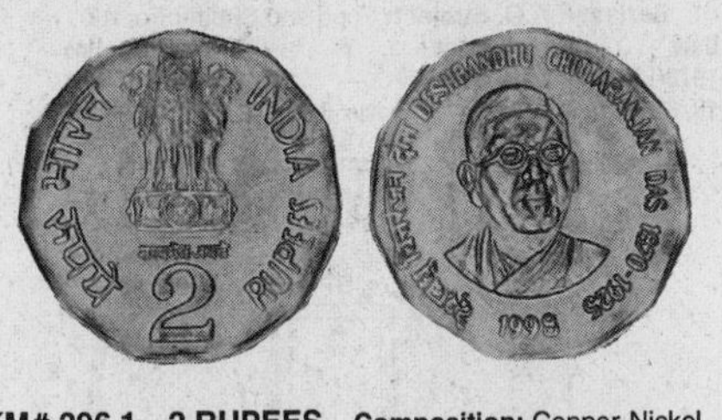

KM# 296.1 2 RUPEES **Composition:** Copper-Nickel **Obverse:** A **Reverse:** Deshbandhu Chittaranjan Das

Date	F	VF	XF	Unc	BU
1998(C)	—	10.00	15.00	25.00	—

KM# 296.2 2 RUPEES **Composition:** Copper-Nickel **Obverse:** B

Date	F	VF	XF	Unc	BU
1998(N)	—	3.00	4.00	6.00	—

KM# 296.3 2 RUPEES **Composition:** Copper-Nickel **Obverse:** C, 7mm, edge flat

Date	F	VF	XF	Unc	BU
1998(C)	—	4.00	6.00	8.00	—

KM# 296.4 2 RUPEES **Composition:** Copper-Nickel **Note:** 5-6mm, edge flat.

Date	F	VF	XF	Unc	BU
1998(C)	—	6.00	8.00	12.00	—

KM# 296.5 2 RUPEES **Composition:** Copper-Nickel **Note:** 3-5mm, edge flat.

Date	F	VF	XF	Unc	BU
1998(C)	—	3.00	4.00	6.00	—

KM# 296.6 2 RUPEES **Composition:** Copper-Nickel **Obverse:** D **Note:** 3-5mm, edge flat.

Date	F	VF	XF	Unc	BU
1998(C)	—	0.75	1.25	2.00	—

KM# 290 2 RUPEES **Composition:** Copper-Nickel **Obverse:** C **Reverse:** Chhatrapati Shivaji

Date	F	VF	XF	Unc	BU
1999(B)	—	0.75	1.25	2.00	—
1999(N)	—	0.75	1.25	2.00	—
1999(C)	—	0.75	1.25	2.00	—
1999(H)	—	1.00	1.75	3.00	—

KM# 291 2 RUPEES **Composition:** Copper-Nickel **Subject:** Supreme Court: 50 Years **Obverse:** C; Lion column above denomination **Reverse:** Wheel above lion column **Edge:** Plain, eleven sided

Date	F	VF	XF	Unc	BU
2000(B)	—	0.75	1.25	2.00	—
2000(C)	—	0.75	1.25	2.00	—

KM# 303 2 RUPEES **Weight:** 6.2400 g. **Composition:** Copper-Nickel **Subject:** Dr. Syama P. Mookerjee **Obverse:** Type B asoka column above denomination **Reverse:** Portrait **Edge:** Plain, seven sided **Size:** 25.7 mm.

Date	F	VF	XF	Unc	BU
2001(C)	—	1.25	2.00	3.00	—

Note: Some specimens exhibit a die defect to the right of the face

KM# 150 5 RUPEES **Composition:** Copper-Nickel **Subject:** Death of Indira Gandhi

Date	Mintage	F	VF	XF	Unc	BU
ND(1985)(B)	59,288,000	—	0.75	1.50	3.00	—
ND(1985)B Proof	Inc. above	Value: 27.50				
ND(1985)(H)	Inc. above	—	3.50	6.00	15.00	—

KM# 151 5 RUPEES **Composition:** Copper-Nickel **Subject:** Centennial - Nehru's Birth

Date	F	VF	XF	Unc	BU
1989(B)	—	1.00	2.00	3.00	—
Note: Short rim teeth.					
1989(B)	—	2.00	3.00	4.50	—
Note: Long rim teeth.					
1989B Proof	—	Value: 25.00			
1989(H)	—	3.50	6.00	15.00	—

KM# 152 5 RUPEES **Composition:** Copper-Nickel **Subject:** Commonwealth Parliamentary Conference **Note:** Similar to 1 Rupee, KM#90.

Date	F	VF	XF	Unc	BU
1991(B) Prooflike	—	—	—	10.00	—
1991B Proof	—	Value: 20.00			

KM# 153 5 RUPEES **Composition:** Copper-Nickel **Subject:** Tourism **Note:** Similar to 1 Rupee, KM#91.

Date	F	VF	XF	Unc	BU
1991(B) Prooflike	—	—	—	10.00	—
1991B Proof	—	Value: 20.00			

KM# 154.1 5 RUPEES **Composition:** Copper-Nickel **Edge:** Security

Date	F	VF	XF	Unc	BU
1992(B)	—	0.20	0.75	1.50	—
1992(C)	—	0.20	0.75	1.50	—
1992(H)	—	0.20	0.75	1.50	—
1993(B)	—	0.20	0.75	1.50	—
1993(C)	—	0.20	0.75	1.50	—
1994(B)	—	0.20	0.75	1.50	—
1994(C)	—	0.20	0.75	1.50	—
1994(H)	—	0.20	0.75	1.50	—
1995(B)	—	0.20	0.75	1.50	—
1995(C)	—	0.20	0.75	1.50	—
1995(H)	—	0.20	0.75	1.50	—
1995(N)	—	0.20	0.75	1.50	—
1996(B)	—	0.20	0.50	1.00	—
1996(C)	—	0.20	0.50	1.00	—
1996(H)	—	0.20	0.50	1.00	—
1996(N)	—	0.20	0.50	1.00	—
1997(B)	—	0.20	0.50	1.00	—
1997(C)	—	0.20	0.50	1.00	—
1997(H)	—	0.20	0.50	1.00	—
1997(N)	—	0.20	0.50	1.00	—
1998(B)	—	0.20	0.50	1.00	—
1998(C)	—	0.20	0.50	1.00	—
1998(H)	—	0.25	0.50	1.00	—
1998(N)	—	0.25	0.50	1.00	—
1999(B)	—	0.50	0.25	1.00	—
1999(C)	—	0.25	0.50	1.00	—

Date	F	VF	XF	Unc	BU
1999(H)	—	0.25	0.50	1.00	—
1999(N)	—	0.25	0.50	1.00	—
1999(R)	—	0.25	0.50	1.00	—
2000(B)	—	0.50	0.25	1.00	—
2000(C)	—	0.25	0.50	1.00	—
2000(H)	—	0.50	1.00	2.00	—
2000(R)	—	0.25	0.50	1.00	—
2000(N)	—	0.25	0.50	1.00	—
2001(C) Plain 1	—	0.25	0.50	1.00	—
2001(C) Serif 1	—	1.00	2.00	3.00	—
2001(H)	—	0.35	0.60	1.50	—
2001(N)	—	0.25	0.50	1.00	—
2002(C)	—	0.25	0.50	1.00	—

KM# 154.2 5 RUPEES **Composition:** Copper-Nickel **Edge:** Milled

Date	F	VF	XF	Unc	BU
1996(C)	—	8.00	10.00	15.00	—
1998(H)	—	8.00	10.00	15.00	—
2000(C)	—	8.00	10.00	15.00	—

KM# 154.3 5 RUPEES **Composition:** Copper-Nickel **Edge:** Plain

Date	F	VF	XF	Unc	BU
1998(H) Error	—	5.00	10.00	15.00	—

KM# 154.4 5 RUPEES **Composition:** Copper Nickel **Obverse:** similar to KM#121.5

Date	F	VF	XF	Unc	BU
1998(B)	—	0.25	0.50	1.00	—
1999(B)	—	0.25	0.50	1.00	—
2000(B)	—	0.25	0.50	1.00	—
2001(B)	—	0.25	0.50	1.00	—
2002(B)	—	0.25	0.50	1.00	—

KM# 155 5 RUPEES **Composition:** Copper-Nickel **Subject:** World of Work **Edge:** Security

Date	F	VF	XF	Unc	BU
ND(1994)(B)	—	0.75	1.00	1.75	—
ND(1994)B Proof	—	Value: 5.00			
ND(1994)(H)	—	1.50	2.25	4.00	—
ND(1994)(N)	—	1.00	1.50	3.00	—

KM# 156 5 RUPEES **Composition:** Copper-Nickel **Series:** 50 Years - United Nations

Date	F	VF	XF	Unc	BU
1995(B)	—	0.75	1.00	1.75	—
1995(N)	—	1.00	1.50	3.00	—

KM# 157 5 RUPEES **Composition:** Copper-Nickel **Series:** 50th Anniversary - F.A.O. **Obverse:** Asoka column **Reverse:** Hand clutching stalks of wheat

Date	F	VF	XF	Unc	BU
1995(B)	—	0.75	1.00	1.75	—
1995(H)	—	1.50	3.00	5.00	—
1995(N)	—	1.00	1.50	3.00	—

KM# 158 5 RUPEES **Composition:** Copper-Nickel **Subject:** Eighth World Tamil Conference **Obverse:** Asoka column **Reverse:** St. Thiruvalluvar

Date	F	VF	XF	Unc	BU
1995(B)	—	0.75	1.00	1.75	—

KM# 159 5 RUPEES **Composition:** Copper-Nickel **Subject:** Mother's Health is Child's Health

Date	F	VF	XF	Unc	BU
1996(B)	—	0.75	1.00	1.50	—
1996(H)	—	0.75	1.00	1.50	—
1996(N)	—	1.00	1.50	2.25	—

KM# 160 5 RUPEES **Composition:** Copper-Nickel **Subject:** 2nd International Crop Science Conference **Note:** This conference was never held.

Date	Mintage	F	VF	XF	Unc	BU
1996(C)	11,000	—	15.00	17.00	20.00	—

KM# 304 5 RUPEES **Weight:** 9.0700 g. **Composition:** Copper-Nickel **Subject:** Bhagwan Mahavir, 2600th Anniversary **Obverse:** Asoka column above denomination **Reverse:** Swastika above hand in irregular frame **Edge:** Security **Size:** 23.2 mm.

Date	F	VF	XF	Unc	BU
2001(B)	—	1.00	2.00	3.00	—

KM# 185 10 RUPEES **Weight:** 15.0000 g. **Composition:** 0.8000 Silver .3858 oz. ASW **Subject:** Centennial - Mahatma Gandhi's Birth **Note:** Struck during 1969 and 1970.

Date	Mintage	F	VF	XF	Unc	BU
ND(1969)(B)	3,160,000	—	—	4.00	6.00	—
ND(1969)B Proof	9,147	Value: 8.50				
ND(1969)(C)	100,000	—	—	7.00	10.00	—

KM# 186 10 RUPEES **Weight:** 15.0000 g. **Composition:** 0.8000 Silver .3858 oz. ASW **Series:** F.A.O.

Date	Mintage	F	VF	XF	Unc	BU
1970(B)	300,000	—	—	4.00	7.50	—
1970B Proof	3,046	Value: 9.00				
1970(C)	100,000	—	—	6.00	10.00	—
1971(B)	—	—	—	6.00	10.00	—
1971B Proof	1,594	Value: 10.00				

KM# 187 10 RUPEES **Weight:** 22.5000 g. **Composition:** 0.5000 Silver .3617 oz. ASW **Subject:** 25th Anniversary of Independence

Date	Mintage	F	VF	XF	Unc	BU
ND(1972)(B)	1,000,000	—	—	—	7.00	—
ND(1972)B Proof	7,895	Value: 9.50				

KM# 187a 10 RUPEES **Composition:** Copper-Nickel

Date	F	VF	XF	Unc	BU
ND(1972)(B)	—	—	—	6.00	—
ND(1972)(C)	—	—	—	6.00	—

Note: Rim thinner, inner flag circle missing on Calcutta issues

KM# 188 10 RUPEES **Weight:** 22.3000 g. **Composition:** 0.5000 Silver .3585 oz. ASW **Series:** F.A.O.

Date	Mintage	F	VF	XF	Unc	BU
1973(B)	64,000	—	—	—	6.50	—
1973B Proof	15,000	Value: 9.50				

KM# 189 10 RUPEES **Composition:** Copper-Nickel **Series:** F.A.O.

Date	Mintage	F	VF	XF	Unc	BU
1974(B)	65,000	—	—	2.00	4.50	—
1974B Proof	12,000	Value: 7.00				

KM# 190 10 RUPEES **Composition:** Copper-Nickel **Series:** F.A.O. **Subject:** Women's Year

Date	Mintage	F	VF	XF	Unc	BU
1975(B)	49,000	—	—	2.00	4.50	—
1975B Proof	2,531	Value: 8.50				

KM# 191 10 RUPEES **Composition:** Copper-Nickel **Series:** F.A.O. **Subject:** Food and Work For All

Date	Mintage	F	VF	XF	Unc	BU
1976(B)	49,000	—	—	2.00	4.50	—
1976B Proof	3,400	Value: 8.50				

KM# 192 10 RUPEES **Composition:** Copper-Nickel **Series:** F.A.O. **Subject:** Save For Development

Date	Mintage	F	VF	XF	Unc	BU
1977(B)	20,000	—	—	2.00	4.50	—
1977B Proof	5,969	Value: 8.50				

KM# 193 10 RUPEES **Composition:** Copper-Nickel **Series:** F.A.O. **Subject:** Food and Shelter For All

Date	Mintage	F	VF	XF	Unc	BU
1978(B)	25,000	—	—	2.00	4.50	—
1978B Proof	—	Value: 8.50				

KM# 194 10 RUPEES **Composition:** Copper-Nickel **Series:** International Year of the Child

Date	F	VF	XF	Unc	BU
1979(B)	—	—	2.50	5.00	—
1979B Proof	—	Value: 9.50			

KM# 195 10 RUPEES **Composition:** Copper-Nickel **Subject:** Rural Women's Advancement

Date	F	VF	XF	Unc	BU
1980(B)	—	—	2.50	5.00	—
1980B Proof	—	Value: 9.50			

KM# 196 10 RUPEES **Composition:** Copper-Nickel **Series:** World Food Day

Date	F	VF	XF	Unc	BU
1981(B)	—	—	2.50	5.00	—
1981B Proof	—	Value: 9.50			

KM# 197 10 RUPEES **Composition:** Copper-Nickel
Subject: IX Asian Games

Date	F	VF	XF	Unc	BU
1982(B)	—	—	2.50	5.00	—
1982B Proof	—	Value: 9.50			

KM# 198 10 RUPEES **Composition:** Copper-Nickel
Subject: National Integration

Date	F	VF	XF	Unc	BU
1982(B)	—	—	—	6.00	—
1982B Proof	—	Value: 10.00			

KM# 199 10 RUPEES **Composition:** Copper-Nickel
Subject: Golden Jubilee - Reserve Bank of India

Date	F	VF	XF	Unc	BU
ND(1985)(B)	—	—	—	65.00	—
ND(1985)B Proof	—	Value: 75.00			

KM# 200 10 RUPEES **Composition:** Copper-Nickel
Subject: Youth Year **Note:** Similar to 1 Rupee, KM#80.

Date	F	VF	XF	Unc	BU
1985(C)	—	—	—	10.00	—
1985(C) Proof	—	Value: 30.00			

KM# 201 10 RUPEES **Composition:** Copper-Nickel
Subject: Commonwealth Parliamentary Conference
Note: Similar to 1 Rupee, KM#90.

Date	F	VF	XF	Unc	BU
1991(B) Prooflike	—	—	—	10.00	—
1991B Proof	—	Value: 20.00			

KM# 202 10 RUPEES **Composition:** Copper-Nickel
Subject: Quit India **Note:** Similar to 1 Rupee, KM#93.

Date	F	VF	XF	Unc	BU
1992(B) Proof	—	Value: 10.00			

KM# 203 10 RUPEES **Composition:** Copper-Nickel
Subject: 100th Anniversary - Birth of Patel **Note:** Similar to 2 Rupee, KM#129.

Date	F	VF	XF	Unc	BU
1996(B)	—	—	—	8.00	—
1996M Proof	—	Value: 12.00			

KM# 204 10 RUPEES **Composition:** Copper-Nickel
Subject: Subhas Chandra Bose **Note:** Similar to 2 Rupees, KM#130.

Date	F	VF	XF	Unc	BU
1997(C)	—	—	—	8.00	—
1997M Proof	—	Value: 12.00			

KM# 205 10 RUPEES **Composition:** Copper-Nickel
Subject: Sri Aurobindo **Note:** Similar to 2 Rupees, KM#131.

Date	F	VF	XF	Unc	BU
1998(B)	—	—	—	8.00	—
1998M Proof	—	Value: 12.00			

KM# 297 10 RUPEES **Weight:** 12.5000 g.
Composition: Copper-Nickel **Subject:** Deshbandhu Chittaranjan Das **Obverse:** Ashoka pillar. **Reverse:** Das portrait. **Edge:** Reeded. **Size:** 31 mm.

Date	F	VF	XF	Unc	BU
1998(C)	—	—	—	7.50	—
1998(C) Proof	—	Value: 12.00			

KM# 240 20 RUPEES **Weight:** 30.0000 g.
Composition: 0.5000 Silver .4823 oz. ASW **Series:** F.A.O.

Date	Mintage	F	VF	XF	Unc	BU
1973(B)	64,000	—	—	—	8.00	—
1973B Proof	12,000	Value: 12.50				

KM# 241 20 RUPEES **Composition:** Copper-Nickel
Subject: Death of Indira Gandhi

Date	F	VF	XF	Unc	BU
ND(1985)(B)	—	—	—	12.50	—
ND(1985)B Proof	—	Value: 50.00			

KM# 242 20 RUPEES **Composition:** Copper-Nickel
Series: F.A.O. **Subject:** Fisheries

Date	F	VF	XF	Unc	BU
1986(B)	—	—	—	10.00	—
1986B Proof	—	Value: 20.00			

KM# 243 20 RUPEES **Composition:** Copper-Nickel
Series: F.A.O. **Subject:** Small Farmers

Date	F	VF	XF	Unc	BU
1987(B)	—	—	—	10.00	—
1987B Proof	—	Value: 20.00			

KM# 244 20 RUPEES **Composition:** Copper-Nickel
Subject: 100th Anniversary of Nehru's Birth

Date	F	VF	XF	Unc	BU
1989(B)	—	—	—	10.00	—
1989B Proof	—	Value: 20.00			

KM# 255 50 RUPEES **Weight:** 34.7000 g.
Composition: 0.5000 Silver .5578 oz. ASW **Series:** F.A.O.

Date	Mintage	F	VF	XF	Unc	BU
1974(B)	82,000	—	—	—	8.00	—
1974B Proof	13,000	Value: 12.50				

KM# 256 50 RUPEES **Weight:** 34.7000 g.
Composition: 0.5000 Silver .5578 oz. ASW **Series:** F.A.O.
Subject: Women's Year

Date	Mintage	F	VF	XF	Unc	BU
1975(B)	65,000	—	—	—	11.50	—
1975B Proof	2,691	Value: 20.00				

KM# 257 50 RUPEES **Weight:** 34.7000 g.
Composition: 0.5000 Silver .5578 oz. ASW **Series:** F.A.O.
Subject: Food and Work For All

Date	Mintage	F	VF	XF	Unc	BU
1976(B)	42,000	—	—	—	12.50	—
1976B Proof	3,385	Value: 20.00				

KM# 258 50 RUPEES **Weight:** 34.7000 g. **Composition:** 0.5000 Silver .5578 oz. ASW **Series:** F.A.O. **Subject:** Save For Development

Date	Mintage	F	VF	XF	Unc	BU
1977(B)	26,000	—	—	—	12.50	—
1977B Proof	2,544	Value: 20.00				

KM# 259 50 RUPEES **Weight:** 34.7000 g. **Composition:** 0.5000 Silver .5578 oz. ASW **Series:** F.A.O. **Subject:** Food and Shelter For All

Date	Mintage	F	VF	XF	Unc	BU
1978(B)	25,000	—	—	—	12.50	—
1978B Proof	—	Value: 20.00				

KM# 260 50 RUPEES **Weight:** 34.7000 g. **Composition:** 0.5000 Silver .5578 oz. ASW **Series:** International Year of the Child

Date	F	VF	XF	Unc	BU
1979(B)	—	—	—	12.50	—
1979B Proof	— Value: 20.00				

KM# 261 50 RUPEES **Composition:** Copper-Nickel **Subject:** Quit India **Note:** Similar to 1 Rupee, KM#93.

Date	F	VF	XF	Unc	BU
1992(B)	—	—	—	12.50	—

KM# 262 50 RUPEES **Composition:** Copper-Nickel **Subject:** International Labor Organizations **Note:** Similar to 100 RUpees, KM#287.

Date	F	VF	XF	Unc	BU
ND(1994)	—	—	—	15.00	—
ND(1994) Proof	— Value: 20.00				

KM# 263 50 RUPEES **Composition:** Copper-Nickel **Subject:** 100th Anniversary - BIrth of Patel **Note:** Similar to 2 Rupees, KM#129.

Date	F	VF	XF	Unc	BU
1996(B)	—	—	—	15.00	—
1996M Proof	— Value: 30.00				

KM# 264 50 RUPEES **Composition:** Copper-Nickel **Subject:** Subhas Chandra Bose **Note:** Similar to 2 Rupees, KM#130.

Date	F	VF	XF	Unc	BU
1997(C)	—	—	—	15.00	—
1997(C) Proof	— Value: 45.00				

KM# 265 50 RUPEES **Weight:** 22.5000 g. **Composition:** 0.5000 Silver .3617 oz. ASW **Subject:** 50th Anniversary of Independence **Note:** Similar to 50 Paise, KM#70.

Date	F	VF	XF	Unc	BU
1997(B)	—	—	—	35.00	—
1997M Proof	— Value: 60.00				

KM# 266 50 RUPEES **Weight:** 22.5000 g. **Composition:** 0.5000 Silver .3617 oz. ASW **Subject:** Sri Aurobindo **Note:** Similar to 2 Rupees, KM#131.

Date	F	VF	XF	Unc	BU
1998(B)	—	—	—	15.00	—
1998M Proof	— Value: 30.00				

KM# 298 50 RUPEES **Weight:** 30.0000 g. **Composition:** Copper-Nickel **Subject:** Deshbandhu Chittaranjan Das **Obverse:** Ashoka pillar **Reverse:** Das portrait **Edge:** Reeded **Size:** 39 mm. **Note:** Similar to 2 Rupees KM#296.3.

Date	F	VF	XF	Unc	BU
1998(C)	—	—	—	15.00	—
1998 Proof	— Value: 30.00				

KM# 300 50 RUPEES **Weight:** 30.0000 g. **Composition:** Copper-Nickel **Subject:** Chhatrapati Shivaji **Obverse:** Ashoka pillar **Reverse:** Turbaned bust of Shivaji right **Edge:** Reeded **Size:** 39 mm.

Date	F	VF	XF	Unc	BU
1999	—	—	—	15.00	—

KM# 275 100 RUPEES **Weight:** 35.0000 g. **Composition:** 0.5000 Silver .5627 oz. ASW **Subject:** Rural Women's Advancement

Date	Mintage	F	VF	XF	Unc	BU
1980(B)	21,000	—	—	—	18.50	—
1980B Proof	5,811	Value: 27.50				

KM# 276 100 RUPEES **Weight:** 35.0000 g. **Composition:** 0.5000 Silver .5627 oz. ASW **Series:** World Food Day

Date	Mintage	F	VF	XF	Unc	BU
1981(B)	22,000	—	—	—	18.50	—
1981B Proof	2,950	Value: 28.50				

KM# 277 100 RUPEES **Weight:** 29.1600 g. **Composition:** 0.9250 Silver .8673 oz. ASW **Series:** International Year of the Child

Date	F	VF	XF	Unc	BU
1981 (1983)B Proof	— Value: 25.00				

KM# 278 100 RUPEES **Weight:** 35.0000 g. **Composition:** 0.5000 Silver .5627 oz. ASW **Subject:** IX Asian Games

Date	F	VF	XF	Unc	BU
1982(B)	—	—	—	17.50	—
1982B Proof	— Value: 27.50				

KM# 279 100 RUPEES **Weight:** 35.0000 g. **Composition:** 0.5000 Silver .5627 oz. ASW **Subject:** National Integration

Date	F	VF	XF	Unc	BU
1982(B)	—	—	—	25.00	—
1982B Proof	— Value: 35.00				

KM# 280 100 RUPEES **Weight:** 35.0000 g. **Composition:** 0.5000 Silver .5627 oz. ASW **Subject:** Golden Jubilee - Reserve Bank of India

Date	F	VF	XF	Unc	BU
1985(B)	—	—	—	75.00	—
1985B Proof	— Value: 85.00				

KM# 281 100 RUPEES **Weight:** 35.0000 g. **Composition:** 0.5000 Silver .5627 oz. ASW **Subject:** Death of Indira Gandhi

Date	F	VF	XF	Unc	BU
ND(1985)(B)	—	—	—	30.00	—
ND(1985)B Proof	—	Value: 70.00			

KM# 282 100 RUPEES **Weight:** 35.0000 g. **Composition:** 0.5000 Silver .5627 oz. ASW **Subject:** Youth Year **Note:** Similar to 1 Rupee, KM#80.

Date	Mintage	F	VF	XF	Unc	BU
1985(C)	16,000	—	—	—	30.00	—
1985(C) Proof	6,267	Value: 50.00				

KM# 283 100 RUPEES **Weight:** 35.0000 g. **Composition:** 0.5000 Silver .5627 oz. ASW **Series:** F.A.O. **Subject:** Fisheries

Date	F	VF	XF	Unc	BU
1986(B)	—	—	—	30.00	—
1986B Proof	—	Value: 50.00			

KM# 284 100 RUPEES **Weight:** 35.0000 g. **Composition:** 0.5000 Silver .5627 oz. ASW **Series:** F.A.O. **Subject:** Small Farmers

Date	F	VF	XF	Unc	BU
1987(B)	—	—	—	30.00	—
1987B Proof	—	Value: 50.00			

KM# 285 100 RUPEES **Weight:** 35.0000 g. **Composition:** 0.5000 Silver .5627 oz. ASW **Subject:** 100th Anniversary of Nehru's Birth

Date	F	VF	XF	Unc	BU
1989(B)	—	—	—	30.00	—
1989B Proof	—	Value: 50.00			

KM# 286 100 RUPEES **Weight:** 35.0000 g. **Composition:** 0.5000 Silver .5627 oz. ASW **Subject:** Quit India **Note:** Similar to 1 Rupee, KM#93.

Date	F	VF	XF	Unc	BU
1992(B)	—	—	—	25.00	—

KM# 287 100 RUPEES **Weight:** 35.0000 g. **Composition:** 0.5000 Silver .5627 oz. ASW **Subject:** World of Work

Date	F	VF	XF	Unc	BU
ND(1994)	—	—	—	25.00	—
ND(1994) Proof	—	Value: 40.00			

KM# 288 100 RUPEES **Weight:** 35.0000 g. **Composition:** 0.5000 Silver .5627 oz. ASW **Subject:** 100th Anniversary - Birth of Patel **Note:** Similar to 2 Rupees, KM#129.

Date	F	VF	XF	Unc	BU
1996(B)	—	—	—	50.00	—
1996M Proof	—	Value: 70.00			

KM# 289 100 RUPEES **Weight:** 35.0000 g. **Composition:** 0.5000 Silver .5627 oz. ASW **Subject:** Subhas Chandra Bose **Note:** Similar to 2 Rupees, KM#130.

Date	F	VF	XF	Unc	BU
1997(C)	—	—	—	35.00	—

KM# 292 100 RUPEES **Weight:** 35.0000 g. **Composition:** 0.5000 Silver .5627 oz. ASW **Subject:** Sri Aurobindo **Note:** Similar to 2 Rupees, KM#131.

Date	F	VF	XF	Unc	BU
1998(B)	—	—	—	30.00	—
1998M Proof	—	Value: 50.00			

KM# 299 100 RUPEES **Weight:** 35.0000 g. **Composition:** 0.5000 Silver 0.5626 oz. ASW **Subject:** Deshbandhu Chittaranjan Das **Obverse:** Ashoka pillar **Reverse:** Das portrait **Edge:** Reeded **Size:** 44 mm.

Date	F	VF	XF	Unc	BU
1998(C)	—	—	—	30.00	—
1998(C) Proof	—	Value: 50.00			

KM# 301 100 RUPEES **Weight:** 35.0000 g. **Composition:** 0.5000 Silver 0.5626 oz. ASW **Subject:** Chhatrapati Shivaji **Obverse:** Ashoka pillar **Reverse:** Bust of turbaned Shivaji right **Edge:** Reeded **Size:** 44 mm.

Date	F	VF	XF	Unc	BU
1999(C)	—	—	—	30.00	—
1999(C) Proof	—	Value: 50.00			

KM# 302 100 RUPEES **Weight:** 35.0000 g. **Composition:** 0.5000 Silver 0.5626 oz. ASW **Subject:** St. Dnyanneshwar **Obverse:** Ashoka pillar **Reverse:** Seated saint **Edge:** Reeded **Size:** 44 mm.

Date	F	VF	XF	Unc	BU
1999(C)	—	—	—	30.00	—
1999(C) Proof	—	Value: 50.00			

PATTERNS

Including off metal strikes

KM#	Date	Mintage	Identification	Mkt Val
Pn1	1946(B)	—	1/4 Rupee. Nickel. KM#548.	—
Pn2	1946(B)	—	1/2 Rupee. Nickel. KM#553.	—
Pn3	1946(B)	—	Rupee. Nickel. KM#559.	—
Pn4	1947(B)	—	1/4 Rupee. Copper-Nickel.	—
Pn5	1947(B)	—	1/2 Rupee. Copper-Nickel.	—
Pn6	1947(B)	—	Rupee. Copper-Nickel.	—
Pn7	1947(B)	—	Rupee. Set of Pn1-3.	1,500
Pn8	1949	—	Pice. Bronze.	—
Pn9	1949	—	Anna. Copper-Nickel.	—
Pn10	1949	—	2 Annas. Copper-Nickel. Profile peacock left.	—
Pn11	1949	—	2 Annas. Copper-Nickel. Facing displayed peacock.	—
Pn12	1949	—	1/4 Rupee. Nickel.	—
Pn13	1949	—	1/2 Rupee. Nickel. Worker with finished background.	—
Pn14	1949	—	1/2 Rupee. Nickel. Worker with plain background.	—
Pn15	1949	—	Rupee. Nickel. Standing figure.	—
Pn16	1949	—	Rupee. Nickel. Similar to Pn9.	—
Pn17	1964(C)	—	Paisa. Copper. Half thickness and weight.	—

PIEFORTS

KM#	Date	Mintage	Identification	Mkt Val
P1	1981	—	100 Rupees. KM#277	250

MINT SETS

KM#	Date	Mintage	Identification	Issue Price	Mkt Val
MS3	1962(B) (6)	—	KM#8a, 11, 16, 24.2, 47.2, 55	1.50	5.00

KM#	Date	Mintage	Identification	Issue Price	Mkt Val
MS4	1962(B) (7)	—	KM#8a, 11, 16, 24.2, 47.2, 55, 75.1(C)	3.60	8.00
MS6	1967(B) (8)	—	KM#10.1, 13.1, 14.1, 18.1, 25, 48.2, 58.1, 75.1 (1962 dated Rupee)	1.00	15.00
MS8	1970(B) (8)	—	KM#10.1, 13.5, 14.2, 18.3, 26.3, 41, 58.2, 75.2 Brown vinyl case	1.00	18.00
MS5	ND(1964) (B) (2)	—	KM#56, 76	1.00	3.75
MS7	ND(1969) (B) (4)	25,281	KM#42.1, 59, 77, 185 Blue plastic case	2.50	10.00
MS9	1970(B) (2)	22,999	KM#43.1, 186	2.00	9.00
MS10	1971(B) (2)	9,987	KM#43.2, 186	—	8.50
MS11	1972(B) (2)	43,121	KM#60, 187	2.00	7.00
MS11a	1972(B (2)	—	KM#60, 187a	2.00	7.50
MS12	1973(B) (2)	48,670	KM#188, 240	—	15.00
MS13	1974(B) (2)	50,219	KM#189, 255	10.00	12.50
MS14	1975(B) (2)	40,279	KM#190, 256	12.00	13.50
MS15	1976(B) (2)	25,105	KM#191, 257	12.00	16.00
MS16	1977(B) (2)	17,071	KM#192, 258	12.00	16.00
MS17	1978(B) (2)	15,041	KM#193, 259	10.00	16.00
MS18	1979(B) (2)	—	KM#194, 260	—	16.50
MS19	1980(B) (2)	—	KM#195, 275	—	21.50
MS20	1981(B) (2)	—	KM#196, 276	—	21.50
MS21	1982(B) (2)	—	KM#197, 278	—	21.50
MS22	1985(B) (2)	—	KM#199, 280	48.00	140
MS23	ND(1985) (B) (2)	—	KM#241, 281	43.00	100
MS24	ND(1985) (C) (2)	—	KM#200, 282	—	40.00
MS25	1986 (2)	—	KM#242, 283	45.00	100
MS26	1987(B) (2)	—	KM#243, 284	45.00	40.00
MS27	1989(B) (2)	—	KM#244, 285	40.00	40.00
MS28	1989(B) (2)	—	KM#83, 285	50.00	45.00
MS29	1991(B) (2)	—	KM#152, 201	—	18.00
MS30	1991(B) (3)	—	KM#90, 152, 201	—	20.00
MS31	1991(B) (2)	—	KM#123, 153	—	20.00
MS32	1991(B) (3)	—	KM#91, 123, 153	—	22.00
MS33	1992(B) (4)	—	KM#92.1, 202, 261, 286	—	45.00
MS34	1994(B) (3)	—	KM#155, 262, 287	—	45.00
MS35	1996(M) (3)	—	KM#203, 263, 288	—	50.00
MS36	1996(M) (2)	—	KM#263, 288	65.00	45.00
MS37	1997(C) (3)	—	KM#204, 264, 289	—	50.00
MS38	1997(B) (2)	—	KM#70, 265	50.00	40.00
MS39	1998(B) (4)	—	KM#131.1, 205, 266, 292	—	55.00
MS40	1998(C) (3)	—	KM#297, 298, 299	—	50.00
MS41	1999(C) (2)	—	KM#295, 302	—	40.00
MS42	1999(B) (3)	—	KM#290, 300, 301	—	50.00
MS43	2000(B) (2)	—	KM#291, 293	—	40.00

PROOF SETS

KM#	Date	Mintage	Identification	Issue Price	Mkt Val
PS2	1954(B) (7)	—	KM#1.3, 2.2, 3.2, 4, 5.1, 6.1, 7.2	8.40	50.00
PS1	1950(B) (7)	—	KM#1.2, 2.1, 3.1, 4, 5.1, 6.1, 7.1	8.40	30.00
PS3	1960(B) (6)	—	KM#8, 11, 16, 24.2, 47.1, 55	7.00	30.00
PS4	1961(B) (6)	—	KM#8, 11, 16, 24.2, 47.2, 55	7.00	40.00
PS5	1962(B) (7)	—	KM#8, 11, 16, 24.2, 47.2, 55, 75.1	8.40	40.00
PS7	1963(B) (6)	—	KM#8a, 11, 16, 24.2, 47.2, 55, 75.1	7.00	30.00
PS8	1963(B) (7)	—	KM#8a, 11, 16, 24.2, 47.2, 55, 75.1	8.40	25.00
PS6	1962(B) (7)	—	KM#8a, 11, 16, 24.1, 47.2, 55, 75.1	8.40	35.00
PS9	ND(1964 (B) (2)	—	KM#56, 76	5.00	7.50
PS10	1969B (9)	9,097	KM#10.1, 13.5, 14.2, 18.3, 26.3, 42.1, 59, 77, 185	15.25	15.00
PS12	1971B (9)	4,161	KM#10.1, 13.5, 14.2, 18.3, 26.3, 43.2, 58.3, 75.2, 186	15.25	15.00
PS11	1970B (9)	2,900	KM#10.1, 13.5, 14.2, 18.3, 26.3, 43.1, 58.3, 75.2, 186	15.25	15.00
PS13	1972B (9)	7,701	KM#10.1, 13.6, 15, 18.6, 27.1, 49.1, 60, 75.2, 187	15.25	15.00
PS14	1973B (10)	7,563	KM#10.1, 13.5, 15, 18.6, 27.1, 49.1, 62, 75.1, 188, 240	26.00	25.00
PS15	1973B (9)	3,326	KM#10.1, 13.6, 15, 18.6, 27.1, 49.1, 62, 75.2, 188	15.25	15.00
PS17	1974B (10)	9,138	KM#10.1, 13.6, 15, 18.6, 28, 49.1, 63, 75.2, 189, 255	29.00	22.00
PS16	1973B (2)	2,408	KM#188, 240	17.50	22.00
PS18	1974B (2)	1,712	KM#189, 255	7.50	20.00
PS19	1975B (10)	2,370	KM#10.1, 13.6, 15, 18.6, 29, 49.1, 63, 78.1	35.00	30.00
PS20	1975B (2)	160	KM#190, 256	22.00	27.50
PS21	1976B (10)	3,209	KM#10.1, 13.6, 15, 19, 30, 49.1, 63, 78.1, 191, 257	35.00	30.00
PS22	1976B (2)	190	KM#191, 257	22.00	27.50
PS23	1977B (10)	2,222	KM#10.1, 13.6, 15, 20, 31, 63, 78.1, 192, 258	35.00	30.00
PS24	1977B (2)	—	KM#192, 258	—	27.50
PS25	1978B (10)	1,390	KM#10.1, 13.6, 15, 21, 32, 49.1, 63, 78.1, 193, 259	35.00	30.00
PS26	1978B (2)	—	KM#193, 259	—	27.50
PS27	1979B (10)	—	KM#10.1, 13.6, 15, 22, 33, 49.2, 63, 78.3, 194, 260	—	35.00
PS28	1979B (2)	—	KM#194, 260	—	28.00
PS29	1980B (4)	—	KM#35, 50, 195, 275	—	40.00
PS30	1980B (2)	—	KM#195, 275	—	35.00
PS31	1981B (4)	—	KM#36, 51, 196, 276	—	40.00
PS32	1981B (2)	—	KM#196, 276	—	35.00
PS-A33	1982B (4)	—	KM#64, 121.1, 198, 279	—	52.50
PS-A34	1982B (2)	—	KM#198, 279	—	45.00
PS33	1982B (4)	—	KM#52, 120, 197, 278	48.00	40.00
PS34	1982B (2)	—	KM#197, 278	38.00	35.00
PS35	1985B (4)	—	KM#66, 122, 199, 280	98.00	235
PS37	ND(1985)B (4)	—	KM#67.1, 150, 241, 281	88.00	150
PS36	1985B (2)	—	KM#199, 280	58.00	160
PS38	ND(1985)B (2)	—	KM#241, 281	48.00	120
PS39	1985(C) (3)	—	KM#80, 200, 282	—	70.00
PS40	1986B (3)	—	KM#68.1, 242, 283	70.00	130
PS41	1986B (2)	—	KM#242, 283	50.00	120
PS42	1987B (3)	—	KM#81, 243, 284	65.00	75.00
PS43	1987B (2)	—	KM#243, 284	60.00	70.00
PS44	1989B (4)	—	KM#83, 151, 244, 285	90.00	100
PS45	1989B (2)	—	KM#244, 285	65.00	70.00
PS46	1991(B) (3)	—	KM#90, 152, 201	—	45.00
PS47	1991(B) (3)	—	KM#91, 123, 153	—	35.00
PS48	ND(1994) (3)	—	KM#155, 262, 287	18.75	55.00
PS49	ND(1994) (2)	—	KM#262, 287	18.05	50.00
PS50	1996M (4)	—	KM#129, 203, 263, 288	110	85.00
PS51	1996M (2)	—	KM#263, 288	100	75.00
PS52	1997(C) (3)	—	KM#24, 264, 289	—	75.00
PS53	1997M (2)	—	KM#70, 265	75.00	60.00
PS55	1998(C) (4)	—	KM#296.3, 298, 299, 297	—	85.00
PS54	1998M (4)	—	KM#131.1, 205, 266, 290	—	85.00

INDONESIA

The Republic of Indonesia, the world's largest archipelago, extends for more than 3,000 miles (4,827 km.) along the equator from the mainland of southeast Asia to Australia. The 17,508 islands comprising the archipelago have a combined area of 788,425 sq. mi. (1,919,440 sq.km.) and a population of 205 million, including East Timor. On August 30, 1999, the Timorese majority voted for independence. The Inter FET (International Forces for East Timor) is now in charge of controlling the chaotic situation. Capitol: Jakarta. Petroleum, timber, rubber, and coffee are exported.

Had Columbus succeeded in reaching the fabled Spice Islands, he would have found advanced civilizations a millennium old, and temples still ranked among the finest examples of ancient art. During the opening centuries of the Christian era, the islands were influenced by Hindu priests and traders who spread their culture and religion. Moslem invasions began in the 13th century, fragmenting the island kingdoms into small states which were unable to resist Western colonial infiltration. Portuguese traders established posts in the 16th century, but they were soon outnumbered by the Dutch who arrived in 1596 and gradually asserted control over the islands comprising present-day Indonesia. Dutch dominance, interrupted by British incursions during the Napoleonic Wars, established the Netherlands East Indies as one of the richest colonial possessions in the world.

The Indonesian independence movement, which began between the two world wars, was encouraged by the Japanese during their 3 1/2-year occupation during World War II. Indonesia proclaimed its independence on Aug. 17,1945, three days after the surrender of Japan and full sovereignty. On Dec. 27, 1949, after four years of guerilla warfare including two large scale campaigns by the Dutch in an effort to reassert control, complete independence was established. Rebellions in Bandung and on the Molluccan Islands occurred in 1950. During the reign of President Mohammad Achmad Sukarno (1950-67) the new Republic not only held together but started to develop. West Irian, formerly Netherlands New Guinea, came under the administration of Indonesia on May 1, 1963. In 1965, the army staged an anti-communist coup in which thousands perished.

On November 28, 1975 the Portuguese Province of Timor, an overseas province occupying the eastern half of the East Indian island of Timor, attained independence as the People's Democratic Republic of East Timor. On December 5, 1975 the government of the People's Democratic Republic was seized by a guerrilla faction sympathetic to the Indonesian territorial claim to East Timor which ousted the constitutional government and replaced it with the Provisional Government of East Timor. On July 17, 1976, the Provisional Government enacted a law that dissolved the free republic and made East Timor the 27th province of Indonesia.

The VOC (United East India Company) struck coins and emergency issues for the Indonesian Archipelago and for the islands at various mints in the Netherlands and the islands. In 1798 the VOC was subsumed by the Dutch government, which issued VOC type transitional and regal types during the Batavian Republic and the Kingdom of the Netherlands until independence. The British issued a coinage during the various occupations by the British East Indian Company, 1811-24. Modern coinage issued by the Republic of Indonesia includes separate series for West Irian and for the Riau Archipelago, an area of small islands between Singapore and Sumatra.

MONETARY SYSTEM

100 Sen = 1 Rupiah

REPUBLIC

STANDARD COINAGE

100 Sen = 1 Rupiah

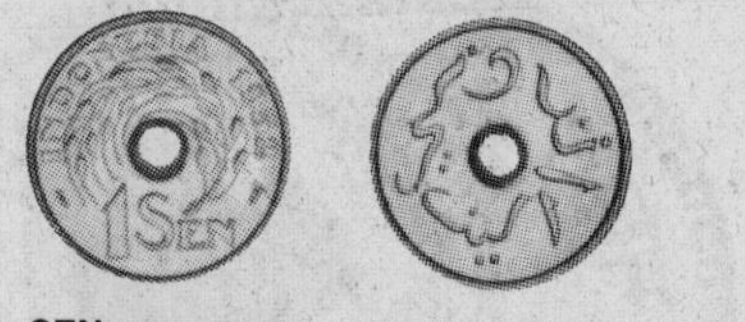

KM# 7 SEN Composition: Aluminum

Date	Mintage	F	VF	XF	Unc	BU
1952(u)	100,000	—	0.25	0.50	1.00	—

KM# 5 5 SEN Composition: Aluminum

Date	F	VF	XF	Unc	BU
1951(u)	—	0.10	0.25	0.50	—
1954	—	0.10	0.25	0.50	—

KM# 6 10 SEN Composition: Aluminum

Date	Mintage	F	VF	XF	Unc	BU
1951(u)	—	—	0.15	0.25	0.45	—
1954	50,000,000	—	0.15	0.25	0.45	—

KM# 12 10 SEN Composition: Aluminum

Date	Mintage	F	VF	XF	Unc	BU
1957	50,224,000	—	0.25	0.50	1.00	—

KM# 8 25 SEN Composition: Aluminum

Date	Mintage	F	VF	XF	Unc	BU
1952(u)	200,000,000	—	0.10	0.20	0.40	—

KM# 11 25 SEN Composition: Aluminum

Date	Mintage	F	VF	XF	Unc	BU
1955	25,767,000	—	0.10	0.20	0.40	—
1957	99,752,000	—	0.10	0.20	0.40	—

KM# 9 50 SEN Composition: Copper-Nickel

Date	Mintage	F	VF	XF	Unc	BU
1952(u)	100,000,000	—	0.15	0.25	0.45	—

KM# 10.1 50 SEN Composition: Copper-Nickel

Date	Mintage	F	VF	XF	Unc	BU
1954	1,290,000	—	1.00	2.25	4.50	—
1955	15,000,000	—	0.15	0.25	0.45	—

KM# 10.2 50 SEN Composition: Copper-Nickel **Reverse:** Different head, larger lettering

Date	Mintage	F	VF	XF	Unc	BU
1957	24,977,000	—	0.15	0.25	0.45	—

KM# 13 50 SEN Composition: Aluminum

Date	Mintage	F	VF	XF	Unc	BU
1958	100,000,000	—	0.15	0.25	0.50	—

KM# 14 50 SEN Composition: Aluminum **Reverse:** Modified eagle

Date	Mintage	F	VF	XF	Unc	BU
1959	100,000,000	—	0.15	0.25	0.50	—
1961	128,528,000	—	0.15	0.25	0.50	—

KM# 20 RUPIAH Composition: Aluminum **Reverse:** Fantail flycatcher, denomination

Date	Mintage	F	VF	XF	Unc	BU
1970	136,010,000	—	—	0.15	0.35	—

KM# 21 2 RUPIAH Composition: Aluminum

Date	Mintage	F	VF	XF	Unc	BU
1970	139,230,000	—	—	0.15	0.25	—

KM# 22 5 RUPIAH Composition: Aluminum **Reverse:** Black drongo, denomination

Date	Mintage	F	VF	XF	Unc	BU
1970	448,000,000	—	0.15	0.30	0.75	—

KM# 37 5 RUPIAH Composition: Aluminum **Subject:** Family Planning Program

Date	Mintage	F	VF	XF	Unc	BU
1974	447,910,000	—	0.10	0.15	0.25	—

KM# 43 5 RUPIAH Composition: Aluminum **Subject:** Family planning program

Date	Mintage	F	VF	XF	Unc	BU
1979	413,200,000	—	0.10	0.15	0.25	—
1995	6,420,000	—	0.20	0.30	0.60	—
1996	—	—	0.20	0.30	0.60	—

KM# 33 10 RUPIAH Composition: Copper-Nickel **Series:** F.A.O.

Date	Mintage	F	VF	XF	Unc	BU
1971	286,360,000	—	0.10	0.20	0.40	—

KM# 38 10 RUPIAH Composition: Brass-Clad Steel **Subject:** National saving program

Date	Mintage	F	VF	XF	Unc	BU
1974	222,910,000	—	0.10	0.20	0.40	—

KM# 44 10 RUPIAH Composition: Aluminum **Series:** F.A.O.

Date	Mintage	F	VF	XF	Unc	BU
1979	285,670,000	—	0.10	0.20	0.40	—

KM# 34 25 RUPIAH Composition: Copper-Nickel **Reverse:** Victoria crowned pigeon, denomination

Date	Mintage	F	VF	XF	Unc	BU
1971	1,221,610,000	—	0.10	0.20	0.50	—

KM# 55 25 RUPIAH Composition: Aluminum **Reverse:** Nutmeg plant

Date	Mintage	F	VF	XF	Unc	BU
1991	30,000,000	—	—	0.40	0.75	—
1992	64,000,000	—	—	0.40	0.75	—
1993	20,000,000	—	—	0.40	0.75	—
1994	250,000,000	—	—	0.25	0.50	—
1995	184,480,000	—	—	0.25	0.50	—
1996	—	—	—	0.25	0.50	—

KM# 35 50 RUPIAH **Composition:** Copper-Nickel **Reverse:** Greater bird of paradise, denomination

Date	Mintage	F	VF	XF	Unc	BU
1971	1,035,435,000	—	0.15	0.30	0.60	—

KM# 52 50 RUPIAH **Composition:** Aluminum-Bronze **Reverse:** Komodo dragon lizard

Date	Mintage	F	VF	XF	Unc	BU
1991	67,000,000	—	0.10	0.20	0.50	—
1992	70,000,000	—	0.10	0.20	0.50	—
1993	120,000,000	—	0.10	0.20	0.45	—
1994	300,000,000	—	0.10	0.20	0.45	—
1995	591,880,000	—	0.10	0.20	0.45	—
1996	—	—	0.10	0.25	0.60	—
1997	150,000	—	0.10	0.25	0.60	—
1998	150,000	—	0.10	0.25	0.60	—

KM# 60 50 RUPIAH **Composition:** Aluminum **Obverse:** National arms **Reverse:** Denomination and black-naped oriole

Date	Mintage	F	VF	XF	Unc	BU
1999		—	—	—	0.40	—
2001		—	—	—	0.30	—

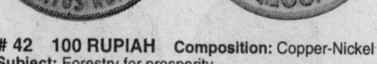

KM# 36 100 RUPIAH **Composition:** Copper-Nickel

Date	Mintage	F	VF	XF	Unc	BU
1973	252,868,000	—	0.30	0.60	1.50	—

KM# 42 100 RUPIAH **Composition:** Copper-Nickel **Subject:** Forestry for prosperity

Date	Mintage	F	VF	XF	Unc	BU
1978	907,773,000	—	0.25	0.50	1.35	—

KM# 53 100 RUPIAH **Composition:** Aluminum-Bronze **Subject:** Cow racing

Date	Mintage	F	VF	XF	Unc	BU
1991	94,000,000	—	0.15	0.30	0.60	—
1992	120,000,000	—	0.15	0.30	0.60	—
1993	300,000,000	—	0.15	0.30	0.60	—
1994	550,000,000	—	0.15	0.30	0.60	—
1995	798,100,000	—	0.15	0.30	0.60	—

Date	Mintage	F	VF	XF	Unc	BU
1996	41,000,000	—	0.15	0.30	0.65	—
1997	150,000,000	—	0.15	0.30	0.65	—
1998	59,000,000	—	0.15	0.30	0.65	—

KM# 61 100 RUPIAH **Composition:** Aluminum **Obverse:** National arms **Reverse:** Denomination and palm cockatoo

Date	Mintage	F	VF	XF	Unc	BU
1999		—	—	—	0.75	—
2000		—	—	—	0.75	—
2001		—	—	—	0.75	—

KM# 23 200 RUPIAH **Weight:** 8.0000 g. **Composition:** 0.9990 Silver .2569 oz. ASW **Subject:** 25th anniversary of independence **Reverse:** Great bird of paradise

Date	Mintage	F	VF	XF	Unc	BU
1970 Proof	5,100	Value: 16.50				

KM# 24 250 RUPIAH **Weight:** 10.0000 g. **Composition:** 0.9990 Silver .3212 oz. ASW **Subject:** 25th anniversary of independence **Obverse:** Manjusri statue from Temple of Tumpang

Date	Mintage	F	VF	XF	Unc	BU
1970 Proof	5,000	Value: 18.50				

KM# 25 500 RUPIAH **Weight:** 20.0000 g. **Composition:** 0.9990 Silver .6424 oz. ASW **Subject:** 25th anniversary of independence **Obverse:** Similar to 10,000 Rupiah, KM#30 **Reverse:** Wayang dancer

Date	Mintage	F	VF	XF	Unc	BU
1970 Proof	4,800	Value: 30.00				

KM# 54 500 RUPIAH **Composition:** Aluminum-Bronze **Reverse:** Jasmine

Date	Mintage	F	VF	XF	Unc	BU
1991	71,000,000	—	—	—	2.50	—
1992	100,000,000	—	—	—	2.50	—
1993	—	—	—	—	2.50	—
1994	—	—	—	—	2.50	—

KM# 59 500 RUPIAH **Composition:** Aluminum-Bronze **Obverse:** National emblem **Reverse:** Denomination

Date	F	VF	XF	Unc	BU
1997	—	—	—	2.25	—
2000	—	—	—	2.00	—
2001	—	—	—	2.00	—

KM# 26 750 RUPIAH **Weight:** 30.0000 g. **Composition:** 0.9990 Silver .9636 oz. ASW **Subject:** 25th Anniversary of Independence **Obverse:** Similar to 20,000 Rupiah, KM#31 **Reverse:** Garuda bird

Date	Mintage	F	VF	XF	Unc	BU
1970 Proof	4,950	Value: 42.50				

KM# 27 1000 RUPIAH **Weight:** 40.0000 g. **Composition:** 0.9990 Silver 1.2848 oz. ASW **Subject:** 25th Anniversary of Independence - Gen. Sudirman **Obverse:** Similar to 25,000 Rupiah, KM#32 **Reverse:** Similar to 750 Rupiah, KM#26

Date	Mintage	F	VF	XF	Unc	BU
1970 Proof	4,250	Value: 55.00				

KM# 56 1000 RUPIAH **Ring Composition:** Copper-Nickel **Center Composition:** Brass **Reverse:** Palm tree

Date	Mintage	F	VF	XF	Unc	BU
1993	5,000,000	—	—	—	4.00	—
1994	6,000,000	—	—	—	4.00	—
1995	19,900,000	—	—	—	4.00	—
1996	—	—	—	—	4.00	—
1997	—	—	—	—	4.00	—
2000	—	—	—	—	4.00	—

KM# 28 2000 RUPIAH **Weight:** 4.9300 g. **Composition:** 0.9000 Gold .1426 oz. AGW **Subject:** 25th Anniversary of Independence **Reverse:** Great bird of paradise

Date	Mintage	F	VF	XF	Unc	BU
1970 Proof	2,970	Value: 110				

KM# 39 2000 RUPIAH **Weight:** 25.6500 g. **Composition:** 0.5000 Silver .4123 oz. ASW **Subject:** Conservation series **Reverse:** Javan tiger

Date	Mintage	F	VF	XF	Unc	BU
1974	43,000	—	—	—	11.50	—

KM# 39a 2000 RUPIAH **Weight:** 28.2800 g. **Composition:** 0.9250 Silver .8411 oz. ASW **Subject:** Conservation series **Reverse:** Javan tiger

Date	Mintage	F	VF	XF	Unc	BU
1974 Proof	18,000	Value: 16.00				

KM# 29 5000 RUPIAH **Weight:** 12.3400 g. **Composition:** 0.9000 Gold .3571 oz. AGW **Subject:** 25th Anniversary of Independence **Obverse:** Manjusri statue from Temple of Tumpang **Reverse:** Similar to 2,000 Rupiah, KM#28

Date	Mintage	F	VF	XF	Unc	BU
1970 Proof	2,150	Value: 245				

KM# 40 5000 RUPIAH **Weight:** 32.0000 g. **Composition:** 0.5000 Silver .5144 oz. ASW **Series:** Conservation **Obverse:** Similar to 100,000 Rupiah, KM#41 **Reverse:** Orangutan

Date	Mintage	F	VF	XF	Unc	BU
1974	43,000	—	—	—	12.50	—

KM# 40a 5000 RUPIAH **Weight:** 35.0000 g. **Composition:** 0.9250 Silver 1.0409 oz. ASW **Series:** Conservation **Obverse:** Similar to 100,000 Rupiah, KM#41 **Reverse:** Orangutan

Date	Mintage	F	VF	XF	Unc	BU
1974 Proof	17,000	Value: 20.00				

KM# 30 10000 RUPIAH **Weight:** 24.6800 g. **Composition:** 0.9000 Gold .7142 oz. AGW **Subject:** 25th Anniversary of Independence **Obverse:** Wayang dancer **Reverse:** Similar to 2,000 Rupiah, KM#28

Date	Mintage	F	VF	XF	Unc	BU
1970 Proof	1,440	Value: 525				

KM# 45 10000 RUPIAH **Weight:** 19.4400 g. **Composition:** 0.9250 Silver .5782 oz. ASW **Subject:** Wildlife **Reverse:** Babi rusa (wild pig)

Date	Mintage	F	VF	XF	Unc	BU
1987 Proof	25,000	Value: 50.00				

KM# 50 10000 RUPIAH **Weight:** 19.4400 g. **Composition:** 0.9250 Silver .5782 oz. ASW **Series:** Save the Child **Reverse:** Playing badminton

Date	Mintage	F	VF	XF	Unc	BU
1990 Proof	20,000	Value: 50.00				

KM# 62 10000 RUPIAH **Weight:** 28.2800 g. **Composition:** 0.9250 Silver 0.841 oz. ASW **Obverse:** The National Coat of Arms of the Republic of Indonesia "Garuda Pancasila" in the center; Above the words BANK INDONESIA; the official UNICEF logo to the left and 1999 to the right **Reverse:** Two girls scouts planting a tree; denomination below and the words "FOR THE CHILDREN OF THE WORLD" above central design **Edge:** Milled **Size:** 38.61 mm. **Note:** Struck at Hungarian Mint.

Date	F	VF	XF	Unc	BU
1999 Proof	—	Value: 45.00			

KM# 31 20000 RUPIAH **Weight:** 49.3700 g. **Composition:** 0.9000 Gold 1.4391 oz. AGW **Subject:** 25th Anniversary of Independence **Obverse:** Garuda bird **Reverse:** Similar to 2,000 Rupiah, KM#28

Date	F	VF	XF	Unc	BU
1970 Proof	—	—	—	1,100	—

KM# 32 25000 RUPIAH **Weight:** 61.7100 g. **Composition:** 0.9000 Gold 1.7858 oz. AGW **Subject:** 25th Anniversary of Independence **Obverse:** Gen. Sudirman **Reverse:** Similar to 20,000 Rupiah, KM#31

Date	Mintage	F	VF	XF	Unc	BU
1970 Proof	970	Value: 1,250				

KM# 64 25000 RUPIAH **Weight:** 28.2800 g. **Composition:** 0.9250 Silver 0.841 oz. ASW **Subject:** Centennial of Sukarno's Birth **Obverse:** National arms. **Reverse:** Uniformed bust of Sukarno. **Edge:** Reeded. **Size:** 38.6 mm.

Date	Mintage	F	VF	XF	Unc	BU
2001 Proof	500	Value: 100				

KM# 41 100000 RUPIAH **Weight:** 33.4370 g. **Composition:** 0.9000 Gold .9676 oz. AGW **Series:** Conservation **Reverse:** Komodo dragon lizard

Date	Mintage	F	VF	XF	Unc	BU
1974	—	—	—	—	400	—
1974 Proof	1,369	Value: 550				

KM# 47 125000 RUPIAH **Weight:** 8.0000 g. **Composition:** 0.9580 Gold .2465 oz. AGW **Subject:** Museum of Struggle '45

Date	Mintage	F	VF	XF	Unc	BU
1990 Proof	16,000	Value: 115				

KM# 63 150000 RUPIAH **Weight:** 6.2200 g. **Composition:** 0.9990 Gold **Subject:** UNICEF - For the Children of the World Children **Obverse:** National coat of arms, UNICEF logo at left, date at right. **Reverse:** Young boy in traditional costume riding a toy horse from East Java, value below. **Edge:** Milled. **Size:** 22 mm.

Date	F	VF	XF	Unc	BU
1999 Proof	—	Value: 200			

KM# 46 200000 RUPIAH **Weight:** 10.0000 g. **Composition:** 0.9170 Gold .2947 oz. AGW **Subject:** Wildlife **Reverse:** Javan rhinoceros

Date	Mintage	F	VF	XF	Unc	BU
1987 Proof	5,000	Value: 300				

KM# 51 200000 RUPIAH **Weight:** 10.0000 g. **Composition:** 0.9170 Gold .2947 oz. AGW **Series:** Save the Children **Reverse:** Balinese dancer

Date	Mintage	F	VF	XF	Unc	BU
1990 Proof	3,000	Value: 300				

KM# 48 250000 RUPIAH **Weight:** 17.0000 g. **Composition:** 0.9580 Gold .5238 oz. AGW **Subject:** 45 years - Indonesian archipelago **Obverse:** Similar to 125,000 Rupiah, KM#47

Date	Mintage	F	VF	XF	Unc	BU
1990 Proof	16,000	Value: 235				

KM# 57 300000 RUPIAH **Weight:** 17.0000 g. **Composition:** 0.9583 Gold .5238 oz. AGW **Subject:** 50th anniversary of independence **Obverse:** National emblem **Reverse:** Presidential talk show

Date	Mintage	F	VF	XF	Unc	BU
1995 Sets only	3,000	—	—	—	800	—

KM# 65 500,000 RUPIAH **Weight:** 15.0000 g. **Composition:** 0.9990 Gold 0.4818 oz. AGW **Subject:** Centennial of Sukarno's Birth **Obverse:** National arms. **Reverse:** Head of Sukarno left. **Edge:** Reeded. **Size:** 28.2 mm.

Date	Mintage	F	VF	XF	Unc	BU
2001 Proof	500	Value: 360				

KM# 49 750000 RUPIAH **Weight:** 45.0000 g. **Composition:** 0.9580 Gold 1.3866 oz. AGW **Subject:** 45 years - arms of generation 1945 **Obverse:** Simlar to 125,000 Rupiah, KM#47

Date	F	VF	XF	Unc	BU
1990 Proof	—	—	—	625	—

KM# 58 850000 RUPIAH **Weight:** 50.0000 g. **Composition:** 0.9583 Gold 1.5405 oz. AGW **Subject:** 50th anniversary of independence **Obverse:** National emblem **Reverse:** President Soeharto's portrait

Date	Mintage	F	VF	XF	Unc	BU
1995 Sets only	3,000	—	—	—	2,200	—

PATTERNS

Including off metal strikes

KM#	Date	Mintage	Identification	Mkt Val
Pn1	1951	—	25 Sen. Aluminum.	275
Pn2	1955	—	50 Sen. Raised SPECIMEN.	325
Pn3	1963	—	2-1/2 Rupiah. Aluminum.	100
Pn4	1970	—	Rupiah. Bronze. KM20.	85.00
Pn5	1970	—	2 Rupiah. Copper. KM21.	85.00
Pn7	1970	—	25 Rupiah. Bronze.	—
Pn6	1970	—	2 Rupiah. Bronze. KM20.	85.00
Pn8	1973	—	100 Rupiah. Aluminum.	120
Pn9	1979	—	10 Rupiah. Copper-Nickel.	—
Pn10	1990	—	125000 Rupiah. Gold-plated base metal. KM#47.	—
Pn11	1990	—	250000 Rupiah. Gold-plated base metal. KM#48.	—
Pn12	1990	—	750000 Rupiah. Gold-plated base metal. KM#49.	—
Pn13	1991	—	500 Rupiah. Copper-Nickel.	—
Pn14	1992	—	500 Rupiah. Bronze.	—
Pn15	1993	—	50 Rupiah. Copper-Nickel.	—
Pn16	1993	—	100 Rupiah. Copper-Nickel.	—

MINT SETS

KM#	Date	Mintage	Identification	Issue Price	Mkt Val
MS1	Mixed dates (14)	—	KM5-6 (1951, 1954), 7-9 (1952), 10.1 (1955), 10.2 (1957), 11 (1955, 1957), 12 (1957), 14 (1961)	—	18.00
MS2	Mixed dates (9)	—	KM20-21 (1970), 33-35 (1971), 36 (1973), 37-38 (1974), 42 (1978)	2.40	6.50
MS3	1970 (3)	—	KM20-22	—	1.50
MS4	1971 (3)	—	KM33-35	—	1.50

PROOF SETS

KM#	Date	Mintage	Identification	Issue Price	Mkt Val
PS1	1970 (10)	970	KM23-32	490	3,400
PS2	1970 (5)	4,250	KM23-27	50.00	170
PS3	1974 (2)	30,000	KM39a-40a	50.00	36.00
PS4	1990 (3)	15,750	KM47-49	755	975
PS5	1990 (2)	—	KM50-51	—	350
PS6	1995 (2)	3,000	KM57-58	2,975	3,000

IRIAN BARAT

(West Irian, Irian Jaya, Netherlands New Guinea)

A province of Indonesia comprising the western half of the island of New Guinea. A special set of coins dated 1962 were issued in 1964, were recalled December 31, 1971 and are no longer legal tender.

INDONESIAN PROVINCE

STANDARD COINAGE

No inscription on edge

KM# 5 SEN **Composition:** Aluminum **Edge:** Plain

Date	F	VF	XF	Unc	BU
1962	0.25	0.50	1.00	2.00	—

KM# 6 5 SEN **Composition:** Aluminum **Edge:** Plain

Date	F	VF	XF	Unc	BU
1962	0.25	0.50	1.25	2.25	—

KM# 7 10 SEN **Composition:** Aluminum **Edge:** Plain

Date	F	VF	XF	Unc	BU
1962	0.25	0.50	1.25	2.25	—

KM# 8.1 25 SEN **Composition:** Aluminum **Edge:** Reeded

Date	F	VF	XF	Unc	BU
1962	—	—	—	—	—

KM# 8.2 25 SEN **Composition:** Aluminum **Reverse:** Different style "5"

Date	F	VF	XF	Unc	BU
1962	0.75	1.50	2.50	4.50	—

KM# 9 50 SEN **Composition:** Aluminum **Edge:** Reeded

Date	F	VF	XF	Unc	BU
1962	0.85	1.60	3.00	7.00	—

PATTERNS

Including off metal strikes

KM#	Date	Mintage	Identification	Mkt Val
Pn1	1962	—	50 Sen. Double reverse as KM#9	125
Pn2	1963	—	2-1/2 Rupiah.	100
Pn3	1965	—	25 Sen. Plain edge. KM#8.2	100
Pn4	1965	—	50 Sen. Reeded edge. KM#9	100
Pn5	1965	—	50 Sen. Plain edge. KM#9	100
Pn6	1965//1962	—	50 Sen. As KM#9.	150

RIAU ARCHIPELAGO

A group of 3,214 islands off the tip of the Malay Peninsula. Coins were issued near the end of 1963 (although dated 1962) and recalled as worthless on Sept. 30, 1964. They were legal tender from Oct. 15, 1963 to July 1, 1964.

INSCRIPTION ON EDGE
KEPULAUAN RIAU

INDONESIAN PROVINCE

STANDARD COINAGE

Inscription on edge: "Kepulauan Riau"

KM# 5 SEN **Composition:** Aluminum

Date	F	VF	XF	Unc	BU
1962	0.35	0.75	1.25	2.50	—

KM# 6 5 SEN Composition: Aluminum

Date	F	VF	XF	Unc	BU
1962	0.30	0.60	1.50	3.00	—

KM# 7 10 SEN Composition: Aluminum

Date	F	VF	XF	Unc	BU
1962	0.35	0.70	1.75	3.50	—

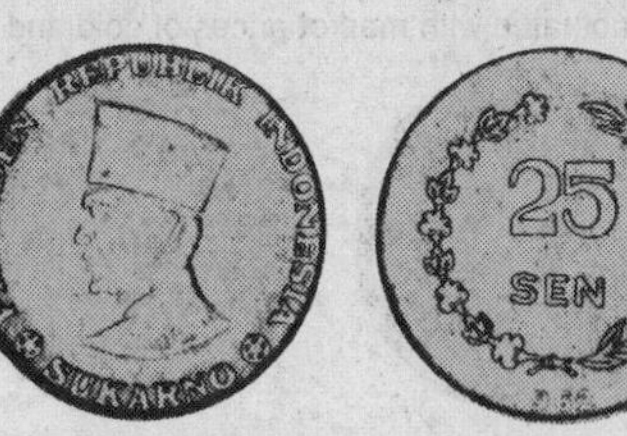

KM# 8.1 25 SEN Composition: Aluminum **Reverse:** "25" style similar to Irian Barat, KM#8.1

Date	F	VF	XF	Unc	BU
1962	—	—	—	—	—

KM# 8.2 25 SEN Composition: Aluminum **Reverse:** Different style "5"

Date	F	VF	XF	Unc	BU
1962	0.85	1.60	2.75	5.50	—

KM# 9 50 SEN Composition: Aluminum **Reverse:** 17 laurel leaves

Date	F	VF	XF	Unc	BU
1962	1.00	2.00	3.50	10.00	—

The Islamic Republic of Iran, located between the Caspian Sea and the Persian Gulf in southwestern Asia, has an area of 636,296 sq. mi. (1,648,000 sq. km.) and a population of 40 million. Capital: Tehran. Although predominantly an agricultural state, Iran depends heavily on oil for foreign exchange. Crude oil, carpets and agricultural products are exported.

Iran (historically known as Persia until 1931AD) is one of the world's most ancient and resilient nations. Strategically astride the lower land gate to Asia, it has been conqueror and conquered, sovereign nation and vassal state, ever emerging from its periods of glory or travail with its culture and political individuality intact. Iran (Persia) was a powerful empire under Cyrus the Great (600-529 B.C.), its borders extending from the Indus to the Nile. It has also been conquered by the predatory empires of antique and recent times - Assyrian, Medean, Macedonian, Seljuq, Turk, Mongol - and more recently been coveted by Russia, the Third Reich and Great Britain. Revolts against the absolute power of the Persian shahs resulted in the establishment of a constitutional monarchy in1906.

With 4,000 troops, Reza Khan marched on the capital arriving in Tehran in the early morning of Feb. 22,1921. The government was taken over with hardly a shot and Zia ad-Din was set up as premier, but the real power was with Reza Khan, although he was officially only the minister of war. In 1923, Reza Khan appointed himself prime minister and summoned the "majlis." Who eventually gave him military powers and he became independent of the shah's authority. In 1925 Reza Khan Pahlavi was elected Shah of Persia. A few weeks later his eldest son, Shahpur Mohammed Reza was appointed Crown Prince and was crowned on April 25, 1926.

In 1931 the Kingdom of Persia became known as the Kingdom of Iran. In 1979 the monarchy was toppled and an Islamic Republic proclaimed.

TITLES

دار الخلافة

Dar al-Khilafat

RULERS

Qajar Dynasty

مظفرالدين

Muzaffar al-Din Shah, AH1313-1324/1896-1907AD

محمد علي

Muhammad Ali Shah, AH1324-1327/1907-1909AD

سلطان احمد

Sultan Ahmad Shah, AH1327-1344/1909-1925AD

Pahlavi Dynasty

رضا

Reza Shah, as prime minister, SH1302-1304/1923-1925AD
as Shah,
SH1304-1320/1925-1941AD

محمد رضا

Mohammad Reza Pahlavi, Shah SH1320-1358/1941-1979AD

جمهوری اسلامی ایران

Islamic Republic, SH1358-/1979-AD

MINTNAME

طهران

Tehran

Tiflis

MINT MARKS

H - Heaton (Birmingham)
L - Leningrad (St. Petersburg)

COIN DATING

Iranian coins were dated according to the Moslem lunar calendar until March 21, 1925 (AD), when dating was switched to a new calendar based on the solar year, indicated by the notation SH. The monarchial calendar system was adopted in 1976 = MS2535 and was abandoned in 1978 = MS2537. The previously used solar year calendar was restored at that time.

MONETARY SYSTEM

1825-1931
(AH1241-1344, SH1304-09)

50 Dinars = 1 Shahi
20 Shahis = 1 Kran (Qiran)
10 Krans = 1 Toman

NOTE: From AD1830-34 (AH1245-50) the gold Toman was known as a 'Keshwarsetan.'

1932-Date (SH1310-Date)

5 Dinars = 1 Shahi
20 Shahis = 1 Rial (100 Dinars)
10 Rials = 1 Toman

NOTE: The Toman ceased to be an official unit in 1932, but continues to be applied in popular usage. Thus, 135 Rials' is always expressed as 13 Toman, 5 Rials'. The term Rial' is often used in conversation, as well as either Kran' or Ezar' (short for Hazar = 1000) is used.

NOTE: The Law of 18 March 1930 fixed the gold Pahlavi at 20 Rials. No gold coins were struck. The Law of 13 March1932 divided the Pahlavi into 100 Rials, instead of 20. The Rial's weight was reduced from 0.3661 grams of pure gold to 0.0732. Since 1937 gold has been allowed to float and the Pahlavi is quoted daily in Rials in the marketplaces.

KINGDOM

NOTE: Other mints also produced local Falus, for which examples were not available to illustrate. Still other mints operated only or largely at earlier dates. These include Damavand, Damghan, Darabjird, Fa'Farafad, Kangan, Ra', Semnan, Tus, Tuy and others.

SILVER AND GOLD COINAGE

The precious metal monetary system of Qajar Persia prior to the reforms of 1878 was the direct descendant of the Mongol system introduced by Ghazan Mahmud in 1297AD, and was the last example of a medieval islamic coinage. It is not a modern system, and cannot be understood as such. It is not possible to list types, dates, and mints as for other countries, both because of the nature of the coinage, and because very little research has been done on the series. The following comments should help elucidate its nature.

STANDARDS: The weight of the primary silver and gold coins was set by law and was expressed in terms of the Mesqal (about 4.61 g) and the Nokhod (24 Nokhod = 1 Mesqal). The primary silver coin was the Rupee from AH1211-1212, the Riyal from AH1212-1241, and the Gheran from AH1241-1344. The standard gold coin was the Toman. Currently the price of gold is quoted in Mesqals.

DENOMINATIONS: In addition to the primary denominations, noted in the last

paragraph, fractional pieces were coined, valued at one-eighth, one-fourth, and one-half the primary denomination, usually in much smaller quantities. These were ordinarily struck from the same dies as the larger pieces, sometimes on broad, thin flans, sometimes on thick, dumpy flans. On the smaller coins, the denomination can best be determined only by weighing the coin. The denomination is almost never expressed on the coin!

DEVALUATIONS: From time to time, the standard for silver and gold was reduced, and the old coin recalled and replaced with lighter coin, the difference going to the government coffers. The effect was that of a devaluation of the primary silver and gold coins, or inversely regarded, an increase in the price of silver and gold. The durations of each standard varied from about 2 to 20 years. The standards are given for each ruler, as the denomination can only be determined when the standard is known.

LIGHTWEIGHT AND ALLOYED PIECES: Most of the smaller denomination coins were issued at lighter weights than those prescribed by law, with the difference going to the pockets of the mintmasters. Other mints, notably Hamadan, added excessive amounts of alloy to the coins, and some mintmasters lost their heads as a result. Discrepancies in weight of as much as 15 percent and more are observed, with the result that it is often quite impossible to determine the denomination of a coin!

OVERSIZE COINS: Occasionally, multiples of the primary denominations were produced, usually on special occasions for presentation by the Shah to his favorites. These 'coins' did not circulate (except as bullion), and were usually worn as ornaments. They were the 'NCLT's' of their day.

MINTS & EPITHETS: Qajar coinage was struck at 34 mints (plus at least a dozen others striking only copper Falus), which are listed previously, with drawings of the mintnames in Persian, as they appear on the coins. However, the Persian script admits of infinite variation and stylistic whimsy, so the forms given are only guides, and not absolute. Only a knowledge of the script will assure correct reading. In addition to the city name, most mintnames were given identifying epithets, which occasionally appear in lieu of the mintname, particularly at Iravan and Mashhad.

TYPES: There were no types in the modern sense, but the arrangement of the legends and the ornamental borders were frequently changed. These changes do not coincide with changes in standards, and cannot be used to determine the mint, which must be found by actually reading the reverse inscriptions.

ARRANGEMENT

The following listings are arranged first by ruler, with various standards explained. Then, the coins are listed by denomination within each reign. For each denomination, one or more pieces, when available, are illustrated, with the mint and date noted beneath each photo. For each type, a date range is given, but this range indicates the years during which the particular type was current, and does not imply that every year of the interval is known on actual coins. Because dates were carelessly engraved, and old dies were used until they wore out or broke, we occasionally find coins of a particular type dated before or after the indicated interval. Such coins command no premium. No attempt has been made to determine which mints actually exist for which types.

KRAN STANDARD

AH1293-1344, SH1304-1309,
1876-1931AD

50 Dinars = 1 Shahi
1000 Dinars = 20 Shahis = 1 Kran (Qiron)
10 Krans = 1 Toman

Special Gold Issue
AH1337/1918-1919AD
1 Ashrafi (= 1 Toman)
SH1305-1309/1927-1931AD

Toman replaced by Pahlavi (light standard). Relationship of Pahlavi to Kran not known.

NOTE: Dated reverse dies lacking the ruler's name were not discarded at the end of a reign (especially from Nasir al-Din to Muzaffar al-Din), but remained in use until broken or worn out. Sometimes the old date was scratched out or changed, but often the die was used with the old date unaltered. Some dies with date below wreath retained the old date but had the new date engraved among the lion's legs.

SHAHI SEFID
(White Shahi)

Called the White (i.e. silver) Shahi to distinguish it from the Black or Copper Shahi, the Shahi Sefid was actually worth 3 Shahis (150 Dinars) or 3 1/8 Shahis (156 ¼ Dinars). It was used primarily for distribution on New Year's Day (now RUZ) as good-luck gifts. Since 1926 special privately struck tokens, having no monetary value, have been used instead of coins. The Shahi Sefid was broader, but much thinner than the ¼ Kran (Rob'l), worth 250 Dinars.

KINGDOM

Anonymous

MILLED COINAGE

KM# 961 50 DINARS **Composition:** Copper-Nickel

Date	Mintage	F	VF	XF	Unc
AH1318 (1900)	10,000,000	0.75	1.50	4.00	8.00
AH1319 (1901)	12,000,000	0.75	1.50	4.00	8.00
AH1321 (1903)	10,000,000	0.75	1.50	4.00	8.00
AH1326 (1908)	8,000,000	1.25	2.50	10.00	20.00
AH1332 (1913)	6,000,000	1.00	2.00	5.00	12.50
AH1337 (1918)	7,000,000	0.75	1.50	3.50	7.50

KM# 1091 50 DINARS **Composition:** Copper-Nickel

Date	Mintage	F	VF	XF	Unc
SH1305 (1926)	11,000,000	0.80	2.00	5.00	12.50
SH1307 (1928)	2,500,000	0.80	2.00	5.00	12.50

KM# 962 100 DINARS (2 Shahi) **Composition:** Copper-Nickel

Date	Mintage	F	VF	XF	Unc
AH1318 (1900)	10,000,000	1.00	1.50	4.00	10.00
AH1319 (1901)	9,000,000	0.75	1.50	4.00	8.00
AH1321/19 (1903)	5,000,000	4.00	6.00	11.50	30.00
AH1321 (1903)	Inc. above	0.75	1.50	4.00	8.00
AH1326 (1908)	6,000,000	1.50	2.50	6.00	15.00
AH1332 (1913)	5,000,000	1.00	2.00	5.00	12.50
AH1337 (1918)	6,500,000	0.75	1.50	3.00	6.50

KM# 1092 100 DINARS (2 Shahi) **Composition:** Copper-Nickel

Date	Mintage	F	VF	XF	Unc
SH1305 (1926)	4,500,000	1.00	1.50	3.50	10.00
SH1307 (1928)	3,750,000	1.00	1.50	3.50	10.00

KM# 1094 500 DINARS (10 Shahis = 1/2 Kran)
Weight: 2.3025 g. **Composition:** 0.9000 Silver .0666 oz. ASW

Date	F	VF	XF	Unc
SH1304 (1925)	100	200	300	500

KM# 1095 1000 DINARS (Kran, Qiran) **Weight:** 4.6050 g. **Composition:** 0.9000 Silver .1332 oz. ASW

Date	Mintage	F	VF	XF	Unc
SH1304 (1925)	2,573,000	3.00	5.00	10.00	20.00
SH1305 (1926)	2,265,000	4.00	7.00	12.50	25.00

KM# 1096 2000 DINARS (2 Kran) **Weight:** 9.2100 g. **Composition:** 0.9000 Silver .2665 oz. ASW **Reverse:** Date below lion

Date	Mintage	F	VF	XF	Unc
SH1304 (1925)	11,920,000	6.00	10.00	15.00	35.00
SH1305 (1926)	9,785,000	5.00	8.00	12.00	25.00

KM# 1007 SHAHI SEFID (White Shahi)
Weight: 0.0691 g. **Composition:** 0.9000 Silver .0200 oz. ASW **Obv. Legend:** "Sahib al-Zaman"

Date	F	VF	XF	Unc
AH1326 (1908)	60.00	125	175	—

KM# 1049 SHAHI SEFID (White Shahi)
Weight: 0.0691 g. **Composition:** 0.9000 Silver .0200 oz. ASW **Rev. Legend:** "Sahib-al-Zaman"

Date	Mintage	F	VF	XF	Unc
ND (1913)	—	10.00	20.00	40.00	—
AH1332 (1913)	—	10.00	18.00	35.00	—
Note: Included in KM#1032					
AH1333 (1914)	—	10.00	20.00	40.00	—
Note: Included in KM#1047					
AH1337 (1918)	—	10.00	20.00	40.00	—
Note: Included in KM#1047					
AH1341 (1922)	3,000	15.00	25.00	50.00	—
AH1342 (1923)	—	15.00	25.00	50.00	—
Note: Included in KM#1047					

KM# 1093 1/4 KRAN (Rob'i = 5 Shahis) **Weight:** 1.1513 g. **Composition:** 0.9000 Silver .0333 oz. ASW **Note:** 8,000 reported struck in SH1305, but that year not yet found and presumed not to exist.

Date	F	VF	XF	Unc
SH1304 (1925)	20.00	50.00	85.00	—

Note: For similar looking coins dated SH1315, see 1/4 Rial, KM#1127.

KM# 1097 5000 DINARS (5 Kran) **Weight:** 23.0251 g. **Composition:** 0.9000 Silver .6662 oz. ASW **Note:** Cross reference Dav.#292.

Date	Mintage	F	VF	XF	Unc
SH1304 (1925)	500,000	10.00	15.00	30.00	80.00
SH1305 (1926)	1,363,000	12.00	20.00	37.50	90.00

REFORM COINAGE

5 Dinars = 1 Shahi; 100 Dinars = 1 Rial;
100 Rials = 1 Pahlavi

The pahlavi was made equal in weight to the British sovereign. It was originally valued at 100 Rials, but has always fluctuated with market prices of gold and silver.

KM# 1126.1 (KM1126) 2-1/2 ABBASI (10 Shahi)
Composition: Copper **Edge:** Reeded

Date	Mintage	F	VF	XF	Unc
SH1314 (1935) Small date	15,714,000	3.00	4.00	12.50	30.00
SH1314 (1935) Small date	15,714,000	3.00	4.00	12.50	30.00
SH1314 (1935) Large date	Inc. above	3.00	4.00	12.50	30.00
SH1314 (1935) Large date	Inc. above	3.00	4.00	12.50	30.00

KM# 1126.2 2-1/2 ABBASI (10 Shahi)
Composition: Copper **Edge:** Plain

Date	F	VF	XF	Unc
SH1314 (1935)	5.00	7.00	15.00	40.00

KM# 1121 DINAR **Composition:** Bronze

Date	Mintage	F	VF	XF	Unc
SH1310 (1931)	10,000,000	10.00	20.00	45.00	100

KM# 1122 2 DINARS **Composition:** Bronze

Date	Mintage	F	VF	XF	Unc
SH1310 (1931)	5,000,000	10.00	20.00	50.00	110

KM# 1123 5 DINARS **Composition:** Copper-Nickel

Date	Mintage	F	VF	XF	Unc
SH1310 (1931)	3,750,000	20.00	40.00	100	200

KM# 1123a 5 DINARS **Composition:** Copper

Date	Mintage	F	VF	XF	Unc
SH1314	480,000	100	225	400	—

KM# 1138 5 DINARS **Composition:** Aluminum-Bronze

Date	Mintage	F	VF	XF	Unc
SH1315 (1936)	5,665,000	2.50	4.00	10.00	20.00
SH1316 (1937)	Inc. above	0.40	0.75	1.50	5.00
SH1317 (1938)	13,025,000	0.40	0.75	1.50	5.00

Date	Mintage	F	VF	XF	Unc
SH1318 (1939)	—	0.40	0.75	1.50	5.00
SH1319 (1940)	—	0.40	0.75	1.50	5.00
SH1320 (1941)	—	0.40	0.75	1.50	4.00
SH1321 (1942)	—	0.40	0.75	1.50	5.00

KM# 1124 10 DINARS Weight: 4.0000 g. **Composition:** Copper-Nickel **Note:** Struck at Berlin.

Date	Mintage	F	VF	XF	Unc
SH1310 (1931)	3,750,000	20.00	40.00	110	220

KM# 1124a 10 DINARS Weight: 3.2000 g. **Composition:** Copper **Note:** Struck at Tehran.

Date	Mintage	F	VF	XF	Unc
SH1314 (1935)	11,350,000	11.50	20.00	45.00	125

KM# 1139 10 DINARS Composition: Aluminum-Bronze

Date	Mintage	F	VF	XF	Unc
SH1315 (1936)	6,195,000	2.00	5.00	15.00	25.00
SH1316 (1937)	Inc. above	0.80	1.50	4.00	10.00
SH1317 (1938)	17,120,000	0.40	0.80	2.00	6.00
SH1318 (1939)	—	0.40	0.80	2.00	6.00
SH1319 (1940)	—	0.40	0.80	2.00	6.00
SH1320 (1941)	—	0.40	0.80	2.00	6.00
SH1321 (1942)	—	0.45	1.00	2.50	6.00

KM# 1125 25 DINARS Composition: Copper-Nickel

Date	Mintage	F	VF	XF	Unc
SH1310 (1931)	750,000	25.00	50.00	100	225

KM# 1125a 25 DINARS Composition: Copper

Date	Mintage	F	VF	XF	Unc
SH1314 (1935)	1,152,000	30.00	60.00	85.00	250

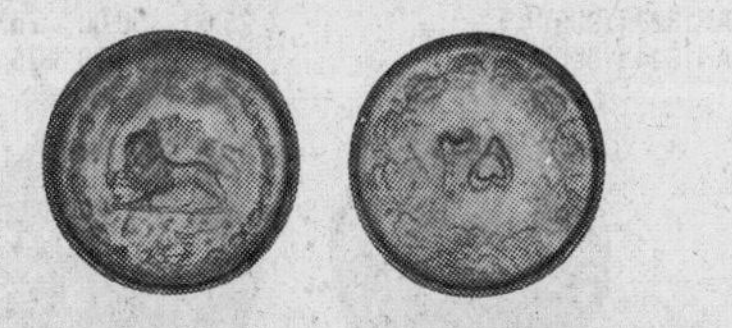

KM# 1140 25 DINARS Composition: Aluminum-Bronze

Date	F	VF	XF	Unc
SH1326 (1947)	10.00	20.00	40.00	80.00
SH1327 (1948)	12.00	30.00	60.00	100
SH1329 (1950)	12.00	30.00	60.00	100

KM# 1141 25 DINARS Composition: Aluminum-Bronze **Obverse:** 25 Dinars, KM#1140 **Reverse:** 1 Rial, KM#1143 **Note:** Mule

Date	F	VF	XF	Unc
SH1329 (1950)	150	200	350	750

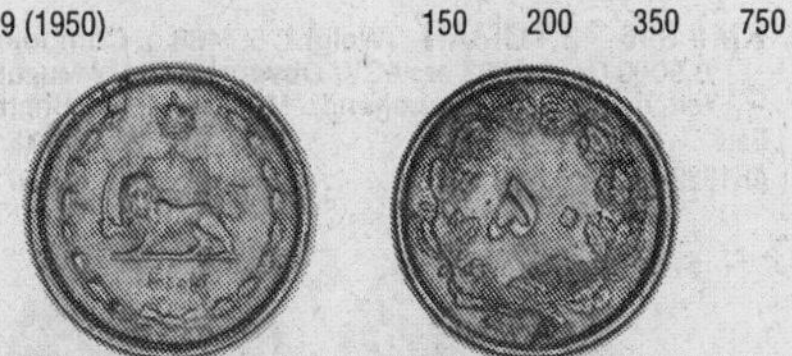

KM# 1142 50 DINARS Composition: Aluminum-Bronze

Date	Mintage	F	VF	XF	Unc
SH1315 (1936)	15,968,000	3.00	4.50	10.00	35.00
SH1316 (1937)	34,200,000	1.25	2.50	6.00	20.00
SH1317 (1938)	17,314,000	0.60	1.50	4.00	15.00
SH1318 (1939)	—	0.60	1.50	4.00	15.00
SH1319 (1940)	—	1.50	2.50	6.00	20.00
SH1320 (1941)	—	0.75	1.50	3.00	10.00
SH1321/0 (1942)	—	0.75	1.50	3.00	15.00
SH1322/10 (1943)	—	0.75	1.50	3.00	15.00
SH1322/12 (1943)	—	0.75	1.50	3.00	10.00
SH1322/0 (1943)	—	0.75	1.50	3.00	10.00
SH1322/1 (1943)	—	0.75	1.50	3.00	10.00
SH1331 (1952)	8,162,000	3.50	4.50	10.00	25.00
SH1332 (1953)	22,892,000	2.00	3.00	5.00	10.00

KM# 1142a 50 DINARS Composition: Copper

Date	F	VF	XF	Unc
SH1322 (1943)	2.00	4.00	7.00	12.00
SH1322/0 (1943)	2.00	6.00	9.00	15.00

KM# 1156 50 DINARS Composition: Aluminum-Bronze **Note:** Reduced thickness.

Date	Mintage	F	VF	XF	Unc
SH1332 (1953)	—	25.00	30.00	40.00	50.00
SH1333 (1954)	4,036,000	0.75	1.50	2.50	8.00
SH1334 (1955)	1,370,000	0.75	1.50	4.00	10.00
SH1335 (1956)	926,000	0.75	1.50	2.50	8.00
SH1336 (1957)	—	1.00	1.25	2.00	8.00

Note: Mint reports record 126,500 in SH1337 and 20,000 in SH1338; these were probably dated SH1336

Date	Mintage	F	VF	XF	Unc
SH1342 (1963)	800,000	0.60	1.00	1.75	6.00
SH1343 (1964)	1,400,000	0.60	1.00	1.75	6.00
SH1344 (1965)	1,600,000	0.35	0.65	1.25	5.00
SH1345 (1966)	1,690,000	0.35	0.65	1.25	5.00
SH1346 (1967)	—	0.20	0.25	0.50	2.00

Note: Mintage report seems excessive for this and all SH1346 coinage

Date	Mintage	F	VF	XF	Unc
SH1347 (1968)	2,000,000	0.20	0.25	0.50	2.00
SH1348 (1969)	1,500,000	0.20	0.25	0.50	2.00
SH1349 (1970)	360,000	2.00	3.00	4.50	12.50
SH1350 (1971)	—	0.30	0.50	0.75	2.00
SH1351 (1972)	—	0.30	0.50	0.75	2.00
SH1353 (1974)	60,000	0.30	0.50	0.75	2.00
SH1354 (1975)	16,000	0.75	1.25	2.00	5.00

KM# 1156a 50 DINARS Composition: Brass-Coated Steel

Date	Mintage	F	VF	XF	Unc
MS2535 (1976)	27,000	0.80	1.00	2.00	3.00
MS2536 (1977)	—	1.00	1.50	2.50	4.00
MS2537 (1978)	—	1.00	1.50	2.50	4.00
SH1357 (1978)	—	1.00	2.00	3.50	6.00
SH1358 (1979)	—	3.00	4.00	6.00	10.00

KM# 1127 1/4 RIAL Weight: 1.2500 g. **Composition:** 0.8280 Silver .0332 oz. ASW

Date	Mintage	F	VF	XF	Unc
SH1315 (1936)	600,000	1.00	1.25	1.75	4.00

Note: The second "1" is often short, so that the date looks like 1305

Nasir al-Din Shah

AH1264-1313/1848-96AD

MILLED COINAGE

KM# 891 SHAHI SEFID (White Shahi) Composition: Copper-Nickel Clad Brass **Obv. Legend:** "Nasir al-Din" (KM#889) **Rev. Legend:** "Shahib alzaman" (obverse of KM#1007)

Date	F	VF	XF	Unc
ND (1908)	50.00	75.00	125	—

Muzaffar al-Din Shah

AH1313-1324/1896-1907AD

MILLED COINAGE

First Nasir al-din legend Second Nasir al-din legend with *Sahibqiran* added

Forms of the denomination:

500 DINARS: ۵۰۰ دینار

or پانصد دینار

ده شاهی

KM# 969 500 DINARS (10 Shahis = 1/2 Kran) Weight: 2.3025 g. **Composition:** 0.9000 Silver .0666 oz. ASW **Obv. Legend:** "Muzaffar al-din", 500 Dinars **Reverse:** Date amidst legs, arranged variously **Note:** Some reverse dies were previously used under Nasir al-Din and show traces of old date beneath wreath on reverse.

Date	F	VF	XF	Unc
ND (1895)	10.00	20.00	35.00	—
AH1298 (sic) (1895)	100	150	250	—

Note: The 1298 is an "undated" variety showing 1298 of the dies previous user

Date	F	VF	XF	Unc
AH1313 (1895)	40.00	75.00	150	—
AH1314 (1896)	20.00	40.00	100	—
AH1315 (1897)	40.00	75.00	150	—
AH1316 (1898)	40.00	75.00	150	—
AH1317 (1899)	—	—	—	—

Note: Reported, not confirmed

Date	F	VF	XF	Unc
AH1318 (1900)	30.00	50.00	125	—
AH1319 (1901)	20.00	40.00	100	—
AH1322 (1904)	20.00	30.00	50.00	—

KM# 977 500 DINARS (10 Shahis = 1/2 Kran) Weight: 2.3025 g. **Composition:** 0.9000 Silver .0666 oz. ASW **Obverse:** Bust of Muzaffar al-Din Shah

Date	Mintage	F	VF	XF	Unc
AH1323 (1905)	130,000	20.00	35.00	80.00	—

Forms of the denomination:

1000 DINARS: یکهزار دینار

1 KRAN: یکقران

KM# 972 1000 DINARS (Kran, Qiran) Weight: 4.6050 g. **Composition:** 0.9000 Silver .1332 oz. ASW **Obverse:** Crown added above legend **Reverse:** Date amidst lion's legs

Date	F	VF	XF	Unc
AH1318 (1900)	100	175	250	—
AH1319 (1901)	150	225	350	—
AH1322 (1904)	75.00	150	225	—

KM# 978 1000 DINARS (Kran, Qiran) **Weight:** 4.6050 g. **Composition:** 0.9000 Silver .1332 oz. ASW **Obverse:** Bust of Muzaffer al-Din Shah, date below sprays

Date	Mintage	F	VF	XF	Unc
AH1323 (1905)	125,000	20.00	30.00	65.00	125

Forms of the denomination:

2 KRANS: دو قران

2000 DINARS: دو هزار دینار

KM# 974 2000 DINARS (2 Kran) **Weight:** 9.2100 g. **Composition:** 0.9000 Silver .2665 oz. ASW **Obverse:** Crown added **Reverse:** Position of date amidst legs varies **Rev. Legend:** "2000 Dinars" **Note:** Blundered dates exist.

Date	Mintage	F	VF	XF	Unc
AH1318 (1900)	—	10.00	20.00	35.00	90.00
AH1319 (1901)	—	10.00	20.00	35.00	90.00
AH1320 (1902)	13,959,000	10.00	20.00	35.00	75.00

KM# 975 2000 DINARS (2 Kran) **Weight:** 9.2100 g. **Composition:** 0.9000 Silver .2665 oz. ASW **Reverse:** Position of digits varies between lion's legs **Rev. Legend:** 2 Krans

Date	Mintage	F	VF	XF	Unc
AH1320 (1902)	Inc. above	12.50	20.00	40.00	100
AH1321 (1903)	18,108,000	15.00	22.50	45.00	100
Note: In blundered form as 13201					
AH1322 (1904)	8,640,000	8.00	15.00	30.00	80.00

KM# 979 2000 DINARS (2 Kran) **Weight:** 9.2100 g. **Composition:** 0.9000 Silver .2665 oz. ASW **Obverse:** Bust of Muzaffer al-Din Shah, date below sprays

Date	F	VF	XF	Unc
AH1322 (1905)	15.00	30.00	60.00	120
Note: Mintage inluded in AH1322 above				
AH'13' (1905)	60.00	100	200	—
Note: 23 of 1323 filled in or never punched				
AH13233 (1905)	45.00	85.00	190	—
Note: Error				

KM# 965 SHAHI SEFID (White Shahi) **Weight:** 0.0691 g. **Composition:** 0.9000 Silver .0200 oz. ASW **Obv. Legend:** "Muzaffar al-Din Shah"

Date	Mintage	F	VF	XF	Unc
ND (1895)	—	8.00	20.00	40.00	—
Note: Some undated issues show traces of an old date (usually AH1301 or AH1303) below wreath on reverse; these are worth slightly more than other undated issues					
AH1313 (1895) Rare	—	—	—	—	—
AH1314 (1896)	—	20.00	40.00	75.00	—
AH1315 (1897)	—	20.00	40.00	75.00	—
AH1316 (1898)	—	20.00	40.00	75.00	—

Date	Mintage	F	VF	XF	Unc
AH1317 (1899)	—	25.00	50.00	100	—
AH1318 (1900)	—	15.00	30.00	60.00	—
AH8310 (1900)	—	15.00	30.00	60.00	—
Note: Error for 1318					
AH1319 (1901)	—	15.00	30.00	60.00	—
AH1039 (1901)	—	25.00	50.00	100	—
Note: Error for 1319					
AH1320 (1902)	150,000	15.00	30.00	60.00	—

KM# 966 SHAHI SEFID (White Shahi) **Weight:** 0.0691 g. **Composition:** 0.9000 Silver .0200 oz. ASW **Reverse:** Denomination omitted

Date	F	VF	XF	Unc
ND (1901)	50.00	80.00	165	—
AH1319 (1901) Rare	—	—	—	—

Note: A number of varieties and mulings of KM#965 and KM#966 with other denominations, especially 1/4 Krans and 500 Dinar pieces, are reported; these command a premium over others of the same types; a total of 58,000 pieces were reported struck in AH1322, 1323 and 1324, but none are known with those dates; the specimens were either struck from old dies or were undated types.

KM# 967 SHAHI SEFID (White Shahi) **Weight:** 0.0691 g. **Composition:** 0.9000 Silver .0200 oz. ASW **Obv. Legend:** "Muzaffar al-Din Shah" **Rev. Legend:** "Sahib al-Zaman" **Note:** Thick and thin lettering varieties exist.

Date	F	VF	XF	Unc
ND (1903)	50.00	85.00	165	—

KM# 976 5000 DINARS (5 Kran) **Weight:** 23.0251 g. **Composition:** 0.9000 Silver .6662 oz. ASW **Obv. Legend:** "Muzaffar al-din Shah" **Note:** Cross reference Dav.#288.

Date	Mintage	F	VF	XF	Unc
AH1320 (1902)	250,000	8.00	11.50	18.50	30.00
Note: Actual mintage must be considerably greater					

KM# 980 5000 DINARS (5 Kran) **Weight:** 23.0251 g. **Composition:** 0.9000 Silver .6662 oz. ASW **Subject:** Royal Birthday **Note:** Cross reference Dav.#287.

Date	F	VF	XF	Unc
AH1322 (1904)	400	550	800	1,200

KM# 981 5000 DINARS (5 Kran) **Weight:** 23.0251 g. **Composition:** 0.9000 Silver .6662 oz. ASW **Obverse:** Without additional inscriptions flanking head **Note:** Cross reference Dav.#289.

Date	Mintage	F	VF	XF	Unc
AH1324 (1906)	3,040	700	1,000	1,750	—

KM# 968 1/4 KRAN (Rob'i = 5 Shahis) **Weight:** 1.1513 g. **Composition:** 0.9000 Silver .0333 oz. ASW **Obv. Legend:** "Muzaffar al-din Shah" **Note:** 300 specimens reportedly struck in AH1322, but none known to exist.

Date	F	VF	XF	Unc
ND (1896)	8.00	15.00	28.00	—
AH1314 (1896)	50.00	100	200	—
AH1316 (1898)	12.50	20.00	35.00	—
AH1318 (1900)	25.00	50.00	85.00	—
AH1319 (1901)	20.00	35.00	65.00	—

MILLED GOLD COINAGE

Modern imitations exist of many types, particularly the small 1/5, 1/2, and 1 Toman coins. These are usually underweight (or rarely overweight), and are sold in the bazaars at a small premium over bullion. They are usually crude and probably not intended to deceive collectors, but some are sold for jewelry and some are dated outside the reign of the ruler whose name or portrait they bear. A few deceptive counterfeits are known of the large 10 Toman pieces.

KM# 986 2000 DINARS (1/5 Toman) **Weight:** 0.6520 g. **Composition:** 0.9000 Gold .0188 oz. AGW **Obv. Legend:** "Mazaffar-al-Din Shah" **Reverse:** Lion and sun

Date	F	VF	XF	Unc
AH9301 (1901) Error for 1319	125	175	275	400

KM# 991 2000 DINARS (1/5 Toman) **Weight:** 0.5749 g. **Composition:** 0.9000 Gold .0166 oz. AGW **Obverse:** Bust of Muzaffar al-Din Shah

Date	F	VF	XF	Unc
ND (1901)	75.00	135	200	300

KM# 992 2000 DINARS (1/5 Toman) **Weight:** 0.5749 g. **Composition:** 0.9000 Gold .0166 oz. AGW **Obverse:** Date and denomination added

Date	F	VF	XF	Unc
AH1319 (1901)	50.00	100	150	250
AH1322 (1904)	50.00	100	150	250
AH1323 (1905)	50.00	100	150	250
AH1324 (1906)	50.00	100	150	250

KM# 922 2000 DINARS (1/5 Toman) **Weight:** 0.6520 g. **Composition:** 0.9000 Gold .0188 oz. AGW **Note:** Mule. Reverse: KM#923, reverse: KM#991.

Date	F	VF	XF	Unc
AH1295 (sic) (1901)	—	—	—	—

KM# 994 5000 DINARS (1/2 Toman) **Weight:** 1.4372 g. **Composition:** 0.9000 Gold .0416 oz. AGW **Obverse:** Bust of Muzaffar right

Date	F	VF	XF	Unc
AH1318 (1900)	25.00	50.00	75.00	150
AH1319 (1901)	30.00	60.00	100	200
AH1320 (1902)	30.00	60.00	100	200
AH1321 (1903)	30.00	60.00	100	200
AH1322 (1904)	30.00	60.00	100	200
AH1323 (1905)	25.00	50.00	75.00	150
AH1324 (1906)	25.00	50.00	75.00	150

KM# 995 TOMAN **Weight:** 2.8744 g. **Composition:** 0.9000 Gold .0832 oz. AGW **Obverse:** Bust of Muzaffer 1/2 right, accession date, AH1314 above left

Date	F	VF	XF	Unc
AH1318 (1900)	45.00	75.00	125	200
AH1319 (1901)	60.00	100	160	250
AH1321 (1903)	60.00	100	160	250

KM# 996 2 TOMAN **Weight:** 5.7488 g. **Composition:** 0.9000 Gold .1663 oz. AGW **Obverse:** Bust of Muzaffer 1/2 left, date at left **Rev. Legend:** "Muzaffer al-Din Shah"

Date	F	VF	XF	Unc
AH1322 (1904)	250	400	750	1,500

KM# 997 2 TOMAN **Weight:** 5.7488 g. **Composition:** 0.9000 Gold .1663 oz. AGW **Subject:** Royal Birthday **Obverse:** Bust with legend at left and right **Rev. Legend:** "Muzaffer al-Din Shah"

Date	F	VF	XF	Unc
AH1322 (1904)	150	300	600	1,250

Muhammad Ali Shah
AH1324-1327/1907-1909AD
MILLED COINAGE

KM# 1010 500 DINARS (10 Shahis = 1/2 Kran) **Weight:** 2.3025 g. **Composition:** 0.9000 Silver .0666 oz. ASW **Obv. Legend:** "Muhammad Ali Shah"

Date	Mintage	F	VF	XF	Unc
AH1325 (1907)	218,000	40.00	75.00	160	—
AH1326 (1908)	218,000	25.00	50.00	110	—
AH1336 (1908) Error for 1326	Inc. above	35.00	60.00	125	—

KM# 1014 500 DINARS (10 Shahis = 1/2 Kran) **Weight:** 2.3025 g. **Composition:** 0.9000 Silver .0666 oz. ASW **Obverse:** KM#1013; date **Reverse:** KM#1010; date

Date	F	VF	XF	Unc
AH1325 (1907)	125	175	320	—
AH1326 (1908)	100	150	240	—

KM# 1013 500 DINARS (10 Shahis = 1/2 Kran) **Weight:** 2.3025 g. **Composition:** 0.9000 Silver .0666 oz. ASW **Obverse:** Bust of Muhammad Ali Shah, date below sprays

Date	F	VF	XF	Unc
AH1326 (1908) Mintage included in KM#1010	40.00	85.00	150	—
AH1327 (1909)	40.00	85.00	150	—

KM# 1011 1000 DINARS (Kran, Qiran) **Weight:** 4.6050 g. **Composition:** 0.9000 Silver .1332 oz. ASW **Obv. Legend:** "Muhammad Ali Shah"

Date	Mintage	F	VF	XF	Unc
AH1325 (1907)	289,000	150	300	600	—
AH1326 (1908)	289,000	150	300	600	—

KM# 1015 1000 DINARS (Kran, Qiran) **Weight:** 4.6050 g. **Composition:** 0.9000 Silver .1332 oz. ASW **Obverse:** Bust of Muhammad Ali Shah, date below sprays

Date	F	VF	XF	Unc
AH1326 (1908)	45.00	70.00	150	375
Note: Mintage included in KM#1011				
AH1327/6 (1909)	—	—	—	—
AH1327 (1909)	40.00	60.00	125	350

KM# 1016 1000 DINARS (Kran, Qiran) **Weight:** 4.6050 g. **Composition:** 0.9000 Silver .1332 oz. ASW **Obverse:** KM#1015; date **Reverse:** KM#1011; date

Date	F	VF	XF	Unc
AH1326 (1908)	125	200	350	—

Note: Mintage included in KM#1011

KM# 1012 2000 DINARS (2 Kran) **Weight:** 9.2100 g. **Composition:** 0.9000 Silver .2665 oz. ASW **Obv. Legend:** "Muhammad Ali Shah" **Reverse:** 2 Krans

Date	Mintage	F	VF	XF	Unc
AH1325 (1907)	3,076,000	15.00	25.00	50.00	100
AH1326 (1908)	3,069,000	7.50	11.50	20.00	50.00
AH1327 (1909)	—	7.50	11.50	20.00	50.00

KM# 1017 2000 DINARS (2 Kran) **Weight:** 9.2100 g. **Composition:** 0.9000 Silver .2665 oz. ASW **Obverse:** Portrait of Muhammad Ali Shah

Date	F	VF	XF	Unc
AH1326 (1908)	1,500	2,000	2,500	—

Note: Mintage included in KM#1012

KM# 1006 SHAHI SEFID (White Shahi) **Weight:** 0.0691 g. **Composition:** 0.9000 Silver .0200 oz. ASW **Obv. Legend:** "Muhammad Ali Shah"

Date	F	VF	XF	Unc
AH1325 (1907)	30.00	60.00	110	—
AH1326 (1908)	25.00	40.00	90.00	—
AH1327 (1909)	20.00	40.00	80.00	—

KM# 1008 SHAHI SEFID (White Shahi) **Weight:** 0.0691 g. **Composition:** 0.9000 Silver .0200 oz. ASW **Obverse:** KM#1006 **Reverse:** Obverse of KM#1007

Date	F	VF	XF	Unc
ND (1909)	50.00	80.00	150	—

KM# 1018 5000 DINARS (5 Kran) **Weight:** 23.0251 g. **Composition:** 0.9000 Silver .6662 oz. ASW **Obverse:** Bust of Muhammad Ali Shah, date below sprays **Note:** Cross reference Dav.#290.

Date	F	VF	XF	Unc
AH1327 (1909)	575	850	1,750	—

Note: Obverse always weakly struck with little detail in head and face

KM# 1009 1/4 KRAN (Rob'i = 5 Shahis) **Weight:** 1.1513 g. **Composition:** 0.9000 Silver .0333 oz. ASW **Obv. Legend:** "Muhammad Ali Shah"

Date	F	VF	XF	Unc
AH1325 (1907)	30.00	50.00	100	—
AH1326 (1908)	15.00	27.50	40.00	—
AH1327 (1909)	10.00	20.00	35.00	—

MILLED GOLD COINAGE

Modern imitations exist of many types, particularly the small 1/5, 1/2, and 1 Toman coins. These are usually underweight (or rarely overweight), and are sold in the bazaars at a small premium over bullion. They are usually crude and probably not intended to deceive collectors, but some are sold for jewelry and some are dated outside the reign of the ruler whose name or portrait they bear. A few deceptive counterfeits are known of the large 10 Toman pieces.

KM# 1024 2000 DINARS (1/5 Toman) **Weight:** 0.5749 g. **Composition:** 0.9000 Gold .0166 oz. AGW **Obverse:** Bust of Muhammad Ali Shah turned half left, divided date **Reverse:** Legend in wreath

Date	F	VF	XF	Unc
AH1326 (1908)	100	190	270	475
AH1327 (1909)	100	190	270	475

KM# 1021 5000 DINARS (1/2 Toman) **Weight:** 1.4372 g. **Composition:** 0.9000 Gold .0416 oz. AGW **Obv. Legend:** Muhammad Ali Shah **Reverse:** Lion and sun

Date	F	VF	XF	Unc
AH1324 (1906)	100	150	250	400
AH1325 (1907)	150	225	350	450

KM# 1025 5000 DINARS (1/2 Toman) **Weight:** 1.4372 g. **Composition:** 0.9000 Gold .0416 oz. AGW **Obverse:** Bust of Muhammad 1/2 left **Rev. Legend:** "Muhammad Ali Shah"

Date	F	VF	XF	Unc
AH1326 (1908)	125	200	300	450
AH1362 (1908) Error for 1326	150	250	350	525
AH1327 (1909)	125	200	300	450

KM# 1022 TOMAN **Weight:** 2.8744 g. **Composition:** 0.9000 Gold .0832 oz. AGW **Obv. Legend:** "Muhammad Ali Shah" **Reverse:** Lion and sun

Date	F	VF	XF	Unc
AH1324 (1906)	250	450	675	900

KM# 1026 TOMAN **Weight:** 2.8744 g. **Composition:** 0.9000 Gold .0832 oz. AGW **Obverse:** Bust of Muhammad 1/2 left, AH1326 **Reverse:** Legend in closed wreath **Rev. Legend:** "Muhammad Ali Shah"

Date	F	VF	XF	Unc
AH1327 (1909)	200	350	500	750

Sultan Ahmad Shah
AH1327-44/1909-25AD
MILLED COINAGE

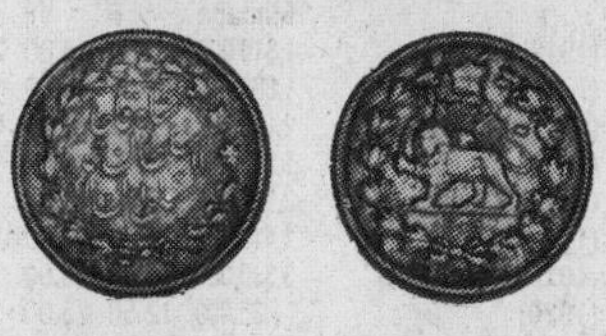

KM# 1036 500 DINARS (10 Shahis = 1/2 Kran) **Weight:** 2.3025 g. **Composition:** 0.9000 Silver .0666 oz. ASW **Obv. Legend:** "Ahmad Shah"

Date	Mintage	F	VF	XF	Unc
AH1327 (1909)	—	5.00	12.50	20.00	—
AH1328 (1910)	—	5.00	12.50	20.00	—
AH1329 (1911)	44,000	10.00	20.00	40.00	—
AH1330 (1911)	627,000	5.00	12.50	20.00	—

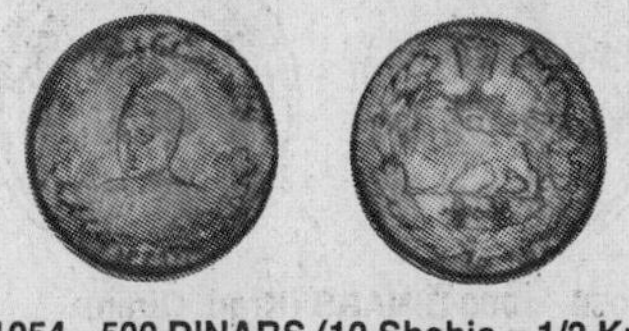

KM# 1054 500 DINARS (10 Shahis = 1/2 Kran) **Weight:** 2.3025 g. **Composition:** 0.9000 Silver .0666 oz. ASW **Obverse:** Portrait of Ahmad Shah, date below sprays

Date	Mintage	F	VF	XF	Unc
AH1331 (1912)	—	3.00	6.00	15.00	—

Note: Mintage included in AH1330 above

Date	Mintage	F	VF	XF	Unc
AH1332 (1913)	560,000	2.00	5.00	10.00	—
AH1333 (1914)	292,000	2.00	5.00	10.00	—
AH1334 (1915)	65,000	3.00	6.00	12.00	—
AH1335 (1916)	150,000	8.00	15.00	30.00	—
AH1336 (1917)	240,000	4.00	8.00	20.00	—
AH1339 (1920)	—	17.50	25.00	40.00	—
AH1343 (1924)	160,000	6.00	10.00	25.00	—

Note: 10,000 reported struck in AH1337 probably dated AH1336

KM# 1055 500 DINARS (10 Shahis = 1/2 Kran)
Weight: 2.3025 g. **Composition:** 0.9000 Silver .0666 oz. ASW **Obverse:** Date **Reverse:** Date

Date	F	VF	XF	Unc
AH1332 (1913)	30.00	50.00	90.00	—

Note: Mintage included in KM#1054

KM# 1038 1000 DINARS (Kran, Qiran)
Weight: 4.6050 g. **Composition:** 0.9000 Silver .1332 oz. ASW **Obv. Legend:** "Sultan Ahmad Shah"

Date	Mintage	F	VF	XF	Unc
AH1327 (1909)	—	15.00	25.00	40.00	70.00
AH1328 (1910)	—	4.00	8.00	15.00	40.00
AH1329 (1911)	3,000,000	4.00	8.00	15.00	40.00
AH1330 (1911)	—	4.00	8.00	15.00	40.00

KM# 1037 1000 DINARS (Kran, Qiran) **Weight:** 4.6050 g. **Composition:** 0.9000 Silver .1332 oz. ASW **Obverse:** KM#1038 **Reverse:** KM#1011 **Note:** Traditional issue.

Date	F	VF	XF	Unc
AH1326 (sic) (1909) Rare	—	—	—	—

KM# 1056 1000 DINARS (Kran, Qiran)
Weight: 4.6050 g. **Composition:** 0.9000 Silver .1332 oz. ASW **Obverse:** Bust of Ahmad Shah, date below sprays

Date	Mintage	F	VF	XF	Unc
AH1331 (1912)	1,310,000	5.00	8.00	25.00	40.00
AH1332 (1913)	1,891,000	3.00	5.00	12.50	30.00
AH1333 (1914)	2,179,000	7.50	12.00	25.00	40.00
AH1334 (1915)	1,273,000	3.00	5.00	12.50	25.00
AH1335 (1916)	2,162,000	3.00	5.00	12.50	25.00
AH1336 (1917)	1,412,000	3.50	6.00	15.00	30.00
AH1337 (1918)	3,330,000	3.00	5.00	12.50	25.00
AH1339 (1920)	35,000	12.50	25.00	55.00	90.00
AH1330 (1921) Error for 1340	—	30.00	65.00	125	175
AH1340 (1921)	28,000	15.00	30.00	60.00	100
AH1341 (1922)	170,000	8.00	15.00	35.00	60.00
AH1342 (1923)	255,000	3.00	6.00	20.00	30.00
AH1343 (1924)	1,345,000	3.00	6.00	20.00	30.00
AH1344 (1925)	2,978,000	4.00	6.00	20.00	35.00

KM# 1059 1000 DINARS (Kran, Qiran)
Weight: 4.6050 g. **Composition:** 0.9000 Silver .1332 oz. ASW **Subject:** 10th Year of Reign

Date	Mintage	F	VF	XF	Unc
AH1337 (1918)	975,000	25.00	40.00	75.00	150

KM# 1040 2000 DINARS (2 Kran) **Weight:** 9.2100 g. **Composition:** 0.9000 Silver .2665 oz. ASW **Obv. Legend:** "Ahmad Shah" **Reverse:** Date below wreath, "2 Krans"

Date	Mintage	F	VF	XF	Unc
AH1327 (1909)	—	4.50	7.00	12.00	30.00

Note: Mintage included in KM#1328

Date	Mintage	F	VF	XF	Unc
AH1328 (1910)	30,000,000	4.50	7.00	12.00	20.00
AH1329 (1911)	29,250,000	4.50	7.00	12.00	20.00

KM# 1041 2000 DINARS (2 Kran) **Weight:** 9.2100 g. **Composition:** 0.9000 Silver .2665 oz. ASW **Reverse:** Date below wreath, "2000 Dinars", fierce triangular face on lion

Date	Mintage	F	VF	XF	Unc
AH1330 (1911)	2,901,000	5.00	8.00	15.00	35.00

KM# 1043 2000 DINARS (2 Kran) **Weight:** 9.2100 g. **Composition:** 0.9000 Silver .2665 oz. ASW **Obv. Legend:** "Ahmad Shah" **Reverse:** Date amidst legs, "2000 Dinars"

Date	Mintage	F	VF	XF	Unc
AH1330 (1911)	—	4.00	7.00	10.00	30.00

Note: Mintage included in KM#1041

Date	Mintage	F	VF	XF	Unc
AH1331 (1912)	13,412,000	5.00	10.00	17.00	40.00

KM# 1057 2000 DINARS (2 Kran) **Weight:** 9.2100 g. **Composition:** 0.9000 Silver .2665 oz. ASW **Obverse:** Bust of Ahmad Shah, date below sprays

Date	Mintage	F	VF	XF	Unc
AH1331 (1912)	—	6.00	12.50	25.00	50.00

Note: Mintage included in KM#1043

Date	Mintage	F	VF	XF	Unc
AH1332 (1913)	12,926,000	5.00	7.50	15.00	30.00
AH1333 (1914)	Inc. above	5.00	7.50	15.00	30.00
AH1334 (1915)	4,299,000	5.00	7.50	15.00	30.00
AH1335 (1916)	9,777,000	5.00	7.50	15.00	30.00
AH1336 (1917)	5,401,000	5.00	7.50	15.00	30.00
AH1337 (1918)	2,951,000	5.00	7.50	15.00	30.00
AH1339 (1920)	1,085,000	6.00	12.50	25.00	50.00
AH1330 (1921) Error for 1340	—	50.00	100	150	250

Note: Mintage included in KM#1043

Date	Mintage	F	VF	XF	Unc
AH1340 (1921)	254,000	9.00	15.00	30.00	65.00
AH1341 (1922)	4,460,000	5.00	7.50	15.00	30.00
AH1342 (1923)	2,245,000	5.00	8.00	20.00	35.00
AH1343 (1924)	5,205,000	5.00	8.00	20.00	35.00
AH1344/34 (1925)	12,354	7.00	12.00	25.00	55.00
AH1344 (1925)	Inc. above	6.00	10.00	20.00	40.00

KM# 1060 2000 DINARS (2 Kran) **Weight:** 9.2100 g. **Composition:** 0.9000 Silver .2665 oz. ASW **Subject:** 10th Anniversary of Reign

Date	Mintage	F	VF	XF	Unc
AH1337 (1918)	3,503,000	25.00	40.00	100	225

KM# 1031 SHAHI SEFID (White Shahi) **Weight:** 0.0691 g. **Composition:** 0.9000 Silver .0200 oz. ASW **Obv. Legend:** "Ahmad Shah" **Reverse:** Date below wreath

Date	Mintage	F	VF	XF	Unc
AH1328 (1910)	—	5.00	10.00	20.00	—
AH1329 (1911)	—	6.00	12.00	25.00	—
AH1330 (1911)	189,000	4.00	10.00	20.00	—

KM# 1032 SHAHI SEFID (White Shahi)
Weight: 0.0691 g. **Composition:** 0.9000 Silver .0200 oz. ASW **Reverse:** Date amidst lion's legs

Date	Mintage	F	VF	XF	Unc
AH1332 (1913)	10,000	30.00	50.00	85.00	—

KM# 1033 SHAHI SEFID (White Shahi) **Weight:** 0.0691 g. **Composition:** 0.9000 Silver .0200 oz. ASW **Obv. Legend:** "Ahmad Shah" **Rev. Legend:** "Sahib-al-Zaman"

Date	F	VF	XF	Unc
ND (1913)	60.00	125	200	—

KM# 1047 SHAHI SEFID (White Shahi)
Weight: 0.0691 g. **Composition:** 0.9000 Silver .0200 oz. ASW **Note:** Varieties exist.

Date	Mintage	F	VF	XF	Unc
AH1333 (1914)	78,000	5.00	10.00	20.00	—
AH1334 (1915)	6,000	12.00	20.00	40.00	—
AH1335 (1916)	73,000	8.00	15.00	30.00	—
AH1335//1337 (1918)	Inc. above	40.00	80.00	165	—
AH1337 (1918)	76,000	8.00	15.00	30.00	—
AH1337//1337 (1918)	—	40.00	75.00	150	—
AH1339 (1920)	10,000	12.00	20.00	40.00	—
AH1342 (1923)	20,000	12.00	20.00	40.00	—

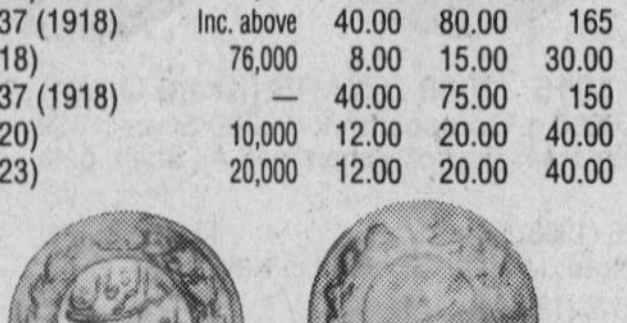

KM# 1048 SHAHI SEFID (White Shahi)
Weight: 0.0691 g. **Composition:** 0.9000 Silver .0200 oz. ASW **Obverse:** KM#1047 **Rev. Legend:** "Sahib-al-Zaman"

Date	F	VF	XF	Unc
AH1335 (1916)	50.00	80.00	150	—

Note: Mintage included in KM#1047 of AH1335

KM# 1050 SHAHI SEFID (White Shahi)
Weight: 0.6908 g. **Composition:** 0.9000 Silver .0200 oz. ASW **Obverse:** KM#1047 dated AH1339 **Reverse:** Similar to KM#1049 with AH1341 between lion's legs, AH1327 below wreath

Date	F	VF	XF	Unc
AH1339//1341 & 1327 (1922)	50.00	80.00	150	—

Note: Numerous silver Nouruz tokens, some with dates SH1328-1346, are available in Tehran for a fraction of the price of true Shahis

KM# 1058 5000 DINARS (5 Kran) **Weight:** 23.0251 g. **Composition:** 0.9000 Silver .6662 oz. ASW **Obverse:** Portrait of Ahmad Shah, date below sprays **Note:** Beware of altered date AH1331 specimens. 9,000 reported minted in AH1336, probably dated earlier. Cross reference Dav.#291.

Date	Mintage	F	VF	XF	Unc
AH1331 (1912)	—	60.00	150	250	500
AH1332 (1913)	3,000,000	8.00	12.00	30.00	85.00
AH1333 (1914)	667,000	10.00	15.00	35.00	90.00
AH1334 (1915)	443,000	10.00	15.00	35.00	90.00
AH1335 (1916)	1,884,000	10.00	15.00	35.00	90.00
AH1337 (1918)	165,000	12.00	25.00	55.00	110
AH1339 (1920)	90,000	20.00	30.00	60.00	125
AH1340 (1921)	303,000	12.00	25.00	55.00	110
AH1341 (1922)	757,000	10.00	15.00	35.00	90.00
AH1342/32 (1923)	546,000	10.00	15.00	35.00	90.00
AH1342 (1923)	Inc. above	10.00	15.00	35.00	90.00
AH1343 (1924)	935,000	10.00	15.00	35.00	90.00
AH1344/34 (1925)	2,284,000	10.00	15.00	30.00	85.00
AH1344 (1925)	Inc. above	15.00	20.00	40.00	95.00

KM# 1035 1/4 KRAN (Rob'i = 5 Shahis)
Weight: 1.1513 g. **Composition:** 0.9000 Silver .0333 oz. ASW **Obv. Legend:** "Ahmad Shah"

Date	Mintage	F	VF	XF	Unc
AH1327 (1909)	—	5.00	10.00	20.00	—
AH1328 (1910)	—	4.00	7.50	15.00	—
AH1329 (1911)	130,000	12.50	20.00	40.00	—
AH1330 (1911)	156,000	4.00	7.50	15.00	—
AH1331 (1912)	30,000	—	—	—	—
Note: Reported, not confirmed.					
AH1313 (1912) Error for 1331	Inc. above	—	—	—	—
Note: Reported, not confirmed.					

KM# 1052 1/4 KRAN (Rob'i = 5 Shahis)
Weight: 1.1513 g. **Composition:** 0.9000 Silver .0333 oz. ASW **Obverse:** KM#1051 **Obv. Legend:** "Ahmad Shah" **Reverse:** KM#1009 **Note:** Mule

Date	F	VF	XF	Unc
ND (1909)	40.00	60.00	115	—
AH1327 (1909)	60.00	125	175	—

KM# 1051 1/4 KRAN (Rob'i = 5 Shahis) **Weight:** 1.1513 g. **Composition:** 0.9000 Silver .0333 oz. ASW **Obv. Legend:** "Ahmad Shah" **Reverse:** Date amidst legs

Date	Mintage	F	VF	XF	Unc
AH1332 (1913)	252,000	5.00	10.00	20.00	—
AH1333 (1914)	Inc. above	6.00	12.00	25.00	—
AH1334 (1915)	70,000	10.00	20.00	50.00	—
AH1335 (1916)	260,000	4.00	8.00	15.00	—
AH1336 (1917)	160,000	4.00	8.00	15.00	—
AH1337 (1918)	80,000	6.00	12.00	25.00	—
AH1339 (1920)	28,000	9.00	15.00	30.00	—
AH1341 (1922)	22,000	12.00	20.00	40.00	—
AH1342 (1923)	110,000	6.00	12.00	25.00	—
AH1343 (1924)	186,000	4.00	8.00	15.00	—

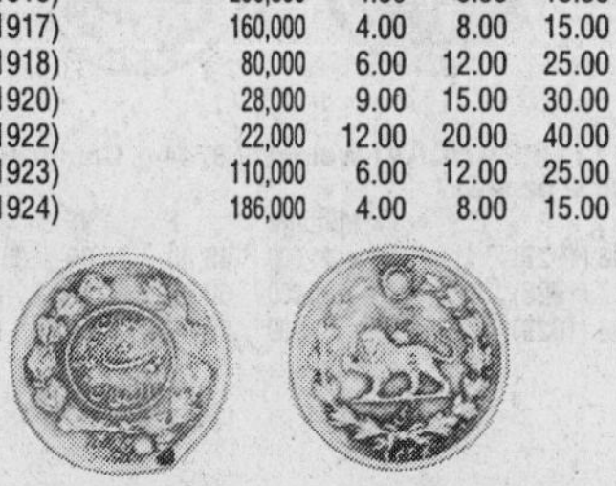

KM# 1053 1/4 KRAN (Rob'i = 5 Shahis)
Weight: 1.1513 g. **Composition:** 0.9000 Silver .0333 oz. ASW **Obverse:** KM#1051, date below wreath

Date	F	VF	XF	Unc
AH1334 (1915) Mintage included with KM#1051	75.00	150	250	—

CLANDESTINE COINAGE

KM# 1039 1000 DINARS (Kran, Qiran) **Composition:** Silver **Note:** KM#1039 differs from KM#1038 in that it is about 1 millimeters broader and has a much thicker rim and more clearly defined denticles. Struck in Germany, without Iranian authorization, for circulation in western Iran during World War I. Also, the lion lacks the triangular face and fierce expression of KM#1038 and the point of the Talwar (scimitar) does not touch the sunburst as it does on Tehran issues.

Date	F	VF	XF	Unc
AH1330 (sic) (1915)	—	7.00	18.00	30.00
AH1330 (sic) (1915) Rare	—	—	—	—

KM# 1042 2000 DINARS (2 Kran) **Composition:** Silver **Reverse:** Lion's face has friendly expression

Date	F	VF	XF	Unc
AH1330 (sic) (1915)	4.00	7.00	10.00	27.00

Note: See general note for KM#1039

MILLED GOLD COINAGE

Modern imitations exist of many types, particularly the small 1/5, 1/2, and 1 Toman coins. These are usually underweight (or rarely overweight), and are sold in the bazaars at a small premium over bullion. They are usually crude and probably not intended to deceive collectors, but some are sold for jewelry and some are dated outside the reign of the ruler whose name or portrait they bear. A few deceptive counterfeits are known of the large 10 Toman pieces.

KM# 1066 2000 DINARS (1/5 Toman)
Weight: 0.5749 g. **Composition:** 0.9000 Gold .0166 oz. AGW **Obv. Legend:** "Ahmad Shah" **Reverse:** Lion and sun

Date	F	VF	XF	Unc
AH1328 (1910)	100	175	250	500
AH1329 (1911)	70.00	125	200	325
AH1330 (1911)	—	—	—	—

KM# 1070 2000 DINARS (1/5 Toman) **Weight:** 0.5749 g. **Composition:** 0.9000 Gold .0166 oz. AGW **Obverse:** Bust of Ahmad Shah **Rev. Legend:** "Ahmad Shah"

Date	F	VF	XF	Unc
AH1332 (1913)	20.00	35.00	60.00	130
AH1333 (1914)	15.00	30.00	55.00	115
AH1334 (1915)	15.00	30.00	40.00	75.00
AH1335 (1916)	12.50	25.00	35.00	50.00
AH1337 (1918)	12.50	25.00	35.00	50.00
AH1339 (1920)	15.00	30.00	40.00	75.00
AH1340 (1921)	17.00	35.00	50.00	90.00
AH1341 (1922)	15.00	30.00	40.00	75.00
AH1342 (1923)	15.00	30.00	40.00	75.00
AH1343 (1924)	15.00	30.00	40.00	60.00

KM# 1067 5000 DINARS (1/2 Toman)
Weight: 1.4372 g. **Composition:** 0.9000 Gold .0416 oz. AGW **Obv. Legend:** "Ahmad Shah" **Reverse:** Lion and sun

Date	F	VF	XF	Unc
AH1328 (1910)	60.00	125	200	275
AH1329 (1911)	60.00	100	150	200
AH1330 (1911)	60.00	100	175	225

KM# 1071 5000 DINARS (1/2 Toman) **Weight:** 1.4372 g. **Composition:** 0.9000 Gold .0416 oz. AGW **Obverse:** Bust of Ahmad Shah divides date **Rev. Legend:** "Ahmad Shah"

Date	F	VF	XF	Unc
AH1331 (1912)	50.00	100	150	300
AH1332 (1913)	40.00	60.00	100	150
AH1333 (1914)	25.00	40.00	75.00	125
AH1334 (1915)	25.00	30.00	40.00	70.00
AH1335 (1916)	25.00	30.00	40.00	70.00
AH1336 (1917)	25.00	35.00	50.00	90.00
AH1337 (1918)	25.00	30.00	40.00	70.00
AH1339 (1920)	25.00	35.00	60.00	110
AH1340 (1921)	25.00	35.00	60.00	110
AH1341 (1922)	25.00	30.00	45.00	90.00
AH1342 (1923)	25.00	30.00	45.00	90.00
AH1343 (1924)	25.00	30.00	45.00	90.00

KM# 1072 5000 DINARS (1/2 Toman)
Weight: 1.4372 g. **Composition:** 0.9000 Gold .0416 oz. AGW **Obverse:** KM#1071 **Rev. Legend:** "Sahib al-Zaman"

Date	F	VF	XF	Unc
AH1340 (1921)	100	150	250	400

KM# 1068 TOMAN **Weight:** 2.8744 g. **Composition:** 0.9000 Gold .0832 oz. AGW **Obv. Legend:** "Ahmad Shah", AH1328-1332 **Reverse:** Lion and sun

Date	F	VF	XF	Unc
AH1329 (1911)	200	300	500	750

KM# 1073 TOMAN **Weight:** 2.8744 g. **Composition:** 0.9000 Gold .0832 oz. AGW **Obverse:** KM#1074 **Reverse:** Ahmad Shah Pattern 2 Toman **Note:** The reverse die used was of an unadopted pattern.

Date	F	VF	XF	Unc
AH1332 (1913)	300	600	900	1,500
AH1333 (1914)	300	600	900	1,500

KM# 1074 TOMAN **Weight:** 2.8744 g. **Composition:** 0.9000 Gold .0832 oz. AGW **Obverse:** Bust of Ahmad Shah 1/2 left **Rev. Legend:** "Ahmad Shah"

Date	F	VF	XF	Unc
AH1334 (1915)	45.00	60.00	100	175
AH1335 (1916)	45.00	70.00	100	175
AH1337 (1918)	45.00	60.00	100	175
AH1339 (1920)	45.00	70.00	100	175
AH1340 (1921)	45.00	70.00	100	175
AH1341 (1922)	40.00	50.00	90.00	150
AH1342 (1923)	40.00	50.00	90.00	150
AH1343 (1924)	40.00	50.00	90.00	150

KM# 1075 5 TOMAN **Weight:** 14.3720 g. **Composition:** 0.9000 Gold .4159 oz. AGW **Obv. Legend:** "Ahmad Shah" **Reverse:** Lion and sun **Note:** A number of gold medals of 5 Toman weight were struck between 1297 and 1326. These bear a couplet which clearly indicates that they are medals awarded by the Shah for bravery.

Date	F	VF	XF	Unc
AH1332/1 (1913)	1,100	1,600	2,000	2,700
AH1334/2/1 (1915)	1,100	1,600	2,000	2,700

KM# 1076 10 TOMAN **Weight:** 28.7440 g. **Composition:** 0.9000 Gold .8317 oz. AGW **Obverse:** Bust of Ahmad Shah **Obv. Legend:** "Ahmad Shah"

Date	F	VF	XF	Unc
AH1331 (1912)	2,400	4,350	6,500	8,500
AH1334 (1915) Rare	—	—	—	—
AH1337//1334 (1918)	—	—	6,500	8,500

Note: The date on the AH1334 reverse die was not changed for use as the reverse to the 1337 issue

KM# 1077 10 TOMAN **Weight:** 28.7440 g. **Composition:** 0.9000 Gold .8317 oz. AGW **Obverse:** Bust of Ahmad Shah **Reverse:** Lion and sun

Date	F	VF	XF	Unc
AH1337 (1918)	1,850	3,000	4,500	5,500

KM# 1080 ASHRAFI **Composition:** Gold **Obverse:** Bust of Ahmad Shah **Reverse:** Lion and sun

Date	F	VF	XF	Unc
AH1337 (1918) Rare	—	—	—	—

KM# A1081 2 ASHRAFI **Composition:** Gold **Obverse:** Bust of Ahmad Shah **Reverse:** Lion and sun

Date	F	VF	XF	Unc
AH1337 (1918) Rare	—	—	—	—

KM# 1081 5 ASHRAFI **Composition:** Gold **Obverse:** Bust of Ahmad Shah **Reverse:** Lion and sun

Date	F	VF	XF	Unc
AH1337 (1918) Rare	—	—	—	—

KM# 1082 10 ASHRAFI **Composition:** Gold **Obverse:** Bust of Ahmad Shah **Reverse:** Lion and sun

Date	F	VF	XF	Unc
AH1337 (1918) Rare	—	—	—	—

Reza Shah

AH1344-60/1925-41AD

MILLED COINAGE

KM# 1098 500 DINARS (10 Shahis = 1/2 Kran) **Weight:** 2.3025 g. **Composition:** 0.9000 Silver .0666 oz. ASW **Obv. Legend:** "Reza Shah"

Date	Mintage	F	VF	XF	Unc
SH1305 (1926)	10,000	200	400	800	1,200

KM# 1102 500 DINARS (10 Shahis = 1/2 Kran) **Weight:** 2.3025 g. **Composition:** 0.9000 Silver .0666 oz. ASW **Obverse:** Bust of Reza Shah, "Julius 1304" left, date below

Date	Mintage	F	VF	XF	Unc
SH1306 (1927)	5,000	40.00	60.00	85.00	120
SH1307 (1928)	46,000	4.50	7.50	15.00	30.00
SH1308 (1929)	464,000	4.50	7.50	15.00	30.00

Note: Some of the coins reported in SH1308 were dated 1307

KM# 1099 1000 DINARS (Kran, Qiran) **Weight:** 4.6050 g. **Composition:** 0.9000 Silver .1332 oz. ASW **Obv. Legend:** "Reza Shah"

Date	Mintage	F	VF	XF	Unc
SH1305 (1926)	—	3.00	5.00	10.00	20.00
Note: Mintage included in KM#1095					
SH1306/5 (1927)	3,130,000	5.00	8.00	15.00	25.00
SH1306 (1927)	Inc. above	3.00	5.00	10.00	20.00

KM# 1103 1000 DINARS (Kran, Qiran) **Weight:** 4.6050 g. **Composition:** 0.9000 Silver .1332 oz. ASW **Obverse:** Bust of Reza Shah, date below sprays

Date	Mintage	F	VF	XF	Unc
SH1306 (1927)	—	4.00	8.00	15.00	30.00
Note: Mintage included in KM#1099					
SH1307 (1928)	4,300,000	4.00	6.00	10.00	20.00
SH1308 (1929)	603,000	4.00	6.00	10.00	20.00

KM# 1100 2000 DINARS (2 Kran) **Weight:** 9.2100 g. **Composition:** 0.9000 Silver .2665 oz. ASW **Obv. Legend:** "Reza Shah" **Reverse:** Date below wreath

Date	Mintage	F	VF	XF	Unc
SH1305 (1926)	—	5.00	10.00	20.00	30.00
SH1306 (1927)	9,380,000	4.00	7.00	12.50	25.00

KM# 1104 2000 DINARS (2 Kran) **Weight:** 9.2100 g. **Composition:** 0.9000 Silver .2665 oz. ASW **Obverse:** Bust of Reza Shah, "Julus 1304" at left, date below

Date	Mintage	F	VF	XF	Unc
SH1306 (1927)	—	4.00	6.00	12.50	25.00
Note: Mintage included in KM#1100					
SH1306 (1927) Proof	—	Value: 375			
SH1306 (1927) H	11,714,000	3.00	5.00	10.00	20.00
SH1306 (1927) L	7,500,000	3.00	5.00	8.00	18.00
SH1307 (1928)	11,146,000	3.00	6.00	15.00	25.00
SH1308 (1929)	1,611,000	4.00	10.00	20.00	30.00

KM# 1105 2000 DINARS (2 Kran) **Weight:** 9.2100 g. **Composition:** 0.9000 Silver .2665 oz. ASW **Obverse:** KM#1104 **Reverse:** KM#1057 **Note:** Mule.

Date	F	VF	XF	Unc
SH1306 (1927)	—	—	—	—

Note: Reported, not confirmed

KM#1101 5000 DINARS (5 Kran) **Weight:** 23.0251 g. **Composition:** 0.9000 Silver .6662 oz. ASW **Obv. Legend:** "Reza Shah" **Note:** Cross reference Dav.#293.

Date	Mintage	F	VF	XF	Unc
SH1305 (1926)	—	10.00	15.00	35.00	100
Note: Mintage included in KM#1097					
SH1306 (1927)	3,186,000	10.00	15.00	30.00	85.00

KM#1106 5000 DINARS (5 Kran) **Weight:** 23.0251 g. **Composition:** 0.9000 Silver .6662 oz. ASW **Obverse:** Portrait of Reza Shah, "Julus 1304" at left, date below **Note:** Cross reference Dav.#294. Mint marks located as on 2000 Dinars, KM#1104.

Date	Mintage	F	VF	XF	Unc
SH1306 (1927)	—	9.00	12.50	20.00	37.50
Note: Mintage including in KM#1101					
SH1306 (1927) Proof	—	Value: 400			
SH1306 (1927) H	4,711,000	6.00	10.00	17.50	32.50
SH1306 (1927) L	3,000,000	6.00	7.50	30.00	45.00
SH1307 (1928)	3,928,000	6.00	7.50	15.00	30.00
SH1308 (1929)	584,000	12.50	25.00	50.00	100

KM#1107 5000 DINARS (5 Kran) **Weight:** 23.0251 g. **Composition:** 0.9000 Silver .6662 oz. ASW **Obverse:** KM#1106 **Reverse:** KM#1058 **Note:** Mule.

Date	F	VF	XF	Unc
SH1306 (1927)	—	—	—	—

Note: Reported, not confirmed

MILLED GOLD COINAGE

Modern imitations exist of many types, particularly the small 1/5, 1/2, and 1 Toman coins. These are usually underweight (or rarely overweight), and are sold in the bazaars at a small premium over bullion. They are usually crude and probably not intended to deceive collectors, but some are sold for jewelry and some are dated outside the reign of the ruler whose name or portrait they bear. A few deceptive counterfeits are known of the large 10 Toman pieces.

KM#1108 TOMAN **Weight:** 2.8744 g. **Composition:** Gold .0832 oz. AGW **Subject:** Reza's First New Year Celebration **Obverse:** Reza type legend **Reverse:** Lion and sun

Date	F	VF	XF	Unc
SH1305 (1926)	125	200	300	450

KM#1111 PAHLAVI **Weight:** 1.9180 g. **Composition:** Gold .0555 oz. AGW

Date	Mintage	F	VF	XF	Unc
SH1305 (1926)	5,000	70.00	100	175	275

KM#1114 PAHLAVI **Weight:** 2.8744 g. **Composition:** Gold .0832 oz. AGW

Date	Mintage	F	VF	XF	Unc
SH1306 (1927)	21,000	45.00	65.00	85.00	125
SH1307 (1928)	5,000	60.00	85.00	120	180
SH1308 (1929)	989	80.00	100	160	275

KM# 1112 2 PAHLAVI **Weight:** 3.8360 g. **Composition:** Gold .1110 oz. AGW

Date	Mintage	F	VF	XF	Unc
SH1305 (1926)	1,134	325	500	750	1,000

KM# 1115 2 PAHLAVI **Weight:** 3.8360 g. **Composition:** Gold .1110 oz. AGW

Date	Mintage	F	VF	XF	Unc
SH1306 (1927)	2,494	60.00	90.00	150	250
SH1307 (1928)	7,000	60.00	90.00	150	230
SH1308 (1929)	789	75.00	115	200	285

KM# 1113 5 PAHLAVI **Weight:** 9.5900 g. **Composition:** Gold .2775 oz. AGW

Date	Mintage	F	VF	XF	Unc
SH1305 (1926)	271	500	700	950	2,000

KM# 1116 5 PAHLAVI **Weight:** 9.5900 g. **Composition:** Gold .2775 oz. AGW

Date	Mintage	F	VF	XF	Unc
SH1306 (1927)	909	400	550	750	1,000
SH1307 (1928)	785	375	500	700	900
SH1308 (1929)	121	450	600	900	1,400

REFORM COINAGE

5 Dinars = 1 Shahi; 100 Dinars = 1 Rial; 100 Rials = 1 Pahlavi

The pahlavi was made equal in weight to the British sovereign. It was originally valued at 100 Rials, but has always fluctuated with market prices of gold and silver.

KM# 1128 1/2 RIAL **Weight:** 2.5000 g. **Composition:** 0.8280 Silver .0665 oz. ASW **Rev. Legend:** "Reza Shah" **Note:** All 1/2 Rials dated SH1311-1315 are recut dies, usually from SH1310.

Date	Mintage	F	VF	XF	Unc
SH1310 (1931)	2,000,000	1.00	3.00	6.00	15.00
SH1311 (1932)	—	30.00	40.00	50.00	90.00
SH1312 (1933)	—	1.00	3.00	5.00	14.00
SH1313 (1934)	1,945,000	1.50	3.00	6.00	15.00
SH1314 (1935)	100,000	3.00	9.00	20.00	40.00
SH1315 (1936)	800,000	2.00	4.00	9.00	20.00

KM# 1130 2 RIALS **Weight:** 10.0000 g. **Composition:** 0.8280 Silver .2662 oz. ASW **Obv. Legend:** "Reza Shah" **Note:** All coins dated SH1311-13 cut or punched over SH1310.

Date	Mintage	F	VF	XF	Unc
SH1310 (1931)	6,145,000	2.00	5.00	10.00	25.00
SH1311 (1932)	8,838,000	2.00	5.00	10.00	22.00
SH1312 (1933)	19,175,000	2.00	5.00	10.00	20.00
SH1313 (1934)	4,015,000	2.00	7.00	15.00	32.00

KM# 1131 5 RIALS **Weight:** 25.0000 g. **Composition:** 0.8280 Silver .6655 oz. ASW **Obv. Legend:** "Reza Shah" **Note:** Most coins dated SH1311-13 are cut or punched over SH1310.

Date	Mintage	F	VF	XF	Unc
SH1310 (1931)	5,471,000	7.50	8.00	12.00	20.00
SH1311 (1932)	4,527,000	7.50	8.00	12.00	20.00
SH1312/0 (1933)	5,502,000	7.50	10.00	15.00	25.00
SH1312 (1933)	Inc. above	7.50	8.00	12.00	20.00
SH1313 (1934)	1,208,000	7.50	10.00	15.00	25.00

KM# 1132 1/2 PAHLAVI **Weight:** 4.0680 g. **Composition:** 0.9000 Gold .1177 oz. AGW **Obverse:** Bust of Reza Shah

Date	Mintage	F	VF	XF	Unc
SH1310 (1931)	696	75.00	150	275	375
SH1311 (1932)	286	75.00	175	300	400
SH1312 (1933)	892	75.00	150	250	350
SH1313 (1934)	531	75.00	175	300	400
SH1314 (1935)	—	75.00	175	300	400
SH1315 (1936)	1,042	75.00	175	275	375

KM# 1133 PAHLAVI **Weight:** 8.1360 g. **Composition:** 0.9000 Gold .2354 oz. AGW **Obverse:** Bust of Reza Shah

Date	Mintage	F	VF	XF	Unc
SH1310 (1931)	304	300	500	850	1,200

Muhammad Reza Pahlavi Shah

SH1320-1358/1941-1979AD

REFORM COINAGE

5 Dinars = 1 Shahi; 100 Dinars = 1 Rial; 100 Rials = 1 Pahlavi

The pahlavi was made equal in weight to the British sovereign. It was originally valued at 100 Rials, but has always fluctuated with market prices of gold and silver

KM# 1143 RIAL (20 Shahi) **Weight:** 1.6000 g. **Composition:** 0.6000 Silver .0308 oz. ASW **Obv. Legend:** "Muhammad Reza Shah Pahlavi"

Date	Mintage	F	VF	XF	Unc
SH1322 (1943)	—	0.50	1.00	2.00	5.00
SH1323/3 (1944)	—	—	—	—	—
SH1323 (1944)	—	0.50	1.00	2.00	5.00
SH1324/3 (1945)	—	—	—	—	—
SH1324 (1945)	—	0.50	1.00	2.00	5.00
SH1424 (1945) Error for 1324	—	—	—	—	—
SH1325 (1946)	—	0.75	1.50	2.00	5.00
SH1326 (1947)	567,000	35.00	40.00	50.00	100
SH1327 (1948)	5,795,000	1.50	2.50	4.00	8.00
SH1328 (1949)	1,565,000	1.50	2.50	4.00	8.00
SH1329 (1950)	144,000	35.00	40.00	50.00	100
SH1330 (1951)	—	2.00	3.00	5.00	15.00

KM#1157 RIAL (20 Shahi) **Composition:** Copper-Nickel **Obv. Legend:** "Muhammad Reza Shah Pahlavi"

Date	Mintage	F	VF	XF	Unc
SH(13)31 (1952)	4,735,000	1.00	2.00	5.00	15.00
SH(13)32 (1953)	3	4.00	8.00	15.00	30.00
Note: Much rarer than mintage would indicate					
SH(13)33 (1954)	16,405,000	0.60	1.00	2.00	5.00
SH(13)34 (1955)	8,980,000	0.60	1.00	2.00	5.00
SH(13)35 (1956)	8,910,000	0.50	1.00	1.00	5.00
SH(13)36 (1957)	4,450,000	1.00	2.00	8.00	20.00

KM# 1171 RIAL (20 Shahi) **Weight:** 2.0000 g. **Composition:** Copper-Nickel **Obv. Legend:** "Muhammad Reza Pahlavi"

Date	Mintage	F	VF	XF	Unc
SH1337 (1958)	8,005,000	0.50	1.00	2.00	5.00

KM# 1171a RIAL (20 Shahi) **Weight:** 1.7500 g. **Composition:** Copper-Nickel **Note:** Date varieties exist.

Date	Mintage	F	VF	XF	Unc
SH1338 (1959)	14,940,000	0.10	0.20	0.40	3.00
SH1339 (1960)	8,400,000	0.25	0.50	1.00	4.00
SH1340 (1961)	8,490,000	0.25	0.50	1.00	4.00
SH1341 (1962)	8,680,000	0.25	0.50	1.00	4.00
SH1342 (1963)	13,332,000	0.10	0.20	0.40	3.00
SH1343 (1964)	14,746,000	0.10	0.15	0.25	2.00
SH1344 (1965)	12,050,000	0.10	0.20	0.50	3.50
SH1345 (1966)	13,786,000	0.10	0.15	0.20	2.00
SH1346 (1967)	155,321,000	0.10	0.15	0.20	2.00
SH1347 (1968)	20,664,000	0.10	0.15	0.25	3.00
SH1348 (1969)	22,960,000	0.10	0.15	0.20	2.00
SH1349 (1970)	19,918,000	0.10	0.15	0.20	2.00
SH1350 (1971)	24,248,000	0.10	0.20	0.65	2.00
SH1351/0 (1972)	21,825,000	0.10	0.25	0.40	3.00
SH1351 (1972)	Inc. above	0.10	0.15	0.20	2.00
SH1352 (1973)	31,449,000	0.10	0.15	0.20	2.00
SH1353 (1974) Large date	33,700,000	0.10	0.20	0.25	3.00
SH1353 (1974) Small date	Inc. above	0.10	0.15	0.20	2.00
SH1354 (1975)	—	0.10	0.15	0.20	2.00
MS2536 (1977)	—	0.10	0.15	0.25	3.00

KM# 1183 RIAL (20 Shahi) Composition: Copper-Nickel **Series:** F.A.O **Obv. Legend:** "Muhammad Reza Shah Pahlavi"

Date	Mintage	F	VF	XF	Unc
SH1350 (1971)	2,770,000	0.10	0.15	0.25	1.00
SH1351 (1972)	8,605,000	0.10	0.15	0.25	1.00
SH1353 (1974)	2,000,000	0.50	0.80	1.25	2.00
SH1354 (1975)	1,000,000	0.50	0.80	1.25	2.00

KM# 1205 RIAL (20 Shahi) Composition: Copper-Nickel **Subject:** 50th Anniversary of Pahlavi Rule

Date	Mintage	F	VF	XF	Unc
MS2535 (1976)	61,945,000	0.50	1.00	1.50	2.50

KM# 1172 RIAL (20 Shahi) Composition: Copper-Nickel **Obverse:** "Aryamehr" added to legend **Obv. Legend:** "Muhammad Reza Shah Pahlavi"

Date	Mintage	F	VF	XF	Unc
MS2536 (1977)	71,150,000	0.10	0.15	0.25	2.00
MS2537 (1978)	—	0.10	0.15	0.25	2.00
MS2537/6537 (1978) Error 2/6	—	—	—	—	6.00
SH1357/6 (1978)	—	0.25	0.50	0.75	5.00
SH1357 (1978)	—	0.25	0.50	0.75	3.00

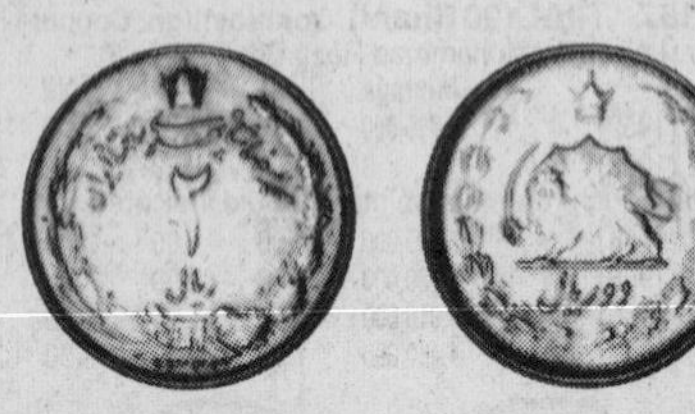

KM# 1144 2 RIALS Weight: 3.2000 g. **Composition:** 0.6000 Silver .0617 oz. ASW **Obv. Legend:** "Muhammad Reza Shah Pahlavi"

Date	Mintage	F	VF	XF	Unc
SH1322 (1943)	—	0.50	1.00	3.50	7.00
SH1323/2 (1944)	—	10.00	20.00	30.00	50.00
SH1323 (1944)	—	0.50	1.00	3.00	6.00
SH1324 (1945)	—	0.50	1.00	3.00	6.00
SH1325 (1946)	—	1.25	3.00	5.00	11.00
SH1326 (1947)	187,000	50.00	60.00	75.00	125
SH1327 (1948)	3,140,000	1.50	3.00	5.00	12.50
SH1328 (1949)	1,198,000	2.50	4.50	7.50	16.00
SH1329 (1950)	—	65.00	80.00	100	150
SH1330 (1951)	—	5.00	8.00	12.50	30.00

KM# 1158 2 RIALS Composition: Copper-Nickel **Obv. Legend:** "Muhammad Reza Shah Pahlavi"

Date	Mintage	F	VF	XF	Unc
SH1331 (1952)	5,335,000	1.25	3.00	7.00	20.00
SH1332 (1953)	6,870,000	1.00	2.00	4.00	8.00
SH1333 (1954)	13,668,000	0.15	0.75	2.00	7.00
SH1334 (1955)	7,185,000	0.15	0.75	2.00	7.00
SH1335 (1956)	2,400,000	0.15	0.75	3.00	12.50
SH1336 (1957)	325,000	15.00	25.00	40.00	75.00

KM# 1173 2 RIALS Composition: Copper-Nickel **Obv. Legend:** "Muhammad Reza Pahlavi"

Date	Mintage	F	VF	XF	Unc
SH1338 (1959)	17,610,000	0.10	0.25	0.75	4.00
SH1339 (1960)	8,575,000	0.10	0.25	0.50	4.00
SH1340 (1961)	5,668,000	0.10	0.25	0.50	4.00
SH1341 (1962)	5,820,000	0.10	0.25	0.75	4.00
SH1342 (1963)	8,570,000	0.10	0.25	0.50	4.00
SH1343 (1964)	11,250,000	0.10	0.25	0.50	3.00
SH1344 (1965)	5,155,000	0.10	0.25	0.50	4.00
SH1345 (1966)	2,267,000	0.15	0.30	1.00	5.00
SH1346 (1967)	92,792,000	—	0.10	0.20	4.00
SH1347 (1968)	10,300,000	—	0.10	1.00	6.00
SH1348 (1969)	9,319,000	0.20	0.45	1.10	4.00
SH1349 (1970)	9,895,000	0.20	0.40	1.00	4.00
SH1350 (1971)	9,545,000	0.15	0.35	1.00	4.00
SH1351 (1972)	13,305,000	0.15	0.35	1.00	3.00
SH1352 (1973)	15,910,000	—	0.10	0.20	3.00
SH1353 (1974)	28,477,000	—	0.10	0.20	3.00
SH1354/3 (1975)	—	0.20	0.40	1.00	5.00
SH1354 (1975)	41,700,000	—	0.10	0.20	3.00
MS2536 (1977)	54,725,000	—	0.10	0.20	3.00

KM# 1206 2 RIALS Composition: Copper-Nickel **Subject:** 50th Anniversary of Pahlavi

Date	Mintage	F	VF	XF	Unc
MS2535 (1976)	59,568,000	0.25	0.50	1.00	2.50

KM# 1174 2 RIALS Composition: Copper-Nickel **Obverse:** "Aryamehr" added to legend **Obv. Legend:** "Muhammad Reza Pahlavi"

Date	F	VF	XF	Unc
MS2536 (1977)	0.25	0.50	1.00	4.00
MS2537 (1978)	0.25	0.50	1.00	4.00
SH1357 (1978)	0.25	0.50	1.00	4.00

KM# 1145 5 RIALS Weight: 8.0000 g. **Composition:** 0.6000 Silver .1543 oz. ASW **Obv. Legend:** "Muhammad Reza Shah Pahlavi"

Date	Mintage	F	VF	XF	Unc
SH1322 (1943)	—	1.00	2.00	3.50	6.00
SH1323 (1944)	—	1.00	2.50	3.50	6.00
SH1324 (1945)	—	1.00	2.00	4.50	10.00
SH1325 (1946)	—	1.00	2.00	3.50	6.00
SH1326 (1947)	61,000	60.00	70.00	85.00	140
SH1327 (1948)	836,000	2.00	5.00	7.50	20.00
SH1328 (1949)	282,000	2.50	10.00	20.00	40.00
SH1329 (1950)	—	75.00	85.00	100	175

KM# 1159 5 RIALS Composition: Copper-Nickel **Obv. Legend:** "Muhammad Reza Shah Pahlavi"

Date	Mintage	F	VF	XF	Unc
SH1331 (1952)	3,660,000	0.50	2.00	5.00	20.00
SH1332 (1953)	16,350,000	0.25	1.00	3.00	10.00
SH1333 (1954)	6,582,000	0.25	1.00	3.00	10.00
SH1334 (1955)	300,000	10.00	15.00	25.00	50.00
SH1336 (1957)	1,410,000	0.50	2.00	5.00	20.00

KM# 1175 5 RIALS Weight: 7.0000 g. **Composition:** Copper-Nickel **Obv. Legend:** "Muhammad Reza Shah Pahlavi"

Date	Mintage	F	VF	XF	Unc
SH1337 (1958)	3,660,000	1.00	2.50	7.50	22.50
SH1338 (1959)	10,467,000	0.50	2.50	8.00	20.00

KM# 1175a 5 RIALS Weight: 5.0000 g. **Composition:** Copper-Nickel

Date	Mintage	F	VF	XF	Unc
SH1338 (1959)	Inc. above	0.25	0.40	1.50	5.00
SH1339 (1960)	3,980,000	0.25	0.40	1.50	5.00
SH1340 (1961)	3,814,000	0.25	0.40	1.50	5.00
SH1341 (1962)	2,332,000	0.25	0.40	1.50	5.00
SH1342 (1963)	7,838,000	0.25	0.40	1.00	4.00
SH1343 (1964)	9,484,000	0.25	0.40	1.00	4.00
SH1344 (1965)	3,468,000	0.25	0.40	1.00	4.00
SH1345 (1966)	6,092,000	0.25	0.40	1.00	4.00
SH1346/36 (1967)	74,781,000	0.25	0.40	1.50	5.00
SH1346 (1967)	Inc. above	0.25	0.40	1.00	4.00

KM# 1176 5 RIALS Weight: 4.6000 g. **Composition:** Copper-Nickel **Obverse:** "Aryamehr" added to legend

Date	Mintage	F	VF	XF	Unc
SH1347 (1968)	7,745,000	0.50	0.85	1.50	4.00
SH1348 (1969)	9,193,000	0.50	0.75	1.25	4.00
SH1349 (1970)	7,300,000	0.50	0.75	1.25	4.00
SH1350 (1971)	10,160,000	0.35	0.75	1.25	3.50
SH1351 (1972)	20,582,000	0.25	0.75	1.25	3.50
SH1352 (1973)	23,590,000	0.25	0.75	1.25	3.50
SH1353 (1974)	28,367,000	0.25	0.75	1.25	3.50
SH1353 (1974) Large date	Inc. above	0.25	0.75	1.25	3.50
SH1354 (1975)	27,294,000	0.25	0.75	1.25	3.50
MS2536 (1977)	47,906,000	0.20	0.50	1.25	3.50
MS2537 (1978)	—	0.35	0.65	1.25	3.50
SH1357 (1978)	—	0.50	0.75	1.25	3.50

KM# 1207 5 RIALS Composition: Copper-Nickel **Subject:** 50th Anniversary of Pahlavi Rule

Date	Mintage	F	VF	XF	Unc
MS2535 (1976)	37,144,000	0.25	0.50	1.25	3.50

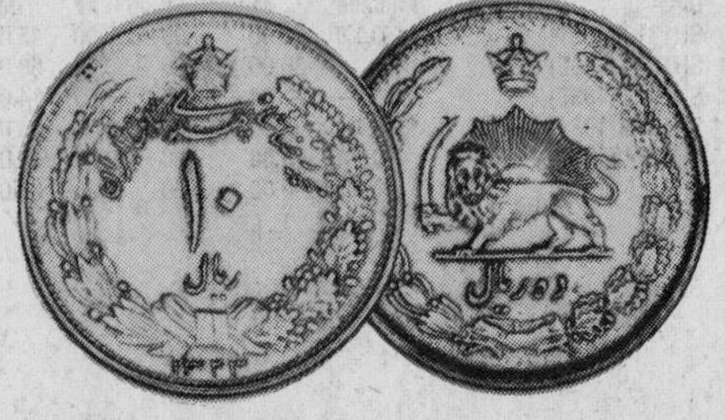

KM# 1146 10 RIALS Weight: 16.0000 g. **Composition:** 0.6000 Silver .3086 oz. ASW **Obv. Legend:** "Muhammad Reza Shah Pahlavi" **Note:** Counterfeits are known dated SH1322.

Date	F	VF	XF	Unc
SH1323/2 (1944)	2.00	3.50	7.00	20.00
SH1323 (1944)	2.00	3.00	5.00	12.00
SH1324 (1945)	2.00	3.00	5.00	15.00
SH1325 (1946)	2.00	3.00	6.00	17.50
SH1326 (1947)	100	125	150	225

KM# 1177 10 RIALS **Weight:** 12.0000 g. **Composition:** Copper-Nickel **Obv. Legend:** "Muhammad Reza Shah Pahlavi"

Date	Mintage	F	VF	XF	Unc
SH1333 (1954)	—	—	—	—	—
SH1335 (1956)	6,225,000	0.50	2.00	4.00	9.00
SH1336 (1957)	4,415,000	1.00	3.00	7.50	15.00
SH1337 (1958)	715,000	3.00	6.00	9.00	20.00
SH1338 (1959)	1,210,000	0.50	2.00	6.00	14.00
SH1339 (1960)	2,775,000	0.50	2.00	4.00	9.00
SH1340 (1961)	3,660,000	0.50	2.00	4.00	9.00
SH1341 (1962)	744,000	20.00	35.00	50.00	75.00
SH1343 (1963)	6,874,000	0.50	2.00	4.00	9.00

KM# 1177a 10 RIALS **Weight:** 9.0000 g. **Composition:** Copper-Nickel **Note:** Thin flan.

Date	Mintage	F	VF	XF	Unc
SH1341 (1962)	—	0.35	1.00	2.50	5.00
Note: Mintage included in KM#1177					
SH1342 (1963)	3,763,000	0.35	1.00	2.00	4.00
SH1343 (1964)	—	0.35	0.75	1.50	2.50
Note: Mintage included in KM#1177					
SH1344 (1965)	1,627,000	0.35	0.75	1.50	2.50

KM# 1178 10 RIALS **Composition:** Copper-Nickel **Obv. Legend:** "Muhammad Reza Shah Pahlavi" **Reverse:** Value in words

Date	Mintage	F	VF	XF	Unc
SH1345 (1966)	1,699,000	0.50	0.60	2.00	5.00
SH1346 (1967)	38,897,000	0.40	0.50	1.00	4.00
SH1347 (1968)	8,220,000	0.40	0.65	1.50	8.00
SH1348 (1969)	7,156,000	0.40	0.50	1.00	4.00
SH1349 (1970)	7,397,000	0.40	0.50	1.00	4.00
SH1350 (1971)	8,972,000	0.40	0.50	1.00	4.00
SH1351 (1972)	9,912,000	0.40	0.50	1.00	4.00
SH1352 (1973)	28,776,000	0.50	2.00	4.50	7.00

KM# 1182 10 RIALS **Composition:** Copper-Nickel **Series:** F.A.O

Date	Mintage	F	VF	XF	Unc
SH1348 (1969)	150,000	0.25	0.50	1.00	3.50

KM# 1179 10 RIALS **Composition:** Copper-Nickel **Reverse:** Value in numerals

Date	Mintage	F	VF	XF	Unc
SH1352 (1973)	Inc. above	0.30	0.60	1.00	4.00
SH1353 (1974)	22,234,000	0.30	0.60	1.00	3.00
SH1354 (1975)	23,482,000	0.30	0.60	1.00	4.00

Date	Mintage	F	VF	XF	Unc
MS2536 (1977)	24,324,000	0.30	0.60	1.00	3.00
MS2537 (1978)	—	0.30	0.60	1.00	4.00
SH1357 (1978)	—	0.30	1.00	1.50	4.00

KM# 1208 10 RIALS **Composition:** Copper-Nickel **Subject:** 50th Anniversary of Pahlavi Rule

Date	Mintage	F	VF	XF	Unc
MS2535 (1976)	29,859,000	0.25	0.50	0.75	3.00

KM# 1180 20 RIALS **Composition:** Copper-Nickel **Obv. Legend:** "Muhammad Reza Shah Pahlavi" **Reverse:** Value in words

Date	Mintage	F	VF	XF	Unc
SH1350 (1971)	2,349,000	0.25	1.00	3.00	6.00
SH1351 (1972)	11,416,000	0.25	0.85	1.00	3.00
SH1352 (1973)	7,172,000	0.25	0.85	1.25	5.00

KM# 1181 20 RIALS **Composition:** Copper-Nickel **Reverse:** Value in numerals **Note:** Varieties exist in date size.

Date	Mintage	F	VF	XF	Unc
SH1352 (1973)	—	0.25	0.75	1.00	3.50
Note: Mintage included in KM#1180					
SH1353 (1974)	12,601,000	0.25	0.75	1.00	3.75
SH1354 (1975)	16,246,000	0.25	0.75	1.00	4.00
MS2536 (1977)	—	0.40	0.75	1.00	4.00
MS2537 (1978)	—	0.50	0.75	1.00	4.00
SH1357 (1978)	—	0.50	1.00	1.50	5.00

KM# 1196 20 RIALS **Composition:** Copper-Nickel **Subject:** 7th Asian Games

Date	F	VF	XF	Unc
SH1353 (1974)	0.75	1.50	2.50	4.50

KM# 1209 20 RIALS **Composition:** Copper-Nickel **Subject:** 50th Anniversary of Pahlavi Rule

Date	F	VF	XF	Unc
MS2535 (1976)	0.50	1.00	2.00	4.50

KM# 1211 20 RIALS **Composition:** Copper-Nickel **Series:** F.A.O

Date	Mintage	F	VF	XF	Unc
MS2535 (1976)	10,000,000	0.50	1.00	2.00	4.50
MS2536 (1977)	23,370,000	0.50	1.00	3.00	5.50

KM# 1214 20 RIALS **Composition:** Copper-Nickel **Subject:** 50th Anniversary of Bank Melli

Date	F	VF	XF	Unc
SH1357 (1978)	4.00	5.00	7.00	13.50

KM# 1215 20 RIALS **Composition:** Copper-Nickel **Series:** F.A.O

Date	Mintage	F	VF	XF	Unc
SH1357 (1978)	5,000,000	0.50	0.75	2.00	6.00

KM# 1184 25 RIALS **Weight:** 7.5000 g. **Composition:** 0.9990 Silver .2409 oz. ASW **Subject:** 2500th Anniversary of Persian Empire **Reverse:** Countermark "1 AR" and 1000 **Note:** Column head from Artaxerxes' Palace in Susa.

Date	Mintage	F	VF	XF	Unc
SH1350 (1971) Proof	18,000	Value: 10.00			

KM# 1185 50 RIALS **Weight:** 15.0000 g. **Composition:** 0.9990 Silver .4818 oz. ASW **Subject:** 2500th Anniversary of Persian Empire **Reverse:** Countermark "1 AR" and 1000 **Note:** Walking griffin with ram antlers

Date	Mintage	F	VF	XF	Unc
SH1350 (1971) Proof	18,000	Value: 15.00			

KM# 1186 75 RIALS **Weight:** 22.5000 g. **Composition:** 0.9990 Silver .7227 oz. ASW **Subject:** 2500th Anniversary of Persian Empire **Obverse:** Similar to 200 Rials, KM#1188 **Reverse:** Countermark with "1 AR" and 1000 **Note:** Stone of Cyrus II

Date	Mintage	F	VF	XF	Unc
SH1350 (1971) Proof	18,000	Value: 16.50			

KM# 1187.1 100 RIALS **Weight:** 30.0000 g. **Composition:** 0.9990 Silver .9636 oz. ASW **Subject:** 2500th Anniversary of Persian Empire **Obverse:** Similar to 200 Rials, KM#1188 **Reverse:** Polished field below palace of Darius I and pillars of reception hall in Persepolis; countermark with "1 AR" and 1000

Date	Mintage	F	VF	XF	Unc
SH1350 (1971) Proof	18,000	Value: 25.00			

KM# 1187.2 100 RIALS **Weight:** 30.0000 g. **Composition:** 0.9990 Silver .9636 oz. ASW **Reverse:** Polished field below palace of Darius I and pillars of reception hall in Persepolis; countermark with "1 AR" and 1000

Date	Mintage	F	VF	XF	Unc
SH1350 (1971) Proof	Inc. above	Value: 25.00			

KM# 1188 200 RIALS **Weight:** 60.0000 g. **Composition:** 0.9990 Silver 1.9273 oz. ASW **Subject:** 2500th Anniversary of Persian Empire **Obverse:** Conjoined busts of royal couple left **Reverse:** Countermark with "1 AR" and 1000

Date	Mintage	F	VF	XF	Unc
SH1350 (1971) Proof	23,000	Value: 42.50			

KM# 1189 500 RIALS **Weight:** 6.5100 g. **Composition:** 0.9000 Gold .1883 oz. AGW **Subject:** 2500th Anniversary of Persian Empire **Reverse:** Walking griffin with ram antlers

Date	Mintage	F	VF	XF	Unc
SH1350 (1971) Proof	11,000	Value: 110			

KM# 1190 750 RIALS **Weight:** 9.7700 g. **Composition:** 0.9000 Gold .2827 oz. AGW **Subject:** 2500th Anniversary of Persian Empire **Reverse:** Stone of Cyrus II

Date	Mintage	F	VF	XF	Unc
SH1350 (1971) Proof	10,000	Value: 135			

KM# 1191.1 1000 RIALS **Weight:** 13.0300 g. **Composition:** 0.9000 Gold .3770 oz. AGW **Subject:** 2500th Anniversary of Persian Empire **Reverse:** Polished fields below Palace of Darius I and pillars of reception hall in Persepolis

Date	Mintage	F	VF	XF	Unc
SH1350 (1971) Proof	10,000	Value: 200			

KM# 1191.2 1000 RIALS **Weight:** 13.0300 g. **Composition:** 0.9000 Gold .3770 oz. AGW **Subject:** 2500th Anniversary of Persian Empire **Reverse:** Polished fields below Palace of Darius I and pillars of reception hall in Persepolis

Date	Mintage	F	VF	XF	Unc
SH1350 (1971) Proof	Inc. above	Value: 200			

KM# 1192 2000 RIALS **Weight:** 26.0600 g. **Composition:** 0.9000 Gold .7541 oz. AGW **Subject:** 2500th Anniversary of Persian Empire **Obverse:** Conjoined busts of Imperial couple left

Date	Mintage	F	VF	XF	Unc
SH1350 (1971) Proof	9,805	Value: 400			

KM# 1160 1/4 PAHLAVI **Weight:** 2.0340 g. **Composition:** 0.9000 Gold .0589 oz. AGW **Obverse:** Bust of Muhammad Reza Pahlavi

Date	Mintage	F	VF	XF	Unc
SH1332 (1953)	41,000	BV	35.00	45.00	60.00
SH1333 (1954)	7,000	35.00	45.00	100	150
SH1334 (1955)	—	BV	35.00	60.00	100
SH1335 (1956)	41,000	BV	35.00	45.00	60.00
SH1336 (1957)	—	30.00	50.00	100	175

KM# 1160a 1/4 PAHLAVI **Weight:** 2.0340 g. **Composition:** 0.9000 Gold .0589 oz. AGW **Note:** Thinner and broader.

Date	Mintage	F	VF	XF	Unc
SH1336 (1957)	7,000	25.00	35.00	70.00	125
SH1337 (1958)	33,000	—	BV	22.00	30.00
SH1338 (1959)	136,000	—	BV	22.00	30.00
SH1339 (1960)	156,000	—	BV	22.00	30.00
SH1340 (1961)	60,000	—	BV	22.00	30.00
SH1342 (1963)	80,000	—	BV	22.00	30.00
SH1343 (1964)	40,000	—	—	—	—
Note: Reported, not confirmed					
SH1344 (1965)	30,000	—	30.00	35.00	55.00
SH1345 (1966)	40,000	—	BV	22.00	30.00
SH1346 (1967)	30,000	—	BV	22.00	30.00
SH1347 (1968)	60,000	—	BV	22.00	30.00
SH1348 (1969)	60,000	—	BV	22.00	30.00
SH1349 (1970)	80,000	—	BV	22.00	30.00
SH1350 (1971)	80,000	—	BV	22.00	30.00

Date	Mintage	F	VF	XF	Unc
SH1351 (1972)	103,000	—	BV	22.00	30.00
SH1353 (1974)	—	—	BV	22.00	30.00

KM# 1198 1/4 PAHLAVI **Weight:** 2.0340 g. **Composition:** 0.9000 Gold .0589 oz. AGW **Obverse:** "Aryamehr" added to legend

Date	Mintage	F	VF	XF	Unc
SH1354 (1975)	106,000	—	BV	22.00	30.00
SH1355 (1976)	186,000	—	BV	22.00	30.00
MS2536 (1977)	—	—	BV	22.00	30.00
MS2537 (1978)	—	—	BV	22.00	30.00
SH1358 (1979)	—	35.00	75.00	125	225

KM# 1147 1/2 PAHLAVI **Weight:** 4.0680 g. **Composition:** 0.9000 Gold .1177 oz. AGW **Obv. Legend:** "Muhammad Reza Shah"

Date	Mintage	F	VF	XF	Unc
SH1320 (1941)	—	150	350	750	1,250
SH1321 (1942)	—	BV	100	200	300
SH1322 (1943)	—	—	BV	40.00	50.00
SH1323 (1944)	76,000	—	BV	40.00	50.00
SH1324 (1945)	—	—	—	—	—
Note: Reported, not confirmed					

KM# 1149 1/2 PAHLAVI **Weight:** 4.0680 g. **Composition:** 0.9000 Gold .1177 oz. AGW **Obverse:** High relief head of Muhammad Reza Pahlavi

Date	Mintage	F	VF	XF	Unc
SH1324 (1945)	—	BV	40.00	50.00	60.00
SH1325 (1946)	—	BV	40.00	50.00	60.00
SH1326 (1947)	36,000	BV	50.00	65.00	110
SH1327 (1948)	36,000	BV	50.00	65.00	110
SH1328 (1949)	—	BV	60.00	75.00	130
SH1329 (1950)	75	—	250	400	750
SH1330 (1951)	98,000	—	—	—	1,350

KM# 1161 1/2 PAHLAVI **Weight:** 4.0680 g. **Composition:** 0.9000 Gold .1177 oz. AGW **Obverse:** Low relief head

Date	Mintage	F	VF	XF	Unc
SH1330 (1951)	—	BV	40.00	50.00	55.00
Note: Mintage included in KM#1149					
SH1332 (1952)	—	—	300	450	750
SH1333 (1954)	—	BV	55.00	70.00	100
SH1334 (1955)	—	—	55.00	70.00	100
SH1335 (1956)	—	—	BV	45.00	55.00
SH1336 (1957)	132,000	—	BV	45.00	55.00
SH1337 (1958)	102,000	—	BV	40.00	50.00
SH1338 (1959)	140,000	—	BV	40.00	50.00
SH1339 (1960)	142,000	—	BV	40.00	50.00
SH1340 (1961)	439,000	—	BV	40.00	50.00
SH1342 (1963)	40,000	—	BV	40.00	50.00
SH1343 (1964)	—	—	—	—	—
Note: Reported, not confirmed					
SH1344 (1965)	30,000	BV	65.00	75.00	110
SH1345 (1966)	40,000	—	BV	45.00	50.00
SH1346 (1967)	40,000	—	BV	45.00	50.00
SH1347 (1968)	50,000	—	BV	45.00	50.00
SH1348 (1969)	40,000	—	BV	45.00	50.00
SH1349 (1970)	80,000	—	BV	45.00	50.00
SH1350 (1971)	80,000	—	BV	45.00	50.00
SH1351 (1972)	103,000	—	BV	45.00	50.00
SH1352 (1973)	67,000	—	BV	45.00	50.00
SH1353 (1974)	—	—	BV	45.00	50.00

KM# 1199 1/2 PAHLAVI **Weight:** 4.0680 g. **Composition:** 0.9000 Gold .1177 oz. AGW **Obverse:** "Aryamehr" added to legend

Date	Mintage	F	VF	XF	Unc
SH1354 (1975)	37,000	—	BV	45.00	50.00
SH1355 (1976)	153,000	—	BV	45.00	50.00
MS2536 (1977)	—	—	BV	45.00	50.00
MS2537 (1978)	—	—	BV	45.00	50.00
SH1358 (1979)	—	100	150	250	500

KM# 1148 PAHLAVI **Weight:** 8.1360 g. **Composition:** 0.9000 Gold .2354 oz. AGW **Obv. Legend:** "Muhammad Reza Shah"

Date	Mintage	F	VF	XF	Unc
SH1320 (1941)	—	250	600	1,250	1,750
Note: Possibly a pattern					
SH1321 (1942)	—	—	—	1,750	2,500
Note: Possibly a pattern					
SH1322 (1943)	—	—	BV	80.00	110
SH1323 (1944)	311,000	—	BV	80.00	110
SH1324 (1945)	—	—	BV	80.00	110

KM# 1150 PAHLAVI **Weight:** 8.1360 g. **Composition:** 0.9000 Gold .2354 oz. AGW **Obverse:** High relief head of Muhammad Reza Pahlavi

Date	Mintage	F	VF	XF	Unc
SH1324 (1945)	—	BV	90.00	100	120
SH1325 (1946)	—	BV	90.00	100	120
SH1326 (1947)	151,000	BV	90.00	100	120
SH1327 (1948)	20,000	BV	90.00	100	120
SH1328 (1949)	4,000	BV	125	185	260
SH1329 (1950)	4,000	BV	125	185	260
SH1330 (1951)	48,000	BV	125	185	260

KM# 1162 PAHLAVI **Weight:** 8.1360 g. **Composition:** 0.9000 Gold .2354 oz. AGW **Obverse:** Low relief head

Date	Mintage	F	VF	XF	Unc
SH1330 (1951)	—	—	BV	80.00	110
SH1331 (1952)	—	—	500	800	1,200
SH1332 (1953)	—	—	500	800	1,200
SH1333 (1954)	—	BV	100	120	160
SH1334 (1955)	—	BV	100	120	160
SH1335 (1956)	—	—	BV	80.00	110
SH1336 (1957)	453,000	—	BV	80.00	110
SH1337 (1958)	665,000	—	BV	80.00	110
SH1338 (1959)	776,000	—	BV	80.00	110
SH1339 (1960)	847,000	—	BV	80.00	110
SH1340 (1961)	528,000	—	BV	80.00	110
SH1342 (1963)	20,000	—	BV	80.00	110
SH1343 (1964)	10,000	—	—	—	—
Note: Reported, not confirmed					
SH1344 (1965)	—	BV	110	110	160
SH1345 (1966)	20,000	—	BV	80.00	110
SH1346 (1967)	30,000	—	BV	80.00	110
SH1347 (1968)	40,000	—	BV	80.00	110
SH1348 (1969)	70,000	—	BV	80.00	110
SH1349 (1970)	70,000	—	BV	80.00	110
SH1350 (1971)	60,000	—	BV	80.00	110
SH1351 (1972)	100,000	—	BV	80.00	110
SH1352 (1973)	320,000	—	BV	80.00	110
SH1353 (1974)	—	—	BV	80.00	110

KM# 1200 PAHLAVI **Weight:** 8.1360 g. **Composition:** 0.9000 Gold .2354 oz. AGW **Obverse:** "Aryamehr" added to legend

Date	Mintage	F	VF	XF	Unc
SH1354 (1975)	21,000	—	BV	80.00	110
SH1355 (1976)	203,000	—	BV	80.00	110
MS2536 (1977)	—	—	BV	80.00	110
MS2537 (1978)	—	—	BV	80.00	110
SH1358 (1979)	—	125	150	250	500

KM# A1163 2-1/2 PAHLAVI **Weight:** 20.3400 g. **Composition:** 0.9000 Gold .5885 oz. AGW **Obverse:** Bust of Mohammad Reza Pahlavi **Reverse:** Lion

Date	F	VF	XF	Unc
SH1338 (1959)	—	—	—	—

KM# 1163 2-1/2 PAHLAVI **Weight:** 20.3400 g. **Composition:** 0.9000 Gold .5885 oz. AGW **Reverse:** Three-line inscription, date below

Date	Mintage	F	VF	XF	Unc
SH1339 (1960)	1,682	BV	200	225	255
SH1340 (1961)	2,788	BV	200	225	255
SH1342 (1963)	30	—	—	—	—
SH1347 (1968)	2,000	—	—	—	—
Note: Reported, not confirmed					
SH1348 (1969)	3,000	BV	200	225	255
SH1349 (1970)	3,000	—	—	—	—
Note: Reported, not confirmed					
SH1350 (1971)	2,000	BV	200	225	255
SH1351 (1972)	2,500	BV	200	225	255
SH1352 (1973)	3,000	BV	200	225	255
SH1353 (1974)	—	BV	200	225	255

KM# 1201 2-1/2 PAHLAVI **Weight:** 20.3400 g. **Composition:** 0.9000 Gold .5885 oz. AGW **Obverse:** "Aryamehr" added to legend **Edge:** Reeded **Size:** 30 mm.

Date	Mintage	F	VF	XF	Unc
SH1354 (1975)	18,000	—	BV	200	235
SH1355 (1976)	16,000	—	BV	200	235
MS2536 (1977)	—	—	BV	200	235
MS2537 (1978)	—	—	BV	200	235
SH1358 (1979) Rare	—	—	—	—	750
MS2538 (1979) Rare	—	—	—	—	750

KM# 1164 5 PAHLAVI **Weight:** 40.6799 g. **Composition:** 0.9000 Gold 1.1772 oz. AGW **Obverse:** Bust of Muhammad Reza Pahlavi **Reverse:** Lion

Date	Mintage	F	VF	XF	Unc
SH1339 (1960)	2,225	BV	400	450	500
SH1340 (1961)	2,430	BV	400	450	500
SH1342 (1963)	20	—	—	—	—
SH1347 (1968)	500	—	—	—	—
Note: Reported, not confirmed					
SH1348 (1969)	2,000	BV	400	450	500
SH1349 (1970)	700	—	—	—	—
Note: Reported, not confirmed					
SH1350 (1971)	2,000	BV	400	450	500
SH1351 (1972)	2,500	BV	400	450	500
SH1352 (1973)	2,100	BV	400	450	500
SH1353 (1974)	—	BV	400	450	500

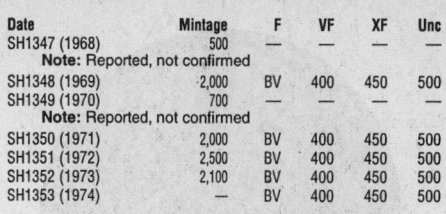

KM# 1202 5 PAHLAVI **Weight:** 40.6799 g. **Composition:** 0.9000 Gold 1.1772 oz. AGW **Obverse:** "Aryamehr" added to legend

Date	Mintage	F	VF	XF	Unc
SH1354 (1975)	10,000	—	BV	425	485
SH1355 (1976)	17,000	—	BV	425	485
MS2536 (1977)	—	—	BV	425	485
MS2537 (1978)	—	—	BV	425	485
SH1358 (1979)	—	—	700	900	1,200

KM# 1210 10 PAHLAVI **Weight:** 81.3598 g. **Composition:** 0.9000 Gold 2.3544 oz. AGW **Subject:** 50th Anniversary of Pahlavi Rule

Date	F	VF	XF	Unc
MS2535 (1976)	—	—	850	1,000

KM# 1212 10 PAHLAVI **Weight:** 81.3598 g. **Composition:** 0.9000 Gold 2.3544 oz. AGW **Subject:** Centenary of Reza Shah's Birth

Date	F	VF	XF	Unc
MS2536 (1977)	—	—	850	1,000

KM# 1213 10 PAHLAVI **Weight:** 81.3598 g. **Composition:** 0.9000 Gold 2.3544 oz. AGW **Obverse:** "Aryamehr" added to legend

Date	F	VF	XF	Unc
MS2537 (1978)	—	—	850	1,000
SH1358 (1979)	—	—	2,000	2,500

ISLAMIC REPUBLIC

MILLED COINAGE

KM# 1231 50 DINARS **Composition:** Brass Clad Steel **Obverse:** Without crown

Date	F	VF	XF	Unc
SH1358 (1979)	6.00	8.00	17.50	25.00

KM# 1232 RIAL (20 Shahi) **Composition:** Copper-Nickel

Date	F	VF	XF	Unc
SH1358 (1979)	—	0.25	0.75	1.75
SH1359 (1980)	—	0.25	0.75	1.75
SH1360 (1981)	—	0.25	0.75	1.75
SH1361 (1982)	—	0.25	0.75	1.75
SH1362 (1983)	—	0.25	0.75	1.75
SH1363 (1984)	0.50	1.00	2.00	3.50
SH1364 (1985)	—	0.25	0.75	1.75
SH1365 (1986)	—	0.15	0.65	1.25
SH1366 (1987)	—	0.15	0.65	1.25
SH1367 (1988)	—	0.15	0.65	1.25

KM# 1245 RIAL (20 Shahi) **Composition:** Bronze Clad Steel **Subject:** World Jerusalem Day **Reverse:** Mosque of Omar

Date	F	VF	XF	Unc
SH1359 (1980)	—	0.50	1.50	2.50

KM# 1263 RIAL (20 Shahi) **Composition:** Brass **Reverse:** Mount Damavand

Date	F	VF	XF	Unc
SH1371 (1992)	—	5.00	7.50	15.00
SH1372 (1993)	—	2.50	5.00	10.00
SH1373 (1994)	—	—	10.00	25.00
SH1374 (1995)	—	—	10.00	25.00

KM# 1233 2 RIALS **Composition:** Copper-Nickel

Date	F	VF	XF	Unc
SH1358 (1979)	—	0.60	1.25	3.50
SH1359 (1980)	—	0.50	1.25	3.50
SH1360 (1981)	—	0.50	1.25	3.50
SH1361 (1982)	—	0.50	1.00	3.00
SH1362 (1983)	—	0.35	0.75	2.75
SH1363 (1984)	—	0.50	1.00	3.00
SH1364 (1985)	—	0.35	0.75	2.75
SH1365 (1986)	—	0.25	0.75	2.50
SH1366 (1987)	—	0.25	0.75	2.50
SH1367 (1988)	—	0.25	0.75	2.50

KM# 1234 5 RIALS **Composition:** Copper-Nickel **Note:** Date varieties exist.

Date	F	VF	XF	Unc
SH1358 (1979)	—	0.75	1.25	3.50
SH1359 (1980)	—	0.75	1.25	3.50
SH1360 (1981)	—	0.75	1.25	3.50
SH1361 (1982)	—	0.75	1.25	3.50
SH1362 (1983)	—	0.75	1.25	3.50
SH1363 (1984)	—	0.75	1.25	3.50
SH1364 (1985)	—	0.75	1.25	3.50
SH1365 (1986)	—	0.75	1.25	3.50
SH1366 (1987)	—	0.75	1.25	3.50
SH1367 (1988)	—	0.75	1.25	3.50
SH1368 (1989)	—	0.75	1.25	3.50

KM# 1258 5 RIALS **Composition:** Brass **Reverse:** Tomb of Hafez

Date	F	VF	XF	Unc
SH1371 (1992)	—	0.50	1.25	3.00
SH1372 (1993)	—	0.50	1.25	3.00
SH1373 (1994)	—	0.50	1.25	3.00
SH1375 (1996)	—	0.50	1.25	3.00
SH1376 (1997)	—	0.50	1.25	3.00
SH1378 (1999)	—	—	2.00	5.00

KM# 1235.1 10 RIALS **Composition:** Copper-Nickel

Date	F	VF	XF	Unc
SH1358 (1979)	—	1.00	2.50	4.50
SH1358 (1979) Large date	—	1.00	2.50	4.50
SH1359 (1980)	—	1.00	2.50	4.50
SH1360 (1981)	—	1.00	2.50	4.50
SH1361 (1982)	—	1.00	2.00	4.00

KM# 1243 10 RIALS **Composition:** Copper-Nickel **Subject:** 1st Anniversary of Revolution

Date	F	VF	XF	Unc
SH1358 (1979)	—	1.50	2.50	4.50

KM# 1249 10 RIALS **Weight:** 6.9700 g. **Composition:** Copper-Nickel **Subject:** Moslem Unity **Edge:** Reeded

Date	F	VF	XF	Unc
SH1361 (1982)	—	1.50	2.50	4.50

KM# 1235.2 10 RIALS **Composition:** Copper-Nickel **Reverse:** Redesigned wreath **Note:** Date varieties exist.

Date	F	VF	XF	Unc
SH1361 (1982)	—	1.00	2.00	4.00
SH1362 (1983)	—	1.00	2.00	4.00
SH1363 (1984)	—	1.00	2.00	4.00
SH1364 (1985)	—	0.90	1.50	4.00
SH1365 (1986)	—	0.90	1.50	4.00
SH1366 (1987)	—	0.90	1.50	4.00
SH1366 (1987) Small date	—	0.90	1.50	4.00
SH1367 (1988)	—	0.65	1.50	3.00

KM# 1253.1 10 RIALS **Weight:** 3.0200 g. **Composition:** Copper-Nickel **Subject:** World Jerusalem Day **Obverse:** Small denomination numerals **Edge:** Plain

Date	F	VF	XF	Unc
SH1368 (1989)	—	1.00	2.00	4.00

KM# 1253.2 10 RIALS **Weight:** 3.0200 g. **Composition:** Copper-Nickel **Obverse:** Large denomination numerals

Date	F	VF	XF	Unc
SH1368 (1989)	—	1.00	2.00	4.00

KM# 1259 10 RIALS **Composition:** Aluminum-Bronze **Reverse:** Tomb of Ferdousi

Date	F	VF	XF	Unc
SH1371 (1992)	—	1.00	2.00	3.75
SH1372 (1993)	—	1.00	2.00	3.75
SH1373 (1994)	—	1.00	2.00	3.75
SH1374 (1995)	—	1.00	2.00	3.75
SH1375 (1996)	—	1.00	2.00	3.75
SH1376 (1996)	—	1.00	2.00	3.75

KM# 1244 20 RIALS **Composition:** Copper-Nickel **Subject:** 1400th Anniversary of Mohammed's Flight

Date	F	VF	XF	Unc
SH1358 (1979)	—	2.50	3.50	5.00

KM# 1236 20 RIALS **Composition:** Copper-Nickel **Note:** Date varieties exist.

Date	F	VF	XF	Unc
SH1358 (1979)	—	1.00	1.75	4.50
SH1359 (1980)	—	1.00	1.75	4.50
SH1360 (1981)	—	1.00	1.75	4.50
SH1361 (1982)	—	1.00	1.75	4.50
SH1362 (1983)	—	1.00	1.75	4.50
SH1363 (1984)	—	1.00	1.75	4.50
SH1364 (1985)	—	1.00	1.75	4.50
SH1365 (1986)	—	1.00	1.75	4.50
SH1366 (1987)	—	1.00	1.75	4.50
SH1367 (1988)	—	1.00	1.75	4.50

KM# 1246 20 RIALS **Composition:** Copper-Nickel **Subject:** 2nd Anniversary of Islamic Revolution

Date	F	VF	XF	Unc
SH1359 (1980)	—	2.50	3.50	5.00

KM# 1247 20 RIALS **Composition:** Copper-Nickel **Subject:** 3rd Anniversary of Islamic Revolution

Date	F	VF	XF	Unc
SH1360 (1981)	—	2.50	3.50	5.00

KM# 1251 20 RIALS **Composition:** Copper-Nickel **Subject:** Islamic Banking Week

Date	F	VF	XF	Unc
SH1367 (1988)	—	2.50	3.50	5.00

KM# 1254.2 20 RIALS **Composition:** Copper-Nickel **Reverse:** Redesigned thick wreath **Note:** 1.70 millimeters thick.

Date	F	VF	XF	Unc
SH1368 (1989)	—	2.50	3.50	5.00

KM# 1254.1 20 RIALS **Composition:** Copper-Nickel **Subject:** 8 Years of Sacred Defense **Obverse:** Twenty-two dots around rim **Note:** 2.00 millimeters thick.

Date	F	VF	XF	Unc
SH1368 (1989)	—	2.50	3.50	5.00

KM# 1237.1 50 RIALS **Composition:** Aluminum-Bronze **Subject:** Oil and Agriculture **Reverse:** Map in relief **Edge:** Lettered **Note:** Two varieties of edge lettering exist.

Date	F	VF	XF	Unc
SH1359 (1980)	—	2.00	3.50	8.00
SH1360 (1981)	—	2.00	3.50	8.00
SH1361 (1982)	—	2.00	3.50	8.00
SH1362 (1983)	—	2.00	3.50	8.00
SH1364 (1985)	—	2.00	3.50	8.00
SH1365 (1986)	—	2.00	3.50	8.00

KM# 1237.2 50 RIALS **Composition:** Aluminum-Bronze **Reverse:** Map incuse

Date	F	VF	XF	Unc
SH1366 (1987)	—	4.00	6.00	9.00
SH1367 (1988)	—	—	4.50	7.00
SH1368 (1989)	—	—	4.50	7.00

KM# 1252 50 RIALS **Composition:** Copper-Nickel **Subject:** 10th Anniversary of Revolution

Date	F	VF	XF	Unc
SH1367 (1988)	—	3.00	5.00	7.50

KM# 1237.1a 50 RIALS **Composition:** Copper-Nickel **Edge:** Lettered

Date	F	VF	XF	Unc
SH1368 (1989)	—	2.00	3.50	7.50

Date	F	VF	XF	Unc
SH1369 (1990)	—	2.00	3.50	7.50
SH1370 (1991)	—	2.00	3.50	7.50

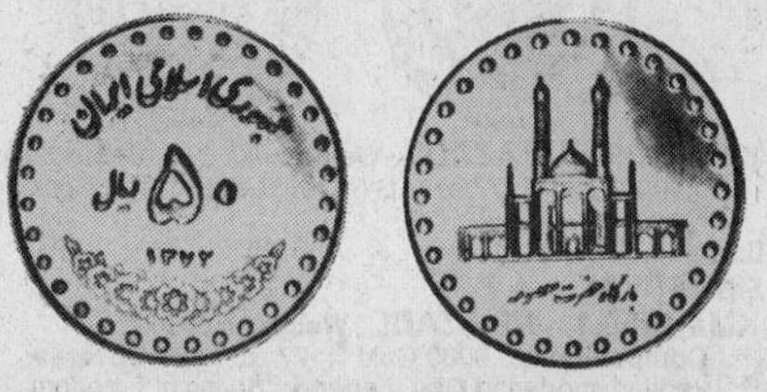

KM# 1260 50 RIALS **Composition:** Copper-Nickel **Reverse:** Shrine of Hazrat Masumah

Date	F	VF	XF	Unc
SH1371 (1992)	—	2.50	3.50	5.00
SH1372 (1993)	—	2.50	3.50	5.00
SH1373 (1994)	—	2.50	3.50	5.00
SH1374 (1995)	—	2.50	3.50	5.00
SH1375 (1996)	—	2.50	3.50	5.00
SH1377 (1998)	—	2.50	3.50	5.00
SH1378 (1999)	—	2.50	3.50	5.00

KM# 1261.1 100 RIALS **Composition:** Copper-Nickel **Obverse:** Thin denomination, numerals **Reverse:** Shrine of Imam Reza

Date	F	VF	XF	Unc
SH1371 (1992)	—	—	—	6.50

KM# 1261.2 100 RIALS **Composition:** Copper-Nickel **Obverse:** Thick denomination, numerals

Date	F	VF	XF	Unc
SH1372 (1993)	—	—	—	6.50
SH1373 (1994)	—	—	—	6.50
SH1375 (1996)	—	—	—	6.50
SH1376 (1997)	—	—	—	6.50
SH1377 (1998)	—	—	—	6.50
SH1378 (1999)	—	—	—	6.50

KM# 1262 250 RIALS **Ring Composition:** Brass **Center Composition:** Copper-Nickel **Reverse:** Stylized flower

Date	F	VF	XF	Unc
SH1372 (1993)	—	—	—	7.50
SH1373 (1994)	—	—	—	7.50
SH1374 (1995)	—	—	—	7.50
SH1375 (1996)	—	—	—	7.50
SH1376 (1997)	—	—	—	7.50
SH1377 (1998)	—	—	—	7.50
SH1378 (1999)	—	—	—	7.50
SH1379 (2000)	—	—	—	7.50

BULLION COINAGE

Issued by the National Bank of Iran

KM# 1238 1/4 AZADI **Weight:** 2.0339 g. **Composition:** 0.9000 Gold .0588 oz. AGW **Obv. Legend:** "1st Spring of Freedom"

Date	F	VF	XF	Unc
SH1358 (1979)	—	—	—	300

KM# 1265 1/4 AZADI **Weight:** 2.0339 g. **Composition:** 0.9000 Gold 0.0589 oz. AGW **Obv. Legend:** "Spring of Freedom"

Date	F	VF	XF	Unc
SH1366	—	—	—	300
SH1368	—	—	—	300
SH1369	—	—	—	200
SH1370	—	—	—	300

KM# 1239 1/2 AZADI **Weight:** 4.0680 g. **Composition:** 0.9000 Gold .1177 oz. AGW **Obv. Legend:** "1st Spring of Freedom"

Date	F	VF	XF	Unc
SH1358 (1979)	—	—	—	100

KM# 1250.1 1/2 AZADI **Weight:** 4.0680 g. **Composition:** 0.9000 Gold .1177 oz. AGW **Obverse:** Legend shortened **Obv. Legend:** "Spring of Freedom"

Date	F	VF	XF	Unc
SH1363 (1984)	—	—	—	100

KM# 1250.2 1/2 AZADI **Weight:** 4.0680 g. **Composition:** 0.9000 Gold .1177 oz. AGW **Obverse:** Legend larger **Obv. Legend:** "Spring of Freedom"

Date	F	VF	XF	Unc
SH1366 (1987)	—	—	—	100
SH1368 (1989)	—	—	—	100
SH1370 (1991)	—	—	—	100

KM# 1240 AZADI **Weight:** 8.1360 g. **Composition:** 0.9000 Gold .2354 oz. AGW **Obv. Legend:** "1st Spring of Freedom"

Date	F	VF	XF	Unc
SH1358 (1979)	—	—	—	125

KM# 1248.1 AZADI **Weight:** 8.1360 g. **Composition:** 0.9000 Gold .2354 oz. AGW **Obverse:** Legend shortened **Obv. Legend:** "Spring of Freedom"

Date	F	VF	XF	Unc
SH1363 (1984)	—	—	—	120

KM# 1248.2 AZADI **Weight:** 8.1360 g. **Composition:** 0.9000 Gold .2354 oz. AGW **Obverse:** Legend larger **Obv. Legend:** "Spring of Freedom"

Date	F	VF	XF	Unc
SH1364 (1985)	—	—	—	120
SH1365 (1986)	—	—	—	120
SH1366 (1987)	—	—	—	120
SH1367 (1988)	—	—	—	120
SH1368 (1989)	—	—	—	120
SH1369 (1990)	—	—	—	120
SH1370 (1991)	—	—	—	120

KM# 1264 AZADI **Weight:** 8.1360 g. **Composition:** 0.9000 Gold .2354 oz. AGW **Obverse:** The Central Bank of Islamic Republic of Iran **Reverse:** Portrait above date

Date	F	VF	XF	Unc
SH1370 (1991)	—	—	—	125
SH1373 (1994)	—	—	—	125
SH1374 (1995)	—	—	—	125
SH1375 (1996)	—	—	—	125

KM# A1264 AZADI **Weight:** 8.1360 g. **Composition:** 0.9000 Gold 0.2354 oz. AGW **Obverse:** Mosque. **Reverse:** Khomeini's portrait. **Edge:** Reeded. **Size:** 23.7 mm.

Date	F	VF	XF	Unc
SH1370 (1991)	—	—	—	180

KM# 1241 2-1/2 AZADI **Weight:** 20.3400 g. **Composition:** 0.9000 Gold .5885 oz. AGW **Obv. Legend:** "1st Spring of Freedom"

Date	Mintage	F	VF	XF	Unc
SH1358 (1979)	6	—	—	—	1,500

Note: A mintage of 6 pieces is reported, but more exist

KM# 1242 5 AZADI **Weight:** 40.6800 g. **Composition:** 0.9000 Gold 1.1770 oz. AGW **Obv. Legend:** "1st Spring of Freedom"

Date	F	VF	XF	Unc
SH1358 (1979)	—	—	—	2,750

PATTERNS

Including off metal strikes

KM#	Date	Mintage	Identification	Mkt Val
Pn25	1318	—	5 Krans. Silver. Struck at Paris Mint.	1,750
Pn29	1319	—	1000 Dinars. Silver. . Plain edgeStruck at Brussels Mint.	700
Pn31	1319	—	5000 Dinars. Silver. . Plain edgeStruck at Brussels Mint.	1,750
Pn32	1319	—	1/4 Toman.	300
Pn26	1319	—	1/4 Kran.	—
Pn27	1319	—	250 Dinars. Silver. . Plain edgeStruck at Brussels Mint. Mouzaffer profile.	550
Pn28	1319	—	500 Dinars. Silver. . Plain edgeStruck at Brussels Mint.	700
Pn30	1319	—	2000 Dinars. Silver. . Plain edgeStruck at Brussels Mint.	800
Pn36	1326	—	2 Toman. . Legend in open wreath	—
Pn35	1326	—	Toman. . Legend in open wreathKM#1026	375
Pn33	1326	—	1/5 Toman. KM#1024	300
Pn34	1326	—	1/2 Toman. . Legend in open wreathKM#1025	300
PnA37	1330	—	2000 Dinars. Nickel. Struck at Berlin.	—
Pn38	1331	—	2 Toman. Gilt Bronze. Portrait of Ahmed Shah	350
Pn37	1331	—	Toman. Gilt Bronze.	300
Pn40	1332	—	2000 Dinars. Gold.	—
Pn39	1332	—	5 Krans. Silver. . Plain edge	1,000
Pn41	1337	—	2 Toman. KM#1080; "2 Ashrafi"	—
Pn44	1337	—	5 Toman. 14.5000 g.KM#1081; "5 Ashrafi"	3,500
Pn45	1337	—	10 Toman. KM#1082	—
Pn42	1337	—	2000 Dinars. Gold. 14.0000 g.	5,000
Pn43	1337	—	2000 Dinars. Gold. 14.0000 g.	5,000
Pn47	1305	—	5 Krans. Silver. . Plain edge	2,500
Pn46	1305	—	2 Krans. Silver. . Plain edge	2,500

MINT SETS

KM#	Date	Mintage	Identification	Issue Price	Mkt Val
MS1	SH1342(1963) (4)	—	KM#1171a, 1173, 1175a, 1177a	2.00	15.00
MSA3	SH1342-1343 (1963-64) (4)	—	KM#1171a, 1173, 1175a, 1177a	—	—
MS2	SH1343(1964) (4)	—	KM#1171a, 1173, 1175a, 1177a	2.00	11.50
MS3	SH1348(1969) (5)	—	KM#1156, 1171a, 1173, 1176, 1178	2.00	17.00
MS4	SH1350(1971) (5)	—	KM#1156, 1171a, 1173, 1176, 1178	2.00	17.00
MS5	SH1353(1974) (6)	—	KM#1156, 1171a, 1173, 1176, 1179, 1181	2.00	19.00
MS6	SH1354(1975) (6)	—	KM#1156, 1171a, 1173, 1176, 1179, 1181	2.00	22.00
MS7	MS2535(1976) (6)	—	KM#1156a, 1205-1209	2.50	21.50
MS8	MS2536(1977) (6)	—	KM#1156a, 1172-1173, 1176, 1179, 1181	2.50	20.00
MS9	SH1358(1989) (8)	—	KM#1243-1244 dated 1358; 1246 dated 1359; 1247 dated 1360; 1252 dated 1367; 1253.1, 1253.2, 1254.1 dated 1368	—	40.00
MS10	SH1366(1989) (7)	—	KM#1232-1234, 1236 dated 1366; 1235.2, 1237.2 dated 1367; 1237.1a dated 1368	—	60.00
MS12	SH1372, 1375, 1378 (1993, 1996, 1999) (6)	—	KM#1258-1260, 1261.2, 1262, 1263	—	75.00
MS13	SH1372, 1375, 1378 (1993, 1996, 1999) (6)	—	KM#1258-1260, 1261.2, 1262, 1263	—	75.00

IRAQ

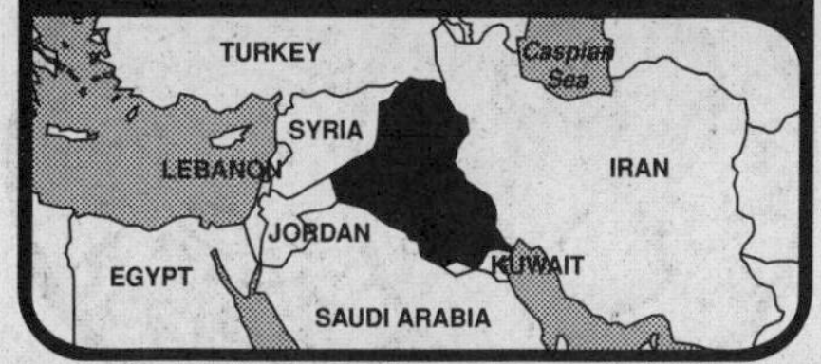

The Republic of Iraq, historically known as Mesopotamia, is located in the Near East and is bordered by Kuwait, Iran, Turkey, Syria, Jordan and Saudi Arabia. It has area of 167,925 sq. mi. (434,920 sq. km.) and a population of 14 million. Capital: Baghdad. The economy of Iraq is based on agriculture and petroleum. Crude oil accounted for 94 percent of the exports before the war with Iran began in 1980.

Mesopotamia was the site of a number of flourishing civilizations of antiquity - Sumeria, Assyria, Babylonia, Parthia, Persia and the Biblical cities of Ur, Ninevehand and Babylon. Desired because of its favored location, which embraced the fertile alluvial plains of the Tigris and Euphrates Rivers, Mesopotamia - 'land between the rivers'- was conquered by Cyrus the Great of Persia, Alexander of Macedonia and by Arabs who made the legendary city of Baghdad the capital of the ruling caliphate. Suleiman the Magnificent conquered Mesopotamia for Turkey in1534, and it formed part of the Ottoman Empire until 1623, and from 1638 to 1917. Great Britain, given a League of Nations mandate over the territory in 1920, recognized Iraq as a kingdom in 1922. Iraq became an independent constitutional monarchy presided over by the Hashemite family, direct descendants of the prophet Mohammed, in 1932. In 1958, the army-led revolution of July 14 overthrew the monarchy and proclaimed a republic.

NOTE: The 'I' mintmark on 1938 and 1943 issues appears on the obverse near the point of the bust. Some of the issues of 1938 have a dot to denote a composition change from nickel to copper-nickel.

RULERS

Ottoman, until 1917
British, 1921-1922
Faisal I, 1921-1933
Ghazi I, 1933-1939
Faisal II, Regency, 1939-1953
As King, 1953-1958

MINT MARKS

I – Bombay

MONETARY SYSTEM

فلسًا فلس فلوس

Falus, Fulus — Fals, Fils — Falsan

50 Fils = 1 Dirham
200 Fils = 1 Riyal
1000 Fils = 1 Dinar (Pound)

TITLES

العراق

Al-Iraq

المملكة العراقية

Al-Mamlaka(t) al-Iraqiya(t)

الجمهورية العرقية

Al-Jumhuriya(t) al-Iraqiya(t)

KINGDOM OF IRAQ

DECIMAL COINAGE

KM# 95 FILS **Weight:** 2.5000 g. **Composition:** Bronze **Ruler:** Faisal I **Size:** 19.5 mm.

Date	Mintage	F	VF	XF	Unc	BU
1931	4,000,000	1.00	3.00	10.00	25.00	—
AH1349 Proof	—	—	—	—	—	—
1931 Proof	—	—	—	—	—	—
1933	6,000,000	1.00	3.00	10.00	25.00	—
1933 Proof	—	—	—	—	—	—

KM# 102 FILS **Weight:** 2.5000 g. **Composition:** Bronze **Ruler:** Ghazi I **Size:** 19.5 mm. **Note:** Struck at Royal and Bombay Mint.

Date	Mintage	F	VF	XF	Unc	BU
1936	3,000,000	1.25	4.00	10.00	25.00	—
1936 Proof	—	—	—	—	—	—
1938	36,000,000	0.25	0.50	1.00	3.00	—
1938 Proof	—	—	—	—	—	—
1938 -I	3,000,000	0.50	2.00	5.00	15.00	—

KM# 109 FILS **Composition:** Bronze **Ruler:** Faisal II, King

Date	Mintage	F	VF	XF	Unc	BU
1953	41,000,000	0.25	0.40	0.60	1.00	—
1953 Proof	200	Value: 75.00				

KM# 96 2 FILS **Weight:** 5.0000 g. **Composition:** Bronze **Ruler:** Faisal I **Size:** 24 mm.

Date	Mintage	F	VF	XF	Unc	BU
1931	2,500,000	1.25	3.50	10.00	25.00	—
1931	2,500,000	1.25	3.50	10.00	25.00	—
1931 Proof	—	—	—	—	—	—
1933	1,000,000	1.50	4.00	15.00	35.00	—
1933 Proof	—	—	—	—	—	—

KM# 110 2 FILS **Composition:** Bronze **Ruler:** Faisal II, King

Date	Mintage	F	VF	XF	Unc	BU
1953	500,000	0.50	1.00	3.00	12.50	—
1953 Proof	200	Value: 100				

KM# 97 4 FILS **Weight:** 4.0000 g. **Composition:** Nickel **Ruler:** Faisal I **Shape:** Scalloped **Size:** 21 mm.

Date	Mintage	F	VF	XF	Unc	BU
1931	4,500,000	1.50	4.00	15.00	50.00	—
1931 Proof	—	—	—	—	—	—
1933	6,500,000	1.50	4.00	15.00	50.00	—
1933 Proof	—	—	—	—	—	—

KM# 105 4 FILS **Weight:** 4.0000 g. **Composition:** Nickel **Ruler:** Ghazi I **Shape:** Scalloped **Size:** 21 mm.

Date	Mintage	F	VF	XF	Unc	BU
1938	1,000,000	1.00	2.00	6.00	15.00	—
1938 Proof	—	—	—	—	—	—
1939	1,000,000	1.25	2.50	10.00	30.00	—
1939 Proof	—	—	—	—	—	—

KM# 105a 4 FILS **Weight:** 21.0000 g. **Composition:** Copper-Nickel **Ruler:** Ghazi I **Shape:** Scalloped **Size:** 21 mm. **Note:** Struck at Royal and Bombay Mint.

Date	Mintage	F	VF	XF	Unc	BU
1938	2,750,000	0.75	1.00	2.00	6.00	—
1938 Proof	—	—	—	—	—	—
1938 -I	2,500,000	1.00	2.00	7.50	15.00	—

KM# 105b 4 FILS **Weight:** 4.0000 g. **Composition:** Bronze **Ruler:** Ghazi I **Shape:** Scalloped **Size:** 21 mm.

Date	Mintage	F	VF	XF	Unc	BU
1938	8,000,000	0.50	1.00	2.00	6.00	—
1938 Proof	—	—	—	—	—	—

KM# 107 4 FILS **Weight:** 4.0000 g. **Composition:** Bronze **Ruler:** Faisal II, Regency **Shape:** Scalloped **Size:** 21 mm.

Date	Mintage	F	VF	XF	Unc	BU
1943 -I	1,500,000	2.00	3.00	7.00	15.00	—

KM# 111 4 FILS **Weight:** 4.0000 g. **Composition:** Copper-Nickel **Ruler:** Faisal II, Regency **Shape:** Scalloped **Size:** 21 mm.

Date	Mintage	F	VF	XF	Unc	BU
1953	20,750,000	0.50	0.75	1.00	2.50	—
1953 Proof	200	Value: 75.00				

KM# 98 10 FILS **Weight:** 6.7500 g. **Composition:** Nickel **Ruler:** Faisal I **Shape:** Scalloped **Size:** 25 mm.

Date	Mintage	F	VF	XF	Unc	BU
1931	2,400,000	2.00	5.00	16.50	50.00	—
1931 Proof	—	—	—	—	—	—
1933	2,200,000	2.00	5.00	16.50	50.00	—
1933 Proof	—	—	—	—	—	—

KM# 103 10 FILS **Weight:** 6.7500 g. **Composition:** Nickel **Ruler:** Ghazi I **Shape:** Scalloped **Size:** 25 mm.

Date	Mintage	F	VF	XF	Unc	BU
1937	400,000	3.00	5.00	16.50	50.00	—
1937 Proof	—	—	—	—	—	—
1938	600,000	2.50	4.00	10.00	35.00	—
1938 Proof	—	—	—	—	—	—

KM# 103a 10 FILS **Weight:** 6.7500 g. **Composition:** Copper-Nickel **Ruler:** Ghazi I **Shape:** Scalloped **Size:** 25 mm. **Note:** Struck at Royal and Bombay Mint.

Date	Mintage	F	VF	XF	Unc	BU
1938	1,100,000	1.00	2.00	4.00	10.00	—
1938 Proof	—	—	—	—	—	—
1938 -I	1,500,000	1.50	2.50	6.00	15.00	—

KM# 103b 10 FILS **Weight:** 6.7500 g. **Composition:** Bronze **Ruler:** Ghazi I **Shape:** Scalloped **Size:** 25 mm.

Date	Mintage	F	VF	XF	Unc	BU
1938	8,250,000	0.50	1.00	2.50	6.50	—
1938 Proof	—	—	—	—	—	—

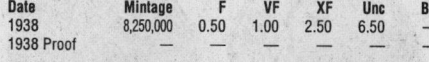

KM# 108 10 FILS Weight: 6.7500 g. **Composition:** Bronze **Ruler:** Faisal II, Regency **Shape:** Scalloped **Size:** 25 mm.

Date	Mintage	F	VF	XF	Unc	BU
1943 -I	1,500,000	3.00	7.00	20.00	50.00	—

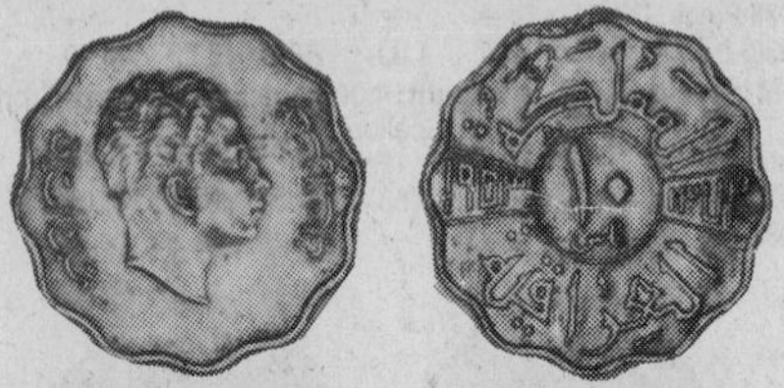

KM# 112 10 FILS Weight: 6.7500 g. **Composition:** Copper-Nickel **Ruler:** Faisal II, Regency **Shape:** Scalloped **Size:** 25 mm.

Date	Mintage	F	VF	XF	Unc	BU
1953	11,400,000	0.50	0.75	1.00	2.50	—
1953 Proof	200	Value: 75.00				

KM# 99 20 FILS Weight: 3.6000 g. **Composition:** 0.5000 Silver .0579 oz. ASW **Ruler:** Faisal I **Size:** 20.5 mm.

Date	Mintage	F	VF	XF	Unc	BU
1931	1,500,000	2.50	9.00	25.00	75.00	—
1931 Proof	—	—	—	—	—	—
1933	1,100,000	2.50	9.00	25.00	75.00	—
1933 Proof	—	—	—	—	—	—
1933 (error) 1252	Inc. above	20.00	60.00	100	200	—

KM# 106 20 FILS Weight: 3.6000 g. **Composition:** 0.5000 Silver .0579 oz. ASW **Ruler:** Ghazi I **Size:** 20.5 mm.

Date	Mintage	F	VF	XF	Unc	BU
1938	1,200,000	2.00	3.50	8.00	22.00	—
1938 -I	1,350,000	2.00	4.00	9.00	26.00	—

KM# 113 20 FILS Weight: 3.6000 g. **Composition:** 0.5000 Silver .0579 oz. ASW **Ruler:** Faisal II, King **Size:** 20.5 mm.

Date	Mintage	F	VF	XF	Unc	BU
1953	250,000	25.00	45.00	70.00	140	—
1953 Proof	200	Value: 300				

KM# 116 20 FILS Weight: 2.8000 g. **Composition:** 0.5000 Silver .0450 oz. ASW **Ruler:** Faisal II, King **Size:** 19 mm.

Date	Mintage	F	VF	XF	Unc	BU
1955	4,000,000	1.50	3.00	5.00	10.00	—
1955 Proof	—	Value: 80.00				

KM# 100 50 FILS Weight: 9.0000 g. **Composition:** 0.5000 Silver .1447 oz. ASW **Ruler:** Faisal I **Size:** 26.5 mm.

Date	Mintage	F	VF	XF	Unc	BU
1931	8,800,000	3.00	10.00	28.00	80.00	—
1931 Proof	—	—	—	—	—	—
1933	800,000	6.00	15.00	35.00	100	—
1933 Proof	—	—	—	—	—	—

KM# 104 50 FILS Weight: 9.0000 g. **Composition:** 0.5000 Silver .1447 oz. ASW **Ruler:** Ghazi I **Size:** 26.5 mm. **Note:** Struck at Royal and Bombay Mint.

Date	Mintage	F	VF	XF	Unc	BU
1937	1,200,000	2.50	7.00	10.00	30.00	—
1937 Proof	—	—	—	—	—	—
1938	5,300,000	2.00	4.00	8.00	25.00	—
1938 Proof	—	—	—	—	—	—
1938 -I	7,500,000	2.00	4.00	8.00	25.00	—

KM# 114 50 FILS Weight: 9.0000 g. **Composition:** 0.5000 Silver .1447 oz. ASW **Ruler:** Faisal II, King **Size:** 26.5 mm.

Date	Mintage	F	VF	XF	Unc	BU
1953	560,000	50.00	100	150	250	—
1953 Proof	200	Value: 450				

KM# 117 50 FILS Weight: 7.0000 g. **Composition:** 0.5000 Silver .1126 oz. ASW **Ruler:** Faisal II, King **Size:** 26 mm.

Date	Mintage	F	VF	XF	Unc	BU
1955	12,000,000	2.50	4.00	6.00	11.50	—
1955 Proof	—	Value: 80.00				

KM# 115 100 FILS Weight: 10.0000 g. **Composition:** 0.9000 Silver .2893 oz. ASW **Ruler:** Faisal II, King **Size:** 29 mm.

Date	Mintage	F	VF	XF	Unc	BU
1953	1,200,000	5.00	7.50	20.00	50.00	—
1953 Proof	200	Value: 250				

KM# 118 100 FILS Weight: 10.0000 g. **Composition:** 0.5000 Silver .1607 oz. ASW **Ruler:** Faisal II, King **Size:** 29 mm.

Date	Mintage	F	VF	XF	Unc	BU
1955	1,000,000	—	700	1,000	1,500	—
1955 Proof	—	Value: 300				

KM# 101 RIYAL (200 Fils) Weight: 20.0000 g. **Composition:** 0.5000 Silver .3215 oz. ASW **Ruler:** Faisal I **Size:** 34 mm. **Note:** Dav. #255.

Date	Mintage	F	VF	XF	Unc	BU
1932		7.50	15.00	35.00	350	—
1932 Proof	Est. 20	Value: 1,600				

REPUBLIC

DECIMAL COINAGE

KM# 119 FILS Weight: 2.5000 g. **Composition:** Bronze **Size:** 19 mm.

Date	Mintage	F	VF	XF	Unc	BU
1959	72,000,000	0.15	0.25	0.50	1.00	—
1959 Proof	400	Value: 30.00				

KM# 120 5 FILS Weight: 5.0000 g. **Composition:** Copper-Nickel **Size:** 22 mm.

Date	Mintage	F	VF	XF	Unc	BU
1959	30,000,000	0.15	0.25	0.50	1.00	—
1959 Proof	400	Value: 30.00				

KM# 125 5 FILS Composition: Copper-Nickel

Date	Mintage	F	VF	XF	Unc	BU
1967	17,000,000	0.15	0.25	0.35	0.50	—
1971	15,000,000	0.15	0.25	0.35	0.50	—

KM# 125a 5 FILS Composition: Stainless Steel

Date	Mintage	F	VF	XF	Unc	BU
1971	2,000,000	0.20	0.30	0.50	0.75	—
1974	15,000,000	0.10	0.15	0.25	0.35	—
1975	94,800,000	0.10	0.15	0.25	0.35	—
1980	20,160,000	0.10	0.15	0.25	0.35	—
1981	29,840,000	0.10	0.15	0.25	0.35	—

KM# 141 5 FILS Composition: Stainless Steel **Series:** F.A.O.

Date	Mintage	F	VF	XF	Unc	BU
1975	2,000,000	0.10	0.15	0.25	0.50	—

KM# 159 5 FILS **Composition:** Stainless Steel
Reverse: Babylon - Ruins

Date	F	VF	XF	Unc	BU
1982	0.10	0.15	0.25	0.50	—

KM# 159a 5 FILS **Composition:** Copper-Nickel

Date	F	VF	XF	Unc	BU
1982 Proof	—	Value: 3.00			

KM# 121 10 FILS **Weight:** 6.7500 g. **Composition:** Copper-Nickel **Size:** 26 mm.

Date	Mintage	F	VF	XF	Unc	BU
1959	24,000,000	0.25	0.35	0.65	1.50	—
1959 Proof	400	Value: 30.00				

KM# 126 10 FILS **Composition:** Copper-Nickel

Date	Mintage	F	VF	XF	Unc	BU
1967	13,400,000	0.20	0.30	0.60	1.25	—
1971	12,000,000	0.20	0.30	0.60	1.25	—

KM# 126a 10 FILS **Composition:** Stainless Steel

Date	Mintage	F	VF	XF	Unc	BU
1971	1,550,000	0.25	0.35	0.65	1.50	—
1974	12,000,000	0.20	0.30	0.50	1.00	—
1975	52,456,000	0.20	0.30	0.50	1.00	—
1979	13,800,000	0.20	0.30	0.50	1.00	—
1980	11,264,000	0.20	0.30	0.50	1.00	—
1981	63,736,000	0.20	0.30	0.50	1.00	—

KM# 142 10 FILS **Composition:** Stainless Steel
Series: F.A.O.

Date	Mintage	F	VF	XF	Unc	BU
1975	1,000,000	0.15	0.25	0.50	0.75	—

KM# 160 10 FILS **Composition:** Stainless Steel
Rev. Legend: Babylon - Ishtar Gate

Date	F	VF	XF	Unc	BU
1982	—	—	—	0.75	—

KM# 160a 10 FILS **Composition:** Copper-Nickel

Date	F	VF	XF	Unc	BU
1982 Proof	—	Value: 3.00			

KM# 122 25 FILS **Weight:** 2.5000 g. **Composition:** 0.5000 Silver .0401 oz. ASW **Size:** 20 mm.

Date	Mintage	F	VF	XF	Unc	BU
1959	12,000,000	0.50	0.75	1.50	3.00	—
1959 Proof	400	Value: 40.00				

KM# 127 25 FILS **Composition:** Copper-Nickel

Date	Mintage	F	VF	XF	Unc	BU
1969	6,000,000	0.20	0.30	0.50	1.00	—
1970	6,000,000	0.20	0.30	0.50	1.00	—
1972	12,000,000	0.20	0.30	0.50	1.00	—
1975	48,000,000	0.20	0.30	0.50	1.00	—
1981	60,000,000	0.20	0.30	0.50	1.00	—

KM# 161 25 FILS **Composition:** Copper-Nickel
Reverse: Babylon - Lion

Date	F	VF	XF	Unc	BU
1982	—	—	—	1.25	—
1982 Proof	—	Value: 4.00			

KM# 123 50 FILS **Weight:** 5.0000 g. **Composition:** 0.5000 Silver .0803 oz. ASW **Size:** 23 mm.

Date	Mintage	F	VF	XF	Unc	BU
1959	24,000,000	0.75	1.25	2.00	4.50	—
1959 Proof	400	Value: 80.00				

KM# 128 50 FILS **Composition:** Copper-Nickel

Date	Mintage	F	VF	XF	Unc	BU
1969	12,000,000	0.25	0.35	0.65	1.25	—
1970	12,000,000	0.25	0.35	0.65	1.25	—
1972	12,000,000	0.25	0.35	0.65	1.25	—
1975	36,000,000	0.25	0.35	0.65	1.25	—
1979	1,500,000	0.25	0.35	0.65	1.75	—
1980	23,520,000	0.25	0.35	0.65	1.25	—
1981	138,995,000	0.25	0.35	0.65	1.00	—
1990	—	0.25	0.35	0.65	1.00	—

KM# 162 50 FILS **Composition:** Copper-Nickel
Reverse: Babylon - Bull

Date	F	VF	XF	Unc	BU
1982	0.25	0.50	0.75	2.50	—
1982 Proof	—	Value: 6.00			

KM# 124 100 FILS **Weight:** 10.0000 g. **Composition:** 0.5000 Silver .1607 oz. ASW **Size:** 29 mm.

Date	Mintage	F	VF	XF	Unc	BU
1959	6,000,000	2.00	3.00	4.50	9.00	—
1959 Proof	400	Value: 150				

KM# 129 100 FILS **Composition:** Copper-Nickel

Date	Mintage	F	VF	XF	Unc	BU
1970	6,000,000	0.35	0.50	0.75	1.50	—
1972	6,000,000	0.35	0.50	0.75	1.50	—
1975	12,000,000	0.35	0.50	0.75	1.50	—
1979	1,000,000	0.35	0.75	1.50	3.00	—

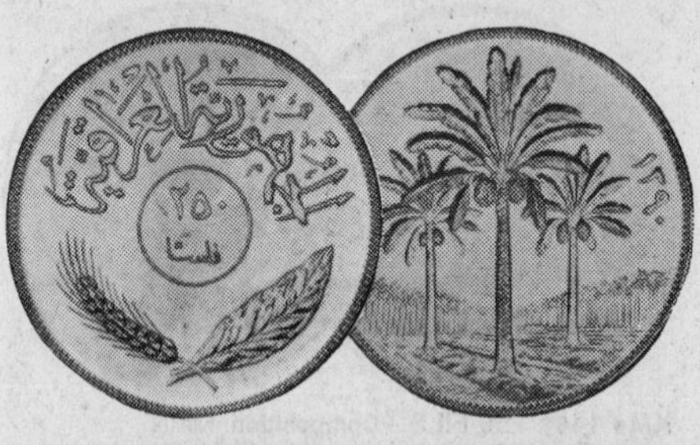

KM# 130 250 FILS **Composition:** Nickel **Series:** F.A.O.
Subject: Agrarian Reform Day

Date	Mintage	F	VF	XF	Unc	BU
1970	500,000	—	1.50	3.00	6.00	—
1970 Proof	1,000	Value: 14.50				

Note: Edge inscription w/FAO-250-repeated three times, relief and incuse varieties reported

KM# 131 250 FILS **Composition:** Nickel **Subject:** 1st Anniversary Peace with Kurds

Date	Mintage	F	VF	XF	Unc	BU
1971	500,000	—	1.50	3.00	6.00	—
1971 Proof	1,000	Value: 14.50				

KM# 135 250 FILS **Composition:** Nickel **Subject:** Silver Jublilee of Al Baath Party

Date	Mintage	F	VF	XF	Unc	BU
1972	250,000	—	1.50	3.00	6.00	—

KM# 136 250 FILS **Composition:** Nickel **Subject:** 25th Anniversary of Central Bank

Date	Mintage	F	VF	XF	Unc	BU
1972	250,000	—	1.50	3.00	6.00	—

KM# 138 250 FILS **Composition:** Nickel **Subject:** Oil Nationalization

Date	Mintage	F	VF	XF	Unc	BU
1973	260,000	—	1.50	3.00	6.50	—
1973 Proof	5,000	Value: 12.00				

KM# 144 250 FILS **Composition:** Nickel **Subject:** International Year of the Child

Date	Mintage	F	VF	XF	Unc	BU
1979 Proof	10,000	Value: 8.00				

KM# 146 250 FILS **Composition:** Copper-Nickel **Subject:** 1st Anniversary of Hussein as President

Date	F	VF	XF	Unc	BU
1980	—	1.00	2.00	5.00	—

KM# 147 250 FILS **Composition:** Copper-Nickel

Date	Mintage	F	VF	XF	Unc	BU
1980	—	—	1.00	2.00	5.00	—
1981	25,568,000	—	1.00	2.00	5.00	—
1990	—	—	1.00	2.00	5.00	—

KM# 152 250 FILS **Composition:** Copper-Nickel **Subject:** World Food Day **Shape:** Octagon

Date	Mintage	F	VF	XF	Unc	BU
1981	46,432,000	—	1.00	2.00	4.00	—

KM# 155 250 FILS **Composition:** Copper-Nickel **Subject:** Nonaligned Nations Baghdad Conference **Shape:** Octagon

Date	F	VF	XF	Unc	BU
1982	—	1.00	2.00	5.00	—

KM# 163 250 FILS **Composition:** Copper-Nickel **Reverse:** Babylon - Top of Hammurabi Stele **Shape:** Octagon

Date	F	VF	XF	Unc	BU
1982	—	1.00	2.00	4.50	—
1982 Proof	—	Value: 8.00			

KM# 132 500 FILS **Composition:** Nickel **Subject:** 50th Anniversary of Iraqi Army

Date	Mintage	F	VF	XF	Unc	BU
1971	100,000	—	2.50	4.50	10.00	—
1971 Proof	5,000	Value: 15.00				

KM# 139 500 FILS **Composition:** Nickel **Subject:** Oil Nationalization

Date	Mintage	F	VF	XF	Unc	BU
1973	260,000	—	2.50	4.50	10.00	—
1973 Proof	5,000	Value: 17.50				

KM# 165 500 FILS **Weight:** 9.0800 g. **Composition:** Nickel **Obverse:** Denomination: "500 Fals" **Shape:** Octagon

Date	F	VF	XF	Unc	BU
1982	—	2.50	4.00	7.00	—

KM# 165a 500 FILS **Composition:** Nickel **Obverse:** Denomination: "500 Falsan" **Shape:** 4-sided **Note:** Reduced weight, 8.98 g.

Date	F	VF	XF	Unc	BU
1982	—	20.00	35.00	85.00	—

KM# 168 500 FILS **Weight:** 9.0800 g. **Composition:** Nickel **Obverse:** Denomination: "500 Fals" **Reverse:** Babylon - Lion of Babylon **Size:** 4-sided mm.

Date	F	VF	XF	Unc	BU
1982	—	2.00	3.50	8.00	—
1982 Proof	—	Value: 12.50			

KM# 168a 500 FILS **Weight:** 9.0800 g. **Composition:** Nickel **Obverse:** Denomination: "500 Falsan"

Date	F	VF	XF	Unc	BU
1982	—	15.00	25.00	75.00	—

KM# 133 DINAR **Weight:** 31.0000 g. **Composition:** 0.9000 Silver .8971 oz. ASW **Subject:** 50th Anniversary of Iraqi Army **Obverse:** Similar to 500 Fils, KM#132

Date	Mintage	F	VF	XF	Unc	BU
1971	20,000	—	—	—	22.50	30.00
1971 Proof	—	Value: 40.00				

KM# 137 DINAR **Weight:** 31.0000 g. **Composition:** 0.5000 Silver .4983 oz. ASW **Subject:** 25th Anniversary of Central Bank **Obverse:** Similar to 250 Fils, KM#136

Date	Mintage	F	VF	XF	Unc	BU
1972	50,000	—	—	—	20.00	—
1972 Proof	—	Value: 35.00				

KM# 140 DINAR **Weight:** 31.0000 g. **Composition:** 0.5000 Silver .4983 oz. ASW **Subject:** Oil Nationalization

Date	Mintage	F	VF	XF	Unc	BU
1973	60,000	—	—	—	20.00	25.00
1973 Proof	5,000	Value: 37.50				

KM# 143 DINAR **Weight:** 31.0000 g. **Composition:** 0.9000 Silver .8971 oz. ASW **Subject:** Inauguaration of Tharthat-Euphrates Canal

Date	Mintage	F	VF	XF	Unc	BU
1977 Proof	7,000	Value: 40.00				

KM# 145 DINAR **Weight:** 31.0000 g. **Composition:** 0.9000 Silver .8971 oz. ASW **Subject:** International Year of the Child

Date	Mintage	F	VF	XF	Unc	BU
1979 Proof	5,000	Value: 47.50				

Note: KM#145 is commonly found impaired. Value listed is for unimpaired Proof

KM# 148 DINAR **Weight:** 30.5300 g. **Composition:** 0.9000 Silver .8835 oz. ASW **Subject:** 15th Century of Hegira

Date	Mintage	F	VF	XF	Unc	BU
1980 Proof	25,000	Value: 50.00				

Note: KM#148 is commonly found impaired. Value listed is for unimpaired Proof

KM# 149 DINAR **Composition:** Nickel **Subject:** Battle of Qadissyiat **Reverse:** Bust of Saddam Hussein left **Shape:** 10-sided

Date	F	VF	XF	Unc	BU
1980	—	—	3.50	8.00	—
1980 Proof	—	Value: 12.50			

KM# 153 DINAR **Composition:** Nickel **Subject:** 50th Anniversary of Iraq Air Force **Reverse:** Bust of Saddam Hussein left **Shape:** 10-sided

Date	F	VF	XF	Unc	BU
1981	—	—	3.50	8.00	—

KM# 170 DINAR **Composition:** Nickel **Subject:** Circulation Coinage **Shape:** 10-sided

Date	F	VF	XF	Unc	BU
1981	—	—	—	6.50	—

KM# 156 DINAR **Composition:** Nickel **Subject:** Nonaligned Nations Baghdad Conference **Shape:** 10-sided

Date	F	VF	XF	Unc	BU
1982	—	—	3.50	8.00	—

KM# 164 DINAR **Composition:** Nickel **Reverse:** Tower of Babylon **Shape:** 10-sided

Date	F	VF	XF	Unc	BU
1982	—	—	3.50	8.00	—
1982 Proof	—	Value: 12.50			

KM# 134 5 DINARS **Weight:** 13.5700 g. **Composition:** 0.9170 Gold .4001 oz. AGW **Subject:** 50th Anniversary of Iraqi Army

Date	Mintage	F	VF	XF	Unc	BU
1971	20,000	—	—	—	225	—
1971 Proof	—	Value: 250				

KM# 171 5 DINARS **Composition:** Bronze **Obverse:** Denomination and legend **Reverse:** Two swords arched above palm tree

Date	F	VF	XF	Unc	BU
1990	—	—	—	—	—

Note: Not released to circulation

KM# 172 10 DINARS **Composition:** Bronze **Obverse:** Denomination and legend **Reverse:** Two swords arched above palm tree

Date	F	VF	XF	Unc	BU
1990	—	—	—	—	—

Note: Not released to circulation

KM# 166 50 DINARS **Weight:** 13.7000 g. **Composition:** 0.9170 Gold .4037 oz. AGW **Subject:** International Year of the Child

Date	Mintage	F	VF	XF	Unc	BU
1979 Proof	10,000 Inc. above	Value: 280				

KM# 150 50 DINARS **Weight:** 13.0000 g. **Composition:** 0.9170 Gold .3832 oz. AGW **Subject:** 15th Century of Hegira

Date	Mintage	F	VF	XF	Unc	BU
1980 Proof	13,000 Inc. above	Value: 225				

KM# 173 50 DINARS **Weight:** 16.9650 g. **Composition:** 0.9170 Gold .5002 oz. AGW **Subject:** 1st Anniversary of Hussein as President

Date	F	VF	XF	Unc	BU
1980 Proof	—	Value: 375			

KM# 157 50 DINARS **Weight:** 13.7000 g. **Composition:** 0.9170 Gold .4040 oz. AGW **Subject:** Nonaligned Nations Baghdad Conference

Date	Mintage	F	VF	XF	Unc	BU
1982 Proof	10,000	Value: 225				

KM# 167 100 DINARS **Weight:** 26.0000 g. **Composition:** 0.9170 Gold .7665 oz. AGW **Subject:** International Year of the Child

Date	Mintage	F	VF	XF	Unc	BU
1979 Proof	10,000 Inc. above	Value: 450				

KM# 151 100 DINARS **Weight:** 26.0000 g. **Composition:** 0.9170 Gold .7665 oz. AGW **Subject:** 15th Century of Hegira

Date	Mintage	F	VF	XF	Unc	BU
1980 Proof	14,000	Value: 400				
	Inc. above					

KM# 174 100 DINARS **Weight:** 33.9300 g. **Composition:** 0.9170 Gold 1.0003 oz. AGW **Subject:** 1st Anniversary of Hussein as President

Date	F	VF	XF	Unc	BU
1980 Proof	—	Value: 725			

KM# 158 100 DINARS **Weight:** 33.9300 g. **Composition:** 0.9170 Gold 1.0003 oz. AGW **Subject:** Nonaligned Nations Baghdad Conference

Date	Mintage	F	VF	XF	Unc	BU
1982 Proof	10,000	Value: 400				

PATTERNS

Including off metal strikes

KM#	Date	Mintage	Identification	Mkt Val
Pn1	1935	—	20 Fils. KM106.	450
Pn2	1935	—	50 Fils. KM104.	450
Pn3	1936	—	2 Fils. KM96.	250
Pn4	1936	—	4 Fils. KM105.	275
Pn5	1936	—	10 Fils. KM103.	325
Pn6	1936	—	20 Fils. KM106.	425
Pn7	1936	—	50 Fils. KM104.	450

PROOF SETS

KM#	Date	Mintage	Identification	Issue Price	Mkt Val
PS1	1953 (7)	200	KM109-115	—	1,325
PS2	1955 (3)	—	KM116-118	—	500
PS3	1959 (6)	400	KM119-124	—	360
PS4	1959 (7)	—	KM119-124, plus medallic crown (M1)	—	400
PS5	1973 (3)	5,000	KM138-140	—	62.00
PS6	1982 (7)	—	KM159a-160a, 161-164, 168	—	50.00

IRELAND REPUBLIC

The Republic of Ireland, which occupies five-sixths of the island of Ireland located in the Atlantic Ocean west of Great Britain, has an area of 27,136 sq. mi. (70,280 sq. km.) and a population of 4.3 million. Capital: Dublin. Agriculture and dairy farming are the principal industries. Meat, livestock, dairy products and textiles are exported.

A race of tall, red-haired Celts from Gaul arrived in Ireland about 400 B.C., assimilated the native Erainn and Picts, and established a Gaelic civilization. After the arrival of St. Patrick in 432AD, Ireland evolved into a center of Latin learning, which sent missionaries to Europe and possibly North America. In 1154, Pope Adrian IV gave all of Ireland to English King Henry II to administer as a Papal fief. Because of the enactment of anti-Catholic laws and the awarding of vast tracts of Irish land to Protestant absentee landowners, English control did not become reasonably absolute until 1800 when England and Ireland became the 'United Kingdom of Great Britain and Ireland'. Religious freedom was restored to the Irish in 1829, but agitation for political autonomy continued until the Irish Free State was established as a dominion on Dec. 6, 1921.Ireland proclaimed itself a republic on April 18, 1949. The government, however, does not use the term 'Republic of Ireland', which tacitly acknowledges the partitioning of the island into Ireland and Northern Ireland, but refers to the country simply as 'Ireland'.

RULERS

British, until 1921

MONETARY SYSTEM

(1928-1971)

4 Farthings = 1 Penny
12 Pence = 1 Shilling
2 Shillings = 1 Florin
20 Shillings = 1 Pound

NOTE: This section has been renumbered to segregate the coinage of the Irish Free State from the earlier crown coinage of Ireland.

IRISH FREE STATE

STERLING COINAGE

KM# 1 FARTHING **Weight:** 2.8300 g. **Composition:** Bronze **Obv. Legend:** SAORSTAT EIREANN = Irish Free State **Reverse:** Woodcock **Size:** 20.3 mm.

Date	Mintage	F	VF	XF	Unc	BU
1928	300,000	0.50	1.50	4.50	10.00	—
1928 Proof	6,001	Value: 15.00				
1930	288,000	0.75	1.50	4.50	16.50	—
1930 Proof; Rare	—	—	—	—	—	—
1931	192,000	4.50	8.00	15.00	35.00	—
1931 Proof	—	—	—	—	—	—
1932	192,000	5.00	10.00	18.00	45.00	—
1932 Proof; Rare	—	—	—	—	—	—
1933	480,000	0.75	1.50	4.00	16.50	—
1933 Proof; Rare	—	—	—	—	—	—
1935	192,000	5.00	8.00	15.00	35.00	—
1935 Proof; Rare	—	—	—	—	—	—
1936	192,000	5.00	8.00	16.50	37.50	—
1936 Proof; Rare	—	—	—	—	—	—
1937	480,000	0.50	1.50	3.00	14.50	—
1937 Proof; Rare	—	—	—	—	—	—

KM# 2 1/2 PENNY **Weight:** 5.6700 g. **Composition:** Bronze **Obv. Legend:** SAORSTATE EIREANN = Irish Free State **Reverse:** Sow with piglets **Size:** 25.5 mm.

Date	Mintage	F	VF	XF	Unc	BU
1928	2,880,000	0.75	2.00	5.00	14.00	—
1928 Proof	6,001	Value: 15.00				
1933	720,000	5.00	15.00	80.00	750	—
1933 Proof; Rare	—	—	—	—	—	—
1935	960,000	2.00	6.00	50.00	275	—
1935 Proof; Rare	—	—	—	—	—	—
1937	960,000	1.00	3.00	15.00	35.00	—

KM# 3 PENNY **Weight:** 9.4500 g. **Composition:** Bronze **Obv. Legend:** SAORSTATE EIREANN = Irish Free State **Reverse:** Hen with chicks **Size:** 30.8 mm.

Date	Mintage	F	VF	XF	Unc	BU
1928	9,000,000	0.50	1.00	4.00	20.00	—
1928 Proof	6,001	Value: 18.50				
1931	2,400,000	1.00	2.00	12.00	50.00	—
1931 Proof	—	Value: 1,500				
1933	1,680,000	1.00	2.50	20.00	125	—
1933 Proof; Rare	—	—	—	—	—	—
1935	5,472,000	0.50	1.00	8.00	32.00	—
1935 Proof; Rare	—	—	—	—	—	—
1937	5,400,000	0.50	1.00	15.00	70.00	—
1937 Proof	—	Value: 12.50				

KM# 4 3 PENCE **Weight:** 3.2400 g. **Composition:** Nickel **Obv. Legend:** SAORSTATE EIREANN = Irish Free State **Reverse:** Hare **Size:** 17.6 mm.

Date	Mintage	F	VF	XF	Unc	BU
1928	1,500,000	0.50	1.00	3.50	10.00	—
1928 Proof	6,001	Value: 20.00				
1933	320,000	3.00	10.00	75.00	400	—
1933 Proof; Rare	—	—	—	—	—	—
1934	800,000	1.00	2.00	12.50	70.00	—
1934 Proof; Rare	—	—	—	—	—	—
1935	240,000	3.00	8.00	35.00	225	—
1935 Proof; Rare	—	—	—	—	—	—

KM# 5 6 PENCE **Weight:** 4.5400 g. **Composition:** Nickel **Obv. Legend:** SAORSTATE EIREANN = Irish Free State **Reverse:** Irish Wolf-hound **Size:** 20.8 mm.

Date	Mintage	F	VF	XF	Unc	BU
1928	3,201,000	0.50	1.00	5.00	17.50	—
1928 Proof	6,001	Value: 25.00				
1933 Proof; Rare	—	—	—	—	—	—
1934	600,000	1.00	2.00	18.00	120	—
1934 Proof; Rare	—	—	—	—	—	—
1935	520,000	1.00	3.00	30.00	320	—
1935 Proof; Rare	—	—	—	—	—	—

KM# 6 SHILLING **Weight:** 5.6552 g. **Composition:** 0.7500 Silver .1364 oz. ASW **Obv. Legend:** SAORSTAT EIREANN = Irish Free State **Reverse:** Bull **Size:** 23.6 mm.

Date	Mintage	F	VF	XF	Unc	BU
1928	2,700,000	1.50	5.00	10.00	22.50	—
1928 Proof	6,001	Value: 27.50				
1930	460,000	5.00	25.00	150	550	—
1930	—	Value: 1,200				
1931	400,000	4.50	18.00	90.00	225	—
1931 Proof; Rare	—	—	—	—	—	—
1933	300,000	5.00	20.00	100	325	—
1933 Proof; Rare	—	—	—	—	—	—
1935	400,000	2.00	7.00	25.00	85.00	—
1935 Proof; Rare	—	—	—	—	—	—
1937	100,000	12.00	65.00	500	2,000	—
1937 Proof; Rare	—	—	—	—	—	—

KM# 7 FLORIN **Weight:** 11.3104 g. **Composition:** 0.7500 Silver .2727 oz. ASW **Obv. Legend:** SAORSTAT EIREANN = Irish Free State **Reverse:** Salmon **Size:** 28.5 mm.

Date	Mintage	F	VF	XF	Unc	BU
1928	2,025,000	3.00	7.00	15.00	40.00	—
1928 Proof	6,001	Value: 42.50				
1930	330,000	6.50	25.00	135	400	—
1930 Proof; Rare	—	—	—	—	—	—
1931	200,000	8.00	35.00	225	500	—
1931 Proof; Rare	—	—	—	—	—	—
1933	300,000	5.00	25.00	195	575	—
1933 Proof; Rare	—	—	—	—	—	—
1934	150,000	10.00	60.00	325	750	—
1934 Proof	—	Value: 2,750				
1935	390,000	5.00	17.50	65.00	185	—
1935 Proof; Rare	—	—	—	—	—	—
1937	150,000	10.00	35.00	210	750	—
1937 Proof; Rare	—	—	—	—	—	—

KM# 8 1/2 CROWN **Weight:** 14.1380 g. **Composition:** 0.7500 Silver .3409 oz. ASW **Obv. Legend:** SAORSTAT EIREANN = Irish Free State **Reverse:** Irish Hunter **Size:** 32.3 mm. **Note:** Close O and I in COROIN. 8 tufts in horse's tail, with 156 beads.

Date	Mintage	F	VF	XF	Unc	BU
1928	2,160,000	3.50	10.00	20.00	45.00	—
1928 Proof	6,001	Value: 55.00				
1930	352,000	4.50	20.00	125	400	—
1930 Proof; Rare	—	—	—	—	—	—
1931	160,000	9.00	30.00	250	650	—
1931 Proof; Rare	—	—	—	—	—	—
1933	336,000	4.50	20.00	125	400	—
1933 Proof; Rare	—	—	—	—	—	—
1934	480,000	4.00	15.00	40.00	150	—
1934 Proof; Rare	—	—	—	—	—	—
1937	40,000	65.00	150	750	1,750	—
1937 Proof; Rare	—	—	—	—	—	—

IRELAND
(Republic)
STERLING COINAGE

KM# 9 FARTHING **Weight:** 2.8300 g. **Composition:** Bronze **Obv. Legend:** EIRE = Ireland **Reverse:** Woodcock **Size:** 20.2 mm.

Date	Mintage	F	VF	XF	Unc	BU
1939	786,000	0.50	1.00	2.00	7.50	—
1939 Proof	—	Value: 815				
1940	192,000	2.00	4.00	8.00	20.00	—
1940 Proof; Rare	—	—	—	—	—	—
1941	480,000	0.50	0.75	2.00	6.50	—
1941 Proof; Rare	—	—	—	—	—	—
1943	480,000	0.50	0.75	2.00	6.50	—
1944	480,000	0.75	1.25	3.00	10.00	—
1946	480,000	0.50	0.75	2.00	6.00	—
1946 Proof	—	—	—	—	—	—
1949	192,000	0.75	3.00	6.00	18.00	—
1949 Proof	—	Value: 300				
1953	192,000	0.25	0.50	1.25	3.00	—
1953 Proof	—	Value: 300				
1959	192,000	0.25	0.50	1.25	3.00	—
1959 Proof; Rare	—	—	—	—	—	—
1966	96,000	0.35	0.75	1.50	3.50	—

KM# 10 1/2 PENNY **Weight:** 5.6700 g. **Composition:** Bronze **Obv. Legend:** EIRE = Ireland **Reverse:** Sow with piglets **Size:** 25.5 mm.

Date	Mintage	F	VF	XF	Unc	BU
1939	240,000	10.00	17.50	60.00	200	—
1939 Proof	—	Value: 1,000				
1940	1,680,000	1.00	4.50	40.00	150	—
1940 Proof; Rare	—	—	—	—	—	—
1941	2,400,000	0.20	0.50	2.50	20.00	—
1941 Proof; Rare	—	—	—	—	—	—
1942	6,931,000	0.10	0.25	1.50	8.00	—
1943	2,669,000	0.20	0.50	3.00	22.00	—
1946	720,000	1.00	2.50	15.00	60.00	—
1946 Proof; Rare	—	—	—	—	—	—
1949	1,344,000	0.10	0.25	1.50	12.50	—
1949 Proof	—	—	—	—	—	—
1953	2,400,000	0.10	0.15	0.25	1.50	—
1953 Proof	—	Value: 400				
1964	2,160,000	0.10	0.15	0.25	1.50	—
1964 Proof; Rare	—	—	—	—	—	—
1965	1,440,000	0.10	0.15	0.75	2.50	—
1966	1,680,000	0.10	0.15	0.25	1.50	—
1967	1,200,000	0.10	0.15	0.25	1.50	—

KM# 11 PENNY **Weight:** 9.4500 g. **Composition:** Bronze **Obv. Legend:** EIRE = Ireland **Reverse:** Hen with chicks **Size:** 30.8 mm. **Note:** Varieties exist.

Date	Mintage	F	VF	XF	Unc	BU
1940	312,000	3.00	10.00	65.00	225	—
1940 Proof; Rare	—	—	—	—	—	—
1941	4,680,000	0.25	0.50	8.00	50.00	—
1941 Proof; Rare	—	—	—	—	—	—
1942	17,520,000	0.25	0.50	2.00	11.50	—
1942 Proof; Rare	—	—	—	—	—	—
1943	3,360,000	0.75	1.50	7.50	45.00	—
1946	4,800,000	0.25	0.50	3.00	20.00	—
1946 Proof; Rare	—	—	—	—	—	—
1948	4,800,000	0.25	0.50	3.00	8.00	—
1948 Proof; Rare	—	—	—	—	—	—
1949	4,080,000	0.25	0.50	3.00	8.00	—
1949 Proof	—	Value: 600				
1950	2,400,000	0.25	0.50	3.50	12.50	—
1950 Proof	—	Value: 600				
1952	2,400,000	0.25	0.50	2.00	6.00	—
1952 Proof; Rare	—	—	—	—	—	—
1962	1,200,000	0.75	2.50	3.50	12.50	—
1962 Proof	—	Value: 175				
1963	9,600,000	0.20	0.40	0.75	2.00	—
1963 Proof	—	Value: 175				
1964	6,000,000	0.20	0.40	0.75	1.50	—
1964 Proof	—	—	—	—	—	—
1965	11,160,000	0.20	0.40	0.75	1.50	—
1966	6,000,000	0.20	0.40	0.75	1.50	—
1967	2,400,000	0.20	0.40	0.75	1.50	—
1968	21,000,000	0.20	0.40	0.75	1.50	—
1968 Proof	—	Value: 350				

KM# 12 3 PENCE **Weight:** 3.2400 g. **Composition:** Nickel **Obv. Legend:** EIRE = Ireland **Reverse:** Hare **Size:** 17.6 mm.

Date	Mintage	F	VF	XF	Unc	BU
1939	64,000	10.00	20.00	70.00	525	—
1939 Proof	—	Value: 1,500				
1940	720,000	1.50	3.00	12.50	50.00	—
1940 Proof; Rare	—	—	—	—	—	—

KM# 12a 3 PENCE **Weight:** 3.2400 g. **Composition:** Copper-Nickel **Obv. Legend:** EIRE = Ireland **Reverse:** Hare

Date	Mintage	F	VF	XF	Unc	BU
1942	4,000,000	0.25	0.75	6.00	30.00	—
1942 Proof	—	Value: 350				
1943	1,360,000	0.50	2.00	15.00	80.00	—
1943 Proof	—	—	—	—	—	—
1946	800,000	1.00	2.00	10.00	45.00	—
1946 Proof	—	Value: 200				
1948	1,600,000	1.00	2.00	35.00	125	—
1948 Proof; Rare	—	—	—	—	—	—
1949	1,200,000	0.25	0.50	3.00	25.00	—
1949 Proof	—	Value: 200				
1950	1,600,000	0.25	0.50	3.00	20.00	—
1950 Proof	—	Value: 400				
1953	1,600,000	0.25	0.50	2.00	10.00	—
1953 Proof; Rare	—	—	—	—	—	—
1956	1,200,000	0.25	0.50	2.00	8.00	—
1956 Proof; Rare	—	—	—	—	—	—
1961	2,400,000	0.15	0.25	0.50	6.00	—
1961 Proof; Rare	—	—	—	—	—	—
1962	3,200,000	0.15	0.25	0.50	8.00	—
1962 Proof; Rare	—	—	—	—	—	—
1963	4,000,000	0.15	0.25	0.50	2.50	—
1963 Proof; Rare	—	—	—	—	—	—
1964	4,000,000	0.10	0.15	0.25	1.50	—
1965	3,600,000	0.10	0.15	0.25	1.50	—
1966	4,000,000	0.10	0.15	0.25	1.50	—
1967	2,400,000	0.10	0.15	0.25	1.50	—
1968	4,000,000	0.10	0.15	0.25	1.50	—
1968 Proof	—	—	—	—	—	—

KM# 13 6 PENCE **Weight:** 4.5400 g. **Composition:** Nickel **Obv. Legend:** EIRE = Ireland **Reverse:** Irish Wolf-hound **Size:** 20.8 mm.

Date	Mintage	F	VF	XF	Unc	BU
1939	876,000	0.75	2.00	8.00	55.00	—
1939 Proof	—	Value: 1,150				
1940	1,120,000	0.75	2.00	6.00	45.00	—
1940 Proof; Rare	—	—	—	—	—	—

KM# 13a 6 PENCE **Weight:** 4.5400 g. **Composition:** Copper-Nickel **Obv. Legend:** EIRE = Ireland **Reverse:** Irish Wolf-hound **Size:** 20.8 mm.

Date	Mintage	F	VF	XF	Unc	BU
1942	1,320,000	0.50	1.00	5.00	40.00	—
1942 Proof; Rare	—	—	—	—	—	—
1945	400,000	2.00	8.00	50.00	160	—
1945 Proof; Rare	—	—	—	—	—	—
1946	720,000	2.00	10.00	100	450	—
1946 Proof; Rare	—	—	—	—	—	—
1947	800,000	1.00	12.00	30.00	70.00	—
1947 Proof; Rare	—	—	—	—	—	—
1948	800,000	1.00	1.50	10.00	55.00	—
1948 Proof; Rare	—	—	—	—	—	—
1949	600,000	1.50	3.50	15.00	65.00	—
1949 Proof; Rare	—	—	—	—	—	—
1950	800,000	1.00	3.00	12.00	60.00	—
1950 Proof; Rare	—	—	—	—	—	—
1952	800,000	0.50	1.00	5.00	20.00	—
1952 Proof	—	Value: 175				
1953	800,000	0.50	1.00	5.00	18.00	—
1953 Proof; Rare	—	—	—	—	—	—
1955	600,000	1.00	2.50	8.00	20.00	—
1955 Proof; Rare	—	—	—	—	—	—
1956	600,000	0.75	2.00	4.00	15.00	—
1956 Proof; Rare	—	—	—	—	—	—
1958	600,000	1.00	2.50	6.00	65.00	—
1958	—	Value: 350				
1959	2,000,000	0.25	0.50	3.00	15.00	—
1959 Proof; Rare	—	—	—	—	—	—
1960	2,020,000	0.25	0.50	2.00	12.00	—
1960 Proof; Rare	—	—	—	—	—	—
1961	3,000,000	0.25	0.25	1.00	6.50	—
1961 Proof; Rare	—	—	—	—	—	—
1962	4,000,000	0.25	0.75	4.00	60.00	—
1962 Proof; Rare	—	—	—	—	—	—
1963	4,000,000	0.15	0.25	0.50	3.00	—
1963 Proof; Rare	—	—	—	—	—	—
1964	6,000,000	0.15	0.25	0.50	3.00	—
1966	2,000,000	0.15	0.25	0.50	3.00	—
1967	4,000,000	0.15	0.25	0.50	3.00	—
1968	8,000,000	0.15	0.25	0.50	3.00	—
1969	2,000,000	0.15	0.25	0.50	3.00	—

KM# 14 SHILLING **Weight:** 5.6552 g. **Composition:** 0.7500 Silver .1364 oz. ASW **Obv. Legend:** EIRE = Ireland **Reverse:** Bull **Size:** 23.6 mm.

Date	Mintage	F	VF	XF	Unc	BU
1939	1,140,000	2.50	4.50	12.50	32.50	—
1939 Proof	—	Value: 775				
1940	580,000	3.00	5.00	15.00	40.00	—
1940 Proof; Rare	—	—	—	—	—	—
1941	300,000	4.00	12.00	22.50	45.00	—
1941 Proof; Rare	—	—	—	—	—	—
1942	286,000	4.00	7.50	15.00	40.00	—
1942 Proof; Rare	—	—	—	—	—	—

KM# 14a SHILLING **Weight:** 5.6600 g. **Composition:** Copper-Nickel **Obv. Legend:** EIRE = Ireland **Reverse:** Bull **Size:** 23.6 mm.

Date	Mintage	F	VF	XF	Unc	BU
1951	2,000,000	0.25	0.50	2.50	15.00	—
1951 Proof	—	Value: 500				
1954	3,000,000	0.25	0.50	2.50	11.50	—
1954 Proof	—	—	—	—	—	—
1955	1,000,000	1.00	2.00	5.00	15.00	—
1955 Proof	—	—	—	—	—	—
1959	2,000,000	0.25	0.50	4.00	35.00	—
1959 Proof; Rare	—	—	—	—	—	—
1962	4,000,000	0.25	0.50	1.00	7.00	—
1962 Proof; Rare	—	—	—	—	—	—
1963	4,000,000	0.25	0.50	1.00	3.00	—
1963 Proof; Rare	—	—	—	—	—	—
1964	4,000,000	0.25	0.50	1.00	2.00	—
1966	3,000,000	0.25	0.50	1.00	2.00	—
1968	4,000,000	0.25	0.50	1.00	3.00	—

KM# 15 FLORIN **Weight:** 11.3104 g. **Composition:** 0.7500 Silver .2727 oz. ASW **Obv. Legend:** EIRE = Ireland **Reverse:** Salmon **Size:** 28.5 mm.

Date	Mintage	F	VF	XF	Unc	BU
1939	1,080,000	2.00	5.00	18.00	40.00	—
1939 Proof	—	Value: 800				
1940	670,000	3.00	6.00	20.00	45.00	—
1940 Proof; Rare	—	—	—	—	—	—
1941	400,000	3.00	8.00	22.50	55.00	—
1941 Proof	—	Value: 800				
1942	109,000	5.00	15.00	25.00	50.00	—
1943	—	1,200	2,000	4,000	8,000	—

Note: Approximately 35 known

KM# 15a FLORIN **Weight:** 11.3100 g. **Composition:** Copper-Nickel **Obv. Legend:** EIRE = Ireland **Reverse:** Salmon **Size:** 28.5 mm.

Date	Mintage	F	VF	XF	Unc	BU
1951	1,000,000	1.00	2.00	6.00	16.00	—
1951 Proof	—	Value: 600				
1954	1,000,000	1.00	2.00	6.00	18.00	—
1954 Proof	—	Value: 450				
1955	1,000,000	1.00	2.00	5.00	15.00	—
1955 Proof	—	Value: 450				
1959	2,000,000	0.50	1.00	2.50	10.00	—
1959 Proof; Rare	—	—	—	—	—	—
1961	2,000,000	0.50	1.00	7.00	22.00	—
1961 Proof; Rare	—	—	—	—	—	—
1962	2,400,000	0.50	1.00	2.00	10.00	—
1962 Proof; Rare	—	—	—	—	—	—
1963	3,000,000	0.25	0.50	0.75	4.00	—
1963 Proof; Rare	—	—	—	—	—	—
1964	4,000,000	0.25	0.50	0.75	2.00	—
1965	2,000,000	0.25	0.50	0.75	2.00	—
1966	3,625,000	0.25	0.50	0.75	2.00	—
1968	1,000,000	0.25	0.35	1.00	4.50	—

KM# 16 1/2 CROWN **Weight:** 14.1380 g. **Composition:** 0.7500 Silver .3409 oz. ASW **Obv. Legend:** EIRE = Ireland **Reverse:** Irish Hunter **Size:** 32.3 mm. **Note:** Normal spacing between O and I in COROIN, 7 tufts in horse's tail, with 151 beads in border.

Date	Mintage	F	VF	XF	Unc	BU
1939	888,000	3.00	8.00	17.50	55.00	—
1939 Proof	—	Value: 800				
1940	752,000	3.00	8.00	15.00	50.00	—
1940 Proof; Rare	—	—	—	—	—	—
1941	320,000	4.00	12.50	30.00	75.00	—
1941 Proof; Rare	—	—	—	—	—	—
1942	286,000	4.00	12.50	25.00	50.00	—

KM# 16a 1/2 CROWN **Weight:** 14.1400 g. **Composition:** Copper-Nickel **Obv. Legend:** EIRE = Ireland **Reverse:** Irish Hunter **Size:** 32.3 mm. **Note:** Normal spacing between O and I on "COROIN", 7 tufts in horse's tail, with 151 beads in border.

Date	Mintage	F	VF	XF	Unc	BU
1951	800,000	1.50	3.00	10.00	35.00	—
1951 Proof	—	Value: 600				
1954	400,000	2.00	4.00	15.00	50.00	—
1954 Proof	—	Value: 500				
1955	1,080,000	1.00	2.00	6.00	25.00	—
1955 Proof	—	Value: 200				
1959	1,600,000	1.00	1.75	3.00	12.50	—
1959 Proof; Rare	—	—	—	—	—	—
1961	1,600,000	1.00	1.75	3.50	20.00	—
1961 Proof	—	—	—	—	—	—
1962	3,200,000	0.50	1.00	2.50	12.50	—
1962 Proof	—	—	—	—	—	—
1963	2,400,000	0.50	1.00	2.00	7.50	—
1963 Proof; Rare	—	—	—	—	—	—
1964	3,200,000	0.50	1.00	2.00	6.00	—
1966	700,000	0.75	1.50	3.00	6.00	—
1967	2,000,000	0.50	1.00	2.00	6.00	—

Note: 1967 exists struck with a polished reverse die; Estimated value is $15.00 in Uncirculated

KM# 17 1/2 CROWN **Composition:** Copper-Nickel **Obverse:** KM#16a **Reverse:** KM#8. **Note:** Mule.

Date	VG	F	VF	XF	Unc
1961	—	8.00	25.00	200	—

KM# 18 10 SHILLING **Weight:** 18.1400 g. **Composition:** 0.8333 Silver .4858 oz. ASW **Subject:** 50th Anniversary of Easter Uprising **Size:** 30.5 mm.

Date		F	VF	XF	Unc	BU
1966		—	—	4.50	9.00	—

Note: Approximately 1.270 melted down

1966 Proof	20,000	Value: 17.50

DECIMAL COINAGE

100 Pence = 1 Pound (Punt)

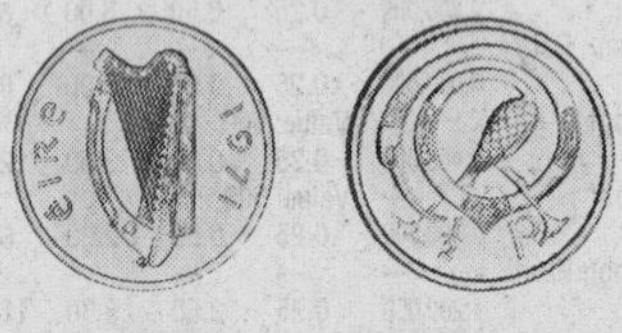

KM# 19 1/2 PENNY **Weight:** 1.7500 g. **Composition:** Bronze **Reverse:** Stylized bird **Size:** 17.1 mm.

Date	Mintage	F	VF	XF	Unc	BU
1971		—	—	0.10	0.30	—
1971 Proof	50,000	Value: 1.00				
1975		—	—	0.10	0.30	—
1976		—	—	0.10	0.30	—
1978		—	—	—	0.25	—
1980		—	—	—	0.25	—
1982		—	—	—	0.30	—
1985		—	—	—	—	—
1986		—	—	—	—	—

Note: This mintage figure represents a surplus of coins minted for Polished Standard Specimen Sets (Proof Sets) later released into circulation. The entire surplus was presumably remelted due to demonitization of this denomination Jan. 1, 1987.

1986 Proof	6,750	Value: 12.50

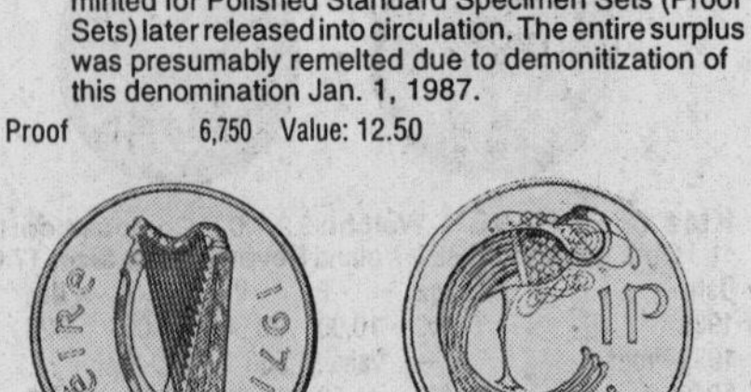

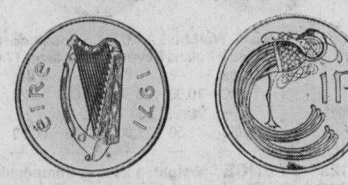

KM# 20 PENNY **Weight:** 3.5600 g. **Composition:** Bronze **Reverse:** Stylized bird **Size:** 20.3 mm.

Date	Mintage	F	VF	XF	Unc	BU
1971	100,500,000	—	—	0.10	0.20	—
1971 Proof	50,000	Value: 1.25				
1974	10,000,000	—	—	0.10	0.25	—
1975	10,000,000	—	—	0.10	0.25	—
1976	38,164,000	—	—	0.10	0.20	—
1978	25,746,000	—	—	0.10	0.20	—
1979	21,766,000	—	—	0.10	0.20	—
1980	86,712,000	—	—	0.10	0.20	—
1982	54,189,000	—	—	0.10	0.20	—
1985	19,242,000	—	—	0.10	0.20	—
1986	36,584,000	—	—	0.10	0.20	—
1986 Proof	6,750	Value: 1.25				
1988	56,772,000	—	—	0.10	0.20	—

KM# 20a PENNY **Weight:** 3.5600 g. **Composition:** Copper-Plated-Steel **Size:** 20.3 mm.

Date	Mintage	F	VF	XF	Unc	BU
1990	65,099,000	—	—	0.10	0.15	—
1992	25,643,000	—	—	0.10	0.15	—
1993	10,000,000	—	—	0.10	0.15	—
1994	45,800,000	—	—	0.10	0.15	—
1995	70,836,000	—	—	0.10	0.15	—
1996	190,092,000	—	—	0.10	0.15	—
1998	40,744,000	—	—	0.10	0.15	—
2000	133,760,000	—	—	0.10	0.15	—

KM# 21 2 PENCE **Weight:** 7.1200 g. **Composition:** Bronze **Reverse:** Stylized bird **Size:** 25.9 mm.

Date	Mintage	F	VF	XF	Unc	BU
1971	75,500,000	—	—	0.10	1.00	—
1971 Proof	50,000	Value: 1.50				
1975	20,010,000	—	—	0.10	0.30	—
1976	5,414,000	—	—	0.10	0.50	—
1978	12,000,000	—	—	0.10	0.30	—
1979	32,373,000	—	—	0.10	0.30	—
1980	59,828,000	—	—	0.10	0.30	—
1982	30,435,000	—	—	0.10	0.30	—
1985	14,469,000	—	—	0.10	0.30	—
1986	23,865,000	—	—	0.10	0.30	—
1986 Proof	6,750	Value: 1.50				
1988	35,868,000	—	—	0.10	0.30	—

KM# 21a 2 PENCE **Weight:** 7.1200 g. **Composition:** Copper-Plated-Steel **Size:** 25.9 mm.

Date	Mintage	F	VF	XF	Unc	BU
1990	34,284,000	—	—	0.10	0.25	—
1992	10,215,000	—	—	0.10	0.25	—
1995	55,459,000	—	—	0.10	0.25	—
1996	69,342,000	—	—	0.10	0.25	—
1998	33,688,000	—	—	0.10	0.25	—
2000	66,960,000	—	—	0.10	0.25	—

KM# 22 5 PENCE **Weight:** 5.6600 g. **Composition:** Copper-Nickel **Reverse:** Bull right **Size:** 23.6 mm.

Date	Mintage	F	VF	XF	Unc	BU
1969	5,000,000	—	0.10	0.15	1.00	—
1970	10,000,000	—	—	0.10	0.50	—
1971	8,000,000	—	—	0.10	0.50	—
1971 Proof	50,000	Value: 2.00				
1974	7,000,000	—	—	0.10	0.50	—
1975	10,000,000	—	—	0.10	0.50	—
1976	20,616,000	—	—	0.10	0.50	—
1978	28,536,000	—	—	0.10	0.50	—
1980	22,190,000	—	—	0.10	0.50	—
1982	24,404,000	—	—	0.10	0.50	—
1985	4,202,000	—	—	0.10	0.50	—
1986	15,298,000	—	0.10	0.15	1.00	—
1986 Proof	6,750	Value: 2.00				
1990	7,547,000	—	—	0.10	0.50	—

KM# 28.1 5 PENCE **Weight:** 3.2500 g. **Composition:** Copper-Nickel **Reverse:** Bull left **Size:** 18.5 mm. **Note:** Reduced size: 18.5mm.

Date	Mintage	F	VF	XF	Unc	BU
1992	74,526,000	—	—	0.10	0.50	—
1993	89,109,000	—	—	0.10	0.50	—
1994	31,058,000	—	—	0.10	0.50	—
1995	14,667,000	—	—	0.10	0.50	—
1996	158,546,000	—	—	0.10	0.50	—
1998	63,247,000	—	—	0.10	0.50	—
2000	58,000,000	—	—	0.10	0.50	—

KM# 28.2 5 PENCE Weight: 3.2400 g. **Composition:** Copper-Nickel **Obverse:** Harp **Reverse:** Bull left **Edge:** Plain **Size:** 18.4 mm.

Date	F	VF	XF	Unc	BU
1995	—	—	—	1.00	—

KM# 23 10 PENCE Weight: 11.3200 g. **Composition:** Copper-Nickel **Reverse:** Salmon right **Size:** 28.5 mm.

Date		F	VF	XF	Unc	BU
1969		—	—	0.40	1.25	—
1971		—	—	0.40	1.25	—
1971 Proof	50,000	Value: 2.50				
1973		—	—	0.40	1.50	—
1974		—	—	0.35	1.25	—
1975		—	—	0.35	1.25	—
1976		—	—	0.35	1.25	—
1978		—	—	0.25	1.00	—
1980		—	—	0.25	1.00	—
1982		—	—	0.25	1.00	—
1985		—	—	0.25	1.25	—
1986		—	2.00	5.00	16.50	—

Note: This mintage figure represents a surplus of coins minted for Polished Standard Specimen Sets (Proof Sets), later released into circulation

1986 Proof	6,750	Value: 16.50

KM# 29 10 PENCE Weight: 5.4500 g. **Composition:** Copper-Nickel **Reverse:** Salmon left **Size:** 22 mm. **Note:** Reduced size.

Date	Mintage	F	VF	XF	Unc	BU
1993	80,061,000	—	—	—	0.75	—
1994	58,510,000	—	—	—	0.75	—
1995	15,781,000	—	—	—	0.75	—
1996	18,402,000	—	—	—	0.75	—
1997	10,033,000	—	—	—	0.75	—
1998	10,000,000	—	—	—	0.75	—
1999	24,500,000	—	—	—	0.75	—
2000	45,679,000	—	—	—	0.75	—

KM# 25 20 PENCE Weight: 8.4700 g. **Composition:** Nickel-Bronze **Reverse:** Irish Hunter **Size:** 27.1 mm.

Date	Mintage	F	VF	XF	Unc	BU
1986	50,430,000	—	—	0.50	1.75	—
1986 Proof	6,750	Value: 3.50				
1988	20,661,000	—	—	0.50	1.75	—
1992	14,761,000	—	—	0.50	1.75	—
1994	11,086,000	—	—	0.50	1.75	—
1995	18,160,000	—	—	0.50	1.75	—
1998	25,024,000	—	—	0.50	1.75	—
1999	11,000,000	—	—	0.50	1.75	—
2000	28,500,000	—	—	0.50	1.75	—

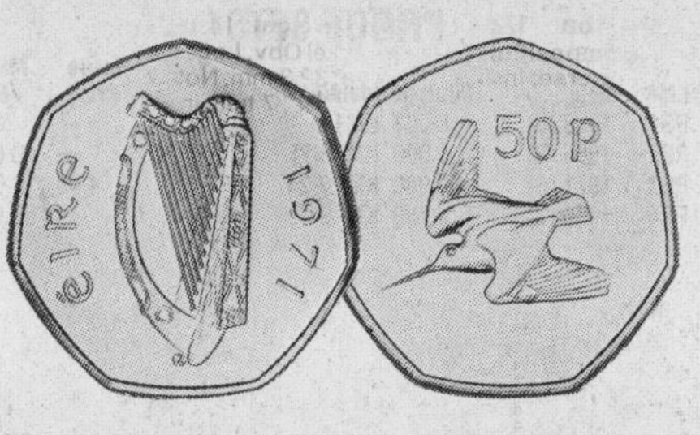

KM# 24 50 PENCE Weight: 13.5000 g. **Composition:** Copper-Nickel **Obverse:** Harp **Reverse:** Woodcock

Date		F	VF	XF	Unc	BU
1970		—	—	1.50	4.00	—
1971		—	1.00	2.00	6.00	—
1971 Proof	50,000	Value: 3.50				
1974		—	1.00	2.00	7.00	—
1975		—	—	1.50	4.00	—
1976		—	—	1.25	3.00	—
1977		—	—	1.25	3.00	—
1978		—	—	1.25	3.00	—
1979		—	—	1.25	3.00	—
1981		—	—	1.00	2.00	—
1982		—	—	1.25	3.00	—
1983		—	—	1.00	1.75	—
1986		—	3.00	6.00	18.50	—

Note: This circulation mintage figure represents a surplus of coins minted for Polished Standard Specimen Sets (Proof Sets), later released into circulation

		F	VF	XF	Unc	BU
1986 Proof	6,750	Value: 18.50				
1988		—	—	1.00	1.75	—
1996		—	—	1.00	1.75	—
1997		—	—	1.00	1.75	—
1998		—	—	1.00	1.75	—
1999		—	—	1.00	1.75	—
2000		—	—	1.00	1.75	—

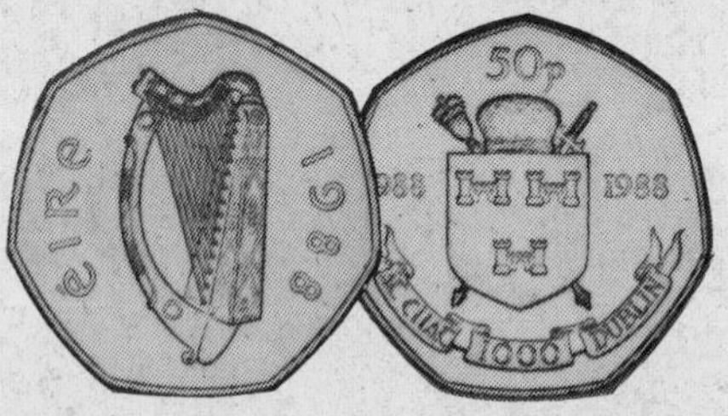

KM# 26 50 PENCE Weight: 13.5000 g. **Composition:** Copper-Nickel **Subject:** Dublin Millennium

Date	Mintage	F	VF	XF	Unc	BU
1988	5,000,000	—	—	—	2.50	—
1988 Proof	50,000	Value: 15.00				

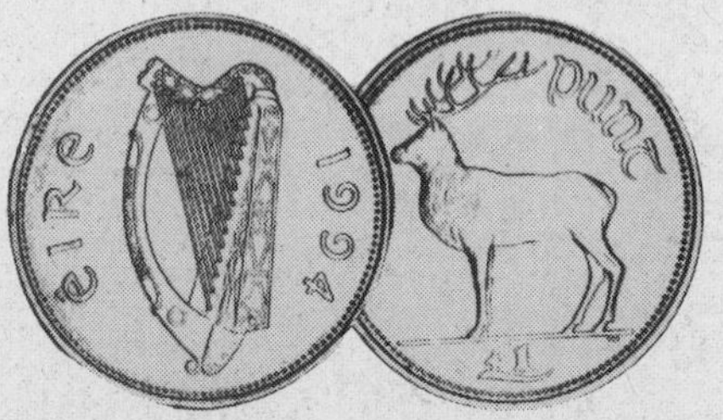

KM# 27 PUNT (Pound) Weight: 13.5000 g. **Composition:** Copper-Nickel **Reverse:** Red Deer left **Note:** The normal KM27 was struck with an engrailed edge. Examples with plain edge, or partial engrailing command a premium of approximately four times the values listed here.

Date	Mintage	F	VF	XF	Unc	BU
1990	62,292,000	—	—	—	7.50	—
1990 Proof	42,000	Value: 27.50				
1994	14,925,000	—	—	—	7.50	—
1995	10,215,000	—	—	—	7.50	—
1996	9,230,000	—	—	—	7.50	—
1998	22,955,000	—	—	—	7.50	—
1999	10,000,000	—	—	—	7.50	—
2000	26,913,000	—	—	—	7.50	—

KM# 30 PUNT (Pound) Weight: 28.2800 g. **Composition:** 0.9250 Silver .8328 oz. ASW **Subject:** 50th Anniversary - United Nations **Obverse:** Harp **Reverse:** Dove and UN logo **Rev. Inscription:** United for Peace **Size:** 38.6 mm.

Date		F	VF	XF	Unc	BU
ND(1995) Proof	—	Value: 40.00				

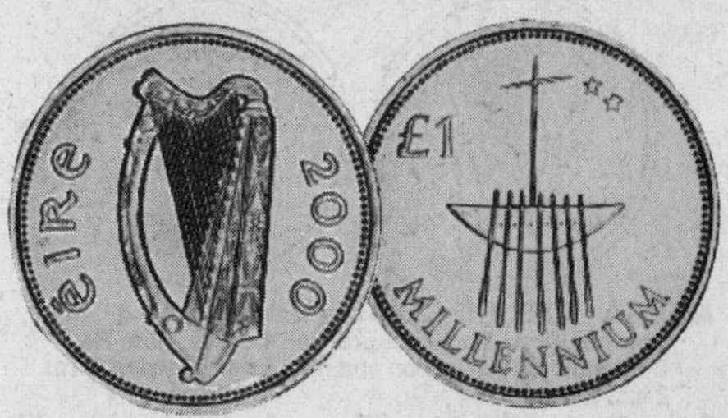

KM# 31 PUNT (Pound) Weight: 10.0000 g. **Composition:** Copper-Nickel **Subject:** Dublin Millennium **Obverse:** Harp **Reverse:** Stylized ancient ship **Note:** Struck at Sandyford.

Date	F	VF	XF	Unc	BU
2000	—	—	—	7.50	—

KM# 31a PUNT (Pound) Weight: 10.5000 g. **Composition:** 0.9250 Silver 0.3123 oz. ASW **Subject:** Dublin Millennium **Obverse:** Harp **Reverse:** Stylized ancient ship

Date		F	VF	XF	Unc	BU
2000 Proof	—	Value: 25.00				

EURO COINAGE

European Economic Community Issues

KM# 32 EURO CENT Weight: 2.2700 g. **Composition:** Copper Plated Steel **Obverse:** Harp **Reverse:** Denomination and globe **Edge:** Plain **Size:** 16.25 mm.

Date	Mintage	VG	F	VF	XF	Unc
2002	464,000,000	—	—	—	—	0.35
2003	—	—	—	—	—	0.35

KM# 33 2 EURO CENTS Weight: 3.0000 g. **Composition:** Copper Plated Steel **Obverse:** Harp **Reverse:** Denomination and globe **Edge:** Grooved **Size:** 18.75 mm.

Date	Mintage	VG	F	VF	XF	Unc
2002	371,000,000	—	—	—	—	0.50
2003	—	—	—	—	—	0.50

KM# 34 5 EURO CENTS Weight: 3.8600 g. **Composition:** Copper-Plated-Steel **Obverse:** Harp. **Reverse:** Denomination and globe. **Edge:** Plain. **Size:** 21.25 mm.

Date	VG	F	VF	XF	Unc
2002	—	—	—	—	1.00
2003	—	—	—	—	1.00

KM# 35 10 EURO CENTS Weight: 4.0700 g. **Composition:** Aluminum-Bronze **Obverse:** Harp **Reverse:** Denomination and map **Edge:** Reeded **Size:** 19.75 mm.

Date	Mintage	VG	F	VF	XF	Unc
2002	217,000,000	—	—	—	—	0.75
2003	—	—	—	—	—	0.75

KM# 36 20 EURO CENTS **Weight:** 5.7300 g. **Composition:** Aluminum-Bronze **Obverse:** Harp **Reverse:** Denomination and map **Edge:** Notched **Size:** 22.25 mm.

Date	Mintage	VG	F	VF	XF	Unc
2002	148,000,000	—	—	—	—	1.25
2003	—	—	—	—	—	1.25

KM# 37 50 EURO CENTS **Weight:** 7.8100 g. **Composition:** Aluminum-Bronze **Obverse:** Harp **Rev. Designer:** Denomination and map **Edge:** Reeded **Size:** 24.25 mm.

Date	Mintage	VG	F	VF	XF	Unc
2002	66,000,000	—	—	—	—	1.50
2003	—	—	—	—	—	1.50

KM# 38 EURO **Ring Weight:** 7.5000 g. **Ring Composition:** Nickel-Brass **Center Composition:** Copper-Nickel Clad Nickel **Obverse:** Harp **Reverse:** Denomination and map **Edge:** Reeded and plain sections **Size:** 23.25 mm.

Date	Mintage	VG	F	VF	XF	Unc
2002	105,000,000	—	—	—	—	2.75
2003	—	—	—	—	—	2.75

KM# 39 2 EUROS **Ring Composition:** Copper-Nickel**Center Weight:** 8.5200 g. **Center Composition:** Nickel-Brass **Obverse:** Harp **Reverse:** Denomination and map **Edge:** Reeded with 2's and stars **Size:** 25.7 mm.

Date	Mintage	VG	F	VF	XF	Unc
2002	66,000,000	—	—	—	—	4.00
2003	—	—	—	—	—	4.00

PATTERNS

Including off metal strikes

KM#	Date	Mintage	Identification	Mkt Val
Pn2	1938	2	1/2 Crown. 0.7500 Silver. KM16.	—
Pn3	1985	—	20 Pence. Nickel-Bronze. Km25.	—
Pn1	1985	—	Penny. Bronze. KM11.	15,000

PROVAS

Public Morbiducci Series

KM#	Date	Mintage	Identification	Mkt Val
Pr8a	1927	—	1/2 Crown. Copper.	—

Note: This series exists in other than standard metals

KM#	Date	Mintage	Identification	Mkt Val
Pr3	1927	—	Penny. Silvered Bronze.	8,000
Pr4	1927	4	3 Pence. Nickel.	5,000
Pr5	1927	4	6 Pence. Nickel.	5,000
Pr6	1927	5	Shilling. Silver.	5,000
Pr7	1927	4	Florin. Silver.	6,500
Pr8	1927	5	1/2 Crown. Silver.	8,500

PIEFORTS

KM#	Date	Mintage	Identification	Mkt Val
P1	2000	—	Punt. Silver. 20.0000 g. Stylized ancient ship. as KM#31	40.00

MINT SETS

KM#	Date	Mintage	Identification	Issue Price	Mkt Val
MS1	1966 (8)	96,000	KM9-11, 12a-16a	—	20.00
MS2	Various dates (6)	—	KM19-21(1971), 22 (1970), 23(1969), 24(1970)	—	6.50
MS3	1971 (6)	—	KM19-24	1.50	9.00
MS4	1978 (6)	—	KM19-24	—	5.00
MS5	1982 (6)	—	KM19-24	—	5.00
MS6	1996 (7)	—	KM20a-21a, 24-25, 27-29	—	12.50
MS7	1998 (7)	—	KM20a-21a, 25-25, 27-29	—	12.50
MS8	2000 (7)	—	KM20a-21a, 24-25, 28-29, 31	—	12.50
MS9	2002 (8)	—	KM#32,33,34,35,36,37,38,39	10.00	10.00
MS10	2003 (8)	—	KM#32-39	10.00	15.00

PROOF SETS

KM#	Date	Mintage	Identification	Issue Price	Mkt Val
PS1	1928 (8)	6,001	KM1-8	—	200
PS2	1966 (2)	1,000	KM18(2)	—	40.00
PS3	1971 (6)	50,000	KM19-24	4.40	12.50
PS4	1986 (7)	6,750	KM19-25	—	55.00

ISLE OF MAN

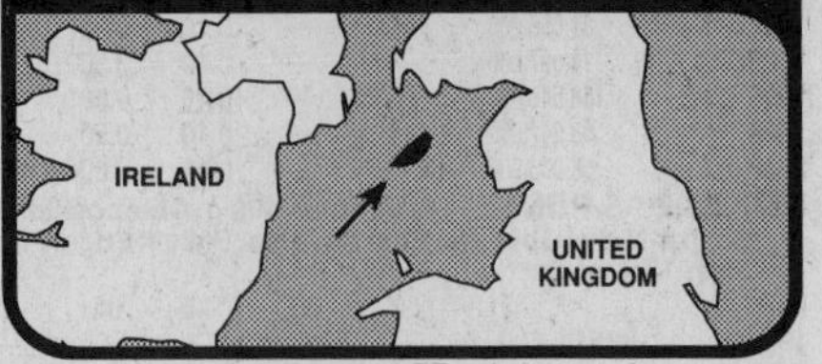

The Isle of Man, a dependency of the British Crown located in the Irish Sea equidistant from Ireland, Scotland and England, has an area of 227 sq. mi. (588 sq. km.) and a population of 68,000. Capital: Douglas. Agriculture, dairy farming, fishing and tourism are the chief industries.

The prevalence of prehistoric artifacts and monuments on the island give evidence that its' mild, almost sub-tropical climate was enjoyed by mankind before the dawn of history. Vikings came to the Isle of Man during the 9th century and remained until ejected by the Scottish in 1266. The island came under the protection of the British Crown in 1288, and in 1406 was granted, in perpetuity, to the earls of Derby, from whom it was inherited, 1736, by the Duke of Atholl. The British Crown purchased the rights and title in 1765; the remaining privileges of the Atholl family were transferred to the crown in 1829. The Isle of Man is ruled by its own legislative council and the House of Keys, the oldest, continuous legislative assembly in the world. Acts of Parliament passed in London do not affect the island unless it is specifically mentioned.

RULERS

James Murray, Duke of Atholl, 1736-1765
British Commencing 1765

MINT MARKS

PM - Pobjoy Mint

PRIVY MARKS

(a) - Big Apple - 1988
(at) - Angel Blowing Trumpet – 1997

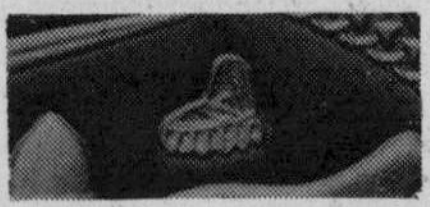

(b) - Baby Crib - 1982
(ba) - Basel Bugle - 1990
(bb) - Big Ben - 1987-1988
(br) - Brooklyn Bridge - 1989
(bs) - Teddy Bear in Stocking - 1996
(c) - Chicago Water Tower CICF - 1990-1991
(cc) - Christmas cracker - 1991
(d) - St. Paul's Cathedral - 1989
(f) - FUN logo - 1988
(fl) - Fleur de Lis - 1990
(fr) - Frauenkirche - Munich Numismata - 1990-1991
(fw) - Fairy w/magic wand - 1999
(h) - Horse - Hong Kong Int. - 1990
(l) - Statue of Liberty - 1987
(lc) - Lion crowned - 1989
(m) - Queen mother's portrait - 1980
(ma) - Maple leaf - CNA - 1990
(mt) - Mistletoe - Christmas - 1987, 1989
(ns) - North Star - 1994
(p) - Carrier Pigeon - Basel - 1988-1989
(pi) - Pine tree - 1986
(pt) - Partridge in a pear tree - 1988
(py) - Poppy - 1995
(s) - Bridge - SINPEX - 1987
(sb) - Soccer ball - 1982
(sc) - Santa Claus - 1995
(sg) - Sleigh - Christmas - 1990
(SL) - St. Louis Arch - 1987
(ss) - Sailing Ship - Sydney - 1988
(t) - Stylized triskelion - 1979
(tb) - Tower Bridge - 1990
(ti) - TICC logo - Tokyo - 1990
(v) - Viking ship - 1990
(vw) - Viking ship in wreath - 1986
(w) - Stylized triskelion - 1985
(x) - Snowman - 1998

PRIVY LETTERS

A - ANA - 1985-1992
C - Coinex, London - 1985-1989
D.M.I.H.E. - Ideal Home Exhibit, London, 1980
D.M.I.H.E.N. - Ideal Home Exhibit, Manchester, 1980
F - FUN - 1987
H - Hong Kong Expo - 1985
L - Long Beach - 1985-1987
T - Torex, Toronto - 1986
U - Uncirculated - 1988, 1990, 1994, 1995
X - Ameripex - 1986

CROWN COLONY

DECIMAL COINAGE

5 New Pence = 1 Shilling; 25 New Pence = 1 Crown; 100 New Pence = 1 Pound

KM# 19 1/2 NEW PENNY Composition: Bronze **Obverse:** Bust of Queen Elizabeth II right **Reverse:** St. James' Weed; Cushaq; Ragwort

Date	Mintage	F	VF	XF	Unc	BU
1971	495,000	—	—	0.10	0.25	—
1971 Proof	10,000	Value: 1.50				
1972	1,000	—	—	—	20.00	—
1973	1,000	—	—	—	20.00	—
1974	1,000	—	—	—	20.00	—
1975	825,000	—	—	0.10	0.15	—

KM# 19a 1/2 NEW PENNY Weight: 2.1000 g. **Composition:** 0.9250 Silver .0624 oz. ASW **Obverse:** Bust of Queen Elizabeth II right **Reverse:** St. James' Weed; Cushaq; Ragwort

Date	Mintage	F	VF	XF	Unc	BU
1975	20,000	—	—	—	2.50	—

KM# 19b 1/2 NEW PENNY Weight: 4.0000 g. **Composition:** 0.9500 Platinum .12214 oz. APW **Obverse:** Bust of Queen Elizabeth II right **Reverse:** St. James' Weed; Cushaq; Ragwort

Date	Mintage	F	VF	XF	Unc	BU
1975 Proof	600	Value: 110				

KM# 32 1/2 PENNY Composition: Bronze **Obverse:** Bust of Queen Elizabeth II right **Reverse:** Atlantic herring

Date	Mintage	F	VF	XF	Unc	BU
1976	600,000	—	—	0.10	0.35	0.50
1978	—	—	—	0.10	0.35	0.50
1978 Proof	—	Value: 1.00				
1979(t) AA	—	—	—	0.10	0.35	0.50
1979(t) AB	—	—	—	0.10	0.35	0.50

KM# 32a 1/2 PENNY Weight: 2.1000 g. **Composition:** 0.9250 Silver .0624 oz. ASW **Obverse:** Bust of Queen Elizabeth II right **Reverse:** Atlantic herring

Date	Mintage	F	VF	XF	Unc	BU
1976	20,000	—	—	—	2.00	—
1978	10,000	—	—	—	2.00	—
1979 (t) Proof	10,000	Value: 2.50				

KM# 32b 1/2 PENNY Weight: 4.0000 g. **Composition:** 0.9500 Platinum .1221 oz. APW **Obverse:** Bust of Queen Elizabeth II right **Reverse:** Atlantic herring

Date	Mintage	F	VF	XF	Unc	BU
1976 Proof	600	Value: 110				
1978 Proof	600	Value: 110				
1979 (t) Proof	500	Value: 110				

KM# 40 1/2 PENNY Composition: Bronze **Series:** F.A.O. **Obverse:** Bust of Queen Elizabeth II right

Date	Mintage	F	VF	XF	Unc	BU
1977 PM on reverse	700,000	—	—	0.10	0.35	0.50
1977 Without PM on reverse	Inc. above	—	—	—	5.00	—

KM# 40a 1/2 PENNY Weight: 2.1000 g. **Composition:** 0.9250 Silver .0624 oz. ASW **Obverse:** Bust of Queen Elizabeth II right

Date	Mintage	F	VF	XF	Unc	BU
1977 Proof	10,000	Value: 4.00				

KM# 58 1/2 PENNY Composition: Bronze **Obverse:** Bust of Queen Elizabeth II right **Reverse:** Atlantic herring

Date	Mintage	F	VF	XF	Unc	BU
1980 AA	—	—	—	0.10	0.35	0.50
1980 AB	—	—	—	0.10	0.35	0.50
1980 Proof	—	Value: 1.00				
1981 AA	—	—	—	0.10	0.35	0.50
1982 AA	—	—	—	0.10	0.35	0.50
1982 (b)	—	—	—	0.10	0.35	0.50
1982 (b) Proof	25,000	Value: 1.00				
1983 AA	—	—	—	0.10	0.35	0.50

KM# 58b 1/2 PENNY Weight: 2.1000 g. **Composition:** 0.9250 Silver .0624 oz. ASW **Obverse:** Bust of Queen Elizabeth II right **Reverse:** Atlantic herring

Date	Mintage	F	VF	XF	Unc	BU
1982 Proof	10,000	Value: 4.00				
1983 Proof	5,000	Value: 5.00				

KM# 58c 1/2 PENNY Weight: 3.5500 g. **Composition:** 0.9170 Gold .1046 oz. AGW **Obverse:** Bust of Queen Elizabeth II right **Reverse:** Atlantic Herring

Date	Mintage	F	VF	XF	Unc	BU
1980 Proof	—	Value: 65.00				
1982 (b) Proof	500	Value: 65.00				
1983 Proof	—	Value: 65.00				

KM# 58d 1/2 PENNY Weight: 4.0000 g. **Composition:** 0.9500 Platinum .1221 oz. APW **Obverse:** Bust of Queen Elizabeth II right **Reverse:** Atlantic herring

Date	Mintage	F	VF	XF	Unc	BU
1980 Proof	500	Value: 110				
1982 (b) Proof	500	Value: 110				
1983 Proof	—	Value: 110				

KM# 58a 1/2 PENNY Weight: 2.1000 g. **Composition:** 0.5000 Silver .0337 oz. ASW **Obverse:** Bust of Queen Elizabeth II right **Reverse:** Atlantic herring

Date	Mintage	F	VF	XF	Unc	BU
1980 Proof	10,000	Value: 4.00				

KM# 72.1 1/2 PENNY Weight: 4.0000 g. **Composition:** 0.9500 Bronze .1221 oz. **Series:** F.A.O. **Obverse:** Bust of Queen Elizabeth II right

Date	F	VF	XF	Unc	BU
1981	—	—	—	0.10	—

KM# 72.2 1/2 PENNY Weight: 4.0000 g. **Composition:** 0.9500 Bronze .1221 oz. **Obverse:** Bust of Queen Elizabeth II right **Reverse:** World Food Day, 16-10-81

Date	Mintage	F	VF	XF	Unc	BU
1981	10,000	—	2.00	5.00	10.00	—

KM# 111 1/2 PENNY Weight: 4.0000 g. **Composition:** 0.9500 Bronze .1221 oz. **Subject:** Quincentenary of the College of Arms **Obverse:** Bust of Queen Elizabeth II right **Reverse:** Fuchsia blossom on garnished and scrolled shield

Date	F	VF	XF	Unc	BU
1984 AA	—	—	—	0.10	—

KM# 111a 1/2 PENNY Weight: 2.1000 g. **Composition:** 0.9250 Silver .0625 oz. ASW **Obverse:** Bust of Queen Elizabeth II right **Reverse:** Fuchsia blossom on garnished and scrolled shield

Date	F	VF	XF	Unc	BU
1984 Proof	— Value: 5.00				

KM# 111b 1/2 PENNY Weight: 3.5500 g. **Composition:** 0.9170 Gold .1046 oz. AGW **Obverse:** Bust of Queen Elizabeth II right **Reverse:** Fuchsia blossom on garnished and scrolled shield

Date	Mintage	F	VF	XF	Unc	BU
1984 Proof	150	Value: 125				

KM# 142 1/2 PENNY Composition: Bronze **Obverse:** Bust of Queen Elizabeth II right **Reverse:** Fuchsia blossom on garnished and scrolled shield

Date	Mintage	F	VF	XF	Unc	BU
1985(w) AA	—	—	—	—	0.10	—
1985 Proof	50,000	Value: 2.00				

KM# 142a 1/2 PENNY Obverse: Bust of Queen Elizabeth II right **Reverse:** Fuchsia blossom on garnished and scrolled shield

Date	Mintage	F	VF	XF	Unc	BU
1985 Proof	10,000	Value: 3.00				

KM# 142b 1/2 PENNY Weight: 3.5500 g. **Composition:** 0.9170 Gold .1046 oz. AGW **Obverse:** Bust of Queen Elizabeth II right **Reverse:** Fuchsia blossom on garnished and scrolled shield

Date	Mintage	F	VF	XF	Unc	BU
1985 Proof	300	Value: 85.00				

KM# 142c 1/2 PENNY Weight: 4.0000 g. **Composition:** 0.9500 Platinum .1221 oz. APW **Obverse:** Bust of Queen Elizabeth II right **Reverse:** Fuchsia blossom on garnished and scrolled shield

Date	Mintage	F	VF	XF	Unc	BU
1985 Proof	200	Value: 110				

KM# 20 NEW PENNY Composition: Bronze **Obverse:** Bust of Queen Elizabeth II right **Reverse:** Celtic cross

Date	Mintage	F	VF	XF	Unc	BU
1971	100,000	—	—	0.10	0.35	—
1971 Proof	10,000	Value: 2.00				
1972	1,000	—	—	—	20.00	—
1973	1,000	—	—	—	20.00	—
1974	1,000	—	—	—	20.00	—
1975	855,000	—	—	0.10	0.20	—

KM# 20a NEW PENNY Weight: 4.2000 g. **Composition:** 0.9250 Silver .1249 oz. ASW **Obverse:** Bust of Queen Elizabeth II right **Reverse:** Celtic cross

Date	Mintage	F	VF	XF	Unc	BU
1975	20,000	—	—	—	5.00	—

KM# 20b NEW PENNY Weight: 8.0000 g. **Composition:** 0.9500 Platinum .2443 oz. APW **Obverse:** Bust of Queen Elizabeth II right **Reverse:** Celtic cross

Date	Mintage	F	VF	XF	Unc	BU
1975 Proof	600	Value: 210				

KM# 33 PENNY Composition: Bronze **Obverse:** Bust of Queen Elizabeth II right **Reverse:** Loaghtyn sheep

Date	Mintage	F	VF	XF	Unc	BU
1976	900,000	—	—	0.25	0.75	1.00
1977	1,000,000	—	—	0.25	0.75	1.00
1978	—	—	—	0.25	0.75	1.00
1978 Proof	—	Value: 1.25				
1979 AA(t)	—	—	—	0.25	0.75	1.00
1979 AB(t)	—	—	—	0.25	0.75	1.00
1979 AC(t)	—	—	—	0.25	0.75	1.00
1979 AD	—	—	—	0.25	0.75	1.00
1979 AE	—	—	—	0.25	0.75	1.00

KM# 33a PENNY Weight: 4.2000 g. **Composition:** 0.9250 Silver .1249 oz. ASW **Obverse:** Bust of Queen Elizabeth II right **Reverse:** Loaghtyn sheep

Date	Mintage	F	VF	XF	Unc	BU
1976	20,000	—	—	—	4.00	—
1977 Proof	10,000	Value: 5.00				
1978	10,000	—	—	—	4.00	—
1979 (t) Proof	10,000	Value: 5.00				

KM# 33b PENNY Weight: 8.0000 g. **Composition:** 0.9500 Platinum .2443 oz. APW **Obverse:** Bust of Queen Elizabeth II right **Reverse:** Loaghtyn sheep

Date	Mintage	F	VF	XF	Unc	BU
1976 Proof	600	Value: 210				
1978 Proof	600	Value: 210				
1979 (t) Proof	500	Value: 210				

KM# 59 PENNY Composition: Bronze **Obverse:** Bust of Queen Elizabeth II right **Reverse:** Manx cat

Date	Mintage	F	VF	XF	Unc	BU
1980 AA	—	—	—	0.25	1.00	1.50
1980 AB	—	—	—	0.25	1.00	1.50
1980 AC	—	—	—	0.25	1.00	1.50
1980 Proof	—	Value: 1.75				
1981 AA	—	—	—	0.25	1.00	1.50
1982 AA	—	—	—	0.25	1.00	1.50
1982 (b)	—	—	—	0.25	1.00	1.50
1982 (b) Proof	25,000	Value: 1.75				
1983 AA	—	—	—	0.25	1.00	1.50
1983 AC	—	—	—	0.25	1.00	1.50
1983 AB	—	—	—	0.25	1.00	1.50

KM# 59a PENNY Weight: 4.2000 g. **Composition:** 0.5000 Silver .0675 oz. ASW **Obverse:** Bust of Queen Elizabeth II right **Reverse:** Manx cat

Date	Mintage	F	VF	XF	Unc	BU
1980 Proof	10,000	Value: 5.00				
1980 AD	—	—	—	—	—	—

KM# 59b PENNY Weight: 4.2000 g. **Composition:** 0.9250 Silver .0675 oz. ASW **Obverse:** Bust of Queen Elizabeth II right **Reverse:** Manx cat

Date	Mintage	F	VF	XF	Unc	BU
1981 Proof	—	Value: 5.00				
1982 (b) Proof	10,000	Value: 5.00				
1983 Proof	5,000	Value: 5.00				

KM# 59c PENNY Weight: 7.1000 g. **Composition:** 0.9170 Gold .2093 oz. AGW **Obverse:** Bust of Queen Elizabeth II right **Reverse:** Manx cat

Date	Mintage	F	VF	XF	Unc	BU
1980 Proof	300	Value: 125				
1982 (b) Proof	500	Value: 125				
1983 Proof	—	Value: 125				

KM# 59d PENNY Weight: 8.0000 g. **Composition:** 0.9500 Platinum .2443 oz. APW **Obverse:** Bust of Queen Elizabeth II right **Reverse:** Manx cat

Date	Mintage	F	VF	XF	Unc	BU
1980 Proof	500	Value: 210				
1982 (b) Proof	500	Value: 210				
1983 Proof	—	Value: 210				

KM# 112 PENNY Composition: Bronze **Subject:** Quincentenary of the College of Arms **Obverse:** Bust of Queen Elizabeth II right **Reverse:** Shag bird on tilting shield

Date	F	VF	XF	Unc	BU
1984 AA	—	—	0.25	0.35	—

KM# 112a PENNY Weight: 4.2000 g. **Composition:** 0.9250 Silver .0675 oz. ASW **Obverse:** Bust of Queen Elizabeth II right **Reverse:** Shag bird on tilting shield

Date	F	VF	XF	Unc	BU
1984 Proof	—	Value: 5.00			

KM# 112b PENNY Weight: 7.1000 g. **Composition:** 0.9170 Gold .2093 oz. AGW **Obverse:** Bust of Queen Elizabeth II right **Reverse:** Puffin

Date	Mintage	F	VF	XF	Unc	BU
1984 Proof	150	Value: 250				

KM# 143 PENNY Composition: Bronze **Obverse:** Head of Queen Elizabeth II right **Reverse:** Shag bird on tilting shield

Date	Mintage	F	VF	XF	Unc	BU
1985 (W) AA	—	—	—	0.10	0.35	—
1985 Proof	50,000	Value: 2.00				
1985 (w) AA	—	—	—	0.10	0.35	—
1986 AA	—	—	—	0.10	0.35	—
1987 AA	—	—	—	0.10	0.35	—
1987 AB	—	—	—	0.10	0.35	—
1987 AC	—	—	—	0.10	0.35	—

KM# 143a PENNY Weight: 4.2000 g. **Composition:** 0.9250 Silver .0675 oz. ASW **Obverse:** Head of Queen Elizabeth II right **Reverse:** Shag bird on tilting shield

Date	Mintage	F	VF	XF	Unc	BU
1985 Proof	10,000	Value: 3.00				

KM# 143b PENNY Weight: 7.1000 g. **Composition:** 0.9170 Gold .2093 oz. AGW **Obverse:** Head of Queen Elizabeth II right **Reverse:** Shag bird on tilting shield

Date	Mintage	F	VF	XF	Unc	BU
1985 Proof	300	Value: 175				

KM# 143c PENNY Weight: 8.0000 g. **Composition:** 0.9500 Platinum .2443 oz. APW **Obverse:** Head of Queen Elizabeth II right **Reverse:** Shag bird on tilting shield

Date	Mintage	F	VF	XF	Unc	BU
1985 Proof	200	Value: 210				

KM# 207 PENNY Composition: Bronze **Obverse:** Head of Queen Elizabeth II right **Reverse:** Precision Tools

Date	F	VF	XF	Unc	BU
1988 AA	—	—	—	0.20	—
1988 AB	—	—	0.10	0.30	—
1988 AC	—	—	0.10	0.30	—
1988 AD	—	—	0.10	0.30	—
1989 AA	—	—	—	0.20	—
1989 AB	—	—	0.10	0.30	—
1989 AC	—	—	0.10	0.30	—
1989 AD	—	—	0.10	0.30	—
1989 AE	—	—	0.10	0.30	—
1990 AA	—	—	—	0.20	—
1991 AA	—	—	—	0.20	—
1991 AE	—	—	—	0.20	—
1992 AA	—	—	—	0.20	—
1993 AA	—	—	—	0.20	—
1994 AA	—	—	—	0.20	—
1995 AA	—	—	—	0.20	—

KM# 588 PENNY Composition: Bronze Plated Steel **Subject:** Sports **Obverse:** Head of Queen Elizabeth II right **Reverse:** Rugby ball

Date	F	VF	XF	Unc	BU
1996 AA	—	—	—	0.20	—
1997 AA	—	—	—	—	—
1998 AA	—	—	—	—	—

KM# 588a PENNY Weight: 4.2000 g. **Composition:** 0.9250 Silver .0675 oz. ASW **Subject:** Sports **Obverse:** Head of Queen Elizabeth II right **Reverse:** Rugby ball

Date	F	VF	XF	Unc	BU
1996 Proof	—	Value: 10.00			

KM# 823 PENNY Composition: Bronze Plated Steel **Obverse:** Rank-Broadley portrait of Queen Elizabeth II **Reverse:** Rugby ball, denomination

Date	F	VF	XF	Unc	BU
1998 AA	—	—	—	0.20	—
1999 AA	—	—	—	—	—

KM# 1036 PENNY Weight: 3.5300 g. **Composition:** Bronze Plated Steel **Obverse:** Queen's portrait **Reverse:** Ruins **Edge:** Plain

Date	F	VF	XF	Unc	BU
2000 AA	—	—	—	0.25	—

KM# 21 2 NEW PENCE Composition: Bronze **Obverse:** Bust of Queen Elizabeth II right **Reverse:** Falcons

Date	Mintage	F	VF	XF	Unc	BU
1971	100,000	—	—	0.25	1.00	—
1971 Proof	10,000	Value: 2.50				
1972	1,000	—	—	—	20.00	—
1973	1,000	—	—	—	20.00	—
1974	1,000	—	—	—	20.00	—
1975	725,000	—	—	0.25	1.00	—

KM# 21a 2 NEW PENCE Weight: 8.4000 g. **Composition:** 0.9250 Silver .2498 oz. ASW **Obverse:** Bust of Queen Elizabeth II right **Reverse:** Falcons

Date	Mintage	F	VF	XF	Unc	BU
1975	20,000	—	—	—	5.00	—

KM# 21b 2 NEW PENCE Weight: 16.0000 g. **Composition:** 0.9500 Platinum .4887 oz. APW **Obverse:** Bust of Queen Elizabeth II right **Reverse:** Falcons

Date	Mintage	F	VF	XF	Unc	BU
1975 Proof	600	Value: 385				

KM# 34 2 PENCE Composition: Bronze **Obverse:** Bust of Queen Elizabeth II right **Reverse:** Manx Shearwater

Date	Mintage	F	VF	XF	Unc	BU
1976	800,000	—	—	0.20	0.50	—
1977	1,000,000	—	—	0.20	0.50	—
1978		—	—	—	0.50	—
1978 Proof	—	Value: 1.25				
1979 AA(t)	10,000	—	—	0.20	0.50	—
1979 AB(t)		—	—	0.20	0.50	—
1979 AC(t)		—	—	0.20	0.50	—
1979 AD(t)		—	—	0.20	0.50	—
1979 AE(t)	—	—	—	0.20	0.50	—
1979 AF(t)	—	—	—	0.20	0.50	—
1979 AG(t)	—	—	—	0.20	0.50	—
1979 AH(t)	—	—	—	0.20	0.50	—

KM# 34a 2 PENCE Weight: 8.4000 g. **Composition:** 0.9250 Silver .2498 oz. ASW **Obverse:** Bust of Queen Elizabeth II right

Date	Mintage	F	VF	XF	Unc	BU
1976	20,000	—	—	—	5.00	—
1977 Proof	10,000	Value: 6.00				
1978	10,000	—	—	—	6.00	—
1979 (t) Proof	10,000	Value: 6.00				

KM# 34b 2 PENCE Weight: 16.0000 g. **Composition:** 0.9500 Platinum .4887 oz. APW **Obverse:** Bust of Queen Elizabeth II right **Reverse:** Manx Shearwater

Date	Mintage	F	VF	XF	Unc	BU
1976 Proof	600	Value: 385				
1977 Proof	600	Value: 385				
1978 Proof	—	Value: 385				
1979 (t) Proof	500	Value: 385				

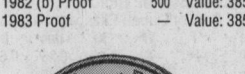

KM# 60 2 PENCE Composition: Bronze **Obverse:** Bust of Queen Elizabeth II right **Reverse:** Red-billed chough

Date	Mintage	F	VF	XF	Unc	BU
1980 AA	—	—	—	0.20	0.50	0.75
1980 AB	—	—	—	0.20	0.50	0.75
1980 AC	—	—	—	0.20	0.50	0.75
1980 AD	—	—	—	0.20	0.50	0.75
1980 Proof	—	Value: 1.25				
1981 AA	—	—	—	0.20	0.50	0.75
1981 AB	—	—	—	0.20	0.50	0.75
1982 AA	—	—	—	0.20	0.50	0.75
1982 (b)	—	—	—	0.20	0.50	0.75
1982 (b) Proof	25,000	Value: 1.25				
1983 AA	—	—	—	0.20	0.50	0.75
1983 AB	—	—	—	0.20	0.50	0.75
1983 AC	—	—	—	0.20	0.50	0.75
1983 AD	—	—	—	0.20	0.50	0.75
1983 AE	—	—	—	0.20	0.50	0.75

KM# 60a 2 PENCE Weight: 8.4000 g. **Composition:** 0.5000 Silver .1350 oz. ASW **Obverse:** Bust of Queen Elizabeth II right **Reverse:** Red-billed chough

Date	Mintage	F	VF	XF	Unc	BU
1980 Proof	10,000	Value: 5.00				

KM# 60b 2 PENCE Weight: 8.4000 g. **Composition:** 0.9250 Silver .2498 oz. ASW **Obverse:** Bust of Queen Elizabeth II right **Reverse:** Red-billed chough

Date	Mintage	F	VF	XF	Unc	BU
1981 Proof	—	—	—	—	—	—
1982 (b) Proof	10,000	Value: 5.00				
1983 Proof	5,000	Value: 6.00				

KM# 60c 2 PENCE Weight: 14.2000 g. **Composition:** 0.9170 Gold .4186 oz. AGW **Obverse:** Bust of Queen Elizabeth II right **Reverse:** Red-billed chough

Date	Mintage	F	VF	XF	Unc	BU
1980 Proof	300	Value: 225				
1982 (b) Proof	500	Value: 225				
1983 Proof	—	Value: 225				

KM# 60d 2 PENCE Weight: 16.0000 g. **Composition:** 0.9500 Platinum .4887 oz. APW **Obverse:** Bust of Queen Elizabeth II right

Date	Mintage	F	VF	XF	Unc	BU
1980 Proof	500	Value: 385				
1982 (b) Proof	500	Value: 385				
1983 Proof	—	Value: 385				

KM# 113 2 PENCE Composition: Bronze **Subject:** Quincentenary of the College of Arms **Obverse:** Bust of Queen Elizabeth II right **Reverse:** Peregrine falcon on ornamented shield

Date	F	VF	XF	Unc	BU
1984 AA	—	—	0.20	0.50	1.00

KM# 113a 2 PENCE Weight: 8.4000 g. **Composition:** 0.9250 Silver .2498 oz. ASW **Obverse:** Bust of Queen Elizabeth II right **Reverse:** Peregrine falcon on ornamented shield

Date	F	VF	XF	Unc	BU
1984 Proof	—	Value: 6.00			

KM# 113b 2 PENCE Weight: 14.2000 g. **Composition:** 0.9170 Gold .4185 oz. AGW **Obverse:** Bust of Queen Elizabeth II right **Reverse:** Peregrine falcon on ornamented shield

Date	Mintage	F	VF	XF	Unc	BU
1984 Proof	150	Value: 450				

KM# 144 2 PENCE **Composition:** Bronze **Obverse:** Head of Queen Elizabeth II right **Reverse:** Peregrine falcon on ornamented shield

Date	Mintage	F	VF	XF	Unc	BU
1985(w) AA	—	—	—	0.20	0.50	1.00
1985(w) AB	—	—	—	0.20	0.50	1.00
1985 Proof	50,000	Value: 3.00				
1986 AA	—	—	—	0.20	0.50	1.00
1986 AB	—	—	—	0.20	0.50	1.00
1986 AC	—	—	—	0.20	0.50	1.00
1986 AD	—	—	—	0.20	0.50	1.00
1987 AA	—	—	—	0.20	0.50	1.00
1987 AB	—	—	—	0.20	0.50	1.00
1987 AC	—	—	—	0.20	0.50	1.00
1987 AD	—	—	—	0.20	0.50	1.00

KM# 144a 2 PENCE **Weight:** 8.4000 g. **Composition:** 0.9250 Silver .2498 oz. ASW **Obverse:** Head of Queen Elizabeth II right **Reverse:** Peregrine falcon on ornamented shield

Date	Mintage	F	VF	XF	Unc	BU
1985 Proof	10,000	Value: 12.00				

KM# 144b 2 PENCE **Weight:** 14.2000 g. **Composition:** 0.9170 Gold .4185 oz. AGW **Obverse:** Head of Queen Eliabeth II right **Reverse:** Peregrine falcon on ornamented shield

Date	Mintage	F	VF	XF	Unc	BU
1985 Proof	300	Value: 325				

KM# 144c 2 PENCE **Weight:** 16.0000 g. **Composition:** 0.9500 Platinum APW **Obverse:** Had of Queen Elizabeth II right **Reverse:** Peregrine falcon on ornamented shield

Date	Mintage	F	VF	XF	Unc	BU
1985 Proof	200	Value: 385				

KM# 208 2 PENCE **Composition:** Bronze **Obverse:** Head of Queen Elizabeth II right **Reverse:** Stone cross with handworking tools

Date	F	VF	XF	Unc	BU
1988 AA	—	—	—	0.30	—
1988 AB	—	—	0.10	0.30	—
1988 AC	—	—	0.10	0.30	—
1988 AD	—	—	0.10	0.30	—
1989 AA	—	—	—	0.30	—
1989 AB	—	—	0.10	0.30	—
1989 AC	—	—	0.10	0.30	—
1989 AE	—	—	0.10	0.30	—
1990 AA	—	—	—	0.30	—
1991 AA	—	—	—	0.30	—
1992 AA	—	—	—	0.30	—
1993 AA	—	—	—	0.30	—
1994 AA	—	—	—	0.30	—
1995 AA	—	—	—	0.30	—

KM# 589 2 PENCE **Composition:** Bronze Clad Steel **Subject:** Sports **Obverse:** Head of Queen Elizabeth II right **Reverse:** Bicyclists

Date	F	VF	XF	Unc	BU
1996	—	—	—	0.20	—
1997 AA	—	—	—	0.20	—

KM# 901 2 PENCE **Composition:** Bronze Clad Steel **Obverse:** Rank-Broadley portrait of Queen Elizabeth II **Reverse:** Two bicyclists

Date	F	VF	XF	Unc	BU
1998	—	—	—	0.20	—
1999	—	—	—	—	—

KM# 1037 2 PENCE **Weight:** 7.1000 g. **Composition:** Brass Plated Steel **Obverse:** Queen's portrait **Reverse:** Sail boat **Edge:** Plain

Date	F	VF	XF	Unc	BU
2000 AA	—	—	—	0.40	—

KM# 22 5 NEW PENCE **Composition:** Copper-Nickel **Obverse:** Bust of Queen Elizabeth II right **Reverse:** Tower of Refuge

Date	Mintage	F	VF	XF	Unc	BU
1971	100,000	—	—	0.10	0.50	—
1971 Proof	10,000	Value: 2.50				
1972	1,000	—	—	—	25.00	—
1973	1,000	—	—	—	25.00	—
1974	1,000	—	—	—	25.00	—
1975	1,400,000	—	—	0.10	0.25	—

KM# 22a 5 NEW PENCE **Weight:** 6.5000 g. **Composition:** 0.9250 Silver .1933 oz. ASW **Obverse:** Bust of Queen Elizabeth II right **Reverse:** Tower of Refuge

Date	Mintage	F	VF	XF	Unc	BU
1975	20,000	—	—	—	5.00	—

KM# 22b 5 NEW PENCE **Weight:** 12.5000 g. **Composition:** 0.9500 Platinum .3818 oz. APW **Obverse:** Bust of Queen Elizabeth II right **Reverse:** Tower of Refuge

Date	Mintage	F	VF	XF	Unc	BU
1975 Proof	600	Value: 310				

KM# 35.1 5 PENCE **Composition:** Copper-Nickel **Obverse:** Bust of Queen Elizabeth II right **Reverse:** Laxey wheel **Note:** Lady Isabella; Mint mark: PM on obverse and reverse.

Date	Mintage	F	VF	XF	Unc	BU
1976	800,000	—	—	0.10	0.60	—
1977	—	—	—	0.10	0.60	—
1978	—	—	—	0.10	0.60	—
1978 Proof	—	Value: 1.50				
1979(t) AA	—	—	—	0.10	0.60	—

KM# 35.1a 5 PENCE **Weight:** 6.5000 g. **Composition:** 0.9250 Silver .1933 oz. ASW **Obverse:** Bust of Queen Elizabeth II right **Reverse:** Laxey wheel

Date	Mintage	F	VF	XF	Unc	BU
1976	20,000	—	—	—	5.50	—
1977 Proof	10,000	Value: 5.50				
1978	10,000	—	—	—	5.50	—
1979(t) AA Proof	10,000	Value: 5.50				

KM# 35.1b 5 PENCE **Weight:** 12.5000 g. **Composition:** 0.9500 Platinum .3818 oz. APW **Obverse:** Bust of Queen Elizabeth II right **Reverse:** Laxey wheel

Date	Mintage	F	VF	XF	Unc	BU
1976 Proof	600	Value: 310				
1978 Proof	600	Value: 310				
1979 Proof	500	Value: 310				

KM# 35.2 5 PENCE **Composition:** Copper-Nickel **Obverse:** Bust of Queen Elizabeth II right **Reverse:** Laxey wheel **Note:** Mint mark: PM on obverse only.

Date	F	VF	XF	Unc	BU
1976	—	—	0.15	0.75	—

KM# 61 5 PENCE **Composition:** Copper-Nickel **Obverse:** Bust of Queen Elizabeth II right **Reverse:** Loagthyn sheep

Date	Mintage	F	VF	XF	Unc	BU
1979 AA	—	—	—	0.15	0.75	—
1979 AA	—	—	—	0.15	0.75	—
1980 AA	—	—	—	0.15	0.75	—
1980 AB	—	—	—	0.15	0.75	—
1980 AC	—	—	—	0.15	0.75	—
1980 Proof	—	Value: 1.50				
1980 AA	—	—	—	0.15	0.75	—
1980 AB	—	—	—	0.15	0.75	—
1980 AC	—	—	—	0.15	0.75	—
1981 AA	—	—	—	0.15	0.75	—
1981 AB	—	—	—	0.15	0.75	—
1982 AA	—	—	—	0.15	0.75	—
1982 (b)	—	—	—	0.15	0.75	—
1982 (b) Proof	25,000	Value: 1.50				
1982 AA	—	—	—	0.15	0.75	—
1982 (b)	—	—	—	0.15	0.75	—
1982 (b) Proof	—	Value: 1.50				
1983 AA	—	—	—	0.15	1.50	—
1983 AA	—	—	—	0.15	0.75	—

KM# 61a 5 PENCE **Weight:** 6.5000 g. **Composition:** 0.5000 Silver .1045 oz. ASW **Obverse:** Bust of Queen Elizabeth II right **Reverse:** Loagthyn sheep

Date	Mintage	F	VF	XF	Unc	BU
1980 Proof	10,000	Value: 5.00				

KM# 61b 5 PENCE **Weight:** 6.5000 g. **Composition:** 0.9250 Silver .1933 oz. ASW **Obverse:** Bust of Queen Elizabeth II right **Reverse:** Loagthyn sheep

Date	Mintage	F	VF	XF	Unc	BU
1981 Proof	—	Value: 5.00				
1982 Proof	10,000	Value: 5.00				
1983 Proof	5,000	Value: 5.00				

KM# 61c 5 PENCE **Weight:** 11.0000 g. **Composition:** 0.9170 Gold .3243 oz. AGW **Obverse:** Bust of Queen Elizabeth II right **Reverse:** Loagthyn sheep

Date	Mintage	F	VF	XF	Unc	BU
1980 Proof	300	Value: 180				
1982 (b) Proof	500	Value: 180				
1983 Proof	—	Value: 180				

KM# 61d 5 PENCE **Weight:** 12.5000 g. **Composition:** 0.9500 Platinum .3818 oz. APW **Obverse:** Bust of Queen Elizabeth II right **Reverse:** Loagthyn sheep

Date	Mintage	F	VF	XF	Unc	BU
1980 Proof	500	Value: 310				
1982 Proof	500	Value: 310				
1983 Proof	—	Value: 310				

KM# 114 5 PENCE **Composition:** Copper-Nickel **Subject:** Quincentenary of the College of Arms **Obverse:** Bust of Queen Elizabeth II right **Reverse:** Cushag

Date	F	VF	XF	Unc	BU
1984 AA	—	—	0.10	0.50	—

KM# 114a 5 PENCE **Weight:** 6.5000 g. **Composition:** 0.9250 Silver .1933 oz. ASW **Obverse:** Bust of Queen Elizabeth II right **Reverse:** Cushag

Date	F	VF	XF	Unc	BU
1984 Proof	Value: 5.00				

KM# 114b 5 PENCE **Weight:** 11.0000 g. **Composition:** 0.9170 Gold .3242 oz. AGW **Obverse:** Bust of Queen Elizabeth II right **Reverse:** Cushag

Date	Mintage	F	VF	XF	Unc	BU
1984 Proof	150	Value: 400				

KM# 145 5 PENCE **Composition:** Copper-Nickel **Obverse:** Head of Queen Elizabeth II right **Reverse:** Cushag

Date	Mintage	F	VF	XF	Unc	BU
1985(w) AA	—	—	—	0.10	0.50	—
1985 Proof	50,000	Value: 3.00				
1986 AA	—	—	—	0.10	0.50	—
1986 AB	—	—	—	0.10	0.50	—
1986 AC	—	—	—	0.10	0.50	—

Date	Mintage	F	VF	XF	Unc	BU
1986 AD	—	—	—	0.10	0.50	—
1987 AA	—	—	—	0.10	0.50	—

KM# 145a 5 PENCE **Weight:** 6.5000 g. **Composition:** 0.9250 Silver .1933 oz. ASW **Obverse:** Head of Queen Elizabeth II right **Reverse:** Cushag

Date	Mintage	F	VF	XF	Unc	BU
1985 Proof	10,000	Value: 8.00				

KM# 145b 5 PENCE **Weight:** 11.0000 g. **Composition:** 0.9170 Gold .3242 oz. AGW **Obverse:** Head of Queen Elizabeth II right **Reverse:** Cushag

Date	Mintage	F	VF	XF	Unc	BU
1985 Proof	300	Value: 180				

KM# 145c 5 PENCE **Weight:** 12.5000 g. **Composition:** 0.9500 Platinum .3818 oz. APW **Obverse:** Head of Queen Elizabeth II right **Reverse:** Cushag

Date	Mintage	F	VF	XF	Unc	BU
1985 Proof	200	Value: 310				

KM# 209.1 5 PENCE **Composition:** Copper-Nickel **Obverse:** Head of Queen Elizabeth II right **Reverse:** Windsurfing

Date	F	VF	XF	Unc	BU
1988 AA	—	—	—	0.50	—
1989 AA	—	—	—	0.50	—
1990	—	—	—	0.50	—

KM# 209.2 5 PENCE **Composition:** Copper-Nickel **Obverse:** Head of Queen Elizabeth II right **Reverse:** Windsurfing **Note:** Reduced size: 18mm.

Date	F	VF	XF	Unc	BU
1990 AA	—	—	—	0.50	—
1991 AA	—	—	—	0.50	—
1991 AB	—	—	—	0.50	—
1992 AA	—	—	—	0.50	—
1993 AA	—	—	—	0.50	—

KM# 392 5 PENCE **Composition:** Copper-Nickel **Obverse:** Head of Queen Elizabeth II right **Reverse:** Golf clubs and ball

Date	F	VF	XF	Unc	BU
1994	—	—	—	0.50	—
1995	—	—	—	0.50	—

KM# 392a 5 PENCE **Weight:** 3.2500 g. **Composition:** 0.9250 Silver .0967 oz. ASW **Obverse:** Head of Queen Elizabeth II right **Reverse:** Golf clubs and ball

Date	F	VF	XF	Unc	BU
1994 Proof	Est. 25,000	Value: 10.00			

KM# 392b 5 PENCE **Weight:** 3.2500 g. **Composition:** 0.9170 Gold .0958 oz. AGW **Obverse:** Head of Queen Elizabeth II right **Reverse:** Golf clubs and ball

Date	Mintage	F	VF	XF	Unc	BU
1994 Proof	10,000	Value: 70.00				

KM# 392c 5 PENCE **Weight:** 3.2500 g. **Composition:** 0.9500 Platinum .0992 oz. APW **Reverse:** Golf clubs and ball

Date	Mintage	F	VF	XF	Unc	BU
1994 Proof	3,500	Value: 90.00				

KM# 590 5 PENCE **Composition:** Copper-Nickel **Subject:** Sports **Obverse:** Head of Queen Elizabeth II right **Reverse:** Golfer

Date	F	VF	XF	Unc	BU
1996 AA	—	—	—	0.50	—
1997 AA	—	—	—	0.50	—

KM# 590a 5 PENCE **Weight:** 3.2500 g. **Composition:** 0.9250 Silver .0967 oz. ASW **Subject:** Sports **Obverse:** Head of Queen Elizabeth II right **Reverse:** Golfer

Date	F	VF	XF	Unc	BU
1996 Proof	—	Value: 10.00			

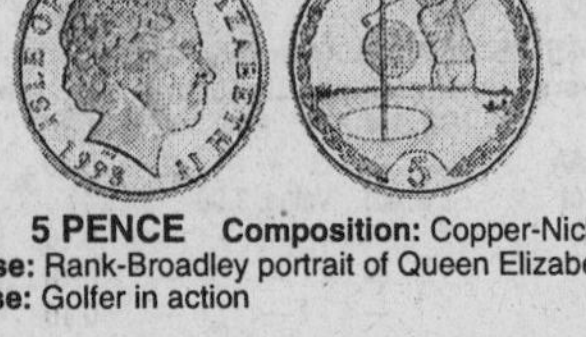

KM# 902 5 PENCE **Composition:** Copper-Nickel **Obverse:** Rank-Broadley portrait of Queen Elizabeth II **Reverse:** Golfer in action

Date	F	VF	XF	Unc	BU
1998 AA	—	—	—	0.50	—
1999 AA	—	—	—	—	—

KM# 1038 5 PENCE **Weight:** 3.2400 g. **Composition:** Copper-Nickel **Obverse:** Queen's portrait **Reverse:** Gaut's Cross **Edge:** Reeded

Date	F	VF	XF	Unc	BU
2000 AC	—	—	—	0.75	—

KM# 23 10 NEW PENCE **Composition:** Copper-Nickel **Obverse:** Bust of Queen Elizabeth II right **Reverse:** Triskelion

Date	Mintage	F	VF	XF	Unc	BU
1971	100,000	—	—	0.20	0.50	—
1971 Proof	10,000	Value: 3.50				
1972	1,000	—	—	—	25.00	—
1973	1,000	—	—	—	25.00	—
1974	1,000	—	—	—	25.00	—
1975	1,500,000	—	—	0.20	0.40	—

KM# 23a 10 NEW PENCE **Weight:** 13.0000 g. **Composition:** 0.9250 Silver .3866 oz. ASW **Obverse:** Bust of Queen Elizabeth II right **Reverse:** Triskelion

Date	Mintage	F	VF	XF	Unc	BU
1975	20,000	—	—	—	10.00	—

KM# 23b 10 NEW PENCE **Weight:** 25.0000 g. **Composition:** 0.9500 Platinum .7636 oz. APW **Obverse:** Bust of Queen Elizabeth II right **Reverse:** Triskelion

Date	Mintage	F	VF	XF	Unc	BU
1975 Proof	600	Value: 615				

KM# 36.1 10 PENCE **Composition:** Copper-Nickel **Obverse:** Bust of Queen Elizabeth II right **Reverse:** Triskelion **Note:** Mintmark: PM on obverse and reverse.

Date	Mintage	F	VF	XF	Unc	BU
1976	2,800,000	—	—	0.20	0.80	—
1977	—	—	—	0.20	0.80	—
1978	—	—	—	0.20	0.80	—
1978 Proof	—	Value: 2.00				
1979(t) AA	—	—	—	0.20	0.80	—
1979(t) AB	—	—	—	0.20	0.80	—

KM# 36.1a 10 PENCE **Weight:** 13.0000 g. **Composition:** 0.9250 Silver .3866 oz. ASW **Obverse:** Bust of Queen Elizabeth II right **Reverse:** Triskelion

Date	Mintage	F	VF	XF	Unc	BU
1976	20,000	—	—	—	10.00	—
1977 Proof	10,000	Value: 10.00				
1978	10,000	—	—	—	10.00	—
1979 (t) Proof	10,000	Value: 10.00				

KM# 36.1b 10 PENCE **Weight:** 25.0000 g. **Composition:** 0.9500 Platinum .7636 oz. APW **Obverse:** Bust of Queen Elizabeth II right **Reverse:** Triskelion

Date	Mintage	F	VF	XF	Unc	BU
1976 Proof	600	Value: 600				
1978 Proof	600	Value: 600				
1979 (t) Proof	500	Value: 600				

KM# 36.2 10 PENCE **Composition:** Copper-Nickel **Obverse:** Bust of Queen Elizabeth II right **Reverse:** Triskelion **Note:** Mintmark: PM on obverse only.

Date	F	VF	XF	Unc	BU
1976	—	—	0.20	1.00	—

KM# 62 10 PENCE **Composition:** Copper-Nickel **Obverse:** Bust of Queen Elizabeth II right **Reverse:** Gyrfalcon

Date	Mintage	F	VF	XF	Unc	BU
1980 AA	—	—	—	0.25	1.00	—
1980 AB	—	—	—	0.25	1.00	—
1980 Proof	—	Value: 2.00				
1981 AA	—	—	—	0.25	1.00	—
1982 AA	—	—	—	0.25	1.00	—
1982 AB	—	—	—	0.25	1.00	—
1982 AB(b)	—	—	—	0.25	1.00	—
1982 AC	—	—	—	0.25	1.00	—
1982 AD	—	—	—	0.25	1.00	—
1982 (b) Proof	25,000	Value: 2.00				
1983 AA	—	—	—	0.25	1.00	—
1983 AB	—	—	—	0.25	1.00	—
1983 AC	—	—	—	0.25	1.00	—
1983 AD	—	—	—	0.25	1.00	—

KM# 62a 10 PENCE **Weight:** 13.0000 g. **Composition:** 0.5000 Silver .2090 oz. ASW **Obverse:** Bust of Queen Elizabeth II right **Reverse:** Gyrfalcon

Date	Mintage	F	VF	XF	Unc	BU
1980 Proof	10,000	Value: 10.00				

KM# 62b 10 PENCE **Weight:** 13.0000 g. **Composition:** 0.9250 Silver .3866 oz. ASW **Obverse:** Bust of Queen Elizabeth II right **Reverse:** Gyrfalcon

Date	Mintage	F	VF	XF	Unc	BU
1981 Proof	—	Value: 10.00				
1982 Proof	10,000	Value: 10.00				
1983 Proof	5,000	Value: 12.50				

KM# 62c 10 PENCE **Weight:** 22.0000 g. **Composition:** 0.9170 Gold .6486 oz. AGW **Obverse:** Bust of Queen Elizabeth II right **Reverse:** Gyrfalcon

Date	Mintage	F	VF	XF	Unc	BU
1980 Proof	300	Value: 350				
1982 (b) Proof	500	Value: 350				
1983 Proof	—	Value: 350				

KM# 62d 10 PENCE **Weight:** 25.0000 g. **Composition:** 0.9500 Platinum .7636 oz. APW **Obverse:** Bust of Queen Elizabeth II right **Reverse:** Gyrfalcon

Date	Mintage	F	VF	XF	Unc	BU
1980 Proof	500	Value: 600				
1982 (b) Proof	500	Value: 600				
1983 Proof	—	Value: 600				

KM# 115 10 PENCE **Composition:** Copper-Nickel **Subject:** Quincentenary of the College of Arms **Obverse:** Bust of Queen Elizabeth II right **Reverse:** Loagthyn ram

Date	F	VF	XF	Unc	BU
1984 AA	—	—	0.25	1.00	—
1984 AB	—	—	0.25	1.00	—
1984 AC	—	—	0.25	1.00	—
1984 AD	—	—	0.25	1.00	—
1984 AE	—	—	0.25	1.00	—
1984 AF	—	—	0.25	1.00	—
1984 AG	—	—	0.25	1.00	—

KM# 115a 10 PENCE **Composition:** Silver **Obverse:** Bust of Queen Elizabeth II right **Reverse:** Loagthyn ram

Date	F	VF	XF	Unc	BU
1984 Proof	—	Value: 10.00			

KM# 115b 10 PENCE **Weight:** 22.0000 g. **Composition:** 0.9170 Gold .6484 oz. AGW **Obverse:** Bust of Queen Elizabeth II right **Reverse:** Loagthyn ram

Date	Mintage	F	VF	XF	Unc	BU
1984 Proof	150	Value: 700				

KM# 146 10 PENCE Composition: Copper-Nickel **Obverse:** Head of Queen Elizabeth II right **Reverse:** Loagthyn ram

Date	Mintage	F	VF	XF	Unc	BU
1985(w) AA	—	—	—	0.20	0.80	—
1985(w) AB	—	—	—	0.20	0.80	—
1985 Proof	50,000	Value: 3.00				
1986 AA	—	—	—	0.20	0.80	—
1987 AA	—	—	—	0.20	0.80	—

KM# 146a 10 PENCE Weight: 13.0000 g. **Composition:** 0.9250 Silver .3866 oz. ASW **Obverse:** Head of Queen Elizabeth II right **Reverse:** Loagthyn ram

Date	Mintage	F	VF	XF	Unc	BU
1985 Proof	10,000	Value: 18.00				

KM# 146b 10 PENCE Weight: 22.0000 g. **Composition:** 0.9170 Gold .6484 oz. AGW **Obverse:** Head of Queen Elizabeth II right **Reverse:** Loagthyn ram

Date	Mintage	F	VF	XF	Unc	BU
1985 Proof	300	Value: 500				

KM# 146c 10 PENCE Weight: 25.0000 g. **Composition:** 0.9500 Platinum .7636 oz. APW **Obverse:** Head of Queen Elizabeth II right **Reverse:** Loagthyn ram

Date	Mintage	F	VF	XF	Unc	BU
1985 Proof	200	Value: 615				

KM# 210 10 PENCE Composition: Copper-Nickel **Obverse:** Head of Queen Elizabeth II right **Reverse:** Island and portcullis on globe

Date	F	VF	XF	Unc	BU
1988 AA	—	—	—	0.75	—
1989 AA	—	—	—	0.75	—
1990 AA	—	—	—	0.75	—
1991 AC	—	—	—	0.75	—
1992	—	—	—	0.75	—

KM# 337 10 PENCE Composition: Copper-Nickel **Obverse:** Head of Queen Elizabeth II right **Reverse:** Triskeles symbol **Note:** Varieties exist.

Date	F	VF	XF	Unc	BU
1992 AE	—	—	—	0.75	—
1992 AA	—	—	—	0.75	—
1992 AB	—	—	—	0.75	—
1993 AA	—	—	—	0.75	—
1994 AA	—	—	—	0.75	—
1995 AA	—	—	—	0.75	—

KM# 337a 10 PENCE Weight: 8.0457 g. **Composition:** 0.9250 Silver .2392 oz. ASW **Obverse:** Head of Queen Elizabeth II right **Reverse:** Triskeles symbol

Date	F	VF	XF	Unc	BU
1992 Proof	—	Value: 13.50			

KM# 337b 10 PENCE Weight: 13.6158 g. **Composition:** 0.9170 Gold .4013 oz. AGW **Obverse:** Head of Queen Elizabeth II right **Reverse:** Triskeles symbol

Date	F	VF	XF	Unc	BU
1992 Proof	—	Value: 285			

KM# 337c 10 PENCE Weight: 15.4725 g. **Composition:** 0.9500 Platinum .4725 oz. APW **Obverse:** Head of Queen Elizabeth II right **Reverse:** Triskeles symbol

Date	F	VF	XF	Unc	BU
1992 Proof	—	Value: 400			

KM# 591 10 PENCE Composition: Copper-Nickel **Subject:** Sports **Obverse:** Head of Queen Elizabeth II right **Reverse:** Sailboat

Date	F	VF	XF	Unc	BU
1996 AA	—	—	—	1.00	—
1997 AA	—	—	—	1.00	—

KM# 591a 10 PENCE Weight: 8.0457 g. **Composition:** 0.9250 Silver .2392 oz. ASW **Subject:** Sports **Obverse:** Head of Queen Elizabeth II right **Reverse:** Sailboat

Date	F	VF	XF	Unc	BU
1996 Proof	—	Value: 22.50			

KM# 903 10 PENCE Composition: Copper-Nickel **Obverse:** Rank-Broadley portrait of Queen Elizabeth II **Reverse:** Sailboat

Date	F	VF	XF	Unc	BU
1998	—	—	—	1.00	—
1999	—	—	—	1.00	—

KM# 1039 10 PENCE Weight: 6.5500 g. **Composition:** Copper-Nickel **Obverse:** Queen's portrait **Reverse:** St. German's Cathedral **Edge:** Reeded

Date	F	VF	XF	Unc	BU
2000 AA	—	—	—	1.00	—

KM# 90 20 PENCE Composition: Copper-Nickel **Subject:** Medieval Norse History **Obverse:** Bust of Queen Elizabeth II right **Shape:** 7-sided

Date	Mintage	F	VF	XF	Unc	BU
1982 BC Proof	—	Value: 1.00				
1982 AA	30,000	—	—	0.35	1.00	—
1982 AB	—	—	—	0.35	1.00	—
1982 AB(b)	—	—	0.50	1.00	5.00	—
1982 AC	—	—	—	0.35	1.00	—
1982 AD	—	—	—	0.35	1.00	—
1982 (b) Proof	25,000	Value: 6.00				
1982 BB Proof	—	Value: 1.00				
1983 AA	—	—	—	0.35	1.00	—

KM# 90a 20 PENCE Weight: 6.0000 g. **Composition:** 0.9250 Silver .1784 oz. ASW **Subject:** Medieval Norse History **Obverse:** Head of Queen Elizabeth II right **Shape:** 7-sided

Date	Mintage	F	VF	XF	Unc	BU
1982 Proof	15,000	Value: 10.00				
1982 (b) Proof	10,000	Value: 10.00				
1983 Proof	5,000	Value: 15.00				

KM# 90b 20 PENCE Weight: 10.0000 g. **Composition:** 0.9170 Gold .2948 oz. AGW **Subject:** Medieval Norse History **Obverse:** Bust of Queen Elizabeth II right **Shape:** 7-sided

Date	Mintage	F	VF	XF	Unc	BU
1982 Proof	1,500	Value: 180				
1982 (b) Proof	500	Value: 180				
1983 Proof	—	Value: 180				

KM# 90c 20 PENCE Weight: 11.3000 g. **Composition:** 0.9500 Platinum .3452 oz. APW **Subject:** Medieval Norse History **Obverse:** Bust of Queen Elizabeth II right **Shape:** 7-sided

Date	Mintage	F	VF	XF	Unc	BU
1982 Proof	250	Value: 280				
1982 (b) Proof	500	Value: 280				
1983 Proof	—	Value: 280				

KM# 116 20 PENCE Composition: Copper-Nickel **Subject:** Quincentenary of the College of Arms **Obverse:** Bust of Queen Elizabeth II right **Reverse:** Atlantic herring **Shape:** 7-sided

Date	F	VF	XF	Unc	BU
1984 AA	—	—	0.35	1.00	—

KM# 116a 20 PENCE Composition: Silver **Subject:** Quincentenary of the College of Arms **Obverse:** Bust of Queen Elizabeth II right **Reverse:** Atlantic herring **Shape:** 7-sided

Date	F	VF	XF	Unc	BU
1984 Proof	—	Value: 20.00			

KM# 116b 20 PENCE Weight: 5.0000 g. **Composition:** 0.9170 Gold .1474 oz. AGW **Subject:** Quincentenary of the College of Arms **Obverse:** Bust of Queen Elizabeth II right **Reverse:** Atlantic herring **Shape:** 7-sided

Date	Mintage	F	VF	XF	Unc	BU
1984 Proof	150	Value: 175				

KM# 147 20 PENCE Composition: Copper-Nickel **Obverse:** Head of Queen Elizabeth II right **Reverse:** Atlantic herring **Shape:** 7-sided

Date	Mintage	F	VF	XF	Unc	BU
1985(w) AA	—	—	—	0.35	1.00	—
1985 Proof	50,000	Value: 3.00				
1986 AA	—	—	—	0.35	1.00	—
1986 AB	—	—	—	0.35	1.00	—
1986 AC	—	—	—	0.35	1.00	—
1987 AA	—	—	—	0.35	1.00	—

KM# 147a 20 PENCE Weight: 5.0000 g. **Composition:** 0.9250 Silver .1487 oz. ASW **Obverse:** Head of Queen Elizabeth II right **Reverse:** Atlantic herring **Shape:** 7-sided

Date	Mintage	F	VF	XF	Unc	BU
1985 Proof	10,000	Value: 8.00				

KM# 147b 20 PENCE Weight: 5.0000 g. **Composition:** 0.9170 Gold .1474 oz. AGW **Obverse:** Head of Queen Elizabeth II right **Reverse:** Atlantic herring **Shape:** 7-sided

Date	Mintage	F	VF	XF	Unc	BU
1985 Proof	300	Value: 100				

KM# 147c 20 PENCE Weight: 5.0000 g. **Composition:** 0.9500 Platinum .1527 oz. APW **Obverse:** Head of Queen Elizabeth II right **Reverse:** Atlantic herring **Shape:** 7-sided

Date	Mintage	F	VF	XF	Unc	BU
1985 Proof	200	Value: 125				

KM# 211 20 PENCE Composition: Copper-Nickel **Obverse:** Head of Queen Elizabeth II right **Reverse:** Farm combine harvester **Shape:** 7-sided

Date	F	VF	XF	Unc	BU
1988 AA	—	—	—	1.00	—
1989 AA	—	—	—	1.00	—
1990 AA	—	—	—	1.00	—
1991 AA	—	—	—	1.00	—
1992 AA	—	—	—	1.00	—
1993 AA	—	—	—	1.00	—

KM# 391 20 PENCE Composition: Copper-Nickel **Obverse:** Head of Queen Elizabeth II right **Reverse:** Farm combine harvester **Shape:** 7-sided **Note:** Obverse and reverse design revised with border.

Date	F	VF	XF	Unc	BU
1993 AA	—	—	—	1.00	—
1994 AA	—	—	—	1.00	—
1995 AA	—	—	—	1.00	—

KM# 592 20 PENCE Composition: Copper-Nickel **Subject:** Sports **Obverse:** Head of Queen Elizabeth II right **Reverse:** Race cars **Shape:** 7-sided

Date	F	VF	XF	Unc	BU
1996 AA	—	—	—	1.25	—
1997 AA	—	—	—	1.25	—

KM# 904 20 PENCE Composition: Copper-Nickel **Obverse:** Rank-Broadley portrait of Queen Elizabeth II **Reverse:** Race cars **Shape:** 7-sided

Date	F	VF	XF	Unc	BU
1998 AA	—	—	—	1.25	—
1999 AA	—	—	—	—	—

KM# 1040 20 PENCE **Weight:** 4.9100 g. **Composition:** Copper-Nickel **Subject:** Rushen Abbey **Obverse:** Queen's portrait **Reverse:** Monk writing **Edge:** Plain **Shape:** 7-sided

Date	F	VF	XF	Unc	BU
2000 AA	—	—	—	1.50	—

KM# 25 25 PENCE **Composition:** Copper-Nickel **Subject:** 25th Wedding Anniversary **Obverse:** Bust of Queen Elizabeth II right **Rev. Designer:** Stuart Devlin **Note:** Struck at the Royal Canadian Mint.

Date	Mintage	F	VF	XF	Unc	BU
1972	70,000	—	—	—	3.00	—

KM# 25a 25 PENCE **Weight:** 28.2800 g. **Composition:** 0.9250 Silver .8411 oz. ASW **Obverse:** Bust of Queen Elizabeth II right **Rev. Designer:** Stuart Devlin **Note:** Struck at the Royal Canadian Mint.

Date	Mintage	F	VF	XF	Unc	BU
1972 Proof	15,000	Value: 10.00				

KM# 31 25 PENCE **Composition:** Copper-Nickel **Obverse:** Bust of Queen Elizabeth II right **Reverse:** Manx cat

Date	Mintage	F	VF	XF	Unc	BU
1975	35,000	—	—	—	3.00	—

KM# 31a 25 PENCE **Weight:** 28.2800 g. **Composition:** 0.9250 Silver .8411 oz. ASW **Obverse:** Bust of Queen Elizabeth II right **Reverse:** Manx cat

Date	Mintage	F	VF	XF	Unc	BU
1975	—	—	—	—	9.00	—
1975 Proof	30,000	Value: 13.50				

KM# 24 50 NEW PENCE **Composition:** Copper-Nickel **Obverse:** Bust of Queen Elizabeth II right **Reverse:** Viking ship sailing right **Shape:** 7-sided

Date	Mintage	F	VF	XF	Unc	BU
1971	100,000	—	—	0.75	1.50	—
1971 Proof	10,000	Value: 7.50				
1972	1,000	—	—	—	30.00	—
1973	1,000	—	—	—	30.00	—
1974	1,000	—	—	—	30.00	—
1975	227,000	—	—	0.75	1.50	—

KM# 24a 50 NEW PENCE **Weight:** 15.5000 g. **Composition:** 0.9250 Silver .4610 oz. ASW **Obverse:** Bust of Queen Elizabeth II right **Reverse:** Viking ship sailing right **Shape:** 7-sided

Date	Mintage	F	VF	XF	Unc	BU
1975	20,000	—	—	—	12.50	—

KM# 24b 50 NEW PENCE **Weight:** 30.4000 g. **Composition:** 0.9500 Platinum .9286 oz. APW **Obverse:** Bust of Queen Elizabeth II right **Reverse:** Viking ship sailing right **Shape:** 7-sided

Date	Mintage	F	VF	XF	Unc	BU
1975 Proof	600	Value: 725				

KM# 39 50 PENCE **Composition:** Copper-Nickel **Obverse:** Bust of Queen Elizabeth II right **Reverse:** Viking ship sailing left **Shape:** 7-sided

Date	Mintage	F	VF	XF	Unc	BU
1976	250,000	—	—	0.75	2.00	—
1977	50,000	—	—	0.75	2.50	—
1978	25,000	—	—	0.75	2.50	—
1978 Proof	—	Value: 3.50				
1979 (t)AA	—	—	—	0.75	3.00	—

KM# 39a 50 PENCE **Weight:** 15.5000 g. **Composition:** 0.9250 Silver .4610 oz. ASW **Obverse:** Bust of Queen Elizabeth II right **Reverse:** Viking ship sailing left **Shape:** 7-sided

Date	Mintage	F	VF	XF	Unc	BU
1976	20,000	—	—	—	12.50	—
1977 Proof	10,000	Value: 12.50				
1978	10,000	—	—	—	12.50	—
1979 (t) Proof	10,000	Value: 12.50				

KM# 39b 50 PENCE **Weight:** 30.4000 g. **Composition:** 0.9500 Platinum .9286 oz. APW **Obverse:** Bust of Queen Elizabeth II right **Reverse:** Viking ship sailing left **Shape:** 7-sided

Date	Mintage	F	VF	XF	Unc	BU
1976 Proof	600	Value: 725				
1978 Proof	600	Value: 725				
1979 (t) Proof	500	Value: 725				

KM# 51.1 50 PENCE **Composition:** Copper-Nickel **Subject:** Manx Day of Tynwald, July 5 **Obverse:** Bust of Queen Elizabeth II right **Reverse:** Viking ship **Edge:** Upright with obverse on top **Edge Lettering:** H.M.Q.E. II ROYAL VISIT I.O.M. JULY 5, 1979 **Shape:** 7-sided

Date	Mintage	F	VF	XF	Unc	BU
1979 AA	50,000	—	—	—	5.00	—
1979 AB	—	—	—	—	5.00	—

KM# 51.2 50 PENCE **Composition:** Copper-Nickel **Obverse:** Bust of Queen Elizabeth II right **Reverse:** Viking ship **Edge:** Lettering upright with reverse on top **Shape:** 7-sided

Date	F	VF	XF	Unc	BU
1979 AA	—	—	—	5.00	—
1979 AB	—	—	—	5.00	—

KM# 51.3 50 PENCE **Composition:** Copper-Nickel **Obverse:** Bust of Queen Elizabeth II right **Reverse:** Viking ship **Shape:** 7-sided **Note:** Inscription not centered in flat sections.

Date	F	VF	XF	Unc	BU
1979 AA	—	—	—	5.00	—
1979 AB	—	—	—	5.00	—

KM# 51a 50 PENCE **Weight:** 15.5000 g. **Composition:** 0.9250 Silver .4610 oz. ASW **Obverse:** Bust of Queen Elizabeth II right **Reverse:** Viking ship **Shape:** 7-sided

Date	Mintage	F	VF	XF	Unc	BU
1979	10,000	—	—	—	10.00	—
1979 Proof	5,000	Value: 15.00				

KM# 51b 50 PENCE **Weight:** 30.4000 g. **Composition:** 0.9500 Platinum .9286 oz. APW **Subject:** Manx Millennium of Tynwald **Obverse:** Bust of Queen Elizabeth II right **Reverse:** Viking ship **Edge:** H.M.Q.E. II ROYAL VISIT I.O.M. JULY 5, 1979 **Shape:** 7-sided

Date	Mintage	F	VF	XF	Unc	BU
1979 Proof	500	Value: 650				

KM# 53 50 PENCE **Composition:** Copper-Nickel **Obverse:** Bust of Queen Elizabeth II right **Reverse:** Odin's raven, Point of Ayre lighthouse **Note:** Same as KM#51.1 with no edge lettering.

Date	F	VF	XF	Unc	BU
1979 AA	—	—	—	3.00	—
1979 AB	—	—	—	3.00	—

KM# 53a 50 PENCE **Weight:** 15.5000 g. **Composition:** 0.9250 Silver .4610 oz. ASW **Obverse:** Bust of Queen Elizabeth II right **Reverse:** Odin's Raven, Point of Ayre lighhouse

Date	F	VF	XF	Unc	BU
1979	—	—	—	10.00	—
1979 Proof	—	Value: 15.00			

KM# 57 50 PENCE **Weight:** 15.5000 g. **Composition:** 0.9250 Silver .4610 oz. ASW **Obverse:** Bust of Queen Elizabeth II right **Reverse:** Carriage **Note:** Mule.

Date	F	VF	XF	Unc	BU
1980	—	—	—	—	—

KM# 69 50 PENCE **Weight:** 15.5000 g. **Composition:** 0.9250 Silver .4610 oz. ASW **Obverse:** Bust of Queen Elizabeth II right **Edge Lettering:** ODINS RAVEN VIKING EXHIBN NEW YORK 1980 **Note:** Same as KM#51.1, different edge lettering.

Date	Mintage	F	VF	XF	Unc	BU
1980 AA	20,000	—	—	—	4.00	—

KM# 69a 50 PENCE **Weight:** 15.5000 g. **Composition:** 0.9250 Silver .4610 oz. ASW **Obverse:** Bust of Queen Elizabeth II right

Date	Mintage	F	VF	XF	Unc	BU
1980 Proof	5,000	Value: 20.00				
1980	—	—	—	—	15.00	—

KM# 69b 50 PENCE **Weight:** 26.0000 g. **Composition:** 0.9170 Gold .7666 oz. AGW **Obverse:** Bust of Queen Elizabeth II right **Edge Lettering:** ODINS RAVEN VIKING EXHIBN NEW YORK 1980

Date	Mintage	F	VF	XF	Unc	BU
1980	250	—	—	—	500	—

KM# 69c 50 PENCE **Weight:** 30.4000 g. **Composition:** 0.9500 Platinum .9286 oz. APW **Obverse:** Bust of Queen Elizabeth II right

Date	Mintage	F	VF	XF	Unc	BU
1980 Proof	50	Value: 775				

KM# 70 50 PENCE **Composition:** Copper-Nickel **Obverse:** Bust of Queen Elizabeth II right **Reverse:** Viking longship **Shape:** Viking ship

Date	Mintage	F	VF	XF	Unc	BU
1980 AB	—	—	—	0.75	2.00	—
1980 Proof	—	Value: 2.50				
1981 AA	—	—	—	0.75	2.00	—
1982 AC	—	—	—	0.75	2.00	—
1982 (b)	—	—	—	0.75	2.00	—
1980 AA	10,000	—	—	0.75	2.00	—
1982 (b) Proof	25,000	Value: 2.50				
1983 AA	—	—	—	0.75	2.00	—
1983 AB	—	—	—	0.75	2.00	—
1984 AA	—	—	—	0.75	2.00	—

KM# 70a 50 PENCE **Weight:** 15.5000 g. **Composition:** 0.5000 Silver .2491 oz. ASW **Obverse:** Bust of Queen Elizabeth II right **Reverse:** Viking longship **Shape:** 7-sided

Date	Mintage	F	VF	XF	Unc	BU
1980 Proof	10,000	Value: 10.00				
1982 (b) Proof	10,000	Value: 15.00				

KM# 70b 50 PENCE **Weight:** 15.5000 g. **Composition:** 0.9250 Silver .4610 oz. ASW **Obverse:** Bust of Queen Elizabeth II right **Reverse:** Viking longship **Shape:** 7-sided

Date	Mintage	F	VF	XF	Unc	BU
1981 Proof	—	Value: 17.50				
1983 Proof	5,000	Value: 17.50				

KM# 70c 50 PENCE **Weight:** 26.0000 g. **Composition:** 0.9170 Gold .7666 oz. AGW **Obverse:** Bust of Queen Elizabeth II right **Reverse:** Viking longship **Shape:** 7-sided

Date	Mintage	F	VF	XF	Unc	BU
1980 Proof	300	Value: 500				
1982 (b) Proof	500	Value: 500				
1983 Proof	—	Value: 500				

KM# 70d 50 PENCE **Weight:** 30.4000 g. **Composition:** 0.9500 Platinum .9286 oz. APW **Obverse:** Bust of Queen Elizabeth II right **Reverse:** Viking longship **Shape:** 7-sided

Date	Mintage	F	VF	XF	Unc	BU
1980 Proof	500	Value: 750				
1982 (b) Proof	500	Value: 750				
1983 Proof	—	Value: 750				

KM# 71 50 PENCE Composition: Copper-Nickel **Subject:** Christmas 1980 **Obverse:** Bust of Queen Elizabeth II right **Reverse:** Carriage **Shape:** 7-sided

Date	Mintage	F	VF	XF	Unc	BU
1980 AB	—	—	—	—	2.50	—
1980 AD	—	—	—	—	2.50	—
1980 AA	30,000	—	—	—	2.50	—

KM# 71a 50 PENCE Weight: 15.5000 g. **Composition:** 0.9250 Silver .4610 oz. ASW **Obverse:** Bust of Queen Elizabeth II right **Reverse:** Carriage **Shape:** 7-sided

Date	Mintage	F	VF	XF	Unc	BU
1980 Proof	5,000	Value: 12.50				

KM# 71b 50 PENCE Weight: 26.0000 g. **Composition:** 0.9170 Gold .7666 oz. AGW **Subject:** Christmas 1980 **Obverse:** Bust of Queen Elizabeth II right **Reverse:** Carriage **Shape:** 7-sided

Date	Mintage	F	VF	XF	Unc	BU
1980 Proof	250	Value: 500				

KM# 71c 50 PENCE Weight: 30.4000 g. **Composition:** 0.9500 Platinum .9286 oz. APW **Obverse:** Bust of Queen Elizabeth II right **Reverse:** Carriage **Shape:** 7-sided

Date	Mintage	F	VF	XF	Unc	BU
1980 Proof	50	Value: 775				

KM# 83 50 PENCE Composition: Copper-Nickel **Subject:** Tourist Trophy Motorcycle Races **Obverse:** Bust of Queen Elizabeth II right **Reverse:** Motorcyclist - Joey Dunlop **Shape:** 7-sided

Date	Mintage	F	VF	XF	Unc	BU
1981 AA	30,000	—	—	—	3.00	—
1981 AB	Inc. above	—	—	—	3.00	—

KM# 83a 50 PENCE Weight: 15.5000 g. **Composition:** 0.9250 Silver .4610 oz. ASW **Subject:** Tourist Trophy Motorcycle Races **Obverse:** Bust of Queen Elizabeth II right **Reverse:** Motorcyclist - Joey Dunlop **Shape:** 7-sided

Date	Mintage	F	VF	XF	Unc	BU
1981 Proof	5,000	Value: 15.00				

KM# 83b 50 PENCE Weight: 26.0000 g. **Composition:** 0.9170 Gold .7666 oz. AGW **Subject:** Tourist Trophy Motorcycle Races **Obverse:** Bust of Queen Elizabeth II right **Reverse:** Motorcyclist - Joey Dunlop **Shape:** 7-sided

Date	Mintage	F	VF	XF	Unc	BU
1981 Proof	250	Value: 500				

KM# 83c 50 PENCE Weight: 30.4000 g. **Composition:** 0.9500 Platinum .9286 oz. APW **Subject:** Tourist Trophy Motorcycle Races **Obverse:** Bust of Queen Elizabeth II right **Reverse:** Motorcyclist - Joey Dunlop **Shape:** 7-sided

Date	Mintage	F	VF	XF	Unc	BU
1981 Proof	50	Value: 775				

KM# 84 50 PENCE Composition: Copper-Nickel **Subject:** Christmas 1981 **Obverse:** Bust of Queen Elizabeth II right **Reverse:** Manx Nickey boat **Shape:** 7-sided

Date	Mintage	F	VF	XF	Unc	BU
1981 AA	30,000	—	—	—	3.00	—
1981 AB	Inc. above	—	—	—	3.00	—
1981 Proof	—	Value: 7.50				

KM# 84a 50 PENCE Weight: 15.5000 g. **Composition:** 0.9250 Silver .4610 oz. ASW **Subject:** Christmas 1981 **Obverse:** Bust of Queen Elizabeth II right **Reverse:** Manx Nickey boat **Shape:** 7-sided

Date	Mintage	F	VF	XF	Unc	BU
1981 Proof	5,000	Value: 12.50				

KM# 84b 50 PENCE Weight: 26.0000 g. **Composition:** 0.9170 Gold .7666 oz. AGW **Subject:** Christmas 1981 **Obverse:** Bust of Queen Elizabeth II right **Reverse:** Manx Nickey boat **Shape:** 7-sided

Date	Mintage	F	VF	XF	Unc	BU
1981 Proof	250	Value: 550				

KM# 84c 50 PENCE Weight: 30.4000 g. **Composition:** 0.9500 Platinum .9286 oz. APW **Subject:** Christmas 1981 **Obverse:** Bust of Queen Elizabeth II right **Reverse:** Manx Nickey boat **Shape:** 7-sided

Date	Mintage	F	VF	XF	Unc	BU
1981 Proof	—	Value: 775				

KM# 101 50 PENCE Composition: Copper-Nickel **Subject:** Tourist Trophy Motorcycle Races **Obverse:** Bust of Queen Elizabeth II right **Reverse:** Motorcyclist **Shape:** 7-sided

Date	Mintage	F	VF	XF	Unc	BU
1982	30,000	—	—	—	3.00	—
1982 Proof	—	Value: 7.50				

KM# 101a 50 PENCE Weight: 15.5000 g. **Composition:** 0.9250 Silver .4610 oz. ASW **Subject:** Tourist Trophy Motorcycle Races **Obverse:** Bust of Queen Elizabeth II right **Reverse:** Motorcyclist **Shape:** 7-sided

Date	Mintage	F	VF	XF	Unc	BU
1982 Proof	5,000	Value: 15.00				

KM# 101b 50 PENCE Weight: 26.0000 g. **Composition:** 0.9170 Gold .7666 oz. AGW **Subject:** Tourist Trophy Motorcycle Races **Obverse:** Bust of Queen Elizabeth II right **Reverse:** Motorcyclist **Shape:** 7-sided

Date	Mintage	F	VF	XF	Unc	BU
1982 Proof	250	Value: 550				

KM# 101c 50 PENCE Weight: 30.4000 g. **Composition:** 0.9500 Platinum .9286 oz. APW **Subject:** Tourist Trophy Motorcycle Races **Obverse:** Bust of Queen Elizabeth II right **Reverse:** Motorcyclist **Shape:** 7-sided

Date	Mintage	F	VF	XF	Unc	BU
1982 Proof	50	Value: 775				

KM# 102 50 PENCE Composition: Copper-Nickel **Subject:** Christmas 1982 **Obverse:** Bust of Queen Elizabeth II right **Reverse:** Victorian carolers around tree, Castle Rushen in background **Shape:** 7-sided

Date	Mintage	F	VF	XF	Unc	BU
1982 AA	30,000	—	—	—	2.50	—
1982 AB	Inc. above	—	—	—	2.50	—
1982 D	Inc. above	—	—	—	2.50	—
1982 Proof	250	Value: 7.50				

KM# 102a 50 PENCE Weight: 15.5000 g. **Composition:** 0.9250 Silver .4610 oz. ASW **Subject:** Christmas 1982 **Obverse:** Bust of Queen Elizabeth II right **Reverse:** Victorian carolers around tree, Castle Rushen in background **Shape:** 7-sided

Date	Mintage	F	VF	XF	Unc	BU
1982 Proof	5,000	Value: 12.50				

KM# 102b 50 PENCE Weight: 26.0000 g. **Composition:** 0.9170 Gold .7666 oz. AGW **Subject:** Christmas 1982 **Obverse:** Bust of Queen Elizabeth II right **Reverse:** Victorian carolers around tree, Castle Rushen in background **Shape:** 7-sided

Date	Mintage	F	VF	XF	Unc	BU
1982 Proof	250	Value: 500				

KM# 102c 50 PENCE Weight: 30.4000 g. **Composition:** 0.9500 Platinum .9286 oz. APW **Subject:** Christmast 1982 **Obverse:** Bust of Queen Elizabeth II right **Reverse:** Victorian carolers around tree, Castle Rushen in background **Shape:** 7-sided

Date	Mintage	F	VF	XF	Unc	BU
1982 Proof	50	Value: 775				

KM# 107 50 PENCE Composition: Copper-Nickel **Subject:** Christmas 1983 **Obverse:** Bust of Queen Elizabeth II right **Reverse:** Ford Model T driving left **Shape:** 7-sided

Date	Mintage	F	VF	XF	Unc	BU
1983 AB	—	—	—	—	4.00	—
1983 AA	—	—	—	—	4.00	—
1983 AC	30,000	—	—	—	4.00	—

KM# 107a 50 PENCE Weight: 15.5000 g. **Composition:** 0.9250 Silver .4610 oz. ASW **Series:** Christmas 1983 **Obverse:** Bust of Queen Elizabeth II right **Reverse:** Ford Model T driving left **Shape:** 7-sided

Date	Mintage	F	VF	XF	Unc	BU
1983 Proof	5,000	Value: 12.50				

KM# 107b 50 PENCE Weight: 26.0000 g. **Composition:** 0.9170 Gold .7666 oz. AGW **Subject:** Christmas 1983 **Obverse:** Bust of Queen Elizabeth II right **Reverse:** Ford Model T driving left **Shape:** 7-sided

Date	Mintage	F	VF	XF	Unc	BU
1983 Proof	250	Value: 500				

KM# 107c 50 PENCE Weight: 30.4000 g. **Composition:** 0.9500 Platinum .9286 oz. APW **Subject:** Christmas 1983 **Obverse:** Bust of Queen Elizabeth II right **Reverse:** Ford Model T driving left **Shape:** 7-sided

Date	Mintage	F	VF	XF	Unc	BU
1983 Proof	50	Value: 775				

KM# 108 50 PENCE Composition: Copper-Nickel **Subject:** Tourist Trophy Motorcycle Races **Obverse:** Bust of Queen Elizabeth II right **Reverse:** Motorcyclist - Ron Haslam **Shape:** 7-sided

Date	Mintage	F	VF	XF	Unc	BU
1983 AA	30,000	—	—	—	3.00	—
1983 AB	Inc. above	—	—	—	3.00	—
1983 AC	Inc. above	—	—	—	3.00	—
1983 AD	Inc. above	—	—	—	3.00	—

KM# 108a 50 PENCE Weight: 15.5000 g. **Composition:** 0.9250 Silver .4610 oz. ASW **Obverse:** Bust of Queen Elizabeth II right **Reverse:** Motorcyclist - Ron Haslam **Edge Lettering:** Tourist Trophy Motorcycle Races **Shape:** 7-sided

Date	Mintage	F	VF	XF	Unc	BU
1983 Proof	5,000	Value: 15.00				

KM# 108b 50 PENCE Weight: 26.0000 g. **Composition:** 0.9170 Gold .7666 oz. AGW **Subject:** Tourist Trophy Motorcycle Races **Obverse:** Bust of Queen Elizabeth II right **Reverse:** Motorcyclist - Ron Haslam **Shape:** 7-sided

Date	Mintage	F	VF	XF	Unc	BU
1983 Proof	250	Value: 500				

KM# 108c 50 PENCE Weight: 30.4000 g. **Composition:** 0.9500 Platinum .9286 oz. APW **Subject:** Tourist Trophy Motorcycle Races **Obverse:** Bust of Queen Elizabeth II right **Reverse:** Motorcyclist - Ron Haslam **Shape:** 7-sided

Date	Mintage	F	VF	XF	Unc	BU
1983 Proof	50	Value: 775				

KM# 125 50 PENCE Composition: Copper-Nickel **Subject:** Quincentenary of the College of Arms **Obverse:** Bust of Queen Elziabeth II right **Reverse:** Viking longship on shield **Shape:** 7-sided

Date	F	VF	XF	Unc	BU
1984 AB	—	—	—	2.00	—
1984 AA	—	—	—	2.00	—

KM# 125a 50 PENCE Weight: 15.5000 g. **Composition:** 0.9250 Silver .4610 oz. ASW **Subject:** Quincentenary ofthe College of Arms **Obverse:** Bust of Queen Elizabeth II right **Reverse:** Viking longship on shield **Shape:** 7-sided

Date	F	VF	XF	Unc	BU
1984 Proof	— Value: 15.00				

KM# 125b 50 PENCE Weight: 26.0000 g. **Composition:** 0.9170 Gold .7666 oz. AGW **Subject:** Quincentenary of the College of Arms **Obverse:** Bust of Queen Elizabeth II right **Reverse:** Viking longship on shield **Shape:** 7-sided

Date	Mintage	F	VF	XF	Unc	BU
1984 Proof	150	Value: 500				

KM# 126 50 PENCE **Composition:** Copper-Nickel **Subject:** Tourist Trophy Motorcycle Races **Obverse:** Bust of Queen Elizabeth II right **Reverse:** Two motorcyclists - Mike Bodine **Shape:** 7-sided

Date	Mintage	F	VF	XF	Unc	BU
1984 AA	30,000	—	—	—	2.25	—

KM# 126a 50 PENCE **Weight:** 15.5000 g. **Composition:** 0.9250 Silver .4610 oz. ASW **Subject:** Tourist Trophy Motorcycle Races **Obverse:** Bust of Queen Elizabeth II right **Reverse:** Two motorcyclists - Mike Bodine **Shape:** 7-sided

Date	Mintage	F	VF	XF	Unc	BU
1984 Proof	5,000	Value: 15.00				

KM# 126b 50 PENCE **Weight:** 26.0000 g. **Composition:** 0.9170 Gold .7666 oz. AGW **Subject:** Tourist Trophy Motorcycle Races **Obverse:** Bust of Queen Elizabeth II right **Reverse:** Two motorcyclists - Mike Bodine **Shape:** 7-sided

Date	Mintage	F	VF	XF	Unc	BU
1984 Proof	250	Value: 500				

KM# 126c 50 PENCE **Weight:** 30.4000 g. **Composition:** 0.9500 Platinum .9286 oz. APW **Subject:** Tourist Trophy Motorcycle Races **Obverse:** Bust of Queen Elizabeth II right **Reverse:** Two motorcyclists - Mike Bodine **Shape:** 7-sided

Date	Mintage	F	VF	XF	Unc	BU
1984 Proof	50	Value: 775				

KM# 127 50 PENCE **Composition:** Copper-Nickel **Subject:** Christmas 1984 **Obverse:** Bust of Queen Elizabeth II right **Reverse:** The "Sutherland" train **Shape:** 7-sided

Date	Mintage	F	VF	XF	Unc	BU
1984 AD	—	—	—	—	2.50	—
1984 AA	—	—	—	—	2.50	—
1984 AB	—	—	—	—	2.50	—
1984 AC	—	—	—	—	2.50	—
1984 BB Proof	30,000	Value: 7.50				

KM# 127a 50 PENCE **Weight:** 15.5000 g. **Composition:** 0.9250 Silver .4610 oz. ASW **Subject:** Christmas 1984 **Obverse:** Bust of Queen Elizabeth II right **Reverse:** The "Sutherland" train **Shape:** 7-sided

Date	F	VF	XF	Unc	BU
1984 Proof	— Value: 25.00				

KM# 127b 50 PENCE **Weight:** 26.0000 g. **Composition:** 0.9170 Gold .7666 oz. AGW **Subject:** Christmas 1984 **Obverse:** Bust of Queen Elizabeth II right **Reverse:** The "Sutherland" train **Shape:** 7-sided

Date	Mintage	F	VF	XF	Unc	BU
1984 Proof	250	Value: 500				

KM# 127c 50 PENCE **Weight:** 30.4000 g. **Composition:** 0.9500 Platinum .9286 oz. APW **Subject:** Christmas 1984 **Obverse:** Bust of Queen Elizabeth II right **Reverse:** The "Sutherland" train **Shape:** 7-sided

Date	F	VF	XF	Unc	BU
1984 Proof	— Value: 750				

KM# 148 50 PENCE **Composition:** Copper-Nickel **Obverse:** Head of Queen Elizabeth II right **Reverse:** Viking longship on shield **Shape:** 7-sided

Date	Mintage	F	VF	XF	Unc	BU
1985(w) AA	—	—	—	—	2.00	—
1985(w) AB	—	—	—	—	2.00	—
1985 (w) Proof	50,000	Value: 4.00				
1986 AA	—	—	—	—	2.00	—
1986 AB	—	—	—	—	2.00	—
1987 AA	—	—	—	—	2.00	—

KM# 148a 50 PENCE **Weight:** 15.5000 g. **Composition:** 0.9250 Silver .4610 oz. ASW **Obverse:** Head of Queen Elizabeth II right **Reverse:** Viking longship on shield **Shape:** 7-sided

Date	Mintage	F	VF	XF	Unc	BU
1985 Proof	Est. 10,000	Value: 15.00				

KM# 148b 50 PENCE **Weight:** 26.0000 g. **Composition:** 0.9170 Gold .7666 oz. AGW **Obverse:** Head of Queen Elizabeth II right **Reverse:** Viking longship on shield **Shape:** 7-sided

Date	Mintage	F	VF	XF	Unc	BU
1985 Proof	Est. 300	Value: 500				

KM# 148c 50 PENCE **Weight:** 30.4000 g. **Composition:** 0.9500 Platinum .9286 oz. APW **Obverse:** Head of Queen Elizabeth II right **Reverse:** Viking longship on shield **Shape:** 7-sided

Date	Mintage	F	VF	XF	Unc	BU
1985 Proof	Est. 200	Value: 750				

KM# 158 50 PENCE **Composition:** Copper-Nickel **Subject:** Christmas 1985 **Obverse:** Head of Queen Elizabeth II right **Reverse:** de Havilland dragon DH84 **Shape:** 7-sided

Date	F	VF	XF	Unc	BU
1985 AA	—	—	—	3.50	—
1985 AB	—	—	—	3.50	—
1985 BB	—	—	—	3.50	—
1985 Proof	Value: 9.50				

KM# 158a 50 PENCE **Weight:** 15.5000 g. **Composition:** 0.9250 Silver .4610 oz. ASW **Subject:** Christmas 1985 **Obverse:** Head of Queen Elizabeth II right **Reverse:** de Havilland Dragon DH84 **Shape:** 7-sided

Date	Mintage	F	VF	XF	Unc	BU
1985 Proof	5,000	Value: 20.00				

KM# 158b 50 PENCE **Weight:** 26.0000 g. **Composition:** 0.9170 Gold .7666 oz. AGW **Subject:** Christmas 1985 **Obverse:** Head of Queen Elizabeth II right **Reverse:** de Havilland Dragon DH84 **Shape:** 7-sided

Date	Mintage	F	VF	XF	Unc	BU
1985 Proof	Est. 250	Value: 500				

KM# 158c 50 PENCE **Weight:** 30.4000 g. **Composition:** 0.9500 Platinum .9286 oz. APW **Subject:** Christmas 1985 **Obverse:** Head of Queen Elizabeth II right **Reverse:** de Havilland Dragon DH84 **Shape:** 7-sided

Date	F	VF	XF	Unc	BU
1985 Proof	— Value: 750				

KM# 172 50 PENCE **Composition:** Copper-Nickel **Subject:** Christmas 1986 **Obverse:** Head of Queen Elizabeth II right **Reverse:** Horse-drawn tram **Shape:** 7-sided

Date	F	VF	XF	Unc	BU
1986 AA	—	—	—	3.50	—
1986 AB	—	—	—	3.50	—
1986 Proof	— Value: 9.50				

KM# 172a 50 PENCE **Weight:** 15.5000 g. **Composition:** 0.9250 Silver .4610 oz. ASW **Subject:** Christmas 1986 **Obverse:** Head of Queen Elizabeth II right **Reverse:** Horse-drawn tram **Shape:** 7-sided

Date	Mintage	F	VF	XF	Unc	BU
1986 Proof	Est. 5,000	Value: 20.00				

KM# 172b 50 PENCE **Weight:** 26.0000 g. **Composition:** 0.9170 Gold .7666 oz. AGW **Subject:** Christmas 1986 **Obverse:** Head of Queen Elizabeth II right **Reverse:** Horse-drawn tram **Shape:** 7-sided

Date	F	VF	XF	Unc	BU
1986 Proof	— Value: 500				

KM# 190 50 PENCE **Composition:** Copper-Nickel **Subject:** Christmas 1987 **Obverse:** Head of Queen Elizabeth II right **Reverse:** Thorneycroft bus **Shape:** 7-sided

Date	F	VF	XF	Unc	BU
1987 AA	—	—	—	2.50	—
1987 D	—	—	—	2.50	—
1987 Proof	— Value: 7.50				

KM# 190a 50 PENCE **Weight:** 15.5000 g. **Composition:** 0.9250 Silver .4610 oz. ASW **Subject:** Christmas 1987 **Obverse:** Head of Queen Elizabeth II right **Reverse:** Thorneycroft bus **Shape:** 7-sided

Date	Mintage	F	VF	XF	Unc	BU
1987 Proof	Est. 5,000	Value: 20.00				

KM# 190b 50 PENCE **Weight:** 26.0000 g. **Composition:** 0.9170 Gold .7666 oz. AGW **Subject:** Christmas 1987 **Obverse:** Head of Queen Elizabeth II right **Reverse:** Thorneycroft bus **Shape:** 7-sided

Date	Mintage	F	VF	XF	Unc	BU
1987 Proof	Est. 250	Value: 500				

KM# 190c 50 PENCE **Weight:** 30.4000 g. **Composition:** 0.9500 Platinum .9286 oz. APW **Subject:** Christmas 1987 **Obverse:** Head of Queen Elizabeth II right **Reverse:** Thorneycroft bus **Shape:** 7-sided

Date	Mintage	F	VF	XF	Unc	BU
1987 Proof	Est. 50	Value: 775				

KM# 212 50 PENCE **Composition:** Copper-Nickel **Obverse:** Head of Queen Elizabeth II right **Reverse:** Computer **Shape:** 7-sided

Date	F	VF	XF	Unc	BU
1988 AA	—	—	—	2.50	—
1989 AA	—	—	—	2.50	—
1990 AA	—	—	—	2.50	—
1991 AA	—	—	—	2.50	—
1992	—	—	—	2.50	—
1993 AA	—	—	—	2.50	—
1994 AA	—	—	—	2.50	—
1995 AA	—	—	—	2.50	—
1997 AA					

KM# 244 50 PENCE **Composition:** Copper-Nickel **Subject:** Christmas 1988 **Obverse:** Head of Queen Elizabeth II right **Reverse:** Motorbike and sidecar **Shape:** 7-sided

Date	F	VF	XF	Unc	BU
1988 AA	—	—	—	2.50	—
1988 BA			—	2.50	—
1988 BB Proof	— Value: 6.50				

KM# 244a 50 PENCE **Weight:** 15.5000 g. **Composition:** 0.9250 Silver .4610 oz. ASW **Subject:** Christmas 1988 **Obverse:** Head of Queen Elizabeth II right **Reverse:** Motorbike and sidecar **Shape:** 7-sided

Date	F	VF	XF	Unc	BU
1988 Proof	— Value: 20.00				

KM# 244b 50 PENCE **Weight:** 26.0000 g. **Composition:** 0.9170 Gold .7666 oz. AGW **Subject:** Christmas 1988 **Obverse:** Head of Queen Elizabeth II right **Reverse:** Motorbike and sidecar **Shape:** 7-sided

Date	F	VF	XF	Unc	BU
1988 Proof	— Value: 500				

KM# 244c 50 PENCE **Weight:** 30.4000 g. **Composition:** 0.9500 Platinum .9286 oz. APW **Subject:** Christmas 1988 **Obverse:** Head of Queen Elizabeth II right **Reverse:** Motorbike and sidecar **Shape:** 7-sided

Date	F	VF	XF	Unc	BU
1988 Proof	— Value: 800				

KM# 259 50 PENCE Composition: Copper-Nickel **Subject:** Christmas 1989 **Obverse:** Head of Queen Elizabeth II right **Reverse:** Electric trolley car **Shape:** 7-sided

Date	F	VF	XF	Unc	BU
1989	—	—	—	2.50	—
1989 BB Proof	—	Value: 6.50			

KM# 259a 50 PENCE Weight: 15.5000 g. **Composition:** 0.9250 Silver .4610 oz. ASW **Subject:** Christmas 1989 **Obverse:** Head of Queen Elizabeth II right **Reverse:** Electric trolly car **Shape:** 7-sided

Date	F	VF	XF	Unc	BU
1989 Proof	—	Value: 40.00			

KM# 259b 50 PENCE Weight: 26.0000 g. **Composition:** 0.9170 Gold .7666 oz. AGW **Subject:** Christmas 1989 **Obverse:** Head of Queen Elizabeth II right **Reverse:** Electric trolley car **Shape:** 7-sided

Date	F	VF	XF	Unc	BU
1989 Proof	—	Value: 835			

KM# 259c 50 PENCE Weight: 30.4000 g. **Composition:** 0.9500 Platinum .9286 oz. APW **Subject:** Christmas 1989 **Obverse:** Head of Queen Elizabeth II right **Reverse:** Electric trolley car **Shape:** 7-sided

Date	F	VF	XF	Unc	BU
1989 Proof	—	Value: 1,150			

KM# 282 50 PENCE Composition: Copper-Nickel **Subject:** Christmas 1990 **Obverse:** Head of Queen Elizabeth II right **Reverse:** Oceanliner **Shape:** 7-sided

Date	Mintage	F	VF	XF	Unc	BU
1990 AA	—	—	—	—	2.50	—
1990 AB	—	—	—	—	2.50	—
1990 Proof	30,000	Value: 6.50				

KM# 282a 50 PENCE Weight: 15.5000 g. **Composition:** 0.9250 Silver .4610 oz. ASW **Subject:** Christmas 1990 **Obverse:** Head of Queen Elizabeth II right **Reverse:** Oceanliner **Shape:** 7-sided

Date	Mintage	F	VF	XF	Unc	BU
1990 Proof	5,000	Value: 40.00				

KM# 282b 50 PENCE Weight: 26.0000 g. **Composition:** 0.9170 Gold .7666 oz. AGW **Subject:** Christmas 1990 **Obverse:** Head of Queen Elizabeth II right **Reverse:** Oceanliner **Shape:** 7-sided

Date	Mintage	F	VF	XF	Unc	BU
1990 Proof	250	Value: 800				

KM# 282c 50 PENCE Weight: 30.4000 g. **Composition:** 0.9500 Platinum .9286 oz. APW **Subject:** Christmas 1990 **Obverse:** Head of Queen Elizabeth II right **Reverse:** Oceanliner **Shape:** 7-sided

Date	Mintage	F	VF	XF	Unc	BU
1990 Proof	50	Value: 1,000				

KM# 303 50 PENCE Composition: Copper-Nickel **Subject:** Christmas 1991 **Obverse:** Head of Queen Elizabeth II right **Reverse:** Nativity scene **Shape:** 7-sided

Date	Mintage	F	VF	XF	Unc	BU
1991	—	—	—	—	2.50	—
1991 Proof	30,000	Value: 6.50				

KM# 303a 50 PENCE Weight: 15.5000 g. **Composition:** 0.9250 Silver .4610 oz. ASW **Subject:** Christmas 1991 **Obverse:** Head of Queen Elizabeth II right **Reverse:** Nativity scene **Shape:** 7-sided

Date	Mintage	F	VF	XF	Unc	BU
1991 Proof	5,000	Value: 40.00				

KM# 303b 50 PENCE Weight: 26.0000 g. **Composition:** 0.9170 Gold .7666 oz. AGW **Subject:** Christmas 1991 **Obverse:** Head of Queen Elizabeth II right **Reverse:** Nativity scene **Shape:** 7-sided

Date	Mintage	F	VF	XF	Unc	BU
1991 Proof	250	Value: 685				

KM# 303c 50 PENCE Weight: 30.4000 g. **Composition:** 0.9500 Platinum .9286 oz. APW **Subject:** Christmas 1991 **Obverse:** Head of Queen Elizabeth II right **Reverse:** Nativity scene **Shape:** 7-sided

Date	Mintage	F	VF	XF	Unc	BU
1991 Proof	50	Value: 860				

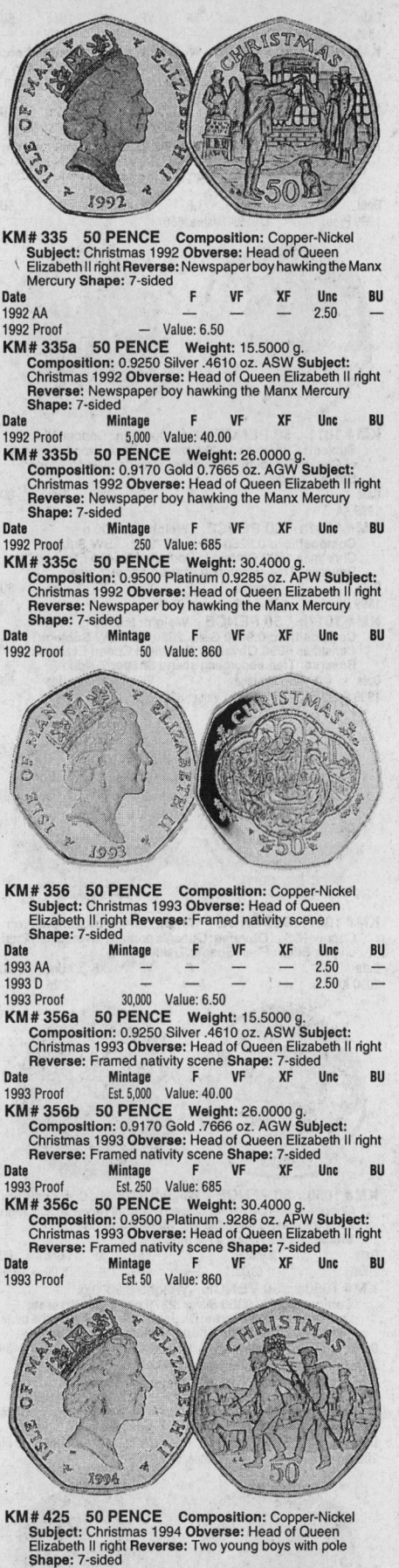

KM# 335 50 PENCE Composition: Copper-Nickel **Subject:** Christmas 1992 **Obverse:** Head of Queen Elizabeth II right **Reverse:** Newspaper boy hawking the Manx Mercury **Shape:** 7-sided

Date	F	VF	XF	Unc	BU
1992 AA	—	—	—	2.50	—
1992 Proof	—	Value: 6.50			

KM# 335a 50 PENCE Weight: 15.5000 g. **Composition:** 0.9250 Silver .4610 oz. ASW **Subject:** Christmas 1992 **Obverse:** Head of Queen Elizabeth II right **Reverse:** Newspaper boy hawking the Manx Mercury **Shape:** 7-sided

Date	Mintage	F	VF	XF	Unc	BU
1992 Proof	5,000	Value: 40.00				

KM# 335b 50 PENCE Weight: 26.0000 g. **Composition:** 0.9170 Gold 0.7665 oz. AGW **Subject:** Christmas 1992 **Obverse:** Head of Queen Elizabeth II right **Reverse:** Newspaper boy hawking the Manx Mercury **Shape:** 7-sided

Date	Mintage	F	VF	XF	Unc	BU
1992 Proof	250	Value: 685				

KM# 335c 50 PENCE Weight: 30.4000 g. **Composition:** 0.9500 Platinum 0.9285 oz. APW **Subject:** Christmas 1992 **Obverse:** Head of Queen Elizabeth II right **Reverse:** Newspaper boy hawking the Manx Mercury **Shape:** 7-sided

Date	Mintage	F	VF	XF	Unc	BU
1992 Proof	50	Value: 860				

KM# 356 50 PENCE Composition: Copper-Nickel **Subject:** Christmas 1993 **Obverse:** Head of Queen Elizabeth II right **Reverse:** Framed nativity scene **Shape:** 7-sided

Date	Mintage	F	VF	XF	Unc	BU
1993 AA	—	—	—	—	2.50	—
1993 D	—	—	—	—	2.50	—
1993 Proof	30,000	Value: 6.50				

KM# 356a 50 PENCE Weight: 15.5000 g. **Composition:** 0.9250 Silver .4610 oz. ASW **Subject:** Christmas 1993 **Obverse:** Head of Queen Elizabeth II right **Reverse:** Framed nativity scene **Shape:** 7-sided

Date	Mintage	F	VF	XF	Unc	BU
1993 Proof	Est. 5,000	Value: 40.00				

KM# 356b 50 PENCE Weight: 26.0000 g. **Composition:** 0.9170 Gold .7666 oz. AGW **Subject:** Christmas 1993 **Obverse:** Head of Queen Elizabeth II right **Reverse:** Framed nativity scene **Shape:** 7-sided

Date	Mintage	F	VF	XF	Unc	BU
1993 Proof	Est. 250	Value: 685				

KM# 356c 50 PENCE Weight: 30.4000 g. **Composition:** 0.9500 Platinum .9286 oz. APW **Subject:** Christmas 1993 **Obverse:** Head of Queen Elizabeth II right **Reverse:** Framed nativity scene **Shape:** 7-sided

Date	Mintage	F	VF	XF	Unc	BU
1993 Proof	Est. 50	Value: 860				

KM# 425 50 PENCE Composition: Copper-Nickel **Subject:** Christmas 1994 **Obverse:** Head of Queen Elizabeth II right **Reverse:** Two young boys with pole **Shape:** 7-sided

Date	F	VF	XF	Unc	BU
1994 AA	—	—	—	2.50	—

KM# 425a 50 PENCE Weight: 15.5000 g. **Composition:** 0.9250 Silver .4610 oz. ASW **Subject:** Christmas 1994 **Obverse:** Head of Queen Elizabeth II right **Reverse:** Two young boys with pole **Shape:** 7-sided

Date	F	VF	XF	Unc	BU
1994 Proof	—	Value: 40.00			

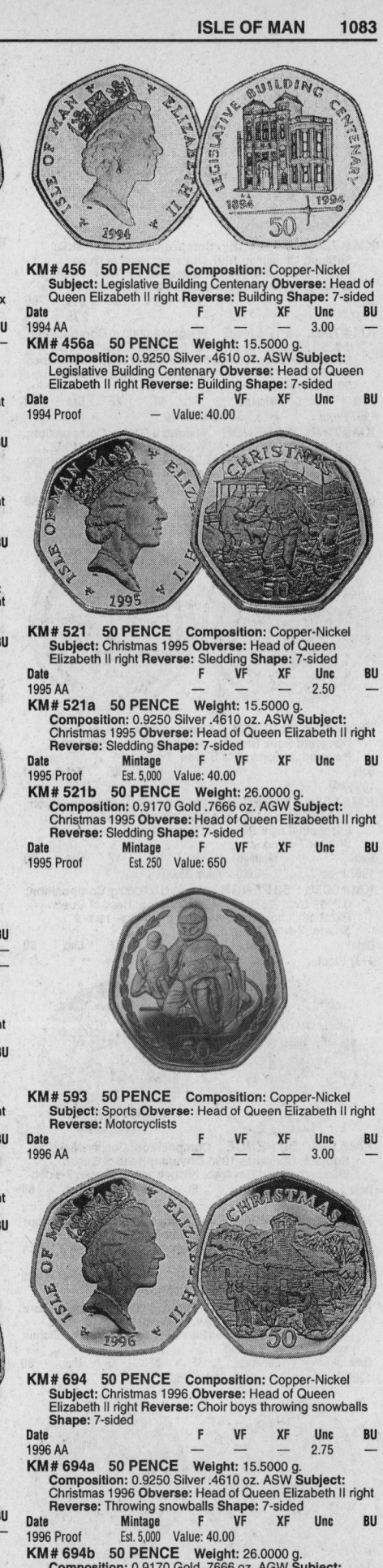

KM# 456 50 PENCE Composition: Copper-Nickel **Subject:** Legislative Building Centenary **Obverse:** Head of Queen Elizabeth II right **Reverse:** Building **Shape:** 7-sided

Date	F	VF	XF	Unc	BU
1994 AA	—	—	—	3.00	—

KM# 456a 50 PENCE Weight: 15.5000 g. **Composition:** 0.9250 Silver .4610 oz. ASW **Subject:** Legislative Building Centenary **Obverse:** Head of Queen Elizabeth II right **Reverse:** Building **Shape:** 7-sided

Date	F	VF	XF	Unc	BU
1994 Proof	—	Value: 40.00			

KM# 521 50 PENCE Composition: Copper-Nickel **Subject:** Christmas 1995 **Obverse:** Head of Queen Elizabeth II right **Reverse:** Sledding **Shape:** 7-sided

Date	F	VF	XF	Unc	BU
1995 AA	—	—	—	2.50	—

KM# 521a 50 PENCE Weight: 15.5000 g. **Composition:** 0.9250 Silver .4610 oz. ASW **Subject:** Christmas 1995 **Obverse:** Head of Queen Elizabeth II right **Reverse:** Sledding **Shape:** 7-sided

Date	Mintage	F	VF	XF	Unc	BU
1995 Proof	Est. 5,000	Value: 40.00				

KM# 521b 50 PENCE Weight: 26.0000 g. **Composition:** 0.9170 Gold .7666 oz. AGW **Subject:** Christmas 1995 **Obverse:** Head of Queen Elizabeeth II right **Reverse:** Sledding **Shape:** 7-sided

Date	Mintage	F	VF	XF	Unc	BU
1995 Proof	Est. 250	Value: 650				

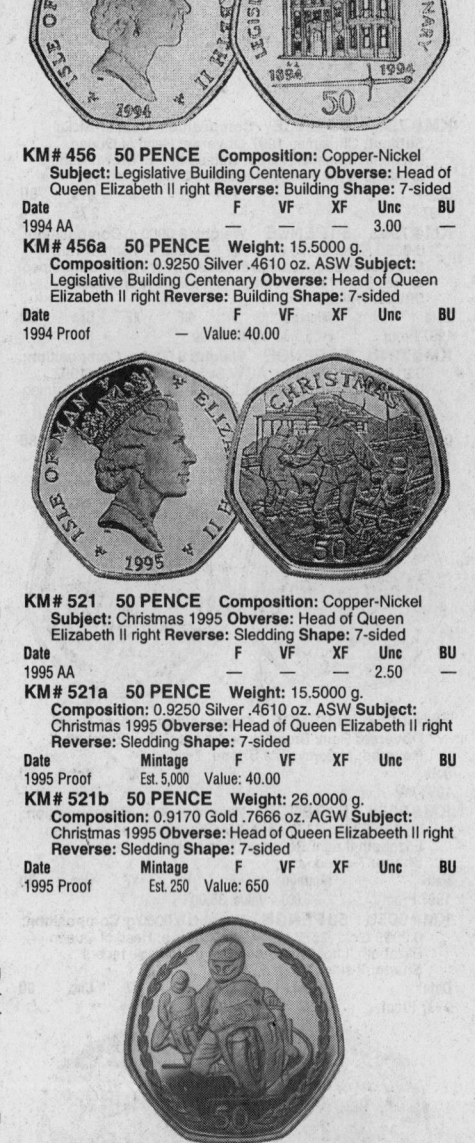

KM# 593 50 PENCE Composition: Copper-Nickel **Subject:** Sports **Obverse:** Head of Queen Elizabeth II right **Reverse:** Motorcyclists

Date	F	VF	XF	Unc	BU
1996 AA	—	—	—	3.00	—

KM# 694 50 PENCE Composition: Copper-Nickel **Subject:** Christmas 1996 **Obverse:** Head of Queen Elizabeth II right **Reverse:** Choir boys throwing snowballs **Shape:** 7-sided

Date	F	VF	XF	Unc	BU
1996 AA	—	—	—	2.75	—

KM# 694a 50 PENCE Weight: 15.5000 g. **Composition:** 0.9250 Silver .4610 oz. ASW **Subject:** Christmas 1996 **Obverse:** Head of Queen Elizabeth II right **Reverse:** Throwing snowballs **Shape:** 7-sided

Date	Mintage	F	VF	XF	Unc	BU
1996 Proof	Est. 5,000	Value: 40.00				

KM# 694b 50 PENCE Weight: 26.0000 g. **Composition:** 0.9170 Gold .7666 oz. AGW **Subject:** Christmas 1996 **Obverse:** Head of Queen Elizabeth II right **Reverse:** Throwing snowballs **Shape:** 7-sided

Date	Mintage	F	VF	XF	Unc	BU
1996 Proof	Est. 250	Value: 650				

KM# 794 50 PENCE **Composition:** Copper-Nickel **Subject:** Christmas 1997 **Obverse:** Head of Queen Elizabeth II right **Reverse:** Cameo of T.E. Brown with montage of his literary characters **Shape:** 7-sided

Date	F	VF	XF	Unc	BU
1997	—	—	—	2.75	—

KM# 794a 50 PENCE **Weight:** 8.0000 g. **Composition:** 0.9250 Silver .2379 oz. ASW **Subject:** Christmas 1987 **Obverse:** Head of Queen Elizabeth II right **Reverse:** Cameo of T.E. Brown with montage of his literacy characters **Shape:** 7-sided

Date	Mintage	F	VF	XF	Unc	BU
1997 Proof	Est. 5,000	Value: 40.00				

KM# 794b 50 PENCE **Weight:** 8.0000 g. **Composition:** 0.9160 Gold .2356 oz. AGW **Subject:** Christmas 1997 **Obverse:** Head of Queen Elizabeth II right **Reverse:** Cameo of T.E. Brown with montage of his literacy characters **Shape:** 7-sided

Date	Mintage	F	VF	XF	Unc	BU
1997 Proof	250	Value: 650				

KM# 905 50 PENCE **Composition:** Copper-Nickel **Obverse:** Rank-Broadley portrait of Queen Elizabeth II **Reverse:** Motorcyclists **Shape:** 7-sided

Date	F	VF	XF	Unc	BU
1998 AA	—	—	—	3.00	—

KM# 905a 50 PENCE **Weight:** 8.0000 g. **Composition:** 0.9250 Silver .2379 oz. ASW **Obverse:** Head of Queen Elizabeth II right **Reverse:** Two motorcycle racers **Shape:** 7-sided

Date	Mintage	F	VF	XF	Unc	BU
1997 Proof	5,000	Value: 35.00				

KM# 905b 50 PENCE **Weight:** 8.0000 g. **Composition:** 0.9999 Gold .2572 oz. AGW **Obverse:** Head of Queen Elizabeth II right **Reverse:** Two motorcycle racers **Shape:** 7-sided

Date	Mintage	F	VF	XF	Unc	BU
1997 Proof	Est. 250	Value: 650				

KM# 908 50 PENCE **Composition:** Copper-Nickel **Subject:** Christmas 1998 **Obverse:** Head of Queen Elizabeth II right **Reverse:** Kitchen scene **Shape:** 7-sided

Date	F	VF	XF	Unc	BU
1998	—	—	—	3.00	—

KM# 908a 50 PENCE **Weight:** 8.0000 g. **Composition:** 0.9250 Silver .2379 oz. ASW **Subject:** Christmas 1998 **Obverse:** Head of Queen Elizabeth II right **Reverse:** Kitchen scene **Shape:** 7-sided

Date	Mintage	F	VF	XF	Unc	BU
1998 Proof	5,000	Value: 35.00				

KM# 908b 50 PENCE **Weight:** 8.0000 g. **Composition:** 0.9167 Gold .2358 oz. AGW **Subject:** Christmas 1998 **Obverse:** Head of Queen Elizabeth II right **Reverse:** Kitchen scene **Shape:** 7-sided

Date	Mintage	F	VF	XF	Unc	BU
1998 Proof	250	Value: 650				

KM# 993 50 PENCE **Composition:** Copper-Nickel **Obverse:** Portrait of Queen Elizabeth II **Reverse:** Motorcycle racer above denomination **Shape:** 7-sided

Date	F	VF	XF	Unc	BU
1999	—	—	—	3.00	—

KM# 993a 50 PENCE **Weight:** 8.0000 g. **Composition:** 0.9250 Silver .2379 oz. ASW **Obverse:** Portrait of Queen Elizabeth II **Reverse:** Motorcycle racer above denomination **Shape:** 7-sided

Date	Mintage	F	VF	XF	Unc	BU
1999 Proof	Est. 5,000	Value: 35.00				

KM# 993b 50 PENCE **Weight:** 8.0000 g. **Composition:** 0.9160 Gold .2356 oz. AGW **Obverse:** Portrait of Queen Elizabeth II **Reverse:** Motorcycle racer above denomination **Shape:** 7-sided

Date	Mintage	F	VF	XF	Unc	BU
1999 Proof	Est. 250	Value: 650				

KM# 1011 50 PENCE **Composition:** Copper-Nickel **Subject:** Christmas 1999 **Obverse:** Rank-Broadley portrait of Queen Elizabeth II **Reverse:** Tree decorating scene **Shape:** 7-sided

Date	F	VF	XF	Unc	BU
1999 AA	—	—	—	3.00	—

KM# 1011a 50 PENCE **Weight:** 8.0000 g. **Composition:** 0.9250 Silver .2379 oz. ASW **Subject:** Christmas 1999 **Obverse:** Portrait of Queen Elizabeth II **Reverse:** Tree decorating scene **Shape:** 7-sided

Date	Mintage	F	VF	XF	Unc	BU
1999 Proof	Est. 5,000	Value: 35.00				

KM# 1011b 50 PENCE **Weight:** 8.0000 g. **Composition:** 0.9160 Gold .2356 oz. AGW **Subject:** Christmas 1999 **Obverse:** Portrait of Queen Elizabeth II **Reverse:** Tree decorating scene **Shape:** 7-sided

Date	Mintage	F	VF	XF	Unc	BU
1999 Proof	Est. 250	Value: 650				

KM# 1041 50 PENCE **Weight:** 7.9400 g. **Composition:** Copper-Nickel **Obverse:** Queen's portrait **Reverse:** Stylized crucifix **Edge:** Plain **Shape:** 7-sided

Date	F	VF	XF	Unc	BU
2000 AA	—	—	—	2.25	—

KM# 1050 50 PENCE **Weight:** 8.0000 g. **Composition:** Copper-Nickel **Obverse:** Queen's portrait **Reverse:** Dr. John Kelly translating the bible into Manx **Edge:** Plain **Shape:** 7-sided **Size:** 27.3 mm.

Date	Mintage	F	VF	XF	Unc	BU
2000	30,000	—	—	—	8.00	—

KM# 1050a 50 PENCE **Weight:** 8.0000 g. **Composition:** 0.9250 Silver .2379 oz. ASW **Obverse:** Queen's portrait **Reverse:** Dr. John Kelly translating the bible into Manx **Edge:** Plain **Shape:** 7-sided **Size:** 27.3 mm.

Date	Mintage	F	VF	XF	Unc	BU
2000 Proof	5,000	Value: 34.00				

KM# 1050b 50 PENCE **Weight:** 8.0000 g. **Composition:** 0.9160 Gold .2356 oz. AGW **Obverse:** Queen's portrait **Reverse:** Dr. John Kelly translating the bible into Manx **Edge:** Plain **Shape:** 7-sided **Size:** 27.3 mm.

Date	Mintage	F	VF	XF	Unc	BU
2000 Proof	250	Value: 645				

KM# 1105 50 PENCE **Weight:** 8.0000 g. **Composition:** Copper-Nickel **Subject:** Christmas **Obverse:** Queen's portrait **Reverse:** Postman and children **Edge:** Plain **Shape:** 7-sided **Size:** 27.3 mm.

Date	Mintage	F	VF	XF	Unc	BU
2001	30,000	—	—	—	10.00	—

KM# 1105a 50 PENCE **Weight:** 8.0000 g. **Composition:** 0.9250 Silver .2379 oz. ASW **Edge:** Plain **Shape:** 7-sided **Size:** 27.3 mm.

Date	Mintage	F	VF	XF	Unc	BU
2001 Proof	5,000	Value: 34.00				

KM# 1105b 50 PENCE **Weight:** 8.0000 g. **Composition:** 0.9167 Gold .2358 oz. AGW **Edge:** Plain **Shape:** 7-sided **Size:** 27.3 mm.

Date	Mintage	F	VF	XF	Unc	BU
2001 Proof	250	Value: 645				

KM# 1160 50 PENCE **Weight:** 8.0000 g. **Composition:** Copper Nickel **Subject:** Christmas **Obverse:** Queen's portrait **Reverse:** Scrooge in bed **Edge:** Plain **Shape:** 7-sided **Size:** 27.3 mm.

Date	Mintage	F	VF	XF	Unc	BU
2002PM	30,000	—	—	—	10.00	—

KM# 1160a 50 PENCE **Weight:** 8.0000 g. **Composition:** 0.9250 Silver 0.2379 oz. ASW **Subject:** Christmas **Obverse:** Queen's portrait **Reverse:** Scrooge in bed **Edge:** Plain **Shape:** 7-sided **Size:** 27.3 mm.

Date	Mintage	F	VF	XF	Unc	BU
2002PM Proof	5,000	Value: 34.00				

KM# 1160b 50 PENCE **Weight:** 8.0000 g. **Composition:** 0.9167 Gold 0.2358 oz. AGW **Subject:** Christmas **Obverse:** Queen's portrait **Reverse:** Scrooge in bed **Edge:** Plain **Shape:** 7-sided **Size:** 27.3 mm.

Date	Mintage	F	VF	XF	Unc	BU
2002PM Proof	250	Value: 645				

KM# 1128 60 PENCE **Subject:** Euro Currency Converter **Obverse:** Bust of Queen Elizabeth II right **Reverse:** Rotating map with cut out arrow revealing the Euro equivalent of the country's currency to which the arrow is pointed **Edge:** Reeded **Size:** 38.6 mm. **Note:** Bronze finished base metal with a silver finished rotator on reverse.

Date	Mintage	F	VF	XF	Unc	BU
2002	15,000	—	—	—	20.00	—

KM# 15 1/2 SOVEREIGN (1/2 Pound) **Weight:** 3.9940 g. **Composition:** 0.9170 Gold .1177 oz. AGW **Subject:** 200th Anniversary of Acquistion **Obverse:** Bust of Queen Elizabeth II right

Date	Mintage	F	VF	XF	Unc	BU
1965	1,500	—	—	—	55.00	—

KM# 15a 1/2 SOVEREIGN (1/2 Pound) **Weight:** 4.0000 g. **Composition:** 0.9800 Gold .1260 oz. AGW **Subject:** 200th Anniversary of Acquistion **Obverse:** Bust of Queen Elizabeth II right

Date	Mintage	F	VF	XF	Unc	BU
1965 Proof	1,000	Value: 60.00				

KM# 26 1/2 SOVEREIGN (1/2 Pound) **Weight:** 3.9813 g. **Composition:** 0.9170 Gold .1173 oz. AGW **Obverse:** Bust of Queen Elizabeth II right

Date	Mintage	F	VF	XF	Unc	BU
1973	14,000	—	—	—	60.00	—
1973 Proof	1,250	Value: 65.00				
1974	6,566	—	—	—	60.00	—
1974 Proof	2,500	Value: 65.00				
1975	1,956	—	—	—	60.00	—
1975 Proof	—	Value: 65.00				
1976	2,558	—	—	—	60.00	—
1976 Proof	—	Value: 65.00				
1977	—	—	—	—	60.00	—
1977 Proof	1,250	Value: 70.00				
1978 Proof	1,250	Value: 70.00				
1979 (t)	8,000	—	—	—	60.00	—
1979 (t) Proof	30,000	Value: 65.00				
1980 (m) Proof	7,500	Value: 65.00				
1980 (v) Proof	—	Value: 65.00				
1982 (b)	40,000	—	—	—	60.00	—
1982 (b) Proof	30,000	Value: 65.00				

KM# 85 1/2 SOVEREIGN (1/2 Pound) **Weight:** 3.9813 g. **Composition:** 0.9170 Gold .1173 oz. AGW **Subject:** Wedding of Prince Charles and Lady Diana **Obverse:** Bust of Queen Elizabeth II right **Reverse:** Portraits of Royal Couple, joined shields

Date	Mintage	F	VF	XF	Unc	BU
1981 Proof	30,000	Value: 100				

KM# 260 1/2 SOVEREIGN (1/2 Pound) **Weight:** 3.9813 g. **Composition:** 0.9170 Gold .1173 oz. AGW **Obverse:** Bust of Queen Elizabeth II right **Note:** Similar to 5 Pounds, KM#263.

Date	Mintage	F	VF	XF	Unc	BU
1984	20	—	—	—	200	—
1984 Proof	20	Value: 250				

KM# 264 1/2 SOVEREIGN (1/2 Pound) **Weight:** 3.9813 g. **Composition:** 0.9170 Gold .1173 oz. AGW **Obverse:** Head of Queen Elizabeth II right **Note:** Similar to 1 Pound, KM#265.

Date	Mintage	F	VF	XF	Unc	BU
1988 Proof	5,879	Value: 85.00				

KM# 16 SOVEREIGN (Pound) **Weight:** 7.9881 g. **Composition:** 0.9170 Gold .2355 oz. AGW **Subject:** 200th Anniversary of Acquisition **Obverse:** Bust of Queen Elizabeth II right **Reverse:** Triskeles symbol in inner circle

Date	Mintage	F	VF	XF	Unc	BU
1965	2,000	—	—	—	115	—

KM# 16a SOVEREIGN (Pound) **Weight:** 8.0000 g. **Composition:** 0.9800 Gold .2520 oz. AGW **Subject:** 200th Anniversary of Acquisition **Obverse:** Bust of Queen Elizabeth II right **Reverse:** Triskeles symbol in inner circle

Date	Mintage	F	VF	XF	Unc	BU
1965 Proof	1,000	Value: 125				

KM# 27 SOVEREIGN (Pound) **Weight:** 7.9627 g. **Composition:** 0.9170 Gold .2347 oz. AGW **Obverse:** Bust of Queen Elizabeth II right

Date	Mintage	F	VF	XF	Unc	BU
1973	40,000	—	—	—	110	—
1973 Proof	1,250	Value: 125				
1974	8,604	—	—	—	115	—
1974 Proof	2,500	Value: 125				
1975	956	—	—	—	140	—
1975 Proof	—	Value: 135				
1976	1,238	—	—	—	120	—
1976 Proof	—	Value: 130				
1977	—	—	—	—	120	—
1977 Proof	1,250	Value: 130				
1978 Proof	1,250	Value: 130				
1979 AA (t)	10,000	—	—	—	110	—
1979 D (t)	—	—	—	—	110	—
1979 (t) Proof	30,000	Value: 120				
1980 D (m) Proof	5,000	Value: 120				
1980 (v) Proof	—	Value: 120				
1982 (b)	30,000	—	—	—	110	—
1982 (b) Proof	40,000	Value: 120				

KM# 44 Pound **Composition:** Virenium **Obverse:** Bust of Queen Elizabeth II right **Reverse:** Triskeles

Date	Mintage	F	VF	XF	Unc	BU
1978 AA	—	—	—	—	3.00	—
1978 AB	—	—	—	—	3.00	—
1978 AC	—	—	—	—	2.50	—
1978 AD	3,780	—	—	—	7.50	—
1978 BB	—	—	—	—	—	—
1978 BC Proof	150,000	Value: 3.50				
1979 AA(t)	—	—	—	—	2.50	—
1979 AB(t)	—	—	—	—	2.50	—
1979 AC(t)	—	—	—	—	2.50	—
1979 BB(t) Proof	—	Value: 3.50				
1979 (t) Crossed oars	—	—	—	—	2.50	—
1980 AA DMIHE	30,000	—	—	—	2.50	—
1980 AA DMIHEN	—	—	—	—	2.50	—
1980 AA TT	—	—	—	—	2.50	—
1980 AB DMIHE	—	—	—	—	2.50	—
1980 AB DHIHEN	—	—	—	—	2.50	—
1980 AB TT	—	—	—	—	5.50	—
1980 AC DMIHE	100,000	—	—	—	2.50	—
1980 Proof	5,000	Value: 10.00				
1980 AA	—	—	—	—	2.50	—
1980 AB	—	—	—	—	2.50	—
1980 AC	—	—	—	—	2.50	—
1981 AA	—	—	—	—	2.50	—

KM# 44a Pound **Weight:** 4.6000 g. **Composition:** 0.9250 Silver .1368 oz. ASW **Obverse:** Bust of Queen Elizabeth II right **Reverse:** Triskeles

Date	Mintage	F	VF	XF	Unc	BU
1978	—	—	—	—	8.00	—
1978 D Proof	100,000	Value: 8.00				
1979 D(t) Proof	75,000	Value: 15.00				
1980 Proof	75,000	Value: 8.00				
1981 Proof	—	Value: 8.00				
1982 (b) Proof	1,000	Value: 35.00				

KM# 44b SOVEREIGN (Pound) **Weight:** 9.0000 g. **Composition:** 0.9500 Platinum .2749 oz. APW **Obverse:** Bust of Queen Elizabeth II right **Reverse:** Triskeles

Date	Mintage	F	VF	XF	Unc	BU
1978 Proof	1,000	Value: 220				
1979 Proof	—	Value: 220				
1980 Proof	1,000	Value: 220				
1982 (b) Proof	100	Value: 250				

KM# 44c SOVEREIGN (Pound) **Weight:** 7.9627 g. **Composition:** 0.9170 Gold .2347 oz. AGW **Obverse:** Bust of Queen Elizabeth II right **Reverse:** Triskeles

Date	Mintage	F	VF	XF	Unc	BU
1980 Proof	5,000	Value: 125				
1980 T.T. Proof	300	Value: 225				
1982 (b)	250	—	—	—	225	—
1982 (b) Proof	750	Value: 200				

KM# 44d SOVEREIGN (Pound) **Weight:** 4.6000 g. **Composition:** 0.5000 Silver .0739 oz. ASW **Obverse:** Bust of Queen Elizabeth II right **Reverse:** Triskeles

Date	Mintage	F	VF	XF	Unc	BU
1980 Proof	10,000	Value: 15.00				

KM# 86 SOVEREIGN (Pound) **Weight:** 7.9627 g. **Composition:** 0.9170 Gold .2347 oz. AGW **Subject:** Wedding of Prince Charles and Lady Diana **Obverse:** Bust of Queen Elizabeth II right **Reverse:** Portraits of Royal Couple, joined shields

Date	Mintage	F	VF	XF	Unc	BU
1981 Proof	40,000	Value: 150				

KM# 109 SOVEREIGN (Pound) **Weight:** 9.5000 g. **Composition:** Nickel-Brass **Obverse:** Bust of Queen Elizabeth II right **Reverse:** Peel

Date	F	VF	XF	Unc	BU
1983 AB	—	—	—	3.50	—
1983 AA	—	—	—	3.50	—

KM# 109a SOVEREIGN (Pound) **Weight:** 4.6000 g. **Composition:** 0.9250 Silver .1368 oz. ASW **Obverse:** Bust of Queen Elizabeth II right **Reverse:** Peel

Date	F	VF	XF	Unc	BU
1983 Proof	— Value: 20.00				

KM# 109b SOVEREIGN (Pound) **Weight:** 9.5000 g. **Composition:** 0.3740 Gold .1142 oz. AGW **Obverse:** Bust of Queen Elizabeth II right **Reverse:** Peel

Date	F	VF	XF	Unc	BU
1983 Proof	— Value: 75.00				

KM# 109c SOVEREIGN (Pound) **Weight:** 7.9627 g. **Composition:** 0.9170 Gold .2347 oz. AGW **Obverse:** Bust of Queen Elizabeth II right **Reverse:** Peel

Date	F	VF	XF	Unc	BU
1983 Proof	— Value: 150				

KM# 109d SOVEREIGN (Pound) **Weight:** 9.0000 g. **Composition:** 0.9500 Platinum .2749 oz. APW **Obverse:** Bust of Queen Elizabeth II right **Reverse:** Peel

Date	F	VF	XF	Unc	BU
1983 Proof	— Value: 220				

KM# 128 SOVEREIGN (Pound) **Weight:** 9.5000 g. **Composition:** Nickel-Brass **Obverse:** Bust of Queen Elizaeth II right **Reverse:** Castletown

Date	F	VF	XF	Unc	BU
1984 D	—	—	—	4.00	—
1984 AA	—	—	—	4.00	—

KM# 128a SOVEREIGN (Pound) **Weight:** 4.6000 g. **Composition:** 0.9250 Silver .1368 oz. ASW **Obverse:** Bust of Queen Elizabeth II right **Reverse:** Castletown

Date	F	VF	XF	Unc	BU
1984	—	—	—	10.00	—
1984 D Proof	— Value: 20.00				

KM# 128b SOVEREIGN (Pound) **Weight:** 9.5000 g. **Composition:** 0.3740 Gold .1142 oz. AGW **Obverse:** Bust of Queen Elizabeth II right **Reverse:** Castletown

Date	Mintage	F	VF	XF	Unc	BU
1984 Proof	4,950	Value: 75.00				

KM# 128c SOVEREIGN (Pound) **Weight:** 7.9627 g. **Composition:** 0.9170 Gold .2347 oz. AGW **Obverse:** Bust of Queen Elizabeth II right **Reverse:** Castletown

Date	Mintage	F	VF	XF	Unc	BU
1984 Proof	950	Value: 150				

KM# 128d SOVEREIGN (Pound) **Weight:** 9.0000 g. **Composition:** 0.9500 Platinum .2749 oz. APW **Obverse:** Bust of Queen Elizabeth II right **Reverse:** Castletown

Date	F	VF	XF	Unc	BU
1984 Proof	— Value: 220				

KM# 261 SOVEREIGN (Pound) **Weight:** 7.9627 g. **Composition:** 0.9170 Gold .2347 oz. AGW **Obverse:** Bust of Queen Elizabeth II right **Reverse:** Four crowned shields

Date	Mintage	F	VF	XF	Unc	BU
1984	20	—	—	—	350	—
1984 Proof	20	Value: 450				

KM# 135 SOVEREIGN (Pound) **Weight:** 4.6000 g. **Composition:** 0.9250 Silver .1368 oz. ASW **Obverse:** Bust of Queen Elizabeth II right **Reverse:** Ramsey

Date	Mintage	F	VF	XF	Unc	BU
1985 D	—	—	—	—	10.00	—
1985 D Proof	Est. 5,000	Value: 22.50				

KM# 135b SOVEREIGN (Pound) **Weight:** 7.9627 g. **Composition:** 0.9170 Gold .2347 oz. AGW **Obverse:** Bust of Queeen Elizabeth II right **Reverse:** Ramsey

Date	Mintage	F	VF	XF	Unc	BU
1985 Proof	Est. 150	Value: 175				

KM# 135c SOVEREIGN (Pound) **Weight:** 9.0000 g. **Composition:** 0.9500 Platinum .2749 oz. APW **Obverse:** Bust of Queen Elizabeth II right **Reverse:** Ramsey

Date	Mintage	F	VF	XF	Unc	BU
1985 Proof	Est. 550	Value: 220				

KM# 151 SOVEREIGN (Pound) **Weight:** 9.5000 g. **Composition:** Nickel-Brass **Obverse:** Head of Queen Elizabeth II right **Reverse:** Ramsey

Date	Mintage	F	VF	XF	Unc	BU
1985 AA	—	—	—	—	3.50	—
1985 AA Proof	25,000	Value: 6.00				
1985(w) AA	—	—	—	—	—	—

KM# 151a SOVEREIGN (Pound) **Weight:** 4.6000 g. **Composition:** 0.9250 Silver .1368 oz. ASW **Obverse:** Head of Queen Elizabeth II right **Reverse:** Ramsey

Date	F	VF	XF	Unc	BU
1985 Proof	— Value: 35.00				

KM# 136 SOVEREIGN (Pound) **Weight:** 4.6000 g. **Composition:** 0.9250 Silver .1368 oz. ASW **Obverse:** Bust of Queen Elizabeth II right **Reverse:** Douglas

Date	F	VF	XF	Unc	BU
1986 AA	—	—	—	10.00	—
1986 D Proof	— Value: 25.00				

KM# 136b SOVEREIGN (Pound) **Weight:** 7.9627 g. **Composition:** 0.9170 Gold .2347 oz. AGW **Obverse:** Bust of Queen Elizabeth II right **Reverse:** Douglas

Date	F	VF	XF	Unc	BU
1986 Proof	— Value: 150				

KM# 136c SOVEREIGN (Pound) **Weight:** 9.0000 g. **Composition:** 0.9500 Platinum .2749 oz. APW **Obverse:** Bust of Queen Elizabeth II right **Reverse:** Douglas

Date	F	VF	XF	Unc	BU
1986 Proof	— Value: 220				

KM# 175 SOVEREIGN (Pound) **Weight:** 9.5000 g. **Composition:** Nickel-Brass **Obverse:** Head of Queen Elizabeth II right **Reverse:** Douglas

Date	Mintage	F	VF	XF	Unc	BU
1986	—	—	—	—	3.50	—
1986 Proof	25,000	Value: 6.00				

KM# 182 SOVEREIGN (Pound) **Weight:** 9.5000 g. **Composition:** Nickel-Brass **Obverse:** Head of Queen Elizabeth II right

Date	F	VF	XF	Unc	BU
1987 AA	—	—	—	3.50	—

KM# 265 SOVEREIGN (Pound) **Weight:** 7.9627 g. **Composition:** 0.9170 Gold .2347 oz. AGW **Obverse:** Head of Queen Elizabeth II right **Reverse:** Four crowned shields

Date	Mintage	F	VF	XF	Unc	BU
1988 Proof	1,600	Value: 150				
1988	5,876	—	—	—	125	—

KM# 213 SOVEREIGN (Pound) **Weight:** 9.5000 g. **Composition:** Nickel-Brass **Obverse:** Head of Queen Elizabeth II right **Reverse:** Telecommunicator

Date	F	VF	XF	Unc	BU
1988 AA	—	—	—	3.50	—
1988 BB	—	—	—	3.50	—
1988 D	—	—	—	3.50	—
1989 AA	—	—	—	3.50	—
1990 AA	—	—	—	3.50	—
1991 AA	—	—	—	3.50	—
1992 AB	—	—	—	3.50	—
1993 AA	—	—	—	3.50	—
1994 AA	—	—	—	3.50	—
1995 AA	—	—	—	3.50	—

KM# 213a SOVEREIGN (Pound) **Weight:** 4.6000 g. **Composition:** 0.9250 Silver .1368 oz. ASW **Obverse:** Head of Queen Elizabeth II right **Reverse:** Telecommunicator

Date	F	VF	XF	Unc	BU
1988 Proof	— Value: 10.00				
1989 Proof	— Value: 10.00				
1990 Proof	— Value: 10.00				
1991 Proof	— Value: 10.00				
1992 Proof	— Value: 10.00				

KM# 594 SOVEREIGN (Pound) **Composition:** Nickel-Brass **Subject:** Sports **Obverse:** Head of Queen Elizabeth II right **Reverse:** Cricket equipment

Date	F	VF	XF	Unc	BU
1996 AA	—	—	—	4.00	—
1997 AA	—	—	—	4.00	—

KM# 594a SOVEREIGN (Pound) **Weight:** 4.6000 g. **Composition:** 0.9250 Silver .1368 oz. ASW **Subject:** Sports **Obverse:** Head of Queen Elizabeth II right **Reverse:** Cricket equipment

Date	F	VF	XF	Unc	BU
1996 Proof	— Value: 25.00				

KM# 655 SOVEREIGN (Pound) **Weight:** 9.5000 g. **Composition:** Nickel-Brass **Subject:** Douglas Centenary **Obverse:** Head of Queen Elizabeth II right **Reverse:** City arms

Date	F	VF	XF	Unc	BU
1996 AA	—	—	—	4.00	—

KM# 655a SOVEREIGN (Pound) **Weight:** 9.5000 g. **Composition:** 0.9250 Silver .2825 oz. ASW **Subject:** Douglas Centenary **Obverse:** Head of Queen Elizabeth II right **Reverse:** City arms

Date	Mintage	F	VF	XF	Unc	BU
1996 Proof	25,000	Value: 15.00				

KM# 655b SOVEREIGN (Pound) **Weight:** 9.5000 g. **Composition:** 0.9160 Gold .2798 oz. AGW **Subject:** Douglas Centenary **Obverse:** Head of Queen Elizabeth II right **Reverse:** City arms

Date		F	VF	XF	Unc	BU
1996 Proof	Est. 10,000	Value: 175				

KM# 665a SOVEREIGN (Pound) **Weight:** 9.5000 g. **Composition:** 0.9250 Silver .2825 oz. ASW **Subject:** Douglas Centenary **Obverse:** Head of Queen Elizabeth II right

Date		F	VF	XF	Unc	BU
1996 Proof	Est. 25,000	Value: 15.00				

KM# 906 SOVEREIGN (Pound) **Weight:** 9.5000 g. **Composition:** Nickel-Brass **Obverse:** Portrait of Queen Elizabeth I **Reverse:** Cricket equipment

Date	F	VF	XF	Unc	BU
1998 AA	—	—	—	4.00	—
1999 AA	—	—	—	—	—

KM# 1042 SOVEREIGN (Pound) **Weight:** 9.5000 g. **Composition:** Brass **Subject:** Millennium Bells **Obverse:** Queen's portrait **Reverse:** Triskeles and three bells **Edge:** Reeded and plain sections

Date	F	VF	XF	Unc	BU
2000 AA	—	—	—	4.00	—

KM# 28 2 POUNDS **Weight:** 15.9253 g. **Composition:** 0.9170 Gold .4695 oz. AGW **Obverse:** Bust of Queen Elizabeth II right

Date	Mintage	F	VF	XF	Unc	BU
1973	3,612	—	—	—	200	—
1973 Proof	1,250	Value: 225				
1974	1,257	—	—	—	200	—
1974 Proof	2,500	Value: 220				
1975	456	—	—	—	200	—
1975 Proof	—	Value: 220				
1976	578	—	—	—	200	—
1976 Proof	—	Value: 220				
1977	—	—	—	—	200	—
1977 Proof	1,250	Value: 225				
1978 Proof	1,250	Value: 225				
1979 (t)	2,000	—	—	—	200	—
1979 (t) Proof	30,000	Value: 215				
1980 (m) Proof	2,000	Value: 220				
1982 (b)	15,000	—	—	—	200	—
1982 (b) Proof	5,000	Value: 220				

KM# 87 2 POUNDS **Weight:** 15.9253 g. **Composition:** 0.9170 Gold .4695 oz. AGW **Subject:** Wedding of Prince Charles and Lady Diana **Obverse:** Bust of Queen Elizabeth II right **Reverse:** Portraits of Royal Couple, joined shields

Date	Mintage	F	VF	XF	Unc	BU
1981 Proof	5,000	Value: 275				

KM# 129 2 POUNDS **Composition:** Virenium **Obverse:** Bust of Queen Elizabeth II right **Reverse:** Tower of Refuge and Manx Shearwater in flight

Date	F	VF	XF	Unc	BU
1984PM	—	—	—	—	—

Note: Reported, not confirmed

KM# 129a 2 POUNDS **Center Composition:** Silver **Obverse:** Bust of Queen Elizabeth II right **Reverse:** Tower of Refuge and Manx Shearwater in flight

Date	F	VF	XF	Unc	BU
1984PM	—	—	—	—	—

Note: Reported, not confirmed

KM# 262 2 POUNDS **Weight:** 15.9200 g. **Composition:** 0.9170 Gold .4695 oz. AGW **Obverse:** Bust of Queen Elizabeth II right **Reverse:** Four crowned shields
Note: Similar to 5 Pounds, KM#263

Date	Mintage	F	VF	XF	Unc	BU
1984	20	—	—	—	650	—
1984 Proof	20	Value: 800				

KM# 149 2 POUNDS **Composition:** Virenium **Obverse:** Head of Queen Elizabeth II right **Reverse:** Tower of Refuge and Manx Shearwater in flight

Date	F	VF	XF	Unc	BU
1985	—	—	—	—	—

Note: Reported, not confirmed

KM# 149a 2 POUNDS **Center Composition:** Silver **Obverse:** Head of Queen Elizabeth II right **Reverse:** Tower of Refuge and Manx Shearwater in flight

Date	F	VF	XF	Unc	BU
1985	—	—	—	—	—

Note: Reported, not confirmed

KM# 167 2 POUNDS **Composition:** Virenium **Obverse:** Head of Queen Elizabeth II right **Reverse:** Tower of Refuge and Manx Shearwater in flight

Date	F	VF	XF	Unc	BU
1986 (VW)	—	—	—	6.50	—
1986 Proof	— Value: 8.50				
1987 AA	—	—	—	6.50	—

KM# 214 2 POUNDS **Composition:** Virenium **Obverse:** Head of Queen Elizabeth II right **Reverse:** Manx Airlines

Date	F	VF	XF	Unc	BU
1988 AA	—	—	—	6.50	—
1988 D	—	—	—	6.50	—
1989	—	—	—	6.50	—
1990 AA	—	—	—	6.50	—
1991 AA	—	—	—	6.50	—
1992 AA	—	—	—	6.50	—
1993	—	—	—	6.50	—

KM# 257a 2 POUNDS **Center Weight:** 9.3000 g. **Center Composition:** 0.9250 Silver .2766 oz. ASW **Obverse:** Head of Queen Elizabeth II right **Reverse:** Manx Airlines dirigible

Date	F	VF	XF	Unc	BU
1989	—	—	—	—	—

Note: Reported, not confirmed

KM# 257b 2 POUNDS **Weight:** 15.9400 g. **Composition:** 0.9170 Gold .4730 oz. AGW **Obverse:** Head of Queen Elizabeth II right **Reverse:** Manx Airlines dirigible

Date	F	VF	XF	Unc	BU
1989	—	—	—	—	—

Note: Reported, not confirmed

KM# 257c 2 POUNDS **Center Weight:** 18.0000 g. **Center Composition:** 0.9500 Platinum .5498 oz. APW **Obverse:** Head of Queen Elizabeth II right **Reverse:** Manx Airlines dirigible

Date	F	VF	XF	Unc	BU
1989 Reported, not confirmed	—	—	—	—	—

Note: Most recalled by government; Few actually issued

KM# 344 2 POUNDS **Composition:** Virenium **Subject:** World Champion - Nigel Mansell **Obverse:** Head of Queen Elizabeth II right **Reverse:** Racecars

Date	F	VF	XF	Unc	BU
1993 AA	—	—	—	6.50	—

KM# 398 2 POUNDS **Composition:** Virenium **Subject:** Indycar World Series Champion - Nigel Mansell **Obverse:** Head of Queen Elizabeth II right **Reverse:** Two racecars

Date	F	VF	XF	Unc	BU
1994 AA	—	—	—	7.50	—

KM# 465 2 POUNDS **Composition:** Virenium **Subject:** 50th Anniversary - VE and VJ Day **Obverse:** Head of Queen Elizabeth II right

Date	F	VF	XF	Unc	BU
1995	—	—	—	7.00	—

KM# 595 2 POUNDS **Composition:** Virenium **Subject:** Sports **Obverse:** Head of Queen Elizabeth II right **Reverse:** Racing cars

Date	F	VF	XF	Unc	BU
1996 AA	—	—	—	7.00	—
1997 AA	—	—	—	7.00	—

KM# 844 2 POUNDS **Ring Composition:** Brass **Center Composition:** Copper-Nickel **Obverse:** Head of Queen Elizabeth II right **Reverse:** Racecars

Date	F	VF	XF	Unc	BU
1997 AA	—	—	—	8.00	—

KM# 858 2 POUNDS **Ring Composition:** Brass **Center Composition:** Copper-Nickel **Obverse:** Portrait of Queen Elizabeth II **Reverse:** Three racecars

Date	F	VF	XF	Unc	BU
1998 AA	—	—	—	8.00	—
1999 AA	—	—	—	8.00	—

KM# 1043 2 POUNDS **Ring Weight:** 12.0000 g. **Ring Composition:** Brass **Center Composition:** Copper-Nickel **Subject:** Thorwald's Cross **Obverse:** Queen's portrait **Reverse:** Ancient drawing **Edge:** Reeded

Date	F	VF	XF	Unc	BU
2000 AA	—	—	—	7.50	—

KM# 17 5 POUNDS **Weight:** 39.9403 g. **Composition:** 0.9170 Gold 1.1776 oz. AGW **Subject:** 200th Anniversary of Acquisition **Obverse:** Bust of Queen Elizabeth II right

Date	Mintage	F	VF	XF	Unc	BU
1965	500	—	—	—	540	—

KM# 17a 5 POUNDS **Center Weight:** 39.9500 g. **Center Composition:** 0.9800 Gold 1.2588 oz. AGW **Subject:** 200th Anniversary of Acquisition **Obverse:** Bust of Queen Elizabeth II right

Date	Mintage	F	VF	XF	Unc	BU
1965 Proof	1,000	Value: 575				

KM# 29 5 POUNDS **Center Weight:** 39.8134 g. **Center Composition:** 0.9170 Gold 1.1739 oz. AGW **Obverse:** Bust of Queen Elizabeth II right

Date	Mintage	F	VF	XF	Unc	BU
1973	3,035	—	—	—	450	—
1973 Proof	1,250	Value: 600				
1974	481	—	—	—	600	—
1974 Proof	2,500	Value: 475				
1975	306	—	—	—	600	—
1975 Proof	—	Value: 500				
1976	370	—	—	—	600	—
1976 Proof	—	Value: 500				
1977	—	—	—	—	475	—
1977 Proof	1,250	Value: 600				
1978 Proof	1,250	Value: 600				
1979 (t)	1,000	—	—	—	600	—
1979 (t) Proof	1,000	Value: 600				
1980 (m)	250	—	—	—	650	—
1982 (b)	10,000	—	—	—	450	—
1982 (b) Proof	500	Value: 600				

KM# 89 5 POUNDS **Center Weight:** 39.8134 g. **Center Composition:** 0.9170 Gold 1.1739 oz. AGW **Subject:** Wedding of Prince Charles and Lady Diana **Obverse:** Bust of Queen Elizabeth II right **Reverse:** Portraits of Royal Couple, joined shields

Date	Mintage	F	VF	XF	Unc	BU
1981 Proof	1,000	Value: 650				

KM# 88 5 POUNDS **Center Composition:** Virenium **Obverse:** Bust of Queen Elizabeth II right **Reverse:** Compass showing geographic location

Date	Mintage	F	VF	XF	Unc	BU
1981 AA	—	—	—	—	10.00	—
1981 AB	—	—	—	—	10.00	—
1981 AC	—	—	—	—	10.00	—
1981 AD	—	—	—	—	10.00	—
1981 Proof	30,000	Value: 12.00				
1982 Proof	—	Value: 12.00				
1983 AA	—	—	—	—	20.00	—
1984 AC	—	—	—	—	10.00	—

KM# 88a 5 POUNDS **Center Weight:** 23.5000 g. **Center Composition:** 0.9250 Silver .6989 oz. ASW **Obverse:** Bust of Queen Elizabeth II right **Reverse:** Compass showing geographic location

Date	Mintage	F	VF	XF	Unc	BU
1981 Proof	500	Value: 40.00				
1982 (b) Proof	1,000	Value: 35.00				
1983 Proof	5,000	Value: 25.00				

KM# 88b 5 POUNDS **Center Weight:** 39.9000 g. **Center Composition:** 0.9170 Gold 1.1764 oz. AGW **Obverse:** Bust of Queen Elizabeth II right **Reverse:** Compass showing geographic location

Date	Mintage	F	VF	XF	Unc	BU
1981 Proof	1,000	Value: 625				
1982 (b) Proof	250	Value: 650				
1982 (b) Proof	750	Value: 650				
1983 Proof	—	Value: 650				

KM# 88c 5 POUNDS **Center Weight:** 45.5000 g. **Center Composition:** 0.9500 Platinum 1.3898 oz. APW **Obverse:** Bust of Queen Elizabeth II right **Reverse:** Compass showing geographic location

Date	Mintage	F	VF	XF	Unc	BU
1981 Proof	500	Value: 1,000				
1982 (b) Proof	100	Value: 1,150				
1983 Proof	—	Value: 1,100				

KM# 134 5 POUNDS **Center Composition:** Virenium **Subject:** Quincentenery of the College of Arms **Obverse:** Bust of Queen Elizabeth II right **Reverse:** Mounted knight in armor with sword, facing right

Date	F	VF	XF	Unc	BU
1984 AA	—	—	—	10.00	—
1984 BB	—	—	—	10.00	—

KM# 134a 5 POUNDS **Center Weight:** 23.5000 g. **Center Composition:** 0.9250 Silver .6989 oz. ASW **Subject:** Quincentenery of the College of Arms **Obverse:** Bust of Queen Elizabeth II right **Reverse:** Mounted knight in armor with sword, facing right

Date	F	VF	XF	Unc	BU
1984 Proof	—	Value: 40.00			

KM# 134b 5 POUNDS **Center Weight:** 39.9000 g. **Center Composition:** 0.9170 Gold 1.1759 oz. AGW **Subject:** Quincentenery of the College of Arms **Obverse:** Bust of Queen Elizabeth II right **Reverse:** Mounted knight in armor with sword, facing right

Date	Mintage	F	VF	XF	Unc	BU
1984 Proof	150	Value: 750				

KM# 134c 5 POUNDS **Center Weight:** 45.5000 g. **Center Composition:** 0.9500 Platinum 1.3898 oz. APW **Subject:** Quincentenery of the College of Arms **Obverse:** Bust of Queen Elizabeth II right **Reverse:** Mounted knight in armor with sword, facing right

Date	F	VF	XF	Unc	BU
1984 Proof	—	Value: 1,100			

KM# 263 5 POUNDS **Center Weight:** 39.8300 g. **Center Composition:** 0.9170 Gold 1.1740 oz. AGW **Obverse:** Bust of Queen Elizabeth II right **Reverse:** Four crowned shields

Date	Mintage	F	VF	XF	Unc	BU
1984	20	—	—	—	1,250	—
1984 Proof	20	Value: 1,650				

KM# 150 5 POUNDS **Center Composition:** Virenium **Obverse:** Head of Queen Elizabeth II right **Reverse:** Similar to KM#134 with sports privy mark

Date	Mintage	F	VF	XF	Unc	BU
1985 AA(w)	—	—	—	—	10.00	—
1985 Proof	25,000	Value: 10.00				
1986 AA	—	—	—	—	10.00	—
1987 AA	—	—	—	—	10.00	—

KM# 150a 5 POUNDS **Center Weight:** 23.5000 g. **Center Composition:** 0.9250 Silver .6989 oz. ASW **Obverse:** Head of Queen Elizabeth II right

Date	F	VF	XF	Unc	BU
1985 Proof	Est. 5,000	Value: 40.00			

KM# 150b 5 POUNDS **Center Weight:** 39.9000 g. **Center Composition:** 0.9170 Gold 1.1759 oz. AGW **Obverse:** Head of Queen Elizabeth II right

Date	F	VF	XF	Unc	BU
1985 Proof	Est. 150	Value: 750			

KM# 150c 5 POUNDS **Center Weight:** 45.5000 g. **Center Composition:** 0.9500 Platinum 1.3898 oz. APW **Obverse:** Head of Queen Elizabeth II right

Date	F	VF	XF	Unc	BU
1985 Proof	Est. 100	Value: 1,200			

KM# 215 5 POUNDS **Center Composition:** Virenium **Obverse:** Head of Queen Elizabeth II right **Reverse:** Lobster fishing boat

Date	F	VF	XF	Unc	BU
1988 AA	—	—	—	10.00	—
1989 AA	—	—	—	10.00	—
1990 AA	—	—	—	10.00	—
1991 AA	—	—	—	10.00	—
1992 AA	—	—	—	10.00	—

KM# 336 5 POUNDS **Center Composition:** Virenium **Subject:** World Champion - Nigel Mansell **Obverse:** Head of Queen Elizabeth II right **Reverse:** Racecars

Date	F	VF	XF	Unc	BU
1993 AA	—	—	—	12.50	—

KM# 399 5 POUNDS **Center Composition:** Virenium **Subject:** Indycar World Series Champion - Nigel Mansell **Obverse:** Head of Queen Elizabeth II right **Reverse:** Two racecars

Date	F	VF	XF	Unc	BU
1994 AA	—	—	—	15.00	—

KM# 466 5 POUNDS **Center Composition:** Virenium **Subject:** 50th Anniversary - End of World War II **Obverse:** Head of Queen Elizabeth II right **Reverse:** Winston Churchill

Date	F	VF	XF	Unc	BU
1995	—	—	—	15.00	—

KM# 466a 5 POUNDS **Center Weight:** 23.5000 g. **Center Composition:** 0.9250 Silver .6989 oz. ASW **Subject:** 50th Anniversary - End of World War II **Obverse:** Head of Queen Elizabeth II right **Reverse:** Winston Churchill

Date	F	VF	XF	Unc	BU
1995 Proof	—	Value: 40.00			

KM# 466b 5 POUNDS **Center Weight:** 39.8300 g. **Center Composition:** 0.9170 Gold 1.1759 oz. AGW **Subject:** 50th Anniversary - End of World War II **Obverse:** Head of Queen Elizabeth II right **Reverse:** Winston Churchill

Date	F	VF	XF	Unc	BU
1995 Proof	Est. 850	Value: 750			

KM# 587 5 POUNDS **Center Composition:** Virenium **Subject:** European Soccer Championships **Obverse:** Head of Queen Elizabeth II right **Reverse:** Players

Date	F	VF	XF	Unc	BU
1996 AA	—	—	—	16.00	—

KM# 587a 5 POUNDS **Center Weight:** 23.5000 g. **Center Composition:** 0.9250 Silver .6989 oz. ASW **Subject:** European Soccer Championships **Obverse:** Head of Queen Elizabeth II right **Reverse:** Players

Date	F	VF	XF	Unc	BU
1996 Proof	Est. 5,000	Value: 40.00			

KM# 587b 5 POUNDS **Center Weight:** 39.0830 g. **Center Composition:** 0.9160 Gold 1.1510 oz. AGW **Subject:** European Soccer Championships **Obverse:** Head of Queen Elizabeth II right **Reverse:** Players

Date	F	VF	XF	Unc	BU
1996 Proof	Est. 850	Value: 900			

KM# 769 5 POUNDS **Center Composition:** Virenium **Subject:** 50th Anniversary - Queen Elizabeth and Prince Philip **Obverse:** Bust of Queen Elizabeth II right **Reverse:** Current portrait of Queen Elizabeth and Prince Philip

Date	F	VF	XF	Unc	BU
1997 AA	—	—	—	16.50	—

KM# 769a 5 POUNDS **Center Weight:** 23.5000 g. **Center Composition:** 0.9250 Silver .6989 oz. ASW **Subject:** 50th Anniversary - Queen Elizabeth and Prince Philip **Obverse:** Bust of Queen Elizabeth II right **Reverse:** Current portrait of Queen Elizabeth and Prince Philip

Date	Mintage	F	VF	XF	Unc	BU
1997 Proof	Est. 5,000	Value: 40.00				

KM# 769b 5 POUNDS **Center Weight:** 39.8300 g. **Center Composition:** 0.9167 Gold 1.1740 oz. AGW **Subject:** 50th Anniversary - Queen Elizabeth and Prince Philip **Obverse:** Bust of Queen Elizabeth II right **Reverse:** Current portrait of Queen Elizabeth and Prince Philip

Date	Mintage	F	VF	XF	Unc	BU
1997 Proof	Est. 850	Value: 900				

KM# 912 5 POUNDS **Center Composition:** Virenium **Subject:** 50th Birthday - Prince Charles **Obverse:** Portrait of Queen Elizabeth II **Reverse:** Portrait of Prince Charles

Date	F	VF	XF	Unc	BU
1998	—	—	—	16.50	—

KM# 912a 5 POUNDS **Center Weight:** 23.5000 g. **Center Composition:** 0.9250 Silver .6989 oz. ASW **Subject:** 50th Birthday - Prince Charles **Obverse:** Portrait of Queen Elizabeth II **Reverse:** Portrait of Prince Charles

Date	Mintage	F	VF	XF	Unc	BU
1998 Proof	Est. 5,000	Value: 50.00				

KM# 912b 5 POUNDS **Center Weight:** 39.8300 g. **Center Composition:** 0.9167 Gold 1.1740 oz. AGW **Subject:** 50th Birthday - Prince Charles **Obverse:** Portrait Queen Elizabeth II **Reverse:** Portrait of Prince Charles

Date	Mintage	F	VF	XF	Unc	BU
1998 Proof	Est. 850	Value: 885				

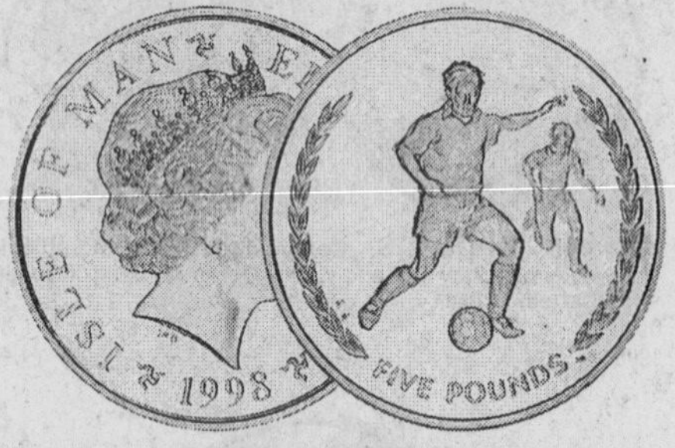

KM# 991 5 POUNDS **Center Composition:** Virenium **Subject:** Soccer **Obverse:** Portrait of Queen Elizabeth II **Reverse:** Two soccer players

Date	F	VF	XF	Unc	BU
1998 AA	—	—	—	16.50	—

KM# 943 5 POUNDS **Center Composition:** Virenium **Subject:** 175th Anniversary of the RN LI **Obverse:** Head of Queen Elizabeth II right **Reverse:** Lifeboat at sea

Date	F	VF	XF	Unc	BU
1999	—	—	—	15.50	—

KM# 943a 5 POUNDS **Center Weight:** 23.5000 g. **Center Composition:** 0.9250 Silver .6989 oz. ASW **Subject:** 175th Anniversary of the RN LI **Obverse:** Head of Queen Elizabeth II right **Reverse:** Lifeboat at sea

Date	F	VF	XF	Unc	BU
1999 Proof	Est. 10,000	Value: 50.00			

KM# 943b 5 POUNDS **Center Weight:** 39.8300 g. **Center Composition:** 0.9167 Gold 1.1739 oz. AGW **Subject:** 175th Anniversary of the RN LI **Obverse:** Head of Queen Elizabeth II right **Reverse:** Lifeboat at sea

Date	Mintage	F	VF	XF	Unc	BU
1999 Proof	850	Value: 885				

KM# 1044 5 POUNDS **Weight:** 20.1000 g. **Composition:** Virenium **Subject:** St. Patrick's Hymn **Obverse:** Queen's portrait **Reverse:** Stylized cross design **Edge:** Reeded and plain sections

Date	F	VF	XF	Unc	BU
2000 AA	—	—	—	16.50	—

KM# 345 10 POUNDS **Weight:** 10.0000 g. **Composition:** 0.9250 Silver .2973 oz. ASW **Subject:** Indycar World Series Champion - Nigel Mansell **Obverse:** Head of Queen Elizabeth II right **Reverse:** Racecar **Note:** Similar to 5 Pounds, KM#336

Date	Mintage	F	VF	XF	Unc	BU
1993 Proof	Est. 20,000	Value: 35.00				

KM# 400 10 POUNDS **Weight:** 10.0000 g. **Composition:** 0.9250 Silver .2973 oz. ASW **Subject:** Indycar World Series Champion - Nigel Mansell **Obverse:** Head of Queen Elizabeth II right **Reverse:** Two race cars **Note:** Similar to 5 Pounds, KM#399

Date	Mintage	F	VF	XF	Unc	BU
1994 Proof	Est. 20,000	Value: 35.00				

KM# 346 25 POUNDS **Weight:** 28.2800 g. **Composition:** 0.9250 Silver .8411 oz. ASW **Subject:** World Champion - Nigel Mansell **Obverse:** Bust of Queen Elizabeth II right **Reverse:** Two racecars

Date	Mintage	F	VF	XF	Unc	BU
1993 Proof	Est. 15,000	Value: 50.00				

KM#347 50 POUNDS **Weight:** 6.2200 g. **Composition:** 0.9990 Gold .2000 oz. AGW **Subject:** World Champion - Nigel Mansell **Obverse:** Head of Queen Elizabeth II right **Reverse:** Two racecars **Note:** Similar to 5 Pounds, KM#336

Date	Mintage	F	VF	XF	Unc	BU
1993 Proof	Est. 5,000	Value: 150				

KM#401 50 POUNDS **Weight:** 6.2200 g. **Composition:** 0.9990 Gold .2000 oz. AGW **Subject:** Indycar World Series Champion - Nigel Mansell **Obverse:** Head of Queen Elizabeth II right **Reverse:** Two racecars **Note:** Similar to 5 Pounds, KM#399

Date	Mintage	F	VF	XF	Unc	BU
1994 Proof	Est. 5,000	Value: 150				

CROWN SERIES

Pobjoy Mint Key

(M) MATTE - Normal circulation strike

(U) SPECIAL UNCIRCULATED - Polished or proof-like in appearance, slightly frosted features.

(P) PROOF - The highest quality obtainable having mirror-like fields and frosted features.

KM# 1129 1/32 CROWN **Weight:** 1.0000 g. **Composition:** 0.9720 Gold 0.0313 oz. AGW **Subject:** Queen's Golden Jubilee **Obverse:** Bust of Queen Elizabeth II right **Reverse:** Seated crowned Queen holding sceptre at her coronation **Edge:** Plain **Size:** 9.8 mm.

Date	F	VF	XF	Unc	BU
2002 Prooflike	—	—	—	—	—

KM# 235 1/25 CROWN **Weight:** 1.2441 g. **Composition:** 0.9990 Gold .0400 oz. AGW **Obverse:** Bust Queen Elizabeth II right **Reverse:** Manx cat

Date	Mintage	F	VF	XF	Unc	BU
1988	40,000	—	—	—	175	—
1988 Proof	5,000	Value: 178				

KM# 252 1/25 CROWN **Weight:** 1.2441 g. **Composition:** 0.9990 Gold .0400 oz. AGW **Obverse:** Bust Queen Elizabeth II **Reverse:** Persian cat

Date	F	VF	XF	Unc	BU
1989	—	—	—	50.00	—
1989 Proof	—	Value: 52.00			

KM# 467 1/25 CROWN **Weight:** 1.2441 g. **Composition:** 0.9995 Platinum .0400 oz. APW **Obverse:** Bust of Queen Elizabeth II right **Reverse:** Persian cat

Date	F	VF	XF	Unc	BU
1989	—	—	—	60.00	—
1989 Proof	—	Value: 62.00			

KM# 277 1/25 CROWN **Weight:** 1.2441 g. **Composition:** 0.9990 Gold .0400 oz. AGW **Obverse:** Bust of Queen Elizabeth II **Reverse:** Alley cat

Date	F	VF	XF	Unc	BU
1990	—	—	—	50.00	—
1990 Proof	—	Value: 52.00			

KM# 294 1/25 CROWN **Weight:** 1.2441 g. **Composition:** 0.9990 Gold .0400 oz. AGW **Obverse:** Bust of Queen Elizabeth II right **Reverse:** Norwegian cat

Date	F	VF	XF	Unc	BU
1991	—	—	—	50.00	—
1991 Proof	—	Value: 52.00			

KM# 322 1/25 CROWN **Weight:** 1.2441 g. **Composition:** 0.9990 Gold .0400 oz. AGW **Subject:** America's Cup **Obverse:** Bust of Queen Elizabeth II right **Reverse:** Sailboat

Date	Mintage	F	VF	XF	Unc	BU
1992 Proof like	50,000	—	—	—	—	—

KM# 328 1/25 CROWN **Weight:** 1.2441 g. **Composition:** 0.9990 Gold .0400 oz. AGW **Obverse:** Bust of Queen Elizabeth II right **Reverse:** Siamese cat

Date	F	VF	XF	Unc	BU
1992	—	—	—	45.00	—
1992 Proof	—	Value: 47.00			

KM# 338 1/25 CROWN **Weight:** 1.2441 g. **Composition:** 0.9990 Gold .0400 oz. AGW **Subject:** Year of the Cockerel **Obverse:** Bust of Queen Elizabeth II right **Reverse:** Cockerel in inner circle

Date	Mintage	F	VF	XF	Unc	BU
1993 Proof	Est. 25,000	Value: 40.00				

KM# 349 1/25 CROWN **Weight:** 1.2441 g. **Composition:** 0.9990 Gold .0400 oz. AGW **Obverse:** Bust of Queen Elizabeth II right **Reverse:** Maine Coon cat

Date	F	VF	XF	Unc	BU
1993	—	—	—	45.00	—
1993 Proof	—	Value: 47.00			

KM# 376 1/25 CROWN **Weight:** 1.2441 g. **Composition:** 0.9990 Gold .0400 oz. AGW **Obverse:** Bust of Queen Elizabeth II right **Reverse:** Japanese Bobtail cat

Date	F	VF	XF	Unc	BU
1994	—	—	—	40.00	—
1994 Proof	—	Value: 42.00			

KM# 402 1/25 CROWN **Weight:** 1.2441 g. **Composition:** 0.9990 Gold .0400 oz. AGW **Obverse:** Bust of Queen Elizabeth II right **Reverse:** Pekingese

Date	Mintage	F	VF	XF	Unc	BU
1994 Proof	Est. 25,000	Value: 50.00				

KM# 473 1/25 CROWN **Weight:** 1.2441 g. **Composition:** 0.9995 Platinum .0400 oz. APW **Obverse:** Bust of Queen Elizabeth II right **Reverse:** Japanese Bobtail cat

Date	F	VF	XF	Unc	BU
1994	—	—	—	60.00	—
1994 Proof	—	Value: 62.00			

KM# 442 1/25 CROWN **Weight:** 1.2441 g. **Composition:** 0.9990 Gold .0400 oz. AGW **Obverse:** Bust of Queen Elizabeth II right **Reverse:** Turkish cat

Date	F	VF	XF	Unc	BU
1995 U	—	—	—	40.00	—
1995 Proof	—	Value: 42.00			

KM# 449 1/25 CROWN **Weight:** 1.2441 g. **Composition:** 0.9990 Gold .0400 oz. AGW **Subject:** Year of the Pig **Obverse:** Bust of Queen Elizabeth II right **Reverse:** Sow with piglets

Date	Mintage	F	VF	XF	Unc	BU
1995 Proof	Est. 25,000	Value: 45.00				

KM# 478 1/25 CROWN **Weight:** 1.2441 g. **Composition:** 0.9995 Platinum .0400 oz. APW **Obverse:** Bust of Queen Elizabeth II right **Reverse:** Turkish cat

Date	F	VF	XF	Unc	BU
1995	—	—	—	50.00	—
1995 Proof	—	Value: 52.00			

KM# 597 1/25 CROWN **Weight:** 1.2441 g. **Composition:** 0.9990 Gold .0400 oz. AGW **Series:** Flower Fairies **Obverse:** Bust of Queen Elizabeth II right **Reverse:** Orchis

Date	Mintage	F	VF	XF	Unc	BU
1996 Proof	Est. 25,000	Value: 40.00				

KM# 598 1/25 CROWN **Weight:** 1.2441 g. **Composition:** 0.9990 Gold .0400 oz. AGW **Series:** Flower Fairies **Obverse:** Bust of Queen Elizabeth II right **Reverse:** Rose

Date	Mintage	F	VF	XF	Unc	BU
1996 Proof	Est. 25,000	Value: 40.00				

KM# 599 1/25 CROWN **Weight:** 1.2441 g. **Composition:** 0.9990 Gold .0400 oz. AGW **Series:** Flower Fairies **Obverse:** Bust of Queen Elizabeth II right **Reverse:** Fuchsia

Date	Mintage	F	VF	XF	Unc	BU
1996 Proof	Est. 25,000	Value: 40.00				

KM# 600 1/25 CROWN **Weight:** 1.2441 g. **Composition:** 0.9990 Gold .0400 oz. AGW **Series:** Flower Fairies **Obverse:** Bust of Queen Elizabeth II right **Reverse:** Pinks

Date	Mintage	F	VF	XF	Unc	BU
1996 Proof	Est. 25,000	Value: 40.00				

KM# 613 1/25 CROWN **Weight:** 1.2441 g. **Composition:** 0.9990 Gold .0400 oz. AGW **Obverse:** Bust of Queen Elizabeth II right **Reverse:** Burmese cat **Note:** #621a.

Date	F	VF	XF	Unc	BU
1996 U	—	—	—	40.00	—
1996 Proof	—	Value: 42.00			

KM# 614 1/25 CROWN **Weight:** 1.2441 g. **Composition:** 0.9995 Platinum .0400 oz. APW **Obverse:** Bust of Queen Elizabeth II right **Reverse:** Burmese cat

Date	F	VF	XF	Unc	BU
1996	—	—	—	50.00	—
1996 Proof	—	Value: 52.00			

KM# 728 1/25 CROWN **Weight:** 1.2441 g. **Composition:** 0.9990 Gold .0400 oz. AGW **Subject:** Year of the Rat **Obverse:** Bust of Queen Elizabeth II right **Reverse:** Rat **Note:** Similar to 1 Crown, KM#732.

Date	F	VF	XF	Unc	BU
1996 Proof	—	—	—	—	—

Note: Entire series purchased by one buyer; Mintage, disposition, and market value unknown

KM# 721 1/25 CROWN **Weight:** 1.2441 g. **Composition:** 0.9990 Gold .0400 oz. AGW **Subject:** Year of the Ox **Obverse:** Bust of Queen Elizabeth II right **Reverse:** Ox laying down

Date	Mintage	F	VF	XF	Unc	BU
1997 Proof	Est. 20,000	Value: 40.00				

KM# 735 1/25 CROWN **Weight:** 1.2441 g. **Composition:** 0.9990 Gold .0400 oz. AGW **Series:** Flower Fairies **Obverse:** Bust of Queen Elizabeth II right **Reverse:** Candytuft

Date	Mintage	F	VF	XF	Unc	BU
1997 Proof	Est. 25,000	Value: 40.00				

KM# 735a 1/25 CROWN **Weight:** 1.2504 g. **Composition:** 0.9950 Platinum .0400 oz. APW

Series: Flower Fairies **Obverse:** Bust of Queen Elizabeth II right **Reverse:** Candytuft

Date	Mintage	F	VF	XF	Unc	BU
1997 Proof	Est. 7,500	Value: 50.00				

KM# 736 1/25 CROWN **Weight:** 1.2441 g. **Composition:** 0.9999 Gold .0400 oz. AGW **Series:** Flower Fairies **Obverse:** Bust of Queen Elizabeth II right **Reverse:** Snowdrop

Date	Mintage	F	VF	XF	Unc	BU
1997 Proof	Est. 25,000	Value: 40.00				

KM# 736a 1/25 CROWN **Weight:** 1.2504 g. **Composition:** 0.9950 Platinum .0400 oz. APW **Series:** Flower Fairies **Obverse:** Bust of Queen Elizabeth II right **Reverse:** Snowdrop

Date	Mintage	F	VF	XF	Unc	BU
1997 Proof	Est. 7,500	Value: 50.00				

KM# 737 1/25 CROWN **Weight:** 1.2441 g. **Composition:** 0.9999 Gold .0400 oz. AGW **Series:** Flower Fairies **Obverse:** Bust of Queen Elizabeth II right **Reverse:** Tulip

Date	Mintage	F	VF	XF	Unc	BU
1997 Proof	Est. 25,000	Value: 40.00				

KM# 737a 1/25 CROWN **Weight:** 1.2504 g. **Composition:** 0.9950 Platinum .0400 oz. APW **Series:** Flower Fairies **Obverse:** Bust of Queen Elizabeth II right **Reverse:** Tulip

Date	Mintage	F	VF	XF	Unc	BU
1997 Proof	Est. 7,500	Value: 50.00				

KM# 738 1/25 CROWN **Weight:** 1.2441 g. **Composition:** 0.9999 Gold .0400 oz. AGW **Series:** Flower Fairies **Obverse:** Bust of Queen Elizabeth II right **Reverse:** Jasmine

Date	Mintage	F	VF	XF	Unc	BU
1997 Proof	Est. 25,000	Value: 40.00				

KM# 738a 1/25 CROWN **Weight:** 1.2504 g. **Composition:** 0.9950 Platinum .0400 oz. APW **Series:** Flower Fairies **Obverse:** Bust of Queen Elizabeth II right **Reverse:** Jasmine

Date	Mintage	F	VF	XF	Unc	BU
1997 Proof	Est. 7,500	Value: 50.00				

KM# 770 1/25 CROWN **Weight:** 1.2440 g. **Composition:** 0.9999 Gold .0400 oz. AGW **Obverse:** Bust of Queen Elizabeth II right **Reverse:** Long-haired Smoke cat **Note:** Similar to 1 Crown, KM#774.

Date	F	VF	XF	Unc	BU
1997	—	—	—	40.00	—
1997 Proof	—	Value: 42.00			

KM# 770a 1/25 CROWN **Weight:** 1.2440 g. **Composition:** 0.9999 Platinum .0400 oz. APW **Obverse:** Bust of Queen Elizabeth II right **Reverse:** Long-haired Smoke cat

Date	F	VF	XF	Unc	BU
1997	—	—	—	50.00	—
1997 Proof	—	Value: 52.00			

KM# 789 1/25 CROWN **Weight:** 1.2440 g. **Composition:** 0.9999 Gold .0400 oz. AGW **Subject:** History of the Cat **Obverse:** Bust of Queen Elizabeth II right **Reverse:** Cat stalking a spider

Date	Mintage	F	VF	XF	Unc	BU
1997 Proof	Est. 25,000	Value: 45.00				

KM# 812 1/25 CROWN **Weight:** 1.2441 g. **Composition:** 0.9999 Gold .0400 oz. AGW **Subject:** Year of the Tiger **Obverse:** Bust of Queen Elizabeth II right **Reverse:** Tiger

Date	Mintage	F	VF	XF	Unc	BU
1998 Proof	Est. 20,000	Value: 45.00				

KM# 828 1/25 CROWN **Weight:** 1.2441 g. **Composition:** 0.9999 Gold .0400 oz. AGW **Series:** Flower Fairies **Obverse:** Bust of Queen Elizabeth II right **Reverse:** Fairy standing, lavender

Date	Mintage	F	VF	XF	Unc	BU
1998 Proof	Est. 25,000	Value: 45.00				

KM# 828a 1/25 CROWN **Weight:** 1.2441 g. **Composition:** 0.9995 Platinum .0400 oz. APW **Series:** Flower Fairies **Obverse:** Bust of Queen Elizabeth II right **Reverse:** Fairy standing, lavender

Date	Mintage	F	VF	XF	Unc	BU
1998 Proof	Est. 7,500	Value: 55.00				

KM# 829 1/25 CROWN **Weight:** 1.2441 g. **Composition:** 0.9999 Gold .0400 oz. AGW **Series:** Flower Fairies **Obverse:** Bust of Queen Elizabeth II right **Reverse:** Two fairies, sweet pea

Date	Mintage	F	VF	XF	Unc	BU
1998 Proof	Est. 25,000	Value: 45.00				

KM# 829a 1/25 CROWN **Weight:** 1.2441 g. **Composition:** 0.9995 Platinum .0400 oz. APW **Series:** Flower Fairies **Obverse:** Bust of Queen Elizabeth II right **Reverse:** Two fairies, sweet pea

Date	Mintage	F	VF	XF	Unc	BU
1998 Proof	Est. 7,500	Value: 55.00				

KM# 830 1/25 CROWN **Weight:** 1.2441 g. **Composition:** 0.9999 Gold .0400 oz. AGW **Series:** Flower Fairies **Obverse:** Bust of Queen Elizabeth II right **Reverse:** Two fairies, sweet pea

Date	F	VF	XF	Unc	BU
1998 Proof	—	—	—	45.00	—

KM# 830a 1/25 CROWN **Weight:** 1.2441 g. **Composition:** 0.9995 Platinum .0400 oz. APW **Series:** Flower Fairies **Obverse:** Bust of Queen Elizabeth II right **Reverse:** Two fairies, sweet pea

Date	Mintage	F	VF	XF	Unc	BU
1998 Proof	Est. 30,000	Value: 55.00				

KM# 831 1/25 CROWN **Weight:** 1.2441 g. **Composition:** 0.9999 Gold .0400 oz. AGW **Series:** Flower Fairies **Obverse:** Bust of Queen Elizabeth II right **Reverse:** Fairy standing, daffodil

Date	Mintage	F	VF	XF	Unc	BU
1998 Proof	Est. 25,000	Value: 45.00				

KM# 831a 1/25 CROWN **Weight:** 1.2441 g. **Composition:** 0.9995 Platinum .0400 oz. APW **Series:** Flower Fairies **Obverse:** Bust of Queen Elizabeth II right **Reverse:** Fairy standing, daffodil

Date	Mintage	F	VF	XF	Unc	BU
1998 Proof	Est. 7,500	Value: 55.00				

KM# 853 1/25 CROWN **Weight:** 1.2440 g. **Composition:** 0.9999 Gold .0400 oz. AGW **Obverse:** Bust of Queen Elizabeth II right **Reverse:** Birman cat **Note:** Similar to 1/5 Crown, KM#857.

Date	Mintage	F	VF	XF	Unc	BU
1998	—	—	—	—	40.00	—
1998 Proof	1,000	Value: 42.00				

KM# 853a 1/25 CROWN **Weight:** 1.2440 g. **Composition:** 0.9995 Platinum .0400 oz. APW **Obverse:** Bust of Queen Elizabeth II right **Reverse:** Birman cat

Date	F	VF	XF	Unc	BU
1998 Proof	—	Value: 50.00			

KM# 859 1/25 CROWN **Weight:** 1.2440 g. **Composition:** 0.9999 Gold .0400 oz. AGW **Subject:** History of the Cat **Obverse:** Bust of Queen Elizabeth II right **Reverse:** Egyptian Mau cat with earring

Date	Mintage	F	VF	XF	Unc	BU
1998 Proof	Est. 25,000	Value: 45.00				

KM# 948 1/25 CROWN **Weight:** 1.2440 g. **Composition:** 0.9999 Gold .0400 oz. AGW **Subject:** Year of the Rabbit **Obverse:** Bust of Queen Elizabeth II right **Reverse:** Two rabbits

Date	Mintage	F	VF	XF	Unc	BU
1999 Proof	Est. 20,000	Value: 45.00				

KM# 958 1/25 CROWN **Weight:** 1.2440 g. **Composition:** 0.9999 Gold .0400 oz. AGW **Obverse:** Bust of Queen Elizabeth II right **Reverse:** British Blue cat

Date	Mintage	F	VF	XF	Unc	BU
1999	—	—	—	—	40.00	—
1999 Proof	—	Value: 42.00				
1999 U Y2K	20,000	—	—	—	40.00	—

KM# 958a 1/25 CROWN **Weight:** 1.2441 g. **Composition:** 0.9995 Platinum .0400 oz. APW **Obverse:** Bust of Queen Elizabeth II right **Reverse:** British Blue cat

Date	F	VF	XF	Unc	BU
1999 Proof	—	Value: 50.00			

KM# 1052 1/25 CROWN **Weight:** 1.2400 g. **Composition:** 0.9999 Gold .0399 oz. AGW **Obverse:** Bust of Queen Elizabeth II right **Reverse:** Scottish fold kitten **Edge:** Reeded **Size:** 13.92 mm.

Date	F	VF	XF	Unc	BU
2000	—	—	—	32.00	—
2000 Proof	—	Value: 45.00			

KM# 1052a 1/25 CROWN **Weight:** 1.2441 g. **Composition:** 0.9995 Platinum .0400 oz. APW

Date	F	VF	XF	Unc	BU
2000	—	—	—	41.00	—

KM# 1012 1/25 CROWN **Weight:** 1.2440 g. **Composition:** 0.9999 Gold .0400 oz. AGW **Subject:** Year of the Dragon **Obverse:** Bust of Queen Elizabeth II right **Reverse:** Dragon, Chinese characters **Note:** Similar to 1/5 Crown, KM#1014.

Date	Mintage	F	VF	XF	Unc	BU
2000 Proof	Est. 20,000	Value: 45.00				

KM# 1058 1/25 CROWN **Weight:** 1.2400 g. **Composition:** 0.9999 Gold .0399 oz. AGW **Subject:** Year of the Snake **Obverse:** Queen's portrait **Reverse:** Snake **Edge:** Reeded **Size:** 13.92 mm.

Date	Mintage	F	VF	XF	Unc	BU
2001 Proof	20,000	Value: 49.50				

KM# 1067 1/25 CROWN **Weight:** 1.2441 g. **Composition:** 0.9999 Gold .0400 oz. AGW **Subject:** Somali Kittens **Obverse:** Queen's portrait **Reverse:** Two kittens **Edge:** Reeded **Size:** 13.9 mm.

Date	Mintage	F	VF	XF	Unc	BU
2001	—	—	—	—	32.00	—
2001 Proof	1,000	Value: 50.00				

KM# 1067a 1/25 CROWN **Weight:** 1.2441 g. **Composition:** 0.9995 Platinum .0400 oz. APW **Subject:** Somali Kittens **Obverse:** Queen's portrait **Reverse:** Two kittens **Edge:** Reeded **Size:** 13.9 mm.

Date	F	VF	XF	Unc	BU
2001	—	—	—	60.00	—

KM# 1086 1/25 CROWN **Weight:** 1.2441 g. **Composition:** 0.9999 Gold .0400 oz. AGW **Subject:** Harry Potter **Obverse:** Queen's portrait **Reverse:** Boy with magic wand **Edge:** Reeded **Size:** 13.9 mm.

Date	Mintage	F	VF	XF	Unc	BU
2001 Proof	10,000	Value: 49.50				

KM# 1088 1/25 CROWN **Weight:** 1.2441 g. **Composition:** 0.9999 Gold .0400 oz. AGW **Series:** Harry Potter **Subject:** Journey to Hogwarts School **Obverse:** Queen's portrait **Reverse:** Boat full of children going to Hogwarts School **Edge:** Reeded **Size:** 13.9 mm.

Date	Mintage	F	VF	XF	Unc	BU
2001 Proof	10,000	Value: 49.50				

KM# 1090 1/25 CROWN **Weight:** 1.2441 g. **Composition:** 0.9999 Gold .0400 oz. AGW **Series:** Harry Potter **Subject:** First Quidditch Match **Obverse:** Queen's portrait **Reverse:** Harry flying a broom **Edge:** Reeded **Size:** 13.9 mm.

Date	Mintage	F	VF	XF	Unc	BU
2001 Proof	10,000	Value: 49.50				

KM# 1092 1/25 CROWN **Weight:** 1.2441 g. **Composition:** 0.9999 Gold .0400 oz. AGW **Series:** Harry Potter **Subject:** Birth of Norbert **Obverse:** Queen's portrait **Edge:** Reeded **Size:** 13.9 mm.

Date	Mintage	F	VF	XF	Unc	BU
2001 Proof	10,000	Value: 49.50				

KM# 1094 1/25 CROWN **Weight:** 1.2441 g. **Composition:** 0.9999 Gold .0400 oz. AGW **Series:** Harry Potter **Subject:** School **Obverse:** Queen's portrait **Reverse:** Harry in Potions class **Edge:** Reeded **Size:** 13.9 mm.

Date	Mintage	F	VF	XF	Unc	BU
2001 Proof	10,000	Value: 49.50				

KM# 1096 1/25 CROWN **Weight:** 1.2441 g. **Composition:** 0.9999 Gold .0400 oz. AGW **Series:** Harry Potter **Subject:** Keys **Obverse:** Queen's portrait **Reverse:** Harry chasing a quiditch **Edge:** Reeded **Size:** 13.9 mm.

Date	Mintage	F	VF	XF	Unc	BU
2001 Proof	10,000	Value: 49.50				

KM# 1098 1/25 CROWN **Weight:** 1.2441 g. **Composition:** 0.9999 Gold .0400 oz. AGW **Subject:** Year of the Horse **Obverse:** Queen's portrait **Reverse:** Two horses **Edge:** Reeded **Size:** 13.9 mm.

Date	Mintage	F	VF	XF	Unc	BU
2002 Proof	20,000	Value: 49.50				

KM# 1107a 1/25 CROWN **Weight:** 1.2440 g. **Composition:** 0.9990 Platinum 0.04 oz. APW **Subject:** Bengal Cat **Obverse:** Bust of Queen Elizabeth II right **Reverse:** Cat and kitten **Edge:** Reeded **Size:** 13.92 mm.

Date	F	VF	XF	Unc	BU
2002 Proof	—	Value: 41.00			

KM# 1143 1/25 CROWN **Weight:** 1.2440 g. **Composition:** 0.9999 Gold 0.04 oz. AGW **Subject:** Harry Potter **Obverse:** Queen's portrait **Reverse:** Tom Riddle twirling Harry's magic wand **Edge:** Reeded **Size:** 13.92 mm.

Date	Mintage	F	VF	XF	Unc	BU
2002PM Proof	10,000	Value: 55.00				

KM# 1147 1/25 CROWN **Subject:** Harry Potter **Obverse:** Queen's portrait **Reverse:** Harry arrives at the Burrow in a flying car **Edge:** Reeded

Date	Mintage	F	VF	XF	Unc	BU
2002PM Proof	10,000	—	—	—	—	—

KM# 1149 1/25 CROWN **Weight:** 1.2440 g. **Composition:** 0.9999 Gold 0.04 oz. AGW **Subject:** Harry Potter Series **Obverse:** Queen's portrait **Reverse:** Harry retrieves Gryffindor sword from snake **Edge:** Reeded **Size:** 13.92 mm.

Date	Mintage	F	VF	XF	Unc	BU
2002PM	10,000	Value: 55.00				

Note: Proof

KM# 1153 1/25 CROWN **Weight:** 1.2440 g. **Composition:** 0.9999 Gold 0.04 oz. AGW **Series:** Harry Potter **Obverse:** Queen's portrait **Reverse:** Harry in hospital **Edge:** Reeded **Size:** 13.92 mm.

Date	Mintage	F	VF	XF	Unc	BU
2002PM	10,000	Value: 55.00				

Note: Proof

KM# 1107 1/25 CROWN **Weight:** 1.2440 g. **Composition:** 0.9990 Gold 0.04 oz. AGW **Subject:** Bengal Cat **Obverse:** Queen Elizabeth's bust right **Reverse:** Cat and kitten **Edge:** Reeded **Size:** 13.92 mm.

Date	Mintage	VG	F	VF	XF	Unc
2002	—	—	—	—	—	32.00
2002 Proof	1,000	Value: 49.50				

KM# 1151 1/25 CROWN **Weight:** 1.2240 g. **Composition:** 0.9999 Gold 0.0393 oz. AGW **Series:** Harry Potter **Obverse:** Queen's portrait **Reverse:** Harry and Ron encounter the spider Aragog **Edge:** Reeded **Size:** 13.92 mm.

Date	Mintage	F	VF	XF	Unc	BU
2002PM Proof	10,000	Value: 55.00				

KM# 1161 1/25 CROWN **Weight:** 1.2440 g. **Composition:** 0.9999 Gold 0.04 oz. AGW **Subject:** Cat **Obverse:** Queen's portrait **Reverse:** Two Balinese kittens **Edge:** Reeded **Size:** 13.92 mm.

Date	F	VF	XF	Unc	BU
2003PM	—	—	—	32.00	—
2003PM Proof	—	Value: 49.50			

KM# 1161a 1/25 CROWN **Weight:** 1.2440 g. **Composition:** 0.9995 Platinum 0.04 oz. APW **Subject:** Cat **Obverse:** Queen's portrait **Reverse:** Two Balinese kittens **Edge:** Reeded **Size:** 13.92 mm.

Date	F	VF	XF	Unc	BU
2003PM	—	—	—	40.00	—

KM# 1167 1/25 CROWN **Weight:** 1.2441 g. **Composition:** 0.9999 Gold 0.04 oz. AGW **Subject:** Year of the Goat **Obverse:** Queen's portrait **Reverse:** Three goats **Edge:** Reeded **Size:** 13.9 mm.

Date	Mintage	F	VF	XF	Unc	BU
2003PM Proof	20,000	Value: 49.50				

KM# 236 1/10 CROWN **Weight:** 3.1100 g. **Composition:** 0.9990 Gold .1000 oz. AGW **Obverse:** Bust of Queen Elizabeth II right **Reverse:** Manx cat

Date	Mintage	F	VF	XF	Unc	BU
1988	12,000	—	—	—	100	—
1988 Proof	5,000	Value: 102				

KM# 253 1/10 CROWN **Weight:** 3.1100 g. **Composition:** 0.9990 Gold .1000 oz. AGW **Obverse:** Bust of Queen Elizabeth II right **Reverse:** Persian cat

Date	F	VF	XF	Unc	BU
1989	—	—	—	85.00	—
1989 Proof	—	Value: 87.00			

KM# 468 1/10 CROWN **Weight:** 3.1100 g. **Composition:** 0.9995 Platinum .1000 oz. APW **Obverse:** Bust of Queen Elizabeth II right **Reverse:** Persian cat

Date	F	VF	XF	Unc	BU
1989	—	—	—	100	—
1989 Proof	—	Value: 102			

KM# 278 1/10 CROWN Weight: 3.1100 g. **Composition:** 0.9990 Gold .1000 oz. AGW **Obverse:** Bust of Queen Elizabeth II right **Reverse:** Alley cat **Note:** Similar to 1 Crown, KM#281.

Date	F	VF	XF	Unc	BU
1990	—	—	—	75.00	—
1990 Proof	—	Value: 77.00			

KM# 295 1/10 CROWN Weight: 3.1100 g. **Composition:** 0.9990 Gold .1000 oz. AGW **Obverse:** Bust of Queen Elizabeth II right **Reverse:** Norwegian cat **Note:** Similar to 1 Crown, KM#292.

Date	F	VF	XF	Unc	BU
1991	—	—	—	75.00	—
1991 Proof	—	Value: 77.00			

KM# 323 1/10 CROWN Weight: 3.1100 g. **Composition:** 0.9990 Gold .1000 oz. AGW **Subject:** America's Cup **Obverse:** Bust of Queen Elizabeth II right

Date	Mintage	F	VF	XF	Unc	BU
1992 Prooflike	25,000	—	—	—	125	—

KM# 323a 1/10 CROWN Weight: 3.1100 g. **Composition:** 0.9995 Platinum .1000 oz. APW **Subject:** America's Cup **Obverse:** Bust of Queen Elizabeth II right **Reverse:** Sailboat

Date	Mintage	F	VF	XF	Unc	BU
1992 Prooflike	5,000	—	—	—	200	—

KM# 329 1/10 CROWN Weight: 3.1100 g. **Composition:** 0.9990 Gold .1000 oz. AGW **Obverse:** Bust of Queen Elizabeth II right **Reverse:** Siamese cat **Note:** Similar to 1 Crown, KM#334.

Date	F	VF	XF	Unc	BU
1992	—	—	—	65.00	—
1992 Proof	—	Value: 67.00			

KM# 339 1/10 CROWN Weight: 3.1100 g. **Composition:** 0.9990 Gold .1000 oz. AGW **Subject:** Year of the Cockerel **Obverse:** Bust of Queen Elizabeth II right **Reverse:** Cockerel in inner circle

Date	Mintage	F	VF	XF	Unc	BU
1993 Proof	Est. 20,000	Value: 85.00				

KM# 350 1/10 CROWN Weight: 3.1100 g. **Composition:** 0.9990 Gold .1000 oz. AGW **Obverse:** Bust of Queen Elizabeth II right **Reverse:** Maine Coon cat **Note:** Similar to 1 Crown, KM#355.

Date	F	VF	XF	Unc	BU
1993	—	—	—	65.00	—
1993 Proof	—	Value: 67.00			

KM# 377 1/10 CROWN Weight: 3.1100 g. **Composition:** 0.9990 Gold .1000 oz. AGW **Obverse:** Bust of Queen Elizabeth II right **Reverse:** Japanese Bobtail cat

Date	F	VF	XF	Unc	BU
1994	—	—	—	60.00	—
1994 Proof	—	Value: 62.00			

KM# 403 1/10 CROWN Weight: 3.1100 g. **Composition:** 0.9990 Gold .1000 oz. AGW **Obverse:** Bust of Queen Elizabeth II right **Reverse:** Pekingese dog

Date	Mintage	F	VF	XF	Unc	BU
1994 Proof	20,000	Value: 95.00				

KM# 474 1/10 CROWN Weight: 3.1100 g. **Composition:** 0.9995 Platinum .1000 oz. APW **Obverse:** Bust of Queen Elizabeth II right **Reverse:** Japanese Bobtail cat

Date	F	VF	XF	Unc	BU
1994	—	—	—	100	—
1994 Proof	—	Value: 102			

KM# 443 1/10 CROWN Weight: 3.1100 g. **Composition:** 0.9990 Gold .1000 oz. AGW **Obverse:** Bust of Queen Elizabeth II right **Reverse:** Turkish cat

Date	F	VF	XF	Unc	BU
1995	—	—	—	60.00	—
1995 Proof	—	Value: 62.00			

KM# 450 1/10 CROWN Weight: 3.1100 g. **Composition:** 0.9990 Gold .1000 oz. AGW **Subject:** Year of the Pig **Obverse:** Bust of Queen Elizabeth II right **Reverse:** Sow with piglets

Date	Mintage	F	VF	XF	Unc	BU
1995 Proof	Est. 20,000	Value: 95.00				

KM# 479 1/10 CROWN Weight: 3.1100 g. **Composition:** 0.9995 Platinum .1000 oz. APW **Obverse:** Bust of Queen Elizabeth II right **Reverse:** Turkish cat

Date	F	VF	XF	Unc	BU
1995	—	—	—	100	—
1995 Proof	—	Value: 102			

KM# 601 1/10 CROWN Weight: 3.1100 g. **Composition:** 0.9990 Gold .1000 oz. AGW **Series:** Flower Fairies **Obverse:** Bust of Queen Elizabeth II right **Reverse:** Orchis

Date	Mintage	F	VF	XF	Unc	BU
1996 Proof	Est. 20,000	Value: 90.00				

KM# 602 1/10 CROWN Weight: 3.1100 g. **Composition:** 0.9990 Gold .1000 oz. AGW **Series:** Flower Fairies **Obverse:** Bust of Queen Elizabeth II right **Reverse:** Rose

Date	Mintage	F	VF	XF	Unc	BU
1996 Proof	Est. 20,000	Value: 90.00				

KM# 603 1/10 CROWN Weight: 3.1100 g. **Composition:** 0.9990 Gold .1000 oz. AGW **Series:** Flower Fairies **Obverse:** Bust of Queen Elizabeth II right **Reverse:** Fuchsia

Date	Mintage	F	VF	XF	Unc	BU
1996 Proof	Est. 20,000	Value: 90.00				

KM# 604 1/10 CROWN Weight: 3.1100 g. **Composition:** 0.9990 Gold .1000 oz. AGW **Obverse:** Bust of Queen Elizabeth II right **Reverse:** Pinks

Date	Mintage	F	VF	XF	Unc	BU
1996 Proof	Est. 20,000	Value: 90.00				

KM# 615 1/10 CROWN Weight: 3.1100 g. **Composition:** 0.9990 Gold .1000 oz. AGW **Obverse:** Bust of Queen Elizabeth II right **Reverse:** Burmese cat

Date	F	VF	XF	Unc	BU
1996	—	—	—	60.00	—
1996 Proof	—	Value: 62.00			

KM# 616 1/10 CROWN Weight: 3.1100 g. **Composition:** 0.9995 Platinum .1000 oz. APW **Obverse:** Bust of Queen Elizabeth II right **Reverse:** Burmese cat

Date	F	VF	XF	Unc	BU
1996	—	—	—	100	—
1996 Proof	—	Value: 102			

KM# 729 1/10 CROWN Weight: 3.1100 g. **Composition:** 0.9990 Gold .1000 oz. AGW **Subject:** Year of the Rat **Obverse:** Bust of Queen Elizabeth II right **Reverse:** Rat

Date	F	VF	XF	Unc	BU
1996 Proof					

Note: Entire series purchased by one buyer. Mintage, disposition and market value unknown

KM# 722 1/10 CROWN Weight: 3.1100 g. **Composition:** 0.9990 Gold .1000 oz. AGW **Subject:** Year of the Ox **Obverse:** Bust of Queen Elizabeth II right **Reverse:** Ox laying down

Date	Mintage	F	VF	XF	Unc	BU
1997 Proof	Est. 15,000	Value: 90.00				

KM# 743 1/10 CROWN Weight: 3.1100 g. **Composition:** 0.9990 Gold .1000 oz. AGW **Series:** Flower Fairies **Obverse:** Bust of Queen Elizabeth II right **Reverse:** Candytuft

Date	Mintage	F	VF	XF	Unc	BU
1997 Proof	Est. 20,000	Value: 80.00				

KM# 743a 1/10 CROWN Weight: 3.1259 g. **Composition:** 0.9950 Platinum .1000 oz. APW **Series:** Flower Fairies **Obverse:** Bust of Queen Elizabeth II right **Reverse:** Candytuft

Date	Mintage	F	VF	XF	Unc	BU
1997 Proof	Est. 5,000	Value: 80.00				

KM# 744 1/10 CROWN Weight: 3.1103 g. **Composition:** 0.9999 Gold .1000 oz. AGW **Obverse:** Bust of Queen Elizabeth II right **Reverse:** Snowdrop

Date	Mintage	F	VF	XF	Unc	BU
1997 Proof	Est. 20,000	Value: 80.00				

KM# 744a 1/10 CROWN Weight: 3.1259 g. **Composition:** 0.9950 Platinum .1000 oz. APW **Series:** Flower Fairies **Obverse:** Bust of Queen Elizabeth II right **Reverse:** Snowdrop

Date	Mintage	F	VF	XF	Unc	BU
1997 Proof	Est. 5,000	Value: 85.00				

KM# 745 1/10 CROWN Weight: 3.1103 g. **Composition:** 0.9999 Gold .1000 oz. AGW **Series:** Flower Fairies **Obverse:** Bust of Queen Elizabeth II right **Reverse:** Tulip

Date	Mintage	F	VF	XF	Unc	BU
1997 Proof	Est. 20,000	Value: 80.00				

KM# 745a 1/10 CROWN Weight: 3.1259 g. **Composition:** 0.9950 Platinum .1000 oz. APW **Series:** Flower Fairies **Obverse:** Bust of Queen Elizabeth II right **Reverse:** Tulip

Date	Mintage	F	VF	XF	Unc	BU
1997 Proof	Est. 5,000	Value: 85.00				

KM# 746 1/10 CROWN Weight: 3.1103 g. **Composition:** 0.9999 Gold .1000 oz. AGW **Series:** Flower Fairies **Obverse:** Bust of Queen Elizabeth II right **Reverse:** Jasmine

Date	Mintage	F	VF	XF	Unc	BU
1997 Proof	Est. 20,000	Value: 80.00				

KM# 746a 1/10 CROWN Weight: 3.1259 g. **Composition:** 0.9950 Platinum .1000 oz. APW **Series:** Flower Fairies **Obverse:** Bust of Queen Elizabeth II right **Reverse:** Jasmine

Date	Mintage	F	VF	XF	Unc	BU
1997 Proof	Est. 5,000	Value: 85.00				

KM# 771 1/10 CROWN Weight: 3.1100 g. **Composition:** 0.9999 Gold .1000 oz. AGW **Obverse:** Bust of Queen Elizabeth II right **Reverse:** Long-haired Smoke cat

Date	F	VF	XF	Unc	BU
1997	—	—	—	60.00	—
1997 Proof	—	Value: 62.00			

KM# 771a 1/10 CROWN Weight: 3.1100 g. **Composition:** 0.9995 Platinum .1000 oz. APW **Obverse:** Bust of Queen Elizabeth II right **Reverse:** Long-haired Smoke cat

Date	F	VF	XF	Unc	BU
1997	—	—	—	100	—
1997 Proof	—	Value: 102			

KM# 790 1/10 CROWN Weight: 3.1100 g. **Composition:** 0.9999 Gold .1000 oz. AGW **Subject:** History of the Cat **Obverse:** Bust of Queen Elizabeth II right **Reverse:** Cat stalking a spider

Date	Mintage	F	VF	XF	Unc	BU
1997 Proof	Est. 20,000	Value: 90.00				

KM# 813 1/10 CROWN Weight: 3.1100 g. **Composition:** 0.9999 Gold .1000 oz. AGW **Subject:** Year of the Tiger **Obverse:** Bust of Queen Elizabeth II right **Reverse:** Tiger

Date	Mintage	F	VF	XF	Unc	BU
1998 Proof	Est. 15,000	Value: 90.00				

KM# 832 1/10 CROWN Weight: 3.1100 g. **Composition:** 0.9999 Gold .1000 oz. AGW **Series:** Flower Fairies **Obverse:** Bust of Queen Elizabeth II right **Reverse:** Standing fairy, lavender

Date	Mintage	F	VF	XF	Unc	BU
1998 Proof	Est. 20,000	Value: 90.00				

KM# 832a 1/10 CROWN Weight: 3.1100 g. **Composition:** 0.9995 Platinum .1000 oz. APW **Series:** Flower Fairies **Obverse:** Bust of Queen Elizabeth II right **Reverse:** Standing fairy, lavender

Date	Mintage	F	VF	XF	Unc	BU
1998 Proof	Est. 5,000	Value: 100				

KM# 833 1/10 CROWN Weight: 3.1100 g. **Composition:** 0.9999 Gold .1000 oz. AGW **Series:** Flower Fairies **Obverse:** Bust of Queen Elizabeth II right **Reverse:** Two fairies, sweet pea

Date	Mintage	F	VF	XF	Unc	BU
1998 Proof	Est. 20,000	Value: 90.00				

KM# 833a 1/10 CROWN Weight: 3.1100 g. **Composition:** 0.9995 Platinum .1000 oz. APW **Series:** Flower Fairies **Obverse:** Bust of Queen Elizabeth II right **Reverse:** Two fairies, sweet pea

Date	Mintage	F	VF	XF	Unc	BU
1998 Proof	Est. 5,000	Value: 100				

KM# 834 1/10 CROWN Weight: 3.1100 g. **Composition:** 0.9999 Gold .1000 oz. AGW **Obverse:** Bust of Queen Elizabeth II right **Reverse:** Fairy looking into flower, White Bindweed

Date	Mintage	F	VF	XF	Unc	BU
1998 Proof	Est. 20,000	Value: 90.00				

KM# 834a 1/10 CROWN Weight: 3.1100 g. **Composition:** 0.9995 Platinum .1000 oz. APW **Series:** Flower Fairies **Obverse:** Bust of Queen Elizabeth II right **Reverse:** Fairy looking into flower, White Bindweed

Date	Mintage	F	VF	XF	Unc	BU
1998 Proof	Est. 5,000	Value: 100				

KM# 835 1/10 CROWN Weight: 3.1100 g. **Composition:** 0.9999 Gold .1000 oz. AGW **Series:** Flower Fairies **Obverse:** Bust of Queen Elizabeth II right **Reverse:** Fairy standing with flower, daffodil

Date	Mintage	F	VF	XF	Unc	BU
1998 Proof	Est. 20,000	Value: 90.00				

KM# 835a 1/10 CROWN Weight: 3.1100 g. **Composition:** 0.9995 Platinum .1000 oz. APW **Obverse:** Bust of Queen Elizabeth II right **Reverse:** Fairy standing with flower, daffodil **Rev. Legend:** Flower Fairies

Date	Mintage	F	VF	XF	Unc	BU
1998 Proof	Est. 5,000	Value: 100				

KM# 854 1/10 CROWN Weight: 3.1100 g. **Composition:** 0.9999 Gold .1000 oz. AGW **Obverse:** Bust of Queen Elizabeth II right **Reverse:** Birman cat

Date	Mintage	F	VF	XF	Unc	BU
1998	—	—	—	—	65.00	—
1998 Proof	1,000	Value: 70.00				

KM# 854a 1/10 CROWN Weight: 3.1100 g. **Composition:** 0.9995 Platinum .1000 oz. APW **Obverse:** Bust of Queen Elizabeth II right **Reverse:** Birman cat

Date	F	VF	XF	Unc	BU
1998 Proof	—	Value: 100			

KM# 860 1/10 CROWN Weight: 3.1100 g. **Composition:** 0.9999 Gold .1000 oz. AGW **Subject:** History of the Cat **Obverse:** Bust of Queen Elizabeth II right **Reverse:** Egyptian Mau cat with earring

Date	Mintage	F	VF	XF	Unc	BU
1998 Proof	Est. 20,000	Value: 90.00				

KM# 949 1/10 CROWN Weight: 3.1100 g. **Composition:** 0.9999 Gold .1000 oz. AGW **Subject:** Year of the Rabbit **Obverse:** Bust of Queen Elizabeth II right **Reverse:** Two rabbits

Date	F	VF	XF	Unc	BU
1999 Proof	—	Value: 90.00			

KM# 960 1/10 CROWN Weight: 3.1100 g. **Composition:** 0.9999 Gold .1000 oz. AGW **Obverse:** Bust of Queen Elizabeth II right **Reverse:** British Blue cat cleaning its paw

Date	Mintage	F	VF	XF	Unc	BU
1999	—	—	—	—	70.00	—
1999 Proof	—	Value: 90.00				
1999 U Y2K	10,000	—	—	—	70.00	—

KM# 960a 1/10 CROWN **Weight:** 3.1104 g. **Composition:** 0.9995 Platinum .1000 oz. APW **Obverse:** Bust of Queen Elizabeth II right **Reverse:** British Blue cat cleaning its paw

Date	F	VF	XF	Unc	BU
1999 Proof	—	Value: 100			

KM# 1053 1/10 CROWN **Weight:** 3.1100 g. **Composition:** 0.9999 Gold .1000 oz. AGW **Obverse:** Bust of Queen Elizabeth II right **Reverse:** Scottish kitten playing with the world **Edge:** Reeded **Size:** 17.95 mm.

Date	F	VF	XF	Unc	BU
2000	—	—	—	70.00	—
2000 Proof	—	Value: 90.00			

KM# 1053a 1/10 CROWN **Weight:** 3.1104 g. **Composition:** 0.9995 Platinum .1000 oz. APW **Reverse:** Scottish kitten playing with the world

Date	F	VF	XF	Unc	BU
2000	—	—	—	80.00	—

KM# 1013 1/10 CROWN **Weight:** 3.1100 g. **Composition:** 0.9999 Gold .1000 oz. AGW **Subject:** Year of the Dragon **Obverse:** Bust of Queen Elizabeth II right **Reverse:** Dragon, Chinese characters

Date	Mintage	F	VF	XF	Unc	BU
2000 Proof	Est. 15,000	Value: 90.00				

KM# 1059 1/10 CROWN **Weight:** 3.1100 g. **Composition:** 0.9999 Gold .1000 oz. AGW **Subject:** Year of the Snake **Obverse:** Queen's portrait **Reverse:** Snake **Edge:** Reeded **Size:** 17.95 mm.

Date	Mintage	F	VF	XF	Unc	BU
2001 Proof	15,000	Value: 95.00				

KM# 1068 1/10 CROWN **Weight:** 3.1100 g. **Composition:** 0.9999 Gold .1000 oz. AGW **Obverse:** Queen's portrait **Reverse:** Somali kittens **Edge:** Reeded **Size:** 18 mm.

Date	Mintage	F	VF	XF	Unc	BU
2001	—	—	—	—	70.00	—
2001 Proof	1,000	Value: 95.00				

KM# 1068a 1/10 CROWN **Weight:** 3.1100 g. **Composition:** 0.9995 Platinum .1000 oz. APW **Reverse:** Somali kittens **Edge:** Reeded **Size:** 18 mm.

Date	F	VF	XF	Unc	BU
2001	—	—	—	130	—

KM# 1099 1/10 CROWN **Weight:** 3.1100 g. **Composition:** 0.9999 Gold .1000 oz. AGW **Subject:** Year of the Horse **Obverse:** Queen's portrait **Reverse:** Two horses **Edge:** Reeded **Size:** 17.95 mm.

Date	Mintage	F	VF	XF	Unc	BU
2002 Proof	15,000	Value: 95.00				

KM# 1108 1/10 CROWN **Weight:** 3.1100 g. **Composition:** 0.9990 Gold 0.0999 oz. AGW **Subject:** Bengal Cat **Obverse:** Queen Elizabeth's bust right **Reverse:** Cat and kitten **Edge:** Reeded **Size:** 17.95 mm.

Date	VG	F	VF	XF	Unc
2002 Proof	—	Value: 95.00			
2002	—	—	—	—	70.00

KM# 1108a 1/10 CROWN **Weight:** 3.1100 g. **Composition:** 0.9990 Platinum 0.0999 oz. APW **Subject:** Bengal Cat **Obverse:** Bust of Queen Elizabeth II right **Reverse:** Cat and kitten **Edge:** Reeded **Size:** 17.95 mm.

Date	F	VF	XF	Unc	BU
2002	—	—	—	80.00	—

KM# 1162 1/10 CROWN **Weight:** 3.1100 g. **Composition:** 0.9999 Gold 0.1 oz. AGW **Subject:** Cat **Obverse:** Queen's portrait **Reverse:** Two Balinese kittens **Edge:** Reeded **Size:** 17.95 mm.

Date	F	VF	XF	Unc	BU
2003PM	—	—	—	70.00	—
2003PM Proof	—	Value: 95.00			

KM# 1168 1/10 CROWN **Weight:** 3.1100 g. **Composition:** 0.9999 Gold 0.1 oz. AGW **Subject:** Year of the Goat **Obverse:** Queen's portrait **Reverse:** Three goats **Edge:** Reeded **Size:** 17.95 mm.

Date	F	VF	XF	Unc	BU
2033PM Proof	—	Value: 95.00			

KM# 237 1/5 CROWN **Weight:** 6.2200 g. **Composition:** 0.9990 Gold .2000 oz. AGW **Obverse:** Bust of Queen Elizabeth II right **Reverse:** Manx cat

Date	Mintage	F	VF	XF	Unc	BU
1988	6,750	—	—	—	200	—
1988 Proof	5,000	Value: 202				

KM# 254 1/5 CROWN **Weight:** 6.2200 g. **Composition:** 0.9990 Gold .2000 oz. AGW **Obverse:** Bust of Queen Elizabeth II right **Reverse:** Persian cat

Date	F	VF	XF	Unc	BU
1989	—	—	—	150	—
1989 Proof	—	Value: 152			

KM# 274 1/5 CROWN **Weight:** 6.2200 g. **Composition:** 0.9990 Gold .2000 oz. AGW **Obverse:** Bust of Queen Elizabeth II right **Reverse:** George Washington

Date	Mintage	F	VF	XF	Unc	BU
1989 Proof	Est. 5,000	Value: 180				

KM# 469 1/5 CROWN **Weight:** 6.2200 g. **Composition:** 0.9990 Platinum .2000 oz. APW **Obverse:** Bust of Queen Elizabeth II right **Reverse:** Persian cat

Date	F	VF	XF	Unc	BU
1989	—	—	—	165	—
1989 Proof	—	Value: 167			

KM# 268 1/5 CROWN **Weight:** 6.2200 g. **Composition:** 0.9990 Gold .2000 oz. AGW **Subject:** 150th Anniversary of "Penny Black" Stamp **Obverse:** Bust of Queen Elizabeth II right **Reverse:** Penny Black Stamp

Date	Mintage	F	VF	XF	Unc	BU
1990 Proof	Est. 5,000	Value: 210				

KM# 279.1 1/5 CROWN **Weight:** 6.2200 g. **Composition:** 0.9990 Gold .2000 oz. AGW **Obverse:** Bust of Queen Elizabeth II right **Reverse:** Alley cat

Date	F	VF	XF	Unc	BU
1990	—	—	—	125	—
1990 Proof	—	Value: 127			

KM# 279.2 1/5 CROWN **Weight:** 6.2200 g. **Composition:** 0.9990 Gold .2000 oz. AGW **Obverse:** Bust of Queen Elizabeth II right **Reverse:** Dies claiming platinum metal content **Note:** Error.

Date	Mintage	F	VF	XF	Unc	BU
1990	467	—	—	—	400	—

KM# 306 1/5 CROWN **Weight:** 6.2200 g. **Composition:** 0.9990 Gold .2000 oz. AGW **Obverse:** Bust of Queen Elizabeth II right **Reverse:** Queen Mother with two daughters

Date	F	VF	XF	Unc	BU
1990 Proof	—	Value: 200			

KM# 306a 1/5 CROWN **Weight:** 6.2200 g. **Composition:** 0.9990 Platinum .2000 oz. APW **Obverse:** Bust of Queen Elizabeth II right **Reverse:** Queen Mother with two daughters

Date	F	VF	XF	Unc	BU
1990 Proof	—	Value: 300			

KM# 472 1/5 CROWN **Weight:** 6.2200 g. **Composition:** 0.9990 Platinum .2000 oz. APW **Obverse:** Bust of Queen Elizabeth II right **Reverse:** Alley cat

Date	F	VF	XF	Unc	BU
1990	—	—	—	165	—
1990 Proof	—	Value: 167			

KM# 819 1/5 CROWN **Weight:** 6.2200 g. **Composition:** 0.9990 Gold .2000 oz. AGW **Subject:** Soccer **Obverse:** Bust of Queen Elizabeth II right **Reverse:** Milano

Date	Mintage	F	VF	XF	Unc	BU
1990 Proof	Est. 500	Value: 115				

KM# 819a 1/5 CROWN **Weight:** 6.2200 g. **Composition:** 0.9990 Platinum .2000 oz. APW **Subject:** Soccer **Obverse:** Bust of Queen Elizabeth II right **Reverse:** Milano

Date	Mintage	F	VF	XF	Unc	BU
1990 Proof	Est. 250	Value: 160				

KM# 820 1/5 CROWN **Weight:** 6.2200 g. **Composition:** 0.9990 Gold .2000 oz. AGW **Subject:** Soccer **Obverse:** Bust of Queen Elizabeth II right **Reverse:** Torino

Date	Mintage	F	VF	XF	Unc	BU
1990 Proof	Est. 500	Value: 115				

KM# 820a 1/5 CROWN **Weight:** 6.2200 g. **Composition:** 0.9990 Platinum .2000 oz. APW **Subject:** Soccer **Obverse:** Bust of Queen Elizabeth II right **Reverse:** Torino

Date	Mintage	F	VF	XF	Unc	BU
1990 Proof	Est. 250	Value: 160				

KM# 821 1/5 CROWN **Weight:** 6.2200 g. **Composition:** 0.9990 Gold .2000 oz. AGW **Subject:** Soccer **Obverse:** Bust of Queen Elizabeth II right **Reverse:** Bologna

Date	Mintage	F	VF	XF	Unc	BU
1990 Proof	Est. 500	Value: 115				

KM# 821a 1/5 CROWN **Weight:** 6.2200 g. **Composition:** 0.9990 Platinum .2000 oz. APW **Subject:** Soccer **Obverse:** Bust of Queen Elizabeth II right **Reverse:** Bologna

Date	Mintage	F	VF	XF	Unc	BU
1990	Est. 250	Value: 160				

KM# 822 1/5 CROWN **Weight:** 6.2200 g. **Composition:** 0.9990 Gold .2000 oz. AGW **Subject:** Soccer **Obverse:** Bust of Queen Elizabeth II right **Reverse:** Palermo

Date	Mintage	F	VF	XF	Unc	BU
1990 Proof	Est. 500	Value: 115				

KM# 822a 1/5 CROWN **Weight:** 6.2200 g. **Composition:** 0.9990 Platinum .2000 oz. APW **Subject:** Soccer **Obverse:** Bust of Queen Elizabeth II right **Reverse:** Palermo

Date	Mintage	F	VF	XF	Unc	BU
1990	Est. 250	Value: 160				

KM# 290 1/5 CROWN **Weight:** 6.2200 g. **Composition:** 0.9990 Gold .2000 oz. AGW **Subject:** 100th Anniversary - American Numismatic Association **Obverse:** Bust of Queen Elizabeth II right **Reverse:** Coins

Date	Mintage	F	VF	XF	Unc	BU
1991 Proof	100	Value: 185				

KM# 296 1/5 CROWN **Weight:** 6.2200 g. **Composition:** 0.9990 Gold .2000 oz. AGW **Obverse:** Bust of Queen Elizabeth II right **Reverse:** Norwegian cat with bushy tail

Date	F	VF	XF	Unc	BU
1991	—	—	—	115	—
1991 Proof	—	Value: 117			

KM# 302 1/5 CROWN **Weight:** 6.2200 g. **Composition:** 0.9990 Gold .2000 oz. AGW **Subject:** America's Cup **Obverse:** Bust of Queen Elizabeth II right **Reverse:** Sailboat

Date	Mintage	F	VF	XF	Unc	BU
1991 Proof	Est. 250	Value: 190				

KM# 324 1/5 CROWN **Weight:** 6.2200 g. **Composition:** 0.9990 Gold .2000 oz. AGW **Subject:** America's Cup **Obverse:** Bust of Queen Elizabeth II right **Reverse:** Sailboat

Date	Mintage	F	VF	XF	Unc	BU
1992 Prooflike	10,000	—	—	—	120	—

KM# 330 1/5 CROWN **Weight:** 6.2200 g. **Composition:** 0.9990 Gold .2000 oz. AGW **Obverse:** Bust of Queen Elizabeth II right **Reverse:** Siamese cat

Date	F	VF	XF	Unc	BU
1992	—	—	—	115	—
1992 Proof	—	Value: 117			

KM# 340 1/5 CROWN **Weight:** 6.2200 g. **Composition:** 0.9990 Gold .2000 oz. AGW **Subject:** Year of the Cockerel **Obverse:** Bust of Queen Elizabeth II right **Reverse:** Cockerel in inner circle

Date	Mintage	F	VF	XF	Unc	BU
1993 Proof	Est. 10,000	Value: 165				

KM# 351 1/5 CROWN **Weight:** 6.2200 g. **Composition:** 0.9990 Gold .2000 oz. AGW **Obverse:** Bust of Queen Elizabeth II right **Reverse:** Maine Coon cat

Date	F	VF	XF	Unc	BU
1993	—	—	—	125	—
1993 Proof	—	Value: 127			

KM# 365 1/5 CROWN **Weight:** 6.2200 g. **Composition:** 0.9990 Gold .2000 oz. AGW **Subject:** World Cup Soccer - Type I **Obverse:** Bust of Queen Elizabeth II right **Reverse:** Player in foreground kicking ball

Date	Mintage	F	VF	XF	Unc	BU
1994 Proof	Est. 5,000	Value: 160				

KM# 367 1/5 CROWN **Weight:** 6.2200 g. **Composition:** 0.9990 Gold .2000 oz. AGW **Subject:** World Cup Soccer - Type II **Obverse:** Bust of Queen Elizabeth II right **Reverse:** Three players

Date	Mintage	F	VF	XF	Unc	BU
1994 Proof	Est. 5,000	Value: 160				

KM# 369 1/5 CROWN **Weight:** 6.2200 g. **Composition:** 0.9990 Gold .2000 oz. AGW **Subject:** World Cup Soccer - Type III **Obverse:** Bust of Queen Eliabeth II right **Reverse:** Player with knee bent, second player in background

Date	Mintage	F	VF	XF	Unc	BU
1994 Proof	Est. 5,000	Value: 160				

KM# 371 1/5 CROWN **Weight:** 6.2200 g. **Composition:** 0.9990 Gold .2000 oz. AGW **Subject:** World Cup Soccer - Type IV **Obverse:** Bust of Queen Elizabeth II right **Reverse:** Three players with one kicking ball

Date	Mintage	F	VF	XF	Unc	BU
1994 Proof	Est. 5,000	Value: 160				

KM# 373 1/5 CROWN **Weight:** 6.2200 g. **Composition:** 0.9990 Gold .2000 oz. AGW **Subject:** World Cup Soccer - Type V **Obverse:** Bust of Queen Elizabeth II right **Reverse:** Goalie catching ball in hand

Date	Mintage	F	VF	XF	Unc	BU
1994 Proof	Est. 5,000	Value: 160				

KM# 375 1/5 CROWN **Weight:** 6.2200 g. **Composition:** 0.9990 Gold .2000 oz. AGW **Subject:** World Cup Soccer - Type VI **Obverse:** Bust of Queen Elizabeth II right **Reverse:** Two players kicking at ball

Date	Mintage	F	VF	XF	Unc	BU
1994 Proof	Est. 5,000	Value: 160				

KM# 378 1/5 CROWN **Weight:** 6.2200 g. **Composition:** 0.9990 Gold .2000 oz. AGW **Obverse:** Bust of Queen Elizabeth II right **Reverse:** Japanese Bobtail cat

Date	F	VF	XF	Unc	BU
1994	—	—	—	90.00	—
1994 Proof	—	Value: 92.00			

KM# 383 1/5 CROWN **Weight:** 6.2200 g. **Composition:** 0.9990 Gold .2000 oz. AGW **Series:** Preserve Planet Earth **Obverse:** Bust of Queen Elizabeth II right **Reverse:** Woolly mammoth

Date	Mintage	F	VF	XF	Unc	BU
1994 Proof	Est. 5,000	Value: 160				

KM# 389 1/5 CROWN **Weight:** 6.2200 g. **Composition:** 0.9990 Gold .2000 oz. AGW **Series:** Preserve Planet Earth **Obverse:** Bust of Queen Elizabeth II right **Reverse:** Mother and pup gray seals

Date	Mintage	F	VF	XF	Unc	BU
1994 Proof	5,000	Value: 160				

KM# 390 1/5 CROWN **Weight:** 6.2200 g. **Composition:** 0.9990 Gold .2000 oz. AGW **Series:** Preserve Planet Earth **Obverse:** Bust of Queen Elizabeth II right **Reverse:** Two deer

Date	Mintage	F	VF	XF	Unc	BU
1994 Proof	5,000	Value: 160				

KM# 404 1/5 CROWN **Weight:** 6.2200 g. **Composition:** 0.9990 Gold .2000 oz. AGW **Obverse:** Bust of Queen Elizabeth II right **Reverse:** Pekingese

Date	Mintage	F	VF	XF	Unc	BU
1994 Proof	10,000	Value: 170				

KM# 409 1/5 CROWN **Weight:** 6.2200 g. **Composition:** 0.9990 Gold .2000 oz. AGW **Series:** Man in Flight **Obverse:** Bust of Queen Elizabeth II right **Reverse:** Manned glider, Otto Lilienthal

Date	Mintage	F	VF	XF	Unc	BU
1994 Proof	Est. 5,000	Value: 170				

KM# 410 1/5 CROWN **Weight:** 6.2200 g. **Composition:** 0.9990 Gold .2000 oz. AGW **Series:** Man in Flight **Obverse:** Bust of Queen Elizabeth II right **Reverse:** Dirigible, Ferdinand von Zeppelin

Date	Mintage	F	VF	XF	Unc	BU
1994 Proof	Est. 5,000	Value: 170				

KM# 411 1/5 CROWN **Weight:** 6.2200 g. **Composition:** 0.9990 Gold .2000 oz. AGW **Series:** Man in Flight **Obverse:** Bust of Queen Elizabeth II right **Reverse:** Bust of Louis Bleriot behind plane flying across channel

Date	Mintage	F	VF	XF	Unc	BU
1994 Proof	Est. 5,000	Value: 170				

KM# 412 1/5 CROWN **Weight:** 6.2200 g. **Composition:** 0.9990 Gold .2000 oz. AGW **Series:** Man in Flight **Obverse:** Bust of Queen Elizabeth II right **Reverse:** Plane flying above ocean, Alcock and Brown

Date	Mintage	F	VF	XF	Unc	BU
1994 Proof	Est. 5,000	Value: 170				

KM# 413 1/5 CROWN **Weight:** 6.2200 g. **Composition:** 0.9990 Gold .2000 oz. AGW **Series:** Man in Flight **Subject:** First England to Australia Flight **Obverse:** Bust of Queen Elizabeth II right **Reverse:** Biplane flying

Date	Mintage	F	VF	XF	Unc	BU
1994 Proof	Est. 5,000	Value: 170				

KM# 414 1/5 CROWN **Weight:** 6.2200 g. **Composition:** 0.9990 Gold .2000 oz. AGW **Series:** Man in Flight **Subject:** 60th Anniversary of Airmail **Obverse:** Bust of Queen Elizabeth II right **Reverse:** Plane flying left above inscription

Date	Mintage	F	VF	XF	Unc	BU
1994 Proof	Est. 5,000	Value: 170				

KM# 415 1/5 CROWN **Weight:** 6.2200 g. **Composition:** 0.9990 Gold .2000 oz. AGW **Series:** Man in Flight **Subject:** 50th Anniversary of International Civil Aviation Organization **Obverse:** Bust of Queen Elizabeth II right **Reverse:** Trademark of ICAO

Date	Mintage	F	VF	XF	Unc	BU
1994 Proof	Est. 5,000	Value: 170				

KM# 416 1/5 CROWN **Weight:** 6.2200 g. **Composition:** 0.9990 Gold .2000 oz. AGW **Series:** Man in Flight **Subject:** First Concorde Flight **Obverse:** Bust of Queen Elizabeth II right **Reverse:** Concorde waiting at airport

Date	Mintage	F	VF	XF	Unc	BU
1994 Proof	Est. 5,000	Value: 170				

KM# 475 1/5 CROWN **Weight:** 6.2200 g. **Composition:** 0.9990 Platinum .2000 oz. APW **Obverse:** Bust of Queen Elizabeth II right **Reverse:** Japanese Bobtail cat

Date	F	VF	XF	Unc	BU
1994	—	—	—	150	—
1994 Proof	—	Value: 155			

KM# 429 1/5 CROWN **Weight:** 6.2200 g. **Composition:** 0.9990 Gold .2000 oz. AGW **Series:** Man in Flight **Obverse:** Bust of Queen Elizabeth II right **Reverse:** Wright Brothers airplane in flight

Date	Mintage	F	VF	XF	Unc	BU
1995 Proof	Est. 5,000	Value: 170				

KM# 426 1/5 CROWN **Weight:** 6.2200 g. **Composition:** 0.9990 Gold .2000 oz. AGW **Series:** Man in Flight **Obverse:** Bust of Queen Elizabeth II right **Reverse:** Icarus' wings melting

Date	Mintage	F	VF	XF	Unc	BU
1995 Proof	Est. 5,000	Value: 170				

KM# 427 1/5 CROWN **Weight:** 6.2200 g. **Composition:** 0.9990 Gold .2000 oz. AGW **Series:** Man in Flight **Obverse:** Bust of Queen Elizabeth II right **Reverse:** Leonardo Da Vinci and aircraft design

Date	Mintage	F	VF	XF	Unc	BU
1995 Proof	Est. 5,000	Value: 170				

KM# 428 1/5 CROWN **Weight:** 6.2200 g. **Composition:** 0.9990 Gold .2000 oz. AGW **Series:** Man in Flight **Obverse:** Bust of Queen Elizabeth II right **Reverse:** Montgolfier Brothers balloon in flight

Date	Mintage	F	VF	XF	Unc	BU
1995 Proof	Est. 5,000	Value: 170				

KM# 430 1/5 CROWN **Weight:** 6.2200 g. **Composition:** 0.9990 Gold .2000 oz. AGW **Series:** Man in Flight **Subject:** 1st Flight Tokyo to Paris by Abe and Kawachi **Obverse:** Bust of Queen Elizabeth II right **Reverse:** Two busts above airplane in flight

Date	Mintage	F	VF	XF	Unc	BU
1995 Proof	Est. 5,000	Value: 170				

KM# 431 1/5 CROWN **Weight:** 6.2200 g. **Composition:** 0.9990 Gold .2000 oz. AGW **Series:** Man in Flight **Subject:** FW109, First Diesel Powered Aircraft **Obverse:** Bust of Queen Elizabeth II right **Reverse:** Airplane on ground

Date	Mintage	F	VF	XF	Unc	BU
1995 Proof	Est. 5,000	Value: 170				

KM# 432 1/5 CROWN **Weight:** 6.2200 g. **Composition:** 0.9990 Gold .2000 oz. AGW **Series:** Man in Flight **Subject:** ME262, First Jet Aircraft **Obverse:** Bust of Queen Elizabeth II right **Reverse:** Jet flying into clouds

Date	Mintage	F	VF	XF	Unc	BU
1995 Proof	Est. 5,000	Value: 170				

KM# 433 1/5 CROWN **Weight:** 6.2200 g. **Composition:** 0.9990 Gold .2000 oz. AGW **Series:** Man in Flight **Subject:** 25th Anniversary of Boeing 747 **Obverse:** Bust of Queen Elizabeth II right **Reverse:** Jumbo jet in flight

Date	Mintage	F	VF	XF	Unc	BU
1995 Proof	Est. 5,000	Value: 170				

KM# 444 1/5 CROWN **Weight:** 6.2200 g. **Composition:** 0.9990 Gold .2000 oz. AGW **Obverse:** Bust of Queen Elizabeth II right **Reverse:** Turkish cat

Date	F	VF	XF	Unc	BU
1995	—	—	—	90.00	—
1995 Proof	—	Value: 92.00			

KM# 451 1/5 CROWN **Weight:** 6.2200 g. **Composition:** 0.9990 Gold .2000 oz. AGW **Subject:** Year of the Pig **Obverse:** Bust of Queen Elizabeth II right **Reverse:** Sow and piglets

Date	Mintage	F	VF	XF	Unc	BU
1995 Proof	Est. 10,000	Value: 170				

KM# 457 1/5 CROWN **Weight:** 6.2200 g. **Composition:** 0.9990 Gold .2000 oz. AGW **Subject:** 95th Birthday of Queen Mother **Obverse:** Bust of Queen Elizabeth II right **Reverse:** Bust of Queen Mother

Date	Mintage	F	VF	XF	Unc	BU
1995 Proof	Est. 5,000	Value: 170				

KM# 459 1/5 CROWN **Weight:** 6.2200 g. **Composition:** 0.9990 Gold .2000 oz. AGW **Series:** Preserve Planet Earth **Obverse:** Bust of Queen Elizabeth II right **Reverse:** Otter

Date	Mintage	F	VF	XF	Unc	BU
1995 Proof	Est. 5,000	Value: 170				

KM# 460 1/5 CROWN **Weight:** 6.2200 g. **Composition:** 0.9990 Gold .2000 oz. AGW **Series:** Preserve Planet Earth **Obverse:** Bust of Queen Elizabeth II right **Reverse:** Egret Birds

Date	Mintage	F	VF	XF	Unc	BU
1995 Proof	Est. 5,000	Value: 170				

KM# 480 1/5 CROWN **Weight:** 6.2200 g. **Composition:** 0.9990 Platinum .2000 oz. APW **Obverse:** Bust of Queen Elizabeth II right **Reverse:** Turkish cat

Date	F	VF	XF	Unc	BU
1995	—	—	—	150	—
1995 Proof	—	Value: 155			

KM# 483 1/5 CROWN **Weight:** 6.2200 g. **Composition:** 0.9990 Gold .2000 oz. AGW **Series:** Aircraft of World War II **Obverse:** Bust of Queen Elizabeth II right **Reverse:** Hawker Hurricane

Date	F	VF	XF	Unc	BU
1995 Proof	Est. 5,000	Value: 185			

KM# 484 1/5 CROWN **Weight:** 6.2200 g. **Composition:** 0.9990 Gold .2000 oz. AGW **Series:** Aircraft of World War II **Obverse:** Bust of Queen Elizabeth II right **Reverse:** P. 51 Munstang

Date	Mintage	F	VF	XF	Unc	BU
1995 Proof	Est. 5,000	Value: 185				

KM# 485 1/5 CROWN **Weight:** 6.2200 g. **Composition:** 0.9990 Gold .2000 oz. AGW **Series:** Aircraft of World War II **Obverse:** Bust of Queen Elizabeth II right **Reverse:** Letrov S328

Date	Mintage	F	VF	XF	Unc	BU
1995 Proof	Est. 5,000	Value: 185				

KM# 486 1/5 CROWN **Weight:** 6.2200 g. **Composition:** 0.9990 Gold .2000 oz. AGW **Series:** Aircraft of World War II **Obverse:** Bust of Queen Elizabeth II right **Reverse:** Messerschmitt ME262

Date	Mintage	F	VF	XF	Unc	BU
1995 Proof	Est. 5,000	Value: 185				

KM# 487 1/5 CROWN **Weight:** 6.2200 g. **Composition:** 0.9990 Gold .2000 oz. AGW **Series:** Aircraft of World War II **Obverse:** Bust of Queen Elizabeth II right **Reverse:** JU87 Stuka

Date	Mintage	F	VF	XF	Unc	BU
1995 Proof	Est. 5,000	Value: 185				

KM# 488 1/5 CROWN **Weight:** 6.2200 g. **Composition:** 0.9990 Gold .2000 oz. AGW **Series:** Aircraft of World War II **Obverse:** Bust of Queen Elizabeth II right **Reverse:** MIG 3

Date	Mintage	F	VF	XF	Unc	BU
1995 Proof	Est. 5,000	Value: 185				

KM# 489 1/5 CROWN **Weight:** 6.2200 g. **Composition:** 0.9990 Gold .2000 oz. AGW **Series:** Aircraft of World War II **Obverse:** Bust of Queen Elizabeth II right **Reverse:** Nakajima Ki-49 Donryu

Date	Mintage	F	VF	XF	Unc	BU
1995 Proof	Est. 5,000	Value: 185				

KM# 490 1/5 CROWN **Weight:** 6.2200 g. **Composition:** 0.9990 Gold .2000 oz. AGW **Series:** Aircraft of World War II **Obverse:** Bust of Queen Elizabeth II right **Reverse:** Vickers Wellington

Date	Mintage	F	VF	XF	Unc	BU
1995 Proof	Est. 5,000	Value: 185				

KM# 491 1/5 CROWN **Weight:** 6.2200 g. **Composition:** 0.9990 Gold .2000 oz. AGW **Series:** Aircraft of World War II **Obverse:** Bust of Queen Elizabeth II right **Reverse:** Spitfire

Date	Mintage	F	VF	XF	Unc	BU
1995 Proof	Est. 5,000	Value: 185				

KM# 492 1/5 CROWN **Weight:** 6.2200 g. **Composition:** 0.9990 Gold .2000 oz. AGW **Series:** Aircraft of World War II **Obverse:** Bust of Queen Elizabeth II right **Reverse:** Fokker G. 1a

Date	Mintage	F	VF	XF	Unc	BU
1995 Proof	Est. 5,000	Value: 185				

KM# 493 1/5 CROWN **Weight:** 6.2200 g. **Composition:** 0.9990 Gold .2000 oz. AGW **Series:** Aircraft of World War II **Obverse:** Bust of Queen Elizabeth II right **Reverse:** Commonwealth Boomerang CA-13

Date	Mintage	F	VF	XF	Unc	BU
1995 Proof	Est. 5,000	Value: 185				

KM# 494 1/5 CROWN **Weight:** 6.2200 g. **Composition:** 0.9990 Gold .2000 oz. AGW **Series:** Aircraft of World War II **Obverse:** Bust of Queen Elizabeth II right **Reverse:** Briston Blenheim 142M

Date	Mintage	F	VF	XF	Unc	BU
1995 Proof	Est. 5,000	Value: 185				

KM# 495 1/5 CROWN **Weight:** 6.2200 g. **Composition:** 0.9990 Gold .2000 oz. AGW **Series:** Aircraft of World War II **Obverse:** Bust of Queen Elizabeth II right **Reverse:** Mitsubishi Zero

Date	Mintage	F	VF	XF	Unc	BU
1995 Proof	Est. 5,000	Value: 185				

KM# 496 1/5 CROWN **Weight:** 6.2200 g. **Composition:** 0.9990 Gold .2000 oz. AGW **Series:** Aircraft of World War II **Obverse:** Bust of Queen Elizabeth II right **Reverse:** Heinkel HE111

Date	Mintage	F	VF	XF	Unc	BU
1995 Proof	Est. 5,000	Value: 185				

KM# 497 1/5 CROWN **Weight:** 6.2200 g. **Composition:** 0.9990 Gold .2000 oz. AGW **Series:** Aircraft of World War II **Obverse:** Bust of Queen Elizabeth II right **Reverse:** Boulton Paul P82 Defiant

Date	Mintage	F	VF	XF	Unc	BU
1995 Proof	Est. 5,000	Value: 185				

KM# 498 1/5 CROWN **Weight:** 6.2200 g. **Composition:** 0.9990 Gold .2000 oz. AGW **Series:** Aircraft of World War II **Obverse:** Bust of Queen Elizabeth II right **Reverse:** Boeing B289 - Enola Gay

Date	Mintage	F	VF	XF	Unc	BU
1995 Proof	Est. 5,000	Value: 185				

KM# 499 1/5 CROWN **Weight:** 6.2200 g. **Composition:** 0.9990 Gold .2000 oz. AGW **Series:** Aircraft of World War II **Obverse:** Bust of Queen Elizabeth II right **Reverse:** Douglas DC-3 (C47)

Date	Mintage	F	VF	XF	Unc	BU
1995 Proof	Est. 5,000	Value: 185				

KM# 500 1/5 CROWN **Weight:** 6.2200 g. **Composition:** 0.9990 Gold .2000 oz. AGW **Series:** Aircraft of World War II **Obverse:** Bust of Queen Elizabeth II right **Reverse:** Fairey Swordfish

Date	Mintage	F	VF	XF	Unc	BU
1995 Proof	Est. 5,000	Value: 185				

KM# 501 1/5 CROWN **Weight:** 6.2200 g. **Composition:** 0.9990 Gold .2000 oz. AGW **Series:** Aircraft of World War II **Obverse:** Bust of Queen Elizabeth II right **Reverse:** Curtiss P40

Date	Mintage	F	VF	XF	Unc	BU
1995 Proof	Est. 5,000	Value: 185				

KM# 523 1/5 CROWN **Weight:** 6.2200 g. **Composition:** 0.9990 Gold .2000 oz. AGW **Subject:** America's Cup **Obverse:** Bust of Queen Elizabeth II right **Reverse:** Two sailing boats

Date	Mintage	F	VF	XF	Unc	BU
1995 Proof	Est. 5,000	Value: 125				

KM# 525 1/5 CROWN **Weight:** 6.2200 g. **Composition:** 0.9999 Gold .2000 oz. AGW **Series:** Inventions of the Modern World **Obverse:** Bust of Queen Elizabeth II right **Reverse:** Cameo of Tsai Lun, paper and tree

Date	Mintage	F	VF	XF	Unc	BU
1995 Proof	Est. 5,000	Value: 165				

KM# 527 1/5 CROWN **Weight:** 6.2200 g. **Composition:** 0.9999 Gold .2000 oz. AGW **Series:** Inventions of the Modern World **Obverse:** Bust of Queen Elizabeth II right **Reverse:** Cameo of Chang Heng and Seismograph

Date	Mintage	F	VF	XF	Unc	BU
1995 Proof	Est. 5,000	Value: 165				

KM# 529 1/5 CROWN **Weight:** 6.2200 g. **Composition:** 0.9999 Gold .2000 oz. AGW **Series:** Inventions of the Modern World **Obverse:** Bust of Queen Elizabeth II right **Reverse:** Cameo of Tsu Chung Chih and compass cart

Date	Mintage	F	VF	XF	Unc	BU
1995 Proof	Est. 5,000	Value: 165				

KM# 531 1/5 CROWN **Weight:** 6.2200 g. **Composition:** 0.9999 Gold .2000 oz. AGW **Series:** Inventions of the Modern World **Obverse:** Bust of Queen Elizabeth II right **Reverse:** Cameo of Pi Sheng and movable type

Date	Mintage	F	VF	XF	Unc	BU
1995 Proof	Est. 5,000	Value: 165				

KM# 533 1/5 CROWN **Weight:** 6.2200 g. **Composition:** 0.9999 Gold .2000 oz. AGW **Series:** Inventions of the Modern World **Obverse:** Bust of Queen Elizabeth II right **Reverse:** Cameo of Charles Babbage and first computer

Date	Mintage	F	VF	XF	Unc	BU
1995 Proof	Est. 5,000	Value: 165				

KM# 535 1/5 CROWN **Weight:** 6.2200 g. **Composition:** 0.9999 Gold .2000 oz. AGW **Series:** Inventions of the Modern World **Obverse:** Bust of Queen Elizabeth II right **Reverse:** Cameo of Fox Talbot, photography

Date	Mintage	F	VF	XF	Unc	BU
1995 Proof	Est. 5,000	Value: 165				

KM# 537 1/5 CROWN **Weight:** 6.2200 g. **Composition:** 0.9999 Gold .2000 oz. AGW **Series:** Inventions of the Modern World **Obverse:** Bust of Queen Elizabeth II right **Reverse:** Cameo of Rudolf Diesel, diesel engine

Date	Mintage	F	VF	XF	Unc	BU
1995 Proof	Est. 5,000	Value: 165				

KM# 539 1/5 CROWN **Weight:** 6.2200 g. **Composition:** 0.9999 Gold .2000 oz. AGW **Series:** Inventions of the Modern World **Obverse:** Bust of Queen Elizabeth II right **Reverse:** Cameo of Wilhelm K. Roentgen and xray of hand

Date	Mintage	F	VF	XF	Unc	BU
1995 Proof	Est. 5,000	Value: 165				

KM# 541 1/5 CROWN **Weight:** 6.2200 g. **Composition:** 0.9999 Gold .2000 oz. AGW **Series:** Inventions of the Modern World **Obverse:** Bust of Queen Elizabeth II right **Reverse:** Cameo of Guglielmo Marconi and radio equipment

Date	Mintage	F	VF	XF	Unc	BU
1995 Proof	Est. 5,000	Value: 165				

KM# 543 1/5 CROWN **Weight:** 6.2200 g. **Composition:** 0.9999 Gold .2000 oz. AGW **Series:** Inventions of the Modern World **Obverse:** Bust of Queen Elizabeth II right **Reverse:** Cameo of John L. Baird and television equipment

Date	Mintage	F	VF	XF	Unc	BU
1995 Proof	Est. 5,000	Value: 165				

KM# 545 1/5 CROWN **Weight:** 6.2200 g. **Composition:** 0.9999 Gold .2000 oz. AGW **Series:** Inventions of the Modern World **Obverse:** Bust of Queen Elizabeth II right **Reverse:** Cameo of Alexander Fleming and microscope

Date	Mintage	F	VF	XF	Unc	BU
1995 Proof	Est. 5,000	Value: 165				

KM# 547 1/5 CROWN **Weight:** 6.2200 g. **Composition:** 0.9999 Gold .2000 oz. AGW **Series:** Inventions of the Modern World **Obverse:** Bust of Queen Elizabeth II right **Reverse:** Cameo of Lazlo Biro and ball-point pen

Date	Mintage	F	VF	XF	Unc	BU
1995 Proof	Est. 5,000	Value: 165				

KM# 549 1/5 CROWN **Weight:** 6.2200 g. **Composition:** 0.9999 Gold .2000 oz. AGW **Series:** Inventions of the Modern World **Obverse:** Bust of Queen Elizabeth II right **Reverse:** Cameo of Wernher von Braun and rocket

Date	Mintage	F	VF	XF	Unc	BU
1996 Proof	Est. 5,000	Value: 165				

KM# 550 1/5 CROWN **Weight:** 6.2200 g. **Composition:** 0.9999 Gold .2000 oz. AGW **Series:** Inventions of the Modern World **Obverse:** Bust of Queen Elizabeth II right **Reverse:** Cameo of Thomas Edison, electricity

Date	Mintage	F	VF	XF	Unc	BU
1996 Proof	Est. 5,000	Value: 165				

KM# 551 1/5 CROWN **Weight:** 6.2200 g. **Composition:** 0.9999 Gold .2000 oz. AGW **Series:** Inventions of the Modern World **Obverse:** Bust of Queen Elizabeth II right **Reverse:** Compass

Date	Mintage	F	VF	XF	Unc	BU
1996 Proof	Est. 5,000	Value: 165				

KM# 552 1/5 CROWN **Weight:** 6.2200 g. **Composition:** 0.9999 Gold .2000 oz. AGW **Series:** Inventions of the Modern World **Obverse:** Bust of Queen Elizabeth II right **Reverse:** Cameo of Michael Faraday, electricity

Date	Mintage	F	VF	XF	Unc	BU
1996 Proof	Est. 5,000	Value: 165				

KM# 553 1/5 CROWN **Weight:** 6.2200 g. **Composition:** 0.9999 Gold .2000 oz. AGW **Series:** Inventions of the Modern World **Obverse:** Bust of Queen Elizabeth II right **Reverse:** Cameo of Emile Berliner and gramophone

Date	Mintage	F	VF	XF	Unc	BU
1996 Proof	Est. 5,000	Value: 165				

KM# 554 1/5 CROWN **Weight:** 6.2200 g. **Composition:** 0.9999 Gold .2000 oz. AGW **Series:** Inventions of the Modern World **Obverse:** Bust of Queen Elizabeth II right **Reverse:** Cameo of Alexander Graham Bell, voice transmission

Date	Mintage	F	VF	XF	Unc	BU
1996 Proof	Est. 5,000	Value: 165				

KM# 561 1/5 CROWN **Weight:** 6.2200 g. **Composition:** 0.9999 Gold .2000 oz. AGW **Series:** 1996 Summer Olympics - Atlanta **Obverse:** Bust of Queen Elizabeth II right **Reverse:** Hurdler

Date	Mintage	F	VF	XF	Unc	BU
1996 Proof	Est. 5,000	Value: 165				

KM# 562 1/5 CROWN **Weight:** 6.2200 g. **Composition:** 0.9999 Gold .2000 oz. AGW **Series:** 1996 Summer Olympics - Atlanta **Obverse:** Bust of Queen Elizabeth II right **Reverse:** Runners

Date	Mintage	F	VF	XF	Unc	BU
1996 Proof	Est. 5,000	Value: 165				

KM# 563 1/5 CROWN **Weight:** 6.2200 g. **Composition:** 0.9999 Gold .2000 oz. AGW **Series:** 1996 Summer Olympics - Atlanta **Obverse:** Bust of Queen Elizabeth II right **Reverse:** Sailing

Date	Mintage	F	VF	XF	Unc	BU
1996 Proof	Est. 5,000	Value: 165				

KM# 564 1/5 CROWN **Weight:** 6.2200 g. **Composition:** 0.9999 Gold .2000 oz. AGW **Series:** 1996 Summer Olympics - Atlanta **Obverse:** Bust of Queen Elizabeth II right **Reverse:** Swimmers

Date	Mintage	F	VF	XF	Unc	BU
1996 Proof	Est. 5,000	Value: 165				

KM# 565 1/5 CROWN **Weight:** 6.2200 g. **Composition:** 0.9999 Gold .2000 oz. AGW **Series:** 1996 Summer Olympics - Atlanta **Obverse:** Bust of Queen Elizabeth II right **Reverse:** Equestrian

Date	Mintage	F	VF	XF	Unc	BU
1996 Proof	Est. 5,000	Value: 165				

KM# 566 1/5 CROWN **Weight:** 6.2200 g. **Composition:** 0.9999 Gold .2000 oz. AGW **Series:** 1996 Summer Olympics - Atlanta **Obverse:** Bust of Queen Elizabeth II right **Reverse:** Cyclists and Nike

Date	Mintage	F	VF	XF	Unc	BU
1996 Proof	Est. 5,000	Value: 165				

KM# 573 1/5 CROWN **Weight:** 6.2200 g. **Composition:** 0.9990 Gold .2000 oz. AGW **Series:** Bicentennial of Robert Burns **Obverse:** Bust of Queen Elizabeth II right **Reverse:** Seated

Date	Mintage	F	VF	XF	Unc	BU
1996 Proof	Est. 5,000	Value: 165				

KM# 574 1/5 CROWN **Weight:** 6.2200 g. **Composition:** 0.9990 Gold .2000 oz. AGW **Series:** Bicentennial of Robert Burns **Obverse:** Bust of Queen Elizabeth II right **Reverse:** Pirate ships

Date	Mintage	F	VF	XF	Unc	BU
1996 Proof	Est. 5,000	Value: 165				

KM# 575 1/5 CROWN **Weight:** 6.2200 g. **Composition:** 0.9990 Gold .2000 oz. AGW **Series:** Bicentennial of Robert Burns **Obverse:** Bust of Queen Elizabeth II right **Reverse:** Auld Lang Syne

Date	Mintage	F	VF	XF	Unc	BU
1996 Proof	Est. 5,000	Value: 165				

KM# 576 1/5 CROWN **Weight:** 6.2200 g. **Composition:** 0.9990 Gold .2000 oz. AGW **Series:** Bicentennial of Robert Burns **Obverse:** Bust of Queen Elizabeth II right **Reverse:** Edinburgh Castle

Date	Mintage	F	VF	XF	Unc	BU
1996 Proof	Est. 5,000	Value: 165				

KM# 581 1/5 CROWN **Weight:** 6.2200 g. **Composition:** 0.9990 Gold .2000 oz. AGW **Subject:** Queen's Birthday **Obverse:** Bust of Queen Elizabeth II right **Reverse:** Flowers

Date	Mintage	F	VF	XF	Unc	BU
1996 Proof	Est. 5,000	Value: 165				

KM# 583 1/5 CROWN **Weight:** 6.2200 g. **Composition:** 0.9990 Gold .2000 oz. AGW **Subject:** Preserve Planet Earth **Obverse:** Bust of Queen Elizabeth II right **Reverse:** Killer whale

Date	Mintage	F	VF	XF	Unc	BU
1996 Proof	Est. 5,000	Value: 165				

KM# 584 1/5 CROWN **Weight:** 6.2200 g. **Composition:** 0.9990 Gold .2000 oz. AGW **Subject:** Preserve Planet Earth **Obverse:** Bust of Queen Elizabeth II right **Reverse:** Razorbill feeding chick

Date	Mintage	F	VF	XF	Unc	BU
1996 Proof	Est. 5,000	Value: 165				

KM# 605 1/5 CROWN **Weight:** 6.2200 g. **Composition:** 0.9990 Gold .2000 oz. AGW **Series:** Flower Fairies **Obverse:** Bust of Queen Elizabeth II right **Reverse:** Orchis

Date	Mintage	F	VF	XF	Unc	BU
1996 Proof	Est. 5,000	Value: 170				

KM# 606 1/5 CROWN **Weight:** 6.2200 g. **Composition:** 0.9990 Gold .2000 oz. AGW **Series:** Flower Fairies **Obverse:** Bust of Queen Elizabeth II right **Reverse:** Rose

Date	Mintage	F	VF	XF	Unc	BU
1996 Proof	Est. 5,000	Value: 170				

KM# 607 1/5 CROWN **Weight:** 6.2200 g. **Composition:** 0.9990 Gold .2000 oz. AGW **Series:** Flower Fairies **Obverse:** Bust of Queen Elizabeth II right **Reverse:** Fuchsia

Date	Mintage	F	VF	XF	Unc	BU
1996 Proof	Est. 5,000	Value: 170				

KM# 608 1/5 CROWN **Weight:** 6.2200 g. **Composition:** 0.9990 Gold .2000 oz. AGW **Series:** Flower Fairies **Obverse:** Bust of Queen Elizabeth II right **Reverse:** Pinks

Date	Mintage	F	VF	XF	Unc	BU
1996 Proof	Est. 5,000	Value: 170				

KM# 617 1/5 CROWN **Weight:** 6.2200 g. **Composition:** 0.9990 Gold .2000 oz. AGW **Obverse:** Bust of Queen Elizabeth II right **Reverse:** Burmese cat

Date	F	VF	XF	Unc	BU
1996	—	—	—	90.00	—
1996 Proof	—	Value: 92.00			

KM# 618 1/5 CROWN **Weight:** 6.2200 g. **Composition:** 0.9990 Platinum .2000 oz. APW **Obverse:** Bust of Queen Elizabeth II right **Reverse:** Burmese cat

Date	F	VF	XF	Unc	BU
1996	—	—	—	150	—
1996 Proof	—	Value: 155			

KM# 625 1/5 CROWN **Weight:** 6.2200 g. **Composition:** 0.9990 Gold .2000 oz. AGW **Obverse:** Bust of Queen Elizabeth II right **Reverse:** Portrait of Ferdinand Magellan, map and ship

Date	Mintage	F	VF	XF	Unc	BU
1996 Proof	Est. 5,000	Value: 165				

KM# 628 1/5 CROWN **Weight:** 6.2200 g. **Composition:** 0.9990 Gold .2000 oz. AGW **Obverse:** Bust of Queen Elizabeth II right **Reverse:** Portrait of Sir Francis Drake, map and ship

Date	Mintage	F	VF	XF	Unc	BU
1996 Proof	Est. 5,000	Value: 165				

KM# 631 1/5 CROWN **Weight:** 6.2200 g. **Composition:** 0.9990 Gold .2000 oz. AGW **Series:** European Football Championship **Obverse:** Bust of Queen Elizabeth II right **Reverse:** Romania vs Bulgaria

Date	Mintage	F	VF	XF	Unc	BU
1996 Proof	Est. 5,000	Value: 165				

KM# 634 1/5 CROWN **Weight:** 6.2200 g. **Composition:** 0.9990 Gold .2000 oz. AGW **Series:** European Football Championship **Obverse:** Bust of Queen Elizabeth II right **Reverse:** Czech Republic vs Italy

Date	Mintage	F	VF	XF	Unc	BU
1996 Proof	Est. 5,000	Value: 165				

KM# 637 1/5 CROWN **Weight:** 6.2200 g. **Composition:** 0.9990 Gold .2000 oz. AGW **Series:** European Football Championship **Obverse:** Bust of Queen Elizabeth II right **Reverse:** Germany vs Russia

Date	Mintage	F	VF	XF	Unc	BU
1996 Proof	Est. 5,000	Value: 165				

KM# 640 1/5 CROWN **Weight:** 6.2200 g. **Composition:** 0.9990 Gold .2000 oz. AGW **Series:** European Football Championship **Obverse:** Bust of Queen Elizabeth II right **Reverse:** Spain vs France

Date	Mintage	F	VF	XF	Unc	BU
1996 Proof	Est. 5,000	Value: 165				

KM# 643 1/5 CROWN **Weight:** 6.2200 g. **Composition:** 0.9990 Gold .2000 oz. AGW **Series:** European Football Championship **Obverse:** Bust of Queen Elizabeth II right **Reverse:** Turkey vs Croatia

Date	Mintage	F	VF	XF	Unc	BU
1996 Proof	Est. 5,000	Value: 165				

KM# 646 1/5 CROWN **Weight:** 6.2200 g. **Composition:** 0.9990 Gold .2000 oz. AGW **Series:** Eurpean Football Championship **Obverse:** Bust of Queen Elizabeth II right **Reverse:** Denmark vs Portugal

Date	Mintage	F	VF	XF	Unc	BU
1996 Proof	Est. 5,000	Value: 165				

KM# 649 1/5 CROWN **Weight:** 6.2200 g. **Composition:** 0.9990 Gold .2000 oz. AGW **Series:** European Football Championship **Obverse:** Bust of Queen Elizabeth II right **Reverse:** Scotland vs England

Date	Mintage	F	VF	XF	Unc	BU
1996 Proof	Est. 5,000	Value: 165				

KM# 652 1/5 CROWN **Weight:** 6.2200 g. **Composition:** 0.9990 Gold .2000 oz. AGW **Series:** European Football Championship **Obverse:** Bust of Queen Elizabeth II right **Reverse:** Holland vs Switzerland

Date	Mintage	F	VF	XF	Unc	BU
1996 Proof	Est. 5,000	Value: 165				

KM# 656 1/5 CROWN **Weight:** 6.2200 g. **Composition:** 0.9990 Gold .2000 oz. AGW **Series:** European Football Championship **Obverse:** Bust of Queen Elizabeth II right **Reverse:** Winner, Germany

Date	Mintage	F	VF	XF	Unc	BU
1996 Proof	Est. 5,000	Value: 165				

KM# 659 1/5 CROWN **Weight:** 6.2200 g. **Composition:** 0.9990 Gold .2000 oz. AGW **Series:** Legend of King Arthur **Obverse:** Bust of Queen Elizabeth II right **Reverse:** King Arthur with sword, orb

Date	Mintage	F	VF	XF	Unc	BU
1996 Proof	Est. 5,000	Value: 165				

KM# 660 1/5 CROWN **Weight:** 6.2200 g. **Composition:** 0.9990 Gold .2000 oz. AGW **Series:** Legend of King Arthur **Obverse:** Bust of Queen Elizabeth II right **Reverse:** Queen Guinevere

Date	Mintage	F	VF	XF	Unc	BU
1996 Proof	Est. 5,000	Value: 165				

KM# 661 1/5 CROWN **Weight:** 6.2200 g. **Composition:** 0.9990 Gold .2000 oz. AGW **Series:** Legend of King Arthur **Obverse:** Bust of Queen Elizabeth II right **Reverse:** Sir Lancelot

Date	Mintage	F	VF	XF	Unc	BU
1996 Proof	Est. 5,000	Value: 165				

KM# 662 1/5 CROWN **Weight:** 6.2200 g. **Composition:** 0.9990 Gold .2000 oz. AGW **Series:** Legend of King Arthur **Obverse:** Bust of Queen Elizabeth II right **Reverse:** Merlin

Date	Mintage	F	VF	XF	Unc	BU
1996 Proof	Est. 5,000	Value: 165				

KM# 663 1/5 CROWN **Weight:** 6.2200 g. **Composition:** 0.9990 Gold .2000 oz. AGW **Series:** Legend of King Arthur **Obverse:** Bust of Queen Elizabeth II right **Reverse:** Camelot Castle

Date	Mintage	F	VF	XF	Unc	BU
1996 Proof	Est. 5,000	Value: 165				

KM# 664 1/5 CROWN **Weight:** 6.2200 g. **Composition:** 0.9990 Platinum .2000 oz. APW **Series:** Legend of King Arthur **Obverse:** Bust of Queen Elizabeth II right **Reverse:** King Arthur with sword, orb

Date	Mintage	F	VF	XF	Unc	BU
1996 Proof	Est. 5,000	Value: 185				

KM# 665 1/5 CROWN **Weight:** 6.2200 g. **Composition:** 0.9990 Platinum .2000 oz. APW **Series:** Legend of King Arthur **Obverse:** Bust of Queen Elizabeth II right **Reverse:** Queen Guinevere

Date	Mintage	F	VF	XF	Unc	BU
1996 Proof	Est. 5,000	Value: 185				

KM# 666 1/5 CROWN **Weight:** 6.2200 g. **Composition:** 0.9990 Platinum .2000 oz. APW **Series:** Legend of King Arthur **Obverse:** Bust of Queen Elizabeth II right **Reverse:** Sir Lancelot

Date	Mintage	F	VF	XF	Unc	BU
1996 Proof	Est. 5,000	Value: 185				

KM# 667 1/5 CROWN **Weight:** 6.2200 g. **Composition:** 0.9990 Platinum .2000 oz. APW **Series:** Legend of King Arthur **Obverse:** Bust of Queen Elizabeth II right **Reverse:** Merlin

Date	Mintage	F	VF	XF	Unc	BU
1996 Proof	Est. 5,000	Value: 185				

KM# 668 1/5 CROWN **Weight:** 6.2200 g. **Composition:** 0.9990 Platinum .2000 oz. APW **Series:** Legend of King Arthur **Obverse:** Bust of Queen Elizabeth II right **Reverse:** Camelot Castle

Date	Mintage	F	VF	XF	Unc	BU
1996 Proof	Est. 5,000	Value: 185				

KM# 730 1/5 CROWN **Weight:** 6.2200 g. **Composition:** 0.9990 Gold .2000 oz. AGW **Subject:** Year of the Rat **Obverse:** Bust of Queen Elizabeth II right **Reverse:** Rat

Date	F	VF	XF	Unc	BU
1996 Proof	—	—	—	—	—

Note: Entire series purchased by one buyer. Mintage, disposition and market value unknown

KM# 766 1/5 CROWN **Weight:** 6.2200 g. **Composition:** 0.9999 Gold .2000 oz. AGW **Subject:** Fridtjof Nansen 1861-1930 **Obverse:** Bust of Queen Elizabeth II right **Reverse:** Portrait, map and ship "The Fram"

Date	Mintage	F	VF	XF	Unc	BU
1997 Proof	Est. 5,000	Value: 175				

KM# 723 1/5 CROWN **Weight:** 6.2200 g. **Composition:** 0.9990 Gold .2000 oz. AGW **Subject:** Year of the Ox **Obverse:** Bust of Queen Elizabeth II right **Reverse:** Ox laying down

Date	Mintage	F	VF	XF	Unc	BU
1997 Proof	Est. 12,000	Value: 170				

KM# 751 1/5 CROWN **Weight:** 6.2200 g. **Composition:** 0.9990 Gold .2000 oz. AGW **Series:** Flower Fairies **Obverse:** Bust of Queen Elizabeth II right **Reverse:** Candytuft

Date	Mintage	F	VF	XF	Unc	BU
1997 Proof	Est. 5,000	Value: 165				

KM# 751a 1/5 CROWN **Weight:** 6.2518 g. **Composition:** 0.9950 Platinum .2000 oz. APW **Series:** Flower Fairies **Obverse:** Bust of Queen Elizabeth II right **Reverse:** Candytuft

Date	Mintage	F	VF	XF	Unc	BU
1997 Proof	Est. 2,500	Value: 175				

KM# 752 1/5 CROWN **Weight:** 6.2200 g. **Composition:** 0.9999 Gold .2000 oz. AGW **Series:** Flower Fairies **Obverse:** Bust of Queen Elizabeth II right **Reverse:** Snowdrop

Date	Mintage	F	VF	XF	Unc	BU
1997 Proof	Est. 5,000	Value: 165				

KM# 752a 1/5 CROWN **Weight:** 6.2518 g. **Composition:** 0.9950 Platinum .2000 oz. APW **Series:** Flower Fairies **Obverse:** Bust of Queen Elizabeth II right **Reverse:** Snowdrop

Date	Mintage	F	VF	XF	Unc	BU
1997 Proof	Est. 2,500	Value: 175				

KM# 753 1/5 CROWN **Weight:** 6.2200 g. **Composition:** 0.9999 Gold .2000 oz. AGW **Series:** Flower Fairies **Obverse:** Bust of Queen Elizabeth II right **Reverse:** Tulip

Date	Mintage	F	VF	XF	Unc	BU
1997 Proof	Est. 5,000	Value: 165				

KM# 753a 1/5 CROWN **Weight:** 6.2518 g. **Composition:** 0.9950 Platinum .2000 oz. APW **Series:** Flower Fairies **Obverse:** Bust of Queen Elizabeth II right **Reverse:** Tulip

Date	Mintage	F	VF	XF	Unc	BU
1997 Proof	Est. 2,500	Value: 175				

KM# 754 1/5 CROWN **Weight:** 6.2200 g. **Composition:** 0.9999 Gold .2000 oz. AGW **Series:** Flower Fairies **Obverse:** Bust of Queen Elizabeth II right **Reverse:** Jasmine

Date	Mintage	F	VF	XF	Unc	BU
1997 Proof	Est. 5,000	Value: 165				

KM# 754a 1/5 CROWN **Weight:** 6.2518 g. **Composition:** 0.9950 Platinum .2000 oz. APW **Series:** Flower Fairies **Obverse:** Bust of Queen Elizabeth II right **Reverse:** Jasmine

Date	Mintage	F	VF	XF	Unc	BU
1997 Proof	Est. 2,500	Value: 175				

KM# 763 1/5 CROWN **Weight:** 6.2200 g. **Composition:** 0.9999 Gold .2000 oz. AGW **Subject:** Leif Eriksson 999-1001 **Obverse:** Bust of Queen Elizabeth II right **Reverse:** Portrait and Viking ship with map sail

Date	Mintage	F	VF	XF	Unc	BU
1997 Proof	Est. 5,000	Value: 175				

KM# 772 1/5 CROWN **Weight:** 6.2200 g. **Composition:** 0.9999 Gold .2000 oz. AGW **Obverse:** Bust of Queen Elizabeth II right **Reverse:** Long-haired Smoke cat

Date	F	VF	XF	Unc	BU
1997	—	—	—	90.00	—
1997 Proof	—	Value: 92.00			

KM# 772a 1/5 CROWN **Weight:** 6.2200 g. **Composition:** 0.9999 Platinum .2000 oz. APW **Obverse:** Bust of Queen Elizabeth II right **Reverse:** Long-haired Smoke cat

Date	F	VF	XF	Unc	BU
1997	—	—	—	150	—
1997 Proof	—	Value: 155			

KM# 776 1/5 CROWN **Weight:** 6.2200 g. **Composition:** 0.9999 Gold .2000 oz. AGW **Subject:** History of the Cat **Obverse:** Bust of Queen Elizabeth II right **Reverse:** Cat stalking a spider

Date	Mintage	F	VF	XF	Unc	BU
1997 Proof	Est. 7,500	Value: 165				

KM# 781 1/5 CROWN **Weight:** 6.2200 g. **Composition:** 0.9999 Gold .2000 oz. AGW **Subject:** 90th Anniversary of the TT - 1907 **Obverse:** Bust of Queen Elizabeth II right **Reverse:** 1907 winner Charlie Collier

Date	Mintage	F	VF	XF	Unc	BU
1997 Proof	Est. 5,000	Value: 165				

KM# 783 1/5 CROWN **Weight:** 6.2200 g. **Composition:** 0.9999 Gold .2000 oz. AGW **Subject:** 90th Anniversary of the TT - 1907 **Obverse:** Bust of Queen Elizabeth II right **Reverse:** 1937 winner Omobono Tenni

Date	Mintage	F	VF	XF	Unc	BU
1997 Proof	Est. 5,000	Value: 165				

KM# 785 1/5 CROWN **Weight:** 6.2200 g. **Composition:** 0.9999 Gold .2000 oz. AGW **Subject:** 90th Anniversary of the TT - 1907 **Obverse:** Bust of Queen Elizabeth II right **Reverse:** 1957 winner Bob McIntyre

Date	Mintage	F	VF	XF	Unc	BU
1997 Proof	Est. 5,000	Value: 165				

KM# 787 1/5 CROWN **Weight:** 6.2200 g. **Composition:** 0.9999 Gold .2000 oz. AGW **Subject:** 90th Anniversary of the TT - 1907 **Obverse:** Bust of Queen Elizabeth II right **Reverse:** 1967 winner Mike Hailwood

Date	Mintage	F	VF	XF	Unc	BU
1997 Proof	Est. 5,000	Value: 165				

KM# 792 1/5 CROWN **Weight:** 6.2200 g. **Composition:** 0.9999 Gold .2000 oz. AGW **Subject:** Golden Wedding Anniversary of Queen Elizabeth II and Prince Philip **Obverse:** Bust of Queen Elizabeth II right **Reverse:** Wedding portrait

Date	Mintage	F	VF	XF	Unc	BU
1997 Proof	Est. 3,500	Value: 165				

KM# 798 1/5 CROWN **Weight:** 6.2200 g. **Composition:** 0.9999 Gold .2000 oz. AGW **Series:** Year 2000 **Subject:** Birth of Christ **Obverse:** Bust of Queen Elizabeth II right **Reverse:** Madonna and child with angels

Date	Mintage	F	VF	XF	Unc	BU
1997 Proof	Est. 2,000	Value: 165				

KM# 800 1/5 CROWN **Weight:** 6.2200 g. **Composition:** 0.9999 Gold .2000 oz. AGW **Series:** Year 2000 **Subject:** Fall of the Roman Empire 476 **Obverse:** Bust of Queen Elizabeth II right **Reverse:** Barbarian defeating Roman soldier

Date	Mintage	F	VF	XF	Unc	BU
1997 Proof	Est. 2,000	Value: 165				

KM# 802 1/5 CROWN **Weight:** 6.2200 g. **Composition:** 0.9999 Gold .2000 oz. AGW **Series:** Year 2000 **Subject:** Flight of Mohammed 622 **Obverse:** Bust of Queen Elizabeth II right **Reverse:** Arabs and camels at an oasis

Date	Mintage	F	VF	XF	Unc	BU
1997 Proof	Est. 2,000	Value: 165				

KM# 804 1/5 CROWN **Weight:** 6.2200 g. **Composition:** 0.9999 Gold .2000 oz. AGW **Series:** Year 2000 **Subject:** Norman Conquest 1066 **Obverse:** Bust of Queen Elizabeth II right **Reverse:** William the Conqueror rallying his troops

Date	Mintage	F	VF	XF	Unc	BU
1997 Proof	Est. 2,000	Value: 165				

KM# 807 1/5 CROWN **Weight:** 6.2200 g. **Composition:** 0.9999 Gold .2000 oz. AGW **Series:** World Cup Soccer

Obverse: Bust of Queen Elizabeth II right **Reverse:** Team captains in pre-game handshake

Date	Mintage	F	VF	XF	Unc	BU
1998 Proof	Est. 5,000	Value: 165				

KM# 814 1/5 CROWN Weight: 6.2200 g. **Composition:** 0.9999 Gold .2000 oz. AGW **Series:** Year of the Tiger **Obverse:** Bust of Queen Elizabeth II right **Reverse:** Tiger

Date	Mintage	F	VF	XF	Unc	BU
1998 Proof	Est. 12,000	Value: 165				

KM# 824 1/5 CROWN Weight: 6.2200 g. **Composition:** 0.9999 Gold .2000 oz. AGW **Obverse:** Bust of Queen Elizabeth II right **Reverse:** Portrait of Marco Polo, caravan and palace

Date	Mintage	F	VF	XF	Unc	BU
1998 Proof	Est. 5,000	Value: 165				

KM# 826 1/5 CROWN Weight: 6.2200 g. **Composition:** 0.9999 Gold .2000 oz. AGW **Obverse:** Bust of Queen Elizabeth II right **Reverse:** Portrait of Vasco da Gama, ship and African map **Note:** Similar to 1 Crown, KM#827.

Date	Mintage	F	VF	XF	Unc	BU
1998 Proof	Est. 5,000	Value: 165				

KM# 836 1/5 CROWN Weight: 6.2200 g. **Composition:** 0.9999 Gold .2000 oz. AGW **Series:** Flower Fairies **Obverse:** Bust of Queen Elizabeth II right **Reverse:** Fairy standing, lavender

Date	Mintage	F	VF	XF	Unc	BU
1998 Proof	Est. 5,000	Value: 165				

KM# 836a 1/5 CROWN Weight: 6.2200 g. **Composition:** 0.9999 Platinum .2000 oz. APW **Series:** Flower Fairies **Obverse:** Bust of Queen Elizabeth II right **Reverse:** Fairy standing, lavender

Date	Mintage	F	VF	XF	Unc	BU
1998 Proof	Est. 2,500	Value: 200				

KM# 837 1/5 CROWN Weight: 6.2200 g. **Composition:** 0.9999 Gold .2000 oz. AGW **Series:** Flower Fairies **Obverse:** Bust of Queen Elizabeth II right **Reverse:** Two fairies, sweet pea

Date	Mintage	F	VF	XF	Unc	BU
1998 Proof	Est. 5,000	Value: 165				

KM# 837a 1/5 CROWN Weight: 6.2200 g. **Composition:** 0.9999 Platinum .2000 oz. APW **Series:** Flower Fairies **Obverse:** Bust of Queen Elizabeth II right **Reverse:** Two fairies, sweet pea

Date	Mintage	F	VF	XF	Unc	BU
1998 Proof	Est. 2,500	Value: 200				

KM# 838 1/5 CROWN Weight: 6.2200 g. **Composition:** 0.9999 Gold .2000 oz. AGW **Series:** Flower Fairies **Obverse:** Bust of Queen Elizabeth II right **Reverse:** Fairy looking into flower, White Bindweed

Date	Mintage	F	VF	XF	Unc	BU
1998 Proof	Est. 5,000	Value: 165				

KM# 838a 1/5 CROWN Weight: 6.2200 g. **Composition:** 0.9999 Platinum .2000 oz. APW **Series:** Flower Fairies **Obverse:** Bust of Queen Elizabeth II right **Reverse:** Fairy looking into flower, White Bindweed

Date	Mintage	F	VF	XF	Unc	BU
1998 Proof	Est. 2,500	Value: 200				

KM# 839 1/5 CROWN Weight: 6.2200 g. **Composition:** 0.9999 Gold .2000 oz. AGW **Series:** Flower Fairies **Obverse:** Bust of Queen Elizabeth II right **Reverse:** Fairy standing, daffodil

Date	Mintage	F	VF	XF	Unc	BU
1998 Proof	Est. 5,000	Value: 165				

KM# 839a 1/5 CROWN Weight: 6.2200 g. **Composition:** 0.9999 Platinum .2000 oz. APW **Series:** Flower Fairies **Obverse:** Bust of Queen Elizabeth II right **Reverse:** Fairy standing, daffodil

Date	Mintage	F	VF	XF	Unc	BU
1998 Proof	Est. 2,500	Value: 200				

KM# 845 1/5 CROWN Weight: 6.2200 g. **Composition:** 0.9999 Gold .2000 oz. AGW **Series:** Winter Olympics - Nagano **Obverse:** Bust of Queen Elizabeth II right **Reverse:** Ski jumper

Date	Mintage	F	VF	XF	Unc	BU
1998 Proof	Est. 5,000	Value: 165				

KM# 846 1/5 CROWN Weight: 6.2200 g. **Composition:** 0.9999 Gold .2000 oz. AGW **Series:** Winter Olympics - Nagano **Obverse:** Bust of Queen Elizabeth II right **Reverse:** Slalom skier

Date	Mintage	F	VF	XF	Unc	BU
1998 Proof	Est. 5,000	Value: 165				

KM# 847 1/5 CROWN Weight: 6.2200 g. **Composition:** 0.9999 Gold .2000 oz. AGW **Series:** Winter Olympics - Nagano **Obverse:** Bust of Queen Elizabeth II right **Reverse:** Figure skaters, Olympic torch

Date	Mintage	F	VF	XF	Unc	BU
1998	Est. 5,000	Value: 165				

KM# 848 1/5 CROWN Weight: 6.2200 g. **Composition:** 0.9999 Gold .2000 oz. AGW **Series:** Winter Olympics - Nagano **Obverse:** Bust of Queen Elizabeth II right **Reverse:** Figure skater, speed skater and skier

Date	Mintage	F	VF	XF	Unc	BU
1998 Proof	Est. 5,000	Value: 165				

KM# 855 1/5 CROWN Weight: 6.2200 g. **Composition:** 0.9999 Gold .2000 oz. AGW **Obverse:** Bust of Queen Elizabeth II right **Reverse:** Birman cat

Date	Mintage	F	VF	XF	Unc	BU
1998 Proof	1,000	Value: 90.00				

KM# 855a 1/5 CROWN Weight: 6.2200 g. **Composition:** 0.9995 Platinum .2000 oz. APW **Obverse:** Bust of Queen Elizabeth II right **Reverse:** Birman cat

Date	F	VF	XF	Unc	BU
1998 Proof	—	Value: 155			

KM# 861 1/5 CROWN Weight: 6.2200 g. **Composition:** 0.9999 Gold .2000 oz. AGW **Series:** History of the Cat **Obverse:** Bust of Queen Elizabeth II right **Reverse:** Egyptian Mau cat with earring

Date	Mintage	F	VF	XF	Unc	BU
1998 Proof	Est. 7,500	Value: 170				

KM# 871 1/5 CROWN Weight: 6.2200 g. **Composition:** 0.9999 Gold .2000 oz. AGW **Subject:** 125th Anniversary of the Steam Railway **Obverse:** Bust of Queen Elizabeth II right **Reverse:** "The General"

Date	Mintage	F	VF	XF	Unc	BU
1998 Proof	Est. 5,000	Value: 170				

KM# 873 1/5 CROWN Weight: 6.2200 g. **Composition:** 0.9999 Gold .2000 oz. AGW **Subject:** 125th Anniversary of the Steam Railway **Obverse:** Bust of Queen Elizabeth II right **Reverse:** "The Rocket" and portrait

Date	Mintage	F	VF	XF	Unc	BU
1998 Proof	Est. 5,000	Value: 170				

KM# 875 1/5 CROWN Weight: 6.2200 g. **Composition:** 0.9999 Gold .2000 oz. AGW **Subject:** 125th Anniversary of the Steam Railway **Obverse:** Bust of Queen Elizabeth II right **Reverse:** Orient Express parlor car, interior view

Date	Mintage	F	VF	XF	Unc	BU
1998 Proof	Est. 5,000	Value: 170				

KM# 877 1/5 CROWN Weight: 6.2200 g. **Composition:** 0.9999 Gold .2000 oz. AGW **Subject:** 125th Anniversary of the Steam Railway **Obverse:** Bust of Queen Elizabeth II right **Reverse:** Mount Pilatus railway

Date	Mintage	F	VF	XF	Unc	BU
1998 Proof	Est. 5,000	Value: 170				

KM# 879 1/5 CROWN Weight: 6.2200 g. **Composition:** 0.9999 Gold .2000 oz. AGW **Subject:** 125th Anniversary of the Steam Railway **Obverse:** Bust of Queen Elizabeth II right **Reverse:** No. 1 Sutherland locomotive

Date	Mintage	F	VF	XF	Unc	BU
1998 Proof	Est. 5,000	Value: 170				

KM# 881 1/5 CROWN Weight: 6.2200 g. **Composition:** 0.9999 Gold .2000 oz. AGW **Subject:** 125th Anniversary of the Steam Railway **Obverse:** Bust of Queen Elizabeth II right **Reverse:** "Flying Scotsman"

Date	Mintage	F	VF	XF	Unc	BU
1998 Proof	Est. 5,000	Value: 170				

KM# 883 1/5 CROWN Weight: 6.2200 g. **Composition:** 0.9999 Gold .2000 oz. AGW **Subject:** 125th Anniversary of the Steam Railway **Obverse:** Bust of Queen Elizabeth II right **Reverse:** Mallard locomotive

Date	Mintage	F	VF	XF	Unc	BU
1998 Proof	Est. 5,000	Value: 170				

KM# 885 1/5 CROWN Weight: 6.2200 g. **Composition:** 0.9999 Gold .2000 oz. AGW **Subject:** 125th Anniversary of the Steam Railway **Obverse:** Bust of Queen Elizabeth II right **Reverse:** The Big Boy locomotive

Date	Mintage	F	VF	XF	Unc	BU
1998 Proof	Est. 5,000	Value: 170				

KM# 887 1/5 CROWN Weight: 6.2200 g. **Composition:** 0.9999 Gold .2000 oz. AGW **Series:** Year 2000 **Obverse:** Bust of Queen Elizabeth II right **Reverse:** American Independence 1776

Date	Mintage	F	VF	XF	Unc	BU
1998 Proof	Est. 2,000	Value: 170				

KM# 889 1/5 CROWN Weight: 6.2200 g. **Composition:** 0.9999 Gold .2000 oz. AGW **Series:** Year 2000 **Obverse:** Bust of Queen Elizabeth II right **Reverse:** French Revolution 1789

Date	Mintage	F	VF	XF	Unc	BU
1998 Proof	Est. 2,000	Value: 170				

KM# 891 1/5 CROWN Weight: 6.2200 g. **Composition:** 0.9999 Gold .2000 oz. AGW **Series:** Year 2000 **Obverse:** Bust of Queen Elizabeth II right **Reverse:** Reformation of the Church 1517

Date	Mintage	F	VF	XF	Unc	BU
1998 Proof	Est. 2,000	Value: 170				

KM# 893 1/5 CROWN Weight: 6.2200 g. **Composition:** 0.9999 Gold .2000 oz. AGW **Series:** Year 2000 **Obverse:** Bust of Queen Elizabeth II right **Reverse:** 400th Anniversary of the Renaissance

Date	Mintage	F	VF	XF	Unc	BU
1998 Proof	Est. 2,000	Value: 170				

KM# 895 1/5 CROWN Weight: 6.2200 g. **Composition:** 0.9999 Gold .2000 oz. AGW **Subject:** 125th Anniversary of the Steam Railway **Obverse:** Bust of Queen Elizabeth II right **Reverse:** Ocean wave and sea gull

Date	Mintage	F	VF	XF	Unc	BU
1998 Proof	Est. 5,000	Value: 170				

KM# 913 1/5 CROWN Weight: 6.2200 g. **Composition:** 0.9999 Gold .2000 oz. AGW **Subject:** Battle of Waterloo 1815 **Obverse:** Bust of Queen Elizabeth II right **Reverse:** Wellington on horse

Date	Mintage	F	VF	XF	Unc	BU
1999 Proof	Est. 2,000	Value: 170				

KM# 915 1/5 CROWN Weight: 6.2200 g. **Composition:** 0.9999 Gold .2000 oz. AGW **Subject:** U.S. Civil War **Obverse:** Bust of Queen Elizabeth II right **Reverse:** Cameos of Lee and Grant, flags, sword and drum

Date	Mintage	F	VF	XF	Unc	BU
1999 Proof	Est. 2,000	Value: 170				

KM# 917 1/5 CROWN Weight: 6.2200 g. **Composition:** 0.9999 Gold .2000 oz. AGW **Subject:** Bolshevik Revolution 1917 **Obverse:** Bust of Queen Elizabeth II right **Reverse:** Lenin above the Aurora

Date	Mintage	F	VF	XF	Unc	BU
1999 Proof	Est. 2,000	Value: 170				

KM# 919 1/5 CROWN Weight: 6.2200 g. **Composition:** 0.9999 Gold .2000 oz. AGW **Subject:** Armistice Day 1918 **Obverse:** Bust of Queen Elizabeth II right **Reverse:** Biplane above tank

Date	Mintage	F	VF	XF	Unc	BU
1999 Proof	Est. 2,000	Value: 170				

KM# 921 1/5 CROWN Weight: 6.2200 g. **Composition:** 0.9999 Gold .2000 oz. AGW **Series:** Summer Olympics - Sydney **Obverse:** Bust of Queen Elizabeth II right **Reverse:** Three javelin throwers

Date	Mintage	F	VF	XF	Unc	BU
1999 Proof	Est. 5,000	Value: 170				

KM# 923 1/5 CROWN Weight: 6.2200 g. **Composition:** 0.9999 Gold .2000 oz. AGW **Series:** Summer Olympics - Sydney **Obverse:** Bust of Queen Elizabeth II right **Reverse:** Female diver

Date	Mintage	F	VF	XF	Unc	BU
1999 Proof	Est. 5,000	Value: 170				

KM# 925 1/5 CROWN Weight: 6.2200 g. **Composition:** 0.9999 Gold .2000 oz. AGW **Series:** Summer Olympics - Sydney **Obverse:** Bust of Queen Elizabeth II right **Reverse:** Sailboat

Date	Mintage	F	VF	XF	Unc	BU
1999 Proof	Est. 5,000	Value: 170				

KM# 927 1/5 CROWN **Weight:** 6.2200 g. **Composition:** 0.9999 Gold .2000 oz. AGW **Series:** Summer Olympics - Sydney **Obverse:** Bust of Queen Elizabeth II right **Reverse:** Two runners

Date	Mintage	F	VF	XF	Unc	BU
1999 Proof	Est. 5,000	Value: 170				

KM# 929 1/5 CROWN **Weight:** 6.2200 g. **Composition:** 0.9999 Gold .2000 oz. AGW **Series:** Summer Olympics - Sydney **Obverse:** Bust of Queen Elizabeth II right **Reverse:** Two hurdlers

Date	Mintage	F	VF	XF	Unc	BU
1999 Proof	Est. 5,000	Value: 170				

KM# 931 1/5 CROWN **Weight:** 6.2200 g. **Composition:** 0.9999 Gold .2000 oz. AGW **Series:** World Cup Rugby 1999 **Obverse:** Bust of Queen Elizabeth II right **Reverse:** Bust of William Webb Ellis

Date	Mintage	F	VF	XF	Unc	BU
1999 Proof	Est. 5,000	Value: 170				

KM# 933 1/5 CROWN **Weight:** 6.2200 g. **Composition:** 0.9999 Gold .2000 oz. AGW **Series:** World Cup Rugby 1999 **Obverse:** Bust of Queen Elizabeth II right **Reverse:** Rugby scrum

Date	Mintage	F	VF	XF	Unc	BU
1999 Proof	Est. 5,000	Value: 170				

KM# 935 1/5 CROWN **Weight:** 6.2200 g. **Composition:** 0.9999 Gold .2000 oz. AGW **Series:** World Cup Rugby 1999 **Obverse:** Bust of Queen Elizabeth II right **Reverse:** Player running for catch

Date	Mintage	F	VF	XF	Unc	BU
1999 Proof	Est. 5,000	Value: 170				

KM# 937 1/5 CROWN **Weight:** 6.2200 g. **Composition:** 0.9999 Gold .2000 oz. AGW **Series:** World Cup Rugby 1999 **Obverse:** Bust of Queen Elizabeth II right **Reverse:** Goal kick

Date	Mintage	F	VF	XF	Unc	BU
1999 Proof	Est. 5,000	Value: 170				

KM# 939 1/5 CROWN **Weight:** 6.2200 g. **Composition:** 0.9999 Gold .2000 oz. AGW **Series:** World Cup Rugby 1999 **Obverse:** Bust of Queen Elizabeth II right **Reverse:** Tackled ball carrier

Date	Mintage	F	VF	XF	Unc	BU
1999 Proof	Est. 5,000	Value: 170				

KM# 941 1/5 CROWN **Weight:** 6.2200 g. **Composition:** 0.9999 Gold .2000 oz. AGW **Series:** World Cup Rugby 1999 **Obverse:** Bust of Queen Elizabeth II right **Reverse:** Player leaping for catch

Date	Mintage	F	VF	XF	Unc	BU
1999 Proof	Est. 5,000	Value: 170				

KM# 950 1/5 CROWN **Weight:** 6.2200 g. **Composition:** 0.9999 Gold .2000 oz. AGW **Series:** Year of the Rabbit **Obverse:** Bust of Queen Elizabeth II right **Reverse:** Two rabbits

Date	Mintage	F	VF	XF	Unc	BU
1999 Proof	Est. 12,000	Value: 170				

KM# 954 1/5 CROWN **Weight:** 6.2200 g. **Composition:** 0.9999 Gold .2000 oz. AGW **Obverse:** Bust of Queen Elizabeth II right **Reverse:** Portrait Sir Walter Raleigh, ship and dates

Date	Mintage	F	VF	XF	Unc	BU
1999 Proof	Est. 5,000	Value: 170				

KM# 956 1/5 CROWN **Weight:** 6.2200 g. **Composition:** 0.9999 Gold .2000 oz. AGW **Obverse:** Bust of Queen Elizabeth II right **Reverse:** Portrait Robert Falcon Scott and compass

Date	Mintage	F	VF	XF	Unc	BU
1999 Proof	Est. 5,000	Value: 170				

KM# 962 1/5 CROWN **Weight:** 6.2200 g. **Composition:** 0.9999 Gold .2000 oz. AGW **Subject:** British Blue Cat **Obverse:** Bust of Queen Elizabeth II right **Reverse:** Cat cleaning paw

Date	F	VF	XF	Unc	BU
1999	—	—	—	90.00	—
1999 Proof	— Value: 92.00				
1999 U Y2K	—	—	—	100	—

KM# 962a 1/5 CROWN **Weight:** 6.2200 g. **Composition:** 0.9995 Platinum .2000 oz. APW **Subject:** British Blue Cat **Obverse:** Bust of Queen Elizabeth II right **Reverse:** Cat cleaning paw

Date	F	VF	XF	Unc	BU
1999 Proof	— Value: 155				

KM# 975 1/5 CROWN **Weight:** 6.2200 g. **Composition:** 0.9999 Gold .2000 oz. AGW **Series:** The Life and Times of the Queen Mother **Obverse:** Bust of Queen Elizabeth II right **Reverse:** Child in chair

Date	Mintage	F	VF	XF	Unc	BU
1999 Proof	Est. 5,000	Value: 170				

KM# 977 1/5 CROWN **Weight:** 6.2200 g. **Composition:** 0.9999 Gold .2000 oz. AGW **Series:** The Life and Times of the Queen Mother **Obverse:** Bust of Queen Elizabeth II right **Reverse:** Engagement portrait

Date	Mintage	F	VF	XF	Unc	BU
1999 Proof	Est. 5,000	Value: 170				

KM# 979 1/5 CROWN **Weight:** 6.2200 g. **Composition:** 0.9999 Gold .2000 oz. AGW **Series:** The Life and Times of the Queen Mother **Obverse:** Bust of Queen Elizabeth II right **Reverse:** Honeymoon departure

Date	Mintage	F	VF	XF	Unc	BU
1999 Proof	Est. 5,000	Value: 170				

KM# 994 1/5 CROWN **Weight:** 6.2200 g. **Composition:** 0.9999 Gold .2000 oz. AGW **Subject:** The Wedding of HRH Prince Edward **Obverse:** Queen's portrait **Reverse:** Portrait of Prince Edward

Date	Mintage	F	VF	XF	Unc	BU
1999 Proof	Est. 5,000	Value: 170				

KM# 995 1/5 CROWN **Weight:** 6.2200 g. **Composition:** 0.9999 Gold .2000 oz. AGW **Series:** The Life and Times of the Queen Mother **Subject:** The Wedding of HRH The Prince Edward **Obverse:** Bust of Queen Elizabeth II right **Reverse:** Head of Prince Edward

Date	Mintage	F	VF	XF	Unc	BU
1999 Proof	Est. 5,000	Value: 170				

KM# 997 1/5 CROWN **Weight:** 6.2200 g. **Composition:** 0.9999 Gold .2000 oz. AGW **Series:** The Life and Times of the Queen Mother **Subject:** The Wedding of HRH The Prince Edward **Obverse:** Bust of Queen Elizabeth II right **Reverse:** Head of Sophie Rhys-Jones

Date	Mintage	F	VF	XF	Unc	BU
1999 Proof	Est. 5,000	Value: 170				

KM# 999 1/5 CROWN **Weight:** 6.2200 g. **Composition:** 0.9999 Gold .2000 oz. AGW **Subject:** 30th Anniversary of First Man on the Moon **Obverse:** Bust of Queen Elizabeth II right **Reverse:** Apollo XI, two moon walkers, date

Date	Mintage	F	VF	XF	Unc	BU
1999 Proof	Est. 2,000	Value: 170				

KM# 1001 1/5 CROWN **Weight:** 6.2200 g. **Composition:** 0.9999 Gold .2000 oz. AGW **Subject:** 30th Anniversary of First Man on the Moon **Obverse:** Bust of Queen Elizabeth II right **Reverse:** Mariner IX, 1971, space craft orbiting Mars

Date	Mintage	F	VF	XF	Unc	BU
1999 Proof	Est. 2,000	Value: 170				

KM# 1003 1/5 CROWN **Weight:** 6.2200 g. **Composition:** 0.9999 Gold .2000 oz. AGW **Subject:** 30th Anniversary of First Man on the Moon **Obverse:** Bust of Queen Elizabeth II right **Reverse:** Apollo-Soyuz link-up

Date	Mintage	F	VF	XF	Unc	BU
1999 Proof	Est. 2,000	Value: 170				

KM# 1005 1/5 CROWN **Weight:** 6.2200 g. **Composition:** 0.9999 Gold .2000 oz. AGW **Subject:** 30th Anniversary of First Man on the Moon **Obverse:** Bust of Queen Elizabeth II right **Reverse:** Viking Mars Lander, 1978

Date	Mintage	F	VF	XF	Unc	BU
1999 Proof	Est. 2,000	Value: 170				

KM# 1007 1/5 CROWN **Weight:** 6.2200 g. **Composition:** 0.9999 Gold .2000 oz. AGW **Subject:** 30th Anniversary of First Man on the Moon **Obverse:** Bust of Queen Elizabeth II right **Reverse:** Shuttle Columbia, 1981

Date	Mintage	F	VF	XF	Unc	BU
1999 Proof	Est. 2,000	Value: 170				

KM# 1009 1/5 CROWN **Weight:** 6.2200 g. **Composition:** 0.9999 Gold .2000 oz. AGW **Subject:** 30th Anniversary of First Man on the Moon **Obverse:** Bust of Queen Elizabeth II right **Reverse:** Mars Pathfinder, 1997

Date	Mintage	F	VF	XF	Unc	BU
1999 Proof	Est. 2,000	Value: 170				

KM# 985 1/5 CROWN **Weight:** 6.2200 g. **Composition:** 0.9999 Gold .2000 oz. AGW **Subject:** First Man on the Moon - Millennium **Obverse:** Bust of Queen Elizabeth II right **Reverse:** Landing scene, date

Date	Mintage	F	VF	XF	Unc	BU
2000 Proof	Est. 2,000	Value: 170				

KM# 987 1/5 CROWN **Weight:** 6.2200 g. **Composition:** 0.9999 Gold .2000 oz. AGW **Subject:** Fall of the Berlin Wall - Millennium **Obverse:** Bust of Queen Elizabeth II right **Reverse:** Crowds surrounding wall

Date	Mintage	F	VF	XF	Unc	BU
2000 Proof	Est. 2,000	Value: 170				

KM# 989 1/5 CROWN **Weight:** 6.2200 g. **Composition:** 0.9999 Gold .2000 oz. AGW **Subject:** Millennium 2000 - The Future **Obverse:** Bust of Queen Elizabeth II right **Reverse:** International space station

Date	Mintage	F	VF	XF	Unc	BU
2000 Proof	Est. 2,000	Value: 170				

KM# 1020 1/5 CROWN **Weight:** 6.2200 g. **Composition:** 0.9999 Gold .2000 oz. AGW **Obverse:** Queen's portrait **Reverse:** Armored portrait of Francisco Pizarro, map and ship **Edge:** Reeded **Size:** 22 mm.

Date	Mintage	F	VF	XF	Unc	BU
2000 Proof	5,000	Value: 175				

KM# 1022 1/5 CROWN **Weight:** 6.2200 g. **Composition:** 0.9999 Gold .2000 oz. AGW **Obverse:** Queen's portrait **Reverse:** Portrait, ship on ice and map, Willem Barents

Date	Mintage	F	VF	XF	Unc	BU
2000 Proof	5,000	Value: 175				

KM# 1024 1/5 CROWN **Weight:** 6.2200 g. **Composition:** 0.9999 Gold .2000 oz. AGW **Series:** Queen Mother **Obverse:** Queen's portrait **Reverse:** 1931 family scene **Edge:** Reeded **Size:** 22 mm.

Date	Mintage	F	VF	XF	Unc	BU
2000 Proof	5,000	Value: 175				

KM# 1026 1/5 CROWN **Weight:** 6.2200 g. **Composition:** 0.9999 Gold .2000 oz. AGW **Series:** Queen Mother **Reverse:** 1937 Coronation scene

Date	Mintage	F	VF	XF	Unc	BU
2000 Proof	5,000	Value: 175				

KM# 1028 1/5 CROWN **Weight:** 6.2200 g. **Composition:** 0.9999 Gold .2000 oz. AGW **Series:** Queen Mother **Reverse:** 1945 Victory Visit scene

Date	Mintage	F	VF	XF	Unc	BU
2000 Proof	5,000	Value: 175				

KM# 1030 1/5 CROWN **Weight:** 6.2200 g. **Composition:** 0.9999 Gold .2000 oz. AGW **Series:** Queen Mother **Reverse:** 1963 Royal Visit scene

Date	Mintage	F	VF	XF	Unc	BU
2000 Proof	175	Value: 175				

KM# 1032 1/5 CROWN **Weight:** 6.2200 g. **Composition:** 0.9990 Gold .2000 oz. AGW **Subject:** Battle of Britain **Obverse:** Queen's portrait **Reverse:** Aerial battle scene **Edge:** Reeded

Date	Mintage	F	VF	XF	Unc	BU
2000 Proof	5,000	Value: 175				

KM# 1034 1/5 CROWN **Weight:** 6.2200 g. **Composition:** 0.9990 Gold .2000 oz. AGW **Subject:** Global Challenge Yacht Race **Obverse:** Queen's portrait **Reverse:** Partial view of ship and map

Date	Mintage	F	VF	XF	Unc	BU
2000 Proof	5,000	Value: 175				

KM# 984 1/5 CROWN **Weight:** 6.2200 g. **Composition:** 0.9999 Gold .2000 oz. AGW **Subject:** Founding of the UN - Millennium **Obverse:** Bust of Queen Elizabeth II right **Reverse:** UN Building, logo

Date	Mintage	F	VF	XF	Unc	BU
2000 Proof	Est. 2,000	Value: 170				

KM# 1014 1/5 CROWN **Weight:** 6.2200 g. **Composition:** 0.9999 Gold .2000 oz. AGW **Subject:** Year of the Dragon **Obverse:** Bust of Queen Elizabeth II right **Reverse:** Dragon, Chinese characters

Date	Mintage	F	VF	XF	Unc	BU
2000 Proof	Est. 12,000	Value: 170				

KM# 1046 1/5 CROWN **Weight:** 6.2200 g. **Composition:** 0.9999 Gold .2000 oz. AGW **Obverse:** Queen's portrait **Reverse:** Prince William's portrait **Edge:** Reeded

Date	Mintage	F	VF	XF	Unc	BU
2000 Proof	5,000	Value: 175				

KM# 1048 1/5 CROWN **Weight:** 6.2200 g. **Composition:** 0.9999 Gold .2000 oz. AGW **Reverse:** Queen Mother's portrait with insert pearl

Date	Mintage	F	VF	XF	Unc	BU
2000 Proof	2,000	Value: 175				

KM# 1054 1/5 CROWN **Weight:** 6.2200 g. **Composition:** 0.9999 Gold .2000 oz. AGW **Obverse:** Bust of Queen Elizabeth II right **Reverse:** Scottish kitten **Edge:** Reeded **Size:** 22 mm.

Date	F	VF	XF	Unc	BU
2000	—	—	—	109	—
2000 Proof	— Value: 175				

KM# 1054a 1/5 CROWN **Weight:** 6.2200 g. **Composition:** 0.9995 Platinum .2000 oz. APW **Reverse:** Scottish kitten

Date	F	VF	XF	Unc	BU
2000	—	—	—	188	—

KM# 1060 1/5 CROWN **Weight:** 6.2200 g. **Composition:** 0.9999 Gold .2000 oz. AGW **Subject:** Year of the Snake **Obverse:** Queen's portrait **Reverse:** Snake **Edge:** Reeded **Size:** 22 mm.

Date	Mintage	F	VF	XF	Unc	BU
2001 Proof	12,000	Value: 175				

KM# 1069 1/5 CROWN **Weight:** 6.2200 g. **Composition:** 0.9999 Gold .2000 oz. AGW **Obverse:** Queen's portrait **Reverse:** Two Somali kittens **Edge:** Reeded **Size:** 22 mm.

Date	Mintage	F	VF	XF	Unc	BU
2001	—	—	—	—	110	—
2001 Proof	1,000	Value: 175				

KM# 1069a 1/5 CROWN **Weight:** 6.2200 g. **Composition:** 0.9995 Platinum .2000 oz. APW **Reverse:** Somali kittens **Edge:** Reeded **Size:** 22 mm.

Date	F	VF	XF	Unc	BU
2001	—	—	—	200	—

KM# 1074 1/5 CROWN **Weight:** 6.2200 g. **Composition:** 0.9999 Gold .2000 oz. AGW **Subject:** Queen Mother **Obverse:** Queen's portrait **Reverse:** 1948 Silver wedding anniversary **Edge:** Reeded **Size:** 22 mm.

Date	Mintage	F	VF	XF	Unc	BU
2001 Proof	5,000	Value: 175				

KM# 1075 1/5 CROWN **Weight:** 6.2200 g. **Composition:** 0.9999 Gold .2000 oz. AGW **Subject:** Queen Mother **Obverse:** Queen's portrait **Reverse:** 1948 holding baby Prince Charles **Edge:** Reeded **Size:** 22 mm.

Date	Mintage	F	VF	XF	Unc	BU
2001 Proof	5,000	Value: 175				

KM# 1078 1/5 CROWN **Weight:** 6.2200 g. **Composition:** 0.9999 Gold .2000 oz. AGW **Subject:** Martin Frobisher **Obverse:** Queen's portrait **Reverse:** Portrait, ship and map **Edge:** Reeded **Size:** 22 mm.

Date	Mintage	F	VF	XF	Unc	BU
2001 Proof	5,000	Value: 175				

KM# 1079 1/5 CROWN **Weight:** 6.2200 g. **Composition:** 0.9999 Gold .2000 oz. AGW **Subject:** Ronald

Amundsen **Obverse:** Queen's portrait **Reverse:** Portrait, ship and dirigible **Edge:** Reeded **Size:** 22 mm.

Date	Mintage	F	VF	XF	Unc	BU
2001 Proof	5,000	Value: 175				

KM# 1082 1/5 CROWN **Weight:** 6.2200 g. **Composition:** 0.9999 Gold .2000 oz. AGW **Subject:** Queen's 75th Birthday **Obverse:** Queen's portrait **Reverse:** Flower bouquet with a tiny diamond mounted on the bow of the ribbon **Edge:** Reeded **Size:** 22 mm.

Date	Mintage	F	VF	XF	Unc	BU
2001 Proof	2,000	Value: 299				

KM# 1117 1/5 CROWN **Weight:** 6.2200 g. **Composition:** 0.9990 Gold 0.1998 oz. AGW **Subject:** Queen Mother's Love of Horses **Obverse:** Bust of Queen Elizabeth II right **Reverse:** Queen Mother and horse **Edge:** Reeded **Size:** 22 mm.

Date	Mintage	F	VF	XF	Unc	BU
2002 Proof	5,000	Value: 175				

KM# 1109 1/5 CROWN **Weight:** 6.2200 g. **Composition:** 0.9990 Gold 0.1998 oz. AGW **Subject:** Bengal Cat **Obverse:** Queen Elizabeth's bust right **Reverse:** Cat and kitten **Edge:** Reeded **Size:** 22 mm.

Date	Mintage	VG	F	VF	XF	Unc
2002 Proof	1,000	Value: 175				
2002	—	—	—	—	—	110

KM# 1109a 1/5 CROWN **Weight:** 6.2200 g. **Composition:** 0.9990 Platinum 0.1998 oz. APW **Subject:** Bengal Cat **Obverse:** Bust of Queen Elizabeth II right. **Reverse:** Cat and kitten **Edge:** Reeded **Size:** 22 mm.

Date	F	VF	XF	Unc	BU
2002	—	—	—	190	—

KM# 1100 1/5 CROWN **Weight:** 6.2200 g. **Composition:** 0.9999 Gold .2000 oz. AGW **Subject:** Year of the Horse **Obverse:** Queen's portrait **Reverse:** Two horses **Edge:** Reeded **Size:** 22 mm.

Date	Mintage	F	VF	XF	Unc	BU
2002 Proof	12,000	Value: 175				

KM# 1113 1/5 CROWN **Weight:** 6.2200 g. **Composition:** 0.9990 Gold 0.1998 oz. AGW **Subject:** Olympics - Salt Lake City **Obverse:** Bust of Queen Elizabeth II right **Reverse:** Skier, torch and flag **Edge:** Reeded **Size:** 22 mm.

Date	Mintage	F	VF	XF	Unc	BU
2002 Proof	5,000	Value: 175				

KM# 1114 1/5 CROWN **Weight:** 6.2200 g. **Composition:** 0.9990 Gold 0.1998 oz. AGW **Subject:** Olympics - Salt Lake City **Obverse:** Bust of Queen Elizabeth II right **Reverse:** Bobsled, torch and stadium **Edge:** Reeded

Date	Mintage	F	VF	XF	Unc	BU
2002 Proof	5,000	Value: 175				

KM# 1120 1/5 CROWN **Weight:** 6.2200 g. **Composition:** 0.9990 Gold 0.1998 oz. AGW **Subject:** World Cup 2002 Japan - Korea **Obverse:** Bust of Queen Elizabeth II right **Reverse:** Player running right **Edge:** Reeded **Size:** 22 mm.

Date	Mintage	F	VF	XF	Unc	BU
2002 Proof	5,000	Value: 175				

KM# 1122 1/5 CROWN **Weight:** 6.2200 g. **Composition:** 0.9990 Gold 0.1998 oz. AGW **Subject:** World Cup 2002 Japan - Korea **Obverse:** Bust of Queen Elizabeth II right **Reverse:** Player kicking to right **Edge:** Reeded **Size:** 22 mm.

Date	Mintage	F	VF	XF	Unc	BU
2002 Proof	5,000	Value: 175				

KM# 1124 1/5 CROWN **Weight:** 6.2200 g. **Composition:** 0.9990 Gold 0.1998 oz. AGW **Subject:** World Cup 2002 Japan - Korea **Obverse:** Bust of Queen Elizabeth II right **Reverse:** Player kicking to left **Edge:** Reeded **Size:** 22 mm.

Date	Mintage	F	VF	XF	Unc	BU
2002 Proof	5,000	Value: 175				

KM# 1126 1/5 CROWN **Weight:** 6.2200 g. **Composition:** 0.9990 Gold 0.1998 oz. AGW **Subject:** World Cup 2002 Japan - Korea **Obverse:** Bust of Queen Elizabeth II right **Reverse:** Player running to left **Edge:** Reeded **Size:** 22 mm.

Date	Mintage	F	VF	XF	Unc	BU
2002 Proof	5,000	Value: 175				

KM# 1130 1/5 CROWN **Weight:** 6.2200 g. **Composition:** 0.3750 Gold 0.075 oz. AGW **Subject:** Queen Elizabeth II's Golden Jubilee **Obverse:** Bust of Queen Elizabeth II right **Reverse:** Seated crowned Queen holding scepter at her coronation **Edge:** Reeded **Size:** 22 mm.

Date	Mintage	F	VF	XF	Unc	BU
2002 Proof	2,002	Value: 60.00				

KM# 1132 1/5 CROWN **Weight:** 6.2200 g. **Composition:** 0.3750 Gold 0.075 oz. AGW **Subject:** Queen Elizabeth II's Golden Jubilee **Obverse:** Bust of Queen Elizabeth II right **Reverse:** Queen on horse **Edge:** Reeded **Size:** 22 mm.

Date	Mintage	F	VF	XF	Unc	BU
2002 Proof	2,002	Value: 60.00				

KM# 1134 1/5 CROWN **Weight:** 6.2200 g. **Composition:** 0.3750 Gold 0.075 oz. AGW **Subject:** Queen Elizabeth II's Golden Jubilee **Obverse:** Bust of Queen Elizabeth II right **Reverse:** Queen with dog **Edge:** Reeded **Size:** 22 mm.

Date	Mintage	F	VF	XF	Unc	BU
2002 Proof	2,002	Value: 60.00				

KM# 1136 1/5 CROWN **Weight:** 6.2200 g. **Composition:** 0.3750 Gold 0.075 oz. AGW **Subject:** Queen Elizabeth II's Golden Jubilee **Obverse:** Bust of Queen Elizabeth II right **Reverse:** Queen at war memorial **Edge:** Reeded **Size:** 22 mm.

Date	Mintage	F	VF	XF	Unc	BU
2002 Proof	2,002	Value: 60.00				

KM# 1138 1/5 CROWN **Weight:** 6.2200 g. **Composition:** 0.9990 Gold 0.1998 oz. AGW **Subject:** Queen Mother **Obverse:** Bust of Queen Elizabeth II right **Reverse:** Queen Mother and Castle May **Edge:** Reeded **Size:** 22 mm.

Date	Mintage	F	VF	XF	Unc	BU
2002 Proof	5,000	Value: 175				

KM# 1140 1/5 CROWN **Weight:** 6.2200 g. **Composition:** 0.9999 Gold 0.2 oz. AGW **Subject:** Princess Diana **Obverse:** Bust of Queen Elizabeth II right **Reverse:** Diana's portrait **Edge:** Reeded **Size:** 22 mm.

Date	Mintage	F	VF	XF	Unc	BU
2002 Proof	5,000	Value: 175				

KM# 1163 1/5 CROWN **Weight:** 6.2200 g. **Composition:** 0.9999 Gold 0.2 oz. AGW **Subject:** Cat **Obverse:** Queen's portrait **Reverse:** Two Balinese kittens **Edge:** Reeded **Size:** 22 mm.

Date	F	VF	XF	Unc	BU
2003PM	—	—	—	109	—
2003PM Proof	—	Value: 175			

KM# 1169 1/5 CROWN **Weight:** 6.2200 g. **Composition:** 0.9999 Gold 0.2 oz. AGW **Subject:** Year of the Goat **Obverse:** Queen's portrait **Reverse:** Three goats **Edge:** Reeded **Size:** 22 mm.

Date	F	VF	XF	Unc	BU
2003PM Proof	—	Value: 175			

KM# 669 1/4 CROWN **Ring Weight:** 3.8880 g. **Ring Composition:** 0.9950 Platinum .1244 oz. APW **Center Weight:** 3.8880 g. **Center Composition:** 0.9990 Gold .1249 oz. AGW **Series:** Legend of King Arthur **Obverse:** Bust of Queen Elizabeth II right **Reverse:** King Arthur with sword and orb

Date	Mintage	F	VF	XF	Unc	BU
1996 Proof	Est. 5,000	Value: 195				

KM# 670 1/4 CROWN **Ring Weight:** 3.8880 g. **Ring Composition:** 0.9950 Platinum .1244 oz. APW **Center Weight:** 3.8880 g. **Center Composition:** 0.9990 Gold .1249 oz. AGW **Series:** Legend of King Arthur **Obverse:** Bust of Queen Elizabeth II right **Reverse:** Queen Guinevere

Date	Mintage	F	VF	XF	Unc	BU
1996 Proof	Est. 5,000	Value: 195				

KM# 671 1/4 CROWN **Ring Weight:** 3.8880 g. **Ring Composition:** 0.9950 Platinum .1244 oz. APW **Center Weight:** 3.8880 g. **Center Composition:** 0.9990 Gold .1249 oz. AGW **Series:** Legend of King Arthur **Obverse:** Bust of Queen Elizabeth II right **Reverse:** Sir Lancelot

Date	Mintage	F	VF	XF	Unc	BU
1996 Proof	Est. 5,000	Value: 195				

KM# 672 1/4 CROWN **Ring Weight:** 3.8880 g. **Ring Composition:** 0.9950 Platinum .1244 oz. APW **Center Weight:** 3.8880 g. **Center Composition:** 0.9990 Gold .1249 oz. AGW **Series:** Legend of King Arthur **Obverse:** Bust of Queen Elizabeth II right **Reverse:** Merlin

Date	Mintage	F	VF	XF	Unc	BU
1996 Proof	Est. 5,000	Value: 195				

KM# 673 1/4 CROWN **Ring Weight:** 3.8880 g. **Ring Composition:** 0.9950 Platinum .1244 oz. APW **Center Weight:** 3.8880 g. **Center Composition:** 0.9990 Gold .1249 oz. AGW **Series:** Legend of King Arthur **Obverse:** Bust of Queen Elizabeth II right **Reverse:** Camelot Castle

Date	Mintage	F	VF	XF	Unc	BU
1996 Proof	Est. 5,000	Value: 195				

KM# 674 1/4 CROWN **Center Weight:** 3.8880 g. **Center Composition:** 0.9950 Platinum .1244 oz. APW **Series:** Legend of King Arthur **Obverse:** Bust of Queen Elizabeth II right **Reverse:** King Arthur with sword and orb

Date	Mintage	F	VF	XF	Unc	BU
1996 Proof	Est. 5,000	Value: 195				

KM# 675 1/4 CROWN **Center Weight:** 3.8880 g. **Center Composition:** 0.9950 Platinum .1244 oz. APW **Series:** Legend of King Arthur **Obverse:** Bust of Queen Elizabeth II right **Reverse:** Queen Guinevere

Date	Mintage	F	VF	XF	Unc	BU
1996 Proof	Est. 5,000	Value: 195				

KM# 676 1/4 CROWN **Center Weight:** 3.8880 g. **Center Composition:** 0.9950 Platinum .1244 oz. APW **Series:** Legend of King Arthur **Obverse:** Bust of Queen Elizabeth II right **Reverse:** Sir Lancelot

Date	Mintage	F	VF	XF	Unc	BU
1996 Proof	Est. 5,000	Value: 195				

KM# 677 1/4 CROWN **Center Weight:** 3.8880 g. **Center Composition:** 0.9950 Platinum .1244 oz. APW **Series:** Legend of King Arthur **Obverse:** Bust of Queen Elizabeth II right **Reverse:** Merlin

Date	Mintage	F	VF	XF	Unc	BU
1996 Proof	Est. 5,000	Value: 195				

KM# 678 1/4 CROWN **Center Weight:** 3.8880 g. **Center Composition:** 0.9950 Platinum .1244 oz. APW **Series:** Legend of King Arthur **Obverse:** Bust of Queen Elizabeth II right **Reverse:** Camelot Castle

Date	Mintage	F	VF	XF	Unc	BU
1996 Proof	Est. 5,000	Value: 195				

KM# 187 1/2 CROWN **Weight:** 15.5500 g. **Composition:** 0.9990 Gold .5000 oz. AGW **Subject:** U.S. Constitution **Obverse:** Bust of Queen Elizabeth II right **Reverse:** Busts of American presidents

Date	Mintage	F	VF	XF	Unc	BU
1987 Proof	12,000	Value: 375				

KM# 187a 1/2 CROWN **Weight:** 15.5500 g. **Composition:** 0.9990 Platinum .5000 oz. APW **Subject:** U.S. Constitution **Obverse:** Bust of Queen Elizabeth II right **Reverse:** Busts of American presidents

Date	Mintage	F	VF	XF	Unc	BU
1987 Proof	250	Value: 600				

KM# 238 1/2 CROWN **Weight:** 15.5500 g. **Composition:** 0.9990 Gold .5000 oz. AGW **Obverse:** Bust of Queen Elizabeth II right **Reverse:** Manx cat

Date	Mintage	F	VF	XF	Unc	BU
1988	6,375	—	—	—	235	—
1988 Proof	5,000	Value: 255				

KM# 286 1/2 CROWN **Weight:** 16.4000 g. **Composition:** 0.9480 Gold .5000 oz. AGW **Subject:** Australian Bicentennial **Obverse:** Bust of Queen Elizabeth II right **Reverse:** Cockatoo

Date	Mintage	F	VF	XF	Unc	BU
1988 Proof	Est. 7,500	Value: 250				

KM# 287 1/2 CROWN **Weight:** 16.4000 g. **Composition:** 0.9480 Gold .5000 oz. AGW **Subject:** Australian Bicentennial **Obverse:** Bust of Queen Elizabeth II right **Reverse:** Koala bear

Date	Mintage	F	VF	XF	Unc	BU
1988 Proof	Est. 7,500	Value: 250				

KM# 288 1/2 CROWN **Weight:** 16.4000 g. **Composition:** 0.9480 Gold .5000 oz. AGW **Subject:** Australian Bicentennial **Obverse:** Bust of Queen Elizabeth II right **Reverse:** Duckbill platypus

Date	Mintage	F	VF	XF	Unc	BU
1988 Proof	Est. 7,500	Value: 250				

KM# 289 1/2 CROWN **Weight:** 16.4000 g. **Composition:** 0.9480 Gold .5000 oz. AGW **Subject:** Australian Bicentennial **Obverse:** Bust of Queen Elizabeth II right **Reverse:** Kangaroo

Date	Mintage	F	VF	XF	Unc	BU
1988 Proof	Est. 7,500	Value: 250				

KM# 359 1/2 CROWN **Weight:** 15.5500 g. **Composition:** 0.9990 Platinum .5000 oz. APW **Subject:** Australian Bicentennial **Obverse:** Bust of Queen Elizabeth II right **Reverse:** Cockatoo

Date	F	VF	XF	Unc	BU
1988 Proof	—	Value: 475			

KM# 360 1/2 CROWN **Weight:** 15.5500 g. **Composition:** 0.9990 Platinum .5000 oz. APW **Subject:** Australian Bicentennial **Obverse:** Bust of Queen Elizabeth II right **Reverse:** Koala bear

Date	F	VF	XF	Unc	BU
1988 Proof	—	Value: 475			

KM# 361 1/2 CROWN **Weight:** 15.5500 g. **Composition:** 0.9990 Platinum .5000 oz. APW **Subject:** Australian Bicentennial **Obverse:** Bust of Queen Elizabeth II right **Reverse:** Duckbill platypus

Date	F	VF	XF	Unc	BU
1988 Proof	—	Value: 475			

KM# 362 1/2 CROWN **Weight:** 15.5500 g. **Composition:** 0.9990 Platinum .5000 oz. APW **Subject:** Australian Bicentennial **Obverse:** Bust of Queen Elizabeth II right **Reverse:** Kangaroo

Date	F	VF	XF	Unc	BU
1988 Proof	—	Value: 475			

KM# 363 1/2 CROWN **Weight:** 15.5500 g. **Composition:** 0.9990 Platinum .5000 oz. APW **Subject:** Australian Bicentennial **Obverse:** Bust of Queen Elizabeth II right **Reverse:** Dingo Dog

Date	F	VF	XF	Unc	BU
1988 Proof	—	Value: 475			

KM# 255 1/2 CROWN **Weight:** 16.4000 g. **Composition:** 0.9480 Gold .5000 oz. AGW **Obverse:** Bust of Queen Elizabeth II right **Reverse:** Persian cat

Date	F	VF	XF	Unc	BU
1989	—	—	—	300	—
1989 Proof	—	Value: 305			

KM# 470 1/2 CROWN **Weight:** 15.5500 g. **Composition:** 0.9990 Platinum .5000 oz. APW **Obverse:** Bust of Queen Elizabeth II right **Reverse:** Persian cat

Date	F	VF	XF	Unc	BU
1989	—	—	—BV+20%		—

KM# 280 1/2 CROWN **Weight:** 16.4000 g. **Composition:** 0.9480 Gold .5000 oz. AGW **Obverse:** Bust of Queen Elizabeth II right **Reverse:** Alley cat

Date	F	VF	XF	Unc	BU
1990	—	—	—	300	—
1990 Proof	—	Value: 310			

KM# 297 1/2 CROWN **Weight:** 15.5500 g. **Composition:** 0.9990 Gold .5000 oz. AGW **Obverse:** Bust of Queen Elizabeth II right **Reverse:** Norwegian cat

Date	F	VF	XF	Unc	BU
1991	—	—	—	250	—
1991 Proof	—	Value: 260			

KM# 325 1/2 CROWN **Center Weight:** 15.5500 g. **Center Composition:** 0.9990 Gold .5000 oz. AGW **Subject:** America's Cup **Obverse:** Bust of Queen Elizabeth II right **Reverse:** Sailboat

Date	Mintage	F	VF	XF	Unc	BU
1992 Proof like	2,000	—	—	—	345	—

KM# 331 1/2 CROWN **Weight:** 15.5500 g. **Composition:** 0.9990 Gold .5000 oz. AGW **Obverse:** Bust of Queen Elizabeth II right **Reverse:** Siamese cat

Date	F	VF	XF	Unc	BU
1992	—	—	—	250	—
1992 Proof	—	Value: 260			

KM# 341 1/2 CROWN **Weight:** 15.5500 g. **Composition:** 0.9990 Gold .5000 oz. AGW **Subject:** Year of the Rooster **Obverse:** Bust of Queen Elizabeth II right **Reverse:** Cockerel in inner circle

Date	Mintage	F	VF	XF	Unc	BU
1993 Proof	Est. 5,000	Value: 365				

KM# 352 1/2 CROWN **Weight:** 15.5500 g. **Composition:** 0.9990 Gold .5000 oz. AGW **Obverse:** Bust of Queen Elizabeth II right **Reverse:** Maine coon cat

Date	F	VF	XF	Unc	BU
1993	—	—	—	225	—
1993 Proof	—	Value: 235			

KM# 379 1/2 CROWN **Weight:** 15.5500 g. **Composition:** 0.9990 Gold .5000 oz. AGW **Obverse:** Bust of Queen Elizabeth II right **Reverse:** Japanese bobtail cat

Date	F	VF	XF	Unc	BU
1994	—	—	—	225	—
1994 Proof	—	Value: 235			

KM# 405 1/2 CROWN **Weight:** 15.5500 g. **Composition:** 0.9990 Gold .5000 oz. AGW **Obverse:** Bust of Queen Elizabeth II right **Reverse:** Pekingese dog

Date	Mintage	F	VF	XF	Unc	BU
1994 Proof	5,000	Value: 360				

KM# 476 1/2 CROWN **Weight:** 15.5500 g. **Composition:** 0.9990 Platinum .5000 oz. APW **Obverse:** Bust of Queen Elizabeth II right **Reverse:** Japanese bobtail cat

Date	F	VF	XF	Unc	BU
1994 Proof	—	—	—	—	—

KM# 445 1/2 CROWN **Weight:** 15.5500 g. **Composition:** 0.9990 Gold .5000 oz. AGW **Obverse:** Bust of Queen Elizabeth II right **Reverse:** Turkish cat looking back

Date	F	VF	XF	Unc	BU
1995 U	—	—	—	225	—
1995 Proof	—	Value: 235			

KM# 452 1/2 CROWN **Weight:** 15.5500 g. **Composition:** 0.9990 Gold .5000 oz. AGW **Subject:** Year of the Pig **Obverse:** Bust of Queen Elizabeth II right **Reverse:** Sow with piglets

Date	Mintage	F	VF	XF	Unc	BU
1995 Proof	Est. 5,000	Value: 360				

KM# 481 1/2 CROWN **Weight:** 15.5500 g. **Composition:** 0.9990 Platinum .5000 oz. APW **Obverse:** Bust of Queen Elizabeth II right **Reverse:** Turkish cat

Date	F	VF	XF	Unc	BU
1995 Proof	—	—	—	—	—

KM# 731 1/2 CROWN **Center Weight:** 15.5517 g. **Center Composition:** 0.9999 Gold .5000 oz. AGW **Subject:** Year of the Rat **Obverse:** Bust of Queen Elizabeth II right **Reverse:** Rat

Date	F	VF	XF	Unc	BU
1996 Proof	—	—	—	—	—

KM# 619 1/2 CROWN **Weight:** 15.5500 g. **Composition:** 0.9990 Gold .5000 oz. AGW **Obverse:** Bust of Queen Elizabeth II right **Reverse:** Burmese cat

Date	F	VF	XF	Unc	BU
1996 U	—	—	—	225	—
1996 Proof	—	Value: 235			

KM# 620 1/2 CROWN **Weight:** 15.5500 g. **Composition:** 0.9990 Platinum .5000 oz. APW **Obverse:** Bust of Queen Elizabeth II right **Reverse:** Burmese cat

Date	F	VF	XF	Unc	BU
1996 U	—	—	—BV+20%		—

KM# 724 1/2 CROWN **Weight:** 15.5517 g. **Composition:** 0.9999 Gold .5000 oz. AGW **Subject:** Year of the Ox **Obverse:** Bust of Queen Elizabeth II right **Reverse:** Ox laying down

Date	Mintage	F	VF	XF	Unc	BU
1996 Proof	Est. 6,000	Value: 360				

KM# 764 1/2 CROWN **Weight:** 15.5517 g. **Composition:** 0.9999 Gold .5000 oz. AGW **Obverse:** Bust of Queen Elizabeth II right **Reverse:** Portrait of Leif Eriksson and Viking ship with map sail

Date	Mintage	F	VF	XF	Unc	BU
1997 Proof	Est. 2,500	Value: 360				

KM# 767 1/2 CROWN **Weight:** 15.5517 g. **Composition:** 0.9999 Gold .5000 oz. AGW **Obverse:** Bust of Queen Elizabeth II right **Reverse:** Portrait of Fridtjof Nansen, map and ship "The Fram"

Date	Mintage	F	VF	XF	Unc	BU
1997 Proof	Est. 2,500	Value: 360				

KM# 767a 1/2 CROWN **Weight:** 15.5500 g. **Composition:** 0.9990 Silver .5 oz. ASW **Obverse:** Bust of Queen Elizabeth II right **Reverse:** Portrait of Fridtjof Nansen, map and ship "The Fram" **Note:** Similar to 1 Crown, KM#768.

Date	F	VF	XF	Unc	BU
1997 Proof	—	Value: 30.00			

KM# 773 1/2 CROWN **Weight:** 15.5517 g. **Composition:** 0.9999 Gold .5000 oz. AGW **Obverse:** Bust of Queen Elizabeth II right **Reverse:** Long-haired Smoke cat

Date	F	VF	XF	Unc	BU
1997 Proof	—	Value: 200			
1997	—	—	—	195	—

KM# 791 1/2 CROWN **Weight:** 15.5517 g. **Composition:** 0.9999 Gold .5000 oz. AGW **Subject:** History of the Cat **Obverse:** Bust of Queen Elizabeth II right **Reverse:** Cat stalking a spider

Date	Mintage	F	VF	XF	Unc	BU
1997 Proof	Est. 2,500	Value: 360				

KM# 815 1/2 CROWN **Weight:** 15.5000 g. **Composition:** 0.9999 Gold .5000 oz. AGW **Subject:** Year of the Tiger **Obverse:** Bust of Queen Elizabeth II right **Reverse:** Tiger

Date	Mintage	F	VF	XF	Unc	BU
1998 Proof	Est. 6,000	Value: 345				

KM# 856 1/2 CROWN **Weight:** 15.5517 g. **Composition:** 0.9999 Gold .5000 oz. AGW **Obverse:** Bust of Queen Elizabeth II right **Reverse:** Birman cat

Date	Mintage	F	VF	XF	Unc	BU
1998	—	—	—	—	195	—
1998 Proof	1,000	Value: 200				

KM# 856a 1/2 CROWN **Weight:** 15.5517 g. **Composition:** 0.9995 Platinum .5000 oz. APW **Obverse:** Bust of Queen Elizabeth II right **Reverse:** Birman cat

Date	F	VF	XF	Unc	BU
1998	—	—	—	—	—

Note: Reported, not confirmed

KM# 862 1/2 CROWN **Weight:** 15.5517 g. **Composition:** 0.9999 Gold .5000 oz. AGW **Subject:** History of the Cat **Obverse:** Bust of Queen Elizabeth II right **Reverse:** Egyptain Mau cat with earring

Date	Mintage	F	VF	XF	Unc	BU
1998 Proof	Est. 250	Value: 375				

KM# 951 1/2 CROWN **Weight:** 15.5517 g. **Composition:** 0.9999 Gold .5000 oz. AGW **Subject:** Year of the Rabbit **Obverse:** Bust of Queen Elizabeth II right **Reverse:** Two rabbits

Date	Mintage	F	VF	XF	Unc	BU
1999 Proof	Est. 6,000	Value: 345				

KM# A994 1/2 CROWN **Ring Weight:** 9.0000 g. **Ring Composition:** 0.9999 Gold .2893 oz. AGW **Center Composition:** Titanium **Subject:** Millennium **Obverse:** Portrait of Queen Elizabeth II **Reverse:** 24-hour clock with world globe center

Date	Mintage	F	VF	XF	Unc	BU
2000 Proof	10,000	Value: 175				

KM# 964 1/2 CROWN **Weight:** 15.5517 g. **Composition:** 0.9999 Gold .5000 oz. AGW **Subject:** British Blue cat **Obverse:** Bust of Queen Elizabeth II right **Reverse:** Cat cleaning paw

Date	F	VF	XF	Unc	BU
1999	—	—	—	195	—
1999 Proof	—	Value: 200			

KM# 964a 1/2 CROWN **Weight:** 15.5518 g. **Composition:** 0.9995 Platinum .5000 oz. APW **Subject:**

British Blue cat **Obverse:** Bust of Queen Elizabeth II right **Reverse:** Cat cleaning paw

Date	F	VF	XF	Unc	BU
1999 Reported, not confirmed	—	—	—	—	—

KM# 1084 1/2 CROWN **Ring Weight:** 9.0000 g. **Ring Composition:** 0.9990 Gold .2891 oz. AGW **Center Weight:** 2.0000 g. **Center Composition:** 0.9900 Titanium **Subject:** Greenwich Meridian Time Clock **Obverse:** Queen's portrait **Reverse:** Greenwich Meridian Line on map clock face **Edge:** Reeded **Size:** 32.25 mm.

Date	Mintage	F	VF	XF	Unc	BU
2000 Proof	10,000	Value: 200				

KM# 1055 1/2 CROWN **Weight:** 15.5517 g. **Composition:** 0.9999 Gold .5000 oz. AGW **Subject:** Scottish Fold Kitten **Obverse:** Bust of Queen Elizabeth II right **Reverse:** Kitten playing with world **Edge:** Reeded **Size:** 30 mm.

Date		F	VF	XF	Unc	BU
2000		—	—	—	250	—
2000 Proof	—	Value: 350				

KM# 1015 1/2 CROWN **Weight:** 15.5517 g. **Composition:** 0.9999 Gold .5000 oz. AGW **Subject:** Year of the Dragon **Obverse:** Bust of Queen Elizabeth II right **Reverse:** Dragon, Chinese characters

Date	Mintage	F	VF	XF	Unc	BU
2000 Proof	Est. 6,000	Value: 345				

KM# 1061 1/2 CROWN **Weight:** 15.5517 g. **Composition:** 0.9999 Gold .5000 oz. AGW **Subject:** Year of the Snake **Obverse:** Queen's portrait **Reverse:** Snake **Edge:** Reeded **Size:** 30 mm.

Date	Mintage	F	VF	XF	Unc	BU
2001 Proof	6,000	Value: 340				

KM# 1070 1/2 CROWN **Weight:** 15.5517 g. **Composition:** 0.9999 Gold .5000 oz. AGW **Obverse:** Queen's portrait **Reverse:** Two Somali kittens **Edge:** Reeded **Size:** 30 mm.

Date	Mintage	F	VF	XF	Unc	BU
2001	—	—	—	—	250	—
2001 Proof	1,000	Value: 340				

KM# 1071 1/2 CROWN **Weight:** 15.5517 g. **Composition:** 0.9995 Platinum .5000 oz. APW **Obverse:** Queen's portrait **Reverse:** Two Somali kittens **Edge:** Reeded **Size:** 27 mm.

Date	F	VF	XF	Unc	BU
2001	—	—	—	450	—

KM# 1110 1/2 CROWN **Weight:** 15.5510 g. **Composition:** 0.9990 Gold 0.4995 oz. AGW **Subject:** Bengal Cat **Obverse:** Queen Elizabeth's bust right **Reverse:** Cat and kitten **Edge:** Reeded **Size:** 30 mm.

Date	Mintage	VG	F	VF	XF	Unc
2002 Proof	1,000	Value: 340				
2002	—	—	—	—	—	250

KM# 1101 1/2 CROWN **Weight:** 15.5500 g. **Composition:** 0.9999 Gold .4999 oz. AGW **Subject:** Year of the Horse **Obverse:** Queen's portrait **Reverse:** Two horses **Edge:** Reeded **Size:** 30 mm.

Date	Mintage	F	VF	XF	Unc	BU
2002 Proof	6,000	Value: 340				

KM# 1110a 1/2 CROWN **Weight:** 6.2200 g. **Composition:** 0.9990 Platinum 0.1998 oz. APW **Subject:** Bengal Cat **Obverse:** Bust of Queen Elizabeth II right **Reverse:** Cat and kitten **Edge:** Reeded **Size:** 30 mm.

Date	F	VF	XF	Unc	BU
2002	—	—	—	375	—

KM# 1164 1/2 CROWN **Weight:** 15.5510 g. **Composition:** 0.9999 Gold 0.4999 oz. AGW **Subject:** Cat **Obverse:** Queen's portrait **Reverse:** Two Balinese kittens **Edge:** Reeded **Size:** 30 mm.

Date		F	VF	XF	Unc	BU
2003PM		—	—	—	250	—
2003PM Proof	—	Value: 340				

KM# 1164a 1/2 CROWN **Weight:** 15.5510 g. **Composition:** 0.9995 Platinum 0.4997 oz. APW **Subject:** Cat **Obverse:** Queen's portrait **Reverse:** Two Balinese kittens **Edge:** Reeded **Size:** 30 mm.

Date	F	VF	XF	Unc	BU
2003PM	—	—	—	365	—

KM# 1170 1/2 CROWN **Weight:** 15.5500 g. **Composition:** 0.9999 Gold 0.4999 oz. AGW **Subject:** Year of the Goat **Obverse:** Queen's portrait **Reverse:** Three goats **Edge:** Reeded **Size:** 30 mm.

Date		F	VF	XF	Unc	BU
2003PM Proof	—	Value: 340				

KM# 18 CROWN **Composition:** Copper-Nickel **Obverse:** Bust of Queen Elizabeth II right **Reverse:** Manx cat

Date	Mintage	F	VF	XF	Unc	BU
1970	150,000	—	—	—	7.50	—

KM# 18a CROWN **Weight:** 28.2800 g. **Composition:** 0.9250 Silver .8411 oz. ASW **Obverse:** Bust of Queen Elizabeth II right **Reverse:** Manx cat

Date	Mintage	F	VF	XF	Unc	BU
1970 Proof	11,000	Value: 16.50				

KM# 30 CROWN **Composition:** Copper-Nickel **Subject:** Centenary - Birth of Winston Churchill **Obverse:** Bust of Queen Elizabeth II right **Reverse:** Bust of Winston Churchill **Note:** Most of this issue are double die.

Date	Mintage	F	VF	XF	Unc	BU
1974	45,000	—	—	—	2.50	—

KM# 30a CROWN **Weight:** 28.2800 g. **Composition:** 0.9250 Silver .8411 oz. ASW **Obverse:** Bust of Queen Elizabeth II right **Reverse:** Bust of Winston Churchill

Date	Mintage	F	VF	XF	Unc	BU
1974	—	—	—	—	8.00	—
1974 Proof	30,000	Value: 9.50				

KM# 37 CROWN **Composition:** Copper-Nickel **Subject:** Bicentenary of American Independence **Obverse:** Bust of Queen Elizabeth II right **Reverse:** Bust of George Washington left **Note:** Doubled die strike exists.

Date	Mintage	F	VF	XF	Unc	BU
1976	50,000	—	—	—	2.50	—

KM# 37a CROWN **Weight:** 28.2800 g. **Composition:** 0.9250 Silver .8411 oz. ASW **Subject:** Bicentenary of American Independence **Obverse:** Bust of Queen Elizabeth II right **Reverse:** Bust of George Washington left

Date	Mintage	F	VF	XF	Unc	BU
1976	—	—	—	—	8.00	—
1976 Proof	30,000	Value: 10.00				

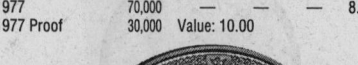

KM# 38 CROWN **Composition:** Copper-Nickel **Obverse:** Bust of Queen Elizabeth II right **Reverse:** Horse-drawn tram **Note:** Doubled die strike exists.

Date	Mintage	F	VF	XF	Unc	BU
1976	50,000	—	—	—	7.50	—

KM# 38a CROWN **Weight:** 28.2800 g. **Composition:** 0.9250 Silver .8411 oz. ASW **Obverse:** Bust of Queen Elizabeth II right **Reverse:** Horse-drawn tram

Date	Mintage	F	VF	XF	Unc	BU
1976	—	—	—	—	12.50	—
1976 Proof	30,000	Value: 15.00				

KM# 41a CROWN **Weight:** 28.2800 g. **Composition:** 0.9250 Silver .8411 oz. ASW **Subject:** Silver Jubilee **Obverse:** Bust of Queen Elizabeth II right **Reverse:** Triskeles at center, three St. Edward's crowns around

Date	Mintage	F	VF	XF	Unc	BU
ND(1977)	—	—	—	—	8.00	—
ND(1977) Proof	30,000	Value: 10.00				

KM# 41 CROWN **Composition:** Copper-Nickel **Subject:** Silver Jubilee **Obverse:** Bust of Queen Elizabeth II right **Reverse:** Triskeles at center, three St. Edward's crowns around

Date	F	VF	XF	Unc	BU
ND(1977)	—	—	—	4.50	—

KM# 42 CROWN **Composition:** Copper-Nickel **Subject:** Queen's Jubilee Appeal **Obverse:** Bust of Queen Elizabeth II right **Reverse:** Crown

Date	F	VF	XF	Unc	BU
1977	—	—	—	2.50	—

Note: Wide and narrow rims exist

KM# 42a CROWN **Weight:** 28.2800 g. **Composition:** 0.9250 Silver .8411 oz. ASW **Subject:** Queen's Jubilee Appeal **Obverse:** Bust of Queen Elizabeth II right **Reverse:** Crown

Date	Mintage	F	VF	XF	Unc	BU
1977	70,000	—	—	—	8.00	—
1977 Proof	30,000	Value: 10.00				

KM# 43 CROWN **Composition:** Copper-Nickel **Subject:** 25th Anniversary of Coronation **Obverse:** Bust of Queen Elizabeth II right **Reverse:** Male and female peregrine falcons

Note: For mule of Isle of Man obverse with Ascension Island KM#1 reverse, refer to Ascension Island listings.

Date		F	VF	XF	Unc	BU
1978		—	—	—	6.50	—
1978 Proof	—	Value: 7.50				

KM# 43a CROWN **Weight:** 28.2800 g. **Composition:** 0.9250 Silver .8411 oz. ASW **Subject:** 25th Anniversary of Coronation **Obverse:** Bust of Queen Elizabeth II right **Reverse:** Male and female peregrine falcons

Date	Mintage	F	VF	XF	Unc	BU
1978	70,000	—	—	—	10.00	—
1978 Proof	30,000	Value: 15.00				

KM# 45 CROWN **Composition:** Copper-Nickel **Subject:** 30th Anniversary of Manx Coinage **Obverse:** Bust of Queen Elizabeth II right **Reverse:** Nine different coins in circle

Date		F	VF	XF	Unc	BU
1979		—	—	—	3.00	—
1979 Proof	—	Value: 7.50				

KM# 45a CROWN **Weight:** 28.2800 g. **Composition:** 0.9250 Silver .8411 oz. ASW **Subject:** 300th Anniversary of Manx Coinage **Obverse:** Bust of Queen Elizabeth II right **Reverse:** Nine coins in circle

Date	Mintage	F	VF	XF	Unc	BU
1979	70,000	—	—	—	10.00	—
1979 Proof	30,000	Value: 12.00				

KM# 46 CROWN **Composition:** Copper-Nickel **Subject:** Millennium of Tynwald **Obverse:** Bust of Queen Elizabeth II right **Reverse:** Viking longship, Godred Cravan

Date	Mintage	F	VF	XF	Unc	BU
1979	100,000	—	—	—	3.50	—

KM# 46a CROWN **Weight:** 28.2800 g. **Composition:** 0.9250 Silver .8411 oz. ASW **Subject:** Millennium of Tynwald **Obverse:** Bust of Queen Elizabeth II right **Reverse:** Viking longship, Godred Cravan

Date	Mintage	F	VF	XF	Unc	BU
1979	25,000	—	—	—	12.00	—
1979 Proof	10,000	Value: 15.00				

KM# 46b CROWN **Weight:** 43.0000 g. **Composition:** 0.9170 Gold 1.2678 oz. AGW **Subject:** Millennium of Tynwald **Obverse:** Bust of Queen Elizabeth II right **Reverse:** Viking longship

Date	Mintage	F	VF	XF	Unc	BU
1979 Proof	300	Value: 700				

KM# 46c CROWN **Weight:** 52.0000 g. **Composition:** 0.9500 Platinum 1.5884 oz. APW **Subject:** Millennium of Tynwald **Obverse:** Bust of Queen Elizabeth II right **Reverse:** Viking longship

Date	Mintage	F	VF	XF	Unc	BU
1979 Proof	100	Value: 1,250				

KM# 47 CROWN **Composition:** Copper-Nickel **Subject:** Millennium of Tynwald **Obverse:** Bust of Queen Elizabeth II right **Reverse:** English cog, Castle Rushen

Date	Mintage	F	VF	XF	Unc	BU
1979	100,000	—	—	—	6.50	—

KM# 47a CROWN **Weight:** 28.2800 g. **Composition:** 0.9250 Silver .8411 oz. ASW **Subject:** Millennium of Tynwald **Obverse:** Bust of Queen Elizabeth II right **Reverse:** Englsih cog, Castle Rushen

Date	Mintage	F	VF	XF	Unc	BU
1979	25,000	—	—	—	9.00	—
1979 Proof	10,000	Value: 12.50				

KM# 47b CROWN **Weight:** 43.0000 g. **Composition:** 0.9170 Gold 1.2678 oz. AGW **Subject:** Millennium of Tynwald **Obverse:** Bust of Queen Elizabeth II right **Reverse:** English cog, Castle Rushen

Date	Mintage	F	VF	XF	Unc	BU
1979 Proof	300	Value: 700				

KM# 47c CROWN **Weight:** 52.0000 g. **Composition:** 0.9500 Platinum 1.5884 oz. APW **Subject:** Millennium of Tynwald **Obverse:** Bust of Queen Elizabeth II right **Reverse:** English cog, Castle Rushen

Date	Mintage	F	VF	XF	Unc	BU
1979 Proof	100	Value: 1,250				

KM# 48 CROWN **Composition:** Copper-Nickel **Subject:** Millennium of Tynwald **Obverse:** Bust of Queen Elizabeth II right **Reverse:** Flemish carrack, St. Michael Island

Date	Mintage	F	VF	XF	Unc	BU
1979	100,000	—	—	—	6.50	—

KM# 48a CROWN **Weight:** 28.2800 g. **Composition:** 0.9250 Silver .8411 oz. ASW **Subject:** Millennium of Tynwald **Obverse:** Bust of Queen Elizabeth II right **Reverse:** Flemish carrack, St. Michael Island

Date	Mintage	F	VF	XF	Unc	BU
1979	25,000	—	—	—	9.00	—
1979 Proof	10,000	Value: 12.50				

KM# 48b CROWN **Weight:** 43.0000 g. **Composition:** 0.9170 Gold 1.2678 oz. AGW **Subject:** Millennium of Tynwald **Obverse:** Bust of Queen Elizabeth II right **Reverse:** Flemish carrack, St. Michael Island

Date	Mintage	F	VF	XF	Unc	BU
1979 Proof	300	Value: 700				

KM# 48c CROWN **Weight:** 52.0000 g. **Composition:** 0.9500 Platinum 1.5884 oz. APW **Subject:** Millennium of Tynwald **Obverse:** Bust of Queen Elizabeth II right **Reverse:** Flemish carrack, St. Michael Island

Date	Mintage	F	VF	XF	Unc	BU
1979 Proof	100	Value: 1,250				

KM# 49 CROWN **Weight:** 28.2800 g. **Composition:** Copper-Nickel **Subject:** Millennium of Tynwald **Obverse:** Bust of Queen Elizabeth II right **Reverse:** Royalist soldier and English Man-of-War

Date	Mintage	F	VF	XF	Unc	BU
1979	100,000	—	—	—	6.50	—

KM# 49a CROWN **Weight:** 28.2800 g. **Composition:** 0.9250 Silver .8411 oz. ASW **Subject:** Millennium of Tynwald **Obverse:** Bust of Queen Elizabeth II right **Reverse:** Royalist soldier and English Man-of-War

Date	Mintage	F	VF	XF	Unc	BU
1979	25,000	—	—	—	9.00	—
1979 Proof	10,000	Value: 12.50				

KM# 49b CROWN **Weight:** 43.0000 g. **Composition:** 0.9170 Gold 1.2678 oz. AGW **Subject:** Millennium of Tynwald **Obverse:** Bust of Queen Elizabeth II right **Reverse:** Royalist soldier and English Man-of-War

Date	Mintage	F	VF	XF	Unc	BU
1979 Proof	300	Value: 700				

KM# 49c CROWN **Weight:** 52.0000 g. **Composition:** 0.9500 Platinum 1.5884 oz. APW **Subject:** Millennium of Tynwald **Obverse:** Bust of Queen Elizabeth II right **Reverse:** Royalist soldier and English Man-of-War

Date	Mintage	F	VF	XF	Unc	BU
1979 Proof	100	Value: 1,250				

KM# 50 CROWN **Weight:** 28.2800 g. **Composition:** Copper-Nickel **Subject:** Millennium of Tynwald **Obverse:** Bust of Queen Elizabeth II right **Reverse:** Lifeboat and Sir William Hillory portrait

Date	Mintage	F	VF	XF	Unc	BU
1979	100,000	—	—	—	6.50	—

KM# 50a CROWN **Weight:** 28.2800 g. **Composition:** 0.9250 Silver .8411 oz. ASW **Subject:** Millennium of Tynwald **Obverse:** Bust of Queen Elizabeth II right **Reverse:** Lifeboat and Sir William Hillory portrait

Date	Mintage	F	VF	XF	Unc	BU
1979	25,000	—	—	—	9.00	—
1979 Proof	10,000	Value: 12.50				

KM# 50b CROWN **Weight:** 43.0000 g. **Composition:** 0.9170 Gold 1.2678 oz. AGW **Subject:** Millennium of Tynwald **Obverse:** Bust of Queen Elizabeth II right **Reverse:** Lifeboat and Sir William Hillory portrait

Date	Mintage	F	VF	XF	Unc	BU
1979 Proof	300	Value: 700				

KM# 50c CROWN **Weight:** 52.0000 g. **Composition:** 0.9500 Platinum 1.5884 oz. APW **Subject:** Millennium of Tynwald **Obverse:** Bust of Queen Elizabeth II right **Reverse:** Lifeboat and Sir William Hillory portrait

Date	Mintage	F	VF	XF	Unc	BU
1979 Proof	100	Value: 1,250				

KM# 63 CROWN **Composition:** Copper-Nickel **Subject:** Derby Bicentennial **Obverse:** Bust of Queen Elizabeth II right **Reverse:** Men racing horses

Date	Mintage	F	VF	XF	Unc	BU
1980	100,000	—	—	—	4.00	—

KM# 63a CROWN **Weight:** 28.2800 g. **Composition:** 0.9250 Silver .8411 oz. ASW **Subject:** Derby Bicentennial **Obverse:** Bust of Queen Elizabeth II right **Reverse:** Men racing horses

Date	Mintage	F	VF	XF	Unc	BU
1980	35,000	—	—	—	8.50	—
1980 Proof	20,000	Value: 12.50				

KM# 63b CROWN **Weight:** 52.0000 g. **Composition:** 0.9500 Platinum 1.5884 oz. APW **Subject:** Derby Bicentennial **Obverse:** Bust of Queen Elizabeth II right **Reverse:** Men racing horses

Date	Mintage	F	VF	XF	Unc	BU
1980 Proof	500	Value: 1,175				

KM# 63c CROWN **Weight:** 43.0000 g. **Composition:** 0.9170 Gold 1.2678 oz. AGW **Subject:** Derby Bicentennial **Obverse:** Bust of Queen Elizabeth II right **Reverse:** Men racing horses

Date		F	VF	XF	Unc	BU
1980 Proof	—	Value: 700				

KM# 64 CROWN **Composition:** Copper-Nickel **Subject:** 1980 Winter Olympics - Lake Placid **Obverse:** Bust of Queen Elizabeth II right **Reverse:** Skater at top, competitors around circle, triskeles within

Date	Mintage	F	VF	XF	Unc	BU
1980	100,000	—	—	—	3.00	—
1980 Proof like	—	—	—	—	7.50	—

KM# 64a CROWN **Weight:** 28.2800 g. **Composition:** 0.9250 Silver .8411 oz. ASW **Subject:** 1980 Winter Olympics - Lake Placid **Obverse:** Bust of Queen Elizabeth II right **Reverse:** Skier at top, competitors around circle, triskeles within

Date	Mintage	F	VF	XF	Unc	BU
1980 Matte	—	—	—	—	16.50	—
1980 Proof	10,000	Value: 17.50				

KM# 64b CROWN **Weight:** 39.8000 g. **Composition:** 0.9170 Gold 1.1735 oz. AGW **Subject:** 1980 Winter Olympics - Lake Placid **Obverse:** Bust of Queen Elizabeth II right **Reverse:** Skier at top, competitors around circle, triskeles within

Date	Mintage	F	VF	XF	Unc	BU
1980	1,500	—	—	—	650	—
1980 Proof	500	Value: 675				

KM# 64c CROWN **Weight:** 52.0000 g. **Composition:** 0.9500 Platinum 1.5884 oz. APW **Subject:** 1980 Winter Olympics - Lake Placid **Obverse:** Bust of Queen Elizabeth II right **Reverse:** Skier at top, competitors around circle, triskeles within

Date	Mintage	F	VF	XF	Unc	BU
1980 Proof	100	Value: 1,250				

KM# 65 CROWN **Composition:** Copper-Nickel **Subject:** 1980 Summer Olympics - Moscow **Obverse:** Bust of Queen Elizabeth II right **Reverse:** Runner at top, competitors around circle, triskeles within

Date	Mintage	F	VF	XF	Unc	BU
1980	30,000	—	—	—	3.00	—
1980 Proof like	—	—	—	—	7.50	—

KM# 65a CROWN **Weight:** 28.2800 g. **Composition:** 0.9250 Silver .8411 oz. ASW **Subject:** 1980 Summer Olympics - Moscow **Obverse:** Bust of Queen Elizabeth II right **Reverse:** Runner at top, competitors around circle, triskeles within

Date	Mintage	F	VF	XF	Unc	BU
1980	—	—	—	—	16.50	—
1980 Proof	10,000	Value: 17.50				

KM# 65b CROWN **Weight:** 39.8000 g. **Composition:** 0.9170 Gold 1.1735 oz. AGW **Subject:** 1980 Summer Olympics - Moscow **Obverse:** Bust of Queen Elizabeth II right **Reverse:** Runner at top, competitors around circle, triskeles within

Date	Mintage	F	VF	XF	Unc	BU
1980	1,500	—	—	—	650	—

KM# 65c CROWN **Weight:** 52.0000 g. **Composition:** 0.9500 Platinum 1.5884 oz. APW **Subject:** 1980 Summer Olympics - Moscow **Obverse:** Bust of Queen Elizabeth II right **Reverse:** Runner at top, competitors around circle, triskeles within

Date	Mintage	F	VF	XF	Unc	BU
1980 Proof	100	Value: 1,250				

KM# 66 CROWN **Composition:** Copper-Nickel **Subject:** 1980 Summer Olympics - Moscow **Obverse:** Bust of Queen Elizabeth II right **Reverse:** Javelin thrower at top, competitors around circle, triskeles within

Date	Mintage	F	VF	XF	Unc	BU
1980	30,000	—	—	—	3.00	—
1980 Proof like	—	—	—	—	7.50	—

KM# 66a CROWN **Weight:** 28.2800 g. **Composition:** 0.9250 Silver .8411 oz. ASW **Subject:** 1980 Summer Olympics - Moscow **Obverse:** Bust of Queen Elizabeth II right **Reverse:** Javelin thrower at top, competitors around circle, triskeles within

Date	Mintage	F	VF	XF	Unc	BU
1980 Matte	—	—	—	—	16.50	—
1980 Proof	10,000	Value: 17.50				

KM# 66b CROWN **Weight:** 39.8000 g. **Composition:** 0.9170 Gold 1.1735 oz. AGW **Subject:** 1980 Summer Olympics - Moscow **Obverse:** Bust of Queen Elizabeth II right **Reverse:** Javelin thrower at top, competitors around circle, triskeles within

Date	Mintage	F	VF	XF	Unc	BU
1980	1,500	—	—	—	650	—

KM# 66c CROWN **Weight:** 52.0000 g. **Composition:** 0.9500 Platinum 1.5884 oz. APW **Subject:** 1980 Summer Olympics - Moscow **Obverse:** Bust of Queen Elizabeth II right **Reverse:** Javelin thrower at top, competitors around circle, triskeles within

Date	Mintage	F	VF	XF	Unc	BU
1980 Proof	100	Value: 1,250				

KM# 67 CROWN **Composition:** Copper-Lead Alloy **Subject:** 1980 Summer Olympics - Moscow **Obverse:** Bust of Queen Elizabeth II right **Reverse:** Judo match at top, competitors around circle, triskeles within

Date	Mintage	F	VF	XF	Unc	BU
1980	30,000	—	—	—	3.00	—
1980 Prooflike	—	—	—	—	7.50	—

KM# 67a CROWN **Weight:** 28.2800 g. **Composition:** 0.9250 Silver .8411 oz. ASW **Subject:** 1980 Summer Olympics - Moscow **Obverse:** Bust of Queen Elizabeth II right **Reverse:** Judo match at top, competitors around circle, triskeles within

Date	Mintage	F	VF	XF	Unc	BU
1980 Matte	—	—	—	—	16.50	—
1980 Proof	10,000	Value: 17.50				

KM# 67b CROWN **Weight:** 39.8000 g. **Composition:** 0.9170 Gold 1.1735 oz. AGW **Subject:** 1980 Summer Olympics - Moscow **Obverse:** Bust of Queen Elizabeth II right **Reverse:** Judo match at top, competitors around circle, triskeles within

Date	Mintage	F	VF	XF	Unc	BU
1980	1,500	—	—	—	650	—

KM# 67c CROWN **Weight:** 52.0000 g. **Composition:** 0.9500 Platinum 1.5884 oz. APW **Subject:** 1980 Summer Olympics - Moscow **Obverse:** Bust of Queen Elizabeth II right **Reverse:** Judo match at top, competitors around circle, triskeles within

Date	Mintage	F	VF	XF	Unc	BU
1980 Proof	100	Value: 1,250				

KM# 68 CROWN **Composition:** Copper-Nickel **Subject:** 80th Birthday of Queen Mother **Obverse:** Bust of Queen Elizabeth II right **Reverse:** Bust of Queen Mother

Date	Mintage	F	VF	XF	Unc	BU
1980	100,000	—	—	—	4.50	—

KM# 68a CROWN **Weight:** 28.2800 g. **Composition:** 0.5000 Silver .4546 oz. ASW **Subject:** 80th Birthday of Queen Mother **Obverse:** Bust of Queen Elizabeth II right **Reverse:** Bust of Queen Mother

Date	Mintage	F	VF	XF	Unc	BU
1980	50,000	—	—	—	10.00	—

KM# 68b CROWN **Weight:** 28.2800 g. **Composition:** 0.9250 Silver .8411 oz. ASW **Subject:** 80th Birthday of Queen Mother **Obverse:** Bust of Queen Elizabeth II right **Reverse:** Bust of Queen Mother

Date	Mintage	F	VF	XF	Unc	BU
1980 Proof	30,000	Value: 15.00				

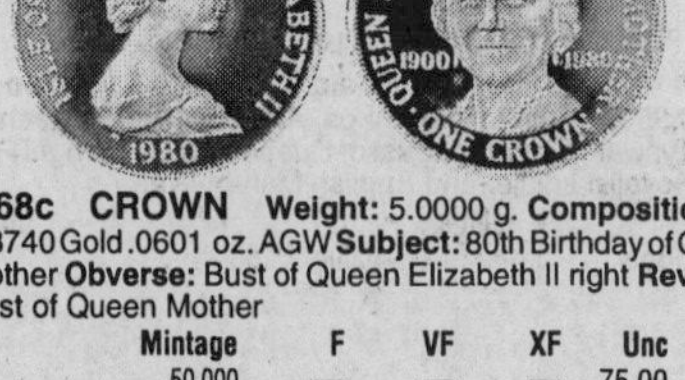

KM# 68c CROWN **Weight:** 5.0000 g. **Composition:** 0.3740 Gold .0601 oz. AGW **Subject:** 80th Birthday of Queen Mother **Obverse:** Bust of Queen Elizabeth II right **Reverse:** Bust of Queen Mother

Date	Mintage	F	VF	XF	Unc	BU
1980	50,000	—	—	—	75.00	—

KM# 68d CROWN **Weight:** 7.9600 g. **Composition:** 0.9170 Gold .2347 oz. AGW **Subject:** 80th Birthday of Queen Mother **Obverse:** Bust of Queen Elizabeth II right **Reverse:** Bust of Queen Mother

Date	Mintage	F	VF	XF	Unc	BU
1980	1,000	—	—	—	150	—

KM# 73 CROWN **Composition:** Copper-Nickel **Subject:** Duke of Edinburgh Award Scheme **Obverse:** Bust of Queen Elizabeth II right **Reverse:** Prince Philip, Duke of Edinburgh bust facing

Date	Mintage	F	VF	XF	Unc	BU
1981	50,000	—	—	—	2.50	—

KM# 73a CROWN **Weight:** 28.2800 g. **Composition:** 0.9250 Silver .8411 oz. ASW **Subject:** Duke of Edinburgh Award Scheme **Obverse:** Bust of Queen Elizabeth II right **Reverse:** Prince Philip, Duke of Edinburgh bust facing

Date	Mintage	F	VF	XF	Unc	BU
1981	20,000	—	—	—	10.00	—
1981 Proof	15,000	Value: 12.50				

KM# 73b CROWN **Weight:** 5.1000 g. **Composition:** 0.3740 Gold 0.613 oz. AGW **Subject:** Duke of Edinburgh Award Scheme **Obverse:** Bust of Queen Elizabeth II right **Reverse:** Prince Philip, Duke of Edinburgh bust facing

Date	Mintage	F	VF	XF	Unc	BU
1981 Proof	10,000	Value: 85.00				

KM# 73c CROWN **Weight:** 7.9600 g. **Composition:** 0.9170 Gold .2347 oz. AGW **Subject:** Duke of Edinburgh Award Scheme **Obverse:** Bust of Queen Elizabeth II right **Reverse:** Prince Philip, Duke of Edinburgh bust facing

Date	Mintage	F	VF	XF	Unc	BU
1981 Proof	1,000	Value: 150				

KM# 73d CROWN **Weight:** 52.0000 g. **Composition:** 0.9500 Platinum 1.5884 oz. APW **Subject:** Duke of Edinburgh Award Scheme **Obverse:** Bust of Queen Elizabeth II right **Reverse:** Prince Philip, Duke of Edinburgh bust facing

Date	Mintage	F	VF	XF	Unc	BU
1981 Proof	100	Value: 1,200				

KM# 74 CROWN **Composition:** Copper-Nickel **Subject:** Duke of Edinburgh Award Scheme **Obverse:** Bust of Queen Elizabeth II right **Reverse:** Monogram within garter

Date	Mintage	F	VF	XF	Unc	BU
1981	50,000	—	—	—	2.50	—

KM# 74a CROWN **Weight:** 28.2800 g. **Composition:** 0.9250 Silver .8411 oz. ASW **Subject:** Duke of Edinburgh Award Scheme **Obverse:** Bust of Queen Elizabeth II right **Reverse:** Monogram within garter

Date	Mintage	F	VF	XF	Unc	BU
1981	20,000	—	—	—	10.00	—
1981 Proof	15,000	Value: 12.00				

KM# 74b CROWN **Weight:** 5.1000 g. **Composition:** 0.3740 Gold .0613 oz. AGW **Subject:** Duke of Edinburgh Award Scheme **Obverse:** Bust of Queen Elizabeth II right **Reverse:** Monogram within garter

Date	Mintage	F	VF	XF	Unc	BU
1981 Proof	10,000	Value: 85.00				

KM# 74c CROWN **Weight:** 7.9600 g. **Composition:** 0.9170 Gold .2347 oz. AGW **Subject:** Duke of Edinburgh Award Scheme **Obverse:** Bust of Queen Elizabeth II right **Reverse:** Monogram within garter

Date	Mintage	F	VF	XF	Unc	BU
1981 Proof	1,000	Value: 150				

KM# 74d CROWN **Weight:** 52.0000 g. **Composition:** 0.9500 Platinum 1.5884 oz. APW **Subject:** Duke of Edinburgh Award Scheme **Obverse:** Bust of Queen Elizabeth II right **Reverse:** Monogram within garter

Date	Mintage	F	VF	XF	Unc	BU
1981 Proof	100	Value: 1,250				

KM# 75 CROWN **Composition:** Copper-Nickel **Subject:** Duke of Edinburgh Award Scheme **Obverse:** Bust of Queen Elizabeth II right **Reverse:** Caring for the bedridden, hiking, swimming

Date	Mintage	F	VF	XF	Unc	BU
1981	50,000	—	—	—	2.50	—

KM# 75a CROWN **Weight:** 28.2800 g. **Composition:** 0.9250 Silver .8411 oz. ASW **Subject:** Duke of Edinburgh Award Scheme **Obverse:** Bust of Queen Elizabeth II right **Reverse:** Caring for the bedridden, hiking, swimming

Date	Mintage	F	VF	XF	Unc	BU
1981	20,000	—	—	—	10.00	—
1981 Proof	15,000	Value: 12.00				

KM# 75b CROWN **Weight:** 5.1000 g. **Composition:** 0.3740 Gold .0613 oz. AGW **Subject:** Duke of Edinburgh Award Scheme **Obverse:** Bust of Queen Elizabeth II right **Reverse:** Caring for the bedridden, hiking, swimming

Date	Mintage	F	VF	XF	Unc	BU
1981 Proof	10,000	Value: 85.00				

KM# 75c CROWN **Weight:** 7.9600 g. **Composition:** 0.9170 Gold .2347 oz. AGW **Subject:** Duke of Edinburgh Award Scheme **Obverse:** Bust of Queen Elizabeth II right **Reverse:** Caring for the bedridden, hiking, swimming

Date	Mintage	F	VF	XF	Unc	BU
1981 Proof	1,000	Value: 150				

KM# 75d CROWN **Weight:** 52.0000 g. **Composition:** 0.9500 Platinum 1.5884 oz. APW **Subject:** Duke of Edinburgh Award Scheme **Obverse:** Bust of Queen Elizabeth II right **Reverse:** Caring for the bedridden, hiking, swimming

Date	Mintage	F	VF	XF	Unc	BU
1981 Proof	100	Value: 1,200				

KM# 76 CROWN **Composition:** Copper-Nickel **Subject:** Duke of Edinburgh Award Scheme **Obverse:** Bust of Queen Elizabeth II right **Reverse:** Rock climbing, sailing, motorcycling

Date	Mintage	F	VF	XF	Unc	BU
1981	50,000	—	—	—	2.50	—

KM# 76a CROWN **Weight:** 28.2800 g. **Composition:** 0.9250 Silver .8411 oz. ASW **Subject:** Duke of Edinburgh Award Scheme **Obverse:** Bust of Queen Elizabeth II right **Reverse:** Rock climbing, sailing, motorcycling

Date	Mintage	F	VF	XF	Unc	BU
1981	20,000	—	—	—	10.00	—
1981 Proof	15,000	Value: 12.00				

KM# 76b CROWN **Weight:** 5.1000 g. **Composition:** 0.3740 Gold .0613 oz. AGW **Subject:** Duke of Edinburgh Award Scheme **Obverse:** Bust of Queen Elizabeth II right **Reverse:** Rock climbing, sailing, motorcycling

Date	Mintage	F	VF	XF	Unc	BU
1981 Proof	10,000	Value: 85.00				

KM# 76c CROWN **Weight:** 7.9600 g. **Composition:** 0.9170 Gold .2347 oz. AGW **Subject:** Duke of Edinburgh Award Scheme **Obverse:** Bust of Queen Elizabeth II right **Reverse:** Rock climbing, sailing, motorcycling

Date	Mintage	F	VF	XF	Unc	BU
1981 Proof	1,000	Value: 150				

KM# 76d CROWN **Weight:** 52.0000 g. **Composition:** 0.9500 Platinum 1.5884 oz. APW **Subject:** Duke of Edinburgh Award Scheme **Obverse:** Bust of Queen Elizabeth II right **Reverse:** Rock climbing, sailing, motorcycling

Date	Mintage	F	VF	XF	Unc	BU
1981 Proof	100	Value: 1,250				

KM# 77 CROWN **Composition:** Copper-Nickel **Subject:** International Year of Disabled **Obverse:** Bust of Queen Elizabeth II right **Reverse:** Braille and bust of Louis Braille

Date	Mintage	F	VF	XF	Unc	BU
1981 Prooflike		—	—	—	5.00	—

KM# 77a CROWN **Weight:** 28.2800 g. **Composition:** 0.9250 Silver .8411 oz. ASW **Subject:** International Year of Disabled **Obverse:** Bust of Queen Elizabeth II right **Reverse:** Braille and bust of Louis Braille

Date	Mintage	F	VF	XF	Unc	BU
1981	20,000	—	—	—	10.00	—
1981 Proof	15,000	Value: 14.00				

KM# 77b CROWN **Weight:** 5.1000 g. **Composition:** 0.3740 Gold .0613 oz. AGW **Subject:** International Year of Disabled **Obverse:** Bust of Queen Elizabeth II right **Reverse:** Braille and bust of Louis Braille

Date	Mintage	F	VF	XF	Unc	BU
1981 Proof	10,000	Value: 100				

KM# 77c CROWN **Weight:** 7.9600 g. **Composition:** 3917.0000 Gold .2347 oz. AGW **Subject:** International Year of Disabled **Obverse:** Bust of Queen Elizabeth II right **Reverse:** Braille and bust of Louis Braille

Date	Mintage	F	VF	XF	Unc	BU
1981 Proof	1,000	Value: 165				

KM# 77d CROWN **Weight:** 52.0000 g. **Composition:** 0.9500 Platinum 1.5884 oz. APW **Subject:** International Year of Disabled **Obverse:** Bust of Queen Elizabeth II right **Reverse:** Braille and bust of Louis Braille

Date	Mintage	F	VF	XF	Unc	BU
1981 Proof	100	Value: 1,250				

KM# 78 CROWN **Composition:** Copper-Nickel **Subject:** International Year of Disabled **Obverse:** Bust of Queen Elizabeth II right **Reverse:** Beethoven, violin and music score

Date	Mintage	F	VF	XF	Unc	BU
1981	50,000	—	—	—	2.50	—
1981 Prooflike	—	—	—	—	—	—

KM# 78a CROWN **Weight:** 28.2800 g. **Composition:** 0.9250 Silver .8411 oz. ASW **Subject:** International Year of Disabled **Obverse:** Bust of Queen Elizabeth II right **Reverse:** Beethoven, violin and music score

Date	Mintage	F	VF	XF	Unc	BU
1981	20,000	—	—	—	12.00	—
1981 Proof	15,000	Value: 16.50				

KM# 78b CROWN **Weight:** 5.1000 g. **Composition:** 0.3740 Gold .0613 oz. AGW **Subject:** International Year of Disabled **Obverse:** Bust of Queen Elizabeth II right **Reverse:** Beethoven, violin and music score

Date	Mintage	F	VF	XF	Unc	BU
1981 Proof	10,000	Value: 100				

KM# 78c CROWN **Weight:** 7.9600 g. **Composition:** 0.9170 Gold .2347 oz. AGW **Subject:** International Year of Disabled **Obverse:** Bust of Queen Elizabeth II right **Reverse:** Beethoven, violin and music score

Date	Mintage	F	VF	XF	Unc	BU
1981 Proof	1,000	Value: 165				

KM# 78d CROWN **Weight:** 52.0000 g. **Composition:** 0.9500 Platinum 1.5884 oz. APW **Subject:** International Year of Disabled **Obverse:** Bust of Queen Elizabeth II right **Reverse:** Beethoven, violin and music score

Date	Mintage	F	VF	XF	Unc	BU
1981 Proof	100	Value: 1,250				

KM# 79 CROWN **Composition:** Copper-Nickel **Subject:** International Year of Disabled **Obverse:** Bust of Queen Elizabeth II right **Reverse:** Sir Douglas Bader

Date	Mintage	F	VF	XF	Unc	BU
1981	50,000	—	—	—	2.50	—
1981 Prooflike	—	—	—	—	5.00	—

KM# 79a CROWN **Weight:** 28.2800 g. **Composition:** 0.9250 Silver .8411 oz. ASW **Subject:** International Year of Disabled **Obverse:** Bust of Queen Elizabeth II right **Reverse:** Sir Douglas Bader

Date	Mintage	F	VF	XF	Unc	BU
1981	20,000	—	—	—	10.00	—
1981 Proof	15,000	Value: 14.00				

KM# 79b CROWN **Weight:** 5.1000 g. **Composition:** 0.3740 Gold 0.613 oz. AGW **Subject:** International Year of Disabled **Obverse:** Bust of Queen Elizabeth II right **Reverse:** Sir Douglas Bader

Date	Mintage	F	VF	XF	Unc	BU
1981 Proof	10,000	Value: 100				

KM# 79c CROWN **Weight:** 7.9600 g. **Composition:** 0.9170 Gold .2347 oz. AGW **Subject:** International Year of Disabled **Obverse:** Bust of Queen Elizabeth II right **Reverse:** Sir Douglas Bader

Date	Mintage	F	VF	XF	Unc	BU
1981 Proof	1,000	Value: 165				

KM# 79d CROWN **Weight:** 52.0000 g. **Composition:** 0.9500 Platinum 1.5884 oz. APW **Subject:** International Year of Disabled **Obverse:** Bust of Queen Elizabeth II right **Reverse:** Sir Douglas Bader

Date	Mintage	F	VF	XF	Unc	BU
1981 Proof	100	Value: 1,250				

KM# 80 CROWN **Composition:** Copper-Nickel **Subject:** International Year of Disabled **Obverse:** Bust of Queen Elizabeth II right **Reverse:** Sir Francis Chichester and sailboat

Date	Mintage	F	VF	XF	Unc	BU
1981	50,000	—	—	—	2.50	—
1981 Proof like	—	—	—	—	5.00	—

KM# 80a CROWN **Weight:** 28.2800 g. **Composition:** 0.9250 Silver .8411 oz. ASW **Subject:** International Year of Disabled **Obverse:** Bust of Queen Elizabeth II right **Reverse:** Sir Francis Chichester and sailboat

Date	Mintage	F	VF	XF	Unc	BU
1981	20,000	—	—	—	14.00	—
1981 Proof	15,000	Value: 20.00				

KM# 80b CROWN **Weight:** 5.1000 g. **Composition:** 0.3740 Gold .0613 oz. AGW **Subject:** International Year of Disabled **Obverse:** Bust of Queen Elizabeth II right **Reverse:** Sir Francis Chichester and sailboat

Date	Mintage	F	VF	XF	Unc	BU
1981 Proof	10,000	Value: 100				

KM# 80c CROWN **Weight:** 7.9600 g. **Composition:** 0.9170 Gold .2347 oz. AGW **Subject:** International Year of Disabled **Obverse:** Bust of Queen Elizabeth II right **Reverse:** Sir Francis Chichester and sailboat

Date	Mintage	F	VF	XF	Unc	BU
1981 Proof	1,000	Value: 165				

KM# 80d CROWN **Weight:** 52.0000 g. **Composition:** 0.9500 Platinum 1.5884 oz. APW **Subject:** International Year of Disabled **Obverse:** Bust of Queen Elizabeth II right **Reverse:** Sir Francis Chichester and sailboat

Date	Mintage	F	VF	XF	Unc	BU
1981 Proof	100	Value: 1,250				

KM# 81 CROWN **Composition:** Copper-Nickel **Subject:** Wedding of Prince Charles and Lady Diana **Obverse:** Bust of Queen Elizabeth II right **Reverse:** Coats of arms

Date	Mintage	F	VF	XF	Unc	BU
1981	50,000	—	—	—	2.25	—

KM# 81a CROWN **Weight:** 28.2800 g. **Composition:** 0.9250 Silver .8411 oz. ASW **Subject:** Wedding of Prince Charles and Lady Diana **Obverse:** Bust of Queen Elizabeth II right **Reverse:** Coats of arms

Date	Mintage	F	VF	XF	Unc	BU
1981	20,000	—	—	—	12.00	—
1981 Proof	15,000	Value: 15.00				

KM# 81b CROWN **Weight:** 5.1000 g. **Composition:** 0.3740 Gold .0613 oz. AGW **Subject:** Wedding of Prince Charles and Lady Diana **Obverse:** Bust of Queen Elizabeth II right **Reverse:** Coats of arms

Date	Mintage	F	VF	XF	Unc	BU
1981 Proof	10,000	Value: 85.00				

KM# 81c CROWN **Weight:** 7.9600 g. **Composition:** 0.9170 Gold .2347 oz. AGW **Subject:** Wedding of Prince Charles and Lady Diana **Obverse:** Bust of Queen Elizabeth II right **Reverse:** Coats of arms

Date	Mintage	F	VF	XF	Unc	BU
1981 Proof	1,000	Value: 150				

KM# 81d CROWN **Weight:** 52.0000 g. **Composition:** 0.9500 Platinum 1.5884 oz. APW **Subject:** Wedding of Prince Charles and Lady Diana **Obverse:** Bust of Queen Elizabeth II right **Reverse:** Coats of arms

Date	Mintage	F	VF	XF	Unc	BU
1981 Proof	100	Value: 1,250				

KM# 82 CROWN **Composition:** Copper-Nickel **Subject:** Wedding of Prince Charles and Lady Diana **Obverse:** Bust of Queen Elizabeth II right **Reverse:** Heads of Prince Charles and Lady Diana

Date	Mintage	F	VF	XF	Unc	BU
1981	50,000	—	—	—	2.25	—

KM# 82a CROWN **Weight:** 28.2800 g. **Composition:** 0.9250 Silver .8411 oz. ASW **Subject:** Wedding of Prince Charles and Lady Diana **Obverse:** Bust of Queen Elizabeth II right **Reverse:** Heads of Prince Charles and Lady Diana

Date	Mintage	F	VF	XF	Unc	BU
1981	20,000	—	—	—	12.00	—
1981	15,000	Value: 15.00				

KM# 82b CROWN Weight: 5.1000 g. **Composition:** 0.3740 Gold .0613 oz. AGW **Subject:** Wedding of Prince Charles and Lady Diana **Obverse:** Bust of Queen Elizabeth II right **Reverse:** Heads of Prince Charles and Lady Diana

Date	Mintage	F	VF	XF	Unc	BU
1981 Proof	10,000	Value: 85.00				

KM# 82c CROWN Weight: 7.9600 g. **Composition:** 0.9170 Gold .2347 oz. AGW **Subject:** Wedding of Prince Charles and Lady Diana **Obverse:** Bust of Queen Elizabeth II right **Reverse:** Heads of Prince Charles and Lady Diana

Date	Mintage	F	VF	XF	Unc	BU
1981 Proof	1,000	Value: 150				

KM# 82d CROWN Weight: 52.0000 g. **Composition:** 0.9500 Platinum 1.5884 oz. APW **Subject:** Wedding of Prince Charles and Lady Diana **Obverse:** Bust of Queen Elizabeth II right **Reverse:** Heads of Prince Charles and Lady Diana

Date	F	VF	XF	Unc	BU
1981 Proof	—	Value: 1,300			

KM# 91 CROWN Composition: Copper-Nickel **Series:** XII World Cup - Spain **Obverse:** Bust of Queen Elizabeth II right **Reverse:** Map, man holding trophy

Date	Mintage	F	VF	XF	Unc	BU
1982	50,000	—	—	—	3.50	—

KM# 91a CROWN Weight: 28.2800 g. **Composition:** 0.9250 Silver .8411 oz. ASW **Series:** XII World Cup - Spain **Obverse:** Bust of Queen Elizabeth II right **Reverse:** Map, man holding trophy

Date	Mintage	F	VF	XF	Unc	BU
1982	20,000	—	—	—	16.50	—
1982 Proof	15,000	Value: 24.00				

KM# 91b CROWN Weight: 5.1000 g. **Composition:** 0.3740 Gold .0613 oz. AGW **Series:** XII World Cup - Spain **Obverse:** Bust of Queen Elizabeth II right **Reverse:** Map, man holding trophy

Date	Mintage	F	VF	XF	Unc	BU
1982 Proof	40,000	Value: 75.00				

KM# 91c CROWN Weight: 7.9600 g. **Composition:** 0.9170 Gold .2347 oz. AGW **Series:** XII World Cup - Spain **Obverse:** Bust of Queen Elizabeth II right **Reverse:** Map, man holding trophy

Date	Mintage	F	VF	XF	Unc	BU
1982 Proof	4,000	Value: 150				

KM# 91d CROWN Weight: 52.0000 g. **Composition:** 0.9500 Platinum 1.5884 oz. APW **Series:** XII World Cup - Spain **Obverse:** Bust of Queen Elizabeth II right **Reverse:** Map, man holding trophy

Date	Mintage	F	VF	XF	Unc	BU
1982 Proof	100	Value: 1,200				

KM# 92 CROWN Composition: Copper-Nickel **Series:** XII World Cup - Spain **Obverse:** Bust of Queen Elizabeth II right **Reverse:** Six country shields

Date	Mintage	F	VF	XF	Unc	BU
1982	50,000	—	—	—	3.50	—

KM# 92a CROWN Weight: 28.2800 g. **Composition:** 0.9250 Silver .8411 oz. ASW **Series:** XII World Cup - Spain **Obverse:** Bust of Queen Elizabeth II right **Reverse:** Six country shields

Date	Mintage	F	VF	XF	Unc	BU
1982	20,000	—	—	—	14.50	—
1982 Proof	15,000	Value: 17.50				

KM# 92b CROWN Weight: 5.1000 g. **Composition:** 0.3740 Gold .0613 oz. AGW **Series:** XII World Cup - Spain **Obverse:** Bust of Queen Elizabeth II right **Reverse:** Six country shields

Date	Mintage	F	VF	XF	Unc	BU
1982 Proof	40,000	Value: 75.00				

KM# 92c CROWN Weight: 7.9600 g. **Composition:** 0.9170 Gold .2347 oz. AGW **Series:** XII World Cup - Spain **Obverse:** Bust of Queen Elizabeth II right **Reverse:** Six country shields

Date	Mintage	F	VF	XF	Unc	BU
1982 Proof	4,000	Value: 150				

KM# 92d CROWN Weight: 52.0000 g. **Composition:** 0.9500 Platinum 1.5884 oz. APW **Series:** XII World Cup - Spain **Obverse:** Bust of Queen Elizabeth II right **Reverse:** Six country shields

Date	Mintage	F	VF	XF	Unc	BU
1982 Proof	100	Value: 1,350				

KM# 93 CROWN Composition: Copper-Nickel **Series:** XII World Cup - Spain **Obverse:** Bust of Queen Elizabeth II right **Reverse:** Three soccer action scenes

Date	Mintage	F	VF	XF	Unc	BU
1982	50,000	—	—	—	3.50	—
1982 (sb)	—	—	—	—	5.00	—

KM# 93a CROWN Weight: 28.2800 g. **Composition:** 0.9250 Silver .8411 oz. ASW **Series:** XII World Cup - Spain **Obverse:** Bust of Queen Elizabeth II right **Reverse:** Three soccer action scenes

Date	Mintage	F	VF	XF	Unc	BU
1982	20,000	—	—	—	14.50	—
1982 Proof	15,000	Value: 20.00				

KM# 93b CROWN Weight: 5.1000 g. **Composition:** 0.3740 Gold .0613 oz. AGW **Series:** XII World Cup - Spain **Obverse:** Bust of Queen Elizabeth II right **Reverse:** Three soccer action scenes

Date	Mintage	F	VF	XF	Unc	BU
1982 Proof	40,000	Value: 75.00				

KM# 93c CROWN Weight: 7.9600 g. **Composition:** 0.9170 Gold .2347 oz. AGW **Series:** XII World Cup - Spain **Obverse:** Bust of Queen Elizabeth II right **Reverse:** Three soccer action scenes

Date	Mintage	F	VF	XF	Unc	BU
1982 Proof	4,000	Value: 150				

KM# 93d CROWN Weight: 52.0000 g. **Composition:** 0.9500 Platinum 1.5884 oz. APW **Series:** XII World Cup - Spain **Obverse:** Bust of Queen Elizabeth II right **Reverse:** Three soccer action scenes

Date	Mintage	F	VF	XF	Unc	BU
1982 Proof	100	Value: 1,200				

KM# 94 CROWN Composition: Copper-Nickel **Series:** XII World Cup - Spain **Obverse:** Bust of Queen Elizabeth II right **Reverse:** Three soccer action scenes

Date	Mintage	F	VF	XF	Unc	BU
1982	50,000	—	—	—	3.50	—

KM# 94a CROWN Weight: 28.2800 g. **Composition:** 0.9250 Silver .8411 oz. ASW **Series:** XII World Cup - Spain **Obverse:** Bust of Queen Elizabeth II right **Reverse:** Three soccer action scenes

Date	Mintage	F	VF	XF	Unc	BU
1982	20,000	—	—	—	14.50	—
1982 Proof	15,000	Value: 20.00				

KM# 94b CROWN Weight: 5.1000 g. **Composition:** 0.3740 Gold .0613 oz. AGW **Series:** XII World Cup - Spain **Obverse:** Bust of Queen Elizabeth II right **Reverse:** Three soccer action scenes

Date	Mintage	F	VF	XF	Unc	BU
1982 Proof	40,000	Value: 75.00				

KM# 94c CROWN Weight: 7.9600 g. **Composition:** 0.9170 Gold .2347 oz. AGW **Series:** XII World Cup - Spain **Obverse:** Bust of Queen Elizabeth II right **Reverse:** Three soccer action scenes

Date	Mintage	F	VF	XF	Unc	BU
1982 Proof	4,000	Value: 150				

KM# 94d CROWN Weight: 52.0000 g. **Composition:** 0.9500 Platinum 1.5884 oz. APW **Series:** XII World Cup - Spain **Obverse:** Bust of Queen Elizabeth II right **Reverse:** Three soccer action scenes

Date	Mintage	F	VF	XF	Unc	BU
1982 Proof	100	Value: 1,200				

KM# 95 CROWN Composition: Copper-Nickel **Series:** XII World Cup - Spain **Obverse:** Bust of Queen Elizabeth II right **Reverse:** Six country shields, with 1982 above Italian shield

Date	F	VF	XF	Unc	BU
1982	—	—	—	3.50	—

KM# 95a CROWN Weight: 28.2800 g. **Composition:** 0.9250 Silver .8411 oz. ASW **Series:** XII World Cup - Spain **Obverse:** Bust of Queen Elizabeth II right **Reverse:** Six country shields, with 1982 above Italian shield

Date	F	VF	XF	Unc	BU
1982	—	Value: 20.00			

KM# 95b CROWN Weight: 5.1000 g. **Composition:** 0.3740 Gold .0613 oz. AGW **Series:** XII World Cup - Spain **Obverse:** Bust of Queen Elizabeth II right **Reverse:** Six country shields, with 1982 above Italian shield

Date	Mintage	F	VF	XF	Unc	BU
1982 Proof	3,000	—	—	—	—	—

KM# 95c CROWN Weight: 7.9600 g. **Composition:** 0.9170 Gold .2347 oz. AGW **Series:** XII World Cup - Spain **Obverse:** Bust of Queen Elizabeth II right **Reverse:** Six country shields, with 1982 above Italian shield

Date	F	VF	XF	Unc	BU
1982 Proof	—	—	—	—	—

KM# 95d CROWN Weight: 52.0000 g. **Composition:** 0.9500 Platinum 1.5884 oz. APW **Series:** XII World Cup - Spain **Obverse:** Bust of Queen Elizabeth II right **Reverse:** Six country shields, with 1982 above Italian shield

Date	F	VF	XF	Unc	BU
1982 Proof	—	—	—	—	—

KM# 96 CROWN Composition: Copper-Nickel **Series:** Maritime Heritage **Obverse:** Bust of Queen Elizabeth II right **Reverse:** "Mayflower" and cameo of Miles Standish

Date	F	VF	XF	Unc	BU
1982	—	—	—	3.00	—
1982 Prooflike	—	—	—	—	—

KM# 96a CROWN Weight: 28.2800 g. **Composition:** 0.9250 Silver .8411 oz. ASW **Series:** Maritime Heritage **Obverse:** Bust of Queen Elizabeth II right **Reverse:** "Mayflower" and cameo of Miles Standish

Date	Mintage	F	VF	XF	Unc	BU
1982	15,000	—	—	—	20.00	—
1982 Proof	10,000	Value: 25.00				

KM# 96b CROWN Weight: 5.1000 g. **Composition:** 0.3740 Gold .0613 oz. AGW **Series:** Maritime Heritage **Obverse:** Bust of Queen Elizabeth II right **Reverse:** "Mayflower" and cameo of Miles Standish

Date	Mintage	F	VF	XF	Unc	BU
1982 Proof	22,000	Value: 75.00				

KM# 96c CROWN Weight: 7.9600 g. **Composition:** 0.9170 Gold .2347 oz. AGW **Series:** Maritime Heritage **Obverse:** Bust of Queen Elizabeth II right **Reverse:** "Mayflower" and cameo of Miles Standish

Date	Mintage	F	VF	XF	Unc	BU
1982 Proof	2,000	Value: 150				

KM# 96d CROWN Weight: 52.0000 g. **Composition:** 0.9500 Platinum 1.5884 oz. APW **Series:** Maritime Heritage **Obverse:** Bust of Queen Elizabeth II right **Reverse:** "Mayflower" and cameo of Miles Standish

Date	Mintage	F	VF	XF	Unc	BU
1982 Proof	50	Value: 1,300				

KM# 97 CROWN Composition: Copper-Nickel **Series:** Maritime Heritage **Obverse:** Bust of Queen Elizabeth II right **Reverse:** "H.M.S. Bounty" and cameo of Fletcher Christian

Date	F	VF	XF	Unc	BU
1982	—	—	—	3.00	—
1982 Prooflike	—	—	—	—	—

KM# 97a CROWN Weight: 28.2800 g. **Composition:** 0.9250 Silver .8411 oz. ASW **Series:** Maritime Heritage **Obverse:** Bust of Queen Elizabeth II right **Reverse:** "H.M.S. Bounty" and cameo of Fletcher Christian

Date	Mintage	F	VF	XF	Unc	BU
1982	15,000	—	—	—	20.00	—
1982 Proof	10,000	Value: 25.00				

KM# 97b CROWN Weight: 5.1000 g. **Composition:** 0.3740 Gold .0613 oz. AGW **Series:** Maritime Heritage **Obverse:** Bust of Queen Elizabeth II right **Reverse:** "H.M.S. Bounty" and cameo of Fletcher Christian

Date	Mintage	F	VF	XF	Unc	BU
1982 Proof	22,000	Value: 75.00				

KM# 97c CROWN Weight: 7.9600 g. **Composition:** 0.9170 Gold .2347 oz. AGW **Series:** Maritime Heritage **Obverse:** Bust of Queen Elizabeth II right **Reverse:** "H.M.S. Bounty" and cameo of Fletcher Christian

Date	Mintage	F	VF	XF	Unc	BU
1982 Proof	2,000	Value: 150				

KM# 97d CROWN Weight: 52.0000 g. **Composition:** 0.9500 Platinum 1.5884 oz. APW **Series:** Maritime Heritage **Obverse:** Bust of Queen Elizabeth II right **Reverse:** "H.M.S. Bounty" and cameo of Fletcher Christian

Date	Mintage	F	VF	XF	Unc	BU
1982 Proof	50	Value: 1,300				

KM# 98 CROWN Composition: Copper-Nickel **Series:** Maritime Heritage **Obverse:** Bust of Queen Elizabeth II right **Reverse:** "H.M.S. Victory" and cameo of John Quilliam

Date	F	VF	XF	Unc	BU
1982	—	—	—	3.00	—
1982 Prooflike	—	—	—	—	—

KM# 98a CROWN Weight: 28.2800 g. **Composition:** 0.9250 Silver .8411 oz. ASW **Series:** Maritime Heritage **Obverse:** Bust of Queen Elizabeth II right **Reverse:** "H.M.S. Victory" and cameo of John Quilliam

Date	Mintage	F	VF	XF	Unc	BU
1982	15,000	—	—	—	20.00	—
1982 Proof	10,000	Value: 25.00				

KM# 98b CROWN Weight: 5.1000 g. **Composition:** 0.3740 Gold .0613 oz. AGW **Series:** Maritime Heritage **Obverse:** Bust of Queen Elizabeth II right **Reverse:** "H.M.S. Victory" and cameo of John Quilliam

Date	Mintage	F	VF	XF	Unc	BU
1982 Proof	22,000	Value: 75.00				

KM# 98c CROWN Weight: 7.9600 g. **Composition:** 0.9170 Gold .2347 oz. AGW **Series:** Maritime Heritage **Obverse:** Bust of Queen Elizabeth II right **Reverse:** "H.M.S. Victory" and cameo of John Quilliam

Date	Mintage	F	VF	XF	Unc	BU
1982 Proof	2,000	Value: 150				

KM# 98d CROWN Weight: 52.0000 g. **Composition:** 0.9500 Platinum 1.5884 oz. APW **Series:** Maritime Heritage **Obverse:** Bust of Queen Elizabeth II right **Reverse:** "H.M.S. Victory" and cameo of John Quilliam

Date	Mintage	F	VF	XF	Unc	BU
1982 Proof	50	Value: 1,300				

KM# 99 CROWN Composition: Copper-Nickel **Series:** Maritime Heritage **Obverse:** Bust of Queen Elizabeth II right **Reverse:** P.S. Mona's "Queen II" and cameo of Capt. William Cain

Date	F	VF	XF	Unc	BU
1982	—	—	—	3.00	—
1982 Prooflike	—	—	—	—	—

KM# 99a CROWN Weight: 28.2800 g. **Composition:** 0.9250 Silver .8411 oz. ASW **Series:** Maritime Heritage **Obverse:** Bust of Queen Elizabeth II right **Reverse:** P.S. Mona's "Queen II" and cameo of Capt. William Cain

Date	Mintage	F	VF	XF	Unc	BU
1982	15,000	—	—	—	20.00	—
1982 Proof	10,000	Value: 25.00				

KM# 99b CROWN Weight: 5.1000 g. **Composition:** 0.3740 Gold .0613 oz. AGW **Series:** Maritime Heritage **Obverse:** Bust of Queen Elizabeth II right **Reverse:** P.S. Mona's "Queen II" and cameo of Capt. William Cain

Date	Mintage	F	VF	XF	Unc	BU
1982 Proof	22,000	Value: 75.00				

KM# 99c CROWN Weight: 7.9600 g. **Composition:** 0.9170 Gold .2347 oz. AGW **Series:** Maritime Heritage **Obverse:** Bust of Queen Elizabeth II right **Reverse:** P.S. Mona's "Queen II" and cameo of Capt. William Cain

Date	Mintage	F	VF	XF	Unc	BU
1982 Proof	2,000	Value: 150				

KM# 99d CROWN Weight: 52.0000 g. **Composition:** 0.9500 Platinum 1.5884 oz. APW **Series:** Maritime Heritage **Obverse:** Bust of Queen Elizabeth II right **Reverse:** P.S. Mona's "Queen II" and cameo of Capt. William Cain

Date	Mintage	F	VF	XF	Unc	BU
1982 Proof	50	Value: 1,300				

KM# 103 CROWN Composition: Copper-Nickel **Series:** Manned Flight **Obverse:** Bust of Queen Elizabeth II right **Reverse:** Hot air balloon

Date	Mintage	F	VF	XF	Unc	BU
1983	50,000	—	—	—	3.75	—
1983 DMIHE	—	—	—	—	15.00	—

KM# 103a CROWN Weight: 28.2800 g. **Composition:** 0.9250 Silver .8411 oz. ASW **Series:** Manned Flight **Obverse:** Bust of Queen Elizabeth II right **Reverse:** Hot air balloon

Date	Mintage	F	VF	XF	Unc	BU
1983	15,000	—	—	—	20.00	—
1983	11,000	Value: 25.00				

KM# 103b CROWN Weight: 5.1000 g. **Composition:** 0.3740 Gold .0613 oz. AGW **Series:** Manned Flight **Obverse:** Bust of Queen Elizabeth II right **Reverse:** Hot air balloon

Date	Mintage	F	VF	XF	Unc	BU
1983 Proof	5,500	Value: 100				

KM# 103c CROWN Weight: 7.9600 g. **Composition:** 0.9170 Gold .2347 oz. AGW **Series:** Manned Flight **Obverse:** Bust of Queen Elizabeth II right **Reverse:** Hot air balloon

Date	Mintage	F	VF	XF	Unc	BU
1983 Proof	500	Value: 175				

KM# 103d CROWN Weight: 52.0000 g. **Composition:** 0.9500 Platinum 1.5884 oz. APW **Series:** Manned Flight **Obverse:** Bust of Queen Elizabeth II right **Reverse:** Hot air balloon

Date	Mintage	F	VF	XF	Unc	BU
1983 Proof	50	Value: 1,275				

KM# 104 CROWN Composition: Copper-Nickel **Series:** Manned Flight **Obverse:** Bust of Queen Elizabeth II right **Reverse:** Biplane

Date	Mintage	F	VF	XF	Unc	BU
1983	50,000	—	—	—	3.75	—
1983 DMIHE	—	—	—	—	15.00	—

KM# 104a CROWN Weight: 28.2800 g. **Composition:** 0.9250 Silver .8411 oz. ASW **Series:** Manned Flight **Obverse:** Bust of Queen Elizabeth II right **Reverse:** Biplane

Date	Mintage	F	VF	XF	Unc	BU
1983	15,000	—	—	—	20.00	—
1983 Proof	11,000	Value: 25.00				

KM# 104b CROWN Weight: 5.1000 g. **Composition:** 0.3740 Gold .0613 oz. AGW **Series:** Manned Flight **Obverse:** Bust of Queen Elizabeth II right **Reverse:** Biplane

Date	Mintage	F	VF	XF	Unc	BU
1983 Proof	5,500	Value: 100				

KM# 104c CROWN Weight: 7.9600 g. **Composition:** 0.9170 Gold .2347 oz. AGW **Series:** Manned Flight **Obverse:** Bust of Queen Elizabeth II right **Reverse:** Biplane

Date	Mintage	F	VF	XF	Unc	BU
1983 Proof	500	Value: 175				

KM# 104d CROWN Weight: 52.0000 g. **Composition:** 0.9500 Platinum 1.5884 oz. APW **Series:** Manned Flight **Obverse:** Bust of Queen Elizabeth II right **Reverse:** Biplane

Date	Mintage	F	VF	XF	Unc	BU
1983 Proof	50	Value: 1,500				

KM# 105 CROWN Composition: Copper-Nickel **Series:** Manned Flight **Obverse:** Bust of Queen Elizabeth II right **Reverse:** Jet

Date	Mintage	F	VF	XF	Unc	BU
1983	50,000	—	—	—	3.75	—
1983 DMIHE	—	—	—	—	15.00	—

KM# 105a CROWN Weight: 28.2800 g. **Composition:** 0.9250 Silver .8411 oz. ASW **Series:** Manned Flight **Obverse:** Bust of Queen Elizabeth II right **Reverse:** Jet

Date	Mintage	F	VF	XF	Unc	BU
1983	15,000	—	—	—	20.00	—
1983 Proof	11,000	Value: 25.00				

KM# 105b CROWN Weight: 5.1000 g. **Composition:** 0.3740 Gold .0613 oz. AGW **Series:** Manned Flight **Obverse:** Bust of Queen Elizabeth II right **Reverse:** Jet

Date	Mintage	F	VF	XF	Unc	BU
1983 Proof	5,500	Value: 100				

KM# 105c CROWN Weight: 7.9600 g. **Composition:** 0.9170 Gold .2347 oz. AGW **Series:** Manned Flight **Obverse:** Bust of Queen Elizabeth II right **Reverse:** Jet

Date	Mintage	F	VF	XF	Unc	BU
1983 Proof	500	Value: 175				

KM# 105d CROWN Weight: 52.0000 g. **Composition:** 0.9500 Platinum 1.5884 oz. APW **Series:** Manned Flight **Obverse:** Bust of Queen Elizabeth II right **Reverse:** Jet

Date	Mintage	F	VF	XF	Unc	BU
1983 Proof	50	Value: 1,500				

KM# 106 CROWN Composition: Copper-Nickel **Series:** Manned Flight **Obverse:** Bust of Queen Elizabeth II right **Reverse:** Space Shuttle

Date	Mintage	F	VF	XF	Unc	BU
1983	50,000	—	—	—	3.75	—
1983 DMIHE	—	—	—	—	15.00	—

KM# 106a CROWN Weight: 28.2800 g. **Composition:** 0.9250 Silver .8411 oz. ASW **Series:** Manned Flight **Obverse:** Bust of Queen Elizabeth II right **Reverse:** Space shuttle

Date	Mintage	F	VF	XF	Unc	BU
1983	15,000	—	—	—	12.00	—
1983 Proof	11,000	Value: 20.00				

KM# 106b CROWN Weight: 5.1000 g. **Composition:** 0.3740 Gold .0613 oz. AGW **Series:** Manned Flight **Obverse:** Bust of Queen Elizabeth II right **Reverse:** Space shuttle

Date	Mintage	F	VF	XF	Unc	BU
1983 Proof	5,500	Value: 100				

KM# 106c CROWN Weight: 7.9600 g. **Composition:** 0.9170 Gold .2347 oz. AGW **Series:** Manned Flight **Obverse:** Bust of Queen Elizabeth II right **Reverse:** Space shuttle

Date	Mintage	F	VF	XF	Unc	BU
1983 Proof	500	Value: 175				

KM# 106d CROWN Weight: 52.0000 g. **Composition:** 0.9500 Platinum 1.5884 oz. APW **Series:** Manned Flight **Obverse:** Bust of Queen Elizabeth II right **Reverse:** Space Shuttle

Date	Mintage	F	VF	XF	Unc	BU
1983 Proof	50	Value: 1,500				

KM# 117 CROWN Composition: Copper-Nickel **Series:** 1984 Olympics - Los Angeles **Obverse:** Bust of Queen Elizabeth II right **Reverse:** Figure skaters Jayne Torvill and Christopher Dean

Date	Mintage	F	VF	XF	Unc	BU
1984	50,000	—	—	—	3.50	—
1984 Proof	—	Value: 8.50				

KM# 117a CROWN Weight: 28.2800 g. **Composition:** 0.9250 Silver .8411 oz. ASW **Series:** 1984 Olympics - Los Angeles **Obverse:** Bust of Queen Elizabeth II right **Reverse:** Figure Skaters Jayne Torvill and Christopher Dean

Date	Mintage	F	VF	XF	Unc	BU
1984 Proof	15,000	Value: 30.00				

KM# 117b CROWN Weight: 5.1000 g. **Composition:** 0.3740 Gold .0613 oz. AGW **Series:** 1984 Olympics - Los Angeles **Obverse:** Bust of Queen Elizabeth II right **Reverse:** Figure skaters Jayne Torvill and Christopher Dean

Date	Mintage	F	VF	XF	Unc	BU
1984 Proof	10,000	Value: 75.00				

KM# 117c CROWN Weight: 7.9600 g. **Composition:** 0.9170 Gold .2347 oz. AGW **Series:** 1984 Olympics - Los Angeles **Obverse:** Bust of Queen Elizabeth II right **Reverse:** Figure skaters Jayne Torvill and Christopher Dean

Date	Mintage	F	VF	XF	Unc	BU
1984 Proof	1,000	Value: 150				

KM# 117d CROWN Weight: 52.0000 g. **Composition:** 0.9500 Platinum 1.5884 oz. APW **Series:** 1984 Olympics - Los Angeles **Obverse:** Bust of Queen Elizabeth II right **Reverse:** Figure skaters Jayne Torvill and Christopher Dean

Date	Mintage	F	VF	XF	Unc	BU
1984 Proof	100	Value: 1,500				

KM# 117e CROWN Composition: Silver Clad Copper-Nickel **Series:** 1984 Olympics - Los Angeles **Obverse:** Bust of Queen Elizabeth II right **Reverse:** Figure skaters Jayne Torvill and Christopher Dean

Date	Mintage	F	VF	XF	Unc	BU
1984	20,000	—	—	—	20.00	—

KM# 118 CROWN Composition: Copper-Nickel **Series:** 1984 Olympics - Los Angeles **Obverse:** Bust of Queen Elizabeth II right **Reverse:** Runners

Date	Mintage	F	VF	XF	Unc	BU
1984	50,000	—	—	—	3.50	—
1984 Proof	—	Value: 8.50				

KM# 118a CROWN Weight: 28.2800 g. **Composition:** 0.9250 Silver .8411 oz. ASW **Series:** 1984 Olympics - Los Angeles **Obverse:** Bust of Queen Elizabeth II right **Reverse:** Runners

Date	Mintage	F	VF	XF	Unc	BU
1984 Proof	15,000	Value: 30.00				

KM# 118b CROWN Weight: 5.1000 g. **Composition:** 0.3740 Gold .0613 oz. AGW **Series:** 1984 Olympics - Los Angeles **Obverse:** Bust of Queen Elizabeth II right **Reverse:** Runners

Date	Mintage	F	VF	XF	Unc	BU
1984 Proof	10,000	Value: 75.00				

KM# 118c CROWN Weight: 7.9600 g. **Composition:** 0.9170 Gold .2347 oz. AGW **Series:** 1984 Olympics - Los Angeles **Obverse:** Bust of Queen Elizabeth II right **Reverse:** Runners

Date	Mintage	F	VF	XF	Unc	BU
1984 Proof	1,000	Value: 150				

KM# 118d CROWN **Weight:** 52.0000 g. **Composition:** 0.9500 Platinum 1.5884 oz. APW **Series:** 1984 Olympics - Los Angeles **Obverse:** Bust of Queen Elizabeth II right **Reverse:** Runners

Date	Mintage	F	VF	XF	Unc	BU
1984 Proof	100	Value: 1,500				

KM# 118e CROWN **Composition:** Silver Clad Copper-Nickel **Series:** 1984 Olympics - Los Angeles **Obverse:** Bust of Queen Elizabeth II right **Reverse:** Runners

Date	Mintage	F	VF	XF	Unc	BU
1984	20,000	—	—	—	20.00	—

KM# 119 CROWN **Composition:** Copper-Nickel **Series:** 1984 Olympics - Los Angeles **Obverse:** Bust of Queen Elizabeth II right **Reverse:** Gymnastics

Date	Mintage	F	VF	XF	Unc	BU
1984	50,000	—	—	—	3.50	—
1984 Proof	—	Value: 8.50				

KM# 119a CROWN **Weight:** 28.2800 g. **Composition:** 0.9250 Silver .8411 oz. ASW **Series:** 1984 Olympics - Los Angeles **Obverse:** Bust of Queen Elizabeth II right **Reverse:** Gymnastics

Date	Mintage	F	VF	XF	Unc	BU
1984 Proof	15,000	Value: 30.00				

KM# 119b CROWN **Weight:** 5.1000 g. **Composition:** 0.3740 Gold .0613 oz. AGW **Series:** 1984 Olympics - Los Angeles **Obverse:** Bust of Queen Elizabeth II right **Reverse:** Gymnastics

Date	Mintage	F	VF	XF	Unc	BU
1984 Proof	10,000	Value: 75.00				

KM# 119c CROWN **Weight:** 7.9600 g. **Composition:** 0.9170 Gold .2347 oz. AGW **Series:** 1984 Olympics - Los Angeles **Obverse:** Bust of Queen Elizabeth II right **Reverse:** Gymnastics

Date	Mintage	F	VF	XF	Unc	BU
1984 Proof	1,000	Value: 150				

KM# 119d CROWN **Weight:** 52.0000 g. **Composition:** 0.9500 Platinum 1.5884 oz. APW **Series:** 1984 Olympics - Los Angeles **Obverse:** Bust of Queen Elizabeth II right **Reverse:** Gymnastics

Date	Mintage	F	VF	XF	Unc	BU
1984 Proof	100	Value: 1,500				

KM# 119e CROWN **Composition:** Silver Clad Copper-Nickel **Series:** 1984 Olympics - Los Angeles **Obverse:** Bust of Queen Elizabeth II right **Reverse:** Gymnastics

Date	Mintage	F	VF	XF	Unc	BU
1984	20,000	—	—	—	20.00	—

KM# 120 CROWN **Composition:** Copper-Nickel **Series:** 1984 Olympics - Los Angeles **Obverse:** Bust of Queen Elizabeth II right **Reverse:** Equestrian

Date	Mintage	F	VF	XF	Unc	BU
1984	50,000	—	—	—	3.50	—
1984 Proof	—	Value: 8.50				

KM# 120a CROWN **Weight:** 28.2800 g. **Composition:** 0.9250 Silver .8411 oz. ASW **Series:** 1984 Olympics - os Angeles **Obverse:** Bust of Queen Elizabeth II right **Reverse:** Equestrian

Date	Mintage	F	VF	XF	Unc	BU
1984 Proof	15,000	Value: 30.00				

KM# 120b CROWN **Weight:** 5.1000 g. **Composition:** 0.3740 Gold .0613 oz. AGW **Series:** 1984 Olympics - Los Angeles **Obverse:** Bust of Queen Elizabeth II right **Reverse:** Equestrian

Date	Mintage	F	VF	XF	Unc	BU
1984 Proof	10,000	Value: 75.00				

KM# 120c CROWN **Weight:** 7.9600 g. **Composition:** 0.9170 Gold .2347 oz. AGW **Series:** 1984 Olympics - Los Angeles **Obverse:** Bust of Queen Elizabeth II right **Reverse:** Equestrian

Date	Mintage	F	VF	XF	Unc	BU
1984 Proof	1,000	Value: 150				

KM# 120d CROWN **Weight:** 52.0000 g. **Composition:** 0.9500 Platinum 1.5884 oz. APW **Series:** 1984 Olympics - Los Angeles **Obverse:** Bust of Queen Elizabeth II right **Reverse:** Equestrian

Date	Mintage	F	VF	XF	Unc	BU
1984 Proof	100	Value: 1,500				

KM# 121 CROWN **Composition:** Copper-Nickel **Subject:** Quincentenary **Obverse:** Bust of Queen Elizabeth II right **Reverse:** The college of arms

Date	F	VF	XF	Unc	BU
1984	—	—	—	2.50	—
1984 Proof like	—	—	—	—	—

KM# 121a CROWN **Weight:** 28.2800 g. **Composition:** 0.9250 Silver .8411 oz. ASW **Subject:** Quincentenary **Obverse:** Bust of Queen Elizabeth II right **Reverse:** The college of arms

Date	F	VF	XF	Unc	BU
1984	—	—	—	12.00	—
1984 Proof	— Value: 18.00				

KM# 121b CROWN **Weight:** 5.1000 g. **Composition:** 0.3740 Gold .0613 oz. AGW **Subject:** Quincentenary **Obverse:** Bust of Queen Elizabeth II right **Reverse:** The college of arms

Date	Mintage	F	VF	XF	Unc	BU
1984 Proof	10,000	Value: 75.00				

KM# 121c CROWN **Weight:** 7.9600 g. **Composition:** 0.9170 Gold .2347 oz. AGW **Subject:** Quincentenary **Obverse:** Bust of Queen Elizabeth II right **Reverse:** The college of arms

Date	Mintage	F	VF	XF	Unc	BU
1984 Proof	1,000	Value: 150				

KM# 121d CROWN **Weight:** 52.0000 g. **Composition:** 0.9500 Platinum 1.5884 oz. APW **Subject:** Quincentenary **Obverse:** Bust of Queen Elizabeth II right **Reverse:** The college of arms

Date	F	VF	XF	Unc	BU
1984 Proof	— Value: 1,200				

KM# 122 CROWN **Composition:** Copper-Nickel **Subject:** Quincentenary **Obverse:** Bust of Queen Elizabeth II right **Reverse:** The college of arms

Date	F	VF	XF	Unc	BU
1984	—	—	—	4.50	—
1984 Prooflike	—	—	—	—	—

KM# 122a CROWN **Weight:** 28.2800 g. **Composition:** 0.9250 Silver .8411 oz. ASW **Subject:** Quincentenary **Obverse:** Bust of Queen Elizabeth II right **Reverse:** The college of arms

Date	F	VF	XF	Unc	BU
1984	—	—	—	12.00	—
1984 Proof	— Value: 18.00				

KM# 122b CROWN **Weight:** 5.1000 g. **Composition:** 0.3740 Gold .0613 oz. AGW **Subject:** Quincentenary **Obverse:** Bust of Queen Elizabeth II right **Reverse:** The college of arms

Date	Mintage	F	VF	XF	Unc	BU
1984 Proof	10,000	Value: 75.00				

KM# 122c CROWN **Weight:** 7.9600 g. **Composition:** 0.9170 Gold .2347 oz. AGW **Subject:** Quincentenary **Obverse:** Bust of Queen Elizabeth II right **Reverse:** The college of arms

Date	Mintage	F	VF	XF	Unc	BU
1984 Proof	1,000	Value: 150				

KM# 122d CROWN **Weight:** 52.0000 g. **Composition:** 0.9500 Platinum 1.5884 oz. APW **Subject:** Quincentenary **Obverse:** Bust of Queen Elizabeth II right **Reverse:** The college of arms

Date	F	VF	XF	Unc	BU
1984 Proof	— Value: 1,200				

KM# 123 CROWN **Composition:** Copper-Nickel **Subject:** Quincentenary **Obverse:** Bust of Queen Elizabeth II right **Reverse:** The college of arms

Date	F	VF	XF	Unc	BU
1984	—	—	—	4.50	—
1984 Prooflike	—	—	—	—	—

KM# 123a CROWN **Weight:** 28.2800 g. **Composition:** 0.9250 Silver .8411 oz. ASW **Subject:** Quincentenary **Obverse:** Bust of Queen Elizabeth II right **Reverse:** The college of arms

Date	F	VF	XF	Unc	BU
1984	—	—	—	12.00	—
1984 Proof	— Value: 18.00				

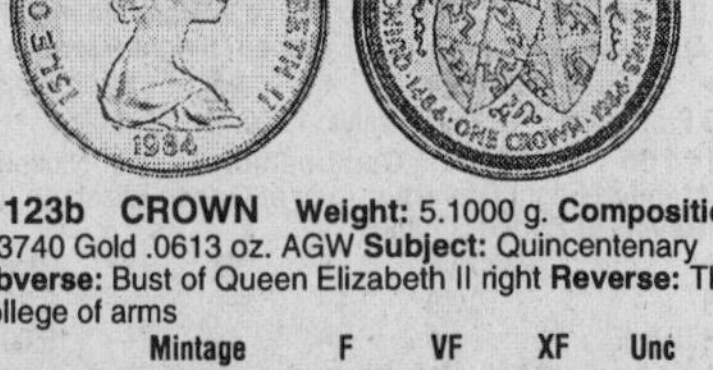

KM# 123b CROWN **Weight:** 5.1000 g. **Composition:** 0.3740 Gold .0613 oz. AGW **Subject:** Quincentenary **Obverse:** Bust of Queen Elizabeth II right **Reverse:** The college of arms

Date	Mintage	F	VF	XF	Unc	BU
1984 Proof	10,000	Value: 75.00				

KM# 123c CROWN **Weight:** 7.9600 g. **Composition:** 0.9170 Gold .2347 oz. AGW **Subject:** Quincentenary **Obverse:** Bust of Queen Elizabeth II right **Reverse:** The college of arms

Date	Mintage	F	VF	XF	Unc	BU
1984 Proof	1,000	Value: 150				

KM# 123d CROWN **Weight:** 52.0000 g. **Composition:** 0.9500 Platinum 1.5884 oz. APW **Subject:** Quincentenary **Obverse:** Bust of Queen Elizabeth II right **Reverse:** The college of arms

Date	F	VF	XF	Unc	BU
1984 Proof	— Value: 1,200				

KM# 124 CROWN **Composition:** Copper-Nickel **Subject:** Quincentenary **Obverse:** Bust of Queen Elizabeth II right **Reverse:** The college of arms

Date	F	VF	XF	Unc	BU
1984	—	—	—	4.50	—
1984 Proof like	—	—	—	—	—

KM# 124a CROWN **Weight:** 28.2800 g. **Composition:** 0.9250 Silver .8411 oz. ASW **Subject:** Quincentenary **Obverse:** Bust of Queen Elizabeth II right **Reverse:** The college of arms

Date	F	VF	XF	Unc	BU
1984	—	—	—	12.00	—
1984 Proof	— Value: 18.00				

KM# 124b CROWN **Weight:** 5.1000 g. **Composition:** 0.3740 Gold .0613 oz. AGW **Subject:** Quincentenary **Obverse:** Bust of Queen Elizabeth II right **Reverse:** The college of arms

Date	Mintage	F	VF	XF	Unc	BU
1984 Proof	10,000	Value: 75.00				

KM# 124c CROWN **Weight:** 7.9600 g. **Composition:** 0.9170 Gold .2347 oz. AGW **Subject:** Quincentenary **Obverse:** Bust of Queen Elizabeth II right **Reverse:** The college of arms

Date	Mintage	F	VF	XF	Unc	BU
1984 Proof	1,000	Value: 150				

KM# 124d CROWN **Weight:** 52.0000 g. **Composition:** 0.9500 Platinum 1.5884 oz. APW **Subject:** Quincentenary **Obverse:** Bust of Queen Elizabeth II right **Reverse:** The college of arms

Date	F	VF	XF	Unc	BU
1984 Proof	— Value: 1,200				

KM# 130 CROWN **Composition:** Copper-Nickel **Subject:** 30th Commonwealth Parliamentary Conference **Obverse:** Bust of Queen Elizabeth II right **Reverse:** Queen Elizabeth II and Prince Philip **Rev. Legend:** Celtic uncial script

Date	F	VF	XF	Unc	BU
1984	—	—	—	3.00	—

KM# 130a CROWN **Weight:** 28.2800 g. **Composition:** 0.9250 Silver .8411 oz. ASW **Subject:** 30th Commonwealth Parliamentary Conference **Obverse:** Bust of Queen Elizabeth II right **Reverse:** Queen Elizabeth II and Prince Philip **Rev. Legend:** Celtic uncial script

Date	F	VF	XF	Unc	BU
1984	—	—	—	15.00	—
1984 Proof	— Value: 20.00				

KM# 130b CROWN **Weight:** 5.1000 g. **Composition:** 0.3740 Gold .0613 oz. AGW **Subject:** 30th Commonwealth Parliamentary Conference **Obverse:** Bust of Queen Elizabeth II right **Reverse:** Queen Elizabeth II and Prince Philip **Rev. Legend:** Celtic uncial script

Date	Mintage	F	VF	XF	Unc	BU
1984 Proof	10,000	Value: 75.00				

KM# 130c CROWN **Weight:** 7.9600 g. **Composition:** 0.9170 Gold .2347 oz. AGW **Subject:** 30th Commonwealth Parliamentary Conference **Obverse:** Bust of Queen Elizabeth II right **Reverse:** Queen Elizabeth II and Prince Philip **Rev. Legend:** Celtic uncial script

Date	Mintage	F	VF	XF	Unc	BU
1984 Proof	1,000	Value: 150				

KM# 130d CROWN **Weight:** 52.0000 g. **Composition:** 0.9500 Platinum 1.5884 oz. APW **Subject:** 30th Commonwealth Parliamentary Conference **Obverse:** Bust of Queen Elizabeth II right **Reverse:** Queen Elizabeth II and Prince Philip **Rev. Legend:** Celtic uncial script

Date	F	VF	XF	Unc	BU
1984 Proof	— Value: 1,200				

KM# 131 CROWN Composition: Copper-Nickel **Subject:** 30th Commonwealth Parliamentary Conference **Obverse:** Bust of Queen Elizabeth II right **Reverse:** Throne, shield and sword

Date	F	VF	XF	Unc	BU
1984	—	—	—	3.00	—

KM# 131a CROWN Weight: 28.2800 g. **Composition:** 0.9250 Silver .8411 oz. ASW **Subject:** 30th Commonwealth Parliamentary Conference **Obverse:** Bust of Queen Elizabeth II right **Reverse:** Throne, sword and shield

Date		F	VF	XF	Unc	BU
1984		—	—	—	15.00	—
1984 Proof	—	Value: 20.00				

KM# 131b CROWN Weight: 5.1000 g. **Composition:** 0.3740 Gold .0613 oz. AGW **Subject:** 30th Commonwealth Parliamentary Conference **Obverse:** Bust of Queen Elizabeth II right **Reverse:** Throne, sword and shield

Date	Mintage	F	VF	XF	Unc	BU
1984 Proof	10,000	Value: 75.00				

KM# 131c CROWN Weight: 7.9600 g. **Composition:** 0.9170 Gold .2347 oz. AGW **Subject:** 30th Commonwealth Parliamentary Conference **Obverse:** Bust of Queen Elizabeth II right **Reverse:** Throne, sword and shield

Date	Mintage	F	VF	XF	Unc	BU
1984 Proof	1,000	Value: 150				

KM# 131d CROWN Weight: 52.0000 g. **Composition:** 0.9500 Platinum 1.5884 oz. APW **Subject:** 30th Commonwealth Parliamentary Conference **Obverse:** Bust of Queen Elizabeth II right **Reverse:** Throne, shield and sword

Date		F	VF	XF	Unc	BU
1984 Proof	—	Value: 1,200				

KM# 132 CROWN Composition: Copper-Nickel **Subject:** 30th Commonwealth Parliamentary Conference **Obverse:** Bust of Queen Elizabeth II right **Reverse:** Princess Anne

Date	F	VF	XF	Unc	BU
1984	—	—	—	3.00	—

KM# 132a CROWN Weight: 28.2800 g. **Composition:** 0.9250 Silver .8411 oz. ASW **Subject:** 30th Commonwealth Parliamentary Conference **Obverse:** Bust of Queen Elizabeth II right **Reverse:** Princess Anne

Date		F	VF	XF	Unc	BU
1984		—	—	—	15.00	—
1984 Proof	—	Value: 20.00				

KM# 132b CROWN Weight: 5.1000 g. **Composition:** 0.3740 Gold .0613 oz. AGW **Subject:** 30th Commonwealth Parliamentary Conference **Obverse:** Bust of Queen Elizabeth II right **Reverse:** Princess Anne

Date	Mintage	F	VF	XF	Unc	BU
1984 Proof	10,000	Value: 75.00				

KM# 132c CROWN Weight: 7.9600 g. **Composition:** 0.9170 Gold .2347 oz. AGW **Subject:** 30th Commonwealth Parliamentary Conference **Obverse:** Bust of Queen Elizabeth II right **Reverse:** Princess Anne

Date	Mintage	F	VF	XF	Unc	BU
1984 Proof	1,000	Value: 150				

KM# 132d CROWN Weight: 52.0000 g. **Composition:** 0.9500 Platinum 1.5884 oz. APW **Subject:** 30th Commonwealth Parliamentary Conference **Obverse:** Bust of Queen Elizabeth II right **Reverse:** Princess Anne

Date		F	VF	XF	Unc	BU
1984 Proof	—	Value: 1,200				

KM# 133 CROWN Composition: Copper-Nickel **Subject:** 30th Commonwealth Parliamentary Conference **Obverse:** Bust of Queen Elizabeth II right **Reverse:** Conference tent

Date	F	VF	XF	Unc	BU
1984	—	—	—	3.00	—

KM# 133a CROWN Weight: 28.2800 g. **Composition:** 0.9250 Silver .8411 oz. ASW **Subject:** 30th Commonwealth Parliamentary Conference **Obverse:** Bust of Queen Elizabeth II right **Reverse:** Conference tent

Date		F	VF	XF	Unc	BU
1984		—	—	—	15.00	—
1984 Proof	—	Value: 20.00				

KM# 133b CROWN Weight: 5.1000 g. **Composition:** 0.3740 Gold .0613 oz. AGW **Subject:** 30th Commonwealth Parliamentary Conference **Obverse:** Bust of Queen Elizabeth II right **Reverse:** Conference tent

Date	Mintage	F	VF	XF	Unc	BU
1984 Proof	10,000	Value: 75.00				

KM# 133c CROWN Weight: 7.9600 g. **Composition:** 0.9170 Gold .2347 oz. AGW **Subject:** 30th Commonwealth Parliamentary Conference **Obverse:** Bust of Queen Elizabeth II right **Reverse:** Conference tent

Date	Mintage	F	VF	XF	Unc	BU
1984 Proof	1,000	Value: 150				

KM# 133d CROWN Weight: 52.0000 g. **Composition:** 0.9500 Platinum 1.5884 oz. APW **Subject:** 30th Commonwealth Parliamentary Conference **Obverse:** Bust of Queen Elizabeth II right **Reverse:** Conference tent

Date		F	VF	XF	Unc	BU
1984 Proof	—	Value: 1,200				

KM# 216 CROWN Composition: Copper-Nickel **Obverse:** Bust of Queen Elizabeth II right **Reverse:** Queen Mother as a young girl

Date	F	VF	XF	Unc	BU
1985	—	—	—	2.50	—

KM# 216a CROWN Composition: Silver Clad Copper-Nickel **Obverse:** Bust of Queen Elizabeth II right **Reverse:** Queen Mother as a young girl

Date	Mintage	F	VF	XF	Unc	BU
1985 Proof	Est. 20,000	Value: 10.00				

KM# 216b CROWN Weight: 28.2800 g. **Composition:** 0.9250 Silver .8411 oz. ASW **Obverse:** Bust of Queen Elizabeth II right **Reverse:** Queen Mother as a young girl

Date	Mintage	F	VF	XF	Unc	BU
1985 Proof	Est. 15,000	Value: 25.00				

KM# 216c CROWN Weight: 5.1000 g. **Composition:** 0.3740 Gold .0613 oz. AGW **Obverse:** Bust of Queen Elizabeth II right **Reverse:** Queen Mother as a young girl

Date	Mintage	F	VF	XF	Unc	BU
1985 Proof	Est. 10,000	Value: 75.00				

KM# 216d CROWN Weight: 7.9600 g. **Composition:** 0.9170 Gold .2347 oz. AGW **Obverse:** Bust of Queen Elizabeth II right **Reverse:** Queen Mother as a young girl

Date	Mintage	F	VF	XF	Unc	BU
1985 Proof	Est. 1,000,000	Value: 150				

KM# 216e CROWN Weight: 52.0000 g. **Composition:** 0.9500 Platinum 1.5884 oz. APW **Obverse:** Bust of Queen Elizabeth II right **Reverse:** Queen Mother as a young girl

Date	Mintage	F	VF	XF	Unc	BU
1985 Proof	Est. 100	Value: 1,200				

KM# 217 CROWN Composition: Copper-Nickel **Obverse:** Bust of Queen Elizabeth II right **Reverse:** Portrait of King George VI and Elizabeth

Date	F	VF	XF	Unc	BU
1985	—	—	—	2.50	—

KM# 217a CROWN Composition: Silver Clad Copper-Nickel **Obverse:** Bust of Queen Elizabeth II right **Reverse:** Portrait of King George VI and Elizabeth

Date	Mintage	F	VF	XF	Unc	BU
1985 Proof	Est. 20,000	Value: 10.00				

KM# 217b CROWN Weight: 28.2800 g. **Composition:** 0.9250 Silver .8411 oz. ASW **Obverse:** Bust of Queen Elizabeth II right **Reverse:** Portrait of King George VI and Elizabeth

Date	Mintage	F	VF	XF	Unc	BU
1985 Proof	Est. 15,000	Value: 25.00				

KM# 217c CROWN Weight: 5.1000 g. **Composition:** 0.3740 Gold .0613 oz. AGW **Obverse:** Bust of Queen Elizabeth II right **Reverse:** Portrait of King George VI and Elizabeth

Date	Mintage	F	VF	XF	Unc	BU
1985 Proof	Est. 10,000	Value: 75.00				

KM# 217d CROWN Weight: 7.9600 g. **Composition:** 0.9170 Gold .2347 oz. AGW **Obverse:** Bust of Queen Elizabeth II right **Reverse:** Portrait of King George VI and Elizabeth

Date	Mintage	F	VF	XF	Unc	BU
1985 Proof	Est. 1,000	Value: 150				

KM# 217e CROWN Weight: 52.0000 g. **Composition:** 0.9500 Platinum 1.5884 oz. APW **Obverse:** Bust of Queen Elizabeth II right **Reverse:** Portrait of King George VI and Elizabeth

Date	Mintage	F	VF	XF	Unc	BU
1985 Proof	Est. 100	Value: 1,200				

KM# 218 CROWN Composition: Copper-Nickel **Obverse:** Bust of Queen Elizabeth II right **Reverse:** Wedding portrait of King George VI and Elizabeth

Date	F	VF	XF	Unc	BU
1985	—	—	—	2.50	—

KM# 218a CROWN Composition: Silver Clad Copper-Nickel **Obverse:** Bust of Queen Elizabeth II right **Reverse:** Wedding portrait of King George VI and Elizabeth

Date	Mintage	F	VF	XF	Unc	BU
1985 Proof	Est. 20,000	Value: 10.00				

KM# 218b CROWN Weight: 28.2800 g. **Composition:** 0.9250 Silver .8411 oz. ASW **Obverse:** Bust of Queen Elizabeth II right **Reverse:** Wedding portrait of King George VI and Elizabeth

Date	Mintage	F	VF	XF	Unc	BU
1985 Proof	Est. 15,000	Value: 25.00				

KM# 218c CROWN Weight: 5.1000 g. **Composition:** 0.3740 Gold .0613 oz. AGW **Obverse:** Bust of Queen Elizabeth II right **Reverse:** Wedding portrait of King George VI and Elizabeth

Date	Mintage	F	VF	XF	Unc	BU
1985 Proof	Est. 10,000	Value: 75.00				

KM# 218d CROWN Weight: 7.9600 g. **Composition:** 0.9170 Gold .2347 oz. AGW **Obverse:** Bust of Queen Elizabeth II right **Reverse:** Wedding portrait of King George VI and Elizabeth

Date	Mintage	F	VF	XF	Unc	BU
1985 Proof	Est. 1,000	Value: 150				

KM# 218e CROWN Weight: 52.0000 g. **Composition:** 0.9500 Platinum 1.5884 oz. APW **Obverse:** Bust of Queen Elizabeth II right **Reverse:** Wedding portrait of King George VI and Elizabeth

Date	Mintage	F	VF	XF	Unc	BU
1985 Proof	Est. 100	Value: 1,200				

KM# 219 CROWN Composition: Copper-Nickel **Obverse:** Bust of Queen Elizabeth II right **Reverse:** Queen Mother and Princess Elizabeth

Date	F	VF	XF	Unc	BU
1985	—	—	—	2.50	—

KM# 219a CROWN Composition: Silver Clad Copper-Nickel **Obverse:** Bust of Queen Elizabeth II right **Reverse:** Queen Mother and Princess Elizabeth

Date	Mintage	F	VF	XF	Unc	BU
1985 Proof	Est. 20,000	Value: 10.00				

KM# 219b CROWN Weight: 28.2800 g. **Composition:** 0.9250 Silver .8411 oz. ASW **Obverse:** Bust of Queen Elizabeth II right **Reverse:** Queen Mother and Princess Elizabeth

Date	Mintage	F	VF	XF	Unc	BU
1985 Proof	Est. 15,000	Value: 25.00				

KM# 219c CROWN **Weight:** 5.1000 g. **Composition:** 0.3740 Gold .0613 oz. AGW **Obverse:** Bust of Queen Elizabeth II right **Reverse:** Queen Mother and Princess Elizabeth

Date	Mintage	F	VF	XF	Unc	BU
1985 Proof	Est. 10,000	Value: 75.00				

KM# 219d CROWN **Weight:** 7.9600 g. **Composition:** 0.9170 Gold .2347 oz. AGW **Obverse:** Bust of Queen Elizabeth II right **Reverse:** Queen Mother and Princess Elizabeth

Date	Mintage	F	VF	XF	Unc	BU
1985 Proof	Est. 1,000	Value: 150				

KM# 219e CROWN **Weight:** 52.0000 g. **Composition:** 0.9500 Platinum 1.5884 oz. APW **Obverse:** Bust of Queen Elizabeth II right **Reverse:** Queen Mother and Princess Elizabeth

Date	Mintage	F	VF	XF	Unc	BU
1985 Proof	Est. 100	Value: 1,200				

KM# 220 CROWN **Composition:** Copper-Nickel **Obverse:** Bust of Queen Elizabeth II right **Reverse:** Queen Mother and Princesses Elizabeth and Margaret

Date	F	VF	XF	Unc	BU
1985	—	—	—	2.50	—
1990	—	—	—	2.50	—

KM# 220a CROWN **Composition:** Silver Clad Copper-Nickel **Obverse:** Bust of Queen Elizabeth II right **Reverse:** Queen Mother and Princesses Elizabeth and Margaret

Date	Mintage	F	VF	XF	Unc	BU
1985 Proof	Est. 20,000	Value: 10.00				

KM# 220b CROWN **Weight:** 28.2800 g. **Composition:** 0.9250 Silver .8411 oz. ASW **Obverse:** Bust of Queen Elizabeth II right **Reverse:** Queen Mother and Princesses Elizabeth and Margaret

Date	Mintage	F	VF	XF	Unc	BU
1985 Proof	Est. 15,000	Value: 25.00				
1990 Proof	—	Value: 28.00				

KM# 220c CROWN **Weight:** 5.1000 g. **Composition:** 0.3740 Gold .0613 oz. AGW **Obverse:** Bust of Queen Elizabeth II right **Reverse:** Queen Mother and Princesses Elizabeth and Margaret

Date	Mintage	F	VF	XF	Unc	BU
1985 Proof	Est. 10,000	Value: 75.00				

KM# 220d CROWN **Weight:** 7.9600 g. **Composition:** 0.9170 Gold .2347 oz. AGW **Obverse:** Bust of Queen Elizabeth II right **Reverse:** Queen Mother and Princess Elizabeth and Margaret

Date	Mintage	F	VF	XF	Unc	BU
1985 Proof	Est. 1,000	Value: 150				

KM# 220e CROWN **Weight:** 52.0000 g. **Composition:** 0.9500 Platinum 1.5884 oz. APW **Obverse:** Bust of Queen Elizabeth II right **Reverse:** Queen Mother and Princess Elizabeth and Margaret

Date	Mintage	F	VF	XF	Unc	BU
1985 Proof	Est. 100	Value: 1,200				

KM# 221 CROWN **Composition:** Copper-Nickel **Subject:** 85th Birthday of Queen Mother **Obverse:** Bust of Queen Elizabeth II right **Reverse:** Queen Mother

Date	F	VF	XF	Unc	BU
1985	—	—	—	2.50	—

KM# 221a CROWN **Composition:** Silver Clad Copper-Nickel **Subject:** 85th Birthday of Queen Mother **Obverse:** Bust of Queen Elizabeth II right **Reverse:** Queen Mother

Date	Mintage	F	VF	XF	Unc	BU
1985 Proof	Est. 20,000	Value: 10.00				

KM# 221b CROWN **Weight:** 28.2800 g. **Composition:** 0.9250 Silver .8411 oz. ASW **Subject:** 85th Birthday of Queen Mother **Obverse:** Bust of Queen Elizabeth II right **Reverse:** Queen Mother

Date	Mintage	F	VF	XF	Unc	BU
1985 Proof	Est. 15,000	Value: 25.00				

KM# 221c CROWN **Weight:** 5.1000 g. **Composition:** 0.3740 Gold .0613 oz. AGW **Subject:** 85th Birthday of Queen Mother **Obverse:** Bust of Queen Elizabeth II right **Reverse:** Queen Mother

Date	Mintage	F	VF	XF	Unc	BU
1985 Proof	Est. 10,000	Value: 75.00				

KM# 221d CROWN **Weight:** 7.9600 g. **Composition:** 0.9170 Gold .2347 oz. AGW **Subject:** 85th Birthday of Queen Mother **Obverse:** Bust of Queen Elizabeth II right **Reverse:** Queen Mother

Date	Mintage	F	VF	XF	Unc	BU
1985 Proof	Est. 1,000,000	Value: 150				

KM# 221e CROWN **Weight:** 52.0000 g. **Composition:** 0.9500 Platinum 1.5884 oz. APW **Subject:** 85th Birthday of Queen Mother **Obverse:** Bust of Queen Elizabeth II right **Reverse:** Queen Mother

Date	Mintage	F	VF	XF	Unc	BU
1985 Proof	Est. 100	Value: 1,200				

KM# 160 CROWN **Composition:** Copper-Nickel **Series:** World Cup Soccer - Mexico **Obverse:** Bust of Queen Elizabeth II right **Reverse:** Map and two players

Date	F	VF	XF	Unc	BU
1986	—	—	—	2.50	—

KM# 160a CROWN **Composition:** Silver Clad Copper-Nickel **Series:** World Cup Soccer - Mexico **Obverse:** Bust of Queen Elizabeth II right **Reverse:** Map and two players

Date	Mintage	F	VF	XF	Unc	BU
1986 Proof	Est. 20,000	Value: 10.00				

KM# 161 CROWN **Composition:** Copper-Nickel **Series:** World Cup Soccer - Mexico **Obverse:** Bust of Queen Elizabeth II right **Reverse:** Three players

Date	F	VF	XF	Unc	BU
1986	—	—	—	2.50	—

KM# 160b CROWN **Weight:** 28.2800 g. **Composition:** 0.9250 Silver .8411 oz. ASW **Series:** World Cup Soccer - Mexico **Obverse:** Bust of Queen Elizabeth II right **Reverse:** Map and two players

Date	Mintage	F	VF	XF	Unc	BU
1986 Proof	Est. 15,000	Value: 17.50				

KM# 161a CROWN **Composition:** Silver Clad Copper-Nickel **Series:** World Cup Soccer - Mexico **Obverse:** Bust of Queen Elizabeth II right **Reverse:** Three players

Date	Mintage	F	VF	XF	Unc	BU
1986 Proof	Est. 20,000	Value: 10.00				

KM# 160c CROWN **Weight:** 5.1000 g. **Composition:** 0.3740 Gold .0613 oz. AGW **Series:** World Cup Soccer - Mexico **Obverse:** Bust of Queen Elizabeth II right **Reverse:** Map and two players

Date	Mintage	F	VF	XF	Unc	BU
1986 Proof	Est. 10,000	Value: 75.00				

KM# 160d CROWN **Weight:** 7.9600 g. **Composition:** 0.9170 Gold .2347 oz. AGW **Series:** World Cup Soccer - Mexico **Obverse:** Bust of Queen Elizabeth II right **Reverse:** Map and two players

Date	Mintage	F	VF	XF	Unc	BU
1986 Proof	Est. 1,000	Value: 150				

KM# 161b CROWN **Weight:** 28.2800 g. **Composition:** 0.9250 Silver .8411 oz. ASW **Series:** World Cup Soccer - Mexico **Obverse:** Bust of Queen Elizabeth II right **Reverse:** Three players

Date	Mintage	F	VF	XF	Unc	BU
1986 Proof	Est. 15,000	Value: 17.50				

KM# 160e CROWN **Weight:** 52.0000 g. **Composition:** 0.9500 Platinum 1.5884 oz. APW **Series:** World Cup Soccer - Mexico **Obverse:** Bust of Queen Elizabeth II right **Reverse:** Map and two players

Date	Mintage	F	VF	XF	Unc	BU
1986 Proof	Est. 200	Value: 1,200				

KM# 161c CROWN **Weight:** 5.1000 g. **Composition:** 0.3740 Gold .0613 oz. AGW **Series:** World Cup Soccer - Mexico **Obverse:** Bust of Queen Elizabeth II right **Reverse:** Three players

Date	Mintage	F	VF	XF	Unc	BU
1986 Proof	Est. 10,000	Value: 75.00				

KM# 161d CROWN **Weight:** 7.9600 g. **Composition:** 0.9170 Gold .2347 oz. AGW **Series:** World Cup Soccer - Mexico **Obverse:** Bust of Queen Elizabeth II right **Reverse:** Three players

Date	Mintage	F	VF	XF	Unc	BU
1986 Proof	Est. 1,000	Value: 150				

KM# 161e CROWN **Weight:** 52.0000 g. **Composition:** 0.9500 Platinum 1.5884 oz. APW **Series:** World Cup Soccer - Mexico **Obverse:** Bust of Queen Elizabeth II right **Reverse:** Three players

Date	Mintage	F	VF	XF	Unc	BU
1986 Proof	Est. 200	Value: 1,200				

KM# 162 CROWN **Composition:** Copper-Nickel **Series:** World Cup Soccer - Mexico **Obverse:** Bust of Queen Elizabeth II right **Reverse:** Two players

Date	F	VF	XF	Unc	BU
1986	—	—	—	2.50	—

KM# 162a CROWN **Composition:** Silver Clad Copper-Nickel **Series:** World Cup Soccer - Mexico **Obverse:** Bust of Queen Elizabeth II right **Reverse:** Two players

Date	Mintage	F	VF	XF	Unc	BU
1986 Proof	Est. 20,000	Value: 10.00				

KM# 162b CROWN **Weight:** 28.2800 g. **Composition:** 0.9250 Silver .8411 oz. ASW **Series:** World Cup Soccer - Mexico **Obverse:** Bust of Queen Elizabeth II right **Reverse:** Two players

Date	Mintage	F	VF	XF	Unc	BU
1986 Proof	Est. 15,000	Value: 17.50				

KM# 162c CROWN **Weight:** 5.1000 g. **Composition:** 0.3740 Gold .0613 oz. AGW **Series:** World Cup Soccer - Mexico **Obverse:** Bust of Queen Elizabeth II right **Reverse:** Two players

Date	Mintage	F	VF	XF	Unc	BU
1986 Proof	Est. 10,000	Value: 75.00				

KM# 162d CROWN **Weight:** 7.9600 g. **Composition:** 0.9170 Gold .2347 oz. AGW **Series:** World Cup Soccer - Mexico **Obverse:** Bust of Queen Elizabeth II right **Reverse:** Two players

Date	Mintage	F	VF	XF	Unc	BU
1986 Proof	Est. 1,000	Value: 150				

KM# 162e CROWN **Weight:** 52.0000 g. **Composition:** 0.9500 Platinum 1.5884 oz. APW **Series:** World Cup Soccer - Mexico **Obverse:** Bust of Queen Elizabeth II right **Reverse:** Two players

Date	Mintage	F	VF	XF	Unc	BU
1986 Proof	Est. 200	Value: 1,200				

KM# 163 CROWN **Composition:** Copper-Nickel **Series:** World Cup Soccer - Mexico **Obverse:** Bust of Queen Elizabeth II right **Reverse:** Net and two players

Date	F	VF	XF	Unc	BU
1986	—	—	—	2.50	—

KM# 163a CROWN **Composition:** Silver Clad Copper-Nickel **Series:** World Cup Soccer - Mexico **Obverse:** Bust of Queen Elizabeth II right **Reverse:** Net and two players

Date	Mintage	F	VF	XF	Unc	BU
1986 Proof	Est. 20,000	Value: 10.00				

KM# 163b CROWN **Weight:** 28.2800 g. **Composition:** 0.9250 Silver .8411 oz. ASW **Series:** World Cup Soccer - Mexico **Obverse:** Bust of Queen Elizabeth II right **Reverse:** Net and two players

Date	Mintage	F	VF	XF	Unc	BU
1986 Proof	Est. 15,000	Value: 17.50				

KM# 163c CROWN **Weight:** 5.1000 g. **Composition:** 0.3740 Gold .0613 oz. AGW **Series:** World Cup Soccer - Mexico **Obverse:** Bust of Queen Elizabeth II right **Reverse:** Net and two players

Date	Mintage	F	VF	XF	Unc	BU
1986 Proof	Est. 10,000	Value: 75.00				

KM# 163d CROWN **Weight:** 7.9600 g. **Composition:** 0.9170 Gold .2347 oz. AGW **Series:** World Cup Soccer - Mexico **Obverse:** Bust of Queen Elizabeth II right **Reverse:** Net and two players

Date	Mintage	F	VF	XF	Unc	BU
1986 Proof	Est. 1,000	Value: 150				

KM# 163e CROWN **Weight:** 52.0000 g. **Composition:** 0.9500 Platinum 1.5884 oz. APW **Series:** World Cup Soccer - Mexico **Obverse:** Bust of Queen Elizabeth II right **Reverse:** Net and two players

Date	Mintage	F	VF	XF	Unc	BU
1986 Proof	Est. 200	Value: 1,200				

KM# 164 CROWN **Composition:** Copper-Nickel **Series:** World Cup Soccer - Mexico **Obverse:** Bust of Queen Elizabeth II right **Reverse:** Globe

Date	F	VF	XF	Unc	BU
1986	—	—	—	2.50	—

KM# 164a CROWN Composition: Silver Clad Copper-Nickel **Series:** World Cup Soccer - Mexico **Obverse:** Bust of Queen Elizabeth II right **Reverse:** Globe

Date	Mintage	F	VF	XF	Unc	BU
1986	Est. 20,000	Value: 10.00				
1989	—	—	—	—	80.00	—

KM# 164b CROWN Weight: 28.2800 g. **Composition:** 0.9250 Silver .8411 oz. ASW **Series:** World Cup Soccer - Mexico **Obverse:** Bust of Queen Elizabeth II right **Reverse:** Globe

Date	Mintage	F	VF	XF	Unc	BU
1986 Proof	Est. 15,000	Value: 17.50				

KM# 164c CROWN Weight: 5.1000 g. **Composition:** 0.3740 Gold .0613 oz. AGW **Series:** World Cup Soccer - Mexico **Obverse:** Bust of Queen Elizabeth II right **Reverse:** Globe

Date	Mintage	F	VF	XF	Unc	BU
1986 Proof	Est. 10,000	Value: 75.00				

KM# 164d CROWN Weight: 7.9600 g. **Composition:** 0.9170 Gold .2347 oz. AGW **Series:** World Cup Soccer - Mexico **Obverse:** Bust of Queen Elizabeth II right **Reverse:** Globe

Date	Mintage	F	VF	XF	Unc	BU
1986 Proof	Est. 1,000	Value: 150				

KM# 164e CROWN Weight: 52.0000 g. **Composition:** 0.9500 Platinum 1.5884 oz. APW **Series:** World Cup Soccer - Mexico **Obverse:** Bust of Queen Elizabeth II right **Reverse:** Globe

Date	Mintage	F	VF	XF	Unc	BU
1986 Proof	Est. 200	Value: 1,200				

KM# 165 CROWN Composition: Copper-Nickel **Series:** World Cup Soccer - Mexico **Obverse:** Bust of Queen Elizabeth II right **Reverse:** Flags

Date	F	VF	XF	Unc	BU
1986	—	—	—	2.50	—

KM# 165a CROWN Composition: Silver Clad Copper-Nickel **Series:** World Cup Soccer - Mexico **Obverse:** Bust of Queen Elizabeth II right **Reverse:** Flags

Date	Mintage	F	VF	XF	Unc	BU
1986	Est. 20,000	Value: 10.00				
1989	—	—	—	—	80.00	—

KM# 165b CROWN Weight: 28.2800 g. **Composition:** 0.9250 Silver .8411 oz. ASW **Series:** World Cup Soccer - Mexico **Obverse:** Bust of Queen Elizabeth II right **Reverse:** Flags

Date	Mintage	F	VF	XF	Unc	BU
1986 Proof	Est. 15,000	Value: 17.50				

KM# 165c CROWN Weight: 5.1000 g. **Composition:** 0.3740 Gold .0613 oz. AGW **Series:** World Cup Soccer - Mexico **Obverse:** Bust of Queen Elizabeth II right **Reverse:** Flags

Date	Mintage	F	VF	XF	Unc	BU
1986 Proof	Est. 10,000	Value: 75.00				

KM# 165d CROWN Weight: 7.9600 g. **Composition:** 0.9170 Gold .2347 oz. AGW **Series:** World Cup Soccer - Mexico **Obverse:** Bust of Queen Elizabeth II right **Reverse:** Flags

Date	Mintage	F	VF	XF	Unc	BU
1986 Proof	Est. 1,000	Value: 150				

KM# 165e CROWN Weight: 52.0000 g. **Composition:** 0.9500 Platinum 1.5884 oz. APW **Series:** World Cup Soccer - Mexico **Obverse:** Bust of Queen Elizabeth II right **Reverse:** Flags

Date	Mintage	F	VF	XF	Unc	BU
1986 Proof	Est. 200	Value: 1,200				

KM# 173 CROWN Composition: Copper-Nickel **Subject:** Prince Andrew's Wedding **Obverse:** Bust of Queen Elizabeth II right **Reverse:** Conjoined busts of Prince Andrew and Sarah Ferguson left

Date	F	VF	XF	Unc	BU
1986	—	—	—	4.00	—
1986 Prooflike	—	—	—	—	—

KM# 173a CROWN Composition: Silver Clad Copper-Nickel **Subject:** Prince Andrew's Wedding **Obverse:** Bust of Queen Elizabeth II right **Reverse:** Conjoined busts of Prince Andrew and Sarah Ferguson left

Date	Mintage	F	VF	XF	Unc	BU
1986 Proof	Est. 20,000	Value: 12.00				

KM# 173b CROWN Weight: 28.2800 g. **Composition:** 0.9250 Silver .8411 oz. ASW **Subject:** Prince Andrew's Wedding **Obverse:** Bust of Queen Elizabeth II right **Reverse:** Conjoined busts of Prince Andrew and Sarah Ferguson left

Date	Mintage	F	VF	XF	Unc	BU
1986	—	—	—	—	15.00	—
1986 Proof	Est. 15,000	Value: 18.00				

KM# 173c CROWN Weight: 5.1000 g. **Composition:** 0.3740 Gold .0613 oz. AGW **Subject:** Prince Andrew's Wedding **Obverse:** Bust of Queen Elizabeth II right **Reverse:** Conjoined busts of Prince Andrew and Sarah Ferguson left

Date	Mintage	F	VF	XF	Unc	BU
1986 Proof	Est. 10,000	Value: 65.00				

KM# 173d CROWN Weight: 7.9600 g. **Composition:** 0.9170 Gold .2347 oz. AGW **Subject:** Prince Andrew's Wedding **Obverse:** Bust of Queen Elizabeth II right **Reverse:** Conjoined busts of Prince Andrew and Sarah Ferguson left

Date	Mintage	F	VF	XF	Unc	BU
1986 Proof	Est. 1,000	Value: 150				

KM# 173e CROWN Weight: 52.0000 g. **Composition:** 0.9500 Platinum 1.5884 oz. APW **Subject:** Prince Andrew's Wedding **Obverse:** Bust of Queen Elizabeth II right **Reverse:** Conjoined busts of Prince Andrew and Sarah Ferguson left

Date	Mintage	F	VF	XF	Unc	BU
1986 Proof	Est. 100	Value: 1,250				

KM# 174 CROWN Composition: Copper-Nickel **Subject:** Prince Andrew's Wedding **Obverse:** Bust of Queen Elizabeth II right **Reverse:** Coat of Arms

Date	F	VF	XF	Unc	BU
1986	—	—	—	4.00	—
1986 Prooflike	—	—	—	—	—

KM# 174a CROWN Composition: Silver Clad Copper-Nickel **Subject:** Prince Andrew's Wedding **Obverse:** Bust of Queen Elizabeth II right **Reverse:** Coat of Arms

Date	Mintage	F	VF	XF	Unc	BU
1986 Proof	Est. 20,000	Value: 12.00				

KM# 174b CROWN Weight: 28.2800 g. **Composition:** 0.9250 Silver .8411 oz. ASW **Subject:** Prince Andrew's Wedding **Obverse:** Bust of Queen Elizabeth II right **Reverse:** Coat of Arms

Date	Mintage	F	VF	XF	Unc	BU
1986	—	—	—	—	15.00	—
1986 Proof	Est. 15,000	Value: 18.00				

KM# 174c CROWN Weight: 5.1000 g. **Composition:** 0.3740 Gold .0613 oz. AGW **Subject:** Prince Andrew's Wedding **Obverse:** Bust of Queen Elizabeth II right **Reverse:** Coat of Arms

Date	Mintage	F	VF	XF	Unc	BU
1986 Proof	Est. 10,000	Value: 75.00				

KM# 174d CROWN Weight: 7.9600 g. **Composition:** 0.9170 Gold .2347 oz. AGW **Subject:** Prince Andrew's Wedding **Obverse:** Bust of Queen Elizabeth II right **Reverse:** Coat of Arms

Date	Mintage	F	VF	XF	Unc	BU
1986 Proof	Est. 1,000	Value: 150				

KM# 174e CROWN Weight: 52.0000 g. **Composition:** 0.9500 Platinum 1.5884 oz. APW **Subject:** Prince Andrew's Wedding **Obverse:** Bust of Queen Elizabeth II right **Reverse:** Coat of Arms

Date	Mintage	F	VF	XF	Unc	BU
1986 Proof	Est. 100	Value: 1,250				

KM# 176 CROWN Composition: Copper-Nickel **Subject:** United States Constitution **Obverse:** Bust of Queen Elizabeth II right **Reverse:** Statue of Liberty surrounded by busts of past presidents

Date	F	VF	XF	Unc	BU
1987 Prooflike	—	—	—	—	—

KM# 176a CROWN Weight: 31.1000 g. **Composition:** 0.9990 Palladium 1.0000 oz. **Subject:** United States Constitution Bicentennial **Obverse:** Bust of Queen Elizabeth II right **Reverse:** Statue of Liberty surrounded by busts of past presidents

Date	Mintage	F	VF	XF	Unc	BU
1987 Proof	Est. 25,000	Value: 750				

KM# 176b CROWN Weight: 31.1000 g. **Composition:** 0.9950 Platinum 1.0000 oz. APW **Subject:** United States Constitution Bicentennial **Obverse:** Bust of Queen Elizabeth II right **Reverse:** Statue of Liberty surrounded by busts of past presidents

Date	Mintage	F	VF	XF	Unc	BU
1987 Proof	Est. 1,000	Value: 850				

KM# 179 CROWN Composition: Copper-Nickel **Series:** Americ'a Cup **Obverse:** Bust of Queen Elizabeth II right **Reverse:** Kookaburra III and map

Date	Mintage	F	VF	XF	Unc	BU
1987	50,000	—	—	—	3.00	—
1987 Prooflike	—	—	—	—	8.00	—

KM# 179b CROWN Weight: 28.2800 g. **Composition:** 0.9250 Silver .8411 oz. ASW **Series:** America's Cup **Obverse:** Bust of Queen Elizabeth II right **Reverse:** Kookaburra III and map

Date	Mintage	F	VF	XF	Unc	BU
1987	—	—	—	—	26.50	—
1987 Proof	Est. 15,000	Value: 40.00				

KM# 179c CROWN Weight: 31.1030 g. **Composition:** 0.9990 Palladium 1.0000 oz. **Series:** America's Cup **Obverse:** Bust of Queen Elizabeth II right **Reverse:** Kookaburra III and map

Date	Mintage	F	VF	XF	Unc	BU
1987 Proof	1,000	Value: 750				

KM# 183 CROWN Composition: Copper-Nickel **Series:** America's Cup **Obverse:** Bust of Queen Elizabeth II right **Reverse:** Sailboats and cup

Date	Mintage	F	VF	XF	Unc	BU
1987	50,000	—	—	—	3.00	—
1987 Prooflike	—	—	—	—	8.00	—

KM# 183b CROWN Weight: 28.2800 g. **Composition:** 0.9250 Silver .8411 oz. ASW **Series:** America's Cup **Obverse:** Bust of Queen Elizabeth II right **Reverse:** Sailboats and cup

Date	Mintage	F	VF	XF	Unc	BU
1987	—	—	—	—	26.50	—
1987 Proof	Est. 15,000	Value: 40.00				

KM# 183c CROWN Weight: 31.1030 g. **Composition:** 0.9990 Palladium 1.0000 oz. **Series:** America's Cup **Obverse:** Bust of Queen Elizabeth II right **Reverse:** Sailboats and cup

Date	Mintage	F	VF	XF	Unc	BU
1987 Proof	1,000	Value: 600				

KM# 184 CROWN Composition: Copper-Nickel **Series:** America's Cup **Obverse:** Bust of Queen Elizabeth II right **Reverse:** Statue of Liberty and sailboats

Date	Mintage	F	VF	XF	Unc	BU
1987	50,000	—	—	—	3.00	—
1987 Prooflike	—	—	—	—	8.00	—

KM# 184b CROWN Weight: 28.2800 g. **Composition:** 0.9250 Silver .8411 oz. ASW **Series:** Americ'a Cup **Obverse:** Bust of Queen Elizabeth II right **Reverse:** Statue of Liberty and sailboats

Date	Mintage	F	VF	XF	Unc	BU
1987	—	—	—	—	26.50	—
1987 Proof	Est. 15,000	Value: 40.00				

KM# 184c CROWN **Weight:** 31.1030 g. **Composition:** 0.9990 Palladium 1.0000 oz. **Series:** America's Cup **Obverse:** Bust of Queen Elizabeth II right **Reverse:** Statue of Liberty and sailboats

Date	Mintage	F	VF	XF	Unc	BU
1987 Proof	1,000	Value: 750				

KM# 185 CROWN **Composition:** Copper-Nickel **Series:** America's Cup **Obverse:** Bust of Queen Elizabeth II right **Reverse:** Bust of George Steers and sailboat

Date	Mintage	F	VF	XF	Unc	BU
1987	50,000	—	—	—	3.00	—
1987 Prooflike	—	—	—	—	8.00	—

KM# 185b CROWN **Weight:** 28.2800 g. **Composition:** 0.9250 Silver .8411 oz. ASW **Series:** America's Cup **Obverse:** Bust of Queen Elizabeth II right **Reverse:** Bust of George Steers and sailboat

Date	Mintage	F	VF	XF	Unc	BU
1987	—	—	—	—	26.50	—
1987 Proof	Est. 15,000	Value: 40.00				

KM# 185c CROWN **Weight:** 31.1030 g. **Composition:** 0.9990 Palladium 1.0000 oz. **Series:** America's Cup **Obverse:** Bust of Queen Elizabeth II right **Reverse:** Bust of George Steers and sailboat

Date	Mintage	F	VF	XF	Unc	BU
1987 Proof	1,000	Value: 750				

KM# 186 CROWN **Composition:** Copper-Nickel **Series:** America's Cup **Obverse:** Bust of Queen Elizabeth II right **Reverse:** Bust of Sir Thomas Lipton and sailboat

Date	Mintage	F	VF	XF	Unc	BU
1987	50,000	—	—	—	3.00	—
1987 Prooflike	—	—	—	—	8.00	—

KM# 186b CROWN **Weight:** 28.2800 g. **Composition:** 0.9250 Silver .8411 oz. ASW **Series:** America's Cup **Obverse:** Bust of Queen Elizabeth II right **Reverse:** Bust of Sir Thomas Lipton and sailboat

Date	Mintage	F	VF	XF	Unc	BU
1987	—	—	—	—	26.50	—
1987 Proof	Est. 15,000	Value: 40.00				

KM# 186c CROWN **Weight:** 31.1030 g. **Composition:** 0.9990 Palladium 1.0000 oz. **Series:** America's Cup **Obverse:** Bust of Queen Elizabeth II right **Reverse:** Bust of Sir Thomas Lipton and sailboat

Date	Mintage	F	VF	XF	Unc	BU
1987 Proof	1,000	Value: 750				

KM# 222 CROWN **Composition:** Copper-Nickel **Subject:** Australian Bicentennial **Obverse:** Bust of Queen Elizabeth II right **Reverse:** Cockatoo on branch

Date	Mintage	F	VF	XF	Unc	BU
1988	—	—	—	—	10.00	—
1988 Proof	500	Value: 15.00				

KM# 222a CROWN **Weight:** 31.1000 g. **Composition:** 0.9990 Silver 1.0000 oz. ASW **Subject:** Australian Bicentennial **Obverse:** Bust of Queen Elizabeth II right **Reverse:** Cockatoo on branch

Date	F	VF	XF	Unc	BU
1988 Proof	—	Value: 175			

KM# 223 CROWN **Composition:** Copper-Nickel **Subject:** Australian Bicentennial **Obverse:** Bust of Queen Elizabeth II right **Reverse:** Koala bear in tree

Date	Mintage	F	VF	XF	Unc	BU
1988	—	—	—	—	10.00	—
1988 Proof	500	Value: 15.00				

KM# 223a CROWN **Weight:** 31.1000 g. **Composition:** 0.9990 Silver 1.0000 oz. ASW **Subject:** Australian Bicentennial **Obverse:** Bust of Queen Elizabeth II right **Reverse:** Koala bear in treee

Date	F	VF	XF	Unc	BU
1988 Proof	—	Value: 175			

KM# 224 CROWN **Composition:** Copper-Nickel **Subject:** Australian Bicentennial **Obverse:** Bust of Queen Elizabeth II right **Reverse:** Duckbill platypus

Date	Mintage	F	VF	XF	Unc	BU
1988	—	—	—	—	10.00	—
1988 Proof	500	Value: 15.00				

KM# 224a CROWN **Weight:** 31.1000 g. **Composition:** 0.9990 Silver 1.0000 oz. ASW **Subject:** Australian Bicentennial **Obverse:** Bust of Queen Elizabeth II right **Reverse:** Duckbill platypus

Date	F	VF	XF	Unc	BU
1988 Proof	—	Value: 175			

KM# 225 CROWN **Composition:** Copper-Nickel **Subject:** Australian Bicentennial **Obverse:** Bust of Queen Elizabeth II right **Reverse:** Kangaroo

Date	Mintage	F	VF	XF	Unc	BU
1988	—	—	—	—	10.00	—
1988 Proof	500	Value: 15.00				

KM# 225a CROWN **Weight:** 31.1000 g. **Composition:** 0.9999 Silver 1.0000 oz. ASW **Subject:** Australian Bicentennial **Obverse:** Bust of Queen Elizabeth II right **Reverse:** Kangaroo

Date	F	VF	XF	Unc	BU
1988 Proof	—	Value: 175			

KM# 226 CROWN **Composition:** Copper-Nickel **Subject:** Australian Bicentennial **Obverse:** Bust of Queen Elizabeth II right **Reverse:** Dingo

Date	F	VF	XF	Unc	BU
1988	—	—	—	11.50	—

KM# 226a CROWN **Weight:** 31.1000 g. **Composition:** 0.9999 Silver 1.0000 oz. ASW **Subject:** Australian Bicentennial **Obverse:** Bust of Queen Elizabeth II right **Reverse:** Dingo

Date	F	VF	XF	Unc	BU
1988 Proof	—	Value: 175			

KM# 227 CROWN Composition: Copper-Nickel **Subject:** Australian Bicentennial **Obverse:** Bust of Queen Elizabeth II right **Reverse:** Tasmanian devil

Date	F	VF	XF	Unc	BU
1988	—	—	—	10.00	—

KM# 227a CROWN Weight: 31.1000 g. **Composition:** 0.9999 Silver 1.0000 oz. ASW **Subject:** Australian Bicentennial **Obverse:** Bust of Queen Elizabeth II right **Reverse:** Tasmanian Devil

Date	F	VF	XF	Unc	BU
1988 Proof	—	Value: 175			

KM# 228 CROWN Composition: Copper-Nickel **Series:** Steam Navigation **Obverse:** Bust of Queen Elizabeth II right **Reverse:** Patrick Miller's Number One

Date	F	VF	XF	Unc	BU
1988	—	—	—	3.50	—

KM# 229 CROWN Composition: Copper-Nickel **Series:** Steam Navigation **Obverse:** Bust of Queen Elizabeth II right **Reverse:** Sirius

Date	F	VF	XF	Unc	BU
1988	—	—	—	3.50	—

KM# 230 CROWN Composition: Copper-Nickel **Series:** Steam Navigation **Obverse:** Bust of Queen Elizabeth II right **Reverse:** Chaperon

Date	F	VF	XF	Unc	BU
1988	—	—	—	3.50	—

KM# 231 CROWN Composition: Copper-Nickel **Series:** Steam Navigation **Obverse:** Bust of Queen Elizabeth II right **Reverse:** Mauretania

Date	F	VF	XF	Unc	BU
1988	—	—	—	3.50	—

KM# 232 CROWN Composition: Copper-Nickel **Series:** Steam Navigation **Obverse:** Bust of Queen Elizabeth II right **Reverse:** Queen Mary

Date	F	VF	XF	Unc	BU
1988	—	—	—	3.50	—

KM# 233 CROWN Composition: Copper-Nickel **Series:** Steam Navigation **Obverse:** Bust of Queen Elizabeth II right **Reverse:** Queen Elizabeth II

Date	F	VF	XF	Unc	BU
1988	—	—	—	3.50	—

KM# 234 CROWN Weight: 31.1000 g. **Composition:** 0.9990 Silver 1.0000 oz. ASW **Obverse:** Bust of Queen Elizabeth II right **Reverse:** Manx cat

Date	Mintage	F	VF	XF	Unc	BU
1988 Proof	15,000	Value: 15.00				

KM# 239 CROWN Weight: 31.1000 g. **Composition:** 0.9990 Gold 1.0000 oz. AGW **Obverse:** Bust of Queen Elizabeth II right **Reverse:** Manx cat

Date	Mintage	F	VF	XF	Unc	BU
1988 U	4,300	—	—	—	500	—
1988 Proof	5,000	Value: 510				

KM# 245 CROWN Composition: Copper-Nickel **Obverse:** Bust of Queen Elizabeth II right **Reverse:** Manx cat

Date	Mintage	F	VF	XF	Unc	BU
1988	—	—	—	—	12.00	—
1988 Proof	250	Value: 25.00				

KM# 240 CROWN Composition: Copper-Nickel **Series:** Mutiny on the Bounty **Obverse:** Bust of Queen Elizabeth II right **Reverse:** Captain Bligh and Elizabeth Betham

Date	F	VF	XF	Unc	BU
1989	—	—	—	3.25	—
1989 Prooflike	—	—	—	15.00	—

KM# 240a CROWN Weight: 28.2800 g. **Composition:** 0.9250 Silver .8411 oz. ASW **Series:** Mutiny on the Bounty **Obverse:** Bust of Queen Elizabeth II right **Reverse:** Captain Bligh and Elizabeth Betham

Date	F	VF	XF	Unc	BU
1989 Proof	—	Value: 45.00			

KM# 241 CROWN Composition: Copper-Nickel **Series:** Mutiny on the Bounty **Obverse:** Bust of Queen Elizabeth II right **Reverse:** H.M.S. Bounty

Date	F	VF	XF	Unc	BU
1989	—	—	—	7.50	—
1989 Prooflike	—	—	—	15.00	—

KM# 241a CROWN Weight: 28.2800 g. **Composition:** 0.9250 Silver .8411 oz. ASW **Series:** Mutiny on the Bounty **Obverse:** Bust of Queen Elizabeth II right **Reverse:** H.M.S. Bounty

Date	F	VF	XF	Unc	BU
1989 Proof	—	Value: 45.00			

KM# 242 CROWN **Composition:** Copper-Nickel **Series:** Mutiny on the Bounty **Obverse:** Bust of Queen Elizabeth II right **Reverse:** Captain Bligh and crew set afloat

Date	F	VF	XF	Unc	BU
1989	—	—	—	7.50	—
1989 Prooflike	—	—	—	15.00	—

KM# 242a CROWN **Weight:** 28.2800 g. **Composition:** 0.9250 Silver .8411 oz. ASW **Series:** Mutiny on the Bounty **Obverse:** Bust of Queen Elizabeth II right **Reverse:** Captain Bligh and crew set afloat

Date	F	VF	XF	Unc	BU
1989 Proof	—	Value: 45.00			

KM# 243 CROWN **Composition:** Copper-Nickel **Series:** Muntiny on the Bounty **Obverse:** Bust of Queen Elizabeth II right **Reverse:** Pitcairn Island

Date	F	VF	XF	Unc	BU
1989	—	—	—	7.50	—
1989 Prooflike	—	—	—	15.00	—

KM# 243a CROWN **Weight:** 28.2800 g. **Composition:** 0.9250 Silver .8411 oz. ASW **Series:** Mutiny on the Bounty **Obverse:** Bust of Queen Elizabeth II right **Reverse:** Pitcairn Island

Date	F	VF	XF	Unc	BU
1989 Proof	—	Value: 45.00			

KM# 246 CROWN **Composition:** Copper-Nickel **Obverse:** Bust of Queen Elizabeth II right **Reverse:** Washington crossing the Delaware

Date	F	VF	XF	Unc	BU
1989	—	—	—	2.75	—
1989 Proof	—	Value: 9.00			

KM# 246a CROWN **Weight:** 28.2800 g. **Composition:** 0.9250 Silver .8411 oz. ASW **Obverse:** Bust of Queen Elizabeth II right **Reverse:** Washington crossing the Delaware

Date	F	VF	XF	Unc	BU
1989 Proof	—	Value: 22.50			

KM# 247 CROWN **Composition:** Copper-Nickel **Subject:** George Washington Inauguration **Obverse:** Bust of Queen Elizabeth II right **Reverse:** Head of George Washington

Date	F	VF	XF	Unc	BU
1989	—	—	—	2.75	—
1989 Proof	—	Value: 9.00			

KM# 247a CROWN **Weight:** 28.2800 g. **Composition:** 0.9250 Silver .8411 oz. ASW **Subject:** George Washington Inauguration **Obverse:** Bust of Queen Elizabeth II right **Reverse:** Head of George Washington

Date	F	VF	XF	Unc	BU
1989 Proof	—	Value: 22.50			

KM# 248 CROWN **Composition:** Copper-Nickel **Subject:** George Washington Inauguration **Obverse:** Bust of Queen Elizabeth II right **Reverse:** Cameo of George Washington with eagle surrounding

Date	F	VF	XF	Unc	BU
1989	—	—	—	2.75	—
1989 Proof	—	Value: 9.00			

KM# 248a CROWN **Weight:** 28.2800 g. **Composition:** 0.9250 Silver .8411 oz. ASW **Subject:** George Washington Inauguration **Obverse:** Bust of Queen Elizabeth II right **Reverse:** Cameo of George Washinton with eagle surrounding

Date	F	VF	XF	Unc	BU
1989 Proof	—	Value: 22.50			

KM# 249 CROWN **Composition:** Copper-Nickel **Subject:** George Washington Inauguration **Obverse:** Bust of Queen Elizabeth II right **Reverse:** George Washington taking oath

Date	F	VF	XF	Unc	BU
1989	—	—	—	2.75	—
1989 Proof	—	Value: 9.00			

KM# 249a CROWN **Weight:** 28.2800 g. **Composition:** 0.9250 Silver .8411 oz. ASW **Subject:** George Washington Inauguration **Obverse:** Bust of Queen Elizabeth II right **Reverse:** George Washington taking oath

Date	F	VF	XF	Unc	BU
1989 Proof	—	Value: 22.50			

KM# 250 CROWN **Composition:** Copper-Nickel **Obverse:** Bust of Queen Elizabeth II right **Reverse:** Persian cat

Date	Mintage	F	VF	XF	Unc	BU
1989	—	—	—	—	9.00	—
1989 Proof	250	Value: 32.00				

KM# 251 CROWN **Weight:** 31.1000 g. **Composition:** 0.9990 Silver 1.0000 oz. ASW **Obverse:** Bust of Queen Elizabeth II right **Reverse:** Persian cat

Date	F	VF	XF	Unc	BU
1989 Proof	—	Value: 28.00			

KM# 256 CROWN **Weight:** 31.1000 g. **Composition:** 0.9990 Gold 1.0000 oz. AGW **Obverse:** Bust of Queen Elizabeth II right **Reverse:** Persian cat

Date	F	VF	XF	Unc	BU
1989	—	—	—	450	—
1989 Proof	—	Value: 460			

KM# 273 CROWN **Composition:** Copper-Nickel **Subject:** Royal Visit **Obverse:** Bust of Queen Elizabeth II right **Reverse:** Three scenes from ship

Date	F	VF	XF	Unc	BU
1989	—	—	—	4.00	—

KM# 273a CROWN **Weight:** 31.1000 g. **Composition:** 0.9990 Silver 1.0000 oz. ASW **Subject:** Royal Visit **Obverse:** Bust of Queen Elizabeth II right **Reverse:** Three scenes from ship

Date	Mintage	F	VF	XF	Unc	BU
1989 Proof	Est. 20,000	Value: 35.00				

KM# 273b CROWN **Weight:** 31.1000 g. **Composition:** 0.9990 Gold 1.0000 oz. AGW **Subject:** Royal Visit **Obverse:** Bust of Queen Elizabeth II right **Reverse:** Three scenes from ship

Date	Mintage	F	VF	XF	Unc	BU
1989 Proof	Est. 7,500	Value: 685				

KM# 471 CROWN **Weight:** 31.1035 g. **Composition:** 0.9995 Platinum .9995 oz. APW **Obverse:** Bust of Queen Elizabeth II right **Reverse:** Persian cat

Date	F	VF	XF	Unc	BU
1989	—	—	—BV+20%		—

KM# 267 CROWN **Composition:** Copper-Nickel **Subject:** 150th Anniversary of "Penny Black" Stamp **Obverse:** Bust of Queen Elizabeth II right **Reverse:** Stamp **Note:** Struck in "pearl black" Copper-Nickel.

Date	Mintage	F	VF	XF	Unc	BU
1990	—	—	—	—	9.00	—
1990 Proof	50,000	Value: 16.50				

KM# 267a CROWN **Weight:** 28.2800 g. **Composition:** 0.9250 Silver .8411 oz. ASW **Subject:** 150th Anniversary of "Penny Black" Stamp **Obverse:** Bust of Queen Elizabeth II right **Reverse:** Stamp

Date	Mintage	F	VF	XF	Unc	BU
1990 Proof	30,000	Value: 30.00				

KM# 267b CROWN Weight: 31.1000 g. **Composition:** 0.9170 Gold 1.0000 oz. AGW **Subject:** 150th Anniversary of "Penny Black" Stamp **Obverse:** Bust of Queen Elizabeth II right **Reverse:** Stamp

Date	Mintage	F	VF	XF	Unc	BU
1990 Proof	Est. 1,000	Value: 685				

KM# 267c CROWN Weight: 52.0000 g. **Composition:** 0.9500 Platinum 1.5884 oz. APW **Subject:** 150th Anniversary of "Penny Black" Stamp **Obverse:** Bust of Queen Elizabeth II right **Reverse:** Stamp

Date	Mintage	F	VF	XF	Unc	BU
1990 Proof	Est. 50	Value: 1,350				

KM# 269 CROWN Composition: Copper-Nickel **Series:** World Cup - Italy **Obverse:** Bust of Queen Elizabeth II right **Reverse:** Milano

Date	Mintage	F	VF	XF	Unc	BU
1990		—	—	—	3.25	—

KM# 269a CROWN Weight: 28.2800 g. **Composition:** 0.9250 Silver .8411 oz. ASW **Series:** World Cup - Italy **Obverse:** Bust of Queen Elizabeth II right **Reverse:** Milano

Date	Mintage	F	VF	XF	Unc	BU
1990 Proof	Est. 30,000	Value: 20.00				

KM# 269b CROWN Weight: 6.2200 g. **Composition:** 0.9990 Gold .2000 oz. AGW **Series:** World Cup - Italy **Obverse:** Bust of Queen Elizabeth II right **Reverse:** Milano

Date	Mintage	F	VF	XF	Unc	BU
1990 Proof	Est. 500	Value: 200				

KM# 269c CROWN Weight: 6.2230 g. **Composition:** 0.9990 Platinum .2000 oz. APW **Series:** World Cup - Italy **Obverse:** Bust of Queen Elizabeth II right **Reverse:** Milano

Date	Mintage	F	VF	XF	Unc	BU
1990 Proof	Est. 100	Value: 250				

KM# 270 CROWN Composition: Copper-Nickel **Series:** World Cup - Italy **Obverse:** Bust of Queen Elizabeth II right **Reverse:** Torino

Date	F	VF	XF	Unc	BU
1990	—	—	—	6.00	—

KM# 270a CROWN Weight: 28.2800 g. **Composition:** 0.9250 Silver .8411 oz. ASW **Series:** World Cup - Italy **Obverse:** Bust of Queen Elizabeth II right **Reverse:** Torino

Date	Mintage	F	VF	XF	Unc	BU
1990 Proof	Est. 30,000	Value: 20.00				

KM# 270b CROWN Weight: 6.2200 g. **Composition:** 0.9990 Gold .2000 oz. AGW **Series:** World Cup - Italy **Obverse:** Bust of Queen Elizabeth II right **Reverse:** Torino

Date	Mintage	F	VF	XF	Unc	BU
1990 Proof	Est. 500	Value: 200				

KM# 270c CROWN Weight: 6.2230 g. **Composition:** 0.9990 Platinum .2000 oz. APW **Series:** World Cup - Italy **Obverse:** Bust of Queen Elizabeth II right **Reverse:** Torino

Date	Mintage	F	VF	XF	Unc	BU
1990 Proof	Est. 100	Value: 250				

KM# 271 CROWN Composition: Copper-Nickel **Series:** World Cup - Italy **Obverse:** Bust of Queen Elizabeth II right **Reverse:** Bologna

Date	F	VF	XF	Unc	BU
1990	—	—	—	6.00	—

KM# 271a CROWN Weight: 28.2800 g. **Composition:** 0.9250 Silver .8411 oz. ASW **Series:** World Cup - Italy **Obverse:** Bust of Queen Elizabeth II right **Reverse:** Bologna

Date	Mintage	F	VF	XF	Unc	BU
1990 Proof	Est. 30,000	Value: 30.00				

KM# 271b CROWN Weight: 6.2200 g. **Composition:** 0.9990 Gold .2000 oz. AGW **Series:** World Cup - Italy **Obverse:** Bust of Queen Elizabeth II right **Reverse:** Bologna

Date	Mintage	F	VF	XF	Unc	BU
1990 Proof	Est. 500	Value: 200				

KM# 271c CROWN Weight: 6.2230 g. **Composition:** 0.9990 Platinum .2000 oz. APW **Series:** World Cup - Italy **Obverse:** Bust of Queen Elizabeth II right **Reverse:** Bologna

Date	Mintage	F	VF	XF	Unc	BU
1990 Proof	Est. 100	Value: 250				

KM# 272 CROWN Composition: Copper-Nickel **Series:** World Cup - Italy **Obverse:** Bust of Queen Elizabeth II right **Reverse:** Palermo

Date	F	VF	XF	Unc	BU
1990	—	—	—	6.00	—

KM# 272a CROWN Weight: 28.2800 g. **Composition:** 0.9250 Silver .8411 oz. ASW **Series:** World Cup - Italy **Obverse:** Bust of Queen Elizabeth II right **Reverse:** Palermo

Date	Mintage	F	VF	XF	Unc	BU
1990 Proof	Est. 30,000	Value: 20.00				

KM# 272b CROWN Weight: 6.2200 g. **Composition:** 0.9990 Gold .2000 oz. AGW **Series:** World Cup - Italy **Obverse:** Bust of Queen Elizabeth II right **Reverse:** Palermo

Date	Mintage	F	VF	XF	Unc	BU
1990 Proof	Est. 500	Value: 200				

KM# 272c CROWN Weight: 6.2230 g. **Composition:** 0.9990 Platinum .2000 oz. APW **Series:** World Cup - Italy **Obverse:** Bust of Queen Elizabeth II right **Reverse:** Palermo

Date	Mintage	F	VF	XF	Unc	BU
1990 Proof	Est. 100	Value: 250				

KM# 275 CROWN Composition: Copper-Nickel **Obverse:** Bust of Queen Elizabeth II right **Reverse:** Alley cat

Date	Mintage	F	VF	XF	Unc	BU
1990	—	—	—	—	10.00	—
1990 Proof	250	Value: 35.00				

KM# 276 CROWN Weight: 31.1000 g. **Composition:** 0.9990 Silver 1.000 oz. ASW **Obverse:** Bust of Queen Elizabeth II right **Reverse:** Alley cat

Date	F	VF	XF	Unc	BU
1990 Proof	— Value: 30.00				

KM# 281 CROWN Weight: 31.1000 g. **Composition:** 0.9990 Gold 1.000 oz. AGW **Obverse:** Bust of Queen Elizabeth II right **Reverse:** Alley cat

Date	F	VF	XF	Unc	BU
1990	—	—	—	500	—
1990 Proof	— Value: 510				

KM# 283 CROWN Composition: Copper-Nickel **Obverse:** Bust of Queen Elizabeth II right **Reverse:** Sir Winston Churchill with cigar

Date	F	VF	XF	Unc	BU
1990	—	—	—	3.25	—

KM# 283a CROWN Weight: 28.2800 g. **Composition:** 0.9250 Silver .8411 oz. ASW **Obverse:** Bust of Queen Elizabeth II right **Reverse:** Sir Winston Churchill with cigar

Date	Mintage	F	VF	XF	Unc	BU
1990 Proof	Est. 25,000	Value: 50.00				

KM# 283b CROWN Weight: 6.2230 g. **Composition:** 0.9990 Gold .2000 oz. AGW **Obverse:** Bust of Queen Elizabeth II right **Reverse:** Sir Winston Churchill with cigar

Date	Mintage	F	VF	XF	Unc	BU
1990 Proof	Est. 500	Value: 200				

KM# 283c CROWN Weight: 6.2230 g. **Composition:** 0.9990 Platinum .2000 oz. APW **Obverse:** Bust of Queen Elizabeth II right **Reverse:** Sir Winston Churchill with cigar

Date	Mintage	F	VF	XF	Unc	BU
1990 Proof	Est. 100	Value: 250				

KM# 284 CROWN Composition: Copper-Nickel **Obverse:** Bust of Queen Elizabeth II right **Reverse:** Sir Winston Churchill in garter robes

Date	F	VF	XF	Unc	BU
1990	—	—	—	3.25	—

KM# 284a CROWN Weight: 28.2800 g. **Composition:** 0.9250 Silver .8411 oz. ASW **Obverse:** Bust of Queen Elizabeth II right **Reverse:** Sir Winston Churchill in garter robes

Date	Mintage	F	VF	XF	Unc	BU
1990 Proof	Est. 25,000	Value: 50.00				

KM# 284b CROWN Weight: 6.2230 g. **Composition:** 0.9990 Gold .2000 oz. AGW **Obverse:** Bust of Queen Elizabeth II right **Reverse:** Sir Winston Churchill in garter robes

Date	Mintage	F	VF	XF	Unc	BU
1990 Proof	Est. 500	Value: 200				

KM# 284c CROWN Weight: 6.2230 g. **Composition:** 0.9990 Platinum .2000 oz. APW **Obverse:** Bust of Queen Elizabeth II right **Reverse:** Sir Winston Churchill in garter robes

Date	Mintage	F	VF	XF	Unc	BU
1990 Proof	Est. 100	Value: 250				

KM# 291 CROWN Composition: Copper-Nickel **Subject:** 100th Anniversary - American Numismatic Association **Obverse:** Bust of Queen Elizabeth II right **Reverse:** Circle of coins

Date	F	VF	XF	Unc	BU
1991	—	—	—	4.50	—

KM# 291a CROWN Weight: 28.2800 g. **Composition:** 0.9250 Silver .8411 oz. ASW **Subject:** 100th Anniversary - American Numismatic Association **Obverse:** Bust of Queen Elizabeth II right **Reverse:** Circle of coins

Date	F	VF	XF	Unc	BU
1991 Proof	— Value: 22.00				

KM# 326 CROWN Composition: Copper-Nickel **Subject:** America's Cup - San Diego **Obverse:** Bust of Queen Elizabeth II right **Reverse:** Cameo of sailing ship above two modern sailboats **Rev. Legend:** AMERICA'S CUP CHALLENGE • SAN DIEGO • 1992

Date	F	VF	XF	Unc	BU
1991	—	—	—	30.00	—
1992	—	—	—	4.75	—
1992 Proof	— Value: 12.50				

KM# 326a CROWN Weight: 28.2800 g. **Composition:** 0.9250 Silver .8411 oz. ASW **Subject:** America's Cup - San Diego **Obverse:** Bust of Queen Elizabeth II right **Reverse:** Cameo of sailing ship above two modern sailboats

Date	Mintage	F	VF	XF	Unc	BU
1992 Proof	25,000	—	—	—	60.00	—

KM# 326b CROWN Weight: 31.0300 g. **Composition:** 0.9990 Gold 1.0000 oz. AGW **Subject:** America's Cup - San Diego **Obverse:** Bust of Queen Elizabeth II right **Reverse:** Cameo of sailing ship above two modern sailboats

Date	F	VF	XF	Unc	BU
1992 Proof	—	—	—	800	—

KM# 292 CROWN **Composition:** Copper-Nickel **Obverse:** Bust of Queen Elizabeth II right **Reverse:** Norwegian cat

Date	Mintage	F	VF	XF	Unc	BU
1991	—	—	—	—	10.00	—
1991 Proof	15	—	—	—	—	—

KM# 293 CROWN **Weight:** 31.1000 g. **Composition:** 0.9990 Silver 1.0000 oz. ASW **Obverse:** Bust of Queen Elizabeth II right **Reverse:** Norwegian cat

Date	Mintage	F	VF	XF	Unc	BU
1991 Proof	50,000	Value: 30.00				

KM# 298 CROWN **Weight:** 31.1000 g. **Composition:** 0.9990 Gold 1.0000 oz. AGW **Obverse:** Bust of Queen Elizabeth II right **Reverse:** Norwegian cat

Date	F	VF	XF	Unc	BU
1991	—	—	—	435	—
1991 Proof	—	Value: 445			

KM# 304 CROWN **Composition:** Copper-Nickel **Subject:** 10th Wedding Anniversary **Obverse:** Bust of Queen Elizabeth II right **Reverse:** Head of Prince Charles

Date	F	VF	XF	Unc	BU
1991	—	—	—	3.75	—

KM# 304a CROWN **Weight:** 28.2800 g. **Composition:** 0.9250 Silver .8411 oz. ASW **Subject:** 10th Wedding Anniversary **Obverse:** Bust of Queen Elizabeth II right **Reverse:** Head of Prince Charles

Date	F	VF	XF	Unc	BU
1991 Proof	—	Value: 40.00			

KM# 304b CROWN **Weight:** 6.2200 g. **Composition:** 0.9990 Gold .2000 oz. AGW **Subject:** 10th Wedding Anniversary **Obverse:** Bust of Queen Elizabeth II right **Reverse:** Head of Prince Charles

Date	F	VF	XF	Unc	BU
1991 Proof	—	Value: 165			

KM# 305 CROWN **Composition:** Copper-Nickel **Subject:** 10th Wedding Anniversary **Obverse:** Bust of Queen Elizabeth II right **Reverse:** Head of Princess Diana

Date	F	VF	XF	Unc	BU
1991	—	—	—	3.75	—

KM# 305a CROWN **Weight:** 28.2800 g. **Composition:** 0.9250 Silver .8411 oz. ASW **Subject:** 10th Wedding Anniversary **Obverse:** Bust of Queen Elizabeth II right **Reverse:** Head of Princess Diana

Date	F	VF	XF	Unc	BU
1991 Proof	—	Value: 40.00			

KM# 305b CROWN **Weight:** 6.2200 g. **Composition:** 0.9990 Gold .2000 oz. AGW **Subject:** 10th Wedding Anniversary **Obverse:** Bust of Queen Elizabeth II right **Reverse:** Head of Princess Diana

Date	F	VF	XF	Unc	BU
1991 Proof	—	Value: 165			

KM#310 CROWN **Composition:** Copper-Nickel **Series:** Discovery of America **Obverse:** Bust of Queen Elizabeth II right **Reverse:** John Casement and train engine

Date	F	VF	XF	Unc	BU
1992	—	—	—	3.75	—
1992 Proof	—	Value: 12.00			

KM# 310a CROWN **Weight:** 28.2800 g. **Composition:** 0.9250 Silver .8411 oz. ASW **Series:** Discovery of America **Obverse:** Bust of Queen Elizabeth II right **Reverse:** John Casement and train engine

Date	F	VF	XF	Unc	BU
1992 Proof	—	Value: 45.00			

KM#311 CROWN **Composition:** Copper-Nickel **Series:** Discovery of America **Obverse:** Bust of Queen Elizabeth II right **Reverse:** Dan Casement and train engine

Date	F	VF	XF	Unc	BU
1992	—	—	—	3.75	—
1992 Proof	—	Value: 12.00			

KM# 311a CROWN **Weight:** 28.2800 g. **Composition:** 0.9250 Silver .8411 oz. ASW **Series:** Discovery of America **Obverse:** Bust of Queen Elizabeth II right **Reverse:** Dan Casement and train engine

Date	F	VF	XF	Unc	BU
1992 Proof	—	Value: 45.00			

KM#312 CROWN **Composition:** Copper-Nickel **Series:** Discovery of America **Obverse:** Bust of Queen Elizabeth II right **Reverse:** Promontory Point, Utah

Date	F	VF	XF	Unc	BU
1992	—	—	—	3.75	—
1992 Proof	—	Value: 10.00			

KM# 312a CROWN **Weight:** 28.2800 g. **Composition:** 0.9250 Silver .8411 oz. ASW **Series:** Discovery of America **Obverse:** Bust of Queen Elizabeth II right **Reverse:** Promontory Point, Utah

Date	F	VF	XF	Unc	BU
1992 Proof	—	Value: 45.00			

KM#313 CROWN **Composition:** Copper-Nickel **Series:** Discovery of America **Obverse:** Bust of Queen Elizabeth II right **Reverse:** Flags of United States and Isle of Man

Date	F	VF	XF	Unc	BU
1992	—	—	—	3.75	—
1992 Proof	—	Value: 10.00			

KM# 313a CROWN **Weight:** 28.2800 g. **Composition:** 0.9250 Silver .8411 oz. ASW **Series:** Discovery of America **Obverse:** Bust of Queen Elizabeth II right **Reverse:** Flags of United States and Isle of Man

Date	F	VF	XF	Unc	BU
1992 Proof	—	Value: 25.00			

KM# 332 CROWN **Composition:** Copper-Nickel **Obverse:** Bust of Queen Elizabeth II right **Reverse:** Seated Siamese cat

Date	F	VF	XF	Unc	BU
1992	—	—	—	11.50	—

KM# 333 CROWN **Weight:** 31.1000 g. **Composition:** 0.9990 Silver 1.0000 oz. ASW **Obverse:** Bust of Queen Elizabeth II right **Reverse:** Seated Siamese cat

Date	Mintage	F	VF	XF	Unc	BU
1992 Proof	50,000	Value: 30.00				

KM# 334 CROWN **Weight:** 31.1000 g. **Composition:** 0.9990 Gold 1.0000 oz. AGW **Obverse:** Bust of Queen Elizabeth II right **Reverse:** Seated Siamese cat

Date	F	VF	XF	Unc	BU
1992	—	—	—	425	—
1992 Proof	—	Value: 435			

KM# 342 CROWN **Weight:** 31.1000 g. **Composition:** 0.9990 Gold 1.0000 oz. AGW **Subject:** Year of the Cockerel **Obverse:** Bust of Queen Elizabeth II right **Reverse:** Cockerel in inner circle

Date	Mintage	F	VF	XF	Unc	BU
1993 Proof	Est. 2,500	Value: 750				

KM# 353 CROWN **Composition:** Copper-Nickel **Obverse:** Bust of Queen Elizabeth II right **Reverse:** Maine coon cat

Date	F	VF	XF	Unc	BU
1993	—	—	—	8.50	—

KM# 354 CROWN **Weight:** 31.1000 g. **Composition:** 0.9990 Silver 1.0000 oz. ASW **Obverse:** Bust of Queen Elizabeth II right **Reverse:** Maine coon cat

Date	Mintage	F	VF	XF	Unc	BU
1993 Proof	50,000	Value: 30.00				

KM# 355 CROWN **Weight:** 31.1000 g. **Composition:** 0.9990 Gold 1.0000 oz. AGW **Obverse:** Bust of Queen Elizabeth II right **Reverse:** Maine coon cat

Date	Mintage	F	VF	XF	Unc	BU
1993		—	—	—	425	—
1993 Proof	—	Value: 435				

KM#357 CROWN **Composition:** Copper-Nickel **Series:** Preserve Planet Earth **Obverse:** Bust of Queen Elizabeth II right **Reverse:** Iquanodon

Date	F	VF	XF	Unc	BU
1993	—	—	—	8.50	—

KM#358 CROWN **Composition:** Copper-Nickel **Series:** Preserve Planet Earth **Obverse:** Bust of Queen Elizabeth II right **Reverse:** Diplodocus

Date	F	VF	XF	Unc	BU
1993	—	—	—	8.50	—

KM#364 CROWN **Composition:** Copper-Nickel **Series:** World Cup Soccer - U.S.A. **Obverse:** Bust of Queen Elizabeth II right **Reverse:** Two players

Date	F	VF	XF	Unc	BU
1994	—	—	—	6.00	—

KM# 364a CROWN **Weight:** 28.2800 g. **Composition:** 0.9250 Silver .8411 oz. ASW **Series:** World Cup Soccer - U.S.A. **Obverse:** Bust of Queen Elizabeth II right **Reverse:** Two players

Date	Mintage	F	VF	XF	Unc	BU
1994 Proof	Est. 30,000	Value: 35.00				

KM#366 CROWN **Composition:** Copper-Nickel **Series:** World Cup Soccer - U.S.A. **Obverse:** Bust of Queen Elizabeth II right **Reverse:** Three players

Date	F	VF	XF	Unc	BU
1994	—	—	—	6.00	—

KM# 366a CROWN **Weight:** 28.2800 g. **Composition:** 0.9250 Silver .8411 oz. ASW **Series:** World Cup Soccer - U.S.A. **Obverse:** Bust of Queen Elizabeth II right **Reverse:** Three players

Date	Mintage	F	VF	XF	Unc	BU
1994 Proof	Est. 30,000	Value: 35.00				

KM#368 CROWN **Composition:** Copper-Nickel **Series:** World Cup Soccer - U.S.A. **Obverse:** Bust of Queen Elizabeth II right **Reverse:** One player with knee bent with second player in background

Date	F	VF	XF	Unc	BU
1994	—	—	—	6.00	—

KM# 368a CROWN **Weight:** 28.2800 g. **Composition:** 0.9250 Silver .8411 oz. ASW **Series:** World Cup Soccer - U.S.A. **Obverse:** Bust of Queen Elizabeth II right **Reverse:** One player with knee bent, second player in background

Date	Mintage	F	VF	XF	Unc	BU
1994 Proof	Est. 30,000	Value: 35.00				

KM#370 CROWN **Composition:** Copper-Nickel **Series:** World Cup Soccer - U.S.A. **Obverse:** Bust of Queen Elizabeth II right **Reverse:** Three players, one kicking ball

Date	F	VF	XF	Unc	BU
1994	—	—	—	6.00	—

KM# 370a CROWN **Weight:** 28.2800 g. **Composition:** 0.9250 Silver .8411 oz. ASW **Series:** World Cup Soccer - U.S.A. **Obverse:** Bust of Queen Elizabeth II right **Reverse:** Three players, one kicking ball

Date	Mintage	F	VF	XF	Unc	BU
1994 Proof	Est. 30,000	Value: 35.00				

KM#372 CROWN **Composition:** Copper-Nickel **Series:** World Cup Soccer - U.S.A. **Obverse:** Bust of Queen Elizabeth II right **Reverse:** Two players, one is goalie blocking shot

Date	F	VF	XF	Unc	BU
1994	—	—	—	6.00	—

KM# 372a CROWN **Weight:** 28.2800 g. **Composition:** 0.9250 Silver .8411 oz. ASW **Series:** World Cup Soccer - U.S.A. **Obverse:** Bust of Queen Elizabeth II right **Reverse:** Two players, one is goalie blocking shot

Date	Mintage	F	VF	XF	Unc	BU
1994 Proof	Est. 30,000	Value: 35.00				

KM#374 CROWN **Composition:** Copper-Nickel **Series:** World Cup Soccer - U.S.A. **Obverse:** Bust of Queen Elizabeth II right **Reverse:** Two players kicking ball right

Date	F	VF	XF	Unc	BU
1994	—	—	—	6.00	—

KM# 374a CROWN **Weight:** 28.2800 g. **Composition:** 0.9250 Silver .8411 oz. ASW **Series:** World Cup Soccer - U.S.A. **Obverse:** Bust of Queen Elizabeth II right **Reverse:** Two players kicking ball right

Date	Mintage	F	VF	XF	Unc	BU
1994 Proof	Est. 30,000	Value: 35.00				

KM# 380 CROWN **Composition:** Copper-Nickel **Obverse:** Bust of Queen Elizabeth II right **Reverse:** Japanese bobtail cat

Date	F	VF	XF	Unc	BU
1994	—	—	—	7.50	—

KM# 381 CROWN **Weight:** 31.1000 g. **Composition:** 0.9990 Silver 1.0000 oz. ASW **Obverse:** Bust of Queen Elizabeth II right **Reverse:** Japanese bobtail cat

Date	Mintage	F	VF	XF	Unc	BU
1994 Proof	—	Value: 30.00				

KM# 382 CROWN **Weight:** 31.1000 g. **Composition:** 0.9990 Gold 1.0000 oz. AGW **Obverse:** Bust of Queen Elizabeth II right **Reverse:** Japanese bobtail cat

Date	Mintage	F	VF	XF	Unc	BU
1994		—	—	—	400	—
1994 Proof	—	Value: 410				

KM#384 CROWN **Composition:** Copper-Nickel **Series:** Preserve Planet Earth **Obverse:** Bust of Queen Elizabeth II right **Reverse:** Woolly mammoth

Date	F	VF	XF	Unc	BU
1994	—	—	—	9.00	—

KM# 384a CROWN **Weight:** 28.2800 g. **Composition:** 0.9250 Silver .8411 oz. ASW **Series:** Preserve Planet Earth **Obverse:** Bust of Queen Elizabeth II right **Reverse:** Woolly mammoth

Date	Mintage	F	VF	XF	Unc	BU
1994 Proof	Est. 30,000	Value: 35.00				

KM# 385 CROWN **Composition:** Copper-Nickel **Series:** Preserve Planet Earth **Obverse:** Bust of Queen Elizabeth II right **Reverse:** Four red-necked wallaby

Date	F	VF	XF	Unc	BU
1994	—	—	—	9.00	—

KM# 385a CROWN **Weight:** 28.2800 g. **Composition:** 0.9250 Silver .8411 oz. ASW **Series:** Preserve Planet Earth **Obverse:** Bust of Queen Elizabeth II right **Reverse:** Four red-necked wallaby

Date	Mintage	F	VF	XF	Unc	BU
1994 Proof	Est. 30,000	Value: 35.00				

KM# 386 CROWN **Composition:** Copper-Nickel **Series:** Preserve Planet Earth **Obverse:** Bust of Queen Elizabeth II right **Reverse:** Grey seal mother and pup

Date	F	VF	XF	Unc	BU
1994	—	—	—	9.00	—

KM# 386a CROWN **Weight:** 28.2800 g. **Composition:** 0.9250 Silver .8411 oz. ASW **Series:** Preserve Planet Earth **Obverse:** Bust of Queen Elizabeth II right **Reverse:** Grey seal mother and pup

Date	Mintage	F	VF	XF	Unc	BU
1994 Proof	Est. 30,000	Value: 35.00				

KM# 387 CROWN **Composition:** Copper-Nickel **Series:** Preserve Planet Earth **Obverse:** Bust of Queen Elizabeth II right **Reverse:** Two fallow deer

Date	F	VF	XF	Unc	BU
1994	—	—	—	9.00	—

KM# 387a CROWN **Weight:** 28.2800 g. **Composition:** 0.9250 Silver .8411 oz. ASW **Series:** Preserve Planet Earth **Obverse:** Bust of Queen Elizabeth II right **Reverse:** Two fallow deer

Date	Mintage	F	VF	XF	Unc	BU
1994 Proof	Est. 30,000	Value: 35.00				

KM# 406 CROWN **Composition:** Copper-Nickel **Subject:** Year of the Dog **Obverse:** Bust of Queen Elizabeth II right **Reverse:** Pekingese dog

Date	F	VF	XF	Unc	BU
1994	—	—	—	8.00	—

KM# 407 CROWN **Weight:** 31.1000 g. **Composition:** 0.9990 Silver 1.000 oz. ASW **Subject:** Year of the Dog **Obverse:** Bust of Queen Elizabeth II right **Reverse:** Pekingese dog

Date	F	VF	XF	Unc	BU
1994 Proof	—	Value: 40.00			

KM# 408 CROWN **Weight:** 31.1000 g. **Composition:** 0.9990 Gold 1.000 oz. AGW **Subject:** Year of the Dog **Obverse:** Bust of Queen Elizabeth II right **Reverse:** Pekingese dog

Date	Mintage	F	VF	XF	Unc	BU
1994 Proof	Est. 5,000	Value: 700				

KM# 417 CROWN **Composition:** Copper-Nickel **Series:** Man in Flight **Obverse:** Bust of Queen Elizabeth II right **Reverse:** Otto Lilienthal

Date	F	VF	XF	Unc	BU
1994	—	—	—	7.00	—

KM# 417a CROWN **Weight:** 28.2800 g. **Composition:** 0.9250 Silver .8411 oz. ASW **Series:** Man in Flight **Obverse:** Bust of Queen Elizabeth II right **Reverse:** Otto Lilienthal

Date	Mintage	F	VF	XF	Unc	BU
1994 Proof	Est. 30,000	Value: 40.00				

KM# 418 CROWN **Composition:** Copper-Nickel **Series:** Man in Flight **Obverse:** Bust of Queen Elizabeth II right **Reverse:** Ferdinand von Zeppelin

Date	F	VF	XF	Unc	BU
1994	—	—	—	9.00	—

KM# 419 CROWN **Composition:** Copper-Nickel **Series:** Man in Flight **Obverse:** Bust of Queen Elizabeth II right **Reverse:** Louis Bleriot **Subject:** First Channel Crossing - 1909

Date	F	VF	XF	Unc	BU
1994	—	—	—	8.00	—

KM# 419a CROWN **Weight:** 28.2800 g. **Composition:** 0.9250 Silver .8411 oz. ASW **Series:** Man in Flight **Subject:** First Channel Crossing - 1909 **Obverse:** Bust of Queen Elizabeth II right **Reverse:** Louis Bleriot

Date	Mintage	F	VF	XF	Unc	BU
1994 Proof	Est. 30,000	Value: 40.00				

KM# 420 CROWN **Composition:** Copper-Nickel **Series:** Man in Flight **Subject:** First Atlantic Crossing - 1919 **Obverse:** Bust of Queen Elizabeth II right **Reverse:** Alcock and Brown

Date	F	VF	XF	Unc	BU
1994	—	—	—	8.00	—

KM# 420a CROWN **Weight:** 28.2800 g. **Composition:** 0.9250 Silver .8411 oz. ASW **Series:** Man in Flight **Subject:** First Atlantic Crossing - 1919 **Obverse:** Bust of Queen Elizabeth II right **Reverse:** Alcock and Brown

Date	Mintage	F	VF	XF	Unc	BU
1994 Proof	Est. 30,000	Value: 40.00				

KM# 421 CROWN **Composition:** Copper-Nickel **Series:** Man in Flight **Subject:** First England to Australia flight **Obverse:** Bust of Queen Elizabeth II right **Reverse:** Biplane

Date	F	VF	XF	Unc	BU
1994	—	—	—	8.00	—

KM# 421a CROWN **Weight:** 28.2800 g. **Composition:** 0.9250 Silver .8411 oz. ASW **Series:** Man in Flight **Subject:** First England to Australia flight **Obverse:** Bust of Queen Elizabeth II right **Reverse:** Biplane

Date	Mintage	F	VF	XF	Unc	BU
1994 Proof	Est. 30,000	Value: 40.00				

KM# 422 CROWN **Composition:** Copper-Nickel **Series:** Man in Flight **Subject:** 60th Anniversary of Airmail **Obverse:** Bust of Queen Elizabeth II right **Reverse:** Airplane

Date	F	VF	XF	Unc	BU
1994	—	—	—	8.00	—

KM# 422a CROWN **Weight:** 28.2800 g. **Composition:** 0.9250 Silver .8411 oz. ASW **Series:** Man in Flight **Subject:** 60th Anniversary of Airmail **Obverse:** Bust of Queen Elizabeth II right **Reverse:** Airplane

Date	Mintage	F	VF	XF	Unc	BU
1994 Proof	Est. 30,000	Value: 40.00				

KM# 423 CROWN **Composition:** Copper-Nickel **Series:** Man in Flight **Subject:** 50th Anniversary of International Civil Aviation Organization **Obverse:** Bust of Queen Elizabeth II right **Reverse:** Emblem

Date	F	VF	XF	Unc	BU
1994	—	—	—	8.00	—

KM# 423a CROWN Weight: 28.2800 g. **Composition:** 0.9250 Silver .8411 oz. ASW **Series:** Man in Flight **Subject:** 50th Anniersary of International Civil Aviation Organization **Obverse:** Bust of Queen Elizabeth II right **Reverse:** Emblem

Date	Mintage	F	VF	XF	Unc	BU
1994 Proof	Est. 30,000	Value: 40.00				

KM# 424 CROWN Composition: Copper-Nickel **Series:** Man in Flight **Subject:** 25th Anniversary of First Concorde Flight **Obverse:** Bust of Queen Elizabeth II right **Reverse:** Concorde

Date	F	VF	XF	Unc	BU
1994	—	—	—	8.00	—

KM# 424a CROWN Weight: 28.2800 g. **Composition:** 0.9250 Silver .8411 oz. ASW **Series:** Man in Flight **Subject:** 25th Anniversary of First Concorde Flight **Obverse:** Bust of Queen Elizabeth II right **Reverse:** Concorde

Date	Mintage	F	VF	XF	Unc	BU
1994 Proof	Est. 30,000	Value: 40.00				

KM# 477 CROWN Weight: 31.1035 g. **Composition:** 0.9995 Platinum .9995 oz. APW **Obverse:** Bust of Queen Elizabeth II right **Reverse:** Japanese bobtail cat

Date	F	VF	XF	Unc	BU
1994	—	—	—BV+20%		—

KM# 695 CROWN Composition: Copper-Nickel **Series:** Normandy Invasion **Obverse:** Bust of Queen Elizabeth II right **Reverse:** Troop ship and landing craft

Date	F	VF	XF	Unc	BU
1994	—	—	—	6.50	—

KM# 695a CROWN Weight: 28.2800 g. **Composition:** 0.9250 Silver .8411 oz. ASW **Series:** Normandy Invasion **Obverse:** Bust of Queen Elizabeth II right **Reverse:** Troop ship and landing craft

Date	Mintage	F	VF	XF	Unc	BU
1994 Proof	Est. 30,000	Value: 26.50				

KM# 696 CROWN Composition: Copper-Nickel **Series:** Normandy Invasion **Obverse:** Bust of Queen Elizabeth II right **Reverse:** American troops landing

Date	F	VF	XF	Unc	BU
1994	—	—	—	6.50	—

KM# 696a CROWN Weight: 28.2800 g. **Composition:** 0.9250 Silver .8411 oz. ASW **Series:** Normandy Invasion **Obverse:** Bust of Queen Elizabeth II right **Reverse:** American troops landing

Date	Mintage	F	VF	XF	Unc	BU
1994 Proof	Est. 30,000	Value: 26.50				

KM# 697 CROWN Composition: Copper-Nickel **Series:** Normandy Invasion **Obverse:** Bust of Queen Elizabeth II right **Reverse:** American soldier behind rock

Date	F	VF	XF	Unc	BU
1994	—	—	—	6.50	—

KM# 697a CROWN Weight: 28.2800 g. **Composition:** 0.9250 Silver .8411 oz. ASW **Series:** Normandy Invasion **Obverse:** Bust of Queen Elizabeth II right **Reverse:** American soldier behind rock

Date	Mintage	F	VF	XF	Unc	BU
1994 Proof	Est. 30,000	Value: 26.50				

KM# 698 CROWN Composition: Copper-Nickel **Series:** Normandy Invasion **Obverse:** Bust of Queen Elizabeth II right **Reverse:** German machine gun nest

Date	F	VF	XF	Unc	BU
1994	—	—	—	6.50	—

KM# 698a CROWN Weight: 28.2800 g. **Composition:** 0.9250 Silver .8411 oz. ASW **Series:** Normandy Invasion **Obverse:** Bust of Queen Elizabeth II right **Reverse:** German machine gun nest

Date	Mintage	F	VF	XF	Unc	BU
1994 Proof	Est. 30,000	Value: 26.50				

KM# 699 CROWN Composition: Copper-Nickel **Series:** Normandy Invasion **Obverse:** Bust of Queen Elizabeth II right **Reverse:** British troops landing

Date	F	VF	XF	Unc	BU
1994	—	—	—	6.50	—

KM# 699a CROWN Weight: 28.2800 g. **Composition:** 0.9250 Silver .8411 oz. ASW **Series:** Normandy Invasion **Obverse:** Bust of Queen Elizabeth II right **Reverse:** British troops landing

Date	Mintage	F	VF	XF	Unc	BU
1994 Proof	Est. 30,000	Value: 26.50				

KM# 700 CROWN Composition: Copper-Nickel **Series:** Normandy Invasion **Obverse:** Bust of Queen Elizabeth II right **Reverse:** General Eisenhower facing left

Date	F	VF	XF	Unc	BU
1994	—	—	—	6.50	—

KM# 700a CROWN Weight: 28.2800 g. **Composition:** 0.9250 Silver .8411 oz. ASW **Series:** Normandy Invasion **Obverse:** Bust of Queen Elizabeth II right **Reverse:** General Eisenhower facing left

Date	Mintage	F	VF	XF	Unc	BU
1994 Proof	Est. 30,000	Value: 26.50				

KM# 701 CROWN Composition: Copper-Nickel **Series:** Normandy Invasion **Obverse:** Bust of Queen Elizabeth II right **Reverse:** General Omar Bradley looking right

Date	F	VF	XF	Unc	BU
1994	—	—	—	6.50	—

KM# 701a CROWN Weight: 28.2800 g. **Composition:** 0.9250 Silver .8411 oz. ASW **Series:** Normandy Invasion **Obverse:** Bust of Queen Elizabeth II right **Reverse:** General Omar Bradley looking right

Date	Mintage	F	VF	XF	Unc	BU
1994 Proof	Est. 30,000	Value: 26.50				

KM# 702 CROWN Composition: Copper-Nickel **Series:** Normandy Invasion **Obverse:** Bust of Queen Elizabeth II right **Reverse:** General Montgomery facing left

Date	F	VF	XF	Unc	BU
1994	—	—	—	6.50	—

KM# 702a CROWN Weight: 28.2800 g. **Composition:** 0.9250 Silver .8411 oz. ASW **Series:** Normandy Invasion **Obverse:** Bust of Queen Elizabeth II right **Reverse:** General Montgomery facing left

Date	Mintage	F	VF	XF	Unc	BU
1994 Proof	Est. 30,000	Value: 26.50				

KM# 703 CROWN Weight: 6.2200 g. **Composition:** 0.9999 Gold .2000 oz. AGW **Series:** Normandy Invasion **Obverse:** Bust of Queen Elizabeth II right **Reverse:** Troop ship and landing craft

Date	Mintage	F	VF	XF	Unc	BU
1994 Proof	Est. 5,000	Value: 165				

KM# 704 CROWN Weight: 6.2200 g. **Composition:** 0.9999 Gold .2000 oz. AGW **Series:** Normandy Invasion **Obverse:** Bust of Queen Elizabeth II right **Reverse:** American troops landing

Date	Mintage	F	VF	XF	Unc	BU
1994 Proof	Est. 5,000	Value: 165				

KM# 705 CROWN Weight: 6.2200 g. **Composition:** 0.9999 Gold .2000 oz. AGW **Series:** Normandy Invasion **Obverse:** Bust of Queen Elizabeth II right **Reverse:** American soldier behind rock

Date	Mintage	F	VF	XF	Unc	BU
1994 Proof	Est. 5,000	Value: 165				

KM# 706 CROWN Weight: 6.2200 g. **Composition:** 0.9999 Gold .2000 oz. AGW **Series:** Normandy Invasion **Obverse:** Bust of Queen Elizabeth II right **Reverse:** German machine gun nest

Date	Mintage	F	VF	XF	Unc	BU
1994 Proof	Est. 5,000	Value: 165				

KM# 707 CROWN **Weight:** 6.2200 g. **Composition:** 0.9999 Gold .2000 oz. AGW **Series:** Normandy Invasion **Obverse:** Bust of Queen Elizabeth II right **Reverse:** British troops landing

Date	Mintage	F	VF	XF	Unc	BU
1994 Proof	Est. 5,000	Value: 165				

KM# 708 CROWN **Weight:** 6.2200 g. **Composition:** 0.9999 Gold .2000 oz. AGW **Series:** Normandy Invasion **Obverse:** Bust of Queen Elizabeth II right **Reverse:** General Eisenhower facing left

Date	Mintage	F	VF	XF	Unc	BU
1994 Proof	Est. 5,000	Value: 165				

KM# 709 CROWN **Weight:** 6.2200 g. **Composition:** 0.9999 Gold .2000 oz. AGW **Series:** Normandy Invasion **Obverse:** Bust of Queen Elizabeth II right **Reverse:** General Omar Bradley facing right

Date	Mintage	F	VF	XF	Unc	BU
1994 Proof	Est. 5,000	Value: 165				

KM# 710 CROWN **Weight:** 6.2200 g. **Composition:** 0.9999 Gold .2000 oz. AGW **Series:** Normandy Invasion **Obverse:** Bust of Queen Elizabeth II right **Reverse:** General Montgomery facing left

Date	Mintage	F	VF	XF	Unc	BU
1994 Proof	Est. 5,000	Value: 165				

KM# 434 CROWN **Composition:** Copper-Nickel **Series:** Man in Flight **Obverse:** Bust of Queen Elizabeth II right **Reverse:** Icarus' wings melting

Date		F	VF	XF	Unc	BU
1995 Proof	—	Value: 7.50				

KM# 434a CROWN **Weight:** 28.2800 g. **Composition:** 0.9250 Silver .8411 oz. ASW **Series:** Man in Flight **Obverse:** Bust of Queen Elizabeth II right **Reverse:** Icarus' wings melting

Date	Mintage	F	VF	XF	Unc	BU
1995 Proof	Est. 30,000	Value: 37.50				

KM# 435 CROWN **Composition:** Copper-Nickel **Series:** Man in Flight **Obverse:** Bust of Queen Elizabeth II right **Reverse:** Leonardo Da Vinci and aircraft design

Date		F	VF	XF	Unc	BU
1995 Proof	—	Value: 6.50				

KM# 435a CROWN **Weight:** 28.2800 g. **Composition:** 0.9250 Silver .8411 oz. ASW **Series:** Man in Flight **Obverse:** Bust of Queen Elizabeth II right **Reverse:** Leonardo da Vinci and aircraft design

Date	Mintage	F	VF	XF	Unc	BU
1995 Proof	Est. 30,000	Value: 37.50				

KM# 436 CROWN **Composition:** Copper-Nickel **Series:** Man in Flight **Obverse:** Bust of Queen Elizabeth II right **Reverse:** Montgolfier Brothers' balloon

Date		F	VF	XF	Unc	BU
1995 Proof	—	Value: 7.50				

KM# 436a CROWN **Weight:** 28.2800 g. **Composition:** 0.9250 Silver .8411 oz. ASW **Series:** Man in Flight **Obverse:** Bust of Queen Elizabeth II right **Reverse:** Montgolfier Brothers' balloon

Date	Mintage	F	VF	XF	Unc	BU
1995 Proof	Est. 30,000	Value: 35.00				

KM# 437 CROWN **Composition:** Copper-Nickel **Series:** Man in Flight **Obverse:** Bust of Queen Elizabeth II right **Reverse:** Wright Brothers' airplane

Date		F	VF	XF	Unc	BU
1995 Proof	—	Value: 6.50				

KM# 437a CROWN **Weight:** 28.2800 g. **Composition:** 0.9250 Silver .8411 oz. ASW **Series:** Man in Flight **Obverse:** Bust of Queen Elizabeth II right **Reverse:** Wright brothers' airplane

Date	Mintage	F	VF	XF	Unc	BU
1995 Proof	Est. 30,000	Value: 38.50				

KM# 438 CROWN **Composition:** Copper-Nickel **Series:** Man in Flight **Subject:** First Flight Toyko to Paris **Obverse:** Bust of Queen Elizabeth II right **Reverse:** Heads of Abe and Kawachi over airplane

Date		F	VF	XF	Unc	BU
1995 Proof	—	Value: 6.50				

KM# 438a CROWN **Weight:** 28.2800 g. **Composition:** 0.9250 Silver .8411 oz. ASW **Series:** Man in Flight **Subject:** First Flight Tokyo to Paris **Obverse:** Bust of Queen Elizabeth II right **Reverse:** Heads of Abe and Kawachi above plane

Date	Mintage	F	VF	XF	Unc	BU
1995 Proof	Est. 30,000	Value: 40.00				

KM# 439.1 CROWN **Composition:** Copper-Nickel **Series:** Man in Flight **Obverse:** Bust of Queen Elizabeth II right **Reverse:** FW190, first diesel powered aircraft

Date	Mintage	F	VF	XF	Unc	BU
1995 Proof	500	Value: 12.50				

KM# 439.1a CROWN **Weight:** 28.2800 g. **Composition:** 0.9250 Silver .8411 oz. ASW **Series:** Man in Flight **Obverse:** Bust of Queen Elizabeth II right **Reverse:** First diesel powered aircraft

Date	Mintage	F	VF	XF	Unc	BU
1995 Proof	Est. 30,000	Value: 40.00				

KM# 439.2 CROWN **Composition:** Copper-Nickel **Series:** Man in Flight **Obverse:** Bust of Queen Elizabeth II right **Reverse:** FW190 BMW injection aero engine

Date	F	VF	XF	Unc	BU
1995	—	—	—	6.50	—

KM# 440.1 CROWN **Composition:** Copper-Nickel **Series:** Man in Flight **Obverse:** Bust of Queen Elizabeth II right **Reverse:** ME262, first jet aircraft 1941

Date	Mintage	F	VF	XF	Unc	BU
1995 Proof	500	Value: 12.50				

KM# 440.1a CROWN **Weight:** 28.2800 g. **Composition:** 0.9250 Silver .8411 oz. ASW **Series:** Man in Flight **Obverse:** Bust of Queen Elizabeth II right **Reverse:** ME262, first jet aircraft 1941

Date	Mintage	F	VF	XF	Unc	BU
1995 Proof	Est. 30,000	Value: 40.00				

KM# 440.2 CROWN **Composition:** Copper-Nickel **Series:** Man in Flight **Obverse:** Bust of Queen Elizabeth II right **Reverse:** Jet powered aircraft 1942

Date	F	VF	XF	Unc	BU
1995	—	—	—	6.50	—

KM# 441 CROWN **Composition:** Copper-Nickel **Series:** Man in Flight **Subject:** 25th Anniversary of Boeing 747 **Obverse:** Bust of Queen Elizabeth II right **Reverse:** Boeing 747

Date		F	VF	XF	Unc	BU
1995 Proof	—	Value: 6.50				

KM# 441a CROWN **Weight:** 28.2800 g. **Composition:** 0.9250 Silver .8411 oz. ASW **Series:** Man in Flight **Subject:** 25th Anniversary of Boeing 747 **Obverse:** Bust of Queen Elizabeth II right **Reverse:** Boeing 747

Date	Mintage	F	VF	XF	Unc	BU
1995 Proof	Est. 30,000	Value: 38.50				

KM# 446 CROWN **Composition:** Copper-Nickel **Obverse:** Bust of Queen Elizabeth II right **Reverse:** Turkish cat

Date	F	VF	XF	Unc	BU
1995	—	—	—	8.50	—

KM# 447 CROWN **Weight:** 31.1000 g. **Composition:** 0.9990 Silver 1.0000 oz. ASW **Obverse:** Bust of Queen Elizabeth II right **Reverse:** Turkish cat

Date		F	VF	XF	Unc	BU
1995 Proof	—	Value: 30.00				

KM# 448 CROWN **Weight:** 31.1000 g. **Composition:** 0.9990 Gold 1.0000 oz. AGW **Obverse:** Bust of Queen Elizabeth II right **Reverse:** Turkish cat

Date	F	VF	XF	Unc	BU
1995 U	—	—	—	400	—
1995 Proof	—	Value: 410			

KM# 453 CROWN **Composition:** Copper-Nickel **Subject:** Year of the Pig **Obverse:** Bust of Queen Elizabeth II right **Reverse:** Mother pig with piglets

Date	F	VF	XF	Unc	BU
1995	—	—	—	8.50	—

KM# 454 CROWN **Weight:** 31.1035 g. **Composition:** 0.9990 Silver 1.0000 oz. ASW **Subject:** Year of the Pig **Obverse:** Bust of Queen Elizabeth II right **Reverse:** Mother pig with piglets

Date	F	VF	XF	Unc	BU
1995 Proof	—	Value: 40.00			

KM# 455 CROWN **Weight:** 31.1035 g. **Composition:** 0.9990 Gold 1.0000 oz. AGW **Subject:** Year of the Pig **Obverse:** Bust of Queen Elizabeth II right **Reverse:** Mother pig with piglets

Date	Mintage	F	VF	XF	Unc	BU
1995 Proof	Est. 2,500	Value: 700				

KM# 458 CROWN **Composition:** Copper-Nickel **Subject:** 95th Birthday of Queen Mother **Obverse:** Bust of Queen Elizabeth II right **Reverse:** Bust of Queen Mother

Date	F	VF	XF	Unc	BU
1995	—	—	—	5.00	—

KM# 458a CROWN **Weight:** 28.2800 g. **Composition:** 0.9250 Silver .8411 oz. ASW **Subject:** 95th Birthday of Queen Mother **Obverse:** Bust of Queen Elizabeth II right **Reverse:** Bust of Queen Mother

Date	Mintage	F	VF	XF	Unc	BU
1995 Proof	Est. 30,000	Value: 35.00				

KM# 461 CROWN **Composition:** Copper-Nickel **Series:** Preserve Planet Earth **Obverse:** Bust of Queen Elizabeth II right **Reverse:** European otter

Date	F	VF	XF	Unc	BU
1995	—	—	—	8.50	—

KM# 461a CROWN **Weight:** 28.2800 g. **Composition:** 0.9250 Silver .8411 oz. ASW **Series:** Preserve Planet Earth **Obverse:** Bust of Queen Elizabeth II right **Reverse:** European otter

Date	Mintage	F	VF	XF	Unc	BU
1995 Proof	Est. 30,000	Value: 40.00				

KM# 462 CROWN **Composition:** Copper-Nickel **Series:** Preserve Planet Earth **Obverse:** Bust of Queen Elizabeth II right **Reverse:** Egrets

Date	F	VF	XF	Unc	BU
1995	—	—	—	8.50	—

KM# 462a CROWN **Weight:** 28.2800 g. **Composition:** 0.9250 Silver .8411 oz. ASW **Series:** Preserve Planet Earth **Obverse:** Bust of Queen Elizabeth II right **Reverse:** Egrets

Date	Mintage	F	VF	XF	Unc	BU
1995 Proof	Est. 30,000	Value: 40.00				

KM# 482 CROWN **Weight:** 31.1035 g. **Composition:** 0.9995 Platinum .9995 oz. APW **Obverse:** Bust of Queen Elizabeth II right **Reverse:** Turkish cat

Date	F	VF	XF	Unc	BU
1995	—	—	—BV+20%		—

KM# 502 CROWN **Composition:** Copper-Nickel **Series:** Aircraft of World War II **Obverse:** Bust of Queen Elizabeth II right **Reverse:** Hawker Hurricane

Date	F	VF	XF	Unc	BU
1995	—	—	—	5.50	—

KM# 502a CROWN **Weight:** 28.2800 g. **Composition:** 0.9250 Silver .8411 oz. ASW **Series:** Aircraft of World War II **Obverse:** Bust of Queen Elizabeth II right **Reverse:** Hawker Hurricane

Date	Mintage	F	VF	XF	Unc	BU
1995 Proof	Est. 30,000	Value: 30.00				

KM# 503 CROWN **Composition:** Copper-Nickel **Series:** Aircraft of World War II **Obverse:** Bust of Queen Elizabeth II right **Reverse:** P-51 Mustang

Date	F	VF	XF	Unc	BU
1995	—	—	—	—	—

KM# 503a CROWN **Weight:** 28.2800 g. **Composition:** 0.9250 Silver .8411 oz. ASW **Series:** Aircraft of World War II **Obverse:** Bust of Queen Elizabeth II right **Reverse:** P-51 Mustang

Date	F	VF	XF	Unc	BU
1995 Proof	—	Value: 30.00			

KM# 504 CROWN **Composition:** Copper-Nickel **Series:** Aircraft of World War II **Obverse:** Bust of Queen Elizabeth II right **Reverse:** Letov 5328

Date	F	VF	XF	Unc	BU
1995	—	—	—	5.50	—

KM# 504a CROWN **Weight:** 28.2800 g. **Composition:** 0.9250 Silver .8411 oz. ASW **Series:** Aircraft of World War II **Obverse:** Bust of Queen Elizabeth II right **Reverse:** Letov 5328

Date	Mintage	F	VF	XF	Unc	BU
1995 Proof	Est. 30,000	Value: 30.00				

KM# 505 CROWN **Composition:** Copper-Nickel **Series:** Aircraft of World War II **Obverse:** Bust of Queen Elizabeth II right **Reverse:** Messerschmitt ME262

Date	F	VF	XF	Unc	BU
1995	—	—	—	5.50	—

KM# 505a CROWN **Weight:** 28.2800 g. **Composition:** 0.9250 Silver .8411 oz. ASW **Series:** Aircraft of World War II **Obverse:** Bust of Queen Elizabeth II right **Reverse:** Messerschmitt ME262

Date	Mintage	F	VF	XF	Unc	BU
1995 Proof	Est. 30,000	Value: 30.00				

KM# 506 CROWN **Composition:** Copper-Nickel **Series:** Aircraft of World War II **Obverse:** Bust of Queen Elizabeth II right **Reverse:** JU87 Stuka

Date	F	VF	XF	Unc	BU
1995	—	—	—	5.50	—

KM# 506a CROWN **Weight:** 28.2800 g. **Composition:** 0.9250 Silver .8411 oz. ASW **Series:** Aircraft of World War II **Obverse:** Bust of Queen Elizabeth II right **Reverse:** JU87 Stuka

Date	Mintage	F	VF	XF	Unc	BU
1995 Proof	Est. 30,000	Value: 30.00				

KM# 507 CROWN **Composition:** Copper-Nickel **Series:** Aircraft of World War II **Obverse:** Bust of Queen Elizabeth II right **Reverse:** MIG 3

Date	F	VF	XF	Unc	BU
1995	—	—	—	5.50	—

KM# 507a CROWN **Weight:** 28.2800 g. **Composition:** 0.9250 Silver .8411 oz. ASW **Series:** Aircraft of World War II **Obverse:** Bust of Queen Elizabeth II right **Reverse:** MIG 3

Date	Mintagd	F	VF	XF	Unc	BU
1995 Proof	Est. 30,000	Value: 30.00				

KM# 508 CROWN **Composition:** Copper-Nickel **Series:** Aircraft of World War II **Obverse:** Bust of Queen Elizabeth II right **Reverse:** Nakajima KI-49 Donryu

Date	F	VF	XF	Unc	BU
1995	—	—	—	5.50	—

KM# 508a CROWN **Weight:** 28.2800 g. **Composition:** 0.9250 Silver .8411 oz. ASW **Series:** Aircraft of World War II **Obverse:** Bust of Queen Elizabeth II right **Reverse:** Nakajima KI-49 Donryu

Date	Mintage	F	VF	XF	Unc	BU
1995 Proof	Est. 30,000	Value: 30.00				

KM# 509 CROWN **Composition:** Copper-Nickel **Series:** Aircraft of World War II **Obverse:** Bust of Queen Elizabeth II right **Reverse:** Vickers Wellington

Date	F	VF	XF	Unc	BU
1995	—	—	—	5.50	—

KM# 509a CROWN **Weight:** 28.2800 g. **Composition:** 0.9250 Silver .8411 oz. ASW **Series:** Aircraft of World War II **Obverse:** Bust of Queen Elizabeth II right **Reverse:** Vickers Wellington

Date	Mintage	F	VF	XF	Unc	BU
1995 Proof	Est. 30,000	Value: 30.00				

KM# 510 CROWN **Composition:** Copper-Nickel **Series:** Aircraft of World War II **Obverse:** Bust of Queen Elizabeth II right **Reverse:** Supermarine Spitfire

Date	F	VF	XF	Unc	BU
1995 (py)	—	—	—	5.50	—
1995	—	—	—	5.50	—

KM# 510a CROWN **Weight:** 28.2800 g. **Composition:** 0.9250 Silver .8411 oz. ASW **Series:** Aircraft of World War II **Obverse:** Bust of Queen Elizabeth II right **Reverse:** Supermarine Spitfire

Date	Mintage	F	VF	XF	Unc	BU
1995 Proof	Est. 30,000	Value: 30.00				

KM# 511 CROWN **Composition:** Copper-Nickel **Series:** Aircraft of World War II **Obverse:** Bust of Queen Elizabeth II right **Reverse:** Fokker G.1a

Date	F	VF	XF	Unc	BU
1995	—	—	—	5.50	—

KM# 511a CROWN **Weight:** 28.2800 g. **Composition:** 0.9250 Silver .8411 oz. ASW **Series:** Aircraft of World War II **Obverse:** Bust of Queen Elizabeth II right **Reverse:** Fokker G.1a

Date	Mintage	F	VF	XF	Unc	BU
1995 Proof	Est. 30,000	Value: 30.00				

KM# 512 CROWN **Composition:** Copper-Nickel **Series:** Aircraft of World War II **Obverse:** Bust of Queen Elizabeth II right **Reverse:** Commonwealth Boomerang CA-13

Date	F	VF	XF	Unc	BU
1995	—	—	—	5.50	—

KM# 512a CROWN **Weight:** 28.2800 g. **Composition:** 0.9250 Silver .8411 oz. ASW **Series:** Aircraft of World War II **Obverse:** Bust of Queen Elizabeth II right **Reverse:** Boomerang CA-13

Date	Mintage	F	VF	XF	Unc	BU
1995 Proof	Est. 30,000	Value: 30.00				

KM# 513 CROWN **Composition:** Copper-Nickel **Series:** Aircraft of World War II **Obverse:** Bust of Queen Elizabeth II right **Reverse:** Bristol Blenheim 142

Date	F	VF	XF	Unc	BU
1995	—	—	—	5.50	—

KM# 513a CROWN **Weight:** 28.2800 g. **Composition:** 0.9250 Silver .8411 oz. ASW **Series:** Aircraft of World War II **Obverse:** Bust of Queen Elizabeth II right **Reverse:** Bristol Blenheim 142

Date	Mintage	F	VF	XF	Unc	BU
1995 Proof	Est. 30,000	Value: 30.00				

KM# 514 CROWN **Composition:** Copper-Nickel **Series:** Aircraft of World War II **Obverse:** Bust of Queen Elizabeth II right **Reverse:** Mitsubishi Zero

Date	F	VF	XF	Unc	BU
1995	—	—	—	5.50	—

KM# 514a CROWN **Weight:** 28.2800 g. **Composition:** 0.9250 Silver .8411 oz. ASW **Series:** Aircraft of World War II **Obverse:** Bust of Queen Elizabeth II right **Reverse:** Mitsubishi Zero

Date	Mintage	F	VF	XF	Unc	BU
1995 Proof	Est. 30,000	Value: 30.00				

KM# 515 CROWN **Composition:** Copper-Nickel **Series:** Aircraft of World War II **Obverse:** Bust of Queen Elizabeth II right **Reverse:** Heinkel HE 111

Date	F	VF	XF	Unc	BU
1995	—	—	—	5.50	—

KM# 515a CROWN **Weight:** 28.2800 g. **Composition:** 0.9250 Silver .8411 oz. ASW **Series:** Aircraft of World War II **Obverse:** Bust of Queen Elizabeth II right **Reverse:** Heinkel HE 111

Date	Mintage	F	VF	XF	Unc	BU
1995 Proof	Est. 30,000	Value: 30.00				

KM# 516 CROWN **Composition:** Copper-Nickel **Series:** Aircraft of World War II **Obverse:** Bust of Queen Elizabeth II right **Reverse:** Boulton Paul P.82 Defiant

Date	F	VF	XF	Unc	BU
1995	—	—	—	5.50	—

KM# 516a CROWN **Weight:** 28.2800 g. **Composition:** 0.9250 Silver .8411 oz. ASW **Series:** Aircraft of World War II **Obverse:** Bust of Queen Elizabeth II right **Reverse:** Boulton Paul P.82 Defiant

Date	Mintage	F	VF	XF	Unc	BU
1995 Proof	Est. 30,000	Value: 30.00				

KM# 517 CROWN **Composition:** Copper-Nickel **Series:** Aircraft of World War II **Obverse:** Bust of Queen Elizabeth II right **Reverse:** Boeing B-29 Enola Gay

Date	F	VF	XF	Unc	BU
1995	—	—	—	5.50	—

KM# 517a CROWN **Weight:** 28.2800 g. **Composition:** 0.9250 Silver .8411 oz. ASW **Series:** Aircraft of World War II **Obverse:** Bust of Queen Elizabeth II right **Reverse:** Boeing B-29 Enola Gay

Date	Mintage	F	VF	XF	Unc	BU
1995 Proof	Est. 30,000	Value: 30.00				

KM# 518 CROWN **Composition:** Copper-Nickel **Series:** Aircraft of World War II **Obverse:** Bust of Queen Elizabeth II right **Reverse:** Douglas DC-3 (C-47) Dakota

Date	F	VF	XF	Unc	BU
1995	—	—	—	5.50	—

KM# 518a CROWN **Weight:** 28.2800 g. **Composition:** 0.9250 Silver .8411 oz. ASW **Series:** Aircraft of World War II **Obverse:** Bust of Queen Elizabeth II right **Reverse:** Douglas DC-3 (C-47) Dakota

Date	Mintage	F	VF	XF	Unc	BU
1995 Proof	Est. 30,000	Value: 30.00				

KM# 519 CROWN Composition: Copper-Nickel **Series:** Aircraft of World War II **Obverse:** Bust of Queen Elizabeth II right **Reverse:** Fairey Swordfish

Date	F	VF	XF	Unc	BU
1995	—	—	—	5.50	—

KM# 519a CROWN Weight: 28.2800 g. **Composition:** 0.9250 Silver .8411 oz. ASW **Series:** Aircraft of World War II **Obverse:** Bust of Queen Elizabeth II right **Reverse:** Fairey Swordfish

Date	Mintage	F	VF	XF	Unc	BU
1995 Proof	Est. 30,000	Value: 30.00				

KM# 520 CROWN Composition: Copper-Nickel **Series:** Aircraft of WW II **Obverse:** Bust of Queen Elizabeth II right **Reverse:** Curtiss P-40 Tomahawk

Date	F	VF	XF	Unc	BU
1995	—	—	—	5.50	—

KM# 520a CROWN Weight: 28.2800 g. **Composition:** 0.9250 Silver .8411 oz. ASW **Series:** Aircraft of WW II **Obverse:** Bust of Queen Elizabeth II right **Reverse:** Curtiss P-40 Tomahawk

Date	Mintage	F	VF	XF	Unc	BU
1995 Proof	Est. 30,000	Value: 30.00				

KM# 524 CROWN Composition: Copper-Nickel **Series:** America's Cup **Obverse:** Bust of Queen Elizabeth II right **Reverse:** Sailboats

Date	F	VF	XF	Unc	BU
1995	—	—	—	5.00	—

KM# 524a CROWN Weight: 28.2800 g. **Composition:** 0.9250 Silver .8411 oz. ASW **Series:** America's Cup **Obverse:** Bust of Queen Elizabeth II right **Reverse:** Sailboats

Date	Mintage	F	VF	XF	Unc	BU
1995 Proof	Est. 30,000	Value: 50.00				

KM# 526 CROWN Composition: Copper-Nickel **Series:** Inventions of the Modern World **Obverse:** Bust of Queen Elizabeth II right **Reverse:** Cameo Tsai Lun, paper and tree

Date	F	VF	XF	Unc	BU
1995	—	—	—	5.00	—

KM# 526a CROWN Weight: 28.2800 g. **Composition:** 0.9250 Silver .8411 oz. ASW **Series:** Inventions of the Modern World **Obverse:** Bust of Queen Elizabeth II right **Reverse:** Cameo of Tsai Lun, paper and tree

Date	Mintage	F	VF	XF	Unc	BU
1995 Proof	Est. 30,000	Value: 40.00				

KM# 528 CROWN Composition: Copper-Nickel **Series:** Inventions of the Modern World **Obverse:** Bust of Queen Elizabeth II right **Reverse:** Cameo of Chang Heng and seismograph

Date	F	VF	XF	Unc	BU
1995	—	—	—	5.00	—

KM# 528a CROWN Weight: 28.2800 g. **Composition:** 0.9250 Silver .8411 oz. ASW **Series:** Inventions of the Modern World **Obverse:** Bust of Queen Elizabeth II right **Reverse:** Cameo of Chang Heng and seismograph

Date	Mintage	F	VF	XF	Unc	BU
1995 Proof	Est. 30,000	Value: 40.00				

KM# 530 CROWN Composition: Copper-Nickel **Series:** Inventions of the Modern World **Obverse:** Bust of Queen Elizabeth II right **Reverse:** Cameo of Tsu Chung Chih and compass cart

Date	F	VF	XF	Unc	BU
1995	—	—	—	5.00	—

KM# 530a CROWN Weight: 28.2800 g. **Composition:** 0.9250 Silver .8411 oz. ASW **Series:** Inventions of the Modern World **Obverse:** Bust of Queen Elizabeth II right **Reverse:** Cameo of Tsu Chung Chih and compass car

Date	Mintage	F	VF	XF	Unc	BU
1995 Proof	Est. 30,000	Value: 40.00				

KM# 532 CROWN Composition: Copper-Nickel **Series:** Inventions of the Modern World **Obverse:** Bust of Queen Elizabeth II right **Reverse:** Cameo of Pi Sheng and movable type

Date	F	VF	XF	Unc	BU
1995	—	—	—	5.00	—

KM# 532a CROWN Weight: 28.2800 g. **Composition:** 0.9250 Silver .8411 oz. ASW **Series:** Inventions of the Modern World **Obverse:** Bust of Queen Elizabeth II right **Reverse:** Cameo of Pi Sheng and movable type

Date	Mintage	F	VF	XF	Unc	BU
1995 Proof	Est. 30,000	Value: 40.00				

KM# 534 CROWN Composition: Copper-Nickel **Series:** Inventions of the Modern World **Obverse:** Bust of Queen Elizabeth II right **Reverse:** Cameo of Charles Babbage and first computer

Date	F	VF	XF	Unc	BU
1995	—	—	—	5.00	—

KM# 534a CROWN Weight: 28.2800 g. **Composition:** 0.9250 Silver .8411 oz. ASW **Series:** Inventions of the Modern World **Obverse:** Bust of Queen Elizabeth II right **Reverse:** Cameo of Charles Babbage and first computer

Date	Mintage	F	VF	XF	Unc	BU
1995 Proof	Est. 30,000	Value: 40.00				

KM# 536 CROWN Composition: Copper-Nickel **Series:** Inventions of the Modern World **Obverse:** Bust of Queen Elizabeth II right **Reverse:** Cameo of Fox Talbot, photography

Date	F	VF	XF	Unc	BU
1995	—	—	—	5.00	—

KM# 536a CROWN Weight: 28.2800 g. **Composition:** 0.9250 Silver .8411 oz. ASW **Series:** Inventions of the Modern World **Obverse:** Bust of Queen Elizabeth II right **Reverse:** Cameo of Fox Talbot, photography

Date	Mintage	F	VF	XF	Unc	BU
1995 Proof	Est. 30,000	Value: 40.00				

KM# 538 CROWN Composition: Copper-Nickel **Series:** Inventions of the Modern World **Obverse:** Bust of Queen Elizabeth II right **Reverse:** Cameo Rudolf Diesel and engine

Date	F	VF	XF	Unc	BU
1995	—	—	—	5.00	—

KM# 538a CROWN Weight: 28.2800 g. **Composition:** 0.9250 Silver .8411 oz. ASW **Series:** Inventions of the Modern World **Obverse:** Bust of Queen Elizabeth II right **Reverse:** Cameo of Rudolf Diesel and engine

Date	Mintage	F	VF	XF	Unc	BU
1995 Proof	Est. 30,000	Value: 40.00				

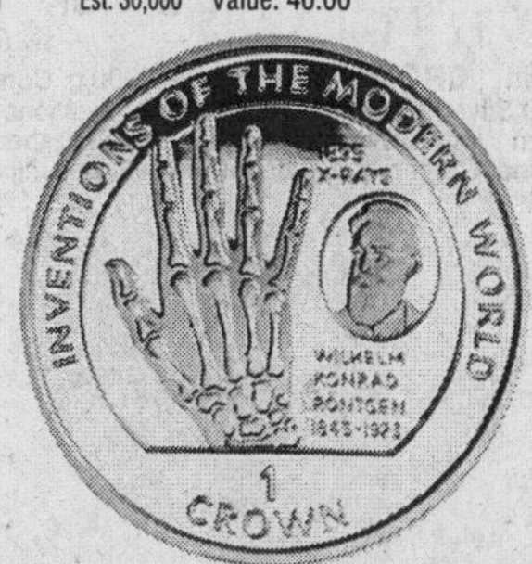

KM# 540 CROWN Composition: Copper-Nickel **Series:** Inventions of the Modern World **Obverse:** Bust of Queen Elizabeth II right **Reverse:** Cameo of Wilhelm K. Roentgern, xray

Date	F	VF	XF	Unc	BU
1995	—	—	—	5.00	—

KM# 540a CROWN **Weight:** 28.2800 g. **Composition:** 0.9250 Silver .8411 oz. ASW **Series:** Inventions of the Modern World **Obverse:** Bust of Queen Elizabeth II right **Reverse:** Cameo of Wilhelm K. Roentgen, xray

Date	Mintage	F	VF	XF	Unc	BU
1995 Proof	Est. 30,000	Value: 40.00				

KM# 542 CROWN **Composition:** Copper-Nickel **Series:** Inventions of the Modern World **Obverse:** Bust of Queen Elizabeth II right **Reverse:** Cameo of Guglielmo Marconi, radio equipment

Date	F	VF	XF	Unc	BU
1995	—	—	—	5.00	—

KM# 542a CROWN **Weight:** 28.2800 g. **Composition:** 0.9250 Silver .8411 oz. ASW **Series:** Inventions of the Modern World **Obverse:** Bust of Queen Elizabeth II right **Reverse:** Cameo of Guglielmo Marconi and radio equipment

Date	Mintage	F	VF	XF	Unc	BU
1995 Proof	Est. 30,000	Value: 40.00				

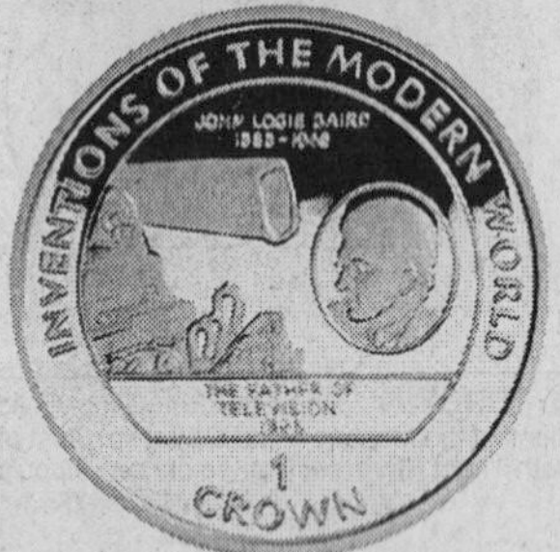

KM# 544 CROWN **Composition:** Copper-Nickel **Series:** Inventions of the Modern World **Obverse:** Bust of Queen Elizabeth II right **Reverse:** Cameo L. Baird and television equipment

Date	F	VF	XF	Unc	BU
1995	—	—	—	5.00	—

KM# 544a CROWN **Weight:** 28.2800 g. **Composition:** 0.9250 Silver .8411 oz. ASW **Series:** Inventions of the Modern World **Obverse:** Bust of Queen Elizabeth II right **Reverse:** Cameo of John L. Baird and television equipment

Date	Mintage	F	VF	XF	Unc	BU
1995 Proof	Est. 30,000	Value: 40.00				

KM# 546 CROWN **Composition:** Copper-Nickel **Series:** Inventions of the Modern World **Obverse:** Bust of Queen Elizabeth II right **Reverse:** Cameo of Alexander Fleming and microscope

Date	F	VF	XF	Unc	BU
1995	—	—	—	5.00	—

KM# 546a CROWN **Weight:** 28.2800 g. **Composition:** 0.9250 Silver .8411 oz. ASW **Series:** Inventions of the Modern World **Obverse:** Bust of Queen Elizabeth II right **Reverse:** Cameo of Alexander Fleming and microscope

Date	F	VF	XF	Unc	BU
1995 Proof	—	—	—	40.00	—

KM# 548 CROWN **Composition:** Copper-Nickel **Series:** Inventions of the Modern World **Obverse:** Bust of Queen Elizabeth II right **Reverse:** Cameo of Lazlo Bird, ball-point pen

Date	F	VF	XF	Unc	BU
1995	—	—	—	5.00	—

KM# 548a CROWN **Weight:** 28.2800 g. **Composition:** 0.9250 Silver .8411 oz. ASW **Series:** Inventions of the Modern World **Obverse:** Bust of Queen Elizabeth II right **Reverse:** Cameo of Lazlo Bird, ball-point pen

Date	Mintage	F	VF	XF	Unc	BU
1995 Proof	Est. 30,000	Value: 40.00				

KM# 555 CROWN **Composition:** Copper-Nickel **Series:** Inventions of the Modern World **Obverse:** Bust of Queen Elizabeth II right **Reverse:** Cameo of Wernher von Braun and rocket

Date	F	VF	XF	Unc	BU
1996	—	—	—	5.00	—

KM# 555a CROWN **Weight:** 28.2800 g. **Composition:** 0.9250 Silver .8411 oz. ASW **Series:** Inventions of the Modern World **Obverse:** Bust of Queen Elizabeth II right **Reverse:** Cameo of Wernher von Braun and rocket

Date	Mintage	F	VF	XF	Unc	BU
1996 Proof	Est. 30,000	Value: 40.00				

KM# 556 CROWN **Composition:** Copper-Nickel **Series:** Inventions of the Modern World **Obverse:** Bust of Queen Elizabeth II right **Reverse:** Cameo of Thomas Edison, electricity

Date	F	VF	XF	Unc	BU
1996	—	—	—	5.00	—

KM# 556a CROWN **Weight:** 28.2800 g. **Composition:** 0.9250 Silver .8411 oz. ASW **Series:** Inventions of the Modern World **Obverse:** Bust of Queen Elizabeth II right **Reverse:** Cameo of Thomas Edison, electricity

Date	F	VF	XF	Unc	BU
1996 Proof	—	—	—	40.00	—

KM# 557a CROWN **Weight:** 28.2800 g. **Composition:** 0.9250 Silver .8411 oz. ASW **Series:** Inventions of the Modern World **Obverse:** Bust of Queen Elizabeth II right **Reverse:** Compass

Date		F	VF	XF	Unc	BU
1996 Proof	—	Value: 40.00				

KM# 558.1 CROWN **Composition:** Copper-Nickel **Series:** Inventions of the Modern World **Obverse:** Bust of Queen Elizabeth II right **Reverse:** Cameo of Michael Faraday, electricity

Date	F	VF	XF	Unc	BU
1996	—	—	—	5.00	—

KM# 558.2 CROWN **Composition:** Copper-Nickel **Series:** Inventions of the Modern World **Obverse:** Bust of Queen Elizabeth II right **Reverse:** Cameo of Michael Faraday, electricity. Error legend: EXRERIMENTAL

Date	F	VF	XF	Unc	BU
1996	—	—	—	12.50	—

KM# 558.2a CROWN **Weight:** 28.2800 g. **Composition:** 0.9250 Silver .8411 oz. ASW **Series:** Inventions of the Modern World **Obverse:** Bust of Queen Elizabeth II right **Reverse:** Cameo of Michael Faraday, electricity. Error legend: EXRERIMENTAL

Date	Mintage	F	VF	XF	Unc	BU
1996 Proof	Est. 30,000	Value: 40.00				

KM# 559 CROWN **Composition:** Copper-Nickel **Series:** Inventions of the Modern World **Obverse:** Bust of Queen Elizabeth II right **Reverse:** Emile Berliner, gramophone

Date	F	VF	XF	Unc	BU
1996	—	—	—	5.00	—

KM# 560 CROWN **Composition:** Copper-Nickel **Series:** Inventions of the Modern World **Obverse:** Bust of Queen Elizabeth II right **Reverse:** Cameo of Alexander Graham Bell, voice transmission

Date	F	VF	XF	Unc	BU
1996	—	—	—	5.00	—

KM# 560a CROWN **Weight:** 28.2800 g. **Composition:** 0.9250 Silver .8411 oz. ASW **Series:** Inventions of the Modern World **Obverse:** Bust of Queen Elizabeth II right **Reverse:** Cameo of Alexander Graham Bell, voice transmission

Date	Mintage	F	VF	XF	Unc	BU
1996 Proof	30,000	Value: 40.00				

KM# 567 CROWN **Composition:** Copper-Nickel **Series:** 1996 Summer Olympics - Atlanta **Obverse:** Bust of Queen Elizabeth II right **Reverse:** Hurdler

Date	F	VF	XF	Unc	BU
1996	—	—	—	6.00	—

KM# 567a CROWN **Weight:** 28.2800 g. **Composition:** 0.9250 Silver .8411 oz. ASW **Series:** 1996 Summer Olympics - Atlanta **Obverse:** Bust of Queen Elizabeth II right **Reverse:** Hurdler

Date	Mintage	F	VF	XF	Unc	BU
1996 Proof	Est. 30,000	Value: 35.00				

KM# 568 CROWN Composition: Copper-Nickel **Series:** 1996 Summer Olympics - Atlanta **Obverse:** Bust of Queen Elizabeth II right **Reverse:** Runners

Date	F	VF	XF	Unc	BU
1996	—	—	—	6.00	—

KM# 568a CROWN Weight: 28.2800 g. **Composition:** 0.9250 Silver .8411 oz. ASW **Series:** 1996 Summer Olympics - Atlanta **Obverse:** Bust of Queen Elizabeth II right **Reverse:** Runners

Date	Mintage	F	VF	XF	Unc	BU
1996 Proof	Est. 30,000	Value: 35.00				

KM# 569 CROWN Composition: Copper-Nickel **Series:** 1996 Summer Olympics - Atlanta **Obverse:** Bust of Queen Elizabeth II right **Reverse:** Sailing

Date	F	VF	XF	Unc	BU
1996	—	—	—	6.00	—

KM# 569a CROWN Weight: 28.2800 g. **Composition:** 0.9250 Silver .8411 oz. ASW **Series:** 1996 Summer Olympics - Atlanta **Obverse:** Bust of Queen Elizabeth II right **Reverse:** Sailing

Date	Mintage	F	VF	XF	Unc	BU
1996 Proof	Est. 30,000	Value: 35.00				

KM# 570 CROWN Composition: Copper-Nickel **Series:** 1996 Summer Olympics - Atlanta **Obverse:** Bust of Queen Elizabeth II right **Reverse:** Swimming

Date	F	VF	XF	Unc	BU
1996	—	—	—	6.00	—

KM# 570a CROWN Weight: 28.2800 g. **Composition:** 0.9250 Silver .8411 oz. ASW **Series:** 1996 Summer Olympics - Atlanta **Obverse:** Bust of Queen Elizabeth II right **Reverse:** Swimming

Date	Mintage	F	VF	XF	Unc	BU
1996 Proof	Est. 30,000	Value: 35.00				

KM# 571 CROWN Composition: Copper-Nickel **Series:** 1996 Summer Olympics - Atlanta **Obverse:** Bust of Queen Elizabeth II right **Reverse:** Equestrian

Date	F	VF	XF	Unc	BU
1996	—	—	—	6.00	—

KM# 571a CROWN Weight: 28.2800 g. **Composition:** 0.9250 Silver .8411 oz. ASW **Series:** 1996 Summer Olympics - Atlanta **Obverse:** Bust of Queen Elizabeth II right **Reverse:** Equestrian

Date	Mintage	F	VF	XF	Unc	BU
1996 Proof	Est. 30,000	Value: 35.00				

KM# 572 CROWN Composition: Copper-Nickel **Series:** 1996 Summer Olympics - Atlanta **Obverse:** Bust of Queen Elizabeth II right **Reverse:** Cyclists and Nike

Date	F	VF	XF	Unc	BU
1996	—	—	—	6.00	—

KM# 572a CROWN Weight: 28.2800 g. **Composition:** 0.9250 Silver .8411 oz. ASW **Series:** 1996 Summer Olympics - Atlanta **Obverse:** Bust of Queen Elizabeth II right **Reverse:** Cyclists and Nike

Date	Mintage	F	VF	XF	Unc	BU
1996 Proof	Est. 30,000	Value: 35.00				

KM# 577 CROWN Composition: Copper-Nickel **Series:** Bicentenary of Robert Burns **Obverse:** Bust of Queen Elizabeth II right **Reverse:** Burns seated

Date	F	VF	XF	Unc	BU
1996	—	—	—	5.00	—

KM# 577a CROWN Weight: 28.2800 g. **Composition:** 0.9250 Silver .8411 oz. ASW **Series:** Bicentenary of Robert Burns **Obverse:** Bust of Queen Elizabeth II right **Reverse:** Burns seated

Date	Mintage	F	VF	XF	Unc	BU
1996 Proof	Est. 30,000	Value: 40.00				

KM# 578 CROWN Composition: Copper-Nickel **Series:** Bicentenary of Robert Burns **Obverse:** Bust of Queen Elizabeth II right **Reverse:** Pirate ship

Date	F	VF	XF	Unc	BU
1996	—	—	—	5.00	—

KM# 578a CROWN Weight: 28.2800 g. **Composition:** 0.9250 Silver .8411 oz. ASW **Series:** Bicentenary of Robert Burns **Obverse:** Bust of Queen Elizabeth II right **Reverse:** Pirate ship

Date	Mintage	F	VF	XF	Unc	BU
1996 Proof	Est. 30,000	Value: 40.00				

KM# 579 CROWN Composition: Copper-Nickel **Series:** Bicentenary of Robert Burns **Obverse:** Bust of Queen Elizabeth II right **Reverse:** Auld Lang Syne

Date	F	VF	XF	Unc	BU
1996	—	—	—	5.00	—

KM# 579a CROWN Weight: 28.2800 g. **Composition:** 0.9250 Silver .8411 oz. ASW **Series:** Bicentenary of Robert Burns **Obverse:** Bust of Queen Elizabeth II right **Reverse:** Auld Lang Syne

Date	Mintage	F	VF	XF	Unc	BU
1996 Proof	Est. 30,000	Value: 40.00				

KM# 580 CROWN Composition: Copper-Nickel **Series:** Bicentenary of Robert Burns **Obverse:** Bust of Queen Elizabeth II right **Reverse:** Edinburgh Castle

Date	F	VF	XF	Unc	BU
1996	—	—	—	5.00	—

KM# 580a CROWN Weight: 28.2800 g. **Composition:** 0.9250 Silver .8411 oz. ASW **Series:** Bicentenary of Robert Burns **Obverse:** Bust of Queen Elizabeth II right **Reverse:** Edinburgh Castle

Date	Mintage	F	VF	XF	Unc	BU
1996 Proof	Est. 30,000	Value: 40.00				

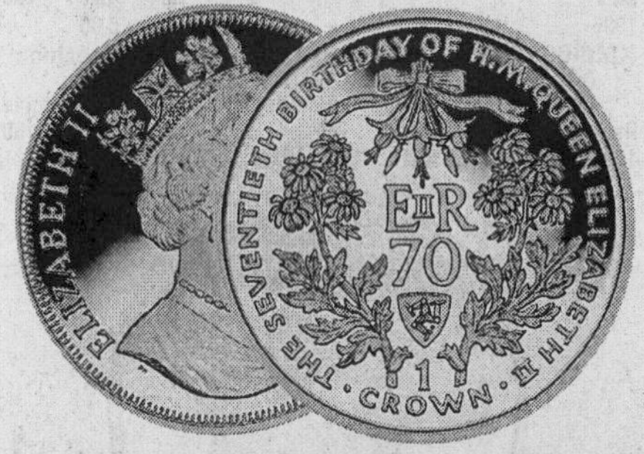

KM# 582 CROWN Weight: 28.2800 g. **Composition:** 0.9250 Silver .8411 oz. ASW **Subject:** 70th Birthday of Queen Elizabeth II **Obverse:** Bust of Queen Elizabeth II right **Reverse:** Flowers

Date	F	VF	XF	Unc	BU
1996	—	—	—	6.00	—

KM# 582a CROWN Weight: 28.2800 g. **Composition:** 0.9250 Silver .8411 oz. ASW **Subject:** 70th Birthday of Queen Elizabeth II **Obverse:** Bust of Queen Elizabeth II right **Reverse:** Flowers

Date	Mintage	F	VF	XF	Unc	BU
1996 Proof	Est. 30,000	Value: 40.00				

KM# 585 CROWN Composition: Copper-Nickel **Series:** Preserve Planet Earth **Obverse:** Bust of Queen Elizabeth II right **Reverse:** Killer whale

Date	F	VF	XF	Unc	BU
1996	—	—	—	8.50	—

KM# 585a CROWN Weight: 28.2800 g. **Composition:** 0.9250 Silver .8411 oz. ASW **Series:** Preserve Planet Earth **Obverse:** Bust of Queen Elizabeth II right **Reverse:** Killer whale

Date	Mintage	F	VF	XF	Unc	BU
1996 Proof	Est. 30,000	Value: 40.00				

KM# 586 CROWN Composition: Copper-Nickel **Series:** Preserve Planet Earth **Obverse:** Bust of Queen Elizabeth II right **Reverse:** Razorbill feeding chick

Date	F	VF	XF	Unc	BU
1996	—	—	—	8.50	—

KM# 586a CROWN Weight: 28.2800 g. **Composition:** 0.9250 Silver .8411 oz. ASW **Series:** Preserve Planet Earth **Obverse:** Bust of Queen Elizabeth II right **Reverse:** Razorbill feeding check

Date	Mintage	F	VF	XF	Unc	BU
1996 Proof	Est. 30,000	Value: 40.00				

KM# 609 CROWN Composition: Copper-Nickel **Series:** Flower Fairies **Obverse:** Bust of Queen Elizabeth II right **Reverse:** Orchis

Date	F	VF	XF	Unc	BU
1996	—	—	—	5.00	—

KM# 609a CROWN Weight: 28.2800 g. **Composition:** 0.9250 Silver .8411 oz. ASW **Series:** Flower Fairies **Obverse:** Bust of Queen Elizabeth II right **Reverse:** Orchis

Date	Mintage	F	VF	XF	Unc	BU
1996 Proof	Est. 30,000	Value: 40.00				

KM# 610 CROWN Composition: Copper-Nickel **Series:** Flower Fairies **Obverse:** Bust of Queen Elizabeth II right **Reverse:** Rose

Date	F	VF	XF	Unc	BU
1996	—	—	—	5.00	—

KM# 610a CROWN Weight: 28.2800 g. **Composition:** 0.9250 Silver .8411 oz. ASW **Series:** Flower Fairies **Obverse:** Bust of Queen Elizabeth II right **Reverse:** Rose

Date	Mintage	F	VF	XF	Unc	BU
1996 Proof	Est. 30,000	Value: 40.00				

KM# 611 CROWN Composition: Copper-Nickel **Series:** Flower Fairies **Obverse:** Bust of Queen Elizabeth II right **Reverse:** Fuchsia

Date	F	VF	XF	Unc	BU
1996	—	—	—	5.00	—

KM# 611a CROWN Weight: 28.2800 g. **Composition:** 0.9250 Silver .8411 oz. ASW **Series:** Flower Fairies **Obverse:** Bust of Queen Elizabeth II right **Reverse:** Fuchsia

Date	Mintage	F	VF	XF	Unc	BU
1996 Proof	Est. 30,000	Value: 40.00				

KM# 612 CROWN Composition: Copper-Nickel **Series:** Flower Fairies **Obverse:** Bust of Queen Elizabeth II right **Reverse:** Pinks

Date	F	VF	XF	Unc	BU
1996	—	—	—	5.00	—

KM# 612a CROWN Weight: 28.2800 g. **Composition:** 0.9250 Silver .8411 oz. ASW **Series:** Flower Fairies **Obverse:** Bust of Queen Elizabeth II right **Reverse:** Pinks

Date	Mintage	F	VF	XF	Unc	BU
1996 Proof	Est. 30,000	Value: 40.00				

KM# 621 CROWN Composition: Copper-Nickel **Obverse:** Bust of Queen Elizabeth II right **Reverse:** Burmese cat

Date	F	VF	XF	Unc	BU
1996	—	—	—	10.00	—

KM# 621a CROWN Weight: 31.1035 g. **Composition:** 0.9990 Silver 1.000 oz. ASW **Obverse:** Bust of Queen Elizabeth II right **Reverse:** Burmese cat

Date	Mintage	F	VF	XF	Unc	BU
1996 Proof	Est. 50,000	Value: 40.00				

KM# 621b CROWN Weight: 31.1000 g. **Composition:** 0.9990 Gold 1.0000 oz. AGW **Obverse:** Bust of Queen Elizabeth II right **Reverse:** Burmese cat

Date	Mintage	F	VF	XF	Unc	BU
1996 U		—	—	—	400	—
1996 Proof	—	Value: 410				

KM# 624 CROWN Weight: 31.1035 g. **Composition:** 0.9995 Platinum .9995 oz. APW **Obverse:** Bust of Queen Elizabeth II right **Reverse:** Burmese cat

Date	F	VF	XF	Unc	BU
1996	—	—	—	BV+20%	—

KM# 626 CROWN Composition: Copper-Nickel **Obverse:** Bust of Queen Elizabeth II right **Reverse:** Bust of Ferdinand Magellan, map and ship

Date	F	VF	XF	Unc	BU
1996	—	—	—	7.50	—

KM# 626a CROWN Weight: 28.2800 g. **Composition:** 0.9250 Silver .8411 oz. ASW **Obverse:** Bust of Queen Elizabeth II right **Reverse:** Bust of Ferdinand Magellan, map and ship

Date	Mintage	F	VF	XF	Unc	BU
1996 Proof	Est. 30,000	Value: 40.00				

KM# 629 CROWN Composition: Copper-Nickel **Obverse:** Bust of Queen Elizabeth II right **Reverse:** Bust of Sir Francis Drake, map and ship

Date	F	VF	XF	Unc	BU
1996	—	—	—	7.50	—

KM# 629a CROWN Weight: 28.2800 g. **Composition:** 0.9250 Silver .8411 oz. ASW **Obverse:** Bust of Queen Elizabeth II right **Reverse:** Bust of Sir Francis Drake, map and ship

Date	Mintage	F	VF	XF	Unc	BU
1996 Proof	Est. 30,000	Value: 40.00				

KM# 632 CROWN Composition: Copper-Nickel **Series:** European Football Championship **Obverse:** Bust of Queen Elizabeth II right **Reverse:** Romania vs Bulgaria

Date	F	VF	XF	Unc	BU
1996	—	—	—	7.00	—

KM# 632a CROWN Weight: 28.2800 g. **Composition:** 0.9250 Silver .8411 oz. ASW **Series:** European Football Championship **Obverse:** Bust of Queen Elizabeth II right **Reverse:** Romania vs Bulgaria

Date	Mintage	F	VF	XF	Unc	BU
1996 Proof	Est. 30,000	Value: 40.00				

KM# 635 CROWN Composition: Copper-Nickel **Series:** European Football Championship **Obverse:** Bust of Queen Elizabeth II right **Reverse:** Czech Republic vs Itay

Date	F	VF	XF	Unc	BU
1996	—	—	—	7.00	—

KM# 635a CROWN Weight: 28.2800 g. **Composition:** 0.9250 Silver .8411 oz. ASW **Series:** European Football Championship **Obverse:** Bust of Queen Elizabeth II right **Reverse:** Czech Republic vs Italy

Date	Mintage	F	VF	XF	Unc	BU
1996 Proof	Est. 30,000	Value: 40.00				

KM# 638 CROWN Composition: Copper-Nickel **Series:** European Football Championship **Obverse:** Bust of Queen Elizabeth II right **Reverse:** Germany vs Russia

Date	F	VF	XF	Unc	BU
1996	—	—	—	7.00	—

KM# 638a CROWN **Weight:** 28.2800 g. **Composition:** 0.9250 Silver .8411 oz. ASW **Series:** European Football Championship **Obverse:** Bust of Queen Elizabeth II right **Reverse:** Germany vs Russia

Date	Mintage	F	VF	XF	Unc	BU
1996 Proof	Est. 30,000	Value: 40.00				

KM# 641 CROWN **Composition:** Copper-Nickel **Series:** European Football Championship **Obverse:** Bust of Queen Elizabeth II right **Reverse:** Spain vs France

Date	F	VF	XF	Unc	BU
1996	—	—	—	7.00	—

KM# 641a CROWN **Weight:** 28.2800 g. **Composition:** 0.9250 Silver .8411 oz. ASW **Series:** European Football Championship **Obverse:** Bust of Queen Elizabeth II right **Reverse:** Spain vs France

Date	Mintage	F	VF	XF	Unc	BU
1996 Proof	Est. 30,000	Value: 40.00				

KM# 644 CROWN **Composition:** Copper-Nickel **Series:** European Football Championship **Obverse:** Bust of Queen Elizabeth II right **Reverse:** Turkey vs Croatia

Date	F	VF	XF	Unc	BU
1996	—	—	—	7.00	—

KM# 644a CROWN **Weight:** 28.2800 g. **Composition:** 0.9250 Silver .8411 oz. ASW **Series:** European Football Championship **Obverse:** Bust of Queen Elizabeth II right **Reverse:** Turkey vs Croatia

Date	Mintage	F	VF	XF	Unc	BU
1996 Proof	Est. 30,000	Value: 40.00				

KM# 647 CROWN **Composition:** Copper-Nickel **Series:** European Football Championship **Obverse:** Bust of Queen Elizabeth II right **Reverse:** Denmark vs Portugal

Date	F	VF	XF	Unc	BU
1996	—	—	—	6.00	—

KM# 647a CROWN **Weight:** 28.2800 g. **Composition:** 0.9250 Silver .8411 oz. ASW **Series:** European Football Championship **Obverse:** Bust of Queen Elizabeth II right **Reverse:** Denmark vs Portugal

Date	Mintage	F	VF	XF	Unc	BU
1996 Proof	Est. 30,000	Value: 40.00				

KM# 650 CROWN **Composition:** Copper-Nickel **Series:** European Football Championship **Obverse:** Bust of Queen Elizabeth II right **Reverse:** Scotland vs England

Date	F	VF	XF	Unc	BU
1996	—	—	—	7.00	—

KM# 650a CROWN **Weight:** 28.2800 g. **Composition:** 0.9250 Silver .8411 oz. ASW **Series:** European Football Championship **Obverse:** Bust of Queen Elizabeth II right **Reverse:** Scotland vs England

Date	Mintage	F	VF	XF	Unc	BU
1996 Proof	Est. 30,000	Value: 40.00				

KM# 653 CROWN **Composition:** Copper-Nickel **Series:** European Football Championship **Obverse:** Bust of Queen Elizabeth II right **Reverse:** Holland vs Switzerland

Date	F	VF	XF	Unc	BU
1996	—	—	—	7.00	—

KM# 653a CROWN **Weight:** 28.2800 g. **Composition:** 0.9250 Silver .8411 oz. ASW **Series:** European Football Championship **Obverse:** Bust of Queen Elizabeth II right **Reverse:** Holland vs Switzerland

Date	Mintage	F	VF	XF	Unc	BU
1996 Proof	Est. 30,000	Value: 40.00				

KM# 657 CROWN **Composition:** Copper-Nickel **Series:** European Football Championship **Obverse:** Bust of Queen Elizabeth II right **Reverse:** German shield, winner

Date	F	VF	XF	Unc	BU
1996	—	—	—	7.00	—

KM# 657a CROWN **Weight:** 28.2800 g. **Composition:** 0.9250 Silver .8411 oz. ASW **Series:** European Football Championship **Obverse:** Bust of Queen Elizabeth II right **Reverse:** German shield, winner

Date	Mintage	F	VF	XF	Unc	BU
1996 Proof	Est. 30,000	Value: 40.00				

KM# 679 CROWN **Composition:** Copper-Nickel **Series:** Legend of King Arthur **Obverse:** Bust of Queen Elizabeth II right **Reverse:** King Arthur with Sword and orb

Date	F	VF	XF	Unc	BU
1996	—	—	—	9.00	—

KM# 679a CROWN **Weight:** 28.2800 g. **Composition:** 0.9250 Silver .8411 oz. ASW **Series:** Legend of King Arthur **Obverse:** Bust of Queen Elizabeth II right **Reverse:** King Arthur with sword and orb

Date	Mintage	F	VF	XF	Unc	BU
1996 Proof	Est. 30,000	Value: 22.50				

KM# 680 CROWN **Composition:** Copper-Nickel **Series:** Legend of King Arthur **Obverse:** Bust of Queen Elizabeth II right **Reverse:** Queen Guinevere

Date	F	VF	XF	Unc	BU
1996	—	—	—	9.00	—

KM# 680a CROWN **Weight:** 28.2800 g. **Composition:** 0.9250 Silver .8411 oz. ASW **Series:** Legend of King Arthur **Obverse:** Bust of Queen Elizabeth II right **Reverse:** Queen Guinevere

Date	Mintage	F	VF	XF	Unc	BU
1996 Proof	Est. 30,000	Value: 22.50				

KM# 681 CROWN **Composition:** Copper-Nickel **Series:** Legend of King Arthur **Obverse:** Bust of Queen Elizabeth II right **Reverse:** Sir Lancelot

Date	F	VF	XF	Unc	BU
1996	—	—	—	9.00	—

KM# 681a CROWN **Weight:** 28.2800 g. **Composition:** 0.9250 Silver .8411 oz. ASW **Series:** Legend of King Arthur **Obverse:** Bust of Queen Elizabeth II right **Reverse:** Sir Lancelot

Date	Mintage	F	VF	XF	Unc	BU
1996 Proof	Est. 30,000	Value: 22.50				

KM# 682 CROWN **Composition:** Copper-Nickel **Series:** Legend of King Arthur **Obverse:** Bust of Queen Elizabeth II right **Reverse:** Merlin

Date	F	VF	XF	Unc	BU
1996	—	—	—	9.00	—

KM# 682a CROWN **Weight:** 28.2800 g. **Composition:** 0.9250 Silver .8411 oz. ASW **Series:** Legend of King Arthur **Obverse:** Bust of Queen Elizabeth II right **Reverse:** Merlin

Date	Mintage	F	VF	XF	Unc	BU
1996 Proof	Est. 30,000	Value: 22.50				

KM# 683 CROWN **Composition:** Copper-Nickel **Series:** Legend of King Arthur **Obverse:** Bust of Queen Elizabeth II right **Reverse:** Camelot Castle

Date	F	VF	XF	Unc	BU
1996	—	—	—	9.00	—

KM# 683a CROWN **Weight:** 28.2800 g. **Composition:** 0.9250 Silver .8411 oz. ASW **Series:** Legend of King Arthur **Obverse:** Bust of Queen Elizabeth II right **Reverse:** Camelot Castle

Date	Mintage	F	VF	XF	Unc	BU
1996 Proof	Est. 30,000	Value: 25.00				

KM# 732 CROWN **Composition:** Copper-Nickel **Subject:** Year of the Rat **Obverse:** Bust of Queen Elizabeth II right **Reverse:** Rat

Date	F	VF	XF	Unc	BU
1996	—	—	—	7.50	—

KM# 732a CROWN **Weight:** 28.2800 g. **Composition:** 0.9250 Silver .8411 oz. ASW **Subject:** Year of the Rat **Obverse:** Bust of Queen Elizabeth II right **Reverse:** Rat

Date	F	VF	XF	Unc	BU
1996 Proof	—	—	—	—	—

Note: Entire silver issue purchased by one buyer. Mintage, disposition and market value unknown

KM# 733 CROWN **Weight:** 31.1035 g. **Composition:** 0.9999 Gold 1.0000 oz. AGW **Subject:** Year of the Rat **Obverse:** Bust of Queen Elizabeth II right **Reverse:** Rat

Date	F	VF	XF	Unc	BU
1996 Proof	—	—	—	—	—

Note: Entire gold issue purchased by one buyer. Mintage, disposition and market value unknown

KM# 725 CROWN **Composition:** Copper-Nickel **Subject:** Year of the Ox **Obverse:** Bust of Queen Elizabeth II right **Reverse:** Ox laying down

Date	F	VF	XF	Unc	BU
1997	—	—	—	8.00	—

KM# 725a CROWN **Weight:** 28.2800 g. **Composition:** 0.9250 Silver .8411 oz. ASW **Subject:** Year of the Ox **Obverse:** Bust of Queen Elizabeth II right **Reverse:** Ox laying down

Date	Mintage	F	VF	XF	Unc	BU
1997 Proof	Est. 30,000	Value: 40.00				

KM# 726 CROWN **Weight:** 31.1035 g. **Composition:** 0.9999 Gold 1.0000 oz. AGW **Subject:** Year of the Ox **Obverse:** Bust of Queen Elizabeth II right **Reverse:** Ox laying down

Date	Mintage	F	VF	XF	Unc	BU
1997 Proof	Est. 2,000	Value: 700				

KM# 759 CROWN **Composition:** Copper-Nickel **Series:** Flower Fairies **Obverse:** Bust of Queen Elizabeth II right **Reverse:** Candytuft

Date	F	VF	XF	Unc	BU
1997	—	—	—	7.50	—

KM# 759a CROWN **Weight:** 28.2800 g. **Composition:** 0.9250 Silver .8411 oz. ASW **Series:** Flower Fairies **Obverse:** Bust of Queen Elizabeth II right **Reverse:** Candytuft

Date	Mintage	F	VF	XF	Unc	BU
1997 Proof	Est. 30,000	Value: 40.00				

KM# 760 CROWN **Composition:** Copper-Nickel **Series:** Flower Fairies **Obverse:** Bust of Queen Elizabeth II right **Reverse:** Snowdrop

Date	F	VF	XF	Unc	BU
1997	—	—	—	7.50	—

KM# 760a CROWN **Weight:** 28.2800 g. **Composition:** 0.9250 Silver .8411 oz. ASW **Series:** Flower Fairies **Obverse:** Bust of Queen Elizabeth II right **Reverse:** Snowdrop

Date	Mintage	F	VF	XF	Unc	BU
1997 Proof	Est. 30,000	Value: 40.00				

KM# 761 CROWN **Composition:** Copper-Nickel **Series:** Flower Fairies **Obverse:** Bust of Queen Elizabeth II right **Reverse:** Tulip

Date	F	VF	XF	Unc	BU
1997	—	—	—	7.50	—

KM# 761a CROWN **Weight:** 28.2800 g. **Composition:** 0.9250 Silver .8411 oz. ASW **Series:** Flower Fairies **Obverse:** Bust of Queen Elizabeth II right **Reverse:** Tulip

Date	Mintage	F	VF	XF	Unc	BU
1997 Proof	Est. 30,000	Value: 40.00				

KM# 762 CROWN **Composition:** Copper-Nickel **Series:** Flower Fairies **Obverse:** Bust of Queen Elizabeth II right **Reverse:** Jasmine

Date	F	VF	XF	Unc	BU
1997	—	—	—	7.50	—

KM# 762a CROWN **Weight:** 28.2800 g. **Composition:** 0.9250 Silver .8411 oz. ASW **Series:** Flower Fairies **Obverse:** Bust of Queen Elizabeth II right **Reverse:** Jasmine

Date	Mintage	F	VF	XF	Unc	BU
1997 Proof	Est. 30,000	Value: 40.00				

KM# 765 CROWN **Composition:** Copper-Nickel **Obverse:** Bust of Queen Elizabeth II right **Reverse:** Leif Eriksson 999-1001, viking ship with map sail

Date	F	VF	XF	Unc	BU
1997	—	—	—	7.50	—

KM# 765a CROWN **Weight:** 28.2800 g. **Composition:** 0.9250 Silver .8411 oz. ASW **Obverse:** Bust of Queen Elizabeth II right **Reverse:** Leif Eriksson 999-1001, viking ship with map sail

Date	Mintage	F	VF	XF	Unc	BU
1997 Proof	Est. 30,000	Value: 40.00				

KM# 768 CROWN **Composition:** Copper-Nickel **Obverse:** Bust of Queen Elizabeth II right **Reverse:** Bust of Fridtjof Nansen, map and his ship "The Fram"

Date	F	VF	XF	Unc	BU
1997	—	—	—	7.50	—

KM# 768a CROWN **Weight:** 28.2800 g. **Composition:** 0.9250 Silver .8411 oz. ASW **Obverse:** Bust of Queen Elizabeth II right **Reverse:** Bust of Fridtjof Nansen, map and his ship "The Fram"

Date	Mintage	F	VF	XF	Unc	BU
1997 Proof	Est. 30,000	Value: 40.00				

KM# 774 CROWN **Composition:** Copper-Nickel **Obverse:** Bust of Queen Elizabeth II right **Reverse:** Long-haired Smoke cat

Date	F	VF	XF	Unc	BU
1997	—	—	—	9.00	—

KM# 774a CROWN **Weight:** 31.1035 g. **Composition:** 0.9999 Silver 1.0000 oz. ASW **Obverse:** Bust of Queen Elizabeth II right **Reverse:** Long-haired Smoke cat

Date	Mintage	F	VF	XF	Unc	BU
1997 Proof	Est. 50,000	Value: 40.00				

KM# 774b CROWN **Weight:** 31.1035 g. **Composition:** 0.9999 Gold 1.0000 oz. AGW **Obverse:** Bust of Queen Elizabeth II right **Reverse:** Long-haired Smoke cat

Date	Mintage	F	VF	XF	Unc	BU
1997		—	—	—	400	—
1997 Proof	—	Value: 410				

KM# 777 CROWN **Weight:** 28.2800 g. **Composition:** 0.9250 Silver .8411 oz. ASW **Series:** History of the Cat **Obverse:** Bust of Queen Elizabeth II right **Reverse:** Ancestry of Felidae, evolution of the cat

Date	Mintage	F	VF	XF	Unc	BU
1997 Proof	Est. 10,000	Value: 40.00				

KM# 778 CROWN **Weight:** 28.2800 g. **Composition:** 0.9250 Silver .8411 oz. ASW **Series:** History of the Cat **Obverse:** Bust of Queen Elizabeth II right **Reverse:** Felis Silvestris Grampia, snarling cat

Date	Mintage	F	VF	XF	Unc	BU
1997 Proof	Est. 10,000	Value: 40.00				

KM# 779 CROWN **Weight:** 28.2800 g. **Composition:** 0.9250 Silver .8411 oz. ASW **Series:** History of the Cat **Obverse:** Bust of Queen Elizabeth II right **Reverse:** Mayalurus Iriomotensis, cat walking left

Date	Mintage	F	VF	XF	Unc	BU
1997 Proof	Est. 10,000	Value: 40.00				

KM# 780 CROWN **Weight:** 28.2800 g. **Composition:** 0.9250 Silver .8411 oz. ASW **Series:** History of the Cat **Obverse:** Bust of Queen Elizabeth II right **Reverse:** Ancient Egyptian Goddess Bast and artifacts

Date	Mintage	F	VF	XF	Unc	BU
1997 Proof	Est. 10,000	Value: 40.00				

KM# 782 CROWN **Composition:** Copper-Nickel **Subject:** 90th Anniversary of the TT **Obverse:** Bust of Queen Elizabeth II right **Reverse:** 1907 winner Charlie Collier

Date	F	VF	XF	Unc	BU
1997	—	—	—	8.50	—

KM# 782a CROWN **Weight:** 28.2800 g. **Composition:** 0.9250 Silver .8411 oz. ASW **Subject:** 90th Anniversary of the TT **Obverse:** Bust of Queen Elizabeth II right **Reverse:** 1907 winner Charlie Collier

Date	Mintage	F	VF	XF	Unc	BU
1997 Proof	Est. 30,000	Value: 42.50				

KM# 784 CROWN **Composition:** Copper-Nickel **Subject:** 90th Anniversary of the TT **Obverse:** Bust of Queen Elizabeth II right **Reverse:** 1937 winner Omobono Tenni

Date	F	VF	XF	Unc	BU
1997	—	—	—	8.50	—

KM# 784a CROWN **Weight:** 28.2800 g. **Composition:** 0.9250 Silver .8411 oz. ASW **Subject:** 90th Anniversary of the TT **Obverse:** Bust of Queen Elizabeth II right **Reverse:** 1937 winner Omobono Tenni

Date	Mintage	F	VF	XF	Unc	BU
1997 Proof	Est. 30,000	Value: 42.50				

KM# 786 CROWN **Composition:** Copper-Nickel **Subject:** 90th Anniversary of the TT **Obverse:** Bust of Queen Elizabeth II right **Reverse:** 1957 winner Bob McIntyre

Date	F	VF	XF	Unc	BU
1997	—	—	—	8.50	—

KM# 786a CROWN **Weight:** 28.2800 g. **Composition:** 0.9250 Silver .8411 oz. ASW **Subject:** 90th Anniversary of the TT **Obverse:** Bust of Queen Elizabeth II right **Reverse:** 1957 winner Bob McIntyre

Date	Mintage	F	VF	XF	Unc	BU
1997 Proof	Est. 30,000	Value: 42.50				

KM# 788 CROWN **Composition:** Copper-Nickel **Subject:** 90th Anniversary of the TT **Obverse:** Bust of Queen Elizabeth II right **Reverse:** 1967 winner Mike Hailwood

Date	F	VF	XF	Unc	BU
1997	—	—	—	8.50	—

KM# 788a CROWN **Weight:** 28.2800 g. **Composition:** 0.9250 Silver .8411 oz. ASW **Subject:** 90th Anniversary of the TT **Obverse:** Bust of Queen Elizabeth II right **Reverse:** 1967 winner Mike Hailwood

Date	Mintage	F	VF	XF	Unc	BU
1997 Proof	Est. 30,000	Value: 42.50				

KM# 793 CROWN **Composition:** Copper-Nickel **Subject:** 50th Wedding Anniversary of Queen Elizabeth II and Prince Philip **Obverse:** Bust of Queen Elizabeth II right **Reverse:** Wedding portrait

Date	F	VF	XF	Unc	BU
1997	—	—	—	8.00	—

KM# 793a CROWN **Weight:** 28.2800 g. **Composition:** 0.9250 Gold Clad Silver .8411 oz. **Subject:** 50th Wedding Anniversary of Queen Elizabeth II and Prince Philip **Obverse:** Bust of Queen Elizabeth II right **Reverse:** Wedding portrait

Date	Mintage	F	VF	XF	Unc	BU
1997 Proof	Est. 10,000	Value: 40.00				

KM# 799 CROWN **Composition:** Copper-Nickel **Series:** Year 2000 **Subject:** Birth of Christ **Obverse:** Bust of Queen Elizabeth II right **Reverse:** Madonna and child with angels

Date	F	VF	XF	Unc	BU
1997	—	—	—	7.50	—

KM# 799a CROWN **Weight:** 28.2800 g. **Composition:** 0.9250 Silver .8411 oz. ASW **Series:** Year 2000 **Subject:** Birth of Christ **Obverse:** Bust of Queen Elizabeth II right **Reverse:** Madonna and child with angels

Date	Mintage	F	VF	XF	Unc	BU
1997 Proof	Est. 10,000	Value: 50.00				

KM# 801 CROWN **Composition:** Copper-Nickel **Series:** Year 2000 **Subject:** Fall of the Roman Empire 476 **Obverse:** Bust of Queen Elizabeth II right **Reverse:** Barbarian defeating soldier

Date	F	VF	XF	Unc	BU
1997	—	—	—	7.50	—

KM# 801a CROWN **Weight:** 28.2800 g. **Composition:** 0.9250 Silver .8411 oz. ASW **Series:** Year 2000 **Subject:** Fall of the Roman Empire 476 **Obverse:** Bust of Queen Elizabeth II right **Reverse:** Barbarian defeating soldier

Date	Mintage	F	VF	XF	Unc	BU
1997 Proof	Est. 10,000	Value: 50.00				

KM# 803 CROWN **Composition:** Copper-Nickel **Series:** Year 2000 **Subject:** Flight of Mohammed 622 **Obverse:** Bust of Queen Elizabeth II right **Reverse:** Arabs and camels at oasis

Date	F	VF	XF	Unc	BU
1997	—	—	—	7.50	—

KM# 803a CROWN **Weight:** 28.2800 g. **Composition:** 0.9250 Silver .8411 oz. ASW **Series:** Year 2000 **Subject:** Flight of Mohammed 622 **Obverse:** Bust of Queen Elizabeth II right **Reverse:** Arabs and camels at oasis

Date	Mintage	F	VF	XF	Unc	BU
1997 Proof	Est. 10,000	Value: 50.00				

KM# 805 CROWN **Composition:** Copper-Nickel **Series:** Year 2000 **Subject:** Norman Conquest 1066 **Obverse:** Bust of Queen Elizabeth II right **Reverse:** William the Conqueror rallying his troops

Date	F	VF	XF	Unc	BU
1997	—	—	—	7.50	—

KM# 805a CROWN **Weight:** 28.2800 g. **Composition:** 0.9250 Silver .8411 oz. ASW **Series:** Year 2000 **Subject:** Norman Conquest 1066 **Obverse:** Bust of Queen Elizabeth II right **Reverse:** William the Conqueror rallying his troops

Date	Mintage	F	VF	XF	Unc	BU
1997 Proof	Est. 10,000	Value: 50.00				

KM# 808 CROWN **Composition:** Copper-Nickel **Series:** World Cup Soccer **Obverse:** Bust of Queen Elizabeth II right **Reverse:** Goalie blocking a shot

Date	F	VF	XF	Unc	BU
1998	—	—	—	7.50	—

KM# 808a CROWN **Weight:** 28.2800 g. **Composition:** 0.9250 Silver .8411 oz. ASW **Series:** World Cup Soccer **Obverse:** Bust of Queen Elizabeth II right **Reverse:** Goalie blocking a shot

Date	Mintage	F	VF	XF	Unc	BU
1998 Proof	Est. 30,000	Value: 45.00				

KM# 809 CROWN **Composition:** Copper-Nickel **Series:** World Cup Soccer **Obverse:** Bust of Queen Elizabeth II right **Reverse:** Two soccer players kicking ball

Date	F	VF	XF	Unc	BU
1998	—	—	—	7.50	—

KM# 809a CROWN **Weight:** 28.2800 g. **Composition:** 0.9250 Silver .8411 oz. ASW **Series:** World Cup Soccer **Obverse:** Bust of Queen Elizabeth II right **Reverse:** Two soccer players kicking ball

Date	Mintage	F	VF	XF	Unc	BU
1998 Proof	Est. 30,000	Value: 45.00				

KM# 810 CROWN **Composition:** Copper-Nickel **Series:** World Cup Soccer **Obverse:** Bust of Queen Elizabeth II right **Reverse:** Two soccer players heading the ball

Date	F	VF	XF	Unc	BU
1998	—	—	—	7.50	—

KM# 810a CROWN **Weight:** 28.2800 g. **Composition:** 0.9250 Silver .8411 oz. ASW **Series:** World Cup Soccer **Obverse:** Bust of Queen Elizabeth II right **Reverse:** Two soccer players heading the ball

Date	Mintage	F	VF	XF	Unc	BU
1998 Proof	Est. 30,000	Value: 45.00				

KM# 811 CROWN **Composition:** Copper-Nickel **Series:** World Cup Soccer **Obverse:** Bust of Queen Elizabeth II right **Reverse:** Three soccer players

Date	F	VF	XF	Unc	BU
1998	—	—	—	7.50	—

KM# 811a CROWN **Weight:** 28.2800 g. **Composition:** 0.9250 Silver .8411 oz. ASW **Series:** World Cup Soccer **Obverse:** Bust of Queen Elizabeth II right **Reverse:** Three soccer players

Date	Mintage	F	VF	XF	Unc	BU
1998 Proof	Est. 30,000	Value: 45.00				

KM# 816 CROWN **Composition:** Copper-Nickel **Subject:** Year of the Tiger **Obverse:** Bust of Queen Elizabeth II right **Reverse:** Tiger in circle

Date	F	VF	XF	Unc	BU
1998	—	—	—	9.00	—

KM# 816a CROWN **Weight:** 28.2800 g. **Composition:** 0.9250 Silver .8411 oz. ASW **Subject:** Year of the Tiger **Obverse:** Bust of Queen Elizabeth II right **Reverse:** Tiger in circle

Date	Mintage	F	VF	XF	Unc	BU
1998 Proof	Est. 30,000	Value: 45.00				

KM# 817 CROWN **Weight:** 31.1035 g. **Composition:** 0.9999 Gold 1.0000 oz. AGW **Subject:** Year of the Tiger **Obverse:** Bust of Queen Elizabeth II right **Reverse:** Tiger

Date	Mintage	F	VF	XF	Unc	BU
1998 Proof	Est. 2,000	Value: 650				

KM# 825 CROWN **Composition:** Copper-Nickel **Obverse:** Bust of Queen Elizabeth II right **Reverse:** Bust of Marco Polo right, caravan and palace

Date	F	VF	XF	Unc	BU
1998	—	—	—	7.50	—

KM# 825a CROWN **Weight:** 28.2800 g. **Composition:** 0.9250 Silver .8411 oz. ASW **Obverse:** Bust of Queen Elizabeth II right **Reverse:** Bust of Marco Polo right, caravan and palace

Date	Mintage	F	VF	XF	Unc	BU
1998 Proof	Est. 30,000	Value: 47.50				

KM# 827 CROWN **Composition:** Copper-Nickel **Obverse:** Bust of Queen Elizabeth II right **Reverse:** Bust of Vasco da Gama, ship and African map

Date	F	VF	XF	Unc	BU
1998	—	—	—	7.50	—

KM# 827a CROWN **Weight:** 28.2800 g. **Composition:** 0.9250 Silver .8411 oz. ASW **Obverse:** Bust of Queen Elizabeth II right **Reverse:** Bust of Vasco da Gama, ship and African map

Date	Mintage	F	VF	XF	Unc	BU
1998 Proof	Est. 30,000	Value: 47.50				

KM# 840 CROWN **Composition:** Copper-Nickel **Series:** Flower Fairies **Obverse:** Bust of Queen Elizabeth II right **Reverse:** Standing fairy, Lavender

Date	F	VF	XF	Unc	BU
1998	—	—	—	7.50	—

KM# 840a CROWN **Weight:** 28.2800 g. **Composition:** 0.9250 Silver .8411 oz. ASW **Series:** Flower Fairies **Obverse:** Bust of Queen Elizabeth II right **Reverse:** Standing fairy, Lavender

Date	Mintage	F	VF	XF	Unc	BU
1998 Proof	Est. 30,000	Value: 47.50				

KM# 841 CROWN **Composition:** Copper-Nickel **Series:** Flower Fairies **Obverse:** Bust of Queen Elizabeth II right **Reverse:** Sweet pea, two fairies

Date	F	VF	XF	Unc	BU
1998	—	—	—	7.50	—

KM# 841a CROWN **Weight:** 28.2800 g. **Composition:** 0.9250 Silver .8411 oz. ASW **Series:** Flower Fairies **Obverse:** Bust of Queen Elizabeth II right **Reverse:** Sweet pea, two fairies

Date	Mintage	F	VF	XF	Unc	BU
1998 Proof	Est. 30,000	Value: 47.50				

KM# 842 CROWN **Composition:** Copper-Nickel **Series:** Flower Fairies **Obverse:** Bust of Queen Elizabeth II right **Reverse:** White bindweed, fairy looking into flower

Date	F	VF	XF	Unc	BU
1998	—	—	—	7.50	—

KM# 842a CROWN **Weight:** 28.2800 g. **Composition:** 0.9250 Silver .8411 oz. ASW **Series:** Flower Fairies **Obverse:** Bust of Queen Elizabeth II right **Reverse:** White bindweed, fairy looking into flower

Date	Mintage	F	VF	XF	Unc	BU
1998 Proof	Est. 30,000	Value: 47.50				

KM# 843 CROWN **Composition:** Copper-Nickel **Series:** Flower Fairies **Obverse:** Bust of Queen Elizabeth II right **Reverse:** Daffodil, fairy standing with flower

Date	F	VF	XF	Unc	BU
1998	—	—	—	7.50	—

KM# 843a CROWN **Weight:** 28.2800 g. **Composition:** 0.9250 Silver .8411 oz. ASW **Series:** Flower Fairies **Obverse:** Bust of Queen Elizabeth II right **Reverse:** Daffodil, fairy standing with flower

Date	Mintage	F	VF	XF	Unc	BU
1998 Proof	Est. 20,000	Value: 47.50				

KM# 849 CROWN **Composition:** Copper-Nickel **Series:** Winter Olympics - Nagano **Obverse:** Bust of Queen Elizabeth II right **Reverse:** Bobsled

Date	F	VF	XF	Unc	BU
1998	—	—	—	7.50	—

KM# 849a CROWN **Weight:** 28.2800 g. **Composition:** 0.9250 Silver .8411 oz. ASW **Series:** Winter Olympics - Nagano **Obverse:** Bust of Queen Elizabeth II right **Reverse:** Bobsled

Date	Mintage	F	VF	XF	Unc	BU
1998 Proof	Est. 30,000	Value: 47.50				

KM# 850 CROWN **Composition:** Copper-Nickel **Series:** Winter Olympics - Nagano **Obverse:** Bust of Queen Elizabeth II right **Reverse:** Cross-country skier

Date	F	VF	XF	Unc	BU
1998	—	—	—	7.50	—

KM# 850a CROWN Weight: 28.2800 g. **Composition:** 0.9250 Silver .8411 oz. ASW **Series:** Winter Olympics - Nagano **Obverse:** Bust of Queen Elizabeth II right **Reverse:** Cross-country skier

Date	Mintage	F	VF	XF	Unc	BU
1998 Proof	Est. 30,000	Value: 47.50				

KM# 851 CROWN Composition: Copper-Nickel **Series:** Winter Olympics - Nagano **Obverse:** Bust of Queen Elizabeth II right **Reverse:** Two hockey players

Date	F	VF	XF	Unc	BU
1998	—	—	—	7.50	—

KM# 851a CROWN Weight: 28.2800 g. **Composition:** 0.9250 Silver .8411 oz. ASW **Series:** Winter Olympics - Nagano **Obverse:** Bust of Queen Elizabeth II right **Reverse:** Two hockey players

Date	Mintage	F	VF	XF	Unc	BU
1998 Proof	Est. 30,000	Value: 47.50				

KM# 852 CROWN Composition: Copper-Nickel **Series:** Winter Olympics - Nagano **Obverse:** Bust of Queen Elizabeth II right **Reverse:** Two speed skaters

Date	F	VF	XF	Unc	BU
1998	—	—	—	7.50	—

KM# 852a CROWN Weight: 28.2800 g. **Composition:** 0.9250 Silver .8411 oz. ASW **Series:** Winter Olympics - Nagano **Obverse:** Bust of Queen Elizabeth II right **Reverse:** Two speed skaters

Date	Mintage	F	VF	XF	Unc	BU
1998 Proof	Est. 30,000	Value: 47.50				

KM# 857 CROWN Composition: Copper-Nickel **Obverse:** Bust of Queen Elizabeth II right **Reverse:** Birman cat

Date	Mintage	F	VF	XF	Unc	BU
1998		—	—	—	8.00	—
1998 Proof	—	Value: 15.00				

KM# 857a CROWN Weight: 31.1035 g. **Composition:** 0.9999 Silver 1.0000 oz. ASW **Obverse:** Bust of Queen Elizabeth II right **Reverse:** Birman cat

Date	Mintage	F	VF	XF	Unc	BU
1998 Proof	Est. 50,000	Value: 47.50				

KM# 857b CROWN Weight: 31.1035 g. **Composition:** 0.9999 Gold 1.0000 oz. AGW **Obverse:** Bust of Queen Elizabeth II right **Reverse:** Birman cat

Date	Mintage	F	VF	XF	Unc	BU
1998	—	—	—	—	400	—
1998 Proof	1,000	Value: 410				

KM# 872 CROWN Composition: Copper-Nickel **Subject:** 125th Anniversary of the Steam Railway **Obverse:** Bust of Queen Elizabeth II right **Reverse:** "The General" locomotive

Date	F	VF	XF	Unc	BU
1998	—	—	—	10.00	—

KM# 872a CROWN Weight: 28.2800 g. **Composition:** 0.9250 Silver .8410 oz. ASW **Subject:** 125th Anniversary of the Steam Railway **Obverse:** Bust of Queen Elizabeth II right **Reverse:** "The General" locomotive

Date	Mintage	F	VF	XF	Unc	BU
1998 Proof	Est. 30,000	Value: 47.50				

KM# 874 CROWN Composition: Copper-Nickel **Subject:** 125th Anniversary of the Steam Railway **Obverse:** Bust of Queen Elizabeth II right **Reverse:** "The Rocket" locomotive and portrtait

Date	F	VF	XF	Unc	BU
1998	—	—	—	10.00	—

KM# 874a CROWN Weight: 28.2800 g. **Composition:** 0.9250 Silver .8410 oz. ASW **Subject:** 125th Anniversary of the Steam Railway **Obverse:** Bust of Queen Elizabeth II right **Reverse:** "The Rocket" and portrait

Date	Mintage	F	VF	XF	Unc	BU
1998 Proof	Est. 30,000	Value: 47.50				

KM# 876 CROWN Composition: Copper-Nickel **Subject:** 125th Anniversary of the Steam Railway **Obverse:** Bust of Queen Elizabeth II right **Reverse:** Orient Express parlor car, interior view

Date	F	VF	XF	Unc	BU
1998	—	—	—	10.00	—

KM# 876a CROWN Weight: 28.2800 g. **Composition:** 0.9250 Silver .8410 oz. ASW **Subject:** 125th Anniversary of the Steam Railway **Obverse:** Bust of Queen Elizabeth II right **Reverse:** Orient Express parlor car, interior view

Date	Mintage	F	VF	XF	Unc	BU
1998 Proof	Est. 30,000	Value: 47.50				

KM# 878 CROWN Composition: Copper-Nickel **Subject:** 125th Anniversary of the Steam Railway **Obverse:** Bust of Queen Elizabeth II right **Reverse:** Mount Pilatus Railway

Date	F	VF	XF	Unc	BU
1998	—	—	—	10.00	—

KM# 878a CROWN Weight: 28.2800 g. **Composition:** 0.9250 Silver .8410 oz. ASW **Subject:** 125th Anniversary of the Steam Railway **Obverse:** Bust of Queen Elizabeth II right **Reverse:** Mount Pilatus Railway

Date	Mintage	F	VF	XF	Unc	BU
1998 Proof	Est. 30,000	Value: 47.50				

KM# 880 CROWN Composition: Copper-Nickel **Subject:** 125th Anniversary of the Steam Railway **Obverse:** Bust of Queen Elizabeth II right **Reverse:** No. 1 Sutherland locomotive

Date	F	VF	XF	Unc	BU
1998	—	—	—	10.00	—

KM# 880a CROWN Weight: 28.2800 g. **Composition:** 0.9250 Silver .8410 oz. ASW **Subject:** 125th Anniversary of the Steam Railway **Obverse:** Bust of Queen Elizabeth II right **Reverse:** No. 1 Sutherland locomotive

Date	Mintage	F	VF	XF	Unc	BU
1998 Proof	Est. 30,000	Value: 47.50				

KM# 882 CROWN Composition: Copper-Nickel **Subject:** 125th Anniversary of the Steam Railway **Obverse:** Bust of Queen Elizabeth II right **Reverse:** "Flying Scotsman" locomotive

Date	F	VF	XF	Unc	BU
1998	—	—	—	10.00	—

KM# 882a CROWN Weight: 28.2800 g. **Composition:** 0.9250 Silver .8410 oz. ASW **Subject:** 125th Anniversary of the Steam Railway **Obverse:** Bust of Queen Elizabeth II right **Reverse:** "Flying Scotsman" locomotive

Date	Mintage	F	VF	XF	Unc	BU
1998 Proof	Est. 30,000	Value: 47.50				

KM# 884 CROWN Composition: Copper-Nickel **Subject:** 125th Anniversary of the Steam Railway **Obverse:** Bust of Queen Elizabeth II right **Reverse:** "The Mallard" locomotive

Date	F	VF	XF	Unc	BU
1998	—	—	—	10.00	—

KM# 884a CROWN Weight: 28.2800 g. **Composition:** 0.9250 Silver .8410 oz. ASW **Subject:** 125th Anniversary of the Steam Railway **Obverse:** Bust of Queen Elizabeth II right **Reverse:** "The Mallard" locomotive

Date	Mintage	F	VF	XF	Unc	BU
1998 Proof	Est. 30,000	Value: 47.50				

KM# 886 CROWN **Composition:** Copper-Nickel **Subject:** 125th Anniversary of the Steam Railway **Obverse:** Bust of Queen Elizabeth II right **Reverse:** "The Big Boy" locomotive

Date	F	VF	XF	Unc	BU
1998	—	—	—	10.00	—

KM# 886a CROWN **Weight:** 28.2800 g. **Composition:** 0.9250 Silver .8410 oz. ASW **Subject:** 125th Anniversary of the Steam Railway **Obverse:** Bust of Queen Elizabeth II right **Reverse:** "The Big Boy" locomotive

Date	Mintage	F	VF	XF	Unc	BU
1998 Proof	Est. 30,000	Value: 47.50				

KM# 888 CROWN **Composition:** Copper-Nickel **Series:** Year 2000 **Obverse:** Bust of Queen Elizabeth II right **Reverse:** American Independence 1776

Date	F	VF	XF	Unc	BU
1998	—	—	—	7.50	—

KM# 888a CROWN **Weight:** 28.2800 g. **Composition:** 0.9250 Silver .8410 oz. ASW **Series:** Year 2000 **Obverse:** Bust of Queen Elizabeth II right **Reverse:** American Independence 1776

Date	Mintage	F	VF	XF	Unc	BU
1998 Proof	Est. 30,000	Value: 28.50				

KM# 890 CROWN **Composition:** Copper-Nickel **Series:** Year 2000 **Obverse:** Bust of Queen Elizabeth II right **Reverse:** French Revolution 1789

Date	F	VF	XF	Unc	BU
1998	—	—	—	7.50	—

KM# 890a CROWN **Weight:** 28.2800 g. **Composition:** 0.9250 Silver .8410 oz. ASW **Series:** Year 2000 **Obverse:** Bust of Queen Elizabeth II right **Reverse:** French Revolution 1789

Date	Mintage	F	VF	XF	Unc	BU
1998 Proof	Est. 30,000	Value: 28.50				

KM# 892 CROWN **Composition:** Copper-Nickel **Series:** Year 2000 **Obverse:** Bust of Queen Elizabeth II right **Reverse:** Reformation of the Church 1517

Date	F	VF	XF	Unc	BU
1998	—	—	—	7.50	—

KM# 892a CROWN **Weight:** 28.2800 g. **Composition:** 0.9250 Silver .8410 oz. ASW **Series:** Year 2000 **Obverse:** Bust of Queen Elizabeth II right **Reverse:** Reformation of the Church 1517

Date	Mintage	F	VF	XF	Unc	BU
1998 Proof	Est. 30,000	Value: 28.50				

KM# 894 CROWN **Composition:** Copper-Nickel **Series:** Year 2000 **Obverse:** Bust of Queen Elizabeth II right **Reverse:** 400th Anniversary of the Renaissance

Date	F	VF	XF	Unc	BU
1998	—	—	—	7.50	—

KM# 894a CROWN **Weight:** 28.2800 g. **Composition:** 0.9250 Silver .8410 oz. ASW **Series:** Year 2000 **Obverse:** Bust of Queen Elizabeth II right **Reverse:** 400th Anniversary of the Renaissance

Date	Mintage	F	VF	XF	Unc	BU
1998 Proof	Est. 30,000	Value: 28.50				

KM# 896 CROWN **Composition:** Copper-Nickel **Series:** Year of the Ocean **Obverse:** Bust of Queen Elizabeth II right **Reverse:** Basking shark

Date	F	VF	XF	Unc	BU
1998	—	—	—	9.00	—

KM# 896a CROWN **Weight:** 28.2800 g. **Composition:** 0.9250 Silver .8410 oz. ASW **Series:** Year of the Ocean **Obverse:** Bust of Queen Elizabeth II right **Reverse:** Basking shark

Date	Mintage	F	VF	XF	Unc	BU
1998 Proof	Est. 30,000	Value: 47.50				

KM# 897 CROWN **Composition:** Copper-Nickel **Series:** Year of the Ocean **Obverse:** Bust of Queen Elizabeth II right **Reverse:** Humpback whale

Date	F	VF	XF	Unc	BU
1998	—	—	—	9.00	—

KM# 897a CROWN **Weight:** 28.2800 g. **Composition:** 0.9250 Silver .8410 oz. ASW **Series:** Year of the Ocean **Obverse:** Bust of Queen Elizabeth II right **Reverse:** Humpback whale

Date	Mintage	F	VF	XF	Unc	BU
1998 Proof	Est. 30,000	Value: 47.50				

KM# 898 CROWN **Composition:** Copper-Nickel **Series:** Year of the Ocean **Obverse:** Bust of Queen Elizabeth II right **Reverse:** Penguins and seals

Date	F	VF	XF	Unc	BU
1998	—	—	—	8.50	—

KM# 898a CROWN **Weight:** 28.2800 g. **Composition:** 0.9250 Silver .8410 oz. ASW **Series:** Year of the Ocean **Obverse:** Bust of Queen Elizabeth II right **Reverse:** Penguins and seals

Date	Mintage	F	VF	XF	Unc	BU
1998 Proof	Est. 30,000	Value: 47.50				

KM# 899 CROWN **Composition:** Copper-Nickel **Series:** Year of the Ocean **Obverse:** Bust of Queen Elizabeth II right **Reverse:** Sailboats

Date	F	VF	XF	Unc	BU
1998	—	—	—	8.50	—

KM# 899a CROWN **Weight:** 28.2800 g. **Composition:** 0.9250 Silver .8410 oz. ASW **Series:** Year of the Ocean **Obverse:** Bust of Queen Elizabeth II right **Reverse:** Sailboats

Date	Mintage	F	VF	XF	Unc	BU
1998 Proof	Est. 30,000	Value: 47.50				

KM# A984 CROWN **Composition:** Copper-Nickel **Subject:** Founding of the UN 1945 **Obverse:** Bust of Queen Elizabeth II right **Reverse:** UN Building and logo

Date	F	VF	XF	Unc	BU
2000	—	—	—	8.50	—

KM# 914 CROWN **Composition:** Copper-Nickel **Subject:** Battle of Waterloo 1815 **Obverse:** Bust of Queen Elizabeth II right **Reverse:** Wellington on horse

Date	F	VF	XF	Unc	BU
1999	—	—	—	7.50	—

KM# 914a CROWN **Weight:** 28.2800 g. **Composition:** 0.9250 Silver .8410 oz. ASW **Subject:** Battle of Waterloo 1815 **Obverse:** Bust of Queen Elizabeth II right **Reverse:** Wellington on horse

Date	Mintage	F	VF	XF	Unc	BU
1999 Proof	Est. 10,000	Value: 50.00				

KM# 918 CROWN **Composition:** Copper-Nickel **Subject:** Russian Revolution 1917 **Obverse:** Bust of Queen Elizabeth II right **Reverse:** Lenin above the Aurora

Date	F	VF	XF	Unc	BU
1999	—	—	—	7.50	—

KM# 918a CROWN **Weight:** 28.2800 g. **Composition:** 0.9250 Silver .8410 oz. ASW **Subject:** Russian Revolution 1917 **Obverse:** Bust of Queen Elizabeth II right **Reverse:** Lenin above the Aurora

Date	Mintage	F	VF	XF	Unc	BU
1999 Proof	Est. 10,000	Value: 50.00				

KM# 916 CROWN **Composition:** Copper-Nickel **Subject:** American Civil War 1865 **Obverse:** Bust of Queen Elizabeth II right **Reverse:** Cameos of Grant and Lee; swords, flag, and drum

Date	F	VF	XF	Unc	BU
1999	—	—	—	7.50	—

KM# 916a CROWN **Weight:** 28.2800 g. **Composition:** 0.9250 Silver .8410 oz. ASW **Subject:** American Civil War 1865 **Obverse:** Bust of Queen Elizabeth II right **Reverse:** Cameos of Grant and Lee; swords, flag, and drum

Date	Mintage	F	VF	XF	Unc	BU
1999 Proof	Est. 10,000	Value: 50.00				

KM# 988 CROWN **Composition:** Copper-Nickel **Subject:** Fall of Berlin Wall 1989 **Obverse:** Bust of Queen Elizabeth II right **Reverse:** Crowds around wall

Date	F	VF	XF	Unc	BU
2000	—	—	—	7.50	—

KM# 988a CROWN **Weight:** 28.2800 g. **Composition:** 0.9250 Silver .8410 oz. ASW **Subject:** Fall of Berlin Wall 1989 **Obverse:** Bust of Queen Elizabeth II right **Reverse:** Crowds around wall

Date	Mintage	F	VF	XF	Unc	BU
2000 Proof	Est. 10,000	Value: 50.00				

KM# 920 CROWN **Composition:** Copper-Nickel **Subject:** World War I Armistice Day 1918 **Obverse:** Bust of Queen Elizabeth II right **Reverse:** Biplane above tank

Date	F	VF	XF	Unc	BU
1999	—	—	—	7.50	—

KM# 920a CROWN **Weight:** 28.2800 g. **Composition:** 0.9250 Silver .8410 oz. ASW **Subject:** World War I Armistice Day 1918 **Obverse:** Bust of Queen Elizabeth II right **Reverse:** Biplane above tank

Date	Mintage	F	VF	XF	Unc	BU
1999 Proof	Est. 10,000	Value: 50.00				

KM# 990 CROWN **Composition:** Copper-Nickel **Subject:** Millennium 2000 - The Future **Obverse:** Bust of Queen Elizabeth II right **Reverse:** International Space Station

Date	F	VF	XF	Unc	BU
2000	—	—	—	7.50	—

KM# 990a CROWN **Weight:** 28.2800 g. **Composition:** 0.9250 Silver .8410 oz. ASW **Subject:** Millennium 2000 - The Future **Obverse:** Bust of Queen Elizabeth II right **Reverse:** International Space Station

Date	Mintage	F	VF	XF	Unc	BU
2000 Proof	Est. 10,000	Value: 50.00				

KM# 922 CROWN **Composition:** Copper-Nickel **Series:** Summer Olympics - Sydney **Obverse:** Bust of Queen Elizabeth II right **Reverse:** Three javelin throwers

Date	F	VF	XF	Unc	BU
1999	—	—	—	7.50	—

KM# 922a CROWN **Weight:** 28.2800 g. **Composition:** 0.9250 Silver .8410 oz. ASW **Series:** Summer Olympics - Sydney **Obverse:** Bust of Queen Elizabeth II right **Reverse:** Three Javelin throwers

Date	Mintage	F	VF	XF	Unc	BU
1999 Proof	Est. 10,000	Value: 50.00				

KM# 924 CROWN **Composition:** Copper-Nickel **Series:** Summer Olympics - Sydney **Obverse:** Bust of Queen Elizabeth II right **Reverse:** Diver and map of Australia

Date	F	VF	XF	Unc	BU
1999	—	—	—	7.50	—

KM# 924a CROWN **Weight:** 28.2800 g. **Composition:** 0.9250 Silver .8410 oz. ASW **Series:** Summer Olympics - Sydney **Obverse:** Bust of Queen Elizabeth II right **Reverse:** Diver and map of Australia

Date	Mintage	F	VF	XF	Unc	BU
1999 Proof	Est. 10,000	Value: 50.00				

KM# 926 CROWN **Composition:** Copper-Nickel **Series:** Summer Olympics - Sydney **Obverse:** Bust of Queen Elizabeth II right **Reverse:** Sailboat and Sydney Opera House

Date	F	VF	XF	Unc	BU
1999	—	—	—	7.50	—

KM# 926a CROWN **Weight:** 28.2800 g. **Composition:** 0.9250 Silver .8410 oz. ASW **Series:** Summer Olympics - Sydney **Obverse:** Bust of Queen Elizabeth II right **Reverse:** Sailboat and Sydney Opera House

Date	Mintage	F	VF	XF	Unc	BU
1999 Proof	Est. 10,000	Value: 50.00				

KM# 928 CROWN **Composition:** Copper-Nickel **Series:** Summer Olympics - Sydney **Obverse:** Bust of Queen Elizabeth II right **Reverse:** Two runners, one with torch

Date	F	VF	XF	Unc	BU
1999	—	—	—	7.50	—

KM# 928a CROWN **Weight:** 28.2800 g. **Composition:** 0.9250 Silver .8410 oz. ASW **Series:** Summer Olympics - Sydney **Obverse:** Bust of Queen Elizabeth II right **Reverse:** Two runners, one with torch

Date	Mintage	F	VF	XF	Unc	BU
1999 Proof	Est. 10,000	Value: 50.00				

KM# 930 CROWN **Composition:** Copper-Nickel **Series:** Summer Olympics - Sydney **Obverse:** Bust of Queen Elizabeth II right **Reverse:** Hurdlers and Sydney Opera House

Date	F	VF	XF	Unc	BU
1999	—	—	—	7.50	—

KM# 930a CROWN **Weight:** 28.2800 g. **Composition:** 0.9250 Silver .8410 oz. ASW **Series:** Summer Olympics - Sydney **Obverse:** Bust of Queen Elizabeth II right **Reverse:** Hurdlers and Sydney Opera House

Date	Mintage	F	VF	XF	Unc	BU
1999 Proof	Est. 10,000	Value: 50.00				

KM# 932 CROWN **Composition:** Copper-Nickel **Series:** World Cup Rugby 1999 **Obverse:** Bust of Queen Elizabeth II right **Reverse:** Bust of William Web Elliss with players behind

Date	F	VF	XF	Unc	BU
1999	—	—	—	8.00	—

KM# 932a CROWN **Weight:** 28.2800 g. **Composition:** 0.9250 Silver .8410 oz. ASW **Series:** World Cup Rugby 1999 **Obverse:** Bust of Queen Elizabeth II right **Reverse:** Bust of William Web Ellis and player behind

Date	Mintage	F	VF	XF	Unc	BU
1999 Proof	Est. 10,000	Value: 50.00				

KM# 934 CROWN **Composition:** Copper-Nickel **Series:** World Cup Rugby 1999 **Obverse:** Bust of Queen Elizabeth II right **Reverse:** Rugby scrum

Date	F	VF	XF	Unc	BU
1999	—	—	—	8.00	—

KM# 934a CROWN **Weight:** 28.2800 g. **Composition:** 0.9250 Silver .8410 oz. ASW **Series:** World Cup Rugby 1999 **Obverse:** Bust of Queen Elizabeth II right **Reverse:** Rugby scrum

Date	Mintage	F	VF	XF	Unc	BU
1999 Proof	Est. 10,000	Value: 50.00				

KM# 936 CROWN **Composition:** Copper-Nickel **Series:** World Cup Rugby 1999 **Obverse:** Bust of Queen Elizabeth II right **Reverse:** Player catching ball

Date	F	VF	XF	Unc	BU
1999	—	—	—	8.00	—

KM# 936a CROWN **Weight:** 28.2800 g. **Composition:** 0.9250 Silver .8410 oz. ASW **Series:** World Cup Rugby 1999 **Obverse:** Bust of Queen Elizabeth II right **Reverse:** Player catching ball

Date	Mintage	F	VF	XF	Unc	BU
1999 Proof	Est. 10,000	Value: 50.00				

KM# 938 CROWN **Composition:** Copper-Nickel **Series:** World Cup Rugby 1999 **Obverse:** Bust of Queen Elizabeth II right **Reverse:** Goal kick

Date	F	VF	XF	Unc	BU
1999	—	—	—	8.00	—

KM# 938a CROWN **Weight:** 28.2800 g. **Composition:** 0.9250 Silver .8410 oz. ASW **Series:** World Cup Rugby 1999 **Obverse:** Bust of Queen Elizabeth II right **Reverse:** Goal kick

Date	Mintage	F	VF	XF	Unc	BU
1999 Proof	Est. 10,000	Value: 50.00				

KM# 940 CROWN **Composition:** Copper-Nickel **Series:** World Cup Rugby 1999 **Obverse:** Bust of Queen Elizabeth II right **Reverse:** Ball runner being tackled

Date	F	VF	XF	Unc	BU
1999	—	—	—	8.00	—

KM# 940a CROWN **Weight:** 28.2800 g. **Composition:** 0.9250 Silver .8410 oz. ASW **Series:** World Cup Rugby 1999 **Obverse:** Bust of Queen Elizabeth II right **Reverse:** Ball runner being tackled

Date	Mintage	F	VF	XF	Unc	BU
1999 Proof	Est. 10,000	Value: 50.00				

KM# 942 CROWN **Composition:** Copper-Nickel **Series:** World Cup Rugby 1999 **Obverse:** Bust of Queen Elizabeth II right **Reverse:** Player jumping for catch

Date	F	VF	XF	Unc	BU
1999	—	—	—	8.00	—

KM# 942a CROWN **Weight:** 28.2800 g. **Composition:** 0.9250 Silver .8410 oz. ASW **Series:** World Cup Rugby 1999 **Obverse:** Bust of Queen Elizabeth II right **Reverse:** Player jumping for catch

Date	Mintage	F	VF	XF	Unc	BU
1999 Proof	Est. 10,000	Value: 50.00				

KM# 952 CROWN **Composition:** Copper-Nickel **Subject:** Year of the Rabbit **Obverse:** Bust of Queen Elizabeth II right **Reverse:** Two rabbits, Chinese characters

Date	F	VF	XF	Unc	BU
1999	—	—	—	8.00	—

KM# 952a CROWN **Weight:** 28.2800 g. **Composition:** 0.9250 Silver .8410 oz. ASW **Subject:** Year of the Rabbit **Obverse:** Bust of Queen Elizabeth II right **Reverse:** Two rabbits, Chinese characters

Date	Mintage	F	VF	XF	Unc	BU
1999 Proof	Est. 10,000	Value: 50.00				

KM# 952b CROWN **Weight:** 31.1035 g. **Composition:** 0.9999 Gold .9999 oz. AGW **Subject:** Year of the Rabbit **Obverse:** Bust of Queen Elizabeth II right **Reverse:** Two rabbits, Chinese characters

Date	Mintage	F	VF	XF	Unc	BU
1999 Proof	Est. 2,000	Value: 650				

KM# 955 CROWN **Composition:** Copper-Nickel **Obverse:** Bust of Queen Elizabeth II right **Reverse:** Bust of Sir Walter Raleigh, map of America and ship

Date	F	VF	XF	Unc	BU
1999	—	—	—	8.50	—

KM# 955a CROWN **Weight:** 28.2800 g. **Composition:** 0.9250 Silver .8410 oz. ASW **Obverse:** Bust of Queen Elizabeth II right **Reverse:** Bust of Sir Walter Raleigh, map of America and ship

Date	Mintage	F	VF	XF	Unc	BU
1999 Proof	Est. 10,000	Value: 50.00				

KM# 957 CROWN **Composition:** Copper-Nickel **Obverse:** Bust of Queen Elizabeth II right **Reverse:** Compass, bust of Robert Falcon Scott and men pulling sled

Date	F	VF	XF	Unc	BU
1999	—	—	—	8.50	—

KM# 957a CROWN **Weight:** 28.2800 g. **Composition:** 0.9250 Silver .8410 oz. ASW **Obverse:** Bust of Queen Elizabeth II right **Reverse:** Compass, bust of Robert Falcon Scott and men pulling sled

Date	Mintage	F	VF	XF	Unc	BU
1999 Proof	Est. 10,000	Value: 50.00				

KM# 966 CROWN **Composition:** Copper-Nickel **Obverse:** Bust of Queen Elizabeth II right **Reverse:** British Blue cat cleaning its paws

Date	F	VF	XF	Unc	BU
1999	—	—	—	8.50	—

KM# 967 CROWN **Weight:** 31.1035 g. **Composition:** 0.9990 Silver 1.0000 oz. ASW **Obverse:** Bust of Queen Elizabeth II right **Reverse:** British Blue cat cleaning its paws

Date	Mintage	F	VF	XF	Unc	BU
1999 Proof	Est. 50,000	Value: 50.00				

KM# 968 CROWN **Weight:** 31.1035 g. **Composition:** 0.9990 Gold 1.0000 oz. AGW **Obverse:** Bust of Queen Elizabeth II right **Reverse:** British Blue cat cleaning its paws

Date	Mintage	F	VF	XF	Unc	BU
1999		—	—	—	400	—
1999 Proof	—	Value: 410				

KM# 976 CROWN **Composition:** Copper-Nickel **Series:** The Life and Times of the Queen Mother **Obverse:** Bust of Queen Elizabeth II right **Reverse:** Queen Mother as a little girl in chair

Date	F	VF	XF	Unc	BU
1999	—	—	—	7.50	—

KM# 976a CROWN **Weight:** 28.2800 g. **Composition:** 0.9250 Silver .8410 oz. ASW **Series:** The Life and Times of the Queen Mother **Obverse:** Bust of Queen Elizabeth II right **Reverse:** Queen Mother as a little girl in chair

Date	Mintage	F	VF	XF	Unc	BU
1999 Proof	Est. 10,000	Value: 50.00				

KM# 978 CROWN **Composition:** Copper-Nickel **Series:** The Life and Times of the Queen Mother **Obverse:** Bust of Queen Elizabeth II right **Reverse:** Royal engagement portrait

Date	F	VF	XF	Unc	BU
1999	—	—	—	7.50	—

KM# 978a CROWN **Weight:** 28.2800 g. **Composition:** 0.9250 Silver .8410 oz. ASW **Series:** The Life and Times of the Queen Mother **Obverse:** Bust of Queen Elizabeth II right **Reverse:** Royal engagement portrait

Date	Mintage	F	VF	XF	Unc	BU
1999 Proof	Est. 10,000	Value: 50.00				

KM# 980 CROWN **Composition:** Copper-Nickel **Series:** The Life and Times of the Queen Mother **Obverse:** Bust of Queen Elizabeth II right **Reverse:** Wedding portrait

Date	F	VF	XF	Unc	BU
1999	—	—	—	7.50	—

KM# 980a CROWN **Weight:** 28.2800 g. **Composition:** 0.9250 Silver .8410 oz. ASW **Series:** The Life and Times of the Queen Mother **Obverse:** Bust of Queen Elizabeth II right **Reverse:** Wedding portrait

Date	Mintage	F	VF	XF	Unc	BU
1999 Proof	Est. 10,000	Value: 50.00				

KM# 982 CROWN **Composition:** Copper-Nickel **Subject:** The Life and Times of the Queen Mother **Obverse:** Queen's portrait **Reverse:** Honeymoon departure

Date	F	VF	XF	Unc	BU
1999	—	—	—	7.50	—

KM# 982a CROWN **Weight:** 28.2800 g. **Composition:** 0.9250 Silver .8410 oz. ASW **Series:** The Life and Times of the Queen Mother **Obverse:** Bust of Queen Elizabeth II right **Reverse:** Honeymoon departure

Date	Mintage	F	VF	XF	Unc	BU
1999 Proof	Est. 10,000	Value: 50.00				

KM# 996 CROWN **Composition:** Copper-Nickel **Subject:** The Wedding of HRH Prince Edward and Sophie Rhys-Jones **Obverse:** Bust of Queen Elizabeth II right **Reverse:** Head of Prince Edward right

Date	F	VF	XF	Unc	BU
1999	—	—	—	8.00	—

KM# 996a CROWN **Weight:** 28.2800 g. **Composition:** 0.9250 Silver .8410 oz. ASW **Subject:** The Wedding of HRH Prince Edward and Sophie Rhys-Jones **Obverse:** Bust of Queen Elizabeth II right **Reverse:** Head of Prince Edward right

Date	Mintage	F	VF	XF	Unc	BU
1999 Proof	Est. 10,000	Value: 50.00				

KM# 998 CROWN **Composition:** Copper-Nickel **Subject:** The Wedding of HRH Prince Edward and Sophie Rhys-Jones **Obverse:** Bust of Queen Elizabeth II right **Reverse:** Head of Sophie Rhys-Jones left

Date	F	VF	XF	Unc	BU
1999	—	—	—	8.00	—

KM# 998a CROWN **Weight:** 28.2800 g. **Composition:** 0.9250 Silver .8410 oz. ASW **Subject:** The Wedding of HRH Prince Edward and Sophie Rhys-Jones **Obverse:** Bust of Queen Elizabeth II right **Reverse:** Head of Sophie Rhys-Jones left

Date	Mintage	F	VF	XF	Unc	BU
1999 Proof	Est. 10,000	Value: 50.00				

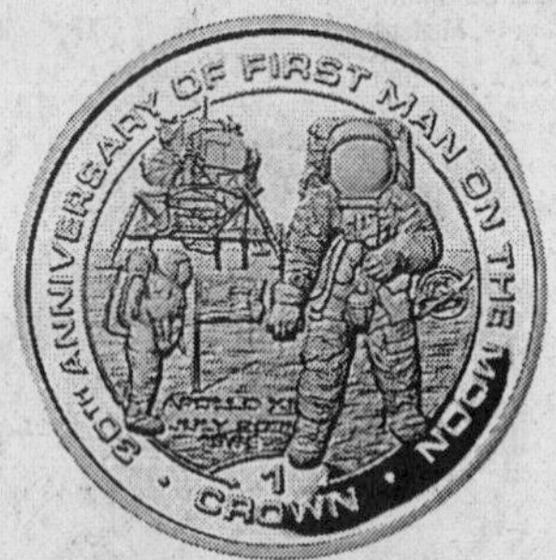

KM# 1000 CROWN **Composition:** Copper-Nickel **Subject:** 30th Anniversary of First Man on the Moon **Obverse:** Bust of Queen Elizabeth II right **Reverse:** Apollo XI, 1969 and moon walkers

Date	F	VF	XF	Unc	BU
1999	—	—	—	7.50	—

KM# 1000a CROWN **Weight:** 28.2800 g. **Composition:** 0.9250 Silver .8410 oz. ASW **Subject:** 30th Anniversary of First Man on the Moon **Obverse:** Bust of Queen Elizabeth II right **Reverse:** Apollo XI, 1969 and two moon walkers

Date	Mintage	F	VF	XF	Unc	BU
1999 Proof	Est. 10,000	Value: 50.00				

KM# 1002 CROWN **Composition:** Copper-Nickel **Subject:** 30th Anniversary of First Man on the Moon **Obverse:** Bust of Queen Elizabeth II right **Reverse:** Mariner IX, 1971 and orbiting Mars

Date	F	VF	XF	Unc	BU
1999	—	—	—	7.50	—

KM# 1002a CROWN **Weight:** 28.2800 g. **Composition:** 0.9250 Silver .8410 oz. ASW **Subject:** 30th Anniversary of First Man on the Moon **Obverse:** Bust of Queen Elizabeth II right **Reverse:** Mariner IX, 1971 and orbiting Mars

Date	Mintage	F	VF	XF	Unc	BU
1999	Est. 10,000	Value: 50.00				

KM# 1004 CROWN **Composition:** Copper-Nickel **Subject:** 30th Anniversary of First Man on the Moon **Obverse:** Bust of Queen Elizabeth II right **Reverse:** Apollo-Soyuz link-up, 1975

Date	F	VF	XF	Unc	BU
1999	—	—	—	7.50	—

KM# 1004a CROWN **Weight:** 28.2800 g. **Composition:** 0.9250 Silver .8410 oz. ASW **Subject:** 30th Anniversary of First Man on the Moon **Obverse:** Bust of Queen Elizabeth II right **Reverse:** Apollo-Soyuz link-up, 1975

Date	Mintage	F	VF	XF	Unc	BU
1999 Proof	Est. 10,000	Value: 50.00				

KM# 1006 CROWN **Composition:** Copper-Nickel **Subject:** 30th Anniversary of First Man on the Moon **Obverse:** Bust of Queen Elizabeth II right **Reverse:** Viking Mars Lander, 1978

Date	F	VF	XF	Unc	BU
1999	—	—	—	7.50	—

KM# 1006a CROWN **Weight:** 28.2800 g. **Composition:** 0.9250 Silver .8410 oz. ASW **Subject:** 30th Anniversary of First Man on the Moon **Obverse:** Bust of Queen Elizabeth II right **Reverse:** Viking Mars lander, 1978

Date	Mintage	F	VF	XF	Unc	BU
1999 Proof	Est. 10,000	Value: 50.00				

KM# 1008 CROWN **Composition:** Copper-Nickel **Subject:** 30th Anniversary of First Man on the Moon **Obverse:** Bust of Queen Elizabeth II right **Reverse:** Shuttle orbiter Columbia, 1981

Date	F	VF	XF	Unc	BU
1999	—	—	—	7.50	—

KM# 1008a CROWN **Weight:** 28.2800 g. **Composition:** 0.9250 Silver .8410 oz. ASW **Subject:** 30th Anniversary of First Man on the Moon **Obverse:** Bust of Queen Elizabeth II right **Reverse:** Shuttle orbiter Columbia, 1981

Date	Mintage	F	VF	XF	Unc	BU
1999 Proof	Est. 10,000	Value: 50.00				

KM# 1010 CROWN **Composition:** Copper-Nickel **Subject:** 30th Anniversary of First Man on the Moon **Obverse:** Bust of Queen Elizabeth II right **Reverse:** Mars Pathfinder, 1997

Date	F	VF	XF	Unc	BU
1999	—	—	—	7.50	—

KM# 1010a CROWN **Weight:** 28.2800 g. **Composition:** 0.9250 Silver .8410 oz. ASW **Subject:** 30th Anniversary of First Man on the Moon **Obverse:** Bust of Queen Elizabeth II right **Reverse:** Mars Pathfinder, 1997

Date	Mintage	F	VF	XF	Unc	BU
1999 Proof	Est. 10,000	Value: 50.00				

KM# 1057 CROWN **Weight:** 31.1035 g. **Composition:** 0.9999 Gold 1.0000 oz. AGW **Subject:** Scottish Fold Kitten **Obverse:** Bust of Queen Elizabeth II right **Reverse:** Kitten playing with world **Edge:** Reeded **Size:** 32.7 mm.

Date	F	VF	XF	Unc	BU
2000	—	—	—	470	—
2000 Proof	— Value: 650				

KM# 1047 CROWN **Weight:** 28.2800 g. **Composition:** Copper-Nickel **Obverse:** Queen's portrait **Reverse:** Prince William's portrait **Edge:** Reeded

Date	F	VF	XF	Unc	BU
2000	—	—	—	10.00	—

KM# 1047a CROWN **Weight:** 28.2800 g. **Composition:** 0.9250 Silver .8410 oz. ASW **Obverse:** Queen's portrait **Reverse:** Prince William's portrait **Edge:** Reeded

Date	Mintage	F	VF	XF	Unc	BU
2000 Proof	10,000	Value: 47.50				

KM# 1049 CROWN **Composition:** Copper-Nickel **Obverse:** Queen's portrait **Reverse:** Queen Mother's portrait

Date	F	VF	XF	Unc	BU
2000	—	—	—	10.00	—

KM# 1049a CROWN **Weight:** 28.2800 g. **Composition:** 0.9250 Silver .8410 oz. ASW **Obverse:** Queen's portrait **Reverse:** Queen Mother's portrait

Date	Mintage	F	VF	XF	Unc	BU
2000 Proof	10,000	Value: 47.50				

KM# 1019 CROWN **Weight:** 28.2800 g. **Composition:** Copper-Nickel **Subject:** Millennium **Obverse:** Queen's portrait **Reverse:** MM Monogram **Edge:** Reeded **Size:** 38.6 mm.

Date	F	VF	XF	Unc	BU
2000	—	—	—	10.00	—

KM# 1019a CROWN **Weight:** 28.2800 g. **Composition:** 0.9250 Silver .8410 oz. ASW **Subject:** Millennium **Obverse:** Queen's portrait **Reverse:** MM monogram **Edge:** Reeded **Size:** 38.6 mm.

Date	Mintage	F	VF	XF	Unc	BU
2000 Proof	10,000	Value: 47.50				

KM# 1055a CROWN **Weight:** 6.2200 g. **Composition:** 0.9995 Platinum .2000 oz. APW

Date	F	VF	XF	Unc	BU
2000	—	—	—	383	—

KM# 1051 CROWN **Weight:** 28.2800 g. **Composition:** 0.9250 Silver .8410 oz. ASW **Subject:** Millennium-Meridian **Obverse:** Queen's portrait **Reverse:** Old Royal Observatory clock face with an embedded brass strip from the original Prime meridian **Edge:** Reeded **Size:** 38.6 mm.

Date	Mintage	F	VF	XF	Unc	BU
2000 Proof	10,000	Value: 47.50				

KM# 1056 CROWN **Composition:** Copper-Nickel **Subject:** Scottish Fold Kitten **Obverse:** Queen's portrait **Reverse:** Kitten playing with world **Edge:** Reeded **Size:** 38.6 mm.

Date	F	VF	XF	Unc	BU
2000	—	—	—	10.00	—

KM# 1056a CROWN **Weight:** 31.1035 g. **Composition:** 0.9999 Silver 1.000 oz. ASW **Subject:** Scottish Fold Kitten **Obverse:** Queen's portrait **Reverse:** Kitten playing with world **Edge:** Reeded **Size:** 38.6 mm.

Date	Mintage	F	VF	XF	Unc	BU
2000 Proof	50,000	Value: 47.50				

KM# 1021 CROWN **Weight:** 28.2800 g. **Composition:** Copper-Nickel **Obverse:** Queen's portrait **Reverse:** Armored portrait of Francisco Pizarro, map and ship **Size:** 38.6 mm.

Date	F	VF	XF	Unc	BU
2000	—	—	—	10.00	—

KM# 1021a CROWN **Weight:** 28.2800 g. **Composition:** 0.9250 Silver .8410 oz. ASW **Obverse:** Queen's portrait **Reverse:** Armored portrait of Francisco Pizarro, map and ship **Size:** 38.6 mm.

Date	Mintage	F	VF	XF	Unc	BU
2000 Proof	10,000	Value: 47.50				

KM# 1023 CROWN **Composition:** Copper-Nickel **Obverse:** Queen's portrait **Reverse:** Portrait of Willem Barents, ship on ice, map

Date	F	VF	XF	Unc	BU
2000	—	—	—	10.00	—

KM# 1023a CROWN **Weight:** 28.2800 g. **Composition:** 0.9250 Silver .8410 oz. ASW **Obverse:** Queen's portrait **Reverse:** Portrait of Willem Barents, ship on ice, map

Date	Mintage	F	VF	XF	Unc	BU
2000 Proof	10,000	Value: 47.50				

KM# 1025 CROWN **Weight:** 28.2800 g. **Composition:** Copper-Nickel **Series:** Queen Mother **Obverse:** Queen's portrait **Reverse:** 1931 family scene **Edge:** Reeded

Date	F	VF	XF	Unc	BU
2000	—	—	—	10.00	—

KM# 1025a CROWN **Weight:** 28.2800 g. **Composition:** 0.9250 Silver .8410 oz. ASW **Series:** Queen Mother **Obverse:** Queen's portrait **Reverse:** 1931 family scene **Edge:** Reeded

Date	Mintage	F	VF	XF	Unc	BU
2000 Proof	10,000	Value: 47.50				

KM# 1027 CROWN **Composition:** Copper-Nickel **Reverse:** 1937 Coronation scene

Date	F	VF	XF	Unc	BU
2000	—	—	—	10.00	—

KM# 1027a CROWN **Weight:** 28.2800 g. **Composition:** 0.9250 Silver .8410 oz. ASW **Reverse:** Coronation scene

Date	Mintage	F	VF	XF	Unc	BU
2000 Proof	10,000	Value: 47.50				

KM# 1029 CROWN **Composition:** Copper-Nickel **Reverse:** 1945 Victory Visit

Date	F	VF	XF	Unc	BU
2000	—	—	—	10.00	—

KM# 1029a CROWN **Weight:** 28.2800 g. **Composition:** 0.9250 Silver .8410 oz. ASW **Reverse:** 1945 Victory Visit

Date	Mintage	F	VF	XF	Unc	BU
2000 Proof	10,000	Value: 47.50				

KM# 1031 CROWN **Composition:** Copper-Nickel **Reverse:** Queen Mother, coach, and man

Date	F	VF	XF	Unc	BU
2000	—	—	—	10.00	—

KM# 1031a CROWN **Weight:** 28.2800 g. **Composition:** 0.9250 Silver .8410 oz. ASW **Reverse:** Queen Mother, coach, and man

Date	Mintage	F	VF	XF	Unc	BU
2000 Proof	10,000	Value: 47.50				

KM# 1033 CROWN **Weight:** 28.2800 g. **Composition:** Copper-Nickel **Subject:** Battle of Britain **Obverse:** Queen's portrait **Reverse:** Aerial battle scene

Date	F	VF	XF	Unc	BU
2000	—	—	—	10.00	—

KM# 1033a CROWN **Weight:** 28.2800 g. **Composition:** 0.9250 Silver .8410 oz. ASW **Subject:** Battle of Britain **Obverse:** Queen's portrait **Reverse:** Aerial battle scene

Date	Mintage	F	VF	XF	Unc	BU
2000 Proof	10,000	Value: 47.50				

KM# 1035 CROWN **Composition:** Copper-Nickel **Subject:** Global Challenge Yacht Race **Obverse:** Queen's portrait **Reverse:** Partial ship and map

Date	F	VF	XF	Unc	BU
2000	—	—	—	10.00	—

KM# 1035a CROWN **Weight:** 28.2800 g. **Composition:** 0.9250 Copper-Nickel Clad Copper .8410 oz. **Subject:** Global Challenge Yacht Race **Obverse:** Queen's portrait **Reverse:** Partial ship and map

Date	Mintage	F	VF	XF	Unc	BU
2000 Proof	10,000	Value: 47.50				

KM# 984a CROWN **Weight:** 28.2800 g. **Composition:** 0.9250 Silver .8410 oz. ASW **Subject:** Founding of the UN 1945 **Obverse:** Bust of Queen Elizabeth II right **Reverse:** UN building and logo

Date	F	VF	XF	Unc	BU
2000 Proof	— Value: 50.00				

KM# 986 CROWN **Composition:** Copper-Nickel **Subject:** First Man on the Moon **Obverse:** Bust of Queen Elizabeth II right **Reverse:** Astronauts on moon and flag

Date	F	VF	XF	Unc	BU
2000	—	—	—	7.50	—

KM# 986a CROWN **Weight:** 28.2800 g. **Composition:** 0.9250 Silver .8410 oz. ASW **Subject:** First Man on the Moon **Obverse:** Bust of Queen Elizabeth II right **Reverse:** Astronauts on moon and flag

Date	Mintage	F	VF	XF	Unc	BU
2000 Proof	Est. 10,000	Value: 50.00				

KM# 1016 CROWN **Composition:** Copper-Nickel **Subject:** Year of the Dragon **Obverse:** Bust of Queen Elizabeth II right **Reverse:** Dragon

Date	F	VF	XF	Unc	BU
2000	—	—	—	8.50	—

KM# 1016a CROWN **Weight:** 28.2800 g. **Composition:** 0.9250 Silver .8410 oz. ASW **Subject:** Year of the Dragon **Obverse:** Bust of Queen Elizabeth II right **Reverse:** Dragon

Date	Mintage	F	VF	XF	Unc	BU
2000 Proof	Est. 30,000	Value: 50.00				

KM# 1017 CROWN **Weight:** 31.1035 g. **Composition:** 0.9999 Gold 1.0000 oz. AGW **Subject:** Year of the Dragon **Obverse:** Bust of Queen Elizabeth II right **Reverse:** Dragon

Date	Mintage	F	VF	XF	Unc	BU
2000 Proof	Est. 2,000	Value: 650				

KM# 1062 CROWN **Weight:** 28.2800 g. **Composition:** Copper-Nickel **Subject:** Year of the Snake **Obverse:** Queen's portrait **Reverse:** Snake **Edge:** Reeded **Size:** 38.6 mm.

Date	F	VF	XF	Unc	BU
2001	—	—	—	10.00	—

KM# 1062a CROWN **Weight:** 28.2800 g. **Composition:** 0.9250 Silver .8410 oz. ASW **Subject:** Year of the Snake **Obverse:** Queen's portrait **Reverse:** Snake **Edge:** Reeded **Size:** 38.6 mm.

Date	Mintage	F	VF	XF	Unc	BU
2001 Proof	30,000	Value: 47.50				

KM# 1063 CROWN **Weight:** 31.1035 g. **Composition:** 0.9999 Gold 1.0000 oz. AGW **Subject:** Year of the Snake **Obverse:** Queen's portrait **Reverse:** Snake **Edge:** Reeded **Size:** 32.7 mm.

Date	Mintage	F	VF	XF	Unc	BU
2001 Proof	2,000	Value: 650				

KM# 1072 CROWN **Weight:** 28.2800 g. **Composition:** Copper-Nickel **Subject:** Somali Kittens **Obverse:** Queen's portrait **Reverse:** Two kittens **Edge:** Reeded **Size:** 38.6 mm.

Date	F	VF	XF	Unc	BU
2001	—	—	—	10.00	—

KM# 1072a CROWN **Weight:** 31.1035 g. **Composition:** 0.9990 Silver 1.0000 oz. ASW **Subject:** Somali Kittens **Obverse:** Queen's portrait **Reverse:** Two kittens **Edge:** Reeded **Size:** 38.6 mm.

Date	Mintage	F	VF	XF	Unc	BU
2001 Proof	50,000	Value: 47.50				

KM# 1073 CROWN **Weight:** 31.1035 g. **Composition:** 0.9999 Gold 1.0000 oz. AGW **Subject:** Somali Kittens **Obverse:** Queen's portrait **Reverse:** Two kittens **Edge:** Reeded **Size:** 32.7 mm.

Date	Mintage	F	VF	XF	Unc	BU
2001	—	—	—	—	470	—
2001 Proof	1,000	Value: 650				

KM# 1076 CROWN **Weight:** 28.2800 g. **Composition:** Copper-Nickel **Subject:** Queen Mother **Obverse:** Queen's portrait **Reverse:** 1948 Silver wedding anniversary **Edge:** Reeded **Size:** 38.6 mm.

Date	F	VF	XF	Unc	BU
2001	—	—	—	10.00	—

KM# 1076a CROWN **Weight:** 28.2800 g. **Composition:** 0.9250 Silver .8410 oz. ASW **Subject:** Queen Mother **Obverse:** Queen's portrait **Reverse:** 1948 Silver wedding anniversary **Edge:** Reeded **Size:** 38.6 mm.

Date	Mintage	F	VF	XF	Unc	BU
2001 Proof	10,000	Value: 47.50				

KM# 1077 CROWN **Composition:** Copper-Nickel **Subject:** Queen Mother **Obverse:** Queen's portrait **Reverse:** 1948 holding baby Prince Charles **Edge:** Reeded **Size:** 38.6 mm.

Date	F	VF	XF	Unc	BU
2001	—	—	—	10.00	—

KM# 1077a CROWN **Weight:** 28.2800 g. **Composition:** 0.9250 Silver .8410 oz. ASW **Subject:** Queen Mother **Obverse:** Queen's portrait **Reverse:** 1948 holding baby Prince Charles **Edge:** Reeded **Size:** 38.6 mm.

Date	Mintage	F	VF	XF	Unc	BU
2001 Proof	10,000	Value: 47.50				

KM# 1080 CROWN **Composition:** Copper-Nickel **Subject:** Martin Frobisher **Obverse:** Queen's portrait **Reverse:** Portrait, ship and map **Edge:** Reeded **Size:** 38.6 mm.

Date	F	VF	XF	Unc	BU
2001	—	—	—	10.00	—

KM# 1080a CROWN **Weight:** 28.2800 g. **Composition:** 0.9250 Silver .8410 oz. ASW **Subject:** Martin Frobisher **Obverse:** Queen's portrait **Reverse:** Portrait, ship and map **Edge:** Reeded **Size:** 38.6 mm.

Date	Mintage	F	VF	XF	Unc	BU
2001 Proof	10,000	Value: 47.50				

KM# 1081 CROWN **Composition:** Copper-Nickel **Subject:** Roald Amundsen **Obverse:** Queen's portrait **Reverse:** Portrait, ship and dirigible **Edge:** Reeded **Size:** 38.6 mm.

Date	F	VF	XF	Unc	BU
2001	—	—	—	10.00	—

KM# 1081a CROWN **Weight:** 28.2800 g. **Composition:** 0.9250 Silver .8410 oz. ASW **Subject:** Roald Amundsen **Obverse:** Queen's portrait **Reverse:** Portrait, ship and dirigible **Edge:** Reeded **Size:** 38.6 mm.

Date	Mintage	F	VF	XF	Unc	BU
2001 Proof	10,000	Value: 47.50				

KM# 1085 CROWN **Weight:** 28.2800 g. **Composition:** Copper-Nickel **Subject:** Joey Dunlop (1952-2000) **Obverse:** Queen Elizabeth's II portrait **Reverse:** Motorcycle racer **Edge:** Reeded **Size:** 38.6 mm.

Date	F	VF	XF	Unc	BU
2001 Black finish	—	—	—	10.00	—

KM# 1085a CROWN **Weight:** 28.2800 g. **Composition:** 0.9250 Silver .8410 oz. ASW **Subject:** Joey Dunlop (1952-2000) **Obverse:** Queen Elizabeth's II portrait **Reverse:** Motorcycle racer **Edge:** Reeded **Size:** 38.6 mm.

Date	Mintage	F	VF	XF	Unc	BU
2001 Proof	10,000	Value: 47.50				

KM# 1083 CROWN **Weight:** 28.2800 g. **Composition:** Copper-Nickel **Subject:** Queen's 75th Birthday **Obverse:** Queen's portrait **Reverse:** Flower bouquet **Edge:** Reeded **Size:** 38.6 mm.

Date	F	VF	XF	Unc	BU
2001	—	—	—	14.00	—

KM# 1083a CROWN **Weight:** 28.2800 g. **Composition:** 0.9250 Silver .8410 oz. ASW **Subject:** Queen's 75th Birthday **Obverse:** Queen's portrait **Reverse:** Flower bouquet **Edge:** Reeded **Size:** 38.6 mm.

Date	Mintage	F	VF	XF	Unc	BU
2001 Proof	10,000	Value: 49.00				

KM# 1087 CROWN **Weight:** 28.2800 g. **Composition:** Copper-Nickel **Series:** Harry Potter **Obverse:** Queen's portrait **Reverse:** Boy with magic wand **Edge:** Reeded **Size:** 38.6 mm.

Date	F	VF	XF	Unc	BU
2001	—	—	—	10.00	—

KM# 1087a CROWN **Weight:** 28.2800 g. **Composition:** 0.9250 Silver .8410 oz. ASW **Series:** Harry Potter **Obverse:** Queen's portrait **Reverse:** Boy with magic wand **Edge:** Reeded **Size:** 38.6 mm.

Date	Mintage	F	VF	XF	Unc	BU
2001 Proof	15,000	Value: 47.50				

KM# 1089 CROWN **Weight:** 28.2800 g. **Composition:** Copper-Nickel **Series:** Harry Potter **Subject:** Journey to

Hogwart's **Obverse:** Queen's portrait **Reverse:** Boat full of children going to Hogwart's **Edge:** Reeded **Size:** 38.6 mm.

Date	F	VF	XF	Unc	BU
2001	—	—	—	10.00	—

KM# 1089a CROWN **Weight:** 28.2800 g. **Composition:** 0.9250 Silver .8410 oz. ASW **Series:** Harry Potter **Obverse:** Queen's portrait **Reverse:** Boat full of children going to Hogwart's **Edge:** Reeded **Size:** 38.6 mm.

Date	Mintage	F	VF	XF	Unc	BU
2001 Proof	15,000	Value: 47.50				

KM# 1091 CROWN **Composition:** Copper-Nickel **Series:** Harry Potter **Subject:** First Quidditch Match **Obverse:** Queen's portrait **Reverse:** Harry flying a broomstick

Date	F	VF	XF	Unc	BU
2001	—	—	—	10.00	—

KM# 1091a CROWN **Weight:** 28.2800 g. **Composition:** 0.9250 Silver .8410 oz. ASW **Series:** Harry Potter **Subject:** First Quidditch Match **Obverse:** Queen's portrait **Reverse:** Harry flying a broomstick

Date	Mintage	F	VF	XF	Unc	BU
2001 Proof	15,000	Value: 47.50				

KM# 1093 CROWN **Composition:** Copper-Nickel **Series:** Harry Potter **Subject:** Birth of Norbert **Obverse:** Queen's portrait **Reverse:** Hagrid and children watching Norbert hatch

Date	F	VF	XF	Unc	BU
2001	—	—	—	10.00	—

KM# 1093a CROWN **Weight:** 28.2800 g. **Composition:** 0.9250 Silver .8410 oz. ASW **Series:** Harry Potter **Subject:** Birth of Norbert **Obverse:** Queen's portrait **Reverse:** Hagrid and children watching Norbert hatch

Date	Mintage	F	VF	XF	Unc	BU
2001 Proof	15,000	Value: 47.50				

KM# 1095 CROWN **Composition:** Copper-Nickel **Series:** Harry Potter **Subject:** School **Obverse:** Queen's portrait **Reverse:** Harry in Potions class

Date	F	VF	XF	Unc	BU
2001	—	—	—	10.00	—

KM# 1095a CROWN **Weight:** 28.2800 g. **Composition:** 0.9250 Silver .8410 oz. ASW **Series:** Harry Potter **Subject:** School **Obverse:** Queen's portrait **Reverse:** Harry in Potions class

Date	Mintage	F	VF	XF	Unc	BU
2001 Proof	15,000	Value: 47.50				

KM# 1097 CROWN **Composition:** Copper-Nickel **Series:** Harry Potter **Subject:** Keys **Obverse:** Queen's portrait **Reverse:** Harry catching a flying key

Date	F	VF	XF	Unc	BU
2001	—	—	—	10.00	—

KM# 1097a CROWN **Weight:** 28.2800 g. **Composition:** 0.9250 Silver .8410 oz. ASW **Series:** Harry Potter **Subject:** Keys **Obverse:** Queen's portrait **Reverse:** Harry catching a flying quidditch

Date	Mintage	F	VF	XF	Unc	BU
2001 Proof	15,000	Value: 47.50				

KM# 1118 CROWN **Weight:** 28.2800 g. **Composition:** Copper-Nickel **Subject:** Queen Mother's Love of Horses **Obverse:** Bust of Queen Elizabeth II right **Reverse:** Queen Mother and horse **Edge:** Reeded **Size:** 38.6 mm.

Date	F	VF	XF	Unc	BU
2002	—	—	—	10.00	—

KM# 1118a CROWN **Weight:** 28.2800 g. **Composition:** Silver **Subject:** Queen Mother's Love of Horses **Obverse:** Bust of Queen Elizabeth II right **Reverse:** Queen Mother and horse **Edge:** Reeded **Size:** 38.6 mm.

Date	Mintage	F	VF	XF	Unc	BU
2002 Proof	10,000	Value: 47.50				

KM# 1119 CROWN **Weight:** 35.0000 g. **Composition:** 0.7500 Gold 0.844 oz. AGW **Subject:** Golden Jubilee **Obverse:** Bust of Queen Elizabeth II right **Reverse:** Queen Elizabeth II's young bust right **Edge:** Reeded **Size:** 38.6 mm. **Note:** Red Gold center in a White Gold inner ring within a Yellow Gold outer ring.

Date	Mintage	F	VF	XF	Unc	BU
2002 Proof	999	Value: 600				

KM# 1144 CROWN **Weight:** 28.2800 g. **Composition:** Copper Nickel **Series:** Harry Potter **Obverse:** Queen's portrait **Reverse:** Tom Riddle twirling Harry's magic wand **Edge:** Reeded **Size:** 38.6 mm.

Date	F	VF	XF	Unc	BU
2002PM	—	—	—	10.00	—

KM# 1144a CROWN **Weight:** 28.2800 g. **Composition:** 0.9250 Silver 0.841 oz. ASW **Series:** Harry Potter **Obverse:** Queen's portrait **Reverse:** Tom Riddle twirling Harry's magic wand **Edge:** Reeded **Size:** 28.6 mm.

Date	Mintage	F	VF	XF	Unc	BU
2002PM Proof	15,000	Value: 49.00				

KM# 1146 CROWN **Weight:** 28.2800 g. **Composition:** Copper-Nickel **Series:** Harry Potter **Obverse:** Queen' portrait **Reverse:** Harry and friends making Polyjuice potion **Edge:** Reeded **Size:** 38.6 mm.

Date	F	VF	XF	Unc	BU
2002PM	—	—	—	10.00	—

KM# 1146a CROWN **Weight:** 28.2800 g. **Composition:** 0.9250 Silver 0.841 oz. ASW **Series:** Harry Potter **Obverse:** Queen's portrait **Reverse:** Harry Potter and friends making Polyjuice potion **Edge:** Reeded **Size:** 38.6 mm.

Date	Mintage	F	VF	XF	Unc	BU
2002PM Proof	15,000	Value: 49.00				

KM# 1148 CROWN **Weight:** 28.2800 g. **Composition:** Copper Nickel **Series:** Harry Potter **Obverse:** Queen's portrait **Reverse:** Harry arrives at the Burrow in a flying car **Edge:** Reeded **Size:** 38.6 mm.

Date	F	VF	XF	Unc	BU
2002PM	—	—	—	10.00	—

KM# 1148a CROWN **Weight:** 28.2800 g. **Composition:** 0.9250 Silver 0.841 oz. ASW **Series:** Harry Potter **Obverse:** Queen's portrait **Reverse:** Harry arrives at the Burrow in a flying car **Edge:** Reeded **Size:** 38.6 mm.

Date	Mintage	F	VF	XF	Unc	BU
2002PM	15,000	Value: 49.00				

Note: Proof

KM# 1150 CROWN **Weight:** 28.2800 g. **Composition:** Copper-Nickel **Series:** Harry Potter **Obverse:** Queen's portrait **Reverse:** Harry retrieves Gryffinder sword from snake **Edge:** Reeded **Size:** 38.6 mm.

Date	F	VF	XF	Unc	BU
2002PM	—	—	—	10.00	—

KM# 1150a CROWN **Weight:** 28.2800 g. **Composition:** 0.9250 Silver 0.841 oz. ASW **Series:** Harry Potter **Obverse:** Queen's portrait **Reverse:** Harry retrieves Gryffindor sword from snake **Edge:** Reeded **Size:** 38.6 mm.

Date	Mintage	F	VF	XF	Unc	BU
2002PM Proof	15,000	Value: 49.00				

KM# 1152 CROWN **Weight:** 28.2800 g. **Composition:** Copper-Nickel **Series:** Harry Potter **Obverse:** Queen'sportrait **Reverse:** Harry and Ron encounter the spider Aragog **Edge:** Reeded **Size:** 38.6 mm.

Date	F	VF	XF	Unc	BU
2002PM	—	—	—	10.00	—

KM# 1152a CROWN **Weight:** 28.2800 g. **Composition:** 0.9250 Silver 0.841 oz. ASW **Series:** Harry Potter **Obverse:** Queen's portrait **Reverse:** Harry and Ron encounter the spider Aragog **Edge:** Reeded **Size:** 38.6 mm.

Date	Mintage	F	VF	XF	Unc	BU
2002PM Proof	15,000	Value: 49.00				

KM# 1154 CROWN **Weight:** 28.2800 g. **Composition:** Copper Nickel **Series:** Harry Potter **Obverse:** Queen's portrait **Reverse:** Harry in hospital **Edge:** Reeded **Size:** 38.6 mm.

Date	F	VF	XF	Unc	BU
2002PM	—	—	—	10.00	—

KM# 1154a CROWN **Weight:** 28.2800 g. **Composition:** 0.9250 Silver 0.841 oz. ASW **Series:** Harry Potter **Obverse:** Queen's portrait **Reverse:** Harry in hospital **Edge:** Reeded **Size:** 38.6 mm.

Date	Mintage	F	VF	XF	Unc	BU
2002PM Proof	15,000	Value: 49.00				

KM# 1102 CROWN **Weight:** 28.2800 g. **Composition:** Copper-Nickel **Subject:** Year of the Horse **Obverse:** Queen's portrait **Reverse:** Two horses **Edge:** Reeded **Size:** 38.6 mm.

Date	F	VF	XF	Unc	BU
2002	—	—	—	10.00	—

KM# 1102a CROWN **Weight:** 28.2800 g. **Composition:** 0.9250 Silver .8410 oz. ASW **Subject:** Year of the Horse **Obverse:** Queen's portrait **Reverse:** Two horses **Edge:** Reeded **Size:** 38.6 mm.

Date	Mintage	F	VF	XF	Unc	BU
2002 Proof	30,000	Value: 47.50				

KM# 1103 CROWN **Weight:** 31.1000 g. **Composition:** 0.9999 Gold .9998 oz. AGW **Subject:** Year of the Horse

Date	Mintage	F	VF	XF	Unc	BU
2002 Proof	2,000	Value: 650				

KM# 1111 CROWN **Weight:** 28.2800 g. **Composition:** Copper-Nickel **Subject:** Bengal Cat **Obverse:** Queen Elizabeth's bust right **Reverse:** Cat and kitten **Edge:** Reeded **Size:** 38.6 mm.

Date	VG	F	VF	XF	Unc
2002	—	—	—	—	10.00

KM# 1111a CROWN **Weight:** 31.1035 g. **Composition:** 0.9990 Silver 0.999 oz. ASW **Subject:** Bengal Cat **Obverse:** Bust of Queen Elizabeth II right **Reverse:** Cat and kitten **Edge:** Reeded **Size:** 38.6 mm.

Date	Mintage	F	VF	XF	Unc	BU
2002 Proof	10,000	Value: 47.50				

KM# 1112 CROWN Weight: 31.1035 g. **Composition:** 0.9990 Gold 0.999 oz. AGW **Subject:** Bengal Cat **Obverse:** Queen Elizabeth's bust right **Reverse:** Cat and kitten **Edge:** Reeded

Date	Mintage	VG	F	VF	XF	Unc
2002	—	—	—	—	—	470
2002 Proof	1,000	Value: 650				

KM# 1115 CROWN Weight: 28.2800 g. **Composition:** Copper-Nickel **Subject:** Olympics - Salt Lake City **Obverse:** Bust of Queen Elizabeth II right **Reverse:** Skier, torch and flag **Edge:** Reeded **Size:** 38.6 mm.

Date	F	VF	XF	Unc	BU
2002	—	—	—	10.00	—

KM# 1115a CROWN Weight: 28.2800 g. **Composition:** 0.9250 Silver 0.841 oz. ASW **Subject:** Olympics - Salt Lake City **Obverse:** Bust of Queen Elizabeth II right **Reverse:** Skier, torch and flag **Edge:** Reeded **Size:** 38.6 mm.

Date	Mintage	F	VF	XF	Unc	BU
2002 Proof	10,000	—	—	—	47.50	—

KM# 1116 CROWN Weight: 28.2800 g. **Composition:** Copper-Nickel **Subject:** Olympics - Salt Lake City **Obverse:** Bust of Queen Elizabeth II right **Reverse:** Bobsled, torch and stadium **Edge:** Reeded **Size:** 38.6 mm.

Date	F	VF	XF	Unc	BU
2002	—	—	—	10.00	—

KM# 1116a CROWN Weight: 28.2800 g. **Composition:** 0.9250 Silver 0.841 oz. ASW **Subject:** Olympics - Salt Lake City **Obverse:** Bust of Queen Elizabeth II right **Reverse:** Bobsled, torch and stadium **Edge:** Reeded **Size:** 38.6 mm.

Date	Mintage	F	VF	XF	Unc	BU
2002 Proof	10,000	Value: 47.50				

KM# 1121 CROWN Weight: 28.2800 g. **Composition:** Copper-Nickel **Subject:** World Cup 2002 Japan - Korea **Obverse:** Bust of Queen Elizabeth II right **Reverse:** Player running right **Edge:** Reeded **Size:** 38.6 mm.

Date	F	VF	XF	Unc	BU
2002	—	—	—	10.00	—

KM# 1121a CROWN Weight: 28.2800 g. **Composition:** 0.9250 Silver 0.841 oz. ASW **Subject:** World Cup 2002 Japan - Korea **Obverse:** Bust of Queen Elizabeth II right **Reverse:** Player running right **Edge:** Reeded **Size:** 38.6 mm.

Date	Mintage	F	VF	XF	Unc	BU
2002 Proof	10,000	Value: 47.50				

KM# 1123 CROWN Weight: 28.2800 g. **Composition:** Copper-Nickel **Subject:** World Cup 2002 Japan - Korea **Obverse:** Bust of Queen Elizabeth II right **Reverse:** Player kicking to right **Edge:** Reeded **Size:** 38.6 mm.

Date	F	VF	XF	Unc	BU
2002	—	—	—	10.00	—

KM# 1123a CROWN Weight: 28.2800 g. **Composition:** 0.9250 Silver 0.841 oz. ASW **Subject:** World Cup 2002 Japan - Korea **Obverse:** Bust of Queen Elizabeth II right **Reverse:** Player kicking to right **Edge:** Reeded **Size:** 38.6 mm.

Date	Mintage	F	VF	XF	Unc	BU
2002 Proof	10,000	Value: 47.50				

KM# 1125 CROWN Weight: 28.2800 g. **Composition:** Copper-Nickel **Subject:** World Cup 2002 Japan - Korea **Obverse:** Bust of Queen Elizabeth II right **Reverse:** Player kicking to left **Edge:** Reeded **Size:** 38.6 mm.

Date	F	VF	XF	Unc	BU
2002	—	—	—	10.00	—

KM# 1125a CROWN Weight: 28.2800 g. **Composition:** 0.9250 Silver 0.841 oz. ASW **Subject:** World Cup 2002 Japan - Korea **Obverse:** Bust of Queen Elizabeth II right **Reverse:** Player kicking to left **Edge:** Reeded **Size:** 38.6 mm.

Date	Mintage	F	VF	XF	Unc	BU
2002 Proof	10,000	Value: 47.50				

KM# 1127 CROWN Weight: 28.2800 g. **Composition:** Copper-Nickel **Subject:** World Cup 2002 Japan - Korea **Obverse:** Bust of Queen Elizabeth II right **Reverse:** Player running to left **Edge:** Reeded **Size:** 38.6 mm.

Date	F	VF	XF	Unc	BU
2002	—	—	—	10.00	—

KM# 1127a CROWN Weight: 28.2800 g. **Composition:** 0.9250 Silver 0.841 oz. ASW **Subject:** World Cup 2002 Japan - Korea **Obverse:** Bust of Queen Elizabeth II right **Reverse:** Player running to left **Edge:** Reeded **Size:** 38.6 mm.

Date	Mintage	F	VF	XF	Unc	BU
2002 Proof	10,000	Value: 47.50				

KM# 1131 CROWN Weight: 28.2800 g. **Composition:** Copper-Nickel **Subject:** Queen Elizabeth II's Golden Jubilee **Obverse:** Bust of Queen Elizabeth II right **Reverse:** Seated crowned Queen holding scepter at her coronation **Edge:** Reeded **Size:** 38.6 mm.

Date	F	VF	XF	Unc	BU
2002	—	—	—	10.00	—

KM# 1131a CROWN Weight: 28.2800 g. **Composition:** Gold Color Base Metal **Subject:** Queen Elizabeth II's Golden Jubilee **Obverse:** Bust of Queen Elizabeth II right **Reverse:** Seated crowned Queen holding scepter at her coronation **Edge:** Reeded **Size:** 38.6 mm.

Date	Mintage	F	VF	XF	Unc	BU
2002	15,000	—	—	—	10.00	—

KM# 1131b CROWN Weight: 28.2800 g. **Composition:** 0.9250 Gold Clad Silver 0.841 oz. **Subject:** Queen Elizabeth II's Golden Jubilee **Obverse:** Bust of Queen Elizabeth II right **Reverse:** Seated crowned Queen holding scepter at her coronation **Edge:** Reeded **Size:** 38.6 mm.

Date	Mintage	F	VF	XF	Unc	BU
2002 Proof	10,000	Value: 47.50				

KM# 1133 CROWN Weight: 28.2800 g. **Composition:** Copper-Nickel **Subject:** Queen Elizabeth II's Golden Jubilee **Obverse:** Bust of Queen Elizabeth II right **Reverse:** Queen on horse **Edge:** Reeded **Size:** 38.6 mm.

Date	F	VF	XF	Unc	BU
2002	—	—	—	10.00	—

KM# 1133a CROWN Weight: 28.2800 g. **Composition:** Gold Color Base Metal **Subject:** Queen Elizabeth II's Golden Jubilee **Obverse:** Bust of Queen Elizabeth II right **Reverse:** Queen on horse **Edge:** Reeded **Size:** 38.6 mm.

Date	Mintage	F	VF	XF	Unc	BU
2002	15,000	—	—	—	10.00	—

KM# 1133b CROWN Weight: 28.2800 g. **Composition:** 0.9250 Gold Clad Silver 0.841 oz. **Subject:** Queen Elizabeth II's Golden Jubilee **Obverse:** Bust of Queen Elizabeth II right **Reverse:** Queen on horse half left **Edge:** Reeded **Size:** 38.6 mm.

Date	Mintage	F	VF	XF	Unc	BU
2002 Proof	10,000	Value: 47.50				

KM# 1135 CROWN Weight: 28.2800 g. **Composition:** Copper-Nickel **Subject:** Queen Elizabeth II's Golden Jubilee **Obverse:** Bust of Queen Elizabeth II right **Reverse:** Queen with her pet Corgi **Edge:** Reeded **Size:** 38.6 mm.

Date	F	VF	XF	Unc	BU
2002	—	—	—	10.00	—

KM# 1135a CROWN Weight: 28.2800 g. **Composition:** Gold Color Base Metal **Subject:** Queen Elizabeth II's Golden Jubilee **Obverse:** Bust of Queen Elizabeth II right **Reverse:** Seated Queen with her pet Corgi **Edge:** Reeded **Size:** 38.6 mm.

Date	Mintage	F	VF	XF	Unc	BU
2002	15,000	—	—	—	10.00	—

KM# 1135b CROWN Weight: 28.2800 g. **Composition:** 0.9250 Gold Clad Silver 0.841 oz. **Subject:** Queen Elizabeth II's Golden Jubilee **Obverse:** Bust of Queen Elizabeth II right **Reverse:** Queen with her pet Corgi **Edge:** Reeded **Size:** 38.6 mm.

Date	Mintage	F	VF	XF	Unc	BU
2002 Proof	10,000	Value: 47.50				

KM# 1137 CROWN **Weight:** 28.2800 g. **Composition:** Copper-Nickel **Subject:** Queen Elizabeth II's Golden Jubilee **Obverse:** Bust of Queen Elizabeth II right **Reverse:** Queen at war memorial **Edge:** Reeded **Size:** 38.6 mm.

Date	F	VF	XF	Unc	BU
2002	—	—	—	10.00	—

KM# 1137a CROWN **Weight:** 28.2800 g. **Composition:** Gold Color Base Metal **Subject:** Queen Elizabeth II's Golden Jubilee **Obverse:** Bust of Queen Elizabeth II right **Reverse:** Queen at war memorial **Edge:** Reeded **Size:** 38.6 mm.

Date	Mintage	F	VF	XF	Unc	BU
2002	15,000	—	—	—	10.00	—

KM# 1137b CROWN **Weight:** 28.2800 g. **Composition:** Gold Clad Silver **Subject:** Queen Elizabeth II's Golden Jubilee **Obverse:** Bust of Queen Elizabeth II right **Reverse:** Queen at war memorial **Edge:** Reeded **Size:** 38.6 mm.

Date	Mintage	F	VF	XF	Unc	BU
2002 Proof	10,000	Value: 47.50				

KM# 1139 CROWN **Composition:** Blackened Copper-Nickel **Subject:** Queen Mother **Obverse:** Bust of Queen Elizabeth II right **Reverse:** Queen Mother and Castle May **Edge:** Reeded **Size:** 38.6 mm.

Date	F	VF	XF	Unc	BU
2002	—	—	—	10.00	—

KM# 1139a CROWN **Weight:** 28.2800 g. **Composition:** 0.9250 Silver 0.841 oz. ASW **Obverse:** Bust of Queen Elizabeth II right with blackened legends **Reverse:** Queen Mother standing at left in front of Castle May with blackened legends **Size:** 38.6 mm.

Date	Mintage	F	VF	XF	Unc	BU
2002 Proof	10,000	Value: 47.50				

KM# 1141 CROWN **Weight:** 28.2800 g. **Composition:** Copper Nickel **Subject:** Princess Diana **Obverse:** Bust of Queen Elizabeth II right **Reverse:** Diana's bust facing **Edge:** Reeded **Size:** 38.6 mm.

Date	F	VF	XF	Unc	BU
2002	—	—	—	10.00	—

KM# 1141a CROWN **Weight:** 28.2800 g. **Composition:** 0.9250 Silver 0.841 oz. ASW **Subject:** Princess Diana **Obverse:** Bust of Queen Elizabeth II right **Reverse:** Diana's bust facing **Edge:** Reeded **Size:** 38.6 mm.

Date	Mintage	F	VF	XF	Unc	BU
2002 Proof	10,000	Value: 47.50				

KM# 1165 CROWN **Weight:** 28.2800 g. **Composition:** Copper-Nickel **Subject:** Cat **Obverse:** Queen's portrait **Reverse:** Two Balinese kittens **Edge:** Reeded **Size:** 38.6 mm.

Date	F	VF	XF	Unc	BU
2003PM	—	—	—	10.00	—

KM# 1165a CROWN **Weight:** 31.1035 g. **Composition:** 0.9990 Silver 0.999 oz. ASW **Subject:** Cat **Obverse:** Queen's portrait **Reverse:** Two Balinese kittens **Edge:** Reeded **Size:** 38.6 mm.

Date	Mintage	F	VF	XF	Unc	BU
2003PM Proof	50,000	Value: 47.50				

KM# 1166 CROWN **Weight:** 31.1035 g. **Composition:** 0.9999 Gold 0.9999 oz. AGW **Subject:** Cat **Obverse:** Queen's portrait **Reverse:** Two Balinese kittens **Edge:** Reeded **Size:** 32.7 mm.

Date	Mintage	F	VF	XF	Unc	BU
2003PM		—	—	—	470	—
2003PM Proof	—	Value: 650				

KM# 1171 CROWN **Weight:** 28.2800 g. **Composition:** Copper-Nickel **Subject:** Year of the Goat **Obverse:** Queen's portrait **Reverse:** Three goats **Edge:** Reeded **Size:** 38.6 mm.

Date	F	VF	XF	Unc	BU
2003PM	—	—	—	10.00	—

KM# 1171a CROWN **Weight:** 28.2800 g. **Composition:** 0.9250 Silver 0.841 oz. ASW **Subject:** Year of the Goat **Obverse:** Queen's portrait **Reverse:** Three goats **Edge:** Reeded **Size:** 38.6 mm.

Date	Mintage	F	VF	XF	Unc	BU
2003PM Proof	30,000	Value: 47.50				

KM# 1172 CROWN **Weight:** 31.1035 g. **Composition:** 0.9999 Gold 0.9999 oz. AGW **Subject:** Year of the Goat **Obverse:** Queen's portrait **Reverse:** Three goats **Edge:** Reeded **Size:** 32.7 mm.

Date	Mintage	F	VF	XF	Unc	BU
2003PM Proof	2,000	Value: 650				

KM# 177 5 CROWN **Weight:** 155.5500 g. **Composition:** 0.9990 Silver 5.0000 oz. ASW **Subject:** Bicentennial of U.S. Constitution **Obverse:** Bust of Queen Elizabeth II right **Reverse:** Busts of U.S. Presidents **Size:** 65 mm. **Note:** Illustration reduced.

Date	Mintage	F	VF	XF	Unc	BU
1987 Proof	9,000	Value: 65.00				

KM# 180 5 CROWN **Weight:** 155.5500 g. **Composition:** 0.9990 Silver 5.0000 oz. ASW **Series:** America's Cup **Obverse:** Bust of Queen Elizabeth II right **Reverse:** Sailboats and trophy **Size:** 65 mm. **Note:** Illustration reduced.

Date	Mintage	F	VF	XF	Unc	BU
1987 Proof	6,000	Value: 90.00				

KM# 299 5 CROWN **Weight:** 155.5500 g. **Composition:** 0.9990 Silver 5.0000 oz. ASW **Series:** America's Cup **Obverse:** Bust of Queen Elizabeth II right **Reverse:** Sailboats and Statue of Liberty **Size:** 65 mm. **Note:** Illustration reduced.

Date	Mintage	F	VF	XF	Unc	BU
1987 Proof	200	Value: 220				

KM# 308 5 CROWN **Weight:** 155.5500 g. **Composition:** 0.9990 Silver 5.0000 oz. ASW **Series:** America's Cup **Obverse:** Bust of Queen Elizabeth II right **Reverse:** Three sailboats and map **Size:** 65 mm. **Note:** Illustration reduced.

Date	F	VF	XF	Unc	BU
1987 Proof	—	Value: 350			

KM#206 5 CROWN **Weight:** 155.5500 g. **Composition:** 0.9990 Silver 5.0000 oz. ASW **Subject:** Steam Navigation **Obverse:** Bust of Queen Elizabeth II right **Reverse:** R.M.S. Queen Mary **Size:** 65 mm. **Note:** Illustration reduced.

Date	F	VF	XF	Unc	BU
1988	—	—	—	150	—

KM#285 5 CROWN **Weight:** 155.5500 g. **Composition:** 0.9990 Silver 5.0000 oz. ASW **Subject:** Australian Bicentennial **Obverse:** Bust of Queen Elizabeth II right **Reverse:** Kangaroo

Date	F	VF	XF	Unc	BU
1988 Proof	—	Value: 150			

KM#321 5 CROWN **Weight:** 155.5500 g. **Composition:** 0.9990 Silver 5.0000 oz. ASW **Series:** America's Cup **Obverse:** Bust of Queen Elizabeth II right **Reverse:** Cameo of sailing ship above two modern sailboats

Date	F	VF	XF	Unc	BU
1991 Proof	—	—	—	—	—

KM#327 5 CROWN **Weight:** 155.5500 g. **Composition:** 0.9990 Silver 5.0000 oz. ASW **Series:** America's Cup **Obverse:** Bust of Queen Elizabeth II right **Reverse:** Sailboat

Date	F	VF	XF	Unc	BU
1992	—	—	—	150	—

KM#348 5 CROWN **Weight:** 155.5500 g. **Composition:** 0.9990 Silver 5.0000 oz. ASW **Obverse:** Bust of Queen Elizabeth II right **Reverse:** Siamese cat **Size:** 65 mm. **Note:** Illustration reduced.

Date	F	VF	XF	Unc	BU
1992 Proof	—	Value: 225			

KM#689 5 CROWN **Weight:** 155.5175 g. **Composition:** 0.9990 Silver 5.0000 oz. ASW **Series:** Legend of King Arthur **Obverse:** Bust of Queen Elizabeth II right **Reverse:** King Arthur with sword and orb

Date	Mintage	F	VF	XF	Unc	BU
1996 Proof	Est. 999	Value: 75.00				

KM#690 5 CROWN **Weight:** 155.5175 g. **Composition:** 0.9990 Silver 5.0000 oz. ASW **Series:** Legend of King Arthur **Obverse:** Bust of Queen Elizabeth II right **Reverse:** Queen Guinevere

Date	Mintage	F	VF	XF	Unc	BU
1996 Proof	Est. 999	Value: 75.00				

KM#691 5 CROWN **Weight:** 155.5175 g. **Composition:** 0.9990 Silver 5.0000 oz. ASW **Series:** Legend of King Arthur **Obverse:** Bust of Queen Elizabeth II right **Reverse:** Sir Lancelot

Date	Mintage	F	VF	XF	Unc	BU
1996	Est. 999	Value: 75.00				

KM#692 5 CROWN **Weight:** 155.5175 g. **Composition:** 0.9990 Silver 5.0000 oz. ASW **Series:** Legend of King Arthur **Obverse:** Bust of Queen Elizabeth II right **Reverse:** Merlin

Date	Mintage	F	VF	XF	Unc	BU
1996	Est. 999	Value: 85.00				

KM#693 5 CROWN **Weight:** 155.5175 g. **Composition:** 0.9990 Silver 5.0000 oz. ASW **Series:** Legend of King Arthur **Obverse:** Bust of Queen Elizabeth II right **Reverse:** Camelot Castle

Date	Mintage	F	VF	XF	Unc	BU
1996	Est. 999	Value: 100				

KM#734 5 CROWN **Weight:** 155.5175 g. **Composition:** 0.9999 Gold 5.0000 oz. AGW **Subject:** Year of the Rat **Obverse:** Bust of Queen Elizabeth II right **Reverse:** Rat

Date	F	VF	XF	Unc	BU
1996 Proof	—	—	—	—	—

Note: Entire series purchased by one buyer. Mintage, disposition, and market value unknown

KM#727 5 CROWN **Weight:** 155.5175 g. **Composition:** 0.9999 Gold 5.0000 oz. AGW **Subject:** Year of the Ox **Obverse:** Bust of Queen Elizabeth II right **Reverse:** Ox laying down

Date	F	VF	XF	Unc	BU
1997 Proof	—	—	—	—	—

KM#818 5 CROWN **Weight:** 155.5175 g. **Composition:** 0.9999 Gold 5.0000 oz. AGW **Subject:** Year of the Tiger **Obverse:** Bust of Queen Elizabeth II right **Reverse:** Tiger

Date	F	VF	XF	Unc	BU
1998 Proof	—	—	—	—	—

KM#953 5 CROWN **Weight:** 155.5175 g. **Composition:** 0.9999 Gold 5.0000 oz. AGW **Subject:** Year of the Rabbit **Obverse:** Bust of Queen Elizabeth II right **Reverse:** Two rabbits

Date	Mintage	F	VF	XF	Unc	BU
1999 Proof	Est. 250	Value: 3,225				

KM# 1018 5 CROWN **Weight:** 155.5175 g. **Composition:** 0.9999 Gold 5.0000 oz. AGW **Subject:** Year of the Dragon **Obverse:** Bust of Queen Elizabeth II right **Reverse:** Dragon, Chinese characters

Date	F	VF	XF	Unc	BU
2000 Proof	—	—	—	—	—

KM# 1064 5 CROWN **Weight:** 155.5175 g. **Composition:** 0.9999 Gold 5.0000 oz. AGW **Subject:** Year of the Snake **Obverse:** Queen's portrait **Reverse:** Snake **Edge:** Reeded **Size:** 65 mm.

Date	Mintage	F	VF	XF	Unc	BU
2001 Proof	250	—	—	—	—	—

KM# 1104 5 CROWN **Weight:** 155.5100 g. **Composition:** 0.9999 Gold 4.9993 oz. AGW **Subject:** Year of the Horse **Obverse:** Queen's portrait **Reverse:** Two horses **Edge:** Reeded **Size:** 65 mm.

Date	Mintage	F	VF	XF	Unc	BU
2002 Proof	250	Value: 3,000				

KM# 1173 5 CROWN **Weight:** 155.5100 g. **Composition:** 0.9999 Gold 4.9993 oz. AGW **Subject:** Year of the Goat **Obverse:** Queen's portrait **Reverse:** Three goats **Edge:** Reeded **Size:** 65 mm.

Date	Mintage	F	VF	XF	Unc	BU
2003PM Proof	250	Value: 3,000				

KM# 181 10 CROWN **Weight:** 311.0350 g. **Composition:** 0.9990 Silver 10.0000 oz. ASW **Series:** America's Cup **Obverse:** Bust of Queen Elizabeth II right **Reverse:** Sailboats and Statue of Liberty **Size:** 75 mm. **Note:** Illustration reduced.

Date	Mintage	F	VF	XF	Unc	BU
1987 Proof	2,000	Value: 125				

KM# 188 10 CROWN **Weight:** 311.0350 g. **Composition:** 0.9990 Silver 10.0000 oz. ASW **Subject:** Bicentenary of America's Constitution **Obverse:** Bust of Queen Elizabeth II right **Reverse:** Busts of Presidents **Size:** 75 mm. **Note:** Illustration reduced.

Date	Mintage	F	VF	XF	Unc	BU
1987 Proof	6,000	Value: 110				

KM# 300 10 CROWN **Weight:** 311.0350 g. **Composition:** 0.9990 Silver 10.0000 oz. ASW **Series:** America's Cup **Obverse:** Bust of Queen Elizabeth II right **Reverse:** Sailboats and trophy **Size:** 75 mm. **Note:** Illustration reduced.

Date	Mintage	F	VF	XF	Unc	BU
1987 Proof	69	Value: 350				

KM# 309 10 CROWN **Weight:** 311.0350 g. **Composition:** 0.9990 Silver 10.0000 oz. ASW **Series:** America's Cup **Obverse:** Bust of Queen Elizabeth II right **Reverse:** Three sailboats and map **Size:** 75 mm. **Note:** Illustration reduced.

Date		F	VF	XF	Unc	BU
1987 Proof	—	Value: 525				

KM# 258 10 CROWN **Weight:** 311.0350 g. **Composition:** 0.9990 Silver 10.0000 oz. ASW **Subject:** Australian Bicentennial **Obverse:** Bust of Queen Elizabeth II right **Reverse:** Koala **Size:** 75 mm. **Note:** Illustration reduced.

Date	Mintage	F	VF	XF	Unc	BU
1988 Proof	Est. 13,000	Value: 150				

KM# 992 10 CROWN **Weight:** 311.0350 g. **Composition:** 0.9990 Silver 10.0000 oz. ASW **Obverse:** Bust of Queen Elizabeth II right **Reverse:** Siamese cat

Date		F	VF	XF	Unc	BU
1992 Proof	—	Value: 300				

KM# 775 10 CROWN **Weight:** 311.0300 g. **Composition:** 0.9250 Silver 9.2499 oz. ASW **Subject:** 10th Anniversary of the Manx Cat **Obverse:** Bust of Queen Elizabeth II right **Reverse:** Cat within inlaid circle of ten cat coin designs **Size:** 75 mm. **Note:** Illustraiton reduced.

Date	Mintage	F	VF	XF	Unc	BU
1997 Proof	Est. 1,997	Value: 350				

KM# 1142 100 CROWNS **Weight:** 3000.0000 g. **Composition:** 0.9999 Silver 96.4425 oz. ASW **Subject:** Queen's Golden Jubilee **Obverse:** Bust of Queen Elizabeth II right. **Reverse:** Queen on horse **Edge:** Reeded **Size:** 130 mm. **Note:** Illustration reduced.

Date	Mintage	F	VF	XF	Unc	BU
2002 Proof	500	Value: 650				

GOLD BULLION COINAGE

Angel Series

KM# 166 1/20 ANGEL **Weight:** 1.6970 g. **Composition:** 0.9170 Gold .0500 oz. AGW **Obverse:** Bust of Queen Elizabeth II right **Reverse:** Archangel Michael

Date	Mintage	F	VF	XF	Unc	BU
1986	—	—	—	—	45.00	—
1986 (pi) Proof	5,000	Value: 60.00				
1987	—	—	—	—	45.00	—
1987 Proof	—	Value: 60.00				

KM# 193 1/20 ANGEL **Weight:** 1.6970 g. **Composition:** 0.9170 Gold .0500 oz. AGW **Obverse:** Bust of Queen Elizabeth II right **Reverse:** Archangel Michael

Date	Mintage	F	VF	XF	Unc	BU
1988		—	—	—	35.00	—
1988 (pi)		—	—	—	50.00	—
1989 (h) Proof	Est. 5,000	Value: 60.00				
1989 (mt) Proof	3,000	Value: 60.00				
1990 (sg) Proof	Est. 3,000	Value: 60.00				
1991 (cc) Proof	1,000	Value: 60.00				
1992 (cb) Proof	1,000	Value: 60.00				
1993 Proof	Est. 1,000	Value: 60.00				

KM# 393 1/20 ANGEL **Weight:** 1.5551 g. **Composition:** 0.9999 Gold .0500 oz. AGW **Obverse:** Bust of Queen Elizabeth II right **Reverse:** Archangel Michael

Date	Mintage	F	VF	XF	Unc	BU
1994 (ns) Proof	—	Value: 50.00				
1995 (sc) Proof	—	Value: 60.00				
1996 (bs) Proof	Est. 1,000	Value: 60.00				
1997 (at) Proof	Est. 1,000	Value: 60.00				
1998 (x) Proof	Est. 1,000	Value: 60.00				
1999 (fw) Proof	Est. 1,000	Value: 60.00				
2000 (ch) Proof	Est. 1,000	Value: 60.00				
2000 Proof	—	Value: 49.50				

Note: Christmas candle privy mark

KM# 1106 1/20 ANGEL **Weight:** 1.5552 g. **Composition:** 0.9999 Gold .0500 oz. AGW **Obverse:** Queen's new portrait **Reverse:** St. Michael slaying dragon, three crown privy mark at right **Edge:** Reeded **Size:** 15 mm.

Date	Mintage	F	VF	XF	Unc	BU
2001 (3c) Proof	1,000	Value: 62.00				
2002 Proof	—	Value: 62.00				

Note: With candy cane privy mark

KM# 138 1/10 ANGEL **Weight:** 3.3900 g. **Composition:** 0.9170 Gold .1000 oz. AGW **Obverse:** Bust of Queen Elizabeth II right **Reverse:** Archangel Michael

Date	Mintage	F	VF	XF	Unc	BU
1984 Proof	5,000	Value: 75.00				

KM# 140 1/10 ANGEL **Weight:** 3.3900 g. **Composition:** 0.9170 Gold .1000 oz. AGW **Obverse:** Bust of Queen Elizabeth II right **Reverse:** Archangel Michael

Date	Mintage	F	VF	XF	Unc	BU
1985 Proof	3,000	Value: 75.00				
1985	8,000	—	—	—	65.00	—
1986	—	—	—	—	65.00	—
1986 Proof	—	Value: 75.00				
1987	—	—	—	—	65.00	—
1987 Proof	—	Value: 75.00				

KM# 159 1/10 ANGEL **Weight:** 3.3900 g. **Composition:** 0.9170 Gold .1000 oz. AGW **Obverse:** Bust of Queen Elizabeth II right **Reverse:** Archangel Michael

Date	Mintage	F	VF	XF	Unc	BU
1985 A	1,000	—	—	—	90.00	—
1985 C	1,000	—	—	—	90.00	—
1985 H	1,000	—	—	—	90.00	—
1985 L	1,000	—	—	—	90.00	—
1985	5,000	—	—	—	65.00	—
1986 A	1,000	—	—	—	90.00	—
1986 T	1,000	—	—	—	90.00	—
1986 X	1,000	—	—	—	90.00	—
1987 A	1,000	—	—	—	90.00	—
1987 F Proof	1,000	Value: 95.00				
1987 L	1,000	—	—	—	90.00	—
1987 (mt) Proof	3,000	Value: 90.00				
1988 A Proof	1,000	Value: 90.00				

KM# 194 1/10 ANGEL **Weight:** 3.3900 g. **Composition:** 0.9170 Gold .1000 oz. AGW **Obverse:** Bust of Queen Elizabeth II right **Reverse:** Archangel Michael

Date	Mintage	F	VF	XF	Unc	BU
1988	—	—	—	—	65.00	—
1989 A Proof	250	Value: 100				
1990 A Proof	1,000	Value: 90.00				
1991 A Proof	400	Value: 95.00				

Note: 299 pieces have been melted

Date	Mintage	F	VF	XF	Unc	BU
1992 A	100	—	—	—	120	—

KM# 394 1/10 ANGEL **Weight:** 3.1103 g. **Composition:** 0.9999 Gold .1000 oz. AGW **Obverse:** Bust of Queen Elizabeth II right **Reverse:** Archangel Michael

Date	F	VF	XF	Unc	BU
1994 Proof	— Value: 75.00				

KM# 152.1 1/4 ANGEL **Weight:** 8.4830 g. **Composition:** 0.9170 Gold .2500 oz. AGW **Obverse:** Bust of Queen Elizabeth II right **Reverse:** Archangel Michael

Date	Mintage	F	VF	XF	Unc	BU
1985	2,117	—	—	—	110	—
1985 Proof	51	Value: 175				
1986 L	1,000	—	—	—	110	—
1986 Proof	—	Value: 125				

KM# 152.2 1/4 ANGEL **Weight:** 8.4830 g. **Composition:** 0.9170 Gold .2500 oz. AGW **Obverse:** Bust of Queen Elizabeth II right **Reverse:** Archangel Michael

Date	Mintage	F	VF	XF	Unc	BU
1987	—	—	—	—	110	—
1987 Proof	—	Value: 125				
1987 (s) Proof	1,000	Value: 125				
1987 (SL) Proof	568	Value: 125				
1987 (bb) Proof	1,000	Value: 125				

KM# 195 1/4 ANGEL **Weight:** 8.4830 g. **Composition:** 0.9170 Gold .2500 oz. AGW **Obverse:** Bust of Queen Elizabeth II right **Reverse:** Archangel Michael

Date	Mintage	F	VF	XF	Unc	BU
1988	—	—	—	—	150	—
1988 (f) Proof	1,000	Value: 200				
1988 (p) Proof	1,000	Value: 200				
1988 (ss) Proof	1,000	Value: 200				
1989 C (d) Proof	1,000	Value: 200				
1989 (p) Proof	500	Value: 200				
1989 (hk) Proof	1,000	Value: 200				
1989 (y)	—	—	—	—	150	—
1990 (ba) Proof	1,000	Value: 200				

Note: 513 pieces melted

Date	Mintage	F	VF	XF	Unc	BU
1990 (c) Proof	250	Value: 220				
1990 (fl)	1,000	—	—	—	150	—

Note: 9 pieces melted

Date	Mintage	F	VF	XF	Unc	BU
1990 (h) Proof	1,000	Value: 155				
1990 (ma) Proof	200	Value: 250				

Note: 40 pieces melted

Date	Mintage	F	VF	XF	Unc	BU
1990 (tb)	1,000	—	—	—	150	—

Note: 10 pieces melted

Date	Mintage	F	VF	XF	Unc	BU
1991 (c) Proof	200	Value: 250				

Note: 57 pieces melted

Date	Mintage	F	VF	XF	Unc	BU
1991 (fr) Proof	500	Value: 200				
1993 Proof	—	Value: 120				

KM# 395 1/4 ANGEL **Weight:** 7.7758 g. **Composition:** 0.9999 Gold .2500 oz. AGW **Obverse:** Bust of Queen Elizabeth II right **Reverse:** Archangel Michael

Date	Mintage	F	VF	XF	Unc	BU
1994 Proof	750	Value: 165				

KM# 1065 1/4 ANGEL **Ring Weight:** 3.8880 g. **Ring Composition:** 0.9995 Platinum .1244 oz. APW **Center Weight:** 3.8880 g. **Center Composition:** 0.9999 Gold .1249 oz. AGW **Obverse:** Queen's portrait **Reverse:** Archangel Michael **Edge:** Reeded **Size:** 22 mm.

Date	F	VF	XF	Unc	BU
1995 Proof	— Value: 250				

KM# 155 1/2 ANGEL **Weight:** 16.9380 g. **Composition:** 0.9170 Gold .5000 oz. AGW **Obverse:** Bust of Queen Elizabeth II right **Reverse:** Archangel Michael

Date	Mintage	F	VF	XF	Unc	BU
1985	1,776	—	—	—	185	—
1985 Proof	51	Value: 275				
1986	—	—	—	—	185	—
1986 Proof	3,000	Value: 225				
1987	—	—	—	—	185	—
1987 Proof	—	Value: 225				

KM# 196 1/2 ANGEL **Weight:** 16.9380 g. **Composition:** 0.9170 Gold .5000 oz. AGW **Obverse:** Bust of Queen Elizabeth II right **Reverse:** Archangel Michael

Date	F	VF	XF	Unc	BU
1988	—	—	—	185	—

KM# 396 1/2 ANGEL **Weight:** 15.5517 g. **Composition:** 0.9999 Gold .5000 oz. AGW **Obverse:** Bust of Queen Elizabeth II right **Reverse:** Archangel Michael

Date	F	VF	XF	Unc	BU
1994 Proof	— Value: 250				

KM# 139 ANGEL **Weight:** 33.9300 g. **Composition:** 0.9170 Gold 1.0000 oz. AGW **Obverse:** Bust of Queen Elizabeth II right **Reverse:** Archangel Michael

Date	Mintage	F	VF	XF	Unc	BU
1984 Proof	3,000	Value: 450				

KM# 141 ANGEL **Weight:** 33.9300 g. **Composition:** 0.9170 Gold 1.0000 oz. AGW **Obverse:** Bust of Queen Elizabeth II right **Reverse:** Archangel Michael

Date	Mintage	F	VF	XF	Unc	BU
1985	28,000	—	—	—	350	—
1985 Proof like	—	—	—	—	—	—
1985 Proof	3,000	Value: 400				
1986	—	—	—	—	350	—
1986 Proof	—	Value: 400				
1987	—	—	—	—	350	—
1987 Proof	—	Value: 400				

KM# 191 ANGEL **Weight:** 33.9300 g. **Composition:** 0.9170 Gold 1.0000 oz. AGW **Subject:** Hong Kong Coin Show **Obverse:** Bust of Queen Elizabeth II right **Reverse:** Archangel Michael

Date	Mintage	F	VF	XF	Unc	BU
1987 Proof	1,000	Value: 500				

KM# 197 ANGEL **Weight:** 33.9300 g. **Composition:** 0.9170 Gold 1.0000 oz. AGW **Obverse:** Bust of Queen Elizabeth II right **Reverse:** Archangel Michael

Date	Mintage	F	VF	XF	Unc	BU
1988	—	—	—	—	375	—
1988 (ss) Proof	1,000	Value: 450				

KM# 397 ANGEL **Weight:** 31.1035 g. **Composition:** 0.9999 Gold 1.0000 oz. AGW **Obverse:** Bust of Queen Elizabeth II right **Reverse:** Archangel Michael

Date	F	VF	XF	Unc	BU
1994 Proof	—	Value: 450			

KM# 522 ANGEL **Weight:** 31.1035 g. **Composition:** 0.9999 Silver 1.0000 oz. ASW **Obverse:** Bust of Queen Elizabeth II right **Reverse:** Archangel Michael

Date	F	VF	XF	Unc	BU
1995 Proof	—	Value: 450			

KM# 156 5 ANGEL **Weight:** 169.6680 g. **Composition:** 0.9170 Gold 5.0000 oz. AGW **Obverse:** Bust of Queen Elizabeth II right **Reverse:** Archangel Michael

Date	Mintage	F	VF	XF	Unc	BU
1985	104	—	—	—	1,950	—
1985 Proof	90	Value: 2,000				
1986	89	—	—	—	1,950	—
1986 Proof	250	Value: 2,000				
1987	150	—	—	—	1,950	—
1987 Proof	27	Value: 2,150				

KM# 198 5 ANGEL **Weight:** 169.6680 g. **Composition:** 0.9170 Gold 5.0000 oz. AGW **Obverse:** Bust of Queen Elizabeth II right **Reverse:** Archangel Michael

Date	Mintage	F	VF	XF	Unc	BU
1988	250	—	—	—	1,950	—

KM# 157 10 ANGEL **Weight:** 339.3350 g. **Composition:** 0.9170 Gold 10.0000 oz. AGW **Obverse:** Bust of Queen Elizabeth II right **Reverse:** Archangel Michael

Date	Mintage	F	VF	XF	Unc	BU
1985	79	—	—	—	3,750	—
1985 Proof	68	Value: 3,800				
1986	47	—	—	—	3,800	—
1986 Proof	250	Value: 3,800				
1987	150	—	—	—	3,750	—
1987 Proof	30	Value: 3,950				

KM# 199 10 ANGEL **Weight:** 339.3350 g. **Composition:** 0.9170 Gold 10.0000 oz. AGW **Obverse:** Bust of Queen Elizabeth II right **Reverse:** Archangel Michael

Date	Mintage	F	VF	XF	Unc	BU
1988 Proof	250	Value: 3,800				

KM# 189 15 ANGEL **Weight:** 508.9575 g. **Composition:** 0.9170 Gold 15.0000 oz. AGW **Obverse:** Bust of Queen Elizabeth II right **Reverse:** Archangel Michael

Date	Mintage	F	VF	XF	Unc	BU
1987	150	—	—	—	5,500	—
1987 Proof	18	Value: 7,500				

KM# 200 15 ANGEL **Weight:** 508.9575 g. **Composition:** 0.9170 Gold 15.0000 oz. AGW **Obverse:** Bust of Queen Elizabeth II right **Reverse:** Archangel Michael

Date	F	VF	XF	Unc	BU
1988 Proof	—	Value: 7,500			

KM# 201 20 ANGEL **Weight:** 678.6720 g. **Composition:** 0.9170 Gold 20.0000 oz. AGW **Obverse:** Bust of Queen Elizabeth II right **Reverse:** Archangel Michael **Size:** 75.2 mm. **Note:** Illustration reduced.

Date	Mintage	F	VF	XF	Unc	BU
1988	250	—	—	—	8,500	—
1988 Proof	100	Value: 9,000				

KM# 201a 20 ANGEL **Composition:** Gilt Silver **Obverse:** Bust of Queen Elizabeth II right **Reverse:** Archangel Michael

Date	F	VF	XF	Unc	BU
1988	—	—	—	—	—

KM# 301 25 ANGEL **Weight:** 848.2750 g. **Composition:** 0.9170 Gold 25.0000 oz. AGW **Obverse:** Bust of Queen Elizabeth II right **Reverse:** Archangel Michael

Date	F	VF	XF	Unc	BU
1989	—	—	—	11,500	—

GOLD BULLION COINAGE

Sovereign Series

KM# 969 1/5 SOVEREIGN **Weight:** 1.0000 g. **Composition:** 0.9999 Gold .0321 oz. AGW **Obverse:** Bust of Queen Elizabeth II right **Reverse:** Triskeles

Date	F	VF	XF	Unc	BU
1999	—	—	—BV+40%		—

KM# 970 1/2 SOVEREIGN **Weight:** 2.5000 g. **Composition:** 0.9999 Gold .0804 oz. AGW **Obverse:** Bust of Queen Elizabeth II right **Reverse:** Triskeles

Date	F	VF	XF	Unc	BU
1999	—	—	—BV+30%		—

KM# 971 3/4 SOVEREIGN **Weight:** 3.5000 g. **Composition:** 0.9999 Gold .1125 oz. AGW **Obverse:** Bust of Queen Elizabeth II right **Reverse:** Triskeles

Date	F	VF	XF	Unc	BU
1999	—	—	—BV+25%		—

KM# 972 SOVEREIGN **Weight:** 5.0000 g. **Composition:** 0.9999 Gold .1607 oz. AGW **Obverse:** Bust of Queen Elizabeth II right **Reverse:** Triskeles

Date	F	VF	XF	Unc	BU
1999	—	—	—BV+20%		—

KM# 973 2 SOVEREIGNS **Weight:** 10.0000 g. **Composition:** 0.9999 Gold .3215 oz. AGW **Obverse:** Bust of Queen Elizabeth II right **Reverse:** Triskeles

Date	F	VF	XF	Unc	BU
1999	—	—	—	—	—

KM# 974 5 SOVEREIGNS **Weight:** 31.1035 g. **Composition:** 0.9999 Gold .9999 oz. AGW **Obverse:** Bust of Queen Elizabeth II right **Reverse:** Triskeles

Date	F	VF	XF	Unc	BU
1999	—	—	— BV+5%		—

GOLD BULLION COINAGE

Platina Series

KM# 944 1/25 PLATINA **Weight:** 1.2447 g. **Composition:** 0.7500 White Gold .0300 oz. AGW **Obverse:** Bust of Queen Elizabeth II right **Reverse:** Crowned arms

Date	Mintage	F	VF	XF	Unc	BU
1999 Proof	Est. 10,000	Value: 40.00				

KM# 945 1/10 PLATINA **Weight:** 3.1103 g. **Composition:** 0.7500 White Gold .0750 oz. AGW **Obverse:** Bust of Queen Elizabeth II right **Reverse:** Crowned arms

Date	Mintage	F	VF	XF	Unc	BU
1999 Proof	Est. 7,500	Value: 75.00				

KM# 946 1/5 PLATINA **Weight:** 6.2200 g. **Composition:** 0.7500 White Gold .1500 oz. AGW **Obverse:** Bust of Queen Elizabeth II right **Reverse:** Crowned arms

Date	Mintage	F	VF	XF	Unc	BU
1999 Proof	Est. 5,000	Value: 135				

KM# 947 1/2 PLATINA **Weight:** 15.5517 g. **Composition:** 0.7500 White Gold .3750 oz. AGW **Obverse:** Bust of Queen Elizabeth II right **Reverse:** Crowned arms

Date	Mintage	F	VF	XF	Unc	BU
1999 Proof	Est. 3,500	Value: 255				

PLATINUM BULLION COINAGE

Noble Series

KM# 266 1/20 NOBLE **Weight:** 1.5551 g. **Composition:** 0.9995 Platinum .0500 oz. APW **Obverse:** Bust of Queen Elizabeth II right **Reverse:** Ship with hologram sail

Date	Mintage	F	VF	XF	Unc	BU
1989	10,000	Value: 65.00				
1992	—	—	—	—	60.00	—

KM# 137 1/10 NOBLE **Weight:** 3.1100 g. **Composition:** 0.9995 Platinum .1000 oz. APW **Obverse:** Bust of Queen Elizabeth II right **Reverse:** Ship with hologram sail

Date	Mintage	F	VF	XF	Unc	BU
1984	—	—	—	—	90.00	—
1984 Proof	5,000	Value: 95.00				

KM# 153 1/10 NOBLE **Weight:** 3.1100 g. **Composition:** 0.9995 Platinum .1000 oz. APW **Obverse:** Bust of Queen Elizabeth II right **Reverse:** Ship with hologram sail

Date	Mintage	F	VF	XF	Unc	BU
1985	99,000	—	—	—	90.00	—
1985 Proof	5,000	Value: 95.00				
1986	—	—	—	—	90.00	—
1986 Proof	5,000	Value: 95.00				
1987	—	—	—	—	90.00	—
1987 Proof	5,000	Value: 95.00				

KM# 202 1/10 NOBLE **Weight:** 3.1100 g. **Composition:** 0.9995 Platinum .1000 oz. APW **Obverse:** Bust of Queen Elizabeth II right **Reverse:** Ship with hologram sail

Date	Mintage	F	VF	XF	Unc	BU
1988	5,000	—	—	—	90.00	—
1989	5,000	—	—	—	90.00	—

KM# 168 1/4 NOBLE **Weight:** 7.7757 g. **Composition:** 0.9995 Platinum .2500 oz. APW **Obverse:** Bust of Queen Elizabeth II right **Reverse:** Ship with hologram sail

Date	Mintage	F	VF	XF	Unc	BU
1986 Proof	2,015	Value: 185				
1987 Proof	3,250	Value: 200				
1987 (1) Proof	750	Value: 185				

KM# 203 1/4 NOBLE **Weight:** 7.7757 g. **Composition:** 0.9995 Platinum .2500 oz. APW **Obverse:** Bust of Queen Elizabeth II right **Reverse:** Ship with hologram sail

Date	Mintage	F	VF	XF	Unc	BU
1988	—	—	—	—	185	—
1988 (a)	—	—	—	—	215	—
1988 (p) Proof	1,000	Value: 185				
1988 (bb) Proof	1,000	Value: 185				
1989 (br) Proof	250	Value: 210				
1989 (p) Proof	500	Value: 200				
1990 (ba) Proof	1,000	Value: 185				
1990 (ti) Proof	Est. 1,000	Value: 185				

KM# 1066 1/4 NOBLE **Ring Weight:** 3.8880 g. **Ring Composition:** 0.9999 Gold .1249 oz. AGW **Center Weight:** 0.9995 g. **Center Composition:** 0.1244 Platinum APW **Obverse:** Queen's portrait **Reverse:** Viking ship **Edge:** Reeded **Size:** 22 mm.

Date	F	VF	XF	Unc	BU
1995 Proof	—	Value: 250			

KM# 717 1/4 NOBLE **Weight:** 7.7757 g. **Composition:** 0.9995 Platinum .2500 oz. APW **Obverse:** Bust of Queen Elizabeth II right **Reverse:** Ship with hologram sail

Date	Mintage	F	VF	XF	Unc	BU
1996 Proof	Est. 10,000	Value: 185				

KM# 169 1/2 NOBLE **Weight:** 15.5514 g. **Composition:** 0.9995 Platinum .5000 oz. APW **Obverse:** Bust of Queen Elizabeth II right **Reverse:** Ship with hologram sail

Date	Mintage	F	VF	XF	Unc	BU
1986 Proof	15	Value: 550				
1987 Proof	3,000	Value: 400				

KM# 204 1/2 NOBLE **Weight:** 15.5514 g. **Composition:** 0.9995 Platinum .5000 oz. APW **Obverse:** Bust of Queen Elizabeth II right **Reverse:** Ship with hologram sail

Date	Mintage	F	VF	XF	Unc	BU
1988	3,000	Value: 400				
1989 Proof	3,000	Value: 400				

KM# 110 NOBLE **Weight:** 31.1030 g. **Composition:** 0.9995 Platinum .9991 oz. APW **Obverse:** Bust of Queen Elizabeth II right **Reverse:** Ship with hologram sail

Date	Mintage	F	VF	XF	Unc	BU
1983	1,700	—	—	—	750	—
1983 Proof	94	Value: 950				
1984	—	—	—	—	750	—
1984 Proof	2,000	Value: 785				

KM# 154 NOBLE **Weight:** 31.1030 g. **Composition:** 0.9995 Platinum .9991 oz. APW **Obverse:** Bust of Queen Elizabeth II right **Reverse:** Ship with hologram sail

Date	Mintage	F	VF	XF	Unc	BU
1985	—	—	—	—	750	—
1985 Proof	3,000	Value: 765				
1986	—	—	—	—	750	—
1986 Proof	3,000	Value: 765				
1987	—	—	—	—	750	—
1987 Proof	3,000	Value: 765				

KM# 205 NOBLE **Weight:** 31.1030 g. **Composition:** 0.9995 Platinum .9991 oz. APW **Obverse:** Bust of Queen Elizabeth II right **Reverse:** Ship with hologram sail

Date	Mintage	F	VF	XF	Unc	BU
1988	3,000	Value: 760				
1989 Proof	3,000	Value: 760				

KM# 170 5 NOBLE **Weight:** 155.5140 g. **Composition:** 0.9995 Platinum 5.0000 oz. APW **Obverse:** Bust of Queen Elizabeth II right **Reverse:** Ship with hologram sail

Date	Mintage	F	VF	XF	Unc	BU
1986 Proof	15	Value: 5,000				
1987 Proof	11	Value: 4,250				
1988 Proof	—	Value: 6,750				

KM# 171 10 NOBLE **Weight:** 311.0280 g. **Composition:** 0.9995 Platinum 10.0000 oz. APW **Obverse:** Bust of Queen Elizabeth II right **Reverse:** Ship with hologram sail **Note:** Illustration reduced. Actual size: 63mm.

Date	Mintage	F	VF	XF	Unc	BU
1986 Proof	15	Value: 9,750				
1987 Proof	11	Value: 9,000				
1988 Proof	—	Value: 12,000				

TRADE COINAGE

Ecu Series

KM# 711 15 ECUS **Weight:** 10.0000 g. **Composition:** 0.9250 Silver .2974 oz. ASW **Obverse:** Bust of Queen Elizabeth II right **Reverse:** Manx cat on shield

Date	F	VF	XF	Unc	BU
1994	—	—	—	40.00	—

KM# 714 15 ECUS **Weight:** 10.0000 g. **Composition:** 0.9250 Silver .2974 oz. ASW **Subject:** 50th Anniversary of United Nations **Obverse:** Bust of Queen Elizabeth II right **Reverse:** Blacksmith

Date	Mintage	F	VF	XF	Unc	BU
1995 Proof	Est. 30,000	Value: 42.50				

KM# 712 25 ECUS **Weight:** 19.2000 g. **Composition:** 0.9250 Silver .5710 oz. ASW **Subject:** 50th Anniversary of United Nations **Obverse:** Bust of Queen Elizabeth II right **Reverse:** Viking boat on helmeted shield

Date	F	VF	XF	Unc	BU
1994	—	—	—	52.50	—

KM# 715 25 ECUS **Weight:** 19.2000 g. **Composition:** 0.9250 Silver .5710 oz. ASW **Subject:** 50th Anniversary of United Nations **Obverse:** Bust of Queen Elizabeth II right **Reverse:** Ram's head shield

Date	Mintage	F	VF	XF	Unc	BU
1995 Proof	Est. 15,000	Value: 55.00				

KM# 713 75 ECUS **Weight:** 6.2200 g. **Composition:** 0.9990 Gold .2000 oz. AGW **Obverse:** Bust of Queen Elizabeth II right **Reverse:** Triskeles on crowned shield

Date	F	VF	XF	Unc	BU
1994	—	—	—	190	—

KM# 716 75 ECUS **Weight:** 6.2200 g. **Composition:** 0.9990 Gold .2000 oz. AGW **Obverse:** Bust of Queen Elizabeth II right **Reverse:** Falcons on shield

Date	Mintage	F	VF	XF	Unc	BU
1995 Proof	Est. 2,000	Value: 200				

TRADE COINAGE

Sterling Euro Series

KM# 718 10 EURO **Weight:** 10.0000 g. **Composition:** 0.9250 Silver .2974 oz. ASW **Subject:** Spain - 10 years Membership E.C. **Obverse:** Bust of Queen Elizabeth II right **Reverse:** Head of De Falla and opera scene

Date	Mintage	F	VF	XF	Unc	BU
1996 Proof	Est. 30,000	Value: 40.00				

KM# 795 10 EURO **Weight:** 10.0000 g. **Composition:** 0.9250 Silver .2974 oz. ASW **Subject:** 200th Anniversary - Birth of Franza Schubert **Obverse:** Bust of Queen Elizabeth II right **Reverse:** Head of Schubert and piano recital scene

Date	Mintage	F	VF	XF	Unc	BU
1997 Proof	Est. 30,000	Value: 40.00				

KM# 796 10 EURO **Weight:** 10.0000 g. **Composition:** 0.9250 Silver .2974 oz. ASW **Obverse:** Bust of Queen Elizabeth II right **Reverse:** Bust of Jan Sweelinck and organ player

Date	Mintage	F	VF	XF	Unc	BU
1997 Proof	Est. 30,000	Value: 40.00				

KM# 909 10 EURO **Weight:** 10.0000 g. **Composition:** 0.9250 Silver .2974 oz. ASW **Subject:** 125th Anniversary of the Isle of Man Railway **Obverse:** Bust of Queen Elizabeth II right **Reverse:** Old steam train

Date	Mintage	F	VF	XF	Unc	BU
1998 Proof	Est. 30,000	Value: 40.00				

KM# 910 10 EURO **Weight:** 10.0000 g. **Composition:** 0.9250 Silver .2974 oz. ASW **Subject:** Myths and Legends - Manannan **Obverse:** Bust of Queen Elizabeth II right **Reverse:** Warrior riding horse

Date	Mintage	F	VF	XF	Unc	BU
1998 Proof	Est. 30,000	Value: 40.00				

KM# 719 15 EURO **Weight:** 19.2000 g. **Composition:** 0.9250 Silver .5710 oz. ASW **Subject:** First Performance - La Boheme **Obverse:** Bust of Queen Elizabeth II right **Reverse:** Head of Puccini and scene

Date	Mintage	F	VF	XF	Unc	BU
1996 Proof	Est. 15,000	Value: 75.00				

KM# 720 50 EURO **Weight:** 6.2200 g. **Composition:** 0.9999 Gold .1999 oz. AGW **Subject:** 125th Anniversary of Aida-Verdi **Obverse:** Bust of Queen Elizabeth II right

Date	Mintage	F	VF	XF	Unc	BU
1996 Proof	Est. 2,000	Value: 165				

KM# 797 50 EURO **Weight:** 6.2200 g. **Composition:** 0.9999 Gold .1999 oz. AGW **Obverse:** Bust of Queen Elizabeth II right **Reverse:** Head of Thomas Moore and harp player

Date	Mintage	F	VF	XF	Unc	BU
1997 Proof	Est. 2,000	Value: 165				

KM# 911 50 EURO **Weight:** 6.2200 g. **Composition:** 0.9999 Gold .1999 oz. AGW **Subject:** St. George **Obverse:** Bust of Queen Elizabeth II right **Reverse:** Rider spearing dragon as captive damsel watches

Date	Mintage	F	VF	XF	Unc	BU
1998 Proof	Est. 2,000	Value: 175				

WW I P.O.W. TOKEN COINAGE

KM# Tn22 6 PENCE **Composition:** Brass **Obverse:** PEEL **Reverse:** 6d in sprays

Date	F	VF	XF	Unc	BU
ND	60.00	100	—	—	—

WW II P.O.W TOKEN COINAGE

KM# Tn23 1/2 PENNY **Composition:** Brass

Date	Mintage	F	VF	XF	Unc	BU
ND	2,000	17.50	35.00	75.00	165	—

KM# Tn24 PENNY Composition: Brass

Date	Mintage	F	VF	XF	Unc	BU
ND	20,000	6.00	15.00	35.00	80.00	—

KM# Tn25 6 PENCE Composition: Brass

Date	Mintage	F	VF	XF	Unc	BU
ND	2,500	12.00	28.00	60.00	135	—

PATTERNS

Including off metal strikes

KM#	Date	Mintage	Identification	Mkt Val
Pn20	1987	30	1/2 Crown. Silver.	300
Pn21	1989	—	Crown. Copper-Nickel. Black finish, first penny postage stamp.	—

KM#	Date	Mintage	Identification	Mkt Val
Pn23	1992	—	5 Pounds. Nigell Mansell, KM336.	—

PIEFORTS

KM#	Date	Mintage	Identification	Mkt Val
P4	1983	4,950	Pound. Silver. KM109.	35.00
P5	1983	4,950	Pound. Silver. KM127	35.00
P6	1983	4,950	Pound. Silver. KM130	40.00
P7	1983	4,950	Pound. Silver. KM131	40.00
P8	1984	1,000	Pound. 0.3740 Gold.	125
P9	1984	250	Pound. 0.9170 Gold.	350
P10	1985	4,950	Pound. Silver.	40.00
P11	1985	950	Pound. 0.3740 Gold.	125
P12	1985	250	Pound. 0.9170 Gold.	350
P13	1985	50	Pound. Platinum.	450

MINT SETS

KM#	Date	Mintage	Identification	Issue Price	Mkt Val
MS1	1965 (3)	1,500	KM15-17	—	700
MS2	1971 (6)	50,000	KM19-24	3.00	3.00
MS3	1973 (4)	2,500	KM26-29	760	820
MS4	1974 (4)	250	KM26-29	—	975
MS5	1975 (6)	20,000	KM19-24	—	3.00
MS6	1975 (6)	20,000	KM19a-24a	56.50	40.00
MS7	1975 (4)	200	KM26-29	—	1,000
MS10	1976 (4)	—	KM26-29	—	980
MS8	1976 (6)	20,000	KM32-34, 35.1,36.2, 39	—	4.00
MS9	1976 (6)	20,000	KM32a-34a, 35.1a-36.1a, 39a	—	37.50
MS11	1977 (6)	50,000	KM33-34, 35.1-36.1, 39-40	—	4.00
MS12	1977 (4)	180	KM26-29	—	850
MS13	1978 (6)	10,000	KM32a-34a, 35.1a-36.1a, 39a	—	50.00
MS14	1978 (6)	—	KM32-34, 35.1-36.1, 39	—	4.00
MS15	1979 (6)	—	KM32-34, 35.1-36.1, 39	—	5.00
MS16	1979 (4)	—	KM26-29	—	970
MS17	1980 (6)	30,000	KM58-62, 70	—	5.00
MS18	1981 (6)	—	KM58-62, 70	—	5.00
MS20	1983 (9)	—	KM58-62, 70, 88, 90, 109	—	27.50
MS21	1983 (6)	—	KM58-62, 70	—	5.00
MS29	1985 (9)	—	KM142-148, 150-151, plus rectangular medal	—	25.00
MS22	1989 (9)	—	KM207-208, 209.1, 210-215	—	25.00
MS23	1990 (9)	—	KM207-208, 209.1, 210-215	25.00	25.00
MS24	1992 (9)	—	KM207-208, 209.2, 210-215	25.00	25.00
MS25	1994 (9)	—	KM207-208, 212-213, 337, 391-392, 398-399	25.00	25.00
MS26	1995 (9)	—	KM207-208, 212-213, 337, 391-392, 465-466	—	—
MS27	1996 (9)	—	KM587-595	—	25.00
MS28	1997 (5)	5,000	KM770-773, 774b	—	785

PROOF SETS

KM#	Date	Mintage	Identification	Issue Price	Mkt Val
PS1	1965 (3)	1,000	KM15a-17a	—	750
PS2	1971 (6)	10,000	KM19-24	20.00	12.50
PS3	1973 (4)	1,250	KM26-29	950	1,025
PS4	1974 (4)	2,500	KM26-29	900	885
PS5	1975 (6)	600	KM19b-24b	1,175	2,200
PS6	1975 (4)	—	KM26-29	—	920
PS8	1976 (4)	—	KM26-29	—	920
PS7	1976 (6)	600	KM32b-34b, 35.1b-36.1b, 39b	—	2,200
PS10	1977 (4)	1,250	KM26-29	—	1,025
PS9	1977 (6)	10,000	KM33a-34a, 35.1a-36.1a, 39a, 40a	—	35.00
PS12	1978 (7)	600	KM32b-34b, 35.1b-36.1b, 39b, 44b	—	24.00
PS16	1980 (7)	10,000	KM44d, 58a-62a, 70a	—	50.00
PS11	1978 (7)	—	KM32-36, 39, 44	—	15.00
PS13	1979 (7)	10,000	KM32a-34a, 35.1a-36.1a, 39a, 44a	110	50.00
PS14	1979 (7)	500	KM32b-34b, 35.1b, 36.1b, 39b, 44b	2,765	2,400
PS15	1979 (4)	1,000	KM26-29	—	1,000
PS19	1982 (9)	1,000	KM44a, 58b-62b, 70a, 88a, 90a	—	130
PS20	1982 (9)	250	KM44c, 58b-62b, 88b, 90b	—	1,050
PS21	1982 (9)	100	KM44b, 58c-62c, 88c, 90c	—	2,570
PS22	1982 (7)	25,000	KM58-62, 70, 90	—	15.00
PS23	1982 (7)	9,000	KM58b-62b, 70a, 90a	—	60.00
PS24	1982 (7)	250	KM58c-62c, 70c, 90b	—	245
PS25	1982 (7)	400	KM58d-62d, 70d, 90c	—	1,720
PS26	1983 (7)	—	KM58d-62d, 90a, 109a	—	1,585
PS27	1983 (7)	—	KM58b-62b, 90b, 109b	—	290
PS28	1983 (7)	—	KM58c-62c, 90c, 109c	—	1,370
PSA16	1980 (7)	—	KM44, 58-62, 70	—	20.00
PSA22	1982 (8)	—	KM44a, 59b-62b, 70a, 88a, 90a	—	—
PSA29	1983 (9)	—	KM59b-62b, 70b, 88a, 90a, 109a	—	—
PSA19	1981 (7)	—	KM44a, 59b-62b, 70b, 88a,	—	—
PS17	1980 (7)	—	KM44c, 58c-62c, 70c	—	170
PS18	1980 (7)	300	KM44b, 58d-62d, 70d	—	1,575
PSA40	1983-1986 (4)	—	KM109a, 128a, 135-136	—	—
PS29	1985 (9)	25,000	KM142-148, 150-151	36.00	36.00
PS37	1985 (6)	51	KM140-141, 152.1, 155-157	—	6,750
PS31	1985 (9)	150	KM135b, 142b-148b, 150b	3,240	2,800
PS32	1985 (9)	100	KM135c, 142c-148c, 150c	3,600	3,850
PS30	1985 (9)	5,000	KM135, 142a-148a, 150a	120	120
PS33	1985 (7)	25,000	KM142-148	20.00	20.00
PS34	1985 (7)	5,000	KM142a-148a	72.00	72.00
PS35	1985 (7)	150	KM142b-148b	2,160	1,875
PS36	1985 (7)	100	KM142c-148c	2,400	2,450
PS38	1986 (7)	17	KM140-141, 152.1, 155-157, 166	—	6,700
PS39	1986 (6)	15	KM153-154, 168-171	—	13,350
PS40	1986 (4)	2,000	KM153-154, 168-169	1,950	1,350
PS41	1986 (5)	2,500	KM140-141, 152.1, 155, 166	—	900
PS43	1987 (6)	30	KM140-141, 152.2, 155-157	—	6,950
PS44	1987 (5)	—	KM140-141, 152.2, 155, 166	—	900
PS45	1987 (4)	3,000	KM140-141, 152.2, 155	—	850
PS46	1987 (6)	11	KM153-154, 168-169, 170-171	—	12,575
PS47	1987 (4)	2,500	KM153-154, 168-169	—	1,325
PS42	1987 (4)	—	KM176a, 177, 187-188	—	1,150
PS48	1988 (5)	611	KM235-239	—	1,250
PS49	1988 (4)	500	KM222-225	—	35.00
PS50	1988 (4)	7,500	KM286-289	—	1,400
PS51	1996 (5)	500	KM613, 615, 617, 619, 621b	—	845
PS52	1998 (5)	1,000	KM853-856, 857b	—	815
PS53	1999 (5)	1,000	KM958, 960, 962, 964, 968	1,300	835
PS54	2000 (5)	1,000	KM1052-1055, 1057	1,300	1,300

PROOF-LIKE SETS (PL)

KM#	Date	Mintage	Identification	Issue Price	Mkt Val
PL1	1980 (4)	—	KM64-67	—	20.00
PL2	1981 (4)	—	KM77-80	—	25.00
PL3	1982 (4)	50,000	KM96-99	—	60.00
PL4	1984 (4)	—	KM121-124	—	20.00
PL5	1986 (2)	—	KM173-174	—	16.00
PL6	1989 (6)	50,000	KM240-243	—	60.00

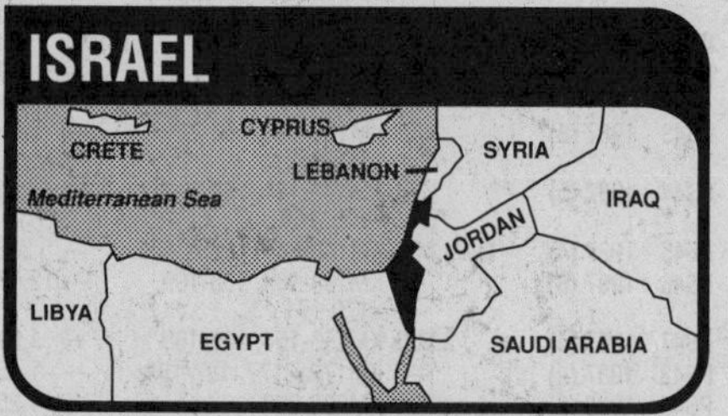

The state of Israel, a Middle Eastern republic at the eastern end of the Mediterranean Sea, bounded by Lebanon on the north, Syria on the northeast, Jordan on the east, and Egypt on the southwest, has an area of 9,000sq. mi. (20,770 sq. km.) and a population of 4.9 million. Capital: Jerusalem. Finished diamonds, chemicals, citrus, textiles, and minerals are exported.

HEBREW COIN DATING

Modern Israel's coins carry Hebrew dating formed from a combination of the 22 consonant letters of the Hebrew alphabet and read from right to left. The Jewish calendar dates back more than 5700 years; but five millenniums are assumed in the dating of coins (until 1981). Thus, the year 5735 (1975AD) appears as 735, with the first two characters from the right indicating the number of years in hundreds; tav (400), plus shin (300). The next is lamedh (30), followed by a separation mark which has the appearance of double quotation marks, then heh (5).

The separation mark - generally similar to a single quotation mark through 5718 (1958 AD), and like a double quotation mark thereafter - serves the purpose of indicating that the letters form a number, not a word, and on some issues can be confused with the character yodh (10), which in a stylized rendering can appear similar, although slightly larger and thicker. The separation mark does not appear in either form on a few commemorative issues.

The Jewish New Year falls in September or October by Christian calendar reckoning. Where dual dating is encountered, with but a few exceptions the Hebrew dating on the coins of modern Israel is 3760 years greater than the Christian dating; 5735 is equivalent to 1975AD, with the 5000 assumed until 1981, when full dates appear on the coins. These exceptions are most of the Hanukka coins, (Feast of Lights), the Bank of Israel gold 50 Pound commemorative of 5725 (1964AD) and others. In such special instances the differential from Christian dating is 3761 years, except in the instance of the 5720 Chanuka Pound, which is dated 1960AD, as is the issue of 5721, an arrangement reflecting the fact that the events fall early in the Jewish year and late in the Christian.

The Star of David is not a mint mark. It appears only on some coins sold by the Israel Government Coins and Medals Corporation Ltd. Which is owned by the Israel government, and is a division of the Prime Minister's office and sole distributor to collectors. The Star of David was first used in 1971 on the science coin to signify that it was minted in Jerusalem, but was later used by different mint facilities.

1948	תש״ח	5708
1949	תש״ט	5709
1952	תשי״ב	5712
1954	תשי״ד	5714
1955	תשט״ו	5715
1957	תשי״ז	5717
1958	תשי״ח	5718
1959	תשי״ט	5719
1960	תש״ך	5720
1960	תשך	5720
1961	תשכ״א	5721
1962	תשכ״ב	5722
1963	תשכ״ג	5723
1964	תשכ״ד	5724
1965	תשכ״ה	5725
1966	תשכ״ו	5726
1967	תשכ״ז	5727
1968	תשכ״ח	5728
1969	תשכ״ט	5729
1970	תש״ל	5730
1971	תשל״א	5731
1972	תשל״ב	5732
1973	תשל״ג	5733
1974	תשל״ד	5734
1975	תשל״ה	5735
1976	תשל״ו	5736
1977	תשל״ז	5737
1978	תשל״ח	5738
1979	תשל״ט	5739
1980	תש״ם	5740
1981	תשמ״א	5741
1981	התשמ״א	5741
1982	התשמ״ב	5742
1983	התשמ״ג	5743
1984	התשמ״ד	5744
1985	התשמ״ה	5745
1986	התשמ״ו	5746
1987	התשמ״ז	5747
1988	התשמ״ח	5748
1989	התשמ״ט	5749
1990	התש״ן	7505
1991	התשנ״א	5751
1992	התשנ״ב	5752
1993	התשנ״ג	5753
1994	התשנ״ד	5754
1995	התשנ״ה	5755
1996	התשנ״ו	5756
1997	התשנ״ז	5757
1998	התשנ״ח	5758
1999	התשנ״ט	5759
2000	התש״ס	5760
2001	התשס״א	5761
2002	התשס״ב	5762
2003	התשס״ג	5763
2004	התשס״ד	5764
2005	התשס״ה	5765

MINT MARKS
(o) - Ottawa
(s) - San Francisco
None – Jerusalem

(M) MATTE - Normal circulation strike or a dull finish produced by sandblasting special uncirculated (polish finish) or proof quality dies.

(U) SPECIAL UNCIRCULATED - Polished or prooflike in appearance without any frosted features.

(P) PROOF - The highest quality obtainable having mirror-like fields and frosted features.

MONETARY SYSTEM
1000 Mils = 1 Pound

REPUBLIC

MIL COINAGE

KM# 8 25 MILS Composition: Aluminum **Note:** Released April 6, 1949.

Date	Mintage	F	VF	XF	Unc	BU
JE5708 (1948)	43,000	—	75.00	200	850	1,000
JE5709 (1949) open link	650,000	—	25.00	75.00	150	—
JE5709 (1949) closed link	—	—	10.00	15.00	25.00	—

REFORM COINAGE

1000 Prutah = 1 Lirah

NOTE: The 1949 Prutah coins, except for the 100 and 500 Prutah values, occur with and without a small pearl under the bar connecting the wreath on the reverse. Only the 50 and 100 Prutah coins were issued in 5709. All later coins were struck with frozen dates.

KM# 9 PRUTA Composition: Aluminum **Obverse:** Anchor

Date	Mintage	F	VF	XF	Unc	BU
JE5709 (1949) With pearl	2,685,000	—	0.50	1.00	2.00	—
JE5709(1949) With Pearl, Prooflike	Inc. above	—	—	—	5.00	—
JE5709 (1949) Without pearl	2,500,000	—	1.00	2.50	20.00	—
JE5709 (1949) Proof	20,000	Value: 500				

KM# 10 5 PRUTAH Composition: Bronze **Obverse:** 4-stringed lyre

Date	Mintage	F	VF	XF	Unc	BU
JE5709 (1949) With pearl	5,045,000	—	0.50	1.00	2.50	—
JE5709 (1949) Proof	25,000	Value: 500				
JE5709 (1949) Without pearl	5,000,000	—	0.50	2.00	20.00	—

KM# 11 10 PRUTAH Composition: Bronze **Obverse:** Amphora

Date	Mintage	F	VF	XF	Unc	BU
JE5709 (1949) With pearl	7,448,000	—	0.75	2.50	20.00	—
JE5709 (1949) Without pearl	7,500,000	—	0.50	1.00	4.00	—
JE5709 (1949) Proof	20,000	Value: 500				

KM# 17 10 PRUTAH **Composition:** Aluminum **Obverse:** Ceremonial pitcher **Shape:** Scalloped

Date	Mintage	F	VF	XF	Unc	BU
JE5712 (1952)	26,042,000	—	0.35	0.75	2.00	—

KM# 20 10 PRUTAH **Composition:** Aluminum **Obverse:** Ceremonial jug

Date	Mintage	F	VF	XF	Unc	BU
JE5717 (1957)	1,000,000	—	0.35	0.75	2.50	—

KM# 20a 10 PRUTAH **Composition:** Copper Electroplated Aluminum **Obverse:** Ceremonial pitcher

Date	Mintage	F	VF	XF	Unc	BU
JE5717 (1957)	1,088,000	—	0.35	0.75	2.00	—

KM# 12 25 PRUTAH **Composition:** Copper-Nickel **Obverse:** Grapes

Date	Mintage	F	VF	XF	Unc	BU
JE5709 (1949) With pearl	10,520,000	—	0.50	0.75	2.00	—
JE5709 (1949) Proof	20,000	Value: 500				
JE5709 (1949) Without pearl	2,500,000	—	5.00	10.00	30.00	—

KM# 12a 25 PRUTAH **Composition:** Nickel-Clad Steel **Obverse:** Grapes

Date	Mintage	F	VF	XF	Unc	BU
JE5714 (1954)	3,697,000	—	0.50	1.00	2.50	—

KM# 13.1 50 PRUTAH **Composition:** Copper-Nickel **Obverse:** Grape leaves **Edge:** Reeded

Date	Mintage	F	VF	XF	Unc	BU
JE5709 (1949) With pearl	12,040,000	—	5.00	10.00	30.00	—
JE5709 (1949) Proof	20,000	Value: 500				
JE5709 (1949) Without pearl	Inc. above	—	0.75	1.50	3.00	—
JE5714 (1954)	250,000	—	8.00	15.00	32.00	—

KM# 13.2 50 PRUTAH **Composition:** Copper-Nickel **Obverse:** Grape leaves **Edge:** Plain

Date	Mintage	F	VF	XF	Unc	BU
JE5714 (1954)	4,500,000	—	0.50	1.00	2.00	—

KM# 13.2a 50 PRUTAH **Composition:** Nickel-Clad Steel **Obverse:** Grape leaves **Edge:** Plain

Date	Mintage	F	VF	XF	Unc	BU
JE5714 (1954)	17,774,000	—	0.50	1.00	2.00	—

KM# 14 100 PRUTAH **Composition:** Copper-Nickel **Obverse:** Date palm

Date	Mintage	F	VF	XF	Unc	BU
JE5709 (1949)	6,062,000	—	0.75	1.25	2.50	—
JE5709 (1949) Proof	20,000	Value: 500				
JE5715 (1949)	5,868,000	—	1.00	1.50	3.00	—

KM# 18 100 PRUTAH **Composition:** Nickel-Clad Steel **Obverse:** Date palm **Reverse:** Large wreath, close to edge **Size:** 25.6 mm. **Note:** Reduced size, Bern die.

Date	Mintage	F	VF	XF	Unc	BU
JE5714 (1954)	700,000	—	1.00	1.50	2.50	—

KM# 19 100 PRUTAH **Composition:** Nickel-Coated Steel **Obverse:** Date palm **Reverse:** Small wreath, away from edge **Size:** 25.6 mm. **Note:** Reduced size, Utrecht die.

Date	Mintage	F	VF	XF	Unc	BU
JE5714 (1954)	20,000	—	250	350	1,000	—

KM# 15 250 PRUTAH **Composition:** Copper-Nickel **Obverse:** Barley spears

Date	Mintage	F	VF	XF	Unc	BU
JE5709 (1949) With pearl	1,496,000	—	2.50	10.00	20.00	—
JE5709 (1949) Without pearl	524,000	—	1.00	2.00	5.00	—

KM# 15a 250 PRUTAH **Weight:** 14.4000 g. **Composition:** 0.5000 Silver .2315 oz. ASW **Obverse:** Barley spears

Date	Mintage	F	VF	XF	Unc	BU
JE5709 (1949) H	44,000	—	4.00	6.50	11.50	—

Note: Not placed into circulation

KM# 16 500 PRUTAH **Weight:** 25.5000 g. **Composition:** 0.5000 Silver .4099 oz. ASW **Obverse:** Pomegranates **Note:** Dav. #257.

Date	Mintage	F	VF	XF	Unc	BU
JE5709 (1949)	34,000	—	8.50	12.50	25.00	50.00

Note: Not placed into circulation

REFORM COINAGE

100 Agorot = 1 Lirah

Commencing January 1, 1958-1980

KM# 24.1 AGORAH **Composition:** Aluminum **Shape:** Scalloped

Date	Mintage	F	VF	XF	Unc	BU
JE5720 (1960) "Lamed" wtih serif	12,768,000	—	5.00	10.00	20.00	—
JE5720 (1960) "Lamed" without lower serif	Inc. above	—	10.00	20.00	100	—
JE5720 (1960) Large date	300	—	150	300	750	—
JE5721 (1961)	19,262,000	—	0.50	2.00	5.00	—
JE5721 (1961) Thick date	Inc. above	—	5.00	15.00	100	—
JE5721 (1961) Wide date	Inc. above	—	5.00	15.00	100	—
JE5722 (1962) Large date	14,500,000	—	0.10	0.40	0.75	—
JE5722 (1962) Small date, small serifs	Inc. above	—	5.00	10.00	20.00	—
JE5723 (1963) Coin alignment	14,804,000	—	0.10	0.40	0.75	—
JE5723 (1963) Medal alignment	10,000	—	4.00	9.00	20.00	35.00
JE5724 (1964)	27,552,000	—	—	—	0.75	—
JE5725 (1965)	20,708,000	—	—	—	0.25	—
JE5726 (1966)	10,165,000	—	—	—	0.25	—
JE5727 (1967)	6,781,000	—	—	—	0.25	—
JE5728 (1968)	20,899,000	—	—	—	0.25	—
JE5729 (1969)	22,120,000	—	—	—	0.25	—
JE5730 (1970)	17,748,000	—	—	—	0.25	—
JE5731 (1971)	10,290,000	—	—	—	0.25	—
JE5732 (1972)	24,512,000	—	—	—	0.25	—
JE5733 (1973)	20,496,000	—	—	—	0.25	—
JE5734 (1974)	42,080,000	—	—	—	0.25	—
JE5735 (1975)	1,574,000	—	—	—	0.25	—
JE5736 (1976)	4,512,000	—	—	—	0.25	—
JE5737 (1977)	9,680,000	—	—	—	0.25	—
JE5738 (1978)	8,864,000	—	—	—	0.25	—
JE5739 (1979)	4,048,000	—	—	—	0.25	—
JE5740 (1980)	2,600,000	—	—	—	1.00	—

KM# 24.2 AGORAH **Composition:** Aluminum **Obverse:** Star of David in field

Date	Mintage	F	VF	XF	Unc	BU
JE5731 (1971)	175,000	—	—	—	1.00	—
JE5732 (1972)	100,000	—	—	—	1.00	—
JE5734 (1974)	100,000	—	—	—	1.00	—
JE5735 (1975)	100,000	—	—	—	1.00	—
JE5736 (1976)	70,000	—	—	—	1.00	—
JE5737 (1977)	60,000	—	—	—	1.00	—
JE5738 (1978)	57,000	—	—	—	1.00	—
JE5739 (1979)	50,000	—	—	—	1.00	—

KM# 63 AGORAH **Composition:** Aluminum **Subject:** 25th Anniversary of Independence **Shape:** Scalloped **Note:** Struck for sets only.

Date	Mintage	F	VF	XF	Unc	BU
JE5733 (1973)	100,000	—	—	—	1.00	—

KM# 96 AGORAH **Composition:** Nickel **Subject:** 25th Anniversary - Bank of Israel **Shape:** Scalloped **Note:** Struck for sets only

Date	Mintage	F	VF	XF	Unc	BU
JE5740 (1980)	35,000	—	—	—	2.00	—

KM# 25 5 AGOROT **Composition:** Aluminum-Bronze **Obverse:** Star of David in field

Date	Mintage	F	VF	XF	Unc	BU
JE5720 (1960)	8,019,000	—	5.00	10.00	25.00	—
JE5721 (1961) Sharp, flat date	15,090,000	—	0.25	0.50	1.50	—
JE5721 (1961) I.C.I. issue; high date with serifs	5,000,000	—	10.00	20.00	75.00	—
JE5722 (1962) Large date	11,198,000	—	0.25	0.50	1.00	—
JE5722 (1962) Small date	Inc. above	—	5.00	10.00	25.00	—
JE5723 (1963)	1,429,000	—	0.25	0.50	1.25	—

Date	Mintage	F	VF	XF	Unc	BU
JE5724 (1964)	21,000	—	12.00	145	450	600
JE5725 (1965)	201,000	—	—	0.10	0.25	—
JE5726 (1966)	291,000	—	—	0.10	0.25	—
JE5727 (1967)	2,195,000	—	—	0.10	0.25	—
JE5728 (1968)	4,019,999	—	—	0.10	0.25	—
JE5729 (1969)	2,200,000	—	—	0.10	0.25	—
JE5730 (1970)	4,003,999	—	—	0.10	0.25	—
JE5731 (1971)	14,010,000	—	—	0.10	0.25	—
JE5732 (1972)	9,005,000	—	—	0.10	0.25	—
JE5733 (1973)	25,720,000	—	—	0.10	0.25	—
JE5734 (1974)	10,470,000	—	—	0.10	0.25	—
JE5735 (1975)	10,232,000	—	—	0.10	0.25	—
JE5736 (1976)	—	—	—	0.10	0.25	—
JE5737 (1977)	—	—	—	0.10	0.25	—

KM# 25a 5 AGOROT Composition: Aluminum-Bronze **Obverse:** Star of David in field

Date	Mintage	F	VF	XF	Unc	BU
JE5731 (1971)	126,000	—	—	—	1.00	—
JE5732 (1972)	69,000	—	—	—	1.00	—

KM# 25b 5 AGOROT Composition: Aluminum **Obverse:** Star of David in field

Date	Mintage	F	VF	XF	Unc	BU
JE5736 (1976) (M)	13,156,000	—	—	0.10	0.50	—
JE5737 (1977) (M)	16,800,000	—	—	0.10	0.50	—
JE5737 (1977)(o)	15,000,000	—	—	0.10	0.50	—
JE5738 (1978) (M)	21,480,000	—	—	0.10	0.50	—
JE5738 (1978)(o) (U)	38,760,000	—	—	0.10	0.50	—
JE5739 (1979) (M)	12,836,000	—	—	0.10	0.50	—

KM# 25c 5 AGOROT Composition: Aluminum-Bronze **Obverse:** Star of David in field

Date	Mintage	F	VF	XF	Unc	BU
JE5734 (1974) In sets only	93,000	—	—	—	1.00	—
JE5735 (1975) In sets only	62,000	—	—	—	1.00	—
JE5736 (1976) In sets only	—	—	—	—	1.00	—
JE5737 (1977) In sets only	60,000	—	—	—	1.00	—
JE5738 (1978)	57,200	—	—	—	1.00	—
JE5739 (1979)	18,000	—	—	—	1.00	—

KM# 64 5 AGOROT Composition: Copper-Nickel **Subject:** 25th Anniversary of Independence

Date	Mintage	F	VF	XF	Unc	BU
JE5733 (1973) In sets only	100,000	—	—	—	1.50	—

KM# 97 5 AGOROT Composition: Nickel **Subject:** 25th Anniversary - Bank of Israel **Note:** Struck for sets only.

Date	Mintage	F	VF	XF	Unc	BU
JE5740 (1980)	35,000	—	—	—	2.00	—

KM# 26 10 AGOROT Composition: Aluminum-Bronze

Date	Mintage	F	VF	XF	Unc	BU
JE5720 (1960)	14,397,000	—	0.50	1.00	10.00	—
JE5721 (1961)	12,821,000	—	0.50	1.00	6.00	—
JE5721 (1961)	Inc. above	—	25.00	80.00	325	—
Note: "Fatha" in Arabic, legend: "Israel"						
JE5722 (1962) Large date, thick letters	8,845,000	—	0.25	0.50	1.00	—
JE5722 (1962) Small date, thin letters	Inc. above	—	5.00	10.00	20.00	—
JE5723 (1963)	3,931,000	—	0.25	0.50	1.00	—
JE5724 (1964) Large date	3,612,000	—	0.25	0.50	1.00	—
JE5724 (1964) Small date	Inc. above	—	10.00	20.00	50.00	—

Date	Mintage	F	VF	XF	Unc	BU
JE5725 (1965)	201,000	—	—	0.20	0.25	—
JE5726 (1966)	7,276,000	—	—	0.10	0.25	—
JE5727 (1967)	6,426,000	—	—	0.10	0.25	—
JE5728 (1968)	4,825,000	—	—	0.10	0.25	—
JE5729 (1969)	6,810,000	—	—	0.10	0.25	—
JE5730 (1970)	6,131,000	—	—	0.10	0.25	—
JE5731 (1971)	6,810,000	—	—	0.10	0.25	—
JE5732 (1972)	19,653,000	—	—	0.10	0.25	—
JE5733 (1973)	16,205,000	—	—	0.10	0.25	—
JE5734 (1974)	22,040,000	—	—	0.10	0.25	—
JE5735 (1975)	25,135,000	—	—	0.10	0.25	—
JE5736 (1976)	54,870,000	—	—	0.10	0.25	—
JE5737 (1977)	27,886,000	—	—	0.10	0.25	—

KM# 26a 10 AGOROT Composition: Aluminum-Bronze **Obverse:** Star of David in field

Date	Mintage	F	VF	XF	Unc	BU
JE5731 (1971)	175,000	—	—	—	0.25	—
JE5732 (1972)	100,000	—	—	—	0.25	—

KM# 26c 10 AGOROT Composition: Copper-Nickel **Obverse:** Star of David in field

Date	Mintage	F	VF	XF	Unc	BU
JE5734 (1974) In sets only	100,000	—	—	—	1.00	—
JE5735 (1975) In sets only	100,000	—	—	—	1.00	—
JE5736 (1976) In sets only	70,000	—	—	—	1.00	—
JE5737 (1977) In sets only	60,000	—	—	—	1.00	—
JE5738 (1978) In sets only	57,000	—	—	—	1.00	—
JE5739 (1979) In sets only	—	—	—	—	1.00	—

KM# 26b 10 AGOROT Composition: Aluminum **Obverse:** Star of David in field

Date	Mintage	F	VF	XF	Unc	BU
JE5737 (1977)(o) (U)	30,100,000	—	—	0.10	0.25	—
JE5738 (1978) (M)	24,050,000	—	—	0.10	0.25	—
JE5738 (1978)(o) (U)	104,336,000	—	—	0.10	0.25	—
JE5739 (1979)	22,201,000	—	—	0.10	0.25	—
JE5740 (1980)	4,752,000	—	—	0.10	0.25	—

Note: Most of the 5740 dated coins were melted down before being issued

KM# 65 10 AGOROT Composition: Copper-Nickel **Subject:** 25th Anniversary of Independence

Date	Mintage	F	VF	XF	Unc	BU
JE5733 (1973) In sets only	100,000	—	—	—	1.00	—

KM# 98 10 AGOROT Composition: Nickel **Subject:** 25th Anniversary - Bank of Israel **Note:** Struck for sets only.

Date	Mintage	F	VF	XF	Unc	BU
JE5740 (1980)	35,000	—	—	—	2.00	—

KM# 27 25 AGOROT Composition: Aluminum-Bronze **Obverse:** Three-string lyre

Date	Mintage	F	VF	XF	Unc	BU
JE5720 (1960)	4,391,000	—	0.25	0.50	3.00	—
JE5721 (1961)	5,009,000	—	0.10	0.20	1.00	—
JE5722 (1962)	882,000	—	0.15	0.30	1.00	—
JE5723 (1963)	194,000	—	0.50	1.00	5.00	—
JE5724 (1964) Five trial pieces only	—	—	—	—	—	—
JE5725 (1965)	187,000	—	0.10	0.20	0.50	—
JE5726 (1966)	320,000	—	—	0.10	0.40	—
JE5727 (1967)	325,000	—	—	0.10	0.40	—
JE5728 (1968)	445,000	—	—	0.10	0.40	—
JE5729 (1969)	432,000	—	—	0.10	0.40	—
JE5730 (1970)	417,000	—	—	0.10	0.40	—
JE5731 (1971)	500,000	—	—	0.10	0.40	—
JE5732 (1972)	1,883,000	—	—	0.10	0.40	—
JE5733 (1973)	3,370,000	—	—	0.10	0.40	—
JE5734 (1974)	2,320,000	—	—	0.10	0.40	—
JE5735 (1975)	3,968,000	—	—	0.10	0.40	—

Date	Mintage	F	VF	XF	Unc	BU
JE5736 (1976)	3,901,000	—	—	0.10	0.40	—
JE5737 (1977)	1,832,000	—	—	0.10	0.40	—
JE5738 (1978)	12,200,000	—	—	0.10	0.40	—
JE5739 (1979)	10,842,000	—	—	0.10	0.40	—

KM# 27a 25 AGOROT Composition: Aluminum-Bronze **Obverse:** Star of David in field, three-string lyre

Date	Mintage	F	VF	XF	Unc	BU
JE5731 (1971)	126,000	—	—	—	0.40	—
JE5732 (1972)	69,000	—	—	—	0.40	—

KM# 27b 25 AGOROT Composition: Copper-Nickel **Obverse:** Star of David in field, three-string lyre **Note:** Struck for sets only.

Date	Mintage	F	VF	XF	Unc	BU
JE5734 (1974)	93,000	—	—	—	1.00	—
JE5735 (1975)	62,000	—	—	—	1.00	—
JE5736 (1976)	—	—	—	—	1.00	—
JE5737 (1977)	60,000	—	—	—	1.00	—
JE5738 (1978)	57,000	—	—	—	1.00	—
JE5739 (1979)	32,000	—	—	—	1.00	—

KM# 66 25 AGOROT Composition: Copper-Nickel **Subject:** 25th Anniversary of Independence **Obverse:** Three-string lyre **Note:** Struck for sets only.

Date	Mintage	F	VF	XF	Unc	BU
JE5733 (1973)	100,000	—	—	—	1.50	—

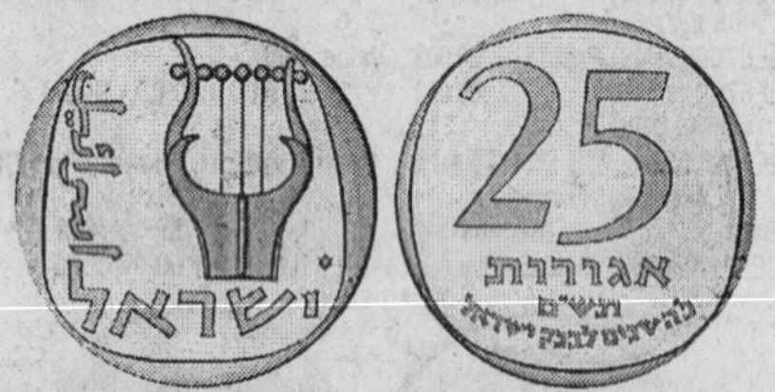

KM# 99 25 AGOROT Composition: Nickel **Subject:** 25th Anniversary - Bank of Israel **Obverse:** Three-string lyre **Note:** Struck for sets only.

Date	Mintage	F	VF	XF	Unc	BU
JE5740 (1980)	35,000	—	—	—	2.00	—

KM# 36.1 1/2 LIRAH Composition: Copper-Nickel **Obverse:** Menorah

Date	Mintage	F	VF	XF	Unc	BU
JE5723 (1963) Large animals	5,593,000	—	0.50	2.00	5.00	—
JE5723 (1963) Small animals	14,000	—	3.00	15.00	30.00	—
JE5724 (1964)	3,762,000	—	0.10	0.75	2.00	—
JE5725 (1965)	1,551,000	—	0.10	0.15	1.00	—
JE5726 (1966)	2,139,000	—	0.10	0.15	0.50	—
JE5727 (1967)	1,942,000	—	0.10	0.15	0.50	—
JE5728 (1968)	1,183,000	—	0.10	0.15	0.50	—
JE5729 (1969)	450,000	—	0.10	0.20	0.60	—
JE5730 (1970)	1,000,999	—	0.10	0.20	0.60	—
JE5731 (1971)	500,000	—	0.10	0.20	0.60	—
JE5732 (1972)	421,000	—	0.10	0.20	0.60	—
JE5733 (1973)	3,225,000	—	0.10	0.15	0.50	—
JE5734 (1974)	4,275,000	—	0.10	0.15	0.50	—
JE5735 (1975)	11,066,000	—	0.10	0.15	0.50	—
JE5736 (1976)	4,959,000	—	0.10	0.15	0.50	—
JE5737 (1977)	4,983,000	—	0.10	0.15	0.50	—
JE5738 (1978)	14,325,000	—	0.10	0.15	0.50	—
JE5739 (1979)	21,391,000	—	0.10	0.15	0.50	—

KM# 36.2 1/2 LIRAH Composition: Copper-Nickel **Obverse:** Star of David in field, menorah **Note:** Stuck for sets only.

Date	Mintage	F	VF	XF	Unc	BU
JE5731 (1971)	175,000	—	—	—	1.00	—
JE5732 (1972)	100,000	—	—	—	1.00	—
JE5734 (1974)	100,000	—	—	—	1.00	—

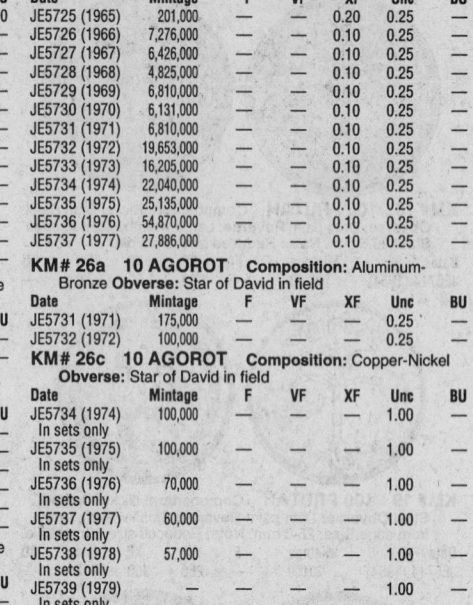

Date	Mintage	F	VF	XF	Unc	BU
JE5735(1975)	100,000	—	—	—	1.00	—
JE5736 (1976)	70,000	—	—	—	1.00	—
JE5737 (1977)	60,000	—	—	—	1.00	—
JE5738 (1978)	57,000	—	—	—	1.00	—
JE5739 (1979)	50,000	—	—	—	1.00	—

KM# 67 1/2 LIRAH Composition: Copper-Nickel **Subject:** 25th Anniversary of Independence **Obverse:** Menorah **Note:** Struck for sets only.

Date	Mintage	F	VF	XF	Unc	BU
JE5733 (1973)	100,000	—	—	—	1.50	—

KM# 100 1/2 LIRAH Composition: Nickel **Subject:** 25th Anniversary - Bank of Israel **Note:** Struck for sets only.

Date	Mintage	F	VF	XF	Unc	BU
JE5740 (1980)	35,000	—	—	—	3.00	—

KM# 101 LIRAH Composition: Nickel **Obverse:** Pomegranates, Star of David in field **Subject:** 25th Anniversary - Bank of Israel **Note:** Struck for sets only.

Date	Mintage	F	VF	XF	Unc	BU
JE5740 (1980)	35,000	—	—	—	4.00	—

KM# 37 LIRAH Composition: Copper-Nickel **Obverse:** Menorah

Date	Mintage	F	VF	XF	Unc	BU
JE5723 (1963) Large animals	4,212,000	—	0.50	1.50	3.00	—
JE5723 (1963) Large animals	4,212,000	—	0.50	1.50	3.00	—
JE5723 (1963) Small animals	Inc. above	—	1.00	10.00	20.00	—
JE5724 (1964) Only ten trial pieces struck	—	—	—	—	—	—
JE5725 (1965)	166,000	—	0.25	0.50	1.25	—
JE5725 (1965)	166,000	—	0.25	0.50	1.25	—
JE5726 (1966)	290,000	—	0.25	0.50	1.25	—
JE5726 (1966)	290,000	—	0.25	0.50	1.25	—
JE5727 (19697)	180,000	—	0.25	0.50	1.25	—
JE5727 (1967)	180,000	—	0.25	0.50	1.25	—

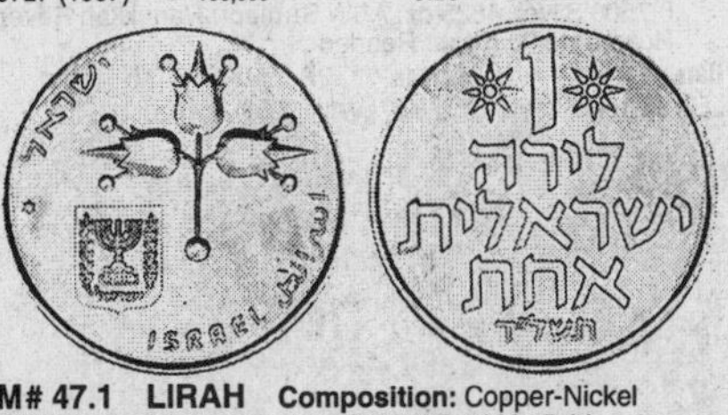

KM# 47.1 LIRAH Composition: Copper-Nickel **Obverse:** Pomegranates, Star of David in field

Date	Mintage	F	VF	XF	Unc	BU
JE5727 (1967)	3,830,000	—	0.10	0.25	1.00	—
JE5728 (1968)	3,932,000	—	0.10	0.25	1.00	—
JE5729 (1969)	12,484,000	—	0.10	0.25	0.75	—

Date	Mintage	F	VF	XF	Unc	BU
JE5730 (1970)	4,794,000	—	0.10	0.25	0.75	—
JE5731 (1971)	2,993,000	—	0.10	0.25	0.75	—
JE5732 (1972)	2,489,000	—	0.10	0.25	0.75	—
JE5733 (1973)	10,265,000	—	0.10	0.25	0.75	—
JE5734 (1974)	6,287,000	—	0.10	0.25	0.75	—
JE5735 (1975)	13,225,000	—	0.10	0.25	0.75	—
JE5736 (1976)	4,268,000	—	0.10	0.25	0.75	—
JE5737 (1977)	11,129,000	—	0.10	0.25	0.75	—
JE5738 (1978)	61,752,000	—	0.10	0.25	0.75	—
JE5739 (1979)	34,815,000	—	0.10	0.25	0.75	—
JE5740 (1980)	10,840,000	—	0.10	0.25	0.75	—

Note: Most of the 5740 dated coins were melted down before being issued

KM# 47.2 LIRAH Composition: Copper-Nickel **Obverse:** Pomegranates, Star of David in field **Note:** Struck for sets only.

Date	Mintage	F	VF	XF	Unc	BU
JE5731 (1971)	126,000	—	—	—	1.50	—
JE5732 (1972)	69,000	—	—	—	1.50	—
JE5734 (1974)	93,000	—	—	—	1.50	—
JE5735 (1975)	62,000	—	—	—	1.50	—
JE5736 (1976)	—	—	—	—	1.50	—
JE5737 (1977)	Inc. above	—	—	—	1.50	—
JE5738 (1978)	Inc. above	—	—	—	1.50	—
JE5739 (1979)	—	—	—	—	1.50	—

KM# 68 LIRAH Composition: Copper-Nickel **Subject:** 25th Anniversary of Independence **Obverse:** Pomegranates, Star of David in field **Note:** Struck for sets only.

Date	Mintage	F	VF	XF	Unc	BU
JE5733 (1973)	100,000	—	—	—	2.00	—

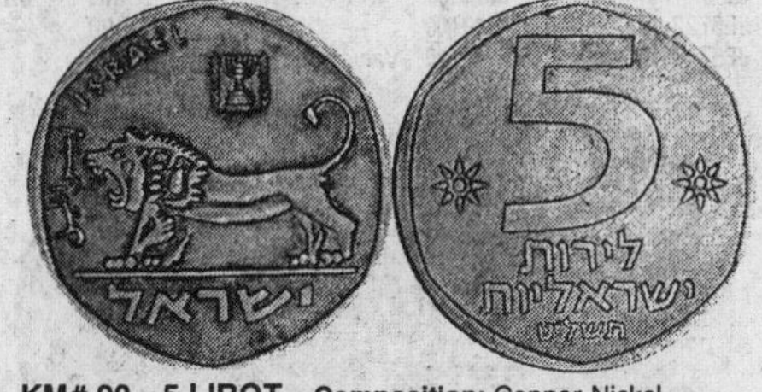

KM# 90 5 LIROT Composition: Copper-Nickel **Obverse:** Roaring lion left, menorah above

Date	Mintage	F	VF	XF	Unc	BU
JE5738 (1978)	8,350,000	—	0.35	0.70	3.00	—
JE5739 (1979)	37,646,000	—	0.35	0.60	2.00	—

KM# 90a 5 LIROT Composition: Copper-Nickel **Obverse:** Star of David in field **Note:** Struck for sets only.

Date	F	VF	XF	Unc	BU
JE5739 (1979)	—	—	—	2.00	—

KM# 102 5 LIROT Composition: Nickel **Subject:** 25th Anniversary - Bank of Israel **Obverse:** Roaring lion left, menorah above **Note:** Struck for sets only.

Date	Mintage	F	VF	XF	Unc	BU
JE5740 (1980)	35,000	—	—	—	6.00	—

COMMEMORATIVE COINAGE

NOTE: All proof commemoratives with the exception of the 1 and 5 Lirot issues of 1958 and the gold 100 Lirot Jerusalem 1968 issues are distinguished from the uncirculated editions by the presence of the Hebrew letter 'mem'.

KM# 31 1/2 LIRAH Composition: Copper-Nickel **Subject:** Feast of Purim

Date	Mintage	F	VF	XF	Unc	BU
JE5721 (1961)	20,000	—	—	—	5.00	—
JE5721 (1961) Proof	4,901	Value: 16.00				
JE5722 (1962)	20,000	—	—	—	5.00	—
JE5722 (1962) Proof	9,894	Value: 10.00				

KM# 22 LIRAH Composition: Copper-Nickel **Subject:** Hanukkah - Law Is Light **Reverse:** Menorah

Date		F	VF	XF	Unc	BU
JE5719-1958 Proof	5,000	Value: 28.00				
JE5719 1958		—	—	—	2.00	—
JE5719 1958	5,000	Value: 20.00				

KM# 28 LIRAH Composition: Copper-Nickel **Subject:** Hanukkah - 50th Anniversary of Deganya

Date	Mintage	F	VF	XF	Unc	BU
JE5720-1960	49,000	—	—	—	6.00	—
JE5720-1960	49,000	—	—	—	6.00	—
JE5720-1960 Proof	4,702	Value: 25.00				

KM# 32 LIRAH Composition: Copper-Nickel **Subject:** Hanukkah **Reverse:** Henrietta Szold

Date	Mintage	F	VF	XF	Unc	BU
JE5721-1960	17,000	—	—	—	17.50	—
JE5721-1960 Proof	3,000	Value: 100				

KM# 34 LIRAH Composition: Copper-Nickel **Subject:** Hanukkah **Reverse:** Death of a Hasmonean Hero

Date	Mintage	F	VF	XF	Unc	BU
JE5722	19,000	—	—	—	10.00	12.00
JE5722 Proof	9,324	Value: 14.50				

KM# 38 LIRAH Composition: Copper-Nickel **Subject:** Hanukkah **Reverse:** Italian lamp

Date	Mintage	F	VF	XF	Unc	BU
JE5722-1962	9,560	—	—	—	15.00	20.00
JE5722-1962 Proof	5,941	Value: 35.00				

KM# 42 LIRAH Composition: Copper-Nickel **Subject:** Hanukkah **Reverse:** 18th Century North African lamp

Date	Mintage	F	VF	XF	Unc	BU
JE5724-1963	9,928	—	—	—	12.50	15.00
JE5724-1963 Proof	5,412	Value: 35.00				

KM# 21 5 LIROT Weight: 25.0000 g. **Composition:** 0.9000 Silver .7234 oz. ASW **Subject:** 10th Anniversary of Independence **Reverse:** Menorah **Note:** Dav. #258

Date	Mintage	F	VF	XF	Unc	BU
JE5718-1958	98,000	—	—	—	10.00	15.00
JE5718-1958 Frosted Proof	2,000	Value: 450				

KM# 23 5 LIROT Composition: Silver **Subject:** 11th Anniversary of Independence **Reverse:** Ingathering of exiles **Note:** Dav. #259.

Date	Mintage	F	VF	XF	Unc	BU
JE5719-1959	27,000	—	—	—	15.00	17.50
JE5719-1959 Proof	4,682	Value: 35.00				

KM# 29 5 LIROT Weight: 25.0000 g. **Composition:** 0.9000 Silver .7234 oz. ASW **Subject:** 12th Anniversary of Independence **Reverse:** Dr. Theodor Herzl **Note:** Dav. #29.

Date	Mintage	F	VF	XF	Unc	BU
JE5720-1960	34,000	—	—	—	12.50	—
JE5720-1960 Proof	4,827	Value: 40.00				

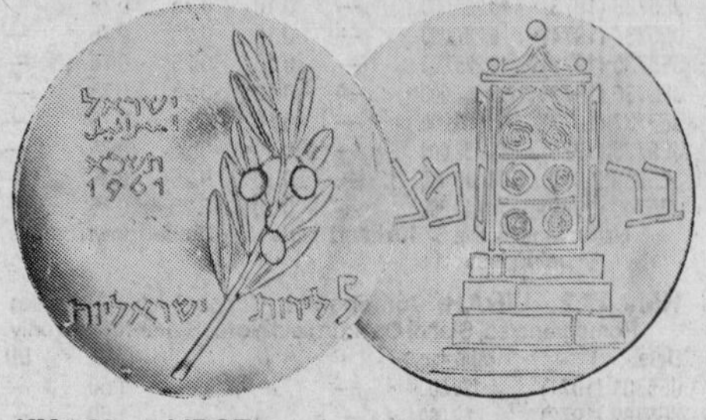

KM# 33 5 LIROT Weight: 25.0000 g. **Composition:** 0.9000 Silver .7234 oz. ASW **Subject:** 13th Anniversary of Independence **Reverse:** Bar Mitzvah **Note:** Dav. #261

Date	Mintage	F	VF	XF	Unc	BU
JE5721-1961	19,000	—	—	—	35.00	40.00
JE5721-1961 Proof	4,455	Value: 60.00				

KM# 35 5 LIROT Weight: 25.0000 g. **Composition:** 0.9000 Silver .7234 oz. ASW **Subject:** 14th Anniversary of Independence **Reverse:** Negev Industrialization **Note:** Dav. #262,

Date	Mintage	F	VF	XF	Unc	BU
JE5722-1962	10,000	—	—	—	25.00	—
JE5722-1962 Proof	4,960	Value: 45.00				

KM# 39 5 LIROT Weight: 25.0000 g. **Composition:** 0.9000 Silver .7234 oz. ASW **Subject:** 15th Anniversary of Independence **Reverse:** Seafaring **Note:** Dav. #263.

Date	Mintage	F	VF	XF	Unc	BU
JE5723-1962	5,960	—	—	—	200	215
JE5723-1962 Proof	4,495	Value: 240				

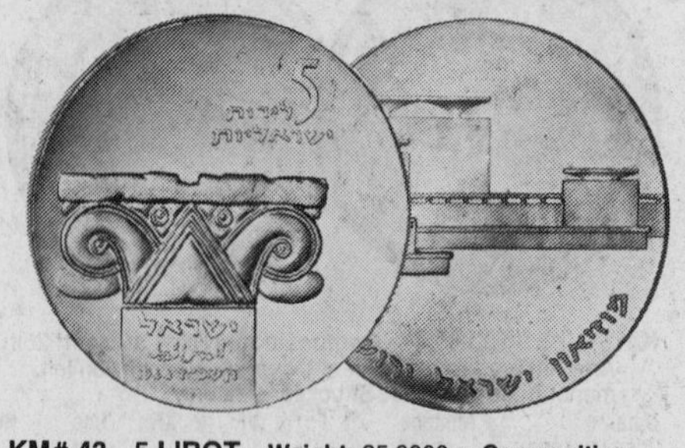

KM# 43 5 LIROT Weight: 25.0000 g. **Composition:** 0.9000 Silver .7234 oz. ASW **Subject:** 16th Anniversary of Independence **Reverse:** Israel Museum **Note:** Dav. #264.

Date	Mintage	F	VF	XF	Unc	BU
JE5724-1964	11,000	—	—	—	25.00	—
JE5724-1964 Proof	4,421	Value: 50.00				

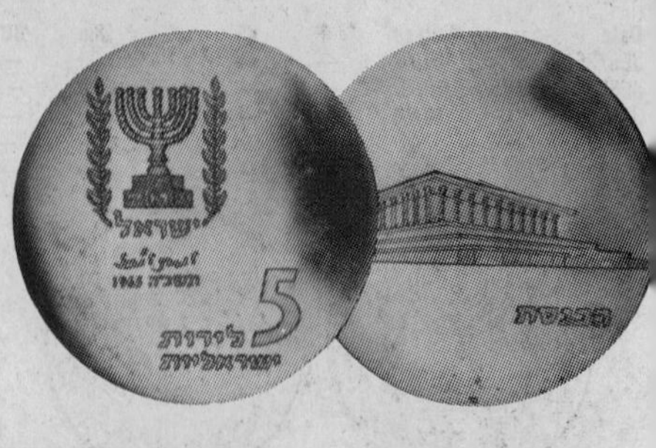

KM# 45 5 LIROT Weight: 25.0000 g. **Composition:** 0.9000 Silver .7234 oz. ASW **Subject:** 17th Anniversary of Independence **Reverse:** Knesset Building **Note:** Dav. #265.

Date	Mintage	F	VF	XF	Unc	BU
JE5725-1965	25,000	—	—	—	11.50	—
JE5725-1965 Proof	7,537	Value: 16.50				

KM# 46 5 LIROT Weight: 25.0000 g. **Composition:** 0.9000 Silver .7234 oz. ASW **Subject:** 18th Anniversary of Independence **Reverse:** Israel lives on **Note:** Dav. #266.

Date	Mintage	F	VF	XF	Unc	BU
JE5726-1966	32,000	—	—	—	8.00	—
JE5726-1966 Proof	10,000	Value: 13.00				

KM# 48 5 LIROT Weight: 25.0000 g. **Composition:** 0.9000 Silver .7234 oz. ASW **Subject:** 19th Anniversary of Independence **Reverse:** Port of Eilat **Note:** Dav. #267.

Date	Mintage	F	VF	XF	Unc	BU
JE5727-1967	30,000	—	—	—	11.50	—
JE5727-1967 Proof	7,680	Value: 17.50				
JE5727-1967 Frosted Proof	Inc. above	Value: 50.00				

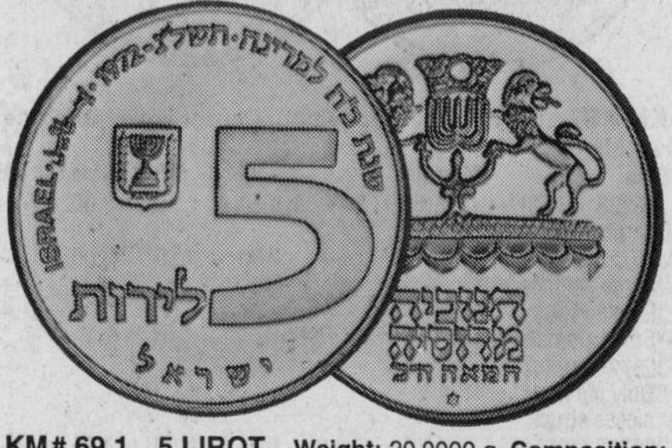

KM# 69.1 5 LIROT Weight: 20.0000 g. **Composition:** 0.7500 Silver .4823 oz. ASW **Subject:** Hanukkah **Reverse:** Russian lamp

Date	Mintage	F	VF	XF	Unc	BU
JE5733-1972	75,000	—	—	—	5.50	—

KM# 69.2 5 LIROT Weight: 20.0000 g. **Composition:** 0.7500 Silver .4823 oz. ASW **Subject:** Hanukkah **Reverse:** Russian lamp **Edge:** Reeded

Date	Mintage	F	VF	XF	Unc	BU
JE5733-1972 Proof	22,000	Value: 7.50				

KM# 75.1 5 LIROT **Weight:** 20.0000 g. **Composition:** 0.5000 Silver .3215 oz. ASW **Subject:** Hanukkah **Reverse:** Babylonian lamp **Edge:** Plain

Date	Mintage	F	VF	XF	Unc	BU
JE5734-1973	95,000	—	—	—	5.50	—

KM# 75.2 5 LIROT **Weight:** 20.0000 g. **Composition:** 0.5000 Silver .3215 oz. ASW **Subject:** Hanukkah **Reverse:** Babylonian lamp **Edge:** Reeded

Date	Mintage	F	VF	XF	Unc	BU
JE5734-1973 Proof	45,000	Value: 7.50				

KM# 49 10 LIROT **Weight:** 26.0000 g. **Composition:** 0.9350 Silver .7524 oz. ASW **Subject:** Victory Commemorative **Note:** Dav. #268

Date	Mintage	F	VF	XF	Unc	BU
JE5727-1967	234,000	—	—	—	10.00	—

KM# 49a 10 LIROT **Weight:** 26.0000 g. **Composition:** 0.9350 Silver .7816 oz. ASW **Subject:** Victory Commemorative **Note:** Dav. #268

Date	Mintage	F	VF	XF	Unc	BU
JE5727-1967 Proof	50,000	Value: 12.00				

KM# 51 10 LIROT **Weight:** 26.0000 g. **Composition:** 0.9000 Silver .7524 oz. ASW **Subject:** 20th Anniversary of Independence **Reverse:** Jerusalem Reunification **Note:** Dav. #269.

Date	Mintage	F	VF	XF	Unc	BU
JE5728-1968	50,000	—	—	—	10.00	—
JE5728-1968 Proof	20,000	Value: 14.00				

KM# 53.1 10 LIROT **Weight:** 26.0000 g. **Composition:** 0.9000 Silver .7524 oz. ASW **Subject:** 21st Anniversary of Independence **Reverse:** Shalom **Note:** Struck at the U.S. Mint(s).

Date	Mintage	F	VF	XF	Unc	BU
JE5729-1969	40,000	—	—	—	10.00	—

KM# 53.2 10 LIROT **Weight:** 26.0000 g. **Composition:** 0.9000 Silver .7524 oz. ASW **Subject:** 21st Anniversary of Independence **Reverse:** K A F to right of helmet

Date	Mintage	F	VF	XF	Unc	BU
JE5729-1969	20,000	—	—	—	10.00	—

Note: Jerusalem Mint

Date	Mintage	F	VF	XF	Unc	BU
JE5729-1969 Proof	20,000	Value: 12.00				

Note: U.S. Mint(s)

KM# 55 10 LIROT **Weight:** 26.0000 g. **Composition:** 0.9000 Silver .7524 oz. ASW **Subject:** 22nd Anniversary of Independence **Reverse:** Mikveh Israel Centenary

Date	Mintage	F	VF	XF	Unc	BU
JE5730-1970	48,000	—	—	—	9.00	—
JE5730-1970 Proof	22,000	Value: 12.00				

KM# 56.1 10 LIROT **Weight:** 26.0000 g. **Composition:** 0.9000 Silver .7524 oz. ASW **Subject:** Pidyon Haben **Edge:** Plain

Date	Mintage	F	VF	XF	Unc	BU
JE5730-1970	49,000	—	—	—	10.00	—

KM# 56.2 10 LIROT **Weight:** 26.0000 g. **Composition:** 0.9000 Silver .7524 oz. ASW **Subject:** Pidyon Haben **Edge:** Reeded **Note:** Struck at the San Francisco Mint.

Date	Mintage	F	VF	XF	Unc	BU
JE5730-1970 Proof	15,000	Value: 12.00				

KM# 57.1 10 LIROT **Weight:** 26.0000 g. **Composition:** 0.9000 Silver .7524 oz. ASW **Subject:** Pidyon Haben **Edge:** Plain

Date	Mintage	F	VF	XF	Unc	BU
JE5731-1971	30,000	—	—	—	10.00	—
JE5731-1971 With Star	—	—	—	—	10.00	—

KM# 57.2 10 LIROT **Weight:** 26.0000 g. **Composition:** 0.9000 Silver .7524 oz. ASW **Subject:** Pidyon Haben **Edge:** Reeded

Date	Mintage	F	VF	XF	Unc	BU
JE5731-1971 Proof	14,000	Value: 12.00				

KM# 58 10 LIROT **Weight:** 26.0000 g. **Composition:** 0.9000 Silver .7524 oz. ASW **Subject:** 23rd Anniversary of Independence **Reverse:** Science and Industry

Date	Mintage	F	VF	XF	Unc	BU
JE5731-1971	30,000	—	—	—	10.00	—

Note: Struck at the Utrecht Mint

Date	Mintage	F	VF	XF	Unc	BU
JE5731-1971 Star	23,000	—	—	—	10.00	—

Date	Mintage	F	VF	XF	Unc	BU

Note: Struck at the Jerusalem Mint

Date	Mintage	F	VF	XF	Unc	BU
JE5731-1971 Proof	18,000	Value: 12.00				

KM# 59.1 10 LIROT **Weight:** 26.0000 g. **Composition:** 0.9000 Silver .7524 oz. ASW **Subject:** Let My People Go **Obverse:** Legend on rim, closed "mem"

Date	Mintage	F	VF	XF	Unc	BU
JE5731-1971	73,000	—	—	—	10.00	—
JE5731-1971 Proof	20,000	Value: 12.00				

KM# 59.2 10 LIROT **Weight:** 26.0000 g. **Composition:** 0.9000 Silver .7524 oz. ASW **Obverse:** Legend away from rim, open "mem" **Note:** Berne die.

Date	Mintage	F	VF	XF	Unc	BU
JE5731-1971 Proof	80	Value: 600				

KM# 61.1 10 LIROT **Weight:** 26.0000 g. **Composition:** 0.9000 Silver .7524 oz. ASW **Subject:** Pidyon Haben **Edge:** Plain

Date	Mintage	F	VF	XF	Unc	BU
JE5732-1972 With star	30,000	—	—	—	10.00	—
JE5732-1972 Without star	15,000	—	—	—	14.00	—

KM# 61.2 10 LIROT **Weight:** 26.0000 g. **Composition:** 0.9000 Silver .7524 oz. ASW **Subject:** Pidyon Haben **Edge:** Reeded

Date	Mintage	F	VF	XF	Unc	BU
JE5732-1972 Proof	12,000	Value: 12.00				

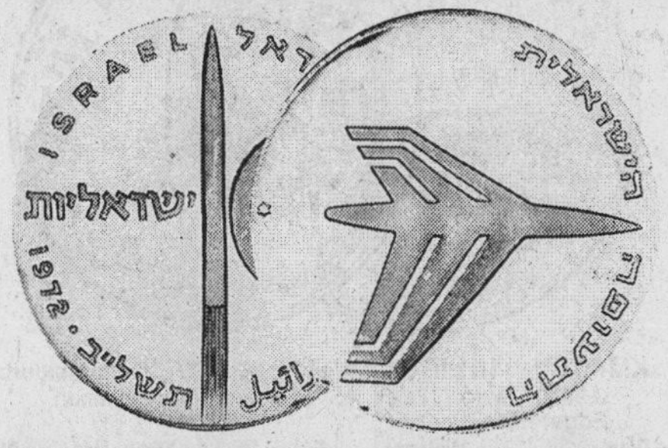

KM# 62 10 LIROT **Weight:** 26.0000 g. **Composition:** 0.9000 Silver .7524 oz. ASW **Subject:** 24th Anniversary of Independence **Reverse:** Aviation **Edge:** Lettered

Date	Mintage	F	VF	XF	Unc	BU
JE5732-1972	50,000	—	—	—	10.00	—
JE5732-1972 Proof	15,000	Value: 15.00				

KM# 70.1 10 LIROT **Weight:** 26.0000 g. **Composition:** 0.9000 Silver .7524 oz. ASW **Subject:** Pidyon Haben **Obverse:** Menorah above inscription **Edge:** Plain

Date	Mintage	F	VF	XF	Unc	BU
JE5733-1973	101,000	—	—	—	10.00	—

KM# 70.2 10 LIROT **Weight:** 26.0000 g. **Composition:** 0.9000 Silver .7524 oz. ASW **Subject:** Pidyon Haben **Obverse:** Menorah above inscription **Edge:** Reeded

Date	Mintage	F	VF	XF	Unc	BU
JE5733-1973 Proof	15,000	Value: 12.00				

KM# 71 10 LIROT **Weight:** 26.0000 g. **Composition:** 0.9000 Silver .7524 oz. ASW **Subject:** 25th Anniversary of Independence **Obverse:** Menorah above inscription **Edge:** Lettered

Date	Mintage	F	VF	XF	Unc	BU
JE5733-1973	124,000	—	—	—	10.00	—
JE5733-1973 Proof	41,000	Value: 12.00				

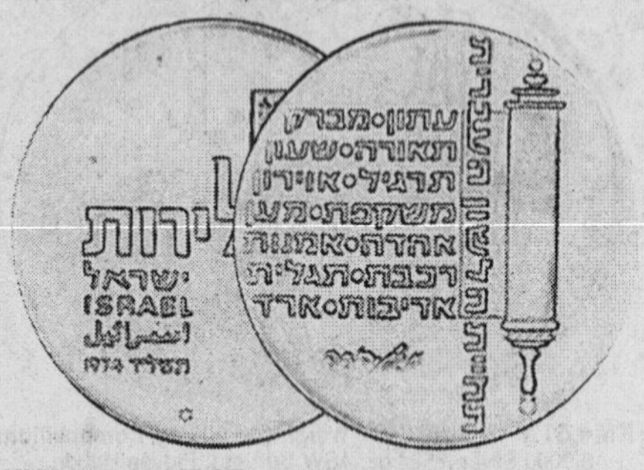

KM# 77 10 LIROT **Weight:** 26.0000 g. **Composition:** 0.9000 Silver .7524 oz. ASW **Subject:** 26th Anniversary of Independence **Edge:** Lettered

Date	Mintage	F	VF	XF	Unc	BU
JE5734-1974	127,000	—	—	—	9.00	—
JE5734-1974 Proof	50,000	Value: 11.00				

KM# 76.1 10 LIROT **Weight:** 26.0000 g. **Composition:** 0.9000 Silver .7524 oz. ASW **Subject:** Pidyon Haben **Edge:** Plain

Date	Mintage	F	VF	XF	Unc	BU
JE5734-1974	109,000	—	—	—	10.00	—

KM# 76.2 10 LIROT **Weight:** 26.0000 g. **Composition:** 0.9000 Silver .7524 oz. ASW **Subject:** Pidyon Haben **Edge:** Reeded

Date	Mintage	F	VF	XF	Unc	BU
JE5734-1974 Proof	44,000	Value: 12.00				

KM# 78.1 10 LIROT **Weight:** 26.0000 g. **Composition:** 0.9000 Silver .7524 oz. ASW **Subject:** Hanukkah **Reverse:** Damascus lamp **Edge:** Plain

Date	Mintage	F	VF	XF	Unc	BU
JE5735-1974	74,000	—	—	—	5.50	—

KM# 78.2 10 LIROT **Weight:** 26.0000 g. **Composition:** 0.9000 Silver .7524 oz. ASW **Subject:** Hanukkah **Reverse:** Damascus lamp **Edge:** Reeded

Date	Mintage	F	VF	XF	Unc	BU
JE5735-1974 Proof	59,000	Value: 7.50				

KM# 84.1 10 LIROT **Weight:** 26.0000 g. **Composition:** 0.9000 Silver .7524 oz. ASW **Subject:** Hanukkah **Reverse:** Holland lamp **Edge:** Plain

Date	Mintage	F	VF	XF	Unc	BU
JE5736-1975	44,000	—	—	—	6.00	—

KM# 84.2 10 LIROT **Weight:** 26.0000 g. **Composition:** 0.9000 Silver .7524 oz. ASW **Subject:** Hanukkah **Reverse:** Holland lamp **Edge:** Reeded

Date	Mintage	F	VF	XF	Unc	BU
JE5736-1975 Proof	34,000	Value: 8.00				

KM# 87.1 10 LIROT **Weight:** 20.0000 g. **Composition:** 0.5000 Silver .3215 oz. ASW **Subject:** Hanukkah **Reverse:** U.S. Hanukkah lamp **Edge:** Plain

Date	Mintage	F	VF	XF	Unc	BU
JE5737-1976	25,000	—	—	—	12.00	—

KM# 87.2 10 LIROT **Weight:** 20.0000 g. **Composition:** 0.5000 Silver .3215 oz. ASW **Subject:** Hanukkah **Reverse:** U.S. Hanukkah lamp **Edge:** Reeded

Date	Mintage	F	VF	XF	Unc	BU
JE5737-1976 Proof	20,000	Value: 15.00				

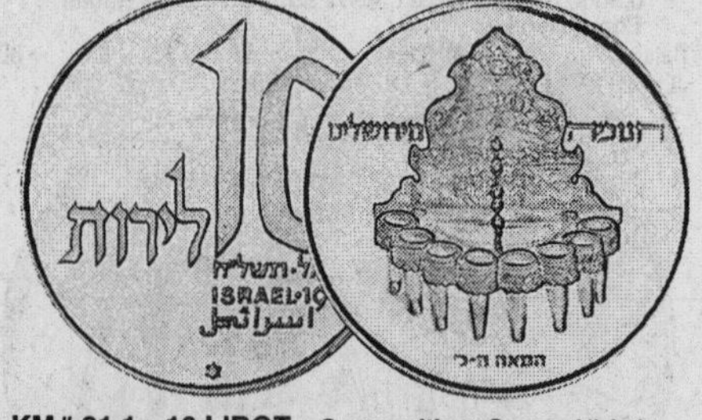

KM# 91.1 10 LIROT **Composition:** Copper-Nickel **Subject:** Hanukkah **Reverse:** Jerusalem lamp **Edge:** Plain

Date	Mintage	F	VF	XF	Unc	BU
JE5738-1977	46,000	—	—	—	4.00	—

KM# 91.2 10 LIROT **Composition:** Copper-Nickel **Subject:** Hanukkah **Reverse:** Jerusalem lamp **Edge:** Reeded **Note:** Open style "mem."

Date	Mintage	F	VF	XF	Unc	BU
JE5738-1977 Proof	30,000	Value: 6.50				

KM# 91.3 10 LIROT **Composition:** Copper-Nickel **Subject:** Hanukkah **Reverse:** Jerusalem lamp **Edge:** Reeded **Note:** Closed style "mem".

Date		F	VF	XF	Unc	BU
JE5738-1977 Proof	Inc. above	Value: 11.00				

KM# 30 20 LIROT **Weight:** 7.9880 g. **Composition:** 0.9170 Gold .2355 oz. AGW **Subject:** 100th Anniversary - Birth of Dr. Theodor Herzl **Obverse:** Menorah **Reverse:** Bust of Herzl left

Date	Mintage	F	VF	XF	Unc	BU
JE5720-1960	10,000	—	—	—	150	—

KM# 79.1 25 LIROT **Weight:** 26.0000 g. **Composition:** 0.9350 Silver .7816 oz. ASW **Subject:** 1st Anniversary - Death of David Ben Gurion **Obverse:** Menorah **Reverse:** Bust of Gurion left **Edge:** Plain

Date	Mintage	F	VF	XF	Unc	BU
JE5735-1974	99,000	—	—	—	11.00	—

KM# 79.2 25 LIROT **Weight:** 26.0000 g. **Composition:** 0.9350 Silver .7816 oz. ASW **Subject:** 1st Anniversary - Death of David Ben Gurion **Edge:** Reeded

Date	Mintage	F	VF	XF	Unc	BU
JE5735-1974 Proof	64,000	Value: 13.00				

KM# 81 25 LIROT **Weight:** 30.0000 g. **Composition:** 0.8000 Silver .7717 oz. ASW **Subject:** 25th Anniversary of Israel Bond Program **Edge:** Lettered

Date	Mintage	F	VF	XF	Unc	BU
JE5735-1975	49,000	—	—	—	10.00	—
JE5735-1975 Proof	40,000	Value: 12.00				

KM# 80.1 25 LIROT **Weight:** 26.0000 g. **Composition:** 0.9000 Silver .7524 oz. ASW **Subject:** Pidyon Haben **Edge:** Plain

Date	Mintage	F	VF	XF	Unc	BU
JE5735-1975	62,000	—	—	—	11.00	—

KM# 80.2 25 LIROT **Weight:** 26.0000 g. **Composition:** 0.9000 Silver .7524 oz. ASW **Subject:** Pidyon Haben **Edge:** Reeded

Date	Mintage	F	VF	XF	Unc	BU
JE5735-1975 Proof	49,000	Value: 12.00				

KM# 85 25 LIROT **Weight:** 26.0000 g. **Composition:** 0.9000 Silver .7534 oz. ASW **Subject:** 28th Anniversary of Independence **Reverse:** Strength **Edge:** Lettered

Date	Mintage	F	VF	XF	Unc	BU
JE5736-1976	38,000	—	—	—	9.00	—
JE5736-1976 Proof	27,000	Value: 11.00				

KM# 86.1 25 LIROT **Weight:** 30.0000 g. **Composition:** 0.8000 Silver .7717 oz. ASW **Subject:** Pidyon Haben **Edge:** Plain

Date	Mintage	F	VF	XF	Unc	BU
JE5736-1976	37,000	—	—	—	10.00	—

KM# 86.2 25 LIROT **Weight:** 30.0000 g. **Composition:** 0.8000 Silver .7717 oz. ASW **Subject:** Pidyon Haben **Edge:** Reeded

Date	Mintage	F	VF	XF	Unc	BU
JE5736-1976 Proof	29,000	Value: 12.00				

KM# 88 25 LIROT **Weight:** 20.0000 g. **Composition:** 0.5000 Silver .3215 oz. ASW **Subject:** 29th Anniversary of Independence **Reverse:** Brotherhood **Edge:** Lettered

Date	Mintage	F	VF	XF	Unc	BU
JE5737-1977	37,000	—	—	—	9.00	—
JE5737-1977 Proof	27,000	Value: 11.00				

KM# 89.1 25 LIROT **Weight:** 26.0000 g. **Composition:** 0.9000 Silver .7534 oz. ASW **Subject:** Pidyon Haben **Edge:** Plain

Date	Mintage	F	VF	XF	Unc	BU
JE5737-1977	32,000	—	—	—	10.00	—

KM# 89.2 25 LIROT **Weight:** 26.0000 g. **Composition:** 0.9000 Silver .7534 oz. ASW **Subject:** Pidyon Haben **Edge:** Reeded

Date	Mintage	F	VF	XF	Unc	BU
JE5737-1977 Proof	19,000	Value: 12,00				

KM# 94.1 25 LIROT **Weight:** 26.0000 g. **Composition:** 0.9000 Silver .7534 oz. ASW **Subject:** Hanukkah **Reverse:** French lamp **Edge:** Plain

Date	Mintage	F	VF	XF	Unc	BU
JE5739-1978	36,000	—	—	—	5.00	—

KM# 94.2 25 LIROT **Weight:** 26.0000 g. **Composition:** 0.9000 Silver .7534 oz. ASW **Subject:** Hanukkah **Reverse:** French lamp **Edge:** Reeded

Date	Mintage	F	VF	XF	Unc	BU
JE5739-1978 Proof	22,000	Value: 8.00				

KM# 40 50 LIROT **Weight:** 13.3400 g. **Composition:** 0.9170 Gold .3933 oz. AGW **Subject:** 10th Anniversary - Death of Weizmann

Date	Mintage	F	VF	XF	Unc	BU
JE5723-1962 Proof	6,202	Value: 225				
JE5723-1962 Without "mem," Proof	10	—	—	—	—	—

KM# 44 50 LIROT **Weight:** 13.3400 g. **Composition:** 0.9170 Gold .3933 oz. AGW **Subject:** 10th Anniversary - Bank of Israel

Date	Mintage	F	VF	XF	Unc	BU
JE5725-1964	6,014	—	—	—	270	—
JE5725-1964 Proof	841	Value: 3,400				

KM# 72 50 LIROT **Weight:** 7.0000 g. **Composition:** 0.9000 Gold .2025 oz. AGW **Subject:** 25th Anniversary of Independence

Date	Mintage	F	VF	XF	Unc	BU
JE5733-1973 Proof	28,000	Value: 110				

KM# 92.1 50 LIROT **Weight:** 20.0000 g. **Composition:** 0.5000 Silver .3215 oz. ASW **Subject:** 30th Anniversary of Independence **Reverse:** Loyalty **Edge:** Lettered

Date	Mintage	F	VF	XF	Unc	BU
JE5738-1978	40,000	—	—	—	9.00	—

KM# 92.2 50 LIROT **Weight:** 20.0000 g. **Composition:** 0.5000 Silver .3215 oz. ASW **Subject:** 30th Anniversary of Independence **Reverse:** Loyalty **Edge:** Reeded

Date	Mintage	F	VF	XF	Unc	BU
JE5738-1978 Proof	22,000	Value: 10.00				

KM# 95 50 LIROT **Weight:** 20.0000 g. **Composition:** 0.5000 Silver .3215 oz. ASW **Subject:** 31st Anniverdary of Independence **Reverse:** Motherhood **Edge:** Lettered

Date	Mintage	F	VF	XF	Unc	BU
JE5739-1979	24,000	—	—	—	10.00	—
JE5739-1979 Proof	16,000	Value: 12.00				

KM# 41 100 LIROT **Weight:** 26.6800 g. **Composition:** 0.9170 Gold .7866 oz. AGW **Subject:** 10th Anniversary - Death of Weizmann **Reverse:** Bust of Weizmann left

Date	Mintage	F	VF	XF	Unc	BU
JE5723-1962 Proof	6,203	Value: 420				
JE5723-1962 Proof	10	—	—	—	—	—

Note: Without "mem" - See KM#40

KM# 50 100 LIROT **Weight:** 26.6800 g. **Composition:** 0.9170 Gold .7866 oz. AGW **Subject:** Victory Commemorative

Date	Mintage	F	VF	XF	Unc	BU
JE5727-1967 Proof	9,004	Value: 375				

KM# 52 100 LIROT **Weight:** 25.0000 g. **Composition:** 0.8000 Gold .6430 oz. AGW **Subject:** 20th Anniversary - Jerusalem Reunification

Date	Mintage	F	VF	XF	Unc	BU
JE5728-1968 Proof	13,000	Value: 300				

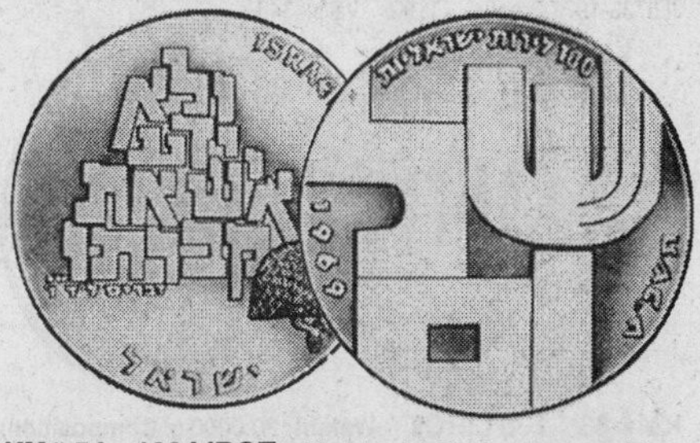

KM# 54 100 LIROT **Weight:** 25.0000 g. **Composition:** 0.8000 Gold .6430 oz. AGW **Subject:** 21st Anniversary of Independence **Reverse:** Shalom

Date	Mintage	F	VF	XF	Unc	BU
JE5729-1969 Proof	13,000	Value: 300				

KM# 60 100 LIROT **Weight:** 22.0000 g. **Composition:** 0.9000 Gold .6366 oz. AGW **Subject:** Let My People Go

Date	Mintage	F	VF	XF	Unc	BU
JE5731-1971 Proof	9,956	Value: 300				

KM# 73 100 LIROT **Weight:** 13.5000 g. **Composition:** 0.9000 Gold .3906 oz. AGW **Subject:** 25th Anniversary of Independence

Date	Mintage	F	VF	XF	Unc	BU
JE5733-1973 Proof	28,000	Value: 185				

KM# 103.1 100 LIROT **Weight:** 20.0000 g. **Composition:** 0.5000 Silver .3215 oz. ASW **Subject:** Hanukkah **Reverse:** Egyptian lamp **Edge:** Plain

Date	Mintage	F	VF	XF	Unc	BU
JE5740-1979	32,000	—	—	—	8.50	—

KM# 103.2 100 LIROT **Weight:** 20.0000 g. **Composition:** 0.5000 Silver .3215 oz. ASW **Subject:** Hanukkah **Reverse:** Egyptian lamp **Edge:** Reeded

Date	Mintage	F	VF	XF	Unc	BU
JE5740-1979 Proof	19,000	Value: 11.50				

KM# 74 200 LIROT **Weight:** 27.0000 g. **Composition:** 0.9000 Gold .7813 oz. AGW **Subject:** 25th Anniversary of Independence

Date	Mintage	F	VF	XF	Unc	BU
JE5733-1973 Proof	18,000	Value: 340				

KM# 83 200 LIROT **Weight:** 20.0000 g. **Composition:** 0.9000 Gold .5787 oz. AGW **Subject:** 25th Anniversary of Israel Bond Program

Date	Mintage	F	VF	XF	Unc	BU
JE5735-1975 Proof	31,000	Value: 245				

KM# 104 200 LIROT **Weight:** 26.0000 g. **Composition:** 0.9000 Silver .7534 oz. ASW **Subject:** 32nd Anniversary of Independence **Reverse:** Egyptian and Israeli Peace Treaty **Edge:** Lettered

Date	Mintage	F	VF	XF	Unc	BU
JE5740-1980	20,000	—	—	—	10.00	—
JE5740-1980 Proof	13,000	Value: 15.00				

KM# 82 500 LIROT **Weight:** 28.0000 g. **Composition:** 0.9000 Gold .8102 oz. AGW **Subject:** 1st Anniversary - Death of David Ben Gurion

Date	Mintage	F	VF	XF	Unc	BU
JE5735-1974 Proof	48,000	Value: 350				

KM# 93 1000 LIROT **Weight:** 12.0000 g. **Composition:** 0.9000 Gold .3473 oz. AGW **Subject:** 30th Anniversary of Independence **Reverse:** Tree of Life

Date	Mintage	F	VF	XF	Unc	BU
JE5738-1978 Proof	12,000	Value: 175				

KM# 105 5000 LIROT **Weight:** 17.2800 g. **Composition:** 0.9000 Gold .50000 oz. AGW **Subject:** 32nd Anniversary of Independence **Reverse:** Egyptian & Israeli Peace Treaty

Date	Mintage	F	VF	XF	Unc	BU
JE5740-1980 Proof	6,382	Value: 250				

REFORM COINAGE

10 Old Agorot = 1 New Agorah; 100 New Agorot = 1 Sheqel

Commencing February 24, 1980-1985

KM# 106 NEW AGORAH **Composition:** Aluminum **Obverse:** Date palm

Date	Mintage	F	VF	XF	Unc	BU
JE5740 (1980)	200,000,000	—	—	—	0.10	—
Note: 110 million coins were reportedly melted down						
JE5741 (1981)	1,000,000	—	—	0.10	0.20	—
JE5742 (1982)	1,000,000	—	—	0.10	0.20	—

KM# 107 5 NEW AGOROT **Composition:** Aluminum **Obverse:** Menorah

Date	Mintage	F	VF	XF	Unc	BU
JE5740 (1980)	69,532,000	—	—	—	0.10	—
JE5741 (1981)	1,000,000	—	—	0.10	0.20	—
JE5742 (1982)	5,000,000	—	—	—	0.10	—

KM# 108 10 NEW AGOROT **Composition:** Bronze **Obverse:** Pomegranate

Date	Mintage	F	VF	XF	Unc	BU
JE5740 (1980)	167,932,000	—	—	—	0.10	—
Note: 70.200 million coins were reportedly melted down						
JE5741 (1981)	241,160,000	—	—	—	0.10	—
JE5742 (1982)	23,000,000	—	—	—	0.10	—
JE5743 (1983)	2,500,000	—	—	0.10	0.15	—
JE5744 (1984)	500,000	—	—	0.10	0.20	—

KM# 109 1/2 SHEQEL **Composition:** Copper-Nickel **Obverse:** Roaring lion left, menorah above

Date	Mintage	F	VF	XF	Unc	BU
JE5740 (1980)	52,308,000	—	—	0.25	0.60	—
JE5741 (1981)	53,272,000	—	—	0.25	0.60	—
JE5742 (1982)	18,808,000	—	—	0.25	0.60	—
JE5743 (1983)	250,000	—	—	0.35	0.75	—
JE5744 (1984)	250,000	—	—	0.35	0.75	—

KM# 121 1/2 SHEQEL **Weight:** 7.2000 g. **Composition:** 0.8500 Silver .1967 oz. ASW **Series:** Holyland Sites **Reverse:** Gumran Caves **Shape:** 12-sided

Date	Mintage	F	VF	XF	Unc	BU
JE5743-1982	15,000	—	—	—	10.00	—

KM# 126 1/2 SHEQEL **Weight:** 7.2000 g. **Composition:** 0.8500 Silver .1967 oz. ASW **Series:** Holyland Sites **Reverse:** Herodion Ruins **Shape:** 12-sided

Date	Mintage	F	VF	XF	Unc	BU
JE5744-1983	11,000	—	—	—	10.00	—

KM# 140 1/2 SHEQEL **Weight:** 7.2000 g. **Composition:** 0.8500 Silver .1967 oz. ASW **Series:** Holyland Sites **Reverse:** Kidron Valley **Shape:** 12-sided

Date	Mintage	F	VF	XF	Unc	BU
JE5745-1984	7,538	—	—	—	16.00	—

KM# 152 1/2 SHEQEL **Weight:** 7.2000 g. **Composition:** 0.8500 Silver .1967 oz. ASW **Series:** Holyland Sites **Reverse:** Capernaum **Shape:** 12-sided

Date	Mintage	F	VF	XF	Unc	BU
JE5746-1985	6,010	—	—	—	16.50	—

KM# 110.1 SHEQEL **Weight:** 14.4000 g. **Composition:** 0.8500 Silver .3935 oz. ASW **Subject:** Hanukkah **Reverse:** Corfu lamp **Edge:** Plain

Date	Mintage	F	VF	XF	Unc	BU
JE5741-1980	24,000	—	—	—	12.00	—

KM# 110.2 SHEQEL **Weight:** 14.4000 g. **Composition:** 0.8500 Silver .3935 oz. ASW **Subject:** Hanukkah **Reverse:** Corfu lamp **Edge:** Reeded

Date	Mintage	F	VF	XF	Unc	BU
JE5741-1980 Proof	15,000	Value: 17.00				

KM# 111 SHEQEL **Composition:** Copper-Nickel **Reverse:** Chalice

Date	Mintage	F	VF	XF	Unc	BU
JE5741(1981)	154,540,000	—	—	0.65	0.85	—
JE5742 (1982)	15,850,000	—	—	0.65	0.85	—
JE5743 (1983)	26,360,000	—	—	0.65	0.85	—
JE5744 (1984)	32,205,000	—	—	0.65	0.85	—
JE5745 (1985)	500,000	—	—	1.00	4.00	—

KM# 116.1 SHEQEL **Weight:** 14.4000 g. **Composition:** 0.8500 Silver .3935 oz. ASW **Subject:** Hanukkah **Reverse:** Polish lamp **Edge:** Plain

Date	Mintage	F	VF	XF	Unc	BU
JE5742 -1981	16,000	—	—	—	10.00	—

KM# 116.2 SHEQEL **Weight:** 14.4000 g. **Composition:** 0.8500 Silver .3935 oz. ASW **Subject:** Hanukkah **Reverse:** Polish lamp **Edge:** Reeded

Date	Mintage	F	VF	XF	Unc	BU
JE5742 -1981 Proof	11,000	Value: 16.50				

KM# 122 SHEQEL **Weight:** 14.4000 g. **Composition:** 0.8500 Silver .3935 oz. ASW **Series:** Holyland Sites **Reverse:** Qumran Caves

Date	Mintage	F	VF	XF	Unc	BU
JE5743-1982 Proof	9,000	Value: 20.00				

KM# 123 SHEQEL **Weight:** 14.4000 g. **Composition:** 0.8500 Silver .3935 oz. ASW **Subject:** Hanukkah **Reverse:** Yeman lamp

Date	Mintage	F	VF	XF	Unc	BU
JE5743-1982 (1982)	14,000	—	—	—	13.50	—

KM# 129 SHEQEL **Weight:** 14.4000 g. **Composition:** 0.8500 Silver .3935 oz. ASW **Subject:** Hanukkah **Reverse:** Prague lamp

Date	Mintage	F	VF	XF	Unc	BU
JE5744-1983	13,000	—	—	—	12.00	—

KM# 128 SHEQEL **Weight:** 14.4000 g. **Composition:** 0.8500 Silver .3935 oz. ASW **Series:** Holyland Sites **Reverse:** Herodion Ruins **Shape:** 12-sided

Date	Mintage	F	VF	XF	Unc	BU
JE5744-1983 Proof	10,000	Value: 22.00				

KM# 127 SHEQEL **Weight:** 14.4000 g. **Composition:** 0.8500 Silver .3935 oz. ASW **Subject:** 35th Anniversary - State of Israel **Reverse:** Valour

Date	Mintage	F	VF	XF	Unc	BU
JE5743-1983	15,000	—	—	—	12.50	—

KM# 135 SHEQEL **Weight:** 14.4000 g. **Composition:** 0.8500 Silver .3935 oz. ASW **Subject:** 36th Anniversary - State of Israel **Reverse:** Kinsmen

Date	Mintage	F	VF	XF	Unc	BU
JE5744-1984	18,000	—	—	—	15.00	—

KM# 141 SHEQEL **Weight:** 14.4000 g. **Composition:** 0.8500 Silver .3935 oz. ASW **Series:** Holyland Sites **Reverse:** Kidron Valley **Shape:** 12-sided

Date	Mintage	F	VF	XF	Unc	BU
JE5745-1984 Proof	6,798	Value: 35.00				

KM# 144 SHEQEL **Weight:** 14.4000 g. **Composition:** 0.8500 Silver .3935 oz. ASW **Subject:** Hanukkah **Reverse:** Theresianstadt lamp

Date	Mintage	F	VF	XF	Unc	BU
JE5745-1984	11,000	—	—	—	15.00	—

KM# 148 SHEQEL **Weight:** 14.4000 g. **Composition:** 0.8500 Silver .3935 oz. ASW **Subject:** 36th Anniversary of Independence **Reverse:** Scientific Achievement

Date	Mintage	F	VF	XF	Unc	BU
JE5745-1985	8,520	—	—	—	14.50	—

KM# 155 SHEQEL **Weight:** 14.4000 g. **Composition:** 0.8500 Silver .3935 oz. ASW **Reverse:** Ancient ship

Date	Mintage	F	VF	XF	Unc	BU
JE5745-1985 Proof Like	13,000	—	—	—	22.00	—

KM# 153 SHEQEL **Weight:** 14.4000 g. **Composition:** 0.8500 Silver .3935 oz. ASW **Series:** Holyland Sites **Reverse:** Capernaum **Shape:** 12-sided

Date	Mintage	F	VF	XF	Unc	BU
JE5746-1985 Proof	6,010	Value: 25.00				

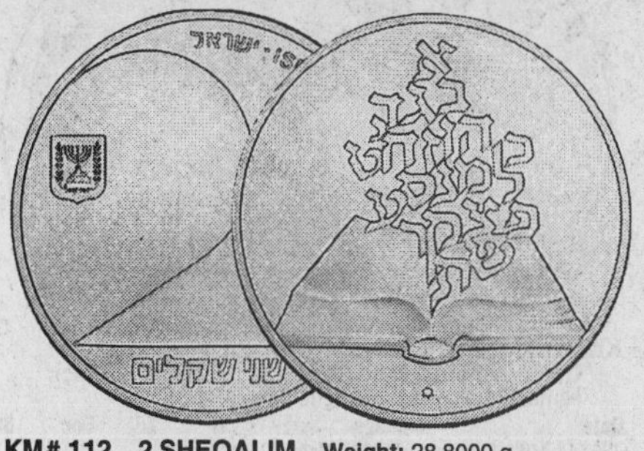

KM# 112 2 SHEQALIM **Weight:** 28.8000 g. **Composition:** 0.8250 Silver .7639 oz. ASW **Subject:** 33rd Anniversary of independence **Reverse:** People of the Book **Edge:** Lettered

Date	Mintage	F	VF	XF	Unc	BU
JE5741-1981	16,000	—	—	—	12.50	—
JE5741-1981 Proof	11,000	Value: 25.00				

KM# 117 2 SHEQALIM **Weight:** 28.8000 g. **Composition:** 0.8500 Silver .7871 oz. ASW **Subject:** 34th Anniversary of Independence **Reverse:** Baron Edmond de Rothschild **Edge:** Lettered

Date	Mintage	F	VF	XF	Unc	BU
JE5742-1982	13,000	—	—	—	18.00	—
JE5742-1982 Proof	9,506	Value: 28.00				

KM# 124 2 SHEQALIM **Weight:** 28.8000 g. **Composition:** 0.8500 Silver .7871 oz. ASW **Subject:** Hanukkah **Reverse:** Yemen lamp

Date	Mintage	F	VF	XF	Unc	BU
JE5743-1982 Proof	8,996	Value: 27.50				

KM# 130 2 SHEQALIM **Weight:** 28.8000 g. **Composition:** 0.8500 Silver .7871 oz. ASW **Subject:** 35th Anniversary of independence **Reverse:** Valour; similar to 1 Shequel, KM#127

Date	Mintage	F	VF	XF	Unc	BU
JE5743-1983 Proof	10,000	Value: 22.50				

KM# 131 2 SHEQALIM **Weight:** 28.8000 g. **Composition:** 0.8500 Silver .7871 oz. ASW **Subject:** Hanukkah **Reverse:** Prague lamp

Date	Mintage	F	VF	XF	Unc	BU
JE5744-1983 Proof	11,000	Value: 25.00				

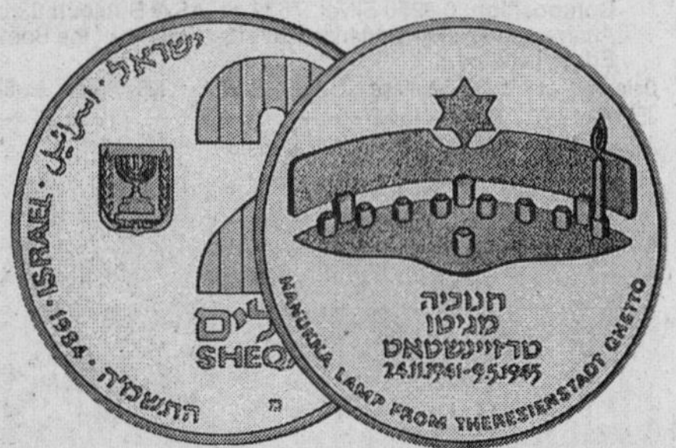

KM# 145 2 SHEQALIM **Weight:** 28.8000 g. **Composition:** 0.8500 Silver .7871 oz. ASW **Subject:** Hanukkah **Reverse:** Theresianstadt lamp

Date	Mintage	F	VF	XF	Unc	BU
JE5745-1984 Proof	10,000	Value: 30.00				

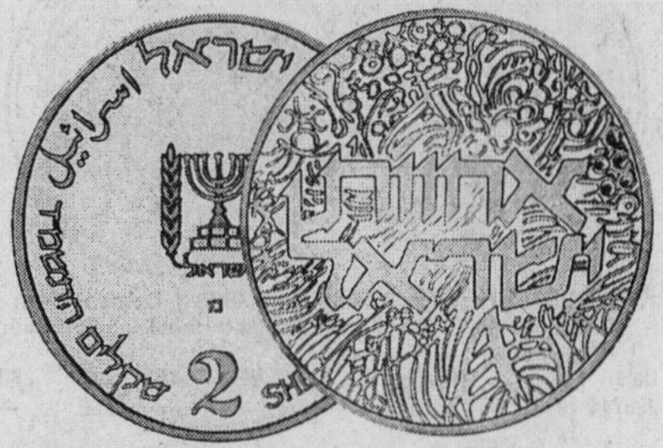

KM# 136 2 SHEQALIM **Weight:** 28.8000 g. **Composition:** 0.8500 Silver .7871 oz. ASW **Subject:** 36th Anniversary of independence **Reverse:** Kinsmen

Date	Mintage	F	VF	XF	Unc	BU
JE5744-1984 Proof	8,526	Value: 25.00				

KM# 149 2 SHEQALIM **Weight:** 28.8000 g. **Composition:** 0.8500 Silver .7871 oz. ASW **Subject:** 37th Anniversary of Independence **Reverse:** Scientific achievement

Date	Mintage	F	VF	XF	Unc	BU
JE5745-1985 Proof	8,330	Value: 28.00				

KM# 118 5 SHEQALIM **Composition:** Aluminum-Bronze **Series:** Cornucopiae

Date	Mintage	F	VF	XF	Unc	BU
JE5742 (1982)	30,000,000	—	—	0.75	1.25	—
JE5743 (1983)	994,000	—	—	1.00	2.00	—
JE5744 (1984)	17,389,000	—	—	0.75	1.25	—
JE5745 (1985)	250,000	—	—	1.00	2.50	—

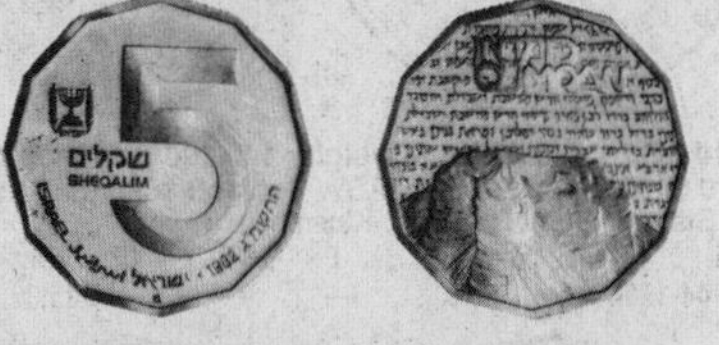

KM# 125 5 SHEQALIM **Weight:** 8.6300 g. **Composition:** 0.9000 Gold .2497 oz. AGW **Series:** Holyland Sites **Reverse:** Qumran Caves **Shape:** 12-sided

Date	Mintage	F	VF	XF	Unc	BU
JE5743-1982 Proof	4,927	Value: 170				

KM# 132 5 SHEQALIM **Weight:** 0.8630 g. **Composition:** 0.9000 Gold .2497 oz. AGW **Series:** Holyland Sites **Reverse:** Herodion Ruins **Shape:** 12-sided

Date	Mintage	F	VF	XF	Unc	BU
JE5744-1983 Proof	4,346	Value: 170				

KM# 142 5 SHEQALIM **Weight:** 8.6300 g. **Composition:** 0.9000 Gold .2497 oz. AGW **Series:** Holyland Sites **Reverse:** Kidron Valley **Shape:** 12-sided

Date	Mintage	F	VF	XF	Unc	BU
JE5745 -1984 Proof	2,601	Value: 370				

KM# 154 5 SHEQALIM **Weight:** 8.6300 g. **Composition:** 0.9000 Gold .2497 oz. AGW **Series:** Holyland Sites **Reverse:** Capernaum **Shape:** 12-sided

Date	Mintage	F	VF	XF	Unc	BU
JE5746-1985 Proof	2,633	Value: 275				

KM# 113 10 SHEQALIM **Weight:** 17.2800 g. **Composition:** 0.9000 Gold .5000 oz. AGW **Subject:** 33rd Anniversary of independence **Reverse:** People of the book

Date	Mintage	F	VF	XF	Unc	BU
JE5741-1981 Proof	5,673	Value: 250				

KM# 120 10 SHEQALIM **Weight:** 17.2800 g. **Composition:** 0.9000 Gold .5000 oz. AGW **Subject:** 34th Anniversary of Independence **Reverse:** Baron Edmond de Rothschild facing

Date	Mintage	F	VF	XF	Unc	BU
JE5742-1982 Proof	4,875	Value: 250				

KM# 119 10 SHEQALIM **Composition:** Copper-Nickel **Obverse:** Ancient Galley

Date	Mintage	F	VF	XF	Unc	BU
JE5742 (1982)	36,084,000	—	—	0.75	1.25	—
JE5743 (1983)	17,851,000	—	—	0.75	1.25	—
JE5744 (1984)	31,950,000	—	—	0.75	1.25	—
JE5745 (1985)	25,864,000	—	—	0.50	0.75	—

KM# 134 10 SHEQALIM **Composition:** Copper-Nickel **Subject:** Hanukkah

Date	Mintage	F	VF	XF	Unc	BU
JE5744 (1983)	2,000,000	—	—	1.00	1.50	—
JE5744 (1984)	—	—	—	1.00	1.50	—

KM# 133 10 SHEQALIM **Weight:** 17.2800 g. **Composition:** 0.9000 Gold .5000 oz. AGW **Subject:** 35th Anniversary of Independence **Reverse:** Valour

Date	Mintage	F	VF	XF	Unc	BU
JE5743-1983 Proof	3,650	Value: 360				

KM# 138 10 SHEQALIM **Weight:** 17.2800 g. **Composition:** 0.9000 Gold .5000 oz. AGW **Subject:** 36th Anniversary of Independence **Reverse:** Kinsmen

Date	Mintage	F	VF	XF	Unc	BU
JE5744-1984 Proof	3,798	Value: 360				

KM# 137 10 SHEQALIM **Composition:** Copper-Nickel **Obverse:** Head of Theodor Herzl left

Date	Mintage	F	VF	XF	Unc	BU
JE5744 (1984)	2,003,000	—	—	1.00	1.50	—

KM# 150 10 SHEQALIM **Weight:** 17.2800 g. **Composition:** 0.9000 Gold .5000 oz. AGW **Subject:** 37th Anniversary of Independence **Reverse:** Scientific Achievement, pomegranate

Date	Mintage	F	VF	XF	Unc	BU
JE5745-1985 Proof	3,240	Value: 375				

KM# 114.1 25 SHEQEL **Weight:** 26.0000 g. **Composition:** 0.9000 Silver .7524 oz. ASW **Subject:** 100th Anniversary - Birth of Zeev Jabotinsky

Date	Mintage	F	VF	XF	Unc	BU
JE5741-1980	14,000	—	—	—	15.00	—

KM# 114.2 25 SHEQEL **Weight:** 26.0000 g. **Composition:** 0.9000 Silver .7524 oz. ASW **Subject:** 100th Anniversary - Birth of Zeev Jabotinsky **Edge:** Reeded

Date	Mintage	F	VF	XF	Unc	BU
JE5741-1980 Proof	12,000	Value: 25.00				

KM# 139 50 SHEQALIM **Composition:** Aluminum-Bronze **Obverse:** Ancient coin

Date	Mintage	F	VF	XF	Unc	BU
JE5744 (1984)	13,994,000	—	—	0.50	1.00	—
JE5745 (1985)	1,000,000	—	—	0.75	1.50	—

KM# 147 50 SHEQALIM **Composition:** Aluminum-Bronze **Obverse:** Head of David Ben Gurion left

Date	Mintage	F	VF	XF	Unc	BU
JE5745 (1985)	1,000,000	—	—	1.00	1.50	—

KM# 143 100 SHEQALIM **Composition:** Copper-Nickel **Obverse:** Menorah

Date	Mintage	F	VF	XF	Unc	BU
JE5744 (1984)	30,028,000	—	—	1.00	2.00	—
JE5745 (1985)	19,638,000	—	—	1.00	2.00	—

KM# 146 100 SHEQALIM **Composition:** Copper-Nickel **Subject:** Hanukkah **Obverse:** Menorah

Date	Mintage	F	VF	XF	Unc	BU
JE5745 (1984)	2,000,000	—	—	1.25	2.25	—
JE5745 (1985)	—	—	—	1.25	2.25	—

KM# 151 100 SHEQALIM **Composition:** Copper-Nickel **Obverse:** Head of Zeev Jabotinsky

Date	Mintage	F	VF	XF	Unc	BU
JE5745 (1985)	2,000,000	—	—	1.25	2.25	—

KM# 115 500 SHEQEL **Weight:** 17.2800 g. **Composition:** 0.9000 Gold .5000 oz. AGW **Subject:** 100th Anniversary - Birth of Zeev Jabotinsky

Date	Mintage	F	VF	XF	Unc	BU
JE5741-1980 Proof	7,471	Value: 250				

REFORM COINAGE

10 Sheqalim = 1 Agorah; 1000 Sheqalim = 1 New Sheqel

September 4, 1985

KM# 156 AGORAH **Composition:** Aluminum-Bronze **Obverse:** Ancient ship

Date	Mintage	F	VF	XF	Unc	BU
JE5745 (1985)	58,144,000	—	—	—	0.50	—
JE5746 (1986)	95,272,000	—	—	—	0.50	—
JE5747 (1987)	1,080,000	—	—	—	0.50	—
JE5748 (1988)	15,768,000	—	—	—	0.50	—
JE5749 (1989)	10,801,000	—	—	—	0.50	—
JE5750 (1990)	4,968,000	—	—	—	0.50	—
JE5751 (1991) In sets only	10,000	—	—	—	1.00	—
JE5754 (1994)	8,000	—	—	—	0.50	—
JE5755 (1995)	10,000	—	—	—	0.50	—
JE5756 (1996)	—	—	—	—	0.50	—

KM# 171 AGORAH **Composition:** Aluminum-Bronze **Subject:** Hanukkah

Date	Mintage	F	VF	XF	Unc	BU
JE5747 (1986)	1,004,000	—	—	0.15	0.75	—
JE5748 (1987)	540,000	—	—	0.15	0.75	—
JE5748 (1988)	504,000	—	—	0.15	0.75	—
JE5749 (1988)	Inc. above	—	—	0.15	0.75	—
JE5750 (1989)	2,160,000	—	—	0.15	0.75	—
JE5751 (1990)	4,968,000	—	—	0.15	0.75	—
JE5752 (1991)	—	—	—	0.15	0.75	—
JE5756 (1996)	—	—	—	0.15	0.75	—

KM# 193 AGORAH **Composition:** Aluminum-Bronze **Subject:** 40th Anniversary of Independence **Obverse:** Ancient ship

Date	Mintage	F	VF	XF	Unc	BU
JE5748 (1988)	504,000	—	—	—	0.25	—

KM# 157 5 AGOROT **Composition:** Aluminum-Bronze

Date	Mintage	F	VF	XF	Unc	BU
JE5745 (1985)	34,504,000	—	—	0.10	0.15	—
JE5746 (1986)	12,384,000	—	—	0.10	0.15	—
JE5747 (1987)	14,257,000	—	—	0.10	0.15	—
JE5748 (1988)	9,360,000	—	—	0.10	0.15	—
JE5749 (1989)	4,896,000	—	—	0.10	0.15	—
JE5750 (1990)	576,000	—	—	0.10	0.15	—
JE5751 (1991)	4,464,000	—	—	0.10	0.15	—
JE5752 (1992)	—	—	—	0.10	0.15	—
JE5753 (1993)	8,000	—	—	0.10	0.15	—
JE5754 (1994)	8,000	—	—	0.10	0.15	—
JE5755 (1995)	7,500	—	—	0.10	0.15	—
JE5757 (1997)	—	—	—	0.10	0.15	—
JE5758 (1998)	—	—	—	0.10	0.15	—
1999	—	—	—	0.10	0.15	—
2000	—	—	—	0.10	0.15	—

KM# 172 5 AGOROT **Composition:** Aluminum-Bronze **Subject:** Hanukkah

Date	Mintage	F	VF	XF	Unc	BU
JE5747 (1986)	1,004,000	—	—	0.10	0.30	—
JE5748 (1987)	536,000	—	—	0.10	0.30	—
JE5749 (1988)	504,000	—	—	0.10	0.30	—
JE5750 (1989)	2,016,000	—	—	0.10	0.30	—
JE5751 (1990)	1,488,000	—	—	0.10	0.30	—
JE5752 (1991)	—	—	—	0.10	0.30	—
JE5753 (1992)	960,000	—	—	0.10	0.30	—

Date	Mintage	F	VF	XF	Unc	BU
JE5753 (1993)	12,000	—	—	0.10	0.30	—
JE5754 (1993)	12,000	—	—	0.10	0.30	—
JE5755 (1994)	—	—	—	0.10	0.30	—
JE5756 (1995)	—	—	—	0.10	0.30	—
JE5757 (1996)	—	—	—	0.10	0.30	—
JE5761 (2000)	—	—	—	—	—	—

KM# 194 5 AGOROT Composition: Aluminum-Bronze **Subject:** 40th Anniversary of Independence

Date	Mintage	F	VF	XF	Unc	BU
JE5748 (1988)	504,000	—	—	—	0.30	—

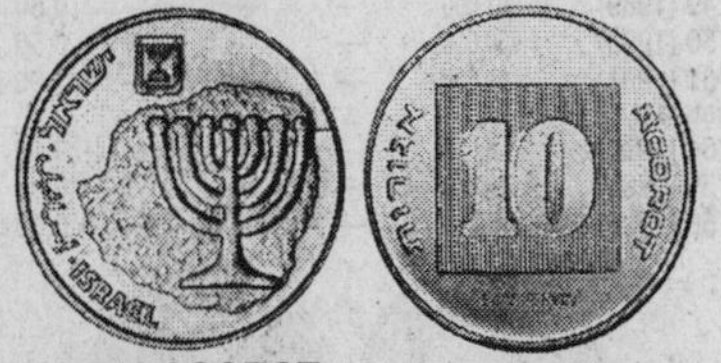

KM# 158 10 AGOROT Composition: Aluminum-Bronze **Obverse:** Menorah

Date	Mintage	F	VF	XF	Unc	BU
JE5745 (1985)	45,000,000	—	—	0.10	0.20	—
JE5746 (1986)	92,754,000	—	—	0.10	0.20	—
JE5747 (1987)	19,351,000	—	—	0.10	0.20	—
JE5748 (1988)	8,640,000	—	—	0.10	0.20	—
JE5749 (1989)	420,000	—	—	0.10	0.20	—
JE5750 (1990)	2,376,000	—	—	0.10	0.20	—
JE5751 (1991)	59,425,000	—	—	0.10	0.20	—

Note: Exist with 6mm or 7mm long date; thick or thin letters; and 7mm or 7.5mm value 10

Date	Mintage	F	VF	XF	Unc	BU
JE5752 (1992)	—	—	—	0.10	0.20	—
JE5753 (1993)	25,920,000	—	—	0.10	0.20	—
JE5754 (1994)	—	—	—	0.10	0.20	—
JE5755 (1995)	—	—	—	0.10	0.20	—
JE5756	—	—	—	0.10	0.20	—
JE5757 (1997)	—	—	—	0.10	0.20	—
JE5758	—	—	—	0.10	0.20	—
JE5759 (1999)	—	—	—	0.10	0.20	—
JE5760(2000)	—	—	—	0.10	0.20	—
JE5761(2001)	—	—	—	0.10	0.20	—

KM# 173 10 AGOROT Composition: Aluminum-Bronze **Subject:** Hanukkah **Obverse:** Menorah

Date	Mintage	F	VF	XF	Unc	BU
JE5747 (1986)	1,004,000	—	—	0.10	0.40	—
JE5748 (1987)	834,000	—	—	0.10	0.40	—
JE5749 (1988)	798,000	—	—	0.10	0.40	—
JE5750 (1989)	2,052,000	—	—	0.10	0.40	—
JE5751 (1990)	1,488,000	—	—	0.10	0.40	—
JE5752 (1991)	—	—	—	0.10	0.40	—
JE5753 (1992)	1,404,000	—	—	0.10	0.40	—
JE5754 (1993)	12,000	—	—	0.10	0.40	—
JE5755 (1994)	12,000	—	—	0.10	0.40	—
JE5756 (1995)	—	—	—	0.10	0.40	—
JE5757 (1996)	—	—	—	0.10	0.40	—
JE5758 (1997)	—	—	—	0.10	0.40	—
JE5761 (2000)	—	—	—	—	—	—

KM# 195 10 AGOROT Composition: Aluminum-Bronze **Subject:** 40th Anniversary of Independence **Obverse:** Menorah

Date	Mintage	F	VF	XF	Unc	BU
JE5748 (1988)	504,000	—	—	—	0.40	—

KM# 356 SHEQEL Weight: 14.4000 g. **Composition:** 0.9250 Silver 0.4282 oz. ASW **Subject:** Independence - Volunteering **Obverse:** Denomination **Reverse:** Heart in hands **Edge:** Plain **Size:** 30 mm.

Date	Mintage	F	VF	XF	Unc	BU
JE5762(2002) Prooflike	3,000	—	—	—	—	—

KM# 159 1/2 NEW SHEQEL Composition: Aluminum-Bronze **Reverse:** Lyre.

Date	Mintage	F	VF	XF	Unc	BU
JE5745 (1985) trimmed thin E	20,328,000	—	—	0.35	0.75	—
JE5745(1985) thick E	—	—	—	0.35	0.75	—
JE5746 (1986)	4,392,000	—	—	0.35	0.75	—
JE5747 (1987)	144,000	—	—	0.35	2.00	—
JE5748 (1988) In sets only	20,000	—	—	—	3.00	—
JE5749 (1989)	756,000	—	—	0.35	0.75	—
JE5750 (1990)	648,000	—	—	0.35	0.75	—
JE5751 (1991)	288,000	—	—	0.35	0.75	—
JE5752 (1992)	—	—	—	0.35	0.75	—
JE5753 (1992)	5,184,000	—	—	0.35	0.75	—
JE5754 (1993)	8,000	—	—	0.35	0.75	—
JE5755 (1994)	8,000	—	—	0.35	0.75	—
JE5755 (1995)	10,000	—	—	0.35	0.75	—
JE5757 (1997)	—	—	—	0.35	0.75	—
JE5758 (1998)	—	—	—	0.35	0.75	—
JE5759 (1999)	—	—	—	0.35	0.75	—
JE5762 (2002)	—	—	—	0.35	0.75	—

KM# 167 1/2 NEW SHEQEL Composition: Aluminum-Bronze **Reverse:** Baron Edmund de Rothschild

Date	Mintage	F	VF	XF	Unc	BU
JE5746 (1986)	2,000,000	—	—	1.00	5.00	—

KM# 168 1/2 NEW SHEQEL Weight: 7.2000 g. **Composition:** 0.8500 Silver .1967 oz. ASW **Series:** Holyland Sites **Reverse:** Akko **Shape:** 12-sided

Date	Mintage	F	VF	XF	Unc	BU
JE5747-1986	6,224	—	—	—	12.50	—

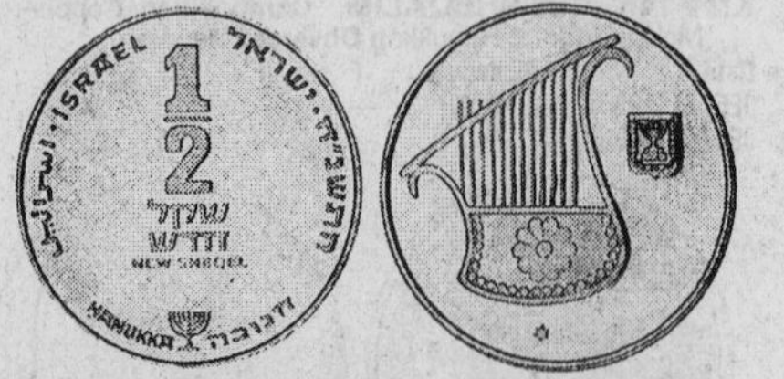

KM# 174 1/2 NEW SHEQEL Composition: Aluminum-Bronze **Subject:** Hanukkah **Reverse:** Lyre

Date	Mintage	F	VF	XF	Unc	BU
JE5747 (1986)	1,004,000	—	—	0.35	0.85	—
JE5748 (1987)	532,000	—	—	0.35	0.85	—
JE5749 (1988)	504,000	—	—	0.35	0.85	—
JE5750 (1989)	2,016,000	—	—	0.35	0.85	—
JE5751 (1990)	960,000	—	—	0.35	0.85	—
JE5752 (1991)	—	—	—	0.35	0.85	—
JE5753 (1992)	304,000	—	—	0.35	0.85	—
JE5754 (1993)	12,000	—	—	0.35	0.85	—
JE5755 (1994)	12,000	—	—	0.35	0.85	—
JE5756 (1995)	—	—	—	0.35	0.85	—
JE5757 (1996)	—	—	—	0.35	0.85	—
JE5758 (1997)	—	—	—	0.35	0.85	—
JE5761 (2000)	—	—	—	—	—	—

KM# 180 1/2 NEW SHEQEL Weight: 7.2000 g. **Composition:** 0.8500 Silver .1967 oz. ASW **Series:** Holyland Sites **Reverse:** Jericho **Shape:** 12-sided

Date	Mintage	F	VF	XF	Unc	BU
JE5748-1987	7,590	—	—	—	13.50	—

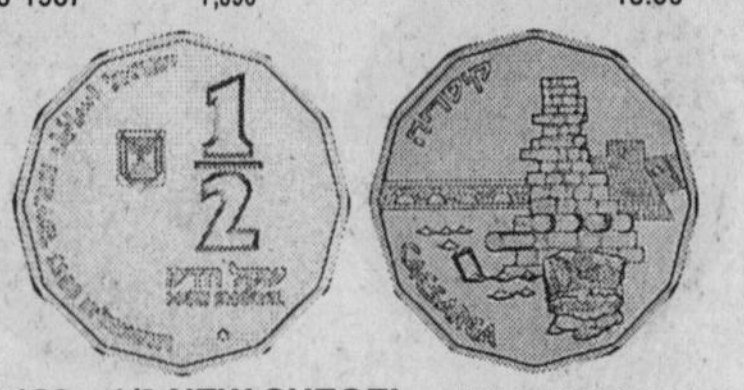

KM# 188 1/2 NEW SHEQEL Weight: 7.2000 g. **Composition:** 0.8500 Silver .1967 oz. ASW **Series:** Holyland Sites **Reverse:** Caesarea **Shape:** 12-sided

Date	Mintage	F	VF	XF	Unc	BU
JE5749-1988	5,865	—	—	—	15.00	—

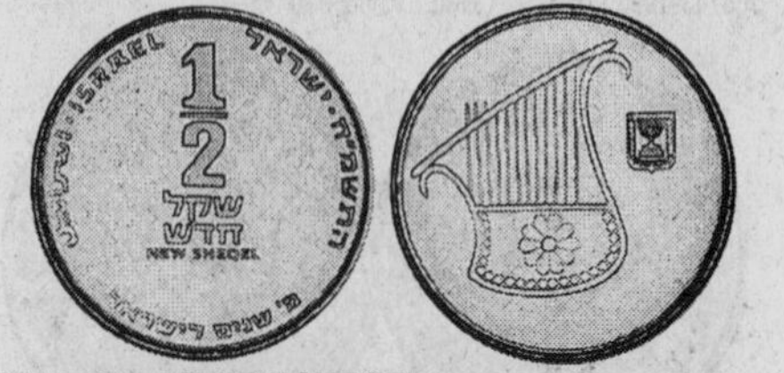

KM# 196 1/2 NEW SHEQEL Composition: Aluminum-Bronze **Subject:** 40th Anniversary of Independence **Reverse:** Lyre

Date	Mintage	F	VF	XF	Unc	BU
JE5748 (1988)	500,000	—	—	—	0.50	—

KM# 202 1/2 NEW SHEQEL Weight: 7.2000 g. **Composition:** 0.8500 Silver .1967 oz. ASW **Subject:** Holyland sites **Reverse:** Jaffa Harbor **Shape:** 12-sided

Date	Mintage	F	VF	XF	Unc	BU
JE5750-1989	4,940	—	—	—	24.00	—

KM# 209 1/2 NEW SHEQEL Weight: 7.2000 g. **Composition:** 0.8500 Silver .1967 oz. ASW **Subject:** Holyland sites **Reverse:** Sea of Galilee sites, map **Shape:** 12-sided

Date	Mintage	F	VF	XF	Unc	BU
JE5751-1990	4,346	—	—	—	25.00	—

KM# 303 1/2 NEW SHEQEL Composition: Copper-Aluminum-Nickel **Series:** Hanukka **Obverse:** Denomination **Reverse:** Theresienstadt lamp **Note:** Struck for sets only.

Date	Mintage	F	VF	XF	Unc	BU
JE5754 (1993)	12,000	—	—	—	8.00	—

KM# 304 1/2 NEW SHEQEL Composition: Copper-Aluminum-Nickel **Series:** Hanukka **Obverse:** Denomination **Reverse:** Early American lamp **Note:** Struck for sets only.

Date	Mintage	F	VF	XF	Unc	BU
JE5755 (1994)	12,000	—	—	—	8.00	—

KM# 305 1/2 NEW SHEQEL Composition: Copper-Aluminum-Nickel **Series:** Hanukka **Obverse:** Denomination **Reverse:** 14th century French lamp **Note:** Struck for sets only.

Date	Mintage	F	VF	XF	Unc	BU
JE5756 (1995)	7,500	—	—	—	10.00	—

KM# 318 1/2 NEW SHEQEL Composition: Copper-Aluminum-Nickel **Series:** Hanukka **Obverse:** Denomination **Reverse:** Russian lamp **Note:** Struck for sets only.

Date	F	VF	XF	Unc	BU
JE5757 (1996)	—	—	—	8.00	—

KM# 314 1/2 NEW SHEQEL Composition: Copper-Aluminum-Nickel **Series:** Hanukka **Obverse:** Denomination **Reverse:** English lamp **Note:** Struck for sets only.

Date	Mintage	F	VF	XF	Unc	BU
JE5758 (1997)	10,000	—	—	—	8.00	—

KM# 331 1/2 NEW SHEQEL Composition: Copper-Aluminum-Nickel **Series:** Hanukka **Obverse:** Menorah **Note:** Struck for sets only.

Date	F	VF	XF	Unc	BU
JE5759 (1998)	—	—	—	8.00	—

KM# 324 1/2 NEW SHEQEL **Composition:** Bronze **Subject:** High Tech in Israel **Obverse:** Cypruss trees, demonimation **Reverse:** Mosaic bouquet **Note:** Struck for sets only.

Date	F	VF	XF	Unc	BU
JE5760 (1999)	—	—	—	8.00	—

KM# 332 1/2 NEW SHEQEL **Composition:** Copper-Aluminum-Nickel **Reverse:** Jerusalem Hanukkah lamp **Note:** Struck for sets only.

Date	F	VF	XF	Unc	BU
JE5760 (1999)	—	—	—	8.00	—

KM# 354 1/2 NEW SHEQEL **Weight:** 6.5000 g. **Composition:** Copper-Aluminum-Nickel **Subject:** Hanukka **Obverse:** Denomination **Reverse:** Curacao Hanukka lamp **Edge:** Plain **Shape:** 12-sided **Size:** 25.5 mm.

Date	Mintage	F	VF	XF	Unc	BU
JE5761 (2000)	4,000	—	—	—	8.00	—

KM# 160 NEW SHEQEL **Composition:** Copper-Nickel

Date	Mintage	F	VF	XF	Unc	BU
JE5745 (1985)	29,088,000	—	—	0.65	1.50	—
JE5746 (1986)	20,960,000	—	—	0.65	1.50	—
JE5747 (1987)	216,000	—	—	0.65	3.00	—
JE5748 (1988)	20,376,000	—	—	0.65	1.50	—
JE5749 (1989)	8,706,000	—	—	0.65	1.50	—
JE5750 (1990)	756,000	—	—	0.65	1.50	—
JE5751 (1991)	1,152,000	—	—	0.65	1.50	—
JE5752 (1992)	—	—	—	0.65	1.50	—
JE5753 (1993)	8,640,000	—	—	0.65	1.50	—
JE5754 (1994)	8,000	—	—	0.65	1.50	—
JE5755 (1995)	10,000	—	—	0.65	1.50	—
JS5757 (1997)	—	—	—	0.65	1.50	—
JS5758 (1998)	—	—	—	0.65	1.50	—
JS5759 (1999)	—	—	—	0.65	1.50	—
JS5760 (2000)	—	—	—	0.65	1.50	—
JS5761 (2001)	—	—	—	0.65	1.50	—
JS5762 (2002)	—	—	—	0.65	1.50	—

KM# 160a NEW SHEQEL **Composition:** Nickel Clad Steel

Date	F	VF	XF	Unc	BU
JE5754 (1994)	—	—	—	1.00	—
JE5754 (1994)(o)	—	—	—	1.00	—
JE5755 (1995)	—	—	—	1.00	—
JE5755 (1995)(o)	—	—	—	1.00	—
JE5756 (1996)(o)	—	—	—	1.00	—
JE5757 (1997)	—	—	—	1.00	—
JE5758 (1998)	—	—	—	1.00	—
JE5759 (1999)	—	—	—	1.00	—
JE5760 (2000)(o)	—	—	—	1.00	—

KM# 161 NEW SHEQEL **Weight:** 14.4000 g. **Composition:** 0.8500 Silver .3935 oz. ASW **Subject:** Hanukkah **Reverse:** Ashkenaz lamp

Date	Mintage	F	VF	XF	Unc	BU
JE5746-1985	9,460	—	—	—	14.00	—

KM# 163 NEW SHEQEL **Composition:** Copper-Nickel **Subject:** Hanukkah

Date	Mintage	F	VF	XF	Unc	BU
JE5746 (1985)	1,056,000	—	—	0.65	1.50	—
JE5747 (1986)	1,004,000	—	—	0.65	1.50	—
JE5748 (1987)	534,000	—	—	0.65	1.50	—
JE5749 (1988)	504,000	—	—	0.65	1.50	—
JE5750 (1989)	2,052,000	—	—	0.65	1.50	—
JE5751 (1990)	1,104,000	—	—	0.65	1.50	—
JE5752 (1991)	—	—	—	0.65	1.50	—
JE5753 (1992)	922,000	—	—	0.65	1.50	—
JE5754 (1993)	12,000	—	—	0.65	1.50	—
JE5755 (1994)	12,000	—	—	0.65	1.50	—
JE5756 (1995)	7,500	—	—	0.65	1.50	—
JE5757 (1996)	—	—	—	0.65	1.50	—
JE5758 (1997)	—	—	—	0.65	1.50	—
JE5761 (2000)	—	—	—	—	—	—

KM# 164 NEW SHEQEL **Weight:** 14.4000 g. **Composition:** 0.8500 Silver .3935 oz. ASW **Subject:** 38th Anniversary of Independence **Reverse:** Tribute to the arts

Date	Mintage	F	VF	XF	Unc	BU
JE5746-1986	8,010	—	—	—	18.00	—

KM# 169 NEW SHEQEL **Weight:** 14.4000 g. **Composition:** 0.8500 Silver .3935 oz. ASW **Series:** Holyland Sites **Reverse:** Akko **Shape:** 12-sided

Date	Mintage	F	VF	XF	Unc	BU
JE5747-1986 Proof	6,117	Value: 22.00				

KM# 175 NEW SHEQEL **Weight:** 14.4000 g. **Composition:** 0.8500 Silver .3935 oz. ASW **Subject:** Hanukkah **Reverse:** Algerian lamp

Date	Mintage	F	VF	XF	Unc	BU
JE5747-1986	8,227	—	—	—	18.00	—

KM# 177 NEW SHEQEL **Weight:** 14.4000 g. **Composition:** 0.8500 Silver .3935 oz. ASW **Subject:** 20th Anniversary - United Jerusalem

Date	Mintage	F	VF	XF	Unc	BU
JE5747-1987	8,107	—	—	—	15.00	—

KM# 181 NEW SHEQEL **Weight:** 14.4000 g. **Composition:** 0.8500 Silver .3935 oz. ASW **Series:** Holyland Sites **Reverse:** Jericho **Shape:** 12-sided

Date	Mintage	F	VF	XF	Unc	BU
JE5748-1987 Proof	8,196	Value: 25.00				

KM# 183 NEW SHEQEL **Weight:** 14.4000 g. **Composition:** 0.8500 Silver .3935 oz. ASW **Subject:** Hanukkah **Reverse:** English lamp

Date	Mintage	F	VF	XF	Unc	BU
JE5748-1987	7,810	—	—	—	22.00	—

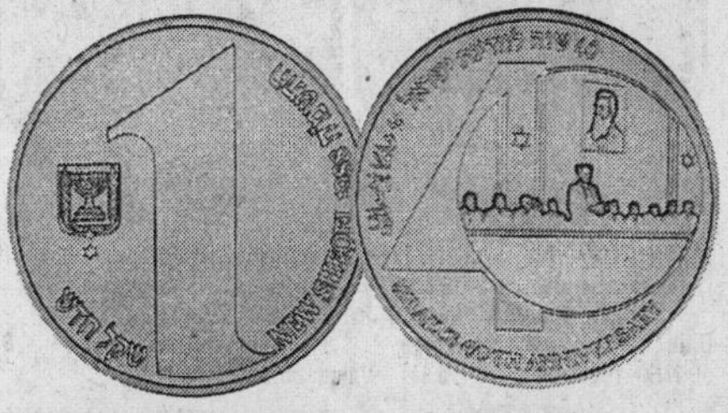

KM# 185 NEW SHEQEL **Weight:** 14.4000 g. **Composition:** 0.8500 Silver .3935 oz. ASW **Subject:** 40th Anniversary of Independence

Date	Mintage	F	VF	XF	Unc	BU
JE5748-1988	8,990	—	—	—	13.50	—

KM# 189 NEW SHEQEL **Weight:** 14.4000 g. **Composition:** 0.8500 Silver .3935 oz. ASW **Series:** Holyland Sites **Reverse:** Caesarea **Shape:** 12-sided

Date	Mintage	F	VF	XF	Unc	BU
JE5749-1988 Proof	6,560	Value: 35.00				

KM# 191 NEW SHEQEL **Weight:** 14.4000 g. **Composition:** 0.8500 Silver .3935 oz. ASW **Subject:** Hanukkah **Reverse:** Tunisian lamp

Date	Mintage	F	VF	XF	Unc	BU
JE5749-1988	6,688	—	—	—	25.00	—

KM# 197 NEW SHEQEL **Composition:** Copper-Nickel **Subject:** 40th Anniversary of Independence

Date	Mintage	F	VF	XF	Unc	BU
JE5748 (1988)	504,000	—	—	—	1.75	—

KM# 198 NEW SHEQEL **Composition:** Copper-Nickel **Reverse:** Maimonides

Date	Mintage	F	VF	XF	Unc	BU
JE5748 (1988)	980,000	—	—	—	1.75	—

KM# 199 NEW SHEQEL **Weight:** 14.4000 g. **Composition:** 0.8500 Silver .3935 oz. ASW **Subject:** 41th Anniversary of Independence

Date	Mintage	F	VF	XF	Unc	BU
JE5749-1989	6,249	—	—	—	22.00	—

KM# 203 NEW SHEQEL **Weight:** 14.4000 g. **Composition:** 0.8500 Silver .3935 oz. ASW **Subject:** Holyland sites **Reverse:** Jaffa Harbor **Shape:** 12-sided

Date	Mintage	F	VF	XF	Unc	BU
JE5750-1989 Proof	5,844	Value: 35.00				

KM# 205 NEW SHEQEL **Weight:** 14.4000 g. **Composition:** 0.8500 Silver .3935 oz. ASW **Subject:** Hanukkah **Reverse:** Persian lamp

Date	Mintage	F	VF	XF	Unc	BU
JE5750-1989	6,171	—	—	—	22.00	—

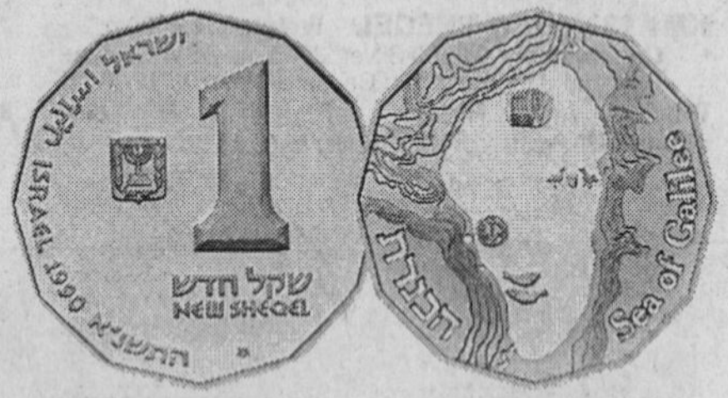

KM# 210 NEW SHEQEL **Weight:** 14.4000 g. **Composition:** 0.8500 Silver .3935 oz. ASW **Subject:** Holyland sites **Reverse:** Sea of Galilee sites, map **Shape:** 12-sided

Date	Mintage	F	VF	XF	Unc	BU
JE5751-1990 Proof	4,735	Value: 40.00				

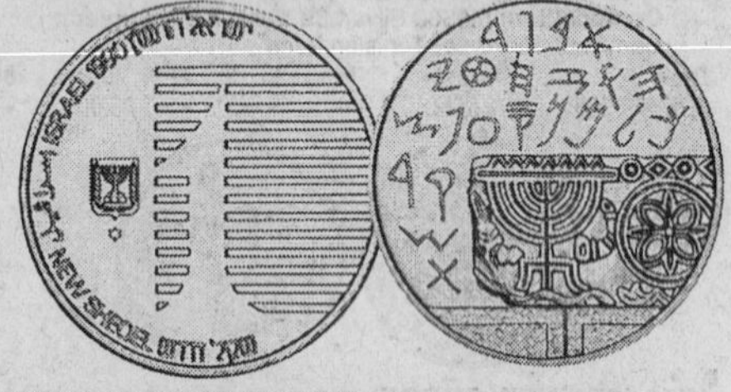

KM# 212 NEW SHEQEL **Weight:** 14.4000 g. **Composition:** 0.8500 Silver .3935 oz. ASW **Subject:** 42th Anniversary of Independence **Reverse:** Archaeology

Date	Mintage	F	VF	XF	Unc	BU
JE5750-1990	5,509	—	—	—	22.50	—

KM# 215 NEW SHEQEL **Weight:** 14.4000 g. **Composition:** 0.8500 Silver .3935 oz. ASW **Subject:** Hanukkah **Reverse:** Cochin lamp

Date	Mintage	F	VF	XF	Unc	BU
JE5751-1990	5,259	—	—	—	22.50	—

KM# 218 NEW SHEQEL **Weight:** 14.4000 g. **Composition:** 0.9250 Silver .4282 oz. ASW **Subject:** 43th Anniversary of independence **Reverse:** Immigration to Israel

Date	F	VF	XF	Unc	BU
JE5751-1991	—	—	—	20.00	—

KM# 220 NEW SHEQEL **Weight:** 14.4000 g. **Composition:** 0.9250 Silver .4282 oz. ASW **Subject:** Wildlife **Reverse:** Cedar trees and dove **Note:** Similar to 2 New Sheqalim, KM#221.

Date	Mintage	F	VF	XF	Unc	BU
JE5752-1991	4,125	—	—	—	25.00	—

KM# 223 NEW SHEQEL **Weight:** 14.4000 g. **Composition:** 0.9250 Silver .4282 oz. ASW **Series:** Judaic **Reverse:** Kiddush cup

Date	Mintage	F	VF	XF	Unc	BU
JE5752-1991	4,876	—	—	—	25.00	—

KM# 342 NEW SHEQEL **Weight:** 3.4600 g. **Composition:** 0.9000 Gold .1001 oz. AGW **Subject:** Wildlife **Reverse:** Cedar trees and dove **Note:** Similar to 2 New Sheqalim, KM#221.

Date	Mintage	F	VF	XF	Unc	BU
JE5752-1991 Proof	2,515	Value: 125				

KM# 225 NEW SHEQEL **Weight:** 14.4000 g. **Composition:** 0.9250 Silver .4282 oz. ASW **Subject:** 44th Anniversary of Independence **Reverse:** Israeli law

Date	Mintage	F	VF	XF	Unc	BU
JE5752-1992	4,047	—	—	—	35.00	—

KM# 231 NEW SHEQEL **Weight:** 14.4000 g. **Composition:** 0.9250 Silver .4282 oz. ASW **Series:** Wildlife **Reverse:** Roe and lily

Date	Mintage	F	VF	XF	Unc	BU
JE5752-1992	4,105	—	—	—	22.50	—

KM# 231a NEW SHEQEL **Weight:** 3.4600 g. **Composition:** 0.9000 Gold .1001 oz. AGW **Series:** Wildlife **Reverse:** Roe and Lily

Date	Mintage	F	VF	XF	Unc	BU
JE5752-1992	2,000	Value: 125				

KM# 234 NEW SHEQEL **Weight:** 14.4000 g. **Composition:** 0.9250 Silver .4282 oz. ASW **Series:** Judaic **Subject:** B'nai B'rith - 150th Anniversary.

Date	Mintage	F	VF	XF	Unc	BU
JE5752-1992	4,034	—	—	—	25.00	—

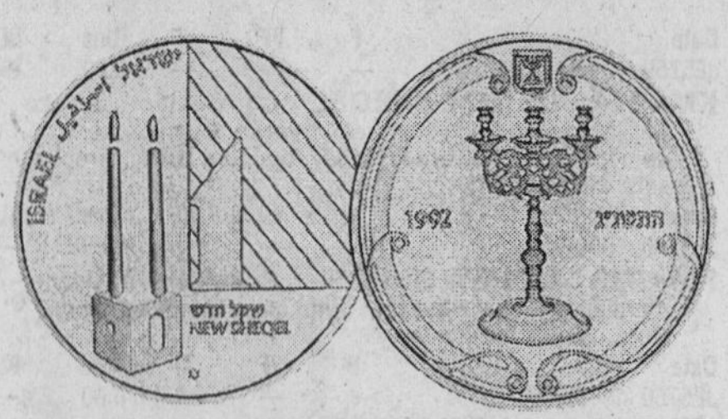

KM# 238 NEW SHEQEL **Weight:** 14.4000 g. **Composition:** 0.9250 Silver .4282 oz. ASW **Series:** Judaic **Reverse:** Shabbat candles

Date	Mintage	F	VF	XF	Unc	BU
JE5753-1992	5,564	—	—	—	25.00	—

KM# 343 NEW SHEQEL **Weight:** 3.4600 g. **Composition:** 0.9000 Gold .1001 oz. AGW **Series:** Wildlife **Reverse:** Roe and lily

Date	Mintage	F	VF	XF	Unc	BU
JE5753-1992 Proof	2,000	Value: 125				

KM# 240 NEW SHEQEL **Weight:** 14.4000 g. **Composition:** 0.9250 Silver .4282 oz. ASW **Subject:** 45th Anniversary of Independence **Reverse:** Tourism

Date	Mintage	F	VF	XF	Unc	BU
JE5753-1993	6,985	—	—	—	22.50	—

KM# 243 NEW SHEQEL **Weight:** 14.4000 g. **Composition:** 0.9250 Silver .4282 oz. ASW **Series:** Wildlife **Reverse:** A young hart

Date	Mintage	F	VF	XF	Unc	BU
JE5754-1993	3,761	—	—	—	25.00	—

KM# 244 NEW SHEQEL **Weight:** 3.4600 g. **Composition:** 0.9000 Gold .1001 oz. AGW **Series:** Wildlife **Reverse:** A young hart

Date	Mintage	F	VF	XF	Unc	BU
JE5754-1993 Proof	1,679	Value: 125				

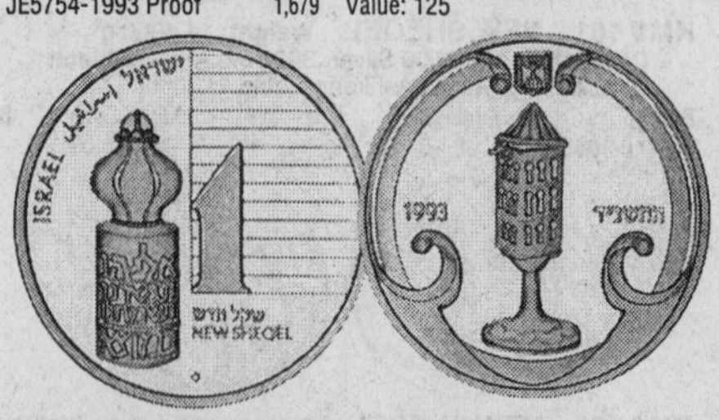

KM# 250 NEW SHEQEL **Weight:** 14.4000 g. **Composition:** 0.9250 Silver .4282 oz. ASW **Series:** Judaic **Reverse:** Havdalah spicebox

Date	Mintage	F	VF	XF	Unc	BU
JE5754-1993	3,288	—	—	—	25.00	—

KM# 247 NEW SHEQEL **Weight:** 14.4000 g. **Composition:** 0.9250 Silver .4282 oz. ASW **Note:** Revolt and Heroism.

Date	Mintage	F	VF	XF	Unc	BU
JE5753-1993	4,642	—	—	—	25.00	—

KM# 252 NEW SHEQEL **Weight:** 14.4000 g. **Composition:** 0.9250 Silver .4282 oz. ASW **Subject:** Enviroment **Reverse:** Globe in flower

Date	Mintage	F	VF	XF	Unc	BU
JE5754-1994	3,490	—	—	—	25.00	—

KM# 256 NEW SHEQEL **Weight:** 14.4000 g. **Composition:** 0.9250 Silver .4282 oz. ASW **Series:** Biblical **Reverse:** Abraham's willingness to sacrifice Isaac

Date	Mintage	F	VF	XF	Unc	BU
JE5754-1994	5,000	—	—	—	25.00	—

KM# 259 NEW SHEQEL **Weight:** 14.4000 g. **Composition:** 0.9250 Silver .4282 oz. ASW **Subject:** Wildlife **Obverse:** Palm tree **Reverse:** Leopard

Date	Mintage	F	VF	XF	Unc	BU
JE5755-1994	3,286	—	—	—	25.00	—

KM# 260 NEW SHEQEL **Weight:** 3.4600 g. **Composition:** 0.9000 Gold .1001 oz. AGW **Subject:** Wildlife **Obverse:** Palm tree **Reverse:** Leopard

Date	Mintage	F	VF	XF	Unc	BU
JE5755-1994	1,355	—	—	—	190	—

KM# 263 NEW SHEQEL **Weight:** 14.4000 g. **Composition:** 0.9250 Silver .4282 oz. ASW **Subject:** Anniversary

Date	Mintage	F	VF	XF	Unc	BU
JE5755-1995	3,468	—	—	—	25.00	—

KM# 267 NEW SHEQEL **Weight:** 14.4000 g. **Composition:** 0.9250 Silver .4282 oz. ASW **Subject:** 50th Anniversary - Defeat of Nazi Germany

Date	Mintage	F	VF	XF	Unc	BU
JE5755-1995 Proof Like	3,450	—	—	—	32.00	—

KM# 271 NEW SHEQEL **Weight:** 14.4000 g. **Composition:** 0.9250 Silver .4282 oz. ASW **Series:** F.A.O.

Date	F	VF	XF	Unc	BU
JE5755-1995 Proof Like	—	—	—	30.00	—

KM# 274 NEW SHEQEL **Weight:** 14.4000 g. **Composition:** 0.9250 Silver .4327 oz. ASW **Subject:** Wildlife **Reverse:** Fox and vineyard

Date	F	VF	XF	Unc	BU
JE5756-1995	—	—	—	25.00	—

KM# 275 NEW SHEQEL **Weight:** 3.4600 g. **Composition:** 0.9000 Gold .1001 oz. AGW **Subject:** Wildlife **Reverse:** Fox and vineyard

Date	F	VF	XF	Unc	BU
JE5756-1995 Proof Est. 2,000 Value: 125					

KM# 278 NEW SHEQEL **Weight:** 14.4000 g. **Composition:** 0.9250 Silver .4282 oz. ASW **Subject:** Peace Treaty with Jordan

Date	F	VF	XF	Unc	BU
JE5755-1995	—	—	—	30.00	—

KM# 281 NEW SHEQEL **Weight:** 14.4000 g. **Composition:** 0.9250 Silver .4282 oz. ASW **Subject:** Biblical Arts - Solomon's Judgment **Note:** Similar to 10 New Sheqalim, KM#283.

Date	F	VF	XF	Unc	BU
JE5755-1995	—	—	—	25.00	—

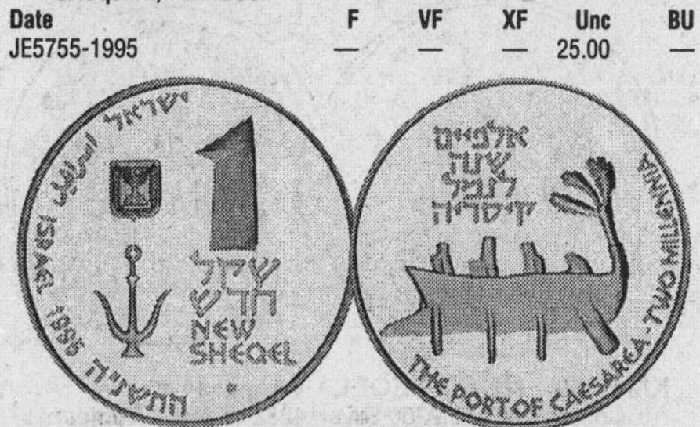

KM# 287 NEW SHEQEL **Weight:** 14.4000 g. **Composition:** 0.9250 Silver .4282 oz. ASW **Subject:** Port of Caesarea **Reverse:** Ancient ship

Date	F	VF	XF	Unc	BU
JE5755-1995	—	—	—	25.00	—

KM# 284 NEW SHEQEL **Weight:** 14.4000 g. **Composition:** 0.9250 Silver .4282 oz. ASW **Subject:** Anniversary **Note:** Similar to 30 New Sheqalim, KM#286.

Date	F	VF	XF	Unc	BU
JE5756-1996	—	—	—	35.00	—

KM# 290 NEW SHEQEL **Weight:** 14.4000 g. **Composition:** 0.9250 Silver .4282 oz. ASW **Subject:** Wildlife **Reverse:** Nightingale

Date	F	VF	XF	Unc	BU
JE5756-1996 Proof Est. 3,500 Value: 25.00					

KM# 291 NEW SHEQEL **Weight:** 3.4600 g. **Composition:** 0.9000 Gold .1001 oz. AGW **Subject:** Wildlife **Reverse:** Nightingale

Date	F	VF	XF	Unc	BU
JE5756-1996 Proof Est. 1,500 Value: 190					

KM# 294 NEW SHEQEL **Weight:** 14.4000 g. **Composition:** 0.9250 Silver .4282 oz. ASW **Subject:** Biblical Arts **Obverse:** Similar to 10 New Sheqalim, KM#296 **Reverse:** Miriam and the women

Date	F	VF	XF	Unc	BU
JE5756-1996	—	—	—	25.00	—

KM# 297 NEW SHEQEL **Weight:** 14.4000 g. **Composition:** 0.9250 Silver .4282 oz. ASW **Obverse:** National arms and denomination **Reverse:** Head of Yitzhak Rabin left

Date	F	VF	XF	Unc	BU
JE5756-1996 BU	—	—	—	—	25.00

KM# 300 NEW SHEQEL **Weight:** 14.4000 g. **Composition:** 0.9250 Silver .4282 oz. ASW **Subject:** First Zionist Congress Centennial **Obverse:** Denomination **Reverse:** Portrait of Herzl

Date	Mintage	F	VF	XF	Unc	BU
JE5757-1997	5,000	—	—	—	25.00	—

KM# 306 NEW SHEQEL Weight: 14.4000 g. **Composition:** 0.9250 Silver .4282 oz. ASW **Subject:** Wildlife **Obverse:** Pomegranates and denomination **Reverse:** Lion

Date	Mintage	F	VF	XF	Unc	BU
JE5758-1997	3,500	—	—	—	25.00	—

KM# 307 NEW SHEQEL Weight: 3.4600 g. **Composition:** 0.9000 Gold .1001 oz. AGW **Subject:** Wildlife **Obverse:** Pomegranates and denomination **Reverse:** Lion **Edge:** Reeded

Date	Mintage	F	VF	XF	Unc	BU
JE5758-1997 Proof	1,500	Value: 120				

KM# 310 NEW SHEQEL Weight: 14.4300 g. **Composition:** 0.9250 Silver .4291 oz. ASW **Subject:** Anniversary **Obverse:** Denominaton **Reverse:** Flag

Date	F	VF	XF	Unc	BU
JE5758-1998 Prooflike	—	—	—	25.00	—

KM# 316 NEW SHEQEL Weight: 14.4300 g. **Composition:** 0.9250 Silver .4291 oz. ASW **Subject:** Biblical - Noah's Ark **Obverse:** Dove, rainbow and denomination **Reverse:** Noah releasing dove

Date	F	VF	XF	Unc	BU
JE5758-1998 Proof like	—	—	—	25.00	—

KM# 320 NEW SHEQEL Weight: 14.4300 g. **Composition:** 0.9250 Silver .4291 oz. ASW **Subject:** Wildlife **Obverse:** Cypress trees, denomination **Reverse:** Stork

Date	F	VF	XF	Unc	BU
JE5759 (1998)	—	—	—	25.00	—

KM# 321 NEW SHEQEL Weight: 3.4600 g. **Composition:** 0.9000 Gold .1001 oz. AGW **Subject:** Wildlife **Obverse:** Cypress trees, denomination **Reverse:** Stork

Date	F	VF	XF	Unc	BU
JE5758 (1998) Proof	Est. 1,500	Value: 140			

KM# 325 NEW SHEQEL Weight: 14.4000 g. **Composition:** 0.9250 Silver .4282 oz. ASW **Subject:** High-Tech in Israel **Obverse:** Denominaton and mosaic **Reverse:** Mosaic bouquet

Date	F	VF	XF	Unc	BU
JE5759 (1999) Prooflike	—	—	—	27.50	—

KM# 328 NEW SHEQEL Weight: 14.4000 g. **Composition:** 0.9250 Silver .4282 oz. ASW **Subject:** The Millenium Coin **Obverse:** Denomination, olive branch **Reverse:** Year 2000 motif incorporating dove with olive branch

Date	F	VF	XF	Unc	BU
JE5759-1999 Prooflike	—	—	—	30.00	—

KM# 333 NEW SHEQEL Weight: 14.4000 g. **Composition:** 0.9250 Silver .4282 oz. ASW **Subject:** Biblical **Reverse:** Abraham looking at the stars

Date	F	VF	XF	Unc	BU
JE5760-1999 Prooflike	—	—	—	25.00	—

KM# 336 NEW SHEQEL Weight: 14.4000 g. **Composition:** 0.9250 Silver .4282 oz. ASW **Subject:** Anniversary - Independence Day **Obverse:** Denomination **Reverse:** Arch above inscription **Edge:** Plain **Size:** 30 mm.

Date	F	VF	XF	Unc	BU
JE5161-2000 Prooflike	—	—	—	25.00	—

KM# 339 NEW SHEQEL Weight: 14.4000 g. **Composition:** 0.9250 Silver .4282 oz. ASW **Subject:** Biblical - Joseph and His Brothers **Obverse:** Denomination **Reverse:** Joseph standing before his kneeling brothers **Edge:** Plain

Date	F	VF	XF	Unc	BU
JE5761-2000 Prooflike	—	—	—	28.00	—

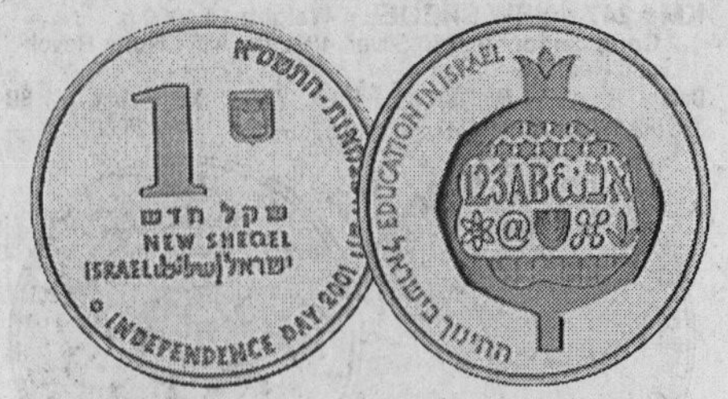

KM# 344 NEW SHEQEL Weight: 14.4000 g. **Composition:** 0.9250 Silver .4282 oz. ASW **Subject:** Anniversary - Independence Day and Education **Obverse:** Denomination **Reverse:** Pomegranate full of symbols - Hebrew 'ABC-123', etc. **Edge:** Plain **Size:** 30 mm.

Date	Mintage	F	VF	XF	Unc	BU
JE5762-2001 Prooflike	3,000	—	—	—	30.00	—

KM# 347 NEW SHEQEL Weight: 14.4000 g. **Composition:** 0.9250 Silver .4282 oz. ASW **Subject:** Wildlife **Obverse:** Shittah tree **Reverse:** Ibex **Edge:** Plain **Size:** 30 mm.

Date	F	VF	XF	Unc	BU
JE5762-2001 Prooflike	—	—	—	25.00	—

KM# 348 NEW SHEQEL Weight: 3.4600 g. **Composition:** 0.9000 Gold .1001 oz. AGW **Subject:** Wildlife **Obverse:** Shittah tree **Reverse:** Ibex **Edge:** Reeded **Size:** 18 mm.

Date	F	VF	XF	Unc	BU
JE5762-2001 Proof	—	Value: 110			

KM# 351 NEW SHEQEL Weight: 14.4000 g. **Composition:** 0.9250 Silver 0.4282 oz. ASW **Subject:** Music **Obverse:** National arms and denomination. **Reverse:** Musical instruments. **Edge:** Plain. **Size:** 30 mm.

Date	F	VF	XF	Unc	BU
JE5761-2001	—	—	—	30.00	—

KM# 357 2 SHEQALIM Weight: 28.8000 g. **Composition:** 0.9250 Silver 0.8565 oz. ASW **Subject:** Independence - Volunteering **Obverse:** Denomination **Reverse:** Heart in hands **Edge:** Reeded **Size:** 38.7 mm.

Date	Mintage	F	VF	XF	Unc	BU
JE5762 (2002)	2,500	Value: 45.00				

KM# 358 10 SHEQALIM Weight: 16.9600 g. **Composition:** 0.9166 Gold 0.4998 oz. AGW **Subject:** Independence - Volunteering **Obverse:** Denomination **Reverse:** Heart in hands **Edge:** Reeded **Size:** 30 mm.

Date	Mintage	F	VF	XF	Unc	BU
JE5762 (2002)	888	Value: 430				

KM# 162 2 NEW SHEQALIM Weight: 28.8000 g. **Composition:** 0.8500 Silver .7871 oz. ASW **Subject:** Hanukkah **Reverse:** Ashkanaz lamp

Date	Mintage	F	VF	XF	Unc	BU
JE5746-1985 Proof	9,225	Value: 25.00				

KM# 176 2 NEW SHEQALIM Weight: 28.8000 g. **Composition:** 0.8500 Silver .7871 oz. ASW **Subject:** Hanukkah **Reverse:** Algerian lamp

Date	Mintage	F	VF	XF	Unc	BU
JE5747-1986 Proof	8,343	Value: 25.00				

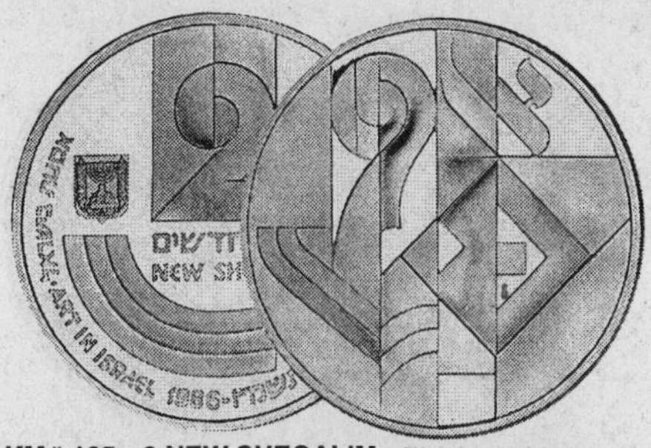

KM# 165 2 NEW SHEQALIM **Weight:** 28.8000 g. **Composition:** 0.8500 Silver .7871 oz. ASW **Subject:** 38th Anniversary of Independence **Reverse:** Tribute to the arts

Date	Mintage	F	VF	XF	Unc	BU
JE5746-1986 Proof	7,344	Value: 25.00				

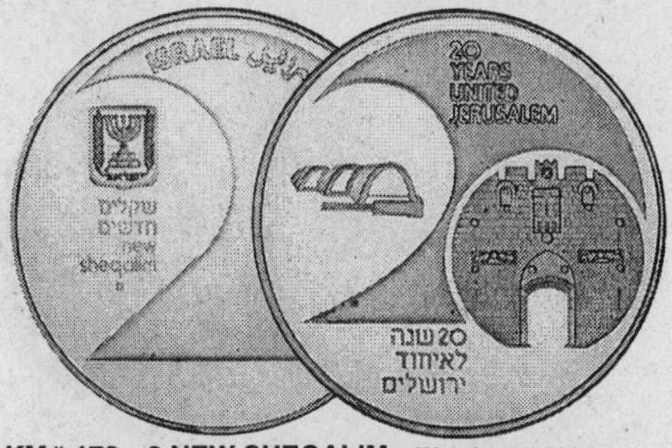

KM# 178 2 NEW SHEQALIM **Weight:** 28.8000 g. **Composition:** 0.8500 Silver .7871 oz. ASW **Subject:** 20th Anniversary - United Jerusalem

Date	Mintage	F	VF	XF	Unc	BU
JE5747-1987 Proof	7,788	Value: 25.00				

KM# 184 2 NEW SHEQALIM **Weight:** 28.8000 g. **Composition:** 0.8500 Silver .7871 oz. ASW **Subject:** Hanukkah **Reverse:** English lamp

Date	Mintage	F	VF	XF	Unc	BU
JE5748-1987 Proof	8,039	Value: 28.00				

KM# 192 2 NEW SHEQALIM **Weight:** 28.8000 g. **Composition:** 0.8500 Silver .7871 oz. ASW **Subject:** Hanukkah **Reverse:** Tunisian lamp

Date	Mintage	F	VF	XF	Unc	BU
JE5749-1988 Proof	7,110	Value: 30.00				

KM# 186 2 NEW SHEQALIM **Weight:** 28.8000 g. **Composition:** 0.8500 Silver .7871 oz. ASW **Subject:** 40th Anniversary of Independence

Date	Mintage	F	VF	XF	Unc	BU
JE5748-1988 Proof	9,100	Value: 25.00				

KM# 200 2 NEW SHEQALIM **Weight:** 28.8000 g. **Composition:** 0.8500 Silver .7871 oz. ASW **Subject:** 41st Anniversary of Independence

Date	Mintage	F	VF	XF	Unc	BU
JE5749-1989 Proof	7,062	Value: 32.00				

KM# 206 2 NEW SHEQALIM **Weight:** 28.8000 g. **Composition:** 0.8500 Silver .7871 oz. ASW **Subject:** Hanukkah **Reverse:** Persian lamp

Date	Mintage	F	VF	XF	Unc	BU
JE5749-1989 Proof	6,282	Value: 30.00				

KM# 216 2 NEW SHEQALIM **Weight:** 28.8000 g. **Composition:** 0.8500 Silver .7871 oz. ASW **Subject:** Hanukkah **Reverse:** Cochin lamp

Date	Mintage	F	VF	XF	Unc	BU
JE5751-1990 Proof	5,383	Value: 42.00				

KM# 213 2 NEW SHEQALIM **Weight:** 28.8000 g. **Composition:** 0.8500 Silver .7871 oz. ASW **Subject:** 42nd Aniversary of Independence **Reverse:** Archaeology

Date	Mintage	F	VF	XF	Unc	BU
JE5750-1990 Proof	5,457	Value: 45.00				

KM# 219 2 NEW SHEQALIM **Weight:** 28.8000 g. **Composition:** 0.9250 Silver .8565 oz. ASW **Subject:** 43rd Aniversary of independence **Reverse:** Immigration to Israel

Date	Mintage	F	VF	XF	Unc	BU
JE5751-1991 Proof	6,693	Value: 40.00				

KM# 221 2 NEW SHEQALIM **Weight:** 28.8000 g. **Composition:** 0.9250 Silver .8565 oz. ASW **Subject:** Wildlife **Obverse:** Trees **Reverse:** Cedar trees and dove

Date	Mintage	F	VF	XF	Unc	BU
JE5751-1991 Proof	5,005	Value: 45.00				

KM# 224 2 NEW SHEQALIM **Weight:** 28.8000 g. **Composition:** 0.9250 Silver .8565 oz. ASW **Series:** Judaic **Reverse:** Kiddush cup

Date	Mintage	F	VF	XF	Unc	BU
JE5752-1991 Proof	6,575	Value: 35.00				

KM# 226 2 NEW SHEQALIM **Weight:** 28.8000 g. **Composition:** 0.9250 Silver .8565 oz. ASW **Subject:** 44th Anniversary of Independence **Reverse:** Israeli law

Date	Mintage	F	VF	XF	Unc	BU
JE5752-1992 Proof	4,486	Value: 47.50				

KM# 228 2 NEW SHEQALIM **Weight:** 28.8000 g. **Composition:** 0.9250 Silver .8565 oz. ASW **Subject:** IX Paralympic Games

Date	Mintage	F	VF	XF	Unc	BU
JE5752-1992 Proof	3,718	Value: 47.50				

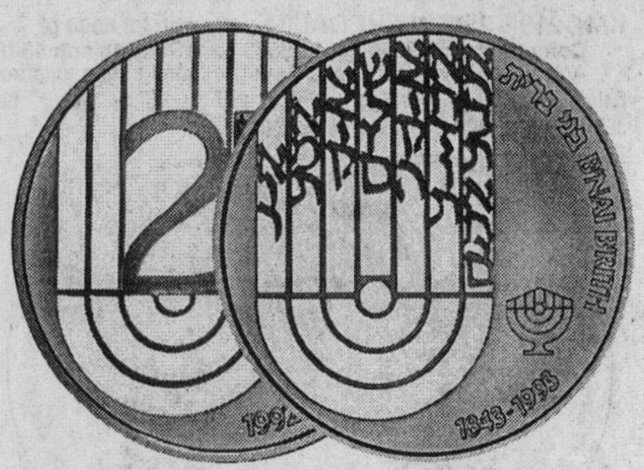

KM# 235 2 NEW SHEQALIM **Weight:** 28.8000 g. **Composition:** 0.9250 Silver .8565 oz. ASW **Reverse:** B'nai B'rith

Date	Mintage	F	VF	XF	Unc	BU
JE5752-1992 Proof	4,622	Value: 40.00				

KM# 232 2 NEW SHEQALIM **Weight:** 28.8000 g. **Composition:** 0.9250 Silver .8565 oz. ASW **Series:** Wildlife **Reverse:** Roe and lily

Date	Mintage	F	VF	XF	Unc	BU
JE5753-1992 Proof	4,724	Value: 45.00				

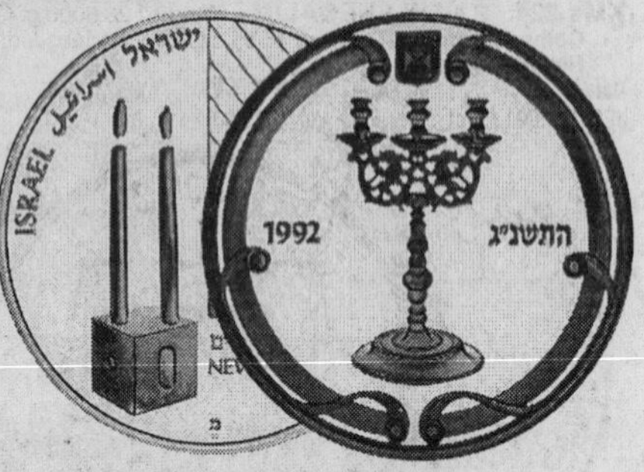

KM# 239 2 NEW SHEQALIM **Weight:** 28.8000 g. **Composition:** 0.9250 Silver .8565 oz. ASW **Series:** Judaic **Reverse:** Shabbat candles

Date	Mintage	F	VF	XF	Unc	BU
JE5753-1992 Proof	4,975	Value: 35.00				

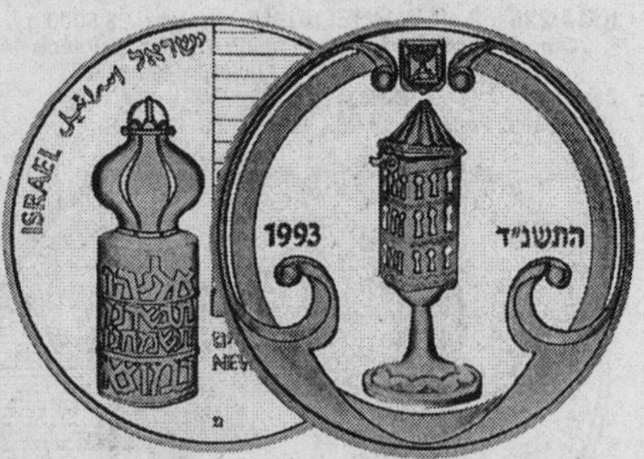

KM# 251 2 NEW SHEQALIM **Weight:** 28.8000 g. **Composition:** 0.9250 Silver .8565 oz. ASW **Series:** Judaic **Reverse:** Havdalah spicebox

Date	Mintage	F	VF	XF	Unc	BU
JE5754-1993 Proof	4,750	Value: 40.00				

KM# 248 2 NEW SHEQALIM **Weight:** 28.8000 g. **Composition:** 0.9250 Silver .8565 oz. ASW **Subject:** Revolt and Heroism

Date	Mintage	F	VF	XF	Unc	BU
JE5753-1993 Proof	4,994	Value: 40.00				

KM# 245 2 NEW SHEQALIM **Weight:** 28.8000 g. **Composition:** 0.9250 Silver .8565 oz. ASW **Series:** Wildlife **Reverse:** A young hart

Date	Mintage	F	VF	XF	Unc	BU
JE5754-1993 Proof	5,382	Value: 45.00				

KM# 241 2 NEW SHEQALIM **Weight:** 28.8000 g. **Composition:** 0.9250 Silver .8565 oz. ASW **Subject:** 45th Anniversary of Independence **Reverse:** Tourism

Date	Mintage	F	VF	XF	Unc	BU
JE5753-1993 Proof	4,570	Value: 42.00				

KM# 253 2 NEW SHEQALIM **Weight:** 28.8000 g. **Composition:** 0.9250 Silver .8565 oz. ASW **Subject:** Environment **Reverse:** World globe and flower

Date	Mintage	F	VF	XF	Unc	BU
JE5754-1994	4,272	—	—	—	45.00	—

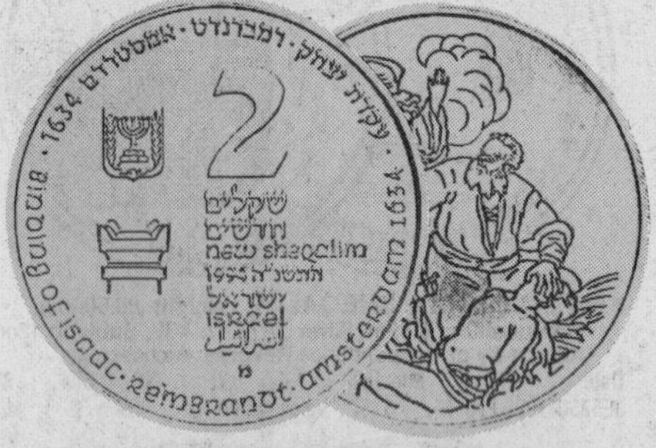

KM# 257 2 NEW SHEQALIM **Weight:** 28.8000 g. **Composition:** 0.9250 Silver .8565 oz. ASW **Series:** Biblical **Reverse:** Abrahams' willingness to sacrifice Isaac

Date	Mintage	F	VF	XF	Unc	BU
JE5755-1994 Proof	5,000	Value: 45.00				

KM# 261 2 NEW SHEQALIM **Weight:** 28.8000 g. **Composition:** 0.9250 Silver .8565 oz. ASW **Subject:** Wildlife **Obverse:** Palm tree **Reverse:** Leopard

Date	Mintage	F	VF	XF	Unc	BU
JE5755-1994 Proof	4,283	Value: 40.00				

KM# 264 2 NEW SHEQALIM **Weight:** 28.8000 g. **Composition:** 0.9250 Silver .8565 oz. ASW **Subject:** Anniversary - Medicine

Date	Mintage	F	VF	XF	Unc	BU
JE5755-1995 Proof	3,698	Value: 45.00				

KM# 268 2 NEW SHEQALIM **Weight:** 28.8000 g. **Composition:** 0.9250 Silver .8565 oz. ASW **Subject:** 50th Anniversary - Defeat of Nazi Germany

Date	Mintage	F	VF	XF	Unc	BU
JE5755-1995 Proof	5,808	Value: 45.00				

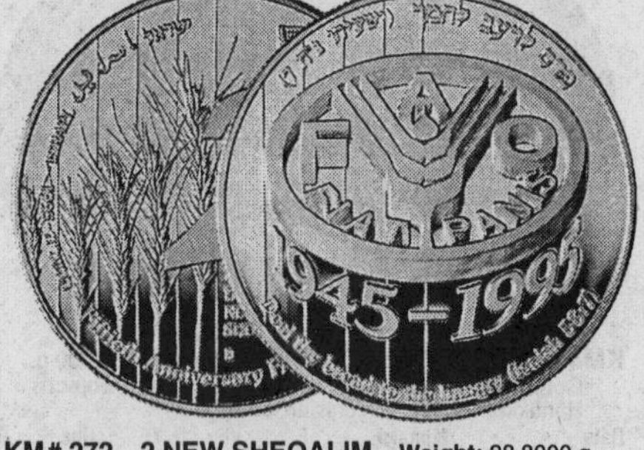

KM# 272 2 NEW SHEQALIM **Weight:** 28.8000 g. **Composition:** 0.9250 Silver .8565 oz. ASW **Series:** F.A.O. **Obverse:** Barley stalks

Date	Mintage	F	VF	XF	Unc	BU
JE5755-1995 Proof	Est. 4,500	Value: 50.00				

KM# 288 2 NEW SHEQALIM **Weight:** 28.8000 g. **Composition:** 0.9250 Silver .8565 oz. ASW **Subject:** Port of Caesarea **Reverse:** Ancient ship

Date	Mintage	F	VF	XF	Unc	BU
JE5755-1995 Proof	Est. 5,000	Value: 40.00				

KM# 279 2 NEW SHEQALIM **Weight:** 28.8000 g. **Composition:** 0.9250 Silver .8565 oz. ASW **Subject:** Peace Treaty with Jordan **Note:** Similar to 1 New Sheqel, KM#178.

Date	Mintage	F	VF	XF	Unc	BU
JE5755-1995 Proof	Est. 5,000	Value: 40.00				

KM# 276 2 NEW SHEQALIM **Weight:** 28.8000 g. **Composition:** 0.9250 Silver .8565 oz. ASW **Series:** Wildlife **Reverse:** Fox and vineyard **Note:** Similar to 1 New Sheqel, KM#274.

Date	Mintage	F	VF	XF	Unc	BU
JE5756-1995 Proof	Est. 4,500	Value: 45.00				
JE5756-1995 Proof	4,500	Value: 45.00				

KM# 282 2 NEW SHEQALIM **Weight:** 28.8000 g. **Composition:** 0.9250 Silver .8565 oz. ASW **Series:** Biblical **Subject:** Solomon's Judgment **Note:** Similar to 10 New Sheqel, KM#283.

Date	Mintage	F	VF	XF	Unc	BU
JE5755-1995 Proof	Est. 5,000	Value: 40.00				

KM# 295 2 NEW SHEQALIM **Weight:** 28.8000 g. **Composition:** 0.9250 Silver .8565 oz. ASW **Subject:** Biblical **Reverse:** Miriam and the women **Note:** Similar to 10 New Sheqalim, KM#296.

Date	Mintage	F	VF	XF	Unc	BU
JE5756-1996 Proof	Est. 4,500	Value: 60.00				

KM# 292 2 NEW SHEQALIM **Weight:** 28.8000 g. **Composition:** 0.9250 Silver .8565 oz. ASW **Subject:** wildlife **Reverse:** Nightingale

Date	Mintage	F	VF	XF	Unc	BU
JE5757-1996 Proof	Est. 3,500	Value: 45.00				

KM# 298 2 NEW SHEQALIM **Weight:** 28.8000 g. **Composition:** 0.9250 Silver .8565 oz. ASW **Obverse:** National arms and denomination **Reverse:** Head of Yitzhak Rabin left

Date	Mintage	F	VF	XF	Unc	BU
JE5756-1996 Proof	Est. 5,300	Value: 45.00				

KM# 301 2 NEW SHEQALIM **Weight:** 28.8000 g. **Composition:** 0.9250 Silver .8565 oz. ASW **Subject:** Anniversary - First Zionist Congress Centennial **Obverse:** Denomination **Reverse:** Portrait of Herzl

Date	Mintage	F	VF	XF	Unc	BU
JE5757-1997 Proof	5,000	Value: 42.50				

KM# 308 2 NEW SHEQALIM **Weight:** 28.8000 g. **Composition:** 0.9250 Silver .8565 oz. ASW **Subject:** Wildlife **Obverse:** Pomegrantes and denomination **Reverse:** Lion walking right

Date	Mintage	F	VF	XF	Unc	BU
JE5758-1997 Proof	3,500	Value: 45.00				

KM# 317 2 NEW SHEQALIM **Weight:** 28.8000 g. **Composition:** 0.9250 Silver .8565 oz. ASW **Subject:** Biblical - Noah's Ark **Obverse:** Dove, rainbow and denomination **Reverse:** Noah releasing dove

Date	Mintage	F	VF	XF	Unc	BU
JE5758-1998 Proof	Est. 4,500	Value: 45.00				

KM# 322 2 NEW SHEQALIM **Weight:** 28.8000 g. **Composition:** 0.9250 Silver .8565 oz. ASW **Subject:** Wildlife **Obverse:** Cypress tree, denomination **Reverse:** Stork

Date	F	VF	XF	Unc	BU
JE5759 (1998) Proof	—	Value: 45.00			

KM# 311 2 NEW SHEQALIM **Weight:** 28.8000 g. **Composition:** 0.9250 Silver .8565 oz. ASW **Series:** Judaic **Subject:** 50th Anniversary of Independence **Obverse:** Denomination **Reverse:** Flag

Date	Mintage	F	VF	XF	Unc	BU
JE5758-1998 Proof	Est. 10,000	Value: 40.00				

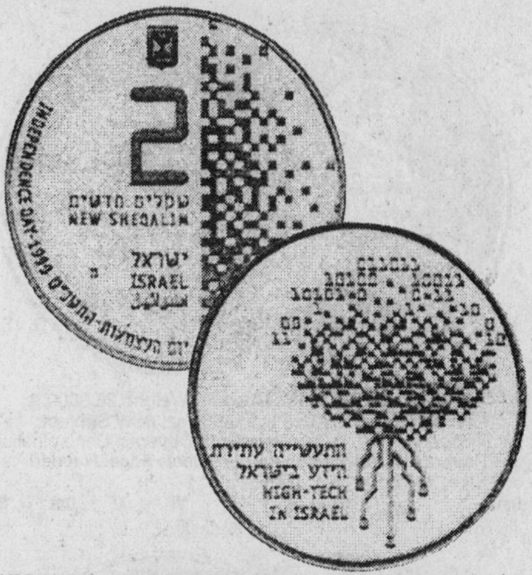

KM# 326 2 NEW SHEQALIM **Weight:** 28.8000 g. **Composition:** 0.9250 Silver .8565 oz. ASW **Subject:** Anniversary - High Tech in Israel **Obverse:** Denomination and mosaic **Reverse:** Mosaic bouquet

Date	Mintage	F	VF	XF	Unc	BU
JE5759 (1999) Proof	6,000	Value: 45.00				

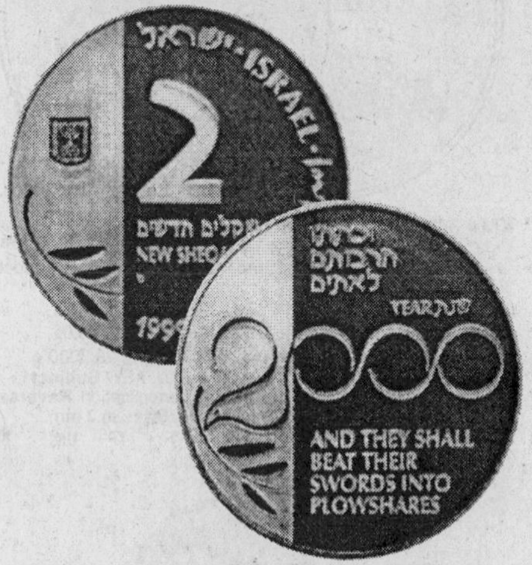

KM# 329 2 NEW SHEQALIM **Weight:** 28.8000 g. **Composition:** 0.9250 Silver .8565 oz. ASW **Obverse:** Denomination, olive branch **Reverse:** Year 2000 motif incorporating dove with olive branch **Edge Lettering:** The Millennium

Date	F	VF	XF	Unc	BU
JE5759-1999 Proof	—	Value: 45.00			

KM# 334 2 NEW SHEQALIM **Weight:** 28.8000 g. **Composition:** 0.9250 Silver .8565 oz. ASW **Series:** Biblical **Reverse:** Abraham looking to stars

Date	F	VF	XF	Unc	BU
JE5759-1999 Proof	—	Value: 45.00			

KM# 337 2 NEW SHEQALIM **Weight:** 28.8000 g. **Composition:** 0.9250 Silver .8565 oz. ASW **Subject:** Anniversary - 'Love Thy Neighbor' **Obverse:** Denomination **Reverse:** Arch above inscription **Edge:** Plain **Size:** 38.7 mm.

Date	F	VF	XF	Unc	BU
JE5760-2000 Proof	—	Value: 45.00			

KM# 340 2 NEW SHEQALIM **Weight:** 28.8000 g. **Composition:** 0.9250 Silver .8565 oz. ASW **Subject:** Biblical - Joseph and his brothers **Obverse:** Denomination **Reverse:** Joseph standing before kneeling brothers **Edge:** Reeded **Size:** 38.7 mm.

Date	F	VF	XF	Unc	BU
JE5760-2000 Proof	—	Value: 45.00			

KM# 345 2 NEW SHEQALIM **Weight:** 28.8000 g. **Composition:** 0.9250 Silver .8564 oz. ASW **Subject:** Independence Day and Education **Obverse:** Denomination **Reverse:** Pomegranate full of symbols **Edge:** Reeded **Size:** 38.7 mm.

Date	Mintage	F	VF	XF	Unc	BU
JE5761-2001 Proof	3,000	Value: 45.00				

KM# 349 2 NEW SHEQALIM **Weight:** 28.8000 g. **Composition:** 0.9250 Silver .8564 oz. ASW **Subject:** Wildlife **Obverse:** Shittah tree **Reverse:** Ibex **Edge:** Reeded **Size:** 38.7 mm.

Date	F	VF	XF	Unc	BU
JE5761-2001 Prooflike	—	—	—	45.00	—

KM# 352 2 NEW SHEQALIM **Weight:** 28.8000 g. **Composition:** 0.9250 Silver 0.8565 oz. ASW **Subject:** Music **Obverse:** National arms and denomination. **Reverse:** Musical instruments. **Edge:** Reeded. **Size:** 38.7 mm.

Date		F	VF	XF	Unc	BU
JE5761-2001 Proof	—	Value: 45.00				

KM# 170 5 NEW SHEQALIM **Weight:** 8.6300 g. **Composition:** 0.9000 Gold .2497 oz. AGW **Series:** Holyland Sites **Reverse:** Akko **Shape:** 12-sided **Note:** Similar to 1 New Sheqel, KM#169.

Date	Mintage	F	VF	XF	Unc	BU
JE5747-1986 Proof	2,800	Value: 225				

KM# 182 5 NEW SHEQALIM **Weight:** 8.6300 g. **Composition:** 0.9000 Gold .2497 oz. AGW **Series:** Holyland Sites **Reverse:** Jericho **Shape:** 12-sided

Date	Mintage	F	VF	XF	Unc	BU
JE5748-1987 Proof	4,000	Value: 185				

KM# 190 5 NEW SHEQALIM **Weight:** 8.6300 g. **Composition:** 0.9000 Gold .2497 oz. AGW **Series:** Holyland Sites **Reverse:** Caesarea **Shape:** 12-sided

Date	Mintage	F	VF	XF	Unc	BU
JE5749-1988 Proof	3,454	Value: 210				

KM# 204 5 NEW SHEQALIM **Weight:** 8.6300 g. **Composition:** 0.9000 Gold .2497 oz. AGW **Series:** Holyland Sites **Reverse:** Jaffa Harbor **Shape:** 12-sided

Date	Mintage	F	VF	XF	Unc	BU
JE5750-1989 Proof	2,402	Value: 250				

KM# 207 5 NEW SHEQALIM **Composition:** Copper-Nickel **Shape:** 12-sided

Date	Mintage	F	VF	XF	Unc	BU
JE5750 (1990)	15,000,000	—	—	—	3.75	—
JE5751 (1991)	324,000	—	—	—	3.75	—
JE5752 (1992)	—	—	—	—	3.75	—
JE5753 (1993)	8,000	—	—	—	3.75	—
JE5754 (1994)	8,000	—	—	—	3.75	—
JE5755 (1995)	10,000	—	—	—	3.75	—
JE5757 (1997)	—	—	—	—	3.75	—
JE5758 (1998)	—	—	—	—	3.75	—
JE5759 (1999)	—	—	—	—	3.75	—

KM# 208 5 NEW SHEQALIM **Composition:** Copper-Nickel **Reverse:** Bust of Levi Eshkol facing

Date	Mintage	F	VF	XF	Unc	BU
JE5750 (1990)	1,500,000	—	—	—	5.00	—

KM# 217 5 NEW SHEQALIM **Composition:** Copper-Nickel **Subject:** Hanukka **Reverse:** Ancient column

Date	Mintage	F	VF	XF	Unc	BU
JE5750 (1990)	500,000	—	—	—	3.75	—
JE5751 (1991)	—	—	—	—	3.75	—
JE5752 (1992)	501,000	—	—	—	3.75	—
JE5753 (1993)	12,000	—	—	—	3.75	—
JE5754 (1994)	12,000	—	—	—	3.75	—
JE5755 (1995)	7,500	—	—	—	3.75	—
JE5761 (2000)	—	—	—	—	—	—

KM# 211 5 NEW SHEQALIM **Weight:** 8.6300 g. **Composition:** 0.9000 Gold .2497 oz. AGW **Series:** Holyland Sites **Reverse:** Sea of Galilee map

Date	Mintage	F	VF	XF	Unc	BU
JE5751-1990 Proof	1,935	Value: 320				

KM# 222 5 NEW SHEQALIM **Weight:** 8.6300 g. **Composition:** 0.9000 Gold .2497 oz. AGW **Subject:** Wildlife **Obverse:** 2 cedar trees, denomination **Reverse:** Dove and tree trunk in legend

Date	Mintage	F	VF	XF	Unc	BU
JE5752-1991 Proof	2,000	Value: 260				

KM# 229 5 NEW SHEQALIM **Weight:** 8.6300 g. **Composition:** 0.9000 Gold .2497 oz. AGW **Subject:** IX Paralympic Games

Date	Mintage	F	VF	XF	Unc	BU
JE5752-1992 Proof	1,629	Value: 375				

KM# 236 5 NEW SHEQALIM **Weight:** 8.6300 g. **Composition:** 0.9000 Gold .2497 oz. AGW **Subject:** B'nai B'rith **Reverse:** Stylized design with inscription

Date	Mintage	F	VF	XF	Unc	BU
JE5752-1992 Proof	2,305	Value: 260				

KM# 233 5 NEW SHEQALIM **Weight:** 8.6300 g. **Composition:** 0.9000 Gold .2497 oz. AGW **Series:** Wildlife **Obverse:** Lily **Reverse:** Roe

Date	Mintage	F	VF	XF	Unc	BU
JE5753-1992 Proof	2,150	Value: 225				

KM# 237 5 NEW SHEQALIM **Composition:** Copper-Nickel **Reverse:** Bust of Chaim Weizmann facing

Date	Mintage	F	VF	XF	Unc	BU
JE5752-1992	1,501,000	—	—	—	5.00	—
JE5753-1993	—	—	—	—	5.00	—

KM# 246 5 NEW SHEQALIM **Weight:** 8.6300 g. **Composition:** 0.9000 Gold .2497 oz. AGW **Series:** Wildlife **Reverse:** A young hart

Date	Mintage	F	VF	XF	Unc	BU
JE5754-1993 Proof	1,782	Value: 235				

KM# 254 5 NEW SHEQALIM **Weight:** 8.6300 g. **Composition:** 0.9000 Gold .2497 oz. AGW **Subject:** Enviroment **Reverse:** World globe in flower

Date	Mintage	F	VF	XF	Unc	BU
JE5754-1994 Proof	1,407	Value: 240				

KM# 262 5 NEW SHEQALIM **Center Weight:** 8.6300 g. **Center Composition:** 0.9000 Gold .2497 oz. AGW **Subject:** Wildlife **Obverse:** Palm tree **Reverse:** Leopard

Date	Mintage	F	VF	XF	Unc	BU
JE5754-1994 Proof	1,535	Value: 265				

KM# 277 5 NEW SHEQALIM **Weight:** 8.6300 g. **Composition:** 0.9000 Gold .2497 oz. AGW **Subject:** Wildlife **Reverse:** Fox and vineyard **Note:** Similar to 1 New Sheqalim, KM#274.

Date		F	VF	XF	Unc	BU
JE5756-1995 Proof	Est. 2,000	Value: 220				

KM# 265 5 NEW SHEQALIM **Weight:** 8.6300 g. **Composition:** 0.9000 Gold .2497 oz. AGW **Subject:** Anniversary - Medicine

Date	Mintage	F	VF	XF	Unc	BU
JE5755-1995 Proof	1,155	Value: 300				

KM# 293 5 NEW SHEQALIM **Weight:** 8.6300 g. **Composition:** 0.9000 Gold .2497 oz. AGW **Subject:** Wildlife **Reverse:** Nightingale **Note:** Similar to 1 New Sheqalim, KM#290.

Date	Mintage	F	VF	XF	Unc	BU
JE5757-1996 Proof	Est. 1,500	Value: 260				

KM# 309 5 NEW SHEQALIM **Weight:** 8.6300 g. **Composition:** 0.9000 Gold .2497 oz. AGW **Subject:** Wildlife **Obverse:** Pomegranates and denominaton **Reverse:** Lion walking right

Date	Mintage	F	VF	XF	Unc	BU
JE5757-1996 Proof	1,500	Value: 240				

KM# 323 5 NEW SHEQALIM **Weight:** 8.6300 g. **Composition:** 0.9000 Gold .2497 oz. AGW **Subject:** Wildlife **Obverse:** Cypress trees, denomination. **Reverse:** Stork

Date		F	VF	XF	Unc	BU
JE5759-1998 Proof	—	Value: 275				

KM# 350 5 NEW SHEQALIM **Weight:** 8.6300 g. **Composition:** 0.9000 Gold .2497 oz. AGW **Subject:** Wildlife **Obverse:** Shittah tree **Reverse:** Ibex **Edge:** Reeded **Size:** 22 mm.

Date		F	VF	XF	Unc	BU
JE5761-2001 Proof	—	Value: 225				

KM# 166 10 NEW SHEQALIM **Weight:** 17.2800 g. **Composition:** 0.9000 Gold .5000 oz. AGW **Subject:** 38th Anniversary of Independence **Reverse:** Tribute to the arts

Date	Mintage	F	VF	XF	Unc	BU
JE5746-1986 Proof	2,485	Value: 425				

KM# 179 10 NEW SHEQALIM **Weight:** 17.2800 g. **Composition:** 0.9000 Gold .5000 oz. AGW **Subject:** 39th Anniversary - United Jerusalem

Date	Mintage	F	VF	XF	Unc	BU
JE5747-1987 Proof	3,200	Value: 325				

KM# 187 10 NEW SHEQALIM **Weight:** 17.2800 g. **Composition:** 0.9000 Gold .5000 oz. AGW **Subject:** 40th Anniversary of Independence

Date	Mintage	F	VF	XF	Unc	BU
JE5748-1988 Proof	Est. 4,575	Value: 245				

KM# 201 10 NEW SHEQALIM **Weight:** 17.2800 g. **Composition:** 0.9000 Gold .5000 oz. AGW **Subject:** 41th Anniversary of Independence **Reverse:** Gazelle in forest, legend at left

Date	Mintage	F	VF	XF	Unc	BU
JE5749-1989 Proof	2,743	Value: 320				

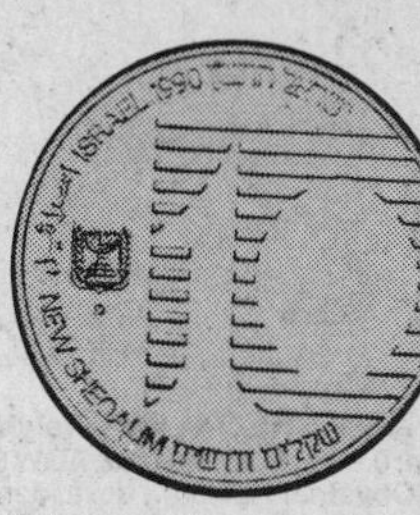

KM# 214 10 NEW SHEQALIM **Weight:** 17.2800 g. **Composition:** 0.9000 Gold .5000 oz. AGW **Subject:** 42nd Anniversary of Independence **Reverse:** Archaeology

Date	Mintage	F	VF	XF	Unc	BU
JE5750-1990 Proof	1,815	Value: 525				

KM# 230 10 NEW SHEQALIM **Weight:** 17.2800 g. **Composition:** 0.9000 Gold .5000 oz. AGW **Subject:** 43rd Anniversary of Independence **Reverse:** Immigration to Israel

Date	Mintage	F	VF	XF	Unc	BU
JE5751-1991 Proof	2,236	Value: 375				

KM# 227 10 NEW SHEQALIM **Weight:** 17.2800 g. **Composition:** 0.9000 Gold .5000 oz. AGW **Subject:** 44th Anniversary of Independence **Reverse:** Israeli law **Note:** Edge varieties exist.

Date	Mintage	F	VF	XF	Unc	BU
JE5752-1992 Proof	2,125	Value: 600				

KM# 242 10 NEW SHEQALIM **Weight:** 17.2800 g. **Composition:** 0.9000 Gold .5000 oz. AGW **Subject:** Tourism

Date	Mintage	F	VF	XF	Unc	BU
JE5753-1993 Proof	1,944	Value: 360				

KM# 249 10 NEW SHEQALIM **Weight:** 17.2800 g. **Composition:** 0.9000 Gold .5000 oz. AGW **Subject:** Revolt and Heroism **Obverse:** State emblem, denomination and legend

Date	Mintage	F	VF	XF	Unc	BU
JE5753-1993 Proof	1,583	Value: 425				

KM# 255 10 NEW SHEQALIM **Weight:** 17.2800 g. **Composition:** 0.9000 Gold .5000 oz. AGW **Subject:** Environment **Reverse:** World globe in flower

Date	Mintage	F	VF	XF	Unc	BU
JE5754-1994 Proof	1,482	Value: 380				

KM# 258 10 NEW SHEQALIM **Weight:** 17.2800 g. **Composition:** 0.9000 Gold .5000 oz. AGW **Subject:** Biblical **Reverse:** Abraham's willingness to sacrifice Isaac

Date	Mintage	F	VF	XF	Unc	BU
JE5754-1994 Proof	Est. 2,000	Value: 360				

KM# 266 10 NEW SHEQALIM **Weight:** 17.2800 g. **Composition:** 0.9000 Gold .5000 oz. AGW **Subject:** Anniversary - Medicine

Date	Mintage	F	VF	XF	Unc	BU
JE5755-1995 Proof	1,230	Value: 420				

KM# 269 10 NEW SHEQALIM **Weight:** 16.9600 g. **Composition:** 0.9170 Gold .4998 oz. AGW **Subject:** 50th Anniversary - Defeat of Nazi Germany

Date	Mintage	F	VF	XF	Unc	BU
JE5755-1995 Proof	1,742	Value: 425				

KM# 270 10 NEW SHEQALIM **Ring Composition:** Nickel Bonded Steel **Center Composition:** Aureate Bonded Bronze

Date	F	VF	XF	Unc	BU
JE5755 (1995)	—	—	—	7.00	—

KM# 273 10 NEW SHEQALIM **Ring Composition:** Nickel Bonded Steel **Center Composition:** Aureate Bonded Bronze **Reverse:** Bust of Golda Meir

Date	Mintage	F	VF	XF	Unc	BU
JE5755 (1995)	1,500,000	—	—	—	10.00	—

KM# 280 10 NEW SHEQALIM **Weight:** 16.9600 g. **Composition:** 0.9170 Gold .4998 oz. AGW **Subject:** Peace Treaty with Jordan

Date	Mintage	F	VF	XF	Unc	BU
JE5755-1995 Proof	Est. 1,500	Value: 400				

KM# 283 10 NEW SHEQALIM **Weight:** 17.2800 g. **Composition:** 0.9000 Gold .5000 oz. AGW **Subject:** Biblical - Solomon's Judgement

Date	Mintage	F	VF	XF	Unc	BU
JE5755(1995) Proof	Est. 2,000	Value: 395				

KM# 289 10 NEW SHEQALIM **Weight:** 16.9600 g. **Composition:** 0.9170 Gold .4998 oz. AGW **Reverse:** Port of Caesarea, ancient ship **Note:** Similar to 1 New Sheqalim, KM#287.

Date	Mintage	F	VF	XF	Unc	BU
JE5755-1995 Proof	Est. 1,700	Value: 400				

KM# 285 10 NEW SHEQALIM **Weight:** 16.9600 g. **Composition:** 0.9170 Gold .4998 oz. AGW **Subject:** Anniversary - Jerusalem's Third Millennium **Note:** Similar to 30 New Sheqalim, KM#286.

Date	Mintage	F	VF	XF	Unc	BU
JE5756-1996 Proof	Est. 1,996	Value: 415				

KM# 296 10 NEW SHEQALIM **Weight:** 17.2800 g. **Composition:** 0.9000 Gold .5000 oz. AGW **Subject:** Biblical **Reverse:** Miriam and the women

Date	Mintage	F	VF	XF	Unc	BU
JE5756-1996 Proof	Est. 1,500	Value: 450				

KM# 302 10 NEW SHEQALIM **Weight:** 17.2800 g. **Composition:** 0.9000 Gold .5000 oz. AGW **Subject:** Anniversary - First Zionist Congress Centennial **Obverse:** Denomination **Reverse:** Portrait of Herzl

Date	Mintage	F	VF	XF	Unc	BU
JE5757-1997 Proof	1,500	Value: 425				

KM# 315 10 NEW SHEQALIM **Ring Composition:** Nickel Bonded Steel **Center Composition:** Aureate **Subject:** Hannukah **Obverse:** Denomination **Reverse:** Palm tree and baskets

Date	Mintage	F	VF	XF	Unc	BU
JE5757 (1997)	10,000	—	—	—	7.00	—
JE5761 (2000)	—	—	—	—	—	—

KM# 312 10 NEW SHEQALIM **Weight:** 15.5500 g. **Composition:** 0.9990 Gold .4994 oz. AGW **Subject:** 50th Anniversary of Independence **Obverse:** Denomination **Reverse:** Flag

Date	Mintage	F	VF	XF	Unc	BU
JE5758 (1998) Proof	Est. 3,000	Value: 400				

KM# 319 10 NEW SHEQALIM **Weight:** 17.2800 g. **Composition:** 0.9000 Gold .5000 oz. AGW **Subject:** Biblical - Noah's Ark **Obverse:** Rainbow, dove, denomination **Reverse:** Noah releasing dove from ark

Date	Mintage	F	VF	XF	Unc	BU
JE5758-1998 Proof	Est. 1,500	Value: 420				

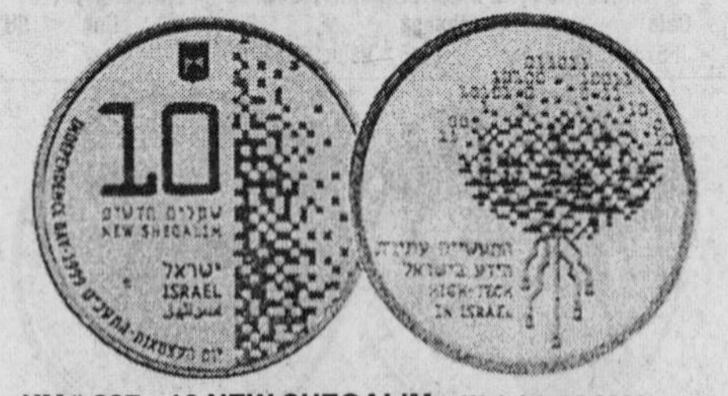

KM# 327 10 NEW SHEQALIM **Weight:** 16.9600 g. **Composition:** 0.9170 Gold .5000 oz. AGW **Subject:** Anniversary - High-Tech in Israel **Obverse:** Denomination and mosaic **Reverse:** Mosaic bouquet

Date	Mintage	F	VF	XF	Unc	BU
JE5759-1999 Proof	2,000	Value: 550				

KM# 330 10 NEW SHEQALIM **Weight:** 16.9600 g. **Composition:** 0.9170 Gold .5000 oz. AGW **Subject:** The Millennium Coin **Obverse:** Denomination, olive branch **Reverse:** Year 2000 motif incorporating dove with olive branch

Date	Mintage	F	VF	XF	Unc	BU
JE5759-1999 Proof	Est. 2,000	Value: 425				

KM# 338 10 NEW SHEQALIM **Weight:** 16.9600 g. **Composition:** 0.9170 Gold .5000 oz. AGW **Subject:** Anniversary - Love Thy Neighbor **Obverse:** Gates of Jerusalem **Reverse:** Back of gate; arch above inscription **Edge:** Reeded

Date	Mintage	F	VF	XF	Unc	BU
JE5760-2000 Proof	—	Value: 400				

KM# 341 10 NEW SHEQALIM **Weight:** 16.9600 g. **Composition:** 0.9170 Gold .5000 oz. AGW **Series:** Biblical **Obverse:** Denomination **Reverse:** Joseph standing before his kneeling brothers **Edge:** Reeded **Size:** 30 mm.

Date	Mintage	F	VF	XF	Unc	BU
JE5760-2000 Proof	1,000	Value: 400				

KM# 346 10 NEW SHEQALIM **Weight:** 16.9600 g. **Composition:** 0.9170 Gold .5000 oz. AGW **Subject:** Independence Day and Education **Obverse:** Denomination **Reverse:** Pomegranate full of symbols - Hebrew for 'ABC - 123', etc. **Edge:** Reeded **Size:** 30 mm.

Date	Mintage	F	VF	XF	Unc	BU
JE5761-2001 Proof	1,200	Value: 420				

KM# 353 10 NEW SHEQALIM **Weight:** 16.9600 g. **Composition:** 0.9170 Gold 0.5 oz. AGW **Subject:** Music **Obverse:** National arms and denomination **Reverse:** Musical instruments **Edge:** Reeded **Size:** 30 mm.

Date	Mintage	F	VF	XF	Unc	BU
JE5761-2001 Proof	—	Value: 430				

KM# 299 20 NEW SHEQALIM **Weight:** 31.1035 g. **Composition:** 0.9990 Gold 1.0000 oz. AGW **Obverse:** Arms above denomination **Reverse:** Head of Yitzhak Rabin left

Date	Mintage	F	VF	XF	Unc	BU
JE5756-1996 Proof	1,999	Value: 900				

KM# 313 20 NEW SHEQALIM **Weight:** 31.1035 g. **Composition:** 0.9990 Gold 1.0000 oz. AGW **Subject:** 50th Anniversary of Independence **Obverse:** Denomination **Reverse:** Flag

Date	Mintage	F	VF	XF	Unc	BU
JE5758-1998 Proof	Est. 3,000	Value: 600				

KM# 286 30 NEW SHEQALIM **Weight:** 155.5175 g. **Composition:** 0.9990 Silver 5.0000 oz. ASW **Subject:** Anniversary - Jerusalem's Third Millennium **Note:** Illustration reduced. Actual size: 65mm.

Date	F	VF	XF	Unc	BU
JE5756-1996 Proof	Est. 4,000	Value: 175			

PATTERNS

KM#	Date	Mintage	Identification	Mkt Val
Pn1	1960	—	Agorah. 8 fat and wide grains. Large 9.50mm 1 and date.	—
Pn2	1960	—	Agorah. 8 thin and narrow grains. Small 9.00mm 1 and large date.	—
Pn3	1960	—	Agorah. 8 thin and narrow grains. Large 9.50mm 1 and date.	—

PIEFORTS

KM#	Date	Mintage	Identification	Mkt Val
P1	JE5741-1981	30,217	New Agorah. Copper-Nickel. KM106.	1.25
P2	JE5741	30,217	5 New Agorot. Copper-Nickel. KM107.	1.50
P3	JE5741-1981	30,217	10 New Agorot. Bronze. KM108.	2.00
P4	JE5741-1981	30,217	1/2 Sheqel. KM109.	2.50
P5	JE5741-1981	30,217	Sheqel. KM111.	3.50
	Note: P1-5 were struck at the Bern Mint			
P6	JE5742-1982	18,735	New Agorah. Copper-Nickel. KM106	3.00
P7	JE5742-1982	19,735	5 New Agorot. Copper-Nickel. KM107.	3.00
P8	JE5742-1982	18,735	10 New Agorot. KM108.	3.00
P9	JE5742-1982	21,735	1/2 Sheqel. KM109.	4.50
P10	JE5742-1982	19,735	Sheqel. KM111.	4.50
P11	JE5742-1982	20,735	5 Sheqalim. KM118.	7.00
P14	JE5743-1983	17,177	10 New Agorot. KM108.	2.00
P15	JE5743-1983	17,177	1/2 Sheqel. KM109.	2.00
P16	JE5743-1983	17,177	Sheqel. KM111.	2.00
P17	JE5743-1983	17,177	5 Sheqalim. KM118.	2.50
P18	JE5743-1983	17,177	10 Sheqalim. KM119.	3.50
P21	JE5744-1984	15,572	10 New Agorot. KM108.	2.00
P22	JE5744-1984	15,572	1/2 Sheqel. KM109.	2.00
P23	JE5744-1984	15,572	Sheqel. KM111.	2.00
P24	JE5744-1984	15,572	5 Sheqalim. KM118.	2.50
P25	JE5744-1984	15,572	10 Sheqalim. KM119.	3.50
	Note: P6-25 were struck at the Rome Mint			
P26	JE5745-1985	14,768	Sheqel. KM111.	2.00
P27	JE5745-1985	14,768	5 Sheqalim. KM118.	2.00
P28	JE5745-1985	14,768	10 Sheqalim. KM119.	2.50
P29	JE5745-1985	14,768	50 Sheqalim. KM139.	3.00
P30	JE5745-1985	14,768	100 Sheqalim. KM143.	3.00
	Note: P26-30 were struck at the Bern Mint			
P31	JE5746-1986	12,665	Agorah. KM156.	1.00
P32	JE5746-1986	12,665	Agorah. KM157.	2.00
P33	JE5746-1986	12,665	10 Agorot. KM158.	2.00
P34	JE5746-1986	12,665	1/2 New Sheqel. KM159.	3.00
P35	JE5746-1986	12,665	New Sheqel. KM160.	3.00
	Note: P31-35 were struck at the Paris Mint			
P36	JE5747-1987	11,529	Agorah. KM156.	1.00
P37	JE5747-1987	11,529	5 Agorot. KM157.	2.00
P38	JE5747-1987	11,529	10 Agorot. KM158.	2.00
P39	JE5747-1987	11,529	1/2 New Sheqel. KM159.	3.00
P40	JE5747-1987	11,529	New Sheqel. KM160.	3.00
P41	JE5748-1988	12,027	5 Agorot. Nickel. KM194.	2.00
P42	JE5748-1988	12,027	10 Agorot. Nickel. KM195.	2.00
P43	JE5748-1988	12,027	1/2 New Sheqel. Nickel. KM196.	3.00
P44	JE5748-1988	12,027	New Sheqel. Nickel. KM197.	3.00
	Note: P36-44 were struck at the Stuttgart Mint			
PA41	JE5748-1988	—	Agorah. KM193.	—
P45	JE5749-1989	9,622	Agorah. Nickel. KM156.	1.00
P46	JE5749-1989	9,622	5 Agorot. KM157.	2.00
P47	JE5749-1989	9,622	10 Agorot. KM155.	2.00
P48	JE5749-1989	9,622	1/2 New Sheqel. KM159.	3.00
P49	JE5749-1989	9,622	New Sheqel. KM160.	3.00
P50	JE5750-1990	—	Agorah. Bronze. KM156.	1.00
P51	JE5750-1990	—	5 Agorot. Bronze. KM157.	2.00
P52	JE5750-1990	—	10 Agorot. Bronze. KM158.	2.00
P53	JE5750-1990	—	1/2 New Sheqel. Bronze. KM159.	3.00
P54	JE5750-1990	—	New Sheqel. KM160.	3.00
P55	JE5750-1990	—	5 New Sheqalim. KM207.	6.00
P56	JE5751-1991	—	Agorah. KM156.	1.00
P57	JE5751-1991	—	5 Agorot. KM157.	2.00
P58	JE5751-1991	—	10 Agorot. KM158.	2.00
P59	JE5751-1991	—	1/2 New Sheqel. KM159.	4.00
P60	JE5751-1991	—	New Sheqel. KM160.	3.00
P61	JE5751	—	5 New Sheqalim. KM207.	—
P62	JE5752-1992	—	Agorah. KM156.	1.00
P63	JE5752-1992	—	5 Agorot. KM157.	2.00
P64	JE5752-1992	—	10 Agorot. KM158.	2.00
P65	JE5752-1992	—	1/2 New Sheqel. KM159.	3.00
P66	JE5752-1992	—	New Sheqel. KM160.	3.00
P67	JE5752-1992	—	5 New Sheqalim. KM207.	8.00
P68	JE5753-1993	8,000	Agorah. KM156.	1.00
P69	JE5753-1993	8,000	5 Agorot. KM157.	—
P70	JE5753-1993	8,000	10 Agorot. KM158.	—
P71	JE5753-1993	8,000	1/2 New Sheqel. KM159.	—
P72	JE5753-1993	8,000	New Sheqel. KM160.	—
P73	JE5753-1993	8,000	5 New Sheqalim. KM161.	—
P74	JE5754-1994	8,000	Agorah. KM156.	—
P75	JE5754-1994	8,000	5 Agorot. KM157.	—
P76	JE5754-1994	8,000	10 Agorot. KM158.	—
P77	JE5754-1994	8,000	1/2 New Sheqel. KM159.	—
P78	JE5754-1994	8,000	1/2 New Sheqel. Bronze. KM306.	—
P79	JE5754-1994	8,000	New Sheqel. KM160.	—
P80	JE5754-1994	8,000	5 New Sheqalim. KM207.	—
P81	JE5755-1995	10,000	Agorah. KM156.	—
P82	JE5755-1995	10,000	5 Agorot. KM157.	—
P83	JE5755-1995	10,000	10 Agorot. KM158.	—
P84	JE5755-1995	10,000	1/2 New Sheqel. KM159.	—
P85	JE5755-1995	10,000	1/2 New Sheqel. Bronze. KM307.	—
P86	JE5755-1995	10,000	New Sheqel. KM160.	—
P87	JE5755-1995	10,000	5 New Sheqalim. KM207.	—
P88	JE5755-1995	10,000	10 New Sheqalim. KM270.	—

MINT SETS

KM#	Date	Mintage	Identification	Issue Price	Mkt Val
MS1	1949 (10)	—	KM8-12,13.1,14-15,15a,16 in muffin tin	—	150
MS2	1962 (16)	4,000	KM12a, 13.2a, 17-20, 20a, 24.1, 25-27	18.50	75.00
MS4	1963 (6)	200	KM24.1, 25-26 (1962), 27, 36.1, 37 (white folder, plastic over card)	2.50	175
MS5	1963 (6)	2,000	KM#24.1, 25, 26, 27, 36.1, 37 (plain white card)	2.50	125
MS6	1963 (6)	10,000	KM#24.1 with inverted reverse, KM#25, 26, 27, 36.1, 37 (card with map).	2.60	35.00
MS7	1963 (6)	10,544	KM#24.1, 25, 26, 27, 36.1, 37 (card with map) - issued in 1964.	2.60	12.00
MS8	1965 (6)	153,424	KM24.1, 25-27, 36.1, 37	3.50	3.00
MS9	1966 (6)	114,714	KM24.1, 25-27, 36.1, 37	3.50	3.00
MS10	1967 (6)	128,124	KM24.1, 25-27, 36.1, 37 (card)	3.50	3.00
MS11	1968 (6)	184,552	KM24.1, 25-27, 36.1, 47.1 (card)	3.50	3.00
MS12	1969 (6)	158,052	KM24.1, 25-27, 36.1, 47.1 (card)	3.50	3.50
MS13	1970 (6)	60,045	KM24.1, 25-27, 36.1, 47.1, in red wallet	3.75	4.00
MS13a	1970 (6)	64,800	KM24.1, 25-27, 36.1, 47.1(card)	3.75	4.00
MS14	1971 (6)	32,543	KM24.1, 25-27, 36.1, 47.1, in blue wallet	3.50	4.00
MS14a	1971 (6)	125,921	KM24.1, 25-27, 36.1, 47.1, with Star of David, in pink plastic case	3.00	3.00
MS15	1972 (6)	21,486	KM24.1, 25-27, 36.1, 47.1, in violet wallet	3.00	5.00
MS15a	1972 (6)	68,513	KM24.1, 25-27, 36.1, 47.1, with Star of David, in violet plastic case	3.50	3.00
MS16	1973 (6)	97,107	KM63-68, in blue plastic case	3.50	4.00

MINT SETS NON-STANDARD METALS

KM#	Date	Mintage	Identification	Issue Price	Mkt Val
MS32	1985 (5)	7,760	KM156-160	10.00	30.00
MS34	1986 (12)	14,305	KM156-160, 163, 167, 171-174 mixed dates	9.00	15.00
MS40	1988 (5)	12,027	KM193-197, piefors	—	30.00
MS41	1988 (5)	15,000	KM193-197, blue holder	6.50	8.50
MS39	1988 (6)	—	KM156-60, 198, green holder	7.50	7.50
MS53	Mixed date (7)	8,000	KM134, 147, 151, 167, 198, 208, 237	15.00	15.00
MS25	1980 (7)	31,348	KM96-102	13.00	15.00
MS17	1974 (6)	92,868	KM24.1, 25a-27a, 36.1, 47.1, in brown plastic case	3.50	3.00
MS21	1978 (6)	57,200	KM#24.2, 25c, 26c, 27b, 36.2, 47.2	3.50	5.00
MS26	1982 (7)	30,000	KM106-109, 111, 118-119	3.50	8.00
MS27	1982 (6)	18,735	KM106-109, 111, 118 pieforts	11.00	20.00
MS28	1983 (7)	17,177	KM106-109, 11, 118-119 pieforts	11.00	22.00
MS28a	1983 (5)	17,478	KM108-109, 111, 118-119	3.50	8.00
MS29	1984 (9)	13,403	KM108-109, 111, 118-119, 134, 137, 143	4.50	10.00
MS29a	1984 (7)	15,572	KM106-109, 111, 118-119 pieforts	10.00	22.00
MS30	1985 (8)	15,224	KM111, 118-119, 139-140, 143, 146, 151	4.50	15.00
MS31	1985 (5)	14,768	KM111, 118-119, 139,143 pieforts	10.00	20.00
MS33	1986 (5)	12,665	KM156-160, pieforts	12.00	30.00
MS35	1986 (5)	—	KM163, 171-174	—	6.00
MS36	1987 (10)	11,094	KM156-160, 163, 171-174 mixed dates	10.00	—
MS37	1987 (5)	30,000	KM163, 171-174	6.50	6.00
MS38	1987 (5)	11,529	KM156-160 pieforts	18.00	30.00
MS42	1988 (5)	20,000	KM163, 171-174	8.00	10.00
MS43	1989 (10)	9,716	KM156-160, 163, 171-174	7.00	12.00
MS44	1989 (5)	15,000	KM156-160, pieforts	15.00	30.00
MS45	1989 (5)	7,562	KM163, 171-174	5.00	10.00
MS46	1990 (6)	12,000	KM156-160, 207	8.00	10.00
MS47	1990 (6)	10,000	KM156-160, 207, pieforts	15.00	35.00
MS48	1990 (6)	7,929	KM163, 171-174, 217	8.00	8.00
MS49	1991 (7)	6,746	KM208 (5750), 156-160, 207 (5751)	10.00	20.00
MS50	1991 (6)	6,617	KM156-160, 207, pieforts	15.00	30.00
MS51	1991 (5)	6,886	KM163, 172-174, 217	8.00	8.00
MS52	1992 (6)	8,000	KM156-160, 207	15.00	15.00
MS54	1992 (5)	8,000	KM157-160, 207	8.00	10.00
MS55	1992 (5)	8,000	KM163, 172-174, 217	9.50	8.00
MS56	1993 (6)	8,000	KM156-160, 207, pieforts	15.00	40.00
MS57	1993 (6)	12,000	KM163, 172-174, 217, 303	16.00	20.00
MS60	1994 (7)	8,000	KM156-160, 207, P78	17.00	20.00
MS59	1994 (6)	12,000	KM163, 172-174, 217, 304	17.00	20.00
MS61	1995 (7)	7,500	KM157-159, 163, 217, 270, 305	29.00	35.00
MS62	1995 (8)	10,000	KM156-160, 207, 270, P85	33.00	35.00
MS63	1996 (6)	—	KM163, 172-174, 217, 318	—	20.00
MS64	1997 (7)	10,000	KM163, 172-174, 217, 314-315	—	35.00
MS65	2000 (7)	4,000	KM163, 172-174, 217, 315,354	—	35.00

PROOF SETS

KM#	Date	Mintage	Identification	Issue Price	Mkt Val
PS3	1996 (2)	—	KM294-295	—	65.00
PS4	1996 (3)	—	KM294-296	—	450

SPECIAL SELECT SETS

KM#	Date	Mintage	Identification	Issue Price	Mkt Val
SS1	1949 (10)	300	KM#8-12 with pearl, 13.1 with pearl, 14-15 with pearl, 15 without pearl, 16 in two-piece heavy plastic case (light blue molded bottom and a clear swivel top)	—	250

Italian Somaliland, a former Italian Colony in East Africa, extended south from Ras Asir to Kenya. Area: 178,218 sq. miles (461,585 sq. km). Capital: Mogadisho. In 1885, Italy obtained commercial concessions in the area of the sultan of Zanzibar, and in 1905 purchased the coast from Warshek to Brava. The Italians then extended their occupation inward. Cession of the Jubaland Province by Britain in 1924, and seizure of the sultanates of Obbia and Mejertein in 1925-27 brought direct Italian administration over the whole territory. Italian dominance continued until WW II. British troops occupied Italian Somaliland in 1941. Britain administered the colony until 1950 when it became a UN trust territory administered by Italy. On July 1, 1960. Italian Somaliland united with British Somaliland to form the Independent Somali Democratic Republic.

TITLES

الصومال الايطليانية

Al-Somal Al-Italiyaniya(t)

MONETARY SYSTEM

100 Bese = 1 Rupia

ITALIAN POSSESSION

STANDARD COINAGE

100 Bese = 1 Rupia

KM# 1 BESA **Composition:** Bronze

Date	Mintage	F	VF	XF	Unc	BU
1909R	2,000,000	10.00	20.00	40.00	145	—
1910R	500,000	10.00	20.00	40.00	145	—
1913R	200,000	15.00	30.00	90.00	300	—
1921R	500,000	12.50	22.50	45.00	175	—

KM# 2 2 BESE **Composition:** Bronze

Date	Mintage	F	VF	XF	Unc	BU
1909R	500,000	12.50	25.00	65.00	250	—
1910R	250,000	12.50	25.00	65.00	275	—
1913R	300,000	15.00	30.00	90.00	300	—
1921R	600,000	12.50	25.00	65.00	235	—
1923R	1,500,000	12.50	22.50	60.00	230	—
1924R	Inc. above	12.50	20.00	55.00	220	—

KM# 3 4 BESE **Composition:** Bronze

Date	Mintage	F	VF	XF	Unc	BU
1909R	250,000	18.00	35.00	90.00	375	—
1910R	250,000	18.00	35.00	90.00	385	—
1913R	50,000	35.00	85.00	250	650	—
1921R	200,000	20.00	40.00	100	400	—
1923R	1,000,000	20.00	40.00	100	400	—
1924R	Inc. above	20.00	50.00	110	420	—

KM# 4 1/4 RUPIA **Weight:** 2.9160 g. **Composition:** 0.9170 Silver .0859 oz. ASW

Date	Mintage	F	VF	XF	Unc	BU
1910R	400,000	12.50	25.00	70.00	175	—
1913R	100,000	35.00	65.00	150	275	—

KM# 5 1/2 RUPIA **Weight:** 5.8319 g. **Composition:** 0.9170 Silver .1719 oz. ASW

Date	Mintage	F	VF	XF	Unc	BU
1910R	400,000	20.00	40.00	90.00	200	—
1912R	100,000	22.50	45.00	100	220	—
1913R	100,000	22.50	45.00	100	220	—
1915R	50,000	35.00	75.00	200	400	—
1919R	200,000	20.00	40.00	90.00	200	—

KM# 6 RUPIA **Weight:** 11.6638 g. **Composition:** 0.9170 Silver .3437 oz. ASW

Date	Mintage	F	VF	XF	Unc	BU
1910R	300,000	25.00	55.00	110	200	—
1912R	600,000	25.00	55.00	110	200	—
1913R	300,000	25.00	50.00	100	185	—
1914R	300,000	25.00	50.00	100	185	—
1915R	250,000	25.00	50.00	100	185	—
1919R	400,000	25.00	50.00	100	185	—
1920R	1,300,000	500	900	2,000	3,500	—
1921R	940,000	950	2,150	3,350	5,750	—

REFORM COINAGE

100 Centesimi = 1 Lira

KM# 7 5 LIRE **Weight:** 6.0000 g. **Composition:** 0.8350 Silver .1611 oz. ASW

Date	Mintage	F	VF	XF	Unc	BU
1925R	400,000	65.00	125	225	350	550

KM# 8 10 LIRE **Weight:** 12.0000 g. **Composition:** 0.8350 Silver .3221 oz. ASW

Date	Mintage	F	VF	XF	Unc	BU
1925R	100,000	100	200	300	500	700

PROVAS

KM#	Date	Mintage	Identification	Mkt Val
Pr1	1909R	—	Besa. Bronze.	250
Pr2	1909R	—	2 Bese. Bronze.	300
Pr3	1909R	—	4 Bese. Bronze.	400
Pr4	1909R	—	4 Bese. Silver.	—
Pr5	1910R	—	4 Bese. Nickel.	—

KM#	Date	Mintage	Identification	Mkt Val
Pr6	1910R	—	1/4 Rupia. Silver.	400

KM#	Date	Mintage	Identification	Mkt Val
Pr7	1910R	—	1/2 Rupia. Silver.	375

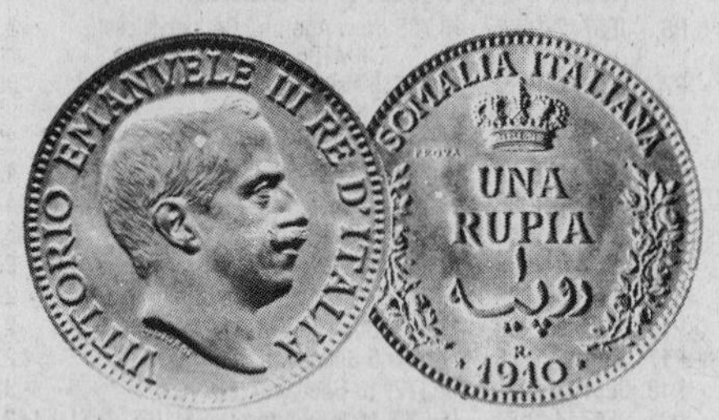

KM#	Date	Mintage	Identification	Mkt Val
Pr8	1910R	—	Rupia. Silver.	400
Pr9	1915R	—	1/2 Rupia. Silver. 1 ANNO/DI GUERRA flanks crown.	—
Pr10	1915R	—	Rupia. Silver. 1 ANNO/DI GUERRA flanks crown.	—
Pr11	1925R	—	5 Lire. Silver. PROVA.	800
Pr13	1925R	—	10 Lire. Silver. PROVA.	1,000
Pr14	1925R	—	10 Lire. Silver. PROVA DI STAMPA.	850
Pr12	1925R	—	5 Lire. Silver. PROVA DI STAMPA.	700

TRIAL STRIKES

KM#	Date	Mintage	Identification	Mkt Val
TS1	1909	—	Besa. Pewter.	375

KM#	Date	Mintage	Identification	Mkt Val
TS2	1909	—	2 Bese. Lead.	—
TS3	1910	—	4 Bese. Pewter.	750

ITALY

The Italian Republic, a 700-mile-long peninsula extending into the heart of the Mediterranean Sea, has an area of 116,304 sq. mi. (301,230 sq. km.) and a population of 60 million. Capital: Rome. The economy centers around agriculture, manufacturing, forestry and fishing. Machinery, textiles, clothing and motor vehicles are exported.

From the fall of Rome until modern times, 'Italy' was little more than a geographical expression. Although nominally included in the Empire of Charlemagne and the Holy Roman Empire, it was in reality divided into a number of independent states and kingdoms presided over by wealthy families, soldiers of fortune or hereditary rulers. The 19th century unification movement fostered by Mazzini, Garibaldi and Cavour attained fruition in 1860-70 with the creation of the Kingdom of Italy and the installation of Victor Emmanuel, king of Sardinia, as king of Italy. Benito Mussolini came to power during the post-World War I period of economic and political unrest, and installed a Fascist dictatorship with a figurehead king as titular Head of State. Mussolini entered Italy into the German-Japanese anti-comitern pact (Tri-Partite Pact) and withdrew from the League of Nations. The war did not go well for Italy and Germany was forced to assist Italy in its failed invasion of Greece. The Allied invasion of Sicily on July 10, 1943 and bombings of Rome brought the Fascist council to a no vote of confidence on July 23, 1943. Mussolini was arrested but soon escaped and set up a government in Salo. Rome fell to the Allied forces in June, 1944 and the country was allowed the status of cobelligerent against Germany. The Germans held northern Italy for another year. Mussolini was eventually captured and executed by partisans.

Following the defeat of the Axis powers, the Italian monarchy was dissolved by plebiscite, and the Italian Republic proclaimed.

KINGDOM

DECIMAL COINAGE

KM# 35 CENTESIMO **Composition:** Copper **Ruler:** Vittorio Emanuele III

Date	Mintage	F	VF	XF	Unc	BU
1902R	26,000	165	450	850	1,650	—
1903R	5,655,000	1.00	2.00	4.00	18.00	—
1904/0R	14,626,000	2.00	3.00	7.50	22.00	—
1904R	Inc. above	1.00	2.00	4.00	10.00	—
1905/0R	8,531,000	2.00	3.00	7.50	22.00	—
1905R	Inc. above	1.00	2.00	4.00	10.00	—
1908R	3,859,000	1.00	2.00	4.00	10.00	—

KM# 40 CENTESIMO **Composition:** Copper **Ruler:** Vittorio Emanuele III

Date	Mintage	F	VF	XF	Unc	BU
1908R	57,000	150	225	450	850	—
1909R	3,539,000	1.00	2.00	4.00	10.00	—
1910R	3,599,000	1.00	2.00	4.00	10.00	—
1911R	700,000	5.00	10.00	15.00	28.00	—
1912R	3,995,000	1.00	2.00	4.00	10.00	—
1913R	3,200,000	1.00	2.00	4.00	10.00	—
1914R	11,585,000	1.00	2.00	4.00	10.00	—
1915R	9,757,000	1.00	2.00	4.00	10.00	—
1916R	9,845,000	1.00	2.00	4.00	10.00	—
1917R	2,400,000	1.00	2.00	4.00	10.00	—
1918R	2,710,000	5.00	10.00	15.00	28.00	—

KM# 38 2 CENTESIMI **Composition:** Copper **Ruler:** Vittorio Emanuele III

Date	Mintage	F	VF	XF	Unc	BU
1903R	5,000,000	0.60	1.50	4.00	15.00	—
1905R	1,260,000	4.00	8.50	18.00	35.00	—
1906R	3,145,000	0.60	1.50	3.50	8.00	—
1907R	230,000	25.00	50.00	75.00	165	—
1908R	1,518,000	1.00	2.50	5.00	18.00	—

KM# 41 2 CENTESIMI **Composition:** Copper **Ruler:** Vittorio Emanuele III

Date	Mintage	F	VF	XF	Unc	BU
1908	298,000	9.00	15.00	25.00	90.00	—
1909	2,419,000	0.60	1.50	3.00	16.50	—
1910	590,000	2.00	4.00	9.00	32.00	—
1911	2,777,000	0.60	1.50	3.00	16.50	—
1912	840,000	0.60	2.00	5.00	17.50	—
1914	1,648,000	0.50	1.30	2.00	16.50	—
1915	4,860,000	0.50	1.30	2.50	16.50	—
1916	1,540,000	0.50	1.30	2.00	16.50	—
1917	3,638,000	0.50	1.30	2.00	16.50	—

KM# 42 5 CENTESIMI **Composition:** Copper **Ruler:** Vittorio Emanuele III

Date	Mintage	F	VF	XF	Unc	BU
1908R	824,000	10.00	25.00	50.00	145	—
1909R	1,734,000	0.75	1.75	3.50	18.00	—
1912R	743,000	1.75	3.00	6.00	35.00	—
1913R Dot after D	1,964,000	4.00	10.00	18.00	55.00	—
1913R Without dot after D	Inc. above	40.00	75.00	150	250	—
1915R	1,038,000	3.50	7.50	12.50	35.00	—
1918R	4,242,000	0.75	1.75	3.50	16.50	—

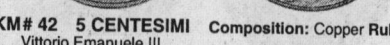

KM# 59 5 CENTESIMI **Composition:** Copper **Ruler:** Vittorio Emanuele III

Date	Mintage	F	VF	XF	Unc	BU
1919R	13,208,000	0.75	2.00	3.00	12.00	—
1920R	33,372,000	0.30	0.75	2.00	5.50	—
1921R	80,111,000	0.30	0.75	2.00	5.50	—
1922R	42,914,000	0.30	0.75	2.00	5.50	—
1923R	29,614,000	0.30	0.75	2.00	5.50	—
1924R	20,352,000	0.30	0.75	2.00	5.50	—
1925R	40,460,000	0.30	0.75	2.00	5.50	—
1926R	21,158,000	0.30	0.75	2.00	5.50	—
1927R	15,800,000	0.30	0.75	2.00	5.50	—
1928R	16,090,000	0.30	0.75	2.00	5.50	—
1929R	29,000,000	0.30	0.75	2.00	5.50	—
1930R	22,694,000	0.30	0.75	2.00	5.50	—
1931R	20,000,000	0.30	0.75	2.00	5.50	—
1932R	11,456,000	0.30	0.75	2.00	5.50	—
1933R	20,720,000	0.30	0.75	2.00	5.50	—
1934R	16,000,000	0.30	0.75	2.00	5.50	—
1935R	11,000,000	0.30	0.75	2.00	5.50	—
1936R	9,462,000	0.30	0.75	2.00	5.50	—
1937R	972,000	4.00	8.00	12.50	27.50	—

KM# 73 5 CENTESIMI **Composition:** Copper **Ruler:** Vittorio Emanuele III

Date	Mintage	F	VF	XF	Unc	BU
1936R Yr. XIV	Inc. above	2.00	4.00	9.00	18.50	—
1937R Yr. XV	7,207,000	0.30	0.75	1.00	3.50	—
1938R Yr. XVI	24,000,000	0.20	0.65	1.00	3.50	—
1939R Yr. XVII	22,000,000	0.20	0.65	1.00	3.50	—

KM# 73a 5 CENTESIMI **Composition:** Aluminum-Bronze **Ruler:** Vittorio Emanuele III

Date	Mintage	F	VF	XF	Unc	BU
1939R Yr. XVII	1,000,000	0.30	0.75	1.25	3.50	—
1940R Yr. XVIII	9,630,000	0.30	0.75	1.00	3.50	—
1941R Yr. XIX	16,340,000	0.30	0.75	1.00	3.50	—
1942R Yr. XX	25,200,000	0.30	0.75	1.25	3.50	—
1943R Yr. XXI	13,922,000	2.00	5.00	10.00	22.00	—

KM# 43 10 CENTESIMI **Composition:** Copper **Ruler:** Vittorio Emanuele III **Note:** Similar to 5 Centesimi, KM#42.

Date	F	VF	XF	Unc	BU
1908R Rare	—	—	—	—	—

KM# 51 10 CENTESIMI **Composition:** Copper **Ruler:** Vittorio Emanuele III **Subject:** 50th Anniversary of the Kingdom

Date	Mintage	F	VF	XF	Unc	BU
1911R	2,000,000	3.50	6.50	12.50	40.00	—

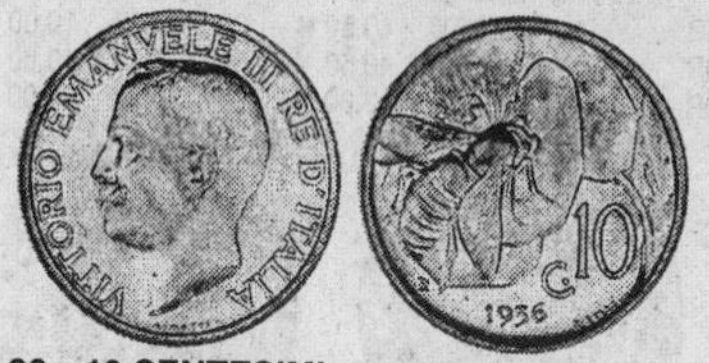

KM# 60 10 CENTESIMI **Composition:** Copper **Ruler:** Vittorio Emanuele III

Date	Mintage	F	VF	XF	Unc	BU
1919R	986,000	20.00	35.00	50.00	110	—
1920R	37,995,000	0.50	1.25	4.00	11.50	—
1921R	66,510,000	0.50	1.25	4.00	11.50	—
1922R	45,217,000	0.50	1.25	4.00	11.50	—
1923R	31,529,000	0.50	1.25	4.00	11.50	—
1924R	35,312,000	0.50	1.25	4.00	11.50	—
1925R	22,370,000	0.50	1.25	4.00	11.50	—
1926R	25,190,000	0.50	1.25	4.00	11.50	—
1927R	22,673,000	0.50	1.25	4.00	11.50	—
1928R	15,680,000	0.50	2.00	7.50	22.00	—
1929R	15,593,000	0.50	1.25	4.00	11.50	—
1930R	17,115,000	0.50	1.25	4.00	11.50	—
1931R	10,750,000	0.50	1.25	4.00	11.50	—
1932R	5,678,000	1.25	2.50	7.50	22.00	—
1933R	10,250,000	0.50	1.25	4.00	11.50	—
1934R	18,300,000	0.50	1.25	4.00	11.50	—
1935R	10,500,000	0.50	1.25	4.00	11.50	—
1936R	8,770,000	0.50	1.50	4.50	13.50	—
1937R	5,500,000	0.50	1.50	4.50	13.50	—

KM# 74 10 CENTESIMI **Composition:** Copper **Ruler:** Vittorio Emanuele III

Date	Mintage	F	VF	XF	Unc	BU
1936R Yr. XIV	Inc. above	0.75	1.50	3.00	13.50	—
1937R Yr. XV	7,212,000	0.25	0.75	1.50	4.50	—
1938R Yr. XVI	18,750,000	0.25	0.75	1.50	4.50	—
1939R Yr. XVII	24,750,000	0.25	0.75	1.50	4.50	—

KM# 74a 10 CENTESIMI **Composition:** Aluminum-Bronze **Ruler:** Vittorio Emanuele III

Date	Mintage	F	VF	XF	Unc	BU
1939R Yr. XVII	750,000	0.50	1.50	2.00	4.50	—
1940R Yr. XVIII	23,355,000	0.20	0.60	1.00	4.50	—
1941R Yr. XIX	27,050,000	0.20	0.60	1.00	4.50	—
1942R Yr. XX	18,100,000	0.20	0.60	1.00	4.50	—
1943R Yr. XXI	25,400,000	0.25	0.60	2.00	5.50	—

KM# 44 20 CENTESIMI **Composition:** Nickel **Ruler:** Vittorio Emanuele III

Date	Mintage	F	VF	XF	Unc	BU
1908R	14,315,000	0.50	1.00	3.00	11.50	—
1909R	19,280,000	0.50	1.00	3.00	11.50	—
1910R	21,887,000	0.50	1.00	3.00	11.50	—
1911R	13,671,000	0.50	1.00	3.00	11.50	—
1912R	21,040,000	0.50	1.00	3.00	11.50	—
1913R	20,729,000	0.50	1.00	3.00	11.50	—
1914R	14,308,000	0.50	1.00	3.00	11.50	—
1919R	3,475,000	1.00	3.50	10.00	28.00	—
1920R	27,284,000	0.50	1.00	3.00	11.50	—
1921R	50,372,000	0.50	1.00	3.00	11.50	—
1922R	17,134,000	0.50	1.00	3.00	11.50	—
1926R	500	—	—	—	175	—
1927R	100	—	—	—	245	—
1928R	50	—	—	—	285	—
1929R	50	—	—	—	285	—
1930R	50	—	—	—	285	—
1931R	50	—	—	—	285	—
1932R	50	—	—	—	285	—
1933R	50	—	—	—	285	—
1934R	50	—	—	—	285	—
1935R	50	—	—	—	285	—

KM# 58 20 CENTESIMI **Composition:** Copper-Nickel **Ruler:** Vittorio Emanuele III **Edge:** Plain and reeded **Note:** Overstruck on KM#28.

Date	Mintage	F	VF	XF	Unc	BU
1918R	43,097,000	0.50	1.00	4.00	10.00	—
1919R	33,432,000	0.50	1.00	4.00	10.00	—
1920R	923,000	3.00	5.00	10.00	32.00	—

KM# 75 20 CENTESIMI **Composition:** Nickel **Ruler:** Vittorio Emanuele III **Size:** 21.5 mm.

Date	Mintage	F	VF	XF	Unc	BU
1936R Yr. XIV	117,000	20.00	45.00	95.00	200	—
1937R Yr. XV	50	—	—	—	375	—
1938R Yr. XVII	20	—	—	—	500	—

KM#75a 20 CENTESIMI **Composition:** Stainless Steel **Ruler:** Vittorio Emanuele III **Edge:** Plain **Size:** 22.5 mm. **Note:** Magnetic.

Date	Mintage	F	VF	XF	Unc	BU
1939R Yr. XVII	10,462,000	2.00	6.00	14.00	38.00	—
1940R Yr. XVIII	35,350,000	1.40	3.50	10.00	28.00	—
1942R Yr. XX	48,500,000	1.40	3.50	10.00	30.00	—

KM#75b 20 CENTESIMI **Composition:** Stainless Steel **Ruler:** Vittorio Emanuele III **Edge:** Reeded **Size:** 21.8 mm. **Note:** Magnetic.

Date	Mintage	F	VF	XF	Unc	BU
1939R Yr. XVIII	Inc. above	0.35	0.70	2.00	8.00	—
1939R Yr. XVII	Inc. above	—	—	—	—	—
1940R Yr. XVIII	Inc. above	0.20	0.40	1.40	4.50	—
1941R Yr. XIX	97,300,000	0.20	0.40	1.40	4.50	—
1942R Yr. XX	Inc. above	0.25	0.50	1.00	4.00	—
1943R Yr. XXI	18,453,000	0.35	0.70	1.75	5.50	—

KM#75c 20 CENTESIMI **Composition:** Stainless Steel **Ruler:** Vittorio Emanuele III **Edge:** Plain **Size:** 22.5 mm. **Note:** Non-magnetic.

Date	F	VF	XF	Unc	BU
1939R Yr. XVII	2.00	6.00	14.00	38.00	—

KM#75d 20 CENTESIMI **Composition:** Stainless Steel **Ruler:** Vittorio Emanuele III **Edge:** Reeded **Size:** 21.8 mm. **Note:** Non-magnetic.

Date	Mintage	F	VF	XF	Unc	BU
1939R Yr. XVII	Inc. above	0.35	0.70	2.00	8.00	—
1939R Yr. XVIII	25,300,000	0.35	1.00	2.75	8.00	—
1940R Yr. XVIII	Inc. above	0.20	0.40	1.40	4.50	—

KM# 36 25 CENTESIMI **Composition:** Nickel **Ruler:** Vittorio Emanuele III

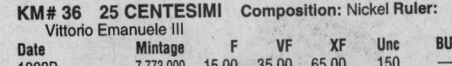

Date	Mintage	F	VF	XF	Unc	BU
1902R	7,773,000	15.00	35.00	65.00	150	—
1903R	5,895,000	12.50	25.00	45.00	120	—

KM# 61.1 50 CENTESIMI **Composition:** Nickel **Ruler:** Vittorio Emanuele III **Edge:** Plain

Date	Mintage	F	VF	XF	Unc	BU
1919R	3,700,000	2.50	5.00	20.00	55.00	—
1920R	29,450,000	0.75	1.50	3.00	20.00	—
1921R	16,849,000	0.75	1.50	3.00	20.00	—
1924R	599,000	50.00	100	285	650	—
1925R	24,884,000	1.50	2.50	8.00	25.00	—
1926R	500	—	—	—	300	—
1927R	100	—	—	—	400	—
1928R	50	—	—	—	500	—

KM# 61.2 50 CENTESIMI **Composition:** Nickel **Ruler:** Vittorio Emanuele III **Edge:** Reeded

Date	Mintage	F	VF	XF	Unc	BU
1919R	Inc. above	2.50	6.25	12.50	110	—
1920R	Inc. above	2.50	6.25	12.50	110	—
1921R	Inc. above	2.50	6.25	12.50	110	—
1924R	Inc. above	25.00	50.00	85.00	285	—
1925R	Inc. above	2.00	4.00	10.00	55.00	—
1929R	50	—	—	—	385	—
1930R	50	—	—	—	385	—
1931R	50	—	—	—	385	—
1932R	50	—	—	—	385	—
1933R	50	—	—	—	385	—
1934R	50	—	—	—	385	—
1935R	50	—	—	—	385	—

KM# 76 50 CENTESIMI **Composition:** Nickel **Ruler:** Vittorio Emanuele III

Date	Mintage	F	VF	XF	Unc	BU
1936R Yr. XIV	118,000	17.50	40.00	90.00	185	—
1937R Yr. XV	50	—	—	—	385	—
1938R Yr. XVII	20	—	—	—	550	—

KM#76a 50 CENTESIMI **Composition:** Stainless Steel **Ruler:** Vittorio Emanuele III **Note:** Non-magnetic.

Date	Mintage	F	VF	XF	Unc	BU
1939R Yr. XVII	9,373,000	0.35	0.75	2.00	8.00	—
1939R Yr. XVIII	10,005,000	0.35	0.75	2.00	8.00	—
1940R Yr. XVIII	19,005,000	0.25	0.60	1.50	5.00	—

KM#76b 50 CENTESIMI **Composition:** Stainless Steel **Ruler:** Vittorio Emanuele III **Note:** Magnetic.

Date	Mintage	F	VF	XF	Unc	BU
1939R Yr. XVII	Inc. above	0.35	0.75	2.00	8.00	—
1940R Yr. XVIII	Inc. above	0.25	0.60	1.50	5.00	—
1941R Yr. XIX	58,100,000	0.25	0.60	1.50	5.00	—
1942R Yr. XX	26,450,000	0.25	0.60	1.50	5.00	—
1943R Yr. XXI	361,000	25.00	45.00	75.00	165	—

KM# 32 LIRA **Weight:** 5.0000 g. **Composition:** 0.8350 Silver .1342 oz. ASW **Ruler:** Vittorio Emanuele III

Date	Mintage	F	VF	XF	Unc	BU
1901R	2,590,000	5.00	12.50	40.00	220	—
1902R	4,084,000	3.50	7.50	30.00	200	—
1905R	700,000	30.00	60.00	175	750	—
1906R	4,665,000	3.50	5.00	20.00	110	—
1907R	8,472,000	2.50	4.50	20.00	110	—

KM# 45 LIRA **Weight:** 5.0000 g. **Composition:** 0.8350 Silver .1342 oz. ASW **Ruler:** Vittorio Emanuele III

Date	Mintage	F	VF	XF	Unc	BU
1908R	2,212,000	20.00	40.00	120	450	—
1909R	3,475,000	3.50	7.50	35.00	220	—
1910R	5,525,000	2.50	5.00	25.00	150	—
1912R	5,865,000	2.50	4.00	15.00	80.00	—
1913R	16,177,000	2.00	3.50	9.00	45.00	—

KM# 57 LIRA **Weight:** 5.0000 g. **Composition:** 0.8350 Silver .1342 oz. ASW **Ruler:** Vittorio Emanuele III

Date	Mintage	F	VF	XF	Unc	BU
1915R	5,229,000	2.75	4.00	20.00	80.00	—
1916R	1,835,000	5.00	10.00	30.00	135	—
1917R	9,744,000	2.75	4.00	12.50	55.00	—

KM# 62 LIRA **Composition:** Nickel **Ruler:** Vittorio Emanuele III

Date	Mintage	F	VF	XF	Unc	BU
1922R	82,267,000	0.60	1.00	7.00	22.00	—
1923R	20,175,000	0.60	1.00	7.00	22.00	—
1924R Closed 2	29,288,000	0.60	1.00	7.00	22.00	—
1926R	500	—	—	—	250	—
1927R	100	—	—	—	350	—
1928R	19,996,000	1.00	2.00	15.00	45.00	—
1929R	50	—	—	—	385	—
1930R	50	—	—	—	385	—
1931R	50	—	—	—	385	—
1932R	50	—	—	—	385	—
1933R	50	—	—	—	385	—
1934R	50	—	—	—	385	—
1935R	50	—	—	—	385	—

KM# 77 LIRA **Composition:** Nickel **Ruler:** Vittorio Emanuele III

Date	Mintage	F	VF	XF	Unc	BU
1936R Yr. XIV	119,000	15.00	35.00	70.00	145	—
1937R Yr. XV	50	—	—	—	400	—
1938R XVII	20	—	—	—	550	—

KM# 77a LIRA **Composition:** Stainless Steel **Ruler:** Vittorio Emanuele III **Note:** Non-magnetic.

Date	Mintage	F	VF	XF	Unc	BU
1939R Yr. XVIII	15,977,000	0.35	0.75	1.50	6.50	—
1939R Yr. XVII	10,034,000	0.40	1.50	4.00	15.00	—
1940R Yr. XVIII	25,997,000	0.30	0.60	1.25	5.50	—

KM# 77b LIRA **Composition:** Stainless Steel **Ruler:** Vittorio Emanuele III **Note:** Magnetic.

Date	Mintage	F	VF	XF	Unc	BU
1939R Yr. XVII	Inc. above	0.40	1.50	4.00	15.00	—
1939R Yr. XVIII	Inc. above	0.35	0.75	1.50	6.50	—
1940R Yr. XVIII	Inc. above	0.30	0.60	1.25	5.50	—
1941R Yr. XIX	8,550,000	0.50	1.75	5.00	17.50	—
1942R Yr. XX	5,700,000	0.35	0.75	1.50	6.50	—
1943R Yr. XXI	11,500,000	10.00	20.00	35.00	85.00	—

KM# 33 2 LIRE **Weight:** 10.0000 g. **Composition:** 0.8350 Silver .2684 oz. ASW **Ruler:** Vittorio Emanuele III

Date	Mintage	F	VF	XF	Unc	BU
1901R	72,000	200	400	1,450	3,200	—
1902R	549,000	50.00	100	320	1,000	—
1903R	54,000	300	500	1,800	5,500	—
1904R	157,000	125	250	800	1,500	—
1905R	1,643,000	10.00	20.00	85.00	450	—
1906R	970,000	12.50	25.00	130	450	—
1907R	1,245,000	10.00	20.00	85.00	450	—

KM# 46 2 LIRE **Weight:** 10.0000 g. **Composition:** 0.8350 Silver .2684 oz. ASW **Ruler:** Vittorio Emanuele III

Date	Mintage	F	VF	XF	Unc	BU
1908R	2,283,000	6.00	15.00	85.00	325	—
1910R	719,000	25.00	50.00	200	650	—
1911R	535,000	30.00	60.00	225	900	—
1912R	2,166,000	6.00	15.00	85.00	325	—

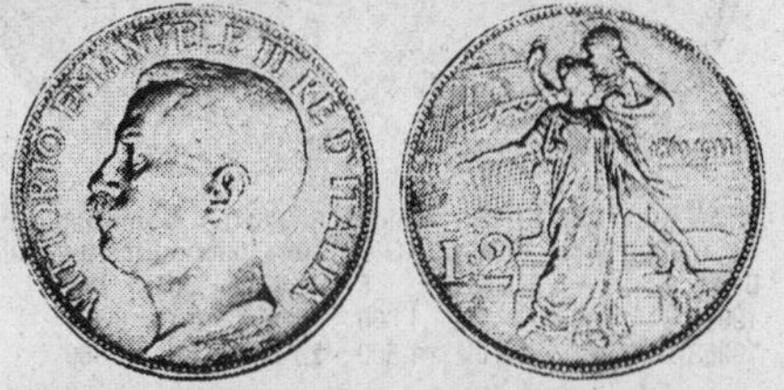

KM# 52 2 LIRE **Weight:** 10.0000 g. **Composition:** 0.8350 Silver .2684 oz. ASW **Ruler:** Vittorio Emanuele III **Subject:** 50th Anniversary of the Kingdom

Date	Mintage	F	VF	XF	Unc	BU
1911R	1,000,000	12.50	25.00	70.00	185	—

KM# 55 2 LIRE **Weight:** 10.0000 g. **Composition:** 0.8350 Silver .2684 oz. ASW **Ruler:** Vittorio Emanuele III

Date	Mintage	F	VF	XF	Unc	BU
1914R	10,390,000	4.00	6.00	12.00	50.00	—
1915R	7,948,000	4.00	6.00	12.00	50.00	—
1916R	10,923,000	4.00	6.00	12.00	50.00	—
1917R	6,123,000	6.00	12.50	25.00	65.00	—

KM# 63 2 LIRE **Composition:** Nickel **Ruler:** Vittorio Emanuele III

Date	Mintage	F	VF	XF	Unc	BU
1923R	32,260,000	1.00	2.50	6.00	22.00	—
1924R	45,051,000	1.00	2.50	6.00	22.00	—
1925R	14,628,000	1.00	2.50	6.00	32.00	—
1926R	5,101,000	5.00	10.00	50.00	165	—
1927R	1,632,000	25.00	50.00	100	325	—
1928R	50	—	—	—	425	—
1929R	50	—	—	—	425	—
1930R	50	—	—	—	425	—
1931R	50	—	—	—	425	—
1932R	50	—	—	—	425	—
1933R	50	—	—	—	425	—
1934R	50	—	—	—	425	—
1935R	50	—	—	—	425	—

KM# 78 2 LIRE **Composition:** Nickel **Ruler:** Vittorio Emanuele III

Date	Mintage	F	VF	XF	Unc	BU
1936R Yr. XIV	120,000	22.50	50.00	100	225	—
1937R Yr. XV	50	—	—	—	425	—
1939R Yr. XVII	20	—	—	—	600	—

KM# 78a 2 LIRE **Composition:** Stainless Steel **Ruler:** Vittorio Emanuele III **Note:** Non-magnetic.

Date	Mintage	F	VF	XF	Unc	BU
1939R Yr. XVIII	4,873,000	0.40	0.90	2.50	10.00	—
1939R Yr. XVII	2,900,000	0.60	1.75	5.00	17.00	—
1940R Yr. XVIII	5,742,000	0.40	0.90	2.00	5.50	—

KM# 78b 2 LIRE **Composition:** Stainless Steel **Ruler:** Vittorio Emanuele III **Note:** Magnetic.

Date	Mintage	F	VF	XF	Unc	BU
1939R Yr. XVII	Inc. above	0.60	1.75	5.00	17.00	—
1939R Yr. XVIII	Inc. above	0.40	0.90	2.50	10.00	—
1940R Yr. XVIII	Inc. above	0.40	0.90	2.00	5.50	—
1941R Yr. XIX	1,865,000	0.50	1.50	3.00	11.50	—
1942R Yr. XX	2,450,000	40.00	80.00	160	350	—
1943R Yr. XXI	600,000	20.00	40.00	100	225	—

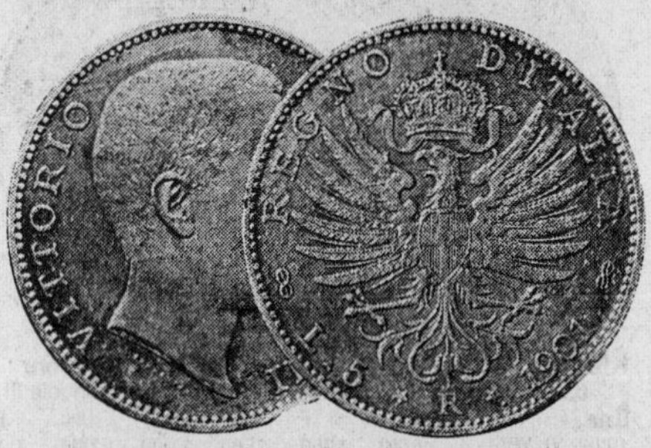

KM# 34 5 LIRE **Weight:** 25.0000 g. **Composition:** 0.9000 Silver .7234 oz. ASW **Ruler:** Vittorio Emanuele III

Date	Mintage	F	VF	XF	Unc	BU
1901R	114	—	—	15,000	20,000	—

KM# 53 5 LIRE **Weight:** 25.0000 g. **Composition:** 0.9000 Silver .7234 oz. ASW **Ruler:** Vittorio Emanuele III **Subject:** 50th Anniversary of the Kingdom

Date	Mintage	F	VF	XF	Unc	BU
1911R	60,000	150	300	500	1,000	—

KM# 56 5 LIRE **Weight:** 25.0000 g. **Composition:** 0.9000 Silver .7234 oz. ASW **Ruler:** Vittorio Emanuele III

Date	Mintage	F	VF	XF	Unc	BU
1914R	273,000	500	850	2,500	4,500	—

KM# 67.1 5 LIRE **Weight:** 5.0000 g. **Composition:** 0.8350 Silver .1342 oz. ASW **Ruler:** Vittorio Emanuele III **Edge Lettering:** *FERT*

Date	Mintage	F	VF	XF	Unc	BU
1926R	5,405,000	5.00	15.00	35.00	175	—
1927R	92,887,000	1.50	3.00	7.00	25.00	—
1928R	9,908,000	6.00	15.00	45.00	200	—
1929R	33,803,000	2.00	4.00	8.00	28.00	—
1930R	19,525,000	2.00	4.00	10.00	30.00	—
1931R	50	—	—	—	450	—
1932R	50	—	—	—	450	—
1933R	50	—	—	—	450	—
1934R	50	—	—	—	450	—
1935R	50	—	—	—	450	—

KM# 67.2 5 LIRE **Weight:** 5.0000 g. **Composition:** 0.8350 Silver .1342 oz. ASW **Ruler:** Vittorio Emanuele III **Edge Lettering:** **FERT**

Date	F	VF	XF	Unc	BU
1927R	2.00	4.00	8.00	38.00	—
1928R	10.00	20.00	50.00	220	—
1929R	3.00	6.00	12.00	45.00	—

KM# 79 5 LIRE **Weight:** 5.0000 g. **Composition:** 0.8350 Silver .1342 oz. ASW **Ruler:** Vittorio Emanuele III

Date	Mintage	F	VF	XF	Unc	BU
1936R Yr. XIV	1,016,000	10.00	20.00	40.00	110	—
1937R Yr. XV	100,000	15.00	30.00	60.00	150	—
1938R Yr. XVIII	20	—	—	—	600	—
1939R Yr. XVIII	20	—	—	—	600	—
1940R Yr. XIX	20	—	—	—	600	—
1941R Yr. XX	20	—	—	—	600	—

KM# 47 10 LIRE **Weight:** 3.2258 g. **Composition:** 0.9000 Gold .0933 oz. AGW **Ruler:** Vittorio Emanuele III **Size:** 18 mm.

Date	Mintage	F	VF	XF	Unc	BU
1910R Rare	—	—	—	—	—	—
Note: All but one piece melted						
1912R	6,796	700	1,250	2,000	3,500	—
1926R	40	—	—	6,000	9,000	—
1927R	30	—	—	5,000	7,000	—

KM# 68.1 10 LIRE **Weight:** 10.0000 g. **Composition:** 0.8350 Silver .2684 oz. ASW **Ruler:** Vittorio Emanuele III **Edge Lettering:** *FERT*

Date	Mintage	F	VF	XF	Unc	BU
1926R	1,748,000	65.00	135	275	600	—
1927R	44,801,000	6.00	12.00	30.00	70.00	—
1928R	6,652,000	20.00	55.00	125	300	—
1929R	6,800,000	30.00	65.00	150	350	—
1930R	3,668,000	60.00	125	250	500	—
1931R	50	—	—	—	750	—
1932R	50	—	—	—	750	—
1933R	50	—	—	—	750	—
1934R	50	—	—	—	750	—

KM# 68.2 10 LIRE **Weight:** 10.0000 g. **Composition:** 0.8350 Silver .2684 oz. ASW **Ruler:** Vittorio Emanuele III **Edge Lettering:** **FERT**

Date	F	VF	XF	Unc	BU
1927R	10.00	20.00	40.00	90.00	—
1928R	75.00	150	300	600	—
1929R	20.00	55.00	125	275	—

KM# 80 10 LIRE **Weight:** 10.0000 g. **Composition:** 0.8350 Silver .2684 oz. ASW **Ruler:** Vittorio Emanuele III

Date	Mintage	F	VF	XF	Unc	BU
1936R Yr. XIV	619,000	15.00	30.00	60.00	125	—
1937R Yr. XV	50	—	—	—	675	—
1938R Yr. XVII	20	—	—	—	850	—
1939R Yr. XVIII	20	—	—	—	850	—
1940R Yr. XIX	20	—	—	—	850	—
1941R Yr. XX	20	—	—	—	850	—

KM# 37.1 20 LIRE **Weight:** 6.4516 g. **Composition:** 0.9000 Gold .1867 oz. AGW **Ruler:** Vittorio Emanuele III

Date	Mintage	F	VF	XF	Unc	BU
1902R	181	—	8,000	15,000	20,000	—
1903R	1,800	350	700	1,200	1,800	—
1905R	8,715	250	400	650	900	—
1908R Rare	—	—	—	—	—	—

KM# 37.2 20 LIRE **Weight:** 6.4516 g. **Composition:** 0.9000 Gold .1867 oz. AGW **Ruler:** Vittorio Emanuele III **Obverse:** Small anchor at bottom indicates gold in coin is from Eritrea

Date	Mintage	F	VF	XF	Unc	BU
1902R	115	4,500	10,000	20,000	30,000	—

KM# 48 20 LIRE **Weight:** 6.4516 g. **Composition:** 0.9000 Gold .1867 oz. AGW **Ruler:** Vittorio Emanuele III **Obverse:** Uniformed bust

Date	F	VF	XF	Unc	BU
1910R	—	—	—	30,000	—
Note: Six pieces currently known to exist					
1912R	275	400	750	1,100	—
1926R	—	—	5,000	8,000	—
1927R	—	—	—	10,000	—

KM# 64 20 LIRE **Weight:** 6.4516 g. **Composition:** 0.9000 Gold .1867 oz. AGW **Ruler:** Vittorio Emanuele III **Subject:** 1st Anniversary of Fascist Government

Date	Mintage	F	VF	XF	Unc	BU
1923R	20,000	200	350	650	850	—

KM# 69 20 LIRE **Weight:** 15.0000 g. **Composition:** 0.8000 Silver .3858 oz. ASW **Ruler:** Vittorio Emanuele III

Date	Mintage	F	VF	XF	Unc	BU
1927R Yr. V	100	—	—	4,000	5,500	—
1927R Yr. VI	3,518,000	40.00	80.00	200	500	—
1928R Yr. VI	2,487,000	65.00	100	320	625	—
1929R Yr. VII	50	—	—	—	1,750	—
1930R Yr. VIII	50	—	—	—	1,750	—
1931R Yr. IX	50	—	—	—	1,750	—
1932R Yr. X	50	—	—	—	1,750	—
1933R Yr. XI	50	—	—	—	1,750	—
1934R Yr. XII	50	—	—	—	1,750	—

KM# 70 20 LIRE **Weight:** 20.0000 g. **Composition:** 0.6000 Silver .3858 oz. ASW **Ruler:** Vittorio Emanuele III **Subject:** 10th Anniversary - End of World War I **Note:** Similar 20 and 100 Lire pieces struck in gold, silver and silvered brass are modern fantasies.

Date	F	VF	XF	Unc	BU
1928R	65.00	125	275	700	—

KM# 81 20 LIRE **Weight:** 20.0000 g. **Composition:** 0.8000 Silver .5145 oz. ASW **Ruler:** Vittorio Emanuele III

Date	Mintage	F	VF	XF	Unc	BU
1936R Yr. XIV	10,000	250	500	1,000	2,000	—
1937R Yr. XV	50	—	—	—	2,500	—
1938R Yr. XVII	20	—	—	—	3,000	—
1939R Yr. XVIII	20	—	—	—	3,000	—
1940R Yr. XIX	20	—	—	—	3,250	—
1941R Yr. XX	20	—	—	—	3,250	—

KM# 49 50 LIRE **Weight:** 16.1290 g. **Composition:** 0.9000 Gold .4667 oz. AGW **Ruler:** Vittorio Emanuele III

Date	Mintage	F	VF	XF	Unc	BU
1910R Rare	2,096	—	—	—	—	—
1912R	11,000	350	650	1,150	1,750	—
1926R	40	—	—	—	15,000	—
1927R	30	—	—	—	18,000	—

KM# 54 50 LIRE **Weight:** 16.1290 g. **Composition:** 0.9000 Gold .4667 oz. AGW **Ruler:** Vittorio Emanuele III **Subject:** 50th Anniversary of the Kingdom

Date	Mintage	F	VF	XF	Unc	BU
1911R	20,000	300	500	750	1,450	—

KM# 71 50 LIRE **Weight:** 4.3995 g. **Composition:** 0.9000 Gold .1273 oz. AGW **Ruler:** Vittorio Emanuele III

Date	Mintage	F	VF	XF	Unc	BU
1931R Yr. IX	32,000	90.00	125	155	250	—
1931R Yr. X	Inc. above	200	300	400	600	—
1932R Yr. X	12,000	200	300	400	600	—
1933R Yr. XI	6,463	300	400	600	800	—

KM# 82 50 LIRE **Weight:** 4.3995 g. **Composition:** 0.9000 Gold .1273 oz. AGW **Ruler:** Vittorio Emanuele III

Date	Mintage	F	VF	XF	Unc	BU
1936R	790	1,000	2,000	4,000	6,000	—

KM# 39 100 LIRE **Weight:** 32.2580 g. **Composition:** 0.9000 Gold .9334 oz. AGW **Ruler:** Vittorio Emanuele III

Date	Mintage	F	VF	XF	Unc	BU
1903R	916	1,800	3,500	7,000	9,500	—
1905R	1,012	1,500	2,700	5,500	7,500	—

KM# 50 100 LIRE **Weight:** 32.2580 g. **Composition:** 0.9000 Gold .9334 oz. AGW **Ruler:** Vittorio Emanuele III

Date	Mintage	F	VF	XF	Unc	BU
1910R Rare	2,013	—	—	—	—	—
1912R	4,946	—	1,800	3,000	4,500	—
1926R	40	—	13,000	18,000	23,000	—
1927R	30	—	15,000	20,000	25,000	—

KM# 65 100 LIRE **Weight:** 32.2580 g. **Composition:** 0.9000 Gold .9334 oz. AGW **Ruler:** Vittorio Emanuele III **Subject:** 1st Anniversary of Fascist Government

Date	Mintage	F	VF	XF	Unc	BU
1923R Matte finish	20,000	750	1,000	1,500	3,000	—
1923R Bright finish, rare	—	—	—	—	—	—

KM# 66 100 LIRE Weight: 32.2580 g. **Composition:** 0.9000 Gold .9334 oz. AGW **Ruler:** Vittorio Emanuele III **Subject:** 25th year of reign, 10th Anniversary - World War I Entry

Date	Mintage	F	VF	XF	Unc	BU
1925R Matte finish	5,000	1,000	1,500	3,000	5,000	—
1925R Bright finish, rare	—	—	—	—	—	—

KM# 72 100 LIRE Weight: 8.7990 g. **Composition:** 0.9000 Gold .2546 oz. AGW **Ruler:** Vittorio Emanuele III

Date	Mintage	F	VF	XF	Unc	BU
1931R Yr. IX	34,000	150	250	350	525	—
1931R Yr. X	Inc. above	150	250	375	600	—
1932R Yr. X	9,081	150	250	375	600	—
1933R Yr. XI	6,464	175	275	425	725	—

KM# 83 100 LIRE Weight: 8.7990 g. **Composition:** 0.9000 Gold .2546 oz. AGW **Ruler:** Vittorio Emanuele III

Date	Mintage	F	VF	XF	Unc	BU
1936R	812	1,250	2,500	4,000	7,000	—

KM# 84 100 LIRE Weight: 5.1900 g. **Composition:** 0.9000 Gold .1502 oz. AGW **Ruler:** Vittorio Emanuele III

Date	Mintage	F	VF	XF	Unc	BU
1937R Yr. XVI	249	—	6,000	12,000	18,000	—
1940R Yr. XVIII, rare	2	—	—	—	—	—

REPUBLIC

DECIMAL COINAGE

KM# 87 LIRA Composition: Aluminum

Date	Mintage	F	VF	XF	Unc	BU
1946R	104,000	10.00	30.00	65.00	125	—
1947R	12,000	60.00	140	250	450	—
1948R	9,000,000	0.40	1.00	3.00	12.00	—
1949R	13,200,000	0.40	1.00	2.50	10.00	—
1950R	1,942,000	1.00	2.00	6.00	17.50	—

KM# 91 LIRA Composition: Aluminum **Note:** The 1968-1969 and 1982-1999 dates were issued in sets only.

Date	Mintage	F	VF	XF	Unc	BU
1951R	3,680,000	0.20	0.50	1.00	8.00	—
1952R	2,720,000	0.20	0.50	1.00	5.00	—
1953R	2,800,000	0.20	0.50	1.00	3.00	—
1954R	41,040,000	0.10	0.25	0.50	1.85	—
1955R	32,640,000	0.10	0.25	0.50	1.85	—
1956R	1,840,000	0.20	0.50	4.00	15.00	—
1957R	7,440,000	0.10	0.25	0.50	2.00	—
1958R	5,280,000	0.10	0.25	0.50	2.00	—
1959R	1,680,000	0.10	0.25	0.50	2.00	—
1968R	100,000	—	—	—	17.00	—
1969R	310,000	—	—	—	5.00	—
1970R	1,011,000	—	—	—	2.50	—
1980R	1,500,000	—	—	—	1.50	—
1981R	500,000	—	—	—	1.50	—
1982R	85,000	—	—	—	2.50	—
1983R	76,000	—	—	—	6.00	—
1984R	77,000	—	—	—	4.00	—
1985R	73,000	—	—	—	2.00	—
1985R Proof	20,000	Value: 4.00				
1986R	—	—	—	—	2.00	—
1986R Proof	—	Value: 4.00				
1987R	177,000	—	—	—	2.50	—
1987R Proof	—	Value: 4.50				
1988R	77,000	—	—	—	2.00	—
1988R Proof	—	Value: 4.50				
1989R	—	—	—	—	2.00	—
1989R Proof	—	Value: 4.50				
1990R	—	—	—	—	2.00	—
1990R Proof	—	Value: 4.50				
1991R	—	—	—	—	2.00	—
1991R Proof	—	Value: 4.50				
1992R	—	—	—	—	2.00	—
1992R Proof	—	Value: 4.50				
1993R	—	—	—	—	2.00	—
1993R Proof	—	Value: 4.50				
1994R	—	—	—	—	2.00	—
1995R	—	—	—	—	2.00	—
1996R	—	—	—	—	2.00	—
1997R	—	—	—	—	2.00	—
1998R	—	—	—	—	2.00	—
1999R	—	—	—	—	2.00	—

KM# 204 LIRA Weight: 14.6000 g. **Composition:** 0.8350 Silver .3919 oz. ASW **Series:** History of the Lira **Subject:** Lira of 1901, KM#32 **Obverse:** King's head right within inner circle **Reverse:** Heraldic eagle design **Edge:** Reeded and plain

Date	F	VF	XF	Unc	BU
1999R	—	—	—	40.00	—

KM# 205 LIRA Weight: 14.6000 g. **Composition:** 0.8350 Silver .3919 oz. ASW **Series:** History of the Lira (reproducing an old coin design in the center of each coin) **Subject:** Lira of 1915, KM#57 **Obverse:** King's portrait

Date	F	VF	XF	Unc	BU
1999R	—	—	—	40.00	—

KM# 206 LIRA Weight: 14.6000 g. **Composition:** 0.8350 Silver .3919 oz. ASW **Series:** History of the Lira **Subject:** Lira of 1922, KM#62 **Obverse:** Seated allegorical figure **Reverse:** Crowned arms and denomination **Edge:** Reeded and plain sections **Size:** 34 mm.

Date	F	VF	XF	Unc	BU
2000	—	—	—	35.00	—

KM# 207 LIRA Weight: 14.6000 g. **Composition:** 0.8350 Silver .3919 oz. ASW **Series:** History of the Lire **Subject:** Lira of 1936, KM#77 **Obverse:** Portrait of Vittorio Emanuele III **Reverse:** Eagle in front of fasces **Edge:** Reeded and plain sections **Size:** 34 mm.

Date	F	VF	XF	Unc	BU
2000	—	—	—	45.00	—

KM# 219 LIRA Weight: 11.0000 g. **Composition:** 0.8350 Silver 0.2953 oz. ASW **Subject:** History of the Lira - Lira of 1946 (KM#87) **Obverse:** Allegorical portrait left **Reverse:** Apple on branch **Edge:** Reeded **Size:** 29 mm. **Note:** This is a Lira Series reproducing an old coin design in the center of each coin.

Date	F	VF	XF	Unc	BU
2001	—	—	—	35.00	—

KM# 220 LIRA Weight: 6.0000 g. **Composition:** 0.8350 Silver 0.1611 oz. ASW **Subject:** History of the Lira - Lira of 1951 (KM#91) **Obverse:** Balance scale **Reverse:** Denomination and cornucopia **Edge:** Reeded **Size:** 24 mm. **Note:** This is a Lira Series reproducing an old coin design in the center of each coin.

Date	F	VF	XF	Unc	BU
2001	—	—	—	35.00	—

KM# 88 2 LIRE Composition: Aluminum

Date	Mintage	F	VF	XF	Unc	BU
1946R	123,000	7.50	20.00	50.00	110	—
1947R	12,000	65.00	150	275	475	—
1948R	7,200,000	0.50	1.50	3.00	9.00	—
1949R	1,350,000	5.00	12.00	25.00	50.00	—
1950R	2,640,000	0.60	1.75	4.00	13.50	—

KM# 94 2 LIRE Composition: Aluminum **Note:** The 1968-1969 and 1982-1999 dates were issued in sets only.

Date	Mintage	F	VF	XF	Unc	BU
1953R	4,125,000	0.25	0.50	0.75	4.00	—
1954R	22,500,000	0.25	0.50	0.75	2.00	—
1955R	2,750,000	0.25	0.50	0.75	3.50	—
1956R	1,500,000	1.00	3.00	5.00	15.00	—
1957R	6,313,000	0.25	0.50	0.75	2.50	—
1958R	125,000	20.00	60.00	140	200	—
1959R	2,000,000	0.25	0.50	0.75	2.50	—
1968R	100,000	—	—	—	15.00	—
1969R	310,000	—	—	—	4.00	—
1970R	1,140,000	—	—	—	2.50	—
1980R	500,000	—	—	—	1.00	—
1981R	500,000	—	—	—	1.00	—
1982R	85,000	—	—	—	2.50	—
1983R	76,000	—	—	—	6.00	—

Date	Mintage	F	VF	XF	Unc	BU
1984R	77,000	—	—	—	4.00	—
1985R	73,000	—	—	—	1.00	—
1985R Proof	20,000	Value: 3.50				
1986R	—	—	—	—	1.00	—
1986R Proof	—	Value: 3.50				
1987R	177,000	—	—	—	1.50	—
1987R Proof	—	Value: 4.00				
1988R	77,000	—	—	—	1.00	—
1988R Proof	—	Value: 4.50				
1989R	—	—	—	—	1.00	—
1989R Proof	—	Value: 4.50				
1990R	—	—	—	—	1.00	—
1990R Proof	—	Value: 4.50				
1991R	—	—	—	—	1.00	—
1991R Proof	—	Value: 4.50				
1992R	—	—	—	—	1.00	—
1992R Proof	—	Value: 4.50				
1993R	—	—	—	—	1.00	—
1993R Proof	—	Value: 4.50				
1994R	—	—	—	—	1.00	—
1995R	—	—	—	—	1.00	—
1996R	—	—	—	—	1.00	—
1997R	—	—	—	—	1.00	—
1998R	—	—	—	—	1.00	—
1999R	—	—	—	—	1.00	—

KM# 89 5 LIRE Composition: Aluminum

Date	Mintage	F	VF	XF	Unc	BU
1946R	81,000	100	200	300	600	—
1947R	17,000	125	275	425	750	—
1948R	25,125,000	0.50	1.50	5.00	15.00	—
1949R	71,100,000	0.30	0.75	2.00	10.00	—
1950	114,790,000	0.30	0.75	2.00	10.00	—

KM# 92 5 LIRE Composition: Aluminum

Date	Mintage	F	VF	XF	Unc	BU
1951R	40,260,000	0.10	0.25	0.50	3.00	—
1952R	57,400,000	0.10	0.25	0.50	4.00	—
1953R	196,200,000	0.10	0.25	0.50	2.00	—
1954R	436,400,000	0.10	0.25	0.50	1.50	—
1955R	159,000,000	0.10	0.25	0.50	2.00	—
1956R	400,000	15.00	50.00	250	800	—
1966R	1,200,000	0.25	0.50	1.00	1.50	—
1967R	10,600,000	0.10	0.25	0.50	1.00	—
1968R	7,500,000	—	—	0.10	0.75	—
1969R	7,910,000	—	—	0.10	0.75	—
1969R Inverted 1 (die break at base of 1)	969,000	1.00	2.00	4.00	22.50	—
1970R	3,200,000	—	—	0.10	0.75	—
1971R	8,600,000	—	—	0.10	0.75	—
1972R	16,400,000	—	—	0.10	0.50	—
1973R	28,800,000	—	—	0.10	0.50	—
1974R	6,600,000	—	—	0.10	0.50	—
1975R	7,000,000	—	—	0.10	0.50	—
1976R	8,800,000	—	—	0.10	0.50	—
1977R	6,700,000	—	—	0.10	0.50	—
1978R	3,600,000	—	—	0.10	0.50	—
1979R	4,200,000	—	—	0.10	0.50	—
1980R	3,663,000	—	—	0.10	0.50	—
1981R	7,788,000	—	—	0.10	0.50	—
1982R	855,000	—	—	0.10	0.50	—
1983R	14,020,000	—	—	0.10	0.50	—
1984R	122,000	—	—	0.10	0.50	—
1985R	3,000,000	—	—	0.10	0.50	—
1985R Proof	20,000	Value: 2.50				
1986R	5,000,000	—	—	0.10	0.50	—
1986R Proof	—	Value: 2.50				
1987R	7,000,000	—	—	0.10	0.50	—
1987R Proof	—	Value: 2.50				
1988R	5,000,000	—	—	0.10	0.50	—
1988R Proof	—	Value: 2.50				
1989R Coin rotation	—	—	—	0.10	0.50	—
1989R Medal rotation	—	—	—	—	10.00	—
1989R Proof	—	Value: 2.50				
1990R	—	—	—	0.10	0.50	—
1990R Proof	—	Value: 2.50				
1991R	—	—	—	0.10	0.50	—
1991R Proof	—	Value: 2.50				
1992R	—	—	—	0.10	0.50	—
1992R Proof	—	Value: 2.50				
1993R	—	—	—	0.10	0.50	—
1993R Proof	—	Value: 2.50				
1994R	—	—	—	0.10	0.50	—

Date	Mintage	F	VF	XF	Unc	BU
1995R	—	—	—	0.10	0.50	—
1996R	—	—	—	0.10	0.50	—
1997R	—	—	—	0.10	0.50	—
1998R	—	—	—	0.10	0.50	—
1999R	—	—	—	0.10	0.50	—
2000R	—	—	—	—	—	—
2001R	—	—	—	—	—	—

KM# 90 10 LIRE Composition: Aluminum

Date	Mintage	F	VF	XF	Unc	BU
1946R	101,000	50.00	100	175	285	—
1947R	12,000	200	600	1,200	1,850	—
1948R	14,400,000	1.00	4.00	25.00	65.00	—
1949R	49,500,000	0.50	1.00	3.00	15.00	—
1950R	53,311,000	0.50	1.00	3.00	15.00	—

KM# 93 10 LIRE Composition: Aluminum

Date	Mintage	F	VF	XF	Unc	BU
1951R	96,600,000	0.10	0.25	2.00	10.00	—
1952R	105,150,000	0.10	0.25	1.50	8.00	—
1953R	151,500,000	0.10	0.25	1.00	6.00	—
1954R	95,250,000	0.50	1.00	5.00	40.00	—
1955R	274,950,000	0.10	0.15	1.00	3.00	—
1956R	76,650,000	0.10	0.25	1.25	6.00	—
1965R	1,050,000	0.25	0.50	1.50	8.00	—
1966R	16,500,000	0.10	0.25	1.00	3.00	—
1967R	29,450,000	0.10	0.25	1.00	2.00	—
1968R	32,200,000	—	—	0.10	0.75	—
1969R	23,710,000	—	—	0.10	0.75	—
1970R	14,100,000	—	—	0.10	0.75	—
1971R	23,550,000	—	—	0.10	0.75	—
1972R	61,300,000	—	—	0.10	0.50	—
1973R	145,800,000	—	—	0.10	0.50	—
1974R	85,000,000	—	—	0.10	0.50	—
1975R	76,800,000	—	—	0.10	0.50	—
1976R	82,000,000	—	—	0.10	0.50	—
1977R	80,750,000	—	—	0.10	0.50	—
1978R	43,800,000	—	—	0.10	0.50	—
1979R	98,000,000	—	—	0.10	0.50	—
1980R	81,109,000	—	—	0.10	0.50	—
1981R	46,967,000	—	—	0.10	0.50	—
1982R	45,986,000	—	—	0.10	0.50	—
1983R	15,110,000	—	—	0.10	0.50	—
1984R	11,122,000	—	—	0.10	0.50	—
1985R	15,000,000	—	—	0.10	0.50	—
1985R Proof	20,000	Value: 3.50				
1986R	16,000,000	—	—	0.10	0.50	—
1986R Proof	—	Value: 3.50				
1987R	13,000,000	—	—	0.10	0.50	—
1987R Proof	—	Value: 3.50				
1988R	13,000,000	—	—	0.10	0.50	—
1988R Proof	—	Value: 3.50				
1989R	—	—	—	0.10	0.50	—
1989R Proof	—	Value: 3.50				
1990R	—	—	—	0.10	0.50	—
1990R Proof	—	Value: 3.50				
1991R	—	—	—	0.10	0.50	—
1991R Proof	—	Value: 3.50				
1992R	—	—	—	0.10	0.50	—
1992R Proof	—	Value: 3.50				
1993R	—	—	—	0.10	0.50	—
1993R Proof	—	Value: 3.50				
1994R	—	—	—	0.10	0.50	—
1995R	—	—	—	0.10	0.50	—
1996R	—	—	—	0.10	0.50	—
1997R	—	—	—	0.10	0.50	—
1998R	—	—	—	0.10	0.50	—
1999R	—	—	—	0.10	0.50	—
2000R	—	—	—	—	—	—
2001R	—	—	—	—	—	—

KM# 97.1 20 LIRE Composition: Aluminum-Bronze

Date	F	VF	XF	Unc	BU
1957R Serifed 7	0.20	0.40	2.00	10.00	—
1957R Plain 7	0.20	0.40	2.00	10.00	—
1958R	0.20	0.40	2.00	10.00	—
1959R	0.50	1.25	5.00	50.00	—

KM# 97.2 20 LIRE Composition: Aluminum-Bronze
Edge: Plain

Date	Mintage	F	VF	XF	Unc	BU
1968R	100,000	—	2.50	5.00	35.00	—
1969R	16,735,000	0.10	0.15	0.25	1.00	—
1970R	31,500,000	0.10	0.15	0.25	0.65	—
1971R	12,375,000	0.10	0.15	0.25	1.00	—
1972R	34,400,000	0.10	0.15	0.25	0.65	—
1973R	20,000,000	0.10	0.15	0.25	0.65	—
1974R	17,000,000	0.10	0.15	0.20	0.65	—
1975R	25,000,000	0.10	0.15	0.20	0.65	—
1976R	15,000,000	0.10	0.15	0.20	0.65	—
1977R	10,000,000	0.10	0.15	0.20	0.65	—
1978R	8,415,000	0.10	0.15	0.20	0.65	—
1979R	32,000,000	0.10	0.15	0.20	0.50	—
1980R	61,795,000	0.10	0.15	0.20	0.50	—
1981R	68,557,000	0.10	0.15	0.20	0.50	—
1982R	44,774,000	0.10	0.15	0.20	0.50	—
1983R	15,110,000	0.10	0.15	0.20	0.50	—
1984R	5,122,000	0.10	0.15	0.20	0.50	—
1985R	15,000,000	0.10	0.15	0.20	0.50	—
1985R Proof	20,000	Value: 3.50				
1986R	13,000,000	0.10	0.15	0.20	0.50	—
1986R Proof	—	Value: 3.50				
1987R	8,234,000	0.10	0.15	0.20	0.50	—
1987R Proof	—	Value: 3.50				
1988R	13,000,000	0.10	0.15	0.20	0.50	—
1988R Proof	—	Value: 3.50				
1989R	—	0.10	0.15	0.20	0.50	—
1989R Proof	—	Value: 3.50				
1990R	—	0.10	0.15	0.20	0.50	—
1990R Proof	—	Value: 3.50				
1991R	—	0.10	0.15	0.20	0.50	—
1991R Proof	—	Value: 3.50				
1992R	—	0.10	0.15	0.20	0.50	—
1992R Proof	—	Value: 3.50				
1993R	—	0.10	0.15	0.20	0.50	—
1993R Proof	—	Value: 3.50				
1994R	—	0.10	0.15	0.20	0.50	—
1995R	—	0.10	0.15	0.20	3.50	—
1996R	—	0.10	0.15	0.20	3.50	—
1997R	—	0.10	0.15	0.20	3.50	—
1998R	—	0.10	0.15	0.20	3.50	—
1999R	—	0.10	0.15	0.20	3.50	—
2000R	—	—	—	—	—	—
2001R	—	—	—	—	—	—

KM# 95 50 LIRE Composition: Stainless Steel

Date	Mintage	F	VF	XF	Unc	BU
1954R	17,600,000	1.00	3.00	20.00	75.00	—
1955R	70,500,000	0.50	1.50	10.00	40.00	—
1956R	69,400,000	0.50	1.50	10.00	40.00	—
1957R	8,925,000	2.00	4.00	25.00	120	—
1958R	825,000	4.00	10.00	50.00	200	—
1959R	8,800,000	0.50	1.50	15.00	80.00	—
1960R	2,025,000	2.00	4.00	20.00	100	—
1961R	11,100,000	0.50	1.50	10.00	40.00	—
1962R	17,700,000	0.50	1.50	10.00	40.00	—
1963R	31,600,000	0.20	0.75	2.50	20.00	—
1964R	37,900,000	0.20	0.75	2.50	18.00	—
1965R	25,300,000	0.20	0.50	1.50	12.00	—
1966R	27,400,000	0.20	0.40	0.80	8.00	—
1967R	28,000,000	0.20	0.40	0.80	6.00	—
1968R	17,800,000	0.20	0.30	0.50	1.50	—
1969R	23,010,000	0.20	0.30	0.50	1.50	—
1970R	21,411,000	0.10	0.20	0.50	1.50	—
1971R	33,410,000	0.10	0.20	0.50	1.50	—
1972R	39,000,000	0.10	0.20	0.50	1.50	—

Date	Mintage	F	VF	XF	Unc	BU
1973R	48,700,000	0.10	0.20	0.50	1.50	—
1974R	65,100,000	0.10	0.20	0.35	1.00	—
1975R	87,000,000	0.10	0.15	0.25	0.75	—
1976R	180,600,000	0.10	0.15	0.25	0.75	—
1977R	293,800,000	0.10	0.15	0.25	0.75	—
1978R	416,808,000	0.10	0.15	0.25	0.75	—
1979R	256,630,000	0.10	0.15	0.25	0.75	—
1980R	—	0.10	0.15	0.25	0.75	—
1981R	—	0.10	0.15	0.25	0.75	—
1982R	—	0.10	0.15	0.25	0.75	—
1983R	—	0.10	0.15	0.25	0.75	—
1984R	—	0.10	0.15	0.25	0.75	—
1985R	—	0.10	0.15	0.25	0.75	—
1985R Proof	20,000	Value: 3.50				
1986R	—	0.10	0.15	0.25	0.75	—
1986R Proof	—	Value: 3.50				
1987R	14,682,000	0.10	0.15	0.25	0.75	—
1987R Proof	—	Value: 3.50				
1988R	20,000,000	0.10	0.15	0.25	0.75	—
1988R Proof	—	Value: 3.50				
1989R	—	0.10	0.15	0.25	0.75	—
1989R Proof	—	Value: 3.50				

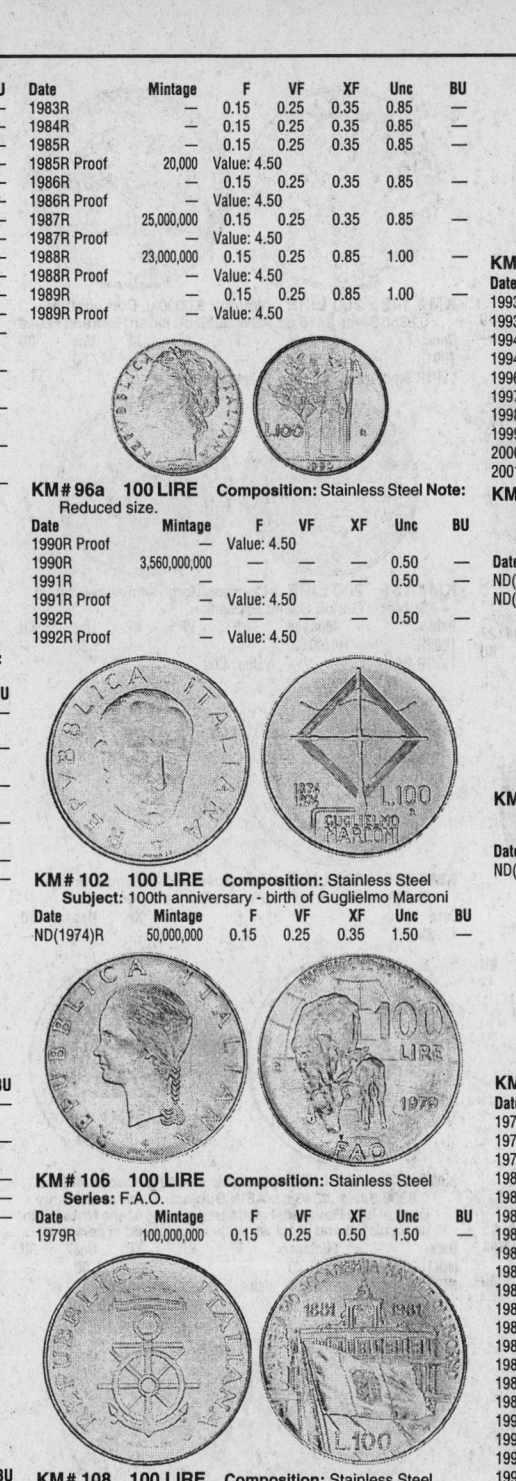

KM# 95a 50 LIRE Composition: Stainless Steel **Note:** Reduced size.

Date	Mintage	F	VF	XF	Unc	BU
1990R	3,600,000,000	—	—	—	0.35	—
1991R	—	—	—	—	0.35	—
1991R Proof	—	Value: 4.00				
1992R	—	—	—	—	0.35	—
1992R Proof	—	Value: 4.00				
1993R	—	—	—	—	0.35	—
1993R Proof	—	Value: 4.00				
1994R	—	—	—	—	0.35	—
1995R	—	—	—	—	0.35	—

KM# 183 50 LIRE Composition: Copper-Nickel

Date		F	VF	XF	Unc	BU
1996R		—	—	—	0.35	—
1996R Proof	—	Value: 4.00				
1997R		—	—	—	0.35	—
1998R Proof	—	Value: 4.00				
1999R		—	—	—	0.35	—
2000R		—	—	—	—	—
2001R		—	—	—	—	—

KM# 96 100 LIRE Composition: Stainless Steel

Date	Mintage	F	VF	XF	Unc	BU
1955R	8,600,000	1.00	3.00	20.00	185	—
1956R	99,800,000	0.25	1.00	4.00	50.00	—
1957R	90,600,000	0.25	1.50	15.00	150	—
1958R	25,640,000	0.25	1.50	15.00	150	—
1959R	19,500,000	0.25	1.50	12.00	120	—
1960R	20,700,000	0.25	1.50	10.00	100	—
1961R	11,860,000	0.25	1.50	10.00	100	—
1962R	21,700,000	0.20	0.50	3.00	40.00	—
1963R	33,100,000	0.20	0.50	2.00	30.00	—
1964R	31,300,000	0.20	0.50	1.50	20.00	—
1965R	37,000,000	0.20	0.50	1.50	20.00	—
1966R	52,500,000	0.15	0.25	1.00	15.00	—
1967R	23,700,000	0.15	0.25	1.00	15.00	—
1968R	34,200,000	0.15	0.25	0.50	3.00	—
1969R	27,710,000	0.15	0.25	0.50	3.00	—
1970R	25,011,000	0.15	0.25	0.50	3.00	—
1971R	25,910,000	0.15	0.25	0.50	3.00	—
1972R	31,170,000	0.15	0.25	0.50	3.00	—
1973R	30,780,000	0.15	0.25	0.50	5.00	—
1974R	83,880,000	0.15	0.25	0.35	0.85	—
1975R	106,650,000	0.15	0.25	0.35	0.85	—
1976R	160,020,000	0.15	0.25	0.35	0.85	—
1977R	253,980,000	0.15	0.25	0.35	0.85	—
1978R	343,626,000	0.15	0.25	0.35	0.85	—
1979R	187,913,000	0.15	0.25	0.35	0.85	—
1980R	—	0.15	0.25	0.35	0.85	—
1981R	—	0.15	0.25	0.35	0.85	—
1982R	—	0.15	0.25	0.35	0.85	—
1983R	—	0.15	0.25	0.35	0.85	—
1984R	—	0.15	0.25	0.35	0.85	—
1985R	—	0.15	0.25	0.35	0.85	—
1985R Proof	20,000	Value: 4.50				
1986R	—	0.15	0.25	0.35	0.85	—
1986R Proof	—	Value: 4.50				
1987R	25,000,000	0.15	0.25	0.35	0.85	—
1987R Proof	—	Value: 4.50				
1988R	23,000,000	0.15	0.25	0.85	1.00	—
1988R Proof	—	Value: 4.50				
1989R	—	0.15	0.25	0.85	1.00	—
1989R Proof	—	Value: 4.50				

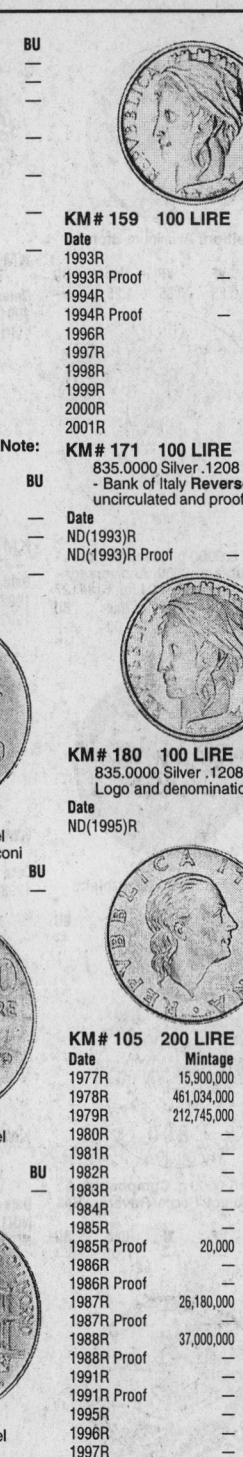

KM# 96a 100 LIRE Composition: Stainless Steel **Note:** Reduced size.

Date	Mintage	F	VF	XF	Unc	BU
1990R Proof	—	Value: 4.50				
1990R	3,560,000,000	—	—	—	0.50	—
1991R	—	—	—	—	0.50	—
1991R Proof	—	Value: 4.50				
1992R	—	—	—	—	0.50	—
1992R Proof	—	Value: 4.50				

KM# 102 100 LIRE Composition: Stainless Steel **Subject:** 100th anniversary - birth of Guglielmo Marconi

Date	Mintage	F	VF	XF	Unc	BU
ND(1974)R	50,000,000	0.15	0.25	0.35	1.50	—

KM# 106 100 LIRE Composition: Stainless Steel **Series:** F.A.O.

Date	Mintage	F	VF	XF	Unc	BU
1979R	100,000,000	0.15	0.25	0.50	1.50	—

KM# 108 100 LIRE Composition: Stainless Steel **Subject:** Centennial of Livorno Naval Academy

Date	Mintage	F	VF	XF	Unc	BU
ND(1981)R	40,000,000	0.15	0.25	0.35	1.50	—

KM# 127 100 LIRE Weight: 8.0000 g. **Composition:** 0.8350 Silver .2148 oz. ASW **Subject:** 900th Anniversary - University of Bologna

Date	Mintage	F	VF	XF	Unc	BU
1988R	44,000	—	—	—	18.00	—
1988R Proof	13,000	Value: 28.00				

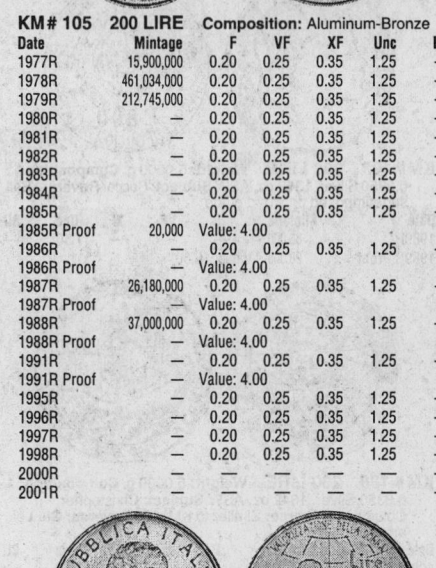

KM# 159 100 LIRE Composition: Copper-Nickel

Date		F	VF	XF	Unc	BU
1993R		—	—	—	0.75	—
1993R Proof	—	Value: 5.00				
1994R		—	—	—	0.75	—
1994R Proof	—	Value: 5.00				
1996R		—	—	—	0.75	—
1997R		—	—	—	0.75	—
1998R		—	—	—	0.75	—
1999R		—	—	—	0.75	—
2000R		—	—	—	—	—
2001R		—	—	—	—	—

KM# 171 100 LIRE Weight: 4.5000 g. **Composition:** 835.0000 Silver .1208 oz. ASW **Subject:** 100th Anniversary - Bank of Italy **Reverse:** Printing press **Note:** Both uncirculated and proof versions were issued in sets only.

Date		F	VF	XF	Unc	BU
ND(1993)R		—	—	—	20.00	—
ND(1993)R Proof	—	Value: 35.00				

KM# 180 100 LIRE Weight: 4.5000 g. **Composition:** 835.0000 Silver .1208 oz. ASW **Series:** F.A.O. **Reverse:** Logo and denomination

Date	F	VF	XF	Unc	BU
ND(1995)R	—	—	—	0.75	—

KM# 105 200 LIRE Composition: Aluminum-Bronze

Date	Mintage	F	VF	XF	Unc	BU
1977R	15,900,000	0.20	0.25	0.35	1.25	—
1978R	461,034,000	0.20	0.25	0.35	1.25	—
1979R	212,745,000	0.20	0.25	0.35	1.25	—
1980R	—	0.20	0.25	0.35	1.25	—
1981R	—	0.20	0.25	0.35	1.25	—
1982R	—	0.20	0.25	0.35	1.25	—
1983R	—	0.20	0.25	0.35	1.25	—
1984R	—	0.20	0.25	0.35	1.25	—
1985R	—	0.20	0.25	0.35	1.25	—
1985R Proof	20,000	Value: 4.00				
1986R	—	0.20	0.25	0.35	1.25	—
1986R Proof	—	Value: 4.00				
1987R	26,180,000	0.20	0.25	0.35	1.25	—
1987R Proof	—	Value: 4.00				
1988R	37,000,000	0.20	0.25	0.35	1.25	—
1988R Proof	—	Value: 4.00				
1991R	—	0.20	0.25	0.35	1.25	—
1991R Proof	—	Value: 4.00				
1995R	—	0.20	0.25	0.35	1.25	—
1996R	—	0.20	0.25	0.35	1.25	—
1997R	—	0.20	0.25	0.35	1.25	—
1998R	—	0.20	0.25	0.35	1.25	—
2000R	—	—	—	—	—	—
2001R	—	—	—	—	—	—

KM# 107 200 LIRE Composition: Aluminum-Bronze **Series:** F.A.O. **Subject:** International Women's Year

Date	Mintage	F	VF	XF	Unc	BU
1980R	50,000,000	0.20	0.25	0.35	1.25	—

KM# 109 200 LIRE **Composition:** Aluminum-Bronze **Subject:** World Food Day

Date	Mintage	F	VF	XF	Unc	BU
1981R	50,000,000	0.20	0.25	0.35	1.25	—

KM# 128 200 LIRE **Weight:** 5.0000 g. **Composition:** 0.8350 Silver .1342 oz. ASW **Subject:** 900th Anniversary - University of Bologna **Obverse:** Similar to 100 Lire, KM#127

Date	Mintage	F	VF	XF	Unc	BU
1988R	68,000	—	—	—	20.00	—
1988R Proof	13,000	Value: 30.00				

KM# 130 200 LIRE **Composition:** Bronzital **Subject:** Taranto Naval Yards

Date	Mintage	F	VF	XF	Unc	BU
ND(1989)R	50,000,000	—	—	—	1.25	—
ND(1989)R Proof	—	Value: 4.00				

KM# 133 200 LIRE **Weight:** 5.0000 g. **Composition:** 0.8350 Silver .1342 oz. ASW **Subject:** Soccer **Reverse:** Ball superimposed on world globe

Date	Mintage	F	VF	XF	Unc	BU
1989R	86,000	—	—	—	11.50	—
1989R Proof	28,000	Value: 16.50				

KM# 138 200 LIRE **Weight:** 5.0000 g. **Composition:** 0.8350 Silver .1342 oz. ASW **Subject:** Christopher Columbus **Obverse:** Similar to KM#139 **Reverse:** Coat of arms and dolphins

Date	Mintage	F	VF	XF	Unc	BU
1989R	75,000	—	—	—	13.50	—
1989R Proof	25,000	Value: 22.50				

KM# 135 200 LIRE **Composition:** Bronzital **Subject:** State Council building

Date	F	VF	XF	Unc	BU
ND(1990)R	—	—	—	1.25	—
ND(1990)R Proof	—	Value: 4.00			

KM# 142 200 LIRE **Weight:** 9.0000 g. **Composition:** 0.8350 Silver .2416 oz. ASW **Subject:** Italian Flora and Fauna

Date	Mintage	F	VF	XF	Unc	BU
1991R	57,000	—	—	—	17.50	—
1991R Proof	10,000	Value: 27.50				

KM# 151 200 LIRE **Composition:** Aluminum-Bronze **Subject:** Genoa Stamp Exposition

Date	Mintage	F	VF	XF	Unc	BU
1992R	110,000,000	—	—	—	1.35	—
1992R Proof	—	Value: 4.00				

KM# 155 200 LIRE **Composition:** Aluminum-Bronze **Subject:** 70th anniversary of military aviation

Date	F	VF	XF	Unc	BU
1993R	—	—	—	1.35	—

KM# 172 200 LIRE **Weight:** 5.0000 g. **Composition:** 0.8350 Silver .1343 oz. ASW **Subject:** 100th anniversary - Bank of Italy **Reverse:** Hammered minting scene **Note:** Both uncirculated and proof versions were issued in sets only.

Date	Mintage	F	VF	XF	Unc	BU
ND(1993)R	52,000	—	—	—	25.00	—
ND(1993)R Proof	10,000	Value: 40.00				

KM# 164 200 LIRE **Composition:** Aluminum-Bronze **Subject:** 180th Anniversary - Carabinieri

Date	F	VF	XF	Unc	BU
ND(1994)R	—	—	—	1.35	—

KM# 184 200 LIRE **Composition:** Brass **Subject:** Centennial - Customs Service Academy **Obverse:** 2 large buildings **Reverse:** Shield above denomination, hat and sword

Date	F	VF	XF	Unc	BU
ND(1996)R	—	—	—	1.00	—

KM# 186 200 LIRE **Composition:** Brass **Subject:** Centennial - Italian Naval League **Reverse:** League seal

Date	F	VF	XF	Unc	BU
ND(1997)	—	—	—	1.00	—

KM# 218 200 LIRE **Weight:** 5.0000 g. **Composition:** Aluminum-Bronze **Ruler:** Umberto II **Subject:** The Carabinieri, Protectors of Art Heritage **Obverse:** Allegorical portrait **Reverse:** Flaming bomb and David statue **Edge:** Reeded **Size:** 24 mm.

Date	F	VF	XF	Unc	BU
ND(1999)	—	—	—	1.50	—

KM# 98 500 LIRE **Weight:** 11.0000 g. **Composition:** 0.8350 Silver .2953 oz. ASW **Edge:** Lettered **Edge Lettering:** Dates in raised lettering

Date	Mintage	F	VF	XF	Unc	BU
1958R	24,240,000	—	BV	4.00	8.00	—
1958R Prooflike	Inc. above	—	—	—	30.00	—
1959R	19,360,000	—	BV	4.00	8.00	—
1959R Prooflike	Inc. above	—	—	—	30.00	—
1960R	24,080,000	—	BV	4.00	8.00	—
1960R Prooflike	Inc. above	—	—	—	30.00	—
1961R	6,560,000	—	BV	10.00	25.00	—
1961R Prooflike	Inc. above	—	—	—	50.00	—
1964R	4,880,000	—	BV	4.50	10.00	—
1964R Prooflike	Inc. above	—	—	—	30.00	—
1965R	3,120,000	—	BV	4.50	10.00	—
1965R Prooflike	Inc. above	—	—	—	30.00	—
1966R	13,120,000	—	BV	3.25	5.00	—
Note: Varieties exist						
1966R Prooflike	Inc. above	—	—	—	25.00	—
1967R	2,480,000	—	BV	3.25	5.00	—
1967R Prooflike	Inc. above	—	—	—	25.00	—
1968R	100,000	—	—	—	110	—
1968R Prooflike	Inc. above	—	—	—	120	—
1969R	310,000	—	—	—	15.00	—
1969R Prooflike	Inc. above	—	—	—	30.00	—
1970R	1,140,000	—	—	—	12.50	—
1970R Prooflike	Inc. above	—	—	—	25.00	—
1980R	500,000	—	—	—	15.00	—
1980R Prooflike	Inc. above	—	—	—	25.00	—
1981R	500,000	—	—	—	16.50	—
1981R Prooflike	Inc. above	—	—	—	30.00	—
1982R	115,000	—	—	—	16.50	—
1982R Prooflike	Inc. above	—	—	—	30.00	—
1983R	76,000	—	—	—	165	—
1984R	77,000	—	—	—	60.00	—
1985R	73,000	—	—	—	30.00	—
1985R Proof	15,000	Value: 60.00				
1986R	95,000	—	—	—	35.00	—
1986R Proof	Inc. above	Value: 60.00				
1987R	60,000	—	—	—	40.00	—
1987R Proof	15,000	Value: 65.00				
1988R	55,000	—	—	—	150	—
1988R Proof	10,000	Value: 185				
1989R	60,000	—	—	—	65.00	—
1989R Proof	10,000	Value: 85.00				
1990R	60,000	—	—	—	75.00	—
1990R Proof	10,000	Value: 75.00				
1991R	—	—	—	—	65.00	—
1991R Proof	—	Value: 85.00				
1992R	—	—	—	—	35.00	—
1992R Proof	—	Value: 60.00				
1993R	—	—	—	—	35.00	—
1993R Proof	—	Value: 60.00				
1994R	—	—	—	—	35.00	—
1995R	—	—	—	—	35.00	—
1996R	—	—	—	—	35.00	—
1997R	—	—	—	—	35.00	—
1998R	—	—	—	—	35.00	—

KM# 99 500 LIRE **Weight:** 11.0000 g. **Composition:** 0.8350 Silver .2953 oz. ASW **Subject:** Italian Unification Centennial

Date	Mintage	F	VF	XF	Unc	BU
ND(1961)R	27,120,000	—	BV	3.00	6.50	—
ND(1961)R Prooflike	Inc. above	—	—	—	25.00	—

KM# 100 500 LIRE **Weight:** 11.0000 g. **Composition:** 0.8350 Silver .2953 oz. ASW **Subject:** 700th Anniversary - Birth of Dante Alighieri

Date	Mintage	F	VF	XF	Unc	BU
1965R	4,272,000	—	BV	4.00	8.50	—
1965R Proof	Inc. above	Value: 15.00				

KM# 103 500 LIRE **Weight:** 11.0000 g. **Composition:** 0.8350 Silver .2953 oz. ASW **Subject:** 100th Anniversary - Birth of Guglielmo Marconi

Date	Mintage	F	VF	XF	Unc	BU
ND(1974)R	670,000	—	—	—	17.50	—
ND(1974)R Proof	Inc. above	Value: 35.00				

KM# 104 500 LIRE **Weight:** 11.0000 g. **Composition:** 0.8350 Silver .2953 oz. ASW **Subject:** 500th Anniversary - Birth of Michelangelo

Date	Mintage	F	VF	XF	Unc	BU
1975R	286,000	—	—	—	20.00	—
1975R Proof	Inc. above	Value: 50.00				

KM# 110 500 LIRE **Weight:** 11.0000 g. **Composition:** 0.8350 Silver .2953 oz. ASW **Subject:** 200th Anniversary - Death of Virgil

Date	Mintage	F	VF	XF	Unc	BU
1981R (1982)	341,000	—	—	—	20.00	—
1981R (1982) Proof	Inc. above	Value: 28.00				

KM# 111 500 LIRE **Center Composition:** Bronzital **Note:** Acmonital ring.

Date	Mintage	F	VF	XF	Unc	BU
1982R	200,000,000	—	0.40	0.60	2.00	—
Note: Obverse portrait varieties exist						
1983R	230,000,000	—	0.40	0.60	2.00	—
1984R	—	—	0.40	0.60	2.00	—
1985R	—	—	0.40	0.60	2.00	—
1985R Proof	20,000	Value: 15.00				
1986R	—	—	0.40	0.60	2.00	—
1986R Proof	—	Value: 12.50				
1987R	200,000,000	—	0.40	0.60	2.00	—
1987R Proof	—	Value: 20.00				
1988R	142,000,000	—	0.40	0.60	2.00	—
1988R Proof	—	Value: 25.00				
1989R	—	—	0.40	0.60	2.00	—
1989R Proof	—	Value: 20.00				
1990R	—	—	0.40	0.60	2.00	—
1990R Proof	—	Value: 20.00				
1991R	—	—	0.40	0.60	2.00	—
1991R Proof	—	Value: 20.00				
1992R	—	—	0.40	0.60	2.00	—
Note: Obverse portrait varieties exist						
1992R Proof	—	Value: 20.00				
1995R	—	—	—	0.60	2.00	—
2000R	—	—	—	—	—	—
2001R	—	—	—	—	—	—

KM# 112 500 LIRE **Weight:** 11.0000 g. **Composition:** 0.8350 Silver .2953 oz. ASW **Subject:** 100th Anniversary - Death of Giuseppe Garibaldi

Date	Mintage	F	VF	XF	Unc	BU
1982R (1983)	193,000	—	—	—	18.00	—
1982R (1983) Proof	Inc. above	Value: 32.00				

KM# 113 500 LIRE **Weight:** 11.0000 g. **Composition:** 0.8350 Silver .2953 oz. ASW **Obverse:** Bust of Galileo Galilei facing

Date	Mintage	F	VF	XF	Unc	BU
ND(1983)R	198,000	—	—	—	18.00	—
ND(1983)R Proof	Inc. above	Value: 32.00				

KM# 114 500 LIRE **Weight:** 11.0000 g. **Composition:** 0.8350 Silver .2953 oz. ASW **Subject:** Los Angeles Olympics

Date	Mintage	F	VF	XF	Unc	BU
1984	193,000	—	—	—	18.50	—

KM# 115 500 LIRE **Weight:** 11.0000 g. **Composition:** 0.8350 Silver .2953 oz. ASW **Subject:** First Italian President of Common Market

Date	Mintage	F	VF	XF	Unc	BU
1985R	103,000	—	—	—	50.00	—
1985R Proof	29,000	Value: 75.00				

KM# 116 500 LIRE **Weight:** 11.0000 g. **Composition:** 0.8350 Silver .2953 oz. ASW **Reverse:** Duino College

Date	Mintage	F	VF	XF	Unc	BU
1985R	126,000	—	—	—	20.00	—
1985R Proof	—	Value: 37.50				

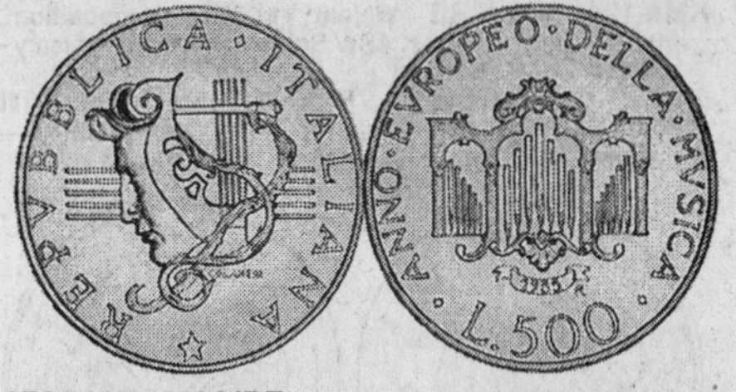

KM# 117 500 LIRE **Weight:** 11.0000 g. **Composition:** 0.8350 Silver .2953 oz. ASW **Subject:** European Year of Music

Date	Mintage	F	VF	XF	Unc	BU
1985R	96,000	—	—	—	20.00	—
1985R Proof	Inc. above	Value: 35.00				

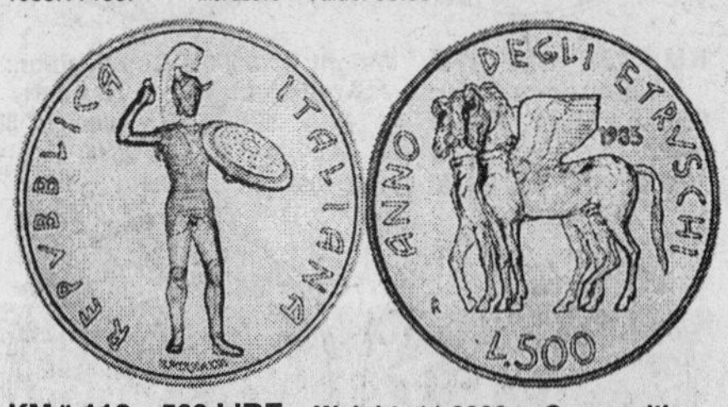

KM# 118 500 LIRE **Weight:** 11.0000 g. **Composition:** 0.8350 Silver .2953 oz. ASW **Subject:** Etruscan Culture

Date	Mintage	F	VF	XF	Unc	BU
1985R	104,000	—	—	—	18.50	—
1985R Proof	Inc. above	Value: 32.50				

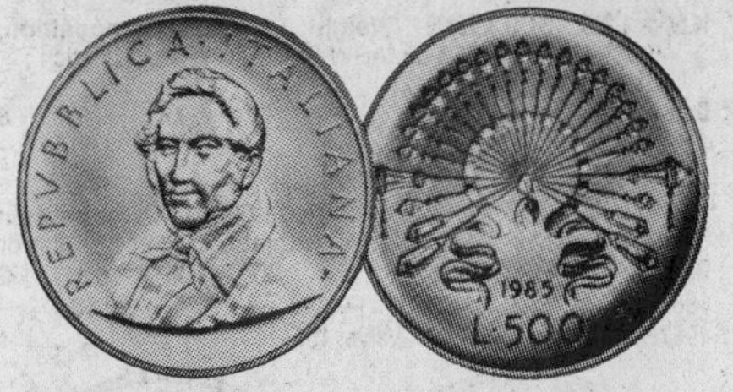

KM# 123 500 LIRE **Weight:** 11.0000 g. **Composition:** 0.8350 Silver .2953 oz. ASW **Subject:** 200th Anniversary - Birth of Alessandro Manzoni

Date	Mintage	F	VF	XF	Unc	BU
1985R	89,000	—	—	—	45.00	—
1985R Proof	20,000	Value: 65.00				

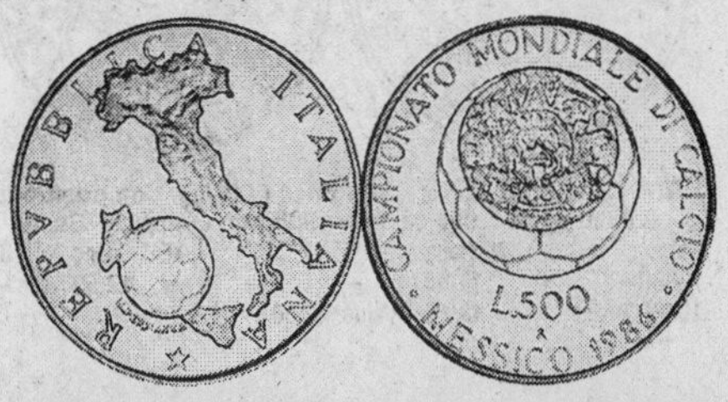

KM# 119 500 LIRE **Weight:** 11.0000 g. **Composition:** 0.8350 Silver .2953 oz. ASW **Subject:** Soccer Championship - Mexico

Date	Mintage	F	VF	XF	Unc	BU
1986R	91,000	—	—	—	20.00	—
1986R Proof	21,000	Value: 35.00				

KM# 120 500 LIRE **Weight:** 11.0000 g. **Composition:** 0.8350 Silver .2953 oz. ASW **Subject:** Year of Peace

Date	Mintage	F	VF	XF	Unc	BU
1986R	90,000	—	—	—	20.00	—
1986R Proof	19,000	Value: 35.00				

KM# 124 500 LIRE **Weight:** 11.0000 g. **Composition:** 0.8350 Silver .2953 oz. ASW **Subject:** 600th Anniversary - Birth of Donatello

Date	Mintage	F	VF	XF	Unc	BU
1986R	60,000	—	—	—	60.00	—
1986R Proof	20,000	Value: 90.00				

KM# 121 500 LIRE **Weight:** 11.0000 g. **Composition:** 0.8350 Silver .2953 oz. ASW **Subject:** Year of the Family

Date	Mintage	F	VF	XF	Unc	BU
1987R	85,000	—	—	—	25.00	—
1987R Proof	20,000	Value: 40.00				

KM# 122 500 LIRE **Weight:** 11.0000 g. **Composition:** 0.8350 Silver .2953 oz. ASW **Subject:** World Athletic Championships

Date	Mintage	F	VF	XF	Unc	BU
1987R	80,000	—	—	—	22.50	—
1987R Proof	20,000	Value: 40.00				

KM# 132 500 LIRE **Weight:** 11.0000 g. **Composition:** 0.8350 Silver .2953 oz. ASW **Subject:** Giacomo Leopardi

Date	Mintage	F	VF	XF	Unc	BU
1987R	58,000	—	—	—	70.00	—
1987R Proof	10,000	Value: 135				

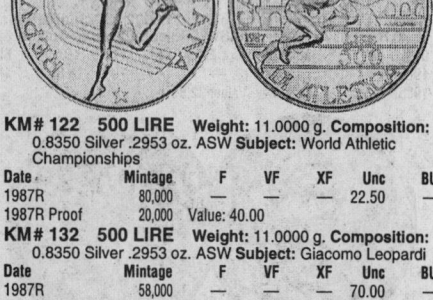

KM# 125 500 LIRE **Weight:** 11.0000 g. **Composition:** 0.8350 Silver .2953 oz. ASW **Subject:** Olympics - Seoul

Date	Mintage	F	VF	XF	Unc	BU
1988R	70,000	—	—	—	27.50	—
1988R Proof	13,000	Value: 42.50				

KM# 126 500 LIRE **Weight:** 11.0000 g. **Composition:** 0.8350 Silver .2953 oz. ASW **Subject:** 40th Anniversary of Constitution

Date	Mintage	F	VF	XF	Unc	BU
ND(1988)R	67,000	—	—	—	27.50	—
ND(1988)R Proof	13,000	Value: 40.00				

KM# 129 500 LIRE **Weight:** 11.0000 g. **Composition:** 0.8350 Silver .2953 oz. ASW **Subject:** 900th Anniversary - University of Bologna **Obverse:** Similar to 100 Lire, KM#127

Date	Mintage	F	VF	XF	Unc	BU
1988R	68,000	—	—	—	40.00	—
1988R Proof	13,000	Value: 70.00				

KM# 144 500 LIRE **Weight:** 11.0000 g. **Composition:** 0.8350 Silver .2953 oz. ASW **Subject:** 100th Anniversary - Death of Giovanni Bosco

Date	Mintage	F	VF	XF	Unc	BU
1988R	51,000	—	—	—	100	—
1988R Proof	9,000	Value: 130				

KM# 131 500 LIRE **Weight:** 11.0000 g. **Composition:** 0.8350 Silver .2953 oz. ASW **Subject:** Fight Against Cancer

Date	Mintage	F	VF	XF	Unc	BU
1989R	46,000	—	—	—	75.00	—
1989R Proof	13,000	Value: 135				

KM# 134 500 LIRE **Weight:** 11.0000 g. **Composition:** 0.8350 Silver .2953 oz. ASW **Subject:** Soccer **Reverse:** Map of Italy on world globe

Date	Mintage	F	VF	XF	Unc	BU
1989R	88,000	—	—	—	25.00	—
1989R	28,000	Value: 30.00				

KM# 139 500 LIRE **Weight:** 11.0000 g. **Composition:** 0.8350 Silver .2953 oz. ASW **Subject:** Christopher Columbus **Reverse:** Ships in dock

Date	Mintage	F	VF	XF	Unc	BU
1989R	75,000	—	—	—	30.00	—
1989R Proof	25,000	Value: 42.50				

KM# 145 500 LIRE **Weight:** 11.0000 g. **Composition:** 0.8350 Silver .2953 oz. ASW **Subject:** 350th Anniversary - Death of Tommaso Campanella

Date	Mintage	F	VF	XF	Unc	BU
1989R	51,000	—	—	—	85.00	—
1989R Proof	9,260	Value: 125				

KM# 136 500 LIRE **Weight:** 11.0000 g. **Composition:** 0.8350 Silver .2953 oz. ASW **Subject:** Soccer

Date	Mintage	F	VF	XF	Unc	BU
1990R	86,000	—	—	—	25.00	—
1990R Proof	28,000	Value: 42.50				

KM# 137 500 LIRE **Weight:** 11.0000 g. **Composition:** 0.8350 Silver .2953 oz. ASW **Subject:** Italian Presidency of the E.E.C. Council

Date	Mintage	F	VF	XF	Unc	BU
1990R	54,000	—	—	—	25.00	—
1990R Proof	10,000	Value: 45.00				

KM# 140 500 LIRE **Weight:** 11.0000 g. **Composition:** 0.8350 Silver .2953 oz. ASW **Subject:** Columbus - Discovery of America

Date	Mintage	F	VF	XF	Unc	BU
1990R	75,000	—	—	—	27.50	—
1990R Proof	25,000	Value: 42.50				

KM# 146 500 LIRE **Weight:** 11.0000 g. **Composition:** 0.8350 Silver .2953 oz. ASW **Subject:** 500th anniversary - birth of Tizian

Date	Mintage	F	VF	XF	Unc	BU
1990R	62,000	—	—	—	60.00	—
1990R Proof	9,450	Value: 100				

KM# 143 500 LIRE **Weight:** 15.0000 g. **Composition:** 0.8350 Silver .4027 oz. ASW **Subject:** Italian Flora and Fauna

Date	Mintage	F	VF	XF	Unc	BU
1991R	50,000	—	—	—	40.00	—
1991R Proof	9,500	Value: 55.00				

KM# 147 500 LIRE **Weight:** 15.0000 g. **Composition:** 0.8350 Silver .4027 oz. ASW **Subject:** 2100th Anniversary of Ponte Milvio

Date	Mintage	F	VF	XF	Unc	BU
1991R	59,000	—	—	—	30.00	—
1991R Proof	14,000	Value: 42.50				

KM# 141 500 LIRE **Weight:** 11.0000 g. **Composition:** 0.8350 Silver .2953 oz. ASW **Subject:** 250th Anniversary - Death of Antonio Vivaldi

Date	Mintage	F	VF	XF	Unc	BU
ND(1991)R	55,000	—	—	—	65.00	—
ND(1991)R Proof	11,000	Value: 110				

KM# 148 500 LIRE **Weight:** 11.0000 g. **Composition:** 0.8350 Silver .2953 oz. ASW **Subject:** Discovery of America **Reverse:** Old map

Date	Mintage	F	VF	XF	Unc	BU
1991R	75,000	—	—	—	28.00	—
1991R Proof	25,000	Value: 47.50				

KM# 149 500 LIRE **Weight:** 15.0000 g. **Composition:** 0.8350 Silver .4027 oz. ASW **Subject:** 500th Anniversary - Death of Lorenzo de' Medici

Date	Mintage	F	VF	XF	Unc	BU
ND(1992)R	50,000	—	—	—	28.00	—
ND(1992)R Proof	10,000	Value: 45.00				

KM# 150 500 LIRE **Weight:** 11.0000 g. **Composition:** 0.8350 Silver .2953 oz. ASW **Subject:** Christopher Columbus

Date	Mintage	F	VF	XF	Unc	BU
1992R	67,000	—	—	—	27.50	—
1992R Proof	18,000	Value: 50.00				

KM# 152 500 LIRE **Weight:** 15.0000 g. **Composition:** 0.8350 Silver .4027 oz. ASW **Subject:** 200th Anniversary - Birth of Gioacchino Rossini

Date	Mintage	F	VF	XF	Unc	BU
1992R	45,000	—	—	—	27.50	—
1992R Proof	9,000	Value: 60.00				

KM# 153 500 LIRE **Weight:** 15.0000 g. **Composition:** 0.8350 Silver .4027 oz. ASW **Subject:** Olympics **Reverse:** Buildings and track

Date	Mintage	F	VF	XF	Unc	BU
1992R	67,000	—	—	—	25.00	—
1992R Proof	12,000	Value: 45.00				

KM# 154 500 LIRE **Weight:** 15.0000 g. **Composition:** 0.8350 Silver .4027 oz. ASW **Subject:** Flora and Fauna

Date	Mintage	F	VF	XF	Unc	BU
1992R	8,650	—	—	—	35.00	—
1992R Proof	6,500	Value: 60.00				

KM# 161 500 LIRE **Weight:** 11.0000 g. **Composition:** 0.8350 Silver .2953 oz. ASW **Subject:** 500th Anniversary - Death of Piero Della Francesca

Date	Mintage	F	VF	XF	Unc	BU
1992R	52,000	—	—	—	65.00	—
1992R Proof	9,500	Value: 110				

KM# 156 500 LIRE **Weight:** 15.0000 g. **Composition:** 0.8350 Silver .4027 oz. ASW **Subject:** 2000th Anniversary - Death of Horace

Date	Mintage	F	VF	XF	Unc	BU
1993R	50,000	—	—	—	28.00	—
1993R Proof	10,000	Value: 45.00				

KM# 157 500 LIRE **Weight:** 15.0000 g. **Composition:** 0.8350 Silver .4027 oz. ASW **Subject:** Wildlife protection **Reverse:** Storks and swordfish

Date	Mintage	F	VF	XF	Unc	BU
1993R	36,000	—	—	—	35.00	—
1993R Proof	10,000	Value: 50.00				

KM# 158 500 LIRE **Weight:** 15.0000 g. **Composition:** 0.8350 Silver .4027 oz. ASW **Subject:** 650th Anniversary - University of Pisa

Date	Mintage	F	VF	XF	Unc	BU
1993R	41,000	—	—	—	28.00	—
1993R Proof	9,080	Value: 45.00				

KM# 160 500 LIRE **Ring Composition:** Stainless Steel **Center Composition:** Brass **Subject:** Centennial - Bank of Italy **Note:** Large and small designer's name, GROSSI, exist.

Date	Mintage	F	VF	XF	Unc	BU
ND(1993)R		—	—	—	3.50	—
ND(1993)R Proof	10,000	Value: 10.00				

KM# 163 500 LIRE **Weight:** 11.0000 g. **Composition:** 0.8350 Silver .2953 oz. ASW **Subject:** 200th anniversary - death of Carolo Goldoni

Date	Mintage	F	VF	XF	Unc	BU
1993R	50,000	—	—	—	35.00	—
1993R Proof	8,500	Value: 60.00				

KM# 173 500 LIRE **Weight:** 11.0000 g. **Composition:** 0.8350 Silver .2953 oz. ASW **Subject:** Centennial - Bank of Italy **Reverse:** Statues and building **Note:** Both uncirculated and proof versions were offered in sets only.

Date	F	VF	XF	Unc	BU
ND(1993)R	—	—	—	40.00	—
ND(1993)R Proof	—	Value: 75.00			

KM# 167 500 LIRE **Ring Composition:** Stainless Steel **Center Composition:** Brass **Subject:** 500th Anniversary - Publication of Mathematical Work by Luca Pacioli

Date	F	VF	XF	Unc	BU
ND(1994)R	—	—	—	2.00	—

KM# 181 500 LIRE **Ring Composition:** Stainless Steel **Center Composition:** Brass **Subject:** Istituto Nazionale di Statistica **Reverse:** Institute building

Date	F	VF	XF	Unc	BU
ND(1996)R	—	—	—	2.00	—

KM# 187 500 LIRE **Ring Composition:** Stainless Steel **Center Composition:** Brass **Subject:** 50th anniversary - National Police Code **Obverse:** Allegorical portrait **Reverse:** Mythological figure above coat of arms

Date	F	VF	XF	Unc	BU
ND(1997)R	—	—	—	2.00	—

KM# 193 500 LIRE **Ring Composition:** Stainless Steel **Center Composition:** Aluminum-Bronze **Series:** F.A.O. **Subject:** F.A.O. - 20 years **Obverse:** Allegorical portrait **Reverse:** Hand and grains

Date	F	VF	XF	Unc	BU
ND(1998)R	—	—	—	2.00	—

KM# 203 500 LIRE **Ring Weight:** 6.8200 g. **Ring Composition:** Stainless Steel **Center Composition:** Aluminum-Bronze **Subject:** European Parliamentary Elections **Obverse:** Allegorical portrait **Reverse:** Ballot box **Edge:** Reeded and plain sections **Size:** 25.9 mm.

Date	F	VF	XF	Unc	BU
ND(1999)R	—	—	—	2.00	—

KM# 101 1000 LIRE **Weight:** 14.6000 g. **Composition:** 0.8350 Silver .392 oz. ASW **Subject:** Centennial of Rome as Italian capital

Date	Mintage	F	VF	XF	Unc	BU
ND(1970)R	3,011,000	—	—	—	16.00	—
ND(1970)R Proof	—	Value: 28.00				

KM# 165 1000 LIRE **Weight:** 14.6000 g. **Composition:** 0.8350 Silver .392 oz. ASW **Subject:** 900th Anniversary - St. Mark's Basilica

Date		F	VF	XF	Unc	BU
1994R		—	—	—	32.00	—
1994R Proof	—	Value: 65.00				

KM# 168 1000 LIRE **Weight:** 14.6000 g. **Composition:** 0.8350 Silver .392 oz. ASW **Subject:** Flora and Fauna Protection

Date		F	VF	XF	Unc	BU
1994R		—	—	—	30.00	—
1994R Proof	—	Value: 65.00				

KM# 169 1000 LIRE **Weight:** 14.6000 g. **Composition:** 0.8350 Silver .392 oz. ASW **Obverse:** Tintoretto in oval **Reverse:** Collage of his paintings

Date		F	VF	XF	Unc	BU
1994R		—	—	—	30.00	—
1994R Proof	—	Value: 55.00				

KM# 185 1000 LIRE **Weight:** 14.6000 g. **Composition:** 0.8350 Silver .392 oz. ASW **Subject:** Pietro Mascagni

Date		F	VF	XF	Unc	BU
1995R		—	—	—	30.00	—
1995R Proof	7,960	Value: 65.00				

KM# 182 1000 LIRE **Weight:** 14.6000 g. **Composition:** 0.8350 Silver .392 oz. ASW **Subject:** Olympics - Atlanta **Reverse:** Torch runner, stadium, denomination

Date		F	VF	XF	Unc	BU
1996R		—	—	—	35.00	—
1996R Proof	—	Value: 60.00				

KM# 199 1000 LIRE **Weight:** 14.6000 g. **Composition:** 0.8350 Silver .392 oz. ASW **Subject:** Montale Commemorative **Note:** Both uncirculated and proof versions were offered in sets only.

Date	Mintage	F	VF	XF	Unc	BU
1996R		—	—	—	32.50	—
1996R Proof	8,000	Value: 65.00				

KM# 200 1000 LIRE **Weight:** 14.6000 g. **Composition:** 0.8350 Silver 0.392 oz. ASW **Subject:** Donizetti Commemorative **Note:** Both uncirculated and proof versions were offered in sets only.

Date	Mintage	F	VF	XF	Unc	BU
1997R		—	—	—	32.50	—
1997R Proof	8,440,000	Value: 65.00				

KM# 190 1000 LIRE **Center Composition:** Copper Nickel **Subject:** European Union **Obverse:** Allegorical portrait **Reverse:** Error map of European Union showing the old West Germany

Date	F	VF	XF	Unc	BU
1997R	—	—	—	5.00	—

KM# 194 1000 LIRE **Center Composition:** Copper Nickel **Subject:** European Union **Obverse:** Allegorical portrait **Reverse:** Corrected map with United Germany

Date	F	VF	XF	Unc	BU
1997R	—	—	—	5.00	—
1998R	—	—	—	5.00	—
1999R	—	—	—	5.00	—
2000R	—	—	—	—	—
2001R	—	—	—	—	—

KM# 201 1000 LIRE **Weight:** 14.6000 g. **Composition:** 0.8350 Silver 0.392 oz. ASW **Subject:** Bernini commemorative **Note:** Both uncirculated and proof versions were offered in sets only.

Date		F	VF	XF	Unc	BU
1998R		—	—	—	32.50	—
1998R Proof	—	Value: 65.00				

KM# 221 1000 LIRE **Weight:** 14.6000 g. **Composition:** 0.8350 Silver 0.3919 oz. ASW **Subject:** Vittorio Alfieri **Obverse:** Portrait **Reverse:** Rope over book **Edge:** Raised ornamentation **Size:** 31.4 mm.

Date		F	VF	XF	Unc	BU
1999R		—	—	—	30.00	—
1999R Proof	—	Value: 50.00				

KM# 195 2000 LIRE Weight: 16.0000 g. **Composition:** 0.8350 Silver .4295 oz. ASW **Subject:** Christian Millennium **Obverse:** Leaves and birds sprouting from globe top **Reverse:** Jesus above denomination

Date	F	VF	XF	Unc	BU
1998R	—	—	—	40.00	—
1998R Proof	—	Value: 75.00			

KM# 196 2000 LIRE Weight: 16.0000 g. **Composition:** 0.8350 Silver .4295 oz. ASW **Obverse:** World globe **Reverse:** Creative brain unraveling DNA

Date	F	VF	XF	Unc	BU
1998R	—	—	—	40.00	—
1998R Proof	—	Value: 75.00			

KM# 202 2000 LIRE Weight: 16.0000 g. **Composition:** 0.8350 Silver .4295 oz. ASW **Subject:** National Museum in Rome **Obverse:** Ancient coin **Reverse:** Seated gladiator

Date	F	VF	XF	Unc	BU
1999R	—	—	—	35.00	—

KM# 170 5000 LIRE Weight: 18.0000 g. **Composition:** 0.8350 Silver .4832 oz. ASW **Subject:** University of Pisa

Date	Mintage	F	VF	XF	Unc	BU
1993R	42,000	—	—	—	35.00	—
1993R Proof	8,500	Value: 75.00				

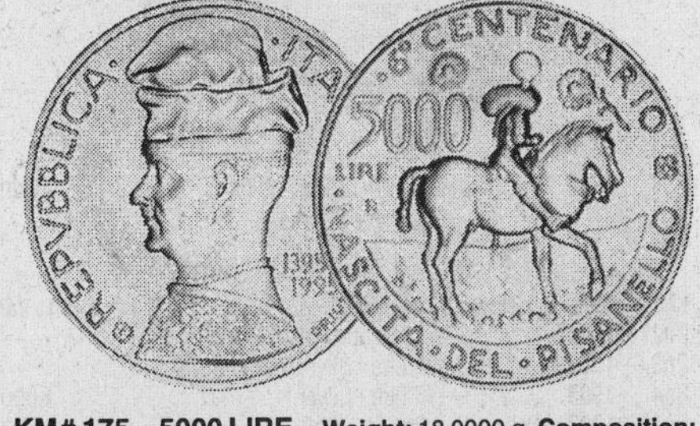

KM# 175 5000 LIRE Weight: 18.0000 g. **Composition:** 0.8350 Silver .4832 oz. ASW **Subject:** 600th Anniversary - Birth of Pisanello

Date	Mintage	F	VF	XF	Unc	BU
1995R	38,000	—	—	—	35.00	—
1995R Proof	9,000	Value: 70.00				

KM# 178 5000 LIRE Weight: 18.0000 g. **Composition:** 0.8350 Silver .4832 oz. ASW **Subject:** Italian presidency of the European Union

Date	Mintage	F	VF	XF	Unc	BU
1996R	38,000	—	—	—	40.00	—
1996R Proof	7,996	Value: 75.00				

KM# 189 5000 LIRE Weight: 18.0000 g. **Composition:** 0.8350 Silver .4832 oz. ASW **Subject:** Giovanni Antonio Canal **Obverse:** Portrait and Venice city view **Reverse:** Harbor full of sailboats

Date	Mintage	F	VF	XF	Unc	BU
ND(1997)R	36,000	—	—	—	35.00	—
ND(1997)R Proof	7,550	Value: 75.00				

KM# 197 5000 LIRE Weight: 18.0000 g. **Composition:** 0.8350 Silver .4832 oz. ASW **Subject:** 1999 **Obverse:** Birds sprouting from globe **Reverse:** Saint and merchant with cloth

Date	F	VF	XF	Unc	BU
1999R	—	—	—	35.00	—
1999R Proof	—	Value: 65.00			

KM# 198 5000 LIRE Weight: 18.0000 g. **Composition:** 0.8350 Silver .4832 oz. ASW **Subject:** 1999 **Obverse:** Three birds and nine stars encircle world **Reverse:** Satellite dish and wheels

Date	F	VF	XF	Unc	BU
1999R	—	—	—	35.00	—
1999R Proof	—	Value: 65.00			

KM# 166 10000 LIRE Weight: 22.0000 g. **Composition:** 0.8350 Silver .5907 oz. ASW **Subject:** World Cup Soccer

Date	Mintage	F	VF	XF	Unc	BU
1994R	43,000	—	—	—	80.00	—
1994R Proof	9,000	Value: 100				

KM# 174 10000 LIRE Weight: 22.0000 g. **Composition:** 0.8350 Silver .5907 oz. ASW **Subject:** 40th Anniversary - Conference of Messina

Date	Mintage	F	VF	XF	Unc	BU
1995R	42,000	—	—	—	60.00	—
1995R Proof	8,050	Value: 85.00				

KM# 179 10000 LIRE Weight: 22.0000 g. **Composition:** 0.8350 Silver .5907 oz. ASW **Subject:** 50th Anniversary of the Republic

Date	Mintage	F	VF	XF	Unc	BU
1996R	38,000	—	—	—	55.00	—
1996R Proof	7,900	Value: 85.00				

KM# 188 10000 LIRE Weight: 22.0000 g. **Composition:** 0.8350 Silver 0.5906 oz. ASW **Subject:** 200th Anniversary - Italian Flag **Obverse:** Allegorical portrait **Reverse:** Woman wearing flag like a cape

Date	Mintage	F	VF	XF	Unc	BU
ND(1997)	36,000	—	—	—	65.00	—
ND(1997) Proof	7,695	Value: 95.00				

KM# 192 10000 LIRE Weight: 22.0000 g. **Composition:** 0.8350 Silver .5907 oz. ASW **Subject:** Soccer **Obverse:** Allegorical portrait **Reverse:** Stylized soccer design

Date	F	VF	XF	Unc	BU
1998R	—	—	—	32.50	—
1998R Proof	—	Value: 55.00			

KM# 208 10000 LIRE Weight: 22.0000 g. **Composition:** 0.8350 Silver .5906 oz. ASW **Obverse:** Birds and grass sprouting **Reverse:** Male figure **Edge:** Reeded and plain sections **Size:** 34 mm.

Date	F	VF	XF	Unc	BU
2000	—	—	—	40.00	—
2000 Proof	—	Value: 60.00			

KM# 209 10000 LIRE Weight: 22.0000 g. **Composition:** 0.8350 Silver .5906 oz. ASW **Obverse:** World Globe **Reverse:** Da Vinci's wing and airplane design **Edge:** Reeded and plain sections **Size:** 34 mm.

Date	F	VF	XF	Unc	BU
2000	—	—	—	40.00	—
2000 Proof	—	Value: 65.00			

KM# 176 50000 LIRE Weight: 7.5000 g. **Composition:** 0.9000 Gold .217 oz. AGW **Subject:** Bank of Italy **Obverse:** Portrait of Bonaldo Stringher **Reverse:** Building and denomination

Date	Mintage	F	VF	XF	Unc	BU
1993R Proof	23,000	Value: 265				

KM# 191 50000 LIRE Weight: 7.5000 g. **Composition:** 0.9000 Gold .217 oz. AGW **Subject:** 1600th Anniversary - Death of St. Ambrose **Obverse:** St. Ambrose Church in Milan **Reverse:** Investiture of St. Ambrose

Date	Mintage	F	VF	XF	Unc	BU
ND(1997)R Proof	5,750	Value: 275				

KM# 177 100000 LIRE Weight: 15.0000 g. **Composition:** 0.9000 Gold .434 oz. AGW **Subject:** Centennial of the Bank of Italy **Obverse:** Portrait of Luigi Einaudi **Reverse:** Denomination and building **Note:** 1996 strikes do not exist.

Date	Mintage	F	VF	XF	Unc	BU
1993 Proof	21,000	Value: 450				

EURO COINAGE

European Economic Community Issues

KM# 210 EURO CENT Weight: 2.2700 g. **Composition:** Copper Plated Steel **Obverse:** Building **Reverse:** Denomination and globe **Edge:** Plain **Size:** 16.2 mm.

Date	Mintage	F	VF	XF	Unc	BU
2002	750,000,000	—	—	—	0.35	—

KM# 211 2 EURO CENTS Weight: 3.0300 g. **Composition:** Copper Plated Steel **Obverse:** Tower **Reverse:** Denomination and globe **Edge:** Grooved **Size:** 18.7 mm.

Date	Mintage	F	VF	XF	Unc	BU
2002	750,000,000	—	—	—	0.50	—

KM# 212 5 EURO CENTS Weight: 3.8600 g. **Composition:** Copper Plated Steel **Obverse:** Colosseum **Reverse:** Denomination and globe **Edge:** Plain **Size:** 21.2 mm.

Date	Mintage	F	VF	XF	Unc	BU
2002	750,000,000	—	—	—	0.75	—

KM# 213 10 EURO CENTS Weight: 4.0700 g. **Composition:** Brass **Obverse:** Allegorical portrait **Reverse:** Denomination and map **Edge:** Reeded **Size:** 19.7 mm.

Date	Mintage	F	VF	XF	Unc	BU
2002	1,200,000,000	—	—	—	0.75	—

KM# 214 20 EURO CENTS Weight: 5.7300 g. **Composition:** Brass **Obverse:** Walking figure **Reverse:** Denomination and map **Edge:** Notched **Size:** 22.1 mm.

Date	Mintage	F	VF	XF	Unc	BU
2002	1,500,000,000	—	—	—	1.00	—

KM# 215 50 EURO CENTS Weight: 7.8100 g. **Composition:** Brass **Obverse:** Ancient Roman on horse **Reverse:** Denomination and map **Edge:** Reeded **Size:** 24.2 mm.

Date	Mintage	F	VF	XF	Unc	BU
2002	900,000,000	—	—	—	1.25	—

KM# 216 EURO Ring Composition: Brass **Center Weight:** 7.5000 g. **Center Composition:** Copper-Nickel **Obverse:** Male figure study **Reverse:** Denomination and map **Edge:** Reeded and plain sections **Size:** 23.2 mm.

Date	Mintage	F	VF	XF	Unc	BU
2002	200,000,000	—	—	—	2.50	—

KM# 217 2 EUROS Ring Composition: Copper-Nickel **Center Weight:** 8.5200 g. **Center Composition:** Brass **Obverse:** Laureled portrait **Reverse:** Denomination and map **Edge:** Reeded **Edge Lettering:** 2's and stars **Size:** 25.7 mm.

Date	Mintage	F	VF	XF	Unc	BU
2002	550,000,000	—	—	—	3.75	—

TRIAL STRIKES

KM#	Date	Mintage	Identification	Mkt Val
TS1	1927R	—	20 Lire. PROVA SENZA RITOCCO. KM69.	1,200
TS2	1927R	—	20 Lire. PROVA TECNICA - R. SENZA RITOCCO. KM69.	1,500
TS3	1940	—	5 Lire. Silver. Uniface.	1,500
TS4	1940	—	5 Lire. Silver. Uniface.	1,500

PATTERNS

Including off metal strikes

KM#	Date	Mintage	Identification	Mkt Val
Pn2	1903R	—	10 Centesimi. Bronze.	—
Pn3	1903R	—	2 Lire. Silver Plated Bronze.	—
Pn4	1903	—	5 Lire. Silver.	1,000
PnA5	1903 (M)	—	20 Lire. Gold.	3,500
Pn5	1903R	—	20 Lire. Gilt Silver.	—
PnA6	1903 (M)	—	100 Lire. Gold.	8,500
Pn6	1903R	—	100 Lire. Gilt Bronze.	225
PnA7	1904	5	Centesimo. Bronze. KM37.	—
PnB7	1904	—	50 Lire. Brass. Head of Vittorio left.. Eagle with spread wings facing, head left, crown above..	—
Pn7	1905R	—	20 Centesimi. Bronze.	—

KM#	Date	Mintage	Identification	Mkt Val
Pn8	1905R	—	20 Centesimi. Nickel.	—
Pn9	1906R	—	20 Lire. Gilt Bronze.	225
Pn10	1907	—	20 Centesimi. Nickel.	—
Pn11	1907	—	100 Lire.	—
PnA12	1908	—	100 Lire. Silver.	775
Pn12	1908	—	100 Lire. Bronze.	250
Pn13	1915R	—	10 Centesimi. Nickel.	—
Pn14	1915R	—	10 Centesimi. Nickel.	—
Pn15	1915R	—	10 Centesimi. Nickel.	—
Pn16	1915	—	10 Centesimi. Nickel.	—
Pn17	1918	—	5 Centesimi. Ferro-nickel.	250
Pn18	1918	—	5 Centesimi. Ferro-nickel.	250
Pn19	1918	—	5 Centesimi. Ferro-nickel.	250
Pn20	1918	—	5 Centesimi. Ferro-nickel.	250
Pn21	1918	—	5 Centesimi. Ferro-nickel.	250
Pn22	1918	—	10 Centesimi. Ferro-nickel.	—
Pn23	1918	—	20 Centesimi. Nickel.	—
Pn24	1918	—	20 Centesimi. Nickel.	—
Pn25	1918	—	20 Centesimi. Nickel.	—
Pn26	1918	—	20 Centesimi. Nickel.	—
Pn27	1918	—	20 Centesimi. Ferro-nickel.	—
Pn28	1918	—	25 Centesimi. Bronze.	—
Pn30	1918	—	50 Centesimi. Nickel.	—
Pn29	1918	—	50 Centesimi.	—
Pn31	1919R	—	5 Centesimi. 17 mm. Ferro-nickel.	—
Pn32	1919	—	5 Centesimi. Bronze.	—
Pn33	ND(1919)	—	10 Centesimi. Bronze.	—
Pn34	1920R	—	Lira. Nickel.	—
Pn35	1920R	—	Lira. Nickel.	—
Pn36	1920R	—	Lira. Nickel.	—
PnA37	1922	—	2 Lire. Nickel.	—
PnA38	1922R	—	2 Lire. Nickel.	—
Pn38	1922R	—	2 Lire. Nickel.	—
Pn37	1922	—	2 Lire. Nickel.	—
Pn39	1926R	—	5 Lire. Silver.	—
Pn40	ND(1927)	—	20 Lire. Silver.	—
Pn41	ND(1927)	—	20 Lire. Silver.	—
Pn42	1950	—	50 Lire. Stainless Steel.	—
Pn43	1950	—	100 Lire. Silver. 20 mm.	—
Pn44	1950	—	100 Lire. Nickel-Silver.	—
Pn45	1950	—	100 Lire. Nickel.	—
Pn46	1951R	—	Lira. Aluminum.	—
Pn47	1951R	—	2 Lire. Aluminum.	—
Pn48	1951R	—	10 Lire. Aluminum.	—
Pn49	1955R	—	20 Lire. Aluminum-Bronze.	—
Pn50	1955R	—	20 Lire. Aluminum-Bronze.	—
Pn51	1956R	—	20 Lire. Aluminum-Bronze. Bottom of neck rounded.	—
Pn52	1956R	1,200	20 Lire. Aluminum-Bronze. Bottom of neck at angle.	—
Pn53	1957R	—	500 Lire. Silver.	—
Pn61	1957R	—	2 Florini. Gilt Bronze.	—
Pn62	1957R	—	2 Florini. Gilt Bronze.	—
Pn59	1957R	—	Florino. Gilt Bronze.	—
Pn60	1957R	—	Florino. Gilt Bronze.	—
Pn54	1957R	—	500 Lire. Silver.	—
Pn55	1957R	—	500 Lire. Silver.	—
Pn56	1957R	—	500 Lire. Silver.	—
Pn57	1957R	—	500 Lire. Silver.	—
Pn58	1957R	—	500 Lire. Silver.	—
Pn65	ND (1970)	—	10000 Lire. Gilt Bronze.	—
Pn63	1970	—	1000 Lire. Silver.	—
Pn64	1970	—	1000 Lire. Silver.	—

PROVAS

PROVA in field; Standard metals unless otherwise noted

Pr2 1903 — 100 Lire. 9,000

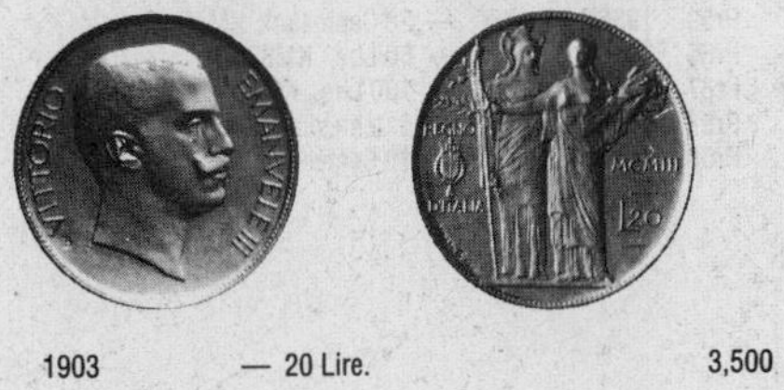

Pr1 1903 — 20 Lire. 3,500

Pr3 1906 (M) — 20 Lire. 9,000

KM#	Date	Mintage	Identification	Mkt Val
Pr4	1906 (M)	—	100 Lire. Gold.	15,000
PrA4	1906	—	20 Lire. Bronze.	—
Pr5	1907R	—	20 Lire. KM48.	4,000

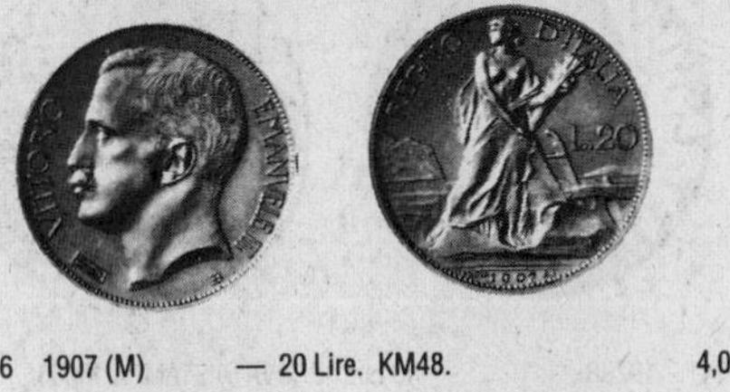

PrA6 1907 (M) — 20 Lire. KM48. 4,000

KM#	Date	Mintage	Identification	Mkt Val
Pr6	1907 (M)	—	50 Lire.	7,000
Pr7	1907R	—	100 Lire. KM50.	12,000
Pr8	1908R	—	2 Centesimi. Bronze. KM41.	325

KM#	Date	Mintage	Identification	Mkt Val
Pr11	1908 (M)	—	100 Lire.	15,000
Pr9	1908R	—	5 Centesimi. KM42.	450

Pr10 1908R — 10 Centesimi. Bronze. KM43. 2,850

KM#	Date	Mintage	Identification	Mkt Val
PrA12	1910R	—	100 Lire. KM50.	8,000
Pr12	1911R	—	2 Lire. KM52.	175

Pr13 1911R — 5 Lire. KM53. 3,250

Pr14 1911R — 50 Lire. KM54. 4,500

PrA15 1912 — 10 Lire. KM47. 3,000

Pr15 1912 — 20 Lire. KM48. 3,500

KM#	Date	Mintage	Identification	Mkt Val
Pr16	1913R	—	5 Lire. KM56.	5,000
Pr18	1914R	—	5 Lire. KM56.	2,500
Pr17	1914	—	2 Lire. KM55.	—
Pr19	1914R	—	5 Lire. Copper. KM56.	—
Pr20	1914R	—	5 Lire. Copper. KM56.	—

KM#	Date	Mintage	Identification	Mkt Val
Pr21	1914R	—	5 Lire. PROVA DI STAMPA. KM56.	2,000
Pr22	1914R	—	5 Lire. PROVA DI STAMPA. KM56.	2,000
Pr25	1919R	—	5 Centesimi. KM59.	—
Pr23	1919R	—	50 Centesimi. KM61.	—
Pr26	1919R	—	10 Centesimi. KM60.	—
Pr24	1919R	—	50 Centesimi. PROVA DI STAMPA. KM61.	—

KM#	Date	Mintage	Identification	Mkt Val
Pr27	1921R	—	Lira. KM62.	—
Pr30	1923R P (for Pova)	—	2 Lire. KM63.	150

KM#	Date	Mintage	Identification	Mkt Val
Pr28	1923R	—	2 Lire. KM63.	325
Pr31	1923R	—	20 Lire. KM64.	3,500

KM#	Date	Mintage	Identification	Mkt Val
Pr32	1923R	—	100 Lire. KM65.	10,000
Pr33	1923R P (for Prova)	—	100 Lire. KM65.	11,000
Pr29	1923R	—	2 Lire. PROVA DI STAMPA. KM63.	—

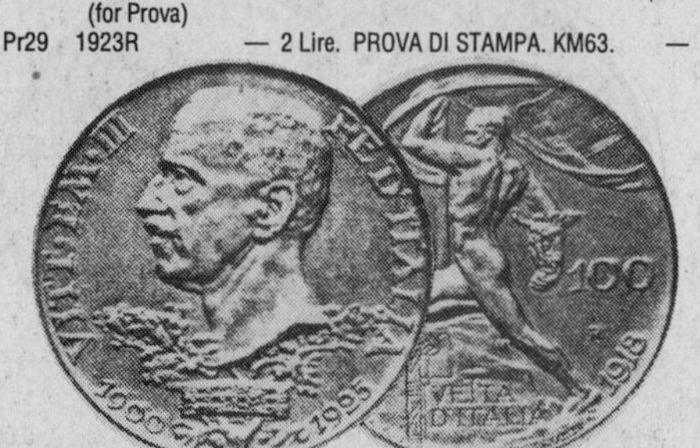

KM#	Date	Mintage	Identification	Mkt Val
Pr34	1925R	—	100 Lire. KM66.	9,500

KM#	Date	Mintage	Identification	Mkt Val
Pr39	1926R	—	10 Lire. PROVA at top. KM68.	500

KM#	Date	Mintage	Identification	Mkt Val
Pr36	1926R	—	5 Lire. KM67.	350
Pr35	1926R	—	50 Centesimi. PROVA TECNICO. KM61.	—

KM#	Date	Mintage	Identification	Mkt Val
Pr37	1926R	—	5 Lire. PROVA DI STAMPA. KM67.	300
Pr40	1926R	—	10 Lire. PROVA beneath horses. KM68.	—

KM#	Date	Mintage	Identification	Mkt Val
Pr41	1926R	—	10 Lire. PROVA DI STAMPA. KM68.	600

KM#	Date	Mintage	Identification	Mkt Val
Pr38	1926R	—	5 Lire. LA PROVA TECNICA. KM67.	350

KM#	Date	Mintage	Identification	Mkt Val
Pr42	1926R	—	10 Lire. 1A PROVA TECNICA. KM68.	500
Pr43	1927R	—	5 Lire. PROVA DI STAMPA above eagle. KM67.	—

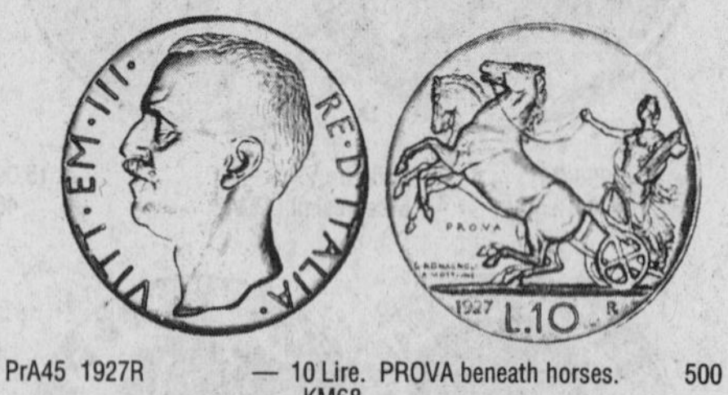

KM#	Date	Mintage	Identification	Mkt Val
PrA45	1927R	—	10 Lire. PROVA beneath horses. KM68.	500
Pr45	1927R	—	20 Lire. KM69.	—
Pr44	1927R	—	5 Lire. PROVA DI STAMPA at right side of eagle. KM67.	—

KM#	Date	Mintage	Identification	Mkt Val
PrB45	1927R	—	10 Lire. PROVA DI STAMPA above. KM68.	400

KM#	Date	Mintage	Identification	Mkt Val
Pr46	1927R	—	20 Lire. PROVA DI STAMPA. KM69.	1,700

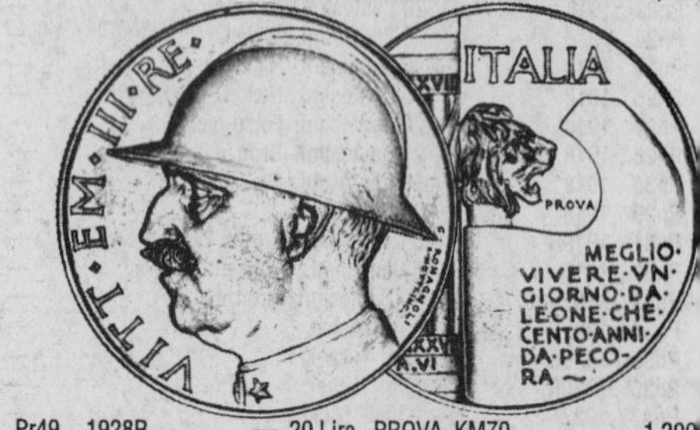

KM#	Date	Mintage	Identification	Mkt Val
Pr49	1928R	—	20 Lire. PROVA. KM70.	1,200

KM#	Date	Mintage	Identification	Mkt Val
Pr50	1928R	—	20 Lire. PROVA DI STAMPA. KM70.	850

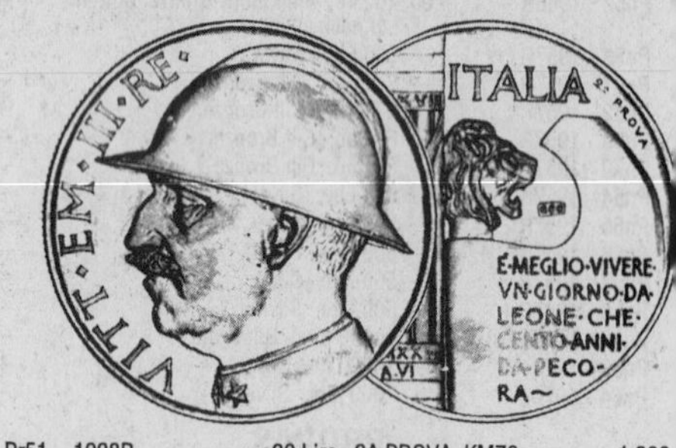

KM#	Date	Mintage	Identification	Mkt Val
Pr51	1928R	—	20 Lire. 2A PROVA. KM70.	1,200
Pr53	1928R	—	20 Lire. Gold. KM70.	18,700

KM#	Date	Mintage	Identification	Mkt Val
Pr54	1928R	—	20 Lire. PROVA behind head. KM70.	1,200
Pr52	1928R	—	20 Lire. PROVA DI STAMPA. KM70.	—
Pr55	1931R	—	50 Lire. KM71.	3,000
Pr56	1931R	—	100 Lire. KM72.	3,000
Pr59	1936R	—	20 Centesimi. KM75.	300
Pr66	1936R	—	50 Lire. KM82.	7,500
Pr67	1936R	—	100 Lire. KM83.	10,500
Pr57	1936R	—	5 Centesimi. KM73.	—
Pr58	1936R	—	10 Centesimi. KM74.	300

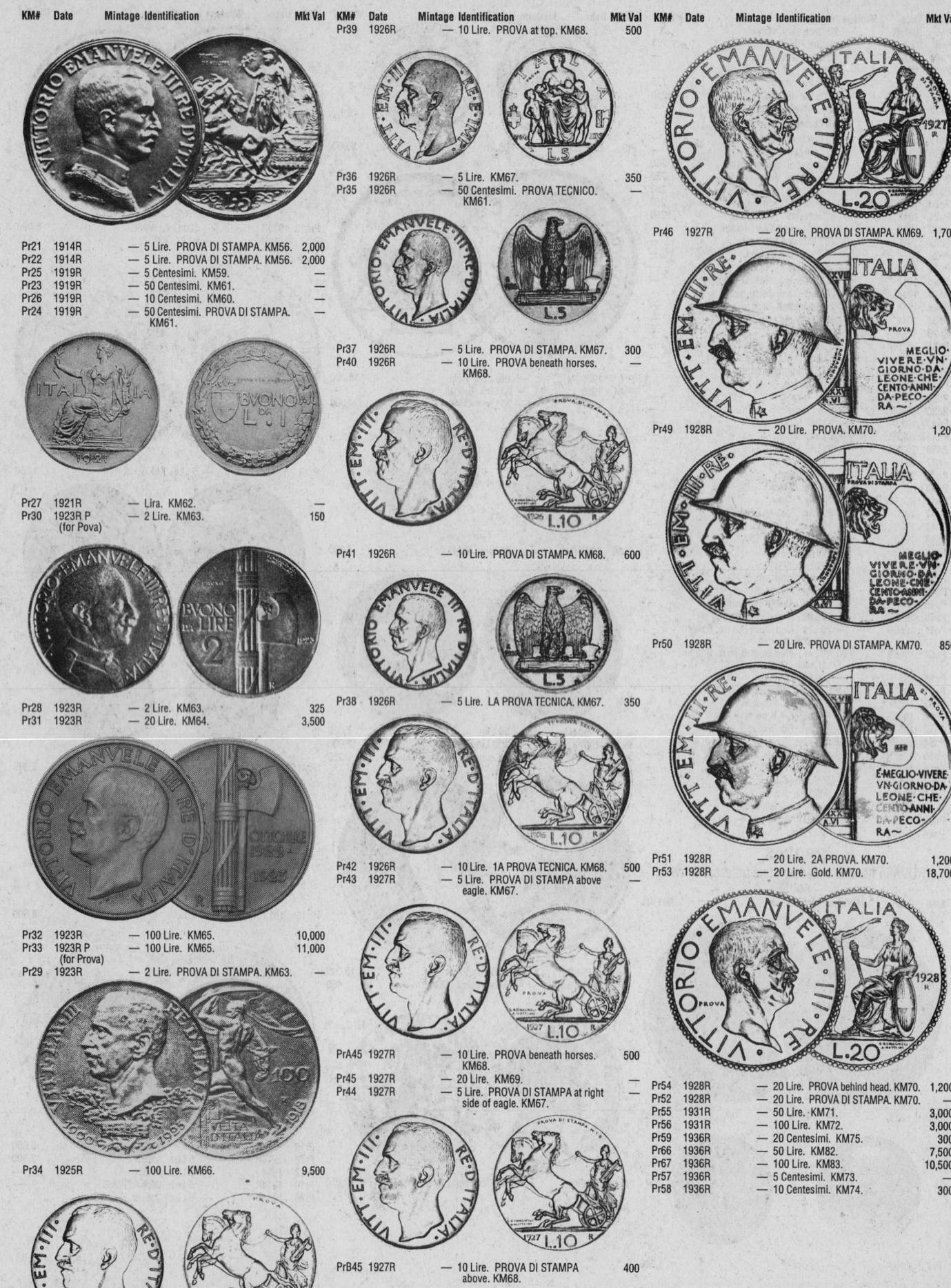

KM#	Date	Mintage	Identification	Mkt Val

KM#	Date	Mintage	Identification	Mkt Val
Pr65	1936R	—	20 Lire. KM81.	1,650
Pr63	1936R	—	5 Lire. KM79.	400

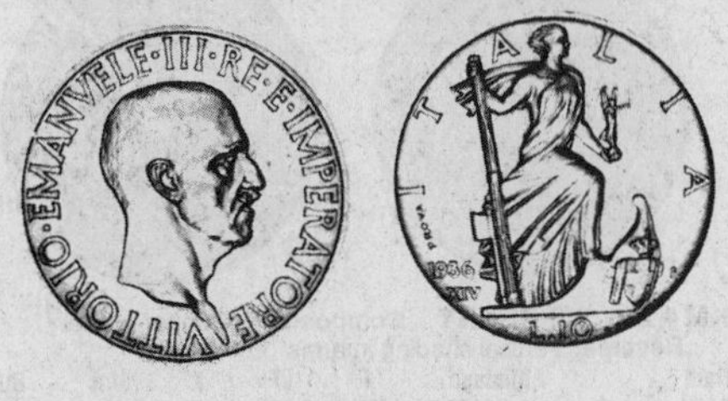

KM#	Date	Mintage	Identification	Mkt Val
Pr64	1936R	—	10 Lire. KM80.	400
Pr60	1936R	—	50 Centesimi. KM76.	300
Pr61	1936R	—	Lira. KM77.	350
Pr62	1936R	—	2 Lire. KM78.	350
Pr69	1939R	—	10 Centesimi. KM74a.	—
Pr72	1939R	—	Lira. KM77a.	—
Pr70	1939R	—	20 Centesimi. KM75a.	—
Pr71	1939R	—	50 Centesimi. KM76a.	—
Pr68	1939R	—	5 Centesimi. KM73a.	—
Pr73	1939R	—	2 Lire. KM78a.	—
Pr74	1946R	—	Lira. KM87.	950
Pr75	1946R	—	2 Lire. KM88.	1,100
Pr76	1946R	—	5 Lire. KM89.	1,150
Pr77	1946R	—	10 Lire. KM90.	1,650
Pr78	1951R	—	Lira. KM91.	1,100
Pr79	1951R	—	5 Lire. KM92.	1,250
Pr80	1951R	—	10 Lire. KM93.	1,350
Pr81	1953R	—	2 Lire. KM94.	950
Pr82	1956R	—	20 Lire. P for PROVA, KM97.1.	750

KM#	Date	Mintage	Identification	Mkt Val
Pr83	1957R	1,004	500 Lire. KM98.	4,500
Pr84	1965R	570	500 Lire. KM100.	1,600
Pr85	1968R	—	20 Lire. KM97.2.	375
Pr86	1970R	2,500	1000 Lire. KM101.	350
Pr91	1974R	730	500 Lire. KM103.	450
Pr87	1974R	—	100 Lire. KM96.	150
Pr88	1974R	—	100 Lire. KM102.	75.00
Pr89	1974R	—	100 Lire. Copper Nickel. KM102.	150
Pr90	1974R	—	100 Lire. Silver. KM102.	400
Pr92	1977R	417	200 Lire. KM105.	300

MINT SETS

KM#	Date	Mintage	Identification	Issue Price	Mkt Val
MS1	1968 (8)	100,000	KM91-96, 97.2, 98	6.50	160
MS2	1969 (8)	310,000	KM91-96, 97.2, 98	6.50	15.00
MS3	1970 (9)	1,011,000	KM91-96, 97.2, 98, 101	—	30.00
MS4	1980 (10)	257,272	KM91-96, 97.2, 98, 105, 107	—	22.50
MS5	1981 (11)	162,794	KM91-96, 97.2, 98, 105, 108-109	—	27.50
MS7	1982 (10)	120,000	KM91-96, 97.2, 98, 105, 111	—	30.00
MS9	1983 (10)	76,000	KM91-96, 97.2, 98, 105, 111	175	—
MS11	1984 (10)	77,000	KM91-96, 97.2, 98, 105, 111	—	70.00
MS13	1985 (10)	17,000	KM91-96, 97.2, 105, 111, 123	—	52.00
MS14	1985 (11)	75,000	KM91-96, 97.2, 98, 105, 111, 123	—	65.00
MS17	1986 (11)	73,000	KM91-96, 97.2, 98, 105, 111, 124	—	75.00
MS18	1987 (11)	58,000	KM91-96, 97.2, 98, 105, 111, 132	—	110
MS19	1988 (11)	51,000	KM91-96, 97.2, 98, 105, 111, 144	46.00	190
MS21	1988 (3)	—	KM127-129	—	85.00
MS22	1989 (11)	51,000	KM91-96, 97.2, 98, 111, 130, 145	—	100
MS23	1989 (2)	—	KM133-134	—	40.00
MS24	1989 (2)	—	KM138-139	—	50.00
MS25	1990 (11)	52,800	KM91-94, 95a-96a, 97.2, 98, 111, 135, 146	—	90.00
MS26	1991 (11)	64,000	KM91-94, 95a-96a, 97.2, 98, 105, 111, 141	50.00	90.00
MS27	1991 (2)	—	KM142-143	—	60.00
MS28	1992 (11)	52,000	KM91-94, 95a-96a, 97.2, 98, 111, 151, 161	50.00	110
MS29	1993 (11)	50,000	KM91-94, 95a, 97.2, 98, 155, 159, 160, 163	—	85.00
MS31	ND (1993) (3)	—	KM171-173	31.00	85.00
MS30	1994 (11)	—	KM91-94, 95a, 97.2, 98, 159, 164, 167, 169	—	175
MS32	1995 (11)	—	KM91-94, 95a, 97.2, 98, 105, 111, 180, 185	—	150
MS33	1996 (11)	—	KM91-94, 97.2, 98, 159, 181, 183-184, 199	—	75.00
MS34	1997 (12)	—	KM91-94, 97.2, 98, 159, 183, 186-187, 196, 200	—	125
MS35	1998 (12)	—	KM91-94, 97.2, 98, 105, 159, 183, 193-194, 201	—	80.00
MS36	1998 (2)	—	KM195-196	—	55.00
MS37	1999 (2)	—	KM197-198	—	65.00

PROOF SETS

KM#	Date	Mintage	Identification	Issue Price	Mkt Val
PS9	1990 (11)	9,400	KM91-94, 95a-96a, 97.2, 98, 111, 135, 146	—	215
PS1	1985 (10)	5,000	KM91-96, 97.2, 105, 111, 123	—	110
PS2	1985 (11)	15,000	KM91-96, 97.2, 98, 105, 111, 123	—	170
PS3	1986 (10)	—	KM91-96, 97.2, 105, 111, 124	—	135
PS4	1986 (11)	18,000	KM91-96, 97.2, 98, 105, 111, 124	—	115
PS5	1987 (11)	10,000	KM91-96, 97.2, 98, 105, 111, 132	—	120
PS6	1988 (11)	9,000	KM91-96, 97.2, 98, 105, 111, 144	100	235
PS7	1988 (3)	—	KM127-129	—	135
PS10	1989 (2)	—	KM133-134	—	50.00
PS8	1989 (11)	9,260	KM91-96, 97.2, 98, 111, 130, 145	—	140
PS11	1989 (2)	—	KM138-139	—	65.00
PS12	1991 (11)	11,000	KM91-94, 95a-96a, 97.2, 98, 105, 111, 141	100	220
PS13	1992 (11)	9,500	KM91-94, 95a-96a, 97.2, 98, 111, 151, 161	90.00	175
PS14	1993 (11)	10,000	KM91-94, 95a, 97.2, 98, 155, 159, 160, 163	—	155
PS15	ND (1993) (3)	—	KM171-173	60.00	150
PS16	1998 (2)	—	KM195-196	—	130
PS17	1999 (2)	—	KM197-198	—	110

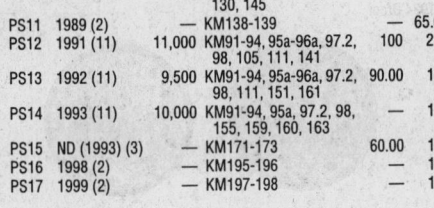

IVORY COAST

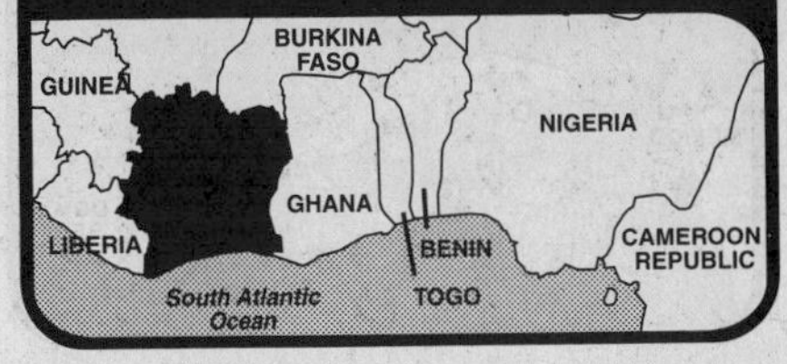

The Republic of the Ivory Coast, (Cote d'Ivoire), a former French Overseas territory located on the south side of the African bulge between Liberia and Ghana, has an area of 124,504 sq. mi. (322,463 sq. km.) and a population of 11.8 million. Capital: Yamoussoukro. The predominantly agricultural economy is one of Africa's most prosperous. Coffee, tropical woods, cocoa, and bananas are exported.

French and Portuguese navigators visited the Ivory Coast in the 15th century. French traders set up establishments in the 19th century, and gradually extended their influence along the coast and inland. The area was organized as a territory in 1893, and from 1904 to 1958 was a constituent unit of the Federation of French West Africa - as a Colony under the Third Republic and an Overseas Territory under the Fourth. In 1958 Ivory Coast became an autonomous republic within the French Community. Independence was attained on Aug. 7, 1960.

REPUBLIC

DECIMAL COINAGE

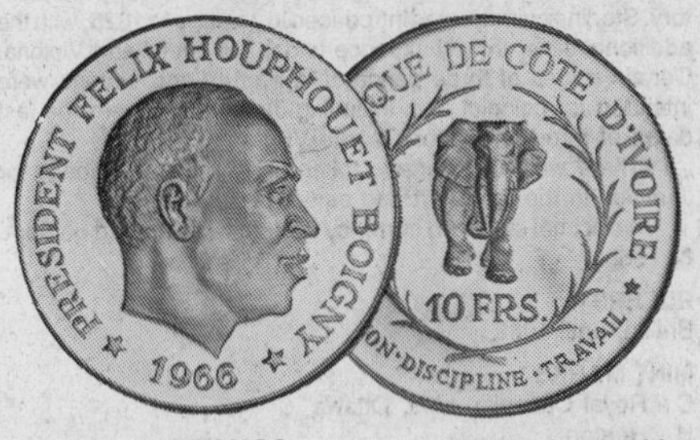

KM# 1 10 FRANCS **Weight:** 25.0000 g. **Composition:** 0.9250 Silver .7434 oz. ASW **Note:** Varieties exist in 2.9-millimeter and 3.5-millimeter planchets.

Date	F	VF	XF	Unc	BU
1966 Proof	—	Value: 55.00			

KM# 2 10 FRANCS **Weight:** 3.2000 g. **Composition:** 0.9000 Gold .0926 oz. AGW

Date	Mintage	F	VF	XF	Unc	BU
1966 Proof	2,000	Value: 85.00				

KM# 3 25 FRANCS **Weight:** 8.0000 g. **Composition:** 0.9000 Gold .2315 oz. AGW

Date	Mintage	F	VF	XF	Unc	BU
1966 Proof	2,000	Value: 135				

KM# 4 50 FRANCS **Weight:** 16.0000 g. **Composition:** 0.9000 Gold .4630 oz. AGW **Note:** Similar to 25 Francs, KM#3.

Date	Mintage	F	VF	XF	Unc	BU
1966 Proof	2,000	Value: 265				

KM# 5 100 FRANCS **Weight:** 32.0000 g. **Composition:** 0.9000 Gold .9260 oz. AGW **Note:** Similar to the 10 Francs, KM#1.

Date	Mintage	F	VF	XF	Unc	BU
1966 Proof	2,000	Value: 525				

ESSAIS

Standard metals unless otherwise noted

KM#	Date	Mintage	Identification	Mkt Val
E1	1966	—	100 Francs. Silver. KM5.	60.00

PIEFORTS WITH ESSAI

KM#	Date	Mintage	Identification	Mkt Val
PE1	1966	—	100 Francs. Silver. KM5.	150

PROOF SETS

KM#	Date	Mintage	Identification	Issue Price	Mkt Val
PS1	1966 (4)	2,000	KM#2-5	—	950

JAMAICA

Jamaica is situated in the Caribbean Sea 90 miles south of Cuba, has an area of 4,244 sq. mi. (10,990 sq. km.) and a population of 2.1 million. Capital: Kingston. The economy is founded chiefly on mining, tourism and agriculture. Aluminum, bauxite, sugar, rum and molasses are exported.

Jamaica was discovered by Columbus on May 3, 1494, and settled by Spain in 1509. The island was captured in1655 by a British naval force under the command of Admiral William Penn, sent by Oliver Cromwell and ceded to Britain by the Treaty of Madrid, 1670. For more than 150 years, the Jamaican economy of sugar, slaves and piracy was one of the most prosperous in the new world. Dissension between the property-oriented island legislature and the home government prompted parliament to establish a crown colony government for Jamaica in 1866. From 1958 to 1961 Jamaica was a member of the West Indies Federation, withdrawing when Jamaican voters rejected the association. The colony attained independence on Aug. 6, 1962. Jamaica is a member of the Commonwealth of Nations. Elizabeth II is the Head of State, as Queen of Jamaica.

In 1758, the Jamaican Assembly authorized stamping a certain amount of Spanish milled coinage. Token coinage by merchants aided the island's monetary supply in the early19th century. Sterling coinage was introduced in Jamaica in 1825, with the additional silver three halfpence under William IV and Victoria. Certain issues of three pence of William IV and Victoria were intended for colonial use, including Jamaica, as were the last dates of three pence for George VI.

There was an extensive token and work tally coinage for Jamaica in the late 19th and early 20th centuries.

A decimal standard currency system was adopted on Sept. 8, 1969.

RULERS

British, until 1962

MINT MARKS

C - Royal Canadian Mint, Ottawa
H - Heaton
FM - Franklin Mint, U.S.A.**
(fm) - Franklin Mint, U.S.A.*
no mint mark - Royal Mint, London

***NOTE:** During 1970 the Franklin Mint produced matte and proof coins (1 cent-1 dollar) using dies similar to/or Royal Mint without the FM mint mark.

NOTE: From 1975-1985 the Franklin Mint produced coinage in up to 3 different qualities. Qualities of issue are designated in ( ) after each date and are defined as follows:

(M) MATTE - Normal circulation strike or a dull finish produced by sandblasting special uncirculated (polish finish) or proof quality dies.

(U) SPECIAL UNCIRCULATED - Polished or proof-like in appearance without any frosted features.

(P) **PROOF** - The highest quality obtainable having mirror-like fields and frosted features.

MONETARY SYSTEM

4 Farthings = 1 Penny
12 Pence = 1 Shilling
8 Reales = 6 Shillings, 8 Pence
(Commencing 1969)
100 Cents = 1 Dollar

BRITISH ADMINISTRATION

REGULAR COINAGE

KM# 18 FARTHING Composition: Copper-Nickel
Reverse: Horizontal shading in arms

Date	Mintage	F	VF	XF	Unc	BU
1902	144,000	2.00	4.00	15.00	45.00	—
1903	144,000	2.00	4.00	15.00	45.00	—

KM# 21 FARTHING Composition: Copper-Nickel
Reverse: Vertical shading in arms

Date	Mintage	F	VF	XF	Unc	BU
1904	192,000	1.00	2.50	12.00	35.00	—
1904 Proof	—	Value: 250				
1905	192,000	1.00	2.50	12.00	35.00	—
1906	528,000	1.00	2.00	8.00	28.00	—
1907	192,000	1.00	2.50	12.00	32.00	—
1909	144,000	2.00	4.00	15.00	45.00	—
1910	48,000	4.00	8.00	25.00	50.00	—

KM# 24 FARTHING Composition: Copper-Nickel

Date	Mintage	F	VF	XF	Unc	BU
1914	192,000	2.00	4.00	12.00	35.00	—
1916H	480,000	0.75	2.00	6.00	20.00	—
1916H Proof	—	Value: 250				
1918C	208,000	1.00	2.00	8.00	25.00	—
1918C Proof	—	Value: 225				
1919C	401,000	0.75	2.00	6.00	20.00	—
1926	240,000	1.00	2.00	8.00	25.00	—
1928	480,000	0.75	2.00	6.00	20.00	—
1928 Proof	—	Value: 225				
1932	480,000	0.75	2.00	6.00	20.00	—
1932 Proof	—	—	—	—	—	—
1934	480,000	0.75	2.00	6.00	20.00	—
1934 Proof	—	—	—	—	—	—

KM# 27 FARTHING Composition: Copper-Nickel

Date	Mintage	F	VF	XF	Unc	BU
1937	480,000	0.50	1.50	5.00	15.00	—
1937 Proof	—	Value: 175				

KM# 30 FARTHING Composition: Copper-Nickel
Obverse: Larger head

Date	Mintage	F	VF	XF	Unc	BU
1938	480,000	0.20	0.40	1.50	8.50	—
1938 Proof	—	—	—	—	—	—
1942	480,000	0.20	0.40	1.50	8.50	—
1945	480,000	0.20	0.40	1.50	8.50	—
1945 Proof	—	Value: 120				
1947	192,000	0.35	1.50	4.00	15.00	—
1947 Proof	—	Value: 120				

KM# 33 FARTHING Composition: Copper-Nickel
Obverse: Without AND EMPEROR OF INIDA in legend

Date	Mintage	F	VF	XF	Unc	BU
1950	288,000	0.10	0.25	0.80	3.25	10.00
1950 Proof	—	Value: 175				
1952	288,000	0.10	0.25	0.80	3.50	12.00
1952 Proof	—	Value: 175				

KM# 19 1/2 PENNY Composition: Copper-Nickel
Reverse: Horizontal shading in arms

Date	Mintage	F	VF	XF	Unc	BU
1902	48,000	2.00	5.00	20.00	50.00	—
1903	48,000	2.00	5.00	20.00	60.00	—

KM# 22 1/2 PENNY Composition: Copper-Nickel
Reverse: Vertical shading in arms

Date	Mintage	F	VF	XF	Unc	BU
1904	48,000	1.50	5.00	25.00	70.00	—
1905	48,000	1.50	5.00	25.00	70.00	—
1906	432,000	0.65	1.50	7.50	25.00	—
1907	504,000	0.65	1.50	7.50	25.00	—
1909	144,000	0.75	2.00	10.00	40.00	—
1910	144,000	0.75	2.00	10.00	40.00	—

KM# 25 1/2 PENNY Composition: Copper-Nickel

Date	Mintage	F	VF	XF	Unc	BU
1914	96,000	3.00	6.00	25.00	75.00	—
1916H	192,000	0.35	1.50	6.00	20.00	—
1918C	251,000	0.35	1.50	6.00	20.00	—
1918C Proof	—	Value: 200				
1919C	312,000	0.35	1.00	5.00	20.00	—
1920	480,000	0.35	1.00	5.00	20.00	—
1926	240,000	0.35	1.00	5.00	30.00	—
1928	120,000	0.35	1.00	5.00	20.00	—
1928 Proof	—	Value: 200				

KM# 28 1/2 PENNY Composition: Nickel-Brass

Date	Mintage	F	VF	XF	Unc	BU
1937	960,000	0.50	1.00	3.50	12.00	—
1937 Proof	—	Value: 175				

KM# 31 1/2 PENNY Composition: Nickel-Brass
Obverse: Larger head

Date	Mintage	F	VF	XF	Unc	BU
1938	960,000	0.25	0.75	3.50	12.00	—
1938 Proof	—	Value: 175				
1940	960,000	0.25	0.75	3.50	12.00	—
1940 Proof	—	Value: 175				
1942	960,000	0.25	0.75	3.50	12.00	—
1945	960,000	0.25	0.75	3.50	12.00	—
1945 Proof	—	Value: 175				
1947	960,000	0.25	0.75	3.50	12.00	—
1947 Proof	—	Value: 200				

KM# 34 1/2 PENNY Composition: Nickel-Brass
Obverse: Without AND EMPEROR OF INIDA in legend

Date	Mintage	F	VF	XF	Unc	BU
1950	1,440,000	0.10	0.20	0.30	3.25	—
1950 Proof	—	Value: 175				
1952	1,200,000	0.10	0.20	0.30	3.25	—
1952 Proof	—	Value: 175				

KM# 36 1/2 PENNY Composition: Nickel-Brass

Date	Mintage	F	VF	XF	Unc	BU
1955	1,440,000	0.10	0.15	0.40	2.00	—
1955 Proof	—	Value: 150				
1957	600,000	1.00	2.00	4.00	6.00	—
1957 Proof	—	—	—	—	—	—
1958	960,000	0.10	0.20	0.50	2.00	—
1958 Proof	—	Value: 150				
1959	960,000	0.10	0.20	0.50	2.00	—
1959 Proof	—	—	—	—	—	—
1961	480,000	0.20	0.40	1.00	4.00	—
1961 Proof	—	—	—	—	—	—
1962	960,000	0.10	0.15	0.30	1.75	—
1962 Proof	—	Value: 150				
1963	960,000	0.10	0.15	0.30	1.75	—
1963 Proof	—	Value: 150				

KM# 38 1/2 PENNY Composition: Nickel-Brass
Reverse: New arms

Date	Mintage	F	VF	XF	Unc	BU
1964	1,440,000	0.10	0.15	0.20	0.80	—
1965	1,200,000	0.10	0.15	0.20	0.80	—
1966	1,680,000	0.10	0.15	0.20	0.80	—

KM# 41 1/2 PENNY Composition: Copper-Nickel-Zinc
Subject: Jamaican Coinage Centennial

Date	Mintage	F	VF	XF	Unc	BU
1969	30,000	0.10	0.15	0.25	0.75	—
1969 Proof	5,000	Value: 2.50				

KM# 20 PENNY Composition: Copper-Nickel **Reverse:** Horizontal shading in arms

Date	Mintage	F	VF	XF	Unc	BU
1902	60,000	2.25	6.00	25.00	70.00	—
1903	60,000	2.25	6.00	25.00	70.00	—

KM# 23 PENNY Composition: Copper-Nickel **Reverse:** Vertical shading in arms

Date	Mintage	F	VF	XF	Unc	BU
1904	24,000	10.00	20.00	50.00	125	—
1904 Proof	—	Value: 250				
1905	48,000	2.00	4.75	22.50	60.00	—
1906	156,000	1.25	2.50	12.00	45.00	—
1907	108,000	1.25	2.50	12.00	45.00	—
1909	144,000	1.25	2.50	12.00	45.00	—
1910	144,000	1.25	2.50	12.00	45.00	—

KM# 26 PENNY Composition: Copper-Nickel

Date	Mintage	F	VF	XF	Unc	BU
1914	24,000	10.00	20.00	65.00	175	—
1916H	24,000	10.00	20.00	60.00	175	—
1918C	187,000	2.00	5.00	15.00	60.00	—
1918C Proof	—	Value: 200				
1919C	251,000	1.25	4.75	12.00	50.00	—
1920	360,000	0.75	2.50	9.50	32.50	—
1926	240,000	0.75	2.50	9.50	35.00	—
1928	360,000	0.75	2.50	9.50	35.00	—
1928 Proof	—	Value: 200				

KM# 29 PENNY Composition: Nickel-Brass

Date	Mintage	F	VF	XF	Unc	BU
1937	1,200,000	1.00	1.75	3.25	12.00	—
1937 Proof	—	Value: 200				

KM# 32 PENNY Composition: Nickel-Brass **Obverse:** Larger head

Date	Mintage	F	VF	XF	Unc	BU
1938	1,200,000	0.35	0.65	3.25	12.00	—
1938 Proof	—	Value: 200				
1940	1,200,000	0.35	0.65	3.25	12.00	—
1940 Proof	—	Value: 200				
1942	1,200,000	0.35	0.65	3.25	12.00	—
1942 Proof	—	Value: 200				
1945	1,200,000	0.35	0.65	3.25	12.00	—
1945 Proof	—	Value: 200				
1947	480,000	0.35	0.65	3.25	12.00	—
1947 Proof	—	Value: 200				

KM# 35 PENNY Composition: Nickel-Brass **Obverse:** Without AND EMPEROR OF INDIA in legend

Date	Mintage	F	VF	XF	Unc	BU
1950	600,000	0.20	0.35	2.00	10.00	—
1950 Proof	—	Value: 200				
1952	725,000	0.20	0.35	2.00	10.00	—
1952 Proof	—	Value: 200				

KM# 37 PENNY Composition: Nickel-Brass

Date	Mintage	F	VF	XF	Unc	BU
1953	1,200,000	0.10	0.20	0.50	1.50	—
1953 Proof	—	Value: 115				
1955	960,000	0.10	0.25	1.00	4.00	—
1955 Proof	—	Value: 115				
1957	600,000	0.10	0.25	1.00	4.00	—
1957 Proof	—	—	—	—	—	—
1958	1,080,000	0.10	0.20	0.30	3.00	—
1958 Proof	—	Value: 100				
1959	1,368,000	0.10	0.20	0.30	2.50	—
1959 Proof	—	—	—	—	—	—
1960	1,368,000	0.10	0.20	0.30	2.50	—
1960 Proof	—	—	—	—	—	—
1961	1,368,000	0.10	0.20	0.30	2.50	—
1961 Proof	—	—	—	—	—	—
1962	1,920,000	0.10	0.20	0.30	2.50	—
1962 Proof	—	Value: 100				
1963	720,000	2.00	4.00	10.00	50.00	—
1963 Proof	—	Value: 100				

KM# 39 PENNY Composition: Nickel-Brass

Date	Mintage	F	VF	XF	Unc	BU
1964	480,000	0.10	0.15	0.25	0.75	—
1965	1,200,000	0.10	0.15	0.20	0.35	—
1966	1,200,000	0.10	0.15	0.20	0.35	—
1967	2,760,000	0.10	0.15	0.20	0.35	—

KM# 42 PENNY Composition: Copper-Nickel-Zinc
Subject: Jamaican Coinage Centennial

Date	Mintage	F	VF	XF	Unc	BU
1969	30,000	0.10	0.15	0.30	0.75	—
1969 Proof	5,000	Value: 2.50				

KM# 40 5 SHILLING **Composition:** Copper-Nickel **Subject:** VIII Commonwealth Games

Date	Mintage	F	VF	XF	Unc	BU
1966	190,000	—	2.00	3.00	5.00	—
1966 Proof	20,000	Value: 6.50				

DECIMAL COINAGE

The Franklin Mint and Royal Mint have both been striking the 1 Cent through 1 Dollar coinage. The 1970 issues were all struck with dies similar to/or Royal Mint without the FM mint mark. The Royal Mint issues have the name JAMAICA extending beyond the native headdress feathers. Those struck after 1970 by the Franklin Mint have the name JAMAICA within the headdress feathers.

KM# 45 CENT **Composition:** Bronze **Reverse:** Ackee fruit

Date	Mintage	F	VF	XF	Unc	BU
1969	30,200,000	—	—	0.10	0.25	—
1969 Proof	19,000	Value: 0.50				
1970 (RM) Small date	10,000,000	—	—	0.10	0.25	—
1970FM (M); Large date	5,000	—	—	0.10	0.25	—
1970FM (P)	12,000	Value: 0.50				
1971 (RM)	5,625,000	—	—	0.10	0.25	—

KM# 51 CENT **Composition:** Bronze

Date	Mintage	F	VF	XF	Unc	BU
1971FM (M)	4,834	—	—	0.10	0.25	—
1971FM (P)	14,000	Value: 0.50				
1972FM (M)	7,982	—	—	0.10	0.25	—
1972FM (P)	17,000	Value: 0.50				
1973FM (M)	29,000	—	—	0.10	0.25	—
1973FM (P)	28,000	Value: 0.50				
1974FM (M)	28,000	—	—	0.10	0.25	—
1974FM (P)	22,000	Value: 0.50				
1975FM (M)	36,000	—	—	0.10	0.25	—
1975FM (U)	4,683	—	—	—	0.25	—
1975FM (P)	16,000	Value: 0.50				

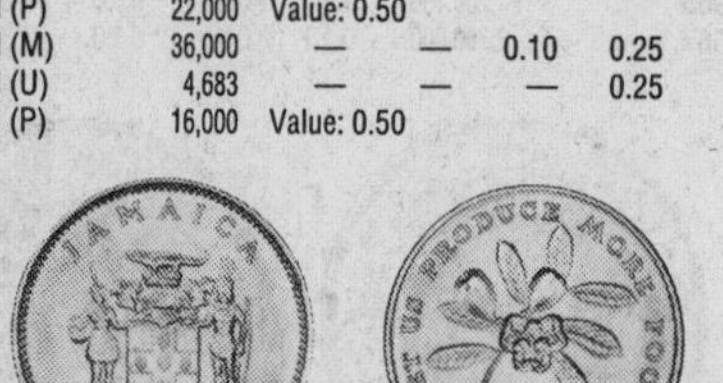

KM# 52 CENT **Composition:** Bronze **Series:** F.A.O.

Date	Mintage	F	VF	XF	Unc	BU
1971	20,000	—	—	0.10	0.30	—
1972	5,000,000	—	—	0.10	0.30	—
1973	5,500,000	—	—	0.10	0.30	—
1974	3,000,000	—	—	0.10	0.30	—

KM# 64 CENT **Composition:** Aluminum **Series:** F.A.O.

Date	Mintage	F	VF	XF	Unc	BU
1975	15,000,000	—	—	0.10	0.20	—
1976	16,000,000	—	—	0.10	0.20	—
1977	—	—	—	0.10	0.20	—
1978	8,400,000	—	—	0.10	0.20	—
1980	10,000,000	—	—	0.10	0.20	—
1981	8,000,000	—	—	0.10	0.20	—
1982	10,000,000	—	—	0.10	0.20	—
1983	1,342,000	—	—	—	0.15	—
1984	8,704,000	—	—	—	0.15	—
1985	5,112,000	—	—	—	0.15	—
1985 Proof	—	Value: 0.50				
1986	17,534,000	—	—	—	0.15	—
1987	9,968,000	—	—	—	0.15	—
1987 Proof	—	Value: 0.50				
1988 Proof	—	Value: 0.50				
1989 Proof	—	Value: 0.50				
1990	—	—	—	—	0.15	—
1990 Proof	—	Value: 0.50				
1991	—	—	—	—	0.15	—
1991 Proof	—	Value: 0.50				
1992 Proof	—	Value: 0.50				
1993 Proof	—	Value: 0.50				
2000	—	—	—	—	—	—
2002	—	—	—	—	0.50	—
2002 Proof	500	Value: 1.00				

KM# 68 CENT **Composition:** Aluminum

Date	Mintage	F	VF	XF	Unc	BU
1976FM (M)	28,000	—	—	—	0.15	—
1976FM (U)	1,802	—	—	—	0.25	—
1976FM (P)	24,000	Value: 0.50				
1977FM (M)	28,000	—	—	—	0.15	—
1977FM (U)	597	—	—	—	1.50	—
1977FM (P)	10,000	Value: 0.50				
1978FM (M)	28,000	—	—	—	0.15	—
1978FM (U)	1,282	—	—	—	0.40	—
1978FM (P)	6,058	Value: 0.60				
1979FM (M)	28,000	—	—	—	0.15	—
1979FM (U)	2,608	—	—	—	0.40	—
1979FM (P)	4,049	Value: 0.60				
1980FM (M)	28,000	—	—	—	0.15	—
1980FM (U)	3,668	—	—	—	0.35	—
1980FM (P)	2,688	Value: 0.75				
1981FM (U)	482	—	—	—	1.50	—
1981FM (P)	1,577	Value: 0.75				
1982FM (U)	—	—	—	—	0.35	—
1982FM (P)	—	Value: 0.75				
1984FM (U)	—	—	—	—	0.35	—
1984FM (P)	—	Value: 0.75				

KM# 136 CENT **Composition:** Aluminum **Note:** Mule. Two obverses of KM#64.

Date	F	VF	XF	Unc	BU
1982FM	—	—	220	250	—

KM# 137 CENT **Composition:** Aluminum **Note:** Mule. Two reverses of KM#64.

Date	F	VF	XF	Unc	BU
1982FM	—	—	250	300	—

KM# 101 CENT **Composition:** Aluminum **Subject:** 21st Anniversary of Independence

Date	F	VF	XF	Unc	BU
ND(1983)M (U)	—	—	—	0.35	—
ND(1983)FM (P)	— Value: 0.75				

KM# 46 5 CENTS **Composition:** Copper-Nickel **Reverse:** American crocodile

Date	Mintage	F	VF	XF	Unc	BU
1969	12,008,000	—	—	0.10	0.50	—
1969 Proof	30,000	Value: 0.65				
1970FM (M)	5,000	—	—	0.10	0.50	—
1970FM (P)	12,000	Value: 0.65				
1972	6,000,000	—	—	0.10	0.50	—
1975	6,010,000	—	—	0.10	0.50	—
1977	2,400,000	—	—	0.10	0.50	—
1978	2,000,000	—	—	0.10	0.50	—
1980	2,272,000	—	—	0.10	0.50	—
1981	2,001,000	—	—	0.10	0.50	—
1982	2,000,000	—	—	0.10	0.50	—
1983	992,000	—	—	0.10	0.50	—
1984	3,508,000	—	—	0.10	0.50	—
1985	4,760,000	—	—	0.10	0.50	—
1985 Proof	—	Value: 0.65				
1986	14,504,000	—	—	0.10	0.50	—
1987	13,166,000	—	—	0.10	0.50	—
1987 Proof	—	Value: 0.65				
1988	9,780,000	—	—	0.10	0.50	—
1988 Proof	—	Value: 0.65				
1989	—	—	—	0.10	0.50	—
1989 Proof	—	Value: 0.65				

KM# 46a 5 CENTS **Composition:** Nickel Plated Steel

Date	F	VF	XF	Unc	BU
1990	—	—	0.10	0.50	—
1990 Proof	— Value: 0.65				
1991	—	—	0.10	0.50	—
1991 Proof	— Value: 0.65				
1992	—	—	0.10	0.50	—
1992 Proof	— Value: 0.65				
1993	—	—	0.10	0.50	—
1993 Proof	— Value: 0.65				

KM# 53 5 CENTS **Composition:** Copper-Nickel

Date	Mintage	F	VF	XF	Unc	BU
1971FM (M)	4,834	—	—	0.10	0.50	—
1971FM (P)	14,000	Value: 0.50				
1972FM (M)	7,982	—	—	0.10	0.50	—
1972FM (P)	17,000	Value: 0.50				
1973FM (M)	17,000	—	—	0.10	0.50	—
1973FM (P)	28,000	Value: 0.50				
1974FM (M)	16,000	—	—	0.10	0.50	—
1974FM (P)	22,000	Value: 0.50				
1975FM (M)	6,240	—	—	0.10	0.50	—
1975FM (U)	4,683	—	—	—	0.50	—
1975FM (P)	16,000	Value: 0.50				
1976FM (M)	5,560	—	—	0.10	0.50	—
1976FM (U)	1,802	—	—	—	0.50	—
1976FM (P)	24,000	Value: 0.50				
1977FM (M)	5,560	—	—	0.10	0.50	—
1977FM (U)	597	—	—	—	1.50	—
1977FM (P)	10,000	Value: 0.50				
1978FM (M)	5,560	—	—	0.10	0.50	—
1978FM (U)	1,282	—	—	—	0.65	—
1978FM (P)	6,058	Value: 0.75				
1979FM (M)	5,560	—	—	0.10	0.50	—
1979FM (U)	2,608	—	—	—	0.60	—
1979FM (P)	4,049	Value: 0.75				
1980FM (M)	5,560	—	—	0.10	0.50	—
1980FM (U)	3,668	—	—	—	0.60	—
1980FM (P)	2,688	Value: 1.00				
1981FM (U)	482	—	—	—	1.50	—
1981FM (P)	1,577	Value: 1.00				
1982FM (U)	—	—	—	—	0.60	—
1982FM (P)	—	Value: 1.00				
1984FM (U)	—	—	—	—	0.60	—
1984FM (P)	—	Value: 1.00				

KM# 102 5 CENTS **Composition:** Copper-Nickel **Subject:** 21st Anniversary of Independence

Date	F	VF	XF	Unc	BU
ND(1983)FM (U)	—	—	—	0.50	—
ND(1983)FM (P)	— Value: 1.00				

KM# 47 10 CENTS **Composition:** Copper-Nickel **Note:** Lignum Vitae

Date	Mintage	F	VF	XF	Unc	BU
1969	19,508,000	—	—	0.10	0.50	—
1969 Proof	30,000	Value: 0.75				
1970FM (M)	5,000	—	—	0.10	0.50	—

Date	Mintage	F	VF	XF	Unc	BU
1970FM (P)	12,000	Value: 0.75				
1972	6,000,000	—	—	0.10	0.50	—
1975	10,010,000	—	—	0.10	0.40	—
1977	8,000,000	—	—	0.10	0.40	—
1981	8,000,000	—	—	0.10	0.30	—
1982	8,000,000	—	—	0.10	0.30	—
1983	2,000,000	—	—	0.10	0.30	—
1984	5,000,000	—	—	0.10	0.30	—
1985	8,310,000	—	—	0.10	0.30	—
1985 Proof	—	Value: 0.75				
1986	21,677,000	—	—	0.10	0.30	—
1987	29,089,000	—	—	0.10	0.30	—
1987 Proof	—	Value: 0.75				
1988	15,660,000	—	—	0.10	0.30	—
1988 Proof	—	Value: 0.75				
1989	—	—	—	0.10	0.30	—
1989 Proof	—	Value: 0.75				

KM# 47a 10 CENTS Composition: Nickel Plated Steel

Date	F	VF	XF	Unc	BU
1990	—	—	0.10	0.30	—
1990 Proof	— Value: 0.75				

KM# 54 10 CENTS Composition: Copper-Nickel

Date	Mintage	F	VF	XF	Unc	BU
1971FM (M)	4,834	—	—	0.10	0.35	—
1971FM (P)	14,000	Value: 0.75				
1972FM (M)	7,982	—	—	0.10	0.35	—
1972FM (P)	17,000	Value: 0.75				
1973FM (M)	15,000	—	—	0.10	0.35	—
1973FM (P)	28,000	Value: 0.75				
1974FM (M)	14,000	—	—	0.10	0.35	—
1974FM (P)	22,000	Value: 0.75				
1975FM (M)	3,120	—	—	0.10	0.35	—
1975FM (U)	4,683	—	—	—	0.35	—
1975FM (P)	16,000	Value: 0.75				
1976FM (M)	2,780	—	—	0.10	0.35	—
1976FM (U)	1,802	—	—	—	0.35	—
1976FM (P)	24,000	Value: 0.75				
1977FM (M)	2,780	—	—	0.10	0.50	—
1977FM (U)	597	—	—	—	1.50	—
1977FM (P)	10,000	Value: 0.75				
1978FM (M)	2,780	—	—	0.10	0.50	—
1978FM (U)	4,062	—	—	—	0.60	—
1978FM (P)	6,058	Value: 1.00				
1979FM (M)	2,780	—	—	0.10	0.50	—
1979FM (U)	2,608	—	—	—	0.60	—
1979FM (P)	4,049	Value: 1.00				
1980FM (M)	2,780	—	—	0.10	0.50	—
1980FM (U)	3,668	—	—	—	0.50	—
1980FM (P)	2,688	Value: 1.50				
1981FM (U)	482	—	—	—	1.50	—
1981FM (P)	1,577	Value: 1.50				
1982FM (U)	—	—	—	—	0.50	—
1982FM (P)	—	Value: 1.50				
1984FM (U)	—	—	—	—	0.50	—
1984FM (P)	—	Value: 1.50				

KM# 103 10 CENTS Composition: Copper-Nickel
Subject: 21st Anniversary of Independence

Date	F	VF	XF	Unc	BU
ND(1983)FM (U)	—	—	—	0.50	—
ND(1983)FM (P)	— Value: 1.50				

KM# 146.1 10 CENTS Composition: Nickel Plated Steel
Note: Paul Bogle

Date	F	VF	XF	Unc	BU
1991	—	—	—	0.50	—
1991 Proof	— Value: 1.50				
1992	—	—	—	0.50	—
1992 Proof	— Value: 1.50				
1993	—	—	—	0.50	—
1993 Proof	— Value: 1.50				
1994	—	—	—	0.50	—
1994 Proof	— Value: 1.50				

KM# 146.2 10 CENTS Composition: Copper Plated Steel **Note:** Reduced size.

Date	Mintage	F	VF	XF	Unc	BU
1995	—	—	—	—	0.25	—
2000	—	—	—	—	0.25	—
2002	—	—	—	—	0.25	—
2002 Proof	500	Value: 2.00				

KM# 48 20 CENTS Composition: Copper-Nickel
Reverse: Mahoe tree

Date	Mintage	F	VF	XF	Unc	BU
1969	3,758,000	—	—	0.20	0.75	—
1969 Proof	30,000	Value: 1.00				
1970FM (M)	5,000	—	—	0.20	0.75	—
1970FM (P)	12,000	Value: 1.00				
1975	10,000	—	—	0.20	0.85	—
1982	1,000,000	—	—	0.20	0.65	—
1984	2,000,000	—	—	0.20	0.65	—
1986	2,530,000	—	—	0.20	0.65	—
1987	5,545,000	—	—	0.20	0.65	—
1987 Proof	—	Value: 1.00				
1988	5,016,000	—	—	0.20	0.65	—
1988 Proof	—	Value: 1.00				
1989	—	—	—	0.20	0.65	—
1989 Proof	—	Value: 1.00				
1990 Proof	—	Value: 1.00				

KM# 55 20 CENTS Composition: Copper-Nickel

Date	Mintage	F	VF	XF	Unc	BU
1971FM (M)	4,834	—	—	0.20	0.50	—
1971FM (P)	14,000	Value: 1.00				
1972FM (M)	7,982	—	—	0.20	0.50	—
1972FM (P)	17,000	Value: 1.00				
1973FM (M)	13,000	—	—	0.20	0.50	—
1973FM (P)	28,000	Value: 1.00				
1974FM (M)	12,000	—	—	0.20	0.50	—
1974FM (P)	22,000	Value: 1.00				
1975FM (M)	1,560	—	—	0.20	0.50	—
1975FM (U)	4,683	—	—	—	0.50	—
1975FM (P)	16,000	Value: 1.00				
1976FM (M)	1,390	—	—	0.20	0.50	—
1976FM (U)	1,802	—	—	—	0.50	—
1976FM (P)	24,000	Value: 1.00				

KM# 69 20 CENTS Composition: Copper-Nickel
Series: F.A.O.

Date	Mintage	F	VF	XF	Unc	BU
1976	3,000,000	—	—	0.20	1.00	—
1981	—	—	—	0.20	1.00	—
1982 Inc. KM#48		—	—	0.20	1.00	—
1984	—	—	—	0.20	1.00	—
1987	—	—	—	0.20	1.00	—

KM# 73 20 CENTS Composition: Copper-Nickel

Date	Mintage	F	VF	XF	Unc	BU
1977FM (M)	1,390	—	—	0.20	0.75	—
1977FM (U)	597	—	—	—	2.00	—
1977FM (P)	10,000	Value: 1.00				
1978FM (M)	1,390	—	—	0.20	0.75	—
1978FM (U)	1,282	—	—	—	0.75	—
1978FM (P)	6,058	Value: 1.50				
1979FM (M)	1,390	—	—	0.20	0.75	—
1979FM (U)	2,608	—	—	—	0.75	—
1979FM (P)	4,049	Value: 1.50				
1980FM (M)	1,390	—	—	0.20	0.60	—
1980FM (U)	3,668	—	—	—	0.60	—
1980FM (P)	2,688	Value: 2.00				
1981FM (U)	482	—	—	—	2.00	—
1981FM (P)	1,577	Value: 2.00				
1982FM (U)	—	—	—	—	0.60	—
1982FM (P)	—	Value: 2.00				
1984FM (U)	—	—	—	—	0.60	—
1984FM (P)	—	Value: 2.00				

KM# 90 20 CENTS Composition: Copper-Nickel
Subject: World Food Day **Obverse:** JAMAICA more compact

Date	F	VF	XF	Unc	BU
1981FM (M)	—	—	—	1.50	—

KM# 120 20 CENTS Composition: Copper-Nickel

Date	Mintage	F	VF	XF	Unc	BU
1981	—	—	—	—	0.60	—
1984	2,000,000	—	—	—	0.60	—
1985	2,988,000	—	—	—	0.60	—
1985 Proof	—	Value: 2.00				
1986	2,530,000	—	—	—	0.60	—
1988	—	—	—	—	0.60	—

KM# 104 20 CENTS Composition: Copper-Nickel
Subject: 21st Anniversary of Independence

Date	F	VF	XF	Unc	BU
ND(1983)FM (U)	—	—	—	0.60	—
ND(1983)FM (P)	— Value: 2.00				

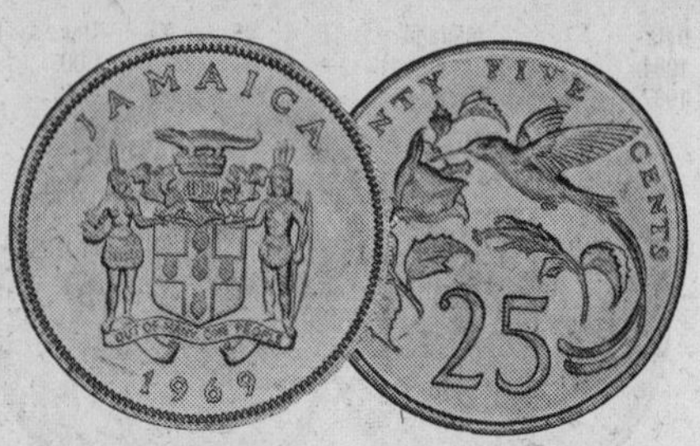

KM# 49 25 CENTS Composition: Copper-Nickel
Reverse: Streamer-tailed hummingbird

Date	Mintage	F	VF	XF	Unc	BU
1969	758,000	—	—	0.60	1.25	—
1969 Proof	30,000	Value: 1.50				
1970FM (M)	5,000	—	—	0.60	1.25	—
1970FM (P)	12,000	Value: 1.50				
1973	160,000	—	—	0.60	1.25	—
1975	3,110,000	—	—	0.60	1.25	—
1982	1,000,000	—	—	0.60	1.25	—
1984	2,002,000	—	—	0.60	1.25	—
1985	1,999,000	—	—	0.60	1.25	—
1985 Proof	—	Value: 1.50				
1986	2,635,000	—	—	0.60	1.25	—
1987	6,006,000	—	—	0.60	1.25	—
1987 Proof	—	Value: 1.50				
1988	3,034,000	—	—	0.60	1.25	—
1988 Proof	—	Value: 1.50				
1989	—	—	—	0.60	1.25	—
1989 Proof	—	Value: 1.50				
1990 Proof	—	Value: 1.50				

KM# 56 25 CENTS Composition: Copper-Nickel

Date	Mintage	F	VF	XF	Unc	BU
1971FM (M)	4,834	—	—	0.60	1.25	—
1971FM (P)	14,000	Value: 1.50				
1972FM (M)	8,382	—	—	0.60	1.25	—
1972FM (P)	17,000	Value: 1.50				
1973FM (M)	13,000	—	—	0.60	1.25	—
1973FM (P)	28,000	Value: 1.50				
1974FM (M)	12,000	—	—	0.60	1.25	—
1974FM (P)	22,000	Value: 1.50				
1975FM (M)	1,503	—	—	0.60	1.25	—
1975FM (U)	4,683	—	—	—	1.25	—
1975FM (P)	16,000	Value: 1.50				
1976FM (M)	1,112	—	—	0.60	1.25	—
1976FM (U)	1,802	—	—	—	1.25	—
1976FM (P)	24,000	Value: 1.50				
1977FM (M)	1,112	—	—	0.60	1.35	—
1977FM (U)	597	—	—	—	3.00	—
1977FM (P)	10,000	Value: 1.50				
1978FM (M)	1,112	—	—	0.60	1.35	—
1978FM (U)	1,282	—	—	—	1.35	—
1978FM (P)	6,058	Value: 2.00				
1979FM (M)	1,112	—	—	0.60	1.35	—
1979FM (U)	2,608	—	—	—	1.35	—
1979FM (P)	4,049	Value: 2.00				
1980FM (M)	1,112	—	—	0.60	1.25	—
1980FM (U)	3,668	—	—	—	1.25	—
1980FM (P)	2,688	Value: 3.00				
1981FM (U)	482	—	—	—	3.00	—
1981FM (P)	1,577	Value: 3.00				
1982FM (U)	—	—	—	—	1.25	—
1982FM (P)	—	Value: 3.00				
1984FM (U)	—	—	—	—	1.25	—
1984FM (P)	—	Value: 3.00				

KM# 105 25 CENTS Composition: Copper-Nickel
Subject: 21st Anniversary of Independence

Date	F	VF	XF	Unc	BU
ND(1983)FM (U)	—	—	—	1.50	—
ND(1983)FM (P)	—	Value: 3.00			

KM# 154 25 CENTS Composition: Copper-Nickel
Subject: 25th Anniversary - Bank of Jamaica

Date	F	VF	XF	Unc	BU
1985	—	—	0.75	3.50	—

KM# 147 25 CENTS Composition: Nickel Plated Steel
Reverse: Marcus Garvey

Date	F	VF	XF	Unc	BU
1991	—	—	—	1.00	—
1991 Proof	—	Value: 3.00			
1992	—	—	—	1.00	—
1992 Proof	—	Value: 3.00			
1993	—	—	—	1.00	—
1993 Proof	—	Value: 3.00			
1994	—	—	—	1.00	—

KM# 167 25 CENTS Composition: Copper Plated Steel

Date	Mintage	F	VF	XF	Unc	BU
1995	—	—	—	—	0.50	—
1996	—	—	—	—	0.50	—
2000	—	—	—	—	0.50	—
2002	—	—	—	—	0.50	—
2002 Proof	500	Value: 3.00				

KM# 65 50 CENTS Composition: Copper-Nickel
Shape: 10-sided **Reverse:** Marcus Garvey

Date	Mintage	F	VF	XF	Unc	BU
1975	12,010,000	—	0.15	0.50	1.50	—
1984	2,000,000	—	0.15	0.50	1.50	—
1985	2,119,000	—	0.15	0.50	1.50	—
1985 Proof	—	Value: 3.00				
1986	3,404,000	—	0.15	0.50	1.50	—
1987	5,545,000	—	0.15	0.50	1.50	—
1988	10,505,000	—	0.15	0.50	1.50	—
1988 Proof	—	Value: 3.00				
1989	—	—	0.15	0.50	1.50	—
1989 Proof	—	Value: 3.00				
1990 Proof	—	Value: 3.00				

KM# 70 50 CENTS Composition: Copper-Nickel
Shape: 10-sided

Date	Mintage	F	VF	XF	Unc	BU
1976FM (M)	1,112	—	—	0.25	1.50	—
1976FM (U)	1,802	—	—	—	1.50	—
1976FM (P)	24,000	Value: 1.50				
1977FM (M)	556	—	—	0.50	3.50	—
1977FM (U)	597	—	—	—	3.50	—
1977FM (P)	10,000	Value: 1.50				
1978FM (M)	556	—	—	0.50	3.50	—
1978FM (U)	1,838	—	—	—	2.00	—
1978FM (P)	6,058	Value: 2.50				
1979FM (M)	556	—	—	0.50	3.50	—
1979FM (U)	1,282	—	—	—	2.50	—
1979FM (P)	4,049	Value: 3.00				
1980FM (M)	556	—	—	0.50	3.50	—
1980FM (U)	3,668	—	—	—	2.00	—
1980FM (P)	2,688	Value: 3.00				
1981FM (U)	482	—	—	—	3.50	—
1981FM (P)	1,577	Value: 3.00				
1982FM (U)	—	—	—	—	2.00	—
1982FM (P)	—	Value: 3.00				
1984FM (U)	—	—	—	—	2.00	—
1984FM (P)	—	Value: 3.00				

KM# 106 50 CENTS Composition: Copper-Nickel
Subject: 21st Anniversary of Independence

Date	F	VF	XF	Unc	BU
ND(1983)FM (U)	—	—	—	2.00	—
ND(1983)FM (P)	—	Value: 4.00			

KM# 132 50 CENTS Composition: Copper-Nickel
Subject: 100th Anniversary - Birth of Marcus Garvey
Obverse: Arms **Reverse:** Bust of Marcus Garvey right

Date	Mintage	F	VF	XF	Unc	BU
1987 Proof	500	Value: 3.50				

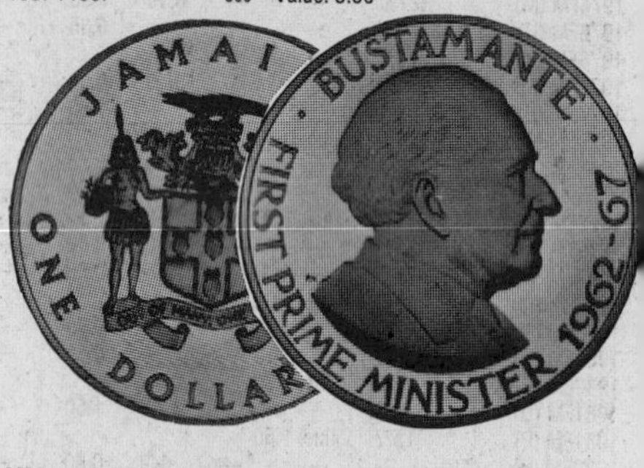

KM# 50 DOLLAR Composition: Copper-Nickel
Reverse: Sir Alexander Bustamante

Date	Mintage	F	VF	XF	Unc	BU
1969	47,000	—	—	1.00	3.00	—
1969 Proof	30,000	Value: 4.50				
1970FM (M)	5,000	—	—	0.30	3.50	—
1970FM (P)	14,000	Value: 4.00				

KM# 57 DOLLAR Composition: Copper-Nickel **Note:** Similar to KM#50.

Date	Mintage	F	VF	XF	Unc	BU
1971FM	5,024	—	—	0.30	3.00	—
1971FM (P)	15,000	Value: 4.00				
1972F (M)	7,982	—	—	0.30	2.00	—
1972FM (P)	17,000	Value: 3.00				
1973FM	10,000	—	—	0.30	2.00	—
1973FM (P)	28,000	Value: 3.00				
1974FM (M)	8,961	—	—	0.30	2.00	—
1974FM (P)	22,000	Value: 3.00				
1975FM (M)	5,312	—	—	0.30	2.50	—
1975FM (U)	4,683	—	—	—	2.50	—
1975FM (P)	16,000	Value: 3.00				
1976FM (M)	284	—	—	—	17.50	—
1976FM (U)	1,802	—	—	—	4.00	—
1976FM (P)	24,000	Value: 2.50				
1977FM (M)	287	—	—	—	17.50	—
1977FM (U)	597	—	—	—	8.00	—
1977FM (P)	10,000	Value: 4.00				
1978FM (U)	1,566	—	—	—	4.00	—
1978FM (P)	6,058	Value: 5.00				
1979FM (M)	284	—	—	—	17.50	—
1979FM (U)	2,608	—	—	—	4.00	—
1979FM (P)	4,049	Value: 5.00				

KM# 84.1 DOLLAR Composition: Copper-Nickel
Obverse: Arms **Reverse:** Bust of Bustamante right

Date	Mintage	F	VF	XF	Unc	BU
1980FM (M)	284	—	—	—	20.00	—
1980FM (U)	3,668	—	—	—	5.00	—
1980FM (P)	2,688	Value: 15.00				

Date	Mintage	F	VF	XF	Unc	BU
1981FM (U)	482	—	—	—	10.00	—
1981FM (P)	1,577	Value: 20.00				
1982FM (U)	—	—	—	—	7.00	—
1982FM (P)	—	Value: 20.00				

KM# 84.2 DOLLAR Composition: Copper-Nickel **Edge:** Reeded

Date	Mintage	F	VF	XF	Unc	BU
1985 Proof	—	Value: 7.50				
1985	—	—	—	—	3.00	—
1987 Proof	—	Value: 7.50				
1988 Proof	—	Value: 7.50				
1989 Proof	—	Value: 7.50				
1990	—	—	—	—	3.00	—

KM# 91 DOLLAR Composition: Copper-Nickel **Subject:** World Food Day

Date	F	VF	XF	Unc	BU
ND(1981)FM (U)	—	—	—	7.50	—

KM# 96 DOLLAR Composition: Copper-Nickel **Subject:** Soccer Games

Date	F	VF	XF	Unc	BU
1982	—	—	—	4.50	—

KM# 107 DOLLAR Composition: Copper-Nickel **Subject:** 21st Anniversary of Independence

Date	Mintage	F	VF	XF	Unc	BU
ND(1983)FM (U)	3,710	—	—	—	7.50	—
ND(1983)FM (P)	609	Value: 20.00				

KM# 134 DOLLAR Composition: Copper-Nickel **Subject:** 21st Anniversary of Independence

Date	F	VF	XF	Unc	BU
ND(1983)FM (P)	—	Value: 14.00			

KM# 113 DOLLAR Composition: Copper-Nickel **Subject:** 100th Anniversary - Birth of Bustamante

Date	Mintage	F	VF	XF	Unc	BU
1984FM (U)	—	—	—	—	3.00	—
1984FM (P)	268	Value: 25.00				

KM# 145 DOLLAR Composition: Nickel-Brass **Subject:** Sir Alexander Bustamante **Edge:** Reeded over "Bank of Jamaica"

Date	F	VF	XF	Unc	BU
1990	—	—	—	2.25	—
1990 Proof	Value: 5.00				
1991	—	—	—	2.25	—
1991 Proof	Value: 5.00				
1992	—	—	—	2.25	—
1992 Proof	Value: 10.00				
1993	—	—	—	2.25	—
1993 Proof	Value: 5.00				
1994	—	—	—	2.25	—

KM# 145a DOLLAR Composition: Brass Plated Steel **Edge:** Reeded, no inscription

Date	Mintage	F	VF	XF	Unc	BU
1993	—	—	—	—	2.25	—
1993 Proof	500	Value: 15.00				
1994	—	—	—	—	2.25	—

KM# 164 DOLLAR Composition: Nickel Clad Steel **Shape:** 7-sided

Date	Mintage	F	VF	XF	Unc	BU
1994	—	—	—	—	1.00	—
1995	—	—	—	—	1.00	—
1996	—	—	—	—	1.00	—
2000	—	—	—	—	1.00	—
2002	—	—	—	—	1.00	—
2002 Proof	500	Value: 4.00				

KM#58 5 DOLLARS Weight: 42.1500 g. **Composition:** 0.9250 Silver 1.2536 oz. ASW **Obverse:** Arms **Reverse:** Norman W. Manley

Date	Mintage	F	VF	XF	Unc	BU
1971FM	4,072	—	—	—	12.00	—
1971FM (P)	13,000	Value: 10.00				

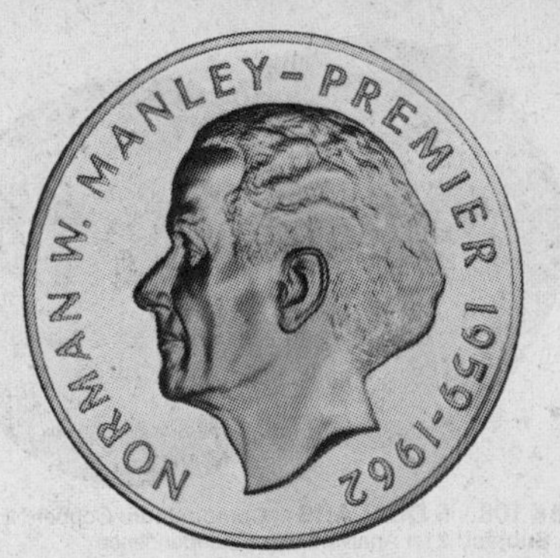

KM#59 5 DOLLARS Weight: 41.4800 g. **Composition:** 0.9250 Silver 1.2336 oz. ASW **Obverse:** Arms

Date	Mintage	F	VF	XF	Unc	BU
1972FM	3,232	—	—	—	14.00	—
1972FM (P)	21,000	Value: 12.00				
1973FM	6,484	—	—	—	14.00	—
1973FM (P)	36,000	Value: 12.00				

KM#62 5 DOLLARS Weight: 41.4800 g. **Composition:** 0.9250 Silver 1.2336 oz. ASW **Reverse:** Norman W. Manley

Date	Mintage	F	VF	XF	Unc	BU
1974FM (M)	8,661	—	—	—	6.00	—
1975FM (M)	65	—	—	—	—	—
1975FM (U)	4,683	—	—	—	7.00	—
1976FM (M)	56	—	—	—	—	—
1976FM (U)	1,802	—	—	—	8.00	—
1977FM (M)	56	—	—	—	—	—
1977FM (U)	597	—	—	—	12.00	—
1978FM (U)	1,338	—	—	—	7.00	—
1979FM (M)	56	—	—	—	—	—
1979FM (U)	2,608	—	—	—	6.00	—

KM#62a 5 DOLLARS Weight: 37.6000 g. **Composition:** 0.5000 Silver .6044 oz. ASW

Date	Mintage	F	VF	XF	Unc	BU
1974FM (P)	22,000	Value: 7.50				
1975FM (P)	16,000	Value: 9.00				
1976FM (P)	23,000	Value: 7.50				
1977FM (P)	10,000	Value: 9.00				
1978FM (P)	6,058	Value: 12.00				
1979FM (P)	4,049	Value: 15.00				

KM# 85.1 5 DOLLARS Composition: Copper-Nickel

Date	Mintage	F	VF	XF	Unc	BU
1980FM (M)	56	—	—	—	—	—
1980FM (U)	3,668	—	—	—	15.00	—
1981FM (U)	482	—	—	—	20.00	—
1982FM (U)	—	—	—	—	10.00	—
1984FM (U)	—	—	—	—	10.00	—

KM#85.1a 5 DOLLARS Weight: 18.5600 g. **Composition:** 0.5000 Silver .2983 oz. ASW

Date	Mintage	F	VF	XF	Unc	BU
1980FM (P)	2,688	Value: 15.00				
1981FM (P)	1,577	Value: 17.00				
1982FM (P)	1,040	Value: 17.00				
1984FM (P)	268	Value: 40.00				

KM#85.2 5 DOLLARS Weight: 18.5600 g. **Composition:** 0.5000 Silver .2983 oz. ASW

Date	Mintage	F	VF	XF	Unc	BU
1985	—	—	—	—	30.00	—
1987 Proof	—	Value: 30.00				
1988 Proof	—	Value: 30.00				
1989 Proof	—	Value: 30.00				
1990 Proof	500	Value: 30.00				
1991 Proof	—	Value: 30.00				
1992 Proof	—	Value: 30.00				
1993 Proof	—	Value: 30.00				

KM# 108 5 DOLLARS **Composition:** Copper-Nickel **Subject:** 21st Anniversary of Independence

Date	F	VF	XF	Unc	BU
1983FM (U)	—	—	—	8.00	—

KM# 108a 5 DOLLARS **Weight:** 18.5600 g. **Composition:** 0.5000 Silver .2983 oz. ASW

Date	F	VF	XF	Unc	BU
1983FM (P)	—	Value: 20.00			

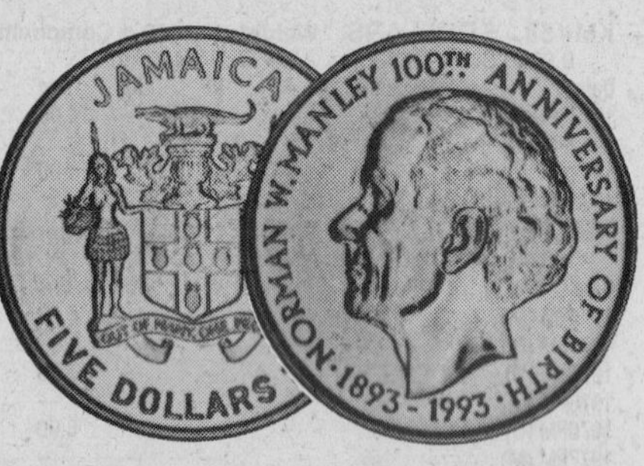

KM# 157 5 DOLLARS **Composition:** Nickel Plated Steel **Subject:** Centennial - Birth of Norman Manley

Date	F	VF	XF	Unc	BU
1993	—	—	—	2.50	—

KM# 157a 5 DOLLARS **Weight:** 18.5000 g. **Composition:** 0.5000 Silver .2984 oz. ASW

Date	F	VF	XF	Unc	BU
1993 Proof	Est. 2,000	Value: 40.00			

KM# 163 5 DOLLARS **Composition:** Steel **Note:** National Hero - Norman Manley

Date	Mintage	F	VF	XF	Unc	BU
1994	—	—	—	—	2.50	—
1995	—	—	—	—	2.50	—
1996	—	—	—	—	2.50	—
2000	—	—	—	—	2.50	—
2002	—	—	—	—	2.50	—
2002 Proof	500	Value: 5.00				

KM# 60 10 DOLLARS **Weight:** 49.2000 g. **Composition:** 0.9250 Silver 1.4632 oz. ASW **Subject:** 10th Anniversary of Independence

Date	Mintage	F	VF	XF	Unc	BU
ND(1972)	42,000	—	—	—	15.00	—
ND(1972) Proof	33,000	Value: 20.00				

KM# 63 10 DOLLARS **Composition:** Copper-Nickel **Obverse:** Arms **Reverse:** Half bust of Sir Henry Morgan facing half left

Date	Mintage	F	VF	XF	Unc	BU
1974FM (M)	15,000	—	—	—	7.50	—

KM# 63a 10 DOLLARS **Weight:** 42.8000 g. **Composition:** 0.9250 Silver 1.2728 oz. ASW **Obverse:** Arms **Reverse:** Half bust of Sir Henry Morgan facing half left

Date	Mintage	F	VF	XF	Unc	BU
1974FM (P)	42,000	Value: 17.00				

KM# 66 10 DOLLARS **Composition:** Copper-Nickel **Obverse:** Arms **Reverse:** Christopher Columbus at right, ship at left

Date	Mintage	F	VF	XF	Unc	BU
1975FM (M)	30	—	—	—	—	—
1975FM (U)	5,758	—	—	—	12.00	—

KM# 66a 10 DOLLARS **Weight:** 42.8000 g. **Composition:** 0.9250 Silver 1.2728 oz. ASW **Obverse:** Arms **Reverse:** Christopher Columbus at right, ship at left

Date	Mintage	F	VF	XF	Unc	BU
1975FM (P)	29,000	Value: 17.00				

KM# 71 10 DOLLARS **Composition:** Copper-Nickel **Obverse:** Arms **Reverse:** Admiral Horatio Nelson at right, ship at left with map above

Date	Mintage	F	VF	XF	Unc	BU
1976FM (M)	27	—	—	—	—	—
1976FM (U)	2,302	—	—	—	15.00	—

KM# 71a 10 DOLLARS **Weight:** 42.8000 g. **Composition:** 0.9250 Silver 1.2728 oz. ASW **Obverse:** Arms **Reverse:** Admiral Horatio Nelson at right, ship at left with map above

Date	Mintage	F	VF	XF	Unc	BU
1976FM (P)	31,000	Value: 16.00				

KM# 74 10 DOLLARS **Composition:** Copper-Nickel **Obverse:** Arms **Reverse:** Admiral George Rodney at right, ship at left

Date	Mintage	F	VF	XF	Unc	BU
1977FM (M)	27	—	—	—	—	—
1977FM (U)	847	—	—	—	30.00	—

KM# 74a 10 DOLLARS **Weight:** 42.8000 g. **Composition:** 0.9250 Silver 1.2728 oz. ASW **Obverse:** Arms **Reverse:** Admiral George Rodney at right, ship at left

Date	Mintage	F	VF	XF	Unc	BU
1977FM (P)	14,000	Value: 20.00				

KM# 75 10 DOLLARS **Composition:** Copper-Nickel **Subject:** Jamaican Unity **Obverse:** Arms **Reverse:** Busts of many different ethnic people in circle

Date	Mintage	F	VF	XF	Unc	BU
1978FM (U)	1,559	—	—	—	20.00	—

KM# 75a 10 DOLLARS **Weight:** 42.8000 g. **Composition:** 0.9250 Silver 1.2728 oz. ASW **Obverse:** Arms **Reverse:** Busts of many different ethnic people in circle **Edge Lettering:** Jamaican Unity

Date	Mintage	F	VF	XF	Unc	BU
1978FM (P)	12,000	Value: 25.00				

KM# 79 10 DOLLARS **Composition:** Copper-Nickel **Obverse:** Arms **Reverse:** Homerus Swallowtails

Date	Mintage	F	VF	XF	Unc	BU
1979FM (M)	27	—	—	—	—	—
1979FM (U)	2,608	—	—	—	30.00	—

KM# 79a 10 DOLLARS **Weight:** 42.8000 g. **Composition:** 0.9250 Silver 1.2728 oz. ASW **Obverse:** Arms **Reverse:** Homerus Swallowtails

Date	Mintage	F	VF	XF	Unc	BU
1979FM (P)	8,308	Value: 35.00				

KM#80 10 DOLLARS Weight: 22.4500 g. **Composition:** 0.9250 Silver .6677 oz. ASW **Subject:** International Year of the Child

Date	Mintage	F	VF	XF	Unc	BU
1979 Proof	20,000	Value: 17.00				

KM# 87 10 DOLLARS Weight: 30.2800 g. **Composition:** 0.5000 Silver .4868 oz. ASW **Subject:** 10th Anniversary of Caribbean Development Bank

Date	Mintage	F	VF	XF	Unc	BU
ND(1980)FM (P)	2,327	Value: 32.00				

KM# 86 10 DOLLARS Composition: Copper-Nickel **Reverse:** Streamer-tailed Hummingbirds

Date	Mintage	F	VF	XF	Unc	BU
1980FM (M)	27	—	—	—	—	—
1980FM (U)	5,668	—	—	—	30.00	—

KM# 86a 10 DOLLARS Weight: 22.4500 g. **Composition:** 0.9250 Silver .6677 oz. ASW **Reverse:** Streamer-tailed Hummingbirds

Date	Mintage	F	VF	XF	Unc	BU
1980FM (P)	5,394	Value: 25.00				

KM# 92 10 DOLLARS Weight: 28.2800 g. **Composition:** 0.9250 Silver .8410 oz. ASW **Subject:** Wedding of Prince Charles and Lady Diana **Reverse:** Conjoined busts of royal couple facing right

Date	Mintage	F	VF	XF	Unc	BU
1981 Proof	40,000	Value: 20.00				

KM# 93 10 DOLLARS Composition: Copper-Nickel **Reverse:** American Crocodile

Date	Mintage	F	VF	XF	Unc	BU
1981FM (U)	804	—	—	—	30.00	—

KM# 93a 10 DOLLARS Weight: 22.4500 g. **Composition:** 0.9250 Silver .6677 oz. ASW **Reverse:** American Crocodile

Date	Mintage	F	VF	XF	Unc	BU
1981FM (P)	3,216	Value: 40.00				

KM# 97 10 DOLLARS Composition: Copper-Nickel **Reverse:** Small Indian Mongoose

Date	F	VF	XF	Unc	BU
1982FM (U)	—	—	—	25.00	—

KM# 97a 10 DOLLARS Weight: 22.4500 g. **Composition:** 0.9250 Silver .6677 oz. ASW **Reverse:** Small Indian Mongoose

Date	Mintage	F	VF	XF	Unc	BU
1982FM (P)	1,852	Value: 40.00				

KM# 98 10 DOLLARS Weight: 22.4500 g. **Composition:** 0.9250 Silver .6677 oz. ASW **Subject:** Soccer - World Championships **Reverse:** Standing player with ball

Date	Mintage	F	VF	XF	Unc	BU
1982 Proof	9,775	Value: 16.50				

KM# 109 10 DOLLARS Composition: Copper-Nickel **Subject:** 21st Anniversary of Independence

Date	Mintage	F	VF	XF	Unc	BU
ND(1983)FM (U)	1,320	—	—	—	15.00	—

KM# 109a 10 DOLLARS Weight: 22.4500 g. **Composition:** 0.9250 Silver .6677 oz. ASW **Subject:** 21st Anniversary of Independence

Date	Mintage	F	VF	XF	Unc	BU
ND(1983)FM (P)	1,187	Value: 30.00				

KM#111 10 DOLLARS Weight: 22.4500 g. **Composition:** 0.9250 Silver .6677 oz. ASW **Subject:** Royal visit **Reverse:** Conjoined busts of Queen Elizabeth II and Prince Philip left

Date	F	VF	XF	Unc	BU
1983	—	Value: 25.00			

KM# 114 10 DOLLARS Composition: Copper-Nickel **Obverse:** Arms **Reverse:** Blue Marlin breaking water

Date	F	VF	XF	Unc	BU
1984FM (U)	—	—	—	28.00	—

KM# 114a 10 DOLLARS Weight: 22.4500 g. **Composition:** 0.9350 Silver .6677 oz. ASW **Reverse:** Blue Marlin breaking water

Date	Mintage	F	VF	XF	Unc	BU
1984FM (P)	335	Value: 70.00				

KM# 115 10 DOLLARS Weight: 22.4500 g. **Composition:** 0.9350 Silver .6677 oz. ASW **Subject:** Decade for Women **Reverse:** Woman with basket on head, map behind

Date	Mintage	F	VF	XF	Unc	BU
1984 Proof	1,100	Value: 30.00				
1985 Proof	610	Value: 42.00				

KM# 125 10 DOLLARS Weight: 22.4500 g. **Composition:** 0.9350 Silver .6677 oz. ASW **Subject:** Summer Olympics - Sprinter

Date	Mintage	F	VF	XF	Unc	BU
1984 Proof	10,000	Value: 22.50				

KM# 123 10 DOLLARS **Weight:** 22.4500 g. **Composition:** 0.9250 Silver .6677 oz. ASW **Subject:** Year of Youth **Reverse:** Collage of many youth's heads

Date	Mintage	F	VF	XF	Unc	BU
1985 Proof	1,000	Value: 40.00				

KM# 121 10 DOLLARS **Weight:** 22.4500 g. **Composition:** 0.9350 Silver .6677 oz. ASW **Subject:** XIII Commonwealth Games - Edinburgh **Reverse:** Relay runners

Date	Mintage	F	VF	XF	Unc	BU
1986	50,000	—	—	—	16.50	—

KM# 121a 10 DOLLARS **Weight:** 28.2800 g. **Composition:** 0.9250 Silver .8411 oz. ASW **Reverse:** Relay runners

Date	Mintage	F	VF	XF	Unc	BU
1986 Proof	20,000	Value: 22.50				

KM# 128 10 DOLLARS **Weight:** 22.4500 g. **Composition:** 0.9250 Silver .6677 oz. ASW **Subject:** 100th Anniversary - Birth of Marcus Garvey **Reverse:** Marcus Garvey

Date	Mintage	F	VF	XF	Unc	BU
1987 Proof	1,000	Value: 40.00				

KM# 133 10 DOLLARS **Weight:** 22.4500 g. **Composition:** 0.9250 Silver .6677 oz. ASW **Subject:** 25th Anniversary of Independence

Date	Mintage	F	VF	XF	Unc	BU
1987 Proof	Est. 500	Value: 45.00				

KM# 138 10 DOLLARS **Composition:** Copper-Nickel **Subject:** Year of the Worker

Date	F	VF	XF	Unc	BU
1988	—	—	—	7.00	—

KM# 138a 10 DOLLARS **Weight:** 22.4500 g. **Composition:** 0.9250 Silver .6677 oz. ASW **Subject:** Year of the Worker

Date	Mintage	F	VF	XF	Unc	BU
1988 Proof	Est. 1,000	Value: 35.00				

KM# 140 10 DOLLARS **Composition:** Copper-Nickel **Subject:** Columbus' Discovery of the New World **Reverse:** Several ships at sea

Date	F	VF	XF	Unc	BU
1989	—	—	—	7.00	—

KM# 140a 10 DOLLARS **Weight:** 22.4500 g. **Composition:** 0.9250 Silver .6677 oz. ASW **Subject:** Columbus' Discovery of the New World **Reverse:** Several ships at sea

Date	Mintage	F	VF	XF	Unc	BU
1989 Proof	Est. 5,500	Value: 37.50				

KM# 144 10 DOLLARS **Composition:** Copper-Nickel **Subject:** Columbus' Arrival in New World **Reverse:** Columbus at left, ship at right in background

Date	F	VF	XF	Unc	BU
1990	—	—	—	7.00	—

KM# 144a 10 DOLLARS **Weight:** 22.4500 g. **Composition:** 0.9250 Silver .6677 oz. ASW **Subject:** Columbus' Arrival in New World **Reverse:** Columbus at left, ship at right in background

Date	Mintage	F	VF	XF	Unc	BU
1990 Proof	Est. 11,000	Value: 35.00				

KM# 148 10 DOLLARS **Composition:** Copper-Nickel **Subject:** Arrival in the New World **Reverse:** Columbus' ship - Pinta

Date	F	VF	XF	Unc	BU
1991	—	—	—	7.00	—

KM# 148a 10 DOLLARS **Weight:** 22.4500 g. **Composition:** 0.9250 Silver .6677 oz. ASW **Subject:** Arrival in the New World **Reverse:** Columbus' ship - Pinta

Date	Mintage	F	VF	XF	Unc	BU
1991 Proof	Est. 5,500	Value: 40.00				

KM# 152 10 DOLLARS **Weight:** 22.4500 g. **Composition:** 0.9250 Silver .6677 oz. ASW **Subject:** 500th Anniversary of Columbus' Arrival **Reverse:** Ship in full sail

Date	Mintage	F	VF	XF	Unc	BU
1992 Proof	5,500	Value: 40.00				

KM# 155 10 DOLLARS **Weight:** 22.4500 g. **Composition:** 0.9250 Silver .6677 oz. ASW **Subject:** 40th Anniversary - Coronation of Queen Elizabeth II

Date	Mintage	F	VF	XF	Unc	BU
1993 Proof	Est. 5,500	Value: 40.00				

KM# 161 10 DOLLARS **Weight:** 28.2800 g. **Composition:** 0.9250 Silver .8411 oz. ASW **Subject:** Royal Visit **Reverse:** Standing sailor beating drum on map of Jamaica at left, ship at right

Date	F	VF	XF	Unc	BU
1994 Proof	—	Value: 35.00			

KM# 168 10 DOLLARS **Weight:** 20.0000 g. **Composition:** 0.5000 Silver .3215 oz. ASW **Reverse:** Ernest Hemingway

Date	F	VF	XF	Unc	BU
1994	—	—	—	20.00	—

KM# 176 10 DOLLARS **Weight:** 28.2800 g. **Composition:** 0.9250 Silver .8411 oz. ASW **Subject:** Olympic Games - 1996 **Reverse:** Relay runner left

Date	Mintage	F	VF	XF	Unc	BU
1996 Proof	Est. 10,000	Value: 30.00				

KM# 181 10 DOLLARS **Composition:** Stainless Steel **Obverse:** National arms **Reverse:** Portrait of George William Gordon **Shape:** Scalloped

Date	Mintage	F	VF	XF	Unc	BU
1999	—	—	—	—	3.00	—
2000	—	—	—	—	3.00	—
2002	—	—	—	—	3.00	—
2002 Proof	500	Value: 9.00				

KM# 61 20 DOLLARS **Weight:** 15.7484 g. **Composition:** 0.5000 Gold .2531 oz. AGW **Subject:** 10th Anniversary of Independence

Date	Mintage	F	VF	XF	Unc	BU
ND(1972)	30,000	—	—	—	100	—
ND(1972) Proof	20,000	Value: 120				

KM# 182 20 DOLLARS **Ring Composition:** Brass **Center Composition:** Copper-Nickel **Obverse:** National arms, denomination above **Reverse:** Marcus Garvey **Edge:** Reeded **Size:** 23 mm.

Date	Mintage	F	VF	XF	Unc	BU
2000	—	—	—	—	3.00	—
2002	—	—	—	—	3.00	—
2002 Proof	500	Value: 15.00				

KM# 76 25 DOLLARS **Weight:** 136.0800 g. **Composition:** 0.9250 Silver 4.0473 oz. ASW **Subject:** 25th Anniversary of Coronation

Date	Mintage	F	VF	XF	Unc	BU
ND(1978)	11,000	—	—	—	40.00	—
ND(1978) Proof	22,000	Value: 42.00				

KM# 81 25 DOLLARS **Weight:** 136.0800 g. **Composition:** 0.9250 Silver 4.0473 oz. ASW **Subject:** 10th Anniversary - Investiture of Prince Charles

Date	Mintage	F	VF	XF	Unc	BU
ND(1979)	16,000	—	—	—	42.00	—
ND(1979) Proof	25,000	Value: 45.00				

KM# 99 25 DOLLARS **Weight:** 136.0800 g. **Composition:** 0.9250 Silver 4.0473 oz. ASW **Subject:** World Championship Soccer Games **Obverse:** Arms **Reverse:** Player kicking ball to right

Date	Mintage	F	VF	XF	Unc	BU
1982 Proof	30,000	Value: 60.00				

KM# 88 25 DOLLARS **Weight:** 136.0800 g. **Composition:** 0.5000 Silver 2.1878 oz. ASW **Subject:** 1980 Olympics **Reverse:** Circle of busts of previous Gold Medal winners

Date	Mintage	F	VF	XF	Unc	BU
1980	—	—	—	—	50.00	—
1980 Proof	6,969	Value: 60.00				

KM# 112 25 DOLLARS **Weight:** 136.0800 g. **Composition:** 0.9250 Silver 4.0473 oz. ASW **Subject:** Royal Visit **Reverse:** Conjoined busts of royal couple facing left

Date	Mintage	F	VF	XF	Unc	BU
1983 Proof	—	Value: 60.00				

KM# 94 25 DOLLARS **Weight:** 136.0800 g. **Composition:** 0.9250 Silver 4.0473 oz. ASW **Subject:** Wedding of Prince Charles and Lady Diana **Obverse:** Bust of Elizabeth II right **Reverse:** Conjoined busts of royal couple

Date	Mintage	F	VF	XF	Unc	BU
1981(T) Proof	6,450	Value: 100				

KM# 116 25 DOLLARS **Weight:** 136.0800 g. **Composition:** 0.9250 Silver 4.0473 oz. ASW **Subject:** Summer Olympics - Sprinter

Date	Mintage	F	VF	XF	Unc	BU
1984 Proof	3,300	Value: 60.00				

KM# 126 25 DOLLARS **Weight:** 23.4400 g. **Composition:** 0.9250 Silver .6677 oz. ASW **Subject:** Decade For Women **Note:** Mule. Denomination error for KM#115.

Date		F	VF	XF	Unc	BU
1984 Proof	—	Value: 160				

KM# 119 25 DOLLARS **Weight:** 136.0800 g. **Composition:** 0.9250 Silver 4.0473 oz. ASW **Subject:** Humpback Whale Protection **Obverse:** Similar to KM#112

Date	Mintage	F	VF	XF	Unc	BU
1985 Proof	2,600	Value: 80.00				

KM# 127 25 DOLLARS **Weight:** 136.0800 g. **Composition:** 0.9250 Silver 4.0473 oz. ASW **Subject:** World Championship Soccer - Mexico

Date	F	VF	XF	Unc	BU
1986	—	—	—	20.00	—

KM# 130 25 DOLLARS **Weight:** 37.7800 g. **Composition:** 0.9250 Silver 1.1236 oz. ASW **Subject:** 25th Anniversary of Independence **Reverse:** Arms

Date	Mintage	F	VF	XF	Unc	BU
1987 Proof	1,900	Value: 45.00				

KM# 141 25 DOLLARS **Weight:** 23.3300 g. **Composition:** 0.9250 Silver .6939 oz. ASW **Subject:** Olympics **Reverse:** Relay runners

Date	Mintage	F	VF	XF	Unc	BU
1988 Proof	Est. 15,000	Value: 22.50				

KM# 142 25 DOLLARS **Weight:** 23.3300 g. **Composition:** 0.9250 Silver .6939 oz. ASW **Subject:** World Championship Soccer **Reverse:** Soccer player

Date		F	VF	XF	Unc	BU
1990 Proof	—	Value: 30.00				

KM# 150 25 DOLLARS **Weight:** 23.3300 g. **Composition:** 0.9250 Silver .6939 oz. ASW **Subject:** Columbus' Jamaican Landfall of 1494

Date	Mintage	F	VF	XF	Unc	BU
1991 Matte	—	—	—	—	60.00	—
1991 Proof	Est. 25,000	Value: 40.00				

KM# 151 25 DOLLARS **Weight:** 23.3300 g. **Composition:** 0.9250 Silver .6939 oz. ASW **Subject:** Discovery of America - Landfall

Date	Mintage	F	VF	XF	Unc	BU
1992 Matte	—	—	—	—	60.00	—
1992 Proof	Est. 25,000	Value: 40.00				

KM# 159 25 DOLLARS **Weight:** 23.3300 g. **Composition:** 0.9250 Silver .6939 oz. ASW **Subject:** Summer Olympic Games **Reverse:** Bicyclists

Date	Mintage	F	VF	XF	Unc	BU
1992 Proof	15,000	Value: 45.00				

KM# 160 25 DOLLARS **Weight:** 23.3300 g. **Composition:** 0.9250 Silver .6939 oz. ASW **Subject:** Summer Olympic Games **Reverse:** Boxers

Date	Mintage	F	VF	XF	Unc	BU
1992 Proof	15,000	Value: 45.00				

KM# 165 25 DOLLARS **Weight:** 28.2000 g. **Composition:** 0.9250 Silver .8386 oz. ASW **Subject:** World Cup Soccer **Reverse:** Soccer player

Date	F	VF	XF	Unc	BU
1994	—	—	—	40.00	—

KM# 169 25 DOLLARS **Weight:** 31.4700 g. **Composition:** 0.9250 Silver .9359 oz. ASW **Subject:** Queen Elizabeth's Wedding Anniversary and Queen Mother's Birthday

Date	Mintage	F	VF	XF	Unc	BU
1994 Proof	Est. 20,000	Value: 32.00				

KM# 166 25 DOLLARS **Weight:** 28.2000 g. **Composition:** 0.9250 Silver .8386 oz. ASW **Subject:** 25th Anniversary - Caribbean Development Bank

Date	F	VF	XF	Unc	BU
1995	—	—	—	50.00	—

KM# 174 25 DOLLARS **Weight:** 28.2800 g. **Composition:** 0.9250 Silver .8411 oz. ASW **Subject:** Endangered Wildlife **Reverse:** Black-billed Amazon Parrots

Date	Mintage	F	VF	XF	Unc	BU
1995 Proof	Est. 10,000	Value: 40.00				

KM# 185 25 DOLLARS **Weight:** 28.2800 g. **Composition:** 0.9250 Silver 0.841 oz. ASW **Subject:** IAAF World Junior Championships **Obverse:** National arms and denomination **Reverse:** Female runner **Edge:** Reeded **Size:** 38.6 mm.

Date	Mintage	F	VF	XF	Unc	BU
2002 Proof	5,500	Value: 60.00				

KM# 171 50 DOLLARS **Weight:** 28.2800 g. **Composition:** 0.9250 Silver .8411 oz. ASW **Reverse:** Robert Marley

Date	Mintage	F	VF	XF	Unc	BU
1995 Proof	30,000	Value: 40.00				

KM# 170 25 DOLLARS **Weight:** 28.2800 g. **Composition:** 0.9250 Silver .8411 oz. ASW **Reverse:** Tycho Brahe at right, world globe at left

Date	Mintage	F	VF	XF	Unc	BU
1995 Proof	Est. 10,000	Value: 40.00				

KM# 177 25 DOLLARS **Weight:** 28.2800 g. **Composition:** 0.9250 Silver .8411 oz. ASW **Subject:** World Cup Soccer **Obverse:** National arms **Reverse:** Soccer player

Date	Mintage	F	VF	XF	Unc	BU
1998 Proof	Est. 10,000	Value: 40.00				

KM# 175 50 DOLLARS **Weight:** 7.7760 g. **Composition:** 0.5833 Gold .1458 oz. AGW **Reverse:** Queen Mother's wedding portrait

Date	Mintage	F	VF	XF	Unc	BU
1995 Proof	Est. 5,000	Value: 90.00				

KM# 173 25 DOLLARS **Weight:** 28.2800 g. **Composition:** 0.9250 Silver .8411 oz. ASW **Subject:** U.N. 50th Anniversary **Reverse:** 3 children embracing

Date	Mintage	F	VF	XF	Unc	BU
ND(1995) Proof	Est. 105,000	Value: 40.00				

KM# 183 25 DOLLARS **Weight:** 28.2800 g. **Composition:** 0.9250 Silver .8410 oz. ASW **Series:** Olympics **Obverse:** National arms **Reverse:** Two women hurdlers **Edge:** Reeded **Size:** 38.6 mm.

Date	Mintage	F	VF	XF	Unc	BU
2000 Proof	5,500	—	—	—	50.00	—

KM# 179 50 DOLLARS **Weight:** 28.2800 g. **Composition:** 0.9250 Silver .8410 oz. ASW **Subject:** 50th Anniversary - University of the West Indies **Obverse:** National arms **Reverse:** University arms

Date	Mintage	F	VF	XF	Unc	BU
1998 Proof	20,000	Value: 45.00				

KM# 184 50 DOLLARS **Weight:** 28.4500 g. **Composition:** 0.9250 Silver .8461 oz. ASW **Subject:** Millennium **Obverse:** National arms **Reverse:** Family and radiant sun **Edge:** Reeded **Size:** 38.6 mm.

Date	Mintage	F	VF	XF	Unc	BU
2002 Proof	5,000	Value: 50.00				

KM# 67 100 DOLLARS **Weight:** 7.8300 g. **Composition:** 0.9000 Gold .2265 oz. AGW **Reverse:** Christopher Columbus

Date	Mintage	F	VF	XF	Unc	BU
1975FM (M)	100	—	—	—	175	—
1975FM (U)	10,000	—	—	—	110	—
1975FM (P)	21,000	Value: 110				

KM# 72 100 DOLLARS **Weight:** 7.8300 g. **Composition:** 0.9000 Gold .2265 oz. AGW **Reverse:** Admiral Horatio Nelson

Date	Mintage	F	VF	XF	Unc	BU
1976FM (M)	100	—	—	—	175	—
1976FM (P)	8,952	Value: 110				

KM# 77 100 DOLLARS **Weight:** 11.3400 g. **Composition:** 0.9000 Gold .3281 oz. AGW **Subject:** 25th Anniversary of Coronation

Date	Mintage	F	VF	XF	Unc	BU
ND(1978)	—	—	—	—	125	—
ND(1978) Proof	5,835	Value: 135				

KM# 82 100 DOLLARS **Weight:** 11.3400 g. **Composition:** 0.9000 Gold .3281 oz. AGW **Subject:** 10th Anniversary - Investiture of Prince Charles

Date	Mintage	F	VF	XF	Unc	BU
ND(1979) Proof	2,891	Value: 160				

KM# 110 100 DOLLARS **Weight:** 7.1300 g. **Composition:** 0.9000 Gold .2063 oz. AGW **Subject:** 21st Anniversary of Independence

Date	Mintage	F	VF	XF	Unc	BU
ND(1983)FM (P)	638	Value: 190				

KM# 117 100 DOLLARS **Weight:** 7.1300 g. **Composition:** 0.9000 Gold .2063 oz. AGW **Subject:** 100th Anniversary - Birth of Bustamante

Date	Mintage	F	VF	XF	Unc	BU
1984FM (P)	531	Value: 150				

KM# 122 100 DOLLARS **Weight:** 136.0800 g. **Composition:** 0.9250 Silver 4.0743 oz. ASW **Subject:** World Championship Soccer - Mexico **Obverse:** Similar to KM#149

Date	Mintage	F	VF	XF	Unc	BU
1986 Proof	20,000	Value: 55.00				

KM# 129 100 DOLLARS **Weight:** 11.3400 g. **Composition:** 0.9000 Gold .3281 oz. AGW **Subject:** 100th Anniversary - Birth of Marcus Garvey **Obverse:** National arms **Reverse:** Portrait of Garvey facing

Date	Mintage	F	VF	XF	Unc	BU
1987 Proof	500	Value: 200				

KM# 139 100 DOLLARS **Weight:** 136.0800 g. **Composition:** 0.9250 Silver 4.0473 oz. ASW **Obverse:** Similar to 250 Dollars KM#124 **Reverse:** Streamer-tailed Hummingbird

Date	F	VF	XF	Unc	BU
1987 Proof	—	Value: 150			

KM# 135 100 DOLLARS **Weight:** 136.0800 g. **Composition:** 0.9250 Silver 4.0473 oz. ASW **Subject:** Summer Olympics - Relay Race **Obverse:** Similar to 10 Dollars, KM#111

Date	Mintage	F	VF	XF	Unc	BU
1988 Proof	15,000	Value: 85.00				

KM# 143 100 DOLLARS **Weight:** 136.0800 g. **Composition:** 0.9250 Silver 4.0473 oz. ASW **Subject:** World Championship Soccer **Reverse:** Soccer player

Date	F	VF	XF	Unc	BU
1990 Proof	—	Value: 150			

KM# 149 100 DOLLARS **Weight:** 137.8000 g. **Composition:** 0.9250 Silver 4.0981 oz. ASW **Subject:** Olympics - Boxing **Reverse:** Boxers

Date	Mintage	F	VF	XF	Unc	BU
1992 Proof	10,000	Value: 90.00				

KM# 158 100 DOLLARS **Weight:** 11.3400 g. **Composition:** 0.9000 Gold .3281 oz. AGW **Subject:** Centennial - Birth of Norman Manley

Date	Mintage	F	VF	XF	Unc	BU
1993 Proof	500	Value: 320				

KM# 172 100 DOLLARS **Weight:** 15.9800 g. **Composition:** 0.9990 Gold .5132 oz. AGW **Reverse:** Robert Marley

Date	Mintage	F	VF	XF	Unc	BU
1995 Proof	2,000	Value: 240				

KM# 178 100 DOLLARS **Weight:** 15.9800 g. **Composition:** 0.9990 Gold .5132 oz. AGW **Subject:** World Cup Soccer **Obverse:** National arms **Reverse:** Soccer player

Date		F	VF	XF	Unc	BU
1998 Proof	Est. 500	Value: 400				

KM# 180 100 DOLLARS **Weight:** 15.9700 g. **Composition:** 0.9167 Gold .4706 oz. AGW **Subject:** 50th Anniversary - University of the West Indies **Obverse:** National arms **Reverse:** University arms

Date	Mintage	F	VF	XF	Unc	BU
1998 Proof	1,000	Value: 300				

KM# 78 250 DOLLARS **Weight:** 43.2200 g. **Composition:** 0.9000 Gold 1.2507 oz. AGW **Subject:** 25th Anniversary of Coronation

Date	Mintage	F	VF	XF	Unc	BU
ND(1978) Proof	3,005	Value: 525				

KM# 83 250 DOLLARS **Weight:** 43.2200 g. **Composition:** 0.9000 Gold 1.2507 oz. AGW **Subject:** 10th Anniversary - Investiture of Prince Charles

Date	Mintage	F	VF	XF	Unc	BU
ND(1979) Proof	1,650	Value: 600				

KM# 89 250 DOLLARS **Weight:** 11.3400 g. **Composition:** 0.9000 Gold .3281 oz. AGW **Subject:** 1980 Olympics **Reverse:** Busts in circle of previous Gold Medal winners

Date	Mintage	F	VF	XF	Unc	BU
1980 Proof	902	Value: 250				

KM# 95 250 DOLLARS **Weight:** 11.3400 g. **Composition:** 0.9000 Gold .3281 oz. AGW **Subject:** Wedding of Prince Charles and Lady Diana **Obverse:** Elizabeth II

Date	Mintage	F	VF	XF	Unc	BU
1981 Proof	1,491	Value: 240				

KM# 100 250 DOLLARS **Weight:** 11.3400 g. **Composition:** 0.9000 Gold .3281 oz. AGW **Subject:** Soccer Games

Date	Mintage	F	VF	XF	Unc	BU
1982 Proof	694	Value: 270				

KM# 124 250 DOLLARS **Weight:** 11.3200 g. **Composition:** 0.9000 Gold .3275 oz. AGW **Subject:** Royal Visit

Date	Mintage	F	VF	XF	Unc	BU
1983 Proof	5,000	Value: 150				

KM# 118 250 DOLLARS **Weight:** 11.3400 g. **Composition:** 0.9000 Gold .3281 oz. AGW **Subject:** Decade for Women **Reverse:** Woman with basket on head, map in background

Date	Mintage	F	VF	XF	Unc	BU
1984 Proof	559	Value: 250				

KM# 131 250 DOLLARS **Weight:** 16.0000 g. **Composition:** 0.9000 Gold .4630 oz. AGW **Subject:** 25th Anniversary of Independence

Date	Mintage	F	VF	XF	Unc	BU
1987 Proof	250	Value: 400				

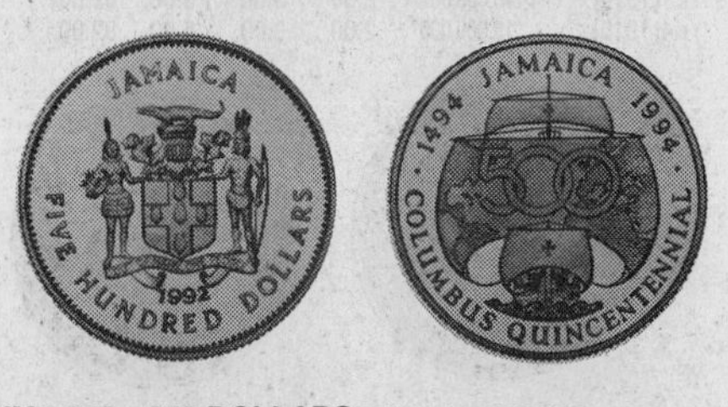

KM# 153 250 DOLLARS **Weight:** 11.3400 g. **Composition:** 0.9000 Gold .3281 oz. AGW **Subject:** Columbus Quincentennial **Reverse:** "500" on ships's sail

Date	Mintage	F	VF	XF	Unc	BU
1992 Proof	500	Value: 500				

KM# 156 250 DOLLARS **Weight:** 11.3400 g. **Composition:** 0.9000 Gold .3281 oz. AGW **Subject:** 40th Anniversary - Coronation of Queen Elizabeth **Obverse:** Portrait of the queen **Reverse:** Arms

Date		F	VF	XF	Unc	BU
1993 Proof	Est. 500	Value: 480				

KM# 162 250 DOLLARS **Weight:** 47.5400 g. **Composition:** 0.9170 Gold 1.4017 oz. AGW **Subject:** Royal Visit **Obverse:** Coat of arms **Reverse:** Drummer on island map with yacht at right

Date	Mintage	F	VF	XF	Unc	BU
1994 Proof	100	Value: 1,000				

PIEFORTS

KM#	Date	Mintage	Identification	Mkt Val
P1	1979	—	10 Dollars. Silver. KM#80	65.00
P2	1983	32	250 Dollars. 0.9000 Gold. Design like 10 Dollars, KM#80	1,250

MINT SETS

KM#	Date	Mintage	Identification	Issue Price	Mkt Val
MS1	1969 (2)	30,000	KM#41-42	0.90	2.00
MS2	1969 (6)	30,000	KM#45-50	—	6.50
MS3	1970 (6)	5,000	KM#45-50	16.00	6.50
MS4	1971 (7)	4,072	KM#51, 53-58	19.50	17.50
MS5	1971 (6)	4,834	KM#51, 53-57	—	10.00
MS6	1972 (7)	2,982	KM#51, 53-57, 59	19.75	25.00
MS7	1972 (6)	4,000	KM#51, 53-57	10.00	10.00
MS8	1973 (7)	6,404	KM#51, 53-57, 59	19.75	20.00
MS9	1973 (6)	3,000	KM#51, 53-57	9.95	10.00
MS10	1974 (8)	8,361	KM#51, 53-57, 59, 63	25.00	20.00
MS11	1975 (8)	4,683	KM#51, 53-57, 62, 66	27.50	20.00
MS12	1976 (9)	1,802	KM#53-57, 62, 68, 70, 71	27.50	27.50
MS13	1977 (9)	597	KM#53-54, 56-57, 62, 68, 70, 73, 74	27.50	45.00
MS14	1978 (9)	1,282	KM#53-54, 56-57, 62, 68, 70, 73, 75	27.50	40.00
MS15	1979 (9)	2,608	KM#53-54, 56-57, 62, 68, 70, 73, 79	27.50	40.00
MS16	1980 (9)	3,668	KM#53-54, 56, 68, 70, 73, 84.1-86	30.00	30.00
MS17	1981 (9)	482	KM#53-54, 56, 68, 70, 73, 84.1, 85.1, 93	31.00	45.00
MS18	1982 (9)	—	KM#53-54, 56, 68, 70, 73, 84.1-85.1, 97	31.00	40.00
MS19	1983 (9)	1,210	KM#101-109	37.00	40.00
MS20	1984 (9)	—	KM#53-54, 56, 68, 70, 73, 85.1, 113-114	37.00	35.00
MS21	2000 (7)	—	KM#64, 146.2, 163, 164, 167, 181-182	25.00	27.50

PROOF SETS

KM#	Date	Mintage	Identification	Issue Price	Mkt Val
PS1	1918C (3)	—	KM#24-26	—	600
PS2	1928 (3)	20	KM#24-26	—	600
PS3	1937 (3)	—	KM#27-29	—	550
PS4	1969 (6)	8,530	KM#45-50	15.00	10.00
PS5	1969 (2)	5,000	KM#41-42	2.70	7.00
PS6	1970 (6)	11,540	KM#45-50	15.00	10.00
PS7	1971 (7)	12,739	KM#51, 53-58	26.50	17.50
PS8	1971 (6)	1,048	KM#51, 53-57	15.00	10.00
PS9	1972 (7)	16,967	KM#51, 53-57, 59	27.50	16.00
PS10	1973 (7)	28,405	KM#51, 53-57, 59	27.50	15.00
PS11	1974 (8)	22,026	KM#51, 53-57, 62a-63a	50.00	30.00
PS12	1975 (8)	15,638	KM#51, 53-57, 62a, 66a	55.00	40.00
PS13	1976 (9)	22,900	KM#53-57, 62a, 68, 70, 71a	55.00	40.00
PS14	1976 (7)	1,503	KM#53-57, 68, 70	22.50	17.00
PS15	1977	10,054	KM#53-54, 56-57, 62a, 68, 70, 73, 74a	55.00	35.00
PS16	1978 (9)	6,058	KM#53-54, 56-57, 62a, 68, 70, 73, 75a	59.00	45.00
PS17	1979 (9)	4,049	KM#53-54, 56-57, 62a, 68, 70, 73, 79a	59.00	50.00
PS23	1985 (9)	—	KM#46-47, 49, 64-65, 84.2-85.2, 120, 123	—	75.00
PS18	1980 (9)	2,688	KM#53-54, 56, 68, 70, 73, 84.1, 85.1a, 86a	90.00	60.00
PS19	1981 (9)	1,577	KM#53-54, 56, 68, 70, 73, 84.1, 85.1a, 93a	92.00	80.00
PS20	1982 (9)	—	KM#53-54, 56, 68, 70, 73, 84.1, 85.1a, 97a	92.00	75.00
PS21	1983 (9)	1,210	KM#101-107, 108a-109a	—	85.00
PS22	1984 (9)	—	KM#53-54, 56, 68, 70, 73, 85.1a, 113, 114a	92.00	75.00
PS24	1987 (9)	500	KM#46-49, 64, 84.2, 85.2, 132, 133	90.00	75.00
PS25	1988 (9)	500	KM#46-49, 64-65, 84.2, 85.2, 138a	115	80.00
PS26	1989 (9)	500	KM#46-49, 64-65, 84.2, 85.2, 140a	120	80.00
PS27	1990 (9)	500	KM#46a-47a, 48-49, 64-65, 85.2, 144, 145	125	100
PS28	1991 (7)	500	KM#46a, 64, 85.2, 145, 146-148	—	100
PS29	1992 (7)	500	KM#46a, 64, 85.2, 145-147, 152	139	140
PS30	1993 (7)	500	KM#46a, 64, 85.2, 145a, 146-147, 155	—	140
PS31	2000 (8)	500	KM#64, 146.2, 163, 164, 167, 181-183	99.00	100
PS33	2002 (8)	500	KM#64, 146.2, 163, 164, 167, 181, 182, 185	99.00	—

JAPAN

Japan, a constitutional monarchy situated off the east coast of Asia, has an area of 145,809 sq. mi. (377,835 sq. km.) and a population of 123.2 million. Capital: Tokyo. Japan, one of the major industrial nations of the world, exports machinery, motor vehicles, electronics and chemicals.

Japan, founded (so legend holds) in 660 B.C. by a direct descendant of the Sun Goddess, was first brought into contact with the west by a storm-blown Portuguese ship in 1542. European traders and missionaries proceeded to enlarge the contact until the Shogunate, sensing a military threat in the foreign presence, expelled all foreigners and restricted relations with the outside world in the 17th century. After Commodore Perry's U.S. flotilla visited in 1854, Japan rapidly industrialized, abolished the Shogunate and established a parliamentary form of government, and by the end of the 19th century achieved the status of a modern economic and military power. A series of wars with China and Russia, and participation with the allies in World War I, enlarged Japan territorially but brought its interests into conflict with the Far Eastern interests of the United States, Britain and the Netherlands, causing it to align with the Axis Powers for the pursuit of World War II. After its defeat in World War II, General Douglas MacArthur forced Japan to renounce military aggression as a political instrument, and he instituted constitutional democratic self-government. Japan quickly gained a position as an economic world power.

Japanese coinage of concern to this catalog includes those issued for the Ryukyu Islands (also called Liuchu), a chain of islands extending southwest from Japan toward Taiwan (Formosa), before the Japanese government converted the islands into a prefecture under the name Okinawa. Many of the provinces of Japan issued their own definitive coinage under the Shogunate.

RULERS

Emperors

Mutsuhito (Meiji), 1867-1912

Years 1-45 明治 or 治明

Yoshihito (Taisho), 1912-1926

Years 1-15 大正 or 正大

Hirohito (Showa), 1926-1989

Years 1-64 昭和 or 和昭

Akihito (Heisei), 1989-

Years 1 - 平成

NOTE: The personal name of the emperor is followed by the name that he chose for his regnal era.

MONETARY SYSTEM

Commencing 1870

10 Rin = 1 Sen
100 Sen = 1 Yen

MONETARY UNITS

Rin 厘

Sen 銭

Yen 円 or 圓 or 圓

DATING

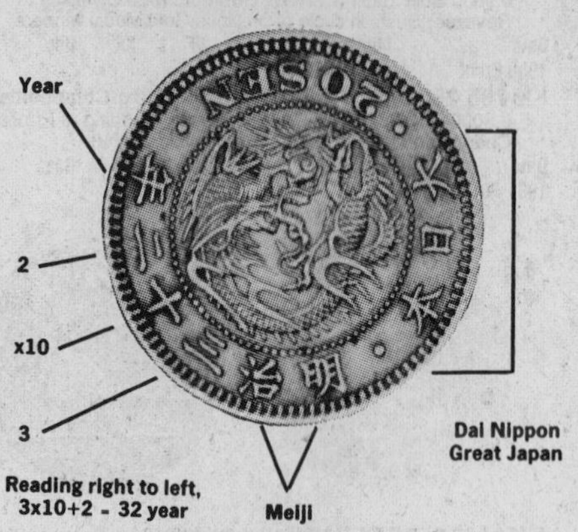

EMPIRE

DECIMAL COINAGE

Y# 41 5 RIN Weight: 2.1000 g. **Composition:** Bronze **Ruler:** Yoshihito (Taisho) **Size:** 12.8 mm.

Date	Mintage	F	VF	XF	Unc	BU
Yr.5(1916)	8,000,000	0.50	2.00	3.50	10.00	—
Yr.6(1917)	5,287,584	0.50	2.00	3.50	10.00	—
Yr.7(1918)	11,661,877	0.25	1.00	2.50	7.50	—
Yr.8(1919)	17,130,539	0.25	1.00	2.50	7.50	—

Y# 20 SEN Weight: 7.1300 g. **Composition:** Bronze **Ruler:** Mutsuhito (Meiji) **Size:** 27.8 mm.

Date	Mintage	F	VF	XF	Unc	BU
Yr.34(1901)	5,555,155	2.00	4.50	16.00	65.00	—
Yr.35(1902)	4,444,845	5.00	10.00	25.00	145	—
Yr.39(1906)	—	—	—	—	—	—

Note: None struck for circulation

Date	Mintage	F	VF	XF	Unc	BU
Yr.42(1909)	—	—	—	—	—	—

Note: None struck for circulation

Y# 35 SEN Weight: 7.1300 g. **Composition:** Bronze **Ruler:** Yoshihito (Taisho) **Size:** 27.8 mm.

Date	Mintage	F	VF	XF	Unc	BU
Yr.2(1913)	15,000,000	2.00	3.00	5.00	32.00	—
Yr.3(1914)	10,000,000	2.00	3.00	5.00	32.00	—
Yr.4(1915)	13,000,000	2.00	3.00	5.00	32.00	—

Y# 42 SEN Weight: 3.7500 g. **Composition:** Bronze **Size:** 23 mm.

Date	Mintage	F	VF	XF	Unc	BU
Yr.5(1916)	19,193,946	0.50	1.00	1.50	30.00	—
Yr.6(1917)	27,183,078	0.25	0.50	1.00	25.00	—
Yr.7(1918)	121,794,756	0.25	0.50	1.00	9.50	—
Yr.8(1919)	209,959,359	0.15	0.25	0.50	4.50	—
Yr.9(1920)	118,829,256	0.15	0.25	0.50	4.50	—
Yr.10(1921)	252,440,000	0.15	0.25	0.50	4.50	—
Yr.11(1922)	253,210,000	0.15	0.25	0.50	4.50	—
Yr.12(1923)	155,500,000	0.15	0.25	0.50	5.50	—
Yr.13(1924)	106,250,000	0.15	0.25	0.50	4.50	—

Y# 47 SEN Weight: 3.7500 g. **Composition:** Bronze **Ruler:** Hirohito (Showa) **Size:** 23 mm.

Date	Mintage	F	VF	XF	Unc	BU
Yr.2(1927)	26,500,000	1.50	2.50	3.50	32.00	—
Yr.4(1929)	3,000,000	3.50	7.50	15.00	45.00	—
Yr.5(1930)	5,000,000	2.50	4.50	7.50	70.00	—
Yr.6(1931)	25,001,222	0.25	0.50	1.50	12.50	—
Yr.7(1932)	35,066,715	0.25	0.50	1.50	9.00	—
Yr.8(1933)	38,936,907	0.15	0.25	0.50	2.50	—
Yr.9(1934)	100,004,950	0.15	0.25	0.50	2.50	—
Yr.10(1935)	200,009,912	0.15	0.25	0.50	1.50	—
Yr.11(1936)	109,170,428	0.15	0.25	0.50	1.50	—
Yr.12(1937)	133,196,568	0.15	0.25	0.50	1.50	—
Yr.13(1938)	87,649,338	0.15	0.25	0.50	1.50	—

Y# 55 SEN Weight: 3.7500 g. **Composition:** Bronze **Size:** 23 mm.

Date	Mintage	F	VF	XF	Unc	BU
Yr.13(1938)	113,600,000	0.15	0.25	0.50	1.50	—

Y# 56 SEN Weight: 0.9000 g. **Composition:** Aluminum **Size:** 17 mm.

Date	Mintage	F	VF	XF	Unc	BU
Yr.13(1938)	45,502,266	—	0.50	2.00	8.50	—
Yr.14(1939) Type A	444,602,146	—	1.50	3.00	12.00	—
Yr.14(1939) Type B	Inc. above	—	0.25	0.50	1.50	—
Yr.15(1940)	601,110,015	—	0.25	0.50	1.50	—

Y# 59 SEN Weight: 0.6500 g. **Composition:** Aluminum **Size:** 16 mm.

Date	Mintage	F	VF	XF	Unc	BU
Yr.16(1941)	1,016,620,734	—	0.15	0.25	0.50	—
Yr.17(1942)	119,709,832	—	0.15	0.25	0.75	—
Yr.18(1943)	1,163,949,434	—	0.15	0.25	0.50	—

Y# 59a SEN Weight: 0.5500 g. **Composition:** Aluminum **Size:** 16 mm. **Note:** Thinner

Date	Mintage	F	VF	XF	Unc	BU
Yr.18(1943)	627,191,000	—	0.15	0.50	1.00	—

Y# 62 SEN Weight: 1.3000 g. **Composition:** Tin-Zinc **Size:** 15 mm.

Date	Mintage	F	VF	XF	Unc	BU
Yr.19(1944)	1,629,580,000	—	0.15	0.25	0.50	—
Yr.20(1945)	Inc. above	—	0.25	0.50	0.75	—

KM# 110 SEN Weight: 0.8000 g. **Composition:** Reddish Brown Baked Clay **Size:** 15 mm.

Date	F	VF	XF	Unc	BU
ND(1945)	4.00	6.00	15.00	20.00	—

Note: Circulated unofficially for a few days before the end of WWII in Central Japan; varieties of color exist

Y# 21 5 SEN **Weight:** 4.6700 g. **Composition:** Copper-Nickel **Ruler:** Mutsuhito (Meiji)

Date	Mintage	F	VF	XF	Unc	BU
Yr.34(1901)	7,124,824	7.50	15.00	25.00	125	—
Yr.35(1902)	24,478,544	12.00	25.00	40.00	285	—
Yr.36(1903)	372,000	150	250	400	2,500	—
Yr.37(1904)	1,628,000	20.00	35.00	75.00	400	—
Yr.38(1905)	6,000,000	5.00	10.00	17.50	115	—
Yr.39(1906)	—	—	—	—	—	—

Note: None struck for circulation; Spink-Taisei Hong Kong sale 9-91 BU realized $10,000

Y# 43 5 SEN **Weight:** 4.2800 g. **Composition:** Copper-Nickel **Ruler:** Yoshihito (Taisho) **Size:** 20.6 mm.

Date	Mintage	F	VF	XF	Unc	BU
Yr.6(1917)	6,781,830	7.50	15.00	25.00	50.00	—
Yr.7(1918)	9,131,201	5.00	10.00	20.00	35.00	—
Yr.8(1919)	44,980,633	3.00	6.00	12.00	20.00	—
Yr.9(1920)	21,906,326	3.00	6.00	12.00	20.00	—

Y# 44 5 SEN **Weight:** 2.6300 g. **Composition:** Copper-Nickel **Ruler:** Yoshihito (Taisho) **Size:** 19.1 mm.

Date	Mintage	F	VF	XF	Unc	BU
Yr.9(1920)	100,455,537	0.35	0.75	2.00	15.00	—
Yr.10(1921)	133,020,000	0.25	0.50	1.50	5.00	—
Yr.11(1922)	163,980,000	0.25	0.50	1.50	5.00	—
Yr.12(1923)	80,000,000	0.25	0.50	1.50	5.00	—

Y# 48 5 SEN **Weight:** 2.6300 g. **Composition:** Copper-Nickel **Ruler:** Hirohito (Showa) **Size:** 19.1 mm.

Date	Mintage	F	VF	XF	Unc	BU
Yr.7(1932)	8,000,394	0.25	0.50	1.75	7.00	—

Y# 53 5 SEN **Weight:** 2.8000 g. **Composition:** Nickel **Ruler:** Hirohito (Showa) **Size:** 19 mm.

Date	Mintage	F	VF	XF	Unc	BU
Yr.8(1933)	16,150,808	0.50	1.50	3.00	5.50	—
Yr.9(1934)	33,851,607	0.50	1.00	2.00	4.50	—
Yr.10(1935)	13,680,677	1.00	2.00	3.50	7.50	—
Yr.11(1936)	36,321,796	0.50	1.00	2.00	4.50	—
Yr.12(1937)	44,402,201	0.50	1.00	2.00	5.50	—
Yr.13(1938) 4 known	10,000,000	—	—	—	—	—

Note: Almost entire mintage remelted

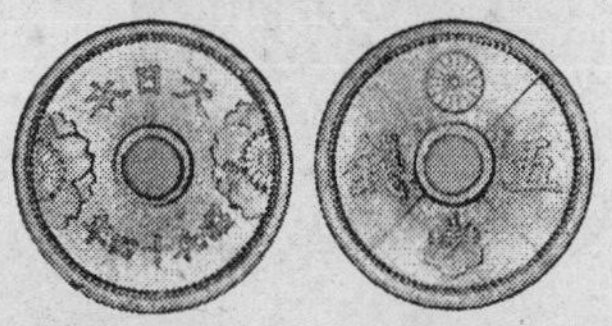

Y# 57 5 SEN **Composition:** Aluminum-Bronze **Ruler:** Hirohito (Showa)

Date	Mintage	F	VF	XF	Unc	BU
Yr.13(1938)	90,001,977	0.50	1.00	1.50	4.00	—
Yr.14(1939)	97,903,873	0.50	1.00	1.50	4.00	—
Yr.15(1940)	34,501,216	0.50	1.00	1.50	5.00	—

Y# 60 5 SEN **Weight:** 1.2000 g. **Composition:** Aluminum **Ruler:** Hirohito (Showa) **Size:** 19 mm. **Note:** Variety I

Date	Mintage	F	VF	XF	Unc	BU
Yr.15(1940)	167,638,000	—	0.25	1.00	3.00	—
Yr.16(1941)	242,361,000	—	0.25	0.75	2.25	—

Y# 60a 5 SEN **Weight:** 1.0000 g. **Composition:** Aluminum **Ruler:** Hirohito (Showa) **Size:** 19 mm. **Note:** Variety 2

Date	Mintage	F	VF	XF	Unc	BU
Yr.16(1941)	478,023,877	1.50	3.50	7.50	37.50	—
Yr.17(1942)	Inc. above	—	0.25	0.75	1.50	—

Y# 60b 5 SEN **Weight:** 0.8000 g. **Composition:** Aluminum **Ruler:** Hirohito (Showa) **Size:** 19 mm. **Note:** Variety 3

Date	Mintage	F	VF	XF	Unc	BU
Yr.18(1943)	276,493,742	—	0.25	0.75	2.00	—

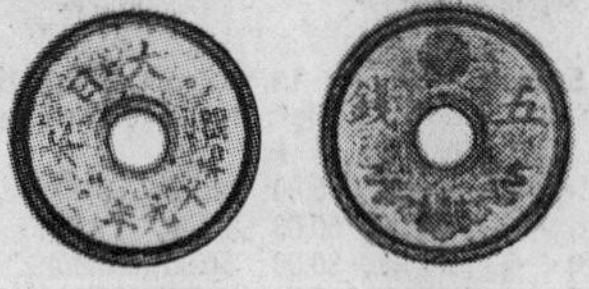

Y# 63 5 SEN **Weight:** 1.9500 g. **Composition:** Tin-Zinc **Ruler:** Hirohito (Showa) **Size:** 17 mm.

Date	Mintage	F	VF	XF	Unc	BU
Yr.19(1944)	70,000,000	—	0.25	0.75	2.50	—

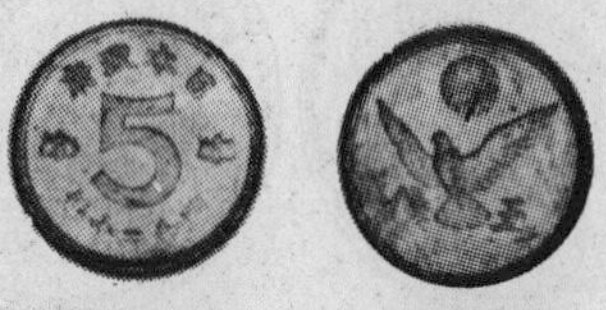

Y# 65 5 SEN **Weight:** 2.0000 g. **Composition:** Tin-Zinc **Ruler:** Hirohito (Showa) **Size:** 17 mm.

Date	Mintage	F	VF	XF	Unc	BU
Yr.20(1945)	180,000,000	—	0.50	1.25	3.50	—
Yr.21(1946)	Inc. above	—	0.50	1.25	3.50	—

KM# 111 5 SEN **Weight:** 1.3000 g. **Composition:** Reddish Brown Baked Clay **Ruler:** Hirohito (Showa) **Size:** 18 mm.

Date	F	VF	XF	Unc	BU
Yr.20(1945)	75.00	125	225	300	—

Note: Not issued for circulation; varieties of color exist

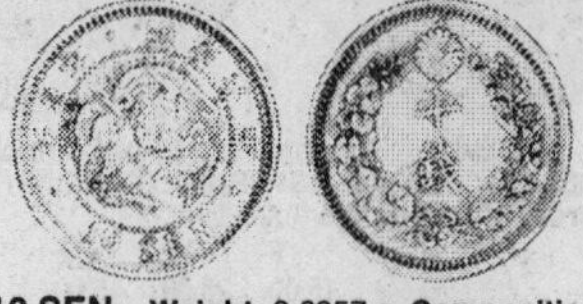

Y# 23 10 SEN **Weight:** 2.6957 g. **Composition:** 0.8000 Silver .070 oz. ASW **Ruler:** Mutsuhito (Meiji)

Date	Mintage	F	VF	XF	Unc	BU
Yr.34(1901)	797,561	125	175	250	800	—
Yr.35(1902)	1,204,439	100	150	200	775	—
Yr.37(1904)	11,106,638	4.50	7.50	10.00	35.00	—
Yr.38(1905)	34,182,194	4.50	7.50	10.00	35.00	—
Yr.39(1906)	4,710,168	4.50	7.50	10.00	35.00	—

Y# 29 10 SEN **Weight:** 2.2500 g. **Composition:** 0.7200 Silver .0521 oz. ASW **Ruler:** Mutsuhito (Meiji)

Date	Mintage	F	VF	XF	Unc	BU
Yr.40(1907)	12,000,000	2.50	5.00	10.00	65.00	—
Yr.41(1908)	12,273,239	2.50	5.00	10.00	60.00	—
Yr.42(1909)	20,279,846	1.00	3.50	5.00	27.50	—
Yr.43(1910)	20,339,816	1.00	3.50	5.00	25.00	—
Yr.44(1911)	38,729,680	1.00	3.50	5.00	27.50	—
Yr.45(1912)	10,755,009	1.00	3.50	5.00	30.00	—

Y# 36.1 10 SEN **Weight:** 2.2500 g. **Composition:** 0.7200 Silver .0521 oz. ASW **Ruler:** Yoshihito (Taisho) **Obverse:** Japanese character "first"

Date	Mintage	F	VF	XF	Unc	BU
Yr.1(1912)	10,344,307	2.50	5.00	10.00	60.00	—

Y# 36.2 10 SEN **Weight:** 2.2500 g. **Composition:** 0.7200 Silver **Ruler:** Yoshihito (Taisho)

Date	Mintage	F	VF	XF	Unc	BU
Yr.2(1913)	13,321,466	1.00	2.50	5.00	12.00	—
Yr.3(1914)	10,325,327	1.00	2.50	5.00	12.00	—
Yr.4(1915)	16,836,225	1.50	3.00	5.00	12.00	—
Yr.5(1916)	10,324,128	1.00	2.50	4.00	12.00	—
Yr.6(1917)	35,170,906	0.75	2.00	3.00	10.00	—

Y# 45 10 SEN **Weight:** 3.7500 g. **Composition:** Copper-Nickel **Ruler:** Yoshihito (Taisho)

Date	Mintage	F	VF	XF	Unc	BU
Yr.9(1920)	4,894,420	0.50	1.00	3.00	25.00	—
Yr.10(1921)	61,870,000	0.25	0.50	1.50	5.00	—
Yr.11(1922)	159,770,000	0.25	0.50	1.50	5.00	—
Yr.12(1923)	190,010,000	0.25	0.50	1.50	4.50	—
Yr.14(1925)	54,475,000	0.25	0.50	1.50	5.00	—
Yr.15(1926)	58,675,000	0.25	0.50	1.50	5.00	—

Y# 49 10 SEN **Weight:** 3.7500 g. **Composition:** Copper-Nickel **Ruler:** Hirohito (Showa)

Date	Mintage	F	VF	XF	Unc	BU
Yr.2(1927)	36,050,000	0.25	0.50	1.50	5.00	—
Yr.3(1928)	41,450,000	0.25	0.50	1.50	5.00	—
Yr.4(1929)	10,050,000	0.50	1.00	2.00	25.00	—
Yr.6(1931)	1,850,087	0.75	1.50	2.50	9.00	—
Yr.7(1932)	23,151,177	0.25	0.50	1.50	5.00	—

Y# 54 10 SEN **Weight:** 4.0200 g. **Composition:** Nickel **Ruler:** Hirohito (Showa)

Date	Mintage	F	VF	XF	Unc	BU
Yr.8(1933)	14,570,714	0.50	1.00	2.00	5.50	—
Yr.9(1934)	37,351,832	0.25	0.75	1.50	4.75	—
Yr.10(1935)	35,586,755	0.30	1.00	1.75	5.25	—
Yr.11(1936)	77,948,804	0.25	0.75	1.50	4.75	—
Yr.12(1937)	40,001,969	0.30	1.00	1.75	5.50	—

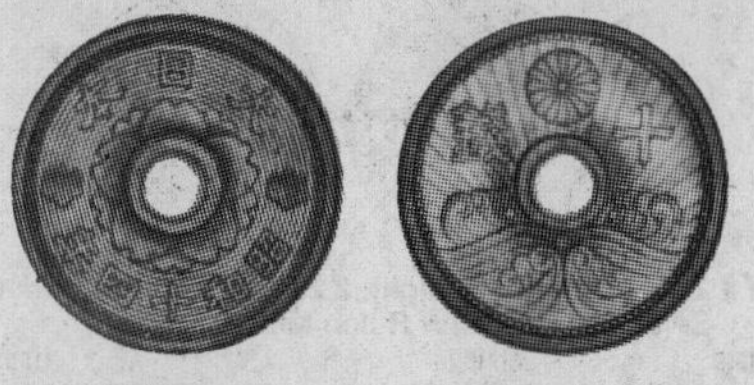

Y# 58 10 SEN Weight: 4.0000 g. **Composition:** Aluminum-Bronze **Ruler:** Hirohito (Showa)

Date	Mintage	F	VF	XF	Unc	BU
Yr.13(1938)	47,077,320	0.35	0.75	1.50	4.75	—
Yr.14(1939)	121,796,011	0.25	0.50	1.00	4.50	—
Yr.15(1940)	16,135,794	0.75	1.50	3.00	12.00	—

Y# 61 10 SEN Weight: 1.5000 g. **Composition:** Aluminum **Ruler:** Hirohito (Showa)

Date	Mintage	F	VF	XF	Unc	BU
Yr.15(1940)	575,600,000	—	0.20	0.35	1.50	—
Yr.16(1941)	Inc. above	—	0.20	0.35	1.50	—

Y# 61a 10 SEN Weight: 1.2000 g. **Composition:** Aluminum **Ruler:** Hirohito (Showa)

Date	Mintage	F	VF	XF	Unc	BU
Yr.16(1941)	94,494,700,000	0.10	0.35	0.50	2.00	—
Yr.17(1942)	Inc. above	—	0.20	0.35	1.50	—
Yr.18(1943)	756,000,000	1.00	3.00	5.00	30.00	—

Y# 61b 10 SEN Weight: 1.0000 g. **Composition:** Aluminum **Ruler:** Hirohito (Showa)

Date	F	VF	XF	Unc	BU
Yr.18(1943)	—	0.20	0.35	1.25	—

Y# 64 10 SEN Weight: 2.4000 g. **Composition:** Tin-Zinc **Ruler:** Hirohito (Showa)

Date	Mintage	F	VF	XF	Unc	BU
Yr.19(1944)	450,000,000	—	0.20	0.35	1.25	—

Y# 68 10 SEN Weight: 1.0000 g. **Composition:** Aluminum **Ruler:** Hirohito (Showa)

Date	Mintage	F	VF	XF	Unc	BU
Yr.20(1945)	237,590,000	—	0.20	0.35	1.00	—
Yr.21(1946)	Inc. above	—	0.20	0.35	1.00	—

KM# 112 10 SEN Weight: 2.0000 g. **Composition:** Reddish Brown Baked Clay **Ruler:** Hirohito (Showa) **Size:** 21.9 mm.

Date	F	VF	XF	Unc	BU
Yr.20(1945)	75.00	135	245	325	—

Note: Not issued for circulation; varieties of color exist

Y# 24 20 SEN Weight: 5.3900 g. **Composition:** 0.8000 Silver .1383 oz. ASW **Ruler:** Mutsuhito (Meiji)

Date	Mintage	F	VF	XF	Unc	BU
Yr.34(1901)	500,000	150	225	350	2,250	—
Yr.37(1904)	5,250,000	5.00	10.00	20.00	70.00	—
Yr.38(1905)	8,444,930	5.00	10.00	20.00	60.00	—

Y# 30 20 SEN Weight: 4.0500 g. **Composition:** 0.8000 Silver .1042 oz. ASW **Ruler:** Mutsuhito (Meiji)

Date	Mintage	F	VF	XF	Unc	BU
Yr.39(1906)	6,555,070	6.50	13.00	25.00	200	—
Yr.40(1907)	20,000,000	2.50	5.50	15.00	75.00	—
Yr.41(1908)	15,000,000	2.50	5.50	15.00	75.00	—
Yr.42(1909)	8,824,702	2.50	5.50	15.00	75.00	—
Yr.43(1910)	21,175,298	2.50	5.50	15.00	75.00	—
Yr.44(1911)	500,000	60.00	120	250	1,150	—

Y# 25 50 SEN Weight: 13.4800 g. **Composition:** 0.8000 Silver .3472 oz. ASW **Ruler:** Mutsuhito (Meiji)

Date	Mintage	F	VF	XF	Unc	BU
Yr.34(1901)	1,790,000	25.00	45.00	80.00	375	—
Yr.35(1902)	1,023,200	50.00	85.00	150	625	—
Yr.36(1903)	1,503,068	30.00	50.00	90.00	425	—
Yr.37(1904)	5,373,652	7.50	12.50	25.00	125	—
Yr.38(1905)	9,566,100	7.50	12.50	25.00	125	—

Y# 31 50 SEN Weight: 10.1000 g. **Composition:** 0.8000 Silver .2597 oz. ASW **Ruler:** Mutsuhito (Meiji)

Date	Mintage	F	VF	XF	Unc	BU
Yr.39(1906)	12,478,264	4.00	8.00	25.00	225	—
Yr.40(1907)	24,062,952	3.50	7.50	18.00	75.00	—
Yr.41(1908)	25,470,321	3.50	7.50	18.00	75.00	—
Yr.42(1909)	21,998,600	3.50	7.50	18.00	75.00	—
Yr.43(1910)	15,323,276	3.50	7.50	18.00	75.00	—
Yr.44(1911)	9,900,437	3.50	7.50	18.00	75.00	—
Yr.45(1912)	3,677,704	8.50	15.00	25.00	100	—

Y# 37.1 50 SEN Weight: 10.1300 g. **Composition:** 0.8000 Silver .2600 oz. ASW **Ruler:** Yoshihito (Taisho) **Obverse:** Japanese character "first"

Date	Mintage	F	VF	XF	Unc	BU
Yr.1(1912)	1,928,649	15.00	25.00	45.00	160	—

Y# 37.2 50 SEN Weight: 10.1300 g. **Composition:** 0.8000 Silver .2600 oz. ASW **Ruler:** Yoshihito (Taisho)

Date	Mintage	F	VF	XF	Unc	BU
Yr.2(1913)	5,910,063	5.00	9.50	22.00	60.00	—
Yr.3(1914)	1,872,331	20.00	35.00	55.00	200	—
Yr.4(1915)	2,011,253	17.50	30.00	50.00	160	—
Yr.5(1916)	8,736,768	4.00	8.00	16.00	35.00	—
Yr.6(1917)	9,963,232	4.00	8.00	16.00	35.00	—

Y# 46 50 SEN Weight: 4.9500 g. **Composition:** 0.7200 Silver .1148 oz. ASW **Ruler:** Yoshihito (Taisho)

Date	Mintage	Good	VG	F	VF	XF
Yr.11(1922)	76,320,000	—	—	BV	1.50	5.00
Yr.12(1923)	185,180,000	—	—	BV	1.50	3.00
Yr.13(1924)	78,520,000	—	—	BV	1.50	3.00
Yr.14(1925)	47,808,000	—	—	BV	1.50	3.00
CDYr.15(1926)	32,572,000	—	—	BV	1.50	3.00

Y# 50 50 SEN Weight: 4.9500 g. **Composition:** 0.7200 Silver .1148 oz. ASW **Ruler:** Yoshihito (Taisho)

Date	Mintage	F	VF	XF	Unc	BU
Yr.3(1928)	38,592,000	BV	1.00	2.50	10.00	—
Yr.4(1929)	12,568,000	BV	1.50	5.00	30.00	—
Yr.5(1930)	10,200,000	BV	2.00	5.50	20.00	—
Yr.6(1931)	27,677,501	BV	1.00	2.50	9.00	—
Yr.7(1932)	24,132,795	BV	1.00	2.50	9.00	—
Yr.8(1933)	10,001,973	BV	2.00	7.00	22.00	—
Yr.9(1934)	20,003,995	BV	1.50	2.50	9.00	—
Yr.10(1935)	11,738,334	BV	1.50	2.50	9.00	—
Yr.11(1936)	44,272,796	BV	1.50	2.50	7.00	—
Yr.12(1937)	48,000,533	BV	1.50	2.50	7.00	—
Yr.13(1938)	3,600,717	50.00	75.00	125	250	—

Y# 67 50 SEN Weight: 4.5000 g. **Composition:** Brass **Ruler:** Yoshihito (Taisho) **Note:** Varieties exist.

Date	Mintage	F	VF	XF	Unc	BU
Yr.21(1946)	268,161,000	0.25	0.50	1.00	2.50	—
Yr.22(1947)	Inc. above	—	650	1,000	1,700	—

Note: Not released to circulation

Y# 69 50 SEN Weight: 2.8000 g. **Composition:** Brass **Ruler:** Yoshihito (Taisho)

Date	Mintage	F	VF	XF	Unc	BU
Yr.22(1947)	849,234,445	0.10	0.20	0.40	1.00	—
Yr.23(1948)	Inc. above	0.10	0.20	0.40	1.00	—

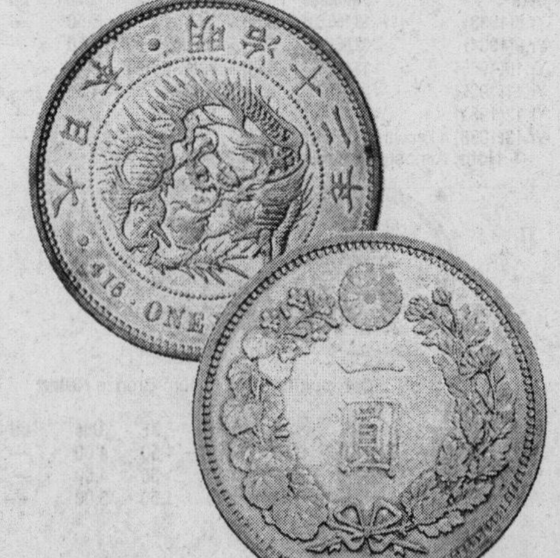

Y# A25.3 YEN Weight: 26.9600 g. **Composition:** 0.9000 Silver .7800 oz. ASW **Ruler:** Mutsuhito (Meiji)

Date	Mintage	F	VF	XF	Unc	BU
Yr.34(1901)	1,256,252	15.00	30.00	50.00	160	—
Yr.35(1902)	668,782	25.00	50.00	75.00	225	—
Yr.36(1903)	5,131,096	15.00	27.50	42.50	140	—
Yr.37(1904)	6,970,843	15.00	27.50	42.50	140	—
Yr.38(1905)	5,031,096	15.00	27.50	42.50	140	—
Yr.39(1906)	3,471,297	25.00	50.00	85.00	275	—
Yr.41(1908)	334,705	50.00	100	150	500	—
Yr.45(1912)	5,000,000	12.50	25.00	42.50	120	—

Y# 38 YEN Weight: 26.9600 g. **Composition:** 0.9000 Silver .7800 oz. ASW **Ruler:** Yoshihito (Taisho)

Date	Mintage	F	VF	XF	Unc	BU
Yr.3(1914)	11,500,000	12.50	22.50	35.00	110	—

REFORM COINAGE

Y# 70 YEN Weight: 3.2000 g. **Composition:** Brass **Ruler:** Hirohito (Showa)

Date	Mintage	F	VF	XF	Unc	BU
Yr.23(1948)	451,170,000	—	0.25	0.50	2.00	—
Yr.24(1949)	Inc. above	—	0.15	0.35	1.25	—
Yr.25(1950)	Inc. above	—	0.15	0.35	1.25	—

Y# 74 YEN Weight: 1.0000 g. **Composition:** Aluminum **Ruler:** Hirohito (Showa)

Date	Mintage	F	VF	XF	Unc	BU
Yr.30(1955)	381,700,000	—	—	—	1.00	—
Yr.31(1956)	500,900,000	—	—	—	1.00	—
Yr.32(1957)	492,000,000	—	—	—	1.00	—
Yr.33(1958)	374,900,000	—	—	—	1.00	—
Yr.34(1959)	208,600,000	—	—	—	1.00	—
Yr.35(1960)	300,000,000	—	—	—	1.00	—
Yr.36(1961)	432,400,000	—	—	—	0.10	—
Yr.37(1962)	572,000,000	—	—	—	0.10	—
Yr.38(1963)	788,700,000	—	—	—	0.10	—
Yr.39(1964)	1,665,100,000	—	—	—	0.10	—
Yr.40(1965)	1,743,256,000	—	—	—	0.10	—
Yr.41(1966)	807,344,000	—	—	—	0.10	—
Yr.42(1967)	220,600,000	—	—	—	0.10	—
Yr.44(1969)	184,700,000	—	—	—	0.10	—
Yr.45(1970)	556,400,000	—	—	—	0.10	—
Yr.46(1971)	904,950,000	—	—	—	0.10	—
Yr.47(1972)	1,274,950,000	—	—	—	0.10	—
Yr.48(1973)	1,470,000,000	—	—	—	0.10	—
Yr.49(1974)	1,750,000,000	—	—	—	0.10	—
Yr.50(1975)	1,656,150,000	—	—	—	0.10	—
Yr.51(1976)	928,800,000	—	—	—	0.10	—
Yr.52(1977)	895,000,000	—	—	—	0.10	—
Yr.53(1978)	864,000,000	—	—	—	0.10	—
Yr.54(1979)	1,015,000,000	—	—	—	0.10	—
Yr.55(1980)	1,145,000,000	—	—	—	0.10	—
Yr.56(1981)	1,206,000,000	—	—	—	0.10	—
Yr.57(1982)	1,017,000,000	—	—	—	0.10	—
Yr.58(1983)	1,086,000,000	—	—	—	0.10	—
Yr.59(1984)	981,850,000	—	—	—	0.10	—
Yr.60(1985)	837,150,000	—	—	—	0.10	—
Yr.61(1986)	417,960,000	—	—	—	0.10	—
Yr.62(1987)	958,520,000	—	—	—	0.10	—

Date	Mintage	F	VF	XF	Unc	BU
Yr.62(1987) Proof	230,000	Value: 1.50				
Yr.63(1988)	1,268,842,000	—	—	—	0.10	—
Yr.63(1988) Proof	200,000	Value: 1.50				
Yr.64(1989)	116,100,000	—	—	—	0.50	—

Y# 95.1 YEN Weight: 1.0000 g. **Composition:** Aluminum **Ruler:** Akihito (Heisei) **Obverse:** Small tree **Reverse:** Large 1 on wide ring in center, date below, with Japanese "first" as third character

Date	Mintage	F	VF	XF	Unc	BU
Yr.1(1989)	2,366,770,000	—	—	—	0.15	—
Yr.1(1989) Proof	200,000	Value: 1.50				

Y# 95.2 YEN Weight: 1.0000 g. **Composition:** Aluminum **Ruler:** Akihito (Heisei)

Date	Mintage	F	VF	XF	Unc	BU
Yr.2(1990)	2,768,753,000	—	—	—	0.15	—
Yr.2(1990) Proof	200,000	Value: 1.50				
Yr.3(1991)	2,300,900,000	—	—	—	0.15	—
Yr.3(1991) Proof	220,000	Value: 1.50				
Yr.4(1992)	1,298,880,000	—	—	—	0.15	—
Yr.4(1992) Proof	250,000	Value: 1.50				
Yr.5(1993)	1,260,990,000	—	—	—	0.15	—
Yr.5(1993) Proof	250,000	Value: 1.50				
Yr.6(1994)	1,040,540,000	—	—	—	0.15	—
Yr.6(1994) Proof	227,000	Value: 1.50				
Yr.7(1995)	1,041,674,000	—	—	—	0.15	—
Yr.7(1995) Proof	200,000	Value: 1.50				
Yr.8(1996)	942,024,000	—	—	—	0.15	—
Yr.8(1996) Proof	189,000	Value: 1.50				
Yr.9(1997)	782,874,000	—	—	—	0.15	—
Yr.9(1997) Proof	212,000	Value: 1.50				
Yr.10(1998)	452,412,000	—	—	—	0.15	—
Yr.10(1998) Proof	200,000	Value: 1.50				
Yr.11(1999)	66,850,000	—	—	—	0.15	—
Yr.11(1999) Proof	280,000	Value: 1.50				
Yr.12(2000)	11,800,000	—	—	—	0.15	—
Yr.12(2000) Proof	226,000	Value: 1.50				
Yr,13(2001)	—	—	—	—	0.15	—
Yr.13(2001) Proof	—	Value: 1.50				

Y# 32 5 YEN Weight: 4.1666 g. **Composition:** 0.9000 Gold .1205 oz. AGW **Ruler:** Mutsuhito (Meiji)

Date	Mintage	F	VF	XF	Unc	BU
Yr.36(1903)	21,956	900	1,000	1,350	2,250	—
Yr.44(1911)	59,880	850	1,000	1,300	2,150	—
Yr.45(1912)	59,880	850	1,000	1,300	2,150	—

Y# 39 5 YEN Weight: 4.1666 g. **Composition:** 0.9000 Gold .1205 oz. AGW **Ruler:** Yoshihito (Taisho)

Date	Mintage	F	VF	XF	Unc	BU
Yr.2(1913)	89,820	750	1,000	1,250	1,850	—
Yr.13(1924)	76,037	650	850	1,000	1,650	—

Y# 51 5 YEN Weight: 4.1666 g. **Composition:** 0.9000 Gold .1205 oz. AGW **Ruler:** Hirohito (Showa)

Date	Mintage	F	VF	XF	Unc	BU
Yr.5(1930)	852,563	20,000	35,000	50,000	65,000	—

Y# 71 5 YEN Weight: 4.0000 g. **Composition:** Brass **Ruler:** Hirohito (Showa)

Date	Mintage	F	VF	XF	Unc	BU
Yr.23(1948)	74,520,000	—	0.50	0.75	12.50	—
Yr.24(1949)	179,692,000	—	0.15	0.40	8.00	—

Y# 72 5 YEN Weight: 3.7500 g. **Composition:** Brass **Ruler:** Hirohito (Showa) **Note:** Old script.

Date	Mintage	F	VF	XF	Unc	BU
Yr.24(1949)	111,896,000	—	0.15	0.25	9.00	—
Yr.25(1950)	181,824,000	—	0.15	0.25	6.50	—
Yr.26(1951)	197,980,000	—	0.15	0.25	6.50	—
Yr.27(1952)	55,000,000	—	0.30	0.60	15.00	—
Yr.28(1953)	45,000,000	—	0.30	0.60	6.50	—
Yr.32(1957)	10,000,000	—	4.00	8.00	15.00	—
Yr.33(1958)	50,000,000	—	0.25	0.50	3.50	—

Y# 72a 5 YEN Weight: 3.7500 g. **Composition:** Brass **Ruler:** Hirohito (Showa) **Note:** New script.

Date	Mintage	F	VF	XF	Unc	BU
Yr.34(1959)	33,000,000	—	0.25	0.50	3.00	—
Yr.35(1960)	34,800,000	—	0.20	0.40	3.00	—
Yr.36(1961)	61,000,000	—	0.15	0.35	2.50	—
Yr.37(1962)	126,700,000	—	0.10	0.30	1.50	—
Yr.38(1963)	171,800,000	—	0.10	0.30	1.50	—
Yr.39(1964)	379,700,000	—	0.10	0.30	1.50	—
Yr.40(1965)	384,200,000	—	0.10	0.30	1.50	—
Yr.41(1966)	163,100,000	—	0.10	0.30	1.50	—
Yr.42(1967)	26,000,000	—	0.25	0.50	1.50	—
Yr.43(1968)	114,000,000	—	—	0.10	1.50	—
Yr.44(1969)	240,000,000	—	—	0.10	1.50	—
Yr.45(1970)	340,000,000	—	—	0.10	1.50	—
Yr.46(1971)	362,050,000	—	—	0.10	1.50	—
Yr.47(1972)	562,950,000	—	—	0.10	0.15	—
Yr.48(1973)	745,000,000	—	—	0.10	0.15	—
Yr.49(1974)	950,000,000	—	—	0.10	0.15	—
Yr.50(1975)	970,000,000	—	—	0.10	0.15	—
Yr.51(1976)	200,000,000	—	—	0.10	0.15	—
Yr.52(1977)	340,000,000	—	—	0.10	0.15	—
Yr.53(1978)	318,000,000	—	—	0.10	0.15	—
Yr.54(1979)	317,000,000	—	—	0.10	0.15	—
Yr.55(1980)	385,000,000	—	—	0.10	0.15	—
Yr.56(1981)	95,000,000	—	—	0.10	0.30	—
Yr.57(1982)	455,000,000	—	—	0.10	0.15	—
Yr.58(1983)	410,000,000	—	—	0.10	0.15	—
Yr.59(1984)	202,850,000	—	—	0.10	0.15	—
Yr.60(1985)	153,150,000	—	—	0.10	0.20	—
Yr.61(1986)	113,960,000	—	—	0.10	0.30	—
Yr.62(1987)	631,545,000	—	—	0.10	0.15	—
Yr.62(1987) Proof	230,000	Value: 1.75				
Yr.63(1988)	368,920,000	—	—	—	0.15	—
Yr.63(1988) Proof	200,000	Value: 1.75				
Yr.64(1989)	67,332,000	—	—	—	0.65	—

Y# 96.1 5 YEN Composition: Brass **Ruler:** Akihito (Heisei) **Obverse:** Inscription and date separated by seed leaf; Japanese character "first" in date **Reverse:** Gear around hole, rice stalk above denomination

Date	Mintage	F	VF	XF	Unc	BU
Yr.1(1989)	960,460,000	—	—	—	0.35	—
Yr.1(1989) Proof	200,000	Value: 1.75				

Y# 96.2 5 YEN Composition: Brass **Ruler:** Akihito (Heisei)

Date		F	VF	XF	Unc	BU
Yr.2(1990)		—	—	—	0.35	—
Yr.2(1990) Proof	200,000	Value: 1.75				
Yr.3(1991)		—	—	—	0.35	—
Yr.3(1991) Proof	220,000	Value: 1.75				
Yr.4(1992)		—	—	—	0.35	—
Yr.4(1992) Proof	250,000	Value: 1.75				
Yr.5(1993)		—	—	—	0.35	—
Yr.5(1993) Proof	250,000	Value: 1.75				
Yr.6(1994)		—	—	—	0.35	—
Yr.6(1994) Proof	227,000	Value: 1.75				
Yr.7(1995)		—	—	—	0.35	—
Yr.7(1995) Proof	200,000	Value: 1.75				
Yr.8(1996)		—	—	—	0.35	—
Yr.8(1996) Proof	189,000	Value: 1.75				
Yr.9(1997)		—	—	—	0.35	—
Yr.9(1997) Proof	212,000	Value: 1.75				
Yr.10(1998)		—	—	—	0.35	—
Yr.10(1998) Proof	200,000	Value: 1.75				
Yr.11(1999)		—	—	—	0.35	—

Date		F	VF	XF	Unc	BU
Yr.11(1999) Proof	280,000	Value: 1.75				
Yr.12(2000)		—	—	—	0.35	—
Yr.12(2000) Proof	226,000	Value: 1.75				
Yr.13(2001)		—	—	—	0.35	—
Yr.13(2001) Proof	—	Value: 1.75				

Y# 33 10 YEN **Weight:** 8.3333 g. **Composition:** 0.9000 Gold .2411 oz. AGW **Ruler:** Mutsuhito (Meiji)

Date	Mintage	F	VF	XF	Unc	BU
Yr.34(1901)	1,654,682	450	600	750	1,250	—
Yr.35(1902)	3,023,940	450	600	750	1,350	—
Yr.36(1903)	2,902,184	450	600	750	1,350	—
Yr.37(1904)	724,548	500	800	1,250	2,500	—
Yr.40(1907)	157,684	500	800	1,250	2,350	—
Yr.41(1908)	1,160,674	450	600	750	1,250	—
Yr.42(1909)	2,165,660	400	600	750	1,200	—
Yr.43(1910)	8,982	7,500	10,000	15,000	25,000	—

Y# 73 10 YEN **Weight:** 4.5000 g. **Composition:** Bronze **Ruler:** Hirohito (Showa) **Obverse:** Ancient phoenix temple Hoo-do surrounded by arabesque pattern **Edge:** Reeded

Date	Mintage	F	VF	XF	Unc	BU
Yr.26(1951)	101,068,000	—	0.20	0.35	35.00	—
Yr.27(1952)	486,632,000	—	0.20	0.35	25.00	—
Yr.28(1953)	466,300,000	—	0.20	0.35	25.00	—
Yr.29(1954)	520,900,000	—	0.20	0.35	35.00	—
Yr.30(1955)	123,100,000	—	0.20	0.35	20.00	—
Yr.32(1957)	50,000,000	—	0.25	0.65	25.00	—
Yr.33(1958)	25,000,000	—	0.40	1.00	38.00	—

Y# 73a 10 YEN **Weight:** 4.5000 g. **Composition:** Bronze **Ruler:** Hirohito (Showa) **Edge:** Plain

Date	Mintage	F	VF	XF	Unc	BU
Yr.34(1959)	62,400,000	—	—	0.20	10.00	—
Yr.35(1960)	225,900,000	—	—	0.20	7.00	—
Yr.36(1961)	229,900,000	—	—	0.20	7.00	—
Yr.37(1962)	284,200,000	—	—	0.20	1.25	—
Yr.38(1963)	411,300,000	—	—	0.20	1.00	—
Yr.39(1964)	479,200,000	—	—	0.20	1.00	—
Yr.40(1965)	387,600,000	—	—	0.20	1.00	—
Yr.41(1966)	395,900,000	—	—	0.20	1.00	—
Yr.42(1967)	158,900,000	—	—	0.20	1.00	—
Yr.43(1968)	363,600,000	—	—	0.20	1.00	—
Yr.44(1969)	414,800,000	—	—	0.20	0.40	—
Yr.45(1970)	382,700,000	—	—	0.20	0.50	—
Yr.46(1971)	610,050,000	—	—	0.20	0.40	—
Yr.47(1972)	634,950,000	—	—	0.20	0.40	—
Yr.48(1973)	1,345,000,000	—	—	0.20	0.35	—
Yr.49(1974)	1,780,000,000	—	—	0.20	0.35	—
Yr.50(1975)	1,280,260,000	—	—	0.20	0.35	—
Yr.51(1976)	1,369,740,000	—	—	0.20	0.35	—
Yr.52(1977)	1,467,000,000	—	—	0.20	0.35	—
Yr.53(1978)	1,435,000,000	—	—	0.20	0.35	—
Yr.54(1979)	1,207,000,000	—	—	0.20	0.35	—
Yr.55(1980)	1,127,000,000	—	—	0.20	0.35	—
Yr.56(1981)	1,369,000,000	—	—	0.20	0.35	—
Yr.57(1982)	890,000,000	—	—	0.20	0.35	—
Yr.58(1983)	870,000,000	—	—	0.20	0.35	—
Yr.59(1984)	533,850,000	—	—	0.20	0.35	—
Yr.60(1985)	335,150,000	—	—	0.20	0.35	—
Yr.61(1986)	68,960,000	—	—	0.25	0.75	—
Yr.62(1987)	165,545,000	—	—	0.20	0.35	—
Yr.62(1987) Proof	230,000	Value: 1.75				
Yr.63(1988)	617,912,000	—	—	—	0.35	—
Yr.63(1988) Proof	200,000	Value: 1.75				
Yr.64(1989)	74,692,000	—	—	0.25	0.75	—

Y# 97.1 10 YEN **Weight:** 4.5000 g. **Composition:** Bronze **Ruler:** Akihito (Heisei) **Reverse:** Japanese character "first" in date

Date	Mintage	F	VF	XF	Unc	BU
Yr.1(1989)	666,108,000	—	—	—	0.45	—
Yr.1(1989) Proof	200,000	Value: 1.75				

Y# 97.2 10 YEN **Weight:** 4.5000 g. **Composition:** Bronze **Ruler:** Akihito (Heisei)

Date	Mintage	F	VF	XF	Unc	BU
Yr.2(1990)		—	—	—	0.45	—
Yr.2(1990) Proof	200,000	Value: 1.75				
Yr.3(1991)		—	—	—	0.45	—
Yr.3(1991) Proof	220,000	Value: 1.75				
Yr.4(1992)		—	—	—	0.45	—
Yr.4(1992) Proof	250,000	Value: 1.75				
Yr.5(1993)		—	—	—	0.45	—
Yr.5(1993) Proof	250,000	Value: 1.75				
Yr.6(1994)		—	—	—	0.45	—
Yr.6(1994) Proof	227,000	Value: 1.75				
Yr.7(1995)		—	—	—	0.45	—
Yr.7(1995) Proof	200,000	Value: 1.75				
Yr.8(1996)		—	—	—	0.45	—
Yr.8(1996) Proof	189,000	Value: 1.75				
Yr.9(1997)		—	—	—	0.45	—
Yr.9(1997) Proof	212,000	Value: 1.75				
Yr.10(1998)		—	—	—	0.45	—
Yr.10(1998) Proof	200,000	Value: 1.75				
Yr.11(1999)		—	—	—	0.45	—
Yr.11(1999) Proof	280,000	Value: 1.75				
Yr.12(2000)		—	—	—	0.45	—
Yr.12(2000) Proof	226,000	Value: 1.75				
Yr.13(2001)		—	—	—	0.45	—
Yr.13(2001) Proof	—	Value: 1.75				

Y# 34 20 YEN **Weight:** 16.6666 g. **Composition:** 0.9000 Gold .4823 oz. AGW **Ruler:** Mutsuhito (Meiji)

Date	Mintage	F	VF	XF	Unc	BU
Yr.36(1903) Rare	—	—	—	—	—	—
Yr.37(1904)	2,759,470	550	1,250	1,750	2,400	—
Yr.38(1905)	1,045,904	550	1,250	1,750	2,400	—
Yr.39(1906)	1,331,332	550	1,250	1,750	2,400	—
Yr.40(1907)	817,363	650	1,350	2,100	2,850	—
Yr.41(1908)	458,082	1,000	1,500	2,250	3,650	—
Yr.42(1909)	557,882	1,000	1,500	2,250	3,750	—
Yr.43(1910)	2,163,644	500	1,000	1,600	2,200	—
Yr.44(1911)	1,470,057	500	1,000	1,600	2,200	—
Yr.45(1912)	1,272,450	525	1,100	1,700	2,300	—

Y# 40.1 20 YEN **Weight:** 16.6666 g. **Composition:** 0.9000 Gold .4823 oz. AGW **Ruler:** Yoshihito (Taisho) **Obverse:** Japanese character "first" used in date

Date	Mintage	F	VF	XF	Unc	BU
Yr.1(1912)	177,644	700	1,400	2,200	3,000	—

Y# 40.2 20 YEN **Weight:** 16.6666 g. **Composition:** 0.9000 Gold .4823 oz. AGW **Ruler:** Yoshihito (Taisho)

Date	Mintage	F	VF	XF	Unc	BU
Yr.2(1913)	869,248	550	1,100	1,700	2,300	—
Yr.3(1914)	1,042,890	550	1,100	1,700	2,300	—
Yr.4(1915)	1,509,960	550	1,100	1,700	2,300	—
Yr.5(1916)	2,376,641	500	1,000	1,600	2,200	—
Yr.6(1917)	6,208,885	475	950	1,550	2,150	—
Yr.7(1918)	3,118,647	500	1,000	1,600	2,200	—
Yr.8(1919)	1,531,217	500	1,000	1,600	2,200	—
Yr.9(1920)	370,366	600	1,300	1,800	2,650	—

Y# 52 20 YEN **Weight:** 16.6666 g. **Composition:** 0.9000 Gold .4823 oz. AGW **Ruler:** Hirohito (Showa)

Date	Mintage	F	VF	XF	Unc	BU
Yr.5(1930)	11,055,500	15,000	25,000	35,000	45,000	—
Yr.6(1931)	7,526,476	17,500	27,500	37,500	47,500	—
Yr.7(1932) Rare	—	—	—	—	—	—

Y# 75 50 YEN **Weight:** 5.5000 g. **Composition:** Nickel **Ruler:** Hirohito (Showa)

Date	Mintage	F	VF	XF	Unc	BU
Yr.30(1955)	63,700,000	—	0.75	1.50	17.50	—
Yr.31(1956)	91,300,000	—	0.75	1.00	17.50	—
Yr.32(1957)	39,000,000	—	0.75	1.50	17.50	—
Yr.33(1958)	18,000,000	—	1.00	2.50	30.00	—

Y# 76 50 YEN **Weight:** 5.0000 g. **Composition:** Nickel **Ruler:** Hirohito (Showa)

Date	Mintage	F	VF	XF	Unc	BU
Yr.34(1959)	23,900,000	—	1.00	2.50	17.50	—
Yr.35(1960)	6,000,000	—	12.50	22.50	40.00	—
Yr.36(1961)	16,000,000	—	2.00	4.00	20.00	—
Yr.37(1962)	50,300,000	—	0.75	1.25	5.00	—
Yr.38(1963)	55,000,000	—	0.75	1.25	5.00	—
Yr.39(1964)	69,200,000	—	0.75	1.25	4.00	—
Yr.40(1965)	189,300,000	—	0.75	1.00	3.00	—
Yr.41(1966)	171,500,000	—	0.75	1.25	2.50	—

Y# 81 50 YEN **Weight:** 4.0000 g. **Composition:** Copper-Nickel **Ruler:** Hirohito (Showa)

Date	Mintage	F	VF	XF	Unc	BU
Yr.42(1967)	238,400,000	—	—	0.75	1.50	—
Yr.43(1968)	200,000,000	—	—	0.75	1.50	—
Yr.44(1969)	210,000,000	—	—	0.75	1.50	—
Yr.45(1970)	269,800,000	—	—	0.75	1.50	—
Yr.46(1971)	80,950,000	—	—	0.75	1.50	—
Yr.47(1972)	138,980,000	—	—	0.75	1.00	—
Yr.48(1973)	200,970,000	—	—	0.75	1.00	—
Yr.49(1974)	470,000,000	—	—	0.75	1.00	—
Yr.50(1975)	238,120,000	—	—	0.75	1.00	—
Yr.51(1976)	241,880,000	—	—	0.75	1.00	—
Yr.52(1977)	176,000,000	—	—	0.75	1.00	—
Yr.53(1978)	234,000,000	—	—	0.75	1.00	—
Yr.54(1979)	110,000,000	—	—	0.75	1.00	—
Yr.55(1980)	51,000,000	—	—	0.75	1.00	—
Yr.56(1981)	179,000,000	—	—	0.75	1.00	—
Yr.57(1982)	30,000,000	—	—	0.75	1.00	—
Yr.58(1983)	30,000,000	—	—	0.75	1.00	—
Yr.59(1984)	29,850,000	—	—	0.75	1.00	—
Yr.60(1985)	10,150,000	—	—	0.75	1.00	—
Yr.61(1986)	9,960,000	—	—	0.75	1.00	—
Yr.62(1987)	545,000	—	—	—	70.00	—
Yr.62(1987) Proof	230,000	Value: 75.00				
Yr.63(1988)	108,912,000	—	—	—	1.00	—
Yr.63(1988) Proof	200,000	Value: 2.00				

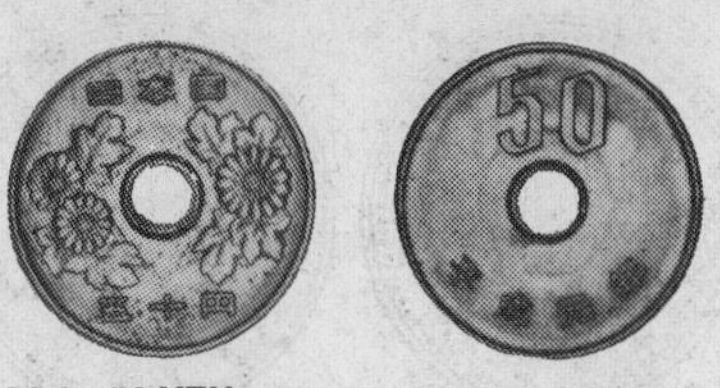

Y# 101.1 50 YEN **Composition:** Copper-Nickel **Ruler:** Akihito (Heisei) **Obverse:** Japanese character "first" in date

Date	Mintage	F	VF	XF	Unc	BU
Yr.1(1989)	244,800,000	—	—	—	1.00	—
Yr.1(1989) Proof	200,000	Value: 2.00				

Y# 101.2 50 YEN **Composition:** Copper-Nickel **Ruler:** Akihito (Heisei)

Date	Mintage	F	VF	XF	Unc	BU
Yr.2(1990)		—	—	—	1.00	—
Yr.2(1990) Proof	200,000	Value: 2.00				
Yr.3(1991)		—	—	—	1.00	—
Yr.3(1991) Proof	220,000	Value: 2.00				
Yr.4(1992)		—	—	—	1.00	—
Yr.4(1992) Proof	250,000	Value: 2.00				
Yr.5(1993)		—	—	—	1.00	—
Yr.5(1993) Proof	250,000	Value: 2.00				
Yr.6(1994)		—	—	—	1.00	—
Yr.6(1994) Proof	227,000	Value: 2.00				
Yr.7(1995)		—	—	—	1.00	—
Yr.7(1995) Proof	200,000	Value: 2.00				
Yr.8(1996)		—	—	—	1.00	—
Yr.8(1996) Proof	189,000	Value: 2.00				
Yr.9(1997)		—	—	—	1.00	—
Yr.9(1997) Proof	212,000	Value: 2.00				
Yr.10(1998)		—	—	—	1.00	—
Yr.10(1998) Proof	200,000	Value: 2.00				
Yr.11(1999)		—	—	—	1.00	—
Yr.11(1999) Proof	280,000	Value: 2.00				
Yr.12(2000)		—	—	—	1.00	—
Yr.12(2000) Proof	226,000	Value: 2.00				
Yr.13(2001)		—	—	—	1.00	—
Yr.13(2001) Proof	—	Value: 2.00				

Y# 77 100 YEN **Weight:** 4.8000 g. **Composition:** 0.6000 Silver .0926 oz. ASW **Ruler:** Hirohito (Showa)

Date	Mintage	F	VF	XF	Unc	BU
Yr.32(1957)	30,000,000	—	1.50	2.50	9.00	—
Yr.33(1958)	70,000,000	—	1.50	2.50	6.00	—

Y# 78 100 YEN **Weight:** 4.8000 g. **Composition:** 0.6000 Silver .0926 oz. ASW **Ruler:** Hirohito (Showa)

Date	Mintage	F	VF	XF	Unc	BU
Yr.34(1959)	110,000,000	—	1.50	2.50	9.00	—
Yr.35(1960)	50,000,000	—	1.50	2.50	9.00	—
Yr.36(1961)	15,000,000	—	1.50	2.50	9.00	—
Yr.38(1963)	45,000,000	—	1.50	2.50	6.00	—
Yr.39(1964)	10,000,000	—	1.75	3.50	7.50	—
Yr.40(1965)	62,500,000	—	1.50	2.50	4.00	—
Yr.41(1966)	97,500,000	—	1.50	2.50	4.00	—

Y# 79 100 YEN **Weight:** 4.8000 g. **Composition:** 0.6000 Silver .0926 oz. ASW **Ruler:** Hirohito (Showa) **Subject:** 1964 Olympic Games

Date	Mintage	F	VF	XF	Unc	BU
Yr.39/1964	80,000,000	—	1.00	2.00	3.50	—

Y# 82 100 YEN **Weight:** 4.2000 g. **Composition:** Copper-Nickel **Ruler:** Hirohito (Showa)

Date	Mintage	F	VF	XF	Unc	BU
Yr.42(1967)	432,200,000	—	—	1.50	2.50	—
Note: Varieties exist						
Yr.43(1968)	471,000,000	—	—	1.50	2.50	—
Yr.44(1969)	323,700,000	—	—	1.50	2.50	—
Yr.45(1970)	237,100,000	—	—	1.50	2.50	—
Yr.46(1971)	481,050,000	—	—	1.50	2.50	—
Yr.47(1972)	468,950,000	—	—	1.50	2.50	—
Yr.48(1973)	680,000,000	—	—	1.50	2.50	—
Yr.49(1974)	660,000,000	—	—	1.50	2.50	—
Yr.50(1975)	437,160,000	—	—	1.50	2.50	—
Yr.51(1976)	322,840,000	—	—	1.50	2.50	—
Yr.52(1977)	440,000,000	—	—	1.50	2.50	—
Yr.53(1978)	292,000,000	—	—	1.50	2.50	—
Yr.54(1979)	382,000,000	—	—	1.50	2.50	—
Yr.55(1980)	588,000,000	—	—	1.50	2.50	—
Yr.56(1981)	348,000,000	—	—	1.50	2.50	—
Yr.57(1982)	110,000,000	—	—	1.50	2.50	—
Yr.58(1983)	50,000,000	—	—	1.50	2.50	—
Yr.59(1984)	41,850,000	—	—	1.50	2.50	—
Yr.60(1985)	58,150,000	—	—	1.50	2.50	—
Yr.61(1986)	99,960,000	—	—	1.50	2.50	—
Yr.62(1987)	193,545,000	—	—	1.50	2.50	—
Yr.62(1987) Proof	230,000	Value: 5.00				
Yr.63(1988)	362,912,000	—	—	1.50	2.50	—
Yr.63(1988) Proof	200,000	Value: 5.00				

Y# 83 100 YEN **Weight:** 9.0000 g. **Composition:** Copper-Nickel **Ruler:** Hirohito (Showa) **Subject:** Osaka Expo '70

Date	Mintage	F	VF	XF	Unc	BU
Yr.45(1970)	40,000,000	—	2.00	3.00	5.50	—

Y# 84 100 YEN **Weight:** 12.0000 g. **Composition:** Copper-Nickel **Ruler:** Hirohito (Showa) **Subject:** 1972 Winter Olympic Games - Sapporo

Date	Mintage	F	VF	XF	Unc	BU
Yr.47/1972	30,000,000	—	2.50	4.00	6.50	—

Y# 85 100 YEN **Weight:** 9.8000 g. **Composition:** Copper-Nickel **Ruler:** Hirohito (Showa) **Subject:** Okinawa Expo '75

Date	Mintage	F	VF	XF	Unc	BU
Yr.50(1975)	120,000,000	—	1.50	2.00	2.50	—

Y# 86 100 YEN **Weight:** 12.0000 g. **Composition:** Copper-Nickel **Ruler:** Hirohito (Showa) **Subject:** 50th Anniversary of Reign

Date	Mintage	F	VF	XF	Unc	BU
Yr.51(1976)	70,000,000	—	2.00	3.00	4.50	—

Y# 98.1 100 YEN **Weight:** 9.8000 g. **Composition:** Copper-Nickel **Ruler:** Akihito (Heisei) **Reverse:** Japanese character "first" in date

Date	Mintage	F	VF	XF	Unc	BU
Yr.1(1989)	368,800,000	—	—	—	2.00	—
Yr.1(1989) Proof	200,000	Value: 5.00				

Y# 98.2 100 YEN **Weight:** 9.8000 g. **Composition:** Copper-Nickel **Ruler:** Akihito (Heisei)

Date	Mintage	F	VF	XF	Unc	BU
Yr.2(1990)	444,753,000	—	—	—	2.00	—
Yr.2(1990) Proof	200,000	Value: 5.00				
Yr.3(1991)	374,900,000	—	—	—	2.00	—
Yr.3(1991) Proof	220,000	Value: 5.00				
Yr.4(1992)	211,050,000	—	—	—	2.00	—
Yr.4(1992) Proof	250,000	Value: 5.00				
Yr.5(1993)	81,990,000	—	—	—	2.00	—
Yr.5(1993) Proof	250,000	Value: 5.00				
Yr.6(1994)	81,540,000	—	—	—	2.00	—
Yr.6(1994) Proof	227,000	Value: 5.00				
Yr.7(1995)	92,674,000	—	—	—	2.00	—
Yr.7(1995) Proof	200,000	Value: 5.00				
Yr.8(1996)	237,024,000	—	—	—	2.00	—
Yr.8(1996) Proof	189,000	Value: 5.00				
Yr.9(1997)	271,876,000	—	—	—	2.00	—
Yr.9(1997) Proof	212,000	Value: 5.00				
Yr.10(1998)	252,412,000	—	—	—	2.00	—
Yr.10(1998) Proof	200,000	Value: 5.00				
Yr.11(1999)	178,850,000	—	—	—	2.00	—
Yr.11(1999) Proof	280,000	Value: 5.00				
Yr.12(2000)		—	—	—	2.00	—
Yr.12(2000) Proof	—	Value: 5.00				
Yr.13(2001)		—	—	—	2.00	—
Yr.13(2001) Proof	—	Value: 5.00				

Y# 87 500 YEN **Weight:** 7.2000 g. **Composition:** Copper-Nickel **Ruler:** Hirohito (Showa) **Obverse:** Pawlownia flower

Date	Mintage	F	VF	XF	Unc	BU
Yr.57(1982)	300,000,000	—	—	7.00	9.00	—
Yr.58(1983)	240,000,000	—	—	7.00	9.00	—
Yr.59(1984)	342,850,000	—	—	7.00	9.00	—
Yr.60(1985)	97,150,000	—	—	7.00	9.00	—
Yr.61(1986)	49,960,000	—	—	7.00	9.00	—
Yr.62(1987)	2,545,000	—	7.00	9.00	15.00	—
Yr.62(1987) Proof	230,000	Value: 25.00				
Yr.63(1988)	148,018,000	—	—	7.00	9.00	—
Yr.63(1988) Proof	200,000	Value: 15.00				
Yr.64(1989)	16,042,000	—	—	7.00	12.00	—

Y# 88 500 YEN **Weight:** 13.0000 g. **Composition:** Copper-Nickel **Ruler:** Hirohito (Showa) **Subject:** 1985 Tsukuba Expo

Date	Mintage	F	VF	XF	Unc	BU
Yr.60(1985)	70,000,000	—	—	7.00	9.00	—

Y# 89 500 YEN **Weight:** 13.0000 g. **Composition:** Copper-Nickel **Ruler:** Hirohito (Showa) **Subject:** 100th Anniversary - Governmental Cabinet System

Date	Mintage	F	VF	XF	Unc	BU
Yr.60(1985)	70,000,000	—	—	7.00	9.00	—

Y# 90 500 YEN **Weight:** 13.0000 g. **Composition:** Copper-Nickel **Ruler:** Hirohito (Showa) **Subject:** 60 Years of Reign of Hirohito

Date	Mintage	F	VF	XF	Unc	BU
Yr.61(1986)	50,000,000	—	—	7.00	10.00	—

Y# 93 500 YEN **Weight:** 13.0000 g. **Composition:** Copper-Nickel **Ruler:** Hirohito (Showa) **Subject:** Opening of Seikan Tunnel

Date	Mintage	F	VF	XF	Unc	BU
Yr.63(1988)	20,000,000	—	—	8.00	11.50	—

Y# 94 500 YEN **Weight:** 13.0000 g. **Composition:** Copper-Nickel **Ruler:** Hirohito (Showa) **Subject:** Opening of Seto Bridge

Date	Mintage	F	VF	XF	Unc	BU
Yr.63(1988)	20,000,000	—	—	8.00	11.50	—

Y# 99.1 500 YEN **Weight:** 7.2000 g. **Composition:** Copper-Nickel **Ruler:** Akihito (Heisei) **Reverse:** Japanese character "first" in date

Date	Mintage	F	VF	XF	Unc	BU
Yr.1(1989)	192,652,000	—	—	7.00	9.00	—
Yr.1(1989) Proof	200,000	Value: 15.00				

Y# 99.2 500 YEN **Weight:** 7.2000 g. **Composition:** Copper-Nickel **Ruler:** Akihito (Heisei)

Date	Mintage	F	VF	XF	Unc	BU
Yr.2(1990)	159,753,000	—	—	7.00	9.00	—
Yr.2(1990) Proof	200,000	Value: 15.00				
Yr.3(1991)	169,900,000	—	—	7.00	9.00	—
Yr.3(1991) Proof	220,000	Value: 15.00				
Yr.4(1992)	87,880,000	—	—	7.00	9.00	—
Yr.4(1992) Proof	250,000	Value: 15.00				
Yr.5(1993)	131,990,000	—	—	7.00	9.00	—
Yr.5(1993) Proof	250,000	Value: 15.00				
Yr.6(1994)	105,545,000	—	—	7.00	9.00	—
Yr.6(1994) Proof	227,000	Value: 15.00				
Yr.7(1995)	182,669,000	—	—	—	9.00	—

Date	Mintage	F	VF	XF	Unc	BU
Yr.7(1995) Proof	200,000	Value: 15.00				
Yr.8(1996)	99,024,000	—	—	—	9.00	—
Yr.8(1996) Proof	189,000	Value: 15.00				
Yr.9(1997)	172,878,000	—	—	—	9.00	—
Yr.9(1997) Proof	212,000	Value: 15.00				
Yr.10(1998)	214,408,000	—	—	—	9.00	—
Yr.10(1998) Proof	200,000	Value: 15.00				
Yr.11(1999)	164,840,000	—	—	—	9.00	—
Yr.11(1999) Proof	280,000	Value: 15.00				

Y# 102 500 YEN **Weight:** 13.0000 g. **Composition:** Copper-Nickel **Ruler:** Akihito (Heisei) **Subject:** Enthronement of Emperor Akihito

Date	Mintage	F	VF	XF	Unc	BU
Yr.2(1990)	30,000,000	—	—	—	12.50	—

Y# 106 500 YEN **Weight:** 13.0000 g. **Composition:** Copper-Nickel **Ruler:** Akihito (Heisei) **Subject:** 20th Anniversary - Reversion of Okinawa

Date	Mintage	F	VF	XF	Unc	BU
Yr.4(1992)	19,953,000	—	—	—	13.00	—
Yr.4(1992) Proof	47,000	Value: 25.00				

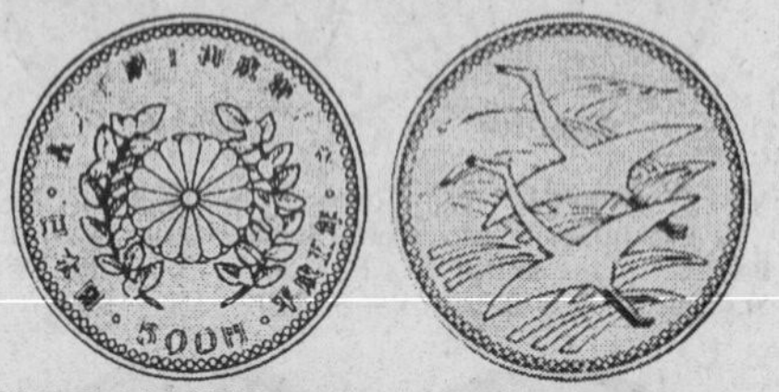

Y# 107 500 YEN **Weight:** 7.2000 g. **Composition:** Copper-Nickel **Ruler:** Akihito (Heisei) **Subject:** Royal wedding of Crown Prince

Date	Mintage	F	VF	XF	Unc	BU
Yr.5(1993)	29,800,000	—	—	—	14.00	—
Yr.5(1993) Proof	200,000	Value: 20.00				

Y# 110 500 YEN **Weight:** 7.2000 g. **Composition:** Copper-Nickel **Ruler:** Akihito (Heisei) **Subject:** Opening of Kansai International Airport

Date	Mintage	F	VF	XF	Unc	BU
Yr.6(1994)	19,900,000	—	—	—	13.00	—
Yr.6(1994) Proof	100,000	Value: 40.00				

Y# 111 500 YEN **Weight:** 7.2000 g. **Composition:** Copper-Nickel **Ruler:** Akihito (Heisei) **Subject:** 12th Asian Games **Reverse:** Runners

Date	Mintage	F	VF	XF	Unc	BU
Yr.6(1994)	9,900,000	—	—	—	12.50	—
Yr.6(1994) Proof	100,000	Value: 30.00				

Y# 112 500 YEN **Weight:** 7.2000 g. **Composition:** Copper-Nickel **Ruler:** Akihito (Heisei) **Subject:** 12th Asian Games **Reverse:** Swimmers

Date	Mintage	F	VF	XF	Unc	BU
Yr.6(1994)	9,900,000	—	—	—	12.50	—
Yr.6(1994) Proof	100,000	Value: 30.00				

Y# 113 500 YEN **Weight:** 7.2000 g. **Composition:** Copper-Nickel **Ruler:** Akihito (Heisei) **Subject:** 12th Asian Games **Reverse:** Jumper

Date	Mintage	F	VF	XF	Unc	BU
Yr.6(1994)	9,900,000	—	—	—	12.50	—
Yr.6(1994) Proof	100,000	Value: 30.00				

Y# 114 500 YEN **Weight:** 7.2000 g. **Composition:** Copper-Nickel **Ruler:** Hirohito (Showa) **Series:** 1998 Nagano Winter Olympics **Obverse:** Snowboarder **Reverse:** Ptarmigan, denomination, dates

Date	Mintage	F	VF	XF	Unc	BU
Yr.9(1997)	19,867,000	—	—	—	10.00	—
Yr.9(1997) Proof	133,000	Value: 35.00				

Y# 117 500 YEN **Weight:** 7.2000 g. **Composition:** Copper-Nickel **Ruler:** Akihito (Heisei) **Series:** 1998 Nagano Winter Olympics **Obverse:** Bobsledding **Reverse:** Ptarmigan, denomination, dates

Date	Mintage	F	VF	XF	Unc	BU
Yr.9(1997)	19,867,000	—	—	—	10.00	—
Yr.9(1997) Proof	133,000	Value: 35.00				

Y# 118 500 YEN **Weight:** 7.2000 g. **Composition:** Copper-Nickel **Ruler:** Akihito (Heisei) **Series:** 1998 Nagano Winter Olympics **Obverse:** Acrobat skier **Reverse:** Ptarmigan, denomination, dates

Date	Mintage	F	VF	XF	Unc	BU
Yr.10(1998)	19,867,000	—	—	—	10.00	—
Yr.10(1998) Proof	133,000	Value: 35.00				

Y# 123 500 YEN **Weight:** 7.2000 g. **Composition:** Copper-Nickel **Ruler:** Akihito (Heisei) **Subject:** 10th

Anniversary of Enthronement **Obverse:** Mt. Fuji and chrysanthemums **Reverse:** Chrysanthemum in wreath

Date		F	VF	XF	Unc	BU
Yr.11(1999)		—	—	—	10.00	—
Yr.11(1999) Proof	100,000	Value: 30.00				

Y# 125 500 YEN **Weight:** 7.0000 g. **Composition:** Nickel-Brass **Ruler:** Akihito (Heisei) **Obverse:** Pawlownia flower and highlighted legends **Reverse:** Denomination with latent denomination in the zeros **Edge:** Slanted reeding **Size:** 26.5 mm.

Date	Mintage	F	VF	XF	Unc	BU
Yr.12(2000)	595,746,000	—	—	—	2.00	—
Yr.12(2000) Proof	226,000	Value: 5.00				
Yr.13(2001)	—	—	—	—	2.00	—
Yr.13(2001) Proof	—	Value: 5.00				

Y# 80 1000 YEN **Weight:** 20.0000 g. **Composition:** 0.9250 Silver .5948 oz. ASW **Ruler:** Hirohito (Showa) **Series:** 1964 Olympic Games **Note:** Dav. #276

Date	Mintage	F	VF	XF	Unc	BU
Yr.39/1964	15,000,000	—	20.00	30.00	50.00	—

Y# 100 5000 YEN **Weight:** 15.0000 g. **Composition:** 0.9250 Silver .4461 oz. ASW **Ruler:** Akihito (Heisei) **Subject:** Osaka Exposition

Date	Mintage	F	VF	XF	Unc	BU
Yr.2/1990	10,000,000	—	—	—	65.00	—

Y# 103 5000 YEN **Weight:** 15.0000 g. **Composition:** 0.9250 Silver .4461 oz. ASW **Ruler:** Akihito (Heisei) **Subject:** Centennial of Parliament

Date	Mintage	F	VF	XF	Unc	BU
Yr.2(1990)	5,000,000	—	—	—	65.00	—

Y# 104 5000 YEN **Weight:** 15.0000 g. **Composition:** 0.9250 Silver .4461 oz. ASW **Ruler:** Akihito (Heisei) **Subject:** Centennial of Judicial System

Date	Mintage	F	VF	XF	Unc	BU
Yr.2(1990)	5,000,000	—	—	—	65.00	—

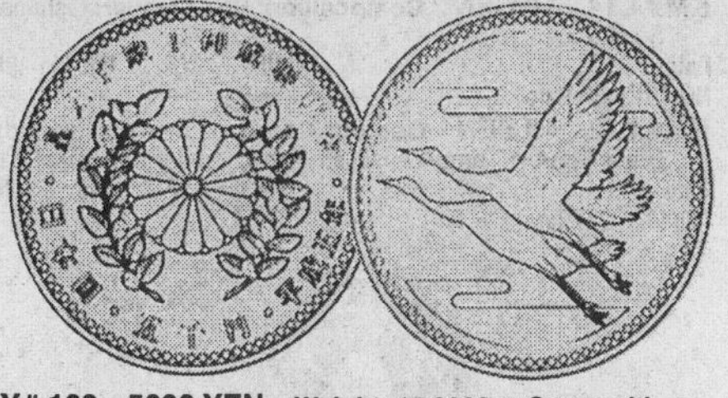

Y# 108 5000 YEN **Weight:** 15.0000 g. **Composition:** 1.0000 Silver .4823 oz. ASW **Ruler:** Akihito (Heisei) **Subject:** Royal wedding of Crown Prince

Date	Mintage	F	VF	XF	Unc	BU
Yr.5(1993)	4,800,000	—	—	—	70.00	—
Yr.5(1993) Proof	200,000	Value: 100				

Y# 115 5000 YEN **Weight:** 15.0000 g. **Composition:** 0.9250 Silver .4461 oz. ASW **Ruler:** Akihito (Heisei) **Series:** 1998 Nagano Winter Olympics **Obverse:** Hockey player **Reverse:** Denomination, dates, and Serow

Date	Mintage	F	VF	XF	Unc	BU
Yr.9(1997)	4,867,000	—	—	—	70.00	—
Yr.9(1997) Proof	133,000	Value: 120				

Y# 119 5000 YEN **Weight:** 15.0000 g. **Composition:** 0.9250 Silver .4461 oz. ASW **Ruler:** Akihito (Heisei) **Series:** 1998 Nagano Winter Olympics **Obverse:** Biathalon **Reverse:** Denomination, dates, and antelope

Date	Mintage	F	VF	XF	Unc	BU
Yr.9(1997)	4,867,000	—	—	—	70.00	—
Yr.9(1997) Proof	133,000	Value: 120				

Y# 120 5000 YEN **Weight:** 15.0000 g. **Composition:** 0.9250 Silver .4461 oz. ASW **Ruler:** Akihito (Heisei) **Series:** 1998 Nagano Winter Olympics **Obverse:** Paralympic skier **Reverse:** Denomination, dates, and antelope

Date	Mintage	F	VF	XF	Unc	BU
Yr.10(1998)	4,867,000	—	—	—	70.00	—
Yr.10(1998) Proof	133,000	Value: 120				

Y# 91 10000 YEN **Weight:** 20.0000 g. **Composition:** 0.9990 Silver .6430 oz. ASW **Ruler:** Hirohito (Showa) **Subject:** 60 Years - Reign of Hirohito

Date	Mintage	F	VF	XF	Unc	BU
Yr.61(1986)	10,000,000	—	—	—	135	—

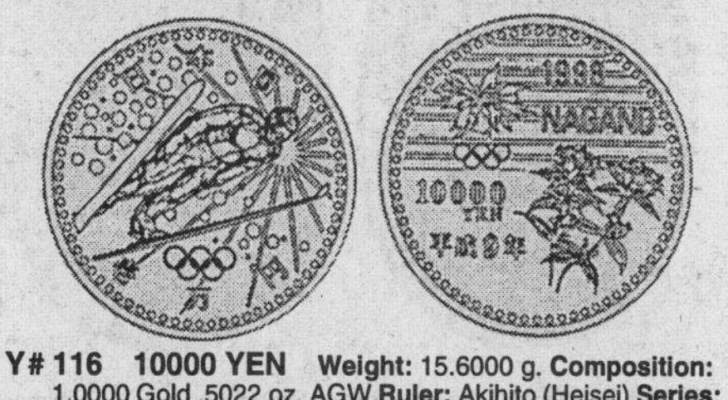

Y# 116 10000 YEN **Weight:** 15.6000 g. **Composition:** 1.0000 Gold .5022 oz. AGW **Ruler:** Akihito (Heisei) **Series:** 1998 Nagano Winter Olympics **Obverse:** Ski jumper **Reverse:** Denomination, dates, and gentian plant

Date	Mintage	F	VF	XF	Unc	BU
Yr.9(1997) Proof	55,000	Value: 650				

Y# 121 10000 YEN **Weight:** 15.6000 g. **Composition:** 1.0000 Gold .5022 oz. AGW **Ruler:** Akihito (Heisei) **Series:** 1998 Nagano Winter Olympics **Obverse:** Figure skater **Reverse:** Denomination, dates, and gentian plant

Date	Mintage	F	VF	XF	Unc	BU
Yr.9(1997) Proof	55,000	Value: 650				

Y# 122 10000 YEN **Weight:** 15.6000 g. **Composition:** 1.0000 Gold .5022 oz. AGW **Ruler:** Akihito (Heisei) **Series:** 1998 Nagano Winter Olympics **Obverse:** Speed skater **Reverse:** Denomination, dates, and gentian plant

Date	Mintage	F	VF	XF	Unc	BU
Yr.10(1998) Proof	55,000	Value: 650				

Y# 124 10000 YEN **Weight:** 20.0000 g. **Composition:** 1.0000 Gold .6430 oz. AGW **Ruler:** Akihito (Heisei) **Subject:** 15th Anniversary of Enthronement **Obverse:** Chrysanthemum in wreath **Reverse:** Stylized Green Pheasant

Date	Mintage	F	VF	XF	Unc	BU
Yr.11(1999) Proof	200,000	Value: 1,200				

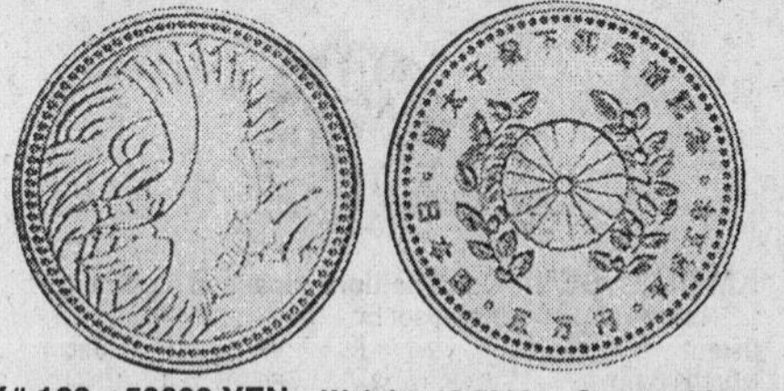

Y# 109 50000 YEN **Weight:** 18.0000 g. **Composition:** 1.0000 Gold .5788 oz. AGW **Ruler:** Akihito (Heisei) **Subject:** Royal wedding of Crown Prince

Date	Mintage	F	VF	XF	Unc	BU
Yr.5(1993)	1,900,000	—	—	—	650	—
Yr.5(1993) Proof	100,000	Value: 850				

Y# 92 100000 YEN **Weight:** 20.0000 g. **Composition:** 1.0000 Gold .6430 oz. AGW **Ruler:** Hirohito (Showa) **Subject:** 60 Years - Reign of Hirohito

Date	Mintage	F	VF	XF	Unc	BU
Yr.61(1986)	10,000,000	—	—	—	1,250	—
Yr.62(1987)	876,000	—	—	—	1,250	—
Yr.62(1987) Proof	124,000	Value: 1,350				

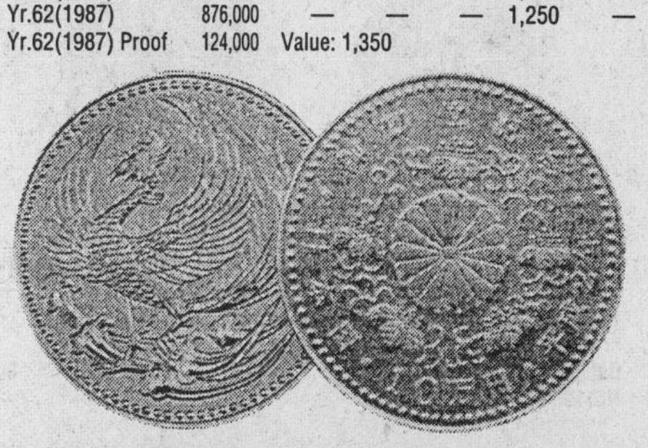

Y# 105 100000 YEN **Weight:** 30.0000 g. **Composition:** 1.0000 Gold .9646 oz. AGW **Ruler:** Akihito (Heisei) **Subject:** Enthronement of Emperor Akihito **Obverse:** Chrysanthemum in wreath **Reverse:** Stylized Green Pheasant

Date	Mintage	F	VF	XF	Unc	BU
Yr.2(1990)	1,900,000	—	—	—	1,250	—
Yr.2(1990) Proof	100,000	Value: 1,350				

PLATINUM BULLION COINAGE

KM# 20 10 MOMME **Weight:** 37.4000 g. **Composition:** Platinum APW **Ruler:** Hirohito (Showa)

Date	Mintage	F	VF	XF	Unc	BU
1937	1,500	—	—	—	1,750	—

LEPROSARIUM COINAGE

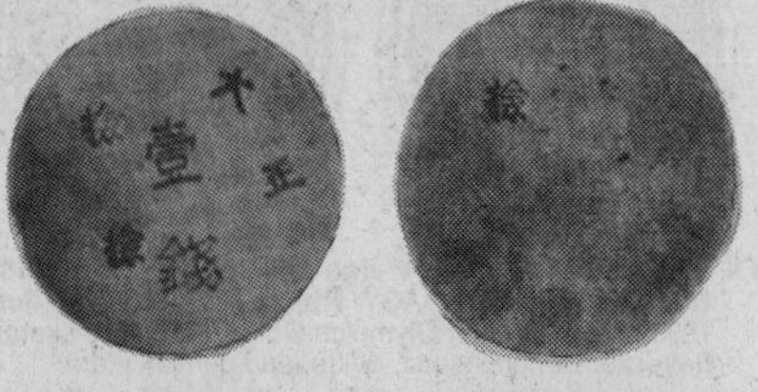

KM# L11 SEN Composition: Brass **Issuer:** Oshima-Seisho En **Obverse:** Denomination with mulitple stamps **Reverse:** "Ken" symbol = inspection

Date	F	VF	XF	Unc	BU
ND(1912-25) Rare	—	—	—	—	—

KM# L20 SEN Composition: Japanned (Lacquered) Brass **Issuer:** Tama-Zensei En **Note:** Uniface. Oval with central hole, denomination, rays at border.

Date	F	VF	XF	Unc	BU
ND(1926-28) Rare	—	—	—	—	—

KM# L1 SEN Composition: Japanned (Lacquered) Brass **Issuer:** Nagashima-Aisei En **Note:** Uniface. Badge of Aisei En above denomination.

Date	F	VF	XF	Unc	BU
ND(1931-48) Rare	—	—	—	—	—

KM# L2 SEN Composition: Japanned Aluminum **Issuer:** Nagashima-Aisei En

Date	F	VF	XF	Unc	BU
ND(1931-48)	—	450	750	—	—

KM# L12 2 SEN Composition: Brass **Issuer:** Oshima-Seisho En

Date	F	VF	XF	Unc	BU
ND(1912-25) Rare	—	—	—	—	—

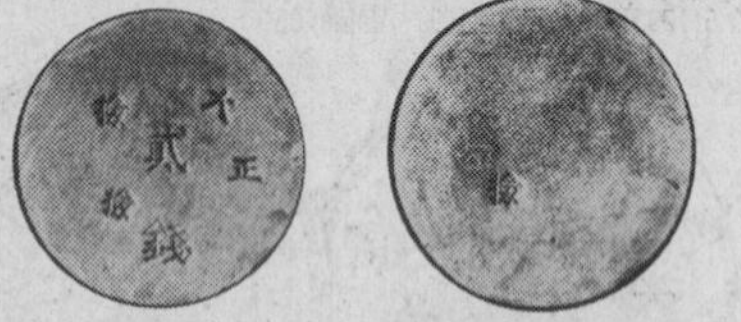

KM# L13 5 SEN Composition: Brass **Issuer:** Oshima-Seisho En

Date	F	VF	XF	Unc	BU
ND(1912-25) Rare	—	—	—	—	—

KM# L21 5 SEN Composition: Japanned (Lacquered) Brass **Issuer:** Tama-Zensei En **Note:** Round with central hole, perpendicular rays fill border from flower.

Date	F	VF	XF	Unc	BU
ND(1926-28) Rare	—	—	—	—	—

KM# L3 5 SEN Composition: Japanned (Lacquered) Brass **Issuer:** Nagashima-Aisei En

Date	F	VF	XF	Unc	BU
ND(1931-48) Rare	—	—	—	—	—

KM# L3a 5 SEN Composition: Japanned Aluminum **Issuer:** Nagashima-Aisei En

Date	F	VF	XF	Unc	BU
ND(1931-48)	—	750	1,250	—	—

KM# L14 10 SEN Composition: Brass **Issuer:** Oshima-Seisho En

Date	F	VF	XF	Unc	BU
ND(1912-25) Rare	—	—	—	—	—

KM# L22 10 SEN Composition: Japanned (Lacquered) Brass **Issuer:** Tama-Zensei En **Note:** Similar to 5 Sen, L21.

Date	F	VF	XF	Unc	BU
ND(1926-28) Rare	—	—	—	—	—

KM# L4 10 SEN Composition: Japanned (Lacquered) Brass **Issuer:** Nagashima-Aisei En

Date	F	VF	XF	Unc	BU
ND(1931-48) Rare	—	—	—	—	—

KM# L4a 10 SEN Composition: Japanned Aluminum **Issuer:** Nagashima-Aisei En

Date	F	VF	XF	Unc	BU
ND(1931-48)	—	750	1,250	—	—

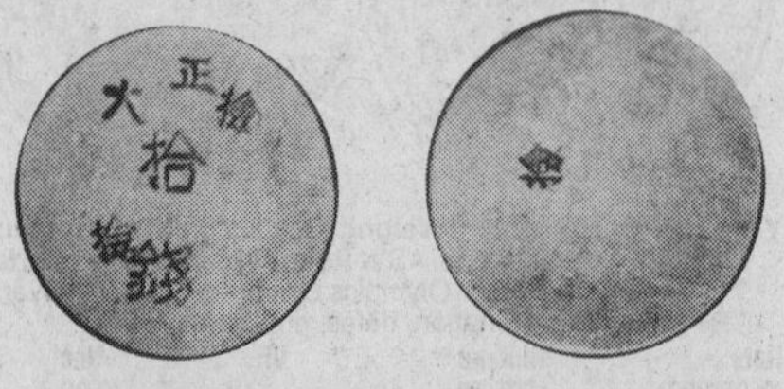

KM# L15 20 SEN Composition: Brass **Issuer:** Oshima-Seisho En

Date	F	VF	XF	Unc	BU
ND(1912-25) Rare	—	—	—	—	—

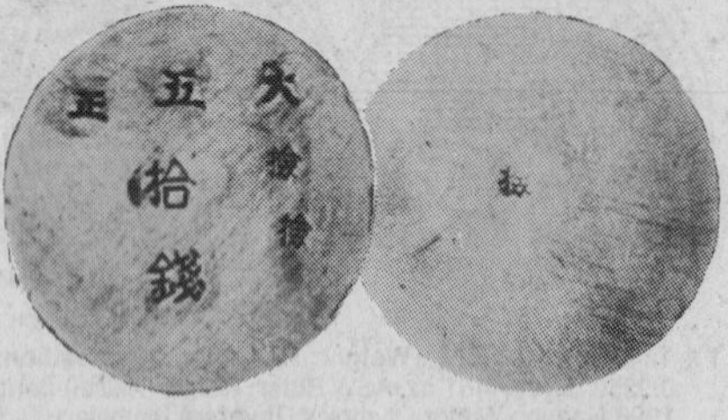

KM# L16 50 SEN Composition: Brass **Issuer:** Oshima-Seisho En

Date	F	VF	XF	Unc	BU
ND(1912-25) Rare	—	—	—	—	—

KM# L23 50 SEN Composition: Japanned (Lacquered) Brass **Issuer:** Tama-Zensei En **Note:** Rectangular with center hole. Sunset with ornate border.

Date	F	VF	XF	Unc	BU
ND(1926-28) Rare	—	—	—	—	—

KM# L5 50 SEN Composition: Japanned (Lacquered) Brass **Issuer:** Nagashima-Aisei En

Date	F	VF	XF	Unc	BU
ND(1931-48)	—	900	1,500	—	—

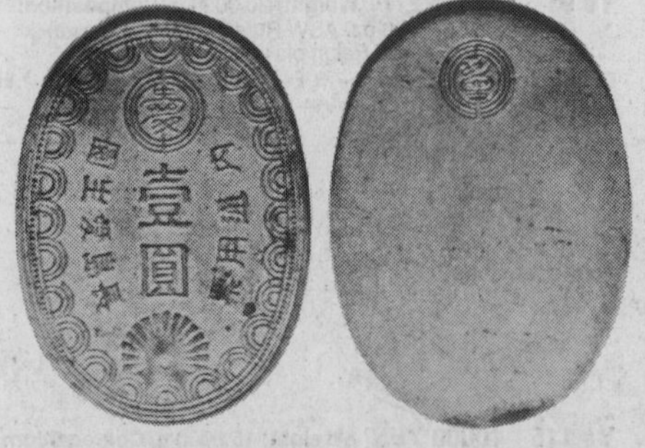

KM# L6 YEN Composition: Brass **Issuer:** Nagashima-Aisei En **Reverse:** Stylized badge of Ansei En

Date	F	VF	XF	Unc	BU
ND(1931-48)	—	1,500	2,500	—	—

OCCUPATION COINAGE

Y# 22 SEN Composition: Aluminum

Date	Mintage	F	VF	XF	Unc	BU
NE2603 (1943)	233,190,000	—	85.00	125	275	—
NE2604 (1944)	66,810,000	—	75.00	110	225	—

Y# A24 10 SEN Composition: Tin Alloy **Note:** Previous number: Y#24

Date	Mintage	F	VF	XF	Unc	BU
NE2603 (1943)	69,490,000	—	40.00	75.00	150	—
NE2604 (1944)	110,510,000	—	35.00	50.00	100	—

PATTERNS

Including off metal strikes

KM#	Date	Mintage	Identification	Mkt Val
Pn31	ND(1901)	—	Yen. Copper. Yr.34	3,250
Pn32	ND(1901)	—	Yen. Silver. Yr.34	—
Pn33	ND(1906)	—	5 Rin. Copper. Yr.39	3,250
Pn34	ND(1908)	—	Sen. Copper. Yr.41	3,250
Pn35	ND(1909)	—	5 Rin. Copper. Yr.42	3,250
Pn36	ND(1911)	—	Sen. Copper. Yr.42	—
Pn37	ND(1911)	—	Sen. Copper. Yr.44	3,250
Pn38	ND(1915)	—	Sen. Copper. Yr.4	3,250
Pn39	ND(1916)	—	5 Rin. Copper. Yr.5	3,250
Pn40	ND(1916)	—	5 Rin. Copper. Yr.5	3,250
Pn43	ND(1916)	—	Sen. Yr.5 of Taisho	—
Pn44	ND(1916)	—	5 Sen. Copper-Nickel. Yr.5	3,250
Pn41	ND(1916)	—	Sen. Copper. Yr.5	3,250
Pn42	ND(1916)	—	Sen. Yr.5	—
Pn45	ND(1918)	—	10 Sen. Silver. Yr.7	8,250
Pn46	ND(1918)	—	20 Sen. Silver. Yr.7	10,000
Pn47	ND(1918)	—	50 Sen. Silver. Yr.7	11,000
Pn48	ND(1918)	—	50 Sen. Yr.7	—
Pn49	ND(1919)	—	10 Sen. Silver. Yr.8	7,500
Pn50	ND(1919)	—	20 Sen. Silver. Yr.8	8,500
Pn51	ND(1919)	—	20 Sen. Silver. Yr.8	12,500
Pn52	ND(1920)	—	25 Sen. Silver. Yr.9	—
Pn53	ND(1920)	—	50 Sen. Silver. Yr.9	—
Pn54	ND(1921)	—	20 Sen. Silver. Yr.10	4,000
Pn55	ND(1923)	—	50 Sen. Tin. Yr.12	850
Pn56	ND(1926)	—	50 Sen. Tin. Yr.15	1,650
Pn57	ND(1927)	—	50 Sen. Brass. Yr.2	625
Pn58	ND(1927)	—	50 Sen. Silver. Yr.2	3,000
Pn59	ND(1927)	—	50 Sen. Brass. Yr.2	575
Pn60	ND(1927)	—	50 Sen. Silver. Yr.2	3,000
Pn61	ND(1928)	—	50 Sen. Tin. Yr.3; Y#50	400
Pn63	ND(1933)	—	10 Sen. Nickel. Yr.8; Y#53	—
Pn62	ND(1933)	—	5 Sen. Nickel. Yr.8; Y#54	—
Pn64	ND(1937)	—	5 Sen. Brass. Yr.12	—
Pn65	ND(1937)	—	10 Sen. Brass. Yr.12	—
Pn66	ND(1938)	—	Sen. Aluminum. Yr.13	—
Pn69	ND(1938)	—	50 Sen. White Metal. Y#50	2,500
Pn67	ND(1938)	—	5 Sen. Yr.13	—
Pn68	ND(1938)	—	10 Sen. Yr.13	—
Pn70	ND(1943)	—	Sen. Tin Alloy. Occupation issue Y#22	—
Pn72	ND(1943)	—	5 Sen. Tin Alloy. Yr. 2603; Y#23	—
PnA73	ND(1943)	—	10 Sen. Silver. Yr. 2603; Y#24	—
Pn71	ND(1943)	—	Sen. Red Fiber. Occupation issue Y#22	—
Pn73	ND(1945)	—	Sen. Brass. Yr.20; Y#62	—
Pn78	ND(1945)	—	10 Sen. White Baked Clay. Yr.20; numerous designs exist.	150
Pn79	ND(1945)	—	10 Sen. Red Baked Clay. Yr.20; numerous designs exist.	150
Pn75	ND(1945)	—	Sen. Red Baked Clay. Yr.20; numerous designs exist.	150
Pn74	ND(1945)	—	Sen. White Baked Clay. Yr.20; numerous designs exist.	150
Pn76	ND(1945)	—	5 Sen. White Baked Clay. Yr.20; numerous designs exist.	150
Pn77	ND(1945)	—	5 Sen. Red Baked Clay. Yr.20; numerous designs exist.	150
Pn80	ND(1946)	—	10 Sen. Brass. Yr.21; small size; Y#68	—
Pn81	ND(1950)	—	Yen. Brass. Yr.25; Y#70	—
Pn82	ND(1950)	—	10 Yen. Aluminum. Yr.25; Y#73	—
Pn83	ND(1950)	—	10 Yen. Copper-Nickel. Yr.25	1,000
Pn84	ND(1951)	—	5 Yen. Aluminum. Yr.26; Y#72	—
Pn85	ND(1951)	—	10 Yen. Copper-Nickel. Yr.26	1,150
Pn86	ND(1958)	—	5 Yen. Brass. Yr.33	—

MINT SETS

KM#	Date	Mintage	Identification	Issue Price	Mkt Val
MS1	1969 (5)	6,162	Y#72a, 73a, 74, 81, 82	1.25	650

KM#	Date	Mintage	Identification	Issue Price	Mkt Val
MS2	1970 (6)	26,000	Y#72a, 73a, 74, 81-83	2.00	50.00
MS3	1971 (5)	14,653	Y#72a, 73a, 74, 81, 82	1.60	110
MS4	1972 (6)	30,000	Y#72a, 73a, 74, 81, 82, 84	2.90	50.00
MS5	1975 (5)	720,000	Y#72a, 73a, 74, 81, 82	2.30	5.00
MS6	1976 (5)	580,000	Y#72a, 73a, 74, 81, 82	2.80	5.00
MS7	1977 (5)	520,000	Y#72a, 73a, 74, 81, 82	3.00	6.50
MS8	1978 (5)	488,000	Y#72a, 73a, 74, 81, 82	3.50	6.50
MS9	1979 (5)	400,000	Y#72a, 73a, 74, 81, 82	3.80	7.50
MS10	1980 (5)	520,000	Y#72a, 73a, 74, 81, 82	3.20	6.50
MS11	1981 (5)	568,000	Y#72a, 73a, 74, 81, 82	4.00	6.50
MS12	1982 (6)	632,000	Y#72a, 73a, 74, 81, 82, 87	6.80	9.00
MS13	1983 (6)	502,000	Y#72a, 73a, 74, 81, 82, 87	6.80	16.00
MS14	1984 (6)	520,000	Y#72a, 73a, 74, 81, 82, 87	7.40	18.00
MS15	1985 (7)	720,000	Y#72a, 73a, 74, 81, 82, 87, 88 Tsukuba Expo box	8.50	18.50
MS16	1985 (7)	100,000	Y#72a, 73a, 74, 81, 82, 87, 88 Tsukuba Expo box, sold on the grounds of the Expo	8.50	90.00
MS17	1985 (7)	746,000	Y#72a, 73a, 74, 81, 82, 87, 89	10.50	18.50
MS18	1986 (7)	642,000	Y#72a, 73a, 74, 81, 82, 87, 90	15.00	18.50
MS19	1986 (6)	517,000	Y#72a, 73a, 74, 81, 82, 87	9.20	12.00
MS20	1987 (6)	496,483	Y#72a, 73a, 74, 81, 82, 87	12.00	175
MS21	1987 (6)	48,537	Y#72a, 73a, 74, 81, 82, 87 Cherry blossom box	12.00	200
MS22	1988 (6)	605,021	Y#72a, 73a, 74, 81, 82, 87	12.40	13.00
MS23	1988 (6)	41,979	Y#72a, 73a, 74, 81, 82, 87 Cherry blossom box	12.40	20.00
MS24	1988 (2)	400,000	Y#93-94	15.20	20.00
MS25	1989 (6)	647,000	Y#95.1-99.1, 101.1	12.80	27.50
MS26	1990 (6)	600,000	Y#95.2-99.2, 101.2	2.00	18.00
MS27	1991 (6)	600,000	Y#95.2-99.2, 101.2	13.00	12.50
MS28	1991 (6)	10,000	Y#95.2-99.2, 101.2 Hiroshima cherry blossom box	13.60	60.00
MS29	1991 (6)	50,000	Y#95.2-99.2, 101.2 Osaka cherry blossom box	13.60	24.00
MS30	1991 (6)	40,000	Y#95.2-99.2, 101.2 "120th Anniversary of the Mint" box	13.60	20.00
MS34	1992 (6)	30,000	Y#95.2-99.2, 101.2 Toyama Expo box	13.60	30.00
MS31	1992 (7)	650,000	Y#95.2-99.2, 101.2, 106	18.40	21.00
MS32	1992 (6)	20,000	Y#95.2-99.2, 101.2 Hiroshima cherry blossom box	13.60	30.00
MS33	1992 (6)	50,000	Y#95.2-99.2, 101.2 Osaka cherry blossom box	13.60	25.00
MS35	1993 (7)	800,000	Y#95.2-99.2, 101.2, 107	22.50	25.00
MS36	1993 (6)	70,000	Y#95.2-99.2, 101.2 Osaka cherry blossom box	17.10	30.00
MS37	1993 (6)	30,000	Y#95.2-99.2, 101.2 Hiroshima cherry blossom box	17.10	30.00
MS38	1993 (6)	10,000	Y#95.2-99.2, 101.2 Tokyo Coin Expo box	17.10	45.00
MS39	1993 (6)	30,000	Y#95.2-99.2, 101.2 Nagano-Shinano expo box	17.10	27.50
MS40	1993 (6)	100,000	Y#95.2-99.2, 101.2 "Respect for the Aged" box	19.80	24.00
MS41	1994 (6)	80,000	Y#95.2-99.2, 101.2 Osaka cherry blossom box	19.00	32.50
MS42	1994 (6)	20,000	Y#95.2-99.2, 101.2 Hiroshima cherry blossom box	19.00	30.00
MS43	1994 (6)	10,000	Y#95.2-99.2, 101.2 "5th International Tokyo Coin Convention" box	19.00	32.50
MS44	1994 (6)	10,000	Y#95.2-99.2, 101.2 "Transfer of the Heian Capitol" box	19.00	125
MS45	1994 (6)	30,000	Y#95.2-99.2, 101.2 "Mie Festival Exposition" box	19.00	30.00
MS46	1994 (6)	800,000	Y#95.2-99.2, 101.2 Mint box	18.00	23.00
MS47	1994 (6)	100,000	Y#95.2-99.2, 101.2 "Respect for the Aged" box	22.00	25.00
MS48	1994 (6)	10,000	Y#95.2-99.2, 101.2 "Toyko Branch Mint Coin Fair" box	19.00	30.00
MSA49	1994 (1)	20,000	Y#99.2 Mint visit souvenir folder	9.00	15.00
MS49	1995 (6)	80,000	Y#95.2-99.2, 101.2 Osaka cherry blossom box	19.00	30.00
MS50	1995 (6)	10,000	Y#95.2-99.2, 101.2 Hiroshima cherry blossom box	19.00	32.50
MS51	1995 (6)	10,000	Y#95.2-99.2, 101.2 6th Tokyo International Coin Convention	19.00	32.50
MS52	1995 (6)	10,000	Y#95.2-99.2, 101.2 "Romantopia '95" box	19.00	35.00
MS53	1995 (6)	10,000	Y#95.2-99.2, 101.2 "Coin and Banknote Fair" box	19.00	32.50
MS54	1995 (6)	12,000	Y#95.2-99.2, 101.2 50th Anniversary Hiroshima Branch Mint	19.00	32.50
MS55	1995 (6)	600,000	Y#95.2-99.2, 101.2 Mint production scenes box	18.00	23.00
MS56	1995 (6)	200,000	Y#95.2-99.2, 101.2 "Respect for the Aged" box	22.00	25.00
MS57	1995 (6)	390,000	Y#95.2-99.2, 101.2 Horyuji Temple folder	19.00	22.50
MS58	1995 (6)	192,500	Y#95.2-99.2, 101.2 Himeji Castle folder	19.00	24.00
MS59	1995 (6)	191,500	Y#95.2-99.2, 101.2 Ancient Kyoto folder	19.00	24.00
MS60	1995 (6)	177,500	Y#95.2-99.2, 101.2 Yakushima folder	19.00	24.00
MS61	1995 (6)	174,500	Y#95.2-99.2, 101.2 Shirakami Mountains folder	19.00	24.00
MS62	1995 (6)	10,000	Y#95.2-99.2, 101.2 "Tokyo Mint Fair" box	18.00	30.00
MS63	1995 (1)	20,000	Y#99.2 Mint visit souvenir folder	8.50	12.00
MS64	1995 (6)	20,000	Y#95.2-99.2, 101.2 Birthday folder	20.00	30.00
MS65	1996 (6)	80,000	Y#95.2-99.2, 101.2 Osaka cherry blossom box	17.00	35.00
MS66	1996 (6)	10,000	Y#95.2-99.2, 101.2 Hiroshima cherry blossom box	17.00	35.00
MS67	1996 (1)	10,000	Y#99.2 Mint visit souvenir folder	8.00	12.00
MS68	1996 (6)	10,000	Y#95.2-99.2, 101.2 Birthday folder	19.00	35.00
MS69	1996 (6)	10,000	Y#95.2-99.2, 101.2 "7th Tokyo International Coin Convention" box	17.00	32.50
MS70	1996 (6)	20,000	Y#95.2-99.2, 101.2 "Saga World Ceramics Expo" box	17.00	30.00
MS71	1996 (6)	8,000	Y#95.2-99.2, 101.2 "Okayama Coin, Banknote, and Stamp Exhibiton" box	17.00	35.00
MS72	1996 (6)	290,000	Y#95.2-99.2, 101.2 Shirakawa district folder	18.00	27.00
MS73	1996 (6)	200,000	Y#95.2-99.2, 101.2 "Respect for the Aged" box	20.00	30.00
MS74	1996 (6)	100,000	Y#95.2-99.2, 101.2 "125th Anniversary Birth of the Yen" folder	27.00	90.00
MS75	1996 (6)	321,000	Y#95.2-99.2, 101.2 Aerial view of old and new mint box	16.00	30.00
MS76	1996 (6)	6,000	Y#95.2-99.2, 101.2 Toyko Branch Mint fair box	17.00	32.50
MS77	1997 (1)	10,000	Y#101.2 Mint visit souvenir folder	8.00	12.00
MS78	1997 (6)	10,000	Y#95.2-99.2, 101.2 Birthday folder	17.00	32.50
MS79	1997 (6)	80,000	Y#95.2-99.2, 101.2 Osaka cherry blossom box	16.00	32.50
MS80	1997 (6)	10,000	Y#95.2-99.2, 101.2 Hiroshima cherry blossom box	16.00	35.00
MS81	1997 (6)	10,000	Y#95.2-99.2, 101.2 "8th Toyko International Coin Convention" box	16.00	30.00
MS82	1997 (6)	20,000	Y#95.2-99.2, 101.2 Tottori '97 Expo box	16.00	35.00
MS83	1997 (6)	10,000	Y#95.2-99.2, 101.2 Yamagata Coin, Note, and Stamp Exibition box	16.00	35.00
MS84	1997 (6)	331,000	Y#95.2-99.2, 101.2 Mint Bureau box	14.00	25.00
MS85	1997 (6)	250,000	Y#95.2-99.2, 101.2 "Respect for the Aged" box	15.50	28.00
MS86	1997 (6)	8,000	Y#95.2-99.2, 101.2 Tokyo Mint Fair box	15.00	30.00
MS87	1997	195,000	Y#95.2-99.2, 101.2 Hiroshima Peace Dome folder	15.50	30.00
MS88	1997 (6)	205,000	Y#95.2-99.2, 101.2 Itsukushima Shrine folder	15.50	30.00
MS89	1998 (1)	10,000	Y#99.2 Mint visit souvenir folder	7.00	12.00
MS90	1998 (6)	10,000	Y#95.2-99.2, 101.2 Birthday folder	16.00	35.00
MS91	1998 (6)	81,000	Y#95.2-99.2, 101.2 Osaka cherry blossom box	14.50	32.50
MS92	1998 (6)	10,000	Y#95.2-99.2, 101.2 Hiroshima cherry blossom box	14.50	32.50
MS93	1998 (6)	13,000	Y#95.2-99.2, 101.2 "9th Tokyo International Coin Convention" box	14.50	30.00
MS94	1998 (6)	257,000	Y#95.2-99.2, 101.2 "Respect for the Aged" box	17.00	28.00
MS95	1998 (6)	10,000	Y#95.2-99.2, 101.2 "World Cup - Japan vs. Argentina" box	17.00	45.00
MS96	1998 (6)	10,000	Y#95.2-99.2, 101.2 "World Cup - Japan vs. Croatia" box	17.00	45.00
MS97	1998 (6)	10,000	Y#95.2-99.2, 101.2 "World Cup - Japan vs. Jamaica" box	17.00	45.00
MS98	1998 (6)	336,000	Y#95.2-99.2, 101.2 Mint Bureau box	17.50	28.00
MS99	1998 (6)	6,000	Y#95.2-99.2, 101.2 Tokyo Mint Fair box	18.05	30.00
MS100	1999 (6)	20,000	Y#95.2-99.2, 101.2 Birthday box	19.95	35.00
MS101	1999 (1)	20,000	Y#99.2 Mint visit souvenir folder	8.55	12.00
MS102	1999 (6)	6,000	Y#95.2-99.2, 101.2 Kumamoto mint box	1,805	45.00
MS103	1999 (6)	80,000	Y#95.2-99.2, 101.2 Osaka cherry blossom box	18.05	32.50
MS104	1999 (6)	10,000	Y#95.2-99.2, 101.2 Hiroshima cherry blossom box	18.05	40.00
MS105	1999 (6)	10,000	Y#95.2-99.2, 101.2 International Coin Convention box	18.05	35.00
MS106	1999 (6)	10,000	Y#95.2-99.2, 101.2 Akita exhibit box	18.55	40.00
MS107	1999 (6)	6,000	Y#95.2-99.2, 101.2 Tokyo Mint Fair box	18.55	40.00
MS108	1999 (6)	200,000	Y#95.2-99.2, 101.2 Nara Monasteries folder	18.55	32.50
MS109	1999 (6)	250,000	Y#95.2-99.2, 101.2 "Respect for the Aged" box	18.55	32.50
MS110	1999 (6)	300,000	Y#95.2-99.2, 101.2 Mint Bureau box	18.55	35.00
MS111	2000 (5)	5,000	Y#95.2-98.2, 101.2 Branch mint in Nagoya box	11.00	30.00
MS112	2000 (5)	65,000	Y#95.2-98.2, 101.2, 125 Osaka cherry blossom box	11.00	25.00
MS113	2000 (5)	10,000	Y#95.2-98.2, 101.2, 125 Hiroshima cherry blossom box	11.00	25.00
MS114	2000 (5)	10,000	Y#95.2-98.2, 101.2, 125 400th Anniversary Japanese-Dutch relation at Nagsaki box	11.00	40.00
MS115	2000 (5)	10,000	Y#95.2-98.2, 101.2, 125 11th Tokyo International Coin Convention box	11.00	25.00
MS116	2000 (5)	7,000	Y#95.2-98.2, 101.2, 125 Otaru Coin and Stamp Show box	11.00	20.00
MS117	2000 (5)	4,000	Y#95.2-98.2, 101.2, 125 Tokyo Mint Fair box	11.00	25.00
MS118	2000 (6)	5,600	Y#95.2-99.2, 101.2 "Japan Coin Set" box	17.00	20.00
MS119	2000 (2)	4,000	Y#96.2, 125 "Japan Coins" short set	8.50	15.00
MS120	2000 (6)	222,300	Y#95.2-99.2, 101.2 Nikko World Cultural Sites	17.00	25.00
MS121	2000 (6)	340,200	Y#95.2-99.2, 101.2 Mint Bureau boX	15.00	18.00
MS122	2000 (2)	4,500	Y#95.2-98.2, 101.2, 125 Birthday box	18.00	25.00
MS123	2000 (6)	155,400	Y#95.2-98.2, 101.2, 125 Millenium Respect for the Aged box	19.00	22.00
MS124	2000 (6)	8,000	Y#95.2-98.2, 101.2, 125 Branch mint in Kanazawa box	16.00	20.00
MS125	2001 (6)	8,000	Y#95.2-98.2, 101.2, 125 Branch mint in Fukuoka box	16.00	—
MS126	2001 (6)	85,000	Y#95.2-98.2, 101.2, 125 Osaka cherry blossoms box	17.00	—
MS127	2001 (6)	10,000	Y#95.2-98.2, 101.2, 125 Hiroshima cherry blossoms box	17.00	—
MS128	2001 (6)	10,000	Y#95.2-98.2, 101.2, 125 12th Tokyo International Coin Convention	17.00	—
MS129	2001 (6)	5,000	Y#95.2-98.2, 101.2, 125 Beautiful Future Exposition	17.00	—
MS130	2001 (6)	8,000	Y#95.2-98.2, 101.2, 125 Kagoshima Coin and Stamp Show	17.00	—
MS131	2001	5,000	Y#95.2-98.2, 101.2, 125 Tokyo Mint Fair	17.00	—
MS132	2001 (6)	5,000	Y#95.2-98.2, 101.2, 125 Yamaguchi Mica Exposition	17.00	—
MS133	2001 (6)	250,000	Y#95.2-98.2, 101.2, 125 21st Century Commemorative Respect for the Aged	17.00	—
MS134	2001 (6)	200,000	Y#95.2-98.2, 101.2, 125 Ryukyu World Cultural Sites	17.00	—
MS135	2001 (6)	10,000	Y#95.2-98.2, 101.2, 125 Birthday folder	18.00	—
MS136	2001 (1)	7,000	Y#125 Mint Visit Commemorative	8.00	—
MS137	2001 (6)	300,000	Y#95.2-98.2, 101.2, 125 Mint Bureau Box	15.00	—
MS138	2001 (6)	3,000	Y#95.2-98.2, 101.2, 125 "Japan Coins"	17.00	—
MS139	2001 (2)	3,000	Y#96.2, 125 "Japan Coins" (short set)	8.50	—
MS140	2001 (6)	150,000	Y#95.2-98.2, 101.2, 125 World Intangible Heritage - Nogaku	17.00	—

PROOF SETS

KM#	Date	Mintage	Identification	Issue Price	Mkt Val
PS1	1987 (6)	230,000	Y#72a, 73a, 74, 81, 82, 87	37.40	150
PS2	1988 (6)	200,000	Y#72a, 73a, 74, 81, 82, 87	46.50	50.00
PS3	1989 (6)	200,000	Y#95.1-99.1, 101.1	47.90	50.00
PS6	1992 (6)	250,000	Y#95.2-99.2, 101.2	55.65	55.00
PS7	1993 (6)	250,000	Y#95.2-99.2, 101.2	72.00	60.00
PS8	1993 (3)	100,000	Y#107-109	100	900
PS9	1993 (2)	100,000	Y#107-108	110	115
PS10	1994 (6)	227,000	Y#95.2-99.2, 101.2	72.00	60.00
PS11	1994 (3)	100,000	Y#111-113	68.00	90.00
PS12	1994 (1)	100,000	Y#110	27.00	40.00
PS13	1995 (6)	200,000	Y#95.2-99.2, 101.2	72.00	65.00
PS14	1996 (6)	189,000	Y#95.2-99.2, 101.2	103	85.00
PS15	1997 (3)	33,000	Y#114-116	413	810
PS16	1997 (2)	100,000	Y#114-115	99.00	160
PS17	1997 (3)	33,000	Y#117, 119, 121	406	810
PS18	1997 (2)	100,000	Y#117, 119	97.00	160
PS19	1997 (6)	1,000	Y#95.2-99.2, 101.2 "Japan Expo Tottori '97" box	59.00	400
PS20	1997 (6)	186,000	Y#95.2-99.2, 101.2	56.00	75.00
PS22	1998 (3)	33,000	Y#118, 120, 122	375	800
PS23	1998 (2)	100,000	Y#118, 120	90.00	100
PS24	1998 (6)	30,000	Y#95.2-99.2, 101.2 Akashi Strait Bridge Opening	59.00	85.00
PS25	1998 (6)	170,000	Y#95.2-99.2, 101.2 Mint Bureau box	62.50	60.00
PS29	1999 (2)	100,000	Y#123, 124	370	400
PS26	1999 (6)	70,000	Y#95.2-99.2, 101.2 Type Coin series	69.85	100
PS27	1999 (6)	50,000	Y#95.2-99.2, 101.2 Coastal Highway	69.85	100
PS28	1999 (6)	150,000	Y#95.2-99.2, 101.2 Bureau box	69.85	100
PS30	2000 (6)	100,000	Y#95.2-98.2, 101.2, 125 Old Type Coin Series	62.50	80.00
PS31	2000 (6)	126,000	Y#95.2-98.2, 101.2, 125 Mint Bureau Box	62,350	80.00
PS32	2000 (6)	150,000	Y#95.2-98.2, 101.2, 125 Mint Bureau Box	62.50	80.00
PS33	2000 (6)	100,000	Y#95.2-98.2, 101.2, 125 Old Type Coin Series	62.50	80.00

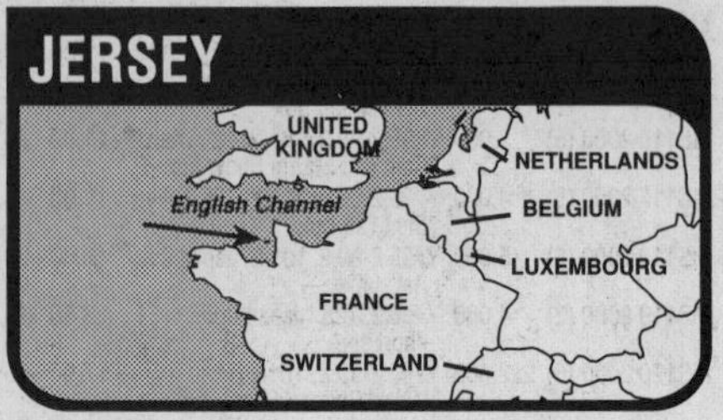

The Bailiwick of Jersey, a British Crown dependency located in the English Channel 12 miles (19 km.) west of Normandy, France, has an area of 45 sq. mi. (117 sq. km.) and a population of 74,000. Capital: St. Helier. The economy is based on agriculture and cattle breeding – the importation of cattle is prohibited to protect the purity of the island's world-famous strain of milch cows.

Jersey was occupied by Neanderthal man by 100,000 B.C., and by Iberians of 2000 B.C. who left their chamber tombs in the island's granite cliffs. Roman legions almost certainly visited the island although they left no evidence of settlement. The country folk of Jersey still speak an archaic form of Norman-French, lingering evidence of the Norman annexation of the island in 933 A.D. Jersey was annexed to England in 1206, 140 years after the Norman Conquest. The dependency is administered by its own laws and customs; laws enacted by the British Parliament do not apply to Jersey unless it is specifically mentioned. During World War II, German troops occupied the island from July1, 1940 until May 9, 1945.

Coins of pre-Roman Gaul and of Rome have been found in abundance on Jersey.

RULERS
British

MINT MARKS
H - Heaton, Birmingham

MONETARY SYSTEM
Commencing 1877
12 Pence = 1 Shilling
5 Shillings = 1 Crown
20 Shillings = 1 Pound
100 New Pence = 1 Pound

BRITISH DEPENDENCY

STANDARD COINAGE

KM# 9 1/24 SHILLING Composition: Bronze **Obverse:** Bust of King Edward VII right **Reverse:** Arms

Date	Mintage	F	VF	XF	Unc	BU
1909	120,000	1.00	2.50	11.50	25.00	—

KM# 11 1/24 SHILLING Composition: Bronze **Obverse:** Bust of King George V left **Reverse:** Arms

Date	Mintage	F	VF	XF	Unc	BU
1911	72,000	1.00	2.50	11.50	25.00	—
1913	72,000	1.00	2.50	11.50	25.00	—
1923	72,000	1.00	2.50	11.50	25.00	—

KM# 13 1/24 SHILLING Composition: Bronze **Obverse:** Bust of King George V left **Reverse:** Arms

Date	Mintage	F	VF	XF	Unc	BU
1923	72,000	0.75	3.00	5.50	22.50	—
1923 Proof	—	Value: 550				
1926	120,000	0.75	2.50	4.50	20.00	—
1926 Proof	—	Value: 550				

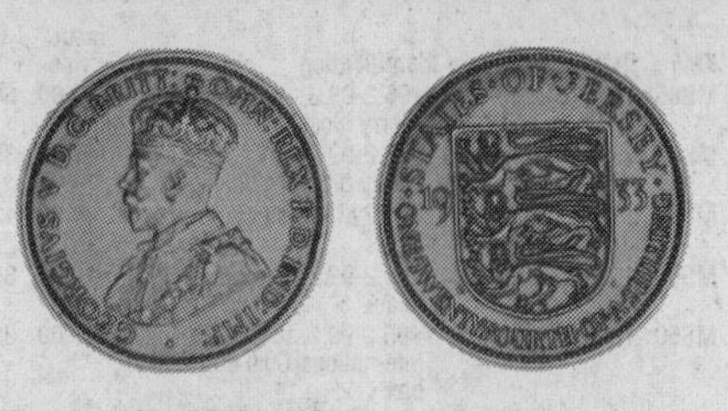

KM# 15 1/24 SHILLING Composition: Bronze **Obverse:** Bust of King George V left **Reverse:** Arms

Date	Mintage	F	VF	XF	Unc	BU
1931	72,000	0.50	1.00	3.00	15.00	—
1931 Proof	—	Value: 165				
1933	72,000	0.50	1.00	3.00	15.00	—
1933 Proof	—	Value: 165				
1935	72,000	0.50	1.00	3.00	15.00	—
1935 Proof	—	Value: 165				

KM# 17 1/24 SHILLING Composition: Bronze **Obverse:** Bust of King George VI left **Reverse:** Arms

Date	Mintage	F	VF	XF	Unc	BU
1937	72,000	0.50	1.00	3.00	15.00	—
1937 Proof	—	Value: 125				
1946	72,000	0.50	1.00	3.00	15.00	—
1946 Proof	—	Value: 125				
1947	72,000	0.50	1.00	3.00	15.00	—
1947 Proof	—	Value: 125				

KM# 10 1/12 SHILLING Composition: Bronze **Obverse:** Bust of King Edward VII right **Reverse:** Arms

Date	Mintage	F	VF	XF	Unc	BU
1909	180,000	0.75	3.50	12.50	60.00	—

KM# 12 1/12 SHILLING Composition: Bronze **Obverse:** Bust of King George V left **Reverse:** Arms

Date	Mintage	F	VF	XF	Unc	BU
1911	204,000	0.50	1.50	5.00	35.00	—
1913	204,000	0.50	1.50	5.00	35.00	—
1923	204,000	0.50	1.50	5.00	35.00	—

KM# 14 1/12 SHILLING Composition: Bronze **Obverse:** Bust of King George V left **Reverse:** Arms

Date	Mintage	F	VF	XF	Unc	BU
1923	301,000	0.50	1.50	5.00	30.00	—
1926	83,000	0.75	2.50	10.00	40.00	—

KM# 16 1/12 SHILLING Composition: Bronze **Obverse:** Bust of King George V left **Reverse:** Arms

Date	Mintage	F	VF	XF	Unc	BU
1931	204,000	0.50	1.25	3.00	12.00	—
1931 Proof	—	Value: 125				
1933	204,000	0.50	1.25	3.00	12.00	—
1933 Proof	—	Value: 125				
1935	204,000	0.50	1.25	3.00	12.00	—
1935 Proof	—	Value: 125				

KM# 18 1/12 SHILLING Composition: Bronze **Obverse:** Bust of King George VI left **Reverse:** Arms

Date	Mintage	F	VF	XF	Unc	BU
1937	204,000	0.50	1.00	2.50	10.00	—
1937 Proof	—	Value: 125				
1946	204,000	0.50	1.00	2.50	10.00	—
1946 Proof	—	Value: 125				
1947	444,000	0.25	0.50	1.50	7.50	—
1947 Proof	—	Value: 125				

KM# 19 1/12 SHILLING Composition: Bronze **Subject:** Liberation Commemorative **Obverse:** Bust of King George VI left **Reverse:** Arms

Date	Mintage	F	VF	XF	Unc	BU
1945	1,000,000	0.25	0.50	1.00	5.00	—
1945 Proof	—	Value: 100				

Note: Struck between 1949-52

KM# 20 1/12 SHILLING Composition: Bronze **Obverse:** Head of Queen Elizabeth II right **Reverse:** Arms

Date	Mintage	F	VF	XF	Unc	BU
ND (1954)	720,000	0.25	0.50	1.00	3.50	—
ND (1954) Proof	—	Value: 100				

KM# 21 1/12 SHILLING Composition: Bronze **Obverse:** Head of Queen Elizabeth II right

Date	Mintage	F	VF	XF	Unc	BU
1957	720,000	0.25	0.45	0.75	2.00	—
1957 Proof	2,100	Value: 7.50				
1964	1,200,000	0.25	0.45	0.75	1.50	—
1964 Proof	20,000	Value: 2.00				

KM# 24 1/12 SHILLING **Composition:** Bronze **Obverse:** Head of Queen Elizabeth II right **Reverse:** KM#23

Date	Mintage	F	VF	XF	Unc	BU
ND Proof	—	Value: 65.00				

KM# 23 1/12 SHILLING **Composition:** Bronze **Subject:** 300th Anniversary - Accession of King Charles II **Obverse:** Head of Queen Elizabeth II right

Date	Mintage	F	VF	XF	Unc	BU
ND (1960)	1,200,000	0.25	0.45	0.75	1.50	—
ND (1960) Proof	4,200	Value: 4.00				

KM#26 1/12 SHILLING **Composition:** Bronze **Subject:** Norman Conquest **Obverse:** Head of Queen Elizabeth II right

Date	Mintage	F	VF	XF	Unc	BU
ND (1966)	1,200,000	0.25	0.45	0.75	1.50	—
ND (1966) Proof	30,000	Value: 2.00				

KM# 22 1/4 SHILLING (3 Pence) **Composition:** Nickel-Brass **Obverse:** Head of Queen Elizabeth II right

Date	Mintage	F	VF	XF	Unc	BU
1957	2,000,000	0.10	0.15	0.50	3.00	—
1957 Proof	6,300	Value: 7.50				
1960 Proof	4,200	Value: 8.50				

KM# 25 1/4 SHILLING (3 Pence) **Composition:** Nickel-Brass **Obverse:** Head of Queen Elizabeth II right

Date	Mintage	F	VF	XF	Unc	BU
1964	1,200,000	0.10	0.15	0.20	0.75	—
1964 Proof	20,000	Value: 2.00				

KM# 27 1/4 SHILLING (3 Pence) **Composition:** Nickel-Brass **Subject:** Norman Conquest **Obverse:** Head of Queen Elizabeth II right

Date	Mintage	F	VF	XF	Unc	BU
ND (1966)	1,200,000	0.10	0.15	0.35	1.25	—
ND (1966) Proof	30,000	Value: 2.00				

KM# 28 5 SHILLING **Composition:** Copper-Nickel **Subject:** Norman Conquest **Obverse:** Head of Queen Elizabeth II right

Date	Mintage	F	VF	XF	Unc	BU
ND (1966)	300,000	—	1.00	2.00	3.50	—
ND (1966) Proof	30,000	Value: 6.00				

DECIMAL COINAGE

100 New Pence = 1 Pound

Many of the following coins are also struck in silver, gold, and platinum for collectors

KM# 29 1/2 NEW PENNY **Composition:** Bronze **Obverse:** Bust of Queen Elizabeth II right

Date	Mintage	F	VF	XF	Unc	BU
1971	3,000,000	—	—	0.10	0.20	—
1980	200,000	—	—	0.10	0.20	—
1980 Proof	10,000	Value: 1.35				

KM# 45 1/2 PENNY **Composition:** Bronze **Obverse:** Bust of Queen Elizabeth II right

Date	Mintage	F	VF	XF	Unc	BU
1981	50,000	—	—	—	0.10	—
1981 Proof	15,000	Value: 0.90				

KM# 30 NEW PENNY **Composition:** Bronze **Obverse:** Bust of Queen Elizabeth II right

Date	Mintage	F	VF	XF	Unc	BU
1971	4,500,000	—	—	0.10	0.20	—
1980	3,000,000	—	—	0.10	0.20	—
1980 Proof	10,000	Value: 1.80				

KM# 46 PENNY **Composition:** Bronze **Obverse:** Bust of Queen Elizabeth II right

Date	Mintage	F	VF	XF	Unc	BU
1981	50,000	—	—	0.10	0.15	—
1981 Proof	15,000	Value: 1.10				

KM# 54 PENNY **Composition:** Bronze **Obverse:** Bust of Queen Elizabeth II right **Reverse:** Le Hocq Watch Tower, St. Clement

Date	Mintage	F	VF	XF	Unc	BU
1983	500,000	—	—	0.10	0.25	—
1984	1,000,000	—	—	0.10	0.25	—
1985	1,000,000	—	—	0.10	0.25	—
1986	2,000,000	—	—	0.10	0.25	—
1987	1,500,000	—	—	0.10	0.25	—
1988	1,000,000	—	—	0.10	0.25	—
1989	1,500,000	—	—	0.10	0.25	—
1990	2,000	—	—	0.10	0.25	—
1992 In sets only	—	—	—	—	0.50	—

KM# 54a PENNY **Weight:** 4.2000 g. **Composition:** 0.9250 Silver .1249 oz. ASW **Obverse:** Bust of Queen Elizabeth II right **Reverse:** Le Hocq Watch Tower, St. Clement

Date	Mintage	F	VF	XF	Unc	BU
1983 Proof	5,000	Value: 7.00				

KM# 54b PENNY **Composition:** Copper Plated Steel **Obverse:** Bust of Queen Elizabeth II right **Reverse:** Le Hocq Watch Tower, St. Clement

Date	Mintage	F	VF	XF	Unc	BU
1994	2,000,000	—	—	0.10	0.50	—
1997	320,000	—	—	0.10	0.50	—

KM# 103 PENNY **Composition:** Copper Plated Steel **Obverse:** Portrait of Queen Elizabeth II **Obv. Designer:** Rank-Broadley

Date	Mintage	F	VF	XF	Unc	BU
1998	9,300,000	—	—	0.10	0.50	—
2002	—	—	—	0.10	0.50	—

KM# 31 2 NEW PENCE **Composition:** Bronze **Obverse:** Bust of Queen Elizabeth II right

Date	Mintage	F	VF	XF	Unc	BU
1971	2,225,000	—	—	0.15	0.30	—
1975	750,000	—	—	0.15	0.40	—
1980	2,000,000	—	—	0.15	0.30	—
1980 Proof	10,000	Value: 2.25				

KM# 47 2 PENCE **Composition:** Bronze **Obverse:** Bust of Queen Elizabeth II right

Date	Mintage	F	VF	XF	Unc	BU
1981	50,000	—	—	0.15	0.25	—
1981 Proof	15,000	Value: 1.35				

KM# 55 2 PENCE Composition: Bronze **Obverse:** Bust of Queen Elizabeth II right **Reverse:** L'Hermitage, St. Helier

Date	Mintage	F	VF	XF	Unc	BU
1983	800,000	—	—	0.15	0.25	—
1984	750,000	—	—	0.15	0.25	—
1985	250,000	—	—	0.15	0.25	—
1986	1,000,000	—	—	0.15	0.25	—
1987	2,000,000	—	—	0.15	0.25	—
1988	750,000	—	—	0.15	0.25	—
1989	1,000,000	—	—	0.15	0.25	—
1990	2,600,000	—	—	0.15	0.25	—
1997	5,500	—	—	—	0.50	—

KM# 55a 2 PENCE Weight: 8.4000 g. **Composition:** 0.9250 Silver .2498 oz. ASW **Obverse:** Bust of Queen Elizabeth II right **Reverse:** L'Hermitage, St. Helier

Date	Mintage	F	VF	XF	Unc	BU
1983 Proof	5,000	Value: 10.00				

KM# 55b 2 PENCE Composition: Bronze Clad Steel **Obverse:** Bust of Queen Elizabeth II right **Reverse:** L'Hermitage, St. Helier **Note:** Released into circulation in 1998.

Date	F	VF	XF	Unc	BU
1992	—	—	0.15	0.50	—

KM# 104 2 PENCE Composition: Copper Plated Steel **Obverse:** Portrait of Queen Elizabeth II **Obv. Designer:** Rank-Broadley **Reverse:** L'Hermitage, St. Helier

Date	Mintage	F	VF	XF	Unc	BU
1998	50,000	—	—	0.15	0.50	—
2002	—	—	—	0.15	0.50	—

KM# 32 5 NEW PENCE Composition: Copper-Nickel **Obverse:** Bust of Queen Elizabeth II right

Date	Mintage	F	VF	XF	Unc	BU
1968	3,600,000	—	0.15	0.25	1.00	—
1980	800,000	—	0.15	0.25	1.00	—
1980 Proof	10,000	Value: 2.75				

KM# 48 5 PENCE Composition: Copper-Nickel **Obverse:** Bust of Queen Elizabeth II right

Date	Mintage	F	VF	XF	Unc	BU
1981	50,000	—	0.15	0.25	1.00	—
1981 Proof	15,000	Value: 1.80				

KM# 56.1 5 PENCE Composition: Copper-Nickel **Obverse:** Bust of Queen Elizabeth II right **Reverse:** Seymour Tower, Grouville, L'Avathison

Date	Mintage	F	VF	XF	Unc	BU
1983	400,000	—	0.10	0.20	1.00	—
1984	300,000	—	0.10	0.20	1.00	—
1985	600,000	—	0.10	0.20	1.00	—
1986	200,000	—	0.10	0.20	1.00	—
1987 In sets only	—	—	—	—	0.50	—
1988	400,000	—	0.10	0.20	1.00	—

KM# 56.1a 5 PENCE Weight: 6.6000 g. **Composition:** 0.9250 Silver .1963 oz. ASW **Obverse:** Bust of Queen Elizabeth II right **Reverse:** Seymour Tower, Grouville, L'Avathison

Date	Mintage	F	VF	XF	Unc	BU
1983 Proof	5,000	Value: 10.00				

KM# 56.2 5 PENCE Composition: Copper-Nickel **Obverse:** Bust of Queen Elizabeth II right **Reverse:** Seymour Tower, Grouville, L'Avathison **Note:** Reduced size.

Date	Mintage	F	VF	XF	Unc	BU
1990	4,000,000	—	—	0.15	0.35	—
1991	2,000,000	—	—	0.15	0.35	—
1992	1,000,000	—	—	0.15	0.50	—
1993	2,000,000	—	—	0.15	0.50	—
1997 In sets only	5,500	—	—	—	1.00	—

KM# 105 5 PENCE Composition: Copper-Nickel **Obverse:** Portrait of Queen Elizabeth II **Obv. Designer:** Rank-Broadley

Date	Mintage	F	VF	XF	Unc	BU
1998	50,000	—	—	0.15	0.50	—
2002	—	—	—	0.15	0.50	—

KM# 33 10 NEW PENCE Composition: Copper-Nickel **Obverse:** Bust of Queen Elizabeth II right

Date	Mintage	F	VF	XF	Unc	BU
1968	1,500,000	—	0.20	0.35	1.00	—
1975	1,022,000	—	0.20	0.30	0.90	—
1980	1,000,000	—	0.20	0.30	0.75	—
1980 Proof	10,000	Value: 5.50				

KM# 49 10 PENCE Composition: Copper-Nickel **Obverse:** Bust of Queen Elizabeth II right

Date	Mintage	F	VF	XF	Unc	BU
1981	50,000	—	—	0.30	1.00	—
1981 Proof	15,000	Value: 2.25				

KM# 57.1 10 PENCE Composition: Copper-Nickel **Obverse:** Bust of Queen Elizabeth II right **Reverse:** La Houque Bie, Faldouet, St. Martin

Date	Mintage	F	VF	XF	Unc	BU
1983	30,000	—	—	0.30	1.00	—
1984	100,000	—	—	0.30	1.00	—
1985	100,000	—	—	0.30	1.00	—
1986	400,000	—	—	0.30	0.75	—
1987	800,000	—	—	0.30	0.75	—
1988	650,000	—	—	0.30	0.75	—
1989	700,000	—	—	0.30	0.75	—
1990	850,000	—	—	0.30	0.75	—

KM# 57.1a 10 PENCE Weight: 13.2000 g. **Composition:** 0.9250 Silver .3926 oz. ASW **Obverse:** Bust of Queen Elizabeth II right **Reverse:** La Houque Bie, Faldouet, St. Martin

Date	Mintage	F	VF	XF	Unc	BU
1983 Proof	5,000	Value: 15.00				

KM# 57.2 10 PENCE Composition: Copper-Nickel **Obverse:** Bust of Queen Elizabeth II right **Reverse:** La Houque Bie, Faldouet, St. Martin **Note:** Reduced size.

Date	Mintage	F	VF	XF	Unc	BU
1992	7,000,000	—	—	0.30	0.50	—
1997 In sets only	5,500	—	—	—	1.00	—
2002	—	—	—	—	—	—

KM# 106 10 PENCE Composition: Copper-Nickel **Obverse:** Portrait of Queen Elizabeth II **Obv. Designer:** Rank-Broadley

Date	Mintage	F	VF	XF	Unc	BU
1998	50,000	—	—	—	1.00	—

Note: In sets only

Date	Mintage	F	VF	XF	Unc	BU
2002	—	—	—	—	1.00	—

KM# 53 20 PENCE Composition: Copper-Nickel **Subject:** 100th Anniversary of Lighthouse at Corbiere **Obverse:** Bust of Queen Elizabeth II right **Reverse:** Date below lighthouse

Date	Mintage	F	VF	XF	Unc	BU
1982	200,000	—	—	0.50	1.50	—

KM# 53a 20 PENCE Weight: 5.8300 g. **Composition:** 0.9250 Silver .1734 oz. ASW **Subject:** 100th Anniversary of Lighthouse at Corbiere **Obverse:** Bust of Queen Elizabeth II right **Reverse:** Date below lighthouse

Date	Mintage	F	VF	XF	Unc	BU
1982 Proof	1,500	Value: 15.00				

KM# 66 20 PENCE Composition: Copper-Nickel **Subject:** 100th Anniversary of Lighthouse at Corbiere **Obverse:** Bust of Queen Elizabeth II right **Reverse:** Date below bust

Date	Mintage	F	VF	XF	Unc	BU
1983	400,000	—	—	0.50	1.00	—
1984	250,000	—	—	0.50	1.00	—
1986	100,000	—	—	0.50	1.00	—
1987	100,000	—	—	0.50	1.00	—
1989	100,000	—	—	0.50	1.00	—
1990	150,000	—	—	0.50	1.00	—
1992 In sets only	—	—	—	—	2.00	—
1994	200,000	—	—	0.50	1.00	—
1996	250,000	—	—	0.50	1.00	—
1997	600,000	—	—	0.50	1.00	—
1998	—	—	—	0.50	1.00	—
2002	—	—	—	—	—	—

KM# 66a 20 PENCE Weight: 5.8300 g. **Composition:** 0.9250 Silver .1734 oz. ASW **Subject:** 100th Anniversary of Lighthouse at Corbiere **Obverse:** Bust of Queen Elizabeth II right **Reverse:** Date below bust

Date	Mintage	F	VF	XF	Unc	BU
1983 Proof	5,000	Value: 15.00				

KM# 107 20 PENCE Weight: 5.8300 g. **Composition:** 0.9250 Silver .1734 oz. ASW **Obverse:** Portrait of Queen Elizabeth II **Obv. Designer:** Rank-Broadley

Date	Mintage	F	VF	XF	Unc	BU
1998	90,000	—	—	0.50	1.00	—
2002	—	—	—	—	1.00	—

KM# 44 25 PENCE **Composition:** Copper-Nickel **Subject:** Queen's Silver Jublilee **Obverse:** Bust of Queen Elizabeth II right

Date	Mintage	F	VF	XF	Unc	BU
ND(1977)	262,000	—	0.75	1.25	3.75	—

KM# 44a 25 PENCE **Weight:** 28.2800 g. **Composition:** 0.9250 Silver .8411 oz. ASW **Subject:** Queen's Silver Jublilee **Obverse:** Bust of Queen Elizabeth II right

Date	Mintage	F	VF	XF	Unc	BU
ND(1977) Proof	25,000	Value: 16.50				

KM# 34 50 PENCE **Composition:** Copper-Nickel **Obverse:** Bust of Queen Elizabeth II right **Shape:** 7-sided

Date	Mintage	F	VF	XF	Unc	BU
1969	480,000	—	—	0.90	1.50	—
1980	100,000	—	—	0.90	1.50	—
1980 Proof	10,000	Value: 9.00				

KM# 35 50 PENCE **Weight:** 5.4200 g. **Composition:** 0.9250 Silver .1612 oz. ASW **Subject:** 25th Wedding Anniversary **Obverse:** Bust of Queen Elizabeth II right

Date	Mintage	F	VF	XF	Unc	BU
1972	24,000	—	—	1.25	3.50	—
1972 Proof	1,500	Value: 6.50				

KM# 50 50 PENCE **Composition:** Copper-Nickel **Obverse:** Bust of Queen Elizabeth II right **Shape:** 7-sided

Date	Mintage	F	VF	XF	Unc	BU
1981	50,000	—	—	1.00	1.75	—
1981 Proof	15,000	Value: 3.00				

KM# 58.1 50 PENCE **Composition:** Copper-Nickel **Obverse:** Bust of Queen Elizabeth II right **Reverse:** Grosnez Castle **Shape:** 7-sided

Date	Mintage	F	VF	XF	Unc	BU
1983	50,000	—	—	1.00	1.75	—
1984	50,000	—	—	1.00	1.75	—
1986	30,000	—	—	1.00	1.75	—
1987	150,000	—	—	1.00	1.75	—
1988	130,000	—	—	1.00	1.75	—
1989	180,000	—	—	1.00	1.75	—
1990	370,000	—	—	1.00	1.75	—
1992 In sets only	—	—	—	—	2.50	—
1994	200,000	—	—	1.00	1.75	—
1997 In sets only	5,500	—	—	—	2.50	—

KM# 58.1a 50 PENCE **Weight:** 15.5000 g. **Composition:** 0.9250 Silver .4609 oz. ASW **Obverse:** Bust of Queen Elizabeth II right **Reverse:** Grosnez Castle **Shape:** 7-sided

Date	Mintage	F	VF	XF	Unc	BU
1983 Proof	5,000	Value: 18.00				

KM# 58.2 50 PENCE **Composition:** Copper-Nickel **Obverse:** Bust of Queen Elizabeth II right **Reverse:** Grosnez Castle **Shape:** 7-sided **Note:** Small size.

Date	Mintage	F	VF	XF	Unc	BU
1997	1,500,000	—	—	—	2.50	—

KM# 63 50 PENCE **Composition:** Copper-Nickel **Subject:** 40th Anniversary - Liberation of 1945 **Obverse:** Bust of Queen Elizabeth II right

Date	Mintage	F	VF	XF	Unc	BU
1985	65,000	—	—	1.25	2.00	—

KM# 108 50 PENCE **Composition:** Copper-Nickel **Obverse:** Bust of Queen Elizabeth II right **Obv. Designer:** Rank-Broadley

Date	Mintage	F	VF	XF	Unc	BU
1998	25,000	—	—	1.00	2.50	—

KM# 36 POUND **Weight:** 10.8400 g. **Composition:** 0.9250 Silver .3224 oz. ASW **Subject:** 25th Wedding Anniversary **Obverse:** Bust of Queen Elizabeth II right

Date	Mintage	F	VF	XF	Unc	BU
1972	24,000	—	—	—	5.00	—
1972 Proof	1,500	Value: 12.00				

KM# 51 POUND **Composition:** Copper-Nickel **Subject:** Bicentennial - Battle of Jersey **Obverse:** Bust of Queen Elizabeth II right **Shape:** Square

Date	Mintage	F	VF	XF	Unc	BU
ND	200,000	—	—	2.00	3.25	—
ND Proof	15,000	Value: 8.00				

KM# 51a POUND **Weight:** 10.4500 g. **Composition:** 0.9250 Silver .3108 oz. ASW **Subject:** Bicentennial - Battle of Jersey **Obverse:** Bust of Queen Elizabeth II right **Shape:** Square

Date	Mintage	F	VF	XF	Unc	BU
ND Proof	10,000	Value: 12.50				

KM# 51b POUND **Weight:** 17.5500 g. **Composition:** 0.9170 Gold .5174 oz. AGW **Subject:** Bicentennial - Battle of Jersey **Obverse:** Bust of Queen Elizabeth II right **Shape:** Square

Date	Mintage	F	VF	XF	Unc	BU
ND Proof	5,000	Value: 250				

KM# 59 POUND **Composition:** Nickel-Brass **Obverse:** Bust of Queen Elizabeth II right **Reverse:** Parish of St. Helier arms

Date	Mintage	F	VF	XF	Unc	BU
1983	100,000	—	—	2.00	3.25	—

KM# 59a POUND **Weight:** 11.6800 g. **Composition:** 0.9250 Silver .3474 oz. ASW **Obverse:** Bust of Queen Elizabeth II right **Reverse:** Parish of St. Helier arms

Date	Mintage	F	VF	XF	Unc	BU
1983 Proof	2,500	Value: 20.00				

KM# 59b POUND **Weight:** 19.6500 g. **Composition:** 0.9170 Gold .5794 oz. AGW **Obverse:** Bust of Queen Elizabeth II right **Reverse:** Parish of St. Helier arms

Date	Mintage	F	VF	XF	Unc	BU
1983 Proof	250	Value: 250				

Note: 497 pieces were remelted

KM# 60 POUND **Composition:** Nickel-Brass **Obverse:** Bust of Queen Elizabeth II right **Reverse:** Parish of St. Saviour arms

Date	Mintage	F	VF	XF	Unc	BU
1984	20,000	—	—	2.00	3.25	—

KM# 60a POUND **Weight:** 11.6800 g. **Composition:** 0.9250 Silver .3474 oz. ASW **Obverse:** Bust of Queen Elizabeth II right **Reverse:** Parish of St. Saviour arms

Date	Mintage	F	VF	XF	Unc	BU
1984 Proof	2,500	Value: 18.50				

KM# 60b POUND **Weight:** 19.6500 g. **Composition:** 0.9170 Gold .5794 oz. AGW **Obverse:** Bust of Queen Elizabeth II right **Reverse:** Parish of St. Saviour arms

Date	Mintage	F	VF	XF	Unc	BU
1984 Proof	250	Value: 275				

KM# 61 POUND **Composition:** Nickel-Brass **Obverse:** Bust of Queen Elizabeth II right **Reverse:** Parish of St. Brelade arms

Date	Mintage	F	VF	XF	Unc	BU
1984	20,000	—	—	2.00	3.25	—

KM# 61a POUND **Weight:** 11.6800 g. **Composition:** 0.9250 Silver .3474 oz. ASW **Obverse:** Bust of Queen Elizabeth II right **Reverse:** Parish of St. Brelade arms

Date	Mintage	F	VF	XF	Unc	BU
1984 Proof	2,500	Value: 20.00				

KM# 61b POUND **Weight:** 19.6500 g. **Composition:** 0.9170 Gold .5794 oz. AGW **Obverse:** Bust of Queen Elizabeth II right **Reverse:** Parish of St. Brelade arms

Date	Mintage	F	VF	XF	Unc	BU
1984 Proof	250	Value: 275				

KM# 62 POUND **Composition:** Nickel-Brass **Obverse:** Bust of Queen Elizabeth II right **Reverse:** Parish of St. Clement arms

Date	Mintage	F	VF	XF	Unc	BU
1985	25,000	—	—	2.00	3.25	—

KM# 62a POUND **Weight:** 11.6800 g. **Composition:** 0.9250 Silver .3474 oz. ASW **Obverse:** Bust of Queen Elizabeth II right **Reverse:** Parish of St. Clement arms

Date	Mintage	F	VF	XF	Unc	BU
1985 Proof	2,500	Value: 18.50				

KM# 62b POUND **Weight:** 19.6500 g. **Composition:** 0.9170 Gold .5794 oz. AGW **Obverse:** Bust of Queen Elizabeth II right **Reverse:** Parish of St. Clement arms

Date	Mintage	F	VF	XF	Unc	BU
1985 Proof	124	Value: 300				

KM# 65 POUND **Composition:** Nickel-Brass **Obverse:** Bust of Queen Elizabeth II right **Reverse:** Parish of St. Lawrence arms

Date	Mintage	F	VF	XF	Unc	BU
1985	10,000	—	—	2.00	3.50	—

KM# 65a POUND **Weight:** 11.6800 g. **Composition:** 0.9250 Silver .3474 oz. ASW **Obverse:** Bust of Queen Elizabeth II right **Reverse:** Parish of St. Lawrence arms

Date	Mintage	F	VF	XF	Unc	BU
1985 Proof	2,500	Value: 20.00				

KM# 65b POUND **Weight:** 19.6500 g. **Composition:** 0.9170 Gold .5794 oz. AGW **Obverse:** Bust of Queen Elizabeth II right **Reverse:** Parish of St. Lawrence arms

Date	Mintage	F	VF	XF	Unc	BU
1985 Proof	108	Value: 325				

KM# 68 POUND **Composition:** Nickel-Brass **Obverse:** Bust of Queen Elizabeth II right **Reverse:** Parish of St. Peter arms

Date	Mintage	F	VF	XF	Unc	BU
1986	10,000	—	—	2.00	3.25	—

KM# 68a POUND **Weight:** 11.6800 g. **Composition:** 0.9250 Silver .3474 oz. ASW **Obverse:** Bust of Queen Elizabeth II right **Reverse:** Parish of St. Peter arms

Date	Mintage	F	VF	XF	Unc	BU
1986 Proof	2,500	Value: 20.00				

KM# 68b POUND **Weight:** 19.6500 g. **Composition:** 0.9170 Gold .5794 oz. AGW **Obverse:** Bust of Queen Elizabeth II right **Reverse:** Parish of St. Peter arms

Date	Mintage	F	VF	XF	Unc	BU
1986 Proof	250	Value: 275				

KM# 69 POUND **Composition:** Nickel-Brass **Obverse:** Bust of Queen Elizabeth II right **Reverse:** Parish of Grouville arms

Date	Mintage	F	VF	XF	Unc	BU
1986	10,000	—	—	2.00	3.25	—

KM# 69a POUND **Weight:** 11.6800 g. **Composition:** 0.9250 Silver .3474 oz. ASW **Obverse:** Bust of Queen Elizabeth II right **Reverse:** Parish of Grouville arms

Date	Mintage	F	VF	XF	Unc	BU
1986 Proof	2,500	Value: 20.00				

KM# 69b POUND **Weight:** 19.6500 g. **Composition:** 0.9170 Gold .5794 oz. AGW **Obverse:** Bust of Queen Elizabeth II right **Reverse:** Parish of Grouville arms

Date	Mintage	F	VF	XF	Unc	BU
1986 Proof	250	Value: 275				

KM# 71 POUND **Composition:** Nickel-Brass **Obverse:** Bust of Queen Elizabeth II right **Reverse:** Parish of St. Martin arms

Date	Mintage	F	VF	XF	Unc	BU
1987	10,000	—	—	2.00	3.50	—

KM# 71a POUND **Weight:** 11.6800 g. **Composition:** 0.9250 Silver .3474 oz. ASW **Obverse:** Bust of Queen Elizabeth II right **Reverse:** Parish of St. Martin arms

Date	Mintage	F	VF	XF	Unc	BU
1987 Proof	2,500	Value: 18.50				

KM# 71b POUND **Weight:** 19.6500 g. **Composition:** 0.9170 Gold .5794 oz. AGW **Obverse:** Bust of Queen Elizabeth II right **Reverse:** Parish of St. Martins arms

Date	Mintage	F	VF	XF	Unc	BU
1987 Proof	250	Value: 275				

KM# 72 POUND **Composition:** Nickel-Brass **Obverse:** Bust of Queen Elizabeth II right **Reverse:** Parish of St. Ouen arms

Date	Mintage	F	VF	XF	Unc	BU
1987	10,000	—	—	2.00	3.25	—

KM# 72a POUND **Weight:** 11.6800 g. **Composition:** 0.9250 Silver .3474 oz. ASW **Obverse:** Bust of Queen Elizabeth II right **Reverse:** Parish of St. Ouen arms

Date	Mintage	F	VF	XF	Unc	BU
1987 Proof	2,500	Value: 18.50				

KM# 72b POUND **Weight:** 19.6500 g. **Composition:** 0.9170 Gold .5794 oz. AGW **Obverse:** Bust of Queen Elizabeth II right **Reverse:** Parish of St. Ouen

Date	Mintage	F	VF	XF	Unc	BU
1987 Proof	250	Value: 285				

KM# 73 POUND **Composition:** Nickel-Brass **Obverse:** Bust of Queen Elizabeth II right **Reverse:** Parish of St. Trinity arms

Date	Mintage	F	VF	XF	Unc	BU
1988	10,000	—	—	2.00	4.00	—

KM# 73a POUND **Weight:** 11.6800 g. **Composition:** 0.9250 Silver .3474 oz. ASW **Obverse:** Bust of Queen Elizabeth II right **Reverse:** Parish of St. Trinity arms

Date	Mintage	F	VF	XF	Unc	BU
1988 Proof	2,500	Value: 18.50				

KM# 73b POUND **Weight:** 19.6500 g. **Composition:** 0.9170 Gold .5794 oz. AGW **Obverse:** Bust of Queen Elizabeth II right **Reverse:** Parish of St. Trinity arms

Date	Mintage	F	VF	XF	Unc	BU
1988 Proof	250	Value: 285				

KM# 74 POUND **Composition:** Nickel-Brass **Obverse:** Bust of Queen Elizabeth II right **Reverse:** Parish of St. John arms

Date	Mintage	F	VF	XF	Unc	BU
1988	10,000	—	—	2.00	3.25	—

KM# 74a POUND **Weight:** 11.6800 g. **Composition:** 0.9250 Silver .3474 oz. ASW **Obverse:** Bust of Queen Elizabeth II right **Reverse:** Parish of St. John arms

Date	Mintage	F	VF	XF	Unc	BU
1988 Proof	2,500	Value: 18.50				

KM# 74b POUND **Weight:** 19.6500 g. **Composition:** 0.9170 Gold .5794 oz. AGW **Obverse:** Bust of Queen Elizabeth II right **Reverse:** Parish of St. John arms

Date	Mintage	F	VF	XF	Unc	BU
1988 Proof	250	Value: 285				

KM# 75 POUND **Composition:** Nickel-Brass **Obverse:** Bust of Queen Elizabeth II right **Reverse:** Parish of St. Mary's arms

Date	Mintage	F	VF	XF	Unc	BU
1989	25,000	—	—	2.00	3.25	—

KM# 75a POUND **Weight:** 11.6800 g. **Composition:** 0.9250 Silver .3474 oz. ASW **Obverse:** Bust of Queen Elizabeth II right **Reverse:** Parish of St. Mary's arms

Date	Mintage	F	VF	XF	Unc	BU
1989 Proof	2,500	Value: 18.50				

KM# 75b POUND **Weight:** 19.6500 g. **Composition:** 0.9170 Gold .5794 oz. AGW **Obverse:** Bust of Queen Elizabeth II right **Reverse:** Parish of St. Mary's arms

Date	Mintage	F	VF	XF	Unc	BU
1989 Proof	250	Value: 285				

KM# 84 POUND **Composition:** Nickel-Brass **Obverse:** Bust of Queen Elizabeth II right **Reverse:** Schooner, The Tickler

Date	Mintage	F	VF	XF	Unc	BU
1991	15,000	—	—	—	3.25	—

KM# 84a POUND **Weight:** 11.6800 g. **Composition:** 0.9250 Silver .3474 oz. ASW **Obverse:** Bust of Queen Elizabeth II right **Reverse:** Schooner, The Tickler

Date	Mintage	F	VF	XF	Unc	BU
1991 Proof	3,000	Value: 20.00				

KM# 84b POUND **Weight:** 19.6500 g. **Composition:** 0.9170 Gold .5794 oz. AGW **Obverse:** Bust of Queen Elizabeth II right **Reverse:** Schooner, The Tickler

Date	Mintage	F	VF	XF	Unc	BU
1991 Proof	Est. 250	Value: 365				

KM# 85 POUND **Composition:** Nickel-Brass **Obverse:** Bust of Queen Elizabeth II right **Reverse:** Sailing ship, Percy Douglas

Date	Mintage	F	VF	XF	Unc	BU
1991	20,000	—	—	—	3.25	—

KM# 85a POUND **Weight:** 11.6800 g. **Composition:** 0.9250 Silver .3474 oz. ASW **Obverse:** Bust of Queen Elizabeth II right **Reverse:** Sailing ship, Percy Douglas

Date	Mintage	F	VF	XF	Unc	BU
1991 Proof	3,000	Value: 20.00				

KM# 85b POUND **Weight:** 19.6500 g. **Composition:** 0.9170 Gold .5794 oz. AGW **Obverse:** Bust of Queen Elizabeth II right **Reverse:** Sailing ship, Percy Douglas

Date	Mintage	F	VF	XF	Unc	BU
1991 Proof	250	Value: 365				

KM# 86 POUND **Composition:** Nickel-Brass **Obverse:** Bust of Queen Elizabeth II right **Reverse:** Sailing ship, Hebe

Date	Mintage	F	VF	XF	Unc	BU
1992	2,000	—	—	—	3.25	—

KM# 86a POUND **Weight:** 11.6800 g. **Composition:** 0.9250 Silver .3474 oz. ASW **Obverse:** Bust of Queen Elizabeth II right **Reverse:** Sailing ship, Hebe

Date	Mintage	F	VF	XF	Unc	BU
1992 Proof	Est. 3,000	Value: 20.00				

KM# 86b POUND **Weight:** 19.6500 g. **Composition:** 0.9170 Gold .5794 oz. AGW **Obverse:** Bust of Queen Elizabeth II right **Reverse:** Sailing ship, Hebe

Date	Mintage	F	VF	XF	Unc	BU
1992 Proof	Est. 250	Value: 365				

KM# 87 POUND **Composition:** Nickel-Brass **Obverse:** Bust of Queen Elizabeth II right **Reverse:** Ornamented coat of arms

Date	Mintage	F	VF	XF	Unc	BU
1992	20,000	—	—	—	3.50	—

KM# 87a POUND **Weight:** 11.6800 g. **Composition:** 0.9250 Silver .3474 oz. ASW **Obverse:** Bust of Queen Elizabeth II right **Reverse:** Ornamented coat of arms

Date	Mintage	F	VF	XF	Unc	BU
1992 Proof	3,000	Value: 20.00				

KM# 87b POUND **Weight:** 19.6500 g. **Composition:** 0.9170 Gold .5794 oz. AGW **Obverse:** Bust of Queen Elizabeth II right **Reverse:** Ornamented coat of arms

Date	Mintage	F	VF	XF	Unc	BU
1992 Proof	250	Value: 300				

KM# 88 POUND **Composition:** Nickel-Brass **Obverse:** Bust of Queen Elizabeth II right **Reverse:** Sailing ship, Gemini

Date	F	VF	XF	Unc	BU
1993	—	—	—	3.25	—

KM# 88a POUND **Weight:** 11.6800 g. **Composition:** 0.9250 Silver .3474 oz. ASW **Obverse:** Bust of Queen Elizabeth II right **Reverse:** Sailing ship, Gemini

Date	Mintage	F	VF	XF	Unc	BU
1993 Proof	3,000	Value: 20.00				

KM# 88b POUND **Weight:** 19.6500 g. **Composition:** 0.9170 Gold .5794 oz. AGW **Obverse:** Bust of Queen Elizabeth II right **Reverse:** Sailing ship, Gemini

Date	Mintage	F	VF	XF	Unc	BU
1993 Proof	250	Value: 375				

KM# 90 POUND **Composition:** Nickel-Brass **Obverse:** Bust of Queen Elizabeth II right **Reverse:** Sailing ship, Century

Date	F	VF	XF	Unc	BU
1993	—	—	—	3.25	—

KM# 90a POUND **Weight:** 11.6800 g. **Composition:** 0.9250 Silver .3474 oz. ASW **Obverse:** Bust of Queen Elizabeth II right **Reverse:** Sailing ship, Century

Date	Mintage	F	VF	XF	Unc	BU
1993 Proof	Est. 3,000	Value: 20.00				

KM# 90b POUND **Weight:** 19.6500 g. **Composition:** 0.9170 Gold .5794 oz. AGW **Obverse:** Bust of Queen Elizabeth II right **Reverse:** Sailing ship, Century

Date	Mintage	F	VF	XF	Unc	BU
1993 Proof	Est. 250	Value: 365				

KM# 91 POUND **Composition:** Nickel-Brass **Obverse:** Bust of Queen Elizabeth II right **Reverse:** Schooner, Resolute

Date	Mintage	F	VF	XF	Unc	BU
1994	60,000	—	—	—	3.25	—
1997	101,000	—	—	—	3.25	—

KM# 91a POUND **Weight:** 11.6800 g. **Composition:** 0.9250 Silver .3474 oz. ASW **Obverse:** Bust of Queen Elizabeth II right **Reverse:** Schooner, Resolute

Date	Mintage	F	VF	XF	Unc	BU
1994 Proof	3,000	Value: 20.00				

KM# 91b POUND **Weight:** 19.6500 g. **Composition:** 0.9170 Gold .5794 oz. AGW **Obverse:** Bust of Queen Elizabeth II right **Reverse:** Schooner, Resolute

Date	Mintage	F	VF	XF	Unc	BU
1994 Proof	250	Value: 365				

KM# 101 POUND **Composition:** Nickel-Brass **Obverse:** Portrait of Queen Elizabeth II **Obv. Designer:** Rank-Broadley **Reverse:** Schooner, Resolute **Edge Lettering:** CAESAREA INSULA

Date	Mintage	F	VF	XF	Unc	BU
1998	174,000	—	—	—	3.25	—

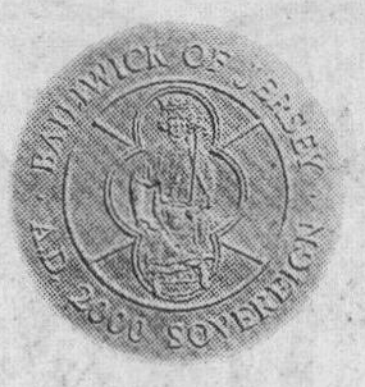

KM# 110 SOVEREIGN **Weight:** 7.9800 g. **Composition:** 0.9167 Gold .2352 oz. AGW **Subject:** William I - Duke of Normandy **Obverse:** Bust of Queen Elizabeth II right **Reverse:** William seated on throne

Date	Mintage	F	VF	XF	Unc	BU
2000	—	—	—	—	125	—
2000 Proof	Est. 2,000	Value: 225				

KM# 37 2 POUNDS **Weight:** 21.9000 g. **Composition:** 0.9250 Silver .6513 oz. ASW **Subject:** 25th Wedding Anniversary **Obverse:** Similar to 1 Pound, KM#36

Date	Mintage	F	VF	XF	Unc	BU
1972	24,000	—	—	—	11.50	—
1972 Proof	1,500	Value: 25.00				

KM# 52 2 POUNDS **Composition:** Copper-Nickel **Subject:** Wedding of Prince Charles and Lady Diana **Obverse:** Bust of Queen Elizabeth II right

Date	Mintage	F	VF	XF	Unc	BU
ND(1981)	150,000	—	—	—	6.00	—

KM# 52a 2 POUNDS **Weight:** 28.2800 g. **Composition:** 0.9250 Silver .8411 oz. ASW **Subject:** Wedding of Prince Charles and Lady Diana **Obverse:** Bust of Queen Elizabeth II right

Date	Mintage	F	VF	XF	Unc	BU
ND(1981) Proof	35,000	Value: 15.00				

KM# 52b 2 POUNDS **Weight:** 15.9800 g. **Composition:** 0.9170 Gold .4712 oz. AGW **Subject:** Wedding of Prince Charles and Lady Diana **Obverse:** Bust of Queen Elizabeth II right

Date	Mintage	F	VF	XF	Unc	BU
ND(1981) Proof	1,500	Value: 225				

KM# 64 2 POUNDS **Composition:** Copper-Nickel **Subject:** 40th Anniversary of Liberation of 1945 **Obverse:** Bust of Queen Elizabeth II right

Date	Mintage	F	VF	XF	Unc	BU
1985	20,000	—	—	—	6.00	—

KM# 64a 2 POUNDS **Weight:** 28.2800 g. **Composition:** 0.9250 Silver .8411 oz. ASW **Subject:** 40th Anniversary of Liberation of 1945 **Obverse:** Bust of Queen Elizabeth II right

Date	Mintage	F	VF	XF	Unc	BU
1985 Proof	2,500	Value: 35.00				

KM# 64b 2 POUNDS **Weight:** 47.5400 g. **Composition:** 0.9170 Gold 1.4011 oz. AGW **Subject:** 40th Anniversary of Liberation of 1945 **Obverse:** Bust of Queen Elizabeth II right

Date	Mintage	F	VF	XF	Unc	BU
1985 Proof	40	Value: 2,000				

KM# 67.1 2 POUNDS **Composition:** Copper-Nickel **Subject:** XIII Commonwealth Games - Edinburgh **Obverse:** Bust of Queen Elizabeth II right **Edge Lettering:** XIII COMMONWEALTH GAMES

Date	Mintage	F	VF	XF	Unc	BU
1986	50,000	—	—	—	6.00	—

KM# 67.2 2 POUNDS **Composition:** Copper-Nickel **Subject:** XIII Commonwealth Games - Edinburgh **Obverse:** Bust of Queen Elizabeth II right **Note:** Without edge inscription.

Date	Mintage	F	VF	XF	Unc	BU
1986	5,000	—	—	—	7.50	—

KM# 67.1a 2 POUNDS **Weight:** 28.2800 g. **Composition:** 0.5000 Silver .4546 oz. ASW **Subject:** XIII Commonwealth Games - Edinburgh **Obverse:** Bust of Queen Elizabeth II right

Date	Mintage	F	VF	XF	Unc	BU
1986	20,000	—	—	—	20.00	—

KM# 67.1b 2 POUNDS **Weight:** 28.2800 g. **Composition:** 0.9250 Silver .8411 oz. ASW **Subject:** XIII Commonwealth Games - Edinburgh **Obverse:** Bust of Queen Elizabeth II right

Date	Mintage	F	VF	XF	Unc	BU
1986 Proof	20,000	Value: 40.00				

KM# 70 2 POUNDS **Composition:** Copper-Nickel **Subject:** World Wildlife Fund **Obverse:** Bust of Queen Elizabeth II right **Reverse:** Mauritius pink pigeon

Date	Mintage	F	VF	XF	Unc	BU
1987	23,000	—	—	—	7.00	—

KM# 70a 2 POUNDS **Weight:** 28.2800 g. **Composition:** 0.9250 Silver .8411 oz. ASW **Subject:** World Wildlife Fund **Obverse:** Bust of Queen Elizabeth II right **Reverse:** Mauritius pink pigeon

Date	Mintage	F	VF	XF	Unc	BU
1987 Proof	25,000	Value: 22.50				

KM# 76 2 POUNDS **Composition:** Copper-Nickel **Subject:** Royal Visit **Obverse:** Bust of Queen Elizabeth II right

Date	Mintage	F	VF	XF	Unc	BU
1989	10,000	—	—	—	6.00	—

KM# 76a 2 POUNDS **Weight:** 28.3000 g. **Composition:** 0.9250 Silver .8411 oz. ASW **Subject:** Royal Visit **Obverse:** Bust of Queen Elizabeth II right

Date	Mintage	F	VF	XF	Unc	BU
1989 Proof	3,000	Value: 30.00				

KM# 77 2 POUNDS **Weight:** 28.3000 g. **Composition:** 0.9250 Silver .8411 oz. ASW **Subject:** 50th Anniversary - The Battle of Britain **Obverse:** Bust of Queen Elizabeth II right **Reverse:** Spitfire

Date	Mintage	F	VF	XF	Unc	BU
ND(1990) Proof	Est. 10,000	Value: 37.50				

KM# 83 2 POUNDS **Composition:** Copper-Nickel **Subject:** 90th Birthday of Queen Mother **Obverse:** Bust of Queen Elizabeth II right **Reverse:** Double "E" monogram

Date	Mintage	F	VF	XF	Unc	BU
ND(1990)	10,000	—	—	—	7.00	—

KM# 83a 2 POUNDS **Weight:** 28.3500 g. **Composition:** 0.9250 Silver .8432 oz. ASW **Subject:** 90th Birthday of Queen Mother **Obverse:** Bust of Queen Elizabeth II right

Date	Mintage	F	VF	XF	Unc	BU
ND(1990) Proof	3,000	Value: 55.00				

KM# 83b 2 POUNDS **Weight:** 15.9800 g. **Composition:** 0.9170 Gold .4708 oz. AGW **Subject:** 90th Birthday of Queen Mother **Obverse:** Bust of Queen Elizabeth II right **Reverse:** Double "E" monogram

Date	Mintage	F	VF	XF	Unc	BU
ND(1990) Proof	90	Value: 750				

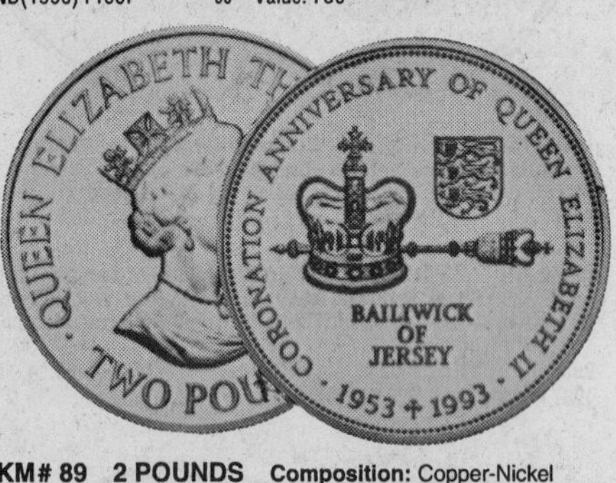

KM# 89 2 POUNDS **Composition:** Copper-Nickel **Subject:** 40th Anniversary - Coronation of Queen Elizabeth II **Obverse:** Bust of Queen Elizabeth II right

Date	Mintage	F	VF	XF	Unc	BU
ND(1993)	12,000	—	—	—	6.00	—

KM# 89a 2 POUNDS **Weight:** 28.2800 g. **Composition:** 0.9250 Silver .8411 oz. ASW **Subject:** 40th Anniversary - Coronation of Queen Elizabeth II **Obverse:** Bust of Queen Elizabeth II right

Date	Mintage	F	VF	XF	Unc	BU
ND(1993) Proof	Est. 10,000	Value: 55.00				

KM# 89b 2 POUNDS **Weight:** 5.9800 g. **Composition:** 0.9167 Gold .4709 oz. AGW **Subject:** 40th Anniversary - Coronation of Queen Elizabeth II **Obverse:** Bust of Queen Elizabeth II right

Date	Mintage	F	VF	XF	Unc	BU
1998 Proof	Est. 500	Value: 500				

KM# 92 2 POUNDS **Composition:** Copper-Nickel **Subject:** 50th Anniversary of Liberation **Obverse:** Bust of Queen Elizabeth II right

Date	Mintage	F	VF	XF	Unc	BU
1995	42,000	—	—	—	8.00	—

Note: Also released in special wallet with 1 Pound commemorative banknote (6,000). Market value: $20.00

KM# 92a 2 POUNDS **Weight:** 28.2800 g. **Composition:** 0.9250 Silver .8411 oz. ASW **Subject:** 50th Anniversary of Liberation **Obverse:** Bust of Queen Elizabeth II right

Date	Mintage	F	VF	XF	Unc	BU
1995 Proof	7,000	Value: 55.00				

KM# 97 2 POUNDS **Composition:** Copper-Nickel **Subject:** Queen Elizabeth's 70th Birthday **Obverse:** Bust of Queen Elizabeth II right **Reverse:** Flowers

Date	F	VF	XF	Unc	BU
1996	—	—	—	8.00	—

KM# 97a 2 POUNDS **Weight:** 28.3800 g. **Composition:** 0.9250 Silver .8411 oz. ASW **Subject:** Queen Elizabeth's 70th Birthday **Obverse:** Bust of Queen Elizabeth II right **Reverse:** Flowers

Date	F	VF	XF	Unc	BU
1996	—	—	—	45.00	—

Note: KM98 and 98a previously listed here, were never produced

KM# 99 2 POUNDS **Ring Composition:** Brass **Center Composition:** Copper-Nickel **Obverse:** Bust of Queen Elizabeth II right **Reverse:** Coats of arms circle denomination

Date	Mintage	F	VF	XF	Unc	BU
1997 In sets only	5,500	—	—	—	9.00	—

KM# 99a 2 POUNDS **Ring Weight:** 12.0000 g. **Ring Composition:** 0.9250 Gold Plated Silver **Center Composition:** Silver **Obverse:** Bust of Queen Elizabeth II right **Reverse:** Coats of arms circle denomination

Date	Mintage	F	VF	XF	Unc	BU
1997 Proof	500	Value: 65.00				

KM# 102 2 POUNDS **Ring Composition:** Nickel-Brass **Center Composition:** Copper-Nickel **Obverse:** Portrait of Queen Elizabeth II **Obv. Designer:** Rank-Broadley **Reverse:** Latent image value in circle of arms **Edge Lettering:** CAESARA INSULA

Date	Mintage	F	VF	XF	Unc	BU
1998	800,000	—	—	—	8.50	—

KM# 38 2 POUNDS 50 PENCE **Weight:** 27.6000 g. **Composition:** 0.9250 Silver .8208 oz. ASW **Subject:** 25th Wedding Anniversary **Obverse:** Similar to 1 Pound, KM#36

Date	Mintage	F	VF	XF	Unc	BU
1972	24,000	—	—	—	12.50	—
1972 Proof	1,500	Value: 27.50				

KM# 39 5 POUNDS **Weight:** 2.6200 g. **Composition:** 0.9170 Gold .0772 oz. AGW **Subject:** 25th Wedding Anniversary **Obverse:** Bust of Queen Elizabeth II right

Date	Mintage	F	VF	XF	Unc	BU
1972	8,500	—	—	—	37.50	—
1972 Proof	1,500	Value: 60.00				

KM# 78 5 POUNDS **Weight:** 155.5600 g. **Composition:** 0.9990 Silver 5 oz. ASW **Subject:** 50th Anniversary - The Battle of Britain **Obverse:** Bust of Queen Elizabeth II right **Reverse:** Spitfire **Note:** Illustration reduced. Actual size: 65mm.

Date	F	VF	XF	Unc	BU
ND Proof	Value: 145				

KM# 100 5 POUNDS **Composition:** Copper-Nickel **Subject:** Queen's Golden Wedding Anniversary **Obverse:** Bust of Queen Elizabeth II right **Reverse:** Conjoined busts of royal couple and coat of arms

Date	Mintage	F	VF	XF	Unc	BU
1997	6,000	—	—	—	15.00	—

KM# 100a 5 POUNDS **Weight:** 28.2800 g. **Composition:** 0.9250 Silver .8411 oz. ASW **Subject:** Queen's Golden Wedding Anniversary **Obverse:** Bust of Queen Elizabeth II right **Reverse:** Conjoined busts of royal couple and gold-plated coat of arms

Date	Mintage	F	VF	XF	Unc	BU
1997 Proof	Est. 30,000	Value: 65.00				

KM# 109 5 POUNDS **Weight:** 28.2800 g. **Composition:** 0.9250 Silver .8411 oz. ASW **Subject:** Millennium **Obverse:** Bust of Queen Elizabeth II right **Reverse:** Gold-plated island map on globe

Date	Mintage	F	VF	XF	Unc	BU
2000 Proof	32,000	Value: 47.50				

KM# 111 5 POUNDS **Weight:** 28.2800 g. **Composition:** Copper-Nickel **Subject:** Princess Diana **Obverse:** Queen's portrait **Reverse:** Diana's cameo portrait above people **Edge:** Reeded **Size:** 38.6 mm.

Date	F	VF	XF	Unc	BU
2002	—	—	—	13.50	—

KM# 111a 5 POUNDS **Weight:** 28.2800 g. **Composition:** 0.9250 Silver 0.841 oz. ASW **Subject:** Princess Dana **Obverse:** Queen's portrait **Reverse:** Diana's cameo portrait above people **Edge:** Reeded **Size:** 38.6 mm.

Date	Mintage	F	VF	XF	Unc	BU
2002 Proof	20,000	Value: 45.00				

KM# 111b 5 POUNDS **Weight:** 39.9400 g. **Composition:** 0.9167 Gold 1.1771 oz. AGW **Subject:** Princess Diana **Obverse:** Queen's portrait **Reverse:** Diana's cameo portrait above people **Edge:** Reeded **Size:** 38.6 mm.

Date	Mintage	F	VF	XF	Unc	BU
2002 Proof	100	Value: 800				

KM# 40 10 POUNDS **Weight:** 4.6400 g. **Composition:** 0.9170 Gold .1368 oz. AGW **Subject:** 25th Wedding Anniversary **Obverse:** Bust of Queen Elizabeth II right

Date	Mintage	F	VF	XF	Unc	BU
1972	8,500	—	—	—	60.00	—
1972 Proof	1,500	Value: 80.00				

KM# 79 10 POUNDS **Weight:** 3.1300 g. **Composition:** 0.9990 Gold .1005 oz. AGW **Subject:** 50th Anniversary - The Battle of Britain **Obverse:** Similar to 50 Pounds, KM#81

Date	Mintage	F	VF	XF	Unc	BU
ND Proof	Est. 500	Value: 120				

KM# 93 10 POUNDS **Weight:** 3.1300 g. **Composition:** 0.9990 Gold .1005 oz. AGW **Subject:** 50th Anniversary of Liberation **Obverse:** Bust of Queen Elizabeth II right

Date	Mintage	F	VF	XF	Unc	BU
1995 Proof sets only	500	—	—	—	85.00	—

KM# 41 20 POUNDS **Weight:** 9.2600 g. **Composition:** 0.9170 Gold .2729 oz. AGW **Subject:** 25th Wedding Anniversary **Obverse:** Bust of Queen Elizabeth II right

Date	Mintage	F	VF	XF	Unc	BU
1972	8,500	—	—	—	125	—
1972 Proof	1,500	Value: 165				

KM# 42 25 POUNDS **Weight:** 11.9000 g. **Composition:** 0.9170 Gold .3507 oz. AGW **Subject:** 25th Wedding Anniversary **Obverse:** Bust of Queen Elizabeth II right

Date	Mintage	F	VF	XF	Unc	BU
1972	8,500	—	—	—	150	—
1972 Proof	1,500	Value: 220				

KM# 80 25 POUNDS **Weight:** 7.8100 g. **Composition:** 0.9990 Gold .2509 oz. AGW **Subject:** 50th Anniversary - The Battle of Britain **Obverse:** Similar to 50 Pounds, KM#81 **Reverse:** Spitfire

Date	Mintage	F	VF	XF	Unc	BU
1990 Proof	Est. 500	Value: 250				

KM# 94 25 POUNDS **Weight:** 7.8100 g. **Composition:** 0.9990 Gold .2509 oz. AGW **Subject:** 50th Anniversary of Liberation **Obverse:** Bust of Queen Elizabeth II right

Date	Mintage	F	VF	XF	Unc	BU
1995 Proof sets only	500	—	—	—	215	—

KM# 112 25 POUNDS **Weight:** 7.9800 g. **Composition:** 0.9167 Gold 0.2352 oz. AGW **Subject:** Princess Diana **Obverse:** Queen's portrait **Reverse:** Diana's portrait **Edge:** Reeded **Size:** 22.05 mm.

Date	Mintage	F	VF	XF	Unc	BU
2002 Proof	2,500	Value: 290				

KM# 43 50 POUNDS **Weight:** 22.6300 g. **Composition:** 0.9170 Gold .6670 oz. AGW **Subject:** 25th Wedding Anniversary **Obverse:** Bust of Queen Elizabeth II right

Date	Mintage	F	VF	XF	Unc	BU
1972	8,500	—	—	—	300	—
1972 Proof	1,500	Value: 375				

KM# 81 50 POUNDS **Weight:** 15.6100 g. **Composition:** 0.9990 Gold .5014 oz. AGW **Subject:** 50th Anniversary - Battle of Britain **Obverse:** Bust of Queen Elizabeth II right **Reverse:** Royal Air Force badge dividing dates

Date	Mintage	F	VF	XF	Unc	BU
ND Proof	Est. 500	Value: 480				

KM# 95 50 POUNDS **Weight:** 15.6100 g. **Composition:** 0.9990 Gold .5014 oz. AGW **Subject:** 50th Anniversary of Liberation **Obverse:** Bust of Queen Elizabeth II right

Date	Mintage	F	VF	XF	Unc	BU
1995 Proof sets only	500	—	—	—	435	—

KM# 82 100 POUNDS **Weight:** 31.2100 g. **Composition:** 0.9990 Gold 1.0025 oz. AGW **Subject:** 50th Anniversary - The Battle of Britain **Obverse:** Bust of Queen Elizabeth II right **Reverse:** Spitfire

Date	Mintage	F	VF	XF	Unc	BU
ND Proof	Est. 500	Value: 900				

KM# 96 100 POUNDS **Weight:** 31.2100 g. **Composition:** 0.9990 Gold 1.0025 oz. AGW **Subject:** 50th Anniversary of Liberation **Obverse:** Bust of Queen Elizabeth II right

Date	Mintage	F	VF	XF	Unc	BU
1995 Proof sets only	500	—	—	—	865	—

PIEFORTS

KM#	Date	Mintage	Identification	Mkt Val
P1	1982	1,500	20 Pence. Silver. Date. KM53a.	25.00
P2	1995	—	2 Pounds. 0.9250 Silver. KM92a.	75.00

MINT SETS

KM#	Date	Mintage	Identification	Issue Price	Mkt Val
MS1	1972 (9)	8,500	KM35-43	348	715
MS2	1972 (4)	15,000	KM35-38	24.00	40.00
MS3	1983 (7)	25,000	KM54-59, 66	—	6.00
MS6	1997 (8)	5,500	KM54b 55b, 56.2-58.2, 66, 91, 99	—	28.00
MS4	1987 (7)	—	KM54-55, 56.1-58.1, 66, 71	—	6.50
MS5	1992 (7)	6,000	KM54,55b, 56.2-57.2, 58.1, 66, 86	22.50	22.50

PROOF SETS

KM#	Date	Mintage	Identification	Issue Price	Mkt Val
PS1	1957 (4)	1,050	KM21-22 two each	—	30.00
PS2.1	1960 (4)	2,100	KM22- 23 two each	—	25.00
PS2.2	1960 (4)	I.A.	KM22, 24 two each	—	150
PS3	1964 (4)	10,000	KM21, 25 two each	—	8.00
PS4	1966 (4)	15,000	KM26-27 two each	—	8.00
PS5	1966 (2)	15,000	KM28 two pieces	—	8.00
PS6	1972 (9)	1,500	KM35-43	648	975
PS7	1980 (6)	10,000	KM29-34	—	20.00
PS8	1981 (7)	15,000	KM45-51	31.00	20.00
PS9	1983 (7)	5,000	KM54a-55a, 56.1a-57.1a, 58a-59a, 66a	—	80.00
PS10	1990 (4)	500	KM79-82	1,595	1,750
PS11	1995 (4)	500	KM93-96	1,600	1,600

The Hashemite Kingdom of Jordan, a constitutional monarchy in southwest Asia, has an area of 37,738 sq. mi.(91,880 sq. km.) and a population of 3.5 million. Capital: Amman. Agriculture and tourism comprise Jordan's economic base. Chief exports are phosphates, tomatoe sand oranges.

Jordan is the Edom and Moab of the time of Moses. It became part of the Roman province of Arabia in 106 A.D., was conquered by the Arabs in 633-36, and was part of the Ottoman Empire from the 16th century until World War I. At that time, the regions presently known as Jordan and Israel were mandated to Great Britain by the League of Nations as Transjordan and Palestine. In 1922 Transjordan was established as the semi-autonomous Emirate of Transjordan, ruled by the Hashemite Prince Abdullah but still nominally a part of the British mandate. The mandate over Transjordan was terminated in 1946, the country becoming the independent Hashemite Kingdom of Transjordan. The kingdom was renamed the Hashemite Kingdom of Jordan in 1950.

Several 1964 and 1965 issues were limited to respective quantities of 3,000 and 5,000 examples struck to make up sets for sale to collectors.

TITLES

المملكة الاردنية الهاشمية

el-Mamlaka(t)el-Urduniya(t)el-Hashemiya(t)

RULERS

Abdullah Ibn Al-Hussein, 1946-1951
Talal Ibn Abdullah, 1951-1952
Hussein Ibn Talal, 1952-1999
Abdullah Ibn Al-Hussein, 1999-

MONETARY SYSTEM

100 Fils = 1 Dirham
1000 Fils = 10 Dirhams = 1 Dinar
Commencing 1992
100 Piastres = 1 Dinar

KINGDOM

DECIMAL COINAGE

KM# 1 FIL Composition: Bronze

Date	Mintage	F	VF	XF	Unc	BU
AH1368 (1949)	350,000	—	1.00	1.50	3.50	—
AH1368 (1949) Proof	—	—	—	—	—	—

Note: "FIL" is an error for "FILS," the correct Arabic singular

KM# 2 FILS Composition: Bronze

Date	Mintage	F	VF	XF	Unc	BU
AH1368 (1949)	Inc. above	—	0.50	0.90	2.25	—
AH1368 (1949) Proof	25	Value: 50.00				

KM# 8 FILS Composition: Bronze

Date	Mintage	F	VF	XF	Unc	BU
AH1374 (1955)	200,000	—	0.35	0.50	1.00	—
AH1374 (1955) Proof	—	—	—	—	—	—
AH1379 (1959)	150,000	—	0.40	0.60	1.25	—
AH1379 (1959) Proof	—	—	—	—	—	—
AH1382 (1962)	200,000	—	0.25	0.50	1.00	—
AH1382 (1962) Proof	—	—	—	—	—	—
AH1383 (1963)	3,000	—	1.50	3.00	5.00	—

Date	Mintage	F	VF	XF	Unc	BU
AH1385 (1965)	5,000	—	1.00	2.00	4.00	—
AH1385 (1965) Proof	10,000	Value: 3.00				

KM# 14 FILS Composition: Bronze **Obverse:** Head of Hussein right

Date	Mintage	F	VF	XF	Unc	BU
AH1387 (1967)	60,000	—	0.15	0.25	0.75	—

KM# 35 FILS Composition: Bronze

Date	Mintage	F	VF	XF	Unc	BU
AH1398 (1978)	—	—	0.15	0.25	0.60	—
AH1398 (1978) Proof	20,000	Value: 0.75				
AH1404 (1984)	100,000	—	0.10	0.20	0.50	—
AH1406 (1986)	—	—	0.10	0.20	0.50	—
AH1406 (1986) Proof	5,000	Value: 0.75				

KM# 3 5 FILS (1/2 Qirsh) Composition: Bronze

Date	Mintage	F	VF	XF	Unc	BU
AH1368 (1949)	3,300	—	0.40	0.75	1.50	—
AH1368 (1949) Proof	25	Value: 60.00				

KM# 9 5 FILS (1/2 Qirsh) Composition: Bronze

Date	Mintage	F	VF	XF	Unc	BU
AH1374 (1955)	3,500,000	—	0.35	0.50	0.75	—
AH1374 (1955) Proof	—	—	—	—	—	—
AH1380 (1960)	540,000	—	0.50	0.70	1.25	—
AH1380 (1960) Proof	—	—	—	—	—	—
AH1382 (1962)	250,000	—	0.45	0.70	1.25	—
AH1382 (1962) Proof	—	—	—	—	—	—
AH1383 (1963)	3,000	—	—	4.50	7.50	—
AH1384 (1964)	2,500,000	—	0.30	0.50	1.00	—
AH1385 (1965)	5,000	—	1.25	2.50	4.00	—
AH1385 (1965) Proof	10,000	Value: 5.00				
AH1387 (1967)	2,000,000	—	0.10	0.20	0.40	—

KM# 15 5 FILS (1/2 Qirsh) Composition: Bronze
Obverse: Head of Hussein right

Date	Mintage	F	VF	XF	Unc	BU
AH1387 (1967)	800,000	—	0.10	0.25	0.50	—
AH1390 (1970)	1,400,000	—	—	0.20	0.40	—
AH1392 (1972)	400,000	—	0.10	0.25	0.65	—
AH1394 (1974)	2,000,000	—	0.10	0.20	0.40	—
AH1395 (1975)	9,000,000	—	0.10	0.15	0.30	—

KM# 36 5 FILS (1/2 Qirsh) Composition: Bronze

Date	Mintage	F	VF	XF	Unc	BU
AH1398 (1978)	60,200,000	—	0.10	0.15	0.30	—
AH1398 (1978) Proof	20,000	Value: 1.25				
AH1406 (1986)	—	—	0.10	0.15	0.30	—
AH1406 (1986) Proof	5,000	Value: 1.25				

KM# 4 10 FILS (Qirsh, Piastre) Composition: Bronze

Date	Mintage	F	VF	XF	Unc	BU
AH1368 (1949)	2,700,000	—	0.75	1.25	2.00	—
AH1368 (1949) Proof	25	Value: 80.00				

KM# 10 10 FILS (Qirsh, Piastre) Composition: Bronze

Date	Mintage	F	VF	XF	Unc	BU
AH1374 (1955)	1,500,000	—	0.60	1.00	2.00	—
AH1374 (1955) Proof	—	—	—	—	—	—
AH1380 (1960)	60,000	—	1.25	2.00	3.50	—
AH1380 (1960) Proof	—	—	—	—	—	—
AH1382 (1962)	2,300,000	—	0.30	0.50	1.00	—
AH1382 (1962) Proof	—	Value: 50.00				
AH1383 (1964)	1,253,000	—	0.30	0.50	1.00	—
AH1385 (1965)	1,003,000	—	0.20	0.40	1.00	—
AH1385 (1965) Proof	10,000	Value: 2.00				
AH1387 (1967)	1,000,000	—	0.20	0.35	1.00	—

KM# 16 10 FILS (Qirsh, Piastre) Composition: Bronze
Obverse: Head of Hussein right

Date	Mintage	F	VF	XF	Unc	BU
AH1387 (1967)	500,000	—	0.20	0.40	0.75	—
AH1390 (1970)	1,000,000	—	0.20	0.35	0.60	—
AH1392 (1972)	600,000	—	0.20	0.40	0.75	—
AH1394 (1974)	1,000,000	—	0.20	0.40	0.65	—
AH1395 (1975)	5,000,000	—	0.20	0.35	0.50	—

KM# 37 10 FILS (Qirsh, Piastre) Composition: Bronze

Date	Mintage	F	VF	XF	Unc	BU
AH1398 (1978)	30,000,000	—	0.10	0.15	0.40	—
AH1398 (1978) Proof	20,000	Value: 1.50				
AH1404 (1984)	10,000,000	—	0.10	0.15	0.40	—
AH1406 (1986)	—	—	0.10	0.15	0.40	—
AH1406 (1986) Proof	5,000	Value: 1.50				
AH1409 (1989)	8,000	—	0.10	0.15	0.40	—

KM# 5 20 FILS Composition: Copper-Nickel

Date	Mintage	F	VF	XF	Unc	BU
AH1368 (1949)	1,570,000	—	0.50	1.00	1.75	—
AH1368 (1949) Proof	25	Value: 90.00				

KM# 13 20 FILS Composition: Copper-Nickel

Date	Mintage	F	VF	XF	Unc	BU
AH1383 (1963)	3,000	—	1.50	3.00	5.00	—
AH1385 (1965)	5,000	—	1.50	3.00	5.00	—
AH1385 (1965) Proof	10,000	Value: 5.00				

KM# 17 25 FILS (1/4 Dirham) Composition: Copper-Nickel **Obverse:** Head of Hussein right

Date	Mintage	F	VF	XF	Unc	BU
AH1387 (1967)	200,000	—	0.15	0.35	0.75	—
AH1390 (1970)	240,000	—	0.15	0.35	0.75	—
AH1394 (1974)	800,000	—	0.15	0.35	0.75	—
AH1395 (1975)	2,000,000	—	0.15	0.35	0.75	—
AH1397 (1977)	1,600,000	—	0.15	0.35	0.75	—

KM# 38 25 FILS (1/4 Dirham) Composition: Copper-Nickel

Date	Mintage	F	VF	XF	Unc	BU
AH1398 (1978)	—	—	0.20	0.30	0.75	—
AH1398 (1978) Proof	20,000	Value: 2.00				
AH1401 (1981)	2,000,000	—	0.20	0.30	0.75	—
AH1404 (1984)	4,000,000	—	0.20	0.30	0.75	—
AH1406 (1986)	—	—	0.20	0.30	0.75	—
AH1406 (1986) Proof	5,000	Value: 2.00				
AH1411 (1990)	5,000,000	—	0.20	0.30	0.75	—

KM# 6 50 FILS (1/2 Dirham) Composition: Copper-Nickel

Date	Mintage	F	VF	XF	Unc	BU
AH1368 (1949)	2,500,000	—	0.75	2.00	3.50	—
AH1368 (1949) Proof	25	Value: 100				

KM# 11 50 FILS (1/2 Dirham) Composition: Copper-Nickel

Date	Mintage	F	VF	XF	Unc	BU
AH1374 (1955)	2,500,000	—	0.75	1.50	3.50	—
AH1374 (1955) Proof	—	—	—	—	—	—
AH1382 (1962)	750,000	—	0.85	1.00	1.50	—
AH1382 (1962) Proof	—	—	—	—	—	—
AH1383 (1964)	1,003,000	—	0.40	0.60	1.00	—
AH1385 (1965)	1,505,000	—	0.40	0.60	1.00	—
AH1385 (1965) Proof	10,000	Value: 3.50				

KM# 18 50 FILS (1/2 Dirham) Composition: Copper-Nickel **Obverse:** Head of Hussein right

Date	Mintage	F	VF	XF	Unc	BU
AH1387 (1967)	400,000	—	0.40	0.75	1.75	—
AH1390 (1970)	1,000,000	—	0.40	0.60	1.25	—
AH1394 (1974)	1,000,000	—	0.40	0.60	1.25	—
AH1395 (1975)	2,000,000	—	0.40	0.60	1.25	—
AH1397 (1977)	6,000,000	—	0.40	0.60	1.25	—

KM# 39 50 FILS (1/2 Dirham) Composition: Copper-Nickel

Date	Mintage	F	VF	XF	Unc	BU
AH1398 (1978)	6,168,000	—	0.25	0.50	1.25	—
AH1398 (1978) Proof	20,000	Value: 2.50				
AH1400 (1980)	—	—	0.25	0.50	1.25	—
AH1401 (1981)	5,000,000	—	0.25	0.50	1.25	—
AH1404 (1984)	10,000,000	—	0.25	0.50	1.25	—
AH1406 (1986)	—	—	0.25	0.50	1.25	—
AH1406 (1986) Proof	5,000	Value: 2.50				
AH1409 (1989)	6,000,000	—	0.25	0.50	1.25	—
AH1411 (1990)	10,000,000	—	0.25	0.50	1.25	—

KM# 7 100 FILS (Dirham) Composition: Copper-Nickel

Date	Mintage	F	VF	XF	Unc	BU
AH1368 (1949)	2,000,000	—	2.00	3.00	5.00	—
AH1368 (1949) Proof	25	Value: 120				

KM# 12 100 FILS (Dirham) Composition: Copper-Nickel

Date	Mintage	F	VF	XF	Unc	BU
AH1374 (1955)	500,000	—	2.00	2.50	4.00	—
AH1374 (1955) Proof	—	—	—	—	—	—
AH1382 (1962)	600,000	—	1.00	1.50	3.00	—
AH1382 (1962) Proof	—	—	—	—	—	—
AH1383 (1963)	3,000	—	1.50	3.00	5.00	—
AH1385 (1965)	405,000	—	1.00	1.25	2.25	—
AH1385 (1965) Proof	10,000	Value: 4.00				

KM# 19 100 FILS (Dirham) Composition: Copper-Nickel **Obverse:** Head of Hussein right

Date	Mintage	F	VF	XF	Unc	BU
AH1387 (1967)	175,000	—	0.75	1.50	2.50	—
AH1395 (1975)	2,500,000	—	0.40	1.00	2.00	—
AH1397 (1977)	2,000,000	—	0.40	1.00	2.00	—

KM# 40 100 FILS (Dirham) Composition: Copper-Nickel

Date	Mintage	F	VF	XF	Unc	BU
AH1398 (1978)	3,000,000	—	0.40	1.00	2.00	—
AH1398 (1978) Proof	20,000	Value: 3.00				
AH1400 (1980)	—	—	0.40	1.00	2.00	—
AH1401 (1981)	4,000,000	—	0.40	1.00	2.00	—
AH1404 (1984)	5,000,000	—	0.40	1.00	1.50	—
AH1406 (1986)	—	—	0.40	1.00	1.50	—
AH1406 (1986) Proof	5,000	Value: 3.00				
AH1409 (1989)	4,000,000	—	0.40	1.00	1.50	—
AH1411 (1990)	6,000,000	—	0.40	1.00	1.50	—

KM# 20 1/4 DINAR Composition: Copper-Nickel **Series:** F.A.O.

Date	Mintage	F	VF	XF	Unc	BU
AH1389 (1969)	60,000	—	2.00	3.00	5.50	—

KM# 28 1/4 DINAR Composition: Copper-Nickel **Series:** F.A.O.

Date	Mintage	F	VF	XF	Unc	BU
AH1390 (1970)	500,000	—	1.00	1.50	4.00	—
AH1394 (1974)	400,000	—	1.00	1.50	4.00	—
AH1395 (1975)	100,000	—	1.00	1.50	4.00	—

KM# 29 1/4 DINAR Weight: 19.0400 g. **Composition:** 0.9250 Silver .5663 oz. ASW **Subject:** 10th Anniversary - Central Bank of Jordan

Date	Mintage	F	VF	XF	Unc	BU
AH1394 (1974) Proof	550	Value: 60.00				

KM# 29a 1/4 DINAR Composition: 0.9170 Gold **Subject:** 10th Anniversary - Central Bank of Jordan

Date	Mintage	F	VF	XF	Unc	BU
AH1394 (1974) Proof	100	Value: 600				

KM# 30 1/4 DINAR **Composition:** Copper-Nickel **Subject:** 25th Anniversary of Reign

Date	Mintage	F	VF	XF	Unc	BU
AH1397 (1977)	200,000	—	1.00	2.00	4.50	—

KM# 41 1/4 DINAR **Composition:** Copper-Nickel

Date	Mintage	F	VF	XF	Unc	BU
AH1398 (1978)	200,000	—	1.00	2.00	4.50	—
AH1398 (1978) Proof	20,000	Value: 5.00				
AH1401 (1981)	800,000	—	0.75	1.50	4.00	—
AH1406 (1986)	—	—	0.75	1.50	4.00	—
AH1406 (1986) Proof	5,000	Value: 5.00				

KM# 21 1/2 DINAR **Weight:** 20.0000 g. **Composition:** 0.9990 Silver .6424 oz. ASW **Reverse:** Al Harraneh Palace

Date	Mintage	F	VF	XF	Unc	BU
AH1389 (1969) Proof	6,100	Value: 20.00				

KM# 42 1/2 DINAR **Composition:** Copper-Nickel **Subject:** 1400th Anniversary of Islam **Shape:** 7-sided

Date	Mintage	F	VF	XF	Unc	BU
AH1400 (1980)	2,006,000	—	1.50	2.50	5.00	—

KM# 22 3/4 DINAR **Weight:** 30.0000 g. **Composition:** 0.9990 Silver .9636 oz. ASW **Obverse:** Similar to 1/2 Dinar, KM#21 **Reverse:** Shrine of the Nativity, Bethlehem

Date	Mintage	F	VF	XF	Unc	BU
AH1389 (1969) Proof	5,800	Value: 40.00				

KM# 23 DINAR **Weight:** 40.0000 g. **Composition:** 0.9990 Silver 1.2848 oz. ASW **Obverse:** Similar to 1/2 Dinar, KM#21 **Reverse:** Temple Hill, Jerusalem

Date	Mintage	F	VF	XF	Unc	BU
AH1389 (1969) Proof	6,800	Value: 60.00				

KM# 47 DINAR **Composition:** Nickel-Bronze **Subject:** King Hussein's 50th Birthday

Date	Mintage	F	VF	XF	Unc	BU
AH1406 (1986)	—	—	—	—	7.50	—
AH1406 (1986) Proof	5,000	Value: 10.00				

KM# 76 DINAR **Weight:** 17.0000 g. **Composition:** 0.9170 Gold .5012 oz. AGW **Note:** Similar to KM#52 but double-size diameter.

Date	F	VF	XF	Unc	BU
AH1413 (1992) Proof	—	Value: 350			

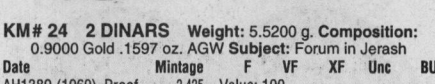

KM# 24 2 DINARS **Weight:** 5.5200 g. **Composition:** 0.9000 Gold .1597 oz. AGW **Subject:** Forum in Jerash

Date	Mintage	F	VF	XF	Unc	BU
AH1389 (1969) Proof	2,425	Value: 100				

KM# 31 2-1/2 DINARS **Weight:** 28.2800 g. **Composition:** 0.9250 Silver .8410 oz. ASW **Subject:** Conservation **Reverse:** Rhim Gazelle

Date	Mintage	F	VF	XF	Unc	BU
AH1397 (1977)	6,265	—	—	—	22.00	—
AH1397 (1977) Proof	5,011	Value: 28.00				

KM# 32 3 DINARS **Weight:** 35.0000 g. **Composition:** 0.9250 Silver 1.0409 oz. ASW **Subject:** Conservation **Obverse:** Similar to 2-1/2 Dinars, KM#31 **Reverse:** Palestine sunbird

Date	Mintage	F	VF	XF	Unc	BU
AH1397 (1977)	6,263	—	—	—	25.00	—
AH1397 (1977) Proof	4,897	Value: 32.50				

KM# 43 3 DINARS **Weight:** 23.3300 g. **Composition:** 0.9250 Silver .6938 oz. ASW **Subject:** International Year of the Child **Obverse:** Similar to 1/4 Dinar, KM#41

Date	Mintage	F	VF	XF	Unc	BU
AH1401 (1981) Proof	21,000	Value: 17.50				

KM# 75 3 DINARS **Weight:** 28.5000 g. **Composition:** Brass **Subject:** Amman: Arabic Culture Capital **Obverse:** King's portrait **Reverse:** Building **Edge:** Reeded **Size:** 40 mm.

Date	Mintage	F	VF	XF	Unc	BU
2002	2,000	—	—	—	15.00	—

KM# 25 5 DINARS **Weight:** 13.8200 g. **Composition:** 0.9000 Gold .3999 oz. AGW **Reverse:** Tomb in Petra

Date	Mintage	F	VF	XF	Unc	BU
AH1389 (1969) Proof	1,950	Value: 250				

Note: KM57 and 57a have been relocated to coinages reflecting the monetary reform

KM# 26 10 DINARS **Weight:** 27.6400 g. **Composition:** 0.9000 Gold .7998 oz. AGW **Subject:** Visit of Pope Paul VI

Date	Mintage	F	VF	XF	Unc	BU
AH1389 (1969) Proof	1,870	Value: 425				

KM# 44 10 DINARS **Weight:** 30.0000 g. **Composition:** 0.9250 Silver .8922 oz. ASW **Reverse:** 15th Century Hijrah calendar

Date	Mintage	F	VF	XF	Unc	BU
AH1400 (1980) Proof	17,000	Value: 37.50				

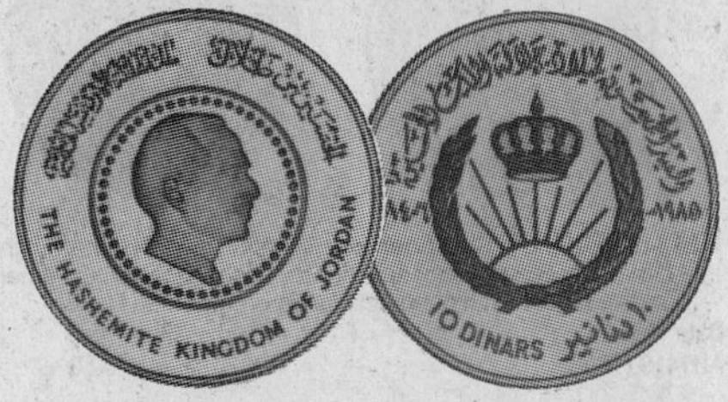

KM# 48 10 DINARS **Weight:** 15.2000 g. **Composition:** 0.9250 Silver .4610 oz. ASW **Subject:** King's 50th Birthday

Date	F	VF	XF	Unc	BU
AH1406 (1986) Proof	—	Value: 27.50			

KM# 72 10 DINARS **Weight:** 31.0000 g. **Composition:** 0.9990 Silver .9957 oz. ASW **Subject:** Millennium and Baptism of Jesus **Obverse:** King's portrait **Reverse:** Baptism scene **Edge:** Reeded **Size:** 40 mm.

Date	F	VF	XF	Unc	BU
AH1420(2000) Matte	—	—	—	45.00	—
AH1420(2000) Proof	—	Value: 55.00			

KM# 27 25 DINARS **Weight:** 69.1100 g. **Composition:** 0.9000 Gold 1.9999 oz. AGW **Reverse:** Dome of the Rock, Jerusalem

Date	Mintage	F	VF	XF	Unc	BU
AH1389 (1969) Proof	1,000	Value: 1,000				

KM# 33 25 DINARS **Weight:** 15.0000 g. **Composition:** 0.9170 Gold .4422 oz. AGW **Subject:** 25th Anniversary of Reign

Date	Mintage	F	VF	XF	Unc	BU
ND(AH1397) (1977) FM Proof	4,724	Value: 225				

KM# 45 40 DINARS **Weight:** 14.3100 g. **Composition:** 0.9170 Gold .4216 oz. AGW **Reverse:** 15th Century Hijrah calendar

Date	Mintage	F	VF	XF	Unc	BU
AH1400 (1980) Proof	9,500	Value: 325				

KM# 50 50 DINARS **Weight:** 15.9800 g. **Composition:** 0.9170 Gold .4710 oz. AGW **Subject:** Five Year Plan

Date	Mintage	F	VF	XF	Unc	BU
AH1396 (1976) Proof	250	Value: 400				

KM# 34 50 DINARS **Weight:** 33.4370 g. **Composition:** 0.9000 Gold .9676 oz. AGW **Subject:** Conservation **Reverse:** Houbara Bustard

Date	Mintage	F	VF	XF	Unc	BU
AH1397 (1977)	829	—	—	—	450	500
AH1397 (1977) Proof	287	Value: 700				

KM# 49 50 DINARS **Weight:** 17.0000 g. **Composition:** 0.9170 Gold .5013 oz. AGW **Subject:** King Husein's 50th Birthday **Note:** Similar to 10 Dinars, KM#48.

Date	Mintage	F	VF	XF	Unc	BU
AH1406 (1985) Proof	2,000	Value: 325				
AH1406 (1985) Proof	2,000	Value: 325				

KM# 77 50 DINARS **Weight:** 33.9200 g. **Composition:** 0.9166 Gold .9996 oz. AGW **Note:** Similar to KM#69 but double-size diameter.

Date	F	VF	XF	Unc	BU
ND(1996) Proof	—	Value: 675			

KM# 46 60 DINARS **Weight:** 17.1700 g. **Composition:** 0.9170 Gold .5062 oz. AGW **Subject:** International Year of the Child **Reverse:** Palace of Culture in Amman

Date	Mintage	F	VF	XF	Unc	BU
AH1401 (1981) Proof	20,000	Value: 235				

REFORM COINAGE

100 Piastres = 1 Dinar; 1/2 Qirsh = 1/2 Piastre

KM# 60 1/2 QIRSH (1/2 Piastre) **Composition:** Copper Plated Steel **Obverse:** Bust of King Hussein facing left **Reverse:** Denomination

Date	F	VF	XF	Unc	BU
AH1416 (1995)	—	—	0.35	0.65	—

KM# 56 QIRSH (Piastre) **Composition:** Bronze Plated Steel

Date	F	VF	XF	Unc	BU
AH1414 (1994)	—	—	0.65	1.25	—
AH1416 (1995)	—	—	0.65	1.25	—

KM# 53 2-1/2 PIASTRES **Composition:** Stainless Steel

Date	F	VF	XF	Unc	BU
AH1412 (1991)	—	—	0.75	1.50	—
AH1413 (1992)	—	—	0.75	1.50	—

KM# 54 5 PIASTRES **Composition:** Nickel Plated Steel

Date	F	VF	XF	Unc	BU
AH1412 (1991)	—	—	1.00	2.00	—
AH1413 (1992)	—	—	1.00	2.00	—
AH1414 (1993)	—	—	1.00	2.00	—
AH1416 (1995)	—	—	1.00	2.00	—
AH1418 (1998)	—	—	1.00	2.00	—

KM# 73 5 PIASTRES **Weight:** 5.0000 g. **Composition:** Nickel-Clad Steel **Ruler:** Abdullah Ibn Al-Hussein **Obverse:** King's portrait **Reverse:** Denomination **Edge:** Reeded **Size:** 25.8 mm.

Date	F	VF	XF	Unc	BU
AH1421-2000	—	—	—	2.00	—

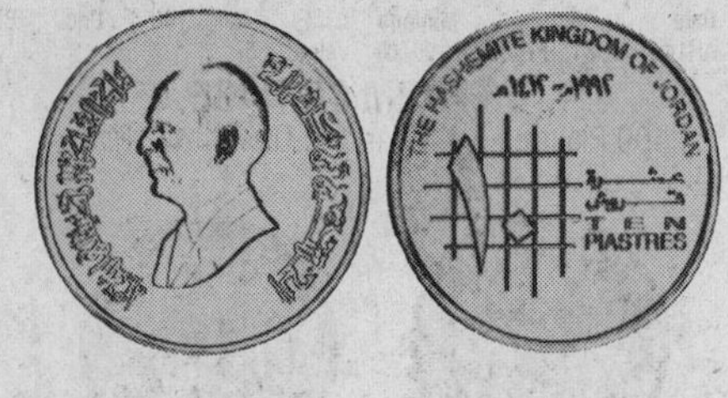

KM# 55 10 PIASTRES **Composition:** Nickel Plated Steel

Date	F	VF	XF	Unc	BU
AH1412 (1991)	—	—	1.25	2.25	—
AH1413 (1992)	—	—	1.25	2.25	—
AH1414 (1993)	—	—	1.25	2.25	—
AH1414 (1994)	—	—	1.25	2.25	—
AH1416 (1995)	—	—	1.25	2.25	—
AH1416 (1996)	—	—	1.25	2.25	—
AH1417 (1996)	—	—	1.25	2.25	—

KM# 74 10 PIASTRES **Weight:** 8.0000 g. **Composition:** Nickel Clad Steel **Ruler:** Abdullah Ibn Al-Hussein **Obverse:** King's portrait **Reverse:** Denomination **Edge:** Reeded **Size:** 27.9 mm.

Date	F	VF	XF	Unc	BU
AH1421-2000	—	—	—	4.00	—

KM# 61 1/4 DINAR **Composition:** Nickel-Brass **Obverse:** King Hussein facing left **Reverse:** Denomination

Date	F	VF	XF	Unc	BU
AH1416 (1995)	—	—	—	3.00	—
AH1417 (1996)	—	—	—	3.00	—

KM# 58 1/2 DINAR **Composition:** Brass **Obverse:** King Hussein facing left

Date	F	VF	XF	Unc	BU
AH1416 (1995)	—	—	—	4.00	—
AH1417 (1996)	—	—	—	4.00	—

KM# 63 1/2 DINAR **Ring Composition:** Aluminum-Bronze **Center Composition:** Copper-Nickel **Obverse:** King Hussein facing left **Reverse:** Denomination **Shape:** 7-sided

Date	F	VF	XF	Unc	BU
AH1417 (1996)	—	—	—	8.00	—

KM# 51 DINAR **Weight:** 15.0000 g. **Composition:** 0.9250 Silver .4461 oz. ASW **Subject:** 40th Year of Reign **Obverse:** King Hussein in uniform

Date	F	VF	XF	Unc	BU
AH1413 (1992)	—	Value: 22.00			

KM# 52 DINAR **Weight:** 8.5000 g. **Composition:** 0.9170 Gold .2505 oz. AGW **Subject:** 40th Year of Reign **Obverse:** King Hussein in uniform

Date	F	VF	XF	Unc	BU
AH1413 (1992) Proof	—	Value: 185			

KM# 62 DINAR **Composition:** Brass **Subject:** 50th Anniversary - F.A.O. **Obverse:** King Hussein facing left **Reverse:** F.A.O. logo **Shape:** 7-sided

Date	F	VF	XF	Unc	BU
AH1415 (1994)	—	—	—	10.00	—

KM# 59 DINAR **Composition:** Brass **Obverse:** King Hussein facing left **Shape:** 7-sided

Date	F	VF	XF	Unc	BU
AH1416 (1995)	—	—	—	8.00	—

KM# 68 DINAR **Weight:** 31.1035 g. **Composition:** 0.9990 Silver 1.0000 oz. ASW **Subject:** 50 Years - Jordanian Independence **Obverse:** Bust of King Hussein facing left **Reverse:** Portrait of former King Abdullah

Date	F	VF	XF	Unc	BU
ND (1996) Proof Est. 2,000	Value: 75.00				

KM# 70 DINAR **Composition:** Brass **Subject:** 50 Years - Jordanian Independence **Obverse:** Bust of King Hussein facing left **Reverse:** Portrait of former King Abdullah

Date	Mintage	F	VF	XF	Unc	BU
AH1417 (1997)	400	—	—	—	8.00	—

KM# 64 DINAR **Center Composition:** Brass **Obverse:** Bust of King Hussein facing left **Reverse:** Denomination in ornamented circle

Date	F	VF	XF	Unc	BU
AH1419 (1998)	—	—	—	5.50	—

KM# 65 DINAR **Composition:** Brass **Subject:** Human Rights **Obverse:** Bust of King Hussein facing left **Reverse:** Commemorative legend with denomination in ornamented circle

Date	F	VF	XF	Unc	BU
AH1419 (1998)	—	—	—	5.50	—

KM# 57 5 DINARS **Composition:** Copper-Nickel **Subject:** UN 50 Years **Obverse:** Bust of King Hussein facing left **Reverse:** Black iris

Date	F	VF	XF	Unc	BU
ND(1995)	—	—	—	10.00	—

KM# 57a 5 DINARS **Weight:** 28.2800 g. **Composition:** 0.9250 Silver .8411 oz. ASW **Subject:** UN 50 Years **Obverse:** Bust of King Hussein facing left **Reverse:** Black iris

Date	Mintage	F	VF	XF	Unc	BU
ND(1995) Proof	100,000	Value: 47.50				

KM# 66 5 DINARS **Weight:** 28.2800 g. **Composition:** 0.9250 Silver .8411 oz. ASW **Subject:** UNICEF: For the Children of the World **Obverse:** Conjoined busts of Hussein and Queen Noor right **Reverse:** Boy, girl, UNICEF logo

Date	Mintage	F	VF	XF	Unc	BU
AH1419 (1999) Proof	25,000	Value: 50.00				

KM# 71 5 DINARS **Weight:** 28.5000 g. **Composition:** Brass **Subject:** Millennium and Baptism of Jesus **Obverse:** King's portrait **Reverse:** Baptism scene **Edge:** Reeded **Size:** 40 mm.

Date	Mintage	F	VF	XF	Unc	BU
AH1420(2000) Prooflike	10,000	—	—	—	20.00	—

KM# 69 50 DINARS **Weight:** 16.9600 g. **Composition:** 0.9166 Gold .4998 oz. AGW **Subject:** 50 Years - Jordanian Independence **Obverse:** King Hussein's portrait **Reverse:** Portrait of former King Abdullah

Date	Mintage	F	VF	XF	Unc	BU
ND(1996) Proof	Est. 1,000	Value: 375				

KM# 67 50 DINARS **Weight:** 6.2200 g. **Composition:** 0.9990 Gold .1998 oz. AGW **Subject:** UNICEF: For the Children of the World **Obverse:** Conjoined busts of King Hussein and Queen Noor **Reverse:** Boy, girl, UNICEF logo

Date	Mintage	F	VF	XF	Unc	BU
AH1419 (1999) Proof	10,000	Value: 175				

PATTERNS

Including off metal strikes

KM#	Date	Mintage	Identification	Mkt Val
Pn1	AH1387	2	Fils. Gold. KM14.	—
Pn2	AH1387	2	5 Fils. Gold. KM15.	—
Pn3	AH1387	2	10 Fils. Gold. KM16.	—
Pn4	AH1387	2	25 Fils. Gold. KM17.	—
Pn5	AH1387	2	50 Fils. Gold. KM18.	700
Pn6	AH1387	2	Dirham. Gold. KM19.	900
Pn7	AH1395	112	Fils. Gold. As KM14.	100
Pn8	AH1395	112	5 Fils. Gold. As KM15.	200
Pn9	AH1395	112	10 Fils. Gold. As KM16.	250
Pn10	AH1395	112	25 Fils. Gold. As KM17.	150
Pn11	AH1395	112	50 Fils. Gold. As KM18.	250
Pn12	AH1395	112	Dirham. Gold. As KM19.	450
Pn13	AH1395	112	1/4 Dinar. Gold. As KM28.	650

PIEFORTS

KM#	Date	Mintage	Identification	Mkt Val
P1	1981	2,050	3 Dinars. KM43.	90.00
P2	1981	450	60 Dinars. KM46.	650
P3	1985	700	50 Dinars. KM49.	700

MINT SETS

KM#	Date	Mintage	Identification	Issue Price	Mkt Val
MS2	Mixed dates (6)	—	KM5 (1949), 8 (1963), 9 (1962), 10-11 (1964), 12 (1962)	—	10.00
MS1	1985 (8)	—	KM35-41, 47	10.75	15.00

PROOF SETS

KM#	Date	Mintage	Identification	Issue Price	Mkt Val
PS1	1949 (6)	25	KM2-7	—	500
PS2	1965 (6)	10,000	KM8-13	14.40	17.50
PS3	1969 (6)	—	KM21-27	396	1,900
PS4	1969 (6)	—	KM21-26	—	900
PS5	1969 (4)	—	KM24-27	—	1,800
PS6	1969 (3)	5,800	KM21-23	36.00	125
PS7	1977 (3)	1,000	KM31-32, 34	780	825
PS8	1977 (2)	9,000	KM31-32	60.00	65.00
PS9	1978 (7)	20,000	KM35-41	27.00	15.00
PS10	1980 (2)	—	KM44-45	365	525
PS11	1985 (8)	5,000	KM35-41, 47	31.00	25.00

SPECIMEN SETS (SS)

KM#	Date	Mintage	Identification	Issue Price	Mkt Val
SS1	1964 (6)	3,000	KM8-13	—	14.00
SS2	1965 (6)	5,000	KM8-13	—	12.00
SS3	1968 (6)	50	KM14-19	—	300
SS4	1968 (6)	2	KMPn1-6	—	—
SS5	1975 (7)	112	KMPn7-13	—	2,000

KATANGA

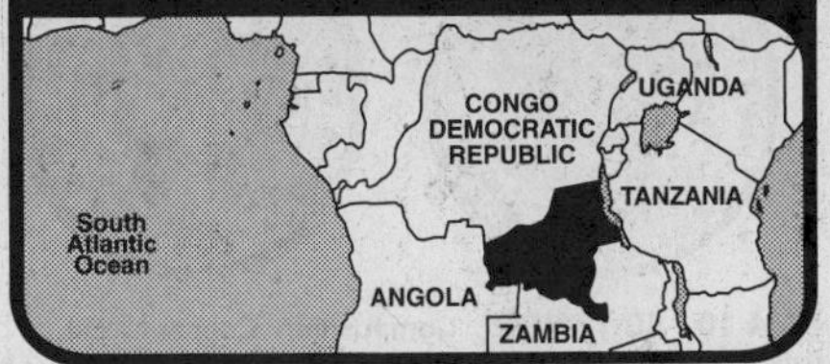

Katanga, the southern province of the former Belgian Congo, had an area of 191,873 sq. mi. (496,951 sq. km.) and was noted for its mineral wealth.

MONETARY SYSTEM
100 Centimes = 1 Franc

PROVINCE

DECIMAL COINAGE

KM# 1 FRANC **Composition:** Bronze

Date	F	VF	XF	Unc	BU
1961	—	1.00	1.75	3.50	—

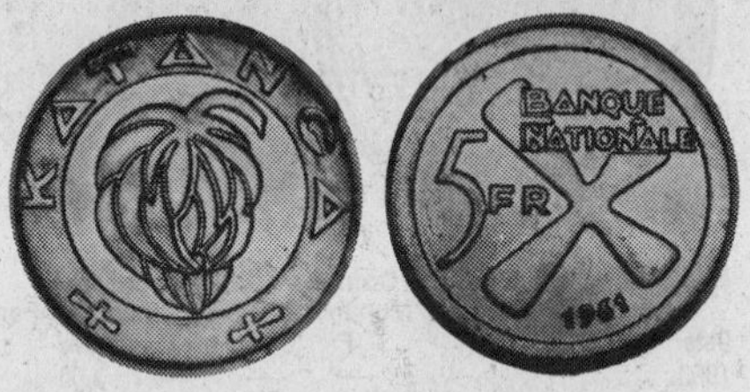

KM# 2 5 FRANCS **Composition:** Bronze

Date	F	VF	XF	Unc	BU
1961	—	2.00	3.75	7.50	—

KM# 2a 5 FRANCS **Weight:** 13.3300 g. **Composition:** 0.9000 Gold .3857 oz. AGW

Date	Mintage	F	VF	XF	Unc	BU
1961	20,000	—	—	—	185	—

KAZAKHSTAN

The Republic of Kazakhstan (formerly Kazakhstan S.S.R.) is bordered to the west by the Caspian Sea and Russia, to the north by Russia, in the east by the Peoples Republic of China and in the south by Uzbekistan and Kirghizia. It has an area of 1,049,155 sq. mi. (2,717,300 sq. km.) and a population of 16.7 million. Capital: Alma-Ata (formerly Verny). Rich in mineral resources including coal, tungsten, copper, lead, zinc and manganese with huge oil and natural gas reserves. Agriculture is very important, (it previously represented 20 percent of the total arable acreage of the combined U.S.S.R.) Non-ferrous metallurgy, heavy engineering and chemical industries are leaders in its economy.

The Kazakhs are a branch of the Turkic peoples which led the nomadic life of herdsmen until WW I. In the 13th century they came under Genghis Khan's eldest son Jujiand. Later they became a part of the Golden Horde, a western Mongol empire. Around the beginning of the 16th century they were divided into 3 confederacies, known as *zhuz* or hordes, in the steppes of Turkestan. At the end of the 17th century an incursion by the Kalmucks, a remnant of the Oirat Mongol confederacy, resulted in heavy losses on both sides which facilitated Russian penetration. Resistance to Russian settlements varied throughout the 1800's, but by 1900 over 100 million acres were declared Czarist state property and used for a planned peasant colonization. After a revolution in 1905 Kazakh deputies were elected. In 1916 the tsarist government ordered mobilization of all males, between 19 and 43, for auxiliary service. The Kazakhs rose in defiance which led the governor general of Turkestan to send troops against the rebels. Shortly after the Russian revolution, Kazakh Nationalists asked for full autonomy. The Communist *coup d'etat* of Nov. 1917 led to civil war. In 1919-20 the Red army defeated the "White" Russian forces and occupied Kazakhstan and fought against the Nationalist government formed on Nov. 17, 1917 by Ali Khan Bukey Khan. The Kazakh Autonomous Soviet Socialist Republic was proclaimed on Aug. 26, 1920 within the R.S.F.S.R. Russian and Ukrainian colonization continued while 2 purges in1927 and 1935 quelled any Kazakh feelings of priority in the matters of their country. On Dec. 5, 1936 Kazakhstan qualified for full status as an S.S.R. and held its first congress in 1937. Independence was declared on Dec. 16, 1991 and Kazakhstan joined the C.I.S.

MONETARY SYSTEM
100 Tyin = 1 Tenge

REPUBLIC

DECIMAL COINAGE

KM# 1 2 TYIN **Composition:** Yellow Brass

Date	F	VF	XF	Unc	BU
1993	—	—	—	0.45	—

KM# 1a 2 TYIN **Composition:** Copper Clad Brass

Date	F	VF	XF	Unc	BU
1993	—	—	—	0.45	—

KM# 2 5 TYIN **Composition:** Yellow Brass

Date	F	VF	XF	Unc	BU
1993	—	—	—	0.60	—

KM# 2a 5 TYIN **Composition:** Copper Clad Brass

Date	F	VF	XF	Unc	BU
1993	—	—	—	0.60	—

KM# 3 10 TYIN **Composition:** Yellow Brass

Date	F	VF	XF	Unc	BU
1993	—	—	—	0.80	—

KM# 3a 10 TYIN **Composition:** Copper Clad Brass

Date	F	VF	XF	Unc	BU
1993	—	—	—	0.80	—

KM# 4 20 TYIN **Composition:** Brass Plated Zinc

Date	F	VF	XF	Unc	BU
1993	—	—	—	1.25	—

KM# 5 50 TYIN **Composition:** Brass Plated Zinc

Date	F	VF	XF	Unc	BU
1993	—	—	—	1.50	—

KM# 6 TENGE **Composition:** Copper-Nickel

Date	F	VF	XF	Unc	BU
1992	—	—	—	1.00	—
1993	—	—	—	0.50	—

KM# 23 TENGE **Composition:** Brass **Obverse:** National emblem **Reverse:** Denomination

Date	F	VF	XF	Unc	BU
1997	—	—	—	0.50	—
2000	—	—	—	0.50	—

KM# 8 3 TENGE **Composition:** Copper-Nickel

Date	F	VF	XF	Unc	BU
1993	—	—	—	0.75	—

KM# 9 5 TENGE **Composition:** Copper-Nickel

Date	F	VF	XF	Unc	BU
1993	—	—	—	1.25	—

KM# 24 5 TENGE **Composition:** Brass **Obverse:** National emblem **Reverse:** Denomination

Date	F	VF	XF	Unc	BU
1997	—	—	—	0.50	—
2000	—	—	—	0.50	—
2002	—	—	—	0.50	—

KM# 10 10 TENGE **Composition:** Copper-Nickel

Date	F	VF	XF	Unc	BU
1993	—	—	—	2.00	—

KM# 25 10 TENGE **Composition:** Brass **Obverse:** National emblem **Reverse:** Denomination

Date	F	VF	XF	Unc	BU
1997	—	—	—	0.75	—
2000	—	—	—	0.75	—
2002	—	—	—	0.75	—

KM# 11 20 TENGE **Composition:** Copper-Nickel **Reverse:** Philosopher Muhammad bin Muhammad-al-Farabi

Date	F	VF	XF	Unc	BU
1993	—	—	—	3.00	—

KM# 12 20 TENGE **Composition:** Copper-Nickel **Subject:** 50th Anniversary - United Nations

Date	F	VF	XF	Unc	BU
1995	—	—	—	3.50	—

KM# 18 20 TENGE **Composition:** Copper-Nickel **Subject:** 150th Anniversary - Jambyl **Obverse:** National emblem **Reverse:** Man with stringed instrument

Date	F	VF	XF	Unc	BU
1996	—	—	—	3.50	—

KM# 19 20 TENGE **Composition:** Copper-Nickel **Subject:** 5th Anniversary - Independence **Obverse:** National emblem **Reverse:** Monument and buildings

Date	F	VF	XF	Unc	BU
1996	—	—	—	3.50	—

KM# 20 20 TENGE **Composition:** Copper-Nickel **Subject:** Centennial - Birth of Muchtar Auezov **Obverse:** National emblem

Date	F	VF	XF	Unc	BU
ND(1997)	—	—	—	3.50	—

KM# 26 20 TENGE **Composition:** Copper-Nickel **Obverse:** National emblem **Reverse:** Denomination

Date	F	VF	XF	Unc	BU
1997	—	—	—	1.00	—
2000	—	—	—	1.00	—

KM# 21 20 TENGE **Composition:** Copper-Nickel **Subject:** Year of Peace and Harmony **Obverse:** National emblem **Reverse:** Stylized dove

Date	F	VF	XF	Unc	BU
1997	—	—	—	3.50	—

KM# 22 20 TENGE **Composition:** Copper-Nickel **Subject:** New Capital - Astana **Obverse:** National emblem **Reverse:** Flower-like design

Date	F	VF	XF	Unc	BU
1998	—	—	—	3.50	—

KM# 28 20 TENGE **Composition:** Copper-Nickel **Subject:** 100th Birthday - K.I. Satbaev **Obverse:** National arms **Reverse:** Portrait of geologist

Date	F	VF	XF	Unc	BU
1999	—	—	—	3.85	—

KM# 27 50 TENGE Composition: Copper-Nickel **Obverse:** National emblem **Reverse:** Denomination

Date	F	VF	XF	Unc	BU
1997	—	—	—	2.00	—
2000	—	—	—	2.00	—

KM# 30 50 TENGE Composition: Copper-Nickel **Subject:** Millennium **Reverse:** Rising sun above three blocks

Date	F	VF	XF	Unc	BU
1999	—	—	—	3.50	—

KM# 31 50 TENGE Weight: 10.7000 g. **Composition:** Copper-Nickel **Subject:** Victorious conclusion of World War II **Obverse:** National arms **Reverse:** Soldiers celebrating **Edge:** Reeded and plain sections **Size:** 31 mm.

Date	F	VF	XF	Unc	BU
ND(2000)	—	—	—	4.00	—

KM# 33 50 TENGE Weight: 11.5000 g. **Composition:** Copper-Nickel **Obverse:** National arms **Reverse:** Portrait **Edge:** Reeded and plain sections

Date	F	VF	XF	Unc	BU
2000	—	—	—	4.00	—

KM# 40 50 TENGE Weight: 11.5000 g. **Composition:** Copper-Nickel **Obverse:** Eagle superimposed on ornate 10 **Edge:** Reeded and plain sections **Size:** 31 mm.

Date	F	VF	XF	Unc	BU
2001	—	—	—	4.00	—

KM# 13 100 TENGE Weight: 24.0000 g. **Composition:** 0.9250 Silver .7137 oz. ASW **Subject:** 150th Anniversary - Birth of Abaj Kunabaev **Reverse:** Mother and child **Edge:** Lettered

Date	Mintage	F	VF	XF	Unc	BU
1995 Proof	6,000	Value: 35.00				

KM# 14 100 TENGE Weight: 24.0000 g. **Composition:** 0.9250 Silver .7137 oz. ASW **Subject:** 150th Anniversary - Birth of Abaj Kunabaev **Reverse:** Falconer

Date	Mintage	F	VF	XF	Unc	BU
1995 Proof	6,000	Value: 37.50				

KM# 15 100 TENGE Weight: 24.0000 g. **Composition:** 0.9250 Silver .7137 oz. ASW **Subject:** 150th Anniversary - Birth of Abaj Kunabaev **Reverse:** Couple on swings

Date	Mintage	F	VF	XF	Unc	BU
1995 Proof	6,000	Value: 35.00				

KM# 16 100 TENGE Weight: 24.0000 g. **Composition:** 0.9250 Silver .7137 oz. ASW **Subject:** 150th Anniversary - Birth of Abaj Kunabaev **Reverse:** Town view

Date	Mintage	F	VF	XF	Unc	BU
1995 Proof	6,000	Value: 35.00				

KM# 17 100 TENGE Weight: 24.0000 g. **Composition:** 0.9250 Silver .7137 oz. ASW **Subject:** 150th Anniversary - Birth of Abaj Kunabaev **Reverse:** Elderly man

Date	Mintage	F	VF	XF	Unc	BU
1995 Proof	6,000	Value: 35.00				

KM# 32 100 TENGE Weight: 24.0000 g. **Composition:** 0.9250 Silver .7137 oz. ASW **Subject:** Millennium **Obverse:** National arms **Reverse:** Ancient and modern technologies **Edge:** Plain **Size:** 37 mm.

Date	Mintage	F	VF	XF	Unc	BU
1999 Proof	2,000	Value: 45.00				

KM# 34 100 TENGE Weight: 24.0000 g. **Composition:** 0.9250 Silver .7137 oz. ASW **Subject:** 1500th Anniversary of Turkestan **Obverse:** Denomination **Reverse:** Domed building **Edge:** Plain **Size:** 37 mm.

Date	F	VF	XF	Unc	BU
2000 Proof	—	—	—	45.00	—

KM# 35 500 TENGE Weight: 24.0000 g. **Composition:** 0.9250 Silver .7137 oz. ASW **Subject:** Snow Leopard **Obverse:** Denomination **Reverse:** Prowling leopard **Edge:** Plain **Size:** 37 mm.

Date	Mintage	F	VF	XF	Unc	BU
2000 Proof	3,000	—	—	—	50.00	—

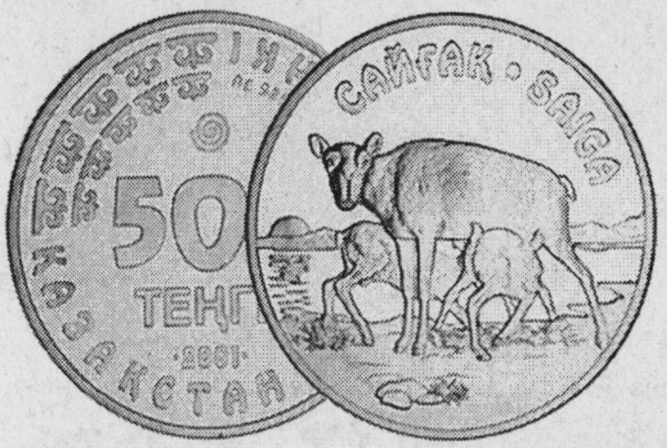

KM# 36 500 TENGE Weight: 24.0000 g. **Composition:** 0.9250 Silver .7137 oz. ASW **Subject:** Petroglyphs of Kazakhstan **Obverse:** Denomination **Reverse:** "Sun God" petroglyph **Edge:** Plain **Size:** 36.9 mm.

Date	Mintage	F	VF	XF	Unc	BU
2000 Proof	3,000	—	—	—	45.00	—

KM# 37 500 TENGE Weight: 23.9000 g. **Composition:** 0.9250 Silver 0.7108 oz. ASW **Subject:** Wildlife **Obverse:** Denomination **Reverse:** Female Saiga with two young **Edge:** Plain **Size:** 37 mm.

Date	Mintage	F	VF	XF	Unc	BU
2001 Proof	—	Value: 50.00				

KM# 38 500 TENGE **Weight:** 23.8100 g. **Composition:** 0.9250 Silver 0.7081 oz. ASW **Subject:** 10 Years of Independence **Obverse:** Monument and flag **Reverse:** Denomination and arms **Edge:** Plain **Size:** 36.9 mm.

Date	Mintage	F	VF	XF	Unc	BU
2001 Proof	3,000	Value: 42.50				

KM# 29 1000 TENGE **Weight:** 3.1200 g. **Composition:** 0.9999 Gold .1003 oz. AGW **Subject:** Silk Road **Reverse:** Caravan around national arms

Date	F	VF	XF	Unc	BU
1995	—	—	—	75.00	—

PROBAS

KM#	Date	Mintage	Identification	Mkt Val
Pr1	1992	—	50 Tenge. Copper Nickel.	—
Pr2	1992	—	50 Tenge. Copper.	—
Pr3	1992	—	50 Tenge. Brass.	—
Pr4	1992	—	50 Tenge. Aluminum.	—

KEELING COCOS

The Territory of Cocos (Keeling) Islands, an Australian territory, comprises a group of 27 coral islands located (see arrow on map of Australia) in the Indian Ocean 1,300 miles northwest of Australia. Only Direction and Home Islands are regularly inhabited. The group has an area of 5.4 sq. mi. and a population of about 569. Calcium, phosphate and coconut products are exported.

The islands were discovered by Capt. William Keeling of the British East India Co. in 1609. Alexander Hare, an English adventurer, established a settlement on one of the southern islands in 1823, but it lasted less than a year. A permanent settlement was established on Direction Island in 1827 by Hare and Capt. John Clunies Ross, a Scot, for the purpose of storing East Indian spices for reshipment to Europe during periods of shortage. When the experiment in spice futures did not develop satisfactorily, Hare left the islands (1829 or 1830), leaving Ross as sole owner. The coral group became a British protectorate in 1856; was attached to the colony of Ceylon in 1878; and was placed under the administration of the Straits Settlements in 1882. In 1903 the group was annexed to the Straits Settlements and incorporated into the colony of Singapore until Nov. of 1955, when it was placed under the administration of Australia.

RULERS
British

MONETARY SYSTEM
100 Cents = 1 Rupee

AUSTRALIAN TERRITORY

DECIMAL COINAGE

KM# 1 5 CENTS **Composition:** Bronze **Obverse:** Palm tree, denomination **Reverse:** Bust of John Clunies Ross facing left

Date	F	VF	XF	Unc	BU
1977	—	—	18.00	35.00	—

KM# 2 10 CENTS **Composition:** Bronze **Obverse:** Palm tree, denomination **Reverse:** Bust of John Clunies Ross facing left

Date	F	VF	XF	Unc	BU
1977	—	—	20.00	40.00	—

KM# 3 25 CENTS **Composition:** Bronze **Obverse:** Palm tree, denomination **Reverse:** Bust of John Clunies Ross facing left

Date	F	VF	XF	Unc	BU
1977	—	—	20.00	40.00	—

KM# 4 50 CENTS **Composition:** Bronze **Obverse:** Palm tree, denomination **Reverse:** Bust of John Clunies Ross facing left

Date	F	VF	XF	Unc	BU
1977	—	—	22.00	45.00	—

KM# 5 RUPEE **Composition:** Copper-Nickel **Obverse:** Palm tree, denomination **Reverse:** Bust of John Clunies Ross facing left

Date	F	VF	XF	Unc	BU
1977	—	—	35.00	70.00	—

KM# 6 2 RUPEE **Composition:** Copper-Nickel **Obverse:** Palm tree, denomination **Reverse:** Bust of John Clunies Ross facing left

Date	F	VF	XF	Unc	BU
1977	—	—	35.00	70.00	—

KM# 7 5 RUPEE **Composition:** Copper-Nickel **Obverse:** Palm tree, denomination **Reverse:** Bust of John Clunies Ross facing left

Date	F	VF	XF	Unc	BU
1977	—	—	40.00	80.00	—

KM# 8 10 RUPEE **Weight:** 6.5000 g. **Composition:** 0.9250 Silver .1933 oz. ASW **Subject:** 150th Anniversary - Keeling-Cocos Islands **Obverse:** Palm tree, denomination **Reverse:** Bust of John Clunies Ross facing left

Date	Mintage	F	VF	XF	Unc	BU
1977	6,000	—	—	—	90.00	—
1977 Proof	4,000	Value: 120				

KM# 9 25 RUPEE **Weight:** 16.2500 g. **Composition:** 0.9250 Silver .4833 oz. ASW **Subject:** 150th Anniversary - Keeling-Cocos Islands **Obverse:** Palm tree, denomination **Reverse:** Bust of John Clunies Ross facing left **Note:** Similar to 10 Rupees, KM#9.

Date	Mintage	F	VF	XF	Unc	BU
1977	6,000	—	—	—	135	—
1977 Proof	4,000	Value: 200				

KM# 10 150 RUPEE **Composition:** 0.7500 Gold **Subject:** 150th Anniversary - Keeling-Cocos Islands **Obverse:** Palm tree, denomination **Reverse:** Bust of John Clunies Ross facing left **Note:** The entire issue of KM#10 was stolen with only 290 pieces being recovered.

Date	Mintage	F	VF	XF	Unc	BU
ND(1977)	2,000	—	—	—	—	—
ND(1977) Proof	2,000	—	—	—	—	—

KM# 10a 150 RUPEE **Weight:** 8.4800 g. **Composition:** 0.9160 Gold .2497 oz. AGW **Obverse:** Palm tree, denomination **Reverse:** Bust of John Clunies Ross facing left

Date	Mintage	F	VF	XF	Unc	BU
ND(1977)	2,000	—	—	—	275	—
ND(1977) Proof	2,000	Value: 375				

TOKEN COINAGE
Plastic Ivory

Tn1-Tn7 were all issued with individual serial numbers.

KM# Tn1 5 CENTS

Date	Mintage	VG	F	VF	XF	Unc
1913	5,000	60.00	100	200	325	425

KM# Tn2 10 CENTS

Date	Mintage	VG	F	VF	XF	Unc
1913	5,000	45.00	75.00	150	275	375

KM# Tn3 25 CENTS

Date	Mintage	VG	F	VF	XF	Unc
1913	5,000	20.00	30.00	50.00	90.00	185

KM# Tn4 50 CENTS

Date	Mintage	VG	F	VF	XF	Unc
1913	2,000	75.00	125	275	475	575

KM# Tn5 RUPEE

Date	Mintage	VG	F	VF	XF	Unc
1913	2,000	25.00	40.00	75.00	125	200

KM# Tn6 2 RUPEE

Date	Mintage	VG	F	VF	XF	Unc
1913	1,000	35.00	50.00	90.00	140	225

KM# Tn7 5 RUPEE

Date	Mintage	VG	F	VF	XF	Unc
1913	1,000	35.00	50.00	100	165	250

TOKEN COINAGE
Modern Plastic

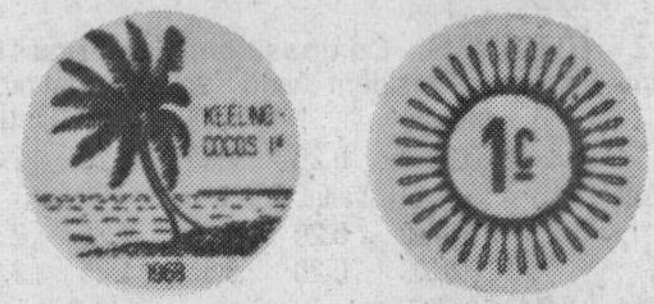

KM# Tn8 CENT **Note:** Aqua-color plastic.

Date	F	VF	XF	Unc	BU
1968	—	—	—	90.00	—

KM# Tn9 5 CENTS **Note:** Aqua-color plastic.

Date	F	VF	XF	Unc	BU
1968	—	—	—	90.00	—

KM# Tn10 10 CENTS **Note:** Aqua-color plastic.

Date	F	VF	XF	Unc	BU
1968	—	—	—	100	—

KM# Tn11 25 CENTS **Note:** Aqua-color plastic.

Date	F	VF	XF	Unc	BU
1968	—	—	—	120	—

KM# Tn12 50 CENTS **Note:** Aqua-color plastic.

Date	F	VF	XF	Unc	BU
1968	—	—	—	135	—

KM# Tn13 RUPEE **Note:** Red-color plastic.

Date	F	VF	XF	Unc	BU
1968	—	—	—	140	—

KM# Tn14 2 RUPEE **Note:** Red-color plastic.

Date	F	VF	XF	Unc	BU
1968	—	—	—	150	—

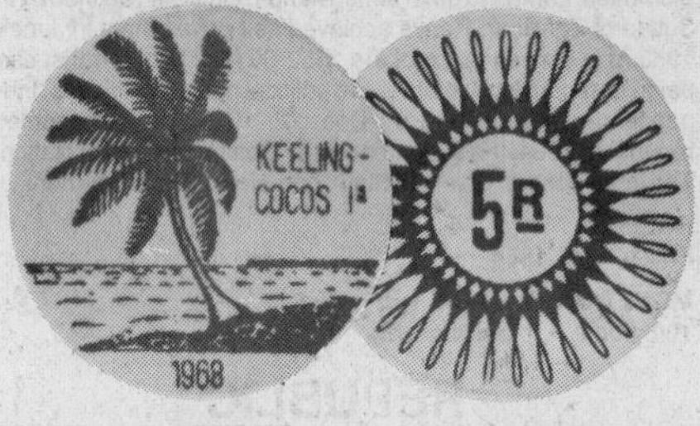

KM# Tn15 5 RUPEE **Note:** Red-color plastic.

Date	F	VF	XF	Unc	BU
1968	—	—	—	175	—

KM# Tn16 10 RUPEE **Note:** Red-color plastic.

Date	F	VF	XF	Unc	BU
1968	—	—	—	210	—

KM# Tn17 25 RUPEE **Note:** Red-color plastic.

Date	F	VF	XF	Unc	BU
1968	—	—	—	245	—

MINT SETS

KM#	Date	Mintage	Identification	Issue Price	Mkt Val
MS1	1977 (7)	—	KM#1-7	—	325
MS2	1977 (2)	6,000	KM#8-9	—	200

PROOF SETS

KM#	Date	Mintage	Identification	Issue Price	Mkt Val
PS1	1977 (2)	4,000	KM#8-9	28.00	275

KENYA

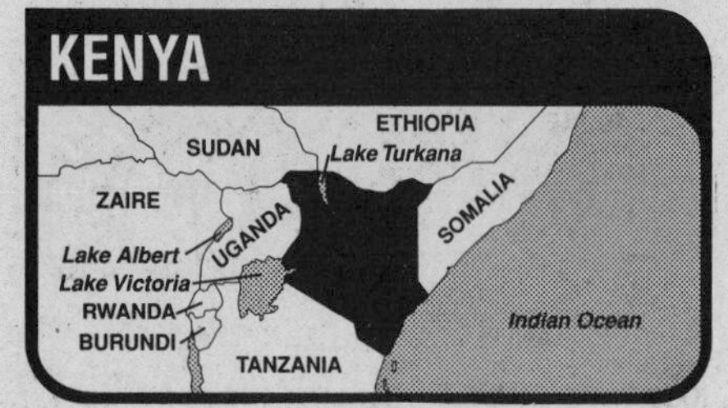

The Republic of Kenya, located on the east coast of Central Africa, has an area of 224,961 sq. mi (582,650 sq. km.) and a population of 20.1 million. Capital: Nairobi. The predominantly agricultural country exports coffee, tea and petroleum products.

The Arabs came to the coast of Kenya in the 8th century and established posts to conduct an ivory and slave trade. The Portuguese, followed in the 16th century. After a lengthy and bitter struggle with the sultans of Zanzibar who controlled much of the southeastern coast of Africa, the Portuguese were driven away (late 17th century) and for many years Kenya was simply a port of call on the route to India. German and British interests in the 19th century produced agreements defining their respective spheres of influence. The British sphere was administrated by the Imperial East Africa Co. until 1895, when the British government purchased the company's rights in the East Africa Protectorate which, in 1920, was designated as Kenya Colony and protectorate - the latter being a 10-mile wide coastal strip together with Mombasa, Lamu and other small islands nominally retained by the Sultan of Zanzibar. Kenya achieved self-government in June of 1963 as a consequence of the 1952-60 Mau Mau terrorist campaign to secure land reforms and political rights for Africans. Independence was attained on Dec. 12, 1963. Kenya became a republic in 1964. It is a member of the Commonwealth of Nations. The president is Chief of State and Head of Government.

RULERS

British, until 1964

MONETARY SYSTEM

100 Cents = 1 Shilling

REPUBLIC

STANDARD COINAGE

KM# 1 5 CENTS **Composition:** Nickel-Brass **Obverse:** Arms **Reverse:** President Jomo Kenyatta bust facing left

Date	Mintage	F	VF	XF	Unc	BU
1966	28,000,000	—	0.25	0.50	1.00	—
1966 Proof	27	Value: 65.00				
1967	9,600,000	—	0.25	0.50	1.00	—
1968	12,000,000	—	0.25	0.50	1.00	—

KM# 10 5 CENTS **Composition:** Nickel-Brass **Obverse:** Arms **Reverse:** President Jomo Kenyatta bust facing left

Date	Mintage	F	VF	XF	Unc	BU
1969	800,000	—	0.50	1.00	2.25	—
1969 Proof	15	Value: 100				
1970	10,000,000	—	0.15	0.25	0.50	—
1971	29,680,000	—	0.15	0.25	0.40	—
1973 Proof	500	Value: 15.00				
1974	5,599,000	—	0.15	0.25	0.40	—
1975	28,000,000	—	0.15	0.25	0.40	—
1978	23,168,000	—	0.15	0.25	0.40	—

KM# 17 5 CENTS **Composition:** Nickel-Brass **Obverse:** Arms **Reverse:** President Arap Moi bust facing right

Date	F	VF	XF	Unc	BU
1978	—	—	—	0.50	—
1978 Proof	—	Value: 10.00			
1980	—	0.15	0.25	0.50	—
1984	—	0.15	0.25	0.75	—
1986	—	0.15	0.25	0.75	—
1987	—	0.15	0.25	0.75	—
1989	—	0.15	0.25	0.50	—
1990	—	0.15	0.25	0.40	—
1991	—	0.15	0.25	0.40	—

KM# 2 10 CENTS **Composition:** Nickel-Brass **Obverse:** Arms **Reverse:** President Jomo Kenyatta bust facing left

Date	Mintage	F	VF	XF	Unc	BU
1966	26,000,000	0.20	0.65	1.25	2.50	—
1966 Proof	27	Value: 65.00				
1967	7,300,000	0.20	0.65	1.25	2.50	—
1968	12,000,000	0.20	0.65	1.25	2.50	—

KM# 11 10 CENTS **Composition:** Nickel-Brass **Obverse:** Arms **Reverse:** President Jomo Kenyatta bust facing left

Date	Mintage	F	VF	XF	Unc	BU
1969	3,900,000	—	0.15	0.25	0.65	—
1969 Proof	15	Value: 100				
1970	7,200,000	—	0.15	0.25	0.65	—
1971	32,400,000	—	0.15	0.25	0.50	—
1973	3,000,000	—	0.15	0.25	0.75	—
1973 Proof	500	Value: 20.00				
1974	3,000,000	—	0.15	0.25	0.75	—
1975	3,000,000	—	0.15	0.25	0.75	—
1977	45,600,000	—	0.15	0.25	0.50	—
1978	22,600,000	—	0.15	0.25	0.50	—

KM# 18 10 CENTS **Composition:** Nickel-Brass **Obverse:** Arms **Reverse:** President Arap Moi bust facing right

Date	F	VF	XF	Unc	BU
1978	—	—	—	1.00	—
1978 Proof	—	Value: 15.00			
1980	—	0.15	0.25	1.00	—
1984	—	0.15	0.25	1.25	—
1986	—	0.15	0.25	1.25	—
1987	—	0.15	0.25	1.25	—
1989	—	0.15	0.25	1.00	—
1990	—	0.15	0.25	1.00	—
1991	—	0.15	0.25	0.75	—

KM# 18a 10 CENTS **Composition:** Brass Plated Steel **Obverse:** Arms **Reverse:** President Arap Moi bust facing right

Date	F	VF	XF	Unc	BU
1994	—	0.20	0.30	1.00	—

KM# 31 10 CENTS **Composition:** Brass Plated Steel **Obverse:** Denomination and arms **Reverse:** President Arap Moi bust facing right

Date	F	VF	XF	Unc	BU
1995	—	0.10	0.20	0.40	—

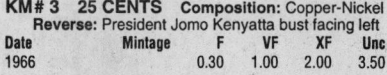

KM# 3 25 CENTS **Composition:** Copper-Nickel **Reverse:** President Jomo Kenyatta bust facing left

Date	Mintage	F	VF	XF	Unc	BU
1966		0.30	1.00	2.00	3.50	—
1966 Proof	27	Value: 75.00				
1967		0.30	1.00	2.00	3.50	—

KM# 12 25 CENTS **Composition:** Copper-Nickel **Reverse:** President Jomo Kenyatta bust facing left

Date	Mintage	F	VF	XF	Unc	BU
1969	200,000	0.50	1.00	2.50	10.00	—
1969 Proof	15	Value: 110				
1973 Proof	500	Value: 18.00				

KM# 4 50 CENTS **Composition:** Copper-Nickel **Reverse:** President Jomo Kenyatta bust facing left

Date	Mintage	F	VF	XF	Unc	BU
1966	4,000,000	0.20	0.40	1.00	2.75	—
1966 Proof	27	Value: 75.00				
1967	5,120,000	0.20	0.40	0.85	2.25	—
1968	6,000,000	0.20	0.40	0.85	2.00	—

KM# 13 50 CENTS **Composition:** Copper-Nickel **Reverse:** President Jomo Kenyatta bust facing left

Date	Mintage	F	VF	XF	Unc	BU
1969	400,000	0.40	0.80	1.50	3.00	—
1969 Proof	15	Value: 110				
1971	9,600,000	—	0.20	0.40	0.75	—
1973	3,360,000	0.20	0.40	0.80	1.75	—
1973 Proof	500	Value: 18.00				
1974	12,640,000	—	0.20	0.40	0.75	—
1975	8,000,000	—	0.20	0.40	0.75	—
1977	16,000,000	—	0.20	0.40	0.75	—
1978	20,480,000	—	0.20	0.40	0.75	—

KM# 19 50 CENTS **Composition:** Copper-Nickel **Reverse:** President Arap Moi bust facing right

Date	F	VF	XF	Unc	BU
1978	—	—	—	0.75	—
1978 Proof	—	Value: 20.00			
1980	—	0.15	0.25	0.75	—
1989	—	0.15	0.25	0.75	—
1990	—	0.15	0.25	0.75	—

KM# 19a 50 CENTS **Composition:** Nickel Plated Steel **Reverse:** President Arap Moi bust facing right

Date	F	VF	XF	Unc	BU
1994	—	0.25	0.35	1.00	—

KM# 28 50 CENTS **Composition:** Brass Plated Steel **Reverse:** President Arap Moi bust facing right

Date	F	VF	XF	Unc	BU
1995	—	0.15	0.25	0.50	—
1997	—	0.15	0.25	0.50	—

KM# 5 SHILLING **Composition:** Copper-Nickel **Reverse:** President Jomo Kenyatta bust facing left

Date	Mintage	F	VF	XF	Unc	BU
1966	20,000,000	0.25	0.50	1.00	3.00	—
1966 Proof	27	Value: 75.00				
1967	4,000,000	0.25	0.50	1.00	2.75	—
1968	8,000,000	0.20	0.40	0.80	2.25	—

KM# 14 SHILLING **Composition:** Copper-Nickel **Reverse:** President Jomo Kenyatta bust facing left

Date	Mintage	F	VF	XF	Unc	BU
1969	4,000,000	0.15	0.30	0.75	2.25	—
1969 Proof	15	Value: 110				
1971	24,000,000	0.10	0.30	0.65	2.00	—
1973	2,480,000	0.20	0.40	0.80	2.75	—
1973 Proof	500	Value: 20.00				
1974	13,520,000	0.10	0.30	0.65	2.00	—
1975	40,856,000	0.10	0.30	0.65	2.00	—
1978	20,000,000	0.10	0.30	0.65	2.00	—

KM# 20 SHILLING **Composition:** Copper-Nickel **Reverse:** President Arap Moi bust facing right

Date	F	VF	XF	Unc	BU
1978	—	—	—	1.50	—
1978 Proof	—	Value: 30.00			
1980	0.15	0.25	0.50	1.50	—
1989	0.15	0.25	0.50	1.50	—

KM# 20a SHILLING **Composition:** Nickel Plated Steel **Reverse:** President Arap Moi bust facing right

Date	F	VF	XF	Unc	BU
1994	0.25	0.35	0.65	1.75	—

KM# 29 SHILLING **Composition:** Brass Plated Steel **Reverse:** Bust of President Arap Moi facing right

Date	F	VF	XF	Unc	BU
1995	0.10	0.20	0.40	0.75	—
1997	0.10	0.20	0.40	0.75	—
1998	0.10	0.20	0.40	0.75	—

KM# 6 2 SHILLINGS **Composition:** Copper-Nickel **Reverse:** President Jomo Kenyatta bust facing left

Date	Mintage	F	VF	XF	Unc	BU
1966	3,000,000	1.00	2.00	3.00	7.00	—
1966 Proof	27	Value: 95.00				
1968	1,100,000	1.00	2.75	4.50	10.00	—

KM# 15 2 SHILLINGS **Composition:** Copper-Nickel **Reverse:** President Jomo Kenyatta bust facing left

Date	Mintage	F	VF	XF	Unc	BU
1969	100,000	2.00	4.00	8.00	12.50	—
1969 Proof	15	Value: 120				
1971	1,920,000	0.60	1.25	3.50	7.50	—
1973 Proof	500	Value: 25.00				

KM# 16 5 SHILLINGS **Composition:** Brass **Subject:** 10th Anniversary of Independence **Shape:** 9-sided

Date	Mintage	F	VF	XF	Unc	BU
1973	100,000	4.50	10.00	17.50	30.00	—
1973 Proof	1,500	Value: 45.00				

KM# 23 5 SHILLINGS **Composition:** Copper-Nickel **Reverse:** President Arap Moi bust facing right **Shape:** 7-sided

Date	F	VF	XF	Unc	BU
1985	0.35	0.75	1.50	3.00	—

KM# 23a 5 SHILLINGS **Composition:** Nickel Plated Steel **Reverse:** President Arap Moi bust facing right **Shape:** 7-sided

Date	F	VF	XF	Unc	BU
1994	0.50	1.00	2.25	4.50	—

KM# 30 5 SHILLINGS **Ring Composition:** Copper-Nickel **Center Composition:** Brass **Reverse:** President Arap Moi bust facing right

Date	F	VF	XF	Unc	BU
1995	—	—	—	4.00	—
1997	—	—	—	4.00	—

KM# 27 10 SHILLINGS **Ring Composition:** Brass **Center Composition:** Copper-Nickel **Reverse:** President Arap Moi bust facing right

Date	F	VF	XF	Unc	BU
1994	—	—	—	5.00	—
1995	—	—	—	5.00	—
1997	—	—	—	5.00	—

KM# 32 20 SHILLINGS **Ring Composition:** Copper-Nickel **Center Composition:** Brass **Obverse:** Denomination above arms **Reverse:** President Arap Moi bust facing right

Date	F	VF	XF	Unc	BU
1998	—	—	—	8.00	—

KM# 7 100 SHILLINGS **Weight:** 7.6000 g. **Composition:** 0.9170 Gold .224 oz. AGW **Subject:** 75th Anniversary - Birth of President Jomo Kenyatta

Date	Mintage	F	VF	XF	Unc	BU
1966	—	—	—	—	110	—
1966 Proof	7,500	Value: 130				

KM# 21 200 SHILLINGS **Weight:** 28.2800 g. **Composition:** 0.9250 Silver .841 oz. ASW **Obverse:** President Moi **Reverse:** Coat of arms

Date	Mintage	F	VF	XF	Unc	BU
1978 Proof	Est. 9,500	Value: 100				

KM# 8 250 SHILLINGS **Weight:** 19.0000 g. **Composition:** 0.9170 Gold .5602 oz. AGW **Subject:** 75th Anniversary - Birth of President Jomo Kenyatta

Date	Mintage	F	VF	XF	Unc	BU
1966	—	—	—	—	250	—
1966 Proof	1,000	Value: 285				

KM# 9 500 SHILLINGS **Weight:** 38.0000 g. **Composition:** 0.9170 Gold 1.1204 oz. AGW **Subject:** 75th Anniversary - Birth of President Jomo Kenyatta

Date	Mintage	F	VF	XF	Unc	BU
1966	—	—	—	—	500	—
1966 Proof	500	Value: 550				

KM# 24 500 SHILLINGS **Weight:** 28.2800 g. **Composition:** 0.9250 Silver .8410 oz. ASW **Subject:** 10th Anniversary of Moi as President **Shape:** 10-sided

Date	F	VF	XF	Unc	BU
ND(1988) Proof	—	Value: 165			

KM# 25 500 SHILLINGS **Weight:** 28.3300 g. **Composition:** 0.9250 Silver .8425 oz. ASW **Subject:** 25th Anniversary of Independence

Date	F	VF	XF	Unc	BU
ND(1988) Proof	—	Value: 185			

KM# 26 1000 SHILLINGS **Weight:** 28.2800 g. **Composition:** 0.9250 Silver .8351 oz. ASW **Subject:** Silver Jubilee of Central Bank

Date	F	VF	XF	Unc	BU
1991 Proof	—	Value: 275			

KM# 22 3000 SHILLING **Weight:** 40.0000 g. **Composition:** 0.9170 Gold 1.1787 oz. AGW **Obverse:** President Moi **Reverse:** Coat of arms

Date	Mintage	F	VF	XF	Unc	BU
1978 Proof	2,000	Value: 750				

MINT SETS

KM#	Date	Mintage	Identification	Issue Price	Mkt Val
MS1	1966 (3)	—	KM7-9	—	865

PROOF SETS

KM#	Date	Mintage	Identification	Issue Price	Mkt Val
PS1	1966 (6)	27	KM1-6	—	450
PS2	1966 (3)	500	KM7-9	153	975
PS3	1969 (6)	15	KM10-15	—	650
PS4	1973 (7)	500	KM10-16	—	160
PS5	1978 (5)	9,500	KM#17-21	—	175

KIAU CHAU

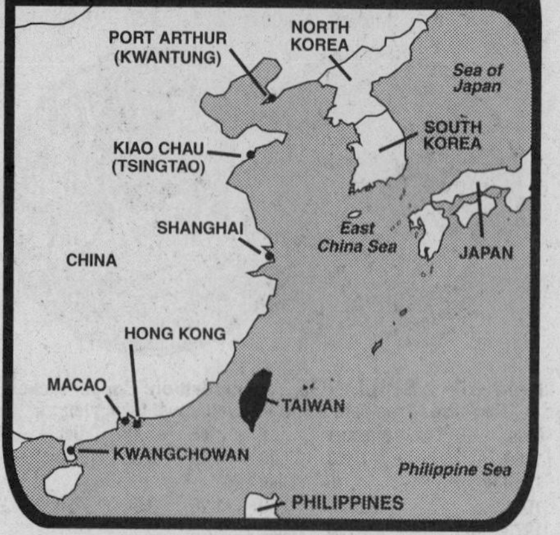

Kiau Chau (Kiao Chau, Kiaochow, Kiautscho, now Jiaozhou), a former German trading enclave, including the port of Tsingtao (Qingdao), was located on the Shantung (Shandong) Peninsula of eastern China. Following the murder of two missionaries in Shantung in 1897, Germany occupied Kiaochow Bay, and during subsequent negotiations with the Chinese government obtained a 99 year lease on 177 sq. mi. of land. The enclave was established as a free port in 1899, and a customs house set up to collect tariffs on goods moving to and from the Chinese interior. The Japanese took seige to the port on Aug. 27, 1914 as their first action in World War I to deprive German sea marauders of their east Asian supply and refitting base. Aided by the British forces, the siege ended Nov. 7. Japan retained possession until 1922, when it was restored to China by the Washington Conference on China and naval armaments. It fell again to Japan in 1938, but not before the Chinese had destroyed its manufacturing facilities. It is presently a part of the Peoples Republic of China. The major city is Tsingtao (Qingdao) and is noted for its beer.

RULERS
Wilhelm II, 1897-1918
Japanese, 1914-1922, 1938-1945

MONETARY SYSTEM
100 Cents = 1 Dollar

GERMAN OCCUPATION

STANDARD COINAGE

Y# 1 5 CENTS **Composition:** Copper-Nickel **Ruler:** Wilhelm II **Obverse:** German Imperial Eagle **Obv. Legend:** DEUTSCH.KIAUTSHAU GEBIET **Rev. Inscription:** Kuang-hsü Yüan-pao

Date	Mintage	F	VF	XF	Unc	BU
1909	610,000	50.00	75.00	115	180	—
1909 Proof	—	Value: 450				

Y# 2 10 CENTS **Ruler:** Wilhelm II **Obverse:** German Imperial Eagle **Obv. Legend:** DEUTSCH.KIAUTSHAU GEBIET **Rev. Inscription:** Kuang-hsü Yüan-pao

Date	Mintage	F	VF	XF	Unc	BU
1909	670,000	30.00	50.00	90.00	150	—
1909 Proof	—	Value: 500				

KIRIBATI

The Republic of Kiribati (formerly the Gilbert Islands), consists of 30 coral atolls and islands spread over more than one million sq. mi. (2,590,000 sq. km.) of the southwest Pacific Ocean, has an area of 332 sq. mi. (717 sq. km.) and a population of 64,200. Capital: Bairiki, on Tarawa. In addition to the Gilbert Islands proper, Kiribati includes Ocean Island, the Central and Southern Line Islands, and the Phoenix Islands, though possession of Canton and Enderbury of the Phoenix Islands is disputed with the United States. Most families engage in subsistence fishing. Copra and phosphates are exported, mostly to Australia and New Zealand.

The Gilbert Islands and the group formerly called the Ellice Islands (now Tuvalu) comprised a single British crown colony, the Gilbert and Ellice Islands.

Spanish mutineers first sighted the islands in 1537, succeeding visits were made by the English navigators John Byron (1764), James Cook (1777), and Thomas Gilbert and John Marshall (1788). An American, Edward Fanning, arrived in 1798. Britain declared a protectorate over the Gilbert and Ellice Islands, and in1915 began the formation of a colony which was completed when the Phoenix Islands were added to the group in 1937. The Central and Southern Line Islands were administratively attached to the Gilbert and Ellice Islands olony in 1972, and remained attached to the Gilberts when Tuvalu was created in 1975. The colony became self-governing in 1971. Kiribati attained independence on July 12, 1979.

RULERS
British, until 1979

MONETARY SYSTEM
100 Cents = 1 Dollar

REPUBLIC

DECIMAL COINAGE

KM# 1 CENT **Composition:** Bronze **Subject:** Christmas Island Frigatebird

Date	Mintage	F	VF	XF	Unc	BU
1979	90,000	—	—	0.15	0.50	—
1979 Proof	10,000	Value: 1.00				
1992	—	—	—	0.15	0.50	—

KM# 2 2 CENTS **Composition:** Bronze **Subject:** B'abal plant

Date	Mintage	F	VF	XF	Unc	BU
1979	25,000	—	—	0.15	0.35	—
1979 Proof	10,000	Value: 1.25				
1992	—	—	—	0.15	0.35	—

KM# 3 5 CENTS **Composition:** Copper-Nickel **Subject:** Tokai lizard

Date	Mintage	F	VF	XF	Unc	BU
1979	20,000	—	0.15	0.30	1.50	—
1979 Proof	10,000	Value: 2.50				

KM# 4 10 CENTS **Composition:** Copper-Nickel **Subject:** Bread fruit

Date	Mintage	F	VF	XF	Unc	BU
1979	20,000	—	0.15	0.25	1.25	—
1979 Proof	10,000	Value: 3.00				

KM# 5 20 CENTS **Composition:** Copper-Nickel **Subject:** Dolphins

Date	Mintage	F	VF	XF	Unc	BU
1979	20,000	—	0.60	1.50	6.00	—
1979 Proof	10,000	Value: 7.50				

KM# 6 50 CENTS **Composition:** Copper-Nickel **Subject:** Panda nut

Date	Mintage	F	VF	XF	Unc	BU
1979	20,000	—	0.50	1.00	3.00	—
1979 Proof	10,000	Value: 6.50				

KM# 7 DOLLAR **Composition:** Copper-Nickel **Subject:** Outrigger sailboat

Date	Mintage	F	VF	XF	Unc	BU
1979	20,000	—	0.85	1.25	4.00	—
1979 Proof	10,000	Value: 8.00				

KM# 14 2 DOLLARS **Composition:** Nickel-Brass **Subject:** 10th Anniversary of Independence

Date	F	VF	XF	Unc	BU
1989	—	—	—	5.00	—

KM#21 2 DOLLARS **Weight:** 10.0000 g. **Composition:** 0.5000 Silver .1607 oz. ASW **Subject:** Titanic sinking **Obverse:** National arms

Date	F	VF	XF	Unc	BU
1998 Proof	—	Value: 15.00			

KM# 8 5 DOLLARS **Weight:** 28.1600 g. **Composition:** 0.5000 Silver .4527 oz. ASW **Subject:** Independence

Date	Mintage	F	VF	XF	Unc	BU
1979	1,545	—	—	—	22.50	—

KM#8a 5 DOLLARS **Weight:** 28.1600 g. **Composition:** 0.9250 Silver .8375 oz. ASW **Subject:** Independence

Date	Mintage	F	VF	XF	Unc	BU
1979 Proof	3,326	Value: 25.00				

KM# 10 5 DOLLARS **Composition:** Copper-Nickel **Subject:** 2nd Anniversary of Independence and wedding of Prince Charles and Lady Diana

Date	Mintage	F	VF	XF	Unc	BU
1981	50,000	—	—	—	7.00	—

KM# 10a 5 DOLLARS **Weight:** 28.6000 g. **Composition:** 0.9250 Silver .8505 oz. ASW **Subject:** 2nd Anniversary of Independence and wedding of Prince Charles and Lady Diana

Date	Mintage	F	VF	XF	Unc	BU
1981 Proof	25,000	Value: 21.50				

KM# 12 5 DOLLARS **Composition:** Copper-Nickel **Subject:** Royal visit

Date	F	VF	XF	Unc	BU
1982	—	—	—	5.00	—

KM# 12a 5 DOLLARS **Composition:** Silver **Subject:** Royal visit

Date	F	VF	XF	Unc	BU
1982 Proof	—	Value: 35.00			

KM#19 5 DOLLARS **Weight:** 31.4700 g. **Composition:** 0.9250 Silver .9359 oz. ASW **Obverse:** National arms **Reverse:** Discoverer of Kiribati - Capt. John Byron, ship

Date	Mintage	F	VF	XF	Unc	BU
1996 Proof	Est. 15,000	Value: 50.00				

KM#20 5 DOLLARS **Weight:** 31.4700 g. **Composition:** 0.9250 Silver .9359 oz. ASW **Obverse:** National arms **Reverse:** High diver

Date	Mintage	F	VF	XF	Unc	BU
1996 Proof	40,000	Value: 32.50				

KM#22 5 DOLLARS **Weight:** 15.5518 g. **Composition:** 0.9250 Silver .4625 oz. ASW **Subject:** Guerra & Paz **Obverse:** Kiribati arms **Reverse:** Dove **Shape:** Jagged half of coin **Note:** Half of two-part coin, combined with Western Samoa KM#115, issued in sets only. Value is determined by combining the two parts.

Date	Mintage	F	VF	XF	Unc	BU
ND(1997) Proof	Est. 10,000	Value: 35.00				

KM#23 5 DOLLARS **Weight:** 15.5518 g. **Composition:** 0.9250 Silver .4625 oz. ASW **Subject:** Powerful empires **Obverse:** Kiribati arms **Reverse:** Helmets and hats **Shape:** Jagged half of coin **Note:** Half of two-part coin, combined with Western Samoa KM#116, issued in sets only. Value is determined by combining the two parts.

Date	Mintage	F	VF	XF	Unc	BU
ND(1997) Proof	Est. 10,000	Value: 35.00				

KM#24 5 DOLLARS **Weight:** 15.5518 g. **Composition:** 0.9250 Silver .4625 oz. ASW **Subject:** Tempora Mutantur **Obverse:** Kiribati arms **Reverse:** Solar system **Shape:** Jagged half of coin **Note:** Half of two-part coin, combined with Western Samoa KM#117, issued in sets only. Value is determined by combining the two parts.

Date	Mintage	F	VF	XF	Unc	BU
ND(1997) Proof	Est. 10,000	Value: 35.00				

KM#25 5 DOLLARS **Weight:** 15.5518 g. **Composition:** 0.9250 Silver .4625 oz. ASW **Subject:** People and monuments - column, compass **Obverse:** Kiribati arms **Shape:** Jagged half of coin **Note:** Half of two-part coin, combined with Western Samoa KM#118, issued in sets only. Value is determined by combining the two parts.

Date	Mintage	F	VF	XF	Unc	BU
ND(1997) Proof	Est. 10,000	Value: 37.50				

KM#30 5 DOLLARS **Weight:** 31.6000 g. **Composition:** 0.9250 Silver 0.9398 oz. ASW **Subject:** Whaling Ship Potomac 1842 **Obverse:** National arms **Reverse:** Ship in background, sailors killing whale scene at bottom above denomination **Edge:** Reeded **Size:** 38.5 mm.

Date	F	VF	XF	Unc	BU
1998 Proof	—	Value: 50.00			

KM#28 5 DOLLARS **Weight:** 31.3000 g. **Composition:** 0.9990 Silver 1.0053 oz. ASW **Subject:** 10th Anniversary of Emperor Akihito's Reign **Obverse:** Kinbati arms **Reverse:** Japan's Imperial couple **Edge:** Reeded **Size:** 38.6 mm.

Date	Mintage	F	VF	XF	Unc	BU
2000 Proof	2,000	Value: 70.00				

KM# 13 10 DOLLARS **Weight:** 28.2800 g. **Composition:** 0.9250 Silver .8411 oz. ASW **Subject:** 5th Anniversary of Independence

Date	Mintage	F	VF	XF	Unc	BU
ND(1984)	—	—	—	—	75.00	—
ND(1984) Proof	2,500	Value: 45.00				

KM# 13a 10 DOLLARS **Weight:** 47.5200 g. **Composition:** 0.9170 Gold 1.4012 oz. AGW **Subject:** 5th Anniversary of Independence

Date	Mintage	F	VF	XF	Unc	BU
ND(1984) Proof	50	Value: 1,250				

KM#27 10 DOLLARS **Weight:** 1.2441 g. **Composition:** 0.9990 Gold .04 oz. AGW **Subject:** Titanic **Obverse:** National arms **Reverse:** Sinking ships and lifeboats

Date	F	VF	XF	Unc	BU
1998 Proof	—	Value: 50.00			

KM# 17 20 DOLLARS **Weight:** 31.4700 g. **Composition:** 0.9250 Silver .9359 oz. ASW **Subject:** Barcelona Olympics - Sailing

Date	Mintage	F	VF	XF	Unc	BU
1992 Proof	40,000	Value: 27.50				

KM# 18 20 DOLLARS **Weight:** 31.4700 g. **Composition:** 0.9250 Silver .9359 oz. ASW **Subject:** Endangered Wildlife **Reverse:** Christmas Island Frigatebird

Date	F	VF	XF	Unc	BU
1992 Proof	—	Value: 40.00			

KM#15 20 DOLLARS **Weight:** 31.4700 g. **Composition:** 0.9250 Silver .9359 oz. ASW **Subject:** Soccer - World Cup '94

Date	Mintage	F	VF	XF	Unc	BU
1993 Proof	Est. 10,000	Value: 32.50				

KM#16 20 DOLLARS **Weight:** 31.4700 g. **Composition:** 0.9250 Silver .9359 oz. ASW **Subject:** First Space Walk

Date	Mintage	F	VF	XF	Unc	BU
1993 Proof	Est. 15,000	Value: 30.00				

KM#26 50 DOLLARS **Weight:** 7.7759 g. **Composition:** 0.9990 Gold .25 oz. AGW **Subject:** Tempora Mutantur **Obverse:** Kiribati arms **Reverse:** Solar system **Shape:** Jagged half of coin **Note:** Similar to KM#24. Half of two-part coin, combined with Western Samoa KM#119, issued in sets only. Value is determined by combining the two parts.

Date	Mintage	F	VF	XF	Unc	BU
ND(1997) Proof	Est. 2,500	Value: 110				

KM# 9 150 DOLLARS **Weight:** 15.9800 g. **Composition:** 0.9170 Gold .4711 oz. AGW **Subject:** Independence - Traditional Meeting House

Date	Mintage	F	VF	XF	Unc	BU
1979	422	—	—	—	250	—
1979 Proof	386	Value: 275				

KM# 11 150 DOLLARS **Weight:** 15.9800 g. **Composition:** 0.9170 Gold .4711 oz. AGW **Subject:** 2nd Anniversary of Independence, and wedding of Prince Charles and Lady Diana

Date	Mintage	F	VF	XF	Unc	BU
1981	750	—	—	—	225	—
1981 Proof	1,500	Value: 250				

KM#29 200 DOLLARS **Weight:** 31.3000 g. **Composition:** 0.9990 Gold 1.0053 oz. AGW **Subject:** 10th Anniversary of Emperor Akihito's Reign **Obverse:** Kinbati arms **Reverse:** Japan's Imperial couple **Edge:** Reeded **Size:** 35 mm.

Date	Mintage	F	VF	XF	Unc	BU
2000 Proof	500	Value: 550				

COMBINED PROOF SETS (CPS)

KM#	Date	Mintage	Identification	Issue Price	Mkt Val
CPS1	1997 (8)	10,000	Kiribati KM#22-25, West Samoa KM#115-118	—	240

PROOF SETS

KM#	Date	Mintage	Identification	Issue Price	Mkt Val
PS1	1979 (7)	10,000	KM1-7	34.00	25.00
PS2	1981 (2)	—	KM10a, 11	—	270

KOREA

Korea, 'Land of the Morning Calm', occupies a mountainous peninsula in northeast Asia bounded by Manchuria, the Yellow Sea and the Sea of Japan.

According to legend, the first Korean dynasty, that of the House of Tangun, ruled from 2333 B.C. to 1122 B.C. It was followed by the dynasty of Kija, a Chinese scholar, which continued until 193 B.C. and brought a high civilization to Korea. The first recorded period in the history of Korea, the period of the Three Kingdoms, lasted from 57 B.C. to 935 A.D. and achieved the first political unification of the peninsula. The Kingdom of Koryo, from which Korea derived its name, was founded in 935 and continued until 1392, when it was superseded by the Yi Dynasty of King Yi. Sung Kye was to last until the Japanese annexation in 1910.

At the end of the 16th century Korea was invaded and occupied for 7 years by Japan, and from 1627 until the late 19th century it was a semi-independent tributary of China. Japan replaced China as the predominant foreign influence at the end of the Sino-Japanese War (1894-95), only to find her position threatened by Russian influence from 1896 to 1904. The Russian threat was eliminated by the Russo-Japanese War (1904-05) and in 1905 Japan established a direct protectorate over Korea. On Aug. 22,1910, the last Korean ruler signed the treaty that annexed Korea to Japan as a government generalcy in the Japanese Empire. Japanese suzerainty was maintained until the end of World War II.

From 1633 to 1891 the monetary system of Korea employed cast coins with a square center hole. Fifty-two agencies were authorized to procure these coins from a lesser number of coin foundries. They exist in thousands of varieties. Seed, or mother coins, were used to make the impressions in the molds in which the regular cash coins were cast. Czarist-Russian Korea experimented with Korean coins when Alexiev of Russia, Korea's Financial Advisor, founded the First Asian Branch of the Russo-Korean Bank on March 1, 1898, and authorized the issuing of a set of new Korean coins with a crowned Russian-style quasi-eagle. British-Japanese opposition and the Russo-Japanese War operated to end the Russian coinage experiment in 1904.

RULERS

Yi Hyong (Kojong), 1864-1897
as Emperor Kuang Mu, 1897-1907
Japanese Puppet
Yung Hi (Sunjong), 1907-1910

DATING

KINGDOM

STANDARD COINAGE

KM# 1116 5 FUN **Weight:** 17.2000 g. **Composition:** Copper **Ruler:** Kuang Mu

Date	F	VF	XF	Unc	BU
6 (1902)	8.00	16.00	32.00	100	—

KM# 1117 1/4 YANG **Composition:** Copper-Nickel **Ruler:** Kuang Mu **Obverse:** Dragon crowded by small tight circle

Date	F	VF	XF	Unc	BU
5 (1901)	200	300	500	1,100	—

RUSSIAN DOMINATION

REFORM COINAGE

KM# 1121 CHON **Weight:** 6.8000 g. **Composition:** Bronze **Ruler:** Kuang Mu

Date	Mintage	F	VF	XF	Unc	BU
2 (1902)	3,001,000	1,650	3,250	5,500	8,500	—

KM# 1122 5 CHON **Weight:** 4.3000 g. **Composition:** Copper-Nickel **Ruler:** Kuang Mu

Date	Mintage	F	VF	XF	Unc	BU
6 (1902)	2,800,000	1,250	2,350	4,000	6,000	—

KM# 1123 1/2 WON **Weight:** 13.5000 g. **Composition:** 0.8000 Silver .3473 oz. ASW **Ruler:** Kuang Mu

Date	Mintage	F	VF	XF	Unc	BU
5 (1901)	1,831,000	2,500	5,500	9,000	14,000	—

Note: Ponterio & Assoc. Witte Museum sale 8-89 choice BU realized $12,500; Heritage Piedmont sale 6-2000 choice BU realized $18,400

JAPANESE PROTECTORATE

REFORM COINAGE

KM# 1124 1/2 CHON **Weight:** 3.5600 g. **Composition:** Bronze **Ruler:** Kuang Mu

Date	Mintage	F	VF	XF	Unc	BU
10 (1906)	24,000,000	3.00	10.00	25.00	90.00	—

KM# 1145 1/2 CHON **Weight:** 2.1000 g. **Composition:** Bronze **Ruler:** Kuang Mu

Date	F	VF	XF	Unc	BU
11 (1907) Rare	—	—	—	—	—

KM# 1136 1/2 CHON **Weight:** 2.1000 g. **Composition:** Bronze **Ruler:** Yung Hi (Sunjong)

Date	Mintage	F	VF	XF	Unc	BU
1 (1907)	Inc. above	125	275	450	750	—

Note: Mintage for year 1 is included in the mintage for Year 11 of KM#1124

Date	Mintage	F	VF	XF	Unc	BU
2 (1908)	21,000,000	6.00	20.00	40.00	140	—
3 (1909)	8,200,000	7.00	22.00	45.00	150	—
4 (1910)	5,070,000	85.00	200	400	750	—

KM# 1125 CHON **Weight:** 7.1300 g. **Composition:** Bronze **Ruler:** Kuang Mu

Date	Mintage	F	VF	XF	Unc	BU
9 (1905)	11,800,000	9.00	15.00	30.00	100	—
10 (1906)	Inc. above	6.50	12.00	25.00	100	—

KM# 1132 CHON **Weight:** 4.2000 g. **Composition:** Bronze **Ruler:** Kuang Mu

Date	Mintage	F	VF	XF	Unc	BU
11 (1907)	11,200,000	3.50	7.50	15.00	85.00	—

KM# 1137 CHON **Weight:** 4.2000 g. **Composition:** Bronze **Ruler:** Yung Hi (Sunjong)

Date	Mintage	F	VF	XF	Unc	BU
1 (1907)	Inc. above	4.50	12.00	27.50	100	—
2 (1908)	6,800,000	3.00	7.00	14.00	75.00	—
3 (1909)	9,200,000	3.00	7.00	12.50	70.00	—
4 (1910)	3,500,000	4.00	11.00	23.00	90.00	—

KM# 1126 5 CHON **Weight:** 4.5000 g. **Composition:** Copper-Nickel **Ruler:** Kuang Mu

Date	Mintage	F	VF	XF	Unc	BU
9 (1905)	20,000,000	7.00	20.00	40.00	80.00	—
9 (1905) Proof	—	Value: 1,500				
11 (1907)	160,000,000	9.00	22.00	45.00	90.00	—

KM# 1138 5 CHON **Weight:** 4.5000 g. **Composition:** Copper-Nickel **Ruler:** Yung Hi (Sunjong)

Date	F	VF	XF	Unc	BU
3 (1909)	900	1,750	3,000	4,000	—

KM# 1127 10 CHON **Weight:** 2.7000 g. **Composition:** 0.8000 Silver .0695 oz. ASW **Ruler:** Kuang Mu **Note:** 1.5 millimeters thick.

Date	Mintage	F	VF	XF	Unc	BU
10 (1906)	2,000,000	15.00	25.00	50.00	100	—

KM# 1133 10 CHON **Weight:** 2.2500 g. **Composition:** 0.8000 Silver .0695 oz. ASW **Ruler:** Kuang Mu **Note:** 1.0 millimeters thick.

Date	Mintage	F	VF	XF	Unc	BU
11 (1907)	2,400,000	15.00	25.00	60.00	120	—

KM# 1139 10 CHON **Weight:** 2.2500 g. **Composition:** 0.8000 Silver .0578 oz. ASW **Ruler:** Yung Hi (Sunjong)

Date	Mintage	F	VF	XF	Unc	BU
2 (1908)	6,300,000	12.00	20.00	35.00	75.00	—
3 (1909) Rare	—	—	—	—	—	—
4 (1910)	9,500,000	10.00	18.00	32.00	65.00	—

KM# 1128 20 CHON **Weight:** 5.3900 g. **Composition:** 0.8000 Silver .1386 oz. ASW **Ruler:** Kuang Mu

Date	Mintage	F	VF	XF	Unc	BU
9 (1905)	1,000,000	30.00	70.00	120	235	—
9 (1905) Proof	—	Value: 2,250				
10 (1906)	2,500,000	25.00	50.00	100	200	—
10 (1906) Proof	—	Value: 1,275				

KM# 1134 20 CHON **Weight:** 4.0500 g. **Composition:** 0.8000 Silver .1042 oz. ASW **Ruler:** Kuang Mu

Date	Mintage	F	VF	XF	Unc	BU
11 (1907)	1,500,000	20.00	40.00	70.00	175	—

KM# 1140 20 CHON **Weight:** 4.0500 g. **Composition:** 0.8000 Silver .1157 oz. ASW **Ruler:** Yung Hi (Sunjong)

Date	Mintage	F	VF	XF	Unc	BU
2 (1908)	3,000,000	16.50	30.00	60.00	135	—
3 (1909)	2,000,000	16.50	30.00	60.00	135	—
4 (1910)	2,000,000	16.50	30.00	60.00	135	—

KM# 1129 1/2 WON **Weight:** 13.4800 g. **Composition:** 0.8000 Silver .3467 oz. ASW **Ruler:** Kuang Mu

Date	Mintage	F	VF	XF	Unc	BU
9 (1905)	600,000	55.00	100	185	385	—
9 (1905) Proof	—	Value: 1,850				
10 (1906)	1,200,000	60.00	110	200	450	—

KM# 1135 1/2 WON **Weight:** 10.1300 g. **Composition:** 0.8000 Silver .2606 oz. ASW **Ruler:** Kuang Mu

Date	Mintage	F	VF	XF	Unc	BU
11 (1907)	1,000,000	65.00	115	225	550	—

KM# 1141 1/2 WON **Weight:** 10.1300 g. **Composition:** 0.8000 Silver .2606 oz. ASW **Ruler:** Yung Hi (Sunjong)

Date	Mintage	F	VF	XF	Unc	BU
2 (1908)	1,400,000	65.00	115	215	475	—

KM# 1142 5 WON **Weight:** 4.1666 g. **Composition:** 0.9000 Gold .1206 oz. AGW **Ruler:** Yung Hi (Sunjong)

Date	Mintage	F	VF	XF	Unc	BU
2 (1908)	10,000	10,000	22,750	32,000	50,000	—
Note: Heritage Piedmont sale 6-2000 Gem BU realized $86,250						
3 (1909) Two known	—	—	—	—	—	—

KM# 1130 10 WON **Weight:** 8.3333 g. **Composition:** 0.9000 Gold .2412 oz. AGW **Ruler:** Kuang Mu

Date	Mintage	F	VF	XF	Unc	BU
10 (1906)	5,012	—	10,000	16,500	27,500	—

KM# A1130 10 WON **Weight:** 8.3333 g. **Composition:** 0.9000 Gold .2412 oz. AGW **Ruler:** Yung Hi (Sunjong)

Date	F	VF	XF	Unc	BU
3 (1909) Two known	—	—	—	—	—

KM# 1131 20 WON **Weight:** 16.6666 g. **Composition:** 0.9000 Gold .4823 oz. AGW **Ruler:** Kuang Mu

Date	Mintage	F	VF	XF	Unc	BU
10 (1906)	2,506	—	22,000	35,000	60,000	—

KM# 1144 20 WON **Weight:** 16.6666 g. **Composition:** 0.9000 Gold .4823 oz. AGW **Ruler:** Yung Hi (Sunjong)

Date	F	VF	XF	Unc	BU
2 (1908) Rare	—	—	—	—	—
3 (1909) Two known	—	—	—	—	—

Note: Reported mintages for Year 2 (1908) of 40,000 and Year 3 (1909) of 25,000 exist, but few are known today

PATTERNS

Including off metal strikes

KM#	Date	Mintage	Identification	Mkt Val
Pn33	5	—	5 Won. Copper.	—
Pn34	5	—	10 Won. Copper.	—
Pn35	6	—	20 Won. Copper.	—
Pn36	6	—	20 Won. Copper.	—
Pn37	7	—	5 Won. Copper.	—
Pn38	7	—	5 Won. Copper.	—

KOREA-NORTH

The Democratic Peoples Republic of Korea, situated in northeastern Asia on the northern half of the Korean peninsula between the Peoples Republic of China and the Republic of Korea, has an area of 46,540 sq. mi. (120,540 sq. km.) and a population of 20 million. Capital: Pyongyang. The economy is based on heavy industry and agriculture. Metals, minerals and farm produce are exported.

Japan replaced China as the predominant foreign influence in Korea in 1895 and annexed the peninsular country in 1910. Defeat in World War II brought an end to Japanese rule. U.S. troops entered Korea from the south and Soviet forces entered from the north. The Cairo conference (1943) had established that Korea should be *free and independent.* The Potsdam conference (1945) set the 38th parallel as the line dividing the occupation forces of the United States and Russia. When Russia refused to permit a U.N. commission designated to supervise reunification elections to enter North Korea, an election was held in South Korea which established the Republic of Korea on Aug. 15,1948. North Korea held an unsupervised election on Aug. 25, 1948, and on Sept. 9, 1948, proclaimed the establishment of the Democratic Peoples Republic of Korea.

NOTE: For earlier coinage see Korea.

MONETARY SYSTEM

100 Chon = 1 Won

CIRCULATION RESTRICTIONS

W/o star: KM#1-4 - General circulation

1 star: KM#5-8 - Issued to visitors from Communist countries.

2 stars: KM#9-12 - Issued to visitors from hard currency countries.

PEOPLES REPUBLIC

DECIMAL COINAGE

KM# 183 1/2 CHON **Weight:** 2.2100 g. **Composition:** Aluminum **Obverse:** State arms **Reverse:** Horse walking left **Edge:** Plain **Size:** 27 mm.

Date	F	VF	XF	Unc	BU
2002	—	—	—	1.25	—

KM# 184 1/2 CHON **Weight:** 2.2100 g. **Composition:** Aluminum **Obverse:** State arms **Reverse:** Chimpanzee **Edge:** Plain **Size:** 27 mm.

Date	F	VF	XF	Unc	BU
2002	—	—	—	1.25	—

KM# 185 1/2 CHON **Weight:** 2.2100 g. **Composition:** Aluminum **Obverse:** State arms **Reverse:** Leopard **Edge:** Plain **Size:** 27 mm.

Date	F	VF	XF	Unc	BU
2002	—	—	—	1.25	—

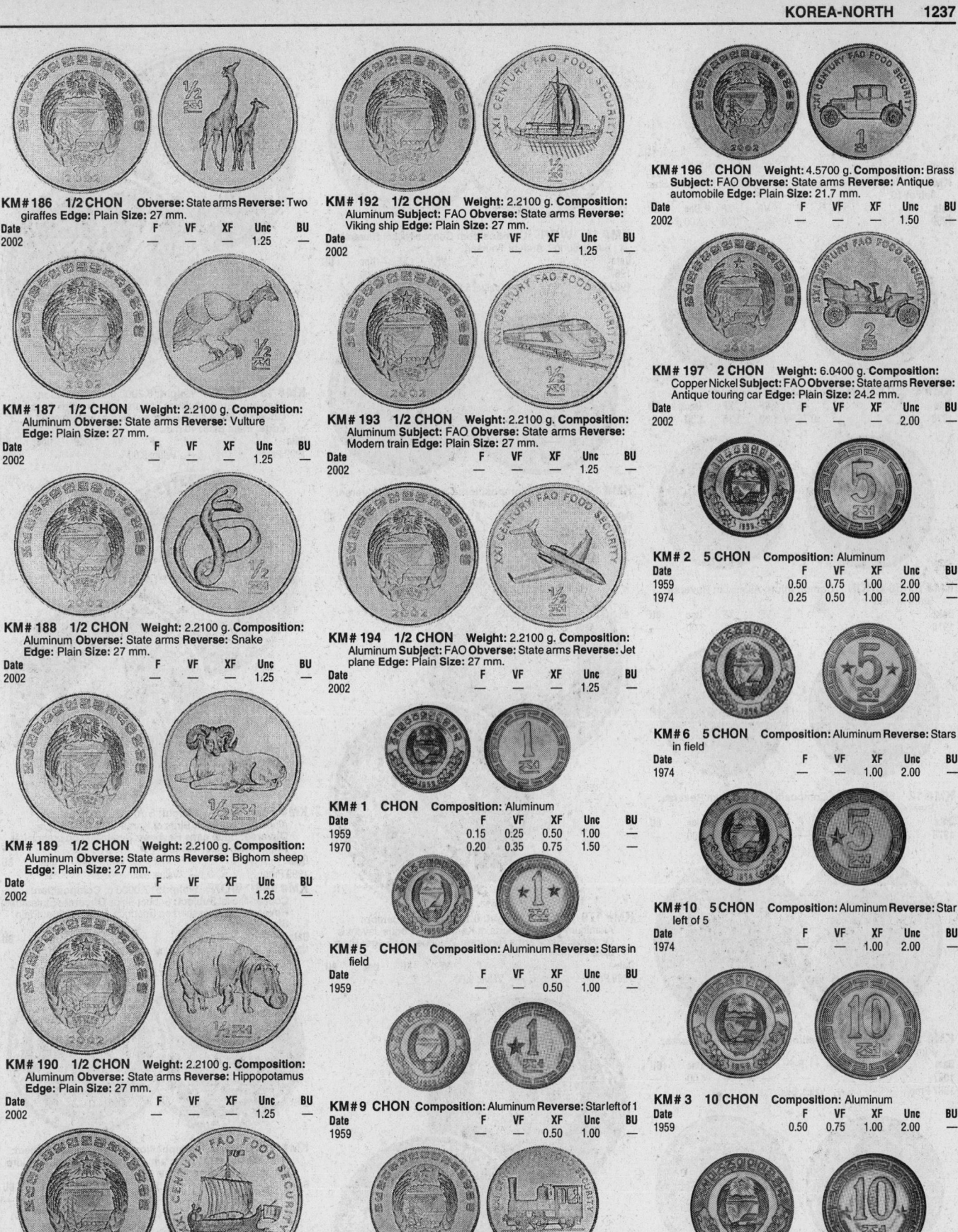

KM# 186 1/2 CHON **Obverse:** State arms **Reverse:** Two giraffes **Edge:** Plain **Size:** 27 mm.

Date	F	VF	XF	Unc	BU
2002	—	—	—	1.25	—

KM# 187 1/2 CHON **Weight:** 2.2100 g. **Composition:** Aluminum **Obverse:** State arms **Reverse:** Vulture **Edge:** Plain **Size:** 27 mm.

Date	F	VF	XF	Unc	BU
2002	—	—	—	1.25	—

KM# 188 1/2 CHON **Weight:** 2.2100 g. **Composition:** Aluminum **Obverse:** State arms **Reverse:** Snake **Edge:** Plain **Size:** 27 mm.

Date	F	VF	XF	Unc	BU
2002	—	—	—	1.25	—

KM# 189 1/2 CHON **Weight:** 2.2100 g. **Composition:** Aluminum **Obverse:** State arms **Reverse:** Bighorn sheep **Edge:** Plain **Size:** 27 mm.

Date	F	VF	XF	Unc	BU
2002	—	—	—	1.25	—

KM# 190 1/2 CHON **Weight:** 2.2100 g. **Composition:** Aluminum **Obverse:** State arms **Reverse:** Hippopotamus **Edge:** Plain **Size:** 27 mm.

Date	F	VF	XF	Unc	BU
2002	—	—	—	1.25	—

KM# 191 1/2 CHON **Weight:** 2.2100 g. **Composition:** Aluminum **Subject:** FAO **Obverse:** State arms **Reverse:** Ancient ship **Edge:** Plain **Size:** 27 mm.

Date	F	VF	XF	Unc	BU
2002	—	—	—	1.25	—

KM# 192 1/2 CHON **Weight:** 2.2100 g. **Composition:** Aluminum **Subject:** FAO **Obverse:** State arms **Reverse:** Viking ship **Edge:** Plain **Size:** 27 mm.

Date	F	VF	XF	Unc	BU
2002	—	—	—	1.25	—

KM# 193 1/2 CHON **Weight:** 2.2100 g. **Composition:** Aluminum **Subject:** FAO **Obverse:** State arms **Reverse:** Modern train **Edge:** Plain **Size:** 27 mm.

Date	F	VF	XF	Unc	BU
2002	—	—	—	1.25	—

KM# 194 1/2 CHON **Weight:** 2.2100 g. **Composition:** Aluminum **Subject:** FAO **Obverse:** State arms **Reverse:** Jet plane **Edge:** Plain **Size:** 27 mm.

Date	F	VF	XF	Unc	BU
2002	—	—	—	1.25	—

KM# 1 CHON **Composition:** Aluminum

Date	F	VF	XF	Unc	BU
1959	0.15	0.25	0.50	1.00	—
1970	0.20	0.35	0.75	1.50	—

KM# 5 CHON **Composition:** Aluminum **Reverse:** Stars in field

Date	F	VF	XF	Unc	BU
1959	—	—	0.50	1.00	—

KM# 9 CHON **Composition:** Aluminum **Reverse:** Star left of 1

Date	F	VF	XF	Unc	BU
1959	—	—	0.50	1.00	—

KM# 195 CHON **Weight:** 4.5700 g. **Composition:** Brass **Subject:** FAO **Obverse:** State arms **Reverse:** Steam locomotive **Edge:** Plain **Size:** 21.7 mm.

Date	F	VF	XF	Unc	BU
2002	—	—	—	1.50	—

KM# 196 CHON **Weight:** 4.5700 g. **Composition:** Brass **Subject:** FAO **Obverse:** State arms **Reverse:** Antique automobile **Edge:** Plain **Size:** 21.7 mm.

Date	F	VF	XF	Unc	BU
2002	—	—	—	1.50	—

KM# 197 2 CHON **Weight:** 6.0400 g. **Composition:** Copper Nickel **Subject:** FAO **Obverse:** State arms **Reverse:** Antique touring car **Edge:** Plain **Size:** 24.2 mm.

Date	F	VF	XF	Unc	BU
2002	—	—	—	2.00	—

KM# 2 5 CHON **Composition:** Aluminum

Date	F	VF	XF	Unc	BU
1959	0.50	0.75	1.00	2.00	—
1974	0.25	0.50	1.00	2.00	—

KM# 6 5 CHON **Composition:** Aluminum **Reverse:** Stars in field

Date	F	VF	XF	Unc	BU
1974	—	—	1.00	2.00	—

KM# 10 5 CHON **Composition:** Aluminum **Reverse:** Star left of 5

Date	F	VF	XF	Unc	BU
1974	—	—	1.00	2.00	—

KM# 3 10 CHON **Composition:** Aluminum

Date	F	VF	XF	Unc	BU
1959	0.50	0.75	1.00	2.00	—

KM# 7 10 CHON **Composition:** Aluminum **Reverse:** Stars in field

Date	F	VF	XF	Unc	BU
1959	—	—	1.00	2.00	—

KM# 11 10 CHON Composition: Aluminum **Reverse:** Star left of 10

Date	F	VF	XF	Unc	BU
1959	—	—	1.00	2.00	—

KM# 4 50 CHON Composition: Aluminum

Date	F	VF	XF	Unc	BU
1978	0.75	1.00	1.75	3.00	—

KM# 8 50 CHON Composition: Aluminum **Reverse:** Stars in field

Date	F	VF	XF	Unc	BU
1978	—	—	1.75	3.00	—

KM# 12 50 CHON Composition: Aluminum **Reverse:** Star behind rider

Date	F	VF	XF	Unc	BU
1978	—	—	1.75	3.00	—

KM# 13 WON Composition: Copper-Nickel **Reverse:** Kim Il Sung's birthplace

Date	F	VF	XF	Unc	BU
1987	—	—	—	4.00	—
1987 Proof	—	Value: 5.00			

KM# 18 WON Composition: Aluminum

Date	F	VF	XF	Unc	BU
1987	—	—	—	3.50	—

KM# 14 WON Composition: Copper-Nickel **Reverse:** Kim Il Sung's Arch of Triumph

Date	F	VF	XF	Unc	BU
1987	—	—	—	4.00	—
1987 Proof	—	Value: 5.00			

KM# 15 WON Composition: Copper-Nickel **Reverse:** Kim Il Sung's Tower of Juche

Date	F	VF	XF	Unc	BU
1987	—	—	—	4.00	—
1987 Proof	—	Value: 5.00			

KM# 179 WON Weight: 6.7000 g. **Composition:** Aluminum **Subject:** Birds of Korea - Dryocopus Javensis **Obverse:** State arms **Reverse:** Woodpecker **Edge:** Plain **Size:** 40 mm.

Date	F	VF	XF	Unc	BU
1999 Proof	—	Value: 9.00			

KM# 180 WON Weight: 6.7000 g. **Composition:** Aluminum **Subject:** Birds of Korea - Lyrurus Tetrix **Obverse:** State arms **Reverse:** Ground bird **Edge:** Plain **Size:** 40 mm.

Date	F	VF	XF	Unc	BU
1999 Proof	—	Value: 9.00			

KM# 181 WON Weight: 6.7000 g. **Composition:** Aluminum **Subject:** Birds of Korea - Syrrhaptes Paradoxus **Obverse:** State arms **Reverse:** Bird at waters edge **Edge:** Plain **Size:** 40 mm.

Date	F	VF	XF	Unc	BU
1999 Proof	—	Value: 9.00			

KM# 182 WON Weight: 6.7000 g. **Composition:** Aluminum **Subject:** Birds of Korea - Pitta Brachyura **Obverse:** State arms **Reverse:** Bird trilling on branch left **Edge:** Plain **Size:** 40 mm.

Date	F	VF	XF	Unc	BU
1999 Proof	—	Value: 9.00			

KM# 198 WON Weight: 17.0000 g. **Composition:** Copper-Nickel **Subject:** School Ships **Obverse:** State arms **Reverse:** SS Grossherzog Friedrich August **Edge:** Plain **Size:** 35 mm.

Date	Mintage	F	VF	XF	Unc	BU
ND Proof	200	Value: 100				

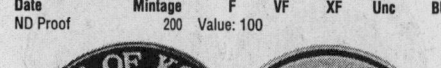

KM# 126 WON Composition: Copper-Nickel **Subject:** Hyonmu **Obverse:** State arms **Reverse:** Mythical creature **Edge:** Reeded **Size:** 32 mm.

Date	F	VF	XF	Unc	BU
2000	—	—	—	6.00	—

KM# 127 WON Composition: Copper-Nickel **Subject:** Blue Dragon **Obverse:** State arms **Reverse:** Dragon over mountains **Edge:** Reeded **Size:** 36 mm.

Date	F	VF	XF	Unc	BU
2000	—	—	—	7.50	—

KM# 128 WON Weight: 22.0000 g. **Composition:** Copper-Nickel **Subject:** Tiger **Obverse:** Tiger in mountains **Reverse:** Tiger head **Edge:** Plain **Size:** 40 mm.

Date	Mintage	F	VF	XF	Unc	BU
ND(1998) Proof	5,000	—	—	—	10.00	—

KM# 156 WON Weight: 16.8600 g. **Composition:** Copper-Nickel **Subject:** Seafaring Ships **Obverse:** State arms **Reverse:** German school ship, Grossherzogin Elisaeth under full sail right **Edge:** Plain **Size:** 35 mm.

Date	F	VF	XF	Unc	BU
ND(2000) Proof	—	Value: 9.00			

KM# 210 WON Weight: 17.0000 g. **Composition:** Copper-Nickel **Subject:** First Nobel Prize Winner in Peace - Henri Dunant **Obverse:** State arms **Reverse:** Bust of Henri Dunant facing at left, war wounded at right **Edge:** Plain **Size:** 35 mm.

Date	Mintage	F	VF	XF	Unc	BU
ND Proof	2,000	Value: 100				

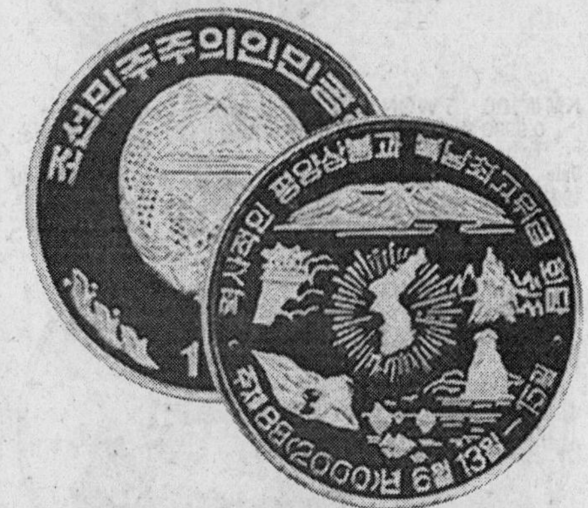

KM# 162 WON Weight: 6.7000 g. **Composition:** Aluminum **Subject:** 3,000 Years of Korean History **Obverse:** State arms **Reverse:** Radiant map and landmarks **Edge:** Plain **Size:** 40 mm.

Date	F	VF	XF	Unc	BU
2000 Proof	—	Value: 9.00			

KM# 155 WON Weight: 16.2000 g. **Composition:** Brass **Subject:** Seafaring Ships **Obverse:** State arms **Reverse:** German school ship, Prinzess Eitel Friedrich with furled sails **Edge:** Plain **Size:** 35 mm.

Date	F	VF	XF	Unc	BU
ND(2000) Proof	—	Value: 9.00			

KM# 155a WON Weight: 17.0000 g. **Composition:** Copper-Nickel **Subject:** School Ships **Obverse:** State arms **Reverse:** SS Prinzess Eitel Friedrich **Edge:** Plain **Size:** 35 mm.

Date	Mintage	F	VF	XF	Unc	BU
ND Proof	200	Value: 100				

KM# 202 WON Weight: 17.0000 g. **Composition:** Copper-Nickel **Subject:** School Ships **Obverse:** State arms. **Reverse:** SS Krusenstern. **Edge:** Plain. **Size:** 35 mm.

Date	Mintage	F	VF	XF	Unc	BU
ND Proof	200	Value: 100				

KM# 157 WON Weight: 6.7000 g. **Composition:** Aluminum **Subject:** Seafaring Ships **Obverse:** State arms **Reverse:** Cruise ship left, conjoined busts in cameo upper right **Edge:** Plain **Size:** 40 mm.

Date	F	VF	XF	Unc	BU
ND(2001) Proof	—	Value: 9.00			

KM# 209 WON Weight: 17.0000 g. **Composition:** Copper-Nickel **Subject:** First Nobel Prize Winner in Medicine - Emil A. von Behring **Obverse:** State arms **Reverse:** von Behring and another man in lab scene **Edge:** Plain **Size:** 35 mm.

Date	Mintage	F	VF	XF	Unc	BU
ND Proof	2,000	Value: 100				

KM# 204 WON Weight: 17.0000 g. **Composition:** Copper-Nickel **Subject:** Wildlife **Obverse:** State arms **Reverse:** Two standing Japanese Ibis birds **Edge:** Plain **Size:** 35 mm.

Date	Mintage	F	VF	XF	Unc	BU
2001 Proof	100	Value: 150				

KM# 207 WON Weight: 17.0000 g. **Composition:** Copper-Nickel **Subject:** Wildlife **Obverse:** State arms **Reverse:** Two Korean Longtail Gorals **Edge:** Plain **Size:** 35 mm.

Date	Mintage	F	VF	XF	Unc	BU
2001 Proof	200	Value: 100				

KM# 211 WON Weight: 17.0000 g. **Composition:** Copper-Nickel **Subject:** First Nobel Prize Winner in Chemistry - Jacobus Van't Hoff **Obverse:** State arms **Reverse:** Van't Hoff and another man in lab scene **Edge:** Plain **Size:** 35 mm.

Date	Mintage	F	VF	XF	Unc	BU
ND Proof	2,000	Value: 100				

KM# 212 WON Weight: 17.0000 g. **Composition:** Copper-Nickel **Subject:** First Nobel Prize Winner in Peace - Frederic Passy **Obverse:** State arms **Reverse:** Bust of Passy at right with allegorical scene at left **Edge:** Plain **Size:** 35 mm.

Date	Mintage	F	VF	XF	Unc	BU
ND Proof	2,000	Value: 100				

KM# 158 WON Weight: 16.2000 g. **Composition:** Brass **Subject:** First Nobel Prize Winner in Literature **Obverse:** State arms **Reverse:** Half bust Sully Prudhomme seated left, shelves and books behind **Edge:** Plain **Size:** 35 mm.

Date	F	VF	XF	Unc	BU
ND(2001) Proof	—	Value: 9.00			

KM# 159 WON Weight: 16.2000 g. **Composition:** Brass **Subject:** First Nobel Prize in Physics **Obverse:** State arms **Reverse:** Bust of Wilhelm C. Rontgen at left facing half right, seated at desk in lab scene at right **Edge:** Plain **Size:** 35 mm.

Date	F	VF	XF	Unc	BU
ND(2001) Proof	—	Value: 9.00			

KM# 160 WON Weight: 16.2000 g. **Composition:** Brass **Subject:** Nipponia Nippon **Obverse:** State arms **Reverse:** Two nest building birds **Edge:** Plain **Size:** 35 mm.

Date	F	VF	XF	Unc	BU
2001 Proof	—	Value: 9.00			

KM# 158a WON Weight: 17.0000 g. **Composition:** Copper-Nickel **Subject:** First Nobel Prize Winner in Literature - Sully Prudhomme **Obverse:** State arms **Reverse:** Seated half bust of Prudhomme, shelves and books behind **Edge:** Plain **Size:** 35 mm.

Date	Mintage	F	VF	XF	Unc	BU
ND Proof	2,000	Value: 100				

KM# 159a WON Weight: 17.0000 g. **Composition:** Copper-Nickel **Subject:** First Nobel Prize Winner in Physics - Wilhelm C. Roentgen **Obverse:** State arms **Reverse:** Bust of Roentgen at left, seated in lab at right **Edge:** Plain **Size:** 35 mm.

Date	Mintage	F	VF	XF	Unc	BU
ND Proof	2,000	Value: 100				

KM# 160a WON Weight: 17.0000 g. **Composition:** Copper-Nickel **Subject:** Wildlife **Obverse:** State arms **Reverse:** Two nesting Japanese Ibis birds **Edge:** Plain **Size:** 35 mm.

Date	Mintage	F	VF	XF	Unc	BU
2001 Proof	200	Value: 100				

KM# 22 5 WON Composition: Copper-Nickel **Reverse:** Kim Il Sung's Arch of Triumph

Date	F	VF	XF	Unc	BU
1987	—	—	—	7.50	—
1987 Proof	—	Value: 10.00			

KM# 23 5 WON Composition: Copper-Nickel **Reverse:** Kim Il Sung's Tower of Juche

Date	F	VF	XF	Unc	BU
1987	—	—	—	7.50	—
1987 Proof	—	Value: 10.00			

KM# 25 5 WON Composition: Copper-Nickel **Reverse:** Kim Il Sung's birthplace

Date	F	VF	XF	Unc	BU
1987	—	—	—	7.50	—
1987 Proof	—	Value: 10.00			

KM# 19 5 WON Composition: Copper-Nickel **Subject:** World Festival of Youth and Students

Date	F	VF	XF	Unc	BU
1989	—	—	—	7.50	—
1989 Proof	—	Value: 10.00			

KM# 92 5 WON Weight: 12.0000 g. **Composition:** 0.9990 Silver .3854 oz. ASW **Subject:** 50th Anniversary of Liberation **Reverse:** Teapot in bowl

Date	Mintage	F	VF	XF	Unc	BU
1995 In proof sets only	300	Value: 50.00				

KM# 129 5 WON Weight: 13.0000 g. **Composition:** Copper Nickel **Subject:** 10th Singapore International Coin Show **Obverse:** State arms **Reverse:** Multicolor logo **Edge:** Plain

Date	Mintage	F	VF	XF	Unc	BU
1996	1,000	—	—	—	12.50	—

KM# 130 5 WON Weight: 27.0000 g. **Composition:** 0.9990 Silver .8672 oz. ASW **Subject:** Kaesong - Sinuiju Railroad **Obverse:** State arms **Reverse:** Multicolor train **Edge:** Plain **Size:** 35 mm.

Date	Mintage	F	VF	XF	Unc	BU
1996	2,000	—	—	—	35.00	—

KM# 131 5 WON Weight: 27.0000 g. **Composition:** 0.9990 Silver .8672 oz. ASW **Subject:** 1st Beijing International Coin Show **Obverse:** State arms **Reverse:** Multicolor panda holding logo **Edge:** Plain **Size:** 35 mm.

Date	Mintage	F	VF	XF	Unc	BU
1996	6,000	—	—	—	30.00	—

KM# 132 5 WON Weight: 27.0000 g. **Composition:** 0.9990 Silver .8672 oz. ASW **Subject:** 11th Singapore International Coin Show **Obverse:** State arms **Reverse:** Multicolor panda holding logo **Edge:** Plain **Size:** 35 mm.

Date	Mintage	F	VF	XF	Unc	BU
1997	1,000	—	—	—	30.00	—

KM# 133 5 WON Weight: 27.0000 g. **Composition:** 0.9990 Silver .8672 oz. ASW **Subject:** World Cup Soccer **Obverse:** State arms **Reverse:** Soccer players **Edge:** Plain **Size:** 35 mm.

Date	Mintage	F	VF	XF	Unc	BU
1997	3,000	—	—	—	30.00	—

KM# 100 5 WON Weight: 26.9400 g. **Composition:** 0.9990 Silver .8644 oz. ASW **Subject:** Olympics **Obverse:** Two speed skaters

Date	Mintage	F	VF	XF	Unc	BU
1997 Proof	3,000	Value: 25.00				

KM# 161 5 WON **Weight:** 26.8400 g. **Composition:** 0.9990 Silver 0.8621 oz. ASW **Subject:** Korean War **Obverse:** State arms **Reverse:** Multicolor flags and flowers in front of monument **Edge:** Reeded **Size:** 40 mm.

Date		F	VF	XF	Unc	BU
1998 Proof	—	Value: 25.00				

KM# 123 5 WON **Weight:** 20.0000 g. **Composition:** 0.9990 Silver .6424 oz. ASW **Subject:** History of Seafaring **Obverse:** State arms **Reverse:** Sailing Junk **Edge:** Reeded and plain sections **Size:** 34.3 mm.

Date	Mintage	F	VF	XF	Unc	BU
1999 Proof	5,000	Value: 35.00				

KM# 172 5 WON **Weight:** 20.0000 g. **Composition:** 0.9990 Silver 0.6424 oz. ASW **Subject:** Endangered Wildlife **Obverse:** State arms **Reverse:** Flying squirrel **Edge:** Reeded and plain sections **Size:** 40 mm.

Date	Mintage	F	VF	XF	Unc	BU
2000 Proof	5,000	Value: 25.00				

KM# 173 5 WON **Weight:** 27.0000 g. **Composition:** 0.9990 Silver 0.8672 oz. ASW **Subject:** King Tongmyong **Obverse:** Mythical bird **Reverse:** Bust of ancient king facing **Edge:** Reeded and plain sections **Size:** 40 mm.

Date	Mintage	F	VF	XF	Unc	BU
2000 Proof	3,000	Value: 25.00				

KM# 174 5 WON **Weight:** 27.0000 g. **Composition:** 0.9990 Silver 0.8672 oz. ASW **Subject:** Olympics **Obverse:** State arms **Reverse:** Female archer drawing back her bow **Edge:** Reeded and plain sections **Size:** 40 mm.

Date	Mintage	F	VF	XF	Unc	BU
2000 Proof	3,000	Value: 25.00				

KM# 175 5 WON **Weight:** 27.0000 g. **Composition:** 0.9990 Silver 0.8672 oz. ASW **Subject:** Olympics **Obverse:** State arms **Reverse:** Handball player **Edge:** Reeded and plain sections **Size:** 40 mm.

Date	Mintage	F	VF	XF	Unc	BU
2000 Proof	3,000	Value: 25.00				

KM# 176 5 WON **Weight:** 27.0000 g. **Composition:** 0.9990 Silver 0.8672 oz. ASW **Subject:** Olympics **Obverse:** State arms **Reverse:** Two wrestlers **Edge:** Reeded and plain sections **Size:** 40 mm.

Date	Mintage	F	VF	XF	Unc	BU
2000 Proof	3,000	Value: 25.00				

KM# 177 5 WON **Weight:** 27.0000 g. **Composition:** 0.9990 Silver 0.8672 oz. ASW **Subject:** Mt. Kumgang **Obverse:** Mythical bird **Reverse:** Buddha statue facing **Edge:** Reeded and plain sections **Size:** 40 mm.

Date	Mintage	F	VF	XF	Unc	BU
2000 Proof	3,000	Value: 25.00				

KM# 199 5 WON **Weight:** 15.0000 g. **Composition:** 0.9990 Silver 0.4818 oz. ASW **Subject:** School Ships **Obverse:** State arms **Reverse:** SS Grossherzogin Elisabeth **Edge:** Plain **Size:** 35 mm.

Date	Mintage	F	VF	XF	Unc	BU
ND Proof	500	Value: 75.00				

KM# 200 5 WON **Weight:** 15.0000 g. **Composition:** 0.9990 Silver 0.4818 oz. ASW **Subject:** School Ships **Obverse:** State arms **Reverse:** SS Prinzess Eitel Friedrich **Edge:** Plain **Size:** 35 mm.

Date	Mintage	F	VF	XF	Unc	BU
ND Proof	500	Value: 75.00				

KM# 201 5 WON **Weight:** 15.0000 g. **Composition:** 0.9990 Silver 0.4818 oz. ASW **Subject:** School Ships **Obverse:** State arms **Reverse:** SS Grossherzog Friedrich August **Edge:** Plain **Size:** 35 mm.

Date	Mintage	F	VF	XF	Unc	BU
ND Proof	500	Value: 75.00				

KM# 213 5 WON **Weight:** 15.0000 g. **Composition:** 0.9990 Silver 0.4818 oz. ASW **Subject:** First Nobel Prize Winners Series - Sully Prudhomme **Obverse:** State arms **Reverse:** Writer's portrait **Edge:** Plain **Size:** 35 mm.

Date	Mintage	F	VF	XF	Unc	BU
ND(2000) Proof	2,000	Value: 100				

KM# 214 5 WON **Weight:** 15.0000 g. **Composition:** 0.9990 Silver 0.4818 oz. ASW **Subject:** First Nobel Prize Winners Series - Wilhelm C. Roentgen **Obverse:** State arms **Reverse:** Portrait and lab scene **Edge:** Plain **Size:** 35 mm.

Date	Mintage	F	VF	XF	Unc	BU
ND(2000) Proof	2,000	Value: 100				

KM# 215 5 WON **Weight:** 15.0000 g. **Composition:** 0.9990 Silver 0.4818 oz. ASW **Subject:** First Nobel Prize Winners Series - Emil A. von Behring **Obverse:** State arms **Reverse:** Two man lab scene **Edge:** Plain **Size:** 35 mm.

Date	Mintage	F	VF	XF	Unc	BU
ND(2000) Proof	2,000	Value: 100				

KM# 216 5 WON **Weight:** 15.0000 g. **Composition:** 0.9990 Silver 0.4818 oz. ASW **Subject:** First Nobel Prize Winners Series - Henri Dunant **Obverse:** State arms **Reverse:** Portrait and war wounded scene **Edge:** Plain **Size:** 35 mm.

Date	Mintage	F	VF	XF	Unc	BU
ND(2000) Proof	2,000	Value: 100				

KM# 217 5 WON **Weight:** 15.0000 g. **Composition:** 0.9990 Silver 0.4818 oz. ASW **Subject:** First Nobel Prize Winners Series - Jacobus Van't Hoff **Obverse:** State arms **Reverse:** Two chemists in lab scene **Edge:** Plain **Size:** 35 mm.

Date	Mintage	F	VF	XF	Unc	BU
ND(2000) Proof	2,000	Value: 100				

KM# 218 5 WON **Weight:** 15.0000 g. **Composition:** 0.9990 Silver 0.4818 oz. ASW **Subject:** First Nobel Prize Winners Series - Frederic Passy **Obverse:** State arms **Reverse:** Portrait and allegorical scene **Edge:** Plain **Size:** 35 mm.

Date	Mintage	F	VF	XF	Unc	BU
ND(2000) Proof	2,000	Value: 100				

KM# 219 5 WON **Weight:** 14.9600 g. **Composition:** 0.9990 Silver 0.4805 oz. ASW **Obverse:** State emblems **Reverse:** Dragon ship **Edge:** Plain **Size:** 35 mm.

Date	Mintage	F	VF	XF	Unc	BU
2001 Proof	5,000	Value: 35.00				

KM# 203 5 WON **Weight:** 15.0000 g. **Composition:** 0.9990 Silver 0.4818 oz. ASW **Subject:** School Ships **Obverse:** State arms **Reverse:** SS Krusenstern **Edge:** Plain **Size:** 35 mm.

Date	Mintage	F	VF	XF	Unc	BU
ND Proof	500	Value: 75.00				

KM# 205 5 WON **Weight:** 15.0000 g. **Composition:** 0.9990 Silver 0.4818 oz. ASW **Subject:** Wildlife **Obverse:** State arms **Reverse:** Two standing Japanese Ibis birds **Edge:** Plain **Size:** 35 mm.

Date	Mintage	F	VF	XF	Unc	BU
2001 Proof	100	Value: 200				

KM# 206 5 WON **Weight:** 15.0000 g. **Composition:** 0.9990 Silver 0.4818 oz. ASW **Subject:** Wildlife **Obverse:** State arms **Reverse:** Two nesting Japanese Ibis birds **Edge:** Plain **Size:** 35 mm.

Date	Mintage	F	VF	XF	Unc	BU
2001 Proof	3,000	Value: 50.00				

KM# 208 5 WON **Weight:** 15.0000 g. **Composition:** 0.9990 Silver 0.4818 oz. ASW **Subject:** Wildlife **Obverse:** State arms **Reverse:** Two Korean Longtail Gorals **Edge:** Plain **Size:** 35 mm.

Date	Mintage	F	VF	XF	Unc	BU
2001 Proof	3,000	Value: 50.00				

KM# 220 7 WON **Weight:** 20.0000 g. **Composition:** 0.9990 Silver 0.6424 oz. ASW **Subject:** 2002 Olympics **Obverse:** State emblem **Reverse:** Two speed skaters **Edge:** Plain **Size:** 38 mm.

Date	Mintage	F	VF	XF	Unc	BU
2001 Proof	10,000	Value: 40.00				

KM# 221 7 WON **Weight:** 20.0000 g. **Composition:** 0.9990 Silver 0.6424 oz. ASW **Subject:** Endangered Wildlife **Obverse:** State emblem **Reverse:** Sea Eagle **Edge:** Plain **Size:** 38 mm.

Date	Mintage	F	VF	XF	Unc	BU
2001 Proof	10,000	Value: 40.00				

KM# 65 10 WON **Composition:** Copper-Nickel **Subject:** 80th Birthday - Kim Il Sung **Reverse:** Kim Il Sung birthplace **Note:** Similar to 50 Won, KM#52.

Date	F	VF	XF	Unc	BU
1992	—	—	—	7.50	—

KM# 66 10 WON **Composition:** Copper-Nickel **Subject:** 50th Birthday - Kim Il Jong **Reverse:** Portrait **Note:** Similar to 50 Won, KM#56.

Date	F	VF	XF	Unc	BU
1992	—	—	—	7.50	—

KM# 73 10 WON **Composition:** Copper-Nickel **Subject:** 80th Birthday - Kim Il Sung **Reverse:** Portrait **Note:** Similar to 50 Won, KM#54.

Date	F	VF	XF	Unc	BU
1992	—	—	—	7.50	—

KM# 87.1 10 WON **Composition:** Copper-Nickel **Subject:** International Sport and Culture Festival **Obverse:** State arms **Reverse:** Multicolor cartoon cat **Edge:** Plain **Size:** 30 mm.

Date	F	VF	XF	Unc	BU
1995	—	—	—	15.00	—

KM# 87.2 10 WON **Weight:** 12.9000 g. **Composition:** Copper-Nickel **Subject:** International Sport and Culture Festival **Obverse:** State arms **Reverse:** Multicolor cartoon cat **Edge:** Plain **Size:** 30 mm.

Date	F	VF	XF	Unc	BU
1995	—	—	—	10.00	—

KM# 134.1 10 WON **Weight:** 12.9000 g. **Composition:** Copper Nickel **Subject:** International Sport and Culture Festival **Obverse:** State arms **Reverse:** Festival logo **Edge:** Plain **Size:** 30 mm.

Date	F	VF	XF	Unc	BU
1995	—	—	—	7.50	—

KM# 134.2 10 WON **Weight:** 12.9000 g. **Composition:** Copper Nickel **Subject:** International Sport and Culture Festival **Obverse:** State arms **Reverse:** Festival logo with pink flame **Edge:** Plain **Size:** 30 mm.

Date	F	VF	XF	Unc	BU
1995	—	—	—	7.50	—

KM# 93 10 WON **Weight:** 28.0000 g. **Composition:** Silver .8993 oz. ASW **Subject:** 50th Anniversary of Liberation **Reverse:** Taedong gatehouse

Date	Mintage	F	VF	XF	Unc	BU
1995 In proof sets only	300	—	—	—	60.00	—

KM# 105 10 WON **Weight:** 31.1035 g. **Composition:** 0.9990 Silver 1 oz. ASW **Subject:** Fauna of Asia - Ducks **Obverse:** National arms **Reverse:** Multicolored pair of Mandarin ducks

Date	Mintage	F	VF	XF	Unc	BU
1996 Proof	1,000	Value: 45.00				

KM# 135 10 WON **Weight:** 31.1035 g. **Composition:** 0.9990 Silver 1.0000 oz. ASW **Subject:** Korean Workers' Party **Obverse:** State arms **Reverse:** Flag and radiant setting sun **Edge:** Plain **Size:** 40 mm.

Date	Mintage	F	VF	XF	Unc	BU
1996	1,000	—	—	—	40.00	—

KM# 115 10 WON **Weight:** 30.9600 g. **Composition:** 0.9990 Silver .9944 oz. ASW **Subject:** Fauna of Asia **Obverse:** National arms **Reverse:** Multicolored parrot

Date	Mintage	F	VF	XF	Unc	BU
1996 Proof	1,000	Value: 75.00				

KM# 120 10 WON **Weight:** 30.9600 g. **Composition:** 0.9990 Silver .9944 oz. ASW **Subject:** Korean War **Obverse:** State arms **Reverse:** Multicolored flags before monument **Edge:** Reeded and plain sections **Size:** 38.6 mm.

Date	Mintage	F	VF	XF	Unc	BU
1997 Proof	20,000	Value: 35.00				

KM# 222 10 WON **Weight:** 30.8000 g. **Composition:** 0.9990 Silver 0.9893 oz. ASW **Subject:** Fauna of Asia **Obverse:** State emblem **Reverse:** Two multicolor water birds **Edge:** Reeded **Size:** 40.2 mm.

Date	F	VF	XF	Unc	BU
1997 Proof	—	Value: 50.00			

KM# 124 10 WON **Weight:** 30.9500 g. **Composition:** 0.9990 Silver .9940 oz. ASW **Subject:** World of Adventure **Obverse:** State arms **Reverse:** Multicolor sailing scene **Edge:** Segmented reeding **Size:** 40.3 mm.

Date	F	VF	XF	Unc	BU
1997 Proof	—	Value: 55.00			

KM# 136 10 WON **Weight:** 31.1035 g. **Composition:** 0.9990 Silver 1.0000 oz. ASW **Subject:** Chou En Lai Centennial of Birth **Obverse:** State arms **Reverse:** Chou's portrait **Edge:** Plain **Size:** 40 mm.

Date	Mintage	F	VF	XF	Unc	BU
1997	8,000	—	—	—	50.00	—

KM# 137 10 WON **Weight:** 31.1035 g. **Composition:** 0.9990 Silver 1.0000 oz. ASW **Subject:** Chinese National Flower **Obverse:** State arms **Reverse:** Multicolor flower **Edge:** Plain **Size:** 40 mm.

Date	Mintage	F	VF	XF	Unc	BU
1997	5,000	—	—	—	55.00	—

KM# 138 10 WON **Weight:** 31.1035 g. **Composition:** 0.9990 Silver 1.0000 oz. ASW **Subject:** Giant Panda **Obverse:** State arms **Reverse:** Multicolor seated panda **Edge:** Plain **Size:** 40 mm.

Date	Mintage	F	VF	XF	Unc	BU
1997	10,000	—	—	—	50.00	—

KM# 98 10 WON **Weight:** 31.0000 g. **Composition:** 0.9990 Silver .9957 oz. ASW **Subject:** Return of Hong Kong to China **Reverse:** Temple of Heaven above Hong Kong city view

Date	Mintage	F	VF	XF	Unc	BU
1997 Proof	2,000	Value: 65.00				

KM# 99 10 WON **Weight:** 31.0000 g. **Composition:** 0.9990 Silver .9957 oz. ASW **Subject:** Ginseng **Obverse:** State emblem **Reverse:** Multicolored ginseng plant including root, leaves, berries

Date	Mintage	F	VF	XF	Unc	BU
1997 Proof	2,000	Value: 45.00				

KM# 121 10 WON **Weight:** 30.9600 g. **Composition:** 0.9990 Silver .9944 oz. ASW **Subject:** Korean War **Obverse:** State arms **Reverse:** Soldier watching bridge bombardment **Edge:** Reeded and plain sections **Size:** 40.3 mm.

Date	Mintage	F	VF	XF	Unc	BU
1997 Proof	20,000	Value: 40.00				

KM# 101 10 WON **Weight:** 30.8800 g. **Composition:** 0.9990 Silver .9918 oz. ASW **Subject:** Shanghai Coin Show **Reverse:** Two multicolored pandas eating bamboo

Date	Mintage	F	VF	XF	Unc	BU
1997 Proof	20,000	Value: 40.00				

KM# 102 10 WON **Weight:** 30.8800 g. **Composition:** 0.9990 Silver .9918 oz. ASW **Subject:** Year of the Tiger **Reverse:** Tiger on mountain ledge

Date	Mintage	F	VF	XF	Unc	BU
ND(1998) Proof	2,000	Value: 37.50				

KM# 163 10 WON **Weight:** 31.0000 g. **Composition:** 0.9990 Silver 0.9957 oz. ASW **Subject:** Intrepid Symbol: Tiger **Obverse:** State arms **Reverse:** Snarling tiger right **Edge:** Reeded and plain sections **Size:** 40 mm.

Date	Mintage	F	VF	XF	Unc	BU
1998 Proof	2,000	Value: 25.00				

KM# 164 10 WON **Weight:** 31.0000 g. **Composition:** 0.9990 Silver 0.9957 oz. ASW **Subject:** 50th Anniversary - People's Republic **Obverse:** State arms **Reverse:** Flag, mountains above **Edge:** Reeded and plain sections **Size:** 40 mm.

Date	Mintage	F	VF	XF	Unc	BU
1998 Proof	1,000	Value: 25.00				

KM# 110 10 WON **Weight:** 30.8800 g. **Composition:** 0.9990 Silver .9918 oz. ASW **Subject:** Korean Folk IV **Obverse:** National arms **Reverse:** Girl on swing

Date	Mintage	F	VF	XF	Unc	BU
1998 Proof	2,000	Value: 40.00				

KM# 111 10 WON **Weight:** 30.8800 g. **Composition:** 0.9990 Silver .9918 oz. ASW **Subject:** Korean Folk I **Obverse:** National arms **Reverse:** Two children flying a kite

Date	Mintage	F	VF	XF	Unc	BU
1998 Proof	2,000	Value: 40.00				

KM# 112 10 WON **Weight:** 30.8800 g. **Composition:** 0.9990 Silver .9918 oz. ASW **Subject:** Korean Folk II **Obverse:** National arms **Reverse:** Two girls see-sawing

Date	Mintage	F	VF	XF	Unc	BU
1998 Proof	2,000	Value: 40.00				

KM# 113 10 WON **Weight:** 30.8800 g. **Composition:** 0.9990 Silver .9918 oz. ASW **Subject:** Korean Folk III **Obverse:** National arms **Reverse:** Wrestling

Date	Mintage	F	VF	XF	Unc	BU
1998 Proof	2,000	Value: 40.00				

KM# 114 10 WON **Weight:** 30.8800 g. **Composition:** 0.9990 Silver .9918 oz. ASW **Subject:** Korean Folk V **Obverse:** National arms **Reverse:** Three girls jumping rope

Date	Mintage	F	VF	XF	Unc	BU
1998 Proof	2,000	Value: 40.00				

KM# 103 10 WON **Weight:** 30.9600 g. **Composition:** 0.9990 Silver .9944 oz. ASW **Subject:** Year of the Rabbit **Obverse:** National arms **Reverse:** Multicolored rabbit with hearts

Date		F	VF	XF	Unc	BU
1999 Proof	5,000	Value: 45.00				

KM# 168 10 WON **Weight:** 31.0000 g. **Composition:** 0.9990 Silver 0.9957 oz. ASW **Subject:** Olympic Games **Obverse:** State arms **Reverse:** Diver **Edge:** Reeded and plain sections **Size:** 40 mm.

Date	Mintage	F	VF	XF	Unc	BU
1999 Proof	3,000	Value: 30.00				

KM# 169 10 WON **Weight:** 31.0000 g. **Composition:** 0.9990 Silver 0.9957 oz. ASW **Subject:** 7th World Track and Field Championships **Obverse:** State arms **Reverse:** Marathon winner Jong Song Ok **Edge:** Reeded and plain sections **Size:** 40 mm.

Date	Mintage	F	VF	XF	Unc	BU
1999 Proof	1,000	Value: 35.00				

KM# 166 10 WON **Weight:** 31.0000 g. **Composition:** 0.9990 Silver 0.9957 oz. ASW **Subject:** Birds of Korea **Obverse:** State arms **Reverse:** Pitta Brachyura on a branch **Edge:** Reeded and plain sections

Date	Mintage	F	VF	XF	Unc	BU
1999 Proof	2,000	Value: 25.00				

KM# 167 10 WON **Weight:** 31.0000 g. **Composition:** 0.9990 Silver 0.9957 oz. ASW **Subject:** Olympic Games **Obverse:** State arms **Reverse:** Man jumping hurdles, kangaroo at bottom right **Edge:** Reeded and plain sections **Size:** 40 mm.

Date	Mintage	F	VF	XF	Unc	BU
1999 Proof	3,000	Value: 30.00				

KM# 170 10 WON **Weight:** 31.0000 g. **Composition:** 0.9990 Silver 0.9957 oz. ASW **Subject:** First North Korean Space Satellite **Obverse:** State arms **Reverse:** Rocket **Edge:** Reeded and plain sections **Size:** 40 mm.

Date	Mintage	F	VF	XF	Unc	BU
1999 Proof	5,000	Value: 30.00				

KM# 171 10 WON Weight: 31.0000 g. **Composition:** 0.9990 Silver 0.9957 oz. ASW **Subject:** Kim Il Sung and Zhou Enlai **Obverse:** State arms **Reverse:** Kim Il Sung and Zhou Enlai shaking hands **Edge:** Reeded and plain sections **Size:** 40 mm.

Date	Mintage	F	VF	XF	Unc	BU
1999 Proof	5,000	Value: 30.00				

KM# 223 10 WON Subject: Birds of Korea **Obverse:** State emblem **Reverse:** Lyrurus Tetrix, bird on ground **Edge:** Reeded

Date	F	VF	XF	Unc	BU
1999	—	—	—	—	—

KM# 224 10 WON Weight: 30.8000 g. **Composition:** 0.9990 Silver 0.9893 oz. ASW **Subject:** Birds of Korea **Obverse:** State emblem **Reverse:** Syrrhaptes Paradoxus, bird on shore **Edge:** Reeded **Size:** 40.2 mm.

Date	F	VF	XF	Unc	BU
1999 Proof	—	Value: 40.00			

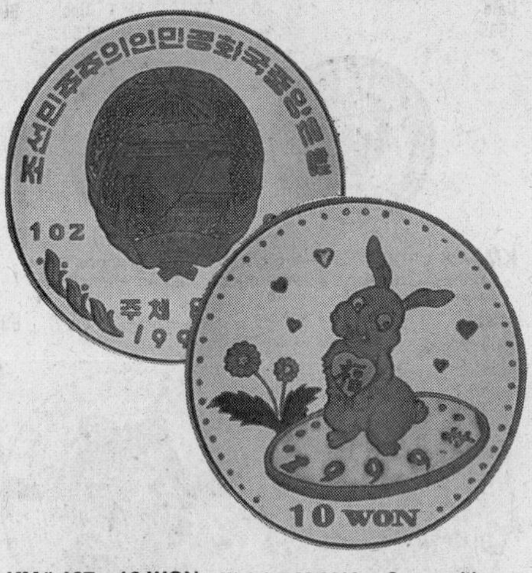

KM# 107 10 WON Weight: 30.9600 g. **Composition:** 0.9990 Silver .9944 oz. ASW **Subject:** Year of the Rabbitt **Obverse:** National arms **Reverse:** Multicolored rabbits with hearts; same as KM#103 but without legend at top

Date	Mintage	F	VF	XF	Unc	BU
1999 Proof	5,000	Value: 40.00				

KM# 108 10 WON Weight: 30.9600 g. **Composition:** 0.9990 Silver .9944 oz. ASW **Subject:** Blue dragon **Obverse:** National arms **Reverse:** Dragon flying right over mountains

Date	Mintage	F	VF	XF	Unc	BU
1999 Proof	5,000	Value: 45.00				

KM# 109.1 (KM109) 10 WON Weight: 30.9600 g. **Composition:** 0.9990 Silver .9944 oz. ASW **Subject:** Birds of Korea **Obverse:** National arms **Reverse:** Woodpecker on tree limb **Edge:** Segmented reeding

Date	Mintage	F	VF	XF	Unc	BU
1999 Proof	3,000	Value: 45.00				

KM# 109.2 10 WON Weight: 30.9600 g. **Composition:** 0.9990 Silver 0.9944 oz. ASW **Subject:** Birds of Korea **Obverse:** National arms **Reverse:** Woodpecker on tree limb **Edge:** Plain

Date	Mintage	F	VF	XF	Unc	BU
1999 Proof	Inc. above	Value: 45.00				

KM# 125 10 WON Weight: 30.9500 g. **Composition:** 0.9990 Silver .9940 oz. ASW **Subject:** One Korea: 3,000 Years of History **Obverse:** State arms **Reverse:** Radiant map and landmarks **Edge:** Segmented reeding **Size:** 40.3 mm.

Date	F	VF	XF	Unc	BU
2000 Proof	—	Value: 50.00			

KM# 178 10 WON Weight: 31.0000 g. **Composition:** 0.9990 Silver 0.9957 oz. ASW **Subject:** King Tangun **Obverse:** State arms **Reverse:** Bust of King Tangun with beard facing **Edge:** Reeded and plain sections **Size:** 40 mm.

Date	Mintage	F	VF	XF	Unc	BU
2000 Proof	5,000	Value: 30.00				

KM# 152 10 WON Weight: 31.0000 g. **Composition:** 0.9990 Silver .9957 oz. ASW **Subject:** Asian Money Fair **Obverse:** State arms **Reverse:** Two snakes **Edge:** Reeded and plain sections **Size:** 39.8 mm.

Date	F	VF	XF	Unc	BU
2001 Proof	—	Value: 50.00			

KM# 153 10 WON Weight: 31.0000 g. **Composition:** 0.9990 Silver .9957 oz. ASW **Subject:** Tortoise-Serpent **Obverse:** State arms **Reverse:** Mythical creature **Edge:** Reeded and plain sections **Size:** 39.8 mm.

Date	F	VF	XF	Unc	BU
2001 Proof	—	Value: 50.00			

KM# 20 20 WON Weight: 14.8000 g. **Composition:** 0.9990 Silver .4758 oz. ASW **Subject:** World Festival of Youth and Students

Date	F	VF	XF	Unc	BU
1989 Proof	—	Value: 25.00			

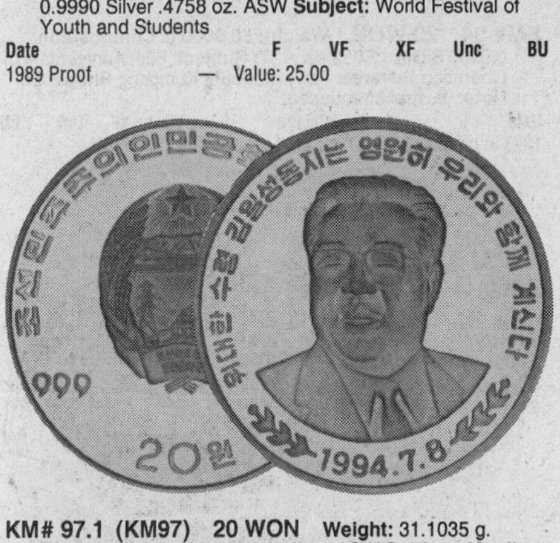

KM# 97.1 (KM97) 20 WON Weight: 31.1035 g. **Composition:** 0.9990 Silver 1 oz. ASW **Subject:** Kim Il Sung's death **Obverse:** State emblem **Edge:** Plain

Date	Mintage	F	VF	XF	Unc	BU
ND(1994) Proof	5,000	Value: 85.00				
ND(1994) Proof	5,000	Value: 85.00				

KM# 97.2 20 WON Weight: 31.1035 g. **Composition:** 0.9990 Silver 1 oz. ASW **Subject:** Kim Il Sung's Death **Obverse:** State emblem **Edge:** Reeded

Date	F	VF	XF	Unc	BU
ND(1994) Proof	—	Value: 50.00			

KM# 74 20 WON **Composition:** Copper-Nickel **Subject:** 1998 World Cup Soccer

Date	Mintage	F	VF	XF	Unc	BU
1995 Proof	10,000	Value: 30.00				

KM# 139 20 WON **Weight:** 31.1035 g. **Composition:** 0.9990 Silver 1.0000 oz. ASW **Subject:** 50th Anniversary - Korean Workers' Party **Obverse:** State arms **Reverse:** Monument **Edge:** Plain **Size:** 40 mm.

Date	F	VF	XF	Unc	BU
1995	—	—	—	40.00	—

KM# 94 20 WON **Weight:** 50.0000 g. **Composition:** 0.9990 Silver 1.6059 oz. ASW **Subject:** 50th Anniversary of Liberation **Reverse:** Fairy of Mount Kumgang **Shape:** 50 **Note:** Illustration reduced.

Date	Mintage	F	VF	XF	Unc	BU
1995 In proof sets only	300	Value: 125				

KM# 140 20 WON **Weight:** 22.0000 g. **Composition:** Copper Nickel **Subject:** 25th Basel International Coin Show **Obverse:** State arms above phone fax and telex numbers **Reverse:** Multicolor island and sea scape **Edge:** Plain **Size:** 40 mm.

Date	Mintage	F	VF	XF	Unc	BU
1996	1,000	—	—	—	15.00	—

KM# 26 30 WON **Weight:** 17.0200 g. **Composition:** 0.9990 Silver .5472 oz. ASW **Subject:** Friendship Art Festival

Date	F	VF	XF	Unc	BU
1989 Proof	—	Value: 40.00			

KM# 52 50 WON **Weight:** 17.0200 g. **Composition:** 0.9990 Silver .5466 oz. ASW **Subject:** 80th Birthday of Kim Il Sung **Reverse:** Kim Il Sung birthplace

Date	Mintage	F	VF	XF	Unc	BU
1992 Proof	1,000	Value: 40.00				

KM# 54 50 WON **Weight:** 17.0200 g. **Composition:** 0.9990 Silver .5466 oz. ASW **Subject:** 80th Birthday of Kim Il Sung **Reverse:** Kim Il Sung portrait

Date	Mintage	F	VF	XF	Unc	BU
1992 Proof	1,000	Value: 45.00				

KM# 56 50 WON **Weight:** 17.0200 g. **Composition:** 0.9990 Silver .5466 oz. ASW **Subject:** 50th Birthday of Kim Jong Il **Reverse:** Kim Jong Il portrait

Date	Mintage	F	VF	XF	Unc	BU
1992 Proof	5,000	Value: 50.00				

KM# 88 50 WON **Composition:** Copper-Nickel **Subject:** Sportsfest **Reverse:** Wrestlers

Date	F	VF	XF	Unc	BU
1995	—	—	—	22.50	—

KM# 141 50 WON **Weight:** 12.9000 g. **Composition:** Copper Nickel **Subject:** International Friendship Exhibition **Obverse:** State arms **Reverse:** Building **Edge:** Plain **Size:** 30 mm.

Date	F	VF	XF	Unc	BU
1995	—	—	—	8.50	—

KM# 142 50 WON **Weight:** 12.9000 g. **Composition:** Copper Nickel **Subject:** May Day Stadium **Obverse:** State arms **Reverse:** Stadium **Edge:** Plain **Size:** 30 mm.

Date	F	VF	XF	Unc	BU
1995	—	—	—	8.50	—

KM# 28 100 WON **Weight:** 3.1300 g. **Composition:** 0.9990 Gold .1 oz. AGW **Subject:** 40th Anniversary of People's Republic

Date	F	VF	XF	Unc	BU
1988 Proof	—	Value: 75.00			

KM# 70 100 WON **Weight:** 7.0000 g. **Composition:** 0.9990 Silver .2248 oz. ASW **Reverse:** Two multicolored Adelle penguins

Date	F	VF	XF	Unc	BU
1995 Proof	—	Value: 35.00			

KM# 71 100 WON **Weight:** 7.0000 g. **Composition:** 0.9990 Silver .2250 oz. ASW **Subject:** 1996 Olympics **Reverse:** Sprinter

Date	Mintage	F	VF	XF	Unc	BU
1995 Proof	30,000	Value: 25.00				

KM# 72 100 WON **Weight:** 7.0000 g. **Composition:** 0.9990 Silver .2250 oz. ASW **Subject:** 1998 World Cup Soccer

Date	Mintage	F	VF	XF	Unc	BU
1995 Proof	30,000	Value: 25.00				

KM# 104 100 WON **Weight:** 7.0000 g. **Composition:** 0.9990 Silver .2250 oz. ASW **Subject:** Aix Galericulata **Obverse:** National arms **Reverse:** Multicolored pair of ducks

Date	Mintage	F	VF	XF	Unc	BU
1995 Proof	Est. 30,000	Value: 35.00				

KM# 122 100 WON **Weight:** 7.0000 g. **Composition:** 0.9990 Silver .2248 oz. ASW **Subject:** Robinson Crusoe **Obverse:** State arms **Reverse:** Multicolor row boat scene **Edge:** Plain **Size:** 30 mm.

Date		F	VF	XF	Unc	BU
1996 Proof	—	Value: 35.00				

KM# 49 200 WON **Weight:** 14.9700 g. **Composition:** 0.9990 Silver .5 oz. ASW **Subject:** Olympics **Obverse:** Silver content statement divided by emblem **Reverse:** Equestrian

Date	Mintage	F	VF	XF	Unc	BU
1991 Proof	25,000	Value: 25.00				

KM# 50 200 WON **Weight:** 14.9700 g. **Composition:** 0.9990 Silver .5 oz. ASW **Subject:** Olympics **Obverse:** Silver content statement below emblem **Reverse:** Equestrian

Date	Mintage	F	VF	XF	Unc	BU
1991 Proof	Inc. above	Value: 22.50				

KM# 64 200 WON **Weight:** 15.0000 g. **Composition:** 0.9990 Silver .481 oz. ASW **Series:** 1992 Olympics **Reverse:** Runner

Date	Mintage	F	VF	XF	Unc	BU
1992 Proof	25,000	Value: 20.00				

KM# 95 200 WON **Weight:** 8.0000 g. **Composition:** Gold .2569 oz. AGW **Subject:** 50th Anniversary of Liberation **Reverse:** Turtle ship

Date	Mintage	F	VF	XF	Unc	BU
1995 In proof sets only	300	Value: 420				

KM# 29 250 WON **Weight:** 7.7800 g. **Composition:** 0.9990 Gold .25 oz. AGW **Subject:** 40th Anniversary of People's Republic

Date		F	VF	XF	Unc	BU
1988 Proof	—	Value: 175				

KM# 21 250 WON **Weight:** 7.7700 g. **Composition:** 0.9990 Gold .25 oz. AGW **Subject:** World Festival of Youth and Students

Date		F	VF	XF	Unc	BU
1989 Proof	—	Value: 275				

KM# 116 250 WON **Weight:** 20.0000 g. **Composition:** 0.9990 Silver .6464 oz. ASW **Subject:** Millennium **Reverse:** Dragon

Date		F	VF	XF	Unc	BU
1998//2000 Proof	—	Value: 40.00				

KM# 225 250 WON **Weight:** 14.9600 g. **Composition:** 0.9990 Silver 0.4805 oz. ASW **Subject:** Beethoven **Obverse:** National arms **Reverse:** Portrait **Edge:** Plain **Size:** 34.9 mm.

Date		F	VF	XF	Unc	BU
1999 Proof	—	Value: 30.00				

KM# 96 400 WON **Weight:** 16.0000 g. **Composition:** Gold .5138 oz. AGW **Subject:** 50th Anniversary of Liberation **Reverse:** Lake on Mount Baektu

Date	Mintage	F	VF	XF	Unc	BU
1995 In proof sets only	100	Value: 700				

KM# 39 500 WON **Weight:** 27.0000 g. **Composition:** 0.9990 Silver .8681 oz. ASW **Subject:** World Championship Soccer - Mexico '96

Date		F	VF	XF	Unc	BU
1987 Proof	—	Value: 35.00				

KM# 16 500 WON **Weight:** 27.0000 g. **Composition:** 0.9990 Silver .8681 oz. ASW **Series:** Winter Olympics **Reverse:** Hockey

Date	Mintage	F	VF	XF	Unc	BU
1988 Proof	20,000	Value: 18.50				

KM# 17 500 WON **Weight:** 27.0000 g. **Composition:** 0.9990 Silver .8681 oz. ASW **Subject:** 30th Anniversary of Gorch Fock

Date		F	VF	XF	Unc	BU
1988 Proof	—	Value: 35.00				

KM# 24 500 WON **Weight:** 27.0000 g. **Composition:** 0.9990 Silver .8681 oz. ASW **Subject:** World Championship Soccer

Date		F	VF	XF	Unc	BU
1988 Proof	—	Value: 25.00				

KM# 30 500 WON **Weight:** 15.5700 g. **Composition:** 0.9990 Gold .5 oz. AGW **Subject:** 40th Anniversary of People's Republic

Date		F	VF	XF	Unc	BU
1988 Proof	—	Value: 300				

KM# 36 500 WON **Weight:** 27.0000 g. **Composition:** 0.9990 Silver .8681 oz. ASW **Series:** F.A.O. **Subject:** Food for all

Date	Mintage	F	VF	XF	Unc	BU
1988 Proof	Est. 2,000	Value: 50.00				

KM# 27 500 WON **Weight:** 27.0000 g. **Composition:** 0.9990 Silver .8681 oz. ASW **Subject:** Amerigo Vespucci

Date	F	VF	XF	Unc	BU
1989 Proof	—	Value: 40.00			

KM# 32 500 WON **Weight:** 31.8200 g. **Composition:** 0.9990 Silver 1.0231 oz. ASW **Reverse:** Fairy of Mount Kumgang

Date	Mintage	F	VF	XF	Unc	BU
1989 Proof	2,000	Value: 55.00				

KM# 33 500 WON **Weight:** 27.0000 g. **Composition:** 0.9990 Silver .8682 oz. ASW **Series:** Calgary Winter Olympics **Reverse:** Figure skater

Date	F	VF	XF	Unc	BU
1989 Proof	—	Value: 35.00			

KM# 34 500 WON **Weight:** 27.0000 g. **Composition:** 0.9990 Silver .8682 oz. ASW **Series:** Barcelona Summer Olympics **Reverse:** Discus thrower

Date	F	VF	XF	Unc	BU
1989 Proof	—	Value: 35.00			

KM# 37 500 WON **Weight:** 27.0000 g. **Composition:** 0.9990 Silver .8682 oz. ASW **Subject:** World Championship Soccer **Obverse:** Similar to KM#33 **Reverse:** Player kicking ball

Date	Mintage	F	VF	XF	Unc	BU
1989 Proof	15,000	Value: 50.00				

KM# 38 500 WON **Weight:** 27.0000 g. **Composition:** 0.9990 Silver .8682 oz. ASW **Subject:** World Championship Soccer **Reverse:** Goalie

Date	F	VF	XF	Unc	BU
1989 Proof	—	Value: 27.50			

KM# 40 500 WON **Weight:** 31.8200 g. **Composition:** 0.9990 Silver .8682 oz. ASW **Subject:** Olympic table tennis

Date	Mintage	F	VF	XF	Unc	BU
1990 Proof	15,000	Value: 27.50				

KM# 41 500 WON **Weight:** 31.8200 g. **Composition:** 0.9990 Silver .8682 oz. ASW **Subject:** Endangered Wildlife **Reverse:** Storks

Date	F	VF	XF	Unc	BU
1990 Proof	—	Value: 45.00			

KM# 44 500 WON **Weight:** 31.1000 g. **Composition:** 0.9990 Silver 1 oz. ASW **Subject:** World Championship Table Tennis **Reverse:** Two male players

Date	Mintage	F	VF	XF	Unc	BU
1991 Proof	5,000	Value: 30.00				

KM# 45 500 WON **Weight:** 31.1000 g. **Composition:** 0.9990 Silver 1 oz. ASW **Subject:** World Championship Table Tennis **Reverse:** Male player

Date	Mintage	F	VF	XF	Unc	BU
1991 Proof	5,000	Value: 30.00				

KM# 46 500 WON **Weight:** 31.1000 g. **Composition:** 0.9990 Silver 1 oz. ASW **Subject:** World Championship Table Tennis **Reverse:** Female player

Date	Mintage	F	VF	XF	Unc	BU
1991 Proof	5,000	Value: 30.00				

KM# 47 500 WON **Weight:** 31.1000 g. **Composition:** 0.9990 Silver 1 oz. ASW **Subject:** World Championship Table Tennis **Reverse:** Korea unified team

Date	Mintage	F	VF	XF	Unc	BU
1991 Proof	10,000	Value: 22.50				

KM# 48 500 WON **Weight:** 27.0000 g. **Composition:** 0.9990 Silver .8682 oz. ASW **Subject:** First armoured ship

Date	Mintage	F	VF	XF	Unc	BU
1991 Proof	Est. 10,000	Value: 50.00				

KM# 63 500 WON **Weight:** 27.0000 g. **Composition:** 0.9990 Silver .8682 oz. ASW **Series:** Olympics **Reverse:** Women's volleyball

Date	Mintage	F	VF	XF	Unc	BU
1991 Proof	15,000	Value: 35.00				

KM# 59 500 WON **Weight:** 27.0000 g. **Composition:** 0.9990 Silver .8682 oz. ASW **Subject:** Environmental protection **Reverse:** Flowers

Date	Mintage	F	VF	XF	Unc	BU
1992 Proof	1,000	Value: 55.00				

KM# 144 500 WON **Weight:** 27.0000 g. **Composition:** 0.9990 Silver .8672 oz. ASW **Subject:** 1994 World Cup Soccer **Obverse:** State arms **Reverse:** Three soccer players **Edge:** Plain **Size:** 35 mm.

Date	F	VF	XF	Unc	BU
1992	—	—	—	35.00	—

KM# 60 500 WON **Weight:** 27.0000 g. **Composition:** 0.9990 Silver .8682 oz. ASW **Series:** 1994 Olympics **Reverse:** Speed skating

Date	Mintage	F	VF	XF	Unc	BU
1993 Proof	1,000	Value: 35.00				

KM# 62.1 (KM62) 500 WON **Weight:** 31.1035 g. **Composition:** 0.9990 Silver 1 oz. ASW **Series:** Prehistoric Animals **Obverse:** State arms **Reverse:** Brontosaurus, more extensive background details **Edge:** Reeded **Size:** 40.3 mm.

Date	F	VF	XF	Unc	BU
1993	—	—	—	—	—
1993	—	—	—	—	—
1993 Proof	—	Value: 45.00			
1993 Proof	—	Value: 45.00			

KM# 61 500 WON **Weight:** 27.0000 g. **Composition:** 0.9990 Silver .8682 oz. ASW **Series:** 1994 Olympics **Reverse:** Two-man bobsled

Date	Mintage	F	VF	XF	Unc	BU
1993 Proof	1,000	Value: 40.00				

KM# 145 500 WON **Weight:** 31.1035 g. **Composition:** 0.9990 Silver 1.0000 oz. ASW **Subject:** 1994 World Cup Soccer **Obverse:** State arms **Reverse:** Two players and trophy cup **Edge:** Plain **Size:** 40 mm.

Date	F	VF	XF	Unc	BU
1994	—	—	—	40.00	—

KM# 146 500 WON **Weight:** 17.0000 g. **Composition:** 0.9990 Silver .5460 oz. ASW **Series:** F.A.O. **Subject:** F.A.O. 50 Years **Obverse:** State arms **Reverse:** F.A.O. logo **Edge:** Plain

Date	F	VF	XF	Unc	BU
1995	—	—	—	30.00	—

KM# 62.2 500 WON **Weight:** 31.1035 g. **Composition:** 0.9990 Silver 0.999 oz. ASW **Series:** Prehistoric Animals **Obverse:** State arms **Reverse:** More vegetation by dinosaur's foot **Edge:** Reeded **Size:** 40.3 mm.

Date	F	VF	XF	Unc	BU
1995 Proof	—	—	—	—	—

KM# 143 500 WON **Weight:** 31.1035 g. **Composition:** 0.9990 Silver 1.0000 oz. ASW **Subject:** International Sport and Culture Festival **Obverse:** State arms **Reverse:** Kim Il Jong portrait **Edge:** Plain **Size:** 40 mm.

Date	F	VF	XF	Unc	BU
1995	—	—	—	40.00	—

KM# 67 500 WON **Weight:** 31.1035 g. **Composition:** 0.9990 Silver 1 oz. ASW **Series:** 1996 Atlanta Olympics **Reverse:** Relay racers

Date	Mintage	F	VF	XF	Unc	BU
1995 Proof	3,000	Value: 35.00				

KM# 79 500 WON **Weight:** 31.1035 g. **Composition:** 0.9990 Silver 1 oz. ASW **Subject:** Fauna of Asia **Reverse:** Multicolor owl

Date	Mintage	F	VF	XF	Unc	BU
1995 Proof	20,000	Value: 45.00				

KM# 68 500 WON **Weight:** 31.1035 g. **Composition:** 0.9990 Silver 1 oz. ASW **Series:** 1996 Atlanta Olympics **Reverse:** Equestrian

Date	Mintage	F	VF	XF	Unc	BU
1995 Proof	3,000	Value: 35.00				

KM# 69 500 WON **Weight:** 31.1035 g. **Composition:** 0.9990 Silver 1 oz. ASW **Subject:** Fauna of Asia **Reverse:** Multicolor tiger

Date	Mintage	F	VF	XF	Unc	BU
1995 Proof	20,000	Value: 45.00				

KM# 75 500 WON **Weight:** 31.1035 g. **Composition:** 0.9990 Silver 1 oz. ASW **Subject:** 1998 World Cup Soccer

Date	Mintage	F	VF	XF	Unc	BU
1995 Proof	10,000	Value: 45.00				

KM# 76 500 WON **Weight:** 31.1035 g. **Composition:** 0.9990 Silver 1 oz. ASW **Subject:** Fauna of Asia **Reverse:** Multicolor panda

Date	Mintage	F	VF	XF	Unc	BU
1995 Proof	20,000	Value: 40.00				

KM# 77 500 WON **Weight:** 31.1035 g. **Composition:** 0.9990 Silver 1 oz. ASW **Subject:** Fauna of Asia **Reverse:** Multicolor parrot

Date	Mintage	F	VF	XF	Unc	BU
1995 Proof	20,000	Value: 40.00				

KM# 78 500 WON **Weight:** 31.1035 g. **Composition:** 0.9990 Silver 1 oz. ASW **Subject:** Fauna of Asia **Reverse:** Multicolor eagle

Date	Mintage	F	VF	XF	Unc	BU
1995 Proof	20,000	Value: 40.00				

KM# 80 500 WON **Weight:** 31.1035 g. **Composition:** 0.9990 Silver 1 oz. ASW **Subject:** Fauna of Asia **Reverse:** Two multicolor Mandarin ducks **Note:** Enameled.

Date	Mintage	F	VF	XF	Unc	BU
1995 Proof	20,000	Value: 40.00				

KM# 154 500 WON **Weight:** 27.0000 g. **Composition:** 0.9990 Silver .8672 oz. ASW **Subject:** First Asian Gymnastic Championship **Obverse:** State arms **Reverse:** Multicolor panda holding logo **Edge:** Coarse and finely reeded sections **Size:** 35.2 mm.

Date	F	VF	XF	Unc	BU
1996 Proof	—	Value: 60.00			

KM# 89 500 WON **Weight:** 31.1035 g. **Composition:** 0.9990 Silver .9969 oz. ASW **Series:** Olympics **Reverse:** Two eurythmic gymnasts

Date	F	VF	XF	Unc	BU
1996	—	—	—	40.00	—

KM# 90 500 WON **Weight:** 31.1035 g. **Composition:** 0.9990 Silver .9969 oz. ASW **Series:** Olympics **Reverse:** Soccer

Date	Mintage	F	VF	XF	Unc	BU
1996	30,000	—	—	—	45.00	—

KM# 91 500 WON **Weight:** 31.1035 g. **Composition:** 0.9990 Silver .9969 oz. ASW **Subject:** Fauna of Asia **Reverse:** Multicolored holographic panda

Date	Mintage	F	VF	XF	Unc	BU
1996 Proof	5,000	Value: 60.00				

KM# 106 500 WON **Weight:** 31.5200 g. **Composition:** 0.9990 Silver 1.0124 oz. ASW **Subject:** Fauna of Asia **Obverse:** National emblem **Reverse:** Multicolored hologram of tiger

Date	F	VF	XF	Unc	BU
1996 Proof	—	Value: 60.00			

KM# 117 500 WON **Weight:** 31.1035 g. **Composition:** 0.9990 Silver 1 oz. ASW **Subject:** Fauna of Asia **Obverse:** National emblem **Reverse:** Multicolored trichogaster leeri fish

Date	F	VF	XF	Unc	BU
1996 Proof	—	Value: 50.00			

KM# 118 500 WON **Weight:** 31.1035 g. **Composition:** 0.9990 Silver 1 oz. ASW **Subject:** Fauna of Asia **Obverse:** National emblem **Reverse:** Multicolored botia macracanthus fish

Date	F	VF	XF	Unc	BU
1996 Proof	—	Value: 50.00			

KM# 119 500 WON **Weight:** 31.1035 g. **Composition:** 0.9990 Silver 1 oz. ASW **Subject:** Fauna of Asia **Obverse:** National emblem **Reverse:** Multicolored long-tailed angelfish

Date		F	VF	XF	Unc	BU
1996 Proof	—	Value: 50.00				

KM# 147 700 WON **Weight:** 31.1035 g. **Composition:** 0.9990 Gold 1.0000 oz. AGW **Subject:** Korean Workers' Party **Obverse:** State arms **Reverse:** Flag and radiant setting sun **Edge:** Plain **Size:** 35 mm.

Date	Mintage	F	VF	XF	Unc	BU
1996	100	—	—	—	750	—

KM# 165 700 WON **Weight:** 31.1000 g. **Composition:** 0.9990 Gold 0.9989 oz. AGW **Subject:** 50th Anniversary of People's Republic **Obverse:** State arms **Reverse:** Flag **Edge:** Plain **Size:** 35 mm.

Date	Mintage	F	VF	XF	Unc	BU
1998 Proof	500	Value: 600				

KM# 31 1000 WON **Weight:** 31.1300 g. **Composition:** 0.9990 Gold 1 oz. AGW **Subject:** 40th Anniversary of People's Republic

Date		F	VF	XF	Unc	BU
1988 Proof	—	Value: 575				

KM# 148 1000 WON **Weight:** 15.5500 g. **Composition:** 0.9990 Gold .4999 oz. AGW **Subject:** Death of Kim Il Sung **Obverse:** State arms **Reverse:** Portrait **Edge:** Plain **Size:** 27 mm.

Date	F	VF	XF	Unc	BU
ND(1994)	—	—	—	400	—

KM# 149 1000 WON **Weight:** 31.1035 g. **Composition:** 0.9990 Gold 1.0000 oz. AGW **Subject:** 50th Anniversary - Korean Workers' Party **Obverse:** State arms **Reverse:** Monument **Edge:** Plain **Size:** 35 mm.

Date	F	VF	XF	Unc	BU
1995	—	—	—	600	—

KM# 58 1500 WON **Weight:** 8.0000 g. **Composition:** 0.9990 Gold .2572 oz. AGW **Series:** Olympics **Reverse:** Gymnast

Date	Mintage	F	VF	XF	Unc	BU
1990 Proof	Est. 3,000	Value: 200				

KM# 42 1500 WON **Weight:** 15.5500 g. **Composition:** 0.9990 Gold .5 oz. AGW **Subject:** Inter-parliamentary Conference

Date	Mintage	F	VF	XF	Unc	BU
1991 Proof	1,000	Value: 400				

KM# 43 1500 WON **Weight:** 15.5500 g. **Composition:** 0.9990 Gold .5 oz. AGW **Subject:** Inter-parliamentary Conference

Date	Mintage	F	VF	XF	Unc	BU
1991 Proof	800	Value: 400				

KM# 51 1500 WON **Weight:** 8.0000 g. **Composition:** 0.9990 Gold .2572 oz. AGW **Subject:** Soccer

Date	Mintage	F	VF	XF	Unc	BU
1991 Proof	1,000	Value: 250				

KM# 150 1500 WON **Weight:** 8.0000 g. **Composition:** 0.9990 Gold .2569 oz. AGW **Series:** Olympics **Obverse:** State arms **Reverse:** Cyclists racing **Edge:** Plain **Size:** 22 mm.

Date	F	VF	XF	Unc	BU
1993	—	—	—	300	—

KM# 53 2000 WON **Weight:** 31.1000 g. **Composition:** 0.9990 Gold 1 oz. AGW **Subject:** 80th Birthday of Kim Il Sung **Reverse:** Kim Il Sung birthplace

Date	Mintage	F	VF	XF	Unc	BU
ND(1992) Proof	500	Value: 725				

KM# 55 2000 WON **Weight:** 31.1000 g. **Composition:** 0.9990 Gold 1 oz. AGW **Subject:** 80th Birthday of Kim Il Sung **Reverse:** Portrait of Kim Il Sung

Date	Mintage	F	VF	XF	Unc	BU
1992 Proof	500	Value: 725				

KM# 57 2000 WON **Weight:** 31.1000 g. **Composition:** 0.9990 Gold 1 oz. AGW **Subject:** 50th Birthday of Kim Jong Il **Reverse:** Portrait of Kim Jong Il

Date	Mintage	F	VF	XF	Unc	BU
1992 Proof	500	Value: 725				

KM# 151 2000 WON **Weight:** 31.1035 g. **Composition:** 0.9990 Gold 1.0000 oz. AGW **Subject:** Death of Kim Il Sung **Obverse:** State arms **Reverse:** Kim's portrait **Edge:** Plain **Size:** 40 mm.

Date	F	VF	XF	Unc	BU
ND(1994)	—	—	—	600	—

KM# 35 2500 WON **Weight:** 15.5500 g. **Composition:** 0.9990 Gold .5 oz. AGW **Subject:** 30th Anniversary of Gorch Fock **Obverse:** State emblem **Reverse:** Sailing ship

Date		F	VF	XF	Unc	BU
1988 Proof	Est. 500	Value: 350				

KM# 81 2500 WON **Weight:** 155.5175 g. **Composition:** 0.9990 Silver 5 oz. ASW **Reverse:** Similar to 500 Won, KM#76 **Size:** 65 mm.

Date	Mintage	F	VF	XF	Unc	BU
1995 Proof	2,500	Value: 150				

KM# 82 2500 WON **Weight:** 155.5175 g. **Composition:** 0.9990 Silver 5 oz. ASW **Reverse:** Similar to 500 Won, KM#69

Date	Mintage	F	VF	XF	Unc	BU
1995 Proof	2,500	Value: 160				

KM# 83 2500 WON **Weight:** 155.5175 g. **Composition:** 0.9990 Silver 5 oz. ASW **Reverse:** Similar to 500 Won, KM#77

Date	Mintage	F	VF	XF	Unc	BU
1995 Proof	2,500	Value: 155				

KM# 85 2500 WON **Weight:** 155.5175 g. **Composition:** 0.9990 Silver 5 oz. ASW **Reverse:** Similar to 500 Won, KM#79

Date	Mintage	F	VF	XF	Unc	BU
1995 Proof	2,500	Value: 160				

KM# 86 2500 WON **Weight:** 155.5175 g. **Composition:** 0.9990 Silver 5 oz. ASW **Reverse:** Similar to 500 Won, KM#80

Date	Mintage	F	VF	XF	Unc	BU
1995 Proof	2,500	Value: 160				

KM# 84 2500 WON **Weight:** 155.5175 g. **Composition:** 0.9990 Silver 5 oz. ASW **Reverse:** Similar to 500 Won, KM#78

Date	Mintage	F	VF	XF	Unc	BU
1995 Proof	2,500	Value: 155				

PROOF SETS

KM#	Date	Mintage	Identification	Issue Price	Mkt Val
PS1	1995 (5)	300	KM92-96	—	1,300

SOUTH KOREA

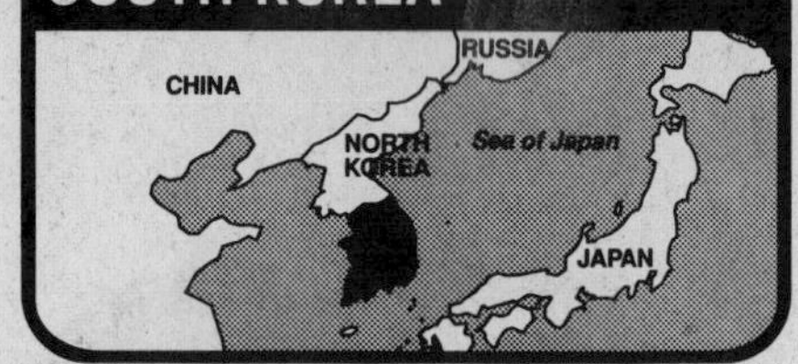

The Republic of Korea, situated in northeastern Asia on the southern half of the Korean peninsula between North Korea and the Korean Strait, has an area of 38,025 sq. mi. (98,480 sq. km.) and a population of 42.5 million. Capital: Seoul. The economy is based on agriculture and light and medium industry. Some of the world's largest oil tankers are built here. Automobiles, plywood, electronics, and textile products are exported.

Japan replaced China as the predominant foreign influence in Korea in 1895 and annexed the peninsular country in 1910. Defeat in World War II brought an end to Japanese rule. U.S. troops entered Korea from the south and Soviet forces entered from the north. The Cairo conference (1943) had established that Korea should be *free and independent*. The Potsdam conference (1945) set the 38th parallel as the line dividing the occupation forces of the United States and Russia. When Russia refused to permit a U.N. commission designated to supervise reunification elections to enter North Korea, an election was held in South Korea on May 10, 1948. By its determination, the Republic of Korea was inaugurated on Aug. 15,1948.

NOTE: For earlier coinage see Korea.

MONETARY SYSTEM
100 Chon = 1 Hwan

REPUBLIC

DECIMAL COINAGE

KM# 1 10 HWAN **Composition:** Bronze **Reverse:** Rose of Sharon

Date	Mintage	F	VF	XF	Unc	BU
KE4292(1959)	100,000,000	1.00	2.00	7.00	12.00	—
KE4294(1961)	100,000,000	0.20	0.35	0.75	2.50	—

KM# 2 50 HWAN **Composition:** Nickel-Brass **Reverse:** Iron-clad turtle boat

Date	Mintage	F	VF	XF	Unc	BU
KE4292(1959)	24,640,000	0.30	0.50	1.00	3.00	—
KE4294(1961)	20,000,000	0.30	0.50	1.00	2.50	—

KM# 3 100 HWAN **Composition:** Copper-Nickel **Reverse:** Bust of Rhee Syngman left

Date	F	VF	XF	Unc	BU
KE4292(1959)	1.25	1.75	2.75	6.00	—

Note: Quantities of KM#1-3 dated 4292 in uncirculated condition were countermarked "SAMPLE" in Korean for distribution to government and banking agencies. See bank samples section at end of listing. KM#3 was withdrawn from circulation June 10, 1962 and melted; KM#1 and KM#2 continued to circulate as 1 Won and 5 Won coins for 13 years respectively until demonitized and withdrawn from circulation March 22, 1975.

REFORM COINAGE

10 Hwan = 1 Won

KM# 4 WON **Composition:** Brass **Obverse:** Rose of Sharon

Date	Mintage	F	VF	XF	Unc	BU
1966	7,000,000	0.20	0.40	1.00	9.00	—
1967	48,500,000	—	0.15	0.25	1.25	—

KM# 4a WON **Composition:** Aluminum

Date	Mintage	F	VF	XF	Unc	BU
1968	66,500,000	—	0.10	0.20	0.85	—
1969	85,000,000	—	—	—	0.25	—
1970	45,000,000	—	—	—	0.25	—
1974	12,000,000	—	0.15	0.25	1.75	—
1975	10,000,000	—	0.10	0.20	0.50	—
1976	20,000,000	—	—	—	0.30	—
1977	30,000,000	—	—	—	0.30	—
1978	30,000,000	—	—	—	0.15	—
1979	30,000,000	—	—	—	0.15	—
1980	20,000,000	—	—	—	0.15	—
1981	20,000,000	—	—	—	0.15	—
1982	30,000,000	—	—	—	0.15	—
1982 Proof	2,000	—	—	—	—	—

KM# 31 WON **Composition:** Aluminum **Obverse:** Rose of Sharon

Date	Mintage	F	VF	XF	Unc	BU
1983	40,000,000	—	—	—	0.15	—
1984	20,000,000	—	—	—	0.15	—
1985	10,000,000	—	—	—	0.15	—
1987	10,000,000	—	—	—	0.15	—
1988	6,500,000	—	—	—	0.15	—
1989	10,000,000	—	—	—	0.15	—
1990	6,000,000	—	—	—	0.15	—
1991	5,000,000	—	—	—	0.15	—
1995	15,000	—	—	—	0.15	—
1996	15,000	—	—	—	0.15	—
1997	15,000	—	—	—	0.15	—
1998	—	—	—	—	0.15	—
1999	—	—	—	—	0.15	—
2000	—	—	—	—	0.15	—
2001	—	—	—	—	0.15	—

KM# 5 5 WON **Composition:** Bronze **Obverse:** Iron-clad turtle boat

Date	Mintage	F	VF	XF	Unc	BU
1966	4,500,000	0.15	0.25	1.50	22.50	—
1967	18,000,000	0.15	0.25	1.00	17.50	—
1968	20,000,000	0.15	0.25	1.00	17.50	—
1969	25,000,000	—	0.10	0.25	3.25	—
1970	50,000,000	—	0.10	0.25	3.00	—

KM# 5a 5 WON **Composition:** Brass **Obverse:** Iron-clad turtle boat

Date	Mintage	F	VF	XF	Unc	BU
1970	Inc. above	—	—	0.10	1.25	—
1971	64,038,000	—	—	—	0.10	—
1972	60,084,000	—	—	—	0.10	—
1977	1,000,000	—	—	0.10	0.75	—
1978	1,000,000	—	—	0.10	0.75	—
1979	1,000,000	—	—	0.10	0.65	—
1980	200,000	—	0.25	0.50	2.50	—
1981	200,000	—	0.25	0.50	1.50	—
1982	200,000	—	0.25	0.50	1.50	—
1982 Proof	2,000	—	—	—	—	—

KM# 32 5 WON **Composition:** Brass **Obverse:** Iron-clad turtle boat

Date	Mintage	F	VF	XF	Unc	BU
1983	6,000,000	—	—	0.10	0.25	—
1987	1,000,000	—	—	0.10	0.25	—
1988	500,000	—	—	0.10	0.25	—
1989	500,000	—	—	0.10	0.25	—
1990	600,000	—	—	0.10	0.25	—
1991	500,000	—	—	0.10	0.25	—
1995	15,000	—	—	0.10	0.25	—

Date	Mintage	F	VF	XF	Unc	BU
1996	15,000	—	—	0.10	0.25	—
1997	15,000	—	—	0.10	0.25	—
1998	—	—	—	0.10	0.25	—
1999	—	—	—	0.10	0.25	—
2000	—	—	—	0.10	0.25	—
2001	—	—	—	0.10	0.25	—

KM# 6 10 WON **Composition:** Bronze **Obverse:** Pagoda at Pul Guk Temple

Date	Mintage	F	VF	XF	Unc	BU
1966	10,600,000	0.15	0.25	1.50	25.00	—
1967	22,500,000	0.15	0.25	1.50	25.00	—
1968	35,000,000	0.15	0.25	1.50	18.50	—
1969	46,500,000	0.15	0.25	1.50	18.50	—
1970	157,000,000	0.15	0.25	1.50	16.50	—

KM# 6a 10 WON **Composition:** Brass **Obverse:** Pagoda at Pul Guk Temple

Date	Mintage	F	VF	XF	Unc	BU
1970	Inc. above	—	0.35	1.25	13.50	—
1971	220,000,000	—	—	0.15	1.75	—
1972	270,000,000	—	—	0.15	1.75	—
1973	30,000,000	—	0.10	0.35	6.50	—
1974	15,000,000	—	0.10	0.35	6.50	—
1975	20,000,000	—	0.10	0.50	11.50	—
1977	1,000,000	—	0.10	0.35	3.50	—
1978	80,000,000	—	0.10	0.15	1.25	—
1979	200,000,000	—	—	0.10	0.55	—
1980	150,000,000	—	—	0.10	0.55	—
1981	100,000	—	0.25	0.75	4.50	—
1982	20,000,000	—	—	0.10	0.60	—
1982 Proof	2,000	—	—	—	—	—

KM# 33.1 10 WON **Composition:** Brass **Obverse:** Pagoda at Pul Guk Temple

Date	Mintage	F	VF	XF	Unc	BU
1983	25,000,000	—	—	0.10	0.35	—
1985	35,000,000	—	—	0.10	0.35	—
1986	195,000,000	—	—	0.10	0.35	—
1987	155,000,000	—	—	0.10	0.35	—
1988	189,000,000	—	—	0.10	0.35	—
1989	310,000,000	—	—	0.10	0.35	—
1990	395,000,000	—	—	0.10	0.35	—
1991	300,000,000	—	—	0.10	0.35	—
1992	150,000,000	—	—	0.10	0.35	—
1993	110,000,000	—	—	0.10	0.35	—
1994	300,000,000	—	—	0.10	0.35	—
1995	380,000,000	—	—	0.10	0.35	—
1996	290,000,000	—	—	0.10	0.35	—
1997	177,000,000	—	—	0.10	0.35	—
1999	—	—	—	0.10	0.35	—
2000	—	—	—	0.10	0.35	—

KM# 33.2 10 WON **Composition:** Brass **Obverse:** Pagoda at Pul Guk Temple **Reverse:** Thick numbers in denomination

Date	F	VF	XF	Unc	BU
1991	—	—	0.10	0.35	—
1997	—	—	0.10	0.35	—
1998	—	—	0.10	0.35	—
1999	—	—	0.10	0.35	—
2000	—	—	0.10	0.35	—
2001	—	—	0.10	0.35	—

KM# 7 50 WON **Weight:** 2.8000 g. **Composition:** 0.9990 Silver .0899 oz. ASW **Obverse:** Yu Kwan-Soon, flag

Date	Mintage	F	VF	XF	Unc	BU
4303 (1970) Proof	4,350	Value: 70.00				
4304 (1971) Rare	—	—	—	—	—	—

KM# 20 50 WON **Composition:** Copper-Nickel **Series:** F.A.O.

Date	Mintage	F	VF	XF	Unc	BU
1972	6,000,000	0.20	0.40	1.00	16.50	—
1973	40,000,000	—	0.15	0.25	3.50	—
1974	25,000,000	—	0.15	0.25	1.50	—
1977	1,000,000	—	0.15	0.25	2.00	—
1978	1,500,000	—	0.15	0.25	1.25	—
1979	20,000,000	—	0.10	0.20	1.25	—
1980	10,000,000	—	0.10	0.20	1.25	—
1981	25,000,000	—	0.10	0.20	1.25	—
1982	40,000,000	—	0.10	0.20	0.75	—
1982 Proof	2,000	—	—	—	—	—

KM# 34 50 WON **Composition:** Copper-Nickel **Series:** F.A.O. **Note:** Die varieties exist.

Date	Mintage	F	VF	XF	Unc	BU
1983	50,000,000	—	—	0.10	0.45	—
1984	40,000,000	—	—	0.10	0.45	—
1985	4,000,000	—	—	0.10	0.45	—
1987	32,000,000	—	—	0.10	0.45	—
1988	53,000,000	—	—	0.10	0.45	—
1989	70,000,000	—	—	0.10	0.45	—
1990	85,000,000	—	—	0.10	0.35	—
1991	80,000,000	—	—	0.10	0.35	—
1992	50,000,000	—	—	0.10	0.35	—
1993	5,000,000	—	—	0.10	0.35	—
1994	102,000,000	—	—	0.10	0.35	—
1995	98,000,000	—	—	0.10	0.35	—
1996	52,000,000	—	—	0.10	0.35	—
1997	129,000,000	—	—	0.10	0.35	—
1998	—	—	—	0.10	0.35	—
1999	—	—	—	0.10	0.35	—
2000	—	—	—	0.10	0.35	—
2001	—	—	—	0.10	0.35	—

KM# 9 100 WON **Composition:** Copper-Nickel

Date	Mintage	F	VF	XF	Unc	BU
1970	1,500,000	0.50	0.75	1.50	18.50	—
1971	13,000,000	0.15	0.25	0.50	13.50	—
1972	20,000,000	—	0.20	0.40	11.50	—
1973	80,000,000	—	0.15	0.30	3.00	—
1974	50,000,000	—	0.15	0.35	4.50	—
Note: Die varieties exist						
1975	75,000,000	—	0.15	0.35	6.00	—
Note: Die varieties exist						
1977	30,000,000	—	0.15	0.35	2.25	—
1978	40,000,000	—	0.15	0.25	1.50	—
1979	130,000,000	—	0.15	0.25	1.50	—
1980	60,000,000	—	0.15	0.25	1.50	—
1981	100,000	—	0.25	0.50	4.00	—
1982	50,000,000	—	0.15	0.25	1.25	—
1982 Proof	2,000	—	—	—	—	—

KM# 8 100 WON **Weight:** 5.6000 g. **Composition:** 0.9990 Silver .1798 oz. ASW **Subject:** Admiral Yi Soon-Shin

Date	Mintage	F	VF	XF	Unc	BU
4303 (1970) Proof	4,350	Value: 125				

KM# 21 100 WON **Composition:** Copper-Nickel **Subject:** 30th Anniersary of Liberation - Yu Kwan Soon

Date	Mintage	F	VF	XF	Unc	BU
ND(1975)	4,998,000	0.20	0.50	0.75	2.25	—
ND(1975) Proof	2,000	Value: 125				

KM# 24 100 WON **Composition:** Copper-Nickel **Subject:** 1st Anniversary of the 5th Republic

Date	Mintage	F	VF	XF	Unc	BU
1981	4,980,000	0.20	0.35	0.65	2.00	—
1981 Unfrosted, Proof	18,000	Value: 25.00				
1981 Proof	2,000	Value: 165				

KM# 35.1 100 WON **Composition:** Copper-Nickel **Obverse:** Admiral Yi Soon-Shin

Date	Mintage	F	VF	XF	Unc	BU
1983	8,000,000	—	0.15	0.25	0.60	—

KM# 35.2 100 WON **Composition:** Copper-Nickel **Obverse:** Admiral Yi Soon-Shin **Reverse:** Modified design

Date	Mintage	F	VF	XF	Unc	BU
1984	40,000,000	—	0.15	0.25	0.60	—
1985	16,000,000	—	0.15	0.30	1.25	—
1986	131,000,000	—	0.15	0.25	0.60	—
1987	170,000,000	—	0.15	0.25	0.60	—
1988	298,000,000	—	0.15	0.25	0.60	—
1989	250,000,000	—	0.15	0.25	0.60	—
1990	185,000,000	—	0.15	0.25	0.60	—
1991	400,000,000	—	0.15	0.25	0.60	—
1992	425,000,000	—	0.15	0.25	0.60	—
1993	185,000,000	—	0.15	0.25	0.60	—
1994	401,000,000	—	0.15	0.25	0.60	—
1995	228,000,000	—	0.15	0.25	0.60	—
1996	447,000,000	—	0.15	0.25	0.60	—
1997	147,000,000	—	0.15	0.25	0.60	—
1999	—	—	0.15	0.25	0.60	—
2000	—	—	0.15	0.25	0.60	—
2001	—	—	0.15	0.25	0.60	—

KM# 10 200 WON **Weight:** 11.2000 g. **Composition:** 0.9990 Silver .3596 oz. ASW **Obverse:** Celadon vase

Date	Mintage	F	VF	XF	Unc	BU
KE4303 (1970) Proof	4,200	Value: 115				

KM# 11 250 WON **Weight:** 14.0000 g. **Composition:** 0.9990 Silver .4497 oz. ASW **Obverse:** Bust of Park Chung-Hee

Date	Mintage	F	VF	XF	Unc	BU
KE4303 (1970) Proof	4,100	Value: 200				

KM# 12 500 WON **Weight:** 28.0000 g. **Composition:** 0.9990 Silver .8994 oz. ASW **Subject:** Kyongji - Bodhisattva from the Cave Temple

Date	Mintage	F	VF	XF	Unc	BU
KE4303 (1970) Proof	4,700	Value: 250				

KM# 22 500 WON **Composition:** Copper-Nickel **Subject:** 42nd World Shooting Championships

Date	Mintage	F	VF	XF	Unc	BU
1978	980,000	0.35	0.75	1.50	4.50	—
1978 Unfrosted, proof	18,000	Value: 27.50				
1978 Proof	2,000	Value: 220				

KM# 27 500 WON **Composition:** Copper-Nickel **Obverse:** Manchurian crane

Date	Mintage	F	VF	XF	Unc	BU
1982	15,000,000	—	—	1.00	3.75	—
1982 Proof	2,000	—	—	—	—	—
1983	64,000,000	—	—	1.00	2.50	—
1984	70,000,000	—	—	1.00	2.50	—
1987	1,000,000	—	—	1.00	2.50	—
1988	27,000,000	—	—	1.00	2.50	—
1989	25,000,000	—	—	1.00	2.50	—
1990	60,000,000	—	—	1.00	2.50	—
1991	90,000,000	—	—	1.00	2.25	—
1992	105,000,000	—	—	1.00	2.25	—
1993	32,000,000	—	—	1.00	2.25	—
1994	50,600,000	—	—	1.00	2.25	—
1995	87,000,000	—	—	1.00	2.25	—
1996	122,000,000	—	—	1.00	2.25	—
1997	62,000,000	—	—	1.00	2.25	—
1998	—	—	—	1.00	2.25	—
1999	—	—	—	1.00	2.25	—
2000	—	—	—	1.00	2.25	—
2001	—	—	—	1.00	2.25	—

KM# 13 1000 WON **Weight:** 56.0000 g. **Composition:** 0.9990 Silver 1.7988 oz. ASW **Subject:** U.N. Forces in South Korea **Reverse:** Similar to 200 Won, KM#10

Date	Mintage	F	VF	XF	Unc	BU
KE4303 (1970) Proof	4,050	Value: 425				

KM# 14.1 1000 WON **Weight:** 3.8700 g. **Composition:** 0.9000 Gold .1119 oz. AGW **Obverse:** Great South Gate in Seoul **Note:** Struck at the Valcambi Mint.

Date	Mintage	F	VF	XF	Unc	BU
KE4303 (1970) Proof	1,500	Value: 350				

KM# 14.2 1000 WON **Weight:** 3.8700 g. **Composition:** 0.9000 Gold .1119 oz. AGW **Obverse:** Great South Gate in Seoul **Note:** Struck at the Paris Mint.

Date	Mintage	F	VF	XF	Unc	BU
KE4303 (1970) Proof	100	Value: 1,250				

KM# 25 1000 WON **Composition:** Nickel **Subject:** 1st Anniversary of the 5th Republic **Reverse:** Imaginary bird, called Bong-hwang, represents a King

Date	Mintage	F	VF	XF	Unc	BU
1981	1,880,000	1.00	1.25	1.50	6.00	—
1981 Unfrosted, proof	18,000	Value: 27.50				
1981 Proof	2,000	Value: 225				

KM# 28 1000 WON **Composition:** Copper-Nickel **Series:** 1988 Olympics **Obverse:** Dancers

Date	Mintage	F	VF	XF	Unc	BU
1982	1,980,000	—	—	1.25	4.00	—
1982 Unfrosted, proof	10,000	Value: 22.50				
1982 Proof	10,000	Value: 37.50				

KM# 36 1000 WON **Composition:** Copper-Nickel **Series:** 1988 Olympics **Obverse:** Drummer (Jangku)

Date	Mintage	F	VF	XF	Unc	BU
1983	330,000	—	—	1.25	4.00	—
1983 Unfrosted, Proof	56,000	Value: 12.50				
1983 Proof	101,000	Value: 18.50				

KM# 39 1000 WON **Composition:** Copper-Nickel **Subject:** 200 Years of Catholic Church in Korea **Reverse:** Myung Dong Cathedral

Date	Mintage	F	VF	XF	Unc	BU
1984	572,000	—	—	1.50	5.00	—

KM# 41 1000 WON **Composition:** Copper-Nickel **Subject:** 10th Asian Games **Reverse:** Lion dance

Date	Mintage	F	VF	XF	Unc	BU
1986	930,000	—	—	1.25	4.00	—
1986 Proof	70,000	Value: 7.00				

KM# 46 1000 WON **Composition:** Copper-Nickel **Series:** 1988 Olympics **Reverse:** Basketball

Date	Mintage	F	VF	XF	Unc	BU
1986	560,000	—	—	—	4.00	—
1986 Proof	140,000	Value: 8.50				

KM# 47 1000 WON **Composition:** Copper-Nickel **Series:** 1988 Olympics **Reverse:** Tennis

Date	Mintage	F	VF	XF	Unc	BU
1987	560,000	—	—	—	4.00	—
1987 Proof	140,000	Value: 7.50				

KM# 48 1000 WON Composition: Copper-Nickel **Series:** 1988 Olympics **Reverse:** Handball

Date	Mintage	F	VF	XF	Unc	BU
1987	560,000	—	—	—	4.00	—
1987 Proof	140,000	Value: 7.50				

KM# 49 1000 WON Composition: Copper-Nickel **Series:** 1988 Olympics **Reverse:** Table tennis

Date	Mintage	F	VF	XF	Unc	BU
1988	560,000	—	—	—	4.00	—
1988 Proof	140,000	Value: 7.50				

KM# 78 1000 WON Composition: Copper-Nickel **Subject:** Taejon International Exposition Kumdori **Reverse:** Mascot of the Expo

Date	Mintage	F	VF	XF	Unc	BU
1993	590,000	—	—	—	5.00	—

KM# 87 1000 WON Composition: Copper-Nickel **Subject:** 50th Anniversary of U.N.

Date	Mintage	F	VF	XF	Unc	BU
1995	5,000	—	—	—	10.00	—

KM# 89 1000 WON Weight: 12.0000 g. **Composition:** Brass **Series:** World Cup Soccer **Obverse:** FIFA World Cup logo **Reverse:** Mascot soccer player **Edge:** Reeded **Size:** 32 mm.

Date	Mintage	F	VF	XF	Unc	BU
2001	102,000	—	—	—	8.50	—

KM# 50 2000 WON Composition: Nickel **Series:** 1988 Olympics **Reverse:** Boxing

Date	Mintage	F	VF	XF	Unc	BU
1986	560,000	—	—	—	6.50	—
1986 Proof	140,000	Value: 8.50				

KM# 51 2000 WON Composition: Nickel **Series:** 1988 Olympics **Reverse:** Tae Kwon Do

Date	Mintage	F	VF	XF	Unc	BU
1987	560,000	—	—	—	5.50	—
1987 Proof	140,000	Value: 8.50				

KM# 52 2000 WON Composition: Nickel **Series:** 1988 Olympics **Reverse:** Wrestling

Date	Mintage	F	VF	XF	Unc	BU
1987	560,000	—	—	—	5.50	—
1987 Proof	140,000	Value: 12.50				

KM# 53 2000 WON Composition: Nickel **Series:** 1988 Olympics **Reverse:** Weight lifting

Date	Mintage	F	VF	XF	Unc	BU
1988	560,000	—	—	—	5.50	—
1988 Proof	140,000	Value: 8.50				

KM# 88 2000 WON Ring Weight: 10.7000 g. **Ring Composition:** Copper-Nickel **Center Composition:** Copper-Aluminum-Nickel **Subject:** New Millennium **Obverse:** Astronomical observation instrument **Reverse:** Stylized design **Edge:** Reeded **Size:** 28 mm. **Note:** Korea Minting and Security Printing Corp.

Date	Mintage	F	VF	XF	Unc	BU
2000	—	—	—	—	9.00	—

KM# 15.1 2500 WON Weight: 9.6800 g. **Composition:** 0.9000 Gold .2801 oz. AGW **Obverse:** Queen Mother Sunduk **Note:** Struck at the Valcambi Mint.

Date	Mintage	F	VF	XF	Unc	BU
KE4303 (1970) Proof	1,750	Value: 500				

KM# 15.2 2500 WON Weight: 9.6800 g. **Composition:** 0.9000 Gold .2801 oz. AGW **Obverse:** Queen Mother Sunduk **Note:** Struck at the Paris Mint.

Date	Mintage	F	VF	XF	Unc	BU
KE4303 (1970) Proof	100	Value: 1,500				

KM# 16.1 5000 WON Weight: 19.3600 g. **Composition:** 0.9000 Gold .5602 oz. AGW **Obverse:** Iron-clad turtle boat **Note:** Struck at the Valcambi Mint.

Date	Mintage	F	VF	XF	Unc	BU
KE4303 (1970) Proof	670	Value: 1,850				

KM# 16.2 5000 WON Weight: 19.3600 g. **Composition:** 0.9000 Gold .5602 oz. AGW **Obverse:** Iron-clad turtle boat **Note:** Struck at the Paris Mint.

Date	Mintage	F	VF	XF	Unc	BU
KE4303 (1970) Proof	70	Value: 2,500				

KM# 23 5000 WON Weight: 23.0000 g. **Composition:** 0.9000 Silver .6655 oz. ASW **Subject:** 42nd World Shooting Championships

Date	Mintage	F	VF	XF	Unc	BU
1978	80,000	—	—	—	35.00	—
1978 Unfrosted, Proof	20,000	Value: 90.00				

KM# 54 5000 WON Weight: 16.8100 g. **Composition:** 0.9250 Silver .5000 oz. ASW **Series:** 1988 Olympics **Reverse:** Tiger mascot

Date	Mintage	F	VF	XF	Unc	BU
1986	92,000	—	—	—	8.50	—
1986 Proof	235,000	Value: 10.00				

KM# 55 5000 WON Weight: 16.8100 g. **Composition:** 0.9250 Silver .5000 oz. ASW **Series:** 1988 Olympics **Reverse:** Tug of war

Date	Mintage	F	VF	XF	Unc	BU
1986	90,000	—	—	—	8.50	—
1986 Proof	217,000	Value: 10.00				

KM# 60 5000 WON Weight: 16.8100 g. **Composition:** 0.9250 Silver .5000 oz. ASW **Series:** 1988 Olympics **Reverse:** Stadium

Date	Mintage	F	VF	XF	Unc	BU
1987	73,000	—	—	—	10.00	—
1987 Proof	199,000	Value: 12.00				

KM# 61 5000 WON **Weight:** 16.8100 g. **Composition:** 0.9250 Silver .5000 oz. ASW **Series:** 1988 Olympics **Reverse:** Chegi - Kicking

Date	Mintage	F	VF	XF	Unc	BU
1987	60,000	—	—	—	9.00	—
1987 Proof	180,000	Value: 12.00				

KM# 66 5000 WON **Weight:** 16.8100 g. **Composition:** 0.9250 Silver .5000 oz. ASW **Series:** 1988 Olympics **Reverse:** Tae Kwon Do

Date	Mintage	F	VF	XF	Unc	BU
1987	58,000	—	—	—	10.00	—
1987 Proof	150,000	Value: 12.00				

KM# 67 5000 WON **Weight:** 16.8100 g. **Composition:** 0.9250 Silver .5000 oz. ASW **Series:** 1988 Olympics **Reverse:** Girls on swing

Date	Mintage	F	VF	XF	Unc	BU
1987	60,000	—	—	—	9.00	—
1987 Proof	147,000	Value: 12.00				

KM# 70 5000 WON **Weight:** 16.8100 g. **Composition:** 0.9250 Silver .5000 oz. ASW **Series:** 1988 Olympics **Reverse:** Wrestling

Date	Mintage	F	VF	XF	Unc	BU
1988	59,000	—	—	—	10.00	—
1988 Proof	136,000	Value: 12.00				

KM# 71 5000 WON **Weight:** 16.8100 g. **Composition:** 0.9250 Silver .5000 oz. ASW **Series:** 1988 Olympics **Reverse:** Boys spinning top

Date	Mintage	F	VF	XF	Unc	BU
1988	59,000	—	—	—	9.00	—
1988 Proof	134,000	Value: 12.00				

KM# 79 5000 WON **Weight:** 16.8100 g. **Composition:** 0.9250 Silver .5000 oz. ASW **Subject:** Taejon International Exposition **Reverse:** Yarn spinners

Date	Mintage	F	VF	XF	Unc	BU
1993	150,000	—	—	—	17.50	—

KM# 80 5000 WON **Weight:** 16.8100 g. **Composition:** 0.9250 Silver .5000 oz. ASW **Subject:** Taejon International Exposition **Reverse:** Folk musicians

Date	Mintage	F	VF	XF	Unc	BU
1993	150,000	—	—	—	17.50	—

KM# 85 5000 WON **Composition:** Nickel **Subject:** 50th Anniversary of Liberation from Japan **Obverse:** Kim-Gu

Date	Mintage	F	VF	XF	Unc	BU
1995	25,000	—	—	—	10.00	—

KM# 96 5000 WON **Weight:** 22.0000 g. **Composition:** Bronze **Obverse:** Head Office of the Bank of Korea old and new buildings. **Reverse:** 50th Anniversary of the Bank of Korea **Size:** 38 mm.

Date	F	VF	XF	Unc	BU
2000	—	—	—	—	—

KM# 17.1 10000 WON **Weight:** 38.7200 g. **Composition:** 0.9000 Gold 1.1205 oz. AGW **Obverse:** Bust of Park Chung-Hee **Note:** Struck at the Valcambi Mint.

Date	Mintage	F	VF	XF	Unc	BU
KE4303 (1970) Proof	435	Value: 5,000				

KM# 17.2 10000 WON **Weight:** 38.7200 g. **Composition:** 0.9000 Gold 1.1205 oz. AGW **Obverse:** Bust of Park Chung-Hee **Note:** Struck at the Paris Mint.

Date	Mintage	F	VF	XF	Unc	BU
KE4303 (1970) Proof	55	Value: 6,000				

KM# 29 10000 WON **Weight:** 15.0000 g. **Composition:** 0.9000 Silver .4340 oz. ASW **Series:** 1988 Olympics **Obverse:** Great South Gate, Soul

Date	Mintage	F	VF	XF	Unc	BU
1982	280,000	—	—	—	14.50	—
1982 Unfrosted, proof	10,000	Value: 32.50				
1982 Proof	10,000	Value: 50.00				

KM# 37 10000 WON **Weight:** 15.0000 g. **Composition:** 0.9000 Silver .4340 oz. ASW **Series:** 1988 Olympics **Obverse:** Pavilion of Kyongbok Palace

Date	Mintage	F	VF	XF	Unc	BU
1983	137,000	—	—	—	14.50	—
1983 Unfrosted, Proof	56,000	Value: 25.00				
1983 Proof	101,000	Value: 30.00				

KM# 40 10000 WON **Weight:** 23.2600 g. **Composition:** 0.5000 Silver .3739 oz. ASW **Subject:** 200 Years of Catholic Church in Korea

Date	Mintage	F	VF	XF	Unc	BU
1984	152,000	—	—	—	20.00	—

KM# 42 10000 WON **Weight:** 23.0000 g. **Composition:** 0.9000 Silver .6655 oz. ASW **Subject:** 10th Asian Games **Obverse:** Similar to 2000 Won, KM#50 **Reverse:** Badminton

Date	Mintage	F	VF	XF	Unc	BU
1986	130,000	—	—	—	14.00	—
1986 Proof	70,000	Value: 24.00				

KM# 43 10000 WON **Weight:** 23.0000 g. **Composition:** 0.9000 Silver .6655 oz. ASW **Subject:** 10th Asian Games **Obverse:** Similar to 2000 Won, KM#50 **Reverse:** Soccer

Date	Mintage	F	VF	XF	Unc	BU
1986	130,000	—	—	—	14.00	—
1986 Proof	70,000	Value: 24.00				

KM# 56 10000 WON **Weight:** 33.6200 g. **Composition:** 0.9250 Silver 1.0000 oz. ASW **Series:** 1988 Olympics **Reverse:** Marathon

Date	Mintage	F	VF	XF	Unc	BU
1986	90,000	—	—	—	15.00	—
1986 Proof	229,000	Value: 16.50				

KM# 57 10000 WON **Weight:** 33.6200 g. **Composition:** 0.9250 Silver 1.0000 oz. ASW **Series:** 1988 Olympics **Reverse:** Diving

Date	Mintage	F	VF	XF	Unc	BU
1987	90,000	—	—	—	15.00	—
1987 Proof	217,000	Value: 16.50				

KM# 62 10000 WON **Weight:** 33.6200 g. **Composition:** 0.9250 Silver 1.0000 oz. ASW **Series:** 1988 Olympics **Reverse:** Archery

Date	Mintage	F	VF	XF	Unc	BU
1987	60,000	—	—	—	17.50	—
1987 Proof	182,000	Value: 16.50				
1988	Inc. above	—	—	—	200	—
1988 Proof	Inc. above	Value: 90.00				

Note: 1988 is an error date

KM# 63 10000 WON **Weight:** 33.6200 g. **Composition:** 0.9250 Silver 1.0000 oz. ASW **Series:** 1988 Olympics **Reverse:** Volleyball

Date	Mintage	F	VF	XF	Unc	BU
1987	72,000	—	—	—	16.00	—
1987 Proof	188,000	Value: 17.50				

KM# 74 10000 WON **Weight:** 33.6200 g. **Composition:** 0.9250 Silver 1.0000 oz. ASW **Series:** 1988 Olympics **Reverse:** Gymnastics

Date	Mintage	F	VF	XF	Unc	BU
1988	9,000	—	—	—	16.50	—
1988 Proof	97,000	Value: 20.00				

KM# 75 10000 WON **Weight:** 33.6200 g. **Composition:** 0.9250 Silver 1.0000 oz. ASW **Series:** 1988 Olympics **Reverse:** Equestrian events

Date	Mintage	F	VF	XF	Unc	BU
1988	9,000	—	—	—	16.50	—
1988 Proof	97,000	Value: 20.00				

KM# 76 10000 WON **Weight:** 33.6200 g. **Composition:** 0.9250 Silver 1.0000 oz. ASW **Series:** 1988 Olympics **Reverse:** Cycling

Date	Mintage	F	VF	XF	Unc	BU
1988	8,700	—	—	—	17.50	—
1988 Proof	95,000	Value: 21.50				

KM# 77 10000 WON **Weight:** 33.6200 g. **Composition:** 0.9250 Silver 1.0000 oz. ASW **Series:** 1988 Olympics **Reverse:** Soccer

Date	Mintage	F	VF	XF	Unc	BU
1988	8,700	—	—	—	17.50	—
1988 Proof	83,000	Value: 21.50				

KM# 81 10000 WON **Weight:** 33.6200 g. **Composition:** 0.9250 Silver 1.0000 oz. ASW **Subject:** Taejon International Exposition **Reverse:** Porcelain celadon

Date	F	VF	XF	Unc	BU
1993	—	—	—	35.00	—

KM# 86 10000 WON **Weight:** 23.0000 g. **Composition:** 0.9000 Silver .6655 oz. ASW **Subject:** 50th Anniversary of Liberation from Japan **Obverse:** Ahn Jong-Kun

Date	Mintage	F	VF	XF	Unc	BU
1995	40,000	—	—	—	35.00	—

KM# 84 10000 WON **Weight:** 22.5000 g. **Composition:** 0.9250 Silver .6691 oz. ASW **Subject:** 50th Anniversary - Republic of Korea **Obverse:** Ahn Jong-Kun **Note:** With multicolor ENAMEL and with GOLD-PLATED center insert.

Date	Mintage	F	VF	XF	Unc	BU
ND(1998)	100,000	—	—	—	35.00	—

KM# 93 10000 WON **Weight:** 31.1035 g. **Composition:** 0.9990 Silver 1.0000 oz. ASW **Series:** World Cup Soccer **Subject:** Daegu Stadium **Obverse:** Multicolor soccer logo **Reverse:** Player controlling the ball **Edge:** Reeded **Size:** 35 mm.

Date	Mintage	F	VF	XF	Unc	BU
2001 Proof	37,000	Value: 40.00				

KM# 94 10000 WON **Weight:** 15.5518 g. **Composition:** 0.9990 Gold .5000 oz. AGW **Series:** World Cup Soccer **Obverse:** Soccer logo **Reverse:** World Cup soccer trophy **Edge:** Reeded **Size:** 28 mm.

Date	Mintage	F	VF	XF	Unc	BU
2001 Proof	20,000	Value: 300				

KM# 90 10000 WON **Weight:** 31.1035 g. **Composition:** 0.9990 Silver 1.0000 oz. ASW **Series:** World Cup Soccer **Subject:** Gwangju Stadium **Obverse:** Multicolor soccer logo **Reverse:** Player heading the ball **Edge:** Reeded **Size:** 35 mm.

Date	Mintage	F	VF	XF	Unc	BU
2001 Proof	37,000	Value: 40.00				

KM# 91 10000 WON **Weight:** 31.1035 g. **Composition:** 0.9990 Silver 1.0000 oz. ASW **Series:** World Sup Soccer **Subject:** Busan Stadium **Obverse:** Multicolor soccer logo **Reverse:** Player kicking the ball **Edge:** Reeded **Size:** 35 mm.

Date	Mintage	F	VF	XF	Unc	BU
2001 Proof	37,000	Value: 40.00				

KM# 92 10000 WON **Weight:** 31.1035 g. **Composition:** 0.9990 Silver 1.0000 oz. ASW **Series:** World Cup Soccer **Subject:** Daegu Stadium **Obverse:** Multicolor soccer logo **Reverse:** Player controlling the ball **Edge:** Reeded **Size:** 35 mm.

Date	Mintage	F	VF	XF	Unc	BU
2001 Proof	37,000	Value: 35.00				

KM# 18.1 20000 WON **Weight:** 77.4000 g. **Composition:** 0.9000 Gold 2.2398 oz. AGW **Obverse:** Gold Crown - Silla Dynasty **Reverse:** Similar to 5000 Won, KM#16.1 **Note:** Struck at the Valcambi Mint.

Date	Mintage	F	VF	XF	Unc	BU
KE4303 (1970) Proof	382	Value: 8,750				

KM# 18.2 20000 WON **Weight:** 77.4000 g. **Composition:** 0.9000 Gold 2.2398 oz. AGW **Obverse:** Gold Crown - Silla Dynasty **Reverse:** Similar to 5000 Won, KM#16.1 **Note:** Struck at the Paris Mint.

Date	Mintage	F	VF	XF	Unc	BU
KE4303 (1970) Proof	52	Value: 10,000				

KM# 26 20000 WON **Weight:** 23.0000 g. **Composition:** 0.9000 Silver .6655 oz. ASW **Subject:** 1st Anniversary of the 5th Repulic

Date	Mintage	F	VF	XF	Unc	BU
1981	80,000	—	—	—	35.00	—
1981 Unfrosted, proof	18,000	Value: 40.00				
1981 Proof	2,000	Value: 320				

KM# 30 20000 WON **Weight:** 23.0000 g. **Composition:** 0.9000 Silver .6655 oz. ASW **Series:** 1988 Olympics **Obverse:** Flame

Date	Mintage	F	VF	XF	Unc	BU
1982	180,000	—	—	—	26.50	—
1982 Unfrosted, proof	10,000	Value: 50.00				
1982 Proof	10,000	Value: 75.00				

KM# 38 20000 WON **Weight:** 23.0000 g. **Composition:** 0.9000 Silver .6655 oz. ASW **Series:** 1988 Olympics **Obverse:** Wrestlers

Date	Mintage	F	VF	XF	Unc	BU
1983	123,000	—	—	—	25.00	—
1983 Unfrosted, proof	56,000	Value: 32.50				
1983 Proof	101,000	Value: 40.00				

KM# 44 20000 WON **Composition:** 0.9000 Silver **Subject:** 10th Asian Games **Obverse:** Similar to 1000 Won, KM#41 **Reverse:** Runner

Date	Mintage	F	VF	XF	Unc	BU
1986	130,000	—	—	—	30.00	—
1986 Proof	70,000	Value: 40.00				

KM# 45 20000 WON **Composition:** 0.9000 Silver **Subject:** 10th Asian Games **Obverse:** Similar to 1000 Won, KM#41 **Reverse:** Pul Guk Temple - Kyong Ju City

Date	Mintage	F	VF	XF	Unc	BU
1986	130,000	—	—	—	28.00	—
1986 Proof	70,000	Value: 40.00				

KM# 19.1 25000 WON **Weight:** 96.8000 g. **Composition:** 0.9000 Gold 2.8012 oz. AGW **Subject:** 10th Asian Games **Obverse:** King Sejong The Great **Reverse:** Similar to 5000 Won, KM#16.1 **Note:** Struck at the Valcambi Mint.

Date	Mintage	F	VF	XF	Unc	BU
KE4303 (1970) Proof	325	Value: 14,000				

KM# 19.2 25000 WON **Weight:** 96.8000 g. **Composition:** 0.9000 Gold 2.8012 oz. AGW **Subject:** 10th Asian Games **Obverse:** King Sejong The Great **Reverse:** Similar to 5000 Won, KM#16.1 **Note:** Struck at the Paris Mint.

Date	Mintage	F	VF	XF	Unc	BU
KE4303(1970) Proof	25	Value: 17,000				

KM# 58 25000 WON **Weight:** 16.8100 g. **Composition:** 0.9250 Gold .5000 oz. AGW **Series:** 1988 Olympics **Reverse:** Folk dancing

Date	Mintage	F	VF	XF	Unc	BU
1986	20,000	—	—	—	200	—
1986 Proof	111,000	Value: 215				

KM# 64 25000 WON **Weight:** 16.8100 g. **Composition:** 0.9250 Gold .5000 oz. AGW **Series:** 1988 Olympics **Reverse:** Fan dancing

Date	Mintage	F	VF	XF	Unc	BU
1987	20,000	—	—	—	200	—
1987 Proof	82,000	Value: 220				

KM# 68 25000 WON **Weight:** 16.8100 g. **Composition:** 0.9250 Gold .5000 oz. AGW **Series:** 1988 Olympics **Reverse:** Kite flying

Date	Mintage	F	VF	XF	Unc	BU
1987	20,000	—	—	—	200	—
1987 Proof	79,000	Value: 225				
1988	—	—	—	—	200	—
1988 Proof	—	Value: 225				

KM# 72 25000 WON **Weight:** 16.8100 g. **Composition:** 0.9250 Gold .5000 oz. AGW **Series:** 1988 Olympics **Reverse:** Korean Seesaw

Date	Mintage	F	VF	XF	Unc	BU
1988	19,000	—	—	—	200	—
1988 Proof	62,000	Value: 225				

KM# 82 25000 WON **Weight:** 16.8100 g. **Composition:** 0.9250 Gold .5000 oz. AGW **Subject:** Taejon International Exposition **Reverse:** Celestial globe

Date	Mintage	F	VF	XF	Unc	BU
1993	40,000	—	—	—	375	—

KM# 95 30000 WON **Weight:** 31.1035 g. **Composition:** 0.9990 Gold 1.0000 oz. AGW **Series:** World Cup Soccer **Obverse:** Soccer logo **Reverse:** Nude soccer player **Edge:** Reeded **Size:** 35 mm.

Date	Mintage	F	VF	XF	Unc	BU
2001 Proof	12,000	Value: 550				

KM# 59 50000 WON **Weight:** 33.6200 g. **Composition:** 0.9250 Gold 1.0000 oz. AGW **Series:** 1988 Olympics **Reverse:** Turtle boat

Date	Mintage	F	VF	XF	Unc	BU
1986 Proof	30,000	Value: 375				

KM# 65 50000 WON **Weight:** 33.6200 g. **Composition:** 0.9250 Gold 1.0000 oz. AGW **Series:** 1988 Olympics **Obverse:** Similar to 10,000 Won, KM#62 **Reverse:** Great South Gate

Date	Mintage	F	VF	XF	Unc	BU
1987 Proof	30,000	Value: 375				

KM# 69 50000 WON **Weight:** 33.6200 g. **Composition:** 0.9250 Gold 1.0000 oz. AGW **Series:** 1988 Olympics **Obverse:** Similar to 10,000 Won, KM#62 **Reverse:** Horse and rider

Date	Mintage	F	VF	XF	Unc	BU
1987 Proof	30,000	Value: 375				

KM# 73 50000 WON **Weight:** 33.6200 g. **Composition:** 0.9250 Gold 1.0000 oz. AGW **Series:** 1988 Olympics **Obverse:** Similar to 10,000 Won, KM#62 **Reverse:** Pul Guk Temple

Date	Mintage	F	VF	XF	Unc	BU
1988 Proof	30,000	Value: 375				

KM# 83 50000 WON **Weight:** 33.6200 g. **Composition:** 0.9250 Gold 1.0000 oz. AGW **Subject:** Taejon International Exposition **Reverse:** Tower of Great Light

Date	Mintage	F	VF	XF	Unc	BU
1993	10,000	—	—	—	550	—

BANK SAMPLES

Korean

NOTE: Bank samples countermarked in Korean Sample have been prepared for government and banking agencies.

견양

KM#	Date	Mintage	Identification	Issue Price	Mkt Val
S1	KE4292	—	10 Hwan. Bronze. KM1.	—	65.00
S2	KE4292	—	50 Hwan. Nickel-Brass. KM2.	—	75.00
S3	KE4292	—	100 Hwan. Copper-Nickel. KM3.	—	90.00
S4	1967	—	Won. Brass. KM4.	—	—
S5	1975	—	100 Won. Copper-Nickel. KM21.	—	—
S6	1978	—	500 Won. Copper-Nickel. KM22.	—	—
S7	1978	—	5000 Won. Silver. KM23.	—	—
S8	1984	—	20000 Won. Silver. KM26.	—	—
S9	1984	—	50000 Won. Silver. KM40.	—	—

MINT SETS

KM#	Date	Mintage	Identification	Issue Price	Mkt Val
MS1	Mixed dates (6)	75,000	KM6a(1980) , 32, 34, 35.1 (1983), 27, 31 (1984)	—	60.00
MS2	1983 (6)	—	KM27, 31-32, 33.1, 34, 35.1	—	60.00
MS3	1986 (5)	130,000	KM41-45	113	100
MS4	1991 (6)	—	KM27, 31-32, 33.1, 34, 35.2	—	12.00
MS5	1993 (6)	10,000	KM78-83	1,180	1,200
MS6	1993 (5)	30,000	KM78-82	443	450
MS7	1993 (4)	50,000	KM78-81	97.00	100
MS8	2001 (7)	—	KM#27, 31, 32, 33.2, 34, 35.2, 89	10.00	—

PROOF SETS

KM#	Date	Mintage	Identification	Issue Price	Mkt Val
PS1	1970 (12)	—	KM7-8, 10-13, 14.1-19.1	752	31,500
PS2	1970 (11)	—	KM7-8, 10-13, 14.2-18.2	—	22,350
PS3	1970 (6)	—	KM7-8, 10-13	53.50	1,100
PS4	1970 (6)	300	KM14.1-19.1	698	32,000
PS5	1970 (6)	25	KM14.2-19.2	—	38,250
PS6	1982 (6)	2,000	KM4a-6a, 9, 20, 27, (presentation set)	—	835
PS7	1986 (6)	350,000	KM#41, 50, 54-56, 58	275	—
PS8	1986 (5)	70,000	KM41-45	170	140
PS9	1986 (2)	—	KM46, 50	—	18.00
PSA9	1986 (6)	160,000	KM#46, 50, 54-56, 58	275	—
PS10	2001 (6)	2,002	KM#90-95	—	1,000

KUWAIT

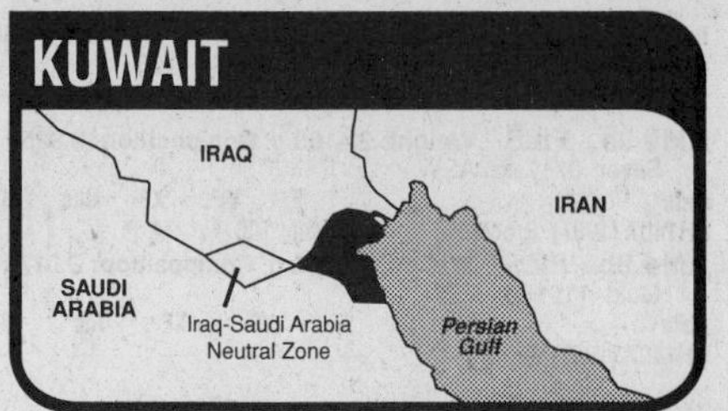

The State of Kuwait, a constitutional monarchy located on the Arabian Peninsula at the northwestern corner of the Persian Gulf, has an area of 6,880 sq. mi. (17,820 sq. km.) and a population of 1.7 million. Capital: Kuwait. Petroleum, the basis of the economy, provides 95 percent of the exports.

The modern history of Kuwait began with the founding of the city of Kuwait, 1740, by tribesmen who wandered northward from the region of the Qatar Peninsula of eastern Arabia. Fearing that the Turks would take over the sheikhdom, Sheikh Mubarak entered into an agreement with Great Britain, 1899, placing Kuwait under the protection of Britain and empowering Britain to conduct its foreign affairs. Britain terminated the protectorate on June19, 1961, giving Kuwait its independence (by a simple exchange of notes) but agreeing to furnish military aid on request.

Kuwait was invaded and occupied by an army from neighboring Iraq Aug. 2, 1990. Soon thereafter Iraq declared that the country would become a province of Iraq. An international coalition of military forces primarily based in Saudi Arabia led by the United States under terms set by the United Nations, attacked Iraqi military installations to liberate Kuwait. This occurred Jan. 17, 1991. Kuwait City was liberated Feb.27, and a cease-fire was declared Feb. 28. New paper currency was introduced March 24, 1991 to replace earlier notes.

TITLES

الكويت

al-Kuwait

RULERS

British Protectorate, until 1961

LOCAL

Al Sabah Dynasty

Mubarak Ibn Sabah, 1896-1915
Jabir Ibn Mubarak, 1915-1917
Salim Ibn Mubarak, 1917-1921
Ahmad Ibn Jabir, 1921-1950
Abdullah Ibn Salim, 1950-1965
Sabah Ibn Salim, 1965-1977
Jabir Ibn Ahmad, 1977-

MONETARY SYSTEM

1000 Fils = 1 Dinar

STATE OF KUWAIT

MODERN COINAGE

KM# 2 FILS **Composition:** Nickel-Brass

Date	Mintage	F	VF	XF	Unc	BU
AH1380 (1960)	2,000,000	—	0.50	1.00	1.50	—
AH1380 (1960) Proof	60	Value: 30.00				

KM# 9 FILS **Composition:** Nickel-Brass

Date	Mintage	F	VF	XF	Unc	BU
AH1382 (1962)	500,000	—	0.10	0.15	0.35	—
AH1382 (1962) Proof	60	Value: 30.00				
AH1384 (1964)	600,000	—	0.25	0.75	1.50	—
AH1385 (1965)	500,000	—	0.25	0.75	1.50	—
AH1386 (1966)	1,875,000	—	0.25	0.75	1.50	—
AH1389 (1969)	375,000	—	0.35	1.00	2.50	—
AH1390 (1970)	500,000	—	0.25	0.75	1.50	—
AH1391 (1971)	500,000	—	0.25	0.75	1.50	—
AH1392 (1972)	500,000	—	0.25	0.75	1.50	—
AH1393 (1973)	375,000	—	0.35	1.00	2.50	—
AH1395 (1975)	500,000	—	0.25	0.75	1.50	—
AH1396 (1976)	2,500,000	—	0.15	0.25	0.50	—
AH1397 (1977)	2,500,000	—	0.15	0.25	0.50	—
AH1399 (1979)	1,500,000	—	0.15	0.25	0.50	—
AH1400 (1980)	—	—	0.15	0.25	0.50	—
AH1403 (1983)	—	—	0.15	0.25	0.50	—

Date	Mintage	F	VF	XF	Unc	BU
AH1407 (1987)	—	—	0.15	0.25	0.50	—
AH1408 (1988)	500,000	—	0.15	0.25	0.50	—

KM# 9a FILS **Weight:** 2.4100 g. **Composition:** 0.9250 Silver .0717 oz. ASW

Date	F	VF	XF	Unc	BU
AH1407 (1987) Proof	—	Value: 100			

KM# 9b FILS **Weight:** 4.0400 g. **Composition:** 0.9170 Gold .1191 oz. AGW

Date	F	VF	XF	Unc	BU
AH1407 (1987) Proof	—	—	—	—	—

KM# 3 5 FILS **Composition:** Nickel-Brass

Date	Mintage	F	VF	XF	Unc	BU
AH1380 (1960)	2,400,000	—	0.60	1.25	2.00	—
AH1380 (1960) Proof	60	Value: 35.00				

KM# 10 5 FILS **Composition:** Nickel-Brass

Date	Mintage	F	VF	XF	Unc	BU
AH1382 (1962)	1,800,000	—	0.10	0.20	0.45	—
AH1382 (1962) Proof	60	Value: 35.00				
AH1384 (1964)	600,000	—	0.30	0.75	2.00	—
AH1386 (1966)	1,600,000	—	0.20	0.35	1.00	—
AH1388 (1968)	800,000	—	0.30	0.75	2.25	—
AH1389 (1969)	—	—	0.30	0.75	2.25	—
AH1389 (1969)	600,000	—	0.30	0.75	2.25	—
AH1390 (1970)	600,000	—	0.30	0.75	2.25	—
AH1391 (1971)	600,000	—	0.30	0.75	2.25	—
AH1392 (1972)	800,000	—	0.25	0.65	1.75	—
AH1393 (1973)	800,000	—	0.25	0.65	1.75	—
AH1394 (1974)	1,200,000	—	0.10	0.20	1.00	—
AH1395 (1975)	5,020,000	—	0.10	0.20	0.50	—
AH1396 (1976)	180,000	—	0.35	1.00	3.00	—
AH1397 (1977)	4,000,000	—	0.10	0.20	0.40	—
AH1399 (1979)	6,700,000	—	0.10	0.20	0.40	—
AH1400 (1980)	—	—	0.10	0.20	0.40	—
AH1401 (1981)	7,000,000	—	0.10	0.20	0.40	—
AH1403 (1983)	—	—	0.10	0.20	0.40	—
AH1405 (1985)	—	—	0.10	0.20	0.40	—
AH1407 (1987)	—	—	0.10	0.20	0.40	—
AH1408 (1988)	3,000,000	—	0.10	0.20	0.40	—
AH1410 (1990)	—	—	0.10	0.20	0.40	—
AH1414 (1993)	—	—	0.10	0.20	0.40	—
AH1415 (1994)	—	—	0.10	0.20	0.40	—
Note: Varieties exist						
AH1417 (1997)	—	—	0.10	0.20	0.40	—

KM# 10a 5 FILS **Weight:** 3.0100 g. **Composition:** 0.9260 Silver .0895 oz. ASW

Date	F	VF	XF	Unc	BU
AH1407 (1987) Proof	—	Value: 100			

KM# 10b 5 FILS **Weight:** 5.0500 g. **Composition:** 0.9170 Gold .1488 oz. AGW

Date	F	VF	XF	Unc	BU
AH1407 (1987) Proof	—	—	—	—	—

KM# 4 10 FILS **Composition:** Nickel-Brass

Date	Mintage	F	VF	XF	Unc	BU
AH1380 (1960)	2,600,000	—	0.65	1.25	2.00	—
AH1380 (1960) Proof	60	Value: 40.00				

KM# 11 10 FILS **Composition:** Nickel-Brass

Date	Mintage	F	VF	XF	Unc	BU
AH1382 (1962)	1,360,000	—	0.15	0.25	0.65	—
AH1382 (1962) Proof	60	Value: 40.00				
AH1384 (1964)	800,000	—	0.35	0.85	2.50	—
AH1386 (1966)	1,360,000	—	0.30	0.75	1.75	—
AH1388 (1968)	672,000	—	0.35	0.85	2.50	—

Date	Mintage	F	VF	XF	Unc	BU
AH1389 (1969)	480,000	—	0.50	1.00	2.75	—
AH1389 (1969)	640,000	—	0.35	0.85	2.50	—
AH1390 (1970)	480,000	—	0.50	1.00	2.75	—
AH1391 (1971)	800,000	—	0.35	0.85	2.50	—
AH1392 (1972)	1,120,000	—	0.15	0.40	2.00	—
AH1393 (1973)	1,440,000	—	0.15	0.40	2.00	—
AH1394 (1974)	1,280,000	—	0.15	0.40	2.00	—
AH1395 (1975)	5,280,000	—	0.15	0.25	0.75	—
AH1396 (1976)	2,400,000	—	0.15	0.25	0.75	—
AH1397 (1977)	—	—	0.15	0.25	0.75	—
AH1399 (1979)	6,160,000	—	0.15	0.25	0.75	—
AH1400 (1980)	—	—	0.15	0.25	0.75	—
AH1401 (1981)	8,320,000	—	0.15	0.25	0.75	—
AH1403 (1983)	—	—	0.15	0.25	0.75	—
AH1405 (1985)	—	—	0.15	0.25	0.75	—
AH1407 (1987)	—	—	0.15	0.25	0.75	—
AH1408 (1988)	5,000,000	—	0.15	0.25	0.75	—
AH1410 (1990)	—	—	0.15	0.25	0.75	—
Note: Varieties exist						
AH1415 (1995)	—	—	0.15	0.25	0.75	—

KM# 11a 10 FILS **Weight:** 4.3500 g. **Composition:** 0.9250 Silver .1294 oz. ASW

Date	F	VF	XF	Unc	BU
AH1407 (1987) Proof	—	Value: 110			

KM# 11b 10 FILS **Weight:** 7.6300 g. **Composition:** 0.9170 Gold .2250 oz. AGW

Date	F	VF	XF	Unc	BU
AH1407 (1987) Proof	—	—	—	—	—

KM# 5 20 FILS **Composition:** Copper-Nickel

Date	Mintage	F	VF	XF	Unc	BU
AH1380 (1960)	2,000,000	—	0.75	1.50	2.50	—
AH1380 (1960) Proof	60	Value: 45.00				

KM# 12 20 FILS **Composition:** Copper-Nickel **Note:** Varieties exist.

Date	Mintage	F	VF	XF	Unc	BU
AH1382 (1962)	1,200,000	—	0.25	0.35	0.75	—
AH1382 (1962) Proof	60	Value: 45.00				
AH1384 (1964)	480,000	—	0.50	1.00	3.00	—
AH1386 (1966)	1,280,000	—	0.35	0.85	2.00	—
AH1388 (1968)	672,000	—	0.35	0.85	2.50	—
AH1389 (1969)	800,000	—	0.35	0.85	2.50	—
AH1389 (1969)	480,000	—	0.50	1.00	3.00	—
AH1390 (1970)	480,000	—	0.50	1.00	3.00	—
AH1391 (1971)	960,000	—	0.35	0.85	2.00	—
AH1392 (1972)	1,440,000	—	0.20	0.45	2.00	—
AH1393 (1973)	1,280,000	—	0.20	0.45	2.00	—
AH1394 (1974)	1,600,000	—	0.20	0.45	1.50	—
AH1395 (1975)	2,400,000	—	0.20	0.30	1.25	—
AH1396 (1976)	3,200,000	—	0.20	0.30	1.25	—
AH1397 (1977)	3,400,000	—	0.20	0.30	1.25	—
AH1399 (1979)	5,520,000	—	0.20	0.30	1.25	—
AH1400 (1980)	—	—	0.20	0.30	1.00	—
AH1401 (1981)	8,960,000	—	0.20	0.30	1.00	—
AH1403 (1983)	—	—	0.20	0.30	1.00	—
AH1405 (1985)	—	—	0.20	0.30	1.00	—
AH1407 (1987)	—	—	0.20	0.30	1.00	—
AH1408 (1988)	5,000,000	—	0.20	0.30	1.00	—
AH1410 (1990)	—	—	0.20	0.30	1.00	—
AH1415 (1994)	—	—	0.20	0.30	1.00	—
AH1417 (1997)	—	—	0.20	0.45	2.00	—

KM# 12a 20 FILS **Weight:** 3.3700 g. **Composition:** 0.9250 Silver .1002 oz. ASW

Date	F	VF	XF	Unc	BU
AH1407 (1987) Proof	—	Value: 110			

KM# 12b 20 FILS **Weight:** 5.6700 g. **Composition:** 0.9170 Gold .1672 oz. AGW

Date	F	VF	XF	Unc	BU
AH1407 (1987) Proof	—	—	—	—	—

KM# 6 50 FILS **Composition:** Copper-Nickel

Date	Mintage	F	VF	XF	Unc	BU
AH1380 (1960)	1,720,000	—	0.85	1.75	2.75	—
AH1380 (1960) Proof	60	Value: 60.00				

KM# 13 50 FILS **Composition:** Copper-Nickel

Date	Mintage	F	VF	XF	Unc	BU
AH1382 (1962)	900,000	—	0.50	0.75	1.25	—
AH1382 (1962) Proof	60	Value: 60.00				
AH1384 (1964)	300,000	—	0.75	1.50	4.00	—
AH1386 (1966)	800,000	—	0.40	0.85	2.50	—
AH1388 (1968)	200,000	—	1.00	2.00	6.00	—
AH1389 (1969)	400,000	—	0.50	1.00	3.00	—
AH1389 (1969)	500,000	—	0.50	1.00	3.00	—
AH1390 (1970)	300,000	—	0.75	1.50	4.00	—
AH1391 (1971)	500,000	—	0.50	1.00	3.00	—
AH1392 (1972)	900,000	—	0.50	0.85	2.50	—
AH1393 (1973)	800,000	—	0.50	0.85	2.50	—
AH1394 (1974)	1,000,000	—	0.35	0.50	2.00	—
AH1395 (1975)	1,950,000	—	0.35	0.50	2.00	—
AH1396 (1976)	2,250,000	—	0.25	0.35	2.00	—
AH1397 (1977)	6,000,000	—	0.25	0.35	1.35	—
AH1399 (1979)	6,050,000	—	0.25	0.35	1.35	—
AH1400 (1980)	—	—	0.25	0.35	1.35	—
AH1401 (1981)	3,000,000	—	0.25	0.35	1.35	—
AH1403 (1983)	—	—	0.25	0.35	1.35	—
AH1405 (1985)	—	—	0.25	0.35	1.35	—
AH1407 (1987)	2,000,000	—	0.25	0.35	1.35	—
AH1408 (1988)	3,000,000	—	0.25	0.35	1.35	—
AH1410 (1990)	—	—	0.25	0.35	1.35	—
AH1413 (1992)	—	—	0.25	0.35	1.35	—
AH1414 (1993)	—	—	0.25	0.35	1.35	—
AH1415 (1994)	—	—	0.25	0.35	1.35	—
Note: Varieties exist						
AH1417 (1997)	—	—	0.25	0.35	1.35	—

KM# 13a 50 FILS **Weight:** 5.0700 g. **Composition:** 0.9250 Silver .1511 oz. ASW

Date	F	VF	XF	Unc	BU
AH1407 (1986) Proof	—	Value: 120			

KM# 13b 50 FILS **Weight:** 8.5200 g. **Composition:** 0.9170 Gold .2512 oz. AGW

Date	F	VF	XF	Unc	BU
AH1407 (1987) Proof	—	—	—	—	—

KM# 7 100 FILS **Composition:** Copper-Nickel

Date	Mintage	F	VF	XF	Unc	BU
AH1380 (1960)	1,260,000	—	1.00	2.00	3.25	—
AH1380 (1960) Proof	60	Value: 90.00				

KM# 14 100 FILS **Composition:** Copper-Nickel

Date	Mintage	F	VF	XF	Unc	BU
AH1382 (1962)	640,000	—	0.50	0.65	1.50	—
AH1382 (1962) Proof	60	Value: 90.00				
AH1384 (1964)	160,000	—	1.75	3.00	6.00	—
AH1386 (1966)	640,000	—	1.00	1.50	3.00	—
AH1388 (1968)	160,000	—	1.75	3.00	6.00	—
AH1389 (1969)	320,000	—	1.00	2.00	4.00	—
AH1391 (1971)	240,000	—	1.25	2.00	4.00	—
AH1392 (1972)	400,000	—	1.00	1.50	3.00	—
AH1393 (1973)	480,000	—	1.00	1.50	3.00	—
AH1394 (1974)	480,000	—	1.00	1.50	3.00	—
AH1395 (1975)	3,040,000	—	0.50	0.75	1.75	—
AH1396 (1976)	—	—	0.50	0.75	1.75	—
AH1397 (1977)	1,600,000	—	0.50	0.75	1.75	—
AH1399 (1979)	3,040,000	—	0.50	0.75	1.75	—
AH1400 (1980)	—	—	0.50	0.75	1.75	—
AH1401 (1981)	2,960,000	—	0.50	0.75	1.75	—
AH1403 (1983)	—	—	0.50	0.75	1.75	—
AH1405 (1985)	—	—	0.50	0.75	1.75	—
AH1407 (1987)	2,000,000	—	0.50	0.75	1.75	—
AH1408 (1988)	2,000,000	—	0.50	0.75	1.75	—
AH1410 (1990)	—	—	0.50	0.75	1.75	—
AH1415 (1994)	—	—	0.50	0.75	1.75	—
Note: Varieties exist						

KM# 14a 100 FILS Weight: 7.3400 g. **Composition:** 0.9250 Silver .2183 oz. ASW

Date	F	VF	XF	Unc	BU
AH1407 (1986) Proof	—	Value: 130			
AH1407 (1987) Proof	—	Value: 130			

KM# 14b 100 FILS Weight: 12.3300 g. **Composition:** 0.9170 Gold .3635 oz. AGW

Date	F	VF	XF	Unc	BU
AH1407 (1987) Proof	—	—	—	—	—

KM# 15 2 DINARS Weight: 28.2800 g. **Composition:** 0.5000 Silver .4546 oz. ASW **Subject:** 15th Anniversary of Independence

Date	Mintage	F	VF	XF	Unc	BU
ND (1975)	70,000	—	—	—	42.50	50.00

KM# 15a 2 DINARS Weight: 28.2800 g. **Composition:** 0.9250 Silver .8411 oz. ASW **Subject:** 15th Anniversary of Independence

Date	Mintage	F	VF	XF	Unc	BU
ND (1976) Proof	53,000	Value: 65.00				

KM# 24 2 DINARS Weight: 28.2800 g. **Composition:** 0.9250 Silver .8411 oz. ASW **Subject:** 50th Anniversary - United Nations

Date	Mintage	F	VF	XF	Unc	BU
ND (1996) Proof	Est. 110,000	Value: 37.50				

KM# 8 5 DINARS Weight: 13.5720 g. **Composition:** 0.9170 Gold .4001 oz. AGW

Date	F	VF	XF	Unc	BU
AH1380 (1960)	—	—	—	—	—

KM# 18 5 DINARS Weight: 28.2800 g. **Composition:** 0.9250 Silver .8411 oz. ASW **Subject:** 20th Anniversary of Independence **Reverse:** Similar to 100 Dinars, KM#19

Date	Mintage	F	VF	XF	Unc	BU
ND (1980) Proof	10,000	Value: 65.00				

KM# 16 5 DINARS Weight: 28.2800 g. **Composition:** 0.9250 Silver .8411 oz. ASW **Subject:** 15th Century of the Hijira

Date	Mintage	F	VF	XF	Unc	BU
AH1401 (1981) Proof	10,000	Value: 65.00				

KM# 20 5 DINARS Weight: 33.6250 g. **Composition:** 0.9250 Silver 1.0000 oz. ASW **Subject:** 25th Anniversary of Kuwait Currency **Obverse:** Arabic denomination, buildings, port scene and refinery **Reverse:** English legend, falcon, dhow, building and map on globe

Date	F	VF	XF	Unc	BU
ND (1985) Proof	—	Value: 85.00			

KM# 21 50 DINARS Weight: 16.9660 g. **Composition:** 0.9170 Gold .5000 oz. AGW **Subject:** 25th Anniversary of Kuwait Independence **Obverse:** Arabic legend, arched design, falcon, tent, dhow and pearl in a shell **Reverse:** Radiant sun, mosque and assembly building, English and Arabic legend

Date	F	VF	XF	Unc	BU
AH1406 (1986) Proof	—	Value: 275			

KM# 19 100 DINARS Weight: 15.9800 g. **Composition:** 0.9170 Gold .4711 oz. AGW **Subject:** 20th Anniversary of Independence

Date	Mintage	F	VF	XF	Unc	BU
ND(AH1401) (1980) Proof	10,000	Value: 400				

KM# 17 100 DINARS Weight: 15.9800 g. **Composition:** 0.9170 Gold .4711 oz. AGW **Subject:** 15th Century of the Hijira

Date	Mintage	F	VF	XF	Unc	BU
AH1401 (1981) Proof	10,000	Value: 375				

Date	F	VF	XF	Unc	BU
ND (1991)	—	Value: 65.00			

PROOF SETS

KM#	Date	Mintage	Identification	Issue Price	Mkt Val
PS1	1961 (6)	60	KM2-7	—	300
PS2	1962 (6)	60	KM9-14	—	300
PS3	1987 (6)	—	KM9a-14a	—	675
PS4	1987 (6)	—	KM9b-14b	—	—

KYRGYZSTAN

The Republic of Kyrgyzstan, (formerly Kirghiz S.S.R., a Union Republic of the U.S.S.R.), independent state since Aug. 31, 1991, is a member of the United Nations and of the C.I.S. It was the last state of the Union Republics to declare its sovereignty. Capital: Bishkek (formerly Frunze).

Originally part of the Autonomous Turkestan S.S.R. founded on May 1, 1918, the Kyrgyz ethnic area was established on October 14, 1924 as the Kara-Kirghiz Autonomous Region within the R.S.F.S.R. Then on May 25, 1925 the name Kara (black) was dropped. It became an A.S.S.R. on Feb. 1, 1926 and a Union Republic of the U.S.S.R. in 1936. On Dec. 12, 1990, the name was then changed to the Republic of Kyrgyzstan.

REPUBLIC

STANDARD COINAGE

KM# 1 10 SOM Weight: 28.2800 g. **Composition:** 0.9250 Silver .8411 oz. ASW **Subject:** Millennium of Manas

Date	Mintage	F	VF	XF	Unc	BU
1995 Proof	Est. 20,000	Value: 55.00				

KM# 3 10 SOM Weight: 28.2800 g. **Composition:** 0.9250 Silver 0.841 oz. ASW **Subject:** Tenth Anniversary of Republic **Obverse:** National arms **Reverse:** Denomination and mountain **Edge:** Reeded **Size:** 38.6 mm.

Date	Mintage	F	VF	XF	Unc	BU
2001 Proof	1,000	Value: 60.00				

KM# 4 10 SOM Weight: 28.2800 g. **Composition:** 0.9250 Silver 0.841 oz. ASW **Subject:** Flora and Fauna **Obverse:** National arms **Reverse:** Edelweiss flower and mountain **Edge:** Reeded **Size:** 38.6 mm.

Date	Mintage	F	VF	XF	Unc	BU
2002	1,000	Value: 60.00				

Note: Proof

KM# 5 10 SOM Weight: 28.2800 g. **Composition:** 0.9250 Silver 0.841 oz. ASW **Subject:** Flora and Fauna **Obverse:** National arms **Reverse:** Bighom sheep and mountain **Edge:** Reeded **Size:** 38.6 mm.

Date	Mintage	F	VF	XF	Unc	BU
2002	1,000	Value: 60.00				

Note: Proof

KM# 2 100 SOM Weight: 6.2200 g. **Composition:** 0.9990 Gold .2000 oz. AGW **Subject:** Millennium of Manas

Date		F	VF	XF	Unc	BU
1995 Proof	Est. 5,000	Value: 185				

LAOS

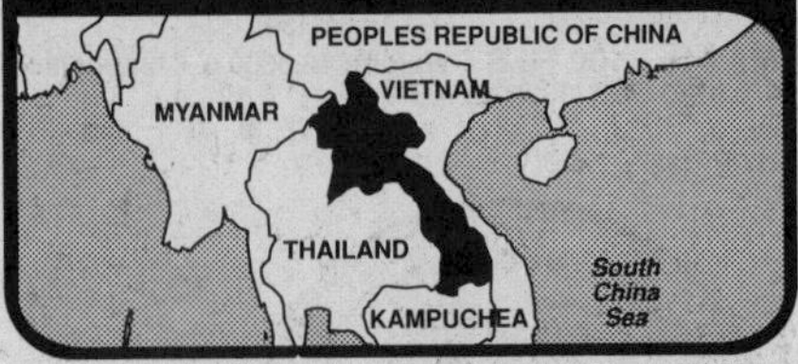

The Lao Peoples Democratic Republic, located on the Indo-Chinese Peninsula between the Socialist Republic of Vietnam and the Kingdom of Thailand, has an area of 91,428 sq. mi. (236,800 km.) and a population of 3.6 million. Capital Vientiane. Agriculture employs 95 per cent of the people. Tin, lumber and coffee are exported.

The first United Kingdom of Lan Xang (Million Elephants) was established in the mid-14th century by King Fa Ngum who ruled an area including present Laos, northeastern Thailand, and the southern part of China's Yunnan province from his capital at Luang Prabang. Thailand and Vietnam obtained control over much of the present Lao territory in the 18th century and remained dominant until France established a protectorate over the area in 1893 and incorporated it into the Union of Indo-China. The Independence of Laos was proclaimed in March of 1945, during the last days of the Japanese occupation of World War II. France reoccupied Laos in 1946, and established it as a constitutional monarchy within the French Union in 1949. In 1953 war erupted between the government and the Pathet Lao, a Communist movement supported by the Vietnamese Communist forces. Peace was declared in 1954 with Laos becoming fully independent in 1955 and the Pathet Lao being permitted to occupy two northern provinces. Civil war broke out again in 1960 with the United States supporting the government of the Kingdom of Laos and the North Vietnamese helping the Communist Pathet Lao, and continued, with intervals of truce and political compromise, until the formation of the Lao Peoples Democratic Republic on Dec. 2, 1975.

NOTE: For earlier coinage see French Indo-China.

RULERS

Sisavang Vong, 1904-1959
Savang Vatthana, 1959-1975

MONETARY SYSTEM

100 Cents = 1 Piastre
Commencing 1955
100 Att = 1 Kip

MINT MARKS

(a) - Paris, privy marks only
Key - Havana
None - Berlin

NOTE: Private bullion issues previously listed here are now listed in *Unusual World Coins,* 3rd Edition, Krause Publications, Inc., 1992.

KINGDOM

STANDARD COINAGE

KM# 4 10 CENTS Composition: Aluminum **Ruler:** Sisavang Vong

Date	Mintage	F	VF	XF	Unc	BU
1952(a)	2,000,000	—	0.25	0.60	1.25	—

KM# 5 20 CENTS Composition: Aluminum **Ruler:** Sisavang Vong

Date	Mintage	F	VF	XF	Unc	BU
1952(a)	3,000,000	—	0.35	0.75	2.00	—

KM# 6 50 CENTS **Composition:** Aluminum **Ruler:** Sisavang Vong

Date	Mintage	F	VF	XF	Unc	BU
1952(a)	1,400,000	—	0.75	1.25	2.50	—

KM# 7 1000 KIP **Weight:** 10.0000 g. **Composition:** 0.9250 Silver .2973 oz. ASW **Ruler:** Savang Vatthana **Subject:** King Savang Vatthana Coronation

Date	Mintage	F	VF	XF	Unc	BU
1971	—	—	—	—	25.00	—
1971 Proof	20,000	Value: 35.00				

KM# 8 2500 KIP **Weight:** 20.0000 g. **Composition:** 0.9250 Silver .5947 oz. ASW **Ruler:** Savang Vatthana **Subject:** King Savang Vatthana Coronation

Date	Mintage	F	VF	XF	Unc	BU
1971	—	—	—	—	35.00	—
1971 Proof	20,000	Value: 45.00				

KM# 9 4000 KIP **Weight:** 4.0000 g. **Composition:** 0.9000 Gold .1157 oz. AGW **Ruler:** Savang Vatthana **Subject:** King Savang Vatthana Coronation

Date	Mintage	F	VF	XF	Unc	BU
1971 Proof	10,000	Value: 120				

KM# 10 5000 KIP **Weight:** 40.0000 g. **Composition:** 0.9250 Silver 1.1895 oz. ASW **Ruler:** Savang Vatthana **Subject:** King Savang Vatthana Coronation **Obverse:** Similar to 2500 Kip, KM#8

Date	Mintage	F	VF	XF	Unc	BU
1971	—	—	—	—	100	—
1971 Proof	20,000	Value: 125				

KM# 16.1 5000 KIP **Weight:** 11.7000 g. **Composition:** 0.9250 Silver .3479 oz. ASW **Ruler:** Savang Vatthana **Subject:** Laotian maiden

Date	Mintage	F	VF	XF	Unc	BU
1975	400	—	—	—	120	—
1975 Proof	775	Value: 125				

KM# 16.2 5000 KIP **Weight:** 11.7000 g. **Composition:** 0.9250 Silver .3479 oz. ASW **Ruler:** Savang Vatthana **Subject:** Laotian maiden

Date	F	VF	XF	Unc	BU
ND(1975)	—	—	—	100	—

KM# 17 5000 KIP **Weight:** 11.7000 g. **Composition:** 0.9250 Silver .3479 oz. ASW **Ruler:** Savang Vatthana **Subject:** Wat Phra Kio Museum, Vientiane

Date	Mintage	F	VF	XF	Unc	BU
1975	400	—	—	—	120	—
1975 Proof	775	Value: 125				

KM# 11 8000 KIP **Weight:** 8.0000 g. **Composition:** 0.9000 Gold .2315 oz. AGW **Ruler:** Savang Vatthana **Subject:** King Savang Vatthana Coronation

Date	Mintage	F	VF	XF	Unc	BU
1971 Proof	10,000	Value: 200				

KM# 12 10000 KIP **Weight:** 80.0000 g. **Composition:** 0.9250 Silver 2.3791 oz. ASW **Ruler:** Savang Vatthana **Subject:** King Savang Vatthana Coronation **Obverse:** Similar to 2500 Kip, KM#8

Date	Mintage	F	VF	XF	Unc	BU
1971	—	—	—	—	150	—
1971 Proof	Est. 20,000	Value: 250				

KM# 18 10000 KIP **Weight:** 23.5000 g. **Composition:** 0.9250 Silver .6988 oz. ASW **Ruler:** Savang Vatthana **Subject:** Wat Xieng - Thong Temple

Date	Mintage	F	VF	XF	Unc	BU
1975	300	—	—	—	170	—
1975 Proof	650	Value: 190				

KM# 13 20000 KIP **Weight:** 20.0000 g. **Composition:** 0.9000 Gold .5787 oz. AGW **Ruler:** Savang Vatthana **Subject:** King Savang Vatthana Coronation

Date	Mintage	F	VF	XF	Unc	BU
1971 Proof	Est. 10,000	Value: 400				

KM# 14 40000 KIP **Weight:** 40.0000 g. **Composition:** 0.9000 Gold 1.1575 oz. AGW **Ruler:** Savang Vatthana **Subject:** King Savang Vatthana Coronation

Date	Mintage	F	VF	XF	Unc	BU
1971 Proof	Est. 10,000	Value: 700				

KM# 19 50000 KIP **Weight:** 3.6000 g. **Composition:** 0.9000 Gold .1041 oz. AGW **Ruler:** Savang Vatthana **Obverse:** Bust of King Savang Vatthana **Reverse:** That Luang Temple

Date	Mintage	F	VF	XF	Unc	BU
1975	100	—	—	—	200	—
1975 Proof	175	Value: 260				

KM# 20 50000 KIP **Weight:** 3.6000 g. **Composition:** 0.9000 Gold .1041 oz. AGW **Ruler:** Savang Vatthana **Obverse:** Similar to 5000 Kip, KM#17 **Reverse:** Bust of King Savang Vatthana

Date	Mintage	F	VF	XF	Unc	BU
1975	100	—	—	—	200	—
1975 Proof	175	Value: 260				

KM# 15 80000 KIP **Weight:** 80.0000 g. **Composition:** 0.9000 Gold 2.3151 oz. AGW **Ruler:** Savang Vatthana **Subject:** King Savang Vatthana Coronation **Obverse:** Similar to 20000 Kip, KM#13

Date	F	VF	XF	Unc	BU
1971 Proof	—	Value: 1,450			

KM# 21 100000 KIP **Weight:** 7.3200 g. **Composition:** 0.9000 Gold .2118 oz. AGW **Ruler:** Savang Vatthana **Obverse:** Bust of King Savang Vatthana **Reverse:** Statue of Buddha

Date	Mintage	F	VF	XF	Unc	BU
1975	100	—	—	—	375	—
1975 Proof	100	Value: 450				

PEOPLES DEMOCRATIC REPUBLIC

STANDARD COINAGE

100 Att = 1 Kip

KM# 22 10 ATT **Composition:** Aluminum

Date	F	VF	XF	Unc	BU
1980	—	0.20	0.40	0.85	—

KM# 23 20 ATT **Composition:** Aluminum

Date	F	VF	XF	Unc	BU
1980	—	0.20	0.40	0.85	—

KM# 24 50 ATT **Composition:** Aluminum

Date	F	VF	XF	Unc	BU
1980	—	0.45	0.90	1.50	—

KM# 37 KIP **Composition:** Copper-Nickel **Subject:** 10th Anniversary of People's Democratic Republic

Date	F	VF	XF	Unc	BU
1985	—	0.50	1.00	2.50	—

KM# 38 5 KIP **Composition:** Copper-Nickel **Subject:** 10th Anniversary of People's Democratic Republic

Date	F	VF	XF	Unc	BU
1985	—	0.75	1.50	4.00	—

KM# 39 10 KIP **Composition:** Copper-Nickel **Subject:** 10th Anniversary of People's Democratic Republic

Date	F	VF	XF	Unc	BU
1985	—	1.25	2.50	6.50	—

KM# 31 10 KIP **Composition:** Copper-Nickel **Reverse:** 5-masted clipper **Size:** 32.5 mm.

Date	Mintage	F	VF	XF	Unc	BU
1988	30,000	—	—	—	9.00	—

KM# 31a 10 KIP **Composition:** Nickel Bonded Steel **Reverse:** 5-masted clipper **Size:** 32.5 mm.

Date	F	VF	XF	Unc	BU
1988	—	—	—	8.50	—

KM#66 10 KIP **Composition:** Copper **Obverse:** National arms **Reverse:** 5-masted clipper

Date	Mintage	F	VF	XF	Unc	BU
1988	—	—	—	—	8.50	—
1988 Proof	100	Value: 75.00				

KM# 30 10 KIP **Composition:** Copper-Nickel **Subject:** World Soccer Championships - Italy 1990

Date	Mintage	F	VF	XF	Unc	BU
1989	2,000	—	—	—	10.00	—

KM#46 10 KIP **Composition:** Nickel Plated Steel **Series:** Olympics **Reverse:** Bicyclists

Date	Mintage	F	VF	XF	Unc	BU
1991	5,000	—	—	—	13.50	—

KM# 51 10 KIP **Composition:** Copper-Nickel **Series:** Endangered Wildife **Reverse:** Tigers

Date	F	VF	XF	Unc	BU
1991	—	—	—	9.00	—

KM# 54 10 KIP **Composition:** Copper **Series:** Endangered Wildife **Reverse:** Tigers

Date	F	VF	XF	Unc	BU
1991	—	—	—	10.00	—

KM# 50 10 KIP **Composition:** Copper-Nickel **Series:** Prehistoric Animals **Reverse:** Tyranosaurus Rex

Date	F	VF	XF	Unc	BU
1993	—	—	—	24.00	—

KM# 52 10 KIP **Composition:** Copper-Nickel **Series:** Prehistoric Animals **Reverse:** Lufengosaurus

Date	F	VF	XF	Unc	BU
1994	—	—	—	24.00	—

KM# 61 10 KIP **Composition:** Copper-Nickel **Subject:** 1996 World Food Summit **Obverse:** National emblem **Reverse:** Farmer plowing with ox

Date	F	VF	XF	Unc	BU
1996	—	—	—	10.00	—

KM# 70 10 KIP **Composition:** Copper Nickel **Series:** XXVII Olympiad **Subject:** Sydney 2000 **Obverse:** National arms **Reverse:** Sailboats, Neptune

Date	Mintage	F	VF	XF	Unc	BU
1999	10,000	—	—	—	7.00	—

KM# 40 20 KIP **Composition:** Copper-Nickel **Subject:** 10th Anniversary of People's Democratic Republic

Date	F	VF	XF	Unc	BU
1985	—	1.50	2.50	7.00	—

KM# 25 50 KIP **Weight:** 38.2000 g. **Composition:** 0.9000 Silver 1.1054 oz. ASW **Subject:** 10th Anniversary of People's Democratic Republic **Reverse:** That Ing Hang

Date	Mintage	F	VF	XF	Unc	BU
1985 Proof	2,000	Value: 42.50				

KM# 26 50 KIP **Weight:** 38.2000 g. **Composition:** 0.9000 Silver 1.1054 oz. ASW **Subject:** 10th Anniversary of People's Democratic Republic **Reverse:** That Luang

Date	Mintage	F	VF	XF	Unc	BU
1985 Proof	2,000	Value: 42.50				

KM# 27 50 KIP **Weight:** 38.2000 g. **Composition:** 0.9000 Silver 1.1054 oz. ASW **Subject:** 10th Anniversary of People's Democratic Republic **Reverse:** Vat Phu

Date	Mintage	F	VF	XF	Unc	BU
1985 Proof	2,000	Value: 42.50				

KM# 28 50 KIP **Weight:** 38.2000 g. **Composition:** 0.9000 Silver 1.1054 oz. ASW **Subject:** 10th Anniversary of People's Democratic Republic **Reverse:** Valley of Jars

Date	Mintage	F	VF	XF	Unc	BU
1985 Proof	2,000	Value: 42.50				

KM# 41 50 KIP **Composition:** Copper-Nickel **Subject:** 10th Anniversary of People's Democratic Republic

Date	F	VF	XF	Unc	BU
1985	—	2.00	3.50	8.50	—

KM# 29 50 KIP **Weight:** 16.0000 g. **Composition:** 0.9990 Silver .5145 oz. ASW **Obverse:** National arms **Reverse:** 5-masted sail ship "Prussia"

Date	Mintage	F	VF	XF	Unc	BU
1988 Proof	2,000	Value: 30.00				

KM# 32 50 KIP **Weight:** 12.0000 g. **Composition:** 0.9990 Silver .3855 oz. ASW **Subject:** European Soccer Championship - Germany

Date	Mintage	F	VF	XF	Unc	BU
1988	5,000	—	—	—	32.50	—

KM# 33 50 KIP **Weight:** 16.0000 g. **Composition:** 0.9990 Silver .5145 oz. ASW **Subject:** World Soccer Championship - Mexico 86

Date	Mintage	F	VF	XF	Unc	BU
ND(1988) Proof	5,000	Value: 26.50				

KM# 34 50 KIP **Weight:** 16.0000 g. **Composition:** 0.9990 Silver .5145 oz. ASW **Subject:** World Soccer Championship - Italy 1990

Date	Mintage	F	VF	XF	Unc	BU
1989 Proof	5,000	Value: 26.50				

KM# 35.1 50 KIP **Weight:** 16.0000 g. **Composition:** 0.9990 Silver .5145 oz. ASW **Series:** Winter Olympics **Subject:** Ice dancing **Note:** Lightly frosted.

Date	F	VF	XF	Unc	BU
1989 Proof	—	Value: 27.50			

KM# 35.2 50 KIP **Weight:** 16.0000 g. **Composition:** 0.9990 Silver .5145 oz. ASW **Series:** Winter Olympics **Subject:** Ice dancing **Note:** Extensive frosting.

Date	F	VF	XF	Unc	BU
1989 Proof	—	Value: 80.00			

KM# 36.1 50 KIP **Weight:** 16.0000 g. **Composition:** 0.9990 Silver .5145 oz. ASW **Series:** Summer Olympics **Subject:** Water polo **Reverse:** Frosted water

Date	Mintage	F	VF	XF	Unc	BU
1989 Proof	5,000	Value: 50.00				

KM# 36.2 50 KIP **Weight:** 16.0000 g. **Composition:** 0.9990 Silver .5145 oz. ASW **Series:** Summer Olympics **Subject:** Water polo **Reverse:** Unfrosted water

Date	F	VF	XF	Unc	BU
1989 Proof	—	Value: 27.50			

KM# 44 50 KIP **Weight:** 12.0000 g. **Composition:** 0.9990 Silver .3858 oz. ASW **Subject:** World Cup Soccer

Date	F	VF	XF	Unc	BU
1991	—	—	—	27.50	—

KM# 45 50 KIP **Weight:** 20.0000 g. **Composition:** 0.9990 Silver .644 oz. ASW **Subject:** Wildlife **Reverse:** Tigers

Date	Mintage	F	VF	XF	Unc	BU
1991	100	—	—	—	175	—
1991 Proof	—	Value: 35.00				

KM# 47 50 KIP **Weight:** 20.0000 g. **Composition:** 0.9990 Silver .643 oz. ASW **Subject:** Soccer **Reverse:** Goalie

Date	F	VF	XF	Unc	BU
1991 Proof	—	Value: 37.50			

KM# 48 50 KIP **Weight:** 20.0000 g. **Composition:** 0.9990 Silver .643 oz. ASW **Subject:** Protection of Nature **Reverse:** Elephant

Date	F	VF	XF	Unc	BU
1993 Proof	—	Value: 40.00			

KM# 49 50 KIP **Weight:** 15.9400 g. **Composition:** 0.9990 Silver .5120 oz. ASW **Series:** Prehistoric Animals **Reverse:** Sauroctonus

Date	F	VF	XF	Unc	BU
1993 Proof	—	Value: 35.00			

KM# 53 50 KIP **Weight:** 16.0000 g. **Composition:** 0.9990 Silver .5145 oz. ASW **Series:** Prehistoric Animals **Reverse:** Elasmosaurus and tylosaurus in combat

Date	F	VF	XF	Unc	BU
1994 Proof	—	Value: 40.00			

KM# 82 50 KIP **Weight:** 16.0000 g. **Composition:** 0.9990 Silver .5145 oz. ASW **Subject:** Prehistoric Animals **Obverse:** State arms **Reverse:** Elmasosaurus fighting a Tylosaurus, type II: similar to KM#53 **Edge:** Plain **Size:** 37.9 mm.

Date	F	VF	XF	Unc	BU
1994 Proof	—	Value: 50.00			

KM# 84 50 KIP **Weight:** 15.9400 g. **Composition:** 0.9990 Silver 0.512 oz. ASW **Obverse:** Megalosaurus

Date	F	VF	XF	Unc	BU
1994 Proof	—	Value: 27.50			

KM# 56 50 KIP **Weight:** 20.0000 g. **Composition:** 0.9990 Silver .6424 oz. ASW **Series:** Olympics **Reverse:** Javelin throwers

Date	Mintage	F	VF	XF	Unc	BU
1995 Proof	Est. 15,000	Value: 25.00				

KM# 57 50 KIP **Weight:** 20.0000 g. **Composition:** 0.9990 Silver .6424 oz. ASW **Subject:** World Cup Soccer **Reverse:** Player and cathedral

Date	Mintage	F	VF	XF	Unc	BU
1996	100	—	—	—	90.00	—
1996 Proof	10,000	Value: 40.00				

KM# 79 50 KIP **Weight:** 15.0000 g. **Composition:** 0.9990 Silver .4818 oz. ASW **Series:** World Cup Soccer **Obverse:** National arms **Reverse:** Soccer player with ball and map background **Edge:** Plain **Size:** 35 mm.

Date	F	VF	XF	Unc	BU
1996 Proof	—	Value: 30.00			

KM# 63 50 KIP **Weight:** 20.0000 g. **Composition:** 0.9990 Silver .6424 oz. ASW **Series:** XXVII Olympiad **Obverse:** State emblem **Reverse:** Gymnastics

Date	F	VF	XF	Unc	BU
1996 Proof	—	Value: 45.00			

KM# 58 50 KIP **Weight:** 20.0000 g. **Composition:** 0.9990 Silver .6424 oz. ASW **Subject:** World Cup Soccer **Reverse:** Stadium, map of France

Date	Mintage	F	VF	XF	Unc	BU
1996 Proof	10,000	Value: 45.00				

KM# 62 50 KIP **Weight:** 20.0000 g. **Composition:** 0.9990 Silver .6424 oz. ASW **Series:** XXVII Olympiad **Obverse:** State emblem **Reverse:** Archer - Diana, goddess of the hunt

Date	F	VF	XF	Unc	BU
1996 Proof	—	Value: 40.00			

KM# 64 50 KIP **Weight:** 15.0000 g. **Composition:** 0.9990 Silver .6423 oz. ASW **Subject:** World of Adventure - Leif Ericson **Obverse:** State emblem **Reverse:** Viking longship

Date	F	VF	XF	Unc	BU
1996 Proof	—	Value: 45.00			

KM# 42 100 KIP **Weight:** 3.1500 g. **Composition:** 0.9990 Gold .1012 oz. AGW **Obverse:** Emblem and legend above denomination **Reverse:** 5-masted sail ship "Prussia"

Date	Mintage	F	VF	XF	Unc	BU
1988	500	—	—	—	125	—

KM# 43 100 KIP **Weight:** 3.1500 g. **Composition:** 0.9990 Gold .1012 oz. AGW **Subject:** 10th Anniversary of People's Democratic Republic **Reverse:** That Louang Temple

Date	F	VF	XF	Unc	BU
1990	—	—	—	145	—

KM# 69 500 KIP **Weight:** 20.0000 g. **Composition:** 0.9250 Silver .5948 oz. ASW **Subject:** Kouprey **Obverse:** State emblem **Reverse:** Wild bull

Date	Mintage	F	VF	XF	Unc	BU
1998 Proof	10,000	Value: 50.00				

KM# 165 1000 KIP **Weight:** 31.6700 g. **Composition:** 0.9990 Silver 1.0172 oz. ASW **Series:** Endangered Wildlife **Obverse:** State emblem **Reverse:** Gibbon

Date	F	VF	XF	Unc	BU
1996 Proof	—	Value: 60.00			

KM# 67 1000 KIP **Weight:** 31.4700 g. **Composition:** 0.9250 Silver .9359 oz. ASW **Series:** Endangered Wildlife **Obverse:** State emblem **Reverse:** 2 long-horned saola

Date	Mintage	F	VF	XF	Unc	BU
1997 Proof	15,000	Value: 40.00				

KM# 59 1200 KIP **Composition:** Nickel Bonded Steel **Subject:** Food for All **Reverse:** Three people harvesting rice

Date	F	VF	XF	Unc	BU
ND(1995)	—	—	—	8.00	—

KM# 68 2000 KIP **Weight:** 1.2441 g. **Composition:** 0.9990 Gold .04 oz. AGW **Subject:** That Luang **Obverse:** State emblem **Reverse:** Temple

Date	F	VF	XF	Unc	BU
1998 Proof	—	Value: 55.00			

KM# 72 3000 KIP **Weight:** 20.0000 g. **Composition:** 0.9250 Silver .5948 oz. ASW **Subject:** Retrospection Rabbit **Obverse:** State arms **Reverse:** Multicolor rabbit looking back **Edge:** Reeded **Size:** 38.6 mm.

Date	F	VF	XF	Unc	BU
1999 Proof	—	Value: 50.00			

KM# 73 3000 KIP **Weight:** 20.0000 g. **Composition:** 0.9250 Silver .5948 oz. ASW **Subject:** Anticipation Rabbit **Obverse:** State arms **Reverse:** Partially gold-plated rabbit

Date	F	VF	XF	Unc	BU
1999 Proof	—	Value: 50.00			

KM# 60 5000 KIP **Weight:** 7.7600 g. **Composition:** 0.5833 Gold .1458 oz. AGW **Series:** Olympics **Reverse:** Two boxers

Date	F	VF	XF	Unc	BU
1996	—	—	—	90.00	—

KM# 80 5000 KIP **Weight:** 15.0000 g. **Composition:** 0.9990 Silver .4818 oz. ASW **Series:** Olympics **Obverse:** National arms **Reverse:** Archer with statue in background - same as 50 Kip KM#62 **Edge:** Plain **Size:** 35 mm.

Date	F	VF	XF	Unc	BU
1998 Proof	—	Value: 30.00			

KM# 81 5000 KIP **Weight:** 15.0000 g. **Composition:** 0.9990 Silver .4818 oz. ASW **Obverse:** National arms **Reverse:** Multicolor torch and athletes - same as 50 Kip KM#63 **Edge:** Plain **Size:** 35 mm.

Date	F	VF	XF	Unc	BU
1998 Proof	—	Value: 50.00			

KM# 71 5000 KIP **Weight:** 20.0500 g. **Composition:** 0.9990 Silver .6584 oz. ASW **Series:** XXVII Olympiad **Subject:** Sydney 2000 **Obverse:** State emblem **Reverse:** Sailboats, Neptune

Date	Mintage	
1999 Proof	5,000	Value: 35.00

KM# 74 5000 KIP **Weight:** 20.0000 g. **Composition:** 0.9250 Silver .5948 oz. ASW **Subject:** Silver Dragon Fish **Obverse:** State emblem **Reverse:** Fish turning to right **Edge:** Reeded **Size:** 39 mm.

Date	Mintage	F	VF	XF	Unc	BU
2000-2001 Proof	10,000	—	—	—	40.00	—

Note: Latent image date

KM# 75 5000 KIP **Weight:** 20.0000 g. **Composition:** 0.9250 Silver .5948 oz. ASW **Subject:** Red Dragon Fish **Obverse:** State emblem **Reverse:** Red colored fish **Edge:** Reeded **Size:** 39 mm.

Date	Mintage	F	VF	XF	Unc	BU
2000-2001 Proof	10,000	—	—	—	40.00	—

Note: Latent image date

KM# 76 5000 KIP **Weight:** 20.0000 g. **Composition:** 0.9250 Silver .5948 oz. ASW **Subject:** Golden Dragon Fish **Obverse:** State emblem **Reverse:** Jumping fish below gold cameo **Edge:** Reeded **Size:** 39 mm.

Date	F	VF	XF	Unc	BU
2000-2001 Proof	—	—	—	50.00	—

Note: Latent image date

KM# 77 10000 KIP **Weight:** 1.2441 g. **Composition:** 0.9999 Gold .0400 oz. AGW **Subject:** Golden Dragon Fish **Obverse:** State emblem **Reverse:** Jumping fish **Edge:** Reeded **Size:** 14 mm.

Date	F	VF	XF	Unc	BU
2000-2001	—	—	—	40.00	—

Note: Latent image date

KM# 83 50000 KIP **Weight:** 7.7750 g. **Composition:** 0.9990 Gold 0.2497 oz. AGW **Obverse:** National arms **Reverse:** Red Dragon Fish **Edge:** Reeded **Size:** 32.2 mm.

Date	Mintage	F	VF	XF	Unc	BU
2000-2001 Proof	3,000	Value: 175				

KM# 78 100000 KIP **Weight:** 15.5518 g. **Composition:** 0.9999 Gold .4999 oz. AGW **Subject:** Golden Dragon Fish **Obverse:** State emblem **Reverse:** Multicolored holographic jumping fish **Edge:** Reeded **Size:** 27 mm.

Date	Mintage	F	VF	XF	Unc	BU
2000-2001 Proof	3,000	—	—	—	400	—

Note: Latent image date

PIEFORTS WITH ESSAI

Standard metals unless otherwise noted

Double Thickness

KM#	Date	Mintage	Identification	Issue Price	Mkt Val
PE1	1952(a)	104	10 Cents.	—	50.00
PE2	1952(a)	104	20 Cents.	—	60.00
PE3	1952(a)	104	50 Cents.	—	75.00

ESSAIS

Standard metals unless otherwise noted

KM#	Date	Mintage	Identification	Issue Price	Mkt Val
e3	1952(a)	1,200	50 Cents.	—	22.50
E1	1952(a)	1,200	10 Cents.	—	20.00
E2	1952(a)	1,200	20 Cents.	—	22.50

PIEFORTS

KM#	Date	Mintage	Identification	Issue Price	Mkt Val
P1	1988	—	50 Kip. Silver.	—	—

MINT SETS

KM#	Date	Mintage	Identification	Issue Price	Mkt Val
MS1	1971 (4)	—	KM7, 8, 10, 12	—	300
MS2	1975 (6)	100	KM16-21	—	1,300
MS3	1975 (3)	300	KM16-18	—	420

PROOF SETS

KM#	Date	Mintage	Identification	Issue Price	Mkt Val
PS1	1971 (5)	10,000	KM9, 11, 13-15	467	2,870
PS2	1971 (4)	20,000	KM7, 8, 10, 12	163	450
PS3	1975 (6)	—	KM16-21	—	1,450
PS4	1975 (3)	650	KM16-18	—	450
PS5	1975 (3)	—	KM19-21	349	960
PS6	1985 (4)	2,000	KM25-28	—	180
PS7	2000-2001 (3)	3,500	KM#74-76	138	200
PS8	2000-2001 (3)	500	KM#74-76	214	300
PS9	2000-2001 (2)	800	KM#78, 83	—	575

LATVIA

The Republic of Latvia, the central Baltic state in east Europe, has an area of 24,749 sq. mi. (43,601 sq. km.) and a population of *2.6 million. Capital: Riga. Livestock raising and manufacturing are the chief industries. Butter, bacon, fertilizers and telephone equipment are exported.

The Latvians, of Aryan descent primarily from the German Order of Livonian Knights, were nomadic tribes-men who settled along the Baltic prior to the 13th century. Ideally situated as a trade route and lacking a central government, conquered in 1561 by Poland and Sweden. Following the third partition of Poland by Austria, Prussia and Russia in 1795, Latvia came under Russian domination and did not experience autonomy until the Russian Revolution of 1917 provided an opportunity for freedom. The Latvian Republic was established on Nov. 18, 1918. The republic was occupied by Soviet troops and annexed to the Soviet Union in 1940. Following the German occupation of 1941-44, it was retaken by Russia and reestablished as a member republic of the Soviet Union. Western countries, including the United States, did not recognize Latvia's incorporation into the Soviet Union.

The coinage issued during the early 20th Century Republic is now obsolete.

Latvia declared their independence from the U.S.S.R. on August 22, 1991.

MONETARY SYSTEM

100 Santimu = 1 Lats

FIRST REPUBLIC
1918-1939

STANDARD COINAGE

100 Santimu = 1 Lats

KM# 1 SANTIMS Weight: 1.6500 g. **Composition:** Bronze **Edge:** Plain **Size:** 17 mm. **Note:** Struck at Huguenin Freres, Le Locle, Switzerland.

Date	Mintage	F	VF	XF	Unc	BU
1922	5,000,000	0.65	1.40	2.75	8.00	—
1923	10	—	—	—	1,500	—
1924	4,990,000	0.65	1.40	2.75	8.00	—
1926	5,000,000	0.65	1.40	2.75	8.00	—
1928	5,000,000	0.65	1.40	2.75	8.00	—
Note: Mint name below ribbon						
1928	Inc. above	2.00	5.00	10.00	32.50	—
Note: Without designer's name below ribbon						
1932	5,000,000	0.65	1.40	2.75	8.00	—
1932 Proof	—	—	—	—	—	—
1935	5,000,000	0.65	1.40	2.75	8.00	—

KM# 10 SANTIMS Weight: 1.8000 g. **Composition:** Bronze **Edge:** Plain **Size:** 17 mm.

Date	Mintage	F	VF	XF	Unc	BU
1937	2,700,000	0.65	1.40	2.75	8.00	—
1938	1,900,000	0.65	1.40	2.75	10.00	—
1939	3,400,000	0.50	1.00	2.00	3.00	—
Note: Most were never placed into circulation						

KM# 2 2 SANTIMI Weight: 2.0000 g. **Composition:** Bronze **Edge:** Plain **Size:** 19.5 mm.

Date	Mintage	F	VF	XF	Unc	BU
1922	10,000,000	1.00	2.00	5.00	10.00	—
Note: Mint name below ribbon						
1922	Inc. above	5.00	10.00	17.50	35.00	—
Note: Without mint name						
1923	2	—	—	—	2,000	—
1926	5,000,000	0.75	1.50	4.00	9.00	—
1928	5,000,000	0.75	1.50	4.00	9.00	—

Date	Mintage	F	VF	XF	Unc	BU
1932	5,000,000	0.75	1.50	4.00	9.00	—
1932 Proof	—	—	—	—	—	—

KM# 11.1 2 SANTIMI Weight: 2.0000 g. **Composition:** Bronze **Edge:** Plain **Size:** 19 mm.

Date	Mintage	F	VF	XF	Unc	BU
1937	45,000	10.00	20.00	30.00	60.00	—

KM# 11.2 2 SANTIMI Weight: 2.0000 g. **Composition:** Bronze **Edge:** Plain **Size:** 19.5 mm.

Date	Mintage	F	VF	XF	Unc	BU
1939	5,000,000	1.00	2.50	4.00	9.00	—
Note: Most were never placed in circulation						

KM# 3 5 SANTIMI Weight: 3.0000 g. **Composition:** Bronze **Size:** 22 mm.

Date	Mintage	F	VF	XF	Unc	BU
1922	15,000,000	0.50	1.00	3.00	8.00	—
Note: Mint name below ribbon						
1922	Inc. above	3.00	6.00	10.00	20.00	—
Note: Without mint name						
1923	2	—	—	—	2,250	—

KM# 4 10 SANTIMU Weight: 3.0000 g. **Composition:** Nickel **Edge:** Plain **Size:** 19 mm. **Note:** Struck at Huguenin.

Date	Mintage	F	VF	XF	Unc	BU
1922	15,000,000	0.50	1.00	3.00	6.00	—

KM# 5 20 SANTIMU Weight: 6.0000 g. **Composition:** Nickel **Edge:** Plain **Size:** 21 mm. **Note:** Struck at Huguenin.

Date	Mintage	F	VF	XF	Unc	BU
1922	15,000,000	0.50	1.00	3.00	8.00	—

KM# 6 50 SANTIMU Weight: 6.5000 g. **Composition:** Nickel **Edge:** Plain **Size:** 25 mm. **Note:** Struck at Huguenin.

Date	Mintage	F	VF	XF	Unc	BU
1922	9,000,000	1.00	3.00	5.00	10.00	—

KM# 7 LATS **Weight:** 5.0000 g. **Composition:** 0.8350 Silver .1342 oz. ASW **Edge:** Milled **Size:** 23 mm.

Date	Mintage	F	VF	XF	Unc	BU
1923	—	—	—	900	—	—
1924	10,000,000	2.00	3.50	7.00	25.00	—

KM# 8 2 LATI **Weight:** 10.0000 g. **Composition:** 0.8350 Silver .2684 oz. ASW **Edge:** Milled **Size:** 27 mm.

Date	Mintage	F	VF	XF	Unc	BU
1925	6,386,000	2.50	3.00	6.00	30.00	—
1926	1,114,000	2.50	3.50	7.00	32.50	—

KM# 9 5 LATI **Weight:** 25.0000 g. **Composition:** 0.8350 Silver .6712 oz. ASW **Edge:** Plain with DIEVS *** SVETI *** LATVOJU *** **Size:** 37 mm.

Date	Mintage	F	VF	XF	Unc	BU
1929	1,000,000	9.00	12.00	20.00	42.50	—
1929 Proof	—	—	—	—	—	—
1931	2,000,000	8.00	11.50	18.00	37.50	—
1931 Proof	—	—	—	—	—	—
1932	600,000	9.00	12.00	20.00	42.50	—
1932 Proof	—	—	—	—	—	—

MODERN REPUBLIC

1991-present

STANDARD COINAGE

100 Santimu = 1 Lats

KM# 15 SANTIMS **Composition:** Copper Plated Iron

Date	F	VF	XF	Unc	BU
1992	—	—	—	0.25	—
1997	—	—	—	0.25	—

KM# 21 2 SANTIMI **Composition:** Bronze Plated Steel

Date	F	VF	XF	Unc	BU
1992	—	—	—	0.50	—
2000	—	—	—	0.50	—

KM# 16 5 SANTIMI **Composition:** Brass

Date	F	VF	XF	Unc	BU
1992	—	—	—	0.75	—

KM# 17 10 SANTIMU **Composition:** Brass

Date	F	VF	XF	Unc	BU
1992	—	—	—	1.25	—

KM# 22 20 SANTIMU **Composition:** Brass

Date	F	VF	XF	Unc	BU
1992	—	—	—	1.50	—

KM# 13 50 SANTIMU **Composition:** Copper-Nickel

Date	F	VF	XF	Unc	BU
1992	—	—	—	2.75	—

KM# 12 LATS **Composition:** Copper-Nickel

Date	F	VF	XF	Unc	BU
1992	—	—	—	3.75	—

KM# 23 LATS **Weight:** 28.2800 g. **Composition:** 0.9250 Silver .8411 oz. ASW **Series:** UN 50th Anniversary **Reverse:** Many people holding hands

Date	Mintage	F	VF	XF	Unc	BU
1995 Proof	100,000	Value: 42.50				

KM# 39 LATS **Weight:** 15.2000 g. **Composition:** 0.9250 Silver .4520 oz. ASW **Subject:** Millennium **Note:** Button design.

Date	Mintage	F	VF	XF	Unc	BU
1999-2000 Proof	35,000	Value: 55.00				

KM# 44 LATS **Weight:** 20.0000 g. **Composition:** 0.9250 Silver .5948 oz. ASW **Series:** Olympics **Obverse:** National arms **Reverse:** Two cyclists **Edge:** Lettered **Size:** 34 mm.

Date	Mintage	F	VF	XF	Unc	BU
1999 Proof	—	Value: 25.00				

KM# 45 LATS **Weight:** 31.4700 g. **Composition:** 0.9250 Silver .9359 oz. ASW **Subject:** European mink **Obverse:** National arms **Reverse:** Mink on rock **Edge:** Lettered **Size:** 38.6 mm.

Date	Mintage	F	VF	XF	Unc	BU
1999 Proof	—	Value: 50.00				

KM# 46 LATS **Weight:** 31.4700 g. **Composition:** 0.9250 Silver .9359 oz. ASW **Subject:** Hanseatic City of Ventspils **Obverse:** City arms above denomination **Reverse:** Building and ship **Edge Lettering:** "LATVIJAS REPUBLIKA LATVIJAS BANKA" **Size:** 38.6 mm.

Date	Mintage	F	VF	XF	Unc	BU
2000 Proof	—	Value: 50.00				

KM# 47 LATS **Weight:** 31.4700 g. **Composition:** 0.9250 Silver .9359 oz. ASW **Subject:** Earth - Roots **Obverse:** Mythological "Roots" pattern **Reverse:** Landscape and denomination **Edge:** Plain **Size:** 38.6 mm.

Date	Mintage	F	VF	XF	Unc	BU
2000 Proof	6,000	Value: 50.00				

KM# 48 LATS **Weight:** 31.4700 g. **Composition:** 0.9250 Silver .9359 oz. ASW **Subject:** UNICEF **Obverse:** National arms **Reverse:** Child art and logo **Edge Lettering:** "LATVIJAS BANKA" twice **Size:** 38.6 mm.

Date	Mintage	F	VF	XF	Unc	BU
2000 Proof	6,000	Value: 50.00				

KM# 49 LATS **Weight:** 31.4700 g. **Composition:** 0.9250 Silver .9359 oz. ASW **Subject:** Hanseatic City of Cesis **Obverse:** City arms **Reverse:** Castle and ship **Edge Lettering:** "LATVIJAS REPUBLIKA.LATVIJAS BANKA" **Size:** 38.6 mm.

Date	Mintage	F	VF	XF	Unc	BU
2001 Proof	25,000	Value: 50.00				

KM# 50 LATS **Weight:** 31.4700 g. **Composition:** 0.9250 Silver .9359 oz. ASW **Series:** Ice Hockey **Obverse:** National arms **Reverse:** Hockey player

Date	Mintage	F	VF	XF	Unc	BU
2001 Proof	25,000	Value: 50.00				

KM# 51 LATS **Weight:** 31.4700 g. **Composition:** 0.9250 Silver 0.9359 oz. ASW **Series:** Roots - Heaven **Obverse:** Stylized Roots pattern **Reverse:** Woman holding the sun **Edge:** Plain **Size:** 38.6 mm.

Date	F	VF	XF	Unc	BU
2001 Proof	—	Value: 50.00			

KM# 54 LATS **Weight:** 4.7500 g. **Composition:** Copper Nickel **Obverse:** National arms **Reverse:** Stork above denomination **Edge Lettering:** "LATVIJAS BANKA" twice **Size:** 21.7 mm.

Date	F	VF	XF	Unc	BU
2001	—	—	—	4.75	—

KM# 55 LATS **Weight:** 31.4700 g. **Composition:** 0.9250 Silver 0.9359 oz. ASW **Subject:** National Library **Obverse:** Country named and diamonds pattern **Reverse:** Library building sketch and diamonds design **Edge Lettering:** "GAISMU SAUCA-GAISMA AUSA" **Size:** 38.6 mm.

Date	Mintage	F	VF	XF	Unc	BU
2002 Proof	5,000	Value: 50.00				

KM# 52 LATS **Weight:** 31.4700 g. **Composition:** 0.9250 Silver 0.9359 oz. ASW **Series:** Roots - Destiny **Obverse:** Stylized Roots pattern **Reverse:** Apple tree and landscape **Edge:** Plain **Size:** 38.6 mm.

Date	F	VF	XF	Unc	BU
2002 Proof	—	Value: 50.00			

KM# 53 LATS **Weight:** 31.4700 g. **Composition:** 0.9250 Silver 0.9359 oz. ASW **Subject:** Hanseatic City of Kuldiga **Obverse:** City arms **Reverse:** City view and ships **Edge:** Lettered **Size:** 38.6 mm.

Date	F	VF	XF	Unc	BU
2002 Proof	—	Value: 50.00			

KM# 14 2 LATI **Composition:** Copper-Nickel

Date	F	VF	XF	Unc	BU
1992	—	—	—	7.00	—

KM# 18 2 LATI **Composition:** Copper-Nickel **Subject:** 75th Anniversary - Declaration of Independence

Date	Mintage	F	VF	XF	Unc	BU
ND(1993)	4,000,000	—	—	—	7.50	—
ND(1993) Proof	200,000	Value: 11.50				

KM# 38 2 LATI **Ring Composition:** Copper-Nickel **Center Composition:** Brass **Reverse:** Cow above denomination

Date	F	VF	XF	Unc	BU
1999	—	—	—	10.00	—

KM# 19 10 LATU **Weight:** 25.1750 g. **Composition:** 0.9250 Silver .7484 oz. ASW **Subject:** 75th Anniversary - Declaration of Independence

Date	Mintage	F	VF	XF	Unc	BU
ND(1993) Proof	30,000	Value: 35.00				

KM# 24 10 LATU **Weight:** 31.4700 g. **Composition:** 0.9250 Silver .9359 oz. ASW **Series:** Olympics **Subject:** Canoeing

Date	Mintage	F	VF	XF	Unc	BU
1994 Proof	30,000	Value: 35.00				

KM# 25 10 LATU **Weight:** 31.4700 g. **Composition:** 0.9250 Silver .9359 oz. ASW **Subject:** Julia Maria **Reverse:** 3-masted schooner

Date	Mintage	F	VF	XF	Unc	BU
1995 Proof	20,000	Value: 42.50				

KM# 27 10 LATU **Weight:** 31.4700 g. **Composition:** 0.9250 Silver .9359 oz. ASW **Subject:** 800th Anniversary - Reiga **Obverse:** Coat of arms from 1368 **Reverse:** The Great Gould's coat of arms from 1354

Date	F	VF	XF	Unc	BU
1995 (1996) Proof	—	—	—	—	—
1995(1996) Proof	—	Value: 47.50			

KM# 26 10 LATU **Weight:** 31.4700 g. **Composition:** 0.9250 Silver .9359 oz. ASW **Subject:** Riga 800 **Reverse:** First city seal

Date		F	VF	XF	Unc	BU
1995 (1996) Proof	Est. 8,000	Value: 50.00				

KM# 33 10 LATU **Weight:** 31.4700 g. **Composition:** 0.9250 Silver .9359 oz. ASW **Series:** Endangered Wildlife **Obverse:** National arms **Reverse:** Grieze (corn-crake) bird **Edge:** Lettered **Edge Lettering:** LATVIJAS BANKA \ (2x)

Date	Mintage	F	VF	XF	Unc	BU
1996 Proof	15,000	Value: 42.50				

KM# 34 10 LATU **Weight:** 31.4700 g. **Composition:** 0.9250 Silver .9359 oz. ASW **Subject:** Riga - XVI Century **Obverse:** Old coin design above denomination **Reverse:** Old city view

Date		F	VF	XF	Unc	BU
1996 Proof	—	Value: 50.00				

KM# 36 10 LATU **Weight:** 31.3500 g. **Composition:** 0.9990 Silver 1.0069 oz. ASW **Subject:** 800th Anniversary of Riga **Obverse:** Old coin design with St. Christopher **Reverse:** Old coin design with city arms **Edge:** Lettered **Edge Lettering:** LATVIJAS REPUBLIKA LATVIJAS BANKA

Date		F	VF	XF	Unc	BU
1996 Proof	—	Value: 50.00				

KM# 28 10 LATU **Weight:** 31.3200 g. **Composition:** 0.9250 Silver .9314 oz. ASW **Obverse:** National arms **Reverse:** 12th-century ship above its sunken remains **Edge:** Lettered **Edge Lettering:** LATIJAS BANKAS

Date	Mintage	F	VF	XF	Unc	BU
1997 Proof	15,000	Value: 42.50				

KM# 35 10 LATU **Weight:** 31.4700 g. **Composition:** 0.9250 Silver .9359 oz. ASW **Subject:** Riga - XVII Century **Obverse:** Old coin design **Reverse:** Aerial view of walled city

Date		F	VF	XF	Unc	BU
1997 Proof	—	Value: 50.00				

KM# 29 10 LATU **Weight:** 1.2441 g. **Composition:** 0.9999 Gold .0400 oz. AGW **Subject:** 800th Anniversary - Riga **Obverse:** City arms on old coin design **Reverse:** City arms and ship on old coin design

Date		F	VF	XF	Unc	BU
1998 Proof	—	Value: 55.00				

KM# 30 10 LATU **Weight:** 31.4700 g. **Composition:** 0.9250 Silver .9359 oz. ASW **Subject:** 800th Anniversary - Riga **Obverse:** National song festival procession **Reverse:** Riga city arms

Date	Mintage	F	VF	XF	Unc	BU
1998 Proof	Est. 8,000	Value: 50.00				

KM# 31 10 LATU **Weight:** 31.4700 g. **Composition:** 0.9250 Silver .9359 oz. ASW **Subject:** 800th Anniversary - Riga **Obverse:** Liberty Monument in Riga **Reverse:** Lions supporting city arms of Riga

Date	Mintage	F	VF	XF	Unc	BU
1998 Proof	Est. 8,000	Value: 55.00				

KM# 32 10 LATU **Weight:** 31.4700 g. **Composition:** 0.9250 Silver .9359 oz. ASW **Obverse:** National arms **Reverse:** 1925 Icebreaker "Krisjanis Valdemara"

Date	Mintage	F	VF	XF	Unc	BU
1998 Proof	10,000	Value: 47.50				

KM# 41 20 LATU **Weight:** 7.7760 g. **Composition:** 0.5830 Gold .1458 oz. AGW **Obverse:** National arms **Reverse:** Sailing ship "Gekronte Ehlendt" **Edge:** Reeded **Size:** 25 mm. **Note:** Struck at Valcambi.

Date		F	VF	XF	Unc	BU
1997 Proof	—	Value: 85.00				

KM# 42 20 LATU **Weight:** 1.2442 g. **Composition:** 0.9990 Gold .0400 oz. AGW **Obverse:** National arms **Reverse:** Sailing ship "Julia Maria" **Edge:** Reeded **Size:** 13.92 mm.

Date		F	VF	XF	Unc	BU
1997 Proof	—	Value: 55.00				

KM# 37 20 LATU **Weight:** 31.4100 g. **Composition:** 0.9210 Silver .9341 oz. ASW **Obverse:** City arms **Reverse:** Melngalvgu **Edge:** Lettered **Edge Lettering:** LATVIJAS REPUBLIKA LATVIJAS BANKA

Date		F	VF	XF	Unc	BU
1997 Proof	—	Value: 50.00				

KM# 43 20 LATU **Weight:** 3.1100 g. **Composition:** 0.5830 Gold .0583 oz. AGW **Series:** Olympics **Obverse:** National arms **Reverse:** Javelin thrower **Edge:** Reeded **Size:** 18.5 mm.

Date		F	VF	XF	Unc	BU
1999 Proof	—	Value: 55.00				

KM# 20 100 LATU **Weight:** 13.3380 g. **Composition:** 0.8330 Gold .2501 oz. AGW **Subject:** 75th Anniversary - Declaration of Independence

Date	Mintage	F	VF	XF	Unc	BU
ND(1993) Proof	5,000	Value: 225				

KM# 40 100 LATU **Weight:** 16.2000 g. **Composition:** 0.9990 Gold .5203 oz. AGW **Subject:** Development **Obverse:** National arms **Reverse:** Partial circle and denomination **Edge:** Reeded and plain sections **Size:** 24 mm.

Date	F	VF	XF	Unc	BU
1998 Proof	—	Value: 350			

PATTERNS

Including off metal strikes

KM#	Date	Mintage	Identification	Mkt Val
Pn1	1922	—	10 Santimu. Silver. KM4.	225
Pn2	1922	—	10 Santimu. Aluminum-Bronze. KM4.	300
Pn3	1924	—	2 Lati. Silver.	300
Pn4	1938	—	2 Santimi. Bronze. KM11.2	600

MINT SETS

KM#	Date	Mintage	Identification	Issue Price	Mkt Val
MS1	1992 (8)	—	KM12-17, 21-22	—	25.00

PROOF SETS

KM#	Date	Mintage	Identification	Issue Price	Mkt Val
PS1	ND (1993) (3)	1,800	KM18-20	—	325

LEBANON

The Republic of Lebanon, situated on the eastern shore of the Mediterranean Sea between Syria and Israel, has an area of 4,015 sq. mi. (10,400 sq. km.) and a population of 3.5 million. Capital: Beirut. The economy is based on agriculture, trade and tourism. Fruit, other foodstuffs and textiles are exported.

Almost at the beginning of recorded history, Lebanon appeared as the well-wooded hinterland of the Phoenicians who exploited its famous forests of cedar. The mountains were a Christian refuge and a Crusader stronghold. Lebanon, the history of which is essentially the same as that of Syria, came under control of the Ottoman Turks early in the 16th century. Following the collapse of the Ottoman Empire after World War I, Lebanon, along with Syria, became a French mandate. The French drew a border around the predominantly Christian Lebanon *Sanjak* or administrative subdivision and on Sept. 1, 1920 proclaimed the area the State of Grand Lebanon (*Etat du Grand Liban*) a republic under French control. France announced the independence of Lebanon on Nov. 26, 1941, but the last British and French troops didn't leave until the end of August 1946.

TITLES

الجمهورية اللبنانية

al-Jomhuriya(t) al-Lubnaniya(t)

MINT MARKS

(a) - Paris, privy marks only
(u) - Utrecht, privy marks only

MONETARY SYSTEM

100 Piastres = 1 Livre (Pound)

FRENCH PROTECTORATE

STANDARD COINAGE

KM# 9 1/2 PIASTRE **Composition:** Copper-Nickel

Date	Mintage	F	VF	XF	Unc	BU
1934(a)	200,000	2.00	5.00	12.50	40.00	—
1936(a)	1,200,000	1.25	3.00	7.50	25.00	—

KM# 9a 1/2 PIASTRE **Composition:** Zinc

Date	Mintage	F	VF	XF	Unc	BU
1941(a)	1,000,000	0.50	1.00	4.00	10.00	—

KM# 3 PIASTRE **Composition:** Copper-Nickel

Date	Mintage	F	VF	XF	Unc	BU
1925(a)	1,500,000	0.50	2.00	7.50	25.00	—
1931(a)	300,000	1.00	4.00	12.50	45.00	—
1933(a)	500,000	1.00	4.00	10.00	45.00	—
1936(a)	2,200,000	0.50	1.00	6.50	20.00	—

KM# 3a PIASTRE **Composition:** Zinc

Date	Mintage	F	VF	XF	Unc	BU
1940(a)	2,000,000	0.50	0.75	4.00	10.00	—

KM# 1 2 PIASTRES **Composition:** Aluminum-Bronze

Date	Mintage	F	VF	XF	Unc	BU
1924(a)	1,800,000	1.25	3.00	12.50	50.00	—

KM# 4 2 PIASTRES **Composition:** Aluminum-Bronze

Date	Mintage	F	VF	XF	Unc	BU
1925(a)	1,000,000	3.00	8.00	20.00	80.00	—

KM# 10 2-1/2 PIASTRES **Composition:** Aluminum-Bronze

Date	Mintage	F	VF	XF	Unc	BU
1940(a)	1,000,000	1.00	2.00	3.50	12.00	—

KM# 2 5 PIASTRES **Composition:** Aluminum-Bronze

Date	Mintage	F	VF	XF	Unc	BU
1924(a)	1,000,000	1.25	3.00	10.00	45.00	—

KM# 5.1 5 PIASTRES **Composition:** Aluminum-Bronze **Reverse:** Both privy marks to left of "5"

Date	Mintage	F	VF	XF	Unc	BU
1925(a)	1,500,000	0.75	1.50	8.00	30.00	—

KM# 5.2 5 PIASTRES **Composition:** Aluminum-Bronze **Reverse:** Privy marks to left and right of "5 Piastres"

Date	Mintage	F	VF	XF	Unc	BU
1925(a)	Inc. above	1.00	2.00	7.50	30.00	—
1931(a)	400,000	1.50	4.00	12.50	40.00	—
1933(a)	500,000	1.50	4.00	12.50	40.00	—
1936(a)	900,000	1.00	2.00	7.50	25.00	—
1940(a)	1,000,000	0.75	1.50	5.00	15.00	—

KM# 6 10 PIASTRES **Weight:** 2.0000 g. **Composition:** 0.6800 Silver .0437 oz. ASW

Date	Mintage	F	VF	XF	Unc	BU
1929	880,000	3.00	7.00	25.00	70.00	—

KM# 7 25 PIASTRES **Weight:** 5.0000 g. **Composition:** 0.6800 Silver .1093 oz. ASW

Date	Mintage	F	VF	XF	Unc	BU
1929	600,000	3.00	7.00	25.00	75.00	—
1933(a)	200,000	4.50	15.00	40.00	125	—
1936(a)	400,000	3.50	10.00	27.50	85.00	—

KM# 8 50 PIASTRES **Weight:** 10.0000 g. **Composition:** 0.6800 Silver .2186 oz. ASW

Date	Mintage	F	VF	XF	Unc	BU
1929	500,000	5.00	10.00	40.00	125	—
1933(a)	100,000	7.00	20.00	65.00	190	—
1936(a)	100,000	7.00	17.50	50.00	140	—

WORLD WAR II COINAGE

KM# 11 1/2 PIASTRE **Composition:** Brass **Note:** Three varieties known. Usually crudely struck, off-center, etc. Perfectly struck, centered uncirculated specimens command a considerable premium. Size of letters also vary.

Date	F	VF	XF	Unc	BU
ND(1941)	1.00	2.50	5.00	12.00	—

KM# 12 PIASTRE **Composition:** Brass **Note:** Two varieties known. Usually crudely struck, off-center, etc. Perfectly struck, centered unc. specimens command a considerable premium.

Date	F	VF	XF	Unc	BU
ND(1941)	1.00	3.00	7.50	18.00	—

KM# 12a PIASTRE **Composition:** Aluminum

Date	F	VF	XF	Unc	BU
ND(1941)	—	—	—	—	—

KM# 13 2-1/2 PIASTRES **Composition:** Aluminum **Note:** Seven varieties known. Usually crudely struck, off-center, etc. Perfectly struck, centered unc. specimens command a considerable premium.

Date	F	VF	XF	Unc	BU
ND(1941)	1.50	3.50	8.00	20.00	—

KM# 13a 2-1/2 PIASTRES **Composition:** Aluminum-Bronze

Date	F	VF	XF	Unc	BU
ND(1941)	—	650	850	—	—

KM# A14 5 PIASTRES **Composition:** Aluminum **Note:** Did not enter circulation in significant numbers.

Date	F	VF	XF	Unc	BU
ND(1941)	—	—	2,000	3,000	—

REPUBLIC

STANDARD COINAGE

KM# 19 PIASTRE **Composition:** Aluminum-Bronze

Date	Mintage	F	VF	XF	Unc	BU
1955(a)	4,000,000	—	0.10	0.20	0.35	—

KM# 20 2-1/2 PIASTRES **Composition:** Aluminum-Bronze

Date	Mintage	F	VF	XF	Unc	BU
1955(a)	5,000,000	—	0.10	0.25	0.50	—

KM# 14 5 PIASTRES **Composition:** Aluminum

Date	Mintage	F	VF	XF	Unc	BU
1952(a)	3,600,000	0.50	1.00	1.50	4.00	—

KM# 18 5 PIASTRES **Composition:** Aluminum

Date	Mintage	F	VF	XF	Unc	BU
1954	4,440,000	0.10	0.30	0.50	1.25	—

KM# 21 5 PIASTRES **Composition:** Aluminum-Bronze

Date	Mintage	F	VF	XF	Unc	BU
1955(a)	3,000,000	0.10	0.20	0.30	0.50	—
1961(a)	—	0.10	0.15	0.20	0.40	—

KM# 25.1 5 PIASTRES **Composition:** Nickel-Brass

Date	Mintage	F	VF	XF	Unc	BU
1968	2,000,000	—	0.10	0.15	0.20	—
1969	4,000,000	—	0.10	0.15	0.20	—
1970	—	—	0.10	0.15	0.25	—

KM# 25.2 5 PIASTRES **Composition:** Nickel-Brass

Date	Mintage	F	VF	XF	Unc	BU
1972(a)	12,000,000	—	—	0.10	0.15	—
1975(a)	—	—	—	0.10	0.15	—
1980	—	—	—	0.10	0.15	—

KM# 15 10 PIASTRES **Composition:** Aluminum

Date	Mintage	F	VF	XF	Unc	BU
1952(a)	3,600,000	0.50	1.00	5.00	15.00	—

KM# 22 10 PIASTRES **Composition:** Aluminum-Bronze

Date	Mintage	F	VF	XF	Unc	BU
1955	2,175,000	0.20	0.40	0.60	1.00	—

KM# 23 10 PIASTRES **Composition:** Aluminum-Bronze

Date	Mintage	F	VF	XF	Unc	BU
1955(a)	6,000,000	0.10	0.25	0.50	0.75	—

KM# 24 10 PIASTRES **Composition:** Copper-Nickel

Date	Mintage	F	VF	XF	Unc	BU
1961	7,000,000	—	0.10	0.25	0.50	—
1961 Proof	—	—	—	—	—	—

KM# 26 10 PIASTRES **Composition:** Nickel-Brass

Date	Mintage	F	VF	XF	Unc	BU
1968(a)	2,000,000	—	0.10	0.15	0.25	—
1969(a)	5,000,000	—	—	0.10	0.20	—
1970(a)	8,000,000	—	—	0.10	0.20	—
1972(a)	12,000,000	—	—	0.10	0.20	—
1975(a)	—	—	—	0.10	0.20	—

KM# 16.1 25 PIASTRES **Composition:** Aluminum-Bronze

Date	Mintage	F	VF	XF	Unc	BU
1952(u)	7,200,000	0.10	0.40	0.60	1.00	—

KM# 16.2 25 PIASTRES **Composition:** Aluminum-Bronze **Note:** Different style of inscription and larger date.

Date	Mintage	F	VF	XF	Unc	BU
1961(u)	5,000,000	0.10	0.40	0.50	0.75	—

KM# 27.1 25 PIASTRES **Composition:** Nickel-Brass

Date	Mintage	F	VF	XF	Unc	BU
1968	1,500,000	0.10	0.15	0.25	0.50	—
1969	2,500,000	0.10	0.15	0.20	0.40	—
1970	—	0.10	0.15	0.20	0.40	—
1972	8,000,000	0.10	0.15	0.20	0.30	—
1975	—	0.10	0.15	0.20	0.30	—

KM# 27.2 25 PIASTRES **Composition:** Nickel-Brass **Reverse:** Thick, plain 25

Date	F	VF	XF	Unc	BU
1980	0.10	0.15	0.20	0.30	—

KM# 17 50 PIASTRES **Weight:** 4.9710 g. **Composition:** 0.6000 Silver .0959 oz. ASW

Date	Mintage	F	VF	XF	Unc	BU
1952(u)	7,200,000	BV	1.00	2.00	4.50	—

KM# 28.1 50 PIASTRES **Composition:** Nickel

Date	Mintage	F	VF	XF	Unc	BU
1968	2,000,000	0.20	0.40	0.60	1.00	—
1969	3,488,000	0.10	0.25	0.40	0.75	—
1970	2,000,000	0.10	0.25	0.40	0.50	—
1971	2,000,000	0.10	0.25	0.40	0.50	—
1975	—	0.10	0.25	0.40	0.50	—
1978	22,400,000	0.10	0.25	0.40	0.50	—

KM# 28.2 50 PIASTRES **Composition:** Nickel **Reverse:** Different "50"

Date	F	VF	XF	Unc	BU
1980	0.10	0.25	0.40	0.50	—

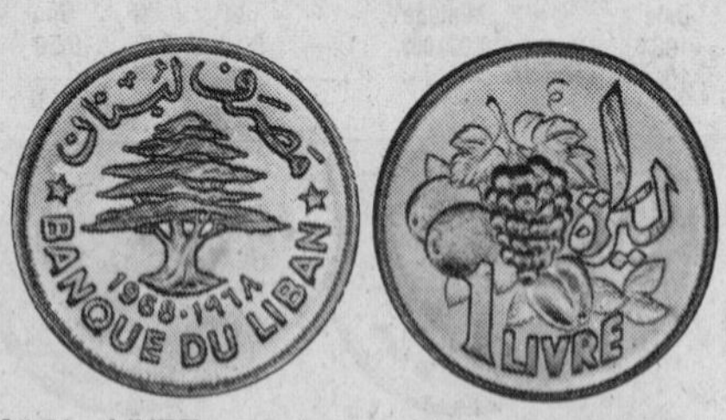

KM# 29 LIVRE **Composition:** Nickel **Series:** F.A.O.

Date	Mintage	F	VF	XF	Unc	BU
1968	300,000	0.25	0.50	1.00	3.00	—

KM# 30 LIVRE **Composition:** Nickel **Note:** Varieties exist.

Date	Mintage	F	VF	XF	Unc	BU
1975	—	0.20	0.40	0.60	1.00	—
1975 Proof	—	—	—	—	—	—
1977	8,000,000	0.20	0.40	0.60	1.00	—
1980	12,000,000	0.20	0.40	0.60	1.00	—
1981	—	0.20	0.40	0.60	1.00	—
1986	—	0.20	0.40	0.60	1.00	—

KM# 32 LIVRE **Composition:** Copper-Nickel **Series:** 1980 Winter Olympics **Subject:** Lake Placid

Date	Mintage	F	VF	XF	Unc	BU
1980 Proof	40,000	Value: 17.50				

KM# 31 5 LIVRES **Composition:** Nickel **Series:** F.A.O.

Date	Mintage	F	VF	XF	Unc	BU
1978	1,000,000	—	—	—	2.50	—

KM# 33 10 LIVRES **Weight:** 19.0000 g. **Composition:** 0.5000 Silver .3054 oz. ASW **Series:** 1980 Winter Olympics **Subject:** Lake Placid

Date	Mintage	F	VF	XF	Unc	BU
1980 Proof	20,000	Value: 40.00				

KM# 35 10 LIVRES **Composition:** Copper-Nickel **Series:** World Food Day

Date	Mintage	F	VF	XF	Unc	BU
1981	15,000	—	—	—	6.50	—

KM# 40 25 LIVRES **Weight:** 2.8200 g. **Composition:** Nickel Plated Steel **Obverse:** Denomination on tree **Reverse:** Denomination in square design **Edge:** Plain **Size:** 20.5 mm.

Date	F	VF	XF	Unc	BU
2002	—	—	—	1.00	—

KM# 37 50 LIVRES **Composition:** Stainless Steel **Obverse:** Arabic legend and denomination **Reverse:** French legend and denomination

Date	F	VF	XF	Unc	BU
1996	—	—	0.45	1.00	—

KM# 38 100 LIVRES **Composition:** Copper-Zinc **Obverse:** Arabic legend and denomination **Reverse:** French legend and denomination

Date	F	VF	XF	Unc	BU
1995	—	—	0.65	1.50	—
1996	—	—	0.65	1.50	—

KM# 36 250 LIVRES **Composition:** Brass **Obverse:** Arabic legend and denomination **Reverse:** French legend and denomination

Date	F	VF	XF	Unc	BU
1995	—	—	0.75	2.00	—
1996	—	—	0.75	2.00	—

KM# 34 400 LIVRES **Weight:** 8.0000 g. **Composition:** 0.9000 Gold .2315 oz. AGW **Series:** 1980 Winter Olympics **Subject:** Lake Placid

Date	Mintage	F	VF	XF	Unc	BU
1980 Proof	1,000	Value: 600				

KM# 39 500 LIVRES **Composition:** Stainless Steel **Obverse:** Arabic legend and denomination **Reverse:** French legend and denomination

Date	F	VF	XF	Unc	BU
1995	—	—	1.00	2.50	—
1996	—	—	1.00	2.50	—
2000	—	—	1.00	2.50	—

ESSAIS

Standard metals unless otherwise noted

KM#	Date	Mintage	Identification	Mkt Val
E1	1924(a)	—	5 Piastres. KM2.	100
E3	1925(a)	—	2 Piastres. KM1.	110
E2	1925(a)	—	Piastre. KM3.	80.00
E4	1925(a)	—	5 Piastres. KM5.1.	90.00
E6	1929	—	10 Piastres. KM6.	120
E7	1929	—	25 Piastres. KM7.	125
E8	1929	—	50 Piastres. KM8.	125
E5	1929(a)	—	Piastre. KM3.	90.00

E9	1934 A	—	1/2 Piastre. KM9.	100

E10	1940(a)	—	2-1/2 Piastres. KM10.	50.00
E12	1972(a)	—	10 Piastres. KM26.	15.00
E11	1972	—	5 Piastres. KM25.	15.00
E13	1980	—	25 Piastres. KM27.	15.00
E15	1980	—	Livre. KM30.	20.00
E14	1980	—	50 Piastres. KM28.	17.50
E16	1981	—	10 Livres. KM35.	40.00

PIEFORTS

KM#	Date	Mintage	Identification	Mkt Val
P2	1980	3,000	10 Livres. KM33.	120
P1	1980	3,000	Livre. KM32.	45.00
P3	1980	750	400 Livres. KM34.	1,400

LESOTHO

The Kingdom of Lesotho, a constitutional monarchy located within the east-central part of the Republic of South Africa, has an area of 11,720 sq. mi. (30,350 sq. km.) and a population of 1.5 million. Capital: Maseru. The economy is based on subsistence agriculture and live stock raising. Wool, mohair, and cattle are exported.

Lesotho (formerly Basutoland) was sparsely populated until the end of the 16th century. Between the 16th and 19th centuries an influx of refugees from tribal wars led to the development of a distinct Basotho group. During the reign of tribal chief Mashoeshoe I (1823-70), a series of wars with the Orange Free State resulted in the loss of large areas of territory to South Africa. Mashoeshoe appealed to the British for help, and Basutoland was constituted a native state under British protection. In 1871 it was annexed to Cape Colony, but was restored to direct control by the Crown in 1884. From 1884 to 1959 legislative and executive authority was vested in a British High Commissioner. The constitution of 1959 recognized the expressed wish of the people for independence, which was attained on Oct.4, 1966.

Lesotho is a member of the Commonwealth of Nations. The king is Head of State.

RULERS
Moshoeshoe II, 1966-1990
Letsie III, 1990-1995
Moshoeshoe II, 1995-

MONETARY SYSTEM
100 Licente/Lisente = 1 Maloti/Loti

KINGDOM

STANDARD COINAGE

100 Licente/Lisente = 1 Maloti/Loti

KM# 16 SENTE Composition: Nickel-Brass **Ruler:** Moshoeshoe II **Reverse:** Traditional house

Date	Mintage	F	VF	XF	Unc	BU
1979	4,500,000	—	—	0.15	0.40	—
1979 Proof	10,000	Value: 0.65				
1980	—	—	—	0.15	0.40	—
1980 Proof	10,000	Value: 0.65				
1981 Proof	2,500	Value: 0.65				
1983	—	—	—	0.15	0.40	—
1985	—	—	—	0.15	0.40	—
1989	—	—	—	0.15	0.40	—

KM# 54 SENTE Composition: Brass **Ruler:** Letsie III

Date	F	VF	XF	Unc	BU
1992	—	—	0.15	0.75	—

KM# 54a SENTE Composition: Brass Plated Steel **Ruler:** Letsie III

Date	F	VF	XF	Unc	BU
1992	—	—	—	—	—

KM# 17 2 LISENTE Composition: Nickel-Brass **Ruler:** Moshoeshoe II **Reverse:** Steer

Date	Mintage	F	VF	XF	Unc	BU
1979	3,000,000	—	—	0.20	0.50	—
1979 Proof	10,000	Value: 1.00				
1980	—	—	—	0.20	0.50	—
1980 Proof	10,000	Value: 1.00				
1981 Proof	2,500	Value: 2.00				
1985	—	—	—	0.20	0.50	—
1989	—	—	—	0.20	0.50	—

KM# 55 2 LISENTE Composition: Brass **Ruler:** Letsie III **Obverse:** National arms **Reverse:** Bull

Date	F	VF	XF	Unc	BU
1992	—	—	0.20	0.50	—

KM# 55a 2 LISENTE Weight: 2.2500 g. **Composition:** Brass Plated Steel **Ruler:** Letsie III **Obverse:** National arms **Reverse:** Bull **Edge:** Plain **Size:** 19.5 mm.

Date	F	VF	XF	Unc	BU
1992	—	—	0.20	0.50	—

KM# 1 5 LICENTE (Lisente) Weight: 2.8900 g. **Composition:** 0.9000 Silver .0836 oz. ASW **Ruler:** Moshoeshoe II **Subject:** Independence attained

Date	Mintage	F	VF	XF	Unc	BU
1966 Proof	5,000	Value: 6.00				

KM# 18 5 LICENTE (Lisente) Composition: Nickel-Brass **Ruler:** Moshoeshoe II **Reverse:** Aloe plant

Date	Mintage	F	VF	XF	Unc	BU
1979	2,700,000	—	—	0.25	0.60	—
1979 Proof	10,000	Value: 1.25				
1980	—	—	—	0.25	0.60	—
1980 Proof	10,000	Value: 1.25				
1981 Proof	2,500	Value: 2.50				
1989	—	—	—	0.25	0.60	—

KM# 56 5 LICENTE (Lisente) Composition: Brass **Ruler:** Letsie III

Date	F	VF	XF	Unc	BU
1994	—	—	0.25	0.60	—

KM# 62 5 LICENTE (Lisente) Composition: Brass Plated Steel **Ruler:** Letsie III

Date	F	VF	XF	Unc	BU
1998	—	—	0.25	0.60	—

KM# 2 10 LICENTE (Lisente) Weight: 5.6800 g. **Composition:** 0.9000 Silver .1643 oz. ASW **Ruler:** Moshoeshoe II **Subject:** Independence Attained

Date	Mintage	F	VF	XF	Unc	BU
1966 Proof	5,000	Value: 6.00				

KM# 19 10 LICENTE (Lisente) Composition: Copper-Nickel **Ruler:** Moshoeshoe II **Reverse:** Angora goat

Date	Mintage	F	VF	XF	Unc	BU
1979	2,000,000	—	0.15	0.30	1.00	—
1979 Proof	10,000	Value: 1.75				
1980	—	—	0.15	0.30	1.00	—
1980 Proof	10,000	Value: 1.75				
1981 Proof	2,500	Value: 3.00				
1983	—	—	0.15	0.30	1.00	—
1989	—	—	0.15	0.30	1.00	—

KM# 61 10 LICENTE (Lisente) Composition: Copper-Nickel **Ruler:** Letsie III **Obverse:** National arms **Reverse:** Angora goat

Date	F	VF	XF	Unc	BU
1992	—	—	—	1.00	—

KM# 63 10 LICENTE (Lisente) Composition: Brass Plated Steel **Ruler:** Moshoeshoe II

Date	F	VF	XF	Unc	BU
1998	—	—	—	1.00	—

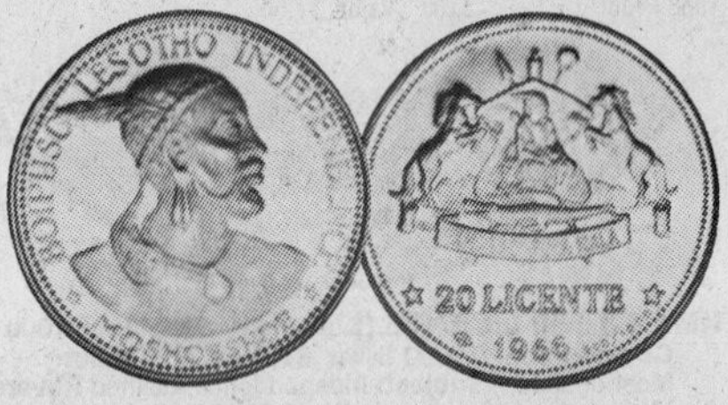

KM# 3.1 20 LICENTE Weight: 11.2800 g. **Composition:** 0.9000 Silver .3263 oz. ASW **Ruler:** Moshoeshoe II **Subject:** Independence Attained **Reverse:** Small 900/1000 at right of date

Date	Mintage	F	VF	XF	Unc	BU
1966 Proof	5,000	Value: 10.00				

KM# 3.2 20 LICENTE Weight: 11.2800 g. **Composition:** 0.9000 Silver .3263 oz. ASW **Ruler:** Moshoeshoe II **Subject:** Independence Attained **Reverse:** Large 900/1000 at right of date

Date	F	VF	XF	Unc	BU
1966 Proof	—	Value: 10.00			

KM# 64 20 LICENTE Composition: Brass Plated Steel **Ruler:** Moshoeshoe II **Reverse:** Flora

Date	F	VF	XF	Unc	BU
1998	—	—	—	0.75	—

KM# 20 25 LISENTE Composition: Copper-Nickel **Ruler:** Moshoeshoe II **Reverse:** Woman in native costume weaving baskets

Date	Mintage	F	VF	XF	Unc	BU
1979	1,200,000	—	0.10	0.20	1.00	—
1979 Proof	10,000	Value: 2.00				
1980	—	—	0.10	0.20	1.00	—
1980 Proof	10,000	Value: 2.00				
1981 Proof	2,500	Value: 3.50				
1985	—	—	0.10	0.20	1.00	—
1989	—	—	0.10	0.20	1.00	—

KM# 4.1 50 LICENTE (Lisente) **Weight:** 28.1000 g. **Composition:** 0.9000 Silver .8131 oz. ASW **Ruler:** Moshoeshoe II **Subject:** Independence Attained **Reverse:** Small 900/1000 at right of date

Date	F	VF	XF	Unc	BU
1966	—	—	—	10.00	—
1966 Proof	—	Value: 17.50			

KM# 4.2 50 LICENTE (Lisente) **Weight:** 28.1000 g. **Composition:** 0.9000 Silver .8131 oz. ASW **Ruler:** Moshoeshoe II **Subject:** Independence Attained **Reverse:** Large 900/1000 at right of date

Date	Mintage	F	VF	XF	Unc	BU
1966	—	—	—	—	10.00	—
1966 Proof	5,000	Value: 17.50				

KM# 4.3 50 LICENTE (Lisente) **Weight:** 28.1000 g. **Composition:** 0.9000 Silver .8131 oz. ASW **Ruler:** Moshoeshoe II **Subject:** Independence Attained **Reverse:** Mint mark and fineness below date

Date	F	VF	XF	Unc	BU
1966	—	—	—	10.00	—
1966 Proof	—	Value: 17.50			

KM# 21 50 LICENTE (Lisente) **Composition:** Copper-Nickel **Ruler:** Moshoeshoe II **Reverse:** Horse and rider

Date	Mintage	F	VF	XF	Unc	BU
1979	480,000	—	0.35	0.50	1.25	—
1979 Proof	10,000	Value: 2.50				
1980	—	—	0.35	0.50	1.25	—
1980 Proof	10,000	Value: 2.50				
1981 Proof	2,500	Value: 4.00				
1983	—	—	0.35	0.50	1.25	—
1989	—	—	0.35	0.50	1.25	—

KM# 65 50 LICENTE (Lisente) **Composition:** Brass Plated Steel **Ruler:** Moshoeshoe II

Date	F	VF	XF	Unc	BU
1998	—	—	—	1.00	—

KM# 5 LOTI **Weight:** 3.9940 g. **Composition:** 0.9170 Gold .1177 oz. AGW **Ruler:** Moshoeshoe II **Subject:** Independence Attained

Date	Mintage	F	VF	XF	Unc	BU
1966 Proof	3,500	Value: 70.00				

KM# 8 LOTI **Weight:** 3.9940 g. **Composition:** 0.9170 Gold .1177 oz. AGW **Ruler:** Moshoeshoe II **Series:** F.A.O.

Date	Mintage	F	VF	XF	Unc	BU
1969 Proof	3,000	Value: 65.00				

KM# 22 LOTI **Composition:** Copper-Nickel **Ruler:** Moshoeshoe II

Date	Mintage	F	VF	XF	Unc	BU
1979	1,275,000	—	0.65	1.25	3.00	—
1979 Proof	10,000	Value: 5.00				
1980	—	—	0.75	1.50	4.00	—
1980 Proof	10,000	Value: 5.00				
1981 Proof	2,500	Value: 7.00				
1989	—	—	0.75	1.50	4.00	—

KM# 46 LOTI **Weight:** 11.3100 g. **Composition:** 0.9250 Silver .3363 oz. ASW **Ruler:** Moshoeshoe II **Subject:** Silver Jubilee of King Moshoeshoe II

Date	Mintage	F	VF	XF	Unc	BU
1985 Proof	2,500	Value: 17.50				

KM# 46a LOTI **Weight:** 18.9800 g. **Composition:** 0.9170 Gold .5626 oz. AGW **Ruler:** Moshoeshoe II **Subject:** Silver Jubilee of King Moshoeshoe II

Date	Mintage	F	VF	XF	Unc	BU
1985 Proof	500	Value: 250				

KM# 60 LOTI **Composition:** Copper-Nickel **Ruler:** Letsie III **Series:** 50th Anniversary - UN

Date	F	VF	XF	Unc	BU
1995	—	—	—	8.00	—

KM# 66 LOTI **Composition:** Nickel Plated Steel **Ruler:** Letsie III **Obverse:** Seated king

Date	F	VF	XF	Unc	BU
1998	—	—	—	1.50	—

KM# 6 2 MALOTI **Weight:** 7.9880 g. **Composition:** 0.9170 Gold .2355 oz. AGW **Ruler:** Moshoeshoe II **Obverse:** Independence Attained

Date	F	VF	XF	Unc	BU
1966 Proof	—	Value: 120			

KM# 9 2 MALOTI **Weight:** 7.9880 g. **Composition:** 0.9170 Gold .2355 oz. AGW **Ruler:** Moshoeshoe II **Series:** F.A.O.

Date	Mintage	F	VF	XF	Unc	BU
1969 Proof	3,000	Value: 120				

KM# 58 2 MALOTI **Composition:** Nickel Clad Steel **Ruler:** Moshoeshoe II **Obverse:** National arms **Reverse:** Maize plants

Date	F	VF	XF	Unc	BU
1996	—	—	—	2.50	—
1998	—	—	—	2.00	—

KM# 7 4 MALOTI **Weight:** 15.9760 g. **Composition:** 0.9170 Gold .471 oz. AGW **Ruler:** Moshoeshoe II **Subject:** Independence Attained

Date	Mintage	F	VF	XF	Unc	BU
1966 Proof	3,500	Value: 235				

KM# 10 4 MALOTI **Weight:** 15.9760 g. **Composition:** 0.9170 Gold .471 oz. AGW **Ruler:** Moshoeshoe II **Series:** F.A.O.

Date	Mintage	F	VF	XF	Unc	BU
1969 Proof	3,000	Value: 250				

KM# 59 5 MALOTI **Composition:** Nickel Clad Steel **Ruler:** Moshoeshoe II **Obverse:** National arms **Reverse:** Five wheat ears

Date	F	VF	XF	Unc	BU
1996	—	—	—	5.50	—
1998	—	—	—	3.50	—

KM# 11 10 MALOTI **Weight:** 39.9400 g. **Composition:** 0.9170 Gold 1.1776 oz. AGW **Ruler:** Moshoeshoe II **Series:** F.A.O. **Reverse:** Farmer leading two oxen

Date	Mintage	F	VF	XF	Unc	BU
1969 Proof	3,000	Value: 550				

KM# 13 10 MALOTI **Weight:** 25.0800 g. **Composition:** 0.9250 Silver .7459 oz. ASW **Ruler:** Moshoeshoe II **Subject:** 10th Anniversary of Independence

Date	Mintage	F	VF	XF	Unc	BU
1976	2,300	—	—	—	20.00	—
1976 Proof	2,100	Value: 30.00				

KM# 23 10 MALOTI **Weight:** 28.2800 g. **Composition:** 0.9250 Silver .8411 oz. ASW **Ruler:** Moshoeshoe II **Subject:** Monument of King Moshoeshoe I

Date	Mintage	F	VF	XF	Unc	BU
1979	10,000	—	—	—	15.00	—
1979 Proof	5,000	Value: 20.00				

KM# 23a 10 MALOTI **Weight:** 12.0000 g. **Composition:** 0.5000 Silver .1929 oz. ASW **Ruler:** Moshoeshoe II **Subject:** Monument of King Moshoeshoe I

Date	Mintage	F	VF	XF	Unc	BU
1980	10,000	—	—	—	10.00	—
1980 Proof	5,000	Value: 15.00				

KM# 24 10 MALOTI **Weight:** 28.2800 g. **Composition:** 0.9250 Silver .8411 oz. ASW **Ruler:** Moshoeshoe II **Series:** International Year of the Child **Note:** Similar to 15 Maloti, KM#25.

Date	Mintage	F	VF	XF	Unc	BU
1979 (1981)	—	—	—	—	11.50	—
1979 (1981) Proof	37,000	Value: 13.50				

KM# 32 10 MALOTI **Weight:** 23.3300 g. **Composition:** 0.9250 Silver .6938 oz. ASW **Ruler:** Moshoeshoe II **Subject:** World Soccer Championship **Reverse:** Goalie in front of goal net

Date	Mintage	F	VF	XF	Unc	BU
1982 Proof	3,582	Value: 22.50				

KM# 34 10 MALOTI **Weight:** 23.3300 g. **Composition:** 0.9250 Silver .6938 oz. ASW **Ruler:** Moshoeshoe II **Subject:** World Soccer Championship

Date	Mintage	F	VF	XF	Unc	BU
1982 Proof	3,000	Value: 20.00				

KM# 40 10 MALOTI **Weight:** 31.1000 g. **Composition:** 0.5000 Silver .5000 oz. ASW **Ruler:** Moshoeshoe II **Subject:** George Washington **Obverse:** Similar to KM#34 **Reverse:** Washington facing left

Date	Mintage	F	VF	XF	Unc	BU
1982 Proof	7,355	Value: 17.50				

KM# 41 10 MALOTI **Weight:** 31.1000 g. **Composition:** 0.5000 Silver .5000 oz. ASW **Ruler:** Moshoeshoe II **Subject:** George Washington **Obverse:** Similar to KM#34 **Reverse:** Washington on bended knee

Date	Mintage	F	VF	XF	Unc	BU
1982 Proof	4,200	Value: 17.50				

KM# 42 10 MALOTI **Weight:** 31.1000 g. **Composition:** 0.5000 Silver .5000 oz. ASW **Ruler:** Moshoeshoe II **Subject:** George Washington **Obverse:** Similar to KM#34 **Reverse:** Washington crossing the Delaware

Date	Mintage	F	VF	XF	Unc	BU
1982 Proof	Est. 15,000	Value: 17.50				

KM# 49 10 MALOTI **Weight:** 23.3300 g. **Composition:** 0.9250 Silver .6939 oz. ASW **Ruler:** Moshoeshoe II **Subject:** Decade for Women

Date	Mintage	F	VF	XF	Unc	BU
1985 Proof	1,000	Value: 35.00				

KM# 50 10 MALOTI **Weight:** 28.2800 g. **Composition:** 0.9250 Silver .8411 oz. ASW **Ruler:** Moshoeshoe II **Subject:** Papal visit

Date	Mintage	F	VF	XF	Unc	BU
1988 Proof	Est. 15,000	Value: 45.00				

KM# 25 15 MALOTI **Weight:** 33.4000 g. **Composition:** 0.9250 Silver .9933 oz. ASW **Ruler:** Moshoeshoe II **Series:** International Year of the Child **Obverse:** Similar to 25 Maloti, KM#35

Date	Mintage	F	VF	XF	Unc	BU
1979	18,000	—	—	—	12.50	—
1979 Proof	7,500	Value: 22.50				

KM# 37 15 MALOTI **Composition:** 0.5000 Silver **Ruler:** Moshoeshoe II **Subject:** 15th Anniversary of Commonwealth Membership **Obverse:** Similar to 50 Maloti, KM#38

Date	Mintage	F	VF	XF	Unc	BU
1981 Proof	2,500	Value: 30.00				

KM# 53 15 MALOTI **Weight:** 12.0000 g. **Composition:** 0.5000 Silver .1929 oz. ASW **Ruler:** Moshoeshoe II **Subject:** 15th Anniversary of Independence

Date	Mintage	F	VF	XF	Unc	BU
1981 Proof	2,500	Value: 35.00				

KM# 12 20 MALOTI **Weight:** 79.8810 g. **Composition:** 0.9170 Gold 2.3553 oz. AGW **Ruler:** Moshoeshoe II **Series:** F.A.O. **Obverse:** Similar to 10 Maloti, KM#11 **Reverse:** Ewe and lamb grazing left

Date	Mintage	F	VF	XF	Unc	BU
1969 Proof	3,000	Value: 1,250				

KM# 35 25 MALOTI **Weight:** 16.8200 g. **Composition:** 0.9250 Silver .5003 oz. ASW **Ruler:** Moshoeshoe II **Obverse:** Duke of Edinburgh Youth Awards

Date	Mintage	F	VF	XF	Unc	BU
1981 Proof	5,000	Value: 35.00				

KM# 44 25 MALOTI **Weight:** 28.2800 g. **Composition:** 0.9250 Silver .8411 oz. ASW **Ruler:** Moshoeshoe II **Series:** International Year of Disabled Persons

Date	F	VF	XF	Unc	BU
1983	—	—	—	32.50	—
1983 Proof	—	Value: 55.00			

KM# 30 30 MALOTI **Composition:** 0.9250 Silver **Ruler:** Moshoeshoe II **Subject:** Wedding of Prince Charles and Lady Diana

Date	Mintage	F	VF	XF	Unc	BU
1981 Proof	10,000	Value: 47.50				

KM# 14 50 MALOTI **Weight:** 4.5000 g. **Composition:** 0.9000 Gold .1302 oz. AGW **Ruler:** Moshoeshoe II **Subject:** 10th Anniversary of Independence

Date	Mintage	F	VF	XF	Unc	BU
ND(1976)	700	—	—	—	125	—
ND(1976) Proof	1,910	Value: 115				

KM# 27 50 MALOTI **Weight:** 33.6200 g. **Composition:** 0.9250 Silver .9999 oz. ASW **Ruler:** Moshoeshoe II **Subject:** 110th Anniversary - Death of King Moshoeshoe I

Date	Mintage	F	VF	XF	Unc	BU
1980	2,500	—	—	—	30.00	—
1980 Proof	1,400	Value: 45.00				

KM# 38 50 MALOTI **Weight:** 33.6200 g. **Composition:** 0.9250 Silver .9999 oz. ASW **Ruler:** Moshoeshoe II **Subject:** 15th Anniversary of Commonwealth Membership

Date	Mintage	F	VF	XF	Unc	BU
1981 Proof	5,000	Value: 60.00				

KM# 15 100 MALOTI **Weight:** 9.0000 g. **Composition:** 0.9000 Gold .2604 oz. AGW **Ruler:** Moshoeshoe II **Subject:** 10th Anniversary of Independence

Date	Mintage	F	VF	XF	Unc	BU
ND(1976)	450	—	—	—	175	—
ND(1976) Proof	1,410	Value: 160				

KM# 45 200 MALOTI **Weight:** 15.9800 g. **Composition:** 0.9000 Gold .4624 oz. AGW **Ruler:** Moshoeshoe II **Series:** International Year of Disabled Persons

Date	Mintage	F	VF	XF	Unc	BU
1983	500	—	—	—	400	—
1983 Proof	500	Value: 450				

KM# 26 250 MALOTI **Weight:** 33.9300 g. **Composition:** 0.9170 Gold 1 oz. AGW **Ruler:** Moshoeshoe II **Series:** International Year of the Child **Obverse:** Similar to 15 Maloti, KM#25

Date	Mintage	F	VF	XF	Unc	BU
1979	2,500	—	—	—	425	—
1979 Proof	2,000	Value: 500				

KM# 28 250 MALOTI **Weight:** 31.1000 g. **Composition:** 0.9170 Gold .917 oz. AGW **Ruler:** Moshoeshoe II **Subject:** 110th Anniversary - Death of King Moshoeshoe I **Obverse:** Similar to 50 Maloti, KM#27

Date	Mintage	F	VF	XF	Unc	BU
1980	1,500	—	—	—	450	—
1980 Proof	3,000	Value: 475				

KM# 31 250 MALOTI **Weight:** 15.9000 g. **Composition:** 0.9170 Gold .4688 oz. AGW **Ruler:** Moshoeshoe II **Subject:** Wedding of Prince Charles and Lady Diana

Date	Mintage	F	VF	XF	Unc	BU
1981	1,000	—	—	—	225	—
1981 Proof	1,500	Value: 275				

KM# 31a 250 MALOTI **Weight:** 15.7500 g. **Composition:** 0.9950 Platinum .5039 oz. APW **Ruler:** Moshoeshoe II **Subject:** Wedding of Prince Charles and Lady Diana

Date	Mintage	F	VF	XF	Unc	BU
1981 Proof	200	Value: 550				

KM# 36 250 MALOTI **Weight:** 16.9600 g. **Composition:** 0.9170 Gold .5001 oz. AGW **Ruler:** Moshoeshoe II **Subject:** Duke of Edinburgh Youth Awards

Date	Mintage	F	VF	XF	Unc	BU
1981 Proof	1,500	Value: 275				

KM# 36a 250 MALOTI **Weight:** 15.7500 g. **Composition:** 0.9950 Platinum .5039 oz. APW **Ruler:** Moshoeshoe II **Subject:** Duke of Edinburgh Youth Awards

Date	Mintage	F	VF	XF	Unc	BU
1981 Proof	200	Value: 550				

KM# 33 250 MALOTI **Weight:** 7.1300 g. **Composition:** 0.9000 Gold .2063 oz. AGW **Ruler:** Moshoeshoe II **Subject:** Soccer Games

Date	Mintage	F	VF	XF	Unc	BU
1982 Proof	551	Value: 250				

KM# 51 250 MALOTI **Weight:** 15.9800 g. **Composition:** 0.9170 Gold .4708 oz. AGW **Ruler:** Moshoeshoe II **Subject:** Papal Visit

Date	Mintage	F	VF	XF	Unc	BU
1988 Proof	Est. 750	Value: 500				

KM# 29 500 MALOTI **Weight:** 33.9300 g. **Composition:** 0.9170 Gold 1 oz. AGW **Ruler:** Moshoeshoe II **Subject:** 110th Anniversary - Death of King Moshoeshoe I **Obverse:** Similar to 50 Maloti, KM#27

Date	Mintage	F	VF	XF	Unc	BU
1980	1,500	—	—	—	475	—
1980 Proof	3,000	Value: 500				

KM# 39 500 MALOTI **Weight:** 33.9300 g. **Composition:** 0.9170 Gold 1 oz. AGW **Ruler:** Moshoeshoe II **Subject:** 15th Anniversary of Commonwealth Membership

Date	Mintage	F	VF	XF	Unc	BU
1981 Proof	500	Value: 550				

KM# 39a 500 MALOTI **Weight:** 31.5000 g. **Composition:** 0.9950 Platinum 1.0078 oz. APW **Ruler:** Moshoeshoe II **Subject:** 15th Anniversary of Commonwealth Membership

Date	Mintage	F	VF	XF	Unc	BU
1981 Proof	200	Value: 825				

KM# 57 500 MALOTI **Weight:** 33.9300 g. **Composition:** 0.9166 Gold 1 oz. AGW **Ruler:** Moshoeshoe II **Subject:** Royal Wedding **Obverse:** Lesotho arms **Reverse:** Conjoined bust of Diana and Charles left

Date	F	VF	XF	Unc	BU
ND(1981) Proof, rare	—	—	—	—	—

KM# 57a 500 MALOTI **Weight:** 33.4800 g. **Composition:** 0.9995 Platinum 1 oz. APW **Ruler:** Moshoeshoe II **Subject:** Royal Wedding **Obverse:** Lesotho arms **Reverse:** Conjoined bust of Diana and Charles left

Date	F	VF	XF	Unc	BU
ND(1981) Proof, rare	—	—	—	—	—

PATTERNS

Including off metal strikes

KM#	Date	Mintage	Identification	Mkt Val
Pn1	1966	2	5 Licente. 0.9000 Silver.	—
Pn2	1966	2	10 Licente. 0.9000 Silver.	—
Pn3	1966	2	20 Licente. 0.9000 Silver.	—
Pn4	1966	2	50 Licente. 0.9000 Silver.	—
Pn6	1966	7	2 Maloti. 0.9160 Gold.	500
Pn7	1966	7	4 Maloti. 0.9160 Gold.	700
Pn8	1966	7	10 Maloti. 0.9160 Gold.	950
Pn9	1966	7	20 Maloti. 0.9160 Gold.	1,250
Pn10	1979	5	15 Maloti. Copper-Nickel. KM25. Medallic alignment.	110
Pn10.2a	1979	—	15 Maloti. 0.9250 Silver. 33.5100 g.	—
Pn11	1979	15	15 Maloti. Copper-Nickel. KM25. Coin alignment.	80.00
Pn12	1979	15	250 Maloti. Brass. KM26.	75.00
Pn13	1979	5	250 Maloti. Copper-Nickel. KM26. Medallic alignment.	110
Pn14	1979	10	250 Maloti. Silver. 20.1500 g. KM26.	115
Pn15	1980	10	50 Maloti. Copper-Nickel. KM27. Medallic alignment.	125
Pn16	1980	10	50 Maloti. Copper-Nickel. Coin alignment.	125
Pn17	1980	10	250 Maloti. Brass. KM28. Coin alignment.	110

KM#	Date	Mintage	Identification	Mkt Val
Pn18	1980	10	250 Maloti. Copper-Nickel. KM28. Medallic alignment.	100
Pn19	1980	10	500 Maloti. Brass. KM29. Coin alignment.	110
Pn20	1980	10	500 Maloti. Copper-Nickel. KM29. Medallic alignment.	110

PIEFORTS

KM#	Date	Mintage	Identification	Mkt Val
P1	1979	50	10 Maloti. KM24.	135
P2	1981	—	250 Maloti. KM31.	550
P3	1983	—	25 Maloti. KM4.	90.00
P4	1983	100	200 Maloti. KM45.	800

MINT SETS

KM#	Date	Mintage	Identification	Issue Price	Mkt Val
MS1	1976 (3)	450	KM13-15	194	315
MS2	1989 (7)	—	KM16-22	—	11.50

PROOF SETS

KM#	Date	Mintage	Identification	Issue Price	Mkt Val
PS1	1966 (7)	1,500	KM1-7	301	475
PS4	1966 (4)	3,500	KM1, 2, 3.1, 4.1	28.00	40.00
PS5	1966 (3)	2,000	KM5-7	301	430
PSA5	1966 (4)	—	KM1, 2, 3.2, 4.2	28.00	40.00
PS3	1966 (4)	2	KMPn1-4	—	—
PS2	1966 (4)	7	KMPn6-9	—	3,000
PS6	1969 (5)	3,000	KM8-12	450	2,450
PS7	1976 (3)	1,410	KM13-15	285	300
PS8	1976 (2)	—	KM14-15	270	270
PS9	1976 (2)	—	KM13-14	—	135
PS10	1979 (7)	10,000	KM16-22	34.00	15.00
PS11	1980 (8)	10,000	KM16-22, 23a	51.00	25.00
PS12	1981 (8)	2,500	KM16-22, 53	55.00	45.00

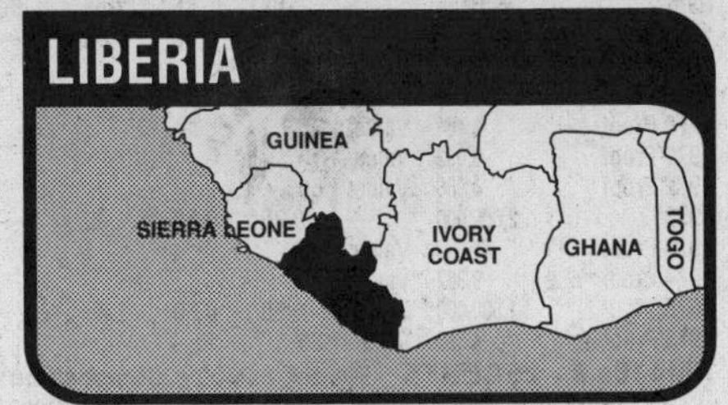

The Republic of Liberia, located on the southern side of the West African bulge between Sierra Leone and Ivory Coast, has an area of 38,250 sq. mi. (111,370 sq. km) and a population of 2.2 million. Capital: Monrovia. The major industries are agriculture, mining and lumbering. Iron ore, diamonds, rubber, coffee and coca are exported.

The Liberian coast was explored and charted by Portuguese navigator Pedro de Cintra in 1461. For the following three centuries Portuguese traders visited the area regularly to trade for gold, slaves and pepper. The modern country of Liberia, Africa's first republic, was settled in1822 by the American Colonization Society as a homeland for American freed slaves, with the U.S. government furnishing funds and assisting in negotiations for procurement of land from the native chiefs. The various settlements united in 1839 to form the Commonwealth of Liberia, and in 1847 established the country as a republic with a constitution modeled after that of the United States.

U.S. money was declared legal tender in Liberia in 1943, replacing British West African currency.

Most of the Liberian pattern series, particularly of the1888-90 period are acknowledged to have been 'unofficial' privately sponsored issues, but they are none-the-less avidly collected by many collectors of Liberian coins. The 'K' number designations on these pieces refer to a listing of Liberian patterns compiled and published by Ernst Kraus.

MINT MARKS

B - Bern, Switzerland
H - Heaton, Birmingham
(l) - London
(s) - San Francisco, U.S.
FM - Franklin Mint, U.S.A.*
PM - Pobjoy Mint

***NOTE:** From 1975-1985 the Franklin Mint produced coinage in up to 3 different qualities. Qualities of issue are designated in ( ) after each date and are defined as follows:

(M) MATTE - Normal circulation strike or a dull finish produced by sandblasting special uncirculated (polish finish) or proof quality dies.

(U) SPECIAL UNCIRCULATED - Polished or prooflike in appearance without any frosted features.

(P) PROOF - The highest quality obtainable having mirror-like fields and frosted features.

MONETARY SYSTEM

100 Cents = 1 Dollar

REPUBLIC

STANDARD COINAGE

100 Cents = 1 Dollar

KM# 10 1/2 CENT Composition: Brass

Date	Mintage	F	VF	XF	Unc	BU
1937	1,000,000	0.10	0.25	0.40	1.00	—

KM# 10a 1/2 CENT Composition: Copper-Nickel

Date	Mintage	F	VF	XF	Unc	BU
1941	250,000	0.15	0.35	0.55	1.25	—

KM# 5 CENT Composition: Bronze

Date	Mintage	F	VF	XF	Unc	BU
1906H	180,000	4.50	10.00	22.00	50.00	—
1906H Proof	—	Value: 130				

KM# 11 CENT Composition: Brass

Date	Mintage	F	VF	XF	Unc	BU
1937	1,000,000	0.20	0.50	1.50	6.00	—

KM# 11a CENT Composition: Copper-Nickel

Date	Mintage	F	VF	XF	Unc	BU
1941	250,000	0.50	2.50	7.50	40.00	—

KM# 13 CENT Composition: Bronze

Date	Mintage	F	VF	XF	Unc	BU
1960	500,000	—	—	0.10	0.50	0.60
1961	7,000,000	—	—	0.10	0.50	0.60
1968(l)	3,000,000	—	—	0.10	0.50	0.60
1968(s) Proof	14,000	Value: 1.00				
1969 Proof	5,056	Value: 1.00				
1970 Proof	3,464	Value: 1.00				
1971 Proof	3,032	Value: 1.00				
1972(d)	10,000,000	—	—	0.10	0.50	0.60
1972(s) Proof	4,866	Value: 1.00				
1973 Proof	11,000	Value: 1.00				
1974 Proof	9,362	Value: 1.00				
1975	5,000,000	—	—	0.10	0.50	0.60
1975 Proof	4,056	Value: 1.00				
1976 Proof	2,131	Value: 1.00				
1977	2,500,000	—	—	0.10	0.50	0.60
1977 Proof	920	Value: 1.00				
1978FM Proof	7,311	Value: 1.00				
1983FM	2,500,000	—	—	0.10	0.50	0.60
1984	2,500,000	—	—	0.10	0.50	0.60

KM# 13a CENT Composition: Bronze **Edge Lettering:** O.A.U. July 1979

Date	Mintage	F	VF	XF	Unc	BU
1979FM Proof	1,857	Value: 1.00				

KM# 6 2 CENTS Composition: Bronze

Date	Mintage	F	VF	XF	Unc	BU
1906H	108,000	5.00	12.00	30.00	75.00	—
1906H Proof	—	Value: 160				

KM# 12 2 CENTS Composition: Brass

Date	Mintage	F	VF	XF	Unc	BU
1937	1,000,000	0.15	0.35	1.00	6.00	—

KM# 12a 2 CENTS Composition: Copper-Nickel

Date	Mintage	F	VF	XF	Unc	BU
1941	810,000	0.10	0.25	0.50	2.50	—
1978FM Proof	7,311	Value: 2.00				

KM# 12b 2 CENTS Composition: Copper-Nickel **Edge Lettering:** O.A.U. July 1979

Date	Mintage	F	VF	XF	Unc	BU
1979FM Proof	1,857	Value: 2.00				

KM# 14 5 CENTS Composition: Copper-Nickel

Date	Mintage	F	VF	XF	Unc	BU
1960	1,000,000	—	0.10	0.15	0.50	0.65
1961	3,200,000	—	0.10	0.15	0.50	0.65
1968 Proof	15,000	Value: 0.85				
1969 Proof	5,056	Value: 0.85				
1970 Proof	3,464	Value: 1.25				
1971 Proof	3,032	Value: 1.25				
1972(d)	3,000,000	—	0.10	0.15	0.40	0.65
1972(s) Proof	4,866	Value: 0.85				
1973 Proof	11,000	Value: 0.85				
1974 Proof	9,362	Value: 0.85				

Date	Mintage	F	VF	XF	Unc	BU
1975	3,000,000	—	0.10	0.15	0.40	0.65
1975 Proof	4,056	Value: 0.85				
1976 Proof	2,131	Value: 0.85				
1977	—	—	0.10	0.15	0.50	0.65
1977 Proof	920	Value: 0.85				
1978FM Proof	7,311	Value: 0.85				
1983FM	1,000,000	—	0.10	0.15	0.40	0.65
1984	1,000,000	—	0.10	0.15	0.40	0.65

KM# 14a 5 CENTS Composition: Copper-Nickel **Edge Lettering:** O.A.U. July 1979

Date	Mintage	F	VF	XF	Unc	BU
1979FM Proof	1,857	Value: 2.00				

KM# 474 5 CENTS Weight: 2.2500 g. **Composition:** Aluminum **Obverse:** National arms **Reverse:** Dragon and denomination **Edge:** Plain **Size:** 26.9 mm.

Date	F	VF	XF	Unc	BU
2000	—	—	—	0.75	—

KM# 7 10 CENTS Weight: 2.3200 g. **Composition:** 0.9250 Silver .0690 oz. ASW

Date	Mintage	F	VF	XF	Unc	BU
1906H	35,000	5.00	12.50	32.50	100	—
1906H Proof	—	Value: 250				

KM# 15 10 CENTS Weight: 2.0700 g. **Composition:** 0.9000 Silver .0599 oz. ASW

Date	Mintage	F	VF	XF	Unc	BU
1960	1,000,000	BV	0.75	1.25	3.00	—
1961	1,200,000	BV	0.75	1.25	3.00	—

KM# 15a.1 10 CENTS Weight: 2.1000 g. **Composition:** Copper-Nickel

Date	Mintage	F	VF	XF	Unc	BU
1966	2,000,000	—	0.15	0.25	0.50	—

KM# 15a.2 10 CENTS Weight: 1.8000 g. **Composition:** Copper-Nickel

Date	Mintage	F	VF	XF	Unc	BU
1968 Proof	14,000	Value: 1.25				
1969 Proof	5,056	Value: 1.25				
1970(d)	2,500,000	—	0.15	0.25	0.50	—
1970(s) Proof	3,464	Value: 1.50				
1971 Proof	3,032	Value: 1.50				
1972 Proof	4,866	Value: 1.25				
1973 Proof	11,000	Value: 1.00				
1974 Proof	9,362	Value: 1.00				
1975	4,500	—	0.15	0.20	0.35	—
1975 Proof	4,056	Value: 1.00				
1976 Proof	2,131	Value: 1.00				
1977	—	—	0.15	0.25	0.75	—
1977 Proof	920	Value: 1.00				
1978FM Proof	7,311	Value: 1.00				
1983FM	500,000	—	0.15	0.25	0.75	—
1984FM	500,000	—	0.15	0.25	0.75	—
1987	10,000,000	—	0.15	0.25	0.75	—

KM# 15b 10 CENTS Weight: 1.8000 g. **Composition:** Copper-Nickel **Edge Lettering:** O.A.U. July 1979

Date	Mintage	F	VF	XF	Unc	BU
1979FM Proof	1,857	Value: 2.00				

KM# 8 25 CENTS Weight: 5.8000 g. **Composition:** 0.9250 Silver .1725 oz. ASW

Date	Mintage	F	VF	XF	Unc	BU
1906H	34,000	6.00	12.50	35.00	120	—
1906H Proof	—	Value: 275				

KM# 16 25 CENTS Weight: 5.1800 g. **Composition:** 0.9000 Silver .1499 oz. ASW

Date	Mintage	F	VF	XF	Unc	BU
1960	900,000	BV	1.50	2.00	4.50	—
1961	1,200,000	BV	1.50	2.00	4.50	—

KM# 16a.1 25 CENTS Weight: 5.2000 g. **Composition:** Copper-Nickel

Date	Mintage	F	VF	XF	Unc	BU
1966	800,000	—	0.25	0.65	1.25	—

KM# 16a.2 25 CENTS Weight: 4.8000 g. **Composition:** Copper-Nickel **Note:** 1 and 1.15mm rim varieties exist.

Date	Mintage	F	VF	XF	Unc	BU
1968(d)	1,600,000	—	0.25	0.50	1.00	—
1968(s) Proof	14,000	Value: 1.50				
1969 Proof	5,056	Value: 1.50				
1970 Proof	3,464	Value: 1.75				
1971 Proof	3,032	Value: 1.75				
1972 Proof	4,866	Value: 1.50				
1973	2,000,000	—	0.25	0.50	1.00	—
1973 Proof	11,000	Value: 1.25				
1974 Proof	9,362	Value: 1.25				
1975	1,600,000	—	0.25	0.50	1.00	—
1975 Proof	4,056	Value: 1.25				

KM# 16a.3 25 CENTS Weight: 5.2000 g. **Composition:** Copper-Nickel **Reverse:** Large letters, higher inscription **Note:** Struck in 1988.

Date	Mintage	F	VF	XF	Unc	BU
1968 Restrike	2,400,000	—	0.25	0.50	1.00	—

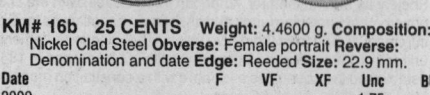

KM# 16b 25 CENTS Weight: 4.4600 g. **Composition:** Nickel Clad Steel **Obverse:** Female portrait **Reverse:** Denomination and date **Edge:** Reeded **Size:** 22.9 mm.

Date	F	VF	XF	Unc	BU
2000	—	—	—	1.75	—

KM# 30 25 CENTS Weight: 5.2000 g. **Composition:** Copper-Nickel **Series:** F.A.O.

Date	Mintage	F	VF	XF	Unc	BU
1976	800,000	—	0.25	0.75	1.75	—
1976 Proof	2,131	Value: 4.00				
1977 Proof	920	Value: 5.00				
1978FM Proof	7,311	Value: 2.50				

KM# 30a 25 CENTS Weight: 5.2000 g. **Composition:** Copper-Nickel **Edge Lettering:** O.A.U. July 1979

Date	Mintage	F	VF	XF	Unc	BU
1979FM Proof	1,857	Value: 3.50				

KM# 9 50 CENTS Weight: 11.6000 g. **Composition:** 0.9250 Silver .3450 oz. ASW

Date	Mintage	F	VF	XF	Unc	BU
1906H	24,000	10.00	20.00	50.00	265	—
1906H Proof	—	Value: 425				

KM# 17 50 CENTS Weight: 10.3700 g. **Composition:** 0.9000 Silver .3001 oz. ASW

Date	Mintage	F	VF	XF	Unc	BU
1960	1,100,000	BV	3.00	4.00	8.00	—
1961	800,000	BV	3.00	4.00	8.00	—

KM# 17a.2 50 CENTS Weight: 8.9000 g. **Composition:** Copper-Nickel

Date	Mintage	F	VF	XF	Unc	BU
1968(l)	1,000,000	—	0.60	0.80	1.50	—
1968(s) Proof	14,000	Value: 1.50				
1969 Proof	5,056	Value: 1.50				
1970 Proof	3,464	Value: 2.50				
1971 Proof	3,032	Value: 2.50				
1972 Proof	4,866	Value: 1.50				
1973	1,000,000	—	0.60	0.75	1.25	—
1973 Proof	11,000	Value: 1.50				
1974 Proof	9,362	Value: 1.50				
1975	800,000	—	0.60	0.75	1.25	—
1975 Proof	4,056	Value: 1.50				

KM# 17a.1 50 CENTS Weight: 10.4000 g. **Composition:** Copper-Nickel

Date	Mintage	F	VF	XF	Unc	BU
1966	200,000	—	0.75	1.00	1.50	—

KM# 17b.2 50 CENTS Weight: 9.0000 g. **Composition:** Nickel-Clad Steel **Obverse:** Portrait **Reverse:** Denomination **Edge:** Reeded **Size:** 28 mm.

Date	F	VF	XF	Unc	BU
2000	—	—	—	3.50	—

KM# 31 50 CENTS Weight: 8.9000 g. **Composition:** Copper-Nickel

Date	Mintage	F	VF	XF	Unc	BU
1976	1,000,000	—	0.60	1.00	2.50	—
1976 Proof	2,131	Value: 5.50				
1977 Proof	920	Value: 6.50				
1978FM Proof	7,311	Value: 4.00				
1987	1,800,000	—	0.60	1.00	2.50	—

KM# 31a 50 CENTS Weight: 8.9000 g. **Composition:** Copper-Nickel **Edge Lettering:** O.A.U. July 1979

Date	Mintage	F	VF	XF	Unc	BU
1979FM Proof	1,857	Value: 4.50				

KM# 18 DOLLAR Weight: 20.7400 g. **Composition:** 0.9000 Silver .6001 oz. ASW

Date	Mintage	F	VF	XF	Unc	BU
1961	200,000	BV	4.50	6.00	12.50	15.00
1962	1,000,000	BV	4.50	5.50	9.00	12.50

KM# 18a.1 DOLLAR Weight: 20.7000 g. **Composition:** Copper-Nickel

Date	Mintage	F	VF	XF	Unc	BU
1966	1,000,000	—	1.00	1.50	2.25	3.50

KM# 18a.2 DOLLAR Weight: 18.0000 g. **Composition:** Copper-Nickel

Date	Mintage	F	VF	XF	Unc	BU
1968(l)	1,000,000	—	1.00	1.50	2.25	3.50
1968(s) Proof	14,000	Value: 2.00				
1969 Proof	5,056	Value: 2.00				
1970(d)	2,000,000	—	1.00	1.50	3.00	4.50
1970(s) Proof	3,464	Value: 6.00				
1971 Proof	3,032	Value: 4.50				
1972 Proof	4,866	Value: 4.50				
1973 Proof	11,000	Value: 3.00				
1974 Proof	9,362	Value: 3.00				
1975	400,000	—	1.25	1.75	3.00	4.50
1975 Proof	4,056	Value: 3.00				

KM# 32 DOLLAR Weight: 18.0000 g. **Composition:** Copper-Nickel

Date	Mintage	F	VF	XF	Unc	BU
1976	2,000,000	—	2.50	4.50	8.00	—
1976 Proof	2,131	Value: 12.00				
1977 Proof	920	Value: 13.50				
1978FM Proof	7,311	Value: 11.00				
1987	1,500,000	—	1.50	3.00	6.00	—

KM# 32a DOLLAR Weight: 18.0000 g. **Composition:** Copper-Nickel **Edge Lettering:** O.A.U. July 1979

Date	Mintage	F	VF	XF	Unc	BU
1979FM Proof	1,857	Value: 10.00				

KM# 98 DOLLAR **Weight:** 18.0000 g. **Composition:** Copper-Nickel **Series:** Preserve Planet Earth **Reverse:** Protoceratops

Date	F	VF	XF	Unc	BU
1993	—	—	—	8.50	—

KM# 109 DOLLAR **Weight:** 28.5200 g. **Composition:** Copper-Nickel **Series:** Preserve Planet Earth **Reverse:** Corythosaurus

Date	F	VF	XF	Unc	BU
1993	—	—	—	8.50	—

KM# 112 DOLLAR **Weight:** 28.5200 g. **Composition:** Copper-Nickel **Series:** Preserve Planet Earth **Reverse:** Atchaeopteryx **Note:** Incorrect spelling.

Date	F	VF	XF	Unc	BU
1993	—	—	—	8.50	—

KM# 101 DOLLAR **Weight:** 18.0000 g. **Composition:** Copper-Nickel **Subject:** Nolan Ryan **Note:** Similar to 10 Dollars, KM#102.

Date	F	VF	XF	Unc	BU
1993	—	—	—	8.50	—

KM# 118 DOLLAR **Weight:** 28.5200 g. **Composition:** Copper-Nickel **Series:** Preserve Planet Earth **Reverse:** Gorillas **Note:** Similar to 10 Dollars, KM#119.

Date	F	VF	XF	Unc	BU
1994	—	—	—	8.50	—

KM# 121 DOLLAR **Weight:** 28.5200 g. **Composition:** Copper-Nickel **Series:** Preserve Planet Earth **Reverse:** Pygmy Hippopotami **Note:** Similar to 10 Dollars, KM#122.

Date	F	VF	XF	Unc	BU
1994	—	—	—	8.50	—

KM# 124 DOLLAR **Weight:** 28.5200 g. **Composition:** Copper-Nickel **Series:** Preserve Planet Earth **Reverse:** Trionyx Turtle **Note:** Similar to 10 Dollars, KM#125.

Date	F	VF	XF	Unc	BU
1994	—	—	—	8.50	—

KM# 115 DOLLAR **Weight:** 28.5200 g. **Composition:** Copper-Nickel **Series:** Preserve Planet Earth **Reverse:** Archaeopteryx **Note:** Correct spelling.

Date	F	VF	XF	Unc	BU
1994	—	—	—	8.00	—

KM# 131 DOLLAR **Weight:** 28.5200 g. **Composition:** Copper-Nickel **Subject:** Centennial - Babe Ruth Sultan of Swat

Date	F	VF	XF	Unc	BU
1994	—	—	—	8.00	—

KM# 131a DOLLAR **Composition:** Gold Plated Copper-Nickel **Note:** Issued in a first day cover.

Date	F	VF	XF	Unc	BU
1994	—	—	—	20.00	—

KM# 139 DOLLAR **Composition:** Copper-Nickel **Subject:** Damon Hill - Formula One Race Car

Date	F	VF	XF	Unc	BU
1994 Prooflike	—	—	—	7.00	—

KM# 248 DOLLAR **Composition:** Copper-Nickel **Subject:** Hall of Fame - Roberto Clemente

Date	F	VF	XF	Unc	BU
1994	—	—	—	8.00	—

KM# 249 DOLLAR **Composition:** Copper-Nickel **Subject:** Hall of Fame - Reggie Jackson

Date	F	VF	XF	Unc	BU
1994	—	—	—	8.00	—

KM# 411 DOLLAR **Composition:** Copper-Nickel **Subject:** President Nelson Mandela **Obverse:** National arms **Reverse:** Portrait and gazelle

Date	F	VF	XF	Unc	BU
1994	—	—	—	8.50	—

KM# 133 DOLLAR **Composition:** Copper-Nickel **Series:** Preserve Planet Earth **Reverse:** Leopard; Similar to 10 Dollars, KM#134.

Date	F	VF	XF	Unc	BU
1995	—	—	—	8.50	—

KM# 136 DOLLAR **Composition:** Copper-Nickel **Series:** Preserve Planet Earth **Reverse:** Storks; Similar to 10 Dollars, KM#137

Date	F	VF	XF	Unc	BU
1995	—	—	—	8.00	—

KM# 140 DOLLAR **Composition:** Copper-Nickel **Subject:** Sir Winston Churchill **Reverse:** Similar to 10 Dollars, KM#145

Date	F	VF	XF	Unc	BU
1995	—	—	—	6.00	—

KM# 141 DOLLAR **Composition:** Copper-Nickel **Subject:** President Franklin D. Roosevelt **Reverse:** Similar to 10 Dollars, KM#146

Date	F	VF	XF	Unc	BU
1995	—	—	—	6.00	—

KM# 142 DOLLAR **Composition:** Copper-Nickel **Subject:** General George Patton **Reverse:** Similar to 10 Dollars, KM#147

Date	F	VF	XF	Unc	BU
1995	—	—	—	6.00	—

KM# 143 DOLLAR **Composition:** Copper-Nickel **Subject:** President Harry S. Truman **Reverse:** Similar to 10 Dollars, KM#148

Date	F	VF	XF	Unc	BU
1995	—	—	—	6.00	—

KM# 144 DOLLAR **Composition:** Copper-Nickel **Subject:** President Charles de Gaulle **Reverse:** Similar to 10 Dollars, KM#149

Date	F	VF	XF	Unc	BU
1995	—	—	—	6.00	—

KM# 158 DOLLAR **Composition:** Copper-Nickel **Subject:** Dr. Sun Yat-sen **Reverse:** Similar to 10 Dollars, KM#159

Date	F	VF	XF	Unc	BU
1995	—	—	—	6.50	—

KM# 161 DOLLAR **Composition:** Copper-Nickel **Subject:** General Chiang Kai-shek **Reverse:** Similar to 10 Dollars, KM#162

Date	F	VF	XF	Unc	BU
1995	—	—	—	6.50	—

KM# 164 DOLLAR **Composition:** Copper-Nickel **Subject:** Cairo Conference - Chiang Kai-shek - Roosevelt - Churchill **Reverse:** Similar to 10 Dollars, KM#165

Date	F	VF	XF	Unc	BU
1995	—	—	—	6.50	—

KM# 167 DOLLAR **Composition:** Copper-Nickel **Subject:** 375th Anniversary - Pilgrim Fathers **Reverse:** The "Mayflower"

Date	F	VF	XF	Unc	BU
1995	—	—	—	6.00	—

KM# 168 DOLLAR **Composition:** Copper-Nickel **Subject:** 375th Anniversary - Pilgrim Fathers **Reverse:** First Thanksgiving scene

Date	F	VF	XF	Unc	BU
1995	—	—	—	6.00	—

KM# 169 DOLLAR **Composition:** Copper-Nickel **Subject:** 375th Anniversary - Pilgrim Fathers **Reverse:** Cape Cod and Pilgrims in skiff

Date	F	VF	XF	Unc	BU
1995	—	—	—	6.00	—

KM# 170 DOLLAR **Composition:** Copper-Nickel **Subject:** 375th Anniversary - Pilgrim Fathers **Reverse:** Pilgrim landing party

Date	F	VF	XF	Unc	BU
1995	—	—	—	6.00	—

KM# 412 DOLLAR **Composition:** Copper-Nickel **Subject:** Nations for Peace **Obverse:** National arms **Reverse:** Paper dolls, UN logo

Date	F	VF	XF	Unc	BU
1995	—	—	—	8.50	—

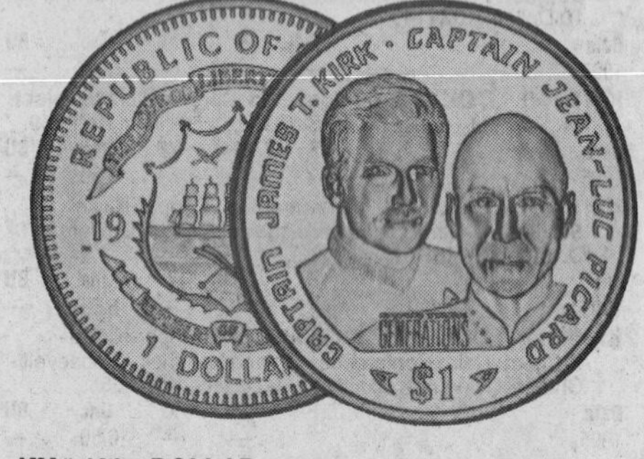

KM# 128 DOLLAR **Composition:** Copper-Nickel **Subject:** Star Trek **Reverse:** Captains Kirk and Picard **Note:** Similar to 10 Dollars, KM#129.

Date	F	VF	XF	Unc	BU
1995	—	—	—	7.50	—

KM# 207 DOLLAR **Composition:** Copper-Nickel **Subject:** Star Trek **Reverse:** Starships NCC-1701 and NCC-1701D **Note:** Similar to 10 Dollars, KM#208.

Date	F	VF	XF	Unc	BU
1996	—	—	—	8.50	—

KM# 210 DOLLAR **Composition:** Copper-Nickel **Subject:** Star Trek **Reverse:** Scott and McCoy **Note:** Similar to 10 Dollars, KM#211.

Date	F	VF	XF	Unc	BU
1996	—	—	—	8.50	—

KM# 213 DOLLAR **Composition:** Copper-Nickel **Subject:** Star Trek **Reverse:** LaForge and Data **Note:** Similar to 10 Dollars, KM#214.

Date	F	VF	XF	Unc	BU
1996	—	—	—	8.50	—

KM# 216 DOLLAR **Composition:** Copper-Nickel **Subject:** Star Trek **Reverse:** Spock and Uhura **Note:** Similar to 10 Dollars, KM#217.

Date	F	VF	XF	Unc	BU
1996	—	—	—	8.50	—

KM# 219 DOLLAR **Composition:** Copper-Nickel **Subject:** Star Trek **Reverse:** Worf and Dr. Crusher **Note:** Similar to 10 Dollars, KM#220.

Date	F	VF	XF	Unc	BU
1996	—	—	—	8.50	—

KM# 222 DOLLAR **Composition:** Copper-Nickel **Series:** Preserve Planet Earth **Reverse:** Grey Parrot **Note:** Similar to 10 Dollars, KM#223.

Date	F	VF	XF	Unc	BU
1996	—	—	—	8.00	—

KM# 225 DOLLAR **Composition:** Copper-Nickel **Series:** Preserve Planet Earth **Reverse:** Love Birds **Note:** Similar to 10 Dollars, KM#226.

Date	F	VF	XF	Unc	BU
1996	—	—	—	8.00	—

KM# 254 DOLLAR **Composition:** Copper-Nickel **Subject:** Chairman Mao Zedong **Note:** Similar to 10 Dollars, KM#256. Issued in first day cover.

Date	Mintage	F	VF	XF	Unc	BU
1996	20,000	—	—	—	7.50	—

KM# 260 DOLLAR **Composition:** Copper-Nickel **Reverse:** Chairman Mao Zedong and President Nixon **Note:** Similar to 10 Dollars, KM#262. Issued in first day cover.

Date	Mintage	F	VF	XF	Unc	BU
1996	20,000	—	—	—	7.50	—

KM# 263 DOLLAR **Composition:** Copper-Nickel **Subject:** Pioneers of the West **Reverse:** Daniel Boone **Note:** Similar to 10 Dollars, KM#264.

Date	F	VF	XF	Unc	BU
1996	—	—	—	7.50	—

KM# 266 DOLLAR **Composition:** Copper-Nickel **Subject:** Pioneers of the West **Reverse:** Davy Crockett **Note:** Similar to 10 Dollars, KM#267.

Date	F	VF	XF	Unc	BU
1996	—	—	—	7.50	—

KM# 269 DOLLAR **Composition:** Copper-Nickel **Subject:** Pioneers of the West **Reverse:** Jim Bowie **Note:** Similar to 10 Dollars, KM#270.

Date	F	VF	XF	Unc	BU
1996	—	—	—	7.50	—

KM# 272 DOLLAR **Composition:** Copper-Nickel **Subject:** Pioneers of the West **Reverse:** Kit Carson **Note:** Similar to 10 Dollars, KM#273.

Date	F	VF	XF	Unc	BU
1996	—	—	—	7.50	—

KM# 275 DOLLAR **Composition:** Copper-Nickel **Subject:** Pioneers of the West **Reverse:** Wild Bill Hickok **Note:** Similar to 10 Dollars, KM#276.

Date	F	VF	XF	Unc	BU
1996	—	—	—	7.50	—

KM# 278 DOLLAR **Composition:** Copper-Nickel **Subject:** Pioneers of the West **Reverse:** Buffalo Bill **Note:** Similar to 10 Dollars, KM#279.

Date	F	VF	XF	Unc	BU
1996	—	—	—	7.50	—

KM# 560 DOLLAR **Composition:** Silver **Reverse:** Multicolored fishes

Date	F	VF	XF	Unc	BU
1996B Proof	— Value: 15.00				

KM# 426 DOLLAR **Weight:** 13.9400 g. **Composition:** Copper **Subject:** AZA Species Survival Plan **Obverse:** National arms **Reverse:** Seated panda eating **Edge:** Reeded **Size:** 32 mm.

Date	F	VF	XF	Unc	BU
1997	—	—	—	6.00	—

KM#313 DOLLAR **Composition:** Copper-Nickel **Subject:** Return of Hong Kong - Dragon **Obverse:** National arms

Date	F	VF	XF	Unc	BU
1997	—	—	—	8.50	—

KM# 320 DOLLAR **Composition:** Copper-Nickel **Subject:** Fiftieth Anniversary of the Kon-Tiki Expedition **Obverse:** National arms

Date	F	VF	XF	Unc	BU
1997	—	—	—	8.50	—

KM# 286 DOLLAR **Composition:** Copper-Nickel **Subject:** WWII - Evacuation of Dunkirk **Note:** Similar to 10 Dollars, KM#287.

Date	F	VF	XF	Unc	BU
1997	—	—	—	8.50	—

KM# 288 DOLLAR **Composition:** Copper-Nickel **Subject:** WWII - Liberation of the Philippines **Note:** Similar to 10 Dollars, KM#289.

Date	F	VF	XF	Unc	BU
1997	—	—	—	8.50	—

KM# 290 DOLLAR **Composition:** Copper-Nickel **Subject:** WWII - Defense of Stalingrad **Note:** Similar to 10 Dollars, KM#291.

Date	F	VF	XF	Unc	BU
1997	—	—	—	8.50	—

KM# 292 DOLLAR **Composition:** Copper-Nickel **Subject:** WWII - Arnhem **Note:** Similar to 10 Dollars, KM#293

Date	F	VF	XF	Unc	BU
1997	—	—	—	8.50	—

KM# 294 DOLLAR **Composition:** Copper-Nickel **Subject** WWII - Raid on the Dams **Note:** Similar to 10 Dollars, KM#295

Date	F	VF	XF	Unc	BU
1997	—	—	—	8.50	—

KM# 296 DOLLAR **Composition:** Copper-Nickel **Subject** WWII - West African Campaign **Note:** Similar to 10 Dollars, KM#297.

Date	F	VF	XF	Unc	BU
1997	—	—	—	8.50	—

KM# 298 DOLLAR **Composition:** Copper-Nickel **Subject:** WWII - North African Campaign **Note:** Similar to 10 Dollars, KM#299.

Date	F	VF	XF	Unc	BU
1997	—	—	—	8.50	—

KM# 300 DOLLAR **Composition:** Copper-Nickel **Subject** WWII - The Dieppe Raid **Note:** Similar to 10 Dollars, KM#301

Date	F	VF	XF	Unc	BU
1997	—	—	—	8.50	—

KM# 302 DOLLAR **Composition:** Copper-Nickel **Subject** WWII - Iwo Jima **Note:** Similar to 10 Dollars, KM#303.

Date	F	VF	XF	Unc	BU
1997	—	—	—	8.50	—

KM# 304 DOLLAR **Composition:** Copper-Nickel **Subject:** WWII - Battle of Britain **Note:** Similar to 10 Dollars, KM#305

Date	F	VF	XF	Unc	BU
1997	—	—	—	8.50	—

KM# 306 DOLLAR **Composition:** Copper-Nickel **Subject:** WWII - Liberation of Paris **Note:** Similar to 10 Dollars, KM#307

Date	F	VF	XF	Unc	BU
1997	—	—	—	8.50	—

KM# 308 DOLLAR **Composition:** Copper-Nickel **Subject:** WWII - Burma Campaign **Note:** Similar to 10 Dollars, KM#309.

Date	F	VF	XF	Unc	BU
1997	—	—	—	8.50	—

KM# 310 DOLLAR **Composition:** Copper-Nickel **Subject:** Mahatma Gandhi **Note:** Similar to 10 Dollars, KM#311.

Date	F	VF	XF	Unc	BU
1997	—	—	—	8.00	—

KM# 324 DOLLAR **Composition:** Copper-Nickel **Subject:** Jurassic Park - Stegosaurus **Obverse:** National arms **Note:** Similar to 10 Dollars, KM#325.

Date	F	VF	XF	Unc	BU
1997	—	—	—	9.00	—

KM# 327 DOLLAR **Composition:** Copper-Nickel **Subject:** Golden Wedding Anniversary **Obverse:** National arms **Reverse:** E & P initials above two shields **Note:** Similar to 10 Dollars, KM#328.

Date	F	VF	XF	Unc	BU
1997	—	—	—	7.50	—

KM# 330 DOLLAR **Composition:** Copper-Nickel **Subject:** Golden Wedding Anniversary **Obverse:** National arms **Reverse:** Royal couple with horse **Note:** Similar to 10 Dollars, KM#331.

Date	F	VF	XF	Unc	BU
1997	—	—	—	7.50	—

KM# 333 DOLLAR **Composition:** Copper-Nickel **Subject:** Golden Wedding Anniversary **Obverse:** National arms **Reverse:** Couple with dogs **Note:** Similar to 10 Dollars, KM#334.

Date	F	VF	XF	Unc	BU
1997	—	—	—	7.50	—

KM# 336 DOLLAR **Composition:** Copper-Nickel **Subject:** Golden Wedding Anniversary **Obverse:** National arms **Reverse:** Royal couple with children **Note:** Similar to 10 Dollars, KM#337.

Date	F	VF	XF	Unc	BU
1997	—	—	—	7.50	—

KM# 344 DOLLAR **Composition:** Copper-Nickel **Subject:** 150th Anniversary of Independence **Obverse:** National arms **Reverse:** The "Ashmon" **Note:** Similar to 10 Dollars, KM#345.

Date	F	VF	XF	Unc	BU
1997	—	—	—	8.50	—

KM# 368 DOLLAR **Composition:** Copper-Nickel **Subject:** Star Trek - The Next Generation **Obverse:** National arms **Reverse:** Romulan Warbird **Note:** Similar to 10 Dollars, KM#369.

Date	F	VF	XF	Unc	BU
1997	—	—	—	7.50	—

KM# 371 DOLLAR **Composition:** Copper-Nickel **Subject:** Star Trek - The Next Generation **Obverse:** National arms **Reverse:** Klingon Attack Cruiser **Note:** Similar to 10 Dollars, KM#372.

Date	F	VF	XF	Unc	BU
1997	—	—	—	7.50	—

KM# 374 DOLLAR **Composition:** Copper-Nickel **Subject:** Star Trek - The Next Generation **Obverse:** National arms **Reverse:** U.S.S. Enterprise NCC-1701-D **Note:** Similar to 10 Dollars, KM#375.

Date	F	VF	XF	Unc	BU
1997	—	—	—	7.50	—

KM# 377 DOLLAR **Composition:** Copper-Nickel **Subject:** Star Trek - The Next Generation **Obverse:** National arms **Reverse:** Klingon Bird of Prey **Note:** Similar to 10 Dollars, KM#378.

Date	F	VF	XF	Unc	BU
1997	—	—	—	7.50	—

KM# 380 DOLLAR **Composition:** Copper-Nickel **Subject:** Star Trek - The Next Generation **Obverse:** National arms **Reverse:** Borg Cube **Note:** Similar to 10 Dollars, KM#381.

Date	F	VF	XF	Unc	BU
1997	—	—	—	7.50	—

KM# 383 DOLLAR **Composition:** Copper-Nickel **Subject:** Star Trek - The Next Generation **Obverse:** National arms **Reverse:** Ferengi Marauder **Note:** Similar to 10 Dollars, KM#384.

Date	F	VF	XF	Unc	BU
1997	—	—	—	7.50	—

KM# 386 DOLLAR **Composition:** Copper-Nickel **Subject:** President Ronald Reagan **Obverse:** National arms **Reverse:** Lincoln statue **Note:** Similar to 10 Dollars, KM#387.

Date	F	VF	XF	Unc	BU
1998	—	—	—	8.50	—

KM# 401 DOLLAR **Composition:** Copper-Nickel **Subject:** Christopher Columbus **Obverse:** National arms **Reverse:** Portrait of Columbus, ship **Note:** Similar to 10 Dollars, KM#402.

Date	F	VF	XF	Unc	BU
1999	—	—	—	8.00	—

KM# 404 DOLLAR **Composition:** Copper-Nickel **Subject:** Captain Cook **Obverse:** National arms **Reverse:** Portrait, ship and map **Note:** Similar to 10 Dollars, KM#403.

Date	F	VF	XF	Unc	BU
1999	—	—	—	8.00	—

KM# 407 DOLLAR **Composition:** Copper-Nickel **Subject:** Return of Macao to China **Obverse:** National arms **Reverse:** Dragon and phoenix **Note:** Similar to 10 Dollars, KM#408.

Date	F	VF	XF	Unc	BU
1999	—	—	—	8.50	—

KM# 413 DOLLAR **Composition:** Copper-Nickel **Subject:** The Wedding of Prince Edward **Obverse:** National arms **Reverse:** Couple in carriage **Note:** Similar to 10 Dollars, KM#413.

Date	F	VF	XF	Unc	BU
1999	—	—	—	8.00	—

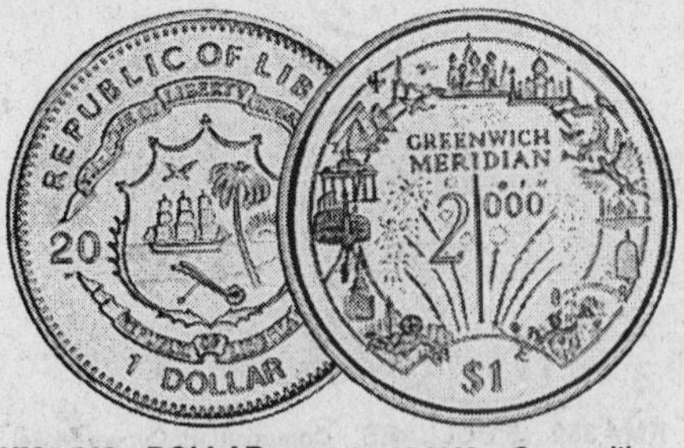

KM# 442 DOLLAR **Weight:** 28.2800 g. **Composition:** Copper-Nickel **Subject:** Greenwich Meridian **Obverse:** National arms **Reverse:** World landmarks and fireworks **Edge:** Reeded **Size:** 38.6 mm.

Date	F	VF	XF	Unc	BU
2000	—	—	—	10.00	—

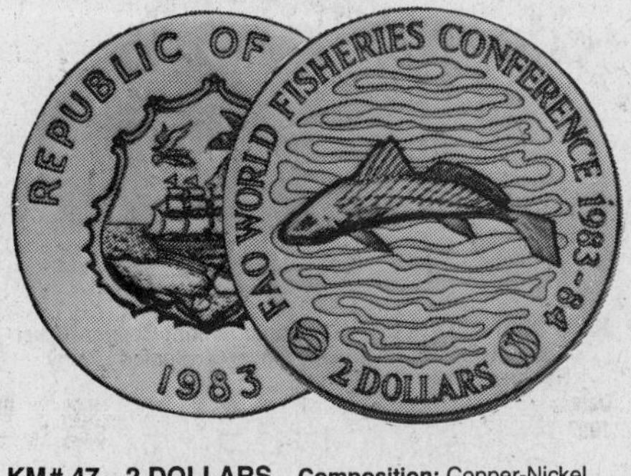

KM# 47 2 DOLLARS **Composition:** Copper-Nickel **Series:** F.A.O. **Subject:** World Fisheries Conference **Reverse:** Longneck croaker fish

Date	Mintage	F	VF	XF	Unc	BU
1983	100,000	—	—	—	15.00	—

KM# 47a 2 DOLLARS **Weight:** 28.2800 g. **Composition:** 0.9250 Silver .8411 oz. ASW **Subject:** World Fisheries Conference

Date	Mintage	F	VF	XF	Unc	BU
1983 Proof	20,000	Value: 50.00				

KM# 47b 2 DOLLARS **Weight:** 47.5400 g. **Composition:** Gold **Series:** F.A.O. **Subject:** World Fisheries Conference

Date	Mintage	F	VF	XF	Unc	BU
1983 Proof	600	Value: 950				

KM# 24 2-1/2 DOLLARS **Weight:** 4.1796 g. **Composition:** 0.9000 Gold .1209 oz. AGW **Subject:** Inauguration of President Tolbert

Date	F	VF	XF	Unc	BU
1972 Proof	—	Value: 80.00			

KM# 62 5 DOLLARS **Weight:** 5.0000 g. **Composition:** 0.9000 Gold .1447 oz. AGW **Subject:** 25th Anniversary of Inter-Continental Hotels

Date	F	VF	XF	Unc	BU
ND(1971) Proof	—	—	—	—	—

KM# 25 5 DOLLARS **Weight:** 8.3592 g. **Composition:** 0.9000 Gold .2419 oz. AGW **Subject:** Inauguration of President Tolbert

Date	F	VF	XF	Unc	BU
1972 Proof	—	Value: 160			

KM# 29 5 DOLLARS **Weight:** 34.1000 g. **Composition:** 0.9000 Silver .9868 oz. ASW

Date	Mintage	F	VF	XF	Unc	BU
1973	500	—	—	—	25.00	—
1973 Proof	28,000	Value: 11.50				
1974 Proof	20,000	Value: 11.50				
1975 Proof	9,017	Value: 12.50				
1976 Proof	3,683	Value: 16.50				
1977 Proof	1,640	Value: 18.50				
1978FM Proof	7,311	Value: 13.50				

KM# 29a 5 DOLLARS **Weight:** 34.1000 g. **Composition:** 0.9000 Silver .9868 oz. ASW **Edge Lettering:** O.A.U. July 1979

Date	Mintage	F	VF	XF	Unc	BU
1979 Proof	1,857	Value: 25.00				

KM# 44 5 DOLLARS **Composition:** Copper-Nickel **Subject:** Military Memorial **Shape:** 7-sided

Date	Mintage	F	VF	XF	Unc	BU
1982	4,000,000	—	5.00	6.50	9.00	—
1985	2,000,000	—	5.00	6.50	9.00	—

KM# 73 5 DOLLARS **Weight:** 15.5500 g. **Composition:** 0.9990 Silver .5000 oz. ASW **Subject:** Formula One - Gerhard Berger

Date	F	VF	XF	Unc	BU
1992 Proof	—	Value: 18.50			

KM# 76 5 DOLLARS **Weight:** 15.5500 g. **Composition:** 0.9990 Silver .5000 oz. ASW **Subject:** Formula One - Nigel Mansell

Date	Mintage	F	VF	XF	Unc	BU
1992 Proof	Est. 50,000	Value: 18.50				

KM# 78 5 DOLLARS **Weight:** 15.5500 g. **Composition:** 0.9990 Silver .5000 oz. ASW **Subject:** Formula One - Ayrton Senna

Date	Mintage	F	VF	XF	Unc	BU
1992 Proof	Est. 50,000	Value: 18.50				

KM# 79 5 DOLLARS **Weight:** 15.5500 g. **Composition:** 0.9990 Silver .5000 oz. ASW **Subject:** Formula One - Riccardo Patrese **Note:** Similar to 10 Dollars, KM#74.

Date	Mintage	F	VF	XF	Unc	BU
1992 Proof	Est. 50,000	Value: 18.50				

KM# 77 5 DOLLARS **Weight:** 15.5500 g. **Composition:** 0.9990 Silver .5000 oz. ASW **Subject:** Formula One - Aguri Suzuki **Note:** Similar to 10 Dollars, KM#84.

Date	Mintage	F	VF	XF	Unc	BU
1992 Proof	Est. 50,000	Value: 18.50				

KM# 80 5 DOLLARS **Weight:** 15.5500 g. **Composition:** 0.9990 Silver .5000 oz. ASW **Subject:** Formula One - Michael Schumacher **Note:** Similar to 10 Dollars, KM#86.

Date	Mintage	F	VF	XF	Unc	BU
1992 Proof	50,000	Value: 18.50				

KM# 81 5 DOLLARS **Weight:** 15.5500 g. **Composition:** 0.9990 Silver .5000 oz. ASW **Subject:** Formula One - Alain Prost **Note:** Similar to 10 Dollars, KM#87.

Date	Mintage	F	VF	XF	Unc	BU
1992 Proof	50,000	Value: 18.50				

KM# 82 5 DOLLARS **Weight:** 15.5500 g. **Composition:** 0.9990 Silver .5000 oz. ASW **Subject:** Formula One - Ukyo Katayama **Note:** Similar to 10 Dollars, KM#88.

Date	Mintage	F	VF	XF	Unc	BU
1992 Proof	50,000	Value: 18.50				

KM# 67 5 DOLLARS **Weight:** 15.5500 g. **Composition:** 0.9990 Silver .5000 oz. ASW **Subject:** President Bill Clinton **Note:** Similar to 10 Dollars, KM#68.

Date	Mintage	F	VF	XF	Unc	BU
1993 Proof	50,000	Value: 25.00				

KM# 97 5 DOLLARS **Weight:** 15.5500 g. **Composition:** 0.9990 Silver .5000 oz. ASW **Subject:** Chancellor Willy Brandt **Note:** Similar to 10 Dollars, KM#72.

Date		F	VF	XF	Unc	BU
1993 Proof	—	Value: 18.50				

KM# 103 5 DOLLARS **Weight:** 15.5500 g. **Composition:** 0.9990 Silver .5000 oz. ASW **Subject:** President John F. Kennedy **Note:** Similar to 10 Dollars, KM#104.

Date	Mintage	F	VF	XF	Unc	BU
1993 Proof	50,000	Value: 20.00				

KM# 562 5 DOLLARS **Weight:** 15.5000 g. **Composition:** 0.9990 Silver 0.4978 oz. ASW **Reverse:** Benz Patent motor car

Date		F	VF	XF	Unc	BU
1995 Proof	—	Value: 24.50				

KM# 563 5 DOLLARS **Weight:** 15.5000 g. **Composition:** 0.9990 Silver **Reverse:** Bughatti Royale **Size:** 32 mm.

Date	F	VF	XF	Unc	BU
1995	—	—	—	25.00	—

KM# 179 5 DOLLARS **Weight:** 15.5500 g. **Composition:** 0.9990 Silver .5000 oz. ASW **Subject:** Formula One - Mika Hakkinen **Reverse:** Similar to 10 Dollars, KM#180

Date	Mintage	F	VF	XF	Unc	BU
1995 Proof	50,000	Value: 20.00				

KM# 182 5 DOLLARS **Weight:** 15.5500 g. **Composition:** 0.9990 Silver .5000 oz. ASW **Subject:** Formula One - Martin Brundle **Reverse:** Similar to 10 Dollars, KM#183

Date	Mintage	F	VF	XF	Unc	BU
1995 Proof	Est. 50,000	Value: 20.00				

KM# 185 5 DOLLARS **Weight:** 15.5500 g. **Composition:** 0.9990 Silver .5000 oz. ASW **Subject:** Formula One - Rubens Barrichello **Reverse:** Similar to 10 Dollars, KM#186

Date	Mintage	F	VF	XF	Unc	BU
1995 Proof	Est. 50,000	Value: 20.00				

KM# 188 5 DOLLARS **Weight:** 15.5500 g. **Composition:** 0.9990 Silver .5000 oz. ASW **Subject:** Formula One - David Coulthard **Reverse:** Similar to 10 Dollars, KM#189

Date	Mintage	F	VF	XF	Unc	BU
1995 Proof	Est. 50,000	Value: 20.00				

KM# 191 5 DOLLARS **Weight:** 15.5500 g. **Composition:** 0.9990 Silver .5000 oz. ASW **Subject:** Formula One - Jean Alesi **Reverse:** Similar to 10 Dollars, KM#192

Date	Mintage	F	VF	XF	Unc	BU
1995 Proof	Est. 50,000	Value: 20.00				

KM# 195 5 DOLLARS **Weight:** 15.5500 g. **Composition:** 0.9990 Silver .5000 oz. ASW **Subject:** Formula One - Mark Blundell **Note:** Similar to 10 Dollars, KM#199.

Date	Mintage	F	VF	XF	Unc	BU
1996 Proof	50,000	Value: 20.00				

KM# 196 5 DOLLARS **Weight:** 15.5500 g. **Composition:** 0.9990 Silver .5000 oz. ASW **Subject:** Formula One - Johnny Herbert **Note:** Similar to 10 Dollars, KM#200.

Date	Mintage	F	VF	XF	Unc	BU
1996 Proof	50,000	Value: 20.00				

KM# 197 5 DOLLARS **Weight:** 15.5500 g. **Composition:** 0.9990 Silver .5000 oz. ASW **Subject:** Formula One - Eddie Irvine **Note:** Similar to 10 Dollars, KM#201.

Date	Mintage	F	VF	XF	Unc	BU
1996 Proof	50,000	Value: 20.00				

KM# 198 5 DOLLARS **Weight:** 15.5500 g. **Composition:** 0.9990 Silver .5000 oz. ASW **Subject:** Formula One - Heinz Frentzen **Note:** Similar to 10 Dollars, KM#202.

Date	Mintage	F	VF	XF	Unc	BU
1996 Proof	50,000	Value: 20.00				

KM# 228 5 DOLLARS **Weight:** 15.5500 g. **Composition:** 0.9990 Silver .5000 oz. ASW **Subject:** Formula One - Ayrton Senna **Note:** Similar to 10 Dollars, KM#229.

Date	Mintage	F	VF	XF	Unc	BU
1996 Proof	50,000	Value: 20.00				

KM# 255 5 DOLLARS **Weight:** 15.5500 g. **Composition:** 0.9990 Silver .5000 oz. ASW **Subject:** Chairman Mao Zedong **Note:** Similar to 10 Dollars, KM#256.

Date	Mintage	F	VF	XF	Unc	BU
1996 Proof	20,000	Value: 20.00				

KM# 261 5 DOLLARS **Weight:** 15.5500 g. **Composition:** 0.9990 Silver .5000 oz. ASW **Subject:** Chairman Mao Zedong and President Nixon **Note:** Similar to 10 Dollars, KM#262.

Date	Mintage	F	VF	XF	Unc	BU
1996 Proof	20,000	Value: 20.00				

KM# 441 5 DOLLARS **Weight:** 20.5600 g. **Composition:** Copper Nickel **Obverse:** National arms **Reverse:** Polar bear **Edge:** Reeded **Size:** 38.5 mm.

Date	F	VF	XF	Unc	BU
1997	—	—	—	7.50	—

KM# 566 5 DOLLARS **Composition:** Copper-Nickel **Reverse:** Elephant

Date	F	VF	XF	Unc	BU
1997	—	—	—	17.50	—

KM# 496 5 DOLLARS **Weight:** 20.5600 g. **Composition:** Copper-Nickel **Obverse:** National arms **Reverse:** Giraffe **Edge:** Reeded **Size:** 38.5 mm.

Date	F	VF	XF	Unc	BU
1997	—	—	—	8.50	—

KM# 452 5 DOLLARS **Composition:** Copper Nickel **Series:** Diana Princess of Wales **Obverse:** National arms **Reverse:** Princess Diana facing left

Date	F	VF	XF	Unc	BU
1997	—	—	—	—	—

KM# 351 5 DOLLARS **Composition:** Copper-Nickel **Subject:** Chinese Astrology **Obverse:** Seated Liberty **Reverse:** Two rats, pumpkin

Date	F	VF	XF	Unc	BU
1997	—	—	—	6.50	—

KM# 352 5 DOLLARS **Composition:** Copper-Nickel **Subject:** Chinese Astrology **Obverse:** Seated Liberty **Reverse:** Ox

Date	F	VF	XF	Unc	BU
1997	—	—	—	6.50	—

KM# 353 5 DOLLARS **Composition:** Copper-Nickel **Subject:** Chinese Astrology **Obverse:** Seated Liberty **Reverse:** Tiger

Date	F	VF	XF	Unc	BU
1997	—	—	—	6.50	—

KM# 354 5 DOLLARS **Composition:** Copper-Nickel **Subject:** Chinese Astrology **Obverse:** Seated Liberty **Reverse:** Rabbits

Date	F	VF	XF	Unc	BU
1997	—	—	—	6.50	—

KM# 355 5 DOLLARS **Composition:** Copper-Nickel **Subject:** Chinese Astrology **Obverse:** Seated Liberty **Reverse:** Dragon

Date	F	VF	XF	Unc	BU
1997	—	—	—	6.50	—

KM# 356 5 DOLLARS **Composition:** Copper-Nickel **Subject:** Chinese Astrology **Obverse:** Seated Liberty **Reverse:** Snake

Date	F	VF	XF	Unc	BU
1997	—	—	—	6.50	—

KM# 357 5 DOLLARS **Composition:** Copper-Nickel **Subject:** Chinese Astrology **Obverse:** Seated Liberty **Reverse:** Horse

Date	F	VF	XF	Unc	BU
1997	—	—	—	7.50	—

KM# 358 5 DOLLARS **Composition:** Copper-Nickel **Subject:** Chinese Astrology **Obverse:** Seated Liberty **Reverse:** Goat

Date	F	VF	XF	Unc	BU
1997	—	—	—	6.50	—

KM# 359 5 DOLLARS **Composition:** Copper-Nickel **Subject:** Chinese Astrology **Obverse:** Seated Liberty **Reverse:** Monkey

Date	F	VF	XF	Unc	BU
1997	—	—	—	6.50	—

KM# 360 5 DOLLARS **Composition:** Copper-Nickel **Subject:** Chinese Astrology **Obverse:** Seated Liberty **Reverse:** Rooster

Date	F	VF	XF	Unc	BU
1997	—	—	—	6.50	—

KM# 361 5 DOLLARS **Composition:** Copper-Nickel **Subject:** Chinese Astrology **Obverse:** Seated Liberty **Reverse:** Dog

Date	F	VF	XF	Unc	BU
1997	—	—	—	6.50	—

KM# 362 5 DOLLARS **Composition:** Copper-Nickel **Subject:** Chinese Astrology **Obverse:** Seated Liberty **Reverse:** Pig

Date	F	VF	XF	Unc	BU
1997	—	—	—	6.50	—

KM# 445 5 DOLLARS **Weight:** 25.1000 g. **Composition:** Copper-Nickel **Subject:** Princess Diana **Obverse:** National arms **Reverse:** Diana memorial portrait **Edge:** Reeded **Size:** 38.5 mm.

Date	F	VF	XF	Unc	BU
1997 Proof	—	Value: 20.00			

KM# 446 5 DOLLARS **Weight:** 25.1000 g. **Composition:** Copper-Nickel **Subject:** Diana Series - Lady Spencer **Obverse:** National arms **Reverse:** Young girl's portrait **Edge:** Reeded **Size:** 38.5 mm.

Date	F	VF	XF	Unc	BU
1997	—	—	—	15.00	—

KM# 447 5 DOLLARS **Weight:** 25.1000 g. **Composition:** Copper-Nickel **Subject:** First TV Interview **Reverse:** Portrait of Diana with microphone

Date	F	VF	XF	Unc	BU
1997	—	—	—	15.00	—

KM# 448 5 DOLLARS **Composition:** Copper-Nickel **Subject:** Diana's Official Portrait **Reverse:** Portrait

Date	F	VF	XF	Unc	BU
1997	—	—	—	15.00	—

KM# 449 5 DOLLARS **Composition:** Copper-Nickel **Subject:** Wedding Day **Reverse:** Diana in wedding dress

Date	F	VF	XF	Unc	BU
1997	—	—	—	15.00	—

KM# 450 5 DOLLARS **Composition:** Copper-Nickel **Subject:** "People's Princess" **Reverse:** Formal portrait

Date	F	VF	XF	Unc	BU
1997	—	—	—	15.00	—

KM# 451 5 DOLLARS **Composition:** Copper-Nickel **Subject:** England's Rose **Reverse:** Diana with bouquet of roses

Date	F	VF	XF	Unc	BU
1997	—	—	—	15.00	—

KM# A452 5 DOLLARS Composition: Copper-Nickel **Subject:** Queen of Hearts **Reverse:** Diana wearing a choker

Date	F	VF	XF	Unc	BU
1997	—	—	—	15.00	—

KM# 453 5 DOLLARS Composition: Copper-Nickel **Subject:** Elegance **Reverse:** Diana wearing a high collar

Date	F	VF	XF	Unc	BU
1997	—	—	—	15.00	—

KM# 454 5 DOLLARS Composition: Copper-Nickel **Subject:** Birth of William **Reverse:** Diana holding Prince William

Date	F	VF	XF	Unc	BU
1997	—	—	—	15.00	—

KM# 455 5 DOLLARS Composition: Copper-Nickel **Subject:** William's Christening **Reverse:** Diana holding Prince William

Date	F	VF	XF	Unc	BU
1997	—	—	—	15.00	—

KM# 456 5 DOLLARS Composition: Copper-Nickel **Subject:** Birth of Prince Harry **Reverse:** Diana holding Prince Harry

Date	F	VF	XF	Unc	BU
1997	—	—	—	15.00	—

KM# 457 5 DOLLARS Composition: Copper-Nickel **Subject:** Loving Mother **Reverse:** Diana with Prince William and Prince Harry

Date	F	VF	XF	Unc	BU
1997	—	—	—	15.00	—

KM# 458 5 DOLLARS Composition: Copper-Nickel **Subject:** Royal Family **Reverse:** Family portrait

Date	F	VF	XF	Unc	BU
1997	—	—	—	15.00	—

KM# 459 5 DOLLARS Composition: Copper-Nickel **Reverse:** Queen Elizabeth II and Diana

Date	F	VF	XF	Unc	BU
1997	—	—	—	15.00	—

KM# 460 5 DOLLARS Composition: Copper-Nickel **Reverse:** Queen Mother and Diana

Date	F	VF	XF	Unc	BU
1997	—	—	—	15.00	—

KM# 461 5 DOLLARS Composition: Copper-Nickel **Subject:** Visit to Wales **Reverse:** Charles and Diana

Date	F	VF	XF	Unc	BU
1997	—	—	—	15.00	—

KM# 462 5 DOLLARS Composition: Copper-Nickel **Reverse:** Charles and Diana dancing

Date	F	VF	XF	Unc	BU
1997	—	—	—	15.00	—

KM# 463 5 DOLLARS Composition: Copper-Nickel **Subject:** Tour of Japan **Reverse:** Emperor Hirohito and Diana

Date	F	VF	XF	Unc	BU
1997	—	—	—	15.00	—

KM# 464 5 DOLLARS Composition: Copper-Nickel **Obverse:** National arms **Reverse:** Diana reading to child **Size:** 38.5 mm.

Date	F	VF	XF	Unc	BU
1997	—	—	—	15.00	—

KM# 465 5 DOLLARS Composition: Copper-Nickel **Subject:** Charity **Reverse:** Diana with poor child

Date	F	VF	XF	Unc	BU
1997	—	—	—	15.00	—

KM# 466 5 DOLLARS Composition: Copper-Nickel **Reverse:** Diana with sick child

Date	F	VF	XF	Unc	BU
1997	—	—	—	15.00	—

KM# 467 5 DOLLARS Composition: Copper-Nickel **Reverse:** Diana's casket on gun carriage

Date	F	VF	XF	Unc	BU
1997	—	—	—	15.00	—

KM# 339 5 DOLLARS Composition: Copper-Nickel **Subject:** Year of the Tiger **Obverse:** National arms **Reverse:** Tiger with three cubs

Date	F	VF	XF	Unc	BU
1998 (1997) Proof	—	Value: 10.00			

KM# 363 5 DOLLARS Composition: Copper-Nickel **Subject:** RMS Titanic **Obverse:** Liberian arms **Reverse:** Ship sinking **Note:** Similar to 20 Dollars, KM#364.

Date	F	VF	XF	Unc	BU
1998	—	—	—	10.00	—

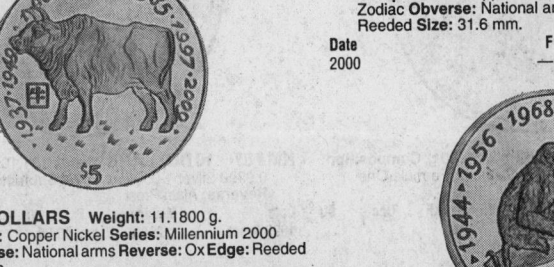

KM# 427 5 DOLLARS Weight: 11.1800 g. **Composition:** Copper Nickel **Series:** Millennium 2000 Zodiac **Obverse:** National arms **Reverse:** Snake **Edge:** Reeded **Size:** 31.6 mm.

Date	F	VF	XF	Unc	BU
2000	—	—	—	3.00	—

KM# 429 5 DOLLARS Weight: 11.1800 g. **Composition:** Copper Nickel **Series:** Millennium 2000 Zodiac **Obverse:** National arms **Reverse:** Ox **Edge:** Reeded **Size:** 31.6 mm.

Date	F	VF	XF	Unc	BU
2000	—	—	—	3.00	—

KM# 428 5 DOLLARS Weight: 11.1800 g. **Composition:** Copper Nickel **Series:** Millennium 2000 Zodiac **Obverse:** National arms **Reverse:** Two rats **Edge:** Reeded **Size:** 31.6 mm.

Date	F	VF	XF	Unc	BU
2000	—	—	—	3.00	—

KM# 430 5 DOLLARS Weight: 11.1800 g. **Composition:** Copper Nickel **Series:** Millennium 2000 Zodiac **Obverse:** National arms **Reverse:** Tiger **Edge:** Reeded **Size:** 31.6 mm.

Date	F	VF	XF	Unc	BU
2000	—	—	—	3.00	—

KM# 431 5 DOLLARS Weight: 11.1800 g. **Composition:** Copper Nickel **Series:** Millennium 2000 Zodiac **Obverse:** National arms **Reverse:** Horse **Edge:** Reeded **Size:** 31.6 mm.

Date	F	VF	XF	Unc	BU
2000	—	—	—	3.00	—

KM# 432 5 DOLLARS Weight: 11.1800 g. **Composition:** Copper Nickel **Series:** Millennium 2000 Zodiac **Obverse:** National arms **Reverse:** Goat **Edge:** Reeded **Size:** 31.6 mm.

Date	F	VF	XF	Unc	BU
2000	—	—	—	3.00	—

KM# 433 5 DOLLARS Weight: 11.1800 g. **Composition:** Copper Nickel **Series:** Millennium 2000 Zodiac **Obverse:** National arms **Reverse:** Monkey **Edge:** Reeded **Size:** 31.6 mm.

Date	F	VF	XF	Unc	BU
2000	—	—	—	3.00	—

KM# 434 5 DOLLARS Weight: 11.1800 g. **Composition:** Copper Nickel **Series:** Millennium 2000 Zodiac **Obverse:** National arms **Reverse:** Rooster **Edge:** Reeded **Size:** 31.6 mm.

Date	F	VF	XF	Unc	BU
2000	—	—	—	3.00	—

KM# 436 5 DOLLARS Weight: 11.1800 g. **Composition:** Copper Nickel **Series:** Millennium 2000 Zodiac **Obverse:** National arms **Reverse:** Pig **Edge:** Reeded **Size:** 31.6 mm.

Date	F	VF	XF	Unc	BU
2000	—	—	—	3.00	—

KM# 437 5 DOLLARS Weight: 11.1800 g. **Composition:** Copper Nickel **Series:** Millennium 2000 Zodiac **Obverse:** National arms **Reverse:** Rabbit **Edge:** Reeded **Size:** 31.6 mm.

Date	F	VF	XF	Unc	BU
2000	—	—	—	3.00	—

KM# 438 5 DOLLARS Weight: 11.1800 g. **Composition:** Copper Nickel **Series:** Millennium 2000 Zodiac **Obverse:** National arms **Reverse:** Dragon **Edge:** Reeded **Size:** 31.6 mm.

Date	F	VF	XF	Unc	BU
2000	—	—	—	4.00	—

KM# 494 5 DOLLARS Weight: 8.5000 g. **Composition:** 0.9999 Silver .2733 oz. ASW **Subject:** Soccer **Obverse:** National arms **Reverse:** Soccer player **Edge:** Reeded **Size:** 30 mm.

Date	Mintage	F	VF	XF	Unc	BU
2002 Proof	3,000	Value: 30.00				

KM# 63 10 DOLLARS Weight: 11.7200 g. **Composition:** 0.9000 Gold .3391 oz. AGW **Subject:** 25th Anniversary of Inter-Continental Hotels

Date	F	VF	XF	Unc	BU
1971 Proof	—	—	—	—	—

KM# 26 10 DOLLARS **Weight:** 16.7185 g. **Composition:** 0.9000 Gold .4838 oz. AGW **Subject:** Inauguration of President Tolbert

Date		F	VF	XF	Unc	BU
1972 Proof	—	Value: 310				

KM# 53 10 DOLLARS **Weight:** 23.3300 g. **Composition:** 0.9250 Silver .6939 oz. ASW **Subject:** Decade For Women **Reverse:** Coat of arms, denomination

Date		F	VF	XF	Unc	BU
1985 Proof	—	Value: 30.00				

KM#54 10 DOLLARS **Weight:** 31.1000 g. **Composition:** 0.9990 Silver 1.0000 oz. ASW **Subject:** President John F. Kennedy

Date	Mintage	F	VF	XF	Unc	BU
1988 Proof	25,000	Value: 37.50				

KM#55 10 DOLLARS **Weight:** 31.1000 g. **Composition:** 0.9990 Silver 1.0000 oz. ASW **Subject:** President Samuel Kanyon Doe **Note:** Similar to 250 Dollars, KM#56.

Date	Mintage	F	VF	XF	Unc	BU
1988 Proof	25,000	Value: 37.50				

KM# 57 10 DOLLARS **Weight:** 31.1000 g. **Composition:** 0.9990 Silver 1.0000 oz. ASW **Subject:** President George Bush **Note:** Similar to 250 Dollars, KM#58.

Date	Mintage	F	VF	XF	Unc	BU
1989 Proof	25,000	Value: 37.50				

KM#59 10 DOLLARS **Weight:** 31.1000 g. **Composition:** 0.9990 Silver 1.0000 oz. ASW **Subject:** Emperor Hirohito **Note:** Similar to 250 Dollars, KM#60.

Date	Mintage	F	VF	XF	Unc	BU
1989 Proof	25,000	Value: 35.00				

KM#72 10 DOLLARS **Weight:** 31.1000 g. **Composition:** 0.9990 Silver 1.0000 oz. ASW **Subject:** Chancellor Willy Brandt - In Memorium **Reverse:** Head of Brandt right

Date		F	VF	XF	Unc	BU
1992 Proof	—	Value: 32.50				

KM#74 10 DOLLARS **Weight:** 31.1000 g. **Composition:** 0.9990 Silver 1.0000 oz. ASW **Subject:** Formula One **Reverse:** Riccardo Patrese

Date	Mintage	F	VF	XF	Unc	BU
1992 Proof	25,000	Value: 40.00				

KM#75 10 DOLLARS **Weight:** 31.1000 g. **Composition:** 0.9990 Silver 1.0000 oz. ASW **Subject:** Formula One **Reverse:** Nigel Mansell

Date	Mintage	F	VF	XF	Unc	BU
1992 Proof	25,000	Value: 40.00				

KM#83 10 DOLLARS **Weight:** 31.1000 g. **Composition:** 0.9990 Silver 1.0000 oz. ASW **Subject:** Formula One **Reverse:** Gerhard Berger

Date	Mintage	F	VF	XF	Unc	BU
1992 Proof	25,000	Value: 40.00				

KM#84 10 DOLLARS **Weight:** 31.1000 g. **Composition:** 0.9990 Silver 1.0000 oz. ASW **Subject:** Formula One **Reverse:** Aguri Suzuki

Date	Mintage	F	VF	XF	Unc	BU
1992 Proof	25,000	Value: 40.00				

KM#85 10 DOLLARS **Weight:** 31.1000 g. **Composition:** 0.9990 Silver 1.0000 oz. ASW **Subject:** Formula One **Reverse:** Ayrton Senna

Date	Mintage	F	VF	XF	Unc	BU
1992 Proof	25,000	Value: 40.00				

KM#86 10 DOLLARS **Weight:** 31.1000 g. **Composition:** 0.9990 Silver 1.0000 oz. ASW **Subject:** Formula One **Reverse:** Michael Schumacher

Date	Mintage	F	VF	XF	Unc	BU
1992 Proof	25,000	Value: 40.00				

KM#87 10 DOLLARS **Weight:** 31.1000 g. **Composition:** 0.9990 Silver 1.0000 oz. ASW **Subject:** Formula One **Reverse:** Alain Prost

Date	Mintage	F	VF	XF	Unc	BU
1992 Proof	25,000	Value: 40.00				

KM#88 10 DOLLARS **Weight:** 31.1000 g. **Composition:** 0.9990 Silver 1.0000 oz. ASW **Subject:** Formula One **Reverse:** Ykyo Katayama

Date	Mintage	F	VF	XF	Unc	BU
1992 Proof	25,000	Value: 40.00				

KM# 68 10 DOLLARS **Weight:** 31.1000 g. **Composition:** 0.9990 Silver 1.0000 oz. ASW **Subject:** President Bill Clinton

Date	Mintage	F	VF	XF	Unc	BU
1993 Proof	25,000	Value: 30.00				

KM# 99 10 DOLLARS **Weight:** 31.1000 g. **Composition:** 0.9990 Silver 1.0000 oz. ASW **Series:** Preserve Planet Earth **Reverse:** Protoceratops

Date	Mintage	F	VF	XF	Unc	BU
1993 Proof	25,000	Value: 35.00				

KM# 102 10 DOLLARS **Weight:** 31.1000 g. **Composition:** 0.9990 Silver 1.0000 oz. ASW **Subject:** Baseball Hall of Fame **Reverse:** Nolan Ryan waving baseball cap

Date	F	VF	XF	Unc	BU
1993 Proof	—	Value: 30.00			

KM# 104 10 DOLLARS **Weight:** 31.1000 g. **Composition:** 0.9990 Silver 1.0000 oz. ASW **Reverse:** President John F. Kennedy

Date	Mintage	F	VF	XF	Unc	BU
1993 Proof	25,000	Value: 40.00				

KM# 110 10 DOLLARS **Weight:** 31.1000 g. **Composition:** 0.9990 Silver 1.0000 oz. ASW **Series:** Preserve Planet Earth **Reverse:** Corythosaurus

Date	Mintage	F	VF	XF	Unc	BU
1993 Proof	25,000	Value: 35.00				

KM# 113 10 DOLLARS **Weight:** 31.1000 g. **Composition:** 0.9990 Silver 1.0000 oz. ASW **Series:** Preserve Planet Earth **Reverse:** Atchaeopteryx **Note:** Incorrect spelling.

Date	Mintage	F	VF	XF	Unc	BU
1993 Proof	25,000	Value: 35.00				

KM# 561 10 DOLLARS **Weight:** 31.1035 g. **Composition:** 0.9990 Silver 1 oz. ASW **Reverse:** Mercedes Benz C-Class car

Date	Mintage	F	VF	XF	Unc	BU
1994 Proof	Est. 25,000	Value: 50.00				

KM# 116 10 DOLLARS **Weight:** 31.1000 g. **Composition:** 0.9990 Silver 1.0000 oz. ASW **Series:** Preserve Planet Earth **Reverse:** Archaeopteryx **Note:** Correct spelling.

Date	Mintage	F	VF	XF	Unc	BU
1994 Proof	25,000	Value: 35.00				

KM# 119 10 DOLLARS **Weight:** 31.1000 g. **Composition:** 0.9990 Silver 1.0000 oz. ASW **Series:** Preserve Planet Earth **Reverse:** Gorillas

Date	Mintage	F	VF	XF	Unc	BU
1994 Proof	25,000	Value: 35.00				

KM# 122 10 DOLLARS **Weight:** 31.1000 g. **Composition:** 0.9990 Silver 1.0000 oz. ASW **Series:** Preserve Planet Earth **Reverse:** Pygmy Hippopotami

Date	Mintage	F	VF	XF	Unc	BU
1994 Proof	25,000	Value: 35.00				

KM# 125 10 DOLLARS **Weight:** 31.1000 g. **Composition:** 0.9990 Silver 1.0000 oz. ASW **Series:** Preserve Planet Earth **Reverse:** Nile Soft-shelled Turtle

Date	Mintage	F	VF	XF	Unc	BU
1994 Proof	25,000	Value: 35.00				

KM# 127 10 DOLLARS **Weight:** 31.1000 g. **Composition:** 0.9990 Silver 1.0000 oz. ASW **Reverse:** President Nelson Mandela left

Date	Mintage	F	VF	XF	Unc	BU
1994 Proof	25,000	Value: 30.00				

KM# 155 10 DOLLARS **Weight:** 31.1000 g. **Composition:** 0.9990 Silver 1.0000 oz. ASW **Reverse:** General Erwin Rommel half left

Date	Mintage	F	VF	XF	Unc	BU
1994 Proof	25,000	Value: 40.00				

KM# 156 10 DOLLARS **Weight:** 31.1000 g. **Composition:** 0.9990 Silver 1.0000 oz. ASW **Reverse:** Field Marshal Montgomery facing

Date	Mintage	F	VF	XF	Unc	BU
1994 Proof	25,000	Value: 40.00				

KM# 157 10 DOLLARS **Weight:** 31.1000 g. **Composition:** 0.9990 Silver 1.0000 oz. ASW **Reverse:** General Dwight D. Eisenhower half left

Date	Mintage	F	VF	XF	Unc	BU
1994 Proof	25,000	Value: 40.00				

KM# 281 10 DOLLARS **Weight:** 31.1000 g. **Composition:** 0.9990 Silver 1.0000 oz. ASW **Subject:** Baseball Hall of Fame **Reverse:** Reggie Jackson hitting the ball

Date		F	VF	XF	Unc	BU
1994 Proof	—	Value: 40.00				

KM# 282 10 DOLLARS **Weight:** 31.1000 g. **Composition:** 0.9990 Silver 1.0000 oz. ASW **Subject:** Baseball Hall of Fame **Reverse:** Roberto Clemente facing

Date		F	VF	XF	Unc	BU
1994 Proof	—	Value: 40.00				

KM# 347 10 DOLLARS **Weight:** 31.1000 g. **Composition:** 0.9990 Silver 1.0000 oz. ASW **Subject:** The History of the Motor Car **Obverse:** National arms **Reverse:** Mercedes-Benz C-Class

Date		F	VF	XF	Unc	BU
1994 Proof	—	Value: 40.00				

KM# 129 10 DOLLARS **Weight:** 31.1000 g. **Composition:** 0.9990 Silver 1.0000 oz. ASW **Subject:** Star Trek **Reverse:** Captains Kirk and Picard

Date		F	VF	XF	Unc	BU
1995 Proof	—	Value: 47.50				

KM# 134 10 DOLLARS **Weight:** 31.1000 g. **Composition:** 0.9990 Silver 1.0000 oz. ASW **Series:** Preserve Planet Earth **Reverse:** Leopard

Date	Mintage	F	VF	XF	Unc	BU
1995 Proof	25,000	Value: 35.00				

KM# 137 10 DOLLARS **Weight:** 31.1000 g. **Composition:** 0.9990 Silver 1.0000 oz. ASW **Series:** Preserve Planet Earth **Reverse:** Storks

Date	Mintage	F	VF	XF	Unc	BU
1995 Proof	25,000	Value: 30.00				

KM# 145 10 DOLLARS **Weight:** 31.1000 g. **Composition:** 0.9990 Silver 1.0000 oz. ASW **Reverse:** Si Winston Churchill

Date	Mintage	F	VF	XF	Unc	B
1995 Proof	25,000	Value: 40.00				

KM# 146 10 DOLLARS **Weight:** 31.1000 g. **Composition:** 0.9990 Silver 1.0000 oz. ASW **Reverse:** President Franklin D. Roosevelt riding in jeep

Date	Mintage	F	VF	XF	Unc	B
1995 Proof	25,000	Value: 40.00				

KM# 147 10 DOLLARS **Weight:** 31.1000 g. **Composition** 0.9990 Silver 1.0000 oz. ASW **Reverse:** General George Patton in front of map

Date	Mintage	F	VF	XF	Unc	B
1995 Proof	25,000	Value: 40.00				

KM# 148 10 DOLLARS **Weight:** 31.1000 g. **Composition:** 0.9990 Silver 1.0000 oz. ASW **Reverse:** President Harry S. Truman facing

Date	Mintage	F	VF	XF	Unc	B
1995 Proof	25,000	Value: 40.00				

KM# 149 10 DOLLARS **Weight:** 31.1000 g. **Composition:** 0.9990 Silver 1.0000 oz. ASW **Reverse:** President Charles de Gaulle on Champs Elysees

Date	Mintage	F	VF	XF	Unc	BU
1995 Proof	25,000	Value: 40.00				

KM# 159 10 DOLLARS **Weight:** 31.1000 g. **Composition:** 0.9990 Silver 1.0000 oz. ASW **Reverse:** Dr. Sun Yat-Sen

Date	Mintage	F	VF	XF	Unc	BU
1995 Proof	25,000	Value: 45.00				
1996 Proof	25,000	Value: 45.00				

KM# 162 10 DOLLARS **Weight:** 31.1000 g. **Composition:** 0.9990 Silver 1.0000 oz. ASW **Reverse:** General Chiang Kai-shék

Date	Mintage	F	VF	XF	Unc	BU
1995 Proof	25,000	Value: 45.00				
1996 Proof	25,000	Value: 45.00				

KM# 165 10 DOLLARS **Weight:** 31.1000 g. **Composition:** 0.9990 Silver 1.0000 oz. ASW **Subject:** Cairo Conference **Reverse:** Chiang Kai-shek - Roosevelt - Churchill

Date	Mintage	F	VF	XF	Unc	BU
1995 Proof	25,000	Value: 45.00				

KM# 171 10 DOLLARS **Weight:** 31.1000 g. **Composition:** 0.9990 Silver 1.0000 oz. ASW **Subject:** 375th Anniversary - Pilgrim Fathers **Reverse:** The "Mayflower"

Date	Mintage	F	VF	XF	Unc	BU
1995 Proof	25,000	Value: 40.00				

KM# 172 10 DOLLARS **Weight:** 31.1000 g. **Composition:** 0.9990 Silver 1.0000 oz. ASW **Subject:** 375th Anniversary - Pilgrim Fathers **Reverse:** Pilgrims in skiff

Date	Mintage	F	VF	XF	Unc	BU
1995 Proof	25,000	Value: 40.00				

KM# 173 10 DOLLARS **Weight:** 31.1000 g. **Composition:** 0.9990 Silver 1.0000 oz. ASW **Subject:** 375th Anniversary - Pilgrim Fathers **Reverse:** Pilgrim landing party

Date	Mintage	F	VF	XF	Unc	BU
1995 Proof	25,000	Value: 40.00				

KM# 174 10 DOLLARS **Weight:** 31.1000 g. **Composition:** 0.9990 Silver 1.0000 oz. ASW **Subject:** 375th Anniversary - Pilgrim Fathers **Reverse:** First Thanksgiving scene

Date	Mintage	F	VF	XF	Unc	BU
1995 Proof	25,000	Value: 40.00				

KM# 180 10 DOLLARS **Weight:** 31.1000 g. **Composition:** 0.9990 Silver 1.0000 oz. ASW **Subject:** Formula One **Reverse:** Mika Hakkinen

Date	Mintage	F	VF	XF	Unc	BU
1995 Proof	25,000	Value: 40.00				

KM# 183 10 DOLLARS **Weight:** 31.1000 g. **Composition:** 0.9990 Silver 1.0000 oz. ASW **Subject:** Formula One **Reverse:** Martin Brundle

Date	Mintage	F	VF	XF	Unc	BU
1995 Proof	25,000	Value: 40.00				

KM# 186 10 DOLLARS **Weight:** 31.1000 g. **Composition:** 0.9990 Silver 1.0000 oz. ASW **Subject:** Formula One **Reverse:** Rubens Barrichello

Date	Mintage	F	VF	XF	Unc	BU
1995 Proof	25,000	Value: 40.00				

KM# 189 10 DOLLARS **Weight:** 31.1000 g. **Composition:** 0.9990 Silver 1.0000 oz. ASW **Subject:** Formula One **Reverse:** David Coulthard

Date	Mintage	F	VF	XF	Unc	BU
1995 Proof	25,000	Value: 40.00				

KM# 192 10 DOLLARS **Weight:** 31.1000 g. **Composition:** 0.9990 Silver 1.0000 oz. ASW **Subject:** Formula One **Reverse:** Jean Alesi

Date	Mintage	F	VF	XF	Unc	BU
1995 Proof	25,000	Value: 40.00				

KM# 194 10 DOLLARS **Weight:** 31.1000 g. **Composition:** 0.9990 Silver 1.0000 oz. ASW **Subject:** Nations United for Peace **Reverse:** Logo, paper dolls

Date	Mintage	F	VF	XF	Unc	BU
1995 Proof	25,000	Value: 37.50				

KM# 564 10 DOLLARS **Weight:** 31.1000 g. **Composition:** 0.9990 Silver 0.9989 oz. ASW **Reverse:** Bugatti Royale **Size:** 38.6 mm.

Date	F	VF	XF	Unc	BU
1995	—	—	—	40.00	—

KM# 132 10 DOLLARS **Weight:** 31.1000 g. **Composition:** 0.9990 Silver 1.0000 oz. ASW **Subject:** Centennial - Babe Ruth - Sultan of Swat **Note:** Similar to 1 Dollar, KM#131.

Date	F	VF	XF	Unc	BU
1995	—	—	—	42.50	—

KM# 199 10 DOLLARS **Weight:** 31.1000 g. **Composition:** 0.9990 Silver 1.0000 oz. ASW **Subject:** Formula One **Reverse:** Mark Blundell

Date	Mintage	F	VF	XF	Unc	BU
1996 Proof	25,000	Value: 40.00				

KM# 200 10 DOLLARS **Weight:** 31.1000 g. **Composition:** 0.9990 Silver 1.0000 oz. ASW **Subject:** Formula One **Reverse:** Johnny Herbert

Date	Mintage	F	VF	XF	Unc	BU
1996 Proof	25,000	Value: 40.00				

KM# 201 10 DOLLARS **Weight:** 31.1000 g. **Composition:** 0.9990 Silver 1.0000 oz. ASW **Subject:** Formula One **Reverse:** Eddie Irvine

Date	Mintage	F	VF	XF	Unc	BU
1996 Proof	25,000	Value: 40.00				

KM# 202 10 DOLLARS **Weight:** 31.1000 g. **Composition:** 0.9990 Silver 1.0000 oz. ASW **Subject:** Formula One **Reverse:** Heinz Frentzen

Date	Mintage	F	VF	XF	Unc	BU
1996 Proof	25,000	Value: 40.00				

KM# 208 10 DOLLARS **Weight:** 31.1000 g. **Composition:** 0.9990 Silver 1.0000 oz. ASW **Subject:** Star Trek **Reverse:** Starships NCC-1701 and NCC-1701D

Date	Mintage	F	VF	XF	Unc	BU
1996 Proof	25,000	Value: 45.00				

KM# 211 10 DOLLARS **Weight:** 31.1000 g. **Composition:** 0.9990 Silver 1.0000 oz. ASW **Subject:** Star Trek **Reverse:** Scott and McCoy

Date	Mintage	F	VF	XF	Unc	BU
1996 Proof	25,000	Value: 45.00				

KM# 214 10 DOLLARS **Weight:** 31.1000 g. **Composition:** 0.9990 Silver 1.0000 oz. ASW **Subject:** Star Trek **Reverse:** LaForge and Data

Date	Mintage	F	VF	XF	Unc	BU
1996 Proof	25,000	Value: 45.00				

KM# 217 10 DOLLARS **Weight:** 31.1000 g. **Composition:** 0.9990 Silver 1.0000 oz. ASW **Subject:** Star Trek **Reverse:** Spock and Uhura

Date	Mintage	F	VF	XF	Unc	BU
1996 Proof	25,000	Value: 45.00				

KM# 220 10 DOLLARS **Weight:** 31.1000 g. **Composition:** 0.9990 Silver 1.0000 oz. ASW **Subject:** Star Trek **Reverse:** Worf and Dr. Crusher

Date	Mintage	F	VF	XF	Unc	BU
1996 Proof	25,000	Value: 45.00				

KM# 223 10 DOLLARS **Weight:** 31.1000 g. **Composition:** 0.9990 Silver 1.0000 oz. ASW **Series:** Preserve Planet Earth **Reverse:** Grey Parrot

Date	Mintage	F	VF	XF	Unc	BU
1996 Proof	25,000	Value: 40.00				

KM# 226 10 DOLLARS **Weight:** 31.1000 g. **Composition:** 0.9990 Silver 1.0000 oz. ASW **Series:** Preserve Planet Earth **Reverse:** Love Birds

Date	Mintage	F	VF	XF	Unc	BU
1996 Proof	25,000	Value: 40.00				

KM# 229 10 DOLLARS **Weight:** 31.1000 g. **Composition:** 0.9990 Silver 1.0000 oz. ASW **Subject:** Formula One **Reverse:** Ayrton Senna

Date	Mintage	F	VF	XF	Unc	BU
1996	25,000	Value: 40.00				

KM# 242 10 DOLLARS **Weight:** 31.1000 g. **Composition:** 0.9990 Silver 1.0000 oz. ASW **Reverse:** President Chiang Ching-kuo

Date	Mintage	F	VF	XF	Unc	BU
1996 Proof	25,000	Value: 42.50				

KM# 245 10 DOLLARS **Weight:** 31.1000 g. **Composition:** 0.9990 Silver 1.0000 oz. ASW **Reverse:** President Lee Ten-hui

Date	Mintage	F	VF	XF	Unc	BU
1996 Proof	25,000	Value: 42.50				

KM# 256 10 DOLLARS **Weight:** 31.1000 g. **Composition:** 0.9990 Silver 1.0000 oz. ASW **Reverse:** Chairman Mao Zedong walking

Date	Mintage	F	VF	XF	Unc	BU
1996 Proof	25,000	Value: 40.00				

KM# 257 10 DOLLARS **Weight:** 31.1000 g. **Composition:** 0.9990 Silver 1.0000 oz. ASW **Reverse:** Chairman Mao Zedong with gate of Heavenly Peace

Date	Mintage	F	VF	XF	Unc	BU
1996 Proof	25,000	Value: 40.00				

KM# 258 10 DOLLARS **Weight:** 31.1000 g. **Composition:** 0.9990 Silver 1.0000 oz. ASW **Reverse:** Chairman Mao Zedong proclaiming People's Republic

Date	Mintage	F	VF	XF	Unc	BU
1996 Proof	25,000	Value: 40.00				

KM# 262 10 DOLLARS **Weight:** 31.1000 g. **Composition:** 0.9990 Silver 1.0000 oz. ASW **Reverse:** Chairman Mao Zedong and President Nixon

Date	Mintage	F	VF	XF	Unc	BU
1996 Proof	25,000	Value: 37.50				

KM# 264 10 DOLLARS **Weight:** 31.1000 g. **Composition:** 0.9990 Silver 1.0000 oz. ASW **Series:** Pioneers of the West **Reverse:** Daniel Boone

Date	Mintage	F	VF	XF	Unc	BU
1996 Proof	25,000	Value: 40.00				

KM# 267 10 DOLLARS **Weight:** 31.1000 g. **Composition:** 0.9990 Silver 1.0000 oz. ASW **Series:** Pioneers of the West **Reverse:** Davy Crockett

Date	Mintage	F	VF	XF	Unc	BU
1996 Proof	25,000	Value: 40.00				

KM# 270 10 DOLLARS **Weight:** 31.1000 g. **Composition:** 0.9990 Silver 1.0000 oz. ASW **Series:** Pioneers of the West **Reverse:** Jim Bowie in front of the Alamo

Date	Mintage	F	VF	XF	Unc	BU
1996 Proof	25,000	Value: 40.00				

KM# 273 10 DOLLARS **Weight:** 31.1000 g. **Composition:** 0.9990 Silver 1.0000 oz. ASW **Series:** Pioneers of the West **Reverse:** Kit Carson

Date	Mintage	F	VF	XF	Unc	BU
1996 Proof	25,000	Value: 40.00				

KM# 276 10 DOLLARS **Weight:** 31.1000 g. **Composition:** 0.9990 Silver 1.0000 oz. ASW **Series:** Pioneers of the West **Reverse:** Wild Bill Hickok

Date	Mintage	F	VF	XF	Unc	BU
1996 Proof	25,000	Value: 40.00				

KM# 279 10 DOLLARS **Weight:** 31.1000 g. **Composition:** 0.9990 Silver 1.0000 oz. ASW **Series:** Pioneers of the West **Reverse:** Buffalo Bill

Date	Mintage	F	VF	XF	Unc	BU
1996 Proof	25,000	Value: 40.00				

KM# 284 10 DOLLARS **Weight:** 31.1000 g. **Composition:** 0.9990 Silver 1.0000 oz. ASW **Subject:** Return of Macao to China **Obverse:** National arms **Reverse:** City views, old and new

Date	Mintage	F	VF	XF	Unc	BU
1996 Proof	Est. 6,000	Value: 32.50				

KM# 285 10 DOLLARS **Weight:** 31.1000 g. **Composition:** 0.9990 Silver 1.0000 oz. ASW **Subject:** Return of Hong Kong to China **Reverse:** City views, old and new **Shape:** Rectangular

Date	Mintage	F	VF	XF	Unc	BU
1996 Proof	Est. 6,000	Value: 32.50				

KM# 287 10 DOLLARS **Weight:** 31.1000 g. **Composition:** 0.9990 Silver 1.0000 oz. ASW **Series:** WWII **Subject:** Evacuation from Dunkirk **Reverse:** Left, British 1939-45 Star Medal, evacuation scene

Date	Mintage	F	VF	XF	Unc	BU
1997 Proof	25,000	Value: 37.50				

KM# 289 10 DOLLARS **Weight:** 31.1000 g. **Composition:** 0.9990 Silver 1.0000 oz. ASW **Series:** WWII **Subject:** Liberation of the Philippines **Reverse:** Right, American Asian-Pacific campaign medal, soldiers in water

Date	Mintage	F	VF	XF	Unc	BU
1997 Proof	25,000	Value: 37.50				

KM# 291 10 DOLLARS **Weight:** 31.1000 g. **Composition:** 0.9990 Silver 1.0000 oz. ASW **Series:** WWII **Subject:** Defense of Stalingrad **Reverse:** Left, Soviet Distinguished Combat Medal, war scene

Date	Mintage	F	VF	XF	Unc	BU
1997 Proof	25,000	Value: 37.50				

KM# 293 10 DOLLARS **Weight:** 31.1000 g. **Composition:** 0.9990 Silver 1.0000 oz. ASW **Series:** WWII **Subject:** Arnhem **Reverse:** Right, Netherlands Bronze Lion Cross, parachutists, bridge and soldier

Date	Mintage	F	VF	XF	Unc	BU
1997 Proof	25,000	Value: 37.50				

KM# 295 10 DOLLARS **Weight:** 31.1000 g. **Composition:** 0.9990 Silver 1.0000 oz. ASW **Series:** WWII **Subject:** Raid on the Dams **Reverse:** Left, British Distinguished Flying Medal

Date	Mintage	F	VF	XF	Unc	BU
1997 Proof	25,000	Value: 37.50				

KM# 297 10 DOLLARS **Weight:** 31.1000 g. **Composition:** 0.9990 Silver 1.0000 oz. ASW **Series:** WWII **Subject:** West African Campaign **Reverse:** Right, WWII Victory Medal

Date	Mintage	F	VF	XF	Unc	BU
1997 Proof	25,000	Value: 37.50				

KM# 299 10 DOLLARS **Weight:** 31.1000 g. **Composition:** 0.9990 Silver 1.0000 oz. ASW **Series:** WWII **Subject:** North African Campaign **Reverse:** Right, British Africa Star Medal, tank in front of pyramid

Date	Mintage	F	VF	XF	Unc	BU
1997 Proof	25,000	Value: 37.50				

KM# 301 10 DOLLARS **Weight:** 31.1000 g. **Composition:** 0.9990 Silver 1.0000 oz. ASW **Series:** WWII **Subject:** The Dieppe Raid **Reverse:** Right, British Victoria Cross, plane over half-track vehicle

Date	Mintage	F	VF	XF	Unc	BU
1997 Proof	25,000	Value: 37.50				

KM# 303 10 DOLLARS **Weight:** 31.1000 g. **Composition:** 0.9990 Silver 1.0000 oz. ASW **Series:** WWII **Subject:** Iwo Jima **Reverse:** Left, Purple Heart Medal

Date	Mintage	F	VF	XF	Unc	BU
1997 Proof	25,000	Value: 37.50				

KM# 305 10 DOLLARS **Weight:** 31.1000 g. **Composition:** 0.9990 Silver 1.0000 oz. ASW **Series:** WWII **Subject:** Battle of Britain **Reverse:** Left, British Distinguished Flying Cross, pilots running to board planes

Date	Mintage	F	VF	XF	Unc	BU
1997 Proof	25,000	Value: 37.50				

KM# 307 10 DOLLARS **Weight:** 31.1000 g. **Composition:** 0.9990 Silver 1.0000 oz. ASW **Series:** WWII **Subject:** Liberation of Paris **Reverse:** Right, Croix de Guerre Medal, soldiers in front of Arch de Triumph

Date	Mintage	F	VF	XF	Unc	BU
1997 Proof	25,000	Value: 37.50				

KM# 309 10 DOLLARS **Weight:** 31.1000 g. **Composition:** 0.9990 Silver 1.0000 oz. ASW **Series:** WWII **Subject:** Burma Campaign **Reverse:** Left, British Burma Star Medal

Date	Mintage	F	VF	XF	Unc	BU
1997 Proof	25,000	Value: 37.50				

KM# 311 10 DOLLARS **Weight:** 31.1000 g. **Composition:** 0.9990 Silver 1.0000 oz. ASW **Obverse:** National arms **Reverse:** Mahatma Gandhi seated in front of Taj Mahal

Date	Mintage	F	VF	XF	Unc	BU
1997 Proof	25,000	Value: 40.00				

KM# 314 10 DOLLARS **Weight:** 31.1000 g. **Composition:** 0.9990 Silver 1.0000 oz. ASW **Subject:** Return of Hong Kong **Obverse:** National arms **Reverse:** Dragon

Date	Mintage	F	VF	XF	Unc	BU
1997 Proof	25,000	Value: 40.00				

KM# 321 10 DOLLARS **Weight:** 31.1000 g. **Composition:** 0.9990 Silver 1.0000 oz. ASW **Subject:** Fiftieth Anniversary of the Kon-Tiki Expedition **Obverse:** National arms **Reverse:** Mask

Date	Mintage	F	VF	XF	Unc	BU
1997 Proof	25,000	Value: 40.00				

KM# 325 10 DOLLARS **Weight:** 31.1000 g. **Composition:** 0.9990 Silver 1.0000 oz. ASW **Subject:** Jurassic Park **Obverse:** National arms **Reverse:** Stegosaurus

Date	Mintage	F	VF	XF	Unc	BU
1997 Proof	10,000	Value: 50.00				

KM# 328 10 DOLLARS **Weight:** 31.1030 g. **Composition:** 0.9250 Gold Clad Silver .9250 oz. **Subject:** Golden Wedding Anniversary **Obverse:** National arms **Reverse:** E & P initials above 2 shields

Date	Mintage	F	VF	XF	Unc	BU
1997 Proof	10,000	Value: 50.00				

KM# 331 10 DOLLARS **Weight:** 31.1030 g. **Composition:** 0.9250 Gold Clad Silver .9250 oz. **Subject:** Queen Elizabeth II and Prince Philip's Golden Wedding Anniversary **Obverse:** National arms **Reverse:** Royal couple with horse

Date	Mintage	F	VF	XF	Unc	BU
1997 Proof	10,000	Value: 50.00				

KM# 334 10 DOLLARS **Weight:** 31.1030 g. **Composition:** 0.9250 Gold Clad Silver .9250 oz. **Subject:** Queen Elizabeth II and Prince Philip's Golden Wedding Anniversary **Obverse:** National arms **Reverse:** Royal couple with dogs

Date	Mintage	F	VF	XF	Unc	BU
1997 Proof	10,000	Value: 50.00				

KM# 337 10 DOLLARS **Weight:** 31.1030 g. **Composition:** 0.9250 Gold Clad Silver .9250 oz. **Subject:** Queen Elizabeth II and Prince Philip's Golden Wedding Anniversary **Obverse:** National arms **Reverse:** Royal couple with children

Date	Mintage	F	VF	XF	Unc	BU
1997 Proof	10,000	Value: 50.00				

KM# 345 10 DOLLARS **Weight:** 31.1035 g. **Composition:** 0.9990 Silver 1.0000 oz. ASW **Subject:** 150th Anniversary - Independence of Liberia **Obverse:** National arms **Reverse:** The "Ashmon"

Date	Mintage	F	VF	XF	Unc	BU
1997 Proof	25,000	Value: 45.00				

KM# 346 10 DOLLARS **Composition:** Copper-Nickel **Subject:** Famous Personalities of the World **Obverse:** National arms with blank ribbons **Reverse:** Marilyn Monroe

Date		F	VF	XF	Unc	BU
ND(1997) Proof	—	Value: 15.00				

KM# 348 10 DOLLARS **Weight:** 31.1035 g. **Composition:** 0.9990 Silver 1.0000 oz. ASW **Subject:** Return of Hong Kong to China **Obverse:** National arms **Reverse:** City view, old and new **Shape:** Rectangular

Date	Mintage	F	VF	XF	Unc	BU
1997 Proof	Est. 8,000	Value: 32.50				

KM# 349 10 DOLLARS **Weight:** 31.1035 g. **Composition:** 0.9990 Silver 1.0000 oz. ASW **Subject:** Pending Return of Macao to China **Obverse:** National arms **Reverse:** City view

Date	Mintage	F	VF	XF	Unc	BU
1997 Proof	Est. 8,000	Value: 32.50				

KM# 350 10 DOLLARS **Weight:** 31.1035 g. **Composition:** 0.9990 Silver 1.0000 oz. ASW **Subject:** Diana - The People's Princess **Obverse:** National arms

Date		F	VF	XF	Unc	BU
1997 Proof	—	Value: 45.00				

KM# 369 10 DOLLARS **Weight:** 31.1035 g. **Composition:** 0.9990 Silver 1.0000 oz. ASW **Subject:** Star Trek - The Next Generation **Obverse:** National arms **Reverse:** Romulan Warbird

Date	Mintage	F	VF	XF	Unc	BU
1997 Proof	25,000	Value: 45.00				

KM# 372 10 DOLLARS **Weight:** 31.1035 g. **Composition:** 0.9990 Silver 1.0000 oz. ASW **Subject:** Star Trek - The Next Generation **Obverse:** National arms **Reverse:** Klingon Attack Cruiser

Date	Mintage	F	VF	XF	Unc	BU
1997 Proof	25,000	Value: 45.00				

KM# 375 10 DOLLARS **Weight:** 31.1035 g. **Composition:** 0.9990 Silver 1.0000 oz. ASW **Subject:** Star Trek - The Next Generation **Obverse:** National arms **Reverse:** U.S.S. Enterprise NCC-1701-D

Date	Mintage	F	VF	XF	Unc	BU
1997 Proof	25,000	Value: 45.00				

KM# 378 10 DOLLARS **Weight:** 31.1035 g. **Composition:** 0.9990 Silver 1.0000 oz. ASW **Subject:** Star Trek - The Next Generation **Obverse:** National arms **Reverse:** Klingon Bird of Prey

Date	Mintage	F	VF	XF	Unc	BU
1997 Proof	25,000	Value: 45.00				

KM# 381 10 DOLLARS **Weight:** 31.1035 g. **Composition:** 0.9990 Silver 1.0000 oz. ASW **Subject:** Star Trek - The Next Generation **Obverse:** National arms **Reverse:** Borg Cube

Date	Mintage	F	VF	XF	Unc	BU
1997 Proof	25,000	Value: 45.00				

KM# 384 10 DOLLARS **Weight:** 31.1035 g. **Composition:** 0.9990 Silver 1.0000 oz. ASW **Subject:** Star Trek - The Next Generation **Obverse:** National arms **Reverse:** Ferengi Marauder

Date	Mintage	F	VF	XF	Unc	BU
1997 Proof	25,000	Value: 45.00				

KM# 387 10 DOLLARS **Weight:** 31.1035 g. **Composition:** 0.9990 Silver 1.0000 oz. ASW **Subject:** President Ronald Reagan **Obverse:** National arms **Reverse:** Lincoln Statue with bust of Reagan right in background

Date	Mintage	F	VF	XF	Unc	BU
1998 Proof	25,000	Value: 50.00				

KM# 402 10 DOLLARS **Weight:** 31.1035 g. **Composition:** 0.9990 Silver 1.0000 oz. ASW **Subject:** Christopher Columbus **Obverse:** National arms **Reverse:** Portrait, ship

Date	Mintage	F	VF	XF	Unc	BU
1999 Proof	25,000	Value: 45.00				

KM# 405 10 DOLLARS **Weight:** 31.1035 g. **Composition:** 0.9990 Silver 1.0000 oz. ASW **Subject:** Captain James Cook **Obverse:** National arms **Reverse:** Portrait, map, ship

Date	Mintage	F	VF	XF	Unc	BU
1999 Proof	25,000	Value: 45.00				

KM# 408 10 DOLLARS **Weight:** 31.1035 g. **Composition:** 0.9990 Silver 1.0000 oz. ASW **Subject:** Return of Macao to China **Obverse:** National arms **Reverse:** Dragon and phoenix

Date	Mintage	F	VF	XF	Unc	BU
1999 Proof	25,000	Value: 50.00				

KM# 414 10 DOLLARS **Weight:** 31.1035 g. **Composition:** 0.9990 Silver 1.0000 oz. ASW **Subject:** The Wedding of Prince Edward and Miss Sophie Rhys-Jones **Obverse:** National arms **Reverse:** Couple in carriage

Date	Mintage	F	VF	XF	Unc	BU
1999 Proof	10,000	Value: 50.00				

KM# 424 10 DOLLARS **Weight:** 15.5517 g. **Composition:** 0.9990 Silver .5000 oz. ASW **Subject:** Liberty **Obverse:** National arms **Reverse:** Conjoined busts of President John F. Kennedy and his son left

Date	F	VF	XF	Unc	BU
1999 Proof	—	Value: 22.50			

KM# 471 10 DOLLARS **Weight:** 30.7500 g. **Composition:** 0.9990 Silver .9876 oz. ASW **Subject:** Transrapid-08 Hamburg-Berlin Monorail **Obverse:** National arms **Reverse:** Monorail train car **Edge:** Reeded **Size:** 37.9 mm.

Date	F	VF	XF	Unc	BU
1999 Proof	—	Value: 35.00			

KM# 468 10 DOLLARS **Weight:** 25.0000 g. **Composition:** 0.9250 Silver .7435 oz. ASW **Obverse:** National arms **Reverse:** Sailing ship "Mayflower" **Edge:** Reeded **Size:** 38.7 mm.

Date	F	VF	XF	Unc	BU
1999 Proof	—	Value: 25.00			

KM# 469 10 DOLLARS **Weight:** 20.5000 g. **Composition:** 0.9250 Silver .6097 oz. ASW **Subject:** Millennium **Obverse:** National arms **Reverse:** Millennium Dome **Edge:** Reeded **Size:** 38.6 mm.

Date	Mintage	F	VF	XF	Unc	BU
2000 Proof	2,000	Value: 32.50				

KM# 470 10 DOLLARS **Weight:** 20.5000 g. **Composition:** 0.9250 Silver .6097 oz. ASW **Subject:** Mutiny on the Bounty **Reverse:** Mutineers setting ship's officers adrift

Date	Mintage	F	VF	XF	Unc	BU
2000 Proof	2,000	Value: 32.50				

KM# 475 10 DOLLARS **Weight:** 8.4500 g. **Composition:** 0.9990 Silver .2714 oz. ASW **Subject:** General Robert E. Lee **Obverse:** National arms **Reverse:** General Lee on horseback facing left **Edge:** Reeded **Size:** 30.1 mm.

Date	F	VF	XF	Unc	BU
2000 Proof	—	Value: 15.00			

KM# 476 10 DOLLARS **Weight:** 8.4500 g. **Composition:** 0.9990 Silver .2714 oz. ASW **Obverse:** National arms **Reverse:** Statue of Liberty

Date	F	VF	XF	Unc	BU
2000 Proof	—	Value: 15.00			

KM# 492 10 DOLLARS **Weight:** 3.3930 g. **Composition:** 0.9167 Gold .1000 oz. AGW **Subject:** US Gold Indian Design Copy **Obverse:** Incuse Indian design **Reverse:** Incuse eagle design **Edge:** Reeded **Size:** 16.5 mm.

Date	F	VF	XF	Unc	BU
2000	—	—	—	130	—

KM# 500 10 DOLLARS **Weight:** 8.5500 g. **Composition:** 0.9990 Silver 0.2746 oz. ASW **Subject:** American History **Obverse:** National arms **Reverse:** Washington crossing the Delaware scene **Edge:** Reeded **Size:** 30 mm. **Note:** The American Mint is not an actual mint.

Date	Mintage	F	VF	XF	Unc	BU
2000 Proof	20,000	Value: 20.00				

KM# 501 10 DOLLARS **Weight:** 8.5500 g. **Composition:** 0.9990 Silver 0.2746 oz. ASW **Subject:** American History - Battle of Gettysburg **Obverse:** National arms **Reverse:** General Lee bust at left, General Meade bust at right, flags in background **Edge:** Reeded **Size:** 30 mm. **Note:** The American Mint is not an actual mint.

Date	Mintage	F	VF	XF	Unc	BU
2000 Proof	20,000	Value: 20.00				

KM# 502 10 DOLLARS **Weight:** 8.5500 g. **Composition:** 0.9990 Silver 0.2746 oz. ASW **Subject:** American History **Obverse:** National arms **Reverse:** B-17 Bomber in action **Edge:** Reeded **Size:** 30 mm. **Note:** The American Mint is not an actual mint.

Date	Mintage	F	VF	XF	Unc	BU
2000 Proof	20,000	Value: 20.00				

KM# 503 10 DOLLARS **Weight:** 8.5500 g. **Composition:** 0.9990 Silver 0.2746 oz. ASW **Subject:** American History - First Man on the Moon **Obverse:** National arms **Reverse:** Astronaut on the moon with American flag **Edge:** Reeded **Size:** 30 mm. **Note:** The American Mint is not an actual mint.

Date	Mintage	F	VF	XF	Unc	BU
2000 Proof	20,000	Value: 20.00				

KM# 499 10 DOLLARS **Weight:** 20.1500 g. **Composition:** 0.9990 Silver 0.6472 oz. ASW **Obverse:** National arms **Reverse:** Two Diana Guenon monkeys **Edge:** Reeded **Size:** 34 mm.

Date	F	VF	XF	Unc	BU
2000 Proof	—	Value: 30.00			

KM# 423 10 DOLLARS **Weight:** 31.1035 g. **Composition:** 0.9990 Silver 1.000 oz. ASW **Subject:** Millennium **Obverse:** Liberty cap, crossed flags of USA and Liberia above Liberian arms **Reverse:** Morgan dollar Liberty portrait

Date	Mintage	F	VF	XF	Unc	BU
2000 Proof	Est. 2,000	Value: 40.00				

KM# 443 10 DOLLARS **Weight:** 31.1035 g. **Composition:** 0.9990 Silver 1.0000 oz. ASW **Subject:** Greenwich Meridian **Obverse:** National arms **Reverse:** World landmarks and fireworks **Edge:** Reeded **Size:** 38.6 mm.

Date	Mintage	F	VF	XF	Unc	BU
2000 Proof	25,000	Value: 47.50				

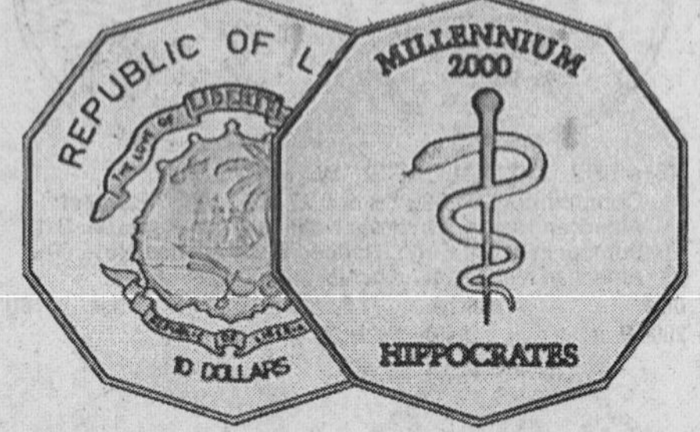

KM# 444 10 DOLLARS **Weight:** 25.0000 g. **Composition:** 0.9250 Silver .7435 oz. ASW **Subject:** Millennium - Hippocrates **Obverse:** National arms **Reverse:** Single snake caduceus **Edge:** Plain **Shape:** 10-sided **Size:** 36.8 mm.

Date	Mintage	F	VF	XF	Unc	BU
2000 Proof	10,000	Value: 35.00				

KM# 513 10 DOLLARS **Composition:** Copper-Nickel **Subject:** Hungarian Revolution of 1848 **Obverse:** Liberian arms **Reverse:** Multicolor heroic scene **Edge:** Reeded **Size:** 38.6 mm.

Date	Mintage	F	VF	XF	Unc	BU
2001 Proof	9,999	Value: 10.00				

KM# 537 10 DOLLARS **Weight:** 28.5000 g. **Composition:** Copper Nickel **Subject:** "Moments of Freedom" Series **Obverse:** National arms **Reverse:** Multicolor Buddha, spelled "Budha" on the coin **Edge:** Reeded **Size:** 38.6 mm.

Date	Mintage	F	VF	XF	Unc	BU
2001 Proof	9,999	Value: 10.00				

KM# 538 10 DOLLARS **Weight:** 28.5000 g. **Composition:** Copper Nickel **Subject:** "Moments of Freedom" Series **Obverse:** National arms **Reverse:** Multicolor Battle of Marathon scene **Edge:** Reeded **Size:** 38.6 mm.

Date	Mintage	F	VF	XF	Unc	BU
2001 Proof	9,999	Value: 10.00				

KM# 539 10 DOLLARS **Weight:** 28.5000 g. **Composition:** Copper Nickel **Series:** "Moments of Freedom" **Obverse:** National arms **Reverse:** Multicolor founding of Liberia design **Edge:** Reeded **Size:** 38.6 mm.

Date	Mintage	F	VF	XF	Unc	BU
2001 Proof	9,999	Value: 10.00				

KM# 540 10 DOLLARS **Weight:** 28.5000 g. **Composition:** Copper Nickel **Series:** "Moments of Freedom" **Obverse:** National arms **Reverse:** Multicolor portrait of Constantine I **Edge:** Reeded **Size:** 38.6 mm.

Date	Mintage	F	VF	XF	Unc	BU
2001 Proof	9,999	Value: 10.00				

KM# 541 10 DOLLARS **Weight:** 28.5000 g. **Composition:** Copper Nickel **Series:** "Moments of Freedom" **Obverse:** National arms **Reverse:** Multicolor William Tell statue **Edge:** Reeded **Size:** 38.6 mm.

Date	Mintage	F	VF	XF	Unc	BU
2001 Proof	9,999	Value: 10.00				

KM# 542 10 DOLLARS **Weight:** 28.5000 g. **Composition:** Copper Nickel **Series:** "Moments of Freedom" **Obverse:** National arms **Reverse:** Multicolor Galileo portrait **Edge:** Reeded **Size:** 38.6 mm.

Date	Mintage	F	VF	XF	Unc	BU
2001 Proof	9,999	Value: 10.00				

KM# 544 10 DOLLARS **Weight:** 28.5000 g. **Composition:** Copper Nickel **Series:** "Moments of Freedom" **Subject:** Fall of Berlin Wall **Obverse:** National arms **Reverse:** Multicolor Brandenburg Gate scene **Edge:** Reeded **Size:** 38.6 mm.

Date	Mintage	F	VF	XF	Unc	BU
2001 Proof	9,999	Value: 10.00				

KM# 545 10 DOLLARS **Weight:** 28.5000 g. **Composition:** Copper Nickel **Series:** "Moments of Freedom" **Obverse:** National arms **Reverse:** Multicolor Dalai Lama portrait **Edge:** Reeded **Size:** 38.6 mm.

Date	Mintage	F	VF	XF	Unc	BU
2001 Proof	9,999	Value: 10.00				

KM# 547 10 DOLLARS **Weight:** 28.5000 g. **Composition:** Copper Nickel **Series:** "Moments of Freedom" **Obverse:** National arms **Reverse:** Multicolor Declaration of Independence scene **Edge:** Reeded **Size:** 38.6 mm.

Date	Mintage	F	VF	XF	Unc	BU
2001 Proof	9,999	Value: 10.00				

KM# 548 10 DOLLARS **Weight:** 28.5000 g. **Composition:** Copper Nickel **Series:** "Moments of Freedom" **Subject:** Women's Rights **Obverse:** National arms **Reverse:** Multicolor allegorical woman **Edge:** Reeded **Size:** 38.6 mm.

Date	Mintage	F	VF	XF	Unc	BU
2001 Proof	9,999	Value: 10.00				

KM# 549 10 DOLLARS **Weight:** 28.5000 g. **Composition:** Copper Nickel **Series:** "Moments of Freedom" **Obverse:** National arms **Reverse:** Multicolor Gandhi portrait **Edge:** Reeded **Size:** 38.6 mm.

Date	Mintage	F	VF	XF	Unc	BU
2001 Proof	9,999	Value: 10.00				

KM# 550 10 DOLLARS **Weight:** 28.5000 g. **Composition:** Copper Nickel **Series:** "Moments of Freedom" **Subject:** Spanish Civil War **Obverse:** National arms **Reverse:** Multicolor picture of a soldier at the moment he is shot in battle **Edge:** Reeded **Size:** 38.6 mm.

Date	Mintage	F	VF	XF	Unc	BU
2001 Proof	9,999	Value: 10.00				

KM# 551 10 DOLLARS **Weight:** 28.5000 g. **Composition:** Copper Nickel **Series:** "Moments of Freedom" **Subject:** End of Holocaust **Obverse:** National arms **Reverse:** Multicolor inmates behind wire fence scene **Edge:** Reeded **Size:** 38.6 mm.

Date	Mintage	F	VF	XF	Unc	BU
2001 Proof	9,999	Value: 10.00				

KM# 552 10 DOLLARS **Weight:** 28.5000 g. **Composition:** Copper Nickel **Series:** "Moments of Freedom" **Subject:** End of WWII **Obverse:** National arms **Reverse:** Multicolor Iwo Jima flag raising scene **Edge:** Reeded **Size:** 38.6 mm.

Date	Mintage	F	VF	XF	Unc	BU
2001 Proof	9,999	Value: 10.00				

KM# 553 10 DOLLARS **Weight:** 28.5000 g. **Composition:** Copper Nickel **Series:** "Moments of Freedom" **Subject:** United Nations **Obverse:** National arms **Reverse:** Multicolor UN logo and dove **Edge:** Reeded **Size:** 38.6 mm.

Date	Mintage	F	VF	XF	Unc	BU
2001 Proof	9,999	Value: 10.00				

KM# 554 10 DOLLARS **Weight:** 28.5000 g. **Composition:** Copper Nickel **Series:** "Moments of Freedom" **Obverse:** National arms **Reverse:** Multicolor Solzhenitsyn portrait **Edge:** Reeded **Size:** 38.6 mm.

Date	Mintage	F	VF	XF	Unc	BU
2001 Proof	9,999	Value: 10.00				

KM# 555 10 DOLLARS **Weight:** 28.5000 g. **Composition:** Copper Nickel **Series:** "Moments of Freedom" **Obverse:** National arms **Reverse:** Multicolor Spartacus and troops **Edge:** Reeded **Size:** 38.6 mm.

Date	Mintage	F	VF	XF	Unc	BU
2001 Proof	9,999	Value: 10.00				

KM# 556 10 DOLLARS **Weight:** 28.5000 g. **Composition:** Copper Nickel **Series:** "Moments of Freedom" **Subject:** Czechoslovakia 1968 **Obverse:** National arms **Reverse:** Multicolor Soviet tank in Prague **Edge:** Reeded **Size:** 38.6 mm.

Date	Mintage	F	VF	XF	Unc	BU
2001 Proof	9,999	Value: 10.00				

KM# 558 10 DOLLARS **Weight:** 28.5000 g. **Composition:** Copper Nickel **Series:** "Moments of Freedom" **Obverse:** National arms **Reverse:** Multicolor Nelson Mandela and fist **Edge:** Reeded **Size:** 38.6 mm.

Date	Mintage	F	VF	XF	Unc	BU
2001 Proof	9,999	Value: 10.00				

KM# 559 10 DOLLARS **Weight:** 28.5000 g. **Composition:** Copper Nickel **Series:** "Moments of Freedom" **Subject:** Freedom of Communication **Obverse:** National arms **Reverse:** Multicolor circuit board and world globe **Edge:** Reeded **Size:** 38.6 mm.

Date	Mintage	F	VF	XF	Unc	BU
2001 Proof	9,999	Value: 10.00				

KM# 510 10 DOLLARS **Weight:** 33.2400 g. **Composition:** Gold-Plated Copper **Subject:** American Eagle **Obverse:** National arms **Reverse:** Multicolor holographic eagle **Edge:** Reeded **Size:** 40.1 mm. **Note:** The American Mint is not an actual mint.

Date	Mintage	F	VF	XF	Unc	BU
2001	20,000	—	—	—	35.00	—

KM# 511 10 DOLLARS **Weight:** 27.6100 g. **Composition:** Copper-Nickel **Subject:** American Eagle **Obverse:** Multicolor holographic Statue of Liberty **Obv. Legend:** LIBERTY 10 DOLLARS **Reverse:** Multicolor holographic eagle **Rev. Legend:** AMERICAN EAGLE 10 DOLLARS **Edge:** Reeded **Size:** 40.1 mm. **Note:** There is not a country name or symbol to be found on this coin. The American Mint is not an actual mint.

Date	Mintage	F	VF	XF	Unc	BU
ND(2001)	20,000	—	—	—	30.00	—

KM# 543 10 DOLLARS **Weight:** 28.5000 g. **Composition:** Copper Nickel **Series:** "Moments of Freedom" **Subject:** Liberation of Vienna **Obverse:** National arms **Reverse:** Multicolor Sultan and battle scene **Edge:** Reeded **Size:** 38.6 mm. **Note:** Vienna was never captured by the Turks.

Date	Mintage	F	VF	XF	Unc	BU
2001 Proof	9,999	Value: 10.00				

KM# 493 10 DOLLARS **Weight:** 770.0000 g. **Composition:** Copper **Subject:** "The Wreck of the Princess Louisa" **Obverse:** National arms **Reverse:** Sailing ship **Edge:** Reeded **Size:** 100 mm. **Note:** Illustration reduced. With an encased glass shard recovered from the wreck site of the Princess Louisa.

Date	Mintage	F	VF	XF	Unc	BU
2001	2,000	—	—	—	200	—

KM# 491 10 DOLLARS **Weight:** 25.2500 g. **Composition:** 0.9250 Silver .7509 oz. ASW **Subject:** Illusion **Obverse:** National arms **Reverse:** Male-female portrait **Edge:** Plain **Shape:** 10-sided **Size:** 36.8mm.

Date	Mintage	F	VF	XF	Unc	BU
2001 Proof	5,000	—	—	—	35.00	—

KM# 20 12 DOLLARS **Weight:** 6.0000 g. **Composition:** 0.9000 Gold .1736 oz. AGW **Subject:** 70th Birthday of President Tubman

Date	Mintage	F	VF	XF	Unc	BU
1965 Proof	400	Value: 125				

KM# 108 15 DOLLARS **Weight:** 1.0000 g. **Composition:** 0.9999 Gold .0321 oz. AGW **Series:** Preserve Planet Earth **Reverse:** Compsognathus

Date		F	VF	XF	Unc	BU
1993 Proof	—	Value: 32.50				

KM# 19 20 DOLLARS **Weight:** 18.6500 g. **Composition:** 0.9000 Gold .5397 oz. AGW **Subject:** William Vacanarat Shadrach Tubman

Date	Mintage	F	VF	XF	Unc	BU
1964B	10,000	—	—	—	250	—

KM# 19a 20 DOLLARS **Composition:** 0.9990 Gold

Date	Mintage	F	VF	XF	Unc	BU
1964B L Proof	100	Value: 350				

Note: Of the total issue, 10,200 were struck of .900 fine gold and bear the "B" mint mark of the Bern Mint below the date, while 100 were struck (restrikes suspected) as proofs of .999 fine gold and are designated by the presence of a small "L" above the date

KM# 64 20 DOLLARS **Weight:** 15.8100 g. **Composition:** 0.9000 Gold .8768 oz. AGW **Subject:** 25th Anniversary of Inter-Continental Hotels

Date	F	VF	XF	Unc	BU
1971 Proof	—	—	—	—	—

KM# 27 20 DOLLARS **Weight:** 33.4370 g. **Composition:** 0.9000 Gold .9675 oz. AGW **Subject:** Inauguration of President Tolbert

Date		F	VF	XF	Unc	BU
1972 Proof	—	Value: 450				

KM# 45 20 DOLLARS **Weight:** 28.2800 g. **Composition:** 0.9250 Silver .8411 oz. ASW **Subject:** Year of the Scout **Obverse:** National arms

Date	Mintage	F	VF	XF	Unc	BU
1983	10,000	—	—	—	30.00	—
1983 Proof	10,000	Value: 48.50				

KM# 48 20 DOLLARS **Weight:** 28.2800 g. **Composition:** 0.9250 Silver .8411 oz. ASW **Series:** International Year of Disabled Persons

Date		F	VF	XF	Unc	BU
1983		—	—	—	32.50	—
1983 Proof	—	Value: 50.00				

KM# 283 20 DOLLARS **Weight:** 1.2700 g. **Composition:** 0.9990 Gold .0408 oz. AGW **Subject:** Formula One **Reverse:** Damon Hill

Date	Mintage	F	VF	XF	Unc	BU
1994 Proof	25,000	Value: 65.00				

KM# 230 20 DOLLARS **Weight:** 1.2700 g. **Composition:** 0.9990 Gold .0408 oz. AGW **Subject:** Formula One **Reverse:** Ayrton Senna **Note:** Similar to 10 Dollars, KM#229.

Date	Mintage	F	VF	XF	Unc	BU
1996 Proof	15,000	Value: 65.00				

KM# 250 20 DOLLARS **Weight:** 1.2700 g. **Composition:** 0.9990 Gold .0408 oz. AGW **Subject:** Dalai Lama **Note:** Similar to 100 Dollars, KM#252.

Date	Mintage	F	VF	XF	Unc	BU
1996 Proof	15,000	Value: 65.00				

KM# 315 20 DOLLARS **Weight:** 1.2400 g. **Composition:** 0.9990 Gold .0400 oz. AGW **Subject:** Return of Hong Kong to China **Note:** Similar to 10 Dollars, KM#314.

Date		F	VF	XF	Unc	BU
1997 Proof	—	Value: 65.00				

KM# 498 20 DOLLARS **Weight:** 31.2200 g. **Composition:** 0.9990 Silver 1.0027 oz. ASW **Subject:** Year of the Ox - Type II **Obverse:** National arms **Reverse:** Ox within inner circle with legend **Edge:** Reeded **Size:** 38.5 mm.

Date		F	VF	XF	Unc	BU
1997 Proof	—	Value: 50.00				

KM# 340 20 DOLLARS **Weight:** 31.1035 g. **Composition:** 0.9990 Silver 1.0000 oz. ASW **Subject:** Year of the Ox **Obverse:** National arms

Date	F	VF	XF	Unc	BU
1997 Proof	—	Value: 32.50			

KM# 341 20 DOLLARS **Weight:** 31.1035 g. **Composition:** 0.9990 Silver 1.0000 oz. ASW **Subject:** Year of the Tiger **Obverse:** National arms **Reverse:** Tiger in bamboo

Date	F	VF	XF	Unc	BU
1998 (1997) Proof	—	Value: 25.00			

KM# 389 20 DOLLARS **Weight:** 31.1035 g. **Composition:** 0.9990 Silver 1.0000 oz. ASW **Subject:** Year of the Rabbit **Obverse:** National arms **Reverse:** Rabbit running left

Date	Mintage	F	VF	XF	Unc	BU
1999 Proof	8,000	Value: 45.00				

KM# 416 20 DOLLARS **Weight:** 31.3500 g. **Composition:** 0.9990 Silver 1.0069 oz. ASW **Subject:** Deng Xiaoping **Obverse:** National arms **Reverse:** Portrait, dates

Date	F	VF	XF	Unc	BU
1997 Proof	—	Value: 22.50			

KM# 342 20 DOLLARS **Weight:** 24.9400 g. **Composition:** Silver **Subject:** Year of the Tiger **Obverse:** National arms **Reverse:** Tiger lying in bamboo

Date	F	VF	XF	Unc	BU
1998 (1997) Proof	—	Value: 37.50			

KM# 390 20 DOLLARS **Weight:** 31.1035 g. **Composition:** 0.9990 Silver 1.0000 oz. ASW **Subject:** Year of the Rabbit **Obverse:** National arms **Reverse:** Rabbit sitting

Date	Mintage	F	VF	XF	Unc	BU
1999 Proof	8,000	Value: 45.00				

KM# 417 20 DOLLARS **Weight:** 31.4000 g. **Composition:** 0.9990 Silver 1.0085 oz. ASW **Subject:** Princess Diana **Obverse:** National arms **Reverse:** Portrait, dates

Date	F	VF	XF	Unc	BU
1997 Proof	—	Value: 32.50			

KM# 343 20 DOLLARS **Weight:** 24.9400 g. **Composition:** Silver **Subject:** Year of the Tiger **Obverse:** National arms **Reverse:** Stalking tiger

Date	F	VF	XF	Unc	BU
1998 (1997) Proof	—	Value: 27.50			

KM# 391 20 DOLLARS **Weight:** 31.1035 g. **Composition:** 0.9990 Silver 1.0000 oz. ASW **Subject:** Year of the Rabbit **Obverse:** National arms **Reverse:** Rabbit running right

Date	Mintage	F	VF	XF	Unc	BU
1999 Proof	8,000	Value: 45.00				

KM# 418 20 DOLLARS **Weight:** 1.2441 g. **Composition:** 0.9999 Gold .0400 oz. AGW **Subject:** Return of Macao to China **Obverse:** National arms **Reverse:** Dragon and phoenix **Note:** Similar to 10 Dollars, KM#408.

Date	Mintage	F	VF	XF	Unc	BU
1999 Proof	25,000	Value: 55.00				

KM# 535 20 DOLLARS **Weight:** 31.1300 g. **Composition:** 0.9990 Silver 0.9999 oz. ASW **Subject:** Princess Diana - Compassion **Obverse:** National arms **Reverse:** Diana with sick child **Edge:** Reeded **Size:** 38.6 mm.

Date	F	VF	XF	Unc	BU
1997 Proof	—	Value: 40.00			

KM# 364 20 DOLLARS **Weight:** 31.1035 g. **Composition:** 0.9990 Silver 1.0000 oz. ASW **Subject:** RMS Titanic **Obverse:** National arms **Reverse:** Ship sinking

Date	Mintage	F	VF	XF	Unc	BU
1998 Proof	25,000	Value: 50.00				

KM# 472 20 DOLLARS **Weight:** 20.1700 g. **Composition:** 0.9990 Silver .6478 oz. ASW **Series:** American History **Obverse:** National arms **Reverse:** The Alamo and defenders **Edge:** Reeded **Size:** 40.3 mm.

Date	F	VF	XF	Unc	BU
2000 Proof	—	Value: 25.00			

KM# 504 20 DOLLARS **Weight:** 20.0000 g. **Composition:** 0.9990 Silver 0.6424 oz. ASW **Subject:** American History **Obverse:** National arms **Reverse:** Treaty of Paris signing scene **Edge:** Reeded **Size:** 40.4 mm. **Note:** The American Mint is not an actual mint.

Date	Mintage	F	VF	XF	Unc	BU
2000 Proof	20,000	Value: 40.00				

KM# 505 20 DOLLARS **Weight:** 20.0000 g. **Composition:** 0.9990 Silver 0.6424 oz. ASW **Subject:** American History - Civil War **Obverse:** National arms **Reverse:** Bombardment of Fort Sumter scene **Edge:** Reeded **Size:** 40.4 mm. **Note:** The American Mint is not an actual mint.

Date	Mintage	F	VF	XF	Unc	BU
2000 Proof	20,000	Value: 40.00				

KM# 506 20 DOLLARS **Weight:** 20.0000 g. **Composition:** 0.9990 Silver 0.6424 oz. ASW **Subject:** American History **Obverse:** National arms **Reverse:** Bust of President Harry S. Truman facing **Edge:** Reeded **Size:** 40.4 mm. **Note:** The American Mint is not an actual mint.

Date	Mintage	F	VF	XF	Unc	BU
2000 Proof	20,000	Value: 40.00				

KM# 507 20 DOLLARS **Weight:** 20.0000 g. **Composition:** 0.9990 Silver 0.6424 oz. ASW **Subject:** American History **Obverse:** National arms**Reverse:** Busts of astronauts Young and Crippen with Space Shuttle model **Edge:** Reeded **Size:** 40.4 mm. **Note:** The American Mint is not an actual mint.

Date	Mintage	F	VF	XF	Unc	BU
2000 Proof	20,000	Value: 40.00				

KM# 508 20 DOLLARS **Weight:** 31.1035 g. **Composition:** 0.9990 Silver 0.999 oz. ASW **Subject:** Millennium **Obverse:** Seated allegorical woman **Reverse:** Y2K design **Edge:** Reeded **Size:** 40.7 mm. **Note:** The American Mint is not an actual mint.

Date	Mintage	F	VF	XF	Unc	BU
2000	2,000	—	—	—	30.00	—

KM# 509.1 20 DOLLARS **Weight:** 31.1035 g. **Composition:** 0.9990 Silver 0.999 oz. ASW **Subject:** Millennium **Obverse:** National arms **Reverse:** Woman with hour glass and dove **Edge:** Reeded **Size:** 39 mm. **Note:** The American Mint is not an actual mint.

Date	F	VF	XF	Unc	BU
2000	—	—	—	30.00	—

KM# 509.2 20 DOLLARS **Weight:** 31.1035 g. **Composition:** 0.9990 Silver 0.999 oz. ASW **Subject:** Millennium **Obverse:** National arms **Reverse:** Multicolor woman with hour glass and dove **Edge:** Reeded **Size:** 39 mm. **Note:** The American Mint is not an actual mint.

Date	F	VF	XF	Unc	BU
2000	—	—	—	30.00	—

KM# 477 20 DOLLARS **Weight:** 20.0400 g. **Composition:** 0.9990 Silver .6437 oz. ASW **Subject:** Admiral David G. Farragut **Obverse:** National arms **Reverse:** Ferragut's portrait **Edge:** Reeded **Size:** 40.3 mm.

Date	Mintage	F	VF	XF	Unc	BU
2000 Proof	Est. 20,000	Value: 25.00				

KM# 478 20 DOLLARS **Weight:** 20.0400 g. **Composition:** 0.9990 Silver .6437 oz. ASW **Subject:** Surrender of Appomattox **Obverse:** National arms **Reverse:** Surrender signing scene

Date	Mintage	F	VF	XF	Unc	BU
2000 Proof	Est. 20,000	Value: 25.00				

KM# 479 20 DOLLARS **Weight:** 20.0400 g. **Composition:** 0.9990 Silver .6437 oz. ASW **Subject:** Abraham Lincoln **Obverse:** National arms **Reverse:** Lincoln's portrait

Date	Mintage	F	VF	XF	Unc	BU
2000 Proof	Est. 20,000	Value: 25.00				

KM# 480 20 DOLLARS **Weight:** 20.0400 g. **Composition:** 0.9990 Silver .6437 oz. ASW **Subject:** Montgolfiere Balloon **Obverse:** National arms **Reverse:** First hot air balloon

Date	Mintage	F	VF	XF	Unc	BU
2000 Proof	Est. 20,000	Value: 25.00				

KM# 481 20 DOLLARS **Weight:** 20.0400 g. **Composition:** 0.9990 Silver .6437 oz. ASW **Subject:** Concorde Supersonic Airliner **Obverse:** National arms **Reverse:** Concorde in flight above runway

Date	Mintage	F	VF	XF	Unc	BU
2000 Proof	Est. 20,000	Value: 25.00				

KM# 482 20 DOLLARS **Weight:** 20.0400 g. **Composition:** 0.9990 Silver .6437 oz. ASW **Subject:** Apollo X **Obverse:** National arms **Reverse:** Rocket launch, space capsule, large X

Date	Mintage	F	VF	XF	Unc	BU
2000 Proof	Est. 20,000	Value: 25.00				

KM# 483 20 DOLLARS **Weight:** 20.0400 g. **Composition:** 0.9990 Silver .6437 oz. ASW **Subject:** Apollo VII **Obverse:** National arms **Reverse:** Space capsule above half-length busts of Schirra, Eisele, and Cunningham facing

Date	Mintage	F	VF	XF	Unc	BU
2000 Proof	Est. 20,000	Value: 25.00				

KM# 484 20 DOLLARS **Weight:** 20.0400 g. **Composition:** 0.9990 Silver .6437 oz. ASW **Subject:** STS-1 **Obverse:** National arms **Reverse:** 3/4-length busts of Young and Crippen facing with shuttle model

Date	Mintage	F	VF	XF	Unc	BU
2000 Proof	Est. 20,000	Value: 25.00				

KM# 485 20 DOLLARS **Weight:** 20.0400 g. **Composition:** 0.9990 Silver .6437 oz. ASW **Subject:** Skylab I **Obverse:** National arms **Reverse:** Half-length busts of Conrad, Kerwin, and Weitz facing below Skylab

Date	Mintage	F	VF	XF	Unc	BU
2000 Proof	Est. 20,000	Value: 25.00				

KM# 486 20 DOLLARS **Weight:** 20.0400 g. **Composition:** 0.9990 Silver .6437 oz. ASW **Series:** Olympics **Obverse:** National arms **Reverse:** Hurdler

Date	Mintage	F	VF	XF	Unc	BU
2000 Proof	Est. 20,000	Value: 25.00				

KM# 487 20 DOLLARS **Weight:** 20.0400 g. **Composition:** 0.9990 Silver .6437 oz. ASW **Series:** Olympics **Obverse:** National arms **Reverse:** Equestrian

Date	Mintage	F	VF	XF	Unc	BU
2000 Proof	Est. 20,000	Value: 25.00				

KM# 488 20 DOLLARS **Weight:** 20.0400 g. **Composition:** 0.9990 Silver .6437 oz. ASW **Series:** Olympics **Obverse:** National arms **Reverse:** Two basketball players in front of flags

Date	Mintage	F	VF	XF	Unc	BU
2000 Proof	Est. 20,000	Value: 25.00				

KM# 489 20 DOLLARS **Weight:** 20.0400 g. **Composition:** 0.9990 Silver .6437 oz. ASW **Series:** Olympics **Obverse:** National arms **Reverse:** Three cyclists

Date	Mintage	F	VF	XF	Unc	BU
2000 Proof	Est. 20,000	Value: 25.00				

KM# 490 20 DOLLARS **Weight:** 20.0400 g. **Composition:** 0.9990 Silver .6437 oz. ASW **Series:** Olympics **Obverse:** National arms **Reverse:** Swimmer, cyclist, and speed walker

Date	Mintage	F	VF	XF	Unc	BU
2000 Proof	Est. 20,000	Value: 25.00				

KM# 514 20 DOLLARS **Weight:** 31.1035 g. **Composition:** 0.9990 Silver 0.999 oz. ASW **Subject:** Bush-Cheney Inauguration **Obverse:** White House **Reverse:** Conjoined busts of President Bush and Vice President Cheney right **Edge:** Reeded **Size:** 38.2 mm.

Date		F	VF	XF	Unc	BU
2001 Proof	—	Value: 40.00				

KM# 21 25 DOLLARS **Weight:** 23.3120 g. **Composition:** 0.9000 Gold .6746 oz. AGW **Subject:** 70th Birthday of President Tubman

Date	Mintage	F	VF	XF	Unc	BU
1965	3,000	—	—	—	325	—

KM# 21a 25 DOLLARS **Composition:** 0.9990 Gold

Date	Mintage	F	VF	XF	Unc	BU
1965B L Proof	100	Value: 400				

KM# 23 25 DOLLARS **Composition:** 0.9990 Gold **Subject:** 75th Birthday of President Tubman

Date		F	VF	XF	Unc	BU
ND(1970)B Proof	—	Value: 300				

KM# 28 25 DOLLARS **Composition:** 0.9990 Gold **Subject:** Sesquicentennial - Founding of Liberia

Date	Mintage	F	VF	XF	Unc	BU
ND(1972)B Proof	3,000	Value: 300				

KM# 323 25 DOLLARS **Weight:** 77.7587 g. **Composition:** 0.9990 Silver 2.5000 oz. ASW **Subject:** 25th Anniversary - Standard Catalog of World Coins **Obverse:** National arms **Reverse:** Children, globe, world coins

Date	Mintage	F	VF	XF	Unc	BU
1997 Proof	2,500	Value: 35.00				

KM# 512 25 DOLLARS **Weight:** 0.7300 g. **Composition:** 0.9990 Gold 0.0234 oz. AGW **Obverse:** National arms **Reverse:** Bust of Egyptian Queen Nefertiti right **Rev. Legend:** NOFRETETE **Edge:** Reeded **Size:** 11.1 mm. **Note:** The American Mint is not an actual mint.

Date	F	VF	XF	Unc	BU
2000 Proof	—	Value: 30.00			

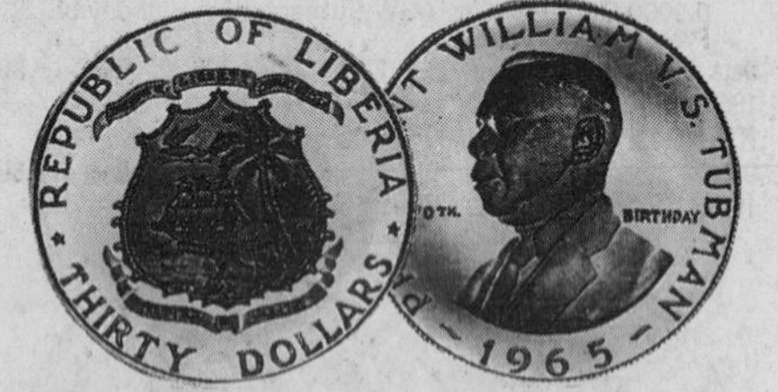

KM# 22 30 DOLLARS **Weight:** 15.0000 g. **Composition:** 0.9000 Gold .4340 oz. AGW **Subject:** 70th Birthday of President Tubman

Date	Mintage	F	VF	XF	Unc	BU
1965 Proof	400	Value: 225				

KM# 69 50 DOLLARS **Weight:** 155.5150 g. **Composition:** 0.9990 Silver 5.0000 oz. ASW **Subject:** President Bill Clinton **Note:** Similar to 10 Dollars, KM#68.

Date	F	VF	XF	Unc	BU
1993 Proof	—	Value: 85.00			

KM# 251 50 DOLLARS **Weight:** 3.1103 g. **Composition:** 0.9990 Gold .1000 oz. AGW **Subject:** Dalai Lama **Note:** Similar to 100 Dollars, KM#252.

Date	Mintage	F	VF	XF	Unc	BU
1996 Proof	10,000	Value: 110				

KM# 410.1 50 DOLLARS **Composition:** Copper-Nickel **Obverse:** National arms **Reverse:** Face on Mars with rough texture

Date	F	VF	XF	Unc	BU
1996	—	—	—	12.00	—

KM# 410.2 50 DOLLARS **Composition:** Copper-Nickel **Obverse:** National arms **Reverse:** Face on Mars with smooth texture

Date	F	VF	XF	Unc	BU
1996	—	—	—	12.00	—

KM# 231 50 DOLLARS **Weight:** 3.1103 g. **Composition:** 0.9990 Gold .1000 oz. AGW **Subject:** Formula One **Reverse:** Ayrton Senna **Note:** Similar to 10 Dollars, KM#229.

Date	Mintage	F	VF	XF	Unc	BU
1996 Proof	10,000	Value: 110				

KM# 316 50 DOLLARS **Weight:** 3.1103 g. **Composition:** 0.9990 Gold .1000 oz. AGW **Subject:** Return of Hong Kong to China **Note:** Similar to 10 Dollars, KM#314.

Date	F	VF	XF	Unc	BU
1997 Proof	—	Value: 100			

KM# 366 50 DOLLARS **Weight:** 3.1103 g. **Composition:** 0.9990 Gold .1000 oz. AGW **Subject:** RMS Titanic **Obverse:** National arms **Reverse:** Ship sinking **Note:** Similar to 20 Dollars, KM#364.

Date	F	VF	XF	Unc	BU
1998 Proof	Est. 2,000	Value: 115			

KM# 419 50 DOLLARS **Weight:** 3.1103 g. **Composition:** 0.9990 Gold .1000 oz. AGW **Subject:** Return of Macao to China **Obverse:** National arms **Reverse:** Dragon and phoenix **Note:** Similar to 10 Dollars, KM#408.

Date	Mintage	F	VF	XF	Unc	BU
1999 Proof	10,000	Value: 100				

KM# 495 50 DOLLARS **Weight:** 907.0000 g. **Composition:** 0.9990 Silver 29.1315 oz. ASW **Subject:** Wreck of the Princess Louisa **Obverse:** National arms, denomination and date **Reverse:** Ship under sail **Edge:** Reeded **Size:** 100 mm. **Note:** Each coin has a cob coin recovered from the wreck site encased in a hole with clear resin. Illustration reduced.

Date	Mintage	F	VF	XF	Unc	BU
2001	500	—	—	—	175	—

KM# 33 100 DOLLARS **Weight:** 6.0000 g. **Composition:** 0.9000 Gold .1736 oz. AGW **Subject:** Inauguration of President Tolbert

Date	Mintage	F	VF	XF	Unc	BU
1976 Proof	175	Value: 225				

KM# 36 100 DOLLARS **Weight:** 10.9300 g. **Composition:** 0.9000 Gold .3163 oz. AGW **Subject:** 130th Anniversary of the Republic

Date	Mintage	F	VF	XF	Unc	BU
1977FM (U)	787	—	—	—	200	—
1977FM (P)	4,250	Value: 145				

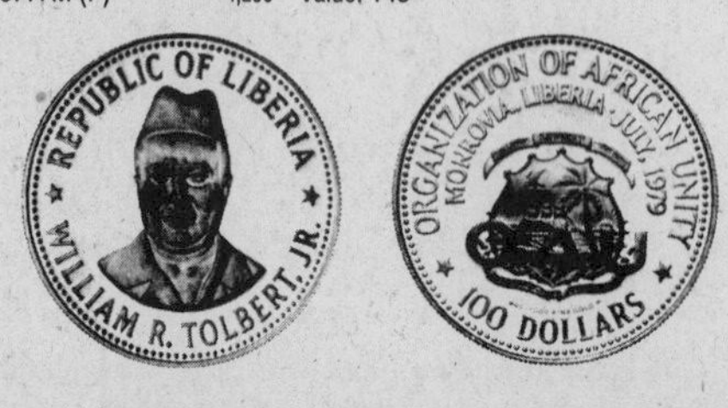

KM# 37 100 DOLLARS **Weight:** 10.9300 g. **Composition:** 0.9000 Gold .3163 oz. AGW **Subject:** Organization of African Unity **Reverse:** Summit Conference

Date	Mintage	F	VF	XF	Unc	BU
1979FM (P)	1,656	Value: 160				

KM# 38 100 DOLLARS **Weight:** 11.2000 g. **Composition:** 0.9000 Gold .3241 oz. AGW **Subject:** Organization of African Unity **Reverse:** Elephant

Date	F	VF	XF	Unc	BU
1979FM (P)	—	Value: 200			

KM# 50 100 DOLLARS **Weight:** 10.9300 g. **Composition:** 0.9000 Gold .3163 oz. AGW **Subject:** 5th Anniversary of Government **Reverse:** Leopard

Date	Mintage	F	VF	XF	Unc	BU
1985FM (P)	409	Value: 450				

KM# 61 100 DOLLARS **Weight:** 7.1300 g. **Composition:** 0.9000 Gold .2063 oz. AGW **Series:** Decade For Women **Reverse:** Woman mashing grain

Date	Mintage	F	VF	XF	Unc	BU
1985 Proof	318	Value: 200				

KM# 70 100 DOLLARS **Weight:** 311.0300 g. **Composition:** 0.9990 Silver 10.0000 oz. ASW **Subject:** President Bill Clinton

Date	F	VF	XF	Unc	BU
1993 Proof	—	Value: 165			

KM# 100 100 DOLLARS **Weight:** 6.2200 g. **Composition:** 0.9990 Gold .2000 oz. AGW **Series:** Preserve Planet Earth **Reverse:** Protoceratops

Date	F	VF	XF	Unc	BU
1993 Proof	Est. 7,500	Value: 165			

KM# 111 100 DOLLARS **Weight:** 6.2200 g. **Composition:** 0.9990 Gold .2000 oz. AGW **Series:** Preserve Planet Earth **Reverse:** Corythosaurus

Date	Mintage	F	VF	XF	Unc	BU
1993 Proof	7,500	Value: 165				

KM# 114 100 DOLLARS **Weight:** 6.2200 g. **Composition:** 0.9990 Gold .2000 oz. AGW **Series:** Preserve Planet Earth **Reverse:** Atchaeopteryx **Note:** Incorrect spelling.

Date	Mintage	F	VF	XF	Unc	BU
1993 Proof	Est. 7,500	Value: 165				

KM# 117 100 DOLLARS Weight: 6.2200 g. **Composition:** 0.9990 Gold .2000 oz. AGW **Series:** Preserve Planet Earth **Reverse:** Archaeopteryx **Note:** Correct spelling.

Date	Mintage	F	VF	XF	Unc	BU
1994 Proof	7,500	Value: 165				

KM# 120 100 DOLLARS Weight: 6.2200 g. **Composition:** 0.9990 Gold .2000 oz. AGW **Series:** Preserve Planet Earth **Reverse:** Gorillas **Note:** Similar to 10 Dollars, KM#120.

Date	Mintage	F	VF	XF	Unc	BU
1994 Proof	Est. 7,500	Value: 165				

KM# 123 100 DOLLARS Weight: 6.2200 g. **Composition:** 0.9990 Gold .2000 oz. AGW **Series:** Preserve Planet Earth **Reverse:** Pygmy Hippopotami **Note:** Similar to 10 Dollars, KM#122.

Date	Mintage	F	VF	XF	Unc	BU
1994 Proof	Est. 7,500	Value: 165				

KM# 126 100 DOLLARS Weight: 6.2200 g. **Composition:** 0.9990 Gold .2000 oz. AGW **Series:** Preserve Planet Earth **Reverse:** Trionyx Turtle **Note:** Similar to 10 Dollars, KM#125.

Date	Mintage	F	VF	XF	Unc	BU
1994 Proof	Est. 7,500	Value: 165				

KM# 130 100 DOLLARS Weight: 6.2200 g. **Composition:** 0.9990 Gold .2000 oz. AGW **Subject:** Star Trek **Reverse:** Captains Kirk and Picard **Note:** Similar to 10 Dollars, KM#129.

Date		F	VF	XF	Unc	BU
1995 Proof	—	Value: 175				

KM# 135 100 DOLLARS Weight: 6.2200 g. **Composition:** 0.9990 Gold .2000 oz. AGW **Series:** Preserve Planet Earth **Reverse:** Leopard; Similar to 10 Dollars, KM#134

Date	Mintage	F	VF	XF	Unc	BU
1995 Proof	Est. 7,500	Value: 165				

KM# 138 100 DOLLARS Weight: 6.2200 g. **Composition:** 0.9990 Gold .2000 oz. AGW **Series:** Preserve Planet Earth **Reverse:** Storks; Similar to 10 Dollars, KM#137

Date	Mintage	F	VF	XF	Unc	BU
1995 Proof	Est. 7,500	Value: 165				

KM# 150 100 DOLLARS Weight: 6.2200 g. **Composition:** 0.9990 Gold .2000 oz. AGW **Subject:** Sir Winston Churchill **Reverse:** Similar to 10 Dollars, KM#145

Date	Mintage	F	VF	XF	Unc	BU
1995 Proof	Est. 7,500	Value: 125				

KM# 151 100 DOLLARS Weight: 6.2200 g. **Composition:** 0.9990 Gold .2000 oz. AGW **Subject:** President Franklin D. Roosevelt **Reverse:** Similar to 10 Dollars, KM#146

Date	Mintage	F	VF	XF	Unc	BU
1995 Proof	Est. 7,500	Value: 125				

KM# 152 100 DOLLARS Weight: 6.2200 g. **Composition:** 0.9990 Gold .2000 oz. AGW **Subject:** General George Patton **Reverse:** Similar to 10 Dollars, KM#147

Date	Mintage	F	VF	XF	Unc	BU
1995 Proof	Est. 7,500	Value: 125				

KM# 153 100 DOLLARS Weight: 6.2200 g. **Composition:** 0.9990 Gold .2000 oz. AGW **Subject:** President Harry S. Truman **Reverse:** Similar to 10 Dollars, KM#148

Date	Mintage	F	VF	XF	Unc	BU
1995 Proof	Est. 7,500	Value: 125				

KM# 154 100 DOLLARS Weight: 6.2200 g. **Composition:** 0.9990 Gold .2000 oz. AGW **Subject:** President Charles de Gaulle **Reverse:** Similar to 10 Dollars, KM#149

Date	Mintage	F	VF	XF	Unc	BU
1995 Proof	Est. 7,500	Value: 125				

KM# 160 100 DOLLARS Weight: 6.2200 g. **Composition:** 0.9990 Gold .2000 oz. AGW **Subject:** Dr. Sun Yat-Sen **Reverse:** Similar to 10 Dollars, KM#159

Date	Mintage	F	VF	XF	Unc	BU
1995 Proof	Est. 7,500	Value: 125				

KM# 163 100 DOLLARS Weight: 6.2200 g. **Composition:** 0.9990 Gold .2000 oz. AGW **Subject:** General Chiang Kai-shek **Reverse:** Similar to 10 Dollars, KM#162

Date	Mintage	F	VF	XF	Unc	BU
1995 Proof	Est. 7,500	Value: 125				

KM# 166 100 DOLLARS Weight: 6.2200 g. **Composition:** 0.9990 Gold .2000 oz. AGW **Subject:** Cairo Conference **Reverse:** Chiang Kai-shek - Roosevelt - Churchill

Date	Mintage	F	VF	XF	Unc	BU
1995 Proof	Est. 7,500	Value: 125				

KM# 175 100 DOLLARS Weight: 6.2200 g. **Composition:** 0.9990 Gold .2000 oz. AGW **Subject:** 375th Anniversary - Pilgrim Fathers **Reverse:** Mayflower; Similar to 10 Dollars, KM#171

Date	Mintage	F	VF	XF	Unc	BU
1995 Proof	7,500	Value: 120				

KM# 176 100 DOLLARS Weight: 6.2200 g. **Composition:** 0.9990 Gold .2000 oz. AGW **Subject:** 375th Anniversary - Pilgrim Fathers **Reverse:** Cape Cod and Pilgrims in skiff

Date	Mintage	F	VF	XF	Unc	BU
1995 Proof	7,500	Value: 120				

KM# 177 100 DOLLARS Weight: 6.2200 g. **Composition:** 0.9990 Gold .2000 oz. AGW **Subject:** 375th Anniversary - Pilgrim Fathers **Reverse:** Pilgrim landing party

Date	Mintage	F	VF	XF	Unc	BU
1995 Proof	7,500	Value: 120				

KM# 178 100 DOLLARS Weight: 6.2200 g. **Composition:** 0.9990 Gold .2000 oz. AGW **Subject:** 375th Anniversary - Pilgrim Fathers **Reverse:** First Thanksgiving scene

Date	Mintage	F	VF	XF	Unc	BU
1995 Proof	7,500	Value: 120				

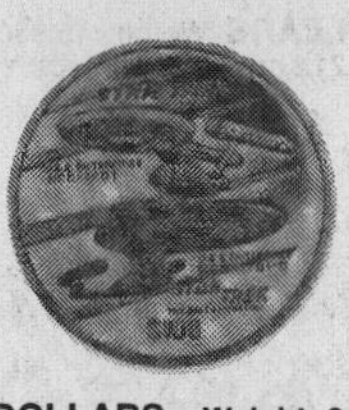

KM# 209 100 DOLLARS Weight: 6.2200 g. **Composition:** 0.9990 Gold .2000 oz. AGW **Subject:** Star Trek **Reverse:** Star ships NCC-1701 and NCC-1701D

Date	Mintage	F	VF	XF	Unc	BU
1996 Proof	Est. 7,500	Value: 150				

KM# 215 100 DOLLARS Weight: 6.2200 g. **Composition:** 0.9990 Gold .2000 oz. AGW **Subject:** Star Trek **Reverse:** LaForge and Data

Date	Mintage	F	VF	XF	Unc	BU
1996 Proof	25,000	Value: 150				

KM# 252 100 DOLLARS Weight: 6.2200 g. **Composition:** 0.9990 Gold .2000 oz. AGW **Subject:** Dalai Lama

Date	Mintage	F	VF	XF	Unc	BU
1996 Proof	Est. 7,500	Value: 115				

KM# 253 100 DOLLARS Weight: 6.2200 g. **Composition:** 0.9990 Gold .2000 oz. AGW **Subject:** Kin Rama IX of Thailand **Reverse:** King seated on radiant throne

Date	Mintage	F	VF	XF	Unc	BU
1996 Proof	Est. 7,500	Value: 115				

KM# 212 100 DOLLARS Weight: 6.2200 g. **Composition:** 0.9990 Gold .2000 oz. AGW **Subject:** Star Trek **Reverse:** Scott and McCoy

Date	Mintage	F	VF	XF	Unc	BU
1996 Proof	7,500	Value: 150				

KM# 240 100 DOLLARS Weight: 6.2200 g. **Composition:** 0.9990 Gold .2000 oz. AGW **Subject:** General Chiang Kai-shek **Note:** Similar to 10 Dollars, KM#162.

Date	Mintage	F	VF	XF	Unc	BU
1996 Proof	Est. 7,500	Value: 120				

KM# 218 100 DOLLARS Weight: 6.2200 g. **Composition:** 0.9990 Gold .2000 oz. AGW **Subject:** Star Trek **Reverse:** Spock and Uhura **Note:** Similar to 10 Dollars, KM#217.

Date	Mintage	F	VF	XF	Unc	BU
1996 Proof	25,000	Value: 150				

KM# 221 100 DOLLARS Weight: 6.2200 g. **Composition:** 0.9990 Gold .2000 oz. AGW **Subject:** Star Trek **Reverse:** Worf and Dr. Crusher **Note:** Similar to 10 Dollars, KM#220.

Date	Mintage	F	VF	XF	Unc	BU
1996 Proof	25,000	Value: 150				

KM# 224 100 DOLLARS Weight: 6.2200 g. **Composition:** 0.9990 Gold .2000 oz. AGW **Subject:** Preserve Planet Earth **Reverse:** Grey Parrot **Note:** Similar to 10 Dollars, KM#223.

Date	Mintage	F	VF	XF	Unc	BU
1996 Proof	25,000	Value: 165				

KM# 227 100 DOLLARS Weight: 6.2200 g. **Composition:** 0.9990 Gold .2000 oz. AGW **Subject:** Preserve Planet Earth **Reverse:** Love Birds **Note:** Similar to 10 Dollars, KM#226.

Date	Mintage	F	VF	XF	Unc	BU
1996 Proof	25,000	Value: 165				

KM# 232 100 DOLLARS Weight: 6.2200 g. **Composition:** 0.9990 Gold .2000 oz. AGW **Subject:** Formula One **Reverse:** Ayrton Senna **Note:** Similar to 10 Dollars, KM#229.

Date	Mintage	F	VF	XF	Unc	BU
1996 Proof	20,000	Value: 165				

KM# 237 100 DOLLARS Weight: 6.2200 g. **Composition:** 0.9990 Gold .2000 oz. AGW **Subject:** Dr. Sun Yat-Sen **Note:** Similar to 10 Dollars, KM#236.

Date	Mintage	F	VF	XF	Unc	BU
1996 Proof	Est. 7,500	Value: 120				

KM# 243 100 DOLLARS Weight: 6.2200 g. **Composition:** 0.9990 Gold .2000 oz. AGW **Subject:** President Chiang Ching-kuo **Note:** Similar to 10 Dollars, KM#242.

Date	Mintage	F	VF	XF	Unc	BU
1996 Proof	Est. 7,500	Value: 120				

KM# 246 100 DOLLARS Weight: 6.2200 g. **Composition:** 0.9990 Gold .2000 oz. AGW **Subject:** President Lee Teng-hui **Note:** Similar to 10 Dollars, KM#245.

Date	Mintage	F	VF	XF	Unc	BU
1996 Proof	Est. 7,500	Value: 120				

KM# 259 100 DOLLARS Weight: 6.2200 g. **Composition:** 0.9990 Gold .2000 oz. AGW **Subject:** Mao Zedong Proclaiming People's Republic **Note:** Similar to 10 Dollars, KM#258.

Date	Mintage	F	VF	XF	Unc	BU
1996 Proof	1,996	Value: 135				

KM# 312 100 DOLLARS Weight: 6.2200 g. **Composition:** 0.9990 Gold .2000 oz. AGW **Subject:** Mahatma Gandhi **Note:** Similar to 10 Dollars, KM#311.

Date	Mintage	F	VF	XF	Unc	BU
1997 Proof	Est. 5,000	Value: 145				

KM# 317 100 DOLLARS Weight: 6.2200 g. **Composition:** 0.9990 Gold .2000 oz. AGW **Subject:** Return of Hong Kong to China **Note:** Similar to 10 Dollars, KM#314.

Date	Mintage	F	VF	XF	Unc	BU
1997 Proof	Est. 5,000	Value: 145				

KM# 326 100 DOLLARS Weight: 6.2200 g. **Composition:** 0.9990 Gold .2000 oz. AGW **Subject:** Jurassic Park **Obverse:** National arms **Reverse:** Stegosaurus **Note:** Similar to 10 Dollars, KM#325.

Date	Mintage	F	VF	XF	Unc	BU
1997 Proof	Est. 2,500	Value: 175				

KM# 329 100 DOLLARS Weight: 6.2200 g. **Composition:** 0.9990 Gold .2000 oz. AGW **Subject:** Golden Wedding Anniversary **Obverse:** National arms **Reverse:** E & P initials above 2 shields **Note:** Similar to 10 Dollars, KM#328.

Date	Mintage	F	VF	XF	Unc	BU
1997 Proof	Est. 3,500	Value: 175				

KM# 332 100 DOLLARS Weight: 6.2200 g. **Composition:** 0.9990 Gold .2000 oz. AGW **Subject:** Golden Wedding Anniversary **Obverse:** National arms **Reverse:** Royal couple with horse **Note:** Similar to 10 Dollars, KM#331.

Date	Mintage	F	VF	XF	Unc	BU
1997 Proof	Est. 3,500	Value: 175				

KM# 335 100 DOLLARS Weight: 6.2200 g. **Composition:** 0.9990 Gold .2000 oz. AGW **Subject:** Golden Wedding Anniversary **Obverse:** National arms **Reverse:** Royal couple with dogs **Note:** Similar to 10 Dollars, KM#334.

Date	Mintage	F	VF	XF	Unc	BU
1997 Proof	Est. 3,500	Value: 175				

KM# 338 100 DOLLARS Weight: 6.2200 g. **Composition:** 0.9990 Gold .2000 oz. AGW **Subject:** Golden Wedding Anniversary **Obverse:** National arms **Reverse:** Royal couple with children **Note:** Similar to 10 Dollars, KM#337.

Date	Mintage	F	VF	XF	Unc	BU
1997 Proof	Est. 3,500	Value: 175				

KM# 370 100 DOLLARS Weight: 6.2200 g. **Composition:** 0.9990 Gold .2000 oz. AGW **Subject:** Star Trek - The Next Generation **Obverse:** National arms **Reverse:** Romulan Warbird **Note:** Similar to 10 Dollars, KM#369.

Date	Mintage	F	VF	XF	Unc	BU
1997 Proof	Est. 7,500	Value: 150				

KM# 373 100 DOLLARS Weight: 6.2200 g. **Composition:** 0.9990 Gold .2000 oz. AGW **Subject:** Star Trek - The Next Generation **Obverse:** National arms **Reverse:** Klingon Attack Cruiser **Note:** Similar to 10 Dollars, KM#372.

Date	Mintage	F	VF	XF	Unc	BU
1997 Proof	Est. 7,500	Value: 150				

KM# 376 100 DOLLARS Weight: 6.2200 g. **Composition:** 0.9990 Gold .2000 oz. AGW **Subject:** Star Trek - The Next Generation **Obverse:** National arms **Reverse:** U.S.S. Enterprise NCC-1701-D **Note:** Similar to 10 Dollars, KM#375.

Date	Mintage	F	VF	XF	Unc	BU
1997 Proof	Est. 7,500	Value: 150				

KM# 379 100 DOLLARS Weight: 6.2200 g. **Composition:** 0.9990 Gold .2000 oz. AGW **Subject:** Star Trek - The Next Generation **Obverse:** National arms **Reverse:** Klingon Bird of Prey **Note:** Similar to 10 Dollars, KM#378.

Date	Mintage	F	VF	XF	Unc	BU
1997 Proof	Est. 7,500	Value: 150				

KM# 382 100 DOLLARS Weight: 6.2200 g. **Composition:** 0.9990 Gold .2000 oz. AGW **Subject:** Star Trek - The Next Generation **Obverse:** National arms **Reverse:** Borg Cube **Note:** Similar to 10 Dollars, KM#381.

Date	Mintage	F	VF	XF	Unc	BU
1997 Proof	Est. 7,500	Value: 150				

KM# 385 100 DOLLARS Weight: 6.2200 g. **Composition:** 0.9990 Gold .2000 oz. AGW **Subject:** Star Trek - The Next Generation **Obverse:** National arms **Reverse:** Ferengi Marauder **Note:** Similar to 10 Dollars, KM#384.

Date	Mintage	F	VF	XF	Unc	BU
1997 Proof	Est. 7,500	Value: 150				

KM# 473 100 DOLLARS Weight: 6.2200 g. **Composition:** 0.9990 Gold .2000 oz. AGW **Subject:** Princess Diana in Memoriam

Date		F	VF	XF	Unc	BU
1997 Proof	—	Value: 165				

KM# 322 100 DOLLARS Weight: 6.2200 g. **Composition:** 0.9990 Gold .2000 oz. AGW **Subject:** Fiftieth Anniversary of the Kon-Tiki Expedition **Note:** Similar to 1 Dollar, KM#320.

Date	Mintage	F	VF	XF	Unc	BU
1997 Proof	Est. 7,500	Value: 145				

KM# 365 100 DOLLARS Weight: 6.2200 g. **Composition:** 0.9990 Gold .2000 oz. AGW **Subject:** RMS Titanic **Obverse:** National arms **Reverse:** Ship sinking **Note:** Similar to 20 Dollars, KM#364.

Date	Mintage	F	VF	XF	Unc	BU
1998 Proof	Est. 5,000	Value: 165				

KM# 388 100 DOLLARS Weight: 6.2200 g. **Composition:** 0.9990 Gold .2000 oz. AGW **Subject:** President Ronald Reagan **Obverse:** National arms **Reverse:** Lincoln Statue **Note:** Similar to 10 Dollars, KM#387.

Date	Mintage	F	VF	XF	Unc	BU
1998 Proof	Est. 7,500	Value: 165				

KM# 403 100 DOLLARS Weight: 6.2200 g. **Composition:** 0.9990 Gold .2000 oz. AGW **Subject:** Christopher Columbus **Obverse:** National arms **Reverse:** Portrait, ship **Note:** Similar to 10 Dollars, KM#402.

Date	Mintage	F	VF	XF	Unc	BU
1999 Proof	10,000	Value: 175				

KM# 406 100 DOLLARS Weight: 6.2200 g. **Composition:** 0.9990 Gold .2000 oz. AGW **Subject:** Captain James Cook **Obverse:** National arms **Reverse:** Portrait, ship, map **Note:** Similar to 10 Dollars, KM#403.

Date	Mintage	F	VF	XF	Unc	BU
1999 Proof	10,000	Value: 175				

KM# 409 100 DOLLARS Weight: 6.2200 g. **Composition:** 0.9990 Gold .2000 oz. AGW **Subject:** Return of Macao to China **Obverse:** National arms **Reverse:** Dragon and phoenix **Note:** Similar to 10 Dollars, KM#408.

Date	Mintage	F	VF	XF	Unc	BU
1999 Proof	10,000	Value: 175				

KM# 415 100 DOLLARS Weight: 6.2200 g. **Composition:** 0.9990 Gold .2000 oz. AGW **Subject:** The Wedding of the Prince **Obverse:** National arms **Reverse:** Couple in carriage **Note:** Similar to 10 Dollars, KM#414.

Date		F	VF	XF	Unc	BU
1999 Proof	Est. 5,000	Value: 175				

KM# 392 100 DOLLARS Weight: 6.2200 g. **Composition:** 0.9990 Gold .2000 oz. AGW **Subject:** Year of the Rabbit **Obverse:** National arms **Reverse:** Rabbit running left **Note:** Similar to 20 Dollars, KM#389.

Date	Mintage	F	VF	XF	Unc	BU
1999 Proof	5,000	Value: 165				

KM# 393 100 DOLLARS Weight: 6.2200 g. **Composition:** 0.9990 Gold .2000 oz. AGW **Subject:** Year of the Rabbit **Obverse:** National arms **Reverse:** Rabbit sitting **Note:** Similar to 20 Dollars, KM#390.

Date	Mintage	F	VF	XF	Unc	BU
1999 Proof	5,000	Value: 165				

KM# 394 100 DOLLARS Weight: 6.2200 g. **Composition:** 0.9990 Gold .2000 oz. AGW **Subject:** Year of the Rabbit **Obverse:** National arms **Reverse:** Rabbit running right **Note:** Similar to 20 Dollars, KM#391.

Date	Mintage	F	VF	XF	Unc	BU
1999 Proof	5,000	Value: 165				

KM# 106 150 DOLLARS Weight: 500.0000 g. **Composition:** 0.9990 Silver 16.0756 oz. ASW **Subject:** Preserve Planet Earth **Reverse:** Two Brachiosauros **Size:** 85 mm. **Note:** Illustration reduced.

Date	Mintage	F	VF	XF	Unc	BU
1993 Proof	121	Value: 300				

KM# 34 200 DOLLARS Weight: 12.0000 g. **Composition:** 0.9000 Gold .3472 oz. AGW **Subject:** Inauguration of President Tolbert

Date	Mintage	F	VF	XF	Unc	BU
1976 Proof	100	Value: 350				

KM# 46 200 DOLLARS Weight: 15.9800 g. **Composition:** 0.9170 Gold .4712 oz. AGW **Subject:** Year of the Scout

Date		F	VF	XF	Unc	BU
ND(1983)		—	—	—	325	—
ND(1983) Proof	—	Value: 425				

KM# 49 200 DOLLARS Weight: 15.9800 g. **Composition:** 0.9000 Gold .4624 oz. AGW **Series:** International Year of Disabled Persons

Date	Mintage	F	VF	XF	Unc	BU
1983	500	—	—	—	325	—
1983 Proof	500	Value: 475				

KM# 395 200 DOLLARS Weight: 12.4444 g. **Composition:** 0.9999 Gold .4000 oz. AGW **Subject:** Year of the Rabbit **Obverse:** National arms **Reverse:** Rabbit running left **Note:** Similar to 20 Dollars, KM#389.

Date	Mintage	F	VF	XF	Unc	BU
1999 Proof	1,500	Value: 325				

KM# 396 200 DOLLARS Weight: 12.4444 g. **Composition:** 0.9999 Gold .4000 oz. AGW **Subject:** Year of the Rabbit **Obverse:** National arms **Reverse:** Rabbit sitting **Note:** Similar to 20 Dollars, KM#390.

Date	Mintage	F	VF	XF	Unc	BU
1999 Proof	1,500	Value: 325				

KM# 397 200 DOLLARS Weight: 12.4444 g. **Composition:** 0.9999 Gold .4000 oz. AGW **Subject:** Year of the Rabbit **Obverse:** National arms **Reverse:** Rabbit running right **Note:** Similar to 20 Dollars, KM#391.

Date	Mintage	F	VF	XF	Unc	BU
1999 Proof	1,500	Value: 325				

KM# 52 250 DOLLARS Weight: 15.5000 g. **Composition:** 0.9990 Gold .5000 oz. AGW **Subject:** President John F. Kennedy

Date	Mintage	F	VF	XF	Unc	BU
1988 Proof	5,000	Value: 350				

KM# 56 250 DOLLARS Weight: 15.5000 g. **Composition:** 0.9990 Gold .5000 oz. AGW **Subject:** President Samuel Kanyon Doe

Date	Mintage	F	VF	XF	Unc	BU
1988 Proof	Est. 5,000	Value: 365				

KM# 58 250 DOLLARS Weight: 15.5000 g. **Composition:** 0.9990 Gold .5000 oz. AGW **Subject:** President George Bush

Date	Mintage	F	VF	XF	Unc	BU
1989 Proof	600	Value: 365				

KM# 60 250 DOLLARS Weight: 15.5000 g. **Composition:** 0.9990 Gold .5000 oz. AGW **Subject:** Emperor Hirohito

Date	Mintage	F	VF	XF	Unc	BU
1989 Proof	600	Value: 365				

KM# 93 250 DOLLARS Weight: 15.5000 g. **Composition:** 0.9990 Gold .5000 oz. AGW **Subject:** Formula One **Reverse:** Riccardo Patrese portrait facing left, car in lower left **Note:** Similar to 10 Dollars, KM#74.

Date	Mintage	F	VF	XF	Unc	BU
1992 Proof	Est. 5,000	Value: 325				

KM# 89 250 DOLLARS Weight: 15.5000 g. **Composition:** 0.9990 Gold .5000 oz. AGW **Subject:** Formula One **Reverse:** Nigel Mansell **Note:** Similar to 10 Dollars, KM#75.

Date	Mintage	F	VF	XF	Unc	BU
1992 Proof	Est. 5,000	Value: 325				

KM# 90 250 DOLLARS Weight: 15.5000 g. **Composition:** 0.9990 Gold .5000 oz. AGW **Subject:** Formula One **Reverse:** Gerhard Berger **Note:** Similar to 10 Dollars, KM#83.

Date	Mintage	F	VF	XF	Unc	BU
1992 Proof	Est. 5,000	Value: 325				

KM# 91 250 DOLLARS Weight: 15.5000 g. **Composition:** 0.9990 Gold .5000 oz. AGW **Subject:** Formula One **Reverse:** Aguri Suzuki portrait facing, car in foreground **Note:** Similar to 10 Dollars, KM#84.

Date	Mintage	F	VF	XF	Unc	BU
1992 Proof	Est. 5,000	Value: 325				

KM# 92 250 DOLLARS Weight: 15.5000 g. **Composition:** 0.9990 Gold .5000 oz. AGW **Subject:** Formula One **Reverse:** Ayrton Senna portrait facing, car in foreground **Note:** Similar to 10 Dollars, KM#85.

Date	Mintage	F	VF	XF	Unc	BU
1992 Proof	Est. 5,000	Value: 325				

KM# 94 250 DOLLARS Weight: 15.5000 g. **Composition:** 0.9990 Gold .5000 oz. AGW **Subject:** Formula One **Reverse:** Michael Schumacher portrait facing left, car at lower left **Note:** Similar to 10 Dollars, KM#86.

Date	Mintage	F	VF	XF	Unc	BU
1992 Proof	Est. 5,000	Value: 325				

KM# 95 250 DOLLARS Weight: 15.5000 g. **Composition:** 0.9990 Gold .5000 oz. AGW **Subject:** Formula One **Reverse:** Alain Prost portrait facing left, car in foreground **Note:** Similar to 10 Dollars, KM#87.

Date	Mintage	F	VF	XF	Unc	BU
1992 Proof	Est. 5,000	Value: 325				

KM# 96 250 DOLLARS Weight: 15.5000 g. **Composition:** 0.9990 Gold .5000 oz. AGW **Subject:** Formula One **Reverse:** Ukyo Katayama portrait facing, car in foreground **Note:** Similar to 10 Dollars, KM#88.

Date	Mintage	F	VF	XF	Unc	BU
1992 Proof	Est. 5,000	Value: 325				

KM# 71 250 DOLLARS Weight: 15.5000 g. **Composition:** 0.9990 Gold .5000 oz. AGW **Subject:** President Bill Clinton **Reverse:** Portrait right **Note:** Similar to 10 Dollars, KM#68.

Date	Mintage	F	VF	XF	Unc	BU
1993 Proof	Est. 5,000	Value: 325				

KM# 105 250 DOLLARS Weight: 15.5000 g. **Composition:** 0.9990 Gold .5000 oz. AGW **Subject:** President John F. Kennedy **Note:** Similar to 10 Dollars, KM#104.

Date	Mintage	F	VF	XF	Unc	BU
1993 Proof	Est. 5,000	Value: 325				

KM# 181 250 DOLLARS Weight: 15.5000 g. **Composition:** 0.9990 Gold .5000 oz. AGW **Subject:** Formula One **Reverse:** Mika Hakkinen; Similar to 10 Dollars, KM#180

Date	Mintage	F	VF	XF	Unc	BU
1995 Proof	Est. 5,000	Value: 325				

KM# 184 250 DOLLARS Weight: 15.5000 g. **Composition:** 0.9990 Gold .5000 oz. AGW **Subject:** Formula One **Reverse:** Martin Brundle; Similar to 10 Dollars, KM#183

Date	Mintage	F	VF	XF	Unc	BU
1995 Proof	Est. 5,000	Value: 325				

KM# 187 250 DOLLARS Weight: 15.5000 g. **Composition:** 0.9990 Gold .5000 oz. AGW **Subject:** Formula One **Reverse:** Rubens Barricchello; Similar to 10 Dollars, KM#186

Date	Mintage	F	VF	XF	Unc	BU
1995 Proof	Est. 5,000	Value: 325				

KM# 190 250 DOLLARS Weight: 15.5000 g. **Composition:** 0.9990 Gold .5000 oz. AGW **Subject:** Formula One **Reverse:** David Coulthard; Similar to 10 Dollars, KM#189

Date	Mintage	F	VF	XF	Unc	BU
1995 Proof	Est. 5,000	Value: 325				

KM# 193 250 DOLLARS Weight: 15.5000 g. **Composition:** 0.9990 Gold .5000 oz. AGW **Subject:** Formula One **Reverse:** Jean Alesi; Similar to 10 Dollars, KM#192

Date	Mintage	F	VF	XF	Unc	BU
1995 Proof	Est. 5,000	Value: 325				

KM# 565 250 DOLLARS Weight: 15.5000 g. **Composition:** 0.9990 Gold 0.4978 oz. AGW **Reverse:** Bugatti Royale **Size:** 33 mm.

Date	F	VF	XF	Unc	BU
1995B	—	—	—	325	—

KM# 203 250 DOLLARS **Weight:** 15.5000 g. **Composition:** 0.9990 Gold .5000 oz. AGW **Subject:** Formula One **Reverse:** Mark Blundell; Similar to 10 Dollars, KM#199

Date	Mintage	F	VF	XF	Unc	BU
1996 Proof	Est. 5,000	Value: 325				

KM# 204 250 DOLLARS **Weight:** 15.5000 g. **Composition:** 0.9990 Gold .5000 oz. AGW **Subject:** Formula One **Reverse:** Johnny Herbert **Note:** Similar to 10 Dollars, KM#200.

Date	Mintage	F	VF	XF	Unc	BU
1996 Proof	Est. 5,000	Value: 325				

KM# 205 250 DOLLARS **Weight:** 15.5000 g. **Composition:** 0.9990 Gold .5000 oz. AGW **Subject:** Formula One **Reverse:** Eddie Irvine **Note:** Similar to 10 Dollars, KM#201.

Date	Mintage	F	VF	XF	Unc	BU
1996 Proof	Est. 5,000	Value: 325				

KM# 206 250 DOLLARS **Weight:** 15.5000 g. **Composition:** 0.9990 Gold .5000 oz. AGW **Subject:** Formula One **Reverse:** Heinz Frentzen **Note:** Similar to 10 Dollars, KM#202.

Date	Mintage	F	VF	XF	Unc	BU
1996 Proof	Est. 5,000	Value: 325				

KM# 233 250 DOLLARS **Weight:** 15.5000 g. **Composition:** 0.9990 Gold .5000 oz. AGW **Subject:** Formula One **Reverse:** Ayrton Senna **Note:** Similar to 10 Dollars, KM#229.

Date	Mintage	F	VF	XF	Unc	BU
1996 Proof	Est. 5,000	Value: 325				

KM# 318 250 DOLLARS **Weight:** 15.5000 g. **Composition:** 0.9990 Gold .5000 oz. AGW **Subject:** Return of Hong Kong **Note:** Similar to 10 Dollars, KM#314.

Date	Mintage	F	VF	XF	Unc	BU
1997 Proof	—	Value: 335				

KM# 420 250 DOLLARS **Weight:** 15.5000 g. **Composition:** 0.9990 Gold .5000 oz. AGW **Subject:** Return of Macao to China **Obverse:** National arms **Reverse:** Dragon and phoenix **Note:** Similar to 10 Dollars, KM#408.

Date	Mintage	F	VF	XF	Unc	BU
1999 Proof	Est. 5,000	Value: 335				

KM# 425 250 DOLLARS **Weight:** 15.5000 g. **Composition:** 0.9990 Gold .5000 oz. AGW **Subject:** Liberty **Obverse:** National arms **Reverse:** Conjoined busts of President J.F. Kennedy and his son **Note:** Similar to 10 Dollars, KM#424.

Date	Mintage	F	VF	XF	Unc	BU
1999 Proof	375	Value: 340				

KM# 439 250 DOLLARS **Weight:** 15.5517 g. **Composition:** 0.9999 Gold .5000 oz. AGW **Subject:** Taipai, Taiwan Rapid Transit System **Obverse:** National arms above hole* and dragon **Reverse:** Subway train, logo and tunnel hole* **Size:** 27 mm. **Note:** Struck at Singapore Mint. *As first done on Albanian coins of 1988.

Date	Mintage	F	VF	XF	Unc	BU
1999 Proof	2,000	Value: 325				

KM# 107 300 DOLLARS **Weight:** 1000.0000 g. **Composition:** 0.9990 Silver 32.1512 oz. ASW **Series:** Preserve Planet Earth **Reverse:** Tyrannosaurus Rex Attaching Triceratops **Size:** 100 mm. **Note:** Illustration reduced.

Date	Mintage	F	VF	XF	Unc	BU
1993 Proof	151	Value: 700				

KM# 367 300 DOLLARS **Weight:** 1000.0000 g. **Composition:** 0.9990 Silver 32.1512 oz. ASW **Subject:** RMS Titanic **Obverse:** National arms **Reverse:** Ship sinking **Note:** Similar to 20 Dollars, KM#364.

Date	Mintage	F	VF	XF	Unc	BU
1998 Proof	Est. 500	Value: 475				

KM# 35 400 DOLLARS **Weight:** 24.0000 g. **Composition:** 0.9000 Gold .6945 oz. AGW **Subject:** Inauguration of President Tolbert

Date	Mintage	F	VF	XF	Unc	BU
1976 Proof	25	Value: 1,250				

KM# 234 500 DOLLARS **Weight:** 31.1035 g. **Composition:** 0.9990 Gold 1.0000 oz. AGW **Subject:** Formula One **Reverse:** Ayrton Senna **Note:** Similar to 10 Dollars, KM#229.

Date	Mintage	F	VF	XF	Unc	BU
1996 Proof	Est. 2,500	Value: 650				

KM# 421 500 DOLLARS **Weight:** 31.1035 g. **Composition:** 0.9990 Gold 1.0000 oz. AGW **Subject:** Return of Macao to China **Obverse:** National arms **Reverse:** Dragon and phoenix **Note:** Similar to 10 Dollars, KM#408.

Date	Mintage	F	VF	XF	Unc	BU
1999 Proof	Est. 1,000	Value: 675				

KM# 241 2500 DOLLARS **Weight:** 155.5175 g. **Composition:** 0.9990 Gold 5.0000 oz. AGW **Subject:** General Chiang Kai-shek **Note:** Similar to 10 Dollars, KM#162.

Date	Mintage	F	VF	XF	Unc	BU
1996 Proof	Est. 250	Value: 3,000				

KM# 235 2500 DOLLARS **Weight:** 155.5175 g. **Composition:** 0.9990 Gold 5.0000 oz. AGW **Subject:** Formula One **Reverse:** Ayrton Senna **Note:** Similar to 10 Dollars, KM#229.

Date	Mintage	F	VF	XF	Unc	BU
1996 Proof	Est. 250	Value: 3,000				

KM# 238 2500 DOLLARS **Weight:** 155.5175 g. **Composition:** 0.9990 Gold 5.0000 oz. AGW **Subject:** Dr. Sun Yat-Sen **Note:** Similar to 10 Dollars, KM#236.

Date	Mintage	F	VF	XF	Unc	BU
1996 Proof	Est. 250	Value: 3,000				

KM# 244 2500 DOLLARS **Weight:** 155.5175 g. **Composition:** 0.9990 Gold 5.0000 oz. AGW **Subject:** President Chiang Ching-kuo **Note:** Similar to 10 Dollars, KM#242.

Date	Mintage	F	VF	XF	Unc	BU
1996 Proof	Est. 250	Value: 3,000				

KM# 247 2500 DOLLARS **Weight:** 155.5175 g. **Composition:** 0.9990 Gold 5.0000 oz. AGW **Subject:** President Lee Teng-hui **Note:** Similar to 10 Dollars, KM#245.

Date	Mintage	F	VF	XF	Unc	BU
1996 Proof	Est. 250	Value: 3,000				

KM# 319 2500 DOLLARS **Weight:** 155.5175 g. **Composition:** 0.9990 Gold 5.0000 oz. AGW **Subject:** Return of Hong Kong **Note:** Similar to 10 Dollars, KM#314.

Date	F	VF	XF	Unc	BU
1997 Proof	—	Value: 3,200			

KM# 422 2500 DOLLARS **Weight:** 155.5175 g. **Composition:** 0.9990 Gold 5.0000 oz. AGW **Subject:** Return of Macao to China **Obverse:** National arms **Reverse:** Dragon and phoenix **Note:** Similar to 10 Dollars, KM#408.

Date	Mintage	F	VF	XF	Unc	BU
1999 Proof	Est. 250	Value: 3,200				

KM# 398 2500 DOLLARS **Weight:** 155.5175 g. **Composition:** 0.9990 Gold 5.0000 oz. AGW **Subject:** Year of the Rabbit **Obverse:** National arms **Reverse:** Rabbit running left **Note:** Similar to 20 Dollars, KM#389.

Date	Mintage	F	VF	XF	Unc	BU
1999 Proof	88	Value: 3,350				

KM# 399 2500 DOLLARS **Weight:** 155.5175 g. **Composition:** 0.9990 Gold 5.0000 oz. AGW **Subject:** Year of the Rabbit **Obverse:** National arms **Reverse:** Rabbit sitting **Note:** Similar to 20 Dollars, KM#390.

Date	Mintage	F	VF	XF	Unc	BU
1999 Proof	88	Value: 3,350				

KM# 400 2500 DOLLARS **Weight:** 155.5175 g. **Composition:** 0.9990 Gold 5.0000 oz. AGW **Subject:** Year of the Rabbit **Obverse:** National arms **Reverse:** Rabbit running right **Note:** Similar to 20 Dollars, KM#391.

Date	Mintage	F	VF	XF	Unc	BU
1999 Proof	88	Value: 3,350				

KM# 440 2500 DOLLARS **Weight:** 155.5175 g. **Composition:** 0.9999 Gold 5.0000 oz. AGW **Subject:** Taipai, Taiwan Rapid Transit System **Obverse:** National arms above dragon **Reverse:** Dragon around subway train viewing sun with diamond inserts **Size:** 55 mm. **Note:** Struck at Singapore Mint.

Date	Mintage	F	VF	XF	Unc	BU
ND(1999) Proof	50	—	—	—	—	—

PATTERNS

Including off metal strikes

KM#	Date	Mintage	Identification	Mkt Val
Pn55	1976	—	100 Dollars. Bronze. KM#33.	150
Pn56	1976	—	200 Dollars. Bronze. KM#34.	175
Pn57	1976	—	400 Dollars. Bronze. KM#35.	200
Pn58	2001	—	10 Dollars. Copper Nickel. 29.2500 g. 38.2 mm. National arms. "9-11" Flag raising scene. Plain edge.	100
Pn59	2001	—	20 Dollars. Silver-Plated Base Metal. 5.3100 g. 20 mm. National arms. "9-11" Flag raising scene. Plain edge.	60.00
Pn60	2001	—	100 Dollars. Gold-Plated Base Metal. 3.4200 g. 16 mm. National arms. "9-11" Flag raising scene. Plain edge.	40.00

PIEFORTS

KM#	Date	Mintage	Identification	Mkt Val
P1	1983	500	2 Dollars. (No Composition). KM#47a.	75.00
P2	1983	—	20 Dollars. (No Composition). KM#48.	100
P3	1983	100	200 Dollars. (No Composition). KM#49.	800

MINT SETS

KM#	Date	Mintage	Identification	Issue Price	Mkt Val
MS1	1997 (2)	4,000	KM#351-352	50.00	60.00

PROOF SETS

KM#	Date	Mintage	Identification	Issue Price	Mkt Val
PS2	1906H (5)	—	KM#5-9	—	1,250
PS3	1968 (6)	14,396	KM#13, 14, 15a.2-18a.2	15.25	8.00
PS4	1969 (6)	5,056	KM#13, 14, 15a.2-18a.2	15.25	8.00
PS5	1970 (6)	3,464	KM#13, 14, 15a.2-18a.2	15.25	12.50
PS6	1971 (6)	3,032	KM#13, 14, 15a.2-18a.2	15.25	10.00
PS7	1972 (6)	4,866	KM#13, 14, 15a.2-18a.2	15.50	9.00
PS8	1972 (4)	—	KM#24-27	—	1,000
PS9	1973 (7)	10,542	KM#13, 14, 15a.2-18a.2, 29	27.00	18.00
PS10	1974 (7)	9,362	KM#13, 14, 15a.2-18a.2, 29	27.00	18.00
PS11	1975 (7)	4,056	KM#13, 14, 15a.2-18a.2, 29	31.50	20.00
PS12	1976 (7)	2,131	KM#13, 14, 15a.2, 29-32	45.00	32.50
PS13	1977 (7)	920	KM#13, 14, 15a.2, 29-32	45.00	37.50
PS14	1978 (8)	7,311	KM#12a, 13, 14, 15a.2, 29-32	47.00	35.00
PS15	1979 (8)	1,857	KM#12b, 13a, 14a, 15b, 29a-32a marked O.A.U. July 1979	45.00	50.00
PS16	1997 (3)	—	KM#417, 445, 473	—	210
PS17	1999 (2)	375	KM#424-425	345	360

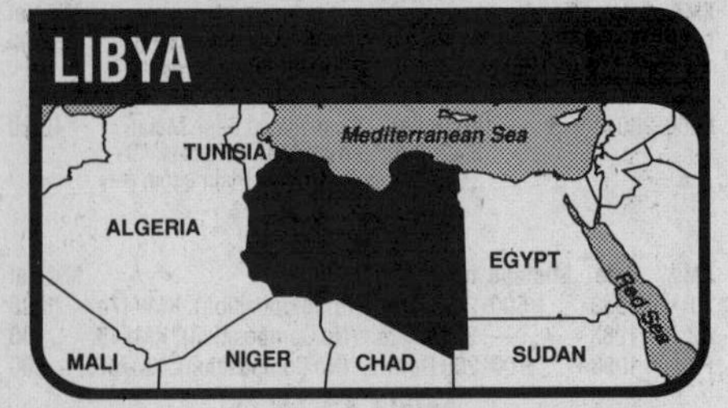

The Socialist People's Libyan Arab Jamahariya, located on the north-central coast of Africa between Tunisia and Egypt, has an area of 679,358 sq. mi. (1,759,540 sq. km.) and a population of 3.9 million. Capital: Tripoli. Crude oil, which accounts for 90 per cent of the export earnings, is the mainstay of the economy.

Libya has been subjected to foreign rule throughout most of its history, various parts of it having been ruled by the Phoenicians, Carthaginians, Vandals, Byzantines, Greeks, Romans, Egyptians, and in the following centuries the Arabs' language, culture and religion were adopted by the indigenous population. Libya was conquered by the Ottoman Turks in 1553, and remained under Turkish domination, becoming a Turkish vilayet in 1835, until it was conquered by Italy and made into a colony in 1911. The name 'Libya', the ancient Greek name for North Africa exclusive of Egypt, was given to the colony by Italy in 1934. Libya came under Allied administration after the fall of Tripoli on Jan. 23, 1943, divided into zones of British and French control. On Dec. 24, 1951, in accordance with a United Nations resolution, Libya proclaimed its independence as a constitutional monarchy, thereby becoming the first country to achieve independence through the United Nations. The monarchy was overthrown by a *coup d'etat* on Sept. 1, 1969, and Libya was established as a republic.

TITLES

المملكة الليبية

al-Mamlaka(t) al-Libiya(t)

الجمهورية العربية الليبية

al-Jomhuriya(t) al-Arabiya(t) al-Libiya(t)

RULERS

Idris I, 1951-1969

MONETARY SYSTEM

10 Milliemes = 1 Piastre
100 Piastres = 1 Pound

MONARCHY

STANDARD COINAGE

10 Milliemes = 1 Piastre; 100 Piastres = 1 Pound

KM# 1 MILLIEME Composition: Bronze Ruler: Idris I

Date	Mintage	F	VF	XF	Unc	BU
ND(1952)	7,750,000	—	0.10	0.15	0.50	—
ND(1952) Proof	32	Value: 75.00				

KM# 6 MILLIEME Composition: Nickel-Brass Ruler: Idris I

Date	Mintage	F	VF	XF	Unc	BU
AH1385(1965)	11,000,000	—	0.10	0.20	0.40	—

KM# 2 2 MILLIEMES Composition: Bronze Ruler: Idris I

Date	Mintage	F	VF	XF	Unc	BU
ND(1952)	6,650,000	—	0.10	0.25	0.75	—
ND(1952) Proof	32	Value: 75.00				

KM# 3 5 MILLIEMES Composition: Bronze Ruler: Idris I

Date	Mintage	F	VF	XF	Unc	BU
ND(1952)	7,680,000	—	0.15	0.35	1.00	—
ND(1952) Proof	32	Value: 75.00				

KM# 7 5 MILLIEMES Composition: Nickel-Brass Ruler: Idris I

Date	Mintage	F	VF	XF	Unc	BU
AH1385(1965)	8,500,000	—	0.15	0.25	0.50	—

KM# 4 PIASTRE Composition: Copper-Nickel Ruler: Idris I

Date	Mintage	F	VF	XF	Unc	BU
ND(1952)	10,200,000	—	0.35	0.60	1.25	—
ND(1952) Proof	32	Value: 100				

KM# 5 2 PIASTRES Composition: Copper-Nickel Ruler: Idris I

Date	Mintage	F	VF	XF	Unc	BU
ND(1952)	6,075,000	—	0.35	0.75	1.50	—
ND(1952) Proof	32	Value: 125				

KM# 8 10 MILLIEMES Composition: Copper-Nickel Ruler: Idris I

Date	Mintage	F	VF	XF	Unc	BU
AH1385(1965)	17,000,000	—	0.15	0.25	0.50	—

KM# 9 20 MILLIEMES Composition: Copper-Nickel Ruler: Idris I

Date	Mintage	F	VF	XF	Unc	BU
AH1385(1965)	8,750,000	—	0.20	0.50	2.00	—

KM# 10 50 MILLIEMES Composition: Copper-Nickel Ruler: Idris I

Date	Mintage	F	VF	XF	Unc	BU
AH1385(1965)	8,000,000	—	0.35	0.75	3.00	—

SOCIALIST PEOPLE'S REPUBLIC

STANDARD COINAGE

1000 Dirhams = 1 Dinar

KM# 12 DIRHAM Composition: Brass Clad Steel

Date	Mintage	F	VF	XF	Unc	BU
AH1395(1975)	20,000,000	—	0.25	0.50	2.00	—

KM# 18 DIRHAM Composition: Brass Clad Steel

Date	Mintage	F	VF	XF	Unc	BU
AH1399(1979)	1,000,000	—	4.00	12.00	20.00	—

KM# 13 5 DIRHAM Composition: Brass Clad Steel

Date	Mintage	F	VF	XF	Unc	BU
AH1395(1975)	23,000,000	—	0.25	0.60	2.50	—

KM# 19 5 DIRHAM Composition: Brass Clad Steel

Date	Mintage	F	VF	XF	Unc	BU
AH1399(1979)	2,000,000	—	3.50	10.00	18.00	—

KM# 14 10 DIRHAMS Composition: Copper-Nickel Clad Steel

Date	Mintage	F	VF	XF	Unc	BU
AH1395(1975)	52,750,000	—	0.25	0.65	2.75	—

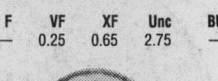

KM# 20 10 DIRHAMS Composition: Copper-Nickel Clad Steel Size: 20 mm.

Date	Mintage	F	VF	XF	Unc	BU
AH1399(1979)	4,000,000	—	3.00	9.00	15.00	—

KM# 15 20 DIRHAMS Composition: Copper-Nickel Clad Steel

Date	Mintage	F	VF	XF	Unc	BU
AH1395(1975)	25,500,000	—	0.50	1.75	5.00	—

KM# 21 20 DIRHAMS Composition: Copper-Nickel Clad Steel

Date	Mintage	F	VF	XF	Unc	BU
AH1399(1979)	6,000,000	—	3.00	9.00	15.00	—

KM# 16 50 DIRHAMS Composition: Copper-Nickel

Date	Mintage	F	VF	XF	Unc	BU
AH1395(1975)	25,640,000	—	1.00	2.50	7.00	—

KM# 22 50 DIRHAMS Composition: Copper-Nickel

Date	Mintage	F	VF	XF	Unc	BU
AH1399(1979)	9,120,000	—	2.50	6.50	12.50	—

KM# 17 100 DIRHAMS Composition: Copper-Nickel

Date	Mintage	F	VF	XF	Unc	BU
AH1395(1975)	15,433,000	—	1.50	3.50	9.00	—

KM# 23 100 DIRHAMS Composition: Copper-Nickel

Date	Mintage	F	VF	XF	Unc	BU
AH1399(1979)	15,000,000	—	2.50	6.50	12.50	—

KM# 24 5 DINARS Weight: 28.2800 g. **Composition:** 0.9250 Silver .8410 oz. ASW **Subject:** International Year of Disabled Persons

Date	Mintage	F	VF	XF	Unc	BU
ND(1981)	20,000	—	—	—	65.00	—
ND(1981) Proof	21,000	Value: 75.00				

KM# 25 70 DINARS Weight: 15.9800 g. **Composition:** 0.9170 Gold .4712 oz. AGW **Subject:** International Year of Disabled Persons

Date	Mintage	F	VF	XF	Unc	BU
ND(1981)	4,000	—	—	—	450	—
ND(1981) Proof	4,000	Value: 550				

PIEFORTS

KM#	Date	Mintage	Identification	Mkt Val
P1	1981	2,150	5 Dinars. KM24.	150
P2	1981	500	70 Dinars. KM25.	1,100

MINT SETS

KM#	Date	Mintage	Identification	Issue Price	Mkt Val
MS1	1975 (6)	—	KM12-17	—	28.00

PROOF SETS

KM#	Date	Mintage	Identification	Issue Price	Mkt Val
PS1	1952 (5)	32	KM1-5	—	450

LIECHTENSTEIN

The Principality of Liechtenstein, located in central Europe on the east bank of the Rhine between Austria and Switzerland, has an area of 62 sq. mi. (160 sq. km.) and a population of 27,200. Capital: Vaduz. The economy is based on agriculture and light manufacturing. Canned goods, textiles, ceramics and precision instruments are exported.

The lordships of Schellenburg and Vaduz were merged into the principality of Liechtenstein. It was a member of the Rhine Confederation from 1806 to 1815, and of the German Confederation from 1815 to 1866 when it became independent. Liechtenstein's long and close association with Austria was terminated by World War I. In 1921 it adopted the coinage of Switzerland, and two years later entered into a customs union with the Swiss, who also operated its postal and telegraph systems and represented it in international affairs. The tiny principality abolished its army in 1868 and has avoided involvement in all European wars since that time.

RULERS

Prince John II, 1858-1929
Prince Franz I, 1929-1938
Prince Franz Josef II, 1938-1990
Prince Hans Adam II, 1990-

MINT MARKS

A - Vienna
B - Bern
M - Munich (restrikes)

MONETARY SYSTEM

100 Heller = 1 Krone

PRINCIPALITY

REFORM COINAGE

100 Heller = 1 Krone

Y# 2 KRONE Weight: 5.0000 g. **Composition:** 0.8350 Silver .1342 oz. ASW **Ruler:** Prince John II

Date	Mintage	F	VF	XF	Unc	BU
1904	75,000	10.00	15.00	20.00	35.00	—
1910	45,000	10.00	15.00	20.00	35.00	—
1915	75,000	10.00	15.00	20.00	35.00	—

Y# 3 2 KRONEN Weight: 10.0000 g. **Composition:** 0:8350 Silver .2684 oz. ASW **Ruler:** Prince John II

Date	Mintage	F	VF	XF	Unc	BU
1912	50,000	12.00	20.00	35.00	65.00	—
1915	38,000	15.00	25.00	40.00	75.00	—

Y# 4 5 KRONEN Weight: 24.0000 g. **Composition:** 0.9000 Silver .6944 oz. ASW **Ruler:** Prince John II

Date	Mintage	F	VF	XF	Unc	BU
1904	15,000	55.00	90.00	150	235	—
1910	10,000	65.00	110	185	300	—
1915	10,000	60.00	100	165	250	—

REFORM COINAGE

100 Rappen = 1 Frank

Y# 7 1/2 FRANK Weight: 2.5000 g. **Composition:** 0.8350 Silver .0751 oz. ASW **Ruler:** Prince John II
Note: 15,745 were melted.

Date	Mintage	F	VF	XF	Unc	BU
1924	30,000	65.00	125	165	225	—

Y# 8 FRANK **Weight:** 5.0000 g. **Composition:** 0.8350 Silver .1342 oz. ASW **Ruler:** Prince John II **Note:** 45,355 were melted.

Date	Mintage	F	VF	XF	Unc	BU
1924	60,000	25.00	45.00	80.00	150	—

Y# 9 2 FRANKEN **Weight:** 10.0000 g. **Composition:** 0.8350 Silver .2684 oz. ASW **Ruler:** Prince John II **Note:** 41,707 were melted.

Date	Mintage	F	VF	XF	Unc	BU
1924	50,000	40.00	90.00	150	215	—

Y# 10 5 FRANKEN **Weight:** 25.0000 g. **Composition:** 0.9000 Silver .7234 oz. ASW **Ruler:** Prince John II **Note:** 11,260 were melted.

Date	Mintage	F	VF	XF	Unc	BU
1924	15,000	250	350	500	900	—

Y# 11 10 FRANKEN **Weight:** 3.2258 g. **Composition:** 0.9000 Gold .0933 oz. AGW **Ruler:** Prince Franz I

Date	Mintage	F	VF	XF	Unc	BU
1930	2,500	—	650	850	1,200	—

Y# 13 10 FRANKEN **Weight:** 3.2258 g. **Composition:** 0.9000 Gold .0933 oz. AGW **Ruler:** Prince Franz Josef II

Date	Mintage	F	VF	XF	Unc	BU
1946B	10,000	—	150	200	265	—

Y# 20 10 FRANKEN **Weight:** 30.0000 g. **Composition:** 0.9000 Silver .8682 oz. ASW **Ruler:** Prince Franz Josef II **Subject:** 50th Anniversary of Reign **Obverse:** Similar to 50 Franken, Y#21

Date	Mintage	F	VF	XF	Unc	BU
1988 Proof	35,000	Value: 45.00				

Y# 22 10 FRANKEN **Weight:** 30.0000 g. **Composition:** 0.9000 Silver .8682 oz. ASW **Ruler:** Prince Hans Adam II **Subject:** Succession of Hans-Adam II

Date	Mintage	F	VF	XF	Unc	BU
1990 Proof	35,000	Value: 40.00				

Y# 12 20 FRANKEN **Weight:** 6.4516 g. **Composition:** 0.9000 Gold .1867 oz. AGW **Ruler:** Prince Franz I

Date	Mintage	F	VF	XF	Unc	BU
1930	2,500	—	650	850	1,500	—

Y# 14 20 FRANKEN **Weight:** 6.4516 g. **Composition:** 0.9000 Gold .1867 oz. AGW **Ruler:** Prince Franz Josef II

Date	Mintage	F	VF	XF	Unc	BU
1946B	10,000	—	125	200	275	—

Y# 15 25 FRANKEN **Weight:** 5.6450 g. **Composition:** 0.9000 Gold .1633 oz. AGW **Ruler:** Prince Franz Josef II **Subject:** Franz Josef II and Princess Gina

Date	Mintage	F	VF	XF	Unc	BU
1956	15,000	—	—	200	250	—

Y# 18 25 FRANKEN **Weight:** 5.6450 g. **Composition:** 0.9000 Gold .1633 oz. AGW **Ruler:** Prince Franz Josef II **Subject:** 100th Anniversary - National Bank

Date	Mintage	F	VF	XF	Unc	BU
1961	20,000	—	—	—	210	—

Y# 16 50 FRANKEN **Weight:** 11.2900 g. **Composition:** 0.9000 Gold .3267 oz. AGW **Ruler:** Prince Franz Josef II **Subject:** Franz Josef II and Princess Gina

Date	Mintage	F	VF	XF	Unc	BU
1956	15,000	—	—	300	350	—

Y# 19 50 FRANKEN **Weight:** 11.2900 g. **Composition:** 0.9000 Gold .3267 oz. AGW **Ruler:** Prince Franz Josef II **Subject:** 100th Anniversary - National Bank

Date	Mintage	F	VF	XF	Unc	BU
1961	20,000	—	—	—	325	—

Y# 21 50 FRANKEN **Weight:** 10.0000 g. **Composition:** 0.9000 Gold .2894 oz. AGW **Ruler:** Prince Franz Josef II **Subject:** 50th Anniversary of Reign

Date	Mintage	F	VF	XF	Unc	BU
1988 Proof	35,000	Value: 220				

Y# 23 50 FRANKEN **Weight:** 10.0000 g. **Composition:** 0.9000 Gold .2894 oz. AGW **Ruler:** Prince Hans Adam II **Subject:** Succession of Hans-Adam II

Date	Mintage	F	VF	XF	Unc	BU
1990 Proof	25,000	Value: 210				

Y# 17 100 FRANKEN **Weight:** 32.2580 g. **Composition:** 0.9000 Gold .9335 oz. AGW **Ruler:** Prince Franz Josef II **Subject:** Franz Josef II and Princess Gina

Date	Mintage	F	VF	XF	Unc	BU
1952	4,000	—	—	3,000	3,600	—

MINT SETS

KM#	Date	Mintage	Identification	Issue Price	Mkt Val
MS1	1930 (2)	2,500	Y11-12	—	2,700
MS2	1946 (2)	10,000	Y13-14	—	540
MS3	1956 (2)	15,000	Y15-16	—	600
MS4	1961 (2)	20,000	Y18-19	—	535

PROOF SETS

KM#	Date	Mintage	Identification	Issue Price	Mkt Val
PS1	1988 (2)	35,000	Y20-21	—	265
PS2	1990 (2)	25,000	Y22-23	—	250

The Republic of Lithuania, southernmost of the Baltic states in east Europe, has an area of 25,174 sq. mi.(65,201 sq. km.) and a population of *3.6 million. Capital: Vilnius. The economy is based on livestock raising and manufacturing. Hogs, cattle, hides and electric motors are exported.

Lithuania emerged as a grand duchy in the 14thcentury. In the 15th century it was a major power of central Europe, stretching from the Baltic to the Black Sea. It was joined with Poland in 1569, but lost Smolensk, Chernihiv, and the right bank of the river Dnepr Ukraina in 1667, while the left bank remained under Polish – Lithuania rule until 1793. Following the third partition of Poland by Austria, Prussia and Russia, 1795,Lithuania came under Russian domination and did not regain its independence until shortly before the end of World War I when it declared itself a sovereign republic on Feb. 16, 1918. In fall of 1920, Poland captured Vilna (Vilnius). The republic was occupied by Soviet troops and annexed to the U.S.S.R. in 1940. Following the German occupation of 1941-44, it was retaken by Russia and reestablished as a member republic of the Soviet Union. Western countries, including the United States, did not recognize Lithuania's incorporation into the Soviet Union.

Lithuania declared its independence March 11, 1990and it was recognized by the United States on Sept. 2,1991, followed by the Soviet government in Moscow on Sept. 6. They were seated in the UN General Assembly on Sept. 17, 1991.

REPUBLIC
1918-1940

STANDARD COINAGE
100 Centas = 1 Litas

KM# 71 CENTAS Weight: 1.6000 g. **Composition:** Aluminum-Bronze **Edge:** Plain **Size:** 16 mm. **Note:** Struck at King's Norton.

Date	Mintage	F	VF	XF	Unc	BU
1925	5,000,000	1.50	3.00	6.00	28.00	—

KM# 79 CENTAS Composition: Bronze **Edge:** Plain **Size:** 16.6 mm.

Date	Mintage	F	VF	XF	Unc	BU
1936	9,995,000	1.50	2.50	5.00	26.00	—

KM# 80 2 CENTAI Weight: 2.3000 g. **Composition:** Bronze **Edge:** Plain **Size:** 18.5 mm.

Date	Mintage	F	VF	XF	Unc	BU
1936	4,951,000	2.00	3.50	9.00	40.00	—

KM# 72 5 CENTAI Composition: Aluminum-Bronze

Date	Mintage	F	VF	XF	Unc	BU
1925	12,000,000	1.50	2.50	5.00	20.00	—

KM# 81 5 CENTAI Weight: 2.5000 g. **Composition:** Bronze **Edge:** Plain **Size:** 20 mm.

Date	Mintage	F	VF	XF	Unc	BU
1936	4,800,000	2.00	3.50	8.00	35.00	—

KM# 73 10 CENTU Weight: 3.0000 g. **Composition:** Aluminum-Bronze **Edge:** Plain **Size:** 21 mm.

Date	Mintage	F	VF	XF	Unc	BU
1925	12,000,000	1.50	2.50	5.00	25.00	—

KM# 74 20 CENTU Weight: 4.0000 g. **Composition:** Aluminum-Bronze **Edge:** Plain **Size:** 23 mm.

Date	Mintage	F	VF	XF	Unc	BU
1925	8,000,000	1.75	2.75	6.50	30.00	—

KM# 75 50 CENTU Weight: 5.0000 g. **Composition:** Aluminum-Bronze **Edge:** Plain **Size:** 25 mm.

Date	Mintage	F	VF	XF	Unc	BU
1925	5,000,000	3.50	5.50	12.00	35.00	—

KM# 76 LITAS Weight: 2.7000 g. **Composition:** 0.5000 Silver .0434 oz. ASW **Edge:** Milled **Size:** 19 mm. **Note:** Struck at Royal Mint of London.

Date	Mintage	F	VF	XF	Unc	BU
1925	5,985,000	2.00	3.00	8.00	30.00	—
1925 Proof	—	Value: 650				

Note: Struck as proof record specimens by the Royal Mint, less than 12 are estimated to exist

KM# 77 2 LITU Weight: 5.4000 g. **Composition:** 0.5000 Silver .0868 oz. ASW **Edge:** Milled **Size:** 22.9 mm.

Date	Mintage	F	VF	XF	Unc	BU
1925	3,000,000	3.50	5.50	12.00	35.00	—
1925 Proof	—	Value: 650				

Note: Struck as proof record specimens by the Royal Mint, less than 12 are estimated to exist

KM# 78 5 LITAI Weight: 13.5000 g. **Composition:** 0.5000 Silver .217 oz. ASW **Edge:** Milled **Size:** 29.5 mm.

Date	Mintage	F	VF	XF	Unc	BU
1925	1,000,000	4.00	8.00	18.00	65.00	—
1925 Proof	—	Value: 650				

Note: Struck as proof record specimens by the Royal Mint, less than 12 are estimated to exist

KM# 82 5 LITAI Weight: 9.0000 g. **Composition:** 0.7500 Silver .217 oz. ASW **Obverse:** Designer's initials below bust **Reverse:** Dr. Jonas Basanavicius bust facing left **Edge:** Lettered. **Edge Lettering:** TAUTOS GEROVE TAVO GEROVE **Size:** 27 mm.

Date	Mintage	F	VF	XF	Unc	BU
1936	2,612,000	3.00	4.50	8.50	20.00	—

KM# 83 10 LITU Weight: 18.0000 g. **Composition:** 0.7500 Silver .434 oz. ASW **Reverse:** Grand Duke Vytautas Didysis (Vytautas the Great) bust facing left **Edge:** Lettered. **Edge Lettering:** VIENYBEJE TAUTOS JEGA **Size:** 32 mm. **Note:** A filled-die variety with the knight riding a mare instead of a stallion exists.

Date	Mintage	F	VF	XF	Unc	BU
1936	720,000	7.50	11.50	20.00	30.00	55.00

KM# 84 10 LITU Weight: 18.0000 g. **Composition:** 0.7500 Silver .434 oz. ASW **Subject:** 20th Anniversary of Republic **Reverse:** President Smetona head facing left **Edge:** Lettered **Edge Lettering:** VIENYBEJE TAUTOS JEGA

Date	Mintage	F	VF	XF	Unc	BU
ND(1938)	170,000	10.00	15.00	25.00	65.00	85.00

MODERN REPUBLIC
1991-present

REFORM COINAGE
100 Centas = 1 Litas

KM# 85 CENTAS Composition: Aluminum

Date	F	VF	XF	Unc	BU
1991	—	—	—	0.20	—

KM# 86 2 CENTAI Composition: Aluminum

Date	F	VF	XF	Unc	BU
1991	—	—	—	0.25	—

KM# 87 5 CENTAI Composition: Aluminum

Date	F	VF	XF	Unc	BU
1991	—	—	—	0.30	—

KM# 88 10 CENTU Composition: Bronze

Date	F	VF	XF	Unc	BU
1991	—	—	—	0.35	—

KM# 106 10 CENTU Weight: 2.6000 g. **Composition:** Brass **Obverse:** Lithuanian knight **Reverse:** Denomination **Edge:** Milled **Size:** 16 mm.

Date		F	VF	XF	Unc	BU
1997		—	—	—	0.40	—
1998		—	—	—	0.40	—
1999		—	—	—	0.40	—
2000 Proof	5,000	Value: 1.00				

KM# 89 20 CENTU Composition: Bronze

Date	F	VF	XF	Unc	BU
1991	—	—	—	0.65	—

KM# 107 20 CENTU Weight: 4.8000 g. **Composition:** Brass **Obverse:** Lithuanian knight **Reverse:** Denomination **Edge:** Milled **Size:** 20 mm.

Date		F	VF	XF	Unc	BU
1997		—	—	—	0.75	—
1998		—	—	—	0.75	—
1999		—	—	—	0.75	—
2000 Proof	5,000	Value: 1.25				

KM# 90 50 CENTU Composition: Bronze

Date	F	VF	XF	Unc	BU
1991	—	—	—	0.85	—

KM# 108 50 CENTU Weight: 6.0000 g. **Composition:** Brass

Date		F	VF	XF	Unc	BU
1997		—	—	—	1.00	—
1998		—	—	—	1.00	—
1999		—	—	—	1.00	—
2000		—	—	—	1.00	—
2000 Proof	5,000	Value: 1.75				

KM# 91 LITAS Composition: Copper-Nickel

Date	F	VF	XF	Unc	BU
1991	—	—	—	2.00	—

KM# 109 LITAS Composition: Copper-Nickel **Subject:** 75th Anniversary - Bank of Lithuania **Obverse:** Knight and denomination **Reverse:** V. Jurgutis

Date	Mintage	F	VF	XF	Unc	BU
1997	200,000	—	—	—	5.00	—

KM# 109a LITAS Weight: 7.7759 g. **Composition:** 0.9990 Gold .25 oz. AGW **Subject:** 75th Anniversary - Bank of Lithuania **Obverse:** Knight and denomination **Reverse:** V. Jurgutis

Date	Mintage	F	VF	XF	Unc	BU
1997 Proof	1,500	Value: 400				

KM# 111 LITAS Composition: Copper-Nickel **Obverse:** Lithuanian knight **Reverse:** Denomination **Edge:** Reeded

Date		F	VF	XF	Unc	BU
1998		—	—	—	1.50	—
1999		—	—	—	1.50	—
2000		—	—	—	1.25	—
2000 Proof	5,000	Value: 2.50				
2001		—	—	—	1.25	—
2002		—	—	—	1.25	—

KM# 117 LITAS Composition: Copper-Nickel **Subject:** The Baltic Highway **Reverse:** Six clasped hands **Edge:** Reeded and plain sections

Date	Mintage	F	VF	XF	Unc	BU
1999	1,000,000	—	—	—	3.00	—

KM# 92 2 LITAI Composition: Copper-Nickel

Date	F	VF	XF	Unc	BU
1991	—	—	—	2.50	—

KM# 112 2 LITAI Ring Composition: Brass **Center Composition:** Copper-Nickel **Obverse:** Lithuanian knight **Reverse:** Denomination **Edge:** Segmented reeding

Date		F	VF	XF	Unc	BU
1998		—	—	—	2.75	—
1999		—	—	—	2.75	—
2000 Proof	5,000	Value: 3.75				
2001		—	—	—	2.75	—
2002		—	—	—	2.75	—

KM# 93 5 LITAI Composition: Copper-Nickel

Date	F	VF	XF	Unc	BU
1991	—	—	—	3.50	—

KM# 113 5 LITAI Ring Composition: Copper Nickel **Center Composition:** Brass **Obverse:** Lithuanian knight **Reverse:** Denomination **Edge:** Lettered **Edge Lettering:** PENKI LITAI

Date	Mintage	F	VF	XF	Unc	BU
1998		—	—	—	4.50	—
1999		—	—	—	4.50	—
2000 Proof	5,000	Value: 5.50				

KM# 127 5 LITAI Series: UNICEF **Subject:** For the Children of the World **Reverse:** Child with pinwheel **Edge:** Lettered **Edge Lettering:** LIETUVOS BANKAS **Size:** 38.6 mm.

Date	Mintage	F	VF	XF	Unc	BU
1998 Proof	3,000	Value: 60.00				

KM# 132 5 LITAI Weight: 28.2800 g. **Composition:** 0.9250 Silver 0.841 oz. ASW **Series:** Endangered Wildlife **Obverse:** Knight on horse **Reverse:** Barn owl in flight **Edge:** Lettered **Edge Lettering:** ILETUVOS BANKAS **Size:** 38.6 mm.

Date	Mintage	F	VF	XF	Unc	BU
2002 Proof	3,000	Value: 32.50				

KM# 94 10 LITU **Composition:** Copper-Nickel **Subject:** 60th Anniversary - Darius and Girenas flight across the Atlantic **Edge:** Lettered **Edge Lettering:** SLOVE ATLANTO NUGALETOJAMS

Date	Mintage	F	VF	XF	Unc	BU
ND(1993)LMK	4,500	—	—	—	50.00	—

KM# 95 10 LITU **Composition:** Copper-Nickel **Subject:** Papal visit **Edge:** Lettered **Edge Lettering:** TIKEJIMAS MEILE VILTIS

Date	Mintage	F	VF	XF	Unc	BU
1993LMK	5,000	—	—	—	45.00	—

KM# 96 10 LITU **Composition:** Copper-Nickel **Subject:** International Song Fest **Edge:** Lettered **Edge Lettering:** SKRISKIT SKAISCIOS DAINOS

Date	Mintage	F	VF	XF	Unc	BU
1994LMK Proof	11,708	Value: 12.00				

KM# 97 10 LITU **Composition:** Copper-Nickel **Subject:** 5th World Sport Games **Edge:** Lettered **Edge Lettering:** LIETUVIAIS ESAME MES GIME

Date	Mintage	F	VF	XF	Unc	BU
1995LMK Proof	10,000	Value: 12.00				

KM# 115 10 LITU **Composition:** Copper-Nickel **Obverse:** National arms above denomination **Reverse:** Vilnus building tops as seen from ground level **Edge:** Lettered **Edge Lettering:** VILNIUS-LIETUVOS SOSTINE

Date	Mintage	F	VF	XF	Unc	BU
1998 Proof	7,500	Value: 15.00				

KM# 116 10 LITU **Composition:** Copper-Nickel **Obverse:** Lithuanian knight **Reverse:** Kaunas city arms and buildings **Edge:** Lettered **Edge Lettering:** LAISUAS BUDAMAS, LAISVES NEISSIZADESI

Date	Mintage	F	VF	XF	Unc	BU
1999 Proof	7,500	Value: 12.00				

KM# 120 10 LITU **Weight:** 1.2440 g. **Composition:** 0.9999 Gold .04 oz. AGW **Subject:** Lithuanian gold coinage **Reverse:** Medieval minter

Date	Mintage	F	VF	XF	Unc	BU
1999 Proof	5,500	Value: 60.00				

KM# 131 10 LITU **Weight:** 13.1500 g. **Composition:** Copper-Nickel **Obverse:** National arms above an aerial harbor view **Reverse:** Klaipeda (Memel) city arms and city view **Edge:** Lettered **Edge Lettering:** KLAIPEDAI - 75 (twice) **Size:** 28.7 mm.

Date	Mintage	F	VF	XF	Unc	BU
2002 Proof	5,000	Value: 15.00				

KM# 98 50 LITU **Weight:** 23.3000 g. **Composition:** 0.9250 Silver .6929 oz. ASW **Subject:** 5th Anniversary - Independence **Edge:** Lettered **Edge Lettering:** TEGUL MEILE LIETUVOS DEGA MUSU SIRDYSE

Date	Mintage	F	VF	XF	Unc	BU
ND(1995)LMK Proof	5,000	Value: 85.00				

KM# 99 50 LITU **Weight:** 23.3000 g. **Composition:** 0.9250 Silver .6929 oz. ASW **Subject:** 120th Birth Anniversary Mikalojaus K. Ciurlionis **Edge:** Lettered **Edge Lettering:** PASAULIS KAIP DIDELE SIMFONIJA

Date	Mintage	F	VF	XF	Unc	BU
1995LMK Proof	6,515	Value: 37.50				

KM# 100 50 LITU **Weight:** 23.3000 g. **Composition:** 0.9250 Silver .6929 oz. ASW **Subject:** 5th Anniversary - 13 January 1991 Assault **Edge:** Lettered **Edge Lettering:** IR KRAUJU KRIKSTYTI TAMPA VEL GYUYBE

Date	Mintage	F	VF	XF	Unc	BU
ND(1996) Proof	Est. 6,000	Value: 37.50				

KM# 103 50 LITU **Weight:** 23.3000 g. **Composition:** 0.9250 Silver .6929 oz. ASW **Reverse:** Grand Duke Gediminas **Edge:** Lettered **Edge Lettering:** IS PRAEITIES TAVO SUNUS TE STIPRYBE SEMIA

Date	Mintage	F	VF	XF	Unc	BU
1996LMK Proof	Est. 4,421	Value: 37.50				

KM# 101 50 LITU **Weight:** 23.3000 g. **Composition:** 0.9250 Silver .6929 oz. ASW **Series:** Altanta Olympics **Reverse:** Basketball players **Edge:** Lettered **Edge Lettering:** CITIUS. ALTIUS. FORTIUS.

Date	Mintage	F	VF	XF	Unc	BU
1996LMK Proof	Est. 6,000	Value: 25.00				

KM# 102 50 LITU **Weight:** 23.3000 g. **Composition:** 0.9250 Silver .6929 oz. ASW **Reverse:** King Mindaugas **Edge:** Lettered **Edge Lettering:** IS PRAEITIES TAVO SUNUS TE STIPRYBE SEMIA

Date	Mintage	F	VF	XF	Unc	BU
1996LMK Proof	Est. 4,982	Value: 35.00				

KM# 104 50 LITU **Weight:** 23.3000 g. **Composition:** 0.9250 Silver .6929 oz. ASW **Subject:** 450th Anniversary - First Lithuanian Book **Obverse:** Mounted Lithuanian knight with sword **Reverse:** Page from book **Edge:** Lettered

Edge Lettering: MARTYNAS MAZVYDAS IMKIT MANE IR SKAITYKIT

Date	Mintage	F	VF	XF	Unc	BU
1997 Proof	Est. 5,000	Value: 37.50				

KM# 105 50 LITU **Weight:** 23.3000 g. **Composition:** 0.9250 Silver .6929 oz. ASW **Subject:** 600th Anniversary - Karaims and Tartars settelment in Lithuania **Obverse:** Mounted Lithuanian knight with sword **Reverse:** Karaim castle guard and Tartar warrior **Edge:** Lettered **Edge Lettering:** LIETUVA TEVYNE MUSU

Date	Mintage	F	VF	XF	Unc	BU
1997 Proof	Est. 5,000	Value: 37.50				

KM# 110 50 LITU **Weight:** 23.3000 g. **Composition:** 0.9250 Silver .6929 oz. ASW **Obverse:** Mounted Grand Duke Algirdas with sword left **Reverse:** Half bust of knight facing and holding scepter

Date	Mintage	F	VF	XF	Unc	BU
1998 Proof	4,000	Value: 37.50				

KM# 114 50 LITU **Weight:** 23.3000 g. **Composition:** 0.9250 Silver .6929 oz. ASW **Subject:** 200th Anniversary - Birth of Adam Mickiewicz **Obverse:** Feather, denomination **Reverse:** Laureated profile of Adomas Mickievicius, building

Date	Mintage	F	VF	XF	Unc	BU
1998 Proof	Est. 5,000	Value: 37.50				

KM# 118 50 LITU **Weight:** 23.1200 g. **Composition:** 0.9250 Silver .6876 oz. ASW **Subject:** Grand Duke Kestutis **Reverse:** Half bust Grand Duke Kestutis facing **Edge:** Lettered **Edge Lettering:** IS PRAEITIES TAVO SUNVS TE STIPRYBE SEMIA **Size:** 34.1 mm. **Note:** Lithuanian Mint.

Date	Mintage	F	VF	XF	Unc	BU
1999 Proof	2,500	Value: 42.00				

KM# 119 50 LITU **Weight:** 28.2800 g. **Composition:** 0.9250 Silver .841 oz. ASW **Subject:** 100th Anniversary - Death of Vincas Kudirka **Obverse:** National arms on stylized bell **Reverse:** Head of Kudirka **Edge:** Lettered **Edge Lettering:** VARDAN TOS LIETUVOS VIENYBE TEZYDI **Size:** 38.6 mm. **Note:** Lithuanian Mint.

Date	Mintage	F	VF	XF	Unc	BU
1999 Proof	4,000	Value: 40.00				

KM# 123 50 LITU **Weight:** 28.2800 g. **Composition:** 0.9250 Silver .841 oz. ASW **Subject:** 10th Anniversary - Baltic Way Highway **Reverse:** Three pairs of clasped hands **Edge:** Lettered **Edge Lettering:** VILNIUS RYGA TALINAS **Size:** 38.6 mm. **Note:** Lithuanian Mint.

Date	Mintage	F	VF	XF	Unc	BU
1999 Proof	4,000	Value: 40.00				

KM# 121 50 LITU **Weight:** 28.2800 g. **Composition:** 0.9250 Silver .841 oz. ASW **Subject:** 350th Anniversary - The Great Art of Artillery Book **Obverse:** National arms on frame **Reverse:** Old rocket designs **Edge:** Lettered **Edge Lettering:** ARS MAGNA ARTILLERIAE * MDCL

Date	Mintage	F	VF	XF	Unc	BU
2000 Proof	2,000	Value: 42.00				

KM# 125 50 LITU **Weight:** 23.3000 g. **Composition:** 0.9250 Silver .6929 oz. ASW **Subject:** Grand Duke Vytautas **Obverse:** National arms above four shields **Reverse:** Crowned portrait holding sword **Edge Lettering:** "IS PRAEITIES TAVO SUNUS TESTIPRYBE SEMIA" **Size:** 34 mm.

Date	Mintage	F	VF	XF	Unc	BU
2000 Proof	2,500	Value: 45.00				

KM# 122 50 LITU **Weight:** 28.2800 g. **Composition:** 0.9250 Silver .841 oz. ASW **Subject:** 10th Anniversary of Independence **Obverse:** Republic of Lithuania coat of arms **Reverse:** Statue of independence **Edge:** Lettered **Edge Lettering:** LAISVE - AMZINOJI TAUTOS VERTYBE **Size:** 38.6 mm. **Note:** Struck at Lietuvos Monetu Vertybe.

Date	Mintage	F	VF	XF	Unc	BU
ND(2000) Proof	3,000	Value: 42.50				

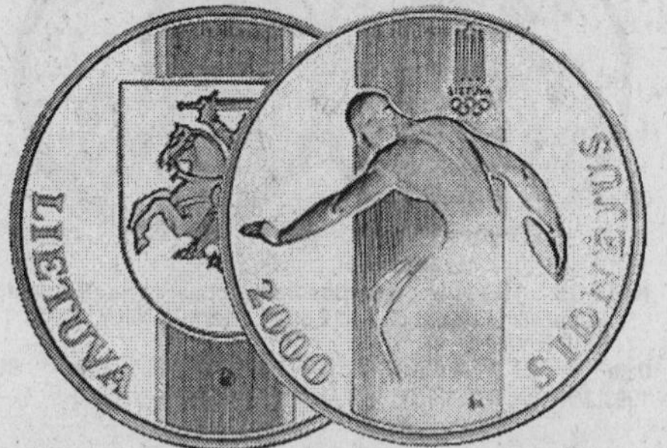

KM# 124 50 LITU **Weight:** 28.2800 g. **Composition:** 0.9250 Silver .841 oz. ASW **Series:** XXVII Summer Olympic Games **Obverse:** Republic of Lithuania coat of arms **Reverse:** Man throwing discus, Olympic emblem, year, and SIDNEJUS (Sydney) **Edge:** Lettered **Edge Lettering:** NUGALI STIPRUS DVASIA IR KUNU

Date	Mintage	F	VF	XF	Unc	BU
2000 Proof	4,000	Value: 40.00				

KM# 128 50 LITU **Weight:** 28.2800 g. **Composition:** 0.9250 Silver .841 oz. ASW **Subject:** Millennium **Obverse:** National arms, denomination **Reverse:** Radiant cross, arch **Edge:** Lettered **Edge Lettering:** SALVE NOVUM MILLENNIUM

Date	Mintage	F	VF	XF	Unc	BU
2000 Proof	3,000	Value: 40.00				

KM# 129 50 LITU **Weight:** 28.2800 g. **Composition:** 0.9250 Silver .8410 oz. ASW **Subject:** Motiejus Valancius' 200th Birthday **Obverse:** National arms and church landscape **Reverse:** Bishop's portrait **Edge Lettering:** "LIETUVISKAS ZODIS RASTAS IR TIKEJMAS TAUTOS GYVASTIS" **Size:** 38.6 mm.

Date	Mintage	F	VF	XF	Unc	BU
2001 Proof	2,000	Value: 45.00				

KM# 130 50 LITU Weight: 28.2800 g. **Composition:** 0.9250 Silver 0.841 oz. ASW **Subject:** Jonas Basanavicius (1851-1927) **Obverse:** Mounted knight left **Reverse:** Jonas Basanavicius **Edge Lettering:** "KAD AUSRAI AUSTANT PRAVISTU IR LIETUVOS DVASIA" **Size:** 38.6 mm.

Date	Mintage	F	VF	XF	Unc	BU
2001 Proof	2,000	Value: 45.00				

KM# 133 50 LITU Composition: 0.9250 Silver **Obverse:** Trakai Island Castle

Date	Mintage	F	VF	XF	Unc	BU
2002 Proof	1,500	Value: 40.00				

KM# 126 100 LITU Weight: 7.7800 g. **Composition:** 0.9999 Gold .2501 oz. AGW **Subject:** Grand Duke Vytautas **Obverse:** Knight on horse **Reverse:** Crowned portrait and sword hilt **Edge Lettering:** IS PRAEITIES TAVO SUNUS TE STIPRYBE SEMIA **Size:** 22.3 mm.

Date	Mintage	F	VF	XF	Unc	BU
2000 Proof	2,000	Value: 250				

PATTERNS

Including off metal strikes

KM#	Date	Mintage	Identification	Mkt Val
Pn3	1936	—	5 Litai. Silver. Plain edge. Coin struck.	700
Pn4	1936	—	5 Litai. Silver. Lettered edge. Coin struck.	700
Pn6	1936	—	10 Litu. Silver. Plain edge. KM83.	800
Pn5	1936	—	5 Litai. Silver. Designer's name (J. ZIKARAS) below bust. Plain edge. KM82. Medal struck.	700
Pn7	1938	—	2 Litai. Brass. Lettered edge.	650
Pn8	1938	—	2 Litai. Silver. Reeded edge.	750
Pn9	1938	—	2 Litai. Silver. Lettered edge.	700
Pn10	1938	—	2 Litai. Silver. Plain edge.	700
Pn11	1938	—	2 Litai. Silver. Plain edge.	750
Pn12	1938	—	2 Litai. Silver. Lettered edge.	750
Pn13	1938	—	10 Litu. Silver. Coin struck.	700
Pn14	1938	2	10 Litu. Gold. Lettered edge. Medal-struck presentation pieces.	—
Pn15	1994	234	50 Litu. Silver. Lettered edge.	—

TRIAL STRIKES

KM#	Date	Mintage	Identification	Mkt Val
TS1	1925	—	Centas. Aluminum-Bronze. Uniface. Obverse.	250
TS2	1925	—	Centas. Aluminum-Bronze. Uniface. Reverse.	250
TS3	1925	—	5 Centai. Aluminum-Bronze. Uniface. Obverse.	250
TS4	1925	—	5 Centai. Aluminum-Bronze. Uniface. Reverse.	250
TS5	1925	—	10 Centu. Aluminum-Bronze. Uniface. Obverse.	275
TS6	1925	—	10 Centu. Aluminum-Bronze. Uniface. Reverse.	275
TS7	1925	—	20 Centu. Aluminum-Bronze. Uniface. Obverse.	275
TS8	1925	—	20 Centu. Aluminum-Bronze. Uniface. Reverse.	275
TS9	1925	—	50 Centu. Aluminum-Bronze. Uniface. Obverse.	285
TS10	1925	—	50 Centu. Aluminum-Bronze. Uniface. Reverse.	285

MINT SETS

KM#	Date	Mintage	Identification	Issue Price	Mkt Val
MS1	1925 (10)	—	KM71-75, 2 of each	—	950
MS2	1991 (9)	100,000	KM85-93	7.50	17.50

PROOF SETS

KM#	Date	Mintage	Identification	Issue Price	Mkt Val
PS1	2000 (6)	5,000	KM106-108, 111-113	7.50	15.00

LUXEMBOURG

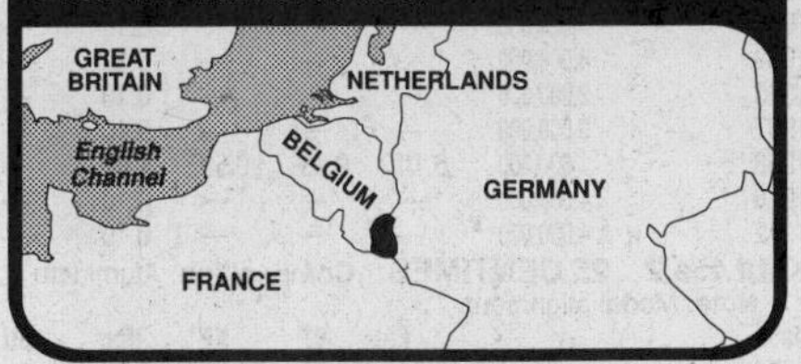

The Grand Duchy of Luxembourg is located in western Europe between Belgium, Germany and France, has an area of 1,103 sq. mi. (2,586 sq. km.) and a population of 377,100. Capital: Luxembourg. The economy is based on steel.

Founded about 963, Luxembourg was a prominent country of the Holy Roman Empire; one of its sovereigns became Holy Roman Emperor as Henry VII, 1308. After being made a duchy by Emperor Charles IV, 1354, Luxembourg passed under the domination of Burgundy, Spain, Austria and France, 1443-1815, regaining autonomy under the Treaty of Vienna, 1815, as a grand duchy in union with the Netherlands, though ostensibly a member of the German Confederation. When Belgium seceded from the Kingdom of the Netherlands, 1830, Luxembourg was forced to cede its greater western section to Belgium. The tiny duchy left the German Confederation in 1867 when the Treaty of London recognized it as an independent state and guaranteed its perpetual neutrality. Luxembourg was occupied by Germany and liberated by American troops in both World Wars.

RULERS

Adolphe, 1890-1905
William IV, 1905-1912
Marie Adelaide, 1912-1919
Charlotte, 1919-1964
Jean, 1964-2000
Henri, 2000-

MINT MARKS

A - Paris
(b) - Brussels, privy marks only
H – Gunzburg
(n) – lion - Namur
(u) - Utrecht, privy marks only

PRIVY MARKS

Angel's head, two headed eagle - Brussels
Sword, Caduceus - Utrecht (1846-74 although struck at Brussels until 1909)

NOTE: Beginning in 1994 the letters "qp" for quality proof appear on Proof coins.

MONETARY SYSTEM

100 Centimes = 1 Franc

DUCHY

STANDARD COINAGE RESUMED

100 Centimes = 1 Franc

KM# 21 2-1/2 CENTIMES Composition: Bronze

Date	Mintage	F	VF	XF	Unc	BU
1901(u)	800,000	1.00	2.00	3.50	12.50	—
Note: BARTH on reverse						
1901(u)	Inc. above	1.00	2.50	4.00	14.00	—
Note: BAPTH on reverse						
1908(u)	400,000	1.00	2.50	4.00	14.00	—

KM# 24 5 CENTIMES Composition: Copper-Nickel

Date	Mintage	F	VF	XF	Unc	BU
1901	2,000,000	0.25	0.75	1.50	6.00	—

KM# 26 5 CENTIMES Composition: Copper-Nickel

Date	Mintage	F	VF	XF	Unc	BU
1908	1,500,000	0.35	1.00	1.75	7.50	—

KM# 27 5 CENTIMES Composition: Zinc

Date	Mintage	F	VF	XF	Unc	BU
1915	1,200,000	1.00	2.50	5.50	15.00	—

KM# 30 5 CENTIMES Composition: Iron

Date	Mintage	F	VF	XF	Unc	BU
1918	1,200,000	1.00	2.50	5.00	15.00	—
1921	600,000	6.00	10.00	20.00	40.00	—
1922	400,000	12.00	20.00	40.00	80.00	—

KM# 33 5 CENTIMES Composition: Copper-Nickel

Date	Mintage	F	VF	XF	Unc	BU
1924	3,000,000	0.20	0.40	0.80	4.50	—

KM# 40 5 CENTIMES Composition: Bronze

Date	Mintage	F	VF	XF	Unc	BU
1930	5,000,000	0.10	0.25	0.60	2.50	—

KM# 25 10 CENTIMES Composition: Copper-Nickel

Date	Mintage	F	VF	XF	Unc	BU
1901	4,000,000	0.25	0.75	1.50	7.50	—

KM# 28 10 CENTIMES Composition: Zinc

Date	Mintage	F	VF	XF	Unc	BU
1915	1,400,000	1.25	3.00	5.00	15.00	—

KM# 31 10 CENTIMES Composition: Iron

Date	Mintage	F	VF	XF	Unc	BU
1918	1,603,000	1.50	3.50	7.50	20.00	—
1921	626,000	2.00	4.50	9.00	22.50	—
1923	350,000	12.00	20.00	40.00	85.00	—

KM# 34 10 CENTIMES Composition: Copper-Nickel

Date	Mintage	F	VF	XF	Unc	BU
1924	3,500,000	0.25	0.50	1.00	4.50	—

KM# 41 10 CENTIMES Composition: Bronze

Date	Mintage	F	VF	XF	Unc	BU
1930	5,000,000	0.10	0.25	0.75	3.00	—

KM# 29 25 CENTIMES Composition: Zinc

Date	Mintage	F	VF	XF	Unc	BU
1916	800,000	1.50	3.50	7.50	15.00	—
1920	—	200	400	600	1,000	—

KM# 32 25 CENTIMES Composition: Iron

Date	Mintage	F	VF	XF	Unc	BU
1919	804,000	2.75	5.50	11.00	30.00	—
1920	800,000	2.25	4.00	8.50	25.00	—
1922	600,000	2.25	4.00	8.50	25.00	—

KM# 37 25 CENTIMES Composition: Copper-Nickel

Date	Mintage	F	VF	XF	Unc	BU
1927	2,500,000	0.35	0.65	1.25	5.00	—

KM# 42 25 CENTIMES Composition: Bronze

Date	Mintage	F	VF	XF	Unc	BU
1930	1,000,000	0.35	0.85	1.75	6.50	—

KM# 42a.1 25 CENTIMES Composition: Copper-Nickel
Note: Coin alignment.

Date	Mintage	F	VF	XF	Unc	BU
1938	2,000,000	1.00	2.00	4.00	7.00	—

KM# 42a.2 25 CENTIMES Composition: Copper-Nickel
Note: Medal alignment.

Date	F	VF	XF	Unc	BU
1938	50.00	75.00	100	200	—

KM# 45 25 CENTIMES Composition: Bronze

Date	Mintage	F	VF	XF	Unc	BU
1946	1,000,000	—	0.15	0.25	0.75	—
1947	1,000,000	—	0.15	0.25	0.75	—

KM# 45a.1 25 CENTIMES Composition: Aluminum
Note: Coin alignment.

Date	Mintage	F	VF	XF	Unc	BU
1954	7,000,000	—	—	—	0.10	—
1957	3,020,000	—	—	—	0.10	—
1960	3,020,000	—	—	—	0.10	—
1963	4,000,000	—	—	—	0.10	—
1965	2,000,000	—	—	—	0.10	—
1967	3,000,000	—	—	—	0.10	—
1968	600,000	0.10	0.25	0.50	1.00	—
1970	4,000,000	—	—	—	0.10	—
1972	4,000,000	—	—	—	0.10	—

KM# 45a.2 25 CENTIMES Composition: Aluminum
Note: Medal alignment.

Date	F	VF	XF	Unc	BU
1954	10.00	20.00	30.00	40.00	—
1960	5.00	10.00	15.00	20.00	—
1963	5.00	10.00	15.00	20.00	—
1965	10.00	20.00	30.00	40.00	—
1967	10.00	20.00	30.00	40.00	—

KM# 45b 25 CENTIMES Weight: 2.9600 g. **Composition:** 0.9250 Silver .088 oz. ASW

Date	Mintage	F	VF	XF	Unc	BU
1980 Proof	3,000	Value: 12.00				

KM# 43 50 CENTIMES Composition: Nickel

Date	Mintage	F	VF	XF	Unc	BU
1930	2,000,000	0.25	0.50	1.00	5.00	—

KM# 35 FRANC Composition: Nickel

Date	Mintage	F	VF	XF	Unc	BU
1924	1,000,000	0.25	0.75	1.25	8.00	—
1928	2,000,000	0.20	0.50	1.00	7.00	—
1935	1,000,000	0.25	0.75	1.25	6.00	—

KM# 44 FRANC Composition: Copper-Nickel

Date	Mintage	F	VF	XF	Unc	BU
1939	5,000,000	0.25	0.75	1.50	5.00	—

KM# 46.1 FRANC Composition: Copper-Nickel

Date	Mintage	F	VF	XF	Unc	BU
1946	4,000,000	0.15	0.35	0.50	1.50	—
1947	2,000,000	0.20	0.40	0.75	2.00	—

KM# 46.2 FRANC Composition: Copper-Nickel

Date	Mintage	F	VF	XF	Unc	BU
1952	5,000,000	0.10	0.25	0.50	1.25	—
1953	2,000,000	0.10	0.25	0.50	1.00	—
1955	1,000,000	0.10	0.25	0.50	1.00	—
1957	2,000,000	—	0.10	0.25	0.50	—
1960	2,000,000	—	0.10	0.25	0.50	—
1962	2,000,000	—	0.10	0.25	0.50	—
1964	2,000,000	—	0.10	0.25	0.50	—

KM# 46.2a FRANC Weight: 4.4500 g. **Composition:** 0.9250 Silver .1323 oz. ASW

Date	Mintage	F	VF	XF	Unc	BU
1980 Proof	3,000	Value: 20.00				

KM# 55 FRANC Composition: Copper-Nickel

Date	Mintage	F	VF	XF	Unc	BU
1965	3,000,000	—	—	0.10	0.20	—
1966	1,000,000	—	—	0.10	0.20	—
1968	3,000,000	—	—	0.10	0.20	—
1970	3,000,000	—	—	0.10	0.20	—
1972	3,000,000	—	—	0.10	0.20	—
1973	3,000,000	—	—	0.10	0.20	—
1976	3,000,000	—	—	0.10	0.20	—
1977	1,000,000	—	—	0.10	0.20	—
1978	3,000,000	—	—	0.10	0.20	—
1979	2,000,000	—	—	0.10	0.20	—
1980	4,000,000	—	—	0.10	0.20	—
1981	5,000,000	—	—	0.10	0.20	—
1982	3,000,000	—	—	0.10	0.20	—
1983	3,000,000	—	—	0.10	0.20	—
1984	3,000,000	—	—	0.10	0.20	—

KM#55a FRANC Weight: 4.4700 g. **Composition:** 0.9250 Silver .1329 oz. ASW

Date	Mintage	F	VF	XF	Unc	BU
1980 Proof	3,000	Value: 20.00				

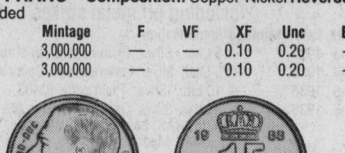

KM#59 FRANC Composition: Copper-Nickel **Reverse:** IML added

Date	Mintage	F	VF	XF	Unc	BU
1986	3,000,000	—	—	0.10	0.20	—
1987	3,000,000	—	—	0.10	0.20	—

KM# 63 FRANC Composition: Nickel-Steel

Date	Mintage	F	VF	XF	Unc	BU
1988	10,000,000	—	—	—	0.40	—
1989	3,000,000	—	—	—	0.40	—
1990	25,010,000	—	—	—	0.40	—
1991	10,010,000	—	—	—	0.40	—
1992 In sets only	10,000	—	—	—	0.50	—
1993 In sets only	10,000	—	—	—	0.50	—
1994 In sets only	10,000	—	—	—	0.50	—
1995 In sets only	10,000	—	—	—	0.50	—

KM# 36 2 FRANCS Composition: Nickel

Date	Mintage	F	VF	XF	Unc	BU
1924	1,000,000	1.00	2.25	4.00	15.00	—

KM# 38 5 FRANCS Weight: 8.0000 g. **Composition:** 0.6250 Silver .1608 oz. ASW

Date	Mintage	F	VF	XF	Unc	BU
1929	2,000,000	BV	3.00	7.00	22.50	—

KM# 50 5 FRANCS **Composition:** Copper-Nickel

Date	Mintage	F	VF	XF	Unc	BU
1949	2,000,000	0.30	0.60	1.00	2.50	—

KM# 51 5 FRANCS **Composition:** Copper-Nickel

Date	Mintage	F	VF	XF	Unc	BU
1962	2,000,000	0.10	0.25	0.40	0.75	—

KM# 51a 5 FRANCS **Weight:** 6.7400 g. **Composition:** 0.9250 Silver .2004 oz. ASW

Date	Mintage	F	VF	XF	Unc	BU
1980 Proof	3,000	Value: 25.00				

KM# 56 5 FRANCS **Composition:** Copper-Nickel

Date	Mintage	F	VF	XF	Unc	BU
1971	1,000,000	—	—	0.15	0.50	—
1976	1,000,000	—	—	0.15	0.50	—
1979	1,000,000	—	—	0.15	0.50	—
1981	1,000,000	—	—	0.15	0.50	—

KM# 56a 5 FRANCS **Weight:** 6.7800 g. **Composition:** 0.9250 Silver .2016 oz. ASW

Date	Mintage	F	VF	XF	Unc	BU
1980 Proof	3,000	Value: 25.00				

KM# 60.1 5 FRANCS **Composition:** Brass **Reverse:** IML added

Date	Mintage	F	VF	XF	Unc	BU
1986	9,000,000	—	—	0.15	0.40	—
1987	7,000,000	—	—	0.15	0.40	—
1988	2,000,000	—	—	0.15	0.40	—

KM# 60.2 5 FRANCS **Composition:** Brass **Reverse:** Larger crown with cross touching rim

Date	F	VF	XF	Unc	BU
1987	—	—	0.15	0.40	—

KM# 65 5 FRANCS **Composition:** Brass

Date	Mintage	F	VF	XF	Unc	BU
1989	2,000,000	—	—	—	0.60	—
1990	4,010,000	—	—	—	0.60	—
1991 In sets only	10,000	—	—	—	0.75	—
1992 In sets only	20,000	—	—	—	0.75	—
1993 In sets only	18,000	—	—	—	0.75	—
1994 In sets only	10,000	—	—	—	0.75	—
1995 In sets only	10,000	—	—	—	0.75	—

KM# 39 10 FRANCS **Weight:** 13.5000 g. **Composition:** 0.7500 Silver .3255 oz. ASW

Date	Mintage	F	VF	XF	Unc	BU
1929	1,000,000	BV	5.00	10.00	32.50	—

KM# 57 10 FRANCS **Composition:** Nickel

Date	Mintage	F	VF	XF	Unc	BU
1971	3,000,000	—	—	0.30	0.60	—
1972	3,000,000	—	—	0.30	0.60	—
1974	3,000,000	—	—	0.30	0.60	—
1976	3,000,000	—	—	0.30	0.60	—
1977	1,000,000	—	—	0.30	0.60	—
1978	1,000,000	—	—	0.30	0.60	—
1979	1,000,000	—	—	0.30	0.60	—
1980	1,000,000	—	—	0.30	0.60	—

KM# 57a 10 FRANCS **Weight:** 8.7900 g. **Composition:** 0.9250 Silver .2614 oz. ASW

Date	Mintage	F	VF	XF	Unc	BU
1980 Proof	3,000	Value: 28.50				

KM# 47 20 FRANCS **Weight:** 8.5000 g. **Composition:** 0.8350 Silver .2282 oz. ASW **Subject:** 600th Anniversary - John the Blind

Date	Mintage	F	VF	XF	Unc	BU
ND(1946)		—	—	7.00	15.00	—
ND(1946) Proof	100	Value: 200				

KM# 58 20 FRANCS **Composition:** Bronze

Date	Mintage	F	VF	XF	Unc	BU
1980	3,000,000	—	—	0.60	1.00	—
1981	3,000,000	—	—	0.60	1.00	—
1982	3,000,000	—	—	0.60	1.00	—
1983	2,000,000	—	—	0.60	1.00	—

KM# 58a 20 FRANCS **Weight:** 10.2100 g. **Composition:** 0.9250 Silver .3036 oz. ASW

Date	Mintage	F	VF	XF	Unc	BU
1980 Proof	3,000	Value: 28.50				

KM# 64 20 FRANCS **Weight:** 6.2200 g. **Composition:** 0.9990 Gold .2 oz. AGW **Subject:** 150th Anniversary of the Grand Duchy

Date	Mintage	F	VF	XF	Unc	BU
ND(1989) Proof	50,000	Value: 100				

KM# 67 20 FRANCS **Composition:** Bronze

Date	Mintage	F	VF	XF	Unc	BU
1990	1,110,000	—	—	—	2.00	—
1991 In sets only	10,000	—	—	—	2.50	—
1992 In sets only	10,000	—	—	—	2.50	—
1993 In sets only	10,000	—	—	—	2.50	—
1994 In sets only	10,000	—	—	—	2.50	—
1995 In sets only	10,000	—	—	—	2.50	—

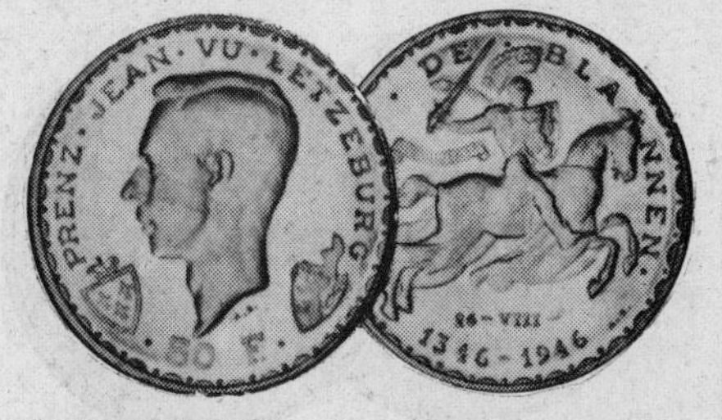

KM# 48 50 FRANCS **Weight:** 12.5000 g. **Composition:** 0.8350 Silver .3356 oz. ASW **Subject:** 600th Anniversary - John the Blind

Date	Mintage	F	VF	XF	Unc	BU
ND(1946)		—	—	12.50	18.00	—
ND(1946) Proof	100	Value: 225				

KM# 62 50 FRANCS **Composition:** Nickel

Date	Mintage	F	VF	XF	Unc	BU
1987	3,000,000	—	—	1.50	3.50	—
1988	1,000,000	—	—	1.50	3.50	—
1989	1,200,000	—	—	1.50	3.50	—

KM# 66 50 FRANCS **Composition:** Nickel **Note:** Similar to 5 Francs, KM#65.

Date	Mintage	F	VF	XF	Unc	BU
1989	2,000,000	—	—	—	3.50	—
1990	2,010,000	—	—	—	3.50	—
1991 In sets only	10,000	—	—	—	3.50	—
1992 In sets only	10,000	—	—	—	4.00	—
1993 In sets only	10,000	—	—	—	4.00	—
1994 In sets only	10,000	—	—	—	4.00	—
1995 In sets only	10,000	—	—	—	4.00	—

KM# 49 100 FRANCS **Weight:** 25.0000 g. **Composition:** 0.8350 Silver .6711 oz. ASW **Subject:** 600th Anniversary - John the Blind

Date	Mintage	F	VF	XF	Unc	BU
ND(1946)	98,000	—	—	20.00	32.50	—
ND(1946) Proof	100	Value: 250				
ND(1946) Restrike	2,000	—	—	—	100	—

Note: Without designer's name

KM# 52 100 FRANCS **Weight:** 18.0000 g. **Composition:** 0.8350 Silver .4832 oz. ASW

Date	Mintage	F	VF	XF	Unc	BU
1963	50,000	—	—	10.00	15.00	—

KM# 54 100 FRANCS **Weight:** 18.0000 g. **Composition:** 0.8350 Silver .4832 oz. ASW

Date	Mintage	F	VF	XF	Unc	BU
1964	50,000	—	—	7.50	12.50	—

KM# 70 100 FRANCS **Weight:** 16.1000 g. **Composition:** 0.9250 Silver .4788 oz. ASW **Subject:** 50th Anniversary - United Nations

Date	Mintage	F	VF	XF	Unc	BU
ND(1995) (qp) Proof	110,000	Value: 28.50				

KM# 53.1 250 FRANCS **Weight:** 25.0000 g. **Composition:** 0.9000 Silver .7234 oz. ASW **Subject:** Millennium of Luxembourg City

Date	Mintage	F	VF	XF	Unc	BU
ND(1963)	11,000	—	—	25.00	40.00	—

KM# 53.2 250 FRANCS **Weight:** 25.0000 g. **Composition:** 0.9000 Silver .7234 oz. ASW **Subject:** Millennium of Luxembourg City **Note:** Darkly toned by the mint.

Date	Mintage	F	VF	XF	Unc	BU
ND(1963)	8,500	—	—	40.00	60.00	—

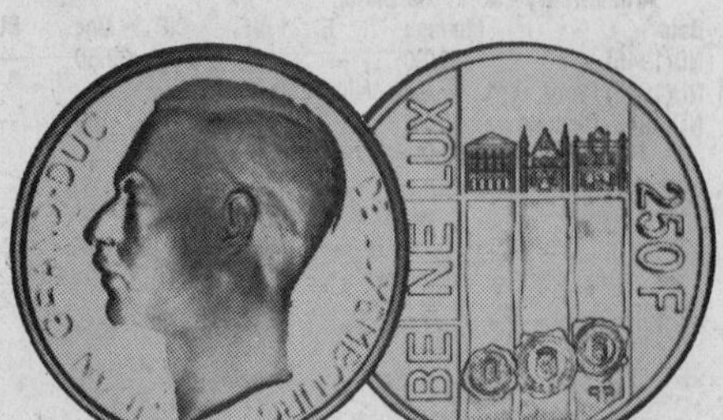

KM# 68 250 FRANCS **Weight:** 18.7500 g. **Composition:** 0.9250 Silver .5577 oz. ASW **Subject:** BE-NE-LUX Treaty

Date	Mintage	F	VF	XF	Unc	BU
ND(1994) (qp) Proof	30,000	Value: 30.00				

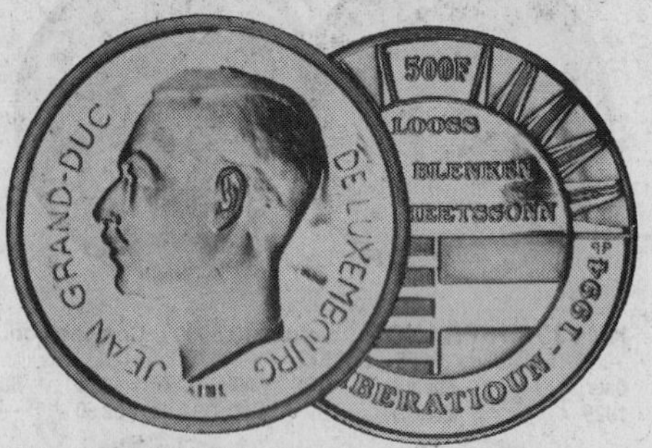

KM# 69 500 FRANCS **Weight:** 22.8500 g. **Composition:** 0.9250 Silver .6795 oz. ASW **Subject:** 50th Anniversary of Liberation

Date	Mintage	F	VF	XF	Unc	BU
ND(1994)	25,000	—	—	—	30.00	—
ND(1994) (qp) Proof	25,000	Value: 42.50				

KM# 71 500 FRANCS **Weight:** 22.8500 g. **Composition:** 0.9250 Silver .6795 oz. ASW **Subject:** Luxembourg - European Cultural City

Date	Mintage	F	VF	XF	Unc	BU
(19)95 (qp) Proof	—	Value: 52.50				

KM# 72 500 FRANCS **Weight:** 22.8500 g. **Composition:** 0.9250 Silver .6795 oz. ASW **Subject:** Presidency of the European Community **Obverse:** Segmented portrait **Reverse:** Symbolic design, dates

Date	Mintage	F	VF	XF	Unc	BU
(19)97 (qp) Proof	10,000	Value: 40.00				
(19)97 (qp) Proof	—	—	—	—	—	—

KM# 73 500 FRANCS **Weight:** 22.8500 g. **Composition:** 0.9250 Silver .6795 oz. ASW **Subject:** 1,300 years of Echternach **Obverse:** Duke's segmented portrait **Reverse:** City seal and anniversary dates

Date	Mintage	F	VF	XF	Unc	BU
ND(1998) (qp) Proof	—	Value: 40.00				

KM# 74 500 FRANCS **Weight:** 22.8500 g. **Composition:** 0.9250 Silver .6795 oz. ASW **Subject:** Coronation of Henry III **Obverse:** Portrait **Reverse:** Crowned "H" **Size:** 37 mm.

Date	Mintage	F	VF	XF	Unc	BU
2000 (qp) Proof	—	Value: 45.00				

EURO COINAGE

European Economic Community Issues

KM# 75 EURO CENT **Weight:** 2.2700 g. **Composition:** Copper Plated Steel **Ruler:** Henri **Obverse:** Prince's portrait **Reverse:** Denominaton and globe **Edge:** Plain **Size:** 16.2 mm.

Date	Mintage	F	VF	XF	Unc	BU
2002	20,000,000	—	—	—	0.35	—

KM# 76 2 EURO CENTS **Weight:** 3.0300 g. **Composition:** Copper Plated Steel **Ruler:** Henri **Obverse:** Prince's portrait **Reverse:** Denomination and globe **Edge:** Grooved **Size:** 18.7 mm.

Date	Mintage	F	VF	XF	Unc	BU
2002	20,000,000	—	—	—	0.50	—

KM# 77 5 EURO CENTS **Weight:** 3.8600 g. **Composition:** Copper Plated Steel **Ruler:** Henri **Obverse:** Prince's portrait **Reverse:** Denomination and globe **Edge:** Plain **Size:** 21.2 mm.

Date	F	VF	XF	Unc	BU

KM# 78 10 EURO CENTS **Weight:** 4.0700 g. **Composition:** Brass **Ruler:** Henri **Obverse:** Prince's portrait **Reverse:** Denomination and map **Edge:** Reeded **Size:** 19.7 mm.

Date	Mintage	F	VF	XF	Unc	BU
2002	20,000,000	—	—	—	0.75	—

KM# 80 50 EURO CENTS **Weight:** 7.8100 g. **Composition:** Brass **Ruler:** Henri **Obverse:** Prince's portrait **Reverse:** Denomination and map **Edge:** Reeded **Size:** 24.1 mm.

Date	Mintage	F	VF	XF	Unc	BU
2002	10,000,000	—	—	—	1.25	—

KM# 81 EURO **Ring Composition:** Brass Center **Weight:** 7.5000 g. **Center Composition:** Copper Nickel **Ruler:** Henri **Obverse:** Prince's portrait **Reverse:** Denomination and map **Edge:** Reeded and plain sections **Size:** 23.2 mm.

Date	Mintage	F	VF	XF	Unc	BU
2002	10,000,000	—	—	—	2.50	—

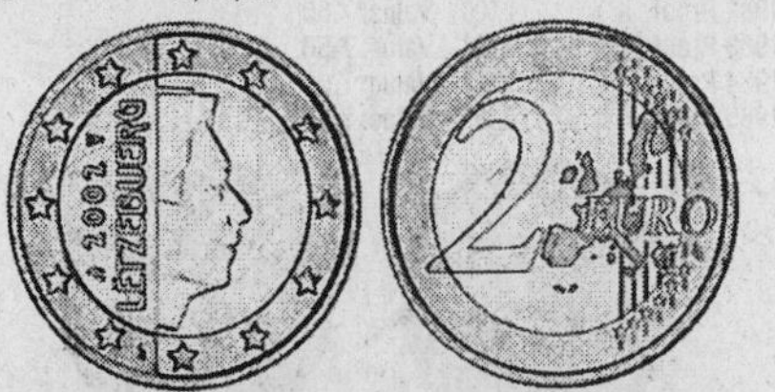

KM# 82 2 EUROS **Center Weight:** 8.5200 g. **Center Composition:** Brass **Ruler:** Henri **Obverse:** Prince's portrait **Reverse:** Denomination and map **Edge:** Reeded with 2's and stars **Size:** 25.7 mm.

Date	Mintage	F	VF	XF	Unc	BU
2002	100,000,000	—	—	—	3.75	—

ESSAIS

KM#	Date	Mintage	Identification	Mkt Val
E23	1901	—	10 Centimes. Gold. Adolph.	1,000
E22	1901	—	5 Centimes. Gold. Adolph.	1,000
E24	1908	—	10 Centimes. Gold. Wilhelm.	1,000
E25	1914	100	50 Centimes. Copper.	60.00

KM#	Date	Mintage	Identification	Mkt Val
E27	1914	100	Franc. Copper.	60.00
E29	1914	100	2 Francs. Copper.	60.00
E30	1914	—	2 Francs. Silver. Restruck after World War I.	45.00
E28	1914	—	Franc. Silver.	45.00
E26	1914	—	50 Centimes. Silver.	45.00
E31	1927	—	25 Centimes. Gold.	—
E32	1929	50	5 Francs. Copper.	150
E35	1929	50	10 Francs. Copper.	150
E33	1929	50	5 Francs. Bronze.	160
E36	1929	50	10 Francs. Bronze.	160
EA37	1929	—	10 Francs. Silver.	1,200
E34	1929	—	5 Francs. Gold.	2,000
E38	1929	—	10 Francs. Gold.	2,000
E39	1939	—	Franc. Gold.	1,500
E40	1945	100	25 Centimes. Copper. 25 at top.	25.00
E41	1945	100	25 Centimes. Copper. 25 at upper right.	25.00
E42	1946	100	25 Centimes. Copper.	15.00
E50	1946	100	20 Francs. Copper.	100
E45	1946	500	Franc. Copper. Plain edge.	15.00
E53	1946	100	50 Francs. Copper.	125
E56	1946	100	100 Francs. Copper.	150
E46	1946	100	Franc. Copper. Milled edge.	20.00
E54	1946	50	50 Francs. Silver.	225
E51	1946	50	20 Francs. Silver.	200
E43	1946	500	25 Centimes. Copper.	15.00
E57	1946	50	100 Francs. Silver.	325
E58	1946	25	100 Francs. Gold.	3,000
E47	1946	500	Franc. Silver. Plain edge.	30.00
E52	1946	25	20 Francs. Gold.	1,200
E55	1946	25	50 Francs. Gold.	2,000
E44	1946	500	25 Centimes. Silver.	25.00
E48	1946	100	Franc. Silver. Milled edge.	40.00
E49	1946	100	Franc. Silver. Small letters.	40.00
E59	1949	50	5 Francs. Copper.	50.00
E60	1949	50	5 Francs. Bronze-Aluminum.	50.00
E61	1962	50	5 Francs. Copper-Nickel.	30.00
E62	1962	—	5 Francs. Silver.	115

KM#	Date	Mintage	Identification	Mkt Val
E63	1962	50	5 Francs. Gold.	1,000
E64	1963	250	20 Francs. Gold.	200
E65	1963	50	100 Francs. Bronze.	70.00

KM#	Date	Mintage	Identification	Mkt Val
E68	ND(1963)	—	250 Francs. Copper-Nickel.	50.00
E66	1963	50	100 Francs. Silver.	60.00
E69	ND(1963)	200	250 Francs. Bronze.	50.00
E70	ND(1963)	200	250 Francs. Silver.	85.00
E67	1963	50	100 Francs. Gold.	1,250
E71	ND(1963)	200	250 Francs. Gold.	1,450
E72	1964	200	20 Francs. Gold.	200

KM#	Date	Mintage	Identification	Mkt Val
E73	1964	—	100 Francs. Copper-Nickel.	20.00
E74	1964	200	100 Francs. Bronze.	20.00
E75	1964	200	100 Francs. Silver.	20.00
E76	1964	200	100 Francs. Gold.	750
E77	1965	—	Franc. Copper-Nickel.	15.00
E78	1965	—	Franc. Silver.	15.00

KM#	Date	Mintage	Identification	Mkt Val
E79	1965	200	Franc. Gold. KM55.	200
EA80	1966	100	40 Francs. Gold.	400
EB81	1967	100	40 Francs. Gold.	400
E85	1971	—	10 Francs. Copper-Nickel.	15.00
E82	1971	—	5 Francs. Copper-Nickel.	15.00
E83	1971	—	5 Francs. Silver.	15.00
E86	1971	—	10 Francs. Silver.	15.00
E87	1971	250	10 Francs. Gold.	325

KM#	Date	Mintage	Identification	Mkt Val
E84	1971	250	5 Francs. Gold. KM56.	315
E88	1980	—	20 Francs. Bronze.	20.00
E89	1980	—	20 Francs. Silver.	45.00
E90	1980	500	20 Francs. Gold.	285

PATTERNS

Including off metal strikes

KM#	Date	Mintage	Identification	Mkt Val
Pn6	1901	—	2-1/2 Centimes. Copper.	125
Pn8	1901	100	5 Centimes. Copper. Without denomination.	125
Pn13	1901	100	10 Centimes. Copper. Without denomination.	90.00
Pn14	1901	100	10 Centimes. Copper-Nickel. Without denomination.	90.00
Pn7	1901	100	2-1/2 Centimes. Silver.	165
Pn9	1901	100	5 Centimes. Copper-Nickel. Without denomination.	125

KM#	Date	Mintage	Identification	Mkt Val
Pn10	1901	100	5 Centimes. Copper-Nickel. Without denomination.	—
Pn15	1901	100	10 Centimes. Copper-Nickel. Plain edge. Large letters.	90.00
Pn16	1901	100	10 Centimes. Copper-Nickel. Milled edge. Large letters.	90.00
Pn11	1901	50	5 Centimes. Silver. Without denomination.	150
Pn12	1901	20	5 Centimes. Gold. Without denomination.	1,000
Pn17	1901	50	10 Centimes. Silver. Large letters.	150
Pn18	1901	20	10 Centimes. Gold. Without denomination.	1,000
Pn19	ND	50	Franc. Nickel. Head of William.	150
Pn20	1917	—	5 Centimes. Copper. Crossed L's.	150

KM#	Date	Mintage	Identification	Mkt Val
Pn21	1917	—	10 Centimes. Copper.	150
Pn26	1923	100	2 Francs. Pewter.	125
Pn22	1923	100	Franc. Aluminum.	90.00
Pn23	1923	100	Franc. Bronze.	100
Pn27	1923	100	2 Francs. Aluminum.	120
Pn28	1923	100	2 Francs. Bronze.	115

KM#	Date	Mintage	Identification	Mkt Val
Pn24	1923	100	Franc. Nickel.	100
Pn25	1923	100	Franc. Silver.	135

KM#	Date	Mintage	Identification	Mkt Val
Pn29	1923	100	2 Francs. Nickel.	135
Pn30	1923	100	2 Francs. Silver.	150
Pn31	1924	—	Franc. Aluminum.	50.00
Pn35	1924	100	2 Francs. Copper.	100
Pn36	1924	100	2 Francs. Bronze.	110
Pn32	1924	100	Franc. Copper.	110
Pn33	1924	100	Franc. Bronze.	110
Pn34	1924	100	Franc. Silver.	110
Pn37	1930	—	5 Centimes. Copper. Crowned value.	85.00

KM#	Date	Mintage	Identification	Mkt Val
Pn40	1930	—	50 Centimes. Copper-Nickel.	150

KM#	Date	Mintage	Identification	Mkt Val
Pn39	1930	—	10 Centimes. Copper.	125

KM#	Date	Mintage	Identification	Mkt Val
Pn41	1930	—	50 Centimes. Copper-Nickel.	160

KM#	Date	Mintage	Identification	Mkt Val
Pn38	1930	—	5 Centimes. Copper.	75.00
Pn42	1939	50	Franc. Silver.	100
Pn43	1939	—	Franc. Gold.	300
Pn44	1942	—	5 Francs. Zinc.	100
Pn45	1942	—	5 Francs. Nickel.	100
Pn46	1947	100	2 Francs. Copper-Nickel.	80.00
Pn47	1947	100	5 Francs. Copper-Nickel.	85.00

PIEFORTS AND PIEFORTS WITH ESSAI

KM#	Date	Mintage	Identification	Mkt Val
PE4	1908	—	10 Centimes. Gold.	1,000
P5	1927	100	25 Centimes. Bronze.	100
P6	1938	100	25 Centimes. Copper-Nickel.	100

MINT SETS

KM#	Date	Mintage	Identification	Issue Price	Mkt Val
MS1	1990 (4)	10,000	KM63, 65-67	—	16.00
MS2	1991 (4)	10,000	KM63, 65-67	—	14.00
MS3	1992 (4)	10,000	KM63, 65-67	—	14.00
MS4	1993 (4)	10,000	KM63, 65-67	—	14.00
MS5	1994 (4)	10,000	KM63, 65-67	—	14.00
MS6	1995 (4)	10,000	KM63, 65-67	—	14.00

PROOF SETS

KM#	Date	Mintage	Identification	Issue Price	Mkt Val
PS1	1980 (7)	3,000	KM45b, 46, 3a, 51a, 55a-58a	—	160

MACAO

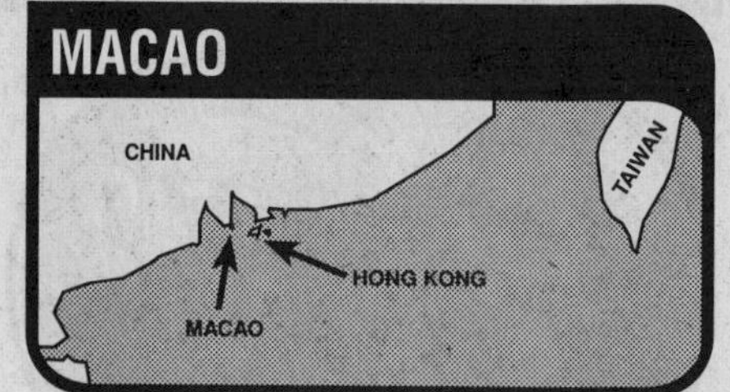

The Province of Macao, a Portuguese overseas province located in the South China Sea 40 miles southwest of Hong Kong, consists of the peninsula of Macao and the islands of Taipa and Coloane. It has an area of 6.2 sq. mi.(16 sq. km.) and a population of 500,000. Capital: Macao. Macao's economy is based on light industry, commerce, tourism, fishing, and gold trading - Macao is one of the entirely free markets for gold in the world. Cement, textiles, fireworks, vegetable oils, and metal products are exported.

Established by the Portuguese in 1557, Macao is the oldest European settlement in the Far East. The Chinese, while agreeing to Portuguese settlement, did not recognize Portuguese sovereign rights and the Portuguese remained largely under control of the Chinese until 1849, when the Portuguese abolished the Chinese customhouse and declared the independence of the port. The Manchu government formally recognized the Portuguese right to *perpetual occupation* of Macao in 1887.

In 1987, Portugal and China agreed that Macao would become a Chinese Territory in 1999. In December of 1999, Macao became a special administrative zone of China.

RULERS
Portuguese 1887-1999

MINT MARKS
(p) - Pobjoy Mint
(s) - Singapore Mint

Pobjoy Mint

Singapore Mint

MONETARY SYSTEM
100 Avos = 1 Pataca

PORTUGUESE COLONY

STANDARD COINAGE

100 Avos = 1 Pataca

KM# 1 5 AVOS Composition: Bronze

Date	Mintage	F	VF	XF	Unc	BU
1952	500,000	—	3.50	15.00	30.00	—

KM# 1a 5 AVOS Composition: Nickel-Brass

Date	Mintage	F	VF	XF	Unc	BU
1967	5,000,000	—	0.50	1.00	2.50	—

KM# 2 10 AVOS Composition: Bronze

Date	Mintage	F	VF	XF	Unc	BU
1952	12,500,000	—	0.50	1.20	4.50	—

KM# 2a 10 AVOS Composition: Nickel-Brass

Date	Mintage	F	VF	XF	Unc	BU
1967	5,525,000	—	0.50	1.00	2.00	—
1968	6,975,000	—	0.25	1.00	2.00	—
1975	20,000,000	—	0.10	0.50	1.50	—
1976	Inc. above	—	0.10	0.50	1.50	—

KM# 20 10 AVOS Composition: Brass

Date	Mintage	F	VF	XF	Unc	BU
1982	24,580,000	—	0.10	0.50	1.50	—
1983	—	—	0.10	0.50	1.50	—
1984	—	—	0.25	0.75	2.50	—
1985	—	—	0.10	0.50	1.50	—
1988	—	—	0.10	0.50	1.50	—

KM# 20a 10 AVOS Weight: 3.2000 g. Composition: 0.9250 Silver .0952 oz. ASW

Date	Mintage	F	VF	XF	Unc	BU
1982 Proof	2,000	Value: 7.50				
1983 Proof	2,500	Value: 7.50				
1984 Proof	2,500	Value: 7.50				
1985 Proof	2,500	Value: 7.50				

KM# 20b 10 AVOS Weight: 4.0000 g. Composition: 0.9170 Gold .1179 oz. AGW Obverse: Low star

Date	Mintage	F	VF	XF	Unc	BU
1982 Proof	150	Value: 100				

KM# 20c 10 AVOS Weight: 4.5000 g. Composition: 0.9500 Platinum .1374 oz. APW

Date	Mintage	F	VF	XF	Unc	BU
1982 Proof	375	Value: 135				

KM# 70 10 AVOS Composition: Brass

Date	F	VF	XF	Unc	BU
1993	—	—	—	0.75	—

KM# 21 20 AVOS Composition: Brass

Date	Mintage	F	VF	XF	Unc	BU
1982	9,960,000	—	0.10	0.50	1.50	—
1983	—	—	0.10	0.50	1.50	—
1984	—	—	0.25	0.75	2.50	—
1985	—	—	0.10	0.50	1.50	—

KM# 21a 20 AVOS Weight: 4.6000 g. Composition: 0.9250 Silver .1368 oz. ASW

Date	Mintage	F	VF	XF	Unc	BU
1982 Proof	2,000	Value: 11.50				
1983 Proof	2,500	Value: 11.50				
1984 Proof	2,500	Value: 11.50				
1985 Proof	2,500	Value: 11.50				

KM# 21b 20 AVOS Weight: 5.5000 g. Composition: 0.9170 Gold .1621 oz. AGW Obverse: Low star

Date	Mintage	F	VF	XF	Unc	BU
1982 Proof	150	Value: 150				

KM# 21c 20 AVOS Weight: 6.2000 g. Composition: 0.9500 Platinum .1893 oz. APW

Date	Mintage	F	VF	XF	Unc	BU
1982 Proof	375	Value: 185				

KM# 71 20 AVOS Composition: Brass

Date	F	VF	XF	Unc	BU
1993	—	—	—	1.00	—

KM# 3 50 AVOS Composition: Copper-Nickel

Date	Mintage	F	VF	XF	Unc	BU
1952	2,560,000	—	0.75	3.50	9.00	—

KM# 7 50 AVOS **Composition:** Copper-Nickel

Date	Mintage	F	VF	XF	Unc	BU
1972	1,600,000	—	0.50	1.50	4.00	—
1973	4,840,000	—	0.50	1.00	3.00	—

KM# 9 50 AVOS **Composition:** Copper-Nickel

Date	Mintage	F	VF	XF	Unc	BU
1978	3,000,000	—	0.50	1.50	4.00	—

KM# 22 50 AVOS **Composition:** Brass

Date	Mintage	F	VF	XF	Unc	BU
1982	16,952,000	—	0.50	1.00	3.00	—
1983	—	—	0.75	4.00	9.00	—
1984	—	—	0.75	3.50	7.00	—
1985	—	—	0.50	2.00	5.00	—

KM# 22a 50 AVOS **Weight:** 5.7000 g. **Composition:** 0.9250 Silver .1695 oz. ASW

Date	Mintage	F	VF	XF	Unc	BU
1982 Proof	2,000	Value: 13.50				
1983 Proof	2,500	Value: 13.50				
1984 Proof	2,500	Value: 13.50				
1985 Proof	2,500	Value: 13.50				

KM# 22b 50 AVOS **Weight:** 7.4000 g. **Composition:** 0.9170 Gold .2181 oz. AGW **Obverse:** Low star

Date	Mintage	F	VF	XF	Unc	BU
1982 Proof	150	Value: 175				

KM# 22c 50 AVOS **Weight:** 8.4000 g. **Composition:** 0.9500 Platinum .2565 oz. APW

Date	Mintage	F	VF	XF	Unc	BU
1982 Proof	375	Value: 245				

KM# 72 50 AVOS **Composition:** Brass

Date	F	VF	XF	Unc	BU
1993	—	—	—	1.50	—

KM# 4 PATACA **Weight:** 3.0000 g. **Composition:** 0.7200 Silver .0694 oz. ASW

Date	Mintage	F	VF	XF	Unc	BU
1952	4,500,000	—	2.50	10.00	20.00	—

KM# 6 PATACA **Composition:** Nickel

Date	Mintage	F	VF	XF	Unc	BU
1968	5,000,000	—	1.00	3.00	6.50	—
1975	6,000,000	—	0.75	2.00	5.00	—

KM# 6a PATACA **Composition:** Copper-Nickel

Date	F	VF	XF	Unc	BU
1980	—	3.50	12.00	25.00	—

KM# 23.1 PATACA **Composition:** Copper-Nickel **Obverse:** High stars

Date	Mintage	F	VF	XF	Unc	BU
1982(s)	6,427,000	—	1.00	2.00	6.00	—
1983(s)	—	—	1.50	3.50	8.00	—
1984(s)	—	—	2.00	4.50	10.00	—
1985(s)	—	—	1.50	3.50	8.00	—

KM# 23.1a PATACA **Weight:** 9.0000 g. **Composition:** 0.9250 Silver .2677 oz. ASW **Obverse:** High stars

Date	Mintage	F	VF	XF	Unc	BU
1982(s) Proof	2,000	Value: 17.50				
1983(s) Proof	2,500	Value: 17.50				
1984(s) Proof	2,500	Value: 17.50				
1985(s) Proof	2,500	Value: 17.50				

KM#23.1b PATACA **Weight:** 11.6000 g. **Composition:** 0.9170 Gold .342 oz. AGW **Obverse:** High stars

Date	Mintage	F	VF	XF	Unc	BU
1982(s) Proof	150	Value: 225				

KM#23.1c PATACA **Weight:** 13.2000 g. **Composition:** 0.9500 Platinum .4032 oz. APW **Obverse:** High stars

Date	Mintage	F	VF	XF	Unc	BU
1982(s) Proof	375	Value: 365				

KM# 23.2 PATACA **Composition:** Copper-Nickel **Obverse:** Low stars

Date	F	VF	XF	Unc	BU
1982(p)	—	1.00	2.00	6.00	—
1983(p)	—	1.50	3.50	8.00	—

KM# 23.2a PATACA **Weight:** 5.7000 g. **Composition:** 0.9250 Silver .1695 oz. ASW **Obverse:** Low stars

Date	F	VF	XF	Unc	BU
1982 Proof	—	Value: 15.00			

KM# 57 PATACA **Composition:** Copper-Nickel

Date	F	VF	XF	Unc	BU
1992	—	—	—	2.50	—
1998	—	—	—	—	—

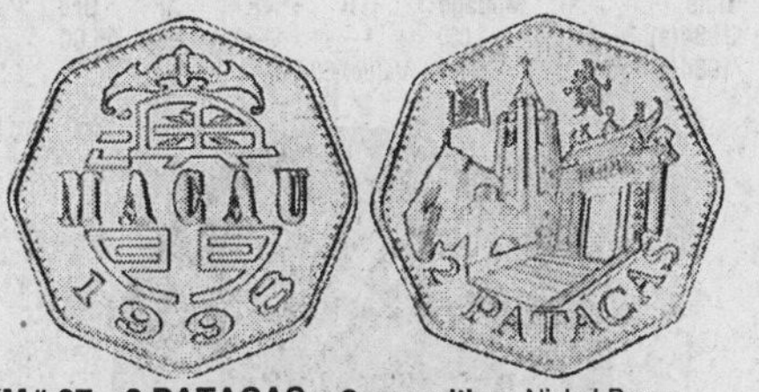

KM# 97 2 PATACAS **Composition:** Nickel-Brass **Obverse:** Name and date **Reverse:** Church and Chinese arch **Edge:** Plain **Shape:** Octagonal **Size:** 27.5 mm.

Date	F	VF	XF	Unc	BU
1998	—	—	—	3.50	—

KM# 5 5 PATACAS **Weight:** 15.0000 g. **Composition:** 0.7200 Silver .3472 oz. ASW

Date	Mintage	F	VF	XF	Unc	BU
1952	900,000	—	5.00	8.50	16.50	—

KM#5a 5 PATACAS **Weight:** 10.0000 g. **Composition:** 0.9500 Silver .2089 oz. ASW

Date	Mintage	F	VF	XF	Unc	BU
1971	500,000	—	4.00	6.50	12.50	—

KM# 24.1 5 PATACAS **Composition:** Copper-Nickel **Obverse:** High stars **Reverse:** Large dragon

Date	Mintage	F	VF	XF	Unc	BU
1982(s)	1,102,000	—	1.00	2.00	6.00	—
1983(s)	—	—	3.50	10.00	20.00	—
1984(s)	—	—	5.00	15.00	30.00	—
1985(s)	—	—	3.50	10.00	20.00	—
1988(s)	—	—	1.00	2.00	6.00	—

KM# 24.1a 5 PATACAS **Weight:** 10.7000 g. **Composition:** 0.9250 Silver .3182 oz. ASW **Obverse:** High stars **Reverse:** Large dragon

Date	Mintage	F	VF	XF	Unc	BU
1982(s) Proof	2,000	Value: 32.50				
1983(s) Proof	2,500	Value: 32.50				
1984(s) Proof	2,500	Value: 32.50				
1985(s) Proof	2,500	Value: 32.50				

KM# 24.1b 5 PATACAS **Weight:** 16.3000 g. **Composition:** 0.9170 Gold .4808 oz. AGW **Obverse:** High stars **Reverse:** Large dragon

Date	Mintage	F	VF	XF	Unc	BU
1982(s) Proof	150	Value: 300				

KM# 24.1c 5 PATACAS **Weight:** 18.4000 g. **Composition:** 0.9500 Platinum .562 oz. APW **Obverse:** High stars **Reverse:** Large dragon

Date	Mintage	F	VF	XF	Unc	BU
1982(s) Proof	375	Value: 520				

KM# 24.2 5 PATACAS **Composition:** Copper-Nickel **Obverse:** Low stars **Reverse:** Small dragon

Date	F	VF	XF	Unc	BU
1982(p)	—	1.00	2.00	6.00	—

KM# 24.2a 5 PATACAS **Weight:** 10.7000 g. **Composition:** 0.9250 Silver .3182 oz. ASW **Obverse:** Low stars **Reverse:** Small dragon

Date	F	VF	XF	Unc	BU
1982(p) Proof	—	Value: 25.00			

KM# 56 5 PATACAS **Composition:** Copper-Nickel

Date	F	VF	XF	Unc	BU
1992	—	—	—	6.50	—

KM# 83 10 PATACAS **Ring Composition:** Brass **Center Composition:** Copper-Nickel **Obverse:** "MACAU" and date **Reverse:** Cathedral and denomination

Date	F	VF	XF	Unc	BU
1997	—	—	—	8.50	—

KM#8 20 PATACAS **Weight:** 18.0000 g. **Composition:** 0.6500 Silver .3762 oz. ASW

Date	Mintage	F	VF	XF	Unc	BU
1974	1,000	—	—	10.00	20.00	—

KM# 10 100 PATACAS **Weight:** 28.2800 g. **Composition:** 0.9250 Silver .8411 oz. ASW **Subject:** 25th Anniversary of Grand Prix

Date	Mintage	F	VF	XF	Unc	BU
1978 Proof	610	Value: 150				

KM# 10a 100 PATACAS **Composition:** Copper-Nickel **Subject:** 25th Anniversary of Grand Prix

Date	Mintage	F	VF	XF	Unc	BU
1978		—	—	—	185	—

KM# 11 100 PATACAS **Weight:** 28.2800 g. **Composition:** 0.9250 Silver .8411 oz. ASW **Reverse:** Racing car with advertising

Date	Mintage	F	VF	XF	Unc	BU
1978 Proof	5,500	Value: 70.00				

KM# 14 100 PATACAS **Weight:** 28.2800 g. **Composition:** 0.9250 Silver .8411 oz. ASW **Subject:** Year of the Goat

Date	Mintage	F	VF	XF	Unc	BU
1979(s) Proof	5,500	Value: 70.00				

KM# 16 100 PATACAS **Weight:** 28.2800 g. **Composition:** 0.9250 Silver .8411 oz. ASW **Subject:** Year of the Monkey **Reverse:** Monkey swinging on a rope

Date	Mintage	F	VF	XF	Unc	BU
1980	1,000	—	—	—	65.00	—
1980 Proof	2,000	Value: 75.00				

KM# 18 100 PATACAS **Weight:** 28.2800 g. **Composition:** 0.9250 Silver .8411 oz. ASW **Subject:** Year of the Rooster

Date	Mintage	F	VF	XF	Unc	BU
1981(p)	1,000	—	—	—	55.00	—
1981(p) Proof	1,000	Value: 70.00				

KM# 25 100 PATACAS **Weight:** 28.2800 g. **Composition:** 0.9250 Silver .8411 oz. ASW **Subject:** Year of the Dog

Date	Mintage	F	VF	XF	Unc	BU
1982(p)	500	—	—	—	65.00	—
1982(p) Proof	500	Value: 75.00				
1982(s)	220	—	—	—	67.50	—
1982(s) Proof	3,500	Value: 70.00				

KM# 27 100 PATACAS **Weight:** 28.2800 g. **Composition:** 0.9250 Silver .8411 oz. ASW **Subject:** Year of the Pig

Date	Mintage	F	VF	XF	Unc	BU
1983(s)	2,500	—	—	—	50.00	—
1983(s) Proof	2,500	Value: 65.00				

KM# 29 100 PATACAS **Weight:** 28.2800 g. **Composition:** 0.9250 Silver .8411 oz. ASW **Subject:** Year of the Rat

Date	Mintage	F	VF	XF	Unc	BU
1984(s)	2,000	—	—	—	55.00	—
1984(s) Proof	5,000	Value: 65.00				

KM# 31 100 PATACAS **Weight:** 28.2800 g. **Composition:** 0.9250 Silver .8411 oz. ASW **Subject:** Year of the Ox

Date	Mintage	F	VF	XF	Unc	BU
1985(s)	10,000	—	—	—	60.00	—
1985(s) Proof	5,000	Value: 65.00				

KM# 33 100 PATACAS **Weight:** 28.2800 g. **Composition:** 0.9250 Silver .8411 oz. ASW **Subject:** Visit of Portugal's President Eanes

Date	Mintage	F	VF	XF	Unc	BU
1985(s)	760	—	—	—	90.00	—
1985(s) Proof	2,000	Value: 65.00				

KM# 34 100 PATACAS **Weight:** 28.2800 g. **Composition:** 0.9250 Silver .8411 oz. ASW **Subject:** Year of the Tiger

Date	Mintage	F	VF	XF	Unc	BU
1986(p)	760	—	—	—	85.00	—
1986(p) Proof	3,000	Value: 60.00				

KM# 36 100 PATACAS **Weight:** 28.2800 g. **Composition:** 0.9250 Silver .8411 oz. ASW **Subject:** Year of the Rabbit

Date	Mintage	F	VF	XF	Unc	BU
1987(p)	—	—	—	—	45.00	—
1987(p) Proof	5,000	Value: 60.00				

KM# 38 100 PATACAS **Weight:** 28.2800 g. **Composition:** 0.9250 Silver .8411 oz. ASW **Subject:** Year of the Dragon **Reverse:** Dragon walking left **Note:** Similar to 1,000 Patacas, KM#39.

Date	Mintage	F	VF	XF	Unc	BU
1988	—	—	—	—	45.00	—
1988 Proof	5,000	Value: 65.00				

KM# 40 100 PATACAS **Weight:** 28.2800 g. **Composition:** 0.9250 Silver .8411 oz. ASW **Subject:** 35th Anniversary of Grand Prix **Reverse:** Racing car, similar to 500 Patacas, KM#42

Date	Mintage	F	VF	XF	Unc	BU
ND(1988) Proof	5,000	Value: 55.00				

KM# 40a 100 PATACAS **Composition:** Platinum APW **Subject:** 35th Anniversary of Grand Prix **Reverse:** Racing car, similar to 500 Patacas, KM#42

Date	Mintage	F	VF	XF	Unc	BU
ND(1988) Proof	10	Value: 2,750				

KM# 44 100 PATACAS **Weight:** 28.2800 g. **Composition:** 0.9250 Silver .8411 oz. ASW **Subject:** Year of the Snake **Reverse:** Coiled snake **Note:** Similar to 1,000 Patacas, KM#45.

Date	Mintage	F	VF	XF	Unc	BU
1989(s)	2,000	—	—	—	47.50	—
1989(s) Proof	3,000	Value: 60.00				

KM# 46 100 PATACAS **Weight:** 28.2800 g. **Composition:** 0.9250 Silver .8411 oz. ASW **Subject:** Year of the Horse

Date	Mintage	F	VF	XF	Unc	BU
1990(s)	1,000	—	—	—	50.00	—
1990(s) Proof	3,364	Value: 75.00				

KM# 48 100 PATACAS **Weight:** 28.2800 g. **Composition:** 0.9250 Silver .8411 oz. ASW **Subject:** Year of the Goat **Reverse:** Facing ram **Note:** Similar to KM#51.

Date	Mintage	F	VF	XF	Unc	BU
1991(s)		—	—	—	45.00	—
1991(s) Proof	Est. 4,000	Value: 50.00				

KM# 52 100 PATACAS **Weight:** 28.2800 g. **Composition:** 0.9250 Silver .8411 oz. ASW **Subject:** Year of the Monkey

Date	Mintage	F	VF	XF	Unc	BU
1992(s)		—	—	—	42.50	—
1992(s) Proof	Est. 4,000	Value: 50.00				

KM# 58 100 PATACAS **Weight:** 28.2800 g. **Composition:** 0.9250 Silver .8411 oz. ASW **Subject:** Year of the Rooster

Date	Mintage	F	VF	XF	Unc	BU
1993		—	—	—	48.50	—
1993 Proof	Est. 4,000	Value: 50.00				

KM# 62 100 PATACAS **Weight:** 28.2800 g. **Composition:** 0.9250 Silver .8411 oz. ASW **Subject:** Macao Grand Prix

Date	Mintage	F	VF	XF	Unc	BU
ND(1993) Proof	5,000	Value: 45.00				

KM# 66 100 PATACAS **Weight:** 28.2800 g. **Composition:** 0.9250 Silver .8411 oz. ASW **Subject:** Year of the Dog

Date	Mintage	F	VF	XF	Unc	BU
1994		—	—	—	45.00	—
1994 Proof	Est. 4,000	Value: 50.00				

KM# 73 100 PATACAS **Weight:** 28.2800 g. **Composition:** 0.9250 Silver .8411 oz. ASW **Subject:** Year of the Pig

Date	Mintage	F	VF	XF	Unc	BU
1995		—	—	—	45.00	—
1995 Proof	Est. 4,000	Value: 50.00				

KM# 77 100 PATACAS **Weight:** 28.2800 g. **Composition:** 0.9250 Silver .8411 oz. ASW **Subject:** Airport

Date	Mintage	F	VF	XF	Unc	BU
1995 Proof	8,000	Value: 42.50				

KM# 79 100 PATACAS **Weight:** 28.2800 g. **Composition:** 0.9250 Silver .8411 oz. ASW **Subject:** Year of the Rat

Date	Mintage	F	VF	XF	Unc	BU
1996		—	—	—	42.50	—
1996 Proof	Est. 4,000	Value: 50.00				

KM# 84 100 PATACAS **Weight:** 28.2800 g. **Composition:** 0.9250 Silver .8411 oz. ASW **Subject:** Year of the Ox **Obverse:** Church facade

Date	Mintage	F	VF	XF	Unc	BU
1997 Proof	4,000	Value: 50.00				

KM# 88 100 PATACAS **Weight:** 28.2800 g. **Composition:** 0.9250 Silver .8411 oz. ASW **Subject:** Year of the Tiger **Obverse:** Church facade

Date	Mintage	F	VF	XF	Unc	BU
1998 Proof	5,000	Value: 50.00				

KM# 106 100 PATACAS **Weight:** 28.4000 g. **Composition:** 0.9250 Silver .8458 oz. ASW **Subject:** 19th East Asian Insurance Conference **Obverse:** Church facade **Reverse:** Two hands holding world **Edge:** Reeded **Size:** 38.4 mm.

Date	F	VF	XF	Unc	BU
1998 Proof	—	—	—	50.00	—

KM# 96 100 PATACAS **Weight:** 31.1035 g. **Composition:** 0.9250 Silver .9250 oz. ASW **Subject:** Macao returns to China **Obverse:** Macao arms **Reverse:** Portuguese and Chinese ships below gold-plated cameo of the Gao Temple

Date	F	VF	XF	Unc	BU
1999	—	—	—	65.00	—

KM# 98 100 PATACAS **Weight:** 28.2800 g. **Composition:** 0.9250 Silver .8410 oz. ASW **Subject:** Year of the Dragon **Obverse:** Church facade **Reverse:** Dragon **Edge:** Reeded **Size:** 38.6 mm.

Date	Mintage	F	VF	XF	Unc	BU
2000	1,000	—	—	—	40.00	—
2000 Proof	4,000	Value: 55.00				

KM# 102 100 PATACAS **Weight:** 28.2800 g. **Composition:** 0.9250 Silver .8410 oz. ASW **Subject:** Year of the Snake **Obverse:** Church facade **Reverse:** Snake

Date	Mintage	F	VF	XF	Unc	BU
2001 Proof	4,000	Value: 55.00				

KM# 107 100 PATACAS **Weight:** 28.2800 g. **Composition:** 0.9250 Silver 0.841 oz. ASW **Subject:** Year of the Horse **Obverse:** Church of St. Paul facade **Reverse:** Horse above denomination **Edge:** Reeded **Size:** 38.6 mm.

Date	Mintage	F	VF	XF	Unc	BU
2002 Proof	4,000	Value: 55.00				

KM# 49 250 PATACAS **Weight:** 3.9900 g. **Composition:** 0.9170 Gold .1176 oz. AGW **Subject:** Year of the Goat **Note:** Similar to 1,000 Patacas, KM#51.

Date	Mintage	F	VF	XF	Unc	BU
1991 Proof	Est. 2,500	Value: 110				

KM# 53 250 PATACAS **Weight:** 3.9900 g. **Composition:** 0.9170 Gold .1176 oz. AGW **Subject:** Year of the Monkey **Note:** Similar to 1,000 Patacas, KM#51.

Date	Mintage	F	VF	XF	Unc	BU
1992 Proof	Est. 2,500	Value: 110				

KM# 59 250 PATACAS **Weight:** 3.9900 g. **Composition:** 0.9170 Gold .1176 oz. AGW **Subject:** Year of the Rooster **Obverse:** St. Paul's Church **Reverse:** Rooster **Note:** Similar to 1,000 Patacas, KM#58.

Date	Mintage	F	VF	XF	Unc	BU
1993 Proof	Est. 2,500	Value: 110				

KM# 67 250 PATACAS **Weight:** 3.9900 g. **Composition:** 0.9170 Gold .1176 oz. AGW **Subject:** Year of the Dog **Note:** Similar to 1,000 Patacas, KM#69.

Date	Mintage	F	VF	XF	Unc	BU
1994 Proof	Est. 2,500	Value: 110				

KM# 74 250 PATACAS **Weight:** 3.9900 g. **Composition:** 0.9170 Gold .1176 oz. AGW **Subject:** Year of the Pig **Obverse:** Building **Reverse:** Pig standing left **Note:** Similar to 100 Patacas, KM#73. In proof sets only.

Date	Mintage	F	VF	XF	Unc	BU
1995 Proof	—	Value: 110				

KM#80 250 PATACAS **Weight:** 3.9900 g. **Composition:** 0.9170 Gold .1176 oz. AGW **Subject:** Year of the Rat

Date	F	VF	XF	Unc	BU
1996	—	Value: 120			

KM# 85 250 PATACAS **Weight:** 3.9900 g. **Composition:** 0.9170 Gold .1176 oz. AGW **Subject:** Year of the Ox **Note:** Similar to 100 Patacas, KM#84.

Date	Mintage	F	VF	XF	Unc	BU
1997 In proof sets only	Est. 2,500	Value: 115				

KM# 89 250 PATACAS **Weight:** 3.9900 g. **Composition:** 0.9170 Gold .1176 oz. AGW **Subject:** Year of the Tiger **Note:** Similar to 100 Patacas, KM#88.

Date	Mintage	F	VF	XF	Unc	BU
1998 In proof sets only	Est. 2,500	Value: 115				

KM# 93 250 PATACAS **Weight:** 3.9900 g. **Composition:** 0.9170 Gold .1176 oz. AGW **Subject:** Year of the Rabbit **Obverse:** Church facade **Reverse:** Rabbit **Note:** Similar to 1,000 Patacas, KM#95.

Date	Mintage	F	VF	XF	Unc	BU
1999 In proof sets only	Est. 2,500	Value: 115				

KM# 99 250 PATACAS **Weight:** 3.9900 g. **Composition:** 0.9167 Gold .1176 oz. AGW **Subject:** Year of the Dragon **Obverse:** Church facade **Reverse:** Dragon **Edge:** Reeded **Size:** 19.3 mm.

Date	Mintage	F	VF	XF	Unc	BU
2000 In Proof sets only	2,500	Value: 125				

KM# 103 250 PATACAS **Weight:** 3.9900 g. **Composition:** 0.9167 Gold .1176 oz. AGW **Subject:** Year of the Snake **Obverse:** Church facade **Reverse:** Snake

Date	Mintage	F	VF	XF	Unc	BU
2001 In Proof sets only	2,500	Value: 125				

KM# 108 250 PATACAS **Weight:** 3.9900 g. **Composition:** 0.9167 Gold 0.1176 oz. AGW **Subject:** Year of the Horse **Obverse:** Church of St. Paul facade **Reverse:** Horse above denomination **Edge:** Reeded **Size:** 19.3 mm.

Date	Mintage	F	VF	XF	Unc	BU
2002	2,500	—	—	—	67.00	—

Note: In proof sets only

KM# 12 500 PATACAS **Weight:** 7.9600 g. **Composition:** 0.9170 Gold .2347 oz. AGW **Subject:** 25th Anniversary of Grand Prix **Obverse:** Church facade

Date	Mintage	F	VF	XF	Unc	BU
1978 Proof	550	Value: 300				

KM# 13 500 PATACAS **Weight:** 7.9600 g. **Composition:** 0.9170 Gold .2347 oz. AGW **Reverse:** Racing car without advertising

Date	Mintage	F	VF	XF	Unc	BU
1978 Proof	5,500	Value: 185				

KM#15 500 PATACAS **Weight:** 7.9600 g. **Composition:** 0.9170 Gold .2347 oz. AGW **Subject:** Year of the Goat

Date	Mintage	F	VF	XF	Unc	BU
1979 Proof	5,500	Value: 145				

KM#41 500 PATACAS **Weight:** 155.5150 g. **Composition:** 0.9990 Silver 5 oz. ASW **Subject:** 35th Anniversary of Grand Prix **Note:** Similar to KM#42.

Date	Mintage	F	VF	XF	Unc	BU
1988 Proof	2,000	Value: 145				

KM# 42 500 PATACAS **Weight:** 7.9881 g. **Composition:** 0.9170 Gold .2354 oz. AGW **Subject:** 35th Anniversary of Grand Prix

Date	Mintage	F	VF	XF	Unc	BU
ND(1988) Proof	4,500	Value: 185				

KM# 50 500 PATACAS **Weight:** 7.9881 g. **Composition:** 0.9170 Gold .2354 oz. AGW **Subject:** Year of the Goat **Note:** Similar to 1,000 Patacas, KM#51.

Date	Mintage	F	VF	XF	Unc	BU
1991 Proof	Est. 2,500	Value: 185				

KM# 54 500 PATACAS **Weight:** 7.9900 g. **Composition:** 0.9170 Gold .2352 oz. AGW **Subject:** Year of the Monkey **Note:** Similar to 1,000 Patacas, KM#51.

Date	Mintage	F	VF	XF	Unc	BU
1992 Proof	Est. 2,500	Value: 200				

KM# 60 500 PATACAS **Weight:** 7.9900 g. **Composition:** 0.9170 Gold .2352 oz. AGW **Subject:** Year of the Rooster **Obverse:** St. Paul's Church **Reverse:** Rooster **Note:** Similar to 100 Patacas, KM#58.

Date	Mintage	F	VF	XF	Unc	BU
1993 Proof	Est. 2,500	Value: 200				

KM#63 500 PATACAS **Weight:** 155.6000 g. **Composition:** 0.9990 Silver 5 oz. ASW **Subject:** Macao Grand Prix

Date	Mintage	F	VF	XF	Unc	BU
1993 Proof	2,000	Value: 145				

KM#64 500 PATACAS **Weight:** 7.9900 g. **Composition:** 0.9170 Gold .2352 oz. AGW **Subject:** Macao Grand Prix

Date	Mintage	F	VF	XF	Unc	BU
ND(1993) Proof	4,500	Value: 185				

KM# 68 500 PATACAS **Weight:** 7.9900 g. **Composition:** 0.9170 Gold .2352 oz. AGW **Subject:** Year of the Dog **Note:** Similar to 1,000 Patacas, KM#69.

Date	Mintage	F	VF	XF	Unc	BU
1994 Proof	Est. 2,500	Value: 210				

KM# 75 500 PATACAS **Weight:** 7.9900 g. **Composition:** 0.9170 Gold .2352 oz. AGW **Subject:** Year of the Pig **Obverse:** Building **Reverse:** Pig standing left **Note:** Similar to 1,000 Patacas, KM#73.

Date	Mintage	F	VF	XF	Unc	BU
1995 In proof sets only	Est. 2,000	Value: 210				

KM# 81 500 PATACAS **Weight:** 7.9900 g. **Composition:** 0.9170 Gold .2352 oz. AGW **Subject:** Year of the Rat

Date	F	VF	XF	Unc	BU
1996 Proof	—	Value: 210			

KM# 86 500 PATACAS **Weight:** 7.9900 g. **Composition:** 0.9170 Gold .2352 oz. AGW **Subject:** Year of the Ox **Note:** Similar to 100 Patacas, KM#84.

Date	Mintage	F	VF	XF	Unc	BU
1997 In proof sets only	2,000	Value: 225				

KM# 90 500 PATACAS **Weight:** 7.9900 g. **Composition:** 0.9170 Gold .2352 oz. AGW **Subject:** Year of the Tiger **Note:** Similar to 100 Patacas, KM#88.

Date	Mintage	F	VF	XF	Unc	BU
1998 In proof sets only	2,500	Value: 225				

KM# 94 500 PATACAS **Weight:** 7.9900 g. **Composition:** 0.9170 Gold .2352 oz. AGW **Subject:** Year of the Rabbit **Obverse:** Church facade **Reverse:** Rabbit **Note:** Similar to 1,000 Patacas, KM#95.

Date	Mintage	F	VF	XF	Unc	BU
1999 In proof sets only	Est. 2,500	Value: 225				

KM# 100 500 PATACAS **Weight:** 7.9900 g. **Composition:** 0.9167 Gold .2355 oz. AGW **Subject:** Year of the Dragon **Obverse:** Church facade **Reverse:** Dragon **Edge:** Reeded **Size:** 22.05 mm.

Date	Mintage	F	VF	XF	Unc	BU
2000 In Proof sets only	2,500	Value: 250				

KM# 104 500 PATACAS **Weight:** 7.9900 g. **Composition:** 0.9167 Gold .2355 oz. AGW **Subject:** Year of the Snake **Obverse:** Church facade **Reverse:** Snake

Date	Mintage	F	VF	XF	Unc	BU
2001 In Proof sets only	2,500	Value: 250				

KM# 109 500 PATACAS **Weight:** 7.9800 g. **Composition:** 0.9167 Gold 0.2352 oz. AGW **Subject:** Year of the Horse **Obverse:** Church of St. Paul facade **Reverse:** Horse above denomination **Edge:** Reeded **Size:** 22.05 mm.

Date	Mintage	F	VF	XF	Unc	BU
2002	2,500	—	—	—	134	—

Note: In proof set only.

KM# 17 1000 PATACAS **Weight:** 15.9760 g. **Composition:** 0.9170 Gold .4711 oz. AGW **Subject:** Year of the Monkey

Date	Mintage	F	VF	XF	Unc	BU
1980 Proof	5,500	Value: 385				

KM#19 1000 PATACAS **Weight:** 15.9760 g. **Composition:** 0.9170 Gold .4711 oz. AGW **Subject:** Year of the Rooster

Date	Mintage	F	VF	XF	Unc	BU
1981	3,500	—	—	—	265	—
1981 Proof	Inc. above	Value: 300				

KM# 26 1000 PATACAS **Weight:** 15.9760 g. **Composition:** 0.9170 Gold .4711 oz. AGW **Subject:** Year of the Dog

Date	Mintage	F	VF	XF	Unc	BU
1982	256	—	—	—	325	—
1982 Proof	255	Value: 470				

KM# 28 1000 PATACAS **Weight:** 15.9760 g. **Composition:** 0.9170 Gold .4711 oz. AGW **Subject:** Year of the Pig

Date	Mintage	F	VF	XF	Unc	BU
1983	400	—	—	—	325	—
1983 Proof	500	Value: 450				

KM# 30 1000 PATACAS **Weight:** 15.9760 g. **Composition:** 0.9170 Gold .4711 oz. AGW **Subject:** Year of the Rat

Date	Mintage	F	VF	XF	Unc	BU
1984	2,000	—	—	—	275	—
1984 Proof	3,000	Value: 350				

KM# 32 1000 PATACAS **Weight:** 15.9760 g. **Composition:** 0.9170 Gold .4711 oz. AGW **Subject:** Year of the Ox

Date	Mintage	F	VF	XF	Unc	BU
1985	10,000	—	—	—	225	—
1985 Proof	5,000	Value: 275				

KM# 35 1000 PATACAS **Weight:** 15.9760 g. **Composition:** 0.9170 Gold .4711 oz. AGW **Subject:** Year of the Tiger

Date	Mintage	F	VF	XF	Unc	BU
1986(p)	2,000	—	—	—	225	—
1986(p) Proof	3,000	Value: 265				

KM# 37 1000 PATACAS **Weight:** 15.9760 g. **Composition:** 0.9170 Gold .4711 oz. AGW **Subject:** Year of the Rabbit

Date	Mintage	F	VF	XF	Unc	BU
1987(p)	—	—	—	—	225	—
1987(p) Proof	5,000	Value: 265				

KM# 39 1000 PATACAS **Weight:** 15.9760 g. **Composition:** 0.9170 Gold .4711 oz. AGW **Subject:** Year of the Dragon

Date	Mintage	F	VF	XF	Unc	BU
1988 Proof	5,000	Value: 265				

KM# 45 1000 PATACAS **Weight:** 15.9760 g. **Composition:** 0.9170 Gold .4711 oz. AGW **Subject:** Year of the Snake

Date	Mintage	F	VF	XF	Unc	BU
1989	2,000	—	—	—	235	—
1989 Proof	3,000	Value: 300				

KM# 47 1000 PATACAS **Weight:** 15.9760 g. **Composition:** 0.9170 Gold .4711 oz. AGW **Subject:** Year of the Horse

Date	Mintage	F	VF	XF	Unc	BU
1990	2,000	—	—	—	235	—
1990 Proof	3,000	Value: 300				

KM# 51 1000 PATACAS **Weight:** 15.9760 g. **Composition:** 0.9170 Gold .4711 oz. AGW **Subject:** Year of the Goat

Date	Mintage	F	VF	XF	Unc	BU
1991	—	—	—	—	375	—
1991 Proof	Est. 4,500	Value: 425				

KM# 55 1000 PATACAS **Weight:** 15.9760 g. **Composition:** 0.9170 Gold .4711 oz. AGW **Subject:** Year of the Monkey

Date	Mintage	F	VF	XF	Unc	BU
1992	—	—	—	—	375	—
1992 Proof	Est. 4,500	Value: 425				

KM# 61 1000 PATACAS **Weight:** 15.9760 g. **Composition:** 0.9170 Gold .4711 oz. AGW **Subject:** Year of the Rooster **Obverse:** St. Paul's Church **Reverse:** Rooster **Note:** Similar to 100 Patacas, KM#58.

Date	Mintage	F	VF	XF	Unc	BU
1993	—	—	—	—	375	—
1993 Proof	Est. 4,500	Value: 425				

KM# 69 1000 PATACAS **Weight:** 15.9760 g. **Composition:** 0.9170 Gold .4711 oz. AGW **Subject:** Year of the Dog

Date	Mintage	F	VF	XF	Unc	BU
1994	—	—	—	—	375	—
1994 Proof	Est. 4,500	Value: 425				

KM# 76 1000 PATACAS **Weight:** 15.9760 g. **Composition:** 0.9170 Gold .4711 oz. AGW **Subject:** Year of the Pig **Obverse:** Building **Reverse:** Pig standing left **Note:** Similar to 100 Patacas, KM#73.

Date	Mintage	F	VF	XF	Unc	BU
1995	—	—	—	—	375	—
1995 Proof	Est. 4,500	Value: 425				

KM# 78 1000 PATACAS **Weight:** 15.9760 g. **Composition:** 0.9170 Gold .4711 oz. AGW **Subject:** Airport **Obverse:** Stylized form **Reverse:** City aerial view **Note:** Similar to 100 Patacas, KM#77.

Date	Mintage	F	VF	XF	Unc	BU
1995 Proof	5,000	Value: 425				

KM# 82 1000 PATACAS **Weight:** 15.9760 g. **Composition:** 0.9170 Gold .4711 oz. AGW **Subject:** Year of the Rat

Date	Mintage	F	VF	XF	Unc	BU
1996 Proof	—	Value: 450				

KM# 87 1000 PATACAS **Weight:** 15.9760 g. **Composition:** 0.9170 Gold .4711 oz. AGW **Subject:** Year of the Ox **Note:** Similar to 100 Patacas, KM#84.

Date	Mintage	F	VF	XF	Unc	BU
1997 Proof	5,000	Value: 500				

KM# 91 1000 PATACAS **Weight:** 15.9760 g. **Composition:** 0.9170 Gold .4711 oz. AGW **Subject:** Year of the Tiger **Note:** Similar to 100 Patacas, KM#88.

Date	Mintage	F	VF	XF	Unc	BU
1998 Proof	5,000	Value: 500				

KM# 95 1000 PATACAS **Weight:** 15.9760 g. **Composition:** 0.9170 Gold .4711 oz. AGW **Subject:** Year of the Rabbit **Obverse:** Church facade **Reverse:** Rabbit **Note:** Similar to 100 Patacas, KM#88.

Date	Mintage	F	VF	XF	Unc	BU
1999 Proof	4,000	Value: 500				

KM# 101 1000 PATACAS **Weight:** 15.9760 g. **Composition:** 0.9167 Gold .4709 oz. AGW **Subject:** Year of the Dragon **Obverse:** Church facade **Reverse:** Dragon **Edge:** Reeded **Size:** 28.4 mm.

Date	Mintage	F	VF	XF	Unc	BU
2000	500	—	—	—	400	—
2000 Proof	4,000	Value: 500				

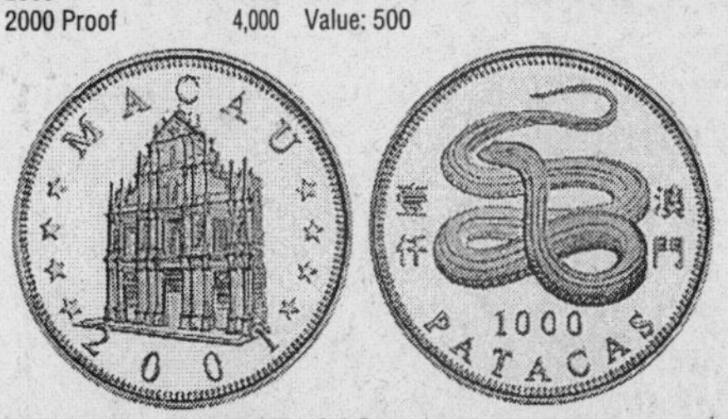

KM# 105 1000 PATACAS **Weight:** 16.9760 g. **Composition:** 0.9167 Gold .4709 oz. AGW **Subject:** Year of the Snake **Obverse:** Church facade **Reverse:** Snake

Date	Mintage	F	VF	XF	Unc	BU
2001 Proof	4,000	Value: 500				

KM# 110 1000 PATACAS **Weight:** 15.9700 g. **Composition:** 0.9167 Gold 0.4707 oz. AGW **Subject:** Year of the Horse **Obverse:** Church of St. Paul facade **Reverse:** Horse above denomination **Edge:** Reeded **Size:** 28.4 mm.

Date	Mintage	F	VF	XF	Unc	BU
2002 Proof	4,000	Value: 499				

KM# 43 10000 PATACAS **Weight:** 155.5150 g. **Composition:** 0.9990 Gold 5 oz. AGW **Subject:** 35th Anniversary of Grand Prix **Note:** Similar to 500 Patacas, KM#42.

Date	Mintage	F	VF	XF	Unc	BU
1988 Proof	500	Value: 3,000				

KM# 65 10000 PATACAS **Weight:** 155.5150 g. **Composition:** 0.9990 Gold 5 oz. AGW **Subject:** Macao Grand Prix **Note:** Similar to 500 Patacas, KM#64.

Date	Mintage	F	VF	XF	Unc	BU
1993 Proof	500	Value: 2,800				

PROVAS

Standard metals

Stamped PROVA in field

KM#	Date	Mintage	Identification	Issue Price	Mkt Val
Pr1	1952	—	5 Avos.	—	20.00
Pr2	1952	—	10 Avos.	—	20.00
Pr3	1952	—	50 Avos.	—	25.00
Pr4	1952	—	Pataca.	—	28.00
Pr5	1952	—	5 Patacas.	—	32.00
Pr6	1967	—	5 Avos.	—	20.00
Pr7	1967	—	10 Avos.	—	20.00
Pr8	1968	—	10 Avos.	—	20.00
Pr9	1968	—	Pataca.	—	25.00
Pr10	1969	—	10 Avos.	—	10.00
Pr11	1971	—	5 Patacas.	—	25.00
Pr12	1972	—	50 Avos.	—	20.00
Pr13	1973	—	50 Avos.	—	20.00
Pr14	1974	—	20 Patacas.	—	35.00
Pr15	1975	—	Pataca.	—	25.00

PROOF SETS

KM#	Date	Mintage	Identification	Issue Price	Mkt Val
PS1	1982 (5)	2,000	KM20a-24a	—	82.50
PS1b	1982 (5)	150	KM20b-24b	—	950
PS1c	1982 (5)	375	KM20c-24c	—	1,450
PS2	1983 (5)	2,500	KM20a-24a	55.00	82.50
PS3	1984 (5)	2,500	KM20a-24a	55.00	82.50
PS4	1985 (5)	2,500	KM20a-24a	55.00	82.50
PS5	1987 (2)	—	KM36-37	—	265
PS6	1988 (2)	—	KM38-39	—	275
PS7	1991 (3)	2,500	KM49-51	775	650
PS8	1992 (3)	2,500	KM53-55	825	700
PS9	1993 (3)	2,500	KM59-61	830	700
PS10	1994 (3)	2,500	KM67-69	825	735
PS11	1995 (3)	2,500	KM74-76	825	735
PS12	1997 (3)	2,500	KM85-87	849	840
PS13	1998 (3)	2,500	KM89-91	855	840
PS14	1999 (3)	2,500	KM93-95	850	840
PS15	2000 (3)	2,500	KM#99-101	849	—
PS16	2001 (3)	2,500	KM#103-105	849	—
PS17	2002 (3)	4,000	KM#108-110	849	—

MACEDONIA

The Republic of Macedonia is land-locked, and is bordered in the north by Yugoslavia, to the east by Bulgaria, in the south by Greece and to the west by Albania and has an area of 9,781 sq. mi. (25,713 sq. km.) and a population at the 1991 census was 2,038,847, of which the predominating ethnic groups were Macedonians. The capital is Skopje.

The Slavs settled in Macedonia since the 6th century, who had been Christianized by Byzantium, were conquered by the non-Slav Bulgars in the 7th century and in the9th century formed a Macedo-Bulgarian empire, the western part of which survived until Byzantine conquest in 1014. In the 14th century, it fell to Serbia, and in1355 to the Ottomans. After the Balkan Wars of 1912-13 Turkey was ousted, and Serbia received the greater part of the territory, the balance going to Bulgaria and Greece. In 1918, Yugoslav Macedonia was incorporated into Serbia as 'South Serbia', becoming a republic in the S.F.R. of Yugoslavia. Claims to the historical Macedonian territory have long been a source of contention between Bulgaria and Greece.

On Nov. 20, 1991 parliament promulgated a new constitution, and declared its independence on Nov.20, 1992, but failed to secure EC and US recognition owing to Greek objections to use of the name *Macedonia*. On Dec. 11, 1992, the UN Security Council authorized the expedition of a small peacekeeping force to prevent hostilities spreading into Macedonia.

There is a 120-member single-chamber National Assembly.

REPUBLIC

STANDARD COINAGE

KM# 1 50 DENI **Composition:** Brass **Obverse:** Seagull flying offshore

Date	F	VF	XF	Unc	BU
1993	—	0.10	0.20	0.50	—

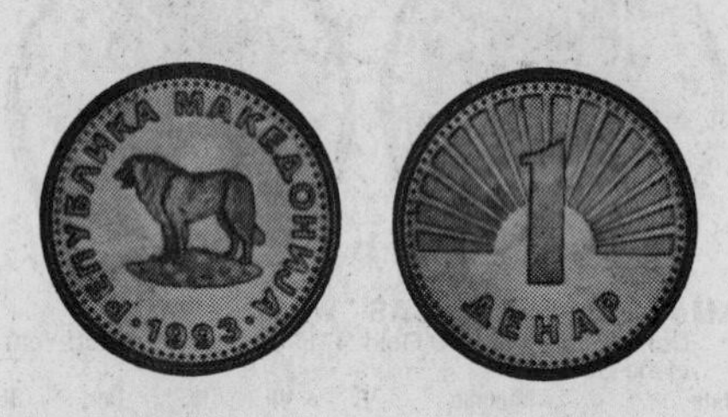

KM# 2 DENAR **Composition:** Brass **Obverse:** Yugoslavian sheep dog standing left

Date	F	VF	XF	Unc	BU
1993	—	0.20	0.35	1.00	—
1997	—	0.20	0.35	1.00	—

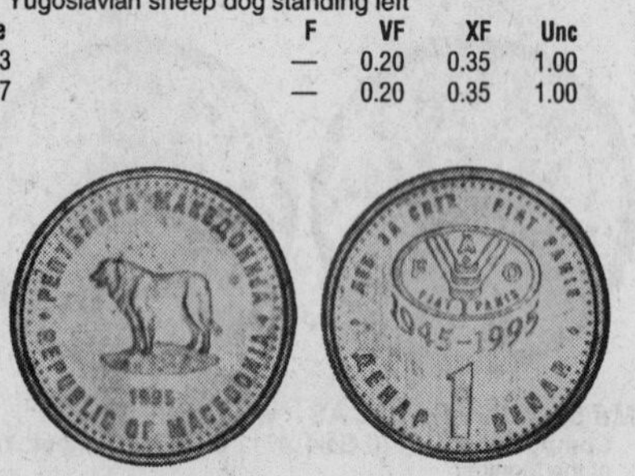

KM# 5 DENAR **Composition:** Brass **Series:** F.A.O. **Obverse:** Yugoslavian sheep dog

Date	Mintage	F	VF	XF	Unc	BU
1995	70,000	—	—	—	0.75	—

KM# 5a DENAR **Composition:** Copper-Nickel-Zinc **Series:** F.A.O. **Obverse:** Yugoslavian sheep dog

Date	F	VF	XF	Unc	BU
1995	—	—	—	0.75	—

KM# 8 DENAR **Weight:** 15.9800 g. **Composition:** 0.9167 Gold .4709 oz. AGW **Subject:** 5th Anniversary - UN Membership **Reverse:** Pair of white storks

Date	Mintage	F	VF	XF	Unc	BU
ND(1996) Proof	1,500	Value: 350				

KM# 9 DENAR **Composition:** Brass **Obverse:** Byzantine coin **Reverse:** Ornamented cross **Edge:** Plain **Size:** 23.8 mm.

Date	F	VF	XF	Unc	BU
2000	—	—	—	1.25	—

KM# 3 2 DENARI **Composition:** Brass **Obverse:** Fish above water

Date	F	VF	XF	Unc	BU
1993	—	0.25	0.50	1.25	—

KM# 6 2 DENARI **Composition:** Brass **Series:** F.A.O. **Obverse:** Fish

Date	Mintage	F	VF	XF	Unc	BU
1995	70,000	—	—	—	1.00	—

KM# 6a 2 DENARI **Composition:** Copper-Nickel-Zinc **Series:** F.A.O. **Obverse:** Fish

Date	F	VF	XF	Unc	BU
1995	—	—	—	1.00	—

KM# 4 5 DENARI **Composition:** Brass **Obverse:** European lynx

Date	F	VF	XF	Unc	BU
1993	—	0.35	0.75	1.75	—

KM# 7 5 DENARI Composition: Brass **Series:** F.A.O. **Obverse:** European lynx

Date	Mintage	F	VF	XF	Unc	BU
1995	70,000	—	—	—	1.25	—

KM# 7a 5 DENARI Composition: Copper-Nickel-Zinc **Series:** F.A.O. **Obverse:** European lynx

Date	F	VF	XF	Unc	BU
1995	—	—	—	1.25	—

MINT SETS

KM#	Date	Mintage	Identification	Issue Price	Mkt Val
MS1	1993 (4)	—	KM1-4	—	6.50
MS2	1995 (3)	—	KM5a-7a	—	5.50

MADAGASCAR

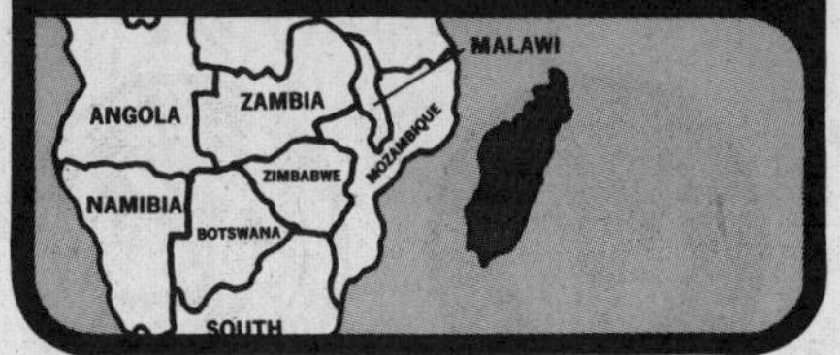

The Democratic Republic of Madagascar, an independent member of the French Community located in the Indian Ocean 250 miles (402 km.) off the southeast coast of Africa, has an area of 226,656 sq. mi. (587,040 sq. km.) and a population of 10 million. Capital: Antananarivo. The economy is primarily agricultural; large bauxite deposits are being developed. Coffee, vanilla, graphite, and rice are exported.

Successive waves of immigrants from south-east Asia, Africa, Arabia and India populated Madagascar beginning about 2,000 years ago. Diago Diaz, a Portuguese navigator, sighted the island of Madagascar on Aug. 10, 1500,when his ship became separated from an India-bound fleet. Attempts at settlement by the British during the reign of Charles I and by the French during the 17th and 18th centuries were of no avail, and the island became a refuge and supply base for Indian Ocean pirates. Despite considerable influence on the island, the British accepted the imposition of a French protectorate in 1886 in return for French recognition of Britain's sphere of influence in Zanzibar. Madagascar was made a French colony in 1896 after absolute control had been established by military force. Britain occupied the island after the fall of France, 1942, to prevent its seizure by the Japanese, returning it to the Free French in 1943. On Oct. 14, 1958, following a decade of intermittent but bitter warfare, Madagascar, as the Malagasy Republic, became an autonomous state within the French Community. On June 27, 1960, it became a sovereign, independent nation, though remaining nominally within the French Community. The Malagasy republic was renamed the Democratic Republic of Madagascar in 1975.

MONETARY SYSTEM

100 Centimes = 1 Franc

MINT MARKS

(a) - Paris, privy marks only
SA - Pretoria

FRENCH COLONY

STANDARD COINAGE

KM# 1 50 CENTIMES Composition: Bronze

Date	Mintage	F	VF	XF	Unc	BU
1943SA	2,000,000	1.50	2.50	10.00	20.00	30.00

KM# 2 FRANC Composition: Bronze

Date	Mintage	F	VF	XF	Unc	BU
1943SA	5,000,000	3.00	6.00	22.00	65.00	—

KM# 3 FRANC Composition: Aluminum

Date	Mintage	F	VF	XF	Unc	BU
1948(a)	7,400,000	0.25	0.35	0.75	2.50	—
1958(a)	2,600,000	0.25	0.35	0.75	2.75	—

KM# 4 2 FRANCS Composition: Aluminum

Date	Mintage	F	VF	XF	Unc	BU
1948(a)	10,000,000	0.25	0.45	0.85	2.25	—

KM# 5 5 FRANCS Composition: Aluminum

Date	Mintage	F	VF	XF	Unc	BU
1953(a)	30,012,000	0.25	0.55	1.00	2.50	—

KM# 6 10 FRANCS Composition: Aluminum-Bronze

Date	Mintage	F	VF	XF	Unc	BU
1953(a)	25,000,000	0.35	0.65	1.25	3.50	—

KM# 7 20 FRANCS Composition: Aluminum-Bronze

Date	Mintage	F	VF	XF	Unc	BU
1953(a)	15,000,000	0.75	1.50	3.00	6.50	—

TOKEN COINAGE

KM# Tn1 25 CENTIMES Composition: Aluminum **Issuer:** Societe des Mines d'Or de Andavakoera. **Obverse:** Legend of issuer around value. **Reverse:** Parakeet head left. **Size:** 21 mm.

Date	VG	F	VF	XF	Unc
ND	10.00	20.00	50.00	120	—

KM# Tn2 50 CENTIMES Composition: Aluminum **Issuer:** Societe des Mines d'Or de Andavakoera **Size:** 28 mm. **Note:** Similar to KM#Tn1.

Date	VG	F	VF	XF	Unc
ND(1920)	7.50	15.00	30.00	100	—

KM# Tn3 FRANC Composition: Aluminum **Issuer:** Societe des Mines d'Or de Andavakoera **Size:** 32 mm. **Note:** Similar to KM#Tn1.

Date	VG	F	VF	XF	Unc
ND(1920)	9.00	18.00	35.00	100	—

MALAGASY REPUBLIC

STANDARD COINAGE

5 Francs = 1 Ariary

KM# 8 FRANC Composition: Stainless Steel

Date	Mintage	F	VF	XF	Unc	BU
1965(a)	1,170,000	0.10	0.15	0.30	1.25	—
1966(a)	—	0.10	0.15	0.30	1.25	—
1970(a)	—	0.10	0.15	0.30	1.25	—
1974(a)	1,250,000	0.10	0.15	0.30	1.25	—
1975(a)	7,355,000	0.10	0.15	0.30	1.25	—
1976(a)	—	0.10	0.15	0.30	1.25	—
1977(a)	—	0.10	0.15	0.30	1.25	—
1979(a)	—	0.10	0.15	0.30	1.25	—
1980(a)	—	0.15	0.20	0.40	1.45	—
1981(a)	—	0.15	0.20	0.40	1.45	—
1982(a)	—	0.15	0.20	0.40	1.45	—
1983(a)	—	0.15	0.20	0.40	1.45	—
1986(a)	—	0.15	0.20	0.40	1.45	—
1987(a)	—	0.15	0.20	0.40	1.45	—
1988(a)	—	0.15	0.20	0.40	1.45	—
1989(a)	—	0.15	0.20	0.40	1.45	—

Date	Mintage	F	VF	XF	Unc	BU
1991(a)	—	0.15	0.20	0.40	1.45	—
1993(a)	—	0.15	0.20	0.40	1.45	—

KM# 9 2 FRANCS **Composition:** Stainless Steel

Date	Mintage	F	VF	XF	Unc	BU
1965(a)	760,000	0.15	0.25	0.50	1.50	—
1970(a)	—	0.15	0.25	0.45	1.25	—
1974(a)	1,250,000	0.15	0.25	0.45	1.25	—
1975(a)	8,250,000	0.15	0.25	0.45	1.25	—
1976(a)	—	0.15	0.25	0.45	1.25	—
1977(a)	—	0.15	0.25	0.45	1.25	—
1979(a)	—	0.15	0.25	0.45	1.25	—
1980(a)	—	0.15	0.25	0.45	1.25	—
1981(a)	—	0.15	0.25	0.45	1.25	—
1982(a)	—	0.15	0.25	0.45	1.25	—
1983(a)	—	0.15	0.25	0.45	1.25	—
1984(a)	—	0.15	0.25	0.45	1.25	—
1986(a)	—	0.15	0.25	0.45	1.25	—
1987(a)	—	0.15	0.25	0.45	1.25	—
1988(a)	—	0.15	0.25	0.45	1.25	—
1989(a)	—	0.15	0.25	0.45	1.25	—

KM# 10 5 FRANCS (Ariary) **Composition:** Stainless Steel

Date	Mintage	F	VF	XF	Unc	BU
1966(a)	—	0.15	0.25	0.60	1.75	—
1967(a)	—	0.15	0.25	0.60	1.75	—
1968(a)	7,500,000	0.15	0.25	0.60	1.75	—
1970(a)	—	0.15	0.25	0.60	1.75	—
1972(a)	19,100,000	0.15	0.25	0.60	1.75	—
1976(a)	—	0.15	0.25	0.60	1.75	—
1977(a)	—	0.15	0.25	0.60	1.75	—
1979(a)	—	0.15	0.25	0.60	1.75	—
1980(a)	—	0.20	0.30	0.65	1.85	—
1981(a)	—	0.20	0.30	0.65	1.85	—
1983(a)	—	0.20	0.30	0.65	1.85	—
1984(a)	—	0.20	0.30	0.65	1.85	—
1986(a)	—	0.20	0.30	0.65	1.85	—
1987(a)	—	0.20	0.30	0.65	1.85	—
1988(a)	—	0.20	0.30	0.65	1.85	—
1989(a)	—	0.20	0.30	0.65	1.85	—

KM# 11 10 FRANCS (2 Ariary) **Composition:** Aluminum-Bronze **Series:** F.A.O.

Date	Mintage	F	VF	XF	Unc	BU
1970(a)	7,000,000	0.20	0.30	0.70	2.00	—
1971(a)	10,000,000	0.20	0.30	0.70	2.00	—
1972(a)	5,050,000	0.20	0.30	0.70	2.00	—
1973(a)	3,000,000	0.20	0.30	0.70	2.00	—
1974(a)	—	0.20	0.30	0.70	2.00	—
1975(a)	—	0.20	0.30	0.70	2.00	—
1976(a)	9,500,000	0.20	0.30	0.70	2.00	—
1977(a)	—	0.20	0.30	0.70	2.00	—
1978(a)	—	0.20	0.30	0.70	2.00	—
1979(a)	—	0.20	0.30	0.70	2.00	—
1980(a)	—	0.25	0.35	0.80	2.25	—
1981(a)	—	0.25	0.35	0.80	2.25	—
1982(a)	—	0.25	0.35	0.80	2.25	—
1983(a)	—	0.25	0.35	0.80	2.25	—
1984(a)	—	0.25	0.35	0.80	2.25	—
1986(a)	—	0.25	0.35	0.80	2.25	—
1987(a)	3,200,000	0.25	0.35	0.80	2.25	—
1988(a)	—	0.25	0.35	0.80	2.25	—
1989(a)	—	0.25	0.35	0.80	2.25	—

KM# 11a 10 FRANCS (2 Ariary) **Composition:** Copper Plated Steel **Series:** F.A.O.

Date	F	VF	XF	Unc	BU
1991	0.25	0.45	1.50	3.50	—

KM# 12 20 FRANCS (4 Ariary) **Composition:** Aluminum-Bronze **Series:** F.A.O.

Date	Mintage	F	VF	XF	Unc	BU
1970(a)	4,000,000	0.25	0.35	0.75	2.50	—
1971(a)	2,000,000	0.25	0.35	0.75	2.50	—
1972(a)	2,000,000	0.30	0.40	0.80	2.75	—
1973(a)	3,000,000	0.30	0.40	0.80	2.75	—
1974(a)	—	0.30	0.40	0.80	2.75	—
1975(a)	—	0.30	0.40	0.80	2.75	—
1976(a)	2,700,000	0.30	0.40	0.80	2.75	—
1977(a)	—	0.30	0.40	0.80	2.75	—
1978(a)	—	0.30	0.40	0.80	2.75	—
1979(a)	—	0.30	0.40	0.80	2.75	—
1980(a)	—	0.35	0.45	0.85	3.00	—
1981(a)	—	0.35	0.45	0.85	3.00	—
1982(a)	—	0.35	0.45	0.85	3.00	—
1983(a)	—	0.35	0.45	0.85	3.00	—
1984(a)	—	0.35	0.45	0.85	3.00	—
1986(a)	—	0.35	0.45	0.85	3.00	—
1987(a)	5,200,000	0.35	0.45	0.85	3.00	—
1988(a)	—	0.35	0.45	0.85	3.00	—
1989(a)	—	0.35	0.45	0.85	3.00	—

DEMOCRATIC REPUBLIC

STANDARD COINAGE

5 Francs = 1 Ariary

KM# 17 5 ARIARY **Composition:** Copper Plated Steel **Obverse:** Star above denomination **Reverse:** Rice plant

Date	F	VF	XF	Unc	BU
1992	0.65	1.25	2.25	4.00	—

KM# 13 10 ARIARY **Composition:** Nickel **Series:** F.A.O. **Obverse:** Star above denomination

Date	Mintage	F	VF	XF	Unc	BU
1978	8,001,000	1.50	2.75	5.00	10.00	—

KM# 13a 10 ARIARY **Weight:** 9.0000 g. **Composition:** 0.9250 Silver .2676 oz. ASW

Date	Mintage	F	VF	XF	Unc	BU
1978 Proof	3,800	Value: 20.00				

KM# 13b 10 ARIARY **Composition:** Copper-Nickel

Date	F	VF	XF	Unc	BU
1983	2.00	4.00	8.00	15.00	—

KM# 16 10 ARIARY **Weight:** 10.0000 g. **Composition:** 0.9170 Gold .2947 oz. AGW **Subject:** World Wildlife Fund **Obverse:** Star above denomination **Reverse:** Ibis

Date	Mintage	F	VF	XF	Unc	BU
1988 Proof	Est. 5,000	Value: 175				

KM# 18 10 ARIARY **Composition:** Stainless Steel **Obverse:** Star above denomination **Reverse:** Man cutting peat **Shape:** 7-sided

Date	F	VF	XF	Unc	BU
1992	0.75	1.50	2.75	5.00	—

KM# 14 20 ARIARY **Composition:** Nickel **Series:** F.A.O. **Obverse:** Star above denomination **Reverse:** Farmer on tractor discing field

Date	Mintage	F	VF	XF	Unc	BU
1978	8,001,000	2.00	4.00	8.00	16.50	—

KM# 14a 20 ARIARY **Weight:** 12.0000 g. **Composition:** 0.9250 Silver .3569 oz. ASW

Date	Mintage	F	VF	XF	Unc	BU
1978 Proof	3,800	Value: 25.00				

KM# 14b 20 ARIARY **Composition:** Copper-Nickel

Date	F	VF	XF	Unc	BU
1983	2.50	4.50	9.00	17.50	—

KM# 15 20 ARIARY **Weight:** 19.4400 g. **Composition:** 0.9250 Silver .5782 oz. ASW **Subject:** World Wildlife Fund **Obverse:** Star above denomination **Reverse:** Lemur

Date	Mintage	F	VF	XF	Unc	BU
1988 Proof	Est. 25,000	Value: 32.50				

KM# 19 (KM19.1) 20 ARIARY **Composition:** Stainless Steel **Obverse:** Star above denomination **Reverse:** Farmer on tractor discing field

Date	F	VF	XF	Unc	BU
1992	1.25	2.50	4.50	10.00	—

KM# 20 (KM20.1) 50 ARIARY **Composition:** Stainless Steel **Obverse:** Star above denomination **Reverse:** Two towering trees

Date	F	VF	XF	Unc	BU
1992	2.00	3.50	6.00	12.50	—

REPUBLIC OF MADAGASCAR

Madagasikara Republic

STANDARD COINAGE

KM# 21 5 FRANCS (Ariary) **Composition:** Stainless Steel **Obverse:** Flower and bank name **Reverse:** Denomination and bovine head

Date	F	VF	XF	Unc	BU
1996	—	—	—	2.50	—

KM# 22 10 FRANCS (2 Ariary) **Composition:** Copper Plated Steel **Obverse:** Bank name and plant **Reverse:** Value, bovine head

Date	F	VF	XF	Unc	BU
1996	—	—	—	3.00	—

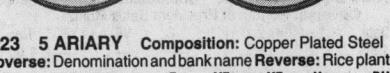

KM# 23 5 ARIARY Composition: Copper Plated Steel **Obverse:** Denomination and bank name **Reverse:** Rice plant

Date	F	VF	XF	Unc	BU
1994	—	—	—	2.50	—
1996	—	—	—	2.50	—

KM# 27 10 ARIARY Composition: Stainless Steel **Obverse:** Star above denomination **Reverse:** Man cutting peat **Edge:** Plain **Shape:** 7-sided

Date	F	VF	XF	Unc	BU
1999	—	—	—	4.50	—

KM# 24 20 ARIARY Composition: Nickel Clad Steel **Obverse:** Denomination and new country name **Reverse:** Farmer on tractor discing field

Date	F	VF	XF	Unc	BU
1994	—	—	—	6.50	—
1999	—	—	—	6.50	—

KM# 26 20 ARIARY Composition: 0.9250 Silver **Series:** UNICEF **Reverse:** Child and ring-tailed lemur

Date	F	VF	XF	Unc	BU
1996 Proof	—	Value: 32.50			

KM# 25 50 ARIARY Composition: Nickel Clad Steel **Obverse:** Denomination and new country name **Reverse:** Two towering trees

Date	F	VF	XF	Unc	BU
1994	—	—	—	8.00	—
1996	—	—	—	8.00	—

ESSAIS

Standard metals unless otherwise noted

KM# E1 FRANC Composition: Copper-Nickel **Note:** KM3.

Date	Mintage
	2,000

KM#	Date	Mintage	Identification	Issue Price	Mkt Val
E1		2,000	Franc. Copper-Nickel. KM3.		

KM#	Date	Mintage	Identification	Issue Price	Mkt Val
E2	1948	2,000	2 Francs. Copper-Nickel. KM4.	—	25.00
E3	1953(a)	1,200	5 Francs. KM5.	—	20.00
E4	1953(a)	1,200	10 Francs. KM6.	—	20.00
E5	1953(a)	1,200	20 Francs. KM7.	—	20.00
E6	1965(a)	—	Franc. KM8.	—	12.00
E7	1965(a)	—	2 Francs. KM9.	—	12.00
E8	1966(a)	—	5 Francs. KM10.	—	12.00
E9	1970(a)	—	10 Francs. KM11.	—	12.00
E10	1970(a)	—	20 Francs. KM12.	—	12.00

PIEFORTS WITH ESSAI

Double thickness; Standard metals unless otherwise noted

KM#	Date	Mintage	Identification	Issue Price	Mkt Val
PE1	1948(a)	104	Franc. KM3.	—	75.00
PE2	1948(a)	104	2 Francs. KM4.	—	85.00
PE3	1953(a)	104	5 Francs. KM5.	—	65.00
PE4	1953(a)	104	10 Francs. KM6.	—	70.00
PE5	1953(a)	104	20 Francs. KM7.	—	90.00

"FDC" SETS

This fleur-de-coin set was issued with New Caledonia and French Polynesia 1967 sets.

KM#	Date	Mintage	Identification	Issue Price	Mkt Val
SS1	1970 (5)	1,500	KM8-12	2.75	11.50

PROOF SETS

KM#	Date	Mintage	Identification	Issue Price	Mkt Val
PS1	1978 (2)	3,800	KM#13a, 14a	38.00	45.00

MADEIRA ISLANDS

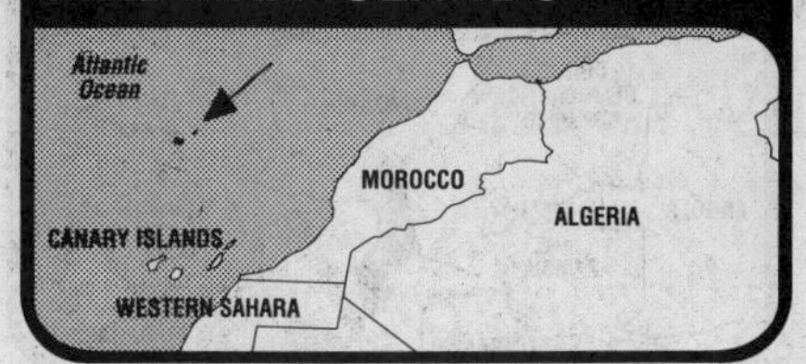

The Madeira Islands, which belong to Portugal, are located 360 miles (492 km.) off the northwest coast of Africa. They have an area of 307 sq. mi. (795 sq. km.) and a population of 270,976. The group consists of two inhabited islands named Madeira and Porto Santo and two groups of uninhabited rocks named Desertas and Selvagens. Capital: Funchal. The two staple products are wine and sugar. Bananas and pineapples are also produced for export.

Although the evidence is insufficient, it is thought that the Phoenicians visited Madeira at an early period. It is also probable that the entire archipelago was explored by Genoese adventurers; an Italian map dated 1351 shows the Madeira Islands quite clearly. The Portuguese navigator Goncalvez Zarco first sighted Porto Santo in 1418, having been driven there by a storm while he was exploring the coast of West Africa. Madeira itself was discovered in 1420. The islands were uninhabited when visited by Zarco, but soon after 1418 Madeira was quickly colonized by Prince Henry the Navigator, aided by the knights of the Order of Christ. British troops occupied the islands in 1801, and again in 1807-14.

RULERS

Portuguese

PORTUGUESE COLONY

MODERN COINAGE

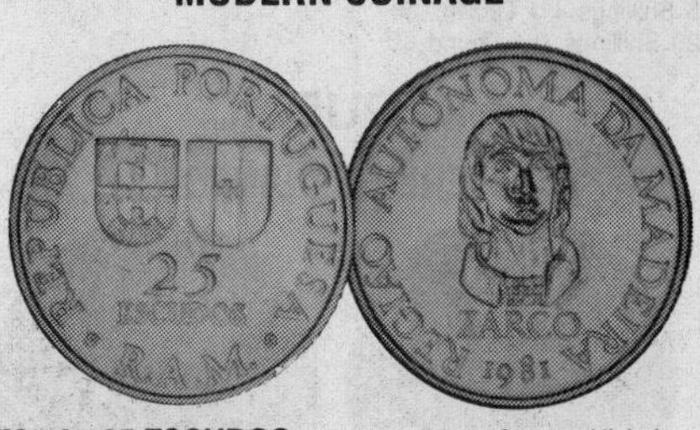

KM# 4 25 ESCUDOS Composition: Copper-Nickel **Subject:** Autonomy of Madeira **Obverse:** Shields of arms over value **Reverse:** Bust of Goncalvez Zarco facing

Date	Mintage	F	VF	XF	Unc	BU
1981	750,000	—	—	—	6.00	—

KM# 4a 25 ESCUDOS Weight: 11.0000 g. **Composition:** 0.9250 Silver .3272 oz. ASW **Subject:** Autonomy of Madeira **Obverse:** Shields of arms over value **Reverse:** Bust of Goncalvez facing

Date	Mintage	F	VF	XF	Unc	BU
1981 Proof	20,000	Value: 15.00				

KM# 5 100 ESCUDOS Composition: Copper-Nickel **Subject:** Autonomy of Madeira **Obverse:** Shields of arms over value **Reverse:** Bust of Goncalvez Zarco facing

Date	Mintage	F	VF	XF	Unc	BU
1981	250,000	—	—	—	12.00	—

KM# 5a 100 ESCUDOS Weight: 16.5000 g. **Composition:** 0.9250 Silver .4908 oz. ASW **Subject:** Autonomy of Madeira **Obverse:** Shields of arms **Reverse:** Bust of Goncalvez Zarco facing

Date	Mintage	F	VF	XF	Unc	BU
1981 Proof	20,000	Value: 22.50				

PROVAS

KM#	Date	Mintage	Identification	Mkt Val
Pr1	1981	—	25 Escudos. KM4.	30.00
Pr2	1981	—	100 Escudos. KM5.	40.00

PROOF SETS

KM#	Date	Mintage	Identification	Issue Price	Mkt Val
PS1	1981 (2)	20,000	KM4a-5a	42.00	37.50

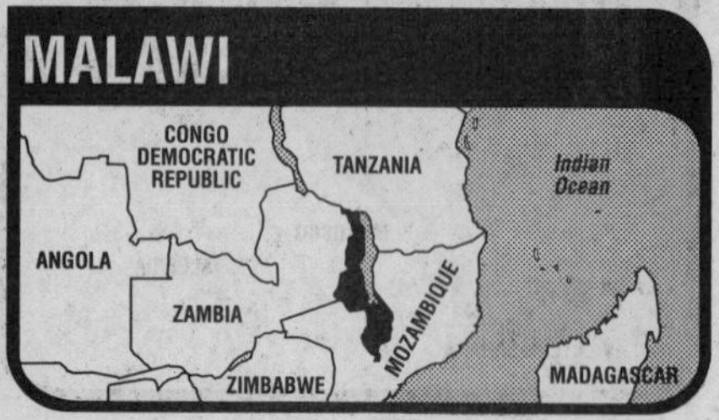

The Republic of Malawi (formerly Nyasaland), located in southeastern Africa to the west of Lake Malawi (Nyasa), has an area of 45,745 sq. mi. (118,480 sq. km.) and a population of 7 million. Capital: Lilongwe. The economy is predominantly agricultural. Tobacco, tea, peanuts and cotton are exported.

Although the Portuguese were the first Europeans to reach the Malawi area, the first meaningful contact was made by missionary-explorer Dr. David Livingstone. He arrived at Lake Malawi on Sept. 16, 1859, and remained to make extensive explorations in the 1860's. Subsequent clashes between settlements of Scottish missionaries and Arab slave traders, and the procurement of development rights by Cecil Rhodes, 1884, stimulated British interest and brought about the establishment of the Nyasaland protectorate in 1891. In 1953 Nyasaland reluctantly joined the Federation of Rhodesia and Nyasaland and, after prolonged protest, was granted self-government within the federation. Nyasaland became the independent nation of Malawi on July 6, 1964, and became a republic two years later. Malawi is a member of the Commonwealth of Nations. The president is the Chief of State and Head of Government.

NOTE: For earlier coinage see Rhodesia and Nyasaland.

MONETARY SYSTEM

12 Pence = 1 Shilling
2 Shillings = 1 Florin
5 Shillings = 1 Crown
20 Shillings = 1 Pound

REPUBLIC

STERLING COINAGE

KM# 6 PENNY Composition: Bronze

Date	Mintage	F	VF	XF	Unc	BU
1967	6,000,000	0.35	0.65	1.25	2.50	—
1968	3,600,000	3.00	6.00	12.00	25.00	—

KM# 1 6 PENCE Composition: Copper-Nickel-Zinc **Obverse:** Dr. Hastings Kamuzu Banda **Reverse:** Rooster

Date	Mintage	F	VF	XF	Unc	BU
1964	14,800,000	0.25	0.50	1.00	2.50	—
1964 Proof	10,000	Value: 1.50				
1967	6,000,000	0.50	1.00	2.50	5.00	—

KM# 2 SCHILLING Composition: Copper-Nickel-Zinc **Obverse:** Dr. Hastings Kamuzu Banda **Reverse:** Bundled cobs of corn

Date	Mintage	F	VF	XF	Unc	BU
1964	11,900,000	0.35	0.65	1.25	2.50	—
1964 Proof	10,000	Value: 1.50				
1968	3,000,000	0.75	1.50	3.00	5.50	—

KM# 3 FLORIN Composition: Copper-Nickel-Zinc **Obverse:** Dr. Hastings Kamuzu Banda **Reverse:** African elephants

Date	Mintage	F	VF	XF	Unc	BU
1964	6,500,000	0.75	1.50	3.00	5.00	—
1964 Proof	10,000	Value: 3.50				

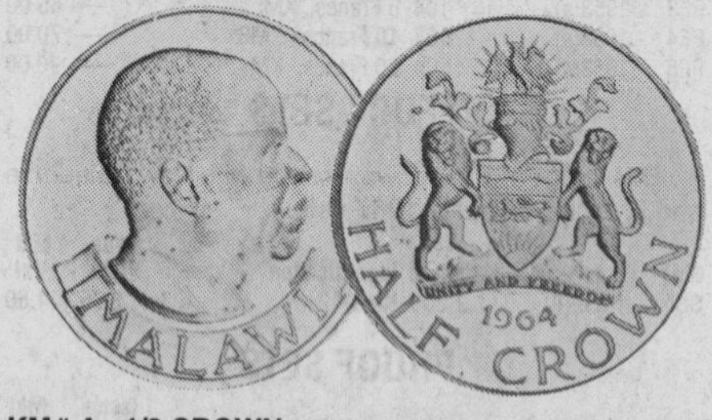

KM# 4 1/2 CROWN Composition: Copper-Nickel-Zinc **Obverse:** Dr. Hastings Kamuzu Banda **Reverse:** Arms

Date	Mintage	F	VF	XF	Unc	BU
1964	6,400,000	1.00	2.00	4.00	6.00	—
1964 Proof	10,000	Value: 4.00				

KM# 5 CROWN Composition: Nickel-Brass **Subject:** Day of the Republic - July 6, 1966

Date	Mintage	F	VF	XF	Unc	BU
1966 Proof	20,000	Value: 7.50				

DECIMAL COINAGE

100 Tambala = 1 Kwacha

KM# 7.1 TAMBALA Composition: Bronze **Obverse:** Dr. Hastings Kamuzu Banda **Reverse:** Rooster

Date	Mintage	F	VF	XF	Unc	BU
1971	15,000,000	0.15	0.20	0.40	0.75	—
1971 Proof	4,000	Value: 1.00				
1973	5,000,000	0.15	0.20	0.40	0.75	—
1974	12,500,000	0.15	0.20	0.40	0.75	—

KM# 7.2 TAMBALA Composition: Bronze **Obverse:** Accent mark above "W" in MALAWI

Date	Mintage	F	VF	XF	Unc	BU
1975	—	0.15	0.20	0.40	0.75	—
1976	10,000,000	0.15	0.20	0.40	0.75	—
1977	10,000,000	0.15	0.20	0.40	0.75	—
1979	15,000,000	0.15	0.20	0.40	0.75	—
1982	15,000,000	0.15	0.20	0.40	0.75	—

KM# 7.2a TAMBALA Composition: Copper Plated Steel

Date	Mintage	F	VF	XF	Unc	BU
1984	201,000	0.20	0.30	0.50	0.80	—
1985	—	0.20	0.30	0.50	0.80	—
1985 Proof	10,000	Value: 3.00				
1987	—	0.20	0.30	0.50	0.80	—
1989	—	0.20	0.30	0.50	0.80	—
1991	—	0.20	0.30	0.50	0.80	—
1994	—	0.20	0.30	0.50	0.80	—

KM# 24 TAMBALA Composition: Copper Plated Steel **Obverse:** Portrait of President Bakili Muluzi

Date	F	VF	XF	Unc	BU
1995	—	—	—	1.00	—

KM# 33 TAMBALA Composition: Bronze **Obverse:** Arms **Reverse:** Two fish **Edge:** Plain **Size:** 17.3 mm.

Date	F	VF	XF	Unc	BU
1995	—	—	—	1.00	—

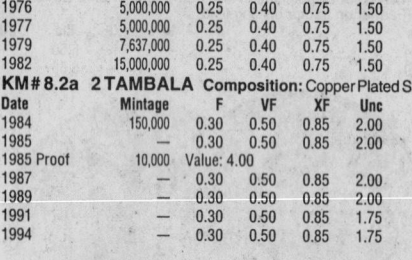

KM# 8.1 2 TAMBALA Composition: Bronze **Obverse:** Dr. Hastings Kamuzu Banda **Reverse:** Paradise Whydah

Date	Mintage	F	VF	XF	Unc	BU
1971	10,000,000	0.25	0.40	0.75	1.50	—
1971 Proof	4,000	Value: 1.75				
1973	5,000,000	0.25	0.40	0.75	1.50	—
1974	5,000,000	0.25	0.40	0.75	1.50	—

KM# 8.2 2 TAMBALA Composition: Bronze **Obverse:** Accent mark above "W" in MALAWI

Date	Mintage	F	VF	XF	Unc	BU
1975	—	0.25	0.40	0.75	1.50	—
1976	5,000,000	0.25	0.40	0.75	1.50	—
1977	5,000,000	0.25	0.40	0.75	1.50	—
1979	7,637,000	0.25	0.40	0.75	1.50	—
1982	15,000,000	0.25	0.40	0.75	1.50	—

KM# 8.2a 2 TAMBALA Composition: Copper Plated Steel

Date	Mintage	F	VF	XF	Unc	BU
1984	150,000	0.30	0.50	0.85	2.00	—
1985	—	0.30	0.50	0.85	2.00	—
1985 Proof	10,000	Value: 4.00				
1987	—	0.30	0.50	0.85	2.00	—
1989	—	0.30	0.50	0.85	2.00	—
1991	—	0.30	0.50	0.85	1.75	—
1994	—	0.30	0.50	0.85	1.75	—

KM# 25 2 TAMBALA Composition: Copper Plated Steel **Obverse:** Portrait of President Bakili Muluzi

Date	F	VF	XF	Unc	BU
1995	—	—	—	1.00	—

KM# 34 2 TAMBALA Composition: Bronze **Obverse:** National arms **Reverse:** Paradise Whydah bird **Edge:** Plain **Size:** 20.3 mm.

Date	F	VF	XF	Unc	BU
1995	—	—	—	1.00	—

KM# 9.1 5 TAMBALA Composition: Copper-Nickel **Obverse:** Dr. Hastings Kamuzu Banda **Reverse:** Purple heron

Date	Mintage	F	VF	XF	Unc	BU
1971	7,000,000	0.25	0.45	0.85	1.75	—
1971 Proof	4,000	Value: 2.00				

KM# 9.2 5 TAMBALA Composition: Copper-Nickel **Obverse:** Accent mark above "W" in MALAWI

Date	Mintage	F	VF	XF	Unc	BU
1985 Proof	10,000	Value: 5.00				

KM# 9.2a 5 TAMBALA **Composition:** Nickel Clad Steel

Date	F	VF	XF	Unc	BU
1989	0.30	0.50	0.85	2.00	—
1994	0.30	0.50	0.85	2.00	—

KM# 26 5 TAMBALA **Composition:** Steel **Obverse:** Portrait of President Bakill Muluzi

Date	F	VF	XF	Unc	BU
1995	—	—	—	1.50	—

KM# 32 5 TAMBALA **Composition:** Steel **Obverse:** Arms **Reverse:** Purple heron

Date	F	VF	XF	Unc	BU
1995	—	—	—	2.50	—

KM# 10.1 10 TAMBALA **Composition:** Copper-Nickel **Obverse:** Dr. Hastings Kamuzu Banda **Reverse:** Bundled cobs of corn

Date	Mintage	F	VF	XF	Unc	BU
1971	4,000,000	0.30	0.50	1.00	2.25	—
1971 Proof	4,000	Value: 2.50				

KM# 10.2 10 TAMBALA **Composition:** Copper-Nickel **Obverse:** Accent mark above "W" in MALAWI

Date	Mintage	F	VF	XF	Unc	BU
1985 Proof	10,000	Value: 6.00				
1989	—	0.40	0.80	1.50	2.75	—

KM# 10.2a 10 TAMBALA **Composition:** Nickel Clad Steel

Date	F	VF	XF	Unc	BU
1989	0.40	0.80	1.50	2.75	—

KM# 27 10 TAMBALA **Composition:** Steel **Obverse:** Portrait of President Bakill Muluzi

Date	F	VF	XF	Unc	BU
1995	—	—	—	2.25	—

KM# 11.1 20 TAMBALA **Composition:** Copper-Nickel **Obverse:** Dr. Hastings Kamuzu Banda **Reverse:** Elephant cow and calf

Date	Mintage	F	VF	XF	Unc	BU
1971	3,000,000	0.75	1.50	2.50	4.00	—
1971 Proof	4,000	Value: 4.50				

KM# 11.2 20 TAMBALA **Composition:** Copper-Nickel **Obverse:** Accent mark above "W" in MALAWI

Date	Mintage	F	VF	XF	Unc	BU
1985 Proof	10,000	Value: 7.00				

KM# 11.2a 20 TAMBALA **Composition:** Nickel Clad Steel

Date	F	VF	XF	Unc	BU
1989	0.60	1.20	2.25	3.75	—
1994	0.60	1.20	2.25	3.75	—

KM# 29 20 TAMBALA **Composition:** Nickel Clad Steel **Obverse:** Portrait of President Bakili Muluzi

Date	F	VF	XF	Unc	BU
1996	—	—	—	3.75	—

KM# 19 50 TAMBALA **Composition:** Copper-Nickel-Zinc **Obverse:** Dr. Hastings Kamuzu Banda **Reverse:** Arms **Note:** The 1989 date for this coin does not exist.

Date	F	VF	XF	Unc	BU
1986	2.00	3.00	5.00	10.00	—
1994	2.00	3.00	5.00	10.00	—

KM# 30 50 TAMBALA **Composition:** Brass Plated Steel **Obverse:** Portrait of President Bakili Muluzi

Date	F	VF	XF	Unc	BU
1996	—	—	—	4.50	—

KM# 12 KWACHA **Composition:** Copper-Nickel **Subject:** Decimalization of coinage **Obverse:** Similar to 5 Kwacha, KM#15

Date	Mintage	F	VF	XF	Unc	BU
1971	20,000	1.00	2.00	3.50	6.00	—
1971 Proof	4,000	Value: 6.50				

KM# 20 KWACHA **Composition:** Copper-Nickel-Zinc **Obverse:** Dr. Hastings Kamuzu Banda **Reverse:** Rooster

Date	F	VF	XF	Unc	BU
1992	1.00	2.00	3.00	5.50	—
1993	2.00	4.00	6.00	10.00	—

KM# 28 KWACHA **Composition:** Brass **Obverse:** Portrait of President Bakili Muluzi

Date	F	VF	XF	Unc	BU
1996	—	—	—	7.00	—

KM# 28.2 KWACHA **Composition:** Brass Plated Steel

Date	F	VF	XF	Unc	BU
1996	—	—	—	7.00	—

KM# 15 5 KWACHA **Weight:** 28.2800 g. **Composition:** 0.9250 Silver .841 oz. ASW **Subject:** Conservation **Reverse:** Burchell's zebras

Date	Mintage	F	VF	XF	Unc	BU
1978	4,048	—	—	—	18.00	—
1978 Proof	3,622	Value: 32.50				

KM# 23 5 KWACHA **Composition:** Copper-Nickel **Subject:** United Nations 50th Anniversary **Reverse:** Child reading

Date	F	VF	XF	Unc	BU
ND(1995)	—	—	—	8.50	—

KM# 23a 5 KWACHA **Weight:** 28.2800 g. **Composition:** 0.9250 Silver .8410 oz. ASW **Subject:** United Nations 50th Anniversary **Reverse:** Child reading

Date	Mintage	F	VF	XF	Unc	BU
ND(1995) Proof	—	Value: 32.50				

KM# 13 10 KWACHA **Weight:** 28.2800 g. **Composition:** 0.9250 Silver .8411 oz. ASW **Subject:** 10th Anniversary of Independence

Date	Mintage	F	VF	XF	Unc	BU
1974	7,556	—	—	—	11.50	—
1974 Proof	4,937	Value: 17.50				

KM# 14 10 KWACHA **Weight:** 28.2800 g. **Composition:** 0.9250 Silver .8411 oz. ASW **Subject:** 10th Anniversary of the Reserve Bank **Obverse:** Similar to KM#13.

Date	Mintage	F	VF	XF	Unc	BU
ND(1975)	6,870	—	—	—	11.50	—
ND(1975) Proof	Inc. above	Value: 18.50				

KM# 14a 10 KWACHA **Composition:** 0.9000 Gold **Subject:** 10th Anniversary of the Reserve Bank

Date	F	VF	XF	Unc	BU
ND(1975)	—	—	—	1,250	—

KM# 16 10 KWACHA **Weight:** 35.0000 g. **Composition:** 0.9250 Silver 1.0409 oz. ASW **Series:** Conservation **Obverse:** Similar to 5 Kwacha, KM#15 **Reverse:** Sable antelope

Date	Mintage	F	VF	XF	Unc	BU
1978	4,009	—	—	—	20.00	—
1978 Proof	3,416	Value: 35.00				

KM# 18 10 KWACHA **Weight:** 28.2800 g. **Composition:** 0.9250 Silver .8410 oz. ASW **Subject:** 20th Anniversary - Reserve Bank

Date	Mintage	F	VF	XF	Unc	BU
ND(1985) Proof	4,000	Value: 22.50				

KM# 18a 10 KWACHA **Weight:** 47.5400 g. **Composition:** 0.9170 Gold 1.4011 oz. AGW **Subject:** 20th Anniversary - Reserve Bank **Obverse:** Similar to 250 Kwacha, KM#17 **Reverse:** Eagle

Date	Mintage	F	VF	XF	Unc	BU
ND(1985) Proof	50	Value: 1,550				

KM# 21 10 KWACHA **Weight:** 28.2800 g. **Composition:** 0.9250 Silver .8411 oz. ASW **Series:** Save the Children **Subject:** Fishing

Date	Mintage	F	VF	XF	Unc	BU
1992 Proof	20,000	Value: 35.00				

KM# 22 20 KWACHA **Weight:** 10.0000 g. **Composition:** 0.9170 Gold .2948 oz. AGW **Series:** Save the Children **Subject:** Mother and children

Date	Mintage	F	VF	XF	Unc	BU
1992 Proof	Est. 3,000	Value: 220				

KM# 35 20 KWACHA **Weight:** 31.4000 g. **Composition:** 0.9250 Silver .9338 oz. ASW **Series:** Endangered Wildlife **Subject:** "The Romans" **Obverse:** National arms **Reverse:** Female elephant with two calves in water **Edge:** Reeded **Size:** 38.6 mm.

Date		F	VF	XF	Unc	BU
1996 Proof	—	Value: 45.00				

KM# 36 20 KWACHA **Weight:** 31.5500 g. **Composition:** 0.9250 Silver 0.9383 oz. ASW **Subject:** Queen Mother **Obverse:** National arms **Reverse:** Queen Mother and two girl scouts **Edge:** Reeded **Size:** 38.6 mm.

Date		F	VF	XF	Unc	BU
1997 Proof	—	Value: 45.00				

KM# 31 20 KWACHA **Weight:** 31.5300 g. **Composition:** 0.9250 Silver .9377 oz. ASW **Subject:** Millennium **Reverse:** People seated below trees, ears of corn, denomination **Shape:** 6-sided.

Date		F	VF	XF	Unc	BU
1999 Proof	—	Value: 40.00				

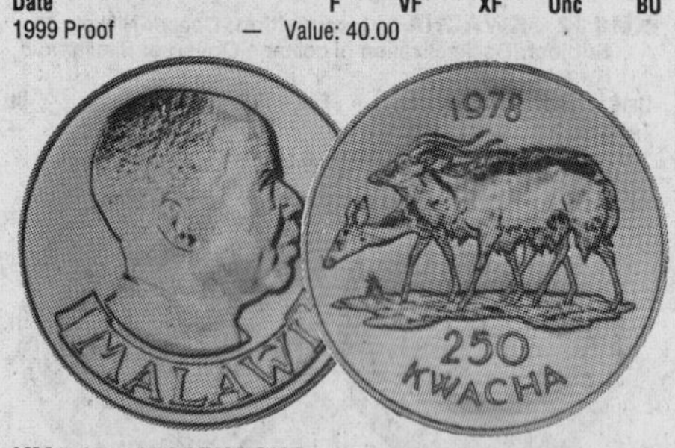

KM# 17 250 KWACHA **Weight:** 33.4370 g. **Composition:** 0.9000 Gold .9676 oz. AGW **Series:** Conservation **Subject:** Nyala

Date	Mintage	F	VF	XF	Unc	BU
1978	566	—	—	—	500	—
1978 Proof	208	Value: 850				

MINT SETS

KM#	Date	Mintage	Identification	Issue Price	Mkt Val
MS1	1971 (6)	10,000	KM7.1-11.1, 12	3.30	16.50
MS2	1978 (2)	—	KM15, 16	—	40.00

PROOF SETS

KM#	Date	Mintage	Identification	Issue Price	Mkt Val
PS1	1964 (4)	10,000	KM1-4	10.00	10.00
PS2	1971 (6)	4,000	KM7.1-11.1, 12	8.70	18.50
PS3	1978 (2)	—	KM15, 16	—	70.00
PS4	1985 (5)	10,000	KM7.2a-8.2a, 9.2-11.2	30.00	25.00

MALAYA

Malaya, a former member of the British Commonwealth located in the southern part of the Malay peninsula, consisted of 11 states: the un-federated Malay states of Johore, Kelantan, Kedah, Perlis and Trengganu; the federated Malay states of Negri-Sembilan, Pahang, Perakand Selangor; former members of the Straits Settlements Penang and Malacca. Malaya was occupied by the Japanese during the years 1942-1945. The only local opposition to the Japanese had come mainly from the Chinese Communists who then continued their guerilla operations after the war, finally being defeated in 1956. Malaya was granted full independence on Aug. 31, 1957, and became part of Malaysia in 1963.

RULERS
British

MINT MARKS
I - Calcutta Mint (1941)
I - Bombay Mint (1945)
No Mint mark - Royal Mint

MONETARY SYSTEM
100 Cents = 1 Dollar

BRITISH COLONY

STANDARD COINAGE

100 Cents = 1 Dollar

KM# 1 1/2 CENT **Composition:** Bronze **Shape:** Square.

Date	Mintage	F	VF	XF	Unc	BU
1940	6,000,000	0.50	1.25	2.00	4.50	—
1940 Proof	—	Value: 150				

KM# 2 CENT **Composition:** Bronze **Shape:** Square.

Date	Mintage	F	VF	XF	Unc	BU
1939	20,000,000	0.25	0.40	0.60	1.75	—
1939 Proof	—	Value: 150				
1940	23,600,000	0.25	0.40	0.60	1.75	—
1940 Proof	—	—	—	—	—	—
1941 I	33,620,000	0.75	1.25	5.00	10.00	—

KM# 6 CENT **Composition:** Bronze **Shape:** Square. **Note:** Reduced size.

Date	Mintage	F	VF	XF	Unc	BU
1943	50,000,000	0.10	0.20	0.45	1.00	—
1943 Proof	—	Value: 150				
1945	40,033,000	0.10	0.20	0.45	1.00	—
1945 Proof	—	Value: 150				

KM# 3 5 CENTS **Weight:** 1.3600 g. **Composition:** 0.7500 Silver .0327 oz. ASW

Date	Mintage	F	VF	XF	Unc	BU
1939	2,000,000	0.50	1.00	1.50	3.00	—
1939 Proof	—	Value: 250				
1941	4,000,000	0.40	0.50	1.20	2.50	—
1941 Proof	—	Value: 250				
1941 I	Inc. above	0.40	0.50	1.20	2.50	—

KM# 3a 5 CENTS **Weight:** 1.3600 g. **Composition:** 0.5000 Silver .0218 oz. ASW

Date	Mintage	F	VF	XF	Unc	BU
1943	10,000,000	0.30	0.40	0.65	1.75	—
1943 Proof	—	Value: 250				
1945	8,800,000	0.30	0.40	0.65	1.75	—
1945 Proof	—	Value: 250				
1945 I	4,600,000	0.50	0.75	1.00	2.50	—

KM# 7 5 CENTS **Composition:** Copper-Nickel

Date	Mintage	F	VF	XF	Unc	BU
1948	30,000,000	0.10	0.25	0.75	2.25	—
1948 Proof	—	Value: 220				
1950	40,000,000	0.10	0.25	0.75	2.25	—
1950 Proof	—	Value: 220				

KM# 4 10 CENTS **Weight:** 2.7100 g. **Composition:** 0.7500 Silver .0653 oz. ASW

Date	Mintage	F	VF	XF	Unc	BU
1939	10,000,000	0.75	1.00	1.25	2.75	—
1939 Proof	—	Value: 280				
1941	17,000,000	0.75	1.00	1.25	2.75	—
1941 Proof	—	Value: 280				
1941 I Proof, rare	—	—	—	—	—	—

KM# 4a 10 CENTS **Weight:** 2.7100 g. **Composition:** 0.5000 Silver .0435 oz. ASW

Date	Mintage	F	VF	XF	Unc	BU
1943	5,000,000	0.75	1.00	1.50	3.00	—
1943 Proof	—	Value: 280				
1945	3,152,000	0.75	1.00	1.50	3.50	—
1945 I Proof, rare	—	—	—	—	—	—

KM# 8 10 CENTS **Composition:** Copper-Nickel

Date	Mintage	F	VF	XF	Unc	BU
1948	23,885,000	0.15	0.30	0.75	2.50	—
1948 Proof	—	Value: 280				
1949	26,115,000	0.25	0.50	1.20	3.50	—
1949 Proof	—	Value: 280				
1950	65,000,000	0.15	0.30	0.75	2.50	—
1950 Proof	—	Value: 280				

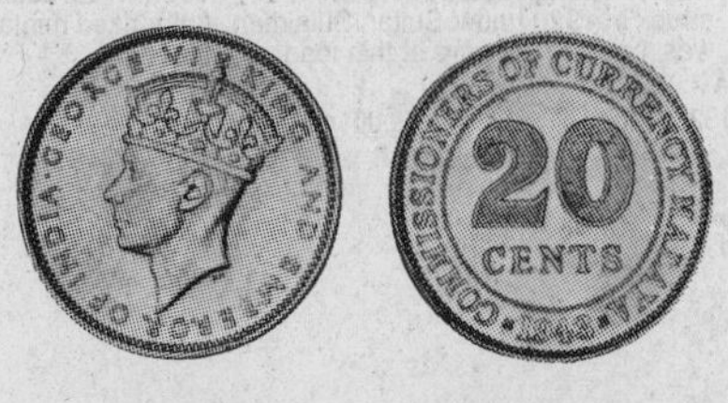

KM# 5 20 CENTS **Weight:** 5.4300 g. **Composition:** 0.7500 Silver .1309 oz. ASW

Date	Mintage	F	VF	XF	Unc	BU
1939	8,000,000	1.25	1.75	2.50	5.00	—
1939 Proof	—	Value: 280				

KM# 5a 20 CENTS **Weight:** 5.4300 g. **Composition:** 0.5000 Silver .0872 oz. ASW

Date	Mintage	F	VF	XF	Unc	BU
1943	5,000,000	1.25	1.75	2.75	5.50	—
1943 Proof	—	Value: 260				
1945	10,000,000	2.00	4.00	8.00	12.00	—
1945 I Proof, rare	—	—	—	—	—	—

KM# 9 20 CENTS **Composition:** Copper-Nickel

Date	Mintage	F	VF	XF	Unc	BU
1948	40,000,000	0.35	0.75	1.75	4.75	—
1948 Proof	—	Value: 280				
1950	20,000,000	0.35	0.75	1.75	4.75	—
1950 Proof	—	Value: 280				

MALAYA & BRITISH BORNEO

Malaya & British Borneo, a Currency Commission named the Board of Commissioners of Currency, Malaya and British Borneo, was initiated on Jan. 1, 1952, for the purpose of providing a common currency for use in Johore, Kelantan, Kedah, Perlis, Trengganu, Negri Sembilan, Pahang, Perak, Selangor, Penang, Malacca, Singapore, North Borneo, Sarawak and Brunei.

RULERS
British

MINT MARKS
KN - King's Norton, Birmingham
H - Heaton, Birmingham
No Mint mark - Royal Mint

MONETARY SYSTEM
100 Cents = 1 Dollar

BRITISH COLONY

STANDARD COINAGE

100 Cents = 1 Dollar

KM# 5 CENT **Composition:** Bronze **Shape:** Square.

Date	Mintage	F	VF	XF	Unc	BU
1956	6,250,000	—	0.10	0.25	0.85	—
1956 Proof	—	Value: 125				
1957	12,500,000	—	0.10	0.25	0.75	—
1957 Proof	—	—	—	—	—	—
1958	5,000,000	—	0.10	0.25	0.85	—
1958 Proof	—	Value: 125				
1961	10,000,000	—	0.10	0.20	0.65	—
1961 Proof	—	Value: 125				

KM# 6 CENT **Composition:** Bronze

Date	Mintage	F	VF	XF	Unc	BU
1962	—	—	—	0.15	0.40	—
1962 Proof	Est. 25	Value: 125				

KM# 1 5 CENTS **Composition:** Copper-Nickel

Date	Mintage	F	VF	XF	Unc	BU
1953	20,000,000	—	0.25	0.50	1.75	—
1953 Proof	—	Value: 200				
1957	10,000,000	—	0.50	0.75	2.25	—
1957 Proof	—	—	—	—	—	—
1957H	10,000,000	—	0.50	0.75	2.25	—
1957KN	Inc. above	—	1.25	1.75	3.50	—
1958	10,000,000	—	0.25	0.50	1.75	—
1958 Proof	—	Value: 200				
1958H	10,000,000	—	0.50	0.75	2.25	—
1961	90,000,000	—	0.15	0.50	1.50	—
1961 Proof	—	—	—	—	—	—
1961H	5,000,000	—	2.00	4.00	10.00	—
1961KN	Inc. above	—	0.50	1.00	2.75	—

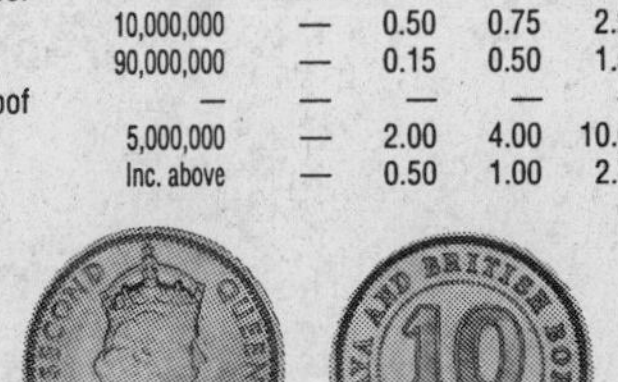

KM# 2 10 CENTS **Composition:** Copper-Nickel

Date	Mintage	F	VF	XF	Unc	BU
1953	20,000,000	—	0.40	0.80	2.25	—
1953 Proof	—	Value: 200				
1956	10,000,000	—	0.40	1.00	2.75	—
1956 Proof	—	Value: 200				
1957H	10,000,000	—	0.40	1.25	3.50	—
1957H Proof	—	Value: 200				
1957KN	10,000,000	—	0.40	1.25	3.50	—
1958	10,000,000	—	0.40	0.80	2.25	—
1958 Proof	—	Value: 200				
1960	10,000,000	—	0.40	0.80	2.25	—
1960 Proof	—	Value: 200				
1961	60,784,000	—	0.20	0.50	1.25	—
1961 Proof	—	Value: 200				
1961H	69,220,000	—	0.20	0.50	1.25	—
1961KN	Inc. above	—	0.50	1.00	3.00	—

KM# 3 20 CENTS **Composition:** Copper-Nickel

Date	Mintage	F	VF	XF	Unc	BU
1954	10,000,000	—	0.80	1.50	3.00	—
1954 Proof	—	Value: 220				
1956	5,000,000	—	0.75	1.25	3.00	—
1956 Proof	—	Value: 220				
1957H	2,500,000	—	1.20	2.00	4.00	—
1957KN	2,500,000	—	1.20	2.00	5.00	—
1961	32,000,000	—	0.50	0.75	2.50	—
1961 Proof	—	Value: 200				
1961H	23,000,000	—	0.75	1.25	2.75	—

KM# 4.1 50 CENTS **Composition:** Copper-Nickel **Edge:** Security

Date	Mintage	F	VF	XF	Unc	BU
1954	8,000,000	—	1.00	2.00	5.00	—
1954 Proof	—	Value: 280				
1955H	4,000,000	—	1.50	2.50	6.00	—
1956	3,440,000	—	1.50	2.25	6.00	—
1956 Proof	—	Value: 280				
1957H	2,000,000	—	1.50	2.50	6.00	—
1957KN	2,000,000	—	2.00	2.75	7.00	—
1958H	4,000,000	—	1.00	1.50	6.00	—
1961	17,000,000	—	1.00	1.50	4.00	—
1961 Proof	—	Value: 280				
1961H	4,000,000	—	1.50	2.50	6.00	—

KM# 4.2 50 CENTS **Composition:** Copper-Nickel **Note:** Error, without security edge.

Date	F	VF	XF	Unc	BU
1954	—	90.00	120	300	—
1957KN	—	90.00	120	300	—
1958H	—	90.00	120	300	—
1961	—	90.00	120	300	—
1961H	—	90.00	120	300	—

MALAY PENINSULA

KELANTAN

A state in northern Malaysia, colonized by the Javanese in 1300's. It was subject to Thailand from 1780 to 1909.

TITLES

كلنتن

Kelantan

خليفة المؤمنين

Khalifa(t) Al-Mu'minin

SULTANS
Muhammed IV, 1902-1919

STATE

STANDARD COINAGE

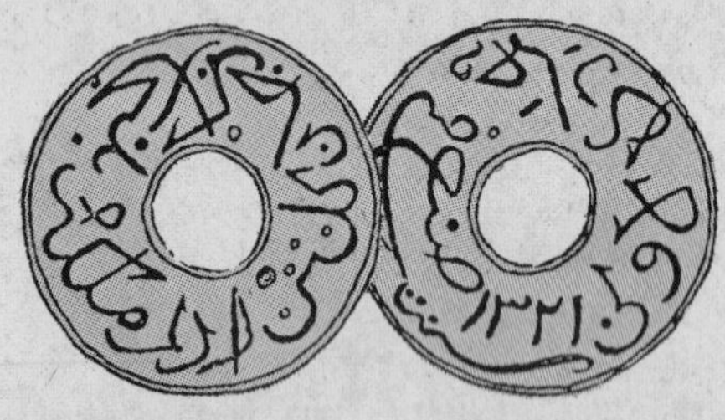

KM# 12 PITIS **Composition:** Tin **Obverse:** Arabic legend **Obv. Legend:** Belanjaan Negri Kelantan Adama Mulkahu **Reverse:** Arabic legend **Rev. Legend:** Duriba Fi Dhul Hijja Sanat 1321 **Size:** 24-29 mm.

Date	F	VF	XF	Unc	BU
AH1321 (1903)	12.00	20.00	30.00	—	—

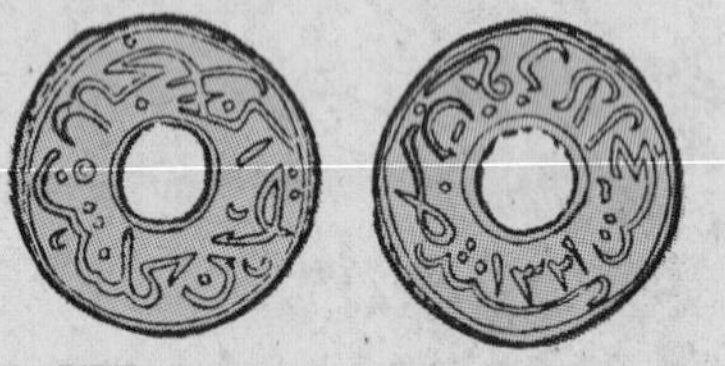

KM# 15 PITIS **Composition:** Tin **Obverse:** Arabic legend **Obv. Legend:** Belanjaan Kerajaan Kelan Tan **Reverse:** Arabic legend **Rev. Legend:** Duriba Fi Dhul Hijja Sanat 1321

Date	F	VF	XF	Unc	BU
AH1321 (1903)	3.00	5.00	9.00	—	—

KM# 18 KEPING **Composition:** Tin **Obverse:** Arabic legend **Obv. Legend:** Negri Kelantan Satu Keping **Reverse:** Uninscribed, but obverse legend shows through in negative form

Date	F	VF	XF	Unc	BU
AH1323 (1905)	25.00	40.00	60.00	—	—

KM# 20 10 KEPINGS **Composition:** Tin **Obverse:** Arabic legend **Obv. Legend:** Belanjaan Kerajaan Kelantin Sepuloh Keping **Reverse:** Border of diamonds around Arabic legend **Rev. Legend:** Sunia Fi Dhul Hijja Sanat 1321

Date	F	VF	XF	Unc	BU
AH1321 (1903)	12.00	25.00	40.00	—	—

TRENGGANU

A state in eastern Malaysia on the shore of the south China Sea. Area of dispute between Malacca and Thailand with the latter emerging with possession. Trengganu became a British dependency in 1909.

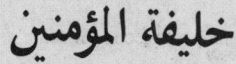

TITLES

ترغكانو

Khalifa(t) al-Mu'minin

خليفة المؤمنين

Trengganu

SULTANS
Zainal Abidin III, 1881-1918
Muhammed, 1918-1920
Sulaiman, 1920-1942

STATE

STANDARD COINAGE

KM# 17 1/4 CENT **Composition:** Tin **Ruler:** Zainal Abidin III **Note:** Similar to 1/2 Cent, KM#16.

Date	F	VF	XF	Unc	BU
AH1325 (1907) Rare	—	—	—	—	—

KM# 16 1/2 CENT **Composition:** Tin **Ruler:** Zainal Abidin III **Note:** Recast.

Date	F	VF	XF	Unc	BU
AH1322 (1904)	—	—	16.50	—	—

KM# 18 1/2 CENT **Composition:** Tin **Ruler:** Zainal Abidin III **Note:** Recast. Originals are rare.

Date	F	VF	XF	Unc	BU
AH1325 (1907)	—	—	16.50	—	—

KM# 19 CENT **Composition:** Tin **Ruler:** Zainal Abidin III

Date	F	VF	XF	Unc	BU
AH1325 (1907)	9.00	16.00	35.00	—	—

KM# 20 CENT **Composition:** Tin **Ruler:** Zainal Abidin III **Note:** Although dated AH1325 (1907), this coin was actually struck in 1920 under Sultan Sulaiman. Authorized mintage was 1 million. Beware of thin lead counterfeits.

Date	F	VF	XF	Unc	BU
AH1325 (1907)	9.00	16.00	35.00	—	—

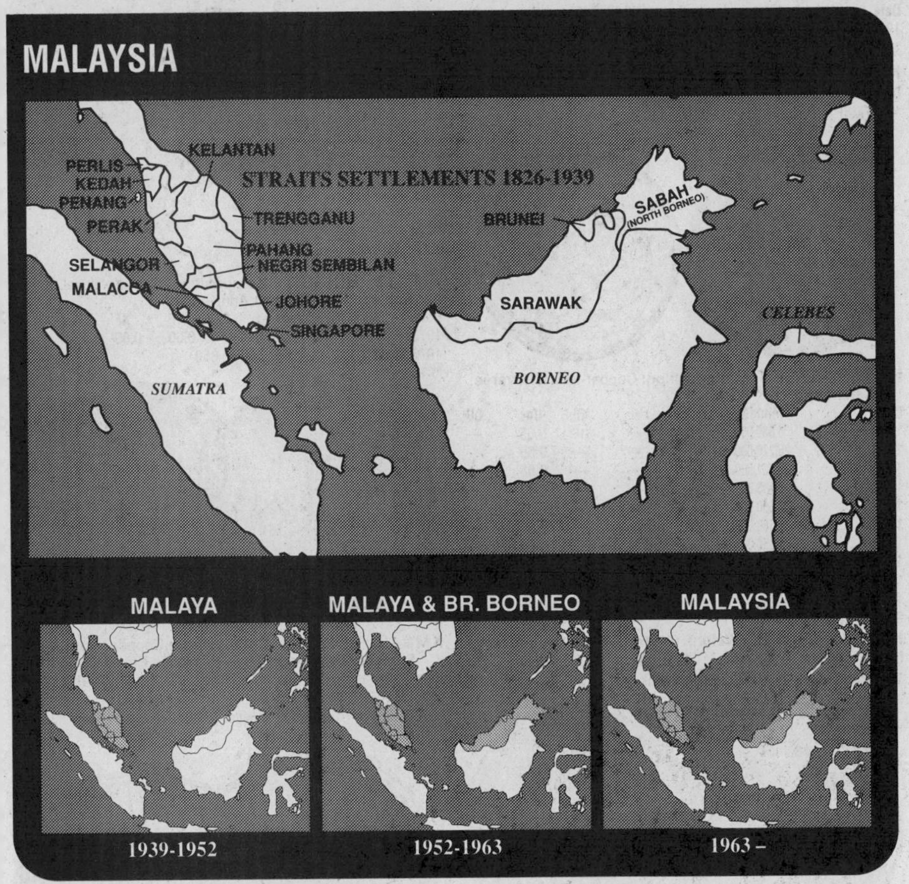

The independent limited constitutional monarchy of Malaysia, which occupies the southern part of the Malay Peninsula in Southeast Asia and the northern part of the island of Borneo, has an area of 127,316 sq. mi. (329,750 sq. km.) and a population of 15.4 million. Capital: Kuala Lumpur. The economy is based on agriculture, mining and forestry. Rubber, tin, timber and palm oil are exported.

Malaysia came into being on Sept. 16, 1963, as a federation of Malaya (Johore, Kelantan, Kedah, Perlis, Trengganu, Negri-Sembilan, Pahang, Perak, Selangor, Penang, Malacca), Singapore, Sabah (British North Borneo) and Sarawak. Following two serious racial riots involving Malays and Chinese, Singapore withdrew from the federation on Aug. 9, 1965. Malaysia is a member of the Commonwealth of Nations.

MINT MARKS

FM - Franklin Mint, U.S.A.

***NOTE:** From 1975-1985 the Franklin Mint produced coinage in up to 3 different qualities. Qualities of issue are designated in ( ) after each date and are defined as follows:

(M) MATTE - Normal circulation strike or a dull finish produced by sandblasting special uncirculated (polish finish) or proof quality dies.

(U) SPECIAL UNCIRCULATED - Polished or prooflike in appearance without any frosted features.

(P) PROOF - The highest quality obtainable having mirror-like fields and frosted features.

MONETARY SYSTEM

100 Sen = 1 Ringgit (Dollar)

CONSTITUTIONAL MONARCHY

STANDARD COINAGE

100 Sen = 1 Ringgit (Dollar)

KM# 1 SEN Composition: Bronze **Reverse:** Parliament building **Note:** Varieties exist.

Date	Mintage	F	VF	XF	Unc	BU
1967	45,000,000	—	—	0.10	0.15	—
1967	500	Value: 5.00				
1968	10,500,000	—	—	0.10	0.15	—
1970	2,535,000	—	0.15	0.50	1.50	—
1971	47,862,000	—	—	0.10	0.15	—
1973	21,400,000	—	—	0.10	0.15	—
1976	100	—	25.00	65.00	125	—
1980FM (P)	5,000	Value: 1.00				
1981FM (P)	6,628	Value: 1.00				

KM# 1a SEN Composition: Copper-Clad Steel

Date	Mintage	F	VF	XF	Unc	BU
1973	Inc. above	—	0.15	0.45	0.65	—
1976	27,406,000	—	—	0.10	0.15	—
1977	21,751,000	—	—	0.10	0.15	—
1978	30,844,000	—	—	0.10	0.15	—
1979	15,714,000	—	—	0.10	0.15	—
1980	16,152,000	—	—	0.10	0.15	—
1981	24,633,000	—	—	0.10	0.15	—
1982	37,295,000	—	—	0.10	0.15	—
1983	19,333,000	—	—	0.10	0.15	—
1984	26,267,000	—	—	0.10	0.15	—
1985	52,402,000	—	—	0.10	0.15	—
1986	48,920,000	—	—	0.10	0.15	—
1987	35,284,000	—	—	0.10	0.15	—
1988	56,749,000	—	—	0.10	0.15	—

KM# 49 SEN Composition: Bronze Clad Steel **Reverse:** Drum

Date	Mintage	F	VF	XF	Unc	BU
1989	28,429,000	—	—	—	0.15	—
1990	102,539,000	—	—	—	0.15	—
1991	100,315,000	—	—	—	0.15	—
1992	122,824,000	—	—	—	0.15	—
1993	153,806,000	—	—	—	0.15	—
1994	185,085,000	—	—	—	0.15	—
1995	208,611,000	—	—	—	0.15	—
1996	—	—	—	—	0.15	—
1997	—	—	—	—	0.15	—
1998	—	—	—	—	0.15	—
1999	—	—	—	—	0.15	—
2000	—	—	—	—	0.15	—

KM# 49a SEN Weight: 0.9250 g. **Composition:** Silver

Date		F	VF	XF	Unc	BU
1992 Proof	—	Value: 15.00				

KM# 2 5 SEN Composition: Copper-Nickel **Note:** Varieties exist.

Date	Mintage	F	VF	XF	Unc	BU
1967	75,464,000	—	—	0.10	0.20	—
1967 Proof	500	Value: 20.00				
1968	74,536,000	—	—	0.10	0.20	—
1971	16,658,000	—	—	0.30	0.50	—
1973	102,942,000	—	—	0.10	0.15	—
1976	65,659,000	—	—	0.10	0.15	—
1977	10,609,000	—	—	0.30	0.50	—
1978	50,044,000	—	—	0.10	0.15	—
1979	38,824,000	—	—	0.10	0.15	—
1980	33,893,000	—	—	0.10	0.15	—
1980FM (P)	6,628	Value: 2.00				
1981	51,490,000	—	—	0.10	0.15	—
1981FM (P)	—	Value: 2.50				
1982	118,594,000	—	—	0.10	0.15	—
1985	15,553,000	—	—	0.10	0.15	—
1987	17,723,000	—	—	0.10	0.15	—
1988	26,788,000	—	—	0.10	0.15	—

KM# 50 5 SEN Composition: Copper-Nickel **Reverse:** Top with string

Date	Mintage	F	VF	XF	Unc	BU
1989	20,484,000	—	—	—	0.15	—
1990	58,909,000	—	—	—	0.15	—
1991	46,092,000	—	—	—	0.15	—
1992	67,844,000	—	—	—	0.15	—
1993	70,703,000	—	—	—	0.15	—
1994	83,026,000	—	—	—	0.15	—
1995	53,069,000	—	—	—	0.15	—
1996	—	—	—	—	0.15	—
1997	—	—	—	—	0.15	—
1998	—	—	—	—	0.15	—
1999	—	—	—	—	0.15	—
2001	—	—	—	—	0.15	—

KM# 50a 5 SEN Weight: 0.9250 g. **Composition:** Silver

Date		F	VF	XF	Unc	BU
1992 Proof	—	Value: 15.00				

KM# 3 10 SEN Composition: Copper-Nickel **Note:** Varieties exist.

Date	Mintage	F	VF	XF	Unc	BU
1967	106,708,000	—	0.10	0.15	0.30	—
1967 Proof	500	Value: 25.00				
1968	128,292,000	—	0.10	0.15	0.30	—
1971	42,000	—	35.00	45.00	65.00	—
1973	214,832,000	—	0.10	0.15	0.30	—
1976	148,841,000	—	0.10	0.15	0.30	—
1977	52,720,000	—	0.10	0.15	0.30	—
1978	21,162,000	—	0.10	0.15	0.30	—
1979	50,633,000	—	0.10	0.15	0.30	—
1980	51,797,000	—	0.10	0.15	0.30	—
1980FM (P)	6,628	Value: 3.00				
1981	236,639,000	—	0.10	0.15	0.30	—
1981FM (P)	—	Value: 3.50				
1982	145,639,000	—	—	0.10	0.25	—
1983	30,832,000	—	—	0.10	0.25	—
1988	17,852,000	—	—	0.10	0.25	—

KM# 51 10 SEN Composition: Copper-Nickel **Reverse:** Ceremonial table

Date	Mintage	F	VF	XF	Unc	BU
1989	32,392,000	—	—	—	0.25	—
1990	132,982,000	—	—	—	0.25	—
1991	133,293,000	—	—	—	0.25	—
1992	89,919,000	—	—	—	0.25	—
1993	44,224,000	—	—	—	0.25	—
1994	7,122,000	—	—	—	0.25	—
1995	82,217,000	—	—	—	0.25	—
1996	—	—	—	—	0.25	—
1997	—	—	—	—	0.25	—
1998	—	—	—	—	0.25	—
1999	—	—	—	—	0.25	—
2000	—	—	—	—	0.25	—

KM# 51a 10 SEN Weight: 0.9250 g. **Composition:** Silver

Date		F	VF	XF	Unc	BU
1992 Proof	—	Value: 15.00				

KM# 4 20 SEN **Composition:** Copper-Nickel **Note:** Varieties exist.

Date	Mintage	F	VF	XF	Unc	BU
1967	49,560,000	—	0.10	0.30	0.45	—
1967 Proof	500	Value: 35.00				
1968	40,440,000	—	0.10	0.30	0.45	—
1969	15,000,000	—	0.15	0.35	0.50	—
1970	1,054,000	—	0.50	0.75	1.00	—
1971	9,958,000	—	0.15	0.35	0.50	—
1973	116,075,000	—	0.10	0.20	0.35	—
1976	47,396,000	—	0.10	0.20	0.35	—
1977	66,139,000	—	0.10	0.20	0.35	—
1978	6,847,000	—	0.15	0.30	0.45	—
1979	17,346,000	—	0.10	0.20	0.35	—
1980	32,837,000	—	0.10	0.20	0.35	—
1980FM (P)	6,628	Value: 4.00				
1981	144,128,000	—	0.10	0.20	0.35	—
1981FM (P)	—	Value: 4.50				
1982	97,905,000	—	—	0.10	0.25	—
1983	8,105,000	—	—	0.10	0.25	—
1987	26,225,000	—	—	0.10	0.25	—
1988	67,218,000	—	—	0.10	0.25	—

KM# 52 20 SEN **Composition:** Copper-Nickel **Reverse:** Basket containing food and utensils

Date	Mintage	F	VF	XF	Unc	BU
1989	28,945,000	—	—	—	0.35	—
1990	56,249,000	—	—	—	0.35	—
1991	82,774,000	—	—	—	0.35	—
1992	48,975,000	—	—	—	0.35	—
1993	55,753,000	—	—	—	0.35	—
1994	2,680,000	—	—	—	0.35	—
1997	—	—	—	—	0.35	—
1998	—	—	—	—	0.35	—
2000	—	—	—	—	0.35	—

KM# 52a 20 SEN **Weight:** 0.9250 g. **Composition:** Silver And Enamel

Date	F	VF	XF	Unc	BU
1992 Proof	—	Value: 17.50			

KM# 5.1 50 SEN **Composition:** Copper-Nickel

Date	Mintage	F	VF	XF	Unc	BU
1967	15,000,000	—	0.25	0.50	1.00	—
1967 Proof	500	Value: 45.00				
1968	12,000,000	—	0.25	0.50	1.00	—
1969	2,000,000	—	0.50	0.75	1.50	—

KM# 5.2 50 SEN **Composition:** Copper-Nickel **Note:** Error with security edge.

Date	F	VF	XF	Unc	BU
1967	—	75.00	140	240	—
1968	—	75.00	140	240	—
1969	—	250	350	550	—

KM# 5.3 50 SEN **Composition:** Copper-Nickel **Edge:** Lettered

Date	Mintage	F	VF	XF	Unc	BU
1971	8,404,000	—	0.30	0.60	1.00	—
1973	50,135,000	—	0.25	0.50	0.75	—
1976	—	—	0.25	0.40	0.60	—
1977	17,720,000	—	0.25	0.40	0.60	—
1978	11,033,000	—	0.25	0.40	0.60	—
1979	5,361,000	—	0.25	0.40	0.60	—
1980	15,911,000	—	0.25	0.40	0.60	—
1980FM Proof	6,628	Value: 4.50				
1981	22,969,000	—	—	0.25	0.50	—
1982	20,585,000	—	—	0.25	0.50	—
1983	11,560,000	—	—	0.25	0.50	—
1984	10,139,000	—	—	0.25	0.50	—
1985	7,115,000	—	—	0.25	0.50	—
1986	8,193,000	—	—	0.25	0.50	—
1987	7,696,000	—	—	0.25	0.50	—
1988	26,788,000	—	—	0.25	0.50	—

KM# 5.4 50 SEN **Composition:** Copper-Nickel **Edge:** Plain

Date	F	VF	XF	Unc	BU
1981FM (P)	—	Value: 8.00			

KM# 53 50 SEN **Composition:** Copper-Nickel **Reverse:** Ceremonial kite

Date	Mintage	F	VF	XF	Unc	BU
1989	6,639,000	—	—	—	0.65	—
1990	26,276,000	—	—	—	0.65	—
1991	20,721,000	—	—	—	0.65	—
1992	15,135,000	—	—	—	0.65	—
1993	7,656,000	—	—	—	0.65	—
1994	6,566,000	—	—	—	0.65	—
1995	1,650,000	—	—	—	0.65	—
1996	—	—	—	—	0.65	—
1997	—	—	—	—	0.65	—
1998	—	—	—	—	0.65	—
2000	—	—	—	—	0.65	—

KM# 53a 50 SEN **Weight:** 0.9250 g. **Composition:** Silver

Date	F	VF	XF	Unc	BU
1992 Proof	—	Value: 20.00			

KM# 7 RINGGIT **Composition:** Copper-Nickel **Subject:** 10th Anniversary - Bank Negara

Date	Mintage	F	VF	XF	Unc	BU
ND(1969)	1,000,000	—	1.00	1.50	2.75	—

KM# 7a RINGGIT **Weight:** 17.0000 g. **Composition:** 0.9250 Silver .5055 oz. ASW

Date	Mintage	F	VF	XF	Unc	BU
ND(1969) Proof	1,000	Value: 275				

KM# 9.1 RINGGIT **Composition:** Copper-Nickel

Date	Mintage	F	VF	XF	Unc	BU
1971	2,000,000	—	0.50	0.75	1.50	—
1971 Proof	500	Value: 800				
1980	472,000	—	0.60	0.85	1.65	—
1980FM (P)	6,628	Value: 8.00				
1981	765,000	—	0.60	0.85	1.65	—
1982	202,000	—	0.60	0.85	1.65	—
1984	355,000	—	0.60	0.85	1.65	—
1985	302,000	—	0.60	0.85	1.65	—
1986	253,000	—	0.60	0.85	1.65	—
1987	177,000	—	0.60	0.85	1.65	—

KM# 9.2 RINGGIT **Composition:** Copper-Nickel **Edge:** Plain

Date	F	VF	XF	Unc	BU
1981FM (P)	—	Value: 16.00			

KM# 12 RINGGIT **Composition:** Copper-Nickel **Subject:** Kuala Lumpur Anniversary

Date	Mintage	F	VF	XF	Unc	BU
1972	500,000	—	0.60	0.85	2.50	—
1972 Proof	500	Value: 350				

KM# 13 RINGGIT **Composition:** Copper-Nickel **Subject:** 25th Anniversary - Employee Provident Fund

Date	Mintage	F	VF	XF	Unc	BU
1976FM (U)	500,000	—	0.60	0.85	2.50	—
1976FM (P)	7,810	Value: 18.00				

KM# 16 RINGGIT **Composition:** Copper-Nickel **Subject:** 3rd Malaysian 5-Year Plan

Date	Mintage	F	VF	XF	Unc	BU
ND(1976)	1,000,000	—	0.60	0.75	2.00	—
ND(1976)FM (P)	17,000	Value: 12.00				

KM# 22 RINGGIT **Composition:** Copper-Nickel **Subject:** 9th Southeast Asian Games

Date	Mintage	F	VF	XF	Unc	BU
1977	1,000,000	—	0.60	0.75	2.00	—
1977FM (P)	11,000	Value: 17.50				

KM# 25 RINGGIT **Composition:** Copper-Nickel **Subject:** 20th Anniversary of Independence

Date	Mintage	F	VF	XF	Unc	BU
ND(1977)	500,000	—	0.60	0.75	2.00	—
ND(1977)FM (P)	3,100	Value: 35.00				

KM# 26 RINGGIT Composition: Copper-Nickel
Subject: 100th Anniversary of Natural Rubber Production

Date	Mintage	F	VF	XF	Unc	BU
ND(1977)	500,000	—	0.60	0.75	2.00	—

KM# 27 RINGGIT Composition: Copper-Nickel
Subject: 20th Anniversary of Bank Negara

Date	Mintage	F	VF	XF	Unc	BU
ND(1979)	300,000	—	0.60	0.75	2.00	—

KM# 27a RINGGIT Weight: 17.0000 g. **Composition:** 0.9250 Silver .5055 oz. ASW

Date	Mintage	F	VF	XF	Unc	BU
ND(1979)	8,000	Value: 16.00				
ND(1979)FM (P)	6,628	Value: 25.00				

KM# 28 RINGGIT Composition: Copper-Nickel
Subject: 15th Centrury of Hejira

Date	Mintage	F	VF	XF	Unc	BU
AH1401(1981)	500,000	—	0.60	0.75	2.00	—

KM# 29 RINGGIT Composition: Copper-Nickel
Subject: 4th Malaysian Plan **Note:** Tun Hussein Onn

Date	Mintage	F	VF	XF	Unc	BU
ND(1981)	1,000,000	—	0.50	0.65	1.85	—
ND(1981) Proof	10,000	Value: 15.00				

KM# 32 RINGGIT Composition: Copper-Nickel
Subject: 25th Anniversary of Independence

Date	Mintage	F	VF	XF	Unc	BU
ND(1982)	1,500,000	—	0.50	0.65	1.85	—
ND(1982) Proof	15,000	Value: 12.00				

KM# 36 RINGGIT Composition: Copper-Nickel
Subject: 5th Malaysian 5-Year Plan

Date	Mintage	F	VF	XF	Unc	BU
ND(1986)	1,000,000	—	0.50	0.65	1.85	—
ND(1986) Proof	8,000	Value: 10.00				

KM# 39 RINGGIT Composition: Copper-Nickel
Subject: 35th Annual PATA Conference

Date	Mintage	F	VF	XF	Unc	BU
ND(1986)	500,000	—	0.50	1.50	5.00	—

KM# 39a RINGGIT Weight: 16.8500 g. **Composition:** 0.5000 Silver .2709 oz. ASW

Date	Mintage	F	VF	XF	Unc	BU
ND(1986) Proof	11,000	Value: 10.00				

KM# 43 RINGGIT Composition: Copper-Zinc **Subject:** 30th Anniversary of Independence

Date	Mintage	F	VF	XF	Unc	BU
ND(1987)	1,000,000	—	—	0.60	1.75	—
ND(1987) Proof	20,000	Value: 10.00				

KM# 54 RINGGIT Composition: Aluminum-Bronze
Reverse: Native dagger and scabbard

Date	Mintage	F	VF	XF	Unc	BU
1989	20,410,000	—	—	—	1.75	—
1990	80,102,000	—	—	—	1.75	—
1991	169,001,000	—	—	—	1.75	—
1992	139,042,000	—	—	—	1.75	—
1993	178,894,000	—	—	—	1.75	—

KM# 54a RINGGIT Composition: 0.9250 Silver

Date	Mintage	F	VF	XF	Unc	BU
1992 Proof	—	Value: 20.00				

KM# 64 RINGGIT Composition: Aluminum-Bronze
Obverse: Denomination spelled out

Date	Mintage	F	VF	XF	Unc	BU
1993	Inc. above	—	—	—	2.00	—
1994	36,899,000	—	—	—	1.75	—
1995	132,173,000	—	—	—	1.75	—
1996	—	—	—	—	1.75	—

KM# 65 RINGGIT Ring Composition: Nickel-Brass**Center Weight:** 8.1500 g. **Center Composition:** Copper-Nickel **Subject:** Thomas-Uber Cup **Obverse:** City view **Reverse:** Two-handled cup on radiant background **Edge:** Reeded **Size:** 26.5 mm.

Date	Mintage	F	VF	XF	Unc	BU
2000	2,000	—	—	—	7.00	—

KM# 71 RINGGIT Weight: 16.8000 g. **Composition:** Copper Nickel **Subject:** XXI SEA Games **Obverse:** Games logo **Reverse:** Cartoon mascot **Edge:** Reeded **Size:** 33.7 mm.

Date	Mintage	F	VF	XF	Unc	BU
2001	200,000	—	—	—	2.00	—

KM# 74 (KM72) RINGGIT Weight: 16.8000 g. **Composition:** Copper Nickel **Subject:** Coronation of Agong XII **Obverse:** King's portrait **Reverse:** National arms **Edge:** Reeded **Size:** 33.7 mm.

Date		F	VF	XF	Unc	BU
ND(2002)		—	—	—	2.00	—
ND(2002)		—	—	—	2.00	—

KM# 10 5 RINGGIT Composition: Copper-Nickel

Date	Mintage	F	VF	XF	Unc	BU
1971	2,000,000	—	2.50	3.00	5.00	—
1971 Proof	500	Value: 850				

KM# 40 5 RINGGIT Weight: 29.0300 g. **Composition:** 0.5000 Silver .4662 oz. ASW **Subject:** PATA Conference

Date	Mintage	F	VF	XF	Unc	BU
ND(1986) Proof	11,000	Value: 27.50				

KM# 47 5 RINGGIT Composition: Copper Plated Zinc
Subject: 15th Southeast Asian Games

Date	Mintage	F	VF	XF	Unc	BU
1989	500,000	—	—	—	6.00	—
1989 Proof	50,000	Value: 12.50				

KM# 55 5 RINGGIT **Composition:** Copper Plated Zinc **Subject:** Commonwealth Heads of State Meeting

Date	Mintage	F	VF	XF	Unc	BU
1989	150,000	—	—	—	6.00	—
1989 Proof	8,000	Value: 12.50				

KM# 59 5 RINGGIT **Composition:** Copper Plated Zinc **Subject:** 100th Anniversary of Kuala Lumpur

Date	Mintage	F	VF	XF	Unc	BU
ND(1990)	100,000	—	—	—	6.00	—

KM# 61 5 RINGGIT **Composition:** Copper-Zinc-Tin **Series:** World Wildlife Fund **Reverse:** Stylized Milky Stork

Date	Mintage	F	VF	XF	Unc	BU
ND(1992)	—	—	—	—	6.00	—
ND(1992) Proof	3,000	Value: 15.00				

KM# 17 10 RINGGIT **Weight:** 10.8200 g. **Composition:** 0.9250 Silver .3218 oz. ASW **Subject:** 3rd Malaysian 5-Year Plan **Shape:** 14-sided.

Date	Mintage	F	VF	XF	Unc	BU
ND(1976)FM (U)	200,000	—	—	—	7.00	—
ND(1980)FM (P)	6,628	Value: 20.00				
ND(1976)FM (P)	10,000	Value: 12.50				

KM# 44 10 RINGGIT **Weight:** 10.8200 g. **Composition:** 0.5000 Silver .1740 oz. ASW **Subject:** 30th Anniversary of Independence

Date	Mintage	F	VF	XF	Unc	BU
ND(1987)	50,000	—	—	—	10.00	—
ND(1987) Proof	10,000	Value: 20.00				

KM# 57 10 RINGGIT **Weight:** 13.6000 g. **Composition:** 0.9250 Silver .4045 oz. ASW **Subject:** Proclamation of Melaka as a Historical City

Date	Mintage	F	VF	XF	Unc	BU
1989 Proof	20,000	Value: 27.00				

KM# 72 10 RINGGIT **Weight:** 21.7000 g. **Composition:** 0.9250 Silver 0.6453 oz. ASW **Subject:** XXI SEA Games **Obverse:** Games logo **Reverse:** Cartoon mascot **Edge:** Reeded **Size:** 35.7 mm.

Date	Mintage	F	VF	XF	Unc	BU
2001 Proof	3,000	Value: 45.00				

KM# 75 (KM775) 10 RINGGIT **Weight:** 21.7000 g. **Composition:** 0.9250 Silver 0.6453 oz. ASW **Subject:** Coronation of Agong XII **Obverse:** King's portrait **Reverse:** National arms **Edge:** Reeded **Size:** 35.7 mm.

Date		F	VF	XF	Unc	BU
ND(2002) Proof	—	Value: 45.00				
ND(2002) Proof	—	Value: 45.00				

KM# 19 15 RINGGIT **Weight:** 28.2800 g. **Composition:** 0.9250 Silver .8411 oz. ASW **Series:** Conservation **Reverse:** Maylasian Gaur

Date	Mintage	F	VF	XF	Unc	BU
1976	40,000	—	—	—	12.50	—
1976 Proof	8,113	Value: 25.00				

KM# 48 15 RINGGIT **Weight:** 16.7300 g. **Composition:** 0.9250 Silver .4986 oz. ASW **Subject:** 15th Southeast Asian Games

Date	Mintage	F	VF	XF	Unc	BU
1989 Prooflike	50,000	—	—	—	—	—
1989 Proof	20,000	Value: 25.00				

KM# 68 15 RINGGIT **Weight:** 17.0000 g. **Composition:** Copper-Nickel **Subject:** First Malaysian Grand Prix **Obverse:** Denomination **Reverse:** Track route above island maps **Edge:** Reeded **Size:** 34 mm.

Date	Mintage	F	VF	XF	Unc	BU
1999 Proof	8,000	Value: 29.00				

KM# 73 100 RINGGIT **Weight:** 8.6000 g. **Composition:** 0.9160 Gold 0.2533 oz. AGW **Subject:** XXI SEA Games **Obverse:** Games logo **Reverse:** Cartoon mascot **Edge:** Reeded **Size:** 22 mm.

Date	Mintage	F	VF	XF	Unc	BU
2001 Proof	500	Value: 250				

KM# 76 100 RINGGIT **Weight:** 8.6000 g. **Composition:** 0.9160 Gold 0.2533 oz. AGW **Subject:** Coronation of Agong XII **Obverse:** King's portrait **Reverse:** National arms **Edge:** Reeded **Size:** 22 mm.

Date		F	VF	XF	Unc	BU
ND(2002) Proof	—	Value: 250				

KM# 30 20 RINGGIT **Weight:** 16.2300 g. **Compositio** 0.5000 Silver .2609 oz. ASW **Subject:** 4th Malaysian 5-Ye Plan **Reverse:** Tun Hussein Onn

Date	Mintage	F	VF	XF	Unc	
ND(1981)FM (U)	100,000	—	—	—	12.50	
ND(1981)FM (P)	5,000	Value: 27.50				

KM# 14 25 RINGGIT **Weight:** 35.0000 g. **Compositio** 0.9250 Silver 1.0409 oz. ASW **Subject:** 25th Anniversary Employee Provident Fund

Date	Mintage	F	VF	XF	Unc	
1976FM (U)	100,000	—	—	—	15.00	
1976FM (P)	7,796	Value: 55.00				

KM# 20 25 RINGGIT **Weight:** 35.0000 g. **Compositior** 0.9250 Silver 1.0409 oz. ASW **Series:** Conservation **Obverse:** Similar to 500 Ringgit, KM#21 **Reverse:** Rhinosceros Hornbill

Date	Mintage	F	VF	XF	Unc	B
1976	40,000	—	—	—	22.50	
1976 Proof	8,008	Value: 32.50				

KM# 23 25 RINGGIT **Weight:** 35.0000 g. **Composition** 0.9250 Silver 1.0409 oz. ASW **Subject:** 9th Southeast Asia Games

Date	Mintage	F	VF	XF	Unc	B
1977FM (U)	100,000	—	—	—	16.50	—
1977FM (P)	5,877	Value: 37.50				
1980FM (P)	5,000	Value: 47.50				

KM# 33 25 RINGGIT **Weight:** 35.0000 g. **Composition:** 0.9250 Silver 1.0409 oz. ASW **Subject:** 25th Anniversary of Independence **Obverse:** Similar to 1 Ringgit, KM#32

Date	Mintage	F	VF	XF	Unc	BU
ND(1982)	154,000	—	—	—	16.50	—
ND(1982) Proof	7,000	Value: 30.00				

KM# 35 25 RINGGIT **Weight:** 35.0000 g. **Composition:** 0.5000 Silver .5627 oz. ASW **Subject:** 25th Anniversary of the National Bank

Date	Mintage	F	VF	XF	Unc	BU
ND(1984)	98,000	—	—	—	16.50	—
ND(1984) Proof	10,000	Value: 30.00				

KM# 41 25 RINGGIT **Weight:** 23.3300 g. **Composition:** 0.9250 Silver .6939 oz. ASW **Subject:** Women's Decade

Date	Mintage	F	VF	XF	Unc	BU
ND(1985) Proof	2,000	Value: 42.50				

KM# 37 25 RINGGIT **Weight:** 35.0000 g. **Composition:** 0.5000 Silver .5627 oz. ASW **Subject:** 5th Malaysian 5-Year Plan

Date	Mintage	F	VF	XF	Unc	BU
ND(1986)	80,000	—	—	—	17.50	—
ND(1986) Proof	5,000	Value: 32.50				

KM# 56 25 RINGGIT **Weight:** 21.9000 g. **Composition:** 0.9250 Silver .6527 oz. ASW **Subject:** Commonwealth Heads of State Meeting

Date	Mintage	F	VF	XF	Unc	BU
1989	30,000	—	—	—	17.50	—
1989 Proof	8,000	Value: 32.50				

KM# 60 25 RINGGIT **Weight:** 21.9000 g. **Composition:** 0.9250 Silver .6527 oz. ASW **Subject:** 100th Anniversary of Kuala Lumpur

Date	Mintage	F	VF	XF	Unc	BU
ND(1990)	25,000	—	—	—	17.50	—
ND(1990) Proof	25,000	Value: 32.50				

KM# 62 25 RINGGIT **Weight:** 21.7700 g. **Composition:** 0.9250 Silver .6474 oz. ASW **Series:** World Wildlife Fund **Subject:** 100th Anniversary of Kuala Lumpur **Reverse:** Reef Fish

Date	Mintage	F	VF	XF	Unc	BU
ND(1992) Proof	Est. 50,000	Value: 32.50				

KM# 69 25 RINGGIT **Weight:** 21.7700 g. **Composition:** 0.9250 Silver 0.6474 oz. ASW **Subject:** First Malaysian Grand Prix **Obverse:** Denomination **Reverse:** Trophy **Edge:** Reeded **Size:** 36.25 mm.

Date	Mintage	F	VF	XF	Unc	BU
1999 Proof	3,000	Value: 50.00				

KM# 46 30 RINGGIT **Weight:** 22.0000 g. **Composition:** 0.9250 Silver .6557 oz. ASW **Subject:** 30th Anniversary of the National Bank

Date	Mintage	F	VF	XF	Unc	BU
1989	47,000	—	—	—	15.00	—
1989 Proof	10,000	Value: 30.00				

KM# 11 100 RINGGIT **Weight:** 18.6600 g. **Composition:** 0.9170 Gold .5502 oz. AGW **Subject:** Prime Minister Abdul Rahman Putra Al-haj

Date	Mintage	F	VF	XF	Unc	BU
1971	100,000	—	—	—	320	—
1971 Proof	500	Value: 900				

KM# 18 200 RINGGIT **Weight:** 7.3000 g. **Composition:** 0.9000 Gold .2212 oz. AGW **Subject:** 3rd Malaysian 5-Year Plan **Shape:** 14-sided.

Date	Mintage	F	VF	XF	Unc	BU
1976FM (U)	51,000	—	—	—	75.00	—
1976FM (P)	3,102	Value: 110				

KM# 24 200 RINGGIT **Weight:** 7.2200 g. **Composition:** 0.9000 Gold .2089 oz. AGW **Subject:** 9th Southeast Asian Games

Date	Mintage	F	VF	XF	Unc	BU
1977FM (U)	12,000	—	—	—	90.00	—
1977FM (P)	975	Value: 165				

KM# 15 250 RINGGIT **Weight:** 10.1100 g. **Composition:** 0.9000 Gold .2925 oz. AGW **Subject:** 25th Anniversary - Employee Provident Fund

Date	Mintage	F	VF	XF	Unc	BU
1976FM (U)	30,000	—	—	—	125	—
1976FM (P)	7,706	Value: 165				

KM# 42 250 RINGGIT **Weight:** 8.1000 g. **Composition:** 0.9000 Gold .2344 oz. AGW **Series:** Womens' Decade

Date	Mintage	F	VF	XF	Unc	BU
1985 Proof	1,500	Value: 230				

KM# 45 250 RINGGIT Weight: 7.4300 g. **Composition:** 0.9000 Gold .2144 oz. AGW **Subject:** 30th Anniversary of Independence

Date	Mintage	F	VF	XF	Unc	BU
1987	5,000	—	—	—	125	—
1987 Proof	2,000	Value: 165				

KM# 58 250 RINGGIT Weight: 7.1300 g. **Composition:** 0.9000 Gold .2063 oz. AGW **Subject:** 15th Southeast Asian Games

Date	Mintage	F	VF	XF	Unc	BU
1989 Proof	2,500	Value: 220				

KM# 63 250 RINGGIT Weight: 8.6000 g. **Composition:** 0.9000 Gold .2489 oz. AGW **Series:** World Wildlife Fund **Obverse:** Panda above World Wildlife Fund **Reverse:** Clouded Leopard

Date	Mintage	F	VF	XF	Unc	BU
1992 Proof	Est. 3,000	Value: 265				

KM# 21 500 RINGGIT Weight: 33.4370 g. **Composition:** 0.9000 Gold .9676 oz. AGW **Series:** Conservation **Reverse:** Malayan Tapir

Date	Mintage	F	VF	XF	Unc	BU
1976	2,894	—	—	—	500	—
1976 Proof	508	Value: 650				

KM# 31 500 RINGGIT Weight: 10.2600 g. **Composition:** 0.9000 Gold .2969 oz. AGW **Subject:** 4th Malaysian 5-Year Plan **Reverse:** Tun Hussein Onn

Date	Mintage	F	VF	XF	Unc	BU
ND(1981)FM (U)	20,000	—	—	—	200	—
ND(1981)FM (P)	1,000	Value: 250				

KM# 34 500 RINGGIT Weight: 10.2600 g. **Composition:** 0.9000 Gold .2969 oz. AGW **Subject:** 25th Anniversary of Independence **Obverse:** Arms **Reverse:** President upholding dagger **Note:** Similar to 1 Ringgit, KM#32.

Date	Mintage	F	VF	XF	Unc	BU
1982	20,000	—	—	—	210	—
1982 Proof	1,000	Value: 285				

KM# 38 500 RINGGIT Weight: 10.2600 g. **Composition:** 0.9000 Gold .2969 oz. AGW **Subject:** 5th Malaysian 5-Year Plan

Date	Mintage	F	VF	XF	Unc	BU
ND(1986)	10,000	—	—	—	220	—
ND(1986) Proof	1,000	Value: 325				

KM# 70 500 RINGGIT Weight: 25.0000 g. **Composition:** 0.9990 Gold 0.803 oz. AGW **Subject:** Millennium **Obverse:** National arms and denomination **Reverse:** Globe **Edge:** Reeded **Size:** 35.25 mm.

Date	Mintage	F	VF	XF	Unc	BU
1999 Proof	10,000	Value: 550				

PATTERNS

Including off metal strikes

KM#	Date	Mintage	Identification	Mkt Val
Pn1	SH2602 (1942)	—	20 Cents. Aluminum. Japanese occupation.	2,500
Pn2	SH2602 (1942)	—	20 Cents. Aluminum. Japanese occupation.	2,500

MINT SETS

KM#	Date	Mintage	Identification	Issue Price	Mkt Val
MS1	1967 (5)	10,000	KM#1-5.1	—	10.00
MS2	1973 (5)	2,000	KM#1-4, 5.3	—	2.50
MS3	1980 (6)	2,000	KM#1a, 2-4, 5.3	—	3.50
MS4	1989 (6)	2,000	KM#49-54	—	4.00
MS5	1990 (6)	2,000	KM#49-54	—	4.00

PROOF SETS

KM#	Date	Mintage	Identification	Issue Price	Mkt Val
PS7	1980 (9)	5,000	KM#1-4, 5.3, 9.1, 17, 23, 27a	132	100
PS4	1976 (3)	2,641	KM#16-18	—	135
PS9	1981 (3)	3,000	KM#29-31	—	320
PS1	1967 (5)	500	KM#1-5.1	—	140
PS8	1981 (6)	—	KM#1-4, 5.4, 9.2	—	35.00
PS2	1976 (3)	508	KM#19-21	808	810
PS3	1976 (2)	7,500	KM#19-20	—	60.00
PS5	1976 (3)	1,000	KM#13-15	—	240
PS6	1977 (3)	975	KM#22-24	164	220
PS10	1982 (3)	4,000	KM#32-34	—	325
PS12	1986 (2)	11,000	KM#39a, 40	—	37.50
PS11	1986	2,000	KM#36-38	—	370
PS13	1987 (3)	1,000	KM#43-45	—	200
PS14	1989 (3)	2,500	KM#47, 48, 58	—	260
PS15	1989 (2)	20,000	KM#47-48	—	37.50
PS16	1989 (2)	15,000	KM#55-56	—	45.00
PS17	1992 (6)	5,000	KM#49a-54a	—	100
PS18	1992 (3)	3,000	KM#61-63	—	300

MALDIVE ISLANDS

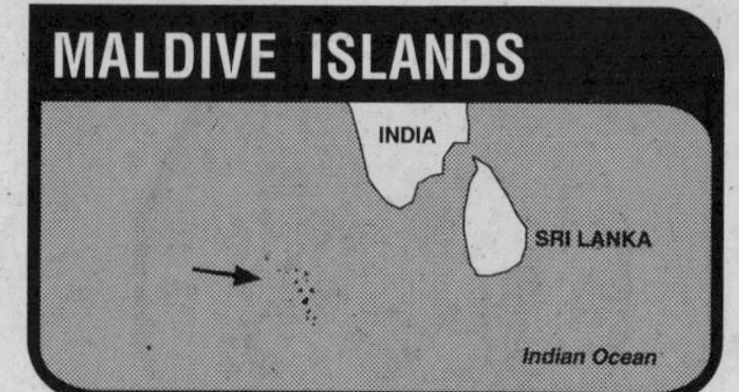

The Republic of Maldives, an archipelago of 2,000 coral isle in the northern Indian Ocean 417 miles (671 km.) west of Ceylo has an area of 116 sq. mi. (298 sq. km.)and a population c 189,000. Capital: Male. Fishing employs 95 % of the male wo force. Dried fish, copra and coir yarn are exported.

The Maldive Islands were visited by Arab traders and cor verted to Islam in 1153. After being harassed in the16th and 17t centuries by Mopla pirates of the Malabar coast and Portugues raiders, the Maldivians voluntarily placed themselves under th suzerainty of Ceylon. In 1887 the islands became an internally sel governing British protectorate and a nominal dependency of Cey lon. Traditionally a sultanate, the Maldives became a republic i 1953 but restored the sultanate in 1954. The Sultanate of th Maldive Islands attained complete internal and external autonom on July 26, 1965, and on Nov. 11,1968, again became a republic The Maldives is a member of the Commonwealth of Nations.

RULERS

Muhammad Imad al-Din V, AH1318-1322/1900-1904AD
Muhammad Shams al-Din III, AH1322-1353/1904-1935AD
Hasan Nur al-Din II, AH1353-1364/1935-1945AD
Abdul-Majid Didi, AH1364-1371/1945-1953AD
First Republic, AH1371-1372/1953-1954AD
Muhammad Farid Didi, AH1372-1388/1954-1968AD
Second Republic, AH1388 to date/1968AD to date*

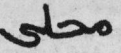

MINTNAME

محلى

Mahle (Male)

MONETARY SYSTEM

100 Lari = 1 Rupee (Rufiyaa)

SULTANATE

STANDARD COINAGE

100 Lari = 1 Rupee (Rufiyaa)

KM# 41 LARIN Weight: 0.9000 g. **Composition:** Bronz **Ruler:** Muhammad Shams al-Din III **Size:** 13 mm. **Note:** Struck at Birmingham, England. Rare mint proof strikes in silver and gold exist.

Date	F	VF	XF	Unc	B
AH1331 (1913)	1.00	1.25	1.75	3.00	–

KM# 39 2 LARIAT Composition: Copper-Brass **Ruler:** Muhammad Imad al-Din V **Size:** 13 mm. **Note:** 1.4-2.2 grams. Previously listed date AH1311 is merely poor die cutting of AH1319. Many die varieties exist.

Date	F	VF	XF	Unc	B
AH1318 (1900)	1.50	3.50	5.00	7.50	–
AH1319 (1901)	1.50	3.50	5.00	7.50	–

KM# 40.1 4 LARIAT Composition: Copper-Brass **Ruler:** Muhammad Imad al-Din V **Edge:** Plain or reeded **Note:** 2.5 4.5 grams. Many die varieties exist; size varies 17 - 18mm.

Date	F	VF	XF	Unc	B
AH1320 (1902)	1.50	2.50	4.50	8.00	–

KM# 40.2 4 LARIAT Composition: Copper-Brass **Ruler:** Muhammad Imad al-Din V **Reverse:** Arabic "Sana(t)" below date **Note:** Silver strikes are most likely presentation pieces; size varies 16.8-18mm.

Date	F	VF	XF	Unc	BU
AH1320 (1902)	3.50	8.00	12.00	16.00	—

KM# 42 4 LARIAT Weight: 3.3000 g. **Composition:** Bronze **Ruler:** Muhammad Shams al-Din III **Size:** 19 mm. **Note:** Struck at Birmingham, England. Rare mint proof strikes in silver and gold exist.

Date	F	VF	XF	Unc	BU
AH1331 (1913)	1.00	1.50	2.75	6.00	—

KM# 43 LAARI Weight: 1.5000 g. **Composition:** Bronze **Ruler:** Muhammad Farid Didi **Size:** 15 mm. **Note:** Similar to Laari, KM#49.

Date	Mintage	F	VF	XF	Unc	BU
AH1379 (1960)	300,000	—	0.15	0.25	0.50	—
AH1379 (1960) Proof	1,270	Value: 3.00				

KM# 44 2 LAARI Weight: 3.1500 g. **Composition:** Bronze **Ruler:** Muhammad Farid Didi **Obverse:** National emblem - crescent moon, star and palm tree flanked by 2 flags. **Note:** 18.2mm square planchet.

Date	Mintage	F	VF	XF	Unc	BU
AH1379 (1960)	600,000	—	0.20	0.35	0.75	—
AH1379 (1960) Proof	1,270	Value: 3.50				

KM# 45 5 LAARI Weight: 2.6000 g. **Composition:** Nickel-Brass **Ruler:** Muhammad Farid Didi **Obverse:** National emblem - crescent moon, star and palm tree flanked by 2 flags. **Size:** 20.4 mm. **Note:** Scalloped flan.

Date	Mintage	F	VF	XF	Unc	BU
AH1379 (1960)	300,000	—	0.25	0.40	0.75	—
AH1379 (1960) Proof	1,270	Value: 4.00				

KM# 46 10 LAARI Weight: 5.2000 g. **Composition:** Nickel-Brass **Ruler:** Muhammad Farid Didi **Obverse:** National emblem - crescent moon, star and palm tree flanked by 2 flags. **Size:** 23 mm. **Note:** Scalloped flan.

Date	Mintage	F	VF	XF	Unc	BU
AH1379 (1960)	600,000	—	0.50	0.75	1.50	—
AH1379 (1960) Proof	1,270	Value: 5.00				

KM# 47.1 25 LAARI Weight: 4.1000 g. **Composition:** Nickel-Brass **Ruler:** Muhammad Farid Didi **Obverse:** National emblem - crescent moon, star and palm tree flanked by 2 flags. **Edge:** Security **Size:** 20.4 mm.

Date	Mintage	F	VF	XF	Unc	BU
AH1379 (1960)	300,000	—	0.60	1.00	1.50	—
AH1379 (1960) Proof	1,270	Value: 6.00				

KM# 47.2 25 LAARI Weight: 4.1000 g. **Composition:** Nickel-Brass **Ruler:** Muhammad Farid Didi **Obverse:** National emblem - crescent moon, star and palm tree flanked by 2 flags. **Edge:** Reeded **Size:** 20.4 mm.

Date	F	VF	XF	Unc	BU
AH1379 (1960)	—	2.00	3.50	6.00	—

KM# 48.1 50 LAARI Weight: 5.6000 g. **Composition:** Nickel-Brass **Ruler:** Muhammad Farid Didi **Obverse:** National emblem - crescent moon, star and palm tree flanked by 2 flags. **Edge:** Security **Size:** 23.5 mm.

Date	Mintage	F	VF	XF	Unc	BU
AH1379 (1960)	300,000	—	1.00	1.75	2.50	—
AH1379 (1960) Proof	1,270	Value: 8.00				

KM# 48.2 50 LAARI Composition: Nickel-Brass **Ruler:** Muhammad Farid Didi **Obverse:** National emblem - crescent moon, star and palm tree flanked by 2 flags. **Edge:** Reeded **Size:** 23.5 mm.

Date	F	VF	XF	Unc	BU
AH1379 (1960)	—	3.00	5.00	8.00	—

STANDARD COINAGE

100 Laari = 1 Rufiyaa

KM# 45b 5 LAARI Composition: Bronze **Ruler:** Muhammad Farid Didi **Obverse:** National emblem - crescent moon, star and palm tree flanked by two flags

Date	F	VF	XF	Unc	BU
AH1379 (1960)	—	0.25	0.40	0.75	—

KM# 46a 10 LAARI Composition: Aluminum **Ruler:** Muhammad Farid Didi **Obverse:** National emblem - crescent moon, star and palm tree flanked by two flags **Size:** 23 mm. **Note:** Similar to 10 Laari, KM#46. Scalloped flan.

Date	F	VF	XF	Unc	BU
AH1399 (1979)	—	—	0.10	0.25	—
AH1399 (1979) Proof	—	Value: 2.50			

REPUBLIC

STANDARD COINAGE

100 Laari = 1 Rufiyaa

KM# 49 LAARI Composition: Aluminum **Obverse:** National emblem - crescent moon, star and palm tree flanked by two flags **Size:** 15 mm.

Date	Mintage	F	VF	XF	Unc	BU
AH1389 (1970)	500,000	—	0.10	0.20	0.40	—
AH1399 (1979)	—	—	0.10	0.20	0.40	—
AH1399 (1979) Proof	100,000	Value: 1.25				

KM# 68 LAARI Composition: Aluminum **Reverse:** Palm tree **Size:** 18.2 mm. **Note:** Square planchet.

Date	Mintage	F	VF	XF	Unc	BU
AH1404 (1984)	—	—	—	0.10	0.15	—
AH1404 (1984) Proof	2,500	Value: 2.50				

KM# 50 2 LAARI Composition: Aluminum **Note:** Similar to 2 Laari, KM#44.

Date	Mintage	F	VF	XF	Unc	BU
AH1389 (1970)	500,000	—	0.15	0.25	0.50	—

KM# 50a 2 LAARI Composition: Aluminum **Size:** 18.2 mm. **Note:** Square planchet.

Date	Mintage	F	VF	XF	Unc	BU
AH1389 (1970)	—	—	—	—	—	—
AH1389 (1970) Proof	—	—	—	—	—	—
AH1399 (1979)	—	—	0.15	0.25	0.50	—
AH1399 (1979) Proof	100,000	Value: 1.25				

KM# 45a 5 LAARI Composition: Aluminum **Obverse:** National emblem - crescent moon, star and palm tree flanked by two flags **Size:** 20.4 mm. **Note:** Similar to 5 Laari, KM#45. Scalloped flan.

Date	Mintage	F	VF	XF	Unc	BU
AH1389 (1970)	300,000	—	0.20	0.30	0.40	—
AH1389 (1970) Proof	—	Value: 3.50				
AH1399 (1979)	—	—	—	0.10	0.20	—
AH1399 (1979) Proof	—	Value: 2.50				

KM# 69 5 LAARI Composition: Aluminum **Reverse:** Two Bonito fish **Size:** 20.4 mm. **Note:** Scalloped flan.

Date	Mintage	F	VF	XF	Unc	BU
AH1404 (1984)	—	—	—	0.10	0.35	—
AH1404 (1984) Proof	2,500	Value: 3.00				
AH1411 (1990)	—	—	—	0.10	0.35	—

KM# 70 10 LAARI Composition: Aluminum **Reverse:** Maldivian sailing ship - Odi **Size:** 23 mm. **Note:** Scalloped flan.

Date	Mintage	F	VF	XF	Unc	BU
AH1404 (1984)	—	—	—	0.10	0.20	—
AH1404 (1984) Proof	2,500	Value: 3.50				

KM# 47.3 25 LAARI Composition: Nickel-Brass **Reverse:** Palm tree **Size:** 20.4 mm. **Note:** Similar to 25 Laari, KM#47.2.

Date	Mintage	F	VF	XF	Unc	BU
AH1399 (1979)	—	—	—	0.10	0.25	—
AH1399 (1979) Proof	100,000	Value: 3.50				

KM# 71 25 LAARI Composition: Nickel-Brass **Reverse:** Mosque **Size:** 20.4 mm.

Date	F	VF	XF	Unc	BU
AH1404 (1984)	—	—	0.15	0.45	—
AH1404 (1984) Proof	—	Value: 4.00			
AH1411 (1990)	—	—	0.15	0.45	—
AH1416 (1995)	—	—	0.15	0.45	—

KM# 48.3 50 LAARI Composition: Nickel-Brass **Reverse:** Palm tree **Size:** 23.5 mm. **Note:** Similar to 50 Laari, KM#48.2.

Date	Mintage	F	VF	XF	Unc	BU
AH1399 (1979)	—	—	0.10	0.20	0.40	—
AH1399 (1979) Proof	100,000	Value: 6.50				

KM# 72 50 LAARI Composition: Nickel-Brass **Reverse:** Loggerhead sea turtle

Date	F	VF	XF	Unc	BU
AH1404 (1984)	—	0.15	0.35	1.50	—
AH1404 (1984) Proof	—	Value: 6.00			
AH1411 (1990)	—	0.15	0.35	1.50	—
AH1415 (1994)	—	0.15	0.35	1.50	—

KM# 73 RUFIYAA Composition: Copper-Nickel Clad Steel **Reverse:** National emblem - crescent moon, star and palm tree flanked by two flags

Date	F	VF	XF	Unc	BU
AH1402 (1982)	—	0.20	0.50	2.00	—

KM# 73a RUFIYAA Composition: Copper-Nickel **Reverse:** National emblem - crescent moon, star and palm tree flanked by two flags

Date	F	VF	XF	Unc	BU
AH1404 (1984)	—	0.20	0.50	2.00	—
AH1404 (1984) Proof	—	Value: 9.00			

Date	F	VF	XF	Unc	BU
AH1411 (1990)	—	0.20	0.50	2.00	—
AH1416 (1995)	—	0.20	0.50	2.00	—

KM# 88 2 RUFIYAA Composition: Brass **Reverse:** Pacific triton sea shell **Edge:** Lettering over reeding **Edge Lettering:** REPUBLIC OF MALDIVES

Date	F	VF	XF	Unc	BU
AH1415 (1995)	—	—	—	6.50	—

KM# 55 5 RUFIYAA Composition: Copper-Nickel **Series:** F.A.O. **Obverse:** National emblem - crescent moon, star and palm tree flanked by two flags **Reverse:** Bonito fish

Date	Mintage	F	VF	XF	Unc	BU
AH1397 (1977)	15,000	—	—	3.50	7.50	—

KM# 57 5 RUFIYAA Composition: Copper-Nickel **Series:** F.A.O. **Obverse:** National emblem - crescent moon, star and palm tree flanked by two flags **Reverse:** Spiny lobster

Date	Mintage	F	VF	XF	Unc	BU
AH1398 (1978)	7,000	—	—	4.00	7.50	—

KM# 57a 5 RUFIYAA Weight: 19.1500 g. **Composition:** 0.9250 Silver .5695 oz. ASW **Series:** F.A.O. **Obverse:** National emblem - crescent moon, star and palm tree flanked by two flags **Reverse:** Spiny lobster

Date	Mintage	F	VF	XF	Unc	BU
AH1398 (1978) Proof	1,887	Value: 25.00				

KM# 57b 5 RUFIYAA Weight: 18.9500 g. **Composition:** 0.9170 Gold .5585 oz. AGW **Series:** F.A.O. **Obverse:** National emblem - crescent moon, star and palm tree flanked by two flags **Reverse:** Spiny lobster

Date	Mintage	F	VF	XF	Unc	BU
AH1398 (1978) Proof	200	Value: 625				

KM# 59 10 RUFIYAA Composition: Copper-Nickel **Series:** F.A.O. **Obverse:** National emblem - crescent moon, star and palm tree flanked by two flags **Reverse:** Woman weaving

Date	F	VF	XF	Unc	BU
AH1399 (1979)	—	—	4.50	10.00	—

KM# 59a 10 RUFIYAA Weight: 25.0000 g. **Composition:** 0.9250 Silver .7435 oz. ASW **Series:** F.A.O. **Obverse:** National emblem - crescent moon, star and palm tree flanked by two flags **Reverse:** Woman weaving

Date	Mintage	F	VF	XF	Unc	BU
AH1399 (1979) Proof	3,000	Value: 16.50				

KM# 62 10 RUFIYAA Composition: Copper-Nickel **Series:** F.A.O. **Obverse:** National emblem - crescent moon, star and palm tree flanked by two flags **Reverse:** Girl making embroidery

Date	F	VF	XF	Unc	BU
AH1400 (1980)	—	—	4.00	9.00	—

KM# 56 20 RUFIYAA Weight: 28.2800 g. **Composition:** 0.5000 Silver .4546 oz. ASW **Series:** F.A.O. **Obverse:** National emblem - crescent moon, star and palm tree flanked by two flags **Reverse:** Bonito and bluefin tuna **Size:** 38.61 mm.

Date	Mintage	F	VF	XF	Unc	BU
AH1397 (1977)	15,000	—	—	—	11.50	—

KM# 61 20 RUFIYAA Weight: 28.2800 g. **Composition:** 0.9250 Silver .8411 oz. ASW **Series:** International Year of the Child **Obverse:** National emblem - crescent moon, star and palm tree flanked by two flags **Reverse:** Three children playing **Size:** 38.61 mm.

Date	Mintage	F	VF	XF	Unc	BU
AH1399 (1979) Proof	12,000	Value: 14.50				

KM# 65 20 RUFIYAA Composition: Copper-Nickel **Subject:** World Fisheries Conference **Obverse:** National emblem - crescent moon, star and palm tree flanked by two flags **Reverse:** Two tuna fish **Size:** 38.61 mm.

Date	Mintage	F	VF	XF	Unc	BU
AH1404 (1984)	100,000	—	—	—	10.00	—

KM# 65a 20 RUFIYAA Weight: 28.2800 g. **Composition:** 0.9250 Silver .8411 oz. ASW **Subject:** World Fisheries Conference **Obverse:** National emblem - crescent moon, star and palm tree flanked by two flags **Reverse:** Two tuna fish **Size:** 38.61 mm.

Date	Mintage	F	VF	XF	Unc	BU
AH1404 (1984) Proof	20,000	Value: 45.00				

KM# 74 20 RUFIYAA Weight: 19.4400 g. **Composition:** 0.9250 Silver .5782 oz. ASW **Series:** Decade for Women **Obverse:** National emblem - crescent moon, star and palm tree flanked by two flags **Reverse:** Woman sewing lace on pillow

Date	Mintage	F	VF	XF	Unc	B
AH1405 (1985) Proof	500	Value: 40.00				

KM# 58 25 RUFIYAA Weight: 28.0500 g. **Composition:** 0.5000 Silver .4509 oz. ASW **Series:** F.A.C **Obverse:** National emblem - crescent moon, star and palr tree flanked by two flags **Reverse:** Sailing ship

Date	Mintage	F	VF	XF	Unc	B
AH1398 (1978)	7,140	—	—	—	22.50	-

KM# 58a 25 RUFIYAA Weight: 28.2800 g. **Composition:** 0.9250 Silver .8411 oz. ASW **Series:** F.A.C **Obverse:** National emblem - crescent moon, star and palr tree flanked by two flags **Reverse:** Sailing ship

Date	Mintage	F	VF	XF	Unc	B
AH1398 (1978) Proof	2,000	Value: 32.50				

KM# 58b 25 RUFIYAA Weight: 28.2500 g. **Composition:** 0.9170 Gold .8326 oz. AGW **Series:** F.A.C **Obverse:** National emblem - crescent moon, star and paln tree flanked by two flags **Reverse:** Sailing ship

Date	Mintage	F	VF	XF	Unc	B
AH1398 (1978) Proof	200	Value: 825				

KM# 95 25 RUFIYAA Composition: Copper-Nickel **Series:** 50th Anniversary - UN **Obverse:** National emblem crescent moon, star and palm tree flanked by two flags **Reverse:** UN building and logo

Date	F	VF	XF	Unc	B
AH1416 (1996)	—	—	—	9.50	-

KM# 89 50 RUFIYAA Weight: 1.2442 g. **Compositior** 0.9999 Gold .04 oz. AGW **Obverse:** National emblem - crescent moon, star and palm tree flanked by two flags **Reverse:** Skylab space station

Date	F	VF	XF	Unc	B
AH1415 (1995)	—	—	—	60.00	-

KM# 90 50 RUFIYAA Weight: 10.0000 g. **Composition:** 0.5000 Silver .1607 oz. ASW **Series:** 1996 Olympics **Obverse:** National emblem - crescent moon, sta and palm tree flanked by two flags **Reverse:** Sailboat

Date	F	VF	XF	Unc	B
AH1416 (1996)	—	—	—	20.00	-

KM# 99 50 RUFIYAA Weight: 31.3000 g. **Composition:** 0.9250 Silver 0.9308 oz. ASW **Subject:** Yea of the Reef **Obverse:** National arms **Reverse:** Multicolor underwater scene **Edge:** Reeded **Size:** 38.5 mm.

Date	F	VF	XF	Unc	B
1998 Proof	—	Value: 50.00			

KM# 60 100 RUFIYAA **Weight:** 28.2800 g. **Composition:** 0.8000 Silver .7274 oz. ASW **Series:** F.A.O. **Obverse:** National emblem - crescent moon, star and palm tree flanked by two flags **Reverse:** Woman making mats

Date	Mintage	F	VF	XF	Unc	BU
AH1399 (1979)	6,000	—	—	—	18.00	—

KM# 60a 100 RUFIYAA **Weight:** 28.2800 g. **Composition:** 0.9250 Silver .8411 oz. ASW **Series:** F.A.O. **Obverse:** National emblem - crescent moon, star and palm tree flanked by two flags **Reverse:** Woman making mats

Date	Mintage	F	VF	XF	Unc	BU
AH1399 (1979) Proof	8,000	Value: 20.00				

KM# 63 100 RUFIYAA **Weight:** 28.2800 g. **Composition:** 0.8000 Silver .7274 oz. ASW **Series:** F.A.O. **Obverse:** National emblem - crescent moon, star and palm tree flanked by two flags **Reverse:** Crown of coconut and palm

Date	Mintage	F	VF	XF	Unc	BU
AH1400 (1980)	6,501	—	—	—	25.00	—

KM# 63a 100 RUFIYAA **Weight:** 28.2800 g. **Composition:** 0.9250 Silver .8411 oz. ASW **Series:** F.A.O. **Obverse:** National emblem - crescent moon, star and palm tree flanked by two flags **Reverse:** Crown of coconut and palm

Date	Mintage	F	VF	XF	Unc	BU
AH1400 (1980) Proof	3,003	Value: 45.00				

KM# 64 100 RUFIYAA **Weight:** 28.2800 g. **Composition:** 0.9250 Silver .8411 oz. ASW **Series:** World Food Day **Obverse:** National emblem - crescent moon, star and palm tree flanked by two flags **Reverse:** 2 women working in a field

Date	Mintage	F	VF	XF	Unc	BU
AH1401 (1981)	10,000	—	—	—	27.50	—
AH1401 (1981) Proof	5,000	Value: 45.00				

KM# 66 100 RUFIYAA **Weight:** 28.2800 g. **Composition:** 0.9250 Silver .8411 oz. ASW **Series:** International Year of Disabled Persons **Obverse:** National emblem - crescent moon, star and palm tree flanked by two flags **Reverse:** Stylized yin and yang symbol **Size:** 38.61 mm.

Date	F	VF	XF	Unc	BU
AH1404 (1984)	—	—	—	25.00	—
AH1404 (1984) Proof	—	Value: 40.00			

KM# 75 100 RUFIYAA **Weight:** 15.9800 g. **Composition:** 0.9170 Gold .4712 oz. AGW **Subject:** Opening of Grand Mosque and Islamic Centre **Obverse:** National emblem - crescent moon, star and palm tree flanked by two flags

Date	Mintage	F	VF	XF	Unc	BU
AH1405 (1984) Proof	100	Value: 600				

KM# 67 100 RUFIYAA **Weight:** 15.9800 g. **Composition:** 0.9170 Gold .4712 oz. AGW **Obverse:** National emblem - crescent moon, star and palm tree flanked by two flags

Date	Mintage	F	VF	XF	Unc	BU
AH1404 (1984)	500	—	—	—	700	—
AH1404 (1984) Proof	500	Value: 800				

KM# 78 100 RUFIYAA **Weight:** 28.2800 g. **Composition:** 0.9250 Silver .8411 oz. ASW **Subject:** Opening of Grand Mosque and Islamic Centre **Obverse:** National emblem - crescent moon, star and palm tree flanked by two flags

Date	Mintage	F	VF	XF	Unc	BU
AH1405 (1984) Proof	500	Value: 70.00				

KM# 76 100 RUFIYAA **Weight:** 28.2800 g. **Composition:** 0.9250 Silver .8411 oz. ASW **Subject:** Commonwealth finance ministers meeting **Obverse:** National emblem - crescent moon, star and palm tree flanked by two flags

Date	Mintage	F	VF	XF	Unc	BU
ND(AH406) (1985) Proof	300	Value: 75.00				

KM# 87 100 RUFIYAA **Weight:** 10.0000 g. **Composition:** 0.5000 Silver .1607 oz. ASW **Obverse:** National emblem - crescent moon, star and palm tree flanked by two flags **Reverse:** Sailing ship "Cutty Sark"

Date	Mintage	F	VF	XF	Unc	BU
AH1413 (1993) Proof	Est. 25,000	Value: 16.50				

KM# 98 100 RUFIYAA **Weight:** 20.0000 g. **Composition:** 0.8350 Silver .5369 oz. ASW **Series:** Olympics **Obverse:** National arms **Reverse:** Swimmer **Edge:** Reeded **Size:** 34 mm.

Date	Mintage	F	VF	XF	Unc	BU
1998 Proof	30,000	—	—	—	35.00	—

KM# 82 250 RUFIYAA **Weight:** 31.4700 g. **Composition:** 0.9250 Silver .9359 oz. ASW **Series:** World Football Championship **Obverse:** National emblem - crescent moon, star and palm tree flanked by two flags **Reverse:** Soccer ball trailing an inscribed ribbon **Size:** 38.61 mm.

Date	F	VF	XF	Unc	BU
AH1410 (1990) Proof	—	Value: 22.50			

KM# 80 250 RUFIYAA **Weight:** 31.4700 g. **Composition:** 0.9250 Silver .9359 oz. ASW **Series:** 1992 Olympics **Subject:** Swimming **Obverse:** National emblem - crescent moon, star and palm tree flanked by two flags

Date	F	VF	XF	Unc	BU
AH1410 (1990) Proof	—	Value: 20.00			

KM# 81 250 RUFIYAA **Weight:** 31.4700 g. **Composition:** 0.9250 Silver .9359 oz. ASW **Obverse:** National emblem - crescent moon, star and palm tree flanked by two flags **Reverse:** Maldivian Schooner - Dhivehi-Odi **Size:** 38.61 mm.

Date	Mintage	F	VF	XF	Unc	BU
AH1410 (1990) Proof	15,000	Value: 28.00				

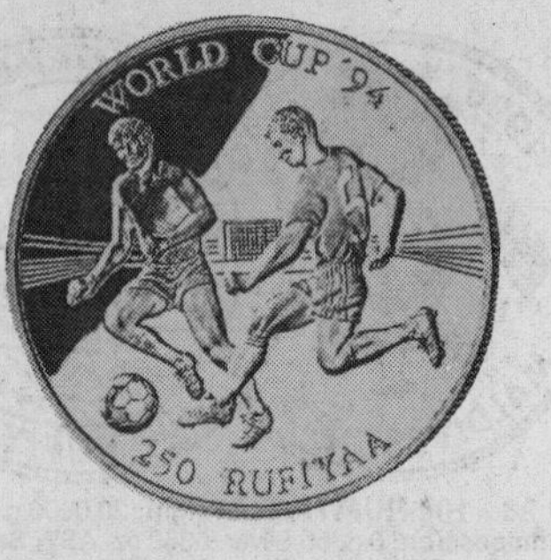

KM# 83 250 RUFIYAA **Weight:** 31.4700 g. **Composition:** 0.9250 Silver .9359 oz. ASW **Subject:** World Cup '94 soccer **Obverse:** National emblem - crescent moon, star and palm tree flanked by two flags **Reverse:** Two football players **Size:** 38.61 mm.

Date	Mintage	F	VF	XF	Unc	BU
AH1413 (1993) Proof	25,000	Value: 36.50				

KM# 84 250 RUFIYAA **Weight:** 31.4700 g. **Composition:** 0.9250 Silver .9359 oz. ASW **Obverse:** National emblem - crescent moon, star and palm tree flanked by two flags **Reverse:** Skylab space station **Size:** 38.61 mm.

Date	Mintage	F	VF	XF	Unc	BU
AH1413 (1993) Proof	1,440	Value: 32.50				

KM# 85 250 RUFIYAA **Weight:** 31.4700 g. **Composition:** 0.9250 Silver .9359 oz. ASW **Series:** 1996 Olympics **Subject:** Sailing **Obverse:** National emblem - crescent moon, star and palm tree flanked by two flags **Size:** 38.61 mm.

Date	Mintage	F	VF	XF	Unc	BU
AH1413 (1993) Proof	25,000	Value: 25.00				

KM# 86 250 RUFIYAA **Weight:** 31.4700 g. **Composition:** 0.9250 Silver .9359 oz. ASW **Series:** Endangered Wildlife **Obverse:** National emblem - crescent moon, star and palm tree flanked by two flags **Reverse:** Turtle **Size:** 38.61 mm.

Date	Mintage	F	VF	XF	Unc	BU
AH1414 (1994) Proof	14,500	Value: 37.50				

KM# 96 250 RUFIYAA **Weight:** 31.2400 g. **Composition:** 0.9250 Silver .9291 oz. ASW **Subject:** Ibn Battuta **Reverse:** Bust of Ibn Battuta, dhow and map **Size:** 38.61 mm.

Date	F	VF	XF	Unc	BU
AH1416 (1995) Proof	—	Value: 37.50			

KM# 91 500 RUFIYAA **Weight:** 28.2800 g. **Composition:** 0.9250 Silver .8411 oz. ASW **Subject:** 25 Years of Independence **Size:** 38.61 mm.

Date	Mintage	F	VF	XF	Unc	BU
AH1410 (1990) Proof	1,000	Value: 60.00				

KM# 92 500 RUFIYAA **Weight:** 28.2800 g. **Composition:** 0.9250 Silver .8411 oz. ASW **Subject:** 25 Years of Republic **Size:** 38.61 mm.

Date	Mintage	F	VF	XF	Unc	BU
AH1413 (1993) Proof	500	Value: 65.00				

KM# 93 1000 RUFIYAA **Weight:** 15.9800 g. **Composition:** 0.9170 Gold .4712 oz. AGW **Subject:** 25 Years of Independence **Size:** 28.4 mm.

Date	Mintage	F	VF	XF	Unc	BU
AH1410 (1990) Proof	1,000	Value: 500				

KM# 94 1000 RUFIYAA **Weight:** 15.9800 g. **Composition:** 0.9170 Gold .4712 oz. AGW **Subject:** 25 Years of Republic **Size:** 28.4 mm.

Date	Mintage	F	VF	XF	Unc	BU
AH1413 (1993) Proof	500	Value: 550				

PATTERNS

Including off metal strikes

KM#	Date	Mintage	Identification	Mkt Val
Pn1	AH1319	—	Larin. Silver. KM38.	—
Pn2	AH1319	—	2 Lariat. Silver. KM39.	—
Pn3	AH1320	—	4 Lariat. Silver. KM40.2.	—

PIEFORTS

KM#	Date	Mintage	Identification	Mkt Val
P1	1979	100	20 Rufiyaa. National emblem - crescent moon, star and palm tree flanked by 2 flags.. 3 children playing. KM61.	80.00
P2	1984	100	100 Rufiyaa. National emblem - crescent moon, star and palm tree flanked by 2 flags.. Stylized Yin-Yang symbol. KM66.	100
P3	1984	100	100 Rufiyaa. National emblem - crescent moon, star and palm tree flanked by 2 flags.. Disabled persons under an umbrella. KM67.	800

MINT SETS

KM#	Date	Mintage	Identification	Issue Price	Mkt Val
MS1	1984 (6)	—	KM68-73	8.75	12.50

PROOF SETS

KM#	Date	Mintage	Identification	Issue Price	Mkt Val
PS2	1979 (6)	—	KM45a, 46a, 47.2, 48.2, 49-50	30.00	18.00
PS1	1960 (6)	1,270	KM43-48	—	30.00
PS3	1979 (2)	3,000	KM59a, 60a	—	42.50
PS4	1984 (6)	2,500	KM68-72, 73a	30.00	28.00

MALI

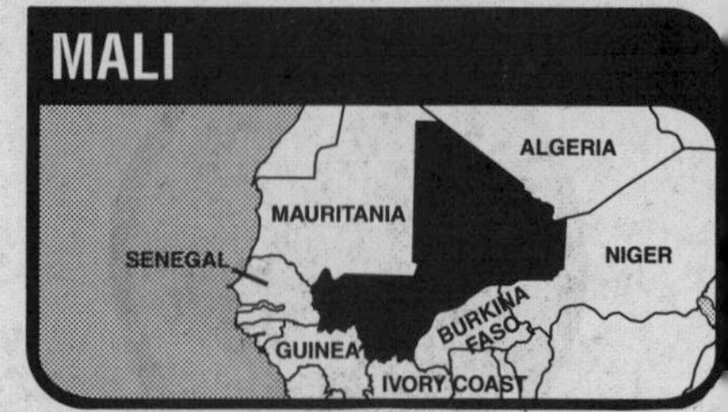

The Republic of Mali, a landlocked country in the interior o West Africa southwest of Algeria, has an area of 482,077 sq. m (1,240,000 sq. km.) and a population of 8.1 million. Capital: Bam ako. Livestock, fish, cotton and peanuts are exported.

Malians are descendants of the ancient Malinke Kingdom c Mali that controlled the middle Niger from the11th to the 17th cer turies. The French penetrated the Sudan (now Mali) about 188C and established their rule in1898 after subduing fierce nativ resistance. In 1904 the area became the colony of Upper Sene gal-Niger (changed to French Sudan in 1920), and became pa of the French Union in 1946. In 1958 French Sudan became th Sudanese Republic with complete internal autonomy. Senega joined with the Sudanese Republic in 1959 to form the Mali Fed eration which, in 1960, became a fully independent member of th French Community. Upon Senegal's subsequent withdrawal fror the Federation, the Sudanese, on Sept. 22, 1960, proclaime their nation the fully independent Republic of Mali and severed a ties with France.

MINT MARKS

(a) - Paris, privy marks only

REPUBLIC

STANDARD COINAGE

KM# 2 5 FRANCS **Composition:** Aluminum

Date	F	VF	XF	Unc	B
1961	0.15	0.25	0.50	1.50	–

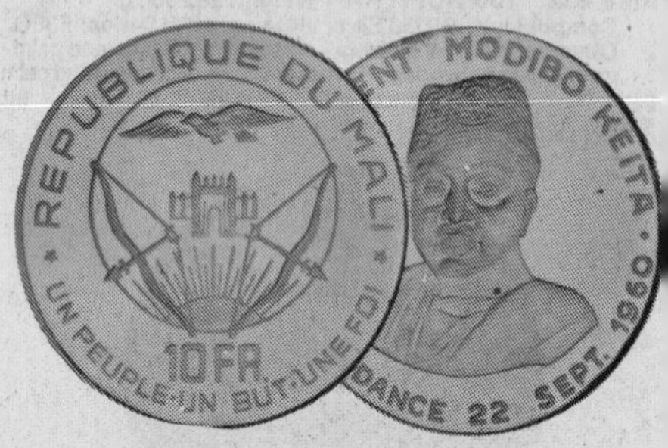

KM# 1 10 FRANCS **Weight:** 25.0000 g. **Composition:** 0.9000 Silver .7234 oz. ASW **Subject:** Independence

Date	Mintage	F	VF	XF	Unc	B
ND(1960) Proof	10,000	Value: 35.00				

KM# 3 10 FRANCS **Composition:** 0.9000 Aluminum

Date	F	VF	XF	Unc	B
1961	0.50	1.00	2.00	5.00	–

KM# 5 10 FRANCS **Weight:** 3.2000 g. **Composition:** 0.9000 Gold .0926 oz. AGW **Subject:** President Modibo Keita **Note:** Similar to 25 Francs, KM#6.

Date	F	VF	XF	Unc	B
1967 Proof	—	Value: 85.00			

KM# 11 10 FRANCS **Composition:** Aluminum

Date	Mintage	F	VF	XF	Unc	BU
1976(a)	5,000,000	1.25	2.50	4.50	12.50	—

KM# 13 10 FRANCS **Weight:** 3.2000 g. **Composition:** 0.9000 Gold .0926 oz. AGW **Subject:** Anniversary of Independence **Note:** Similar to 50 Francs, KM#15.

Date	F	VF	XF	Unc	BU
ND Proof	—	—	—	—	—

Note: Reported not confirmed

KM# 4 25 FRANCS **Composition:** Aluminum

Date	F	VF	XF	Unc	BU
1961	0.35	0.65	1.50	4.00	—

KM# 6 25 FRANCS **Weight:** 8.0000 g. **Composition:** 0.9000 Gold .2315 oz. AGW **Subject:** President Modibo Keita

Date	F	VF	XF	Unc	BU
1967 Proof	—	Value: 145			

KM# 12 25 FRANCS **Composition:** Aluminum

Date	Mintage	F	VF	XF	Unc	BU
1976(a)	5,000,000	2.50	4.00	8.00	18.00	—

KM# 14 25 FRANCS **Weight:** 8.0000 g. **Composition:** 0.9000 Gold .2315 oz. AGW **Subject:** Anniversary of Independence

Date	F	VF	XF	Unc	BU
ND Proof	—	Value: 325			

KM# 7 50 FRANCS **Weight:** 16.0000 g. **Composition:** 0.9000 Gold .4630 oz. AGW **Subject:** President Modibo Keita

Date	F	VF	XF	Unc	BU
1967 Proof	—	Value: 265			

KM# 9 50 FRANCS **Composition:** Nickel-Brass **Series:** F.A.O.

Date	Mintage	F	VF	XF	Unc	BU
1975(a)	10,000,000	0.25	0.50	1.00	2.50	—
1977(a)	—	0.25	0.50	1.00	2.50	—

KM# 15 50 FRANCS **Weight:** 16.0000 g. **Composition:** 0.9000 Gold .463 oz. AGW **Subject:** Anniversary of Independence

Date	F	VF	XF	Unc	BU
ND Proof	—	Value: 575			

KM# 8 100 FRANCS **Weight:** 32.0000 g. **Composition:** 0.9000 Gold .926 oz. AGW **Subject:** President Modibo Keita

Date	F	VF	XF	Unc	BU
1967 Proof	—	Value: 500			

KM# 10 100 FRANCS **Composition:** Nickel-Brass **Series:** F.A.O.

Date	Mintage	F	VF	XF	Unc	BU
1975(a)	23,000,000	0.65	1.25	2.50	5.00	—

KM# 16 100 FRANCS **Weight:** 32.0000 g. **Composition:** 0.9000 Gold .926 oz. AGW **Subject:** Anniversary of Independence

Date	F	VF	XF	Unc	BU
ND Proof	—	Value: 950			

ESSAIS

Standard metals unless otherwise noted

Some essais have surnames stamped (from die) on them. Purpose is unknown.

KM#	Date	Mintage	Identification	Issue Price	Mkt Val
E1	1975	—	50 Francs. KM9.	—	17.50
E2	1975	—	100 Francs. KM10.	—	20.00
E3	1976	—	10 Francs. KM11.	—	17.50
E4	1976	—	25 Francs. KM12.	—	20.00

PIEFORTS WITH ESSAIS

Standard metlas unliess otherwise noted

KM#	Date	Mintage	Identification	Issue Price	Mkt Val
PE1	1960	10	10 Francs. KM1.	—	250

PROOF SETS

KM#	Date	Mintage	Identification	Issue Price	Mkt Val
PS1	1967 (4)	—	KM5-8	—	1,000

MALTA

The Republic of Malta, an independent parliamentary democracy, is situated in the Mediterranean Sea between Sicily and North Africa. With the islands of Gozo and Comino, Malta has an area of 124 sq. mi. (320 sq. km.) and a population of 386,000.Capital: Valletta. Malta has no proven mineral resources, an agriculture insufficient to its needs, and a small, but expanding, manufacturing facility. Clothing, textile yarns and fabrics, and knitted wear are exported.

For more than 3,500 years Malta was ruled, in succession by Phoenicians, Carthaginians, Romans, Arabs, Normans, the Knights of Malta, France and Britain. Napoleon seized Malta by treachery in 1798. The French were ousted by a Maltese insurrection assisted by Britain, and in 1814 Malta, of its own free will, became a part of the British Empire. Malta obtained full independence in Sept., 1964; electing to remain within the Commonwealth with the British monarch as the nominal head of state.

Malta became a republic on Dec. 13, 1974, but remained a member of the Commonwealth of Nations. The president is Chief of State. The prime minister is the Head of Government.

RULERS

British, until 1964

REPUBLIC

DECIMAL COINAGE

10 Mils = 1 Cent; 100 Cents = 1 Pound

KM# 5 2 MILS **Composition:** Aluminum **Obverse:** Maltese cross

Date	Mintage	F	VF	XF	Unc	BU
1972	30,000	—	0.10	0.15	0.30	—
1972 Proof	13,000	Value: 0.50				
1976FM (M)	5,000	—	—	—	2.00	—
1976FM (P)	26,000	Value: 0.50				
1977FM (U)	5,252	—	—	—	1.00	—
1977FM (P)	6,884	Value: 1.00				
1978FM (U)	5,252	—	—	—	1.00	—
1978FM (P)	3,244	Value: 1.00				
1979FM (U)	537	—	—	—	3.00	—
1979FM (P)	6,577	Value: 1.00				
1980FM (U)	385	—	—	—	3.00	—
1980FM (P)	3,451	Value: 1.00				
1981FM (U)	444	—	—	—	3.00	—
1981FM (P)	1,453	Value: 1.00				

KM# 54 2 MILS **Composition:** Aluminum **Subject:** 10th Anniversary of Decimalization **Obverse:** Maltese cross

Date	Mintage	F	VF	XF	Unc	BU
1982FM (U)	850	—	—	—	3.00	—
1982FM (P)	1,793	Value: 1.00				

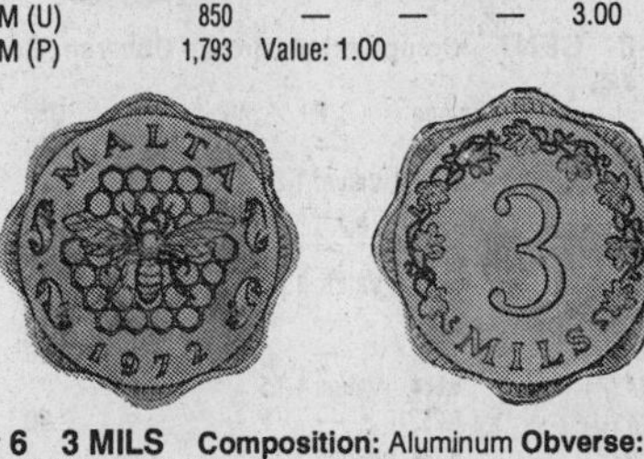

KM# 6 3 MILS **Composition:** Aluminum **Obverse:** Bee and honeycomb

Date	Mintage	F	VF	XF	Unc	BU
1972	—	—	0.10	0.15	0.50	—
1972 Proof	8,000	Value: 1.00				
1976FM (M)	5,000	—	—	—	2.50	—
1976FM (P)	26,000	Value: 1.00				
1977FM (U)	5,252	—	—	—	1.50	—
1977FM (P)	6,884	Value: 1.25				
1978FM (U)	5,252	—	—	—	2.50	—

Date	Mintage	F	VF	XF	Unc	BU
1978FM (P)	3,244	Value: 1.25				
1979FM (U)	537	—	—	—	5.00	—
1979FM (P)	6,577	Value: 1.25				
1980FM (U)	385	—	—	—	5.00	—
1980FM (P)	3,451	Value: 1.25				
1981FM (U)	449	—	—	—	5.00	—
1981FM (P)	1,453	Value: 1.25				

KM# 55 3 MILS Composition: Aluminum **Subject:** 10th Anniversary of Decimalization **Obverse:** Bea and honeycomb

Date	Mintage	F	VF	XF	Unc	BU
1982FM (U)	850	—	—	—	4.00	—
1982FM (P)	1,793	Value: 1.25				

KM# 7 5 MILS Composition: Aluminum **Obverse:** Earthen lampstand

Date	Mintage	F	VF	XF	Unc	BU
1972	4,320,000	—	0.10	0.15	0.40	—
1972 Proof	13,000	Value: 1.00				
1976FM (M)	5,000	—	—	—	3.00	—
1976FM (P)	26,000	Value: 1.00				
1977FM (U)	5,252	—	—	—	2.00	—
1977FM (P)	6,884	Value: 1.50				
1978FM (U)	5,252	—	—	—	2.00	—
1978FM (P)	3,244	Value: 1.50				
1979FM (U)	537	—	—	—	7.00	—
1979FM (P)	6,577	Value: 1.50				
1980FM (U)	385	—	—	—	7.00	—
1980FM (P)	3,451	Value: 1.50				
1981FM (U)	449	—	—	—	7.00	—
1981FM (P)	1,453	Value: 1.50				

KM# 56 5 MILS Composition: Aluminum **Subject:** 10th Anniversary of Decimalization **Obverse:** Earthen lampstand

Date	Mintage	F	VF	XF	Unc	BU
1982FM (U)	850	—	—	—	5.00	—
1982FM (P)	1,793	Value: 1.50				

KM# 8 CENT Composition: Bronze **Obverse:** George Cross

Date	Mintage	F	VF	XF	Unc	BU
1972	5,650,000	—	0.10	0.15	0.40	—
1972 Proof	13,000	Value: 1.25				
1975	1,500,000	—	0.10	0.20	0.50	—
1976FM (M)	5,000	—	—	—	3.50	—
1976FM (P)	26,000	Value: 1.25				
1977	2,793,000	—	0.10	0.15	0.40	—
1977FM (U)	5,252	—	—	—	2.50	—
1977FM (P)	6,884	Value: 1.75				
1978FM (U)	5,252	—	—	—	2.50	—
1978FM (P)	3,244	Value: 1.75				
1979FM (U)	537	—	—	—	9.00	—
1979FM (P)	6,577	Value: 1.75				
1980FM (U)	385	—	—	—	9.00	—
1980FM (P)	3,451	Value: 1.75				
1981FM (U)	449	—	—	—	9.00	—
1981FM (P)	1,453	Value: 1.75				
1982	—	—	0.10	0.15	0.25	—

KM# 57 CENT Composition: Bronze **Subject:** 10th Anniversary of Decimalization **Obverse:** The George Cross military award

Date	Mintage	F	VF	XF	Unc	BU
1982FM (U)	850	—	—	—	7.50	—
1982FM (P)	1,793	Value: 1.75				

KM# 9 2 CENTS Composition: Copper-Zinc **Subject:** Penthesilea, Queen of the Amazons

Date	Mintage	F	VF	XF	Unc	BU
1972		—	0.10	0.15	0.40	—
1972 Proof	13,000	Value: 1.50				
1976		—	0.15	0.20	0.60	—
1976FM (M)		—	—	—	4.50	—
1976FM (P)	26,000	Value: 1.50				
1977		—	0.10	0.15	0.40	—
1977FM (U)		—	—	—	4.50	—
1977FM (P)	6,884	Value: 2.50				
1978FM (U)		—	—	—	4.50	—
1978FM (P)	3,244	Value: 2.50				
1979FM (U)		—	—	—	12.00	—
1979FM (P)	6,577	Value: 2.50				
1980FM (U)		—	—	—	12.00	—
1980FM (P)	3,451	Value: 2.50				
1981FM (U)		—	—	—	12.00	—
1981FM (P)	1,453	Value: 2.50				
1982		—	0.10	0.15	0.30	—

KM# 58 2 CENTS Composition: Copper-Zinc **Subject:** 10th Anniversary of Decimalization

Date	Mintage	F	VF	XF	Unc	BU
1982FM (U)	850	—	—	—	10.00	—
1982FM (P)	1,793	Value: 2.50				

KM# 10 5 CENTS Composition: Copper-Nickel **Obverse:** Floral altar in the Temple of Hagar Qim

Date	Mintage	F	VF	XF	Unc	BU
1972	4,180,000	—	0.20	0.30	0.50	—
1972 Proof	13,000	Value: 1.75				
1976	1,009,000	—	0.20	0.30	0.60	—
1976FM (M)	2,500	—	—	—	5.00	—
1976FM (P)	26,000	Value: 2.00				
1977	—	—	0.20	0.30	0.50	—
1977FM (U)	2,752	—	—	—	5.00	—
1977FM (P)	6,884	Value: 3.00				
1978FM (U)	2,752	—	—	—	5.00	—
1978FM (P)	3,244	Value: 3.00				
1979FM (U)	537	—	—	—	15.00	—
1979FM (P)	6,577	Value: 3.00				
1980FM (U)	385	—	—	—	15.00	—
1980FM (P)	3,451	Value: 3.00				
1981FM (U)	449	—	—	—	15.00	—
1981FM (P)	1,453	Value: 3.00				

KM# 59 5 CENTS Composition: Copper-Nickel **Subject:** 10th Anniversary of Decimalization **Obverse:** Floral altar in the Temple of Hagar Qim

Date	Mintage	F	VF	XF	Unc	BU
1982FM (U)	850	—	—	—	12.50	—
1982FM (P)	1,793	Value: 3.00				

KM# 11 10 CENTS Composition: Copper-Nickel **Obverse:** Barge of the grand master

Date	Mintage	F	VF	XF	Unc	BU
1972	10,680,000	—	0.40	0.60	1.00	—
1972 Proof	13,000	Value: 2.25				
1976FM (M)	1,000	—	—	—	6.00	—
1976FM (P)	26,000	Value: 2.50				
1977FM (U)	1,252	—	—	—	6.00	—
1977FM (P)	6,884	Value: 3.50				
1978FM (U)	1,252	—	—	—	6.00	—
1978FM (P)	3,244	Value: 3.50				
1979FM (U)	537	—	—	—	17.50	—
1979FM (P)	6,577	Value: 3.50				
1980FM (U)	385	—	—	—	15.00	—
1980FM (P)	3,451	Value: 3.50				
1981FM (U)	449	—	—	—	15.00	—
1981FM (P)	1,453	Value: 3.50				

KM# 60 10 CENTS Composition: Copper-Nickel **Subject:** 10th Anniversary of Decimalization **Obverse:** Barge of the grand master

Date	Mintage	F	VF	XF	Unc	BU
1982FM (U)	850	—	—	—	14.00	—
1982FM (P)	1,793	Value: 3.50				

KM# 29 25 CENTS Composition: Brass **Subject:** 1st Anniversary - Republic of Malta

Date	Mintage	F	VF	XF	Unc	BU
1975	4,750,000	—	1.00	1.50	2.50	—
1975 Matte proof	—	—	—	—	150	—

KM# 29a 25 CENTS Composition: Bronze

Date	Mintage	F	VF	XF	Unc	BU
1975 Proof	6,000	Value: 12.50				

KM# 29b 25 CENTS Composition: Copper-Nickel

Date	Mintage	F	VF	XF	Unc	BU
1976FM (M)	300	—	—	—	40.00	—
1976FM (P)	26,000	Value: 3.00				
1977FM (U)	552	—	—	—	20.00	—
1977FM (P)	6,884	Value: 4.50				
1978FM (U)	552	—	—	—	20.00	—
1978FM (P)	3,244	Value: 4.50				
1979FM (U)	537	—	—	—	20.00	—
1979FM (P)	6,577	Value: 4.50				
1980FM (U)	385	—	—	—	20.00	—
1980FM (P)	3,451	Value: 4.50				
1981FM (U)	449	—	—	—	20.00	—
1981FM (P)	1,453	Value: 4.50				

KM# 61 25 CENTS Composition: Copper-Nickel
Subject: 10th Anniversary of Decimalization

Date	Mintage	F	VF	XF	Unc	BU
1982FM (U)	850	—	—	—	15.00	—
1982FM (P)	1,793	Value: 4.50				

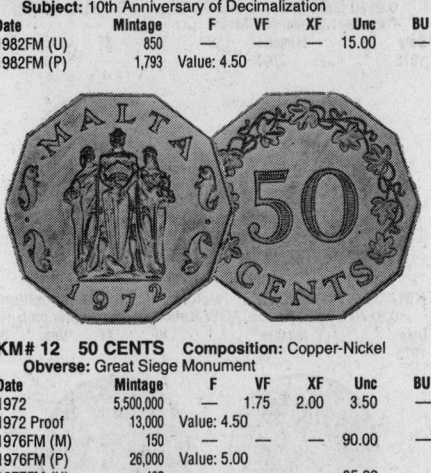

KM# 12 50 CENTS Composition: Copper-Nickel
Obverse: Great Siege Monument

Date	Mintage	F	VF	XF	Unc	BU
1972	5,500,000	—	1.75	2.00	3.50	—
1972 Proof	13,000	Value: 4.50				
1976FM (M)	150	—	—	—	90.00	—
1976FM (P)	26,000	Value: 5.00				
1977FM (U)	402	—	—	—	25.00	—
1977FM (P)	6,884	Value: 6.00				
1978FM (U)	402	—	—	—	25.00	—
1978FM (P)	3,244	Value: 6.00				
1979FM (U)	537	—	—	—	25.00	—
1979FM (P)	6,577	Value: 6.00				
1980FM (U)	385	—	—	—	25.00	—
1980FM (P)	3,451	Value: 6.00				
1981FM (U)	449	—	—	—	25.00	—
1981FM (P)	1,453	Value: 6.00				

KM# 62 50 CENTS Composition: Copper-Nickel
Subject: 10th Anniversary of Decimalization **Obverse:** Great Siege Monument

Date	Mintage	F	VF	XF	Unc	BU
1982FM (U)	850	—	—	—	20.00	—
1982FM (P)	1,793	Value: 6.00				

KM# 13 POUND Weight: 10.0000 g. **Composition:** 0.9870 Silver .3173 oz. ASW **Reverse:** Manwel Dimech bust facing left

Date	Mintage	F	VF	XF	Unc	BU
1972	55,000	—	—	4.00	7.00	—

KM# 19 POUND Weight: 10.0000 g. **Composition:** 0.9870 Silver .3173 oz. ASW **Reverse:** Sir Temi Zammit bust facing left

Date	Mintage	F	VF	XF	Unc	BU
1973	30,000	—	—	4.00	7.00	—

KM# 45 POUND Weight: 5.6600 g. **Composition:** 0.9250 Silver .1683 oz. ASW **Reverse:** Kelb tal-Fenek, an ancient Maltese dog

Date	Mintage	F	VF	XF	Unc	BU
1977	66,000	—	—	8.00	25.00	—
1977 Proof	2,500	Value: 45.00				

KM# 51 POUND Weight: 5.6600 g. **Composition:** 0.9250 Silver .1683 oz. ASW **Subject:** Departure of foreign forces

Date	Mintage	F	VF	XF	Unc	BU
1979FM (U)	50,000	—	—	4.00	7.00	—
1979FM (P)	7,871	Value: 16.50				

KM# 14 2 POUNDS Weight: 20.0000 g. **Composition:** 0.9870 Silver .6347 oz. ASW **Reverse:** Fort St. Angelo

Date	Mintage	F	VF	XF	Unc	BU
1972	53,000	—	—	6.50	12.50	—

KM# 20 2 POUNDS Weight: 20.0000 g. **Composition:** 0.9870 Silver .6347 oz. ASW **Obverse:** Similar to KM#14 **Reverse:** Tal-Imdina Gate

Date	Mintage	F	VF	XF	Unc	BU
1973	30,000	—	—	8.00	14.50	—

KM# 24 2 POUNDS Weight: 10.0000 g. **Composition:** 0.9870 Silver .3173 oz. ASW **Reverse:** Giovanni Francesco Abela bust facing forward

Date	Mintage	F	VF	XF	Unc	BU
1974	25,000	—	—	6.50	8.50	—

KM# 30 2 POUNDS Weight: 10.0000 g. **Composition:** 0.9870 Silver .3173 oz. ASW **Obverse:** Similar to KM#24 **Reverse:** Similar to KM#31

Date	Mintage	F	VF	XF	Unc	BU
1975	2,000	—	—	8.00	15.00	—

KM# 31 2 POUNDS Weight: 10.0000 g. **Composition:** 0.9870 Silver .3173 oz. ASW **Reverse:** Alfonso Maria Galea bust facing left

Date	Mintage	F	VF	XF	Unc	BU
1975	18,000	—	—	6.50	8.50	—

KM# 40 2 POUNDS Weight: 10.0000 g. **Composition:** 0.9870 Silver .3173 oz. ASW **Reverse:** Guze Ellul Mercer bust facing right

Date	Mintage	F	VF	XF	Unc	BU
1976	11,000	—	—	8.00	10.00	—

KM# 46 2 POUNDS Weight: 11.3100 g. **Composition:** 0.9250 Silver .3363 oz. ASW **Reverse:** Sir Luigi Preziosi bust facing left

Date	Mintage	F	VF	XF	Unc	BU
1977	15,000	—	—	—	9.00	—
1977 Proof	3,692	Value: 12.50				

KM# 52 2 POUNDS Weight: 11.3100 g. **Composition:** 0.9250 Silver .3363 oz. ASW **Series:** World Food Day

Date	Mintage	F	VF	XF	Unc	BU
1981	1,500	—	—	—	15.00	—
1981 Proof	12,000	Value: 10.00				

KM# 25 4 POUNDS Weight: 20.0000 g. **Composition:** 0.9870 Silver .6347 oz. ASW **Reverse:** Cottonera Gate

Date	Mintage	F	VF	XF	Unc	BU
1974	24,000	—	—	10.00	15.00	—

KM# 32 4 POUNDS Weight: 20.0000 g. **Composition:** 0.9870 Silver .6347 oz. ASW **Obverse:** Same as KM#25 **Reverse:** Similar to KM#33

Date	Mintage	F	VF	XF	Unc	BU
1975	2,000	—	—	15.00	27.50	—

KM# 33 4 POUNDS **Weight:** 20.0000 g. **Composition:** 0.9870 Silver .6347 oz. ASW **Reverse:** St. Agatha's Tower at Gammieh

Date	Mintage	F	VF	XF	Unc	BU
1975	18,000	—	—	13.50	17.50	—

KM# 41 4 POUNDS **Weight:** 20.0000 g. **Composition:** 0.9870 Silver .6347 oz. ASW **Reverse:** Fort Manoel Gate

Date	Mintage	F	VF	XF	Unc	BU
1976	10,000	—	—	14.50	18.50	—

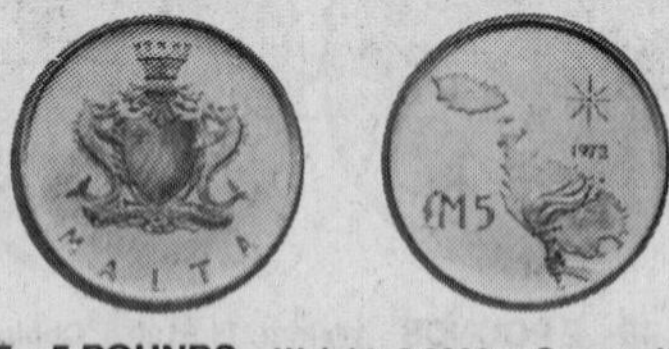

KM# 15 5 POUNDS **Weight:** 3.0000 g. **Composition:** 0.9160 Gold .0883 oz. AGW **Reverse:** Hand holding torch, map of Malta

Date	Mintage	F	VF	XF	Unc	BU
1972	18,000	—	—	—	65.00	—

KM# 47 5 POUNDS **Weight:** 28.2800 g. **Composition:** 0.9250 Silver .8411 oz. ASW **Reverse:** Windmill of Xarolla

Date	Mintage	F	VF	XF	Unc	BU
1977	15,000	—	—	—	22.50	—
1977 Proof	3,938	Value: 37.50				

KM# 53 5 POUNDS **Weight:** 28.2800 g. **Composition:** 0.9250 Silver .8411 oz. ASW **Subject:** International Youth Conference - UNICEF

Date	Mintage	F	VF	XF	Unc	BU
1981 Proof	11,000	Value: 13.50				

KM# 16 10 POUNDS **Weight:** 6.0000 g. **Composition:** 0.9170 Gold .1767 oz. AGW **Reverse:** Kenur, a Maltese stone charcoal stove

Date	Mintage	F	VF	XF	Unc	BU
1972	16,000	—	—	—	95.00	—

KM# 21 10 POUNDS **Weight:** 3.0000 g. **Composition:** 0.9170 Gold .0883 oz. AGW **Reverse:** Watchtower

Date	Mintage	F	VF	XF	Unc	BU
1973	9,078	—	—	—	55.00	—

KM# 26 10 POUNDS **Weight:** 3.0000 g. **Composition:** 0.9170 Gold .0883 oz. AGW **Reverse:** Zerafa flower

Date	Mintage	F	VF	XF	Unc	BU
1974	9,124	—	—	—	55.00	—

KM# 34 10 POUNDS **Weight:** 3.0000 g. **Composition:** 0.9170 Gold .0883 oz. AGW **Obverse:** Similar to KM#26 **Reverse:** Similar to KM#35

Date	Mintage	F	VF	XF	Unc	BU
1975	2,000	—	—	—	75.00	—

KM# 35 10 POUNDS **Weight:** 3.0000 g. **Composition:** 0.9170 Gold .0883 oz. AGW **Reverse:** Maltese falcon

Date	Mintage	F	VF	XF	Unc	BU
1975	6,448	—	—	—	90.00	—

KM# 17 20 POUNDS **Weight:** 12.0000 g. **Composition:** 0.9170 Gold .3534 oz. AGW **Reverse:** Merill bird

Date	Mintage	F	VF	XF	Unc	BU
1972	16,000	—	—	—	185	—

KM# 22 20 POUNDS **Weight:** 6.0000 g. **Composition:** 0.9170 Gold .1767 oz. AGW **Reverse:** Dolphins Fountain at Floriana

Date	Mintage	F	VF	XF	Unc	BU
1973	9,075	—	—	—	110	—

KM# 27 20 POUNDS **Weight:** 6.0000 g. **Composition:** 0.9170 Gold .1767 oz. AGW **Reverse:** Gozo boat

Date	Mintage	F	VF	XF	Unc	BU
1974	8,700	—	—	—	110	—

KM# 36 20 POUNDS **Weight:** 6.0000 g. **Composition:** 0.9170 Gold .1767 oz. AGW **Obverse:** Similar to KM#27 **Reverse:** Similar to KM#37

Date	Mintage	F	VF	XF	Unc	BU
1975	2,000	—	—	—	150	—

KM# 37 20 POUNDS **Weight:** 6.0000 g. **Composition:** 0.9170 Gold .1767 oz. AGW **Reverse:** Freshwater crab

Date	Mintage	F	VF	XF	Unc	BU
1975	5,698	—	—	—	125	—

KM# 43 20 POUNDS **Weight:** 6.0000 g. **Composition:** 0.9170 Gold .1767 oz. AGW **Reverse:** Storm petrel bird

Date	Mintage	F	VF	XF	Unc	BU
1976	4,098	—	—	—	135	—

KM# 42 20 POUNDS **Weight:** 3.0000 g. **Composition:** 0.9170 Gold .0883 oz. AGW **Reverse:** Swallow-tail butterfly

Date	Mintage	F	VF	XF	Unc	BU
1976	4,448	—	—	—	100	—

KM# 48 25 POUNDS **Weight:** 7.9900 g. **Composition:** 0.9170 Gold .2353 oz. AGW **Subject:** First Gozo coin

Date	Mintage	F	VF	XF	Unc	BU
1977	4,000	—	—	—	125	—
1977 Proof	3,249	Value: 150				

KM# 18 50 POUNDS **Weight:** 30.0000 g. **Composition:** 0.9170 Gold .8836 oz. AGW **Reverse:** Neptune

Date	Mintage	F	VF	XF	Unc	BU
1972	16,000	—	—	—	425	—

KM# 23 50 POUNDS **Weight:** 15.0000 g. **Composition:** 0.9170 Gold .4418 oz. AGW **Subject:** Auberge de Castille at Valletta

Date	Mintage	F	VF	XF	Unc	BU
1973	9,075	—	—	—	225	—

KM# 28 50 POUNDS **Weight:** 15.0000 g. **Composition:** 0.9170 Gold .4418 oz. AGW **Subject:** First Maltese coin

Date	Mintage	F	VF	XF	Unc	BU
1974	8,667	—	—	—	225	—

KM# 38 50 POUNDS **Weight:** 15.0000 g. **Composition:** 0.9170 Gold .4418 oz. AGW **Reverse:** Ornamental stone balcony

Date	Mintage	F	VF	XF	Unc	BU
1975	2,000	—	—	—	325	—

KM# 39 50 POUNDS **Weight:** 15.0000 g. **Composition:** 0.9170 Gold .4418 oz. AGW **Reverse:** Ornamental stone balcony

Date	Mintage	F	VF	XF	Unc	BU
1975	5,500	—	—	—	225	—

KM# 44 50 POUNDS **Weight:** 15.0000 g. **Composition:** 0.9170 Gold .4418 oz. AGW **Reverse:** Ornamental door knocker

Date	Mintage	F	VF	XF	Unc	BU
1976	3,748	—	—	—	225	—

KM# 49 50 POUNDS **Weight:** 15.9800 g. **Composition:** 0.9170 Gold .4707 oz. AGW **Subject:** Mnara

Date	Mintage	F	VF	XF	Unc	BU
1977	4,000	—	—	—	225	—
1977 Proof	846	Value: 350				

KM# 50 100 POUNDS **Weight:** 31.9600 g. **Composition:** 0.9170 Gold .9413 oz. AGW **Reverse:** "Les Gavroches" sculpture

Date	Mintage	F	VF	XF	Unc	BU
1977	4,000	—	—	—	500	—
1977 Proof	846	Value: 650				

REFORM COINAGE

1982 - Present

100 Cents = 1 Lira

KM# 78 CENT **Composition:** Copper-Zinc **Obverse:** Similar to Lira, KM#82 **Reverse:** Common weasel

Date	Mintage	F	VF	XF	Unc	BU
1986	21,526,000	—	0.15	0.25	0.50	—
1986 Proof	10,000	Value: 2.00				

KM# 93 CENT **Composition:** Copper-Zinc **Reverse:** Common weasel

Date	F	VF	XF	Unc	BU
1991	—	0.15	0.25	0.50	—
1995	—	0.15	0.25	0.50	—
1998	—	0.15	0.25	0.50	—

KM# 79 2 CENTS **Composition:** Copper-Zinc **Obverse:** Similar to Lira, KM#82 **Reverse:** Olive branch

Date	Mintage	F	VF	XF	Unc	BU
1986	280,000	—	0.15	0.25	0.45	—
1986 Proof	10,000	Value: 3.00				

KM# 94 2 CENTS **Composition:** Copper-Zinc

Date	F	VF	XF	Unc	BU
1991	—	0.15	0.25	0.45	—
1992	—	0.15	0.25	0.45	—
1993	—	0.15	0.25	0.45	—
1995	—	0.15	0.25	0.45	—
1998	—	0.15	0.25	0.45	—

KM# 77 5 CENTS **Composition:** Copper-Nickel **Reverse:** Fresh-water crab

Date	Mintage	F	VF	XF	Unc	BU
1986	150,000	—	0.25	0.45	1.00	—
1986 Proof	10,000	Value: 3.50				

KM# 95 5 CENTS **Composition:** Copper-Nickel **Reverse:** Fresh-water crab

Date	F	VF	XF	Unc	BU
1991	—	0.25	0.45	1.00	—
1995	—	0.25	0.45	1.00	—
1998	—	0.25	0.45	1.00	—

KM# 76 10 CENTS **Composition:** Copper-Nickel **Reverse:** Dolphin fish

Date	Mintage	F	VF	XF	Unc	BU
1986	4,188,000	—	0.40	0.70	1.50	—
1986 Proof	10,000	Value: 4.00				

KM# 96 10 CENTS **Composition:** Copper-Nickel **Obverse:** Crowned shield **Reverse:** Dolphin fish

Date	F	VF	XF	Unc	BU
1991	—	0.40	0.70	1.50	—
1992	—	0.40	0.70	1.50	—
1995	—	0.40	0.70	1.50	—
1998	—	0.40	0.70	1.50	—

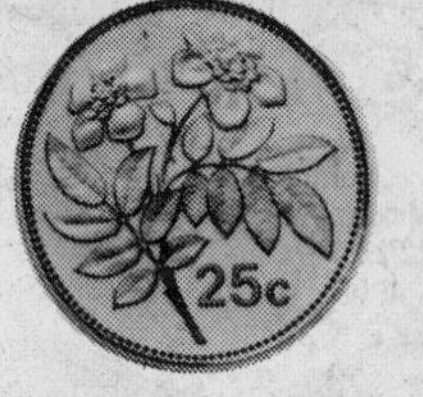

KM# 80 25 CENTS **Composition:** Copper-Nickel **Reverse:** Ghirlanda flower

Date	Mintage	F	VF	XF	Unc	BU
1986	3,090,000	—	1.00	1.80	2.50	—
1986 Proof	10,000	Value: 5.00				

KM# 97 25 CENTS **Composition:** Copper-Nickel **Obverse:** Crowned shield **Reverse:** Ghirlanda flower

Date	F	VF	XF	Unc	BU
1991	—	1.00	1.50	2.50	—
1993	—	1.00	1.50	2.50	—
1995	—	1.00	1.50	2.50	—
1998	—	1.00	1.50	2.50	—

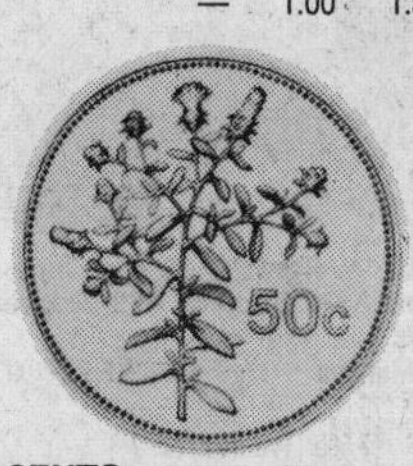

KM# 81 50 CENTS **Composition:** Copper-Nickel **Obverse:** Similar to Lira, KM#82 **Reverse:** Tulliera plant

Date	Mintage	F	VF	XF	Unc	BU
1986	2,086,000	—	1.75	2.25	4.50	—
1986 Proof	10,000	Value: 7.00				

KM# 98 50 CENTS **Composition:** Copper-Nickel **Obverse:** Similar to 5 Cents, KM#95 **Reverse:** Tulliera plant

Date	F	VF	XF	Unc	BU
1991	—	1.75	2.25	4.50	—
1992	—	1.75	2.25	4.50	—
1995	—	1.75	2.25	4.50	—

KM# 116 50 CENTS Composition: Copper Nickel Shape: 8-sided Size: 25 mm.

Date	F	VF	XF	Unc	BU
1995	—	—	—	—	—

KM# 63 LIRA Composition: Copper-Nickel Subject: World Fisheries Conference

Date	Mintage	F	VF	XF	Unc	BU
ND(1984)	120,000	—	—	4.00	7.50	—

KM# 82 LIRA Composition: Nickel Reverse: Merill bird

Date	Mintage	F	VF	XF	Unc	BU
1986	2,272,000	—	—	4.00	8.00	—
1986 Proof	10,000	Value: 10.00				

KM# 99 LIRA Composition: Nickel

Date	F	VF	XF	Unc	BU
1991	—	—	4.00	6.00	7.50
1992	—	—	4.00	6.00	7.50
1994	—	—	4.00	6.00	7.50
1995	—	—	4.00	6.00	7.50

KM# 88 2 LIRI Weight: 17.0000 g. Composition: 0.9250 Silver .5056 oz. ASW Subject: 25th Anniversary of Independence

Date	Mintage	F	VF	XF	Unc	BU
1989	75,000	—	—	—	10.00	—
1989 Proof	7,500	Value: 17.50				

KM# 65 5 LIRI Weight: 28.2800 g. Composition: 0.9250 Silver .8411 oz. ASW Series: International Year of Disabled Persons

Date	F	VF	XF	Unc	BU
1983	—	—	—	22.50	—
1983 Proof	—	Value: 40.00			

KM# 67 5 LIRI Weight: 20.0000 g. Composition: 0.9250 Silver .5949 oz. ASW Subject: Maritime history "Strangier" (1813)

Date	Mintage	F	VF	XF	Unc	BU
1984 Prooflike	15,000	—	—	—	22.50	—

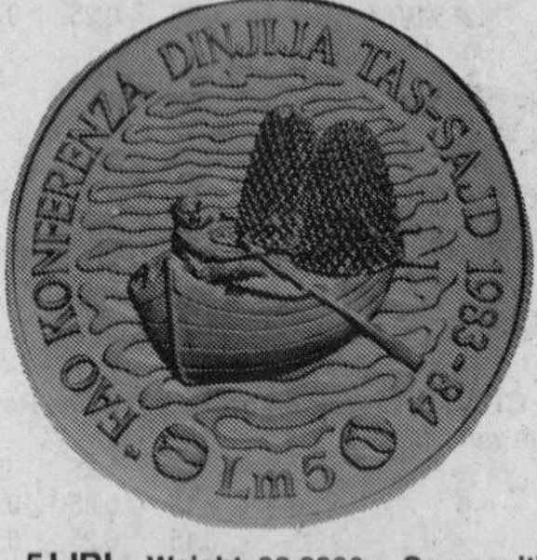

KM# 64 5 LIRI Weight: 28.2800 g. Composition: 0.9250 Silver .8411 oz. ASW Subject: World Fisheries Conference

Date	Mintage	F	VF	XF	Unc	BU
ND(1984) Proof	20,000	Value: 50.00				

KM# 68 5 LIRI Weight: 20.0000 g. Composition: 0.9250 Silver .5949 oz. ASW Subject: Maritime history "Tigre" (1839)

Date	Mintage	F	VF	XF	Unc	BU
1984 Prooflike	15,000	—	—	—	22.50	—

KM# 69 5 LIRI Weight: 20.0000 g. Composition: 0.9250 Silver .5949 oz. ASW Subject: Maritime history "Wignacourt" (1844)

Date	Mintage	F	VF	XF	Unc	BU
1984 Prooflike	15,000	—	—	—	22.50	—

KM# 70 5 LIRI Weight: 20.0000 g. Composition: 0.9250 Silver .5949 oz. ASW Subject: Maritime history "Providenza" (1848)

Date	Mintage	F	VF	XF	Unc	BU
1984 Prooflike	15,000	—	—	—	22.50	—

KM# 71 5 LIRI Weight: 28.2800 g. Composition: 0.9250 Silver .8411 oz. ASW Series: Decade for Women

Date	Mintage	F	VF	XF	Unc	BU
1984 Proof	17,000	Value: 35.00				

KM# 72 5 LIRI Weight: 20.0000 g. Composition: 0.9250 Silver .5949 oz. ASW Subject: Maritime history "Malta" (1862)

Date	Mintage	F	VF	XF	Unc	BU
1985 Prooflike	15,000	—	—	—	22.50	—

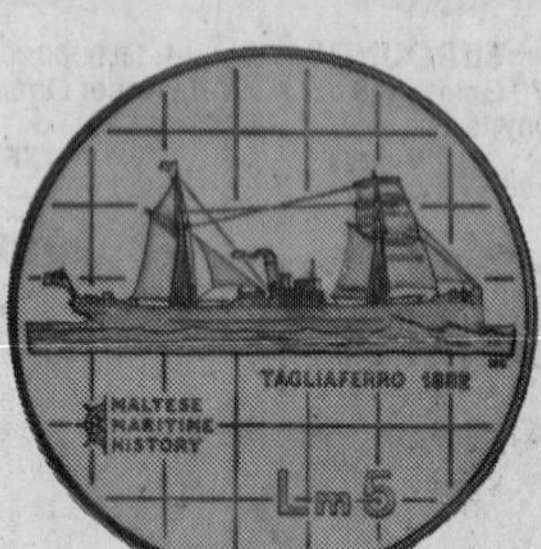

KM# 73 5 LIRI Weight: 20.0000 g. Composition: 0.9250 Silver .5949 oz. ASW Subject: Maritime history "Tagliaferro" (1882)

Date	Mintage	F	VF	XF	Unc	BU
1985 Prooflike	15,000	—	—	—	22.50	—

KM# 74 5 LIRI Weight: 20.0000 g. Composition: 0.9250 Silver .5949 oz. ASW Subject: Maritime history "L'Isle Adam" (1883)

Date	Mintage	F	VF	XF	Unc	BU
1985 Prooflike	15,000	—	—	—	22.50	—

KM# 75 5 LIRI **Weight:** 20.0000 g. **Composition:** 0.9250 Silver .5949 oz. ASW **Subject:** Maritime history "Maria Dacoutros" (1902)

Date	Mintage	F	VF	XF	Unc	BU
1985 Prooflike	15,000	—	—	—	22.50	—

KM# 83 5 LIRI **Weight:** 20.0000 g. **Composition:** 0.9250 Silver .5949 oz. ASW **Subject:** Maritime history "Valetta City" (1917)

Date	Mintage	F	VF	XF	Unc	BU
1986 Prooflike	15,000	—	—	—	22.50	—

KM# 84 5 LIRI **Weight:** 20.0000 g. **Composition:** 0.9250 Silver .5949 oz. ASW **Subject:** Maritime history "Knight of Malta" (1929)

Date	Mintage	F	VF	XF	Unc	BU
1986 Prooflike	15,000	—	—	—	22.50	—

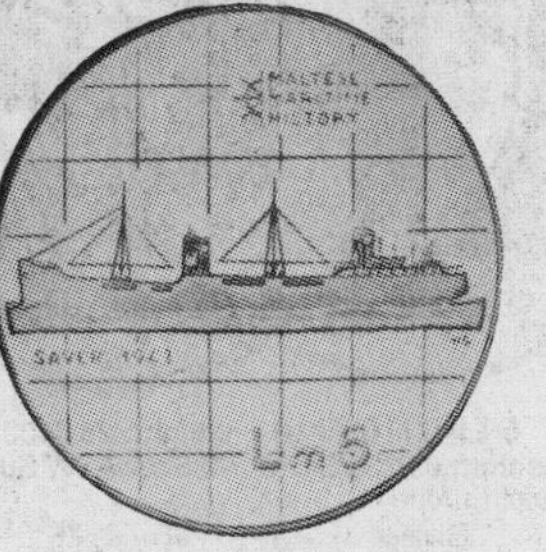

KM# 85 5 LIRI **Weight:** 20.0000 g. **Composition:** 0.9250 Silver .5949 oz. ASW **Subject:** Maritime history "Saver" (1943)

Date	Mintage	F	VF	XF	Unc	BU
1986 Prooflike	15,000	—	—	—	22.50	—

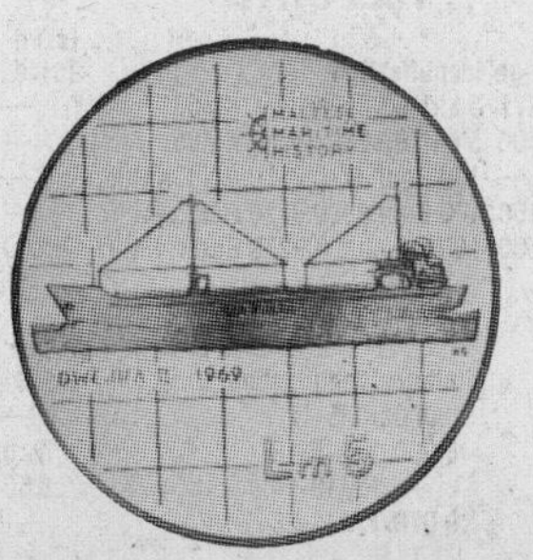

KM# 86 5 LIRI **Weight:** 20.0000 g. **Composition:** 0.9250 Silver .5949 oz. ASW **Subject:** Maritime history "Dwejra II" (1969)

Date	Mintage	F	VF	XF	Unc	BU
1986 Prooflike	15,000	—	—	—	22.50	—

KM# 87 5 LIRI **Weight:** 28.2800 g. **Composition:** 0.9250 Silver .8411 oz. ASW **Subject:** 20th Anniversary - Central Bank of Malta

Date	Mintage	F	VF	XF	Unc	BU
1988	—	—	—	—	25.00	—
1988 Proof	Est. 2,000	Value: 40.00				

KM# 90 5 LIRI **Weight:** 28.6000 g. **Composition:** 0.9250 Silver .8506 oz. ASW **Subject:** Papal visit

Date	Mintage	F	VF	XF	Unc	BU
1990	500	—	—	—	45.00	—
1990 Proof	4,000	Value: 55.00				

KM# 91 5 LIRI **Weight:** 28.2800 g. **Composition:** 0.9250 Silver .8411 oz. ASW **Subject:** Entry of Malta to European Economic Community

Date	Mintage	F	VF	XF	Unc	BU
1990	—	—	—	—	30.00	—
1990 Proof	Est. 4,000	Value: 50.00				

KM# 92 5 LIRI **Weight:** 28.2800 g. **Composition:** 0.9250 Silver .8411 oz. ASW **Series:** Save the Children

Date	Mintage	F	VF	XF	Unc	BU
1991 Proof	20,000	Value: 30.00				

KM# 100 5 LIRI **Weight:** 28.2800 g. **Composition:** 0.9250 Silver .8411 oz. ASW **Subject:** 50th Anniversary of George Cross Award

Date	Mintage	F	VF	XF	Unc	BU
1992 Proof	Est. 10,000	Value: 37.50				

KM# 102 5 LIRI **Weight:** 28.2800 g. **Composition:** 0.9250 Silver .8411 oz. ASW **Subject:** 25th Anniversary of Central Bank

Date	Mintage	F	VF	XF	Unc	BU
ND(1993)	—	—	—	—	32.50	—
ND(1993) Proof	Est. 1,500	Value: 55.00				

KM# 106 5 LIRI **Weight:** 28.2800 g. **Composition:** 0.9250 Silver .8411 oz. ASW **Subject:** 400th Anniversary - University of Malta

Date	Mintage	F	VF	XF	Unc	BU
ND(1993) Proof	Est. 1,000	Value: 40.00				

KM# 107 5 LIRI **Weight:** 28.2800 g. **Composition:** 0.9250 Silver .8411 oz. ASW **Subject:** World Cup Soccer

Date	Mintage	F	VF	XF	Unc	BU
1993 Proof	Est. 20,000	Value: 32.50				

KM# 108 5 LIRI **Weight:** 31.4700 g. **Composition:** 0.9250 Silver .9359 oz. ASW **Reverse:** Sailing ship "Valletta" and fortress

Date	Mintage	F	VF	XF	Unc	BU
1994 Proof	Est. 20,000	Value: 32.50				

KM# 109 5 LIRI **Weight:** 28.2800 g. **Composition:** 0.9250 Silver .8411 oz. ASW **Series:** 50th Anniversary - United Nations

Date	Mintage	F	VF	XF	Unc	BU
1995 Proof	Est. 125,000	Value: 30.00				

KM# 110 5 LIRI **Weight:** 31.4700 g. **Composition:** 0.9250 Silver .9359 oz. ASW **Series:** Olympic Games **Subject:** Water polo **Obverse:** National arms

Date	Mintage	F	VF	XF	Unc	BU
1996 Proof	Est. 35,000	Value: 28.50				

KM# 115 5 LIRI **Weight:** 28.2800 g. **Composition:** 0.9250 Silver 0.841 oz. ASW **Subject:** UNICEF **Obverse:** National arms. **Reverse:** Boy with dog and computer. **Edge:** Reeded. **Size:** 38.6 mm.

Date	Mintage	F	VF	XF	Unc	BU
1997 Proof	25,000	Value: 17.50				

KM# 111 5 LIRI **Weight:** 28.2800 g. **Composition:** 0.9250 Silver .841 oz. ASW **Obverse:** National arms **Reverse:** Bank's pyramid fountain

Date	Mintage	F	VF	XF	Unc	BU
1998 Proof	Est. 5,000	Value: 60.00				

KM# 112 5 LIRI **Weight:** 28.2800 g. **Composition:** 0.9250 Silver .841 oz. ASW **Subject:** 200th Anniversary - Anti-French Revolution **Obverse:** National arms **Reverse:** "Blockade" medal of 1798

Date	Mintage	F	VF	XF	Unc	BU
1998 Proof	Est. 5,000	Value: 60.00				

KM# 113 5 LIRI **Weight:** 28.3500 g. **Composition:** 0.9250 Silver .8431 oz. ASW **Subject:** Mattia Preti **Obverse:** National arms **Reverse:** Portrait of Preti and John the Baptist **Edge:** Reeded **Size:** 38.4 mm.

Date	F	VF	XF	Unc	BU
1999 Proof	—	—	—	50.00	—

KM# 114 5 LIRI **Weight:** 15.0000 g. **Composition:** 0.9250 Silver .4461 oz. ASW **Subject:** Millennium **Obverse:** Two modern gold-plated coin designs **Reverse:** Two ancient gold-plated coin designs and map **Edge:** Plain **Note:** 40x20 milimeters.

Date	Mintage	F	VF	XF	Unc	BU
2000 Proof	32,000	—	—	—	50.00	—

KM# 101 25 LIRI **Weight:** 7.9900 g. **Composition:** 0.9170 Gold .2353 oz. AGW **Subject:** 50th Anniversary of George Cross Award

Date	Mintage	F	VF	XF	Unc	BU
1992 Proof	Est. 500	Value: 185				

KM# 66 100 LIRI **Weight:** 15.9800 g. **Composition:** 0.9170 Gold .4709 oz. AGW **Series:** International Year of Disabled Persons

Date	Mintage	F	VF	XF	Unc	BU
1983	700	—	—	—	400	—
1983 Proof	600	Value: 500				

KM# 89 100 LIRI **Weight:** 17.0000 g. **Composition:** 0.9170 Gold .5007 oz. AGW **Subject:** 25th Anniversary of Independence

Date	Mintage	F	VF	XF	Unc	BU
1989	5,000	—	—	—	250	—
1989 Proof	2,500	Value: 300				

EUROPEAN CURRENCY UNIT

ECU

KM# 103 LIRA (2 Ecu) **Composition:** Copper-Nickel **Subject:** Defense of Europe

Date	Mintage	F	VF	XF	Unc	BU
1993	25,000	—	—	—	11.50	—

KM# 104 5 LIRI (10 Ecu) **Weight:** 25.0000 g. **Composition:** 0.9250 Silver .7435 oz. ASW **Subject:** Defense of Europe

Date	Mintage	F	VF	XF	Unc	BU
1993 Proof	35,000	Value: 28.50				

KM# 105 25 LIRI (55 Ecu) **Weight:** 6.7200 g. **Composition:** 0.9000 Gold .1945 oz. AGW **Subject:** Defense of Europe

Date	Mintage	F	VF	XF	Unc	BU
1993 Proof	2,500	Value: 175				

PIEFORTS

KM#	Date	Mintage	Identification	Issue Price	Mkt Val
P1	1981	177	5 Liri. 0.9250 Silver. KM53.	—	120
P2	1983	700	5 Liri. 0.9250 Silver. KM65.	—	70.00
P3	1983	—	100 Pounds. 0.9170 Gold. KM66.	—	800
P3	1983	150	100 Pounds. 0.9170 Gold. KM66.	—	800
P4	1988	500	100 Pounds. 0.9250 Silver. KM87.	80.00	100

MINT SETS

KM#	Date	Mintage	Identification	Issue Price	Mkt Val
MS1	1972 (8)	8,000	KM5-12	—	7.50
MS2	1972 (4)	8,000	KM15-18	210	800
MS3	1972 (2)	—	KM13-14	8.50	27.50
MS4	1973 (3)	9,078	KM21-23	—	400

KM#	Date	Mintage	Identification	Issue Price	Mkt Val
MS5	1973 (2)	—	KM19-20	—	27.50
MS6	1974 (3)	—	KM26-28	256	400
MS7	1974 (2)	—	KM24-25	19.60	22.50
MS10	1975 (2)	—	KM30, 32	20.00	45.00
MS8	1975 (5)	2,000	KM30, 32, 34, 36, 38	276	600
MS9	1975 (3)	—	KM34, 36, 38	256	550
MS11	1975 (3)	—	KM35, 37, 39	—	425
MSA10	1975 (2)	—	KM31, 33	—	28.00
MS12	1976 (3)	—	KM42-44	—	425
MS13	1976 (2)	—	KM40-41	—	25.00
MS14	1977 (9)	252	KM5-12, 29b	—	60.00
MS15	1977 (3)	4,000	KM48-50	610	900
MS16	1977 (3)	15,000	KM45-47	34.50	36.50
MS17	1978 (9)	252	KM5-12, 29b	—	60.00
MS18	1979 (9)	537	KM5-12, 29b	—	110
MS19	1980 (9)	385	KM5-12, 29b	11.00	110
MS20	1981 (9)	449	KM5-12, 29b	13.25	110
MS21	1982 (9)	850	KM54-62	13.25	120
MS22	1984 (4)	15,000	KM67-70	72.00	90.00
MS23	1985 (4)	15,000	KM72-75	72.00	90.00
MS24	1986 (4)	15,000	KM83-86	72.00	90.00

PROOF SETS

KM#	Date	Mintage	Identification	Issue Price	Mkt Val
PS1	1972 (8)	8,000	KM5-12; plastic case	—	12.50
PS2	1976 (9)	26,248	KM5-12, 29b	27.50	15.00
PS3	1977 (9)	6,884	KM5-12, 29b	31.50	21.50
PS4	1977 (3)	750	KM48-50	909	1,150
PS5	1977 (3)	2,500	KM45-47	72.00	80.00
PS6	1978 (9)	3,244	KM5-12, 29b	—	18.00
PS7	1979 (10)	6,577	KM5-12, 29b, 51	41.50	30.00
PS8	1980 (9)	3,451	KM5-12, 29b	30.00	25.00
PS9	1981 (9)	1,453	KM5-12, 29b	25.30	45.00
PS10	1982 (9)	1,793	KM54-62	32.00	45.00
PS11	1986 (7)	10,000	KM76-82	29.75	30.00

MARSHALL ISLANDS

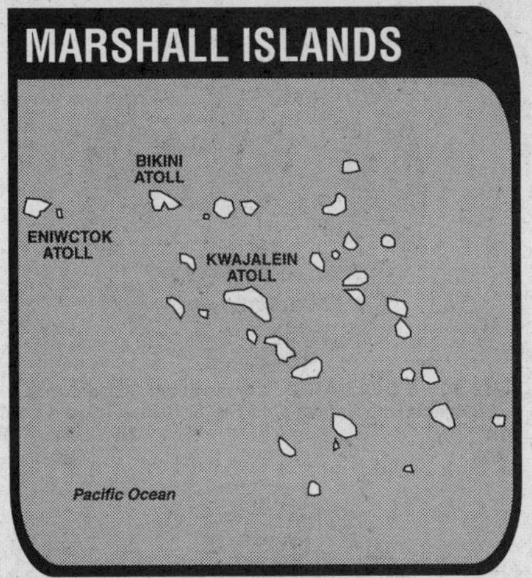

The Republic of the Marshall Islands, an archipelago which is one of the four island groups that make up what is commonly known as Micronesia, consists of 33 coral atolls comprised of over 1,150 islands or islets. It is located east of the Caroline Islands and west-northwest of the Gilbert Islands half way between Hawaii and Australia. The Ratak chain to the east and the Ralik chain to the west comprise a total land area of 70 sq. mi. (181 sq. km.) with a population of 25,000 of which about 10 % includes Americans who work at the Kwajalein Missile Range. Majuro Atoll is the government and commercial center of the Republic.

Very little is known of the history of the islands before the 16th century. It is believed that many countries vessels visited the islands while searching for new trade routes to the East. In 1788, John Marshall, a British sea captain for whom the islands were named, explored them. The Islands have undergone successive domination by the Spanish, Germans, Japanese and Americans. It was the site of some of the fiercest fighting of the entire Pacific theater during World War II. At the conclusion of the war, the United States, under the direction of the United Nations administered the affairs of the Marshall Islands.

A constitutional government was formed on May 1,1979 with Amata Kabua being elected as the head of the government. On October 1, 1986, the United States notified the United Nations that the Marshall Islands were to be recognized as a separate nation.

The USA dollar is the current monetary system. Recently, the coinage has had limited redemption policies enforced.

MINT MARKS

M - Medallic Art Co.
R - Roger Williams Mint, Rhode Island
S - Sunshine Mining Co. Mint, Idaho

REPUBLIC

NON-CIRCULATING COLLECTOR COINAGE

The USA dollar is the current monetary system. Recently, the coinage has had limited redemption policies enforced.

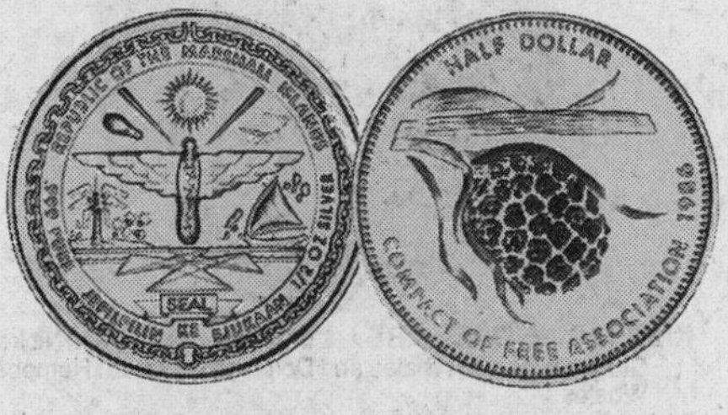

KM# 1 1/2 DOLLAR **Weight:** 15.5510 g. **Composition:** 0.9990 Silver .5000 oz. ASW **Reverse:** Pandanus Fruit

Date	Mintage	F	VF	XF	Unc	BU
1986 Proof	10,000	Value: 12.50				

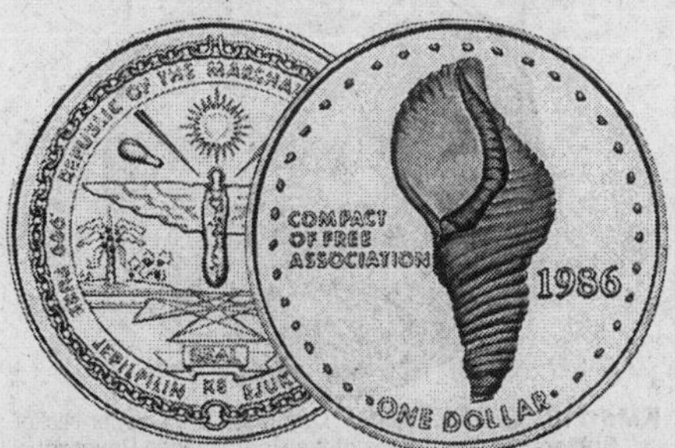

KM# 2 DOLLAR **Weight:** 31.1030 g. **Composition:** 0.9990 Silver 1.0000 oz. ASW **Obverse:** Similar to 1/2 Dollar, KM#1 **Reverse:** Triton Shell

Date	Mintage	F	VF	XF	Unc	BU
1986 Proof	10,000	Value: 25.00				

KM# 293 DOLLAR **Weight:** 1.5552 g. **Composition:** 0.9990 Gold .0499 oz. AGW **Obverse:** Lion **Note:** Similar to 5 Dollars, KM#295.

Date	F	VF	XF	Unc	BU
1996	—	—	—	45.00	—

KM# 294 2-1/2 DOLLARS **Weight:** 3.1103 g. **Composition:** 0.9990 Gold .0999 oz. AGW **Obverse:** Lion **Note:** Similar to 5 Dollars, KM#295.

Date	F	VF	XF	Unc	BU
1996	—	—	—	85.00	—

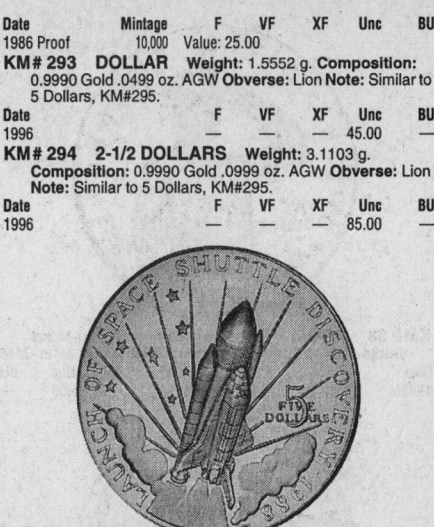

KM# 6 5 DOLLARS **Composition:** Copper-Nickel **Subject:** U.S. Space Shuttle - Discovery

Date	Mintage	F	VF	XF	Unc	BU
1988	756,000	—	—	—	3.50	—
1988M	431,000	—	—	—	4.50	—

KM# 13 5 DOLLARS **Composition:** Copper-Nickel **Subject:** 20th Anniversary - First Men on the Moon

Date	F	VF	XF	Unc	BU
1989	—	—	—	3.50	—

KM# 18 5 DOLLARS **Composition:** Copper-Nickel **Subject:** 50th Anniversary - Battle of Britain

Date	F	VF	XF	Unc	BU
1990M	—	—	—	4.50	—

KM# 33 5 DOLLARS **Composition:** Copper-Nickel **Subject:** German Unification

Date	F	VF	XF	Unc	BU
1990M	—	—	—	8.00	—

KM# 38 5 DOLLARS **Composition:** Copper-Nickel
Subject: Dwight David Eisenhower **Obverse:** Sim.ilar to KM#6

Date	F	VF	XF	Unc	BU
1990M	—	—	—	5.00	—

KM# 35 5 DOLLARS **Composition:** Copper-Nickel
Subject: To the Heroes of Pearl Harbor

Date	F	VF	XF	Unc	BU
1991M	—	—	—	4.00	—

KM# 37 5 DOLLARS **Composition:** Copper-Nickel
Subject: Space Shuttle Columbia

Date	F	VF	XF	Unc	BU
1991M	—	—	—	5.00	—

KM# 40 5 DOLLARS **Composition:** Copper-Nickel
Subject: To the Heroes of Desert Storm

Date	F	VF	XF	Unc	BU
1991R	—	—	—	6.00	—

KM# 81 5 DOLLARS **Composition:** Copper-Nickel
Subject: Reaching For New Horizons - Tipnol

Date	F	VF	XF	Unc	BU
1992R	—	—	—	6.00	—

KM# 84 5 DOLLARS **Composition:** Copper-Nickel
Subject: To the Heroes of the First Air Raid on Tokyo - Doolittle

Date	F	VF	XF	Unc	BU
1992R	—	—	—	5.50	—

KM# 87 5 DOLLARS **Composition:** Copper-Nickel
Subject: To the Heroes of Corregidor

Date	F	VF	XF	Unc	BU
1992R	—	—	—	8.00	—

KM# 90 5 DOLLARS **Composition:** Copper-Nickel
Subject: To the Heroes of Battle of Midway

Date	F	VF	XF	Unc	BU
1992R	—	—	—	8.00	—

KM# 110 5 DOLLARS **Composition:** Copper-Nickel
Subject: Pacific Whales and Dolphins **Reverse:** Humpback Whales

Date	F	VF	XF	Unc	BU
1993R Prooflike	—	—	—	10.00	—

KM# 118 5 DOLLARS **Composition:** Copper-Nickel
Subject: To the Heroes of the North Atlantic **Reverse:** Submarine

Date	F	VF	XF	Unc	BU
1993R Prooflike	—	—	—	6.00	—

KM# 121 5 DOLLARS **Composition:** Copper-Nickel
Subject: To the Heroes of Guadalcanal **Reverse:** Marine, battleship and airplanes

Date	F	VF	XF	Unc	BU
1993R Prooflike	—	—	—	6.00	—

KM# 124 5 DOLLARS **Composition:** Copper-Nickel
Reverse: Elvis Presley

Date	F	VF	XF	Unc	BU
1993R Prooflike	—	—	—	8.00	—

KM# 126 5 DOLLARS **Composition:** Copper-Nickel
Subject: Pacific Whales and Dolphins **Reverse:** Common Dolphin

Date	F	VF	XF	Unc	BU
1993R Prooflike	—	—	—	10.00	—

KM# 144 5 DOLLARS **Composition:** Copper-Nickel
Subject: Christmas 1993

Date	F	VF	XF	Unc	BU
1993	—	—	—	8.50	—

KM# 148 5 DOLLARS **Composition:** Copper-Nickel
Subject: Flight at Kitty Hawk

Date	F	VF	XF	Unc	BU
1993	—	—	—	8.50	—

KM# 151 5 DOLLARS **Composition:** Copper-Nickel
Subject: First Men on the Moon

Date	F	VF	XF	Unc	BU
1994	—	—	—	8.50	—

KM# 179 5 DOLLARS **Composition:** Copper-Nickel
Subject: To the Heroes of D-Day - Normandy Invasion

Date	F	VF	XF	Unc	BU
1994	—	—	—	8.50	—

KM# 182 5 DOLLARS **Composition:** Copper-Nickel
Subject: To the Heroes of the Philippines **Reverse:** MacArthur and staff

Date	F	VF	XF	Unc	BU
1994	—	—	—	6.50	—

KM# 263 5 DOLLARS **Composition:** Copper-Nickel
Subject: To the Heroes of the Battle of The Bulge

Date	F	VF	XF	Unc	BU
1994	—	—	—	5.50	—

KM# 187 5 DOLLARS **Composition:** Copper-Nickel
Subject: World Cup Soccer

Date	F	VF	XF	Unc	BU
1994	—	—	—	5.50	—

KM# 260 5 DOLLARS **Composition:** Copper-Nickel
Subject: Christmas - Cherub

Date	F	VF	XF	Unc	BU
1994	—	—	—	5.50	—

KM# 270 5 DOLLARS **Composition:** Copper-Nickel
Reverse: Tornado F. MK 3 - Bomber

Date	F	VF	XF	Unc	BU
1995	—	—	—	6.00	—

KM# 271 5 DOLLARS **Composition:** Copper-Nickel
Subject: Christmas **Reverse:** Cherub

Date	F	VF	XF	Unc	BU
1995	—	—	—	5.50	—

KM# 395 5 DOLLARS **Composition:** Copper-Nickel
Obverse: State seal **Reverse:** F-80 Shooting Star

Date	F	VF	XF	Unc	BU
1995	—	—	—	6.50	—

KM# 185 5 DOLLARS **Composition:** Copper-Nickel
Reverse: F-100 Super Sabre

Date	F	VF	XF	Unc	BU
1995	—	—	—	5.50	—

KM# 186 5 DOLLARS **Composition:** Copper-Nickel
Reverse: F-16 Fighting Falcon

Date	F	VF	XF	Unc	BU
1995	—	—	—	5.50	—

KM# 216 5 DOLLARS **Composition:** Copper-Nickel
Subject: Peace - Victory in Europe

Date	F	VF	XF	Unc	BU
1995	—	—	—	5.50	—

KM# 219 5 DOLLARS **Composition:** Copper-Nickel
Subject: To the Heroes of the Vietnam War

Date	F	VF	XF	Unc	BU
1995	—	—	—	5.50	—

KM# 222 5 DOLLARS **Composition:** Copper-Nickel
Reverse: Elvis Presley

Date	F	VF	XF	Unc	BU
1995	—	—	—	9.00	—

KM# 253 5 DOLLARS **Composition:** Copper-Nickel
Reverse: Marilyn Monroe

Date	F	VF	XF	Unc	BU
1995	—	—	—	7.00	—

KM# 257 5 DOLLARS **Composition:** Copper-Nickel **Series:** 50th Anniversary United Nations **Subject:** Peace

Date	F	VF	XF	Unc	BU
1995	—	—	—	5.50	—

KM# 266 5 DOLLARS **Composition:** Copper-Nickel **Subject:** Peace - VJ Day

Date	F	VF	XF	Unc	BU
1995	—	—	—	5.50	—

KM# 269 5 DOLLARS **Composition:** Copper-Nickel **Reverse:** Mirage 2000C Jet Fighter

Date	F	VF	XF	Unc	BU
1995	—	—	—	6.00	—

KM# 225 5 DOLLARS **Composition:** Copper-Nickel **Subject:** War in the Pacific **Note:** Similar to 10 Dollars, KM#226.

Date	F	VF	XF	Unc	BU
1995	—	—	—	9.50	—

KM# 308 5 DOLLARS **Composition:** Copper-Nickel **Subject:** Classic Cars **Reverse:** Ford Quadricycle **Note:** Similar to 10 Dollars, KM#309.

Date	F	VF	XF	Unc	BU
1996	—	—	—	7.50	—

KM# 331 5 DOLLARS **Composition:** Copper-Nickel **Subject:** Steam Locomotive **Reverse:** "Big Boy" **Note:** Similar to 50 Dollar, KM#292.

Date	F	VF	XF	Unc	BU
1996	—	—	—	6.00	—

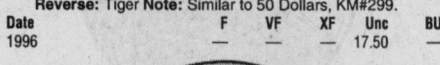

KM# 297 5 DOLLARS **Composition:** Copper-Nickel **Reverse:** Tiger **Note:** Similar to 50 Dollars, KM#299.

Date	F	VF	XF	Unc	BU
1996	—	—	—	17.50	—

KM# 280 5 DOLLARS **Composition:** Copper-Nickel **Subject:** Year of the Rat

Date	F	VF	XF	Unc	BU
1996	—	—	—	8.00	—

KM# 288 5 DOLLARS **Composition:** Copper-Nickel **Reverse:** Space Shuttle Columbia

Date	F	VF	XF	Unc	BU
1996	—	—	—	5.50	—

KM# 295 5 DOLLARS **Weight:** 7.7759 g. **Composition:** 0.9990 Gold .2497 oz. AGW **Obverse:** State seal **Reverse:** Lion

Date	F	VF	XF	Unc	BU
1996	—	—	—	200	—

KM# 300 5 DOLLARS **Composition:** Copper-Nickel **Reverse:** Elvis Presley

Date	F	VF	XF	Unc	BU
1996	—	—	—	9.00	—

KM# 303 5 DOLLARS **Composition:** Copper-Nickel **Reverse:** James Dean

Date	F	VF	XF	Unc	BU
1996	—	—	—	8.00	—

KM# 311 5 DOLLARS **Composition:** Copper-Nickel **Subject:** Classic Cars **Reverse:** Model A Ford

Date	F	VF	XF	Unc	BU
1996	—	—	—	7.00	—

KM# 314 5 DOLLARS **Composition:** Copper-Nickel **Subject:** Classic Cars **Reverse:** Model T Ford

Date	F	VF	XF	Unc	BU
1996	—	—	—	7.00	—

KM# 317 5 DOLLARS **Composition:** Copper-Nickel **Subject:** Classic Cars **Reverse:** 1955 Thunderbird

Date	F	VF	XF	Unc	BU
1996	—	—	—	8.50	—

KM# 320 5 DOLLARS **Composition:** Copper-Nickel **Subject:** Classic Cars **Reverse:** 1964 Mustang

Date	F	VF	XF	Unc	BU
1996	—	—	—	8.50	—

KM# 323 5 DOLLARS **Composition:** Copper-Nickel
Subject: Classic Cars **Reverse:** Ford Taurus

Date	F	VF	XF	Unc	BU
1996	—	—	—	7.00	—

KM# 330 5 DOLLARS **Composition:** Copper-Nickel
Subject: Steam Locomotive **Reverse:** Pennsylvania K4

Date	F	VF	XF	Unc	BU
1996	—	—	—	6.00	—

KM# 344 5 DOLLARS **Composition:** Copper-Nickel
Reverse: Lion

Date	F	VF	XF	Unc	BU
1996	—	—	—	15.00	—

KM# 345 5 DOLLARS **Composition:** Copper-Nickel
Reverse: Cheetah

Date	F	VF	XF	Unc	BU
1996	—	—	—	15.00	—

KM# 346 5 DOLLARS **Composition:** Copper-Nickel
Reverse: Jaguar

Date	F	VF	XF	Unc	BU
1996	—	—	—	15.00	—

KM# 353 5 DOLLARS **Composition:** Copper-Nickel
Subject: Christmas **Reverse:** Two angels

Date	F	VF	XF	Unc	BU
1996	—	—	—	7.50	—

KM# 362 5 DOLLARS **Composition:** Copper-Nickel
Subject: Year of the Ox **Obverse:** State seal **Reverse:** Stylized Ox

Date	F	VF	XF	Unc	BU
1997	—	—	—	7.50	—

KM# 364 5 DOLLARS **Composition:** Copper-Nickel
Reverse: Elvis Presley

Date	F	VF	XF	Unc	BU
1997	—	—	—	10.00	—

KM# 398 5 DOLLARS **Composition:** Copper-Nickel
Subject: History's Great Fighting Ships **Obverse:** State seal
Reverse: USS Constitution

Date	F	VF	XF	Unc	BU
1997	—	—	—	6.50	—

KM# 403 5 DOLLARS **Composition:** Copper-Nickel
Subject: Christmas **Obverse:** State seal **Reverse:** Two cherubs

Date	F	VF	XF	Unc	BU
1997	—	—	—	6.00	—

KM# 407 5 DOLLARS **Composition:** Copper-Nickel
Subject: Sermon on the Mount **Obverse:** State seal
Reverse: Jesus preaching

Date	F	VF	XF	Unc	BU
1997	—	—	—	6.00	—

KM# 369 5 DOLLARS **Composition:** Copper-Nickel
Subject: The Last Supper **Obverse:** State seal

Date	F	VF	XF	Unc	BU
1997	—	—	—	6.00	—

KM# 371 5 DOLLARS **Composition:** Copper-Nickel
Subject: To the Heroes of the Korean War **Obverse:** State seal **Reverse:** Soldier in poncho

Date	F	VF	XF	Unc	BU
1997	—	—	—	6.00	—

KM# 374 5 DOLLARS **Composition:** Copper-Nickel
Obverse: State seal **Reverse:** Gray wolf

Date	F	VF	XF	Unc	BU
1997	—	—	—	15.00	—

KM# 413 5 DOLLARS **Composition:** Copper-Nickel **Subject:** Year of the Tiger **Obverse:** State seal **Reverse:** Stylized tiger

Date	F	VF	XF	Unc	BU
1998	—	—	—	6.00	—

KM# 463 5 DOLLARS **Composition:** Copper-Nickel **Subject:** History's Great Fighting Ships **Obverse:** State seal **Reverse:** USS Missouri

Date	F	VF	XF	Unc	BU
1998	—	—	—	5.50	—

KM# 464 5 DOLLARS **Composition:** Copper-Nickel **Subject:** To the Heroes of the Berlin Airlift **Obverse:** State seal **Reverse:** C-54 landing

Date	F	VF	XF	Unc	BU
1998	—	—	—	5.50	—

KM# 466 5 DOLLARS **Composition:** Copper-Nickel **Subject:** Classic Cars **Obverse:** State seal **Reverse:** 1912 Chevy Classic Six

Date	F	VF	XF	Unc	BU
1998	—	—	—	6.00	—

KM# 468 5 DOLLARS **Composition:** Copper-Nickel **Subject:** Classic Cars **Obverse:** State seal **Reverse:** 1931 Chevy Roadster

Date	F	VF	XF	Unc	BU
1998	—	—	—	6.00	—

KM# 470 5 DOLLARS **Composition:** Copper-Nickel **Subject:** Classic Cars **Obverse:** State seal **Reverse:** Cameo Carrier

Date	F	VF	XF	Unc	BU
1998	—	—	—	6.00	—

KM# 472 5 DOLLARS **Composition:** Copper-Nickel **Subject:** Classic Cars **Obverse:** State seal **Reverse:** 1957 Chevy Bel Air

Date	F	VF	XF	Unc	BU
1998	—	—	—	6.00	—

KM# 474 5 DOLLARS **Composition:** Copper-Nickel **Subject:** Classic Cars **Obverse:** State seal **Reverse:** 1957 Chevy Corvette

Date	F	VF	XF	Unc	BU
1998	—	—	—	6.00	—

KM# 476 5 DOLLARS **Composition:** Copper-Nickel **Subject:** Classic Cars **Obverse:** State seal **Reverse:** 1967 Chevy Camaro

Date	F	VF	XF	Unc	BU
1998	—	—	—	6.00	—

KM# 478 5 DOLLARS **Composition:** Copper-Nickel **Obverse:** State seal **Reverse:** Babe Ruth at bat

Date	F	VF	XF	Unc	BU
1998	—	—	—	6.50	—

KM# 481 5 DOLLARS **Composition:** Copper-Nickel **Subject:** Christmas **Obverse:** State seal **Reverse:** Angel

Date	F	VF	XF	Unc	BU
1998	—	—	—	6.00	—

KM# 484 5 DOLLARS **Composition:** Copper-Nickel **Reverse:** Friendship 7 and Discovery blasting off

Date	F	VF	XF	Unc	BU
1998	—	—	—	6.00	—

KM# 486 5 DOLLARS **Composition:** Copper-Nickel **Subject:** USS United States **Obverse:** National seal **Reverse:** Sailing ship **Edge:** Reeded **Size:** 38.4 mm.

Date	F	VF	XF	Unc	BU
1998	—	—	—	10.00	—

KM# 487 5 DOLLARS **Composition:** Copper-Nickel **Obverse:** National seal **Reverse:** USS Monitor and Merrimack battle scene **Edge:** Reeded **Size:** 38.4 mm.

Date	F	VF	XF	Unc	BU
1998	—	—	—	10.00	—

KM# 488 5 DOLLARS **Composition:** Copper-Nickel **Subject:** USS Olympia **Obverse:** National seal **Reverse:** Battleship steaming left **Edge:** Reeded **Size:** 38.4 mm.

Date	F	VF	XF	Unc	BU
1998	—	—	—	10.00	—

KM# 489 5 DOLLARS **Composition:** Copper-Nickel **Obverse:** National seal **Reverse:** USS Fanning and USS Nicholson **Edge:** Reeded **Size:** 38.4 mm.

Date	F	VF	XF	Unc	BU
1998	—	—	—	10.00	—

KM# 490 5 DOLLARS **Composition:** Copper-Nickel **Obverse:** National seal **Reverse:** USS Enterprise **Edge:** Reeded **Size:** 38.4 mm.

Date	F	VF	XF	Unc	BU
1998	—	—	—	10.00	—

KM# 491 5 DOLLARS **Composition:** Copper-Nickel **Obverse:** National seal **Reverse:** Battleship USS New Jersey **Edge:** Reeded **Size:** 38.4 mm.

Date	F	VF	XF	Unc	BU
1998	—	—	—	10.00	—

KM# 492 5 DOLLARS **Composition:** Copper-Nickel **Obverse:** National seal **Reverse:** Heavy Cruiser USS Juneau **Edge:** Reeded **Size:** 38.4 mm.

Date	F	VF	XF	Unc	BU
1998	—	—	—	10.00	—

KM# 147 10 DOLLARS **Weight:** 11.0000 g. **Composition:** 0.9990 Silver .3533 oz. ASW **Reverse:** Greg Louganis

Date	F	VF	XF	Unc	BU
1988 Proof	—	Value: 185			

KM#41 10 DOLLARS **Composition:** Brass **Subject:** To the Heroes of Desert Storm

Date	F	VF	XF	Unc	BU
1991R	—	—	—	8.00	—

KM# 59 10 DOLLARS **Composition:** Brass **Reverse:** WWII American P-51 Mustang

Date	F	VF	XF	Unc	BU
1991S Prooflike	—	—	—	12.50	—

KM# 60 10 DOLLARS **Composition:** Brass **Reverse:** WWII American B-29 Superfortress

Date	F	VF	XF	Unc	BU
1991S Prooflike	—	—	—	12.50	—

KM# 61 10 DOLLARS **Composition:** Brass **Reverse:** WWII American B-25 Mitchell

Date	F	VF	XF	Unc	BU
1991S Prooflike	—	—	—	12.50	—

KM# 62 10 DOLLARS **Composition:** Brass **Reverse:** WWII American PBY Catalina

Date	F	VF	XF	Unc	BU
1991S Prooflike	—	—	—	12.50	—

KM# 63 10 DOLLARS **Composition:** Brass **Reverse:** WWII German BF 109 Messerschmitt

Date	F	VF	XF	Unc	BU
1991S Prooflike	—	—	—	12.50	—

KM# 64 10 DOLLARS **Composition:** Brass **Reverse:** WWII British Spitfire

Date	F	VF	XF	Unc	BU
1991S Prooflike	—	—	—	12.50	—

KM# 65 10 DOLLARS **Composition:** Brass **Reverse:** WWII Japanaese A6M Reisen

Date	F	VF	XF	Unc	BU
1991S Prooflike	—	—	—	12.50	—

KM# 66 10 DOLLARS **Composition:** Brass **Reverse:** WWII American F6F Hellcat

Date	F	VF	XF	Unc	BU
1991S Prooflike	—	—	—	12.50	—

KM# 67 10 DOLLARS **Composition:** Brass **Reverse:** WWII Soviet Yak 9

Date	F	VF	XF	Unc	BU
1991S Prooflike	—	—	—	12.50	—

KM# 68 10 DOLLARS **Composition:** Brass **Reverse:** WWII American B-17 Flying Fortress

Date	F	VF	XF	Unc	BU
1991S Prooflike	—	—	—	12.50	—

KM# 69 10 DOLLARS **Composition:** Brass **Reverse:** WWII British Hawker Hurricane

Date	F	VF	XF	Unc	BU
1991S Prooflike	—	—	—	12.50	—

KM# 73 10 DOLLARS **Composition:** Brass **Subject:** To the Heroes of Pearl Harbor **Obverse:** National seal

Date	F	VF	XF	Unc	BU
1991 Prooflike	—	—	—	12.50	—

KM# 70 10 DOLLARS **Composition:** Brass **Reverse:** WWII British Mosquito

Date	F	VF	XF	Unc	BU
1991S Prooflike	—	—	—	12.50	—

KM# 71 10 DOLLARS **Composition:** Brass **Reverse:** WWII British Lancaster

Date	F	VF	XF	Unc	BU
1991S Prooflike	—	—	—	12.50	—

KM# 96 10 DOLLARS **Composition:** Brass **Reverse:** WWII American C-47 Skytrain

Date	F	VF	XF	Unc	BU
1991S Prooflike	—	—	—	12.50	—

KM# 98 10 DOLLARS **Composition:** Brass **Reverse:** WWII American F4U Corsair

Date	F	VF	XF	Unc	BU
1991S Prooflike	—	—	—	12.50	—

KM# 101 10 DOLLARS **Composition:** Brass **Reverse:** WWII American P-38 Lightning

Date	F	VF	XF	Unc	BU
1991 Prooflike	—	—	—	12.50	—

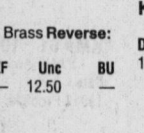

KM# 103 10 DOLLARS **Composition:** Brass **Reverse:** WWII Japanese G4M "Betty" Bomber

Date	F	VF	XF	Unc	BU
1991S Prooflike	—	—	—	12.50	—

KM# 107 10 DOLLARS **Composition:** Brass **Reverse:** WWII Japanese KI-61 Kien "Tony"

Date	F	VF	XF	Unc	BU
1991S Prooflike	—	—	—	12.50	—

KM# 109 10 DOLLARS **Composition:** Brass **Reverse:** WWII French D.520 Fighter

Date	F	VF	XF	Unc	BU
1991S Prooflike	—	—	—	12.50	—

KM# 125 10 DOLLARS **Composition:** Brass **Reverse:** WWII German FW 190 Fighters

Date	F	VF	XF	Unc	BU
1991S Prooflike	—	—	—	12.50	—

KM# 131 10 DOLLARS **Composition:** Brass **Reverse:** WWII American B-24 Liberator

Date	F	VF	XF	Unc	BU
1991S Prooflike	—	—	—	12.50	—

KM# 140 10 DOLLARS **Composition:** Brass **Reverse:** WWII Italian S.M. 79 Sparviero

Date	F	VF	XF	Unc	BU
1991S Prooflike	—	—	—	12.50	—

KM# 141 10 DOLLARS **Composition:** Brass **Reverse:** WWII German HE III Bombers

Date	F	VF	XF	Unc	BU
1991S Prooflike	—	—	—	12.50	—

KM# 142 10 DOLLARS Composition: Brass **Reverse:** WWII Sovient IL-2 Shturmovik ground attack

Date	F	VF	XF	Unc	BU
1991S Prooflike	—	—	—	12.50	—

KM# 143 10 DOLLARS Composition: Brass **Reverse:** WWII American P-51 Mustang

Date	F	VF	XF	Unc	BU
1991S Prooflike	—	—	—	12.50	—

KM# 82 10 DOLLARS Composition: Brass **Subject:** Legends of Discovery **Reverse:** Santa Maria

Date	F	VF	XF	Unc	BU
1992R	—	—	—	12.50	—

KM# 85 10 DOLLARS Composition: Brass **Subject:** First Air Raid on Tokyo **Reverse:** Doolittle

Date	F	VF	XF	Unc	BU
1992R	—	—	—	12.50	—

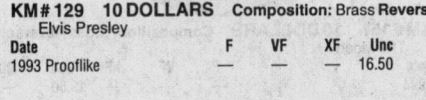

KM# 88 10 DOLLARS Composition: Brass **Subject:** To the Heroes of Corregidor

Date	F	VF	XF	Unc	BU
1992R	—	—	—	12.50	—

KM# 91 10 DOLLARS Composition: Brass **Subject:** To the Heroes of Battle of Midway

Date	F	VF	XF	Unc	BU
1992R	—	—	—	12.50	—

KM# 119 10 DOLLARS Composition: Brass **Subject:** To the Heroes of the North Atlantic **Reverse:** Submarine

Date	F	VF	XF	Unc	BU
1993R Prooflike	—	—	—	14.00	—

KM# 122 10 DOLLARS Composition: Brass **Subject:** To the Heroes of Guadalcanal **Reverse:** Marine, battleship and airplanes

Date	F	VF	XF	Unc	BU
1993R Prooflike	—	—	—	12.50	—

KM# 127 10 DOLLARS Composition: Brass **Subject:** Pacific Whales and Dolphins **Reverse:** Common Dolphin

Date	F	VF	XF	Unc	BU
1993R Prooflike	—	—	—	15.00	—

KM# 129 10 DOLLARS Composition: Brass **Reverse:** Elvis Presley

Date	F	VF	XF	Unc	BU
1993 Prooflike	—	—	—	16.50	—

KM# 132 10 DOLLARS Composition: Brass **Subject:** Pacific Whales and Dolphins **Reverse:** Humpback Whales

Date	F	VF	XF	Unc	BU
1993	—	—	—	15.00	—

KM# 133 10 DOLLARS Composition: Brass **Subject:** Pacific Whales and Dolphins **Reverse:** Risso's Dolphins

Date	F	VF	XF	Unc	BU
1993	—	—	—	15.00	—

KM# 134 10 DOLLARS Composition: Brass **Subject:** Pacific Whales and Dolphins **Reverse:** Beluga Whales

Date	F	VF	XF	Unc	BU
1993	—	—	—	15.00	—

KM# 135 10 DOLLARS Composition: Brass **Subject:** Pacific Whales and Dolphins **Reverse:** Hector's Dolphins

Date	F	VF	XF	Unc	BU
1993	—	—	—	15.00	—

KM# 136 10 DOLLARS Composition: Brass **Subject:** Pacific Whales and Dolphins **Reverse:** Blue Whale

Date	F	VF	XF	Unc	BU
1993	—	—	—	15.00	—

KM# 137 10 DOLLARS Composition: Brass **Subject:** Pacific Whales and Dolphins **Reverse:** Bottlenose Dolphin

Date	F	VF	XF	Unc	BU
1993	—	—	—	15.00	—

KM# 138 10 DOLLARS Composition: Brass **Subject:** Pacific Whales and Dolphins **Reverse:** Killer Whale

Date	F	VF	XF	Unc	BU
1993	—	—	—	15.00	—

KM# 139 10 DOLLARS Composition: Brass **Subject:** Pacific Whales and Dolphins **Reverse:** Baiji Dolphins

Date	F	VF	XF	Unc	BU
1993	—	—	—	15.00	—

KM# 145 10 DOLLARS Composition: Brass **Subject:** Christmas 1993

Date	F	VF	XF	Unc	BU
1993	—	—	—	12.50	—

KM# 149 10 DOLLARS Composition: Brass **Subject:** Flight of the Kitty Hawk

Date	F	VF	XF	Unc	BU
1993	—	—	—	12.50	—

KM# 408 10 DOLLARS Composition: Brass **Subject:** Pacific Whales and Dolphins **Reverse:** Indo-Pacific Humpbacked Dolphin

Date	F	VF	XF	Unc	BU
1993	—	—	—	15.00	—

KM# 409 10 DOLLARS Composition: Brass **Subject:** Pacific Whales and Dolphins **Obverse:** State seal **Reverse:** Long-Snouted Spinner Dolphin

Date	F	VF	XF	Unc	BU
1993	—	—	—	15.00	—

KM# 410 10 DOLLARS Composition: Brass **Subject:** Pacific Whales and Dolphins **Reverse:** Two Sperm whales

Date	F	VF	XF	Unc	BU
1993	—	—	—	15.00	—

KM# 411 10 DOLLARS Composition: Brass **Subject:** Pacific Whales and Dolphins **Reverse:** Minke Whale

Date	F	VF	XF	Unc	BU
1993	—	—	—	15.00	—

KM# 152 10 DOLLARS Composition: Brass **Subject:** First Men on the Moon

Date	F	VF	XF	Unc	BU
1994	—	—	—	12.50	—

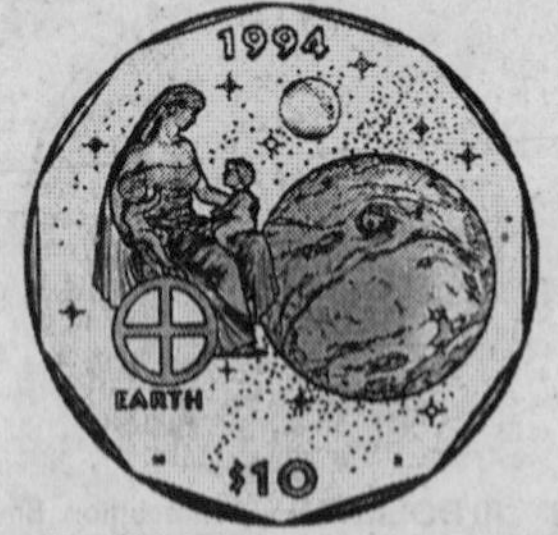

KM# 155 10 DOLLARS Composition: Brass **Subject:** Mythological Mother Earth

Date	F	VF	XF	Unc	BU
1994R	—	—	—	12.50	—

KM# 156 10 DOLLARS Composition: Brass **Reverse:** The Sun

Date	F	VF	XF	Unc	BU
1994	—	—	—	14.50	—

KM# 157 10 DOLLARS Composition: Brass **Reverse:** The Moon

Date	F	VF	XF	Unc	BU
1994	—	—	—	13.50	—

KM# 158 10 DOLLARS Composition: Brass **Reverse:** Pluto

Date	F	VF	XF	Unc	BU
1994	—	—	—	13.50	—

KM# 159 10 DOLLARS Composition: Brass **Reverse:** Mercury

Date	F	VF	XF	Unc	BU
1994	—	—	—	12.50	—

KM# 160 10 DOLLARS Composition: Brass **Reverse:** Venus

Date	F	VF	XF	Unc	BU
1994	—	—	—	15.50	—

KM# 161 10 DOLLARS Composition: Brass **Reverse:** Mars

Date	F	VF	XF	Unc	BU
1994	—	—	—	12.50	—

KM# 162 10 DOLLARS Composition: Brass **Reverse:** Saturn

Date	F	VF	XF	Unc	BU
1994	—	—	—	13.50	—

KM# 163 10 DOLLARS **Composition:** Brass **Reverse:** Jupiter

Date	F	VF	XF	Unc	BU
1994	—	—	—	14.50	—

KM# 164 10 DOLLARS **Composition:** Brass **Reverse:** Uranus

Date	F	VF	XF	Unc	BU
1994	—	—	—	12.50	—

KM# 165 10 DOLLARS **Composition:** Brass **Reverse:** Neptune

Date	F	VF	XF	Unc	BU
1994	—	—	—	14.50	—

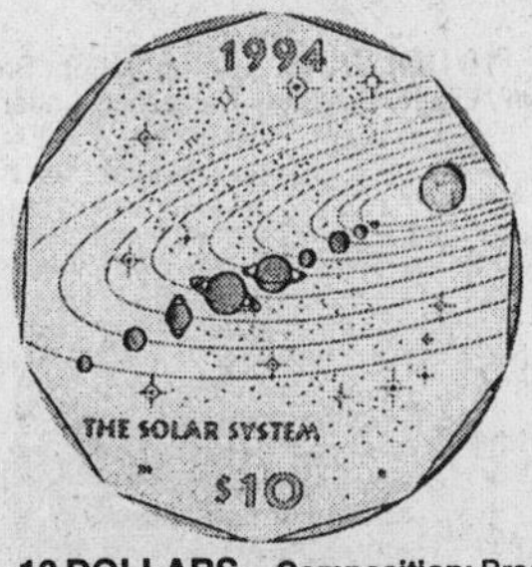

KM# 166 10 DOLLARS **Composition:** Brass **Reverse:** Solar System

Date	F	VF	XF	Unc	BU
1994	—	—	—	13.50	—

KM# 180 10 DOLLARS **Composition:** Brass **Subject:** To the Heroes of D-Day - Normandy Invasion

Date	F	VF	XF	Unc	BU
1994 Prooflike	—	—	—	12.50	—

KM# 183 10 DOLLARS **Composition:** Brass **Subject:** Heroes of the Philippines **Reverse:** MacArthur and staff

Date	F	VF	XF	Unc	BU
1994 Prooflike	—	—	—	12.50	—

KM# 188 10 DOLLARS **Composition:** Brass **Subject:** World Cup Soccer

Date	F	VF	XF	Unc	BU
1994	—	—	—	12.50	—

KM# 264 10 DOLLARS **Composition:** Brass **Reverse:** To the Heroes of the Battle of the Bulge

Date	F	VF	XF	Unc	BU
1994 Prooflike	—	—	—	12.50	—

KM# 261 10 DOLLARS **Composition:** Brass **Subject:** Christmas **Reverse:** Cherub **Note:** Similar to 5 Dollars, KM#271.

Date	F	VF	XF	Unc	BU
1994	—	—	—	12.50	—

KM# 217 10 DOLLARS **Composition:** Brass **Subject:** Peace - Victory in Europe

Date	F	VF	XF	Unc	BU
1995	—	—	—	12.50	—

KM# 220 10 DOLLARS **Composition:** Brass **Subject:** To the Heroes of Vietnam

Date	F	VF	XF	Unc	BU
1995 Prooflike	—	—	—	12.50	—

KM# 223 10 DOLLARS **Composition:** Brass **Reverse:** Elvis Presley

Date	F	VF	XF	Unc	BU
1995	—	—	—	12.50	—

KM# 226 10 DOLLARS **Composition:** Brass **Subject:** To the Heroes of the War in the Pacific

Date	F	VF	XF	Unc	BU
1995 Prooflike	—	—	—	12.50	—

KM# 228 10 DOLLARS **Composition:** Brass **Reverse:** F-14 Tomcat

Date	F	VF	XF	Unc	BU
1995R	—	—	—	12.50	—

KM# 229 10 DOLLARS **Composition:** Brass **Reverse:** F-16 Fighting Falcon

Date	F	VF	XF	Unc	BU
1995R	—	—	—	12.50	—

KM# 230 10 DOLLARS **Composition:** Brass **Reverse:** Me 262A-1a Schwalbe

Date	F	VF	XF	Unc	BU
1995R	—	—	—	12.50	—

KM# 231 10 DOLLARS **Composition:** Brass **Reverse:** F-104 Starfighter

Date	F	VF	XF	Unc	BU
1995R	—	—	—	12.50	—

KM# 232 10 DOLLARS **Composition:** Brass **Reverse:** Mirage 2000C

Date	F	VF	XF	Unc	BU
1995R	—	—	—	12.50	—

KM# 233 10 DOLLARS **Composition:** Brass **Reverse:** F-4 Phantom II

Date	F	VF	XF	Unc	BU
1995R	—	—	—	12.50	—

KM# 234 10 DOLLARS **Composition:** Brass **Reverse:** Sea Harrier

Date	F	VF	XF	Unc	BU
1995R	—	—	—	12.50	—

KM# 235 10 DOLLARS **Composition:** Brass **Reverse:** F-117 Nighthawk

Date	F	VF	XF	Unc	BU
1995R	—	—	—	12.50	—

KM# 236 10 DOLLARS **Composition:** Brass **Reverse:** F-100 Super Sabre

Date	F	VF	XF	Unc	BU
1995R	—	—	—	12.50	—

KM# 237 10 DOLLARS **Composition:** Brass **Reverse:** F-86 Sabre

Date	F	VF	XF	Unc	BU
1995R	—	—	—	12.50	—

KM# 238 10 DOLLARS **Composition:** Brass **Reverse:** MIG-15

Date	F	VF	XF	Unc	BU
1995R	—	—	—	12.50	—

KM# 239 10 DOLLARS **Composition:** Brass **Reverse:** G91R

Date	F	VF	XF	Unc	BU
1995R	—	—	—	12.50	—

KM# 240 10 DOLLARS **Composition:** Brass **Reverse:** SAAB 35 Draken

Date	F	VF	XF	Unc	BU
1995R	—	—	—	12.50	—

KM# 241 10 DOLLARS **Composition:** Brass **Reverse:** Meteor FMK8

Date	F	VF	XF	Unc	BU
1995R	—	—	—	12.50	—

KM# 242 10 DOLLARS **Composition:** Brass **Reverse:** F-105 Thunderbird

Date	F	VF	XF	Unc	BU
1995R	—	—	—	12.50	—

KM# 243 10 DOLLARS **Composition:** Brass **Reverse:** Tornado FMK3

Date	F	VF	XF	Unc	BU
1995R	—	—	—	12.50	—

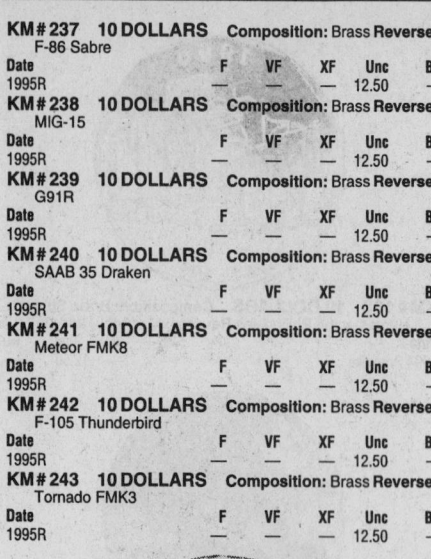

KM# 254 10 DOLLARS **Composition:** Brass **Reverse:** Marilyn Monroe

Date	F	VF	XF	Unc	BU
1995	—	—	—	12.50	—

KM# 258 10 DOLLARS **Composition:** Brass **Series:** 50th Anniversary United Nations **Subject:** Peace

Date	F	VF	XF	Unc	BU
1995	—	—	—	12.50	—

KM# 267 10 DOLLARS **Composition:** Brass **Subject:** Peace - VJ Day

Date	F	VF	XF	Unc	BU
1995	—	—	—	12.50	—

KM# 272 10 DOLLARS **Composition:** Brass **Subject:** Christmas **Reverse:** Cherub

Date	F	VF	XF	Unc	BU
1995	—	—	—	12.50	—

KM# 282 10 DOLLARS **Composition:** Brass **Subject:** Freedom / Liberty **Reverse:** Torpedo Boat PT109

Date	F	VF	XF	Unc	BU
1995	—	—	—	12.00	—

KM# 283 10 DOLLARS **Composition:** Brass **Subject:** Freedom / Liberty **Reverse:** President John F. Kennedy takes oath of office

Date	F	VF	XF	Unc	BU
1995	—	—	—	12.50	—

KM# 284 10 DOLLARS **Composition:** Brass **Subject:** Freedom / Liberty **Reverse:** Peace Corps worker and native

Date	F	VF	XF	Unc	BU
1995	—	—	—	12.50	—

KM# 285 10 DOLLARS **Composition:** Brass **Subject:** Freedom / Liberty **Reverse:** Battleships under starry sky

Date	F	VF	XF	Unc	BU
1995	—	—	—	12.50	—

KM# 286 10 DOLLARS **Composition:** Brass **Subject:** Freedom / Liberty **Reverse:** President John F. Kennedy working at desk

Date	F	VF	XF	Unc	BU
1995	—	—	—	12.50	—

KM# 287 10 DOLLARS **Composition:** Brass **Subject:** Freedom / Liberty **Reverse:** President John F. Kennedy's Eternal Flame

Date	F	VF	XF	Unc	BU
1995	—	—	—	12.50	—

KM# 396 10 DOLLARS **Composition:** Brass **Subject:** F-16 Fighting Falcon **Obverse:** National seal **Reverse:** Jet fighter

Date	F	VF	XF	Unc	BU
1995	—	—	—	12.00	—

KM# 289 10 DOLLARS **Composition:** Brass **Reverse:** Space Shuttle Columbia

Date	F	VF	XF	Unc	BU
1996	—	—	—	12.50	—

KM# 301 10 DOLLARS **Composition:** Brass **Reverse:** Elvis Presley

Date	F	VF	XF	Unc	BU
1996	—	—	—	13.50	—

KM# 306 10 DOLLARS **Composition:** Brass **Subject:** Steam Locomotive **Reverse:** "Pennsylvania K4"

Date	F	VF	XF	Unc	BU
1996	—	—	—	14.00	—

KM# 307 10 DOLLARS **Composition:** Brass **Subject:** Steam Locomotive **Reverse:** "Big Boy"

Date	F	VF	XF	Unc	BU
1996	—	—	—	14.00	—

KM# 309 10 DOLLARS **Composition:** Brass **Subject:** Classic Cars **Reverse:** Ford Quadricycle

Date	F	VF	XF	Unc	BU
1996 Prooflike	—	—	—	12.50	—

KM# 312 10 DOLLARS **Composition:** Brass **Subject:** Classic Cars **Reverse:** Model A Ford

Date	F	VF	XF	Unc	BU
1996 Prooflike	—	—	—	12.50	—

KM# 321 10 DOLLARS **Composition:** Brass **Subject:** Classic Cars **Reverse:** 1964 Mustang

Date	F	VF	XF	Unc	BU
1996 Prooflike	—	—	—	12.50	—

KM# 336 10 DOLLARS **Composition:** Brass **Reverse:** Space Shuttle - Challenger

Date	F	VF	XF	Unc	BU
1996	—	—	—	12.50	—

KM# 337 10 DOLLARS **Composition:** Brass **Reverse:** Space Shuttle - Discovery

Date	F	VF	XF	Unc	BU
1996	—	—	—	12.50	—

KM# 338 10 DOLLARS **Composition:** Brass **Reverse:** Space Shuttle - Atlantis

Date	F	VF	XF	Unc	BU
1996	—	—	—	12.50	—

KM# 339 10 DOLLARS **Composition:** Brass **Reverse:** Space Shuttle - Endeavor

Date	F	VF	XF	Unc	BU
1996	—	—	—	12.50	—

KM# 354 10 DOLLARS **Composition:** Brass **Subject:** Christmas **Reverse:** Two angels

Date	F	VF	XF	Unc	BU
1996	—	—	—	12.50	—

KM# 356 10 DOLLARS **Composition:** Brass **Subject:** Steam Locomotive **Reverse:** "DB Class 01"

Date	F	VF	XF	Unc	BU
1996	—	—	—	14.00	—

KM# 359 10 DOLLARS **Composition:** Brass **Subject:** Steam Locomotive **Reverse:** "RENFE Class 242"

Date	F	VF	XF	Unc	BU
1996	—	—	—	14.50	—

KM# 361 10 DOLLARS **Composition:** Brass **Subject:** Steam Locomotive **Reverse:** "FS Group 691"

Date	F	VF	XF	Unc	BU
1996	—	—	—	14.50	—

KM# 368 10 DOLLARS **Composition:** Brass **Subject:** Steam Locomotive **Reverse:** "SNCF 232. U1"

Date	F	VF	XF	Unc	BU
1996	—	—	—	14.50	—

KM# 378 10 DOLLARS **Composition:** Brass **Subject:** Steam Locomotive **Reverse:** "SAR 520 Class"

Date	F	VF	XF	Unc	BU
1996	—	—	—	14.50	—

KM# 379 10 DOLLARS **Composition:** Brass **Subject:** Steam Locomotive **Reverse:** "Evening Star"

Date	F	VF	XF	Unc	BU
1996	—	—	—	14.50	—

KM# 393 10 DOLLARS **Composition:** Brass **Subject:** Steam Locomotive **Reverse:** QJ "Advance Forward"

Date	F	VF	XF	Unc	BU
1996	—	—	—	14.50	—

KM# 394 10 DOLLARS **Composition:** Brass **Subject:** Steam Locomotive **Obverse:** State seal **Reverse:** "Royal Hudson"

Date	F	VF	XF	Unc	BU
1996	—	—	—	14.50	—

KM# 402 10 DOLLARS **Composition:** Brass **Subject:** Steam Locomotive **Obverse:** State seal **Reverse:** C62 "Swallow"

Date	F	VF	XF	Unc	BU
1996	—	—	—	14.50	—

KM# 304 10 DOLLARS **Composition:** Brass **Reverse:** James Dean **Note:** Similar to 5 Dollars, KM#303.

Date	F	VF	XF	Unc	BU
1996	—	—	—	13.50	—

KM# 315 10 DOLLARS **Composition:** Brass **Subject:** Classic Cars **Reverse:** Model T Ford **Note:** Similar to 5 Dollars, KM#314.

Date	F	VF	XF	Unc	BU
1996 Prooflike	—	—	—	—	—

KM# 318 10 DOLLARS **Composition:** Brass **Subject:** Classic Cars **Reverse:** 1955 Thunderbird **Note:** Similar to 5 Dollars, KM#317.

Date	F	VF	XF	Unc	BU
1996 Prooflike	—	—	—	12.50	—

KM# 324 10 DOLLARS **Composition:** Brass **Subject:** Classic Cars **Reverse:** Ford Taurus **Note:** Similar to 5 Dollars, KM#323.

Date	F	VF	XF	Unc	BU
1996 Prooflike	—	—	—	12.50	—

KM# 347 10 DOLLARS **Composition:** Brass **Reverse:** Lion **Note:** Similar to 5 Dollars, KM#344.

Date	F	VF	XF	Unc	BU
1996	—	—	—	15.00	—

KM# 348 10 DOLLARS **Composition:** Brass **Reverse:** Cheetah **Note:** Similar to 5 Dollars, KM#345.

Date	F	VF	XF	Unc	BU
1996	—	—	—	15.00	—

KM# 349 10 DOLLARS **Composition:** Brass **Reverse:** Jaguar **Note:** Similar to 5 Dollars, KM#346.

Date	F	VF	XF	Unc	BU
1996	—	—	—	15.00	—

KM# 326 10 DOLLARS **Composition:** Brass **Subject:** Steam Locomotive **Reverse:** "Mallard" **Note:** Similar to 50 Dollars, KM#296.

Date	F	VF	XF	Unc	BU
1996	—	—	—	14.00	—

KM# 298 10 DOLLARS **Composition:** Brass **Reverse:** Tiger **Note:** Similar to 50 Dollars, KM#299.

Date	F	VF	XF	Unc	BU
1996	—	—	—	13.50	—

KM# 372 10 DOLLARS **Composition:** Brass **Subject:** To the Heroes of the Korean War **Note:** Siimilar to 5 Dollars, KM#371.

Date	F	VF	XF	Unc	BU
1997	—	—	—	12.00	—

KM# 365 10 DOLLARS **Composition:** Brass **Reverse:** Elvis Presley **Note:** Similar to 5 Dollars, KM#364.

Date	F	VF	XF	Unc	BU
1997	—	—	—	12.50	—

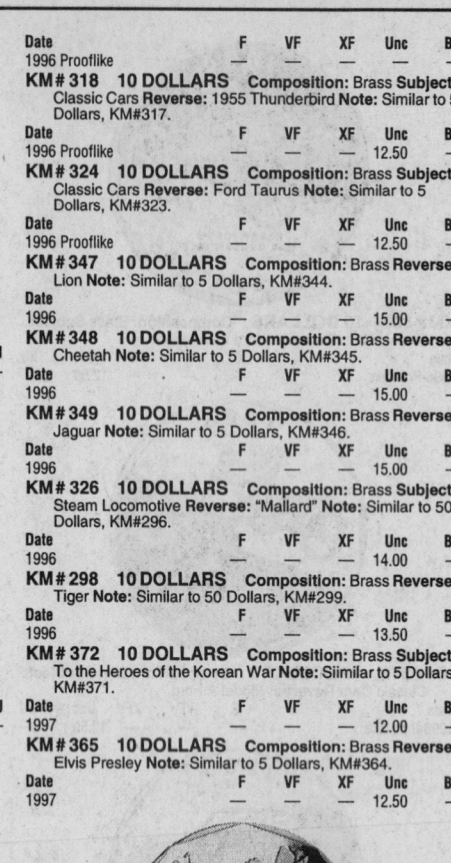

KM# 381 10 DOLLARS **Composition:** Brass **Subject:** Twelve Apostles Series **Obverse:** State seal **Reverse:** Andrew

Date	F	VF	XF	Unc	BU
1997	—	—	—	12.00	—

KM# 382 10 DOLLARS **Composition:** Brass **Subject:** Twelve Apostles Series **Obverse:** State seal **Reverse:** Bartholomew

Date	F	VF	XF	Unc	BU
1997	—	—	—	12.00	—

KM# 383 10 DOLLARS **Composition:** Brass **Subject:** Twelve Apostles Series **Obverse:** State seal **Reverse:** James, Son of Zebedee

Date	F	VF	XF	Unc	BU
1997	—	—	—	12.00	—

KM# 384 10 DOLLARS **Composition:** Brass **Subject:** Twelve Apostles Series **Obverse:** State seal **Reverse:** James, Son of Alphaeus

Date	F	VF	XF	Unc	BU
1997	—	—	—	12.00	—

KM# 385 10 DOLLARS **Composition:** Brass **Subject:** Twelve Apostles Series **Obverse:** State seal **Reverse:** John

Date	F	VF	XF	Unc	BU
1997	—	—	—	12.00	—

KM# 386 10 DOLLARS **Composition:** Brass **Subject:** Twelve Apostles Series **Obverse:** State seal **Reverse:** Paul

Date	F	VF	XF	Unc	BU
1997	—	—	—	12.00	—

KM# 387 10 DOLLARS **Composition:** Brass **Subject:** Twelve Apostles Series **Obverse:** State seal **Reverse:** Matthew

Date	F	VF	XF	Unc	BU
1997	—	—	—	12.00	—

KM# 388 10 DOLLARS **Composition:** Brass **Subject:** Twelve Apostles Series **Obverse:** State seal **Reverse:** Peter

Date	F	VF	XF	Unc	BU
1997	—	—	—	12.00	—

KM# 389 10 DOLLARS **Composition:** Brass **Subject:** Twelve Apostles Series **Obverse:** State seal **Reverse:** Philip

Date	F	VF	XF	Unc	BU
1997	—	—	—	12.00	—

KM# 390 10 DOLLARS **Composition:** Brass **Subject:** Twelve Apostles Series **Obverse:** State seal **Reverse:** Simon

Date	F	VF	XF	Unc	BU
1997	—	—	—	12.00	—

KM# 391 10 DOLLARS **Composition:** Brass **Subject:** Twelve Apostles Series **Obverse:** State seal **Reverse:** Thaddaeus

Date	F	VF	XF	Unc	BU
1997	—	—	—	12.00	—

KM# 392 10 DOLLARS **Composition:** Brass **Subject:** Twelve Apostles Series **Obverse:** State seal **Reverse:** Thomas

Date	F	VF	XF	Unc	BU
1997	—	—	—	12.00	—

KM# 404 10 DOLLARS **Composition:** Brass **Subject:** Christmas **Obverse:** State seal **Reverse:** Two cherubs

Date	F	VF	XF	Unc	BU
1997	—	—	—	12.00	—

KM# 406 10 DOLLARS **Composition:** Brass **Obverse:** National seal **Reverse:** Charging bull elephant

Date	F	VF	XF	Unc	BU
1997	—	—	—	13.50	—

KM# 400 10 DOLLARS **Composition:** Brass **Obverse:** State seal **Reverse:** Deng Ziaoping

Date	F	VF	XF	Unc	BU
1997	—	—	—	12.00	—

KM# 415 10 DOLLARS **Composition:** Brass **Subject:** History's Great Fighting Ships **Obverse:** State seal **Reverse:** Viking Longship

Date	F	VF	XF	Unc	BU
1998	—	—	—	12.00	—

KM# 417 10 DOLLARS **Composition:** Brass **Subject:** History's Great Fighting Ships **Obverse:** State seal **Reverse:** Greek Trireme

Date	F	VF	XF	Unc	BU
1998	—	—	—	12.00	—

KM# 419 10 DOLLARS **Composition:** Brass **Subject:** History's Great Fighting Ships **Obverse:** State seal **Reverse:** Roman Trireme

Date	F	VF	XF	Unc	BU
1998	—	—	—	12.00	—

KM# 421 10 DOLLARS **Composition:** Brass **Subject:** History's Great Fighting Ships **Obverse:** State seal **Reverse:** Chinese Ming Treasure Ship

Date	F	VF	XF	Unc	BU
1998	—	—	—	12.00	—

KM# 423 10 DOLLARS **Composition:** Brass **Subject:** History's Great Fighting Ships **Obverse:** State seal **Reverse:** Korean Turtle Ship

Date	F	VF	XF	Unc	BU
1998	—	—	—	12.00	—

KM# 425 10 DOLLARS **Composition:** Brass **Subject:** History's Great Fighting Ships **Obverse:** State seal **Reverse:** Fijan War Canoe

Date	F	VF	XF	Unc	BU
1998	—	—	—	12.00	—

KM# 427 10 DOLLARS **Composition:** Brass **Subject:** History's Great Fighting Ships **Obverse:** State seal **Reverse:** The Bismarck

Date	F	VF	XF	Unc	BU
1998	—	—	—	12.00	—

KM# 429 10 DOLLARS **Composition:** Brass **Subject:** History's Great Fighting Ships **Obverse:** State seal **Reverse:** The Graf Spee

Date	F	VF	XF	Unc	BU
1998	—	—	—	12.00	—

KM# 431 10 DOLLARS **Composition:** Brass **Subject:** History's Great Fighting Ships **Obverse:** State seal **Reverse:** The Yamato

Date	F	VF	XF	Unc	BU
1998	—	—	—	12.00	—

KM# 433 10 DOLLARS **Composition:** Brass **Subject:** History's Great Fighting Ships **Obverse:** State seal **Reverse:** HMS Victory

Date	F	VF	XF	Unc	BU
1998	—	—	—	12.00	—

KM# 435 10 DOLLARS **Composition:** Brass **Subject:** History's Great Fighting Ships **Reverse:** HMS Mary Rose

Date	F	VF	XF	Unc	BU
1998	—	—	—	12.00	—

KM# 437 10 DOLLARS **Composition:** Brass **Subject:** History's Great Fighting Ships **Reverse:** HMS Dreadnought

Date	F	VF	XF	Unc	BU
1998	—	—	—	12.00	—

KM# 439 10 DOLLARS **Composition:** Brass **Subject:** History's Great Fighting Ships **Obverse:** State Seal **Reverse:** HMS Dorsetshire

Date	F	VF	XF	Unc	BU
1998	—	—	—	12.00	—

KM# 441 10 DOLLARS **Composition:** Brass **Subject:** History's Great Fighting Ships **Obverse:** State Seal **Reverse:** Nuestra Senora del Rosario

Date	F	VF	XF	Unc	BU
1998	—	—	—	12.00	—

KM# 443 10 DOLLARS **Composition:** Brass **Subject:** History's Great Fighting Ships **Obverse:** State Seal **Reverse:** Santisima Trinidad

Date	F	VF	XF	Unc	BU
1998	—	—	—	12.00	—

KM# 445 10 DOLLARS **Composition:** Brass **Subject:** History's Great Fighting Ships **Obverse:** State Seal **Reverse:** USS Bonhomme Richard

Date	F	VF	XF	Unc	BU
1998	—	—	—	12.00	—

KM# 447 10 DOLLARS **Composition:** Brass **Subject:** History's Great Fighting Ships **Obverse:** State Seal **Reverse:** USS Constellation

Date	F	VF	XF	Unc	BU
1998	—	—	—	12.00	—

KM# 449 10 DOLLARS **Composition:** Brass **Subject:** History's Great Fighting Ships **Obverse:** State Seal **Reverse:** USS Hartford

Date	F	VF	XF	Unc	BU
1998	—	—	—	12.00	—

KM# 451 10 DOLLARS **Composition:** Brass **Subject:** History's Great Fighting Ships **Obverse:** State Seal **Reverse:** USS Hornet

Date	F	VF	XF	Unc	BU
1998	—	—	—	12.00	—

KM# 453 10 DOLLARS **Composition:** Brass **Subject:** History's Great Fighting Ships **Obverse:** State Seal **Reverse:** USS Missouri

Date	F	VF	XF	Unc	BU
1998	—	—	—	12.00	—

KM# 455 10 DOLLARS **Composition:** Brass **Subject:** History's Great Fighting Ships **Obverse:** State Seal **Reverse:** USS Tautog

Date	F	VF	XF	Unc	BU
1998	—	—	—	12.00	—

KM# 457 10 DOLLARS **Composition:** Brass **Subject:** History's Great Fighting Ships **Obverse:** State Seal **Reverse:** Brederode

Date	F	VF	XF	Unc	BU
1998	—	—	—	12.00	—

KM# 459 10 DOLLARS **Composition:** Brass **Subject:** History's Great Fighting Ships **Obverse:** State Seal **Reverse:** Ville de Paris

Date	F	VF	XF	Unc	BU
1998	—	—	—	12.00	—

KM# 461 10 DOLLARS **Composition:** Brass **Subject:** History's Great Fighting Ships **Obverse:** State Seal **Reverse:** Galera Veneziana

Date	F	VF	XF	Unc	BU
1998	—	—	—	12.00	—

KM# 479 10 DOLLARS **Composition:** Brass **Subject:** Babe Ruth at bat **Obverse:** State Seal

Date	F	VF	XF	Unc	BU
1998	—	—	—	12.00	—

KM# 482 10 DOLLARS **Composition:** Brass **Subject:** Christmas **Obverse:** State Seal **Reverse:** Angel

Date	F	VF	XF	Unc	BU
1998	—	—	—	12.00	—

KM# 3 20 DOLLARS **Weight:** 3.1100 g. **Composition:** 0.9990 Gold .1000 oz. AGW **Reverse:** Sun

Date	F	VF	XF	Unc	BU
1986 Proof	Est. 5,000	Value: 50.00			

KM# 153 20 DOLLARS Weight: 15.5517 g. **Composition:** 0.9990 Silver .5000 oz. ASW **Subject:** First Men on the Moon

Date	F	VF	XF	Unc	BU
1994 Proof	—	Value: 20.00			

KM# 189 20 DOLLARS Weight: 15.5517 g. **Composition:** 0.9990 Silver .5000 oz. ASW **Subject:** World Cup Soccer

Date	F	VF	XF	Unc	BU
1994 Proof	—	Value: 17.50			

KM# 255 20 DOLLARS Weight: 15.5517 g. **Composition:** 0.9990 Silver .5000 oz. ASW **Subject:** Marilyn Monroe

Date	F	VF	XF	Unc	BU
1995 Proof	—	Value: 25.00			

KM# 401 20 DOLLARS Weight: 10.3678 g. **Composition:** 0.9990 Silver .3330 oz. ASW **Subject:** Deng Xiaoping **Obverse:** State seal

Date	F	VF	XF	Unc	BU
1997 Proof	—	Value: 25.00			

KM# 20 25 DOLLARS Weight: 33.9600 g. **Composition:** 0.9250 Silver 1.0100 oz. ASW **Subject:** Greg Louganis **Reverse:** Back dive

Date	Mintage	F	VF	XF	Unc	BU
1988		—	—	—	75.00	—
1988 Proof	Est. 350,000	Value: 100				

KM# 21 25 DOLLARS Weight: 33.9600 g. **Composition:** 0.9250 Silver 1.0100 oz. ASW **Subject:** Greg Louganis **Reverse:** Twister

Date	Mintage	F	VF	XF	Unc	BU
1988		—	—	—	75.00	—
1988 Proof	Est. 350,000	Value: 100				

KM# 22 25 DOLLARS Weight: 33.9600 g. **Composition:** 0.9250 Silver 1.0100 oz. ASW **Subject:** Greg Louganis **Reverse:** Jackknife

Date	F	VF	XF	Unc	BU
1988	—	—	—	75.00	—
1988 Proof	Est. 350,000	Value: 100			

KM# 4 50 DOLLARS Weight: 7.7750 g. **Composition:** 0.9990 Gold .2500 oz. AGW **Reverse:** Coconut

Date	Mintage	F	VF	XF	Unc	BU
1986 Proof	Est. 5,000	Value: 125				

KM# 7 50 DOLLARS Weight: 31.1000 g. **Composition:** 0.9990 Silver 1.0000 oz. ASW **Subject:** John Glenn in Space Orbit

Date	Mintage	F	VF	XF	Unc	BU
1989 Proof	Est. 25,000	Value: 27.50				
1989S Proof	Inc. above	Value: 23.50				

KM# 8 50 DOLLARS Weight: 31.1000 g. **Composition:** 0.9990 Silver 1.0000 oz. ASW **Subject:** Neil Armstrong on the Moon **Obverse:** Similar to KM#12

Date	Mintage	F	VF	XF	Unc	BU
1989 Proof	Est. 25,000	Value: 27.50				
1989S Proof	Inc. above	Value: 23.50				

KM# 9 50 DOLLARS Weight: 31.1000 g. **Composition:** 0.9990 Silver 1.0000 oz. ASW **Subject:** American Space Station - Skylab **Obverse:** Similar to KM#12

Date	Mintage	F	VF	XF	Unc	BU
1989 Proof	Est. 25,000	Value: 22.50				
1989S Proof	Inc. above	Value: 20.00				

KM# 10 50 DOLLARS Weight: 31.1000 g. **Composition:** 0.9990 Silver 1.0000 oz. ASW **Subject:** Apollo - Sojus Joint Mission

Date	Mintage	F	VF	XF	Unc	BU
1989 Proof	Est. 25,000	Value: 27.50				
1989S Proof	Inc. above	Value: 23.50				

KM# 11 50 DOLLARS Weight: 31.1000 g. **Composition:** 0.9990 Silver 1.0000 oz. ASW **Subject:** First Space Shuttle Flight

Date	Mintage	F	VF	XF	Unc	BU
1989 Proof	Est. 25,000	Value: 27.50				
1989S Proof	Inc. above	Value: 23.50				

KM# 12 50 DOLLARS Weight: 31.1000 g. **Composition:** 0.9990 Silver 1.0000 oz. ASW **Subject:** U.S. Space Shuttle - Discovery

Date	Mintage	F	VF	XF	Unc	BU
1989 Proof	Est. 50,000	Value: 18.50				
1989S Proof	Inc. above	Value: 16.50				

KM# 14 50 DOLLARS Weight: 31.1000 g. **Composition:** 0.9990 Silver 1.0000 oz. ASW **Subject:** 20th Anniversary - First Men on the Moon

Date	Mintage	F	VF	XF	Unc	BU
1989 Proof	Est. 50,000	Value: 18.50				
1989S Proof	Inc. above	Value: 16.50				

KM# 15 50 DOLLARS **Weight:** 31.1000 g. **Composition:** 0.9990 Silver 1.0000 oz. ASW **Subject:** First American Space Walk

Date	Mintage	F	VF	XF	Unc	BU
1989 Proof	Est. 25,000	Value: 27.50				
1989S Proof	Inc. above	Value: 23.50				

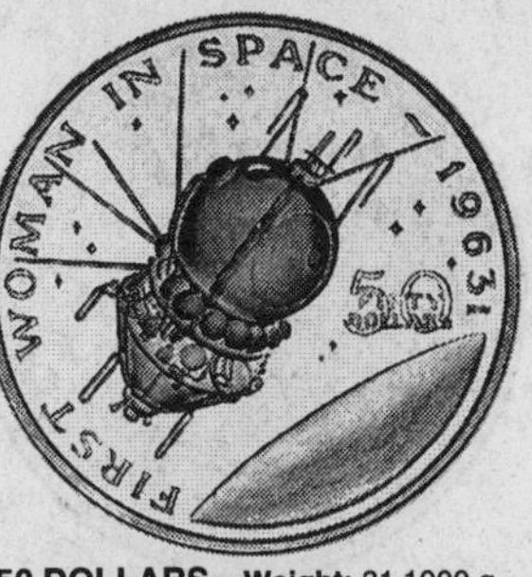

KM# 26 50 DOLLARS **Weight:** 31.1000 g. **Composition:** 0.9990 Silver 1.0000 oz. ASW **Subject:** First Woman In Space - 1963

Date	Mintage	F	VF	XF	Unc	BU
1989 Proof	Est. 25,000	Value: 27.50				
1989S Proof	Inc. above	Value: 23.50				

KM# 30 50 DOLLARS **Weight:** 31.1000 g. **Composition:** 0.9990 Silver 1.0000 oz. ASW **Subject:** First Probe of Venus - 1967

Date	Mintage	F	VF	XF	Unc	BU
1989 Proof	Est. 25,000	Value: 27.50				
1989S Proof	Inc. above	Value: 23.50				

KM# 23 50 DOLLARS **Weight:** 31.1000 g. **Composition:** 0.9990 Silver 1.0000 oz. ASW **Subject:** First Docking In Space

Date	Mintage	F	VF	XF	Unc	BU
1989 Proof	Est. 25,000	Value: 27.50				
1989S Proof	Inc. above	Value: 23.50				

KM# 27 50 DOLLARS **Weight:** 31.1000 g. **Composition:** 0.9990 Silver 1.0000 oz. ASW **Subject:** First Rendezvous In Space - 1965

Date	Mintage	F	VF	XF	Unc	BU
1989 Proof	Est. 25,000	Value: 27.50				
1989S Proof	Inc. above	Value: 23.50				

KM# 31 50 DOLLARS **Weight:** 31.1000 g. **Composition:** 0.9990 Silver 1.0000 oz. ASW **Subject:** First Manned Orbit of the Moon - 1968

Date	Mintage	F	VF	XF	Unc	BU
1989 Proof	Est. 25,000	Value: 27.50				
1989S Proof	Inc. above	Value: 23.50				

KM# 24 50 DOLLARS **Weight:** 31.1000 g. **Composition:** 0.9990 Silver 1.0000 oz. ASW **Subject:** First Man-made Satellite - 1957

Date	Mintage	F	VF	XF	Unc	BU
1989 Proof	Est. 25,000	Value: 22.50				
1989S Proof	Inc. above	Value: 20.00				

KM# 28 50 DOLLARS **Weight:** 31.1000 g. **Composition:** 0.9990 Silver 1.0000 oz. ASW **Subject:** First Space Walk - 1965

Date	Mintage	F	VF	XF	Unc	BU
1989 Proof	Est. 25,000	Value: 27.50				
1989S Proof	Inc. above	Value: 23.50				

KM# 32 50 DOLLARS **Weight:** 31.1000 g. **Composition:** 0.9990 Silver 1.0000 oz. ASW **Subject:** First Space Station Crew - 1971

Date	Mintage	F	VF	XF	Unc	BU
1989 Proof	Est. 25,000	Value: 27.50				
1989S Proof	Inc. above	Value: 23.50				

KM# 25 50 DOLLARS **Weight:** 31.1000 g. **Composition:** 0.9990 Silver 1.0000 oz. ASW **Subject:** First Man In Space - 1961

Date	Mintage	F	VF	XF	Unc	BU
1989 Proof	Est. 25,000	Value: 27.50				
1989S Proof	Inc. above	Value: 23.50				

KM# 29 50 DOLLARS **Weight:** 31.1000 g. **Composition:** 0.9990 Silver 1.0000 oz. ASW **Subject:** First Soft Landing on the Moon - 1966

Date	Mintage	F	VF	XF	Unc	BU
1989 Proof	Est. 25,000	Value: 27.50				
1989S Proof	Inc. above	Value: 23.50				

KM# 50 50 DOLLARS **Weight:** 31.1000 g. **Composition:** 0.9990 Silver 1.0000 oz. ASW **Subject:** First Manned Lunar Vehicle - 1971

Date	Mintage	F	VF	XF	Unc	BU
1989 Proof	Est. 25,000	Value: 27.50				
1989S Proof	Inc. above	Value: 23.50				

KM# 51 50 DOLLARS **Weight:** 31.1000 g. **Composition:** 0.9990 Silver 1.0000 oz. ASW **Subject:** First American Satellite - 1958

Date	Mintage	F	VF	XF	Unc	BU
1989 Proof	Est. 25,000	Value: 27.50				
1989S Proof	Inc. above	Value: 23.50				

KM# 52 50 DOLLARS **Weight:** 31.1000 g. **Composition:** 0.9990 Silver 1.0000 oz. ASW **Subject:** First Liquid Fuel Rocket Launch - 1926

Date	Mintage	F	VF	XF	Unc	BU
1989 Proof	Est. 25,000	Value: 27.50				
1989S Proof	Inc. above	Value: 23.50				

KM# 53 50 DOLLARS **Weight:** 31.1000 g. **Composition:** 0.9990 Silver 1.0000 oz. ASW **Subject:** First Untethered Space Walk - 1984

Date	Mintage	F	VF	XF	Unc	BU
1989 Proof	Est. 25,000	Value: 27.50				
1989S Proof	Inc. above	Value: 23.50				

KM# 54 50 DOLLARS **Weight:** 31.1000 g. **Composition:** 0.9990 Silver 1.0000 oz. ASW **Subject:** First Landing on Mars - 1976

Date	Mintage	F	VF	XF	Unc	BU
1989 Proof	Est. 25,000	Value: 27.50				
1989S Proof	Inc. above	Value: 23.50				

KM# 55 50 DOLLARS **Weight:** 31.1000 g. **Composition:** 0.9990 Silver 1.0000 oz. ASW **Subject:** First Flyby of Saturn - 1979

Date	Mintage	F	VF	XF	Unc	BU
1989 Proof	Est. 25,000	Value: 27.50				
1989S Proof	Inc. above	Value: 23.50				

KM# 56 50 DOLLARS **Weight:** 31.1000 g. **Composition:** 0.9990 Silver 1.0000 oz. ASW **Subject:** First Probe Beyond the Solar System - 1983

Date	Mintage	F	VF	XF	Unc	BU
1989 Proof	Est. 25,000	Value: 27.50				
1989S Proof	Inc. above	Value: 23.50				

KM# 57 50 DOLLARS **Weight:** 31.1000 g. **Composition:** 0.9990 Silver 1.0000 oz. ASW **Subject:** First Flyby of Jupiter - 1973

Date	Mintage	F	VF	XF	Unc	BU
1989 Proof	Est. 25,000	Value: 27.50				
1989S Proof	Inc. above	Value: 23.50				

KM# 19 50 DOLLARS **Weight:** 31.1000 g. **Composition:** 0.9990 Silver 1.0000 oz. ASW **Subject:** 50th Anniversary - Battle of Britain

Date	Mintage	F	VF	XF	Unc	BU
1990M Proof	Est. 50,000	Value: 35.00				

KM# 34 50 DOLLARS **Weight:** 31.1000 g. **Composition:** 0.9990 Silver 1.0000 oz. ASW **Subject:** German Unification

Date	Mintage	F	VF	XF	Unc	BU
1990M Proof	Est. 50,000	Value: 50.00				

KM# 39 50 DOLLARS **Weight:** 31.1000 g. **Composition:** 0.9990 Silver 1.0000 oz. ASW **Subject:** Dwight David Eisenhower

Date	Mintage	F	VF	XF	Unc	BU
1990M Proof	Est. 50,000	Value: 25.00				

KM# 36 50 DOLLARS **Weight:** 31.1000 g. **Composition:** 0.9990 Silver 1.0000 oz. ASW **Subject:** Pearl Harbor

Date	Mintage	F	VF	XF	Unc	BU
1991M Proof	Est. 50,000	Value: 27.50				

KM# 42 50 DOLLARS **Weight:** 31.1000 g. **Composition:** 0.9990 Silver 1.0000 oz. ASW **Subject:** To the Heroes of Desert Storm.

Date	F	VF	XF	Unc	BU
1991R Proof	— Value: 22.50				

KM# 43 50 DOLLARS **Weight:** 31.1000 g. **Composition:** 0.9990 Silver 1.0000 oz. ASW **Reverse:** WWII American P-51 Mustang

Date	Mintage	F	VF	XF	Unc	BU
1991 Proof	Est. 25,000	Value: 27.50				

KM# 44 50 DOLLARS **Weight:** 31.1000 g. **Composition:** 0.9990 Silver 1.0000 oz. ASW **Reverse:** WWII American B-29 Superfortress

Date	Mintage	F	VF	XF	Unc	BU
1991M Proof	Est. 25,000	Value: 27.50				

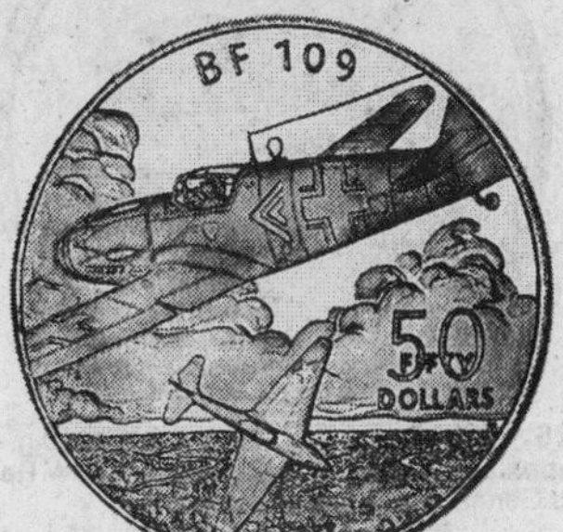

KM# 45 50 DOLLARS **Weight:** 31.1000 g. **Composition:** 0.9990 Silver 1.0000 oz. ASW **Reverse:** WWII German BF-109 Messerschmitt

Date	Mintage	F	VF	XF	Unc	BU
1991 Proof	Est. 25,000	Value: 27.50				

KM# 46 50 DOLLARS **Weight:** 31.1000 g. **Composition:** 0.9990 Silver 1.0000 oz. ASW **Reverse:** WWII British Spitfire

Date	Mintage	F	VF	XF	Unc	BU
1991M Proof	Est. 25,000	Value: 27.50				

KM# 47 50 DOLLARS **Weight:** 31.1000 g. **Composition:** 0.9990 Silver 1.0000 oz. ASW **Reverse:** WWII American PBY Catalina

Date	Mintage	F	VF	XF	Unc	BU
1991M Proof	Est. 25,000	Value: 25.00				

KM# 48 50 DOLLARS **Weight:** 31.1000 g. **Composition:** 0.9990 Silver 1.0000 oz. ASW **Reverse:** WWII Japanese A6M Reisen

Date	Mintage	F	VF	XF	Unc	BU
1991M Proof	Est. 25,000	Value: 27.50				

KM# 58 50 DOLLARS **Weight:** 31.1000 g. **Composition:** 0.9990 Silver 1.0000 oz. ASW **Reverse:** WWII American P-40 Warhawk

Date	Mintage	F	VF	XF	Unc	BU
1991M Proof	Est. 25,000	Value: 27.50				

KM# 72 50 DOLLARS **Weight:** 31.1000 g. **Composition:** 0.9990 Silver 1.0000 oz. ASW **Reverse:** Space Shuttle Columbia - 1981

Date	Mintage	F	VF	XF	Unc	BU
1991M Proof	Est. 25,000	Value: 40.00				

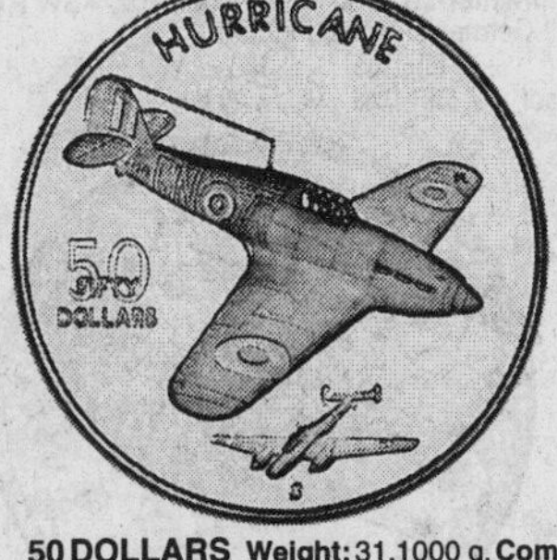

KM# 74 50 DOLLARS **Weight:** 31.1000 g. **Composition:** 0.9990 Silver 1.0000 oz. ASW **Reverse:** WWII British Hurricane

Date	Mintage	F	VF	XF	Unc	BU
1991S Proof	Est. 24,000	Value: 25.00				

KM# 75 50 DOLLARS **Weight:** 31.1000 g. **Composition:** 0.9990 Silver 1.0000 oz. ASW **Reverse:** WWII British Mosquito

Date	Mintage	F	VF	XF	Unc	BU
1991S Proof	Est. 24,000	Value: 25.00				

KM# 76 50 DOLLARS **Weight:** 31.1000 g. **Composition:** 0.9990 Silver 1.0000 oz. ASW **Reverse:** WWII American B-24 Liberator

Date	Mintage	F	VF	XF	Unc	BU
1991S Proof	Est. 25,000	Value: 22.50				

KM# 77 50 DOLLARS **Weight:** 31.1000 g. **Composition:** 0.9990 Silver 1.0000 oz. ASW **Reverse:** WWII American B-25 Mitchell

Date	Mintage	F	VF	XF	Unc	BU
1991S Proof	Est. 25,000	Value: 27.50				

KM# 78 50 DOLLARS **Weight:** 31.1000 g. **Composition:** 0.9990 Silver 1.0000 oz. ASW **Reverse:** WWII American C-47 Skytrain

Date	Mintage	F	VF	XF	Unc	BU
1991S Proof	Est. 24,000	Value: 27.50				

KM# 79 50 DOLLARS **Weight:** 31.1000 g. **Composition:** 0.9990 Silver 1.0000 oz. ASW **Reverse:** WWII American B-17 Flying Fortress

Date	Mintage	F	VF	XF	Unc	BU
1991S Proof	Est. 24,000	Value: 27.50				

KM# 80 50 DOLLARS **Weight:** 31.1000 g. **Composition:** 0.9990 Silver 1.0000 oz. ASW **Reverse:** WWII American F4U Corsair

Date	Mintage	F	VF	XF	Unc	BU
1991S Proof	Est. 24,000	Value: 27.50				

KM# 93 50 DOLLARS **Weight:** 31.1000 g. **Composition:** 0.9990 Silver 1.0000 oz. ASW **Reverse:** WWII American P-38 Lightning

Date	Mintage	F	VF	XF	Unc	BU
1991S Proof	Est. 25,000	Value: 27.50				

KM# 94 50 DOLLARS **Weight:** 31.1000 g. **Composition:** 0.9990 Silver 1.0000 oz. ASW **Reverse:** WWII American F6F Hellcat

Date	Mintage	F	VF	XF	Unc	BU
1991S Proof	Est. 24,000	Value: 25.00				

KM# 95 50 DOLLARS **Weight:** 31.1000 g. **Composition:** 0.9990 Silver 1.0000 oz. ASW **Reverse:** WWII Japanese G4M "Betty" Bomber

Date	Mintage	F	VF	XF	Unc	BU
1991S Proof	Est. 25,000	Value: 25.00				

KM# 97 50 DOLLARS **Weight:** 31.1000 g. **Composition:** 0.9990 Silver 1.0000 oz. ASW **Reverse:** WWII Soviet Yak-9

Date	Mintage	F	VF	XF	Unc	BU
1991S Proof	Est. 24,000	Value: 25.00				

KM# 99 50 DOLLARS **Weight:** 31.1000 g. **Composition:** 0.9990 Silver 1.0000 oz. ASW **Reverse:** WWII Japanese K1-61 Hien "Tony"

Date	Mintage	F	VF	XF	Unc	BU
1991S Proof	Est. 25,000	Value: 25.00				

KM# 100 50 DOLLARS **Weight:** 31.1000 g. **Composition:** 0.9990 Silver 1.0000 oz. ASW **Reverse:** WWII French D-520 Fighter

Date	Mintage	F	VF	XF	Unc	BU
1991S Proof	Est. 25,000	Value: 25.00				

KM# 102 50 DOLLARS **Weight:** 31.1000 g. **Composition:** 0.9990 Silver 1.0000 oz. ASW **Reverse:** WWII German FW 190 Fighters

Date	Mintage	F	VF	XF	Unc	BU
1991S Proof	Est. 24,000	Value: 25.00				

KM# 104 50 DOLLARS **Weight:** 31.1000 g. **Composition:** 0.9990 Silver 1.0000 oz. ASW **Reverse:** WWII British Lancaster

Date	Mintage	F	VF	XF	Unc	BU
1991S Proof	Est. 25,000	Value: 25.00				

KM# 105 50 DOLLARS **Weight:** 31.1000 g. **Composition:** 0.9990 Silver 1.0000 oz. ASW **Reverse:** WWII Italian S.M. 79 Sparviero Bombers

Date	Mintage	F	VF	XF	Unc	BU
1991S Proof	Est. 24,000	Value: 27.50				

KM# 106 50 DOLLARS **Weight:** 31.1000 g. **Composition:** 0.9990 Silver 1.0000 oz. ASW **Reverse:** WWII German HE 111 Bombers

Date	Mintage	F	VF	XF	Unc	BU
1991S Proof	Est. 25,000	Value: 25.00				

KM# 108 50 DOLLARS **Weight:** 31.1000 g. **Composition:** 0.9990 Silver 1.0000 oz. ASW **Reverse:** WWII Soviet IL-2 Shturmovik

Date	Mintage	F	VF	XF	Unc	BU
1991S Proof	Est. 24,000	Value: 22.50				

KM# 83 50 DOLLARS **Weight:** 31.1000 g. **Composition:** 0.9990 Silver 1.0000 oz. ASW **Subject:** Reaching for the Stars **Reverse:** Greek ship Argo

Date	F	VF	XF	Unc	BU
1992R Proof	—	Value: 42.50			

KM# 86 50 DOLLARS **Weight:** 31.1000 g. **Composition:** 0.9990 Silver 1.0000 oz. ASW **Subject:** To the Heroes of the Raid on Tokyo - Doolittle

Date		F	VF	XF	Unc	BU
1992R Proof	—	Value: 45.00				

KM# 89 50 DOLLARS **Weight:** 31.1000 g. **Composition:** 0.9990 Silver 1.0000 oz. ASW **Subject:** Heroes of Corregidor

Date		F	VF	XF	Unc	BU
1992R Proof	—	Value: 45.00				

KM# 92 50 DOLLARS **Weight:** 31.1000 g. **Composition:** 0.9990 Silver 1.0000 oz. ASW **Subject:** To the Heroes of Battle of Midway

Date		F	VF	XF	Unc	BU
1992R Proof	—	Value: 40.00				

KM# 111 50 DOLLARS **Weight:** 31.1000 g. **Composition:** 0.9990 Silver 1.0000 oz. ASW **Subject:** Pacific Whales and Dolphins **Reverse:** Humpback Whale

Date	Mintage	F	VF	XF	Unc	BU
1993R Proof	Est. 25,000	Value: 42.50				

KM# 112 50 DOLLARS **Weight:** 31.1000 g. **Composition:** 0.9990 Silver 1.0000 oz. ASW **Subject:** Pacific Whales and Dolphins **Reverse:** Risso's Dolphins

Date	Mintage	F	VF	XF	Unc	BU
1993R Proof	Est. 25,000	Value: 42.50				

KM# 113 50 DOLLARS **Weight:** 31.1000 g. **Composition:** 0.9990 Silver 1.0000 oz. ASW **Subject:** Pacific Whales and Dolphins **Reverse:** Beluga Whale

Date	Mintage	F	VF	XF	Unc	BU
1993R Proof	Est. 25,000	Value: 42.50				

KM# 114 50 DOLLARS **Weight:** 31.1000 g. **Composition:** 0.9990 Silver 1.0000 oz. ASW **Subject:** Pacific Whales and Dolphins **Reverse:** Hector's Dolphin

Date	Mintage	F	VF	XF	Unc	BU
1993R Proof	Est. 25,000	Value: 42.50				

KM# 115 50 DOLLARS **Weight:** 31.1000 g. **Composition:** 0.9990 Silver 1.0000 oz. ASW **Subject:** Pacific Whales and Dolphins **Reverse:** Blue Whales

Date	Mintage	F	VF	XF	Unc	BU
1993R Proof	Est. 25,000	Value: 42.50				

KM# 116 50 DOLLARS **Weight:** 31.1000 g. **Composition:** 0.9990 Silver 1.0000 oz. ASW **Subject:** Pacific Whales and Dolphins **Reverse:** Baiji Dolphins

Date	Mintage	F	VF	XF	Unc	BU
1993R Proof	Est. 25,000	Value: 42.50				

KM# 117 50 DOLLARS **Weight:** 31.1000 g. **Composition:** 0.9990 Silver 1.0000 oz. ASW **Subject:** Pacific Whales and Dolphins **Reverse:** Killer Whales

Date	Mintage	F	VF	XF	Unc	BU
1993R Proof	Est. 25,000	Value: 42.50				

KM# 120 50 DOLLARS **Weight:** 31.1000 g. **Composition:** 0.9990 Silver 1.0000 oz. ASW **Subject:** To the Heroes of the North Atlantic **Reverse:** Submarine

Date		F	VF	XF	Unc	BU
1993R Proof	—	Value: 60.00				

KM# 123 50 DOLLARS **Weight:** 31.1000 g. **Composition:** 0.9990 Silver 1.0000 oz. ASW **Subject:** To the Heroes of Guadalcanal **Reverse:** Marine, battleship and airplanes

Date		F	VF	XF	Unc	BU
1993R Proof	—	Value: 60.00				

KM# 128 50 DOLLARS **Weight:** 31.1000 g. **Composition:** 0.9990 Silver 1.0000 oz. ASW **Subject:** Pacific Whales and Dolphins **Reverse:** Common Dolphins

Date		F	VF	XF	Unc	BU
1993R Proof	—	Value: 42.50				

KM# 130 50 DOLLARS **Weight:** 31.1000 g. **Composition:** 0.9990 Silver 1.0000 oz. ASW **Reverse:** Elvis Presley

Date		F	VF	XF	Unc	BU
1993S Proof	—	Value: 37.50				

KM# 146 50 DOLLARS **Weight:** 31.1000 g. **Composition:** 0.9990 Silver 1.0000 oz. ASW **Subject:** Christmas 1993

Date		F	VF	XF	Unc	BU
1993R Proof	—	Value: 32.50				

KM# 150 50 DOLLARS **Weight:** 31.1000 g. **Composition:** 0.9990 Silver 1.0000 oz. ASW **Subject:** Flight of the Kitty Hawk

Date		F	VF	XF	Unc	BU
1993 Proof	—	Value: 37.50				

KM# 493 50 DOLLARS **Weight:** 31.1300 g. **Composition:** 0.9990 Silver 0.9999 oz. ASW **Subject:** Indo-Pacific Humpbacked Dolphin **Obverse:** State seal **Reverse:**

Two dolphins and island **Edge:** Reeded **Size:** 38.6 mm. **Note:** Legal tender status in question.

Date	Mintage	F	VF	XF	Unc	BU
1993 Proof	25,000	Value: 60.00				

KM# 494 50 DOLLARS Weight: 31.1300 g. **Composition:** 0.9990 Silver 0.9999 oz. ASW **Subject:** Minke Whale **Obverse:** State seal **Reverse:** Two Minke whales and ship with coastline in background **Edge:** Reeded **Size:** 38.6 mm. **Note:** Legal tender status in question.

Date	Mintage	F	VF	XF	Unc	BU
1993 Proof	25,000	Value: 60.00				

KM# 154 50 DOLLARS Weight: 31.1000 g. **Composition:** 0.9990 Silver 1.0000 oz. ASW **Subject:** First Men on the Moon

Date	F	VF	XF	Unc	BU
1994 Proof	—	Value: 28.50			

KM# 167 50 DOLLARS Weight: 31.1000 g. **Composition:** 0.9990 Silver 1.0000 oz. ASW **Reverse:** Mythological Mother Earth

Date	Mintage	F	VF	XF	Unc	BU
1994 Proof	Est. 25,000	Value: 30.00				

KM# 168 50 DOLLARS Weight: 31.1000 g. **Composition:** 0.9990 Silver 1.0000 oz. ASW **Reverse:** Sun

Date	Mintage	F	VF	XF	Unc	BU
1994 Proof	Est. 25,000	Value: 30.00				

KM# 169 50 DOLLARS Weight: 31.1000 g. **Composition:** 0.9990 Silver 1.0000 oz. ASW **Reverse:** Moon

Date	Mintage	F	VF	XF	Unc	BU
1994 Proof	Est. 25,000	Value: 30.00				

KM# 170 50 DOLLARS Weight: 31.1000 g. **Composition:** 0.9990 Silver 1.0000 oz. ASW **Reverse:** Pluto

Date	Mintage	F	VF	XF	Unc	BU
1994 Proof	Est. 25,000	Value: 30.00				

KM# 171 50 DOLLARS Weight: 31.1000 g. **Composition:** 0.9990 Silver 1.0000 oz. ASW **Reverse:** Mercury

Date	Mintage	F	VF	XF	Unc	BU
1994 Proof	Est. 25,000	Value: 30.00				

KM# 172 50 DOLLARS Weight: 31.1000 g. **Composition:** 0.9990 Silver 1.0000 oz. ASW **Reverse:** Venus

Date	Mintage	F	VF	XF	Unc	BU
1994 Proof	Est. 25,000	Value: 30.00				

KM# 173 50 DOLLARS Weight: 31.1000 g. **Composition:** 0.9990 Silver 1.0000 oz. ASW **Reverse:** Mars

Date	Mintage	F	VF	XF	Unc	BU
1994 Proof	Est. 25,000	Value: 30.00				

KM# 174 50 DOLLARS Weight: 31.1000 g. **Composition:** 0.9990 Silver 1.0000 oz. ASW **Reverse:** Saturn

Date	Mintage	F	VF	XF	Unc	BU
1994 Proof	Est. 25,000	Value: 30.00				

KM# 175 50 DOLLARS Weight: 31.1000 g. **Composition:** 0.9990 Silver 1.0000 oz. ASW **Reverse:** Jupiter

Date	Mintage	F	VF	XF	Unc	BU
1994 Proof	Est. 25,000	Value: 30.00				

KM# 176 50 DOLLARS Weight: 31.1000 g. **Composition:** 0.9990 Silver 1.0000 oz. ASW **Reverse:** Uranus

Date	Mintage	F	VF	XF	Unc	BU
1994 Proof	Est. 25,000	Value: 30.00				

KM# 177 50 DOLLARS Weight: 31.1000 g. **Composition:** 0.9990 Silver 1.0000 oz. ASW **Reverse:** Neptune

Date	Mintage	F	VF	XF	Unc	BU
1994 Proof	Est. 25,000	Value: 30.00				

KM# 178 50 DOLLARS Weight: 31.1000 g. **Composition:** 0.9990 Silver 1.0000 oz. ASW **Reverse:** Solar System

Date	Mintage	F	VF	XF	Unc	BU
1994 Proof	Est. 25,000	Value: 30.00				

KM# 181 50 DOLLARS Weight: 31.1000 g. **Composition:** 0.9990 Silver 1.0000 oz. ASW **Subject:** To the Heroes of D-Day - Normandy Invasion

Date	F	VF	XF	Unc	BU
1994 Proof	—	Value: 32.50			

KM# 184 50 DOLLARS Weight: 31.1000 g. **Composition:** 0.9990 Silver 1.0000 oz. ASW **Subject:** Heroes of the Philippines **Reverse:** MacArthur and Staff

Date	F	VF	XF	Unc	BU
1994 Proof	—	Value: 50.00			

KM# 190 50 DOLLARS Weight: 31.1000 g. **Composition:** 0.9990 Silver 1.0000 oz. ASW **Subject:** World Cup Soccer

Date	F	VF	XF	Unc	BU
1994 Proof	—	Value: 37.50			

KM# 262 50 DOLLARS Weight: 31.1000 g. **Composition:** 0.9990 Silver 1.0000 oz. ASW **Subject:** Christmas **Reverse:** Angel

Date	F	VF	XF	Unc	BU
1994 Proof	—	Value: 30.00			

KM# 265 50 DOLLARS Weight: 31.1000 g. **Composition:** 0.9990 Silver 1.0000 oz. ASW **Subject:** To the Heroes of Battle of the Bulge

Date	F	VF	XF	Unc	BU
1994 Proof	—	Value: 32.50			

KM# 191 50 DOLLARS **Weight:** 31.1000 g. **Composition:** 0.9990 Silver 1.0000 oz. ASW **Reverse:** Jet Fighter - F-4 Phantom II

Date	Mintage	F	VF	XF	Unc	BU
1995 Proof	25,000	Value: 28.50				

KM# 192 50 DOLLARS **Weight:** 31.1000 g. **Composition:** 0.9990 Silver 1.0000 oz. ASW **Reverse:** Jet Fighter - F-100 Super Sabre

Date	Mintage	F	VF	XF	Unc	BU
1995 Proof	25,000	Value: 27.50				

KM# 193 50 DOLLARS **Weight:** 31.1000 g. **Composition:** 0.9990 Silver 1.0000 oz. ASW **Reverse:** Jet Fighter - Mirage 2000C

Date	Mintage	F	VF	XF	Unc	BU
1995 Proof	25,000	Value: 27.50				

KM# 194 50 DOLLARS **Weight:** 31.1000 g. **Composition:** 0.9990 Silver 1.0000 oz. ASW **Reverse:** Jet Fighter - F-14 Tomcat

Date	Mintage	F	VF	XF	Unc	BU
1995 Proof	25,000	Value: 27.50				

KM# 195 50 DOLLARS **Weight:** 31.1000 g. **Composition:** 0.9990 Silver 1.0000 oz. ASW **Reverse:** Jet Fighter - F-86 Sabre

Date	Mintage	F	VF	XF	Unc	BU
1995 Proof	25,000	Value: 27.50				

KM# 196 50 DOLLARS **Weight:** 31.1000 g. **Composition:** 0.9990 Silver 1.0000 oz. ASW **Reverse:** Jet Fighter - MIG 15

Date	Mintage	F	VF	XF	Unc	BU
1995 Proof	25,000	Value: 27.50				

KM# 197 50 DOLLARS **Weight:** 31.1000 g. **Composition:** 0.9990 Silver 1.0000 oz. ASW **Reverse:** Jet Fighter - G91R

Date	Mintage	F	VF	XF	Unc	BU
1995 Proof	25,000	Value: 30.00				

KM# 198 50 DOLLARS **Weight:** 31.1000 g. **Composition:** 0.9990 Silver 1.0000 oz. ASW **Reverse:** Jet Fighter - Saab J35 Draken

Date	Mintage	F	VF	XF	Unc	BU
1995 Proof	25,000	Value: 27.50				

KM# 199 50 DOLLARS **Weight:** 31.1000 g. **Composition:** 0.9990 Silver 1.0000 oz. ASW **Reverse:** Jet Fighter - Meteor F.MK8

Date	Mintage	F	VF	XF	Unc	BU
1995 Proof	25,000	Value: 27.50				

KM# 200 50 DOLLARS **Weight:** 31.1000 g. **Composition:** 0.9990 Silver 1.0000 oz. ASW **Reverse:** Jet Fighter - F-105 Thunderchief

Date	Mintage	F	VF	XF	Unc	BU
1995 Proof	25,000	Value: 27.50				

KM# 201 50 DOLLARS **Weight:** 31.1000 g. **Composition:** 0.9990 Silver 1.0000 oz. ASW **Reverse:** Jet Fighter - Tornado F.MK3

Date	Mintage	F	VF	XF	Unc	BU
1995 Proof	25,000	Value: 27.50				

KM# 202 50 DOLLARS **Weight:** 31.1000 g. **Composition:** 0.9990 Silver 1.0000 oz. ASW **Reverse:** Jet Fighter - F-16 Fighting Falcon

Date	Mintage	F	VF	XF	Unc	BU
1995 Proof	25,000	Value: 27.50				

KM# 203 50 DOLLARS **Weight:** 31.1000 g. **Composition:** 0.9990 Silver 1.0000 oz. ASW **Reverse:** Me 262A-la Schwable

Date	Mintage	F	VF	XF	Unc	BU
1995 Proof	25,000	Value: 27.50				

KM# 204 50 DOLLARS **Weight:** 31.1000 g. **Composition:** 0.9990 Silver 1.0000 oz. ASW **Reverse:** Sea Harrier FRS. MK 1

Date	Mintage	F	VF	XF	Unc	BU
1995 Proof	25,000	Value: 27.50				

KM# 205 50 DOLLARS **Weight:** 31.1000 g. **Composition:** 0.9990 Silver 1.0000 oz. ASW **Reverse:** F-117 Nighthawk

Date	Mintage	F	VF	XF	Unc	BU
1995 Proof	25,000	Value: 28.50				

KM# 206 50 DOLLARS **Weight:** 31.1000 g. **Composition:** 0.9990 Silver 1.0000 oz. ASW **Reverse:** MIG - 21MF

Date	Mintage	F	VF	XF	Unc	BU
1995 Proof	25,000	Value: 28.50				

KM# 207 50 DOLLARS **Weight:** 31.1000 g. **Composition:** 0.9990 Silver 1.0000 oz. ASW **Reverse:** F-104 Starfighter

Date	Mintage	F	VF	XF	Unc	BU
1995 Proof	25,000	Value: 27.50				

KM# 208 50 DOLLARS **Weight:** 31.1000 g. **Composition:** 0.9990 Silver 1.0000 oz. ASW **Reverse:** Sukhoi SU-27 UB

Date	Mintage	F	VF	XF	Unc	BU
1995 Proof	25,000	Value: 28.50				

KM# 209 50 DOLLARS **Weight:** 31.1000 g. **Composition:** 0.9990 Silver 1.0000 oz. ASW **Reverse:** F-80 Shooting Star

Date	Mintage	F	VF	XF	Unc	BU
1995 Proof	25,000	Value: 27.50				

KM# 210 50 DOLLARS **Weight:** 31.1000 g. **Composition:** 0.9990 Silver 1.0000 oz. ASW **Reverse:** Swedish Saab JA 37 Viggen

Date	Mintage	F	VF	XF	Unc	BU
1995 Proof	25,000	Value: 27.50				

KM# 211 50 DOLLARS **Weight:** 31.1000 g. **Composition:** 0.9990 Silver 1.0000 oz. ASW **Reverse:** F8U Crusader

Date	Mintage	F	VF	XF	Unc	BU
1995 Proof	25,000	Value: 27.50				

KM# 212 50 DOLLARS **Weight:** 31.1000 g. **Composition:** 0.9990 Silver 1.0000 oz. ASW **Reverse:** Fiat-G91Y Jet Fighter

Date	Mintage	F	VF	XF	Unc	BU
1995 Proof	25,000	Value: 30.00				

KM# 213 50 DOLLARS **Weight:** 31.1000 g. **Composition:** 0.9990 Silver 1.0000 oz. ASW **Reverse:** Mirage FIC

Date	Mintage	F	VF	XF	Unc	BU
1995 Proof	Est. 25,000	Value: 27.50				

KM# 214 50 DOLLARS **Weight:** 31.1000 g. **Composition:** 0.9990 Silver 1.0000 oz. ASW **Reverse:** F-15 Eagle

Date	Mintage	F	VF	XF	Unc	BU
1995 Proof	Est. 25,000	Value: 27.50				

KM# 215 50 DOLLARS **Weight:** 31.1000 g. **Composition:** 0.9990 Silver 1.0000 oz. ASW **Obverse:** State seal **Reverse:** F9F-2 Panther

Date	Mintage	F	VF	XF	Unc	BU
1995 Proof	Est. 25,000	Value: 27.50				

KM# 224 50 DOLLARS **Weight:** 31.1000 g. **Composition:** 0.9990 Silver 1.0000 oz. ASW **Reverse:** Elvis Presley

Date	F	VF	XF	Unc	BU
1995 Proof	—	Value: 60.00			

KM# 256 50 DOLLARS **Weight:** 31.1000 g. **Composition:** 0.9990 Silver 1.0000 oz. ASW **Reverse:** Marilyn Monroe

Date	F	VF	XF	Unc	BU
1995 Proof	—	Value: 56.00			

KM# 259 50 DOLLARS **Weight:** 31.1000 g. **Composition:** 0.9990 Silver 1.0000 oz. ASW **Series:** 50th Anniversary United Nations **Subject:** Peace

Date	F	VF	XF	Unc	BU
1995 Proof	—	Value: 45.00			

KM# 268 50 DOLLARS **Weight:** 31.1000 g. **Composition:** 0.9990 Silver 1.0000 oz. ASW **Subject:** Peace - VJ Day

Date	F	VF	XF	Unc	BU
1995 Proof	—	Value: 45.00			

KM# 273 50 DOLLARS **Weight:** 31.1000 g. **Composition:** 0.9990 Silver 1.0000 oz. ASW **Subject:** Christmas **Reverse:** Cherub

Date	F	VF	XF	Unc	BU
1995 Proof	—	Value: 35.00			

KM# 274 50 DOLLARS **Weight:** 31.1000 g. **Composition:** 0.9990 Silver 1.0000 oz. ASW **Subject:** Freedom / Liberty **Reverse:** Torpedo Boat PT-109

Date	Mintage	F	VF	XF	Unc	BU
1995 Proof	Est. 25,000	Value: 56.00				

KM# 275 50 DOLLARS **Weight:** 31.1000 g. **Composition:** 0.9990 Silver 1.0000 oz. ASW **Subject:** Freedom / Liberty **Reverse:** President John F. Kennedy takes oath of office

Date	Mintage	F	VF	XF	Unc	BU
1995 Proof	Est. 25,000	Value: 56.00				

KM# 276 50 DOLLARS **Weight:** 31.1000 g. **Composition:** 0.9990 Silver 1.0000 oz. ASW **Subject:** Freedom / Liberty **Reverse:** Peace Corps worker and native

Date	Mintage	F	VF	XF	Unc	BU
1995 Proof	Est. 25,000	Value: 56.00				

KM# 367 50 DOLLARS **Weight:** 31.1000 g. **Composition:** 0.9990 Silver 1.0000 oz. ASW **Obverse:** State seal **Reverse:** F-102A Delta Dagger

Date	Mintage	F	VF	XF	Unc	BU
1995 Proof	25,000	Value: 27.50				

KM# 397 50 DOLLARS **Weight:** 31.1000 g. **Composition:** 0.9990 Silver 1.0000 oz. ASW **Obverse:** State seal **Reverse:** B-52 Stratofortress

Date	Mintage	F	VF	XF	Unc	BU
1995 Proof	25,000	Value: 30.00				

KM# 277 50 DOLLARS **Weight:** 31.1000 g. **Composition:** 0.9990 Silver 1.0000 oz. ASW **Subject:** Freedom / Liberty **Reverse:** Battleship and freighter

Date	Mintage	F	VF	XF	Unc	BU
1995 Proof	Est. 25,000	Value: 56.00				

KM# 278 50 DOLLARS **Weight:** 31.1000 g. **Composition:** 0.9990 Silver 1.0000 oz. ASW **Subject:** Freedom / Liberty **Reverse:** President John F. Kennedy working at desk

Date	Mintage	F	VF	XF	Unc	BU
1995 Proof	Est. 25,000	Value: 56.00				

KM# 279 50 DOLLARS **Weight:** 31.1000 g. **Composition:** 0.9990 Silver 1.0000 oz. ASW **Subject:** Freedom / Liberty **Reverse:** President John F. Kennedy's Eternal Flame

Date	Mintage	F	VF	XF	Unc	BU
1995 Proof	Est. 25,000	Value: 56.00				

KM# 227 50 DOLLARS **Weight:** 31.1000 g. **Composition:** 0.9990 Silver 1.0000 oz. ASW **Subject:** War in the Pacific **Note:** Similar to 10 Dollars, KM#226.

Date		F	VF	XF	Unc	BU
1995 Proof	—	Value: 32.50				

KM# 218 50 DOLLARS **Weight:** 31.1000 g. **Composition:** 0.9990 Silver 1.0000 oz. ASW **Subject:** Victory in Europe **Note:** Similar to 5 Dollars, KM#216.

Date		F	VF	XF	Unc	BU
1995 Proof	—	Value: 40.00				

KM# 221 50 DOLLARS **Weight:** 31.1000 g. **Composition:** 0.9990 Silver 1.0000 oz. ASW **Subject:** Vietnam Veterans **Note:** Similar to 5 Dollars, KM#219.

Date		F	VF	XF	Unc	BU
1995 Proof	—	Value: 32.50				

KM# 281 50 DOLLARS **Weight:** 31.1000 g. **Composition:** 0.9990 Silver 1.0000 oz. ASW **Subject:** Year of the Rat **Note:** Similar to 5 Dollars, KM#280.

Date		F	VF	XF	Unc	BU
1996 Proof	—	Value: 40.00				

KM# 305 50 DOLLARS **Weight:** 31.1000 g. **Composition:** 0.9990 Silver 1.0000 oz. ASW **Reverse:** James Dean **Note:** Similar to 5 Dollars, KM#303.

Date		F	VF	XF	Unc	BU
1996 Proof	—	Value: 50.00				

KM# 350 50 DOLLARS **Weight:** 31.1000 g. **Composition:** 0.9990 Silver 1.0000 oz. ASW **Reverse:** Lion **Note:** Similar to 5 Dollars, KM#344.

Date		F	VF	XF	Unc	BU
1996 Proof	—	Value: 42.50				

KM# 352 50 DOLLARS **Weight:** 31.1000 g. **Composition:** 0.9990 Silver 1.0000 oz. ASW **Reverse:** Jaguar **Note:** Similar to 5 Dollars, KM#346.

Date		F	VF	XF	Unc	BU
1996 Proof	—	Value: 42.50				

KM# 313 50 DOLLARS **Weight:** 31.1000 g. **Composition:** 0.9990 Silver 1.0000 oz. ASW **Subject:** Classic Cars **Reverse:** Model A Ford **Note:** Similar to 10 Dollars, KM#312.

Date		F	VF	XF	Unc	BU
1996 Proof	—	Value: 32.50				

KM# 340 50 DOLLARS **Weight:** 31.1000 g. **Composition:** 0.9990 Silver 1.0000 oz. ASW **Reverse:** Space Shuttle Challenger **Note:** Similar to 10 Dollars, KM#336.

Date		F	VF	XF	Unc	BU
1996 Proof	—	Value: 32.50				

KM# 341 50 DOLLARS **Weight:** 31.1000 g. **Composition:** 0.9990 Silver 1.0000 oz. ASW **Reverse:** Space Shuttle Discovery **Note:** Similar to 10 Dollars, KM#338.

Date		F	VF	XF	Unc	BU
1996 Proof	—	Value: 32.50				

KM# 290 50 DOLLARS **Weight:** 31.1000 g. **Composition:** 0.9990 Silver 1.0000 oz. ASW **Reverse:** Space Shuttle Columbia

Date		F	VF	XF	Unc	BU
1996 Proof	—	Value: 37.50				

KM# 291 50 DOLLARS **Weight:** 31.1000 g. **Composition:** 0.9990 Silver 1.0000 oz. ASW **Reverse:** "Pennsylvania K4"

Date		F	VF	XF	Unc	BU
1996 Proof	—	Value: 32.50				

KM# 292 50 DOLLARS **Weight:** 31.1000 g. **Composition:** 0.9990 Silver 1.0000 oz. ASW **Subject:** Steam Locomotive **Reverse:** "Big Boy"

Date		F	VF	XF	Unc	BU
1996 Proof	—	Value: 32.50				

KM# 296 50 DOLLARS **Weight:** 31.1000 g. **Composition:** 0.9990 Silver 1.0000 oz. ASW **Subject:** Steam Locomotive **Reverse:** "Mallard"

Date		F	VF	XF	Unc	BU
1996 Proof	—	Value: 32.50				

KM# 299 50 DOLLARS **Weight:** 31.1000 g. **Composition:** 0.9990 Silver 1.0000 oz. ASW **Reverse:** Tiger

Date	F	VF	XF	Unc	BU
1996 In set only	—	—	—	42.50	—

KM# 302 50 DOLLARS **Weight:** 31.1000 g. **Composition:** 0.9990 Silver 1.0000 oz. ASW **Reverse:** Elvis Presley

Date	F	VF	XF	Unc	BU
1996 Proof	—	Value: 50.00			

KM# 310 50 DOLLARS **Weight:** 31.1000 g. **Composition:** 0.9990 Silver 1.0000 oz. ASW **Subject:** Classic Cars **Reverse:** Ford Quadricycle

Date	F	VF	XF	Unc	BU
1996 Proof	—	Value: 32.50			

KM# 316 50 DOLLARS **Weight:** 31.1000 g. **Composition:** 0.9990 Silver 1.0000 oz. ASW **Subject:** Classic Cars **Reverse:** Model T Ford

Date	F	VF	XF	Unc	BU
1996 Proof	—	Value: 32.50			

KM# 319 50 DOLLARS **Weight:** 31.1000 g. **Composition:** 0.9990 Silver 1.0000 oz. ASW **Subject:** Classic Cars **Reverse:** 1955 Thunderbird

Date	F	VF	XF	Unc	BU
1996 Proof	—	Value: 50.00			

KM# 322 50 DOLLARS **Weight:** 31.1000 g. **Composition:** 0.9990 Silver 1.0000 oz. ASW **Subject:** Classic Cars **Reverse:** 1964 Mustang

Date	F	VF	XF	Unc	BU
1996 Proof	—	Value: 32.50			

KM# 325 50 DOLLARS **Weight:** 31.1000 g. **Composition:** 0.9990 Silver 1.0000 oz. ASW **Subject:** Classic Cars **Reverse:** Ford Taurus

Date	F	VF	XF	Unc	BU
1996 Proof	—	Value: 32.50			

KM# 327 50 DOLLARS **Weight:** 31.1000 g. **Composition:** 0.9990 Silver 1.0000 oz. ASW **Subject:** Steam Locomotive **Reverse:** "DB Class 01"

Date	Mintage	F	VF	XF	Unc	BU
1996 Proof	Est. 25,000	Value: 32.50				

KM# 328 50 DOLLARS **Weight:** 31.1000 g. **Composition:** 0.9990 Silver 1.0000 oz. ASW **Subject:** Steam Locomotive **Reverse:** "RENFE Class 242"

Date	F	VF	XF	Unc	BU
1996 Proof	—	Value: 32.50			

KM# 329 50 DOLLARS **Weight:** 31.1000 g. **Composition:** 0.9990 Silver 1.0000 oz. ASW **Subject:** Steam Locomotive **Reverse:** "S Group 691"

Date	F	VF	XF	Unc	BU
1996 Proof	—	Value: 32.50			

KM# 342 50 DOLLARS **Weight:** 31.1000 g. **Composition:** 0.9990 Silver 1.0000 oz. ASW **Reverse:** Space Shuttle Atlantis

Date	F	VF	XF	Unc	BU
1996 Proof	—	Value: 32.50			

KM# 343 50 DOLLARS **Weight:** 31.1000 g. **Composition:** 0.9990 Silver 1.0000 oz. ASW **Reverse:** Space Shuttle Endeavor

Date	F	VF	XF	Unc	BU
1996 Proof	—	Value: 32.50			

KM# 351 50 DOLLARS **Weight:** 31.1000 g. **Composition:** 0.9990 Silver 1.0000 oz. ASW **Reverse:** Cheetah

Date	F	VF	XF	Unc	BU
1996 Proof	—	Value: 40.00			

KM# 355 50 DOLLARS **Weight:** 31.1000 g. **Composition:** 0.9990 Silver 1.0000 oz. ASW **Subject:** Christmas **Reverse:** Two angels

Date	F	VF	XF	Unc	BU
1996 Proof	—	Value: 35.00			

KM# 357 50 DOLLARS **Weight:** 31.1000 g. **Composition:** 0.9990 Silver 1.0000 oz. ASW **Subject:** Steam Locomotive **Reverse:** "SNCF 232.U1"

Date	F	VF	XF	Unc	BU
1996 Proof	—	Value: 40.00			

KM# 358 50 DOLLARS **Weight:** 31.1000 g. **Composition:** 0.9990 Silver 1.0000 oz. ASW **Subject:** Steam Locomotive **Reverse:** "SAR 520 Class"

Date	F	VF	XF	Unc	BU
1996 Proof	—	Value: 40.00			

KM# 360 50 DOLLARS **Weight:** 31.1000 g. **Composition:** 0.9990 Silver 1.0000 oz. ASW **Subject:** Steam Locomotive **Reverse:** "Evening Star"

Date	F	VF	XF	Unc	BU
1996	—	—	—	40.00	—

KM# 376 50 DOLLARS **Weight:** 31.1000 g. **Composition:** 0.9990 Silver 1.0000 oz. ASW **Subject:** Steam Locomotive **Reverse:** C62 "Swallow"

Date	F	VF	XF	Unc	BU
1996 Proof	—	Value: 40.00			

KM# 377 50 DOLLARS **Weight:** 31.1000 g. **Composition:** 0.9990 Silver 1.0000 oz. ASW **Subject:** Steam Locomotive **Reverse:** QJ "Advance Forward"

Date	F	VF	XF	Unc	BU
1996 Proof	—	Value: 40.00			

KM# 380 50 DOLLARS **Weight:** 31.1000 g. **Composition:** 0.9990 Silver 1.0000 oz. ASW **Subject:** Steam Locomotive **Reverse:** "Royal Hudson"

Date	F	VF	XF	Unc	BU
1996 Proof	—	Value: 40.00			

KM# 363 50 DOLLARS **Weight:** 31.1000 g. **Composition:** 0.9990 Silver 1.0000 oz. ASW **Subject:** Year of the Ox **Obverse:** State seal **Reverse:** Stylized ox

Date	F	VF	XF	Unc	BU
1997 Proof	—	Value: 57.50			

KM# 375 0 DOLLARS **Weight:** 31.1000 g. **Composition:** 0.9990 Silver 1.0000 oz. ASW **Reverse:** Gray wolf

Date	F	VF	XF	Unc	BU
1997 Proof	—	Value: 45.00			

KM# 399 50 DOLLARS **Weight:** 31.1000 g. **Composition:** 0.9990 Silver 1.0000 oz. ASW **Subject:** History's Great Fightintg Ships **Reverse:** USS Constitution; ship, dates

Date	F	VF	XF	Unc	BU
1997 Proof	—	Value: 56.00			

KM# 405 50 DOLLARS **Weight:** 31.1000 g. **Composition:** 0.9990 Silver 1.0000 oz. ASW **Subject:** Christmas **Reverse:** Two cherubs

Date	F	VF	XF	Unc	BU
1997	—	—	—	35.00	—

KM# 366 50 DOLLARS **Weight:** 31.1000 g. **Composition:** 0.9990 Silver 1.0000 oz. ASW **Reverse:** Elvis Presley **Note:** Similar to 5 Dollars, KM#362.

Date	F	VF	XF	Unc	BU
1997 Proof	—	Value: 57.50			

KM# 370 50 DOLLARS **Weight:** 31.1000 g. **Composition:** 0.9990 Silver 1.0000 oz. ASW **Subject:** The Last Supper **Note:** Similar to 5 Dollars, KM#369.

Date	F	VF	XF	Unc	BU
1997 Proof	—	Value: 50.00			

KM# 373 50 DOLLARS **Weight:** 31.1000 g. **Composition:** 0.9990 Silver 1.0000 oz. ASW **Subject:** To the Heroes of the Korean War **Note:** Similar to 5 Dollars, KM#371.

Date	F	VF	XF	Unc	BU
1997 Proof	—	Value: 40.00			

KM# 467 50 DOLLARS **Weight:** 31.1000 g. **Composition:** 0.9990 Silver 1.0000 oz. ASW **Subject:** Classic Cars **Obverse:** State seal **Reverse:** 1912 Chevy Classic Six **Note:** Similar to 5 Dollars, KM#466.

Date	F	VF	XF	Unc	BU
1998 Proof	—	Value: 56.00			

KM# 469 50 DOLLARS **Weight:** 31.1000 g. **Composition:** 0.9990 Silver 1.0000 oz. ASW **Subject:** Classic Cars **Obverse:** State seal **Reverse:** 1931 Chevy Roadster **Note:** Similar to 5 Dollars, KM#468.

Date	F	VF	XF	Unc	BU
1998 Proof	—	Value: 56.00			

KM# 471 50 DOLLARS **Weight:** 31.1000 g. **Composition:** 0.9990 Silver 1.0000 oz. ASW **Subject:** Classic Cars **Obverse:** State seal **Reverse:** Cameo Carrier **Note:** Similar to 5 Dollars, KM#470.

Date	F	VF	XF	Unc	BU
1998 Proof	—	Value: 56.00			

KM# 473 50 DOLLARS **Weight:** 31.1000 g. **Composition:** 0.9990 Silver 1.0000 oz. ASW **Subject:** Classic Cars **Obverse:** State seal **Reverse:** 1957 Chevy Bel Air **Note:** Similar to 5 Dollars, KM#472.

Date	F	VF	XF	Unc	BU
1998 Proof	—	Value: 56.00			

KM# 475 50 DOLLARS **Weight:** 31.1000 g. **Composition:** 0.9990 Silver 1.0000 oz. ASW **Subject:** Classic Cars **Obverse:** State seal **Reverse:** 1957 Chevy Corvette **Note:** Similar to 5 Dollars, KM#474.

Date	F	VF	XF	Unc	BU
1998 Proof	—	Value: 56.00			

KM# 477 50 DOLLARS **Weight:** 31.1000 g. **Composition:** 0.9990 Silver 1.0000 oz. ASW **Subject:** Classic Cars **Obverse:** State seal **Reverse:** 1967 Chevy Camaro **Note:** Similar to 5 Dollars, KM#476.

Date	F	VF	XF	Unc	BU
1998 Proof	—	Value: 50.00			

KM# 414 50 DOLLARS **Weight:** 31.1000 g. **Composition:** 0.9990 Silver 1.0000 oz. ASW **Subject:** Year of the Tiger **Reverse:** Stylized tiger

Date	F	VF	XF	Unc	BU
1998 Proof	—	Value: 50.00			

KM# 416 50 DOLLARS **Weight:** 31.1000 g. **Composition:** 0.9990 Silver 1.0000 oz. ASW **Subject:** History's Great Fighting Ships **Reverse:** Viking Longship

Date	Mintage	F	VF	XF	Unc	BU
1998 Proof	Est. 25,000	Value: 56.00				

KM# 418 50 DOLLARS **Weight:** 31.1000 g. **Composition:** 0.9990 Silver 1.0000 oz. ASW **Subject:** History's Great Fighting Ships **Reverse:** Greek Trireme

Date	Mintage	F	VF	XF	Unc	BU
1998 Proof	Est. 25,000	Value: 56.00				

KM# 420 50 DOLLARS **Weight:** 31.1000 g. **Composition:** 0.9990 Silver 1.0000 oz. ASW **Subject:** History's Great Fighting Ships **Reverse:** Roman Trireme

Date	Mintage	F	VF	XF	Unc	BU
1998 Proof	Est. 25,000	Value: 56.00				

KM# 422 50 DOLLARS **Weight:** 31.1000 g. **Composition:** 0.9990 Silver 1.0000 oz. ASW **Subject:** History's Great Fighting Ships **Reverse:** Chinese Ming Treasure Ship

Date	Mintage	F	VF	XF	Unc	BU
1998 Proof	Est. 25,000	Value: 56.00				

KM# 424 50 DOLLARS **Weight:** 31.1000 g. **Composition:** 0.9990 Silver 1.0000 oz. ASW **Subject:** History's Great Fighting Ships **Reverse:** Korean Turtle Ship

Date	Mintage	F	VF	XF	Unc	BU
1998 Proof	Est. 25,000	Value: 56.00				

KM# 426 50 DOLLARS **Weight:** 31.1000 g. **Composition:** 0.9990 Silver 1.0000 oz. ASW **Subject:** History's Great Fighting Ships **Reverse:** Fijan War Canoe

Date	Mintage	F	VF	XF	Unc	BU
1998 Proof	Est. 25,000	Value: 56.00				

KM# 428 50 DOLLARS **Weight:** 31.1000 g. **Composition:** 0.9990 Silver 1.0000 oz. ASW **Subject:** History's Great Fighting Ships **Reverse:** The Bismarck

Date	Mintage	F	VF	XF	Unc	BU
1998 Proof	Est. 25,000	Value: 56.00				

KM# 430 50 DOLLARS **Weight:** 31.1000 g. **Composition:** 0.9990 Silver 1.0000 oz. ASW **Subject:** History's Great Fighting Ships **Reverse:** The Graf Spee

Date	Mintage	F	VF	XF	Unc	BU
1998 Proof	Est. 25,000	Value: 56.00				

KM# 432 50 DOLLARS **Weight:** 31.1000 g. **Composition:** 0.9990 Silver 1.0000 oz. ASW **Subject:** History's Great Fighting Ships **Reverse:** The Yamato

Date	Mintage	F	VF	XF	Unc	BU
1998 Proof	Est. 25,000	Value: 56.00				

KM# 434 50 DOLLARS **Weight:** 31.1000 g. **Composition:** 0.9990 Silver 1.0000 oz. ASW **Subject:** History's Great Fighting Ships **Reverse:** HMS Victory

Date	Mintage	F	VF	XF	Unc	BU
1998 Proof	Est. 25,000	Value: 56.00				

KM# 436 50 DOLLARS Weight: 31.1000 g. **Composition:** 0.9990 Silver 1.0000 oz. ASW **Subject:** History's Great Fighting Ships **Reverse:** HMS Mary Rose

Date	Mintage	F	VF	XF	Unc	BU
1998 Proof	Est. 25,000	Value: 56.00				

KM# 438 50 DOLLARS Weight: 31.1000 g. **Composition:** 0.9990 Silver 1.0000 oz. ASW **Subject:** History's Great Fighting Ships **Reverse:** HMS Dreadnought

Date	Mintage	F	VF	XF	Unc	BU
1998 Proof	Est. 25,000	Value: 56.00				

KM# 440 50 DOLLARS Weight: 31.1000 g. **Composition:** 0.9990 Silver 1.0000 oz. ASW **Subject:** History's Great Fighting Ships **Reverse:** HMS Dorsetshire

Date	Mintage	F	VF	XF	Unc	BU
1998 Proof	Est. 25,000	Value: 56.00				

KM# 442 50 DOLLARS Weight: 31.1000 g. **Composition:** 0.9990 Silver 1.0000 oz. ASW **Subject:** History's Great Fighting Ships **Obverse:** State seal **Reverse:** Spanish Galleon Nuestra Senora del Rosario

Date	Mintage	F	VF	XF	Unc	BU
1998 Proof	Est. 25,000	Value: 56.00				

KM# 444 50 DOLLARS Weight: 31.1000 g. **Composition:** 0.9990 Silver 1.0000 oz. ASW **Subject:** History's Great Fighting Ships **Obverse:** State seal **Reverse:** Spanish Galleon Santisima Trinidad

Date	Mintage	F	VF	XF	Unc	BU
1998 Proof	Est. 25,000	Value: 56.00				

KM# 446 50 DOLLARS Weight: 31.1000 g. **Composition:** 0.9990 Silver 1.0000 oz. ASW **Subject:** History's Great Fighting Ships **Obverse:** State seal **Reverse:** USS Bonhomme Richard

Date	Mintage	F	VF	XF	Unc	BU
1998 Proof	Est. 25,000	Value: 56.00				

KM# 448 50 DOLLARS Weight: 31.1000 g. **Composition:** 0.9990 Silver 1.0000 oz. ASW **Subject:** History's Great Fighting Ships **Obverse:** State seal **Reverse:** USS Constellation

Date	Mintage	F	VF	XF	Unc	BU
1998 Proof	Est. 25,000	Value: 56.00				

KM# 450 50 DOLLARS Weight: 31.1000 g. **Composition:** 0.9990 Silver 1.0000 oz. ASW **Subject:** History's Great Fighting Ships **Obverse:** State seal **Reverse:** USS Hartford

Date	Mintage	F	VF	XF	Unc	BU
1998 Proof	Est. 25,000	Value: 56.00				

KM# 452 50 DOLLARS Weight: 31.1000 g. **Composition:** 0.9990 Silver 1.0000 oz. ASW **Subject:** History's Great Fighting Ships **Obverse:** State seal **Reverse:** USS Hornet

Date	Mintage	F	VF	XF	Unc	BU
1998 Proof	Est. 25,000	Value: 56.00				

KM# 454 50 DOLLARS Weight: 31.1000 g. **Composition:** 0.9990 Silver 1.0000 oz. ASW **Subject:** History's Great Fighting Ships **Obverse:** State seal **Reverse:** USS Missouri

Date	Mintage	F	VF	XF	Unc	BU
1998 Proof	Est. 25,000	Value: 56.00				

KM# 456 50 DOLLARS Weight: 31.1000 g. **Composition:** 0.9990 Silver 1.0000 oz. ASW **Subject:** History's Great Fighting Ships **Obverse:** State seal **Reverse:** USS Tautog

Date	Mintage	F	VF	XF	Unc	BU
1998 Proof	Est. 25,000	Value: 56.00				

KM# 458 50 DOLLARS Weight: 31.1000 g. **Composition:** 0.9990 Silver 1.0000 oz. ASW **Subject:** History's Great Fighting Ships **Obverse:** State seal **Reverse:** Dutch Ship Brederode

Date	Mintage	F	VF	XF	Unc	BU
1998 Proof	Est. 25,000	Value: 56.00				

KM# 460 50 DOLLARS Weight: 31.1000 g. **Composition:** 0.9990 Silver 1.0000 oz. ASW **Subject:** History's Great Fighting Ships **Obverse:** State seal **Reverse:** French Ship Ville de Paris

Date	Mintage	F	VF	XF	Unc	BU
1998 Proof	Est. 25,000	Value: 56.00				

KM# 462 50 DOLLARS Weight: 31.1000 g. **Composition:** 0.9990 Silver 1.0000 oz. ASW **Subject:** History's Great Fighting Ships **Obverse:** State seal **Reverse:** Italian Ship Galera Veneziana

Date	Mintage	F	VF	XF	Unc	BU
1998 Proof	Est. 25,000	Value: 56.00				

KM# 465 50 DOLLARS Weight: 31.1000 g. **Composition:** 0.9990 Silver 1.0000 oz. ASW **Subject:** To the Heroes of the Berlin Airlift **Obverse:** State seal **Reverse:** C-54 Landing

Date	F	VF	XF	Unc	BU
1998 Proof	—	Value: 56.00			

KM# 480 50 DOLLARS Weight: 31.1000 g. **Composition:** 0.9990 Silver 1.0000 oz. ASW **Subject:** Babe Ruth at bat **Obverse:** State seal

Date	F	VF	XF	Unc	BU
1998 Proof	—	Value: 45.00			

KM# 483 50 DOLLARS Weight: 31.1000 g. **Composition:** 0.9990 Silver 1.0000 oz. ASW **Subject:** Christmas **Obverse:** State seal **Reverse:** Angel

Date	F	VF	XF	Unc	BU
1998 Proof	—	Value: 45.00			

KM# 485 50 DOLLARS Weight: 31.1000 g. **Composition:** 0.9990 Silver 1.0000 oz. ASW **Reverse:** Friendship 7 and Discovery blasting off **Edge:** Reeded

Date	F	VF	XF	Unc	BU
1998 Proof	—	Value: 56.00			

KM# 16 75 DOLLARS Weight: 155.6700 g. **Composition:** 0.9990 Silver 5.0055 oz. ASW **Subject:** Greg Louganis - World's Greatest Diver **Size:** 65 mm. **Note:** Illustration reduced. An actual mintage of 20 pieces has been reported for KM#16.

Date	Mintage	F	VF	XF	Unc	BU
1988 Proof	Est. 175,000	Value: 800				

KM# 17 100 DOLLARS Weight: 13.3300 g. **Composition:** 0.5830 Gold .2499 oz. AGW **Subject:** Greg Louganis - World's Greatest Diver **Obverse:** State seal and legend **Reverse:** Diver

Date	Mintage	F	VF	XF	Unc	BU
1988		—	—	—	275	—
1988 Proof	Est. 350,000	Value: 300				

KM# 5 200 DOLLARS Weight: 31.1030 g. **Composition:** 0.9990 Gold 1.0000 oz. AGW **Reverse:** Stick chart

Date	Mintage	F	VF	XF	Unc	BU
1986 Proof	Est. 5,000	Value: 425				

MINT SETS

KM#	Date	Mintage	Identification	Issue Price	Mkt Val
MS2	1988 (4)	—	KM#17, 20-22	—	550
MS1	1988 (3)	—	KM#20-22	—	250
MS3	1992R (3)	—	KM#81-83	71.00	75.00
MS4	1992R (3)	—	KM#84-86	71.00	75.00
MS5	1992R (3)	—	KM#87-89	71.00	75.00
MS6	1992R (3)	—	KM#90-92	71.00	75.00
MS7	1992R (3)	—	KM#84, 87, 90	17.50	20.00
MS8	1992R (3)	—	KM#85, 88, 91	34.00	35.00
MS9	1992R (3)	—	KM#86, 89, 92	156	160
MS10	1995 (6)	—	KM#282-287	66.00	75.00

M#	Date	Mintage	Identification	Issue Price	Mkt Val
1S11	1998 (24)	25,000	KM#415, 417, 419, 421, 423, 425, 427, 429, 431, 433, 435, 437, 439, 441, 443, 445, 447, 449, 451, 453, 455, 457, 459, 461	288	290

PROOF SETS

M#	Date	Mintage	Identification	Issue Price	Mkt Val
S1	1986 (3)	5,000	KM#3-5	1,095	600
S2	1986 (2)	10,000	KM#1-2	45.00	50.00
S3	1988 (3)	—	KM#20-22	—	375
S4	1988 (4)	—	KM#17, 20-22	—	700
S5	1991 (3)	—	KM#40-42	71.00	75.00
S6	1993 (3)	—	KM#124, 129-130	—	85.00
S7	1994 (3)	—	KM#179-180 BU, 181	71.00	75.00
S8	1994 (3)	—	KM#182 BU, 183 P/L, 184	71.00	75.00
S9	1994 (3)	—	KM#260 BU, 261, 262	—	75.00
S10	1994 (3)	—	KM#263 BU, 264, 265	—	75.00
S11	1995 (6)	25,000	KM#274-279	—	340
PS12	1995 (3)	—	KM#216 BU, 217, 218	—	75.00
PS13	1995 (3)	—	KM#219 BU, 220, 221	—	75.00
PS14	1995 (3)	—	KM#222 BU, 223, 224	—	75.00
PS15	1995 (3)	—	KM#225 BU, 226, 227	—	75.00
PS16	1995 (3)	—	KM#253 BU, 254, 255	—	95.00
PS17	1995 (3)	—	KM#257 BU, 258, 259	—	75.00
PS18	1995 (3)	—	KM#266 BU, 267, 268	—	75.00
PS19	1996 (6)	—	KM#308, 311, 314, 317, 320, 323	33.00	40.00
PS20	1996 (6)	—	KM#309, 312, 315, 318, 321, 324	66.00	80.00
PS21	1996 (6)	—	KM#310, 313, 316, 319, 322, 325	306	325
PS22	1996 (3)	—	KM#288-290	71.00	75.00
PS23	1996 (3)	—	KM#297-299	71.00	78.00
PS24	1996 (3)	—	KM#300-302	71.00	78.00
PS25	1996 (3)	—	KM#303-305	71.00	75.00
PS26	1996 (3)	—	KM#308-310	71.00	75.00
PS27	1996 (3)	—	KM#311-313	71.00	75.00
PS28	1996 (3)	—	KM#314-316	71.00	75.00
PS29	1996 (3)	—	KM#317-319	71.00	75.00
PS30	1996 (3)	—	KM#320-322	71.00	75.00
PS31	1996 (4)	—	KM#322-325	71.00	75.00
PS32	1996 (3)	—	KM#353-355	71.00	75.00
PS33	1997 (2)	—	KM#362-363	61.00	65.00
PS34	1997 (3)	—	KM#364-366	71.00	77.50
PS35	1997 (2)	—	KM#369-370	61.00	62.50
PS36	1997 (3)	—	KM#371-373	71.00	75.00
PS37	1997 (2)	—	KM#374-375	61.00	65.00
PS38	1997 (2)	—	KM#398-399	61.00	62.50
PS39	1997 (2)	—	KM#400-401	—	37.50
PS40	1997 (3)	—	KM#403-405	71.00	75.00
PS41	1998 (24)	—	KM#416, 418, 420, 422, 424, 426, 428, 430, 432, 434, 436, 438, 440, 442, 444, 446, 448, 450, 452, 454, 456, 458, 460, 462	1,344	1,345
PS42	1998 (3)	—	KM#478-480	71.00	72.00
PS43	1998 (3)	—	KM#481-483	71.00	72.00

MARTINIQUE

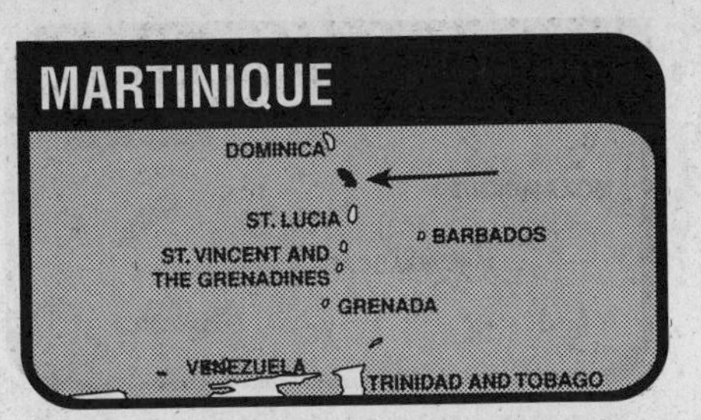

The French Overseas Department of Martinique, located in the Lesser Antilles of the West Indies between Dominica and Saint Lucia, has an area of 425 sq. mi.(1,100 sq. km.) and a population of 290,000. Capital: Fort-de-France. Agriculture and tourism are the major sources of income. Bananas, sugar, and rum are exported.

Christopher Columbus discovered Martinique, probably on June 15, 1502. France took possession on June 25, 1635, and has maintained possession since that time except for three short periods of British occupation during the Napoleonic Wars. A French department since 1946, Martinique voted a reaffirmation of that status in 1958, remaining within the new French Community. Martinique was the birthplace of Napoleon's Empress Josephine, and the site of the eruption of Mt. Pelee in 1902 that claimed 40,000 lives.

The official currency of Martinique is the French franc. The 1897-1922 coinage of the Colony of Martinique is now obsolete.

MONETARY SYSTEM

15 Sols = 1 Escalin
20 Sols = 1 Livre
66 Livres = 4 Escudos = 6400 Reis

FRENCH COLONY

DECIMAL COINAGE

KM# 40 50 CENTIMES Composition: Copper-Nickel

Date	Mintage	VG	F	VF	XF	Unc
1922	500,000	12.00	22.00	40.00	125	300

KM# 41 FRANC Composition: Copper-Nickel

Date	Mintage	VG	F	VF	XF	Unc
1922	350,000	15.00	25.00	50.00	150	320

MAURITANIA

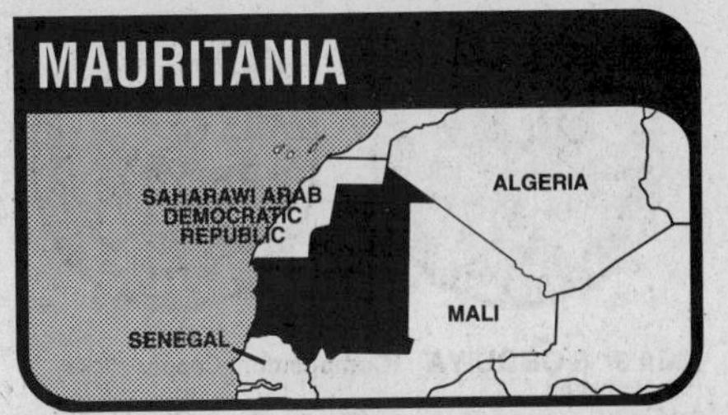

The Islamic Republic of Mauritania, located in northwest Africa bounded by Western Sahara, Mali, Algeria, Senegal and the Atlantic Ocean, has an area of 397,955 sq. mi.(1,030,700 sq. km.) and a population of 1.9 million. Capital: Nouakchott. The economy centers about herding, agriculture, fishing and mining. Iron ore, copper concentrates and fish products are exported.

The indigenous Negroid inhabitants were driven out of Mauritania by Berber invaders of the Islamic faith in the11th century. The Berbers in turn were conquered by Arab invaders, the Beni Hassan, in the 16th century. Arab traders carried on a gainful trade in gum arabic, gold and slaves with Portuguese, Dutch, English and French traders until late in the 19th century when France took control of the area and made it a part of French West Africa, in 1920.Mauritania became a part of the French Union in 1946 and was made an autonomous republic within the new French Community in 1958, when the Islamic Republic of Mauritania was proclaimed. The republic became independent on November 28, 1960, and withdrew from the French Community in 1966.

On June 28, 1973, in a move designed to emphasize its non-alignment with France, Mauritania converted its currency from the old French-supported C.F.A. franc unit to a new unit called the Ouguiya.

MONETARY SYSTEM

5 Khoums = 1 Ouguiya

REPUBLIC

STANDARD COINAGE

KM# 1 1/5 OUGUIYA (Khoums) Composition: Aluminum

Date	Mintage	VG	F	VF	XF	Unc
AH1393	1,000,000	—	0.35	0.75	1.50	3.00

KM# 2 OUGUIYA Composition: Copper-Nickel-Aluminum **Reverse:** Arabic legend below value in one line

Date	VG	F	VF	XF	Unc
AH1393	—	5.00	10.00	17.50	30.00

KM# 6 OUGUIYA Composition: Copper-Nickel-Aluminum **Reverse:** Arabic legend below value in two lines

Date	VG	F	VF	XF	Unc
AH1394	—	2.50	5.50	10.00	18.50
AH1401	—	1.50	3.00	4.50	7.50
AH1403	—	1.00	2.00	3.50	6.50
AH1406	—	0.75	1.50	2.50	4.50
AH1407	—	0.50	1.00	2.00	4.00
AH1410	—	0.50	1.00	2.00	4.00
AH1414	—	0.50	1.00	2.00	4.00
AH1416	—	0.50	1.00	2.00	4.00

KM# 3 5 OUGUIYA **Composition:** Copper-Nickel-Aluminum

Date	VG	F	VF	XF	Unc
AH1393	—	2.50	5.50	10.00	15.00
AH1394	—	2.50	5.50	10.00	17.50
AH1401	—	2.00	4.00	6.00	12.50
AH1404	—	1.50	2.50	4.50	10.00
AH1407	—	0.75	1.50	2.50	5.00
AH1410	—	0.50	1.00	2.00	4.00
AH1414	—	0.50	1.00	2.00	4.00
AH1416	—	0.50	1.00	2.00	4.00
AH1418	—	0.50	1.00	2.00	4.00
AH1420	—	0.50	1.00	2.00	4.00

KM# 4 10 OUGUIYA **Composition:** Copper-Nickel

Date	VG	F	VF	XF	Unc
AH1393	—	2.50	5.50	10.00	17.50
AH1394	—	2.50	5.50	10.00	17.50
AH1401	—	2.00	5.00	7.50	15.00
AH1403	—	1.25	2.50	4.00	8.00
AH1407	—	1.25	2.50	4.00	8.00
AH1410	—	0.75	1.50	2.50	4.50
AH1411	—	0.75	1.50	2.50	4.50
AH1414	—	0.75	1.50	2.50	4.50
AH1416	—	0.75	1.50	2.50	4.50
AH1418	—	0.75	1.50	2.50	4.50
AH1420	—	—	—	—	—
AH1420	—	0.75	1.50	2.50	4.50

KM# 5 20 OUGUIYA **Composition:** Copper-Nickel

Date	VG	F	VF	XF	Unc
AH1393	—	2.00	5.00	10.00	18.00
AH1394	—	2.00	5.00	10.00	18.00
AH1403	—	1.25	2.50	4.00	8.00
AH1407	—	1.25	2.50	4.00	8.00
AH1410	—	1.25	2.50	4.00	8.00
AH1414	—	1.25	2.50	4.00	8.00
AH1416	—	1.25	2.50	4.00	8.00
AH1418	—	1.25	2.50	4.00	8.00
AH1420	—	1.25	2.50	4.00	8.00

KM# 7 500 OUGUIYA **Weight:** 26.0800 g. **Composition:** 0.9200 Gold .7714 oz. AGW **Subject:** 15th Anniversary of Independence

Date	Mintage	F	VF	XF	Unc	BU
1975 (a)	1,800	—	—	—	525	—

MINT SETS

KM#	Date	Mintage	Identification	Issue Price	Mkt Val
MS1	1973 (10)	—	KM1-5, two each	20.00	150

MAURITIUS

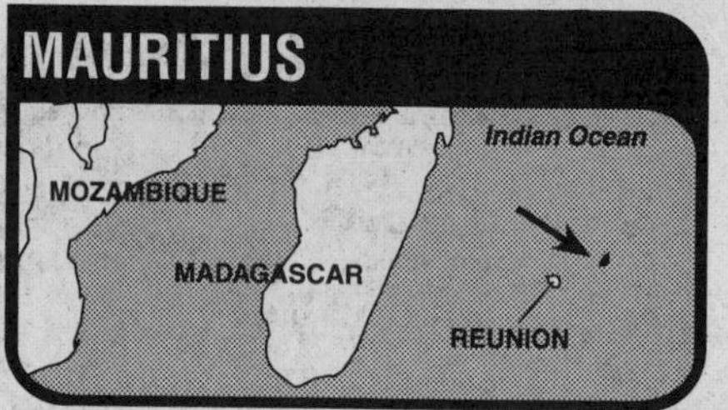

The Republic of Mauritius, is located in the Indian Ocean 500 miles (805 km.) east of Madagascar, has an area of 790 sq. mi. (1,860 sq. km.) and a population of 1 million. Capital: Port Louis. Sugar provides 90 percent of the export revenue.

Cartographic evidence indicates that Arabs and Malays arrived at Mauritius during the Middle Ages. Domingo Fernandez, a Portuguese navigator, visited the island in the early 16th century, but Portugal made no attempt at settlement. The Dutch took possession, and named the island, in 1598. Their colony failed to prosper and was abandoned in 1710. France claimed Mauritius in 1715 and developed a strong and prosperous colony that endured until the island was captured by the British, 1810, during the Napoleonic Wars. British possession was confirmed by the 1814 Treaty of Paris. Mauritius became independent on March 12, 1968. It is a member of the Commonwealth of Nations.

The first coins struck under British auspices for Mauritius were undated (1822) and bore French legends.

RULERS
British, until 1968

MINT MARKS
H - Heaton, Birmingham
SA - Pretoria Mint

MONETARY SYSTEM
100 Cents = 1 Rupee

REPUBLIC

STANDARD COINAGE

100 Cents = 1 Rupee

KM# 12 CENT **Composition:** Bronze

Date	Mintage	F	VF	XF	Unc	BU
1911	1,000,000	1.00	2.00	12.00	40.00	—
1912	500,000	1.25	2.50	18.50	55.00	—
1917	500,000	1.00	2.00	12.00	35.00	—
1920	500,000	1.50	3.00	22.50	60.00	—
1921	500,000	2.00	4.00	22.50	60.00	—
1922	1,800,000	0.75	1.50	9.00	25.00	—
1923	200,000	3.00	7.00	35.00	75.00	—
1924	200,000	3.00	7.00	35.00	75.00	—

KM# 21 CENT **Composition:** Bronze

Date	Mintage	F	VF	XF	Unc	BU
1943SA	520,000	0.50	1.25	4.00	10.00	22.00
1944SA	500,000	0.50	1.25	4.00	10.00	22.00
1945SA	500,000	0.50	1.25	4.00	10.00	22.00
1946SA	500,000	0.50	1.25	4.00	10.00	22.00
1947SA	500,000	0.50	1.25	4.00	10.00	22.00

KM# 25 CENT **Composition:** Bronze

Date	Mintage	F	VF	XF	Unc	BU
1949	500,000	0.75	1.25	2.50	7.50	15.00
1949 Proof	—	Value: 100				
1952	500,000	0.75	1.25	2.50	7.50	15.00
1952 Proof	—	Value: 100				

KM# 31 CENT **Composition:** Bronze

Date	Mintage	F	VF	XF	Unc	BU
1953	500,000	0.10	0.25	0.50	1.50	—
1953 Proof	—	Value: 75.00				
1955	501,000	0.10	0.25	0.50	2.50	—
1955 Proof	—	Value: 75.00				
1956	500,000	0.10	0.20	0.50	2.50	—
1956 Proof	—	Value: 75.00				
1957	501,000	0.10	0.20	0.50	2.50	—
1959	501,000	0.10	0.20	0.50	2.50	—
1959 Proof	—	Value: 75.00				
1960	500,000	0.10	0.20	0.50	2.50	—
1960 Proof	—	Value: 75.00				
1961	500,000	0.10	0.20	0.50	2.50	—
1961 Proof	—	Value: 75.00				
1962	500,000	0.10	0.20	0.50	1.50	—
1962 Proof	—	Value: 50.00				
1963	500,000	0.10	0.20	0.50	1.50	—
1963 Proof	—	Value: 50.00				
1964	1,500,000	—	0.10	0.20	0.50	—
1964 Proof	—	Value: 50.00				
1965	1,500,000	—	0.10	0.20	0.50	—
1969	500,000	—	0.10	0.15	0.30	—
1970	1,500,000	—	—	0.10	0.20	—
1971	1,000,000	—	—	0.10	0.20	—
1971 Proof	750	Value: 17.50				
1975	400,000	—	—	0.10	0.20	—
1978	—	—	—	0.10	0.20	—

KM# 13 2 CENTS **Composition:** Bronze

Date	Mintage	F	VF	XF	Unc	BU
1911	500,000	2.00	4.00	15.00	40.00	—
1911 Proof	—	Value: 300				
1912	250,000	3.00	5.00	30.00	70.00	—
1917	250,000	1.25	2.50	12.00	35.00	—
1920	250,000	1.50	3.00	20.00	45.00	—
1921	250,000	1.50	3.00	20.00	45.00	—
1922	900,000	0.50	1.00	8.00	30.00	—
1923	400,000	1.25	2.50	18.50	45.00	—
1924	400,000	1.25	2.50	18.50	45.00	—

KM# 22 2 CENTS **Composition:** Bronze

Date	Mintage	F	VF	XF	Unc	BU
1943SA	290,000	0.75	2.00	4.00	10.00	22.00
1944SA	500,000	0.75	2.00	4.00	10.00	22.00
1945SA	250,000	0.75	2.00	4.00	10.00	22.00
1946SA	400,000	0.75	2.00	4.00	10.00	22.00
1947SA	250,000	0.75	2.00	4.00	10.00	22.00

KM# 26 2 CENTS **Composition:** Bronze

Date	Mintage	F	VF	XF	Unc	BU
1949	250,000	0.75	1.25	2.50	6.50	12.50
1949 Proof	—	Value: 120				
1952	250,000	0.75	1.25	2.50	6.50	12.50
1952 Proof	—	Value: 120				

KM# 32 2 CENTS Composition: Bronze

Date	Mintage	F	VF	XF	Unc	BU
1953	250,000	0.10	0.25	0.50	2.50	—
1953 Proof	—	Value: 100				
1954 Proof	—	Value: 300				
1955	501,000	0.10	0.25	0.50	2.50	—
1955 Proof	—	Value: 100				
1956	250,000	0.10	0.25	0.50	3.50	—
1956 Proof	—	Value: 100				
1957	501,000	0.10	0.25	0.50	3.50	—
1959	503,000	0.10	0.25	0.50	3.50	—
1959 Proof	—	Value: 100				
1960	250,000	0.10	0.25	0.50	3.50	—
1960 Proof	—	Value: 100				
1961	500,000	0.10	0.25	0.50	3.50	—
1961 Proof	—	Value: 100				
1962	500,000	0.10	0.25	0.50	1.50	—
1962 Proof	—	Value: 75.00				
1963	500,000	0.10	0.25	0.50	1.50	—
1963 Proof	—	Value: 75.00				
1964	1,000,000	—	0.10	0.25	0.50	—
1964 Proof	—	Value: 50.00				
1965	750,000	0.10	0.20	0.40	0.60	—
1966	500,000	0.10	0.20	0.40	0.50	—
1967	250,000	0.10	0.20	0.40	0.50	—
1969	500,000	0.10	0.20	0.40	0.50	—
1971	1,000,000	—	0.10	0.20	0.40	—
1971 Proof	750	Value: 17.50				
1975	5,200,000	—	—	0.10	0.35	—
1978	—	—	—	0.10	0.35	—
1978 Proof	9,268	Value: 1.50				

KM# 14 5 CENTS Composition: Bronze

Date	Mintage	F	VF	XF	Unc	BU
1917	600,000	2.00	4.50	27.50	80.00	—
1920	200,000	2.00	4.50	32.50	100	—
1921	100,000	3.00	6.50	35.00	120	—
1922	360,000	2.00	4.50	32.50	100	—
1923	400,000	3.00	6.50	35.00	120	—
1924	400,000	2.00	4.50	32.50	100	—

KM# 20 5 CENTS Composition: Bronze

Date	Mintage	F	VF	XF	Unc	BU
1942SA	940,000	1.50	2.50	6.50	15.00	35.00
1944SA	1,000,000	1.25	1.75	4.00	10.00	22.00
1945SA	500,000	1.25	1.75	4.00	12.00	30.00

KM# 34 5 CENTS Composition: Bronze

Date	Mintage	F	VF	XF	Unc	BU
1956	201,000	0.25	0.50	0.75	5.00	—
1956 Proof	—	Value: 100				
1957	203,000	0.25	0.50	2.00	8.00	—
1957 Proof	—	Value: 100				
1959	801,000	0.25	0.50	1.00	4.00	—
1959 Proof	—	Value: 75.00				
1960	400,000	0.25	0.50	1.00	4.00	—
1960 Proof	—	Value: 75.00				

Date	Mintage	F	VF	XF	Unc	BU
1963	200,000	0.25	0.50	1.00	2.00	—
1963 Proof	—	Value: 70.00				
1964	600,000	0.25	0.50	1.00	2.00	—
1964 Proof	—	Value: 70.00				
1965	200,000	0.25	0.50	0.75	2.00	—
1966	200,000	0.25	0.50	0.75	1.50	—
1967	200,000	0.25	0.50	0.75	2.00	—
1969	500,000	0.10	0.15	0.25	0.50	—
1970	800,000	0.10	0.15	0.25	0.50	—
1971	500,000	0.10	0.15	0.25	0.50	—
1971 Proof	750	Value: 17.50				
1975	3,700,000	0.10	0.15	0.25	0.50	—
1978	8,000,000	—	0.10	0.20	0.50	—
1978 Proof	9,268	Value: 2.00				

KM# 24 10 CENTS Composition: Copper-Nickel

Date	Mintage	F	VF	XF	Unc	BU
1947	500,000	0.75	1.50	8.00	35.00	—
1947 Proof	—	Value: 200				

KM# 30 10 CENTS Composition: Copper-Nickel

Date	Mintage	F	VF	XF	Unc	BU
1952	250,000	0.50	0.75	1.50	6.50	—
1952 Proof	—	Value: 150				

KM# 33 10 CENTS Composition: Copper-Nickel

Date	Mintage	F	VF	XF	Unc	BU
1954	252,000	0.20	0.35	0.75	2.50	—
1954 Proof	—	Value: 150				
1957	250,000	0.20	0.35	0.75	2.50	—
1959	253,000	0.20	0.35	0.75	2.50	—
1959 Proof	—	Value: 175				
1960	50,000	0.20	0.35	0.75	2.00	—
1960 Proof	—	Value: 175				
1963	200,000	0.15	0.30	0.60	1.50	—
1963 Proof	—	Value: 175				
1964	200,000	0.15	0.30	0.60	1.00	—
1965	200,000	0.15	0.30	0.60	1.00	—
1966	200,000	0.10	0.25	0.50	0.75	—
1969	200,000	0.10	0.25	0.50	0.75	—
1970	500,000	0.10	0.25	0.50	0.75	—
1971	300,000	0.10	0.25	0.50	0.75	—
1971 Proof	750	Value: 17.50				
1975	6,675,000	0.10	0.25	0.50	0.75	—
1978	13,000,000	0.10	0.25	0.50	0.75	—
1978 Proof	9,268	Value: 2.50				

KM# 15 1/4 RUPEE Weight: 2.9200 g. Composition: 0.9160 Silver .0816 oz. ASW

Date	Mintage	F	VF	XF	Unc	BU
1934	400,000	2.00	7.00	20.00	60.00	—
1934 Proof	—	Value: 600				
1935	400,000	2.00	7.00	20.00	60.00	—
1935 Proof	—	Value: 750				
1936	400,000	2.00	6.00	18.00	50.00	—
1936 Proof	—	Value: 650				

KM# 18 1/4 RUPEE Weight: 2.9200 g. Composition: 0.9160 Silver .0816 oz. ASW

Date	Mintage	F	VF	XF	Unc	BU
1938	2,000,000	3.00	10.00	30.00	80.00	—
1938 Proof	—	Value: 375				

KM# 18a 1/4 RUPEE Weight: 2.9200 g. Composition: 0.5000 Silver .047 oz. ASW

Date	Mintage	F	VF	XF	Unc	BU
1946	2,000,000	7.50	20.00	40.00	100	—
1946 Proof	—	Value: 400				

KM# 27 1/4 RUPEE Composition: Copper-Nickel

Date	Mintage	F	VF	XF	Unc	BU
1950	2,000,000	0.50	1.00	2.00	9.50	18.00
1950 Proof	—	Value: 175				
1951	1,000,000	0.50	1.00	2.00	9.50	18.00
1951 Proof	—	Value: 175				

KM# 36 1/4 RUPEE Composition: Copper-Nickel

Date	Mintage	F	VF	XF	Unc	BU
1960	1,000,000	0.35	0.75	1.00	2.00	—
1960 Proof	—	Value: 100				
1964	400,000	0.25	0.50	0.75	1.50	—
1964 Proof	—	Value: 100				
1965	400,000	0.25	0.50	0.75	1.25	—
1970	400,000	0.20	0.35	0.65	1.25	—
1971	540,000	0.25	0.50	0.75	1.25	—
1971 Proof	750	Value: 17.50				
1975	8,940,000	0.15	0.30	0.60	1.00	—
1978	8,800,000	0.15	0.30	0.60	1.00	—

Note: Variety exists with lower hole in 8 filled

Date	Mintage	F	VF	XF	Unc	BU
1978 Proof	9,268	Value: 3.50				

KM# 16 1/2 RUPEE Weight: 5.8300 g. Composition: 0.9160 Silver .1717 oz. ASW

Date	Mintage	F	VF	XF	Unc	BU
1934	1,000,000	2.50	5.00	15.00	50.00	—
1934 Proof	—	Value: 450				

KM# 23 1/2 RUPEE Weight: 5.8300 g. Composition: 0.5000 Silver .0937 oz. ASW

Date	Mintage	F	VF	XF	Unc	BU
1946	1,000,000	10.00	25.00	125	200	—
1946 Proof	—	Value: 700				

KM# 28 1/2 RUPEE Composition: Copper-Nickel

Date	Mintage	F	VF	XF	Unc	BU
1950	1,000,000	0.50	1.00	1.75	7.50	—
1950 Proof	—	Value: 175				
1951	570,000	0.75	1.25	2.00	8.50	—
1951 Proof	—	Value: 225				

KM# 37.1 1/2 RUPEE **Composition:** Copper-Nickel

Date	Mintage	F	VF	XF	Unc	BU
1965	200,000	0.50	1.00	2.00	6.50	—
1971	400,000	0.25	0.50	0.75	2.50	—
1971 Proof	750	Value: 22.50				
1975	4,160,000	0.25	0.50	0.75	2.50	—
1978	400,000	0.25	0.50	0.75	2.50	—
1978 Proof	9,268	Value: 4.00				

KM# 37.2 1/2 RUPEE **Composition:** Copper-Nickel **Edge:** Without security feature **Note:** Error.

Date	F	VF	XF	Unc	BU
1971	—	—	—	—	—

KM# 17 RUPEE **Weight:** 11.6600 g. **Composition:** 0.9160 Silver .3434 oz. ASW

Date	Mintage	F	VF	XF	Unc	BU
1934	1,500,000	4.00	8.00	20.00	55.00	75.00
1934 Proof	—	Value: 600				

KM# 19 RUPEE **Weight:** 11.6600 g. **Composition:** 0.9160 Silver .3434 oz. ASW

Date	Mintage	F	VF	XF	Unc	BU
1938	200,000	10.00	20.00	60.00	175	—
1938 Proof	—	Value: 550				

KM# 29.1 RUPEE **Composition:** Copper-Nickel

Date	Mintage	F	VF	XF	Unc	BU
1950	1,500,000	0.75	1.50	3.00	16.00	—
1950 Proof	—	Value: 200				
1951	1,000,000	0.50	1.25	2.00	12.00	—
1951 Proof	—	Value: 300				

KM# 29.2 RUPEE **Composition:** Copper-Nickel **Edge:** Without security feature **Note:** Error.

Date	F	VF	XF	Unc	BU
1951	—	—	—	—	—

KM# 35.1 RUPEE **Composition:** Copper-Nickel

Date	Mintage	F	VF	XF	Unc	BU
1956	1,000,000	0.25	0.75	1.50	7.50	—
1956 Proof	—	Value: 200				
1964	200,000	0.50	1.00	3.00	5.00	—
1971	600,000	0.25	0.60	1.00	2.00	—
1971 Proof	750	Value: 45.00				
1975	4,525,000	0.25	0.60	1.00	2.00	—
1978	2,000,000	0.25	0.60	1.00	2.00	—
1978 Proof	9,268	Value: 5.00				

KM# 35.2 RUPEE **Composition:** Copper-Nickel **Edge:** Without security feature **Note:** Error.

Date	F	VF	XF	Unc	BU
1971	0.25	0.75	1.25	2.50	—

KM# 38 10 RUPEES **Composition:** Copper-Nickel **Subject:** Independence **Obverse:** Young Queen Elizabeth **Reverse:** Dodo bird

Date	Mintage	F	VF	XF	Unc	BU
1971	50,000	—	1.50	4.00	8.00	—

KM# 38a 10 RUPEES **Weight:** 20.0000 g. **Composition:** 0.9250 Silver .5948 oz. ASW **Subject:** Independence **Obverse:** Young Queen Elizabeth **Reverse:** Dodo bird

Date	Mintage	F	VF	XF	Unc	BU
1971 Proof	750	Value: 125				

KM# 46 10 RUPEES **Composition:** Copper-Nickel **Subject:** Wedding of Prince Charles and Lady Diana

Date	F	VF	XF	Unc	BU
ND(1981)	—	1.25	2.25	6.50	—

KM# 46a 10 RUPEES **Weight:** 28.2800 g. **Composition:** 0.9250 Silver .8411 oz. ASW **Subject:** Wedding of Prince Charles and Lady Diana

Date	Mintage	F	VF	XF	Unc	BU
ND(1981) Proof	2,090	Value: 22.50				

KM# 48 10 RUPEES **Weight:** 28.2800 g. **Composition:** 0.9250 Silver .8411 oz. ASW **Series:** World Food Day **Obverse:** Similar to KM#46

Date	Mintage	F	VF	XF	Unc	BU
1981	10,000	—	—	—	17.50	—
1981 Proof	5,000	Value: 27.50				

KM# 40 25 RUPEES **Weight:** 25.5000 g. **Composition:** 0.5000 Silver .4099 oz. ASW **Series:** Conservation **Reverse:** Blue swallowtail

Date	F	VF	XF	Unc	BU
1975	—	—	—	15.00	—

KM# 40a 25 RUPEES **Weight:** 28.2800 g. **Composition:** 0.9250 Silver .8411 oz. ASW **Series:** Conservation **Reverse:** Blue swallowtail

Date	Mintage	F	VF	XF	Unc	BU
1975	12	—	—	—	100	—
1975 Proof	9,869	Value: 20.00				

KM# 43 25 RUPEES **Weight:** 28.4000 g. **Composition:** 0.5000 Silver .4565 oz. ASW **Subject:** Queen's silver jubilee

Date	F	VF	XF	Unc	BU
ND(1977)	—	—	—	9.00	—

KM# 43a 25 RUPEES **Weight:** 28.2800 g. **Composition:** 0.9250 Silver .8411 oz. ASW **Subject:** Queen's silver jubilee

Date	Mintage	F	VF	XF	Unc	BU
ND(1977) Proof	47,000	Value: 12.50				

KM# 44 25 RUPEES **Weight:** 28.2800 g. **Composition:** 0.9250 Silver .8411 oz. ASW **Subject:** 10th Anniversary of Independence **Obverse:** Similar to 1,000 Rupees, KM#45

Date	Mintage	F	VF	XF	Unc	BU
1978	20,000	—	—	—	12.50	—
1978 Proof	5,100	Value: 25.00				

KM# 49 25 RUPEES **Weight:** 28.2800 g. **Composition:** 0.9250 Silver .8411 oz. ASW **Series:** International Year of Disabled Persons

Date	Mintage	F	VF	XF	Unc	BU
1982	11,000	—	—	—	18.50	—
1982 Proof	10,000	Value: 23.50				

KM# 41 50 RUPEES **Weight:** 32.1500 g. **Composition:** 0.5000 Silver .5168 oz. ASW **Series:** Conservation **Reverse:** Mauritius Kestrel

Date	F	VF	XF	Unc	BU
1975	—	—	—	16.50	—

KM# 41a 50 RUPEES **Weight:** 35.0000 g. **Composition:** 0.9250 Silver 1.0409 oz. ASW **Series:** Conservation **Obverse:** Similar to 1,000 Rupees, KM#42 **Reverse:** Mauritius Kestrel

Date	Mintage	F	VF	XF	Unc	BU
1975	12	—	—	—	125	—
1975 Proof	9,513	Value: 22.50				

KM# 39 200 RUPEES **Weight:** 15.5600 g. **Composition:** 0.9170 Gold .4587 oz. AGW **Subject:** Independence

Date	Mintage	F	VF	XF	Unc	BU
1971	2,500	—	—	—	160	—
1971 Proof	750	Value: 275				

KM# 42 1000 RUPEES **Weight:** 33.4370 g. **Composition:** 0.9000 Gold .9676 oz. AGW **Series:** Conservation **Subject:** Mauritius flycatcher

Date	Mintage	F	VF	XF	Unc	BU
1975	1,966	—	—	—	375	—
1975 Proof	716	Value: 525				

KM# 45 1000 RUPEES **Weight:** 15.9800 g. **Composition:** 0.9170 Gold .4711 oz. AGW **Subject:** 10th Anniversary of Independence

Date	Mintage	F	VF	XF	Unc	BU
1978	1,000	—	—	—	200	—
1978 Proof	1,016	Value: 250				

KM# 47 1000 RUPEES **Weight:** 15.9800 g. **Composition:** 0.9170 Gold .4711 oz. AGW **Subject:** Wedding of Prince Charles and Lady Diana

Date	Mintage	F	VF	XF	Unc	BU
ND(1981)	28	—	—	—	600	—
ND(1981) Proof	22	Value: 950				

KM# 50 1000 RUPEES **Weight:** 15.9800 g. **Composition:** 0.9170 Gold .4711 oz. AGW **Series:** International Year of Disabled Persons

Date	Mintage	F	VF	XF	Unc	BU
1982	45	—	—	—	550	—
1982 Proof	48	Value: 925				

REFORM COINAGE

KM# 51 CENT **Composition:** Copper Plated Steel

Date	Mintage	F	VF	XF	Unc	BU
1987	—	—	—	—	0.20	—
1987 Proof	Est. 2,500	Value: 1.00				

KM# 52 5 CENTS **Composition:** Copper Plated Steel

Date	Mintage	F	VF	XF	Unc	BU
1987	—	—	—	—	0.30	—
1987 Proof	Est. 2,500	Value: 2.00				
1990	—	—	—	—	0.30	—
1991	—	—	—	—	0.30	—
1993	—	—	—	—	0.30	—
1994	—	—	—	—	0.30	—
1995	—	—	—	—	0.30	—
1996	—	—	—	—	0.30	—

KM# 53 20 CENTS **Composition:** Nickel Plated Steel

Date	Mintage	F	VF	XF	Unc	BU
1987	—	—	—	—	0.50	—
1987 Proof	Est. 2,500	Value: 3.00				
1990	—	—	—	—	0.50	—
1991	—	—	—	—	0.50	—
1993	—	—	—	—	0.50	—
1994	—	—	—	—	0.50	—
1995	—	—	—	—	0.50	—
1996	—	—	—	—	0.50	—
1999	—	—	—	—	0.50	—

KM# 54 1/2 RUPEE **Composition:** Nickel Plated Steel

Date	Mintage	F	VF	XF	Unc	BU
1987	—	—	—	—	1.50	—
1987 Proof	Est. 2,500	Value: 5.00				
1990	—	—	—	—	1.50	—
1997	—	—	—	—	1.50	—
1999	—	—	—	—	1.50	—

KM# 55 RUPEE **Composition:** Copper-Nickel

Date	Mintage	F	VF	XF	Unc	BU
1987	—	—	—	—	1.65	—
1987 Proof	Est. 2,500	Value: 10.00				
1990	—	—	—	—	1.65	—
1991	—	—	—	—	1.65	—
1993	—	—	—	—	1.65	—
1994	—	—	—	—	1.65	—
1997	—	—	—	—	1.65	—

KM# 56 5 RUPEES **Composition:** Copper-Nickel

Date	Mintage	F	VF	XF	Unc	BU
1987	—	—	—	—	3.00	—
1987 Proof	Est. 2,500	Value: 16.00				
1991	—	—	—	—	3.00	—
1992	—	—	—	—	3.00	—

KM# 61 10 RUPEES **Composition:** Copper-Nickel **Obverse:** Portrait **Reverse:** Sugar cane harvesting

Date	F	VF	XF	Unc	BU
1997	—	—	—	4.00	—

GOLD BULLION COINAGE

KM# 57 100 RUPEES **Weight:** 3.4120 g. **Composition:** 0.9170 Gold .1 oz. AGW **Obverse:** Similar to 1,000 Rupees, KM#60 **Reverse:** Dodo bird

Date	F	VF	XF	Unc	BU
1988	—	—	—	75.00	—

KM# 58 250 RUPEES **Weight:** 8.5130 g. **Composition:** 0.9170 Gold .25 oz. AGW **Obverse:** Similar to 1,000 Rupees, KM#60 **Reverse:** Dodo bird

Date	F	VF	XF	Unc	BU
1988	—	—	—	150	—

KM# 59 500 RUPEES **Weight:** 17.0250 g. **Composition:** 0.9170 Gold .5 oz. AGW **Obverse:** Similar to 1,000 Rupees, KM#60 **Reverse:** Dodo bird

Date	F	VF	XF	Unc	BU
1988	—	—	—	275	—

KM# 60 1000 RUPEES **Weight:** 34.0500 g.
Composition: 0.9170 Gold 1 oz. AGW **Reverse:** Dodo bird

Date	F	VF	XF	Unc	BU
1988	—	—	—	475	—

PIEFORTS

KM#	Date	Mintage	Identification	Issue Price	Mkt Val
P2	1981	—	1000 Rupees. Gold. KM47.	—	—
P3	1982	1,100	25 Rupees. 0.9250 Silver. KM49.	—	100
P4	1982	—	1000 Rupees. Gold. KM50.	—	1,850

MINT SETS

KM#	Date	Mintage	Identification	Issue Price	Mkt Val
MS1	1987 (6)	5,000	KM51-56	16.95	17.50
MS2	1988 (4)	—	KM57-60	1,250	1,000

PROOF SETS

KM#	Date	Mintage	Identification	Issue Price	Mkt Val
PS1	1934 (3)	20	KM15-17	—	2,100
PS2	1971 (9)	750	KM31-37, 38a, 39	200	645
PS3	1975 (2)	9,268	KM40a-41a	50.00	40.00
PS4	1978 (7)	30,000	KM31-37	22.00	20.00
PS5	1981 (2)	—	KM46a, 47	—	975
PS6	1987 (6)	2,500	KM51-56	36.95	37.50

MEXICO

The United States of Mexico, located immediately south of the United States has an area of 759,529 sq. mi. (1,967,183 sq. km.) and an estimated population of 88 million. Capital: Mexico City. The economy is based on agriculture, manufacturing and mining. Oil, cotton, silver, coffee, and shrimp are exported.

Mexico was the site of highly advanced Indian civilizations 1,500 years before conquistador Hernando Cortes conquered the wealthy Aztec empire of Montezuma,1519-21, and founded a Spanish colony which lasted for nearly 300 years. During the Spanish period, Mexico, then called New Spain, stretched from Guatemala to the present states of Wyoming and California, its present northern boundary having been established by the secession of Texas during 1836 and the war of 1846-48 with the United States.

Independence from Spain was declared by Father Miguel Hidalgo on Sept. 16, 1810, (Mexican Independence Day) and was achieved by General Agustin de Iturbide in1821. Iturbide became emperor in 1822 but was deposed when a republic was established a year later. For more than fifty years following the birth of the republic, the political scene of Mexico was characterized by turmoil which saw two emperors (including the unfortunate Maximilian), several dictators and an average of one new government every nine months passing swiftly from obscurity to oblivion. The land, social, economic and labor reforms promulgated by the Reform Constitution of Feb. 5, 1917 established the basis for sustained economic development and participative democracy that have made Mexico one of the most politically stable countries of modern Latin America.

REPUBLIC
Second

MINT MARKS

A, AS - Alamos
CE - Real de Catorce
CA,CH - Chihuahua
C, Cn, Gn(error) - Culiacan
D, Do - Durango
EoMo - Estado de Mexico
Ga - Guadalajara
GC - Guadalupe y Calvo
G, Go - Guanajuato
H, Ho - Hermosillo
M, Mo - Mexico City
O, OA - Oaxaca
SLP, PI, P, I/P - San Luis Potosi
Z, Zs – Zacatecas

ASSAYERS INITIALS

CULIACAN MINT

Initials	Years	Mint Officials
JQ, Q	1899-1903	Jesus S. Quiroz
FV, V	1903	Francisco Valdez
MH, H	1904	Merced Hernandez
RP, P	1904-05	Ramon Ponce de Leon

MEXICO CITY MINT

Because of the great number of assayers for this mint (Mexico City is a much larger mint than any of the others) there is much confusion as to which initial stands for which assayer at any one time. Therefore we feel that it would be of no value to list the assayers.

ZACATECAS MINT

Initials	Years	Mint Officials
FZ	1886-1905	Francisco de P. Zarate
FM	1904-05	Francisco Mateos

DECIMAL COINAGE
100 Centavos = 1 Peso

KM# 394 CENTAVO **Composition:** Copper **Note:** Struck at Culiacan Mint, mint mark C, Cn. Reduced size. Varieties exist.

Date	Mintage	F	VF	XF	Unc	BU
1901	220,000	15.00	22.50	35.00	65.00	—
1902	320,000	15.00	22.50	50.00	90.00	—
1903	536,000	7.50	12.50	20.00	50.00	—
1904/3	148,000	35.00	50.00	75.00	125	—
1905	110,000	100	150	250	550	—

KM# 394.1 CENTAVO **Composition:** Copper **Note:** Struck at Mexico City Mint, mint mark M, Mo. Reduced size. Varieties exist.

Date	Mintage	F	VF	XF	Unc	BU
1901	1,494,000	3.00	8.00	17.50	50.00	—
1901	1,494,000	3.00	8.00	17.50	50.00	—
1902/899	2,090,000	30.00	60.00	100	175	—
1902	Inc. above	2.25	4.00	10.00	40.00	—
1903	8,400,000	1.50	3.00	7.00	20.00	—
1904/3	10,250,000	1.50	10.00	20.00	55.00	—
1904	Inc. above	1.50	3.00	7.00	25.00	—
1905	3,643,000	2.25	4.00	10.00	40.00	—

KM# 400 5 CENTAVOS **Composition:** 0.9030 Silver **Obverse:** Restyled eagle **Note:** Struck at Culiacan Mint, mint mark Cn. Varieties exist.

Date	Mintage	F	VF	XF	Unc	BU
1901Cn Q	148,000	1.75	2.50	4.50	15.00	—
1902Cn Q Narrow C, heavy serifs	262,000	1.75	3.00	6.00	16.50	—
1902Cn Q Wide C, light serifs	Inc. above	1.75	3.00	6.00	16.50	—
1903/1Cn Q	331,000	2.00	3.00	6.00	16.50	—
1903Cn Q	Inc. above	1.75	2.50	4.50	15.00	—
1903/1898Cn V	Inc. above	3.50	4.50	9.00	22.50	—
1903Cn V	Inc. above	1.75	2.50	4.50	15.00	—
1904Cn H	352,000	1.75	2.25	5.00	16.50	—
1904Cn H 0/9	—	1.75	2.50	5.00	16.50	—
1904Cn H/C	—	1.75	2.50	5.00	16.50	—

KM# 400.2 5 CENTAVOS **Composition:** 0.9030 Silver **Obverse:** Restyled eagle **Note:** Struck at Mexico City Mint, mint mark Mo.

Date	Mintage	F	VF	XF	Unc	BU
1901Mo M	100,000	1.75	2.50	4.50	15.00	—
1902Mo M	144,000	1.25	2.00	3.75	12.00	—
1902/1Mo MoM	—	1.75	3.00	6.00	16.50	—
1903Mo M	500,000	1.25	2.00	3.75	12.00	—
1904/804Mo M	1,090,000	1.75	3.00	6.00	16.50	—
1904/94Mo M	Inc. above	1.75	3.00	6.00	16.50	—
1904Mo M	Inc. above	1.75	3.00	6.00	15.00	—
1905Mo M	344,000	1.75	3.75	7.50	18.50	—

KM# 400.3 5 CENTAVOS **Composition:** 0.9030 Silver **Obverse:** Restyled eagle **Note:** Struck at Zacatecas Mint, mint mark Zs.

Date	Mintage	F	VF	XF	Unc	BU
1901Zs Z	40,000	1.75	2.50	5.00	16.50	—
1902/1Zs Z	34,000	2.00	4.50	9.00	22.50	—
1902Zs Z	Inc. above	1.75	3.75	7.50	18.50	—
1903Zs Z	217,000	1.25	2.00	5.00	12.50	—
1904Zs Z	191,000	1.75	2.50	5.00	12.50	—
1904Zs M	Inc. above	1.75	2.50	5.00	16.50	—
1905Zs M	46,000	2.00	4.50	9.00	22.50	—
1905Zs M Repullica - Rare	Inc. above	—	—	—	—	—

KM# 404 10 CENTAVOS **Weight:** 2.7070 g. **Composition:** 0.9030 Silver .0785 oz. ASW **Obverse:** Restyled eagle **Note:** Struck at Culiacan Mint, mint mark Cn. Varieties exist.

Date	Mintage	F	VF	XF	Unc	BU
1901Cn Q	235,000	1.50	2.50	5.00	20.00	—
1902Cn Q	186,000	1.50	2.50	5.00	20.00	—
1903Cn Q	256,000	1.50	2.50	6.00	20.00	—
1903Cn V	Inc. above	1.50	2.50	5.00	15.00	—
1904Cn H	307,000	1.50	2.50	5.00	15.00	—

KM# 404.2 10 CENTAVOS **Weight:** 2.7070 g. **Composition:** 0.9030 Silver .0785 oz. ASW **Obverse:** Restyled eagle **Note:** Struck at Mexico City Mint, mint mark Mo.

Date	Mintage	F	VF	XF	Unc	BU
1901Mo M	80,000	2.50	3.50	7.00	22.50	—
1902Mo M	181,000	1.50	2.50	5.00	20.00	—
1903Mo M	581,000	1.50	2.50	5.00	20.00	—
1904Mo M	1,266,000	1.25	2.00	4.50	18.00	—
1904Mo MM (Error)	Inc. above	2.50	5.00	10.00	25.00	—
1905Mo M	266,000	2.00	3.75	7.50	20.00	—

KM# 404.3 10 CENTAVOS **Weight:** 2.7070 g. **Composition:** 0.9030 Silver .0785 oz. ASW **Obverse:** Restyled eagle **Note:** Struck at Zacatecas Mint, mint mark Zs.

Date	Mintage	F	VF	XF	Unc	BU
1901Zs Z	70,000	2.50	5.00	10.00	25.00	—
1902Zs Z	120,000	2.50	5.00	10.00	25.00	—
1903Zs Z	228,000	1.50	3.00	10.00	20.00	—
1904Zs Z	368,000	1.50	3.00	10.00	20.00	—
1904Zs M	Inc. above	1.50	3.00	10.00	25.00	—
1905Zs M	66,000	7.50	20.00	50.00	200	—

KM# 405 20 CENTAVOS **Weight:** 5.4150 g. **Composition:** 0.9030 Silver .1572 oz. ASW **Obverse:** Restyled eagle **Note:** Struck at Culiacan Mint, mint mark Cn.

Date	Mintage	F	VF	XF	Unc	BU
1901Cn Q	185,000	5.00	10.00	30.00	120	—
1902/802Cn Q	98,000	6.00	10.00	30.00	120	—
1902Cn Q	Inc. above	4.00	9.00	30.00	120	—
1903Cn Q	93,000	4.00	9.00	30.00	120	—
1904/3Cn H	258,000	—	—	—	—	—
1904Cn H	Inc. above	5.00	10.00	30.00	120	—

KM# 405.2 20 CENTAVOS **Weight:** 5.4150 g. **Composition:** 0.9030 Silver .1572 oz. ASW **Obverse:** Restyled eagle **Note:** Struck at Mexico City Mint, mint mark Mo. Varieties exist.

Date	Mintage	F	VF	XF	Unc	BU
1901Mo M	110,000	4.00	8.00	20.00	90.00	—
1902Mo M	120,000	4.00	8.00	20.00	90.00	—
1903Mo M	213,000	4.00	8.00	20.00	90.00	—
1904Mo M	276,000	4.00	8.00	20.00	90.00	—
1905Mo M	117,000	6.50	20.00	50.00	150	—

KM# 405.3 20 CENTAVOS **Weight:** 5.4150 g. **Composition:** 0.9030 Silver .1572 oz. ASW **Obverse:** Restyled eagle **Note:** Struck at Zacatecas Mint, mint mark Zs.

Date	Mintage	F	VF	XF	Unc	BU
1901Zs Z	Inc. above	5.00	10.00	20.00	100	—
1901/0Zs Z	130,000	25.00	50.00	100	250	—
1902Zs Z	105,000	5.00	10.00	20.00	100	—
1903Zs Z	143,000	5.00	10.00	20.00	100	—
1904Zs Z	246,000	5.00	10.00	20.00	100	—
1904Zs M	Inc. above	5.00	10.00	50.00	300	—
1905Zs M	59,000	10.00	70.00	50.00	400	—

KM# 409 PESO **Weight:** 27.0730 g. **Composition:** 0.9030 Silver .7860 oz. ASW **Reverse:** Liberty cap **Note:** Struck at Culiacan Mint, mint mark Cn.

Date	Mintage	F	VF	XF	Unc	BU
1901Cn JQ	1,473,000	10.00	15.00	25.00	75.00	—
1902Cn JQ	1,194,000	10.00	15.00	45.00	125	—
1903Cn JQ	1,514,000	10.00	15.00	30.00	85.00	—
1903Cn FV	Inc. above	25.00	50.00	100	225	—
1904Cn MH	1,554,000	10.00	15.00	25.00	75.00	—
1904Cn RP	Inc. above	50.00	100	150	350	—
1905Cn RP	598,000	25.00	50.00	100	250	—

KM# 410.2 PESO **Weight:** 1.6920 g. **Composition:** 0.8750 Gold .0476 oz. AGW **Note:** Struck at Culiacan Mint, mint mark Cn.

Date	Mintage	F	VF	XF	Unc	BU
1901/0Cn Q	2,350	65.00	100	150	225	—
1902Cn Q	2,480	65.00	100	150	225	—
1902Cn/MoQ/C	Inc. above	65.00	100	150	225	—
1904Cn H	3,614	65.00	100	150	225	—
1904Cn/Mo/ H	Inc. above	65.00	100	150	250	—
1905Cn P	1,000	—	—	—	—	—

Note: Reported, not confirmed

KM# 410.5 PESO **Weight:** 1.6920 g. **Composition:** 0.8750 Gold .0476 oz. AGW **Note:** Struck at Mexico City Mint, mint mark Mo.

Date	Mintage	F	VF	XF	Unc	BU
1901Mo M Small date	Inc. above	40.00	60.00	90.00	185	—
1901/801Mo M Large date	8,293	40.00	60.00	90.00	185	—
1902Mo M Large date	11,000	40.00	60.00	90.00	185	—
1902Mo M Small date	Inc. above	40.00	60.00	90.00	185	—
1903Mo M Large date	10,000	40.00	60.00	90.00	185	—
1903Mo M Small date	Inc. above	50.00	80.00	120	200	—
1904Mo M	9,845	40.00	60.00	90.00	185	—
1905Mo M	3,429	40.00	60.00	90.00	185	—

KM# 409.2 PESO **Weight:** 27.0730 g. **Composition:** 0.9030 Silver .7860 oz. ASW **Reverse:** Liberty cap **Note:** Struck at Mexico City Mint, mint mark Mo. Varieties exist.

Date	Mintage	F	VF	XF	Unc	BU
1901Mo AM	14,505,000	9.00	11.50	20.00	70.00	—
1902/1Mo AM	16,224,000	150	300	500	950	—
1902Mo AM	Inc. above	9.00	11.50	20.00	70.00	—
1903Mo AM	22,396,000	9.00	11.50	20.00	70.00	—
1903Mo AM (Error)	Inc. above	1,500	2,500	3,500	7,500	—
1904Mo AM	14,935,000	9.00	11.50	20.00	70.00	—
1905Mo AM	3,557,000	15.00	25.00	55.00	125	—
1908Mo AM	7,575,000	10.00	12.50	20.00	60.00	—
1908Mo GV	Inc. above	10.00	12.50	18.50	40.00	—
1909Mo GV	2,924,000	10.00	12.50	18.50	40.00	—

KM# 409.3 PESO **Weight:** 27.0730 g. **Composition:** 0.9030 Silver .7860 oz. ASW **Reverse:** Liberty cap **Note:** Struck at Zacatecas Mint, mint mark Zs. Varieties exist.

Date	Mintage	F	VF	XF	Unc	BU
1901Zs FZ	Inc. above	10.00	12.50	20.00	55.00	—
1901Zs AZ	5,706,000	4,000	6,500	10,000	—	—
1902Zs FZ	7,134,000	10.00	12.50	20.00	55.00	—
1903/2Zs FZ	3,080,000	12.50	15.00	50.00	125	—
1903Zs FZ	Inc. above	10.00	12.50	20.00	65.00	—
1904Zs FZ	2,423,000	10.00	15.00	25.00	85.00	—
1904Zs FM	Inc. above	10.00	15.00	25.00	75.00	—
1905Zs FM	995,000	20.00	40.00	60.00	150	—

KM# 412.6 5 PESOS **Weight:** 8.4600 g. **Composition:** 0.8750 Gold .2380 oz. AGW **Note:** Struck at Mexico City Mint, mint mark Mo.

Date	Mintage	F	VF	XF	Unc	BU
1901Mo M	1,071	150	300	400	650	—
1902Mo M	1,478	150	300	400	650	—
1903Mo M	1,162	150	300	400	650	—
1904Mo M	1,415	150	300	400	650	—
1905Mo M	563	200	400	550	1,500	—

KM# 412.2 5 PESOS **Weight:** 8.4600 g. **Composition:** 0.8750 Gold .2380 oz. AGW **Note:** Struck at Culiacan Mint, mint mark Cn.

Date	Mintage	F	VF	XF	Unc	BU
1903Cn Q	1,000	150	300	400	750	—

KM# 413.7 10 PESOS **Weight:** 16.9200 g. **Composition:** 0.8750 Gold .4760 oz. AGW **Reverse:** Balance scale **Note:** Struck at Mexico City Mint, mint mark Mo.

Date	Mintage	F	VF	XF	Unc	BU
1901Mo M	562	350	500	800	1,250	—
1902Mo M	719	350	500	800	1,250	—
1903Mo M	713	350	500	800	1,250	—
1904Mo M	694	350	500	800	1,250	—
1905Mo M	401	400	600	950	1,500	—

KM# 413.2 10 PESOS **Weight:** 16.9200 g. **Composition:** 0.8750 Gold .4760 oz. AGW **Reverse:** Balance scale **Note:** Struck at Culiacan Mint, mint mark Cn.

Date	Mintage	F	VF	XF	Unc	BU
1903Cn Q	774	400	600	1,000	1,750	—

KM# 414.2 20 PESOS **Weight:** 33.8400 g. **Composition:** 0.8750 Gold .9520 oz. AGW **Reverse:** Balance scale **Note:** Struck at Culiacan Mint, mint mark Cn.

Date	Mintage	F	VF	XF	Unc	BU
1901Cn Q	Inc. above	450	675	950	2,000	—
1901/0Cn Q	1,496	—	—	—	—	—
1902Cn Q	1,059	450	675	950	2,000	—
1903Cn Q	1,121	450	675	950	2,000	—
1904Cn H	4,646	450	675	950	2,000	—
1905Cn P	1,738	500	900	1,200	2,250	—

KM# 414.6 20 PESOS **Weight:** 33.8400 g. **Composition:** 0.8750 Gold .9520 oz. AGW **Reverse:** Balance scale **Note:** Struck at Mexico City Mint, mint mark Mo.

Date	Mintage	F	VF	XF	Unc	BU
1901Mo M	29,000	400	600	850	1,450	—
1902Mo M	38,000	400	600	850	1,450	—
1903/2Mo M	31,000	400	600	850	1,450	—
1903Mo M	Inc. above	400	600	850	1,450	—
1904Mo M	52,000	400	600	850	1,450	—
1905Mo M	9,757	400	600	850	1,450	—

UNITED STATES

MINT MARK

o

M - Mexico City

DECIMAL COINAGE

100 Centavos = 1 Peso

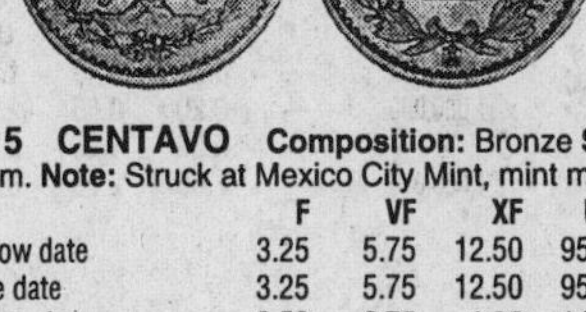

KM# 415 CENTAVO **Composition:** Bronze **Size:** 20 mm. **Note:** Struck at Mexico City Mint, mint mark Mo.

Date	F	VF	XF	Unc	BU
1905 Narrow date	3.25	5.75	12.50	95.00	—
1905 Wide date	3.25	5.75	12.50	95.00	—
1906 Narrow date	0.50	0.75	1.25	14.00	—

Note: 50,000,000 pcs. were struck at the Birmingham Mint

Date	F	VF	XF	Unc	BU
1906 Wide date	0.65	1.25	2.25	22.00	—
1910 Narrow date	1.50	2.50	6.50	90.00	—

Date	F	VF	XF	Unc	BU
1910 Wide date	1.50	2.50	6.50	90.00	—
1911 Narrow date	0.60	1.00	2.75	22.50	—
1911 Wide date	0.75	1.25	5.00	32.00	—
1912	0.75	1.25	3.00	32.00	—
1913	0.65	1.00	2.75	33.00	—
1914 Narrow date	0.60	0.85	2.50	14.50	—
1914 Wide date	0.60	0.85	2.50	14.50	—
1915	9.00	21.50	65.00	250	—
1916	30.00	65.00	165	1,200	—
1920	15.00	30.00	65.00	400	—
1921	4.25	13.50	42.50	275	—
1922	8.00	15.00	45.00	300	—
1923	0.50	0.75	1.75	11.50	—
1924/3	50.00	140	250	500	—
1924	4.00	10.00	20.00	220	—
1925	3.75	9.25	20.00	210	—
1926	0.90	1.75	3.50	26.00	—
1927/6	25.00	40.00	60.00	140	—
1927	0.60	1.25	4.50	36.00	—
1928	0.60	0.80	3.25	16.50	—
1929	0.60	0.80	1.75	18.00	—
1930	0.75	1.00	2.25	19.00	—
1933	0.25	0.35	1.75	16.50	—
1934	0.40	0.95	3.25	35.00	—
1935	0.15	0.25	0.40	11.50	—
1936	0.15	0.20	0.30	8.00	—
1937	0.15	0.25	0.35	3.50	—
1938	0.10	0.15	0.30	2.25	—
1939	0.10	0.20	0.30	1.25	—
1940	0.20	0.30	0.60	6.50	—
1941	0.15	0.25	0.35	2.25	—
1942	0.15	0.20	0.30	1.25	—
1943	0.30	0.50	0.75	9.00	—
1944	0.15	0.25	0.50	7.00	—
1945	0.10	0.15	0.25	1.00	—
1946	—	0.15	0.20	0.60	—
1947	—	0.10	0.15	0.80	—
1948	—	0.15	0.30	1.10	—
1949	0.10	0.15	0.30	1.75	—

Note: Varieties exist.

KM# 416 CENTAVO Composition: Bronze **Size:** 16 mm. **Note:** Zapata issue. Struck at Mexico City Mint, mint mark Mo. Reduced size.

Date	Mintage	F	VF	XF	Unc	BU
1915	179,000	16.00	27.50	50.00	75.50	—

KM# 417 CENTAVO Composition: Brass **Size:** 16 mm. **Note:** Struck at Mexico City Mint, mint mark Mo.

Date	Mintage	F	VF	XF	Unc	BU
1950	12,815,000	—	0.15	0.30	1.75	2.00
1951	25,740,000	—	0.15	0.25	0.65	1.10
1952	24,610,000	—	0.10	0.25	0.40	0.75
1953	21,160,000	—	0.10	0.25	0.40	0.85
1954	25,675,000	—	0.10	0.15	0.85	1.20
1955	9,820,000	—	0.15	0.25	0.85	1.50
1956	11,285,000	—	0.15	0.25	0.80	1.45
1957	9,805,000	—	0.15	0.25	0.85	1.35
1958	12,155,000	—	0.10	0.25	0.45	0.80
1959	11,875,000	—	0.10	0.25	0.75	1.25
1960	10,360,000	—	0.10	0.15	0.40	0.65
1961	6,385,000	—	0.10	0.15	0.45	0.85
1962	4,850,000	—	0.10	0.15	0.55	0.90
1963	7,775,000	—	0.10	0.15	0.25	0.45
1964	4,280,000	—	0.10	0.15	0.20	0.35
1965	2,255,000	—	0.10	0.15	0.25	0.40
1966	1,760,000	—	0.10	0.25	0.60	0.75
1967	1,290,000	—	0.10	0.15	0.40	0.70
1968	1,000,000	—	0.10	0.20	0.85	1.25
1969	1,000,000	—	0.10	0.15	0.75	1.25

KM# 418 CENTAVO Composition: Brass **Size:** 13 mm. **Note:** Reduced size.

Date	Mintage	F	VF	XF	Unc	BU
1970	1,000,000	—	0.20	0.40	1.30	1.80
1972	1,000,000	—	0.20	0.45	2.50	3.25
1972/2	—	—	0.50	1.25	3.25	5.00
1973	1,000,000	—	1.65	2.75	8.00	9.75

KM# 419 2 CENTAVOS Composition: Bronze **Size:** 25 mm. **Note:** Struck at Mexico City Mint, mint mark Mo.

Date	Mintage	F	VF	XF	Unc	BU
1905	50,000	125	275	425	1,200	—
1906 Inverted 6	9,998,000	25.00	50.00	110	375	—
1906 Wide date	Inc. above	4.00	10.00	21.50	80.00	—
1906 Narrow date	Inc. above	6.50	12.50	25.00	85.00	—

Note: 5,000,000 pieces were struck at the Birmingham Mint

Date	Mintage	F	VF	XF	Unc	BU
1920	1,325,000	6.50	21.50	60.00	350	—
1921	4,275,000	2.50	4.75	10.00	90.00	—
1922	—	225	550	1,350	4,000	—
1924	750,000	8.50	20.00	50.00	450	—
1925	3,650,000	2.50	3.50	9.00	40.00	—
1926	4,750,000	1.00	2.25	5.50	35.00	—
1927	7,250,000	0.60	1.00	4.50	22.75	—
1928	3,250,000	0.75	1.50	3.75	25.00	—
1929	250,000	45.00	120	500	1,000	—
1935	1,250,000	4.25	9.25	22.50	200	—
1939	5,000,000	0.60	0.90	2.25	20.00	—
1941	3,550,000	0.45	0.60	1.25	18.00	—

KM# 420 2 CENTAVOS Composition: Bronze **Size:** 20 mm. **Note:** Zapata issue. Struck at Mexico City Mint, mint mark Mo. Reduced size.

Date	Mintage	F	VF	XF	Unc	BU
1915	487,000	6.50	9.00	13.50	65.00	—

KM# 421 5 CENTAVOS Composition: Nickel **Note:** Struck at Mexico City Mint, mint mark Mo. Varieties exist.

Date	Mintage	F	VF	XF	Unc	BU
1905	1,420,000	6.00	9.50	22.50	290	—
1906/5	10,615,000	12.00	23.50	60.00	375	—
1906	Inc. above	0.75	1.20	3.25	50.00	—
1907	4,000,000	1.25	3.50	10.00	350	—
1909	2,052,000	3.25	9.50	42.50	360	—
1910	6,181,000	1.15	3.20	5.50	77.00	115
1911 Narrow date	4,487,000	0.75	3.00	5.00	85.00	125
1911 Wide date	Inc. above	2.50	4.25	9.00	110	160
1912 Small mint mark	420,000	97.50	120	210	725	—
1912 Large mint mark	Inc. above	60.00	85.00	160	575	—
1913	2,035,000	1.65	3.75	9.00	100	150

Note: Wide and narrow dates exist for 1913

Date	Mintage	F	VF	XF	Unc	BU
1914	2,000,000	0.75	1.75	3.50	60.00	90.00

Note: 5,000,000 pieces appear to have been struck at the Birmingham Mint in 1914 and all of 1909-1911. The Mexican Mint report does not mention receiving the 1914 dated coins

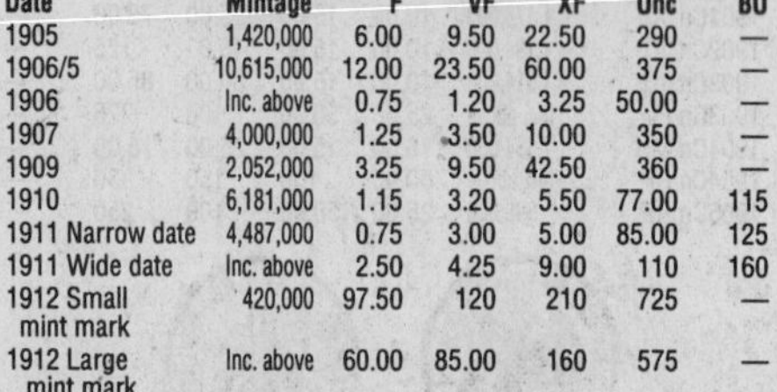

KM# 422 5 CENTAVOS Composition: Bronze **Note:** Struck at Mexico City Mint, mint mark Mo.

Date	Mintage	F	VF	XF	Unc	BU
1914	2,500,000	10.00	21.50	45.00	225	—
1915	11,424,000	2.50	4.50	14.50	125	—
1916	2,860,000	13.50	32.00	150	690	—
1917	800,000	60.00	150	320	820	—
1918	1,332,000	28.00	70.00	175	625	—
1919	400,000	100	190	335	925	—
1920	5,920,000	3.00	7.50	40.00	285	—
1921	2,080,000	9.00	21.50	70.00	275	—
1924	780,000	35.00	80.00	235	625	—
1925	4,040,000	4.75	10.00	42.50	225	—
1926	3,160,000	5.50	11.00	43.50	300	—
1927	3,600,000	3.25	6.75	27.50	220	—
1928 Large date	1,740,000	10.00	17.50	68.00	250	—
1928 Small date	Inc. above	25.00	45.00	90.00	385	—
1929	2,400,000	4.75	10.00	40.00	180	—
1930 Large oval 0 in date	2,600,000	4.00	7.50	27.50	210	—
1930 Small square 0 in date	Inc. above	50.00	115	220	565	—
1931	—	475	675	1,000	3,250	—
1933	8,000,000	1.25	2.00	3.25	25.00	—
1934	10,000,000	1.00	1.50	2.50	22.50	—
1935	21,980,000	0.75	1.20	2.25	20.00	—

KM# 423 5 CENTAVOS Composition: Copper-Nickel **Note:** Struck at Mexico City Mint, mint mark Mo.

Date	Mintage	F	VF	XF	Unc	BU
1936	46,700,000	—	0.65	1.25	6.50	9.00
1937	49,060,000	—	0.50	1.00	6.00	9.00
1938	3,340,000	—	5.00	12.50	65.00	250
1940	22,800,000	—	0.75	1.50	8.00	12.00
1942	7,100,000	—	1.50	3.20	35.00	45.00

KM# 424 5 CENTAVOS Ring Composition: Bronze **Reverse:** "Josefa" Ortiz de Dominguez **Note:** Struck at Mexico City Mint, mint mark Mo.

Date	Mintage	F	VF	XF	Unc	BU
1942	900,000	—	20.00	60.00	350	500
1943	54,660,000	—	0.40	0.65	3.00	4.00
1944	53,463,000	—	0.25	0.35	0.75	1.00
1945	44,262,000	—	0.25	0.35	0.90	1.65
1946	49,054,000	—	0.50	0.75	2.00	2.75
1951	50,758,000	—	0.60	0.85	3.00	4.75
1952	17,674,000	—	1.25	2.25	9.25	11.50
1953	31,568,000	—	1.10	1.75	7.00	10.00
1954	58,680,000	—	0.40	0.75	2.75	4.00
1955	31,114,000	—	1.85	2.50	10.00	14.00

KM# 425 5 CENTAVOS Composition: Copper-Nickel **Reverse:** White Josefa **Note:** Struck at Mexico City Mint, mint mark Mo.

Date	Mintage	F	VF	XF	Unc	BU
1950	5,700,000	—	0.75	1.50	6.25	8.00

Note: 5,600,000 pieces struck at Connecticut melted

KM# 426 5 CENTAVOS Composition: Brass **Reverse:** White Josefa **Note:** Struck at Mexico City Mint, mint mark Mo.

Date	Mintage	F	VF	XF	Unc	BU
1954 Dot	—	—	9.00	32.00	325	375
1954 Without dot	—	—	12.00	25.00	250	290
1955	12,136,000	—	0.75	1.50	9.00	12.50
1956	60,216,000	—	0.20	0.30	0.90	1.50
1957	55,288,000	—	0.15	0.20	0.90	1.50
1958	104,624,000	—	0.15	0.20	0.60	1.00
1959	106,000,000	—	0.15	0.25	0.90	1.50
1960	99,144,000	—	0.10	0.15	0.50	0.75
1961	61,136,000	—	0.10	0.15	0.40	0.70
1962	47,232,000	—	0.10	0.15	0.30	0.55
1963	156,680,000	—	—	0.15	0.20	0.35
1964	71,168,000	—	—	0.15	0.20	0.40
1965	155,720,000	—	—	0.15	0.25	0.35
1966	124,944,000	—	—	0.15	0.40	0.65
1967	118,816,000	—	—	0.15	0.25	0.40
1968	189,588,000	—	—	0.15	0.50	0.75
1969	210,492,000	—	—	0.15	0.55	0.80

KM# 426a 5 CENTAVOS Composition: Copper-Nickel **Reverse:** White Josefa **Note:** Struck at Mexico City Mint, mint mark Mo.

Date	Mintage	F	VF	XF	Unc	BU
1960	—	—	300	450	—	—
1962	19	—	300	450	—	—
1965	—	—	300	450	—	—

KM# 427 5 CENTAVOS **Composition:** Brass **Reverse:** White Josefa **Size:** 18 mm. **Note:** Due to some minor alloy variations this type is often encountered with a bronze color toning. Reduced size.

Date	Mintage	F	VF	XF	Unc	BU
1970	163,368,000	—	0.10	0.15	0.35	0.45
1971	198,844,000	—	0.10	0.15	0.25	0.30
1972	225,000,000	—	0.10	0.15	0.25	0.30
1973 Flat top 3	595,070,000	—	0.10	0.15	0.25	0.40
1973 Round top 3	Inc. above	—	0.10	0.15	0.20	0.30
1974	401,584,000	—	0.10	0.15	0.30	0.40
1975	342,308,000	—	0.10	0.15	0.25	0.35
1976	367,524,000	—	0.10	0.15	0.40	0.60

KM# 428 10 CENTAVOS **Weight:** 2.5000 g. **Composition:** 0.8000 Silver .0643 oz. ASW **Note:** Struck at Mexico City Mint, mint mark Mo.

Date	Mintage	F	VF	XF	Unc	BU
1905	3,920,000	—	5.25	7.00	35.00	50.00
1906	8,410,000	—	4.75	6.25	25.00	35.00
1907/6	5,950,000	—	45.00	115	275	350
1907	Inc. above	—	5.50	7.75	35.00	42.50
1909	2,620,000	—	8.00	12.50	70.00	85.00
1910/00	3,450,000	—	10.00	32.00	75.00	100
1910	Inc. above	—	8.00	12.50	25.00	30.00
1911 Narrow date	2,550,000	—	10.00	15.00	88.00	125
1911 Wide date	Inc. above	—	6.00	8.50	42.50	60.00
1912	1,350,000	—	9.00	16.00	120	135
1912 Low 2	Inc. above	—	8.00	15.00	110	130
1913/2	1,990,000	—	7.50	14.00	35.00	65.00
1913	Inc. above	—	6.00	8.50	30.00	40.00
1914	3,110,000	—	4.50	5.75	13.50	20.00

Note: Wide and narrow dates exist for 1914

KM# 430 10 CENTAVOS **Composition:** Bronze **Note:** Struck at Mexico City Mint, mint mark Mo.

Date	Mintage	F	VF	XF	Unc	BU
1919	1,232,000	—	20.00	60.00	450	525
1920	6,612,000	—	12.50	40.00	400	475
1921	2,255,000	—	30.00	75.00	650	800
1935	5,970,000	—	12.00	25.00	125	175

KM# 429 10 CENTAVOS **Weight:** 1.8125 g. **Composition:** 0.8000 Silver .0466 oz. ASW **Size:** 15 mm. **Note:** Struck at Mexico City Mint, mint mark Mo. Reduced size.

Date	Mintage	F	VF	XF	Unc	BU
1919	8,360,000	—	6.00	12.00	70.00	100

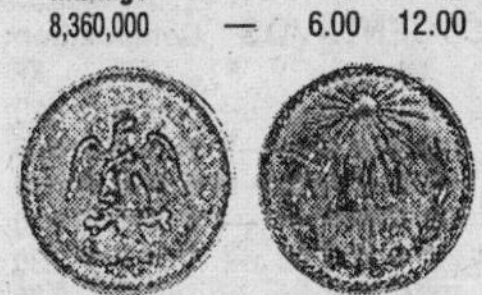

KM# 431 10 CENTAVOS **Weight:** 1.6600 g. **Composition:** 0.7200 Silver .0384 oz. ASW **Note:** Struck at Mexico City Mint, mint mark Mo.

Date	Mintage	F	VF	XF	Unc	BU
1925/15	5,350,000	—	18.00	35.00	110	125
1925/3	Inc. above	—	18.00	35.00	115	130
1925	Inc. above	—	2.00	4.00	35.00	47.50
1926/16	2,650,000	—	25.00	55.00	160	175
1926	Inc. above	—	3.50	6.00	62.50	80.00
1927	2,810,000	—	2.25	3.00	17.50	21.50
1928	5,270,000	—	1.75	2.25	12.00	14.25
1930	2,000,000	—	3.75	5.00	18.75	22.50
1933	5,000,000	—	1.50	3.00	10.00	12.50
1934	8,000,000	—	1.75	2.25	8.00	9.50
1935	3,500,000	—	2.75	4.00	11.00	13.50

KM# 432 10 CENTAVOS **Composition:** Copper-Nickel **Note:** Struck at Mexico City Mint, mint mark Mo.

Date	Mintage	F	VF	XF	Unc	BU
1936	33,030,000	—	0.65	2.25	8.25	10.00
1937	3,000,000	—	2.75	42.50	200	250
1938	3,650,000	—	1.75	5.50	60.00	75.00
1939	6,920,000	—	1.00	3.50	30.00	40.00
1940	12,300,000	—	0.40	1.00	5.00	6.50
1942	14,380,000	—	0.60	1.50	7.00	8.50
1945	9,558,000	—	0.40	0.70	3.50	4.00
1946	46,230,000	—	0.25	0.45	2.25	3.10

KM# 433 10 CENTAVOS **Composition:** Bronze **Reverse:** Benito Juarez **Note:** Struck at Mexico City Mint, mint mark Mo.

Date	Mintage	F	VF	XF	Unc	BU
1955	1,818,000	—	0.60	3.00	22.00	30.00
1956	5,255,000	—	0.50	3.00	22.00	35.00
1957	11,925,000	—	0.20	0.40	5.50	8.00
1959	26,140,000	—	0.20	0.35	0.65	1.25
1966	5,873,000	—	0.15	0.25	0.65	1.50
1967	32,318,000	—	0.10	0.15	0.30	0.40

KM# 434.1 10 CENTAVOS **Composition:** Copper-Nickel **Reverse:** Five full rows of kernels, sharp stem, wide date **Note:** Variety I

Date	Mintage	F	VF	XF	Unc	BU
1974	6,000,000	—	—	0.35	0.85	1.00
1975	5,550,000	—	0.10	0.35	0.85	1.75
1976	7,680,000	—	0.10	0.20	0.30	0.40
1977	144,650,000	—	1.25	2.25	3.50	4.50
1978	271,870,000	—	—	1.00	1.50	2.25
1979	375,660,000	—	—	0.50	1.00	1.75
1980/79	21,290,000	—	2.45	3.75	6.00	7.00
1980	Inc. above	—	1.50	2.00	4.50	5.00

KM# 434.2 10 CENTAVOS **Composition:** Copper-Nickel **Reverse:** Five full, plus one partial row at left, blunt stem, narrow date **Note:** Variety II

Date	F	VF	XF	Unc	BU
1974	—	—	0.10	0.25	0.35
1977	—	—	0.10	0.30	0.35
1978	—	—	0.10	0.30	0.40
1979	—	0.15	0.50	1.00	2.00
1980	—	—	0.10	0.30	0.35

KM# 434.4 10 CENTAVOS **Composition:** Copper-Nickel **Reverse:** Five full, plus one partial row, sharp stem and narrow date **Note:** Variety IV

Date	F	VF	XF	Unc	BU
1974	—	—	—	1.50	2.50
1979	—	—	—	1.50	2.50

KM# 434.3 10 CENTAVOS **Composition:** Copper-Nickel **Reverse:** Five full, plus one partial row, blunt stem and wide date **Note:** Variety III

Date	F	VF	XF	Unc	BU
1980/79	—	—	—	—	—

KM# 435 20 CENTAVOS **Weight:** 5.0000 g. **Composition:** 0.8000 Silver .1286 oz. ASW **Note:** Struck at Mexico City Mint, mint mark Mo.

Date	Mintage	F	VF	XF	Unc	BU
1905	2,565,000	—	9.00	15.00	145	175
1906	6,860,000	—	7.25	14.50	60.00	80.00
1907 Straight 7	4,000,000	—	8.50	17.50	65.00	95.00
1907 Curved 7	5,435,000	—	7.50	13.50	70.00	90.00
1908	350,000	—	85.00	200	1,500	—
1910	1,135,000	—	9.50	15.00	80.00	95.00
1911	1,150,000	—	14.00	32.00	125	150
1912	625,000	—	25.00	70.00	335	375
1913	1,000,000	—	14.50	30.00	95.00	115
1914	1,500,000	—	10.00	21.50	62.50	75.00

KM# 436 20 CENTAVOS **Weight:** 3.6250 g. **Composition:** 0.8000 Silver .0932 oz. ASW **Size:** 19 mm. **Note:** Struck at Mexico City Mint, mint mark Mo. Reduced size.

Date	Mintage	F	VF	XF	Unc	BU
1919	4,155,000	—	25.00	50.00	190	245

KM# 437 20 CENTAVOS **Composition:** Bronze **Note:** Struck at Mexico City Mint, mint mark Mo.

Date	Mintage	F	VF	XF	Unc	BU
1920	4,835,000	—	40.00	110	575	700
1935	20,000,000	—	5.50	8.50	85.00	125

KM# 438 20 CENTAVOS **Weight:** 3.3333 g. **Composition:** 0.7200 Silver .0772 oz. ASW **Note:** Struck at Mexico City Mint, mint mark Mo.

Date	Mintage	F	VF	XF	Unc	BU
1920	3,710,000	—	4.75	10.00	165	215
1921	6,160,000	—	4.50	10.00	100	145
1925	1,450,000	—	8.00	17.00	125	150
1926/5	1,465,000	—	18.00	45.00	325	375
1926	Inc. above	—	4.50	6.25	80.00	110
1927	1,405,000	—	3.75	6.25	80.00	115
1928	3,630,000	—	2.50	4.50	14.50	19.50
1930	1,000,000	—	3.50	6.25	22.00	30.00
1933	2,500,000	—	2.25	2.75	10.00	11.50
1934	2,500,000	—	2.25	3.00	11.00	12.50
1935	2,460,000	—	2.25	2.75	10.00	11.50
1937	10,000,000	—	2.25	2.50	4.75	5.50
1939	8,800,000	—	1.75	2.00	4.00	5.00
1940	3,000,000	—	1.75	2.00	3.50	5.00
1941	5,740,000	—	1.50	2.00	3.00	3.50
1942	12,460,000	—	1.50	2.00	3.25	3.80
1943	3,955,000	—	2.00	2.50	3.50	4.25

KM# 439 20 CENTAVOS **Composition:** Bronze **Note:** Struck at Mexico City Mint, mint mark Mo.

Date	Mintage	F	VF	XF	Unc	BU
1943	46,350,000	—	0.75	2.75	18.00	25.00
1944	83,650,000	—	0.40	0.65	8.00	10.00
1945	26,801,000	—	1.10	3.50	9.50	12.00
1946	25,695,000	—	0.90	2.00	6.00	8.25
1951	11,385,000	—	2.50	5.50	80.00	100
1952	6,560,000	—	2.50	4.50	25.00	32.50
1953	26,948,000	—	0.35	0.75	7.25	11.00
1954	40,108,000	—	0.35	0.80	8.00	11.50
1955	16,950,000	—	2.50	6.00	60.00	75.00

KM# 440 20 CENTAVOS **Composition:** Bronze **Note:** Struck at Mexico City Mint, mint mark Mo.

Date	Mintage	F	VF	XF	Unc	BU
1955 Inc. KM#439	Inc. above	—	0.65	1.50	13.50	18.50
1956	22,431,000	—	0.30	0.35	3.00	5.00
1957	13,455,000	—	0.45	1.25	9.00	12.00
1959	6,017,000	—	4.00	7.50	65.00	95.00
1960	39,756,000	—	0.15	0.25	0.85	1.25
1963	14,869,000	—	0.25	0.35	0.90	1.25
1964	28,654,000	—	0.25	0.40	0.90	1.25
1965	74,162,000	—	0.20	0.40	0.85	1.20
1966	43,745,000	—	0.15	0.25	0.90	1.30
1967	46,487,000	—	0.20	0.55	1.20	1.50
1968	15,477,000	—	0.30	0.55	1.35	1.65
1969	63,647,000	—	0.20	0.40	1.00	1.50
1970	76,287,000	—	0.15	0.20	0.90	1.30
1971	49,892,000	—	0.30	0.50	1.40	1.75

KM# 441 20 CENTAVOS **Composition:** Bronze

Date	Mintage	F	VF	XF	Unc	BU
1971 Inc. KM#440	Inc. above	—	0.20	0.35	1.75	2.35
1973	78,398,000	—	0.25	0.35	0.95	1.50
1974	34,200,000	—	0.20	0.35	1.25	1.75

KM# 442 20 CENTAVOS **Composition:** Copper-Nickel **Reverse:** Francisco Madero

Date	Mintage	F	VF	XF	Unc	BU
1974	112,000,000	—	0.10	0.15	0.25	0.30
1975	611,000,000	—	0.10	0.15	0.30	0.35
1976	394,000,000	—	0.10	0.15	0.35	0.45
1977	394,350,000	—	0.10	0.15	0.40	0.45
1978	527,950,000	—	0.10	0.15	0.25	0.30
1979	524,615,000	—	0.10	0.15	0.30	0.40
1979 Doubled die obv. large/small letters	—	—	1.25	2.00	4.00	8.00
1980	326,500,000	—	0.15	0.25	0.40	0.60
1981 Open 8	106,205,000	—	0.30	0.50	1.00	2.00
1981 Closed 8, high date	248,500,000	—	0.30	0.50	1.00	2.00
1981 Closed 8, low date	—	—	1.00	1.50	3.50	4.25
1981/1982	—	—	30.00	75.00	160	190

Note: The 1981/1982 overdate is often mistaken as 1982/1981

Date	Mintage	F	VF	XF	Unc	BU
1982	286,855,000	—	0.40	0.60	0.90	1.10
1983 Round top 3	100,930,000	—	0.25	0.40	1.75	2.25
1983 Flat top 3	Inc. above	—	0.25	0.50	1.25	1.75
1983 Proof	998	Value: 15.00				

KM# 491 20 CENTAVOS **Composition:** Bronze **Subject:** Olmec Culture

Date	Mintage	F	VF	XF	Unc	BU
1983	260,000,000	—	0.20	0.25	0.90	1.10
1984	180,320,000	—	0.20	0.25	1.50	1.70

KM# 443 25 CENTAVOS **Weight:** 3.3330 g. **Composition:** 0.3000 Silver .0321 oz. ASW **Note:** Struck at Mexico City Mint, mint mark Mo.

Date	Mintage	F	VF	XF	Unc	BU
1950	77,060,000	—	0.50	0.75	1.75	2.25
1951	41,172,000	—	0.50	0.75	1.60	2.00
1952	29,264,000	—	0.75	1.10	1.80	2.50
1953	38,144,000	—	0.60	0.70	1.50	2.00

KM# 444 25 CENTAVOS **Composition:** Copper-Nickel **Reverse:** Francisco Madero

Date	Mintage	F	VF	XF	Unc	BU
1964	20,686,000	—	—	0.15	0.25	0.40
1966 Closed beak	180,000	—	0.65	1.00	2.50	3.00
1966 Open beak	Inc. above	—	1.75	3.50	10.00	14.00

KM# 445 50 CENTAVOS **Weight:** 12.5000 g. **Composition:** 0.8000 Silver .3215 oz. ASW **Note:** Struck at Mexico City Mint, mint mark Mo.

Date	Mintage	F	VF	XF	Unc	BU
1905	2,446,000	—	12.50	20.00	150	225
1906 Open 9	16,966,000	—	5.00	10.00	30.00	50.00
1906 Closed 9	Inc. above	—	4.50	8.50	27.50	40.00
1907 Straight 7	18,920,000	—	4.50	7.25	25.00	28.50
1907 Curved 7	14,841,000	—	5.25	8.00	25.00	28.50
1908	488,000	—	65.00	150	525	625
1912	3,736,000	—	10.00	12.50	45.00	60.00
1913/07	10,510,000	—	30.00	70.00	225	275
1913/2	Inc. above	—	18.00	22.50	65.00	85.00
1913	Inc. above	—	5.50	8.50	25.00	30.00
1914	7,710,000	—	6.75	13.50	30.00	40.00
1916 Narrow date	480,000	—	50.00	75.00	200	290
1916 Wide date	Inc. above	—	50.00	75.00	200	290
1917	37,112,000	—	5.50	8.50	20.00	22.50
1918	1,320,000	—	60.00	110	250	335

KM# 446 50 CENTAVOS **Weight:** 9.0625 g. **Composition:** 0.8000 Silver .2331 oz. ASW **Size:** 27 mm. **Note:** Struck at Mexico City Mint, mint mark Mo. Reduced size.

Date	Mintage	F	VF	XF	Unc	BU
1918/7	2,760,000	—	525	625	1,250	—
1918	Inc. above	—	15.00	50.00	300	385
1919	29,670,000	—	7.00	16.50	85.00	110

KM# 447 50 CENTAVOS **Weight:** 8.3333 g. **Composition:** 0.7200 Silver .1929 oz. ASW **Note:** Struck at Mexico City Mint, mint mark Mo.

Date	Mintage	F	VF	XF	Unc	BU
1919	10,200,000	—	8.00	18.50	87.50	110
1920	27,166,000	—	6.00	8.50	65.00	80.00
1921	21,864,000	—	6.50	9.00	80.00	95.00
1925	3,280,000	—	14.00	30.00	120	160
1937	20,000,000	—	3.75	5.00	7.50	8.50
1938	100,000	—	40.00	75.00	225	300
1939	10,440,000	—	5.25	7.25	14.00	16.50
1942	800,000	—	5.50	7.50	15.00	17.00
1943	41,512,000	—	2.75	4.00	5.50	6.50
1944	55,806,000	—	3.00	3.75	5.50	6.50
1945	56,766,000	—	3.00	3.75	6.00	6.50

KM# 448 50 CENTAVOS **Weight:** 7.9730 g. **Composition:** 0.4200 Silver .1076 oz. ASW **Note:** Struck at Mexico City Mint, mint mark Mo.

Date	Mintage	F	VF	XF	Unc	BU
1935	70,800,000	—	2.20	2.75	5.00	6.00

KM# 449 50 CENTAVOS **Weight:** 6.6600 g. **Composition:** 0.3000 Silver .0642 oz. ASW **Reverse:** Cuauhtemoc **Note:** Struck at Mexico City Mint, mint mark Mo.

Date	Mintage	F	VF	XF	Unc	BU
1950	13,570,000	—	1.50	1.80	3.00	4.00
1951	3,650,000	—	2.00	2.50	3.75	5.00

KM# 450 50 CENTAVOS **Composition:** Bronze **Note:** Struck at Mexico City Mint, mint mark Mo.

Date	Mintage	F	VF	XF	Unc	BU
1955	3,502,000	—	1.20	2.20	27.50	35.00
1956	34,643,000	—	0.65	1.00	3.25	4.50
1957	9,675,000	—	1.00	2.00	6.50	7.50
1959	4,540,000	—	0.35	0.50	1.50	2.00

KM# 451 50 CENTAVOS **Composition:** Copper-Nickel

Date	Mintage	F	VF	XF	Unc	BU
1964	43,806,000	—	0.15	0.20	0.45	0.65
1965	14,326,000	—	0.20	0.25	0.45	0.65
1966	1,726,000	—	0.20	0.40	1.30	1.75
1967	55,144,000	—	0.20	0.30	0.65	1.00
1968	80,438,000	—	0.15	0.30	0.65	0.80
1969	87,640,000	—	0.20	0.35	0.80	1.15

KM# 452 50 CENTAVOS **Composition:** Copper-Nickel **Obverse:** Stylized eagle **Note:** Coins dated 1975 and 1976 exist with and without dots in centers of three circles on plumage on reverse. Edge varieties exist.

Date	Mintage	F	VF	XF	Unc	BU
1970	76,236,000	—	0.15	0.20	0.90	1.25
1971	125,288,000	—	0.15	0.20	0.90	1.30

Date	Mintage	F	VF	XF	Unc	BU
1972	16,000,000	—	1.25	2.00	3.00	4.75
1975 Dots	177,958,000	—	0.60	1.25	3.50	6.00
1975 No dots	Inc. above	—	0.15	0.20	0.50	0.75
1976 Dots	37,480,000	—	0.75	1.25	5.00	6.00
1976 No dots	Inc. above	—	0.15	0.20	0.50	0.75
1977	12,410,000	—	6.50	10.00	32.50	42.50
1978	85,400,000	—	0.15	0.25	0.50	0.75
1979 Round 2nd 9 in date	229,000,000	—	0.15	0.25	0.50	0.65
1979 Square 9's in date	Inc. above	—	0.20	0.40	1.60	2.10
1980 Narrow date, square 9	89,978,000	—	0.45	0.75	1.00	2.00
1980 Wide date, round 9	178,188,000	—	0.20	0.25	1.00	1.15
1981 Rectangular 9, narrow date	142,212,000	—	0.50	0.75	1.75	2.50
1981 Round 9, wide date	Inc. above	—	0.30	0.50	1.25	1.75
1982	45,474,000	—	0.20	0.40	1.50	2.40
1983	90,318,000	—	0.50	0.75	2.25	2.85
1983 Proof	998	Value: 16.00				

KM# 492 50 CENTAVOS **Composition:** Stainless Steel **Subject:** Palenque Culture **Obverse:** Stylized eagle **Reverse:** Cuauhtemoc

Date	Mintage	F	VF	XF	Unc	BU
1983	99,540,000	—	—	0.30	1.50	2.50
1983 Proof	53	Value: 165				

KM# 453 PESO **Weight:** 27.0700 g. **Composition:** 0.9030 Silver .7859 oz. ASW **Subject:** Caballito **Note:** Struck at Mexico City Mint, mint mark Mo.

Date	Mintage	F	VF	XF	Unc	BU
1910	3,814,000	—	30.00	45.00	155	250
1911 Long lower left ray on reverse	1,227,000	—	45.00	75.00	200	275
1911 Short lower left ray on reverse	Inc. above	—	135	225	600	800
1912	322,000	—	95.00	200	350	500
1913/2	2,880,000	—	45.00	75.00	265	400
1913	Inc. above	—	45.00	70.00	160	250

Note: 1913 coins exist with even and unevenly spaced date

Date	Mintage	F	VF	XF	Unc	BU
1914	120,000	—	600	950	3,000	—

KM# 454 PESO **Weight:** 18.1300 g. **Composition:** 0.8000 Silver .4663 oz. ASW **Subject:** Caballito **Note:** Struck at Mexico City Mint, mint mark Mo.

Date	Mintage	F	VF	XF	Unc	BU
1918	3,050,000	—	30.00	100	1,350	2,100
1919	6,151,000	—	18.00	45.00	900	1,600

KM# 455 PESO **Weight:** 16.6600 g. **Composition:** 0.7200 Silver .3856 oz. ASW **Note:** Struck at Mexico City Mint, mint mark Mo.

Date	Mintage	F	VF	XF	Unc	BU
1920/10	8,830,000	—	50.00	90.00	320	—
1920	Inc. above	—	6.50	18.00	150	200
1921	5,480,000	—	8.00	20.00	160	200
1922	33,620,000	—	3.25	5.00	20.00	26.00
1923	35,280,000	—	3.25	5.00	20.00	28.00
1924	33,060,000	—	3.25	5.00	20.00	26.00
1925	9,160,000	—	4.50	9.50	60.00	75.00
1926	28,840,000	—	3.25	5.00	20.00	25.00
1927	5,060,000	—	5.00	10.00	55.00	75.00
1932 Open 9	50,770,000	—	2.75	4.00	5.00	7.00
1932 Closed 9	Inc. above	—	2.75	4.00	5.00	7.00
1933/2	43,920,000	—	15.00	25.00	80.00	—
1933	Inc. above	—	2.75	4.00	5.00	7.00
1934	22,070,000	—	3.25	4.50	9.00	10.50
1935	8,050,000	—	4.50	6.00	11.50	13.50
1938	30,000,000	—	2.75	4.00	6.00	7.50
1940	20,000,000	—	2.75	3.50	5.00	6.50
1943	47,662,000	—	2.75	3.25	4.50	6.00
1944	39,522,000	—	2.75	3.50	4.50	6.00
1945	37,300,000	—	2.75	3.50	4.50	6.00

KM# 456 PESO **Weight:** 14.0000 g. **Composition:** 0.5000 Silver .2250 oz. ASW **Reverse:** Jose Morelos y Pavon **Note:** Struck at Mexico City Mint, mint mark Mo.

Date	Mintage	F	VF	XF	Unc	BU
1947	61,460,000	—	1.75	2.50	4.50	5.50
1948	22,915,000	—	2.25	3.50	5.50	6.50
1949	4,000,000	—	—	1,200	1,600	2,500

Note: Not released for circulation

Date	Mintage	F	VF	XF	Unc	BU
1949 Proof	—	Value: 5,000				

KM# 457 PESO **Weight:** 13.3300 g. **Composition:** 0.3000 Silver .1285 oz. ASW **Reverse:** Jose Morelos y Pavon **Note:** Struck at Mexico City Mint, mint mark Mo.

Date	Mintage	F	VF	XF	Unc	BU
1950	3,287,000	—	2.50	4.00	7.00	8.50

KM# 458 PESO **Weight:** 16.0000 g. **Composition:** 0.1000 Silver .0514 oz. ASW **Subject:** 100th Anniversary of Constitution **Note:** Struck at Mexico City Mint, mint mark Mo.

Date	Mintage	F	VF	XF	Unc	BU
1957	500,000	—	3.50	5.00	13.50	18.00

KM# 459 PESO **Weight:** 16.0000 g. **Composition:** 0.1000 Silver .0514 oz. ASW **Subject:** 100th Anniversary of Constitution **Reverse:** Jose Morelos y Pavon **Note:** Struck at Mexico City Mint, mint mark Mo.

Date	Mintage	F	VF	XF	Unc	BU
1957	28,273,000	—	0.65	1.00	2.25	3.00
1958	41,899,000	—	0.65	0.85	1.85	2.50
1959	27,369,000	—	1.25	2.00	5.50	7.00
1960	26,259,000	—	0.65	1.10	3.25	3.50
1961	52,601,000	—	0.50	0.90	2.25	3.00
1962	61,094,000	—	0.50	0.90	2.10	2.75
1963	26,394,000	—	BV	0.80	2.00	2.40
1964	15,615,000	—	BV	0.75	2.00	2.40
1965	5,004,000	—	BV	0.60	1.85	2.00
1966	30,998,000	—	BV	0.60	1.85	2.00
1967	9,308,000	—	BV	0.60	2.75	3.50

KM# 460 PESO **Composition:** Copper-Nickel **Reverse:** Jose Morelos y Pavon

Date	Mintage	F	VF	XF	Unc	BU
1970 Narrow date	102,715,000	—	0.25	0.35	0.75	0.90
1970 Wide date	Inc. above	—	1.25	2.50	8.00	10.00
1971	426,222,000	—	0.20	0.25	0.50	0.65
1972	120,000,000	—	0.20	0.25	0.40	0.65
1974	63,700,000	—	0.20	0.25	0.65	0.90
1975 Tall narrow date	205,979,000	—	0.25	0.45	1.00	1.35
1975 Short wide date	Inc. above	—	0.30	0.40	0.75	1.00
1976	94,489,000	—	0.15	0.20	0.50	0.75
1977 Thick date	94,364,000	—	0.25	0.45	1.00	1.25
1977 Thin date	Inc. above	—	1.00	2.00	6.50	13.50
1978 Closed 8	208,300,000	—	0.20	0.30	0.65	1.15
1978 Open 8	55,140,000	—	0.75	1.50	11.00	16.50
1979 Thin date	117,884,000	—	0.20	0.30	1.00	1.50
1979 Thick date	Inc. above	—	0.40	0.60	1.25	1.75
1980 Closed 8	318,800,000	—	0.25	0.35	1.00	1.20
1980 Open 8	23,865,000	—	0.75	1.50	9.00	12.75
1981 Closed 8	413,349,000	—	0.20	0.30	0.85	1.00
1981 Open 8	58,616,000	—	0.50	1.25	7.00	8.50
1982	235,000,000	—	0.25	0.75	2.25	2.50
1983 Wide date	100,000,000	—	0.50	1.10	3.00	3.50
1983 Narrow date	Inc. above	—	0.30	0.45	3.25	3.75
1983 Proof	1,051,000	Value: 15.00				

KM# 496 PESO **Composition:** Stainless Steel **Reverse:** Jose Morelos y Pavon

Date	Mintage	F	VF	XF	Unc	BU
1984	722,802,000	—	0.10	0.25	0.65	0.85
1985	985,000,000	—	0.10	0.25	0.50	0.75
1986	740,000,000	—	0.10	0.25	0.50	0.75
1987	250,000,000	—	—	0.25	0.50	0.80
1987 Proof; 2 known	—	Value: 1,250				

KM# 461 2 PESOS **Weight:** 1.6666 g. **Composition:** 0.9000 Gold .0482 oz. AGW **Note:** Struck at Mexico City Mint, mint mark Mo.

Date	F	VF	XF	Unc	BU
1919	—	BV	25.00	32.00	—
1920	—	BV	25.00	32.00	—

Date	F	VF	XF	Unc	BU
1944	27.50	35.00	50.00	80.00	—
1945	—	—	—BV+20%		—
1946	30.00	45.00	55.00	80.00	—
1947	27.50	35.00	50.00	65.00	—
1948 No specimens known	—	—	—	—	—

Note: During 1951-1972 a total of 4,590,493 pieces were restruck, most likely dated 1945. In 1996 matte restrikes were produced

KM# 462 2 PESOS **Weight:** 26.6667 g. **Composition:** 0.9000 Silver .7717 oz. ASW **Subject:** Centennial of Independence **Note:** Struck at Mexico City Mint, mint mark Mo.

Date	Mintage	F	VF	XF	Unc	BU
1921	1,278,000	—	30.00	55.00	265	400

KM# 463 2-1/2 PESOS **Weight:** 2.0833 g. **Composition:** 0.9000 Gold .0602 oz. AGW **Note:** Struck at Mexico City Mint, mint mark Mo.

Date	F	VF	XF	Unc	BU
1918	—	BV	28.00	45.00	—
1919	—	BV	28.00	45.00	—
1920/10	—	BV	55.00	100	—
1920	—	BV	28.00	45.00	—
1944	—	BV	28.00	45.00	—
1945	—	—	—BV+18%		—
1946	—	BV	28.00	45.00	—
1947	200	265	325	400	—
1948	BV	35.00	40.00	65.00	—

Note: During 1951-1972 a total of 5,025,087 pieces were restruck, most likely dated 1945. In 1996 matte restrikes were produced

KM# 464 5 PESOS **Weight:** 4.1666 g. **Composition:** 0.9000 Gold .1205 oz. AGW **Note:** Struck at Mexico City Mint, mint mark Mo.

Date	F	VF	XF	Unc	BU
1905	100	150	200	400	—
1906	—	BV	50.00	70.00	—
1907	—	BV	50.00	70.00	—
1910	BV	55.00	70.00	120	—
1918/7	BV	55.00	70.00	120	—
1918	—	BV	50.00	70.00	—
1919	—	BV	50.00	70.00	—
1920	—	BV	50.00	70.00	—
1955	—	—	—BV+11%		—

Note: During 1955-1972 a total of 1,767,645 pieces were restruck, most likely dated 1955. In 1996 matte restrikes were produced

KM# 465 5 PESOS **Weight:** 30.0000 g. **Composition:** 0.9000 Silver .8681 oz. ASW **Reverse:** Head of Cuauhtemoc left **Note:** Struck at Mexico City Mint, mint mark Mo.

Date	Mintage	F	VF	XF	Unc	BU
1947	5,110,000	—	BV	6.25	8.75	10.00
1948	26,740,000	—	BV	6.00	8.00	9.00

KM# 466 5 PESOS **Weight:** 27.7800 g. **Composition:** 0.7200 Silver .06431 oz. ASW **Subject:** Opening of Southern Railroad **Note:** Struck at Mexico City Mint, mint mark Mo.

Date	Mintage	F	VF	XF	Unc	BU
1950	200,000	—	22.50	27.50	35.00	45.00

Note: It is recorded that 100,000 pieces were melted to be used for the 1968 Mexican Olympic 25 Pesos

KM# 467 5 PESOS **Weight:** 27.7800 g. **Composition:** 0.7200 Silver .6431 oz. ASW **Subject:** Opening of Southern Railroad **Reverse:** Miguel Hidalgo y Costilla **Note:** Struck at Mexico City Mint, mint mark Mo.

Date	Mintage	F	VF	XF	Unc	BU
1951	4,958,000	—	BV	5.75	7.00	10.00
1952	9,595,000	—	BV	5.50	6.75	9.00
1953	20,376,000	—	BV	5.25	6.75	9.00
1954	30,000	—	27.50	45.00	65.00	80.00

KM# 468 5 PESOS **Weight:** 27.7800 g. **Composition:** 0.7200 Silver .6431 oz. ASW **Subject:** Bicentennial of Hidalgo's Birth **Note:** Struck at Mexico City Mint, mint mark Mo.

Date	Mintage	F	VF	XF	Unc	BU
1953	1,000,000	—	BV	5.50	7.50	10.00

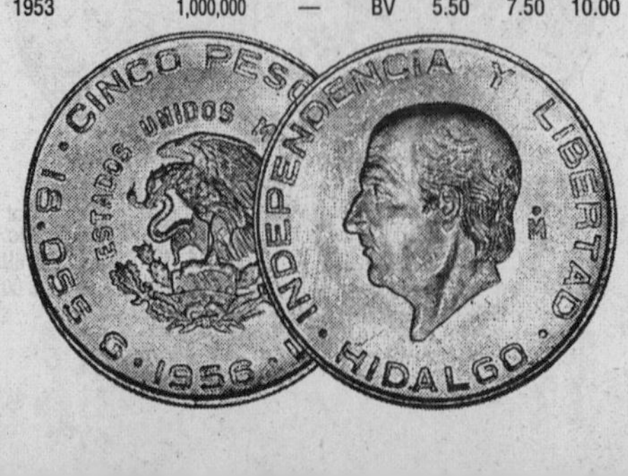

KM# 469 5 PESOS **Weight:** 18.0500 g. **Composition:** 0.7200 Silver .4170 oz. ASW **Note:** Struck at Mexico City Mint, mint mark Mo.

Date	Mintage	F	VF	XF	Unc	BU
1955	4,271,000	—	3.25	4.00	4.75	7.00
1956	4,596,000	—	3.25	4.00	4.75	7.00
1957	3,464,000	—	3.25	4.00	4.75	7.00

KM# 470 5 PESOS **Weight:** 18.0500 g. **Composition:** 0.7200 Silver .4170 oz. ASW **Subject:** 100th Anniversary of Constitution **Note:** Struck at Mexico City Mint, mint mark Mo.

Date	Mintage	F	VF	XF	Unc	BU
1957	200,000	—	5.50	7.50	13.50	15.50

KM# 471 5 PESOS **Weight:** 27.7800 g. **Composition:** 0.7200 Silver .6431 oz. ASW **Subject:** Centennial of Carranza's Birth **Note:** Struck at Mexico City Mint, mint mark Mo.

Date	Mintage	F	VF	XF	Unc	BU
1959	1,000,000	—	BV	4.50	6.50	9.50

KM# 472 5 PESOS **Composition:** Copper-Nickel **Reverse:** Vicente Guerrero **Note:** Small date, large date varieties.

Date	Mintage	F	VF	XF	Unc	BU
1971	28,457,000	—	0.50	0.95	2.50	3.25
1972	75,000,000	—	0.60	1.25	2.00	2.50
1973	19,405,000	—	1.25	2.10	5.00	7.50
1974	34,500,000	—	0.50	0.80	1.75	2.25
1976 Small date	26,121,000	—	0.75	1.45	3.50	4.25
1976 Large date	121,550,000	—	0.35	0.50	1.50	1.75
1977	102,000,000	—	0.50	0.75	1.50	2.00
1978	25,700,000	—	1.00	1.50	5.25	6.75

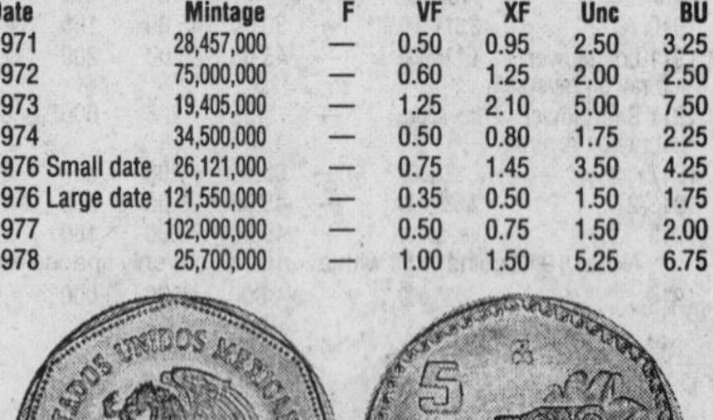

KM# 485 5 PESOS **Composition:** Copper-Nickel **Subject:** Quetzalcoatl

Date	Mintage	F	VF	XF	Unc	BU
1980	266,899,999	—	0.25	0.50	1.75	2.25
1981	30,500,000	—	0.45	0.65	2.75	3.25
1982	20,000,000	—	1.50	2.35	4.25	5.25
1982 Proof	1,051	Value: 18.00				
1983 Proof; 7 known	—	Value: 1,150				
1984	16,300,000	—	1.25	2.00	4.75	6.00
1985	76,900,000	—	2.25	4.00	4.50	5.25

KM# 502 5 PESOS **Composition:** Brass **Subject:** Quetzalcoatl **Note:** Circulation coinage.

Date	Mintage	F	VF	XF	Unc	BU
1985	30,000,000	—	—	0.15	0.35	0.50
1987	81,900,000	—	8.00	9.50	12.50	15.00
1988	76,600,000	—	—	0.10	0.25	0.35
1988 Proof; 2 known	—	Value: 600				

KM# 473 10 PESOS **Weight:** 8.3333 g. **Composition:** 0.9000 Gold .2411 oz. AGW **Reverse:** Miguel Hidalgo **Note:** Struck at Mexico City Mint, mint mark Mo.

Date	F	VF	XF	Unc	BU
1905	110	125	155	200	—
1906	—	BV	100	150	—
1907	—	BV	100	150	—
1908	—	BV	100	150	—
1910	—	BV	100	150	—
1916	110	120	150	275	—
1917	—	BV	100	150	—
1919	—	BV	100	150	—
1920	150	250	400	650	—
1959	—	—	—	BV+7%	—

Note: *During 1961-1972 a total of 954,983 pieces were restruck, most likely dated 1959. In 1996 matte restrikes were produced

KM# 474 10 PESOS **Weight:** 28.8800 g. **Composition:** 0.9000 Silver .8357 oz. ASW **Reverse:** Miguel Hidalgo **Note:** Struck at Mexico City Mint, mint mark Mo.

Date	Mintage	F	VF	XF	Unc	BU
1955	585,000	—	BV	6.00	8.75	12.00
1956	3,535,000	—	BV	5.50	8.50	12.50

KM# 475 10 PESOS **Weight:** 28.8800 g. **Composition:** 0.9000 Silver .8357 oz. ASW **Subject:** 100th Anniversary of Constutution **Note:** Struck at Mexico City Mint, mint mark Mo.

Date	Mintage	F	VF	XF	Unc	BU
1957	100,000	—	12.50	22.50	37.50	45.00

KM# 476 10 PESOS **Weight:** 28.8800 g. **Composition:** 0.9000 Silver .8357 oz. ASW **Subject:** 150th Anniversary - War of Independence **Note:** Struck at Mexico City Mint, mint mark Mo.

Date	Mintage	F	VF	XF	Unc	BU
1960	1,000,000	—	BV	6.00	9.00	13.50

KM# 477.1 10 PESOS **Composition:** Copper-Nickel **Reverse:** Miguel Hidalgo **Shape:** 7-sided **Note:** Thin flan - 1.6mm

Date	Mintage	F	VF	XF	Unc	BU
1974	3,900,000	—	0.50	1.00	3.50	4.25
1974 Proof	—	Value: 625				
1975	1,000,000	—	2.25	3.25	7.75	15.00
1976	74,500,000	—	0.25	0.75	1.75	2.25
1977	79,620,000	—	0.50	1.00	2.00	3.00

KM# 477.2 10 PESOS **Composition:** Copper-Nickel **Reverse:** Miguel Hidalgo **Note:** Thick flan - 2.3mm

Date	Mintage	F	VF	XF	Unc	BU
1978	124,850,000	—	0.50	0.75	2.50	2.75
1979	57,200,000	—	0.50	0.75	2.25	2.50
1980	55,200,000	—	0.50	0.75	2.50	3.75
1981	222,768,000	—	0.40	0.60	2.25	2.60
1982	151,770,000	—	0.50	0.80	2.50	3.50
1982 Proof	1,051	Value: 18.00				
1985	58,000,000	—	1.25	1.75	5.75	7.50

KM# 512 10 PESOS **Composition:** Stainless Steel **Reverse:** Miguel Hidalgo **Note:** Date varieties exist.

Date	Mintage	F	VF	XF	Unc	BU
1985	257,000,000	—	—	0.15	0.50	0.75
1986	392,000,000	—	—	0.15	0.50	1.50
1987	305,000,000	—	—	0.15	0.35	0.50
1988	500,300,000	—	—	0.15	0.25	0.35
1989	—	—	0.20	0.25	0.75	1.50
1990	—	—	—	0.25	0.75	1.25
1990 Proof; 2 known	—	Value: 500				

KM# 478 20 PESOS **Weight:** 16.6666 g. **Composition:** 0.9000 Gold .4823 oz. AGW **Note:** Struck at Mexico City Mint, mint mark Mo.

Date	F	VF	XF	Unc	BU
1917	—	BV	155	185	—
1918	—	BV	155	185	—
1919	—	BV	155	185	—
1920/10	—	BV	160	195	—
1920	—	BV	155	185	—
1921/11	—	BV	160	195	—
1921/10	—	—	—	—	—
1921	—	BV	155	185	—
1959	—	—	—	—	—

Note: During 1960-1971 a total of 1,158,414 pieces were restruck, most likely dated 1959. In 1996 matte restrikes were produced

KM# 486 20 PESOS **Composition:** Copper-Nickel

Date	Mintage	F	VF	XF	Unc	BU
1980	84,900,000	—	0.50	0.85	2.50	3.40
1981	250,573,000	—	0.60	0.80	2.50	3.50
1982	236,892,000	—	1.00	1.75	2.75	3.85
1982 Proof	1,051	Value: 18.00				
1983 Proof; 3 known	—	—	—	—	—	—
1984	55,000,000	—	1.00	1.50	3.75	7.50

KM# 508 20 PESOS **Composition:** Brass **Reverse:** Guadalupe Victoria, First President

Date	Mintage	F	VF	XF	Unc	BU
1985 Wide date	25,000,000	—	0.10	0.20	1.00	1.25
1985 Narrow date	Inc. above	—	0.10	0.25	1.50	2.00
1986	10,000,000	—	1.00	1.75	5.00	6.00
1988	355,200,000	—	0.10	0.20	0.50	1.00
1989	—	—	0.15	0.30	1.50	2.00
1990	—	—	0.15	0.30	1.50	2.50

KM# 479.1 25 PESOS **Weight:** 22.5000 g. **Composition:** 0.7200 Silver .5209 oz. ASW **Note:** Type I, Rings aligned.

Date	Mintage	F	VF	XF	Unc	BU
1968	27,182,000	—	BV	4.00	4.75	6.00

KM# 479.2 25 PESOS **Weight:** 22.5000 g. **Composition:** 0.7200 Silver .5209 oz. ASW **Subject:** Summer Olympics - Mexico City **Note:** Type II, center ring low.

Date	F	VF	XF	Unc	BU
1968	—	4.00	5.00	9.00	10.50

KM# 479.3 25 PESOS Weight: 22.5000 g. **Composition:** 0.7200 Silver .5209 oz. ASW **Subject:** Summer Olympics - Mexico City **Note:** Normal tongue and long curved tongue Type III, center rings low. Snake with long curved tongue.

Date	F	VF	XF	Unc	BU
1968	—	4.25	5.25	9.50	11.00

KM# 480 25 PESOS Weight: 22.5000 g. **Composition:** 0.7200 Silver .5209 oz. ASW **Reverse:** Benito Juarez

Date	Mintage	F	VF	XF	Unc	BU
1972	2,000,000	—	—	4.00	6.00	9.00

KM# 497 25 PESOS Weight: 7.7760 g. **Composition:** 0.7200 Silver .1800 oz. ASW **Subject:** 1986 World Cup Soccer Games

Date	Mintage	F	VF	XF	Unc	BU
1985	354,000	—	—	—	—	6.50

KM# 503 25 PESOS Weight: 8.4060 g. **Composition:** 0.9250 Silver .2450 oz. ASW **Subject:** 1986 World Cup Soccer Games

Date	Mintage	F	VF	XF	Unc	BU
1985 Proof	277,000	Value: 9.00				

KM# 514 25 PESOS Weight: 8.4060 g. **Composition:** 0.9250 Silver .2450 oz. ASW **Subject:** 1986 World Cup Soccer Games

Date	Mintage	F	VF	XF	Unc	BU
1985 Proof	234,000	Value: 9.00				

KM# 519 25 PESOS Weight: 8.4060 g. **Composition:** 0.9250 Silver .2450 oz. ASW **Subject:** 1986 World Cup Soccer Games

Date	F	VF	XF	Unc	BU
1986 Proof	—	Value: 9.00			

KM# 497a 25 PESOS Weight: 8.4060 g. **Composition:** 0.9250 Silver .2450 oz. ASW **Subject:** 1986 World Cup Soccer Games **Reverse:** Without fineness statement

Date	F	VF	XF	Unc	BU
1986 Proof	—	Value: 9.00			

KM# 554 25 PESOS Weight: 7.7758 g. **Composition:** 0.9990 Silver .2500 oz. ASW **Reverse:** Eagle warrior

Date	Mintage	F	VF	XF	Unc	BU
1992	50,000	—	—	—	6.50	—
1992 Proof	3,000	Value: 10.50				

KM# 481 50 PESOS Weight: 41.6666 g. **Composition:** 0.9000 Gold 1.2057 oz. AGW **Subject:** Centennial of Independence **Note:** During 1949-1972 a total of 3,975,654 pieces were restruck, most likely dated 1947. In 1996 matte restrikes were produced. Struck at Mexico City Mint, mint mark Mo.

Date	Mintage	F	VF	XF	Unc	BU
1921	180,000	—	—	BV	525	—
1922	463,000	—	—	BV	460	—
1923	432,000	—	—	BV	460	—
1924	439,000	—	—	BV	460	—
1925	716,000	—	—	BV	460	—
1926	600,000	—	—	BV	460	—
1927	606,000	—	—	BV	460	—
1928	538,000	—	—	BV	460	—
1929	458,000	—	—	BV	460	—
1930	372,000	—	—	BV	460	—
1931	137,000	—	—	BV	475	—
1944	593,000	—	—	BV	450	—
1945	1,012,000	—	—	BV	450	—
1946	1,588,000	—	—	BV	450	—
1947	309,000	—	—	—	BV+3%	—
1947 Specimen	—	—	—	—	—	—

Note: Value, $6,500

KM# 490 50 PESOS Composition: Copper-Nickel **Subject:** Coyolxauhqui **Note:** Doubled die examples of 1982 and 1983 dates exist.

Date	Mintage	F	VF	XF	Unc	BU
1982	222,890,000	—	1.00	2.50	5.00	6.25
1983	45,000,000	—	1.50	3.00	6.00	6.50
1983 Proof	1,051	Value: 22.00				
1984	73,537,000	—	1.00	1.35	3.50	4.00
1984 Proof; 4 known	—	Value: 750				

KM# 495 50 PESOS Composition: Copper-Nickel **Subject:** Benito Juarez

Date	Mintage	F	VF	XF	Unc	BU
1984	94,216,000	—	0.65	1.25	2.75	3.50
1985	296,000,000	—	0.25	0.45	1.50	2.25
1986	50,000,000	—	5.00	7.00	11.00	12.50
1987	210,000,000	—	0.25	0.45	1.00	1.25
1988	80,200,000	—	6.25	9.00	12.50	14.50

KM# 498 50 PESOS Weight: 15.5520 g. **Composition:** 0.7200 Silver .3601 oz. ASW **Subject:** 1986 World Cup Soccer Games

Date	Mintage	F	VF	XF	Unc	BU
1985	347,000	—	—	—	—	7.50

KM# 504 50 PESOS Weight: 16.8310 g. **Composition:** 0.9250 Silver .5000 oz. ASW **Subject:** 1986 World Cup Soccer Games **Reverse:** Without fineness statement

Date	Mintage	F	VF	XF	Unc	BU
1985 Proof	347,000	Value: 13.50				

KM# 515 50 PESOS Weight: 16.8310 g. **Composition:** 0.9250 Silver .5000 oz. ASW **Subject:** 1986 World Cup Soccer Games

Date	Mintage	F	VF	XF	Unc	BU
1985 Proof	234,000	Value: 13.50				

KM# 523 50 PESOS Weight: 16.8310 g. **Composition:** 0.9250 Silver .5000 oz. ASW **Subject:** 1986 World Cup Soccer Games

Date	Mintage	F	VF	XF	Unc	BU
1986 Proof	190,000	Value: 13.50				

KM# 498a 50 PESOS Weight: 16.8310 g. **Composition:** 0.9250 Silver .5000 oz. ASW **Subject:** 1986 World Cup Soccer Games **Reverse:** Without fineness statement

Date	Mintage	F	VF	XF	Unc	BU
1986 Proof	10,000	Value: 13.50				

KM# 532 50 PESOS Weight: 15.5500 g. **Composition:** 0.9990 Silver .5000 oz. ASW **Subject:** 50th Anniversary - Nationalization of Oil Industry

Date	Mintage	F	VF	XF	Unc	BU
ND(1988)	30,000	—	—	—	12.00	15.00

KM# 495a 50 PESOS Composition: Stainless Steel **Subject:** Benito Juarez **Edge:** Plain.

Date	Mintage	F	VF	XF	Unc	BU
1988	353,300,000	—	—	0.20	0.75	1.50
1989	—	—	—	—	—	—
1990	—	—	—	0.30	1.00	2.00
1991	—	—	—	—	—	—
1992	—	—	—	0.25	1.00	2.75

KM# 555 50 PESOS **Weight:** 15.5517 g. **Composition:** 0.9990 Silver .5000 oz. ASW **Subject:** 50th Anniversary - Nationalization of Oil Industry **Reverse:** Eagle warrior

Date	Mintage	F	VF	XF	Unc	BU
1992	50,000	—	—	—	8.50	—
1992 Proof	3,000	Value: 18.50				

KM# 483.1 100 PESOS **Weight:** 27.7700 g. **Composition:** 0.7200 Silver .6429 oz. ASW **Reverse:** Jose Morelos y Pavon **Note:** Low 7's and high 7's.

Date	Mintage	F	VF	XF	Unc	BU
1977 Low 7's, sloping shoulder	5,225,000	—	BV	4.00	6.00	10.00
1977 High 7's, sloping shoulder	Inc. above	—	BV	4.00	6.00	10.50

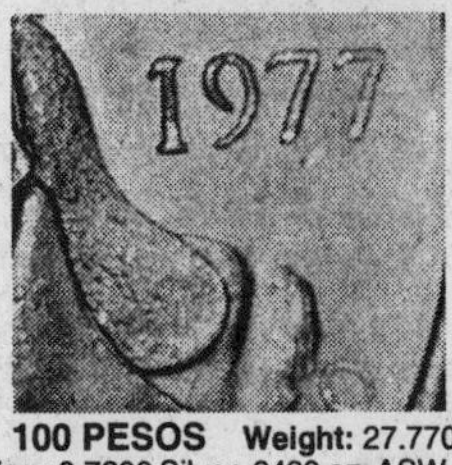

KM# 483.2 100 PESOS **Weight:** 27.7700 g. **Composition:** 0.7200 Silver .6429 oz. ASW **Reverse:** Jose Morelos y Pavon **Note:** Low 7's and high 7's.

Date	Mintage	F	VF	XF	Unc	BU
1978	9,879,000	—	BV	4.00	6.50	8.50
1979	784,000	—	BV	4.00	6.50	8.50
1979 Proof	—	Value: 550				

KM# 493 100 PESOS **Composition:** Aluminum-Bronze **Reverse:** Venustiano Carranza

Date	Mintage	F	VF	XF	Unc	BU
1984	227,809,000	—	0.45	0.60	2.75	4.00
1985	377,423,000	—	0.30	0.50	2.00	3.00
1986	43,000,000	—	1.00	2.50	4.75	7.50

Date	Mintage	F	VF	XF	Unc	BU
1987	165,000,000	—	0.60	1.25	2.50	3.50
1988	433,100,000	—	0.30	0.50	2.00	2.75
1989	—	—	0.35	0.65	2.00	2.75
1990	—	—	0.15	0.40	1.50	2.50
1990 Proof; 1 known	—	Value: 650				
1991	—	—	0.15	0.25	1.00	2.50
1992	—	—	0.30	0.75	1.75	3.00

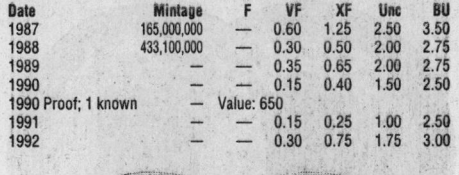

KM# 499 100 PESOS **Weight:** 31.1030 g. **Composition:** 0.7200 Silver .7201 oz. ASW **Subject:** 1986 World Cup Soccer Games

Date	Mintage	F	VF	XF	Unc	BU
1985	302,000	—	—	—	—	11.50

KM# 499a 100 PESOS **Weight:** 32.6250 g. **Composition:** 0.9250 Silver 1.0000 oz. ASW **Subject:** 1986 World Cup Soccer Games **Reverse:** Without fineness statement

Date	Mintage	F	VF	XF	Unc	BU
1985 Proof	9,006	Value: 18.50				

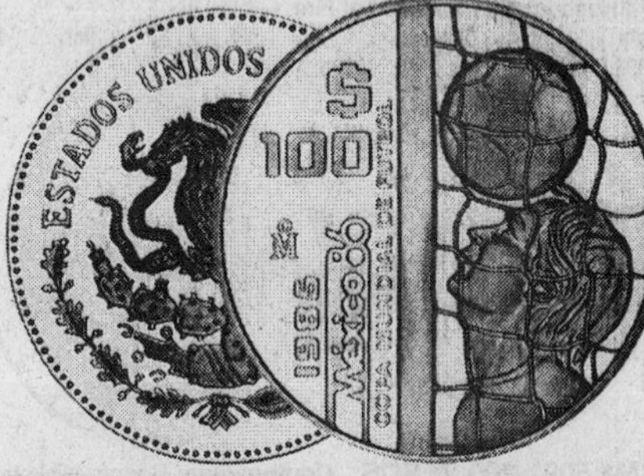

KM# 505 100 PESOS **Weight:** 32.6250 g. **Composition:** 0.9250 Silver 1.0000 oz. ASW **Subject:** 1986 World Cup Soccer Games **Reverse:** Without fineness statement

Date	Mintage	F	VF	XF	Unc	BU
1985 Proof	9,006	Value: 18.50				

KM# 521 100 PESOS **Weight:** 32.6250 g. **Composition:** 0.9250 Silver 1.0000 oz. ASW **Subject:** 1986 World Cup Soccer Games **Reverse:** Without fineness statement

Date	Mintage	F	VF	XF	Unc	BU
1986 Proof	208,000	Value: 18.50				

KM# 524 100 PESOS **Weight:** 32.6250 g. **Composition:** 0.9250 Silver 1.0000 oz. ASW **Subject:** 1986 World Cup Soccer Games **Reverse:** Without fineness statement

Date	Mintage	F	VF	XF	Unc	BU
1986 Proof	190,000	Value: 18.50				

KM# 537 100 PESOS **Weight:** 32.6250 g. **Composition:** 0.9250 Silver 1.0000 oz. ASW **Subject:** World Wildlife Fund **Reverse:** Monarch butterflies

Date	Mintage	F	VF	XF	Unc	BU
1987 Proof	Est. 30,000	Value: 40.00				

KM# 533 100 PESOS **Weight:** 31.1030 g. **Composition:** 0.9990 Silver 1.0000 oz. ASW **Subject:** 50th Anniversary - Nationalization of Oil Industry

Date	Mintage	F	VF	XF	Unc	BU
1988	10,000	—	—	—	28.00	35.00

KM# 539 100 PESOS **Weight:** 33.6250 g. **Composition:** 0.9250 Silver 1.0000 oz. ASW **Subject:** Save the Children

Date	Mintage	F	VF	XF	Unc	BU
1991 Proof	30,000	Value: 35.00				

KM# 540 100 PESOS **Weight:** 27.0000 g. **Composition:** 0.9250 Silver .8029 oz. ASW **Subject:** Ibero - American Series **Reverse:** Pillars

Date	Mintage	F	VF	XF	Unc	BU
1991 Proof	50,000	Value: 47.50				
1992 Proof	75,000	Value: 42.50				

KM# 566 100 PESOS **Weight:** 31.1035 g. **Composition:** 0.9990 Silver 1.0000 oz. ASW **Subject:** Save the Vaquita Porpoise

Date		F	VF	XF	Unc	BU
1992 Proof	—	Value: 40.00				

KM# 556 100 PESOS **Weight:** 31.1035 g. **Composition:** 0.9990 Silver 1.0000 oz. ASW **Reverse:** Eagle warrior

Date	Mintage	F	VF	XF	Unc	BU
1992	205,000	—	—	—	11.50	—
1992	4,000	Value: 37.50				

KM# 562 100 PESOS **Weight:** 31.1035 g. **Composition:** 0.9990 Silver 1.0000 oz. ASW **Reverse:** Xochipilli - The God of Joy, Music and Dance

Date	Mintage	F	VF	XF	Unc	BU
1992 Proof	4,000	Value: 37.50				

KM# 563 100 PESOS **Weight:** 31.1035 g. **Composition:** 0.9990 Silver 1.0000 oz. ASW **Reverse:** Brasero Efigie - The God of Rain

Date	Mintage	F	VF	XF	Unc	BU
1992 Proof	4,000	Value: 37.50				

KM# 564 100 PESOS **Weight:** 31.1035 g. **Composition:** 0.9990 Silver 1.0000 oz. ASW **Reverse:** Huehueteotl - The God of Fire

Date	Mintage	F	VF	XF	Unc	BU
1992 Proof	4,000	Value: 37.50				

KM# 509 200 PESOS **Composition:** Copper-Nickel **Subject:** 175th Anniversary of Independence

Date	Mintage	F	VF	XF	Unc	BU
1985	75,000,000	—	—	0.25	3.25	4.75

KM# 510 200 PESOS **Composition:** Copper-Nickel **Subject:** 175th Anniversary of 1910 Revolution

Date	Mintage	F	VF	XF	Unc	BU
1985	98,590,000	—	—	0.25	3.25	4.25

KM# 525 200 PESOS **Composition:** Copper-Nickel **Subject:** 1986 World Cup Soccer Games

Date	Mintage	F	VF	XF	Unc	BU
1986	50,000,000	—	—	1.00	3.50	4.50

KM# 526 200 PESOS **Weight:** 62.2060 g. **Composition:** 0.9990 Silver 2.0000 oz. ASW **Subject:** 1986 World Cup Soccer Games

Date	Mintage	F	VF	XF	Unc	BU
1986	50,000	—	—	—	40.00	50.00

KM# 500.1 250 PESOS **Weight:** 8.6400 g. **Composition:** 0.9000 Gold .2500 oz. AGW **Subject:** 1986 World Cup Soccer Games

Date	Mintage	F	VF	XF	Unc	BU
1985	100,000	—	—	—	—	100
1986	—	—	—	—	—	100

KM# 500.2 250 PESOS **Weight:** 8.6400 g. **Composition:** 0.9000 Gold .2500 oz. AGW **Subject:** 1986 World Cup Soccer Games **Reverse:** Without fineness statement

Date	Mintage	F	VF	XF	Unc	BU
1985 Proof	4,506	Value: 110				
1986 Proof	—	Value: 135				

KM# 506.1 250 PESOS **Weight:** 8.6400 g. **Composition:** 0.9000 Gold .2500 oz. AGW **Subject:** 1986 World Cup Soccer Games

Date	Mintage	F	VF	XF	Unc	BU
1985	88,000	—	—	—	—	110

KM# 506.2 250 PESOS **Weight:** 8.6400 g. **Composition:** 0.9000 Gold .2500 oz. AGW **Subject:** 1986 World Cup Soccer Games **Reverse:** Without fineness statement

Date	Mintage	F	VF	XF	Unc	BU
1985 Proof	Est. 80,000	Value: 115				

KM# 558 250 PESOS **Weight:** 7.7758 g. **Composition:** 0.9990 Gold .2500 oz. AGW **Subject:** Native Culture **Reverse:** Sculpture of jaguar head

Date	Mintage	F	VF	XF	Unc	BU
1992	10,000	—	—	—	145	—
1992 Proof	2,000	Value: 250				

KM# 501.1 500 PESOS **Weight:** 17.2800 g. **Composition:** 0.9000 Gold .5000 oz. AGW **Subject:** 1986 World Cup Soccer Games **Obverse:** Eagle facing left with snake in beak

Date	Mintage	F	VF	XF	Unc	BU
1985	102,000	—	—	—	—	210
1986	—	—	—	—	—	210

KM# 501.2 500 PESOS **Weight:** 17.2800 g. **Composition:** 0.9000 Gold .5000 oz. AGW **Subject:** 1986 World Cup Soccer Games **Obverse:** Eagle facing left with snake in beak **Reverse:** Without fineness statement

Date	Mintage	F	VF	XF	Unc	BU
1985 Proof	5,506	Value: 225				
1986 Proof	—	Value: 225				

KM# 507.1 500 PESOS **Weight:** 17.2800 g. **Composition:** 0.9000 Gold .5000 oz. AGW **Subject:** 1986 World Cup Soccer Games **Obverse:** Eagle facing left with snake in beak

Date	F	VF	XF	Unc	BU
1985	—	—	—	—	225

KM# 507.2 500 PESOS **Weight:** 17.2800 g. **Composition:** 0.9000 Gold .5000 oz. AGW **Subject:** 1986 World Cup Soccer Games **Obverse:** Eagle facing left with snake in beak **Reverse:** Without fineness statement

Date	F	VF	XF	Unc	BU
1985 Proof	—	Value: 225			

KM# 511 500 PESOS **Weight:** 3334500.0000 g. **Composition:** 0.9250 Silver 1.0000 oz. ASW **Subject:** 17th Anniversary of 1910 Revolution **Obverse:** Eagle facing left with snake in beak

Date	Mintage	F	VF	XF	Unc	BU
1985 Proof	40,000	Value: 30.00				

KM# 529 500 PESOS **Composition:** Copper-Nickel **Reverse:** Francisco Madero

Date	Mintage	F	VF	XF	Unc	BU
1986	20,000,000	—	—	1.00	2.50	3.00
1987	180,000,000	—	—	0.75	2.00	2.50
1988	230,000,000	—	—	0.50	2.00	2.50
1988 Proof; 2 known	—	Value: 650				
1989	—	—	—	0.75	2.00	3.00
1992	—	—	—	1.00	2.25	3.50

KM# 534 500 PESOS **Weight:** 17.2800 g. **Composition:** 0.9000 Gold .5000 oz. AGW **Subject:** 50th Anniversary - Nationalization of Oil Industry **Reverse:** Monument **Note:** Similar to 5000 Pesos, KM#531.

Date	F	VF	XF	Unc	BU
1988	—	—	—	—	225

KM# 559 500 PESOS **Weight:** 15.5517 g. **Composition:** 0.9990 Gold .5000 oz. AGW **Subject:** Native Culture - Sculpture of Jaguar Head

Date	Mintage	F	VF	XF	Unc	BU
1992	10,000	—	—	—	200	—
1992 Proof	2,000	Value: 400				

KM# 513 1000 PESOS **Weight:** 17.2800 g. **Composition:** 0.9000 Gold .5000 oz. AGW **Subject:** 175th Anniversary of Independence

Date	F	VF	XF	Unc	BU
1985 Proof	—	Value: 325			

KM# 527 1000 PESOS **Weight:** 31.1030 g. **Composition:** 0.9990 Gold 1.0000 oz. AGW **Subject:** 1986 World Cup Soccer Games

Date	F	VF	XF	Unc	BU
1986	—	—	—	—	550

KM# 536 1000 PESOS **Composition:** Aluminum-Bronze **Note:** Juana de Asbaje

Date	Mintage	F	VF	XF	Unc	BU
1988	229,300,000	—	0.85	1.25	3.75	4.25
1989	—	—	0.85	1.25	3.45	4.25
1990	—	—	0.85	1.25	2.25	4.25
1990 Proof; 2 known	—	Value: 550				
1991	—	—	1.00	1.50	2.50	4.25
1992	—	—	1.00	1.50	2.25	3.50

KM# 535 1000 PESOS **Weight:** 34.5590 g. **Composition:** 0.9000 Gold 1.0000 oz. AGW **Subject:** 50th Anniversary - Nationalization of Oil Industry **Reverse:** Portrait of Cardenas **Note:** Similar to 5000 Pesos, KM#531.

Date	F	VF	XF	Unc	BU
1988 Proof	—	Value: 440			

KM# 643 1000 PESOS **Composition:** Aluminum-Bronze **Subject:** Unissed type **Obverse:** National emblem **Reverse:** Stylized boat and "ATLAN" above denomination **Size:** 22 mm. **Note:** Unissued type due to currency reform.

Date	F	VF	XF	Unc	BU
1991Mo	—	—	—	25.00	—

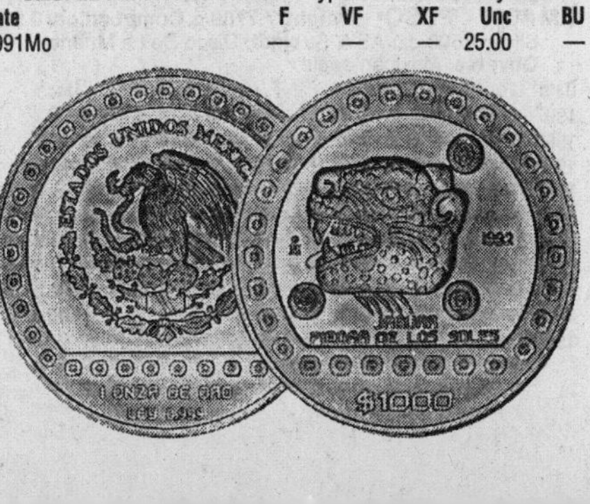

KM# 560 1000 PESOS **Weight:** 31.1035 g. **Composition:** 0.9990 Gold 1.0000 oz. AGW **Subject:** Native Culture **Reverse:** Sculpture of jaguar head

Date	Mintage	F	VF	XF	Unc	BU
1992	18,000	—	—	—	400	—
1992 Proof	2,000	Value: 600				

KM# 528 2000 PESOS **Weight:** 62.2000 g. **Composition:** 0.9990 Gold 2.0000 oz. AGW **Subject:** 1986 World Cup Soccer Games

Date	F	VF	XF	Unc	BU
1986	—	—	—	—	900

KM# 531 5000 PESOS **Composition:** Copper-Nickel **Subject:** 50th Anniversary - Nationalization of Oil Industry

Date	Mintage	F	VF	XF	Unc	BU
ND(1988)	50,000,000	—	—	4.75	7.75	10.00

KM# 557 10000 PESOS **Weight:** 155.5175 g. **Composition:** 0.9990 Silver 5.0000 oz. ASW **Subject:** Pieora De Tizoc **Reverse:** Native warriors taking female captive **Size:** 64 mm. **Note:** Illustration reduced.

Date	Mintage	F	VF	XF	Unc	BU
1992	52,000	—	—	—	46.00	—
1992 Proof	3,005	Value: 80.00				

REFORM COINAGE

1 New Peso = 1000 Old Pesos

KM# 546 5 CENTAVOS **Composition:** Stainless Steel

Date	F	VF	XF	Unc	BU
1992	—	—	0.15	0.25	—
1993	—	—	0.15	0.25	—
1994	—	—	0.15	0.25	—
1995	—	—	0.15	0.25	—
1995 Proof	—	Value: 0.50			
1996	—	—	0.15	0.25	—
1997	—	—	0.15	0.25	—
2000Mo	—	—	0.15	0.25	—

KM# 547 10 CENTAVOS **Composition:** Stainless Steel

Date	F	VF	XF	Unc	BU
1992	—	—	0.20	0.30	—
1993	—	—	0.20	0.30	—
1994	—	—	0.20	0.30	—
1995	—	—	0.20	0.30	—
1995 Proof	—	Value: 0.60			
1996	—	—	0.20	0.30	—
1997	—	—	0.20	0.30	—
2001Mo	—	—	0.20	0.30	—

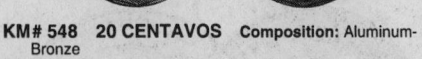

KM# 548 20 CENTAVOS **Composition:** Aluminum-Bronze

Date	F	VF	XF	Unc	BU
1992	—	—	0.25	0.35	—
1993	—	—	0.25	0.35	—
1994	—	—	0.25	0.35	—
1995	—	—	0.25	0.35	—
1995 Proof	—	Value: 0.75			
1996	—	—	0.25	0.35	—

KM# 549 50 CENTAVOS **Composition:** Aluminum-Bronze

Date	F	VF	XF	Unc	BU
1992	—	—	0.45	0.85	—
1993	—	—	0.45	0.75	—
1994	—	—	0.45	0.75	—
1995	—	—	0.45	0.75	—
1995 Proof	—	Value: 0.90			
1996	—	—	0.45	0.75	—
1997	—	—	0.45	0.75	—

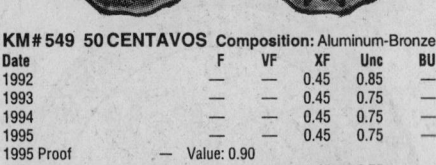

KM# 550 NUEVO PESO **Ring Composition:** Stainless Steel **Center Composition:** Aluminum-Bronze

Date	F	VF	XF	Unc	BU
1992	—	—	0.60	1.25	—
1993	—	—	0.60	1.25	—
1994	—	—	0.60	1.25	—
1995	—	—	0.60	1.25	—
1995 Proof	—	Value: 2.50			

KM# 644 NUEVO PESO **Weight:** 7.7700 g. **Composition:** 0.9990 Silver .2496 oz. ASW **Subject:** Eagle Warrior **Obverse:** National arms **Reverse:** Costumed warrior **Edge:** Reeded **Size:** 26.8 mm.

Date	F	VF	XF	Unc	BU
1993 Proof	—	—	—	11.50	—

KM# 567 NUEVO PESO **Weight:** 7.7601 g. **Composition:** 0.9990 Silver .2498 oz. ASW **Subject:** Bajorrelieve Del El Tajin

Date	Mintage	F	VF	XF	Unc	BU
1993	100,000	—	—	—	6.50	—
1993 Proof	3,000	Value: 10.50				

KM# 572 NUEVO PESO **Weight:** 7.7601 g. **Composition:** 0.9990 Silver .2498 oz. ASW **Subject:** Chaac Mool

Date	Mintage	F	VF	XF	Unc	BU
1994 Proof	2,000	Value: 10.50				

KM# 593 PESO **Weight:** 7.7750 g. **Composition:** 0.9990 Silver .2500 oz. ASW **Subject:** Senor De Las Limas **Note:** Similar to 5 Pesos, KM#595.

Date	Mintage	F	VF	XF	Unc	BU
1996	10,000	—	—	—	4.00	—
1996 Proof	—	Value: 25.00				
1998 Matte	—	—	—	—	3.25	—

KM# 603 PESO **Ring Composition:** Stainless Steel **Center Composition:** Aluminum-Bronze **Note:** Similar to KM#550 but without N.

Date	F	VF	XF	Unc	BU
1996Mo	—	—	—	1.25	—
1998Mo	—	—	—	1.25	—
2001Mo	—	—	—	1.25	—
2002Mo	—	—	—	1.25	—

KM# 617 PESO **Weight:** 7.7759 g. **Composition:** 0.9990 Silver .2500 oz. ASW **Subject:** Disco De La Muerte **Obverse:** Mexican eagle

Date	F	VF	XF	Unc	BU
1997	—	—	—	4.00	—
1997 Proof	—	Value: 10.50			
1998 Matte	—	—	—	10.50	—

KM# 661 PESO **Weight:** 7.7759 g. **Composition:** 0.9990 Silver .2500 oz. ASW **Subject:** Jaguar **Obverse:** National emblem **Reverse:** Jaguar carving **Edge:** Reeded **Size:** 27 mm.

Date	F	VF	XF	Unc	BU
1998	—	—	—	4.00	—
1998 Proof	—	Value: 8.00			

KM# 551 2 NUEVO PESOS **Ring Composition:** Stainless Steel **Center Composition:** Aluminum-Bronze

Date	F	VF	XF	Unc	BU
1992	—	—	1.50	2.50	—
1993	—	—	1.00	2.35	—
1994	—	—	1.00	2.35	—
1995	—	—	1.00	2.35	—
1995 Proof	—	Value: 4.50			

KM# 645 2 NUEVO PESOS **Weight:** 15.4200 g. **Composition:** 0.9990 Silver .4953 oz. ASW **Subject:** Eagle Warrior **Obverse:** National arms **Reverse:** Costumed warrior **Edge:** Reeded **Size:** 32.9 mm.

Date	F	VF	XF	Unc	BU
1993 Proof	—	—	—	23.00	—

KM# 568 2 NUEVO PESOS **Weight:** 15.5516 g. **Composition:** 0.9990 Silver .4995 oz. ASW **Subject:** Bajorrelieve Del El Tajin

Date	Mintage	F	VF	XF	Unc	BU
1993	100,000	—	—	—	6.50	—
1993 Proof	3,000	Value: 10.50				

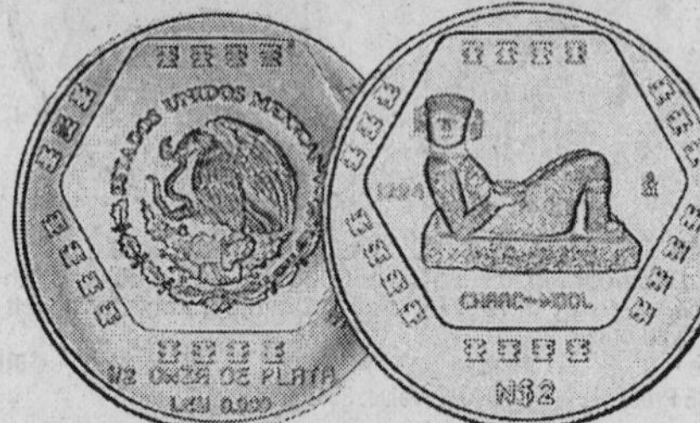

KM# 573 2 NUEVO PESOS **Weight:** 15.5516 g. **Composition:** 0.9990 Silver .4995 oz. ASW **Subject:** Chaac Mool

Date	Mintage	F	VF	XF	Unc	BU
1994 Matte	30,000	—	—	—	6.50	—
1994 Proof	2,000	Value: 10.50				

KM# 594 2 PESOS **Weight:** 15.5517 g. **Composition:** 0.9990 Silver .5000 oz. ASW **Subject:** Senor De Las Limasl **Note:** Similar to 5 Pesos, KM#595.

Date	Mintage	F	VF	XF	Unc	BU
1996	10,000	—	—	—	6.00	—
1996 Proof	—	Value: 18.50				
1998 Matte	—	—	—	—	8.50	—

KM# 604 2 PESOS **Ring Composition:** Stainless Steel **Center Composition:** Aluminum-Bronze **Note:** Similar to KM#551, but denomination without N.

Date	F	VF	XF	Unc	BU
1996Mo	—	—	—	2.50	—
1998Mo	—	—	—	2.50	—
2001Mo	—	—	—	2.50	—
2002Mo	—	—	—	2.50	—

KM# 618 2 PESOS **Weight:** 15.5517 g. **Composition:** 0.9990 Silver .5000 oz. ASW **Subject:** Disco De La Muerte **Obverse:** Mexican eagle

Date	F	VF	XF	Unc	BU
1997	—	—	—	6.00	—
1997 Proof	—	Value: 10.50			
1998	—	—	—	6.50	—

KM# 662 2 PESOS **Weight:** 15.5517 g. **Composition:** 0.9990 Silver .5000 oz. ASW **Subject:** Jaguar **Obverse:** National emblem **Reverse:** Jaguar carving **Edge:** Reeded **Size:** 33 mm.

Date	F	VF	XF	Unc	BU
1998	—	—	—	8.00	—
1998 Proof	—	Value: 16.00			

KM# 552 5 NUEVO PESOS **Ring Composition:** Stainless Steel **Center Composition:** Aluminum-Bronze

Date	F	VF	XF	Unc	BU
1992	—	—	2.00	4.00	—
1993	—	—	2.00	4.00	—
1994	—	—	2.00	4.00	—
1995 Proof	—	Value: 25.00			

KM# 583 5 NUEVO PESOS **Weight:** 31.1035 g. **Composition:** 0.9990 Silver .9991 oz. ASW **Subject:** Anciano Con Brasero **Reverse:** Kneeling figure sculpture

Date	Mintage	F	VF	XF	Unc	BU
1993	—	—	—	—	12.00	—
1993 Proof	2,655	Value: 37.50				

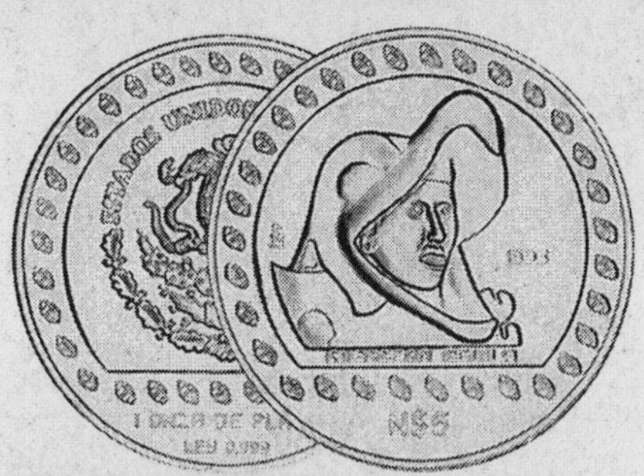

KM# 646 5 NUEVO PESOS **Weight:** 31.0500 g. **Composition:** 0.9990 Silver .9973 oz. ASW **Subject:** Eagle Warrior **Obverse:** National arms **Reverse:** Costumed warrior **Edge:** Reeded **Size:** 40 mm.

Date	F	VF	XF	Unc	BU
1993 Proof	—	Value: 46.00			

KM# 647 5 NUEVO PESOS **Weight:** 31.0000 g. **Composition:** 0.9990 Silver .9957 oz. ASW **Subject:** Xochipilli **Obverse:** National arms **Reverse:** Seated figure sculpture **Edge:** Reeded **Size:** 40 mm.

Date	F	VF	XF	Unc	BU
1993 Proof	—	Value: 45.00			

KM# 648 5 NUEVO PESOS **Weight:** 31.0000 g. **Composition:** 0.9990 Silver .9957 oz. ASW **Subject:** Brasco Efigie **Obverse:** National arms **Reverse:** Sculpture **Edge:** Reeded **Size:** 40 mm.

Date	F	VF	XF	Unc	BU
1993 Proof	—	Value: 45.00			

KM# 649 5 NUEVO PESOS **Weight:** 31.0000 g. **Composition:** 0.9990 Silver .9957 oz. ASW **Subject:** Huchucteotl **Obverse:** National arms **Reverse:** Aztec sculpture **Edge:** Reeded **Size:** 40 mm.

Date	F	VF	XF	Unc	BU
1993 Proof	—	Value: 45.00			

KM# 584 5 NUEVO PESOS **Weight:** 31.1035 g. **Composition:** 0.9990 Silver .9991 oz. ASW **Subject:** Carita Sonriente **Reverse:** Sculptured head

Date	Mintage	F	VF	XF	Unc	BU
1993	—	—	—	—	12.00	—
1993 Proof	3,000	Value: 36.00				

KM# 582 5 NUEVO PESOS **Weight:** 31.1035 g. **Composition:** 0.9990 Silver .9991 oz. ASW **Subject:** Palma Con Cecodrilo **Obverse:** National emblem **Reverse:** Aerial view of crocodile

Date	Mintage	F	VF	XF	Unc	BU
1993	—	—	—	—	12.00	—
1993 Proof	2,655	Value: 37.50				

KM# 569 5 NUEVO PESOS **Weight:** 31.1035 g. **Composition:** 0.9990 Silver .9991 oz. ASW **Subject:** Bajorrelieve Del El Tajin **Obverse:** Mexican eagle

Date	Mintage	F	VF	XF	Unc	BU
1993	100,000	—	—	—	12.00	—
1993 Proof	2,200	Value: 37.50				

KM# 574 5 NUEVO PESOS **Weight:** 31.1035 g. **Composition:** 0.9990 Silver .9991 oz. ASW **Subject:** Chaac Mool **Reverse:** Sculptured head

Date	Mintage	F	VF	XF	Unc	BU
1994 Matte	50,000	—	—	—	12.00	—
1994 Proof	2,200	Value: 37.50				

KM# 575 5 NUEVO PESOS **Weight:** 31.1035 g. **Composition:** 0.9990 Silver .9991 oz. ASW **Subject:** Chaac Mool **Reverse:** Tomb of Palenque Memorial Stone

Date	Mintage	F	VF	XF	Unc	BU
1994	—	—	—	—	12.00	—
1994 Proof	2,200	Value: 37.50				

KM# 577 5 NUEVO PESOS **Weight:** 31.1035 g. **Composition:** 0.9990 Silver .9991 oz. ASW **Subject:** Mascaron Del Dios Chaac **Reverse:** Elaborately carved wall segment

Date	Mintage	F	VF	XF	Unc	BU
1994	—	—	—	—	12.00	—
1994 Proof	2,200	Value: 37.50				

KM# 578 5 NUEVO PESOS **Weight:** 31.1035 g. **Composition:** 0.9990 Silver .9991 oz. ASW **Subject:** Dintel 26 **Reverse:** Two seated figures wall carving

Date	Mintage	F	VF	XF	Unc	BU
1994	—	—	—	—	12.00	—
1994 Proof	2,200	Value: 37.50				

KM# 588 5 NUEVO PESOS **Weight:** 27.0000 g. **Composition:** 0.9250 Silver .8030 oz. ASW **Subject:** Environmental Protection **Reverse:** Pacific Ridley Sea Turtle

Date	Mintage	F	VF	XF	Unc	BU
1994 Proof	20,000	Value: 37.50				

KM# 657 5 NUEVO PESOS **Weight:** 31.1710 g. **Composition:** 0.9990 Silver 1.0012 oz. ASW **Series:** Endangered Wildlife - Berrendo **Obverse:** National arms past and present **Reverse:** Peninsula antelope, giant cardon cactus in back **Size:** 40 mm.

Date	Mintage	F	VF	XF	Unc	BU
2000	50,000	—	—	—	27.50	—

KM# 652 5 NUEVO PESOS **Weight:** 31.1710 g. **Composition:** 0.9990 Silver 1.0012 oz. ASW **Series:** Endangered Wildlife **Subject:** Aguila Real **Obverse:** National arms past and present **Reverse:** Eagle on branch **Size:** 40 mm.

Date	Mintage	F	VF	XF	Unc	BU
2000	50,000	—	—	—	27.50	—

KM# 655 5 NUEVO PESOS **Weight:** 31.1710 g. **Composition:** 0.9990 Silver 1.0012 oz. ASW **Series:** Endangered Wildlife **Subject:** Cocodrilo de Rio **Obverse:** National arms past and present **Reverse:** Crocodile **Size:** 40 mm.

Date	Mintage	F	VF	XF	Unc	BU
2000	50,000	—	—	—	27.50	—

KM# 656 5 NUEVO PESOS **Weight:** 31.1710 g. **Composition:** 0.9990 Silver 1.0012 oz. ASW **Series:** Endangered Wildlife **Subject:** Nutria de Rio **Obverse:** National arms past and present **Reverse:** Nutria **Size:** 40 mm.

Date	Mintage	F	VF	XF	Unc	BU
2000	50,000	—	—	—	27.50	—

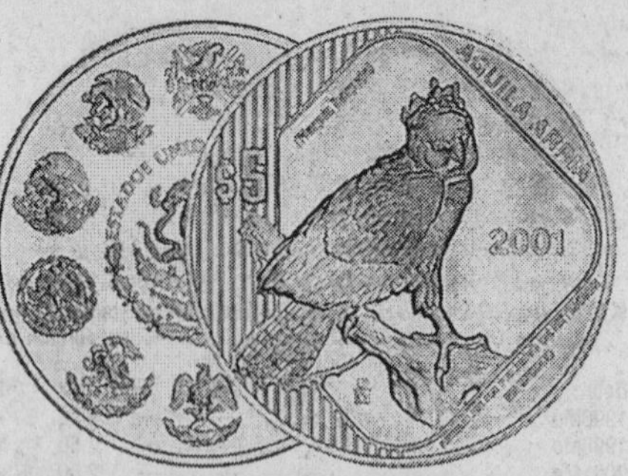

KM# 653 5 NUEVO PESOS **Weight:** 31.1710 g. **Composition:** 0.9990 Silver 1.0012 oz. ASW **Subject:** Aguila Arpia **Obverse:** National arms past and present **Reverse:** Harpie Eagle **Size:** 40 mm.

Date	Mintage	F	VF	XF	Unc	BU
2001	50,000	—	—	—	27.50	—

KM# 654 5 NUEVO PESOS **Weight:** 31.1710 g. **Composition:** 0.9990 Silver 1.0012 oz. ASW **Series:** Endangered Wildlife **Subject:** Oso Negro **Obverse:** National arms past and present **Reverse:** Black bear **Size:** 40 mm.

Date	Mintage	F	VF	XF	Unc	BU
2001	50,000	—	—	—	27.50	—

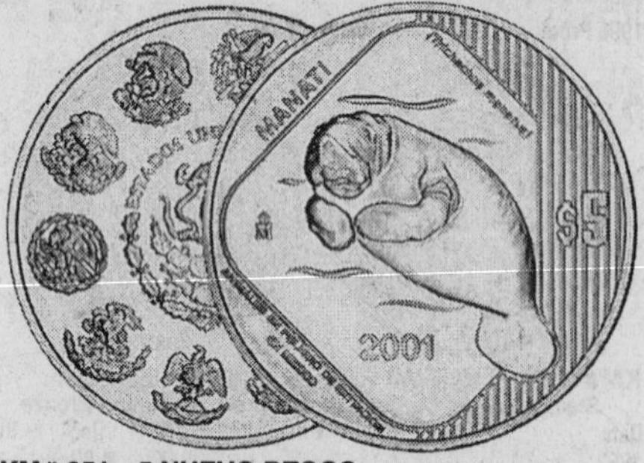

KM# 651 5 NUEVO PESOS **Weight:** 31.1710 g. **Composition:** 0.9990 Silver 1.0012 oz. ASW **Series:** Endangered Wildlife **Obverse:** National arms past and present **Reverse:** West Indian Manati **Edge:** Reeded **Size:** 40 mm.

Date	Mintage	F	VF	XF	Unc	BU
2001	50,000	—	—	—	27.50	—

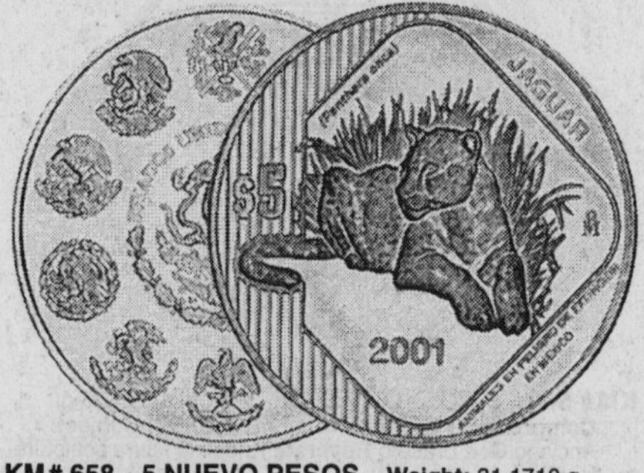

KM# 658 5 NUEVO PESOS **Weight:** 31.1710 g. **Composition:** 0.9990 Silver 1.0012 oz. ASW **Series:** Endangered Wildlife **Obverse:** National arms past and present **Reverse:** Jaguar resting **Size:** 40 mm.

Date	Mintage	F	VF	XF	Unc	BU
2001	50,000	—	—	—	27.50	—

KM# 659 5 NUEVO PESOS **Weight:** 31.1710 g. **Composition:** 0.9990 Silver 1.0012 oz. ASW **Series:** Endangered Wildlife **Obverse:** National arms past and present **Reverse:** Black-tailed Prairie dog **Size:** 40 mm.

Date	Mintage	F	VF	XF	Unc	BU
2001	50,000	—	—	—	27.50	—

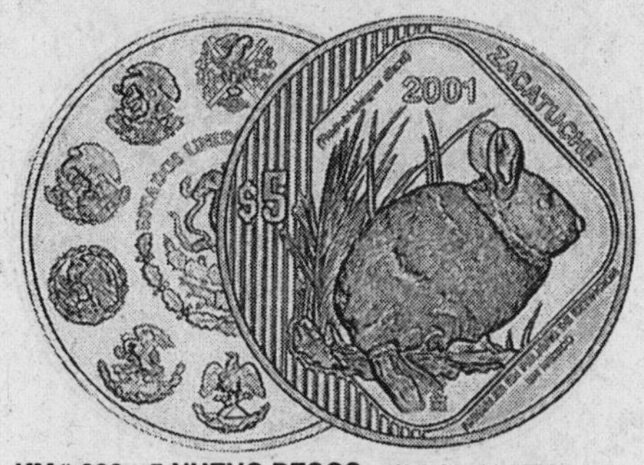

KM# 660 5 NUEVO PESOS **Weight:** 31.1710 g. **Composition:** 0.9990 Silver 1.0012 oz. ASW **Series:** Endangered Wildlife **Obverse:** National arms past and present **Reverse:** Volcano Rabbit **Size:** 40 mm.

Date	Mintage	F	VF	XF	Unc	BU
2001	50,000	—	—	—	27.50	—

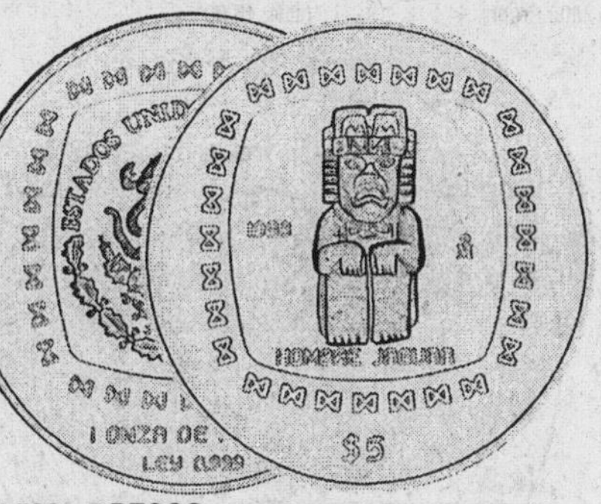

KM# 596 5 PESOS **Weight:** 31.1035 g. **Composition:** 0.9990 Silver 1.0000 oz. ASW **Subject:** Hombre Jaguar

Date	Mintage	F	VF	XF	Unc	BU
1996	30,000	—	—	—	13.50	—
1996 Proof	—	Value: 36.00				
1998 Matte	—	—	—	—	10.00	—

KM# 595 5 PESOS **Weight:** 31.1035 g. **Composition:** 0.9990 Silver 1.0000 oz. ASW **Subject:** Senor De Las Limas

Date	Mintage	F	VF	XF	Unc	BU
1996	30,000	—	—	—	12.00	—
1996 Proof	30,000	Value: 36.00				
1998 Matte	—	—	—	—	16.25	—

KM# 597 5 PESOS **Weight:** 31.1035 g. **Composition:** 0.9990 Silver 1.0000 oz. ASW **Subject:** El Luchador

Date	Mintage	F	VF	XF	Unc	BU
1996	30,000	—	—	—	13.50	—
1996 Proof	—	Value: 36.00				
1998 Matte	—	—	—	—	10.00	—

KM# 598 5 PESOS **Weight:** 31.1035 g. **Composition:** 0.9990 Silver 1.0000 oz. ASW **Subject:** Hacha Ceremonial

Date	Mintage	F	VF	XF	Unc	BU
1996 Proof	30,000	Value: 36.00				
1998 Matte	—	—	—	—	10.00	—

KM# 619 5 PESOS **Weight:** 31.1035 g. **Composition:** 0.9990 Silver 1.0000 oz. ASW **Subject:** Teohituacan - Disco de la Muerte **Obverse:** Eagle and snake

Date	Mintage	F	VF	XF	Unc	BU
1997 Proof	Est. 30,000	Value: 36.00				
1998	—	—	—	—	13.50	—

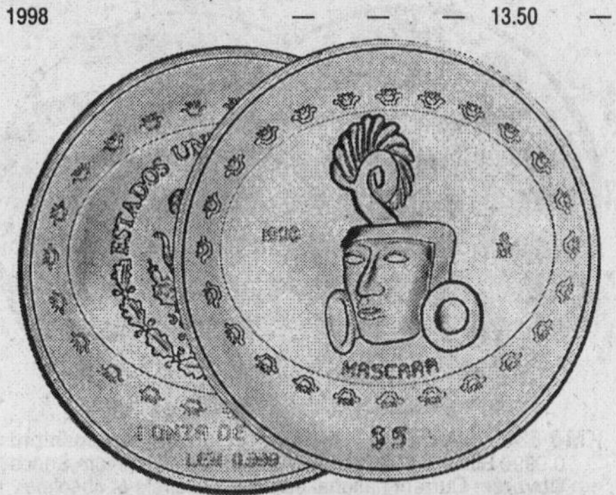

KM# 620 5 PESOS **Weight:** 31.1035 g. **Composition:** 0.9990 Silver 1.0000 oz. ASW **Subject:** Teohituacan - Mascara **Obverse:** Eagle and snake

Date	Mintage	F	VF	XF	Unc	BU
1997 Proof	Est. 30,000	Value: 36.00				
1998	—	—	—	—	13.50	—

KM# 621 5 PESOS **Weight:** 31.1035 g. **Composition:** 0.9990 Silver 1.0000 oz. ASW **Subject:** Teohituacan - Vasija **Obverse:** Eagle and snake

Date	Mintage	F	VF	XF	Unc	BU
1997	—	—	—	—	9.00	—
1997 Proof	Est. 30,000	Value: 36.00				
1998 Matte	—	—	—	—	13.50	—

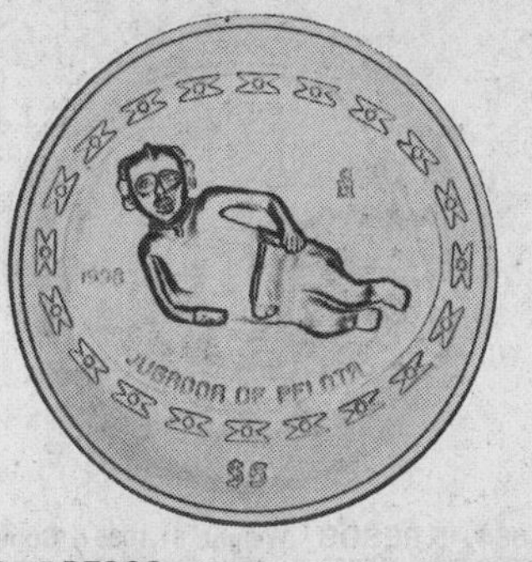

KM# 622 5 PESOS **Weight:** 31.1035 g. **Composition:** 0.9990 Silver 1.0000 oz. ASW **Subject:** Teohituacan - Jugador of Pelota **Obverse:** Eagle and snake

Date	Mintage	F	VF	XF	Unc	BU
1997	—	—	—	—	9.00	—
1997 Proof	Est. 30,000	Value: 36.50				
1998 Matte	—	—	—	—	10.00	—

KM# 629 5 PESOS **Weight:** 27.0000 g. **Composition:** 0.9250 Silver .8030 oz. ASW **Subject:** Jarabe Tapatio **Obverse:** Mexican emblem within circle of arms **Reverse:** Two dancers

Date	Mintage	F	VF	XF	Unc	BU
1997 Proof	20,000	Value: 30.00				

KM# 605 5 PESOS **Ring Composition:** Stainless Steel **Center Composition:** Aluminum-Bronze **Note:** Similar to KM#552 but deonomination without N.

Date	F	VF	XF	Unc	BU
1997Mo	—	—	—	5.50	—
1998Mo	—	—	—	5.50	—
2001Mo	—	—	—	5.50	—
2002Mo	—	—	—	5.50	—

KM# 663 5 PESOS **Weight:** 31.1035 g. **Composition:** 0.9990 Silver 1.0000 oz. ASW **Subject:** Jaguar **Obverse:** National emblem **Reverse:** Jaguar carving **Edge:** Reeded **Size:** 40 mm.

Date	F	VF	XF	Unc	BU
1998	—	—	—	18.00	—
1998 Proof	—	Value: 40.00			

KM# 664 5 PESOS **Weight:** 31.1035 g. **Composition:** 0.9990 Silver 1.0000 oz. ASW **Obverse:** National emblem **Reverse:** Sacerdote sculpture **Edge:** Reeded **Size:** 40 mm.

Date	F	VF	XF	Unc	BU
1998	—	—	—	18.00	—
1998 Proof	—	Value: 40.00			

KM# 630 5 PESOS **Weight:** 31.1800 g. **Composition:** 0.9990 Silver 1.0025 oz. ASW **Subject:** Millennium Series **Obverse:** Current national eagle within circle of obsolete versions **Reverse:** Butterfly, dates

Date	Mintage	F	VF	XF	Unc	BU
1999-2000 Proof	75,000	Value: 30.00				

KM# 640 5 PESOS **Weight:** 31.1030 g. **Composition:** 0.9990 Silver .9990 oz. ASW **Subject:** UNICEF **Obverse:** National arms **Reverse:** Two children flying kite **Edge:** Reeded **Size:** 40 mm.

Date	F	VF	XF	Unc	BU
1999	—	Value: 37.50			

KM# 666 5 PESOS **Weight:** 31.1035 g. **Composition:** 0.9990 Silver 1.0000 oz. ASW **Subject:** Serpiente con Craneo **Obverse:** National emblem **Reverse:** Large sculpture **Edge:** Reeded **Size:** 40 mm.

Date	F	VF	XF	Unc	BU
1998	—	—	—	18.00	—
1998 Proof	—	Value: 40.00			

KM# 631 5 PESOS **Weight:** 31.1800 g. **Composition:** 0.9990 Silver 1.0025 oz. ASW **Subject:** Millennium Series **Obverse:** Current national eagle within circle of obsolete versions **Reverse:** Stylized dove/hand of peace

Date	Mintage	F	VF	XF	Unc	BU
1999-2000 Proof	75,000	Value: 30.00				

KM# 670 5 PESOS **Weight:** 27.0000 g. **Composition:** 0.9250 Silver 0.803 oz. ASW **Series:** Ibero-America **Obverse:** Mexican arms within circle of other national arms **Reverse:** Cowboy trick riding two horses **Edge:** Reeded **Size:** 40 mm.

Date	F	VF	XF	Unc	BU
2000 Proof	—	Value: 45.00			

KM# 665 5 PESOS **Weight:** 31.1035 g. **Composition:** 0.9990 Silver 1.0000 oz. ASW **Subject:** Quetzalcoatle **Obverse:** National emblem **Reverse:** Quetzalcoatle sculpture **Edge:** Reeded **Size:** 40 mm.

Date	F	VF	XF	Unc	BU
1998	—	—	—	18.00	—
1998 Proof	—	Value: 40.00			

KM# 632 5 PESOS **Weight:** 31.1800 g. **Composition:** 0.9990 Silver 1.0025 oz. ASW **Subject:** Millennium Series **Obverse:** Current national eagle within circle of obsolete versions **Reverse:** Aztec bird design, denomination

Date	Mintage	F	VF	XF	Unc	BU
1999-2000 Proof	75,000	Value: 30.00				

KM# 627 5 PESOS **Weight:** 31.1035 g. **Composition:** 0.9990 Silver 1.0000 oz. ASW **Subject:** World Wildlife Fund **Obverse:** Mexican eagle

Date	Mintage	F	VF	XF	Unc	BU
1998 Proof	Est. 15,000	Value: 42.50				

KM# 635 5 PESOS **Weight:** 19.6000 g. **Composition:** 0.9250 Silver .6411 oz. ASW **Subject:** Millennium Series **Obverse:** Current national eagle within circle of obsolete versions **Reverse:** Naval training ship Cuauhtemoc

Date	F	VF	XF	Unc	BU
1999	—	Value: 35.00			

KM# 650 10 NUEVO PESOS **Weight:** 155.3100 g. **Composition:** 0.9990 Silver 4.9883 oz. ASW **Subject:** Piedra de Tizoc **Obverse:** National arms **Reverse:** Warrior capturing woman **Edge:** Reeded **Size:** 64 mm. **Note:** Illustration reduced.

Date	F	VF	XF	Unc	BU
1992 Proof	—	Value: 85.00			
1993	—	—	—	55.00	—

KM# 553 10 NUEVO PESOS **Ring Composition:** Aluminum-Bronze**Center Weight:** 11.1400 g. **Center Composition:** 0.9250 Silver .1666 oz. ASW

Date	F	VF	XF	Unc	BU
1992	—	—	—	7.50	—
1993	—	—	—	7.50	—
1994	—	—	—	7.50	—
1995	—	—	—	7.50	—

KM# 570 10 NUEVO PESOS **Center Weight:** 115.5175 g. **Center Composition:** 0.9990 Silver 4.9956 oz. ASW **Subject:** Piramide Del El Tajin **Size:** 64 mm. **Note:** Illustration reduced.

Date	Mintage	F	VF	XF	Unc	BU
1993	50,000	—	—	—	46.00	—
1993 Proof	3,000	Value: 78.00				

KM# 576 10 NUEVO PESOS **Center Weight:** 115.5175 g. **Center Composition:** 0.9990 Silver 4.9956 oz. ASW **Subject:** Piramide del Castillo **Size:** 64 mm. **Note:** Illustration reduced.

Date	Mintage	F	VF	XF	Unc	BU
1994	20,000	—	—	—	46.50	—
1994 Proof	1,000	Value: 80.00				

KM# 599 10 PESOS **Center Weight:** 1555.5175 g. **Center Composition:** 0.9990 Silver 5.0000 oz. ASW **Subject:** Cabeza Olmeca **Size:** 64 mm. **Note:** Illustration reduced.

Date	Mintage	F	VF	XF	Unc	BU
1996 Proof	10,000	Value: 80.00				
1998 Matte	—	—	—	—	46.00	—

KM# 606 10 PESOS **Center Weight:** 11.1400 g. **Center Composition:** 0.9250 Silver .1666 oz. ASW **Note:** Similar to KM#553, but denomination without N.

Date	F	VF	XF	Unc	BU
1996	—	—	—	7.50	—

KM# 623 10 PESOS **Weight:** 1555.5175 g. **Composition:** 0.9990 Silver 5.0000 oz. ASW **Subject:** Piramide Del Sol **Obverse:** Mexican eagle **Size:** 64 mm. **Note:** Illustration reduced.

Date	Mintage	F	VF	XF	Unc	BU
1997	—	—	—	—	50.00	—
1997 Proof	10,000	Value: 95.00				
1998 Matte	—	—	—	—	46.00	—

KM# 616 10 PESOS **Ring Composition:** Brass **Center Composition:** Copper-Nickel-Zinc **Subject:** Cabeza Olmeca **Obverse:** National emblem **Reverse:** Aztec design

Date	F	VF	XF	Unc	BU
1997	—	—	—	7.50	—
1998	—	—	—	7.50	—
1998	—	—	—	7.50	—

Note: Small date, date on brass ring

Date	F	VF	XF	Unc	BU
1998	—	—	—	7.50	—

Note: Large date, date partially on copper-nickel center

KM# 634 10 PESOS **Weight:** 155.7300 g. **Composition:** 0.9990 Silver 5.0018 oz. ASW **Subject:** Atlantes **Obverse:** National arms **Reverse:** Three curved statues

Date	F	VF	XF	Unc	BU
1998	—	—	—	50.00	—
1998 Proof	—	Value: 95.00			

KM# 633 10 PESOS **Weight:** 62.0300 g. **Composition:** 0.9990 Silver 1.9923 oz. ASW **Subject:** Millennium Series **Obverse:** Current national eagle within circle of obsolete versions **Reverse:** Old and modern buildings, dates

Date	Mintage	F	VF	XF	Unc	BU
1999-2000 Proof	75,000	Value: 55.00				

KM# 636 10 PESOS **Ring Composition:** Brass **Center Composition:** Copper-Nickel **Subject:** Millennium Series **Reverse:** Aztec carving

Date	F	VF	XF	Unc	BU
2000Mo	—	—	—	7.00	—
2001Mo	—	—	—	7.00	—

KM# 561 20 NUEVO PESOS **Ring Composition:** Aluminum-Bronze .2499 oz. **Center Composition:** Silver

Date	F	VF	XF	Unc	BU
1993	—	—	—	12.00	—
1994	—	—	—	12.00	—
1995	—	—	—	12.00	—

KM# 641 20 PESOS **Weight:** 6.2210 g. **Composition:** 0.9990 Gold .1998 oz. AGW **Subject:** UNICEF **Obverse:** National arms **Reverse:** Child playing with lasso **Edge:** Reeded **Size:** 21.9 mm.

Date	F	VF	XF	Unc	BU
1999	—	—	—	170	—

KM# 637 20 PESOS **Ring Composition:** Brass **Center Composition:** Copper-Nickel **Subject:** Xiutecuhtli **Reverse:** Aztec with torch

Date	F	VF	XF	Unc	BU
2000	—	—	—	15.00	—

KM# 638 20 PESOS **Ring Composition:** Brass **Center Composition:** Copper-Nickel **Subject:** Octavio Paz **Reverse:** Aztec with torch

Date	F	VF	XF	Unc	BU
2000	—	—	—	15.00	—

KM# 585 25 NUEVO PESOS **Weight:** 7.7758 g. **Composition:** 0.9990 Gold .2500 oz. AGW **Subject:** Hacha Ceremonial **Note:** Similar to 100 New Pesos, KM#587.

Date	Mintage	F	VF	XF	Unc	BU
1993	16,000	—	—	—	145	—
1993 Proof	800	Value: 250				

KM# 579 25 NUEVO PESOS **Weight:** 7.7758 g. **Composition:** 0.9990 Gold .2500 oz. AGW **Subject:** Personaje de Jaina **Reverse:** Seated figure

Date	Mintage	F	VF	XF	Unc	BU
1994	2,000	—	—	—	165	—
1994 Proof	500	Value: 300				

KM# 600 25 PESOS **Weight:** 7.7758 g. **Composition:** 0.9990 Gold .2500 oz. AGW **Subject:** Sacerdote **Note:** Similar to 100 Pesos, KM#602.

Date	Mintage	F	VF	XF	Unc	BU
1996	10,000	—	—	—	200	—
1996 Proof	—	Value: 250				

KM# 624 25 PESOS **Weight:** 7.7758 g. **Composition:** 0.9990 Gold .2500 oz. AGW **Subject:** Serpiente Emplumada **Obverse:** Mexican eagle **Note:** Similar to 100 Pesos, KM#626.

Date	Mintage	F	VF	XF	Unc	BU
1997	—	—	—	—	200	—
1997 Proof	10,000	Value: 250				

KM# 667 25 PESOS **Weight:** 7.7759 g. **Composition:** 0.9990 Gold 0.2498 oz. AGW **Subject:** Aguila **Obverse:** Mexican arms **Reverse:** Eagle sculpture **Edge:** Reeded **Size:** 23 mm.

Date	F	VF	XF	Unc	BU
1998	—	—	—	200	—
1998 Proof	—	Value: 265			

KM# 571 50 NUEVO PESOS **Ring Composition:** Brass **Center Weight:** 34.0000 g. **Center Composition:** 0.9250 Silver .5051 oz. ASW **Subject:** Nino Heroes

Date	F	VF	XF	Unc	BU
1993	—	—	—	28.00	—
1994	—	—	—	28.00	—
1995	—	—	—	28.00	—

KM# 586 50 NUEVO PESOS **Weight:** 15.5517 g. **Composition:** 0.9990 Gold .5000 oz. AGW **Subject:** Hacha Ceremonial **Note:** Similar to 100 New Pesos, KM#587.

Date	Mintage	F	VF	XF	Unc	BU
1993	16,000	—	—	—	275	—
1993 Proof	500	Value: 425				

KM# 580 50 NUEVO PESOS **Weight:** 15.5517 g. **Composition:** 0.9990 Gold .5000 oz. AGW **Subject:** Personaje de Jaina **Reverse:** Seated figure

Date	Mintage	F	VF	XF	Unc	BU
1994	1,000	—	—	—	300	—
1994 Proof	500	Value: 475				

KM# 482 50 PESOS **Weight:** 41.6666 g. **Composition:** 0.9000 Gold 1.2057 oz. AGW

Date	Mintage	F	VF	XF	Unc	BU
1943	89,000	—	—	—	BV	525

KM# 601 50 PESOS **Weight:** 15.5517 g. **Composition:** 0.9990 Gold .5000 oz. AGW **Subject:** Sacerdote **Note:** Similar to 100 Pesos, KM#602.

Date	Mintage	F	VF	XF	Unc	BU
1996	10,000	—	—	—	375	—
1996 Proof	—	Value: 425				

KM# 608 50 PESOS **Weight:** 15.5517 g. **Composition:** 0.9990 Silver .5000 oz. ASW **Note:** Similar to 50 New Pesos, KM#571 without "N" before denomination.

Date	F	VF	XF	Unc	BU
1996	—	—	—	22.00	—

KM# 625 50 PESOS **Weight:** 15.5517 g. **Composition:** 0.9990 Gold .5000 oz. AGW **Subject:** Serpiente Emplumada **Obverse:** Mexican eagle **Note:** Similar to 100 Pesos, KM#626.

Date	Mintage	F	VF	XF	Unc	BU
1997	—	—	—	—	350	—
1997 Proof	10,000	Value: 450				

KM# 668 50 PESOS **Weight:** 15.5517 g. **Composition:** 0.9990 Gold 0.4995 oz. AGW **Subject:** Aguila **Obverse:** Mexican arms **Reverse:** Eagle sculpture **Edge:** Reeded **Size:** 29 mm.

Date	F	VF	XF	Unc	BU
1998	—	—	—	350	—
1998 Proof	—	Value: 420			

KM# 587 100 NUEVO PESOS **Weight:** 31.1035 g. **Composition:** 0.9990 Gold 1.0000 oz. AGW **Subject:** Hacha Ceremonial

Date	Mintage	F	VF	XF	Unc	BU
1993	7,158	—	—	—	525	—
1993 Proof	500	Value: 650				

KM# 581 100 NUEVO PESOS **Weight:** 31.1035 g. **Composition:** 0.9990 Gold 1.0000 oz. AGW **Subject:** Personaje de Jaina

Date	Mintage	F	VF	XF	Unc	BU
1994	1,000	—	—	—	575	—
1994 Proof	500	Value: 700				

KM# 602 100 PESOS **Weight:** 31.1035 g. **Composition:** 0.9990 Gold 1.0000 oz. AGW **Subject:** Sacerdote

Date	Mintage	F	VF	XF	Unc	BU
1996	10,000	—	—	—	575	—
1996 Proof	—	Value: 600				

KM# 626 100 PESOS **Weight:** 31.1035 g. **Composition:** 0.9990 Gold 1.0000 oz. AGW **Subject:** Teohituacan - Serpiente Emplumada **Obverse:** Eagle and snake

Date	Mintage	F	VF	XF	Unc	BU
1997	—	—	—	—	600	—
1997 Proof	Est. 10,000	Value: 650				

KM# 669 100 PESOS **Weight:** 31.1035 g. **Composition:** 0.9990 Gold 0.999 oz. AGW **Subject:** Aguila **Obverse:** Mexican arms **Reverse:** Eagle sculpture **Edge:** Reeded **Size:** 34.5 mm.

Date	F	VF	XF	Unc	BU
1998	—	—	—	600	—
1998 Proof	—	Value: 670			

SILVER BULLION COINAGE

KM# 542 1/20 ONZA (1/20 Troy Ounce of Silver) **Weight:** 1.5551 g. **Composition:** 0.9990 Silver .0500 oz. ASW

Date	Mintage	F	VF	XF	Unc	BU
1991	50,017	—	—	—	—	3.50
1992	295,783	—	—	—	—	3.50
1992 Proof	5,000	Value: 10.00				
1993	100,000	—	—	—	—	3.50
1993 Proof	—	Value: 10.00				
1994	90,100	—	—	—	—	3.50
1994 Proof	10,000	Value: 10.00				
1995	50,000	—	—	—	—	3.50
1995 Proof	2,000	Value: 10.00				

KM# 609 1/20 ONZA (1/20 Troy Ounce of Silver) **Weight:** 1.5551 g. **Composition:** 0.9990 Silver .0500 oz. ASW **Obverse:** Mexican eagle **Reverse:** Winged Victory

Date	Mintage	F	VF	XF	Unc	BU
1996	50,000	—	—	—	—	3.50
1996 Proof	1,000	Value: 10.00				
1997	20,000	—	—	—	—	3.50
1997 Proof	800	Value: 10.00				
1998	6,400	—	—	—	—	3.50
1998 Proof	300	Value: 12.00				
1999	8,001	—	—	—	—	3.50
1999 Proof	600	Value: 10.00				
2000	57,500	—	—	—	—	3.50
2000 Proof	900	Value: 10.00				
2001	—	—	—	—	—	3.50
2001 Proof	—	Value: 10.00				
2002	—	—	—	—	—	3.50
2002 Proof	—	Value: 10.00				

KM# 543 1/10 ONZA (1/10 Troy Ounce of Silver)
Weight: 3.1103 g. **Composition:** 0.9990 Silver .1000 oz. ASW **Obverse:** Mexican eagle **Reverse:** Winged Victory

Date	Mintage	F	VF	XF	Unc	BU
1991	50,017	—	—	—	—	4.00
1992	299,983	—	—	—	—	4.00
1992 Proof	5,000	Value: 12.00				
1993	100,000	—	—	—	—	4.00
1993 Proof	—	Value: 12.00				
1994	90,100	—	—	—	—	4.00
1994 Proof	10,000	Value: 12.00				
1995	50,000	—	—	—	—	4.00
1995 Proof	2,000	Value: 12.00				

KM# 610 1/10 ONZA (1/10 Troy Ounce of Silver)
Weight: 3.1103 g. **Composition:** 0.9990 Silver .1000 oz. ASW **Obverse:** Mexican eagle **Reverse:** Winged Victory

Date	Mintage	F	VF	XF	Unc	BU
1996	50,000	—	—	—	—	4.00
1996 Proof	1,000	Value: 12.00				
1997	20,000	—	—	—	—	4.00
1997 Proof	800	Value: 12.00				
1998	6,400	—	—	—	—	4.00
1998 Proof	300	Value: 15.00				
1999	8,000	—	—	—	—	4.00
1999 Proof	600	Value: 12.00				
2000	27,500	—	—	—	—	4.00
2000 Proof	1,000	Value: 12.00				
2001	—	—	—	—	—	4.00
2001 Proof	—	Value: 12.00				
2002	—	—	—	—	—	4.00
2002 Proof	—	Value: 12.00				

KM# 544 1/4 ONZA (1/4 Troy Ounce of Silver)
Weight: 7.7758 g. **Composition:** 0.9990 Silver .2500 oz. ASW **Obverse:** Mexican eagle **Reverse:** Winged Victory

Date	Mintage	F	VF	XF	Unc	BU
1991	50,017	—	—	—	—	5.50
1992	104,000	—	—	—	—	5.50
1992 Proof	5,000	Value: 15.00				
1993	86,500	—	—	—	—	5.50
1993 Proof	—	Value: 15.00				
1994	90,100	—	—	—	—	5.50
1994 Proof	15,000	Value: 15.00				
1995	50,000	—	—	—	—	5.50
1995 Proof	2,000	Value: 15.00				

KM# 611 1/4 ONZA (1/4 Troy Ounce of Silver)
Weight: 7.7758 g. **Composition:** 0.9990 Silver .2500 oz. ASW **Obverse:** Mexican eagle **Reverse:** Winged Victory

Date	Mintage	F	VF	XF	Unc	BU
1996	50,000	—	—	—	—	5.50
1996 Proof	1,000	Value: 15.00				
1997	20,000	—	—	—	—	5.50
1997 Proof	800	Value: 15.00				
1998	6,400	—	—	—	—	5.50
1998 Proof	300	Value: 20.00				
1999	7,000	—	—	—	—	5.50
1999 Proof	600	Value: 15.00				
2000	21,000	—	—	—	—	5.50
2000 Proof	700	Value: 15.00				
2001	—	—	—	—	—	5.50
2001 Proof	—	Value: 15.00				
2002	—	—	—	—	—	5.50
2002 Proof	—	Value: 15.00				

KM# 545 1/2 ONZA (1/2 Troy Ounce of Silver)
Weight: 15.5517 g. **Composition:** 0.9990 Silver .5000 oz. ASW **Obverse:** Mexican eagle **Reverse:** Winged Victory

Date	Mintage	F	VF	XF	Unc	BU
1991	50,618	—	—	—	—	7.50
1992	119,000	—	—	—	—	7.50
1992 Proof	5,000	Value: 17.50				
1993	71,500	—	—	—	—	7.50
1993 Proof	—	Value: 17.50				
1994	90,100	—	—	—	—	7.50
1994 Proof	15,000	Value: 17.50				
1995	50,000	—	—	—	—	7.50
1995 Proof	2,000	Value: 17.50				

KM# 612 1/2 ONZA (1/2 Troy Ounce of Silver)
Weight: 15.5517 g. **Composition:** 0.9990 Silver .5000 oz. ASW **Obverse:** Mexican eagle **Reverse:** Winged Victory

Date	Mintage	F	VF	XF	Unc	BU
1996	50,000	—	—	—	—	7.50
1996 Proof	1,000	Value: 17.50				
1997	20,000	—	—	—	—	7.50
1997 Proof	800	Value: 17.50				
1998	6,400	—	—	—	—	7.50
1998 Proof	300	Value: 25.00				
1999	7,000	—	—	—	—	7.50
1999 Proof	600	Value: 17.50				
2000	20,000	—	—	—	—	7.50
2000 Proof	700	Value: 17.50				
2001	—	—	—	—	—	7.50
2001 Proof	—	Value: 17.50				
2002	—	—	—	—	—	7.50
2002 Proof	—	Value: 17.50				

KM# 494.1 ONZA (Troy Ounce of Silver) **Weight:** 31.1000 g. **Composition:** 0.9990 Silver 1.0000 oz. ASW **Subject:** Libertad

Date	Mintage	F	VF	XF	Unc	BU
1982	1,050,000	—	—	—	BV	12.00
1983	1,002,000	—	—	—	BV	12.00
1983 Proof	998	Value: 185				
1984	1,014,000	—	—	—	BV	12.00
1985	2,017,000	—	—	—	BV	12.00
1986	1,699,000	—	—	—	BV	12.50
1986 Proof	30,000	Value: 22.00				
1987	500,000	—	—	—	BV	35.00
1987 Proof	12,000	Value: 40.00				
1988	1,500,500	—	—	—	BV	30.00
1989	1,397,000	—	—	—	BV	22.00
1989 Proof	10,000	Value: 35.00				

KM# 494.2 ONZA (Troy Ounce of Silver) **Weight:** 31.1000 g. **Composition:** 0.9990 Silver 1.0000 oz. ASW **Edge:** Reeded

Date	Mintage	F	VF	XF	Unc	BU
1988 Proof	10,000	Value: 42.50				
1990	1,200,000	—	—	—	BV	12.50
1990 Proof	10,000	Value: 35.00				
1991	1,651,000	—	—	—	BV	14.50

KM# 494.3 ONZA (Troy Ounce of Silver) **Weight:** 31.1000 g. **Composition:** 0.9990 Silver 1.0000 oz. ASW **Subject:** Libertad **Obverse:** Eight dots below eagle's left talons **Reverse:** Revised design and lettering **Edge:** Reeded edge **Note:** Mule

Date	Mintage	F	VF	XF	Unc	BU
1991	Inc. above	—	—	—	BV	20.00
1992	2,458,000	—	—	—	BV	11.50
1992 Proof	10,000	Value: 32.00				

KM# 494.4 ONZA (Troy Ounce of Silver) **Weight:** 31.1000 g. **Composition:** 0.9990 Silver 1.0000 oz. ASW **Subject:** Libertad **Obverse:** Seven dots below eagle's left talons, dull claws on right talon, thick letters **Reverse:** Revised design and lettering **Edge:** Reeded edge **Note:** Mule

Date	Mintage	F	VF	XF	Unc	BU
1993	1,000,000	—	—	—	BV	11.50
1993 Proof	—	Value: 34.00				
1994	400,000	—	—	—	BV	14.00
1994 Proof	10,000	Value: 34.00				
1995	500,000	—	—	—	BV	12.50
1995 Proof	2,000	Value: 35.00				

KM# 494.5 ONZA (Troy Ounce of Silver) **Weight:** 31.1000 g. **Composition:** 0.9990 Silver 1.0000 oz. ASW **Subject:** Libertad **Obverse:** KM#494.3 **Reverse:** KM#494.2 **Edge:** Reeded edge **Note:** Mule

Date	Mintage	F	VF	XF	Unc	BU
1991 Proof	10,000	Value: 32.00				

KM# 613 ONZA (Troy Ounce of Silver) **Weight:** 33.6250 g. **Composition:** 0.9250 Silver 1.0000 oz. ASW **Obverse:** Mexican eagle **Reverse:** Winged Victory

Date	Mintage	F	VF	XF	Unc	BU
1996	300,000	—	—	—	—	12.00
1996 Proof	2,000	Value: 35.00				
1997	100,000	—	—	—	—	14.00
1997 Proof	1,500	Value: 35.00				
1998	67,000	—	—	—	—	17.50
1998 Proof	500	Value: 40.00				
1999	95,000	—	—	—	—	14.50
1999 Proof	600	Value: 40.00				
2000	340,000	—	—	—	—	14.00
2000 Proof	1,600	Value: 35.00				
2001	—	—	—	—	—	12.00
2001 Proof	—	Value: 32.50				
2002	—	—	—	—	—	12.00
2002 Proof	—	Value: 32.50				

KM# 639 ONZA (Troy Ounce of Silver) **Weight:** 31.1000 g. **Composition:** 0.9990 Silver 1.0000 oz. ASW **Subject:** Libertad **Obverse:** Modern Mexican eagle within circle of obsolete versions **Edge:** Reeded edge **Note:** Mule

Date	F	VF	XF	Unc	BU
2000	—	—	—	—	10.00
2000	— Value: 35.00				

KM# 614 2 ONZAS (2 Troy Ounces of Silver)
Weight: 62.2070 g. **Composition:** 0.9990 Silver 2.0000 oz. ASW **Subject:** Libertad **Obverse:** Mexican eagle **Reverse:** Winged Victory

Date	Mintage	F	VF	XF	Unc	BU
1996	50,000	—	—	—	—	22.00
1996 Proof	1,200	Value: 45.00				
1997	15,000	—	—	—	—	20.00
1997 Proof	1,300	Value: 45.00				
1998	7,000	—	—	—	—	28.50
1998 Proof	400	Value: 50.00				
1999	5,000	—	—	—	—	32.50
1999 Proof	280	Value: 70.00				
2000	7,500	—	—	—	—	30.00
2000 Proof	500	Value: 47.50				
2001	—	—	—	—	—	22.50
2001 Proof	—	Value: 45.00				
2002	—	—	—	—	—	22.50
2002 Proof	—	Value: 45.00				

KM# 615 5 ONZAS (5 Troy Ounces of Silver)
Weight: 155.5175 g. **Composition:** 0.9990 Silver 5.0000 oz. ASW **Subject:** Libertad **Obverse:** Mexican eagle **Reverse:** Winged Victory

Date	Mintage	F	VF	XF	Unc	BU
1996	20,000	—	—	—	—	50.00
1996 Proof	1,200	Value: 85.00				
1997	10,000	—	—	—	—	50.00
1997 Proof	1,300	Value: 85.00				
1998	3,500	—	—	—	—	60.00
1998 Proof	400	Value: 100				
1999	2,800	—	—	—	—	60.00
1999 Proof	100	Value: 150				
2000	4,000	—	—	—	—	48.50
2000 Proof	500	Value: 80.00				
2001	—	—	—	—	—	48.50
2001 Proof	—	Value: 80.00				
2002	—	—	—	—	—	48.50
2002 Proof	—	Value: 80.00				

GOLD BULLION COINAGE

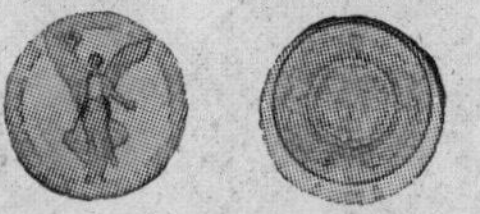

KM# 530 1/20 ONZA (1/20 Ounce of Pure Gold)
Weight: 1.7500 g. **Composition:** 0.9000 Gold .0500 oz. AGW **Obverse:** Winged Victory **Reverse:** Calendar stone

Date	F	VF	XF	Unc	BU
1987	—	—	—	—	BV+ 30%
1988	—	—	—	—	BV+30%

KM# 589 1/20 ONZA (1/20 Ounce of Pure Gold)
Weight: 1.5551 g. **Composition:** 0.9990 Gold .500 oz. AGW **Obverse:** Winged Victory **Reverse:** Eagle and snake

Date	Mintage	F	VF	XF	Unc	BU
1991	10,000	—	—	—	—	BV+30%
1992	65,225	—	—	—	—	BV+30%
1993	10,000	—	—	—	—	BV+30%
1994	10,000	—	—	—	—	BV+30%

KM# 642 1/20 ONZA (1/20 Ounce of Pure Gold)
Weight: 1.5551 g. **Composition:** 0.9990 Gold .500 oz. AGW **Obverse:** Winged Victory **Reverse:** Teocuitlatl and an indian working

Date	F	VF	XF	Unc	BU
2000 Proof	— Value: 50.00				

KM# 671 1/20 ONZA (1/20 Ounce of Pure Gold)
Weight: 1.5551 g. **Composition:** 0.9990 Gold 0.0499 oz. AGW **Obverse:** Mexican arms **Reverse:** Winged Victory facing left **Edge:** Reeded **Size:** 16 mm. **Note:** Design similar to KM#609. Value estimates do not include the high taxes and surcharges added to the issue prices by the Mexican Government.

Date	Mintage	F	VF	XF	Unc	BU
2000	5,300	—	—	—	—	—

KM# 628 1/15 ONZA (1/15 Ounce of Pure Gold)
Composition: 0.9990 Gold **Obverse:** Winged Victory above legend

Date	F	VF	XF	Unc	BU
1987	—	—	—	—	BV+25%

KM# 541 1/10 ONZA (1/10 Ounce of Pure Gold)
Weight: 3.1103 g. **Composition:** 0.9990 Gold .1000 oz. AGW

Date	Mintage	F	VF	XF	Unc	BU
1991	10,000	—	—	—	—	BV+20%
1992	50,777	—	—	—	—	BV+20%
1993	10,000	—	—	—	—	BV+20%
1994	10,000	—	—	—	—	BV+20%

KM# 672 1/10 ONZA (1/10 Ounce of Pure Gold)
Weight: 3.1103 g. **Composition:** 0.9990 Gold 0.0999 oz. AGW **Obverse:** Mexican arms **Reverse:** Winged Victory facing left **Edge:** Reeded **Size:** 20 mm. **Note:** Design similar to KM#610. Value estimates do not include the high taxes and surcharges added to the issue prices by the Mexican Government.

Date	Mintage	F	VF	XF	Unc	BU
2000	3,500	—	—	—	—	—

KM# 487 1/4 ONZA (1/4 Ounce of Pure Gold)
Weight: 8.6396 g. **Composition:** 0.9000 Gold .2500 oz. AGW **Note:** Similar to KM#488.

Date	Mintage	F	VF	XF	Unc	BU
1981	313,000	—	—	—	—	BV+11%

KM# 590 1/4 ONZA (1/4 Ounce of Pure Gold)
Weight: 7.7758 g. **Composition:** 0.9990 Gold .2500 oz. AGW **Obverse:** Winged Victory above legend **Reverse:** Eagle and snake

Date	Mintage	F	VF	XF	Unc	BU
1991	10,000	—	—	—	—	BV+11%
1992	28,106	—	—	—	—	BV+11%
1993	2,500	—	—	—	—	BV+11%
1994	2,500	—	—	—	—	BV+11%

KM# 673 1/4 ONZA (1/4 Ounce of Pure Gold)
Weight: 7.7758 g. **Composition:** 0.9990 Gold 0.2497 oz. AGW **Obverse:** Mexican arms **Reverse:** Winged Victory facing left **Edge:** Reeded **Size:** 26.9 mm. **Note:** Design similar to KM#611. Value estimates do not include the high taxes and surcharges added to the issue prices by the Mexican Government.

Date	Mintage	F	VF	XF	Unc	BU
2000	2,500	—	—	—	—	—

KM# 488 1/2 ONZA (1/2 Ounce of Pure Gold) **Weight:** 17.2792 g. **Composition:** 0.9000 Gold .5000 oz. AGW

Date	Mintage	F	VF	XF	Unc	BU
1981	193,000	—	—	—	—	BV+8%
1989 Proof	704	Value: 500				

KM# 591 1/2 ONZA (1/2 Ounce of Pure Gold)
Weight: 15.5517 g. **Composition:** 0.9990 Gold .5000 oz. AGW **Obverse:** Winged Victory above legend **Reverse:** Eagle and snake

Date	Mintage	F	VF	XF	Unc	BU
1991	10,000	—	—	—	—	BV+8%
1992	25,220	—	—	—	—	BV+8%
1993	2,500	—	—	—	—	BV+8%
1994	2,500	—	—	—	—	BV+8%

KM# 674 1/2 ONZA (1/2 Ounce of Pure Gold)
Weight: 15.5517 g. **Composition:** 0.9990 Gold 0.4995 oz. AGW **Obverse:** Mexican arms **Reverse:** Winged Victory facing left **Edge:** Reeded **Size:** 32.9 mm. **Note:** Design similar to KM#612. Value estimates do not include the high taxes and surcharges added to the issue prices by the Mexican Government.

Date	Mintage	F	VF	XF	Unc	BU
2000	1,500	—	—	—	—	—

KM# 489 ONZA (Ounce of Pure Gold) **Weight:** 34.5585 g. **Composition:** 0.9000 Gold 1.0000 oz. AGW **Note:** Similar to KM#488.

Date	Mintage	F	VF	XF	Unc	BU
1981	596,000	—	—	—	—	BV+3%
1985	—	—	—	—	—	BV+3%
1988	—	—	—	—	—	BV+3%

KM# 592 ONZA (Ounce of Pure Gold) **Weight:** 31.1035 g. **Composition:** 0.9990 Gold 1.0000 oz. AGW **Obverse:** Winged Victory above legend **Reverse:** Eagle and snake

Date	Mintage	F	VF	XF	Unc	BU
1991	109,193	—	—	—	—	BV+3%
1992	46,281	—	—	—	—	BV+3%
1993	10,000	—	—	—	—	BV+3%
1995	1,000	—	—	—	—	BV+3%

KM# 675 ONZA (Ounce of Pure Gold) **Weight:** 31.1035 g. **Composition:** 0.9990 Gold 0.999 oz. AGW **Obverse:** Mexican arms **Reverse:** Winged Victory facing left **Edge:** Reeded **Size:** 40 mm. **Note:** Design similar to KM#639. Value estimates do not include the high taxes and surcharges added to the issue prices by the Mexican Government.

Date	Mintage	F	VF	XF	Unc	BU
2000	2,730	—	—	—	—	—

PLATINUM BULLION COINAGE

KM# 538 1/4 ONZA (1/4 Ounce) **Weight:** 7.7775 g. **Composition:** 0.9990 Platinum .2500 oz. APW

Date	Mintage	F	VF	XF	Unc	BU
1989	704	Value: 300				

MEDALLIC COINAGE

KM# M49a ONZA (Troy Ounce of Silver) **Weight:** 33.6250 g. **Composition:** 0.9250 Silver 1.0000 oz. ASW **Obverse:** Mint mark above coin press

Date	Mintage	F	VF	XF	Unc	BU
1949	1,000,000	—	10.00	12.50	17.50	27.50

KM# M49b.1 ONZA (Troy Ounce of Silver) Weight: 33.6250 g. **Composition:** 0.9250 Silver 1.0000 oz. ASW **Obverse:** Wide spacing between DE MONEDA **Reverse:** Mint mark below balance scale **Note:** Type I

Date	Mintage	F	VF	XF	Unc	BU
1978	280,000	—	—	BV	7.50	16.50

KM# M49b.2 ONZA (Troy Ounce of Silver) Weight: 33.6250 g. **Composition:** 0.9250 Silver 1.0000 oz. ASW **Obverse:** Close spacing between DE MONEDA **Reverse:** Mint mark below balance scale **Note:** Type II

Date	F	VF	XF	Unc	BU
1978	—	—	BV	7.50	15.00

KM# M49b.3 ONZA (Troy Ounce of Silver) Weight: 33.6250 g. **Composition:** 0.9250 Silver 1.0000 oz. ASW **Obverse:** Close spacing between DE MONEDA **Reverse:** Left scale pan points to U in UNA **Note:** Type III

Date	Mintage	F	VF	XF	Unc	BU
1979	4,508,000	—	—	BV	6.75	13.50

KM# M49b.4 ONZA (Troy Ounce of Silver) Weight: 33.6250 g. **Composition:** 0.9250 Silver 1.0000 oz. ASW **Obverse:** Close spacing between DE MONEDA **Reverse:** Left scale pan points between U and N of UNA **Note:** Type IV

Date	F	VF	XF	Unc	BU
1979	—	—	BV	6.75	13.50

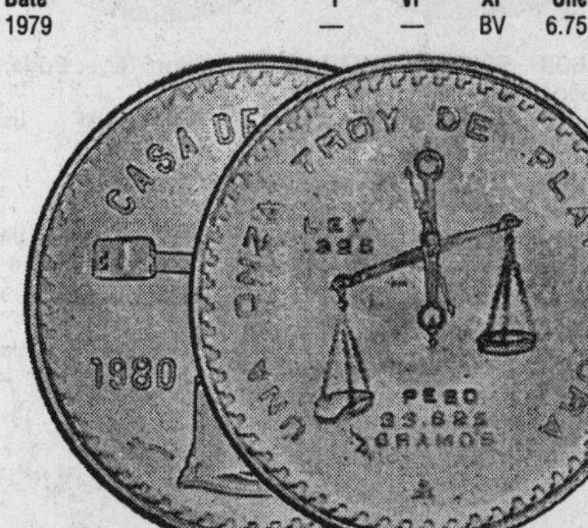

KM# M49b.5 ONZA (Troy Ounce of Silver) Weight: 33.6250 g. **Composition:** 0.9250 Silver 1.0000 oz. ASW **Obverse:** Close spacing between DE MONEDA **Reverse:** Left scale pan points between U and N of UNA **Note:** Type V

Date	Mintage	F	VF	XF	Unc	BU
1980	6,104,000	—	—	BV	6.75	11.00
1980/70	Inc. above	—	—	BV	6.75	14.50

PATTERNS

Including off metal strikes

KM#	Date	Mintage	Identification	Mkt Val
Pn170	1901	—	20 Centavos. Bronze.	425
Pn171	1904Zs FZ	—	Peso. Aluminum.	—
Pn172	1906Z	—	2 Centavos. Silver.	—
Pn173	1907Mo	—	50 Centavos. Silver. Plain edge.	4,000
Pn174	1907Mo	—	50 Centavos. Silver. Incuse lettered edge.	3,500
Pn175	1907	—	50 Centavos. Silver. Raised lettered edge.	3,500
Pn176	1908Mo	—	50 Centavos. Silver. Plain edge.	3,000
Pn177	1908Mo	—	Peso. Silver. Plain edge.	—
Pn178	1909Mo	—	Peso. Silver. Plain edge.	7,000
Pn179	1909Mo	—	Peso. Silver. Incuse lettered edge.	—
Pn180	1909Mo	—	Peso. Brass. Incuse lettered edge.	3,250
Pn181	1909Mo	—	Peso. Brass. Raised lettered edge.	3,250
Pn182	1909Mo	—	Peso. Bronzed Lead. Raised lettered edge.	—
Pn183	1909	—	Peso. Silver. Raised lettered edge.	—
Pn185	1911Mo	—	Peso. Silver. Plain edge.	2,500
Pn186	1911Mo	—	Peso. Bronze. Plain edge.	2,500
Pn187	1911	—	Peso. Brass. Plain edge.	2,500
Pn188	1914Mo	—	5 Centavos. Copper.	200
Pn189	1916Mo	—	20 Pesos. Copper.	1,150
Pn190	1936Mo	—	Centavo. Copper-Nickel.	—
Pn191	1936Mo	—	Peso. Silver.	3,200
Pn192	1945Mo	—	50 Centavos. Nickel.	1,250
Pn193	1947Mo	—	Peso. Silver.	2,500
Pn194	1947Mo	—	Peso. Silver.	2,500
Pn195	1947Mo	—	5 Pesos. Silver.	4,250
Pn196	1947Mo	—	Onza. 0.9250 Silver.	1,250
Pn197	1950Mo	—	5 Pesos. Silver.	1,650
Pn198	1951Mo	2	Onza. Silver.	4,000
Pn199	1954Mo	—	50 Centavos. Bronze.	—
Pn200	1954Mo	—	50 Centavos. Copper-Nickel.	—
Pn201	1955Mo	—	50 Centavos. Bronze.	625
Pn202	1955Mo	—	Peso. Copper-Nickel.	1,800
Pn203	1962Mo	—	5 Centavos. Copper-Nickel.	60.00
Pn204	1969Mo	—	Peso. Copper-Nickel.	2,000
Pn205	1969Mo	—	Peso. Copper-Nickel.	1,650
Pn206	1970Mo	—	10 Centavos. Bronze.	400
Pn207	1970Mo	—	25 Centavos. Copper-Nickel.	750
Pn208	1973Mo	—	10 Pesos. Aluminum-Bronze.	800
Pn209	1974Mo	—	10 Pesos. Copper-Nickel.	600
Pn210	1976Mo	16	100 Pesos. 0.7200 Silver.	—
Pn211	1978Mo	—	Onza. Silver.	3,000
Pn212	1978Mo	—	Onza. 0.9250 Silver.	2,500
Pn214	1978Mo	—	Onza. 0.9250 Silver.	2,000
Pn215	1978Mo	—	Onza. 0.9250 Silver.	1,750
Pn216	1979Mo	—	Onza. 0.9250 Silver.	2,000
Pn217	1979	—	20 Pesos.	—
Pn218	1980Mo	8	20 Centavos. Copper-Nickel.	—
Pn219	1980Mo	—	Peso. Brass.	350
Pn220	1980	—	10 Pesos.	—
Pn221	1980Mo	—	10 Pesos. Bronze.	750
Pn222	1980Mo	—	20 Pesos. Copper-Nickel.	300
Pn223	1980Mo	—	1/10 Onza. Silver.	90.00
Pn224	1981Mo	—	20 Centavos. Copper-Nickel. Small obverse design.	165
Pn225	1981Mo	—	20 Centavos. Copper-Nickel. Modified portrait.	135
Pn226	19xx	—	20 Centavos. Copper.	350
Pn227	1983Mo	—	50 Centavos.	650
Pn228	1983Mo	12	Peso. Stainless Steel.	550
Pn229	1983	—	5 Pesos. Bronze.	350
Pn230	1983	—	Onza. Silver. Libertad.	1,350
Pn231	1984Mo	—	50 Pesos. Copper-Nickel.	400
Pn232	ND	—	50 Pesos. Gold.	—
Pn233	1985	—	Peso. Copper.	325
pnA235	1985	—	Peso. Silver.	350
Pn235	1986Mo	—	Peso. Stainless Steel.	65.00
Pn236	1986	—	500 Pesos. Stainless Steel.	500
Pn237	1987	3	100 Pesos. Copper.	—
Pn238	1987	3	100 Pesos. Copper-Nickel.	—
Pn239	1988	3	100 Pesos. Brass.	—
Pn240	1988Mo	3	500 Pesos. Aluminum-Brass.	500
Pn241	1988Mo	—	Onza. Silver. Plain edge.	—
Pn242	1990Mo	—	50000 Pesos. Copper-Nickel.	650
Pn243	1990	—	100000 Pesos. Bronze.	650
pnA243	1990	—	50000 Pesos. Silver.	800
Pn244	1991	—	100 Pesos. Aluminum.	275
Pn245	1991	—	200 Pesos. Aluminum.	200
Pn246	1991	—	500 Pesos. Bronze.	400
Pn247	1991	—	1000 Pesos. Bronze.	35.00
Pn248	1991Mo	—	2000 Pesos. Bronze.	400
Pn249	1991Mo	—	2000 Pesos. Steel.	400
Pn250	1991Mo	—	2000 Pesos.	275

TRIAL STRIKES

KM#	Date	Mintage	Identification	Mkt Val
TS15	190-	—	8 Reales. Bronze-Plated Lead.	—

KM#	Date	Mintage	Identification	Mkt Val
TS16	1980	—	1/10 Onza. Copper.	75.00
TS17	1980	—	1/10 Onza. Silver.	125

MINT SETS

KM#	Date	Mintage	Identification	Issue Price	Mkt Val
MSA2	1977 (9)	—	434.1, 434.2, 442, 452, 460 thick date, 460 thin date, 472, 477.1, 483.2, Type II for 3-ring binder	—	85.00
MS2	1978 (9)	500	434.1, 434.2, 442, 452, 460 open 8, 460 closed 8, 472, 477.2, 483.2, Type I flat pack	—	150
MS3	1978 (9)	—	KM434.1, 434.2, 442, 452, 460 open 8, 460 closed 8, 472, 477.2, 483.2, Type II for 3-ring binder	—	65.00
MS4	1979 (8)	—	KM434.2, 442, 452 square 9, 452 round 9, 460 (2), 477.2, 483.2, Type I flat pack	11.00	8.00
MS5	1979 (8)	—	KM434.1, 434.2, 442, 452 square 9, 452 round 9, 460, 477.2, 483.2, Type II for 3-ring binder	11.00	9.00
MS6	1980 (9)	—	KM434.2, 442, 452 square 9, 452 round 9, 460 open 8, 460 closed 8, 477.2, 485-486	4.20	11.00
MS7	1981 (9)	—	KM442 open 8, 442 closed 8, 452 rectangular 9, 452 round 9, 460 open 8, 460 closed 8, 477.2, 485, 486	4.20	11.00
MS8	1982 (7)	—	KM442, 452, 460, 477.2, 485, 486, 490	—	15.00
MS10	1983 (11)	—	KM442 (2), 452 (2), 460 (2), 490 (1), 491 (2), 492 (2) for 3-ring plastic set	—	12.50
MS9	1983 (11)	—	KM442 (2), 452 (2), 460 (2), 490 (1), 491 (2), 492 (2), hard case set	—	12.50
MS11	1984 (8)	—	KM485, 486, 490, 491, 493, 495 (2), 496	—	17.50
MS12	1985 (12)	—	KM477.2, 485, 493 (2), 495 (2), 496, 502, 508, 509, 510, 512	—	16.00
MS14	1985/1986 (7)	—	KM493, 495, 496, 502, 508, 509, 512	—	18.50
MS13	1986 (7)	—	KM493, 495, 496, 508, 512, 525, 529	—	18.00
MS15	1987 (9)	—	KM493, 495 (2), 496, 502 (2), 512, 529 (2)	—	35.00
MS16	1988 (8)	—	KM493, 495a, 502, 508, 512, 529, 531, 536	—	20.00
MS17	1996 (6)	—	KM546-549, 603-604	12.00	15.00

PROOF SETS

KM#	Date	Mintage	Identification	Issue Price	Mkt Val
PS1	1982/1983 (8)	998	KM442, 452, 460, 485, 477.2, 486, 490, 494.1	495	275
PS2	1982/1983 (8)	—	KM460, 477.2, 485, 486, 490, 491, 492, PnB169 (in white box with Mo. in gold)	—	—
PS3	1982/1983 (7)	23	KM460, 477.2, 485, 486, 490, 491, 492 (in white box with Mo in gold)	—	500
PS4	1982/1983 (7)	17	KM460, 477.2, 485, 486, 490, 491, 492 (in white box)	—	500
PS5	1982/1983 (7)	8	KM460, 477.2, 485, 486, 490, 491, 492 (in white box)	—	500
PS6	1983 (7)	3	KM460, 477.2, 485, 486, 490, 491, 492	—	—
PS10	1985 (3)	—	KM503-505 (in blue box)	—	60.00
PS11	1985 (2)	—	KM511, 513	—	350
PS7	1985/1986 (12)	—	KM497a-499a, 503-505, 514-515, 519, 521, 523-524	—	250
PS8	1985 (4)	—	KM500.2-501.2, 506.2, 507.2	—	700
PS9	1985 (3)	—	KM499a, 514, 515 (in blue box)	—	60.00
PS12	1989 (3)	704	KM488, 494.1, 538, Rainbow	730	850
PS13	1992 (5)	5,000	KM494.3, 542-545	—	87.50
PS14	1993 (5)	5,000	KM494.4, 542-545	—	87.50
PS15	1994 (5)	5,000	KM494.4, 542-545	—	85.00
PS16	1995 (7)	—	KM546-550, 552, 553, 555	45.00	45.00

MEXICO-REVOLUTIONARY

Revolution, 1910-1917

The Mexican independence movement, which is of interest and concern to collectors because of the warfare induced activity of local and state mints, began with the Sept. 16, 1810 march on the capital led by Father Miguel Hidalgo, a well-intentioned man of imagination and courage who proved to be an inept organizer and leader. Hidalgo was captured and executed within 10 months. His revolution, led by such as Morelos, Guerrero and Iturbide, continued and culminated in Mexican independence in 1821. Turbulent years followed. From 1821 to 1877 there were two emperors, several dictators and enough presidents to provide a change of government on the average of once every nine months. Porfirio Diaz, who had the longest tenure of any 19th century dictator in Latin American history, seized power in 1877 and did not relinquish it until 1911.

The final phase of Mexico's lengthy revolutionary period began in 1910 and lasted through the adoption of a liberal constitution and the election of a new congress in 1917. The 1910-1917 revolution was agrarian in character and intended to destroy the regime of Diaz and make Mexico economically and diplomatically independent. The republic experienced a state of upheaval that saw most of the leading figures of the revolution (Villa, Carranza, Obregon, Zapata, Calles) fighting each other at one time or another. Carranza eventually emerged as the most powerful figure of the early revolution. As *de-facto* president in 1916, he convened a constitutional convention, which produced a constitution in which the aims of the revolution were formulized. Obregon, perhaps the ablest general and wiliest politician of the lot, became Mexico's elected president in 1920, bringing the most disastrous but significant decade in Mexico's history to an end.

AGUASCALIENTES

Aguascalientes is a state in central Mexico. Its coin issues, struck by authority of Pancho Villa, represent his deepest penetration into the Mexican heartland. Lack of silver made it necessary to make all denominations in copper.

FRANCISCO "PANCHO" VILLA

FRANCISCO PACHO VILLA REVOLUTIONARY COINAGE

KM# 601 CENTAVO **Composition:** Copper

Date	VG	F	VF	XF	Unc
1915 Large date, reeded edge	25.00	40.00	60.00	90.00	—
1915 Large date, plain edge	250	350	450	—	—
1915 Small date, reeded edge	20.00	30.00	50.00	75.00	—
1915 Small date, plain edge	30.00	50.00	75.00	115	—

KM# 601a CENTAVO **Composition:** Silver

Date	Mintage	F	VF	XF	Unc	BU
1915 Large date	50	—	325	525	—	—
1915 Small date	Inc. above	—	325	525	—	—

KM# 602.1 2 CENTAVOS **Composition:** Copper

Date	VG	F	VF	XF	Unc
1915 Round front 2, plain edge	40.00	100	200	350	—

KM# 602.2 2 CENTAVOS **Composition:** Copper

Date	VG	F	VF	XF	Unc
1915 Square front 2, reeded edge	35.00	60.00	85.00	200	—
1915 Square front 2, plain edge	40.00	70.00	100	225	—

KM# 602a 2 CENTAVOS **Composition:** Silver

Date	Mintage	F	VF	XF	Unc	BU
1915	50	—	600	1,000	—	—

KM# 603 5 CENTAVOS **Composition:** Copper

Date	VG	F	VF	XF	Unc
1915 Plain edge; Rare	—	—	—	—	—
1915 Reeded edge	10.00	20.00	30.00	45.00	—

KM# 604.1 5 CENTAVOS **Composition:** Copper
Reverse: Vertically shaded 5

Date	VG	F	VF	XF	Unc
1915 Reeded edge	10.00	15.00	25.00	35.00	—
1915 Plain edge	100	150	225	325	—

KM# 604.2 5 CENTAVOS **Composition:** Copper
Reverse: Horizontally shaded 5

Date	VG	F	VF	XF	Unc
1915 Reeded edge	15.00	20.00	35.00	50.00	—
1915 Plain edge	20.00	30.00	50.00	80.00	—

KM# 604a 5 CENTAVOS **Composition:** Silver

Date	Mintage	F	VF	XF	Unc	BU
1915	50	—	1,000	2,000	—	—

KM# 606 20 CENTAVOS **Composition:** Copper **Obverse:** Blunt winged eagle **Reverse:** With wavy-bottomed 2

Date	VG	F	VF	XF	Unc
1915 Reeded edge	4.50	6.00	12.00	35.00	—

KM# 605 20 CENTAVOS **Composition:** Copper
Obverse: Blunt winged eagle **Reverse:** With flat-bottomed 2

Date	VG	F	VF	XF	Unc
1915 Reeded edge	4.50	8.00	12.00	35.00	—

KM# 605a 20 CENTAVOS **Composition:** Silver
Obverse: Blunt winged eagle **Reverse:** With flat-bottomed 2
Note: Piedfort.

Date	Mintage	F	VF	XF	Unc	BU
1915 Plain edge	50	—	1,200	2,000	—	—

KM# 600 20 CENTAVOS **Composition:** Copper
Obverse: Pointed winged eagle **Reverse:** With wavy-bottomed 2

Date	VG	F	VF	XF	Unc
1915 Reeded edge	15.00	20.00	35.00	60.00	—

KM# 600a 20 CENTAVOS **Composition:** Silver
Obverse: Pointed winged eagle **Reverse:** With wavy-bottomed 2

Date	VG	F	VF	XF	Unc
1915	800	1,200	1,600	2,000	—

Note: Varieties exist with both plain and milled edges and many variations in the shading of the numerals

CHIHUAHUA

Chihuahua is a northern state of Mexico bordering the U.S. It was the arena that introduced Pancho Villa to the world. Villa, an outlaw, was given a title when asked by Madero to participate in maintaining order during Madero's presidency. After Madero's death in February 1913, Villa became a persuasive leader. Chihuahua was where he made his first coins - the Parral series. The *Army of the North* pesos also came from this state. This coin helped Villa recruit soldiers because of his ability to pay in silver while others were paying in worthless paper money.

HIDALGO DEL PARRAL
Fuerzas Constitucionalistas

REVOLUTIONARY COINAGE

KM# 607 2 CENTAVOS **Composition:** Copper

Date	VG	F	VF	XF	Unc
1913	2.50	4.00	8.00	15.00	—

KM# 607a 2 CENTAVOS **Composition:** Brass

Date	VG	F	VF	XF	Unc
1913	80.00	100	125	250	—

KM# 608 50 CENTAVOS **Composition:** Silver **Edge:** Reeded edge

Date	VG	F	VF	XF	Unc
1913	9.00	20.00	30.00	60.00	—

KM# 609 50 CENTAVOS **Composition:** Silver
Edge: Plain edge

Date	VG	F	VF	XF	Unc
1913	40.00	60.00	80.00	100	—

KM# 609a 50 CENTAVOS **Composition:** Copper
Edge: Plain edge

Date	VG	F	VF	XF	Unc
1913 rare	100	200	275	350	—

KM# 610 PESO **Composition:** Silver **Reverse:** 1 through PESO and ball, BOLITA

Date	VG	F	VF	XF	Unc
1913	1,000	1,400	2,000	2,400	—

KM# 611 PESO **Composition:** Silver **Obverse:** Similar to KM#610 **Reverse:** 1 above PESO

Date	VG	F	VF	XF	Unc
1913	35.00	40.00	55.00	135	—

Note: Well struck counterfeits of this coin exist with the dot at the end of the word Peso even with the bottom of the O. On legitimate pieces the dot is slightly higher

CONSTITUTIONALIST ARMY

Ejercito Constitucionalista

REVOLUTIONARY COINAGE

KM# 612 5 CENTAVOS **Composition:** Copper **Reverse:** Small rosettes at date

Date	VG	F	VF	XF	Unc
1914	20.00	30.00	50.00	80.00	—

KM# 613 5 CENTAVOS **Composition:** Copper **Reverse:** Large ornamental spear heads at date **Note:** Numerous varieties exist.

Date	VG	F	VF	XF	Unc
1914	1.00	2.50	4.00	8.00	—
1915	1.00	2.50	40.00	8.00	—

KM# 613a 5 CENTAVOS **Composition:** Brass **Reverse:** Large ornamental spear heads at date **Note:** Numerous varieties exist.

Date	VG	F	VF	XF	Unc
1914	2.00	3.00	8.00	10.00	—
1915	2.00	3.00	8.00	10.00	—

KM# 613b 5 CENTAVOS **Composition:** Cast Copper **Reverse:** Large ornamental spear heads at date

Date	VG	F	VF	XF	Unc
1914	75.00	150	250	350	—

KM# 614 5 CENTAVOS **Composition:** Copper **Reverse:** Double lined V

Date	VG	F	VF	XF	Unc
1915 MS	150	250	325	500	—
1915 SS Unique	—	—	—	—	—

KM# 614a 5 CENTAVOS **Composition:** Copper **Reverse:** Solid V

Date	VG	F	VF	XF	Unc
1915 Rare	—	—	—	—	—

KM# 614b 5 CENTAVOS **Composition:** Copper **Obverse:** KM#614 **Reverse:** Reverse of KM#613 **Note:** Mule.

Date	VG	F	VF	XF	Unc
1915	—	350	—	—	—

KM# 614c 5 CENTAVOS **Composition:** Copper **Obverse:** KM#614 **Reverse:** Obverse of KM#612 **Note:** Mule.

Date	VG	F	VF	XF	Unc
1915 Rare	—	—	—	—	—

KM# 615 10 CENTAVOS **Composition:** Copper

Date	VG	F	VF	XF	Unc
1915	1.25	2.50	3.50	5.00	—

KM# 615a 10 CENTAVOS **Composition:** Brass

Date	VG	F	VF	XF	Unc
1915	1.75	5.00	15.00	20.00	—

Note: Many varieties exist

ARMY OF THE NORTH

Ejercito Del Norte

REVOLUTIONARY COINAGE

KM# 619 PESO **Composition:** Silver

Date	VG	F	VF	XF	Unc
1915	15.00	25.00	35.00	65.00	—

KM# 619a PESO **Composition:** Copper

Date	VG	F	VF	XF	Unc
1915	450	750	1,000	1,500	—

KM# 619b PESO **Composition:** Brass **Note:** Uniface obverse

Date	VG	F	VF	XF	Unc
1915 Rare	—	—	—	—	—

PATTERNS

Constitutionalist Army

KM#	Date	Mintage	Identification	Mkt Val
Pn1	1913	—	Peso. Silver.	11,000
Pn2.1	1914	—	50 Centavos. Copper. Reeded edge.	1,000
Pn2.2	1914	—	50 Centavos. Copper. Plain edge.	1,200

Note: Specimens exist in silver plated copper

KM#	Date	Mintage	Identification	Mkt Val
Pn3	1914	—	Peso. Copper.	2,000
Pn4	1914	—	Peso. Silver.	—

Note: Silver or silver-plated copper pieces are modern fantasies

DURANGO

A state in north central Mexico. Another area of operation for Pancho Villa. The *Muera Huerta* peso originates in this state. The coins were made in Cuencame under the orders of Generals Cemceros and Contreras.

CUENCAME

Muera Huerta (Death to Huerta)

REVOLUTIONARY COINAGE

KM# 620 PESO **Composition:** Silver **Reverse:** 1914 below UN PESO with three stars at each side

Date	VG	F	VF	XF	Unc
1914	800	1,400	1,800	3,500	—

KM# 621 PESO **Composition:** Silver **Obverse:** Continuous border **Reverse:** Continuous border

Date	VG	F	VF	XF	Unc
1914	60.00	90.00	120	200	450

KM# 621a PESO **Composition:** Copper **Obverse:** Continuous border **Reverse:** Continuous border **Note:** Varieties exist.

Date	VG	F	VF	XF	Unc
1914	250	425	650	1,200	—

KM# 621b PESO **Composition:** Brass

Date	VG	F	VF	XF	Unc
1914	—	600	800	1,500	—

KM# 622 PESO **Composition:** Silver **Obverse:** Dot and dash border **Reverse:** Continuous border

Date	VG	F	VF	XF	Unc
1914	60.00	100	150	225	500

Note: The so-called 20 Pesos gold Muera Huerta pieces are modern fantasies. Refer to Unusual World Coins, 3rd edition, ©1989, Krause Publications, Inc

ESTADO DE DURANGO

REVOLUTIONARY COINAGE

KM# 625 CENTAVO **Composition:** Copper

Date	VG	F	VF	XF	Unc
1914	2.00	3.00	5.00	7.50	—

KM# 625a CENTAVO **Composition:** Brass

Date	VG	F	VF	XF	Unc
1914	9.00	15.00	20.00	30.00	—

KM# 625b CENTAVO **Composition:** Lead

Date	VG	F	VF	XF	Unc
1914	20.00	40.00	65.00	90.00	—

KM# 625c CENTAVO **Composition:** Copper **Obverse:** Obverse of KM#625 **Reverse:** Obverse of KM#625

Date	VG	F	VF	XF	Unc
1914	25.00	50.00	80.00	125	—

KM# 624 CENTAVO **Composition:** Cast Lead **Reverse:** Retrograde N

Date	VG	F	VF	XF	Unc
1914	45.00	75.00	100	200	—

KM# 626 CENTAVO **Composition:** Copper

Date	VG	F	VF	XF	Unc
1914	15.00	20.00	35.00	45.00	—

KM# 626a CENTAVO **Composition:** Brass

Date	VG	F	VF	XF	Unc
1914	50.00	75.00	100	250	—

KM# 626b CENTAVO **Composition:** Lead

Date	VG	F	VF	XF	Unc
1914	20.00	25.00	40.00	60.00	—

Note: Varieties in size exist

KM# 627 CENTAVO **Composition:** Copper **Obverse:** Three stars below date **Reverse:** Retrograde N

Date	VG	F	VF	XF	Unc
1914	6.00	10.00	15.00	20.00	—

KM# 627a CENTAVO **Composition:** Lead **Obverse:** Three stars below date **Reverse:** Retrograde N

Date	VG	F	VF	XF	Unc
1914	20.00	30.00	40.00	50.00	—

KM# 628 CENTAVO **Composition:** Aluminum **Obverse:** Eagle on cactus

Date	VG	F	VF	XF	Unc
1914	0.65	1.00	2.00	3.00	—

KM# 629 5 CENTAVOS **Composition:** Copper **Obv. Legend:** ESTADO DE DURANGO **Reverse:** Large 5

Date	VG	F	VF	XF	Unc
1914	1.25	2.00	4.00	7.00	—

KM# 630 5 CENTAVOS **Composition:** Copper **Obv. Legend:** E. DE DURANGO **Reverse:** Thin 5

Date	VG	F	VF	XF	Unc
1914	125	275	375	600	—

KM# 631 5 CENTAVOS **Composition:** Copper **Obv. Legend:** E. DE DURANGO **Reverse:** Thick 5

Date	VG	F	VF	XF	Unc
1914	1.25	2.00	4.00	7.50	—

KM# 631a 5 CENTAVOS **Composition:** Brass **Obv. Legend:** E. DE DURANGO **Reverse:** Thick 5

Date	VG	F	VF	XF	Unc
1914	30.00	40.00	50.00	85.00	—

KM# 631b 5 CENTAVOS **Composition:** Lead **Obv. Legend:** E. DE DURANGO **Reverse:** Thick 5

Date	VG	F	VF	XF	Unc
1914	45.00	70.00	100	180	—

KM# 632 5 CENTAVOS **Composition:** Copper **Obv. Legend:** E. DE DURANGO **Reverse:** Denomination V

Date	VG	F	VF	XF	Unc
1914	3.00	5.00	9.00	20.00	—

KM# 632a 5 CENTAVOS **Composition:** Lead **Obv. Legend:** E. DE DURANGO **Reverse:** Denomination V

Date	VG	F	VF	XF	Unc
1914	50.00	75.00	100	150	—

KM# 633 5 CENTAVOS **Composition:** Lead **Obverse:** Three stars below 1914 **Reverse:** 5 CVS

Date	VG	F	VF	XF	Unc
1914	—	400	800	—	—

KM# 634 5 CENTAVOS **Composition:** Brass

Date	VG	F	VF	XF	Unc
1914	0.50	1.00	2.00	3.50	—

KM# 634a 5 CENTAVOS **Composition:** Copper

Date	VG	F	VF	XF	Unc
1914	75.00	100	145	175	—

Note: There are numerous varieties of these general types of the Durango 1 and 5 Centavo pieces

GUERRERO

Guerrero is a state on the southwestern coast of Mexico. It was one of the areas of operation of Zapata and his forces in the south of Mexico. The Zapata forces operated seven different mints in this state. The date ranges were from 1914 to 1917 and denominations from 2 Centavos to 2 Pesos. Some were cast but most were struck and the rarest coin of the group is the Suriana 1915 2 Pesos.

EMILIANO ZAPATA
(General Salgado)

REVOLUTIONARY COINAGE

KM# 638 2 CENTAVOS **Composition:** Copper

Date	VG	F	VF	XF	Unc
1915	75.00	125	175	250	—

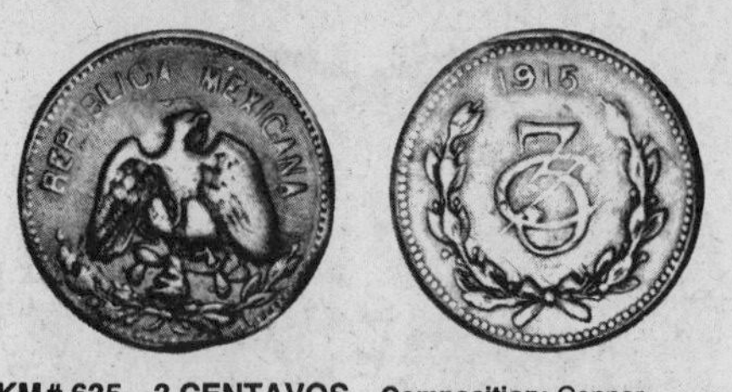

KM# 635 3 CENTAVOS **Composition:** Copper

Date	VG	F	VF	XF	Unc
1915	500	1,000	1,500	2,000	—

KM# 636 5 CENTAVOS **Composition:** Copper

Date	VG	F	VF	XF	Unc
1915GRO	800	1,200	1,800	2,600	—

KM# 637.1 10 CENTAVOS **Composition:** Copper **Obverse:** Snake head ends at L in REPUBLICA

Date	VG	F	VF	XF	Unc
1915GRO	600	800	1,000	1,500	—

KM# 637.2 10 CENTAVOS **Composition:** Copper **Obverse:** Snake head ends at C in REPUBLICA

Date	VG	F	VF	XF	Unc
1915GRO	2.00	3.00	6.50	7.50	—

KM# 637.2a 10 CENTAVOS **Composition:** Brass **Obverse:** Snake head ends at C in REPUBLICA

Date	VG	F	VF	XF	Unc
1915GRO	8.00	15.00	25.00	50.00	—

KM# 637.2b 10 CENTAVOS **Composition:** Lead **Obverse:** Snake head ends at C in REPUBLICA

Date	VG	F	VF	XF	Unc
1915GRO	50.00	75.00	175	275	—

KM# 637.3 10 CENTAVOS **Composition:** Copper **Obverse:** Snake head ends before A in REPUBLICA **Reverse:** Dot after date

Date	VG	F	VF	XF	Unc
1915GRO	2.00	3.00	6.50	7.50	—

KM# 637.3a 10 CENTAVOS **Composition:** Brass **Obverse:** Snake head ends before A in REPUBLICA **Reverse:** Dot after date

Date	VG	F	VF	XF	Unc
1915GRO	8.00	15.00	25.00	50.00	—

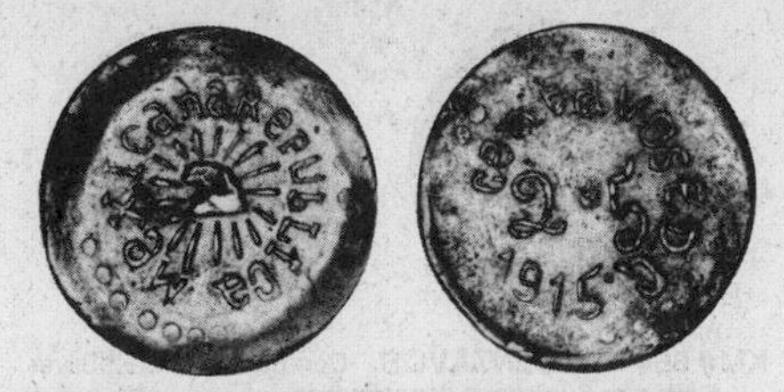

KM# 639 25 CENTAVOS **Composition:** Silver
Obverse: Cap and rays

Date	VG	F	VF	XF	Unc
1915	100	200	400	500	—

KM# 640 50 CENTAVOS **Composition:** Silver
Obverse: Cap and rays

Date	VG	F	VF	XF	Unc
1915	900	1,500	2,100	3,000	—

KM# 641a PESO (UN) **Composition:** Copper

Date	Good	VG	F	VF	XF
1914	—	100	150	225	900

KM# 641 PESO (UN) **Weight:** 0.3000 g. **Composition:** 1.0000 Gold-Silver **Obverse:** Star before UN PESO
Reverse: Cap and rays

Date	VG	F	VF	XF	Unc
1914	15.00	25.00	35.00	65.00	—

Note: Many die varieties exist

KM# 642 PESO (UN) **Weight:** 0.3000 g. **Composition:** 1.0000 Gold-Silver **Obverse:** Star before and after UN PESO
Reverse: Cap and rays

Date	VG	F	VF	XF	Unc
1914	50.00	75.00	100	150	—
1915	600	1,000	1,500	1,800	—

KM# 643 2 PESOS (Dos) **Weight:** 0.5950 g. **Composition:** 1.0000 Gold-Silver **Reverse:** Sun and mountains

Date	VG	F	VF	XF	Unc
1914GRO	12.00	20.00	32.00	60.00	—

Note: Many varieties exist

KM# 643a 2 PESOS (Dos) **Composition:** Copper

Date	Good	VG	F	VF	XF
1914	—	—	600	700	1,000

KM# 644 2 PESOS (Dos) **Weight:** 0.5950 g. **Composition:** 1.0000 Gold-Silver **Reverse:** Sun and mountains

Date	VG	F	VF	XF	Unc
1915GRO	65.00	85.00	160	200	—

KM# 644a 2 PESOS (Dos) **Composition:** Copper
Reverse: Sun and mountains

Date	VG	F	VF	XF	Unc
1915GRO	400	600	800	1,000	—

ATLIXTAC

REVOLUTIONARY COINAGE

KM# 645 10 CENTAVOS **Composition:** Copper

Date	VG	F	VF	XF	Unc
1915	3.00	4.00	6.50	10.00	—

KM# 646 10 CENTAVOS **Composition:** Copper
Obverse: Stars in legend

Date	VG	F	VF	XF	Unc
1915	3.00	4.00	6.50	10.00	—

CACAHUATEPEC

REVOLUTIONARY COINAGE

KM# 648 5 CENTAVOS **Composition:** Copper

Date	VG	F	VF	XF	Unc
1917	12.00	25.00	40.00	75.00	—

KM# 649 20 CENTAVOS **Composition:** Silver
Reverse: Cap and rays above denomination

Date	VG	F	VF	XF	Unc
1917	75.00	125	200	250	—

KM# 650 50 CENTAVOS **Composition:** Silver
Reverse: Cap and rays above denomination

Date	VG	F	VF	XF	Unc
1917	10.00	30.00	45.00	90.00	—

KM# 651 PESO (UN) **Composition:** Silver **Reverse:** Cap and rays

Date	VG	F	VF	XF	Unc
1917 L.V. Go	1,250	2,250	3,500	5,000	—

CACALOTEPEC

REVOLUTIONARY COINAGE

KM# 652 20 CENTAVOS **Composition:** Silver
Reverse: Cap and rays above denomination

Date	VG	F	VF	XF	Unc
1917	800	1,400	1,800	2,250	—

CAMPO MORADO

REVOLUTIONARY COINAGE

KM# 653 5 CENTAVOS **Composition:** Copper

Date	VG	F	VF	XF	Unc
1915 C.M.	9.00	15.00	22.50	35.00	—

KM# 654 10 CENTAVOS **Composition:** Copper

Date	VG	F	VF	XF	Unc
1915 C.M. GRO	6.00	10.00	17.50	27.50	—

KM# 655 20 CENTAVOS **Composition:** Copper

Date	VG	F	VF	XF	Unc
1915 C.M. GRO	15.00	25.00	35.00	50.00	—

KM# 656 50 CENTAVOS **Composition:** Copper **Obverse:** UN PESO effaced below eagle

Date	VG	F	VF	XF	Unc
1915 C.M. GRO	12.00	20.00	30.00	60.00	—

KM# 657 50 CENTAVOS **Composition:** Copper **Note:** Regular obverse.

Date	VG	F	VF	XF	Unc
1915 C.M. GRO	6.00	10.00	15.00	25.00	—

KM# 657a 50 CENTAVOS **Composition:** Base Silver **Note:** Regular obverse.

Date	VG	F	VF	XF	Unc
1915 C.M. GRO	165	275	400	575	—

KM# 658 PESO (UN) **Weight:** 0.3000 g. **Composition:** 1.0000 Gold-Silver **Obverse:** Date below eagle

Date	VG	F	VF	XF	Unc
1914 Co Mo Gro	450	500	800	1,000	—

KM# 658a PESO (UN) **Composition:** Brass **Obverse:** Date below eagle

Date	VG	F	VF	XF	Unc
1914 Co Mo Gro Unique	—	—	—	—	—

KM# 659 PESO (UN) **Weight:** 0.3000 g. **Composition:** 1.0000 Gold-Silver **Reverse:** Date below Liberty cap

Date	VG	F	VF	XF	Unc
1914 CAMPO Mo	15.00	30.00	45.00	60.00	—

KM# 660 2 PESOS (Dos) **Weight:** 0.5950 g. **Composition:** 1.0000 Gold-Silver **Reverse:** Sun over mountains

Date	VG	F	VF	XF	Unc
1915 Co. Mo.	12.00	20.00	30.00	50.00	—

KM# 660a 2 PESOS (Dos) **Composition:** Copper **Reverse:** Sun over mountains

Date	VG	F	VF	XF	Unc
1915 Co. Mo.	—	600	800	1,000	—

KM# 661 2 PESOS (Dos) **Weight:** 0.5950 g. **Composition:** 1.0000 Gold-Silver **Reverse:** Star before and after Co. Mo

Date	VG	F	VF	XF	Unc
1915 Co. Mo.	1,200	1,500	2,000	3,000	—

KM# 662 2 PESOS (Dos) **Weight:** 0.5950 g. **Composition:** 1.0000 Gold-Silver **Reverse:** Cap and rays

Date	VG	F	VF	XF	Unc
1915 C. M. GRO	15.00	25.00	35.00	60.00	—

KM# 662a.1 2 PESOS (Dos) **Composition:** Copper **Reverse:** Cap and rays

Date	VG	F	VF	XF	Unc
1915 C. M. GRO	—	—	—	900	—

KM# 662a.2 2 PESOS (Dos) **Composition:** Copper **Obverse:** Star between spray and R in REPUBLICA **Reverse:** Cap and rays

Date	VG	F	VF	XF	Unc
1915 C. M. GRO unique	—	—	—	—	—

CHILPANCINGO

REVOLUTIONARY COINAGE

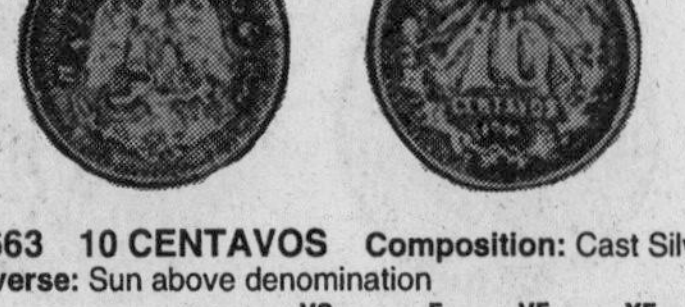

KM# 663 10 CENTAVOS **Composition:** Cast Silver **Reverse:** Sun above denomination

Date	VG	F	VF	XF	Unc
1914	700	1,000	1,200	1,500	—

Note: Counterfeits exist

KM# 664 20 CENTAVOS **Composition:** Cast Silver **Reverse:** Sun above denomination

Date	VG	F	VF	XF	Unc
1914	700	1,000	1,200	1,500	—

Note: Counterfeits exist

SURIANA

REVOLUTIONARY COINAGE

KM# 665 2 PESOS (Dos) **Composition:** 1.0000 Gold-Silver .595 oz. **Reverse:** Sun over mountains

Date	VG	F	VF	XF	Unc
1915 Rare	—	—	—	—	—

Note: Spink America Gerber sale part 2, 6-96 VF realized $16,500

TAXCO

REVOLUTIONARY COINAGE

KM# 667 2 CENTAVOS **Composition:** Copper **Obv. Legend:** EDO.DE.GRO

Date	VG	F	VF	XF	Unc
1915 O/T	25.00	40.00	60.00	90.00	—

KM# 668 5 CENTAVOS **Composition:** Copper

Date	VG	F	VF	XF	Unc
1915	9.00	15.00	20.00	25.00	—

KM# 669 10 CENTAVOS **Composition:** Copper

Date	VG	F	VF	XF	Unc
1915	9.00	20.00	30.00	40.00	—

KM# 670 50 CENTAVOS **Composition:** Copper **Obverse:** Legend in large letters

Date	VG	F	VF	XF	Unc
1915	15.00	25.00	50.00	65.00	—

KM# 671 50 CENTAVOS **Composition:** Silver **Reverse:** Sun above denomination

Date	VG	F	VF	XF	Unc
1915	20.00	30.00	40.00	70.00	—

KM# 672 PESO (UN) **Weight:** 0.3000 g. **Composition:** 1.0000 Gold-Silver **Obverse:** Star before UN PESO **Reverse:** Star before G

Date	VG	F	VF	XF	Unc
1915	12.00	20.00	30.00	45.00	—

KM# 672a PESO (UN) **Composition:** Brass **Obverse:** Star before UN PESO **Reverse:** Star before G

Date	VG	F	VF	XF	Unc
1915	100	200	350	450	—

KM# 672b PESO (UN) **Composition:** Lead **Obverse:** Star before UN PESO **Reverse:** Star before G

Date	VG	F	VF	XF	Unc
1915	50.00	100	200	350	—

KM# 672c PESO (UN) **Composition:** Copper **Obverse:** Star before UN PESO **Reverse:** Star before G

Date	VG	F	VF	XF	Unc
1915	100	200	350	450	—

KM# 673 PESO (UN) **Weight:** 0.3000 g. **Composition:** 1.0000 Gold-Silver **Obverse:** Star before UN PESO **Reverse:** Without star before G

Date	VG	F	VF	XF	Unc
1915	250	300	400	500	—

KM# 674 PESO (UN) **Weight:** 0.3000 g. **Composition:** 1.0000 Gold-Silver **Obverse:** Without star before UN PESO **Reverse:** Without star before G

Date	VG	F	VF	XF	Unc
1915	75.00	150	275	400	—

PATTERNS

Including off-metal strikes

KM#	Date	Mintage	Identification	Mkt Val
Pn647	1914	—	2 Pesos. Gold-Silver. 0.3000 g. Atlixtac.	—

JALISCO

Jalisco is a state on the west coast of Mexico. The few coins made for this state show that the *Army of the North* did not restrict their operations to the northern border states. The coins were made in Guadalajara under the watchful eye of General Dieguez, commander of this segment of Villa's forces.

GUADALAJARA

REVOLUTIONARY COINAGE

KM# 675 CENTAVO **Composition:** Copper **Obverse:** Cap and rays

Date	VG	F	VF	XF	Unc
1915	9.50	15.00	20.00	30.00	—

KM# 675a CENTAVO **Composition:** Brass **Obverse:** Cap and rays

Date	VG	F	VF	XF	Unc
1915	—	—	300	450	—

KM# A676 CENTAVO **Composition:** Copper **Obverse:** Cap and rays **Reverse:** Retrograde

Date	VG	F	VF	XF	Unc
1915	75.00	125	250	600	—

Note: Varieties exist.

KM# 676.1 2 CENTAVOS **Composition:** Copper **Obverse:** Cap and rays

Date	VG	F	VF	XF	Unc
1915	9.50	15.00	17.50	27.50	—

Note: Varieties exist.

KM# 676.2 2 CENTAVOS **Composition:** Copper **Obverse:** Retrograde date, smaller Liberty cap and shorter rays

Date	VG	F	VF	XF	Unc
1915	125	150	200	300	—

KM# 677 5 CENTAVOS **Composition:** Copper **Obverse:** Cap and rays

Date	VG	F	VF	XF	Unc
1915	6.50	12.00	15.00	25.00	—

KM# 677a 5 CENTAVOS **Composition:** Brass **Obverse:** Cap and rays

Date	VG	F	VF	XF	Unc
1915 rare	—	—	—	—	—

KM# 678 10 CENTAVOS **Composition:** Copper **Obverse:** Cap and rays above denomination **Reverse:** Arms

Date	VG	F	VF	XF	Unc
1915	—	—	2,200	3,500	—

KM# A678 PESO **Composition:** Copper

Date	VG	F	VF	XF	Unc
1915	—	—	—	8,000	—

MEXICO, ESTADO DE

Estado de Mexico is a state in central Mexico that surrounds the Federal District on three sides. The issues by the Zapata forces in this state have two distinctions – the Amecameca pieces are the crudest and the Toluca cardboard piece is the most unusual. General Tenorio authorized the crude incuse Amecameca pieces.

AMECAMECA

REVOLUTIONARY COINAGE

KM# 679 5 CENTAVOS **Composition:** Brass **Obv. Legend:** EJERCITO CONVENCIONISTA

Date	VG	F	VF	XF	Unc
ND unique	—	—	—	—	—

KM# 680 5 CENTAVOS **Composition:** Brass **Obverse:** Eagle above RM **Note:** Hand stamped.

Date	VG	F	VF	XF	Unc
ND	100	200	300	400	—

KM# 681 10 CENTAVOS **Composition:** Brass **Obverse:** Eagle above RM **Note:** Hand stamped.

Date	VG	F	VF	XF	Unc
ND	60.00	90.00	150	200	—

Note: Varieties exist.

KM# 681a 10 CENTAVOS **Composition:** Copper **Obverse:** Eagle above RM **Note:** Hand stamped.

Date	VG	F	VF	XF	Unc
ND	75.00	125	225	350	—

KM# 682 20 CENTAVOS **Composition:** Brass **Obverse:** Eagle above RM **Note:** Hand stamped.

Date	VG	F	VF	XF	Unc
ND	15.00	22.50	35.00	60.00	—

Note: Varieties exist

KM# 682a 20 CENTAVOS **Composition:** Copper **Obverse:** Eagle above RM **Note:** Hand stamped.

Date	VG	F	VF	XF	Unc
ND	25.00	50.00	175	250	—

KM# 683 20 CENTAVOS **Composition:** Copper **Obverse:** Eagle over A. D. J.

Date	VG	F	VF	XF	Unc
ND	7.50	12.50	20.00	35.00	—

KM# 683a 20 CENTAVOS **Composition:** Brass **Obverse:** Eagle over A. D. J.

Date	VG	F	VF	XF	Unc
ND	—	—	125	175	—

KM# 684 25 CENTAVOS **Composition:** Brass **Obv. Legend:** EJERCITO CONVENCIONISTA

Date	VG	F	VF	XF	Unc
ND unique	—	—	—	—	—

KM# 685 25 CENTAVOS **Composition:** Copper **Obverse:** Eagle over sprays **Note:** Hand stamped. Many modern counterfeits exist in all metals.

Date	VG	F	VF	XF	Unc
ND	15.00	20.00	30.00	40.00	—

KM# 685a 25 CENTAVOS **Composition:** Brass **Obverse:** Eagle over sprays **Note:** Hand stamped.

Date	VG	F	VF	XF	Unc
ND	—	—	50.00	100	—

KM# 685b 25 CENTAVOS **Composition:** Silver **Obverse:** Eagle over sprays **Note:** Hand stamped.

Date	VG	F	VF	XF	Unc
ND	—	—	175	250	—

KM# 686 50 CENTAVOS **Composition:** Copper **Obverse:** Eagle over sprays **Note:** Hand stamped.

Date	VG	F	VF	XF	Unc
ND	5.00	8.00	12.00	20.00	—

KM# 686a 50 CENTAVOS **Composition:** Brass **Obverse:** Eagle over sprays **Note:** Hand stamped.

Date	VG	F	VF	XF	Unc
ND	75.00	100	150	200	—

KM# 687 50 CENTAVOS **Composition:** Copper **Note:** Contemporary counterfeit, hand engraved.

Date	VG	F	VF	XF	Unc
ND	12.00	30.00	50.00	80.00	—

Note: KM#687 - ¢ clears top of 5 while KM#686a has the stem of ¢ above the 5

TENANCINGO, TOWN

(Distrito Federal Mexico)

REVOLUTIONARY COINAGE

KM# 688.1 2 CENTAVOS **Composition:** Copper **Reverse:** Without TM below deonomination

Date	VG	F	VF	XF	Unc
1915	—	—	350	1,500	—

KM# 688.2 2 CENTAVOS **Composition:** Copper **Reverse:** With TM below deonomination

Date	VG	F	VF	XF	Unc
1915	—	200	300	1,500	—

KM# 689.1 5 CENTAVOS **Composition:** Copper **Reverse:** Lined C

Date	VG	F	VF	XF	Unc
1915	5.00	10.00	18.00	30.00	—

KM# 689.2 5 CENTAVOS **Composition:** Copper **Reverse:** Solid C

Date	VG	F	VF	XF	Unc
1915	75.00	125	300	400	—

KM# 690.1 10 CENTAVOS **Composition:** Copper **Reverse:** Without dot in C

Date	VG	F	VF	XF	Unc
1916	10.00	15.00	20.00	30.00	—

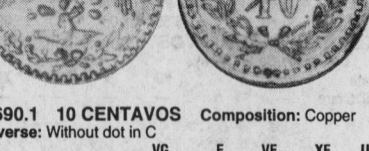

KM# 690.2 10 CENTAVOS **Composition:** Copper **Reverse:** Dot in C

Date	VG	F	VF	XF	Unc
1916	75.00	125	300	400	—

KM# 691 20 CENTAVOS **Composition:** Copper

Date	VG	F	VF	XF	Unc
1915	25.00	40.00	55.00	75.00	—

TOLUCA, CITY

(Distrito Federal Mexico)

REVOLUTIONARY COINAGE

KM# 692.1 5 CENTAVOS **Composition:** Grey Cardboard **Obverse:** Without dot after TOLUCA

Date	VG	F	VF	XF	Unc
1915	15.00	30.00	40.00	55.00	—

KM# 692.2 5 CENTAVOS **Composition:** Grey Cardboard **Obverse:** Dot after TOLUCA

Date	VG	F	VF	XF	Unc
1915	15.00	30.00	40.00	55.00	—

COUNTERMARKED COINAGE

KM# 693.2 20 CENTAVOS **Composition:** Copper **Countermark:** 20 within C **Note:** Countermark on 1 Centavo, KM#394.1.

CM Date	Host Date	Good	VG	F	VF	XF
(1915)	1904	—	200	400	800	1,000

KM# 693.1 20 CENTAVOS **Composition:** Copper **Countermark:** 20 within C **Note:** Countermark on 1 Centavo, KM#415.

CM Date	Host Date	Good	VG	F	VF	XF
ND(1915)	ND	—	20.00	30.00	45.00	60.00

Note: Varieties exist

KM# 694 40 CENTAVOS **Composition:** Copper **Countermark:** 40 within C **Note:** Countermark on 2 Centavos, KM#419.

CM Date	Host Date	Good	VG	F	VF	XF
ND(1915)	ND	—	25.00	40.00	60.00	80.00

Note: Varieties exist

MORELOS

Morelos is a state in south central Mexico, adjoining the federal district on the south. It was the headquarters of Emiliano Zapata. His personal quarters were at Tlatizapan in Morelos. The Morelos coins from 2 Centavos to 1 Peso were all copper except one type of 1 Peso in silver. The two operating Zapatista mints in Morelos were Atlihuayan and Tlaltizapan.

EMILIANO ZAPATA
(Zapatista)
REVOLUTIONARY COINAGE

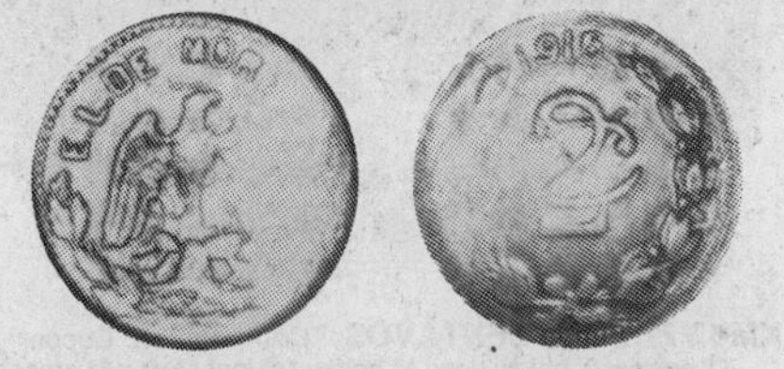

KM# 695 2 CENTAVOS Composition: Copper **Obv. Legend:** E.L. DE MORELOS

Date	VG	F	VF	XF	Unc
1915	1,000	1,400	1,800	2,250	—

KM# 696 5 CENTAVOS Composition: Copper **Rev. Legend:** E. DE MOR. 1915

Date	VG	F	VF	XF	Unc
1915	300	500	1,000	3,500	—

KM# 697 10 CENTAVOS Composition: Copper

Date	VG	F	VF	XF	Unc
1915	12.00	20.00	30.00	40.00	—

KM# 698 10 CENTAVOS Composition: Copper **Reverse:** Date effaced from die

Date	VG	F	VF	XF	Unc
ND	12.00	20.00	35.00	55.00	—

KM# 699 10 CENTAVOS Composition: Copper **Rev. Legend:** E. DE MOR

Date	VG	F	VF	XF	Unc
1915	1,000	2,000	2,500	3,000	—

KM# 700 10 CENTAVOS Composition: Copper **Rev. Legend:** MOR

Date	VG	F	VF	XF	Unc
1916	5.00	10.00	17.50	25.00	—

KM# 701 20 CENTAVOS Composition: Copper

Date	VG	F	VF	XF	Unc
1915	9.00	15.00	25.00	35.00	—

KM# 702 50 CENTAVOS Composition: Copper **Obverse:** MOR beneath eagle **Reverse:** 50C monogram

Date	VG	F	VF	XF	Unc
1915	300	500	900	1,300	—

KM# 703 50 CENTAVOS Composition: Copper **Obverse:** Sprays beneath eagle **Reverse:** 50C monogram

Date	VG	F	VF	XF	Unc
1915	12.50	17.50	30.00	42.00	—

Note: The above exists with a silver and also a brass wash

KM# 703a 50 CENTAVOS Composition: Brass **Obverse:** Sprays beneath eagle **Reverse:** 50C monogram

Date	VG	F	VF	XF	Unc
1915	100	200	400	600	—

KM# 706 50 CENTAVOS Composition: Copper **Obverse:** Sprays beneath eagle **Rev. Legend:** REFORMA LIBERTAD JUSTICIA Y LEY

Date	VG	F	VF	XF	Unc
1915	350	500	800	1,000	—

KM# 704 50 CENTAVOS Composition: Copper **Obverse:** MORELOS below eagle

Date	VG	F	VF	XF	Unc
1916	12.50	20.00	30.00	50.00	—

KM# 708 PESO (UN) Composition: Silver **Reverse:** Cap and rays

Date	VG	F	VF	XF	Unc
1916	450	750	1,000	1,500	—

KM# 708a PESO (UN) Composition: Copper **Reverse:** Cap and rays

Date	VG	F	VF	XF	Unc
1916	450	750	1,000	1,500	—

PATTERNS
Including off-metal strikes

KM#	Date	Mintage	Identification	Issue Price	Mkt Val
Pn1	1915	—	50 Centavos. Silver. KM#705.	—	1,500
Pn2	1915	—	50 Centavos. Copper. KM#705.	—	450
Pn3	191x	—	Peso. Silver. KM#707.	—	4,000
Pn4	191x	—	Peso. Copper. KM#707a.	—	4,000
Pn5	1916	—	Peso. Copper. KM#707b.	—	4,250

OAXACA

Oaxaca is one of the southern states in Mexico. The coins issued in this state represent the most prolific series of the Revolution. Most of the coins bear the portrait of Benito Juarez, have corded or plain edges and were issued by a provisional government in the state. The exceptions are the rectangular 1 and 3 Centavos pieces that begin the series.

PROVISIONAL GOVERNMENT
REVOLUTIONARY COINAGE

KM# 709 CENTAVO (UN) Composition: Copper **Note:** Rectangular flan.

Date	VG	F	VF	XF	Unc
1915	60.00	90.00	125	225	—

KM# 710 CENTAVO (UN) Composition: Copper **Obverse:** Bust of Juarez left

Date	VG	F	VF	XF	Unc
1915	12.00	17.50	25.00	40.00	—

KM# 710a CENTAVO (UN) Composition: Brass **Obverse:** Bust of Juarez left

Date	VG	F	VF	XF	Unc
1915	50.00	100	175	225	—

KM# 711 3 CENTAVOS (Tres) Composition: Copper **Rev. Legend:** PROVISIO... **Note:** Rectangular flan.

Date	VG	F	VF	XF	Unc
1915	60.00	100	125	200	—

KM# 712 3 CENTAVOS (Tres) Composition: Copper **Rev. Legend:** PROVISI... **Note:** Rectangular flan.

Date	VG	F	VF	XF	Unc
1915	600	1,200	1,800	3,000	—

KM# 713.1 3 CENTAVOS (Tres) Composition: Copper **Obverse:** Bust of Juarez left **Reverse:** Without TM below denomination

Date	VG	F	VF	XF	Unc
1915	3.00	5.00	10.00	15.00	—

KM# 713.2 3 CENTAVOS (Tres) Composition: Copper **Reverse:** Without TM below denomination **Edge:** Plain

Date	VG	F	VF	XF	Unc
1915	—	—	70.00	100	—

KM# 713.3 3 CENTAVOS (Tres) Composition: Copper **Reverse:** With TM below denomination

Date	VG	F	VF	XF	Unc
1915	100	150	250	350	—

KM# 714 3 CENTAVOS (Tres) Composition: Copper **Reverse:** Small 3

Date	VG	F	VF	XF	Unc
1915	6.00	9.00	14.00	20.00	—

KM# 715 5 CENTAVOS Composition: Copper **Note:** JAN. 15 1915. incuse lettering

Date	VG	F	VF	XF	Unc
1915 Rare	—	—	—	—	—

KM# 716 5 CENTAVOS Composition: Copper **Obverse:** Facing bust of Juarez

Date	VG	F	VF	XF	Unc
1915	—	—	—	5,000	—

KM# 717 5 CENTAVOS Composition: Copper **Obverse:** Second bust, low relief with long, pointed truncation

Date	VG	F	VF	XF	Unc
1915	1.50	3.00	4.50	7.00	—

KM# 718 5 CENTAVOS Composition: Copper **Obverse:** Fifth bust, heavy with short unfinished lapels

Date	VG	F	VF	XF	Unc
1915	1.50	2.50	4.00	6.00	—

KM# 719 5 CENTAVOS Composition: Copper **Obverse:** Sixth bust, curved bottom

Date	VG	F	VF	XF	Unc
1915	1.50	2.50	4.00	6.00	—

KM# 720 5 CENTAVOS Composition: Copper **Obverse:** Seventh bust, short truncation with closed lapels

Date	VG	F	VF	XF	Unc
1915	1.50	3.00	4.50	7.00	—

KM# 721 5 CENTAVOS Composition: Copper **Obverse:** Eighth bust, short curved truncation

Date	VG	F	VF	XF	Unc
1915	1.50	2.50	4.00	6.00	—

KM# 722 10 CENTAVOS Composition: Copper **Obverse:** Second bust, low relief with long, pointed truncation

Date	VG	F	VF	XF	Unc
1915	1.50	2.50	4.00	6.00	—

KM# 723 10 CENTAVOS Composition: Copper **Note:** Obverse and reverse legend retrograde.

Date	VG	F	VF	XF	Unc
1915 Rare	—	—	—	—	—

KM# 724 10 CENTAVOS Composition: Copper **Obverse:** Fourth bust, bold, unfinished truncation using 1 Peso obverse die of KM#740

Date	VG	F	VF	XF	Unc
1915	3.00	5.00	7.00	9.00	—

KM# 725 10 CENTAVOS Composition: Copper **Obverse:** Fifth bust, heavy with short unfinished lapels centered high

Date	VG	F	VF	XF	Unc
1915	1.50	2.50	4.00	6.00	—

KM# 726 10 CENTAVOS Composition: Copper **Obverse:** Sixth bust, curved bottom

Date	VG	F	VF	XF	Unc
1915	1.50	2.50	4.00	6.00	—

KM# 727.1 10 CENTAVOS Composition: Copper **Obverse:** Seventh bust, short truncation with closed lapels

Date	VG	F	VF	XF	Unc
1915	1.50	2.50	4.00	6.00	—

KM# 727.2 10 CENTAVOS Composition: Copper **Obverse:** T below bow, M below 1st leaf **Note:** At present, only four pieces of this type are known. All are VF or better.

Date	VG	F	VF	XF	Unc
1915	—	—	300	450	—

KM# 727.3 10 CENTAVOS Composition: Copper **Obverse:** Counterstamp GV on seventh bust, short truncation with closed lapels **Reverse:** Similar to KM#727.1 **Note:** Letters GV correspond to General Garcia Vigil.

Date	VG	F	VF	XF	Unc
1915	100	200	250	350	—

Note: This counter stamp appears on several different type host 10 cent coins

KM# 728 20 CENTAVOS Composition: Silver **Obverse:** Second bust, low relief with long pointed truncation

Date	VG	F	VF	XF	Unc
1915	500	750	1,200	1,500	—

KM# 728a 20 CENTAVOS Composition: Copper **Obverse:** Second bust, low relief with long pointed truncation

Date	VG	F	VF	XF	Unc
1915 Rare	—	—	—	—	—

KM# 729.1 20 CENTAVOS Composition: Copper **Obverse:** Fourth bust, unfinished truncation using 1 Peso obverse die

Date	VG	F	VF	XF	Unc
1915	1.50	3.00	4.50	7.00	—

KM# 729.2 20 CENTAVOS Composition: Copper **Counterstamp:** Liberty cap **Obverse:** Counterstamp liberty cap and rays on fourth bust, bold unfinished truncation using 1 Peso obverse die

Date	VG	F	VF	XF	Unc
1915	100	150	200	275	—

KM# 730 20 CENTAVOS Composition: Copper **Obverse:** 5th bust, heavy with short unfinished lapels using 20 Pesos obverse die

Date	VG	F	VF	XF	Unc
1915	5.00	7.00	10.00	15.00	—

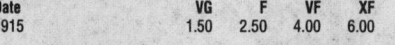

KM# 731.1 20 CENTAVOS **Composition:** Copper
Obverse: Sixth bust, curved bottom

Date	VG	F	VF	XF	Unc
1915	1.50	2.50	4.00	6.00	—

KM# 731.2 20 CENTAVOS **Composition:** Copper
Note: Similar to KM#731.1 but with fourth bust.

Date	VG	F	VF	XF	Unc
1915 Unique	—	—	—	—	—

KM# 732 20 CENTAVOS **Composition:** Copper
Obverse: Sixth bust

Date	VG	F	VF	XF	Unc
1915	1.50	2.50	4.00	6.00	—

KM# 733 20 CENTAVOS **Composition:** Copper
Obverse: 7th bust, short truncation with closed lapels

Date	VG	F	VF	XF	Unc
1915	1.50	3.00	4.50	7.00	—

KM# 734 50 CENTAVOS **Composition:** Silver
Obverse: Fifth bust, heavy, with short unfinished lapels, centered high

Date	VG	F	VF	XF	Unc
1915	10.00	20.00	40.00	85.00	—

KM# 735 50 CENTAVOS **Composition:** Silver
Obverse: Sixth bust, curved bottom

Date	VG	F	VF	XF	Unc
1915	6.00	9.00	14.00	22.50	—

KM# 736 50 CENTAVOS **Composition:** Silver
Obverse: Seventh bust, short truncation with closed lapels

Date	VG	F	VF	XF	Unc
1915	6.00	9.00	15.00	25.00	—

KM# 737 50 CENTAVOS **Composition:** Silver
Obverse: Eighth bust, short truncation with pronounced curve

Date	VG	F	VF	XF	Unc
1915	6.50	10.00	16.00	30.00	—

KM# 739 50 CENTAVOS **Composition:** Billon
Obverse: Ninth bust, high nearly straight truncation

Date	VG	F	VF	XF	Unc
1915	—	—	—	2,000	—

KM# 739a 50 CENTAVOS **Composition:** Copper
Obverse: Ninth bust, high nearly straight truncation

Date	VG	F	VF	XF	Unc
1915	—	—	—	—	—

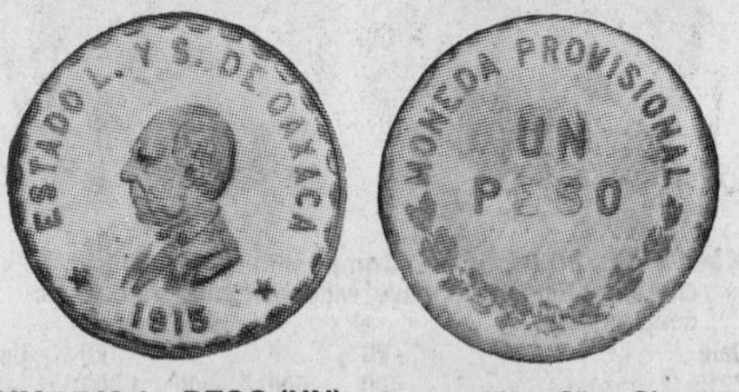

KM# 740.1 PESO (UN) **Composition:** Silver **Obverse:** Fourth bust, with heavy unfinished truncation

Date	VG	F	VF	XF	Unc
1915	3.00	5.00	8.50	14.00	—

KM# 740.2 PESO (UN) **Composition:** Silver **Obverse:** Fourth bust, with heavy unfinished truncation **Reverse:** TM below bow on wreath

Date	VG	F	VF	XF	Unc
1915	150	200	250	350	—

KM# 741 PESO (UN) **Composition:** Silver **Obverse:** Fifth bust, heavy, with short unfinished lapels, centered high

Date	VG	F	VF	XF	Unc
1915	6.00	9.00	14.00	22.50	—

KM# 742 PESO (UN) **Composition:** Silver **Obverse:** Sixth bust, curved bottom line

Date	VG	F	VF	XF	Unc
1915	6.00	9.00	14.00	22.50	—

KM# 742a PESO (UN) **Composition:** Copper **Obverse:** Sixth bust, curved bottom line

Date	VG	F	VF	XF	Unc
1915	—	—	—	500	—

KM# 743 PESO (UN) **Composition:** Silver **Obverse:** Seventh bust, short truncation with closed lapels

Date	VG	F	VF	XF	Unc
1915	4.00	6.00	10.00	16.00	—

KM# 743a PESO (UN) **Composition:** Silver **Obverse:** Seventh bust, short truncation with closed lapels **Reverse:** TM below bow on wreath

Date	VG	F	VF	XF	Unc
1915	35.00	75.00	150	200	—

KM# 744 2 PESOS (Dos) **Composition:** Silver
Obverse: Fourth bust, using 1 Peso obverse die

Date	VG	F	VF	XF	Unc
1915	12.00	20.00	25.00	35.00	—

KM# 744a 2 PESOS (Dos) **Composition:** Copper
Obverse: Fourth bust, using 1 Peso obverse die

Date	VG	F	VF	XF	Unc
1915 Rare	—	—	—	—	—

KM# 745 2 PESOS (Dos) **Obverse:** Fifth bust **Reverse:** Curved bottomed 2 over PESOS **Size:** 22 mm. **Note:** 0.9020 Silver, 0.0100 Gold.

Date	VG	F	VF	XF	Unc
1915	12.00	20.00	30.00	50.00	—

KM# 745a 2 PESOS (Dos) **Composition:** Copper
Obverse: Fifth bust **Reverse:** Curved bottomed 2 over PESOS

Date	VG	F	VF	XF	Unc
1915	50.00	75.00	110	160	—

KM# A746 2 PESOS (Dos) **Composition:** Copper
Obverse: Seventh bust, short truncation with closed lapels

Date	VG	F	VF	XF	Unc
1915 Unique	—	—	—	—	—

KM# 746 2 PESOS (Dos) **Composition:** Silver
Obverse: Sixth bust **Reverse:** 2 PESOS

Date	VG	F	VF	XF	Unc
1915	10.00	15.00	27.50	45.00	—

KM# A747 2 PESOS (Dos) **Composition:** Silver
Obverse: Sixth bust **Reverse:** Dos PESOS **Note:** Obverse die is free hand engraved.

Date	VG	F	VF	XF	Unc
1915	—	—	185	275	—

KM# 746a 2 PESOS (Dos) **Composition:** Copper
Obverse: Sixth bust **Reverse:** 2 PESOS

Date	Good	VG	F	VF	XF
1915	—	150	200	600	900

KM# 747.1 2 PESOS (Dos) **Composition:** Silver
Obverse: Sixth bust **Reverse:** DOS PESOS

Date	VG	F	VF	XF	Unc
1915	10.00	15.00	25.00	40.00	—

KM# 747.2 2 PESOS (Dos) **Composition:** Silver
Obverse: Sixth bust, dot after date **Reverse:** DOS PESOS

Date	VG	F	VF	XF	Unc
1915	10.00	15.00	25.00	40.00	—

KM# 747.3 2 PESOS (Dos) **Composition:** Silver
Obverse: Sixth bust, dot after date, periods after L and S **Reverse:** DOS PESOS

Date	VG	F	VF	XF	Unc
1915	10.00	15.00	25.00	40.00	—

KM# 748 2 PESOS (Dos) **Composition:** 0.9020 Silver
Obverse: Seventh bust, short truncation with closed lapels **Size:** 22 mm.

Date	VG	F	VF	XF	Unc
1915	12.00	20.00	40.00	60.00	—

KM# 749 2 PESOS (Dos) **Composition:** Silver
Obverse: Tenth, small nude bust

Date	VG	F	VF	XF	Unc
1915 Unique	—	—	—	2,300	—

KM# 750 5 PESOS **Composition:** 0.1750 Gold
Obverse: Third bust, heavy, with short unfinished lapels

Date	VG	F	VF	XF	Unc
1915	150	200	275	375	—

KM# 750a 5 PESOS **Composition:** Copper **Obverse:** Third bust, heavy, with short unfinished lapels

Date	VG	F	VF	XF	Unc
1915 Unique	—	—	—	—	—

KM# 751 5 PESOS **Composition:** 0.9020 Silver
Obverse: Seventh bust, short truncation with closed lapels

Date	VG	F	VF	XF	Unc
1915	30.00	50.00	100	150	—

KM# 751a 5 PESOS **Composition:** Copper **Obverse:** Seventh bust, short truncation with closed lapels

Date	VG	F	VF	XF	Unc
1915	125	200	300	800	—

KM# A752 10 PESOS **Composition:** 0.1500 Gold
Obverse: Fourth bust

Date	VG	F	VF	XF	Unc
1915 Rare	—	—	—	—	—

KM# 752 10 PESOS **Composition:** 0.1750 Gold
Obverse: Fifth bust

Date	VG	F	VF	XF	Unc
1915	200	275	375	500	—

KM# 752a 10 PESOS **Composition:** Copper **Obverse:** Fifth bust

Date	VG	F	VF	XF	Unc
1915	300	800	1,200	2,500	—

KM# A753 20 PESOS **Composition:** 0.1500 Gold
Obverse: Fourth bust

Date	VG	F	VF	XF	Unc
1915 Unique	—	—	—	—	—

KM# 753 20 PESOS **Composition:** 0.1750 Gold
Obverse: Fifth bust, heavy, with short unfinished lapels, centered high

Date	VG	F	VF	XF	Unc
1915	400	600	800	1,000	—

KM# 754 20 PESOS **Composition:** 0.1750 Gold
Obverse: Seventh bust, short truncation with closed lapels

Date	VG	F	VF	XF	Unc
1915	200	300	400	625	—

KM# 755 60 PESOS **Composition:** 0.8590 Gold
Edge: Reeded

Date	F	VF	XF	Unc	BU
1916 Rare	—	6,000	13,000	20,000	—

KM# 755a 60 PESOS **Composition:** Silver
Edge: Reeded

Date	F	VF	XF	Unc	BU
1916	—	—	—	1,800	—

KM# 755b 60 PESOS **Composition:** Copper
Edge: Plain

Date	F	VF	XF	Unc	BU
1916	—	—	1,000	1,800	—

PUEBLA

A state of central Mexico. Puebla was a state that occasionally saw Zapata forces active within its boundaries. Also active, and an issuer of coins, was the Madero brigade who issued coins with their name two years after Madero's death. The state issue of 2, 5, 10 and 20 Centavos saw limited circulation and recent hoards have been found of some values.

CHICONCUAUTLA
Madero Brigade
REVOLUTIONARY COINAGE

KM# 756 10 CENTAVOS **Composition:** Copper

Date	VG	F	VF	XF	Unc
1915	7.50	12.50	17.50	25.00	—

KM# 757 20 CENTAVOS **Composition:** Copper
Reverse: TRANSITORIO between rosettes

Date	VG	F	VF	XF	Unc
1915	2.50	4.00	6.50	12.00	—

Note: Varieties exist

KM# 758 20 CENTAVOS **Composition:** Copper
Reverse: TRANSITORIO without rosettes

Date	VG	F	VF	XF	Unc
1915	2.50	4.00	6.50	12.00	—

TETELA DEL ORO Y OCAMPO
REVOLUTIONARY COINAGE

KM# 759 2 CENTAVOS **Composition:** Copper

Date	VG	F	VF	XF	Unc
1915	12.50	20.00	28.00	45.00	—
1915 Restrikes	—	1.00	1.50	2.00	—

KM# 760 2 CENTAVOS **Composition:** Copper
Rev. Legend: E. DE PU.

Date	VG	F	VF	XF	Unc
1915	15.00	25.00	35.00	75.00	—

KM# 761 2 CENTAVOS **Composition:** Copper
Rev. Legend: E. DE PUE.

Date	VG	F	VF	XF	Unc
1915	9.00	15.00	22.50	35.00	—

KM# 762 5 CENTAVOS **Composition:** Copper

Date	VG	F	VF	XF	Unc
1915	50.00	100	150	250	—

KM# 764 20 CENTAVOS **Composition:** Copper

Date	VG	F	VF	XF	Unc
1915	50.00	100	150	225	—

TRIAL STRIKES

KM#	Date	Mintage	Identification	Mkt Val
TS1	1915	—	10 Centavos. Copper. Uniface, KM#763.	475
TS2	1915	—	10 Centavos. Brass. Uniface, KM#763.	750
TS3	1915	—	10 Centavos. Copper. KM#761. Eagle.	1,600

SINALOA

A state along the west coast of Mexico. The cast pieces of this state have been attributed to two people - Generals Rafael Buelna and Juan Carrasco. The cap and rays 8 Reales is usually attributed to General Buelna and the rest of the series to Carrasco. Because of their crude nature it is questionable whether separate series or mints can be determined.

BUELNA / CARRASCO

MOLDED OR CAST COINAGE

Revolutionary

KM# 765 20 CENTAVOS **Composition:** Cast Silver
Note: Sand molded using regular 20 Centavos.

Date	Good	VG	F	VF	XF
ND(1898-1905)	200	300	—	—	—

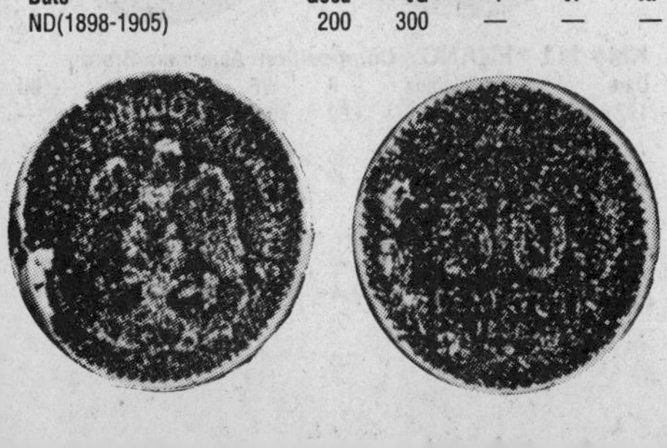

KM# 766 50 CENTAVOS **Composition:** Cast Silver
Note: Sand molded using regular 50 Centavos, KM#445.

Date	Good	VG	F	VF	XF
ND(1905-1918)	200	300	—	—	—

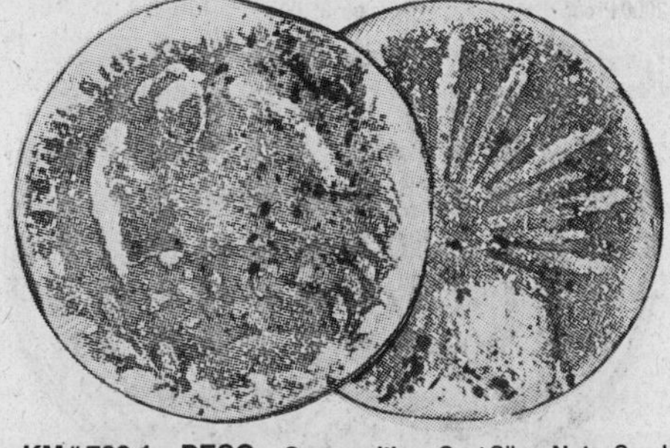

KM# 768.1 PESO **Composition:** Cast Silver **Note:** Sand molded using regular 8 Reales, KM#377.

Date	Good	VG	F	VF	XF
ND(1824-1897)	17.50	35.00	45.00	55.00	—

KM# 768.2 PESO **Composition:** Cast Silver
Countermark: G.C. **Obverse:** With additional countermark
Note: Sand molded using regular 8 Reales, KM#377.

Date	Good	VG	F	VF	XF
ND(1824-1897)	25.00	45.00	100	150	—

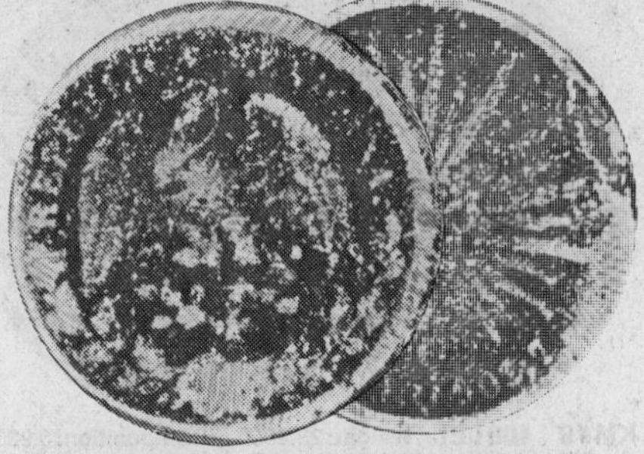

KM# 769 PESO **Composition:** Cast Silver
Countermark: G.C **Obverse:** With additional countermark
Note: Sand molded using regular Peso, KM#409.

Date	Good	VG	F	VF	XF
ND(1898-1909)	10.00	20.00	30.00	40.00	—

COUNTERMARKED COINAGE

Revolutionary

These are all crude sand cast coins using regular coins to prepare the mold. Prices below give a range for how much of the original coin from which the mold was prepared is visible.

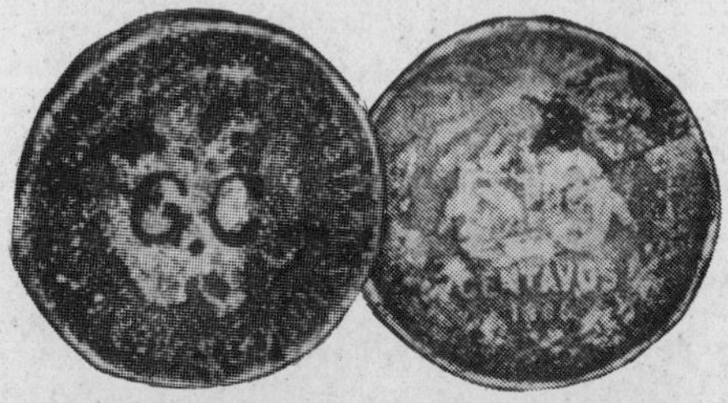

KM# 767 50 CENTAVOS **Composition:** Cast Silver
Countermark: G.C. **Obverse:** With additional countermark
Note: Sand molded using regular 50 Centavos, KM#445.

CM Date	Host Date	Good	VG	F	VF	XF
ND	ND(1905-1918)	100	150	200	300	—

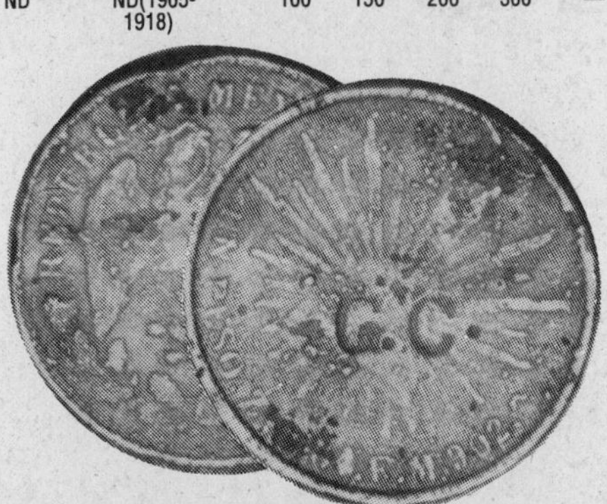

KM# 770 PESO **Composition:** Cast Silver
Countermark: G.C **Obverse:** With additional countermark
Note: Sand molded using regular Peso, KM#409.

CM Date	Host Date	Good	VG	F	VF	XF
ND	ND(1898-1909)	30.00	60.00	140	175	—

MOLDOVA

The Republic of Moldova (formerly the Moldavian S.S.R.) is bordered in the north, east and south by the Ukraine and on the west by Romania. It has an area of 13,000 sq.mi. (33,700 sq.km.) and a population of 4.4 million. The capital is Chisinau. Agricultural products are mainly cereals, grapes, tobacco, sugar beets and fruits. Food processing, clothing, building materials and agricultural machinery manufacturing dominate industry.

The historical Romanian principality of Moldova was established in the 14th century. It fell under Turkish suzerainty in the 16th century. From 1812 to 1918 Russians occupied the eastern portion of Moldova, which they named Bessarabia. In March 1918the Bessarabian legislature voted in favor of reunification with Romania. At the Paris Peace Conference in 1920 United States, France, U.K., and Italy a.s.o officially recognized the union. The new Soviet government did not accept the union. In 1924, due to Soviet pressure against Romania a Moldavian Autonomous Soviet Socialist Republic (A.S.S.R.) was established within the USSR on border strip that extends east of Nistru River (today it is Transdniestra or Transdniester).

Following the Molotov-Ribbentrop Pact (1939), the Soviet - German agreement, which divided Eastern Europe, the Soviet forces, reoccupied the region in June 1940 and the Moldavian S.S.R. was proclaimed. The Transdniestra region was transferred to the new republic, while Ukrainian S.S.R. obtained possession of southern part of Bessarabia. Romanian forces liberated the region in 1941. The Soviets reconquered the territory in (1944).

A declaration of republican sovereignty was adopted in June 1990 and in Aug. 1991 the area was renamed Moldova, an independent republic. In Dec. 1991Moldova became a member of the C.I.S. In 1992, as a result of Russian involvement, Transdniestra seceded from Moldova. In May 1992 fighting began between Moldavian separatists (Romanians) and rebels aided by contingents of Cossacks and the Russian14th Army. The Moldavian government made several futile requests for United Nations intervention. On July 3, 1992, Russian and Moldavian presidents agreed upon a neutral demarcation line with the withdrawal of Russian forces from Transdniestra. This status will remain until a more feasible constitution is proclaimed.

RULERS
Romanian, until 1940

MONETARY SYSTEM
100 Bani = 1 Leu

REPUBLIC

DECIMAL COINAGE

KM# 1 BAN **Composition:** Aluminum

Date	F	VF	XF	Unc	BU
1993	—	—	—	0.20	—
1995	—	—	—	0.20	—
1996	—	—	—	0.25	—
2000	—	—	—	0.25	—

KM# 2 5 BANI **Composition:** Aluminum

Date	F	VF	XF	Unc	BU
1993	—	—	—	0.30	—
1995	—	—	—	0.30	—
1996	—	—	—	0.30	—
1999	—	—	—	0.30	—
2000	—	—	—	0.30	—
2001	—	—	—	0.30	—
2002	—	—	—	0.30	—

KM# 7 10 BANI **Composition:** Aluminum

Date	F	VF	XF	Unc	BU
1995	—	—	—	0.40	—
1996	—	—	—	0.40	—
1997	—	—	—	0.40	—
1998	—	—	—	0.40	—
2000	—	—	—	0.40	—
2001	—	—	—	0.40	—
2002	—	—	—	0.40	—

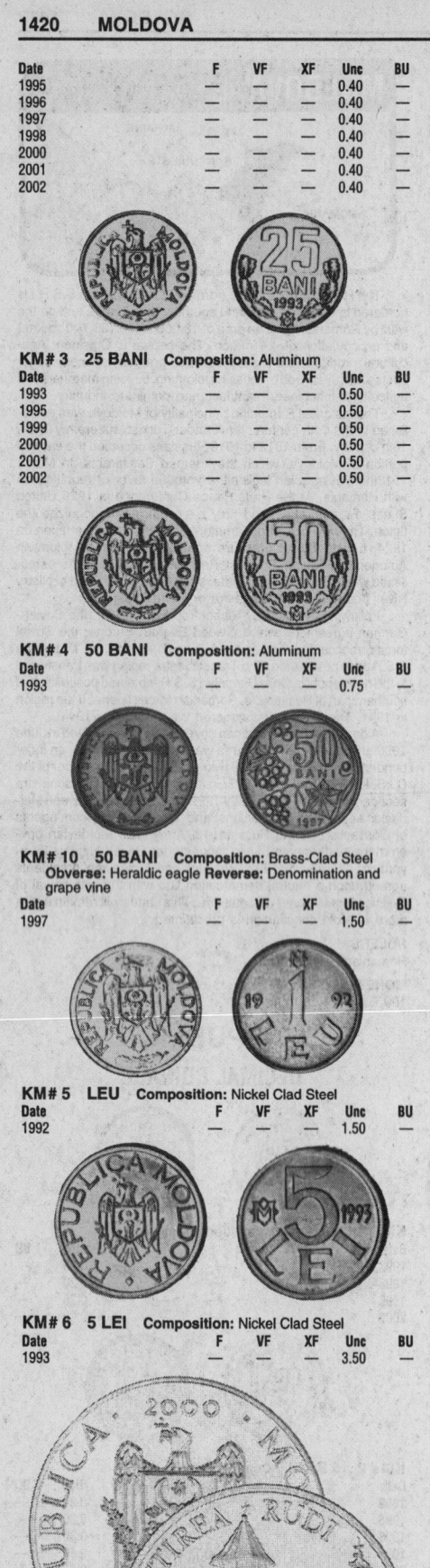

KM# 3 25 BANI **Composition:** Aluminum

Date	F	VF	XF	Unc	BU
1993	—	—	—	0.50	—
1995	—	—	—	0.50	—
1999	—	—	—	0.50	—
2000	—	—	—	0.50	—
2001	—	—	—	0.50	—
2002	—	—	—	0.50	—

KM# 4 50 BANI **Composition:** Aluminum

Date	F	VF	XF	Unc	BU
1993	—	—	—	0.75	—

KM# 10 50 BANI **Composition:** Brass-Clad Steel **Obverse:** Heraldic eagle **Reverse:** Denomination and grape vine

Date	F	VF	XF	Unc	BU
1997	—	—	—	1.50	—

KM# 5 LEU **Composition:** Nickel Clad Steel

Date	F	VF	XF	Unc	BU
1992	—	—	—	1.50	—

KM# 6 5 LEI **Composition:** Nickel Clad Steel

Date	F	VF	XF	Unc	BU
1993	—	—	—	3.50	—

KM# 11 50 LEI **Weight:** 16.6300 g. **Composition:** 0.9850 Silver 0.5266 oz. ASW **Subject:** Manastirea Rudi **Obverse:** National arms **Reverse:** Monastary building **Edge:** Plain **Size:** 30 mm.

Date	F	VF	XF	Unc	BU
2000 Proof	— Value: 35.00				

KM# 8 100 LEI **Weight:** 28.2800 g. **Composition:** 0.9250 Silver .8411 oz. ASW **Subject:** 5th Anniversary of Independence **Obverse:** National arms **Reverse:** Flying stork with grapes

Date	Mintage	F	VF	XF	Unc	BU
1996	20,000	Value: 55.00				

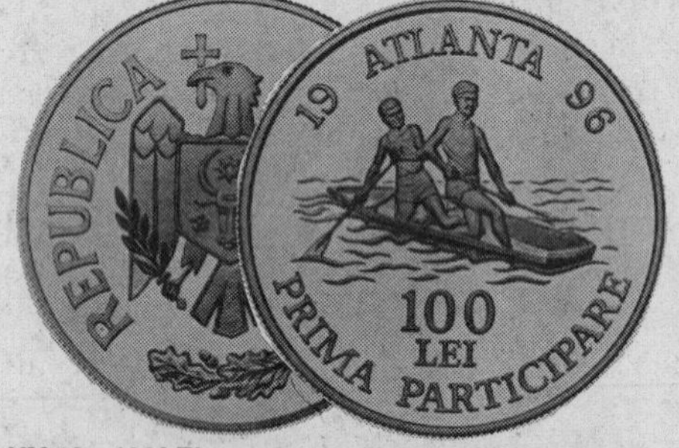

KM# 9 100 LEI **Weight:** 28.2800 g. **Composition:** 0.9250 Silver .8411 oz. ASW **Subject:** First Olympic Games Participation **Obverse:** National arms **Reverse:** 2 man canoe

Date	Mintage	F	VF	XF	Unc	BU
1996	20,000	Value: 55.00				

MONACO

The Principality of Monaco, located on the Mediterranean coast nine miles from Nice, has an area of 0.58 sq. mi. (1.9 sq. km.) and a population of 26,000. Capital: Monaco-Ville. The economy is based on tourism and the manufacture of cosmetics, gourmet foods and highly specialized electronics. Monaco also derives its revenue from a tobacco monopoly and the sale of postage stamps for philatelic purpose. Gambling in Monte Carlo accounts for only a small fraction of the country's revenue.

Monaco derives its name from Monoikos', the Greek surname for Hercules, the mythological strong man who, according to legend, formed the Monacan headland during one of his twelve labors. Monaco has been ruled by the Grimaldi dynasty since 1297 - Prince Rainier III, the present and 31st monarch of Monaco, is still of that line - except for a period during the French Revolution until Napoleon's downfall when the Principality was annexed to France. Since 1865, Monaco has maintained a customs union with France which guarantees its privileged position as long as the royal line remains intact. Under the new constitution proclaimed on December 17, 1962, the Prince shares his power with an 18-member unicameral National Council.

RULERS

Albert I, 1889-1922
Louis II, 1922-1949
Rainier III, 1949-

MINT MARKS

M - Monaco
A – Paris

MINT PRIVY MARKS

(a) - Paris (privy marks only)
(p) - Thunderbolt - Poissy

MONETARY SYSTEM

10 Centimes = 1 Decime
10 Decimes = 1 Franc

PRINCIPALITY

DECIMAL COINAGE

10 Centimes = 1 Decime; 10 Decimes = 1 Franc

KM# 110 50 CENTIMES **Composition:** Aluminum-Bronze

Date	Mintage	F	VF	XF	Unc	BU
1924 (p)	150,000	3.50	8.00	18.00	45.00	—

KM# 113 50 CENTIMES **Composition:** Aluminum-Bronze

Date	Mintage	F	VF	XF	Unc	BU
1926 (p)	100,000	4.00	9.00	20.00	50.00	—

KM# 111 FRANC **Composition:** Aluminum-Bronze

Date	Mintage	F	VF	XF	Unc	BU
1924 (p)	150,000	3.00	7.00	14.00	30.00	—

KM# 114 FRANC Composition: Aluminum-Bronze

Date	Mintage	F	VF	XF	Unc	BU
1926 (p)	100,000	4.00	9.00	16.00	35.00	—

KM# 120 FRANC Composition: Aluminum

Date	Mintage	F	VF	XF	Unc	BU
ND(1943) (a)	2,500,000	0.50	1.00	2.00	4.50	—

KM# 120a FRANC Composition: Aluminum-Bronze

Date	Mintage	F	VF	XF	Unc	BU
ND(1945) (a)	1,509,000	0.50	1.00	2.00	5.00	—

KM# 112 2 FRANCS Composition: Aluminum-Bronze

Date	Mintage	F	VF	XF	Unc	BU
1924 (p)	75,000	8.00	14.00	30.00	75.00	—

KM# 115 2 FRANCS Composition: Aluminum-Bronze

Date	Mintage	F	VF	XF	Unc	BU
1926 (p)	75,000	7.00	12.00	25.00	70.00	—

KM# 121 2 FRANCS Composition: Aluminum

Date	Mintage	F	VF	XF	Unc	BU
ND(1943) (a)	1,250,000	0.75	1.50	5.00	10.00	—

KM# 121a 2 FRANCS Composition: Aluminum-Bronze

Date	Mintage	F	VF	XF	Unc	BU
ND(1945) (a)	1,080,000	0.50	1.00	2.50	6.00	—

KM# 122 5 FRANCS Composition: Aluminum

Date	Mintage	F	VF	XF	Unc	BU
1945 (a)	1,000,000	1.50	3.00	7.00	15.00	—

KM# 123 10 FRANCS Composition: Copper-Nickel

Date	Mintage	F	VF	XF	Unc	BU
1946 (a)	1,000,000	1.50	3.00	6.00	12.50	—

KM# 130 10 FRANCS Composition: Aluminum-Bronze

Date	Mintage	F	VF	XF	Unc	BU
1950 (a)	500,000	0.50	1.00	2.00	4.00	—
1951 (a)	500,000	0.50	1.00	2.00	4.00	—

KM# 124 20 FRANCS (Vingt) Composition: Copper-Nickel

Date	Mintage	F	VF	XF	Unc	BU
1947 (a)	1,000,000	2.00	4.00	8.00	20.00	—

KM# 131 20 FRANCS (Vingt) Composition: Aluminum-Bronze

Date	Mintage	F	VF	XF	Unc	BU
1950 (a)	500,000	0.65	1.25	2.50	6.00	—
1951 (a)	500,000	0.65	1.25	2.50	6.00	—

KM# 132 50 FRANCS (Cinquante) Composition: Aluminum-Bronze

Date	Mintage	F	VF	XF	Unc	BU
1950 (a)	500,000	1.50	3.00	5.00	12.00	—

KM# 105 100 FRANCS (Cent) Weight: 32.2580 g. Composition: 0.9000 Gold .9335 oz. AGW

Date	Mintage	F	VF	XF	Unc	BU
1901A	15,000	BV	420	500	775	—
1904A	10,000	BV	420	500	775	—

KM# 133 100 FRANCS (Cent) Composition: Copper-Nickel

Date	Mintage	F	VF	XF	Unc	BU
1950 (a)	500,000	2.00	4.00	8.00	18.00	—

KM# 134 100 FRANCS (Cent) Composition: Copper-Nickel

Date	Mintage	F	VF	XF	Unc	BU
1956 (a)	500,000	1.50	2.50	5.50	15.00	—

REFORM COINAGE

100 Old Francs = 1 New Franc

KM# 155 CENTIME Composition: Stainless Steel

Date	Mintage	F	VF	XF	Unc	BU
1976 (a)	25,000	—	0.15	0.30	4.00	—
1977 (a)	25,000	—	0.15	0.30	4.00	—
1978 (a)	75,000	—	0.15	0.30	4.00	—
1979 (a)	75,000	—	0.15	0.30	4.00	—
1982 (a)	10,000	—	0.15	0.30	4.00	—
1995 (a)	—	—	0.15	0.30	4.00	—

KM# 156 5 CENTIMES Composition: Copper-Aluminum-Nickel

Date	Mintage	F	VF	XF	Unc	BU
1976 (a)	25,000	—	0.20	0.40	4.50	—
1977 (a)	25,000	—	0.20	0.40	4.50	—
1978 (a)	75,000	—	0.20	0.40	4.50	—
1979 (a)	75,000	—	0.20	0.40	4.50	—
1982 (a)	10,000	—	0.20	0.40	4.50	—
1995 (a)	—	—	0.20	0.40	4.50	—

KM# 142 10 CENTIMES Composition: Aluminum-Bronze

Date	Mintage	F	VF	XF	Unc	BU
1962 (a)	750,000	—	0.15	0.30	1.50	—
1974 (a)	179,000	—	0.15	0.30	2.25	—
1975 (a)	172,000	—	0.15	0.30	2.25	—
1976 (a)	178,000	—	0.15	0.30	2.25	—
1977 (a)	172,000	—	0.15	0.30	2.25	—
1978 (a)	112,000	—	0.15	0.30	2.50	—
1979 (a)	112,000	—	0.15	0.30	2.50	—
1982 (a)	100,000	—	0.15	0.30	2.50	—
1995 (a)	—	—	0.15	0.30	2.50	—

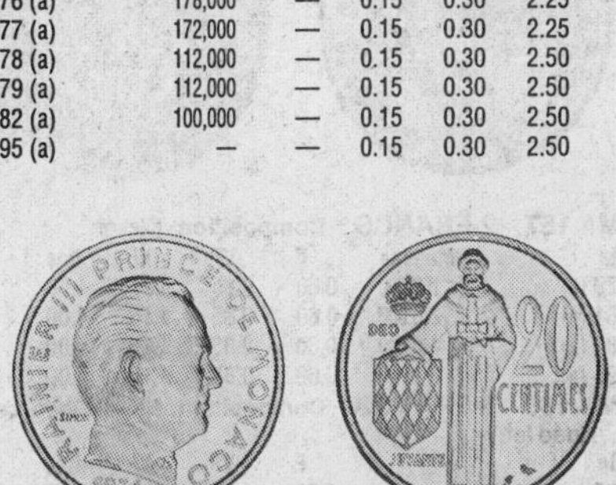

KM# 143 20 CENTIMES **Composition:** Aluminum-Bronze

Date	Mintage	F	VF	XF	Unc	BU
1962 (a)	750,000	—	0.25	0.50	1.75	—
1974 (a)	104,000	—	0.25	0.50	2.75	—
1975 (a)	97,000	—	0.25	0.50	2.75	—
1976 (a)	103,000	—	0.25	0.50	2.75	—
1977 (a)	97,000	—	0.25	0.50	2.75	—
1978 (a)	81,000	—	0.25	0.50	2.75	—
1979 (a)	81,000	—	0.25	0.50	2.75	—
1982 (a)	100,000	—	0.25	0.50	2.75	—
1995 (a)	—	—	0.25	0.50	2.75	—

KM# 144 50 CENTIMES **Composition:** Aluminum-Bronze

Date	Mintage	F	VF	XF	Unc	BU
1962 (a)	375,000	—	1.25	2.50	4.50	—

KM# 145 1/2 FRANC **Composition:** Nickel

Date	Mintage	F	VF	XF	Unc	BU
1965 (a)	375,000	0.30	0.60	1.25	2.50	—
1968 (a)	250,000	0.30	0.60	1.25	2.50	—
1974 (a)	69,000	0.35	0.70	1.50	3.50	—
1975 (a)	70,000	0.35	0.70	1.50	3.50	—
1976 (a)	68,000	0.35	0.70	1.50	3.50	—
1977 (a)	62,000	0.35	0.70	1.50	3.50	—
1978 (a)	414,000	0.30	0.60	1.25	2.75	—
1979 (a)	414,000	0.30	0.60	1.25	2.75	—
1982 (a)	457,000	0.30	0.60	1.25	2.75	—
1989 (a)	—	0.30	0.60	1.25	2.75	—
1995 (a)	—	0.30	0.60	1.25	2.75	—

KM# 140 FRANC **Composition:** Nickel

Date	Mintage	F	VF	XF	Unc	BU
1960 (a)	500,000	0.35	0.70	1.50	3.25	—
1966 (a)	175,000	0.40	0.80	1.75	4.00	—
1968 (a)	250,000	0.40	0.80	1.75	4.00	—
1974 (a)	194,000	0.40	0.80	1.75	4.00	—
1975 (a)	195,000	0.40	0.80	1.75	4.00	—
1976 (a)	193,000	0.40	0.80	1.75	4.00	—
1977 (a)	188,000	0.40	0.80	1.75	4.00	—
1978 (a)	783,000	0.40	0.80	1.75	3.50	—
1979 (a)	783,000	0.40	0.80	1.75	3.50	—
1982 (a)	525,000	0.40	0.80	1.75	3.50	—
1986 (a)	—	0.35	0.70	1.50	3.00	—
1989 (a)	—	0.35	0.70	1.50	2.75	—
1995 (a)	—	0.35	0.70	1.50	2.75	—

KM# 157 2 FRANCS **Composition:** Nickel

Date	Mintage	F	VF	XF	Unc	BU
1979 (a)	162,000	0.60	0.85	1.75	4.00	—
1981 (a)	275,000	0.60	0.85	1.75	4.00	—
1982 (a)	446,000	0.60	0.85	1.75	4.00	—
1995 (a)	—	0.60	0.85	1.75	4.00	—

KM# 166 2 FRANCS **Composition:** Nickel **Obverse:** Head left

Date	F	VF	XF	Unc	BU
1995 (a)	0.60	0.85	1.75	4.00	—

KM# 141 5 FRANCS **Weight:** 12.0000 g. **Composition:** 0.8350 Silver .3221 oz. ASW

Date	Mintage	F	VF	XF	Unc	BU
1960 (a)	125,000	—	—	7.50	10.00	—
1966 (a)	125,000	—	—	7.50	10.00	—

KM# 150 5 FRANCS **Composition:** Nickel Clad Copper-Nickel

Date	Mintage	F	VF	XF	Unc	BU
1971 (a)	250,000	—	1.50	2.50	4.50	—
1974 (a)	152,000	—	1.50	2.50	4.50	—
1975 (a)	8,000	—	2.50	6.00	12.50	—
1976 (a)	8,000	—	2.50	6.00	12.50	—
1977 (a)	42,000	—	2.00	5.00	10.00	—
1978 (a)	22,000	—	2.00	5.00	10.00	—
1979 (a)	22,000	—	2.00	5.00	10.00	—
1982 (a)	152,000	—	2.00	5.00	10.00	—
1989	—	—	2.00	5.00	10.00	—
1995 (a)	—	—	2.00	5.00	10.00	—

KM# 146 10 FRANCS **Weight:** 25.0000 g. **Composition:** 0.9000 Silver .7234 oz. ASW **Subject:** 100th anniversary - Accession of Charles III

Date	Mintage	F	VF	XF	Unc	BU
1966 (a)	38,000	—	—	—	21.50	30.00

KM# 151 10 FRANCS **Composition:** Copper-Nickel-Aluminum **Subject:** 25th anniversary of reign

Date	Mintage	F	VF	XF	Unc	BU
ND(1974) (a)	25,000	—	2.50	4.50	8.00	—

KM# 154 10 FRANCS **Composition:** Copper-Nickel-Aluminum

Date	Mintage	F	VF	XF	Unc	BU
1975 (a)	25,000	—	2.25	3.75	8.00	—
1976 (a)	16,000	—	2.50	4.00	9.00	—
1977 (a)	50,000	—	2.25	3.25	5.50	—
1978 (a)	228,000	—	2.25	3.25	5.50	—
1979 (a)	228,000	—	2.25	3.25	5.50	—
1981 (a)	235,000	—	2.25	3.25	5.50	—
1982 (a)	230,000	—	2.25	3.25	5.50	—

KM# 160 10 FRANCS **Composition:** Copper-Nickel-Aluminum **Obverse:** Princess Grace bust facing left

Date	Mintage	F	VF	XF	Unc	BU
1982 (a)	30,000	—	—	—	12.50	—

KM# 162 10 FRANCS **Composition:** Nickel-Aluminum-Bronze **Subject:** Prince Pierre Foundation

Date	F	VF	XF	Unc	BU
1989 (a)	—	—	—	6.50	—

KM# 163 10 FRANCS **Ring Composition:** Aluminum-Bronze **Center Composition:** Steel

Date	F	VF	XF	Unc	BU
1989 (a)	—	—	—	9.00	—
1991 (a)	—	—	—	14.00	—
1992 (a)	—	—	—	12.50	—
1993 (a)	—	—	—	14.00	—
1994 (a)	—	—	—	14.00	—
1995 (a)	—	—	—	9.00	—
1996 (a)	—	—	—	9.00	—
1997 (a)	—	—	—	9.00	—
1998 (a)	—	—	—	9.00	—
2000 (a)	—	—	—	9.00	—

KM# 165 20 FRANCS **Ring Composition:** Nickel **Center Composition:** Copper-Aluminum-Nickel **Reverse:** Prince's palace

Date	F	VF	XF	Unc	BU
1992 (a)	—	—	—	15.00	—
1995 (a)	—	—	—	15.00	—
1997 (a)	—	—	—	15.00	—

KM# 152.1 50 FRANCS **Weight:** 30.0000 g. **Composition:** 0.9000 Silver .8681 oz. ASW **Subject:** 25th anniversary of reign **Edge:** Commemorative inscription

Date	Mintage	F	VF	XF	Unc	BU
1974 (a)	25,000	—	—	—	42.00	55.00

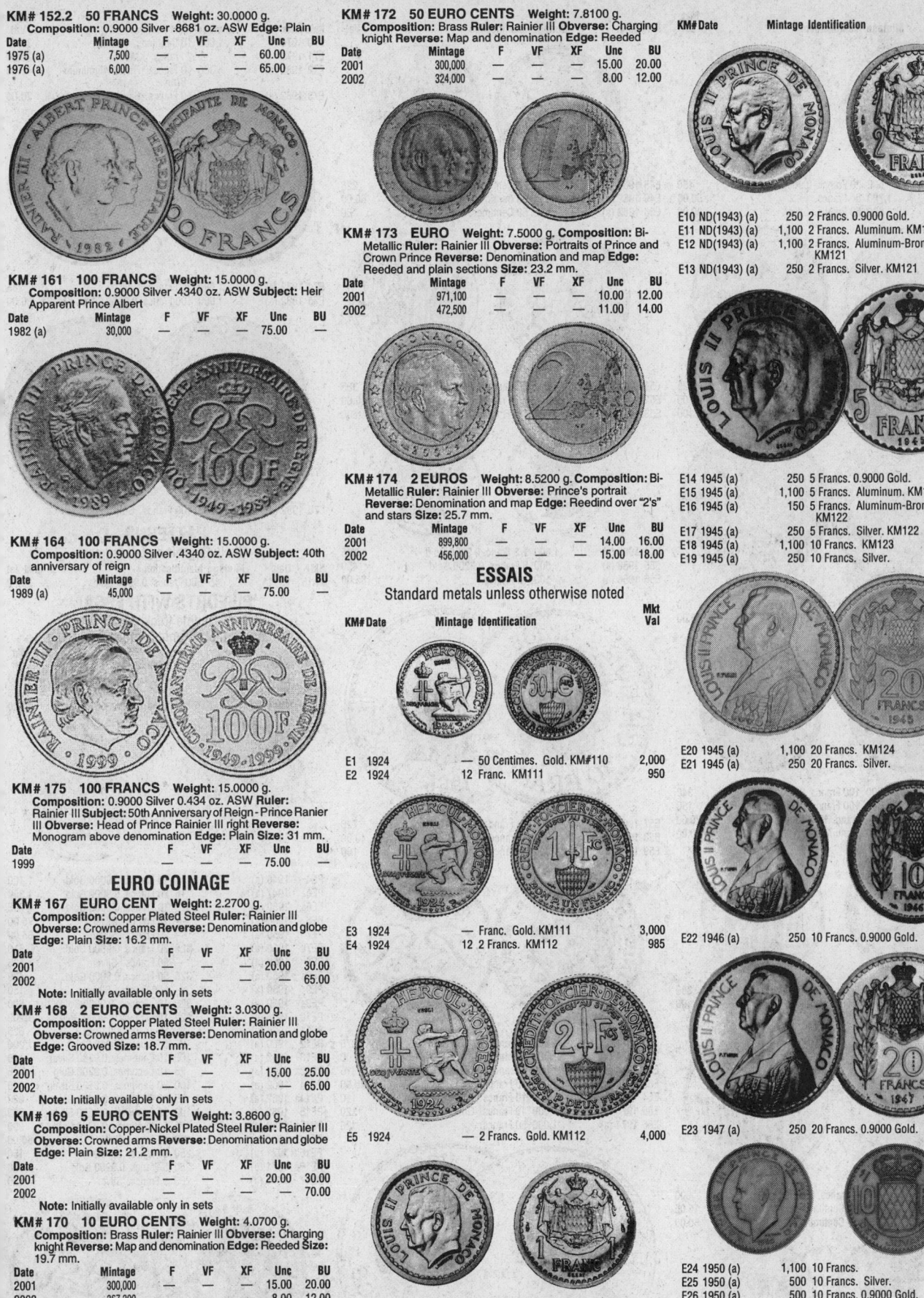

KM# 152.2 50 FRANCS **Weight:** 30.0000 g. **Composition:** 0.9000 Silver .8681 oz. ASW **Edge:** Plain

Date	Mintage	F	VF	XF	Unc	BU
1975 (a)	7,500	—	—	—	60.00	—
1976 (a)	6,000	—	—	—	65.00	—

KM# 161 100 FRANCS **Weight:** 15.0000 g. **Composition:** 0.9000 Silver .4340 oz. ASW **Subject:** Heir Apparent Prince Albert

Date	Mintage	F	VF	XF	Unc	BU
1982 (a)	30,000	—	—	—	75.00	—

KM# 164 100 FRANCS **Weight:** 15.0000 g. **Composition:** 0.9000 Silver .4340 oz. ASW **Subject:** 40th anniversary of reign

Date	Mintage	F	VF	XF	Unc	BU
1989 (a)	45,000	—	—	—	75.00	—

KM# 175 100 FRANCS **Weight:** 15.0000 g. **Composition:** 0.9000 Silver 0.434 oz. ASW **Ruler:** Rainier III **Subject:** 50th Anniversary of Reign - Prince Ranier III **Obverse:** Head of Prince Rainier III right **Reverse:** Monogram above denomination **Edge:** Plain **Size:** 31 mm.

Date	F	VF	XF	Unc	BU
1999	—	—	—	75.00	—

EURO COINAGE

KM# 167 EURO CENT **Weight:** 2.2700 g. **Composition:** Copper Plated Steel **Ruler:** Rainier III **Obverse:** Crowned arms **Reverse:** Denomination and globe **Edge:** Plain **Size:** 16.2 mm.

Date	F	VF	XF	Unc	BU
2001	—	—	—	20.00	30.00
2002	—	—	—	—	65.00

Note: Initially available only in sets

KM# 168 2 EURO CENTS **Weight:** 3.0300 g. **Composition:** Copper Plated Steel **Ruler:** Rainier III **Obverse:** Crowned arms **Reverse:** Denomination and globe **Edge:** Grooved **Size:** 18.7 mm.

Date	F	VF	XF	Unc	BU
2001	—	—	—	15.00	25.00
2002	—	—	—	—	65.00

Note: Initially available only in sets

KM# 169 5 EURO CENTS **Weight:** 3.8600 g. **Composition:** Copper-Nickel Plated Steel **Ruler:** Rainier III **Obverse:** Crowned arms **Reverse:** Denomination and globe **Edge:** Plain **Size:** 21.2 mm.

Date	F	VF	XF	Unc	BU
2001	—	—	—	20.00	30.00
2002	—	—	—	—	70.00

Note: Initially available only in sets

KM# 170 10 EURO CENTS **Weight:** 4.0700 g. **Composition:** Brass **Ruler:** Rainier III **Obverse:** Charging knight **Reverse:** Map and denomination **Edge:** Reeded **Size:** 19.7 mm.

Date	Mintage	F	VF	XF	Unc	BU
2001	300,000	—	—	—	15.00	20.00
2002	367,200	—	—	—	8.00	12.00

KM# 171 20 EURO CENTS **Weight:** 5.7300 g. **Composition:** Brass **Ruler:** Rainier III **Obverse:** Charging knight **Reverse:** Map and denomination **Edge:** Notched **Size:** 22.1 mm.

Date	Mintage	F	VF	XF	Unc	BU
2001	366,400	—	—	—	15.00	20.00
2002	336,000	—	—	—	12.00	15.00

KM# 172 50 EURO CENTS **Weight:** 7.8100 g. **Composition:** Brass **Ruler:** Rainier III **Obverse:** Charging knight **Reverse:** Map and denomination **Edge:** Reeded

Date	Mintage	F	VF	XF	Unc	BU
2001	300,000	—	—	—	15.00	20.00
2002	324,000	—	—	—	8.00	12.00

KM# 173 EURO **Weight:** 7.5000 g. **Composition:** Bi-Metallic **Ruler:** Rainier III **Obverse:** Portraits of Prince and Crown Prince **Reverse:** Denomination and map **Edge:** Reeded and plain sections **Size:** 23.2 mm.

Date	Mintage	F	VF	XF	Unc	BU
2001	971,100	—	—	—	10.00	12.00
2002	472,500	—	—	—	11.00	14.00

KM# 174 2 EUROS **Weight:** 8.5200 g. **Composition:** Bi-Metallic **Ruler:** Rainier III **Obverse:** Prince's portrait **Reverse:** Denomination and map **Edge:** Reedind over "2's" and stars **Size:** 25.7 mm.

Date	Mintage	F	VF	XF	Unc	BU
2001	899,800	—	—	—	14.00	16.00
2002	456,000	—	—	—	15.00	18.00

ESSAIS

Standard metals unless otherwise noted

KM#	Date	Mintage	Identification	Mkt Val
E1	1924	—	50 Centimes. Gold. KM#110	2,000
E2	1924	12	Franc. KM111	950

KM#	Date	Mintage	Identification	Mkt Val
E3	1924	—	Franc. Gold. KM111	3,000
E4	1924	12	2 Francs. KM112	985

KM#	Date	Mintage	Identification	Mkt Val
E5	1924	—	2 Francs. Gold. KM112	4,000

KM#	Date	Mintage	Identification	Mkt Val
E6	ND(1943) (a)	250	Franc. 0.9000 Gold.	625
E7	ND(1943) (a)	1,100	Franc. Aluminum. KM120	28.00
E8	ND(1943) (a)	—	Franc. Aluminum-Bronze. KM120	25.00
E9	ND(1943) (a)	250	Franc. Silver. KM120	140

KM#	Date	Mintage	Identification	Mkt Val
E10	ND(1943) (a)	250	2 Francs. 0.9000 Gold.	725
E11	ND(1943) (a)	1,100	2 Francs. Aluminum. KM121	35.00
E12	ND(1943) (a)	1,100	2 Francs. Aluminum-Bronze. KM121	37.00
E13	ND(1943) (a)	250	2 Francs. Silver. KM121	165

KM#	Date	Mintage	Identification	Mkt Val
E14	1945 (a)	250	5 Francs. 0.9000 Gold.	800
E15	1945 (a)	1,100	5 Francs. Aluminum. KM122	50.00
E16	1945 (a)	150	5 Francs. Aluminum-Bronze. KM122	145
E17	1945 (a)	250	5 Francs. Silver. KM122	225
E18	1945 (a)	1,100	10 Francs. KM123	40.00
E19	1945 (a)	250	10 Francs. Silver.	190

KM#	Date	Mintage	Identification	Mkt Val
E20	1945 (a)	1,100	20 Francs. KM124	60.00
E21	1945 (a)	250	20 Francs. Silver.	180

KM#	Date	Mintage	Identification	Mkt Val
E22	1946 (a)	250	10 Francs. 0.9000 Gold.	800

KM#	Date	Mintage	Identification	Mkt Val
E23	1947 (a)	250	20 Francs. 0.9000 Gold.	850

KM#	Date	Mintage	Identification	Mkt Val
E24	1950 (a)	1,100	10 Francs.	25.00
E25	1950 (a)	500	10 Francs. Silver.	50.00
E26	1950 (a)	500	10 Francs. 0.9000 Gold.	365
E27	1950 (a)	1,700	20 Francs.	32.00

KM#	Date	Mintage	Identification	Mkt Val
E29	1950 (a)	500	20 Francs. 0.9000 Gold.	450
E30	1950 (a)	1,700	50 Francs.	50.00
E31	1950 (a)	500	50 Francs. Silver.	90.00

KM#	Date	Mintage	Identification	Mkt Val
E32	1950 (a)	500	50 Francs. 0.9000 Gold.	725
E33	1950 (a)	1,700	100 Francs.	50.00
E34	1950 (a)	500	100 Francs. Silver.	100

KM#	Date	Mintage	Identification	Mkt Val
E35	1950 (a)	500	100 Francs. 0.9000 Gold.	750
E28	1950 (a)	—	20 Francs. Silver.	70.00

KM#	Date	Mintage	Identification	Mkt Val
E36	1956 (a)	500	100 Francs. 0.9000 Gold.	340
E37	1956 (a)	500	100 Francs. Silver. KM134	150
E38	1960 (a)	—	Franc. KM140	70.00
E39	1960 (a)	500	Franc. Silver.	70.00

KM#	Date	Mintage	Identification	Mkt Val
E40	1960 (a)	500	Franc. 0.9200 Gold.	300
E41	1960 (a)	500	5 Francs. Silver.	100

KM#	Date	Mintage	Identification	Mkt Val
E42	1960 (a)	500	5 Francs. 0.9200 Gold.	600
E43	1962 (a)	1,200	10 Centimes.	15.00
E44	1962 (a)	502	10 Centimes. 0.9500 Silver.	60.00

KM#	Date	Mintage	Identification	Mkt Val
E45	1962 (a)	502	10 Centimes. 0.9200 Gold.	180
E46	1962 (a)	1,200	20 Centimes.	40.00
E47	1962 (a)	502	20 Centimes. 0.9500 Silver.	75.00

KM#	Date	Mintage	Identification	Mkt Val
E48	1962 (a)	502	20 Centimes. 0.9200 Gold.	225
E49	1962 (a)	1,200	50 Centimes.	60.00
E50	1962 (a)	502	50 Centimes. 0.9500 Silver.	150

KM#	Date	Mintage	Identification	Mkt Val
E51	1962 (a)	502	50 Centimes. 0.9200 Gold.	385
E52	1965 (a)	2,000	1/2 Franc. Nickel.	40.00
E53	1965 (a)	1,000	1/2 Franc. Silver.	60.00

KM#	Date	Mintage	Identification	Mkt Val
E54	1965 (a)	1,000	1/2 Franc. 0.9200 Gold.	185
E55	1966 (a)	500	5 Francs. 0.9200 Gold.	450
E56	1966 (a)	100	10 Francs.	85.00

KM#	Date	Mintage	Identification	Mkt Val
E57	1966 (a)	1,000	10 Francs. 0.9200 Gold.	725
E58	1971 (a)	1,000	5 Francs.	40.00
E59	1971 (a)	1,000	5 Francs. Silver.	100

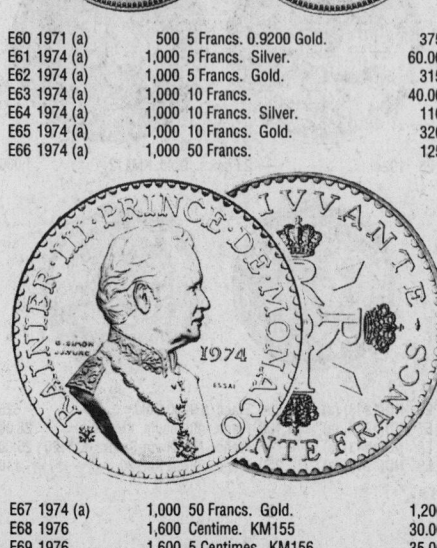

KM#	Date	Mintage	Identification	Mkt Val
E60	1971 (a)	500	5 Francs. 0.9200 Gold.	375
E61	1974 (a)	1,000	5 Francs. Silver.	60.00
E62	1974 (a)	1,000	5 Francs. Gold.	315
E63	1974 (a)	1,000	10 Francs.	40.00
E64	1974 (a)	1,000	10 Francs. Silver.	110
E65	1974 (a)	1,000	10 Francs. Gold.	320
E66	1974 (a)	1,000	50 Francs.	125

KM#	Date	Mintage	Identification	Mkt Val
E67	1974 (a)	1,000	50 Francs. Gold.	1,200
E68	1976	1,600	Centime. KM155	30.00
E69	1976	1,600	5 Centimes. KM156	35.00
E70	1976	1,600	10 Centimes. KM142	35.00
E71	1979	—	2 Francs. KM157	70.00
E72	1982 (a)	4,000	10 Francs. Nickel-Aluminum-Bronze.	45.00
E73	1982 (a)	30,000	10 Francs. Silver.	20.00

KM#	Date	Mintage	Identification	Mkt Val
E74	1982 (a)	1,000	10 Francs. Gold.	385
E75	1982 (a)	1,000	100 Francs. 0.9000 Silver. KM161	60.00

KM#	Date	Mintage	Identification	Mkt Val
E76	1982 (a)	1,000	100 Francs. Gold.	400

PATTERNS

Including off metal strikes

KM#	Date	Mintage	Identification	Mkt Val
Pn15	1934A	15	500 Francs. 0.9000 Gold.	3,220

PIEFORTS WITH ESSAI

Double thickness;
Standard metals unless otherwise noted

KM#	Date	Mintage	Identification	Mkt Val
PE1	ND(1943) (a)	15	Franc. 0.9000 Gold.	850
PE2	ND(1943) (a)	15	2 Francs. 0.9000 Gold.	950
PE3	1945 (a)	15	5 Francs. 0.9000 Gold.	1,500

KM#	Date	Mintage	Identification	Mkt Val
PE4	1946 (a)	16	10 Francs. 0.9000 Gold.	1,100
PE5	1947 (a)	16	20 Francs. 0.9000 Gold.	1,350
PE6a	1950 (a)	325	10 Francs. 0.9000 Gold.	265
PE6	1950 (a)	—	10 Francs. Silver.	75.00
PE7	1950 (a)	—	20 Francs. Silver.	65.00
PE7a	1950 (a)	325	20 Francs. 0.9000 Gold.	310
PE8	1950 (a)	—	50 Francs. Silver.	125
PE8a	1950 (a)	325	50 Francs. 0.9000 Gold.	425
PE9	1950 (a)	—	100 Francs. Silver.	150
PE9a	1950 (a)	325	100 Francs. 0.9000 Gold.	500
PE10	1956 (a)	20	100 Francs. 0.9000 Gold.	1,200
PE11	1960 (a)	25	Franc. 0.9200 Gold.	625
PE12	1960 (a)	25	5 Francs. 0.9200 Gold.	1,200
PE13	1962 (a)	100	10 Centimes. 0.9500 Silver.	140
PE13a	1962 (a)	25	10 Centimes. 0.9200 Gold.	725
PE14	1962 (a)	100	20 Centimes. 0.9500 Silver.	140
PE14a	1962 (a)	25	20 Centimes. 0.9200 Gold.	820
PE15	1962 (a)	100	50 Centimes. 0.9500 Silver.	200
PE15a	1962 (a)	25	50 Centimes. 0.9200 Gold.	900
PE16	1966 (a)	150	5 Francs. Nickel.	60.00
PE16a	1971 (a)	250	5 Francs. Silver.	150
PE16b	1971 (a)	250	5 Francs. 0.9200 Gold.	600
PE17	1974 (a)	250	5 Francs. Silver.	150

KM#	Date	Mintage	Identification	Mkt Val
PE17a	1974 (a)	250	5 Francs. Gold.	600
PE18	1974 (a)	250	10 Francs. Silver.	200

KM#	Date	Mintage	Identification	Mkt Val

KM#	Date	Mintage	Identification	Mkt Val
PE18a	1974 (a)	250	10 Francs. Gold.	500
P18a	1974 (a)	—	10 Francs. Gold. Without Essai	600
PE19	1974 (a)	250	50 Francs. Without Essai	100

KM#	Date	Mintage	Identification	Mkt Val
PE19a	1974 (a)	250	50 Francs. Gold.	1,750
P19a	1974 (a)	250	50 Francs. Gold. Without Essai	1,500
PE20	1982 (a)	250	10 Francs. Silver.	150
PE20a	1982 (a)	250	10 Francs. Gold.	500
PE21	1982 (a)	250	100 Francs. Silver.	200
PE21a	1982 (a)	250	100 Francs. Gold.	700

MINT SETS

KM#	Date	Mintage	Identification	Issue Price	Mkt Val
MS1	2001 (8)	20,000	KM#167-174, exercise caution, as privately packaged and deceptively false sets are known	35.00	375
MS2	2002 (8)	40,000	KM#167-174, exercise caution, as partial sets, privately packaged and deceptively false sets are known	35.00	350

SPECIMEN SETS (SS)

KM#	Date	Mintage	Identification	Issue Price	Mkt Val
SS1	1974 (7)	7	KM140, 142, 143, 145, 150, 151, 152.1. 3,000 sets not released.	45.00	120
SS2	1975 (7)	8	KM140, 142, 143, 145, 150, 152.2, 154	—	100
SS3	1976 (9)	6,000	KM140, 142, 143, 145, 150, 152.2, 154-156	—	120
SS6	1982 (11)	10,000	KM140, 142, 143, 145, 150, 154-157, 160, 161	—	150
SS7	1995 (9)	—	KM140, 142, 143, 150, 155, 156, 163, 165, 166	—	120

MONGOLIA

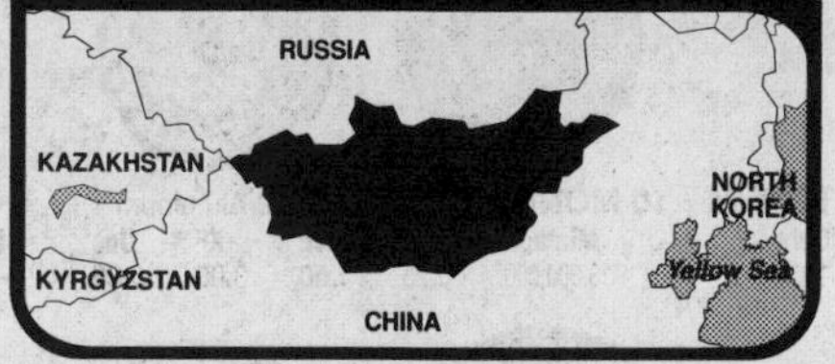

The State of Mongolia, (formerly the Mongolian Peoples Republic) a landlocked country in central Asia between Russia and the People's Republic of China, has an area of 604,250 sq. mi. (1,565,000 sq. km.) and a population of 2.26 million. Capital: Ulaan Baator. Animal herds and flocks are the chief economic asset. Wool, cattle, butter, meat and hides are exported.

Mongolia (often referred to as Outer Mongolia), one of the world's oldest countries, attained its greatest power in the 13th century when Genghis Khan and his successors conquered all of China and extended their influence westward as far as Hungary and Poland. The empire dissolved in later centuries and in 1691 was brought under suzeraintyof the Manchus, who had conquered China in 1644. After the Chinese republican movement led by Sun-Yat-sen overthrew the Manchus and set up the Chinese Republic in 1911. Mongolia, with the support of Russia, proclaimed their independence from China and, on March 13, 1921 a Provisional Peoples Government was established and later, on Nov. 26, 1924 the government proclaimed the Mongolian Peoples Republic.

Although nominally a dependency of China, Outer Mongolia voted at a plebiscite Oct. 20, 1945 to sever all ties with China and become an independent nation. Opposition to the communist party developed in late 1989 and after demonstrations and hunger strikes, the Politburo resigned on March 12, 1990 and the new State of Mongolia was organized.

On Feb. 12, 1992 it became the first to discard communism as the national political system by adopting a new constitution.

For earlier issues see Russia - Tannu Tuva.

MONETARY SYSTEM
100 Mongo = 1 Tugrik

PEOPLE'S REPUBLIC

DECIMAL COINAGE

KM# 1 MONGO Composition: Copper

Date	F	VF	XF	Unc	BU
AH15 (1925)	5.00	8.00	12.00	20.00	—

KM# 9 MONGO Composition: Aluminum-Bronze

Date	F	VF	XF	Unc	BU
AH27 (1937)	2.50	3.50	7.00	15.00	—

KM# 15 MONGO Composition: Aluminum-Bronze

Date	F	VF	XF	Unc	BU
AH35 (1945)	2.00	3.00	5.50	11.50	—

KM# 21 MONGO Composition: Aluminum

Date	Mintage	F	VF	XF	Unc	BU
1959	9,000,000	0.25	0.60	1.00	1.75	—

KM# 27 MONGO Composition: Aluminum

Date	F	VF	XF	Unc	BU
1970	0.25	0.60	0.85	1.25	—
1977	0.25	0.60	0.85	1.25	—
1980	0.25	0.60	0.85	1.25	—
1981	0.25	0.60	0.85	1.25	—

KM# 2 2 MONGO Composition: Copper

Date	F	VF	XF	Unc	BU
AH15 (1925)	3.50	6.50	12.00	20.00	—

KM# 10 2 MONGO Composition: Aluminum-Bronze

Date	F	VF	XF	Unc	BU
AH27 (1937)	2.50	3.50	6.00	12.00	—

KM# 16 2 MONGO Composition: Aluminum-Bronze

Date	F	VF	XF	Unc	BU
AH35 (1945)	1.00	2.00	4.00	7.00	—

KM# 22 2 MONGO Composition: Aluminum

Date	Mintage	F	VF	XF	Unc	BU
1959	4,000,000	0.25	0.65	1.50	3.00	—

KM# 28 2 MONGO Composition: Aluminum

Date	F	VF	XF	Unc	BU
1970	0.25	0.65	1.20	2.25	—
1977	0.25	0.65	1.20	2.25	—
1980	0.25	0.65	1.20	2.25	—
1981	0.25	0.65	1.20	2.25	—

KM# 3 5 MONGO Composition: Copper

Date	F	VF	XF	Unc	BU
AH15 (1925)	5.00	10.00	20.00	35.00	—

Note: Variety in obverse legend exists

KM# 11 5 MONGO **Composition:** Aluminum-Bronze

Date	F	VF	XF	Unc	BU
AH27 (1937)	2.75	3.50	6.00	12.00	—

KM# 17 5 MONGO **Composition:** Aluminum-Bronze

Date	F	VF	XF	Unc	BU
AH35 (1945)	1.75	2.50	5.00	10.00	—

KM# 23 5 MONGO **Composition:** Aluminum

Date	Mintage	F	VF	XF	Unc	BU
1959	2,400,000	0.25	1.00	2.00	3.00	—

KM# 29 5 MONGO **Composition:** Aluminum

Date	F	VF	XF	Unc	BU
1970	0.25	0.85	1.75	2.75	—
1977	0.25	0.85	1.75	2.75	—
1980	0.25	0.85	1.75	2.75	—
1981	0.25	0.85	1.75	2.75	—

KM# 4 10 MONGO **Weight:** 1.7996 g. **Composition:** 0.5000 Silver .0289 oz. ASW

Date	Mintage	VG	F	VF	XF	Unc
AH15 (1925)	1,500,000	—	3.00	5.00	9.00	17.50

KM# 12 10 MONGO **Composition:** Copper-Nickel

Date	F	VF	XF	Unc	BU
AH27 (1937)	2.00	3.50	7.00	14.00	—

KM# 18 10 MONGO **Composition:** Copper-Nickel

Date	F	VF	XF	Unc	BU
AH35 (1945)	1.50	3.00	5.00	9.00	—

KM# 24 10 MONGO **Composition:** Aluminum

Date	Mintage	F	VF	XF	Unc	BU
1959	3,000,000	0.75	1.50	3.00	5.00	—

KM# 30 10 MONGO **Composition:** Copper-Nickel

Date	F	VF	XF	Unc	BU
1970	0.35	0.85	1.75	2.75	—
1977	0.35	0.85	1.75	2.75	—
1980	0.35	0.85	1.75	2.75	—
1981	0.35	0.85	1.75	2.75	—

KM# 5 15 MONGO **Weight:** 2.6994 g. **Composition:** 0.5000 Silver .0433 oz. ASW

Date	Mintage	VG	F	VF	XF	Unc
AH15 (1925)	417,000	—	3.50	6.00	12.00	20.00

KM# 13 15 MONGO **Composition:** Copper-Nickel

Date	F	VF	XF	Unc	BU
AH27 (1937)	2.00	3.00	6.00	12.00	—

KM# 19 15 MONGO **Composition:** Copper-Nickel

Date	F	VF	XF	Unc	BU
AH35 (1945)	1.50	2.25	4.00	8.00	—

KM# 25 15 MONGO **Composition:** Aluminum

Date	Mintage	F	VF	XF	Unc	BU
1959	4,600,000	0.35	0.85	1.75	3.50	—

KM# 31 15 MONGO **Composition:** Copper-Nickel

Date	F	VF	XF	Unc	BU
1970	0.25	0.65	1.25	2.50	—
1977	0.25	0.65	1.25	2.50	—
1980	0.25	0.65	1.25	2.50	—
1981	0.25	0.65	1.25	2.50	—

KM# 6 20 MONGO **Weight:** 3.5992 g. **Composition:** 0.5000 Silver .0578 oz. ASW

Date	Mintage	VG	F	VF	XF	Unc
AH15 (1925)	1,625,000	—	4.00	7.50	14.00	25.00

KM# 14 20 MONGO **Composition:** Copper-Nickel

Date	F	VF	XF	Unc	BU
AH27 (1937)	2.50	4.50	10.00	18.00	—

KM# 20 20 MONGO **Composition:** Copper-Nickel

Date	F	VF	XF	Unc	BU
AH35 (1945)	1.50	2.50	5.00	10.00	—

KM# 26 20 MONGO **Composition:** Aluminum

Date	Mintage	F	VF	XF	Unc	BU
1959	3,600,000	0.60	1.25	2.25	3.50	—

KM# 32 20 MONGO **Composition:** Copper-Nickel

Date	F	VF	XF	Unc	BU
1970	0.40	0.80	1.50	2.50	—
1977	0.40	0.80	1.50	2.50	—
1980	0.40	0.80	1.50	2.50	—
1981	0.40	0.80	1.50	2.50	—

KM# 7 50 MONGO **Weight:** 9.9979 g. **Composition:** 0.9000 Silver .2893 oz. ASW

Date	Mintage	VG	F	VF	XF	Unc
AH15 (1925)	920,000	—	7.50	12.00	18.50	30.00

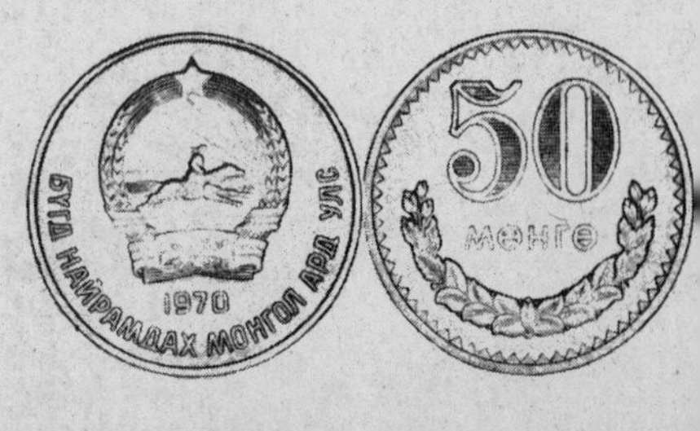

KM# 33 50 MONGO Composition: Copper-Nickel

Date	F	VF	XF	Unc	BU
1970	0.50	1.00	1.75	3.00	—
1977	0.50	1.00	1.75	3.00	—
1980	0.50	1.00	1.75	3.00	—
1981	0.50	1.00	1.75	3.00	—

KM# 8 TUGRIK Weight: 19.9957 g. **Composition:** 0.9000 Silver .5786 oz. ASW

Date	Mintage	VG	F	VF	XF	Unc
AH15 (1925)	400,000	—	10.00	15.00	20.00	35.00

KM# 34 TUGRIK Composition: Aluminum-Bronze **Subject:** 50th Anniversary of the Revolution **Note:** Date on edge.

Date	F	VF	XF	Unc	BU
ND(1971)	—	4.00	6.00	10.00	—

KM# 34a TUGRIK Composition: Copper-Nickel

Date	F	VF	XF	Unc	BU
ND(1971)	6.00	8.00	12.00	18.00	—

KM# 34b TUGRIK Weight: 18.4000 g. **Composition:** Silver

Date	F	VF	XF	Unc	BU
(1971) Proof	—	Value: 50.00			

KM# 34c TUGRIK Weight: 30.0000 g. **Composition:** Gold **Subject:** 50th Anniversary of the Revolution **Note:** Mintage: 5-10.

Date	F	VF	XF	Unc	BU
(1971) Proof	—	Value: 2,500			

KM# 41 TUGRIK Composition: Aluminum-Bronze **Subject:** 60th Anniversary of the Revolution

Date	F	VF	XF	Unc	BU
1981	—	—	4.00	7.50	—

KM# 42 TUGRIK Composition: Aluminum-Bronze **Subject:** Soviet - Mongolian Space Flight

Date	F	VF	XF	Unc	BU
1981	—	—	3.00	6.00	—

KM# 43 TUGRIK Composition: Aluminum-Bronze **Subject:** 60th Anniversary of the State Bank

Date	F	VF	XF	Unc	BU
1984	—	—	3.00	6.00	—

Note: Edge varieties exist

KM# 44 TUGRIK Composition: Aluminum-Bronze **Subject:** 60th Anniversary of the People's Republic

Date	F	VF	XF	Unc	BU
1984	—	—	3.00	5.50	—

KM# 48 TUGRIK Composition: Aluminum-Bronze **Subject:** Year of Peace

Date	F	VF	XF	Unc	BU
1986	—	—	3.00	5.50	—

KM# 49 TUGRIK Composition: Aluminum-Bronze **Subject:** 65th Anniversary of the Revolution

Date	F	VF	XF	Unc	BU
1986	—	—	3.00	5.50	—

KM# 52 TUGRIK Composition: Aluminum-Bronze **Subject:** 170th Anniversary - Birth of Karl Marx

Date	F	VF	XF	Unc	BU
ND(1988)	—	—	4.00	12.50	—
ND(1988)	—	—	4.00	12.50	—

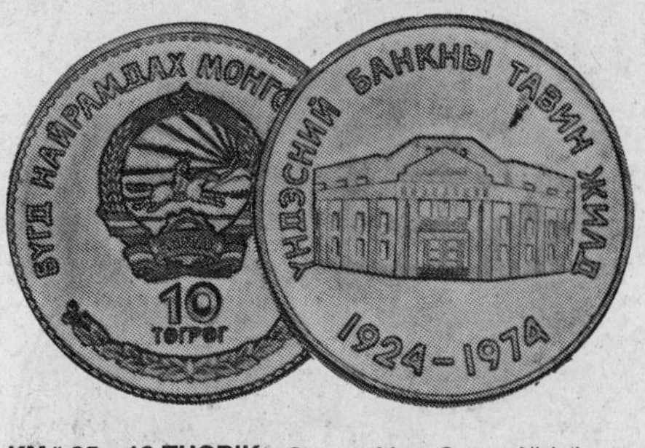

KM# 35 10 TUGRIK Composition: Copper-Nickel **Subject:** 50th Anniversary of State Bank

Date	F	VF	XF	Unc	BU
ND(1974)	—	—	—	9.00	—
ND(1974)	—	—	—	9.00	—

KM# 36 25 TUGRIK Weight: 28.2800 g. **Composition:** 0.9250 Silver .8411 oz. ASW **Subject:** Conservation **Reverse:** Arfali sheep

Date	Mintage	F	VF	XF	Unc	BU
1976	5,348	—	—	—	15.00	—
1976 Proof	6,096	Value: 20.00				

KM# 39 25 TUGRIK Weight: 19.4400 g. **Composition:** 0.9250 Silver .5781 oz. ASW **Series:** International Year of the Child

Date	Mintage	F	VF	XF	Unc	BU
1980 Proof	14,000	Value: 20.00				

KM# 47 25 TUGRIK Weight: 19.4400 g. **Composition:** 0.9250 Silver .5781 oz. ASW **Series:** Decade for Women

Date	Mintage	F	VF	XF	Unc	BU
1984 Proof	1,249	Value: 37.50				

KM# 50 25 TUGRIK **Weight:** 28.2800 g. **Composition:** 0.9250 Silver .8411 oz. ASW **Series:** World Wildlife Fund **Reverse:** Snow leopard

Date	Mintage	F	VF	XF	Unc	BU
1987 Matte	850	—	—	—	45.00	—
1987 Proof	25,000	Value: 27.50				

KM# 54 25 TUGRIK **Weight:** 28.2800 g. **Composition:** 0.9250 Silver .8411 oz. ASW **Series:** Save the Children Fund

Date	Mintage	F	VF	XF	Unc	BU
1989 Proof	20,000	Value: 28.50				

KM# 37 50 TUGRIK **Weight:** 35.0000 g. **Composition:** 0.9250 Silver 1.0409 oz. ASW **Subject:** Conservation **Obverse:** Siimilar to 25 Tugrik, KM#36 **Reverse:** Bactrian camel

Date	Mintage	F	VF	XF	Unc	BU
1976	5,328	—	—	—	20.00	—
1976 Proof	5,900	Value: 25.00				

KM# 57 50 TUGRIK **Weight:** 31.1000 g. **Composition:** 0.9990 Silver 1.0000 oz. ASW **Subject:** Discovery of America **Reverse:** Columbus

Date	Mintage	F	VF	XF	Unc	BU
1992 Proof	20,000	Value: 32.50				

Note: KM#57.2, previously listed here, has been correctly identified as belonging with coinage of The People's Republic.

KM# 170 50 TUGRIK **Weight:** 31.1000 g. **Composition:** 0.9990 Silver 1 oz. ASW **Subject:** Year of the Monkey **Obverse:** Similar to KM#57 **Reverse:** Similar to KM#86

Date	F	VF	XF	Unc	BU
1992	—	—	—	80.00	—

KM# 53 100 TUGRIK **Weight:** 28.0000 g. **Composition:** 0.9000 Silver .8102 oz. ASW **Subject:** Dinosaurs **Reverse:** Nemectosaurus

Date	Mintage	F	VF	XF	Unc	BU
1989	1,000	—	—	—	80.00	—

KM# 55 100 TUGRIK **Weight:** 28.0000 g. **Composition:** 0.9000 Silver .8102 oz. ASW **Subject:** Secret history of the Mongols **Obverse:** State emblem above denomination within English legend **Reverse:** Portrait of Genghis Khan in light clothing

Date	Mintage	F	VF	XF	Unc	BU
1990	4,000	—	—	—	50.00	—

KM# 58 100 TUGRIK **Weight:** 1.5600 g. **Composition:** 0.9990 Gold .0500 oz. AGW **Subject:** Discovery of America - Columbus **Obverse:** Similar to KM#53 **Reverse:** Portrait of Columbus and ship within circle and legend **Note:** Similar to 50 Tugrik, KM#57.

Date	Mintage	F	VF	XF	Unc	BU
1992 Proof	Est. 10,000	Value: 45.00				

KM# 59 200 TUGRIK **Weight:** 3.1100 g. **Composition:** 0.9990 Gold .1000 oz. AGW **Subject:** Discovery of America - Columbus **Obverse:** Similar to KM#53 **Reverse:** Portrait of Columbus and ship within circle and legend **Note:** Similar to 50 Tugrik, KM#57

Date	Mintage	F	VF	XF	Unc	BU
1992 Proof	Est. 10,000	Value: 60.00				

KM# 45 250 TUGRIK **Weight:** 7.1300 g. **Composition:** 0.9000 Gold .2026 oz. AGW **Series:** Decade for Women

Date	Mintage	F	VF	XF	Unc	BU
1984 Proof	510	Value: 150				

KM# 72 300 TUGRIK **Weight:** 7.7700 g. **Composition:** 0.9990 Gold .25 oz. AGW **Subject:** Japanese royal wedding **Note:** Similar to 500 Tugrik, KM#73

Date	Mintage	F	VF	XF	Unc	BU
1993 Proof	Est. 500	Value: 235				

KM# 38 750 TUGRIK **Weight:** 33.4370 g. **Composition:** 0.9000 Gold .9676 oz. AGW **Subject:** Conservation **Reverse:** Przewalski horses

Date	Mintage	F	VF	XF	Unc	BU
1976	929	—	—	—	500	—
1976 Proof	374	Value: 750				

KM# 40 750 TUGRIK **Weight:** 18.7900 g. **Composition:** 0.9000 Gold .5437 oz. AGW **Series:** International Year of the Child

Date	Mintage	F	VF	XF	Unc	BU
1980 Proof	32,000	Value: 225				

KM# 56 1000 TUGRIK **Weight:** 20.7000 g. **Composition:** 0.9000 Gold .5990 oz. AGW **Subject:** Secret history of the Mongols **Obverse:** State emblem above denomination within English legend **Reverse:** Portrait of Genghis Khan in heavy clothing

Date	F	VF	XF	Unc	BU
1990	—	—	—	325	—

KM# 60 1000 TUGRIK **Weight:** 31.1000 g. **Composition:** 0.9990 Gold 1.0000 oz. AGW **Subject:** Discovery of America **Reverse:** Columbus

Date	Mintage	F	VF	XF	Unc	BU
1992 Proof	2,000	Value: 450				

KM# 171 1000 TUGRIK **Subject:** Year of the Monkey **Obverse:** Similar to KM#60 **Reverse:** Similar to KM#91

Date	F	VF	XF	Unc	BU
1992	—	—	—	650	—

STATE OF MONGOLIA

DECIMAL COINAGE

KM# 122 20 TUGRIK **Composition:** Aluminum **Obverse:** National emblem **Reverse:** Denomination

Date	F	VF	XF	Unc	BU
1994	—	—	—	1.50	—

KM# 84 50 TUGRIK **Weight:** 15.0000 g. **Composition:** 0.9990 Silver .4818 oz. ASW **Reverse:** Ugedei Khan, son of Genghis

Date	Mintage	F	VF	XF	Unc	BU
1992 Proof	Est. 1,000	Value: 30.00				

KM# 86 50 TUGRIK **Weight:** 31.1035 g. **Composition:** 0.9990 Silver 1.0000 oz. ASW **Subject:** Year of the Monkey

Date	Mintage	F	VF	XF	Unc	BU
1992 Proof	20,000	Value: 40.00				

KM# 166 50 TUGRIK **Weight:** 31.1035 g. **Composition:** 0.9990 Silver 1 oz. ASW **Subject:** Discovery of America - Columbus **Obverse:** Similar to KM#86 **Reverse:** Similar to KM#57

Date	F	VF	XF	Unc	BU
1992 Proof	—	Value: 42.50			

KM# 61 50 TUGRIK **Weight:** 31.1035 g. **Composition:** 0.9990 Silver 1 oz. ASW **Subject:** Year of the Rooster

Date	Mintage	F	VF	XF	Unc	BU
1993 Proof	20,000	Value: 40.00				

KM# 69 50 TUGRIK **Weight:** 31.1035 g. **Composition:** 0.9990 Silver 1 oz. ASW **Subject:** Japanese royal wedding

Date	Mintage	F	VF	XF	Unc	BU
1993 Proof	1,962	Value: 47.50				

KM# 75 50 TUGRIK **Subject:** Year of the Dog

Date	Mintage	F	VF	XF	Unc	BU
1994 Proof	4,000	Value: 45.00				

KM# 123 50 TUGRIK **Composition:** Aluminum **Obverse:** National emblem **Reverse:** Denomination

Date	F	VF	XF	Unc	BU
1994	—	—	—	1.75	—

KM# 94 50 TUGRIK **Composition:** Copper-Nickel **Subject:** Year of the Pig **Obverse:** National emblem

Date	Mintage	F	VF	XF	Unc	BU
1995 Proof	50,000	Value: 15.00				

KM# 104 50 TUGRIK **Composition:** Copper-Nickel **Subject:** Year of the Rat

Date	Mintage	F	VF	XF	Unc	BU
1996 Proof	50,000	Value: 15.00				

KM# 126 50 TUGRIK **Composition:** Copper-Nickel **Subject:** Year of the Ox **Obverse:** National emblem

Date	Mintage	F	VF	XF	Unc	BU
1997 Proof	25,000	Value: 15.00				

KM# 172 50 TUGRIK **Composition:** Copper-Nickel **Subject:** Year of the Tiger

Date	Mintage	F	VF	XF	Unc	BU
1998	25,000	—	—	—	15.00	—

KM# 159 50 TUGRIK **Weight:** 20.0000 g. **Composition:** Copper-Nickel **Subject:** Year of the Rabbit **Obverse:** National emblem **Reverse:** Rabbit **Edge:** Plain **Size:** 38 mm.

Date	Mintage	F	VF	XF	Unc	BU
1999 Prooflike	25,000	—	—	—	15.00	—

KM# 87 100 TUGRIK **Weight:** 1.5600 g. **Composition:** 0.9990 Gold .0500 oz. AGW **Subject:** Year of the Monkey **Note:** Similar to 50 Tugrik, KM#86.

Date	Mintage	F	VF	XF	Unc	BU
1992 Proof	10,000	Value: 75.00				

KM# 167 100 TUGRIK **Weight:** 1.5600 g. **Composition:** 0.9990 Gold .0500 oz. AGW **Subject:** Discovery of America - Columbus **Obverse:** Similar to KM#126 **Reverse:** Similar to KM#57

Date	F	VF	XF	Unc	BU
1992 Proof	—	Value: 45.00			

KM# 62.1 100 TUGRIK **Weight:** 1.5600 g. **Composition:** 0.9990 Gold .0500 oz. AGW **Subject:** Year of the Rooster **Note:** Similar to 50 Tugrik, KM#61.

Date	Mintage	F	VF	XF	Unc	BU
1993 Proof	30,000	Value: 50.00				

KM# 62.2 100 TUGRIK **Weight:** 1.5600 g. **Composition:** 0.9990 Gold .0500 oz. AGW **Note:** Handstruck.

Date	Mintage	F	VF	XF	Unc	BU
1993 Proof	500	Value: 250				

Note: Strikes tend to be crude and do not have ".999" on them.

KM# 70 100 TUGRIK **Weight:** 1.5600 g. **Composition:** 0.9990 Gold .0500 oz. AGW **Subject:** Japanese Royal Wedding **Note:** Similar to 50 Tugrik, KM#69.

Date	Mintage	F	VF	XF	Unc	BU
1993 Proof	Est. 3,000	Value: 75.00				

KM# 124 100 TUGRIK **Composition:** Copper-Nickel **Obverse:** National emblem **Reverse:** Denomination

Date	F	VF	XF	Unc	BU
1994	—	—	—	3.50	—

KM# 168 200 TUGRIK **Weight:** 3.1100 g. **Composition:** 0.9990 Gold .1000 oz. AGW **Subject:** Discovery of America - Columbus **Obverse:** Similar to KM#86 **Reverse:** Similar to KM#57

Date	F	VF	XF	Unc	BU
1992 Proof	—	Value: 60.00			

KM# 63 200 TUGRIK **Weight:** 3.1100 g. **Composition:** 0.9990 Gold .1000 oz. AGW **Subject:** Year of the Rooster **Obverse:** National emblem above denomination at left, country name at right **Reverse:** Rooster **Note:** Similar to 50 Tigrik, KM#61

Date	Mintage	F	VF	XF	Unc	BU
1993 Proof	500	Value: 200				

KM# 71 200 TUGRIK **Weight:** 3.1100 g. **Composition:** 0.9990 Gold .1000 oz. AGW **Subject:** Japanese Royal Wedding **Note:** Similar to 50 Tigrik, KM#69.

Date	Mintage	F	VF	XF	Unc	BU
1993 Proof	100	Value: 300				

KM# 76 200 TUGRIK **Weight:** 3.1100 g. **Composition:** 0.9990 Gold .1000 oz. AGW **Subject:** Year of the Dog.

Date	Mintage	F	VF	XF	Unc	BU
1994 Proof	500	Value: 175				

KM# 125 200 TUGRIK **Composition:** Copper-Nickel **Obverse:** Similar to 100 Tugrik KM#124

Date	F	VF	XF	Unc	BU
1994	—	—	—	3.50	—

KM# 80 250 TUGRIK **Weight:** 31.4700 g. **Composition:** 0.9250 Silver .9359 oz. ASW **Subject:** Wildlife **Reverse:** Wolves

Date	Mintage	F	VF	XF	Unc	BU
1993 Proof	Est. 15,000	Value: 32.50				

Note: KM#89 previously listed here has been reported as never released.

Date	Mintage	F	VF	XF	Unc	BU
1993 Proof	15,000	Value: 32.50				

Note: KM#89 previously listed here has been reported as never released

KM# 100 250 TUGRIK **Weight:** 31.4700 g. **Composition:** 0.9250 Silver .9359 oz. ASW **Subject:** Wildlife **Obverse:** National emblem **Reverse:** Przewalski's Horses

Date	Mintage	F	VF	XF	Unc	BU
1992 Proof	20,000	Value: 30.00				

KM# 110 250 TUGRIK **Weight:** 31.4700 g. **Composition:** 0.9250 Silver .9359 oz. ASW **Series:** Endangered Wildlife **Reverse:** Saiga Antelope

Date	Mintage	F	VF	XF	Unc	BU
1993 Proof	Est. 10,000	Value: 28.00				

KM# 64 250 TUGRIK **Weight:** 155.5000 g. **Composition:** 0.9990 Silver 5.000 oz. ASW **Subject:** Year of the Rooster **Note:** Similar to 50 Tugrik, KM#61.

Date	Mintage	F	VF	XF	Unc	BU
1993	300	Value: 150				

KM# 77 250 TUGRIK Weight: 155.5000 g. **Composition:** 0.9990 Silver 5.0000 oz. ASW **Subject:** Year of the Dog **Size:** 65 mm. **Note:** Illustration reduced.

Date	Mintage	F	VF	XF	Unc	BU
1994 Proof	200	Value: 300				

KM# 112 250 TUGRIK Weight: 31.4700 g. **Composition:** 0.9250 Silver .9359 oz. ASW **Series:** Olympics **Subject:** Archery

Date	Mintage	F	VF	XF	Unc	BU
1994 Proof	—	Value: 27.50				
1995 Proof	Est. 40,000	Value: 30.00				

KM# 111 250 TUGRIK Weight: 31.4700 g. **Composition:** 0.9250 Silver .9359 oz. ASW **Series:** Olympics **Subject:** Boxing **Obverse:** National emblem

Date	Mintage	F	VF	XF	Unc	BU
1994 Proof	Est. 5,000	Value: 50.00				

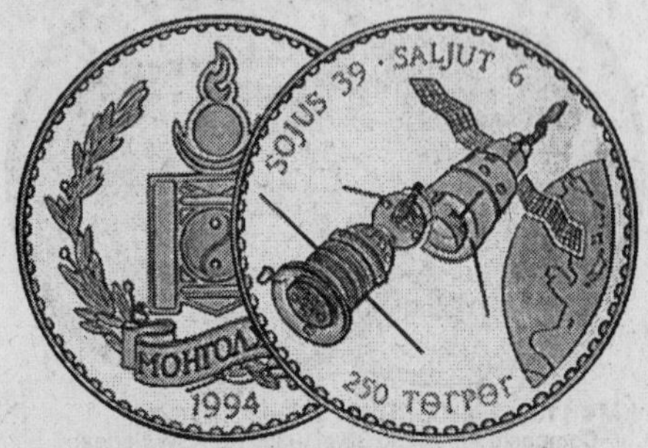

KM# 186 250 TUGRIK Weight: 31.4000 g. **Composition:** 0.9250 Silver .9338 oz. ASW **Subject:** Sojus 39 and Saljut 6 **Obverse:** National arms **Reverse:** 2 space capsules **Edge:** Reeded **Size:** 38.4 mm.

Date	F	VF	XF	Unc	BU
1994 Proof	—	Value: 55.00			

KM#103 250 TUGRIK Weight: 31.4700 g. **Composition:** 0.9250 Silver .9359 oz. ASW **Subject:** World Cup soccer

Date	F	VF	XF	Unc	BU
1994 Proof	—	Value: 30.00			

KM# 73 500 TUGRIK Weight: 15.5500 g. **Composition:** 0.9990 Gold .5000 oz. AGW **Subject:** Japanese Royal Wedding

Date	Mintage	F	VF	XF	Unc	BU
1993 Proof	160	Value: 285				

KM# 95 500 TUGRIK Weight: 31.1035 g. **Composition:** 0.9990 Silver 1.0000 oz. ASW **Subject:** Year of the Pig

Date	Mintage	F	VF	XF	Unc	BU
1995 Proof	3,000	Value: 45.00				

KM# 101 500 TUGRIK Weight: 31.1035 g. **Composition:** 0.9990 Silver 1.0000 oz. ASW **Subject:** Moscow - Bejing Railroad

Date	Mintage	F	VF	XF	Unc	BU
1995 Proof	20,000	Value: 30.00				

KM#187 500 TUGRIK Weight: 31.6000 g. **Composition:** 0.9250 Silver .9398 oz. ASW **Series:** Endangered Wildlife **Obverse:** National emblem **Reverse:** Pelican

Date	F	VF	XF	Unc	BU
1996 Proof	—	—	—	45.00	—

KM#105 500 TUGRIK Weight: 31.1035 g. **Composition:** 0.9990 Silver 1.0000 oz. ASW **Subject:** Year of the Rat **Note:** Similar to 50 Tugrik, KM#104, but with gold plated rat.

Date	Mintage	F	VF	XF	Unc	BU
1996 Proof	500	Value: 90.00				

KM# 132 500 TUGRIK Weight: 25.0000 g. **Composition:** 0.9250 Silver .7435 oz. ASW **Subject:** Aquila Rapax **Obverse:** National emblem

Date	Mintage	F	VF	XF	Unc	BU
1996 Proof	3,500	Value: 35.00				

KM# 133 500 TUGRIK Weight: 25.0000 g. **Composition:** 0.9250 Silver .7435 oz. ASW **Subject:** Equus Ferus **Obverse:** National emblem

Date	Mintage	F	VF	XF	Unc	BU
1996 Proof	3,500	Value: 35.00				

KM# 134 500 TUGRIK Weight: 25.0000 g. **Composition:** 0.9250 Silver .7435 oz. ASW **Subject:** Cameleus Ferus **Obverse:** National emblem

Date	Mintage	F	VF	XF	Unc	BU
1996 Proof	3,500	Value: 35.00				

KM# 135 500 TUGRIK Weight: 25.0000 g. **Composition:** 0.9250 Silver .7435 oz. ASW **Subject:** Panthera Tigris Altaica **Obverse:** National emblem

Date	Mintage	F	VF	XF	Unc	BU
1996 Proof	3,500	Value: 35.00				

KM# 193 500 TUGRIK Weight: 19.4400 g. **Composition:** 0.9250 Silver 0.5781 oz. ASW **Subject:** UNICEF **Obverse:** National arms. **Reverse:** Three costumed children. **Edge:** Reeded. **Size:** 36 mm.

Date	Mintage	F	VF	XF	Unc	BU
1997 Proof	25,000	Value: 25.00				

KM#127 500 TUGRIK Weight: 31.1035 g. **Composition:** 0.9990 Silver With Partial Gold Plating .1000 oz. **Subject:** Year of the Ox **Note:** Similar to 50 Tugrik, KM#126.

Date	Mintage	F	VF	XF	Unc	BU
1997 Proof	3,000	Value: 50.00				

KM# 197 500 TUGRIK Composition: Gold **Reverse:** Sumo wrestling

Date	F	VF	XF	Unc	BU
1998 Proof	—	Value: 40.00			

KM# 155 500 TUGRIK **Weight:** 15.0000 g. **Composition:** 0.9250 Silver .4461 oz. ASW **Series:** 1988 Olympics **Obverse:** National emblem **Reverse:** Skier

Date	F	VF	XF	Unc	BU
1998	—	Value: 30.00			

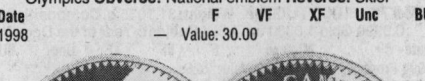

KM# 156 500 TUGRIK **Weight:** 20.0000 g. **Composition:** 0.5000 Silver .3215 oz. ASW **Series:** 2000 Olympics **Obverse:** National emblem **Reverse:** 2 wrestlers

Date	VG	F	VF	XF	Unc
1998 Proof	—	Value: 28.00			

KM# 157 500 TUGRIK **Weight:** 31.4700 g. **Composition:** 0.9990 Silver 1.0108 oz. ASW **Subject:** Endangered wildlife **Obverse:** National emblem **Reverse:** Tiger and cubs

Date	F	VF	XF	Unc	BU
1998 Proof	—	Value: 50.00			

KM# 158 500 TUGRIK **Weight:** 1.2241 g. **Composition:** 0.9990 Gold .0400 oz. AGW **Subject:** Buddhist Diety Maitreya **Obverse:** National emblem

Date	F	VF	XF	Unc	BU
1998 Proof	—	Value: 50.00			

KM# 173 500 TUGRIK **Weight:** 31.1045 g. **Composition:** 0.9990 Silver 1.0000 oz. ASW **Subject:** Year of the Tiger

Date	Mintage	F	VF	XF	Unc	BU
1998	25,000	—	—	—	25.00	—

KM# 173a 500 TUGRIK **Weight:** 31.1045 g. **Composition:** 0.9990 Silver 1.0000 oz. ASW **Subject:** Year of the Tiger **Note:** Gold plated tiger.

Date	Mintage	F	VF	XF	Unc	BU
1998	3,000	—	—	—	50.00	—

KM# 174 500 TUGRIK **Weight:** 1.2441 g. **Composition:** 0.9990 Gold .0400 oz. AGW **Subject:** Year of the TIger

Date	F	VF	XF	Unc	BU
1998	—	—	—	40.00	—

KM# 178 500 TUGRIK **Weight:** 31.6100 g. **Composition:** 0.9250 Silver .9400 oz. ASW **Subject:** Millennium 2000 **Obverse:** National emblem **Reverse:** Rider and multicolored speckled hologram

Date	Mintage	F	VF	XF	Unc	BU
1998 Proof	Est. 10,000	Value: 37.50				

KM# 160 500 TUGRIK **Weight:** 31.1045 g. **Composition:** 0.9990 Silver 1.0000 oz. ASW **Subject:** Year of the Rabbit

Date	Mintage	F	VF	XF	Unc	BU
1999	3,000	—	—	—	30.00	—

KM# 196 500 TUGRIK **Weight:** 19.8200 g. **Composition:** 0.5000 Silver 0.3186 oz. ASW **Obverse:** National emblem. **Reverse:** Two Bactrian camels. **Edge:** Reeded. **Size:** 34 mm.

Date	F	VF	XF	Unc	BU
1999 Proof	—	—	—	30.00	—

KM# 160a 500 TUGRIK **Weight:** 31.1045 g. **Composition:** 0.9990 Silver 1.0000 oz. ASW **Subject:** Year of the Rabbit **Note:** Gold plated rabbit.

Date	Mintage	F	VF	XF	Unc	BU
1999	3,000	—	—	—	50.00	—

KM# 161 500 TUGRIK **Weight:** 1.2441 g. **Composition:** 0.9990 Gold .0400 oz. AGW **Subject:** Year of the Rabbit

Date	Mintage	F	VF	XF	Unc	BU
1999	5,000	—	—	—	55.00	—

KM# 179 500 TUGRIK **Weight:** 25.2700 g. **Composition:** 0.9250 Silver .7515 oz. ASW **Subject:** Sita Tara **Obverse:** National emblem above denomination **Reverse:** Gold colored seated figure of Undur Geghen Zanabazar

Date	Mintage	F	VF	XF	Unc	BU
1999 Proof	2,500	Value: 46.50				

KM# 180 500 TUGRIK **Ring Weight:** 25.0000 g. **Ring Composition:** 0.9250 Silver .7435 oz. ASW **Center Composition:** Goldine **Subject:** Genius of the Millennium - Gutenberg **Obverse:** National emblem **Reverse:** Open book, dates **Note:** Goldine center is square.

Date	Mintage	F	VF	XF	Unc	BU
1999 Proof	2,500	Value: 43.50				

KM# 181 500 TUGRIK **Ring Weight:** 25.0000 g. **Ring Composition:** 0.9250 Silver .7435 oz. ASW **Center Composition:** Goldine **Subject:** Genius of the Millennium - Da Vinci **Obverse:** National emblem **Reverse:** Male figure study **Note:** Goldine center is triangular.

Date	Mintage	F	VF	XF	Unc	BU
1999 Proof	2,500	Value: 46.50				

KM# 182 500 TUGRIK **Ring Weight:** 25.0000 g. **Ring Composition:** 0.9250 Silver .7435 oz. ASW **Center Composition:** Goldine **Subject:** Genius of the Millennium - Newton **Obverse:** National emblem **Reverse:** Solar system diagram **Note:** Goldine center is round.

Date	Mintage	F	VF	XF	Unc	BU
1999 Proof	2,500	Value: 46.50				

KM# 183 500 TUGRIK **Ring Weight:** 25.0000 g. **Ring Composition:** 0.9250 Silver .7435 oz. ASW **Subject:** Genius of the Millennium - von Goethe **Obverse:** National emblem **Reverse:** Goethe's portrait **Note:** Goldine center is round.

Date	Mintage	F	VF	XF	Unc	BU
1999 Proof	2,500	Value: 43.50				

KM# 184 500 TUGRIK **Ring Weight:** 25.0000 g. **Ring Composition:** 0.9250 Silver .7435 oz. ASW **Center Composition:** Goldine **Subject:** Genius of the Millennium - Edison **Obverse:** National emblem **Reverse:** Light bulb, telephone, record player **Note:** Goldine center is square.

Date	Mintage	F	VF	XF	Unc	BU
1999 Proof	2,500	Value: 43.50				

Note: KM#90, previously listed here, has been reported as never released.

KM# 195 500 TUGRIK **Composition:** Copper-Nickel **Subject:** Sukhe-Bataar **Obverse:** National emblem and denomination. **Reverse:** Bataars portrait. **Edge:** Plain. **Size:** 22.1 mm.

Date	F	VF	XF	Unc	BU
2001	—	—	—	2.50	—

KM# 189 500 TUGRIK **Weight:** 25.0000 g. **Composition:** 0.9250 Silver .7435 oz. ASW **Subject:** Protoceratops Andrewsi **Obverse:** National arms above denomination **Reverse:** Dinosaur **Edge:** Reeded **Size:** 38.7 mm.

Date	Mintage	F	VF	XF	Unc	BU
2001 Proof	2,500	—	—	—	42.50	—

KM# 190 500 TUGRIK **Weight:** 25.0000 g. **Composition:** 0.9250 Silver .7435 oz. ASW **Subject:** Velociraptor Mongoliensis **Obverse:** National arms above denomination **Reverse:** Dinosaur

Date	Mintage	F	VF	XF	Unc	BU
2001 Proof	2,500	Value: 45.00				

KM# 191 500 TUGRIK **Weight:** 25.0000 g. **Composition:** 0.9250 Silver .7435 oz. ASW **Series:** Olympics **Obverse:** National arms above denomination **Reverse:** Speed skater

Date	Mintage	F	VF	XF	Unc	BU
2001 Proof	15,000	—	—	—	32.50	—

KM# 192 500 TUGRIK **Weight:** 25.0000 g. **Composition:** 0.9250 Silver .7435 oz. ASW **Series:** Olympics **Obverse:** National arms above denomination **Reverse:** Three cross-country skiers

Date	Mintage	F	VF	XF	Unc	BU
2001 Proof	20,000	—	—	—	32.50	—

KM# 65 600 TUGRIK **Weight:** 373.2000 g. **Composition:** 0.9990 Silver 12.0000 oz. ASW **Subject:** Year of the Rooster **Note:** Similar to 50 Tugrik, KM#61

Date	Mintage	F	VF	XF	Unc	BU
1993 Proof	200	Value: 500				

KM# 91 1000 TUGRIK **Weight:** 31.1000 g. **Composition:** 0.9990 Gold 1.0000 oz. AGW **Subject:** Year of the Monkey **Note:** Similar to 50 Tugrik, KM#86.

Date	Mintage	F	VF	XF	Unc	BU
1992 Proof	2,000	Value: 475				

KM# 85 1000 TUGRIK **Weight:** 20.0000 g. **Composition:** 0.9000 Gold .5788 oz. AGW **Reverse:** Ugedei Khan, Son of Genghis

Date	Mintage	F	VF	XF	Unc	BU
1992 Proof	500	Value: 300				

KM# 169 1000 TUGRIK **Weight:** 20.0000 g. **Composition:** 0.9000 Gold .5788 oz. AGW **Subject:** Discovery of American - Columbus **Obverse:** Similar to KM#74 **Reverse:** Similar to KM#60

Date	Mintage	F	VF	XF	Unc	BU
1992 Proof	Est. 2,000	Value: 450				

KM# 66 1000 TUGRIK **Weight:** 31.1000 g. **Composition:** 0.9990 Gold 1.0000 oz. AGW **Subject:** Year of the Rooster **Obverse:** National emblem above denomination at left, country name at right **Reverse:** Rooster **Note:** Similar to 50 Tugrik, KM#61.

Date	Mintage	F	VF	XF	Unc	BU
1993 Proof	1,000	Value: 650				

KM# 74 1000 TUGRIK **Weight:** 20.0000 g. **Composition:** 0.9000 Gold .5788 oz. AGW **Subject:** Japanese Royal Wedding

Date	Mintage	F	VF	XF	Unc	BU
1993 Proof	145	Value: 700				

KM# 78 1000 TUGRIK **Weight:** 31.1035 g. **Composition:** 0.9990 Gold 1.0000 oz. AGW **Subject:** Year of the Dog

Date	Mintage	F	VF	XF	Unc	BU
1994 Proof	500	Value: 525				

KM# 96 1000 TUGRIK **Weight:** 3.1100 g. **Composition:** 0.9990 Gold 1.0000 oz. AGW **Subject:** Year of the Pig **Obverse:** National emblem **Reverse:** Wild boar **Note:** Similar to 500 Tugrik, KM#95.

Date	Mintage	F	VF	XF	Unc	BU
1995 Proof	500	Value: 200				

KM# 148 1000 TUGRIK **Weight:** 4.4100 g. **Composition:** 0.9000 Gold .1276 oz. AGW **Subject:** Moscow - Ulaan Blaatar - Bejing Railroad **Obverse:** National emblem **Reverse:** Steam locomotive

Date	Mintage	F	VF	XF	Unc	BU
1995 Proof	—	Value: 100				

KM# 106 1000 TUGRIK **Weight:** 3.1100 g. **Composition:** 0.9990 Gold 1.0000 oz. AGW **Subject:** Year of the Rat **Note:** Similar to 50 Tugrik, KM#104.

Date	Mintage	F	VF	XF	Unc	BU
1996 Proof	500	Value: 150				

KM# 115 1000 TUGRIK **Weight:** 156.6100 g. **Composition:** 0.9990 Silver 5.0000 oz. ASW **Series:** Olympics **Reverse:** Ancient runners **Size:** 65.5 mm. **Note:** With gold inlay. Illustation reduced.

Date	F	VF	XF	Unc	BU
1996 Matte	—	—	—	225	—

KM# 128 1000 TUGRIK **Weight:** 3.1100 g. **Composition:** 0.9990 Gold .1000 oz. AGW **Subject:** Year of the Ox **Note:** Similar to 50 Tugrik, KM#126.

Date	Mintage	F	VF	XF	Unc	BU
1997 Proof	500	Value: 100				

KM# 185 1000 TUGRIK **Weight:** 1.2441 g. **Composition:** 0.9999 Gold .0400 oz. AGW **Subject:** Genius of the Millennium - Da Vinci **Obverse:** National arms **Reverse:** Male figure study **Note:** Similar to 500 Tugrik, KM#181.

Date	Mintage	F	VF	XF	Unc	BU
1999 Proof	25,000	Value: 45.00				

KM# 116 1200 TUGRIK **Weight:** 7.7000 g. **Composition:** 0.9990 Silver .2496 oz. ASW **Subject:** Chinnggis Khan **Note:** Similar to 5,000 Tugrik, KM#118.

Date	Mintage	F	VF	XF	Unc	BU
1996	—	—	—	—	10.00	—
1996 Proof	Est. 10,000	Value: 15.00				

KM# 149 1200 TUGRIK **Weight:** 7.7000 g. **Composition:** 0.9990 Silver .2496 oz. ASW **Subject:** Ugedei Khan **Obverse:** National emblem **Reverse:** Portrait dates

Date	Mintage	F	VF	XF	Unc	BU
1997 Proof	Est. 10,000	Value: 15.00				

KM# 113 2000 TUGRIK **Weight:** 7.7760 g. **Composition:** 0.5830 Gold .1458 oz. AGW **Series:** Endangered Wildlife **Reverse:** Snow leopard

Date	Mintage	F	VF	XF	Unc	BU
1994 Proof	Est. 5,000	Value: 150				

KM# 114 2000 TUGRIK **Weight:** 7.7760 g. **Composition:** 0.5830 Gold .1458 oz. AGW **Series:** Olympics **Reverse:** Boxer

Date	Mintage	F	VF	XF	Unc	BU
1994 Proof	Est. 5,000	Value: 150				

KM# 175 2000 TUGRIK **Weight:** 7.7760 g. **Composition:** 0.5830 Gold .1458 oz. AGW **Subject:** Year of the Tiger

Date	F	VF	XF	Unc	BU
1998	—	—	—	65.00	—

KM# 97 2500 TUGRIK **Weight:** 155.5150 g. **Composition:** 0.9990 Silver 5.0000 oz. ASW **Subject:** Year of the Pig **Size:** 65 mm. **Note:** Illustration reduced.

Date	Mintage	F	VF	XF	Unc	BU
1995 Proof	300	Value: 160				

KM# 102 2500 TUGRIK **Weight:** 155.5150 g. **Composition:** 0.9990 Silver 5.0000 oz. ASW **Subject:** Moscow - Bejing Railroad **Note:** Similar 500 Tugrik, KM#101

Date	Mintage	F	VF	XF	Unc	BU
1995 Proof	5,000	Value: 125				

KM# 107 2500 TUGRIK **Weight:** 155.5150 g. **Composition:** 0.9990 Silver 5.0000 oz. ASW **Subject:** Year of the Rat **Reverse:** Gold plated rat **Size:** 65 mm. **Note:** Illustration reduced.

Date	Mintage	F	VF	XF	Unc	BU
1996 Proof	300	Value: 250				

KM# 117 2500 TUGRIK **Weight:** 15.5500 g. **Composition:** 0.9990 Silver .4994 oz. ASW **Reverse:** Chinggis Khan **Note:** Similar to 5000 Tugrik, KM#118

Date	Mintage	F	VF	XF	Unc	BU
1996	—	—	—	—	20.00	—
1996 Proof	Est. 10,000	Value: 30.00				

KM# 129 2500 TUGRIK **Weight:** 155.5150 g. **Composition:** 0.9990 Silver With Partial Gold Plating 5.0000 oz. **Subject:** Year of the Ox **Obverse:** National emblem

Date	Mintage	F	VF	XF	Unc	BU
1997 Proof	300	Value: 200				

KM# 150 2500 TUGRIK **Weight:** 15.5517 g. **Composition:** 0.9990 Silver 5.0000 oz. ASW **Obverse:** National emblem **Reverse:** Ugedei Khan

Date	Mintage	F	VF	XF	Unc	BU
1997 Proof	Est. 10,000	Value: 30.00				

KM# 162 2500 TUGRIK **Weight:** 155.1750 g. **Composition:** 0.9990 Silver 4.984 oz. ASW **Subject:** Year of the Rabbit **Obverse:** National emblem **Reverse:** Rabbit **Edge:** Plain **Size:** 65 mm. **Note:** Struck at B.H. Mayer's.

Date	Mintage	F	VF	XF	Unc	BU
1999 Proof	1,500	Value: 175				

KM# 163 2500 TUGRIK **Weight:** 7.7759 g. **Composition:** 0.9990 Gold 0.2498 oz. AGW **Subject:** Year of the Rabbit **Obverse:** National emblem **Reverse:** Rabbit **Edge:** Plain **Size:** 22.5 mm. **Note:** Struck at B.H. Mayer's.

Date	Mintage	F	VF	XF	Unc	BU
1999 Proof	1,500	Value: 200				

KM# 81 4000 TUGRIK **Weight:** 15.5940 g. **Composition:** 0.9999 Gold 5.0000 oz. AGW **Reverse:** Chinggis Khan on horse

Date	Mintage	F	VF	XF	Unc	BU
1992 Proof	Est. 9,000	Value: 650				

KM# 67 5000 TUGRIK **Weight:** 155.5000 g. **Composition:** 0.9990 Gold 5.0000 oz. AGW **Subject:** Year of the Rooster **Obverse:** National emblem above denomination at left, country name at right **Reverse:** Rooster **Note:** Similar to 50 Tugrik, KM#51.

Date	Mintage	F	VF	XF	Unc	BU
1993 Proof	50	Value: 3,750				

KM# 79 5000 TUGRIK **Weight:** 155.5000 g. **Composition:** 0.9990 Gold 5.0000 oz. AGW **Subject:** Year of the dog

Date	Mintage	F	VF	XF	Unc	BU
1994 Proof	25	Value: 5,000				

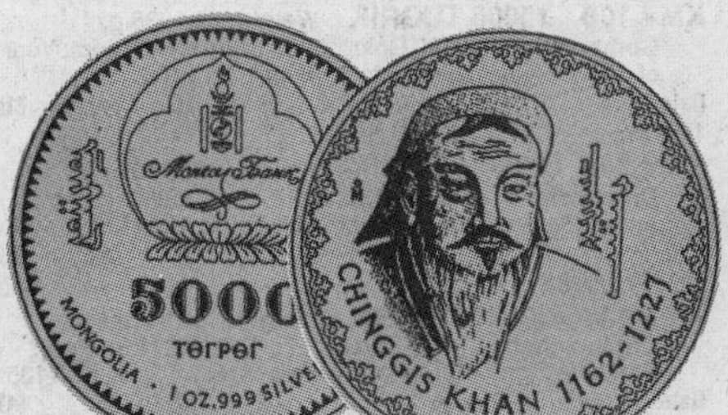

KM# 118 5000 TUGRIK **Weight:** 3.1000 g. **Composition:** 0.9990 Silver .9989 oz. ASW **Reverse:** Chinggis Khan

Date	Mintage	F	VF	XF	Unc	BU
1996		—	—	—	30.00	—
1996 Proof	Est. 10,000	Value: 50.00				

KM# 194 5000 TUGRIK **Weight:** 6.2200 g. **Composition:** 0.9990 Gold 0.1998 oz. AGW **Subject:** UNICEF **Obverse:** National emblem and denomination. **Reverse:** Three costumed children. **Edge:** Reeded.

Date	Mintage	F	VF	XF	Unc	BU
1997 Proof	10,000	Value: 120				

KM# 136 5000 TUGRIK **Weight:** 155.5175 g. **Composition:** 0.9990 Silver 5.0000 oz. ASW **Subject:** Aquila Rapax **Note:** Similar to 500 Tugrik, KM#132.

Date	Mintage	F	VF	XF	Unc	BU
1997 Proof	750	Value: 225				

KM# 137 5000 TUGRIK **Weight:** 155.5175 g. **Composition:** 0.9990 Silver 5.0000 oz. ASW **Subject:** Eguus Fergus **Note:** Similar to 500 Tugrik, KM#133.

Date	Mintage	F	VF	XF	Unc	BU
1997 Proof	750	Value: 225				

KM# 139 5000 TUGRIK **Weight:** 155.5175 g. **Composition:** 0.9990 Silver 5.0000 oz. ASW **Subject:** Panthera Tigris Altaica **Note:** Similar to 500 Tugrik, KM#135.

Date	Mintage	F	VF	XF	Unc	BU
1997 Proof	750	Value: 225				

KM# 151 5000 TUGRIK **Weight:** 31.1035 g. **Composition:** 0.9990 Silver 1.0000 oz. ASW **Obverse:** National emblem **Reverse:** Ugedei Khan

Date	Mintage	F	VF	XF	Unc	BU
1997 Proof	Est. 10,000	Value: 50.00				

KM# 138 5000 TUGRIK **Weight:** 155.5175 g. **Composition:** 0.9990 Silver 5 oz. ASW **Subject:** Camelus Ferus **Note:** Similar to 500 Tugrik, KM#134.

Date	Mintage	F	VF	XF	Unc	BU
1997 Proof	750	Value: 225				

KM# 82 8000 TUGRIK **Weight:** 31.1620 g. **Composition:** 0.9999 Gold 1.0000 oz. AGW **Reverse:** Chinggis Khan

Date	Mintage	F	VF	XF	Unc	BU
1992 Proof	Est. 3,000	Value: 1,200				

KM# 98 10000 TUGRIK **Weight:** 31.1035 g. **Composition:** 0.9990 Gold 1.0000 oz. AGW **Subject:** Year of the Pig **Obverse:** National emblem **Reverse:** Wild boar **Note:** Similar to 500 Tugrik, KM#95.

Date	Mintage	F	VF	XF	Unc	BU
1995 Proof	300	Value: 600				

KM# 108 10000 TUGRIK **Weight:** 31.1035 g. **Composition:** 0.9990 Gold 1.0000 oz. AGW **Subject:** Year of the Rat **Note:** Siimilar to 50 Tugrik, KM#104.

Date	Mintage	F	VF	XF	Unc	BU
1996 Proof	300	Value: 550				

KM# 140 10000 TUGRIK **Weight:** 1000.1000 g. **Composition:** 0.9990 Silver 32.1575 oz. ASW **Subject:** Aquila Rapax **Note:** Similar to 500 Tugrik, KM#132.

Date	Mintage	F	VF	XF	Unc	BU
1996 Prooflike	333	—	—	—	—	600

KM# 143 10000 TUGRIK **Weight:** 1000.1000 g. **Composition:** 0.9990 Silver 32.1575 oz. ASW **Subject:** Panthera Tigris Alaica **Note:** Siimilar to 500 Tugrik, KM#135.

Date	Mintage	F	VF	XF	Unc	BU
1996 Proof	333	—	—	—	—	600

KM# 141 10000 TUGRIK **Weight:** 1000.1000 g. **Composition:** 0.9990 Silver 32.1575 oz. ASW **Subject:** Equus Ferus **Note:** Similar to 500 Tugrik, KM#133.

Date	Mintage	F	VF	XF	Unc	BU
1996 Prooflike	333	—	—	—	—	600

KM# 142 10000 TUGRIK **Weight:** 1000.1000 g. **Composition:** 0.9990 Silver 32.1575 oz. ASW **Subject:** Camelus Ferus **Note:** Similar to 500 Tugrik, KM#134.

Date	Mintage	F	VF	XF	Unc	BU
1996 Prooflike	333	—	—	—	—	600

KM# 130 10000 TUGRIK **Weight:** 31.1035 g. **Composition:** 0.9990 Gold 1.0000 oz. AGW **Subject:** Year of the Ox **Note:** Siimilar to 2,500 Tugrik, KM#129.

Date	Mintage	F	VF	XF	Unc	BU
1997 Proof	300	Value: 525				

KM# 176 10000 TUGRIK **Weight:** 31.1035 g. **Composition:** 0.9990 Gold 1.0000 oz. AGW **Subject:** Year of the Tiger

Date	Mintage	F	VF	XF	Unc	BU
1998	250	—	—	—	525	—

KM# 164 10000 TUGRIK **Weight:** 31.1035 g. **Composition:** 0.9990 Gold 1 oz. AGW **Subject:** Year of the Rabbit

Date	Mintage	F	VF	XF	Unc	BU
1999	250	—	—	—	525	—

KM# 68 12000 TUGRIK **Weight:** 373.2000 g. **Composition:** 0.9990 Gold 12.0000 oz. AGW **Subject:** Year of the Rooster **Obverse:** National emblem above denomination at left, country name at right **Reverse:** Rooster **Note:** Similar to 50 Tugrik, KM#61.

Date	Mintage	F	VF	XF	Unc	BU
1993 Proof	25	Value: 6,000				

KM# 119 12000 TUGRIK **Weight:** 7.7700 g. **Composition:** 0.9999 Gold .2498 oz. AGW **Subject:** Chinggis Khan **Note:** Similar to 50,000 Tugrik, KM#121.

Date	F	VF	XF	Unc	BU
1996 Rare	—	—	—	—	—
1996 Proof, rare	—	—	—	—	—

KM# 119a 12000 TUGRIK **Weight:** 7.7700 g. **Composition:** 0.9990 Gold .2495 oz. AGW **Subject:** Chinggis Khan

Date	Mintage	F	VF	XF	Unc	BU
1996	—	—	—	—	150	—
1996 Proof	Est. 10,000	Value: 175				

KM# 152 12000 TUGRIK **Weight:** 7.7750 g. **Composition:** 0.9990 Gold .2500 oz. AGW **Obverse:** National emblem **Reverse:** Ugedei Khan

Date	Mintage	F	VF	XF	Unc	BU
1997 Proof	Est. 10,000	Value: 300				

KM# 120 25000 TUGRIK **Weight:** 15.5500 g. **Composition:** 0.9999 Gold .4999 oz. AGW **Subject:** Chinggis Khan **Note:** Similar to 50,000 Tugrik, KM#121.

Date	Mintage	F	VF	XF	Unc	BU
1996 Rare	10	—	—	—	—	—
1996 Proof, Rare	10	—	—	—	—	—

KM# 120a 25000 TUGRIK **Weight:** 15.5500 g. **Composition:** 0.9990 Gold .4994 oz. AGW

Date	Mintage	F	VF	XF	Unc	BU
1996	—	—	—	—	250	—
1996 Proof	Est. 10,000	Value: 350				

KM# 144 25000 TUGRIK **Weight:** 15.5940 g. **Composition:** 0.9999 Gold .5000 oz. AGW **Subject:** Aquila Rapaz **Note:** Similar to 500 Tugrik, KM#132.

Date	Mintage	F	VF	XF	Unc	BU
1996 Proof	300	Value: 385				

KM# 145 25000 TUGRIK **Weight:** 15.5940 g. **Composition:** 0.9999 Gold .5000 oz. AGW **Subject:** Equus Fergus **Note:** Similar to 500 Tugrik, KM#133.

Date	Mintage	F	VF	XF	Unc	BU
1996 Proof	300	Value: 385				

KM# 146 25000 TUGRIK **Weight:** 15.5940 g. **Composition:** 0.9999 Gold .5000 oz. AGW **Subject:** Cameleus Ferus **Note:** Similar to 500 Tugrik, KM#134.

Date	Mintage	F	VF	XF	Unc	BU
1996 Proof	300	Value: 385				

KM# 147 25000 TUGRIK **Weight:** 15.5940 g. **Composition:** 0.9999 Gold .5000 oz. AGW **Subject:** Panthera Tigris Altaica **Note:** Similar to 500 Tugrik, KM#135.

Date	Mintage	F	VF	XF	Unc	BU
1996 Proof	300	Value: 385				

KM# 153 25000 TUGRIK **Weight:** 15.5517 g. **Composition:** 0.9990 Gold .5 oz. AGW **Subject:** Ugedei Khan **Obverse:** National arms

Date	Mintage	F	VF	XF	Unc	BU
1997 Proof	Est. 10,000	Value: 600				

KM# 99 50000 TUGRIK **Weight:** 155.5150 g. **Composition:** 0.9990 Gold 5.0000 oz. AGW **Subject:** Year of the Pig **Obverse:** National emblem **Reverse:** Pigs in field **Note:** Similar to 2500 Tigrik, KM#97

Date	Mintage	F	VF	XF	Unc	BU
1995 Proof	25	Value: 5,000				

KM# 109 50000 TUGRIK **Weight:** 155.5150 g. **Composition:** 0.9990 Gold 5.0000 oz. AGW **Subject:** Year of the Rat **Note:** Similar to 50 Tugrik, KM#104.

Date	Mintage	F	VF	XF	Unc	BU
1996 Proof	25	Value: 4,250				

KM# 121 50000 TUGRIK **Weight:** 31.1000 g. **Composition:** 0.9999 Gold .9998 oz. AGW **Reverse:** Chinggis Khan

Date	Mintage	F	VF	XF	Unc	BU
1996 Rare	10	—	—	—	—	—
1996 Proof, rare	10	—	—	—	—	—

KM# 121a 50000 TUGRIK **Weight:** 31.1000 g. **Composition:** 0.9990 Gold .9998 oz. AGW **Subject:** Chinggis Khan

Date	Mintage	F	VF	XF	Unc	BU
1996	—	—	—	—	600	—
1996 Proof	Est. 10,000	Value: 800				

KM# 131 50000 TUGRIK **Weight:** 155.5150 g. **Composition:** 0.9999 Gold 5.0000 oz. AGW **Subject:** Year of the Ox **Note:** Similar to 2,500 Tugrik, KM#129.

Date	Mintage	F	VF	XF	Unc	BU
1997 Proof	25	Value: 4,000				

KM# 154 50000 TUGRIK **Weight:** 31.1035 g. **Composition:** 0.9990 Gold 1.0000 oz. AGW **Obverse:** National emblem **Reverse:** Ugedei Khan

Date	Mintage	F	VF	XF	Unc	BU
1997 Proof	Est. 10,000	Value: 1,200				

KM# 177 50000 TUGRIK **Weight:** 155.5150 g. **Composition:** 0.9999 Gold 5.0000 oz. AGW **Subject:** Year of the Tiger

Date	Mintage	F	VF	XF	Unc	BU
1998	99	—	—	—	3,500	—

KM# 165 50000 TUGRIK **Weight:** 155.5150 g. **Composition:** 0.9999 Gold 5.0000 oz. AGW **Subject:** Year of the Rabbit

Date	Mintage	F	VF	XF	Unc	BU
1999	99	—	—	—	3,500	—

KM# 83 250000 TUGRIK **Weight:** 1000.1000 g. **Composition:** 0.9999 Gold 32.1575 oz. AGW **Reverse:** Chinggis Khan **Size:** 85 mm. **Note:** Illustration reduced.

Date	Mintage	F	VF	XF	Unc	BU
1992 Proof	Est. 300	Value: 25,000				

PIEFORTS

KM#	Date	Mintage	Identification	Mkt Val
P1	1980	92	25 Tugrik. KM39.	135
P2	1980	550	750 Tugrik. KM40.	750

MINT SETS

KM#	Date	Mintage	Identification	Issue Price	Mkt Val
MS1	1980 (8)	—	KM27-33, 41	—	25.00
MS2	1996 (3)	10,000	KM116-118	—	40.00
MS3	1996 (3)	10	KM119-121	—	—
MS4	1996 (3)	10,000	KM119a-121a	—	1,100

PROOF SETS

KM#	Date	Mintage	Identification	Issue Price	Mkt Val
PS1	1996 (3)	—	KM105, 106, 108	—	700
PS2	1996 (3)	10,000	KM116-118. The *10,000 mintage limit is per denomination including proof and BU single coins as well as coins included in sets.	—	70.00
PS3	1996 (3)	10	KM119-121	—	—
PS5	1996 (4)	10	KM116-118, 121	—	—
PS6	1996 (4)	10,000	KM116-118, 121a. The *10,000 mintage limit is per denomination including proof and BU single coins as well as coins included in sets.	—	975
PS7	1996 (4)	10	KM118, 119-121	—	—
PS8	1996 (4)	10,000	KM118, 119a-121a. The *10,000 mintage limit is per denomination including proof and BU single coins as well as coins included in sets.	—	1,650
PS4	1996	10,000	KM119a-121a. The *10,000 mintage limit is per denomination including proof and BU single coins as well as coins included in sets.	—	1,600
PS10	1997 (3)	10,000	KM152-154	—	2,100
PS9	1997 (3)	10,000	KM149-151	—	100

MONTENEGRO

The former independent kingdom of Montenegro, now one of the nominally autonomous federated units of Yugoslavia, was located in southeastern Europe north of Albania. As a kingdom, it had an area of 5,333 sq. mi. (13,812 sq. km.) and a population of about 250,000. Capital: Podgorica.

Montenegro became an independent state in 1355 following the break-up of the Serb empire. During the Turkish invasion of Albania and Herzegovina in the 15th century, the Montenegrins moved their capital to the remote mountain village of Cetinje where they maintained their independence through two centuries of intermittent attack, emerging as the only one of the Balkan states not subjugated by the Turks. When World War I began, Montenegro joined with Serbia and was subsequently invaded and occupied by the Austrians. Austria withdrew upon the defeat of the Central Powers, permitting the Serbians to move in and maintain the occupation. Montenegro then joined the kingdom of the Serbs, Croats and Slovenes, which later became Yugoslavia.

The coinage, issued under the autocratic rule of Prince Nicholas, is obsolete.

RULERS

Nicholas I, as Prince, 1860-1910 as King, 1910-1918

MINT MARKS

(a) - Paris, privy marks only

MONETARY SYSTEM

100 Para, ПАРА ПАРА = 1 Perper, ПЕРПЕР

KINGDOM

STANDARD COINAGE

KM# 1 PARA Composition: Bronze **Ruler:** Nicholas I

Date	Mintage	F	VF	XF	Unc	BU
1906	200,000	8.00	16.00	35.00	75.00	—

KM# 16 PARA Composition: Bronze **Ruler:** Nicholas I

Date	Mintage	F	VF	XF	Unc	BU
1913	100,000	12.50	25.00	60.00	125	—
1914	200,000	6.00	12.00	25.00	70.00	—

KM# 2 2 PARE Composition: Bronze **Ruler:** Nicholas I

Date	Mintage	F	VF	XF	Unc	BU
1906	600,000	4.00	8.00	18.00	35.00	—
1908	250,000	8.00	18.00	32.00	75.00	—

KM# 17 2 PARE Composition: Bronze **Ruler:** Nicholas I

Date	Mintage	F	VF	XF	Unc	BU
1913	500,000	4.00	7.50	15.00	30.00	—
1914	400,000	4.50	9.00	18.00	45.00	—

KM# 3 10 PARA Composition: Nickel **Ruler:** Nicholas I

Date	Mintage	F	VF	XF	Unc	BU
1906	750,000	2.50	5.00	12.00	25.00	—
1908	250,000	3.00	6.50	16.00	32.00	—

KM# 18 10 PARA Composition: Nickel **Ruler:** Nicholas I

Date	Mintage	F	VF	XF	Unc	BU
1913	200,000	3.50	8.00	18.00	40.00	—
1914	800,000	2.50	5.00	12.00	25.00	—

KM# 4 20 PARA Composition: Nickel **Ruler:** Nicholas I

Date	Mintage	F	VF	XF	Unc	BU
1906	600,000	3.00	6.00	12.00	25.00	—
1908	400,000	3.00	7.00	15.00	32.00	—

KM# 19 20 PARA Composition: Nickel **Ruler:** Nicholas I

Date	Mintage	F	VF	XF	Unc	BU
1913	200,000	4.00	8.00	18.00	40.00	—
1914	800,000	3.00	6.00	12.00	25.00	—

KM# 5 PERPER Weight: 5.0000 g. **Composition:** 0.8350 Silver .1342 oz. ASW **Ruler:** Nicholas I **Note:** Approximately 30 percent melted.

Date	Mintage	F	VF	XF	Unc	BU
1909(a)	500,000	12.00	22.00	42.00	95.00	—

KM# 14 PERPER Weight: 5.0000 g. **Composition:** 0.8350 Silver .1342 oz. ASW **Ruler:** Nicholas I

Date	Mintage	F	VF	XF	Unc	BU
1912	520,000	8.00	14.00	30.00	85.00	—
1914	500,000	9.00	18.00	35.00	90.00	—

KM# 7 2 PERPERA Weight: 10.0000 g. **Composition:** 0.8350 Silver .2685 oz. ASW **Ruler:** Nicholas I

Date	Mintage	F	VF	XF	Unc	BU
1910	300,000	15.00	30.00	65.00	165	—

KM# 20 2 PERPERA Weight: 10.0000 g. **Composition:** 0.8350 Silver .2685 oz. ASW **Ruler:** Nicholas I

Date	Mintage	F	VF	XF	Unc	BU
1914	200,000	15.00	35.00	75.00	175	—

KM# 6 5 PERPERA Weight: 24.0000 g. **Composition:** 0.9000 Silver .6944 oz. ASW **Ruler:** Nicholas I **Note:** Approximately 50 percent melted.

Date	Mintage	F	VF	XF	Unc	BU
1909(a)	60,000	60.00	120	250	700	—

KM# 15 5 PERPERA Weight: 24.0000 g. **Composition:** 0.9000 Silver .6944 oz. ASW **Ruler:** Nicholas I

Date	Mintage	F	VF	XF	Unc	BU
1912	40,000	80.00	160	280	700	—
1914	20,000	85.00	160	300	950	—

KM# 8 10 PERPERA Weight: 3.3875 g. **Composition:** 0.9000 Gold .0980 oz. AGW **Ruler:** Nicholas I

Date	Mintage	F	VF	XF	Unc	BU
1910	40,000	110	220	300	450	—

KM# 9 10 PERPERA Weight: 3.3875 g. **Composition:** 0.9000 Gold .0980 oz. AGW **Ruler:** Nicholas I **Subject:** 50th year of reign

Date	Mintage	F	VF	XF	Unc	BU
1910	35,000	125	250	325	500	—

KM# 10 20 PERPERA Weight: 6.7751 g. **Composition:** 0.9000 Gold .1960 oz. AGW **Ruler:** Nicholas I

Date	Mintage	F	VF	XF	Unc	BU
1910	30,000	150	275	450	650	—

KM# 11 20 PERPERA **Weight:** 6.7751 g. **Composition:** 0.9000 Gold .1960 oz. AGW **Ruler:** Nicholas I **Subject:** 50th year of reign

Date	Mintage	F	VF	XF	Unc	BU
1910	30,000	150	275	450	650	—

KM# 12 100 PERPERA **Weight:** 33.8753 g. **Composition:** 0.9000 Gold .9802 oz. AGW **Ruler:** Nicholas I

Date	Mintage	F	VF	XF	Unc	BU
1910	300	—	4,500	6,500	10,000	—
1910 Proof	25	Value: 12,500				

KM# 13 100 PERPERA **Weight:** 33.8753 g. **Composition:** 0.9000 Gold .9802 oz. AGW **Ruler:** Nicholas I **Subject:** 50th year of reign

Date	Mintage	F	VF	XF	Unc	BU
1910	500	—	4,500	6,500	10,000	—
1910 Proof	Inc. above	Value: 15,000				

PATTERNS

KM#	Date	Mintage	Identification	Mkt Val
Pn1	1915	—	Para. With ESSAI. Struck at Paris.	1,200
Pn2	1915	—	2 Pare. With ESSAI. Struck at Paris.	1,200
Pn3	1915	—	10 Para. With ESSAI. Struck at Paris.	—
Pn4	1915	—	20 Para. With ESSAI. Struck at Paris.	—
Pn5	1915	—	Perper. With ESSAI. Struck at Paris.	1,500
Pn6	1915	—	2 Perpera. With ESSAI. Struck at Paris.	2,000
Pn7	1915	—	5 Perpera. With ESSAI. Struck at Paris. Bears the monogram EL for Edmond Lindauer, who copied the work of S. Schwarz of the Vienna Mint, where the regular issue coinage was struck.	8,000

TRIAL STRIKES

KM#	Date	Mintage	Identification	Mkt Val
TS1	ND(1910)	—	100 Perpera. Hallmarked edge. Uniface.	6,000
TS2	ND(1910)	—	100 Perpera. TITRE ZZK ESSAI.	5,000

MONTSERRAT

Montserrat, a British crown colony located in the Lesser Antilles of the West Indies 27 miles (43 km.) southwest of Antigua, has an area of 38 sq. mi. (100 sq. km.) and a population of 18,500. Capital: Plymouth. The island - actually a range of volcanic peaks rising from the Caribbean - exports cotton, limes and vegetables.

Columbus discovered Montserrat in 1493 and named it after Monserrado, a mountain in Spain. It was colonized by the English in 1632 and, except for brief periods of French occupancy in 1667 and 1782-83, has remained a British possession from that time. Currency of the British Caribbean Territories (Eastern Group) was used until later when the East Caribbean States coinage was introduced. Until becoming a separate colony in 1956, Montserrat was a presidency of the Leeward Islands.

The early 19th century countermarks of a crowned 3, 4,7, 9 or 18 over M as documented by Major Pridmore have been more correctly listed under St. Bartholomew.

RULERS
British

MONETARY SYSTEM
100 Cents = 1 Dollar

CROWN COLONY

MODERN COINAGE

KM# 30 4 DOLLARS **Composition:** Copper-Nickel **Series:** F.A.O.

Date	Mintage	F	VF	XF	Unc	BU
1970	13,000	—	—	7.50	14.50	—
1970 Proof	2,000	Value: 32.50				

MOROCCO

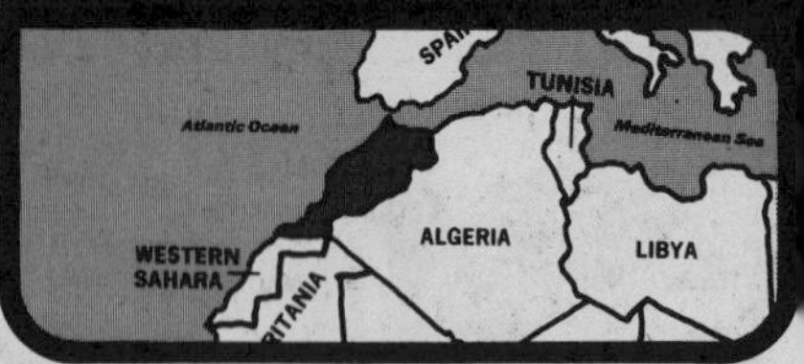

The Kingdom of Morocco, situated on the northwest corne of Africa, has an area of 275,117 sq. mi. (446,550 sq. km.) an a population of 22.5 million. Capital: Rabat. The economy essentially agricultural. Phosphates, fresh and preserved ve etables, canned fish, and raw materials are exported.

Morocco's strategic position at the gateway to western Europ has been the principal determinant of its violent, frequently unfo tunate history. Time and again the fertile plain between the rugge Atlas Mountains and the sea has echoed the battle's trumpet a Phoenicians, Romans, Vandals, Visigoths, Byzantine Greeks an Islamic Arabs successively conquered and occupied the land. Mod em Morocco is a remnant of an early empire formed by the Arab at the close of the 7th century which encompassed all of northwe Africa and most of the Iberian Peninsula. During the 17th and 18 centuries, while under the control of native dynasties, it was th headquarters of the famous Sale pirates. Morocco's strategic pos tion involved it in the competition of 19th century European powe for political influence in Africa, and resulted in the division of Morocc into French and Spanish spheres of interest which were establishe as protectorates in 1912. Morocco became independent on Marc 2, 1956, after France agreed to end its protectorate. Spain signe similar agreements on April 7 of the same year.

TITLES

المعربية

Al-Maghribiya(t)

المملكة المغربية

Al-Mamlaka(t) al-Maghribiya(t)

المحمدية الشريفة

Al-Mohammediya(t) esh-Sherifiya(t)

RULERS
'Abd al-Aziz, AH1311-1326/1894-1908AD
al-Hafiz, AH1326-1330/1908-1912AD
French Protectorate, AH1330/1912AD
Yusuf, AH1330-1346/1912-1927AD
Mohammed V, AH1346-1375/1927-1955AD

Kingdom
Mohammed V, AH1376-1381/1956-1962AD
al-Hasan II, AH1381-1420/1962-1999AD
Sidi Mohammed, AH1420- /1999- AD

MINTS
(a) - Paris privy marks only

بانكلند

Bi - England (Birmingham)

بانكلند

Ln = bi-England (London)

باريز

Pa = bi-Bariz (Paris)

فاس

Fs = Fes (Fas, Fez)

Py - Poissy Inscribed "Paris" but with thunderbolt privy mark.

NOTE: Some of the above forms of the mintnames are show as they appear on the coins, not in regular Arabic script.

NOTES:

On the silver coins the denominations are written in word and each series has its own characteristic names:
Y#9-13 (1313-1319) Denomination in 'Preferred' Dirhams.
Y#18-22 (1320-1323) Denomination in fractions of a Rial, but or the 3 larger sizes, the equivalent is given in "Urti parts", 1 Rial 20 = Urti parts.
Y#23-25 (1329) Denomination in Dirhams and in fraction of a Rial
Y#30-33 (1331-1336) Denomination in Yusuti or "Treasury" Dirhams

On most of the larger denominations, the denomination i given in the form of a rhymed couplet.

NOTE: Various copper and silver coins dated AH1297-131 are believed to be patterns. Copper coins similar to Y#14-17, bu without denomination on reverse, are patterns.

On the silver coins the denominations are written in word and each series has its own characteristic name: Y#4-8 (1299 1314) Denomination in Shar i Dirhams. Y#9-13 (1313-1319 Denomination in "Preferred" Dirhams. Y#18-22 (1320-1323 Denomination in fractions of a Rial, but on the 3 larger sizes, th equivalent is given in "Urti parts", 1 Rial 20 = Urti parts. Y#23-2 (1329) Denomination in Dirhams and in fraction of a Rial. Y#30 33 (1331-1336) Denomination in Yusuti or "Treasury Dirhams"

On most of the larger denominations, the denomination i given in the form of a rhymed couplet.

KINGDOM

Filali Sharifs - Alawi Dynasty

Abd al-Aziz

AH1311-1326 / 1894-1908AD

REFORM COINAGE

50 Muzunas = 1 Dirham; 10 Dirhams = 1 Rial

Y# 14 MUZUNA **Weight:** 29.1160 g. **Composition:** 0.9000 Silver .8425 oz. ASW **Note:** 5 million examples of 1320Pa were struck and melted, but at least one specimen is known to exist.

Date	Mintage	F	VF	XF	Unc
AH1320Be Rare	5	—	—	—	—
AH1320Bi	3,000,000	4.50	9.00	20.00	40.00
AH1320Bi Proof	—	Value: 275			
AH1320Fs	—	30.00	70.00	150	300
AH1321Bi	900,000	6.50	13.50	32.50	60.00

Y# 15.1 2 MUZUNAS **Composition:** Bronze **Note:** Varieties exist.

Date	Mintage	F	VF	XF	Unc
AH1320Bi	1,500,000	8.50	18.50	35.00	75.00
AH1320Bi Proof	—	Value: 275			
AH1320Fs	—	20.00	40.00	80.00	150
AH1320Pa Proof	—	—	—	—	—
AH1320Be Rare	5	—	—	—	—
AH1321Bi	450,000	12.50	25.00	50.00	90.00
AH1321Pa	6,500,000	2.00	5.00	10.00	25.00
AH1322Fs	—	40.00	90.00	200	400
AH1323Fs	—	25.00	60.00	120	200

Y# 15.2 2 MUZUNAS **Composition:** Bronze **Reverse:** Rim design reversed

Date	F	VF	XF	Unc
AH1320Fs	30.00	75.00	150	275

Y# 16 5 MUZUNAS **Composition:** Bronze **Note:** Varieties exist.

Date	F	VF	XF	Unc
AH1320Be Proof	—	—	—	—

Note: An additional 799,764 pieces are reported struck, but very few are known

Date	Mintage	F	VF	XF	Unc
AH1320Bi		2.00	5.00	10.00	25.00
AH1320Bi Proof	—	Value: 325			
AH1320Fs		15.00	30.00	60.00	150
AH1320Pa Proof	—	Value: 375			
AH1321Bi		4.00	8.00	15.00	30.00
AH1321Pa		2.00	5.00	10.00	25.00
AH1322Fs		30.00	60.00	150	250

Y# 17 10 MUZUNAS **Composition:** Bronze

Date	Mintage	F	VF	XF	Unc
AH1320Be		2.00	5.00	10.00	25.00
AH1320Be Proof; Rare		—	—	—	—
AH1320Bi		3.00	6.00	12.00	28.00
AH1320Bi Proof	—	Value: 400			
AH1320Fs Large letters		20.00	40.00	80.00	160
AH1321Be		2.00	5.00	10.00	25.00
AH1321Bi		4.00	8.00	16.00	35.00
AH1321Fs		18.00	35.00	75.00	150
AH1323Fs Large 10		50.00	100	250	450
AH1323Fs Small 10		50.00	100	250	450

Y# 20 1/4 RIAL **Weight:** 6.2500 g. **Composition:** 0.8350 Silver .1678 oz. ASW

Date	Mintage	F	VF	XF	Unc
AH1320	1,380,000	4.00	12.50	20.00	50.00
AH1320Be	1,380,000	4.00	12.50	20.00	50.00
AH1320Ln	3,056,000	4.00	10.00	12.50	40.00
AH1320Pa	480,000	12.00	25.00	50.00	100
AH1321Be	4,450,000	4.00	7.00	10.00	32.50
AH1321Be Proof	5	—	—	—	—
AH1321Ln	1,889,000	4.00	7.00	10.00	32.50
AH1321Pa	160,000	40.00	75.00	150	300

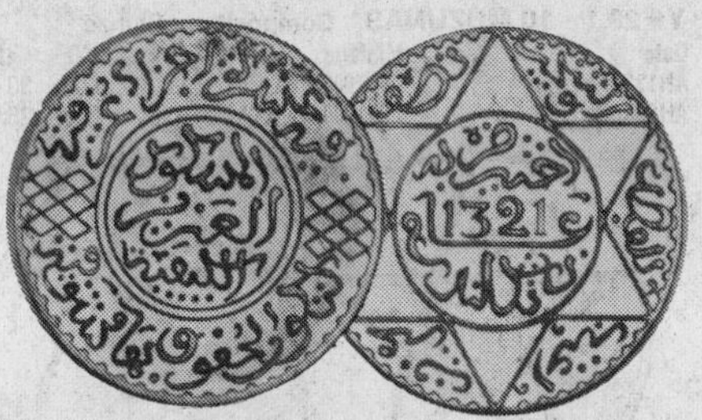

Y# 21 1/2 RIAL **Weight:** 12.5000 g. **Composition:** 0.8350 Silver .3356 oz. ASW

Date	Mintage	F	VF	XF	Unc
AH1320Be	2,510,000	7.00	15.00	30.00	75.00
AH1320Ln	900,000	7.00	15.00	30.00	75.00
AH1321Be Rare	—	—	—	—	—
AH1321Ln	1,041,000	7.00	15.00	30.00	75.00
AH1321Pa	1,800,000	7.00	17.50	35.00	85.00
AH1322Pa	540,000	15.00	30.00	75.00	150
AH1323Pa	1,090,000	12.00	25.00	50.00	110

Y# 22 RIAL **Weight:** 25.0000 g. **Composition:** 0.9000 Silver .7234 oz. ASW

Date	Mintage	F	VF	XF	Unc
AH1320Ln	330,000	17.50	35.00	75.00	150
AH1321Pa	300,000	20.00	35.00	75.00	150

Y# 9.2 1/2 DIRHAM **Weight:** 1.4558 g. **Composition:** 0.8350 Silver .0391 oz. ASW **Reverse:** Arrow heads point inward

Date	F	VF	XF	Unc
AH1319Pa	8.50	17.50	32.50	60.00

Y# 18 1/2 DIRHAM **Weight:** 1.2500 g. **Composition:** 0.8350 Silver .0336 oz. ASW

Date	Mintage	F	VF	XF	Unc
AH1320Ln	3,920,000	1.25	4.00	10.00	20.00
AH1320Pa	2,400,000	1.50	4.00	10.00	20.00
AH1321Ln	2,105,000	3.00	5.00	10.00	20.00

Y# 19 DIRHAM **Weight:** 2.5000 g. **Composition:** 0.8350 Silver .0671 oz. ASW

Date	Mintage	F	VF	XF	Unc
AH1320Ln	2,940,000	3.00	8.00	15.00	40.00
AH1321Ln	770,000	5.00	12.00	25.00	60.00

al-Hafiz

AH1326-1330 / 1908-1912AD

REFORM COINAGE

50 Muzunas = 1 Dirham; 10 Dirhams = 1 Rial

Y# 23 1/4 RIAL (2-1/2 Dirhams) **Weight:** 6.2500 g. **Composition:** 0.8350 Silver .1678 oz. ASW

Date	Mintage	F	VF	XF	Unc
AH1329Pa	3,130,000	4.00	8.50	18.00	40.00

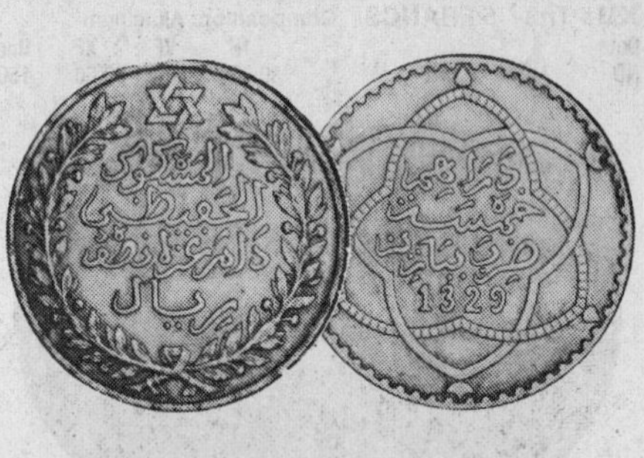

Y# 24 1/2 RIAL (5 Dirhams) **Weight:** 12.5000 g. **Composition:** 0.8350 Silver .3356 oz. ASW

Date	Mintage	F	VF	XF	Unc
AH1329Pa	4,660,000	7.00	10.00	25.00	90.00

Y# 25 10 DIRHAMS (Rial) **Weight:** 25.0000 g. **Composition:** 0.9000 Silver .7234 oz. ASW

Date	Mintage	F	VF	XF	Unc
AH1329Pa	7,040,000	10.00	20.00	40.00	100

PRIVATE TOKEN COINAGE

Enterprise Collet et Gouvernet

KM# Tn1 FRANC **Composition:** Aluminum **Issuer:** Entreprise Collet et Gouvernet **Shape:** Hexagon

Date	F	VF	XF	Unc
ND	18.00	30.00	50.00	100

KM# Tn2 2 FRANCS **Composition:** Aluminum **Shape:** Scalloped

Date	F	VF	XF	Unc
ND	20.00	35.00	60.00	100

KM# Tn3 5 FRANCS **Composition:** Aluminum

Date	F	VF	XF	Unc
ND	30.00	50.00	80.00	150

KM# Tn4 5 FRANCS **Composition:** Aluminum

Date	F	VF	XF	Unc
ND	35.00	60.00	100	175

Yusuf

AH1330-1346 / 1912-1927AD

REFORM COINAGE

50 Muzunas = 1 Dirham; 10 Dirhams = 1 Rial

Y# 26 MUZUNA **Composition:** Bronze

Date	Mintage	F	VF	XF	Unc
AH1330Pa	1,850,000	2.00	5.00	15.00	30.00

Y# 27 2 MUZUNAS **Composition:** Bronze

Date	Mintage	F	VF	XF	Unc
AH1330Pa	2,790,000	2.00	4.00	12.00	30.00

Note: Coins reportedly dated 1331Pa probably bore date AH1330

Y# 28.1 5 MUZUNAS **Composition:** Bronze

Date	Mintage	F	VF	XF	Unc
AH1330Pa	2,983,000	2.00	5.00	11.00	25.00
AH1340Pa	2,000,000	2.00	5.00	11.00	25.00

Y# 28.2 5 MUZUNAS **Composition:** Bronze **Reverse:** Privy marks on Py. mint examples.

Date	Mintage	F	VF	XF	Unc
AH1340Pa	2,000,000	1.00	2.00	5.00	25.00
AH1340Py	2,010,000	2.00	5.00	8.00	27.50

Y# 29.1 10 MUZUNAS **Composition:** Bronze

Date	Mintage	F	VF	XF	Unc
AH1330Pa	1,500,000	0.75	2.50	10.00	30.00
AH1340Pa	1,000,000	0.75	1.50	7.50	25.00

Y# 29.2 10 MUZUNAS **Composition:** Bronze **Reverse:** Privy marks

Date	Mintage	F	VF	XF	Unc
AH1340Py	1,000,000	1.00	3.00	12.00	30.00

Y# 30 1/10 RIAL (Dirham) **Weight:** 2.5000 g. **Composition:** 0.8350 Silver .0671 oz. ASW

Date	Mintage	F	VF	XF	Unc
AH1331Pa	500,000	30.00	45.00	75.00	200
AH1331Pa Proof	—	Value: 800			

Y# 31 1/4 RIAL (2-1/2 Dirhams) **Weight:** 6.2500 g. **Composition:** 0.8350 Silver .1678 oz. ASW

Date	Mintage	F	VF	XF	Unc
AH1331Pa	2,500,000	30.00	45.00	90.00	225

Y# 32 1/2 RIAL (5 Dirhams) **Composition:** 0.8350 Silver

Date	Mintage	F	VF	XF	Unc
AH1331Pa	1,500,000	7.00	16.00	25.00	60.00
AH1336Pa	11,500,000	6.00	11.00	20.00	50.00

Y# 33 RIAL (10 Dirhams) **Weight:** 25.0000 g. **Composition:** 0.9000 Silver .7234 oz. ASW

Date	Mintage	F	VF	XF	Unc
AH1331Pa	7,000,000	9.00	20.00	35.00	70.0
AH1336Pa	2,600,000	9.00	17.50	25.00	55.0

FRENCH PROTECTORATE

Yusuf

AH1330-1346 / 1912-1927AD

STANDARD COINAGE

100 Centimes = 1 Franc

Y# 34.1 25 CENTIMES **Composition:** Copper-Nickel **Obverse:** Without privy marks **Reverse:** Without privy mark

Date	Mintage	F	VF	XF	Unc
ND(1921)Pa	8,000,000	1.00	3.00	8.00	40.0

Y# 34.2 25 CENTIMES **Composition:** Copper-Nickel **Reverse:** Thunderbolt above CENTIMES

Date	Mintage	F	VF	XF	Unc
ND(1924)Py	2,037,000	2.00	4.00	19.00	45.0

Y# 34.3 25 CENTIMES **Composition:** Copper-Nickel **Reverse:** Thunderbolt and torch at left and right of CENTIME

Date	F	VF	XF	Unc
ND(1924)Py	3.00	8.00	15.00	60.0

Y# 35.1 50 CENTIMES **Composition:** Nickel **Obverse:** Without privy marks **Reverse:** Without privy marks

Date	Mintage	F	VF	XF	Unc
ND(1921)Pa	7,976,000	0.50	1.00	6.50	45.0

Y# 35.2 50 CENTIMES **Composition:** Nickel **Reverse:** Thunderbolt at bottom

Date	Mintage	F	VF	XF	Unc
ND(1924)Py	3,000,000	1.00	2.00	8.00	45.0

Y# 36.1 FRANC **Composition:** Nickel **Obverse:** Without privy marks **Reverse:** Without privy marks

Date	Mintage	F	VF	XF	Unc
AHND(1921)Pa	8,325,000	0.50	1.00	6.50	37.50

Y# 36.2 FRANC **Composition:** Nickel **Reverse:** Thunderbolt below 1

Date	Mintage	F	VF	XF	Unc
ND(1924)Py	3,000,000	1.25	2.50	10.00	55.00

Mohammed V

AH1346-1381 / 1927-1962AD

STANDARD COINAGE

100 Centimes = 1 Franc

Y# 40 50 CENTIMES **Composition:** Aluminum-Bronze

Date	Mintage	F	VF	XF	Unc
AH1364-1945(a)	24,000,000	—	0.25	1.50	2.50

Y# 41 FRANC **Composition:** Aluminum-Bronze

Date	Mintage	F	VF	XF	Unc
AH1364-1945(a)	24,000,000	—	0.25	1.50	2.50

Y# 46 FRANC **Composition:** Aluminum

Date	Mintage	F	VF	XF	Unc
AH1370-1951(a)	33,000,000	—	0.15	0.35	1.25

Note: Note: Y#46-51 were struck for more than 20 years without change of date, until a new currency was introduced in 1974; Final mintage statistics not yet available

Y# 42 2 FRANCS **Composition:** Aluminum-Bronze

Date	Mintage	F	VF	XF	Unc
AH1364-1945(a)	12,000,000	—	0.75	2.50	6.00

Y# 47 2 FRANCS **Composition:** Aluminum

Date	Mintage	F	VF	XF	Unc
AH1370-1951(a)	20,000,000	—	0.15	0.50	2.00

Y# 37 5 FRANCS **Weight:** 5.0000 g. **Composition:** 0.6800 Silver .1093 oz. ASW

Date	Mintage	F	VF	XF	Unc
AH1347(a)	4,000,000	—	2.50	7.00	32.00
AH1352(a)	5,000,000	—	1.50	4.00	18.00

Y# 43 5 FRANCS **Composition:** Aluminum-Bronze

Date	Mintage	F	VF	XF	Unc
AH1365(a)	20,000,000	0.25	0.50	0.75	2.00

Y# 48 5 FRANCS **Composition:** Aluminum

Date	Mintage	F	VF	XF	Unc
AH1370(a)	23,000,000	0.15	0.30	0.65	1.75

Y# 38 10 FRANCS **Weight:** 10.0000 g. **Composition:** 0.6800 Silver .2186 oz. ASW

Date	Mintage	F	VF	XF	Unc
AH1347(a)	1,600,000	4.00	10.00	22.00	80.00
AH1352(a)	2,900,000	2.25	3.00	8.00	27.50

Y# 44 10 FRANCS **Composition:** Copper-Nickel

Date	Mintage	F	VF	XF	Unc
AH1366(a)	20,000,000	0.50	1.00	1.50	2.50

Y# 49 10 FRANCS **Composition:** Aluminum-Bronze

Date	Mintage	F	VF	XF	Unc
AH1371(a)	40,000,000	0.15	0.40	0.85	2.00

Y# 39 20 FRANCS **Weight:** 20.0000 g. **Composition:** 0.6800 Silver .4372 oz. ASW

Date	Mintage	F	VF	XF	Unc
AH1347(a)	177,000	5.00	12.00	32.50	80.00
AH1352(a)	2,000,000	5.00	8.00	25.00	50.00

Y# 45 20 FRANCS **Composition:** Copper-Nickel

Date	Mintage	F	VF	XF	Unc
AH1366(a)	6,000,000	0.35	0.65	1.25	2.50
AH1366(a) Proof	—	Value: 50.00			

Y# 50 20 FRANCS **Composition:** Aluminum-Bronze

Date	Mintage	F	VF	XF	Unc
AH1371(a)	20,000,000	0.25	0.50	1.00	2.00

Y# 51 50 FRANCS **Composition:** Aluminum-Bronze

Date	Mintage	F	VF	XF	Unc
AH1371(a)	10,000,000	0.35	0.65	1.25	2.25

Y# 51a 50 FRANCS **Composition:** Gold

Date	F	VF	XF	Unc
AH1371(a) Rare	—	—	—	—

Y# A54 100 FRANCS **Weight:** 2.5000 g. **Composition:** 0.7200 Silver .0579 oz. ASW

Date	Mintage	F	VF	XF	Unc
AH1370(a)	10,000,000	—	—	—	400

Note: Most were remelted, about 50 known

Y# 52 100 FRANCS **Weight:** 2.5000 g. **Composition:** 0.7200 Silver .0579 oz. ASW

Date	Mintage	F	VF	XF	Unc
AH1372(a)	20,000,000	—	2.75	3.75	6.50

Y# 53 200 FRANCS **Weight:** 8.0000 g. **Composition:** 0.7200 Silver .1851 oz. ASW

Date	Mintage	F	VF	XF	Unc
AH1372 (1953) (a)	10,176,000	—	2.75	4.25	9.00

KINGDOM
Resumed

Mohammed V
AH1346-1381 / 1927-1962AD

STANDARD COINAGE
100 Centimes = 1 Franc

Y# 54 500 FRANCS **Weight:** 22.5000 g. **Composition:** 0.9000 Silver .6511 oz. ASW

Date	Mintage	F	VF	XF	Unc
AH1376-1956(a)	2,000,000	—	8.00	10.00	20.00

REFORM COINAGE
100 Francs = 1 Dirham

Y# 55 DIRHAM **Weight:** 6.0000 g. **Composition:** 0.6000 Silver .1157 oz. ASW

Date	Mintage	F	VF	XF	Unc
AH1380-1960(a)	18,830,000	—	1.25	2.75	5.50

al-Hassan II
AH1381-1420 / 1962-1999AD

REFORM COINAGE
100 Francs = 1 Dirham

Y# 57 1/2 MITQAL (5 Dirhams) **Weight:** 11.7500 g. **Composition:** 0.7200 Silver .2720 oz. ASW

Date	Mintage	F	VF	XF	Unc
AH1384-1965 (a)	2,000,000	—	5.00	7.50	14.50
AH1384-1965 (a) Proof	200	Value: 60.00			

Y# 56 DIRHAM **Composition:** Nickel

Date	Mintage	F	VF	XF	Unc
AH1384-1965(a)	22,190,000	—	0.50	0.75	1.00
AH1388-1968(a)	5,000,000	—	0.50	0.75	1.00
AH1389-1969(a)	10,000,000	—	0.50	0.75	1.00

REFORM COINAGE
100 Santimat = 1 Dirham

Y# 58 SANTIM **Composition:** Aluminum **Obverse:** Royal arms

Date	Mintage	F	VF	XF	Unc
AH1394-1974	10,240,000	—	—	0.50	1.25
AH1394-1974 Proof	34,000	Value: 1.00			
AH1395-1975	1,700,000	—	—	0.10	1.00
AH1395-1975	14,000	Value: 2.50			

Y# 58a SANTIM **Composition:** 0.9170 Gold

Date	Mintage	F	VF	XF	Unc
AH1394-1974 Proof	30	Value: 400			

Y# 93 SANTIM **Composition:** Aluminum **Obverse:** Royal arms **Reverse:** Fish and denomination

Date	F	VF	XF	Unc
AH1407-1987	—	—	20.00	40.00

Note: Most were remelted

Y# 59 5 SANTIMAT **Composition:** Brass **Series:** F.A.O.

Date	Mintage	F	VF	XF	Unc
AH1394-1974	54,820,000	—	—	0.15	0.30
AH1394-1974 Proof	20,000	Value: 1.25			
AH1395-1975	11,000,000	—	—	0.10	0.25
AH1398-1978	12,600,000	—	—	0.10	0.25

Y# 59a 5 SANTIMAT **Composition:** 0.9170 Gold **Series:** F.A.O.

Date	Mintage	F	VF	XF	Unc
AH1394-1974 Proof	30	Value: 475			

Y# 83 5 SANTIMAT **Composition:** Brass **Series:** F.A.O.

Date	F	VF	XF	Unc
AH1407-1987	—	—	—	0.30

Y# 60 10 SANTIMAT **Composition:** Brass **Series:** F.A.O.

Date	Mintage	F	VF	XF	Unc
AH1394-1974	67,950,000	—	—	0.15	0.30
AH1394-1974 Proof	20,000	Value: 1.75			
AH1395-1975	10,900,000	—	—	0.10	0.20
AH1398-1978	1,000,000	—	—	0.10	0.30

Y# 60a 10 SANTIMAT **Composition:** 0.9170 Gold **Series:** F.A.O.

Date	Mintage	F	VF	XF	Unc
AH1394-1974 Proof	30	Value: 575			

Y# 84 10 SANTIMAT **Composition:** Brass **Series:** F.A.O.

Date	F	VF	XF	Unc
AH1407-1987	—	—	—	0.40

Y# 61 20 SANTIMAT **Composition:** Brass

Date	Mintage	F	VF	XF	Unc
AH1394-1974	59,840,000	—	0.30	0.40	0.50
AH1394-1974 Proof	—	Value: 2.50			
AH1395-1975	10,700,000	—	0.10	0.15	0.35
AH1397-1975	22,800,000	—	0.10	0.15	0.35
AH1398-1978	2,200,000	—	0.10	0.15	0.35

Y# 61a 20 SANTIMAT **Composition:** 0.9170 Gold

Date	Mintage	F	VF	XF	Unc
AH1394-1974 Proof	30	Value: 575			

Y# 85 20 SANTIMAT **Composition:** Brass **Series:** F.A.O.

Date	F	VF	XF	Unc
AH1407-1987	—	—	—	0.50

Y# 62 50 SANTIMAT **Composition:** Copper-Nickel

Date	Mintage	F	VF	XF	Unc
AH1394-1974	40,380,000	—	0.20	0.40	0.60
AH1394-1974 Proof	20,000	Value: 3.00			
AH1398-1978	1,100,000	—	0.25	0.50	0.75

Y# 62a 50 SANTIMAT **Composition:** 0.9170 Gold

Date	Mintage	F	VF	XF	Unc
AH1394-1974 Proof	30	Value: 575			

Y# 87 1/2 DIRHAM **Composition:** Copper-Nickel **Obverse:** Portrait of King **Reverse:** Arms above denomination

Date	F	VF	XF	Unc
AH1407-1987	—	—	—	1.25

Y# 63 DIRHAM **Composition:** Copper-Nickel

Date	Mintage	F	VF	XF	Unc
AH1394 (1974)	32,850,000	—	0.30	0.50	0.75
AH1394 (1974) Proof	37,850,000	Value: 5.00			
AH1398 (1977)	18,100,000	—	0.15	0.35	0.75

Y# 63a DIRHAM **Composition:** 0.9170 Gold

Date	Mintage	F	VF	XF	Unc
AH1394 (1974) Proof	30	Value: 675			

Y# 88 DIRHAM **Composition:** Copper-Nickel

Date	F	VF	XF	Unc
AH1407 (1986)	—	—	—	2.75

Y# 64 5 DIRHAMS **Composition:** Copper-Nickel **Series:** World Food Conference

Date	Mintage	F	VF	XF	Unc
AH1395-1975	500,000	—	—	2.00	6.00
AH1395-1975 Proof	500	Value: 80.00			

Y# 64a 5 DIRHAMS **Weight:** 12.0000 g. **Composition:** 0.9250 Silver .3569 oz. ASW

Date	Mintage	F	VF	XF	Unc
AH1395-1975 Proof	200	Value: 150			

Y# 64b 5 DIRHAMS **Weight:** 23.6500 g. **Composition:** 0.9000 Gold .6844 oz. AGW **Series:** World Food Conference

Date	Mintage	F	VF	XF	Unc
AH1395-1975 Proof	20	Value: 1,000			

Y# 72 5 DIRHAMS **Composition:** Copper-Nickel

Date	Mintage	F	VF	XF	Unc
AH1400-1980	10,000,000	—	1.50	4.00	6.50

Y# 82 5 DIRHAMS **Ring Composition:** Stainless Steel **Center Composition:** Aluminum-Bronze

Date	F	VF	XF	Unc
AH1407-1987	—	2.00	4.50	7.50

Y# 92 10 DIRHAMS (Rial) **Ring Composition:** Brass **Center Composition:** Copper-Nickel **Obverse:** Hassan II **Reverse:** National arms

Date	F	VF	XF	Unc
AH1415-1995	—	—	—	8.00

Y# 65 50 DIRHAMS **Weight:** 35.0000 g. **Composition:** 0.9250 Silver 1.0409 oz. ASW **Subject:** 20th Anniversary of Independence

Date	Mintage	F	VF	XF	Unc
AH1395-1975	6,000	—	—	—	30.00
AH1395-1975 Proof	4,400	Value: 50.00			

Y# 65a 50 DIRHAMS **Weight:** 60.1400 g. **Composition:** 0.9000 Gold 1.7404 oz. AGW **Subject:** 20th Anniversary of Independence

Date	Mintage	F	VF	XF	Unc
AH1395-1975 Proof	40	Value: 1,200			

Y# 67 50 DIRHAMS **Weight:** 35.0000 g. **Composition:** 0.9250 Silver 1.0409 oz. ASW **Series:** International Women's Year **Obverse:** Similar to Y#65

Date	Mintage	F	VF	XF	Unc
AH1395-1975	6,000	—	—	—	30.00
AH1395-1975 Proof	4,400	Value: 50.00			

Y# 67a 50 DIRHAMS **Weight:** 60.1400 g. **Composition:** 0.9000 Gold 1.7404 oz. AGW **Series:** International Women's Year **Obverse:** Similar to Y#65a

Date	Mintage	F	VF	XF	Unc
AH1395-1975 Proof	20	Value: 1,500			

Y# 68 50 DIRHAMS **Weight:** 35.0000 g. **Composition:** 0.9250 Silver 1.0409 oz. ASW **Subject:** Anniversary - Green March **Obverse:** Similar to Y#65

Date	Mintage	F	VF	XF	Unc
AH1396-1976	11,000	—	—	—	25.00
AH1396-1976 Proof	4,400	Value: 50.00			
AH1397-1977	3,500	—	—	—	50.00
AH1397-1977 Proof	200	Value: 150			
AH1398-1978	5,000	—	—	—	40.00
AH1398-1978 Proof	300	Value: 120			
AH1399-1979	3,000	—	—	—	50.00
AH1399-1979 Proof	300	Value: 150			
AH1400-1980	1,000	—	—	—	80.00
AH1400-1980 Proof	200	Value: 200			

Y# 68a 50 DIRHAMS **Weight:** 60.1400 g. **Composition:** 0.9000 Gold 1.7404 oz. AGW **Subject:** Anniversary - Green March **Obverse:** Similar to Y#65a

Date	Mintage	F	VF	XF	Unc
AH1396-1976 Proof	20	Value: 1,750			
AH1397-1977 Proof	20	Value: 1,700			
AH1398-1978 Proof	70	Value: 1,200			
AH1399-1979 Proof	70	Value: 1,200			
AH1400-1980 Proof	30	Value: 1,450			

Y# 70 50 DIRHAMS **Weight:** 35.0000 g. **Composition:** 0.9250 Silver 1.0409 oz. ASW **Series:** International Year of the Child **Obverse:** Similar to Y#65

Date	Mintage	F	VF	XF	Unc
AH1399-1979	5,000	—	—	—	30.00
AH1399-1979 Proof	500	Value: 75.00			

Y# 70a 50 DIRHAMS **Weight:** 60.1400 g. **Composition:** 0.9000 Gold 1.7404 oz. AGW **Series:** International Year of the Child **Obverse:** Similar to 250 Dirhams, Y#66

Date	Mintage	F	VF	XF	Unc
AH1399-1979 Proof	70	Value: 1,200			

Y# 76 50 DIRHAMS **Weight:** 35.0000 g. **Composition:** 0.9250 Silver 1.0409 oz. ASW **Subject:** 50th Birthday - King Hassan

Date	Mintage	F	VF	XF	Unc
AH1399-1979	5,000	—	—	—	40.00
AH1399-1979 Proof	500	Value: 100			

Y# 76a 50 DIRHAMS **Weight:** 60.1400 g. **Composition:** 0.9000 Gold 1.7404 oz. AGW **Subject:** 50th Birthday - King Hassan **Obverse:** Similar to Y#65a

Date	Mintage	F	VF	XF	Unc
AH1399-1979 Proof	70	Value: 1,400			

Y# 75 100 DIRHAMS **Weight:** 25.0000 g. **Composition:** 0.9250 Silver .7436 oz. ASW **Subject:** 9th Mediterranean Games

Date	Mintage	F	VF	XF	Unc
AH1403-1983	5,000	—	—	—	35.00
AH1403-1983 Proof	500	Value: 75.00			

Y#77 100 DIRHAMS **Weight:** 15.0000 g. **Composition:** 0.9250 Silver .4461 oz. ASW **Series:** 6th Panarab Sports Games - Olympics **Reverse:** Olympic rings above map

Date	Mintage	F	VF	XF	Unc
AH1405-1985	2,300	—	—	—	40.00
AH1405-1985 Proof	300	Value: 150			

Y#78 100 DIRHAMS **Weight:** 15.0000 g. **Composition:** 0.9250 Silver .4461 oz. ASW **Subject:** 10th Anniversary of Green March

Date	Mintage	F	VF	XF	Unc
AH1406-1985	1,200	—	—	—	50.00
AH1406-1985 Proof	200	Value: 200			

Y#79 100 DIRHAMS **Weight:** 15.0000 g. **Composition:** 0.9250 Silver .4461 oz. ASW **Subject:** 25th Year - Reign of King Hassan

Date	F	VF	XF	Unc
AH1406-1986	—	—	—	35.00

Y#80 100 DIRHAMS **Weight:** 15.0000 g. **Composition:** 0.9250 Silver .4461 oz. ASW **Subject:** Visit of the Pope

Date	Mintage	F	VF	XF	Unc
AH1406-1986 Proof	2,000	Value: 60.00			

Y#86 100 DIRHAMS **Weight:** 15.0000 g. **Composition:** 0.9250 Silver .4461 oz. ASW **Subject:** Opening of the Rabat Mint

Date		F	VF	XF	Unc
AH1407-1987		—	—	—	25.00
AH1407-1987 Proof	—	Value: 50.00			

Y#74 150 DIRHAMS **Weight:** 35.0000 g. **Composition:** 0.9250 Silver 1.0409 oz. ASW **Subject:** 15th Hejira Calendar Century **Obverse:** Similar to Y#73

Date	Mintage	F	VF	XF	Unc
AH1401-1980	3,000	—	—	—	50.00
AH1401-1980 Proof	300	Value: 150			

Y# 74a 150 DIRHAMS **Weight:** 60.1400 g. **Composition:** 0.9000 Gold 1.7404 oz. AGW **Subject:** 15th Hejira Calendar Century **Obverse:** Similar to Y#73a

Date	Mintage	F	VF	XF	Unc
AH1401-1980 Proof	30	Value: 1,800			

Y#73 150 DIRHAMS **Weight:** 35.0000 g. **Composition:** 0.9250 Silver 1.0409 oz. ASW **Subject:** 20th Anniversary - King Hassan's Coronation

Date	Mintage	F	VF	XF	Unc
AH1401-1981	3,000	—	—	—	50.00
AH1401-1981 Proof	300	Value: 150			

Y# 73a 150 DIRHAMS **Weight:** 60.1400 g. **Composition:** 0.9000 Gold 1.7404 oz. AGW **Subject:** 20th Anniversary - King Hassan's Coronation

Date	Mintage	F	VF	XF	Unc
AH1401-1981 Proof	30	Value: 1,700			

Y#81 200 DIRHAMS **Weight:** 15.0000 g. **Composition:** 0.9250 Silver .4461 oz. ASW **Subject:** Moroccan - American Friendship Treaty

Date	Mintage	F	VF	XF	Unc
AH1408-1987 Proof	Est. 5,000	Value: 40.00			

Y#97 200 DIRHAMS **Weight:** 15.0000 g. **Composition** 0.9250 Silver 0.4461 oz. ASW **Subject:** African Cup Socce Games **Obverse:** King's portrait **Reverse:** Games logo **Edge:** Reeded **Size:** 31.3 mm.

Date	F	VF	XF	Un
AH1408-1988	—	—	—	40.0

Y#91 200 DIRHAMS **Weight:** 15.0000 g. **Composition** 0.9250 Silver .4461 oz. ASW **Subject:** First Francophone Games

Date	Mintage	F	VF	XF	Un
AH1409-1989	5,000	—	—	—	30.0
AH1409-1989 Proof	500	Value: 95.00			

Y#90 200 DIRHAMS **Weight:** 15.0000 g. **Composition** 0.9250 Silver 0.4461 oz. ASW **Subject:** King's Tunisian Visi **Obverse:** King's portrait **Reverse:** Inscription **Edge:** Reedec **Size:** 31.3 mm.

Date		F	VF	XF	Un
AH1441-1990 Proof	—	Value: 95.00			
AH1411-1990		—	—	—	50.0

Y#89 200 DIRHAMS **Weight:** 15.0000 g. **Composition** 0.9250 Silver 0.4461 oz. ASW **Subject:** Independence 35th Anniversary **Obverse:** King's portrait **Reverse:** National arms **Edge:** Reeded **Size:** 31.3 mm.

Date		F	VF	XF	Un
AH1411-1990		—	—	—	40.0
AH1411-1990 Proof	—	Value: 75.00			

Y#96 200 DIRHAMS **Weight:** 15.0000 g. **Composition** 0.9250 Silver 0.4461 oz. ASW **Subject:** 30th Anniversary o Reign **Obverse:** National arms **Reverse:** King on horse amidst a crowd **Edge:** Reeded **Size:** 31.3 mm.

Date		F	VF	XF	Un
AH1411-1991 Proof	—	Value: 95.00			
AH1411-1991		—	—	—	50.0

Y#98 200 DIRHAMS **Weight:** 15.0000 g. **Composition:** 0.9250 Silver 0.4461 oz. ASW **Subject:** Revolution, 40th Anniversary **Obverse:** King's portrait **Reverse:** Building **Edge:** Reeded **Size:** 31.3 mm.

Date	Mintage	F	VF	XF	Unc
AH1414-1993	2,000	—	—	—	40.00
AH1414-1993 Proof	300	Value: 85.00			

Y#99 200 DIRHAMS **Weight:** 15.0000 g. **Composition:** 0.9250 Silver 0.4461 oz. ASW **Subject:** Hassan's 33rd Inauguration Anniversary **Obverse:** King's portrait **Reverse:** Mosque **Edge:** Reeded **Size:** 31.3 mm.

Date	Mintage	F	VF	XF	Unc
AH1414-1993	2,000	—	—	—	40.00
AH1414-1993 Proof	300	Value: 85.00			

Y# 100 200 DIRHAMS **Weight:** 15.0000 g. **Composition:** 0.9250 Silver 0.4461 oz. ASW **Subject:** GATT Agreement **Obverse:** King's portrait **Reverse:** Tower with world globe background **Edge:** Reeded **Size:** 31.3 mm.

Date	Mintage	F	VF	XF	Unc
AH1414-1993 Proof	300	Value: 80.00			
AH1414-1994	2,000	—	—	—	40.00

Y# 101 200 DIRHAMS **Weight:** 15.0000 g. **Composition:** 0.9250 Silver 0.4461 oz. ASW **Subject:** 40th Anniversary Independence **Obverse:** King's portrait **Reverse:** National arms **Edge:** Reeded **Size:** 31.3 mm.

Date	F	VF	XF	Unc
AH1416-1995	—	—	—	40.00
AH1416-1995 Proof	— Value: 75.00			

Y# 102 200 DIRHAMS **Weight:** 15.0000 g. **Composition:** 0.9250 Silver 0.4461 oz. ASW **Subject:** United Nations 50th Anniversary **Obverse:** King's portrait **Reverse:** UN logo **Edge:** Reeded **Size:** 31.3 mm.

Date	F	VF	XF	Unc
AH1416-1995	—	—	—	40.00
AH1416-1995 Proof	— Value: 75.00			

Y# 103 200 DIRHAMS **Weight:** 15.0000 g. **Composition:** 0.9250 Silver 0.4461 oz. ASW **Subject:** Rabat 800th Anniversary **Obverse:** King's portrait **Reverse:** City view **Edge:** Reeded **Size:** 31.3 mm.

Date	F	VF	XF	Unc
AH1416-1995	—	—	—	40.00
AH1416-1995 Proof	— Value: 75.00			

Y# 104 200 DIRHAMS **Weight:** 15.0000 g. **Composition:** 0.9250 Silver 0.4461 oz. ASW **Subject:** Green March 20th Anniversary **Obverse:** King's portrait **Reverse:** Arabic inscription **Edge:** Reeded **Size:** 31.3 mm.

Date	F	VF	XF	Unc
AH1416-1995	—	—	—	40.00
AH1416-1995 Proof	— Value: 75.00			

Y# 105 200 DIRHAMS **Weight:** 15.0000 g. **Composition:** 0.9250 Silver 0.4461 oz. ASW **Subject:** 50th Anniversary Human Rights Declaration **Obverse:** King's portrait **Reverse:** Logo, legend and inscription **Edge:** Reeded **Size:** 31.3 mm.

Date	F	VF	XF	Unc
AH1419-1998	—	—	—	40.00

Y# 66 250 DIRHAMS **Weight:** 6.4500 g. **Composition:** 0.9000 Gold .1867 oz. AGW **Subject:** Birthday of King Hassan

Date	Mintage	F	VF	XF	Unc
AH1395-1975	5,000	—	—	—	120
AH1395-1975 Proof	1,270	Value: 150			
AH1396-1976	3,200	—	—	—	120
AH1396-1976 Proof	450	Value: 175			
AH1397-1977	3,000	—	—	—	120
AH1397-1977 Proof	800	Value: 125			
AH1398-1978	2,000	—	—	—	120
AH1398-1978 Proof	150	Value: 200			

Y#71 500 DIRHAMS **Weight:** 12.9000 g. **Composition:** 0.9000 Gold .3733 oz. AGW **Subject:** Birthday of King Hassan

Date	Mintage	F	VF	XF	Unc
AH1399-1979	3,000	—	—	—	210
AH1399-1979 Proof	300	Value: 300			
AH1400-1980	100	—	—	—	400
AH1400-1980 Proof	100	Value: 500			
AH1401-1981	100	—	—	—	400
AH1401-1981 Proof	100	Value: 500			
AH1402-1982	100	—	—	—	400
AH1402-1982 Proof	100	Value: 500			
AH1403-1983	2,500	—	—	—	210
AH1403-1983 Proof	Inc. above	Value: 220			
AH1404-1984	100	—	—	—	400
AH1404-1984 Proof	100	Value: 500			
AH1405-1985	275	—	—	—	250
AH1405-1985 Proof	125	Value: 475			
AH1406-1986 Proof	—	Value: 450			
AH1407-1987 Proof	—	Value: 450			

Mohammed VI
AH1420 / 1999AD

REFORM COINAGE

100 Santimat = 1 Dirham

Y#94 250 DIRHAMS **Weight:** 25.0000 g. **Composition:** 0.9250 Silver .7435 oz. ASW **Subject:** First Anniversary of Mohammed VI's Enthronement **Obverse:** King's portrait **Reverse:** National arms **Edge:** Reeded **Size:** 37 mm.

Date	F	VF	XF	Unc
AH1421-2000	—	—	—	50.00

Y# 106 250 DIRHAMS **Weight:** 25.0000 g. **Composition:** 0.9250 Silver 0.7435 oz. ASW **Subject:** Green March 25th Anniversary **Obverse:** King's portrait **Reverse:** Map **Edge:** Reeded **Size:** 37 mm.

Date	F	VF	XF	Unc
AH1421-2000	—	—	—	40.00

Y#107 250 DIRHAMS **Weight:** 25.0000 g. **Composition:** 0.9250 Silver 0.7435 oz. ASW **Subject:** Inauguration of Mohammed VI 2nd Anniversary **Obverse:** King's portrait **Reverse:** National arms **Edge:** Reeded **Size:** 37 mm.

Date	F	VF	XF	Unc
AH1422-2001	—	—	—	50.00

Y#95 250 DIRHAMS **Weight:** 25.0000 g. **Composition:** 0.9250 Silver 0.7435 oz. ASW **Subject:** World Children's Day **Obverse:** King's portrait **Reverse:** Children standing on open book with a globe background **Edge:** Reeded **Size:** 37 mm.

Date	F	VF	XF	Unc
AH1422-2001	—	—	—	50.00

Y# 95a (Y95) 250 DIRHAMS **Weight:** 25.0000 g. **Composition:** 0.9999 Gold .8037 oz. AGW **Subject:** World Children's Day **Obverse:** King's portrait **Reverse:** Two children on an open book and a world globe **Edge:** Reeded **Size:** 37 mm.

Date	Mintage	F	VF	XF	Unc
AH1422-2001 Proof	2,800	Value: 500			
AH1422-2001 Proof	2,800	Value: 500			

Y# 108 250 DIRHAMS **Weight:** 25.0000 g. **Composition:** 0.9250 Silver 0.7435 oz. ASW **Subject:** Mohammed VI's Inauguration 3rd Anniversary **Obverse:** King's portrait **Reverse:** National arms, legend differs slightly from the legend of Y-107 **Edge:** Reeded **Size:** 37 mm.

Date	F	VF	XF	Unc
AH1423-2002	—	—	—	45.00

BULLION COINAGE

Y# 250 500 DIRHAMS **Weight:** 33.9100 g. **Composition:** 0.9170 Gold 1.0000 oz. AGW **Issuer:** First Banking Corporation, Tangier **Obverse:** Hercules

Date	F	VF	XF	Unc
ND(1954)	—	—	475	650

ESSAIS

KM#	Date	Mintage	Identification	Mkt Val
E1	1329	—	5 Dirhams. Y24.	375
E2	1330	—	Muzuna. Y26.	175
E3	1330	—	2 Muzunas. Y15.	185

KM#	Date	Mintage	Identification	Mkt Val
E4	1330	—	5 Muzunas. Y16.	200
E5	1330	—	10 Muzunas. Y17.	250
E6	1331	—	5 Dirhams. Nickel.	350
E7	1331	—	5 Dirhams. Aluminum-Bronze.	350
E8	1331	—	5 Dirhams. Aluminum. Y32.	325
E8a	1331	—	5 Dirhams. Nickel. Y32.	325

KM#	Date	Mintage	Identification	Mkt Val
E10		—	50 Centimes.	130
E10a	ND	—	50 Centimes. Y35.	—

KM#	Date	Mintage	Identification	Mkt Val
E11		—	Franc. Y36.	140

KM#	Date	Mintage	Identification	Mkt Val
E12	1340	—	5 Muzunas. Y28,	200

KM#	Date	Mintage	Identification	Mkt Val
E13	1340	—	10 Muzunas. Y29.	250

KM#	Date	Mintage	Identification	Mkt Val
E9		—	25 Centimes. Without hole or ESSAI, Y34.	180

KM#	Date	Mintage	Identification	Mkt Val
E9a		—	25 Centimes. With hole, Y34.	150

KM#	Date	Mintage	Identification	Mkt Val
E14	1346	—	10 Francs. Nickel.	500
E15	1346	—	10 Francs. Nickel. Without ESSAI.	500

KM#	Date	Mintage	Identification	Mkt Val
E21	1347	—	10 Francs. Silver.	450

KM#	Date	Mintage	Identification	Mkt Val
E16		—	5 Dirhams. Nickel.	900
E17		—	5 Dirhams. Nickel. Without ESSAI.	900
E18		—	5 Dirhams. Aluminum-Bronze.	900
E19		—	5 Dirhams. Aluminum-Bronze. Without ESSAI.	900

KM#	Date	Mintage	Identification	Mkt Val
E20	1347	—	5 Francs. Y37.	180
E22	1347	—	10 Francs. Silver. Without ESSAI.	450
E23	1347	—	10 Francs. Y38.	200

KM#	Date	Mintage	Identification	Mkt Val
E24	1347	—	20 Francs.	650
E25	1347	—	20 Francs. Without ESSAI.	650

KM#	Date	Mintage	Identification	Mkt Val
E26	1347	—	20 Francs. Y39.	25
E28	1361	—	50 Centimes. Y40.	40.0

KM#	Date	Mintage	Identification	Mkt Val
E29	1361	—	Franc. Y41.	40.0
E30	1361	—	2 Francs. Y42.	45.0
E31	1365	—	50 Centimes. Y40.	20.0
E32	1365	—	Franc. Y41.	22.0
E33	1365	—	2 Francs. Y42.	25.0
E34	1365	—	5 Francs. Y43.	30.0
E35	1366	1,100	10 Francs. Y44.	25.0
E36	1366	1,100	20 Francs. Y45.	30.0
E37	1370	1,100	Franc. Y46.	21.0
E38	1370	1,100	2 Francs. Y47.	24.0
E39	1370	1,100	5 Francs. Y48.	30.0

KM#	Date	Mintage	Identification	Mkt Val
E40	1370	1,100	100 Francs. 0.7200 Silver. Y-A54.	70.0

Note: KM#E37-E40 were issued in a set with Tunisia, KM#E28-E30.

KM#	Date	Mintage	Identification	Mkt Val
E41	1371	1,100	10 Francs. Y49.	30.0

KM#	Date	Mintage	Identification	Mkt Val
E42	1371	1,100	20 Francs. Y50.	30.0

KM#	Date	Mintage	Identification	Mkt Val
E43	1371	1,100	50 Francs. Y51.	35.0

Note: KM#E41-43 also issued in 3-piece boxed sets.

KM#	Date	Mintage	Identification	Mkt Val
E44	1372	1,100	100 Francs. Y52.	75.0
E45	1372	1,100	200 Francs. Y53.	90.0

PIEFORTS

Double thickness

KM#	Date	Mintage	Identification	Mkt Val
P1	1395	10	5 Dirhams. Gold. Y64b	70
P2	1395	40	50 Dirhams. Silver. Y65	–
P3	1395	10	50 Dirhams. Gold. Y65a.	2,10
P4	1395	10	50 Dirhams. Gold. Y67a	2,10
P5	1395	10	250 Dirhams. Gold. Y66	20

KM#	Date	Mintage	Identification	Mkt Val
P7	1396	10	250 Dirhams. Gold. Y66	200
P6	1395	10	50 Dirhams. Gold. Y68a.	2,100
P8	1396	10	50 Dirhams. Gold. Y68a.	2,100
P9	1397	15	250 Dirhams. Gold. Y66.	—
P10	1397	15	250 Dirhams. Gold. Y68a.	—
P11	1398	20	250 Dirhams. Gold. Y66.	—
P12	1399	20	50 Dirhams. Gold. Y68a.	2,000
P13	1399	20	50 Dirhams. Silver. Y70.	350
P14	1399	20	50 Dirhams. 0.9250 Silver. Y76	—
P15	1399	20	50 Dirhams. Gold. Y76a.	2,000
P16	1399	20	500 Dirhams. Gold. Y71.	—
P17	1400	10	50 Dirhams. Gold. Y68a.	2,100
P18	1400	10	150 Dirhams. 0.9000 Gold. Y74a.	2,200
P19	1401	10	150 Dirhams. 0.9000 Gold. Y73a.	2,200

PIEFORTS WITH ESSAI

KM#	Date	Mintage	Identification	Mkt Val
PEA1	1361	—	50 Centimes. Y40.	90.00
PE1	1361	—	Franc. Y41.	110
PE2	1361	—	2 Francs. Y42.	120
PE3	1364	104	50 Centimes. Y40.	70.00
PE4	1364	104	Franc. Y41	85.00
PE5	1364	104	2 Francs. Y42.	90.00
PE6	1365	104	5 Francs. Y43.	100
PE7	1366	104	10 Francs. Y44.	95.00
PE8	1366	104	20 Francs. Y45.	95.00
PE9	1372	104	100 Francs. Y52.	100
PE10	1372	104	200 Francs. Y53.	125
PE11	1372	—	200 Francs. Gold. Y53.	1,000

TRIAL STRIKES

Uniface

KM#	Date	Mintage	Identification	Mkt Val
TS1	1347	—	10 Francs. Silvered Bronze.	500

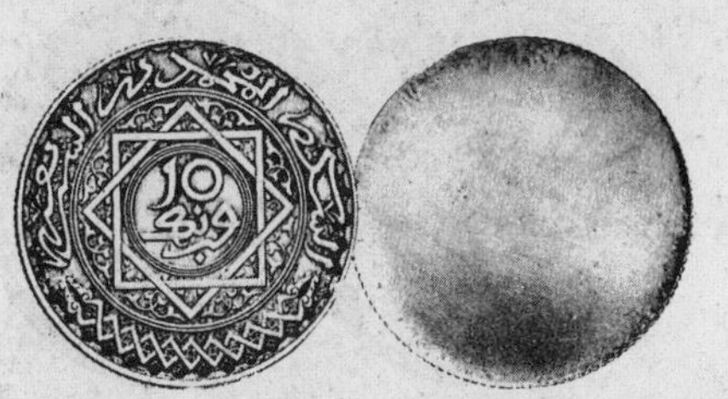

KM#	Date	Mintage	Identification	Mkt Val
TS2	1347	—	10 Francs. Silvered Bronze.	500
TS3	1347	—	20 Francs. Silvered Bronze.	750

KM#	Date	Mintage	Identification	Mkt Val
TS4	1347	—	20 Francs. Silvered Bronze.	750

MINT SETS

KM#	Date	Mintage	Identification	Issue Price	Mkt Val
MS1	AH1370-84 (8)	—	Y#46-48(AH1370), 49-51(AH1371), 56-57(AH1384)	—	17.50

PROOF SETS

KM#	Date	Mintage	Identification	Issue Price	Mkt Val
PS1	AH1320 (4)	5	Y#14, 15.1, 16, 17	—	—
PS3	1974 (6)	30	Y#58a-63a	—	3,650
PS2	1974-1975 (7)	20,000	Y#58-63 (1974), 64 (1975)	20.00	25.00

MOZAMBIQUE

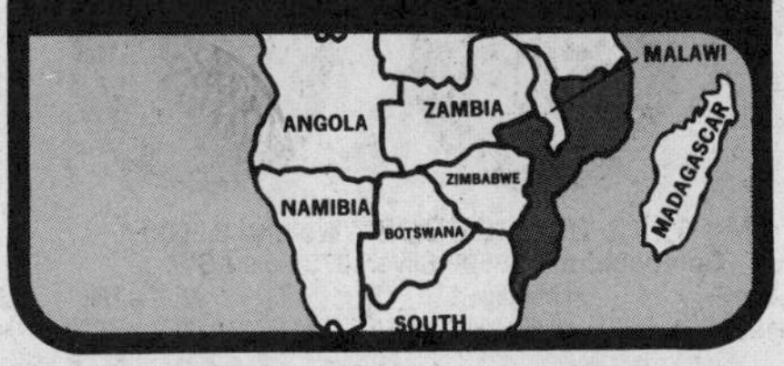

The Republic of Mozambique, a former overseas province of Portugal, stretches for 1,430 miles (2,301 km.) along the southeast coast of Africa, has an area of 302,330 sq. mi. (801,590 sq. km.) and a population of 14.1 million, 99 % of whom are native Africans of the Bantu tribes. Capital: Maputo. Agriculture is the chief industry. Cashew nuts, cotton, sugar, copra and tea are exported.

Vasco de Gama explored all the coast of Mozambique in 1498 and found Arab trading posts already established along the coast. Portuguese settlement dates from the establishment of the trading post of Mozambique in 1505. Within five years Portugal absorbed all the former Arab sultanates along the east African coast. The area was organized as a colony in 1907 and became an overseas province in 1952. In Sept. of 1974, after more than a decade of guerrilla warfare with the forces of the Mozambique Liberation Front, Portugal agreed to the independence of Mozambique, effective June 25, 1975. The Socialist party, led by President Joaquim Chissano was in power until the 2nd of November, 1990 when they became a republic.

Mozambique became a member of the Commonwealth of Nations in November 1995. The President is Head of State; the Prime Minister is Head of Government.

RULERS

Portuguese, until 1975

MONETARY SYSTEM

100 Centavos = 1 Escudo

PORTUGUESE COLONY

DECIMAL COINAGE

100 Centavos = 1 Escudo

KM# 63 10 CENTAVOS Composition: Bronze

Date	Mintage	F	VF	XF	Unc	BU
1936	2,000,000	2.00	4.00	22.00	50.00	—

KM# 72 10 CENTAVOS Composition: Bronze

Date	Mintage	F	VF	XF	Unc	BU
1942	2,000,000	1.00	2.50	7.50	20.00	—

KM# 83 10 CENTAVOS Composition: Bronze

Date	Mintage	F	VF	XF	Unc	BU
1960	3,750,000	—	0.50	1.25	3.00	—
1961	10,300,000	—	0.25	1.00	2.50	—

KM# 64 20 CENTAVOS Composition: Bronze

Date	Mintage	F	VF	XF	Unc	BU
1936	2,500,000	2.00	4.50	50.00	90.00	—

KM# 71 20 CENTAVOS Composition: Bronze

Date	Mintage	F	VF	XF	Unc	BU
1941	2,000,000	1.75	4.50	50.00	90.00	—

KM# 75 20 CENTAVOS Composition: Bronze

Date	Mintage	F	VF	XF	Unc	BU
1949	8,000,000	0.75	1.50	4.00	10.00	—
1950	12,500,000	0.75	1.50	3.00	8.50	—

KM# 85 20 CENTAVOS Composition: Bronze

Date	Mintage	F	VF	XF	Unc	BU
1961	12,500,000	—	0.25	1.00	2.50	—

KM# 88 20 CENTAVOS Composition: Bronze **Size:** 16 mm. **Note:** Reduced size.

Date	Mintage	F	VF	XF	Unc	BU
1973	1,798,000	1.00	2.00	3.00	7.50	—
1974	13,044,000	1.00	2.50	3.75	9.00	—

KM# 65 50 CENTAVOS Composition: Copper-Nickel

Date	Mintage	F	VF	XF	Unc	BU
1936	2,500,000	5.00	45.00	125	225	—

KM# 73 50 CENTAVOS Composition: Bronze

Date	Mintage	F	VF	XF	Unc	BU
1945	2,500,000	1.50	3.50	25.00	50.00	—

KM# 76 50 CENTAVOS Composition: Nickel-Bronze

Date	Mintage	F	VF	XF	Unc	BU
1950	20,000,000	1.00	3.00	12.00	22.00	—
1951	16,000,000	1.00	3.00	10.00	20.00	—

KM# 81 50 CENTAVOS **Composition:** Bronze

Date	Mintage	F	VF	XF	Unc	BU
1953	5,010,000	0.50	1.50	4.00	10.00	—
1957	24,990,000	—	0.50	1.25	4.50	—

KM# 89 50 CENTAVOS **Composition:** Bronze

Date	Mintage	F	VF	XF	Unc	BU
1973	6,841,000	—	0.50	1.00	3.00	—
1974	23,810,000	—	0.50	1.00	4.00	—

KM# 66 ESCUDO **Composition:** Copper-Nickel

Date	Mintage	F	VF	XF	Unc	BU
1936	2,000,000	4.00	25.00	100	210	—

KM# 74 ESCUDO **Composition:** Bronze

Date	Mintage	F	VF	XF	Unc	BU
1945	2,000,000	2.00	15.00	45.00	110	—

KM# 77 ESCUDO **Composition:** Nickel-Bronze

Date	Mintage	F	VF	XF	Unc	BU
1950	10,000,000	2.00	15.00	45.00	90.00	—
1951	10,000,000	1.50	3.00	12.50	30.00	—

KM# 82 ESCUDO **Composition:** Bronze

Date	Mintage	F	VF	XF	Unc	BU
1953	2,013,000	0.75	1.50	10.00	25.00	—
1957	2,987,000	0.75	1.50	17.50	35.00	—
1962	600,000	0.50	1.25	11.50	22.50	—
1963	3,258,000	0.50	0.75	4.00	12.50	—
1965	5,000,000	—	0.25	1.50	3.50	—
1968	4,500,000	—	0.25	1.50	3.50	—
1969	1,642,000	—	0.50	1.75	4.00	—
1973	501,000	0.20	0.50	2.00	6.50	—
1974	25,281,000	—	0.25	1.50	3.00	—

KM# 61 2-1/2 ESCUDOS **Weight:** 3.5000 g. **Composition:** 0.6500 Silver .0731 oz. ASW

Date	Mintage	F	VF	XF	Unc	BU
1935	1,200,000	4.50	12.50	40.00	100	—

KM# 68 2-1/2 ESCUDOS **Weight:** 3.5000 g. **Composition:** 0.6500 Silver .0731 oz. ASW

Date	Mintage	F	VF	XF	Unc	BU
1938	1,000,000	3.50	10.00	25.00	65.00	—
1942	1,200,000	2.50	7.50	20.00	55.00	—
1950	4,000,000	1.25	2.50	7.50	20.00	—
1951	4,000,000	2.00	6.50	18.00	50.00	—

KM# 78 2-1/2 ESCUDOS **Composition:** Copper-Nickel

Date	Mintage	F	VF	XF	Unc	BU
1952	4,000,000	0.50	8.00	20.00	50.00	—
1953	4,000,000	0.30	5.00	20.00	45.00	—
1954	4,000,000	0.25	3.00	12.00	22.00	—
1955	4,000,000	0.30	1.50	13.50	42.50	—
1965	8,000,000	0.10	0.25	1.00	4.00	—
1973	1,767,000	0.25	0.65	2.50	6.50	—

KM# 62 5 ESCUDOS **Weight:** 7.0000 g. **Composition:** 0.6500 Silver .1463 oz. ASW

Date	Mintage	F	VF	XF	Unc	BU
1935	1,000,000	5.50	22.50	45.00	100	—

KM# 69 5 ESCUDOS **Weight:** 7.0000 g. **Composition:** 0.6500 Silver .1463 oz. ASW

Date	Mintage	F	VF	XF	Unc	BU
1938	800,000	7.50	20.00	67.50	130	—
1949	8,000,000	2.00	5.50	17.50	45.00	—

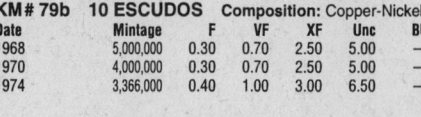

KM# 84 5 ESCUDOS **Weight:** 4.0000 g. **Composition:** 0.6500 Silver .0835 oz. ASW

Date	Mintage	F	VF	XF	Unc	BU
1960	8,000,000	1.00	2.00	3.25	7.00	—

KM# 86 5 ESCUDOS **Composition:** Copper-Nickel

Date	Mintage	F	VF	XF	Unc	BU
1971	8,000,000	0.20	0.50	1.00	3.00	—
1973	3,352,000	0.20	0.50	1.75	4.50	—

KM# 67 10 ESCUDOS **Weight:** 12.5000 g. **Composition:** 0.8350 Silver .3356 oz. ASW

Date	Mintage	F	VF	XF	Unc	BU
1936	497,000	10.00	20.00	67.50	130	—

KM# 70 10 ESCUDOS **Weight:** 12.5000 g. **Composition:** 0.8350 Silver .3356 oz. ASW

Date	Mintage	F	VF	XF	Unc	BU
1938	530,000	20.00	35.00	75.00	160	—

KM# 79 10 ESCUDOS **Weight:** 5.0000 g. **Composition:** 0.7200 Silver .1157 oz. ASW

Date	Mintage	VG	F	VF	XF	Unc
1952	1,503,000	—	2.00	4.50	15.00	35.00
1954	1,335,000	—	2.00	4.50	20.00	50.00
1955	1,162,000	—	2.00	4.50	15.00	35.00
1960	2,000,000	—	1.00	2.00	5.00	12.00

KM# 79a 10 ESCUDOS **Weight:** 5.0000 g. **Composition:** 0.6800 Silver .1093 oz. ASW

Date	Mintage	F	VF	XF	Unc	BU
1966	500,000	1.00	2.00	5.50	12.50	—

KM# 79b 10 ESCUDOS **Composition:** Copper-Nickel

Date	Mintage	F	VF	XF	Unc	BU
1968	5,000,000	0.30	0.70	2.50	5.00	—
1970	4,000,000	0.30	0.70	2.50	5.00	—
1974	3,366,000	0.40	1.00	3.00	6.50	—

KM# 80 20 ESCUDOS Weight: 10.0000 g. Composition: 0.7200 Silver .2315 oz. ASW

Date	Mintage	F	VF	XF	Unc	BU
1952	1,004,000	1.50	3.00	10.00	25.00	—
1955	996,000	1.75	3.50	12.50	30.00	—
1960	2,000,000	1.25	2.50	5.00	11.50	—

KM# 80a 20 ESCUDOS Weight: 10.0000 g. Composition: 0.6800 Silver .2186 oz. ASW

Date	Mintage	F	VF	XF	Unc	BU
1966	250,000	2.75	4.50	8.50	17.50	—

KM# 87 20 ESCUDOS Composition: Nickel

Date	Mintage	F	VF	XF	Unc	BU
1971	2,000,000	0.35	0.75	1.75	5.00	—
1972	1,158,000	0.50	1.00	2.50	6.00	—

REFORM COINAGE

100 Centavos = 1 Metical

KM# 116 5 METICAIS Composition: Brass Clad Steel

Date	F	VF	XF	Unc	BU
1994	—	—	—	1.00	—

PEOPLE'S REPUBLIC

DECIMAL COINAGE

100 Centimos = 1 Metica

KM# 90 CENTIMO Composition: Aluminum

Date	Mintage	F	VF	XF	Unc	BU
1975	15,050,000	—	—	120	225	—

KM# 91 2 CENTIMOS Composition: Copper-Zinc

Date	Mintage	F	VF	XF	Unc	BU
1975	8,242,000	—	—	70.00	120	—

KM# 92 5 CENTIMOS Composition: Copper-Zinc

Date	Mintage	F	VF	XF	Unc	BU
1975	14,898,000	—	—	60.00	110	—

KM# 93 10 CENTIMOS Composition: Copper-Zinc

Date	Mintage	F	VF	XF	Unc	BU
1975	18,000,000	—	—	50.00	90.00	—

KM# 94 20 CENTIMOS Composition: Copper-Nickel

Date	Mintage	F	VF	XF	Unc	BU
1975	8,050,000	—	—	125	225	—

KM# 95 50 CENTIMOS Composition: Copper-Nickel

Date	Mintage	F	VF	XF	Unc	BU
1975	3,050,000	—	—	160	275	—

KM# 96 METICA Composition: Copper-Nickel

Date	Mintage	F	VF	XF	Unc	BU
1975	2,550,000	—	—	50.00	85.00	—

KM# 97 2-1/2 METICAS Composition: Copper-Nickel Shape: 7-sided

Date	Mintage	F	VF	XF	Unc	BU
1975	1,500,000	—	—	125	200	—

REFORM COINAGE

100 Centavos = 1 Metical

KM# 98 50 CENTAVOS Composition: Aluminum Reverse: Musical instrument

Date	Mintage	F	VF	XF	Unc	BU
1980	5,160,000	0.15	0.30	0.60	1.25	—
1982	—	0.15	0.30	0.60	1.25	—

KM# 100 2-1/2 METICAS Composition: Aluminum Reverse: Ship and crane in harbor Note: 1.80-2.00 grams.

Date	Mintage	F	VF	XF	Unc	BU
1980	1,088,000	0.25	0.50	1.00	1.75	—
1982	—	0.25	0.50	1.00	1.75	—
1986	—	0.25	0.50	1.00	1.75	—

Note: Edge varieties exist

KM# 99 METICAL Composition: Brass Reverse: Female student

Date	Mintage	F	VF	XF	Unc	BU
1980	32,000	1.50	3.00	5.00	10.00	—
1982	—	1.50	3.00	5.00	10.00	—

KM# 99a METICAL Composition: Aluminum Reverse: Female student

Date	F	VF	XF	Unc	BU
1986	0.20	0.40	0.60	1.00	—

KM# 115 METICAL Composition: Brass Clad Steel

Date	F	VF	XF	Unc	BU
1994	—	—	—	0.50	—

KM# 101 5 METICAIS Composition: Aluminum Reverse: Tractor

Date	Mintage	F	VF	XF	Unc	BU
1980	7,736,000	0.35	0.75	1.25	2.00	—
1982	—	0.35	0.75	1.25	2.00	—
1986	—	0.35	0.75	1.25	2.00	—

KM# 102 10 METICAIS Composition: Copper-Nickel Reverse: Industrial skyline

Date	Mintage	F	VF	XF	Unc	BU
1980	152,000	0.75	1.50	2.50	6.00	—
1981	—	0.75	1.50	2.50	6.00	—

KM# 102a 10 METICAIS Composition: Aluminum Reverse: Industrial skyline

Date	F	VF	XF	Unc	BU
1986	0.25	0.45	1.00	2.00	—

KM# 117 10 METICAIS **Composition:** Brass Clad Steel **Reverse:** Cotton plant

Date	F	VF	XF	Unc	BU
1994	—	—	—	1.25	—

KM# 103 20 METICAIS **Composition:** Copper-Nickel **Reverse:** Panzer tank

Date	Mintage	F	VF	XF	Unc	BU
1980	78,000	1.00	2.00	4.00	9.00	—

KM# 103a 20 METICAIS **Composition:** Aluminum **Reverse:** Panzer tank

Date	F	VF	XF	Unc	BU
1986	0.40	0.80	1.50	3.00	—

KM# 118 20 METICAIS **Composition:** Brass Clad Steel **Reverse:** Pepper plant

Date	F	VF	XF	Unc	BU
1994	—	—	—	1.50	—

KM# 106 50 METICAIS **Composition:** Copper-Nickel **Subject:** World Fisheries Conference

Date	Mintage	F	VF	XF	Unc	BU
1983	130,000	2.50	5.00	8.00	12.50	—

KM# 106a 50 METICAIS **Weight:** 22.0000 g. **Composition:** 0.9250 Silver .6543 oz. ASW **Subject:** World Fisheries Conference

Date	Mintage	F	VF	XF	Unc	BU
1983 Proof	21,000	Value: 50.00				

KM# 106b 50 METICAIS **Weight:** 22.0000 g. **Composition:** 0.9000 Gold .6366 oz. AGW **Subject:** World Fisheries Conference

Date	Mintage	F	VF	XF	Unc	BU
1983 Proof	135	Value: 1,000				

KM# 112 50 METICAIS **Composition:** Aluminum **Reverse:** Woman and soldier with provisions

Date	F	VF	XF	Unc	BU
1986	0.75	1.50	2.50	5.50	—

KM# 119 50 METICAIS **Composition:** Nickel Clad Steel **Reverse:** Leopard's head

Date	F	VF	XF	Unc	BU
1994	—	—	—	2.75	—

KM# 120 100 METICAIS **Composition:** Nickel Clad Steel **Reverse:** Lobster

Date	F	VF	XF	Unc	BU
1994	—	—	—	3.50	—

KM# 107 250 METICAIS **Weight:** 28.2800 g. **Composition:** 0.9250 Silver .8411 oz. ASW **Subject:** 10th Anniversary of Independence

Date	Mintage	F	VF	XF	Unc	BU
1985 Proof	2,000	Value: 42.50				

KM# 107a 250 METICAIS **Composition:** Copper-Nickel

Date	F	VF	XF	Unc	BU
1985	—	—	—	—	—

KM# 104 500 METICAIS **Weight:** 19.4000 g. **Composition:** 0.8000 Silver .4990 oz. ASW **Subject:** 5th Anniversary of Independence

Date	Mintage	F	VF	XF	Unc	BU
1980 Proof	5,000	Value: 35.00				

KM# 110 500 METICAIS **Weight:** 16.0000 g. **Composition:** 0.9990 Silver .5145 oz. ASW **Subject:** Defense of Nature **Reverse:** Lions

Date	Mintage	F	VF	XF	Unc	BU
1989 Proof	2,500	Value: 32.50				

KM# 111 500 METICAIS **Weight:** 16.0000 g. **Composition:** 0.9990 Silver .5145 oz. ASW **Subject:** Defense of Nature **Reverse:** Moorish Idol Fish

Date	Mintage	F	VF	XF	Unc	BU
1989 Proof	2,000	Value: 32.50				

KM# 113 500 METICAIS **Weight:** 16.0000 g. **Composition:** 0.9990 Silver .5145 oz. ASW **Subject:** Defense of Nature **Reverse:** Giraffes

Date	Mintage	F	VF	XF	Unc	BU
1990 Proof	2,000	Value: 32.50				

KM# 121 500 METICAIS **Composition:** Nickel Clad Steel

Date	F	VF	XF	Unc	BU
1994	—	—	—	4.50	—

KM# 127 500 METICAIS **Composition:** Nickel Clad Steel **Series:** 2000 Summer Olympics - Sydney

Date	Mintage	F	VF	XF	Unc	BU
1998 Proof	10,000	Value: 7.50				

KM# 109 1000 METICAIS **Composition:** Copper-Nickel **Subject:** Visit of Pope John Paul II

Date	F	VF	XF	Unc	BU
1988	—	—	—	8.00	—

KM# 109a 1000 METICAIS **Weight:** 28.2800 g. **Composition:** 0.9250 Silver .8411 oz. ASW

Date	Mintage	F	VF	XF	Unc	BU
1988 Proof	Est. 3,500	Value: 42.50				

KM# 122 1000 METICAIS **Composition:** Nickel Clad Steel

Date	F	VF	XF	Unc	BU
1994	—	—	—	5.00	—

KM# 128 1000 METICAIS **Weight:** 24.6200 g. **Composition:** 0.9250 Silver .7322 oz. ASW **Series:** 2000 Summer Olympics - Sydney

Date	Mintage	F	VF	XF	Unc	BU
1998 Proof	10,000	Value: 32.50				

KM# 108 2000 METICAIS **Weight:** 17.5000 g. **Composition:** 0.9170 Gold .5158 oz. AGW **Subject:** 10th Anniversary of Independence

Date	Mintage	F	VF	XF	Unc	BU
1985 Proof	100	Value: 650				

KM# 105 5000 METICAIS **Weight:** 17.2790 g. **Composition:** 0.9000 Gold .5000 oz. AGW **Subject:** 5th Anniversary of Independence **Obverse:** State emblem above denomination **Reverse:** Figure at left, corn plants in background, tractor above

Date	Mintage	F	VF	XF	Unc	BU
1980 Proof	2,000	Value: 325				

KM# 125 5000 METICAIS **Weight:** 411.4224 g. **Composition:** 0.9990 Silver 13.2143 oz. ASW **Obverse:** National arms **Reverse:** Rhinoceros right **Edge:** Reeded **Size:** 97 mm. **Note:** Illustration reduced.

Date	Mintage	F	VF	XF	Unc	BU
1997 Proof	2,000	Value: 300				

KM# 124 5000 METICAIS **Composition:** Nickel Clad Steel **Obverse:** State emblem **Reverse:** High power electric lines

Date	F	VF	XF	Unc	BU
1998	—	—	—	5.00	—

KM# 114.1 10000 METICAIS **Weight:** 20.0000 g. **Composition:** 0.9990 Silver .6430 oz. ASW **Subject:** World Cup Soccer

Date	F	VF	XF	Unc	BU
1994 Proof	—	Value: 65.00			

KM# 114.2 10000 METICAIS **Weight:** 20.0000 g. **Composition:** 0.9990 Silver .6430 oz. ASW **Reverse:** Without 999

Date	F	VF	XF	Unc	BU
1994 Proof	—	Value: 65.00			

KM# 123 10000 METICAIS **Weight:** 21.0600 g. **Composition:** 0.9990 Silver .6764 oz. ASW **Subject:** World Cup Soccer

Date	F	VF	XF	Unc	BU
1994 Proof	—	Value: 65.00			

KM# 126 10000 METICAIS **Weight:** 822.8449 g. **Composition:** 0.9990 Silver 26.4286 oz. ASW **Obverse:** National arms **Reverse:** Elephant charging **Edge:** Reeded **Size:** 100 mm. **Note:** Illustration reduced.

Date	Mintage	F	VF	XF	Unc	BU
1997 Proof	2,000	Value: 500				

KM# 129 10000 METICAIS **Weight:** 822.8449 g. **Composition:** 0.9990 Silver 26.4286 oz. ASW **Series:** 2000 Summer Olympics - Sydney

Date	Mintage	F	VF	XF	Unc	BU
1998 Proof	2,000	Value: 365				

PATTERNS

Including off metal strikes

KM#	Date	Mintage	Identification	Mkt Val
Pn1	1994	—	10000 Meticais. Copper-Nickel. KM#114.1.	—
Pn2	1994	—	10000 Meticais. Copper-Nickel. KM#123.	—

PIEFORTS

KM#	Date	Mintage	Identification	Issue Price	Mkt Val
P1	1983	600	50 Meticais. 0.9250 Silver.	—	70.00

PROVAS

Standard Metals

KM#	Date	Mintage	Identification	Issue Price	Mkt Val
Pr1	1935	—	2-1/2 Escudos. KM#61	—	125
Pr2	1935	—	5 Escudos. KM62.	—	145
Pr3	1936	—	10 Centavos. KM63.	—	60.00
Pr4	1936	—	20 Centavos. KM64.	—	60.00
Pr5	1936	—	50 Centavos. KM65.	—	90.00
Pr6	1936	—	Escudo. KM66	—	90.00
Pr7	1936	—	10 Escudos. KM67.	—	180
Pr8	1938	—	2-1/2 Escudos. KM61.	—	100
Pr9	1938	—	5 Escudos. KM69.	—	120
Pr10	1938	—	10 Escudos. KM70.	—	130
Pr11	1941	—	10 Centavos. KM71.	—	65.00
Pr12	1942	—	10 Centavos. KM72.	—	40.00
Pr13	1942	—	2-1/2 Escudos. KM68.	—	75.00
Pr14	1945	—	50 Centavos. KM73.	—	40.00
Pr15	1945	—	Escudo. KM74.	—	40.00
Pr16	1948	—	2-1/2 Escudos.	—	—
Pr17	1949	—	20 Centavos. KM75.	—	40.00
Pr18	1949	—	5 Escudos. KM69.	—	75.00
PrA19	1950	—	20 Centavos. KM75.	—	85.00
Pr19	1950	—	50 Centavos. KM76.	—	45.00
Pr20	1950	—	Escudo. KM77.	—	45.00
Pr21	1950	—	2-1/2 Escudos. KM68.	—	80.00
Pr22	1951	—	50 Centavos. KM76.	—	35.00
Pr23	1951	—	Escudo. KM77.	—	35.00
Pr24	1951	—	2-1/2 Escudos. KM68.	—	65.00
Pr25	1951	—	5 Escudos.	—	—
Pr26	1952	—	2-1/2 Escudos. KM78.	—	65.00
Pr27	1952	—	5 Escudos.	—	—
Pr28	1952	—	10 Escudos. KM79	—	65.00
Pr29	1952	—	20 Escudos. KM80.	—	75.00
Pr30	1953	—	50 Centavos. KM81.	—	35.00
Pr31	1953	—	Escudo. KM82.	—	35.00
Pr32	1953	—	2-1/2 Escudos. KM78.	—	45.00
Pr34	1954	—	10 Escudos. KM79.	—	65.00
Pr35	1955	—	2-1/2 Escudos. KM78.	—	45.00
Pr36	1955	—	10 Escudos. KM79.	—	65.00
Pr37	1955	—	20 Escudos. KM80.	—	65.00
Pr38	1957	—	50 Centavos. KM81.	—	35.00
Pr39	1957	—	Escudo. KM82.	—	35.00
Pr40	1960	—	10 Centavos. KM83.	—	35.00
Pr41	1960	—	5 Escudos. KM84	—	65.00
Pr42	1960	—	10 Escudos. KM79.	—	65.00
Pr43	1960	—	20 Escudos. KM80.	—	65.00
Pr44	1961	—	10 Centavos. KM83.	—	35.00
Pr45	1961	—	20 Centavos. KM85.	—	35.00
Pr46	1962	—	Escudo. KM82.	—	35.00
Pr47	1963	—	Escudo. KM82.	—	35.00
Pr48	1965	—	Escudo. KM82.	—	35.00
Pr49	1965	—	2-1/2 Escudos. KM78.	—	45.00
Pr50	1966	—	10 Escudos. KM79a.	—	65.00
Pr51	1966	—	20 Escudos. KM80a	—	75.00
Pr52	1968	—	Escudo. KM82.	—	35.00
Pr53	1968	—	10 Escudos. KM79b.	—	45.00
Pr54	1968	—	20 Escudos.	—	45.00
Pr55	1969	—	Escudo. KM82.	—	35.00
Pr56	1969	—	20 Escudos.	—	45.00
Pr57	1970	—	10 Escudos. KM79b.	—	45.00
Pr58	1970	—	20 Escudos.	—	45.00
Pr59	1971	—	5 Escudos. KM86.	—	45.00
Pr60	1971	—	20 Escudos. KM87.	—	45.00
Pr61	1972	—	20 Escudos. KM87.	—	85.00
Pr62	1973	—	20 Centavos. KM88.	—	65.00
Pr63	1973	—	50 Centavos. KM89.	—	85.00
Pr64	1973	—	Escudo. KM82.	—	65.00
Pr65	1973	—	2-1/2 Escudos. KM78.	—	85.00
Pr66	1973	—	5 Escudos. KM86.	—	85.00
Pr67	1973	—	20 Escudos.	—	85.00
Pr68	1974	—	20 Centavos. KM88.	—	65.00
Pr69	1974	—	50 Centavos. KM89.	—	85.00
Pr70	1974	—	Escudo. KM82.	—	65.00

MINT SETS

KM#	Date	Mintage	Identification	Issue Price	Mkt Val
MS1	1980 (6)	—	KM#98-103	—	30.00

SPECIMEN SETS (SS)

KM#	Date	Mintage	Identification	Issue Price	Mkt Val
SS1	1975 (8)	—	KM#90-97	—	2,250

MUSCAT & OMAN

RULERS

al-Bu Sa'id Dynasty

Faisal bin Turkee, AH1306-1332/1888-1913AD
Taimur bin Faisal, AH1332-1351/1913-1932AD
Sa'id bin Taimur, AH1351-1390/1932-1970AD
Qabus bin Sa'id, AH1390-/1970-AD

MONETARY SYSTEM

Until 1970

4 Baiza = 1 Anna
64 Baiza = 1 Rupee
200 Baiza = 1 Saidi (Dasin Dog)/Dhofari Rial

1970-1972

1000 (new) Baisa = 1 Saidi Rial

Commencing 1972

1000 Baisa = 1 Omani Rial

SULTANATE OF MUSCAT AND OMAN

COUNTERMARKED COINAGE

C# 19.1 1/4 ANNA Composition: Copper **Countermark:** ST **Note:** Countermark in Arabic on 1/4 Anna, KM#3.

CM Date	Host Date	Good	VG	F	VF	XF
AH	AH1315	15.00	25.00	40.00	60.00	—

C# 19.2 1/4 ANNA Composition: Copper **Countermark:** ST **Note:** Countermark in Arabic on 1/4 Anna, KM#8. Countermark for Sultan Taimur or Sayyid Taimur.

CM Date	Host Date	Good	VG	F	VF	XF
AH	AH1312	15.00	25.00	45.00	70.00	—

C# 20.1 1/4 ANNA Composition: Copper **Countermark:** SS **Note:** Large 10mm countermark in Arabic on 1/4 Anna, KM#3.

CM Date	Host Date	Good	VG	F	VF	XF
AH	AH1312	30.00	50.00	80.00	120	—
AH	AH1315	30.00	50.00	80.00	120	—

C# 20.2 1/4 ANNA Composition: Copper **Countermark:** SS **Note:** Large 10mm countermark in Arabic on 1/4 Anna, KM#8.

CM Date	Host Date	Good	VG	F	VF	XF
AH	AH1312	30.00	50.00	80.00	120	—

C# 21.1 1/4 ANNA Composition: Copper **Countermark:** SS **Note:** Small 8mm countermark in Arabic on 1/4 Anna, KM#3.

CM Date	Host Date	Good	VG	F	VF	XF
AH	AH1312	30.00	50.00	80.00	120	—

C# 21.2 1/4 ANNA Composition: Copper **Countermark:** SS **Note:** Small 8mm countermark in Arabic on 1/4 Anna, KM#8. Countermark for Sultan Sa'id or Sayyid Sa'id.

CM Date	Host Date	Good	VG	F	VF	XF
AH	AH1312	30.00	50.00	80.00	120	—

REFORM COINAGE

1000 (new) Baisa = 1 Saidi Rial

KM# 25 2 BAISA (Baiza) Composition: Copper-Nickel **Ruler:** Sa'id bin Taimur **Shape:** Square

Date	Mintage	F	VF	XF	Unc	BU
AH1365	1,500,000	0.50	0.75	1.00	2.00	—
AH1365 Proof	—	Value: 4.00				

Note: Coins of AH1365 have the monetary unit spelled "Baiza", on all other coins it is spelled "Baisa". Most of the proof issues of the AH1359 and 1365 dated coins of Muscat and Oman now on the market are probably later restrikes produced by the Bombay Mint

KM# 36 2 BAISA (Baiza) Composition: Bronze **Ruler:** Sa'id bin Taimur

Date	Mintage	F	VF	XF	Unc	BU
AH1390	4,000,000	0.10	0.15	0.25	0.50	—
AH1390 Proof	—	Value: 2.50				

KM# 30 3 BAISA Composition: Bronze **Ruler:** Sa'id bin Taimur

Date	Mintage	F	VF	XF	Unc	BU
AH1378	8,000,000	0.75	1.00	1.50	2.50	—
AH1378 Proof	—	—	—	—	—	—

Note: Struck for use in Dhofar Province

KM# 32 3 BAISA Composition: Bronze **Ruler:** Sa'id bin Taimur

Date	Mintage	F	VF	XF	Unc	BU
AH1380	10,000,000	0.35	0.50	0.60	1.25	—
AH1380 Proof	Inc. above	—	—	—	—	—

Note: Struck for use in Muscat Province

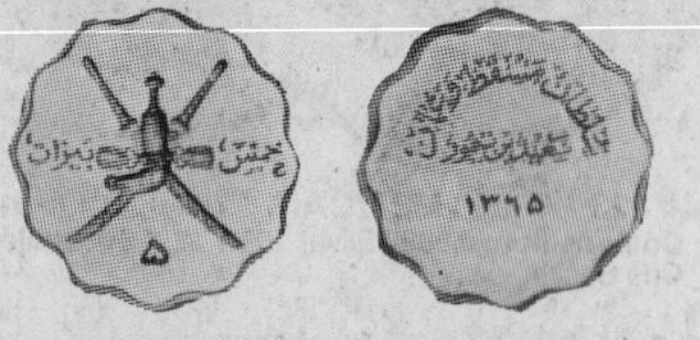

KM# 26 5 BAISA (Baiza) Composition: Copper-Nickel **Ruler:** Sa'id bin Taimur **Shape:** Scalloped

Date	Mintage	F	VF	XF	Unc	BU
AH1365	3,849,000	1.00	1.25	1.50	2.50	—
AH1365 Proof	—	Value: 5.00				

Note: Coins of AH1365 have the monetary unit spelled "Baiza", on all other coins it is spelled "Baisa"

KM# 33 5 BAISA (Baiza) Composition: Copper-Nickel **Ruler:** Sa'id bin Taimur

Date	Mintage	F	VF	XF	Unc	BU
AH1381	5,000,000	0.40	0.60	1.00	2.00	—
AH1381 Proof	Inc. above	—	—	—	—	—

Note: Struck for use in Muscat Province

KM# 37 5 BAISA (Baiza) Composition: Bronze **Ruler:** Sa'id bin Taimur

Date	Mintage	F	VF	XF	Unc	BU
AH1390	3,400,000	0.10	0.15	0.25	0.50	—
AH1390 Proof	—	Value: 2.00				

KM# 22 10 BAISA Composition: Copper-Nickel **Ruler:** Sa'id bin Taimur

Date	Mintage	F	VF	XF	Unc	BU
AH1359	572,000	2.50	3.25	4.00	6.00	—
AH1359 Proof	—	Value: 8.50				

Note: Struck for use in Dhofar Province

KM# 22a 10 BAISA Composition: Gold **Ruler:** Sa'id bin Taimur

Date	F	VF	XF	Unc	BU
AH1359 Proof	—	Value: 1,850			

KM# 38 10 BAISA Composition: Bronze **Ruler:** Sa'id bin Taimur

Date	Mintage	F	VF	XF	Unc	BU
AH1390	4,500,000	0.10	0.15	0.25	0.50	—
AH1390 Proof	—	Value: 2.50				

KM# 23 20 BAISA (Baiza) Composition: Copper-Nickel **Ruler:** Sa'id bin Taimur **Shape:** Square

Date	Mintage	F	VF	XF	Unc	BU
AH1359	35,000	3.00	5.00	7.50	11.50	—
AH1359 Proof	—	Value: 14.50				

Note: Struck for use in Dhofar Province

KM# 23a 20 BAISA (Baiza) Composition: Gold **Ruler:** Sa'id bin Taimur

Date	F	VF	XF	Unc	BU
AH1359 Proof	—	Value: 1,650			

KM# 27 20 BAISA (Baiza) Composition: Copper-Nickel **Ruler:** Sa'id bin Taimur **Shape:** Square

Date	Mintage	F	VF	XF	Unc	BU
AH1365	1,135,000	1.00	2.00	2.75	4.50	—
AH1365 Proof	—	Value: 7.00				

KM# 28 20 BAISA (Baiza) Composition: Gold **Ruler:** Sa'id bin Taimur **Obverse:** KM#23 **Reverse:** KM#27 **Note:** Mule.

Date	F	VF	XF	Unc	BU
AH1359/1365 Restrike	—	—	—	17.50	—

KM# 39 25 BAISA Composition: Copper-Nickel **Ruler:** Sa'id bin Taimur

Date	Mintage	F	VF	XF	Unc	BU
AH1390	2,000,000	0.15	0.20	0.35	0.75	—
AH1390 Proof	—	Value: 2.75				

KM# 39a 25 BAISA Weight: 6.0100 g. **Composition:** 0.9160 Gold .1771 oz. AGW **Ruler:** Sa'id bin Taimur

Date	Mintage	F	VF	XF	Unc	BU
AH1390 Proof	350	Value: 100				

KM# 24 50 BAISA Composition: Copper-Nickel **Ruler:** Sa'id bin Taimur **Shape:** Octagon

Date	Mintage	F	VF	XF	Unc	BU
AH1359	65,000	0.20	6.50	8.50	12.50	—
AH1359 Proof	—	Value: 16.50				

Note: Struck for use in Dhofar Province

KM# 24a 50 BAISA Comp.: Gold **Ruler:** Sa'id bin Taimur

Date		F	VF	XF	Unc	BU
AH1359 Proof	—	Value: 1,750				

KM# 40 50 BAISA Composition: Copper-Nickel **Ruler:** Sa'id bin Taimur

Date	Mintage	F	VF	XF	Unc	BU
AH1390	1,600,000	0.20	0.35	0.60	1.25	—
AH1390 Proof	—	Value: 3.50				

KM# 40a 50 BAISA Weight: 12.8100 g. **Composition:** 0.9160 Gold .3775 oz. AGW **Ruler:** Sa'id bin Taimur

Date	Mintage	F	VF	XF	Unc	BU
AH1390 Proof	350	Value: 200				

KM# 41 100 BAISA Composition: Copper-Nickel **Ruler:** Sa'id bin Taimur

Date	Mintage	F	VF	XF	Unc	BU
AH1390	1,000,000	0.30	0.45	0.70	1.50	—
AH1390 Proof	—	Value: 5.00				

KM# 41a 100 BAISA Weight: 22.6300 g. **Composition:** 0.9160 Gold .6670 oz. AGW **Ruler:** Sa'id bin Taimur

Date	Mintage	F	VF	XF	Unc	BU
AH1390 Proof	350	Value: 325				

KM# 29 1/2 DHOFARI RIAL Weight: 14.0300 g. **Composition:** 0.5000 Silver .2256 oz. ASW **Ruler:** Sa'id bin Taimur

Date	Mintage	F	VF	XF	Unc	BU
AH1367	200,000	12.00	14.00	18.00	28.00	—
AH1367 Proof	—	Value: 45.00				

Note: Struck for use in Dhofar Province

KM# 29a 1/2 DHOFARI RIAL Weight: 24.0300 g. **Composition:** 0.9170 Gold .6780 oz. AGW **Ruler:** Sa'id bin Taimur

Date	Mintage	F	VF	XF	Unc	BU
AH1367 Proof	2	Value: 5,500				

Note: Struck for presentation purposes

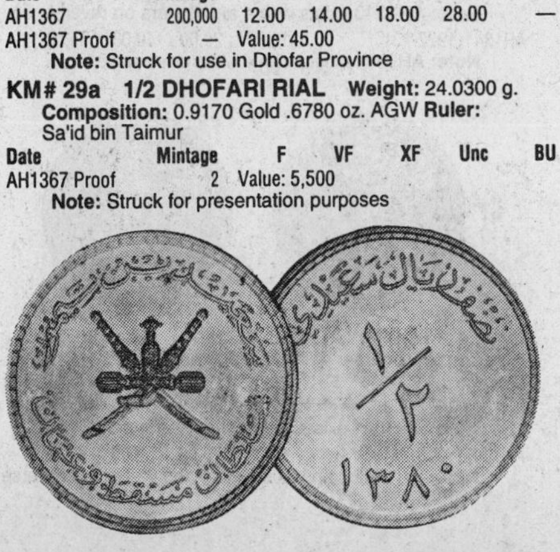

KM# 34 1/2 SAIDI RIAL Weight: 14.0300 g. **Composition:** 0.5000 Silver .2256 oz. ASW **Ruler:** Sa'id bin Taimur

Date	Mintage	F	VF	XF	Unc	BU
AH1380	300,000	3.00	3.50	4.75	8.00	—
AH1380 Proof	—	Value: 75.00				
AH1381	850,000	3.00	3.50	4.75	8.00	—

KM# 34a 1/2 SAIDI RIAL Weight: 25.6000 g. **Comp.:** 0.9160 Gold .7540 oz. AGW **Ruler:** Sa'id bin Taimur

Date	Mintage	F	VF	XF	Unc	BU
AH1381 Proof	150	Value: 450				
AH1382 Proof	100	Value: 475				
AH1390 Proof	350	Value: 350				

Note: Struck for presentation purposes

KM# 31 SAIDI RIAL Weight: 28.0700 g. **Composition:** 0.8330 Silver .7518 oz. ASW **Ruler:** Sa'id bin Taimur

Date	Mintage	F	VF	XF	Unc	BU
AH1378	1,000,000	—	12.00	15.00	20.00	—
AH1378 Proof	100	Value: 650				

KM# 31a SAIDI RIAL Weight: 28.0700 g. **Composition:** 0.5000 Silver .4512 oz. ASW **Ruler:** Sa'id bin Taimur

Date	Mintage	F	VF	XF	Unc	BU
AH1378	400,000	—	10.00	12.50	15.00	—

KM# 31b SAIDI RIAL Weight: 46.6500 g. **Composition:** 0.9160 Gold 1.3740 oz. AGW **Ruler:** Sa'id bin Taimur **Size:** 33.7 mm.

Date	Mintage	F	VF	XF	Unc	BU
AH1978 Proof	100	Value: 1,100				
AH1390 Proof	350	Value: 750				

Note: Struck for presentation purposes

KM# 35 15 SAIDI RIALS Weight: 7.9900 g. **Composition:** 0.9160 Gold .2353 oz. AGW **Ruler:** Sa'id bin Taimur

Date	Mintage	F	VF	XF	Unc	BU
AH1381	2,000	—	—	—	150	—
AH1381 Proof	100	Value: 575				

Note: Struck for presentation purposes

MINT SETS

KM#	Date	Mintage	Identification	Issue Price	Mkt Val
MS1	AH1390 (1970) (6)	5,500	KM#36-41	—	6.00

PROOF SETS

KM#	Date	Mintage	Identification	Issue Price	Mkt Val
PS1	AH1359, 65, 57 (1940, 45, 47) (6)	—	KM#22-26, 29	—	75.00
PS2	AH1359, 65, 57 (1940, 45, 47) (6)	—	KM#22, 24-27, 29	—	70.00
PS4	AH1390 (1970) (3)	350	KM#39a-41a	—	625
PS3	AH1390 (1970) (6)	2,102	KM#36-41	11.00	16.50

MUTAWAKKILITE

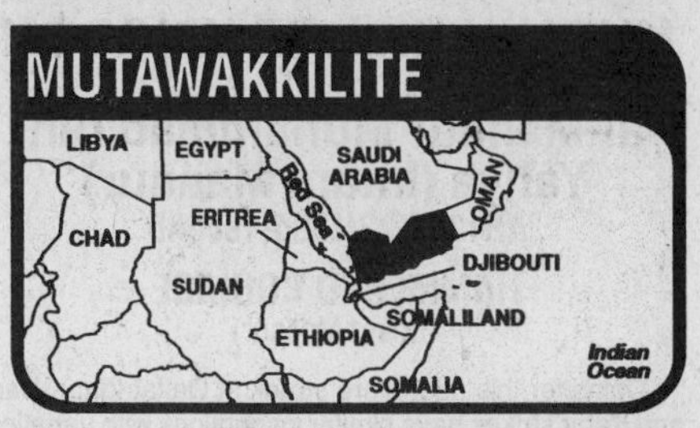

One of the oldest centers of civilization in the Middle East, Yemen was once part of the Minaean Kingdom and of the ancient Kingdom of Sheba, after which it was captured successively by Egyptians, Ethiopians and Romans. It was converted to Islam in 628 A.D. and administered as a caliphate until 1538, when it came under Ottoman occupation in 1849. The second Ottoman occupation which began in 1872 was maintained until 1918 when autonomy was achieved through revolution.

TITLES

المملكة المتوكلية اليمنية

al-Mamlaka(t) al-Mutawakkiliya(t) al-Yamaniya(t)

RULERS

Ottoman, until 1625

QASIMID IMAMS

al-Mansur Muhammad bin Yahya, (Imam Mansur) AH1307-1322/1890-1904AD

al Hadi al-Hasan bin Yahya (Counter Imam, in Sa'da) AH1322/1904AD

al-Mutawakkil Yahya bin Muhammad (Imam Yahya) AH1322-1367/1904-1948AD

al-Nasir Ahmad bin Yahya, (Imam Ahmad) AH1367-1382/ 1948-1962AD

al-Badr Muhammad bin Ahmad, (Imam Badr) AH1382-1388/ 1962-1968AD (mostly in exile)

MINTNAME

San'a صنعاء

MONETARY SYSTEM

After Accession of Iman Yahya AH1322/1904AD

1 Zalat = 1/160 Riyal
2 Zalat = 1 Halala = 1/80 Riyal
2 Halala = 1 Buqsha = 1/40 Riyal
40 Buqsha = 1 Riyal

NOTE: The Riyal was called an IMADI (RIYAL) during the reign of Imam Yahya "Imadi" honorific name for Yahyawi and an AHMADI (RIYAL) during the reign of Imam Ahmad. The 1 Zalat, Y#2.1, D1, A3, A4 and all Imam Yahya gold strikes except Y#F10, bear no indication of value. Many of the Mutawakkilite coins after AH1322/1904AD bear the denomination expressed as fraction of the Riyal as follows.

BRONZE and ALUMINUM

Thumn ushr = 1/80 Riyal = 1/2 Buqsha = 1 Halala
Rub ushr = 1/40 Riyal = 1 Buqsha
Nisf ushr = 1/20 Riyal = 2 Buqsha = 1/2 Bawlah
Nisf thumn = 1/16 Riyal = 2-1/2 Buqsha
Ushr = 1/10 Riyal = 4 Buqsha = 1 Bawlah
Thumn = 1/8 Riyal = 5 Buqsha
Rub = 1/4 Riyal = 10 Buqsha
Nisf = 1/2 Riyal = 20 Buqsha
1 Riyal (Imadi, Ahmadi) = 40 Buqsha

DATING

All coins of Imam Yahya have accession date AH1322 on obverse and actual date of issue on reverse. All coins of Imam Ahmad bear accession date AH1367 on obverse and actual date on reverse.

If not otherwise noted, all coins of Imam Yahya and Imam Ahad as well as the early issues of the Republic (Y#20 through Y#A25 and Y#32), were struck at the mint in Sana'a. The Sana'a Mint was essentially a medieval mint, using hand-cut dies and crudely machined blanks. There is a large amount of variation from one die to the next in arrangement of legends and ornaments, form of crescents, number of stars, size of the circle, etc., and literally hundreds of subtypes could be identified. Types are divided only when there are changes in the inscriptions, or major variations in the basic type, such as the presence or absence of "Rabb al-Alamin" in the legend or the position of the word *Sana* (= year) in relation to the year.

NOTE: All "ZALAT" coins are without mint name or denomination.

MUTAWAKKILITE KINGDOM

al-Mansur Muhammad bin Yahya (Imam Mansur)

AH1307-22/1890-1904AD

HAMMERED COINAGE

(Imam Mansur)

Coins for this ruler were struck at Qaflat Idhar. Harf and Kabir strikes have similar inscriptions with varieties in position of date, legend arrangements, and ornamentation. No indication of value on coins.

KM# 408.1 KABIR Composition: Silver **Obverse:** Ornament below legend **Obv. Legend:** "Bilah/al-Mansu/r" **Reverse:** Legend as circle **Rev. Legend:** "Allah/", date, "Abd" **Note:** Weight varies: 0.40-0.80 grams. Size varies: 15-17 millimeters. Varieties of shape of ornaments exist.

Date	Good	VG	F	VF	XF
AH1312 (1894)	—	—	—	—	—
AH1316 (1898)	—	—	—	—	—
AH1318 (1900)	—	—	—	—	—

KM# 410 KABIR Composition: Silver **Obverse:** Similar to KM#409 **Reverse:** "Allah/Abd/" date, divided by ornament, wtih four circular segments **Note:** Wright varies: 0.60-1.00 gram. Size varies: 15-16 millimeters. Varieties with three and four stars on reverse exist.

Date	Good	VG	F	VF	XF
AH1316 (1898)	15.00	30.00	50.00	85.00	—
AH1319 (1901)	15.00	30.00	50.00	85.00	—
AH1320 (1902)	15.00	30.00	50.00	85.00	—
AH1321 (1903)	15.00	30.00	50.00	85.00	—

KM# 407.2 KABIR Composition: Silver **Reverse:** Date at bottom **Note:** Weight varies: 0.60-0.70 grams.

Date	Good	VG	F	VF	XF
AH1318 (1900)	—	—	—	—	—

KM# 403 HARF Composition: Bronze **Note:** Similar to 1 Kabir, KM#410.

Date	Good	VG	F	VF	XF
AH1320 (1902)	—	—	—	—	—

al Hadi al-Hasan

AH1322/1904AD

MILLED COINAGE

Y# C1 HALALA Weight: 1.9300 g. **Composition:** Bronze **Obverse:** Al-Hasan/bin Yahya/Sana 1322 **Reverse:** Al-Hadi/Li-din Allah

Date	Good	VG	F	VF	XF
AH1322 (1904)	—	—	—	—	—

al-Mutawakkil Yahya bin Muhammad (Imam Yahya)

AH1322-67/1904-48AD

MILLED COINAGE

Y# 1.1 ZALAT Composition: Bronze **Obverse:** Inscription in three lines above regnal year **Edge:** Plain **Note:** Weight varies: 0.90-1.60 grams. Varieties with two stars. Reverse with eight stars. Size of inner circle varies, various planchet thicknesses.

Date	Good	VG	F	VF	XF
AH1341(1922-23)	15.00	30.00	100	160	—
AH1342(1923-24)	5.00	12.00	30.00	50.00	—
AH1343(1924-25)	4.00	10.00	20.00	40.00	—
Note: 1343 also known with seven stars					
AH1344(1925-26)	5.00	12.00	30.00	50.00	—
Note: 1344 also exists with traces of reeded edges					
AH1345(1926-27)	10.00	25.00	75.00	125	—
AH1346(1927-28)	4.00	10.00	20.00	40.00	—

Y# 1.2 ZALAT Composition: Bronze **Obverse:** Inscription in two lines above regnal year

Date	Good	VG	F	VF	XF
AH1342(1923-24)	5.00	12.00	30.00	50.00	—

Note: Obverse varieties with 1, 2, and 4 stars, and reverse with 8, 11, 12, 13, 14, 15, 16, 17, 20, and 22 stars exist; Some specimens show traces of reeded edges; Various planchet thicknesses exist

Y# 1.7 ZALAT Composition: Bronze **Reverse:** Date in margin at bottom

Date	Good	VG	F	VF	XF
AH1342(1923-24) Rare	—	—	—	—	—

Note: Obverse varieties with 1 and 2 stars, Reverse with 11 stars, various planchet thicknesses

Y# 1.4 ZALAT Composition: Bronze **Obverse:** Crescent design

Date	Good	VG	F	VF	XF
AH1342(1923-24)	300	425	650	1,000	—

Note: Varieties exist with 11, 14, 15, 16, and 17 stars on reverse and with 1, 2, and 4 stars on obverse; Various planchet thicknesses

Y# B1 ZALAT Composition: Bronze **Note:** Dated accessionally (AH1322) on reverse. Probably struck at Shaharah about 1925. Dies were reportedly prepared in Italy. For silver strikes, see Y#A4.

Date	Good	VG	F	VF	XF
NDAH1322(ca.1925)	30.00	60.00	125	200	—
Note: This issue is believed to be a pattern					
ND(ca.1925)	30.00	60.00	125	200	—

Y# 2.1 1/80 RIYAL (1/2 Buqsha) Composition: Bronze **Note:** Accession date: AH1322.

Date	Good	VG	F	VF	XF
ND(ca.1911-21)	12.50	25.00	50.00	85.00	—

Note: Probably struck at Shaharah

Y# D1 1/80 RIYAL (1/2 Buqsha) Composition: Bronze **Obverse:** "Rabb al-Alamin" **Reverse:** Toughra design **Note:** Accession date: AH1322. Without denomination or mint name.

Date	Good	VG	F	VF	XF
ND(ca.1911-21) Rare; Accessional date only	—	—	—	—	—

Y# 2.8 1/80 RIYAL (1/2 Buqsha) Composition: Bronze **Note:** Mule, two obverses.

Date	Good	VG	F	VF	XF
ND(1911-21)	20.00	30.00	60.00	100	—

Y# 2.2 1/80 RIYAL (1/2 Buqsha) Composition: Bronze **Note:** Thin flan, 1.50-3.00 grams. The number and arrangement of stars and the size of the circle on the reverse vary as well as the exact arrangement of the legends which sometimes vary within each year. The reverse exists with 10, 12, 14, 20, 22, 24, 28, and 34 stars. Obverse varieties exist with 1, 2, or 3 stars and without stars. Struck at Shaharah.

Date	Good	VG	F	VF	XF
AH1330(1911-12)	20.00	35.00	60.00	100	—
AH1331(1912-13)	20.00	35.00	75.00	150	—
AH1332(1913-14)	10.00	15.00	25.00	40.00	—
AH1333(1914-15)	10.00	15.00	25.00	40.00	—
AH1337(1918-19)	10.00	15.00	25.00	40.00	—
AH1338(1919-20)	10.00	15.00	25.00	40.00	—
AH1339(1920-21)	—	—	—	—	—

Y# 2.7 1/80 RIYAL (1/2 Buqsha) Composition: Bronze **Note:** Thick flan. Weight varies: 4.00-4.50 grams. Varieties with 10 and 14 stars on reverse. Obverse with 1, 2, and 3 stars. Varieties of legend distribution. Some coins occur with light silver wash. Struck at Shaharah.

Date	Good	VG	F	VF	XF
AH1332(1913-14)	10.00	15.00	25.00	40.00	—
AH1333(1914-15)	10.00	15.00	25.00	40.00	—
AH1338(1919-20)	10.00	15.00	25.00	40.00	—

Y# 2.6 1/80 RIYAL (1/2 Buqsha) Weight: 3.0000 g. **Composition:** Bronze **Reverse:** "Sana" below date **Note:** Thin flan. Struck at Shaharah.

Date	Good	VG	F	VF	XF
AH1333(1914-15)	80.00	100	200	300	—

Y# 2.5 1/80 RIYAL (1/2 Buqsha) Composition: Bronze (Red To Yellow) **Obverse:** "Rabb al-Alamin" **Reverse:** "Sana" above date **Note:** Number and arrangement of stars on reverse (4, 5, 6, 7, or 8) as well as the size of the inner circle vary. Varieties exist in the form of crescent and arrangement of legends and planchet thicknesses.

Date	Good	VG	F	VF	XF
AH1339(1920-21)	7.00	12.00	25.00	40.00	—
AH1341(1922-23)	7.00	12.00	25.00	40.00	—
AH1342(1923-24)	2.00	5.00	12.00	20.00	—
AH1343(1924-25)	2.00	5.00	12.00	20.00	—
AH1344(1925-26)	2.00	5.00	12.00	20.00	—
AH1345(1926-27)	1.50	4.00	8.00	15.00	—
AH1346(1927-28)	1.50	3.00	6.00	12.00	—
Note: Some examples of AH1346 show the 6 re-engraved over low I					
AH1347(1928-29)	1.50	4.00	8.00	15.00	—
AH1348(1929-30)	1.50	4.00	8.00	15.00	—
AH1349(1930-31)	1.50	4.00	8.00	15.00	—
AH1350(1931-32)	1.50	4.00	8.00	15.00	—
AH135x(1932)	1.50	4.00	8.00	15.00	—
AH1351(1932-33)	2.00	6.00	12.00	20.00	—
AH1352(1933-34)	2.00	6.00	12.00	20.00	—
AH1353(1934-35)	2.00	6.00	12.00	20.00	—
AH1358(1939-40)	—	—	—	—	—
Note: Reported, not confirmed					
AH1359(1940-41)	2.50	6.00	12.00	20.00	—
AH1360(1941-42)	2.50	4.00	8.00	15.00	—
AH1361(1942-43)	4.00	8.00	15.00	25.00	—

Y# 2.3 1/80 RIYAL (1/2 Buqsha) Composition: Bronze **Reverse:** "Duriba Bi Sana'a" added

Date	Good	VG	F	VF	XF
AH1340(1921-22)	10.00	20.00	40.00	75.00	—
Note: AH1340 exists with 4 and 8 stars on reverse					
AH1341(1922-23)	10.00	20.00	40.00	75.00	—
Note: AH1341 exists with 4 stars on reverse					

Y# 2.4 1/80 RIYAL (1/2 Buqsha) Composition: Bronze **Obverse:** Without "Rabb al-Alamin"

Date	Good	VG	F	VF	XF
AH1341(1922-23)	12.00	25.00	50.00	85.00	—
Note: AH1341 exists with 4 stars on reverse					
AH1342(1923-24)	12.00	25.00	50.00	85.00	—
Note: AH1342 coins exist with 4 and 6 stars on reverse					

Y# A3 1/40 RIYAL (1 Buqsha) **Composition:** Billon/Silver **Note:** Weight varies: 0.65-1.25 grams. Size varies: 15-16 millimeters. Accession date: AH1322.

Date	VG	F	VF	XF	Unc
ND(ca.1911-21)	275	550	1,100	1,650	—

Note: Minted at Qaflat Idhar, without mint name or denomination

Y# 3.1 1/40 RIYAL (1 Buqsha) **Composition:** Bronze **Obverse:** Without "Rabb al-Alamin" **Reverse:** "Sana" below date **Note:** Accession date: AH1322.

Date	VG	F	VF	XF	Unc
AH1341(1922-23)	10.00	20.00	40.00	80.00	—

Note: Varieties of borders, arrangement of legends, and thickness of planchets exist

Y# 3.2 1/40 RIYAL (1 Buqsha) **Composition:** Bronze (Red To Yellow) **Obverse:** "Rabb al-Alamin" **Reverse:** "Sana" above date, small "Sana'a" and three leaf ornaments plus star in border legend

Date	VG	F	VF	XF	Unc
AH1342(1923-24)	4.00	10.00	20.00	60.00	—
Note: AH1342 exists with 4 leaf ornaments and without star in border legend					
AH13442(1923)	65.00	125	—	—	—
AH1343(1924-25)	4.00	10.00	20.00	60.00	—
AH1344(1925-26)	15.00	30.00	50.00	75.00	—

Y# 3.3 1/40 RIYAL (1 Buqsha) **Composition:** Bronze (Red To Yellow) **Reverse:** Large "Sana'a" in legend **Note:** Varieties in arrangement of legends, ornaments, form of the crescent, and size of the circle on reverse exist.

Date	VG	F	VF	XF	Unc
AH1344(1925-26)	12.00	20.00	35.00	100	—
AH1345(1926-27)	12.00	20.00	35.00	100	—
AH1349(1930-31)	1.50	3.50	10.00	25.00	—
AH1353(1934-35)	—	—	—	—	—
Note: Reported, not confirmed					
AH1358(1939-40)	2.00	4.00	10.00	25.00	—
AH1359(1940-41)	2.00	4.00	10.00	25.00	—
AH1360(1941-42)	2.00	4.00	10.00	25.00	—
AH1361/0(1942-43)	10.00	20.00	50.00	75.00	—
AH1362/0(1943)	2.50	5.00	10.00	35.00	—
AH1362(1943)	1.50	3.50	10.00	30.00	—
AH1363(1943)	1.50	5.00	12.00	35.00	—
AH1364(1944-45)	1.50	5.00	12.00	35.00	—
AH1365/4(1945)	2.25	5.00	12.00	35.00	—
AH1365(1945-46)	2.50	5.00	12.00	35.00	—
AH1366(1946-47)	1.50	3.50	12.00	30.00	—
AH1366/x(1946)	2.50	5.00	12.00	35.00	—
AH1367(1947-48)	10.00	20.00	50.00	75.00	—

Y# A4 1/20 IMADI RIYAL **Composition:** Silver **Note:** Accession date: AH1322.

Date	VG	F	VF	XF	Unc
ND(1911-21)	60.00	120	250	400	—

Note: Dated accessionally on obverse without mint name or denomination; Probably struck at Shaharah about 1925; dies were reportedly prepared in Italy; Strikes in nickel reported; See Y#B1;This issue is believed to be a pattern

Y# B4 1/20 IMADI RIYAL **Composition:** Silver **Obverse:** "Rabb al-Alamin" **Reverse:** Without "Sana"

Date	VG	F	VF	XF	Unc
AH1337(1918-19) Rare	—	—	—	—	—

Note: Three stars on reverse

Y# 4.1 1/20 IMADI RIYAL **Composition:** Silver **Obverse:** Without "Rabb al-Alamin" **Note:** Varieties in arrangement of legends, size of circle, and with 3 and 4 stars on reverse exist. Variety of Y#4 dated with 2 digits AH(13)22 of the accessional year are considered local contemporary counterfeits by leading authorities. They are reported having been produced by the Zaraing tribe at Bait Al-Faqih. See note below Y#5.5.

Date	VG	F	VF	XF	Unc
AH1337(1918-19)	40.00	80.00	150	250	—
AH1338(1919-20) Rare	—	—	—	—	—
AH1339(1920-21)	40.00	80.00	150	250	—
Note: Some strikes show accessional year as 322 only					
AH1340(1921-22)	20.00	30.00	60.00	100	—
Note: Some strikes show accessional year as 322 only					
AH1342(1923-24)	5.00	12.00	30.00	60.00	—
AH1343(1924-25)	4.00	10.00	25.00	50.00	—
AH1344(1925-26)	4.00	10.00	25.00	50.00	—
AH1345/2(1926)	4.00	10.00	25.00	50.00	—
AH1345(1926-27)	4.00	10.00	25.00	50.00	—
AH1347(1928-29)	5.00	12.00	30.00	60.00	—
AH1348(1929-30)	4.00	10.00	25.00	50.00	—
AH1349(1930-31)	4.00	10.00	25.00	50.00	—
AH1350(1931-32)	4.00	12.00	30.00	60.00	—
AH1351(1932-33)	5.00	15.00	35.00	75.00	—
AH1352(1933-34)	4.00	12.00	30.00	60.00	—
AH1353(1934-35)	4.00	12.00	30.00	60.00	—
AH1358(1939-40)	3.00	8.00	20.00	40.00	—
AH1359(1940-41)	3.00	8.00	20.00	40.00	—
AH1362/58(1943)	5.00	15.00	30.00	60.00	—
AH1362/59(1943)	5.00	15.00	30.00	60.00	—
AH1363(1943)	4.00	10.00	30.00	60.00	—
AH1364/46(1944)	3.00	8.00	20.00	40.00	—
AH1364(1944-45)	3.00	8.00	20.00	40.00	—
AHx364(1944)	3.00	8.00	20.00	40.00	—
AH1365(1945-46)	3.00	10.00	25.00	50.00	—
AH1366/44(1946)	4.00	12.00	30.00	60.00	—
AH1366(1946-47)	4.00	12.00	30.00	60.00	—

Y# 4.4 1/20 IMADI RIYAL **Composition:** Silver **Reverse:** Border legend shifted to left

Date	VG	F	VF	XF	Unc
AH1340(1921-22) Rare	—	—	—	—	—

Note: Three stars on reverse

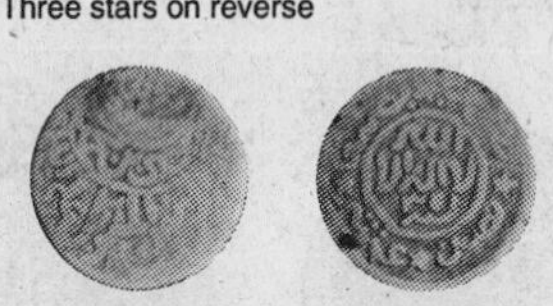

Y# 4.2 1/20 IMADI RIYAL **Composition:** Silver **Reverse:** "Sana" below date, normal legend position **Note:** Four stars on reverse.

Date	VG	F	VF	XF	Unc
AH1341(1922-23)	40.00	80.00	150	250	—
AHx341(1922)	40.00	80.00	150	250	—

Y# 5.1 1/10 IMADI RIYAL **Composition:** Silver **Obverse:** "Rabb al-Alamin" **Reverse:** Without "Sana" **Note:** Accession date: AH1322.

Date	VG	F	VF	XF	Unc
AH1337(1918-19)	30.00	60.00	100	175	—

Note: Reverse varieties with 3, 4, and 5 stars. Size of circle and form of crescent varies

Y# 5.2 1/10 IMADI RIYAL **Composition:** Silver **Obverse:** Without "Rabb al-Alamin"

Date	VG	F	VF	XF	Unc
AH1339(1920-21)	20.00	40.00	75.00	150	—
Note: Some AH1339 strikes show accession date as 322					
AH1340(1921-22)	20.00	40.00	75.00	150	—
Note: AH1340 also exists with three stars, others with six stars on reverse					
AH1341(1922-23)	20.00	40.00	75.00	150	—
AH1348(1929-30)	100	150	350	500	—

Y# 5.3 1/10 IMADI RIYAL **Composition:** Silver **Reverse:** "Sana" below date **Note:** Varieties with three and six stars on the reverse exist.

Date	VG	F	VF	XF	Unc
AH1341(1922-23)	20.00	40.00	75.00	150	—
AH1342(1923-24)	20.00	40.00	75.00	150	—

Y# 5.5 1/10 IMADI RIYAL **Composition:** Silver **Obverse:** Without "Rabb al-Alamin" **Reverse:** "Sana" above date **Note:** Form of crescent, size of circle on reverse, and arrangement of legends vary. Varieties with 6, 7, 8, 9, 10, and 12 stars on reverse exist. Some earlier dates show traces of reeded edges.

Date	VG	F	VF	XF	Unc
AH1342(1923-24)	4.00	10.00	25.00	50.00	—
AH1343(1924-25)	4.00	10.00	25.00	50.00	—
AH1344(1925-26)	3.00	8.00	20.00	40.00	—
AH1345(1926-27)	3.00	8.00	20.00	40.00	—
AH1347(1928-29)	3.00	8.00	20.00	40.00	—
AH1348(1929-30)	3.00	8.00	20.00	35.00	—
AH1349(1930-31)	3.00	6.00	15.00	30.00	—
AH1351(1932-33)	4.00	10.00	25.00	40.00	—
AH1352(1933-34)	4.00	10.00	25.00	40.00	—
AH1358/49(1939)	3.00	8.00	15.00	30.00	—
AH1358(1939-40)	3.00	8.00	15.00	30.00	—
AH1359/3(1940)	3.00	8.00	15.00	30.00	—
AH1359/49(1940-41)	3.00	8.00	15.00	30.00	—
AH1362/44(1943)	4.00	10.00	25.00	40.00	—
AH1362/59(1943)	4.00	10.00	25.00	40.00	—
AH1363(1943)	3.00	8.00	25.00	45.00	—
AH1364/43(1944)	3.00	8.00	20.00	40.00	—
AH1364/3(1944)	3.00	8.00	25.00	45.00	—
AH1364/52(1944)	3.00	8.00	25.00	45.00	—
AH1364(1944-45)	3.00	8.00	15.00	35.00	—
AH1365(1945-46)	3.00	8.00	15.00	35.00	—
AH1366/5(1945)	3.00	10.00	20.00	50.00	—
AH1366/5x(1945)	3.00	10.00	20.00	50.00	—

Y# 5.4 1/10 IMADI RIYAL **Composition:** Silver **Obverse:** "Rabb al-Alamin" **Reverse:** "Sana" above date **Note:** Varieties with 8, 9, and 10 stars on reverse exist.

Date	VG	F	VF	XF	Unc
AH1342(1923-24)	20.00	40.00	75.00	150	—

Y# 8 1/8 IMADI RIYAL **Composition:** Silver **Obverse:** One or no stars in crescent **Reverse:** "Thumn" in place of "Ushr" below date, 6 stars

Date	VG	F	VF	XF	Unc
AH1339(1920-21)	325	550	1,100	1,650	—

Y#6.1 1/4 IMADI RIYAL **Composition:** Silver **Obverse:** Without "Rabb al-Alamin" **Reverse:** "Sana" below date

Date	VG	F	VF	XF	Unc
AH1341(1922-23)	20.00	45.00	75.00	150	—
Note: AH1341 with 4 stars on reverse					
AH1342(1923-24)	25.00	50.00	100	175	—
Note: AH1342 with 6 stars on reverse					

Y#6.2 1/4 IMADI RIYAL **Composition:** Silver **Obverse:** "Rabb al-Alamin" **Reverse:** "Sana" above date, two stars and two ornaments in border

Date	VG	F	VF	XF	Unc
AH1342(1923-24)	70.00	100	300	450	—

Y# 6.3 1/4 IMADI RIYAL **Composition:** Silver **Obverse:** Ten crescents and stars in border

Date	VG	F	VF	XF	Unc
AH1342(1923-24)	30.00	50.00	100	175	—

Note: Plain and traces of reeded edges known

Y# 6.5 1/4 IMADI RIYAL **Composition:** Silver **Reverse:** "Sana" below date, eight stars in border

Date	VG	F	VF	XF	Unc
AH1342(1923-24)	100	150	300	500	—

Y# 6.6 1/4 IMADI RIYAL **Composition:** Silver **Reverse:** "Sana" below date, one star in border

Date	VG	F	VF	XF	Unc
AH1342(1923-24)	100	150	300	500	—

Note: Obverse varieties with one and two stars exist

Y# 6.4 1/4 IMADI RIYAL **Composition:** Silver **Obverse:** With crescents only in border **Note:** Number and form of crescents on obverse vary. 14, 15, and 16 crescents known in border. Plain and traces of reeded edges known.

Date	VG	F	VF	XF	Unc
AH1342(1923-24)	20.00	40.00	75.00	150	—
AH1343(1924-25)	20.00	40.00	75.00	150	—

Y# 10 1/4 IMADI RIYAL **Composition:** Silver **Reverse:** Redesigned, date moved to margin **Note:** The size of the reverse inner circle varies, 12 to 16 crescents on obverse. Plain and traces of reeded edges are known.

Date	VG	F	VF	XF	Unc
AH1343(1924-25)	20.00	60.00	100	175	—
AH1344(1925-26)	4.25	10.00	25.00	75.00	—
AH1345(1926-27)	4.25	10.00	25.00	60.00	—
AH1349(1930-31)	—	—	—	—	—
Note: Reported, not confirmed					
AH1351(1932-33)	20.00	30.00	50.00	100	—
AH1352(1933-34)	5.00	12.00	20.00	40.00	—
AH1358(1939-40)	3.50	5.50	15.00	35.00	—
AH1359(1940-41)	3.50	5.50	15.00	35.00	—
AH1363(1943)	3.50	8.00	20.00	40.00	—
AH1364/3(1944)	4.25	8.00	20.00	40.00	—
AH1364(1944-45)	3.50	5.00	20.00	40.00	—
AH1365/4(1945)	4.25	6.00	20.00	40.00	—
AH1365(1945-46)	3.50	5.00	20.00	40.00	—
AH1366(1946)	3.50	5.00	20.00	40.00	—

Y# 7 IMADI RIYAL **Weight:** 28.0700 g. **Composition:** Silver **Note:** Accession date: AH1322. Several die varieties exist, possibly struck over a number of years with frozen date AH1344. Edge varieties exist.

Date	VG	F	VF	XF	Unc
AH1342(1923-24)	—	—	—	—	—
Note: Reported, not confirmed					
AH1344(1925-26)	7.00	12.00	18.00	28.00	40.00
Note: Copper trial strikes dated AH1344 reported					
AH1365(1945-46) Two known	—	—	—	1,000	—

GOLD PRESENTATION COINAGE

All Imam Yahya gold strikes are considered presentation issues which were based on the gold standard of the Turkish Lira.

Y# A10 1/8 LIRA (1/40 Riyal) **Weight:** 0.9200 g. **Composition:** Gold **Note:** Accession date: AH1322.

Date	VG	F	VF	XF	Unc
AH(13)44(1925-26)	—	—	—	1,350	—

Y# B10 1/4 LIRA (1/20 Riyal) **Weight:** 1.7000 g. **Composition:** Gold **Note:** Accession date: AH1322.

Date	VG	F	VF	XF	Unc
AH(13)44(1925-26)	—	—	—	1,500	—

Y# C10 1/2 LIRA (1/10 Riyal) **Weight:** 3.3100 g. **Composition:** Gold **Note:** Accession date: AH1322.

Date	VG	F	VF	XF	Unc
AH(13)44(1925-26)	—	—	—	1,650	—

Y# D10 LIRA (1/5 Riyal) **Weight:** 6.8000 g. **Composition:** Gold **Note:** Accession date: AH1322.

Date	VG	F	VF	XF	Unc
AH(13)44(1925-26)	—	—	—	2,000	—

Y# E10 2-1/2 LIRA (1/2 Riyal) **Weight:** 17.7000 g. **Composition:** Gold **Note:** Accession date: AH1322.

Date	VG	F	VF	XF	Unc
AH(13)44(1925-26)	—	—	—	3,500	—

Y# K10 2-1/2 LIRA (1/2 Riyal) **Composition:** Gold **Note:** Weight varies: 17.44-17.82 grams. Accession date: AH1322.

Date	VG	F	VF	XF	Unc
AH1352(1933-34)	—	—	—	2,500	—

Y# P10 5 LIRA (1 Riyal) **Weight:** 34.2400 g. **Composition:** Gold **Note:** Thin planchet strike of 10 Lira (2 Riyal), Y#N10.

Date	VG	F	VF	XF	Unc
AH1358(1939-40) 2 known	—	—	—	3,250	—

Y# F10 5 LIRA (1 Riyal) **Weight:** 35.5000 g. **Composition:** Gold **Note:** Similar to 1 Imadi Riyal, Y#7.

Date	VG	F	VF	XF	Unc
AH1344(1925-26) Rare	—	—	—	—	—

Note: Dies of AH1344 Riyal silver and gold strikes are not identical

Y# M10 10 LIRA (2 Riyal) **Weight:** 69.8300 g. **Composition:** Gold **Obverse:** Similar to Gold 2-1/2 Lira, Y#K10 **Note:** Accession date: AH1322.

Date	VG	F	VF	XF	Unc
AH1352(1933-34)	—	—	—	6,500	—

Y# N10 10 LIRA (2 Riyal) **Weight:** 69.8300 g. **Composition:** Gold **Reverse:** Two crossed flags in center **Rev. Legend:** "Duriba bi-dar al-khilafa al-mutawakkiliya bi Sana'a 'asimat al-Yamam sana 1358"

Date	VG	F	VF	XF	Unc
AH1358(1939-40) 4 known	—	—	—	5,500	—

al-Nasir Ahmad bin Yahya (Imam Ahmad)

AH1367-82/1948-62AD

MILLED COINAGE

Y# 18 1/80 RIYAL (1 Halala = 1/2 Buqsha)
Composition: Aluminum **Note:** Accession date: AH1367.

Date	VG	F	VF	XF	Unc
ND(1948)	0.15	0.25	0.50	1.00	—

Note: Struck privately in Lebanon in 1955 and 1956 and released into circulation in 1956

Y# 11.1 1/80 RIYAL (1 Halala = 1/2 Buqsha) **Composition:** Bronze (Red To Yellow) **Reverse:** "Sana" above date **Note:** Accession date: AH1367. There is a variation in the number of stars on reverse, as follows: AH1368 - 8 stars; AH1371-74 and some AH1381 (not overdate) - 7 stars; AH1375-81 including some AH1381, and all AH1381 overdates - 8 stars. Varieties of arrangement of legends, form of crescent, and size of circle on reverse exist. Some earlier dates exist on thinner planchets.

Date	VG	F	VF	XF	Unc
AH1368(1948-49)	1.00	2.00	5.00	10.00	—
AH1371(1951-52)	0.30	1.00	3.00	8.00	—
AH1372(1952-53)	0.30	1.00	3.00	8.00	—
AH1373(1953-54)	0.30	0.60	1.00	3.00	—
AH1374(1954-55)	0.30	1.00	3.00	8.00	—
AH1275(1955) Error for 1375	1.00	2.00	6.00	12.00	—
AH1375(1955-56)	—	—	—	—	—
AH1376(1956-57)	—	—	—	—	—
AH1376/86(1956) Error	—	—	—	—	—
AH1278(1958) Error for 1378	1.00	2.00	6.00	12.00	—
AH1378(1958-59)	—	—	—	—	—
AHx379(1959)	1.00	2.00	6.00	12.00	—
AH1379(1959-60)	0.50	1.00	2.50	5.00	—
AH1380/1(1960)	1.00	2.00	6.00	12.00	—
AH1380/79(1960)	0.50	1.00	2.50	5.00	—
AH1380/9(1960)	0.50	1.00	2.50	5.00	—
AH1380(1960-61)	0.50	1.00	2.50	5.00	—
AH1381/80/79(1961)	0.40	0.85	1.50	2.50	—
AH1381/79(1961)	0.40	0.85	1.50	2.50	—
AH1381(1961-62)	0.20	0.40	0.75	1.25	—
AH1382(1962-63)	5.00	10.00	15.00	20.00	—

Y# 11a 1/80 RIYAL (1 Halala = 1/2 Buqsha)
Composition: Aluminum **Reverse:** "Sana" above date **Note:** AH1374 and some AH1380 have 7 stars, the rest have 8 stars on reverse. Dies of 1/80 Riyal, Y#11.1, were used.

Date	VG	F	VF	XF	Unc
AH1374(1954-55)	0.25	1.00	2.50	5.00	—
AH1375(1955-56)	0.75	2.50	5.50	10.00	—
AH1376(1956-57)	0.25	1.50	4.00	8.00	—
AH1377(1957-58)	0.75	2.50	5.50	10.00	—
AH1378(1958-59)	0.25	1.00	2.50	5.00	—
AH1378/6(1958)	0.25	1.00	2.50	5.00	—
AH1379/5(1959)	0.75	2.50	5.50	10.00	—
AH1379/8(1959)	0.75	2.50	5.50	10.00	—
AH1379(1959-60)	0.25	1.00	2.50	5.00	—
AH1380(1960-61)	0.25	1.00	2.50	5.00	—

Y# 11.2 1/80 RIYAL (1 Halala = 1/2 Buqsha)
Composition: Bronze **Reverse:** Without "Sana"

Date	VG	F	VF	XF	Unc
AH1373(1953-54) Rare	—	—	—	—	—

Y# 11.3 1/80 RIYAL (1 Halala = 1/2 Buqsha)
Composition: Bronze **Note:** Struck with dies of 1/4 Ahmadi Riyal, Y#15 on 1/8 Riyal planchet.

Date	VG	F	VF	XF	Unc
AH(13)80(1960-61) Rare	—	—	—	—	—

Y# 19 1/40 RIYAL (1 Buqsha) **Composition:** Aluminum **Note:** Accession date: AH1367.

Date	VG	F	VF	XF	Unc
ND(1948)	0.15	0.25	0.40	0.75	—

Y# 12.1 1/40 RIYAL (1 Buqsha) **Composition:** Bronze (Red To Yellow) **Reverse:** "Sana" above date, large "Sana'a" in border legend **Note:** Accession date: AH1367. Some earlier dates exist on thinner planchets.

Date	VG	F	VF	XF	Unc
AH1368(1948-49)	0.50	1.00	4.00	12.00	—
Note: AH1368 also exists with accession date 13776 (error) known					
AH1369(1949-50)	0.75	1.25	5.00	15.00	—
AH1370(1950-51)	0.35	0.75	3.00	6.00	—
AH1371(1951-52)	0.35	0.75	3.00	6.00	—
AH1372(1952-53)	0.35	0.75	2.00	4.00	—
AH1373/1(1953)	—	—	—	—	—
AH1373/2(1953)	0.85	1.80	3.00	6.00	—
AH1373(1953-54)	0.35	0.75	2.00	4.00	—
AH1374(1954-55)	0.35	0.75	2.00	4.00	—
AH1375/4(1955-56)	0.50	1.00	3.00	6.00	—
AH1377(1957-58)	—	—	—	—	—

Note: Reported, not confirmed

Y# 12a.1 1/40 RIYAL (1 Buqsha) **Composition:** Aluminum **Reverse:** "Sana" above date, large "Sana'a" in border legend **Note:** Dies of 1/40 Riyal, Y#12.1, were used.

Date	VG	F	VF	XF	Unc
AH1371(1951-52)	0.50	1.00	4.00	10.00	—
AH1373(1953-54)	0.50	1.00	4.00	10.00	—
AH1374(1954-55)	0.50	1.00	4.00	10.00	—
AH1375(1955-56)	0.50	1.00	4.00	10.00	—
AH1377(1957-58)	15.00	30.00	50.00	90.00	—

Y# 12.3 1/40 RIYAL (1 Buqsha) **Composition:** Bronze (Red To Yellow) **Reverse:** Large "Sana'a" in legend, without "Sana" above date

Date	VG	F	VF	XF	Unc
AH1371(1951-52)	0.50	1.00	4.00	12.00	—

Y# 12.2 1/40 RIYAL (1 Buqsha) **Composition:** Bronze (Red To Yellow) **Reverse:** Small "Sana'a" in legend **Note:** Varieties of arrangement of legends, form of crescent, and size of circle exist.

Date	VG	F	VF	XF	Unc
AH1371(1951-52)	0.35	0.75	3.00	6.00	—
AH1374(1954-55)	0.35	0.75	2.00	4.00	—
AH1375(1955-56)	0.35	0.75	2.00	4.00	—
AH1376(1956-57)	0.50	1.00	5.00	12.00	—
Note: Exists with accession date 1376 instead of 1367 on obverse					
AH1377/6(1957-58)	0.85	1.75	4.00	8.00	—
Note: Exists with accession date 1376 instead of 1367 on obverse					
AH1378/5(1958-59)	—	—	—	—	—
AH1379/7(1959-60)	0.85	1.75	4.00	8.00	—
AH1380/79(1960)	10.00	20.00	50.00	75.00	—
AH1380(1960-61)	0.85	1.75	4.00	8.00	—

Y# 12a.2 1/40 RIYAL (1 Buqsha) **Composition:** Aluminum **Reverse:** Small "Sana'a" in legend **Note:** Dies of 1/40 Riyal, Y#12.2, were used. AH1376 and AH1377 plain dates also exist with accession date AH1376 instead of AH1367 on obverse. Varieties exist.

Date	VG	F	VF	XF	Unc
AH1375(1955-56)	0.50	1.00	4.00	10.00	—
AH1376(1956-57)	0.50	1.00	4.00	10.00	—
AH1377/6(1957)	10.00	20.00	40.00	75.00	—
AH1377(1957-58)	15.00	30.00	50.00	90.00	—

Y# 13 1/16 AHMADI RIYAL **Composition:** Silver **Obv. Legend:** "Amir al-Mu'minin" **Shape:** 5-sided **Note:** Accession date: AH1367. Arrangement of legends and size of inner circle on reverse vary.

Date	VG	F	VF	XF	Unc
AH1367(1948)	0.75	1.50	6.00	12.00	—
AH1368(1948-49)	0.75	1.50	5.00	10.00	—
AH1371(1951-52)	0.75	1.50	5.00	10.00	—
AH1374(1954-55)	0.75	1.50	4.00	8.00	—

Y# 13.1 1/16 AHMADI RIYAL **Composition:** Silver **Obverse:** 1/8 Ahmadi Riyal, Y#14 **Reverse:** Y#13 **Shape:** 5-sided **Note:** Mule. Accession date: AH1367. Ends of crescents cut off on reverse.

Date	VG	F	VF	XF	Unc
AH1374(1954-55)	20.00	40.00	100	150	—

Y# A14 1/10 AHMADI RIYAL **Composition:** Silver **Note:** Accession date: AH1367.

Date	VG	F	VF	XF	Unc
AH1370(1950-51)	400	750	1,250	1,500	—

Y# 14a 1/8 AHMADI RIYAL **Composition:** Silver **Shape:** Hexagonal

Date	VG	F	VF	XF	Unc
AH1368(1948-49)	350	650	1,250	1,850	—

Y# 14 1/8 AHMADI RIYAL Composition: Silver **Note:** Accession date: AH1367. Pentagonal planchet. Arrangement of legends and size of inner circle on reverse vary.

Date	VG	F	VF	XF	Unc
AH1367(1948)	4.00	8.00	15.00	30.00	—
AH1368(1948-49)	2.75	3.50	8.00	20.00	—
AH1370(1950-51)	2.75	3.50	8.00	20.00	—
AH1371(1951-52)	1.75	2.50	6.00	15.00	—
AH1372(1952-53)	1.75	2.50	4.00	10.00	—
AH1373(1953-54)	1.75	2.50	4.00	10.00	—
AH1374(1954-55)	1.75	2.50	5.00	15.00	—
AH1375/1(1955-56)	4.00	10.00	40.00	80.00	—
AH1379/x(1959)	1.75	2.50	5.00	15.00	—
AH1379/5(1959)	1.75	2.50	5.00	15.00	—
AH1379(1959-60)	1.75	2.50	6.00	15.00	—
AH1380(1960-61)	1.75	2.50	7.00	20.00	—

Y# 15 1/4 AHMADI RIYAL Composition: Silver **Edge:** Reeded **Note:** Accession date: 1367. The size of inner circle as well as the arrangement of legends on reverse vary. All dates have only the final 2 digits on the coin.

Date	VG	F	VF	XF	Unc
AH(13)67(1948)	3.50	5.00	7.50	15.00	—
AH(13)68(1949-50)	3.50	5.00	7.50	15.00	—
AH(13)70(1950-51)	3.00	4.00	6.00	12.00	—
AH(13)71/68(1951)	6.00	8.00	12.50	20.00	—
AH(13)71/0(1951)	4.50	6.00	9.00	15.00	—
AH(13)71(1951-52)	3.00	4.00	6.00	10.00	—
AH(13)72(1952-53)	3.00	4.00	6.00	10.00	—
AH(13)74(1954-55)	3.00	4.00	6.00	10.00	—
AH(13)75/3(1955)	4.50	6.00	9.00	15.00	—
AH(13)75(1955-56)	3.00	4.00	6.00	10.00	—
AH(13)77/5(1957-58)	4.50	6.00	9.00	15.00	—
AH(13)80(1960-61)	30.00	60.00	100	175	—

Y# 15a 1/4 AHMADI RIYAL Composition: Copper

Date	VG	F	VF	XF	Unc
AH(13)81(1961-61) Rare	—	—	—	—	—

Note: This issue is considered a pattern

Y# 16.1 1/2 AHMADI RIYAL Composition: Silver **Reverse:** Full dates; denomination and mint name read inward **Note:** Accession date: 1367.

Date	VG	F	VF	XF	Unc
AH1367(1948)	6.00	10.00	15.00	35.00	—
AH1368(1948-49)	6.00	10.00	15.00	35.00	—
AH1369(1949-50)	5.00	8.00	12.50	20.00	—
AH1370(1950-51)	7.50	12.50	20.00	40.00	—
AH1371(1951/52)	7.50	12.50	20.00	40.00	—
AH1372/68(1952-53)	6.00	10.00	15.00	30.00	—
AH1373(1953-54)	9.00	15.00	25.00	45.00	—
AH1375((1955-56)	—	—	—	—	—
Note: Reported, not confirmed					
AH(13)75(1955)	30.00	50.00	80.00	100	—
AH1377(1957-58)	—	—	—	—	—

Y# 16.2 (prevY16.3) 1/2 AHMADI RIYAL Composition: Silver **Reverse:** Full dates; denomination and mint name read outward **Edge:** Reeded **Note:** Arrangement of legends and size of circle on reverse vary. These coins were struck over blanks punched from Maria Theresa Thalers. The outer rings are reported to have circulated as currency, but this is doubtful, as they are found only counterstamped "Void" in Arabic.

Date	VG	F	VF	XF	Unc
AH1377(1957-58)	5.00	8.00	12.50	20.00	—
AH1377(1957-58)	5.00	8.00	12.50	20.00	—
AH1378(1958-59)	6.00	10.00	15.00	25.00	—
AH1378(1958-59)	6.00	10.00	15.00	25.00	—
AH1379(1959-60)	5.00	8.00	12.50	20.00	—
AH1379(1959-60)	5.00	8.00	12.50	20.00	—
AH1380(1960-61)	17.50	30.00	40.00	75.00	—
AH1380(1960-61)	17.50	30.00	40.00	75.00	—
AH1381(1961-62)	12.50	22.50	30.00	50.00	—
AH1381(1961-62)	12.50	22.50	30.00	50.00	—
AH1382(1962-63)	7.50	12.50	25.00	40.00	—
AH1382(1962-63)	7.50	12.50	25.00	40.00	—

Y# 16a 1/2 AHMADI RIYAL Composition: Copper

Date	VG	F	VF	XF	Unc
AH1381(1961-62) Rare	—	—	—	—	—

Note: This issue is considered a pattern

Y# 17 AHMADI RIYAL Composition: Silver **Note:** Accession date: AH1367. These are usually found struck over Austrian Maria Theresa Talers and occasionally over other foreign crowns. All Y-17s have 1367 in the center obverse. The date for each piece is located in the lower left of the reverse. Varieties exist.

Date	F	VF	XF	Unc
AH1367(1948)	20.00	30.00	45.00	75.00
AH1370(1950-51)	12.50	20.00	28.50	45.00
AH1371(1951-52)	12.50	20.00	28.50	45.00
AH1372/68(1952-53)	—	—	—	—
Note: Reported, not confirmed				
AH1373(1953-54)	8.50	13.50	20.00	30.00
Note: Most AH1373 Riyals appear to be weakly struck from recut AH1372 dies, and the dates are easily confused				
AH1374(1954-55)	10.00	15.00	22.50	35.00
AH1375(1955-56)	10.00	15.00	22.50	35.00
AH1377(1957-58)	—	—	—	—
Note: Reported, not confirmed				
AH1378(1958-59)	10.00	15.00	22.50	35.00
AH1380(1960-61)	10.00	15.00	22.50	35.00
AH1381(1961-62)	10.00	15.00	22.50	35.00

GOLD COINAGE

Imam Ahmad gold strikes were based on the gold standard of the Turkish Lira (7.2164 g gold). Strikes on the British Gold Standard can have an additional countermark of an Arabic 1, 2, or 4, probably indicating the equivalence to 1, 2, or 4 British Sovereigns.

Y# G15 GOLD 1/4 RIYAL (1 Lira - Sovereign) Composition: Gold **Note:** Accession date: AH1367. Weight varies: 6.30-8.90 grams. Dies of silver 1/4 Ahmadi riyal, (Y#15) were used.

Date	F	VF	XF	Unc
AH(13)71(1951-52)	—	450	850	1,500
AH(13)75/3(1955)	—	450	850	1,500
AH(13)75(1955)	—	450	850	1,500
AH(13)77/5(1957-58)	—	450	850	1,500

Y# G16.1 GOLD 1/2 RIYAL (2-1/2 Lira - 2 Sovereigns) Composition: Gold **Reverse:** Full dates; denomination and mint name read inward **Note:** Accession date: AH1367. Weight varies: 15.57-17.99 grams.

Date	F	VF	XF	Unc
AH1370(1950-51)	425	650	1,150	2,000
AH1371(1951-52)	425	650	1,150	2,000
AH1375(1955-56)	425	650	1,150	2,000
AH(13)75(1955)	425	650	1,150	2,000
AH1377(1957-58)	425	650	1,150	2,000

Y# G16.2 (YG16.3) GOLD 1/2 RIYAL (2-1/2 Lira - 2 Sovereigns) Composition: Gold **Reverse:** Full date; denomination and mint name read outward **Note:** Dies of silver 1/2 Ahmadi Riyal, (Y#16) were used.

Date	F	VF	XF	Unc
AH1377(1957-58)	425	650	1,150	2,000
AH1377(1957-58)	425	650	1,150	2,000
AH1378(1958-59)	425	650	1,150	2,000
AH1378(1958-59)	425	650	1,150	2,000
AH1379(1959-60)	425	650	1,150	2,000
AH1379(1959-60)	425	650	1,150	2,000
AH1380(1960-61)	425	650	1,150	2,000
AH1380(1960-61)	425	650	1,150	2,000
AH1381(1961-62)	425	650	1,150	2,000
AH1381(1961-62)	425	650	1,150	2,000

Y# G17 GOLD RIYAL (5 Lira - 4 Sovereigns) Composition: Gold **Note:** Weight varies: 30.46-39.06 grams. Accession date: AH1367. Dies of silver Ahmadi Riyal (Y#17) were used.

Date	F	VF	XF	Unc
AH1371(1951-52) Rare	—	—	—	—
AH1372(1952-53) Rare	—	—	—	—
AH1373(1953-54)	—	675	1,000	1,750
AH1374(1954-55)	—	675	1,000	1,750
AH1375(1955-56)	—	675	1,000	1,750
AH1377(1957-58)	—	675	1,000	1,750
AH1378(1958-59)	—	675	1,000	1,750
AH1381(1961-62)	—	675	1,000	1,750

MYANMAR (Burma)

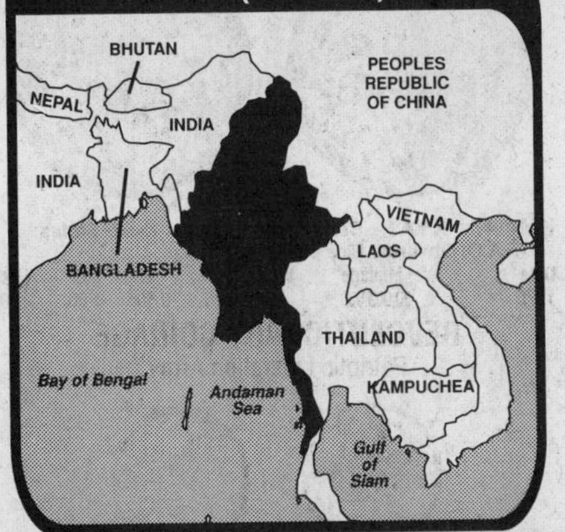

The Union of Myanmar, formerly Burma, a country of Southeast Asia fronting on the Bay of Bengal and the Andaman Sea, has an area of 261,218 sq. mi. (678,500 sq. km.) and a population of 38.8 million. Capital: Yangon (Rangoon). Myanmar is an agricultural country heavily dependent on its leading product (rice) which occupies two-thirds of the cultivated area and accounts for 40 % of the value of exports. Mineral resources are extensive, but production is low. Petroleum, lead, tin, silver, zinc, nickel cobalt, and precious stones are exported.

The first European to reach Burma, in about 1435, was Nicolo Di Conti, a Venetian merchant. During the beginning of the reign of Bodawpaya (1781-1819AD) the kingdom comprised most of the same area as it does today including Arakan which was taken over in 1784-85. The British East India Company, while unsuccessful in its1612 effort to establish posts along the Bay of Bengal, was enabled by the Anglo-Burmese Wars of 1824-86 to expand to the whole of Burma and to secure its annexation to British India. In 1937, Burma was separated from India, becoming a separate British colony with limited self-government. Burma became an independent nation outside the British Commonwealth on Jan. 4, 1948, the constitution of 1948 providing for a parliamentary democracy and the nationalization of certain industries. However, political and economic problems persisted, and on March 2, 1962, Gen. Ne Win took over the government, suspended the constitution, installed himself as chief of state, and pursued a socialistic program with nationalization of nearly all industry and trade. On Jan. 4, 1974, a new constitution adopted by referendum established Burma as a socialist republic under one-party rule. The country name was changed to Myanmar in 1989.

The coins issued by kings Mindon and Thibaw between1 852 and 1885 circulated in Upper Burma. Indian coins were current in Lower Burma, which was annexed in 1852. Burmese coins are frequently known by the equivalent Indian denominations, although their values are inscribed in Burmese units. Upper Burma was annexed in 1885 and the Burmese coinage remained in circulation until 1889,when Indian coins became current throughout Burma. Coins were again issued in the old Burmese denominations after independence in 1948, but these were replaced by decimal issues in 1952. The Chula-Sakarat (CS) dating is sometimes referred to as BE-Burmese Era and began in 638AD.

RULERS

British, 1886-1948

MONETARY SYSTEM

(Until 1952)

4 Pyas = 1 Pe
2 Pe = 1 Mu
2 Mu = 1 Mat

5 Mat = 1 Kyat

NOTE: Originally 10 light Mu = 1 Kyat, eventually 8 heavy Mu = 1 Kyat.

Indian Equivalents

1 Silver Kyat = 1 Rupee = 16 Annas
1 Gold Kyat = 1 Mohur = 16 Rupees

UNION OF BURMA

STANDARD COINAGE

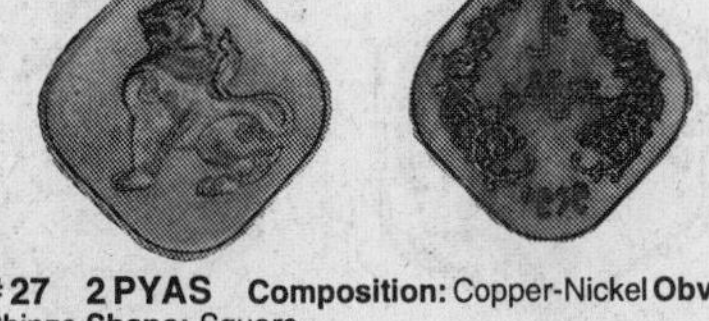

KM# 27 2 PYAS Composition: Copper-Nickel **Obverse:** Chinze **Shape:** Square

Date	Mintage	F	VF	XF	Unc	BU
1949	7,000,000	0.25	0.50	1.00	3.00	—
1949 Proof	100	Value: 100				

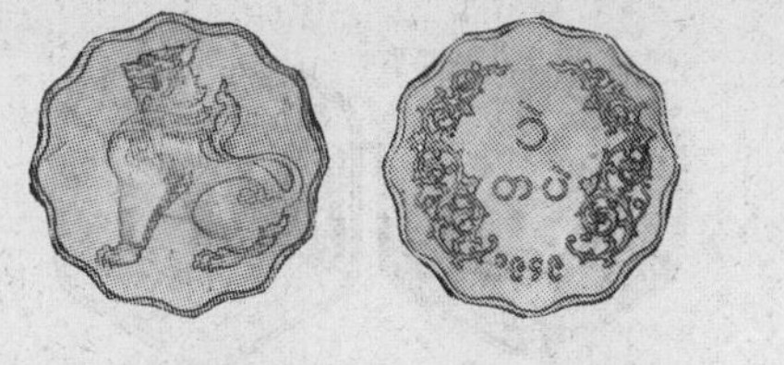

KM# 28 PE Composition: Copper-Nickel **Obverse:** Chinze **Shape:** Scalloped

Date	Mintage	F	VF	XF	Unc	BU
1949	8,000,000	0.35	0.75	1.50	4.00	—
1949 Proof	100	Value: 100				
1950	9,500,000	0.35	0.75	1.50	4.00	—
1950 Proof	—	—	—	—	—	—
1951	6,500,000	0.50	1.00	2.00	5.00	—
1951 Proof	—	—	—	—	—	—

KM# 29 2 PE Composition: Copper-Nickel **Obverse:** Chinze **Shape:** Square

Date	Mintage	F	VF	XF	Unc	BU
1949	7,100,000	0.50	1.00	2.00	5.00	—
1949 Proof	100	Value: 100				
1950	8,500,000	0.50	1.00	2.00	5.00	—
1950 Proof	—	—	—	—	—	—
1951	7,480,000	0.50	1.00	2.00	5.00	—
1951 Proof	—	—	—	—	—	—

KM# 30 4 PE Composition: Nickel **Obverse:** Chinze

Date	Mintage	F	VF	XF	Unc	BU
1949	6,500,000	1.25	2.50	5.00	15.00	—
1949 Proof	100	Value: 100				
1950	6,120,000	1.00	2.00	4.00	12.00	—

KM# 31 8 PE Composition: Nickel **Obverse:** Chinze

Date	Mintage	F	VF	XF	Unc	BU
1949	3,270,000	1.50	3.00	6.00	25.00	—
1949 Proof	100	Value: 100				
1950	3,900,000	1.25	2.50	5.00	20.00	—
1950 Proof	—	—	—	—	—	—

KM# 31a 8 PE Composition: Copper-Nickel **Obverse:** Chinze

Date	Mintage	VG	F	VF	XF	Unc
CS1314 (1952)	1,642,000	—	50.00	100	150	200
CS1314 (1952) Proof	—	Value: 400				

DECIMAL COINAGE

100 Pyas = 1 Kyat

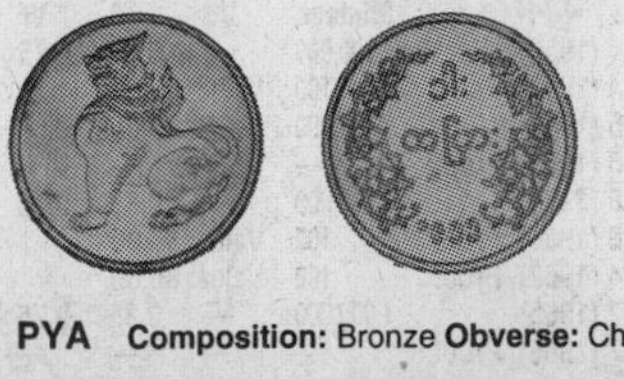

KM# 32 PYA Composition: Bronze **Obverse:** Chinze

Date	Mintage	VG	F	VF	XF	Unc
CS1314 (1952)	500,000	—	0.10	0.15	0.20	0.35
CS1314 (1952) Proof	100	Value: 60.00				
CS1315 (1953)	14,000,000	—	0.10	0.15	0.20	0.35
CS1315 (1953) Proof	—	—	—	—	—	—
CS1317 (1955)	30,000,000	—	0.10	0.15	0.20	0.35
CS1317 (1955) Proof	—	—	—	—	—	—
CS1318 (1956) Proof	100	Value: 60.00				
CS1324 (1962) Proof	100	Value: 60.00				
CS1327 (1965)	15,000,000	—	0.10	0.15	0.20	0.35
CS1327 (1965) Proof	—	—	—	—	—	—

KM# 38 PYA Composition: Aluminum **Subject:** Aung San

Date	Mintage	VG	F	VF	XF	Unc
CS1328 (1966)	8,000,000	—	0.10	0.15	0.25	0.50

KM# 33 5 PYAS Composition: Copper-Nickel **Obverse:** Chinze **Shape:** Scalloped

Date	Mintage	VG	F	VF	XF	Unc
CS1314 (1952)	20,000,000	—	0.10	0.15	0.35	0.75
CS1314 (1952) Proof	100	Value: 65.00				
CS1315 (1953)	59,700,000	—	0.10	0.15	0.35	0.75
CS1315 (1953) Proof	—	—	—	—	—	—
CS1317 (1955)	40,272,000	—	0.10	0.15	0.35	0.75
CS1317 (1955) Proof	—	—	—	—	—	—
CS1318 (1956)	20,000,000	—	0.10	0.15	0.35	0.75
CS1318 (1956) Proof	100	Value: 65.00				
CS1323 (1961)	12,000,000	—	0.10	0.15	0.35	0.75
CS1323 (1961) Proof	—	—	—	—	—	—
CS1324 (1962)	10,000,000	—	0.10	0.15	0.35	0.75
CS1324 (1962) Proof	100	Value: 65.00				
CS1325 (1963)	40,400,000	—	0.10	0.15	0.25	0.60
CS1325 (1963) Proof	—	—	—	—	—	—
CS1327 (1965)	43,600,000	—	0.10	0.15	0.20	0.40
CS1327 (1965) Proof	—	—	—	—	—	—
CS1328 (1966)	20,000,000	—	0.10	0.15	0.20	0.40
CS1328 (1966) Proof	—	—	—	—	—	—

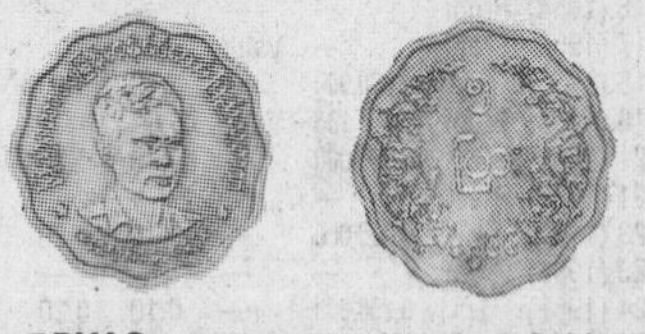

KM# 39 5 PYAS Composition: Aluminum **Subject:** Aung San **Shape:** Scalloped

Date	VG	F	VF	XF	Unc
CS1328 (1966)	—	0.10	0.20	0.35	0.60

KM# 51 5 PYAS Composition: Aluminum-Bronze **Series:** F.A.O. **Obverse:** Rice plant

Date	F	VF	XF	Unc	BU
1987	0.10	0.20	0.40	1.00	—

KM# 34 10 PYAS Composition: Copper-Nickel **Obverse:** Chinze **Shape:** Square

Date	Mintage	VG	F	VF	XF	Unc
CS1314 (1952)	20,000,000	—	0.10	0.20	0.40	1.00
CS1314 (1952) Proof	100	Value: 70.00				
CS1315 (1953)	37,250,000	—	0.10	0.20	0.40	1.00
CS1315 (1953) Proof	—	—	—	—	—	—
CS1317 (1955)	22,750,000	—	0.10	0.20	0.40	1.00
CS1317 (1955) Proof	—	—	—	—	—	—
CS1318 (1956)	35,000,000	—	0.10	0.15	0.40	1.00

Date	Mintage	VG	F	VF	XF	Unc
CS1318 (1956) Proof	100	Value: 70.00				
CS1324 (1962)	6,000,000	—	0.10	0.20	0.40	1.00
CS1324 (1962) Proof	100	Value: 70.00				
CS1325 (1963)	10,750,000	—	0.10	0.20	0.40	1.00
CS1325 (1963) Proof	10,750,000	—	—	—	—	—
CS1327 (1965)	32,619,999	—	0.10	0.20	0.40	1.00
CS1327 (1965) Proof	—	—	—	—	—	—

KM# 40 10 PYAS **Composition:** Aluminum **Subject:** Aung San **Shape:** Square

Date	VG	F	VF	XF	Unc
CS1328 (1966)	—	0.15	0.30	0.60	1.00

KM# 49 10 PYAS **Composition:** Brass **Series:** F.A.O. **Obverse:** Rice plant

Date	VG	F	VF	XF	Unc
1983	—	0.15	0.30	0.60	1.00

KM# 35 25 PYAS **Composition:** Copper-Nickel **Obverse:** Chinze **Shape:** Scalloped

Date	Mintage	VG	F	VF	XF	Unc
CS1314 (1952)	13,540,000	—	0.10	0.20	0.50	1.25
CS1314 (1952) Proof	100	Value: 75.00				
CS1316 (1954)	18,000,000	—	0.10	0.20	0.50	1.25
CS1316 (1954) Proof	—	—	—	—	—	—
CS1317 (1955) Proof	—	Value: 75.00				
CS1318 (1956)	14,000,000	—	0.10	0.20	0.50	1.25
CS1318 (1956) Proof	100	Value: 75.00				
CS1321 (1959)	6,000,000	—	0.10	0.20	0.50	1.25
CS1321 (1959) Proof	—	—	—	—	—	—
CS1323 (1961)	4,000,000	—	0.10	0.20	0.50	1.25
CS1323 (1961) Proof	—	—	—	—	—	—
CS1324 (1962)	3,200,000	—	0.10	0.20	0.50	1.25
CS1324 (1962) Proof	100	Value: 75.00				
CS1325 (1963)	16,000,000	—	0.10	0.15	0.30	0.75
CS1325 (1963) Proof	—	—	—	—	—	—
CS1327 (1965)	26,000,000	—	0.10	0.15	0.30	0.75
CS1327 (1965) Proof	—	—	—	—	—	—

KM# 41 25 PYAS **Composition:** Aluminum **Subject:** Aung San **Shape:** Scalloped

Date	VG	F	VF	XF	Unc
CS1328 (1966)	—	0.15	0.30	0.60	1.00

KM# 48 25 PYAS **Composition:** Bronze **Series:** F.A.O. **Obverse:** Rice plant

Date	VG	F	VF	XF	Unc
1980	—	0.15	0.30	0.60	1.00

KM# 50 25 PYAS **Composition:** Bronze **Series:** F.A.O. **Obverse:** Rice plant **Shape:** Hexagon

Date	VG	F	VF	XF	Unc
1986	—	0.10	0.20	0.35	0.60

KM# 36 50 PYAS **Composition:** Copper-Nickel **Obverse:** Chinze

Date	Mintage	VG	F	VF	XF	Unc
CS1314 (1952)	2,500,000	—	0.20	0.50	0.75	1.75
CS1314 (1952) Proof	100	Value: 80.00				
CS1316 (1954)	12,000,000	—	0.20	0.50	0.75	1.75
CS1316 (1954) Proof	—	—	—	—	—	—
CS1318 (1956)	8,000,000	—	0.20	0.50	0.75	1.75
CS1318 (1956) Proof	100	Value: 80.00				
CS1323 (1961)	2,000,000	—	0.15	0.40	0.75	1.75
CS1323 (1961) Proof	—	—	—	—	—	—
CS1324 (1962)	600,000	—	0.25	0.75	1.25	2.25
CS1324 (1962) Proof	100	Value: 80.00				
CS1325 (1963)	4,800,000	—	0.15	0.25	0.65	1.25
CS1325 (1963) Proof	—	—	—	—	—	—
CS1327 (1965)	2,800,000	—	0.15	0.40	0.75	1.75
CS1327 (1965) Proof	—	—	—	—	—	—
CS1328 (1966)	3,400,000	—	0.10	0.30	0.75	1.75
CS1328 (1966) Proof	—	—	—	—	—	—

KM# 42 50 PYAS **Composition:** Aluminum **Subject:** Aung San

Date	VG	F	VF	XF	Unc
CS1328 (1966)	—	0.15	0.40	1.00	2.00

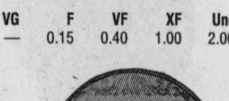

KM# 46 50 PYAS **Composition:** Brass **Series:** F.A.O. **Obverse:** Rice plant

Date	VG	F	VF	XF	Unc
1975	—	0.15	0.35	0.70	1.25
1976	—	0.15	0.35	0.70	1.25

KM# 37 KYAT **Composition:** Copper-Nickel

Date	Mintage	VG	F	VF	XF	Unc
CS1314 (1952)	2,500,000	—	0.35	0.75	1.50	3.00
CS1314 (1952) Proof	100	Value: 85.00				
CS1315 (1953)	7,500,000	—	0.25	0.50	1.00	2.00
CS1315 (1953) Proof	—	—	—	—	—	—
CS1318 (1956)	3,500,000	—	0.35	0.75	1.50	3.00
CS1318 (1956) Proof	100	Value: 85.00				
CS1324 (1962) Proof	100	Value: 85.00				
CS1327 (1965)	1,000,000	—	0.35	0.75	1.50	3.00
CS1327 (1965) Proof	—	—	—	—	—	—

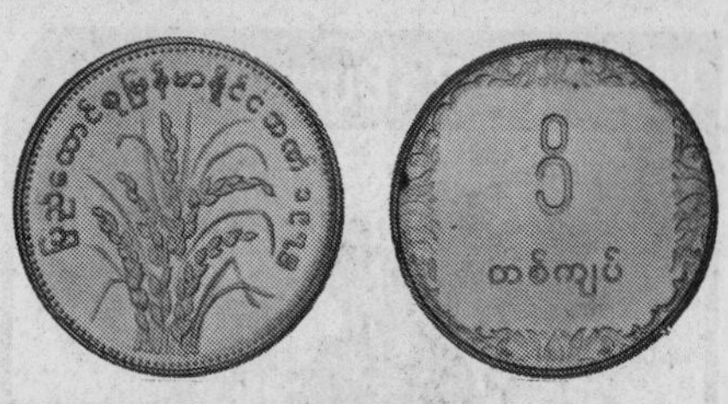

KM# 47 KYAT **Composition:** Copper-Nickel **Series:** F.A.O. **Obverse:** Rice plant

Date	Mintage	VG	F	VF	XF	Unc
1975	20,000,000	—	0.25	0.50	1.00	2.00

REVOLUTIONARY COINAGE

Patriotic Liberation Army

KM# 43 MU **Weight:** 2.0000 g. **Composition:** 1.0000 Gold .0643 oz. AGW **Obverse:** UNION OF BURMA GOVERNMENT 1970-1971 around peacock **Reverse:** Legend: U NU in star SHWE MUZI below

Date	F	VF	XF	Unc	BU
1970-71	—	—	—	135	—

KM# 44 2 MU **Weight:** 4.0000 g. **Composition:** 1.0000 Gold .1286 oz. AGW

Date	F	VF	XF	Unc	BU
1970-71	—	—	—	260	—
1970-71	—	—	—	260	—

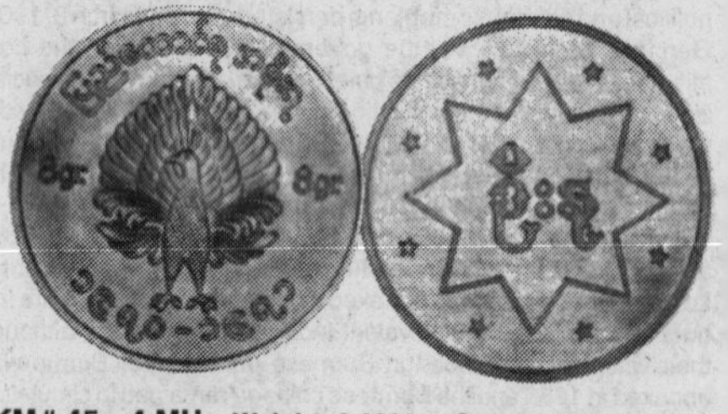

KM# 45 4 MU **Weight:** 8.0000 g. **Composition:** 1.0000 Gold .2572 oz. AGW

Date	F	VF	XF	Unc	BU
1970-71	—	—	—	485	—

UNION OF MYANMAR

DECIMAL COINAGE

100 Pyas = 1 Kyat

KM# 57 10 PYAS **Composition:** Brass **Obv. Legend:** Myanmar Central Bank **Note:** Similar to KM#49.

Date	VG	F	VF	XF	Unc
1991	—	0.15	0.30	0.60	1.00

KM# 58 25 PYAS **Composition:** Chrome Plated Steel **Obv. Legend:** Myanmar Central Bank **Shape:** Hexagon

Date	VG	F	VF	XF	Unc
1991	—	0.15	0.30	0.60	1.00

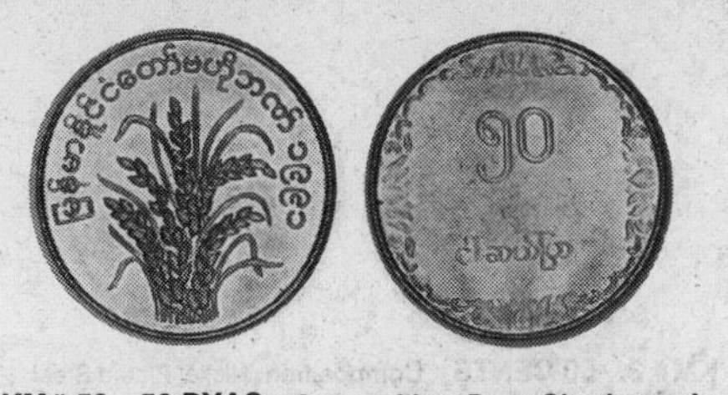

KM# 59 50 PYAS **Composition:** Brass **Obv. Legend:** Myanmar Central Bank **Reverse:** Denomination **Edge:** Reeded **Size:** 24.6 mm. **Note:** Struck at Prome.

Date	VG	F	VF	XF	Unc
1991	—	0.15	0.35	0.70	1.25

KM# 61 5 KYATS **Weight:** 2.7300 g. **Composition:** Brass **Obverse:** Seated lion **Reverse:** Denomination **Edge:** Plain **Size:** 20 mm.

Date	F	VF	XF	Unc	BU
1999	—	—	—	0.50	—

KM# 62 10 KYATS **Composition:** Brass

Date	F	VF	XF	Unc	BU
1999	—	—	—	0.75	—

KM# 63 50 KYATS **Weight:** 5.0600 g. **Composition:** Copper-Nickel **Obverse:** Seated lion **Reverse:** Denomination **Edge:** Reeded **Size:** 23.85 mm.

Date	F	VF	XF	Unc	BU
1999	—	—	—	1.75	—

KM# 64 100 KYATS **Weight:** 7.5200 g. **Composition:** Copper-Nickel **Obverse:** Seated lion **Reverse:** Denomination **Edge:** Reeded **Size:** 26.8 mm. **Note:** Struck at Prome.

Date	F	VF	XF	Unc	BU
1999	—	—	—	3.00	—

KM# A51 300 KYAT **Weight:** 1.2441 g. **Composition:** 0.9990 Gold .04 oz. AGW **Subject:** Year of the Tiger **Obverse:** Lotus flower

Date	F	VF	XF	Unc	BU
1998	—	—	—	35.00	—

KM# 52 500 KYAT **Weight:** 20.0000 g. **Composition:** 0.9250 Silver .5948 oz. ASW **Subject:** Year of the Tiger **Obverse:** Lotus flower

Date	Mintage	F	VF	XF	Unc	BU
1987 Proof	Est. 15,000	Value: 50.00				

KM# 53 500 KYAT **Weight:** 20.0000 g. **Composition:** 0.9250 Silver .5948 oz. ASW **Subject:** Year of the Tiger **Obverse:** Lotus flower

Date	Mintage	F	VF	XF	Unc	BU
1998 Proof	Est. 15,000	Value: 50.00				

KM# 54 500 KYAT **Weight:** 20.0000 g. **Composition:** 0.9250 Silver .5948 oz. ASW **Subject:** Year of the Tiger **Obverse:** Lotus flower

Date	Mintage	F	VF	XF	Unc	BU
1998 Proof	1,014,999	Value: 37.50				

KM# 55 2000 KYAT **Weight:** 7.7759 g. **Composition:** 0.9999 Gold .2500 oz. AGW **Subject:** Year of the Tiger **Obverse:** Lotus flower

Date	Mintage	F	VF	XF	Unc	BU
1998 Proof	1,998	Value: 250				

Note: In sets only

KM# 56 5000 KYAT **Weight:** 15.5518 g. **Composition:** 0.9999 Gold .5000 oz. AGW **Subject:** Year of the Tiger **Obverse:** Lotus flower

Date	Mintage	F	VF	XF	Unc	BU
1998 Proof	5,798	Value: 425				

PATTERNS

Including off metal strikes

KM#	Date	Mintage	Identification	Mkt Val
Pn10	BE2602	—	4 Annas. Aluminum. 25 mm.	—
Pn11	BE2602	—	4 Annas. Aluminum. 19 mm.	—
Pn12	BE2602	—	4 Annas. Aluminum. 16 mm.	—

PROOF SETS

KM#	Date	Mintage	Identification	Issue Price	Mkt Val
PS1	1949 (5)	100	KM#27-31	—	500
PS2	1952 (6)	100	KM#32-37	—	435
PS3	1956 (6)	100	KM#32-37	—	435
PS4	1962 (6)	100	KM#32-37	—	435
PS5	1998 (3)	3,998	KM#52-54	—	145
PS6	1998 (2)	1,998	KM#55-56	—	675

NAGORNO-KARABAKH

Nagorno-Karabakh, an ethnically Armenian enclave inside Azerbaijan (pop., 1991 est.: 193,000), SW region. It occupies an area of 1,700 sq mi (4,400 square km) on the NE flank of the Karabakh Mountain Range, with the capital city of Stepanakert.

Russia annexed the area from Persia in 1813, and in 1923 it was established as an autonomous province of the Azerbaijan S.S.R. In 1988 the region's ethnic Armenian majority demonstrated against Azerbaijani rule, and in 1991, after the breakup of the U.S.S.R. brought independence to Armenia and Azerbaijan, war broke out between the two ethnic groups. On January 8, 1992 the leaders of Nagorno-Karabakh declared independence as the Republic of Mountainous Karabakh (RMK). Since 1994, following a cease-fire, ethnic Armenians have held Karabakh, though officially it remains part of Azerbaijan. Karabakh remains sovereign, but the political and military condition is volatile and tensions frequently flare into skirmishes.

It's marvelous nature and geographic situation, have all facilitated Karabakh to be a center of science, poetry and, especially, of the musical culture of Azerbaijan.

REPUBLIC

STANDARD COINAGE

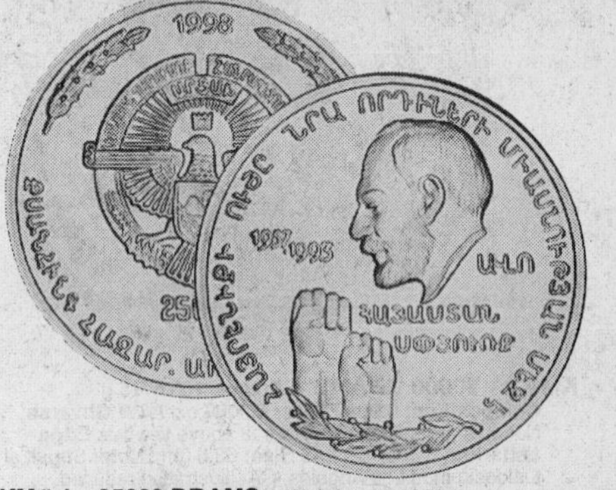

KM# 1 25000 DRAMS **Weight:** 31.2000 g. **Composition:** 0.9990 Silver 1.0021 oz. ASW **Obverse:** National arms **Reverse:** Portrait above two fists **Edge:** Reeded **Size:** 39 mm. **Note:** Struck at Lialoosin Inc., Los Angeles, CA.

Date	F	VF	XF	Unc	BU
1998 Proof	—	Value: 55.00			

KM# 5 25000 DRAMS **Weight:** 30.8000 g. **Composition:** 0.9990 Silver .9893 oz. ASW **Obverse:** National arms **Reverse:** Two stone faces monument **Edge:** Plain **Note:** Struck at Lialoosin Inc., Los Angeles, CA.

Date	F	VF	XF	Unc	BU
1998(2000) Proof	—	Value: 55.00			

KM# 1a 25000 DRAMS **Composition:** Gold Plated Silver

Date	F	VF	XF	Unc	BU
1998 Proof	—	Value: 60.00			

KM# 5a 25000 DRAMS **Composition:** Gold Plated Silver **Size:** 38.8 mm.

Date	F	VF	XF	Unc	BU
1998(2000) Proof	—	Value: 60.00			

KM# 3 50000 DRAMS **Weight:** 7.8000 g. **Composition:** 0.9000 Gold .2257 oz. AGW **Obverse:** National arms **Reverse:** Portrait above two fists **Edge:** Plain **Size:** 22 mm. **Note:** Struck at Lialoosin Inc., Los Angeles, CA.

Date	F	VF	XF	Unc	BU
1998 Proof	—	Value: 200			

KM# 2 50000 DRAMS **Weight:** 155.5175 g. **Composition:** 0.9990 Silver 5.0000 oz. ASW **Obverse:** National arms **Reverse:** Portrait above two fists **Edge Lettering:** 5 T.O. .999 A6 **Size:** 63.8 mm. **Note:** Struck at Lialoosin Inc., Los Angeles, CA. Illustration reduced.

Date	F	VF	XF	Unc	BU
1998 Proof	—	Value: 235			

KM# 4 50000 DRAMS **Weight:** 155.5175 g. **Composition:** 0.9990 Silver 5.0000 oz. ASW **Obverse:** National arms **Reverse:** Two monumental portraits **Edge Lettering:** 5.T.O. .999 AG **Size:** 63.8 mm. **Note:** Struck at Lialoosin Inc., Los Angeles, CA. Illustration reduced.

Date	F	VF	XF	Unc	BU
1998 Proof	—	Value: 235			

KM# 2a 50000 DRAMS **Composition:** Gold Plated Silver

Date	F	VF	XF	Unc	BU
1998 Proof	—	—	—	—	—

KM# 4a 50000 DRAMS **Composition:** Gold Plated Silver

Date	F	VF	XF	Unc	BU
1998 Proof	—	Value: 250			

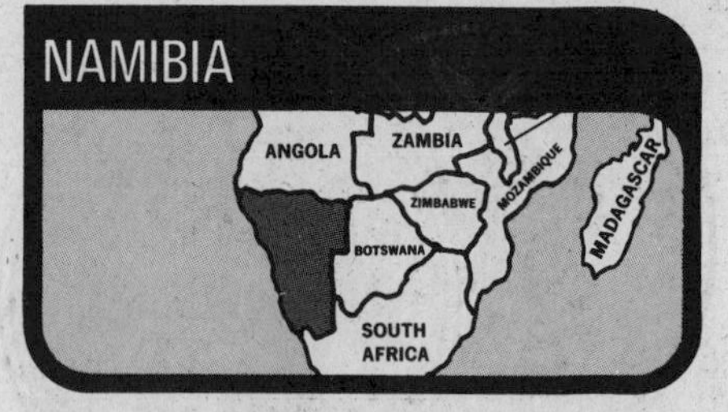

The Republic of Namibia, once the German colonial territory of German South West Africa, and later South West Africa, is situated on the Atlantic coast of southern Africa, bounded on the north by Angola, on the east by Botswana, and on the south by South Africa. It has an area of 318,261 sq. mi. (824,290 sq. km.) and a population of *1.4 million. Capital: Windhoek. Diamonds, copper, lead, zinc, and cattle are exported.

South Africa undertook the administration of South West Africa under the terms of a League of Nations mandate on Dec. 17, 1920. When the League of Nations was dissolved in 1946, its supervisory authority for South West Africa was inherited by the United Nations. In 1946 the UN denied South Africa's request to annex South West Africa. South Africa responded by refusing to place the territory under a UN trusteeship. In 1950 the International Court of Justice ruled that South Africa could not unilaterally modify the international status of South West Africa. A 1966 UN resolution declaring the mandate terminated was rejected by South Africa, and the status of the area remained in dispute. In June 1968 the UN General Assembly voted to rename the territory Namibia. In 1971 the International Court of Justice ruled that South Africa's presence in Namibia was illegal. In Dec. 1973 the UN appointed a UN Commissioner and a multi-racial Advisory Council was appointed. An interim government was formed in 1977 and independence was to be declared by Dec. 31, 1978. This resolution was rejected by major UN powers. In April 1978 South Africa accepted a plan for UN-supervised elections, which led to a political abstention by the South West Africa People's Organization (SWAPO) party leading to dissolving of the Minister's Council and National Assembly in Jan.1983. A Multi-Party Conference (MPC) was formed in May 1984, which held talks with SWAPO. The MPC petitioned South Africa for self-government and on June 17, 1985 the Transitional Government of National Unity was installed. Negotiations were held in 1988between Angola, Cuba, and South Africa reaching a peaceful settlement on Aug. 5, 1988. By April 1989 Cuban troops were to withdraw from Angola and South African troops from Namibia. The Transitional Government resigned on Feb. 28, 1988 for the upcoming elections of the constituent assembly in Nov. 1989.Independence was finally achieved on March 12, 1990 within the Commonwealth of Nations. The President is the Head of State; the Prime Minister is Head of Government.

MONETARY SYSTEM

100 Cents = 1 Namibia Dollar

1 Namibia Dollar = 1 South African Rand

REPUBLIC OF NAMIBIA

DECIMAL COINAGE

KM# 1 5 CENTS **Composition:** Nickel Plated Steel **Obverse:** National arms

Date	F	VF	XF	Unc	BU
1993 (1993)	—	—	0.20	0.50	—

KM# 16 5 CENTS **Composition:** Stainless Steel **Obverse:** National arms **Reverse:** Horse mackerel fish, denomination

Date	F	VF	XF	Unc	BU
2000 (1999)	—	—	—	1.00	—

KM# 2 10 CENTS **Composition:** Nickel Plated Steel **Obverse:** National arms

Date	F	VF	XF	Unc	BU
1993	—	—	0.35	1.00	—
1996	—	—	0.35	1.00	—
1998	—	—	0.35	1.00	—

KM# 3 50 CENTS **Composition:** Nickel Plated Steel **Obverse:** National arms

Date	F	VF	XF	Unc	BU
1993	—	—	0.75	1.75	—
1996	—	—	0.75	1.75	—

KM# 4 DOLLAR **Composition:** Brass **Obverse:** National arms

Date	F	VF	XF	Unc	BU
1993	—	—	1.25	3.50	—
1996	—	—	1.25	3.50	—

KM# 6 DOLLAR **Composition:** Copper-Nickel **Subject:** 5th Year of Independence **Obverse:** National arms

Date	Mintage	F	VF	XF	Unc	BU
1995	50,000	—	—	—	10.00	—

KM# 7 DOLLAR **Composition:** Copper-Nickel **Subject:** Miss Universe **Obverse:** National arms **Reverse:** Multicolored gemsbok

Date	Mintage	F	VF	XF	Unc	BU
1995	50,000	—	—	—	9.00	—

KM# 12 DOLLAR **Composition:** Copper-Nickel **Subject:** Marine Life Protection **Obverse:** National arms **Reverse:** Multicolored whale and calf

Date	Mintage	F	VF	XF	Unc	BU
1998 Proof	7,500	Value: 25.00				

KM# 5 5 DOLLARS **Composition:** Brass **Obverse:** National arms

Date	F	VF	XF	Unc	BU
1993	—	—	4.00	7.00	—

KM# 18 5 DOLLARS **Weight:** 1.2700 g. **Composition:** 0.9999 Gold .0408 oz. AGW **Subject:** 10 Years of Independence **Obverse:** National arms **Reverse:** Two lions **Edge:** Reeded **Size:** 13.9 mm. **Note:** Struck at the Huguenin Mint.

Date	Mintage	F	VF	XF	Unc	BU
2000 Proof	8,000	Value: 35.00				

KM# 8 10 DOLLARS **Weight:** 25.0000 g. **Composition:** 0.9250 Silver .7435 oz. ASW **Subject:** 5th Year of Independence **Obverse:** National arms **Reverse:** Multicolored desert view

Date	Mintage	F	VF	XF	Unc	BU
1995 Proof	10,000	Value: 32.50				

KM# 9 10 DOLLARS **Composition:** Copper-Nickel **Subject:** U.N. 50th Anniversary **Obverse:** National arms **Reverse:** Farm scene

Date	F	VF	XF	Unc	BU
1995	—	—	—	12.50	—

KM# 9a 10 DOLLARS **Weight:** 28.2800 g. **Composition:** 0.9250 Silver .8410 oz. ASW **Subject:** U.N. 50th Anniversary **Obverse:** National arms **Reverse:** Farm scene

Date	F	VF	XF	Unc	BU
1995 Proof	—	Value: 50.00			

KM# 10 10 DOLLARS **Weight:** 25.0000 g. **Composition:** 0.9250 Silver .7435 oz. ASW **Subject:** Miss Universe **Obverse:** National arms **Reverse:** Multicolored leopard

Date	Mintage	F	VF	XF	Unc	BU
1995 Proof	10,000	Value: 35.00				

KM# 11 10 DOLLARS **Weight:** 25.0000 g. **Composition:** 0.9250 Silver .7435 oz. ASW **Series:** Olympic Games 1996 **Obverse:** National arms **Reverse:** Runner, cheetah

Date	F	VF	XF	Unc	BU
1996 Proof	—	Value: 35.00			

KM# 13 10 DOLLARS **Weight:** 25.0000 g. **Composition:** 0.9250 Silver .7435 oz. ASW **Subject:** Marine Life Protection **Obverse:** National arms **Reverse:** Multicolored whale and calf **Note:** Similar to 1 Dollar, KM#12.

Date	F	VF	XF	Unc	BU
1998 Proof	—	Value: 60.00			

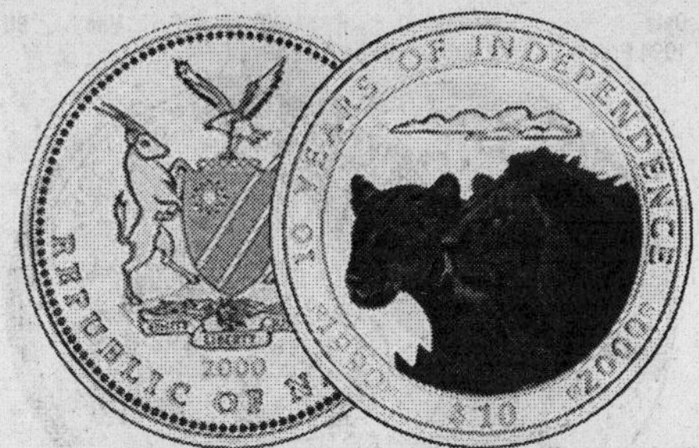

KM# 19 10 DOLLARS **Weight:** 25.0000 g. **Composition:** 0.9000 Silver .7234 oz. ASW **Subject:** 10 Years of Independence **Obverse:** National arms **Reverse:** Two multicolored lions **Edge:** Reeded **Size:** 37.3 mm. **Note:** Struck at Huguenin.

Date	Mintage	F	VF	XF	Unc	BU
2000 Proof	3,000	Value: 40.00				

KM# 14 20 DOLLARS **Weight:** 155.5175 g. **Composition:** 0.9990 Silver 4.9950 oz. ASW **Obverse:** National arms **Reverse:** Multicolored whale and calf **Note:** Similar to 1 Dollar, KM#12.

Date	F	VF	XF	Unc	BU
1998 Proof	—	Value: 350			

KM# 17 100 DOLLARS **Weight:** 31.1035 g. **Composition:** 0.9999 Gold 1.0000 oz. AGW **Series:** Olympic Games 1996 **Reverse:** Runner, cheetah **Note:** Similar to 10 Dollar, KM#11.

Date	Mintage	F	VF	XF	Unc	BU
1996 Proof	400	Value: 750				

KM# 15 100 DOLLARS **Weight:** 31.1035 g. **Composition:** 0.9999 Gold 1.0000 oz. AGW **Subject:** Marine Life Protection **Obverse:** National arms **Reverse:** Multicolored whale and calf **Note:** Similar to 1 Dollar, KM#12.

Date	Mintage	F	VF	XF	Unc	BU
1998 Proof	125	Value: 800				

ESSAIS

KM#	Date	Mintage	Identification	Mkt Val
E2	1996	30	100 Dollars. Copper-Nickel. Multi-color, KM#17.	220
E1	1996	30	10 Dollars. Copper-Nickel. Multi-color, KM#11.	200

NAURU ISLAND

The Republic of Nauru, formerly Pleasant Island, is an island republic in the western Pacific Ocean west of the Gilbert Islands. It has an area of 8-1/2 sq. mi. and a population of 7,254. It is known for its phosphate deposits.

The island was discovered in 1798. It was annexed by Germany in 1888 and made a part of the Marshall Island protectorate. In 1914 the island was occupied by Australia and placed under mandate in 1919. During World War II it was seized by the Japanese in August, 1942.It became a joint Australian, British and New Zealand trust territory in 1947 and remained as such until it became an independent republic in 1968. Nauru has a unique relationship with the Commonwealth of Nations.

RULERS

British, until 1968

MONETARY SYSTEM

100 Cents = 1 (Australian) Dollar

REPUBLIC OF NAURU

DECIMAL COINAGE

KM# 12 DOLLAR **Composition:** Copper-Nickel **Subject:** British Queen Mother **Obverse:** National arms **Reverse:** Queen Mother and Churchill **Edge:** Reeded **Size:** 38.6 mm. **Note:** Struck at the Royal Australian Mint.

Date	F	VF	XF	Unc	BU
1996	—	—	—	12.00	—

KM# 1 10 DOLLARS **Weight:** 38.7000 g. **Composition:** 0.9250 Silver 1.1508 oz. ASW **Subject:** Silver Jubilee of Independence

Date	Mintage	F	VF	XF	Unc	BU
1993 Proof	1,000	Value: 85.00				

KM# 2 10 DOLLARS **Weight:** 31.4700 g. **Composition:** 0.9250 Silver .9359 oz. ASW **Subject:** Noah's Ark

Date	Mintage	F	VF	XF	Unc	BU
1993 Proof	Est. 15,000	Value: 65.00				

KM#5 10 DOLLARS **Weight:** 31.4700 g. **Composition:** 0.9250 Silver .9359 oz. ASW **Series:** Endangered Wildlife **Reverse:** Songbirds

Date	Mintage	F	VF	XF	Unc	BU
1993 Proof	Est. 10,000	Value: 50.00				

KM#3 10 DOLLARS **Weight:** 31.4700 g. **Composition:** 0.9250 Silver .9359 oz. ASW **Subject:** World Cup Soccer

Date	Mintage	F	VF	XF	Unc	BU
1994 Proof	30,000	Value: 45.00				

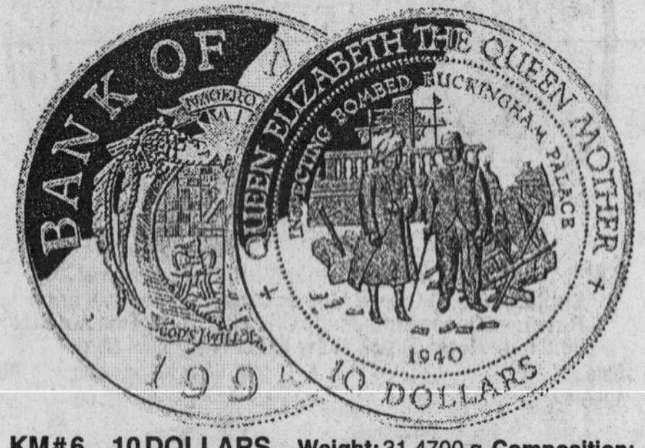

KM#6 10 DOLLARS **Weight:** 31.4700 g. **Composition:** 0.9250 Silver .9359 oz. ASW **Subject:** Queen Mother Visits Bombed Palace

Date	Mintage	F	VF	XF	Unc	BU
1994 Proof	Est. 30,000	Value: 45.00				

KM#7 10 DOLLARS **Weight:** 31.4700 g. **Composition:** 0.9250 Silver .9359 oz. ASW **Subject:** John Fearn **Reverse:** Ship

Date	Mintage	F	VF	XF	Unc	BU
1994 Proof	Est. 15,000	Value: 50.00				

KM#8 10 DOLLARS **Weight:** 31.4700 g. **Composition:** 0.9250 Silver .9359 oz. ASW **Reverse:** Galileo Galilei with telescope

Date	Mintage	F	VF	XF	Unc	BU
1994 Proof	Est. 10,000	Value: 52.50				

KM#9 10 DOLLARS **Weight:** 31.4700 g. **Composition:** 0.9250 Silver .9359 oz. ASW **Series:** Olympics **Reverse:** Weight lifter

Date	Mintage	F	VF	XF	Unc	BU
1995 Proof	Est. 30,000	Value: 45.00				

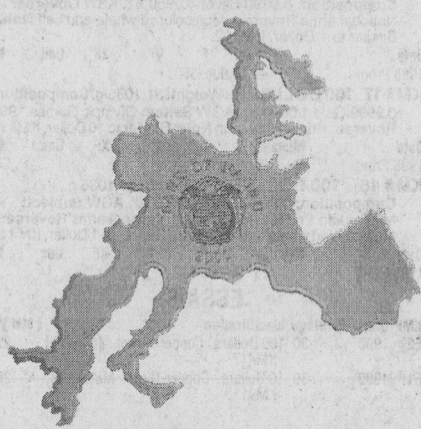

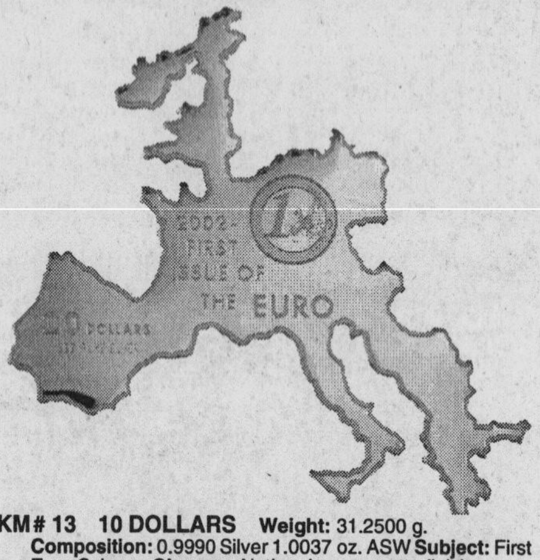

KM# 13 10 DOLLARS **Weight:** 31.2500 g. **Composition:** 0.9990 Silver 1.0037 oz. ASW **Subject:** First Euro Coinage **Obverse:** National arms, matte finish **Reverse:** Denomination, inscription and partially gold-plated 1 euro reverse coin design, Proof finish **Edge:** Plain **Shape:** Like a map **Size:** 72 mm. **Note:** Illustration reduced.

Date	Mintage	F	VF	XF	Unc	BU
2002 Proof	—	Value: 50.00				

KM# 4 50 DOLLARS **Weight:** 8.0500 g. **Composition:** 0.9000 Gold .2329 oz. AGW **Series:** 1996 Olympics **Reverse:** Javelin throwing

Date	Mintage	F	VF	XF	Unc	BU
1994 Proof	3,000	Value: 165				

KM#10 50 DOLLARS **Weight:** 7.7760 g. **Composition:** 0.5833 Gold .1458 oz. AGW **Reverse:** German eagle above steamship "Kaiser Wilhelm II"

Date	Mintage	F	VF	XF	Unc	BU
1994 Proof	Est. 3,000	Value: 145				

KM#11 50 DOLLARS **Weight:** 7.7760 g. **Composition:** 0.5833 Gold .1458 oz. AGW **Subject:** Endangered Wildlife **Reverse:** Dugong (Manatee-like creature)

Date	Mintage	F	VF	XF	Unc	BU
1995 Proof	Est. 2,000	Value: 145				

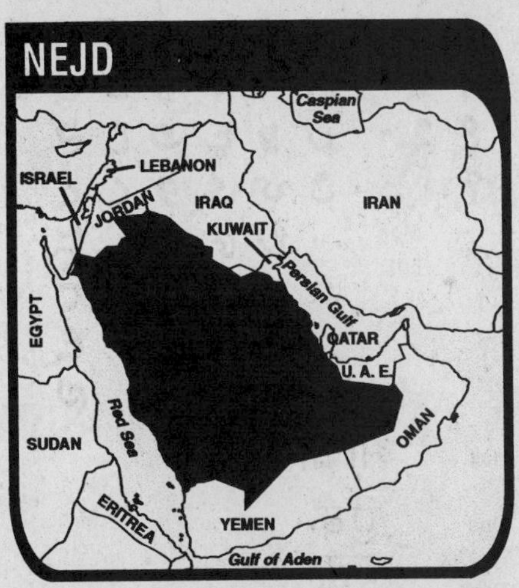

Nejd, a province of Saudi Arabia which may be described as an open steppe, occupies the core of the Arabian peninsula. The province became a nominal dependency of the Turkish empire in 1871 and a sultanate of King Abd Al-Aziz Bin Sa'ud in 1905.

TITLES

نجد

Nejd

RULERS

Abd Al-Aziz Bin Sa'ud, AH1322-1373/1905-1953AD
(Over all of Hejaz after 1925, and then in all Saudi Arabia after 1932).

MONETARY SYSTEM

40 Para = 1 Piastre (Ghirsh)
20 Piastres = 1 Riyal

KINGDOM

COUNTERMARKED COINAGE

Silver Coins

Following the defeat of the Ottomans in 1916, silver coins of various sizes were also countermarked Nejd. The most common host coins include the Maria Theresa thalers of Austria, British India Rupees, and 5, 10, and 20 Kurush or Qirsh of Turkey and Egypt. The countermark occurs in various sizes and styles of script. These countermarks may have been applied by local silversmiths to discourage re-exportation of the badly needed hard currency and silver of known fineness.

Some crown-sized examples exist with both the al-Hejaz and Nejd countermarks. The authenticity of the silver countermarked coins has long been discussed, and it is likely that most were privately produced. Other host coins are considered local or spurious.

KM# 1 5 PIASTRES **Composition:** Silver **Ruler:** Abd Al-Aziz Bin Sa'ud **Countermark:** "Nejd" **Note:** Accession date: AH1327. Countermark on Egypt 5 Piastres, KM#308.

CM Date	Host Date	Good	VG	F	VF	XF
AH(1918)	AH1327/2H	30.00	60.00	120	180	—
AH(1918)	AH1327/3H	25.00	50.00	100	150	—
AH(1918)	AH1327/4H	25.00	50.00	100	150	—
AH(1918)	AH1327/6H	25.00	50.00	100	150	—

KM# 2.1 (KM2) 5 PIASTRES **Composition:** Silver **Countermark:** "Nejd" **Note:** Countermark on Egypt 5 Piastres, KM#318.1. Accession date: AH1335.

CM Date	Host Date	Good	VG	F	VF	XF
AH(1918)	AH1335-1916	25.00	50.00	100	150	—
AH(1918)	AH1335-1916	25.00	50.00	100	150	—
AH(1918)	AH1335-1917	25.00	50.00	100	150	—
AH(1918)	AH1335-1917	25.00	50.00	100	150	—

KM# 2.2 5 PIASTRES **Composition:** Silver **Ruler:** Abd Al-Aziz Bin Sa'ud **Countermark:** "Nejd" **Note:** Countermark on Egypt 5 Piastres, KM#318.2. Accession date: AH1333. Previous KM#2.

CM Date	Host Date	Good	VG	F	VF	XF
AH(1918)	AH1335-1917H	25.00	50.00	100	150	—

KM# 3 5 PIASTRES **Composition:** Silver **Ruler:** Abd Al-Aziz Bin Sa'ud **Countermark:** "Nejd" **Note:** Countermark on Turkey 5 Kurush, KM#750. Accession date: AH1327.

CM Date	Host Date	Good	VG	F	VF	XF
AH(1918)	AH1327/1-7	25.00	50.00	100	150	—

KM# 4 5 PIASTRES **Composition:** Silver **Ruler:** Abd Al-Aziz Bin Sa'ud **Countermark:** "Nejd" **Note:** Countermark on Turkey 5 Kurush, KM#771. Accession date: AH1327.

CM Date	Host Date	Good	VG	F	VF	XF
AH(1918)	AH1327/7-9	25.00	50.00	100	150	—

KM# 5 RUPEE **Composition:** Silver **Ruler:** Abd Al-Aziz Bin Sa'ud **Countermark:** "Nejd" **Note:** Countermark on India Rupee, KM#450.

CM Date	Host Date	Good	VG	F	VF	XF
(1918)	1835	25.00	50.00	100	150	—

KM# 6 RUPEE **Composition:** Silver **Ruler:** Abd Al-Aziz Bin Sa'ud **Countermark:** "Nejd" **Note:** Countermark on India Rupee, KM#457.

CM Date	Host Date	Good	VG	F	VF	XF
(1918)	1840	25.00	50.00	125	275	—

KM# 7 RUPEE **Composition:** Silver **Ruler:** Abd Al-Aziz Bin Sa'ud **Countermark:** "Nejd" **Note:** Countermark on India Rupee, KM#458.

CM Date	Host Date	Good	VG	F	VF	XF
(1918)	1840	25.00	50.00	125	225	—

KM# 8 RUPEE **Composition:** Silver **Ruler:** Abd Al-Aziz Bin Sa'ud **Countermark:** "Nejd" **Note:** Countermark on India Rupee, KM#473.

CM Date	Host Date	Good	VG	F	VF	XF
(1918)	1862-76	25.00	50.00	100	150	—

KM# A9 RUPEE **Composition:** Silver **Ruler:** Abd Al-Aziz Bin Sa'ud **Countermark:** "Nejd" **Note:** Countermark on India Rupee, KM#492.

CM Date	Host Date	Good	VG	F	VF	XF
(1918)	1877-1901	25.00	50.00	100	150	—

KM# 9 10 PIASTRES **Composition:** Silver **Ruler:** Abd Al-Aziz Bin Sa'ud **Countermark:** "Nejd" **Note:** Countermark on Egypt 10 Qirsh, KM#295. Accession date: AH1293.

CM Date	Host Date	Good	VG	F	VF	XF
AH(1918)	AH1293/27 w	50.00	70.00	125	200	—
AH(1918)	AH1293/29 w	50.00	70.00	125	200	—
AH(1918)	AH1293/29H	50.00	70.00	125	200	—
AH(1918)	AH1293/30H	50.00	70.00	125	200	—
AH(1918)	AH1293/31H	60.00	90.00	150	250	—
AH(1918)	AH1293/32H	50.00	70.00	125	200	—
AH(1918)	AH1293/33H	50.00	70.00	125	200	—

KM# 10 10 PIASTRES **Composition:** Silver **Ruler:** Abd Al-Aziz Bin Sa'ud **Countermark:** "Nejd" **Note:** Countermark on Turkey 10 Kurush, KM#751. Accession date: AH1327.

CM Date	Host Date	Good	VG	F	VF	XF
AH(1918)	AH1327/1-7	50.00	70.00	125	200	—

KM# A11.1 10 PIASTRES **Composition:** Silver **Ruler:** Abd Al-Aziz Bin Sa'ud **Countermark:** "Nejd" **Note:** Countermark on Egypt 10 Piastres, KM#319. Accession date: AH1333. Previous KM#A11.

CM Date	Host Date	Good	VG	F	VF	XF
AH(1918)	AH1335-1916	50.00	85.00	125	200	—
AH(1918)	AH1335-1917	50.00	85.00	125	200	—

KM# A11.2 10 PIASTRES **Composition:** Silver **Ruler:** Abd Al-Aziz Bin Sa'ud **Countermark:** "Nejd" **Note:** Countermark on Egypt 10 Piastres, KM#320. Accession date: AH1333. Previous KM#A11.

CM Date	Host Date	Good	VG	F	VF	XF
AH(1918)	AH1335-1917H	50.00	85.00	125	200	—

KM# 11 10 PIASTRES **Composition:** Silver **Ruler:** Abd Al-Aziz Bin Sa'ud **Countermark:** "Nejd" **Note:** Countermark on Turkey 10 Kurush, KM#772. Accession date: AH1327.

CM Date	Host Date	Good	VG	F	VF	XF
AH(1918)	AH1327/7-10	50.00	70.00	125	200	—

KM# A12 20 PIASTRES **Composition:** Silver **Ruler:** Abd Al-Aziz Bin Sa'ud **Countermark:** "Nejd" **Note:** Countermark on Turkey 20 Kurush, KM#722. Accession date: AH1293.

CM Date	Host Date	Good	VG	F	VF	XF
AH(1918)	AH1293/1-3	75.00	125	200	350	—

KM# 12 20 PIASTRES **Composition:** Silver **Ruler:** Abd Al-Aziz Bin Sa'ud **Countermark:** "Nejd" **Note:** Countermark on Egypt 20 Qirsh, KM#310. Accession date: AH1327.

CM Date	Host Date	Good	VG	F	VF	XF
AH(1918)	AH1327/2H	75.00	125	200	350	—
AH(1918)	AH1327/3H	75.00	125	200	350	—
AH(1918)	AH1327/4H	75.00	125	200	350	—
AH(1918)	AH1327/6H	75.00	125	200	350	—

KM# B12.1 (KMB12) 20 PIASTRES **Composition:** Silver **Ruler:** Abd Al-Aziz Bin Sa'ud **Countermark:** "Nejd" **Note:** Countermark on Turkey 20 Kurush, KM#675. Accession date: AH1255.

CM Date	Host Date	Good	VG	F	VF	XF
AH(1918)	AH1255/6-15	75.00	125	200	350	—
AH(1918)	AH1255/6-15	75.00	125	200	350	—

KM# B12.2 20 PIASTRES **Composition:** Silver **Ruler:** Abd Al-Aziz Bin Sa'ud **Countermark:** "Nejd" **Note:** Countermark on Turkey 20 Kurush, KM#676. Accession date: AH1255. Previous KM#B12.

CM Date	Host Date	Good	VG	F	VF	XF
AH(1918)	AH1255/15-23	75.00	125	200	350	—

KM# C12 20 PIASTRES **Composition:** Silver **Ruler:** Abd Al-Aziz Bin Sa'ud **Countermark:** "Nejd" **Note:** Countermark on Turkey 20 Kurush, KM#693. Accession date: AH1277.

CM Date	Host Date	Good	VG	F	VF	XF
AH(1918)	AH1277/1-15	75.00	125	200	350	—

KM# A13.1 20 PIASTRES **Composition:** Silver **Ruler:** Abd Al-Aziz Bin Sa'ud **Countermark:** "Nejd" **Note:** Countermark on Egypt 20 Piastres, KM#321. Accession date: 1333.

CM Date	Host Date	Good	VG	F	VF	XF
AH(1918)	AH1335-1916	75.00	125	200	350	—
AH(1918)	AH1335-1917	75.00	125	200	350	—

KM# A13.2 20 PIASTRES **Composition:** Silver **Ruler:** Abd Al-Aziz Bin Sa'ud **Countermark:** "Nejd" **Note:** Countermark on Egypt 20 Piastres, KM#322. Accession date: 1333.

CM Date	Host Date	Good	VG	F	VF	XF
AH(1918)	AH1335-1917H	90.00	150	250	425	—

KM# 13 20 PIASTRES **Composition:** Silver **Ruler:** Abd Al-Aziz Bin Sa'ud **Countermark:** "Nejd" **Note:** Countermark on Turkey 20 Kurush, KM#780. Accession date: AH1327.

CM Date	Host Date	Good	VG	F	VF	XF
AH(1918)	AH1327/8-10	75.00	125	200	350	—

KM# 14 20 PIASTRES **Composition:** Silver **Ruler:** Abd Al-Aziz Bin Sa'ud **Countermark:** "Nejd" **Note:** Countermark on Austria Maria Theresa Thaler, KM#T1.

CM Date	Host Date	Good	VG	F	VF	XF
(1918)	1780 Restrike	40.00	80.00	200	425	—

The Kingdom of Nepal, the world's only surviving Hindu kingdom, is a landlocked country occupying the southern slopes of the Himalayas. It has an area of 56,136 sq. mi. (140,800 sq. km.) and a population of 18 million. Capital: Kathmandu. Nepal has deposits of coal, copper, iron and cobalt, but they are largely unexploited. Agriculture is the principal economic activity. Rice, timber and jute are exported, with tourism being the other major foreign exchange earner.

Apart from a brief Muslim invasion in the 14th century, Nepal was able to avoid the mainstream of Northern Indian politics, due to its impregnable position in the mountains. It is therefore a unique survivor of the medieval Hindu and Buddhist culture of Northern India, which was largely destroyed by the successive waves of Muslim invasions.

Prior to the late 18th century, Nepal, as we know it today, was divided among a number of small states. Unless otherwise stated, the term *Nepal* applies to the small fertile valley, about 4,500 ft. above sea level, in which the three main cities of Kathmandu, Patan and Bhatgaon are situated.

During the reign of King Yaksha Malla (1428-1482AD), the Nepalese kingdom, with capital at Bhatgaon, was extended northwards into Tibet, and also controlled a considerable area to the south of the hills. After Yaksha Malla's death, the Kingdom was divided among his sons, so four kingdoms were established with capitals at Bhatgaon, Patan, Kathmandu and Banepa, all situated within the small valley, less than 20 miles square. Banepa was quickly absorbed within the territory of Bhatgaon, but the other three kingdoms remained until 1769. The internecine strife between the three kings effectively stopped Nepal from becoming a major military force during this period, although with its fertile land and strategic position, it was by far the wealthiest and most powerful of the Himalayan states.

Apart from agriculture, Nepal owed its prosperity to its position on one of the easiest trade routes between the great monasteries of central Tibet, and India. Nepal made full use of this, and a trading community was set up in Lhasa during the 16th century, and Nepalese coins became the accepted currency medium in Tibet.

The seeds of discord between Nepal and Tibet were sown during the first half of the 18th century, when the Nepalese debased the coinage, and the fate of the Malla kings of Nepal was sealed when Prithvi Narayan Shah, King of the small state of Gorkha, to the west of Kathmandu, was able to gain control of the trans-himalayan trade routes during the years after 1750.

Prithvi Narayan spent several years consolidating his position in hill areas before he finally succeeded in conquering the Kathmandu Valley in 1768, where he established the Shah dynasty, and moved his capital to Kathmandu.

After Prithvi Narayan's death a period of political instability ensued which lasted until the 1840's when the Rana family reduced the monarch to a figurehead and established the post of hereditary Prime Minister. A popular revolution in 1950 toppled the Rana family and reconstituted power in the throne. In 1959 King Mahendra declared Nepal a constitutional monarchy, and in 1962 a new constitution set up a system of *panchayat* (village council) democracy. In 1990, following political unrest, the king's powers were reduced. The country then adopted a system of parliamentary democracy.

On June 2, 2001 tragedy struck the royal family when Crown Prince Dipendra used an assault rifle to kill his father, mother and other members of the royal family as the result of a dispute over his current lady friend. He died 48 hours later, as King, from self inflicted gunshot wounds. Gyanendra began his second reign as King (his first was a short time as a toddler, 1950-51).

DATING

Saka Era (SE)

Up until 1888AD all coins of the Gorkha Dynasty were dated in the Saka era (SE). To convert from Saka to AD take Saka date and add 78 to arrive at the AD date. Coins dated with this era have SE before the date in the following listing.

Bikram Samvat Era (VS)

From 1888AD most copper coins were dated in the Bikram Samvat (VS) era. To convert take VS date - 57 =AD date. Coins with this era have VS before the year in the listing. With the exception of a few gold coins struck in 1890 & 1892, silver and gold coins only changed to the VS era in 1911AD, but now this era is used for all coins struck in Nepal.

RULERS

SHAH DYNASTY

Prithvi Bir Bikram

पृथ्वी वीर विक्रम

SE1803-1833/1881-1911AD, VS1938-1968/
Queen of Prithvi Bir Bikram: Lakshmi Divyeswari

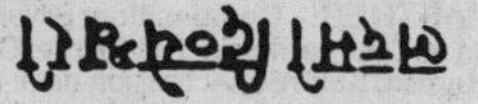

Tribhuvana Bir Bikram

त्रिभुवनवीर विक्रम

VS1968-2007, 2007-2011/1911-1950, 1951-1955AD (first reign)
VS2058- / 2001- AD (second reign)
Gyanendra Bir Bikram

ज्ञानेन्द्रवीर विक्रम

VS2007/1950-1951AD
Mahendra Bir Bikram

महेन्द्रवीर विक्रम

VS2012-2028/1955-1971AD
Queen of Mahendra Bir Bikram: Ratna Rajya Lakshmi

रत्न राज लक्ष्मी

Birendra Bir Bikram

वीरेन्द्र वीर विक्रम

VS2028-2058 /1971-2001AD
Queen of Birendra Bir Bikram: Aishvarya Rajya Lakshmi

ऐश्वर्य राज्य लक्ष्मी देवी

VS2028-2058 /1971-2001AD

VS2058 / 2001AD (reign of 48 hours)
Dipendra Bir Bikram

MONETARY SYSTEM

Many of the mohars circulated in Tibet as well as in Nepal, and on a number of occasions coins were struck from bullion supplied by the Tibetan authorities. The smaller denominations never circulated in Tibet, but some of the mohars were cut for use as small change in Tibet.

In these listings only major changes in design have been noted. There are numerous minor varieties of ornamentation or spelling.

With a few exceptions, most all coins were struck at Kathmandu.

COPPER

Initially the copper paisa was not fixed in value relative to the silver coins, and generally fluctuated in value from1/32 mohar in 1865AD to around 1/50 mohar afterc1880AD, and was fixed at that value in 1903AD.

4 Dam = 1 Paisa
2 Paisa = 1 Dyak, Adhani

COPPER and SILVER

Decimal Series

100 Paisa = 1 Rupee

Although the value of the copper paisa was fixed at 100 paisa to the rupee in 1903, it was not until 1932 that silver coins were struck in the decimal system.

GOLD COINAGE

Nepalese gold coinage, until recently, did not carry any denominations and was traded for silver, etc. at the local bullion exchange rate. The three basic weight standards used in the following listing are distinguished for convenience, although all were known as Asarphi (gold coin) locally as follows:

GOLD MOHAR

5.60 g multiples and fractions

TOLA

12.48 g multiples and fractions

GOLD RUPEE or ASHRPHI/ASARFI

11.66 g multiples and fractions
(Reduced to 10.00 g in 1966)

NOTE: In some instances the gold and silver issues were struck from the same dies.

NUMERALS

Nepal has used more variations of numerals on their coins than any other nation. The most common are illustrated in the numeral chart in the introduction. The chart below illustrates some variations encompassing the last four centuries.

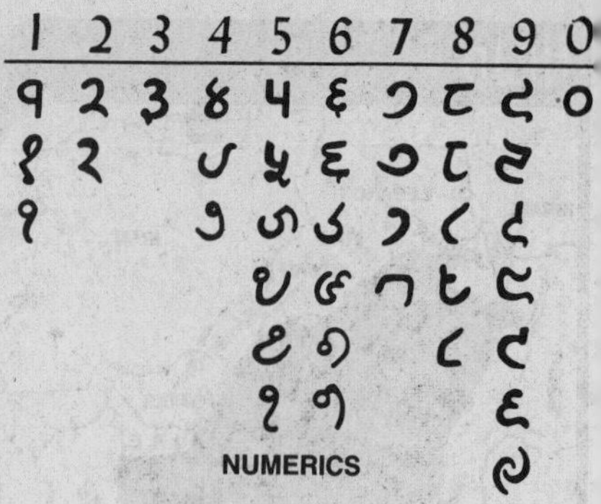

NUMERICS

Half	आधा
One	एक
Two	दुइ
Four	चार
Five	पाँच
Ten	दस
Twenty	विस
Twenty-five	पचीस
Fifty	पचास
Hundred	सय

DENOMINATIONS

Paisa	पैसा
Dam	दाम
Mohar	मोहर
Rupee	रुपैयाँ
Ashrapi	अश्रफी
Asarfi	असर्फी

DIE VARIETIES

Although the same dies were usually used both for silver and gold minor denominations, the gold Mohar is easily recognized being less ornate. The following illustrations are of a silver Mohar, KM#602 and a gold Mohar KM#615 issued by Surendra Bikram Saha Deva in the period SE1769-1803/1847-1881AD. Note the similar reverse legend. The obverse usually will start with the character for the word Shri either in single or multiples, the latter as Shri Shri Shri or Shri 3.

OBVERSE

SILVER SE1791 | GOLD SE1793

LEGEND

श्री श्रीश्री सुरेन्द्र विक्रम साहदेव

Shri Shri Shri Surendra Bikrama Saha Deva (date).

REVERSE

SILVER GOLD

LEGEND
(in center)

श्री ३ भवानी

Shri 3 Bhavani
(around outer circle)

श्री श्री श्री गोरषनाथ

Shri Shri Shri Gorakhanatha

SHAH DYNASTY

KINGDOM
Shah Dynasty

Prithvi Bir Bikram
VS1938-1968 / 1881-1911AD

COPPER COINAGE

KM# 620.2 DAM Composition: Copper **Rev. Inscription:** "Sarkar"

Date	F	VF	XF	Unc
VS(19)64 (1907)	7.50	12.00	15.00	20.00

KM# 621 DAM Composition: Copper

Date	F	VF	XF	Unc
VS(19)68 (1911)	4.50	7.50	10.00	17.50

KM# 622 1/2 PAISA Composition: Copper

Date	F	VF	XF	Unc
VS(19)64 (1907)	4.50	7.50	10.00	17.50
VS(19)68 (1911)	4.50	7.50	10.00	17.50

KM# 629 PAISA Composition: Copper **Obverse:** Legend within squares **Reverse:** Legend within squares

Date	Good	VG	F	VF	XF
VS1959 (1902)	1.00	1.50	2.50	4.00	—
VS1962 (1905)	1.00	1.50	2.50	4.00	—
VS1963 (1906)	1.00	1.50	2.50	4.00	—
VS1964 (1907)	1.00	1.50	2.50	4.00	—
VS1965 (1908)	1.00	1.50	2.50	4.00	—
VS1966 (1909)	1.00	1.50	2.50	4.00	—
VS1967 (1910)	1.00	1.50	2.50	4.00	—
VS1968 (1911)	1.00	1.50	2.50	4.00	—

KM# 630 PAISA Composition: Copper-Iron Alloy **Obverse:** Legend within square **Reverse:** Legend within circle

Date	Good	VG	F	VF	XF
VS1959 (1902)	7.50	12.50	20.00	33.50	—

KM# 628 PAISA Composition: Copper **Obverse:** Legend within sprays **Reverse:** Legend within sprays **Note:** Varieties in sprays exist. Coin and medal alignment varieties exist.

Date	Good	VG	F	VF	XF
VS1959 (1902)	1.00	1.50	3.00	5.00	—
VS1960 (1903)	1.00	1.50	3.00	5.00	—
VS1961 (1904)	1.00	1.50	3.00	5.00	—
VS1962 (1905)	1.00	1.50	3.00	5.00	—
VS(19)62 (1905)	—	—	—	—	—
VS1963 (1906)	1.00	1.50	3.00	5.00	—
VS1964 (1907)	1.00	1.50	3.00	5.00	—
VS(19)64 (1907)	—	—	—	—	—

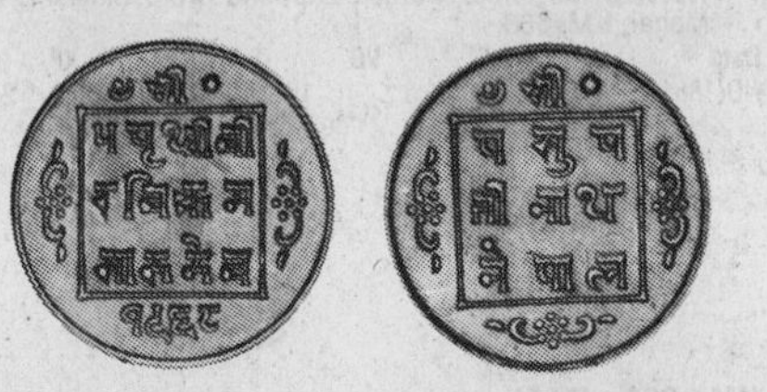

KM# 631 PAISA Composition: Copper **Note:** Also Tribhuvana Bir Bikram struck a Paisa VS1968, see KM#685.1.

Date	F	VF	XF	Unc
VS1964 (1907)	5.50	9.00	15.00	22.50
VS1968 (1911)	8.50	13.50	20.00	30.00

KM# 633 2 PAISA (Dak) Composition: Copper **Obverse:** Legend within square **Reverse:** Legend within circle

Date	Good	VG	F	VF	XF
VS1959 (1902)	12.50	17.50	25.00	50.00	—

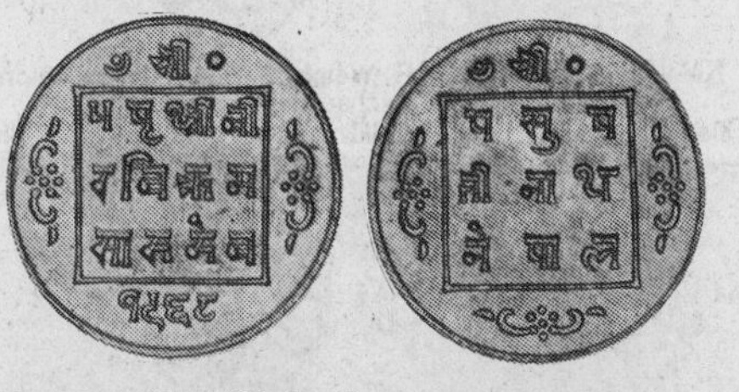

KM# 634 2 PAISA (Dak) Composition: Copper

Date	F	VF	XF	Unc
VS1964 (1907)	8.50	13.50	20.00	30.00
VS1968 (1911)	9.00	15.00	22.50	35.00

SILVER COINAGE

KM# 635 DAM Weight: 0.0400 g. **Composition:** Silver **Note:** Uniface. Five characters around sword.

Date	VG	F	VF	XF	Unc
ND(1881-1911)	—	8.00	10.00	15.00	25.00

KM# 636 DAM Weight: 0.0400 g. **Composition:** Silver **Note:** Four characters around sword.

Date	VG	F	VF	XF	Unc
ND(1881-1911)	—	15.00	25.00	30.00	40.00

KM# 637 1/32 MOHAR Weight: 0.1800 g. **Composition:** Silver **Obverse:** Sun and moon

Date	VG	F	VF	XF	Unc
ND(1881-1911)	5.00	8.50	12.50	16.50	—

KM# 638 1/32 MOHAR Weight: 0.1800 g. **Composition:** Silver **Obverse:** Without sun and moon

Date	VG	F	VF	XF	Unc
ND(1881-1911)	5.00	8.50	12.50	16.50	—

KM# 639 1/16 MOHAR Weight: 0.3500 g. **Composition:** Silver **Note:** Varieties exist.

Date	VG	F	VF	XF	Unc
ND(1881-1911)	—	6.00	10.00	13.50	20.00

KM# 640 1/8 MOHAR Weight: 0.7000 g. **Composition:** Silver **Note:** Varieties exist.

Date	VG	F	VF	XF	Unc
ND(1881-1911)	—	7.50	12.50	18.50	27.50

KM# 643 1/4 MOHAR Weight: 1.4000 g. **Composition:** Silver **Reverse:** Moon and dot for sun **Note:** Machine struck.

Date	VG	F	VF	XF	Unc
SE1827 (1905)	1.75	3.00	5.00	7.00	—

KM# 644 1/4 MOHAR Weight: 1.4000 g. **Composition:** Silver **Note:** Machine struck.

Date	VG	F	VF	XF	Unc
SE1833 (1911)	1.75	3.00	5.00	7.00	—
SE1833 Proof	—	Value: 25.00			

KM# 647 1/2 MOHAR Weight: 2.7700 g. **Composition:** Silver **Edge:** Plain **Note:** Machine struck. Varieties exist.

Date	F	VF	XF	Unc
SE1824 (1902)	20.00	25.00	30.00	35.00

KM# 648 1/2 MOHAR Weight: 2.7700 g. **Composition:** Silver **Note:** Machine struck.

Date	F	VF	XF	Unc
SE1826 (1904)	3.00	5.00	7.00	10.00
SE1827 (1905)	3.00	5.00	7.00	10.00
SE1829 (1907)	3.50	5.50	8.50	11.50

KM# 649 1/2 MOHAR Weight: 2.7700 g. **Composition:** Silver **Edge:** Milled **Note:** Machine struck.

Date	F	VF	XF	Unc
SE1832 (1910)	20.00	25.00	30.00	35.00
SE1833 (1911)	2.25	3.50	5.00	7.00
SE1833 (1911) Proof	—	Value: 35.00		

KM# 651.1 MOHAR **Weight:** 5.6000 g. **Composition:** Silver **Edge:** Plain **Note:** Machine struck.

Date	F	VF	XF	Unc
SE1823 (1901)	4.50	6.50	8.00	10.00
SE1824 (1902)	4.50	6.50	8.00	10.00
SE1825 (1903)	4.50	6.50	8.00	10.00
SE1826 (1904)	4.50	6.50	8.00	10.00
SE1827 (1905)	4.50	6.50	8.00	10.00

KM# 652 MOHAR **Weight:** 5.6000 g. **Composition:** Silver **Reverse:** Gold die, in error

Date	F	VF	XF	Unc
SE1825 (1903)	10.00	15.00	25.00	32.50

KM# 651.2 MOHAR **Weight:** 5.6000 g. **Composition:** Silver **Edge:** Milled **Note:** Machine struck.

Date	F	VF	XF	Unc
SE1826 (1904)	4.50	6.50	8.00	10.00
SE1827 (1905)	4.50	6.50	8.00	10.00
SE1828 (1906)	4.50	6.50	8.00	10.00
SE1829 (1907)	4.50	6.50	8.00	10.00
SE1830 (1908)	4.50	6.50	8.00	10.00
SE1831 (1909)	4.50	6.50	8.00	10.00
SE1832 (1910)	4.50	6.50	8.00	10.00
SE1833 (1911)	—	25.00	35.00	50.00

Note: The date SE1833 was only issued in presentation sets

KM# 655 2 MOHARS **Weight:** 11.2000 g. **Composition:** Silver **Edge:** Milled **Size:** 27 mm. **Note:** Machine struck.

Date	F	VF	XF	Unc
SE1829 (1907)	15.00	27.50	40.00	60.00
SE1831 (1909)	6.00	9.00	12.50	20.00

KM# 656 2 MOHARS **Composition:** Silver **Size:** 29 mm. **Note:** Machine struck.

Date	F	VF	XF	Unc
SE1832 (1910)	7.00	9.00	11.50	18.50
SE1833 (1911)	6.00	8.00	10.00	16.50

KM# 658 4 MOHARS **Weight:** 22.4000 g. **Composition:** Silver **Edge:** Milled

Date	F	VF	XF	Unc
SE1833 (1911)	60.00	100	140	200

GOLD COINAGE

KM# 661 DAM **Weight:** 0.0400 g. **Composition:** Gold **Note:** Uniface. Circle around characters.

Date	VG	F	VF	XF	Unc
ND(1881-1911)	—	10.00	14.00	20.00	27.50

KM# 659 DAM **Weight:** 0.0400 g. **Composition:** Gold **Note:** Uniface. Five characters around sword. Similar to 1/64 Mohar, KM#664.

Date	VG	F	VF	XF	Unc
ND(1881-1911)	—	10.00	14.00	20.00	27.50

KM# 660 DAM **Weight:** 0.0400 g. **Composition:** Gold **Note:** Uniface. Four characters around sword. Similar to 1/64 Mohar, KM#663.

Date	VG	F	VF	XF	Unc
ND(1881-1911)	—	10.00	14.00	20.00	27.50

KM# 662 DAM **Weight:** 0.0400 g. **Composition:** Gold **Note:** Uniface. Two characters below sword. Varieties exist.

Date	VG	F	VF	XF	Unc
ND(1881-1911)	—	10.00	14.00	20.00	27.50

KM# 664 1/64 MOHAR **Weight:** 0.0900 g. **Composition:** Gold **Note:** Uniface. Five characters around sword.

Date	VG	F	VF	XF	Unc
ND(1881-1911)	—	12.50	17.50	22.50	30.00

KM# 663 1/64 MOHAR **Weight:** 0.0900 g. **Composition:** Gold **Note:** Uniface. Four characters around sword.

Date	VG	F	VF	XF	Unc
ND(1881-1911)	—	12.50	17.50	22.50	30.00

KM# 665 1/32 MOHAR **Weight:** 0.1800 g. **Composition:** Gold **Note:** Uniface. Five characters around sword.

Date	VG	F	VF	XF	Unc
ND(1881-1911)	—	20.00	40.00	75.00	100

KM# 666 1/32 MOHAR **Weight:** 0.1800 g. **Composition:** Gold **Note:** Uniface. Four characters around sword.

Date	VG	F	VF	XF	Unc
ND(1881-1911)	—	15.00	30.00	75.00	100

KM# 667 1/16 MOHAR **Weight:** 0.3500 g. **Composition:** Gold

Date	VG	F	VF	XF	Unc
ND(1881-1911)	—	15.00	40.00	75.00	100

KM# 668 1/16 MOHAR **Weight:** 0.3500 g. **Composition:** Gold

Date	F	VF	XF	Unc
SE(18)33 (1911)	15.00	30.00	75.00	100

KM# 669.1 1/8 MOHAR **Weight:** 0.7000 g. **Composition:** Gold **Obverse:** Six characters

Date	F	VF	XF	Unc
ND (1881)	22.50	40.00	75.00	100

KM# 669.2 1/8 MOHAR **Weight:** 0.7000 g. **Composition:** Gold **Obverse:** Five characters **Note:** Varieties exist.

Date	F	VF	XF	Unc
ND (1881)	22.50	40.00	75.00	100

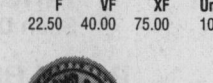

KM# 670 1/8 MOHAR **Weight:** 0.7000 g. **Composition:** Gold

Date	F	VF	XF	Unc
SE(18)33 (1911)	22.50	40.00	75.00	100

KM# 671.1 1/4 MOHAR **Weight:** 1.4000 g. **Composition:** Gold

Date	F	VF	XF	Unc
SE1823 (1901)	45.00	60.00	80.00	100
SE1829 (1907)	40.00	50.00	60.00	80.00

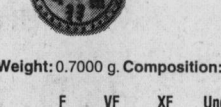

KM# 671.2 1/4 MOHAR **Weight:** 1.4000 g. **Composition:** Gold

Date	F	VF	XF	Unc
SE1833 (1911)	40.00	50.00	60.00	80.00

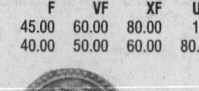

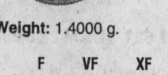

KM# 672.3 1/2 MOHAR **Weight:** 2.8000 g. **Composition:** Gold

Date	F	VF	XF	Unc
SE1823 (1901)	70.00	80.00	100	125

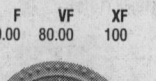

KM# 672.4 1/2 MOHAR **Weight:** 2.8000 g. **Composition:** Gold

Date	F	VF	XF	Unc
SE1829 (1907)	65.00	75.00	85.00	100

KM# 672.5 1/2 MOHAR Weight: 2.8000 g.
Composition: Gold

Date	F	VF	XF	Unc
SE1833 (1911)	65.00	75.00	85.00	100

KM# 673.1 MOHAR Weight: 5.6000 g. Composition: Gold

Date	F	VF	XF	Unc
SE1823 (1901)	115	125	150	200
SE1825 (1903)	115	125	150	200
SE1826 (1904)	115	125	150	200
SE1827 (1905)	115	125	150	200

KM# 673.2 MOHAR Weight: 5.6000 g. Composition: Gold Edge: Milled

Date	F	VF	XF	Unc
SE1828 (1906)	115	125	150	200
SE1829 (1907)	115	125	150	200
SE1831 (1909)	115	125	150	200
SE1833 (1911)	115	125	150	200

KM# 674.3 TOLA Weight: 12.4800 g. Composition: Gold Edge: Plain

Date	F	VF	XF	Unc
SE1823 (1901)	235	255	275	300
SE1824 (1902)	235	255	275	300
SE1825 (1903)	235	255	275	300
SE1826 (1904)	235	255	275	300

KM# 675.1 TOLA Weight: 12.4800 g. Composition: Gold Edge: Vertical milling

Date	F	VF	XF	Unc
SE1828 (1906)	235	255	275	300
SE1829 (1907)	235	255	275	300
SE1831 (1909)	235	255	275	300
SE1832 (1910)	235	255	275	300
SE1833 (1911)	235	255	275	300

KM# 678 DUITOLA ASARPHI Weight: 23.3200 g.
Composition: Gold Edge: pLAIN

Date	F	VF	XF	Unc
SE1825 (1902)	600	700	800	1,000

KM# 679 DUITOLA ASARPHI Weight: 23.3200 g.
Composition: Gold Edge: Milled

Date	F	VF	XF	Unc
SE1829 (1907)	550	600	700	800

KM# 680 DUITOLA ASARPHI Weight: 23.3200 g.
Composition: Gold Edge: Milled

Date	F	VF	XF	Unc
SE1833 (1911)	550	600	700	800

TOKEN COINAGE

KM# Tn1 12 PAISA Composition: Iron

Date	VG	F	VF	XF	Unc
ND(ca.1902)	3.50	8.50	15.00	25.00	—

KM# Tn2 14 PAISA Composition: Iron

Date	VG	F	VF	XF	Unc
ND(ca.1902)	3.50	8.50	15.00	25.00	—

KM# Tn3 16 PAISA Composition: Brass Note: Occasionally found with various numbers stamped.

Date	VG	F	VF	XF	Unc
SE1824 (1902)	5.00	10.00	20.00	35.00	—

Tribhuvana Bir Bikram
VS1968-2007 / 1911-1950AD

COPPER COINAGE

KM# 684 1/2 PAISA Composition: Copper Note: Struck only for presentation sets.

Date	F	VF	XF	Unc
VS1978 (1921)	—	—	50.00	75.00
VS1985 (1928)	—	—	50.00	75.00

KM# 685.1 PAISA Composition: Copper Note: Machine struck. Also Prithvi Bir Bikram struck a Paisa VS1968, see KM#631.

Date	Good	VG	F	VF	XF
VS1968 (1911)	10.00	20.00	50.00	75.00	—

KM# 685.2 PAISA Composition: Copper Note: Hand struck.

Date	Good	VG	F	VF	XF
VS1969 (1912)	1.00	1.50	2.25	3.50	—
VS1970 (1913)	1.00	1.50	2.25	3.50	—
VS1971 (1914)	1.00	1.50	2.25	3.50	—
VS1972 (1915)	1.00	1.50	2.25	3.50	—
VS1973 (1916)	1.00	1.50	2.25	3.50	—
VS1974 (1917)	1.00	1.50	2.25	3.50	—
VS1975 (1918)	1.00	1.50	2.25	3.50	—
VS1976 (1919)	1.00	1.50	2.25	3.50	—
VS1977 (1920)	1.00	1.50	2.25	3.50	—

KM# 687.1 PAISA Weight: 3.7500 g. Composition: Copper Size: 21.5 mm. Note: Machine struck. Fine style. Varieties of the Khukris exist.

Date	F	VF	XF	Unc
VS1975 (1918)	1.25	1.75	3.00	6.00
VS1976 (1919)	1.25	1.75	3.00	6.00

KM# 686.1 PAISA Composition: Copper Size: 23.5 mm.

Date	F	VF	XF	Unc
VS1975 (1918)	—	—	37.50	50.00

KM# 686.2 PAISA Composition: Copper Size: 21.5 mm.

Date	Good	VG	F	VF	XF
VS1975 (1918)	—	—	60.00	90.00	—

Note: The above issues are believed to be patterns

KM# 687.2 PAISA Weight: 3.7500 g. Composition: Copper Size: 21 mm. Note: Crude, hand struck. Varieties of the Khukris exist, left over right and right over left.

Date	Good	VG	F	VF	XF
VS1977 (1920)	1.25	1.75	3.00	6.00	—
VS1977 (1920)	1.25	1.75	3.00	6.00	—
Note: Inverted date					
VS1978 (1921)	2.00	3.00	4.50	7.50	—
VS1979 (1922)	2.00	3.00	4.50	7.50	—
VS1980 (1923)	4.00	5.00	7.50	12.50	—
VS1981 (1924)	4.00	5.00	7.50	12.50	—
VS1982 (1925)	4.00	5.00	7.50	12.50	—
VS1983 (1926)	4.00	5.00	7.50	12.50	—

KM# 688 PAISA Composition: Copper Size: 22 mm. Note: Machine struck. Weight varies: 2.6-3.1 grams. Varieties of the Khukris exist, always right over left.

Date	F	VF	XF	Unc
VS1978 (1921)	1.25	1.75	3.00	6.00
VS1979 (1922)	1.25	1.75	3.00	6.00
VS1980 (1923)	1.50	3.00	5.00	10.00
VS1981 (1924)	1.50	3.00	5.00	10.00
VS1982 (1925)	1.25	1.75	3.00	6.00
VS1984 (1927)	1.25	1.75	3.00	6.00
VS1985 (1928)	1.25	1.75	3.00	6.00
VS1986 (1929)	1.25	1.75	3.00	6.00
VS1987 (1930)	1.25	1.75	3.00	6.00

KM# 689.2 2 PAISA Composition: Copper Note: Crude struck. Varieties of the Khukris exist, left over right and right over left. Weight varies: 4.6-5.5 grams.

Date	Good	VG	F	VF	XF
VS1978 (1919)	1.00	2.00	3.50	6.50	—
VS1979 (1922)	1.00	2.00	3.50	6.50	—
VS1980 (1923)	1.00	2.00	3.50	6.50	—
VS1981 (1924)	1.00	2.00	3.50	6.50	—
VS1982 (1925)	1.00	2.00	3.50	6.50	—
VS1983 (1926)	1.00	2.00	3.50	6.50	—
VS1984 (1927)	1.00	2.00	3.50	6.50	—
VS1985 (1928)	1.00	2.00	3.50	6.50	—
VS1986 (1929)	1.50	2.50	4.00	7.50	—
VS1987 (1930)	1.50	2.50	4.00	7.50	—
VS1988 (1931)	2.00	3.00	5.00	9.00	—

KM# 689.1 2 PAISA **Composition:** Copper **Size:** 26 mm. **Note:** Machine struck. Varieties of the Khukris exist. Weight varies: 6.9-7.5 grams.

Date	VG	F	VF	XF	Unc
VS1976 (1919)	1.00	2.00	3.00	5.00	—
VS1977 (1920)	1.00	2.00	3.00	5.00	—
VS1977 (1920) Inverted date	3.50	5.00	8.50	13.50	—

KM# 689.3 2 PAISA **Weight:** 5.0000 g. **Composition:** Copper **Note:** Machine struck. Weight varies: 5.00-5.700 grams. Varieties of the Khukris exist, always right over left.

Date	VG	F	VF	XF	Unc
VS1978 (1919)	1.00	2.00	3.00	4.50	—
VS1979 (1922)	1.00	2.00	3.00	4.50	—
VS1980 (1923)	1.00	2.00	3.00	4.50	—
VS1981 (1924)	1.00	2.00	3.00	4.50	—
VS1982 (1925)	1.00	2.00	3.00	4.50	—
VS1983 (1926)	1.00	2.00	3.00	4.50	—
VS1984 (1927)	1.00	2.00	3.00	4.50	—
VS1991 (1934)	1.50	2.50	4.00	6.00	—

KM# 690.1 5 PAISA **Weight:** 18.0000 g. **Composition:** Copper **Size:** 29.5 mm. **Note:** Varieties of the Khukris exist. VS1976 crude style is plain or reeded (scarce), all other years are plain.

Date	F	VF	XF	Unc
VS1976 (1919)	6.00	10.00	14.00	20.00
Note: Fine style				
VS1976 (1919)	1.25	2.25	3.50	6.00
Note: Crude style				
VS1977 (1920)	1.25	2.25	3.50	6.00
VS1977 (1920) Inverted date	3.00	5.00	8.50	12.50

KM# 690.2 5 PAISA **Weight:** 18.0000 g. **Composition:** Copper **Note:** Crude hand struck. Varieties of the Khukris exist, left over right and right over left. Weight varies: 11.0-13.2 grams. Size varies: 29.0-32.5 millimeters.

Date	F	VF	XF	Unc
VS1978 (1921)	1.75	3.00	5.00	8.00
VS1979 (1922)	1.75	3.00	5.00	8.00
VS1980 (1923)	1.75	3.00	5.00	8.00
VS1981 (1924)	1.75	3.00	5.00	8.00
VS1982 (1925)	1.75	3.00	5.00	8.00
VS1983 (1926)	1.75	3.00	5.00	8.00
VS1984 (1927)	1.75	3.00	5.00	8.00
VS1985 (1928)	1.75	3.00	5.00	8.00
VS1986 (1929)	1.75	3.00	5.00	8.00
VS1987 (1930)	1.75	3.00	5.00	8.00
VS1988 (1931)	6.00	10.00	14.00	20.00

KM# 690.3 5 PAISA **Weight:** 14.0000 g. **Composition:** Copper **Note:** Machine struck. Weight varies: 13.5-14.0 grams. Varieties exist with both open and closed handles on Khukris, always right over left. Size varies: 29.0-30.0 millimeters.

Date	F	VF	XF	Unc
VS1978 (1921)	1.25	2.25	3.50	5.00
VS1979 (1922)	1.25	2.25	3.50	5.00
VS1979 (1922) Backwards date	1.25	2.25	3.50	5.00
VS1980 (1923)	1.25	2.25	3.50	5.00
VS1981 (1924)	1.25	2.25	3.50	5.00
VS1982 (1925)	1.25	2.25	3.50	5.00
VS1983 (1926)	1.25	2.25	3.50	5.00
VS1984 (1927)	1.25	2.25	3.50	5.00
VS1991 (1934)	15.00	20.00	25.00	30.00

SILVER COINAGE

KM# 691 DAM **Weight:** 0.0400 g. **Composition:** Silver **Note:** Uniface.

Date	F	VF	XF	Unc
ND (1911)	15.00	25.00	30.00	50.00

KM# 692 1/4 MOHAR **Weight:** 1.4000 g. **Composition:** Silver

Date	VG	F	VF	XF	Unc
VS1969 (1912)	1.75	3.00	5.00	7.00	—
VS1970 (1913)	1.75	3.00	5.00	7.00	—

KM# 693 1/2 MOHAR **Weight:** 2.8000 g. **Composition:** Silver

Date	F	VF	XF	Unc
VS1968 (1911)	2.25	3.50	5.00	7.00
VS1970 (1913)	2.25	3.50	5.00	7.00
VS1971 (1914)	2.25	3.50	5.00	7.00

KM# 681 1/2 MOHAR **Weight:** 2.7700 g. **Composition:** Silver **Note:** In the name of "Queen Lakshmi Divyeswari" - Regent for Tribhuvana Bir Bikram.

Date	F	VF	XF	Unc
VS1971 (1914)	4.00	6.00	9.00	11.50

KM# 694 MOHAR **Weight:** 5.6000 g. **Composition:** Silver

Date	F	VF	XF	Unc
VS1968 (1911)	4.50	6.50	8.00	10.00
VS1969 (1912)	4.50	6.50	8.00	10.00
VS1971 (1914)	4.50	6.50	8.00	10.00

KM# 682 MOHAR **Weight:** 5.6000 g. **Composition:** Silver **Note:** In the name of "Queen Lakshmi Divyeswari" - Regent for Tribhuvana Bir Bikram.

Date	F	VF	XF	Unc
VS1971 (1914)	4.50	6.50	9.00	11.50

KM# 695 2 MOHARS **Weight:** 11.2000 g. **Composition:** Silver **Note:** Varieties exist for this type.

Date	F	VF	XF	Unc
VS1968 (1911)	BV	7.50	10.00	16.50
VS1969 (1912)	BV	7.50	10.00	16.50
VS1970 (1913)	BV	7.50	10.00	16.50
VS1971 (1914)	BV	7.50	10.00	16.50
VS1972 (1915)	BV	7.50	10.00	16.50
VS1973 (1916)	BV	7.50	10.00	16.50
VS1974 (1917)	BV	7.50	10.00	16.50
VS1975 (1918)	BV	7.50	10.00	16.50
VS1976 (1919)	BV	7.50	10.00	16.50
VS1977 (1920)	BV	7.50	10.00	16.50
VS1978 (1921)	BV	7.50	10.00	16.50
VS1979 (1922)	BV	7.50	10.00	16.50

Date	F	VF	XF	U
VS1980 (1923)	BV	7.50	10.00	16.
VS1982 (1925)	BV	7.50	10.00	16.
VS1983 (1926)	BV	7.50	10.00	16.
VS1984 (1927)	BV	7.50	10.00	16.
VS1985 (1928)	BV	7.50	10.00	16.
VS1986 (1929)	BV	7.50	10.00	16.
VS1987 (1930)	BV	7.50	10.00	16.
VS1988 (1931)	BV	7.50	10.00	16.
VS1989 (1932)	BV	7.50	10.00	16.

KM# 696 4 MOHARS **Weight:** 22.4000 g. **Compositior** Silver

Date	F	VF	XF	U
VS1971 (1914)	40.00	75.00	125	1

GOLD COINAGE

KM# 697 DAM **Weight:** 0.0400 g. **Composition:** Gold **Note:** Uniface.

Date	F	VF	XF	U
ND (1911)	25.00	40.00	75.00	1

KM# 697a DAM **Weight:** 0.0400 g. **Composition:** Gol **Note:** Uniface, machine struck.

Date	F	VF	XF	U
ND (1911)	25.00	40.00	70.00	1

KM# 698 1/32 MOHAR **Weight:** 0.1800 g. **Compositior** Gold **Note:** Uniface.

Date	F	VF	XF	U
ND (1911)	35.00	60.00	90.00	12

KM# 699 1/16 MOHAR **Weight:** 0.3500 g. **Compositior** Gold

Date	F	VF	XF	Ur
VS(19)77 (1920)	50.00	90.00	120	15

KM# 700 1/8 MOHAR **Weight:** 0.7000 g. **Composition** Gold

Date	F	VF	XF	Ur
VS(19)76 (1919)	75.00	120	150	20

KM# 701 1/2 MOHAR **Weight:** 2.8000 g. **Composition** Gold

Date	F	VF	XF	Ur
VS1969 (1912)	—	—	—	-

KM# 717 1/2 MOHAR **Weight:** 2.8000 g. **Composition** Gold

Date	F	VF	XF	Ur
VS1995 (1938)	—	—	—	-

KM# 702 MOHAR Weight: 5.6000 g. Composition: Gold

Date	F	VF	XF	Unc
VS1969 (1912)	100	125	150	200
VS1975 (1918)	100	125	150	200
VS1978 (1921)	100	125	150	200
VS1979 (1922)	100	125	150	200
VS1981 (1924)	100	125	150	200
VS1983 (1926)	100	125	150	200
VS1985 (1928)	100	125	150	200
VS1986 (1929)	100	125	150	200
VS1987 (1930)	100	125	150	200
VS1989 (1932)	100	125	150	200
VS1990 (1933)	100	125	150	200
VS1991 (1934)	100	125	150	200
VS1998 (1941)	100	125	150	200
VS1999 (1942)	100	125	150	200
VS2000 (1943)	100	125	150	200
VS2003 (1946)	100	125	150	200
VS2005 (1948)	100	125	150	200

KM# 683 MOHAR Weight: 5.6000 g. Composition: Gold Note: In the name of "Queen Lakshmi Divyeswari" - Regent for Tribhuvana Bir Bikram.

Date	F	VF	XF	Unc
VS1971 (1914)	100	125	145	175

KM# 722 MOHAR Weight: 5.6000 g. Composition: Gold

Date	Mintage	F	VF	XF	Unc
VS1993 (1936)	376,000	—	—	—	—
VS1994 (1937)	283,000	—	—	—	—

KM# 703.1 ASHRAPHI (Tola) Composition: Gold

Date	F	VF	XF	Unc
VS1969 (1912)	225	245	275	300
VS1974 (1917)	225	245	275	300
VS1975 (1918)	225	245	275	300
VS1976 (1919)	225	245	275	300
VS1977 (1920)	225	245	275	300
VS1978 (1921)	225	245	275	300
VS1979 (1922)	225	245	275	300
VS1980 (1923)	225	245	275	300
VS1981 (1924)	225	245	275	300
VS1982 (1925)	225	245	275	300
VS1983 (1926)	225	245	275	300
VS1984 (1927)	225	245	275	300
VS1985 (1928)	225	245	275	300
VS1986 (1929)	225	245	275	300
VS1987 (1930)	225	245	275	300
VS1988 (1931)	225	245	275	300
VS1989 (1932)	225	245	275	300
VS1990 (1933)	225	245	275	300
VS1991 (1934)	225	245	275	300
VS1998 (1941)	225	245	275	300
VS1999 (1942)	225	245	275	300
VS2000 (1943)	225	245	275	300
VS2003 (1946)	225	245	275	300

KM# 727 ASHRAPHI (Tola) Composition: Gold
Obverse: Trident between moon and sun above crossed Khukris in center

Date	F	VF	XF	Unc
VS1992 (1935)	235	250	285	350

KM# 703.2 ASHRAPHI (Tola) Composition: Gold

Date	F	VF	XF	Unc
VS2005 (1948)	225	245	275	300

KM# 728 DUITOLA ASARPHI Composition: Gold
Note: Similar to 1 Tola, KM#703.

Date	F	VF	XF	Unc
VS2005 (1948)	450	500	550	650

ANONYMOUS COINAGE

KM# 733 PAISA Composition: Brass

Date	F	VF	XF	Unc
VS2010 (1953)	8.00	15.00	20.00	25.00
VS2011 (1954)	17.50	25.00	35.00	40.00
VS2012 (1955) Restrike	—	1.00	1.50	2.00

KM# 734 PAISA Composition: Brass

Date	F	VF	XF	Unc
VS2012 (1955)	1.25	2.00	2.50	3.50

KM# 735 2 PAISA Composition: Brass

Date	F	VF	XF	Unc
VS2010 (1953)	12.50	20.00	37.50	60.00
VS2011 (1954)	30.00	40.00	50.00	75.00
VS2011 (1954) Restrike	—	—	1.50	2.50

KM# 749 2 PAISA Composition: Brass

Date	F	VF	XF	Unc
VS2012 (1955)	0.30	0.50	0.75	1.50
VS2013 (1956)	0.30	0.50	0.75	1.50
VS2014 (1957)	0.30	0.50	0.75	1.50

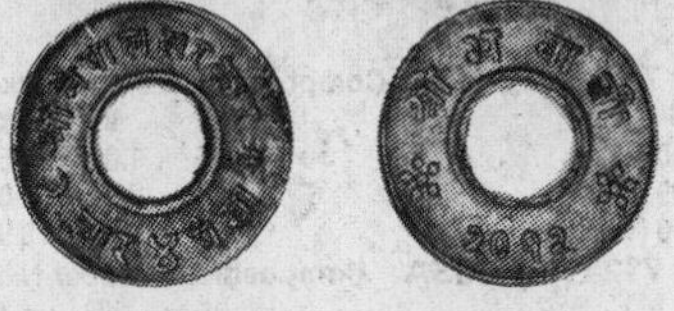

KM# 754 4 PAISA Composition: Brass

Date	F	VF	XF	Unc
VS2012 (1955)	1.00	1.75	3.00	5.00

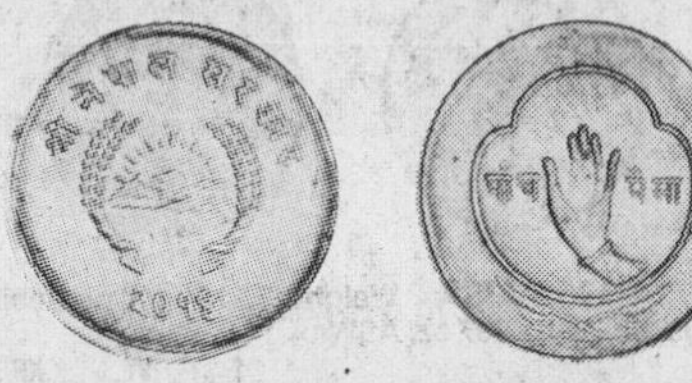

KM# 736 5 PAISA Weight: 3.8900 g. Composition: Brass

Date	F	VF	XF	Unc
VS2010 (1953)	2.75	4.50	7.00	10.00
VS2011 (1954)	0.65	1.00	2.75	5.00
VS2012 (1955)	0.30	0.50	0.75	1.25
VS2013 (1956)	0.30	0.50	0.75	1.25
VS2014 (1957)	0.30	0.50	0.75	1.25

KM# 736a 5 PAISA Weight: 4.0400 g. Composition: Copper-Nickel

Date	F	VF	XF	Unc
VS2014 (1957)	—	—	—	—

KM# 737 10 PAISA Composition: Bronze

Date	F	VF	XF	Unc
VS2010 (1953)	2.75	4.50	7.00	10.00
VS2011 (1954)	0.15	0.25	0.50	1.00
VS2011 (1954) Restrike	—	—	0.15	0.25
VS2012 (1955)	0.15	0.25	0.50	1.00

KM# 738 20 PAISA Composition: Copper-Nickel

Date	F	VF	XF	Unc
VS2010 (1953)	12.50	20.00	30.00	40.00
VS2010 (1953) Restrike	—	—	2.50	3.00
VS2011 (1954)	32.50	40.00	50.00	60.00

KM# 739 25 PAISA Composition: Copper-Nickel

Date	F	VF	XF	Unc
VS2010 (1953)	2.00	3.50	4.50	6.00
VS2011 (1954)	2.00	3.50	4.50	6.00
VS2012 (1955)	1.25	2.00	2.50	3.50
VS2014 (1957)	1.25	2.00	2.50	3.50

KM# 768 1/5 ASARPHI Weight: 2.3300 g. Composition: Gold

Date	F	VF	XF	Unc
VS2010 (1953)	—	50.00	60.00	100

Note: Coins dated VS2010 are normally found as restrikes ca. 1968

Date	F	VF	XF	Unc
VS2012 (1955)	—	—	—	—

KM# 774 1/4 ASARPHI Weight: 2.9000 g. Composition: Gold

Date	F	VF	XF	Unc
VS2010 (1953)	60.00	70.00	80.00	120

Note: Coins dated VS2010 are normally found as restrikes ca. 1968

Date	F	VF	XF	Unc
VS2012 (1955)	—	—	—	—

DECIMAL COINAGE

100 Paisa = 1 Rupee

KM# 704 1/4 PAISA Composition: Copper

Date	F	VF	XF	Unc
VS2000 (1943)	15.00	25.00	30.00	40.00
VS2004 (1947)	15.00	25.00	30.00	40.00

KM# 705 1/2 PAISA Composition: Copper

Date	F	VF	XF	Unc
VS2004 (1947)	—	25.00	30.00	40.00

KM# 706.1 (KM706) PAISA Composition: Copper
Reverse: Right wreath with sharp end

Date	F	VF	XF	Unc
VS1990 (1933)	0.75	1.50	3.00	5.00
VS1990 (1933)	0.75	1.50	3.00	5.00
VS1991 (1934)	0.75	1.50	3.00	5.00
VS1991 (1934)	0.75	1.50	3.00	5.00
VS1992 (1935)	0.75	1.50	3.00	5.00
VS1992 (1935)	0.75	1.50	3.00	5.00

KM# 706.2 PAISA Composition: Copper Reverse: Right wreath with round end

Date	Mintage	F	VF	XF	Unc
VS1993 (1936)	—	0.75	1.50	3.00	5.00
VS1994 (1937)	456,000	0.75	1.50	3.00	5.00
VS1995 (1938)	—	0.75	1.50	3.00	5.00
VS1996 (1939)	—	0.75	1.50	3.00	5.00

KM# 707a PAISA Composition: Brass

Date	F	VF	XF	Unc
VS2003 (1946)	0.30	0.50	0.75	1.00
VS2004 (1947)	3.00	5.00	7.00	10.00
VS2005 (1948)	0.30	0.50	0.75	1.00
VS2001 (1948)	0.30	0.50	0.75	1.00
VS2006 (1949)	0.60	1.00	1.25	1.75

KM# 707 PAISA Composition: Copper

Date	F	VF	XF	Unc
VS2005 (1948)	0.75	1.25	1.75	2.50

KM# 708 2 PAISA Composition: Copper

Date	VG	F	VF	XF	Unc
VS1992 (1935)	3.00	5.00	8.50	13.50	—

KM# 709.1 2 PAISA Composition: Copper

Date	Mintage	F	VF	XF	Unc
VS1993 (1936)	473,000	1.00	2.00	3.00	5.00
VS1994 (1937)	1,133,000	1.00	2.00	3.00	5.00
VS1995 (1938)	—	1.00	2.00	3.00	5.00
VS1996 (1939)	—	1.00	2.00	3.00	5.00

KM# 709.2 2 PAISA Composition: Copper

Date	F	VF	XF	Unc
VS1992 (1936)	0.60	1.00	1.75	3.00
VS1994 (1937)	0.50	0.75	1.50	2.50
VS1995 (1938)	2.00	3.50	5.00	7.50
VS1996 (1939)	0.30	0.50	1.00	1.50
VS1997 (1940)	0.50	0.75	1.50	2.50
VS1998 (1941)	0.50	0.75	1.50	2.50
VS1999 (1942)	0.50	0.75	1.50	2.50

KM# 710 2 PAISA Composition: Copper

Date	F	VF	XF	Unc
VS1999 (1942)	0.30	0.50	1.00	2.00
VS2000 (1943)	0.30	0.50	1.00	2.00
VS2003 (1946)	0.30	0.50	1.00	2.00
VS2005 (1948)	3.00	5.00	7.00	10.00

KM# 710a 2 PAISA Composition: Brass

Date	F	VF	XF	Unc
VS1999 (1942)	0.30	0.50	1.00	2.00
VS2000 (1943)	0.30	0.50	1.00	2.00
VS2001 (1944)	0.30	0.50	1.00	2.00
VS2005 (1948)	1.75	3.00	5.00	7.50
VS2008 (1951)	0.30	0.50	1.00	2.00
VS2009 (1952)	0.30	0.50	1.00	2.00
VS2010 (1953)	0.30	0.50	1.00	2.00

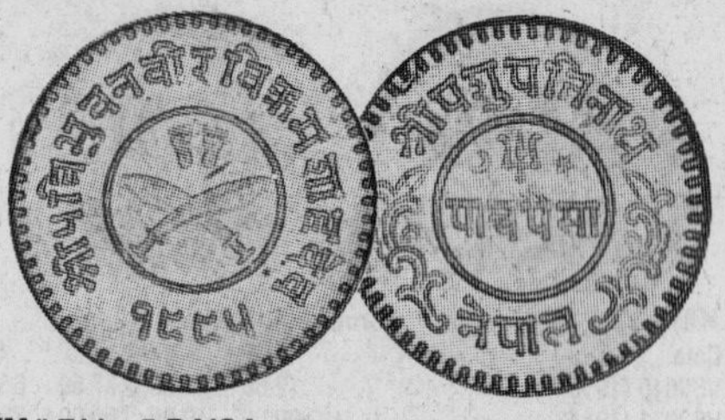

KM# 711 5 PAISA Composition: Copper

Date	Mintage	F	VF	XF	Unc
VS1992 (1935)	—	1.50	3.00	4.50	6.50
VS1993 (1936)	878,000	1.50	3.00	4.50	6.50
VS1994 (1937)	403,000	1.50	3.00	4.50	6.50
VS1995 (1938)	—	1.00	2.00	3.00	5.00
VS1996 (1939)	—	1.50	3.00	4.50	6.50
VS1997 (1940)	—	1.50	3.00	4.50	6.50
VS1998 (1941)	—	—	—	—	—

KM# 712 5 PAISA Composition: Copper-Nickel-Zinc

Date	F	VF	XF	Unc
VS2000 (1943)	0.65	1.00	1.50	2.50
VS2009 (1952)	1.75	3.00	5.00	8.50
VS2010 (1953)	1.25	2.00	3.00	5.00

KM# 712a 5 PAISA Composition: Copper-Nickel

Date	F	VF	XF	Unc
VS2010 (1953) Restrike	0.65	1.00	1.50	2.50

KM# 714 20 PAISA Weight: 2.2161 g. Composition: 0.3330 Silver .0237 oz. ASW

Date	F	VF	XF	Unc
VS1989 (1932)	2.25	4.00	5.00	6.50
VS1991 (1934)	1.75	3.50	4.50	6.00
VS1992 (1935)	1.75	3.50	4.50	6.00
VS1993 (1936)	1.75	3.50	4.50	6.00
VS1994 (1937)	3.75	6.50	10.00	15.00
VS1995 (1938)	1.75	3.50	4.50	6.00
VS1996 (1939)	1.75	3.50	4.50	6.00
VS1997 (1940)	1.75	3.50	4.50	6.00
VS1998 (1941)	1.75	3.50	4.50	6.00
VS1999 (1942)	1.75	3.50	4.50	6.00
VS2000 (1943)	1.75	3.50	4.50	6.00
VS2001 (1944)	1.75	3.50	4.50	6.00
VS2003 (1946)	1.75	3.50	4.50	6.00
VS2004 (1947)	1.75	3.50	4.50	6.00

KM# 715 20 PAISA Weight: 2.2161 g. Composition: 0.3330 Silver .0237 oz. ASW

Date	F	VF	XF	Unc
VS1989 (1932)	2.25	4.00	6.00	8.50

Note: The date VS1989 is given in different style characters. Refer to 50 Paisa KM#719 and 1 Rupee, KM#724 for style

KM# 716 20 PAISA Weight: 2.2161 g. Composition: 0.3330 Silver .0237 oz. ASW

Date	F	VF	XF	Unc
VS2006 (1949)	0.75	1.00	1.25	1.75
VS2007 (1950)	—	—	—	—
VS2009 (1952)	0.75	1.00	1.50	2.50
VS2010 (1953)	0.75	1.00	1.50	2.50

KM# 718 50 PAISA Weight: 5.5403 g. Composition: 0.8000 Silver .1425 oz. ASW

Date	F	VF	XF	Unc
VS1989 (1932)	5.50	6.50	8.00	10.00
VS1991 (1934)	2.50	4.50	7.00	10.00
VS1992 (1935)	2.50	4.50	7.00	10.00
VS1993 (1936)	2.50	4.50	7.00	10.00
VS1994 (1937)	2.50	4.50	7.00	10.00
VS1995 (1938)	2.50	4.50	7.00	10.00
VS1996 (1939)	2.50	4.50	7.00	10.00
VS1997 (1940)	2.50	4.50	7.00	10.00
VS1998 (1941)	2.50	4.50	7.00	10.00
VS1999 (1942)	2.50	4.50	7.00	10.00
VS2000 (1943)	2.50	4.50	7.00	10.00
VS2001 (1944)	2.50	4.50	7.00	10.00
VS2003 (1946)	2.50	4.50	7.00	10.00
VS2004 (1947)	2.50	4.50	7.00	10.00
VS2005 (1948)	2.50	4.50	7.00	10.00

KM# 719 50 PAISA Weight: 5.5403 g. Composition: 0.8000 Silver .1425 oz. ASW

Date	F	VF	XF	Unc
VS1989 (1932)	2.50	4.50	7.00	9.0

Note: The date is given in different style characters

KM# 720 50 PAISA Weight: 5.5403 g. Composition: 0.3330 Silver .0593 oz. ASW Obverse: Four dots around trident

Date	F	VF	XF	Unc
VS2005 (1948)	45.00	65.00	90.00	125

KM# 721 50 PAISA Weight: 5.5403 g. Composition: 0.3330 Silver .0593 oz. ASW Obverse: Without dots around trident

Date	F	VF	XF	Unc
VS2006 (1949)	1.50	2.00	2.75	4.50
VS2007 (1950)	1.50	2.00	2.75	4.50
VS2009/7 (1952)	1.50	2.25	3.00	5.00
VS2009 (1952)	1.50	2.00	2.75	4.50
VS2010 (1953)	1.50	2.00	2.75	4.50

KM# 713 1/16 RUPEE Composition: Silver

Date	F	VF	XF	Unc
VS(19)96 (1939)	12.50	20.00	32.50	50.00

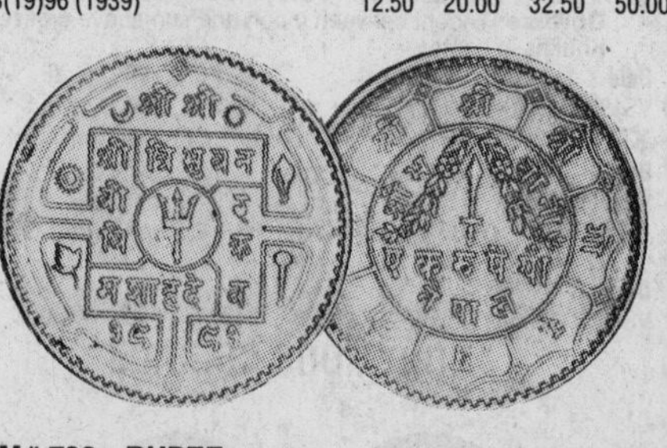

KM# 723 RUPEE Weight: 11.0806 g. Composition: 0.8000 Silver .2850 oz. ASW

Date	Mintage	F	VF	XF	Unc
VS1989 (1932)	—	2.50	5.00	8.00	20.00
VS1991 (1934)	—	2.50	5.00	8.00	16.50
VS1992 (1935)	—	2.50	5.00	8.00	16.50
VS1993 (1936)	1,717,000	2.50	5.00	8.00	16.50
VS1994 (1937)	2,097,000	2.50	5.00	8.00	16.50
VS1995 (1938)	—	2.50	5.00	8.00	16.50

Date	Mintage	F	VF	XF	Unc
VS1996 (1939)	—	2.50	5.00	8.00	16.50
VS1997 (1940)	—	2.50	5.00	8.00	16.50
VS1998 (1941)	—	2.50	5.00	8.00	16.50
VS1999 (1942)	—	2.50	5.00	8.00	16.50
VS2000 (1943)	—	2.50	5.00	8.00	16.50
VS2001 (1944)	—	2.50	5.00	8.00	16.50
VS2003 (1946)	—	2.50	5.00	8.00	16.50
VS2005 (1948)	—	2.50	5.00	8.00	16.50

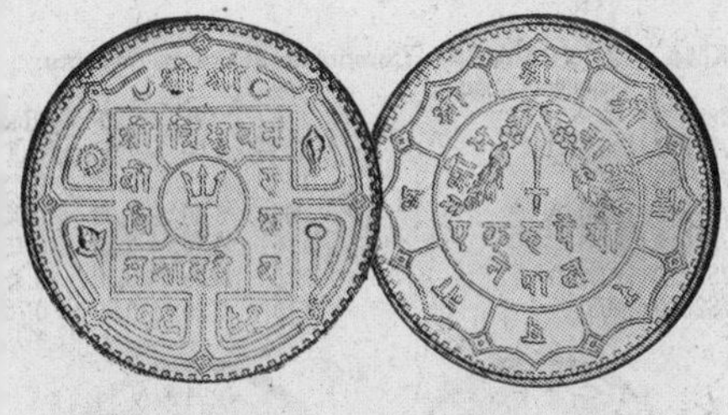

KM# 724 RUPEE **Weight:** 11.0806 g. **Composition:** 0.8000 Silver .2850 oz. ASW

Date	F	VF	XF	Unc
VS1989 (1932)	7.50	10.00	12.50	15.00

Note: The date is given in different style characters

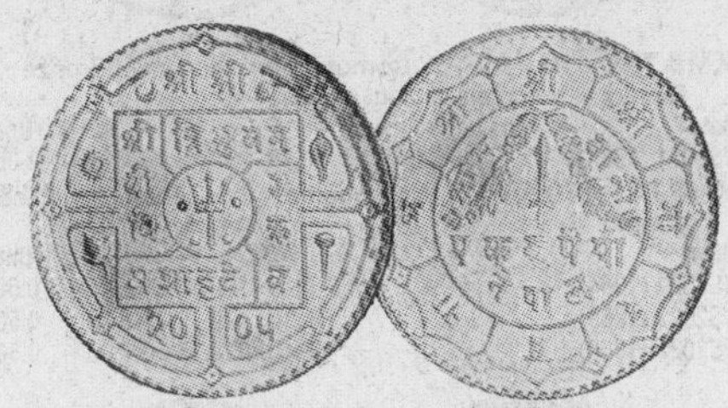

KM# 725 RUPEE **Weight:** 11.0806 g. **Composition:** 0.3330 Silver .1186 oz. ASW **Obverse:** Four dots around trident

Date	F	VF	XF	Unc
VS2005 (1948)	5.00	7.50	10.00	13.50

KM# 726 RUPEE **Weight:** 11.0806 g. **Composition:** 0.3330 Silver .1186 oz. ASW **Obverse:** Without dots around trident

Date	F	VF	XF	Unc
VS2006 (1949)	2.50	3.50	5.00	7.50
VS2007 (1950)	2.50	3.50	5.00	7.50
VS2008 (1951)	2.50	3.50	5.00	7.50
VS2009 (1951)	2.50	3.50	5.00	7.50
VS2010 (1952)	2.50	3.50	5.00	7.50

KM# 741 1/2 ASARPHI **Weight:** 5.8000 g. **Composition:** Gold **Obverse:** Head of Tribhuvan Bir Bikram right on 5-pointed star **Note:** Portrait type.

Date	F	VF	XF	Unc
VS2010 (1953)	—	120	140	170

Note: KM#741 is normally found as a restrike ca. 1968

Gyanendra Bir Bikram
VS2007 / 1950-51AD (first reign)

DECIMAL COINAGE
100 Paisa = 1 Rupee

KM# 729 50 PAISA **Weight:** 5.5403 g. **Composition:** 0.3330 Silver .0593 oz. ASW

Date	Mintage	F	VF	XF	Unc
VS2007 (1950)	26	—	175	275	350

KM# 731 MOHAR **Composition:** Gold

Date	F	VF	XF	Unc
VS2007 (1950) Rare	—	—	—	—

KM# 730 RUPEE **Weight:** 11.0806 g. **Composition:** 0.3330 Silver .1186 oz. ASW

Date	F	VF	XF	Unc
VS2007 (1950)	4.50	6.50	9.00	12.50

KM# 732 TOLA **Composition:** Gold

Date	F	VF	XF	Unc
VS2007 (1950) Rare	—	—	—	—

Trivhuvan Bir Bikram
VS2007-2011 / 1951-1955AD (second reign)

DECIMAL COINAGE
100 Paisa = 1 Rupee

KM# 740 50 PAISA **Composition:** Copper-Nickel **Obverse:** Head of Tribhuvan Bir Bikram right on 5-pointed star

Date	F	VF	XF	Unc
VS2010 (1953)	0.50	1.00	2.00	4.00
VS2011 (1954)	0.35	0.75	1.50	3.00

KM# 742 RUPEE **Composition:** Copper-Nickel **Obverse:** Head of Tribhuvan Bir Bikram right on 5-pointed star **Note:** Equal denticles at rim.

Date	F	VF	XF	Unc
VS2010 (1953)	0.75	1.25	2.25	4.50
VS2011 (1954)	0.75	1.25	2.25	4.50

KM# 743 RUPEE **Composition:** Copper-Nickel **Obverse:** Head of Tribhuvan Bir Bikram right on 5-pointed star **Note:** Unequal denticles at rim.

Date	F	VF	XF	Unc
VS2011 (1954)	0.75	1.25	2.25	4.50

KM# 744 ASARPHI **Weight:** 11.6600 g. **Composition:** Gold **Obverse:** Head of Tribhuvan Bir Bikram right on 5-pointed star

Date	F	VF	XF	Unc
VS2010 (1953)	—	175	200	250

Note: KM#744 normally found as a restrike ca. 1968

Mahendra Bir Bikram
VS2012-2028 / 1955-1971AD

DECIMAL COINAGE
100 Paisa = 1 Rupee

KM# 745.1 (KM745) PAISA **Composition:** Brass **Subject:** Mahendra Coronation

Date	F	VF	XF	Unc
VS2013 (1956) Narrow rim	0.30	0.50	0.75	1.00
VS2013 (1956) Narrow rim	0.30	0.50	0.75	1.00

KM# 745.2 PAISA **Composition:** Brass **Subject:** Mahendra coronation

Date	F	VF	XF	Unc
VS2015 (1956) Wide rim	0.30	0.50	0.75	1.00

KM# 746 PAISA **Composition:** Brass **Reverse:** Numerals with shading

Date	F	VF	XF	Unc
VS2014 (1957)	0.10	0.15	0.25	0.40
VS2015 (1958)	0.10	0.15	0.25	0.40
VS2018 (1961)	0.10	0.15	0.25	0.40
VS2019 (1962)	0.10	0.15	0.25	0.40
VS2020 (1963)	0.10	0.15	0.25	0.40

KM# 747 PAISA **Composition:** Brass **Reverse:** Numerals without shading

Date	F	VF	XF	Unc
VS2021 (1964)	0.10	0.15	0.20	0.30
VS2022 (1965)	0.10	0.15	0.25	0.40

KM# 748 PAISA **Composition:** Aluminum **Reverse:** National flower

Date	Mintage	F	VF	XF	Unc
VS2023 (1966)	—	—	0.10	0.15	0.25
VS2025 (1968)	—	—	0.10	0.15	0.25
VS2026 (1969)	—	—	0.10	0.15	0.25
VS2027 (1970) Proof	2,187	Value: 1.25			
VS2028 (1971)	—	—	0.10	0.15	0.25
VS2028 (1971) Proof	2,380	Value: 1.25			

KM# 750.1 2 PAISA **Composition:** Brass **Subject:** Mahendra Coronation **Note:** Narrow rim.

Date	F	VF	XF	Unc
VS2013 (1956)	0.30	0.50	0.75	1.00

KM# 750.2 2 PAISA **Composition:** Brass **Subject:** Mahendra coronation **Note:** Wide rim.

Date	F	VF	XF	Unc
VS2013 (1956)	0.30	0.50	0.75	1.00

KM# 751 2 PAISA **Composition:** Brass **Reverse:** Numerals wtih shading

Date	F	VF	XF	Unc
VS2014 (1957)	0.10	0.15	0.25	0.40
VS2015 (1958)	0.10	0.15	0.25	0.40
VS2016 (1959)	0.10	0.15	0.25	0.40
VS2018 (1961)	0.10	0.15	0.25	0.40
VS2019 (1962)	0.10	0.15	0.25	0.40
VS2020 (1963)	0.10	0.15	0.25	0.40

KM# 752 2 PAISA **Composition:** Brass **Reverse:** Numerals wtihout shading

Date	F	VF	XF	Unc
VS2021 (1964)	0.10	0.15	0.20	0.35
VS2022 (1965)	0.10	0.15	0.25	0.50
VS2023 (1966)	0.10	0.15	0.25	0.50

KM# 753 2 PAISA **Composition:** Aluminum **Reverse:** Himalayan Monal pheasant

Date	Mintage	F	VF	XF	Unc
VS2023 (1966)	—	—	0.10	0.15	0.25
VS2024 (1967)	—	—	0.10	0.15	0.25
VS2025 (1968)	—	—	0.10	0.15	0.25
VS2026 (1969)	—	—	0.10	0.15	0.25
VS2027 (1970)	—	—	0.10	0.15	0.25
VS2027 (1970) Proof	2,187	Value: 1.50			
VS2028 (1971)	—	—	0.10	0.15	0.25
VS2028 (1971) Proof	2,380	Value: 1.50			

KM# 756.1 5 PAISA **Composition:** Bronze **Subject:** Mahendra Coronation **Note:** Wide rim with accent mark.

Date	F	VF	XF	Unc
VS2013 (1955)	10.00	20.00	30.00	40.00

KM# 756.2 5 PAISA **Composition:** Bronze **Subject:** Mahendra coronation **Note:** Narrow rim.

Date	F	VF	XF	Unc
VS2013 (1955) Restrike	0.35	0.60	1.00	1.50

KM# 756.3 5 PAISA **Composition:** Bronze **Subject:** Mahendra coronation **Note:** Without accent mark.

Date	F	VF	XF	Unc
VS2013 (1955)	1.00	2.00	3.00	5.00

KM# 757 5 PAISA **Composition:** Bronze **Reverse:** Numerals with shading

Date	F	VF	XF	Unc
VS2014 (1957)	0.10	0.20	0.30	0.75
VS2015 (1958)	0.10	0.20	0.30	0.75
VS2016 (1959)	0.10	0.30	0.50	1.00
VS2017 (1960)	0.10	0.20	0.30	0.75
VS2018 (1961)	0.10	0.20	0.30	0.75
VS2019 (1962)	0.10	0.20	0.30	0.75
VS2020 (1963)	0.10	0.20	0.30	0.75

KM# 758 5 PAISA **Composition:** Aluminum-Bronze **Reverse:** Numerals without shading

Date	F	VF	XF	Unc
VS2021 (1964)	0.50	1.00	1.50	2.50

KM# 758a 5 PAISA **Composition:** Bronze

Date	F	VF	XF	Unc
VS2021 (1964)	0.10	0.15	0.25	0.50
VS2022 (1965)	0.10	0.15	0.30	0.60
VS2023 (1966)	0.10	0.15	0.30	0.60

KM# 759 5 PAISA **Composition:** Aluminum

Date	Mintage	F	VF	XF	Unc
VS2023 (1966)	—	—	0.15	0.25	0.50
VS2024 (1967)	—	—	0.10	0.20	0.35
VS2025 (1968)	—	—	0.10	0.20	0.35
VS2026 (1969)	—	—	0.10	0.20	0.25
VS2027 (1970)	—	—	0.10	0.20	0.35
VS2027 (1970) Proof	2,187	Value: 1.75			
VS2028 (1971)	—	—	0.10	0.20	0.35
VS2028 (1971) Proof	2,038	Value: 1.75			

KM# 761 10 PAISA **Composition:** Bronze **Subject:** Mahendra Coronation

Date	F	VF	XF	Unc
VS2013 (1956)	0.25	0.50	0.75	1.50

KM# 762 10 PAISA **Composition:** Bronze **Reverse:** Numerals with shading

Date	F	VF	XF	Unc
VS2014 (1957)	2.75	4.50	7.00	10.00
VS2015 (1958)	0.15	0.25	0.50	0.75
VS2016 (1959)	3.00	5.00	7.00	10.00
VS2018 (1961)	0.15	0.25	0.50	0.75
VS2019 (1962)	0.15	0.25	0.50	0.75
VS2020 (1963)	0.15	0.25	0.50	0.75

KM# 763 10 PAISA **Composition:** Aluminum-Bronze **Reverse:** Numerals without shading

Date	F	VF	XF	Unc
VS2021 (1964)	0.75	1.25	2.00	3.00

KM# 764 10 PAISA **Composition:** Bronze **Note:** Modified design.

Date	F	VF	XF	Unc
VS2021 (1964)	0.10	0.15	0.25	0.50
VS2022 (1965)	0.10	0.15	0.25	0.50
VS2023 (1966)	0.10	0.15	0.25	0.50

KM# 765 10 PAISA **Composition:** Brass

Date	Mintage	F	VF	XF	Unc
VS2023 (1966)	—	—	0.15	0.25	0.50
VS2024 (1967)	—	—	0.15	0.25	0.50
VS2025 (1968)	—	—	15.00	17.50	20.00
VS2026 (1969)	—	—	0.10	0.20	0.35
VS2027 (1970)	—	—	0.10	0.20	0.35
VS2027 (1970) Proof	2,187	Value: 2.00			
VS2028 (1971)	—	—	0.10	0.20	0.35
VS2028 (1971) Proof	2,380	Value: 2.00			

Note: Birendra Bir Bikram also struck a 10 Paisa VS2028, see KM#806

KM# 766 10 PAISA **Composition:** Brass **Series:** F.A.O.

Date	Mintage	F	VF	XF	Unc
VS2028 (1971)	1,500,000	—	0.10	0.15	0.20

KM# 770 25 PAISA **Composition:** Brass **Subject:** Mahendra Coronation

Date	F	VF	XF	Unc
VS2013 (1956)	0.30	0.50	0.70	1.00

KM# 771 25 PAISA **Composition:** Brass **Obverse:** Four characters in line above trident **Reverse:** Small character at bottom (outer circle)

Date	F	VF	XF	Unc
VS2015 (1958)	1.50	2.50	4.00	6.00
VS2018 (1961)	0.25	0.40	0.60	0.80
VS2020 (1963)	0.25	0.40	0.60	0.80
VS2022 (1965)	2.00	3.50	6.00	9.00

KM# 771a 25 PAISA **Weight:** 2.9900 g. **Composition:** 840.0000 Silver .0913 oz. ASW

Date	F	VF	XF	Unc
VS2017/615 (1960)	—	—	—	100

KM# 772 25 PAISA **Composition:** Copper-Nickel **Reverse:** Large different character at bottom **Note:** Two varieties of moon (obverse at upper left) exist as open crescent and almost closed circle.

Date	F	VF	XF	Unc
VS2021 (1964)	0.30	0.50	0.70	1.00
VS2022 (1965)	0.30	0.50	0.70	1.00
VS2023 (1966)	0.30	0.50	0.70	1.00

KM# 773 25 PAISA **Composition:** Copper-Nickel **Obverse:** Five characters in line above trident

Date		Mintage	F	VF	XF	Unc
VS2024 (1967)		—	—	0.35	0.50	0.75
VS2025 (1968)		—	—	15.00	20.00	25.00
VS2026 (1969)		—	—	0.35	0.50	0.75
VS2027 (1970)		—	—	0.35	0.50	0.75
VS2027 (1970)	Proof	2,187	Value: 2.50			
VS2028 (1971)		—	—	0.35	0.50	0.75
VS2028 (1971)	Proof	2,380	Value: 2.50			
VS2030 (1973)		—	—	0.35	0.50	0.75

KM# 777 50 PAISA **Composition:** Copper-Nickel **Reverse:** Small character at bottom

Date	F	VF	XF	Unc
VS2011 (1954)	0.50	1.00	1.50	3.00
VS2012 (1955)	0.25	0.50	0.75	1.00
VS2013 (1956)	0.25	0.50	1.00	2.00
VS2014 (1957)	0.25	0.50	1.00	2.00
VS2015 (1958)	0.25	0.50	1.00	2.00
VS2016 (1959)	0.25	0.50	1.00	2.00
VS2017 (1960)	0.25	0.30	0.75	1.25
VS2018 (1961)	0.25	0.50	1.00	2.00
VS2020 (1963)	0.25	0.30	0.75	1.50

KM# 795 50 PAISA **Composition:** Copper-Nickel **Note:** In the name of "Queen Ratna Rajya Lakshmi".

Date	F	VF	XF	Unc
VS2012 (1955)	3,000	100	125	150

KM# 776 50 PAISA **Composition:** Copper-Nickel **Subject:** Mahendra Coronation

Date	F	VF	XF	Unc
VS2013 (1956)	0.35	0.75	1.00	1.50

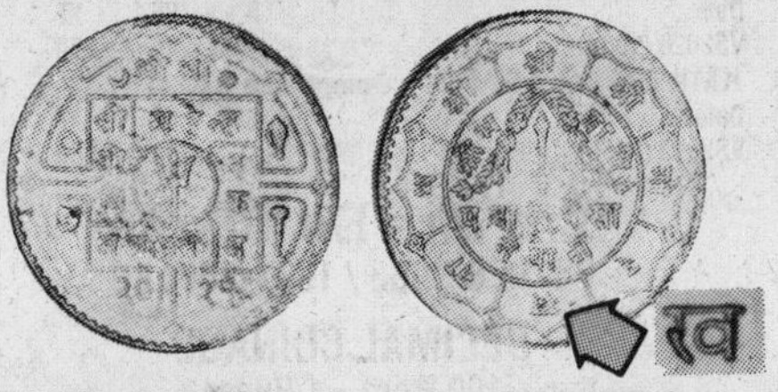

KM# 778 50 PAISA **Composition:** Copper-Nickel **Reverse:** Large different character at bottom

Date	F	VF	XF	Unc
VS2021 (1964)	0.25	0.35	0.50	0.75
VS2022 (1965)	0.25	0.50	0.75	1.50
VS2023 (1966)	0.25	0.50	0.75	1.00

KM# 779 50 PAISA **Composition:** Copper-Nickel **Obverse:** Four characters in line above trident **Size:** 23.5 mm. **Note:** Reduced size.

Date	F	VF	XF	Unc
VS2023 (1966)	0.25	0.50	0.75	1.50

KM# 780 50 PAISA **Composition:** Copper-Nickel **Obverse:** Five characters in line above trident

Date		Mintage	F	VF	XF	Unc
VS2025 (1968)		—	—	0.30	0.50	1.00
VS2026 (1969)		—	—	0.30	0.50	0.85
VS2027 (1970)	Proof	2,187	Value: 3.00			
VS2028 (1971)	Proof	2,380	Value: 3.00			
VS2030 (1973)		—	—	0.30	0.50	0.85

KM# 784 RUPEE **Composition:** Copper-Nickel

Date	F	VF	XF	Unc
VS2011 (1954)	1.25	2.25	3.50	5.00
VS2012 (1955)	1.00	1.75	2.50	4.00

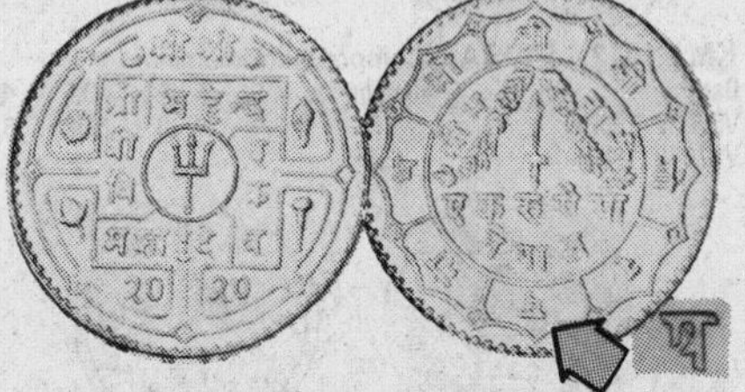

KM# 785 RUPEE **Composition:** Copper-Nickel **Reverse:** Small character at bottom **Note:** Reduced size.

Date	F	VF	XF	Unc
VS2012 (1955)	0.50	0.85	1.25	1.75
VS2013 (1956)	0.50	0.85	1.25	1.75
VS2014 (1957)	0.50	0.85	1.25	1.75
VS2015 (1958)	0.50	0.85	1.25	1.75
VS2016 (1959)	0.50	0.85	1.25	1.75
VS2018 (1961)	0.50	0.85	1.25	1.75
VS2020 (1963)	0.50	0.85	1.25	1.75

KM# 797 RUPEE **Composition:** Copper-Nickel **Note:** In the name of "Queen Ratna Rajya Lakshmi".

Date	Mintage	F	VF	XF	Unc
VS2012 (1955)	2,000	—	100	150	175

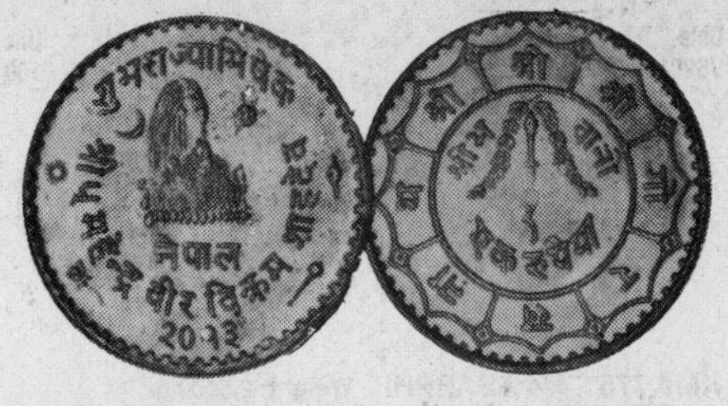

KM# 790 RUPEE **Composition:** Copper-Nickel **Subject:** Mahendra Coronation

Date	F	VF	XF	Unc
VS2013 (1956)	—	1.25	1.75	2.50

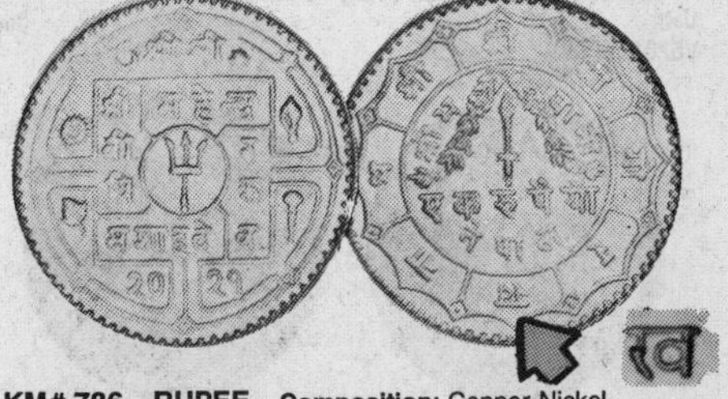

KM# 786 RUPEE **Composition:** Copper-Nickel **Reverse:** Large character at bottom

Date	F	VF	XF	Unc
VS2021 (1964)	0.50	0.75	1.00	1.50
VS2022 (1965)	0.50	1.00	1.50	2.50
VS2023 (1966)	4.50	7.50	10.00	15.00

KM# 787 RUPEE **Composition:** Copper-Nickel **Obverse:** Four characters in line above trident **Size:** 27 mm. **Note:** Reduced size.

Date	F	VF	XF	Unc
VS2023 (1966)	0.75	1.00	1.35	2.00

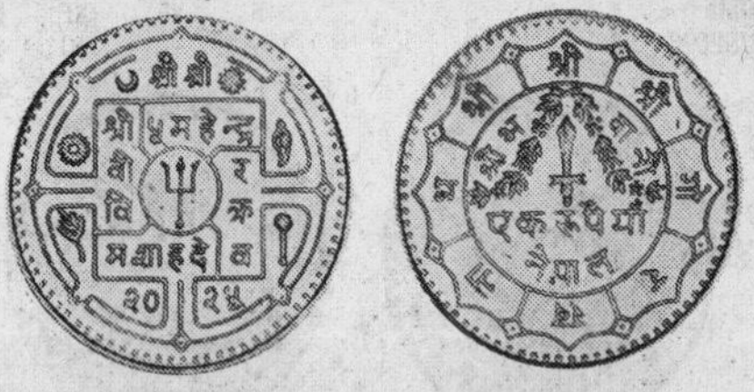

KM# 788 RUPEE **Composition:** Copper-Nickel **Obverse:** Five characters in line above trident

Date		Mintage	F	VF	XF	Unc
VS2025 (1968)		—	—	1.00	1.50	2.00
VS2026 (1969)		—	—	1.00	1.40	2.00
VS2027 (1970)	Proof	2,187	Value: 4.50			
VS2028 (1971)	Proof	2,380	Value: 4.50			

KM# 794 10 RUPEE **Weight:** 15.6000 g. **Composition:** 0.6000 Silver .3009 oz. ASW **Series:** F.A.O. **Obverse:** Bust of Mahendra Bir Bikram left

Date	Mintage	F	VF	XF	Unc
VS2025 (1968)	1,000,000	—	2.50	3.50	6.00

KM# 767 1/6 ASARPHI **Weight:** 1.9000 g. **Composition:** Gold **Subject:** Mahendra Coronation

Date	F	VF	XF	Unc
VS2013 (1956)	—	50.00	60.00	100

KM# 775 1/4 ASARPHI **Weight:** 2.5000 g. **Composition:** Gold **Note:** Reduced weight

Date	F	VF	XF	Unc
VS2026 (1969)	—	—	75.00	110

KM# 796 1/2 ASARPHI **Composition:** Gold **Note:** In the name of "Queen Ratna Rajya Lakshmi".

Date	F	VF	XF	Unc
VS2012 (1955)	—	—	—	—

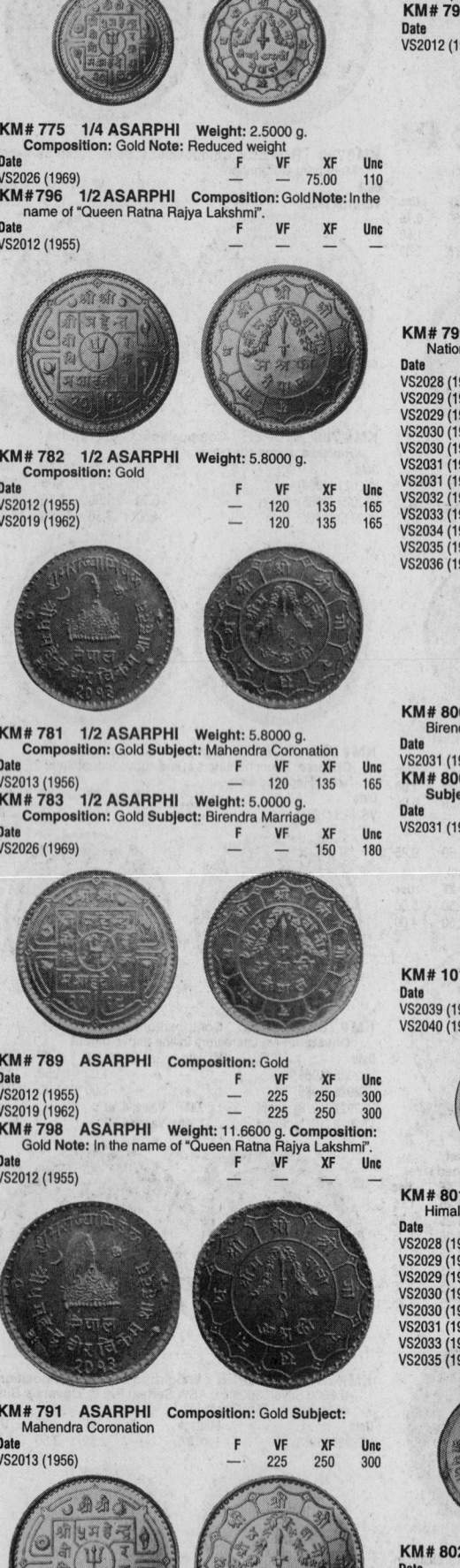

KM# 782 1/2 ASARPHI **Weight:** 5.8000 g. **Composition:** Gold

Date	F	VF	XF	Unc
VS2012 (1955)	—	120	135	165
VS2019 (1962)	—	120	135	165

KM# 781 1/2 ASARPHI **Weight:** 5.8000 g. **Composition:** Gold **Subject:** Mahendra Coronation

Date	F	VF	XF	Unc
VS2013 (1956)	—	120	135	165

KM# 783 1/2 ASARPHI **Weight:** 5.0000 g. **Composition:** Gold **Subject:** Birendra Marriage

Date	F	VF	XF	Unc
VS2026 (1969)	—	—	150	180

KM# 789 ASARPHI **Composition:** Gold

Date	F	VF	XF	Unc
VS2012 (1955)	—	225	250	300
VS2019 (1962)	—	225	250	300

KM# 798 ASARPHI **Weight:** 11.6600 g. **Composition:** Gold **Note:** In the name of "Queen Ratna Rajya Lakshmi".

Date	F	VF	XF	Unc
VS2012 (1955)	—	—	—	—

KM# 791 ASARPHI **Composition:** Gold **Subject:** Mahendra Coronation

Date	F	VF	XF	Unc
VS2013 (1956)	—	225	250	300

KM# 792 ASARPHI **Weight:** 10.0000 g. **Composition:** Gold

Date	F	VF	XF	Unc
VS2026 (1969)	—	225	250	300

KM# 793 2 ASARFI **Composition:** Gold

Date	F	VF	XF	Unc
VS2012 (1955)	—	500	550	625

Birendra Bir Bikram
VS2028-2058 / 1971-2001AD

DECIMAL COINAGE
100 Paisa = 1 Rupee

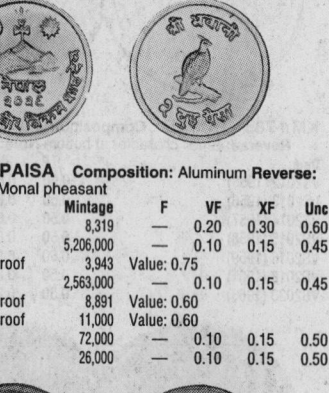

KM# 799 PAISA **Composition:** Aluminum **Reverse:** National flower

Date	Mintage	F	VF	XF	Unc
VS2028 (1971)	10,000	—	0.20	0.30	0.40
VS2029 (1972)	3,036,000	—	0.10	0.15	0.25
VS2029 (1972) Proof	3,943	Value: 0.60			
VS2030 (1973)	1,279,000	—	0.10	0.15	0.25
VS2030 (1973) Proof	8,891	Value: 0.40			
VS2031 (1974)	430,000	—	0.10	0.15	0.25
VS2031 (1974) Proof	11,000	Value: 0.40			
VS2032 (1975)	324,000	—	0.10	0.15	0.25
VS2033 (1976)	217,000	—	—	0.10	0.25
VS2034 (1977)	1,040,000	—	0.10	0.15	0.25
VS2035 (1978)	394,000	—	0.10	0.15	0.25
VS2036 (1979)	—	—	0.10	0.15	0.25

KM# 800 PAISA **Composition:** Aluminum **Subject:** Birendra Coronation

Date	Mintage	F	VF	XF	Unc
VS2031 (1974)	75,000	—	0.10	0.15	0.25

KM# 800a PAISA **Composition:** Copper-Nickel **Subject:** Birendra Coronation

Date	Mintage	F	VF	XF	Unc
VS2031 (1974) Proof	1,000	Value: 2.50			

KM# 1012 PAISA **Composition:** Aluminum

Date	Mintage	F	VF	XF	Unc
VS2039 (1982)	—	—	4.00	6.00	8.00
VS2040 (1983)	42,000	—	—	—	—

KM# 801 2 PAISA **Composition:** Aluminum **Reverse:** Himalayan Monal pheasant

Date	Mintage	F	VF	XF	Unc
VS2028 (1971)	8,319	—	0.20	0.30	0.60
VS2029 (1972)	5,206,000	—	0.10	0.15	0.45
VS2029 (1972) Proof	3,943	Value: 0.75			
VS2030 (1973)	2,563,000	—	0.10	0.15	0.45
VS2030 (1973) Proof	8,891	Value: 0.60			
VS2031 (1974) Proof	11,000	Value: 0.60			
VS2033 (1976)	72,000	—	0.10	0.15	0.50
VS2035 (1978)	26,000	—	0.10	0.15	0.50

KM# 802 5 PAISA **Composition:** Aluminum

Date	Mintage	F	VF	XF	Unc
VS2028 (1971)	3,700,000	—	0.10	0.20	0.50
VS2029 (1972)	23,578,000	—	0.10	0.20	0.50
VS2029 (1972) Proof	3,943	Value: 0.85			
VS2030 (1973)	12,320,000	—	0.10	0.20	0.50
VS2030 (1973) Proof	8,891	Value: 0.60			
VS2031 (1974)	15,730,000	—	0.10	0.20	0.5
VS2031 (1974) Proof	11,000	Value: 0.60			
VS2032 (1975)	19,747,000	—	0.10	0.20	0.5
VS2033 (1976)	29,619,000	—	0.10	0.20	0.5
VS2034 (1977)	27,222,000	—	0.10	0.20	0.5
VS2035 (1978)	27,613,000	—	0.10	0.20	0.5
VS2036 (1979)	—	—	0.10	0.20	0.5
VS2037 (1980)	13,235,000	—	0.10	0.20	0.5
VS2038 (1981)	15,137,000	—	0.10	0.20	0.5
VS2039 (1982)	8,971,000	—	0.10	0.20	0.5

KM# 803 5 PAISA **Composition:** Aluminum **Series:** F.A.O

Date	Mintage	F	VF	XF	Unc
VS2031 (1974)	4,584,000	—	0.10	0.15	0.2

KM# 804 5 PAISA **Composition:** Aluminum **Subject:** Birendra Coronation

Date	Mintage	F	VF	XF	Unc
VS2031 (1974)	2,869,000	—	0.10	0.25	0.50

KM# 804a 5 PAISA **Composition:** Copper-Nickel **Subject:** Birendra Coronation

Date	Mintage	F	VF	XF	Unc
VS2031 (1974) Proof	1,000	Value: 3.00			

KM# 1013 5 PAISA **Composition:** Aluminum

Date	Mintage	F	VF	XF	Unc
VS2039 (1982)	8,971,000	—	7.00	10.00	15.00
VS2040 (1983)	6,430,000	—	—	0.10	0.25
VS2041 (1984)	9,634,000	—	—	0.10	0.25
VS2042 (1985)	58,000	—	—	0.10	0.25
VS2043 (1986)	2,937,000	—	—	0.10	0.25
VS2044 (1987)	3,126,000	—	—	0.10	0.25
VS2045 (1988)	1,030,000	—	—	0.10	0.25
VS2046 (1989)	—	—	—	0.10	0.25
VS2047 (1990)	—	—	—	0.10	0.25

KM# 806 10 PAISA **Composition:** Brass

Date	Mintage	F	VF	XF	Unc
VS2028 (1971)	5,035,000	—	0.25	0.40	1.00

Note: Birendra Bir Bikram also struck a 10 Paisa VS2028, see KM#765

KM# 807 10 PAISA **Composition:** Brass

Date	Mintage	F	VF	XF	Unc
VS2029 (1972)	3,297,000	—	0.15	0.25	0.40
VS2029 (1972) Proof	3,943	Value: 1.00			
VS2030 (1973)	5,670,000	—	0.15	0.25	0.40
VS2030 (1973) Proof	8,891	Value: 0.70			
VS2031 (1974) Proof	11,000	Value: 0.70			

KM# 808 10 PAISA **Composition:** Aluminum **Subject:** Birendra Coronation

Date	Mintage	F	VF	XF	Unc
VS2031 (1974)	192,000	—	0.10	0.20	0.35

KM# 808a 10 PAISA **Composition:** Copper-Nickel **Subject:** Birendra Coronation

Date	Mintage	F	VF	XF	Unc
VS2031 (1974) Proof	1,000	Value: 3.50			

KM# 809 10 PAISA **Composition:** Brass **Series:** F.A.O. International Women's Year

Date	Mintage	F	VF	XF	Unc
VS2032 (1975)	2,500,000	—	0.10	0.15	0.25

KM# 810 10 PAISA **Composition:** Brass **Subject:** Agricultural Developement

Date	Mintage	F	VF	XF	Unc
VS2033 (1976)	10,000,000	—	0.10	0.15	0.25

KM# 811 10 PAISA **Composition:** Aluminum **Series:** International Year of the Child

Date	Mintage	F	VF	XF	Unc
VS2036 (1979)	213,000	—	0.10	0.15	0.25

KM# 812 10 PAISA **Composition:** Aluminum **Subject:** Education for Village Women

Date	F	VF	XF	Unc
VS2036 (1979)	—	0.10	0.15	0.50

KM# 1014.1 10 PAISA **Composition:** Aluminum **Reverse:** Large ears of grain

Date	Mintage	F	VF	XF	Unc
VS2039 (1982)	796	—	7.00	10.00	15.00
VS2040 (1983)	—	—	—	0.10	0.30
VS2041 (1984)	7,834,000	—	—	0.10	0.30
VS2042 (1985)	99,000	—	—	0.10	0.30

KM# 1014.2 10 PAISA **Composition:** Aluminum **Reverse:** Small ears of grain

Date	Mintage	F	VF	XF	Unc
VS2041 (1984)	—	—	—	0.10	0.30
VS2042 (1985)	Inc. above	—	—	0.10	0.30
VS2043 (1986)	10,000	—	—	0.10	0.30
VS2044 (1987)	30,172,000	—	—	0.10	0.30
VS2045 (1988)	4,140,000	—	—	0.10	0.30
VS2046 (1989)	—	—	—	0.10	0.30
VS2047 (1990)	—	—	—	0.10	0.30
VS2048 (1991)	—	—	—	0.10	0.30

KM# 1014.3 10 PAISA **Composition:** Aluminum **Size:** 17 mm. **Note:** Reduced size.

Date	F	VF	XF	Unc
VS2051 (1994)	—	—	0.10	0.30
VS2052 (1995)	—	—	0.10	0.30
VS2053 (1996)	—	—	0.10	0.30
VS2054 (1997)	—	—	0.10	0.30
VS2055 (1998)	—	—	0.10	0.30
VS2056 (1999)	—	—	0.10	0.30
VS2057 (2000)	—	—	0.10	0.30

KM# 813 20 PAISA **Composition:** Brass **Series:** F.A.O.

Date	Mintage	F	VF	XF	Unc
VS2035 (1978)	234,000	—	0.35	0.75	1.00

KM# 814 20 PAISA **Composition:** Brass **Series:** International Year of the Child

Date	Mintage	F	VF	XF	Unc
VS2036 (1979)	30,000	—	0.35	0.75	1.00

KM# 815 25 PAISA **Weight:** 3.0000 g. **Composition:** Copper-Nickel **Note:** Varieties exist.

Date	Mintage	F	VF	XF	Unc
VS2028 (1971)	5,691	—	0.40	0.60	0.80
Note: Line missing					
VS2029 (1972) Proof	3,943	Value: 1.25			
VS2030 (1973)	8,676,000	—	0.30	0.40	0.50
VS2030 (1973) Proof	8,891	Value: 0.80			
VS2031 (1974)	1,172,000	—	0.35	0.50	0.75
VS2031 (1974) Proof	11,000	Value: 0.80			
VS2032 (1975)	4,584,000	—	0.30	0.40	0.50
VS2033 (1976)	1,837,000	—	0.30	0.40	0.50
VS2034 (1977)	3,808,000	—	0.30	0.40	0.50
VS2035 (1978)	5,964,000	—	0.30	0.40	0.50
VS2036 (1979)	—	—	0.30	0.40	0.50
VS2037 (1980)	2,047,000	—	0.30	0.40	0.50
VS2038 (1981)	1,580,000	—	0.30	0.40	0.50
VS2039 (1982)	7,185,000	—	0.30	0.40	0.50

KM# 816.1 25 PAISA **Composition:** Copper-Nickel **Subject:** Birendra Coronation

Date	Mintage	F	VF	XF	Unc
VS2031 (1974)	431,000	—	0.35	0.50	0.75

KM# 816.2 25 PAISA **Composition:** Copper-Nickel **Subject:** Birendra Coronation **Edge:** Reeded

Date	Mintage	F	VF	XF	Unc
VS2031 (1974) Proof	1,000	Value: 4.00			

KM# 817 25 PAISA **Composition:** Brass **Series:** World Food Day

Date	Mintage	F	VF	XF	Unc
VS2038 (1981)	2,000,000	—	—	0.10	0.30

KM# 818 25 PAISA **Composition:** Brass **Series:** International Year of Disabled Persons

Date	F	VF	XF	Unc
VS2038 (1981)	—	0.10	0.25	0.50

KM# 1015.1 25 PAISA **Composition:** Aluminum **Obverse:** Royal crown

Date	Mintage	F	VF	XF	Unc
VS2039 (1982)	—	—	4.00	6.00	8.00
VS2040 (1983)	7,603,000	—	0.10	0.25	0.50
VS2041 (1984)	15,534,000	—	0.10	0.25	0.50
VS2042 (1985)	12,586,000	—	0.10	0.25	0.50
VS2043 (1986)	54,000	—	0.10	0.25	0.50
VS2044 (1987)	13,633,000	—	0.10	0.25	0.50
VS2045 (1988)	13,046,000	—	0.10	0.25	0.50
VS2046 (1989)	—	—	0.10	0.25	0.50
VS2047 (1990)	—	—	0.10	0.25	0.50
VS2048 (1991)	—	—	0.10	0.25	0.50
VS2049 (1992)	—	—	0.10	0.25	0.50
VS2050 (1993)	—	—	0.10	0.25	0.50

KM# 1015.2 25 PAISA **Composition:** Aluminum **Obverse:** Royal crown **Size:** 20 mm. **Note:** Reduced size.

Date	F	VF	XF	Unc
VS2051 (1994)	—	0.10	0.25	0.50
VS2052 (1995)	—	0.10	0.25	0.50
VS2053 (1996)	—	0.10	0.25	0.50
VS2054 (1997)	—	0.10	0.25	0.50
VS2055 (1998)	—	0.10	0.25	0.50
VS2056 (1999)	—	0.10	0.25	0.50
VS2057 (2000)	—	0.10	0.25	0.50

KM# 821a 50 PAISA **Composition:** Copper-Nickel **Size:** 19 mm.

Date	Mintage	F	VF	XF	Unc
VS2039 (1971)	Inc. above	—	0.10	0.25	0.50
VS2040 (1983)	72,000	—	0.10	0.25	0.50
VS2041 (1984)	5,917,000	—	0.10	0.25	0.50

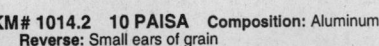

KM# 821 50 PAISA **Weight:** 5.0000 g. **Composition:** Copper-Nickel **Note:** Obverse die variations are known to exist.

Date	Mintage	F	VF	XF	Unc
VS2028 (1971)	5,343	—	0.35	0.50	1.00
VS2029 (1972)	347,000	—	0.35	0.50	0.90
VS2029 (1972) Proof	3,943	Value: 1.50			
VS2030 (1973)	998,000	—	0.35	0.50	0.90
VS2030 (1973) Proof	8,891	Value: 1.00			
VS2031 (1974)	16,000	—	0.35	0.50	1.00
VS2031 (1974) Proof	11,000	Value: 1.00			
VS2032 (1975)	227,000	—	0.35	0.50	0.90
VS2033 (1976)	3,446,000	—	0.35	0.50	0.75
VS2034 (1977)	6,016,000	—	0.35	0.50	0.75
VS2035 (1978)	2,355,000	—	0.35	0.50	0.75
VS2036 (1979)	—	—	0.35	0.50	0.75
VS2037 (1980)	4,861,000	—	0.35	0.50	0.75
VS2038 (1981)	929,000	—	0.35	0.50	0.75
VS2039 (1982)	2,954,000	—	0.35	0.50	0.75

KM# 822.1 50 PAISA **Composition:** Copper-Nickel **Subject:** Birendra Coronation **Note:** One millimeter thick.

Date	Mintage	F	VF	XF	Unc
VS2031 (1974)	136,000	—	0.50	0.75	1.25

KM# 822.2 50 PAISA **Composition:** Copper-Nickel **Subject:** Birendra Coronation **Edge:** Reeded **Note:** 1.5 millimeters thick.

Date	Mintage	F	VF	XF	Unc
VS2031 (1974) Proof	1,000	Value: 5.00			

KM# 846 50 PAISA **Composition:** Copper-Nickel **Note:** In the name of Queen Aishvarya Rajya Lakshmi

Date	F	VF	XF	Unc
VS2031 (1974)	—	—	—	100

KM# 823 50 PAISA **Composition:** Copper-Nickel **Series:** World Food Day

Date	Mintage	F	VF	XF	Unc
VS2038 (1981)	2,000,000	—	0.10	0.30	0.60

KM# 824 50 PAISA **Composition:** Copper-Nickel **Series:** Internatinal Year of Disabled Persons

Date	F	VF	XF	Unc
VS2038 (1981)	—	0.50	0.75	1.25

KM# 1016 50 PAISA **Composition:** Copper-Nickel **Subject:** Family Planning

Date	F	VF	XF	Unc
VS2041 (1984)	—	0.10	0.25	0.50

KM# 1018.1 50 PAISA **Composition:** Stainless Steel **Obverse:** Smaller trident in center **Size:** 23.5 mm.

Date	Mintage	F	VF	XF	Unc
VS2044 (1987)	6,341,000	—	0.10	0.25	0.50
VS2045 (1988)	7,350,000	—	0.10	0.25	0.50

Note: Varieties with small and large Nepalese "5" exist

Date	Mintage	F	VF	XF	Unc
VS2046 (1989)	—	—	0.10	0.25	0.50

KM# 1018.2 50 PAISA **Composition:** Stainless Steel **Obverse:** Larger trident in center

Date	F	VF	XF	Unc
VS2047 (1990)	—	0.10	0.25	0.50
VS2048 (1991)	—	0.10	0.25	0.50
VS2049 (1992)	—	0.10	0.25	0.50

KM# 1072 50 PAISA **Composition:** Aluminum **Obverse:** Royal crown **Size:** 22.5 mm. **Note:** Coins dated VS2051 exist in two minor varieties being struck at Kathmandu (round edge) and Singapore (sharp edge).

Date	F	VF	XF	Unc
VS2051 (1994)	—	0.10	0.20	0.40
VS2052 (1995)	—	0.10	0.20	0.40
VS2053 (1996)	—	0.10	0.20	0.40
VS2054 (1997)	—	0.10	0.20	0.40
VS2055 (1998)	—	0.10	0.20	0.40
VS2056 (1999)	—	0.10	0.20	0.40
VS2057 (2000)	—	0.10	0.20	0.40

KM# 828 RUPEE **Weight:** 10.2000 g. **Composition:** Copper-Nickel

Date	Mintage	F	VF	XF	Unc
VS2028 (1971)	5,030	—	0.50	1.00	2.00
VS2029 (1972)	22,000	—	0.50	1.00	1.50
VS2029 (1972) Proof	3,943	Value: 2.50			
VS2030 (1973)	5,667	—	0.50	1.00	2.00
VS2030 (1973) Proof	8,891	Value: 2.00			
VS2031 (1974) Proof	11,000	Value: 1.50			

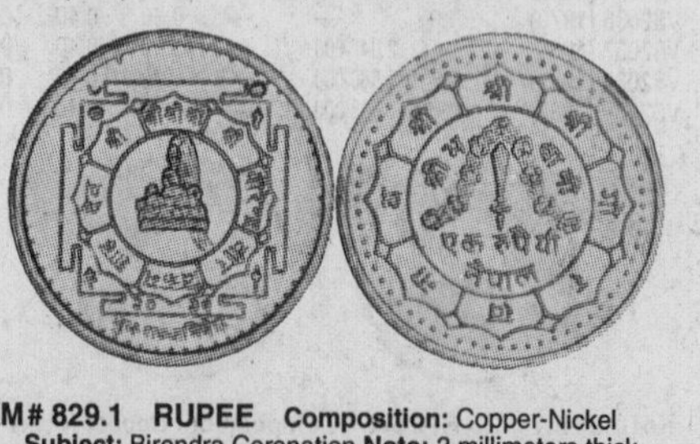

KM# 829.1 RUPEE **Composition:** Copper-Nickel **Subject:** Birendra Coronation **Note:** 2 millimeters thick.

Date	F	VF	XF	Unc
VS2031 (1973)	—	0.75	1.25	1.75

KM# 829.2 RUPEE **Composition:** Copper-Nickel **Subject:** Birendra Coronation **Edge:** Reeded **Note:** 2.5 millimeters thick.

Date	Mintage	F	VF	XF	Unc
VS2031 (1973) Proof	1,000	Value: 6.00			

KM# 848 RUPEE **Composition:** Copper-Nickel **Note:** Ir the name of Queen Aishvarya Rajya Lakshmi

Date	F	VF	XF	Un
VS2031 (1974)	—	—	—	15

KM# 831 RUPEE **Composition:** Copper-Nickel **Series:** F.A.O. International Women's Year

Date	Mintage	F	VF	XF	Un
VS2032 (1975)	1,500,000	—	0.25	0.50	1.2

KM# 828a RUPEE **Weight:** 7.5000 g. **Composition:** Copper-Nickel **Note:** Reduced weight. Coins dated VS2036 and 2034 were struck at the Canberra Mint and have a very shiny surface.

Date	Mintage	F	VF	XF	Un
VS2033 (1976)	58,000	—	0.50	1.00	1.5
VS2034 (1977)	30,000,000	—	0.25	0.50	1.0
VS2035 (1978)	—	—	0.25	0.50	1.0
VS2036 (1979)	—	—	0.25	0.50	1.0
VS2036 (1979)	30,000,000	—	0.25	0.50	1.0

KM# 1019 RUPEE **Composition:** Copper-Nickel **Subject:** Family Planning

Date	Mintage	F	VF	XF	Un
VS2041 (1984)	21,000	—	—	—	0.7

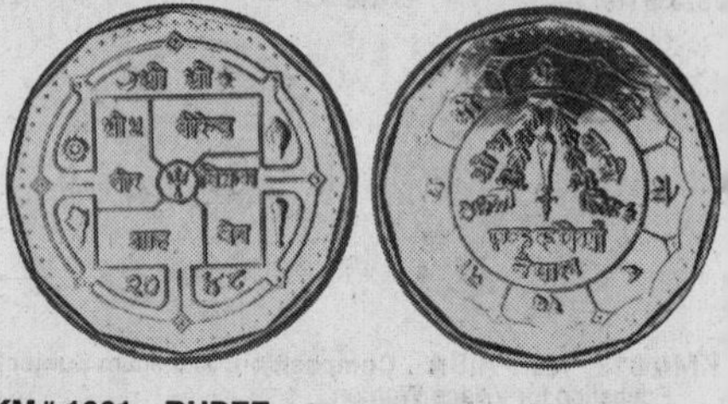

KM# 1061 RUPEE **Composition:** Stainless Steel **Obverse:** Smaller trident in center

Date	F	VF	XF	Unc
VS2045 (1988) Prooflike	—	0.25	0.50	1.00
VS2048 (1991) Prooflike	—	0.25	0.50	1.00

Note: Varieties exist

Date	F	VF	XF	Unc
VS2049 (1992) Prooflike	—	0.25	0.50	1.25

KM# 1073 RUPEE **Composition:** Brass Plated Steel **Reverse:** Large legends **Size:** 22 mm. **Note:** Sharp and round edge varieties.

Date	F	VF	XF	Unc
VS2051 (1994)	—	0.25	0.50	1.00
VS2052 (1995)	—	0.25	0.50	1.00

KM# 1152 RUPEE **Weight:** 28.1600 g. **Composition:** Copper-Nickel **Subject:** 50th Anniversary of United Nations **Obverse:** Traditional design, same design as KM#1092 **Reverse:** Anniversary logo **Edge:** Reeded **Size:** 38.5 mm.

Date	F	VF	XF	Unc
VS2052 (1995)	—	—	—	8.00

KM# 1073a RUPEE Composition: Brass **Obverse:** Traditional design **Reverse:** Small legends **Size:** 20 mm.

ate	F	VF	XF	Unc
S2052 (1995)	—	—	—	1.00
S2053 (1996)	—	—	—	1.00
'S2054 (1997)	—	—	—	1.00
'S2055 (1998)	—	—	—	1.00
S2056 (1999)	—	—	—	1.00
'S2057 (2000)	—	—	—	1.00

KM# 1092.1 RUPEE Composition: Brass Plated Steel **Series:** U.N. 50th Anniversary **Size:** 22 mm.

Date	F	VF	XF	Unc
VS2052 (1995)	—	—	—	1.75

KM# 1115 RUPEE Composition: Brass **Subject:** Visit Nepal '98 **Obverse:** Traditional design **Reverse:** Moon and sun flanking mountaintop **Size:** 20 mm.

Date	F	VF	XF	Unc
VS2054 (1997)	—	—	—	1.00

KM# 1139 RUPEE Composition: Brass **Subject:** Gorkhapatra Centenary **Reverse:** Inscription within wreath of ten people reading newspapers **Rev. Inscription:** "Gorkhapata 1958-VS2057" **Size:** 20 mm.

Date	F	VF	XF	Unc
VS2057 (2000)	—	—	—	1.00

KM# 832 2 RUPEES Composition: Copper-Nickel **Series:** World Food Day

Date	Mintage	F	VF	XF	Unc
VS2038 (1981)	1,000,000	—	0.50	0.75	1.50

KM# 1025 2 RUPEES Composition: Copper-Nickel **Series:** F.A.O. **Note:** Size of obverse square varies. With or without dot in reverse sun.

Date	Mintage	F	VF	XF	Unc
VS2039 (1982)	366,000	—	0.50	0.75	1.50

KM# 1020 2 RUPEES Composition: Copper-Nickel **Subject:** Family Planning

Date	Mintage	F	VF	XF	Unc
VS2041 (1984)	11,000	—	0.50	0.75	1.50

KM# 1074 2 RUPEES Composition: Brass Plated Steel **Size:** 24.5 mm. **Note:** Sharp and round edge varieties exist.

Date	F	VF	XF	Unc
VS2051 (1994)	—	0.35	0.60	1.25
VS2052 (1995)	—	0.35	0.60	1.25
VS2053 (1996)	—	0.35	0.60	1.25

KM# 1116 2 RUPEES Composition: Brass Plated Steel **Subject:** Visit Nepal '98 **Obverse:** Traditional design **Reverse:** Moon and sun flanking mountaintop **Size:** 25 mm.

Date	F	VF	XF	Unc
VS2053(1996) (1996)	—	—	—	—
VS2054 (1997)	—	—	—	1.25

KM# 833 5 RUPEE Composition: Copper-Nickel **Subject:** Rural Women's Advancement

Date	Mintage	F	VF	XF	Unc
VS2037 (1980)	50,000	—	0.75	1.50	3.00

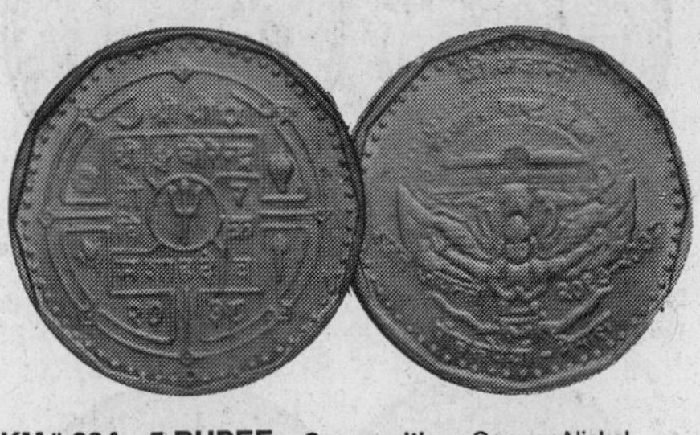

KM# 834 5 RUPEE Composition: Copper-Nickel **Subject:** National Bank Silver Jubilee **Note:** Size varies: 28.7-30.0 millimeters.

Date	Mintage	F	VF	XF	Unc
VS2038 (1981)	64,000	—	0.75	1.50	3.00

KM# 1009 5 RUPEE Composition: Copper-Nickel **Note:** Circulation coinage

Date	Mintage	F	VF	XF	Unc
VS2039 (1982)	Inc. above	—	0.50	1.00	2.00
VS2040 (1983)	478,000	—	0.30	0.50	1.00

KM# 1017 5 RUPEE Composition: Copper-Nickel **Subject:** Family Planning

Date	Mintage	F	VF	XF	Unc
VS2041 (1984)	458,000	—	0.50	1.00	2.00

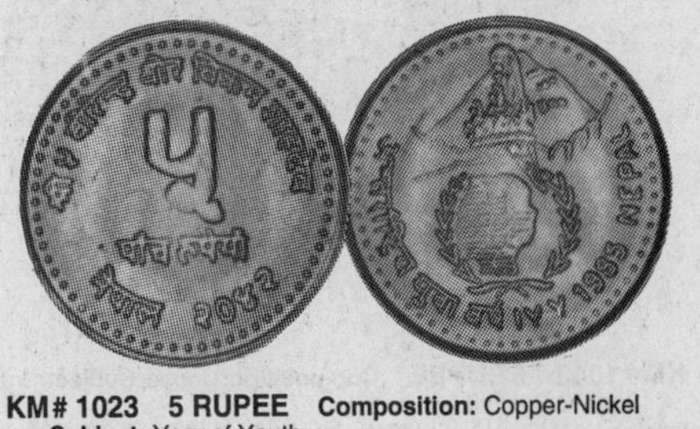

KM# 1023 5 RUPEE Composition: Copper-Nickel **Subject:** Year of Youth

Date	Mintage	F	VF	XF	Unc
VS2042 (1985)	1,124,000	—	—	—	2.50

KM# 1047 5 RUPEE Composition: Copper-Nickel **Subject:** Social Services

Date	F	VF	XF	Unc
VS2042 (1985)	—	—	—	3.50

KM# 1028 5 RUPEE Composition: Copper-Nickel **Series:** World Food Day

Date	Mintage	F	VF	XF	Unc
VS2043 (1986)	99,000	—	—	—	3.50

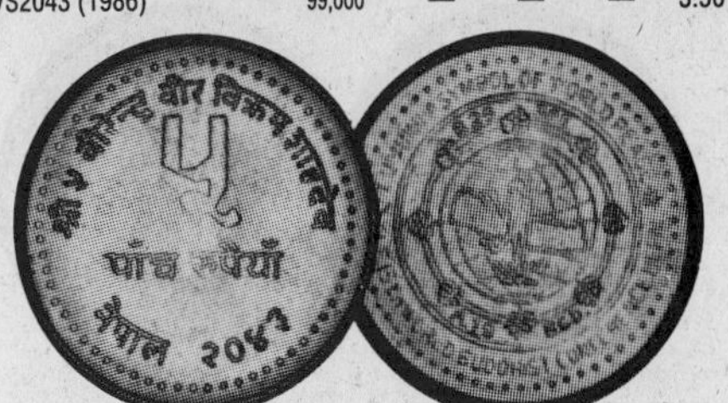

KM# 1042 5 RUPEE Composition: Copper-Nickel **Subject:** 15th World Buddhist Conference **Note:** Two different obverse dies exist.

Date	Mintage	F	VF	XF	Unc
VS2043//1986 (1986)	135,000	—	—	—	3.50

KM# 1030 5 RUPEE **Composition:** Copper-Nickel **Subject:** 10th Year of National Social Security Administration

Date	Mintage	F	VF	XF	Unc
VS2044 (1987)	104,000	—	—	—	3.50
VS2045 (1988)	—	—	—	—	3.50

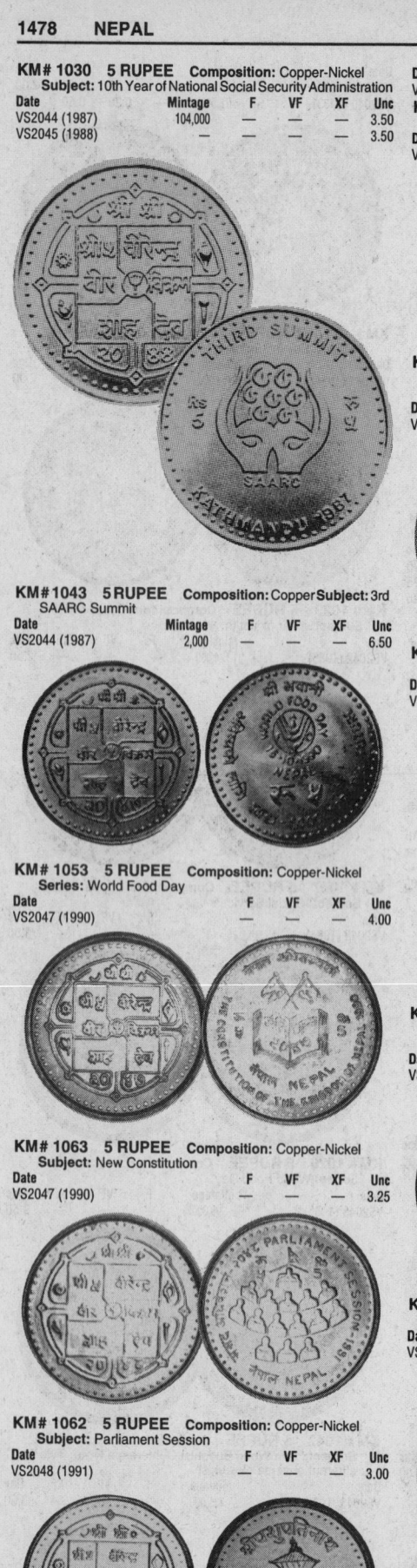

KM# 1043 5 RUPEE **Composition:** Copper **Subject:** 3rd SAARC Summit

Date	Mintage	F	VF	XF	Unc
VS2044 (1987)	2,000	—	—	—	6.50

KM# 1053 5 RUPEE **Composition:** Copper-Nickel **Series:** World Food Day

Date	F	VF	XF	Unc
VS2047 (1990)	—	—	—	4.00

KM# 1063 5 RUPEE **Composition:** Copper-Nickel **Subject:** New Constitution

Date	F	VF	XF	Unc
VS2047 (1990)	—	—	—	3.25

KM# 1062 5 RUPEE **Composition:** Copper-Nickel **Subject:** Parliament Session

Date	F	VF	XF	Unc
VS2048 (1991)	—	—	—	3.00

KM# 1075.1 5 RUPEE **Composition:** Brass Plated Steel **Edge:** Plain **Size:** 27 mm.

Date	F	VF	XF	Unc
VS2051 (1994)	—	—	—	1.50

KM# 1075.2 5 RUPEE **Composition:** Brass **Edge:** Reeded **Size:** 25 mm.

Date	F	VF	XF	Unc
VS2053 (1996)	—	—	—	1.50

KM# 1117 5 RUPEE **Composition:** Copper **Subject:** Visit Nepal '98 **Obverse:** Traditional design **Reverse:** Sun and moon flanking mountaintop **Edge:** Reeded **Size:** 25 mm.

Date	F	VF	XF	Unc
VS2054 (1997)	—	—	—	1.50

KM# 835 10 RUPEE **Weight:** 8.0000 g. **Composition:** 0.2500 Silver .0643 oz. ASW **Series:** F.A.O.

Date	Mintage	F	VF	XF	Unc
VS2031 (1974)	39,000	—	—	4.00	6.00

KM# 1004 10 RUPEE **Composition:** Copper-Nickel **Subject:** 30th Anniversary - Ascent of Mt. Everest **Obverse:** Similar to 5 Rupee, KM#833

Date	Mintage	F	VF	XF	Unc
VS2040 (1983)	2,000	—	—	—	12.50

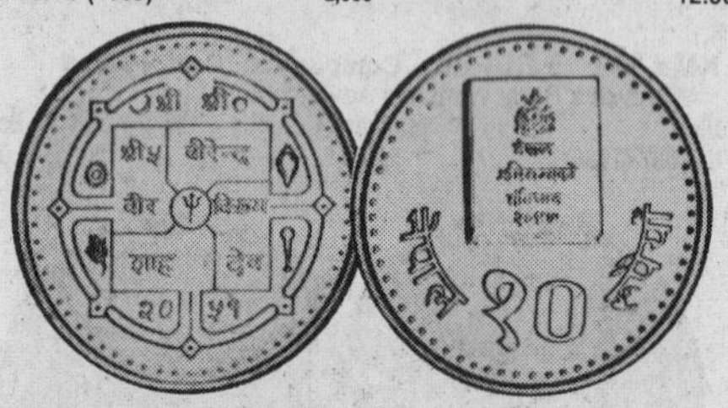

KM# 1076 10 RUPEE **Composition:** Brass Plated Steel **Size:** 29 mm.

Date	F	VF	XF	Unc
VS2051 (1994)	—	—	—	2.50

KM# 1083 10 RUPEE **Composition:** Copper-Nickel **Subject:** 75th Anniversary - International Labor Organization

Date	F	VF	XF	Unc
VS2051 (1994)	—	—	—	4.50

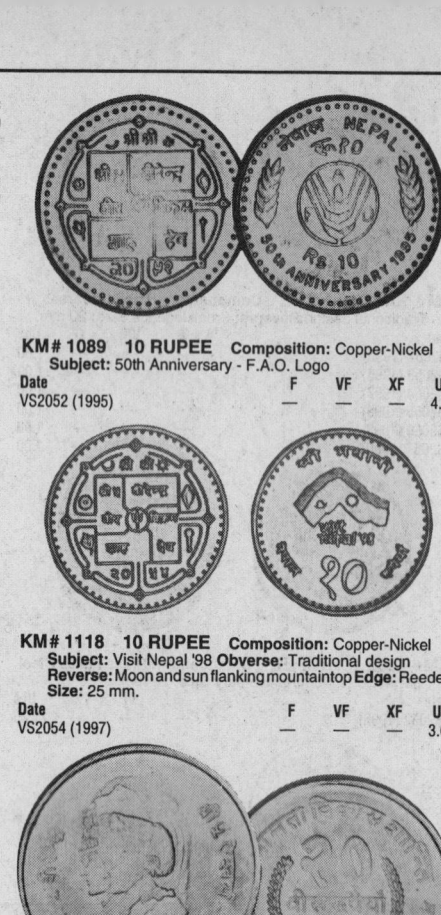

KM# 1089 10 RUPEE **Composition:** Copper-Nickel **Subject:** 50th Anniversary - F.A.O. Logo

Date	F	VF	XF	Unc
VS2052 (1995)	—	—	—	4.0

KM# 1118 10 RUPEE **Composition:** Copper-Nickel **Subject:** Visit Nepal '98 **Obverse:** Traditional design **Reverse:** Moon and sun flanking mountaintop **Edge:** Reede **Size:** 25 mm.

Date	F	VF	XF	Un
VS2054 (1997)	—	—	—	3.0

KM# 836 20 RUPEE **Weight:** 14.8500 g. **Composition:** 0.5000 Silver .2387 oz. ASW **Series:** F.A.O. International Women's Year

Date	Mintage	F	VF	XF	Un
VS2032 (1975)	50,000	—	—	3.50	7.5

KM# 837 20 RUPEE **Weight:** 14.8500 g. **Composition:** 0.5000 Silver .2387 oz. ASW **Series:** International Year of the Child

Date	F	VF	XF	Unc
VS2036 (1979)	—	—	2.50	5.00

KM# 837a 20 RUPEE **Weight:** 15.0000 g. **Composition:** 0.9250 Silver .4461 oz. ASW

Date	Mintage	F	VF	XF	Unc
VS2036 (1979) Proof	1,000	Value: 27.50			

 # 839 25 RUPEE **Weight:** 25.6000 g. **Composition:** 0.5000 Silver .4115 oz. ASW **Series:** Conservation **Obverse:** Bust of Birendra Bir Bikram right **Reverse:** Himalayan Monal Pheasant

e	Mintage	F	VF	XF	Unc
2031 (1974)	11,000	—	—	6.00	11.50

 # 839a 25 RUPEE **Weight:** 28.2800 g. **Composition:** 0.9250 Silver .8411 oz. ASW **Reverse:** Himalayan Monal Pheasant

e	Mintage	F	VF	XF	Unc
2031 (1974) Proof	11,000	Value: 20.00			

M# 838 25 RUPEE **Weight:** 25.6000 g. **Composition:** 0.5000 Silver .4115 oz. ASW **Subject:** Birendra Coronation **Edge:** Reeded **Note:** 2 millimeters thick.

ate	Mintage	F	VF	XF	Unc
S2031 (1974)	75,000	—	—	4.00	9.00

M# 838a 25 RUPEE **Weight:** 28.2800 g. **Composition:** 0.9250 Silver .8411 oz. ASW **Edge:** Reeded **Note:** 3 millimeters thick.

ate	Mintage	F	VF	XF	Unc
S2031 (1974) Proof	2,000	Value: 22.50			

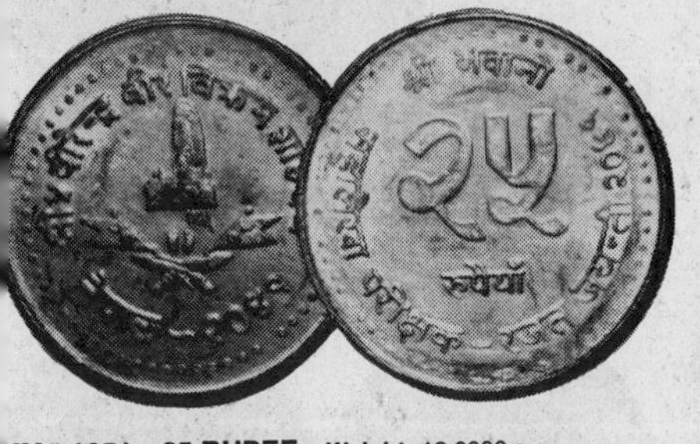

KM# 1051 25 RUPEE **Weight:** 12.0000 g. **Composition:** 0.2500 Silver .0965 oz. ASW

ate	F	VF	XF	Unc
VS2041 (1984)	—	—	—	15.00

KM# 1048 25 RUPEE **Weight:** 12.0000 g. **Composition:** 0.2500 Silver .0965 oz. ASW **Subject:** 25th Anniversary of Panchayat **Note:** Varieties exist with hollow or solid hand-like symbol below on obverse.

Date	Mintage	F	VF	XF	Unc
VS2042 (1985)	9,962,000	—	—	—	10.00

KM# 1135 25 RUPEE **Weight:** 8.5000 g. **Composition:** Copper Nickel **Subject:** Silver Jubilee of King's Accession **Obverse:** Traditional design **Reverse:** Crown on radiant emblem **Edge:** Plain **Size:** 29 mm.

Date	F	VF	XF	Unc
VS2053 (1996)	—	—	—	3.50

KM# 1126 25 RUPEE **Composition:** Copper-Nickel **Subject:** Silver Jubilee **Obverse:** Traditional design **Reverse:** Stylized face design

Date	F	VF	XF	Unc
VS2055 (1998)	—	—	—	4.50

KM# 841 50 RUPEE **Weight:** 31.8000 g. **Composition:** 0.5000 Silver .5112 oz. ASW **Series:** Conservation **Obverse:** Similar to 25 Rupee, KM#839 **Reverse:** Red panda

Date	Mintage	F	VF	XF	Unc
VS2031 (1974)	11,000	—	—	10.00	15.00

KM# 841a 50 RUPEE **Weight:** 35.0000 g. **Composition:** 0.9250 Silver 1.0409 oz. ASW

Date	Mintage	F	VF	XF	Unc
VS2031 (1974) Proof	10,000	Value: 22.50			

KM# 842 50 RUPEE **Weight:** 25.0000 g. **Composition:** 0.5000 Silver .4018 oz. ASW **Subject:** Education for Village Women

Date	Mintage	F	VF	XF	Unc
VS2036 (1979)	15,000	—	—	—	12.50

KM# 842a 50 RUPEE **Weight:** 25.0000 g. **Composition:** 0.9250 Silver .7436 oz. ASW

Date	Mintage	F	VF	XF	Unc
VS2036 (1979) Proof	1,000	Value: 40.00			

KM# 843 50 RUPEE **Weight:** 14.9000 g. **Composition:** 0.5000 Silver .2395 oz. ASW **Series:** International Year of Disabled Persons

Date	Mintage	F	VF	XF	Unc
VS2038 (1981)	16,000	—	—	—	8.50

KM# A851 50 RUPEE **Weight:** 15.0000 g. **Composition:** 0.4000 Silver .1929 oz. ASW **Series:** International Year of the Child **Note:** Similar to 100 Rupee, KM#851.

Date	F	VF	XF	Unc
VS2038 (1981)	—	—	—	—

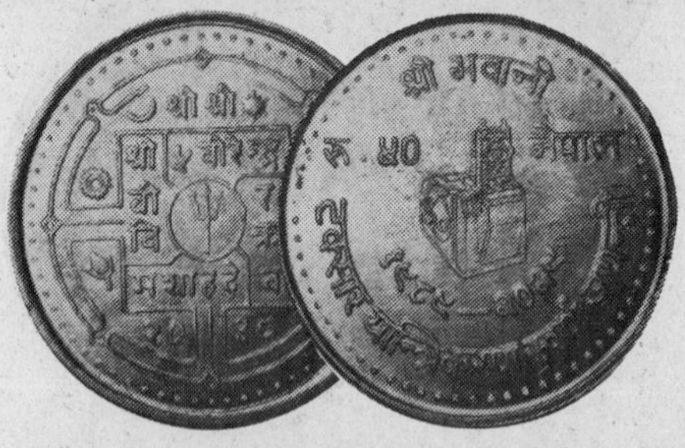

KM# 1046 50 RUPEE **Weight:** 15.0000 g. **Composition:** 0.5000 Silver .2406 oz. ASW **Subject:** 50th Anniversary of Kathmandu Mint

Date	Mintage	F	VF	XF	Unc
VS2039 (1982)	8,765	—	—	13.50	17.50

KM# 1119 50 RUPEE **Composition:** Bronze **Obverse:** Traditional square in circle design **Reverse:** Buddha's portrait and Ashoka pillar **Note:** Lord Buddha; Similar to 1500 Rupee, KM#1120.

Date	Mintage	F	VF	XF	Unc
VS2055 (1998)	30,000	—	—	—	10.00

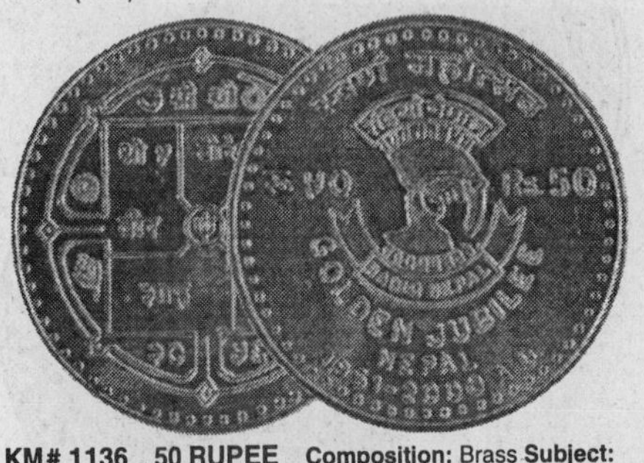

KM# 1136 50 RUPEE **Composition:** Brass **Subject:** 50th Anniversary - Radio Nepal **Obverse:** Traditional design **Reverse:** Stylized design **Edge:** Plain **Size:** 37.5 mm.

Date	F	VF	XF	Unc
VS2056 (1999)	—	—	—	10.00

KM# 1137 50 RUPEE Composition: Brass **Subject:** St. Xavier's Golden Jubilee **Obverse:** Traditional design **Reverse:** Coat of arms **Edge:** Plain **Size:** 37.5 mm.

Date	F	VF	XF	Unc
VS2057 (2000)	—	—	—	10.00

KM# 1127 50 RUPEE Composition: Bronze **Subject:** Buddha **Obverse:** Traditional square design **Reverse:** Buddha and four figures **Edge:** Reeded **Size:** 38.7 mm.

Date	Mintage	F	VF	XF	Unc
2000 (2000)	30,000	—	—	—	10.00

KM# 850.1 100 RUPEE Weight: 25.4900 g. **Composition:** 0.5000 Silver .4050 oz. ASW **Series:** World Food Day

Date	Mintage	F	VF	XF	Unc
VS2038 (1981)	18,000	—	—	—	22.50

KM# 850.2 100 RUPEE Weight: 25.4900 g. **Composition:** 0.9250 Silver .7580 oz. ASW **Series:** World Food Day

Date	F	VF	XF	Unc
VS2038 (1981)	—	Value: 80.00		

KM# 851 100 RUPEE Weight: 19.4400 g. **Composition:** 0.5000 Silver .3125 oz. ASW **Series:** International Year of the Child

Date	Mintage	F	VF	XF	Unc
VS2031(1974) Proof	9,270	Value: 17.50			

Note: Struck in 1981

KM# 1005 100 RUPEE Weight: 31.1000 g. **Composition:** 0.9250 Silver .9250 oz. ASW **Subject:** 30th Anniversary Ascent of Mt. Everest **Obverse:** Similar to 5 Rupee, KM#833

Date	Mintage	F	VF	XF	Unc
VS2040 (1983) Proof	1,500	Value: 50.00			

KM# 1024 100 RUPEE Weight: 15.0000 g. **Composition:** 0.5000 Silver .2411 oz. ASW **Subject:** Year of Youth

Date	Mintage	F	VF	XF	Unc
VS2042 (1985)	8,199	—	—	—	12.00

KM# 1114 100 RUPEE Weight: 12.0400 g. **Composition:** 0.6000 Silver .2323 oz. ASW **Series:** 50th Anniversary - F.A.O.

Date	F	VF	XF	Unc
VS2052 (1995)	—	—	—	15.00

KM# 1102 100 RUPEE Composition: Copper-Nicke **Series:** Nepal Wildlife **Reverse:** Multicolored tiger

Date	Mintage	F	VF	XF	U
VS2054-1998	25,000	—	—	—	25
VS2054-1998	25,000	—	—	—	25

KM# 1103 100 RUPEE Composition: Copper-Nickel **Series:** Nepal Wildlife **Reverse:** Multicolored rhino

Date	Mintage	F	VF	XF	U
VS2054-1998	25,000	—	—	—	25.

KM# 1141 100 RUPEE Weight: 12.5000 g. **Composition:** 0.5000 Silver .200 oz. ASW **Series:** International Year of Older Persons

Date	F	VF	XF	Ur
VS2056 (1999)	—	—	—	10.0

KM# 1031 200 RUPEE Weight: 15.0000 g. **Composition:** 0.6000 Silver .2894 oz. ASW **Subject:** 10th Anniversary of National Social Security Administration

Date	Mintage	F	VF	XF	Ur
VS2044 (1987)	4,145	—	—	—	25.0

KM# 1007 250 RUPEE **Weight:** 28.2800 g. **Composition:** 0.9250 Silver .8411 oz. ASW **Subject:** 10th Anniversary of Reign

Date	Mintage	F	VF	XF	Unc
VS2038 (1981) Proof	10,000	Value: 95.00			

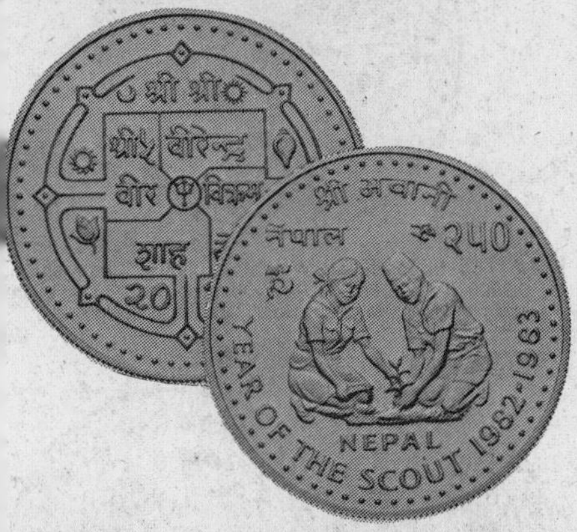

KM# 1010 250 RUPEE **Weight:** 28.2800 g. **Composition:** 0.9250 Silver .8411 oz. ASW **Subject:** Year of the Scout

Date	Mintage	F	VF	XF	Unc
VS2039 (1982)	10,000	—	—	—	45.00
VS2039 (1982) Proof	Inc. above	Value: 55.00			

KM# 1026 250 RUPEE **Weight:** 19.4400 g. **Composition:** 0.9250 Silver .5782 oz. ASW **Series:** Wildlife Preservation **Reverse:** Deer

Date	Mintage	F	VF	XF	Unc
VS2043 (1986) Proof	20,000	Value: 22.50			

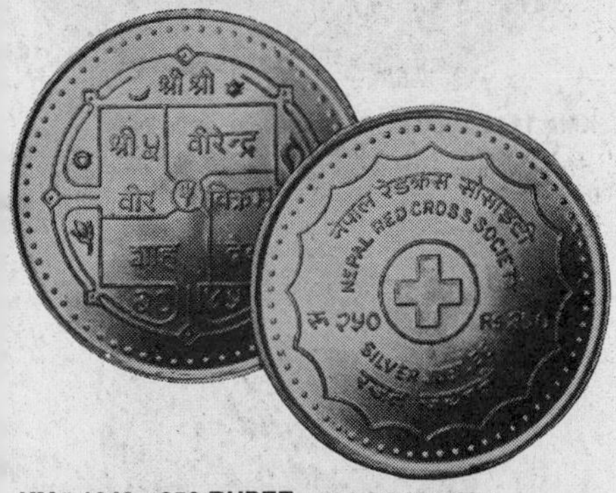

KM# 1049 250 RUPEE **Weight:** 19.4400 g. **Composition:** 0.9250 Silver .5782 oz. ASW **Subject:** Silver Jubilee of Nepal Red Cross Society

Date	Mintage	F	VF	XF	Unc
VS2045 (1988)	6,360	—	—	—	23.50

KM# 1052 250 RUPEE **Weight:** 19.4400 g. **Composition:** 0.9250 Silver .5782 oz. ASW **Subject:** 25th Anniversary of Nepalese Power Company

Date	F	VF	XF	Unc
VS2046 (1989)	—	—	—	23.50

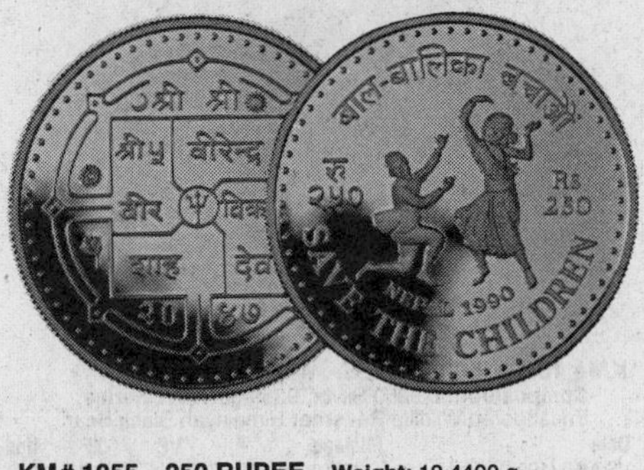

KM# 1055 250 RUPEE **Weight:** 19.4400 g. **Composition:** 0.9250 Silver .5782 oz. ASW **Series:** Save the Children

Date	Mintage	F	VF	XF	Unc
VS2047 (1990) Proof	20,000	Value: 22.50			

KM# 1134 250 RUPEE **Weight:** 19.4400 g. **Composition:** 0.9250 Silver .5782 oz. ASW **Subject:** Nepal Disabled Association

Date	F	VF	XF	Unc
VS2052 (1995)	—	—	—	27.50

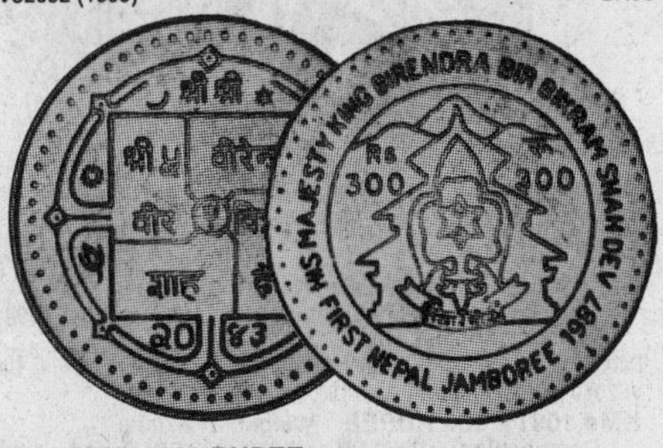

KM# 1029 300 RUPEE **Weight:** 25.2900 g. **Composition:** 0.5000 Silver .4066 oz. ASW **Subject:** First Scout Jamboree in Nepal

Date	Mintage	F	VF	XF	Unc
VS2043 (1986)	6,967	—	—	—	27.50

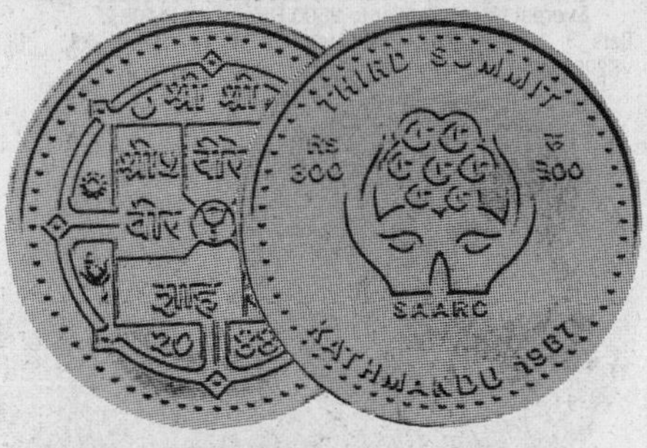

KM# 1044 300 RUPEE **Weight:** 25.0000 g. **Composition:** 0.9250 Silver .7436 oz. ASW **Subject:** 3rd SAARC Summit

Date	Mintage	F	VF	XF	Unc
VS2044 (1987)	5,000	—	—	—	22.50

KM# 1057 300 RUPEE **Weight:** 18.0500 g. **Composition:** 0.9250 Silver .5368 oz. ASW **Reverse:** Rastriya Banijya Bank logo

Date	F	VF	XF	Unc
VS2047 (1990)	—	—	—	22.50

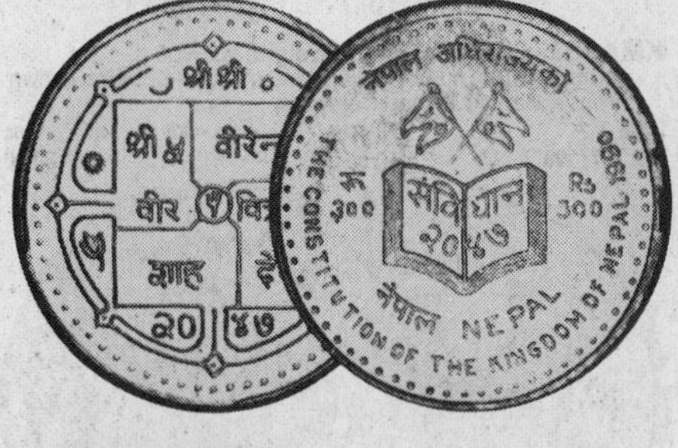

KM# 1064 300 RUPEE **Weight:** 18.3150 g. **Composition:** 0.9250 Silver .5447 oz. ASW **Subject:** New Constitution

Date	F	VF	XF	Unc
VS2047 (1990)	—	—	—	22.50

KM# 1065 300 RUPEE **Weight:** 18.3150 g. **Composition:** 0.9250 Silver .5447 oz. ASW **Subject:** Parliament Session

Date	F	VF	XF	Unc
VS2048 (1991)	—	—	—	22.50

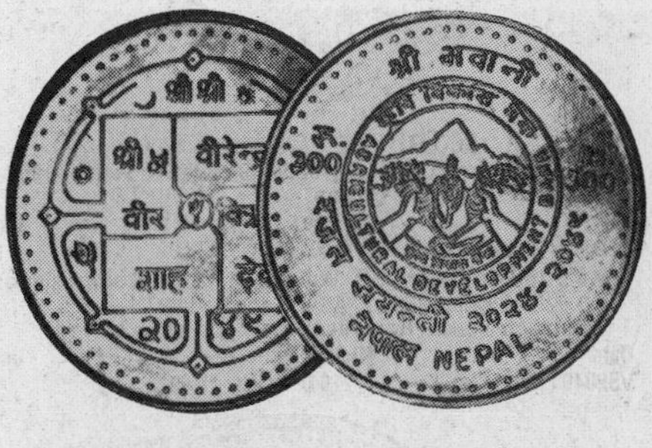

KM# 1068 300 RUPEE **Weight:** 17.8100 g. **Composition:** 0.9250 Silver .5297 oz. ASW **Reverse:** Agricultural Development Bank

Date	F	VF	XF	Unc
VS2049 (1992)	—	—	—	22.50

KM# 1094 300 RUPEE **Weight:** 18.1300 g. **Composition:** 0.9250 Silver .5392 oz. ASW **Subject:** Rastriya Beema Sansthan Silver Jubilee

Date	F	VF	XF	Unc
VS2049 (1992)	—	—	—	22.50

KM# 1142 300 RUPEE **Weight:** 18.0000 g. **Composition:** 0.9250 Silver .5353 oz. ASW **Subject:** 75th Anniversary of I.L.O.

Date	F	VF	XF	Unc
VS2051 (1994)	—	—	—	22.50

KM# 1032 350 RUPEE **Weight:** 23.3000 g. **Composition:** 0.5000 Silver .3746 oz. ASW **Subject:** Crown Prince, Sacred Thread Ceremony

Date	Mintage	F	VF	XF	Unc
VS2044 (1987)	5,217	—	—	—	30.00

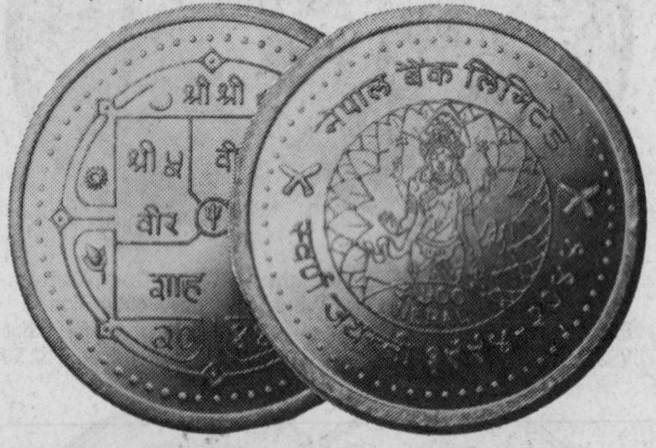

KM# 1035 500 RUPEE **Weight:** 35.0000 g. **Composition:** 0.5000 Silver .5627 oz. ASW **Subject:** 50th Anniversary of National Bank

Date	Mintage	F	VF	XF	Unc
VS2044 (1987)	19,000	—	—	—	45.00

KM# 1058 500 RUPEE **Weight:** 31.4700 g. **Composition:** 0.9250 Silver .9359 oz. ASW **Series:** 1992 Olympics **Reverse:** Boxers

Date	Mintage	F	VF	XF	Unc
VS2049 (1992) Proof	Est. 40,000	Value: 17.50			

KM# 1069 500 RUPEE **Weight:** 31.4700 g. **Composition:** 0.9250 Silver .9359 oz. ASW **Series:** 1992 Olympics **Subject:** Soccer **Reverse:** Soccer goal being scored

Date	Mintage	F	VF	XF	Unc
VS2049 (1992) Proof	20,000	Value: 28.50			

KM# 1071 500 RUPEE **Weight:** 31.8300 g. **Composition:** 0.9250 Silver .9466 oz. ASW **Series:** 1992 Olympics - Ski Jumping

Date	Mintage	F	VF	XF	Unc
VS2049 (1992) Proof	Est. 40,000	Value: 16.50			

KM# 1090 500 RUPEE **Weight:** 31.4700 g. **Composition:** 0.9250 Silver .9359 oz. ASW **Series:** Endangered Wildlife **Reverse:** Red Panda

Date	Mintage	F	VF	XF	Unc
VS2049 (1992) Proof	Est. 15,000	Value: 30.00			

KM# 1070 500 RUPEE **Weight:** 31.4700 g. **Composition:** 0.9250 Silver .9359 oz. ASW **Series:** Endangered Wildlife **Reverse:** Himalayan Black Bear

Date	Mintage	F	VF	XF	Unc
VS2050 (1993) Proof	10,000	Value: 37.50			

KM# 1066 500 RUPEE **Weight:** 31.7500 g. **Composition:** 0.9250 Silver .9443 oz. ASW **Series:** 1994 Olympics **Subject:** Cross-country Skiing

Date	Mintage	F	VF	XF	Unc
VS2050 (1993) Proof	40,000	Value: 22.50			

KM# 1091 500 RUPEE **Weight:** 31.4700 g. **Composition:** 0.9250 Silver .9359 oz. ASW **Series:** Endangered Wildlife **Reverse:** Tiger

Date	Mintage	F	VF	XF	Unc
VS2050 (1993) Proof	Est. 15,000	Value: 35.00			

KM# 1084 500 RUPEE **Weight:** 28.2800 g. **Composition:** 0.9250 Silver .8411 oz. ASW **Subject:** Conquest of Mt. Everest **Note:** Similar to 2500 Rupee, KM#1085.

Date	Mintage	F	VF	XF	Unc
VS2050 (1993) Proof	Est. 10,000	Value: 32.50			

KM# 1133 500 RUPEE **Weight:** 35.2000 g. **Composition:** 0.9000 Silver 1.0000 oz. ASW **Subject:** International Monetary Fund

Date	F	VF	XF	Unc
VS2051 (1994)	—	—	—	45.00

KM# 1077 500 RUPEE **Weight:** 31.1035 g. **Composition:** 0.9250 Silver .9250 oz. ASW **Reverse:** Buddha

Date	Mintage	F	VF	XF	Unc
VS2052 (1995) Proof	15,000	Value: 37.50			

KM# 1125 500 RUPEE **Weight:** 31.3500 g. **Composition:** 0.9990 Silver 1.0069 oz. ASW **Obverse:** Traditional square in circle design **Reverse:** Gold-plated lotus flowers

Date	Mintage	F	VF	XF	Unc
VS2052 (1995) Proof	Est. 7,000	Value: 45.00			

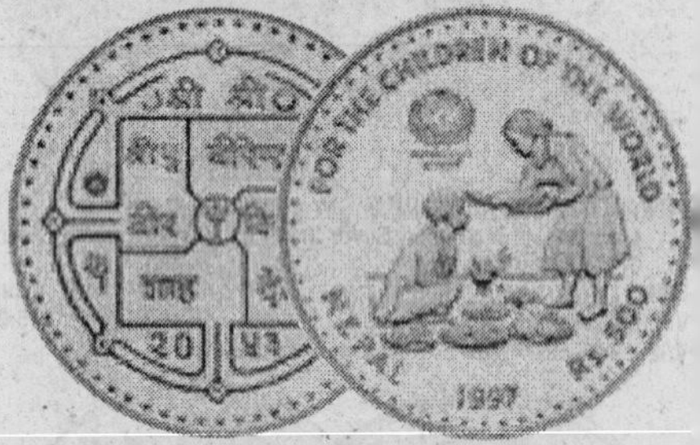

KM# 1138 500 RUPEE **Weight:** 19.4400 g. **Composition:** 0.9250 Silver 0.5781 oz. ASW **Series:** UNICEF **Obverse:** Traditional design **Reverse:** Standing girl serving seated boy **Edge:** Reeded **Size:** 36 mm.

Date	Mintage	F	VF	XF	Unc
1997 Proof	25,000	Value: 25.00			

KM# 1143 500 RUPEE **Weight:** 25.2000 g. **Composition:** 0.9250 Silver .7494 oz. ASW **Subject:** 50th Anniversary of Universal Declaration of Human Rights

Date	F	VF	XF	Unc
VS2055 (1998)	—	—	—	22.50

KM# 1041 600 RUPEE **Weight:** 31.1030 g. **Composition:** 0.9990 Silver 1.0000 oz. ASW **Subject:** 60th Birthday - Queen Mother

Date	Mintage	F	VF	XF	Unc
VS2045 (1988) Proof	5,000	Value: 60.00			

KM# 844 1000 RUPEE **Weight:** 33.4370 g. **Composition:** 0.9000 Gold .9676 oz. AGW **Series:** Conservation **Reverse:** Great Indian Rhinoceros **Note:** Very small quantity restruck in 1979.

Date	Mintage	F	VF	XF	Unc
VS2031 (1974)	2,176	—	—	—	450
VS2031 (1974) Proof	671	Value: 650			

KM# 1000 1000 RUPEE **Weight:** 33.4370 g. **Composition:** 0.9000 Gold .9676 oz. AGW **Subject:** Rural Women's Advancement

Date	Mintage	F	VF	XF	Unc
VS2037 (1980) Proof	500	Value: 150			

KM# 1036 1000 RUPEE **Weight:** 155.5150 g. **Composition:** 0.9990 Silver 5.0000 oz. ASW **Reverse:** Snow Leopard **Size:** 65 mm. **Note:** Illustration reduced.

Date	Mintage	F	VF	XF	Unc
VS2045 (1988) Proof	Est. 5,000	Value: 150			

KM# 1095 1500 RUPEE **Weight:** 31.1035 g. **Composition:** 0.9250 Silver .9250 oz. ASW **Subject:** Buddha's Birth **Obverse:** Traditional square in circle design

Date	F	VF	XF	Unc
VS2054 (1997) Proof	—	Value: 35.00		

KM# 1120 1500 RUPEE **Weight:** 20.0000 g. **Composition:** 0.9250 Silver .5948 oz. ASW **Subject:** Lord Buddha **Obverse:** Traditional square in circle design **Reverse:** Portrait of Buddha, Ashoka pillar, portrait halo glows under ultraviolet light

Date	Mintage	F	VF	XF	Unc
VS2055 (1998) Proof	15,000	Value: 50.00			

KM# 1128 1500 RUPEE **Weight:** 20.0000 g. **Composition:** 0.9250 Silver .5948 oz. ASW **Subject:** Buddha **Obverse:** Traditional square design **Reverse:** Buddha with golden aura **Edge:** Reeded **Size:** 38.7 mm.

Date	F	VF	XF	Unc
VS2057 (2000)	—	—	—	50.00

KM# 1100 2000 RUPEE **Weight:** 31.2400 g. **Composition:** 0.9990 Silver 1.0034 oz. ASW **Subject:** Silver Jubilee of King's Accession **Obverse:** Traditional design **Reverse:** Multicolor crown **Size:** 40 mm.

Date	Mintage	F	VF	XF	Unc
VS2053 (1996) Proof	Est. 5,000	Value: 40.00			

KM# 1121 2000 RUPEE **Weight:** 20.0000 g. **Composition:** 0.9250 Silver .5948 oz. ASW **Obverse:** Traditional square in circle design **Reverse:** Buddha's portrait with gold insert halo, Ashoka pillar at right **Note:** Lord Buudha; Similar to 1500 Rupee, KM#1120.

Date	Mintage	F	VF	XF	Unc
VS2055 (1998) Proof	5,000	Value: 75.00			

KM# 1104 2000 RUPEE **Weight:** 31.1700 g. **Composition:** 0.9990 Silver 1.011 oz. ASW **Series:** Nepal Wildlife **Obverse:** Traditional design **Reverse:** Multicolored leopard

Date	Mintage	F	VF	XF	Unc
VS2054-1998 Proof	8,000	Value: 42.50			

KM# 1105 2000 RUPEE **Weight:** 31.1700 g. **Composition:** 0.9990 Silver 1.011 oz. ASW **Series:** Nepal Wildlife **Reverse:** Multicolored elephants

Date	Mintage	F	VF	XF	Unc
VS2054-1998 Proof	8,000	Value: 42.50			

KM# 1085 2500 RUPEE **Weight:** 155.5100 g. **Composition:** 0.9990 Silver 5.0000 oz. ASW **Subject:** Conquest of Mt. Everest **Note:** Illustration reduced.

Date	Mintage	F	VF	XF	Unc
VS2050 (1993) Proof	Est. 3,000	Value: 145			

KM# 1078 2500 RUPEE **Weight:** 155.5100 g. **Composition:** 0.9990 Silver 5.0000 oz. ASW **Reverse:** Buddha **Note:** Similar to 500 Rupee, KM#1077.

Date	Mintage	F	VF	XF	Unc
VS2052 (1995) Proof	3,000	Value: 200			

KM# 1101 5000 RUPEE **Weight:** 155.5000 g. **Composition:** 0.9990 Silver 4.9944 oz. ASW **Subject:** Silver Jubilee of King's Accession **Obverse:** Traditional design **Reverse:** Multicolored crown **Size:** 65 mm.

Date	Mintage	F	VF	XF	Unc
VS2053 (1996) Proof	Est. 2,500	Value: 200			

KM# 1106 5000 RUPEE **Weight:** 155.5518 g. **Composition:** 0.9990 Silver 4.9961 oz. ASW **Series:** Nepal Wildlife **Reverse:** Multicolored elephants **Note:** Similar to 2000 Rupee, KM#1105.

Date	Mintage	F	VF	XF	Unc
VS2054 (1997) Proof	500	Value: 250			

ASARFI GOLD COINAGE

(Asarphi)

Fractional designations are approximate for this series. Actual Gold Weight (AGW) is used to identify each type.

KM# 1050a 0.3G ASARPHI **Weight:** 0.2500 g. **Composition:** 0.9990 Gold .804 oz. AGW

Date	F	VF	XF	Unc
VS2051 (1994)	—	—	—	40.00
VS2052 (1995)	—	—	—	40.00
VS2053 (1996)	—	—	—	35.00

Date	F	VF	XF	Unc
VS2054 (1997)	—	—	—	35.00
VS2055 (1998)	—	—	—	35.00
VS2056 (1999)	—	—	—	35.00
VS2057 (2000)	—	—	—	35.00

KM# 1129 0.3G ASARPHI **Weight:** 0.3000 g. **Composition:** 0.9999 Gold .0096 oz. AGW **Subject:** Buddha **Obverse:** Traditional square design **Reverse:** Buddha with halo **Edge:** Reeded **Size:** 7 mm.

Date	Mintage	F	VF	XF	Unc
VS2057 (2000)	25,000	—	—	—	10.00

KM# 825 5.0G ASARPHI **Weight:** 5.0000 g. **Composition:** 0.9990 Gold .1607 oz. AGW

Date	Mintage	F	VF	XF	Unc
VS2028 (1971)	4	—	—	—	—
VS2030 (1973)	—	—	—	—	160
VS2031 (1974)	—	—	—	—	160
VS2036 (1979)	36	—	—	—	160
VS2037 (1980)	45	—	—	—	160
Note: Reports indicate a mintage of 44 pieces struck in .960 gold in 1980					
VS2038 (1981)	—	—	—	—	160

KM# 822a 5.0G ASARPHI **Weight:** 5.0000 g. **Composition:** 0.9990 Gold .1607 oz. AGW **Subject:** Birendra Coronation

Date	Mintage	F	VF	XF	Unc
VS2031 (1974)	500	—	—	—	150

KM# 1021 5.0G ASARPHI **Weight:** 5.0000 g. **Composition:** 0.9000 Gold .1447 oz. AGW

Date	Mintage	F	VF	XF	Unc
VS2039 (1982)	23	—	—	—	—

KM# 1021a 5.0G ASARPHI **Weight:** 0.5000 g. **Composition:** 0.9990 Gold .1607 oz. AGW

Date	F	VF	XF	Unc
VS2042 (1985)	—	—	—	100
VS2043 (1986)	—	—	—	100
VS2044 (1987)	—	—	—	100
VS2045 (1988)	—	—	—	90.00
VS2046 (1989)	—	—	—	90.00
VS2048 (1991)	—	—	—	90.00
VS2049 (1992)	—	—	—	90.00
VS2050 (1993)	—	—	—	80.00
VS2051 (1994)	—	—	—	80.00
VS2052 (1995)	—	—	—	70.00
VS2053 (1996)	—	—	—	70.00
VS2054 (1997)	—	—	—	70.00
VS2056 (1999)	—	—	—	70.00

KM# 1060 5.0G ASARPHI **Weight:** 5.0000 g. **Composition:** 0.9990 Gold .1600 oz. AGW **Subject:** The New Constitution **Note:** Similar to 10 Asarphi, KM#1054.

Date	F	VF	XF	Unc
VS2047 (1990)	—	—	—	150

KM# 1144 5.0G ASARPHI **Weight:** 5.0000 g. **Composition:** 0.9990 Gold .1606 oz. AGW **Subject:** New Parliament Session

Date	F	VF	XF	Unc
VS2048 (1991)	—	—	—	100

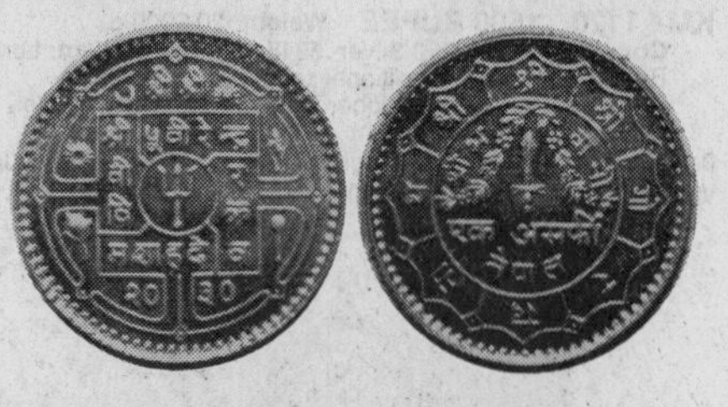

KM# 827 10.0G ASARPHI **Weight:** 10.0000 g. **Composition:** 0.9990 Gold .3215 oz. AGW

Date	F	VF	XF	Unc
VS2028 (1971)	—	—	—	—
VS2030 (1973)	—	—	—	350
VS2031 (1974)	—	—	—	350
VS2033 (1976)	—	—	—	350
VS2035 (1978)	—	—	—	3.50
VS2036 (1979)	—	—	—	350
VS2037 (1980)	—	—	—	350
Note: Reports indicate a mintage of 44 pieces struck in .960 gold in 1980				
VS2038 (1981)	—	—	—	3.50

KM# 829a 10.0G ASARPHI **Weight:** 10.0000 g. **Composition:** 0.9990 Gold .3215 oz. AGW **Subject:** Birendra Coronation

Date	Mintage	F	VF	XF	Unc
VS2031 (1974) Proof	Est. 500	Value: 285			

KM# 829b 10.0G ASARPHI **Weight:** 10.0000 g. **Composition:** 0.5000 White Gold .1608 oz. AGW

Date	Mintage	F	VF	XF	Unc
VS2031 (1974) Proof	Est. 250	Value: 350			

Note: Sometimes referred to as 1000 Rupees

KM# 852 10.0G ASARPHI **Weight:** 11.6600 g. **Composition:** 0.9000 Gold .3374 oz. AGW **Series:** International Year of the Child

Date	Mintage	F	VF	XF	Unc
VS2038 (1974) Proof	4,055	Value: 185			

Note: Struck in 1981

KM# 1022 10.0G ASARPHI **Weight:** 10.0000 g. **Composition:** 0.9000 Gold .2894 oz. AGW

Date	Mintage	F	VF	XF	Unc
VS2039 (1982)	25	—	—	—	—

KM# 1006 10.0G ASARPHI **Weight:** 10.0000 g. **Composition:** 0.5000 Gold .1608 oz. AGW **Subject:** 30th Anniversary Ascent of Mt. Everest **Obverse:** Similar to 5 Rupees, KM#833

Date	Mintage	F	VF	XF	Unc
VS2040 (1983) Proof	350	Value: 225			

KM# 1022a 10.0G ASARPHI **Weight:** 10.0000 g. **Composition:** 0.9990 Gold .3212 oz. AGW

Date	F	VF	XF	Unc
VS2042 (1985)	—	—	—	180
VS2046 (1989)	—	—	—	150
VS2048 (1991)	—	—	—	150
VS2049 (1992)	—	—	—	150
VS2050 (1993)	—	—	—	130
VS2052 (1995)	—	—	—	130
VS2054 (1997)	—	—	—	130
VS2056 (1999)	—	—	—	130

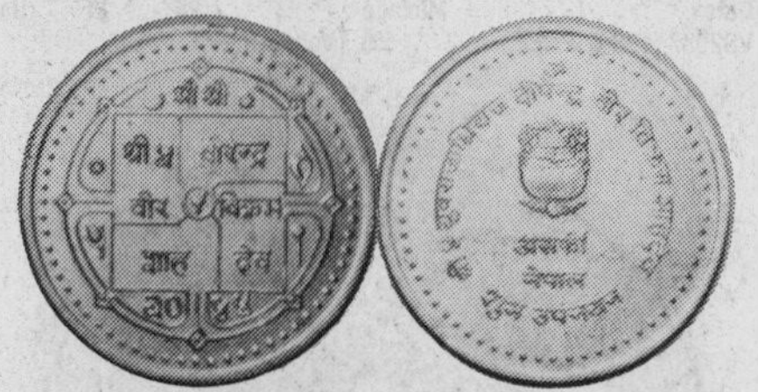

KM# 1034 10.0G ASARPHI **Weight:** 10.0000 g. **Composition:** Gold **Subject:** Crown Prince, Sacred Thread Ceremony

Date	Mintage	F	VF	XF	Unc
VS2044 (1987)	1,962	—	—	—	225

KM# 1054 10.0G ASARPHI **Weight:** 10.0000 g. **Composition:** 0.9990 Gold .3215 oz. AGW **Subject:** The New Constitution

Date	F	VF	XF	Unc
VS2047 (1990)	—	—	—	240

KM# 1145 10.0G ASARPHI **Weight:** 10.0000 g. **Composition:** 0.9990 Gold .3212 oz. AGW **Subject:** 50th Anniversary International Monetary Fund

Date	F	VF	XF	Unc
VS2051 (1994)	—	—	—	150

KM# 1146 10.0G ASARPHI **Weight:** 10.0000 g. **Composition:** 0.9990 Gold .3212 oz. AGW **Subject:** 50th Anniversary World Bank

Date	F	VF	XF	Unc
VS2051 (1994)	—	—	—	150

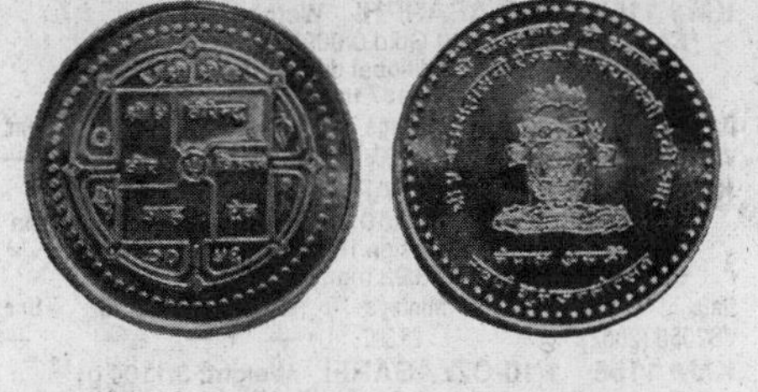

KM# 1147 10.0G ASARPHI **Weight:** 10.0000 g. **Composition:** 0.9990 Gold .3212 oz. AGW **Subject:** Queen Aishwariya Golden Anniversary

Date	F	VF	XF	Unc
VS2056 (1999)	—	—	—	150

KM# 1122 1/25-OZ. ASARFI **Weight:** 1.2441 g. **Composition:** 0.9999 Gold .0400 oz. AGW **Obverse:** Traditional square in circle design **Reverse:** Buddha's portrait and Ashoka pillar **Note:** Lord Buddha; Similar to Asarfi KM#1124.

Date	Mintage	F	VF	XF	Unc
VS2055 (1998) Proof	30,000	Value: 35.00			

KM# 1130 1/25-OZ. ASARFI **Weight:** 1.2441 g. **Composition:** 0.9999 Gold .0400 oz. AGW **Subject:** Buddha **Obverse:** Traditional square design **Reverse:** Buddha with halo **Edge:** Reeded **Size:** 18 mm.

Date	Mintage	F	VF	XF	Unc
VS2057 (2000)	30,000	—	—	—	30.00

KM# 1033 1/20-OZ. ASARFI **Weight:** 5.8300 g. **Composition:** 0.9600 Gold .1800 oz. AGW **Subject:** Crown Prince, Sacred Thread Ceremony

Date	Mintage	F	VF	XF	Unc
VS2044 (1987)	2,774	—	—	—	110

KM# 1079 1/20-OZ. ASARFI **Weight:** 1.5532 g. **Composition:** 0.9990 Gold .0500 oz. AGW **Reverse:** Buddha **Note:** Similar to 1-oz. Asarfi, KM#1082.

Date	Mintage	F	VF	XF	Unc
VS2052 (1995)	15,000	—	—	—	35.00

KM# 1096 1/20-OZ. ASARFI **Weight:** 1.5532 g. **Composition:** 0.9990 Gold .0500 oz. AGW **Subject:** Buddha's Birth **Note:** Similar to 1500 Rupee, KM#1095.

Date	F	VF	XF	Unc
VS2054 (1997)	—	—	—	35.00

KM# 1107 1/20-OZ. ASARFI **Weight:** 1.5552 g. **Composition:** 0.9990 Gold .0500 oz. AGW **Series:** Nepal Wildlife **Reverse:** Multicolored leopard **Note:** Similar to 2000 Rupees, KM#1104.

Date	Mintage	F	VF	XF	Unc
VS2054 (1998) Proof	15,000	Value: 75.00			

KM# 1108 1/20-OZ. ASARFI **Weight:** 1.5552 g. **Composition:** 0.9990 Gold .0500 oz. AGW **Series:** Nepal Wildlife **Reverse:** Multicolored tiger **Note:** Similar to 100 Rupees, KM#1102.

Date	Mintage	F	VF	XF	Unc
VS2054 (1998) Proof	15,000	Value: 75.00			

KM# 1050 1/10-OZ. ASARFI **Weight:** 2.5000 g. **Composition:** 0.9000 Gold .0724 oz. AGW

Date	Mintage	F	VF	XF	Unc
VS2039 (1982)	11	—	—	—	—

KM# 1037 1/10-OZ. ASARFI **Weight:** 3.1100 g. **Composition:** 0.9990 Gold .1000 oz. AGW **Reverse:** Snow leopard **Note:** Similar to 1-oz. Asarphi, KM#1040.

Date	Mintage	F	VF	XF	Unc
VS2045 (1988)	—	—	—	—	50.00
VS2045 (1988) Proof	2,000	Value: 65.00			

KM# 1080 1/10-OZ. ASARFI **Weight:** 3.1100 g. **Composition:** 0.9990 Gold .1000 oz. AGW **Reverse:** Buddha **Note:** Similar to 1-oz. Asarphi, KM#1082.

Date	Mintage	F	VF	XF	Unc
VS2052 (1995)	15,000	—	—	—	60.00

KM# 1097 1/10-OZ. ASARFI **Weight:** 3.1100 g. **Composition:** 0.9990 Gold .1000 oz. AGW **Subject:** Buddha's Birth **Note:** Similar to 1500 Rupee, KM#1095.

Date	F	VF	XF	Unc
VS2054 (1997)	—	—	—	60.00

KM# 1109 1/10-OZ. ASARFI **Weight:** 3.1104 g. **Composition:** 0.9990 Gold .1000 oz. AGW **Series:** Nepal Wildlife **Reverse:** Multicolored leopard **Note:** Similar to 2000 Rupees, KM#1104.

Date	Mintage	F	VF	XF	Unc
VS2054 (1998) Proof	10,000	Value: 100			

KM# 1123 1/10-OZ. ASARFI **Weight:** 3.1104 g. **Composition:** 0.9999 Gold .1000 oz. AGW **Obverse:** Traditional square in circle design **Reverse:** Buddha's portrait and Ashoka pillar **Note:** Lord Buddha; Similar to Asarfi KM#1124.

Date	Mintage	F	VF	XF	Unc
VS2055 (1998) Proof	15,000	Value: 65.00			

KM# 1131 1/10-OZ. ASARFI **Weight:** 3.1100 g. **Composition:** 0.9990 Gold .1000 oz. AGW **Subject:** Buddha **Obverse:** Traditional square design **Reverse:** Buddha with halo **Edge:** Reeded **Size:** 18 mm.

Date	Mintage	F	VF	XF	Unc
VS2057 (2000)	30,000	—	—	—	50.00

KM# 819 1/4-OZ. ASARFI **Weight:** 2.5000 g. **Composition:** 0.9990 Gold .804 oz. AGW

Date	Mintage	F	VF	XF	Unc
VS2028 (1971)	4	—	—	—	—
VS2030 (1973)	—	—	—	—	110
VS2031 (1974)	—	—	—	—	110
VS2036 (1979)	—	—	—	—	110
VS2037 (1980)	48	—	—	—	110

KM# 816a 1/4-OZ. ASARFI **Weight:** 2.5000 g. **Composition:** 0.9990 Gold .804 oz. AGW **Subject:** Birendra Coronation

Date	Mintage	F	VF	XF	Unc
VS2031 (1974)	500	—	—	—	100

KM# 1038 1/4-OZ. ASARFI **Weight:** 7.7700 g. **Composition:** 0.9990 Gold .2500 oz. AGW **Reverse:** Snow leopard **Note:** Similar to 1-oz. Asarphi, KM#1040, Bullion Series.

Date	Mintage	F	VF	XF	Unc
VS2045 (1988)	—	—	—	—	145
VS2045 (1988) Proof	Est. 2,000	Value: 175			

KM# 1059 1/4-OZ. ASARFI **Weight:** 2.5000 g. **Composition:** 0.9990 Gold .0804 oz. AGW **Note:** Similar to 1-oz. Asarphi, KM#1054.

Date	F	VF	XF	Unc
VS2047 (1990)	—	—	—	90.00

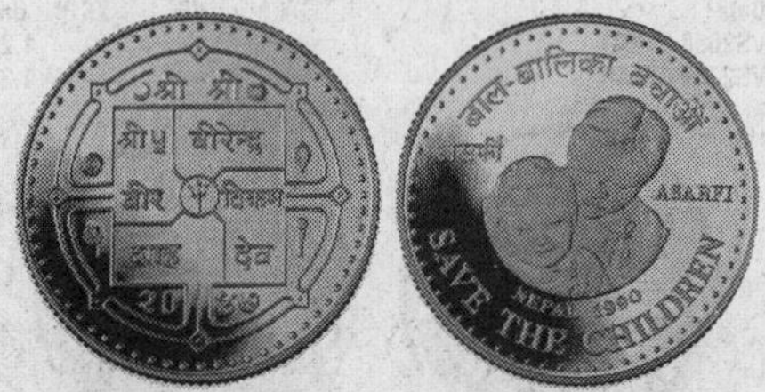

KM# 1056 1/4-OZ. ASARFI **Weight:** 11.6600 g. **Composition:** 0.9000 Gold .3374 oz. AGW **Series:** Save the Children

Date	Mintage	F	VF	XF	Unc
VS2047 (1990) Proof	3,000	Value: 240			

KM# 1093 1/4-OZ. ASARFI **Weight:** 7.7760 g. **Composition:** 0.5830 Gold .1457 oz. AGW **Series:** Olympics **Reverse:** Runner and temple

Date	F	VF	XF	Unc
VS2052 (1995)	—	—	—	150

KM# 1081 1/4-OZ. ASARFI **Weight:** 7.7759 g. **Composition:** 0.9990 Gold .2500 oz. AGW **Reverse:** Buddha **Note:** Similar to 1-oz. Asarphi, KM#1082.

Date	Mintage	F	VF	XF	Unc
VS2052 (1995)	15,000	—	—	—	125

KM# 1098 1/4-OZ. ASARFI **Weight:** 7.7759 g. **Composition:** 0.9990 Gold .2500 oz. AGW **Subject:** Buddha's Birth **Note:** Similar to 1500 Rupees, KM#1095.

Date	F	VF	XF	Unc
VS2054 (1997)	—	—	—	125

KM# 1110 1/4-OZ. ASARFI **Weight:** 7.7759 g. **Composition:** 0.9990 Gold .2500 oz. AGW **Series:** Nepal Wildlife **Reverse:** Multicolored elephants **Note:** Similar to 2000 Rupees, KM#1105.

Date	Mintage	F	VF	XF	Unc
VS2054 (1998) Proof	2,000	Value: 175			

KM# 1111 1/4-OZ. ASARFI **Weight:** 7.7759 g. **Composition:** 0.9990 Gold .2500 oz. AGW **Series:** Nepal Wildlife **Reverse:** Multicolored tiger **Note:** Similar to 100 Rupees, KM#1102.

Date	Mintage	F	VF	XF	Unc
VS2054 (1998) Proof	2,000	Value: 175			

KM# 1112 1/4-OZ. ASARFI **Weight:** 7.7759 g. **Composition:** 0.9990 Gold .2500 oz. AGW **Series:** Nepal Wildlife **Reverse:** Multicolored rhinoceros **Note:** Similar to 100 Rupees, KM#1103.

Date	Mintage	F	VF	XF	Unc
VS2054 (1998) Proof	2,000	Value: 175			

KM# 1113 1/4-OZ. ASARFI **Weight:** 7.7759 g. **Composition:** 0.9990 Gold .2500 oz. AGW **Series:** Nepal Wildlife **Reverse:** Multicolored leopard **Note:** Similar to 100 Rupees, KM#1104.

Date	Mintage	F	VF	XF	Unc
VS2054 (1998) Proof	2,000	Value: 175			

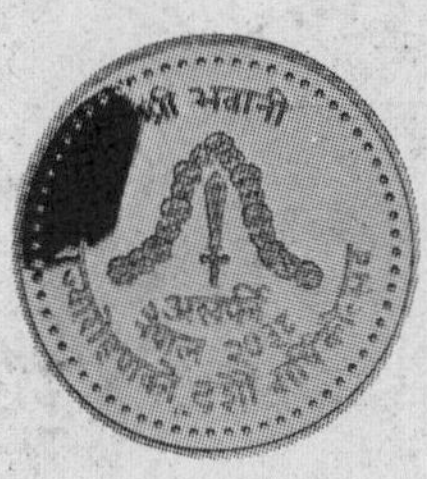

KM# 1008 1/2-OZ. ASARFI **Weight:** 15.9800 g. **Composition:** 0.9000 Gold .4624 oz. AGW **Subject:** 10th Anniversary of Reign

Date	Mintage	F	VF	XF	Unc
VS2038 (1981)	27	—	—	—	450
VS2038 (1981) Proof	5,092	Value: 235			

KM# 1011 1/2-OZ. ASARFI **Weight:** 15.9800 g. **Composition:** 0.9170 Gold .4712 oz. AGW **Series:** Year of the Scout

Date	Mintage	F	VF	XF	Unc
VS2039 (1982)	2,000	—	—	—	400

KM# 1045 1/2-OZ. ASARFI **Weight:** 15.0000 g. **Composition:** 0.9000 Gold .4340 oz. AGW **Subject:** 3rd SAARC Summit **Note:** Similar to 300 Rupees, KM#1044.

Date	Mintage	F	VF	XF	Unc
VS2044 (1987)	1,000	—	—	—	350

KM# 1039 1/2-OZ. ASARFI **Weight:** 15.5500 g. **Composition:** 0.9990 Gold .5000 oz. AGW **Reverse:** Snow leopard **Note:** Similar to 1-oz. Asarphi, KM#1040.

Date	Mintage	F	VF	XF	Unc
VS2045 (1988)	—	—	—	—	220
VS2045 (1988) Proof	Est. 2,000	Value: 265			

KM# 1124 1/2-OZ. ASARFI **Weight:** 15.5518 g. **Composition:** 0.9999 Gold .5000 oz. AGW **Obverse:** Traditional square in circle design **Reverse:** Lord Buddha, Ashoka pillar

Date	Mintage	F	VF	XF	Unc
VS2055 (1998) Proof	2,500	Value: 285			

KM# 1132 1/2-OZ. ASARFI **Weight:** 15.5518 g. **Composition:** 0.9999 Gold .5000 oz. AGW **Subject:** Buddha **Obverse:** Traditional square design **Reverse:** Buddha with halo **Edge:** Reeded **Size:** 27 mm.

Date	Mintage	F	VF	XF	Unc
VS2057 (2000) Proof	2,500	Value: 285			

KM# 1027 1-OZ. ASARFI **Weight:** 10.0000 g. **Composition:** Gold **Series:** Wildlife Protection **Reverse:** Ganges River Dolphins

Date	Mintage	F	VF	XF	Unc
VS2043 (1986) Proof	5,000	Value: 185			

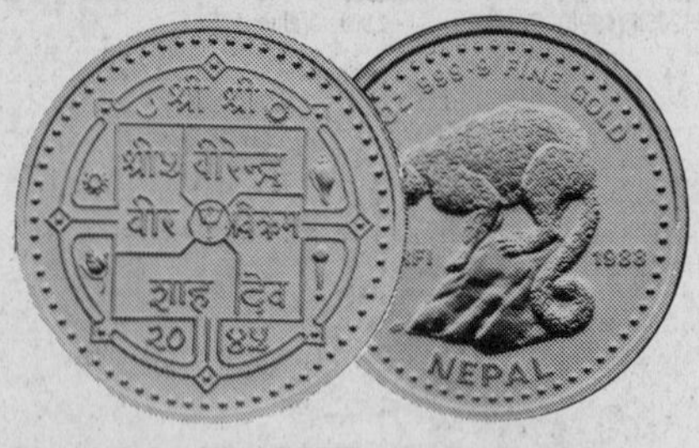

KM# 1040 1-OZ. ASARFI **Weight:** 31.1000 g. **Composition:** 0.9999 Gold 1.0000 oz. AGW **Reverse:** Snow leopard

Date	Mintage	F	VF	XF	Unc
VS2045 (1988)	—	—	—	—	425
VS2045 (1988) Proof	2,000	Value: 550			

KM# 1082 1-OZ. ASARFI **Weight:** 31.1035 g. **Composition:** 0.9999 Gold 1.0000 oz. AGW **Reverse:** Buddha

Date	Mintage	F	VF	XF	Unc
VS2052 (1995) Proof	2,500	Value: 600			

KM# 1099 1-OZ. ASARFI **Weight:** 31.1035 g. **Composition:** 0.9999 Gold 1.0000 oz. AGW **Subject:** Buddha's Birth **Obverse:** Traditional square in circle design **Reverse:** Woman holding onto a tree

Date	F	VF	XF	Unc
VS2054 (1997) Proof	—	Value: 600		

KM# 1086 1-1/2 OZ. ASARFI **Weight:** 44.6400 g. **Composition:** 0.9167 Gold 1.3156 oz. AGW **Subject:** Conquest of Mt. Everest

Date		F	VF	XF	Unc
VS2050 (1993) Proof	Est. 100	Value: 995			

Gyanendra Bir Bikram

VS2058- / 2001- AD (second reign)

DECIMAL COINAGE

100 Paisa = 1 Rupee

KM# 1148 25 PAISA **Composition:** Aluminum **Obverse:** Royal crown **Edge:** Plain **Size:** 20 mm.

Date	F	VF	XF	Unc
VS2058 (2001)	—	—	—	0.50
VS2053 (2002)	—	—	—	0.50

KM# 1149 50 PAISA **Composition:** Aluminum **Obverse:** Royal crown **Edge:** Plain **Size:** 22.5 mm.

Date	F	VF	XF	Unc
VS2058 (2001)	—	—	—	0.50
VS2059 (2002)	—	—	—	0.50

KM# 1150.2 RUPEE **Composition:** Brass **Reverse:** 3 millimeter "1", small temple **Edge:** Reeded **Size:** 30 mm.

Date	F	VF	XF	Unc
VS2058 (2001)	—	—	—	1.00
VS2059 (2002)	—	—	—	1.00

KM# 1050.1 RUPEE **Composition:** Brass **Reverse:** 4 millimeter "1", large temple **Edge:** Reeded

Date	F	VF	XF	Unc
VS2058 (2001)	—	—	—	1.00

KM# 1151.2 2 RUPEES **Composition:** Brass Plated Steel **Reverse:** Thick dots, larger central trident **Edge:** Plain **Size:** 25 mm.

Date	F	VF	XF	Unc
VS2058 (2001)	—	—	—	1.25
VS2059 (2002)	—	—	—	1.25

KM# 1151.1 (KM1151) 2 RUPEES **Composition:** Brass Plated Steel **Reverse:** Thin dots, small central trident **Edge:** Plain **Size:** 25 mm. **Note:** Edge varieties exist.

Date	F	VF	XF	Unc
VS2058 (2001)	—	—	—	1.25
VS2058 (2001)	—	—	—	1.25

KM# 1157 100 RUPEE **Weight:** 20.0000 g. **Composition:** Brass **Subject:** Buddha **Obverse:** Traditional design **Reverse:** Seated Buddha teaching five seated monks **Edge:** Reeded **Size:** 38.7 mm.

Date	Mintage	F	VF	XF	Unc
VS2058 (2002)	30,000	—	—	—	—

KM# 1158 1500 RUPEE **Weight:** 20.0000 g. **Composition:** 0.9250 Silver 0.5948 oz. ASW **Subject:** Buddha **Obverse:** Traditional design **Reverse:** Seated Buddha teaching five seated monks **Edge:** Reeded **Size:** 38.7 mm.

Date	Mintage	F	VF	XF	Unc
VS2058 (2002) Proof	15,000	Value: 31.50			

ASARFI GOLD COINAGE

(Asarphi)

Fractional designations are approximate for this series. Actual Gold Weight (AGW) is used to identify each type.

KM# 1153 0.3G ASARPHI **Weight:** 0.3000 g. **Composition:** 0.9999 Gold 0.0096 oz. AGW **Subject:** Buddha **Obverse:** Traditional design **Reverse:** Seated Buddha **Edge:** Plain **Size:** 7 mm.

Date	Mintage	F	VF	XF	Unc
VS2058 (2002)	30,000	—	—	—	—

KM# 1154 1/25-OZ. ASARFI **Weight:** 1.2441 g. **Composition:** 0.9999 Gold 0.04 oz. AGW **Subject:** Buddha **Obverse:** Traditional design **Reverse:** Seated Buddha **Edge:** Reeded **Size:** 13.92 mm.

Date	Mintage	F	VF	XF	Unc
VS2058 (2002)	25,000	—	—	—	—

KM# 1155 1/10-OZ. ASARFI **Weight:** 3.1104 g. **Composition:** 0.9999 Gold 0.1 oz. AGW **Subject:** Buddha **Obverse:** Traditional design **Reverse:** Seated Buddha **Edge:** Reeded **Size:** 17.95 mm.

Date	Mintage	F	VF	XF	Unc
VS2058 (2002)	15,000	—	—	—	—

KM# 1156 1/2-OZ. ASARFI **Weight:** 15.5518 g. **Composition:** 0.9999 Gold 0.5 oz. AGW **Subject:** Buddha **Obverse:** Traditional design **Reverse:** Seated Buddha **Edge:** Reeded **Size:** 27 mm.

Date	Mintage	F	VF	XF	Unc
VS2058 (2002) Proof	2,500	Value: 315			

PATTERNS

Including off metal strikes

KM#	Date	Mintage	Identification	Mkt Val
Pn3	1975	—	5 Paisa. KM#690.1	—

PIEFORTS

KM#	Date	Mintage	Identification	Mkt Val
P1	2038	88	100 Rupee. KM#851.	100
P2	2039	48	Asarphi.	1,250

MINT SETS

KM#	Date	Mintage	Identification	Issue Price	Mkt Val
MSA4	1996, 1995, 2011 (3)	—	KM#709.2 (1996); 711 (1995); 737 (2011)	—	7.00
MS8	1957 (6)	—	KM#709.1 (1996), 755 (2014), 760 (2011); 2 pieces each	0.85	7.00
MS4	1955 (3)	—	KM#712 (2000); 733; 749 (2012)	0.85	5.00
MS2	1949 (3)	—	KM#716, 718, 723 (restrikes)	—	8.00
MS3	1953 (8)	—	KM#733, 735-740, 742	—	160
MS7	1957 (4)	—	KM#740 (2011), 742, 738 (2010), 769 (2014)	2.05	12.00
MS10	1964 (7)	—	KM#747, 752, 758a, 764, 772, 778, 785	—	50.00
MS5	1956 (7)	—	KM#745.1, 750.1, 756.2, 761, 770, 776, 790	—	50.00
MS6	1956 (7)	—	KM#745.1, 750.1, 756.3, 761, 770, 776, 790 (restrikes)	—	13.50
MS9	1964 (7)	—	KM#747, 752, 758, 763, 772, 778, 785	—	10.00
MS11	1965 (7)	—	KM#747, 752 (2022), 758, 763, 772, 778, 786 (2021)	2.75	10.00
MS12	1966 (7)	—	KM#748, 753, 759, 765, 772, 779, 787	—	7.00
MS13	1967 (7)	—	KM#748, 753, 759, 765, 772, 779, 787	—	5.00
MS14	1971 (7)	—	KM#799, 801, 802, 806, 815, 821, 828	—	5.00
MS15	1974 (7)	—	KM#800, 804, 808, 816.1, 822.1, 829.1, 838	—	12.50
MS16	1974 (2)	—	KM#829.1, 841	32.50	30.00
MS17	1975 (5)	—	KM#808, 816.1, 822.1, 829.1, 838	—	13.00
MS18	1975 (3)	—	KM#809, 831, 836	—	9.00
MS19	1997 (3)	—	KM#1096-1098	—	225

PROOF SETS

KM#	Date	Mintage	Identification	Issue Price	Mkt Val
PS3	1970 (7)	2,187	KM#748, 753, 759, 765, 733, 780, 788	10.00	15.00
PS4	1971 (7)	2,380	KM#748, 753, 759, 765, 773, 780, 788	10.00	15.00
PS5	1972 (7)	3,943	KM#799, 801, 802, 807, 815, 821, 828	10.00	8.50
PS6	1973 (7)	8,891	KM#799, 801, 802, 807, 815, 821, 828	10.00	6.00
PS9	1981 (7)	1,000	KM#800a, 804a, 808a, 816.2, 822.2, 829.2, 838a (dated 1974)Coins dated 2031 (1974) but this set was issued in 1981 to celebrate the 7th Anniversary of the Coronation.	62.00	50.00
PS7	1974 (7)	10,543	KM#799, 801, 802, 807, 815, 821, 828	10.00	5.50
PS8	1974 (2)	30,000	KM#839a, 841a	50.00	42.00
PS10	1988 (4)	2,000	KM#1037-1040	—	1,050
PS11	1995-97 (2)	—	KM#1077, 1099	—	645

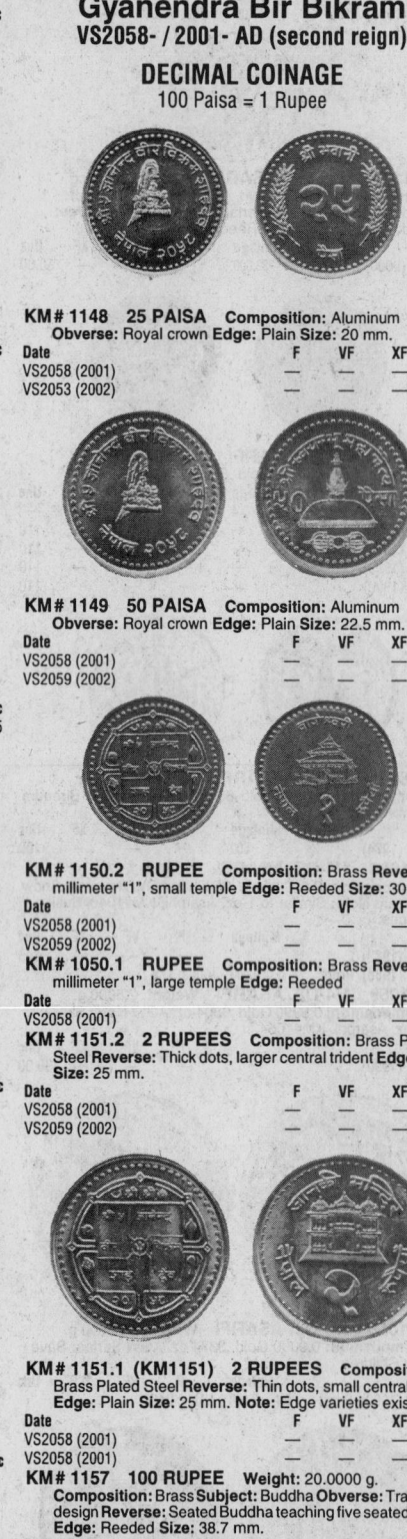

NETHERLANDS

The Kingdom of the Netherlands, a country of western Europe fronting on the North Sea and bordered by Belgium and Germany, has an area of 15,770 sq. mi. (41,500 sq. km.) and a population of 16.1 million. Capital: Amsterdam, but the seat of government is at The Hague. The economy is based on dairy farming and a variety of industrial activities. Chemicals, yarns and fabrics, and meat products are exported.

After being a part of Charlemagne's empire in the 8th and 9th centuries, the Netherlands came under control of Burgundy and the Austrian Hapsburgs, and finally was subjected to Spanish domination in the 16th century. Led by William of Orange, the Dutch revolted against Spain in 1568. The seven northern provinces formed the Union of Utrecht and declared their independence in 1581, becoming the Republic of the United Netherlands. In the following century, the *Golden Age* of Dutch history, the Netherlands became a great sea and colonial power, a patron of the arts and a refuge for the persecuted. The United Dutch Republic ended in 1795 when the French formed the Batavian Republic. Napoleon made his brother Louis, the King of Holland in 1806, however he abdicated in 1810 when Napoleon annexed Holland. The French were expelled in 1813, and all the provinces of Holland and Belgium were merged into the Kingdom of the United Netherlands under William I, in 1814. The Belgians withdrew in 1830 to form their own kingdom, the last substantial change in the configuration of European Netherlands. German forces invaded in 1940 as the royal family fled to England where a government-in-exile was formed.

WORLD WAR II COINAGE

U.S. mints in the name of the government in exile and its remaining Curacao and Surinam Colonies during the years 1941-45 minted coinage of the Netherlands Homeland Types -KM #152, 153, 163, 164, 161.1 and 161.2 -. The Curacao and Surinam strikes, distinguished by the presence of a palm tree in combination with a mint mark (P-Philadelphia; D-Denver; S-San Francisco) flanking the date, are incorporated under those titles in this volume. Pieces of this period struck in the name of the homeland bear an acorn and mint mark and are incorporated in the following tabulation.

NOTE: Excepting the World War II issues struck at U.S. mints, all of the modern coins were struck at the Utrecht Mint and bear the caduceus mint mark of that facility. They also bear the mintmasters marks.

RULERS

KINGDOM OF THE NETHERLANDS

Wilhelmina I, 1890-1948
Juliana, 1948-1980
Beatrix, 1980—

MINT MARKS

D - Denver, 1943-1945
P - Philadelphia, 1941-1945
S - San Francisco, 1944-1245

MINT PRIVY MARKS
Utrecht

Date	Privy Mark
1806-present	Caduceus

MINTMASTERS PRIVY MARKS

U. S. Mints

Date	Privy Mark
1941-45	Palm tree

Utrecht Mint

Date	Privy Mark
1888-1909	Halberd
1909	Halberd and star
1909-1933	Seahorse
1933-42	Grapes
1943-1945	No privy mark
1945-69	Fish
1969-79	Cock
1980	Cock and star (temporal)
1980-88	Anvil with hammer
1989-99	Bow and arrow
2000-	Bow, arrow and star
2001	Wine tendril w/grapes
2002	Wine tendril w/grapes and star
2003	Sails of a clipper

NOTE: A star adjoining the privy mark indicates that the piece was struck at the beginning of the term of office of a successor. (The star was used only if the successor had not chosen his own mark yet.)

NOTE: Since October, 1999, the Dutch Mint has taken the title of Royal Dutch Mint.

MONETARY SYSTEM

Until January 29, 2002
100 Cents = 1 Gulden
Since January 1, 2002
100 Cents = 1 Euro

KINGDOM OF THE NETHERLANDS

DECIMAL COINAGE

KM# 109 1/2 CENT Composition: Bronze **Obverse:** 17 small shields in field **Obv. Legend:** KONINGRIJK. . .

Date	Mintage	F	VF	XF	Unc	BU
1901	6,000,000	1.50	3.00	6.00	17.50	35.00

KM# 133 1/2 CENT Composition: Bronze **Obverse:** 17 small shields in field **Obv. Legend:** KONINGRIJK. . .

Date	Mintage	F	VF	XF	Unc	BU
1903	10,000,000	1.00	2.00	3.00	10.00	15.00
1906	10,000,000	1.00	2.00	3.00	10.00	15.00

KM# 138 1/2 CENT Composition: Bronze **Obverse:** 15 large shields in field around larger lion, smaller date and legend **Reverse:** CENT in larger letters

Date	Mintage	F	VF	XF	Unc	BU
1909	5,000,000	1.00	2.00	3.00	10.00	15.00
1911	5,000,000	1.00	2.00	3.00	10.00	15.00
1912	5,000,000	1.00	2.00	3.00	10.00	15.00
1914	5,000,000	1.00	2.00	3.00	10.00	15.00
1915	2,500,000	5.00	10.00	15.00	25.00	45.00
1916	4,000,000	2.00	4.00	7.00	15.00	25.00
1917	5,000,000	1.00	2.00	4.00	10.00	15.00
1921	1,500,000	5.00	10.00	15.00	25.00	45.00
1922/1	—	25.00	55.00	100	225	350
1922	2,500,000	5.00	10.00	15.00	25.00	45.00
1928	4,000,000	1.00	2.00	3.00	8.00	15.00
1930	6,000,000	1.00	1.50	2.50	6.00	12.00
1934	5,000,000	0.75	1.75	2.50	5.00	8.00
1936	5,000,000	0.75	1.75	2.50	5.00	8.00
1937	1,600,000	1.00	2.50	4.00	8.00	12.50
1938	8,400,000	0.75	1.50	2.00	3.00	5.00
1940	6,000,000	0.75	1.50	2.00	3.00	5.00

KM# 130 CENT Composition: Bronze **Obverse:** 15 large shields in field **Obv. Legend:** KONINKRIJK

Date	Mintage	F	VF	XF	Unc	BU
1901	10,000,000	1.00	2.50	5.00	20.00	—

KM# 131 CENT Composition: Bronze **Obverse:** 10 large shields in field **Obv. Legend:** KONINGRIJK

Date	Mintage	F	VF	XF	Unc	BU
1901	10,000,000	1.00	2.50	5.00	20.00	—

KM# 132.1 CENT Composition: Bronze **Obverse:** 15 medium shields in field **Obv. Legend:** KONINGRIJK

Date	Mintage	F	VF	XF	Unc	BU
1902	10,000,000	1.00	2.00	3.00	15.00	25.00
1904	15,000,000	1.00	2.00	3.00	15.00	25.00
1905	10,000,000	1.00	2.00	3.00	15.00	25.00
1906	9,000,000	1.00	2.00	3.00	15.00	25.00
1907	6,000,000	6.00	12.00	30.00	60.00	85.00

KM# 132.2 CENT Composition: Bronze **Obverse:** 15 medium shields in field **Obv. Legend:** KONINGRIJK **Edge:** Plain

Date	F	VF	XF	Unc	BU
1906 Proof	—	Value: 875			

KM# 152 CENT Composition: Bronze

Date	Mintage	F	VF	XF	Unc	BU
1913	5,000,000	2.50	6.00	12.00	28.00	50.00
1914	9,000,000	1.00	2.00	3.00	15.00	25.00
1915	10,800,000	1.00	2.00	3.00	12.00	18.00
1916	21,700,000	0.75	1.00	2.00	10.00	15.00
1916 Proof	—	Value: 110				
1917	20,000,000	0.75	1.00	2.00	10.00	15.00
1918	10,000,000	1.00	2.00	4.00	12.00	20.00
1919	6,000,000	2.75	5.00	10.00	20.00	30.00
1920	11,400,000	0.75	1.50	2.00	10.00	15.00
1921	12,600,000	0.75	1.50	2.00	10.00	15.00
1922	20,000,000	0.75	1.50	2.00	10.00	15.00
1924	1,400,000	15.00	30.00	55.00	100	145
1925	18,600,000	0.75	1.50	2.00	10.00	15.00
1926	10,000,000	0.75	1.50	2.00	10.00	15.00
1927	10,000,000	0.75	1.50	2.00	10.00	15.00
1928	10,000,000	0.75	1.50	2.00	10.00	15.00
1929	20,000,000	0.75	1.50	2.00	8.00	12.00
1930	10,000,000	0.75	1.50	2.00	8.00	12.00
1931	3,400,000	3.50	7.50	12.50	35.00	50.00
1937	10,000,000	0.50	1.00	1.50	5.00	8.00
1938	16,600,000	0.50	1.00	1.50	5.00	8.00
1939	22,000,000	0.50	1.00	1.50	5.00	7.00
1940	24,600,000	0.50	1.00	1.50	5.00	7.00
1941	66,600,000	0.25	0.60	1.00	2.50	4.00

Note: For similar coins dated 1942P see Curacao; 1943P, 1957-1960 see Suriname

KM# 170 CENT Composition: Zinc

Date	Mintage	F	VF	XF	Unc	BU
1941	31,800,000	1.00	2.00	4.00	15.00	25.00
1942	241,000,000	0.25	0.50	1.00	3.00	8.00
1943	71,000,000	0.50	1.00	2.00	5.00	15.00
1944	29,600,000	1.00	2.00	4.00	15.00	25.00

KM# 175 CENT Composition: Bronze

Date	Mintage	F	VF	XF	Unc	BU
1948	130,400,000	0.10	0.25	0.50	1.50	9.00
1948 Proof	—	Value: 80.00				

large date small date

KM# 180 CENT Composition: Bronze

Date	Mintage	F	VF	XF	Unc	BU
1950	91,000,000	—	0.10	0.25	0.75	5.50
1950 Proof	—	Value: 50.00				
1951	45,800,000	—	0.10	0.25	0.75	5.50
1951 Proof	—	Value: 45.00				
1952	68,000,000	—	0.10	0.25	0.75	5.50
1952 Proof	—	Value: 45.00				
1953	54,000,000	—	0.10	0.25	0.75	5.50
1953 Proof	—	Value: 45.00				
1954	54,000,000	—	0.10	0.25	0.75	5.50
1954 Proof	—	Value: 45.00				
1955	52,000,000	—	0.10	0.25	0.75	5.50
1955 Proof	—	Value: 45.00				
1956	34,800,000	—	0.10	0.25	0.75	5.50
1956 Proof	—	Value: 45.00				
1957	48,000,000	—	0.10	0.25	0.75	5.50
1957 Proof	—	Value: 45.00				
1958	34,000,000	—	0.10	0.25	0.75	5.50
1958 Proof	—	Value: 40.00				
1959	36,000,000	—	0.10	0.25	0.75	5.50
1959 Proof	—	Value: 35.00				
1960	40,000,000	—	0.10	0.25	0.75	4.50

Date	Mintage	F	VF	XF	Unc	BU
1960 Proof	—	Value: 35.00				
1961	52,000,000	—	—	0.10	0.35	3.00
1961 Proof	—	Value: 35.00				
1962	57,000,000	—	—	0.10	0.35	3.00
1962 Proof	—	Value: 35.00				
1963	70,000,000	—	—	0.10	0.35	3.00
1963 Proof	—	Value: 35.00				
1964	73,000,000	—	—	0.10	0.35	3.00
1964 Proof	—	Value: 35.00				
1965	91,000,000	—	—	0.10	0.35	3.00
1965 Proof	—	Value: 35.00				
1966 large date	104,000,000	—	—	0.10	0.25	1.50
1966 Proof, large date	—	Value: 35.00				
1966 small date	Inc. above	—	—	0.10	0.25	1.50
1966 Proof, small date	—	Value: 20.00				
1967	140,000,000	—	—	0.10	0.25	1.50
1967 Proof	—	Value: 25.00				
1968	28,000,000	—	—	0.10	0.25	1.50
1968 Proof	—	Value: 20.00				
1969 fish privy mark	50,000,000	—	—	0.10	0.25	1.50
1969 Proof, fish privy mark	—	Value: 20.00				
1969 cock privy mark	50,000,000	—	—	0.10	0.25	1.50
1969 Proof, cock privy mark	—	Value: 20.00				
1970	100,000,000	—	—	0.10	0.15	1.50
1970 Proof	—	Value: 20.00				
1971	70,000,000	—	—	0.10	0.15	1.50
1972	40,000,000	—	—	—	0.10	1.00
1973	34,000,000	—	—	—	0.10	1.00
1974	46,000,000	—	—	—	0.10	1.00
1975	25,000,000	—	—	—	0.10	1.00
1976	15,000,000	—	—	—	0.10	1.00
1977	15,000,000	—	—	—	0.10	1.00
1978	15,000,000	—	—	—	0.10	1.00
1979	15,000,000	—	—	—	0.10	1.00
1980 cock and star privy mark	15,300,000	—	—	—	0.10	0.50

KM# 134 2-1/2 CENT Composition: Bronze **Obverse:** 15 large shields in field **Obv. Legend:** KONINGRIJK.

Date	Mintage	F	VF	XF	Unc	BU
1903	4,000,000	2.00	3.50	6.50	20.00	35.00
1904	4,000,000	2.00	3.50	6.50	20.00	35.00
1905	4,000,000	2.00	3.50	6.50	20.00	35.00
1906	8,000,000	2.00	3.50	6.50	20.00	35.00

KM# 150 2-1/2 CENT Composition: Bronze **Obverse:** 15 large shields in field **Obv. Legend:** KONINGRIJK.

Date	Mintage	F	VF	XF	Unc	BU
1912	2,000,000	4.00	8.00	16.50	42.50	75.00
1913	4,000,000	2.50	4.50	8.00	20.00	40.00
1914	2,000,000	4.00	8.00	16.50	42.50	75.00
1915	3,000,000	3.00	6.00	12.00	25.00	45.00
1916	8,000,000	2.00	3.50	6.00	15.00	25.00
1918	4,000,000	2.50	4.00	8.00	22.50	45.00
1919	2,000,000	3.00	6.00	12.00	25.00	50.00
1929	8,000,000	2.00	3.50	6.00	10.00	15.00
1941	19,800,000	1.25	2.00	3.00	6.50	10.00

KM# 171 2-1/2 CENT Composition: Zinc

Date	F	VF	XF	Unc	BU
1941	1.00	3.00	5.00	15.00	30.00
1942	750	3,500	5,500	8,500	11,000

Note: Almost entire issue melted, about 30 pieces known

KM# 137 5 CENTS Composition: Copper-Nickel

Date	Mintage	F	VF	XF	Unc	BU
1907	6,000,000	3.00	6.00	10.00	20.00	35.00
1908	5,430,000	4.00	8.00	12.50	22.50	40.00
1909	2,570,000	20.00	30.00	50.00	90.00	135

KM# 153 5 CENTS Composition: Copper-Nickel **Shape:** Square

Date	Mintage	F	VF	XF	Unc	BU
1913	6,000,000	1.50	3.00	5.00	15.00	30.00
1914	7,400,000	1.50	3.00	5.00	15.00	30.00
1923	10,000,000	1.50	3.00	5.00	15.00	30.00
1929	8,000,000	1.50	3.00	5.00	15.00	30.00
1932	2,000,000	5.50	12.00	20.00	35.00	65.00
1933	1,400,000	20.00	30.00	50.00	90.00	150
1934	2,600,000	4.00	6.00	10.00	20.00	40.00
1936	2,600,000	4.00	6.00	10.00	20.00	40.00
1938	4,200,000	2.00	3.50	4.50	10.00	20.00
1939	4,600,000	2.00	3.50	4.50	10.00	20.00
1940	7,200,000	2.00	3.00	4.00	9.00	15.00

Note: For a similar coin dated 1943, see Curacao

KM# 172 5 CENTS Composition: Zinc **Shape:** Square

Date	Mintage	F	VF	XF	Unc	BU
1941	32,200,000	1.00	2.50	6.00	18.00	35.00
1942	11,800,000	2.00	3.50	9.00	22.00	40.00
1943	7,000,000	5.00	8.00	16.50	42.50	75.00

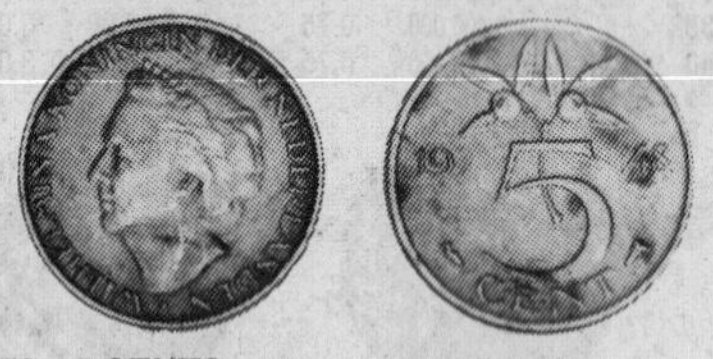

KM# 176 5 CENTS Composition: Bronze

Date	Mintage	F	VF	XF	Unc	BU
1948	23,600,000	0.50	0.75	7.00	16.50	
1948 Proof	—	Value: 100				

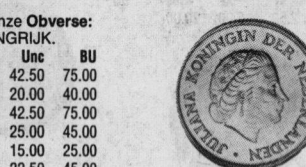

KM# 181 5 CENTS Composition: Bronze

Date	Mintage	F	VF	XF	Unc	BU
1950	20,000,000	—	0.10	0.25	3.50	8.00
1950 Proof	—	Value: 50.00				
1951	16,200,000	—	0.10	0.25	3.50	8.00
1951 Proof	—	Value: 50.00				
1952	14,400,000	—	0.10	0.25	3.50	8.00
1952 Proof	—	Value: 50.00				
1953	12,000,000	—	0.10	0.25	3.50	8.00
1953 Proof	—	Value: 50.00				
1954	14,000,000	—	0.10	0.25	3.50	8.00
1954 Proof	—	Value: 50.00				
1955	11,400,000	—	0.10	0.25	3.50	8.00
1955 Proof	—	Value: 50.00				
1956	7,400,000	—	0.15	0.35	4.50	10.00
1956 Proof	—	Value: 50.00				
1957	16,000,000	—	0.10	0.25	3.50	8.00
1957 Proof	—	Value: 50.00				
1958	9,000,000	—	0.10	0.25	4.50	10.00
1958 Proof	—	Value: 50.00				
1960	11,000,000	—	0.10	0.25	2.50	6.50
1960 Proof	—	Value: 40.00				
1961	12,000,000	—	0.10	0.25	2.50	6.50
1961 Proof	—	Value: 40.00				
1962	15,000,000	—	0.10	0.25	2.00	4.5
1962 Proof	—	Value: 40.00				
1963	18,000,000	—	0.10	0.25	2.00	4.5
1963 Proof	—	Value: 40.00				
1964	21,000,000	—	0.10	0.25	2.00	4.5
1964 Proof	—	Value: 40.00				
1965	28,000,000	—	0.10	0.25	1.50	3.0
1965 Proof	—	Value: 40.00				
1966	22,000,000	—	0.10	0.25	2.00	4.5
1966 Proof	—	Value: 40.00				
1967 leaves far from rim	32,000,000	—	—	0.20	1.50	3.5
1967 Proof, leaves far from rim	—	Value: 50.00				
1967 leaves touching rim	Inc. above	—	0.15	0.50	1.50	3.5
1967 Proof, leaves touching rim	—	Value: 40.00				
1969 fish privy mark	5,000,000	—	0.15	0.50	3.50	10.0
1969 Proof, fish privy mark	—	Value: 40.00				
1969 cock privy mark	11,000,000	—	—	0.10	1.00	4.0
1969 Proof, cock privy mark	—	Value: 40.00				
1970	22,000,000	—	—	0.10	0.75	3.0
1970 Proof	—	Value: 25.00				
1970 date close to rim	Inc. above	—	—	0.10	0.75	3.0
1970 Proof, date close to rim	—	Value: 20.00				
1971	25,000,000	—	—	0.10	0.50	2.0
1972	25,000,000	—	—	0.10	0.50	2.0
1973	22,000,000	—	—	0.10	0.50	2.0
1974	20,000,000	—	—	—	0.50	2.0
1975	46,000,000	—	—	—	0.25	1.5
1976	50,000,000	—	—	—	0.25	1.5
1977	50,000,000	—	—	—	0.25	1.5
1978	60,000,000	—	—	—	0.25	1.5
1979	80,000,000	—	—	—	0.25	1.5
1980 cock and star privy mark	252,500,000	—	—	—	0.10	0.3

KM# 202 5 CENTS Composition: Bronze

Date	Mintage	F	VF	XF	Unc	BU
1982		—	—	—	0.10	0.40
1982 Proof	10,000	Value: 10.00				
1983		—	—	—	0.10	0.40
1983 Proof	15,000	Value: 7.50				
1984		—	—	—	0.10	0.40
1984 Proof	20,000	Value: 4.00				
1985		—	—	—	0.10	0.40
1985 Proof	17,000	Value: 4.00				
1986		—	—	—	0.50	1.50
1986 Proof	20,000	Value: 4.00				
1987		—	—	—	—	0.40
1987 Proof	18,000	Value: 4.00				
1988		—	—	—	—	0.40
1988 Proof	20,000	Value: 4.00				
1989		—	—	—	—	0.40
1989 Proof	15,000	Value: 4.00				
1990		—	—	—	—	0.40
1990 Proof	15,000	Value: 4.00				
1991		—	—	—	—	0.40
1991 Proof	14,000	Value: 4.00				
1992		—	—	—	—	0.40
1992 Proof	13,000	Value: 4.00				
1993		—	—	—	—	0.40
1993 Proof	12,000	Value: 4.00				
1994		—	—	—	—	1.50
1994 Proof	13,000	Value: 4.00				
1995		—	—	—	0.75	3.00
1995 Proof	12,000	Value: 4.00				
1996		—	—	—	—	0.40
1996 Proof	14,000	Value: 4.00				
1997		—	—	—	—	0.40
1997 Proof	12,000	Value: 4.00				
1998		—	—	—	—	0.40
1998 Proof	12,000	Value: 4.00				
1999		—	—	—	—	0.40
1999 Proof	15,000	Value: 4.00				
2000		—	—	—	—	0.40
2000 Proof	15,000	Value: 4.00				
2001		—	—	—	—	0.40
2001 Proof	—	Value: 4.00				

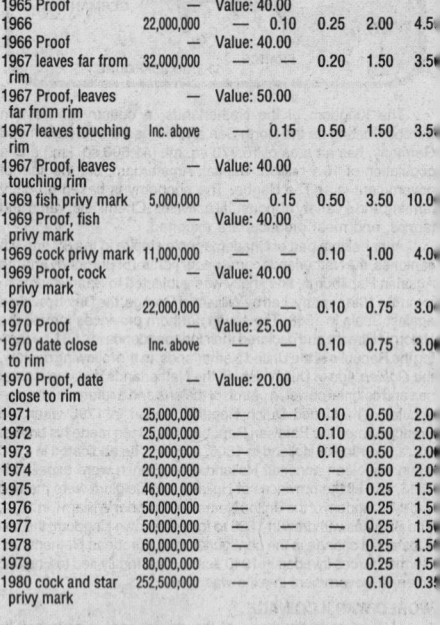

KM# 119 10 CENTS **Weight:** 1.4000 g. **Composition:** 0.6400 Silver .0288 oz. ASW **Obverse:** Small head, divided legend

Date	Mintage	F	VF	XF	Unc	BU
1901	2,000,000	10.00	25.00	60.00	135	200

KM# 135 10 CENTS **Weight:** 1.4000 g. **Composition:** 0.6400 Silver .0288 oz. ASW **Obverse:** Large head

Date	Mintage	F	VF	XF	Unc	BU
1903	6,000,000	4.00	12.00	30.00	50.00	65.00

KM# 136 10 CENTS **Weight:** 1.4000 g. **Composition:** 0.6400 Silver .0288 oz. ASW **Obverse:** Small head, continous legend

Date	Mintage	F	VF	XF	Unc	BU
1904	3,000,000	6.00	16.50	30.00	70.00	120
1905	2,000,000	8.00	22.50	40.00	85.00	135
1906	4,000,000	4.00	14.50	25.00	55.00	100

KM# 145 10 CENTS **Weight:** 1.4000 g. **Composition:** 0.6400 Silver .0288 oz. ASW **Obverse:** Small head, continuous legend

Date	Mintage	F	VF	XF	Unc	BU
1910	2,250,000	10.00	25.00	45.00	85.00	140
1911	4,000,000	4.00	9.00	22.00	45.00	75.00
1912	4,000,000	4.00	9.00	22.00	45.00	75.00
1913	5,000,000	3.00	7.00	15.00	40.00	65.00
1914	9,000,000	1.50	4.00	10.00	25.00	45.00
1915	5,000,000	1.75	5.00	12.00	30.00	50.00
1916	5,000,000	1.75	5.00	12.00	30.00	50.00
1917	10,000,000	1.50	3.50	8.00	16.00	25.00
1918	20,000,000	1.00	2.50	5.00	13.50	20.00
1919	10,000,000	1.50	3.50	8.00	16.00	25.00
1921	5,000,000	2.00	6.00	10.00	22.00	42.00
1925	5,000,000	2.00	6.00	10.00	22.00	42.00

KM# 163 10 CENTS **Weight:** 1.4000 g. **Composition:** 0.6400 Silver .0288 oz. ASW **Obverse:** Small head, continous legend

Date	Mintage	F	VF	XF	Unc	BU
1926	2,700,000	2.50	6.00	15.00	35.00	55.00
1927	2,300,000	2.50	6.00	15.00	35.00	55.00
1928	10,000,000	0.75	2.00	5.00	16.00	35.00
1930	5,000,000	1.00	3.50	7.50	22.00	40.00
1934	2,000,000	2.50	6.00	15.00	40.00	65.00
1935	8,000,000	0.50	1.50	3.50	10.00	15.00
1936	15,000,000	0.25	0.75	2.00	5.00	10.00
1937	18,600,000	0.25	0.75	2.00	3.50	5.00
1938	21,400,000	0.25	0.75	2.00	3.50	5.00
1939	20,000,000	0.25	0.75	2.00	3.50	5.00
1941	43,000,000	0.25	0.50	1.50	2.25	3.00
1943P Acorn privy mark	—	0.50	1.00	2.00	7.00	10.00
1944P	120,000,000	0.25	0.75	1.25	2.00	3.00
1944D	25,400,000	1,100	2,500	3,500	5,500	8,500
Note: Almost entire issue melted						
1944S	64,040,000	0.75	2.00	4.50	12.00	15.00
1945P	90,560,000	120	300	550	850	1,000

Note: For similar coins dated 1941P-1943P with palm tree privy mark, see Curacao and Suriname

KM# 173 10 CENTS **Composition:** Zinc

Date	Mintage	F	VF	XF	Unc	BU
1941	29,800,000	0.75	1.50	3.50	10.00	20.00
1942	95,600,000	0.25	0.50	2.00	5.00	10.00
1943	29,000,000	0.75	1.50	3.50	10.00	20.00

KM# 177 10 CENTS **Composition:** Nickel

Date	Mintage	F	VF	XF	Unc	BU
1948	69,200,000	—	0.25	0.50	1.00	6.50
1948 Proof	—	Value: 100				

KM# 182 10 CENTS **Composition:** Nickel

Date	Mintage	F	VF	XF	Unc	BU
1950	56,600,000	—	0.10	0.35	0.75	3.50
1950 Proof	—	Value: 80.00				
1951	54,200,000	—	0.10	0.35	0.75	3.50
1951 Proof	—	Value: 60.00				
1954	8,200,000	—	0.20	0.50	1.00	5.50
1954 Proof	—	Value: 60.00				
1955	18,200,000	—	0.10	0.35	0.75	4.00
1955 Proof	—	Value: 60.00				
1956	12,000,000	—	0.10	0.35	0.75	4.00
1956 Proof	—	Value: 60.00				
1957	18,600,000	—	0.10	0.35	0.75	4.00
1957 Proof	—	Value: 60.00				
1958	34,000,000	—	0.10	0.35	0.75	3.00
1958 Proof	—	Value: 60.00				
1959	44,000,000	—	0.10	0.35	0.75	3.00
1959 Proof	—	Value: 50.00				
1960	12,000,000	—	0.10	0.35	0.75	4.00
1960 Proof	—	Value: 50.00				
1961	25,000,000	—	—	0.10	0.25	2.50
1961 Proof	—	Value: 50.00				
1962	30,000,000	—	—	0.10	0.25	1.50
1962 Proof	—	Value: 50.00				
1963	35,000,000	—	—	0.10	0.25	1.50
1963 Proof	—	Value: 60.00				
1964	41,000,000	—	—	0.10	0.25	1.50
1964 Proof	—	Value: 60.00				
1965	59,000,000	—	—	0.10	0.25	1.50
1965 Proof	—	Value: 60.00				
1966	44,000,000	—	—	—	0.10	1.00
1966 Proof	—	Value: 50.00				
1967	39,000,000	—	—	—	0.10	1.00
1967 Proof	—	Value: 50.00				
1968	42,000,000	—	—	—	0.10	1.00
1968 Proof	—	Value: 40.00				
1969 fish privy mark	29,100,000	—	—	—	0.10	1.50
1969 Proof, fish privy mark	—	Value: 40.00				
1969 cock privy mark	24,000,000	—	—	—	0.10	1.50
1969 Proof, cock privy mark	—	Value: 40.00				
1970	50,000,000	—	—	—	0.10	1.00
1970 Proof	—	Value: 40.00				
1971	55,000,000	—	—	—	0.10	1.00
1972	60,000,000	—	—	—	0.10	1.00
1973	90,000,000	—	—	—	0.10	1.00
1974	75,000,000	—	—	—	0.10	2.00
1975	110,000,000	—	—	—	0.10	1.00
1976	85,000,000	—	—	—	0.10	1.00
1977	100,000,000	—	—	—	0.10	1.00
1978	110,000,000	—	—	—	0.10	1.00
1979	120,000,000	—	—	—	0.10	1.00
1980 cock and star privy mark	195,300,000	—	—	—	0.10	0.50

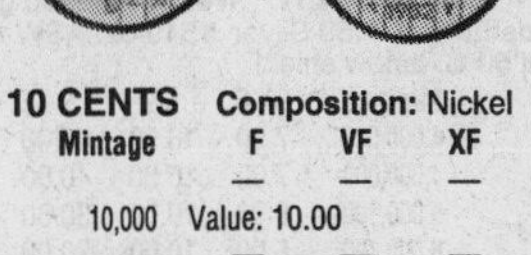

KM# 203 10 CENTS **Composition:** Nickel

Date	Mintage	F	VF	XF	Unc	BU
1982	—	—	—	—	0.10	0.50
1982 Proof	10,000	Value: 10.00				
1983	—	—	—	—	—	0.50
1983 Proof	15,000	Value: 8.00				
1984	—	—	—	—	0.10	0.50
1984 Proof	20,000	Value: 4.00				
1985	—	—	—	—	0.10	0.50
1985 Proof	17,000	Value: 4.00				
1986	—	—	—	—	0.10	0.50
1986 Proof	20,000	Value: 4.00				
1987	—	—	—	—	0.10	0.50
1987 Proof	18,000	Value: 4.00				
1988	—	—	—	—	0.25	2.00
1988 Proof	20,000	Value: 6.00				
1989	—	—	—	—	—	1.50
1989 Proof	15,000	Value: 5.00				

Date	Mintage	F	VF	XF	Unc	BU
1990	—	—	—	—	—	0.50
1990 Proof	15,000	Value: 4.00				
1991	—	—	—	—	—	0.50
1991 Proof	14,000	Value: 4.00				
1992	—	—	—	—	—	0.50
1992 Proof	13,000	Value: 4.00				
1993	—	—	—	—	—	0.50
1993 Proof	12,000	Value: 4.00				
1994	—	—	—	—	—	0.50
1994 Proof	13,000	Value: 4.00				
1995	—	—	—	—	—	0.50
1995 Proof	12,000	Value: 4.00				
1996	—	—	—	—	—	0.50
1996 Proof	14,000	Value: 4.00				
1997	—	—	—	—	—	0.50
1997 Proof	12,000	Value: 4.00				
1998	—	—	—	—	—	0.50
1998 Proof	12,000	Value: 4.00				
1999	—	—	—	—	—	0.50
1999 Proof	15,000	Value: 4.00				
2000	—	—	—	—	—	0.50
2000 Proof	15,000	Value: 4.00				
2001	—	—	—	—	—	0.50
2001 Proof	17,000	Value: 4.00				

KM# 120.1 25 CENTS **Weight:** 3.5750 g. **Composition:** 0.6400 Silver .0736 oz. ASW **Obverse:** Bust with wide truncation

Date	Mintage	F	VF	XF	Unc	BU
1901	1,600,000	40.00	85.00	175	450	750

KM# 120.2 25 CENTS **Weight:** 3.5750 g. **Composition:** 0.6400 Silver .0736 oz. ASW **Obverse:** Bust with narrow truncation

Date	Mintage	F	VF	XF	Unc	BU
1901	Inc. above	8.00	22.00	45.00	110	150
1901 Proof	3	Value: 1,500				
1902	1,200,000	8.00	25.00	50.00	120	160
1903	1,200,000	8.00	25.00	50.00	120	160
1904	1,600,000	7.00	20.00	40.00	100	135
1905	1,200,000	8.00	25.00	50.00	120	160
1906	2,000,000	6.00	18.00	35.00	85.00	125

KM# 146 25 CENTS **Weight:** 3.5750 g. **Composition:** 0.6400 Silver .0736 oz. ASW

Date	Mintage	F	VF	XF	Unc	BU
1910	880,000	18.00	35.00	75.00	165	250
1910 Proof	—	Value: 400				
1911	1,600,000	8.00	20.00	40.00	135	200
1912	1,600,000	8.00	20.00	40.00	135	200
1913	1,200,000	20.00	40.00	75.00	150	245
1914	5,600,000	3.50	8.00	20.00	50.00	75.00
1915	2,000,000	4.50	12.00	25.00	60.00	85.00
1916	2,000,000	4.50	12.00	25.00	60.00	85.00
1917	4,000,000	3.50	8.00	20.00	50.00	75.00
1918	6,000,000	2.00	6.00	12.00	32.00	50.00
1919	4,000,000	3.50	8.00	20.00	50.00	75.00
1925	2,000,000	4.50	12.00	20.00	55.00	80.00

KM# 164 25 CENTS **Weight:** 3.5750 g. **Composition:** 0.6400 Silver .0736 oz. ASW

Date	Mintage	F	VF	XF	Unc	BU
1926	2,000,000	6.00	12.00	30.00	65.00	90.00
1928	8,000,000	0.75	1.50	5.00	18.00	28.00
1939	4,000,000	0.75	1.00	2.00	5.00	8.00
1940	9,000,000	0.50	1.00	2.00	5.00	8.00
1941	40,000,000	0.35	0.60	1.50	2.50	4.50
1943P acorn privy mark	—	0.65	1.25	3.50	12.50	20.00
1944P acorn privy mark	40,000,000	0.35	0.60	1.50	2.50	4.50
1945 acorn privy mark	92,000,000	40.00	110	165	250	375

Note: For similar coins dated 1941P and 1943P with palm tree privy mark, see Curacao

KM# 174 25 CENTS **Composition:** Zinc

Date	Mintage	F	VF	XF	Unc	BU
1941	34,600,000	0.75	1.50	3.50	12.00	25.00
1942	27,800,000	0.75	1.50	3.50	12.00	25.00
1943	13,600,000	2.50	6.00	12.00	35.00	50.00

KM# 178 25 CENTS **Composition:** Nickel

Date	Mintage	F	VF	XF	Unc	BU
1948	27,400,000	—	0.25	0.50	1.50	7.50
1948 Proof	—	Value: 100				

KM# 183 25 CENTS **Composition:** Nickel

Date	Mintage	F	VF	XF	Unc	BU
1950	43,000,000	—	0.20	0.30	1.50	4.50
1950 Proof	—	Value: 75.00				
1951	33,200,000	—	0.20	0.30	1.50	4.50
1951 Proof	—	Value: 65.00				
1954	6,400,000	—	0.50	1.50	2.00	8.00
1954 Proof	—	Value: 65.00				
1955	10,000,000	—	0.20	0.30	1.50	3.00
1955 Proof	—	Value: 65.00				
1956	8,000,000	—	0.20	0.30	1.50	4.00
1956 Proof	—	Value: 65.00				
1957	8,000,000	—	0.20	0.30	1.50	4.00
1957 Proof	—	Value: 65.00				
1958	15,000,000	—	0.20	0.30	1.00	2.00
1958 Proof	—	Value: 65.00				
1960	9,000,000	—	0.20	0.30	1.50	4.00
1960 Proof	—	Value: 60.00				
1961	6,000,000	—	0.40	1.25	1.50	5.00
1961 Proof	—	Value: 50.00				
1962	12,000,000	—	0.20	0.30	1.00	2.00
1962 Proof	—	Value: 50.00				
1963	18,000,000	—	0.20	0.30	1.00	2.00
1963 Proof	—	Value: 50.00				
1964	25,000,000	—	0.20	0.30	1.00	2.00
1964 Proof	—	Value: 50.00				
1965	18,000,000	—	0.20	0.30	1.00	1.50
1965 Proof	—	Value: 50.00				
1966	25,000,000	—	—	0.20	0.75	1.50
1966 Proof	—	Value: 50.00				
1967	18,000,000	—	—	0.20	0.75	1.50
1967 Proof	—	Value: 60.00				
1968	26,000,000	—	—	0.20	0.75	1.00
1968 Proof	—	Value: 60.00				
1969 fish privy mark	14,000,000	—	—	0.20	0.30	1.00
1969 Proof, fish privy mark	—	Value: 60.00				
1969 cock privy mark	21,000,000	—	—	0.20	0.75	1.00
1969 Proof, cock privy mark	—	Value: 60.00				
1970	39,000,000	—	—	0.20	0.30	1.00
1970 Proof	—	Value: 60.00				
1971	40,000,000	—	—	0.20	0.30	1.00
1972	50,000,000	—	—	0.20	0.30	1.00
1973	45,000,000	—	—	0.20	0.30	1.00
1974	10,000,000	—	—	0.20	0.50	1.50
1975	25,000,000	—	—	0.20	0.30	1.00
1976	64,000,000	—	—	0.20	0.30	1.00
1977	55,000,000	—	—	0.20	0.30	1.00
1978	35,000,000	—	—	0.20	0.30	1.00
1979	45,000,000	—	—	0.20	0.30	1.00
1980 cock and star privy mark	159,300,000	—	—	—	0.20	0.50

KM# 183a 25 CENTS **Composition:** Aluminum

Date	Mintage	F	VF	XF	Unc	BU
1980	15	—	—	—	—	500

KM# 204 25 CENTS **Weight:** 3.0000 g. **Composition:** Nickel

Date	Mintage	F	VF	XF	Unc	BU
1982	—	—	—	—	0.20	0.60
1982 Proof	10,000	Value: 15.00				
1983	—	—	—	—	0.20	0.60
1983 Proof	15,000	Value: 12.00				
1984	—	—	—	—	0.20	0.60
1984 Proof	20,000	Value: 6.00				
1985	—	—	—	—	0.20	0.60
1985 Proof	17,000	Value: 6.00				
1986	—	—	—	—	0.20	0.60
1986 Proof	20,000	Value: 6.00				
1987	—	—	—	—	0.20	0.60
1987 Proof	18,000	Value: 6.00				
1988	—	—	—	—	0.20	0.60
1988 Proof	20,000	Value: 6.00				
1989	—	—	—	—	0.20	0.60
1989 Proof	15,000	Value: 6.00				
1990	—	—	—	—	0.20	0.60
1990 Proof	15,000	Value: 6.00				
1991	—	—	—	—	0.20	0.60
1991 Proof	14,000	Value: 6.00				
1992	—	—	—	—	0.20	0.60
1992 Proof	13,000	Value: 6.00				
1993	—	—	—	—	0.25	1.00
1993 Proof	12,000	Value: 6.00				
1994	—	—	—	—	1.00	4.00
1994 Proof	13,000	Value: 10.00				
1995	—	—	—	—	0.50	1.25
1995 Proof	12,000	Value: 8.00				
1996	—	—	—	—	0.20	0.60
1996 Proof	14,000	Value: 6.00				
1997	—	—	—	—	0.20	0.60
1997 Proof	12,000	Value: 6.00				
1998	—	—	—	—	0.20	0.60
1998 Proof	12,000	Value: 6.00				
1999	—	—	—	—	0.20	0.80
1999 Proof	15,000	Value: 6.00				
2000	—	—	—	—	0.20	0.60
2000 Proof	15,000	Value: 6.00				
2001	—	—	—	—	0.20	0.60
2001 Proof	17,000	Value: 6.00				

KM# 121.2 1/2 GULDEN **Weight:** 5.0000 g. **Composition:** 0.9450 Silver .1519 oz. ASW **Reverse:** Without 50 C. below shield

Date	Mintage	F	VF	XF	Unc	BU
1904	1,000,000	25.00	60.00	110	225	375
1905	4,000,000	7.00	15.00	35.00	90.00	135
1906	1,000,000	25.00	60.00	110	225	375
1907	3,300,000	7.00	15.00	35.00	90.00	135
1907 Proof	—	Value: 400				
1908	4,000,000	7.00	15.00	35.00	90.00	135
1909	3,000,000	7.00	15.00	35.00	90.00	135

KM# 147 1/2 GULDEN **Weight:** 5.0000 g. **Composition:** 0.9450 Silver .1519 oz. ASW **Reverse:** Without 50 C. below shield

Date	Mintage	F	VF	XF	Unc	BU
1910	4,000,000	7.00	16.50	40.00	90.00	135
1912	4,000,000	7.00	16.50	40.00	90.00	135
1913	8,000,000	6.00	10.00	30.00	65.00	90.00
1919	8,000,000	6.00	10.00	30.00	65.00	90.00

KM# 160 1/2 GULDEN **Weight:** 5.0000 g. **Composition:** 0.7200 Silver .1157 oz. ASW **Reverse:** Without 50 C. below shield

Date	Mintage	F	VF	XF	Unc	BU
1921	5,000,000	1.00	2.50	5.00	22.00	30.00
1921 Proof	—	Value: 250				
1922	11,240,000	0.75	1.50	3.50	15.00	22.00
1928	5,000,000	1.00	2.50	5.00	22.00	30.00
1929	9,500,000	0.75	2.00	3.00	12.00	18.00
1930	18,500,000	0.75	1.50	2.50	9.00	15.00

KM# 122.1 GULDEN **Weight:** 10.0000 g. **Composition:** 0.9450 Silver .3038 oz. ASW

Date	Mintage	F	VF	XF	Unc	BU
1901	2,000,000	22.00	45.00	90.00	225	325
1901 Proof	—	Value: 650				

KM# 122.2 GULDEN **Weight:** 10.0000 g. **Composition:** 0.9450 Silver .3038 oz. ASW **Reverse:** Without 100 C. below shield

Date	Mintage	F	VF	XF	Unc	BU
1904	2,000,000	12.00	30.00	60.00	125	200
1905	1,000,000	22.00	55.00	100	220	325
1905 Proof	—	Value: 800				
1906	500,000	100	200	450	750	1,250
1906 Proof	—	Value: 1,350				
1907	5,100,000	8.00	20.00	35.00	90.00	120
1908	4,700,000	8.00	20.00	35.00	90.00	120
1908 Proof	—	Value: 475				
1909	2,000,000	10.00	25.00	50.00	135	275

KM# 148 GULDEN **Weight:** 10.0000 g. **Composition:** 0.9450 Silver .3038 oz. ASW **Obv. Legend:** Without 100 C. below shield

Date	Mintage	F	VF	XF	Unc	BU
1910	1,000,000	30.00	75.00	200	375	500
1910	—	Value: 850				
1911	2,000,000	20.00	45.00	150	275	400
1912	3,000,000	10.00	35.00	65.00	115	175
1913	8,000,000	7.00	20.00	45.00	80.00	120
1914	15,785,000	5.00	15.00	32.50	60.00	90.00
1915	14,215,000	5.00	16.50	35.00	65.00	95.00
1916	5,000,000	16.00	40.00	65.00	125	185
1917	2,300,000	20.00	45.00	75.00	135	190

KM# 161.1 GULDEN **Weight:** 10.0000 g. **Composition:** 0.7200 Silver .2315 oz. ASW **Obv. Legend:** Ends below truncation

Date	Mintage	F	VF	XF	Unc	BU
1922	9,550,000	2.00	3.50	10.00	30.00	55.00
1922 Proof	—	Value: 450				
1923	8,050,000	2.00	3.50	10.00	30.00	55.00
1924	8,000,000	2.00	4.50	10.00	30.00	55.00
1928	6,150,000	BV	2.50	8.00	25.00	65.00
1929	32,350,000	BV	2.50	4.00	10.00	18.00
1930	13,500,000	BV	2.50	5.00	12.00	30.00
1931	38,100,000	BV	2.50	4.00	10.00	15.00
1938	5,000,000	2.00	4.00	7.00	18.00	25.00

Date	Mintage	F	VF	XF	Unc	BU
1939	14,200,000	BV	BV	2.50	7.00	12.00
1940	21,300,000	BV	BV	2.50	7.00	12.00
1940 Proof	—	Value: 200				
1944P acorn privy mark	Inc. above	60.00	150	250	325	500

KM# 161.2 GULDEN **Weight:** 10.0000 g. **Composition:** 0.7200 Silver .2315 oz. ASW **Obv. Legend:** Ends at right of truncation **Note:** For similar coins dated 1943D with palm tree privy mark, see Netherlands East Indies

Date	Mintage	F	VF	XF	Unc	BU
1944P acorn privy mark	105,125,000	7.50	20.00	35.00	55.00	80.00
1945P acorn privy mark	25,375,000	225	425	700	1,100	1,650

Note: Only a small number placed into circulation

KM# 184 GULDEN **Weight:** 6.5000 g. **Composition:** 0.7200 Silver .1504 oz. ASW

Date	Mintage	F	VF	XF	Unc	BU
1954	6,600,000	—	—	BV	3.00	6.00
1954 Proof	—	Value: 65.00				
1955	37,500,000	—	—	BV	2.00	5.00
1955 Proof	—	Value: 65.00				
1956	38,900,000	—	—	BV	2.00	5.00
1956 Proof	—	Value: 65.00				
1957	27,000,000	—	—	BV	2.00	5.00
1957 Proof	—	Value: 65.00				
1958	30,000,000	—	—	BV	2.50	5.00
1958 Proof	—	Value: 65.00				
1963	5,000,000	—	—	BV	3.50	7.50
1963 Proof	—	Value: 80.00				
1964	9,000,000	—	—	BV	2.00	5.00
1964 Proof	—	Value: 80.00				
1965	21,000,000	—	—	BV	2.00	4.00
1965 Proof	—	Value: 80.00				
1966	5,000,000	—	—	BV	2.00	5.00
1966 Proof	—	Value: 80.00				
1967	7,000,000	—	—	BV	2.50	6.00
1967 Proof	—	Value: 110				

KM# 184a GULDEN **Weight:** 6.0000 g. **Composition:** Nickel

Date	Mintage	F	VF	XF	Unc	BU
1967	31,000,000	—	—	0.75	2.00	5.00
1967 Proof	—	Value: 55.00				
1968	61,000,000	—	—	0.75	2.00	5.00
1969 fish	27,500,000	—	—	—	2.50	6.00
1969 Proof, fish	—	Value: 50.00				
1969 cock	15,500,000	—	—	—	2.50	6.00
1969 Proof, cock	—	Value: 50.00				
1970	18,000,000	—	—	0.75	2.00	5.00
1970 Proof	—	Value: 50.00				
1971	50,000,000	—	—	—	0.75	2.00
1972	60,000,000	—	—	—	0.75	2.00
1973	27,000,000	—	—	—	0.75	3.00
1975	9,000,000	—	—	—	2.00	5.00
1976	32,000,000	—	—	—	0.75	2.00
1977	38,000,000	—	—	—	0.75	2.00
1978	30,000,000	—	—	—	0.75	2.00
1979	25,000,000	—	—	—	0.75	2.00
1980 cock and star privy mark	118,300,000	—	—	—	0.65	1.00

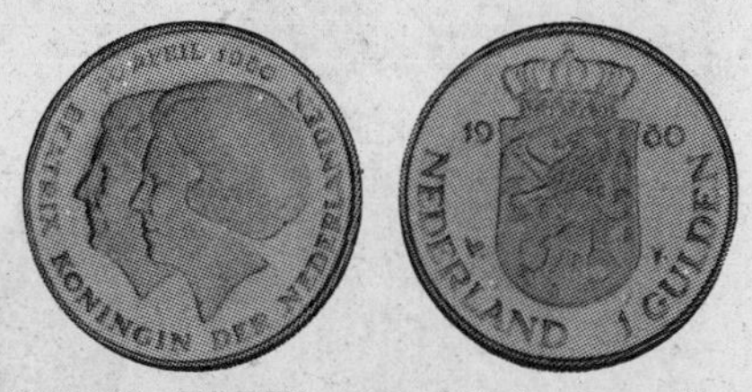

KM# 200 GULDEN **Weight:** 6.0000 g. **Composition:** Nickel **Subject:** Investiture of New Queen **Obverse:** Conjoined busts of Queens Juliana and Beatrix left

Date	Mintage	F	VF	XF	Unc	BU
1980	30,500,000	—	—	—	0.65	1.00

KM# 200a GULDEN **Composition:** Silver **Subject:** Investiture of New Queen **Obverse:** Conjoined busts of Queens Juliana and Beatrix left

Date	Mintage	F	VF	XF	Unc	BU
1980	157	—	—	—	—	700

KM# 200b GULDEN **Composition:** Gold **Subject:** Investiture of New Queen **Obverse:** Conjoined busts of Queens Juliana and Beatrix left

Date	Mintage	F	VF	XF	Unc	BU
1980 Rare	7	—	—	—	—	—

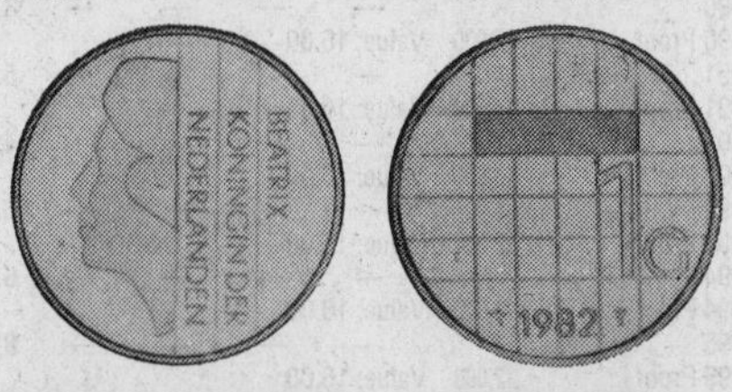

KM# 205 GULDEN **Weight:** 6.0000 g. **Composition:** Nickel

Date		F	VF	XF	Unc	BU
1982		—	—	—	—	1.25
1982 Proof	10,000	Value: 20.00				
1983		—	—	—	—	1.50
1983 Proof	15,000	Value: 15.00				
1984		—	—	—	—	1.50
1984 Proof	20,000	Value: 7.50				
1985		—	—	—	—	2.50
1985 Proof	17,000	Value: 7.50				
1986		—	—	—	—	1.75
1986 Proof	18,000	Value: 7.50				
1987		—	—	—	—	1.75
1987 Proof	20,000	Value: 7.50				
1988		—	—	—	—	1.75
1988 Proof	20,000	Value: 7.50				
1989		—	—	—	—	3.50
1989 Proof	15,000	Value: 7.50				
1990		—	—	—	—	3.50
1990 Proof	15,000	Value: 7.50				
1991		—	—	—	—	4.00
1991 Proof	14,000	Value: 7.50				
1992		—	—	—	—	1.50
1992 Proof	13,000	Value: 7.50				
1993		—	—	—	—	1.50
1993 Proof	12,000	Value: 7.50				
1994		—	—	—	—	1.50
1994 Proof	13,000	Value: 7.50				
1995		—	—	—	—	1.50
1995 Proof	12,000	Value: 7.50				
1996		—	—	—	—	1.50
1996 Proof	14,000	Value: 7.50				
1997		—	—	—	—	1.50
1997 Proof	12,000	Value: 7.50				
1998		—	—	—	—	1.75
1998 Proof	12,000	Value: 7.50				
1999		—	—	—	—	1.25
1999 Proof	15,000	Value: 7.50				
2000		—	—	—	—	1.25
2000 Proof	15,000	Value: 7.50				
2001		—	—	—	—	1.25
2001 Proof	17,000	Value: 7.50				

KM# 205b (KM205a) GULDEN **Weight:** 13.2000 g. **Composition:** 0.9990 Gold .4243 oz. AGW

Date	Mintage	F	VF	XF	Unc	BU
2001 Prooflike	25,500	—	—	—	250	—
2001 Prooflike	25,500	—	—	—	250	—

KM# 230 GULDEN **Weight:** 11.0000 g. **Composition:** 0.7500 Gold .2652 oz. AGW **Reverse:** Small tulip, "750" added **Note:** Similar to KM#205.

Date	Mintage	F	VF	XF	Unc	BU
1999 Proof	1,000	Value: 500				

Note: Approximately 480 of the mintage were melted down

KM# 205a GULDEN **Weight:** 7.1000 g. **Composition:** 0.9250 Silver 0.2111 oz. ASW

Date	Mintage	F	VF	XF	Unc	BU
2001 Prooflike	200,000	—	—	—	17.50	—

KM# 233 GULDEN **Weight:** 6.0400 g. **Composition:** Nickel **Obverse:** Queen's portrait **Reverse:** Child art design **Edge Lettering:** GOD ZUI MET ONS **Size:** 25 mm.

Date	Mintage	F	VF	XF	Unc	BU
2001	16,000,000	—	—	—	2.50	—

KM# 233a GULDEN **Weight:** 13.2000 g. **Composition:** 0.9250 Silver .3926 oz. ASW **Obverse:** Queen's portrait **Reverse:** Child art design **Edge Lettering:** GOD ZUI MET ONS **Size:** 25 mm.

Date	Mintage	F	VF	XF	Unc	BU
2001 Prooflike	400	—	—	—	—	—

Note: Given as gifts to workers at the mint

KM# 233b GULDEN **Weight:** 13.2000 g. **Composition:** 0.9990 Gold .4240 oz. AGW **Obverse:** Queen's portrait **Reverse:** Child art design **Size:** 25 mm.

Date	Mintage	F	VF	XF	Unc	BU
2001 Prooflike	100	—	—	—	—	—

KM# 165 2-1/2 GULDEN **Weight:** 25.0000 g. **Composition:** 0.7200 Silver .5787 oz. ASW

Date	Mintage	F	VF	XF	Unc	BU
1929	4,400,000	5.00	8.00	15.00	35.00	60.00
1930	11,600,000	4.00	7.50	12.00	20.00	30.00
1931	4,400,000	4.00	7.50	12.00	20.00	30.00
1932	6,320,000	4.00	7.50	12.00	20.00	30.00
1932 deep hair lines	Inc. above	70.00	125	200	300	350
1933	3,560,000	5.00	8.00	15.00	25.00	50.00
1937	4,000,000	5.00	7.00	10.00	20.00	30.00
1938	2,000,000	6.00	10.00	18.00	30.00	45.00
1938 deep hair lines	Inc. above	35.00	75.00	135	225	325
1939	3,760,000	4.00	7.00	10.00	20.00	30.00
1940	4,640,000	12.00	20.00	30.00	50.00	75.00

Note: For similar coins dated 1943D with palm tree privy mark, see Netherlands East Indies

KM# 185 2-1/2 GULDEN **Weight:** 15.0000 g. **Composition:** 0.7200 Silver .3472 oz. ASW

Date	Mintage	F	VF	XF	Unc	BU
1959	7,200,000	—	1.50	2.00	4.00	9.00
1959 Proof	—	Value: 175				
1960	12,800,000	—	1.50	2.00	4.00	9.00
1960 Proof	—	Value: 175				
1961	10,000,000	—	1.50	2.00	4.00	9.00
1961 Proof	—	Value: 175				
1962	5,000,000	—	1.50	2.00	4.00	10.00
1962 Proof	—	Value: 175				
1963	4,000,000	—	2.00	5.00	10.00	15.00
1963 Proof	—	Value: 175				
1964	2,800,000	—	4.00	8.00	15.00	20.00
1964 Proof	—	Value: 175				
1966	5,000,000	—	1.50	2.00	4.00	9.00
1966 Proof	—	Value: 175				

KM# 191 2-1/2 GULDEN **Composition:** Nickel

Date	Mintage	F	VF	XF	Unc	BU
1969 fish privy mark	1,200,000	—	—	1.00	2.00	5.00
1969 Proof, fish privy mark with front hair lock	—	Value: 90.00				
1969 Proof, Rare, fish privy mark without front hair lock	—	—	—	—	—	—
1969 cock privy mark	15,600,000	—	—	—	2.00	5.00
1969 Proof, cocky privy mark	—	Value: 90.00				
1970	22,000,000	—	—	—	1.50	2.00
1970 Proof	—	Value: 90.00				
1971	8,000,000	—	—	—	1.50	2.00
1972	20,000,000	—	—	—	1.50	2.00
1978	5,000,000	—	—	—	1.50	2.00
1980 cock and star privy mark	37,300,000	—	—	—	1.50	2.00

KM# 197 2-1/2 GULDEN **Weight:** 10.0000 g. **Composition:** Nickel **Subject:** 400th Anniversary - The Union of Utrecht

Date	Mintage	F	VF	XF	Unc	BU
1979	25,000,000	—	—	—	1.50	2.00

KM# 201 2-1/2 GULDEN **Weight:** 10.0000 g. **Composition:** Nickel **Subject:** Investiture of New Queen **Obverse:** Conjoined busts of Queens Juliana and Beatrix left

Date	Mintage	F	VF	XF	Unc	BU
1980	30,500,000	—	—	—	1.50	2.00

KM# 201a 2-1/2 GULDEN **Composition:** Silver **Subject:** Investiture of New Queen **Obverse:** Conjoined busts of Queens Juliana and Beatrix left

Date	Mintage	F	VF	XF	Unc	BU
1980	157	—	—	—	—	500

KM# 201b 2-1/2 GULDEN **Composition:** Gold **Subject:** Investiture of New Queen **Obverse:** Conjoined busts of Queens Juliana and Beatrix left

Date	Mintage	F	VF	XF	Unc	BU
1980 Rare	7	—	—	—	—	—

KM# 206 2-1/2 GULDEN **Weight:** 10.0000 g. **Composition:** Nickel

Date	Mintage	F	VF	XF	Unc	BU
1982		—	—	—	—	2.00
1982 Proof	10,000	Value: 35.00				
1983		—	—	—	—	2.50
1983 Proof	15,000	Value: 27.50				
1984		—	—	—	—	2.50
1984 Proof		—	—	—	—	—
1985		—	—	—	—	3.50
1985 Proof	17,000	Value: 16.00				
1986		—	—	—	—	3.50
1986 Proof	20,000	Value: 16.00				
1987		—	—	—	—	3.50
1987 Proof	18,000	Value: 16.00				
1988		—	—	—	—	3.50
1988 Proof	20,000	Value: 16.00				
1989		—	—	—	—	3.00
1989 Proof	15,000	Value: 16.00				
1990		—	—	—	—	3.00
1990 Proof	15,000	Value: 16.00				
1991		—	—	—	—	5.00
1991 Proof	14,000	Value: 16.00				
1992		—	—	—	—	4.00
1992 Proof	13,000	Value: 16.00				
1993		—	—	—	—	6.00
1993 Proof	12,000	Value: 16.00				
1994		—	—	—	—	6.00
1994 Proof	13,000	Value: 16.00				
1995		—	—	—	—	8.00
1995 Proof	12,000	Value: 16.00				
1996		—	—	—	—	7.00
1996 Proof	14,000	Value: 16.00				
1997		—	—	—	—	7.00
1997 Proof	12,000	Value: 16.00				
1998		—	—	—	—	7.00
1998 Proof	12,000	Value: 16.00				
1999		—	—	—	—	4.00
1999 Proof	15,000	Value: 16.00				
2000		—	—	—	—	4.00
2000 Proof	15,000	Value: 16.00				
2001		—	—	—	—	4.00
2001 Proof	17,000	Value: 16.00				

KM# 151 5 GULDEN **Weight:** 3.3645 g. **Composition:** 0.9000 Gold .0973 oz. AGW

Date	Mintage	F	VF	XF	Unc	BU
1912	1,000,000	40.00	60.00	90.00	150	175
1912 Matte Proof	120	Value: 800				

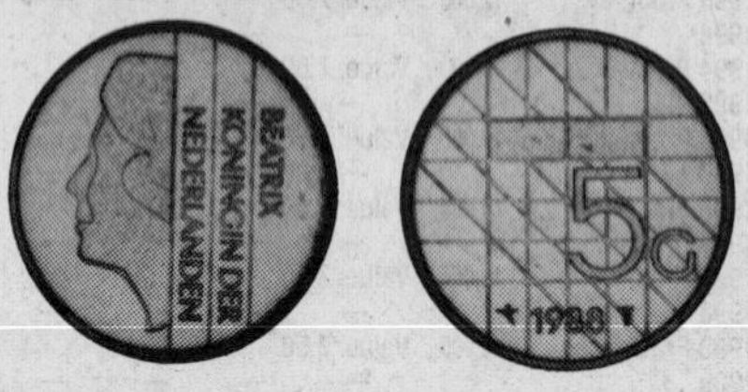

KM# 210 5 GULDEN **Weight:** 9.2500 g. **Composition:** Bronze Clad Nickel

Date	Mintage	F	VF	XF	Unc	BU
1987 Proof		—	—	—	—	—
1988		—	—	—	—	4.50
1988 Proof	20,000	Value: 12.50				
1989		—	—	—	—	4.50
1989 Proof	15,000	Value: 12.50				
1990		—	—	—	—	4.50
1990 Proof	15,000	Value: 15.00				
1991		—	—	—	—	4.00
1991 Proof	14,000	Value: 15.00				
1992		—	—	—	—	4.00
1992 Proof	13,000	Value: 15.00				
1993		—	—	—	—	4.00
1993 Proof	12,000	Value: 15.00				
1994		—	—	—	—	6.00
1994 Proof	13,000	Value: 17.50				
1995		—	—	—	—	6.00
1995 Proof	12,000	Value: 17.50				
1996		—	—	—	—	6.00
1996 Proof	14,000	Value: 17.50				
1997		—	—	—	—	6.00
1997 Proof	12,000	Value: 17.50				
1998		—	—	—	—	8.00
1998 Proof	12,000	Value: 16.00				
1999		—	—	—	—	6.50
1999 Proof	15,000	Value: 16.00				
2000		—	—	—	—	3.50
2000 Proof	15,000	Value: 16.00				
2001		—	—	—	—	3.50
2001 Proof	17,000	Value: 15.50				

KM# 231 5 GULDEN **Weight:** 9.2500 g. **Composition:** Brass Plated Nickel **Subject:** Soccer **Edge:** Reeded **Edge Lettering:** GOD * ZIJ * MET * ONS *

Date	Mintage	F	VF	XF	Unc	BU
2000		—	—	—	4.00	8.50
2000 Proof, small mm	Est. 1,000	Value: 250				
2000 Proof, large mm	19,000	Value: 12.50				

Note: A joint issue proof set exists containing the Netherlands KM#231, Belgium KM#213-214 plus a medal

KM# 149 10 GULDEN **Weight:** 6.7290 g. **Composition:** 0.9000 Gold .1947 oz. AGW

Date	Mintage	F	VF	XF	Unc	BU
1911	774,544	—	BV	60.00	80.00	90.00
1911 Proof	8	Value: 1,750				
1912	3,000,000	—	BV	60.00	80.00	90.00
1912 Proof	20	Value: 1,500				
1913	1,133,476	—	BV	60.00	80.00	90.00
1917	4,000,000	—	BV	60.00	80.00	90.00

KM# 162 10 GULDEN **Weight:** 6.7290 g. **Composition:** 0.9000 Gold .1947 oz. AGW

Date	Mintage	F	VF	XF	Unc	BU
1925	2,000,000	—	BV	60.00	80.00	90.00
1925 Proof	12	Value: 1,500				
1926	2,500,000	—	BV	60.00	80.00	90.00
1926 Proof	—	Value: 1,300				
1927	1,000,000	—	BV	60.00	80.00	90.00
1932	4,323,954	—	BV	60.00	80.00	90.00
1933	2,462,101	—	BV	60.00	80.00	90.00

KM# 195 10 GULDEN **Weight:** 25.0000 g. **Composition:** 0.7200 Silver .5787 oz. ASW **Subject:** 25th Anniversary of Liberation

Date	Mintage	F	VF	XF	Unc	BU
ND(1970)	5,910,000	—	—	—	8.00	10.00
ND(1970) Prooflike	20,000	—	—	—	—	30.00
ND(1970) Proof	40	Value: 700				

KM# 196 10 GULDEN **Weight:** 25.0000 g. **Composition:** 0.7200 Silver .5787 oz. ASW **Subject:** 25th Anniversary of Reign

Date	Mintage	F	VF	XF	Unc	BU
1973	4,505,000	—	—	—	8.00	10.00
1973 Proof	105,570	Value: 20.00				

KM# 216 10 GULDEN **Weight:** 15.0000 g. **Composition:** 0.7200 Silver .3473 oz. ASW **Subject:** BENE-LUX Treaty

Date	Mintage	F	VF	XF	Unc	BU
1994	2,000,000	—	—	—	—	12.50

Note: 100,000 pieces melted.

Date	Mintage	F	VF	XF	Unc	BU
1994 Proof	66,500	Value: 25.00				

Note: 25,000 pieces issued in sets only

KM# 220 10 GULDEN **Weight:** 15.0000 g. **Composition:** 0.8000 Silver **Subject:** 300th Anniversary - Death of Hugo de Groot

Date	Mintage	F	VF	XF	Unc	BU
1995	1,500,000	—	—	—	—	12.50

Note: 110,000 pieces melted.

Date	Mintage	F	VF	XF	Unc	BU
1995 Proof	37,500	Value: 22.50				

KM# 223 10 GULDEN **Weight:** 15.0000 g. **Composition:** 0.8000 Silver **Subject:** Artist Jan Steen - Mandolin Player

Date	Mintage	F	VF	XF	Unc	BU
1996	1,500,000	—	—	—	—	12.50

Note: 395,000 pieces melted.

Date	Mintage	F	VF	XF	Unc	BU
1996 Proof	25,000	Value: 22.50				

KM# 224 10 GULDEN **Weight:** 15.0000 g. **Composition:** 0.8000 Silver .3858 oz. ASW **Subject:** Marshall Plan **Obverse:** Head of Queen Beatrix left

Date	Mintage	F	VF	XF	Unc	BU
1997	1,010,000	—	—	—	—	20.00

Note: 55,000 pieces melted.

Date	Mintage	F	VF	XF	Unc	BU
1997 Proof	27,000	Value: 28.00				

KM# 228 10 GULDEN **Weight:** 15.0000 g. **Composition:** 0.8000 Silver .3858 oz. ASW **Subject:** Millennium **Obverse:** Head of Queen above 12 concentric rings, 1999 **Reverse:** Head of Queen above 12 concentric rings, 2000 **Edge:** GOD ZIJ MED ONS

Date	Mintage	F	VF	XF	Unc	BU
1999	1,250,000	—	—	—	—	20.00
1999 Proof	50,000	Value: 28.00				

KM# 207 50 GULDEN **Weight:** 25.0000 g. **Composition:** 0.9250 Silver .7435 oz. ASW **Subject:** Dutch-American Friendship

Date	Mintage	F	VF	XF	Unc	BU
ND(1982)	189,900	—	—	—	—	22.50
ND(1982) Proof	69,900	Value: 45.00				

KM# 207a 50 GULDEN **Composition:** Gold **Subject:** Dutch-American Friendship

Date	Mintage	F	VF	XF	Unc	BU
ND(1982) Rare	2	—	—	—	—	—

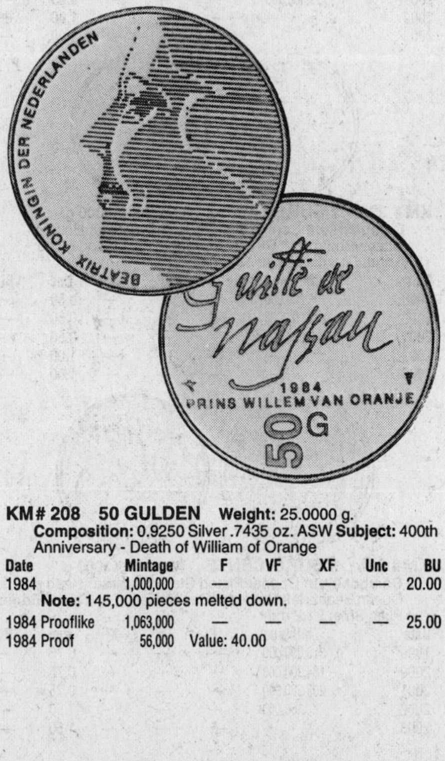

KM# 208 50 GULDEN **Weight:** 25.0000 g. **Composition:** 0.9250 Silver .7435 oz. ASW **Subject:** 400th Anniversary - Death of William of Orange

Date	Mintage	F	VF	XF	Unc	BU
1984	1,000,000	—	—	—	—	20.00

Note: 145,000 pieces melted down.

Date	Mintage	F	VF	XF	Unc	BU
1984 Prooflike	1,063,000	—	—	—	—	25.00
1984 Proof	56,000	Value: 40.00				

KM# 209 50 GULDEN **Weight:** 25.0000 g. **Composition:** 0.9250 Silver .7435 oz. ASW **Subject:** Golden Wedding Anniversary - Queen Mother and Prince Bernhard

Date	Mintage	F	VF	XF	Unc	BU
1987	1,500,000	—	—	—	—	20.00

Note: 535,000 pieces melted down.

Date	Mintage	F	VF	XF	Unc	BU
1987 Prooflike	81,000	—	—	—	—	25.00
1987 Proof	52,800	Value: 40.00				

KM# 212 50 GULDEN **Weight:** 25.0000 g. **Composition:** 0.9250 Silver .7435 oz. ASW **Subject:** 300th Anniversary of William and Mary

Date	Mintage	F	VF	XF	Unc	BU
1988	900,000	—	—	—	—	20.00

Note: 235,000 pieces melted.

Date	Mintage	F	VF	XF	Unc	BU
1988 Prooflike	52,500	—	—	—	—	25.00
1988 Proof	35,500	Value: 42.50				

KM# 212a 50 GULDEN **Composition:** Gold **Subject:** 300th Anniversary of William and Mary

Date	Mintage	F	VF	XF	Unc	BU
1988 Rare	4	—	—	—	—	—

KM# 214 50 GULDEN **Weight:** 25.0000 g. **Composition:** 0.9250 Silver .7435 oz. ASW **Subject:** 100 Years of Queens **Obverse:** Heads of Queens Emma, Wilhelmina, Juliana, and Beatrix in circle

Date	Mintage	F	VF	XF	Unc	BU
1990	800,000	—	—	—	—	20.00
Note: 210,000 pieces melted.						
1990 Prooflike	50,400	—	—	—	—	30.00
1990 Proof	34,500	Value: 50.00				

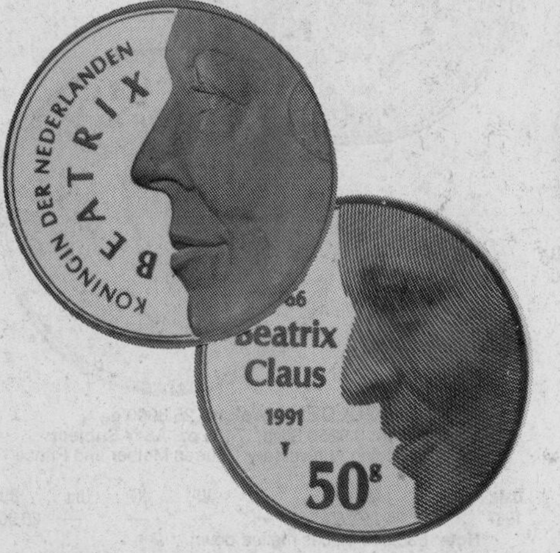

KM# 215 50 GULDEN **Weight:** 25.0000 g. **Composition:** 0.9250 Silver .7435 oz. ASW **Subject:** Silver Wedding Anniversary

Date	Mintage	F	VF	XF	Unc	BU
1991	600,000	—	—	—	—	20.00
Note: 60,000 pieces melted.						
1991 Prooflike	45,800	—	—	—	—	30.00
1991 Proof	34,700	Value: 50.00				

KM# 217 50 GULDEN **Weight:** 25.0000 g. **Composition:** 0.9250 Silver .7435 oz. ASW **Subject:** Maastricht Treaty

Date	Mintage	F	VF	XF	Unc	BU
1994	550,000	—	—	—	—	25.00
Note: 170,000 pieces melted.						
1994 Prooflike	28,000	—	—	—	—	40.00
1994 Proof	24,500	Value: 60.00				

KM# 219 50 GULDEN **Weight:** 25.0000 g. **Composition:** 0.9250 Silver .7435 oz. ASW **Subject:** 50th Anniversary of Liberation

Date	Mintage	F	VF	XF	Unc	BU
ND(1995)	650,000	—	—	—	—	25.00
Note: 220,000 pieces melted.						
ND(1995) Prooflike	27,500	—	—	—	—	40.00
ND(1995) Proof	26,000	Value: 55.00				

KM# 227 50 GULDEN **Weight:** 25.0000 g. **Composition:** 0.9250 Silver .7435 oz. ASW **Subject:** 350th Anniversary - Treaty of Munster **Obverse:** Head of Queen left **Reverse:** Mirror image of obverse **Edge Lettering:** GOD*ZIJ*MET*ONS*

Date	Mintage	F	VF	XF	Unc	BU
1998	450,000	—	—	—	—	30.00
Note: 180,000 pieces melted.						
1998 Prooflike	20,000	—	—	—	—	50.00
1998 Proof	20,000	Value: 65.00				

EURO COINAGE

European Economic Community Issues

KM# 234 EURO CENT **Weight:** 2.3000 g. **Composition:** Copper Plated Steel **Obverse:** Head of Queen Beatrix left **Reverse:** Denomination and globe **Edge:** Plain **Size:** 16.2 mm.

Date	Mintage	F	VF	XF	Unc	BU
1999	47,800,000	—	—	—	0.50	—
2000	276,700,000	—	—	—	0.35	—
2001	179,300,000	—	—	—	0.35	—
2002	—	—	—	—	1.00	—
2003	—	—	—	—	1.00	—

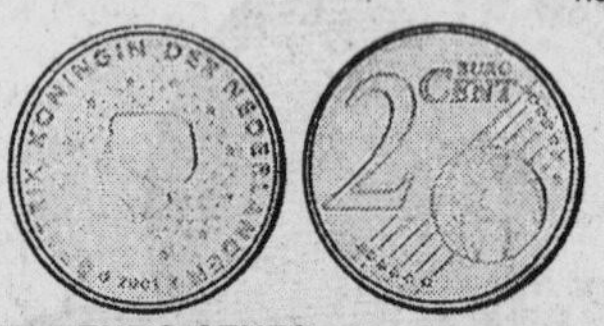

KM# 235 2 EURO CENTS **Weight:** 3.0000 g. **Composition:** Copper Plated Steel **Obverse:** Head of Queen Beatrix left **Reverse:** Denomination and globe **Edge:** Grooved **Size:** 18.7 mm.

Date	Mintage	F	VF	XF	Unc	BU
1999	109,000,000	—	—	—	0.50	—
2000	122,000,000	—	—	—	0.50	—
2001	148,000,000	—	—	—	0.50	—
2002	—	—	—	—	1.00	—
2003	—	—	—	—	1.00	—

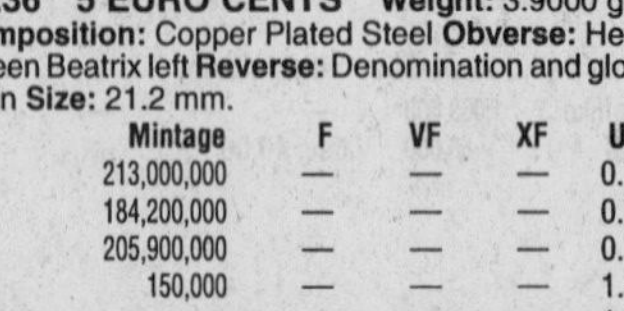

KM# 236 5 EURO CENTS **Weight:** 3.9000 g. **Composition:** Copper Plated Steel **Obverse:** Head of Queen Beatrix left **Reverse:** Denomination and globe **Edge:** Plain **Size:** 21.2 mm.

Date	Mintage	F	VF	XF	Unc	BU
1999	213,000,000	—	—	—	0.75	—
2000	184,200,000	—	—	—	0.75	—
2001	205,900,000	—	—	—	0.75	—
2002	150,000	—	—	—	1.50	—
2003	—	—	—	—	1.50	—

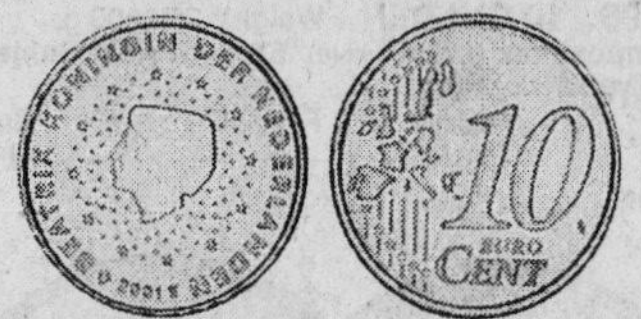

KM# 237 10 EURO CENTS **Weight:** 4.1000 g. **Composition:** Brass **Obverse:** Head of Queen Beatrix left **Reverse:** Denomination and map **Size:** 19.7 mm.

Date	Mintage	F	VF	XF	Unc	BU
1999	149,700,000	—	—	—	0.75	—
2000	156,700,000	—	—	—	0.75	—
2001	193,500,000	—	—	—	0.75	—
2002	—	—	—	—	1.50	—
2003	—	—	—	—	1.50	—

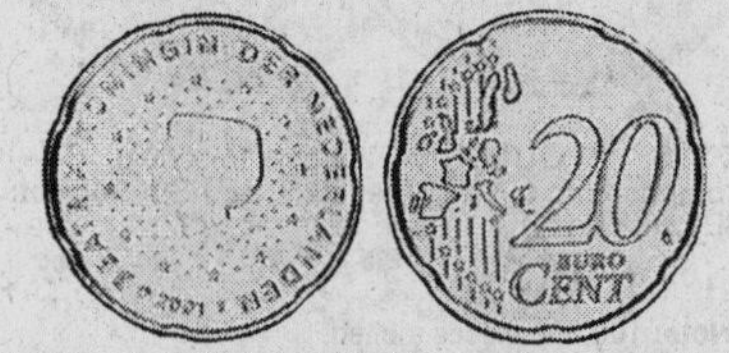

KM# 238 20 EURO CENTS **Weight:** 5.7000 g. **Composition:** Brass **Obverse:** Head of Queen Beatrix left **Reverse:** Denomination and map **Edge:** Notched **Size:** 22.2 mm.

Date	Mintage	F	VF	XF	Unc	BU
1999	86,500,000	—	—	—	1.00	—
2000	67,500,000	—	—	—	1.00	—
2001	97,600,000	—	—	—	1.00	—
2002	—	—	—	—	2.00	—
2003	—	—	—	—	2.00	—

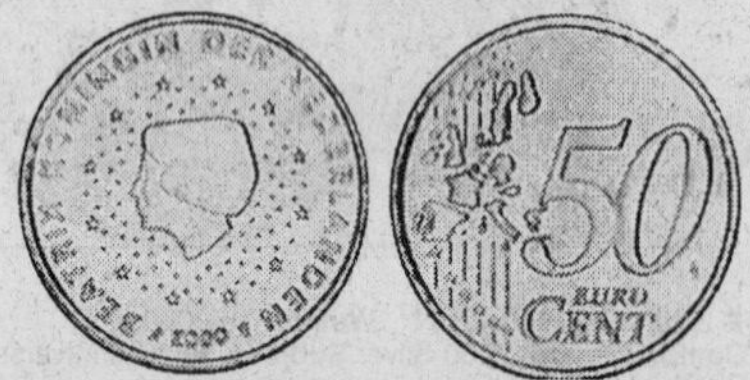

KM# 239 50 EURO CENTS **Weight:** 7.8000 g. **Composition:** Brass **Obverse:** Head of Queen Beatrix left **Reverse:** Denomination and map **Edge:** Notched **Size:** 24.2 mm.

Date	Mintage	F	VF	XF	Unc	BU
1999	99,600,000	—	—	—	1.25	—
2000	87,000,000	—	—	—	1.25	—
2001	94,500,000	—	—	—	1.25	—
2002	—	—	—	—	2.25	—
2003	—	—	—	—	2.25	—

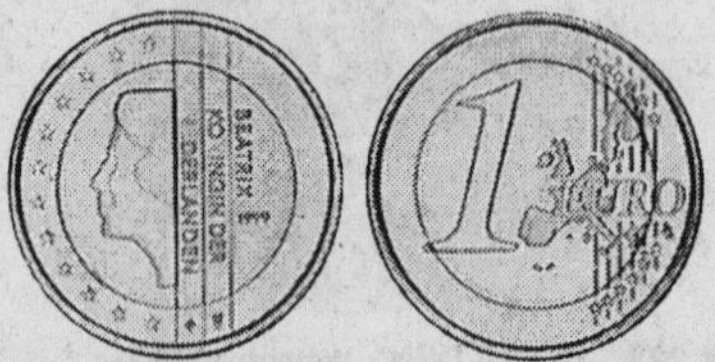

KM# 240 EURO **Ring Weight:** 7.5000 g. **Ring Composition:** Brass **Center Composition:** Copper-Nickel **Obverse:** Queen's profile left **Reverse:** Denomination and map **Edge:** Plain and reeded sections **Size:** 23.2 mm.

Date	Mintage	F	VF	XF	Unc	BU
1999	63,500,000	—	—	—	2.50	—
2000	62,800,000	—	—	—	2.50	—
2001	67,900,000	—	—	—	2.50	—
2002	—	—	—	—	3.25	—
2003	—	—	—	—	3.25	—

KM# 241 2 EURO **Ring Weight:** 8.5000 g. **Ring Composition:** Copper-Nickel **Center Composition:** Brass **Obverse:** Queen's profile left **Reverse:** Denomination and map **Edge:** Reeded **Edge Lettering:** "GOD*ZIJ*MET*ONS*" **Size:** 25.7 mm.

Date	Mintage	F	VF	XF	Unc	BU
1999	9,900,000	—	—	—	6.00	—
2000	24,400,000	—	—	—	5.00	—
2001	140,500,000	—	—	—	4.00	—
2002	—	—	—	—	6.00	—
2003	—	—	—	—	6.00	—

KM# 245 5 EURO **Weight:** 11.9900 g. **Composition:** 0.9250 Silver 0.3566 oz. ASW **Subject:** Vincent Van Gogh **Obverse:** Queen's portrait **Reverse:** Van Gogh's portrait **Edge:** Lettered: "GOD ZIJ MET ONS" **Size:** 29 mm.

Date	F	VF	XF	Unc	BU
ND(2003) Proof-like	—	—	—	—	—

KM# 243 10 EURO **Weight:** 17.8000 g. **Composition:** 0.9250 Silver 0.5294 oz. ASW **Subject:** Crown Prince's Wedding **Obverse:** Head of Queen Beatrix left **Reverse:** Two facing silhouettes **Edge:** Plain **Size:** 33 mm.

Date	F	VF	XF	Unc	BU
2002 Prooflike	—	—	—	—	32.50

KM# 244 10 EURO **Weight:** 6.7200 g. **Composition:** 0.9000 Gold 0.1944 oz. AGW **Subject:** Crown Prince's Wedding **Obverse:** Head of Queen Beatrix right **Reverse:** Two facing silhouettes of Willem Alexander and Maxima **Edge:** Reeded **Size:** 22.5 mm.

Date	F	VF	XF	Unc	BU
2002 Prooflike	—	—	—	—	130

KM# 246 10 EURO **Weight:** 6.7200 g. **Composition:** 0.9000 Gold 0.1944 oz. AGW **Subject:** Vincent Van Gogh **Obverse:** Queen's portrait **Reverse:** Van Gogh's portrait **Edge:** Reeded **Size:** 22.5 mm.

Date	F	VF	XF	Unc	BU
ND(2003) Proof	—	Value: 155			

TRADE COINAGE

KM# 83.1 DUCAT **Weight:** 3.5000 g. **Composition:** 0.9830 Gold .1106 oz. AGW

Date	Mintage	F	VF	XF	Unc	BU
1901	29,284	200	450	750	1,500	2,000
1903/1	91,000	200	450	750	1,500	2,000
1903	Inc. above	150	400	600	800	1,200
1905	87,995	150	400	600	800	1,200
1906	29,379	200	450	750	1,500	2,000
1908	91,006	125	250	400	600	1,100
1909 halberd with star privy mark	106,021	125	250	400	700	1,200
1909 sea horse privy mark	30,182	175	475	850	1,750	2,500
1910	421,447	125	275	425	650	850
1910 Proof	—	Value: 1,000				
1912	147,860	125	275	425	650	850
1912 Proof	—	Value: 1,000				
1913	205,464	125	275	425	650	850
1914	246,560	125	275	425	650	850
1916	116,997	125	275	425	650	850
1916 Proof	—	Value: 1,250				
1917	216,892	BV	65.00	90.00	125	150
1920	293,389	BV	65.00	90.00	125	150
1920 Proof	—	Value: 800				
1921	409,001	BV	60.00	70.00	90.00	110
1922	49,837	100	250	400	600	800
1923	106,674	BV	75.00	150	250	350
1924	84,206	BV	75.00	150	250	350
1925	573,071	BV	60.00	70.00	90.00	110
1925 Proof	Inc. above	Value: 450				
1926	191,311	BV	60.00	80.00	110	150
1927	654,424	—	BV	40.00	50.00	60.00
1928	571,801	—	BV	40.00	50.00	60.00
1932	88,268	200	500	900	1,500	1,800
1937	116,660	BV	70.00	90.00	110	125

KM# 190.1 DUCAT **Weight:** 3.5000 g. **Composition:** 0.9830 Gold .1106 oz. AGW **Obverse:** Knight with right leg bent, larger letters in legend

Date	F	VF	XF	Unc	BU
1960	50.00	100	200	300	400
1972 Prooflike	—	—	—	—	70.00
1974 Prooflike	—	—	—	—	70.00
1974 medal struck	65.00	125	250	350	475
1975 Prooflike	—	—	—	—	60.00
1976 Prooflike	—	—	50.00	100	150

Note: Of 37,844 pieces struck, 32,000 were melted

Date	F	VF	XF	Unc	BU
1978 Prooflike	—	—	—	60.00	90.00
1985 Prooflike	—	—	—	—	55.00

KM# 190.2 DUCAT **Weight:** 3.5000 g. **Composition:** 0.9830 Gold .1106 oz. AGW **Obverse:** Knight with left leg bent, larger letters in legend

Date	Mintage	F	VF	XF	Unc	BU
1986 Prooflike		—	—	—	—	60.00
1989 Proof	24,478	Value: 80.00				
1990 Proof	17,500	Value: 90.00				
1991 Proof	11,500	Value: 85.00				
1992 Proof	14,400	Value: 85.00				
1993 Proof	11,100	Value: 95.00				
1994 Proof	11,500	Value: 90.00				
1995 Proof	11,000	Value: 90.00				
1996 Proof	12,000	Value: 90.00				
1997 Proof	12,000	Value: 90.00				
1998 Proof	12,000	Value: 90.00				
1999 Proof	11,000	Value: 90.00				
2000 Proof	12,000	Value: 90.00				
2001 Proof	12,000	Value: 90.00				
2002 Proof	12,000	Value: 90.00				

KM# 211 2 DUCAT **Weight:** 6.9880 g. **Composition:** 0.9830 Gold .2209 oz. AGW

Date	Mintage	F	VF	XF	Unc	BU
1988 Prooflike		—	—	—	—	130
1989 Proof	17,862	Value: 130				
1991 Proof	10,000	Value: 140				
1992 Proof	12,000	Value: 140				
1996 Proof	11,000	Value: 140				
1999 Proof	9,300	Value: 150				
2000 Proof	9,000	Value: 140				
2002 Proof	Est. 6,000	Value: 140				

SILVER BULLION COINAGE

KM# 213 SILVER DUCAT **Weight:** 28.2500 g. **Composition:** 0.8730 Silver .7948 oz. ASW

Date	Mintage	F	VF	XF	Unc	BU
1989 Proof	35,797	Value: 25.00				
1992 Proof	17,200	Value: 40.00				
1993 Proof	12,500	Value: 50.00				

KM# 218 SILVER DUCAT **Weight:** 28.2500 g. **Composition:** 0.8730 Silver .7948 oz. ASW **Subject:** Seven Provinces - Groningen

Date	Mintage	F	VF	XF	Unc	BU
1994 Proof	11,000	Value: 75.00				

KM# 221 SILVER DUCAT **Weight:** 28.2500 g. **Composition:** 0.8730 Silver .7948 oz. ASW **Subject:** Seven Provinces - Zeeland

Date	Mintage	F	VF	XF	Unc	BU
1995 Proof	11,000	Value: 50.00				

KM# 222 SILVER DUCAT **Weight:** 28.2500 g. **Composition:** 0.8730 Silver .7948 oz. ASW **Subject:** Seven Provinces - Holland

Date	Mintage	F	VF	XF	Unc	BU
1996 Proof	12,500	Value: 50.00				

KM# 225 SILVER DUCAT **Weight:** 28.2500 g. **Composition:** 0.8730 Silver .7948 oz. ASW **Subject:** Seven Provinces - Gelderland

Date	Mintage	F	VF	XF	Unc	BU
1997 Proof	11,500	Value: 50.00				

KM# 226 SILVER DUCAT **Weight:** 28.2500 g. **Composition:** 0.8730 Silver .7948 oz. ASW **Subject:** Seven Provinces - Friesland

Date	Mintage	F	VF	XF	Unc	BU
1998 Proof	11,100	Value: 50.00				

KM# 229 SILVER DUCAT **Weight:** 28.2500 g. **Composition:** 0.8730 Silver .7948 oz. ASW **Subject:** Seven Provinces - Utrecht

Date	Mintage	F	VF	XF	Unc	BU
1999 Proof	9,500	Value: 50.00				

KM# 232 SILVER DUCAT **Weight:** 28.2500 g. **Composition:** 0.8730 Silver .7948 oz. ASW **Obverse:** Crowned arms **Reverse:** Standing knight with the arms of Overijssel **Edge:** Reeded **Size:** 40 mm.

Date	Mintage	F	VF	XF	Unc	BU
2000 Proof	10,100	Value: 45.00				
2002 Proof	—	Value: 45.00				

KM# 242 SILVER DUCAT **Weight:** 28.2500 g. **Composition:** 0.8730 Silver 0.7929 oz. ASW **Obverse:** Standing knight with sword and arms **Reverse:** Crowned arms **Edge:** Reeded **Size:** 40 mm. **Note:** Utrecht coin design circa 1659 based on KM#48.

Date	Mintage	F	VF	XF	Unc	BU
2001 Proof	9,000	Value: 45.00				

PATTERNS

Including off metal strikes

KM#	Date	Mintage	Identification	Mkt Val
PnA101	190x	—	5 Cents. Small 5. Reverse small 5.	—
Pn101	190x	—	5 Cents. Bronze. Large 5. Reverse large 5.	—
Pn101a	190x	—	5 Cents. Silver.	—
Pn103	190x	—	10 Cents. Nickel.	—
Pn102	190x	—	5 Cents. Bronze. 29 mm.	—
PnA124	1928	—	Gulden. Gold. 19 mm.	550
Pn95	190x	—	5 Cents. Nickel.	—
PNA102	190x	—	5 Cents. Bronze. 27 mm.	—
Pn96	1902	—	Cent. Gold. KM132.	—
Pn99	1903	—	10 Cents. Gold. KM135.	—
Pn98	1903	—	2-1/2 Cent. Gold. KM134.	—
Pn97	1903	—	1/2 Cent. Gold. KM133.	—
Pn100	1903	—	25 Cents. Gold. KM120.2	—
Pn109	1904	—	5 Cents. Nickel. Holed.	—
Pn104	1904	—	Cent. Bronze-Nickel Plug.	—
PnA110	1904	—	5 Cents.	—
Pn105	1904	—	5 Cents. Bronze.	—
Pn106	1904	—	5 Cents. Bronze.	—
Pn107	1904	—	5 Cents. Bronze. Holed.	—
Pn108	1904	—	5 Cents. Nickel.	—
Pn110	1905	—	1/2 Gulden. Gold. KM121.2	—
Pn114	1906	—	5 Cents. Nickel.	—
Pn116	1906	—	10 Cents. Nickel.	—
Pn115	1906	—	5 Cents. Silver.	—
Pn111	1906	—	5 Cents. Bronze.	—
Pn112	1906	—	5 Cents. Nickel.	—
Pn113	1906	—	5 Cents. Nickel.	—
PnA111	1906	—	5 Cents. Silver. Plain edge.	1,000
PnA117	1906	—	10 Cents.	—
Pn117	1907	—	5 Cents. Bronze. Crown.	—
Pn118	1907	—	5 Cents. Nickel. Small crown.	—
Pn119	1908	—	Gulden. Bronze. KM122.	—
Pn120	1910	—	10 Cents. Gold. KM145.	—
PnA121	1911	—	Gulden. Bronze.	1,100
PnB121	1912	—	5 Cents. Nickel. "Proof".	—
Pn121	1913	—	2-1/2 Gulden. Silver. KM148.	—
Pn122	1928	—	Gulden. Silver. 28 mm.	350
Pn123	1928	—	Gulden. Silver. 19 mm.	250
PnA123	1928	—	Gulden. Gold. 28 mm.	700
Pn124	1929	—	Gulden. Silver.	—
PnA125	1929	—	2-1/2 Gulden. Bronze.	1,200
Pn125	1929	—	2-1/2 Gulden. Silver.	550
PnA126	1929	—	2-1/2 Gulden. Gold.	1,000
Pn126	1934	—	10 Cents. Bronze. KM163.	—
PnA127	1935	—	5 Cents. Gold.	2,000
Pn127	1941	—	Cent. Zinc. KM170 with center hole.	550
Pn128	1941	—	2-1/2 Cent. Zinc. KM171 with center hole.	550
Pn129	1941	—	10 Cents. Zinc.	160
PnA134	1969	—	10 Cents. Nickel-Brass.	—
PnA130	1969	—	Cent. Nickel.	—
Pn130	1969	—	5 Cents. Nickel. Plain edge.	—
Pn132	1969	—	5 Cents. Aluminum. 1.5000 g.	—
Pn133	1969	—	5 Cents. Aluminum. 1.2200 g.	—
PnB134	1969	—	25 Cents. Brass.	—
Pn131	1969	—	5 Cents. Nickel.	—
PnC134	1970	—	Cent. Aluminum.	—
Pn134	1973	—	10 Gulden. Silver.	—
Pn135	1979	—	10 Gulden. Nickel.	—
Pn137	1980	—	Gulden. Nickel. KM200b error, shield on both sides.	—
Pn138	1980	—	Gulden. Gold. KM200b.	—
Pn139	1980	—	Gulden. Silver. KM200a.	500
Pn140	1980	—	2-1/2 Gulden. Gold. KM201b.	—
Pn136	1980	—	25 Cents. Aluminum. KM183a.	—
Pn141	1980	—	2-1/2 Gulden. Silver. KM201a.	500
Pn146	1982	—	Gulden. Nickel.	—
Pn142	1982	—	5 Cents. Bronze. 17 mm.	—
Pn143	1982	—	5 Cents. Tombac.	—
Pn145	1982	—	5 Cents. Copper Clad Steel.	—
Pn147	1982	—	50 Gulden. Gold. KM207.	—
Pn144	1982	—	5 Cents. Brass.	—
Pn148	1984	—	5 Cents. Tombac.	200
Pn149	1984	—	10 Cents. Bronze.	200
Pn150	1985	—	5 Cents. Nickel. Plain edge.	200
Pn151	1986	—	25 Cents. Brass. KM204.	300
Pn152	1986	—	25 Cents. Aluminum. KM204.	300
Pn153	1986	—	Ducat. Tombac. KM190.2.	500
Pn154	1987	—	5 Cents. Nickel. KM202.	—
Pn155	1988	—	5 Cents. Nickel Clad Steel.	—
PnB158	1988	—	50 Gulden. Silver.	850
PnA158	1988	—	50 Gulden. Tombac.	750
Pn158	1988	—	50 Gulden. Gold. KM212.	—
Pn156	1988	—	5 Cents. Copper Clad Steel.	—
Pn157	1988	—	5 Cents. Brass Clad Steel.	—
Pn159	1990	—	5 Cents. Aluminum.	—
Pn161	1991	—	50 Gulden. Silver. 1/4 Circle. Queen Beatrix and Prince Claus	—
Pn160	1991	—	5 Cents. Nickel. KM202.	—
Pn162	2001	—	Gulden. Nickel. Medal rotation	—

PIEFORTS

KM#	Date	Mintage	Identification	Mkt Val
P19	1905	—	1/2 Gulden. Silver. KM121.2	900
P20	1905	—	Gulden. Silver. KM122.2	—
P21	1910	—	25 Cents. Bronze. KM146.	—
P22	1948	—	Cent. Silver. KM175.	—
P23	1948	—	5 Cents. Silver. KM176.	—
P24	1948	—	10 Cents. Silver. KM177.	—
P25	1948	—	25 Cents. Silver. KM178.	—
PA26	1956	—	Gulden. Silver. similar to KM#184	—
P26	1958	—	Gulden. Silver. KM184.	—

MINT SETS

KM#	Date	Mintage	Identification	Issue Price	Mkt Val
MS1	1999 (8)	—	KM#234-241	15.00	17.00
MS2	2000 (6)	50,000	KM#202-206, 210	12.00	18.00
MS3	2000 (8)	—	KM#234-241	15.00	17.00
MS4	2001 (6)	85,000	KM#202-206, 210	12.00	15.00
MS5	2001 (8)	—	KM#234-241	15.00	17.00
MS10	2002 (8)	3,500	KM#234-241	20.00	110
MS11	2002 (8)	2,002	KM#234-241	22.00	180
MS12	2002 (8)	10,000	KM#234-241	22.00	35.00
MS13	2002 (8)	10,000	KM#234-241	22.00	25.00
MS14	2002 (8)	10,000	KM#234-241	22.00	25.00
MS15	2002 (8)	10,000	KM#234-241	22.00	25.00
MS16	2002 (8)	3,000	KM#234-241	30.00	40.00
MS17	2002 (1)	—	KM#243	30.00	30.00
MS18	2002 (8)	1,000	KM#234-241	99.00	99.00
MS6	2002 (8)	—	KM#234-241	15.00	17.00
MS7	2002 (8)	—	KM#234-241	15.00	17.00
MS8	2002 (8)	—	KM#234-241	15.50	25.00
MS9	2002 (8)	—	KM#234-241	15.50	35.00
MS19	2003 (8)	10,000	KM#234-241	22.00	25.00
MS20	2003 (8)	10,000	KM#234-241	22.00	25.00

PROOF SETS

KM#	Date	Mintage	Identification	Issue Price	Mkt Val
PS1	1948 (4)	50	KM175-178 with PROEF	—	1,800
PS2	1948 (4)	—	KM175-178	—	400
PS4	1950 (4)	—	KM180-183 with PROEF	—	1,250
PS5	1950 (4)	—	KM180-183	—	325
PS6	1951 (4)	—	KM180-183	—	275
PS7	1952 (2)	—	KM180-181	—	275
PS8	1953 (2)	—	KM180-181	—	275
PS9	1954 (5)	—	KM180-184	—	300
PS10	1955 (5)	—	KM180-184	—	250
PS11	1956 (5)	—	KM180-184	—	250
PS12	1957 (5)	—	KM18-184	—	250
PS13	1958 (5)	—	KM180-184	—	250
PS14	1959 (3)	—	KM180, 182, 185	—	450
PS15	1960 (5)	—	KM180-183, 185	—	450
PS16	1961 (5)	—	KM180-183, 185	—	450
PS17	1962 (5)	40	KM180-183, 185	—	450
PS18	1963 (6)	40	KM180-185	—	475
PS19	1964 (6)	40	KM180-185	—	475
PS20	1965 (5)	—	KM180-184	—	250
PS21	1966 (6)	—	KM180-185	—	450
PS22	1967 (5)	—	KM180-183, 184a	—	200
PD23	1968 (3)	—	KM180, 182-183	—	175
PS25	1969 (6)	—	KM180-183, 184a, 191. Fish.	—	250
PS24	1969 (6)	—	KM180-183, 184a, 191. Cock.	—	250
PS26	1970 (6)	—	KM180-183, 184a, 191	—	250
PS27	1982 (5)	10,000	KM202-206	35.00	85.00
PS28	1983 (5)	15,000	KM202-206	35.00	35.00
PS29	1984 (5)	20,406	KM202-206	35.00	22.50
PS30	1985 (5)	17,100	KM202-206	35.00	22.50
PS31	1986 (5)	19,500	KM202-206	35.00	32.50
PS32	1987 (5)	18,100	KM202-206, Utrecht medal	35.00	32.50
PS33	1988 (6)	19,550	KM202-206, 210, Groningen medal	5.50	32.50
PS34	1989 (6)	15,300	KM202-206,210, Flevoland medal	50.00	45.00
PS35	1989 (3)	6,400	LM190.2, 211, 213	260	200
PS36	1990 (6)	15,100	KM202-206, 210, N. Brabant medal. Set also includes 1974 25 Cents.	50.00	45.00
PS37	1991 (6)	14,240	KM202-206, 210,Drenthe medal	50.00	45.00
PS38	1992 (6)	12,600	KM202-206, 210, Zeeland medal	53.50	50.00
PS39	1992 (3)	6,300	KM190.2, 211, 213	270	235
PS40	1993 (6)	12,000	KM202-206, 210, Limburg medal	53.50	55.00
PS41	1994 (6)	12,500	KM202-206, 210, Friesland medal	59.50	55.00
PS43	1995 (6)	11,500	KM202-206, 210, Zuid-Holland medal	59.50	55.00
PS44	1996 (6)	13,500	KM202-206, 210 Booklet, 5 cents, Stuiver	60.00	75.00
PS45	1996 (2)	6,500	KM190.2, 211	247	225
PS46	1997 (6)	12,000	KM202-206, 210 Booklet, 10 Cents	60.00	70.00
PS47	1998 (6)	—	KM202-206, 210 Booklet, 25 Cents	60.00	70.00
PS48	1999 (6)	—	KM202-206, 210, Booklet, 1 Guilden	50.00	50.00
PS49	1999 (3)	2,500	KM190.2, 211, 229	—	280
PS50	1999 (2)	1,800	KM190.2, 211	—	240
PS51	2000 (6)	15,000	KM#202-206, 210	50.00	60.00
PS52	2000 (2)	500	KM#190.2, 211	—	230
PS53	2000 (3)	1,000	KM#190.2, 211, 232	—	270
PS54	2001 (6)	17,000	KM#202-206, 210	50.00	60.00
PS55	2001 (2)	500	KM#190.2, 242	50.00	60.00
PS56	2002 (2)	—	KM#190.2, 211	—	230
PS57	2002 (3)	—	KM#190.2, 211, 232	—	270

KM# 245 5 EURO **Weight:** 11.9900 g. **Composition:** 0.9250 Silver 0.3566 oz. ASW **Subject:** Vincent Van Gogh **Obverse:** Queen's portrait **Reverse:** Van Gogh's portrait **Edge:** Lettered: "GOD ZIJ MET ONS" **Size:** 29 mm.

Date	F	VF	XF	Unc	BU
ND(2003) Proof-like	—	—	—	—	—

KM# 243 10 EURO **Weight:** 17.8000 g. **Composition:** 0.9250 Silver 0.5294 oz. ASW **Subject:** Crown Prince's Wedding **Obverse:** Head of Queen Beatrix left **Reverse:** Two facing silhouettes **Edge:** Plain **Size:** 33 mm.

Date	F	VF	XF	Unc	BU
2002 Prooflike	—	—	—	—	32.50

KM# 244 10 EURO **Weight:** 6.7200 g. **Composition:** 0.9000 Gold 0.1944 oz. AGW **Subject:** Crown Prince's Wedding **Obverse:** Head of Queen Beatrix right **Reverse:** Two facing silhouettes of Willem Alexander and Maxima **Edge:** Reeded **Size:** 22.5 mm.

Date	F	VF	XF	Unc	BU
2002 Prooflike	—	—	—	—	130

KM# 246 10 EURO **Weight:** 6.7200 g. **Composition:** 0.9000 Gold 0.1944 oz. AGW **Subject:** Vincent Van Gogh **Obverse:** Queen's portrait **Reverse:** Van Gogh's portrait **Edge:** Reeded **Size:** 22.5 mm.

Date	F	VF	XF	Unc	BU
ND(2003) Proof	—	Value: 155			

TRADE COINAGE

KM# 83.1 DUCAT **Weight:** 3.5000 g. **Composition:** 0.9830 Gold .1106 oz. AGW

Date	Mintage	F	VF	XF	Unc	BU
1901	29,284	200	450	750	1,500	2,000
1903/1	91,000	200	450	750	1,500	2,000
1903	Inc. above	150	400	600	800	1,200
1905	87,995	150	400	600	800	1,200
1906	29,379	200	450	750	1,500	2,000
1908	91,006	125	250	400	600	1,100
1909 halberd with star privy mark	106,021	125	250	400	700	1,200
1909 sea horse privy mark	30,182	175	475	850	1,750	2,500
1910	421,447	125	275	425	650	850
1910 Proof	—	Value: 1,000				
1912	147,860	125	275	425	650	850
1912 Proof	—	Value: 1,000				
1913	205,464	125	275	425	650	850
1914	246,560	125	275	425	650	850
1916	116,997	125	275	425	650	850
1916 Proof	—	Value: 1,250				
1917	216,892	BV	65.00	90.00	125	150
1920	293,389	BV	65.00	90.00	125	150
1920 Proof	—	Value: 800				
1921	409,001	BV	60.00	70.00	90.00	110
1922	49,837	100	250	400	600	800
1923	106,674	BV	75.00	150	250	350
1924	84,206	BV	75.00	150	250	350
1925	573,071	BV	60.00	70.00	90.00	110
1925 Proof	Inc. above	Value: 450				
1926	191,311	BV	60.00	80.00	110	150
1927	654,424	—	BV	40.00	50.00	60.00
1928	571,801	—	BV	40.00	50.00	60.00
1932	88,268	200	500	900	1,500	1,800
1937	116,660	BV	70.00	90.00	110	125

KM# 190.1 DUCAT **Weight:** 3.5000 g. **Composition:** 0.9830 Gold .1106 oz. AGW **Obverse:** Knight with right leg bent, larger letters in legend

Date	F	VF	XF	Unc	BU
1960	50.00	100	200	300	400
1972 Prooflike	—	—	—	—	70.00
1974 Prooflike	—	—	—	—	70.00
1974 medal struck	65.00	125	250	350	475
1975 Prooflike	—	—	—	—	60.00
1976 Prooflike	—	—	50.00	100	150

Note: Of 37,844 pieces struck, 32,000 were melted

Date	F	VF	XF	Unc	BU
1978 Prooflike	—	—	—	60.00	90.00
1985 Prooflike	—	—	—	—	55.00

KM# 190.2 DUCAT **Weight:** 3.5000 g. **Composition:** 0.9830 Gold .1106 oz. AGW **Obverse:** Knight with left leg bent, larger letters in legend

Date	Mintage	F	VF	XF	Unc	BU
1986 Prooflike		—	—	—	—	60.00
1989 Proof	24,478	Value: 80.00				
1990 Proof	17,500	Value: 90.00				
1991 Proof	11,500	Value: 85.00				
1992 Proof	14,400	Value: 85.00				
1993 Proof	11,100	Value: 95.00				
1994 Proof	11,500	Value: 90.00				
1995 Proof	11,000	Value: 90.00				
1996 Proof	12,000	Value: 90.00				
1997 Proof	12,000	Value: 90.00				
1998 Proof	12,000	Value: 90.00				
1999 Proof	11,000	Value: 90.00				
2000 Proof	12,000	Value: 90.00				
2001 Proof	12,000	Value: 90.00				
2002 Proof	12,000	Value: 90.00				

KM# 211 2 DUCAT **Weight:** 6.9880 g. **Composition:** 0.9830 Gold .2209 oz. AGW

Date	Mintage	F	VF	XF	Unc	BU
1988 Prooflike		—	—	—	—	130
1989 Proof	17,862	Value: 130				
1991 Proof	10,000	Value: 140				
1992 Proof	12,000	Value: 140				
1996 Proof	11,000	Value: 140				
1999 Proof	9,300	Value: 150				
2000 Proof	9,000	Value: 140				
2002 Proof	Est. 6,000	Value: 140				

SILVER BULLION COINAGE

KM# 213 SILVER DUCAT **Weight:** 28.2500 g. **Composition:** 0.8730 Silver .7948 oz. ASW

Date	Mintage	F	VF	XF	Unc	BU
1989 Proof	35,797	Value: 25.00				
1992 Proof	17,200	Value: 40.00				
1993 Proof	12,500	Value: 50.00				

KM# 218 SILVER DUCAT **Weight:** 28.2500 g. **Composition:** 0.8730 Silver .7948 oz. ASW **Subject:** Seven Provinces - Groningen

Date	Mintage	F	VF	XF	Unc	BU
1994 Proof	11,000	Value: 75.00				

KM# 221 SILVER DUCAT **Weight:** 28.2500 g. **Composition:** 0.8730 Silver .7948 oz. ASW **Subject:** Seven Provinces - Zeeland

Date	Mintage	F	VF	XF	Unc	BU
1995 Proof	11,000	Value: 50.00				

KM# 222 SILVER DUCAT Weight: 28.2500 g. **Composition:** 0.8730 Silver .7948 oz. ASW **Subject:** Seven Provinces - Holland

Date	Mintage	F	VF	XF	Unc	BU
1996 Proof	12,500	Value: 50.00				

KM# 225 SILVER DUCAT Weight: 28.2500 g. **Composition:** 0.8730 Silver .7948 oz. ASW **Subject:** Seven Provinces - Gelderland

Date	Mintage	F	VF	XF	Unc	BU
1997 Proof	11,500	Value: 50.00				

KM# 226 SILVER DUCAT Weight: 28.2500 g. **Composition:** 0.8730 Silver .7948 oz. ASW **Subject:** Seven Provinces - Friesland

Date	Mintage	F	VF	XF	Unc	BU
1998 Proof	11,100	Value: 50.00				

KM# 229 SILVER DUCAT Weight: 28.2500 g. **Composition:** 0.8730 Silver .7948 oz. ASW **Subject:** Seven Provinces - Utrecht

Date	Mintage	F	VF	XF	Unc	BU
1999 Proof	9,500	Value: 50.00				

KM# 232 SILVER DUCAT Weight: 28.2500 g. **Composition:** 0.8730 Silver .7948 oz. ASW **Obverse:** Crowned arms **Reverse:** Standing knight with the arms of Overijssel **Edge:** Reeded **Size:** 40 mm.

Date	Mintage	F	VF	XF	Unc	BU
2000 Proof	10,100	Value: 45.00				
2002 Proof	—	Value: 45.00				

KM# 242 SILVER DUCAT Weight: 28.2500 g. **Composition:** 0.8730 Silver 0.7929 oz. ASW **Obverse:** Standing knight with sword and arms **Reverse:** Crowned arms **Edge:** Reeded **Size:** 40 mm. **Note:** Utrecht coin design circa 1659 based on KM#48.

Date	Mintage	F	VF	XF	Unc	BU
2001 Proof	9,000	Value: 45.00				

PATTERNS

Including off metal strikes

KM#	Date	Mintage	Identification	Mkt Val
PnA101	190x	—	5 Cents. Small 5. Reverse small 5.	—
Pn101	190x	—	5 Cents. Bronze. Large 5. Reverse large 5.	—
Pn101a	190x	—	5 Cents. Silver.	—
Pn103	190x	—	10 Cents. Nickel.	—
Pn102	190x	—	5 Cents. Bronze. 29 mm.	—
PnA124	1928	—	Gulden. Gold. 19 mm.	550
Pn95	190x	—	5 Cents. Nickel.	—
PNA102	190x	—	5 Cents. Bronze. 27 mm.	—
Pn96	1902	—	Cent. Gold. KM132.	—
Pn99	1903	—	10 Cents. Gold. KM135.	—
Pn98	1903	—	2-1/2 Cent. Gold. KM134.	—
Pn97	1903	—	1/2 Cent. Gold. KM133.	—
Pn100	1903	—	25 Cents. Gold. KM120.2	—
Pn109	1904	—	5 Cents. Nickel. Holed.	—
Pn104	1904	—	Cent. Bronze-Nickel Plug.	—
PnA110	1904	—	5 Cents.	—
Pn105	1904	—	5 Cents. Bronze.	—
Pn106	1904	—	5 Cents. Bronze.	—
Pn107	1904	—	5 Cents. Bronze. Holed.	—
Pn108	1904	—	5 Cents. Nickel.	—
Pn110	1905	—	1/2 Gulden. Gold. KM121.2	—
Pn114	1906	—	5 Cents. Nickel.	—
Pn116	1906	—	10 Cents. Nickel.	—
Pn115	1906	—	5 Cents. Silver.	—
Pn111	1906	—	5 Cents. Bronze.	—
Pn112	1906	—	5 Cents. Nickel.	—
Pn113	1906	—	5 Cents. Nickel.	—
PnA111	1906	—	5 Cents. Silver. Plain edge.	1,000
PnA117	1906	—	10 Cents.	—
Pn117	1907	—	5 Cents. Bronze. Crown.	—
Pn118	1907	—	5 Cents. Nickel. Small crown.	—
Pn119	1908	—	Gulden. Bronze. KM122.	—
Pn120	1910	—	10 Cents. Gold. KM145.	—
PnA121	1911	—	Gulden. Bronze.	1,100
PnB121	1912	—	5 Cents. Nickel. "Proof".	—
Pn121	1913	—	2-1/2 Gulden. Silver. KM148.	—
Pn122	1928	—	Gulden. Silver. 28 mm.	350
Pn123	1928	—	Gulden. Silver. 19 mm.	250
PnA123	1928	—	Gulden. Gold. 28 mm.	700
Pn124	1929	—	Gulden. Silver.	—
PnA125	1929	—	2-1/2 Gulden. Bronze.	1,200
Pn125	1929	—	2-1/2 Gulden. Silver.	550
PnA126	1929	—	2-1/2 Gulden. Gold.	1,000
Pn126	1934	—	10 Cents. Bronze. KM163.	—
PnA127	1935	—	5 Cents. Gold.	2,000
Pn127	1941	—	Cent. Zinc. KM170 with center hole.	550
Pn128	1941	—	2-1/2 Cent. Zinc. KM171 with center hole.	550
Pn129	1941	—	10 Cents. Zinc.	160
PnA134	1969	—	10 Cents. Nickel-Brass.	—
PnA130	1969	—	Cent. Nickel.	—
Pn130	1969	—	5 Cents. Nickel. Plain edge.	—
Pn132	1969	—	5 Cents. Aluminum. 1.5000 g.	—
Pn133	1969	—	5 Cents. Aluminum. 1.2200 g.	—
PnB134	1969	—	25 Cents. Brass.	—
Pn131	1969	—	5 Cents. Nickel.	—
PnC134	1970	—	Cent. Aluminum.	—
Pn134	1973	—	10 Gulden. Silver.	—
Pn135	1979	—	10 Gulden. Nickel.	—
Pn137	1980	—	Gulden. Nickel. KM200b error, shield on both sides.	—
Pn138	1980	—	Gulden. Gold. KM200b.	—
Pn139	1980	—	Gulden. Silver. KM200a.	500
Pn140	1980	—	2-1/2 Gulden. Gold. KM201b.	—
Pn136	1980	—	25 Cents. Aluminum. KM183a.	—
Pn141	1980	—	2-1/2 Gulden. Silver. KM201a.	500
Pn146	1982	—	Gulden. Nickel.	—
Pn142	1982	—	5 Cents. Bronze. 17 mm.	—
Pn143	1982	—	5 Cents. Tombac.	—
Pn145	1982	—	5 Cents. Copper Clad Steel.	—
Pn147	1982	—	50 Gulden. Gold. KM207.	—
Pn144	1982	—	5 Cents. Brass.	—
Pn148	1984	—	5 Cents. Tombac.	200
Pn149	1984	—	10 Cents. Bronze.	200
Pn150	1985	—	5 Cents. Nickel. Plain edge.	200
Pn151	1986	—	25 Cents. Brass. KM204.	300
Pn152	1986	—	25 Cents. Aluminum. KM204.	300
Pn153	1986	—	Ducat. Tombac. KM190.2.	500
Pn154	1987	—	5 Cents. Nickel. KM202.	—
Pn155	1988	—	5 Cents. Nickel Clad Steel.	—
PnB158	1988	—	50 Gulden. Silver.	850
PnA158	1988	—	50 Gulden. Tombac.	750
Pn158	1988	—	50 Gulden. Gold. KM212.	—
Pn156	1988	—	5 Cents. Copper Clad Steel.	—
Pn157	1988	—	5 Cents. Brass Clad Steel.	—
Pn159	1990	—	5 Cents. Aluminum.	—
Pn161	1991	—	50 Gulden. Silver. 1/4 Circle. Queen Beatrix and Prince Claus	—
Pn160	1991	—	5 Cents. Nickel. KM202.	—
Pn162	2001	—	Gulden. Nickel. Medal rotation	—

PIEFORTS

KM#	Date	Mintage	Identification	Mkt Val
P19	1905	—	1/2 Gulden. Silver. KM121.2	900
P20	1905	—	Gulden. Silver. KM122.2	—
P21	1910	—	25 Cents. Bronze. KM146.	—
P22	1948	—	Cent. Silver. KM175.	—
P23	1948	—	5 Cents. Silver. KM176.	—
P24	1948	—	10 Cents. Silver. KM177.	—
P25	1948	—	25 Cents. Silver. KM178.	—
PA26	1956	—	Gulden. Silver. similar to KM#184	—
P26	1958	—	Gulden. Silver. KM184.	—

MINT SETS

KM#	Date	Mintage	Identification	Issue Price	Mkt Val
MS1	1999 (8)	—	KM#234-241	15.00	17.00
MS2	2000 (6)	50,000	KM#202-206, 210	12.00	18.00
MS3	2000 (8)	—	KM#234-241	15.00	17.00
MS4	2001 (6)	85,000	KM#202-206, 210	12.00	15.00
MS5	2001 (8)	—	KM#234-241	15.00	17.00
MS10	2002 (8)	3,500	KM#234-241	20.00	110
MS11	2002 (8)	2,002	KM#234-241	22.00	180
MS12	2002 (8)	10,000	KM#234-241	22.00	35.00
MS13	2002 (8)	10,000	KM#234-241	22.00	25.00
MS14	2002 (8)	10,000	KM#234-241	22.00	25.00
MS15	2002 (8)	10,000	KM#234-241	22.00	25.00
MS16	2002 (8)	3,000	KM#234-241	30.00	40.00
MS17	2002 (1)	—	KM#243	30.00	30.00
MS18	2002 (8)	1,000	KM#234-241	99.00	99.00
MS6	2002 (8)	—	KM#234-241	15.00	17.00
MS7	2002 (8)	—	KM#234-241	15.00	17.00
MS8	2002 (8)	—	KM#234-241	15.50	25.00
MS9	2002 (8)	—	KM#234-241	15.50	35.00
MS19	2003 (8)	10,000	KM#234-241	22.00	25.00
MS20	2003 (8)	10,000	KM#234-241	22.00	25.00

PROOF SETS

KM#	Date	Mintage	Identification	Issue Price	Mkt Val
PS1	1948 (4)	50	KM175-178 with PROEF	—	1,800
PS2	1948 (4)	—	KM175-178	—	400
PS4	1950 (4)	—	KM180-183 with PROEF	—	1,250
PS5	1950 (4)	—	KM180-183	—	325
PS6	1951 (4)	—	KM180-183	—	275
PS7	1952 (2)	—	KM180-181	—	275
PS8	1953 (2)	—	KM180-181	—	275
PS9	1954 (5)	—	KM180-184	—	300
PS10	1955 (5)	—	KM180-184	—	250
PS11	1956 (5)	—	KM180-184	—	250
PS12	1957 (5)	—	KM18-184	—	250
PS13	1958 (5)	—	KM180-184	—	250
PS14	1959 (3)	—	KM180, 182, 185	—	450
PS15	1960 (5)	—	KM180-183, 185	—	450
PS16	1961 (5)	—	KM180-183, 185	—	450
PS17	1962 (5)	40	KM180-183, 185	—	450
PS18	1963 (6)	40	KM180-185	—	475
PS19	1964 (6)	40	KM180-185	—	475
PS20	1965 (5)	—	KM180-184	—	250
PS21	1966 (6)	—	KM180-185	—	450
PS22	1967 (5)	—	KM180-183, 184a	—	200
PD23	1968 (3)	—	KM180, 182-183	—	175
PS25	1969 (6)	—	KM180-183, 184a, 191. Fish.	—	250
PS24	1969 (6)	—	KM180-183, 184a, 191. Cock.	—	250
PS26	1970 (6)	—	KM180-183, 184a, 191	—	250
PS27	1982 (5)	10,000	KM202-206	35.00	85.00
PS28	1983 (5)	15,000	KM202-206	35.00	35.00
PS29	1984 (5)	20,406	KM202-206	35.00	22.50
PS30	1985 (5)	17,100	KM202-206	35.00	22.50
PS31	1986 (5)	19,500	KM202-206	35.00	32.50
PS32	1987 (5)	18,100	KM202-206, Utrecht medal	35.00	32.50
PS33	1988 (6)	19,550	KM202-206, 210, Groningen medal	5.50	32.50
PS34	1989 (6)	15,300	KM202-206,210, Flevoland medal	50.00	45.00
PS35	1989 (3)	6,400	LM190.2, 211, 213	260	200
PS36	1990 (6)	15,100	KM202-206, 210, N. Brabant medal. Set also includes 1974 25 Cents.	50.00	45.00
PS37	1991 (6)	14,240	KM202-206, 210,Drenthe medal	50.00	45.00
PS38	1992 (6)	12,600	KM202-206, 210, Zeeland medal	53.50	50.00
PS39	1992 (3)	6,300	KM190.2, 211, 213	270	235
PS40	1993 (6)	12,000	KM202-206, 210, Limburg medal	53.50	55.00
PS41	1994 (6)	12,500	KM202-206, 210, Friesland medal	59.50	55.00
PS43	1995 (6)	11,500	KM202-206, 210, Zuid-Holland medal	59.50	55.00
PS44	1996 (6)	13,500	KM202-206, 210 Booklet, 5 cents, Stuiver	60.00	75.00
PS45	1996 (2)	6,500	KM190.2, 211	247	225
PS46	1997 (6)	12,000	KM202-206, 210 Booklet, 10 Cents	60.00	70.00
PS47	1998 (6)	—	KM202-206, 210 Booklet, 25 Cents	60.00	70.00
PS48	1999 (6)	—	KM202-206, 210, Booklet, 1 Guilden	50.00	50.00
PS49	1999 (3)	2,500	KM190.2, 211, 229	—	280
PS50	1999 (2)	1,800	KM190.2, 211	—	240
PS51	2000 (6)	15,000	KM#202-206, 210	50.00	60.00
PS52	2000 (2)	500	KM#190.2, 211	—	230
PS53	2000 (3)	1,000	KM#190.2, 211, 232	—	270
PS54	2001 (6)	17,000	KM#202-206, 210	50.00	60.00
PS55	2001 (2)	500	KM#190.2, 242	50.00	60.00
PS56	2002 (2)	—	KM#190.2, 211	—	230
PS57	2002 (3)	—	KM#190.2, 211, 232	—	270

Date	Mintage	F	VF	XF	Unc	BU
1956 Proof	500	Value: 40.00				
1957	200,000	1.00	2.00	4.00	10.00	15.00
1957 Proof	250	Value: 40.00				
1960	240,000	0.50	1.00	2.00	5.00	8.00
1960 Proof	300	Value: 40.00				
1962	240,000	0.50	1.00	2.00	5.00	8.00
1962 Proof	200	Value: 45.00				
1963	300,000	0.50	1.00	2.00	5.00	8.00
1963 Proof	—	Value: 45.00				
1965	500,000	0.50	1.00	2.00	5.00	8.00
1965 Proof	—	Value: 45.00				
1967 fish	310,000	0.50	1.00	2.00	5.00	8.00
1967 Proof, fish	—	Value: 45.00				
1967 fish and star	200,000	0.50	1.00	2.00	5.00	8.00
1970	150,000	0.50	1.00	2.00	5.00	8.00
1970 Proof	—	Value: 35.00				

KM# 11 25 CENTS **Weight:** 3.0000 g. **Composition:** Nickel **Obverse:** Arms **Reverse:** Value, 6 stars

Date	Mintage	F	VF	XF	Unc	BU
1970	750,000	0.30	0.50	1.00	2.00	—
1970 Proof	—	Value: 30.00				
1971	3,000,000	—	0.20	0.40	0.80	—
1971 Proof	—	Value: 30.00				
1975	1,000,000	—	0.20	0.40	0.80	—
1975 Proof	—	Value: 30.00				
1976	1,000,000	—	0.10	0.25	0.50	—
1977	1,000,000	—	0.10	0.25	0.50	—
1978	1,000,000	—	0.10	0.25	0.50	—
1979	1,012,000	—	0.10	0.25	0.50	—
1979 Proof	—	Value: 17.50				
1980 cock and star	1,018,000	—	0.10	0.25	0.50	—
1981	1,022,999	—	0.10	0.25	0.50	—
1982	1,010,000	—	0.10	0.25	0.50	—
1983	1,024,999	—	0.10	0.25	0.50	—
1984	1,026,000	—	0.10	0.25	0.50	—
1985	774,000	—	0.10	0.25	0.50	—

KM# 35 25 CENTS **Weight:** 3.5000 g. **Composition:** Nickel Bonded Steel **Obverse:** Orange blossom **Reverse:** Geometric design

Date	Mintage	F	VF	XF	Unc	BU
1989	915,000	—	—	—	0.50	—
1990	1,811,000	—	—	—	0.50	—
1991	2,013,000	—	—	—	0.50	—
1992	898,000	—	—	—	0.50	—
1993	997,000	—	—	—	0.50	—
1994	997,000	—	—	—	0.50	—
1995	297,000	—	—	—	0.50	—
1996	420,000	—	—	—	0.50	—
1997	1,297,000	—	—	—	0.50	—
1998	2,007,000	—	—	—	0.50	—
1999		—	—	—	0.50	—
2000		—	—	—	0.50	—

KM# 36 50 CENTS **Weight:** 5.0000 g. **Composition:** Aureate Steel **Obverse:** Orange blossom, geometric design **Reverse:** Value, pearls, shells **Shape:** Square

Date	Mintage	F	VF	XF	Unc	BU
1989	315,000	—	—	—	1.00	—
1990	611,000	—	—	—	1.00	—
1991	513,000	—	—	—	1.00	—
1992	48,000	—	—	—	1.00	—
1993 In sets only	8,560	—	—	—	2.00	—
1994 In sets only	9,000	—	—	—	1.50	—
1995 In sets only	9,000	—	—	—	1.50	—
1996 In sets only	7,500	—	—	—	1.50	—
1997	32,000	—	—	—	1.00	—
1998	132,000	—	—	—	1.00	—
1999	—	—	—	—	1.00	—
2000	—	—	—	—	1.00	—

KM# 2 GULDEN **Weight:** 10.0000 g. **Composition:** 0.7200 Silver .2315 oz. ASW **Obv. Designer:** Queen Juliana **Reverse:** Arms

Date	Mintage	F	VF	XF	Unc	BU
1952	1,000,000	1.50	2.50	4.00	7.00	12.00
1952 Proof	100	Value: 110				
1963	100,000	2.00	3.00	5.00	12.00	20.00
1963 Proof	—	Value: 100				
1964 fish	300,000	1.50	2.50	4.00	7.00	12.00
1964 Proof	—	Value: 100				
1964 fish and star	200,000	1.50	2.50	4.00	7.00	12.00
1970	50,000	2.00	3.50	6.00	10.00	16.00
1970 Proof	—	Value: 100				

KM# 12 GULDEN **Weight:** 9.0000 g. **Composition:** Nickel **Obverse:** Bust of Queen Juliana right **Reverse:** Arms

Date	Mintage	F	VF	XF	Unc	BU
1970	500,000	0.65	0.85	1.65	3.25	—
1970 Proof	—	Value: 50.00				
1971	3,000,000	—	0.60	1.25	2.50	—
1971 Proof	—	Value: 50.00				
1978	500,000	—	0.50	1.00	2.00	—
1979	512,000	—	0.50	1.00	2.00	—
1979 Proof	—	Value: 25.00				
1980 cock and star	518,000	—	0.40	0.75	1.50	—

Note: 1969 date is now listed in the Patterns section

KM# 24 GULDEN **Weight:** 9.0000 g. **Composition:** Nickel **Obverse:** Bust of Queen Beatrix left **Reverse:** Arms

Date	Mintage	F	VF	XF	Unc	BU
1980 anvil	223,000	—	0.40	0.75	1.50	—
1981	223,000	—	0.40	0.75	1.50	—
1982	510,000	—	0.40	0.75	1.50	—
1983	525,000	—	0.40	0.75	1.50	—
1984	526,000	—	0.40	0.75	1.50	—
1985	424,000	—	0.40	0.75	1.50	—

KM# 37 GULDEN **Weight:** 6.0000 g. **Composition:** Aureate Steel **Obverse:** Queen Beatrix **Reverse:** Arms

Date	Mintage	F	VF	XF	Unc	BU
1989	715,000	—	—	0.50	1.00	—
1990	1,411,000	—	—	0.50	1.00	—
1991	2,013,000	—	—	0.50	1.00	—
1992	1,198,000	—	—	0.50	1.00	—
1993	1,986,000	—	—	0.50	1.00	—
1994	997,000	—	—	0.50	1.00	—
1995 In sets only	9,000	—	—	—	2.00	—
1996 In sets only	7,500	—	—	—	2.00	—
1997	2,507,000	—	—	0.50	1.00	—
1998	12,507,000	—	—	0.50	1.00	—
1999		—	—	0.50	1.00	—
2000		—	—	0.50	1.00	—

KM# 7 2-1/2 GULDEN **Weight:** 25.0000 g. **Composition:** 0.7200 Silver .5787 oz. ASW **Obverse:** Queen Juliana **Reverse:** Arms

Date	F	VF	XF	Unc	BU
1964	—	BV	5.00	10.00	12.00
1964 Proof	—	Value: 200			

KM# 19 2-1/2 GULDEN **Weight:** 12.0000 g. **Composition:** Nickel **Obverse:** Bust of Queen Juliana **Reverse:** Arms

Date	Mintage	F	VF	XF	Unc	BU
1978	100,000	—	—	1.75	3.50	—
1979	212,000	—	—	1.75	3.50	—
1979 Proof	—	Value: 35.00				
1980 cock and star	200,000	—	—	1.75	3.50	—

KM#25 2-1/2 GULDEN **Weight:** 12.0000 g. **Composition:** Nickel **Obverse:** Bust of Queen Beatrix **Reverse:** Arms

Date	Mintage	F	VF	XF	Unc	BU
1980 anvil	80,000	—	—	1.65	3.25	—
1981	30,000	—	—	1.65	3.25	—
1982	44,000	—	—	1.65	3.25	—
1984	30,000	—	—	1.65	3.25	—
1985	37,000	—	—	1.65	3.25	—

KM#38 2-1/2 GULDEN **Weight:** 9.0000 g. **Composition:** Aureate Steel **Obverse:** Queen Beatrix **Reverse:** Arms

Date	Mintage	F	VF	XF	Unc	BU
1989	35,000	—	—	—	2.50	—
1990	60,000	—	—	—	2.50	—
1991	63,000	—	—	—	2.50	—
1992	23,000	—	—	—	2.50	—
1993 In sets only	8,560	—	—	—	4.25	—
1994 In sets only	9,000	—	—	—	3.50	—
1995 In sets only	9,000	—	—	—	3.50	—
1996 In sets only	7,500	—	—	—	3.50	—
1997	9,500	—	—	—	3.50	—
1998	20,000	—	—	—	3.50	—
1999	—	—	—	—	3.50	—
2000	—	—	—	—	3.50	—

KM# 26 5 GULDEN **Weight:** 3.3600 g. **Composition:** 0.9000 Gold .0972 oz. AGW **Obverse:** Bust of Queen Beatrix left

Date	Mintage	F	VF	XF	Unc	BU
1980(1982) Proof, cock and star	16,000	Value: 50.00				

KM# 43 5 GULDEN **Weight:** 11.0000 g. **Composition:** Brass Plated Steel **Obverse:** Head of Queen Beatrix left **Reverse:** Crowned arms divide denomination **Edge Lettering:** GOD ZIJ MET ONS

Date	Mintage	F	VF	XF	Unc	BU
1998	607,000	—	—	—	5.50	—
1999	—	—	—	—	5.50	—
2000	—	—	—	—	5.50	—

KM# 20 10 GULDEN **Weight:** 25.0000 g. **Composition:** 0.7200 Silver .5787 oz. ASW **Subject:** 150th Anniversary of Bank **Obverse:** Queen Juliana **Reverse:** Arms

Date	Mintage	F	VF	XF	Unc	BU
1978	35,000	—	—	—	7.00	—
1978 Proof	15,000	Value: 10.00				

KM# 27 10 GULDEN **Weight:** 6.7200 g. **Composition:** 0.9000 Gold .1945 oz. AGW **Obverse:** Head of Queen Beatrix left **Reverse:** Arms of the Antilles and Netherlands joined

Date	Mintage	F	VF	XF	Unc	BU
1980 Proof, cock and star	6,000	Value: 100				

KM# 49 10 GULDEN **Weight:** 31.1035 g. **Composition:** 0.9250 Silver .9250 oz. ASW **Ruler:** Beatrix **Series:** Gold Trade Coins: Sulla Aureus **Obverse:** National arms and denomination **Reverse:** Bust of Sulla facing two gold inserts replicating the aureus coin issued by Manlius and Sulla in 82-81 BC **Edge:** Reeded **Size:** 40 mm.

Date	F	VF	XF	Unc	BU
2001 Proof	—	Value: 50.00			

KM# 50 10 GULDEN **Weight:** 31.1035 g. **Composition:** 0.9250 Silver .9250 oz. ASW **Ruler:** Beatrix **Series:** Gold Trade Coins: Constantin I Solidus **Obverse:** National arms and denomination **Reverse:** Bust of Constantin I the Great facing, two gold inserts replicating a solidus coin issued during his reign **Edge:** Reeded **Size:** 40 mm.

Date	F	VF	XF	Unc	BU
2001 Proof	—	Value: 50.00			

KM# 51 10 GULDEN **Weight:** 31.1035 g. **Composition:** 0.9250 Silver .9250 oz. ASW **Ruler:** Beatrix **Series:** Gold Trade Coins: Clovis I Tremissisfiorino d'oro **Obverse:** National arms and denomination **Reverse:** Bust of Clovis I facing two gold inserts replicating the tremissisfioeino d'oro coin issued during his reign **Edge:** Reeded **Size:** 40 mm.

Date	F	VF	XF	Unc	BU
2001 Proof	—	Value: 50.00			

KM# 52 10 GULDEN **Weight:** 31.1035 g. **Composition:** 0.9250 Silver .9250 oz. ASW **Ruler:** Beatrix **Series:** Gold Trade Coins: Cosimo de'Medici Fiorino d'oro **Obverse:** National arms and denomination **Reverse:** Bust of Cosimo de'Medici facing two gold inserts replicating the Fiorino d'oro coin issued during his reign **Edge:** Reeded **Size:** 40 mm.

Date	F	VF	XF	Unc	BU
2001 Proof	—	Value: 50.00			

KM# 53 10 GULDEN **Weight:** 31.1035 g. **Composition:** 0.9250 Silver .9250 oz. ASW **Ruler:** Beatrix **Series:** Gold Trade Coins: Dandolo Ducato d'oro **Obverse:** National arms and denomination **Reverse:** Bust of Dandolo facing two gold inserts replicating the Ducato d'oro coin issued during his reign **Edge:** Reeded **Size:** 40 mm.

Date	F	VF	XF	Unc	BU
2001 Proof	—	Value: 50.00			

KM# 54 10 GULDEN **Weight:** 31.1035 g. **Composition:** 0.9250 Silver .9250 oz. ASW **Ruler:** Beatrix **Series:** Gold Trade Coins: Philips IV Ecu d'or la chaise **Obverse:** National arms and denomination **Reverse:** Bust of Philips IV facing two gold inserts replicating the Ecu d'or la chaise coin issued during his reign **Edge:** Reeded **Size:** 40 mm.

Date	F	VF	XF	Unc	BU
2001 Proof	—	Value: 50.00			

KM# 55 10 GULDEN **Weight:** 31.1035 g. **Composition:** 0.9250 Silver .9250 oz. ASW **Ruler:** Beatrix **Series:** Gold Trade Coins: Edward III Nobel **Obverse:** National arms and denomination **Reverse:** Bust of Edward III facing two gold inserts replicating the Nobel coin issued during his reign **Edge:** Reeded **Size:** 40 mm.

Date	F	VF	XF	Unc	BU
2001 Proof	—	Value: 50.00			

KM# 56 10 GULDEN **Weight:** 31.1035 g. **Composition:** 0.9250 Silver .9250 oz. ASW **Ruler:** Beatrix **Series:** Gold Trade Coins: Carolus IV Rhine Gold Guilder **Obverse:** National arms and denomination **Reverse:** Bust of Carolus IV facing two gold inserts replicating the Rhine Gold Guilder coin issued during his reign **Edge:** Reeded **Size:** 40 mm.

Date	F	VF	XF	Unc	BU
2001 Proof	—	Value: 50.00			

KM# 57 10 GULDEN **Weight:** 31.1035 g. **Composition:** 0.9250 Silver .9250 oz. ASW **Ruler:** Beatrix **Series:** Gold Trade Coins: John II Franc d'or a cheval **Obverse:** National arms and denomination **Reverse:** Bust of John II the Good facing two gold inserts replicating the Franc d'or a cheval coin issued during his reign **Edge:** Reeded **Size:** 40 mm.

Date	F	VF	XF	Unc	BU
2001 Proof	—	Value: 50.00			

KM# 58 10 GULDEN **Weight:** 31.1035 g. **Composition:** 0.9250 Silver .9250 oz. ASW **Ruler:** Beatrix **Series:** Gold Trade Coins: Philip the Good Adriesguilder **Obverse:** National arms and denomination **Reverse:** Bust of Philip the Good facing two gold inserts replicating the Adriesguilder coin issued during his reign **Edge:** Reeded **Size:** 40 mm.

Date	F	VF	XF	Unc	BU
2001 Proof	—	Value: 50.00			

KM# 59 10 GULDEN **Weight:** 31.1035 g. **Composition:** 0.9250 Silver .9250 oz. ASW **Ruler:** Beatrix **Series:** Gold Trade Coins: Louis XI Ecu d'or au soleil **Obverse:** National arms and denomination **Reverse:** Bust of Louis XI facing two gold inserts replicating the Ecu d'or au soleil coin issued during his reign **Edge:** Reeded **Size:** 40 mm.

Date	F	VF	XF	Unc	BU
2002 Proof	—	Value: 50.00			

KM# 60 10 GULDEN **Weight:** 31.1035 g. **Composition:** 0.9250 Silver .9250 oz. ASW **Ruler:** Beatrix **Series:** Gold Trade Coins: Elisabeth I Sovereign **Obverse:** National arms and denomination **Reverse:** Bust of Elisabeth I facing two gold inserts replicating the Sovereign coin issued during her reign **Edge:** Reeded **Size:** 40 mm.

Date	F	VF	XF	Unc	BU
2002 Proof	—	Value: 50.00			

KM# 61 10 GULDEN **Weight:** 31.1035 g. **Composition:** 0.9250 Silver .9250 oz. ASW **Ruler:** Beatrix **Series:** Gold Trade Coins: Carolus V Carolus Guilder **Obverse:** National arms and denomination **Reverse:** Bust of Carolus V facing two gold inserts replicating the Carolus Guilder coin issued during his reign **Edge:** Reeded **Size:** 40 mm.

Date	F	VF	XF	Unc	BU
2002 Proof	—	Value: 50.00			

KM# 62 10 GULDEN **Weight:** 31.1035 g. **Composition:** 0.9250 Silver .9250 oz. ASW **Ruler:** Beatrix **Series:** Gold Trade Coins: Philips II Real **Obverse:** National arms and denomination **Reverse:** Bust of Philips II facing two gold inserts replicating the Real coin issued during his reign **Edge:** Reeded **Size:** 40 mm.

Date	F	VF	XF	Unc	BU
2002 Proof	—	Value: 50.00			

KM# 63 10 GULDEN **Weight:** 31.1035 g. **Composition:** 0.9250 Silver .9250 oz. ASW **Ruler:** Beatrix **Series:** Gold Trade Coins: Maurits Ducat **Obverse:** National arms and denomination **Reverse:** Bust of Maurits (Orange-Nassau) facing two gold inserts replicating the Ducat coin issued during his reign **Edge:** Reeded **Size:** 40 mm.

Date	F	VF	XF	Unc	BU
2002 Proof	—	Value: 50.00			

KM# 64 10 GULDEN **Weight:** 31.1035 g. **Composition:** 0.9250 Silver .9250 oz. ASW **Ruler:** Beatrix **Series:** Gold Trade Coins: Isabella and Albrecht Double Albertin **Obverse:** National arms and denomination **Reverse:** Bust of Isabella and Albrecht facing two gold inserts replicating Double Albertin issued during their reign **Edge:** Reeded **Size:** 40 mm.

Date	F	VF	XF	Unc	BU
2002 Proof	—	Value: 50.00			

KM# 65 10 GULDEN **Weight:** 31.1035 g. **Composition:** 0.9250 Silver .9250 oz. ASW **Ruler:** Beatrix **Series:** Gold Trade Coins: William III Golden Rider **Obverse:** National arms and denomination **Reverse:** Bust of William III facing two gold inserts replicating Golden Rider issued during his reign **Edge:** Reeded **Size:** 40 mm.

Date	F	VF	XF	Unc	BU
2002 Proof	—	Value: 50.00			

KM# 66 10 GULDEN **Weight:** 31.1035 g. **Composition:** 0.9250 Silver .9250 oz. ASW **Ruler:** Beatrix **Series:** Gold Trade Coins: Louis XIII Louis d'or **Obverse:** National arms and denomination **Reverse:** Bust of Louis XIII facing two gold inserts replicating Louis d'or issued during his reign **Edge:** Reeded **Size:** 40 mm.

Date	F	VF	XF	Unc	BU
2003 Proof	—	Value: 50.00			

KM# 67 10 GULDEN **Weight:** 31.1035 g. **Composition:** 0.9250 Silver .9250 oz. ASW **Ruler:** Beatrix **Series:** Gold Trade Coins: Catharina the Great Rubel **Obverse:** National arms and denomination **Reverse:** Bust of Catharina the Great facing two gold inserts replicating a Rubel coin issued during her reign **Edge:** Reeded **Size:** 40 mm.

Date	F	VF	XF	Unc	BU
2003 Proof	—	Value: 50.00			

KM# 68 10 GULDEN **Weight:** 31.1035 g. **Composition:** 0.9250 Silver .9250 oz. ASW **Ruler:** Beatrix **Series:** Gold Trade Coins: Maria Theresia Double Sovereign **Obverse:** National arms and denomination **Reverse:** Bust of Maria Theresia facing two gold inserts replicating a double sovereign coin issued during her reign **Edge:** Reeded **Size:** 40 mm.

Date	F	VF	XF	Unc	BU
2003 Proof	—	Value: 50.00			

KM# 69 10 GULDEN **Weight:** 31.1035 g. **Composition:** 0.9250 Silver .9250 oz. ASW **Ruler:** Beatrix **Series:** Gold Trade Coins: Napolean Bonaparte 20 Franc **Obverse:** National arms and denomination **Reverse:** Bust of Napolean Bonaparte facing two gold inserts replicating a 20 franc coin issued during his rule **Edge:** Reeded **Size:** 40 mm.

Date	F	VF	XF	Unc	BU
2003 Proof	—	Value: 50.00			

KM# 70 10 GULDEN **Weight:** 31.1035 g. **Composition:** 0.9250 Silver .9250 oz. ASW **Ruler:** Beatrix **Series:** Gold Trade Coins: Wilhelmina Golden 10 Guilder **Obverse:** National arms and denomination **Reverse:** Bust of Wilhelmina facing two gold inserts replicating a Golden 10 Guilder issued during her reign **Edge:** Reeded **Size:** 40 mm.

Date	F	VF	XF	Unc	BU
2003 Proof	—	Value: 50.00			

KM# 71 10 GULDEN **Weight:** 31.1035 g. **Composition:** 0.9250 Silver .9250 oz. ASW **Ruler:** Beatrix **Series:** Gold Trade Coins: George III Souvereign **Obverse:** National arms and denomination **Reverse:** Bust of George III facing two gold inserts replicating a gold sovereign coin issued during his reign **Edge:** Reeded **Size:** 40 mm.

Date	F	VF	XF	Unc	BU
2003 Proof	—	Value: 50.00			

KM# 72 10 GULDEN **Weight:** 31.1035 g. **Composition:** 0.9250 Silver .9250 oz. ASW **Ruler:** Beatrix **Series:** Gold Trade Coins: Albert I Belgium 20 Franc **Obverse:** National arms and denomination **Reverse:** Bust of Albert I facing two gold inserts replicating a Belgian 20 franc coin issued during his reign **Edge:** Reeded **Size:** 40 mm.

Date	F	VF	XF	Unc	BU
2003 Proof	—	Value: 50.00			

KM# 14 25 GULDEN **Weight:** 41.7000 g. **Composition:** 0.9250 Silver 1.2401 oz. ASW **Subject:** 25th Anniversary of Reign **Obverse:** Queen Juliana **Reverse:** Royal carriage and Paramaribo pontoon bridge

Date	Mintage	F	VF	XF	Unc	BU
1973	40,000	—	—	—	15.00	—
1973 Proof	20,000	Value: 18.00				

KM# 39 25 GULDEN **Weight:** 25.0000 g. **Composition:** 0.9250 Silver .7435 oz. ASW **Subject:** Visit of Pope John Paul II **Obverse:** Pope John Paul II head right **Reverse:** Curacao map, Juliana bridge

Date	Mintage	F	VF	XF	Unc	BU
1990	10,000	—	—	—	35.00	—
1990 Proof	6,500	Value: 37.50				

KM# 42 25 GULDEN **Weight:** 25.0000 g. **Composition:** 0.9250 Silver .7435 oz. ASW **Subject:** Fort Nassau 1797-1997 **Obverse:** Queen Beatrix **Reverse:** Old stem sail ship Curacao, dates

Date	Mintage	F	VF	XF	Unc	BU
ND(1997) Proof	25,000	Value: 35.00				

KM# 15 25 GULDEN **Weight:** 41.7000 g. **Composition:** 0.9250 Silver 1.2401 oz. ASW **Subject:** U.S. Bicentennial **Obverse:** Queen Juliana **Reverse:** Saling ship Andrrew Doria

Date	Mintage	F	VF	XF	Unc	BU
1976 FM(M)	200	—	—	—	165	—
1976 FM(U)	9,425	—	—	—	20.00	—
1976 FM(P)	13,000	Value: 35.00				

KM# 40 25 GULDEN **Weight:** 25.0000 g. **Composition:** 0.9250 Silver .7435 oz. ASW **Subject:** First Amsterdam to Curacao Flight in 1934 **Obverse:** Queen Beatrix **Reverse:** Folker FXVIII plane over route map

Date	F	VF	XF	Unc	BU
1994 Proof	—	Value: 35.00			

KM# 44 25 GULDEN **Weight:** 25.0000 g. **Composition:** 0.9250 Silver .7435 oz. ASW **Series:** World Wildlife Fund **Obverse:** Crowned arms, denomination **Reverse:** Whitetail buck and doe, WWF logo

Date	Mintage	F	VF	XF	Unc	BU
1998 Proof like	500	—	—	—	—	30.00
1998 Proof	—	Value: 35.00				

KM# 17 25 GULDEN **Weight:** 41.7000 g. **Composition:** 0.9250 Silver 1.2401 oz. ASW **Subject:** Peter Stuyvesant

Date	F	VF	XF	Unc	BU
1977	—	—	80.00	160	—

KM# 22 25 GULDEN **Weight:** 27.2200 g. **Composition:** 0.9250 Silver .8095 oz. ASW **Series:** International Year of the Child **Obverse:** Queen Juliana **Reverse:** Children dancing

Date	Mintage	F	VF	XF	Unc	BU
1979	1,000	—	—	—	75.00	—
1979 Prooflike	4,000	—	—	—	—	32.50
1979 Proof	17,000	Value: 20.00				

KM# 41 25 GULDEN **Weight:** 25.0000 g. **Composition:** 0.9250 Silver .7435 oz. ASW **Series:** Olympics **Obverse:** Crowned arms **Reverse:** Weight lifter, dates

Date	F	VF	XF	Unc	BU
1995 Proof	—	Value: 22.50			

KM# 45 25 GULDEN **Weight:** 25.0000 g. **Composition:** 0.9250 Silver .7435 oz. ASW **Subject:** 1499 Discovery of Curacao **Obverse:** Crowned arms, date **Reverse:** Sailing ship - Nina **Edge Lettering:** DIOS KU NOS **Note:** Edge inscription repeats three times.

Date	Mintage	F	VF	XF	Unc	BU
1999 Proof	9,500	Value: 35.00				

KM# 48 25 GULDEN **Weight:** 25.0000 g. **Composition:** 0.9250 Silver 0.7435 oz. ASW **Ruler:** Beatrix **Subject:** Olympics **Obverse:** National arms and denomination **Reverse:** Swimmer **Edge:** Lettered **Size:** 38 mm.

Date	F	VF	XF	Unc	BU
2000 Proof	—	Value: 35.00			

KM# 23 50 GULDEN **Weight:** 3.3600 g. **Composition:** 0.9000 Gold .0972 oz. AGW **Subject:** 75th Anniversary of the Royal Convenant **Obverse:** Queen Juliana

Date	Mintage	F	VF	XF	Unc	BU
1979	11,000	—	—	—	40.00	—
1979 Proof	64,000	Value: 45.00				

KM# 28 50 GULDEN **Weight:** 24.0000 g. **Composition:** 0.5000 Silver .3859 oz. ASW **Obverse:** Queen Beatrix **Reverse:** Joined arms of the Antilles and Netherlands

Date	Mintage	F	VF	XF	Unc	BU
1980 cock and star	8,600	—	—	—	17.50	—
1980 Proof, cock and star	16,000	Value: 20.00				

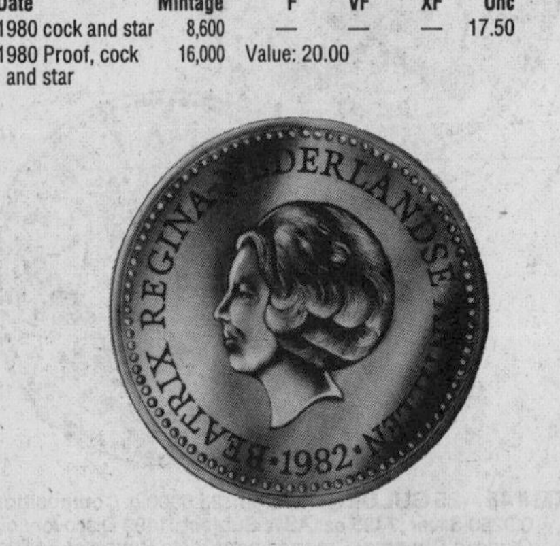

KM# 30 50 GULDEN **Weight:** 25.0000 g. **Composition:** 0.9250 Silver .7435 oz. ASW **Subject:** Dutch American Friendship **Obverse:** Queen Beatrix **Reverse:** Peter Stuyvesant, three flags as banners below

Date	Mintage	F	VF	XF	Unc	BU
1982 Y Proof	40,000	Value: 30.00				

KM# 31 50 GULDEN **Weight:** 25.0000 g. **Composition:** 0.9250 Silver .7435 oz. ASW **Obverse:** Queen Beatrix **Reverse:** Mikve Israel Emanuel Synagogue

Date	Mintage	F	VF	XF	Unc	BU
ND(1982) Proof	10,000	Value: 45.00				

KM# 47 75 GULDEN **Composition:** Bi-Metallic Gold And Silver **Subject:** Enkuentro Di Pueblonan **Obverse:** Arms **Reverse:** Globe above five heads

Date	F	VF	XF	Unc	BU
1999 Proof	—	Value: 200			

KM# 21 100 GULDEN **Weight:** 6.7200 g. **Composition:** 0.9000 Gold .1944 oz. AGW **Subject:** 150th Anniversary of Bank **Obverse:** Queen Juliana **Reverse:** King William

Date	Mintage	F	VF	XF	Unc	BU
1978	27,000	—	—	—	75.00	—
1978 Proof	24,000	Value: 80.00				

KM# 46 100 GULDEN **Weight:** 7.7700 g. **Composition:** 0.9990 Gold .2500 oz. AGW **Obverse:** Arms **Obv. Legend:** YEGADA DI SPAÑONAN. **Reverse:** Sailing ship Santa Maria

Date	F	VF	XF	Unc	BU
1999 Proof	—	Value: 175			

KM# 16 200 GULDEN **Weight:** 7.9500 g. **Composition:** 0.9000 Gold .2300 oz. AGW **Subject:** U.S. Bicentennial **Shape:** Octagon

Date	Mintage	F	VF	XF	Unc	BU
1976 FM(M)	100	—	—	—	300	—
1976 FM(U)	5,626	—	—	—	120	—
1976 FM(P)	15,000	Value: 100				

KM# 18 200 GULDEN **Weight:** 7.9500 g. **Composition:** 0.9000 Gold .2300 oz. AGW **Obverse:** Queen Juliana **Reverse:** Peter Stuyvesant **Shape:** Octagon

Date	Mintage	F	VF	XF	Unc	BU
1977 FM(M)	1,000	—	—	—	150	—
1977 FM(U)	645	—	—	—	275	—
1977 FM(P)	6,878	Value: 120				

KM# 29.1 300 GULDEN **Weight:** 5.0400 g. **Composition:** 0.9000 Gold .1458 oz. AGW **Subject:** Abdication of Queen Juliana **Obverse:** Queen Juliana **Reverse:** Joined arms of the Antilles and Netherlands **Shape:** Square

Date	Mintage	F	VF	XF	Unc	BU
1980 (u) cock and star	—	—	—	—	60.00	—
1980 (u) Proof, cock and star	29,000	Value: 65.00				

KM# 29.2 300 GULDEN **Weight:** 5.0400 g. **Composition:** 0.9000 Gold .1458 oz. AGW **Subject:** Abdication of Queen Juliana **Obverse:** Queen Juliana **Reverse:** Without mint mark

Date	Mintage	F	VF	XF	Unc	BU
1980 Proof	Inc. above	Value: 250				

PATTERNS

Including off metal strikes

KM#	Date	Mintage	Identification	Mkt Val
Pn1	1969	200	Cent. Nickel. KM8.	550
Pn2	1969	200	2-1/2 Cents. Nickel. KM9.	550
Pn3	1969	200	5 Cents. Nickel. KMA13.	550
Pn4	1969	200	10 Cents. Nickel. KM10.	550
Pn5	1969	200	25 Cents. Nickel. KM11.	550
Pn6	1969	200	Gulden. Nickel. (KM12).	550
Pn7	1981 Y	—	125 Gulden. Gilt Bronze.	750
Pn8	1981 Y	—	125 Gulden. Gold.	3,000
Pn9	1981 Y	—	250 Gulden. Gilt Bronze.	850
Pn10	1981 Y	—	250 Gulden. Gold.	4,000
Pn11	1981 Y	—	500 Gulden. Gilt Bronze.	950
Pn12	1981 Y	—	500 Gulden. Gold.	5,000
Pn13	1983	—	50 Guilder. 0.9250 Silver. 25.0000 g. 38 mm. Head of Beatrix Regina left. Arms and banner above six islands of the Antilles, value 50G below. Struck at a private mint.	—

PIEFORT

KM#	Date	Mintage	Identification	Mkt Val
P1	1979	7,162	25 Gulden. KM22.	75.00

MINT SETS

KM#	Date	Mintage	Identification	Issue Price	Mkt Val
MS1	1971 (7)	—	KM8-13 and Curacao KM46	—	22.00
MS2	1979 (7)	12,000	KM8a-9a, 10-13, 19	—	14.50
MS3	1980 (7)	18,000	KM8a-9a, 10-13, 19	—	11.50
MS4	1980 (2)	23,000	KM24-25	—	6.00
MS5	1981 (7)	23,000	KM8a-9a, 10-12, 24, 25	—	14.50
MS6	1982 (7)	10,000	KM8a-9a, 10-12, 24, 25	—	14.50
MS7	1983 (6)	25,000	KM8a-9a, 10-12, 24 and medallion	14.00	11.50

KM#	Date	Mintage	Identification	Issue Price	Mkt Val
MS8	1984 (7)	26,000	KM8a-9a, 10-12, 24, 25	14.50	11.50
MS9	1985 (7)	24,000	KM8a-9a, 10-12, 24, 25	—	11.50
MS10	1989 (7)	15,000	KM32-38	—	14.50
MS11	1990 (7)	10,000	KM32-38	13.00	14.50
MS12	1991 (7)	12,500	KM32-38	13.50	14.50
MS13	1992 (7)	10,500	MS32-38	—	14.50
MS14	1993 (7)	8,560	KM32-38	—	14.50
MS15	1994 (7)	9,000	KM32-38	17.00	14.50
MS16	1995 (7)	9,000	KM32-38	17.50	14.50
MS17	1996 (7)	7,500	KM32-38	18.50	14.50
MS18	1997 (7)	7,000	KM32-38	—	14.50
MS19	1998 (8)	7,000	KM32-38, 43	—	14.50
MS20	1999 (8)	—	KM32-38, 43	—	14.50
MS21	2000 (8)	—	KM32-38, 43	—	14.50

PROOF SETS

KM#	Date	Mintage	Identification	Issue Price	Mkt Val
PS1	1952 (2)	100	KM1-2	—	180
PS2	1954 (3)	200	KM1, 3-4	—	120
PS3	1956 (3)	500	KM3-5	—	120
PS4	1957 (4)	250	KM1, 3-4, 6	—	160
PS5	1959 (3)	250	KM1, 3, 5	—	100
PS6	1960 (3)	300	KM1, 3-4	—	110
PS7	1962 (3)	200	KM3-4, 6	—	110
PS8	1963 (5)	—	KM1-4, 6	—	235
PS9	1964 (3)	—	KM1-2, 7	—	325
PS10	1965 (4)	—	KM1, 4-6	—	125
PS11	1967 (3)	—	KM1, 4, 6	—	100
PS12	1969 (6)	200	KM8-12, A13, Pattern set	—	650
PS13	1970 (10)	—	KM1-4, 6, 8-12	—	350
PS14	1971 (6)	—	KM8-13	—	165
PS15	1973 (3)	—	KM8-9, 14	—	87.50
PS16	1974 (4)	—	KM8-10, 13	—	85.00
PS17	1975 (4)	—	KM8, 10-11, 13	—	240
PS18	1976 (2)	13,000	KM15-16	187	325
PS19	1979 (7)	—	KM8a-9a, 10-13, 19	—	120
PS20	1999 (5)	—	KM45-47, with Aruba KM18-19	—	625

NETHERLANDS EAST INDIES

Netherlands East Indies, (Kingdom of the Netherlands) is the world's largest archipelago extending for more than 3,000 mi. along the equator from the mainland of southeast Asia to Australia. At present time, since the late 1940's, it is known as Indonesia. The Dutch were in control until 1945 when Indonesia declared its independence from the Netherlands.

RULERS

Dutch, 1816-1942

MINT

Utrecht

Privy Marks
(a) - Halberd
(b) - Halberd and star
(c) - Sea horse
(d) - Grapes

KINGDOM

DECIMAL COINAGE

KM# 306 1/2 CENT Weight: 2.3000 g. Composition: Copper

Date	Mintage	F	VF	XF	Unc	BU
1855(u) Proof	—	Value: 125				
1856(u)	10,800,000	12.50	20.00	35.00	60.00	—
1857(u)	36,800,000	10.00	15.00	25.00	40.00	—
1858(u)	53,588,000	3.50	6.00	12.50	25.00	—
1858(u) Proof	—	—	—	—	—	—
1859(u)	219,600,000	2.50	4.00	10.00	20.00	—
1860(u)	107,124,000	2.50	4.00	10.00	20.00	—
1902(u)	20,000,000	1.00	3.00	8.00	15.00	25.00
1902(u) Proof	—	Value: 25.00				
1908(u)	10,600,000	2.00	5.00	15.00	30.00	60.00
1908(u) Proof	—	Value: 65.00				
1909(u)	4,400,000	5.00	9.00	18.00	25.00	40.00

KM# 314.1 1/2 CENT Weight: 2.3000 g. Composition: Bronze Note: Mintmaster's mark: Sea horse.

Date	Mintage	F	VF	XF	Unc	BU
1914(u)	50,000,000	1.00	1.50	3.00	5.00	8.00
1916(u)	10,000,000	1.50	2.50	5.00	10.00	15.00
1921(u)	4,000,000	5.00	9.00	18.00	25.00	40.00
1932(u)	10,000,000	1.50	2.50	5.00	9.00	15.00
1933(u)	15,000,000	1.50	2.50	5.00	9.00	15.00

KM# 314.2 1/2 CENT Weight: 2.3000 g. Composition: Bronze Note: Mintmaster's mark: Grapes.

Date	Mintage	F	VF	XF	Unc	BU
1933(u)	5,000,000	10.00	20.00	50.00	80.00	110
1934(u)	30,000,000	0.75	1.50	2.50	5.00	8.00
1935(u)	14,000,000	1.50	2.50	5.00	9.00	12.00
1936(u)	12,000,000	1.50	2.50	5.00	9.00	12.00
1936(u) Proof	—	Value: 35.00				
1937(u)	8,400,000	1.50	2.50	5.00	9.00	15.00
1937(u) Proof	—	Value: 35.00				
1938(u)	3,600,000	2.50	5.00	10.00	20.00	30.00
1939(u)	2,000,000	5.00	10.00	20.00	30.00	50.00
1945P	400,000,000	0.15	0.30	0.65	1.25	2.00

KM# 307.2 CENT Composition: Copper Obverse: Legend begins and ends beside date

Date	Mintage	F	VF	XF	Unc	BU
1901(u)	15,000,000	4.00	8.00	15.00	40.00	55.00
1901(u) Proof	—	Value: 65.00				
1902(u)	10,000,000	4.00	8.00	15.00	30.00	40.00
1907(u)	7,500,000	4.00	8.00	15.00	30.00	40.00
1907(u) Proof	—	Value: 100				
1908(u)	12,500,000	4.00	8.00	15.00	30.00	40.00
1908(u) Proof	—	Value: 55.00				
1909(u)	7,500,000	4.00	8.00	15.00	30.00	40.00
1912(u)	25,000,000	1.50	3.00	6.00	12.00	18.00

KM# 315 CENT Composition: Bronze

Date	Mintage	F	VF	XF	Unc	BU
1914(u)	85,000,000	1.00	2.00	4.00	8.00	15.00
1914(u) Proof	—	Value: 50.00				
1916(u)	16,440,000	2.00	4.00	8.00	15.00	20.00
1919(u)	20,000,000	2.00	4.00	8.00	15.00	20.00
1919(u) Proof	—	Value: 65.00				
1920(u)	120,000,000	1.00	2.00	3.00	6.00	10.00
1926(u)	10,000,000	3.00	6.00	10.00	20.00	30.00
1929(u)	50,000,000	1.00	2.00	4.00	8.00	15.00
1929(u) Proof	—	Value: 100				

KM# 317 CENT Composition: Bronze

Date	Mintage	F	VF	XF	Unc	BU
1936(u)	52,000,000	0.50	1.00	2.00	3.00	5.00
1937(u)	120,400,000	0.45	0.75	1.50	2.50	4.00
1937(u) Proof	—	Value: 40.00				
1938(u)	150,000,000	0.40	0.75	1.50	2.50	4.00
1939(u)	81,400,000	0.45	0.75	1.50	3.00	5.00
1942P	100,000,000	0.10	0.25	0.50	1.00	2.00
1945P	335,000,000	0.10	0.25	0.50	1.00	1.50
1945D	133,800,000	0.10	0.25	0.50	1.00	2.00
1945S	102,568,000	0.10	0.25	0.50	1.00	2.00

KM# 308 2-1/2 CENTS Composition: Copper

Date	Mintage	F	VF	XF	Unc	BU
1902	6,000,000	5.00	10.00	20.00	30.00	50.00
1907	3,000,000	8.00	15.00	25.00	40.00	60.00
1908	5,940,000	5.00	10.00	20.00	30.00	50.00
1908 Proof	—	Value: 135				
1909	3,060,000	8.00	12.50	30.00	50.00	65.00
1913	4,000,000	8.00	12.50	30.00	50.00	65.00
1913 Proof	—	Value: 135				

KM# 316 2-1/2 CENTS Composition: Bronze

Date	Mintage	F	VF	XF	Unc	BU
1914(u)	22,000,000	2.50	5.00	8.00	12.00	20.00
1914(u)	—	Value: 165				
1915(u)	6,000,000	3.75	7.50	15.00	30.00	45.00
1920(u)	48,000,000	2.00	4.00	7.00	12.00	18.00
1920(u)	—	Value: 165				
1945P	200,000,000	0.25	0.50	1.00	2.00	3.50

KM# 313 5 CENTS Composition: Copper-Nickel

Date	Mintage	F	VF	XF	Unc	BU
1913(u)	60,000,000	0.75	1.75	3.50	7.00	18.00
1913(u) Proof	—	Value: 90.00				
1921(u)	40,000,000	0.75	1.75	3.50	7.00	18.00
1921(u) Proof	—	Value: 220				
1922(u)	20,000,000	1.00	2.50	5.00	10.00	25.00

KM# 304 1/10 GULDEN **Weight:** 1.2500 g. **Composition:** 0.7200 Silver .0289 oz. ASW

Date	Mintage	F	VF	XF	Unc	BU
1901(u)	5,000,000	2.00	4.00	7.50	15.00	20.00
1901(u) Proof	—	Value: 120				

KM# 309 1/10 GULDEN **Weight:** 1.2500 g. **Composition:** 0.7200 Silver .0289 oz. ASW

Date	Mintage	F	VF	XF	Unc	BU
1903(u)	5,000,000	2.00	4.00	7.50	15.00	20.00
1903(u) Proof	—	Value: 110				
1904(u)	5,000,000	2.00	4.00	8.00	16.50	20.00
1905(u)	5,000,000	2.00	4.00	8.00	16.50	20.00
1906(u)	7,500,000	1.00	2.25	4.50	9.00	15.00
1907(u)	14,000,000	1.00	2.25	4.50	9.00	15.00
1907(u) Proof	—	Value: 55.00				
1908(u)	3,000,000	2.00	4.00	8.00	20.00	30.00
1909(u)	10,000,000	0.75	1.50	3.00	8.00	15.00
1909(u) Proof	—	Value: 110				

KM# 311 1/10 GULDEN **Weight:** 1.2500 g. **Composition:** 0.7200 Silver .0289 oz. ASW **Obverse:** Wide rims and small legend **Reverse:** Wide rims and small legend

Date	Mintage	F	VF	XF	Unc	BU
1910(u)	15,000,000	0.75	1.50	3.00	8.00	15.00
1910(u) Proof	—	Value: 140				
1911(u)	10,000,000	0.75	1.50	3.00	8.00	15.00
1912(u)	25,000,000	0.50	1.00	2.00	6.00	10.00
1913(u)	15,000,000	0.75	1.50	3.00	7.00	12.00
1914(u)	25,000,000	0.50	1.00	2.00	6.00	10.00
1915(u)	15,000,000	0.50	1.50	3.00	7.00	12.00
1918(u)	30,000,000	0.50	1.00	2.00	6.00	10.00
1919(u)	20,000,000	0.50	1.00	2.00	6.00	10.00
1920(u)	8,500,000	0.75	1.50	3.50	8.00	15.00
1928(u)	30,000,000	0.50	1.00	2.00	6.00	10.00
1930(u)	15,000,000	0.50	1.00	2.00	6.00	10.00

KM# 318 1/10 GULDEN **Weight:** 1.2500 g. **Composition:** 0.7200 Silver .0289 oz. ASW **Obverse:** Narrow rims and large legend **Reverse:** Narrow rims and large legend

Date	Mintage	F	VF	XF	Unc	BU
1937(u)	20,000,000	0.35	0.75	1.50	2.50	4.00
1937(u) Proof	—	Value: 130				
1938(u)	30,000,000	0.35	0.75	1.50	2.50	4.00
1939(u)	5,400,000	0.75	1.50	3.00	5.00	9.00
1939(u) Proof	—	Value: 130				
1940(u)	10,000,000	0.40	0.85	1.75	3.50	5.00
1941P	41,850,000	0.20	0.35	0.75	1.25	2.00
1941S	58,150,000	0.20	0.35	0.75	1.25	2.00
1942S	75,000,000	0.20	0.35	0.75	1.25	2.00
1945P	100,720,000	0.20	0.35	0.75	1.25	2.00
1945S	19,280,000	0.25	0.40	0.75	1.50	3.00

KM# 305 1/4 GULDEN **Weight:** 3.1800 g. **Composition:** 0.7200 Silver .0736 oz. ASW

Date	Mintage	F	VF	XF	Unc	BU
1901(u)	2,000,000	8.00	15.00	25.00	4.00	60.00
1901(u) Proof	—	Value: 100				

KM# 310 1/4 GULDEN **Weight:** 3.1800 g. **Composition:** 0.7200 Silver .0736 oz. ASW

Date	Mintage	F	VF	XF	Unc	BU
1903(u)	2,000,000	8.00	15.00	25.00	40.00	60.00
1903(u) Proof	—	Value: 115				
1904(u)	2,000,000	5.00	12.00	20.00	30.00	50.00
1904(u) Proof	—	Value: 115				
1905(u)	2,000,000	5.00	12.00	20.00	30.00	50.00
1905(u) Proof	—	Value: 170				
1906(u)	4,000,000	2.50	5.00	10.00	20.00	35.00
1907(u)	4,400,000	2.50	5.00	10.00	20.00	35.00
1907(u) Proof	—	Value: 100				
1908(u)	2,000,000	3.00	12.00	20.00	30.00	50.00
1909(u)	4,000,000	2.50	5.00	10.00	20.00	35.00
1909(u) Proof	—	Value: 80.00				

KM# 312 1/4 GULDEN **Weight:** 3.1800 g. **Composition:** 0.7200 Silver .0736 oz. ASW **Obverse:** Wide rims and small legend **Reverse:** Wide rims and small legend

Date	Mintage	F	VF	XF	Unc	BU
1910(u)	6,000,000	3.75	7.50	15.00	30.00	50.00
1911(u)	4,000,000	3.75	7.50	15.00	30.00	50.00
1911(u) Proof	—	Value: 80.00				
1912(u)	10,000,000	2.50	5.00	10.00	20.00	35.00
1913(u)	6,000,000	2.50	5.00	10.00	20.00	35.00
1914(u)	10,000,000	2.50	5.00	10.00	20.00	35.00
1915(u)	6,000,000	2.50	5.00	10.00	20.00	35.00
1917(u)	12,000,000	1.25	2.50	5.00	10.00	20.00
1919(u)	6,000,000	2.50	5.00	10.00	20.00	35.00
1920(u)	20,000,000	0.75	1.50	4.00	8.00	12.00
1921(u)	24,000,000	0.75	1.50	4.00	8.00	12.00
1929(u)	5,000,000	1.25	2.50	5.00	10.00	15.00
1930(u)	7,000,000	1.25	2.50	5.00	10.00	15.00
1930(u) Proof	—	Value: 160				

KM# 319 1/4 GULDEN **Weight:** 3.1800 g. **Composition:** 0.7200 Silver .0736 oz. ASW **Obverse:** Narrow rims and large legend **Reverse:** Narrow rims and large legend

Date	Mintage	F	VF	XF	Unc	BU
1937(u)	8,000,000	1.00	2.00	3.50	6.00	8.00
1938(u)	12,000,000	1.00	2.00	3.50	6.00	8.00
1939(u)	10,400,000	1.00	2.00	3.50	6.00	8.00
1939 Proof	—	Value: 65.00				
1941P	34,947,000	0.25	0.50	1.00	2.00	3.00
1941S	5,053,000	0.50	1.00	2.00	7.50	10.00
1942S	32,000,000	0.25	0.50	1.00	2.00	3.00
1945S	56,000,000	0.25	0.50	1.00	2.00	3.00

WORLD WAR II COINAGE

Netherlands and Netherlands East Indies coins of the 1941-45 period were struck at U.S. Mints (P-Philadelphia, D-Denver, S-San Francisco) and bear the mint mark and a palm tree (acorn on Homeland issues) flanking the date. The following issues, KM#330 and KM#331, are of the usual Netherlands type, being distinguished from similar 1944-45 issues produced in the name of the Homeland by the presence of the palm tree, but were produced for release in the colony. See other related issues under Curacao and Suriname.

TRADE COINAGE

These gold coins, intended primarily for circulation in the Netherlands East Indies, will be found listed as KM#83.1 in the Netherlands section.

KM# T1 DUCAT **Composition:** 0.9860 Gold

Date	VG	F	VF	XF	Unc
ND(1901-37)	—	—	—	—	—

HOMELAND COINAGE

KM# 330 GULDEN **Weight:** 10.0000 g. **Composition:** 0.7200 Silver .2315 oz. ASW

Date	Mintage	F	VF	XF	Unc	BU
1943D	20,000,000	2.00	3.50	6.50	15.00	20.00

KM# 331 2-1/2 GULDEN **Weight:** 25.0000 g. **Composition:** 0.7200 Silver .5787 oz. ASW

Date	Mintage	F	VF	XF	Unc	BU
1943D	2,000,000	6.00	9.00	12.00	18.50	25.00

OCCUPATION COINAGE

Japan

These coins were struck primarily for circulation in the East Indies. The Sen, 5 Sen and 10 Sen are inscribed DAI NIPON (Great Japan) and are found listed under Japan - Occupation issues as Y#22, Y#24 and Pn48.

KM# J1 10 SEN **Composition:** Tin Alloy

Date	VG	F	VF	XF	Unc
ND(1943-45)	—	—	—	—	—

PATTERNS

KM#	Date	Mintage	Identification	Mkt Val
Pn11	1902(u)	—	1/2 Cent. Silver. KM#306	—
Pn12	1902(u)	—	1/2 Cent. Gold. KM#306	—
Pn13	1902(u)	—	Cent. Silver. KM#307	—
Pn14	1902(u)	—	Cent. Gold. KM#307	—
Pn15	1902(u)	—	2-1/2 Cents. Silver. 13.5000 g. KM#308	—
Pn16	1902(u)	—	2-1/2 Cents. Gold. KM#308	—
Pn18	1903(u)	—	1/4 Gulden. Gold. KM#310	—
Pn17	1908(u)	—	1/10 Gulden. Gold. KM#309	—
Pn19	1908	—	1/2 Cent. Silver.	—
Pn20	1908	—	1/2 Cent. Gold.	—
Pn21	1908	—	Cent. Iron.	—
Pn22	1908	—	Cent. Silver.	—
Pn23	1908	—	Cent. Gold.	—
Pn24	1908	—	2-1/2 Cents. Silver. KM#308	—
Pn25	1908	—	2-1/2 Cents. Gold. 22.1220 g. KM#308	—
Pn27	1914	—	10 Sen. Tin.	—
Pn28	1914	5	5 Cents. Tin.	—
Pn29	1914	—	5 Cents. Gold.	—
Pn26	1934(u)	—	5 Cents. Copper-Nickel. KM#313	—
PnA30	1934	—	1/4 Cent. Copper.	—
Pn30	1934	—	1/4 Cent. Copper. Holed	—
Pn31	1934	—	1/2 Cent. Copper. KM#314	—
Pn32	1934	—	1/4 Cent. Copper. KM#320	—
Pn33	1945	—	1/4 Gulden. Gold. KM#319	50.00

NEW CALEDONIA

The French Overseas Territory of New Caledonia, are a group of about 25 islands in the South Pacific. It is situated about 750 miles (1,207 km.) east of Australia. The territory, which includes the dependencies of Ile des Pins, Loyalty Islands, Ile Huon, Isles Belep, Isles Chesterfield, and Ile Walpole, has a total land area of 7,358 sq. mi.(19,060 sq. km.) and a population of *156,000. Capital: Noumea. The islands are rich in minerals; New Caledonia has the world's largest known deposit of nickel. Nickel, nickel castings, coffee and copra are exported.

The first European to sight New Caledonia was the British navigator Capt. James Cook in 1774. The French took possession in 1853, and established a penal colony on the island in 1854. The European population of the colony remained disproportionately convict until 1894.New Caledonia became an overseas territory within the French Community in 1946, and in 1958 and 1972 chose to remain affiliated with France.

MINT MARKS
Paris, privy marks only

MONETARY SYSTEM
100 Centimes = 1 Franc

FRENCH OVERSEAS TERRITORY

DECIMAL COINAGE

KM# 1 50 CENTIMES **Composition:** Aluminum **Reverse:** Kagu bird

Date	Mintage	F	VF	XF	Unc	BU
1949(a)	1,000,000	—	0.50	1.00	3.50	—

KM# 2 FRANC **Composition:** Aluminum **Reverse:** Kagu bird

Date	Mintage	F	VF	XF	Unc	BU
1949(a)	4,000,000	—	0.25	0.75	3.00	—

KM# 8 FRANC **Composition:** Aluminum **Reverse:** Kagu bird

Date	Mintage	F	VF	XF	Unc	BU
1971(a)	1,000,000	—	0.25	0.75	2.00	—

KM# 10 FRANC **Composition:** Aluminum **Obverse:** Legend added **Obv. Legend:** I. E. O. M. **Reverse:** Kagu bird

Date	Mintage	F	VF	XF	Unc	BU
1972(a)	600,000	—	0.25	0.75	2.50	—
1973(a)	1,000,000	—	0.15	0.25	1.00	—
1977(a)	1,500,000	—	0.15	0.25	1.00	—

Date	Mintage	F	VF	XF	Unc	BU
1979(a)	—	—	0.10	0.20	1.00	—
1981(a)	1,000,000	—	0.10	0.20	0.75	—
1982(a)	1,000,000	—	0.10	0.20	0.75	—
1983(a)	2,000,000	—	0.10	0.20	0.65	—
1984(a)	—	—	0.10	0.20	0.65	—
1985(a)	2,000,000	—	0.10	0.20	0.65	—
1988(a)	2,000,000	—	0.10	0.20	0.65	—
1989(a)	1,000,000	—	0.10	0.20	0.65	—
1990(a)	—	—	0.10	0.20	0.65	—
1991(a)	—	—	0.10	0.20	0.65	—
1994(a)	—	—	0.10	0.20	0.65	—

KM# 3 2 FRANCS **Composition:** Aluminum **Reverse:** Kagu bird

Date	Mintage	F	VF	XF	Unc	BU
1949(a)	3,000,000	—	0.50	1.75	5.00	—

KM# 9 2 FRANCS **Composition:** Aluminum **Reverse:** Kagu bird

Date	Mintage	F	VF	XF	Unc	BU
1971(a)	1,000,000	—	0.35	1.25	3.00	—

KM# 14 2 FRANCS **Composition:** Aluminum **Obverse:** Legend added **Obv. Legend:** I. E. O. M. **Reverse:** Kagu bird

Date	Mintage	F	VF	XF	Unc	BU
1973(a)	400,000	—	0.20	0.75	2.50	—
1977(a)	1,500,000	—	0.20	0.50	1.50	—
1979(a)	—	—	0.20	0.40	1.50	—
1982(a)	1,000,000	—	0.20	0.35	1.00	—
1983(a)	2,000,000	—	0.20	0.35	0.75	—
1987(a)	2,000,000	—	0.20	0.35	0.75	—
1989(a)	1,200,000	—	0.20	0.35	0.75	—
1990(a)	—	—	0.20	0.35	0.75	—
1991(a)	—	—	0.20	0.35	0.75	—
1995(a)	—	—	0.20	0.35	0.75	—
1996(a)	—	—	0.20	0.35	0.75	—
1998(a)	—	—	0.20	0.35	0.75	—
1999(a)	—	—	0.20	0.35	0.75	—

KM# 4 5 FRANCS **Composition:** Aluminum **Reverse:** Kagu bird

Date	Mintage	F	VF	XF	Unc	BU
1952(a)	4,000,000	—	0.50	1.50	4.00	—

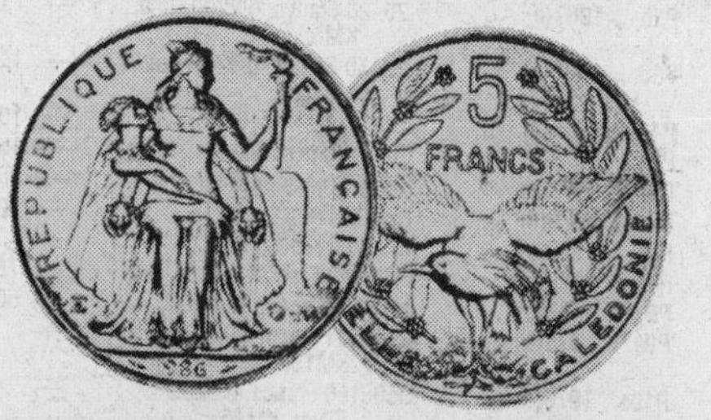

KM# 16 5 FRANCS **Composition:** Aluminum **Obverse:** Legend added **Obv. Legend:** I. E. O. M. **Reverse:** Kagu bird

Date	Mintage	F	VF	XF	Unc	BU
1983(a)	500,000	—	0.50	1.00	3.00	—
1986(a)	1,000,000	—	0.50	1.00	3.00	—
1989(a)	500,000	—	0.50	1.00	3.00	—
1990(a)	—	—	0.50	1.00	3.00	—
1991(a)	—	—	0.50	1.00	3.00	—

Date	Mintage	F	VF	XF	Unc	BU
1992(a)	—	—	0.50	1.00	2.50	—
1994(a)	—	—	0.50	1.00	2.50	—
1997(a)	—	—	0.50	1.00	2.50	—
1999(a)	—	—	0.50	1.00	2.50	—

KM# 5 10 FRANCS **Composition:** Nickel

Date	Mintage	F	VF	XF	Unc	BU
1967(a)	400,000	—	1.00	2.00	4.50	—
1970(a)	1,000,000	—	0.50	0.75	2.50	—

KM# 11 10 FRANCS **Composition:** Nickel **Obverse:** Legend added **Obv. Legend:** I. E. O. M.

Date	Mintage	F	VF	XF	Unc	BU
1972(a)	600,000	—	0.50	0.75	2.00	—
1973(a)	400,000	—	0.50	0.75	2.00	—
1977(a)	1,000,000	—	0.50	0.75	1.50	—
1979(a)	—	—	0.35	0.50	1.50	—
1983(a)	800,000	—	0.35	0.50	1.50	—
1986(a)	1,000,000	—	0.35	0.50	1.00	—
1989(a)	500,000	—	0.35	0.50	1.00	—
1990(a)	—	—	0.35	0.50	1.00	—
1991(a)	—	—	0.35	0.50	1.00	—
1995(a)	—	—	0.35	0.50	1.00	—
1996(a)	—	—	0.35	0.50	1.00	—

KM# 6 20 FRANCS **Composition:** Nickel

Date	Mintage	F	VF	XF	Unc	BU
1967(a)	300,000	—	1.25	2.50	5.00	—
1970(a)	1,200,000	—	0.60	1.00	2.00	—

KM# 12 20 FRANCS **Composition:** Nickel **Obverse:** Legend added **Obv. Legend:** I. O. E. M.

Date	Mintage	F	VF	XF	Unc	BU
1972(a)	700,000	—	0.75	1.00	2.00	—
1977(a)	350,000	—	0.75	1.00	3.00	—
1979(a)	—	—	0.50	0.85	2.00	—
1983(a)	600,000	—	0.50	0.85	2.00	—
1986(a)	800,000	—	0.50	0.85	1.50	—
1990(a)	—	—	0.50	0.85	1.50	—
1991(a)	—	—	0.50	0.85	1.50	—
1992(a)	—	—	0.50	0.85	1.50	—

KM# 7 50 FRANCS Composition: Nickel

Date	Mintage	F	VF	XF	Unc	BU
1967(a)	700,000	—	1.50	3.00	7.00	—

KM# 13 50 FRANCS Composition: Nickel **Obverse:** Legend added **Obv. Legend:** I. E. O. M.

Date	Mintage	F	VF	XF	Unc	BU
1972(a)	300,000	—	1.50	2.00	5.00	—
1979(a)	—	—	1.50	2.00	6.00	—
1983(a)	300,000	—	1.50	2.00	5.00	—
1987(a)	300,000	—	1.50	2.00	5.00	—
1991(a)	—	—	1.50	2.00	3.50	—
1992(a)	—	—	1.50	2.00	3.50	—

KM# 15 100 FRANCS Composition: Nickel-Bronze

Date	Mintage	F	VF	XF	Unc	BU
1976(a)	2,000,000	—	1.50	2.50	6.00	—
1979(a)	—	—	1.50	2.75	7.00	—
1984(a)	600,000	—	1.50	2.50	6.00	—
1987(a)	800,000	—	1.50	2.50	6.00	—
1988(a)	—	—	1.50	2.50	6.00	—
1991(a)	—	—	1.50	2.50	5.00	—
1994	—	—	1.50	2.50	5.00	—
1995(a)	—	—	1.50	2.50	4.50	—
1997	—	—	1.50	2.50	4.50	—

ESSAIS

KM#	Date	Mintage	Identification	Issue Price	Mkt Val
E1	1948(a)	1,100	50 Centimes. Nickel-Bronze. Incuse design, flat rim	—	15.00

KM#	Date	Mintage	Identification	Issue Price	Mkt Val
E3	1948(a)	1,100	Franc. Nickel-Bronze. Incuse design, flat rim.	—	17.50

KM#	Date	Mintage	Identification	Issue Price	Mkt Val
E5	1948(a)	1,100	2 Francs. Nickel-Bronze. Incuse design, flat rim.	—	20.00
E5a	1948(a)	—	2 Francs. Aluminum. Incuse design, flat rim.	—	40.00
E3a	1948(a)	—	Franc. Aluminum. Incuse design, flat rim.	—	35.00
E1a	1948(a)	—	50 Centimes. Aluminum. Incuse design, flat rim	—	30.00

KM#	Date	Mintage	Identification	Issue Price	Mkt Val
E2	1948(a)	1,100	50 Centimes. Nickel-Bronze. Incuse design, raised rim.	—	15.00

KM#	Date	Mintage	Identification	Issue Price	Mkt Val
E4	1948(a)	1,100	Franc. Nickel-Bronze. Incuse design, raised rim.	—	20.00

KM#	Date	Mintage	Identification	Issue Price	Mkt Val
E6	1948(a)	1,100	2 Francs. Nickel-Bronze. Incuse design, raised rim.	—	15.00
E6a	1948(a)	—	2 Francs. Aluminum. Incuse design, raised rim.	—	40.00
E4a	1948(a)	—	Franc. Aluminum. Incuse design, raised rim.	—	35.00
E2a	1948(a)	—	50 Centimes. Aluminum. Incuse design, raised rim.	—	30.00
E7	1949(a)	2,000	50 Centimes. Copper Nickel. KM1.	—	12.00
E8	1949(a)	2,000	Franc. Copper Nickel. KM2.	—	15.00
E9	1949(a)	2,000	2 Francs. Copper Nickel. KM3.	—	18.00
E10	1952(a)	1,200	5 Francs. KM4.	—	20.00
E11	1967(a)	1,700	10 Francs. KM5.	—	10.00
E12	1967(a)	1,700	20 Francs. KM6.	—	10.00
E13	1967(a)	1,700	50 Francs. KM7.	—	12.50
E14	1976(a)	1,900	100 Francs. KM15.	—	22.50

PIEFORTS

Several gold pieforts were melted in 1983.

KM#	Date	Mintage	Identification	Issue Price	Mkt Val
P9b	1979(a)	96	50 Francs. 0.9200 Gold. KM13.	—	1,350
P1	1967(a)	500	10 Francs. KM5.	—	25.00
P2	1967(a)	500	20 Francs. KM6.	—	30.00
P3	1967(a)	500	50 Francs. KM7.	—	35.00
P3a	1967(a)	50	50 Francs. 0.9500 Silver. KM7.	—	200
P2a	1967(a)	50	20 Francs. 0.9500 Silver. KM6.	—	175
P1a	1967(a)	50	10 Francs. 0.9500 Silver. KM5.	—	150
P1b	1967(a)	20	10 Francs. 0.9200 Gold. KM5.	—	800
P2b	1967(a)	20	20 Francs. 0.9200 Gold. KM6.	—	1,000
P3b	1967(a)	20	50 Francs. 0.9200 Gold. KM7.	—	1,350
P4	1979(a)	150	Franc. KM10.	—	10.00
P5	1979(a)	150	2 Francs. KM14.	—	15.00
P6	1979(a)	150	5 Francs. KM4.	—	25.00
P7	1979(a)	150	10 Francs. KM11.	—	40.00
P8	1979(a)	150	20 Francs. KM12.	—	40.00
P10	1979(a)	150	100 Francs. KM15.	—	75.00
P9	1979(a)	150	50 Francs. KM13.	—	50.00
P9a	1979(a)	250	50 Francs. 0.9250 Silver. KM13.	—	100
P10a	1979(a)	350	100 Francs. 0.9250 Silver. KM15.	—	125
P8a	1979(a)	250	20 Francs. 0.9250 Silver.	—	100
P7a	1979(a)	250	10 Francs. 0.9250 Silver. KM11.	—	100
P6a	1979(a)	250	5 Francs. 0.9250 Silver. KM4.	—	75.00
P5a	1979(a)	250	2 Francs. 0.9250 Silver. KM14.	—	50.00
P4a	1979(a)	250	Franc. 0.9250 Silver. KM10.	—	25.00
P4b	1979(a)	94	Franc. 0.9200 Gold. KM10.	—	550
P5b	1979(a)	96	2 Francs. 0.9200 Gold. KM14.	—	925
P6b	1979(a)	94	5 Francs. 0.9200 Gold. KM4.	—	1,300
P7b	1979(a)	93	10 Francs. 0.9200 Gold. KM11.	—	850
P8b	1979(a)	95	20 Francs. 0.9200 Gold.	—	1,200
P10b	1979(a)	96	100 Francs. 0.9200 Gold. KM15.	—	1,250

PIEFORTS WITH ESSAI

Double thickness

KM#	Date	Mintage	Identification	Issue Price	Mkt Val
PE2	1949(a)	104	Franc. Double thickness. KM2.	—	70.00
PE3	1949(a)	104	2 Francs. Double thickness. KM3.	—	80.00
PE4	1952(a)	104	5 Francs. Double thickness. KM4.	—	90.00

SPECIMEN SETS (SS)

KM#	Date	Mintage	Identification	Issue Price	Mkt Val
SS1	1967 (3)	2,200	KM5-7. This set issued with New Hebrides and French Polynesia 1967 set.	10.00	20.00

NEWFOUNDLAND

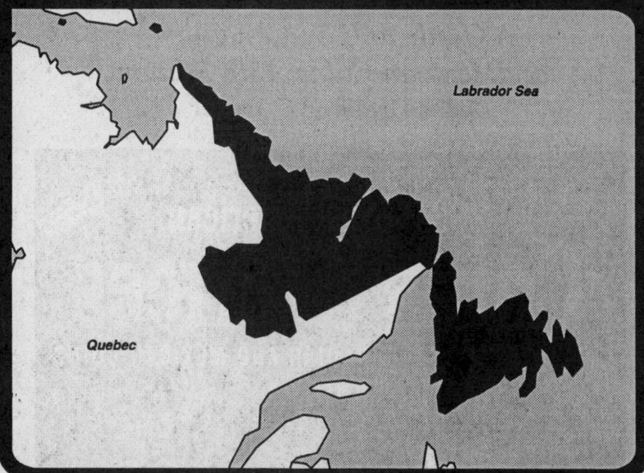

Canadian province discovered by John Cabot in 1497, formally occupied by Sir Humphrey Gilbert in 1583, on behalf of the British Crown. Attempts to colonize this area were unsuccessful until 1904, though British sovereignty was recognized by the Treaty of Utrecht in 1713. Newfoundland remained outside the Canadian Confederation in 1867 and continued to govern itself until 1934, when the British assumed responsibility for governing the colony and Labrador. This continued until the union with Canada in 1949. The province comprises an area of 143,501 sq. miles to the north and east of Quebec, with an estimated population of 564,000. The capital city is St. John.

PROVINCE

CIRCULATION COINAGE

CENT (Large) **Composition:** Bronze.

KM#	Date	Mintage	VG-8	F-12	VF-20	XF-40	MS-60	MS-63	Proof
9	1904 H	100,000	7.00	11.00	22.00	37.50	275	650	—
	1904 H Proof	—	—	—	—	—	—	—	4,000
	1907	200,000	1.50	2.50	4.00	12.00	110	375	—
	1909	200,000	1.50	2.50	4.00	10.50	90.00	150	—
	1909 Proof	—	—	—	—	—	—	—	400

CENT (Large) **Composition:** Bronze. **Obverse:** George V bust facing left. **Reverse:** Similar to KM#9.

KM#	Date	Mintage	VG-8	F-12	VF-20	XF-40	MS-60	MS-63	Proof
16	1913	400,000	0.75	1.50	2.00	4.00	40.00	75.00	—
	1917 C	702,350	0.75	1.50	2.00	4.00	65.00	185	—
	1917 C Proof	—	—	—	—	—	—	—	800
	1919 C	300,000	0.80	1.60	2.25	5.00	100	275	—
	1919 C Proof	—	—	—	—	—	—	—	1,000
	1920 C	302,184	0.75	1.50	3.50	12.00	200	1,000	—
	1929 C	300,000	0.75	1.50	2.00	4.00	55.00	100	—
	1929 C Proof	—	—	—	—	—	—	—	1,000
	1936	300,000	0.75	1.25	1.75	3.00	28.00	75.00	—

CENT (Small) **Composition:** Bronze.

KM#	Date	Mintage	VG-8	F-12	VF-20	XF-40	MS-60	MS-63	Proof
18	1938	500,000	0.50	0.75	1.50	2.50	16.00	40.00	—
	1938 Proof	—	—	—	—	—	—	—	1,000
	1940	300,000	1.25	2.00	3.00	7.00	35.00	175	—
	1940 re-engraved date	—	16.00	27.50	40.00	70.00	185	500	—
	1940 Proof	—	—	—	—	—	—	—	1,000
	1941 C	827,662	0.35	0.45	0.70	1.50	13.50	120	—
	1941 C re-engraved date	—	9.00	13.00	20.00	35.00	100	400	—
	1942	1,996,889	0.35	0.45	0.70	1.50	13.50	70.00	—
	1943 C	1,239,732	0.35	0.45	0.70	1.50	13.50	70.00	—
	1944 C	1,328,776	1.00	2.00	3.00	7.00	90.00	335	—
	1947 C	313,772	0.90	1.65	2.50	6.00	35.00	200	—
	1947 C Proof	—	—	—	—	—	—	—	2,000

5 CENTS **Weight:** 1.1782 g. **Composition:** 0.9250 Silver., .0350 oz. ASW.

KM#	Date	Mintage	VG-8	F-12	VF-20	XF-40	MS-60	MS-63	Proof
7	1903	100,000	3.00	6.00	18.00	45.00	425	1,200	—
	1903 Proof	—	—	—	—	—	—	—	2,000
	1904 H	100,000	2.00	5.00	14.00	35.00	160	275	—
	1904 H Proof	—	—	—	—	—	—	—	1,200
	1908	400,000	1.75	3.50	11.50	25.00	160	400	—

5 CENTS **Weight:** 1.1782 g. **Composition:** 0.9250 Silver., .0350 oz. ASW. **Obverse:** George V bust facing left. **Reverse:** Similar to KM#7.

KM#	Date	Mintage	VG-8	F-12	VF-20	XF-40	MS-60	MS-63	Proof
13	1912	300,000	1.00	2.00	5.00	20.00	125	275	—
	1912 Proof	—	—	—	—	—	—	—	2,000
	1917 C	300,319	1.00	2.00	4.00	14.00	200	450	—
	1917 C Proof	—	—	—	—	—	—	—	2,000
	1919 C	100,844	1.25	3.00	10.00	30.00	750	1,250	—
	1919 C Proof	—	—	—	—	—	—	—	2,000
	1929	300,000	1.00	1.75	3.25	12.00	165	350	—

5 CENTS **Weight:** 1.1782 g. **Composition:** 0.9250 Silver., .0350 oz. ASW.

KM#	Date	Mintage	VG-8	F-12	VF-20	XF-40	MS-60	MS-63	Proof
19	1938	100,000	0.80	0.90	1.50	4.00	65.00	150	—
	1938 Proof	—	—	—	—	—	—	—	1,000
	1940 C	200,000	0.80	0.90	1.50	4.00	60.00	200	—
	1940 C Proof	—	—	—	—	—	—	—	2,000
	1941 C	621,641	0.60	0.90	1.50	2.50	15.00	30.00	—
	1942 C	298,348	0.85	0.90	2.00	2.50	15.00	30.00	—
	1943 C	351,666	0.55	0.85	1.25	2.50	15.00	27.50	—

5 CENTS **Weight:** 1.1664 g. **Composition:** 0.8000 Silver., .0300 oz. ASW.

KM#	Date	Mintage	VG-8	F-12	VF-20	XF-40	MS-60	MS-63	Proof
19a	1944 C	286,504	1.25	1.75	3.00	4.00	25.00	50.00	—
	1945 C	203,828	0.55	0.85	1.25	2.50	13.00	26.00	—
	1946 C	2,041	200	225	325	400	1,100	1,750	—
	1946 C Prooflike	—	—	—	—	—	—	2,500	—
	1947 C	38,400	2.00	3.00	5.00	10.00	60.00	100	—
	1947 C Prooflike	—	—	—	—	—	—	350	—

10 CENTS **Weight:** 2.3564 g. **Composition:** 0.9250 Silver., .0701 oz. ASW.

KM#	Date	Mintage	VG-8	F-12	VF-20	XF-40	MS-60	MS-63	Proof
8	1903	100,000	5.00	10.00	35.00	110	850	2,000	—
	1903 Proof	—	—	—	—	—	—	—	2,500
	1904 H	100,000	2.50	6.50	20.00	55.00	175	250	—
	1904 H Proof	—	—	—	—	—	—	—	1,500

10 CENTS **Weight:** 2.3564 g. **Composition:** 0.9250 Silver., .0701 oz. ASW.

KM#	Date	Mintage	VG-8	F-12	VF-20	XF-40	MS-60	MS-63	Proof
20	1938	100,000	0.75	1.50	2.75	7.00	80.00	300	—
	1938 Proof	—	—	—	—	—	—	—	2,000
	1940	100,000	0.65	1.20	2.50	6.00	80.00	300	—
	1940 Proof	—	—	—	—	—	—	—	2,500
	1941 C	483,630	0.60	1.40	2.20	3.50	27.00	125	—
	1942 C	293,736	0.60	1.50	2.20	3.50	30.00	130	—
	1943 C	104,706	0.60	1.50	2.40	3.50	60.00	200	—
	1944 C	151,471	2.50	3.50	5.00	7.50	90.00	250	—

10 CENTS **Weight:** 2.3328 g. **Composition:** 0.8000 Silver., .0600 oz. ASW.

KM#	Date	Mintage	VG-8	F-12	VF-20	XF-40	MS-60	MS-63	Proof
20a	1945 C	175,833	0.65	1.25	2.00	4.00	27.00	185	—
	1946 C	38,400	2.00	4.00	7.00	15.00	60.00	250	—
	1946 C Proof	—	—	—	—	—	—	—	700
	1947 C	61,988	1.50	3.00	4.50	9.00	45.00	245	—

20 CENTS **Weight:** 4.7127 g. **Composition:** 0.9250 Silver., .1401 oz. ASW.

KM#	Date	Mintage	VG-8	F-12	VF-20	XF-40	MS-60	MS-63	Proof
10	1904 H	75,000	6.00	16.00	50.00	175	2,000	4,250	—
	1904 H Proof	—	—	—	—	—	—	—	1,750

20 CENTS Weight: 4.7127 g. Composition: 0.9250 Silver., .1401 oz. ASW. Obverse: George V bust facing left. Reverse: Similar to KM#10.

KM#	Date	Mintage	VG-8	F-12	VF-20	XF-40	MS-60	MS-63	Proof
15	1912	350,000	2.00	3.00	8.00	30.00	275	650	—
	1912 Proof	—	—	—	—	—	—	—	2,500

25 CENTS Weight: 5.8319 g. Composition: 0.9250 Silver., .1734 oz. ASW.

KM#	Date	Mintage	VG-8	F-12	VF-20	XF-40	MS-60	MS-63	Proof
17	1917 C	464,779	1.50	2.00	4.00	8.00	120	250	—
	1917 C Proof	—	—	—	—	—	—	—	2,500
	1919 C	163,939	1.50	2.25	4.25	12.00	220	700	—
	1919 C Proof	—	—	—	—	—	—	—	2,500

50 CENTS Weight: 11.7800 g. Composition: 0.9250 Silver., .3504 oz. ASW.

KM#	Date	Mintage	VG-8	F-12	VF-20	XF-40	MS-60	MS-63	Proof
11	1904 H	140,000	3.25	5.00	13.00	35.00	225	650	—
	1904 H Proof	—	—	—	—	—	—	—	5,000
	1907	100,000	3.00	5.00	13.00	45.00	250	800	—
	1908	160,000	3.25	4.50	12.50	32.50	175	600	—
	1909	200,000	3.25	4.50	12.50	35.00	200	600	—

50 CENTS Weight: 11.7800 g. Composition: 0.9250 Silver., .3504 oz. ASW.

KM#	Date	Mintage	VG-8	F-12	VF-20	XF-40	MS-60	MS-63	Proof
12	1911	200,000	2.75	3.25	6.00	20.00	175	450	—
	1917 C	375,560	2.75	3.25	6.00	16.50	125	285	—
	1917 C Proof	—	—	—	—	—	—	—	2,500
	1918 C	294,824	2.75	3.25	6.00	16.50	125	285	—
	1919 C	306,267	2.75	3.25	6.00	16.50	125	380	—
	1919 C Proof	—	—	—	—	—	—	—	2,500

TRIAL STRIKES

KM#	Date	Mintage	Identification	MktVal
TS3	1945C	—	10 Cents. Nickel.	—

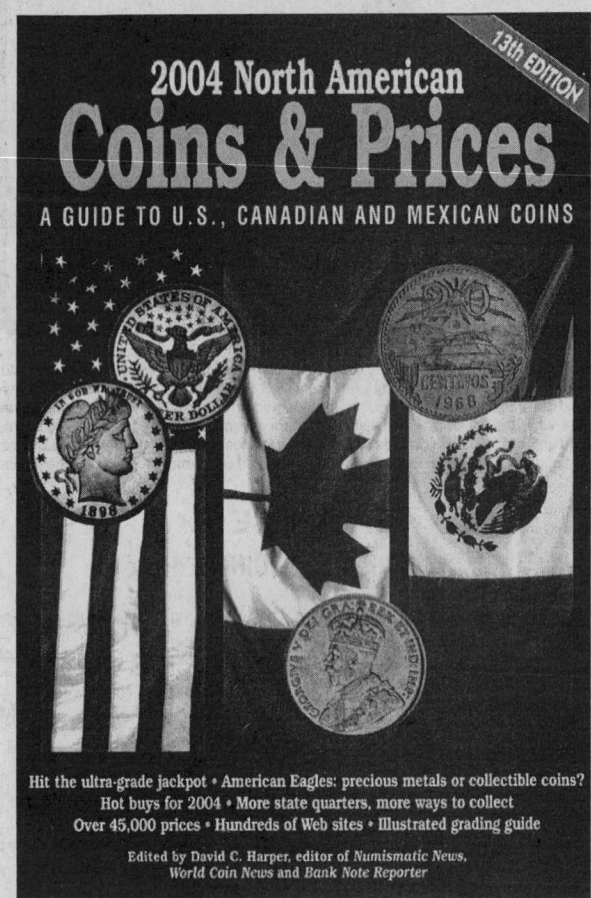

NEW GUINEA

Spanish navigator Jorge de Menezes, who landed on the northwest shore in 1527, discovered New Guinea, the world's largest island after Greenland. European interests, attracted by exaggerated estimates of the resources of the area, resulted in the island being claimed in part by Spain, the Netherlands, Great Britain and Germany.

RULERS
British, 1910-1952

MONETARY SYSTEM
12 Pence = 1 Shilling
20 Shillings = 1 Pound

BRITISH ADMINISTRATION
1910-1952

STANDARD COINAGE

12 Pence = 1 Shilling; 20 Shillings = 1 Pound

KM# 1a 1/2 PENNY **Composition:** Nickel

Date		F	VF	XF	Unc	BU
1929 Proof	—	Value: 650				

KM# 1 1/2 PENNY **Composition:** Copper-Nickel **Note:** Entire mintage returned to Melbourne Mint which later sold 400 pcs. in sets with KM#2. The balance of mintage was destroyed.

Date	Mintage	F	VF	XF	Unc	BU
1929	25,000	—	—	225	375	—
1929 Proof	—	Value: 450				

KM# 2a PENNY **Composition:** Nickel

Date		F	VF	XF	Unc	BU
1929 Proof	—	Value: 650				

KM# 2 PENNY **Composition:** Copper-Nickel **Note:** Entire mintage returned to Melbourne Mint which later sold 400 pcs. in sets with KM#1. The balance of mintage was destroyed.

Date	Mintage	F	VF	XF	Unc	BU
1929	63,000	—	—	225	375	—
1929 Proof	—	Value: 450				

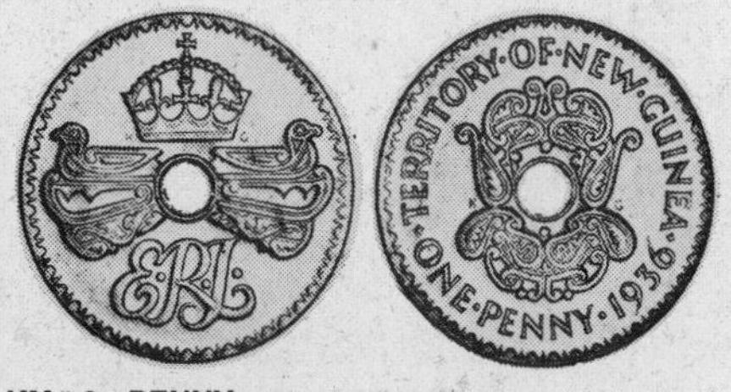

KM# 6 PENNY **Composition:** Bronze

Date	Mintage	F	VF	XF	Unc	BU
1936	360,000	0.75	1.00	2.00	6.00	—
1936 Proof	—	Value: 275				

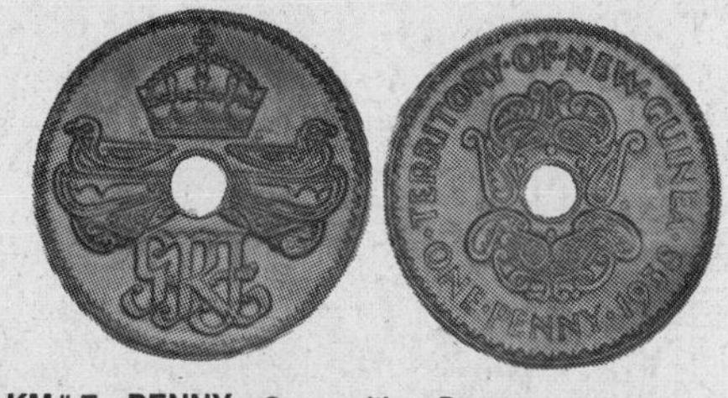

KM# 7 PENNY **Composition:** Bronze

Date	Mintage	F	VF	XF	Unc	BU
1938	360,000	1.75	4.00	7.00	16.50	—
1944	240,000	1.00	2.00	4.00	9.00	—

KM# 3 3 PENCE **Composition:** Copper-Nickel

Date	Mintage	F	VF	XF	Unc	BU
1935	1,200,000	3.00	6.00	10.00	32.00	—
1935 Proof	—	Value: 225				

KM# 10 3 PENCE **Composition:** Copper-Nickel

Date	Mintage	F	VF	XF	Unc	BU
1944	500,000	2.00	4.00	8.50	30.00	—

KM# 4 6 PENCE **Composition:** Copper-Nickel

Date	Mintage	F	VF	XF	Unc	BU
1935	2,000,000	2.50	4.00	8.00	32.00	—
1935 Proof	—	Value: 225				

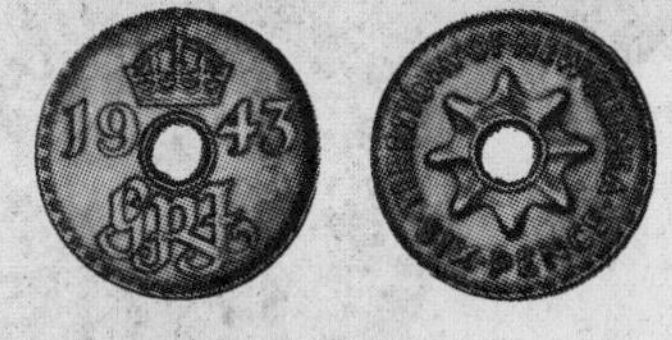

KM# 9 6 PENCE **Composition:** Copper-Nickel

Date	Mintage	F	VF	XF	Unc	BU
1943	130,000	3.00	6.00	12.50	40.00	—

KM# 5 SHILLING **Weight:** 5.3800 g. **Composition:** 0.9250 Silver .16 oz. ASW

Date	Mintage	F	VF	XF	Unc	BU
1935	2,100,000	BV	2.00	3.00	7.50	—
1936	1,360,000	BV	2.00	3.00	7.50	—

KM# 8 SHILLING **Weight:** 5.3800 g. **Composition:** 0.9250 Silver .16 oz. ASW

Date	Mintage	F	VF	XF	Unc	BU
1938	3,400,000	BV	2.00	3.00	7.50	—
1945	2,000,000	BV	2.00	3.00	7.50	—

PROOF SETS

KM#	Date	Mintage	Identification	Issue Price	Mkt Val
PS2	1929	20	KM#1a, 2a	—	1,300
PS1	1929 (2)	—	KM#1, 2	—	900

NEW HEBRIDES

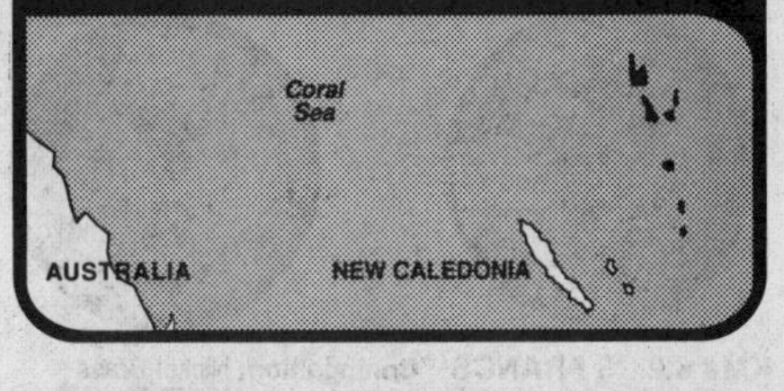

The New Hebrides were discovered by Portuguese navigator Pedro de Quiros in 1606, visited by French explorer Bougainville in 1768, and named by British navigator Capt. James Cook in 1774. Ships of all nations converged on the islands to trade for sandalwood, prompting France and Britain to relinquish their individual claims and declare the islands a neutral zone in 1878. The New Hebrides were placed under the control of a mixed Anglo-French commission of naval officers during the native uprisings of 1887, and established as a condominium under the joint sovereignty of France and Great Britain in 1906.

MINT MARKS
(a) - Paris, privy marks only

MONETARY SYSTEM
100 Centimes = 1 Franc

FRENCH/BRITISH CONDOMINIUM
(Jointly Governed Territory)

STANDARD COINAGE

KM# 4.1 FRANC **Composition:** Nickel-Brass

Date	Mintage	F	VF	XF	Unc	BU
1970(a)	435,000	—	0.25	0.50	0.85	—

KM# 4.2 FRANC **Composition:** Nickel-Brass **Obverse:** Legend added **Obv. Legend:** I.E.O.M.

Date	Mintage	F	VF	XF	Unc	BU
1975(a)	350,000	—	0.20	0.40	0.75	—
1978(a)	200,000	—	0.20	0.40	0.75	—
1979(a)	350,000	—	0.20	0.40	0.75	—
1982(a)	—	—	0.20	0.40	0.75	—

KM# 5.1 2 FRANCS **Composition:** Nickel-Brass

Date	Mintage	F	VF	XF	Unc	BU
1970(a)	264,000	—	0.60	1.25	2.25	—

KM# 5.2 2 FRANCS **Composition:** Nickel-Brass **Obverse:** Legend added **Obv. Legend:** I.E.O.M.

Date	Mintage	F	VF	XF	Unc	BU
1973(a)	200,000	—	0.20	0.40	0.75	—
1975(a)	300,000	—	0.20	0.40	0.75	—
1978(a)	150,000	—	0.20	0.40	0.75	—
1979(a)	250,000	—	0.20	0.40	0.75	—
1982(a)	—	—	0.20	0.40	0.75	—

KM# 6.1 5 FRANCS **Composition:** Nickel-Brass

Date	Mintage	F	VF	XF	Unc	BU
1970(a)	375,000	—	0.50	0.75	1.65	—

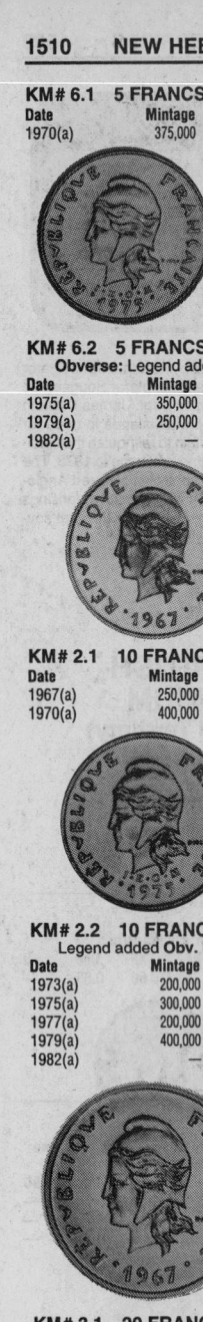

KM# 6.2 5 FRANCS **Composition:** Nickel-Brass **Obverse:** Legend added **Obv. Legend:** I.E.O.M.

Date	Mintage	F	VF	XF	Unc	BU
1975(a)	350,000	—	0.30	0.60	1.25	—
1979(a)	250,000	—	0.30	0.60	1.25	—
1982(a)	—	—	0.30	0.60	1.25	—

KM# 2.1 10 FRANCS **Composition:** Nickel

Date	Mintage	F	VF	XF	Unc	BU
1967(a)	250,000	—	0.30	0.65	1.50	—
1970(a)	400,000	—	0.30	0.65	1.50	—

KM# 2.2 10 FRANCS **Composition:** Nickel **Obverse:** Legend added **Obv. Legend:** I.E.O.M.

Date	Mintage	F	VF	XF	Unc	BU
1973(a)	200,000	—	0.30	0.65	1.50	—
1975(a)	300,000	—	0.30	0.65	1.50	—
1977(a)	200,000	—	0.30	0.65	1.50	—
1979(a)	400,000	—	0.30	0.65	1.50	—
1982(a)	—	—	0.30	0.65	1.50	—

KM# 3.1 20 FRANCS **Composition:** Nickel

Date	Mintage	F	VF	XF	Unc	BU
1967(a)	250,000	—	0.60	1.25	2.25	—
1970(a)	300,000	—	0.60	1.25	2.25	—

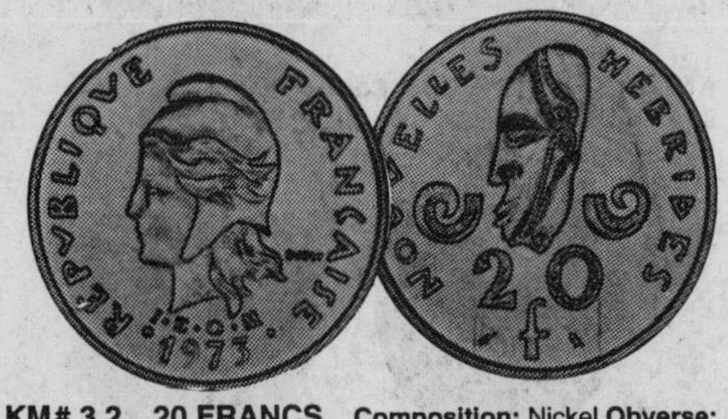

KM# 3.2 20 FRANCS **Composition:** Nickel **Obverse:** Legend added **Obv. Legend:** I.E.O.M.

Date	Mintage	F	VF	XF	Unc	BU
1973(a)	200,000	—	0.60	1.25	2.25	—
1975(a)	150,000	—	0.60	1.25	2.25	—
1977(a)	150,000	—	0.60	1.25	2.25	—
1979(a)	300,000	—	0.60	1.25	2.25	—
1982(a)	—	—	0.60	1.25	2.25	—

KM# 7 50 FRANCS **Composition:** Nickel

Date	Mintage	F	VF	XF	Unc	BU
1972(a)	200,000	—	1.50	2.50	4.00	—

KM# 1 100 FRANCS **Weight:** 25.0000 g. **Composition:** 0.8350 Silver .6712 oz. ASW

Date	Mintage	F	VF	XF	Unc	BU
1966(a)	200,000	—	—	—	15.00	—
1979(a)	—	—	—	—	20.00	—

ESSAIS

KM#	Date	Mintage	Identification	Issue Price	Mkt Val
E1	1966(a)	3,000	100 Francs.	—	35.00
E2	1967(a)	1,700	10 Francs.	—	15.00
E3	1967(a)	1,700	20 Francs.	—	15.00
E4	1970(a)	1,700	Franc.	—	15.00
E5	1970(a)	1,700	2 Francs.	—	15.00
E6	1970(a)	1,700	5 Francs.	—	15.00
E7	1972(a)	1,300	50 Francs.	—	17.50

PATTERNS

Including off metal strikes

KM#	Date	Mintage	Identification	Mkt Val
Pn1	1979	60	500 Francs. Copper-Nickel-Aluminum.	300
Pn2	1979	60	500 Francs. 0.9990 Silver.	450
Pn3	1979	—	500 Francs. 0.9990 Gold. 62.2000 g.	5,000
Pn4	1979	1	500 Francs. 0.9990 Platinum. 62.2000 g.	9,000

PIEFORTS WITH ESSAI

Double thickness

KM#	Date	Mintage	Identification	Issue Price	Mkt Val
PE1	1966(a)	500	100 Francs.	—	140
PE2	1966(a)	50	100 Francs. 0.9200 Gold.	—	3,500

KM#	Date	Mintage	Identification	Issue Price	Mkt Val
PE3	1967(a)	500	10 Francs.	—	15.00
PE4	1967(a)	50	10 Francs. 0.9500 Silver.	—	75.00
PE5	1967(a)	20	10 Francs. 0.9200 Gold.	—	500
PE6	1967(a)	500	20 Francs.	—	15.00

KM#	Date	Mintage	Identification	Issue Price	Mkt Val
PE7	1967(a)	50	20 Francs. 0.9500 Silver.	—	125
PE8	1967(a)	20	20 Francs. 0.9200 Gold.	—	1,000
PE10	1974(a)	500	100 Francs. 0.9250 Silver.	—	100
PE11	1974(a)	119	100 Francs. 0.9200 Gold.	—	2,850
PE12	1979(a)	150	Franc.	—	10.00
PE13	1979	250	Franc. 0.9250 Silver.	—	20.00
PE14	1979(a)	123	Franc. 0.9200 Gold.	—	200
PE15	1979(a)	150	2 Francs.	—	12.50
PE16	1979(a)	250	2 Francs. 0.9250 Silver.	—	20.00
PE17	1979(a)	115	2 Francs. 0.9200 Gold.	—	250
PE18	1979(a)	150	5 Francs.	—	15.00
PE19	1979(a)	250	5 Francs. 0.9250 Silver.	—	20.00
PE20	1979(a)	116	5 Francs. 0.9200 Gold.	—	350
PE21	1979(a)	150	10 Francs.	—	17.50
PE22	1979(a)	250	10 Francs. 0.9250 Silver.	—	20.00
PE23	1979(a)	116	10 Francs. 0.9200 Gold.	—	500
PE24	1979(a)	150	20 Francs.	—	20.00
PE25	1979(a)	250	20 Francs. 0.9250 Silver.	—	20.00
PE26	1979(a)	115	20 Francs. 0.9200 Gold.	—	600
PE27	1979(a)	150	50 Francs.	—	25.00
PE28	1979(a)	250	50 Francs. 0.9250 Silver.	—	100
PE29	1979(a)	116	50 Francs. 0.9200 Gold.	—	1,250

"FDC" SETS

This fleur-de-coin set was issued with New Caledonia and French Polynesia 1967 sets.

KM#	Date	Mintage	Identification	Issue Price	Mkt Val
SS1	1966-67 (3)	2,200	KM#1, 2.1, 3.1	10.00	10.00

NEW ZEALAND

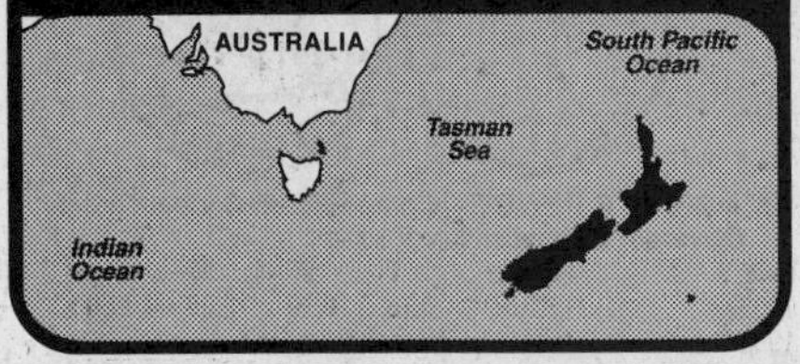

New Zealand, a parliamentary state located in the Southwest Pacific 1,250 miles (2,011 km.) east of Australia, has an area of 103,883 sq. mi. (268,680 sq. km.) and a population of *3.4 million. Capital: Wellington. Wool, meat, dairy products and some manufactured items are exported.

The first European to sight New Zealand was the Dutch navigator Abel Tasman in 1642. The islands were explored by British navigator Capt. James Cook who surveyed it in 1769 and annexed the land to Great Britain. The British government disavowed the annexation and for the next 70years the only white settlers to arrive were adventurers attracted by the prospects of lumbering, sealing and whaling. Great Britain annexed the land in 1840 by treaty with the native chiefs and made it a dependency of New South Wales. The colony was granted self-government in1852, a ministerial form of government in 1856, and full dominion status on Sept. 26, 1907. Full internal and external autonomy, which New Zealand had in effect possessed for many years, was formally extended in 1947.New Zealand is a member of the Commonwealth of Nations. Elizabeth II is Head of State as Queen of New Zealand.

Prior to 1933 English coins were the official legal tender but Australian coins were accepted in small transactions. Currency fluctuations caused a distinctive New Zealand coinage to be introduced in 1933. The 1935 Waitangi crown and proof set were originally intended to mark the introduction but delays caused their date to be changed to 1935. The 1940 half crown marked the centennial of British rule, the 1949 and 1953 crowns commemorated Royal visits and the 1953 proof set marked the coronation of Queen Elizabeth.

Decimal Currency was introduced in 1967 with special sets commemorating the last issued of pound sterling (1965) and the first of the decimal issues. Since then dollars and set of coins have been issued nearly every year.

RULERS
British

MINTS
(L) – British Royal Mint (Llantrisant)
(C) – Royal Australian Mint (Canberra)
(O) – Royal Canadian Mint
(N) – Norwegian Mint
(P) – South African Mint (Pretoria)

MONETARY SYSTEM
4 Farthings = 1 Penny
12 Pence = 1 Shilling
20 Shillings = 1 Pound

BRITISH PARLIAMENTARY STATE

POUND STERLING COINAGE

KM# 12 1/2 PENNY Composition: Bronze **Subject:** Hei Tiki

Date	Mintage	F	VF	XF	Unc	BU
1940	3,432,000	0.25	0.65	2.00	15.00	—
1940 Proof; 5 known	—	Value: 800				
1941	960,000	0.25	0.65	2.00	15.00	—
1941	—	Value: 225				
1942	1,960,000	0.35	0.75	6.00	30.00	—
1944	2,035,000	0.50	1.00	5.00	15.00	—
1945	1,516,000	0.50	1.00	3.50	15.00	—
1945 Proof	—	Value: 175				
1946	3,120,000	0.50	1.00	3.50	15.00	—
1946 Proof	—	Value: 175				
1947	2,726,000	0.25	0.50	1.50	12.50	—
1947 Proof	—	Value: 150				

KM# 20 1/2 PENNY Composition: Bronze

Date	Mintage	F	VF	XF	Unc	BU
1949	1,766,000	0.10	0.25	3.50	15.00	—
1949 Proof	—	Value: 150				
1950	1,426,000	0.10	0.25	2.50	12.50	—
1950 Proof	—	Value: 175				
1951	2,342,000	0.10	0.25	1.50	7.50	—
1951 Proof	—	Value: 150				
1952	2,400,000	0.10	0.20	1.50	6.00	—
1952 Proof	—	Value: 150				

KM# 23.1 1/2 PENNY Composition: Bronze **Obverse:** Without shoulder strap

Date	Mintage	F	VF	XF	Unc	BU
1953	720,000	0.10	0.25	1.50	7.50	—
1953 Proof	7,000	Value: 5.00				
1953 Matte proof	—	Value: 100				
1954	240,000	0.75	1.25	7.00	27.50	—
1954 Proof	—	Value: 135				
1955	240,000	0.75	1.25	7.00	27.50	—
1955	—	Value: 135				

KM# 23.2 1/2 PENNY Composition: Bronze **Obverse:** With shoulder strap

Date	F	VF	XF	Unc	BU
1956	0.10	0.35	0.80	7.50	—
1956 Proof	— Value: 135				
1957	0.10	0.35	0.80	7.50	—
1957 Proof	— Value: 135				
1958	0.10	0.30	0.75	5.00	—
1958 Proof	— Value: 135				
1959	0.10	0.20	0.50	5.00	—
1959 Proof	— Value: 135				
1960	0.10	0.20	0.50	5.00	—
1960 Proof	— Value: 135				
1961	0.10	0.15	0.40	3.50	—
1961 Proof	— Value: 135				
1962	0.10	0.15	0.40	3.50	—
1962 Proof	— Value: 135				
1963	0.10	0.15	0.30	2.50	—
1963 Proof	— Value: 135				
1964	0.10	0.15	0.20	1.50	—
1964 Proof	— Value: 135				
1965	0.10	0.15	0.20	0.80	—
1965 Prooflike	—	—	—	—	1.25
1965 Proof	—	—	—	—	—

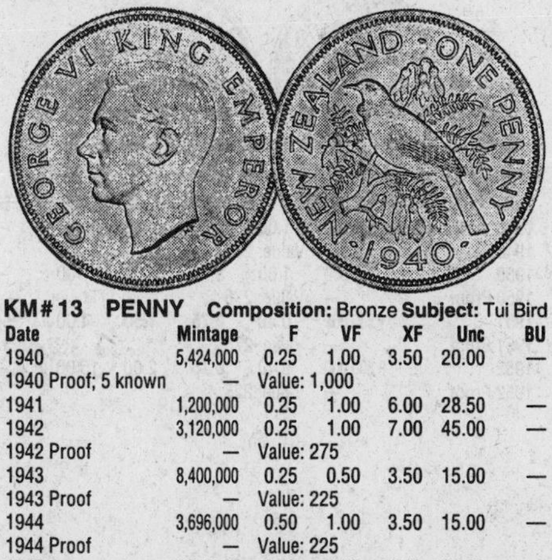

KM# 13 PENNY Composition: Bronze **Subject:** Tui Bird

Date	Mintage	F	VF	XF	Unc	BU
1940	5,424,000	0.25	1.00	3.50	20.00	—
1940 Proof; 5 known	—	Value: 1,000				
1941	1,200,000	0.25	1.00	6.00	28.50	—
1942	3,120,000	0.25	1.00	7.00	45.00	—
1942 Proof	—	Value: 275				
1943	8,400,000	0.25	0.50	3.50	15.00	—
1943 Proof	—	Value: 225				
1944	3,696,000	0.50	1.00	3.50	15.00	—
1944 Proof	—	Value: 225				
1945	4,764,000	0.25	0.50	3.50	20.00	—
1945 Proof	—	Value: 225				
1946	6,720,000	0.25	0.50	3.00	15.00	—
1946 Proof	—	Value: 225				
1947	5,880,000	0.25	0.50	3.00	15.00	—
1947 Proof	—	Value: 225				

KM# 13a PENNY Composition: Bronze **Note:** Burnished

Date	F	VF	XF	Unc	BU
1945	—	—	80.00	250	—

Note: Struck in error by the Royal Mint on Great Britain blanks

KM# 21 PENNY Composition: Bronze

Date	Mintage	F	VF	XF	Unc	BU
1949	2,016,000	0.20	0.60	3.50	20.00	—
1949 Proof	—	Value: 225				
1950	5,784,000	0.15	0.50	2.50	15.00	—
1950 Proof	—	Value: 175				
1951	6,888,000	0.15	0.50	1.50	12.50	—
1951 Proof	—	Value: 175				
1952	10,800,000	0.15	0.50	1.25	10.00	—
1952 Proof	—	Value: 150				

KM# 24.1 PENNY Composition: Bronze **Obverse:** Without shoulder strap

Date	Mintage	F	VF	XF	Unc	BU
1953	2,400,000	0.10	0.25	2.50	10.00	—
1953 Proof	7,000	Value: 10.00				
1953 Matte proof	—	Value: 100				
1954	1,080,000	0.25	1.00	7.50	28.50	—
1954 Proof	—	Value: 175				
1955	3,720,000	0.10	0.25	2.50	12.50	—
1955 Proof	—	Value: 150				
1956	Inc. below	25.00	40.00	125	425	—

KM# 24.2 PENNY Composition: Bronze **Obverse:** With shoulder strap

Date	F	VF	XF	Unc	BU
1956	0.10	0.20	2.00	10.00	—
1956 Proof	— Value: 150				
1957	0.20	0.50	1.50	7.50	—
1957 Proof	— Value: 150				
1958	0.10	0.20	1.25	8.00	—
1958 Proof	— Value: 150				
1959	0.10	0.20	1.25	8.00	—
1959 Proof	— Value: 150				
1960	0.10	0.20	0.50	4.00	—
1960 Proof	— Value: 135				
1961	0.10	0.20	0.50	3.50	—
1961 Proof	— Value: 135				
1962	—	0.10	0.45	2.50	—
1962 Proof	— Value: 135				
1963	—	0.10	0.20	1.75	—
1963 Proof	— Value: 135				
1964	—	0.10	0.15	1.00	—
1964 Proof	— Value: 135				
1965	—	0.50	1.00	2.50	—
1965 Prooflike	—	—	—	—	2.00
1965 Proof	—	—	—	—	—

KM# 1 3 PENCE **Composition:** 0.5000 Silver .0226 oz. ASW **Subject:** Crossed Patu

Date	Mintage	F	VF	XF	Unc	BU
1933		0.35	0.75	3.25	15.00	—
1933 Proof	Est. 20	Value: 450				
1934		0.35	0.75	3.25	15.00	—
1934 Proof	Est. 20	Value: 1,500				
1935		40.00	100	175	625	—
1935 Proof	364	Value: 550				
1936		0.35	0.75	3.50	20.00	—
1936 Proof	—	Value: 450				

KM# 7 3 PENCE **Composition:** 0.5000 Silver .0226 oz. ASW **Subject:** Crossed Patu

Date	Mintage	F	VF	XF	Unc	BU
1937		0.35	0.75	2.50	15.00	—
1937 Proof	Est. 200	Value: 400				
1939		0.35	0.60	2.25	15.00	—
1939 Proof	—	Value: 400				
1940		0.35	1.00	3.50	25.00	—
1940 Proof	—	Value: 400				
1941		0.40	1.50	12.50	75.00	—
1941 Proof	—	Value: 350				
1942		0.30	0.60	2.00	12.50	—
1942 With 1 dot		4.00	8.00	100	300	—
1943		0.30	0.50	1.25	10.00	—
1944		0.30	0.50	1.25	12.50	—
1944 Proof	—	Value: 350				
1945		0.30	0.50	1.25	7.50	—
1945 Proof	—	Value: 350				
1946		0.30	0.50	1.25	7.50	—
1946 Proof	—	Value: 350				

KM# 7a 3 PENCE **Composition:** Copper-Nickel

Date		F	VF	XF	Unc	BU
1947		0.15	0.35	2.50	12.50	
1947 Proof	Est. 20	Value: 300				

KM# 15 3 PENCE **Composition:** Copper-Nickel

Date	Mintage	F	VF	XF	Unc	BU
1948	4,000,000	0.30	0.70	3.25	15.00	—
1948 Proof	—	Value: 175				
1950	800,000	0.50	2.00	12.50	75.00	—
1950 Proof	—	Value: 225				
1951	3,600,000	0.30	0.70	2.50	10.00	—
1951 Proof	—	Value: 175				
1952	8,000,000	0.30	0.70	2.00	7.50	—
1952 Proof	—	Value: 175				

KM# 25.1 3 PENCE **Composition:** Copper-Nickel **Obverse:** Without shoulder strap

Date	Mintage	F	VF	XF	Unc	BU
1953	4,000,000	0.15	0.35	0.75	6.00	—
1953 Proof	7,000	Value: 7.00				
1953 Matte proof	—	Value: 125				
1954	4,000,000	0.15	0.35	1.00	8.00	—
1954 Proof	—	Value: 175				
1955	4,000,000	0.15	0.35	1.00	8.00	—
1955 Proof	—	Value: 175				
1956	Inc. below	2.50	4.00	35.00	150	—
1956 Proof	—	Value: 250				

KM# 25.2 3 PENCE **Composition:** Copper-Nickel **Obverse:** With shoulder strap

Date		F	VF	XF	Unc	BU
1956		0.10	0.20	0.50	4.00	—
1956 Proof	—	Value: 175				
1957		0.10	0.20	0.30	3.50	—
1957 Proof	—	Value: 175				
1958		0.10	0.20	0.30	2.50	—
1958 Proof	—	Value: 175				
1959		0.10	0.20	0.30	2.50	—
1959 Proof	—	Value: 175				
1960		0.10	0.20	0.30	2.50	—
1960 Proof	—	Value: 175				
1961		0.10	0.15	0.30	1.25	—
1961 Proof	—	Value: 175				
1962		0.10	0.15	0.30	1.50	—
1962 Proof	—	Value: 175				
1963		0.10	0.15	0.25	0.50	—
1963 Proof	—	Value: 175				
1964		0.10	0.15	0.25	0.50	—
1964 Proof	—	Value: 175				
1965		—	0.10	0.15	0.50	—
1965 Prooflike		—	—	—	—	0.75
1965 Proof		—	—	—	—	—

KM# 2 6 PENCE **Weight:** 2.8300 g. **Composition:** 0.5000 Silver .0454 oz. ASW **Reverse:** Huia Bird

Date	Mintage	F	VF	XF	Unc	BU
1933	3,000,000	0.60	1.50	10.00	40.00	—
1933 Proof	20	Value: 450				
1934	3,600,000	0.60	1.50	10.00	40.00	—
1934 Proof	20	Value: 1,500				
1935	560,000	2.00	6.00	40.00	225	—
1935 Proof	364	Value: 275				
1936	1,480,000	0.75	2.25	10.00	40.00	—
1936 Proof	—	—	—	—	—	—

KM# 8 6 PENCE **Weight:** 2.8300 g. **Composition:** 0.5000 Silver .0454 oz. ASW

Date		F	VF	XF	Unc	BU
1937		0.50	1.50	7.00	50.00	—
1937 Proof	Est. 200	Value: 350				
1939		0.50	1.50	7.50	50.00	—
1939 Proof	—	Value: 350				
1940		0.50	2.25	12.50	60.00	—
1940 Proof	—	Value: 350				
1941		2.00	4.00	40.00	275	—
1941 Proof	—	Value: 550				
1942		2.00	4.00	40.00	275	—
1943		0.50	1.00	7.00	30.00	—
1944		1.00	2.00	8.00	30.00	—
1944 Proof	—	Value: 300				
1945		1.50	3.50	10.00	30.00	—
1945 Proof	—	Value: 300				
1946		0.75	1.50	4.00	15.00	—
1946	—	Value: 300				

KM# 8a 6 PENCE **Composition:** Copper-Nickel

Date	Mintage	F	VF	XF	Unc	BU
1947		1.00	2.00	7.50	40.00	—
1947 Proof	Est. 20	Value: 300				

KM# 16 6 PENCE **Composition:** Copper-Nickel

Date	Mintage	F	VF	XF	Unc	BU
1948	2,000,000	1.00	2.00	4.00	35.00	—
1948 Proof	—	Value: 275				
1950	800,000	1.00	3.50	16.00	100	—
1950 Proof	—	Value: 275				
1951	1,800,000	0.40	0.75	1.50	4.00	—
1951 Proof	—	Value: 275				
1952	3,200,000	0.40	0.75	2.00	15.00	—
1952 Proof	—	Value: 225				

KM# 26.1 6 PENCE **Composition:** Copper-Nickel **Obverse:** Without shoulder strap

Date	Mintage	F	VF	XF	Unc	BU
1953	1,200,000	0.15	0.30	2.50	7.50	—
1953 Proof	14,000	Value: 6.50				
1953 Matte proof	—	—	—	—	125	—
1954	1,200,000	0.15	0.30	2.50	14.00	—
1954 Proof	—	Value: 175				
1955	1,600,000	0.15	0.30	2.50	15.00	—
1957	Inc. below	1.50	3.50	60.00	175	—
1957 Proof	—	Value: 600				

KM# 26.2 6 PENCE **Composition:** Copper-Nickel **Obverse:** With shoulder strap

Date		F	VF	XF	Unc	BU
1955 Proof	—	Value: 2,800				
1956		0.20	0.50	1.50	4.00	—
1956 Proof	—	Value: 200				
1957		0.20	0.50	0.75	4.00	—
1957 Proof	—	Value: 200				
1958		0.15	0.50	0.75	4.00	—
1958 Proof	—	Value: 200				
1959		0.15	0.50	0.75	2.50	—
1959 Proof	—	Value: 200				
1960		0.15	0.25	0.40	1.50	—
1960 Proof	—	Value: 200				
1961		0.10	0.15	0.25	2.50	—
1961 Proof	—	Value: 200				
1962		0.10	0.15	0.25	2.50	—
1962 Proof	—	Value: 200				
1963		0.10	0.15	0.25	2.00	—
1963 Proof	—	Value: 200				
1964		—	0.10	0.15	2.00	—
1964 Proof	—	Value: 175				
1965		—	—	0.10	0.75	—
1965 Broken wing		—	15.00	25.00	60.00	—
1965 Prooflike		—	—	—	—	1.00
1965 Proof		—	—	—	—	—

KM# 3 SHILLING **Weight:** 5.6500 g. **Composition:** 0.5000 Silver .0908 oz. ASW **Subject:** Maori Warrior

Date	Mintage	F	VF	XF	Unc	BU
1933		1.50	3.00	20.00	100	—
1933 Proof	Est. 20	Value: 600				
1934		1.50	3.50	15.00	75.00	—
1934 Proof	Est. 20	Value: 1,800				
1935		2.50	4.00	28.50	150	—
1935 Proof	364	Value: 275				

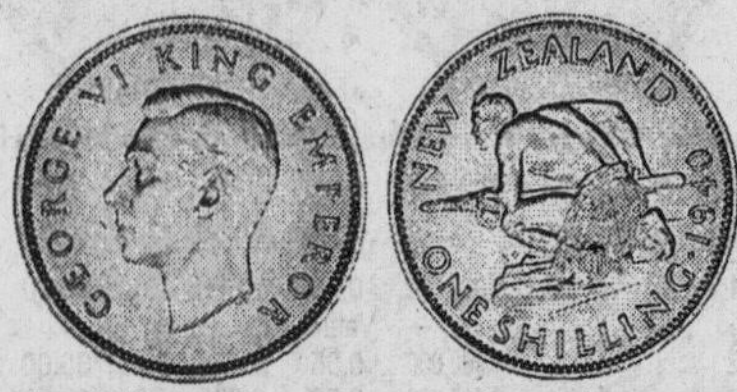

KM# 9 SHILLING **Weight:** 5.6500 g. **Composition:** 0.5000 Silver .0908 oz. ASW

Date	Mintage	F	VF	XF	Unc	BU
1937		1.25	3.00	12.50	70.00	—
1937 Proof	Est. 200	Value: 550				
1940		1.25	2.00	10.00	90.00	—
1940 Proof	—	Value: 550				
1941		1.75	4.00	40.00	225	—
1941 Proof	—	Value: 550				
1942		1.75	4.00	40.00	225	—
1943		2.00	4.00	12.50	55.00	—
1944		2.00	4.00	12.50	55.00	—
1944 Proof	—	Value: 550				
1945		1.00	3.00	8.00	45.00	—
1945 Proof	—	Value: 550				
1946		1.00	3.00	8.00	45.00	—
1946 Proof	—	Value: 550				

KM# 9a SHILLING **Composition:** Copper-Nickel

Date	Mintage	F	VF	XF	Unc	BU
1947		1.50	3.00	25.00	75.00	—
1947 Proof	Est. 20	Value: 350				

KM# 17 SHILLING **Composition:** Copper-Nickel

Date	Mintage	F	VF	XF	Unc	BU
1948	1,000,000	2.00	5.00	20.00	70.00	—
1948 Proof	—	Value: 350				
1950	600,000	2.00	5.00	15.00	70.00	—
1950 Proof	—	Value: 350				
1951	1,200,000	2.00	5.00	15.00	70.00	—
1951 Proof	—	Value: 350				
1952	600,000	2.00	5.00	15.00	70.00	—
1952 Proof	—	Value: 350				

KM# 27.1 SHILLING **Composition:** Copper-Nickel
Obverse: Without shoulder strap

Date	Mintage	F	VF	XF	Unc	BU
1953	200,000	0.60	1.00	4.00	12.00	—
1953 Proof	14,000	Value: 8.00				
1953 Matte proof	—	Value: 125				
1955	200,000	1.00	2.00	10.00	60.00	—
1955 Proof	—	Value: 350				

KM# 27.2 SHILLING **Composition:** Copper-Nickel
Obverse: With shoulder strap

Date	F	VF	XF	Unc	BU
1956	1.00	2.00	3.50	15.00	—
1956 Proof	Value: 350				
1957	1.00	2.00	3.50	15.00	—
1957 Proof	Value: 350				
1958	0.50	1.00	2.50	12.50	—
1958 Proof	Value: 350				
1959	0.75	1.50	3.00	12.50	—
1959 Proof	Value: 350				
1960	0.75	1.50	3.00	12.50	—
1960 Proof	Value: 350				
1961	0.15	0.30	0.60	8.00	—
1961 Proof	Value: 350				
1962	0.15	0.30	0.50	6.00	—
1962 Proof	Value: 350				
1963	0.15	0.30	0.50	4.00	—
1963 Proof	Value: 350				
1964	0.10	0.15	0.30	1.25	—
1964 Proof	Value: 350				
1965	0.10	0.15	0.30	1.00	—
1965 Prooflike	—	—	—	—	1.25
1965 Proof	—	—	—	—	—

KM# 4 FLORIN **Weight:** 11.3100 g. **Composition:** 0.5000 Silver .1818 oz. ASW **Reverse:** Kiwi

Date	Mintage	F	VF	XF	Unc	BU
1933		1.50	3.00	25.00	120	—
1933 Proof	Est. 20	Value: 600				
1934		1.50	3.00	25.00	100	—
1934 Proof	Est. 20	Value: 2,000				
1935		2.00	5.00	40.00	150	—
1935 Proof	364	Value: 300				
1936		6.00	12.50	85.00	775	—
1936 Proof	—	Value: 1,250				

KM# 10.1 FLORIN **Weight:** 11.3100 g. **Composition:** 0.5000 Silver .1818 oz. ASW

Date	Mintage	F	VF	XF	Unc	BU
1937		1.50	2.50	8.00	80.00	—
1937 Proof	Est. 200	Value: 600				
1940		3.00	10.00	80.00	600	—
1940 Proof	—	Value: 800				
1941		1.50	3.00	8.00	70.00	—
1941 Proof	—	Value: 600				
1942		1.50	4.00	25.00	90.00	—
1943		1.25	2.50	8.00	55.00	—
1944		3.00	10.00	35.00	160	—
1944 Proof	—	Value: 800				
1945		2.00	4.00	8.00	55.00	—
1945 Proof	—	Value: 650				
1946		2.00	5.00	10.00	70.00	—
1946 Proof	—	Value: 650				

KM# 10.2 FLORIN **Weight:** 11.3100 g. **Composition:** 0.5000 Silver .1818 oz. ASW **Reverse:** Flat back on Kiwi

Date	F	VF	XF	Unc	BU
1946	6.00	15.00	125	450	—

KM# 10.2a FLORIN **Composition:** Copper-Nickel

Date	Mintage	F	VF	XF	Unc	BU
1947		1.00	2.00	30.00	125	—
1947 Proof	Est. 20	Value: 450				

KM# 18 FLORIN **Composition:** Copper-Nickel

Date	Mintage	F	VF	XF	Unc	BU
1948	1,750,000	1.00	2.00	17.50	100	—
1948 Proof	—	Value: 400				
1949	3,500,000	1.00	2.00	17.50	80.00	—
1949 Proof	—	Value: 400				
1950	3,500,000	1.00	2.00	7.00	25.00	—
1950 Proof	—	Value: 400				
1951	1,000,000	1.00	2.00	7.00	25.00	—
1951 Proof	—	Value: 400				

KM# 28.1 FLORIN **Composition:** Copper-Nickel
Obverse: Without shoulder strap

Date	Mintage	F	VF	XF	Unc	BU
1953	250,000	1.00	1.50	2.50	10.00	—
1953 Proof	7,000	Value: 12.50				
1953 Matte proof	—	Value: 180				

KM# 28.2 FLORIN **Composition:** Copper-Nickel
Obverse: With shoulder strap

Date	Mintage	F	VF	XF	Unc	BU
1961		0.15	0.25	1.00	8.00	—
1961 Proof	—	Value: 375				
1962		0.15	0.25	1.00	8.00	—
1962 Proof	—	Value: 375				
1963		0.15	0.60	1.25	10.00	—
1963 Proof	—	Value: 375				
1964		0.15	0.20	0.35	3.50	—
1964 Proof	—	Value: 375				
1965		0.15	0.20	0.35	1.75	—
1965 Prooflike		—	—	—	—	2.00
1965 Proof		—	—	—	—	—

KM# 5 1/2 CROWN **Weight:** 14.1400 g. **Composition:** 0.5000 Silver .2273 oz. ASW

Date	Mintage	F	VF	XF	Unc	BU
1933		2.50	8.00	25.00	125	—
1933 Proof	Est. 20	Value: 650				
1934		2.50	8.00	20.00	120	—
1934 Proof	Est. 20	Value: 2,250				
1935		3.50	10.00	45.00	275	—
1935 Proof	364	Value: 600				

KM# 11 1/2 CROWN **Weight:** 14.1400 g. **Composition:** 0.5000 Silver .2273 oz. ASW

Date	Mintage	F	VF	XF	Unc	BU
1937	672,000	2.25	5.00	17.50	100	—
1937 Proof	200	Value: 700				
1941	776,000	2.25	6.00	17.50	100	—
1941 Proof	—	Value: 700				
1942	240,000	2.25	6.00	20.00	100	—
1943	1,120,000	1.75	3.50	12.50	80.00	—
1944	180,000	5.00	10.00	60.00	350	—
1944 Proof	—	Value: 700				
1945	420,000	3.00	6.00	17.50	120	—
1945 Proof	—	Value: 700				
1946	960,000	3.00	6.00	17.50	120	—
1946 Proof	—	Value: 700				

KM# 11a 1/2 CROWN **Composition:** Copper-Nickel

Date	Mintage	F	VF	XF	Unc	BU
1947		0.40	2.00	7.00	110	—
1947 Proof	Est. 20	Value: 550				

KM# 14 1/2 CROWN **Weight:** 14.1400 g. **Composition:** 0.5000 Silver .2273 oz. ASW **Subject:** New Zealand Centennial **Reverse:** Maori Wahine

Date	Mintage	F	VF	XF	Unc	BU
1940	101,000	2.50	4.00	10.00	32.00	—
1940 Proof	—	Value: 5,000				

KM# 19 1/2 CROWN **Composition:** Copper-Nickel

Date	Mintage	F	VF	XF	Unc	BU
1948	1,400,000	0.40	1.50	7.00	100	—
1948 Proof	—	Value: 500				
1949	2,800,000	0.40	1.50	7.00	90.00	—
1949 Proof	—	Value: 500				
1950 K. G. close to dots	3,600,000	0.40	1.00	2.00	20.00	—
1950 Proof	—	Value: 500				
1950 K. G. close to rim	Inc. above	0.40	1.00	2.00	20.00	—
1950 Proof	—	Value: 500				
1951	1,200,000	0.40	1.00	2.00	20.00	—
1951 Proof	—	Value: 500				

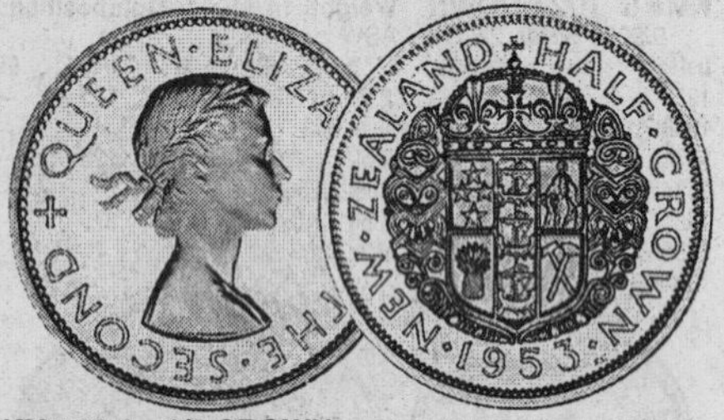

KM# 29.1 1/2 CROWN **Composition:** Copper-Nickel **Reverse:** Without shoulder strap

Date	Mintage	F	VF	XF	Unc	BU
1953	120,000	1.00	2.50	4.00	15.00	—
1953 Proof	7,000	Value: 10.00				
1953 Matte proof	—	Value: 245				

KM# 29.2 1/2 CROWN **Composition:** Copper-Nickel **Obverse:** With shoulder strap

Date	Mintage	F	VF	XF	Unc	BU
1961	80,000	0.40	0.80	2.00	10.00	—
1961 Proof	—	Value: 450				
1962	600,000	0.30	0.70	1.50	7.50	—
1962 Proof	—	Value: 450				
1963	400,000	0.50	0.70	1.50	6.00	—
1963 Proof	—	Value: 450				
1965	175,000	0.50	0.70	1.00	2.50	—
1965 Prooflike	25,000	—	—	—	—	3.00
1965 Proof	10	—	—	—	—	—

KM# 6 CROWN **Weight:** 28.2800 g. **Composition:** 0.5000 Silver .4546 oz. ASW **Subject:** Treaty of Waitangi in 1840. **Reverse:** Woka Nene and Govemor Hobson

Date	Mintage	F	VF	XF	Unc	BU
1935	764	1,100	1,350	2,250	2,750	—
1935 Proof	364	Value: 2,500				

KM# 22 CROWN **Weight:** 28.2800 g. **Composition:** 0.5000 Silver .4546 oz. ASW **Subject:** Proposed Royal visit **Reverse:** Silver Fern Leaf

Date	Mintage	F	VF	XF	Unc	BU
1949	—	2.50	4.00	12.00	—	
1949 Proof	Est. 3	Value: 4,250				

KM# 30 CROWN **Composition:** Copper-Nickel **Subject:** Queen Elizabeth II Coronation

Date	Mintage	F	VF	XF	Unc	BU
1953	250,000	—	—	2.00	4.00	—
1953 Proof	7,000	Value: 20.00				

DECIMAL COINAGE

100 Cents = 1 Dollar

(c) Royal Australian Mint, Canberra

(l) Royal Mint, Llantrisant

(o) Royal Canadian Mint, Ottawa

KM# 31 CENT **Composition:** Bronze **Reverse:** Silver Fern Leaf

Date	Mintage	F	VF	XF	Unc	BU
1967(l)	250,000	—	—	0.10	0.15	—
1967(l) Prooflike	50,000	—	—	—	—	0.80
1967 Proof	10	—	—	—	—	—
1968	35,000	—	—	0.15	1.00	—
1968 Prooflike	40,000	—	—	—	—	1.25
1969	50,000	—	—	0.15	1.00	—
1969 Prooflike	50,000	—	—	—	—	1.25
1970	30,000	—	—	0.15	0.60	—
1970 Prooflike	20,010	—	—	—	—	1.00
1971(c) Serifs on date numerals	10,000,000	—	—	0.20	4.00	—
1971(l) Without serifs	15,000	—	—	0.15	2.75	—
1971(l) Proof	5,000	Value: 12.50				
1972(c)	10,055,000	—	—	0.15	2.75	—
1972(c) Proof	8,045	Value: 5.00				
1973(c)	15,055,000	—	—	0.10	2.50	—
1973(c) Proof	8,000	Value: 5.00				
1974(c)	35,035,000	—	—	0.10	2.00	—
1974(c) Proof	8,000	Value: 4.00				
1975(l)	60,015,000	—	—	0.10	1.00	—
1975(l) Proof	10,000	Value: 4.00				
1976(l)	20,016,000	—	—	0.10	0.60	—
1976(l) Proof	11,000	Value: 4.00				
1977	20,000	—	—	0.20	6.00	—
1977 Proof	12,000	Value: 5.00				
1978(o)	15,023,000	—	—	0.10	1.25	—
1978(o) Proof	15,000	Value: 3.50				
1979(o)	35,025,000	—	—	0.10	0.60	—
1979(o) Proof	16,000	Value: 3.50				
1980(l) Smooth shoulder folds in gown	27,000	—	—	0.10	1.25	—
1980(l) Proof	17,000	Value: 3.50				
1980(o) Incised shoulder folds in gown	4,000,000	—	—	0.10	0.80	—
1981(o) Incised shoulder folds in gown.	10,000,000	—	—	0.10	0.40	—
1981(l) Smooth shoulder folds in gown.	25,000	—	—	0.10	1.00	—
1981(l) Proof; Smooth shoulder folds in gown	18,000	Value: 3.50				
1982(o) Blunt tipped 2	10,000,000	—	—	0.10	0.40	—
1982(l) Round tipped 2	25,000	—	—	0.10	0.80	—
1982(l) Proof; Round tipped 2	18,000	Value: 2.50				
1983(o) Round top 3	40,000,000	—	—	0.10	0.40	—
1983(l) Flat top 3	25,000	—	—	0.10	0.80	—
1983(l) Proof; Flat top 3	18,000	Value: 2.50				
1984(o) Wiry hair, bushy eyebrow	30,000,000	—	—	0.10	0.25	—
1984(l) Smooth shoulder folds	25,000	—	—	—	0.80	—
1984(l) Proof; Smooth shoulder folds	15,000	Value: 1.50				
1985(o) Wiry hair, bush eyebrow	40,000,000	—	—	—	0.25	—
1985(c) Smooth shoulder folds	20,000	—	—	—	1.25	—
1985(c) Proof	12,000	Value: 1.00				

KM# 58 CENT **Composition:** Bronze **Obverse:** Similar to 1 Dollar, KM# 57

Date	Mintage	F	VF	XF	Unc	BU
1986(o)	25,000,000	—	—	—	0.25	—
1986(l)	18,000	—	—	—	1.25	—
1986(l) Proof	10,000	Value: 1.00				
1987(o)	27,500,000	—	—	—	0.25	—
1987(l)	18,000	—	—	—	1.25	—
1987(l) Proof	10,000	Value: 1.00				
1988(l)	15,000	—	—	—	7.00	—
1988(l) Proof	9,000	Value: 2.00				

Note: 1988 cent was struck for sets only.

KM# 32 2 CENTS **Composition:** Bronze **Reverse:** Kowhai Leaves

Date	Mintage	F	VF	XF	Unc	BU
1967(l)	250,000	—	—	0.10	0.15	—
1967(l) Prooflike	50,000	—	—	—	—	0.7
1967(l) Proof	10	—	—	—	—	—
1968	35,000	—	—	0.15	0.75	—
1968 Prooflike	40,000	—	—	—	—	1.2
1969	50,000	—	—	0.15	0.50	—
1969 Prooflike	50,000	—	—	—	—	1.2
1970	30,000	—	—	0.15	2.75	—
1970 Prooflike	20,010	—	—	—	—	1.2
1971(c) Serifs on date numerals	15,050,000	—	—	0.20	3.50	—
1971(l) Without serifs	15,000	—	—	0.20	3.50	—
1971(l) Proof	5,000	Value: 12.50				
1972(c)	17,525,000	—	—	0.15	2.50	—
1972(c) Proof	8,045	Value: 5.00				
1973(c)	38,565,000	—	—	0.10	2.25	—
1973(c) Proof	8,000	Value: 5.25				
1974(c)	50,015,000	—	—	0.10	2.25	—
1974(c) Proof	8,000	Value: 3.25				
1975(l)	20,015,000	—	—	0.10	1.00	—
1975(l) Proof	10,000	Value: 3.25				
1976(l)	15,016,000	—	—	0.10	0.60	—
1976(l) Proof	11,000	Value: 3.25				
1977(l)	20,000,000	—	—	0.10	0.75	—
1977(l) Proof	12,000	Value: 3.25				
1978	23,000	—	—	0.10	6.00	—
1978 Proof	15,000	Value: 3.25				
1979	25,000	—	—	0.10	4.00	—
1979	16,000	Value: 3.25				
1980(l) Smooth shoulder folds on gown	27,000	—	—	0.10	0.80	—
1980(l) Proof	17,000	Value: 2.75				
1980(o) Incised shoulder folds on gown	10,000,000	—	—	0.10	1.00	—
1981(o) Incised shoulder folds on gown	25,000,000	—	—	0.10	1.00	—

Date	Mintage	F	VF	XF	Unc	BU
1981(l) Smooth shoulder folds on gown	25,000	—	—	0.10	1.00	—
1981(l) Proof	18,000	Value: 2.75				
1982(o) Blunt open 2	50,000,000	—	—	0.10	0.75	—
1982(l) Pointed tight 2	25,000	—	—	0.10	0.60	—
1982(l) Proof	18,000	Value: 2.75				
1983(o) Round topped 3	15,000,000	—	—	0.10	0.75	—
1983(l) Flat topped 3	25,000	—	—	0.10	0.60	—
1983(l) Proof	18,000	Value: 2.75				
1984(o) Wiry hair, bushy eyebrow	10,000,000	—	—	0.10	0.60	—
1984(l) Smooth shoulder folds	25,000	—	—	0.10	2.00	—
1984(l) Proof	15,000	Value: 1.75				
1985(o) Wiry hair, bushy eyebrow	22,500,000	—	—	0.10	0.60	—
1985(c) Smooth shoulder folds	20,000	—	—	0.10	2.00	—
1985(c) Proof	12,000	Value: 1.25				

KM# 33 2 CENTS Composition: Bronze **Obverse:** Bahamas 5 Cent, KM#3 **Reverse:** KM#32 **Note:** Mule.

Date	F	VF	XF	Unc	BU
ND(1967)	—	7.50	10.00	20.00	—

KM# 59 2 CENTS Composition: Bronze **Obverse:** Similar to 1 Dollar, KM#57

Date	Mintage	F	VF	XF	Unc	BU
1986(l)	18,000	—	—	—	5.00	—
1986(l) Proof	10,000	Value: 1.25				
1987(o)	36,250,000	—	—	—	0.35	—
1987(l)	18,000	—	—	—	1.50	—
1987(l) Proof	10,000	Value: 1.25				
1988(l)	15,000	—	—	—	5.00	—
1988(l) Proof	9,000	Value: 1.25				

KM# 34 5 CENTS Composition: Copper-Nickel **Subject:** Tuatara

Date	Mintage	F	VF	XF	Unc	BU
1967(l)	250,000	—	—	0.10	0.25	—
1967(l) Without sea line	Inc. above	—	3.00	7.50	28.50	—
1967(l) Prooflike	50,000	—	—	—	—	1.00
1967(l) Proof	10	—	—	—	—	—
1968	35,000	—	—	0.15	1.25	—
1968 Prooflike	40,000	—	—	—	—	1.50
1969	50,000	—	—	0.15	0.50	—
1969 Prooflike	50,000	—	—	—	—	—
1970	30,000	—	—	0.15	0.50	—
1970 Prooflike	20,010	—	—	—	—	1.50
1971(c) Serifs on date numerals	11,520,000	—	—	0.15	3.75	—
1971(l) Without serifs	15,000	—	—	0.15	3.75	—
1971(l) Proof	5,000	Value: 15.00				
1972(c)	20,015,000	—	—	0.10	2.75	—
1972(c) Proof	8,045	Value: 5.00				
1973(c)	4,038,999	—	—	0.10	2.00	—
1973(c) Proof	8,000	Value: 4.50				
1974(c)	18,015,000	—	—	0.10	2.75	—
1974(c) Proof	8,000	Value: 4.00				
1975(c)	32,015,000	—	—	0.10	1.50	—
1975(c) Proof	10,000	Value: 4.50				
1976	16,000	—	—	0.20	7.50	—
1976 Proof	11,000	Value: 4.00				
1977	20,000	—	—	0.15	5.50	—
1977 Proof	12,000	Value: 4.00				
1978(o)	20,023,000	—	—	0.10	0.40	—
1978(o) Proof	15,000	Value: 4.00				
1979	25,000	—	—	0.15	6.00	—
1979 Proof	16,000	Value: 4.00				
1980(l) Smooth shoulder folds on gown	27,000	—	—	0.10	1.00	—
1980(l) Proof	17,000	Value: 4.00				
1980(o) Incised shoulder folds on gown	12,000,000	—	—	0.10	0.75	—
1981(o) Incised shoulder folds on gown	20,000,000	—	—	0.10	0.75	—
1981(l) Smooth shoulder folds on gown	25,000	—	—	0.10	1.00	—
1981(l) Proof	18,000	Value: 3.00				
1982(o) Blunt 2	50,000,000	—	—	0.10	0.75	—
1982(l) Pointed 2	25,000	—	—	0.10	1.00	—
1982(l) Proof	18,000	Value: 3.00				
1983(l)	25,000	—	—	0.10	3.00	—
1983(l) Proof	18,000	Value: 2.75				
1984(l)	25,000	—	—	0.10	4.00	—
1984(l) Proof	15,000	Value: 3.00				
1985(o) Wiry hair, bushy eyebrow	14,000,000	—	—	0.10	0.75	—
1985(c)	20,000	—	—	0.10	2.00	—
1985(c) Proof	12,000	Value: 3.00				

KM# 64 5 CENTS Composition: Copper-Nickel **Obverse:** KM#34 **Reverse:** Canada 10 Cent, KM#77 **Note:** Mule.

Date	F	VF	XF	Unc	BU
1981(o) Rare; Serif on 1	—	—	—	—	—

KM# 60 5 CENTS Composition: Copper-Nickel

Date	Mintage	F	VF	XF	Unc	BU
1986(o)		—	—	0.10	0.25	—
1986(l)		—	—	—	1.50	—
1986(l) Proof	10,000	Value: 3.00				
1987(o)		—	—	0.10	0.25	—
1987(l)		—	—	—	1.50	—
1987(l) Proof	10,000	Value: 3.00				
1988(c) Round topped numerals		—	—	0.10	0.50	—
1988(l) Flat topped numerals		—	—	—	1.50	—
1988(l) Proof	9,000	Value: 3.00				
1989(o)		—	—	—	0.25	—
1989(c)		—	—	—	1.50	—
1989(c) Proof	8,500,000	Value: 3.00				
1990(l)		—	—	—	0.75	
1990(l) Proof	10,000	Value: 3.00				
1991(c)		—	—	—	1.50	—
1991(c) Proof	9,000	Value: 3.00				
1992(l)		—	—	—	2.75	—
1992(l) Proof	9,000	Value: 3.00				
1993(l)		—	—	—	1.50	—
1993(l) Proof	10,000	Value: 3.00				
1994(l)		—	—	—	0.25	—
1994(l) Proof	10,000	Value: 3.00				
1995(l)		—	—	—	0.25	—
1995(l) Proof	Est. 4,000	Value: 3.00				
1996(n)		—	—	—	0.25	—
1997(n)		—	—	—	0.25	—
1997(n) Proof	—	Value: 3.00				
1998(n)		—	—	—	0.25	—
1998(n) Proof	Est. 2,000	Value: 3.00				

KM# 72 5 CENTS Composition: Copper-Nickel **Subject:** 1990 Anniversary Celebrations

Date	Mintage	F	VF	XF	Unc	BU
1990	10,000	—	—	—	1.00	—

KM# 72a 5 CENTS Weight: 3.2700 g. **Composition:** 0.9250 Silver .0973 oz. ASW

Date	Mintage	F	VF	XF	Unc	BU
1990 Proof	7,000	Value: 10.00				

KM# 116 5 CENTS Composition: Copper-Nickel **Obverse:** Rank-Broadley portrait of Queen Elizabeth II **Reverse:** Similar to KM#60

Date	Mintage	F	VF	XF	Unc	BU
1999(p)		—	—	0.10	0.50	—
1999(p) Proof	Est. 2,000	Value: 3.00				
2000(o)		—	—	0.10	0.50	—
2000 Proof	—	Value: 3.00				
2001(l)		—	—	0.10	0.50	—
2002(l)		—	—	0.10	0.50	—

KM# 35 10 CENTS Composition: Copper-Nickel **Reverse:** Maori Mask

Date	Mintage	F	VF	XF	Unc	BU
1967(l)	250,000	—	—	0.10	0.25	—
1967(l) Prooflike	50,000	—	—	—	—	1.25
1967(l) Proof	10	—	—	—	—	—
1968	35,000	—	—	0.15	1.50	—
1968 Prooflike	40,000	—	—	—	—	2.00
1969	3,050,000	—	—	0.15	0.75	—
1969 Proof	50,000	Value: 1.50				

KM# 41 10 CENTS Composition: Copper-Nickel

Date	Mintage	F	VF	XF	Unc	BU
1970	30,000	—	—	0.15	0.75	—
1970 Prooflike	20,010	—	—	—	—	1.50
1971(c) Serifs on date numerals	2,800,000	—	1.00	3.50	25.00	—
1971(l) Without serifs	15,000	—	—	0.15	4.00	—
1971(l) Proof	5,000	Value: 25.00				
1972(c)	2,039,000	—	—	0.15	2.00	—
1972(c) Proof	8,000	Value: 15.00				
1973(c)	3,525,000	—	—	0.10	2.00	—
1973(c) Proof	8,000	Value: 6.00				
1974(c)	4,619,000	—	—	0.10	2.00	—
1974(c) Proof	8,000	Value: 6.00				
1975(l)	7,015,000	—	—	0.10	2.00	—
1975(l) Proof	10,000	Value: 5.00				
1976(l)	5,016,000	—	—	0.10	1.50	—
1976(l) Proof	11,000	Value: 5.00				
1977(l)	5,000,000	—	—	0.10	1.00	—
1977(o) Proof	12,000	Value: 5.00				
1978(o)	16,023,000	—	—	0.10	2.00	—
1978(o) Proof	15,000	Value: 4.00				
1979(o)	6,000,000	—	—	0.10	0.60	—
1979(o) Proof	16,000	Value: 4.00				
1980(l) Smooth shoulder folds on gown	27,000	—	—	0.10	0.80	—
1980(l) Proof	17,000	Value: 4.00				
1980(o) Incised shoulder folds on gown	28,000,000	—	—	0.10	2.50	—
1981(o) Oval holes in 8	5,000,000	—	—	0.10	2.50	—
1981(l) Round holes in 8	25,000	—	—	0.10	1.00	—
1981(l) Proof	18,000	Value: 4.00				
1982(o) Blunt open 2	18,000,000	—	—	0.10	2.50	—
1982(l) Point tipped 2	25,000	—	—	0.10	1.75	—
1982(l) Proof	18,000	Value: 4.00				
1983(l)	25,000	—	—	0.10	3.00	—
1983(l) Proof	18,000	Value: 4.00				
1984(l)	25,000	—	—	0.10	3.00	—
1984(l) Proof	15,000	Value: 4.00				
1985(o) Wiry hair, bushy eyebrow	8,000,000	—	—	0.10	3.50	—
1985(c) Smooth shoulder folds on gown	20,000	—	—	0.10	2.75	—
1985(c) Proof	12,000	Value: 3.50				

KM# 61 10 CENTS Composition: Copper-Nickel

Date	Mintage	F	VF	XF	Unc	BU
1986(l)		—	—	0.15	5.00	—
1986(l) Proof	10,000	Value: 3.50				
1987(o)		—	—	0.10	1.50	—
1987(l)		—	—	0.10	1.50	—
1987(l) Proof	10,000	Value: 3.75				
1988(c)		—	—	0.10	0.25	—
1988(l)		—	—	0.10	1.50	—
1988(l) Proof	9,000	Value: 3.75				
1989(c)		—	—	—	0.25	—
1989(c) Proof	8,500	Value: 3.75				
1989(o)		—	—	—	1.50	—
1990(c)		—	—	—	1.25	—
1990(c) Proof	10,000	Value: 3.75				

Date	Mintage	F	VF	XF	Unc	BU
1991(c)		—	—	—	1.50	—
1991(c) Proof	15,000	Value: 3.75				
1992		—	—	—	1.50	—
1992 Proof	9,000	Value: 3.75				
1993		—	—	—	0.80	—
1993 Proof	10,000	Value: 3.75				
1994		—	—	—	0.80	—
1994 Proof	10,000	Value: 3.75				
1995		—	—	—	0.80	—
1995 Proof	Est. 4,000	Value: 3.75				
1996(n)		—	—	—	0.80	—
1997		—	—	—	0.80	—
1997 Proof	—	Value: 3.75				
1998		—	—	—	0.80	—
1998 Proof	Est. 2,000	Value: 3.75				

KM# 73 10 CENTS **Composition:** Copper-Nickel **Subject:** 1990 Anniversary Celebrations **Obverse:** Similar to 1 Dollar, KM#76

Date	Mintage	F	VF	XF	Unc	BU
1990	10,000	—	—	—	1.50	—

KM# 73a 10 CENTS **Weight:** 6.5300 g. **Composition:** 0.9250 Silver .1942 oz. ASW

Date	Mintage	F	VF	XF	Unc	BU
1990 Proof	7,000	Value: 10.00				

KM# 117 10 CENTS **Composition:** Copper-Nickel **Obverse:** Rank-Broadley portrait of Queen Elizabeth II **Reverse:** Similar to KM#61

Date	Mintage	F	VF	XF	Unc	BU
1999		—	—	—	0.50	—
1999 Proof	Est. 2,000	Value: 4.00				
2000(o)		—	—	—	0.50	—
2000(o) Proof	—	Value: 4.00				
2001(l)		—	—	—	0.50	—
2002(l)		—	—	—	0.50	—

KM# 36 20 CENTS **Composition:** Copper-Nickel **Subject:** Kiwi

Date	Mintage	F	VF	XF	Unc	BU
1967(l)	250,000	—	—	0.20	0.40	—
1967(l) Prooflike	50,000	—	—	—	—	1.25
1967(l) Proof	10	—	—	—	—	—
1968	35,000	—	—	0.20	1.50	—
1968 Prooflike	40,000	—	—	—	—	2.50
1969	50,000	—	—	0.20	0.60	—
1969 Prooflike	50,000	—	—	—	—	2.00
1970	30,000	—	—	0.25	4.00	—
1970 Prooflike	20,010	—	—	—	—	2.50
1971(c) Serifs on date numerals	1,600,000	—	1.00	4.00	20.00	—
1971(l) Without serifs	15,000	—	—	0.25	4.00	—
1971(l) Proof	5,000	Value: 40.00				
1972(c)	1,531,000	—	—	0.15	2.00	—
1972(c) Proof	8,000	Value: 12.50				
1973(c)	3,043,000	—	—	0.15	2.00	—
1973(c) Proof	8,000	Value: 7.00				
1974(c)	4,527,000	—	—	0.15	4.00	—
1974(c) Proof	8,000	Value: 8.00				
1975(l)	5,015,000	—	—	0.15	2.00	—
1975(l) Proof	12,000	Value: 6.50				
1976(l)	7,516,000	—	—	0.15	2.00	—
1976(l) Proof	11,000	Value: 6.00				
1977(l)	7,500,000	—	—	0.15	2.00	—
1977(l) Proof	12,000	Value: 6.50				
1978(o)	2,523,000	—	—	0.15	2.00	—
1978(o) Proof	15,000	Value: 5.00				
1979(o)	8,000,000	—	—	0.15	1.00	—
1979(o) Proof	16,000	Value: 5.00				

Date	Mintage	F	VF	XF	Unc	BU
1980(l) Smooth shoulder folds on gown	27,000	—	—	0.15	1.00	—
1980(l) Proof	17,000	Value: 5.00				
1980(o) Incised shoulder folds on gown	9,000,000	—	—	0.15	5.00	—
1981(o) Incised shoulder folds on gown	7,500,000	—	—	0.15	5.00	—
1981(l) Smooth shoulder folds on gown	25,000	—	—	0.15	1.00	—
1981(l) Proof	18,000	Value: 4.00				
1982(o) Blunt 2	17,500,000	—	—	0.15	5.00	—
1982(l) Pointed 2	25,000	—	—	0.15	1.00	—
1982(l) Proof	18,000	Value: 5.00				
1983(o) Round topped 3	2,500,000	—	—	0.15	5.00	—
1983(l) Flat topped 3	25,000	—	—	0.15	1.00	—
1983(l) Proof	18,000	Value: 4.00				
1984(o) Wiry hair, bushy eyebrows	1,500,000	—	—	0.15	5.00	—
1984(l) Smooth shoulder folds on gown	25,000	—	—	0.15	0.60	—
1984(l) Proof	18,000	Value: 4.00				
1985(o) Pointed tip 5	6,000,000	—	—	0.15	7.00	—
1985(c) Round tip 5	20,000	—	—	0.15	1.50	—
1985(c) Proof	12,000	Value: 4.00				

KM# 62 20 CENTS **Composition:** Copper-Nickel **Obverse:** Similar to 1 Dollar, KM#57

Date	Mintage	F	VF	XF	Unc	BU
1986(o)	12,500,000	—	—	0.15	0.50	—
1986(l)	18,000	—	—	0.25	1.50	—
1986(l) Proof	10,000	Value: 4.00				
1987(o)	14,000,000	—	—	0.15	0.40	—
1987(l)	18,000	—	—	0.25	1.50	—
1987(l) Proof	10,000	Value: 4.00				
1988(c)	12,500,000	—	—	0.15	0.40	—
1988(l)	15,000	—	—	0.25	1.50	—
1988(l) Proof	9,000	Value: 4.00				
1989(o)	5,000,000	—	—	—	0.40	—
1989(o) Proof	8,500	Value: 4.00				
1989(c)	15,000	—	—	—	1.50	—

KM# 74 20 CENTS **Composition:** Copper-Nickel **Subject:** 1990 Anniversary Celebrations

Date	Mintage	F	VF	XF	Unc	BU
1990(c)	10,000	—	—	—	1.75	—

KM# 74a 20 CENTS **Weight:** 13.0700 g. **Composition:** 0.9250 Silver .3887 oz. ASW

Date	Mintage	F	VF	XF	Unc	BU
1990(c) Proof	7,000	Value: 10.00				

KM# 81 20 CENTS **Composition:** Copper-Nickel

Date	Mintage	F	VF	XF	Unc	BU
1990(l)		—	—	—	0.40	—
1990(c)		—	—	—	1.50	—
1990(c) Proof	10,000	Value: 4.00				
1991(c)		—	—	—	1.50	—
1991(c) Proof	15,000	Value: 4.00				
1992(l)		—	—	—	1.50	—
1992(l) Proof	9,000	Value: 4.00				
1993(l)		—	—	—	1.50	—
1993(l) Proof	10,000	Value: 4.00				
1994(l)		—	—	—	1.50	—
1994(l) Proof	10,000	Value: 4.00				
1995(l)		—	—	—	1.50	—
1995(l) Proof	Est. 4,000	Value: 4.00				
1996(l)		—	—	—	1.50	—
1997(l)		—	—	—	1.50	—
1997(l) Proof	—	Value: 4.00				
1998(l)		—	—	—	1.50	—
1998(l) Proof	Est. 2,000	Value: 4.00				

KM# 81a 20 CENTS **Weight:** 13.0700 g. **Composition:** 0.9250 Silver .3887 oz. ASW

Date	Mintage	F	VF	XF	Unc	BU
1995 Proof	Est. 2,500	Value: 12.50				

KM# 118 20 CENTS **Composition:** Copper-Nickel **Obverse:** Rank-Broadley portrait of Queen Elizabeth II **Reverse:** Similar to KM#81

Date	Mintage	F	VF	XF	Unc	BU
1999		—	—	—	0.75	—
1999 Proof	Est. 2,000	Value: 4.00				
2000		—	—	—	0.75	—
2000 Proof	—	Value: 4.00				
2002(l)		—	—	—	0.75	—

KM# 37 50 CENTS **Composition:** Copper-Nickel **Subject:** H.M.B. Endeavour

Date	Mintage	F	VF	XF	Unc	BU
1967(l)	250,000	—	—	0.40	0.60	—
1967(l) Dot above 1	Inc. above	—	2.50	5.00	25.00	—
1967(l) Prooflike	50,000	—	—	—	—	1.50
1967(l)	10	—	—	—	—	—
1968	35,000	—	—	0.45	2.00	—
1968 Prooflike	40,000	—	—	—	—	3.00
1970	30,000	—	—	0.45	3.50	—
1970 Prooflike	20,010	—	—	—	—	3.50
1971(c) Serifs on date numerals	1,123,000	—	1.00	4.50	30.00	—
1971(l) Without serifs	15,000	—	—	0.35	3.50	—
1971(l) Proof	5,000	Value: 40.00				
1972(c)	1,423,000	—	—	0.35	4.00	—
1972(c) Proof	8,045	Value: 15.00				
1973(c)	2,523,000	—	—	0.35	3.50	—
1973(c) Proof	8,000	Value: 10.00				
1974(c)	1,215,000	—	—	0.35	3.50	—
1974(c) Proof	8,000	Value: 10.00				
1975(l)	3,815,000	—	—	0.35	3.50	—
1975(l) Proof	10,000	Value: 7.50				
1976(l)	2,016,000	—	—	0.35	3.50	—
1976(l) Proof	11,000	Value: 7.50				
1977(l)	2,000,000	—	—	0.35	2.00	—
1977(l) Proof	12,000	Value: 7.50				
1978(o)	2,023,000	—	—	0.35	2.00	—
1978(o) Proof	15,000	Value: 6.00				
1979(o)	2,400,000	—	—	0.35	2.00	—
1979(o) Proof	16,000	Value: 6.00				
1980(l) Smooth back line to hair	27,000	—	—	0.35	2.00	—
1980(l) Proof	17,000	Value: 6.00				
1980(o) Strong back line to hair	8,000,000	—	—	0.50	10.00	—
1981(o) Blunt end on 9	4,000,000	—	—	0.50	10.00	—
1981(l) Pointed end on 9	25,000	—	—	0.35	1.25	—
1981(l) Proof	18,000	Value: 6.00				
1982(o) Blunt end on 2	6,000,000	—	—	0.50	10.00	—
1982(l) Pointed end on 2	25,000	—	—	0.35	3.00	—
1982(l) Proof	18,000	Value: 6.00				
1983(l)	25,000	—	—	0.35	3.00	—
1983(l) Proof	18,000	Value: 6.00				
1984(o) Wiry hair, bushy eyebrows	2,000,000	—	—	0.50	10.00	—
1984(l) Incised shoulder folds on gown	25,000	—	—	0.35	3.00	—
1984(l) Proof	15,000	Value: 5.00				
1985(o) Wiry hair, bushy eyebrows	2,000,000	—	—	0.50	10.00	—
1985(c)	20,000	—	—	0.35	3.00	—
1985(c) Proof	12,000	Value: 5.00				

KM# 39 50 CENTS **Composition:** Copper-Nickel **Subject:** 200th Anniversary - Captain Cook's Voyage **Edge Lettering:** Cook Bi-Centenary 1769-1969 **Note:** Similar to KM#37.

Date	Mintage	F	VF	XF	Unc	BU
1969	50,000	—	—	0.75	3.00	—
1969 Prooflike	50,000	—	—	—	—	3.50

KM# 95 50 CENTS Composition: Nickel **Obverse:** KM#37 **Reverse:** Canada 1 Dollar KM#120 **Note:** Mule.

Date	F	VF	XF	Unc	BU
1985 6 known	—	1,200	1,900	—	—

KM# 63 50 CENTS Composition: Copper-Nickel

Date	Mintage	F	VF	XF	Unc	BU
1986(o)		—	—	0.35	0.75	—
1986(l)		—	—	0.50	1.00	—
1986(l) Proof	10,000	Value: 5.00				
1987(o)		—	—	0.35	0.75	—
1987(l)		—	—	0.50	1.00	—
1987(l) Proof	10,000	Value: 5.00				
1988(c)		—	—	0.35	0.75	—
1988(l)		—	—	0.50	1.50	—
1988(l) Proof	9,000	Value: 5.00				
1989(c)		—	—	—	1.00	—
1989(c) Proof	8,500	Value: 5.00				
1990(l)		—	—	—	1.00	—
1990(l) Proof	10,000	Value: 5.00				
1991(c)		—	—	—	1.00	—
1991(c) Proof	15,000	Value: 5.00				
1992(l)		—	—	—	1.00	—
1992(l) Proof	9,000	Value: 5.00				
1993(l)		—	—	—	1.00	—
1993(l) Proof	10,000	Value: 5.00				
1995(l)		—	—	—	1.00	—
1995(l) Proof	Est. 4,000	Value: 5.00				
1996(l)		—	—	—	1.00	—
1997(l)		—	—	—	1.00	—
1997(l) Proof	—	Value: 5.00				
1998(l)		—	—	—	1.00	—
1998(l) Proof	Est. 2,000	Value: 5.00				

KM# 75 50 CENTS Composition: Nickel **Subject:** 1990 Anniversary Celebrations

Date	Mintage	F	VF	XF	Unc	BU
1990(c)	10,000	—	—	—	5.00	—

KM# 75a 50 CENTS Weight: 15.7400 g. **Composition:** 0.9250 Silver .4682 oz. ASW

Date	Mintage	F	VF	XF	Unc	BU
1990(c) Proof	7,000	Value: 20.00				

KM# 90 50 CENTS Ring Composition: Copper-Nickel **Center Composition:** Aluminum-Bronze **Subject:** H.M.B. Endeavour

Date	Mintage	F	VF	XF	Unc	BU
1994	53,000	—	—	—	20.00	—

KM# 90a 50 CENTS Ring Composition: 0.9250 Silver **Center Composition:** Aluminum-Bronze

Date	Mintage	F	VF	XF	Unc	BU
1994 Proof	10,000	Value: 25.00				

KM# 90b 50 CENTS Ring Composition: 0.3750 Gold **Center Composition:** 0.9160 Gold **Subject:** H.M.B. Endeavour

Date	Mintage	F	VF	XF	Unc	BU
1994 Proof	500	Value: 400				

KM# 119 50 CENTS Composition: Copper-Nickel **Obverse:** Rank-Broadley portrait of Queen Elizabeth II **Reverse:** Similar to KM#81

Date	Mintage	F	VF	XF	Unc	BU
1999		—	—	—	1.00	—
1999 Proof	Est. 2,000	Value: 5.00				
2000		—	—	—	1.00	—
2000 Proof	—	Value: 5.00				
2001(l)		—	—	—	1.00	—
2002(l)		—	—	—	1.00	—

KM# 38.1 DOLLAR Composition: Copper-Nickel **Subject:** Decimalization Commemorative **Edge:** Lettered

Date	Mintage	F	VF	XF	Unc	BU
1967	250,000	—	—	0.75	1.00	—
1967 Prooflike	50,000	—	—	—	—	2.50
1967 Proof	10	—	—	—	—	—

KM# 38.2 DOLLAR Composition: Copper-Nickel **Subject:** Regular Issue **Edge:** Reeded

Date	Mintage	F	VF	XF	Unc	BU
1971	45,000	—	—	2.00	3.00	—
1971 Proof	5,000	Value: 25.00				
1972	42,000	—	—	2.00	3.00	—
1972 Proof	8,045	Value: 12.50				
1972 RAM case; Proof	3,000	Value: 27.50				
1973	37,000	—	—	2.00	3.00	—
1973 Proof	16,000	Value: 5.00				
1975	30,000	—	—	2.00	3.00	—
1975 Proof	20,000	Value: 5.00				
1976	36,000	—	—	2.00	3.00	—
1976 Proof	22,000	Value: 5.00				

KM# 40.1 DOLLAR Composition: Copper-Nickel **Subject:** 200th Anniversary - Captain Cook's Voyage

Date	Mintage	F	VF	XF	Unc	BU
1969	400,000	—	—	0.75	1.25	—
1969 Prooflike	50,000	—	—	—	—	3.00

KM# 40.2 DOLLAR Composition: Copper-Nickel **Edge:** No hyphen in edge inscription

Date	F	VF	XF	Unc	BU
1969	—	—	—	7.50	—

KM# 42 DOLLAR Composition: Copper-Nickel **Subject:** Royal Visit **Reverse:** Mount Cook

Date	Mintage	F	VF	XF	Unc	BU
1970	285,000	—	—	0.75	1.00	—
1970 Prooflike	20,000	—	—	—	—	4.00

KM# 43 DOLLAR Composition: Copper-Nickel **Subject:** Cook Islands

Date	Mintage	F	VF	XF	Unc	BU
1970	25,000	—	—	4.00	9.00	—
1970 Proof	5,030	Value: 22.50				

KM# 44 DOLLAR Composition: Copper-Nickel **Subject:** Commonwealth Games

Date	Mintage	F	VF	XF	Unc	BU
1974	515,000	—	—	1.00	1.75	—

KM# 44a DOLLAR Weight: 27.2160 g. **Composition:** 0.9250 Silver .8095 oz. ASW

Date	Mintage	F	VF	XF	Unc	BU
1974 Proof	18,000	Value: 15.00				

KM# 45 DOLLAR Composition: Copper-Nickel **Subject:** New Zealand Day **Reverse:** Great Egret

Date	Mintage	F	VF	XF	Unc	BU
1974	50,000	—	—	3.00	10.00	—
1974 Proof	5,000	Value: 65.00				

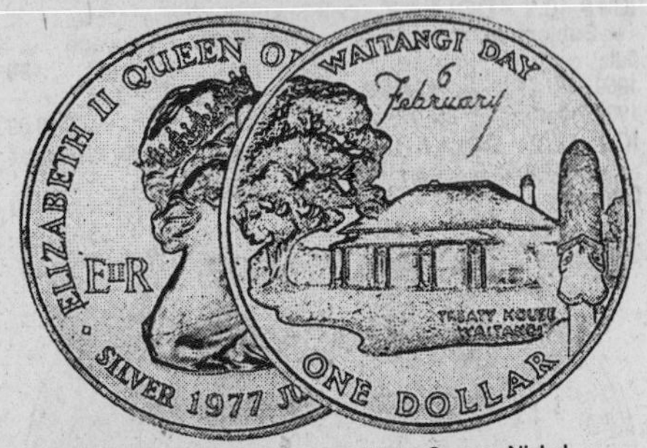

KM# 46 DOLLAR Composition: Copper-Nickel **Subject:** Waitangi Day **Reverse:** Treaty House

Date	Mintage	F	VF	XF	Unc	BU
1977	90,000	—	—	1.50	3.00	—

KM# 46a DOLLAR Weight: 27.2160 g. **Composition:** 0.9250 Silver .8095 oz. ASW

Date	Mintage	F	VF	XF	Unc	BU
1977 Proof	27,000	Value: 10.00				

KM# 50 DOLLAR Composition: Copper-Nickel **Subject:** Royal Visit **Reverse:** English Oak and N.Z. Kauri

Date	Mintage	F	VF	XF	Unc	BU
1981	100,000	—	—	0.75	2.00	—

KM# 50a DOLLAR Weight: 27.2160 g. **Composition:** 0.9250 Silver .8095 oz. ASW

Date	Mintage	F	VF	XF	Unc	BU
1981 Proof	38,000	Value: 8.50				

KM# 54 DOLLAR Composition: Copper-Nickel **Subject:** Chatham Island Black Robin

Date	Mintage	F	VF	XF	Unc	BU
1984	65,000	—	—	2.00	8.50	—

KM# 54a DOLLAR Weight: 27.2160 g. **Composition:** 0.9250 Silver .8095 oz. ASW

Date	Mintage	F	VF	XF	Unc	BU
1984 Proof	30,000	Value: 15.00				

KM# 47 DOLLAR Composition: Copper-Nickel **Subject:** 25th Anniversary of Coronation **Reverse:** Parliament

Date	Mintage	F	VF	XF	Unc	BU
1978	123,000	—	—	0.75	1.75	—

KM# 47a DOLLAR Weight: 27.2160 g. **Composition:** 0.9250 Silver .8095 oz. ASW

Date	Mintage	F	VF	XF	Unc	BU
1978 Proof	33,000	Value: 7.50				

KM# 51 DOLLAR Composition: Copper-Nickel **Reverse:** Takahe

Date	Mintage	F	VF	XF	Unc	BU
1982	65,000	—	—	1.50	7.00	—

KM# 51a DOLLAR Weight: 27.2160 g. **Composition:** 0.9250 Silver .8095 oz. ASW

Date	Mintage	F	VF	XF	Unc	BU
1982 Proof	35,000	Value: 15.00				

KM# 55 DOLLAR Composition: Copper-Nickel **Subject:** Black Stilt **Obverse:** Similar to KM#38.1

Date	Mintage	F	VF	XF	Unc	BU
1985	60,000	—	—	1.00	3.50	—

KM# 55a DOLLAR Weight: 27.2160 g. **Composition:** 0.9250 Silver .8095 oz. ASW

Date	Mintage	F	VF	XF	Unc	BU
1985 Proof	25,000	Value: 13.50				

KM# 48 DOLLAR Composition: Copper-Nickel

Date	Mintage	F	VF	XF	Unc	BU
1979	110,000	—	—	0.75	1.75	—

KM# 48a DOLLAR Weight: 27.2160 g. **Composition:** 0.9250 Silver .8095 oz. ASW

Date	Mintage	F	VF	XF	Unc	BU
1979 Proof	35,000	Value: 10.00				

KM# 52 DOLLAR Composition: Copper-Nickel **Subject:** Royal Visit

Date	Mintage	F	VF	XF	Unc	BU
1983	40,000	—	—	0.75	2.00	—

KM# 52a DOLLAR Weight: 27.2160 g. **Composition:** 0.9250 Silver .8095 oz. ASW

Date	Mintage	F	VF	XF	Unc	BU
1983 Proof	17,000	Value: 16.00				

KM# 56 DOLLAR Composition: Copper-Nickel **Subject:** Royal Visit

Date	Mintage	F	VF	XF	Unc	BU
1986	40,000	—	—	1.00	2.50	—

KM# 56a DOLLAR Weight: 27.2160 g. **Composition:** 0.9250 Silver .8095 oz. ASW

Date	Mintage	F	VF	XF	Unc	BU
1986 Proof	13,000	Value: 12.50				

KM# 49 DOLLAR Composition: Copper-Nickel **Reverse:** Fantail

Date	Mintage	F	VF	XF	Unc	BU
1980	112,000	—	—	1.25	6.00	—

KM# 49a DOLLAR Weight: 27.2160 g. **Composition:** 0.9250 Silver .8095 oz. ASW

Date	Mintage	F	VF	XF	Unc	BU
1980 Proof	37,000	Value: 14.00				

KM# 53 DOLLAR Composition: Copper-Nickel **Subject:** 50 Years of New Zealand Coinage

Date	Mintage	F	VF	XF	Unc	BU
1983	65,000	—	—	1.25	4.00	—

KM# 53a DOLLAR Weight: 27.2160 g. **Composition:** 0.9250 Silver .8095 oz. ASW

Date	Mintage	F	VF	XF	Unc	BU
1983 Proof	35,000	Value: 10.00				

KM# 57 DOLLAR Composition: Copper-Nickel **Reverse:** Kakapo

Date	Mintage	F	VF	XF	Unc	BU
1986	53,000	—	—	2.00	6.00	—

KM# 57a DOLLAR Weight: 27.2160 g. **Composition:** 0.9250 Silver .8095 oz. ASW

Date	Mintage	F	VF	XF	Unc	BU
1986 Proof	21,000	Value: 15.50				

KM# 65 DOLLAR **Composition:** Copper-Nickel **Subject:** National Parks Centennial

Date	Mintage	F	VF	XF	Unc	BU
1987	53,000	—	—	1.00	2.50	—

KM# 65a DOLLAR **Weight:** 27.2160 g. **Composition:** 0.9250 Silver .8095 oz. ASW

Date	Mintage	F	VF	XF	Unc	BU
1987 Proof	21,000	Value: 12.50				

KM# 66 DOLLAR **Composition:** Copper-Nickel **Reverse:** Yellow-eyed Penguin

Date	F	VF	XF	Unc	BU
1988	—	—	2.50	10.00	—

KM# 66a DOLLAR **Weight:** 27.2160 g. **Composition:** 0.9250 Silver .8095 oz. ASW

Date	Mintage	F	VF	XF	Unc	BU
1988 Proof	Est. 19,000	Value: 40.00				

KM# 67 DOLLAR **Composition:** Copper-Nickel **Subject:** XIV Commonwealth Games **Obverse:** Similar to KM#66 **Reverse:** Runner

Date	Mintage	F	VF	XF	Unc	BU
1989	140,000	—	—	1.25	3.00	—

KM# 67a DOLLAR **Weight:** 27.2160 g. **Composition:** 0.9250 Silver .8095 oz. ASW

Date	Mintage	F	VF	XF	Unc	BU
1989 Proof	80,000	Value: 15.00				

KM# 68 DOLLAR **Composition:** Copper-Nickel **Subject:** XIV Commonwealth Games **Obverse:** Similar to KM#66 **Reverse:** Gymnast

Date	Mintage	F	VF	XF	Unc	BU
1989	140,000	—	—	1.25	3.00	—

KM# 68a DOLLAR **Weight:** 27.2160 g. **Composition:** 0.9250 Silver .8095 oz. ASW

Date	Mintage	F	VF	XF	Unc	BU
1989 Proof	80,000	Value: 15.00				

KM# 69 DOLLAR **Composition:** Copper-Nickel **Subject:** XIV Commonwealth Games **Obverse:** Similar to KM#66 **Reverse:** Swimmer

Date	Mintage	F	VF	XF	Unc	BU
1989	140,000	—	—	1.25	3.00	—

KM# 69a DOLLAR **Weight:** 27.2160 g. **Composition:** 0.9250 Silver .8095 oz. ASW

Date	Mintage	F	VF	XF	Unc	BU
1989 Proof	80,000	Value: 15.00				

KM# 70 DOLLAR **Composition:** Copper-Nickel **Subject:** XIV Commonwealth Games **Obverse:** Similar to KM#66 **Reverse:** Weightlifter

Date	Mintage	F	VF	XF	Unc	BU
1989	140,000	—	—	1.25	3.00	—

KM# 70a DOLLAR **Weight:** 27.2160 g. **Composition:** 0.9250 Silver .8095 oz. ASW

Date	Mintage	F	VF	XF	Unc	BU
1989 Proof	80,000	Value: 15.00				

KM# 76 DOLLAR **Composition:** Copper-Nickel **Subject:** 1990 Anniversary Celebrations - Treaty of Waitangi

Date	Mintage	F	VF	XF	Unc	BU
1990	50,000	—	—	1.25	3.00	—

KM# 76a DOLLAR **Weight:** 27.2160 g. **Composition:** 0.9250 Silver .8095 oz. ASW

Date	Mintage	F	VF	XF	Unc	BU
1990 Proof	14,000	Value: 22.50				

KM# 78 DOLLAR **Composition:** Aluminum-Bronze **Reverse:** Kiwi Bird

Date	Mintage	F	VF	XF	Unc	BU
1990(l)	—	—	—	—	1.00	—
1990(l) Proof	18,000	Value: 2.25				
1990(c)	—	—	—	—	4.00	—
1991(l)	—	—	—	—	1.00	—
1991(c)	—	—	—	—	2.25	—
1991(c) Proof	15,000	Value: 4.00				
1992(l)	—	—	—	—	2.25	—
1992(l) Proof	9,000	Value: 4.00				
1993(l)	—	—	—	—	2.25	—
1993(l) Proof	10,000	Value: 4.00				
1994(l)	—	—	—	—	2.50	—
1994(l) Proof	10,000	Value: 4.00				
1995(l)	—	—	—	—	2.50	—
1995(l) Proof	Est. 4,000	Value: 4.00				
1996(l)	—	—	—	—	1.50	—
1997(l)	—	—	—	—	1.50	—
1997(l) Proof	—	Value: 4.00				
1998(l)	—	—	—	—	1.50	—
1998(l) Proof	Est. 2,000	Value: 4.00				

KM# 78a DOLLAR **Weight:** 8.0000 g. **Composition:** 0.9250 Silver .2380 oz. ASW

Date	Mintage	F	VF	XF	Unc	BU
1990 Proof	10,000	Value: 20.00				

KM# 120 DOLLAR **Composition:** Aluminum-Bronze **Obverse:** Rank-Broadley portrait of Queen Elizabeth II **Reverse:** Similar to KM#78

Date	Mintage	F	VF	XF	Unc	BU
1999	—	—	—	—	1.75	2.00
1999 Proof	Est. 2,000	Value: 5.00				
2000(o)	—	—	—	—	1.75	2.00
2000 Proof	—	Value: 5.00				
2002(l)	—	—	—	—	1.75	2.00

KM# 79 2 DOLLARS **Composition:** Aluminum-Bronze **Reverse:** Great Egret

Date	Mintage	F	VF	XF	Unc	BU
1990(l)	—	—	—	—	2.00	—
1990(c)	—	—	—	—	2.50	—
1990(l) Proof	10,000	Value: 4.00				
1991(l)	—	—	—	—	2.00	—
1991(c)	—	—	—	—	2.50	—
1991(c) Proof	15,000	Value: 6.00				
1992(l)	—	—	—	—	2.50	—
1992(l) Proof	9,000	Value: 7.50				
1994(l)	—	—	—	—	2.50	—
1994(l) Proof	10,000	Value: 7.50				
1995(l)	—	—	—	—	3.00	—
1995(l) Proof	Est. 4,000	Value: 7.00				
1996(l)	—	—	—	—	2.50	—
1997(l) Proof	—	Value: 7.00				
1998(l)	—	—	—	—	2.50	—
1998(l) Proof	Est. 2,000	Value: 7.00				

KM# 79a 2 DOLLARS **Weight:** 10.0000 g. **Composition:** 0.9250 Silver .2974 oz. ASW

Date	Mintage	F	VF	XF	Unc	BU
1990 Proof	10,000	Value: 20.00				

KM# 87 2 DOLLARS **Composition:** Copper-Aluminum-Nickel **Reverse:** Sacred Kingfisher

Date	Mintage	F	VF	XF	Unc	BU
1993	40,000	—	—	—	7.50	—

KM# 87a 2 DOLLARS **Weight:** 10.0000 g. **Composition:** 0.9250 Silver .2974 oz. ASW

Date	Mintage	F	VF	XF	Unc	BU
1993 Proof	10,000	Value: 15.00				

KM# 121 2 DOLLARS **Composition:** Aluminum-Bronze **Obverse:** Rank-Broadley portrait of Queen Elizabeth II **Reverse:** Similar to KM#79

Date	Mintage	F	VF	XF	Unc	BU
1999	—	—	—	—	2.50	3.00
1999 Proof	Est. 2,000	Value: 7.50				
2000	—	—	—	—	2.50	3.00

Date	Mintage	F	VF	XF	Unc	BU
2000 Proof	—	Value: 7.50				
2001		—	—	—	2.50	3.00

KM# 71 5 DOLLARS **Composition:** Aluminum-Bronze **Reverse:** ANZAC Memorial

Date	Mintage	F	VF	XF	Unc	BU
1990 Proof	60,000	Value: 27.50				

KM# 80 5 DOLLARS **Composition:** Copper-Nickel **Subject:** Rugby World Cup

Date	Mintage	F	VF	XF	Unc	BU
1991	120,000	—	—	—	3.50	—

KM# 80a 5 DOLLARS **Weight:** 27.6000 g. **Composition:** 0.9250 Silver .8208 oz. ASW

Date	Mintage	F	VF	XF	Unc	BU
1991 Proof	Est. 15,000	Value: 15.00				

KM# 82 5 DOLLARS **Composition:** Copper-Nickel **Subject:** 25th Anniversary of Decimal Currency

Date	Mintage	F	VF	XF	Unc	BU
1992	19,000	—	—	—	6.50	—

KM# 82a 5 DOLLARS **Weight:** 27.2200 g. **Composition:** 0.9250 Silver .8096 oz. ASW

Date	Mintage	F	VF	XF	Unc	BU
1992 Proof	8,000	Value: 15.00				

KM# 83 5 DOLLARS **Composition:** Copper-Nickel **Subject:** Mythological Maori Hero - Kupe

Date	Mintage	F	VF	XF	Unc	BU
1992	40,000	—	—	—	3.50	—

KM# 84 5 DOLLARS **Composition:** Copper-Nickel **Subject:** Abel Tasman

Date	Mintage	F	VF	XF	Unc	BU
1992	40,000	—	—	—	3.50	—

KM# 85 5 DOLLARS **Composition:** Copper-Nickel **Subject:** Captain James Cook

Date	Mintage	F	VF	XF	Unc	BU
1992	40,000	—	—	—	3.50	—

KM# 86 5 DOLLARS **Composition:** Copper-Nickel **Subject:** Christopher Columbus

Date	Mintage	F	VF	XF	Unc	BU
1992	40,000	—	—	—	3.50	—

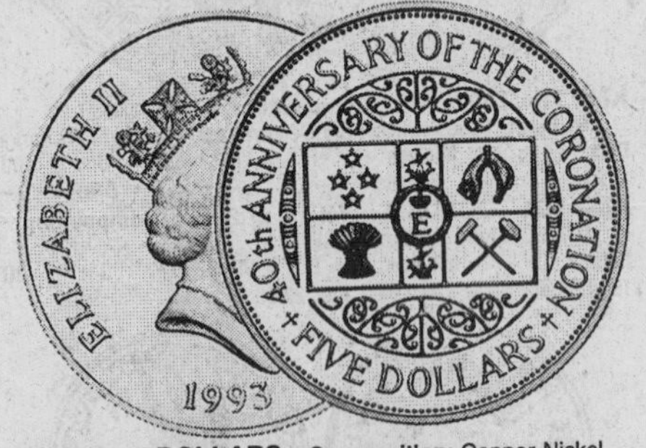

KM# 88 5 DOLLARS **Composition:** Copper-Nickel **Subject:** 40th Anniversary of Coronation

Date	Mintage	F	VF	XF	Unc	BU
1993	15,000	—	—	—	5.00	—

KM# 88a 5 DOLLARS **Weight:** 27.2200 g. **Composition:** 0.9250 Silver .8095 oz. ASW

Date	Mintage	F	VF	XF	Unc	BU
1993 Proof	Est. 15,000	Value: 20.00				

KM# 88b 5 DOLLARS **Weight:** 47.5250 g. **Composition:** 0.9170 Gold 1.4010 oz. AGW **Subject:** 40th Anniversary of Coronation

Date	Mintage	F	VF	XF	Unc	BU
1993 Proof	Est. 500	Value: 775				

KM# 89 5 DOLLARS **Weight:** 31.4700 g. **Composition:** 0.9250 Silver .9357 oz. ASW **Reverse:** Hooker Sea Lion **Size:** Endangered Wildlife mm.

Date	Mintage	F	VF	XF	Unc	BU
1993 Proof	18,000	Value: 40.00				

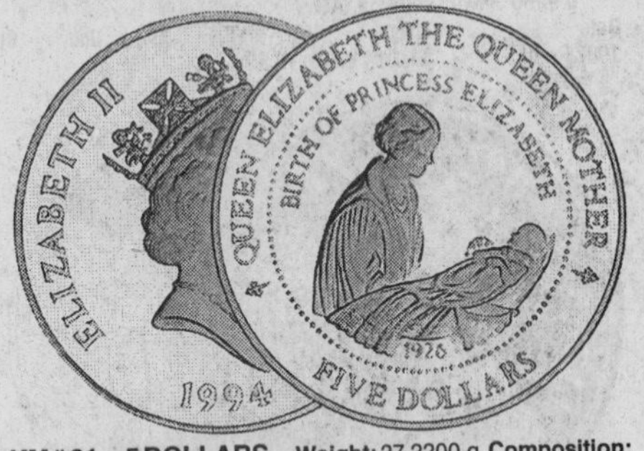

KM# 91 5 DOLLARS **Weight:** 27.2200 g. **Composition:** 0.9250 Silver .8096 oz. ASW **Reverse:** Queen Mother and Infant Elizabeth

Date	Mintage	F	VF	XF	Unc	BU
1994 Proof	Est. 35,000	Value: 25.00				

KM# 96 5 DOLLARS **Weight:** 27.2200 g. **Composition:** 0.9250 Silver **Series:** Winter Olympics - 1994 **Obverse:** Queen's portrait **Reverse:** Downhill skier

Date		F	VF	XF	Unc	BU
1994 Proof	—	Value: 20.00				

KM# 92 5 DOLLARS **Weight:** 27.2200 g. **Composition:** 0.9250 Silver **Subject:** Antarctica **Reverse:** James Clark Ross

Date	Mintage	F	VF	XF	Unc	BU
1995 Proof	Est. 12,000	Value: 28.50				

KM# 93 5 DOLLARS **Composition:** Copper-Nickel **Reverse:** Bird - Tui

Date	F	VF	XF	Unc	BU
1995	—	—	—	8.50	—

KM# 93a 5 DOLLARS **Weight:** 28.2800 g. **Composition:** 0.9250 Silver .8411 oz. ASW

Date	Mintage	F	VF	XF	Unc	BU
1995 Proof	Est. 7,000	Value: 25.00				

KM# 97 5 DOLLARS **Composition:** Copper-Nickel **Reverse:** Kaka (Bush Parrot)

Date	F	VF	XF	Unc	BU
1996	—	—	—	15.00	—

KM# 97a 5 DOLLARS **Weight:** 28.2800 g. **Composition:** 0.9250 Silver .8410 oz. ASW

Date	F	VF	XF	Unc	BU
1996 Proof	—	Value: 40.00			

KM# 99 5 DOLLARS **Composition:** Copper-Nickel **Subject:** Auckland City of Sails **Reverse:** Bridge, Boats

Date	F	VF	XF	Unc	BU
1996	—	—	—	12.50	—

KM# 99a 5 DOLLARS **Weight:** 28.2800 g. **Composition:** 0.9250 Silver .8410 oz. ASW

Date	Mintage	F	VF	XF	Unc	BU
1996 Proof	Est. 3,000	Value: 32.50				

KM# 101 5 DOLLARS **Weight:** 28.4500 g. **Composition:** 0.9250 Silver .8461 oz. ASW **Obverse:** Queen Elizabeth II

Date	F	VF	XF	Unc	BU
1996	—	—	—	50.00	—

Note: In sets only with $20 commemorative banknote.

KM# 102 5 DOLLARS **Weight:** 25.2200 g. **Composition:** 0.9250 Silver .8096 oz. ASW **Subject:** De Heemskerck **Obverse:** Queen Elizabeth II **Reverse:** Sail ship on globe with map

Date	Mintage	F	VF	XF	Unc	BU
1996 Proof	Est. 18,000	Value: 45.00				

KM# 103 5 DOLLARS **Composition:** Copper-Nickel **Subject:** WWF Conserving Nature **Obverse:** Queen Elizabeth II **Reverse:** Saddleback

Date	F	VF	XF	Unc	BU
1997	—	—	—	8.00	—

KM# 103a 5 DOLLARS **Weight:** 28.2800 g. **Composition:** 0.9250 Silver .8411 oz. ASW

Date	F	VF	XF	Unc	BU
1997 Proof	—	Value: 25.00			

KM# 105 5 DOLLARS **Composition:** Copper-Nickel **Subject:** Queen's Golden Wedding Anniversary **Obverse:** Queen Elizabeth II

Date	F	VF	XF	Unc	BU
1997	—	—	—	10.00	—

KM# 106 5 DOLLARS **Subject:** City of Christchurch **Obverse:** Queen Elizabeth II **Reverse:** Cathedral

Date	F	VF	XF	Unc	BU
1997	—	—	—	10.00	—

KM# 106a 5 DOLLARS **Weight:** 28.2800 g. **Composition:** 0.9250 Silver .8410 oz. ASW

Date	Mintage	F	VF	XF	Unc	BU
1997	Est. 3,000	Value: 45.00				

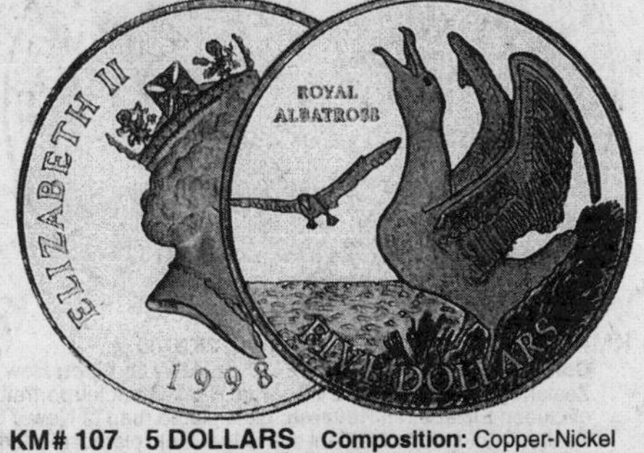

KM# 107 5 DOLLARS **Composition:** Copper-Nickel **Obverse:** Queen Elizabeth II **Reverse:** Royal Albatross

Date	F	VF	XF	Unc	BU
1998	—	—	—	12.00	—

KM# 107a 5 DOLLARS **Weight:** 29.2000 g. **Composition:** 0.9250 Silver .8684 oz. ASW

Date	Mintage	F	VF	XF	Unc	BU
1998 Proof	Est. 4,000	Value: 65.00				

KM# 109 5 DOLLARS **Composition:** Copper-Nickel **Subject:** Pride in New Zealand **Obverse:** Queen Elizabeth II **Reverse:** Four stars

Date	Mintage	F	VF	XF	Unc	BU
1998 In mint sets only	2,000	—	—	—	10.00	—

KM# 109a 5 DOLLARS **Weight:** 6.0000 g. **Composition:** 0.9990 Silver .1927 oz. ASW

Date	Mintage	F	VF	XF	Unc	BU
1998 In proof sets only	1,200	—	—	—	15.00	—

KM# 110 5 DOLLARS **Composition:** Copper-Nickel **Subject:** Pride in New Zealand **Obverse:** Queen Elizabeth II **Reverse:** Fleece

Date	Mintage	F	VF	XF	Unc	BU
1998 In mint sets only	2,000	—	—	—	10.00	—

KM# 110a 5 DOLLARS **Weight:** 6.0000 g. **Composition:** 0.9990 Silver .1927 oz. ASW

Date	Mintage	F	VF	XF	Unc	BU
1998 In proof sets only	1,200	—	—	—	15.00	—

KM# 111 5 DOLLARS **Composition:** Copper-Nickel **Subject:** Pride in New Zealand **Obverse:** Queen Elizabeth II **Reverse:** Wheat sheaf

Date	Mintage	F	VF	XF	Unc	BU
1998 In mint sets only	2,000	—	—	—	10.00	—

KM# 111a 5 DOLLARS **Weight:** 6.0000 g. **Composition:** 0.9990 Silver .1927 oz. ASW

Date	Mintage	F	VF	XF	Unc	BU
1998 In proof sets only	1,200	—	—	—	15.00	—

KM# 112 5 DOLLARS **Composition:** Copper-Nickel **Subject:** Pride in New Zealand **Obverse:** Queen Elizabeth II **Reverse:** Crossed hammers

Date	Mintage	F	VF	XF	Unc	BU
1998 In mint sets only	2,000	—	—	—	10.00	—

KM# 112a 5 DOLLARS **Weight:** 6.0000 g. **Composition:** 0.9990 Silver .1927 oz. ASW

Date	Mintage	F	VF	XF	Unc	BU
1998 In proof sets only	1,200	—	—	—	15.00	—

KM# 113 5 DOLLARS **Composition:** Copper-Nickel **Subject:** Dunedin **Obverse:** Queen Elizabeth II **Reverse:** Larnach Castle

Date	Mintage	F	VF	XF	Unc	BU
1998	4,000	—	—	—	10.00	—

KM# 113a 5 DOLLARS **Weight:** 28.2800 g. **Composition:** 0.9250 Silver .8684 oz. ASW

Date	Mintage	F	VF	XF	Unc	BU
1998 Proof	2,500	Value: 30.00				

KM# 115 5 DOLLARS **Composition:** Copper-Nickel **Obverse:** Rank-Broadley portrait of Queen Elizabeth II **Reverse:** Morepork owl

Date	F	VF	XF	Unc	BU
1999	—	—	—	12.00	—

KM# 115a 5 DOLLARS **Weight:** 28.2800 g. **Composition:** 0.9990 Silver .9083 oz. ASW

Date	Mintage	F	VF	XF	Unc	BU
1999 Proof	Est. 7,000	Value: 35.00				

KM# 123 5 DOLLARS **Weight:** 31.0500 g. **Composition:** 0.9250 Silver .9234 oz. ASW **Subject:** Wellington Harbour Capital **Obverse:** Queen's head right **Reverse:** City view with ship **Edge:** Reeded **Size:** 38.7 mm.

Date	F	VF	XF	Unc	BU
1999 Proof	—	Value: 30.00			

KM# 125 5 DOLLARS **Weight:** 32.2000 g. **Composition:** Copper-Nickel **Obverse:** Queen's head right **Reverse:** Perching cormorant **Edge:** Reeded **Size:** 38.6 mm. **Note:** Struck at Valcombi.

Date	Mintage	F	VF	XF	Unc	BU
2000 Frosted finish	5,500	—	—	—	12.00	—

KM# 125a 5 DOLLARS **Weight:** 31.1300 g. **Composition:** 0.9990 Silver .9998 oz. ASW **Note:** Heavier than the official weight of 28.28 grams.

Date	Mintage	F	VF	XF	Unc	BU
2000 Proof	5,000	Value: 35.00				

KM# 128 5 DOLLARS **Weight:** 28.2800 g. **Composition:** Copper-Nickel **Subject:** Kereru Bird **Obverse:** Queen's portrait **Reverse:** Pigeon on branch **Edge:** Reeded **Size:** 38.6 mm.

Date	Mintage	F	VF	XF	Unc	BU
2001	7,500	—	—	—	12.50	—

KM# 128a 5 DOLLARS **Weight:** 28.2800 g. **Composition:** 0.9990 Silver .9083 oz. ASW

Date	Mintage	F	VF	XF	Unc	BU
2001 Proof	4,500	Value: 35.00				

KM# 131 5 DOLLARS **Weight:** 28.2800 g. **Composition:** Copper-Nickel **Subject:** Architectural Heritage **Obverse:** Bust of Queen Elizabeth II right. **Reverse:** Auckland Sky Tower. **Edge:** Reeded. **Size:** 38.6 mm.

Date	Mintage	F	VF	XF	Unc	BU
2002	3,000	—	—	—	12.50	—

Note: 500 of which are issued in Numismatic-Philatelic covers.

KM# 131a 5 DOLLARS **Weight:** 28.2800 g. **Composition:** 0.9250 Silver 0.841 oz. ASW **Subject:** Architectural Heritage **Obverse:** Bust of Queen Elizabeth II right. **Reverse:** Auckland Sky Tower. **Edge:** Reeded. **Size:** 38.6 mm.

Date	Mintage	F	VF	XF	Unc	BU
2002	2,000	Value: 37.50				

Note: 500 of which are issued in Numismatic-Philatelic covers.

KM# 94 10 DOLLARS **Composition:** Aluminum-Bronze **Reverse:** Gold Prospector

Date	Mintage	F	VF	XF	Unc	BU
1995	5,400	—	—	—	15.00	—

KM# 94a 10 DOLLARS **Composition:** Gold .5000 oz. AGW

Date	Mintage	F	VF	XF	Unc	BU
1995 Proof	600	Value: 325				

KM# 98 10 DOLLARS **Subject:** Sinking of General Grant

Date	Mintage	F	VF	XF	Unc	BU
1996 Prooflike	6,000	—	—	—	—	15.00

KM# 98a 10 DOLLARS **Composition:** Gold .5000 oz. AGW

Date	Mintage	F	VF	XF	Unc	BU
1996 Proof	650	Value: 350				

KM# 104 10 DOLLARS **Composition:** Aluminum-Bronze **Subject:** Gabriel's Gully **Obverse:** Queen Elizabeth II **Reverse:** Prospector

Date	F	VF	XF	Unc	BU
1997	—	—	—	17.50	—

KM# 104a 10 DOLLARS **Composition:** Gold .5000 oz. AGW

Date	F	VF	XF	Unc	BU
1997 Proof	—	Value: 325			

KM# 114 10 DOLLARS **Composition:** Aluminum-Bronze **Subject:** Century of Motoring **Obverse:** Queen Elizabeth II **Reverse:** Karl Benz driving his automobile

Date	Mintage	F	VF	XF	Unc	BU
1998	2,000	—	—	—	15.00	—

KM# 114a 10 DOLLARS **Composition:** Gold Plated Aluminum-Bronze

Date	Mintage	F	VF	XF	Unc	BU
1998 Proof	1,500	Value: 45.00				

KM# 124 10 DOLLARS **Weight:** 15.4500 g. **Composition:** 0.9990 Silver .4962 oz. ASW **Obverse:** Queen's head right **Reverse:** Kiwi bird **Edge:** Reeded **Size:** 29.9 mm.

Date	F	VF	XF	Unc	BU
1998	—	—	—	17.50	—

KM# 122 10 DOLLARS **Weight:** 28.3700 g. **Composition:** 0.9250 Silver .8437 oz. ASW **Subject:** New Zealand - First to the Future **Obverse:** Rank-Broadley portrait of Queen Elizabeth II **Reverse:** Gold plated map of New Zealand, gold printed radiant sun **Edge:** Gold plated, reeded

Date	Mintage	F	VF	XF	Unc	BU
2000(1999) Proof	Est. 33,000	Value: 40.00				

KM# 129 10 DOLLARS **Weight:** 3.8879 g. **Composition:** 0.9990 Gold .1250 oz. AGW **Obverse:** Queen's portrait **Reverse:** Salvage ship "Claymore" **Edge:** Reeded **Size:** 18 mm.

Date	Mintage	F	VF	XF	Unc	BU
2001 Proof	600	Value: 102				

KM# 130 10 DOLLARS **Weight:** 7.7759 g. **Composition:** 0.9990 Gold .2500 oz. AGW **Obverse:** Queen's portrait **Reverse:** R.M.S. "Niagara" **Edge:** Reeded **Size:** 22 mm.

Date	Mintage	F	VF	XF	Unc	BU
2001 Proof	600	Value: 205				

KM# 100 20 DOLLARS **Weight:** 31.1030 g. **Composition:** 0.9250 Silver .9250 oz. ASW **Subject:** Salute to Bravery **Obverse:** Queen Elizabeth II **Reverse:** Charles H Upham

Date	Mintage	F	VF	XF	Unc	BU
1995 Proof	3,500	Value: 40.00				

KM# 108 20 DOLLARS **Weight:** 28.2800 g. **Composition:** 0.9250 Silver .8410 oz. ASW **Subject:** Queen's Golden Wedding Anniversary **Note:** Similar to 5 Dollars, KM#105.

Date	Mintage	F	VF	XF	Unc	BU
1997 Proof	Est. 2,000	Value: 40.00				

KM# 77 150 DOLLARS **Weight:** 16.9500 g. **Composition:** 0.9170 Gold .4996 oz. AGW **Reverse:** Kiwi

Date	Mintage	F	VF	XF	Unc	BU
1990 Proof	10,000	Value: 250				

KM# 126 150 DOLLARS **Weight:** 15.6000 g. **Composition:** 0.9950 Platinum .4990 oz. APW **Obverse:** Queen's portrait. **Reverse:** Two Kiwi and fern. **Edge:** Reeded. **Size:** 30 mm.

Date	F	VF	XF	Unc	BU
1998 Proof	—	Value: 400			

PATTERNS

Including off metal strikes

KM#	Date	Mintage	Identification	Mkt Va
Pn2	1933	—	3 Pence. Silver.	—
Pn3	1933	—	Shilling. Silver.	20,000
Pn4	1935	—	Crown. Silver.	50,000

PIEFORTS

KM#	Date	Mintage	Identification	Mkt Va
P1	1992	3,300	Dollar. 0.9250 Silver. KM78.	100
P2	1995	2,500	20 Cents. Silver. KM81	95.00

MINT SETS

KM#	Date	Mintage	Identification	Issue Price	Mkt Val
MS1	1965 (7)	100,000	KM23.2-29.2, pink label, flat pack	2.00	3.00
MSA1	1965 (7)	75,000	KM23.2-29.2, green label, flat pack	2.50	10.00
MS2	1967 (7)	250,000	KM31-32, 34-37, 38.1	4.50	2.00

KM#	Date	Mintage	Identification	Issue Price	Mkt Val
MS4	1968 (6)	35,000	KM31-32, 34-37	2.15	3.00
MS5	1969 (7)	50,000	KM31-32, 34-36, 39-40	3.25	5.00
MS7	1970 (7)	30,000	KM31-32, 34, 36-37, 41-42	3.50	5.00
MS10	1971 (7)	15,000	KM31-32, 36-37, 38.2, 41	3.50	10.00
MS12	1972 (7)	15,000	KM31-32, 34, 36-37, 38.2, 41	3.50	5.00
MS14	1973 (7)	15,000	KM31-32, 34, 36-37, 38.2, 41	3.50	7.00
MS17	1974 (7)	15,000	KM31-32, 34, 36-37, 41, 44	4.35	8.00
MS20	1975 (7)	15,000	KM31-32, 34, 36-37, 38.2, 41	4.50	5.00
MS22	1976 (7)	16,000	KM31-32, 34, 36-37, 38.2, 41	4.75	7.50
MS23	1977 (7)	20,000	KM31-32, 34, 36-37, 41, 46	4.75	7.00
MS24	1978 (7)	23,000	KM31-32, 34, 36-37, 41, 47	5.25	4.00
MS25	1979 (7)	25,000	KM31-32, 34, 36-37, 41, 48	5.50	4.00
MS26	1980 (7)	27,000	KM31-32, 34, 36-37, 41, 49	5.75	6.00
MS27	1981 (7)	25,000	KM31-32, 34, 36-37, 41, 50	5.75	4.00
MS28	1982 (7)	25,000	KM31-32, 34, 36-37, 41, 51	6.00	4.00
MS29	1983 (7)	25,000	KM31-32, 34, 36-37, 41, 53	6.25	4.00
MS30	1984 (7)	25,000	KM31-32, 34, 36-37, 41, 54	4.75	6.50
MS31	1985 (7)	20,000	KM31-32, 34, 36-37, 41, 55	4.00	8.00
MS32	1986	18,000	KM57-63	5.00	7.00
MS33	1987 (7)	18,000	KM58-63, 65	7.50	7.00
MS34	1988 (7)	15,000	KM58-63, 66	8.00	15.00
MS35	1989 (5)	10	KM60-63, 67	14,600	11.00
MS37	1990 (5)	10,000	KM72-76	11.00	25.00
MS36	1990 (6)	18,000	KM60-61, 63, 78-79, 81	13.00	12.50
MS38	1991 (7)	20,000	KM60-61, 63, 78-81	16.00	12.50
MS39	1992 (4)	15,000	KM60-61, 63, 78-79, 81-82	15.00	12.50
MS40	1992 (4)	24,000	KM83-86	—	12.50
MS41	1993 (6)	15,000	KM60-61, 63, 78, 81, 87	—	10.00
MS42	1994 (6)	16,000	KM60-61, 78-79,81,90	20.00	10.00
MS43	1995 (7)	6,000	KM60-61, 63, 78-79, 81, 93	17.00	12.50
MS44	1996 (7)	—	KM60-61, 63, 78-79, 81, 97	17.00	16.00
MS45	1997 (7)	—	KM60-63, 78-79, 81, 103	—	15.00
MS46	1998	4,000	KM60-61, 63, 78-79, 81, 107	15.00	18.00
MS47	1998 (4)	2,000	KM109-112	—	50.00
MS48	1999 (7)	5,000	KM115-121	20.00	18.00
MS49	2000 (7)	3,000	KM116-121, 127	18.00	18.00

PROOF SETS

KM#	Date	Mintage	Identification	Issue Price	Mkt Val
PS1	1933 (5)	20	KM1-5	—	2,850
PS2	1934 (5)	20	KM1-5	—	9,000
PS3	1935 (6)	364	KM1-6	—	4,650
PS4	1937 (5)	200	KM7-11	—	2,700
PS5	1947 (5)	20	KM7a-11a	—	2,150
PSA6	1950 (7)	—	KM15-21	—	2,100
PS6	1953 (8)	7,000	KM23-30	—	75.00
PS7	1953 (8)	—	KM23-30, Matte Proof	—	1,350
PS10	1965 (7)	10	KM23.2-29.2	—	—
PS11	1967 (7)	10	KM31-32,34-38	—	—
PS12	1971 (7)	5,000	KM31-32, 34, 36-37, 38.2, 41	15.00	70.00
PS13	1972 (7)	8,000	KM31-32, 34, 36-37, 38.2, 41	16.00	15.00
PS14	1973 (7)	8,000	KM31-32, 34, 36-37, 38.2, 41	16.00	12.50
PS15	1974 (7)	8,000	KM31-32, 34, 36-37, 41, 44a	14.00	20.00
PS16	1975 (7)	10,000	KM31-32, 34, 36-37, 38.2, 41	18.50	7.00
PS17	1976 (7)	11,000	KM31-32, 34, 36-37, 38.2, 41	19.00	7.00
PS18	1977 (7)	12,000	KM31-32, 34, 36-37, 41, 46a	19.50	12.50
PS19	1977 (7)	10	KM31-32, 34, 36-37, 41, 46a, Official card	—	—
PS20	1978 (7)	15,000	KM31-32, 34, 36-37, 41, 47a	23.50	12.50
PS21	1979 (7)	16,000	KM31-32, 34, 36-37, 41, 48a	25.50	10.00
PS22	1980 (7)	17,000	KM31-32, 34, 36-37, 41, 49a	42.00	12.50
PS23	1981 (7)	18,000	KM31-32, 34, 36-37, 41, 50a	37.00	10.00
PS24	1982 (7)	18,000	KM31-32, 34, 36-37, 41, 51a	33.00	12.50
PS25	1983 (7)	18,000	KM31-32, 34, 36-37, 41, 53a	40.00	14.00
PS26	1984 (7)	15,000	KM31-32, 34, 36-37, 41, 54a	28.00	15.00
PS27	1985 (7)	11,500	KM31-32, 34, 36-37, 41, 55a	27.00	15.00
PS28	1986 (7)	10,000	KM57a, 58-63	30.00	20.00
PS29	1987 (7)	10,000	KM58-63, 65a	38.00	20.00
PS30	1988 (7)	9,000	KM58-63, 66a	43.00	35.00
PS31	1989 (5)	8,500	KM60-63, 67a	44.50	30.00
PS32	1989 (4)	8,600	KM67a-70a	132	55.00
PS33	1990 (6)	10,000	KM60-61, 63, 78a-79a, 81	52.00	60.00
PS34	1990 (5)	7,000	KM72a-76a	110	80.00
PS35	1991 (7)	12,000	KM60-61, 63, 78-79, 80a, 81	61.00	30.00
PS36	1992 (7)	9,000	KM60-61, 63, 78-79, 81, 82a	58.00	37.50
PS37	1993 (6)	10,000	KM60-61, 63, 78, 81, 87a	75.00	37.50
PS38	1994 (6)	10,000	KM60-61, 78-79, 81, 90a	45.00	30.00
PS39	1995 (7)	4,000	KM60-61, 63, 78-79, 81, 93a	57.50	35.00
PS40	1997 (7)	—	KM60-63, 78-79, 81, 103a	—	35.00
PS41	1998 (7)	2,000	KM60-61, 63, 78-79, 81, 107a	55.00	85.00
PS42	1998 (4)	1,200	KM109a-112a	—	75.00
PS43	1999 (7)	2,000	KM115a, 116-121	59.00	70.00
PS44	2000 (7)	1,500	KM116-121, 125a	54.00	55.00

PROOF-LIKE SETS (PL)

KM#	Date	Mintage	Identification	Issue Price	Mkt Val
PLS1	1965 (7)	25,000	KM23.2-29.2 flat pack	—	7.00
PLS2	1965 (7)	400	KM23.2-29.2 red plush case; reported, not confirmed	—	—
PLS3	1967 (7)	49,500	KM31-32, 34-38 flat pack	10.00	3.00
PLS4	1967	500	KM31-32, 34-38 blue plush case	—	110
PLS5	1967 (7)	10	KM31-32, 34-38	—	—
PLS6	1968 (6)	40,000	KM31-32, 34-37 flat pack	7.00	2.50
PLS7	1968 (6)	I.A.	KM31-32, 34-37 blue plush case	—	7.50
PLS8	1969 (7)	50,000	KM31-32, 34-36, 39-40 flat packet	7.00	4.00
PLS9	1969 (7)	I.A.	KM31-32, 34-36, 39-40 blue plush case	—	10.00
PLS10	1970 (7)	20,000	KM31-32, 34, 36-37, 41-42, flat pack	7.00	7.00
PLS11	1970 (7)	I.A.	KM31-32, 34, 36-37, 41-42, blue plush case	—	12.50
PLS12	1970 (7)	10	KM31-32, 34, 36-37, 41-42, official card, red plush case	—	—

NICARAGUA

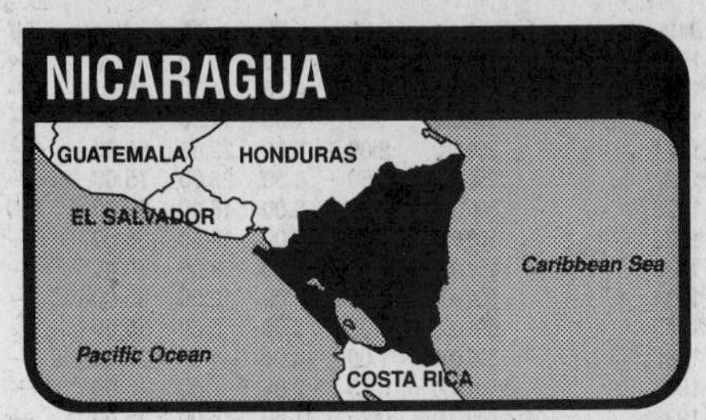

The Republic of Nicaragua, situated in Central America between Honduras and Costa Rica, has an area of 50,193 sq. mi. (129,494 sq. km.) and a population of *3.7 million. Capital: Managua. Agriculture, mining (gold and silver) and hardwood logging are the principal industries. Cotton, meat, coffee and sugar are exported.

Columbus sighted the coast of Nicaragua on Sept. 12,1502 during the course of his last voyage of discovery. It was first visited in 1522 by conquistadors from Panama, under the command of Gil Gonzalez. Francisco Hernandez de Cordoba established the first settlements in 1524 at Granada and Leon. Nicaragua was incorporated, for administrative purpose, in the Captaincy General of Guatemala, which included every Central American state but Panama. On September 15, 1821 the Captaincy General of Guatemala declared itself and all the Central American provinces independent of Spain. The next year Nicaragua united with the Mexican Empire of Augustin de Iturbide, only to join in 1823 the federation of the Central American Republic. Within Nicaragua rival cities or juntas such as Leon, Granada and El Viejo vied for power, wealth and influence, often attacking each other at will. To further prove their legitimacy as well as provide an acceptable circulating coinage in those turbulent times (1821-1825), provisional mints functioned intermittently at Granada, Leon and ElViejo. The early coinage reflected traditional but crude Spanish colonial cob-style designs. Nicaragua's first governor was Pedro Arias Davila, appointed on June 1, 1827. When the federation was dissolved, Nicaragua declared itself an independent republic on April 30, 1838.

Dissension between the Liberals and Conservatives of the contending cities kept Nicaragua in turmoil, which made it possible for William Walker to make himself President in 1855. The two major political parties finally united to drive him out and in 1857 he was expelled. A relative peace followed, but by1912, Nicaragua had requested the U.S. Marines to restore order, which began a U.S. involvement that lasted until the Good Neighbor Policy was adopted in 1933. Anastasio Somoza Garcia assumed the Presidency in 1936. This family dynasty dominated Nicaragua until its overthrow in 1979. Formal elections in 1990 renewed a democratic government in power.

MINT MARKS

H - Heaton, Birmingham
HF - Huguenin Freres, Le Locle, Switzerland
Mo - Mexico City
-Philadelphia, Pa.
-Sherritt Mint, Canada
-Waterbury, Ct.

MONETARY SYSTEM

100 Centavos = 1 Peso

REPUBLIC

DECIMAL COINAGE

KM# 10 1/2 CENTAVO Composition: Bronze

Date	Mintage	F	VF	XF	Unc	BU
1912H	900,000	1.00	2.50	15.00	40.00	—
1912H Proof	—	Value: 275				
1915H	320,000	1.50	4.00	30.00	100	—
1916H	720,000	1.50	4.00	30.00	100	—
1917	720,000	1.50	4.00	20.00	65.00	—
1922	400,000	2.00	5.00	20.00	80.00	—
1924	400,000	1.00	3.00	12.00	70.00	—
1934	500,000	1.00	3.00	10.00	45.00	—
1936	600,000	0.50	0.75	5.00	35.00	—
1937	1,000,000	0.40	0.60	4.00	20.00	—

KM# 11 CENTAVO Composition: Bronze

Date	Mintage	F	VF	XF	Unc	BU
1912H	450,000	1.00	3.00	10.00	45.00	—
1912H Proof	—	Value: 275				
1914H	300,000	5.00	10.00	30.00	85.00	—
1915H	500,000	5.00	10.00	35.00	100	—
1916H	450,000	5.00	10.00	35.00	100	—
1917	450,000	3.00	7.00	28.00	75.00	—

Date	Mintage	F	VF	XF	Unc	BU
1919	750,000	2.00	6.00	18.00	50.00	—
1920	700,000	1.00	4.50	14.50	45.00	—
1922	500,000	1.00	4.50	14.50	45.00	—
1924	300,000	2.00	6.00	22.00	65.00	—
1927	250,000	3.50	8.50	28.00	75.00	—
1928	500,000	2.00	6.00	18.00	45.00	—
1929	500,000	2.00	5.00	13.50	35.00	—
1930	250,000	3.00	8.00	25.00	70.00	—
1934	500,000	1.50	4.00	12.00	35.00	—
1935	500,000	1.00	3.00	8.00	25.00	—
1936	500,000	1.00	3.00	8.00	25.00	—
1937	1,000,000	0.75	2.00	7.00	20.00	—
1938	2,000,000	0.75	1.50	5.00	15.00	—
1940	2,000,000	0.75	1.50	5.00	15.00	—

KM# 20 CENTAVO **Composition:** Brass

Date	Mintage	F	VF	XF	Unc	BU
1943	1,000,000	0.50	1.50	4.50	18.00	—

KM# 12 5 CENTAVOS **Composition:** Copper-Nickel

Date	Mintage	F	VF	XF	Unc	BU
1912H	460,000	4.00	10.00	25.00	75.00	—
1912H Proof	—	Value: 300				
1914H	300,000	4.00	10.00	30.00	85.00	—
1915H	160,000	8.00	20.00	50.00	225	—
1919	100,000	4.00	10.00	30.00	110	—
1920	150,000	4.00	10.00	30.00	100	—
1927	100,000	4.00	10.00	30.00	100	—
1928	100,000	4.00	10.00	30.00	100	—
1929	100,000	—	—	—	—	—
1930	100,000	4.00	10.00	30.00	100	—
1934	200,000	3.00	10.00	25.00	90.00	—
1935	200,000	2.00	5.00	20.00	85.00	—
1936	300,000	1.50	3.00	15.00	65.00	—
1937	300,000	1.50	3.00	10.00	40.00	—
1938	800,000	1.00	2.00	8.00	30.00	—
1940	800,000	1.00	2.00	6.00	20.00	—

KM# 21 5 CENTAVOS **Composition:** Brass **Edge:** Plain

Date	Mintage	F	VF	XF	Unc	BU
1943	2,000,000	0.75	2.50	10.00	60.00	—

KM# 24.1 5 CENTAVOS **Composition:** Copper-Nickel **Edge Lettering:** B. N. N **Note:** Reduced size.

Date	Mintage	F	VF	XF	Unc	BU
1946	4,000,000	0.10	0.25	2.50	18.00	—
1946 Proof	—	Value: 200				
1950	—	0.10	0.25	2.50	18.00	—
1952	4,000,000	0.10	0.25	3.50	25.00	—
1952 Proof	—	Value: 250				
1954	4,000,000	0.10	0.15	0.25	5.00	—
1954 Proof	—	Value: 250				
1956	5,000,000	0.10	0.15	0.50	5.00	—
1956 Proof	—	Value: 250				

KM# 24.2 5 CENTAVOS **Composition:** Copper-Nickel **Edge Lettering:** B. C. N

Date	Mintage	F	VF	XF	Unc	BU
1962	3,000,000	—	0.10	0.15	2.00	—
1962 Proof	—	Value: 150				
1964	4,000,000	—	0.10	0.15	2.00	—
1965	10,000,000	—	0.10	0.15	2.00	—

KM# 24.2a 5 CENTAVOS **Composition:** Nickel Clad Steel

Date	Mintage	F	VF	XF	Unc	BU
1972	10,020,000	—	—	0.10	0.50	—

KM# 24.3 5 CENTAVOS **Composition:** Copper-Nickel **Edge:** Reeded

Date	Mintage	F	VF	XF	Unc	BU
1972 Proof	20,000	Value: 2.50				

KM# 27 5 CENTAVOS **Composition:** Aluminum

Date	Mintage	F	VF	XF	Unc	BU
1974	18,000,000	—	—	0.10	0.50	—

KM# 28 5 CENTAVOS **Composition:** Aluminum **Series:** F.A.O.

Date	Mintage	F	VF	XF	Unc	BU
1974	2,000,000	—	—	0.40	2.00	—

KM# 49 5 CENTAVOS **Composition:** Aluminum

Date	Mintage	F	VF	XF	Unc	BU
1981	5,000,000	—	—	0.40	1.50	—

KM# 55 5 CENTAVOS **Composition:** Aluminum

Date	Mintage	F	VF	XF	Unc	BU
1987	38,000,000	—	—	0.40	1.00	—

KM# 80 5 CENTAVOS **Composition:** Chromium Plated Steel

Date	Mintage	F	VF	XF	Unc	BU
1994	20,000,000	—	—	—	0.50	—

KM# 97 5 CENTAVOS **Weight:** 3.0000 g. **Composition:** Copper Plated Steel **Obverse:** National arms **Reverse:** Denomination **Edge:** Plain **Size:** 18.5 mm.

Date	F	VF	XF	Unc	BU
2002	—	—	—	0.25	—

KM# 13 10 CENTAVOS **Weight:** 2.5000 g. **Composition:** 0.8000 Silver .0643 oz. ASW **Note:** All dates struck with medal rotation except 1935, which appears only in coin rotation.

Date	Mintage	F	VF	XF	Unc	BU
1912H	230,000	2.00	7.00	25.00	100	—
1912H Proof	—	Value: 250				
1914H	220,000	3.00	10.00	35.00	115	—
1914H Proof	—	Value: 375				
1927	500,000	2.00	4.00	20.00	85.00	—
1928	1,000,000	1.00	3.00	15.00	65.00	—
1930	150,000	1.50	4.00	30.00	95.00	—
1935	250,000	1.00	3.00	12.50	45.00	—
1936	250,000	1.00	3.00	10.00	30.00	—

KM# 17.1 10 CENTAVOS **Composition:** Copper-Nickel **Edge Lettering:** B.N.N

Date	Mintage	F	VF	XF	Unc	BU
1939	2,500,000	1.00	3.00	8.00	25.00	—
1939 Proof	—	Value: 200				
1946	2,000,000	1.00	3.00	8.00	25.00	—
1946 Proof	—	Value: 200				
1950	2,000,000	0.25	0.50	3.00	20.00	—
1950 Proof	—	Value: 200				
1952	1,500,000	0.25	0.50	3.00	25.00	—
1952 Proof	—	Value: 200				
1954	3,000,000	0.10	0.25	1.50	10.00	—
1954 Proof	—	Value: 200				
1956	5,000,000	0.10	0.20	1.00	6.00	—
1956 Proof	—	Value: 200				

KM# 17.2 10 CENTAVOS **Composition:** Copper-Nickel **Edge Lettering:** B.C.N

Date	Mintage	F	VF	XF	Unc	BU
1962	4,000,000	—	0.10	0.15	5.00	—
1962 Proof	—	Value: 225				
1964	4,000,000	—	0.10	0.15	5.00	—
1965	12,000,000	—	0.10	0.15	1.00	—

KM# 17.2a (KM17.3a) 10 CENTAVOS **Composition:** Nickel Clad Steel

Date	Mintage	F	VF	XF	Unc	BU
1972	10,020,000	—	0.10	0.15	0.30	—
1972	10,020,000	—	0.10	0.15	0.30	—

KM# 17.3 10 CENTAVOS **Composition:** Copper-Nickel **Edge:** Reeded

Date	Mintage	F	VF	XF	Unc	BU
1972 Proof	20,000	Value: 2.50				

KM# 22 10 CENTAVOS **Composition:** Brass **Edge:** Reeded

Date	Mintage	F	VF	XF	Unc	BU
1943	2,000,000	0.50	1.00	5.00	50.00	—

KM# 29 10 CENTAVOS **Composition:** Aluminum **Series:** F.A.O.

Date	Mintage	F	VF	XF	Unc	BU
1974	2,000,000	—	—	0.10	1.00	—

KM# 30 10 CENTAVOS **Composition:** Aluminum

Date	Mintage	F	VF	XF	Unc	BU
1974	18,000,000	—	—	0.10	0.20	—

KM# 31 10 CENTAVOS **Composition:** Copper-Nickel

Date	Mintage	F	VF	XF	Unc	BU
1978	20,000,000	—	—	0.40	2.00	—

KM# 50 10 CENTAVOS **Composition:** Aluminum

Date	Mintage	F	VF	XF	Unc	BU
1981	10,000,000	—	—	0.15	1.00	—

KM# 56 10 CENTAVOS **Composition:** Aluminum

Date	Mintage	F	VF	XF	Unc	BU
1987	16,000,000	—	—	0.15	0.40	—

KM# 81 10 CENTAVOS **Composition:** Chromium Plated Steel

Date	Mintage	F	VF	XF	Unc	BU
1994	6,439,000	—	—	—	0.75	—

KM# 98 10 CENTAVOS **Weight:** 4.0000 g. **Composition:** Brass Plated Steel **Obverse:** National arms **Reverse:** Denomination **Edge:** Reeded and plain sections **Size:** 20.5 mm.

Date	F	VF	XF	Unc	BU
2002	—	—	—	0.40	—

KM# 14 25 CENTAVOS **Weight:** 6.2500 g. **Composition:** 0.8000 Silver .1607 oz. ASW

Date	Mintage	F	VF	XF	Unc	BU
1912H	320,000	3.00	10.00	35.00	90.00	—
1912H Proof	—	Value: 350				
1914H	100,000	5.00	15.00	50.00	170	—
1928	200,000	3.00	10.00	30.00	90.00	—
1929	20,000	8.00	35.00	90.00	275	—
1930	20,000	8.00	35.00	90.00	250	—
1936	100,000	2.00	8.00	20.00	65.00	—

KM# 18.1 25 CENTAVOS **Composition:** Copper-Nickel **Edge Lettering:** B. N. N

Date	Mintage	F	VF	XF	Unc	BU
1939	1,000,000	2.00	6.00	15.00	50.00	—
1939 Proof	—	Value: 250				
1946	1,000,000	1.50	4.00	12.00	40.00	—
1946 Proof	—	Value: 280				
1950	1,000,000	0.25	0.50	1.50	20.00	—
1950 Proof	—	Value: 300				
1952	1,000,000	0.25	0.50	1.50	15.00	—
1952 Proof	—	Value: 280				
1954	2,000,000	0.10	0.20	0.50	6.00	—
1954 Proof	—	Value: 280				
1956	3,000,000	0.10	0.20	0.50	5.00	—
1956 Proof	—	Value: 280				

KM# 18.2 25 CENTAVOS **Composition:** Copper-Nickel **Edge Lettering:** B. C. N.

Date	Mintage	F	VF	XF	Unc	BU
1964	3,000,000	0.10	0.20	0.40	4.00	—
1965	4,400,000	0.10	0.20	0.30	4.00	—

KM# 18.3 25 CENTAVOS **Composition:** Copper-Nickel **Edge:** Reeded

Date	Mintage	F	VF	XF	Unc	BU
1972	4,000,000	—	0.10	0.15	2.00	—
1972 Proof	20,000	Value: 2.50				
1974	6,000,000	—	0.10	0.15	2.00	—

KM# 23 25 CENTAVOS **Composition:** Brass **Edge:** Reeded

Date	Mintage	F	VF	XF	Unc	BU
1943	1,000,000	0.50	1.50	8.50	50.00	—

KM# 51 25 CENTAVOS **Composition:** Nickel Clad Steel **Note:** Struck at Sherritt Mint.

Date	Mintage	F	VF	XF	Unc	BU
1981	10,000,000	—	—	0.25	1.50	—
1985	8,000,000	5.00	10.00	20.00	30.00	—

KM# 57 25 CENTAVOS **Composition:** Aluminum

Date	F	VF	XF	Unc	BU
1987	—	—	0.25	2.00	—

KM# 82 25 CENTAVOS **Composition:** Chromium Plated Steel

Date	Mintage	F	VF	XF	Unc	BU
1994	2,500,000	—	—	—	1.00	—

KM# 99 25 CENTAVOS **Weight:** 5.0000 g. **Composition:** Brass Plated Steel **Obverse:** National arms **Reverse:** Denomination **Edge:** Reeded and plain sections **Size:** 23.2 mm.

Date	F	VF	XF	Unc	BU
2002	—	—	—	0.60	—

KM# 15 50 CENTAVOS **Weight:** 12.5000 g. **Composition:** 0.8000 Silver .3215 oz. ASW

Date	Mintage	F	VF	XF	Unc	BU
1912H	260,000	4.00	12.00	50.00	175	—
1912H Proof	—	Value: 500				
1929	20,000	5.00	15.00	65.00	275	—

KM# 19.1 50 CENTAVOS **Composition:** Copper-Nickel **Edge Lettering:** B. N. N

Date	Mintage	F	VF	XF	Unc	BU
1939	1,000,000	3.00	8.00	20.00	65.00	—
1939 Proof	—	Value: 250				
1946	500,000	2.00	5.00	12.50	50.00	—
1946 Proof	—	Value: 300				
1950	500,000	1.00	2.00	10.00	50.00	—
1950 Proof	—	Value: 300				
1952	1,000,000	0.75	1.50	5.00	30.00	—
1952 Proof	—	Value: 300				
1954	2,000,000	0.50	1.00	4.00	15.00	—
1954 Proof	—	Value: 300				
1956	2,000,000	0.50	1.00	4.00	15.00	—
1956 Proof	—	Value: 300				

KM# 19.2 50 CENTAVOS **Composition:** Copper-Nickel **Edge Lettering:** B. C. N

Date	Mintage	F	VF	XF	Unc	BU
1965	600,000	0.50	1.25	4.50	15.00	—
1965 Proof	—	Value: 150				

KM# 19.3 50 CENTAVOS **Composition:** Copper-Nickel **Edge:** Reeded

Date	Mintage	F	VF	XF	Unc	BU
1972	—	—	—	—	—	—
1972 Proof	20,000	Value: 2.50				
1974	2,000,000	0.10	0.25	0.50	3.50	—

KM# 42 50 CENTAVOS **Composition:** Copper-Nickel

Date	Mintage	F	VF	XF	Unc	BU
1980Mo	15,000,000	0.10	0.25	0.50	1.75	—

KM# 42a 50 CENTAVOS **Composition:** Nickel Clad Steel

Date	Mintage	F	VF	XF	Unc	BU
1983	10,000,000	—	—	0.40	2.50	—
1985	10,000,000	3.50	7.50	15.00	25.00	—

KM# 58 50 CENTAVOS **Composition:** Aluminum-Bronze

Date	Mintage	F	VF	XF	Unc	BU
1987	12,000,000	—	—	0.40	2.50	—

KM# 83 50 CENTAVOS **Composition:** Chromium Plated Steel

Date	Mintage	F	VF	XF	Unc	BU
1994	12,000,000	—	—	—	1.25	—

KM# 88 50 CENTAVOS **Composition:** Nickel Clad Steel **Obverse:** National emblem **Reverse:** Denomination

Date	Mintage	F	VF	XF	Unc	BU
1997	24,000,000	—	—	—	1.25	—

KM# 16 CORDOBA **Weight:** 25.0000 g. **Composition:** 0.9000 Silver .7234 oz. ASW

Date	Mintage	F	VF	XF	Unc	BU
1912H	35,000	30.00	75.00	285	1,900	—
1912H Proof	—	Value: 2,850				

KM# 26 CORDOBA **Composition:** Copper-Nickel **Edge:** Reeded

Date	Mintage	F	VF	XF	Unc	BU
1972	20,000,000	0.10	0.20	2.00	4.00	—
1972 Proof	40,000	Value: 5.00				

KM# 43 CORDOBA **Composition:** Copper-Nickel

Date	Mintage	F	VF	XF	Unc	BU
1980Mo	10,000,000	0.10	0.20	0.50	2.00	—
1983Mo	10,000,000	0.10	0.20	0.50	2.00	—

KM# 43a CORDOBA **Composition:** Nickel Clad Steel

Date	Mintage	F	VF	XF	Unc	BU
1984	10,000,000	—	0.10	0.50	2.00	—
1985	10,000,000	1.00	2.00	7.00	35.00	—

KM# 59 CORDOBA **Composition:** Aluminum-Bronze

Date	Mintage	F	VF	XF	Unc	BU
1987	23,000,000	—	0.75	1.00	3.75	—

KM# 77 CORDOBA **Weight:** 27.0000 g. **Composition:** 0.9250 Silver .8029 oz. ASW **Subject:** Ibero - American Series **Reverse:** 2 figures

Date	Mintage	F	VF	XF	Unc	BU
1991 Proof	10,000	Value: 65.00				

KM# 84 CORDOBA **Weight:** 13.8200 g. **Composition:** 0.9250 Silver .4110 oz. ASW **Subject:** National Ruben Dario Theater

Date	Mintage	F	VF	XF	Unc	BU
1994 Proof	2,000	Value: 42.50				

KM# 85 CORDOBA **Weight:** 14.1700 g. **Composition:** 0.9250 Silver .4214 oz. ASW **Subject:** 100th Anniversary - City of Boaco

Date	Mintage	F	VF	XF	Unc	BU
1995 Proof	1,000	Value: 45.00				

KM# 87 CORDOBA **Weight:** 13.9600 g. **Composition:** 0.8250 Silver .3703 oz. ASW **Subject:** 50th Anniversary - F.A.O **Obverse:** National emblem **Reverse:** F.A.O. logo

Date	Mintage	F	VF	XF	Unc	BU
1995 Proof	2,200	Value: 37.50				

KM# 89 CORDOBA **Composition:** Nickel Clad Steel **Obverse:** National emblem **Reverse:** Denomination

Date	Mintage	F	VF	XF	Unc	BU
1997	39,000,000	—	—	—	2.50	—
2000	35,000,000	—	—	—	2.50	—

KM# 44 5 CORDOBAS **Composition:** Copper-Nickel

Date	Mintage	F	VF	XF	Unc	BU
1980	10,000,000	0.15	0.25	1.00	3.00	—

KM# 44a 5 CORDOBAS **Composition:** Nickel Clad Steel

Date	Mintage	F	VF	XF	Unc	BU
1984	8,000,000	—	0.25	1.00	3.50	—

KM# 60 5 CORDOBAS **Composition:** Aluminum-Bronze

Date	Mintage	F	VF	XF	Unc	BU
1987	23,000,000	—	1.00	2.50	4.00	—

KM# 86 5 CORDOBAS **Weight:** 27.0000 g. **Composition:** 0.9250 Silver .8030 oz. ASW **Subject:** Wildlive Protection **Obverse:** Howler Monkey

Date	Mintage	F	VF	XF	Unc	B
1994 Proof	20,000	Value: 45.00				

KM# 90 5 CORDOBAS **Composition:** Nickel Clad Stee **Obverse:** National emblem **Reverse:** Denomination

Date	Mintage	F	VF	XF	Unc	B
1997	11,000,000	—	—	—	4.00	–
2000	25,000,000	—	—	—	4.00	–

KM# 96 5 CORDOBAS **Weight:** 27.0000 g. **Composition:** 0.9250 Silver 0.803 oz. ASW **Subject:** Ibero America **Obverse:** National arms within circle of arms. **Reverse:** Two folk dancers. **Edge:** Reeded. **Size:** 40 mm.

Date	F	VF	XF	Unc	B
1997 Proof	—	Value: 60.00			

KM# 76 10 CORDOBAS **Weight:** 25.7000 g. **Composition:** 0.9990 Silver .8263 oz. ASW **Subject:** Soccer

Date	Mintage	F	VF	XF	Unc	B
1991 Proof	10,000	Value: 65.00				

KM# 78 10 CORDOBAS **Weight:** 19.9500 g. **Composition:** 0.9990 Silver .6408 oz. ASW **Subject:** Spanish Royal Visit

Date	Mintage	F	VF	XF	Unc	B
1991 Proof	5,000	Value: 55.00				

M# 95 10 CORDOBAS **Weight:** 27.2000 g. **Composition:** 0.9250 Silver 0.8089 oz. ASW **Subject:** Ibero-America Series **Obverse:** National arms within circle of arms **Reverse:** Man on horse with two milk cans **Edge:** Reeded **Size:** 40 mm.

ate	F	VF	XF	Unc	BU
99 Proof	—	Value: 75.00			

KM# 32 20 CORDOBAS **Weight:** 5.0300 g. **Composition:** 0.9250 Silver .1496 oz. ASW **Subject:** Earthquake Relief Issue

ate	Mintage	F	VF	XF	Unc	BU
975	2,491	—	—	—	14.50	—
975 Proof	1,750	Value: 20.00				

KM# 25 50 CORDOBAS **Weight:** 35.6000 g. **Composition:** 0.9000 Gold 1.0300 oz. AGW **Subject:** 100th Anniversary - Birth of Ruben Dario

ate	Mintage	F	VF	XF	Unc	BU
967HF Prooflike	16,000	—	—	—	—	450

Note: 500 pieces were issued in blue boxes with certificates. Boxed examples command a premium

KM# 33 50 CORDOBAS **Weight:** 12.5700 g. **Composition:** 0.9250 Silver .3738 oz. ASW **Subject:** U.S. Bicentennial **Note:** Mintages are included with KM#34.

ate	F	VF	XF	Unc	BU
975	—	—	—	21.50	—
975 Proof	—	Value: 30.00			

KM# 34 50 CORDOBAS **Weight:** 12.5700 g. **Composition:** 0.9250 Silver .3738 oz. ASW **Subject:** Earthquake Relief Issue

Date	Mintage	F	VF	XF	Unc	BU
1975	4,482	—	—	—	18.00	—
1975 Proof	3,500	Value: 27.50				

KM# 61 50 CORDOBAS **Weight:** 16.6000 g. **Composition:** 0.8250 Silver .4403 oz. ASW **Series:** Winter Olympics **Reverse:** Skier

Date	Mintage	F	VF	XF	Unc	BU
1988 Proof	10,000	Value: 22.50				

KM# 62 50 CORDOBAS **Weight:** 16.6000 g. **Composition:** 0.8250 Silver .4403 oz. ASW **Series:** Olympics **Reverse:** Sailboat

Date	Mintage	F	VF	XF	Unc	BU
1988 Proof	10,000	Value: 22.50				

KM# 91 50 CORDOBAS **Weight:** 27.0000 g. **Composition:** 0.9250 Silver 0.803 oz. ASW **Subject:** Central Bank 40th Anniversary **Obverse:** National arms **Reverse:** Portrait of Cordoba **Edge:** Reeded **Size:** 40 mm.

Date	Mintage	F	VF	XF	Unc	BU
2000 Proof	1,000	Value: 75.00				

KM# 35 100 CORDOBAS **Weight:** 25.1400 g. **Composition:** 0.9250 Silver .6668 oz. ASW **Subject:** U.S. Bicentennial **Note:** Mintages included with KM#36.

Date	F	VF	XF	Unc	BU
1975	—	—	—	35.00	—
1975 Proof	—	Value: 45.00			

KM# 36 100 CORDOBAS **Weight:** 25.1400 g. **Composition:** 0.9250 Silver .6668 oz. ASW **Subject:** Earthquake Relief Issue

Date	Mintage	F	VF	XF	Unc	BU
1975	4,682	—	—	—	35.00	—
1975 Proof	3,500	Value: 45.00				

KM# 37 200 CORDOBAS **Weight:** 2.1000 g. **Composition:** 0.9000 Gold .0608 oz. AGW **Subject:** Pieta

Date	Mintage	F	VF	XF	Unc	BU
1975	1,200	—	—	—	55.00	—
1975 Proof	1,650	Value: 70.00				

KM# 79 250 CORDOBAS **Weight:** 171.0700 g. **Composition:** 0.9990 Silver 5.4946 oz. ASW **Subject:** Spanish Royal Visit **Obverse:** Similar to KM#78

Date	F	VF	XF	Unc	BU
1992 Proof	—	Value: 135			

KM# 38 500 CORDOBAS **Weight:** 5.4000 g. **Composition:** 0.9000 Gold .1563 oz. AGW **Subject:** Colonial Church

Date	Mintage	F	VF	XF	Unc	BU
1975	200	—	—	—	300	—
1975 Proof	100	Value: 600				

KM# 39 500 CORDOBAS **Weight:** 5.4000 g. **Composition:** 0.9000 Gold .1563 oz. AGW **Subject:** Earthquake Relief Issue

Date	Mintage	F	VF	XF	Unc	BU
1975	1,750	—	—	—	135	—
1975 Proof	1,120	Value: 190				

KM# 45 500 CORDOBAS **Weight:** 14.0000 g. **Composition:** 0.9250 Silver .4164 oz. ASW **Subject:** A. C. Sandino

Date	Mintage	F	VF	XF	Unc	BU
1980Mo Proof	7,000	Value: 35.00				

KM# 46 500 CORDOBAS **Weight:** 14.0000 g. **Composition:** 0.9250 Silver .4164 oz. ASW **Subject:** Dobas Carlos Fonseca

Date	Mintage	F	VF	XF	Unc	BU
1980Mo Proof	7,000	Value: 35.00				

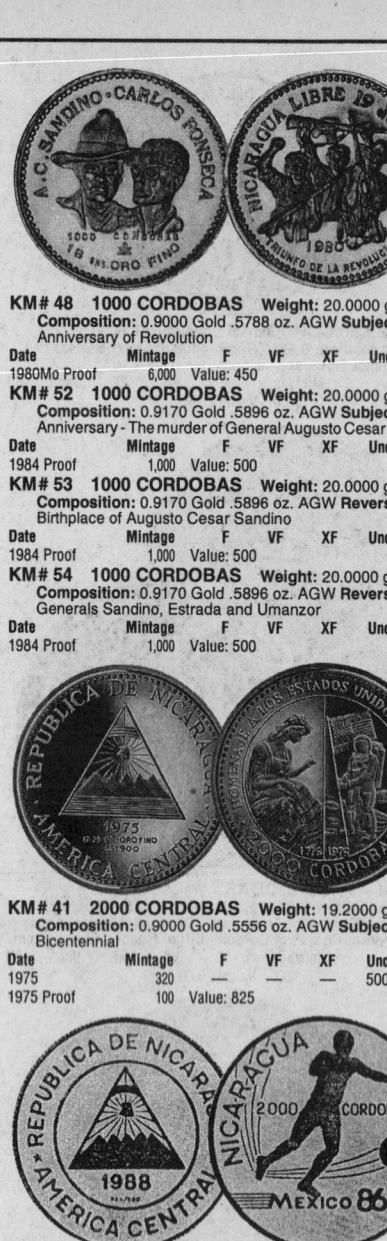

KM# 47 500 CORDOBAS **Weight:** 14.0000 g. **Composition:** 0.9250 Silver .4164 oz. ASW **Subject:** Rigoberto Lopez Perez

Date	Mintage	F	VF	XF	Unc	BU
1980Mo Proof	7,000	Value: 35.00				

KM# 69 500 CORDOBAS **Weight:** 14.0000 g. **Composition:** 0.9990 Silver .4502 oz. ASW **Subject:** Birthplace of Augusto Cesar Sandino

Date	Mintage	F	VF	XF	Unc	BU
ND(1984) Proof	1,000	Value: 45.00				

KM# 70 500 CORDOBAS **Weight:** 14.0000 g. **Composition:** 0.9990 Silver .4502 oz. ASW **Subject:** Generals Sandino, Estrada and Umanzor

Date	Mintage	F	VF	XF	Unc	BU
ND(1984) Proof	1,000	Value: 45.00				

KM# 73 500 CORDOBAS **Weight:** 14.0000 g. **Composition:** 0.9990 Silver .4502 oz. ASW **Subject:** 50th Anniversary - The murder of General Augusto Cesar Sandino

Date	Mintage	F	VF	XF	Unc	BU
ND(1984) Proof	1,000	Value: 45.00				

KM# 63 500 CORDOBAS **Composition:** Aluminum

Date	F	VF	XF	Unc	BU
1987	—	—	2.50	6.50	—

KM# 40 1000 CORDOBAS **Weight:** 9.5000 g. **Composition:** 0.9000 Gold .2749 oz. AGW **Subject:** U.S. Bicentennial

Date	Mintage	F	VF	XF	Unc	BU
1975	3,380	—	—	—	165	—
1975 Proof	2,270	Value: 220				

KM# 48 1000 CORDOBAS **Weight:** 20.0000 g. **Composition:** 0.9000 Gold .5788 oz. AGW **Subject:** 1st Anniversary of Revolution

Date	Mintage	F	VF	XF	Unc	BU
1980Mo Proof	6,000	Value: 450				

KM# 52 1000 CORDOBAS **Weight:** 20.0000 g. **Composition:** 0.9170 Gold .5896 oz. AGW **Subject:** 50th Anniversary - The murder of General Augusto Cesar Sandino

Date	Mintage	F	VF	XF	Unc	BU
1984 Proof	1,000	Value: 500				

KM# 53 1000 CORDOBAS **Weight:** 20.0000 g. **Composition:** 0.9170 Gold .5896 oz. AGW **Reverse:** Birthplace of Augusto Cesar Sandino

Date	Mintage	F	VF	XF	Unc	BU
1984 Proof	1,000	Value: 500				

KM# 54 1000 CORDOBAS **Weight:** 20.0000 g. **Composition:** 0.9170 Gold .5896 oz. AGW **Reverse:** Generals Sandino, Estrada and Umanzor

Date	Mintage	F	VF	XF	Unc	BU
1984 Proof	1,000	Value: 500				

KM# 41 2000 CORDOBAS **Weight:** 19.2000 g. **Composition:** 0.9000 Gold .5556 oz. AGW **Subject:** U.S. Bicentennial

Date	Mintage	F	VF	XF	Unc	BU
1975	320	—	—	—	500	—
1975 Proof	100	Value: 825				

KM# 65 2000 CORDOBAS **Weight:** 16.6000 g. **Composition:** 0.8250 Silver .4404 oz. ASW **Subject:** Soccer - 1 player

Date	Mintage	F	VF	XF	Unc	BU
1988 Proof	5,000	Value: 40.00				

KM# 64 10000 CORDOBAS **Weight:** 20.0000 g. **Composition:** 0.9990 Silver .6431 oz. ASW **Subject:** Discovery of Nicaragua by Columbus

Date	Mintage	F	VF	XF	Unc	BU
1989 Proof	Est. 10,000	Value: 45.00				

KM# 66 10000 CORDOBAS **Weight:** 26.4000 g. **Composition:** 0.9990 Silver .8480 oz. ASW **Subject:** Soccer **Reverse:** 2 soccer players

Date	Mintage	F	VF	XF	Unc	BU
1990 Proof	5,000	Value: 45.00				

KM# 67 10000 CORDOBAS **Weight:** 26.0000 g. **Composition:** 0.9990 Silver .8352 oz. ASW **Subject:** Discovery of America **Reverse:** Sailing ship

Date	Mintage	F	VF	XF	Unc	BU
1990 Proof	10,000	Value: 47.50				

KM# 68 10000 CORDOBAS **Weight:** 26.0000 g. **Composition:** 0.9990 Silver .8352 oz. ASW **Series:** 1992 Summer Olympics **Reverse:** Bicyclist

Date	Mintage	F	VF	XF	Unc	BU
1990 Proof	10,000	Value: 40.00				

KM# 71 10000 CORDOBAS **Weight:** 26.0000 g. **Composition:** 0.9990 Silver .8352 oz. ASW **Subject:** Wildlife Protection **Reverse:** Ocelot

Date	Mintage	F	VF	XF	Unc	BU
1990 Proof	5,000	Value: 42.50				

KM# 72.1 10000 CORDOBAS **Weight:** 20.4000 g. **Composition:** 0.9990 Silver .6553 oz. ASW **Series:** 1992 Summer Olympics **Reverse:** Equestrian

Date	Mintage	F	VF	XF	Unc	BU
1990 Proof	10,000	Value: 60.00				

KM# 72.2 10000 CORDOBAS **Weight:** 20.0000 g. **Composition:** 0.9990 Silver .6431 oz. ASW **Reverse:** "999" added at 4 o'clock

Date		F	VF	XF	Unc	BU
1990 Proof	Inc. above	Value: 42.50				

KM# 74 10000 CORDOBAS **Weight:** 25.9000 g. **Composition:** 0.9990 Silver .8320 oz. ASW **Series:** 1992 Summer Olympics **Reverse:** Tennis player proclaiming victory

Date	Mintage	F	VF	XF	Unc	BU
1990 Proof	10,000	Value: 50.00				

KM# 75 10000 CORDOBAS **Weight:** 20.0000 g. **Composition:** 0.9990 Silver .6431 oz. ASW **Series:** 1992 Winter Olympics **Reverse:** Figure skater

Date	Mintage	F	VF	XF	Unc	BU
1990 Proof	10,000	Value: 47.50				

REVOLUTIONARY TOKEN COINAGE

KM# Tn1 10 PESOS **Weight:** 18.0000 g. **Composition:** Lead **Issuer:** General Augusto Cesar Sandino, 1925-1934

Date		VG	F	VF	XF	Unc
ND(1927)		400	700	1,200	2,500	—

PATTERNS

Including off metal strikes.

KM#	Date	Mintage	Identification	Mkt Val
Pn10	1912H	2	1/2 Centavo. Silver. KM10; 2 known.	—
Pn11	1912H	1	1/2 Centavo. Gold. KM10; unique.	—
Pn13	1912H	1	Centavo. Gold. KM#11.	—
Pn14	1912H	2	5 Centavos. Silver. KM12.	—
Pn15	1912H	1	5 Centavos. Gold. KM12.	—
Pn16	1912H	1	10 Centavos. Gold. KM13.	—
Pn17	1912H	1	25 Centavos. Gold. KM14.	—
Pn19	1912H	1	Cordoba. Gold. KM16.	—
Pn18	1912H	1	50 Centavos. Gold. KM#15.	—
Pn12	1912H	2	Centavo. Silver. KM11; 2 known.	4,000
Pn20	1975	—	20 Cordobas. KM32 with 4.65 gram Plata Fino, LEY 925 below date.	—
Pn21	1975	—	50 Cordobas. KM34 with 11.63 gram. Plata Fino, LEY 925 below date.	—
Pn22	1975	—	100 Cordobas. KM36 with 23.25 gram. Plata Fino, LEY 925 below date.	—

TRIAL STRIKES

KM#	Date	Mintage	Identification	Mkt Val
TS7	ND(1912)	—	Cordoba. 18.0000 Aluminum. Obverse.	—
TS8	ND(1912)	—	Cordoba. 18.0000 Aluminum. Reverse.	—
TS1	ND(1912)	—	10 Centavos. Aluminum. Obverse.	350

KM#	Date	Mintage	Identification	Mkt Val
TS2	ND(1912)	—	10 Centavos. Aluminum. Reverse.	350
TS3	ND(1912)	—	25 Centavos. Aluminum. Obverse.	360
TS4	ND(1912)	—	25 Centavos. Aluminum. Reverse.	360

KM#	Date	Mintage	Identification	Mkt Val
TS5	ND(1912)	—	50 Centavos. Aluminum. Obverse.	375

KM#	Date	Mintage	Identification	Mkt Val
TS6	ND(1912)	—	50 Centavos. Aluminum.	375
TS9	1965	—	5 Centavos. Nickel. Raised "Trial" left of bust on obverse, above rays on reverse. KM24.2.	—
TS10	1965	—	10 Centavos. Nickel. Raised "Trial" left of bust on obverse, above rays on reverse. KM17.2.	—

MINT SETS

KM#	Date	Mintage	Identification	Issue Price	Mkt Val
MS1	1975 (5)	—	KM37-41	—	1,150
MS2	1975 (5)	2,250	KM#32-36	—	110

PROOF SETS

KM#	Date	Mintage	Identification	Issue Price	Mkt Val
PS1	1912 (7)	10	KM10-16	—	4,500
PS2	1912 (3)	2	Pn10, Pn12, Pn14	—	4,500
PS3	1912 (7)	1	Pn11, Pn13, Pn15-19	—	—
PS4	1972 (5)	20,000	KM17.3-19.3, 24.3, 26	8.00	15.00
PS5	1975 (7)	—	KM32, 33, 35, 37, 38, 40, 41	—	1,750
PS6	1975 (5)	2,000	KM32-36	—	160
PS7	1975 (3)	—	KM32, 33, 35	115	90.00
PS8	1975 (3)	—	KM34, 36, 39	—	255
PS9	1975 (2)	—	KM37, 39	—	255

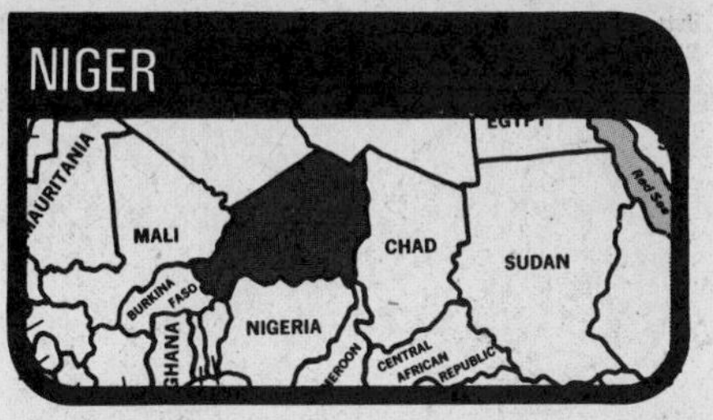

The Republic of Niger, located in West Africa's Sahara region 1,000 miles (1,609 km.) from the Mediterranean shore, has an area of 489,191 sq. mi. (1,267,000 sq. km.) and a population of *7.4 million. Capital: Niamey. The economy is based on subsistence agriculture and raising livestock.. Peanuts, peanut oil, and livestock are exported.

Although four-fifths of Niger is arid desert, it was, some 6,000 years ago inhabited and an important economic crossroads. Its modern history began in the 19th century with the beginning of contacts with British and German explorers searching for the mouth of the Niger River. Niger was incorporated into French West Africa in 1896, but it was 1922 before all native resistance was quelled and Niger became a French colony. In 1958 the voters approved the new French Constitution and elected to become an autonomous republic within the French Community. On Aug. 3, 1960, Niger withdrew from the Community and proclaimed its independence.

REPUBLIC

DECIMAL COINAGE

KM# 1 10 FRANCS **Weight:** 4.2000 g. **Composition:** 0.9000 Gold .1215 oz. AGW **Subject:** Independence Commemorataive

Date	Mintage	F	VF	XF	Unc	BU
ND(1960) Proof	1,000	Value: 85.00				

KM# 7 10 FRANCS **Weight:** 3.2000 g. **Composition:** 0.9000 Gold .0926 oz. AGW **Obverse:** Ostriches

Date	Mintage	F	VF	XF	Unc	BU
1968 Proof	1,000	Value: 120				

KM# 8.1 10 FRANCS **Weight:** 20.0000 g. **Composition:** 0.9000 Silver .5845 oz. ASW **Note:** Sharp details, raised rim.

Date	Mintage	F	VF	XF	Unc	BU
1968 Proof	1,000	Value: 65.00				

KM# 8.2 10 FRANCS **Weight:** 24.5400 g. **Composition:** 0.9000 Silver .7100 oz. ASW **Obverse:** Exists with and without accent marks above first E in REPUBLIQUE **Note:** Dull details, machined-down rim

Date	F	VF	XF	Unc	BU
1968 Proof	—	—	—	40.00	—

KM# 2 25 FRANCS **Weight:** 8.0000 g. **Composition:** 0.9000 Gold .2315 oz. AGW **Subject:** Independence Commemorative

Date	Mintage	F	VF	XF	Unc	BU
ND(1960) Proof	1,000	Value: 135				

KM# 9 25 FRANCS **Weight:** 8.0000 g. **Composition:** 0.9000 Gold .2315 oz. AGW **Obverse:** Barbary sheep

Date	Mintage	F	VF	XF	Unc	BU
1968 Proof	1,000	Value: 175				

KM# 3 50 FRANCS **Weight:** 16.0000 g. **Composition:** 0.9000 Gold .4630 oz. AGW **Subject:** Independence Commemorative

Date	Mintage	F	VF	XF	Unc	BU
ND(1960) Proof	1,000	Value: 250				

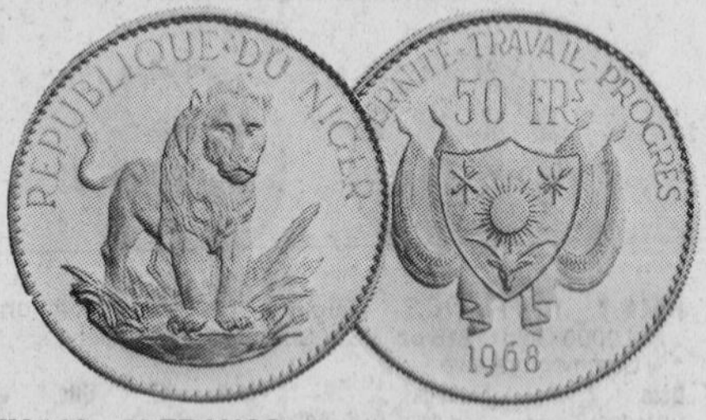

KM# 10 50 FRANCS **Weight:** 16.0000 g. **Composition:** 0.9000 Gold .4630 oz. AGW **Subject:** Independence Commemorative

Date	Mintage	F	VF	XF	Unc	BU
1968 Proof	1,000	Value: 400				

KM# 4 100 FRANCS **Weight:** 32.0000 g. **Composition:** 0.9260 Gold .9260 oz. AGW **Subject:** Independence Commemorative

Date	Mintage	F	VF	XF	Unc	BU
ND(1960) Proof	1,000	Value: 400				

KM# 11 100 FRANCS **Weight:** 32.0000 g. **Composition:** 0.9000 Gold .9260 oz. AGW **Subject:** Independence Commemorative

Date	Mintage	F	VF	XF	Unc	BU
1968 Proof	1,000	Value: 550				

KM# 5 500 FRANCS **Weight:** 10.0000 g. **Composition:** 0.9000 Silver .2893 oz. ASW **Subject:** Independence Commemorative

Date	F	VF	XF	Unc	BU
ND(1960) Proof	—	Value: 35.00			

KM# 6 1000 FRANCS **Weight:** 20.0000 g. **Composition:** 0.9000 Silver .5787 oz. ASW **Subject:** Independence Commemorative

Date	F	VF	XF	Unc	BU
ND(1960) Proof	—	Value: 55.00			

ESSAIS

KM#	Date	Mintage	Identification	Issue Price	Mkt Val
E1	1960	—	10 Francs. Silver. 39.4000 g. Lion facing. Arms. Thick planchet.	—	110
E2	1960	—	25 Francs.	—	200
E3	1960	—	50 Francs.	—	325
E4	1960	—	100 Francs.	—	650
E5	1960	1,000	500 Francs. KM5.	—	40.00
E6	ND(1960)	1,000	1000 Francs. KM5.	—	60.00

KM#	Date	Mintage	Identification	Issue Price	Mkt Val
E7	1968	—	10 Francs. Gold. 31.7800 g. KM8.	—	1,750
E8	1968	—	10 Francs. Silver.	—	35.00
E9	1968	—	25 Francs. Silver.	—	40.00
E10	1968	—	50 Francs. Silver.	—	45.00
E11	1968	—	100 Francs. Silver.	—	50.00

PATTERNS

Including off metal strikes

KM#	Date	Mintage	Identification	Mkt Val
Pn1	1968	—	10 Francs. Copper. 18.8200 g. Reeded edge. KM8.1.	200

PROOF SETS

KM#	Date	Mintage	Identification	Issue Price	Mkt Val
PS1	1960 (4)	1,000	KM1-4	—	870
PS2	1968 (4)	—	KM7, 9-11	—	1,250

NIGERIA

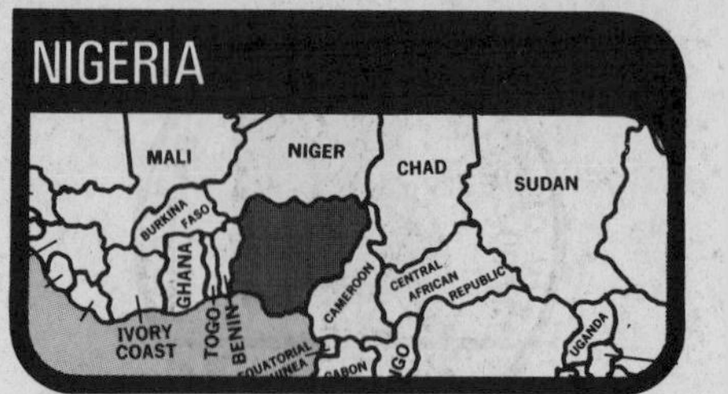

The Federal Republic of Nigeria, situated on the Atlantic coast of West Africa has an area of 356,669 sq. mi. (923,770 sq. km.) and a population of *115.2 million. Capital: Abuja. The economy is based on petroleum and agriculture. Crude oil, cocoa, natural gas, tobacco and tin are exported.

Following the Napoleonic Wars, the British expanded their trade with the interior of Nigeria. The Berlin Conference of 1885 recognized British claims to a sphere of influence in that area, and in the following year the Royal Niger Company was chartered. Direct British control of the territory was initiated in 1900, and in 1914 the amalgamation of Northern and Southern Nigeria into the Colony and Protectorate of Nigeria was effected. In 1960, following a number of territorial and constitutional changes, Nigeria was granted independence within the British Commonwealth as a federation of the Northern, Western and Eastern regions. Nigeria altered its political relationship with Great Britain on Oct. 1, 1963, by proclaiming itself a republic. It did, however, elect to remain a member of the Commonwealth of Nations.

On May 30, 1967, the Eastern Region of the republic -an area occupied principally by the proud and resourceful Ibo tribe - seceded from Nigeria and proclaimed itself the independent Republic of Biafra with Odumegwu Ojukwu as Chief of State. Civil war erupted and raged for 31 months. Casualties, including civilian, were about two million, the majority succumbing to malnutrition and disease. Biafra surrendered to the federal government on January 15, 1970.

As of November 1995, Nigeria has been suspended from the Commonwealth. Presidential democratic elections continue to be held.

For earlier coinage refer to British West Africa.

RULERS

Elizabeth II, 1952-1963

MONETARY SYSTEM

12 Pence = 1 Shilling
20 Shillings = 1 Pound

BRITISH PROTECTORATE OF NIGERIA

POUND STERLING COINAGE

KM# 1 1/2 PENNY **Composition:** Bronze

Date	Mintage	F	VF	XF	Unc	BU
1959	52,800,000	—	0.15	0.25	0.75	—
1959 Proof	6,031	Value: 2.50				

KM# 2 PENNY **Composition:** Bronze

Date	Mintage	F	VF	XF	Unc	BU
1959	93,368,000	—	0.15	0.25	1.25	—
1959 Proof	6,031	Value: 2.50				

KM# 3 3 PENCE **Composition:** Nickel-Brass

Date	Mintage	F	VF	XF	Unc	BU
1959	52,000,000	—	0.20	0.40	1.50	—
1959 Proof	6,031	Value: 3.50				

KM# 4 6 PENCE Composition: Copper-Nickel

Date	Mintage	F	VF	XF	Unc	BU
1959	35,000,000	—	0.40	0.80	2.50	—
1959 Proof	6,031	Value: 5.00				

KM# 5 SHILLING Composition: Copper-Nickel

Date	Mintage	F	VF	XF	Unc	BU
1959	18,000,000	—	0.65	1.45	3.50	—
1959 Proof	6,031	Value: 6.50				
1961	48,584,000	—	0.65	1.45	3.50	—
1961 Reported, not confirmed	—	—	—	—	—	—
1962	39,416,000	—	0.65	1.45	3.50	—

KM# 6.1 2 SHILLING Composition: Copper-Nickel
Edge: Security

Date	Mintage	F	VF	XF	Unc	BU
1959	15,000,000	—	1.25	2.50	6.00	—
1959 Proof	6,031	Value: 9.00				

KM# 6.2 2 SHILLING Composition: Copper-Nickel
Edge: Reeded

Date	F	VF	XF	Unc	BU
1959	—	1.25	2.50	6.00	—

REPUBLIC

DECIMAL COINAGE

KM# 7 1/2 KOBO Composition: Bronze

Date	Mintage	F	VF	XF	Unc	BU
1973	166,618,000	—	0.45	1.00	3.50	—
1973 Proof	10,000	Value: 3.50				

KM# 8.1 KOBO Composition: Bronze **Obverse:** Arms **Obv. Legend:** Unity and faith

Date	Mintage	F	VF	XF	Unc	BU
1973	586,944,000	—	0.25	0.50	2.00	—
1973 Proof	10,000	Value: 3.50				
1974	14,500,000	—	0.25	0.50	3.00	—

KM# 8.2 KOBO Composition: Bronze **Obverse:** Arms **Obv. Legend:** Unity and faith, peace and progress

Date	F	VF	XF	Unc	BU
1987	—	0.50	1.50	6.00	—
1988	—	0.50	1.50	6.00	—

KM# 8.2a KOBO Composition: Copper Plated Steel

Date	F	VF	XF	Unc	BU
1991	—	—	—	0.25	—

KM# 9.1 5 KOBO Composition: Copper-Nickel **Obverse:** Arms **Obv. Legend:** Unity and faith

Date	Mintage	F	VF	XF	Unc	BU
1973	96,920,000	—	0.35	0.75	2.75	—
1973 Proof	10,000	Value: 4.00				
1974	—	—	0.45	0.85	3.00	—
1976	9,800,000	—	0.45	0.85	3.00	—
1986	—	—	0.45	0.85	3.00	—

KM# 9.2 5 KOBO Composition: Copper-Nickel **Obverse:** Arms **Obv. Legend:** Unity and faith, peace and progress

Date	F	VF	XF	Unc	BU
1987	—	1.00	2.50	7.00	—
1988	—	1.00	2.50	7.00	—
1989	—	1.00	2.50	7.00	—

KM# 10.1 10 KOBO Composition: Copper-Nickel **Obverse:** Arms **Obv. Legend:** Unity and faith

Date	Mintage	F	VF	XF	Unc	BU
1973	340,870,000	—	0.50	1.00	3.50	—
1973 Proof	10,000	Value: 5.00				
1974	—	—	0.60	1.20	3.75	—
1976	7,000,000	—	0.60	1.20	3.75	—

KM# 10.2 10 KOBO Composition: Copper-Nickel **Obverse:** Arms **Obv. Legend:** Unity and faith, peace and progress

Date	F	VF	XF	Unc	BU
1987	—	1.25	3.50	9.00	—
1988	—	1.25	3.50	9.00	—
1989	—	1.25	3.50	9.00	—
1990	—	1.25	3.50	9.00	—

KM# 12 10 KOBO Composition: Copper Plated Steel

Date	F	VF	XF	Unc	BU
1991	—	—	—	0.45	—

KM# 11 25 KOBO Composition: Copper-Nickel

Date	Mintage	F	VF	XF	Unc	BU
1973	4,616,000	—	1.00	2.50	7.50	—
1973 Proof	10,000	Value: 8.50				
1975	—	—	1.00	2.50	7.50	—

KM# 11a 25 KOBO Composition: Copper Plated Steel

Date	F	VF	XF	Unc	BU
1991	—	—	—	0.65	—

KM# 13 50 KOBO Composition: Nickel Plated Steel

Date	F	VF	XF	Unc	BU
1991	—	—	—	1.25	—
1993	—	—	—	1.25	—

KM# 14 NAIRA Composition: Nickel Plated Steel

Date	F	VF	XF	Unc	BU
1991	—	—	—	1.75	—
1993	—	—	—	1.75	—

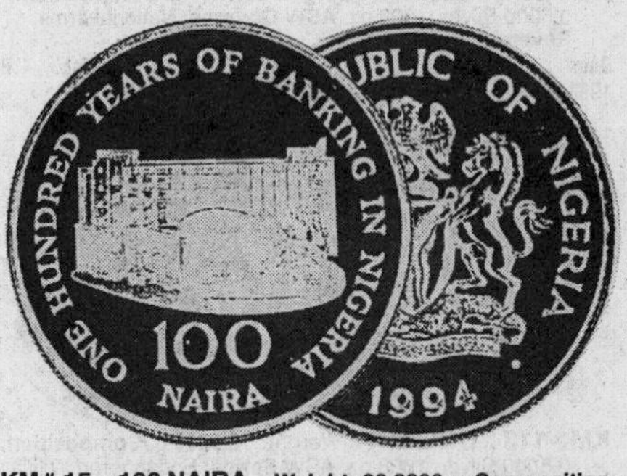

KM# 15 100 NAIRA Weight: 28.2800 g. **Composition:** 0.9250 Silver .8410 oz. ASW **Subject:** 100 Years - Baning in Nigeria **Obverse:** National arms **Reverse:** Bank building **Edge:** Reeded

Date	Mintage	F	VF	XF	Unc	BU
1994 Proof	5,000	Value: 600				

Note: Issue price at Bank in Lagos approximately $1,400.

KM# 16 1000 NAIRA Weight: 47.5400 g. **Composition:** 0.9166 Gold 1.4010 oz. AGW **Subject:** 100 Years - Banking in Nigeria **Obverse:** National arms **Reverse:** Bank building **Edge:** Reeded

Date	Mintage	F	VF	XF	Unc	BU
1994 Proof	100	Value: 2,250				

PATTERNS

Including off metal strikes

KM#	Date	Mintage	Identification	Mkt Val
Pn1	1962	—	Shilling. Bronze. KM5.	200
Pn2	1973	—	10 Kobo. Bronze. KM10.	175

TRIAL STRIKES

KM#	Date	Mintage	Identification	Mkt Val
TS1	1962	—	Shilling. Copper-Nickel. "TRIAL" in field on obverse and reverse.	80.00

PROOF SETS

KM#	Date	Mintage	Identification	Issue Price	Mkt Val
PS1	1959 (6)	1,031	KM1-5, 6.1, red case, originals	—	30.00
PS2	1959 (6)	5,000	KM1-5, 6.1, blue case, restirkes	—	16.50
PS3	1973 (5)	102,000	KM7, 8.1-10.1,11	14.70	25.00

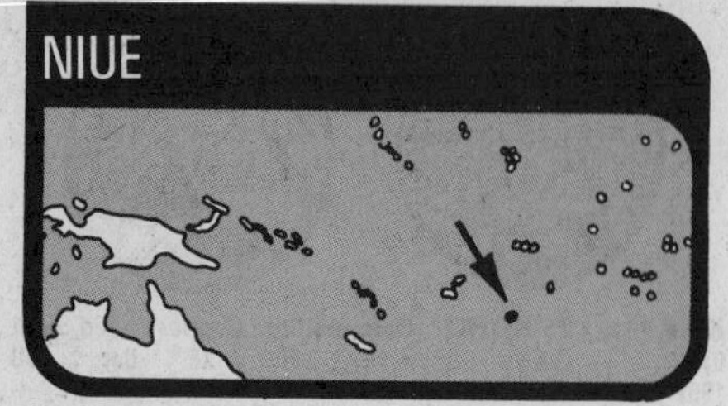

Niue, or Savage Island, a dependent state of New Zealand is located in the Pacific Ocean east of Tonga and southeast of Samoa. The size is 100 sq. mi. (260 sq. km.) with a population of *2,000. Chief village and port is Alofi. Bananas and copra are exported.

Discovered by Captain Cook in 1774, it was originally part of the Cook Islands administration but has been separate since 1922.

MINT MARKS

PM - Pobjoy Mint

NEW ZEALAND DEPENDENT STATE

DECIMAL COINAGE

KM# 85 DOLLAR Weight: 10.0200 g. **Composition:** 0.5000 Silver .1608 oz. ASW **Obverse:** National arms **Reverse:** The Bounty

Date	F	VF	XF	Unc	BU
1996 Proof	—	Value: 20.00			

KM# 113 DOLLAR Weight: 10.0200 g. **Composition:** 0.5000 Silver .1608 oz. ASW **Series:** Endangered Wildlife **Obverse:** Arms **Reverse:** Jaguar on tree limb

Date	F	VF	XF	Unc	BU
1996 Proof	—	Value: 20.00			

KM# 122 DOLLAR Weight: 10.0000 g. **Composition:** 0.5000 Silver .1608 oz. ASW **Series:** Protect Our World **Obverse:** National arms **Reverse:** Oak tree **Edge:** Reeded **Size:** 30 mm.

Date	F	VF	XF	Unc	BU
1996 Proof	—	—	—	15.00	—

KM# 88 DOLLAR Composition: Copper-Nickel **Obverse:** Arms **Reverse:** Diana **Rev. Legend:** . . . Princess of Wales **Note:** Similar to 10 Dollars, KM#91.

Date	F	VF	XF	Unc	BU
1997	—	—	—	10.00	—

KM# 89 DOLLAR Composition: Copper-Nickel **Obverse:** Arms **Reverse:** Diana, sprays below bust **Rev. Legend:** . . . Princess of Wales **Note:** Similar to 10 Dollars, KM#92.

Date	F	VF	XF	Unc	BU
1997	—	—	—	10.00	—

KM# 87 DOLLAR Composition: Copper-Nickel **Obverse:** Arms **Reverse:** Diana **Rev. Legend:** . . . The People's Princess

Date	F	VF	XF	Unc	BU
1997	—	—	—	10.00	—

KM# 102 DOLLAR Composition: Copper-Nickel **Obverse:** Queen Elizabethh II **Reverse:** Diana **Rev. Legend:** . . . In Memoriam **Note:** Similar to 10 Dollars, KM#104.

Date	F	VF	XF	Unc	BU
1998	—	—	—	10.00	—

KM# 103 DOLLAR Composition: Copper-Nickel **Obverse:** Queen Elizabethh II **Reverse:** Diana **Rev. Legend:** . . . Princess of Wales **Note:** Similar to 10 Dollars, KM#105.

Date	F	VF	XF	Unc	BU
1998	—	—	—	10.00	—

KM# 115 DOLLAR Composition: Copper-Nickel **Subject:** 50th Anniversary of Peanuts **Obverse:** Queen's portrait **Reverse:** Snoopy and Woodstock **Note:** Similar to 10 Dollars, KM#116.

Date	F	VF	XF	Unc	BU
2000	—	—	—	12.00	—

KM# 123 DOLLAR Weight: 28.2800 g. **Composition:** Copper-Nickel **Subject:** Snoopy as an Ace **Obverse:** Queen's portrait **Reverse:** Snoopy flying his dog house **Edge:** Reeded **Size:** 38.6 mm.

Date	Mintage	F	VF	XF	Unc	BU
2001	100,000	—	—	—	10.00	—

KM# 128 DOLLAR Weight: 28.2800 g. **Composition:** Copper-Nickel **Series:** Pokemon **Obverse:** National arms **Reverse:** "Bulbasaur" **Edge:** Reeded **Size:** 38.6 mm.

Date	Mintage	F	VF	XF	Unc	BU
2001	100,000	—	—	—	9.00	—

KM# 129 DOLLAR Weight: 7.7700 g. **Composition:** 0.9990 Silver .2496 oz. ASW **Series:** Pokemon **Obverse:** National arms **Reverse:** "Bulbasaur" **Edge:** Reeded **Size:** 22 mm.

Date	Mintage	F	VF	XF	Unc	BU
2001 Proof	20,000	Value: 12.50				

KM# 131 DOLLAR Weight: 28.2800 g. **Composition:** Copper-Nickel **Series:** Pokemon **Obverse:** National arms **Reverse:** "Charmander" **Edge:** Reeded **Size:** 38.6 mm.

Date	Mintage	F	VF	XF	Unc	BU
2001	100,000	—	—	—	9.00	—

KM# 132 DOLLAR Weight: 7.7700 g. **Composition:** 0.9990 Silver .2496 oz. ASW **Series:** Pokemon **Obverse:** National arms **Reverse:** "Charmander" **Edge:** Reeded **Size:** 22 mm.

Date	Mintage	F	VF	XF	Unc	BU
2001 Proof	20,000	Value: 12.50				

KM# 134 DOLLAR Weight: 28.2800 g. **Composition:** Copper-Nickel **Series:** Pokemon **Obverse:** National arms **Reverse:** "Meowth" **Edge:** Reeded **Size:** 38.6 mm.

Date	Mintage	F	VF	XF	Unc	BU
2001	100,000	—	—	—	9.00	—

KM# 135 DOLLAR Weight: 7.7700 g. **Composition:** 0.9990 Silver .2496 oz. ASW **Series:** Pokemon **Obverse:** National arms **Reverse:** "Meowth" **Edge:** Reeded **Size:** 22 mm.

Date	Mintage	F	VF	XF	Unc	BU
2001 Proof	20,000	Value: 12.50				

KM# 137 DOLLAR Weight: 28.2800 g. **Composition:** Copper-Nickel **Series:** Pokemon **Obverse:** National arms **Reverse:** "Pikachu" **Edge:** Reeded **Size:** 38.6 mm.

Date	Mintage	F	VF	XF	Unc	BU
2001	100,000	—	—	—	9.00	—

KM# 138 DOLLAR Weight: 7.7700 g. **Composition:** 0.9990 Silver .2496 oz. ASW **Series:** Pokemon **Obverse:** National arms **Reverse:** "Pikachu" **Edge:** Reeded **Size:** 22 mm.

Date	Mintage	F	VF	XF	Unc	BU
2001 Proof	20,000	Value: 12.50				

KM# 140 DOLLAR Weight: 28.2800 g. **Composition:** Copper-Nickel **Series:** Pokemon **Obverse:** National arms **Reverse:** "Squirtle" **Edge:** Reeded **Size:** 38.6 mm.

Date	Mintage	F	VF	XF	Unc	BU
2001	100,000	—	—	—	9.00	—

KM# 141 DOLLAR Weight: 7.7700 g. **Composition:** 0.9990 Silver .2496 oz. ASW **Series:** Pokemon **Obverse:** National arms **Reverse:** "Squirtle" **Edge:** Reeded **Size:** 22 mm.

Date	Mintage	F	VF	XF	Unc	BU
2001 Proof	20,000	Value: 12.50				

KM# 146 DOLLAR Weight: 28.2800 g. **Composition:** Copper-Nickel **Subject:** Pokemon Series **Obverse:** National arms **Reverse:** Pikachu **Edge:** Reeded **Size:** 38.6 mm.

Date	Mintage	F	VF	XF	Unc	BU
2002PM	100,000	—	—	—	10.00	—

KM# 151 DOLLAR Weight: 28.2800 g. **Composition:** Copper-Nickel **Subject:** Pokemon Series **Obverse:** National arms **Reverse:** Pichu **Edge:** Reeded **Size:** 38.6 mm.

Date	Mintage	F	VF	XF	Unc	BU
2002PM	100,000	—	—	—	10.00	—

KM# 156 DOLLAR Weight: 28.2800 g. **Composition:** Copper-Nickel **Subject:** Pokemon Series **Obverse:** National arms **Reverse:** Mewtwo **Edge:** Reeded **Size:** 38.6 mm.

Date	Mintage	F	VF	XF	Unc	BU
2002PM	100,000	—	—	—	10.00	—

M# 161 DOLLAR **Weight:** 28.2800 g. **Composition:** Copper-Nickel **Subject:** Pokemon Series **Obverse:** National arms **Reverse:** Entei **Edge:** Reeded **Size:** 38.6 mm.

ate	Mintage	F	VF	XF	Unc	BU
02PM	100,000	—	—	—	10.00	—

M# 166 DOLLAR **Weight:** 28.2800 g. **Composition:** Copper Nickel **Subject:** Pokemon Series **Obverse:** National arms **Reverse:** Celebi **Edge:** Reeded **Size:** 38.6 mm.

ate	Mintage	F	VF	XF	Unc	BU
02PM	100,000	—	—	—	10.00	—

:M# 1 5 DOLLARS **Composition:** Copper-Nickel **Series:** Olympics **Subject:** Tennis **Obverse:** Arms **Reverse:** Boris Becker

ate	Mintage	F	VF	XF	Unc	BU
987	80,000	—	—	—	5.50	—

:M# 5 5 DOLLARS **Composition:** Copper-Nickel **Series:** Olympics **Subject:** Tennis **Obverse:** Arms **Reverse:** Steffi Graf

ate	Mintage	F	VF	XF	Unc	BU
987	50,000	—	—	—	5.50	—

:M# 11 5 DOLLARS **Composition:** Copper-Nickel **Series:** Olympics **Subject:** Tennis **Obverse:** Arms **Reverse:** Steffi Graf

ate	Mintage	F	VF	XF	Unc	BU
988	80,000	—	—	—	5.50	—

KM# 12 5 DOLLARS **Composition:** Copper-Nickel **Series:** Olympics **Subject:** Soccer **Obverse:** Arms **Reverse:** Franz Beckenbauer

Date	Mintage	F	VF	XF	Unc	BU
1988	50,000	—	—	—	5.50	—

KM# 15 5 DOLLARS **Composition:** Copper-Nickel **Series:** Olympics **Subject:** Tennis **Obverse:** Arms **Reverse:** Navratilova, Graf and Evert

Date	Mintage	F	VF	XF	Unc	BU
1988	80,000	—	—	—	5.50	—

KM# 17 5 DOLLARS **Composition:** Copper-Nickel **Obverse:** Arms **Reverse:** President John F. Kennedy

Date	Mintage	F	VF	XF	Unc	BU
1988	80,000	—	—	—	6.50	—

KM# 22 5 DOLLARS **Composition:** Copper-Nickel **Obverse:** Arms **Reverse:** General Douglas MacArthur

Date		F	VF	XF	Unc	BU
1989		—	—	—	7.00	—

KM# 24 5 DOLLARS **Composition:** Copper-Nickel **Obverse:** Arms **Reverse:** Davis Cup Tennis

Date		F	VF	XF	Unc	BU
1989		—	—	—	6.00	—

KM# 67 5 DOLLARS **Composition:** Copper-Nickel **Series:** Olympics **Subject:** Tennis **Obverse:** Arms **Reverse:** Steffi Graf

Date		F	VF	XF	Unc	BU
1989		—	—	—	6.50	—

KM# 29 5 DOLLARS **Composition:** Copper-Nickel **Obverse:** Arms **Reverse:** General Dwight D. Eisenhower

Date		F	VF	XF	Unc	BU
1990		—	—	—	6.00	—

KM# 31 5 DOLLARS **Composition:** Copper-Nickel **Obverse:** Arms **Reverse:** General George S. Patton

Date		F	VF	XF	Unc	BU
1990		—	—	—	6.00	—

KM# 33 5 DOLLARS **Composition:** Copper-Nickel **Obverse:** Arms **Reverse:** Admiral William Halsey

Date		F	VF	XF	Unc	BU
1990		—	—	—	6.00	—

KM# 35 5 DOLLARS **Composition:** Copper-Nickel **Obverse:** Arms **Reverse:** President Franklin D. Roosevelt

Date	F	VF	XF	Unc	BU
1990	—	—	—	6.00	—

KM# 37 5 DOLLARS **Composition:** Copper-Nickel **Obverse:** Arms **Reverse:** Sir Winston Churchill

Date	F	VF	XF	Unc	BU
1990	—	—	—	6.00	—

KM# 143 5 DOLLARS **Weight:** 28.3400 g. **Composition:** Copper-Nickel **Subject:** XIV Football World Championship Italy '90 **Obverse:** National arms. **Reverse:** Bust at left, player and Italian map. **Edge:** Reeded. **Size:** 38.6 mm.

Date	Mintage	F	VF	XF	Unc	BU
1990	60,000	—	—	—	10.00	—

KM# 144 5 DOLLARS **Weight:** 28.1500 g. **Composition:** Copper-Nickel **Subject:** Basketball Centennial **Obverse:** National arms. **Reverse:** Two female players circa 1891. **Edge:** Reeded. **Size:** 38.5 mm.

Date	Mintage	F	VF	XF	Unc	BU
1991	28,000	—	—	—	10.00	—

KM# 58 5 DOLLARS **Weight:** 9.9300 g. **Composition:** 0.5000 Silver .1596 oz. ASW **Series:** World Cup Soccer **Obverse:** Arms **Reverse:** Player and Statue of Liberty

Date	Mintage	F	VF	XF	Unc	BU
1991	150,000	—	—	—	15.00	—

KM# 55 5 DOLLARS **Weight:** 10.0000 g. **Composition:** 0.5000 Silver .1608 oz. ASW **Obverse:** Arms **Reverse:** The HMS Bounty

Date	F	VF	XF	Unc	BU
1992	—	—	—	17.50	—

KM# 60 5 DOLLARS **Weight:** 10.0000 g. **Composition:** 0.5000 Silver .1608 oz. ASW **Series:** Endangered Wildlife **Obverse:** Arms **Reverse:** Jaguar

Date	Mintage	F	VF	XF	Unc	BU
1992 Proof	Est. 25,000	Value: 17.50				

KM# 61 5 DOLLARS **Weight:** 10.0000 g. **Composition:** 0.5000 Silver .1608 oz. ASW **Series:** Olympics 1996 **Obverse:** Arms **Reverse:** Sprinter

Date	Mintage	F	VF	XF	Unc	BU
1992 Proof	100,000	Value: 16.50				

KM# 68 5 DOLLARS **Weight:** 9.8500 g. **Composition:** 0.5000 Silver .1584 oz. ASW **Subject:** First Moon Landing **Obverse:** Arms

Date	F	VF	XF	Unc	BU
1992 Proof	—	Value: 16.50			

KM# 76 5 DOLLARS **Weight:** 10.0000 g. **Composition:** 0.9250 Silver .1607 oz. ASW **Obverse:** Arms **Reverse:** Kennedy, Brandenburg Gate

Date	Mintage	F	VF	XF	Unc	BU
1992 Proof	Est. 50,000	Value: 16.50				

KM# 80 5 DOLLARS **Weight:** 9.9500 g. **Composition:** 0.5000 Silver .1599 oz. ASW **Series:** Endangered Wildlife **Obverse:** Arms **Reverse:** Commerson's dolphins

Date	F	VF	XF	Unc	BU
1992 Proof	—	Value: 17.50			

KM# 62 5 DOLLARS **Weight:** 9.9500 g. **Composition:** 0.5000 Silver .1599 oz. ASW **Series:** Protect Our World **Obverse:** Arms **Reverse:** Oak tree

Date	F	VF	XF	Unc	BU
1993 Proof	—	Value: 16.00			

KM# 114 5 DOLLARS **Weight:** 31.5000 g. **Composition:** 0.9250 Silver .9368 oz. ASW **Subject:** The Resolution **Obverse:** Crowned arms **Reverse:** Sail ship above denomination

Date	F	VF	XF	Unc	BU
1996 Proof	—	Value: 45.00			

KM# 145 5 DOLLARS **Weight:** 31.3600 g. **Composition:** 0.9250 Silver 0.9326 oz. ASW **Subject:** Queen Mother **Obverse:** Bust of Queen Elizabeth II right. **Reverse:** Queen Mother's Silver Wedding scene. **Edge:** Reeded. **Size:** 38.4 mm.

Date	F	VF	XF	Unc	BU
1998 Proof	—	Value: 45.00			

KM# 171 5 DOLLARS **Weight:** 31.2500 g. **Composition:** 0.9250 Silver 0.9294 oz. ASW **Subject:** Pygoplites Diacantus **Obverse:** Queen's portrait **Reverse:** Three gold plated fish **Edge:** Plain, seven sided **Size:** 35.5 mm.

Date	F	VF	XF	Unc	BU
1999 Proof	—	Value: 75.00			

KM# 120 5 DOLLARS **Weight:** 31.4200 g. **Composition:** 0.9250 Silver .9344 oz. ASW **Subject:** Pterois Radiata **Obverse:** Queen's head right **Reverse:** Gold colored Clearfin lion fish **Edge:** Plain **Note:** 7-sided.

Date		F	VF	XF	Unc	BU
1999 Proof	—	Value: 50.00				

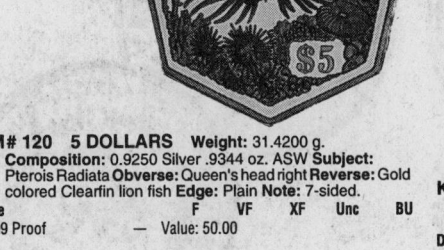

KM# 121 5 DOLLARS **Weight:** 31.4200 g. **Composition:** 0.9250 Silver .9344 oz. ASW **Subject:** Fourcipiger Longirostris **Obverse:** Queen's head right **Reverse:** Gold colored big long nosed Butterfly fish **Edge:** Plain **Note:** 7-sided.

Date		F	VF	XF	Unc	BU
1999 Proof	—	Value: 50.00				

KM# 172 5 DOLLARS **Weight:** 28.4000 g. **Composition:** 0.9250 Silver 0.8446 oz. ASW **Subject:** Queen Mother **Obverse:** Queen's portrait **Reverse:** Queen Mother's engagement portrait **Edge:** Reeded **Size:** 38.5 mm.

Date		F	VF	XF	Unc	BU
2000 Proof	—	Value: 50.00				

KM# 46 10 DOLLARS **Weight:** 10.0000 g. **Composition:** 0.9250 Silver .2974 oz. ASW **Series:** Summer Olympics **Obverse:** Crowned arms **Reverse:** Runners

Date	Mintage	F	VF	XF	Unc	BU
1991	150,000	—	—	—	17.50	—

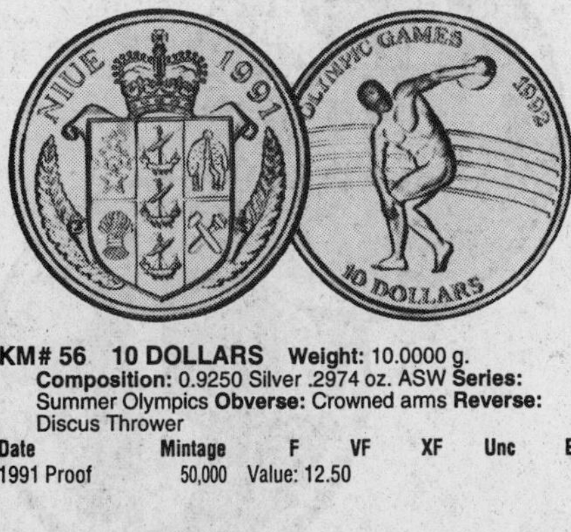

KM# 56 10 DOLLARS **Weight:** 10.0000 g. **Composition:** 0.9250 Silver .2974 oz. ASW **Series:** Summer Olympics **Obverse:** Crowned arms **Reverse:** Discus Thrower

Date	Mintage	F	VF	XF	Unc	BU
1991 Proof	50,000	Value: 12.50				

KM# 59 10 DOLLARS **Weight:** 31.5300 g. **Composition:** 0.9999 Silver 1.0128 oz. ASW **Series:** World Cup Soccer **Obverse:** Crowned arms **Reverse:** Handshake

Date	Mintage	F	VF	XF	Unc	BU
1991 Proof	20,000	Value: 17.50				

KM# 69 10 DOLLARS **Weight:** 31.4300 g. **Composition:** 0.9999 Silver 1.0106 oz. ASW **Subject:** Cook's Pacific Voyages **Obverse:** Crowned arms

Date		F	VF	XF	Unc	BU
1992 Proof	—	Value: 30.00				

KM# 70 10 DOLLARS **Weight:** 31.4300 g. **Composition:** 0.9999 Silver 1.0106 oz. ASW **Subject:** Moon Landing **Obverse:** Crowned arms **Reverse:** Luna 9

Date	Mintage	F	VF	XF	Unc	BU
1992 Proof	Est. 15,000	Value: 30.00				

KM# 74 10 DOLLARS **Weight:** 31.4700 g. **Composition:** 0.9250 Silver .9359 oz. ASW **Series:** Endangered Wildlife **Obverse:** Crowned arms **Reverse:** Whales

Date	Mintage	F	VF	XF	Unc	BU
1992 Proof	25,000	Value: 28.50				

KM# 78 10 DOLLARS **Weight:** 31.4700 g. **Composition:** 0.9250 Silver .9359 oz. ASW **Subject:** The Resolution **Obverse:** Crowned arms **Reverse:** 3 masted ship

Date	Mintage	F	VF	XF	Unc	BU
1992 Proof	Est. 15,000	Value: 37.50				

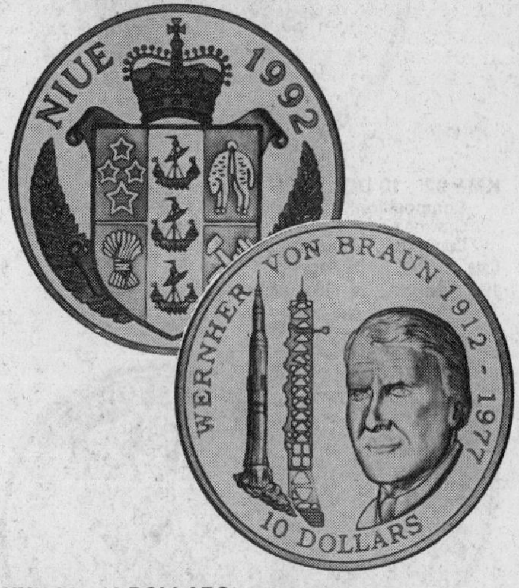

KM# 86 10 DOLLARS **Weight:** 31.0400 g. **Composition:** 0.9250 Silver .9231 oz. ASW **Obverse:** Crowned arms **Reverse:** Dr. Wernher von Braun, rocket launch

Date		F	VF	XF	Unc	BU
1992 Proof	—	Value: 30.00				

KM# 81 10 DOLLARS **Weight:** 1.2440 g. **Composition:** 0.9990 Gold .0400 oz. AGW **Subject:** Liberty Gold Bullion **Obverse:** Head of Queen Elizabeth II right **Reverse:** Statue of Liberty

Date		F	VF	XF	Unc	BU
1997		—	—	—	30.00	—

KM# 90 10 DOLLARS **Weight:** 28.2800 g. **Composition:** 0.9250 Silver .8411 oz. ASW **Obverse:** Crowned arms **Reverse:** Diana **Rev. Legend:** . . . The People's Princess

Date	Mintage	F	VF	XF	Unc	BU
1997 Proof	Est. 10,000	Value: 47.50				

KM# 91 10 DOLLARS Weight: 28.2800 g. **Composition:** 0.9250 Silver .8411 oz. ASW **Obverse:** Crowned arms **Reverse:** Diana **Rev. Legend:** . . . Princess of Wales

Date	Mintage	F	VF	XF	Unc	BU
1997 Proof	Est. 10,000	Value: 47.50				

KM# 92 10 DOLLARS Weight: 28.2800 g. **Composition:** 0.9250 Silver .8411 oz. ASW **Obverse:** Crowned arms **Reverse:** Diana, sprays below bust **Rev. Legend:** . . . Princess of Wales

Date	Mintage	F	VF	XF	Unc	BU
1997 Proof	Est. 10,000	Value: 47.50				

KM# 104 10 DOLLARS Weight: 28.2800 g. **Composition:** 0.9250 Silver .8411 oz. ASW **Obverse:** Head of Queen Elizabeth II right **Reverse:** Diana **Rev. Legend:** . . . In Memoriam

Date	Mintage	F	VF	XF	Unc	BU
1998 Proof	Est. 10,000	Value: 47.50				

KM# 105 10 DOLLARS Weight: 28.2800 g. **Composition:** 0.9250 Silver .8411 oz. ASW **Obverse:** Head of Queen Elizabeth II right **Reverse:** Diana **Rev. Legend:** . . . Princess of Wales

Date	Mintage	F	VF	XF	Unc	BU
1998 Proof	Est. 10,000	Value: 47.50				

KM# 116 10 DOLLARS Weight: 28.2800 g. **Composition:** 0.9250 Silver .8411 oz. ASW **Subject:** 50th Anniversary of Peanuts **Obverse:** Head of Queen Elizabeth II right **Reverse:** Snoopy and Woodstock

Date	Mintage	F	VF	XF	Unc	BU
2000 Proof	Est. 10,000	Value: 50.00				

KM# 124 10 DOLLARS Weight: 28.2800 g. **Composition:** 0.9250 Silver .8410 oz. ASW **Subject:** Snoopy as an Ace **Obverse:** Queen's portrait **Reverse:** Snoopy flying his dog house **Edge:** Reeded **Size:** 38.6 mm.

Date	Mintage	F	VF	XF	Unc	BU
2001 Proof	10,000	Value: 47.50				

KM# 130 10 DOLLARS Weight: 28.2800 g. **Composition:** 0.9250 Silver .8410 oz. ASW **Series:** Pokeman **Obverse:** National arms **Reverse:** "Bulbasaur" **Edge:** Reeded **Size:** 38.6 mm.

Date	Mintage	F	VF	XF	Unc	BU
2001 Proof	10,000	Value: 47.50				

KM# 133 10 DOLLARS Weight: 28.2800 g. **Composition:** 0.9250 Silver .8410 oz. ASW **Series:** Pokeman **Obverse:** National arms **Reverse:** "Charmander" **Edge:** Reeded **Size:** 38.6 mm.

Date	Mintage	F	VF	XF	Unc	BU
2001 Proof	10,000	Value: 47.50				

KM# 136 10 DOLLARS Weight: 28.2800 g. **Composition:** 0.9250 Silver .8410 oz. ASW **Series:** Pokeman **Obverse:** National arms **Reverse:** "Meowth" **Edge:** Reeded **Size:** 38.6 mm.

Date	Mintage	F	VF	XF	Unc	BU
2001 Proof	10,000	Value: 47.50				

KM# 139 10 DOLLARS Weight: 28.2800 g. **Composition:** 0.9250 Silver .8410 oz. ASW **Series:** Pokeman **Obverse:** National arms **Reverse:** "Pikachu" **Edge:** Reeded **Size:** 38.6 mm.

Date	Mintage	F	VF	XF	Unc	BU
2001 Proof	10,000	Value: 47.50				

KM# 142 10 DOLLARS Weight: 28.2800 g. **Composition:** 0.9250 Silver .8410 oz. ASW **Series:** Pokeman **Obverse:** National arms **Reverse:** "Squirtle" **Edge:** Reeded **Size:** 38.6 mm.

Date	Mintage	F	VF	XF	Unc	BU
2001 Proof	10,000	Value: 47.50				

KM# 147 10 DOLLARS Weight: 28.2800 g. **Composition:** 0.9250 Silver 0.841 oz. ASW **Subject:** Pokemon Series **Obverse:** National arms **Reverse:** Pikachu **Edge:** Reeded **Size:** 38.6 mm.

Date	Mintage	F	VF	XF	Unc	BU
2002PM Proof	10,000	Value: 47.50				

KM# 152 10 DOLLARS Weight: 28.2800 g. **Composition:** 0.9250 Silver 0.841 oz. ASW **Subject:** Pokemon Series **Obverse:** National arms **Reverse:** Pichu **Edge:** Reeded **Size:** 38.6 mm.

Date	Mintage	F	VF	XF	Unc	BU
2002PM Proof	10,000	Value: 47.50				

KM# 157 10 DOLLARS Weight: 28.2800 g. **Composition:** 0.9250 Silver 0.841 oz. ASW **Subject:** Pokemon Series **Reverse:** Mewtwo **Edge:** Reeded **Size:** 38.6 mm.

Date	Mintage	F	VF	XF	Unc	BU
2002PM Proof	10,000	Value: 47.50				

KM# 162 10 DOLLARS Weight: 28.2800 g. **Composition:** 0.9250 Silver 0.841 oz. ASW **Subject:** Pokemon Series **Obverse:** National arms **Reverse:** Entei **Edge:** Reeded **Size:** 38.6 mm.

Date	Mintage	F	VF	XF	Unc	BU
2002PM Proof	10,000	Value: 47.50				

KM# 167 10 DOLLARS Weight: 28.2800 g. **Composition:** 0.9250 Silver 0.841 oz. ASW **Subject:** Pokemon Series **Obverse:** National arms **Reverse:** Celebi **Edge:** Reeded **Size:** 38.6 mm.

Date	Mintage	F	VF	XF	Unc	BU
2002PM Proof	10,000	Value: 47.50				

KM# 57 20 DOLLARS Weight: 31.4700 g. **Composition:** 0.9250 Silver .9359 oz. ASW **Subject:** 40th Anniversary of Coronation **Obverse:** Head of Queen Elizabeth II right

Date	Mintage	F	VF	XF	Unc	BU
1993 Proof	Est. 10,000	Value: 55.00				

KM# 63 20 DOLLARS Weight: 31.4700 g. **Composition:** 0.9250 Silver .9359 oz. ASW **Series:** Protect Our World **Obverse:** Crowned arms **Reverse:** Hand ho;lding seedling

Date	Mintage	F	VF	XF	Unc	BU
1993 Proof	Est. 10,000	Value: 27.50				

KM# 64 20 DOLLARS **Weight:** 31.4700 g. **Composition:** 0.9250 Silver .9359 oz. ASW **Obverse:** Crowned arms **Reverse:** Kennedy and Statue of Liberty

Date		F	VF	XF	Unc	BU
1993 Proof	—	Value: 37.50				

KM# 93 20 DOLLARS **Weight:** 1.2440 g. **Composition:** 0.9990 Gold .0400 oz. AGW **Obverse:** Crowned arms **Reverse:** Diana **Rev. Legend:** . . . The people's Princess

Date	Mintage	F	VF	XF	Unc	BU
1997 Proof	Est. 10,000	Value: 40.00				

KM# 94 20 DOLLARS **Weight:** 1.2440 g. **Composition:** 0.9990 Gold .0400 oz. AGW **Obverse:** Crowned arms **Reverse:** Diana **Rev. Legend:** . . . Princess of Wales

Date	Mintage	F	VF	XF	Unc	BU
1997 Proof	Est. 10,000	Value: 45.00				

KM# 95 20 DOLLARS **Weight:** 1.2440 g. **Composition:** 0.9990 Gold .0400 oz. AGW **Obverse:** Crowned arms **Reverse:** Diana, sprays below bust **Rev. Legend:** . . . Princess of Wales

Date	Mintage	F	VF	XF	Unc	BU
1997 Proof	Est. 10,000	Value: 45.00				

KM# 106 20 DOLLARS **Weight:** 1.2440 g. **Composition:** 0.9990 Gold .0400 oz. AGW **Obverse:** Head of Queen Elizabeth II right **Reverse:** Diana **Rev. Legend:** . . . In Memoriam

Date	Mintage	F	VF	XF	Unc	BU
1998 Proof	Est. 10,000	Value: 45.00				

KM# 107 20 DOLLARS **Weight:** 1.2440 g. **Composition:** 0.9990 Gold .0400 oz. AGW **Obverse:** Head of Queen Elizabeth II right **Reverse:** Diana **Rev. Legend:** . . . Princess of Wales

Date	Mintage	F	VF	XF	Unc	BU
1998 Proof	Est. 10,000	Value: 45.00				

KM# 117 20 DOLLARS **Weight:** 1.2400 g. **Composition:** 0.9990 Gold .0395 oz. AGW **Subject:** 50th Anniversary of Peanuts **Obverse:** Head of Queen Elizabeth II right **Reverse:** Snoppy and Woodstock

Date	Mintage	F	VF	XF	Unc	BU
2000 Proof	Est. 10,000	Value: 50.00				

KM# 125 20 DOLLARS **Weight:** 1.2400 g. **Composition:** 0.9999 Gold .0399 oz. AGW **Subject:** Snoopy as an Ace **Obverse:** Queen's portrait **Reverse:** Snoopy flying his dog house **Edge:** Reeded **Size:** 13.9 mm.

Date	Mintage	F	VF	XF	Unc	BU
2001 Proof	10,000	Value: 58.00				

KM# 148 20 DOLLARS **Weight:** 1.2400 g. **Composition:** 0.9999 Gold 0.0399 oz. AGW **Subject:** Pokemon Series **Obverse:** National arms **Reverse:** Pikachu **Edge:** Reeded **Size:** 13.92 mm.

Date	Mintage	F	VF	XF	Unc	BU
2002PM Proof	10,000	Value: 49.50				

KM# 158 20 DOLLARS **Weight:** 1.2400 g. **Composition:** 0.9999 Gold 0.0399 oz. AGW **Subject:** Pokemon Series **Reverse:** Mewtwo **Edge:** Reeded **Size:** 13.92 mm.

Date	Mintage	F	VF	XF	Unc	BU
2002PM Proof	10,000	Value: 49.50				

KM# 163 20 DOLLARS **Subject:** Pokemon Series **Obverse:** National arms **Reverse:** Entei **Edge:** Reeded **Size:** 13.9 mm.

Date	Mintage	F	VF	XF	Unc	BU
2002PM Proof	10,000	—	—	—	—	—

KM# 168 20 DOLLARS **Weight:** 1.2400 g. **Composition:** 0.9999 Gold 0.0399 oz. AGW **Subject:** Pokemon Series **Obverse:** National arms **Reverse:** Celebi **Edge:** Reeded **Size:** 13.9 mm.

Date	Mintage	F	VF	XF	Unc	BU
2002PM Proof	10,000	Value: 49.50				

KM# 153 20 DOLLARS **Weight:** 1.2400 g. **Composition:** 0.9999 Gold 0.0399 oz. AGW **Subject:** Pokemon Series **Obverse:** National arms **Reverse:** Pichu **Edge:** Reeded **Size:** 13.9 mm.

Date	Mintage	F	VF	XF	Unc	BU
2002PM Proof	10,000	Value: 49.50				

KM# 79 25 DOLLARS **Weight:** 1.2441 g. **Composition:** 0.9990 Gold .0400 oz. AGW **Obverse:** Crowned arms **Reverse:** Kennedy taking oath

Date	Mintage	F	VF	XF	Unc	BU
1994 Proof	Est. 25,000	Value: 50.00				

KM# 82 25 DOLLARS **Weight:** 3.1000 g. **Composition:** 0.9990 Gold .1000 oz. AGW **Series:** Liberty Gold Bullion **Obverse:** Head of Queen Elizabeth II right **Reverse:** Statue of Liberty

Date	F	VF	XF	Unc	BU
1997	—	—	—	65.00	—

KM# 96 25 DOLLARS **Weight:** 3.1000 g. **Composition:** 0.9990 Gold .1000 oz. AGW **Obverse:** Crowned arms **Reverse:** Diana **Rev. Legend:** . . . The People's Princess

Date	Mintage	F	VF	XF	Unc	BU
1997 Proof	Est. 7,500	Value: 95.00				

KM# 97 25 DOLLARS **Weight:** 3.1000 g. **Composition:** 0.9990 Gold .1000 oz. AGW **Obverse:** Crowned arms **Reverse:** Diana **Rev. Legend:** . . . Princess of Wales

Date	Mintage	F	VF	XF	Unc	BU
1997 Proof	Est. 7,500	Value: 95.00				

KM# 98 25 DOLLARS **Weight:** 3.1000 g. **Composition:** 0.9990 Gold .1000 oz. AGW **Obverse:** Crowned arms **Reverse:** , sprays below bust **Rev. Legend:** . . . Princess of Wales

Date	Mintage	F	VF	XF	Unc	BU
1997 Proof	Est. 7,500	Value: 95.00				

KM# 2 50 DOLLARS **Weight:** 27.1000 g. **Composition:** 0.6250 Silver .5446 oz. ASW **Series:** Olympics **Subject:** Tennis **Obverse:** Crowned arms **Reverse:** Boris Becker

Date	Mintage	F	VF	XF	Unc	BU
1987 Proof	20,000	Value: 18.50				

KM# 6 50 DOLLARS **Weight:** 27.1000 g. **Composition:** 0.6250 Silver .5446 oz. ASW **Series:** Olympics **Subject:** Tennis **Obverse:** Crowned arms **Reverse:** Steffi Graf

Date	Mintage	F	VF	XF	Unc	BU
1987 Proof	20,000	Value: 17.50				

KM# 13 50 DOLLARS **Weight:** 27.1000 g. **Composition:** 0.6250 Silver .5446 oz. ASW **Series:** Olympics **Subject:** Tennis **Obverse:** Crowned arms **Reverse:** Steffi Graf **Note:** Similar to 5 Dollars, KM#11.

Date	Mintage	F	VF	XF	Unc	BU
1988 Proof	Est. 20,000	Value: 35.00				

KM# 14 50 DOLLARS **Weight:** 27.1000 g. **Composition:** 0.6250 Silver .5446 oz. ASW **Series:** Olympics **Subject:** Soccer **Obverse:** Crowned arms **Reverse:** Franz Beckenbauer

Date	Mintage	F	VF	XF	Unc	BU
1988 Proof	Est. 20,000	Value: 25.00				

KM# 16 50 DOLLARS **Weight:** 27.1000 g. **Composition:** 0.6250 Silver .5446 oz. ASW **Series:** Olympics **Subject:** Tennis **Obverse:** Crowned arms **Reverse:** Navratilova, Graf and Evert

Date	Mintage	F	VF	XF	Unc	BU
1988 Proof	Est. 20,000	Value: 32.50				

KM# 18 50 DOLLARS **Weight:** 28.2800 g. **Composition:** 0.9250 Silver .8411 oz. ASW **Obverse:** Crowned arms **Reverse:** President John F. Kennedy

Date	Mintage	F	VF	XF	Unc	BU
1988 Proof	20,000	Value: 27.50				

KM# 43 50 DOLLARS **Weight:** 28.2800 g. **Composition:** 0.9250 Silver .8411 oz. ASW **Subject:** Soccer **Obverse:** Crowned arms **Reverse:** 2 players

Date	F	VF	XF	Unc	BU
1988 Proof	—	Value: 25.00			

KM# 23 50 DOLLARS **Weight:** 31.1030 g. **Composition:** 0.9990 Silver 1.0000 oz. ASW **Obverse:** Crowned arms **Reverse:** General Douglas MacArthur

Date	Mintage	F	VF	XF	Unc	BU
1989 Proof	Est. 50,000	Value: 27.50				

KM# 25 50 DOLLARS **Weight:** 28.2800 g. **Composition:** 0.9250 Silver .8411 oz. ASW **Series:** Davis Cup Tennis **Obverse:** Crowned arms **Reverse:** 4 players

Date	Mintage	F	VF	XF	Unc	BU
1989 Proof	Est. 20,000	Value: 35.00				

KM# 27 50 DOLLARS **Weight:** 28.2800 g. **Composition:** 0.9250 Silver .8411 oz. ASW **Series:** 1992 Olympics **Subject:** Rowing **Obverse:** Crowned arms **Reverse:** 2 men rowing

Date	Mintage	F	VF	XF	Unc	BU
1989 Proof	Est. 30,000	Value: 25.00				

KM# 44 50 DOLLARS **Weight:** 28.2800 g. **Composition:** 0.9250 Silver .8411 oz. ASW **Series:** Olympics **Subject:** Tennis **Obverse:** Crowned arms **Reverse:** Steffi Graf

Date	Mintage	F	VF	XF	Unc	BU
1989 Proof	20,000	Value: 22.50				

KM# 30 50 DOLLARS **Weight:** 31.1030 g. **Composition:** 0.9990 Silver 1.000 oz. ASW **Obverse:** Crowned arms **Reverse:** General Dwight D. Eisenhower

Date	Mintage	F	VF	XF	Unc	BU
1990 Proof	Est. 50,000	Value: 25.00				

KM# 32 50 DOLLARS **Weight:** 31.1030 g. **Composition:** 0.9990 Silver 1.000 oz. ASW **Obverse:** Crowned arms **Reverse:** General George S. Patton

Date	Mintage	F	VF	XF	Unc	BU
1990 Proof	Est. 50,000	Value: 25.00				

KM# 34 50 DOLLARS **Weight:** 31.1030 g. **Composition:** 0.9990 Silver 1.000 oz. ASW **Obverse:** Crowned arms **Reverse:** Admiral William Halsey

Date	Mintage	F	VF	XF	Unc	BU
1990 Proof	Est. 50,000	Value: 30.00				

KM# 36 50 DOLLARS **Weight:** 31.1030 g. **Composition:** 0.9990 Silver 1.000 oz. ASW **Obverse:** Crowned arms **Reverse:** President Franklin D. Roosevelt

Date	Mintage	F	VF	XF	Unc	BU
1990 Proof	Est. 50,000	Value: 25.00				

KM# 38 50 DOLLARS **Weight:** 31.1030 g. **Composition:** 0.9990 Silver 1.000 oz. ASW **Obverse:** Crowned arms **Reverse:** Sir Winston Churchill

Date	Mintage	F	VF	XF	Unc	BU
1990 Proof	Est. 50,000	Value: 25.00				

KM# 47 50 DOLLARS **Weight:** 38.2000 g. **Composition:** 0.9250 Silver 1.1361 oz. ASW **Subject:** Soccer **Obverse:** Crowned arms **Reverse:** Player kicking ball

Date	Mintage	F	VF	XF	Unc	BU
1990 Proof	20,000	Value: 22.50				

KM# 75 50 DOLLARS **Weight:** 28.5600 g. **Composition:** 0.9250 Silver .8984 oz. ASW **Subject:** Soccer **Obverse:** Crowned arms **Reverse:** 2 players

Date	Mintage	F	VF	XF	Unc	BU
1990 Proof	20,000	Value: 25.00				

KM#71 50 DOLLARS **Weight:** 7.7000 g. **Composition:** 0.5830 Gold .1444 oz. AGW **Series:** Olympics **Obverse:** Crowned arms **Reverse:** Discus thrower

Date	Mintage	F	VF	XF	Unc	BU
1992 Proof	6,000	Value: 125				

KM# 65 50 DOLLARS **Weight:** 155.5175 g. **Composition:** 0.9990 Silver 5.000 oz. ASW **Obverse:** Crowned arms **Reverse:** Bust of President Kennedy left, Apollo rocket

Date	F	VF	XF	Unc	BU
1993 Proof	—	Value: 200			

KM# 66 50 DOLLARS **Weight:** 7.7760 g. **Composition:** 0.5830 Gold .1458 oz. AGW **Obverse:** Crowned arms **Reverse:** Bust of President John F. Kennedy left, Apollo rocket

Date	F	VF	XF	Unc	BU
1993 Proof	—	Value: 110			

KM# 72 50 DOLLARS **Weight:** 156.1700 g. **Composition:** 0.9990 Silver 5.0247 oz. ASW **Series:** World Cup Soccer **Obverse:** Crowned arms **Size:** 65 mm. **Note:** Illustration reduced.

Date	Mintage	F	VF	XF	Unc	BU
1994 Proof	Est. 3,000	Value: 175				

KM#83 50 DOLLARS **Weight:** 6.2200 g. **Composition:** 0.9990 Gold .2000 oz. AGW **Series:** Liberty Gold Bullion **Obverse:** Bust of Queen Elizabeth II right **Reverse:** Statue of Liberty

Date	F	VF	XF	Unc	BU
1997	—	—	—	110	—

KM# 108 50 DOLLARS **Weight:** 3.1100 g. **Composition:** 0.9999 Gold .1000 oz. AGW **Obverse:** Bust of Queen Elizabeth II right **Reverse:** Diana **Rev. Legend:** . . . In Memoriam

Date	Mintage	F	VF	XF	Unc	BU
1998 Proof	Est. 7,500	Value: 95.00				

KM# 109 50 DOLLARS **Weight:** 3.1100 g. **Composition:** 0.9999 Gold .1000 oz. AGW **Obverse:** Bust of Queen Elizabeth II right **Reverse:** Diana **Rev. Legend:** . . . Princess of Wales

Date	Mintage	F	VF	XF	Unc	BU
1998 Proof	Est. 7,500	Value: 95.00				

KM# 118 50 DOLLARS **Weight:** 3.1103 g. **Composition:** 0.9990 Gold .1000 oz. AGW **Subject:** 50th Anniversary of Peanuts **Obverse:** Head of Queen Elizabeth II right **Reverse:** Snoopy and Woodstock

Date	Mintage	F	VF	XF	Unc	BU
2000 Proof	Est. 7,500	Value: 100				

KM# 126 50 DOLLARS **Weight:** 3.1100 g. **Composition:** 0.9999 Gold .1000 oz. AGW **Subject:** Snoopy as an Ace **Obverse:** Queen's portrait **Reverse:** Snoopy flying his dog house **Edge:** Reeded **Size:** 17.9 mm.

Date	Mintage	F	VF	XF	Unc	BU
2001 Proof	7,500	Value: 95.00				

KM# 149 50 DOLLARS **Weight:** 3.1100 g. **Composition:** 0.9999 Gold 0.1 oz. AGW **Subject:** Pokemon

Series **Obverse:** National arms **Reverse:** Pikachu **Edge:** Reeded **Size:** 17.9 mm.

	Mintage	F	VF	XF	Unc	BU
2PM Proof	7,500	Value: 95.00				

 # 154 50 DOLLARS **Weight:** 3.1100 g. **Composition:** 0.9999 Gold 0.1 oz. AGW **Subject:** Pokemon Series **Obverse:** National arms **Reverse:** Pichu **Edge:** Reeded **Size:** 17.9 mm.

	Mintage	F	VF	XF	Unc	BU
2PM Proof	7,500	Value: 95.00				

 # 159 50 DOLLARS **Weight:** 3.1100 g. **Composition:** 0.9999 Gold 0.1 oz. AGW **Subject:** Pokemon Series **Obverse:** National arms **Reverse:** Mewtwo **Edge:** Reeded **Size:** 17.9 mm.

	Mintage	F	VF	XF	Unc	BU
2PM Proof	7,500	Value: 95.00				

 # 164 50 DOLLARS **Weight:** 3.1100 g. **Composition:** 0.9999 Gold 0.1 oz. AGW **Subject:** Pokemon Series **Obverse:** National arms **Reverse:** Entei **Edge:** Reeded **Size:** 17.9 mm.

	Mintage	F	VF	XF	Unc	BU
2PM Proof	7,500	Value: 95.00				

 # 169 50 DOLLARS **Weight:** 3.1100 g. **Composition:** 0.9999 Gold 0.1 oz. AGW **Subject:** Pokemon Series **Obverse:** National arms **Reverse:** Celebi **Edge:** Reeded **Size:** 17.9 mm.

	Mintage	F	VF	XF	Unc	BU
2PM Proof	7,500	Value: 95.00				

 # 7 100 DOLLARS **Weight:** 155.5175 g. **Composition:** 0.9990 Silver 5.0000 oz. ASW **Series:** Olympics **Subject:** Tennis **Obverse:** Crowned arms **Reverse:** Steffi Graf

	Mintage	F	VF	XF	Unc	BU
7	Est. 5,000	Value: 100				

 # 3 100 DOLLARS **Weight:** 155.5175 g. **Composition:** 0.9990 Silver 5.0000 oz. ASW **Series:** Olympics **Subject:** Tennis **Obverse:** Crowned arms **Reverse:** Boris Becker **Size:** 65 mm. **Note:** Illustration reduced.

	Mintage	F	VF	XF	Unc	BU
7 Proof	Est. 5,000	Value: 80.00				

 # 77 100 DOLLARS **Composition:** Silver **Note:** Similar to $5 KM#11.

	F	VF	XF	Unc	BU
8	—	—	—	150	—

 # 19 100 DOLLARS **Weight:** 155.5175 g. **Composition:** 0.9990 Silver 5.0000 oz. ASW **Obverse:** Crowned arms **Reverse:** Head of President John F. Kennedy left

	Mintage	F	VF	XF	Unc	BU
8 Proof	3,000	Value: 85.00				

 # 21 100 DOLLARS **Weight:** 155.5175 g. **Composition:** 0.9990 Silver 5.0000 oz. ASW **Subject:** Soccer **Obverse:** Crowned arms **Reverse:** Franz Beckenbauer

	Mintage	F	VF	XF	Unc	BU
8 Proof	3,000	Value: 125				

 # 40 100 DOLLARS **Weight:** 155.5175 g. **Composition:** 0.9990 Silver 5.0000 oz. ASW **Series:** Olympics **Subject:** Tennis **Obverse:** Crowned arms **Reverse:** Navratilova, Graf and Evert

Date	Mintage	F	VF	XF	Unc	BU
1988 Proof	Est. 3,000	Value: 120				

KM# 28 100 DOLLARS **Weight:** 155.5175 g. **Composition:** 0.9990 Silver 5.0000 oz. ASW **Series:** Olympics **Subject:** Tennis **Obverse:** Crowned arms **Reverse:** Steffi Graf **Size:** 65 mm. **Note:** Illustration reduced.

Date	Mintage	F	VF	XF	Unc	BU
1989 Proof	3,000	Value: 120				

KM# 73 100 DOLLARS **Weight:** 154.8500 g. **Composition:** 0.9990 Silver 4.9791 oz. ASW **Subject:** Soccer **Obverse:** Crowned arms **Reverse:** 1990 World Champion Italian soccer team **Size:** 65 mm. **Note:** Illustration reduced.

Date	Mintage	F	VF	XF	Unc	BU
1990 Proof	Est. 3,000	Value: 175				

KM# 84 100 DOLLARS **Weight:** 15.5517 g. **Composition:** 0.9990 Gold .5000 oz. AGW **Series:** Liberty Gold Bullion **Obverse:** Head of Queen Elizabeth II right **Reverse:** Statue of Liberty

Date	F	VF	XF	Unc	BU
1997	—	—	—	225	—

KM# 99 100 DOLLARS **Weight:** 6.2200 g. **Composition:** 0.9990 Gold .2000 oz. AGW **Obverse:** Crowned arms **Reverse:** Diana **Rev. Legend:** . . . The People's Princess

Date	Mintage	F	VF	XF	Unc	BU
1997 Proof	Est. 5,000	Value: 150				

KM# 100 100 DOLLARS **Weight:** 6.2200 g. **Composition:** 0.9990 Gold .2000 oz. AGW **Obverse:** Crowned arms **Reverse:** Diana **Rev. Legend:** . . . Princess of Wales

Date	Mintage	F	VF	XF	Unc	BU
1997 Proof	Est. 5,000	Value: 150				

KM# 101 100 DOLLARS **Weight:** 6.2200 g. **Composition:** 0.9990 Gold .2000 oz. AGW **Obverse:** Crowned arms **Reverse:** Diana, sprays below bust **Rev. Legend:** . . . Princess of Wales

Date	Mintage	F	VF	XF	Unc	BU
1997 Proof	Est. 5,000	Value: 150				

KM# 110 100 DOLLARS **Weight:** 6.2200 g. **Composition:** 0.9990 Gold .2000 oz. AGW **Obverse:** Bust of Queen Elizabeth II right **Reverse:** Diana **Rev. Legend:** . . . In Memoriam

Date	Mintage	F	VF	XF	Unc	BU
1998 Proof	Est. 5,000	Value: 150				

KM# 111 100 DOLLARS **Weight:** 6.2200 g. **Composition:** 0.9990 Gold .2000 oz. AGW **Obverse:** Bust of Queen Elizabeth II right **Reverse:** Diana **Rev. Legend:** . . . Princess of Wales

Date	Mintage	F	VF	XF	Unc	BU
1998 Proof	Est. 5,000	Value: 150				

KM# 119 100 DOLLARS **Weight:** 6.2200 g. **Composition:** 0.9990 Gold .2000 oz. AGW **Subject:** 50th Anniversary of Peanuts **Obverse:** Bust of Queen Elizabeth II right **Reverse:** Snoopy and Woodstock

Date	Mintage	F	VF	XF	Unc	BU
2000 Proof	Est. 5,000	Value: 175				

KM# 127 100 DOLLARS **Weight:** 6.2200 g. **Composition:** 0.9990 Gold .2000 oz. AGW **Subject:** Snoopy as an Ace **Obverse:** Queen's portrait **Reverse:** Snoopy flying his dog house **Edge:** Reeded **Size:** 22 mm.

Date	Mintage	F	VF	XF	Unc	BU
2001 Proof	5,000	Value: 205				

KM# 150 100 DOLLARS **Weight:** 6.2200 g. **Composition:** 0.9999 Gold 0.2 oz. AGW **Subject:** Pokemon Series **Obverse:** National arms **Reverse:** Pikachu **Edge:** Reeded **Size:** 22 mm.

Date	Mintage	F	VF	XF	Unc	BU
2002PM Proof	5,000	—	—	—	—	—

KM# 155 100 DOLLARS **Weight:** 6.2200 g. **Composition:** 0.9999 Gold 0.2 oz. AGW **Subject:** Pokemon Series **Obverse:** National arms **Reverse:** Pichu **Edge:** Reeded **Size:** 22 mm.

Date	Mintage	F	VF	XF	Unc	BU
2002PM Proof	5,000	Value: 175				

KM# 160 100 DOLLARS **Weight:** 6.2200 g. **Composition:** 0.9999 Gold 0.2 oz. AGW **Subject:** Pokemon Series **Obverse:** National arms **Reverse:** Mewtwo **Edge:** Reeded **Size:** 22 mm.

Date	Mintage	F	VF	XF	Unc	BU
2002PM Proof	5,000	Value: 175				

KM# 165 100 DOLLARS **Weight:** 6.2200 g. **Composition:** 0.9999 Gold 0.2 oz. AGW **Subject:** Pokemon Series **Obverse:** National arms **Reverse:** Entei **Edge:** Reeded **Size:** 22 mm.

Date	Mintage	F	VF	XF	Unc	BU
2002PM Proof	5,000	Value: 175				

KM# 170 100 DOLLARS **Weight:** 3.1100 g. **Composition:** 0.9999 Gold 0.1 oz. AGW **Subject:** Pokemon Series **Obverse:** National arms **Reverse:** Celebi **Edge:** reeded **Size:** 22 mm.

Date	Mintage	F	VF	XF	Unc	BU
2002PM Proof	5,000	Value: 175				

KM# 4 200 DOLLARS **Weight:** 311.0350 g. **Composition:** 0.9990 Silver 10.000 oz. ASW **Series:** Olympics **Subject:** Tennis **Obverse:** Crowned arms **Reverse:** Boris Becker

Date	Mintage	F	VF	XF	Unc	BU
1987 Proof	Est. 3,000	Value: 165				

KM# 8 200 DOLLARS **Weight:** 311.0350 g. **Composition:** 0.9990 Silver 10.000 oz. ASW **Series:** Olympics **Subject:** Tennis **Obverse:** Crowned arms **Reverse:** Steffi Graf

Date	Mintage	F	VF	XF	Unc	BU
1987 Proof	Est. 3,000	Value: 165				

KM# 42 200 DOLLARS **Weight:** 6.9117 g. **Composition:** 0.9000 Gold .2000 oz. AGW **Obverse:** Crowned arms **Reverse:** General Douglas MacArthur

Date	Mintage	F	VF	XF	Unc	BU
1989 Proof	Est. 2,500	Value: 150				

KM# 50 200 DOLLARS **Weight:** 6.9117 g. **Composition:** 0.9000 Gold .2000 oz. AGW **Obverse:** Crowned arms **Reverse:** General George S. Patton

Date		F	VF	XF	Unc	BU
1989 Proof	—	Value: 150				

KM# 45 200 DOLLARS **Weight:** 6.9117 g. **Composition:** 0.9000 Gold .2000 oz. AGW **Obverse:** Crowned arms **Reverse:** General Dwight D. Eisenhower

Date	Mintage	F	VF	XF	Unc	BU
1990 Proof	2,500	Value: 150				

KM# 51 200 DOLLARS **Weight:** 6.9117 g. **Composition:** 0.9000 Gold .2000 oz. AGW **Obverse:** Crowned arms **Reverse:** Admiral William Halsey

Date		F	VF	XF	Unc	BU
1990 Proof	—	Value: 150				

KM# 52 200 DOLLARS **Weight:** 6.9117 g. **Composition:** 0.9000 Gold .2000 oz. AGW **Obverse:** Crowned arms **Reverse:** President Franklin D. Roosevelt

Date		F	VF	XF	Unc	BU
1990 Proof	—	Value: 150				

KM# 53 200 DOLLARS **Weight:** 6.9117 g. **Composition:** 0.9000 Gold .2000 oz. AGW **Obverse:** Crowned arms **Reverse:** Sir Winston Churchill

Date		F	VF	XF	Unc	BU
1990 Proof	—	Value: 150				

KM# 9 250 DOLLARS **Weight:** 8.4830 g. **Composition:** 0.9170 Gold .2500 oz. AGW **Series:** Olympics **Subject:** Tennis **Obverse:** Crowned arms **Reverse:** Boris Becker

Date	Mintage	F	VF	XF	Unc	BU
1987 Proof	1,000	Value: 200				

KM# 10 250 DOLLARS **Weight:** 8.4830 g. **Composition:** 0.9170 Gold .2500 oz. AGW **Series:** Olympics **Subject:** Tennis **Obverse:** Crowned arms **Reverse:** Steffi Graf

Date	Mintage	F	VF	XF	Unc	BU
1987 Proof	1,000	Value: 275				

KM# 20 250 DOLLARS **Weight:** 10.0000 g. **Composition:** 0.9170 Gold .2948 oz. AGW **Obverse:** Crowned arms **Reverse:** Head of President John F. Kennedy left

Date	Mintage	F	VF	XF	Unc	BU
1988 Proof	5,000	Value: 175				

KM# 39 250 DOLLARS **Weight:** 10.0000 g. **Composition:** 0.9170 Gold .2948 oz. AGW **Subject:** Soccer **Obverse:** Crowned arms **Reverse:** Beckenbauer

Date	Mintage	F	VF	XF	Unc	BU
1988 Proof	Est. 5,000	Value: 150				

KM# 41 250 DOLLARS **Weight:** 10.0000 g. **Composition:** 0.9170 Gold .2948 oz. AGW **Series:** Olympics **Subject:** Tennis **Obverse:** Crowned arms **Reverse:** Navratilova, Graf and Evert

Date	Mintage	F	VF	XF	Unc	BU
1988 Proof	Est. 5,000	Value: 200				

KM# 48 250 DOLLARS **Weight:** 10.0000 g. **Composition:** 0.9170 Gold .2948 oz. AGW **Series:** Olympics **Subject:** Tennis **Obverse:** Crowned arms **Reverse:** Steffi Graf

Date	Mintage	F	VF	XF	Unc	BU
1988 Proof	5,000	Value: 190				

KM# 26 250 DOLLARS **Weight:** 10.0000 g. **Composition:** 0.9170 Gold .2948 oz. AGW **Series:** Davis Cup Tennis **Obverse:** Crowned arms

Date	Mintage	F	VF	XF	Unc	BU
1989 Proof	500	Value: 245				

KM# 49 250 DOLLARS **Weight:** 10.0000 g. **Composition:** 0.9170 Gold .2948 oz. AGW **Series:** Olympics **Subject:** Tennis **Obverse:** Crowned arms **Reverse:** Steffi Graf

Date	Mintage	F	VF	XF	Unc	BU
1989 Proof	3,000	Value: 225				

KM# 54 250 DOLLARS **Weight:** 10.0000 g. **Composition:** 0.9170 Gold .2948 oz. AGW **Subject:** Soccer - Italian **Obverse:** Crowned arms

Date	Mintage	F	VF	XF	Unc	BU
1990 Proof	Est. 2,500	Value: 225				

KM# 112 250 DOLLARS **Weight:** 15.5500 g. **Composition:** 0.9999 Gold .5000 oz. AGW **Obverse:** Head of Queenf Elizabeth II right **Reverse:** Diana **Rev. Legend:** . . . In Memoriam

Date	Mintage	F	VF	XF	Unc	BU
1998 Proof	Est. 3,000	Value: 340				

KM# A113 250 DOLLARS **Weight:** 15.5500 g. **Composition:** 0.9999 Gold .5 oz. AGW **Obverse:** Head of Queen Elizabeth II right **Reverse:** Diana **Rev. Legend:** ... Princess of Wales

Date	Mintage	F	VF	XF	Unc	BU
1998 Proof	3,000	Value: 340				

PATTERNS

Including off metal strikes

KM#	Date	Mintage	Identification	Mkt Val
Pn2	1990	2	5 Dollars. (No Composition). Silver Proof, KM35.	—
Pn3	1990	2	5 Dollars. (No Composition). Silver Proof, KM37.	—

NORWAY

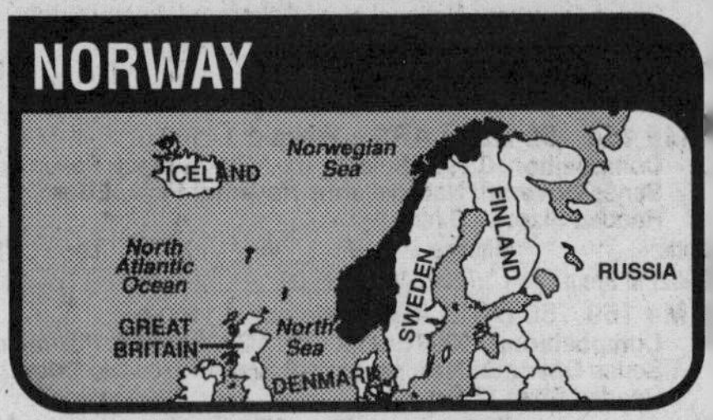

The Kingdom of Norway (*Norge, Noreg*), a constitutiona monarchy located in northwestern Europe, has an area c 150,000sq. mi. (324,220 sq. km.), including the island territorie of Spitzbergen (Svalbard) and Jan Mayen, and a population c *4.2 million. Capital: Oslo (Christiana). The diversified economi base of Norway includes shipping, fishing, forestry, agriculture and manufacturing. Nonferrous metals, paper and paperboarc paper pulp, iron, steel and oil are exported.

A united Norwegian kingdom was established in the 9th century, the era of the indomitable Norse Vikings who ranged far and wide, visiting the coasts of northwestern Europe, the Mediterranean, Greenland and North America. In the 13th century the Norse kingdom was united briefly with Sweden, then passed through inheritance in 1380 to the rule of Denmark which wa maintained until 1814. In 1814 Norway fell again under the rul of Sweden. The union lasted until 1905 when the Norwegian Parliament arranged a peaceful separation and invited a Danis prince (King Haakon VII) to ascend the throne of an independer Kingdom of Norway.

RULERS

Swedish, 1814-1905
Haakon VII, 1905-1957
Olav V, 1957-1991
Harald V, 1991-

MINT MARKS

(h) - Crossed hammers – Kongsberg

MINT OFFICIALS INITIALS

Letter	Date	Name
AB, B	1961-1980	Arne Jon Bakken
AB*	1980	Ole R. Kolberg
I, IT	1880-1918	Ivar Trondsen, engraver
IAR		Angrid Austlid Rise, engraver
K	1981	Ole R. Kolberg
OH	1959	Oivind Hansen, engraver

MONETARY SYSTEM

100 Ore = 1 Krone (30 Skilling)

KINGDOM

DECIMAL COINAGE

KM# 352 ORE **Weight:** 2.0000 g. **Composition:** Bronz **Note:** Varieties exist.

Date	Mintage	VG	F	VF	XF	B
1902	4,500,000	—	2.00	4.00	12.00	45.0

KM# 361 ORE **Weight:** 2.0000 g. **Composition:** Bronz

Date	Mintage	VG	F	VF	XF	B
1906	3,000,000	—	2.00	3.00	10.00	25.0
1907	2,550,000	—	2.00	3.00	10.00	25.0

KM# 367 ORE **Weight:** 2.0000 g. **Composition:** Bronz

Date	Mintage	VG	F	VF	XF	B
1908	1,450,000	—	10.00	16.00	45.00	16
1910	2,480,000	—	1.00	2.50	12.00	40.0
1911	3,270,000	—	1.00	2.50	12.00	50.0
1912	2,850,000	—	3.00	7.00	35.00	17
1913	2,840,000	—	1.00	2.50	6.00	32.5
1914	5,020,000	—	1.00	2.50	6.00	40.0
1915	1,540,000	—	10.00	22.00	60.00	27
1921	3,805,000	—	20.00	40.00	95.00	27
1922	Inc. above	—	0.50	2.00	15.00	55.0
1923	770,000	—	6.00	14.00	35.00	16
1925	3,000,000	—	0.50	1.50	15.00	60.0
1926	2,200,000	—	0.50	1.50	15.00	60.0
1927	800,000	—	3.00	10.00	28.00	16
1928	3,000,000	—	0.25	0.75	4.50	25.0
1929	4,990,000	—	0.25	0.75	4.50	20.0
1930 large date	2,009,999	—	0.50	1.00	6.00	27.5

Date	Mintage	VG	F	VF	XF	BU
1930 small date	Inc. above	—	0.50	1.00	6.00	27.50
1931	2,000,000	—	0.50	1.00	6.00	25.00
1932	2,500,000	—	0.50	1.00	6.00	25.00
1933	2,000,000	—	0.50	1.00	6.00	20.00
1934	2,000,000	—	0.50	1.00	6.00	25.00
1935	5,495,000	—	0.25	0.75	2.50	12.50
1936	6,855,000	—	0.25	0.75	2.50	12.50
1937	6,020,000	—	0.20	0.50	1.50	8.00
1938	4,920,000	—	0.20	0.50	1.50	8.00
1939	2,500,000	—	0.20	0.50	1.50	12.50
1940	5,010,000	—	0.20	0.50	1.50	8.00
1941	12,260,000	—	0.10	0.25	1.50	8.00
1946	2,200,000	—	0.10	0.25	1.50	8.00
1947	4,870,000	—	0.10	0.25	0.90	6.00
1948	9,405,000	—	0.10	0.25	0.90	5.00
1949	2,785,000	—	0.10	0.25	0.90	8.00
1950	5,730,000	—	0.10	0.25	0.90	5.00
1951	16,670,000	—	0.10	0.25	0.90	5.00
1952	Inc. above	—	0.10	0.25	0.90	4.00

KM# 367a ORE **Weight:** 1.7400 g. **Composition:** Iron

Date	Mintage	VG	F	VF	XF	BU
1918	6,000,000	—	5.00	8.00	17.50	65.00
1919	12,930,000	—	1.50	3.50	12.00	30.00
1920	4,445,000	—	6.00	10.00	25.00	150
1921	2,270,000	—	30.00	35.00	65.00	185

KM# 387 ORE **Weight:** 1.7400 g. **Composition:** Iron
Subject: World War II German occupation

Date	Mintage	VG	F	VF	XF	BU
1941	13,410,000	—	0.15	0.50	1.75	12.50
1942	37,710,000	—	0.15	0.50	1.75	6.00
1943	33,030,000	—	0.15	0.50	1.75	6.00
1944	8,820,000	—	0.25	0.75	2.25	6.50
1945	1,740,000	—	4.00	8.00	15.00	32.50

KM# 398 ORE **Weight:** 2.0000 g. **Composition:** Bronze

Date	Mintage	VG	F	VF	XF	BU
1952		—	—	0.10	1.00	6.50
Note: Mintage included with KM#367.						
1953	7,440,000	—	—	0.10	0.75	4.50
1954	7,650,000	—	—	0.10	0.75	4.50
1955	8,635,000	—	—	0.10	0.75	4.50
1956	11,705,000	—	—	0.10	0.75	4.50
1957	15,750,000	—	—	0.10	0.50	3.25

KM# 403 ORE **Weight:** 2.0000 g. **Composition:** Bronze
Note: Varieties exist.

Date	Mintage	VG	F	VF	XF	BU
1958	2,820,000	—	0.25	0.50	2.25	9.00
1959	9,120,000	—	0.10	0.20	0.85	7.50
1960	7,890,000	—	—	0.10	0.30	3.00
1961	5,670,600	—	—	0.10	0.30	3.00
1962	12,180,000	—	—	0.10	0.25	1.50
1963	8,010,000	—	—	0.10	0.30	3.00
1964	11,020,000	—	—	—	0.10	0.75
1965	8,081,000	—	—	—	0.15	2.00
1966	12,431,000	—	—	—	0.15	1.25
1967	13,026,000	—	—	—	0.10	0.75
1968	125,500	—	0.50	1.00	2.25	8.50
1969	6,290,500	—	—	—	0.10	0.50
1970	6,607,500	—	—	—	0.10	0.50
1971	18,966,000	—	—	—	0.10	0.40
1972	21,102,984	—	—	—	0.10	0.40

KM# 353 2 ORE **Weight:** 4.0000 g. **Composition:** Bronze

Date	Mintage	VG	F	VF	XF	BU
1902	1,005,000	—	1.50	4.00	12.00	115

KM# 362 2 ORE **Weight:** 4.0000 g. **Composition:** Bronze

Date	Mintage	VG	F	VF	XF	BU
1906	500,000	—	5.00	10.00	40.00	250
1907	980,000	—	3.00	4.00	20.00	120

KM# 371 2 ORE **Weight:** 4.0000 g. **Composition:** Bronze

Date	Mintage	VG	F	VF	XF	BU
1909	520,000	—	6.00	15.00	45.00	240
1910	500,000	—	6.00	15.00	45.00	450
1911	195,000	—	6.00	15.00	45.00	275
1912	805,000	—	6.00	15.00	45.00	275
1913	2,010,000	—	0.75	2.00	12.00	95.00
1914	2,990,000	—	0.75	2.00	12.00	95.00
1915	Inc. above	—	5.00	10.00	70.00	400
1921	2,028,000	—	0.50	1.00	12.00	65.00
1922	2,288,000	—	0.50	1.00	12.00	65.00
1923	745,000	—	1.00	2.00	30.00	145
1928	2,250,000	—	0.50	1.00	10.00	60.00
1929	750,000	—	1.00	2.00	18.00	100
1931	1,570,000	—	0.50	1.00	6.00	60.00
1932	630,000	—	3.50	6.00	35.00	210
1933	750,000	—	0.50	1.50	7.00	60.00
1934	500,000	—	0.50	1.50	7.00	60.00
1935	2,223,000	—	0.25	1.00	5.00	45.00
1936	4,533,000	—	0.25	1.00	5.00	45.00
1937	3,790,000	—	0.20	0.50	2.75	20.00
1938	3,765,000	—	0.20	0.50	2.75	20.00
1939	4,420,000	—	0.20	0.50	2.75	20.00
1940	2,655,000	—	0.20	0.50	2.75	20.00
1946	1,575,000	—	0.20	0.50	3.50	20.00
1947	4,679,000	—	0.10	0.25	1.25	12.50
1948	1,002,999	—	1.00	3.00	5.00	12.50
1949	1,455,000	—	0.10	0.25	1.00	9.00
1950	5,790,000	—	0.10	0.25	1.00	6.00
1951	10,540,000	—	0.10	0.25	1.00	5.00
1952	Inc. above	—	0.10	0.25	1.00	5.00

KM# 371a 2 ORE **Weight:** 3.4800 g. **Composition:** Iron

Date	Mintage	VG	F	VF	XF	BU
1917	720,000	—	75.00	120	240	425
1918	1,280,000	—	25.00	45.00	100	225
1919	3,365,000	—	10.00	15.00	40.00	150
1920	2,635,000	—	10.00	15.00	55.00	250

KM# 394 2 ORE **Weight:** 3.4700 g. **Composition:** Iron
Note: World War II German occupation issue.

Date	Mintage	VG	F	VF	XF	BU
1943	6,575,000	—	0.50	0.75	1.75	9.00
1944	9,805,000	—	0.50	0.75	1.75	9.00
1945	2,520,000	—	1.50	3.00	6.00	20.00

KM# 399 2 ORE **Weight:** 4.0000 g. **Composition:** Bronze

Date	Mintage	VG	F	VF	XF	BU
1952	Inc. above	—	—	0.10	0.85	8.50
1953	6,705,000	—	—	0.10	0.85	7.00
1954	2,805,000	—	—	0.10	0.85	7.00
1955	3,600,000	—	—	0.10	0.85	7.00
1956	6,780,000	—	—	0.10	0.85	7.00
1957	6,090,000	—	—	0.10	0.85	7.00

KM# 404 2 ORE **Weight:** 4.0000 g. **Composition:** Bronze **Reverse:** Small lettering

Date	Mintage	VG	F	VF	XF	BU
1958	2,700,000	—	0.20	0.50	1.75	10.00

KM# 410 2 ORE **Weight:** 4.0000 g. **Composition:** Bronze **Reverse:** Large lettering

Date	Mintage	VG	F	VF	XF	BU
1959	4,125,000	—	0.10	0.20	1.25	7.00
1960	3,735,000	—	—	0.10	0.85	12.50
1961	4,477,000	—	—	0.10	0.35	2.75
1962	6,205,000	—	—	0.10	0.35	2.75
1963	4,840,000	—	—	0.10	0.35	2.75
1964	7,250,000	—	—	0.10	0.20	1.50
1965	6,241,000	—	—	0.10	0.30	3.00
1966	10,485,000	—	—	—	0.15	2.75
1967	11,993,000	—	—	—	0.15	1.50
1968	3,467	—	—	—	—	900
Note: In mint sets only						
1969	315,600	—	0.50	1.00	1.75	6.00
1970	6,794,000	—	—	—	0.10	1.00
1971	15,462,000	—	—	—	0.10	0.85
1972	15,897,984	—	—	—	0.10	0.85

KM# 349 5 ORE **Weight:** 8.0000 g. **Composition:** Bronze

Date	Mintage	VG	F	VF	XF	BU
1902	705,000	—	2.50	6.00	40.00	275

KM# 364 5 ORE **Weight:** 8.0000 g. **Composition:** Bronze

Date	Mintage	VG	F	VF	XF	BU
1907	200,000	—	3.50	10.00	50.00	285

KM# 368 5 ORE **Composition:** Bronze

Date	Mintage	VG	F	VF	XF	BU
1908	600,000	—	20.00	40.00	120	520
1911	480,000	—	2.00	10.00	45.00	260
1912	520,000	—	4.00	25.00	90.00	650
1913	1,000,000	—	1.25	2.50	25.00	145
1914	1,000,000	—	1.25	2.50	25.00	145
1915	Inc. above	—	8.00	30.00	110	675
1916	300,000	—	6.00	12.50	40.00	285
1921	683,000	—	1.50	6.00	60.00	280
1922	2,296,000	—	1.25	5.00	30.00	150
1923	456,000	—	2.50	7.50	60.00	260
1928	848,000	—	0.60	3.00	18.00	110
1929	452,000	—	3.00	9.00	60.00	280
1930	1,292,000	—	0.60	2.50	25.00	120
1931	808,000	—	0.60	2.50	25.00	120
1932	500,000	—	3.00	10.00	35.00	190
1933	300,000	—	3.00	10.00	60.00	285
1935	496,000	—	1.50	5.00	18.00	160
1936	760,000	—	1.00	2.50	15.00	90.00
1937	1,552,000	—	0.50	1.50	12.00	50.00
1938	1,332,000	—	0.50	1.50	12.00	50.00
1939	1,370,000	—	0.50	1.50	9.00	50.00
1940	2,554,000	—	0.30	1.00	7.00	32.50
1941	3,576,000	—	0.30	1.00	6.00	25.00
1951	8,128,000	—	0.25	0.50	2.25	20.00
1952	Inc. above	—	1.50	3.50	9.00	50.00

KM# 368a 5 ORE **Weight:** 6.6900 g. **Composition:** Iron

Date	Mintage	VG	F	VF	XF	BU
1917	1,700,000	—	20.00	35.00	60.00	125
1918/7	432,000	—	120	200	375	850
1918	Inc. above	—	120	200	375	850
1919	3,464,000	—	8.00	25.00	60.00	200
1920	1,629,000	—	25.00	55.00	120	325

KM# 388 5 ORE Weight: 6.9400 g. **Composition:** Iron **Note:** World War II German occupation issue.

Date	Mintage	VG	F	VF	XF	BU
1941	6,608,000	—	0.50	1.50	5.50	40.00
1942	10,312,000	—	0.50	1.50	5.00	20.00
1943	6,184,000	—	0.75	2.00	7.00	32.50
1944	4,256,000	—	1.25	3.00	9.00	32.50
1945	408,000	—	145	165	270	520

KM# 400 5 ORE Weight: 8.0000 g. **Composition:** Bronze

Date	Mintage	VG	F	VF	XF	BU
1952	—	—	0.10	0.50	2.50	32.50

Note: Mintage included with KM#368.

Date	Mintage	VG	F	VF	XF	BU
1953	6,216,000	—	0.10	0.35	2.25	20.00
1954	4,536,000	—	0.10	0.35	2.25	20.00
1955	6,570,000	—	0.10	0.35	2.25	20.00
1956	2,959,000	—	0.10	0.35	2.25	25.00
1957	5,624,000	—	0.10	0.35	2.25	12.50

KM# 405 5 ORE Weight: 8.0000 g. **Composition:** Bronze

Date	Mintage	VG	F	VF	XF	BU
1958	2,205,000	—	1.00	2.00	6.00	40.00
1959	3,208,000	—	0.10	0.50	2.25	20.00
1960	5,519,000	—	0.10	0.20	1.25	12.50
1961	4,554,000	—	0.10	0.20	1.25	12.50
1962	7,764,000	—	0.10	0.15	0.75	6.50
1963	3,204,000	—	0.10	0.15	0.75	6.50
1964	6,108,000	—	—	0.10	0.50	3.00
1965	6,841,000	—	—	0.10	0.50	3.00
1966	8,415,000	—	—	0.10	0.50	3.00
1967	9,071,000	—	—	0.10	0.45	3.00
1968	4,286,000	—	—	0.10	0.85	4.50
1969	4,328,000	—	—	0.10	0.35	1.25
1970	7,350,600	—	—	0.10	0.35	1.25
1971	13,450,100	—	—	0.10	0.35	1.25
1972	19,001,784	—	—	—	0.15	1.00
1973	9,584,175	—	—	—	0.15	1.00

KM# 415 5 ORE Weight: 3.0000 g. **Composition:** Bronze **Note:** Varieties exist.

Date	Mintage	VG	F	VF	XF	BU
1973	52,886,175	—	—	—	0.10	0.45
1974	37,150,223	—	—	—	0.10	0.45
1975	32,478,744	—	—	—	0.10	0.45
1976	24,232,824	—	—	—	0.10	0.25
1977	29,646,000	—	—	—	0.10	0.25
1978	13,838,000	—	—	—	0.10	0.25
1979	25,255,000	—	—	—	0.10	0.25
1980	12,315,000	—	—	—	0.10	0.25
1980 Without star	27,515,000	—	—	—	0.10	0.25
1981	24,529,000	—	—	—	0.10	0.25
1982	16,849,000	—	—	—	0.10	0.25

KM# 350 10 ORE Weight: 1.5000 g. **Composition:** 0.4000 Silver .0192 oz. ASW

Date	Mintage	VG	F	VF	XF	BU
1901	2,021,100	—	5.00	10.00	22.50	50.00
1903	1,500,700	—	5.00	10.00	22.50	50.00

KM# 372 10 ORE Weight: 1.4500 g. **Composition:** 0.4000 Silver

Date	Mintage	VG	F	VF	XF	BU
1909	2,000,000	—	4.00	7.50	20.00	60.00
1911	1,650,000	—	5.00	10.00	30.00	175
1912	2,350,000	—	4.00	6.00	17.50	60.00
1913	2,000,000	—	4.00	6.00	17.50	50.00
1914	1,180,000	—	7.00	15.00	30.00	115
1915	2,820,000	—	1.50	3.00	7.00	50.00
1916	1,500,000	—	6.00	9.00	30.00	90.00
1917	5,950,000	—	1.00	2.00	5.00	10.00
1918/7	1,650,000	—	15.00	35.00	75.00	—
1918	Inc. above	—	1.50	2.50	6.00	25.00
1919/7	7,800,000	—	—	—	—	—
1919/7	7,800,000	—	15.00	35.00	75.00	—
1919	Inc. above	—	1.00	2.00	5.00	10.00

KM# 378 10 ORE Weight: 1.5000 g. **Composition:** Copper-Nickel

Date	Mintage	VG	F	VF	XF	BU
1920	2,535,000	—	10.00	15.00	25.00	55.00
1921	6,465,000	—	5.00	10.00	18.00	50.00
1922	3,965,000	—	5.00	10.00	18.00	50.00
1923	7,135,000	—	10.00	15.00	25.00	55.00

KM# 383 10 ORE Weight: 1.5000 g. **Composition:** Copper-Nickel

Date	Mintage	VG	F	VF	XF	BU
1924	12,079,100	—	0.30	0.75	9.00	40.00
1925	7,050,700	—	0.30	0.75	9.00	55.00
1926	11,764,200	—	0.30	0.75	9.00	40.00
1927	526,000	5.00	10.00	20.00	120	600
1937	5,000,000	—	0.30	0.75	5.00	27.50
1938	3,412,600	—	0.30	0.75	5.00	25.00
1939	1,538,400	—	1.00	2.50	9.50	50.00
1940	4,800,000	—	0.30	0.75	1.75	12.50
1941	10,150,000	—	0.30	0.75	1.75	10.00
1945	1,718,000	—	0.10	0.25	1.75	12.50
1946	3,723,200	—	0.10	0.25	1.75	9.00
1947	7,256,700	—	0.10	0.25	1.75	6.50
1948	3,104,500	—	0.10	0.25	2.00	7.00
1949	11,545,500	—	0.10	0.25	1.75	7.00
1951	5,150,000	—	0.10	0.25	1.75	7.00

KM# 389 10 ORE Weight: 1.2500 g. **Composition:** Zinc **Note:** World War II German occupation issue.

Date	Mintage	VG	F	VF	XF	BU
1941	15,309,900	—	0.75	2.00	6.00	32.50
1942	50,387,600	—	0.35	1.00	3.50	12.50
1943	13,377,700	—	0.75	2.00	5.50	25.00
1944	3,549,400	—	7.50	12.50	30.00	115
1945	5,645,500	—	4.00	8.00	18.00	50.00

KM# 391 10 ORE Weight: 1.1500 g. **Composition:** Nickel-Brass **Note:** World War II government in exile issue.

Date	Mintage	VG	F	VF	XF	BU
1942	6,000,000	—	—	—	120	200

Note: All except 9,667 were melted

KM# 396 10 ORE Weight: 1.5000 g. **Composition:** Copper-Nickel

Date	Mintage	VG	F	VF	XF	BU
1951	17,400,000	—	0.10	0.30	2.50	50.00
1952	Inc. above	—	0.10	0.20	1.50	20.00
1953	7,700,000	—	0.10	0.20	1.50	20.00
1954	10,105,000	—	0.10	0.20	1.50	20.00
1955	9,829,500	—	0.10	0.20	1.50	40.00
1956	10,066,000	—	0.10	0.20	1.50	20.00
1957	22,900,000	—	0.10	0.20	1.50	12.00

KM# 406 10 ORE Weight: 1.5000 g. **Composition:** Copper-Nickel **Reverse:** Small lettering

Date	Mintage	VG	F	VF	XF	BU
1958	1,425,000	—	0.50	1.50	3.00	20.00

KM# 411 10 ORE Weight: 1.5000 g. **Composition:** Copper-Nickel **Reverse:** Large lettering

Date	Mintage	VG	F	VF	XF	BU
1959	2,500,000	—	—	0.75	3.00	20.00
1960	12,490,200	—	—	0.10	0.60	7.00
1961	10,385,000	—	—	0.10	0.60	20.00
1962	16,210,000	—	—	0.10	0.60	4.00
1963	17,560,000	—	—	0.10	0.60	4.00
1964	9,781,000	—	—	0.10	0.35	1.35
1965	10,561,000	—	—	0.10	0.60	7.00
1966	16,610,000	—	—	0.10	0.50	3.00
1967	18,243,000	—	—	0.10	0.35	3.00
1968	24,998,300	—	—	0.10	0.35	5.00
1969	27,157,200	—	—	0.10	0.25	2.50
1970	639,300	—	0.50	1.00	2.25	4.00
1971	8,903,800	—	—	0.10	0.25	1.35
1972	24,834,484	—	—	—	0.25	1.00
1973	22,300,925	—	—	—	0.25	1.00

KM# 416 10 ORE Weight: 1.2500 g. **Composition:** Copper-Nickel **Note:** Varieties exist in monogram.

Date	Mintage	VG	F	VF	XF	BU
1974	30,995,223	—	—	—	0.10	0.60
1975	21,845,496	—	—	—	0.10	0.60
1976	42,403,074	—	—	—	0.10	0.40
1977	43,304,000	—	—	—	0.10	0.40
1978	37,395,000	—	—	—	0.10	0.40
1979	25,808,000	—	—	—	0.10	0.40
1980	28,620,000	—	—	—	0.10	0.40
1980 Without star	14,050,000	—	—	—	0.10	0.40
1981	43,083,400	—	—	—	0.10	0.40
1982	40,974,256	—	—	—	0.10	0.40
1983	45,637,300	—	—	—	0.10	0.40
1984	100,066,000	—	—	—	0.10	0.35
1985	103,108,000	—	—	—	0.10	0.35
1986	146,392,000	—	—	—	0.10	0.35
1987	166,040,000	—	—	—	0.10	0.35
1988	94,677,000	—	—	—	0.10	0.35
1989	97,273,500	—	—	—	0.10	0.35
1990	150,290,000	—	—	—	0.10	0.35
1991	56,383,000	—	—	—	0.10	0.35

KM# 360 25 ORE Weight: 2.4200 g. **Composition:** 0.6000 Silver .0463 oz. ASW

Date	Mintage	VG	F	VF	XF	BU
1901	606,900	5.00	10.00	22.00	42.00	11[illegible]
1902	611,700	5.00	10.00	22.00	42.00	11[illegible]
1904	600,000	5.00	10.00	22.00	42.00	11[illegible]

KM# 373 25 ORE Weight: 2.4200 g. **Composition:** 0.6000 Silver .0463 oz. ASW

Date	Mintage	VG	F	VF	XF	BU
1909	600,000	5.00	10.00	20.00	50.00	90.00
1911	400,000	10.00	20.00	30.00	70.00	190
1912	200,000	35.00	70.00	125	270	600
1913	400,000	8.00	16.50	27.50	65.00	140
1914	399,600	8.00	16.50	27.50	65.00	165
1915	1,032,300	3.00	6.00	10.00	25.00	65.00
1916	368,000	10.00	20.00	42.00	75.00	225
1917	400,000	10.00	20.00	40.00	70.00	150
1918/6	800,000	6.00	10.00	17.50	35.00	65.00
1918	Inc. above	3.00	7.00	10.00	25.00	60.00
1919	1,600,000	2.00	5.00	8.00	17.50	45.00

KM# 381 25 ORE **Weight:** 4.4000 g. **Composition:** Copper-Nickel

Date	Mintage	VG	F	VF	XF	BU
1921	4,800,000	4.00	7.50	10.00	20.00	40.00
1922	14,200,000	4.00	7.50	10.00	20.00	40.00
1923	5,200,000	8.00	16.50	22.00	32.50	55.00

KM# 382 25 ORE **Weight:** 2.4000 g. **Composition:** Copper-Nickel

Date	VG	F	VF	XF	BU
1921	1.50	3.00	5.00	45.00	520
1922	1.50	3.00	4.00	35.00	325
1923	1.75	1.50	3.00	25.00	190

Note: Respective mintages included with KM#381.

KM# 384 25 ORE **Weight:** 2.4000 g. **Composition:** Copper-Nickel

Date	Mintage	VG	F	VF	XF	BU
1924	4,000,000	—	0.50	2.00	7.00	60.00
1927	6,200,000	—	0.50	1.50	7.00	60.00
1929	800,000	—	1.50	6.00	42.00	250
1939	1,220,000	—	0.25	0.75	3.50	50.00
1940	1,160,000	—	0.25	0.75	3.50	50.00
1946	1,850,000	—	0.20	0.50	1.75	20.00
1947	2,592,000	—	0.20	0.50	1.75	12.00
1949	2,602,000	—	0.20	0.50	1.75	12.00
1950	2,800,000	—	0.20	0.50	1.75	12.00

KM# 392 25 ORE **Weight:** 2.4000 g. **Composition:** Nickel-Brass **Note:** World War II government in exile issue.

Date	Mintage	VG	F	VF	XF	BU
1942	2,400,000	—	—	—	120	225

Note: All but 10,300 were melted

KM# 395 25 ORE **Weight:** 2.0000 g. **Composition:** Zinc **Note:** World War II German occupation.

Date	Mintage	VG	F	VF	XF	BU
1943	14,104,800	—	1.00	1.50	4.00	25.00
1944	3,030,500	2.00	4.00	7.50	20.00	50.00
1945	3,010,000	3.00	6.00	10.00	22.00	60.00

KM# 401 25 ORE **Weight:** 2.4000 g. **Composition:** Copper-Nickel **Note:** Mint marks exist with mint mark on square or without square.

Date	Mintage	VG	F	VF	XF	BU
1952	4,060,000	—	0.10	0.25	1.20	25.00
1953	3,320,000	—	0.10	0.25	1.20	32.50
1954	3,140,000	—	0.10	0.25	1.20	25.00
1955	2,000,000	—	0.10	0.25	1.20	60.00
1956	3,980,000	—	0.10	0.25	1.20	20.00
1957	7,660,000	—	0.10	0.25	1.20	20.00

KM# 407 25 ORE **Weight:** 2.4000 g. **Composition:** Copper-Nickel

Date	Mintage	VG	F	VF	XF	BU
1958	1,316,000	—	0.50	1.00	3.00	32.50
1959	1,184,000	—	0.50	1.00	3.00	25.00
1960	3,964,200	—	—	0.10	1.25	12.00
1961	4,656,000	—	—	0.10	1.00	6.50
1962	6,304,000	—	—	0.10	1.00	6.50
1963	3,640,000	—	—	0.10	1.00	6.50
1964	4,953,000	—	—	0.10	0.50	2.75
1965	2,798,000	—	—	0.10	0.65	32.50
1966	6,075,000	—	—	0.10	0.65	3.00
1967	6,641,000	—	—	0.10	0.65	3.00
1968	4,963,400	—	—	0.10	0.50	2.50
1969	12,426,500	—	—	0.10	0.15	2.00
1970	1,545,400	—	—	0.15	0.75	6.50
1971	5,247,200	—	—	—	0.10	1.25
1972	7,928,584	—	—	—	0.10	1.25
1973	8,516,175	—	—	—	0.10	1.25

KM# 417 25 ORE **Weight:** 2.0000 g. **Composition:** Copper-Nickel

Date	Mintage	VG	F	VF	XF	BU
1974	8,048,223	—	—	—	0.10	0.65
1975	15,594,696	—	—	—	0.10	0.65
1976	24,721,074	—	—	—	0.10	0.50
1977	20,150,000	—	—	—	0.10	0.50
1978	11,259,000	—	—	—	0.10	0.50
1979	16,666,000	—	—	—	0.10	0.50
1980	6,289,000	—	—	—	0.10	0.50
1980 Without star	8,176,000	—	—	—	0.10	0.50
1981	17,971,000	—	—	—	0.10	0.50
1982	16,863,000	—	—	—	0.10	0.50

KM# 356 50 ORE **Weight:** 5.0000 g. **Composition:** 0.6000 Silver .0964 oz. ASW **Reverse:** Without 15 SK

Date	Mintage	VG	F	VF	XF	BU
1901	404,000	4.00	8.00	22.00	65.00	185
1902	301,200	4.00	8.00	22.00	65.00	185
1904	100,500	35.00	70.00	120	260	350

KM# 374 50 ORE **Weight:** 5.0000 g. **Composition:** 0.6000 Silver .0964 oz. ASW

Date	Mintage	VG	F	VF	XF	BU
1909	200,000	7.50	15.00	30.00	65.00	160
1911	200,000	12.50	25.00	40.00	90.00	220
1912	200,000	20.00	40.00	60.00	120	325
1913	200,000	12.50	25.00	40.00	90.00	225
1914	800,000	2.25	5.00	9.00	20.00	90.00
1915	300,000	7.50	15.00	20.00	40.00	135
1916	700,000	3.00	6.00	10.00	25.00	90.00
1918	3,090,000	1.00	2.00	4.00	12.00	70.00
1919	1,219,000	1.25	2.50	4.50	12.00	35.00

KM# 379 50 ORE **Weight:** 4.8000 g. **Composition:** Copper Nickel

Date	Mintage	VG	F	VF	XF	BU
1920	1,236,000	15.00	25.00	35.00	60.00	95.00
1921	7,345,000	4.00	8.00	10.00	25.00	50.00
1922	3,000,000	4.00	8.00	10.00	25.00	50.00
1923	4,540,000	22.00	45.00	65.00	100	185

KM# 380 50 ORE **Weight:** 4.8000 g. **Composition:** Copper Nickel **Note:** Respective mintages are included with KM#379.

Date	VG	F	VF	XF	BU
1920	—	30.00	60.00	180	1,000
1921	—	3.00	8.00	95.00	650
1922	—	2.50	6.00	60.00	445
1923	—	2.50	6.00	42.50	325

KM# 386 50 ORE **Weight:** 4.8000 g. **Composition:** Copper Nickel

Date	Mintage	VG	F	VF	XF	BU
1926	2,000,000	—	0.35	1.50	17.50	95.00
1927	2,502,100	—	0.35	1.50	12.00	75.00
1928/7	1,458,200	—	0.50	2.50	16.50	100
1928	Inc. above	—	0.35	1.50	15.00	95.00
1929	600,000	—	1.50	6.00	70.00	520
1939	900,000	—	0.25	0.60	5.00	125
1940	2,193,000	—	0.20	0.50	3.50	25.00
1941	2,373,000	—	0.20	0.50	3.50	20.00
1945	1,354,000	—	0.20	0.50	2.50	32.50
1946	1,532,500	—	0.20	0.50	3.50	20.00
1947	2,465,300	—	0.20	0.50	3.50	12.50
1948	5,911,400	—	0.20	0.40	1.75	12.50
1949	1,029,600	—	0.25	1.00	5.00	25.00

KM# 390 50 ORE **Composition:** Zinc **Note:** World War II German occupation issue.

Date	Mintage	VG	F	VF	XF	BU
1941	7,760,800	—	1.25	3.00	10.00	65.00
1942	7,605,550	—	1.00	2.50	7.00	40.00
1943	3,348,500	7.00	15.00	20.00	60.00	165
1944	1,542,400	5.00	10.00	15.00	35.00	65.00
1945	226,000	90.00	180	285	400	675

KM# 393 50 ORE **Weight:** 4.8000 g. **Composition:** Nickel-Brass **Note:** World War II government in exile issue.

Date	Mintage	VG	F	VF	XF	BU
1942	1,600,000	—	—	—	125	250

Note: All but 9,238 were melted

KM# 402 50 ORE **Weight:** 4.8000 g. **Composition:** Copper-Nickel

Date	Mintage	VG	F	VF	XF	BU
1953	2,370,000	—	0.20	0.60	1.75	32.50
1954	230,000	1.25	3.75	10.00	70.00	450
1955	1,930,000	—	0.10	0.40	2.25	65.00
1956	1,630,000	—	0.10	0.40	2.25	65.00
1957	1,800,000	—	0.10	0.40	2.25	32.50

KM# 408 50 ORE **Weight:** 4.8000 g. **Composition:** Copper-Nickel

Date	Mintage	VG	F	VF	XF	BU
1958	1,560,000	—	0.25	0.75	3.00	65.00
1959	340,000	—	1.00	2.00	12.00	65.00
1960	1,584,200	—	—	0.10	1.75	22.50
1961	2,424,600	—	—	0.10	0.85	12.50
1962	3,064,000	—	—	0.10	0.85	12.50
1963	2,168,000	—	—	0.10	0.85	12.50
1964	2,692,000	—	—	0.10	0.60	6.50
1965	1,248,000	—	0.25	0.75	3.00	40.00
1966	4,262,000	—	—	0.10	0.25	6.50
1967	4,001,000	—	—	0.10	0.25	6.50
1968	5,430,800	—	—	0.10	0.25	10.00
1969	7,591,000	—	—	0.10	0.25	2.75
1970	481,000	—	0.25	0.75	2.25	6.50
1971	2,489,300	—	—	0.10	0.15	2.50
1972	4,452,784	—	—	0.10	0.15	2.50
1973	3,317,175	—	—	0.10	0.15	2.50

KM# 418 50 ORE **Weight:** 4.8000 g. **Composition:** Copper-Nickel **Note:** Varieties in shield exist.

Date	Mintage	VG	F	VF	XF	BU
1974	8,494,223	—	—	0.10	0.15	0.75
1975	10,123,196	—	—	0.10	0.15	0.75
1976	15,172,324	—	—	0.10	0.15	0.65
1977	19,411,750	—	—	0.10	0.15	0.50
1978	15,305,000	—	—	0.10	0.15	0.50
1979	10,152,000	—	—	0.10	0.15	0.50
1980	7,082,000	—	—	0.10	0.15	0.50
1980 Without star	7,066,000	—	—	0.10	0.15	0.50
1981	3,402,000	—	—	0.10	0.15	0.50
1982	11,156,650	—	—	0.10	0.15	0.40
1983	15,762,300	—	—	0.10	0.15	0.40
1984	8,615,000	—	—	0.10	0.15	0.40
1985	4,444,000	—	—	0.10	0.15	0.40
1986	4,178,000	—	—	0.10	0.15	0.40
1987	5,167,000	—	—	0.10	0.15	0.40
1988	9,610,000	—	—	0.10	0.15	0.40
1989	5,785,000	—	—	0.10	0.15	0.40
1990	1,729,000	—	—	0.10	0.15	0.50
1991	2,924,008	—	—	0.10	0.15	0.40
1992	6,802,027	—	—	0.10	0.15	0.40
1992 Proof	20,000	Value: 10.00				
1993	8,056,000	—	—	0.10	0.15	0.40
1994	7,173,000	—	—	0.10	0.15	0.40
1994 Proof	12,000	Value: 10.00				
1995	6,835,000	—	—	—	—	0.40
1995 Proof	—	Value: 10.00				
1996	4,500,000	—	—	—	—	0.40
1996 Proof	—	Value: 10.00				

KM# 460 50 ORE **Weight:** 3.6000 g. **Composition:** Bronze **Obverse:** Crown **Reverse:** Stylized animal, denomination

Date	Mintage	VG	F	VF	XF	BU
1996	86,456,200	—	—	—	—	0.65
1997	24,089,823	—	—	—	—	0.45
1997 Proof	—	Value: 10.00				
1998	30,913,000	—	—	—	—	0.45
1998 Proof	—	Value: 10.00				
1999	25,314,273	—	—	—	—	0.45
1999 Proof	—	Value: 10.00				
2000	18,979,552	—	—	—	—	0.45
2000 Proof	—	Value: 10.00				
2001 without star	16,848,250	—	—	—	—	0.45
2001 with star	13,291,750	—	—	—	—	0.45
2001 Proof	—	Value: 10.00				

KM# 357 KRONE **Weight:** 7.5000 g. **Composition:** 0.8000 Silver .1929 oz. ASW **Note:** Without 30 SK

Date	Mintage	VG	F	VF	XF	BU
1901	151,800	10.00	20.00	50.00	120	420
1904	100,100	30.00	60.00	100	200	500

KM# 369 KRONE **Weight:** 7.5000 g. **Composition:** 0.8000 Silver .1929 oz. ASW

Date	Mintage	VG	F	VF	XF	BU
1908 Crossed hammers on shield	180,000	17.50	35.00	50.00	120	250
1908 Crossed hammers without shield	170,000	10.00	20.00	40.00	90.00	190
1910	100,000	28.00	55.00	100	225	500
1912	200,000	17.50	35.00	60.00	120	285
1913	230,000	12.50	25.00	50.00	120	285
1914	602,000	7.00	10.00	20.00	50.00	110
1915	498,000	7.50	12.50	22.50	55.00	125
1916	400,000	8.00	15.00	25.00	60.00	250
1917	600,000	7.00	10.00	17.50	30.00	95.00

KM# 385 KRONE **Weight:** 7.0000 g. **Composition:** Copper-Nickel

Date	Mintage	VG	F	VF	XF	BU
1925	8,686,000	—	0.30	3.00	18.00	140
1926	1,984,000	—	0.50	4.00	25.00	240
1927	1,000,000	—	1.00	5.00	55.00	425
1936	700,000	—	1.25	5.50	60.00	435
1937	1,000,000	—	1.00	4.00	35.00	290
1938	926,000	—	0.60	2.50	18.00	120
1939	2,253,000	—	0.60	1.50	9.00	85.00
1940	3,890,000	—	0.30	1.00	6.00	65.00
1946	5,499,000	—	0.25	0.50	3.00	20.00
1947	802,000	—	1.00	2.00	12.00	65.00
1949	7,846,000	—	0.20	0.50	3.00	15.00
1950	9,942,000	—	0.20	0.50	3.00	15.00
1951	4,761,000	—	0.20	0.50	3.00	15.00

KM# 397 KRONE **Weight:** 7.0000 g. **Composition:** Copper-Nickel

Date	Mintage	VG	F	VF	XF	BU
1951	3,819,000	—	0.20	0.50	2.50	32.50
1953	1,465,000	—	0.20	0.50	2.50	65.00
1954	3,045,000	—	0.20	0.50	2.50	65.00
1955	1,970,000	—	0.20	0.50	2.50	95.00
1956	4,300,000	—	0.20	0.50	2.50	55.00
1957	7,630,000	—	0.20	0.50	2.50	32.50

KM# 409 KRONE **Weight:** 7.0000 g. **Composition:** Copper-Nickel

Date	Mintage	VG	F	VF	XF	BU
1958	540,000	—	3.00	7.00	35.00	350
1959	4,450,000	—	—	0.20	2.50	40.00
1960	1,790,200	—	—	0.20	2.50	32.50
1961	3,933,600	—	—	0.20	0.85	15.00
1962	6,015,000	—	—	0.20	0.85	15.00
1963	4,677,000	—	—	0.20	0.85	15.00
1964	3,469,000	—	—	0.20	0.60	6.50
1965	3,222,000	—	—	0.20	1.20	55.00
1966	3,084,000	—	—	0.20	0.85	20.00
1967	6,680,000	—	—	0.20	0.85	20.00
1968	6,149,200	—	—	0.20	0.85	50.00
1969	5,185,500	—	—	0.20	0.40	4.00
1970	8,637,900	—	—	0.20	0.50	12.50
1971	10,257,800	—	—	0.20	0.40	4.00
1972	13,179,394	—	—	0.20	0.40	4.00
1973	9,140,175	—	—	0.20	0.40	4.00

KM# 419 KRONE **Weight:** 7.0000 g. **Composition:** Copper-Nickel **Note:** Varieties with and without star mint mark exist.

Date	Mintage	VG	F	VF	XF	BU
1974	16,537,223	—	—	0.20	0.35	1.25
1975	26,043,966	—	—	0.20	0.35	1.25
1976	35,926,574	—	—	0.20	0.35	0.85
1977	26,263,500	—	—	0.20	0.35	0.85
1978	23,360,000	—	—	0.20	0.35	0.85
1979	15,896,500	—	—	0.20	0.35	0.85
1980	5,918,000	—	—	0.20	0.35	2.75
1981	16,308,150	—	—	0.20	0.35	0.75
1982	29,187,000	—	—	0.20	0.35	0.75
1983	24,293,300	—	—	0.20	0.35	0.75
1984	3,677,000	—	—	0.20	0.35	1.50
1985	10,985,000	—	—	0.20	0.35	0.75
1986	5,612,500	—	—	0.20	0.35	0.75
1987	11,015,500	—	—	0.20	0.35	0.75
1988	14,880,000	—	—	0.20	0.35	0.75
1989	5,605,000	—	—	0.20	0.35	0.65
1990	8,804,000	—	—	0.20	0.35	0.65
1990 Proof	15,110	Value: 85.00				
1991	15,080,000	—	—	0.20	0.35	0.65

KM# 436 KRONE **Weight:** 7.0000 g. **Composition:** Copper-Nickel

Date	Mintage	VG	F	VF	XF	BU
1992	7,415,527	—	—	0.20	0.35	0.65
1992 Proof	20,000	Value: 10.00				
1993	10,916,500	—	—	0.20	0.35	0.65
1994	25,951,000	—	—	0.20	0.35	0.65
1994 Proof	12,000	Value: 10.00				
1995	12,883,000	—	—	0.20	0.35	0.65
1995 Proof	—	Value: 10.00				
1996	20,736,000	—	—	0.20	0.35	0.65
1996 Proof	—	Value: 10.00				

KM# 462 KRONE **Weight:** 4.3000 g. **Composition:** Copper-Nickel **Obverse:** Monogram cross **Reverse:** Bird or vine above date and denomination

Date	Mintage	VG	F	VF	XF	BU
1997	141,099,823	—	—	—	—	0.6
1997 Proof	—	Value: 10.00				
1998	139,493,000	—	—	—	—	0.6
1998 Proof	—	Value: 10.00				
1999	74,454,273	—	—	—	—	0.6
1999 Proof	—	Value: 10.00				
2000	42,689,277	—	—	—	—	0.6
2000 Proof	—	Value: 10.00				
2001 without star	43,128,650	—	—	—	—	0.6
2001 with star	7,355,350	—	—	—	—	0.6
2001 Proof	—	Value: 10.00				

KM# 359 2 KRONER **Weight:** 15.0000 g. **Composition:** 0.8000 Silver .3858 oz. ASW **Note:** Restrikes are made by the Royal Mint, Norway, in gold, silver and bronze.

Date	Mintage	VG	F	VF	XF	BU
1902	153,100	15.00	30.00	55.00	140	450
1904	75,600	22.00	45.00	85.00	200	500

KM# 363 2 KRONER **Weight:** 15.0000 g. **Composition:** 0.8000 Silver .3858 oz. ASW **Subject:** Norway independence **Obverse:** Large shield

Date	Mintage	VG	F	VF	XF	BU
1906	100,000	5.00	10.00	15.00	30.00	75.00

KM# 365 2 KRONER **Weight:** 15.0000 g. **Composition:** 0.8000 Silver .3858 oz. ASW **Obverse:** Smaller shield

Date	Mintage	VG	F	VF	XF	BU
1907	54,600	10.00	20.00	30.00	60.00	120

KM# 366 2 KRONER **Weight:** 15.0000 g. **Composition:** 0.8000 Silver .3858 oz. ASW **Subject:** Border watch

Date	Mintage	VG	F	VF	XF	BU
1907	27,500	—	60.00	125	270	650

KM# 370 2 KRONER **Weight:** 15.0000 g. **Composition:** 0.8000 Silver .3858 oz. ASW

Date	Mintage	VG	F	VF	XF	BU
1908	200,000	—	20.00	30.00	65.00	175
1910	150,000	—	35.00	60.00	120	350
1912	150,000	—	30.00	55.00	120	350
1913	270,000	—	15.00	25.00	60.00	160
1914	255,000	—	17.50	30.00	70.00	195
1915	225,000	—	17.50	30.00	70.00	195
1916	250,000	—	30.00	45.00	90.00	250
1917	377,500	—	10.00	15.00	35.00	120

KM# 377 2 KRONER **Weight:** 15.0000 g. **Composition:** 0.8000 Silver .3858 oz. ASW **Subject:** Constitution centennial

Date	Mintage	VG	F	VF	XF	BU
1914	225,600	3.00	6.00	10.00	20.00	90.00

KM# 412 5 KRONER **Weight:** 11.5000 g. **Composition:** Copper-Nickel

Date	Mintage	VG	F	VF	XF	BU
1963	7,074,000	—	—	1.00	3.50	25.00
1964	7,346,000	—	—	1.00	2.25	12.00
1965	2,233,000	—	—	1.00	3.00	90.00
1966	2,502,000	—	—	1.00	3.00	45.00
1967	583,000	—	1.00	1.75	6.50	50.00
1968	1,813,400	—	—	1.00	2.25	40.00
1969	2,403,700	—	—	1.00	2.25	12.00
1970	202,300	—	1.50	2.50	6.50	20.00
1971	177,900	—	1.50	2.50	7.00	25.00
1972	2,208,704	—	—	—	1.25	3.50
1973	2,778,055	—	—	—	1.25	7.50

KM# 420 5 KRONER **Weight:** 11.5000 g. **Composition:** Copper-Nickel **Note:** Varieties exist with large and small shields.

Date	Mintage	VG	F	VF	XF	BU
1974	1,983,423	—	—	—	1.00	7.50
1975	2,946,442	—	—	—	1.00	5.00
1976	9,055,574	—	—	—	1.00	2.25
1977	4,629,600	—	—	—	1.00	1.50
1978	5,853,000	—	—	—	1.00	1.50
1979	6,818,000	—	—	—	1.00	1.50
1980	1,578,400	—	—	—	1.00	2.50
1981	1,104,800	—	—	—	1.00	2.25
1982	3,919,890	—	—	—	1.00	1.50
1983	2,932,260	—	—	—	1.00	1.50
1984	1,233,000	—	—	—	1.00	2.25
1985	1,399,600	—	—	—	1.00	1.50
1987	900,200	—	—	—	1.00	2.50
1988	865,200	—	—	—	1.00	2.50

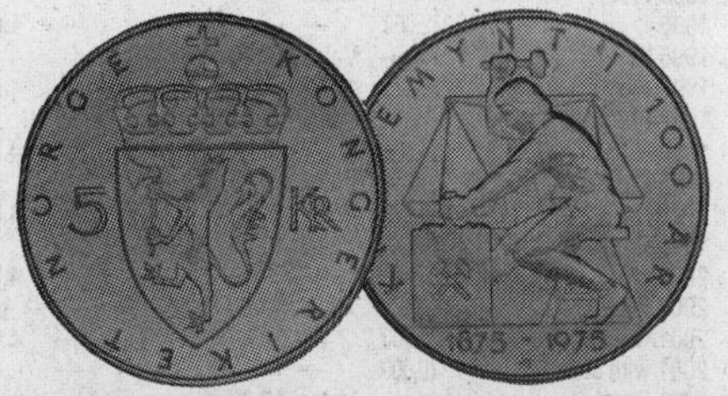

KM# 421 5 KRONER **Weight:** 11.5000 g. **Composition:** Copper-Nickel **Subject:** 100th anniversary of krone system

Date	Mintage	VG	F	VF	XF	BU
ND(1975)	1,191,813	—	—	1.00	1.50	3.50

KM# 422 5 KRONER **Weight:** 11.5000 g. **Composition:** Copper-Nickel **Subject:** 150th anniversary - immigration to America

Date	Mintage	VG	F	VF	XF	BU
ND(1975)	1,222,827	—	—	1.00	1.50	3.50

KM# 423 5 KRONER **Weight:** 11.5000 g. **Composition:** Copper-Nickel **Subject:** 350th anniversary of Norwegian army

Date	Mintage	VG	F	VF	XF	BU
ND(1978)	2,989,768	—	—	1.00	1.50	3.00

KM# 428 5 KRONER **Weight:** 11.5000 g. **Composition:** Copper-Nickel **Subject:** 300th anniversary of the mint

Date	Mintage	VG	F	VF	XF	BU
1986	2,345,500	—	—	1.00	1.50	3.00
1986 Prooflike	5,000	—	—	—	—	—

KM# 430 5 KRONER **Weight:** 11.5000 g. **Composition:** Copper-Nickel **Subject:** 175th anniversary of the national bank

Date	Mintage	VG	F	VF	XF	BU
1991	532,008	—	—	—	—	7.00

KM# 437 5 KRONER **Weight:** 11.5000 g. **Composition:** Copper-Nickel **Obverse:** Harald V

Date	Mintage	VG	F	VF	XF	BU
1992	500,022	—	—	—	—	2.50
Note: 100,000 are in mint sets.						
1992 Proof	20,000	Value: 10.00				
1993	509,600	—	—	—	—	3.00
1994	2,112,000	—	—	—	—	2.50
1994 Proof	12,000	Value: 10.00				

KM# 456 5 KRONER **Weight:** 11.5000 g. **Composition:** Copper-Nickel **Obverse:** 1,000 years of Norwegian coinage

Date	Mintage	VG	F	VF	XF	BU
1995	500,000	—	—	—	—	3.50
1995 Proof	12,000	Value: 22.50				

KM# 458 5 KRONER **Weight:** 11.5000 g. **Composition:** Copper-Nickel **Subject:** 50th anniversary - United Nations

Date	Mintage	VG	F	VF	XF	BU
ND(1995)	500,000	—	—	—	—	3.50

KM# 459 5 KRONER **Weight:** 11.5000 g. **Composition:** Copper-Nickel **Subject:** Centennial - Nasen's return from the Arctic

Date	Mintage	VG	F	VF	XF	BU
1996	1,381,909	—	—	—	—	3.00
1996 Proof	12,000	Value: 22.50				

KM# 461 5 KRONER **Weight:** 11.5000 g. **Composition:** Copper-Nickel **Subject:** 350th anniversary - Norwegian postal service

Date	Mintage	VG	F	VF	XF	BU
ND(1997)	1,742,073	—	—	—	—	3.00
ND(1997) Proof	12,000	Value: 10.00				

KM# 463 5 KRONER **Weight:** 7.8500 g. **Composition:** Copper-Nickel **Subject:** Order of St. Olaf **Reverse:** Denomination and date

Date		VG	F	VF	XF	BU
1998		—	—	—	—	1.75
1998 Proof	10,000	Value: 12.50				
1999		—	—	—	—	1.75
1999 Proof	10,000	Value: 12.50				
2000		—	—	—	—	1.75
2000 Proof	10,000	Value: 12.50				
2001		—	—	—	—	1.75
2001 Proof		—	—	—	—	—

KM# 358 10 KRONER **Weight:** 4.4803 g. **Composition:** 0.9000 Gold .1296 oz. AGW

Date	Mintage	F	VF	XF	Unc	BU
1902	24,100	100	200	375	600	—

KM# 375 10 KRONER **Weight:** 4.4803 g. **Composition:** 0.9000 Gold .1296 oz. AGW

Date	Mintage	F	VF	XF	Unc	BU
1910	52,600	80.00	165	275	450	—

KM# 413 10 KRONER **Weight:** 20.0000 g. **Composition:** 0.9000 Silver .5707 oz. ASW **Subject:** Constitution sesquicentennial **Note:** Edge lettering varieties exist.

Date	Mintage	VG	F	VF	XF	BU
ND(1964)	1,408,000	—	—	—	3.50	8.00

KM# 427 10 KRONER **Weight:** 9.0000 g. **Composition:** Copper-Zinc-Nickel

Date	Mintage	VG	F	VF	XF	BU
1983	20,193,060	—	—	—	2.00	5.50
1984	11,073,500	—	—	—	1.75	3.50
1985	22,457,550	—	—	—	1.75	3.00
1986	29,060,950	—	—	—	1.75	3.00
1987	8,809,750	—	—	—	1.75	3.50
1988	2,630,500	—	—	—	1.75	3.50
1989	3,259,000	—	—	—	1.75	3.50
1990	3,004,000	—	—	—	1.75	3.50
1991	14,413,030	—	—	—	1.75	3.00

KM# 457 10 KRONER **Weight:** 6.8000 g. **Composition:** Copper-Zinc-Nickel **Reverse:** Church rooftop

Date	Mintage	VG	F	VF	XF	BU
1995	56,825,022	—	—	—	—	4.00
1995 Proof	—	Value: 10.00				
1996	36,372,000	—	—	—	—	4.00
1996 Proof	—	Value: 10.00				
1997	1,229,873	—	—	—	—	4.00
1997 Proof	—	Value: 10.00				
1998	1,058,000	—	—	—	—	4.00
1998 Proof	—	Value: 10.00				
1999	1,059,273	—	—	—	—	4.00
1999 Proof	—	Value: 10.00				
2000	1,096,727	—	—	—	—	4.00
2000 Proof	—	Value: 10.00				
2001 without star	9,837,500	—	—	—	—	4.00
2001 with star	10,000	—	—	—	—	—
2001 Proof	—	Value: 10.00				

KM# 355 20 KRONER **Weight:** 8.9600 g. **Composition:** 0.9000 Gold .2593 oz. AGW

Date	Mintage	F	VF	XF	Unc	BU
1902	50,400	80.00	120	200	350	—

KM# 376 20 KRONER **Weight:** 8.9600 g. **Composition:** 0.9000 Gold .2593 oz. AGW

Date	Mintage	F	VF	XF	Unc	B
1910	250,000	125	165	300	475	-

KM# 453 20 KRONER **Composition:** Copper-Zinc-Nick

Date		F	VF	XF	Unc	B
1994		—	—	—	6.50	-
1994 Proof	12,000	Value: 25.00				
1995		—	—	—	6.50	-
1995 Proof	—	Value: 25.00				
1996		—	—	—	6.50	-
1996 Proof	—	Value: 25.00				
1997		—	—	—	6.50	-
1997 Proof	—	Value: 25.00				
1998		—	—	—	6.50	-
1998 Proof	—	Value: 25.00				
1999		—	—	—	6.50	-
1999 Proof	—	Value: 25.00				
2000		—	—	—	6.50	-
2000 Proof	10,000	Value: 10.00				
2001		—	—	—	—	6.5
2001 Proof		—	—	—	—	

KM# 464 20 KRONER **Weight:** 9.9000 g. **Composition:** Copper-Zinc-Nickel **Subject:** 700th anniversary - Akershus Fortress **Obverse:** Seal of King Hakon V **Reverse:** Fortress

Date	Mintage	F	VF	XF	Unc	B
1999	5,121,986	—	—	—	7.50	-

KM# 465 20 KRONER **Weight:** 9.9000 g. **Composition:** Nickel-Bronze **Subject:** Vinland **Obverse:** King's portrait **Reverse:** Viking ship hull

Date	Mintage	F	VF	XF	Unc
1999	1,048,700	—	—	—	7.50
1999 Proof	2,500	Value: 30.00			

Note: In sets only.

KM# 468 20 KRONER **Weight:** 9.9000 g. **Composition:** Nickel-Brass **Subject:** Millennium **Obvers** King's head right **Reverse:** Unknown road into the future

Date	Mintage	F	VF	XF	Unc
2000	1,032,307	—	—	—	12.50

KM# 471 20 KRONER **Weight:** 9.7300 g. **Composition:** Nickel-Brass **Ruler:** Harald V **Subject:** Nie

Henrik Abel **Obverse:** King's portrait **Reverse:** Mathematical graphs **Edge:** Plain **Size:** 27.4 mm.

Date	F	VF	XF	Unc	BU
2002	—	—	—	10.00	—

KM# 414 25 KRONER Weight: 29.0000 g. **Composition:** 0.8750 Silver .8159 oz. ASW **Subject:** 25th anniversary of liberation

Date	Mintage	VG	F	VF	XF	BU
1970	1,203,700	—	—	—	—	8.00

KM# 424 50 KRONER Weight: 27.0000 g. **Composition:** 0.9250 Silver .8030 oz. ASW **Subject:** 75th birthday of King Olav V

Date	Mintage	VG	F	VF	XF	BU
ND (1978)	800,000	—	—	—	—	11.50

KM# 431 50 KRONER Weight: 16.8100 g. **Composition:** 0.9250 Silver .5000 oz. ASW **Subject:** 1994 Olympics **Reverse:** Skiers

Date	Mintage	VG	F	VF	XF	BU
1991	80,016	—	—	—	—	37.50

KM# 432 50 KRONER Weight: 16.8100 g. **Composition:** 0.9250 Silver .5000 oz. ASW **Subject:** 1994 Olympics **Reverse:** Child skiing

Date	Mintage	VG	F	VF	XF	BU
1991	120,000	—	—	—	—	37.50

KM# 438 50 KRONER Weight: 16.8100 g. **Composition:** 0.9250 Silver .5000 oz. ASW **Subject:** 1994 Olympics **Reverse:** Grandfather and child

Date	Mintage	VG	F	VF	XF	BU
1992	74,000	—	—	—	—	37.50

KM# 439 50 KRONER Weight: 16.8100 g. **Composition:** 0.9250 Silver .5000 oz. ASW **Subject:** 1994 Olympics **Reverse:** 2 children on sled

Date	Mintage	VG	F	VF	XF	BU
1992	88,000	—	—	—	—	37.50

KM# 447 50 KRONER Weight: 16.8100 g. **Composition:** 0.9250 Silver .5000 oz. ASW **Subject:** 1994 Olympics **Reverse:** Cross-country skiers

Date	Mintage	VG	F	VF	XF	BU
1993	65,000	—	—	—	—	37.50

KM# 448 50 KRONER Weight: 16.8100 g. **Composition:** 0.9250 Silver .5000 oz. ASW **Subject:** 1994 Olympics **Reverse:** Children ice skating

Date	Mintage	VG	F	VF	XF	BU
1993	77,000	—	—	—	—	37.50

KM# 454 50 KRONER Weight: 16.8100 g. **Composition:** 0.9250 Silver .5000 oz. ASW **Subject:** 50th anniversary - United Nations

Date	Mintage	VG	F	VF	XF	BU
ND(1995) Proof	200,000	Value: 42.50				

KM# 455 50 KRONER Weight: 16.8100 g. **Composition:** 0.9250 Silver .5000 oz. ASW **Subject:** 50th anniversary - end of World War II

Date	Mintage	VG	F	VF	XF	BU
ND(1995) Proof	50,000	Value: 47.50				

KM# 426 100 KRONER Weight: 24.7300 g. **Composition:** 0.9250 Silver .7355 oz. ASW **Subject:** 25th anniversary of King Olaf's reign

Date	Mintage	VG	F	VF	XF	BU
1982	800,000	—	—	—	—	25.00

KM# 433 100 KRONER **Weight:** 33.6200 g. **Composition:** 0.9250 Silver 1 oz. ASW **Subject:** 1994 Olympics **Obverse:** Similar to 50 Kroner, KM#431 **Reverse:** Cross-country skier

Date	Mintage	VG	F	VF	XF	BU
1991	88,000	—	—	—	—	60.00

KM# 441 100 KRONER **Weight:** 33.6200 g. **Composition:** 0.9250 Silver 1 oz. ASW **Subject:** 1994 Olympics **Reverse:** Hockey players

Date	Mintage	VG	F	VF	XF	BU
1992	81,000	—	—	—	—	60.00

KM# 449 100 KRONER **Weight:** 33.6200 g. **Composition:** 0.9250 Silver 1 oz. ASW **Subject:** 1984 Olympics **Reverse:** Female figure skater

Date	Mintage	VG	F	VF	XF	BU
1993	96,000	—	—	—	—	60.00

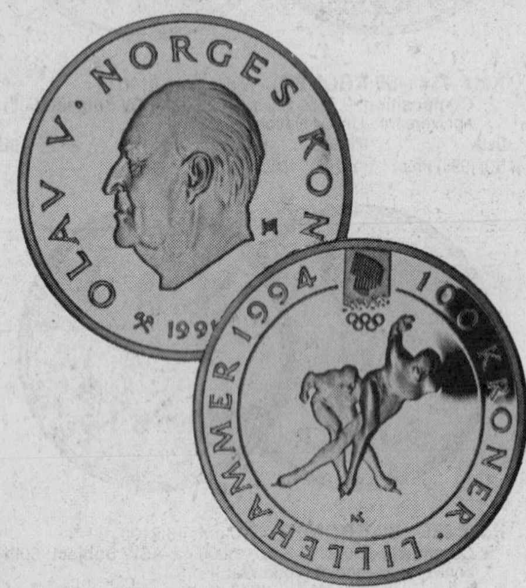

KM# 434 100 KRONER **Weight:** 33.6200 g. **Composition:** 0.9250 Silver 1 oz. ASW **Subject:** 1994 Olympics **Reverse:** 2 speed skaters

Date	Mintage	VG	F	VF	XF	BU
1991	116,000	—	—	—	—	60.00

KM# 443 100 KRONER **Weight:** 33.6200 g. **Composition:** 0.9250 Silver 1 oz. ASW **Subject:** World Cycling Championships **Reverse:** Cyclist

Date	Mintage	VG	F	VF	XF	BU
1993	9,288	—	—	—	—	75.00

KM# 450 100 KRONER **Weight:** 33.6200 g. **Composition:** 0.9250 Silver 1 oz. ASW **Subject:** 1984 Olympics **Reverse:** Alpine skier

Date	Mintage	VG	F	VF	XF	BU
1993	85,000	—	—	—	—	60.0

KM# 440 100 KRONER **Weight:** 33.6200 g. **Composition:** 0.9250 Silver 1 oz. ASW **Subject:** 1994 Olympics **Reverse:** Ski jumper

Date	Mintage	VG	F	VF	XF	BU
1992	85,000	—	—	—	—	60.00

KM# 444 100 KRONER **Weight:** 33.6200 g. **Composition:** 0.9250 Silver 1 oz. ASW **Subject:** World Cycling Championships **Reverse:** 7 cyclists

Date	Mintage	VG	F	VF	XF	BU
1993	9,288	—	—	—	—	75.00

KM# 466 100 KRONER **Weight:** 33.8000 g. **Composition:** 0.9250 Silver 1.0052 oz. ASW **Subject:** Yea 2000 **Obverse:** National arms **Reverse:** Cut tree trunk exposing rings

Date	Mintage	F	VF	XF	Unc	B
1999 Proof	50,000	Value: 70.00				

KM# 469 100 KRONER Weight: 33.6000 g. **Composition:** 0.9250 Silver .9992 oz. ASW **Subject:** Nobel Peace Prize Centennial **Obverse:** National arms **Reverse:** Nobel's portrait **Edge:** Plain **Size:** 39 mm.

Date	Mintage	F	VF	XF	Unc	BU
2001 Proof	Est. 50,000	Value: 60.00				

KM# 429 175 KRONER Weight: 26.5000 g. **Composition:** 0.9250 Silver .7882 oz. ASW **Subject:** 175th anniversary of constitution

Date	Mintage	VG	F	VF	XF	BU
ND(1989)	85,000	—	—	—	—	80.00
ND(1989) Proof	15,000	Value: 285				

KM# 425 200 KRONER Weight: 26.8000 g. **Composition:** 0.6250 Silver .5385 oz. ASW **Subject:** 35th anniversary of liberation

Date	Mintage	VG	F	VF	XF	BU
1980	298,399	—	—	—	—	45.00

KM# 435 1500 KRONER Weight: 17.0000 g. **Composition:** 0.9170 Gold .5 oz. AGW **Subject:** 1994 Olympics **Obverse:** Head of King Olav V right **Reverse:** Ancient Norwegian skier

Date	Mintage	VG	F	VF	XF	BU
1991 Proof	30,000	Value: 385				

KM# 442 1500 KRONER Weight: 17.0000 g. **Composition:** 0.9170 Gold .5 oz. AGW **Subject:** 1994 Olympics **Reverse:** Birkebeiners

Date	Mintage	VG	F	VF	XF	BU
1992 Proof	30,000	Value: 385				

KM# 445 1500 KRONER Weight: 17.0000 g. **Composition:** 0.9170 Gold .5 oz. AGW **Subject:** World Cycling Championships **Reverse:** 2 19th century cyclists

Date	Mintage	VG	F	VF	XF	BU
1993 Proof	6,390	Value: 525				

KM# 446 1500 KRONER Weight: 17.0000 g. **Composition:** 0.9170 Gold .5 oz. AGW **Subject:** Edvard Grieg

Date	Mintage	VG	F	VF	XF	BU
1993 Proof	5,139	Value: 575				

KM# 451 1500 KRONER Weight: 17.0000 g. **Composition:** 0.9170 Gold .5 oz. AGW **Subject:** 1994 Olympics **Reverse:** Telemark skier

Date	Mintage	VG	F	VF	XF	BU
1993 Proof	30,000	Value: 385				

KM# 452 1500 KRONER Weight: 17.0000 g. **Composition:** 0.9170 Gold .5 oz. AGW **Subject:** Roald Amundsen

Date	Mintage	VG	F	VF	XF	BU
1993 Proof	22,000	Value: 450				

KM# 467 1500 KRONER Weight: 16.9600 g. **Composition:** 0.9170 Gold .4994 oz. AGW **Subject:** Year 2000 **Obverse:** King Harald V right **Reverse:** Tree and roots

Date	Mintage	VG	F	VF	XF	BU
2000 Proof	7,500	Value: 425				

KM# 470 1500 KRONER Weight: 16.9600 g. **Composition:** 0.9170 Gold .5000 oz. AGW **Ruler:** Harald V **Subject:** Nobel Peace Prize Centennial **Obverse:** King's portrait **Reverse:** Reverse design of the prize medal **Edge:** Plain **Size:** 27 mm.

Date	Mintage	VG	F	VF	XF	BU
ND(2001) Matte Proof	7,500	Value: 385				

PATTERNS

Including off metal strikes

KM#	Date	Mintage	Identification	Mkt Val
Pn40	1958	6	Ore.	—

MINT SETS

KM#	Date	Mintage	Identification	Issue Price	Mkt Val
MS1	1960 (7)	200	KM403, 405, 407-411	—	—
MS2	1961 (7)	475	KM403, 405, 407-411	—	—
MS3	1962 (7)	570	KM403, 405, 407-411	—	—
MS4	1963 (8)	430	KM403, 405, 407-412	—	—
MS6	1964 (8)	1,200	KM403, 405, 407-412	—	—
MS7	1965 (8)	1,800	KM403, 405, 407-412. Plastic.	—	200
MS8	1966 (8)	1,400	KM403, 405, 407-412. Plastic.	—	175
MS9	1967 (8)	2,490	KM403, 405, 407-412. Soft plastic.	—	165
MS11	1968 (8)	1,167	KM403, 405, 407-412. Soft plastic.	—	950
MS12	1968 (8)	2,300	KM403, 405, 407-412. Sandhill.	—	1,000
MS13	1969 (8)	3,140	KM403, 405, 407-412	—	32.50
MS14	1969 (8)	7,450	KM403, 405, 407-412. Sandhill.	—	65.00
MS15	1970 (8)	2,005	KM403, 405, 407-412. Soft plastic.	—	60.00
MS16	1970 (8)	7,311	KM403, 405, 407-412. Sandhill.	—	110
MS17	1971 (8)	2,010	KM403, 405, 407-412. Soft plastic.	—	60.00
MS18	1971 (8)	4,055	KM403, 405, 407-412. Sandhill.	—	125
MS19	1972 (8)	6,549	KM403, 405, 407-412. Soft plastic.	—	17.50
MS20	1972 (8)	6,435	KM403, 405, 407-412. Sandhill.	—	60.00
MS21	1973 (7)	7,085	KM405, 407-409, 411-412, 415. Soft plastic.	—	16.50
MS22	1973 (7)	13,090	KM405, 407-409, 411-412, 415. Sandhill.	—	40.00
MS23	1974 (6)	10,275	KM415-420. Soft plastic.	—	10.00
MS24	1974 (6)	29,695	KM415-420. Sandhill.	—	15.00
MS25	1975 (8)	30,207	KM415-422. Sandhill.	5.00	40.00
MS26	1975 (7)	5,287	KM415-421. Soft plastic.	5.00	25.00
MS27	1976 (6)	5,000	KM415-420. Soft plastic.	3.00	9.00
MS28	1976 (6)	25,000	KM415-420. Sandhill.	3.00	12.00
MS29	1977 (6)	5,000	KM415-420. Soft plastic.	3.40	15.00
MS30	1977 (6)	25,000	KM415-420. Sandhill.	3.40	32.50
MS31	1978 (6)	5,000	KM415-420. Soft plastic.	3.40	18.00
MS32	1978 (6)	30,000	KM415-420. Sandhill.	3.40	32.50
MS33	1979 (6)	8,000	KM415-420. Soft plastic.	3.40	7.00
MS34	1979 (6)	50,000	KM415-420. Sandhill.	3.40	11.50
MS35	1980 (6)	10,000	KM415-420. Soft plastic.	3.40	9.00
MS36	1980 (6)	70,000	KM415-420. Sandhill.	3.40	20.00

KM#	Date	Mintage	Identification	Issue Price	Mkt Val
MS37	1981 (6)	100,000	KM415-420. Hard plastic.	4.25	10.00
MS38	1982 (6)	102,650	KM415-420	4.50	12.50
MS39	1983 (4)	102,300	KM416, 418-420	5.00	10.00
MS40	1984 (5)	101,000	KM416, 418-420, 427	5.00	10.00
MS41	1985 (5)	110,000	KM416, 418-420, 427	5.00	10.00
MS42	1986 (5)	100,000	KM416, 418-419, 427-428	7.00	15.00
MS43	1987 (5)	85,000	KM416, 418-420, 427	7.00	15.00
MS44	1988 (4)	102,000	KM416, 418, 420, 427	7.00	12.50
MS45	1989 (4)	101,000	KM416, 418-419, 427	8.00	15.00
MS46	1990 (4)	103,000	KM416, 418-419, 427	8.00	15.00
MS47	1991/1992 (5)	100,000	KM416, 418, 427, 436-437	—	10.00
MS48	1991/1993 (5)	100,000	KM416, 418, 427, 436-437	—	20.00
MS49	1994 (5)	100,000	KM418, 427, 436-437, 453	—	18.00
MS50	1995 (5)	100,000	KM418, 436, 453, 456, 457	—	20.00
MS51	1996 (5)	90,000	KM418, 436, 453, 457, 459	—	25.00
MS52	1997 (5)	90,000	KM453, 457, 460, 461, 462	—	25.00
MS53	1998 (5)	90,000	KM453, 457, 460, 462, 463	—	25.00
MS54	1999 (5)	—	KM453, 457, 460, 462, 463	—	25.00
MS55	1999 (5)	50,000	KM457, 460 462-464. Souvenir folder.	13.00	15.00
MS56	1999 (5)	35,000	KM457, 460, 462-464. Baby coin set.	14.30	15.00
MS57	1999 (5)	—	KM457, 460, 462-464 plus medal.	26.00	26.00
MS58	2000 (5)	—	KM453, 457, 460, 462, 463. Hard case.	—	27.50
MS59	2001 (5)	55,000	KM453, 457, 460, 462, 463. Folder.	20.00	22.00
MS60	2001 (5)	30,000	KM453, 457, 460, 462, 463. Baby gift set.	18.00	20.00
MS61	2001 (5)	2,000	KM453, 457, 460, 462, 463 plus medal.	27.00	27.00
MS62	2001 (5)	—	KM453, 457, 460, 462, 463. Sandhill.	—	20.00

PROOF SETS

KM#	Date	Mintage	Identification	Issue Price	Mkt Val
PS1	1992 (3)	20,000	KM418, 436-437	—	35.00
PS2	1993 (3)	12,000	KM443-445	—	650
PS3	1994 (4)	15,000	KM418, 436-437, 453	—	60.00
PS4	1995 (5)	14,459	KM418, 436, 453, 456, 457	—	80.00
PS5	1996 (5)	11,551	KM418, 436, 453, 457, 459	—	80.00
PS6	1997 (5)	15,000	KM453, 457, 460, 461, 462. Norwegian Heritage Set.	—	65.00
PS7	1997 (5)	12,000	KM453, 457, 460, 461, 462	—	70.00
PS8	1998 (5)	14,097	KM453, 457, 460, 462, 463. Norwegian Heritage Set.	—	65.00
PS9	1998 (5)	12,000	KM453, 457, 460, 462, 463	—	70.00
PS10	1999 (5)	15,000	KM453, 457, 460, 462, 463	60.00	80.00
PS11	1999 (5)	2,500	KM457, 460, 462-463, 465	—	90.00
PS12	2000 (5)	10,000	KM453, 457, 460, 462, 463	—	65.00

The Sultanate of Oman (formerly Muscat and Oman), an independent monarchy located in the southeastern part of the Arabian Peninsula, has an area of 82,030 sq. mi. (212,460 sq. km.) and a population of *1.3 million. Capital: Muscat. The economy is based on agriculture, herding and petroleum. Petroleum products, dates, fish and hides are exported.

The Portuguese who captured Muscat, the capital and chief port, in 1508, made the first European contact with Muscat and Oman. They occupied the city, utilizing it as a naval base and factory and holding it against land and sea attacks by Arabs and Persians until finally ejected by local Arabs in 1650. It was next occupied by the Persians who maintained control until 1741, when it was taken by Ahmed ibn Sa'id of the present ruling family. Muscat and Oman was the most powerful state in Arabia during the first half of the 19th century, until weakened by the persistent attack of interior nomadic tribes. British influence, initiated by the signing of a treaty of friendship with the Sultanate in 1798, remains a dominant fact of the civil and military phases of the government, although Britain recognizes the Sultanate as a sovereign state.

Sultan Sa'id bin Taimur was overthrown by his son, Qabus bin Sa'id, on July 23, 1970. The new sultan changed the nation's name to Sultanate of Oman.

TITLES

Muscat مسقط

Oman عمان

SULTANATE

DECIMAL COINAGE

1000 (new) Baisa = 1 Saidi Rial

KM# 42 1/2 SAIDI RIAL Weight: 25.6000 g. **Composition:** 0.9170 Gold .7548 oz. AGW

Date	Mintage	F	VF	XF	Unc	BU
AH1391 (1971) Proof	100	Value: 650				

Note: Struck for presentation purposes

KM# 44 SAIDI RIAL Weight: 46.6500 g. **Composition:** 0.9170 Gold 1.3755 oz. AGW

Date	Mintage	F	VF	XF	Unc	BU
AH1391 (1971) Proof	100	Value: 750				
AH1394 (1974) Proof	250	Value: 750				

Note: Struck for presentation purposes

KM# 43 15 SAIDI RIALS Weight: 5.8100 g. **Composition:** 0.9170 Gold .1713 oz. AGW

Date	Mintage	F	VF	XF	Unc	BU
AH1391 (1971) Proof	112	Value: 650				

Note: Struck for presentation purposes

KM# 53 15 SAIDI RIALS Weight: 7.9800 g. **Composition:** 0.9170 Gold .2353 oz. AGW

Date	Mintage	F	VF	XF	Unc	BU
AH1391 (1971) Proof	224	Value: 550				

Note: Struck for presentation purposes

REFORM COINAGE

1000 Baisa = 1 Omani Rial

KM# 50 5 BAISA Composition: Bronze

Date	Mintage	F	VF	XF	Unc	BU
AH1395 (1975)	6,000,000	—	0.10	0.20	0.45	—
AH1400 (1979)	3,000,000	—	0.10	0.20	0.45	—
AH1406 (1985)	2,000,000	—	0.10	0.20	0.45	—
AH1410 (1989)	5,000,000	—	0.10	0.20	0.45	—

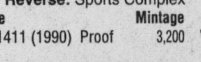

KM# 76 5 BAISA Composition: Bronze **Subject:** 20th National Day - Sultan Qaboos **Obverse:** National emblem **Reverse:** Sports Complex

Date	Mintage	F	VF	XF	Unc	BU
AH1411 (1990) Proof	3,200	Value: 5.00				

KM# 51 10 BAISA Composition: Bronze **Series:** F.A.O.

Date	Mintage	F	VF	XF	Unc	BU
AH1395 (1975)	1,000,000	—	0.15	0.30	0.65	—

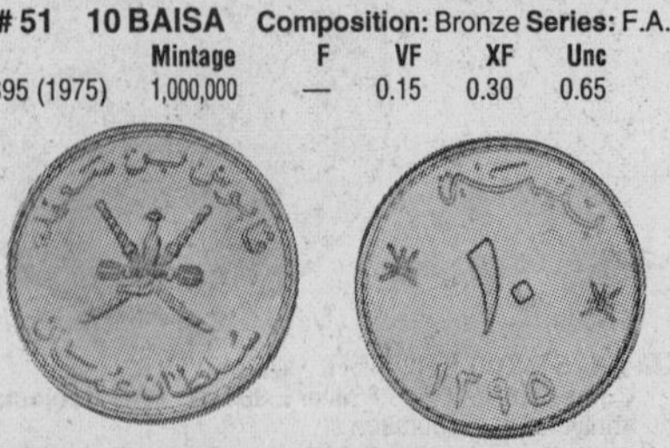

KM# 52.1 10 BAISA Composition: Bronze **Series:** F.A.O.

Date	Mintage	F	VF	XF	Unc	BU
AH1395 (1975)	6,000,000	—	0.15	0.30	0.65	—
AH1400 (1979)	5,250,000	—	0.15	0.30	0.65	—
AH1406 (1985)	3,000,000	—	0.15	0.30	0.65	—
AH1410 (1989)	6,000,000	—	0.15	0.30	0.65	—
AH1418 (1997)	—	—	0.15	0.30	0.65	—

KM# 52.2 10 BAISA Composition: Bronze Clad Steel

Date	F	VF	XF	Unc	BU
AH1420 (1975)	—	0.15	0.30	0.65	—

KM# 77 10 BAISA **Composition:** Bronze Clad Steel **Subject:** 20th National Day - Central Bank of Oman **Obverse:** National emblem

Date	Mintage	F	VF	XF	Unc	BU
AH1411 (1990) Proof	3,200	Value: 5.00				

KM# 94 10 BAISA **Composition:** Bronze Clad Steel **Series:** F.A.O. **Subject:** 50 Years

Date	Mintage	F	VF	XF	Unc	BU
ND (1995)	—	—	—	—	1.25	—
ND (1995)	224	—	—	—	1.25	—

KM# 75 15 BAISA **Weight:** 20.0000 g. **Composition:** 0.9250 Silver .5949 oz. ASW **Subject:** 15th Anniversary - Reign of Sultan

Date	Mintage	F	VF	XF	Unc	BU
AH1406 (1985) Proof	2,000	Value: 160				

KM# 45 25 BAISA **Weight:** 5.9600 g. **Composition:** 0.9170 Gold .1757 oz. AGW

Date	Mintage	F	VF	XF	Unc	BU
AH1392 (1972)	100	—	—	—	100	—
AH1392 (1972) Proof	50	Value: 150				
AH1394 (1974) Proof	250	Value: 100				
AH1395 (1975) Proof	250	Value: 100				

Note: Struck for presentation purposes

KM# 45a 25 BAISA **Composition:** Copper-Nickel

Date	Mintage	F	VF	XF	Unc	BU
AH1395 (1975)	4,500,000	—	0.20	0.40	0.85	—
AH1400 (1979)	5,250,000	—	0.20	0.40	0.85	—
AH1406 (1985)	4,000,000	—	0.20	0.40	0.85	—
AH1410 (1989)	7,000,000	—	0.20	0.40	0.85	—
AH1418 (1997)	—	—	0.20	0.40	0.85	—

KM# 78 25 BAISA **Composition:** Copper-Nickel **Subject:** 20th National Day - Royal Hospital **Obverse:** National emblem

Date	Mintage	F	VF	XF	Unc	BU
AH1411 (1990) Proof	3,200	Value: 7.00				

KM# 46 50 BAISA **Weight:** 12.8900 g. **Composition:** 0.9170 Gold .3801 oz. AGW

Date	Mintage	F	VF	XF	Unc	BU
AH1392 (1972)	200	—	—	—	200	—
AH1392 (1972) Proof	50	Value: 250				
AH1394 (1974) Proof	250	Value: 200				
AH1395 (1975) Proof	250	Value: 200				

Note: Struck for presentation purposes

KM# 46a 50 BAISA **Composition:** Copper-Nickel

Date	Mintage	F	VF	XF	Unc	BU
AH1395 (1975)	2,500,000	—	0.30	0.60	1.50	—
AH1400 (1979)	2,750,000	—	0.30	0.60	1.50	—
AH1406 (1985)	4,000,000	—	0.30	0.60	1.50	—
AH1410 (1989)	4,000,000	—	0.30	0.60	1.50	—
AH1418 (1997)	—	—	0.30	0.60	1.50	—

KM# 79 50 BAISA **Composition:** Copper-Nickel **Subject:** 20th National Day - Irrigation Canal **Obverse:** National emblem

Date	Mintage	F	VF	XF	Unc	BU
AH1411 (1990) Proof	3,200	Value: 8.00				

KM# 95 50 BAISA **Composition:** Copper-Nickel **Subject:** U.N. - 50 Years

Date	F	VF	XF	Unc	BU
ND (1995)	—	—	—	3.00	—

KM# 47 100 BAISA **Weight:** 22.7400 g. **Composition:** 0.9170 Gold .6705 oz. AGW

Date	Mintage	F	VF	XF	Unc	BU
AH1392 (1972)	200	—	—	—	320	—
AH1392 (1972) Proof	50	Value: 375				
AH1394 (1974) Proof	250	Value: 320				
AH1395 (1975) Proof	250	Value: 320				

Note: Struck for presentation purposes

KM# 68 100 BAISA **Composition:** Copper-Nickel

Date	Mintage	F	VF	XF	Unc	BU
AH1404 (1983)	4,000,000	—	0.40	0.80	2.25	—

KM# 80 100 BAISA **Composition:** Copper-Nickel **Subject:** 20th National Day - Sultan Qaboos University **Obverse:** National emblem

Date	Mintage	F	VF	XF	Unc	BU
AH1411 (1990) Proof	3,200	Value: 10.00				

KM# 82 100 BAISA **Ring Composition:** Copper-Nickel **Center Composition:** Aluminum-Bronze

Date	Mintage	F	VF	XF	Unc	BU
AH1411 (1990)	—	—	—	—	5.00	—
AH1411 (1990) Proof	1,000	Value: 20.00				

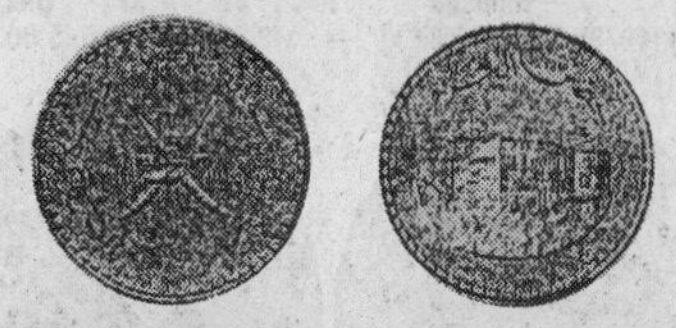

KM# 57 1/4 OMANI RIAL **Weight:** 12.8900 g. **Composition:** 0.9170 Gold .3799 oz. AGW **Subject:** Fort al Hazam **Obverse:** Similar to 1/2 Omani Rial, KM#58 **Reverse:** Fort

Date	Mintage	F	VF	XF	Unc	BU
AH1397 (1976) Proof	1,000	Value: 250				
AH1408 (1987) Proof	250	Value: 400				

KM# 66 1/4 OMANI RIAL **Composition:** Aluminum-Bronze

Date	Mintage	F	VF	XF	Unc	BU
AH1400 (1980)	4,000,000	—	0.75	1.00	2.00	—

KM# 48 1/2 OMANI RIAL **Weight:** 25.6000 g. **Composition:** 0.9170 Gold .7548 oz. AGW

Date	Mintage	F	VF	XF	Unc	BU
AH1392 (1972) Proof	124	Value: 650				
AH1394 (1974)	250	—	—	—	650	—
AH1395 (1975)	250	—	—	—	600	—

Note: Struck for presentation purposes

KM# 58 1/2 OMANI RIAL **Weight:** 19.6700 g. **Composition:** 0.9170 Gold .5797 oz. AGW **Subject:** Fort Mirbat

Date	Mintage	F	VF	XF	Unc	BU
AH1397 (1976) Proof	1,000	Value: 350				
AH1408 (1987) Proof	250	Value: 500				

KM# 64 1/2 OMANI RIAL **Composition:** Copper-Nickel **Series:** F.A.O.

Date	Mintage	F	VF	XF	Unc	BU
AH1398 (1978)	15,000	—	2.75	3.50	5.00	—

KM# 69 1/2 OMANI RIAL **Weight:** 19.6700 g. **Composition:** 0.9170 Gold .5800 oz. AGW **Subject:** 10th National Day

Date	Mintage	F	VF	XF	Unc	BU
AH1400 (1979) Proof	600	Value: 450				

Note: Struck for presentation purposes

KM# 67 1/2 OMANI RIAL **Composition:** Aluminum-Bronze

Date	Mintage	F	VF	XF	Unc	BU
AH1400 (1980)	2,000,000	—	2.75	3.50	5.00	—

KM# 87 1/2 OMANI RIAL **Weight:** 10.0000 g. **Composition:** 0.9170 Gold .2947 oz. AGW **Subject:** Youth Year

Date	Mintage	F	VF	XF	Unc	BU
AH1403 (1982) Proof	1,000	Value: 225				

KM# 85 1/2 OMANI RIAL **Weight:** 28.2800 g. **Composition:** 0.9250 Silver .8411 oz. ASW **Subject:** Year of Agriculture

Date	Mintage	F	VF	XF	Unc	BU
AH1409 (1988) Proof	300	Value: 135				

KM# 86 1/2 OMANI RIAL **Weight:** 28.2800 g. **Composition:** 0.9250 Silver .8411 oz. ASW **Subject:** Year of Industry

Date	Mintage	F	VF	XF	Unc	BU
AH1411 (1990) Proof	810	Value: 110				

KM# 134 1/2 OMANI RIAL **Weight:** 15.0000 g. **Composition:** 0.9250 Silver .4461 oz. ASW **Subject:** Youth Year **Obverse:** Crown above crossed swords **Reverse:** Radiant design. Similar to KM#91

Date	Mintage	F	VF	XF	Unc	BU
AH1413 (1992) Proof; Rare	310	—	—	—	—	—

KM# 91 1/2 OMANI RIAL **Weight:** 15.0000 g. **Composition:** 0.9250 Silver .4461 oz. ASW **Subject:** Youth Year **Reverse:** Radiant design

Date	Mintage	F	VF	XF	Unc	BU
AH1413 (1992) Proof	600	Value: 85.00				

KM# 92 1/2 OMANI RIAL **Weight:** 28.2800 g. **Composition:** 0.9250 Silver .8411 oz. ASW **Subject:** Heritage Year **Reverse:** Radiant design

Date	Mintage	F	VF	XF	Unc	BU
AH1414 (1993) Proof	840	Value: 100				

KM# 111 1/2 OMANI RIAL **Weight:** 28.2800 g. **Composition:** 0.9250 Silver .8411 oz. ASW **Subject:** 250th Anniversary - Al Bu Sa'id Dynasty

Date	Mintage	F	VF	XF	Unc	BU
AH1414 (1993) Proof	500	Value: 110				

KM# 54 OMANI RIAL **Weight:** 46.6500 g. **Composition:** 0.9170 Gold 1.3755 oz. AGW

Date	Mintage	F	VF	XF	Unc	BU
AH1392 (1972) Proof	124	Value: 750				
AH1394 (1974) Proof	250	Value: 750				
AH1395 (1975) Proof	250	Value: 750				

Note: Struck for presentation purposes

KM# 59 OMANI RIAL **Weight:** 25.6000 g. **Composition:** 0.9170 Gold .7545 oz. AGW **Subject:** Fort Buraimi

Date	Mintage	F	VF	XF	Unc	BU
AH1397 (1976) Proof	1,000	Value: 450				
AH1408 (1987) Proof	250	Value: 600				

KM# 65 OMANI RIAL **Weight:** 15.0000 g. **Composition:** 0.5000 Silver .2412 oz. ASW **Series:** F.A.O.

Date	Mintage	F	VF	XF	Unc	BU
AH1398 (1978)	15,000	—	—	7.50	12.50	—

KM# 70 OMANI RIAL **Weight:** 25.6000 g. **Composition:** 0.9170 Gold .7548 oz. AGW **Subject:** 10th National Day

Date	Mintage	F	VF	XF	Unc	BU
AH1400 (1979) Proof	300	Value: 600				

Note: Struck for presentation purposes

KM# 84 OMANI RIAL **Weight:** 14.8400 g. **Composition:** 0.9250 Silver .4413 oz. ASW **Subject:** Youth Year

Date	Mintage	F	VF	XF	Unc	BU
AH1403 (1982) Proof	1,200	Value: 75.00				

KM# 84a OMANI RIAL **Weight:** 20.0000 g. **Composition:** 0.9170 Gold .5894 oz. AGW **Subject:** Youth Year **Size:** 30 mm.

Date	Mintage	F	VF	XF	Unc	BU
AH1403 (1982) Proof	900	Value: 350				

KM# 135 OMANI RIAL **Weight:** 20.0000 g. **Composition:** 0.9170 Gold .5894 oz. AGW **Subject:** Youth Year **Obverse:** Crown above crossed swords **Note:** Similar to 1/2 Omani Rial, KM#91.

Date	Mintage	F	VF	XF	Unc	BU
AH1413 (1992) Proof; Rare	110	—	—	—	—	—

KM# 112 OMANI RIAL **Weight:** 20.0000 g. **Composition:** 0.9170 Gold .5894 oz. AGW **Subject:** Youth Year **Obverse:** Without crown above crossed swords **Note:** Similar to 1/2 Omani Rial, KM#91.

Date	Mintage	F	VF	XF	Unc	BU
AH1413 (1992) Proof	900	Value: 400				

KM# 93 OMANI RIAL **Weight:** 39.9400 g. **Composition:** 0.9167 Gold 1.1771 oz. AGW **Subject:** Heritage Year **Note:** Similar to 1/2 Omani Rial, KM#92.

Date	Mintage	F	VF	XF	Unc	BU
AH1414 (1993) Proof	1,000	Value: 900				

KM# 146 OMANI RIAL **Weight:** 39.9400 g. **Composition:** 0.9167 Gold 1.1771 oz. AGW **Subject:** 250th Anniversary - Al Bu Sa'id Dynasty **Note:** Similar to 1/2 Omani Rial, KM#111.

Date	Mintage	F	VF	XF	Unc	BU
AH1414 (1993) Proof	500	Value: 975				

KM# 96 OMANI RIAL **Weight:** 10.0000 g. **Composition:** 0.9250 Silver .2974 oz. ASW **Subject:** F.A.O. - 50 Years **Size:** 30 mm.

Date	F	VF	XF	Unc	BU
ND (1995) Proof	—	Value: 30.00			

KM# 114 OMANI RIAL **Weight:** 28.2800 g. **Composition:** 0.9250 Silver .8410 oz. ASW **Subject:** Al-Hazm Castle **Obverse:** National arms **Reverse:** Al-Hazm castle

Date	F	VF	XF	Unc	BU
AH1416 (1995) Proof	—	Value: 37.50			

KM# 115 OMANI RIAL **Weight:** 28.2800 g. **Composition:** 0.9250 Silver .8410 oz. ASW **Subject:** Al-Jalali Fort **Obverse:** National arms **Reverse:** Al-Jalali fort

Date	F	VF	XF	Unc	BU
AH1416 (1995) Proof	—	Value: 37.50			

KM# 116 OMANI RIAL **Weight:** 28.2800 g. **Composition:** 0.9250 Silver .8410 oz. ASW **Subject:** Al-Mirani Fort **Obverse:** National arms **Reverse:** Al-Mirani fort

Date	F	VF	XF	Unc	BU
AH1416 (1995) Proof	—	Value: 37.50			

KM# 117 OMANI RIAL **Weight:** 28.2800 g. **Composition:** 0.9250 Silver .8410 oz. ASW **Subject:** Al-Rustaq Fort **Obverse:** National arms **Reverse:** Al-Rustaq fort

Date	F	VF	XF	Unc	BU
AH1416 (1995) Proof	—	Value: 37.50			

KM# 118 OMANI RIAL **Weight:** 28.2800 g. **Composition:** 0.9250 Silver .8410 oz. ASW **Subject:** Al-Wafi Castle **Obverse:** National arms **Reverse:** Al-Wafi castle

Date	F	VF	XF	Unc	BU
AH1416 (1995) Proof	—	Value: 37.50			

KM# 119 OMANI RIAL **Weight:** 28.2800 g. **Composition:** 0.9250 Silver .8410 oz. ASW **Subject:** Bait Al-Falaj Fort **Obverse:** National arms **Reverse:** Bait Al-Falaj fort

Date	F	VF	XF	Unc	BU
AH1416 (1995) Proof	—	Value: 37.50			

KM# 120 OMANI RIAL **Weight:** 28.2800 g. **Composition:** 0.9250 Silver .8410 oz. ASW **Subject:** Bait Al-Na'Aman Castle **Obverse:** National arms **Reverse:** Bait Al-Na'Aman castle

Date	F	VF	XF	Unc	BU
AH1416 (1995) Proof	—	Value: 37.50			

KM# 121 OMANI RIAL **Weight:** 28.2800 g. **Composition:** 0.9250 Silver .8410 oz. ASW **Subject:** Bahla Fort **Obverse:** National arms **Reverse:** Bahla fort

Date	F	VF	XF	Unc	BU
AH1416 (1995) Proof	—	Value: 37.50			

KM# 122 OMANI RIAL **Weight:** 28.2800 g. **Composition:** 0.9250 Silver .8410 oz. ASW **Subject:** Barka Fort **Obverse:** National arms **Reverse:** Barka fort

Date	F	VF	XF	Unc	BU
AH1416 (1995) Proof	—	Value: 37.50			

KM# 126 OMANI RIAL **Weight:** 28.2800 g. **Composition:** 0.9250 Silver .8410 oz. ASW **Subject:** Jabrin Castle **Obverse:** National arms **Reverse:** Jabrin castle

Date	F	VF	XF	Unc	BU
AH1416 (1995) Proof	—	Value: 37.50			

KM# 130 OMANI RIAL **Weight:** 28.2800 g. **Composition:** 0.9250 Silver .8410 oz. ASW **Subject:** Nakhl Fort **Obverse:** National arms **Reverse:** Nakhl fort

Date	F	VF	XF	Unc	BU
AH1416 (1995) Proof	—	Value: 37.50			

KM# 123 OMANI RIAL **Weight:** 28.2800 g. **Composition:** 0.9250 Silver .8410 oz. ASW **Subject:** Barkat-Al-Mauz Castle **Obverse:** National arms **Reverse:** Barkat-Al-Mauz castle

Date	F	VF	XF	Unc	BU
AH1416 (1995) Proof	—	Value: 37.50			

KM# 127 OMANI RIAL **Weight:** 28.2800 g. **Composition:** 0.9250 Silver .8410 oz. ASW **Subject:** Khasab Fort **Obverse:** National arms **Reverse:** Khasab fort

Date	F	VF	XF	Unc	BU
AH1416 (1995) Proof	—	Value: 37.50			

KM# 131 OMANI RIAL **Weight:** 28.2800 g. **Composition:** 0.9250 Silver .8410 oz. ASW **Subject:** Nizwa Fort **Obverse:** National arms **Reverse:** Nizwa fort

Date	F	VF	XF	Unc	BU
AH1416 (1995) Proof	—	Value: 37.50			

KM# 124 OMANI RIAL **Weight:** 28.2800 g. **Composition:** 0.9250 Silver .8410 oz. ASW **Subject:** Buraimi Fort **Obverse:** National arms **Reverse:** Buraimi fort

Date	F	VF	XF	Unc	BU
AH1416 (1995) Proof	—	Value: 37.50			

KM# 128 OMANI RIAL **Weight:** 28.2800 g. **Composition:** 0.9250 Silver .8410 oz. ASW **Subject:** Matrah Fort **Obverse:** National arms **Reverse:** Matrah fort

Date	F	VF	XF	Unc	BU
AH1416 (1995) Proof	—	Value: 37.50			

KM# 132 OMANI RIAL **Weight:** 28.2800 g. **Composition:** 0.9250 Silver .8410 oz. ASW **Subject:** Sohar Fort **Obverse:** National arms **Reverse:** Sohar fort

Date	F	VF	XF	Unc	BU
AH1416 (1995) Proof	—	Value: 37.50			

KM# 125 OMANI RIAL **Weight:** 28.2800 g. **Composition:** 0.9250 Silver .8410 oz. ASW **Subject:** Ja'Alan Bani Bu Hassan Castle **Obverse:** National arms **Reverse:** Ja'Alan Bani Bu Hassan castle

Date	F	VF	XF	Unc	BU
AH1416 (1995) Proof	—	Value: 37.50			

KM# 129 OMANI RIAL **Weight:** 28.2800 g. **Composition:** 0.9250 Silver .8410 oz. ASW **Subject:** Mirbat Castle **Obverse:** National arms **Reverse:** Mirbat castle

Date	F	VF	XF	Unc	BU
AH1416 (1995) Proof	—	Value: 37.50			

KM# 133 OMANI RIAL **Weight:** 28.2800 g. **Composition:** 0.9250 Silver .8410 oz. ASW **Subject:** Sur Castle **Obverse:** National arms **Reverse:** Sur castle

Date	F	VF	XF	Unc	BU
AH1416 (1995) Proof	—	Value: 37.50			

KM# 140 OMANI RIAL **Weight:** 13.9000 g. **Composition:** 0.9250 Silver .4134 oz. ASW **Subject:** 25th National Day Anniversary - Burj Al Nahda

Date	F	VF	XF	Unc	BU
1995 Proof	—	Value: 65.00			

KM# 140a OMANI RIAL Weight: 22.8000 g. **Composition:** 0.9160 Gold .6715 oz. AGW

Date	F	VF	XF	Unc	BU
1995 Proof	—	Value: 450			

KM# 145 OMANI RIAL Weight: 28.2800 g. **Composition:** 0.9250 Silver .8410 oz. ASW **Subject:** U.N. - 50 Years **Size:** 30 mm.

Date	Mintage	F	VF	XF	Unc	BU
ND(1995) Proof	25,000	Value: 40.00				

KM# 101 OMANI RIAL Weight: 31.4700 g. **Composition:** 0.9250 Silver .9359 oz. ASW **Subject:** 26th National Day Anniversary - Sultanah **Obverse:** Omani arms

Date	F	VF	XF	Unc	BU
1996 Proof	—	Value: 45.00			

KM# 102 OMANI RIAL Weight: 37.8000 g. **Composition:** 0.9160 Gold 1.1132 oz. AGW **Subject:** 26th National Day Anniversary - Sultanah **Obverse:** Omani arms

Date	F	VF	XF	Unc	BU
1996 Proof	—	Value: 625			

KM# 103 OMANI RIAL Weight: 28.2800 g. **Composition:** 0.9250 Silver .8411 oz. ASW **Subject:** 26th National Day Anniversary - Al Battil **Obverse:** Omani arms

Date	F	VF	XF	Unc	BU
1996 Proof	—	Value: 35.00			

KM# 104 OMANI RIAL Weight: 28.2800 g. **Composition:** 0.9250 Silver .8411 oz. ASW **Subject:** 26th National Day Anniversary - Al Badan **Obverse:** Omani arms

Date	F	VF	XF	Unc	BU
1996 Proof	—	Value: 35.00			

KM# 105 OMANI RIAL Weight: 28.2800 g. **Composition:** 0.9250 Silver .8411 oz. ASW **Subject:** 26th National Day Anniversary - Al Baglah **Obverse:** Omani arms

Date	F	VF	XF	Unc	BU
1996 Proof	—	Value: 35.00			

KM# 106 OMANI RIAL Weight: 28.2800 g. **Composition:** 0.9250 Silver .8411 oz. ASW **Subject:** 26th National Day Anniversary - Al Boum **Obverse:** Omani arms

Date	F	VF	XF	Unc	BU
1996 Proof	—	Value: 35.00			

KM# 107 OMANI RIAL Weight: 28.2800 g. **Composition:** 0.9250 Silver .8411 oz. ASW **Subject:** 26th National Day Anniversary - Al Jalbout **Obverse:** Omani arms

Date	F	VF	XF	Unc	BU
1996 Proof	—	Value: 35.00			

KM# 108 OMANI RIAL Weight: 28.2800 g. **Composition:** 0.9250 Silver .8411 oz. ASW **Subject:** 26th National Day Anniversary - Al Sanbuq **Obverse:** Omani arms

Date	F	VF	XF	Unc	BU
1996 Proof	—	Value: 35.00			

KM# 109 OMANI RIAL Weight: 28.2800 g. **Composition:** 0.9250 Silver .8411 oz. ASW **Subject:** 26th National Day Anniversary - Al Ghanjah **Obverse:** Omani arms

Date	F	VF	XF	Unc	BU
1996 Proof	—	Value: 35.00			

KM# 110 OMANI RIAL Weight: 28.2800 g. **Composition:** 0.9250 Silver .8411 oz. ASW **Subject:** 26th National Day Anniversary - Al Lateen **Obverse:** Omani arms

Date	F	VF	XF	Unc	BU
1996 Proof	—	Value: 35.00			

KM# 136 OMANI RIAL Weight: 28.2800 g. **Composition:** 0.9250 Silver .8411 oz. ASW **Subject:** 27th National Day Anniversary - Al Nahdha **Reverse:** Al Nahdha Tower, coconut tree and Frankincense tree from the Dhofar Region. **Size:** 38.6 mm. **Note:** Struck by Royal Mint - London.

Date	F	VF	XF	Unc	BU
AH1417 (1996) Proof	—	Value: 45.00			

KM# 136a OMANI RIAL Weight: 37.8000 g. **Composition:** 0.9167 Gold 1.1141 oz. AGW **Subject:** 27th National Day Anniversary - Al Nahdha **Reverse:** Al Nahdha Tower, coconut tree and Frankincense tree from the Dhofar Region. **Size:** 38.6 mm. **Note:** Struck by Royal Mint - London.

Date	F	VF	XF	Unc	BU
AH1417 (1996) Proof	—	Value: 650			

KM# 138 OMANI RIAL Weight: 28.2800 g. **Composition:** 0.9250 Silver .8411 oz. ASW **Series:** World Wildlife Fund **Reverse:** Leopard

Date	Mintage	F	VF	XF	Unc	BU
1997 Proof	15,000	Value: 37.50				

KM# 113 OMANI RIAL Weight: 28.2800 g. **Composition:** 0.9250 Silver .8411 oz. ASW **Series:** World Wildlife Fund **Obverse:** National emblem **Reverse:** Mountain gazelle **Size:** 38.6 mm. **Note:** Struck at Royal Norwegian Mint.

Date	Mintage	F	VF	XF	Unc	BU
1997 Proof	15,000	Value: 37.50				

KM# 139 OMANI RIAL **Weight:** 28.2800 g. **Composition:** 0.9250 Silver .8411 oz. ASW **Subject:** 28th National Day Anniversary - Private Sector Year **Size:** 38.6 mm.

Date	F	VF	XF	Unc	BU
AH1418 (1997) Proof	—	Value: 45.00			

KM# 139a OMANI RIAL **Weight:** 37.8000 g. **Composition:** 0.9167 Gold 1.1141 oz. AGW **Subject:** 28th National Day Anniversary - Private Sector Year **Size:** 38.6 mm.

Date	F	VF	XF	Unc	BU
AH1418 (1997)	—	—	—	650	—

KM# 149 OMANI RIAL **Weight:** 28.2800 g. **Composition:** 0.9250 Silver .8410 oz. ASW **Subject:** 29th National Day Anniversary - 1420/1999 **Obverse:** National arms. **Reverse:** Palm tree (Khalas) and camels caravan. **Size:** 38.61 mm. **Note:** Struck by Royal Mint - London.

Date	F	VF	XF	Unc	BU
ND(1999)	—	—	—	—	—

KM# 149a OMANI RIAL **Weight:** 37.8000 g. **Composition:** 0.9167 Gold 1.1141 oz. AGW **Subject:** 29th National Day Anniversary - 1420/1999 **Obverse:** National arms. **Reverse:** Palm tree (Khalas) and camels caravan. **Size:** 38.61 mm. **Note:** Struck by Royal Mint - London.

Date	F	VF	XF	Unc	BU
ND(1999)	—	—	—	—	—

KM# 148 OMANI RIAL **Weight:** 27.8700 g. **Composition:** 0.9250 Silver .8288 oz. ASW **Subject:** Central Bank's 25th Anniversary **Obverse:** National arms **Reverse:** Central Bank of Oman **Size:** 38.6 mm.

Date	F	VF	XF	Unc	BU
ND(2000) Proof	—	—	—	100	—

KM# 147 OMANI RIAL **Weight:** 27.8700 g. **Composition:** 0.9250 Silver .8288 oz. ASW **Subject:** 30th National Day **Obverse:** National arms **Reverse:** Factory and various items **Edge:** Reeded **Size:** 38.61 mm. **Note:** Struck by Huguenin & Kramer - Switzerland.

Date	F	VF	XF	Unc	BU
2000 Proof	—	—	—	100	—

KM# 147a OMANI RIAL **Weight:** 37.8000 g. **Composition:** 0.9160 Gold 1.1141 oz. AGW **Subject:** 30th National Day **Obverse:** National arms. **Reverse:** Factory and various items. **Edge:** Reeded. **Size:** 38.61 mm. **Note:** Struck by Huguenin & Kramer - Switzerland.

Date	F	VF	XF	Unc	BU
2000	—	—	—	—	—

KM# 154 OMANI RIAL **Weight:** 28.2800 g. **Composition:** 0.9250 Silver 0.841 oz. ASW **Subject:** 31st National Day and Environment Year **Obverse:** National arms **Reverse:** Multicolor map design **Edge:** Reeded **Size:** 38.6 mm.

Date	Mintage	F	VF	XF	Unc	BU
2001	500	—	—	—	60.00	—
2001 Proof	105	Value: 100				

KM# 154a OMANI RIAL **Weight:** 37.8000 g. **Composition:** 0.9160 Gold 1.1132 oz. AGW **Subject:** 31st National Day and Environment Year **Obverse:** National arms **Reverse:** Multicolor map design **Edge:** Reeded **Size:** 38.6 mm.

Date	Mintage	F	VF	XF	Unc	BU
2001	350	—	—	—	750	—
2001 Proof	105	Value: 850				

KM# 81 2 OMANI RIALS **Weight:** 20.0000 g. **Composition:** 0.9250 Silver .5948 oz. ASW **Subject:** 20th National Day - Sultan Sa'id

Date	Mintage	F	VF	XF	Unc	BU
AH1411 (1990) Proof	3,200	Value: 50.00				

KM# 60 2-1/2 OMANI RIALS **Weight:** 28.2800 g. **Composition:** 0.9250 Silver .8411 oz. ASW **Subject:** Conservation **Reverse:** Caracal Lynx

Date	Mintage	F	VF	XF	Unc	BU
AH1397 (1976)	4,539	—	—	—	25.00	—
AH1397 (1976) Proof	4,407	Value: 30.00				

KM# 71 2-1/2 OMANI RIALS **Weight:** 28.2800 g. **Composition:** 0.9250 Silver .8411 oz. ASW **Obverse:** Crown above crossed swords **Reverse:** Verreaux's eagle

Date	F	VF	XF	Unc	BU
AH1407 (1986) Proof; Rare	—	—	—	—	—

Note: Struck for presentation purposes

KM# 73 2-1/2 OMANI RIALS **Weight:** 28.2800 g. **Composition:** 0.9250 Silver .8411 oz. ASW **Series:** World Wildlife Fund **Reverse:** Verreaux's eagle

Date	Mintage	F	VF	XF	Unc	BU
AH1407 (1987) Proof	25,000	Value: 30.00				

KM# 83 2-1/2 OMANI RIALS **Weight:** 28.2800 g. **Composition:** 0.9250 Silver .8411 oz. ASW **Series:** Save the Children

Date	Mintage	F	VF	XF	Unc	BU
AH1411 (1990) Proof	Est. 20,000	Value: 37.50				

KM# 97 2-1/2 OMANI RIALS **Weight:** 28.2800 g. **Composition:** 0.9250 Silver .8411 oz. ASW **Obverse:** Similar to KM#71 **Reverse:** KM#83

Date	F	VF	XF	Unc	BU
AH1411 (1990) Proof; Rare	—	—	—	—	—

Note: Struck for presentation purposes

KM# 61 5 OMANI RIALS **Weight:** 35.0000 g. **Composition:** 0.9250 Silver 1.0409 oz. ASW **Subject:** Conservation **Reverse:** Arabian White Oryx

Date	Mintage	F	VF	XF	Unc	BU
AH1397 (1976)	4,359	—	—	—	27.50	—
AH1397 (1976) Proof	4,401	Value: 35.00				

KM# 62 5 OMANI RIALS Weight: 45.6500 g. **Composition:** 0.9170 Gold 1.3454 oz. AGW **Subject:** 7th Anniversary - Reign of Sultan Qabus bin Sa'id

Date	Mintage	F	VF	XF	Unc	BU
AH1397 (1976) Proof	1,000	Value: 850				
AH1408 (1987) Proof	250	Value: 950				

KM# 89 5 OMANI RIALS Weight: 20.0000 g. **Composition:** 0.9170 Gold .5894 oz. AGW **Subject:** Agricultural Year **Note:** Similar to 1/2 Omani Rial, KM#85.

Date	Mintage	F	VF	XF	Unc	BU
AH1409 (1988) Proof	200	Value: 350				

KM# 90 5 OMANI RIALS Weight: 20.0000 g. **Composition:** 0.9170 Gold .5894 oz. AGW **Subject:** Industry Year **Note:** Similar to 1/2 Omani Rial, KM#86.

Date	Mintage	F	VF	XF	Unc	BU
AH1411 (1990) Proof	410	Value: 350				

KM# 141 5 OMANI RIALS Weight: 18.8000 g. **Composition:** 0.9250 Silver .5591 oz. ASW **Subject:** 25th National Day Anniversary - Burj Al Sahwa

Date	F	VF	XF	Unc	BU
1995 Proof	—	Value: 75.00			

KM# 141a 5 OMANI RIALS Weight: 31.0000 g. **Composition:** 0.9160 Gold .9130 oz. AGW

Date	F	VF	XF	Unc	BU
1995 Proof	—	Value: 550			

KM# 142 10 OMANI RIALS Weight: 23.2000 g. **Composition:** 0.9250 Silver .6900 oz. ASW **Subject:** 25th National Day Anniversary - Central Bank

Date	F	VF	XF	Unc	BU
1995 Proof	—	Value: 85.00			

KM# 142a 10 OMANI RIALS Weight: 36.4000 g. **Composition:** 0.9160 Gold 1.0720 oz. AGW

Date	F	VF	XF	Unc	BU
1995 Proof	—	Value: 650			

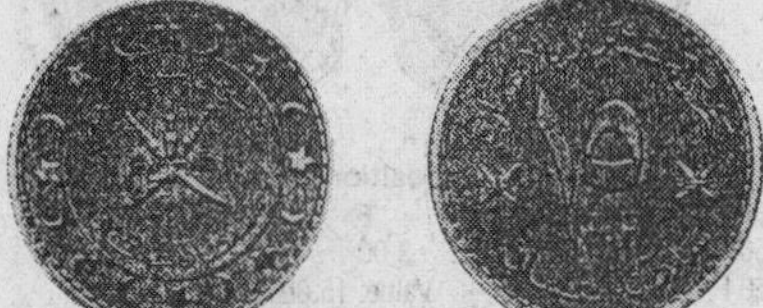

KM# 49 15 OMANI RIALS Weight: 7.9900 g. **Composition:** 0.9170 Gold .2355 oz. AGW

Date	Mintage	F	VF	XF	Unc	BU
AH1392 (1972) Proof	124	Value: 350				
AH1394 (1974)	300	—	—	—	200	—

Note: Struck for presentation purposes

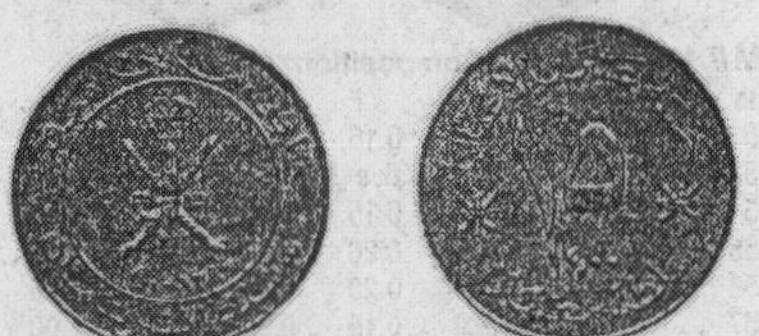

KM# 55 15 OMANI RIALS Weight: 7.9900 g. **Composition:** 0.9170 Gold .2355 oz. AGW **Subject:** 10th National Day

Date	Mintage	F	VF	XF	Unc	BU
AH1400 (1979) Proof	1,000	Value: 400				

Note: Struck for presentation purposes

KM# 56 15 OMANI RIALS Weight: 20.0000 g. **Composition:** 0.9170 Gold .5897 oz. AGW **Subject:** 15th Anniversary - Reign of Sultan

Date	Mintage	F	VF	XF	Unc	BU
AH1406 (1985) Proof	2,000	Value: 350				

KM# 56a 15 OMANI RIALS Weight: 31.0100 g. **Composition:** 0.9170 Gold .9144 oz. AGW

Date	Mintage	F	VF	XF	Unc	BU
AH1406 (1985) Proof	200	Value: 800				

KM# 98 20 OMANI RIALS Weight: 20.0000 g. **Composition:** 0.9170 Gold .5897 oz. AGW **Subject:** 20th National Day - Sultan Sa'id **Note:** Similar to 2 Omani Rials, KM#81.

Date	Mintage	F	VF	XF	Unc	BU
AH1411 (1990) Proof	1,200	Value: 375				

KM# 137.1 20 OMANI RIALS Weight: 48.6500 g. **Composition:** 0.9167 Gold 1.4338 oz. AGW

Date	Mintage	F	VF	XF	Unc	BU
AH1411 (1990)	500	—	—	—	—	—

KM# 137.2 (KM137) 20 OMANI RIALS Weight: 65.3700 g. **Composition:** 0.9170 Gold 1.9273 oz. AGW **Subject:** 20th Anniversary of Sultan's Reign

Date	F	VF	XF	Unc	BU
ND(AH1411) (1990) Proof	—	—	—	—	—
ND(AH1411) (1990) Proof	—	—	—	—	—

KM# 143 20 OMANI RIALS Weight: 27.4000 g. **Composition:** 0.9250 Silver .8149 oz. ASW **Subject:** 25th National Day Anniversary **Reverse:** Emblem

Date	F	VF	XF	Unc	BU
1995 Proof	—	Value: 95.00			

KM# 143a 20 OMANI RIALS Weight: 41.2000 g. **Composition:** 0.9160 Gold 1.2133 oz. AGW

Date	F	VF	XF	Unc	BU
1995 Proof	—	Value: 750			

KM# 74 25 OMANI RIALS Weight: 10.0000 g. **Composition:** 0.9170 Gold .2947 oz. AGW **Series:** World Wildlife Fund **Reverse:** Masked Booby

Date	Mintage	F	VF	XF	Unc	BU
AH1407 (1986) Proof	5,000	Value: 165				

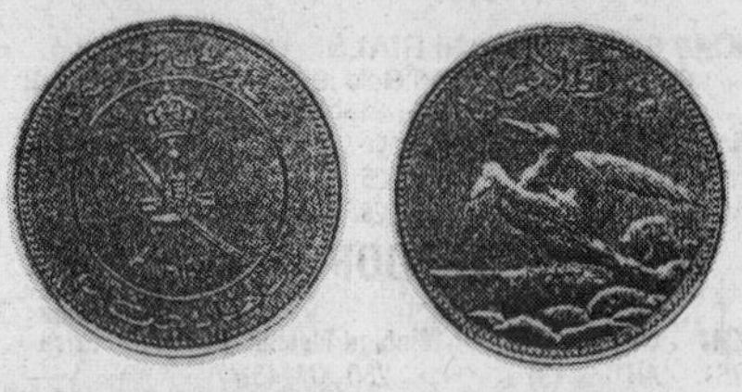

KM# 99 25 OMANI RIALS Weight: 10.0000 g. **Composition:** 0.9170 Gold .2947 oz. AGW **Obverse:** Crown above crossed swords

Date	F	VF	XF	Unc	BU
AH1407 (1986) Proof; Rare	—	—	—	—	—

Note: Struck for presentation purposes

KM# 88 25 OMANI RIALS Weight: 10.0000 g. **Composition:** 0.9170 Gold .2947 oz. AGW **Series:** Save the Children **Reverse:** School Master, Pupils

Date	Mintage	F	VF	XF	Unc	BU
AH1411 (1990) Proof	Est. 3,000	Value: 200				

KM# 100 25 OMANI RIALS Weight: 10.0000 g. **Composition:** 0.9170 Gold .2947 oz. AGW **Obverse:** Crown above crossed swords

Date	F	VF	XF	Unc	BU
AH1411 (1990) Proof; Rare	—	—	—	—	—

Note: Struck for presentation purposes

KM# 144 25 OMANI RIALS Weight: 31.7000 g. **Composition:** 0.9250 Silver .9427 oz. ASW **Subject:** 25th National Day Anniversary - Sultan Qaboos bin Said **Reverse:** Multicolor portrait

Date		F	VF	XF	Unc	BU
1995 Proof	—	Value: 100				

KM# 144a 25 OMANI RIALS Weight: 50.2000 g. **Composition:** 0.9160 Gold 1.4784 oz. AGW

Date		F	VF	XF	Unc	BU
1995 Proof	—	Value: 900				

KM# 63 75 OMANI RIALS Weight: 33.4370 g. **Composition:** 0.9000 Gold .9676 oz. AGW **Subject:** Conservation **Reverse:** Arabian Tahr

Date	Mintage	F	VF	XF	Unc	BU
AH1397 (1976)	825	—	—	—	475	—
AH1397 (1976) Proof	325	Value: 700				

PROOF SETS

KM#	Date	Mintage	Identification	Issue Price	Mkt Val
PS1	AH1394 (3)	250	KM#45-47	—	620
PS2	AH1395 (3)	250	KM#45-47	—	620
PS3	AH1397 (3)	—	KM#60, 61, 63	780	765
PS4	AH1397 (2)	—	KM#60, 61	60.00	65.00
PS5	AH1411 (6)	3,200	KM#76-81	84.50	95.00
PS6	AH1416 (20)	—	KM#114-133	—	750
PSA6	1996 (2)	—	KM#101-102	640	670
PS7	1996 (4)	—	KM#103-106	125	140
PS9	1996 (8)	—	KM#103-110	247	280
PS8	1996 (4)	—	KM#107-110	125	140

PAKISTAN

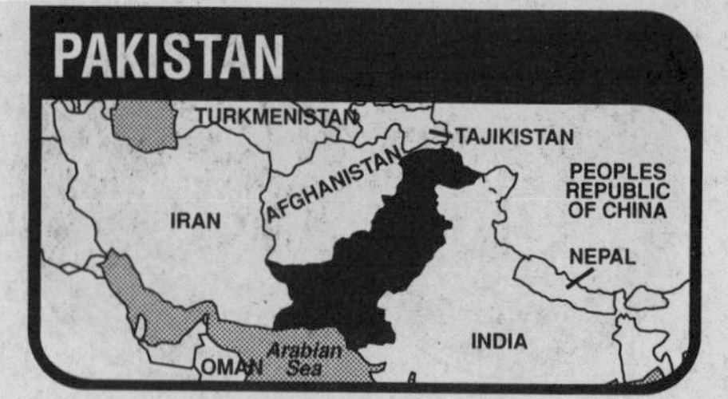

The Islamic Republic of Pakistan, located on the Indian subcontinent between India and Afghanistan, has an area of 310,404 sq. mi. (803,940 sq. km.) and a population of130 million. Capital: Islamabad. Pakistan is mainly an agricultural land although the industrial base is expanding rapidly. Yarn, textiles, cotton, rice, medical instruments, sports equipment and leather are exported.

Afghan and Turkish intrusions into northern India between the 11th and 18th centuries resulted in large numbers of Indians being converted to Islam. The idea of a separate Moslem state independent of Hindu India developed in the 1930's and was agreed to by Britain in1946. The Islamic majority areas of India, consisting of the separate geographic entities known as East and West Pakistan, achieved self-government as Pakistan, with dominion status in the British Commonwealth, when the British withdrew from India on Aug. 14, 1947. Pakistan became a republic in 1956. When a basic constitutional crisis initiated by the election of Dec. 1, 1970 - the first direct general election in Pakistani history - could not be resolved by the leaders of East and West Pakistan, the East Pakistanis seceded from the Islamic Republic of Pakistan (March 26, 1971) and formed the independent People's Republic of Bangladesh. After many years of vacillation between civilian and military regimes, the people of Pakistan held a free national election in November, 1988 and installed the first of a series of democratic governments under a parliamentary system.

TITLE

پاکستان

Pakistan

MONETARY SYSTEM
100 Paisa = 1 Rupee

ISLAMIC REPUBLIC

STANDARD COINAGE

3 Pies = 1 Pice; 4 Pice = 1 Anna; 16 Annas = 1 Rupee

KM# 1 PAISA Composition: Bronze **Note:** Varieties exist.

Date	Mintage	F	VF	XF	Unc	BU
1948	101,070,000	0.20	0.40	0.75	1.50	—
1948 Proof	—	Value: 2.00				
1949	25,740,000	0.20	0.40	0.75	1.50	—
1949 Proof	—	Value: 2.00				
1951	14,050,000	0.20	0.45	0.85	1.75	—
1952	41,680,000	0.20	0.40	0.75	1.50	—

KM# 11 PAISA Composition: Bronze

Date	Mintage	F	VF	XF	Unc	BU
1951	2,950,000	0.25	0.50	1.00	2.50	—
1951 Proof	—	Value: 4.00				
1953	110,000	0.25	0.75	1.50	3.00	—
1953 Proof	—	Value: 5.00				
1955	211,000	0.25	0.75	1.50	3.00	—
1955 Proof	—	Value: 15.00				
1956	3,390,000	0.25	0.50	1.00	2.50	—
1957	—	0.25	0.50	1.00	2.50	—

KM# 12 PAISA Composition: Nickel-Brass

Date	Mintage	F	VF	XF	Unc	BU
1953	47,540,000	0.15	0.30	0.50	1.00	—
1953 Proof	—	Value: 1.50				
1955	31,280,000	0.15	0.30	0.50	1.00	—
1956	9,710,000	0.20	0.35	0.60	1.15	—
1957	57,790,000	0.15	0.30	0.50	1.00	—
1958	52,470,000	0.15	0.30	0.50	1.00	—
1959	41,620,000	0.15	0.30	0.50	1.00	—

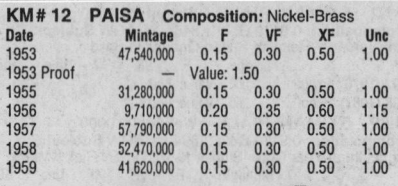

KM# 2 1/2 ANNA Composition: Copper-Nickel

Date	Mintage	F	VF	XF	Unc	BU
1948	73,920,000	0.15	0.30	0.50	1.00	—
1948 Proof	—	Value: 1.50				
1949 Dot after date	16,940,000	0.20	0.35	0.60	1.15	—
1951	75,360,000	0.15	0.30	0.50	1.00	—

KM# 13 1/2 ANNA Composition: Nickel-Brass

Date	Mintage	F	VF	XF	Unc	BU
1953	8,350,000	0.20	0.35	0.60	1.15	—
1953 Proof	—	Value: 1.50				
1955	17,310,000	0.15	0.30	0.50	1.00	—
1958	38,250,000	0.15	0.30	0.50	1.00	—

KM# 3 ANNA Composition: Copper-Nickel

Date	Mintage	F	VF	XF	Unc	BU
1948	73,460,000	0.15	0.30	0.50	1.00	—
1948 Proof	—	Value: 1.50				
1949	11,140,000	0.20	0.35	0.60	1.15	—
1949 Dot after date	—	0.15	0.30	0.50	1.00	—

Note: Mintage included with KM#8.

Date	Mintage	F	VF	XF	Unc	BU
1951	40,800,000	0.15	0.30	0.50	1.00	—
1952	15,430,000	0.20	0.35	0.60	1.15	—

KM# 8 ANNA Composition: Copper-Nickel

Date	Mintage	F	VF	XF	Unc	BU
1950	94,830,000	3.00	4.50	6.50	10.00	—
1950 Proof	—	Value: 15.00				

KM# 14 ANNA Composition: Copper-Nickel

Date	Mintage	F	VF	XF	Unc	BU
1953	9,350,000	0.15	0.30	0.50	1.00	—
1953 Proof	—	Value: 1.50				
1954	35,360,000	0.15	0.30	0.50	1.00	—
1955	6,230,000	0.20	0.35	0.60	1.15	—
1956	4,580,000	0.20	0.35	0.60	1.15	—
1957	12,500,000	0.15	0.30	0.50	1.00	—
1958	44,320,000	0.15	0.30	0.50	1.00	—

KM# 4 2 ANNAS Composition: Copper-Nickel

Date	Mintage	F	VF	XF	Unc	BU
1948	55,930,000	0.15	0.30	0.50	1.00	—
1948 Proof	—	Value: 1.50				
1949	19,720,000	0.15	0.30	0.50	1.00	—
1949 Dot after date	—	0.20	0.35	0.60	1.15	—

Note: Mintage included with KM#9.

Date	Mintage	F	VF	XF	Unc	BU
1951	33,130,000	0.15	0.30	0.50	1.00	—

KM# 9 2 ANNAS Composition: Copper-Nickel

Date	Mintage	F	VF	XF	Unc	BU
1950	21,190,000	3.50	5.00	7.50	12.50	—
1950 Proof	—	Value: 20.00				

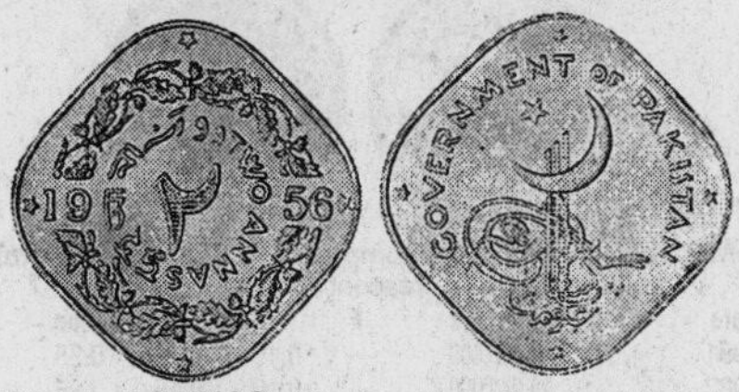

KM# 15 2 ANNAS Composition: Copper-Nickel

Date	Mintage	F	VF	XF	Unc	BU
1953	7,910,000	0.15	0.30	0.50	1.00	—
1953 Proof	—	Value: 1.50				
1954	5,740,000	0.15	0.30	0.50	1.00	—
1955	6,230,000	0.15	0.30	0.50	1.00	—
1956	1,370,000	0.20	0.35	0.60	1.15	—
1957	2,570,000	0.20	0.35	0.60	1.15	—
1958	6,200,000	0.15	0.30	0.50	1.00	—
1959	8,010,000	0.15	0.30	0.50	1.00	—

KM# 5 1/4 RUPEE Composition: Nickel

Date	Mintage	F	VF	XF	Unc	BU
1948	52,680,000	0.20	0.30	0.50	1.00	—
1948 Proof	—	Value: 2.25				
1949	46,000,000	0.20	0.30	0.50	1.00	—
1951	19,120,000	0.20	0.35	0.60	1.15	—

KM# 10 1/4 RUPEE Composition: Nickel

Date	Mintage	F	VF	XF	Unc	BU
1950	19,400,000	5.00	7.50	12.00	20.00	—
1950 Proof	—	Value: 25.00				

KM# 6 1/2 RUPEE Composition: Nickel

Date	Mintage	F	VF	XF	Unc	BU
1948	33,260,000	0.40	0.60	0.75	1.50	—
1948 Proof	—	Value: 2.00				
1949	20,300,000	0.40	0.60	0.75	1.50	—
1951	11,430,000	0.40	0.65	0.90	1.75	—

KM# 7 RUPEE Composition: Nickel **Note:** Varieties exist.

Date	Mintage	F	VF	XF	Unc	BU
1948	46,200,000	0.75	1.25	2.00	3.50	—
1948 Proof	—	Value: 5.00				
1949	37,100,000	0.75	1.25	2.00	3.50	—

DECIMAL COINAGE

100 Paisa (Pice) = 1 Rupee

KM# 16 PAISA Composition: Bronze

Date	Mintage	F	VF	XF	Unc	BU
1961	74,910,000	0.15	0.30	0.50	1.00	—

KM# 17 PAISA Composition: Bronze

Date	Mintage	F	VF	XF	Unc	BU
1961	134,650,000	0.15	0.25	0.40	0.80	—
1961 Proof	—	Value: 1.50				
1962	149,380,000	0.15	0.25	0.40	0.80	—
1963	127,810,000	0.15	0.25	0.40	0.80	—

KM# 24 PAISA Composition: Bronze

Date	Mintage	F	VF	XF	Unc	BU
1964	39,890,000	0.20	0.35	0.50	1.00	—
1964 Proof	—	Value: 1.50				
1965	69,660,000	0.20	0.35	0.50	1.00	—

KM# 24a PAISA Composition: Nickel-Brass

Date	Mintage	F	VF	XF	Unc	BU
1965	32,950,000	0.20	0.35	0.50	1.00	—
1966	179,370,000	0.15	0.25	0.40	0.80	—

KM# 29 PAISA Composition: Aluminum

Date	Mintage	F	VF	XF	Unc	BU
1967	170,070,000	—	0.10	0.15	0.30	—
1968	—	—	0.10	0.15	0.30	—
1969	—	—	0.10	0.15	0.30	—
1970	204,606,000	—	0.10	0.15	0.30	—
1971	191,880,000	—	0.10	0.15	0.30	—
1972	108,510,000	—	0.10	0.15	0.30	—
1973	Inc. above	—	0.10	0.15	0.30	—

KM# 33 PAISA Composition: Aluminum **Series:** F.A.O. **Reverse:** Abstract cotton plant

Date	Mintage	F	VF	XF	Unc	BU
1974	14,230,000	—	0.10	0.15	0.30	—
1975	43,000,000	—	0.10	0.15	0.30	—
1976	49,180,000	—	0.10	0.15	0.30	—
1977	62,750,000	—	0.10	0.15	0.30	—
1978	20,380,000	—	0.10	0.15	0.30	—
1979	5,630,000	—	0.10	0.15	0.30	—

KM# 25 2 PAISA Composition: Bronze

Date	Mintage	F	VF	XF	Unc	BU
1964	67,660,000	0.15	0.25	0.35	0.70	—
1964 Proof	—	Value: 1.50				
1965	27,880,000	0.15	0.25	0.35	0.70	—
1966	50,590,000	0.15	0.25	0.35	0.70	—

KM# 28 2 PAISA Composition: Aluminum

Date	Mintage	F	VF	XF	Unc	BU
1966	11,940,000	—	0.10	0.15	0.30	—
1967	73,970,000	—	0.10	0.15	0.30	—
1968	—	—	0.10	0.15	0.30	—

KM# 25a 2 PAISA Composition: Aluminum

Date	Mintage	F	VF	XF	Unc	BU
1968	—	—	0.10	0.15	0.30	—
1969	—	—	0.10	0.15	0.30	—
1970	24,401,000	—	0.10	0.15	0.30	—
1971	10,140,000	—	0.10	0.15	0.30	—
1972	4,040,000	0.10	0.15	0.20	0.40	—

KM# 34 2 PAISA Composition: Aluminum **Series:** F.A.O. **Reverse:** Rice plant

Date	Mintage	F	VF	XF	Unc	BU
1974	3,600,000	0.10	0.15	0.20	0.40	—
1975	4,020,000	0.10	0.15	0.20	0.40	—
1976	5,750,000	0.10	0.15	0.20	0.40	—

KM# 18 5 PAISA Composition: Nickel-Brass

Date	Mintage	F	VF	XF	Unc	BU
1961	40,050,000	0.20	0.30	0.40	0.80	—

KM# 19 5 PAISA Composition: Nickel-Brass

Date	Mintage	F	VF	XF	Unc	BU
1961	40,790,000	0.15	0.25	0.35	0.70	—
1961 Proof	—	Value: 1.50				
1962	48,200,000	0.15	0.25	0.35	0.70	—
1963	45,020,000	0.15	0.25	0.35	0.70	—

KM# 26 5 PAISA Composition: Nickel-Brass

Date	Mintage	F	VF	XF	Unc	BU
1964	82,730,000	0.15	0.25	0.35	0.70	—
1965	72,570,000	0.15	0.25	0.35	0.70	—
1966	32,900,000	0.15	0.25	0.35	0.70	—
1967	24,470,000	0.15	0.25	0.35	0.70	—
1968	—	0.15	0.25	0.35	0.70	—
1969	5,690,000	0.20	0.30	0.40	0.80	—
1970	24,655,000	0.15	0.25	0.35	0.70	—
1971	23,860,000	0.15	0.25	0.35	0.70	—
1972	40,345,000	0.15	0.25	0.35	0.70	—
1973	Inc. above	0.15	0.25	0.35	0.70	—
1974	7,695,000	0.20	0.30	0.40	0.80	—

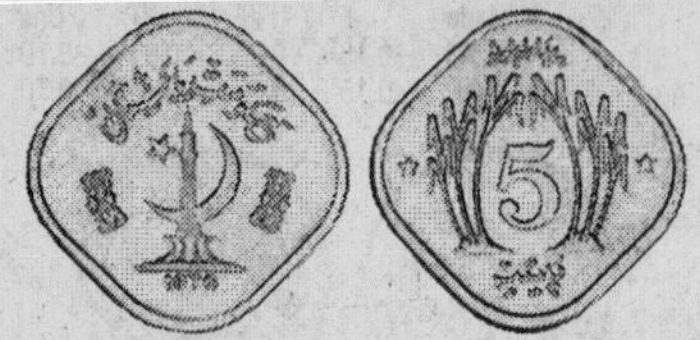

KM# 35 5 PAISA **Composition:** Aluminum **Series:** F.A.O. **Reverse:** Sugar cane

Date	Mintage	F	VF	XF	Unc	BU
1974	23,395,000	—	0.10	0.15	0.30	—
1975	50,030,000	—	0.10	0.15	0.30	—
1976	58,255,000	—	0.10	0.15	0.30	—
1977	32,840,000	—	0.10	0.15	0.30	—
1978	61,940,000	—	0.10	0.15	0.30	—
1979	65,485,000	—	0.10	0.15	0.30	—
1980	55,940,000	—	0.10	0.15	0.30	—
1981	18,290,000	—	0.10	0.15	0.30	—

KM# 52 5 PAISA **Composition:** Aluminum

Date	Mintage	F	VF	XF	Unc	BU
1981	16,730,000	—	0.10	0.15	0.30	—
1982	51,210,000	—	0.10	0.15	0.30	—
1983	42,915,000	—	0.10	0.15	0.30	—
1984	45,105,000	—	0.10	0.15	0.30	—
1985	46,555,000	—	0.10	0.15	0.30	—
1986	20,065,000	—	—	0.10	0.20	—
1987	37,710,000	—	—	0.10	0.20	—
1988	40,150,000	—	—	0.10	0.20	—
1989	—	—	—	0.10	0.20	—
1990	—	—	—	0.10	0.20	—
1991	—	—	—	0.10	0.20	—
1992	—	—	—	0.10	0.20	—
1993	—	—	—	0.10	0.20	—
1994	—	—	—	0.10	0.20	—
1996	—	—	—	0.10	0.20	—

KM# 20 10 PAISA **Composition:** Copper-Nickel

Date	Mintage	F	VF	XF	Unc	BU
1961	22,230,000	0.20	0.30	0.50	1.00	—

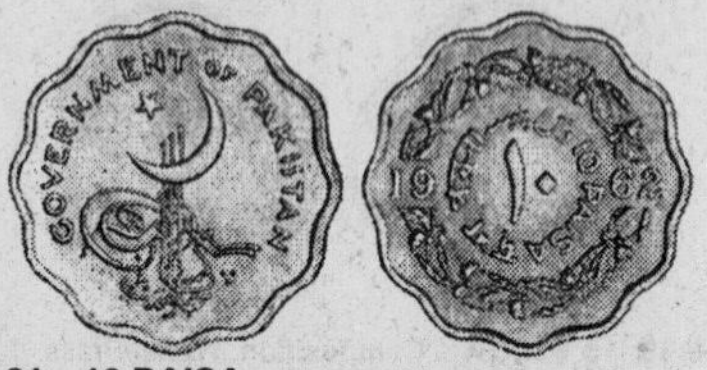

KM# 21 10 PAISA **Composition:** Copper-Nickel

Date	Mintage	F	VF	XF	Unc	BU
1961	31,090,000	0.15	0.25	0.35	0.70	—
1961 Proof	—	Value: 2.00				
1962	29,440,000	0.15	0.25	0.35	0.70	—
1963	19,760,000	0.15	0.25	0.35	0.70	—

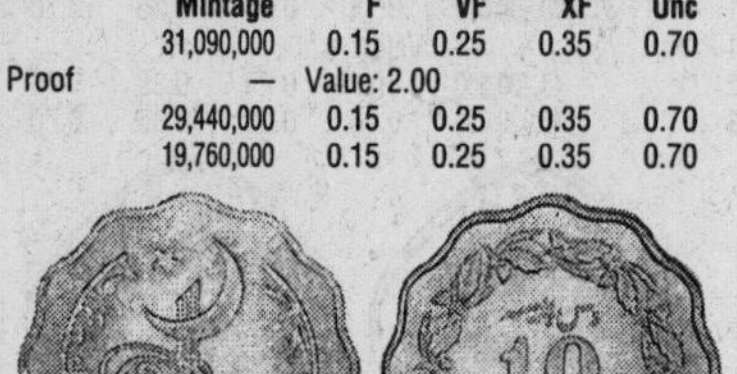

KM# 27 10 PAISA **Composition:** Copper-Nickel

Date	Mintage	F	VF	XF	Unc	BU
1964	52,580,000	0.15	0.25	0.35	0.70	—
1965	51,540,000	0.15	0.25	0.35	0.70	—
1966	—	0.15	0.25	0.35	0.70	—
1967	16,430,000	0.15	0.25	0.35	0.70	—
1968	—	0.15	0.25	0.35	0.70	—

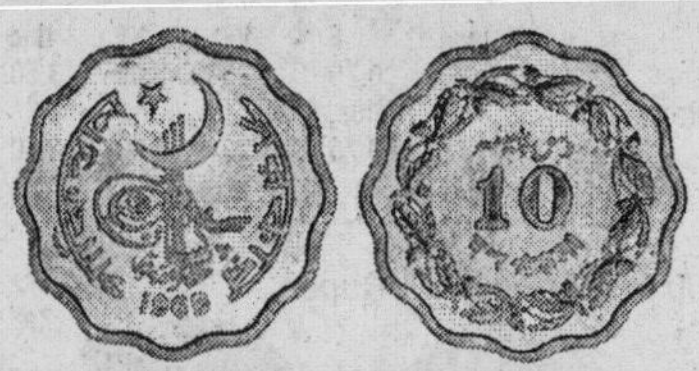

KM# 31 10 PAISA **Composition:** Copper-Nickel **Note:** Reduced size.

Date	Mintage	F	VF	XF	Unc	BU
1969	—	0.15	0.25	0.35	0.70	—
1970	30,250,000	0.15	0.25	0.35	0.70	—
1971	26,270,000	0.15	0.25	0.35	0.70	—
1972	24,845,000	0.15	0.25	0.35	0.70	—
1973	Inc. above	0.15	0.25	0.35	0.70	—
1974	4,780,000	0.20	0.30	0.40	0.80	—

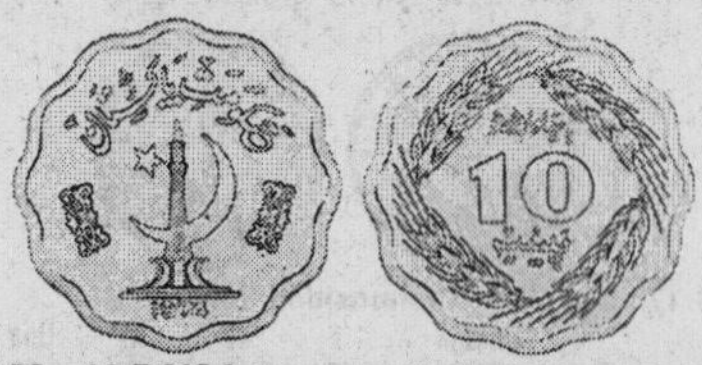

KM# 36 10 PAISA **Composition:** Aluminum **Series:** F.A.O. **Reverse:** Wheat ears

Date	Mintage	F	VF	XF	Unc	BU
1974	18,640,000	—	0.10	0.15	0.30	—
1975	28,875,000	—	0.10	0.15	0.30	—
1976	43,755,000	—	0.10	0.15	0.30	—
1977	29,045,000	—	0.10	0.15	0.30	—
1978	55,185,000	—	0.10	0.15	0.30	—
1979	56,100,000	—	0.10	0.15	0.30	—
1980	40,985,000	—	0.10	0.15	0.30	—
1981	15,500,000	—	0.10	0.15	0.30	—

KM# 53 10 PAISA **Composition:** Aluminum

Date	Mintage	F	VF	XF	Unc	BU
1981	7,995,000	0.10	0.15	0.20	0.40	—
1982	39,770,000	—	0.10	0.15	0.30	—
1983	44,705,000	—	0.10	0.15	0.30	—
1984	35,255,000	—	0.10	0.15	0.30	—
1985	41,545,000	—	0.10	0.15	0.30	—
1986	43,280,000	—	—	0.10	0.20	—
1987	39,090,000	—	—	0.10	0.20	—
1988	42,510,000	—	—	0.10	0.20	—
1989	—	—	—	0.10	0.20	—
1990	—	—	—	0.10	0.20	—
1991	—	—	—	0.10	0.20	—
1992	—	—	—	0.10	0.20	—
1993	—	—	—	0.10	0.20	—
1994	—	—	—	0.10	0.20	—
1995	—	—	—	0.10	0.20	—

KM# 22 25 PAISA **Composition:** Nickel

Date	Mintage	F	VF	XF	Unc	BU
1963	16,900,000	0.15	0.25	0.35	0.70	—
1964	7,990,000	0.15	0.25	0.35	0.70	—
1965	9,290,000	0.15	0.25	0.35	0.70	—
1966	6,650,000	0.15	0.25	0.35	0.70	—
1967	3,740,000	0.20	0.30	0.40	0.80	—

KM# 30 25 PAISA **Composition:** Copper-Nickel

Date	Mintage	F	VF	XF	Unc	BU
1967	5,500,000	0.10	0.15	0.25	0.50	—
Note: Mintage unconfirmed.						
1968	5,500,000	0.10	0.15	0.25	0.50	—
Note: Mintage unconfirmed.						
1969	—	0.10	0.15	0.25	0.50	—
1970	30,392,000	0.10	0.15	0.25	0.50	—
1971	12,664,000	0.10	0.15	0.25	0.50	—
1972	10,824,000	0.10	0.15	0.25	0.50	—

Date	Mintage	F	VF	XF	Unc	BU
1973	—	0.10	0.15	0.25	0.50	—
1974	9,756,000	0.10	0.20	0.30	0.55	—

KM# 37 25 PAISA **Composition:** Copper-Nickel

Date	Mintage	F	VF	XF	Unc	BU
1975	14,264,000	0.10	0.15	0.20	0.40	—
1976	20,440,000	0.10	0.15	0.20	0.40	—
1977	22,092,000	0.10	0.15	0.20	0.40	—
1978	33,544,000	0.10	0.15	0.20	0.40	—
1979	29,648,000	0.10	0.15	0.20	0.40	—
1980	49,556,000	0.10	0.15	0.20	0.40	—
1981	33,952,000	0.10	0.15	0.20	0.40	—

KM# 58 25 PAISA **Composition:** Copper-Nickel **Note:** Varieties in date and crescent size exist.

Date	Mintage	F	VF	XF	Unc	BU
1981	5,648,000	—	0.10	0.15	0.35	—
1982	28,940,000	—	0.10	0.15	0.35	—
1983	40,844,000	—	0.10	0.15	0.35	—
1984	50,988,000	—	0.10	0.15	0.35	—
1985	53,748,000	—	0.10	0.15	0.35	—
1986	75,764,000	—	0.10	0.15	0.35	—
1987	53,560,000	—	0.10	0.15	0.35	—
1988	58,900,000	—	0.10	0.15	0.35	—
1989	—	—	0.10	0.15	0.35	—
1990	—	—	0.10	0.15	0.35	—
1991	—	—	0.10	0.15	0.35	—
1992	—	—	0.10	0.15	0.35	—
1993	—	—	0.10	0.15	0.35	—
1994	—	—	0.10	0.15	0.35	—
1995	—	—	0.10	0.15	0.35	—
1996	—	—	0.10	0.15	0.35	—

KM# 23 50 PAISA **Composition:** Nickel

Date	Mintage	F	VF	XF	Unc	BU
1963	8,110,000	0.15	0.25	0.40	0.80	—
1964	4,580,000	0.20	0.30	0.50	1.00	—
1965	8,980,000	0.15	0.25	0.40	0.80	—
1966	2,860,000	0.20	0.30	0.50	1.00	—
1968	—	0.15	0.25	0.40	0.80	—
1969	—	0.15	0.25	0.40	0.80	—

KM# 32 50 PAISA **Composition:** Copper-Nickel

Date	Mintage	F	VF	XF	Unc	BU
1970	9,240,000	0.15	0.25	0.35	0.70	—
1971	4,670,000	0.15	0.25	0.35	0.70	—
1972	4,900,000	0.15	0.25	0.35	0.70	—
1974	1,128,000	0.20	0.30	0.40	0.80	—

KM# 38 50 PAISA **Composition:** Copper-Nickel **Note:** Varieties in date size exist.

Date	Mintage	F	VF	XF	Unc	BU
1975	9,180,000	0.15	0.20	0.30	0.60	—
1976	—	0.15	0.20	0.30	0.60	—
1977	5,548,000	0.15	0.20	0.30	0.60	—
1978	18,252,000	0.15	0.20	0.30	0.60	—
1979	14,596,000	0.15	0.20	0.30	0.60	—
1980	22,332,000	0.15	0.20	0.30	0.60	—
1981	13,552,000	0.15	0.20	0.30	0.60	—

KM# 39 50 PAISA **Composition:** Copper-Nickel
Subject: 100th anniversary - birth of Mohammad Ali Jinnah

Date	Mintage	F	VF	XF	Unc	BU
1976	5,600,000	0.15	0.25	0.50	1.00	—

KM# 54 50 PAISA **Composition:** Copper-Nickel

Date	Mintage	F	VF	XF	Unc	BU
1981	4,612,000	0.10	0.15	0.25	0.55	—
1982	15,844,000	0.10	0.15	0.25	0.55	—
1983	9,608,000	0.10	0.15	0.25	0.55	—
1984	17,520,000	0.10	0.15	0.25	0.55	—
1985	20,144,000	0.10	0.15	0.25	0.55	—
1986	14,116,000	—	0.10	0.15	0.50	—
1987	23,044,000	—	0.10	0.15	0.50	—
1988	37,140,000	—	0.10	0.15	0.50	—
1989	—	—	0.10	0.15	0.50	—
1990	—	—	0.10	0.15	0.50	—
1991	—	—	0.10	0.15	0.50	—
1992	—	—	0.10	0.15	0.50	—
1993	—	—	0.10	0.15	0.50	—
1994	—	—	0.10	0.15	0.50	—
1995	—	—	0.10	0.15	0.50	—
1996	—	—	0.10	0.15	0.50	—

KM# 51 50 PAISA **Composition:** Copper-Nickel
Subject: 1,400th Hejira anniversary

Date	F	VF	XF	Unc	BU
AH1401 (1981)	—	0.25	0.50	1.00	—

KM# 45 RUPEE **Composition:** Copper-Nickel **Subject:** Islamic Summit Conference

Date	Mintage	F	VF	XF	Unc	BU
1977	5,074,000	0.25	0.50	1.00	2.00	—

KM# 46 RUPEE **Composition:** Copper-Nickel **Subject:** 100th anniversary - birth of Allama Mohammad Iqbal

Date	Mintage	F	VF	XF	Unc	BU
1977	5,000,000	0.25	0.50	1.00	2.00	—

KM# 57.1 RUPEE **Composition:** Copper-Nickel **Size:** 26.5 mm.

Date	Mintage	F	VF	XF	Unc	BU
1979	—	0.30	0.40	0.55	1.15	—
1980	14,522,000	0.30	0.40	0.55	1.15	—
1981	12,038,000	0.30	0.40	0.55	1.15	—

KM# 57.2 RUPEE **Composition:** Copper-Nickel **Size:** 25 mm.

Date	Mintage	F	VF	XF	Unc	BU
1981	4,084,000	0.25	0.40	0.55	1.00	—
1982	27,878,000	0.20	0.35	0.50	1.00	—
1983	18,746,000	0.20	0.35	0.50	1.00	—
1984	14,562,000	0.20	0.35	0.50	1.00	—
1985	4,934,000	0.25	0.40	0.55	1.00	—
1986	11,840,000	0.15	0.25	0.40	0.80	—
1987	50,416,000	0.15	0.25	0.40	0.80	—
1988	10,644,000	0.15	0.25	0.40	0.80	—
1990	—	0.15	0.25	0.40	0.80	—

KM# 55 RUPEE **Composition:** Copper-Nickel **Subject:** 1,400th Hejira anniversary

Date	Mintage	F	VF	XF	Unc	BU
AH1401 (1981)	45,000	—	0.60	1.25	2.50	—

KM# 56 RUPEE **Composition:** Copper-Nickel **Series:** World Food Day

Date	Mintage	F	VF	XF	Unc	BU
1981	45,000	0.35	0.75	1.50	3.00	—

KM# 62 RUPEE **Composition:** Bronze **Obverse:** Portrait of Mohammad Ali Jinnah **Reverse:** Mosque and denomination

Date	F	VF	XF	Unc	BU
1998	0.15	0.25	0.35	0.65	—
1999	0.15	0.25	0.35	0.65	—
2000	0.15	0.25	0.35	0.65	—
2001	—	0.25	0.35	0.60	—

KM# 63 2 RUPEES **Composition:** Nickel-Brass **Obverse:** National emblem **Reverse:** Mosque

Date	F	VF	XF	Unc	BU
1998	0.20	0.30	0.45	0.85	—

KM# 64 2 RUPEES **Weight:** 5.0000 g. **Composition:** Nickel-Brass **Obverse:** National emblem **Reverse:** Clouds above mosque **Edge:** Reeded **Size:** 22.75 mm.

Date	F	VF	XF	Unc	BU
1999	0.20	0.30	45.00	0.85	—
2000	0.20	0.30	0.45	0.85	—

KM# 59 5 RUPEES **Composition:** Copper **Subject:** United Nations 50th year **Reverse:** 50, UN logo **Note:** Four die varieties are reported to exist.

Date	Mintage	F	VF	XF	Unc	BU
1995	500,000	—	—	—	5.50	—

KM# 61 10 RUPEES **Composition:** Copper-Nickel **Subject:** 25th anniversary - Pakistan's senate **Obverse:** Star and crescent

Date	Mintage	F	VF	XF	Unc	BU
1998	100,000	—	—	—	6.50	—

KM# 60 50 RUPEES **Composition:** Copper-Nickel **Subject:** 50th anniversary - national independence **Obverse:** Star and crescent

Date	Mintage	F	VF	XF	Unc	BU
1997	500,000	—	—	—	7.50	—

KM# 40 100 RUPEES **Weight:** 28.2800 g. **Composition:** 0.9250 Silver .8411 oz. ASW **Series:** Conservation **Reverse:** Tropogan pheasant

Date	Mintage	F	VF	XF	Unc	BU
1976	5,120	—	—	—	32.50	—
1976 Proof	5,837	Value: 37.50				

KM# 41 100 RUPEES **Weight:** 20.4400 g. **Composition:** 0.9250 Silver .6079 oz. ASW **Subject:** 100th anniversary - birth of Mohammad Ali Jinnah

Date	Mintage	F	VF	XF	Unc	BU
ND(1976)	1,300	—	—	—	30.00	—
ND(1976) Proof	2,800	Value: 35.00				

KM# 47 100 RUPEES **Weight:** 20.4400 g. **Composition:** 0.9250 Silver .6079 oz. ASW **Subject:** Islamic Summit Conference

Date	Mintage	F	VF	XF	Unc	BU
1977	1,500	—	—	—	30.00	—
1977 Proof	2,500	Value: 35.00				

KM# 48 100 RUPEES **Weight:** 20.4400 g. **Composition:** 0.9250 Silver .6079 oz. ASW **Subject:** 100th anniversary - birth of Allama Mohammad Iqbal **Obverse:** Iqbal bust leaning on hand

Date	Mintage	F	VF	XF	Unc	BU
1977	3,000	—	—	—	30.00	—
1977 Proof	300	Value: 50.00				

KM# 42 150 RUPEES **Weight:** 35.0000 g. **Composition:** 0.9250 Silver 1.0409 oz. ASW **Series:** Conservation **Obverse:** Similar to 100 Rupees, KM#40 **Reverse:** Gavial crocodile

Date	Mintage	F	VF	XF	Unc	BU
1976	5,119	—	—	—	37.50	—
1976 Proof	5,637	Value: 42.50				

KM# 43 500 RUPEES **Weight:** 4.5000 g. **Composition:** 0.9170 Gold .1325 oz. AGW **Subject:** 100th anniversary - birth of Mohammad Ali Jinnah

Date	Mintage	F	VF	XF	Unc	BU
ND(1976)	500	—	—	—	125	—
ND(1976) Proof	500	Value: 150				

KM# 49 500 RUPEES **Weight:** 3.6400 g. **Composition:** 0.9170 Gold .1073 oz. AGW **Subject:** 100th anniversary - birth of Allama Mohammad Iqbal

Date	Mintage	F	VF	XF	Unc	BU
1977	500	—	—	—	125	—
1977 Proof	200	Value: 150				

KM# 50 1000 RUPEES **Weight:** 9.0000 g. **Composition:** 0.9170 Gold .2650 oz. AGW **Subject:** Islamic Summit Conference

Date	Mintage	F	VF	XF	Unc	BU
1977	400	—	—	—	200	—
1977 Proof	400	Value: 275				

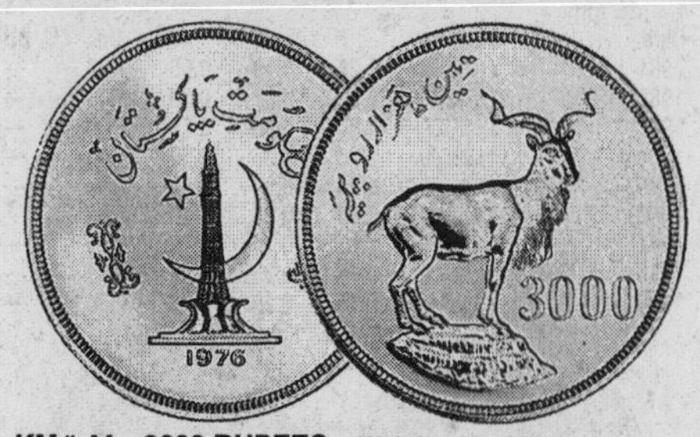

KM# 44 3000 RUPEES **Weight:** 33.4370 g. **Composition:** 0.9000 Gold .9676 oz. AGW **Reverse:** Astor Markhor

Date	Mintage	F	VF	XF	Unc	BU
1976	902	—	—	—	475	—
1976 Proof	273	Value: 750				

MINT SETS

KM#	Date	Mintage	Identification	Issue Price	Mkt Val
MS1	1948 (7)	—	KM1-7	—	10.00
MS2	1948, 1951, 1953 (8)	—	KM5-7 (1948), 11 (1951), 12-15 (1953). Restrikes have been issued.	4.00	12.50
MS3	1948, 1961 (6)	—	KM5-7 (1948), 17, 19, 21 (1961). Restrikes have been issued.	2.00	6.50
MS4	1948, 1964 (7)	—	KM7 (1948), 22-27 (1964). Restrikes have been issued.	2.00	6.50
MS5	1948, 1975 (7)	—	KM7 (1948), 33-38 (1975). Restrikes have been issued.	—	5.00
MS6	1951, 1953 (5)	—	KM11 (1951), 12-15 (1953). Restrikes have been issued.	—	8.00
MS7	1961 (3)	—	KM17, 19, 21	—	3.50
MS8	1976 (2)	—	KM41, 43	63.00	155
MS9	1976 (2)	—	KM40, 42	—	68.00
MS10	1977 (2)	—	KM47, 50	—	225

PROOF SETS

KM#	Date	Mintage	Identification	Issue Price	Mkt Val
PS1	1948 (7)	5,000	KM1-7	4.00	15.50
PS3	1950 (3)	—	KM8-10	—	60.00
PS4	1953 (5)	—	KM11-15	2.00	11.50
PS5	1961 (3)	—	KM17, 19, 21	1.00	5.00
PS6	1976 (2)	—	KM41, 43	90.50	185
PS7	1976 (2)	—	KM40, 42	—	78.00
PS8	1977 (2)	—	KM47, 50	—	300

PALAU

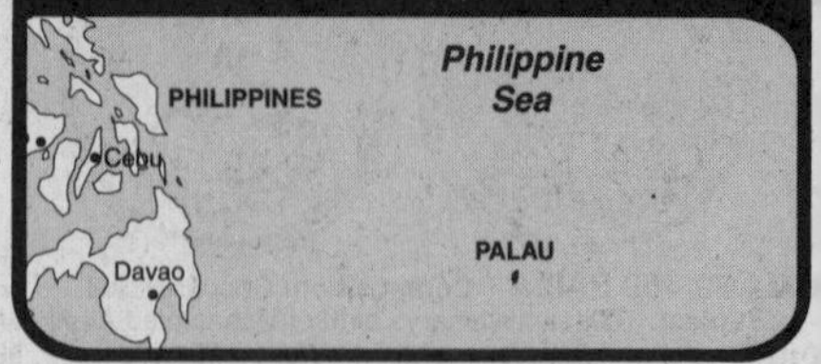

The Republic of Palau, a group of about 100 islands an islets, is generally considered a part of the Caroline Islands. It i located about 1,000 miles southeast of Manila and about th same distance southwest of Saipan and has an area of 179 sq mi. and a population of 12,116. Capital: Koror.

The islands were administered as part of the Caroline Island under the Spanish regime until they were sold to Germany i 1899. Seized by Japan in 1914, it was mandated to them in 191 and Koror was made the administrative headquarters of all th Japanese mandated islands in 1921. During World War II th islands were taken by the Allies, in 1944, with the heaviest fightin taking place on Peleliu. They became part of the U.S. Trust Ter ritory of the Pacific Islands in 1947. In 1980 they became internall self-governing and independent. Control over foreign policy except defense, was approved in 1986. Palau became an inde pendent nation in 1995.

REPUBLIC

COLLECTOR COINAGE

KM# 1 DOLLAR **Composition:** Copper-Nickel **Subject** Year of Marine Life protection **Reverse:** Multicolor

Date	Mintage	F	VF	XF	Unc	B
1992 Proof	Est. 50,000	Value: 40.00				

KM# 3 DOLLAR **Composition:** Copper-Nickel **Series:** Marine Life Protection **Reverse:** Multicolor

Date	Mintage	F	VF	XF	Unc	B
1993 Proof	50,000	Value: 25.00				

KM# 5 DOLLAR **Composition:** Copper-Nickel **Series:** Marine Life Protection **Reverse:** Multicolor

Date		F	VF	XF	Unc	BU
1994 Proof	—	Value: 30.00				

KM# 14 DOLLAR **Composition:** Copper-Nickel **Subject:** United Nations 50th Anniversary

Date	Mintage	F	VF	XF	Unc	BU
1995 Proof	30,000	Value: 27.50				

KM# 31 DOLLAR **Weight:** 1.2441 g. **Composition:** 0.9999 Gold .0400 oz. AGW **Series:** Marine Life Protection **Obverse:** Mermaid with cockatoo **Reverse:** Multicolored high-relief turtle

Date		F	VF	XF	Unc	BU
1998 Proof	—	Value: 50.00				

KM# 35 DOLLAR **Composition:** Copper-Nickel **Series:** Marine Life Protection **Obverse:** Mermaid and dolphin **Reverse:** Multicolored high-relief manta ray

Date		F	VF	XF	Unc	BU
1999 Proof	—	Value: 25.00				

KM# 36 DOLLAR **Weight:** 1.2441 g. **Composition:** 0.9999 Gold .0400 oz. AGW **Series:** Marine Life Protection **Obverse:** Mermaid and dolphin **Reverse:** Multicolored high-relief manta ray

Date		F	VF	XF	Unc	BU
1999 Proof	—	Value: 50.00				

KM# 8 DOLLAR **Composition:** Copper-Nickel **Subject:** Independence **Obverse:** Neptune and mermaid **Reverse:** Multicolor

Date		F	VF	XF	Unc	BU
1994 Proof	—	Value: 30.00				

KM# 25 DOLLAR **Composition:** Copper-Nickel **Series:** Marine Life Protection **Obverse:** 2 mermaids **Reverse:** Multicolored high-relief dolphin

Date	Mintage	F	VF	XF	Unc	BU
1998 Proof	13,000	Value: 27.50				

KM# 26 DOLLAR **Weight:** 1.2441 g. **Composition:** 0.9999 Gold .0400 oz. AGW **Series:** Marine Life Protection **Obverse:** 2 mermaids **Reverse:** Multicolored high-relief dolphin

Date	Mintage	F	VF	XF	Unc	BU
1998 Proof	10,000	Value: 50.00				

KM# 40 DOLLAR **Composition:** Copper-Nickel **Series:** Marine Life Protection **Obverse:** Mermaid and dolphin **Reverse:** Multicolored shark

Date		F	VF	XF	Unc	BU
1999 Proof	—	Value: 28.50				

KM# 11 DOLLAR **Composition:** Copper-Nickel **Subject:** Marine Life Protection **Reverse:** Multicolor sea horse and lion fish

Date	Mintage	F	VF	XF	Unc	BU
1995 Proof	50,000	Value: 32.00				

KM# 30 DOLLAR **Composition:** Copper-Nickel **Series:** Marine Life Protection **Obverse:** Mermaid with cockatoo **Reverse:** Multicolored high-relief turtle

Date		F	VF	XF	Unc	BU
1998 Proof	—	Value: 30.00				

KM# 43 DOLLAR **Weight:** 26.6500 g. **Composition:** Copper-Nickel **Series:** Marine Life Protection **Obverse:** Mermaid and ship **Reverse:** Multicolored fish and coral

Date		F	VF	XF	Unc	BU
2000 Proof	—	Value: 30.00				

KM# 52 DOLLAR **Weight:** 26.8600 g. **Composition:** Copper Nickel **Subject:** Marine Life Protection **Obverse:** Mermaid figurehead. **Reverse:** Multicolor jellyfish. **Edge:** Reeded. **Size:** 37.3 mm.

Date	F	VF	XF	Unc	BU
2001	—	—	—	30.00	—

KM# 2 5 DOLLARS **Weight:** 25.0000 g. **Composition:** 0.9000 Silver .7234 oz. ASW **Series:** Marine Life Protection **Reverse:** Multicolor

Date	Mintage	F	VF	XF	Unc	BU
1992 Proof	Est. 6,000	Value: 125				

KM# 4 5 DOLLARS **Weight:** 25.0000 g. **Composition:** 0.9000 Silver .7234 oz. ASW **Series:** Marine Life Protection **Obverse:** Neptune in shell **Reverse:** Similar to Dollar, KM#3

Date	Mintage	F	VF	XF	Unc	BU
1993 Proof	6,000	Value: 75.00				

KM# 6 5 DOLLARS **Weight:** 25.0000 g. **Composition:** 0.9000 Silver .7234 oz. ASW **Series:** Marine Life Protection **Obverse:** Neptune and sea scape

Date	Mintage	F	VF	XF	Unc	BU
1994 Proof	6,000	Value: 55.00				

KM# 9 5 DOLLARS **Weight:** 25.0000 g. **Composition:** 0.9000 Silver .7234 oz. ASW **Series:** Independence **Obverse:** Mermaid and Neptune **Reverse:** Nautilus and sea scape

Date	F	VF	XF	Unc	BU
1994 Proof	—	Value: 55.00			

KM#12 5 DOLLARS **Weight:** 25.0000 g. **Composition:** 0.9000 Silver .7234 oz. ASW **Series:** Marine Life Protection **Reverse:** Seahorse and lion fish

Date	Mintage	F	VF	XF	Unc	BU
1995 Proof	7,500	Value: 50.00				

KM#15 5 DOLLARS **Weight:** 25.0000 g. **Composition:** 0.9000 Silver .7234 oz. ASW **Subject:** United Nations 50th Anniversary

Date	F	VF	XF	Unc	BU
1995 Proof	—	Value: 50.00			

KM#46 5 DOLLARS **Weight:** 24.6400 g. **Composition:** 0.9000 Silver .7130 oz. ASW **Series:** Marine Life Protection **Obverse:** Mermaid and sailboat **Reverse:** Multicolored shark

Date	F	VF	XF	Unc	BU
1998 Proof	—	Value: 70.00			
1999 Proof	—	Value: 70.00			

KM#27 5 DOLLARS **Weight:** 25.0000 g. **Composition:** 0.9000 Silver .7234 oz. ASW **Series:** Marine Life Protection **Obverse:** 2 mermaids **Reverse:** Multicolored high-relief dolphin **Note:** Similar to Dollar, KM#25.

Date	Mintage	F	VF	XF	Unc	BU
1998 Proof	5,000	Value: 70.00				

KM#32 5 DOLLARS **Weight:** 25.0000 g. **Composition:** 0.9000 Silver .7234 oz. ASW **Series:** Marine Life Protection **Obverse:** Mermaid holding cockatoo **Reverse:** Multicolored high-relief turtle **Note:** Similar to Dollar, KM#30.

Date	F	VF	XF	Unc	BU
1998 Proof	—	Value: 70.00			

KM#44 5 DOLLARS **Weight:** 24.6400 g. **Composition:** 0.9000 Silver .7130 oz. ASW **Series:** Marine Life Protection **Obverse:** Neptune and ship **Reverse:** Multicolored dolphin jumping **Edge:** Reeded

Date	F	VF	XF	Unc	BU
1998 Proof	—	Value: 65.00			

KM#45 5 DOLLARS **Weight:** 24.6400 g. **Composition:** 0.9000 Silver .7130 oz. ASW **Series:** Marine Life Protection **Obverse:** Neptune and 2 dolphins **Reverse:** Multicolored sea turtle

Date	F	VF	XF	Unc	BU
1998 Proof	—	Value: 70.00			

KM#37 5 DOLLARS **Weight:** 25.0000 g. **Composition:** 0.9000 Silver .7234 oz. ASW **Subject:** Marine Life Protection **Obverse:** Mermaid and dolphin **Reverse:** Multicolor high relief manta ray **Edge:** Reeded **Size:** 37 mm.

Date	F	VF	XF	Unc	BU
1999 Proof	—	Value: 70.00			

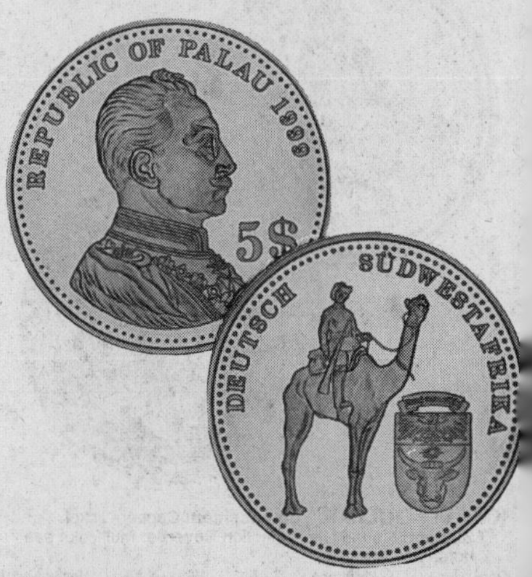

KM#23 5 DOLLARS **Weight:** 25.0000 g. **Composition:** 0.9250 Silver .7435 oz. ASW **Series:** International Coins **Subject:** German South West Africa **Obverse:** Whilhelm II portrait from Prussian 5 Mark coin of 1913-1914 **Reverse:** Colonial arms and trooper on camel

Date	F	VF	XF	Unc	BU
1999 Proof	—	Value: 40.00			

KM# 47 5 DOLLARS **Weight:** 24.6400 g. **Composition:** 0.9000 Silver .7130 oz. ASW **Series:** Marine Life Protection **Obverse:** Mermaid in profile, sailboat **Reverse:** Multicolored manta ray

Date	F	VF	XF	Unc	BU
1999 Proof	—	Value: 65.00			

KM# 16 5 DOLLARS **Weight:** 25.0000 g. **Composition:** 0.9250 Silver .7435 oz. ASW **Series:** International Coins **Subject:** Spanish 5 Peseta - 1896-1899 **Obverse:** Spanish arms **Reverse:** Portrait of Alfonso XIII

Date	F	VF	XF	Unc	BU
1999 Proof	—	Value: 37.50			

KM# 17 5 DOLLARS **Weight:** 25.0000 g. **Composition:** 0.9250 Silver .7435 oz. ASW **Series:** International Coins **Subject:** Prussian 5 Mark - 1891-1908 **Obverse:** German heraldic eagle **Reverse:** Portrait of Wilhelm II

Date	F	VF	XF	Unc	BU
1999 Proof	—	Value: 40.00			

KM# 18 5 DOLLARS **Weight:** 25.0000 g. **Composition:** 0.9250 Silver .7435 oz. ASW **Series:** International Coins **Subject:** German East Africa **Obverse:** Elephant based on G.E.A. 15 Rupien of 1916 **Reverse:** Portrait of V. Lettow-Vorbeck, colonial arms

Date	F	VF	XF	Unc	BU
1999 Proof	—	Value: 40.00			

KM# 19 5 DOLLARS **Weight:** 25.0000 g. **Composition:** 0.9250 Silver .7435 oz. ASW **Series:** International Coins **Subject:** German Cameroon **Obverse:** Portrait of Wilhelm I **Reverse:** Germania and colonial arms

Date	F	VF	XF	Unc	BU
1999 Proof	—	Value: 37.50			

KM# 20 5 DOLLARS **Weight:** 25.0000 g. **Composition:** 0.9250 Silver .7435 oz. ASW **Series:** International Coins **Subject:** Kiau Chau **Obverse:** Ships in harbor **Reverse:** Emblem based on 1909 coinage

Date	F	VF	XF	Unc	BU
1999 Proof	—	Value: 42.50			

KM# 21 5 DOLLARS **Weight:** 25.0000 g. **Composition:** 0.9250 Silver .7435 oz. ASW **Series:** International Coins **Subject:** German New Guinea **Obverse:** Large ship **Reverse:** Colonial arms

Date	F	VF	XF	Unc	BU
1999 Proof	—	Value: 42.50			

KM# 22 5 DOLLARS **Weight:** 25.0000 g. **Composition:** 0.9250 Silver .7435 oz. ASW **Series:** International Coins **Subject:** German Samoa **Obverse:** Whilhelm II portrait from German East African coinage **Reverse:** Colonial arms

Date	F	VF	XF	Unc	BU
1999 Proof	—	Value: 37.50			

KM# 24 5 DOLLARS **Weight:** 25.0000 g. **Composition:** 0.9250 Silver .7435 oz. ASW **Series:** International Coins **Subject:** German Togo **Obverse:** Seated Germania from the German 100 Mark notes of 1908-1910 **Reverse:** Colonial arms

Date	F	VF	XF	Unc	BU
1999 Proof	—	Value: 37.50			

KM# 48 5 DOLLARS **Weight:** 24.6400 g. **Composition:** 0.9000 Silver .7130 oz. ASW **Series:** Marine Life Protection **Obverse:** Neptune seated **Reverse:** Multicolored 3 fish and coral

Date		F	VF	XF	Unc	BU
2000 Proof	—	Value: 65.00				

KM# 51 5 DOLLARS **Weight:** 24.9400 g. **Composition:** 0.9000 Silver .7217 oz. ASW **Subject:** Our world - our future **Obverse:** Dancer **Reverse:** Multicolored world map **Edge:** Reeded **Size:** 38.6 mm.

Date		F	VF	XF	Unc	BU
2000 Proof	—	Value: 50.00				

KM# 53 5 DOLLARS **Weight:** 25.0000 g. **Composition:** 0.9000 Silver .7234 oz. ASW **Series:** Marine Life Protection **Obverse:** Neptune. **Reverse:** Multicolored jellyfish. **Edge:** Reeded. **Size:** 37.2 mm.

Date	F	VF	XF	Unc	BU
2001	—	—	—	90.00	—

KM# 7 20 DOLLARS **Weight:** 155.5175 g. **Composition:** 0.9990 Silver 5.0000 oz. ASW **Series:** Marine Life Protection **Subject:** Marine to outer space **Size:** 63.9 mm. **Note:** Illustration reduced.

Date	Mintage	F	VF	XF	Unc	BU
1994 Proof	3,000	Value: 150				

KM# 42 20 DOLLARS **Weight:** 155.5175 g. **Composition:** 0.9990 Silver 5.0000 oz. ASW **Subject:** Independence - October 1994 **Obverse:** Similar to 200 Dollars, KM#10 **Reverse:** Multicolored sea scape with rautilus **Size:** 63.9 mm. **Note:** Illustration reduced.

Date		F	VF	XF	Unc	BU
ND(1994) Proof	—	Value: 190				

KM# 13 20 DOLLARS **Weight:** 155.5175 g. **Composition:** 0.9990 Silver 5.0000 oz. ASW **Series:** Marine Life Protection **Reverse:** Seahorse and lion fish **Note:** Similar to Dollar, KM#11.

Date	Mintage	F	VF	XF	Unc	BU
1995 Proof	3,000	Value: 165				

KM# 41 20 DOLLARS **Weight:** 15.6500 g. **Composition:** 0.9990 Silver 4.9993 oz. ASW **Series:** 50th Anniversary - United Nations Member **Obverse:** Mermaid driving quadrigia **Reverse:** Multicolored sea scape, globe of earth below **Size:** 64.5 mm. **Note:** Illustration reduced.

Date		F	VF	XF	Unc	BU
1995 Proof	—	Value: 155				

KM# 28 20 DOLLARS **Weight:** 155.5175 g. **Composition:** 0.9990 Silver 4.9950 oz. ASW **Series:** Marine Life Protection **Obverse:** 2 mermaids **Reverse:** Multicolored high-relief dolphin **Note:** Similar to Dollar, KM#25.

Date	Mintage	F	VF	XF	Unc	BU
1998 Proof	700	Value: 190				

KM# 33 20 DOLLARS **Weight:** 155.5175 g. **Composition:** 0.9990 Silver 4.9950 oz. ASW **Series:** Marine Life Protection **Obverse:** Mermaid with cockatoo **Reverse:** Multicolored high-relief turtle **Note:** Similar to Dollar, KM#30.

Date	Mintage	F	VF	XF	Unc	BU
1998 Proof	500	Value: 200				

KM# 38 20 DOLLARS **Weight:** 155.5175 g. **Composition:** 0.9990 Silver 4.9950 oz. ASW **Series:** Marine Life Protection **Obverse:** Mermaid with dolphin **Reverse:** Multicolored high-relief manta ray **Note:** Similar to Dollar, KM#35.

Date	Mintage	F	VF	XF	Unc	BU
1999 Proof	500	Value: 200				

KM# 49 20 DOLLARS **Weight:** 153.9400 g. **Composition:** 0.9990 Silver 4.9443 oz. ASW **Series:** Marine Life Protection **Obverse:** Seated mermaid and sailboat **Reverse:** Multicolored shark **Edge:** Reeded

Date	Mintage	F	VF	XF	Unc	BU
1999 Proof	500	Value: 200				

KM# 50 20 DOLLARS **Weight:** 153.9400 g. **Composition:** 0.9990 Silver 4.9443 oz. ASW **Series:** Marine Life Protection **Obverse:** Mermaid and ship **Reverse:** Multicolored 3 fish and coral

Date		F	VF	XF	Unc	BU
2000 Proof	500	Value: 200				

KM# 54 20 DOLLARS Weight: 154.8400 g. **Composition:** 0.9990 Silver 4.9732 oz. ASW **Subject:** Marine Life Protection **Obverse:** Seated mermaid. **Reverse:** Multicolor sunken ship and fish scene. **Edge:** Reeded. **Size:** 64.5 mm. **Note:** Illustration reduced. Actual size: 64.5mm.

Date	Mintage	F	VF	XF	Unc	BU
2000 Proof	500	Value: 200				

KM# 55 20 DOLLARS Weight: 154.8400 g. **Composition:** 0.9990 Silver 4.9732 oz. ASW **Subject:** Marine Life Protection **Obverse:** Seated mermaid. **Reverse:** Multicolor jumping swordfish scene. **Edge:** Reeded. **Size:** 64.5 mm. **Note:** Illustration reduced. Actual size: 64.5mm.

Date	Mintage	F	VF	XF	Unc	BU
2000 Proof	500	Value: 200				

KM# 10 200 DOLLARS Weight: 31.1035 g. **Composition:** 0.9990 Gold 1.0000 oz. AGW **Subject:** Independence **Obverse:** Mermaid and Neptune **Reverse:** Nautilus and sea scape, similar to Dollar, KM#8

Date	F	VF	XF	Unc	BU
1994 Proof	—	Value: 775			

KM# 29 200 DOLLARS Weight: 31.1035 g. **Composition:** 0.9990 Gold 1.0000 oz. AGW **Series:** Marine Life Protection **Obverse:** 2 mermaids **Reverse:** Multicolored high-relief dolphin **Note:** Similar to Dollar, KM#25.

Date	Mintage	F	VF	XF	Unc	BU
1998 Proof	200	Value: 775				

KM# 34 200 DOLLARS Weight: 31.1035 g. **Composition:** 0.9990 Gold 1.0000 oz. AGW **Series:** Marine Life Protection **Obverse:** Mermaid with cockatoo **Reverse:** Multicolored high-relief turtle **Note:** Similar to Dollar, KM#30.

Date	F	VF	XF	Unc	BU
1998 Proof	—	Value: 775			

KM# 39 200 DOLLARS Weight: 31.1035 g. **Composition:** 0.9990 Gold 1.0000 oz. AGW **Series:** Marine Life Protection **Obverse:** Mermaid with dolphin **Reverse:** Multicolored high-relief manta ray **Note:** Similar to Dollar, KM#35.

Date	F	VF	XF	Unc	BU
1999 Proof	—	Value: 775			

ESSAIS

Standard metals unless otherwise noted

KM#	Date	Mintage	Identification	Issue Price	Mkt Val
E1	1992	—	Dollar. 0.9990 Gold. 25.9600 g. Seated mermaid and sailboat. Multicolor sea life. KM1.	—	1,500

KM#	Date	Mintage	Identification	Issue Price	Mkt Val
E2	1992	—	5 Dollars. 0.9990 Gold. 25.9700 g. Seated Neptune and ship. Multicolor sea life. Reeded edge. KM2.	—	1,500

KM#	Date	Mintage	Identification	Issue Price	Mkt Val
E3	1995	30	Dollar. Silver. KM41.	—	125

KM#	Date	Mintage	Identification	Issue Price	Mkt Val
E4	1995	30	5 Dollars. Copper-Nickel. KM41.	—	100

KM#	Date	Mintage	Identification	Issue Price	Mkt Val
E5	1995	30	200 Dollars. Copper-Nickel. KM41.	—	120
E6	1995	30	200 Dollars. Silver. KM41.	—	185

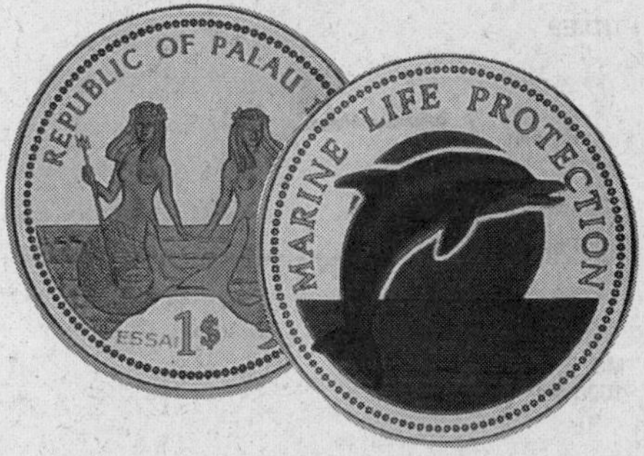

KM#	Date	Mintage	Identification	Issue Price	Mkt Val
E7	1998		20 Dollar. Silver. KM25.	—	145

KM#	Date	Mintage	Identification	Issue Price	Mkt Val
E8	1998	20	5 Dollars. Copper-Nickel. KM25.	—	145

KM#	Date	Mintage	Identification	Issue Price	Mkt Val
E9	1998	20	200 Dollars. Silver. KM25.	—	145

PROOF SETS

KM#	Date	Mintage	Identification	Issue Price	Mkt Val
PS1	1992	—	KME1, E2	—	3,000
PS2	1995 (4)	20	KME3, E4, E5, E6	—	600
PS3	1998 (3)	20	KME7, E8, E9	—	450

PALESTINE

Palestine, which corresponds to Canaan of the Bible, was settled by the Philistines about the 12th century B.C. and shortly thereafter was settled by the Jews who established the kingdoms of Israel and Judah. Because of its position as part of the land bridge connecting Asia and Africa, Palestine was invaded and conquered by nearly all of the historic empires of ancient Europe and Asia. In the16th century it became a part of the Ottoman Empire. After falling to the British in World War I, it, together with Transjordan, was mandated to Great Britain by the League of Nations, 1922.

For more than half a century prior to the termination of the British mandate over Palestine, 1948, Zionist leaders had sought to create a Jewish homeland for Jews who were dispersed throughout the world. For almost as long, Jews fleeing persecution had immigrated to Palestine. The Nazi persecutions of the 1930s and 1940s increased the Jewish movement to Palestine and generated international support for the creation of a Jewish state, first promulgated by the Balfour Declaration of 1917, which asserted British support for the endeavor. The dream of a Jewish homeland was realized on May 14, 1948 when Palestine was proclaimed the State of Israel.

TITLES

Filastin فلسطين

Paleshtina (E.I.) פלשתינה (א"י).

MONETARY SYSTEM
1000 Mils = 1 Pound

BRITISH ADMINISTRATION

MIL COINAGE

KM# 1 MIL Composition: Bronze **Obv. Inscription:** PALESTINE, 1927 (In English and Arabic) **Reverse:** Value, plant.

Date		F	VF	XF	Unc	BU
1927		0.50	2.00	3.00	20.00	—
1927 Proof	66	Value: 650				
1935		2.00	3.00	5.00	25.00	—
1937		1.50	2.00	10.00	100	200
1939		1.00	2.00	10.00	30.00	—
1939 Proof	—	Value: 400				
1940		6.50	12.50	50.00	150	—
1941		1.00	2.00	5.00	20.00	—
1942		1.00	2.00	5.00	25.00	—
1943		0.75	2.00	5.00	35.00	—
1944		0.75	2.00	5.00	20.00	—
1946		2.00	4.00	8.00	30.00	—
1946 Proof	—	Value: 500				
1947		—	—	—	10,000	—

Note: Only 5 known. The entire issue was to be melted down.

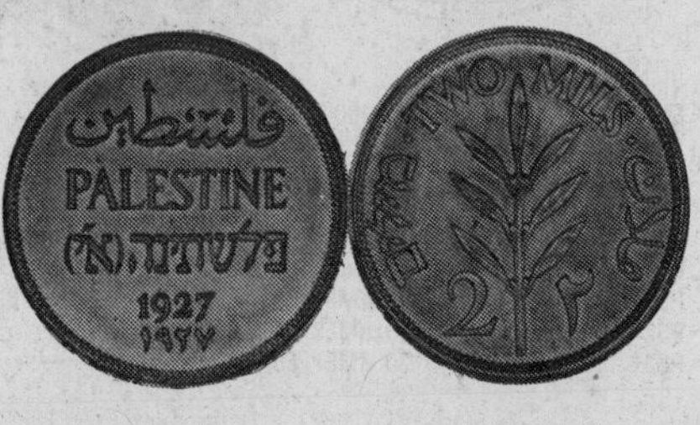

KM# 2 2 MILS Composition: Bronze **Obv. Inscription:** PALESTINE, 1927 (In English and Arabic) **Reverse:** Value, plant.

Date	Mintage	F	VF	XF	Unc	BU
1927	5,000,000	2.00	3.00	5.00	35.00	—
1927 Proof	66	Value: 700				
1941	1,600,000	1.00	2.00	6.00	40.00	—
1941 Proof	—	Value: 400				
1942	2,400,000	1.00	2.50	10.00	40.00	—
1945	960,000	2.00	5.00	20.00	150	—
1946	960,000	4.00	10.00	30.00	175	—
1947	480,000	—	—	—	—	—

Note: The entire issue was melted down.

KM# 3 5 MILS Composition: Copper-Nickel

Date	Mintage	F	VF	XF	Unc	BU
1927	10,000,000	0.75	2.00	5.00	35.00	—
1927 Proof	66	Value: 550				
1934	500,000	6.50	12.50	50.00	175	—
1935	2,700,000	0.75	2.00	7.00	60.00	—
1939	2,000,000	0.75	2.00	5.00	30.00	—
1939 Proof	—	Value: 425				
1941	400,000	10.00	20.00	35.00	175	—
1941 Proof	—	Value: 375				
1946	1,000,000	2.00	4.00	8.00	30.00	—
1946 Proof	—	Value: 450				
1947	1,000,000	—	—	—	—	—

Note: Almost the entire issue was melted down, with only 2 remaining pieces known to exist

KM# 3a 5 MILS Composition: Bronze

Date	Mintage	F	VF	XF	Unc	BU
1942	2,700,000	1.50	2.00	8.00	60.00	—
1944	1,000,000	2.00	5.00	10.00	60.00	—

KM# 4 10 MILS Composition: Copper-Nickel

Date	Mintage	F	VF	XF	Unc	BU
1927	5,000,000	2.00	6.00	10.00	60.00	—
1927 Proof	66	Value: 575				
1933	500,000	4.00	8.00	65.00	220	—
1933 Proof	—	Value: 350				
1934	500,000	5.00	12.00	85.00	400	—
1934 Proof	—	Value: 375				
1935	1,150,000	1.00	10.00	35.00	250	—
1935 Proof	—	Value: 425				
1937	750,000	2.00	5.00	15.00	150	—
1937 Proof	—	Value: 425				
1939	1,000,000	1.00	5.00	15.00	100	—
1939 Proof	—	Value: 350				
1940	1,500,000	1.00	5.00	15.00	100	—
1940 Proof	—	Value: 100				
1941	400,000	6.00	15.00	50.00	200	—
1941 Proof	—	Value: 350				
1942	600,000	4.00	10.00	25.00	175	—
1946	1,000,000	2.00	15.00	25.00	75.00	—
1946 Proof	—	Value: 300				
1947	1,000,000	—	—	—	—	—

KM# 4a 10 MILS Composition: Bronze

Date	Mintage	F	VF	XF	Unc	BU
1942	1,000,000	4.00	5.00	15.00	100	—
1943	1,000,000	7.00	10.00	20.00	125	—

KM# 5 20 MILS Composition: Copper-Nickel

Date	Mintage	F	VF	XF	Unc	BU
1927	1,500,000	7.00	12.00	35.00	100	—
1927 Proof	66	Value: 800				
1933	250,000	10.00	20.00	50.00	400	—
1934	125,000	40.00	70.00	175	600	—
1934 Proof	—	—	—	—	—	—
1935	575,000	5.00	15.00	50.00	225	—
1940	200,000	10.00	15.00	50.00	350	—
1940 Proof	—	Value: 500				
1941	100,000	50.00	75.00	150	850	—
1941 Proof	—	Value: 1,200				

KM# 5a 20 MILS Composition: Bronze

Date	Mintage	F	VF	XF	Unc	BU
1942	1,100,000	6.00	12.00	30.00	175	—
1944	1,000,000	20.00	50.00	80.00	200	—

KM# 6 50 MILS Weight: 5.8319 g. **Composition:** 0.720 Silver 0.135 oz. ASW

Date	Mintage	F	VF	XF	Unc	B
1927	8,000,000	3.50	10.00	15.00	110	—
1927 Proof	66	Value: 775				
1931	500,000	12.00	30.00	75.00	500	—
1933	1,000,000	5.00	10.00	25.00	125	—
1934	399,000	10.00	25.00	50.00	125	—
1935	5,600,000	4.00	5.00	10.00	50.00	—
1939	3,000,000	4.00	6.00	12.00	40.00	—
1939 Proof	—	Value: 275				
1940	2,000,000	5.00	20.00	30.00	75.00	—
1940 Proof	—	Value: 150				
1942	5,000,000	4.00	6.00	12.00	60.00	—

KM# 7 50 MILS Weight: 11.6638 g. **Composition:** 0.7200 Silver 0.27 oz. ASW

Date	Mintage	F	VF	XF	Unc	BU
1927	2,000,000	5.00	10.00	25.00	120	—
1927 Proof	66	Value: 850				
1931	250,000	40.00	75.00	175	1,000	1,50
1931 Proof	—	Value: 1,400				
1933	500,000	15.00	30.00	100	350	—
1934	200,000	60.00	85.00	175	450	—
1935	2,850,000	5.00	10.00	20.00	100	—
1939	1,500,000	6.00	12.00	25.00	120	—
1939 Proof	—	Value: 250				
1940	1,000,000	8.50	15.00	25.00	110	—
1942	2,500,000	8.50	15.00	25.00	90.00	—

TOKEN COINAGE

KM# Tn1 SOUVENIR MIL Composition: Bronze

Date	F	VF	XF	Unc	BU
1927	—	100	175	300	—

Note: This souvenir which incorporates an appropriate reproduction of a 1927 1 Mil coin of Palestine was privately created for sale to pilgrims as a souvenir of their visit to the Holy Land. The Arabic translates to Souvenir of the Holy Land. It is not known who produced them nor how many were produced.

MINT SETS

KM#	Date	Mintage	Identification	Issue Price	Mkt Val
MS1	1927 (14)	—	KM1-7, two each	—	1,750

PROOF SETS

KM#	Date	Mintage	Identification	Issue Price	Mkt Val
PS1	1927 (14)	34	KM1-7, two each, original case	—	7,500
PS2	1927 (7)	4	KM1-7, original case	—	5,000

PANAMA

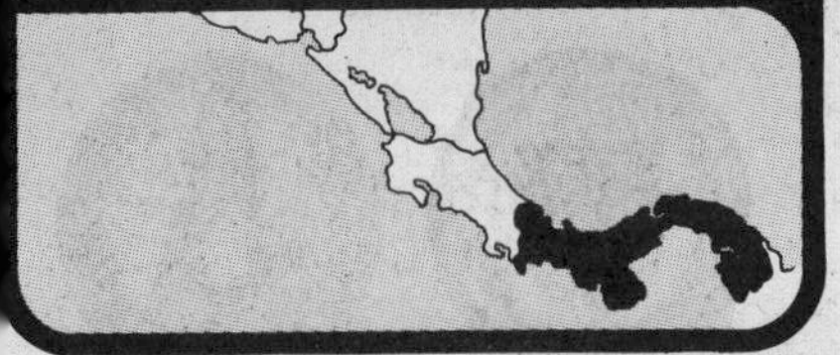

The Republic of Panama, a Central American Country situated between Costa Rica and Colombia, has an area of 29,762 sq. mi. (78,200 sq. km.) and a population of *2.4 million. Capital: Panama City. The Panama Canal is the country's biggest asset; servicing world related transit trade and international commerce. Bananas, refined petroleum, sugar and shrimp are exported.

Discovered in 1501 by the Spanish conquistador Rodrigo Galvan de Bastidas, the land of Panama was soon explored and after a few attempts at settlement was successfully colonized by the Spanish. It was in Panama in 1513 that Vasco Nunez de Balboa became the first European to see the Pacific Ocean. The first Pacific-coast settlement, founded in 1519 on the site of a village the natives called Panama, was named *Nuestra Senora de la Asuncion de Panama* (Our Lady of the Assumption of Panama). The settlement soon became a city and eventually, albeit briefly, an Audiencia (judicial tribunal).

In 1578 the city of Panama, being a primary transshipment center for treasure and supplies to and from Spain's South Pacific-coast colonies, was chosen for a new mint, and minting had begun there by 1580. By late 1582 or 1583 production was halted, possibly due to the fact that there were no nearby silver mines to sustain it. In it's brief operation, the Panama Mint must not have made many coins, as the corpus of surviving specimens known today from this colonial mint is less than 40.

The city of Panama, known today as the Old City of Panama, was sacked and burned in 1671 by the famous Henry Morgan in one of the greatest pirate victories against the Spanish Main.

Panama declared its independence in 1821 and joined the Confederation of Greater Colombia. In 1903, after Colombia rejected a treaty enabling the United States to build a canal across the Isthmus, Panama with the support of the United States proclaimed its independence from Colombia and became a sovereign republic.

The 1904 2-1/2 centesimos known as the 'Panama Pill' or 'Panama Pearl' is one of the world's smaller silver coins and a favorite with collectors.

MINT MARKS

FM - Franklin Mint, U.S.A.*

CHI in circle - Valcambi Mint, Balerna, Switzerland

***NOTE:** From 1975-1985 the Franklin Mint produced coinage in up to 3 different qualities. Qualities of issue are designated in ( ) after each date and are defined as follows:

(M) MATTE - Normal circulation strike or a dull finish produced by sandblasting special uncirculated (polish finish) or proof quality dies.

(U) SPECIAL UNCIRCULATED - Polished or proof-like in appearance without any frosted features.

(P) PROOF - The highest quality obtainable having mirror-like fields and frosted features.

MONETARY SYSTEM

100 Centesimos = 1 Balboa

REPUBLIC

DECIMAL COINAGE

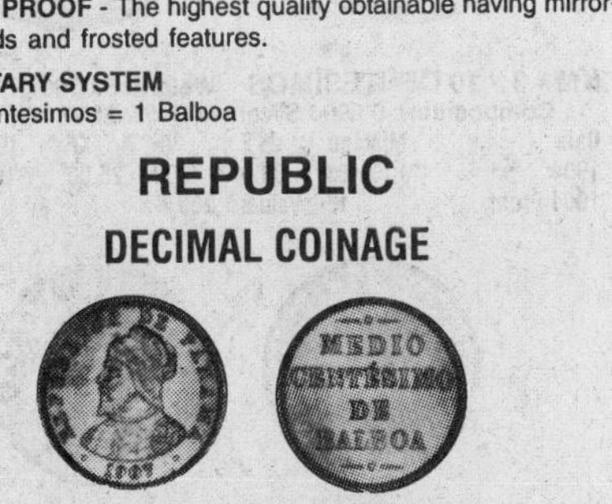

KM# 6 1/2 CENTESIMO Composition: Copper-Nickel **Note:** Previously listed re-engraved overdates were struck from very common doubled dies. The plain date in unc. is scarcer.

Date	Mintage	F	VF	XF	Unc	BU
1907	1,000,000	1.00	2.00	3.00	7.00	12.00
1907 Proof	—	Value: 200				

KM# 14 CENTESIMO Composition: Bronze **Subject:** Uracca

Date	Mintage	F	VF	XF	Unc	BU
1935	200,000	2.00	5.00	15.00	35.00	60.00
1937	200,000	1.50	3.50	10.00	25.00	50.00

KM# 17 CENTESIMO Composition: Bronze **Subject:** 50th Anniversary of the Republic

Date	Mintage	F	VF	XF	Unc	BU
1953	1,500,000	0.10	0.25	0.75	2.00	5.00

KM# 22 CENTESIMO Composition: Bronze **Note:** Varieties exist.

Date	Mintage	F	VF	XF	Unc	BU
1961		—	0.15	0.25	1.50	2.50
1962		—	0.15	0.25	1.50	2.50
1962 Proof	Est. 50	Value: 160				
1966		—	0.15	0.25	1.25	—
1966 Proof	13,000	Value: 1.00				
1967		—	0.15	0.25	1.00	—
1967 Proof	20,000	Value: 1.00				
1968		—	0.10	0.15	0.85	—
1968 Proof	23,000	Value: 1.00				
1969 Proof	14,000	Value: 1.00				
1970 Proof	9,528	Value: 1.00				
1971 Proof	11,000	Value: 1.00				
1972 Proof	13,000	Value: 1.00				
1973 Proof	17,000	Value: 1.00				
1974		—	0.10	0.15	0.75	1.00

Note: The 1974 circulation coins were stuck at West Point, NY.

Date	Mintage	F	VF	XF	Unc	BU
1974 Proof	Est. 18,000	Value: 1.00				

Note: The 1974 proof coins were struck at San Francisco

Date	Mintage	F	VF	XF	Unc	BU
1975		—	0.10	0.15	0.85	1.50
1977		—	0.10	0.15	0.75	1.00
1978		—	0.10	0.15	0.75	1.00
1979		—	0.10	0.15	0.75	1.00
1980		—	0.10	0.15	0.75	1.00
1982		—	0.10	0.15	0.75	1.00
1983FM (P)	—	Value: 2.00				
1983		—	0.15	0.25	1.00	1.50
1984FM (P)	—	Value: 2.00				
1986		—	0.10	0.15	0.75	1.00
1987		—	0.10	0.15	0.75	1.00

KM# 33.1 CENTESIMO Composition: Copper Coated Zinc

Date	Mintage	F	VF	XF	Unc	BU
1975 (RCM)	500,000	—	0.10	0.20	0.75	—
1975FM (M)	125,000	—	0.10	0.25	1.00	—
1975FM (U)	1,410	—	—	—	3.00	—
1975FM (P)	41,000	Value: 1.00				
1976 (RCM)	50,000	—	0.10	0.20	1.00	—
1976FM (M)	63,000	—	0.10	0.20	1.00	—
1976FM (P)	12,000	Value: 1.00				
1977FM (U)	63,000	—	0.10	0.20	1.00	—
1977FM (P)	9,548	Value: 1.00				
1979FM (U)	20,000	—	0.10	0.20	1.00	—
1979FM (P)	5,949	Value: 1.00				
1980FM (U)	40,000	—	0.10	0.20	1.00	—
1981FM (P)	1,973	Value: 1.00				
1982FM (U)	5,000	—	0.75	1.50	3.50	—
1982FM (P)	1,480	Value: 1.00				

KM# 33.2 CENTESIMO Composition: Copper Coated Zinc **Edge Lettering:** 1830 BOLIVAR 1980

Date	Mintage	F	VF	XF	Unc	BU
1980FM (P)	2,629	Value: 1.00				

KM# 45 CENTESIMO Composition: Copper Coated Zinc **Subject:** 75th Anniversary of Independence

Date	Mintage	F	VF	XF	Unc	BU
1978FM (U)	50,000	—	0.10	0.20	1.00	—
1978FM (P)	11,000	Value: 1.25				

KM# 22a CENTESIMO Composition: Copper Coated Zinc

Date	Mintage	F	VF	XF	Unc	BU
1983	45,000,000	—	0.10	0.15	0.75	—

KM# 124 CENTESIMO Composition: Copper Plated Zinc

Date	Mintage	F	VF	XF	Unc	BU
1991	—	—	—	—	0.35	—
1993	30,000,000	—	—	—	0.35	—

KM# 125 CENTESIMO Composition: Copper Plated Zinc

Date	Mintage	F	VF	XF	Unc	BU
1996	180,000,000	—	—	—	0.15	—

KM# 132 CENTESIMO Weight: 1.6400 g. **Composition:** Aluminum **Series:** F.A.O **Subject:** XXI Century F.A.O. Food Security **Obverse:** National arms **Reverse:** Ship in canal **Edge:** Plain **Size:** 22.8 mm.

Date	F	VF	XF	Unc	BU
2000	—	—	—	1.00	—

KM# 15 1-1/4 CENTESIMOS Composition: Bronze

Date	Mintage	F	VF	XF	Unc	BU
1940	1,600,000	0.50	1.00	2.50	10.00	15.00

KM# 1 2-1/2 CENTESIMOS Weight: 1.2500 g. **Composition:** 0.9000 Silver .0362 oz. ASW **Note:** This coin is popularly referred to as the "Panama Pill."

Date	Mintage	F	VF	XF	Unc	BU
1904	400,000	6.00	9.00	12.50	20.00	35.00

KM# 7.1 2-1/2 CENTESIMOS Composition: Copper-Nickel **Rev. Legend:** DOS Y MEDIOS

Date	Mintage	F	VF	XF	Unc	BU
1907	800,000	1.25	4.00	12.50	40.00	75.00

KM# 7.2 2-1/2 CENTESIMOS Composition: Copper-Nickel **Rev. Legend:** DOS Y MEDIO

Date	Mintage	F	VF	XF	Unc	BU
1916	800,000	1.25	5.00	20.00	80.00	120
1918 7 Known	—	—	1,600	2,400	—	—

Note: Unauthorized issue, 1 million pieces melted June 1918.

KM# 8 2-1/2 CENTESIMOS **Composition:** Copper-Nickel

Date	Mintage	F	VF	XF	Unc	BU
1929	1,000,000	1.00	4.00	20.00	120	—
1929 Proof	—	—	—	—	—	—

KM# 16 2-1/2 CENTESIMOS **Composition:** Copper-Nickel

Date	Mintage	F	VF	XF	Unc	BU
1940	1,200,000	0.50	1.00	3.50	10.00	15.00

KM# 32 2-1/2 CENTESIMOS **Composition:** Copper-Nickel Clad Copper **Series:** F.A.O.

Date	Mintage	F	VF	XF	Unc	BU
1973	2,000,000	—	—	0.10	0.35	0.50
1975	1,000,000	—	—	0.10	0.50	1.00

KM# 34.1 2-1/2 CENTESIMOS **Composition:** Copper-Nickel Clad Copper **Subject:** Victoriano Lorenzo

Date	Mintage	F	VF	XF	Unc	BU
1975 (RCM)	40,000	—	0.50	0.75	1.50	—
1975FM (M)	50,000	—	0.50	0.75	1.50	—
1975FM (U)	1,410	—	1.00	2.00	3.00	—
1975FM (P)	41,000	Value: 1.00				
1976 (RCM)	20,000	—	0.50	0.75	2.25	—
1976FM (M)	25,000	—	0.50	0.75	2.00	—
1976FM (P)	24,000	Value: 1.00				
1977FM (U)	25,000	—	0.50	0.75	2.00	—
1977FM (P)	9,548	Value: 1.00				
1979FM (U)	12,000	—	0.50	0.75	2.50	—
1979FM (P)	5,949	Value: 1.00				
1980FM (U)	40,000	—	0.50	0.75	1.50	—
1981FM (P)	1,973	Value: 2.50				
1982FM (U)	2,000	—	1.00	2.00	3.50	—
1982FM (P)	1,480	Value: 3.00				

KM# 34.2 2-1/2 CENTESIMOS **Composition:** Copper-Nickel Clad Copper **Edge Lettering:** 1830 BOLIVAR 1980

Date	Mintage	F	VF	XF	Unc	BU
1980FM (P)	2,629	Value: 2.00				

KM# 46 2-1/2 CENTESIMOS **Composition:** Copper-Nickel Clad Copper **Subject:** 75th Anniversary of Independence

Date	Mintage	F	VF	XF	Unc	BU
1978FM (U)	40,000	—	0.25	0.50	2.00	—
1978FM (P)	11,000	Value: 1.50				

KM# 85 2-1/2 CENTESIMOS **Composition:** Copper-Nickel Clad Copper

Date	F	VF	XF	Unc	BU
1983FM (P)	—	Value: 3.00			
1984FM (P)	—	Value: 3.00			

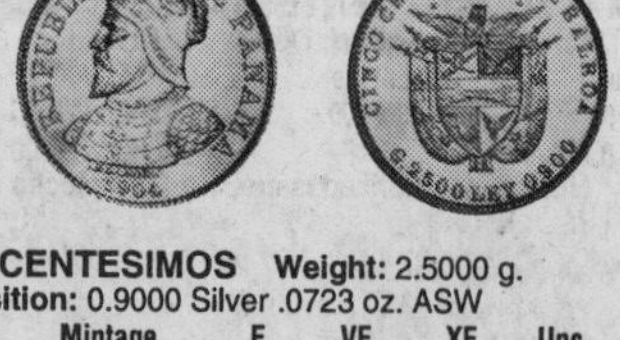

KM# 2 5 CENTESIMOS **Weight:** 2.5000 g. **Composition:** 0.9000 Silver .0723 oz. ASW

Date	Mintage	F	VF	XF	Unc	BU
1904	1,500,000	2.50	4.00	12.50	35.00	60.00
1904 Proof	12	Value: 1,250				
1916	100,000	40.00	70.00	130	200	350

KM# 9 5 CENTESIMOS **Composition:** Copper-Nickel

Date	Mintage	F	VF	XF	Unc	BU
1929	500,000	2.50	4.50	12.00	60.00	80.00
1932	332,000	3.00	5.00	13.50	70.00	100

KM# 23.1 5 CENTESIMOS **Composition:** Copper-Nickel

Date	Mintage	F	VF	XF	Unc	BU
1961	1,000,000	—	0.50	1.00	2.50	—

KM# 23.2 5 CENTESIMOS **Composition:** Copper-Nickel **Note:** The 1962 & 1966 Royal Mint strikes are normally sharper in detail. The stars on the reverse above the eagle are flat while previous dates are raised. Varieties exist.

Date	Mintage	F	VF	XF	Unc	BU
1962	—	0.25	0.50	2.00	—	
1962 Proof	Est. 25	Value: 350				
1966	—	0.10	0.20	1.00	—	
1966 Proof	13,000	Value: 1.00				
1967	—	0.10	0.20	1.00	—	
1967 Proof	20,000	Value: 1.00				
1968	—	0.10	0.20	1.00	—	
1968 Proof	23,000	Value: 1.00				
1969 Proof	14,000	Value: 1.00				
1970	—	0.10	0.20	1.00	—	
1970 Proof	9,528	Value: 1.00				
1971 Proof	11,000	Value: 1.00				
1972 Proof	13,000	Value: 1.00				
1973	—	0.10	0.20	1.50	—	
1973 Proof	17,000	Value: 1.00				
1974 Proof	19,000	Value: 1.00				
1975	—	0.10	0.15	1.00	—	
1982	—	0.10	0.15	1.00	—	
1983	—	0.10	0.15	1.00	—	
1993	—	0.10	0.15	1.00	—	
1993 Proof	—	Value: 250				

Note: The 1993 proof strike was not authorized by the Panamanian government

KM# 35.1 5 CENTESIMOS **Composition:** Copper-Nickel Clad Copper **Subject:** Carlos J. Finlay

Date	Mintage	F	VF	XF	Unc	BU
1975 (RCM)	80,000	—	0.25	0.50	1.00	—
1975FM (M)	15,000	—	0.25	0.50	1.00	—
1975FM (U)	1,410	—	—	—	2.50	—
1975FM (P)	41,000	Value: 1.00				
1976 (RCM)	20,000	—	0.25	0.50	1.25	—
1976FM (M)	13,000	—	0.25	0.50	1.50	—
1976FM (P)	12,000	Value: 1.00				
1977FM (U)	13,000	—	0.25	0.50	1.50	—
1977FM (P)	9,548	Value: 1.00				
1979FM (U)	12,000	—	0.25	0.50	1.50	—
1979FM (P)	5,949	Value: 1.00				
1980FM (U)	43,000	—	0.25	0.50	1.50	—
1981FM (P)	1,973	Value: 1.50				
1982FM (U)	3,000	—	2.50	5.00	10.00	—
1982FM (P)	1,480	Value: 1.50				

KM# 47 5 CENTESIMOS **Composition:** Copper-Nickel Clad Copper **Subject:** 75th Anniversary of Independence

Date	Mintage	F	VF	XF	Unc	BU
1978FM (U)	30,000	—	—	—	1.00	—
1978FM (P)	11,000	Value: 1.00				

KM# 35.2 5 CENTESIMOS **Composition:** Copper-Nickel Clad Copper **Edge Lettering:** 1830 BOLIVAR 1980

Date	Mintage	F	VF	XF	Unc	BU
1980FM (P)	2,629	Value: 1.50				

KM# 86 5 CENTESIMOS **Composition:** Copper-Nickel Clad Copper

Date	F	VF	XF	Unc	BU
1983FM (P)	—	Value: 2.50			
1984FM (P)	—	Value: 2.50			

KM# 126 5 CENTESIMOS **Composition:** Copper-Nickel **Obverse:** National arms **Rev. Legend:** Denomination

Date	Mintage	F	VF	XF	Unc	BU
1996	4,000,000	—	—	—	0.40	—

KM# 133 5 CENTESIMOS **Weight:** 5.0000 g. **Composition:** Copper Nickel **Subject:** Sara Sotillo **Obverse:** National arms **Reverse:** Portrait **Edge:** Plain **Size:** 21.2 mm.

Date	Mintage	F	VF	XF	Unc	BU
2001	8,000,000	—	—	—	0.25	—

KM# 3 10 CENTESIMOS **Weight:** 5.0000 g. **Composition:** 0.9000 Silver .1447 oz. ASW

Date	Mintage	F	VF	XF	Unc	BU
1904	1,100,000	3.50	8.00	25.00	100	15[illegible]
1904 Proof	12	Value: 1,250				

KM# 36.1 10 CENTESIMOS **Composition:** Copper-Nickel Clad Copper **Subject:** Manuel E. Amador

Date	Mintage	F	VF	XF	Unc	BU
1975 (RCM)	50,000	—	0.25	0.50	1.00	—
1975 FM (M)	13,000	—	0.25	0.50	1.50	—
1975 FM (U)	1,410	—	—	—	2.50	—
1975 FM (P)	41,000	Value: 1.00				
1976 (RCM)	20,000	—	0.25	1.00	1.50	—
1976 FM (M)	6,250	—	0.50	1.25	2.50	—
1976 FM (P)	12,000	Value: 1.50				
1977 FM (U)	6,250	—	0.50	1.25	2.50	—
1977 FM (P)	9,548	Value: 1.50				
1979 FM (U)	10,000	—	0.50	1.00	2.00	—
1979 FM (P)	5,949	Value: 2.00				
1980 FM (U)	40,000	—	0.50	1.00	2.00	—
1981 FM (P)	1,973	Value: 1.50				
1982 FM (U)	2,500	—	0.75	1.50	3.00	—
1982 Proof	1,480	Value: 2.50				

KM# 36.2 10 CENTESIMOS **Composition:** Copper-Nickel Clad Copper **Edge Lettering:** 1830 BOLIVAR 1980

Date	Mintage	F	VF	XF	Unc	BU
1980 FM (P)	2,629	Value: 2.50				

KM# 48 10 CENTESIMOS **Composition:** Copper-Nickel Clad Copper **Subject:** 75th Anniversary of Independence

Date	Mintage	F	VF	XF	Unc	BU
978 FM (U)	20,000	—	0.20	0.50	1.50	—
978 FM (P)	11,000	Value: 1.50				

KM# 10.1 1/10 BALBOA **Weight:** 2.5000 g. **Composition:** 0.9000 Silver .0723 oz. ASW **Note:** High relief.

Date	Mintage	F	VF	XF	Unc	BU
1930	500,000	2.00	4.00	8.00	30.00	50.00
1930 Matte proof	20	—	—	—	1,000	—
1931	200,000	2.50	5.00	17.50	75.00	120
1932	150,000	3.00	6.00	18.00	85.00	150
1933	100,000	6.50	12.50	30.00	120	200
1934	75,000	8.00	16.00	40.00	150	250
1947	1,000,000	1.00	2.00	4.00	12.00	20.00

KM# 10.2 1/10 BALBOA **Weight:** 2.5000 g. **Composition:** 0.9000 Silver .0723 oz. ASW **Note:** Low relief.

Date	Mintage	F	VF	XF	Unc	BU
1962		BV	—	1.00	3.00	—
1962 Proof	Est. 25	Value: 500				

KM# 18 1/10 BALBOA **Weight:** 2.5000 g. **Composition:** 0.9000 Silver .0723 oz. ASW **Subject:** 50th Anniversary of rhe Republic

Date	Mintage	F	VF	XF	Unc	BU
1953	3,300,000	BV	0.75	1.50	4.00	—

KM# 24 1/10 BALBOA **Weight:** 2.5000 g. **Composition:** 0.9000 Silver .0723 oz. ASW

Date	Mintage	F	VF	XF	Unc	BU
1961	2,500,000	BV	0.65	1.25	3.00	—

KM# 10a 1/10 BALBOA **Composition:** Copper-Nickel Clad Copper

Date	Mintage	F	VF	XF	Unc	BU
1966 Type 1	6,955,000	—	0.50	0.85	3.00	—

Note: The Type I is similar to the 1962 strike on a thick flan (London) with diamonds on both sides of DE

Date	Mintage	F	VF	XF	Unc	BU
1966 Type 2	1,000,000	—	0.75	2.00	10.00	—

Note: The Type II strike similar to the 1947 strikes on a thin flan (U.S.) with elongated diamonds on both sides of DE

Date	Mintage	F	VF	XF	Unc	BU
1966	6,955,000	—	0.50	0.85	3.00	—

Note: The type 1 variety is similar to the 1962 strike (London) on a thick flan with diamonds on both sides of DE

Date	Mintage	F	VF	XF	Unc	BU
1966	1,000,000	—	0.75	2.00	10.00	—

Note: The type 2 variety is similar to the 1947 strike (U.S.) on a thin flan with elongated diamonds on both sides of DE

Date	Mintage	F	VF	XF	Unc	BU
1966 Proof	13,000	Value: 1.00				
1967 Proof	20,000	Value: 1.00				
1968	5,000,000	—	0.20	0.30	1.50	—
1968 Proof	23,000	Value: 1.00				
1969 Proof	14,000	Value: 1.00				
1970	7,500,000	—	0.15	0.25	1.00	—
1970 Proof	9,528	Value: 1.00				
1971 Proof	11,000	Value: 1.00				
1972 Proof	13,000	Value: 1.00				
1973	10,000,000	—	0.15	0.20	1.50	—
1973 Proof	17,000	Value: 1.00				
1974 Proof	18,000	Value: 1.00				
1975	500,000	—	0.25	0.50	2.00	—
1980	5,000,000	—	0.20	0.30	1.25	—
1982	7,740,000	—	0.15	0.25	1.25	—
1983 (RCM)	7,750,000	—	0.15	0.25	1.00	—
1986 (RCM)	1,000,000	—	0.15	0.25	1.50	—
1993	7,000,000	—	0.15	0.25	1.00	—
1993 Proof	—	Value: 300				

Note: Unorthorized striking.

KM# 87 1/10 BALBOA **Composition:** Copper-Nickel Clad Copper

Date		F	VF	XF	Unc	BU
1983 FM (P)	—	Value: 3.00				
1984 FM (P)	—	Value: 3.00				

KM# 127 1/10 BALBOA **Composition:** Copper-Nickel Clad Copper **Obverse:** National arms **Reverse:** Balboa's portrait

Date	Mintage	F	VF	XF	Unc	BU
1996	21,000,000	—	—	—	0.50	—

KM# 4 25 CENTESIMOS **Weight:** 12.5000 g. **Composition:** 0.9000 Silver .3617 oz. ASW

Date	Mintage	F	VF	XF	Unc	BU
1904	16,000,000	5.00	12.00	35.00	100	150
1904 Proof	12	Value: 2,000				

KM# 37.1 25 CENTESIMOS **Composition:** Copper-Nickel Clad Copper

Date	Mintage	F	VF	XF	Unc	BU
1975 (RCM)	40,000	—	0.35	0.50	1.00	—
1975 FM (M)	5,000	—	1.00	1.75	3.00	—
1975 FM (U)	1,410	—	—	—	4.00	—
1975 FM (P)	41,000	Value: 1.50				
1976 (RCM)	12,000	—	0.45	0.60	1.50	—
1976 FM (M)	2,500	—	0.75	1.50	3.00	—
1976 FM (P)	12,000	Value: 1.50				
1977 FM (U)	2,500	—	0.75	1.50	2.50	—
1977 FM (P)	9,548	Value: 1.50				
1979 FM (U)	4,000	—	1.00	1.50	3.50	—
1979 FM (P)	5,949	Value: 1.50				
1980 FM (U)	4,000	—	1.00	1.50	3.50	—
1981 FM (P)	1,973	Value: 2.00				
1982 FM (U)	2,000	—	1.50	2.50	4.50	—
1982 Proof	1,480	Value: 2.00				

KM# 37.2 25 CENTESIMOS **Composition:** Copper-Nickel Clad Copper **Edge Lettering:** 1830 BOLIVAR 1980

Date	Mintage	F	VF	XF	Unc	BU
1980 FM (P)	2,629	Value: 2.00				

KM# 49 25 CENTESIMOS **Composition:** Copper-Nickel Clad Copper **Subject:** 75th Anniversary of Independence

Date	Mintage	F	VF	XF	Unc	BU
1978 FM (U)		—	0.75	1.25	2.50	—
1978 FM (P)	11,000	Value: 2.00				
1978 FM (P)	11,000	Value: 2.00				

KM# 11.1 1/4 BALBOA **Weight:** 6.2500 g. **Composition:** 0.9000 Silver .1809 oz. ASW

Date	Mintage	F	VF	XF	Unc	BU
1930	400,000	2.00	3.00	25.00	45.00	80.00
1930 Matte proof	20	—	—	—	2,000	—
1931	48,000	15.00	30.00	300	1,000	1,800
1932	126,000	3.00	7.00	65.00	325	650
1933	120,000	3.00	6.00	30.00	150	250
1934	90,000	3.00	6.00	20.00	120	200
1947	700,000	1.50	2.00	5.00	20.00	35.00

KM# 11.2 1/4 BALBOA **Weight:** 6.2500 g. **Composition:** 0.9000 Silver .1809 oz. ASW **Note:** Low relief.

Date	Mintage	F	VF	XF	Unc	BU
1962	4,000,000	BV	1.00	2.00	4.00	—
1962 Proof	25	Value: 500				

KM# 19 1/4 BALBOA **Weight:** 6.2500 g. **Composition:** 0.9000 Silver .1809 oz. ASW

Date	Mintage	F	VF	XF	Unc	BU
1953		BV	1.50	4.00	18.50	—
1953 Proof	Est. 5	Value: 1,350				

KM# 25 1/4 BALBOA **Weight:** 6.2500 g. **Composition:** 0.9000 Silver ,1809 oz. ASW

Date	Mintage	F	VF	XF	Unc	BU
1961	2,000,000	BV	1.25	1.75	3.75	—

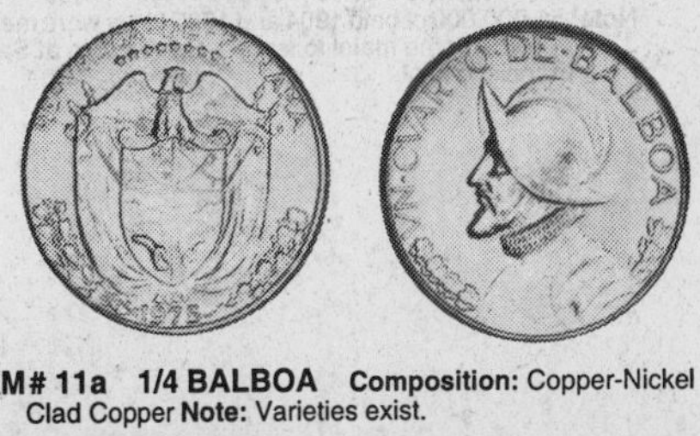

KM# 11a 1/4 BALBOA **Composition:** Copper-Nickel Clad Copper **Note:** Varieties exist.

Date	Mintage	F	VF	XF	Unc	BU
1966 (RCM)	7,400,000	—	0.35	0.50	1.00	—
1966 (RCM) Proof	13,000	Value: 2.00				
1967 Proof	20,000	Value: 1.50				
1968	1,200,000	—	0.35	0.60	1.50	—
1968 Proof	23,000	Value: 1.50				
1969 Proof	14,000	Value: 1.50				
1970	2,000,000	—	0.35	0.60	1.25	—
1970 Proof	9,528	Value: 2.00				
1971 Proof	11,000	Value: 2.00				
1972 Proof	13,000	Value: 2.00				
1973	800,000	—	0.40	1.00	2.00	—
1973 Proof	17,000	Value: 2.00				
1974 Proof	18,000	Value: 2.00				
1975	1,500,000	—	0.35	0.50	2.00	—
1979	2,000,000	—	0.25	0.45	1.50	—
1980	2,000,000	—	0.25	0.45	2.00	—
1982	3,000,000	—	0.25	0.45	2.00	—
1983 (RCM)	6,000,000	—	0.25	0.45	1.50	—
1986 (RCM)	3,000,000	—	0.25	0.50	1.50	—
1993	4,000,000	—	0.25	0.45	1.00	—
1993 Proof	—	Value: 350				

Note: The 1993 Proof strikes were not authorized by the Panamanian government

KM# 88 1/4 BALBOA Composition: Copper-Nickel Clad Copper

Date		F	VF	XF	Unc	BU
1983 FM (P)	—	Value: 4.00				
1984 FM (P)	—	Value: 4.00				

KM# 128 1/4 BALBOA Composition: Copper-Nickel Clad Copper **Obverse:** National arms **Reverse:** Balboa's portrait

Date	Mintage	F	VF	XF	Unc	BU
1996	7,200,000	—	—	—	0.75	—

KM# 5 50 CENTESIMOS Weight: 25.0000 g. **Composition:** 0.9000 Silver .7235 oz. ASW

Date	Mintage	F	VF	XF	Unc	BU
1904	1,000,000	15.00	30.00	60.00	185	250
1904 Proof	12	Value: 2,500				
1905	1,800,000	25.00	50.00	135	350	500

Note: 51,000,000 of both 1904 and 1905 dates were melted in 1931 for the metal to issue 1 Balboa coin at San Francisco Mint

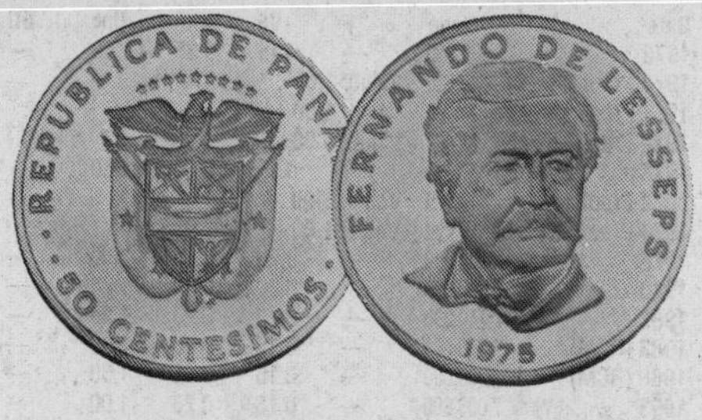

KM# 38.1 50 CENTESIMOS Composition: Copper-Nickel Clad Copper **Subject:** Fernando de Lesseps

Date	Mintage	F	VF	XF	Unc	BU
1975 (RCM)	20,000	—	1.00	1.50	2.00	—
1975FM (M)	2,000	—	1.50	3.00	5.00	—
1975FM (U)	1,410	—	—	—	6.50	—
1975FM (P) Proof	41,000	Value: 2.00				
1976 (RCM)	12,000	—	1.25	1.75	3.00	—
1976FM (M)	1,250	—	1.00	2.25	8.00	—
1976FM (P) Proof	12,000	Value: 2.50				
1977FM (U)	1,250	—	1.00	2.25	8.00	—
1977FM (P) Proof	9,548	Value: 2.50				
1979FM (U)	2,000	—	2.00	3.50	9.00	—
1979FM (P) Proof	5,949	Value: 2.50				
1980FM (U)	2,000	—	2.00	3.50	9.00	—
1981FM (P) Proof	1,973	Value: 5.00				
1982FM (U)	1,000	—	3.00	5.00	11.50	—
1982FM (P) Proof	1,480	Value: 5.00				

Note: (Error) Without edge lettering

KM# 38.2 50 CENTESIMOS Composition: Copper-Nickel Clad Copper **Edge Lettering:** 1830 BOLIVAR 1980

Date	Mintage	F	VF	XF	Unc	BU
1980 FM (P)	2,629	Value: 5.00				
1980 Proof	Inc. above	Value: 125				

Note: (error) without edge lettering

KM# 50 50 CENTESIMOS Composition: Copper-Nickel Clad Copper **Subject:** 75th Anniversary of Independence

Date	Mintage	F	VF	XF	Unc	BU
1978FM (U)	8,000	—	1.50	3.00	5.00	—
1978FM (P)	11,000	Value: 5.00				

KM# 12.1 1/2 BALBOA Weight: 12.5000 g. **Composition:** 0.9000 Silver .3617 oz. ASW **Note:** High relief.

Date	Mintage	F	VF	XF	Unc	BU
1930	300,000	3.50	8.00	30.00	75.00	100
1930 Matte proof	20	Value: 2,200				
1932	63,000	5.00	10.00	125	400	750
1933	120,000	4.00	6.00	40.00	275	400
1934	90,000	4.00	6.00	40.00	250	300
1947	450,000	2.00	3.50	10.00	35.00	55.00

KM# 12.2 1/2 BALBOA Weight: 12.5000 g. **Composition:** 0.9000 Silver .3617 oz. ASW **Note:** Low relie

Date	Mintage	F	VF	XF	Unc	B
1962	700,000	BV	2.50	3.50	6.00	9.
1962 Proof	25	Value: 750				

KM# 20 1/2 BALBOA Weight: 12.5000 g. **Composition:** 0.9000 Silver .3617 oz. ASW

Date	Mintage	F	VF	XF	Unc	B
1953		BV	3.50	4.50	6.00	10.0
1953 Proof	Est. 5	Value: 1,850				

KM# 26 1/2 BALBOA Weight: 12.5000 g. **Composition:** 0.9000 Silver .3617 oz. ASW

Date	Mintage	F	VF	XF	Unc	B
1961	350,000	BV	3.50	5.00	8.00	10.0

KM# 12a.1 1/2 BALBOA Weight: 12.5000 g. **Composition:** 0.4000 Silver Clad .1608 oz. ASW **Obverse:** Normal helmet **Note:** Varieties exist.

Date	Mintage	F	VF	XF	Unc	B
1966 (RCM)	1,000,000	1.00	1.50	2.00	5.00	–
1966 (RCM) Proof	13,000	Value: 3.00				
1967	300,000	1.00	1.50	2.00	5.00	–
1967 Proof	20,000	Value: 3.00				
1968	1,000,000	1.00	1.50	2.00	4.00	–
1968 Proof	23,000	Value: 3.00				
1969 Proof	14,000	Value: 3.00				
1970	610,000	1.00	1.50	2.00	5.00	–
1970 Proof	9,528	Value: 4.00				
1971 Proof	11,000	Value: 3.00				
1972 Proof	13,000	Value: 3.00				
1993 Proof	—	Value: 450				

Note: The 1993 Proof strike was not authorized by the Pan amanian government

KM# 12a.2 1/2 BALBOA Weight: 12.5000 g. **Composition:** 0.4000 Silver Clad .1608 oz. ASW **Note:** Error: Type II helmet rim incomplete.

Date		F	VF	XF	Unc	BU
1966		1.50	3.50	7.50	15.00	25.0

KM# 12b 1/2 BALBOA Composition: Copper-Nickel Clad Copper **Note:** Varieties exist.

te	Mintage	F	VF	XF	Unc	BU
73	1,000,000	—	1.00	1.25	2.00	—
73 Proof	17,000	Value: 2.00				
74 Proof	18,000	Value: 2.00				
75	1,200,000	—	0.75	1.25	1.75	—
79	1,000,000	—	—	0.75	1.50	—
30	400,000	—	—	0.75	2.00	—
32	400,000	—	—	0.75	2.00	—
33 (RCM)	1,850,000	—	—	0.75	1.50	—
36 (RCM)	200,000	—	0.75	1.50	5.00	—
93	600,000	—	0.75	1.25	2.00	—

M# 89 1/2 BALBOA **Composition:** Copper-Nickel Clad Copper

ate		F	VF	XF	Unc	BU
983FM (P) Proof	—	Value: 6.00				
984FM (P) Proof	—	Value: 6.00				

M# 129 1/2 BALBOA **Composition:** Copper-Nickel Clad Copper **Obverse:** National arms **Reverse:** Balboa's Portrait

ate	Mintage	F	VF	XF	Unc	BU
996	200,000	—	0.75	1.00	3.00	—

M# 13 BALBOA **Weight:** 26.7300 g. **Composition:** 0.9000 Silver .7735 oz. ASW **Subject:** Vasco Nunez de Balboa

Date	Mintage	F	VF	XF	Unc	BU
1931	200,000	6.00	8.00	20.00	60.00	90.00
1931 Proof	20	Value: 3,000				
1934	225,000	6.00	7.50	17.50	50.00	80.00
1947	500,000	4.00	5.00	8.00	16.00	25.00

KM# 21 BALBOA **Weight:** 26.7300 g. **Composition:** 0.9000 Silver .7735 oz. ASW **Subject:** 50th Anniversary of the Republic **Obverse:** Similar to KM#13

Date	Mintage	F	VF	XF	Unc	BU
1953	50,000	6.50	8.00	12.00	25.00	35.00

KM# 27 BALBOA **Weight:** 26.7300 g. **Composition:** 0.9000 Silver .7735 oz. ASW **Note:** More than 200,000 of 1966 dates were melted down in 1971 for silver for the 20 Balboas. Varieties exist.

Date	Mintage	F	VF	XF	Unc	BU
1966 (RCM)	300,000	—	—	—	10.00	—
1966 (RCM) Proof	13,000	Value: 15.00				
1967 Proof	20,000	Value: 12.00				
1968	23,000	Value: 12.00				
1969 Proof	14,000	Value: 12.00				
1970 Proof	13,000	Value: 15.00				
1971 Proof	18,000	Value: 13.50				
1972 Proof	23,000	Value: 12.00				
1973 Proof	30,000	Value: 12.00				
1974 Proof	30,000	Value: 12.00				

KM# 39.1 BALBOA **Composition:** Copper-Nickel Clad Copper

Date	Mintage	F	VF	XF	Unc	BU
1975FM (M)	4,035	—	—	—	18.00	—
1975FM (U)	1,410	—	—	—	35.00	—
1976FM (M)	625	—	—	—	75.00	—
1977FM (U)	625	—	—	—	75.00	—
1979FM (U)	1,000	—	—	—	50.00	—
1980FM (U)	1,000	—	—	—	50.00	—
1982FM (U)	500	—	—	—	65.00	—

KM# 39.1a BALBOA **Weight:** 26.7300 g. **Composition:** 0.9250 Silver .7950 oz. ASW

Date	Mintage	F	VF	XF	Unc	BU
1975FM (P)	45,000	Value: 10.00				
1976FM (P)	14,000	Value: 12.00				
1977FM (P)	11,000	Value: 12.00				
1979FM (P)	7,160	Value: 20.00				

KM# 39.1b BALBOA **Weight:** 20.7400 g. **Composition:** 0.5000 Silver .3334 oz. ASW

Date	Mintage	F	VF	XF	Unc	BU
1981FM (P)	2,633	Value: 20.00				
1982FM (P)	1,837	Value: 22.00				

KM# 39.2 BALBOA **Composition:** Copper-Nickel Clad Copper **Obverse:** Erroneous silver content (LEY .925) below arms

Date	Mintage	F	VF	XF	Unc	BU
1975 (RCM)	10,000	—	—	—	8.00	—
1976 (RCM)	12,000	—	—	—	8.00	—

KM# 39.3 BALBOA **Weight:** 2.7400 g. **Composition:** 0.5000 Silver .3334 oz. ASW **Edge Lettering:** 1830 BALBOA 1980

Date	Mintage	F	VF	XF	Unc	BU
1980FM (P)	2,629	Value: 20.00				

KM# 39.4 BALBOA **Composition:** Copper-Nickel Clad Copper **Obverse:** Erroneous silver content (LEY .500) below arms

Date	Mintage	F	VF	XF	Unc	BU
1982FM (U)	11	—	—	—	600	—

KM# 51 BALBOA **Composition:** Copper-Nickel Clad Copper **Subject:** 75th Anniversary of Independence

Date	Mintage	F	VF	XF	Unc	BU
1978FM (U)	4,000	—	—	—	15.00	—

KM# 51a BALBOA **Composition:** 0.9250 Silver

Date	Mintage	F	VF	XF	Unc	BU
1978FM (P)	13,000	Value: 20.00				

KM# 76 BALBOA **Composition:** Copper Nickel **Subject:** Death of General Omar Torrijos

Date	Mintage	F	VF	XF	Unc	BU
1982	200,000	—	—	1.50	3.00	5.00
1982 Frosted obverse and reverse. Proof	200	Value: 125				
1982 Frosted obverse. Proof	50	Value: 200				
1983	200,000	—	—	1.50	3.00	5.00
1984	200,000	—	—	1.50	3.00	5.00

KM# 90 BALBOA Weight: 20.7400 g. **Composition:** 0.5000 Silver .3334 oz. ASW

Date	Mintage	F	VF	XF	Unc	BU
1983FM (P)	1,602	Value: 27.50				
1984FM (P)	1,044	Value: 30.00				
1985FM (P)	954	Value: 40.00				

KM# 28 5 BALBOAS Weight: 35.7000 g. **Composition:** 0.9250 Silver 1.0617 oz. ASW **Subject:** 11th Central American and Caribbean Games

Date	Mintage	F	VF	XF	Unc	BU
1970FM	1,647,000	—	—	—	8.00	9.00
1970FM (U)	603,000	—	—	—	—	—
1970FM (P)	59,000	Value: 10.00				

KM# 30 5 BALBOAS Weight: 35.0000 g. **Composition:** 0.9000 Silver 1.0128 oz. ASW **Subject:** F.A.O. **Obverse:** Similar to KM#28

Date	Mintage	F	VF	XF	Unc	BU
1972	70,000	—	—	—	9.00	10.00
1972 Proof	10,000	Value: 20.00				

KM# 40.1 5 BALBOAS Composition: Copper-Nickel Clad Copper **Subject:** Belisario Porras **Obverse:** Similar to KM#28

Date	Mintage	F	VF	XF	Unc	BU
1975FM (M)	5,125	—	—	—	12.00	—
1975FM (U)	1,410	—	—	—	20.00	—
1976FM (M)	125	—	—	—	175	—
1977FM (U)	125	—	—	—	175	—
1979FM (U)	1,000	—	—	—	25.00	—
1980FM (U)	1,000	—	—	—	25.00	—
1982FM (U)	1,200	—	—	—	22.50	—

KM# 40.1a 5 BALBOAS Weight: 35.1200 g. **Composition:** 0.9250 Silver 1.0446 oz. ASW

Date	Mintage	F	VF	XF	Unc	BU
1975FM (P)	41,000	Value: 15.00				
1976FM (P)	12,000	Value: 20.00				
1977FM (P)	9,548	Value: 20.00				
1979FM (P)	5,949	Value: 30.00				

KM# 40.1b 5 BALBOAS Weight: 23.3300 g. **Composition:** 0.5000 Silver .3751 oz. ASW

Date	Mintage	F	VF	XF	Unc	BU
1981FM (P)	1,973	Value: 30.00				
1982FM (P)	1,480	Value: 30.00				

KM# 40.2 5 BALBOAS Composition: Copper-Nickel Clad Copper **Obverse:** Erroneous silver content (LEY .925) below arms

Date	Mintage	F	VF	XF	Unc	BU
1975	4,000	—	—	—	8.50	—
1976	5,000	—	—	—	8.50	—

KM# 40.3 5 BALBOAS Weight: 23.3300 g. **Composition:** 0.5000 Silver .3751 oz. ASW **Edge Lettering:** 1830 BALBOA 1980

Date	Mintage	F	VF	XF	Unc	BU
1980FM (P)	2,629	Value: 20.00				

KM# 40.4 5 BALBOAS Weight: 23.3300 g. **Composition:** 0.5000 Silver .3751 oz. ASW **Obverse:** Erroneous silver content (LEY .925) below arms

Date		F	VF	XF	Unc	BU
1982FM (P)	—	Value: 65.00				

KM# 40.5 5 BALBOAS Composition: Copper-Nickel Clad Copper 500 oz. **Obverse:** Erroneous silver content (LEY .500) below arms

Date	Mintage	F	VF	XF	Unc	BU
1982FM (U)	200	—	—	—	135	—

KM# 52 5 BALBOAS Composition: Copper-Nickel Clad Copper 500 oz. **Subject:** 75th Anniversary of Independence

Date	Mintage	F	VF	XF	Unc
1978FM (U)	2,000	—	—	—	20.00

KM# 52a 5 BALBOAS Weight: 35.1200 g. **Composition:** 0.9250 Silver 1.0466 oz. ASW

Date	Mintage	F	VF	XF	Unc
1978FM (P)	11,000	Value: 22.50			

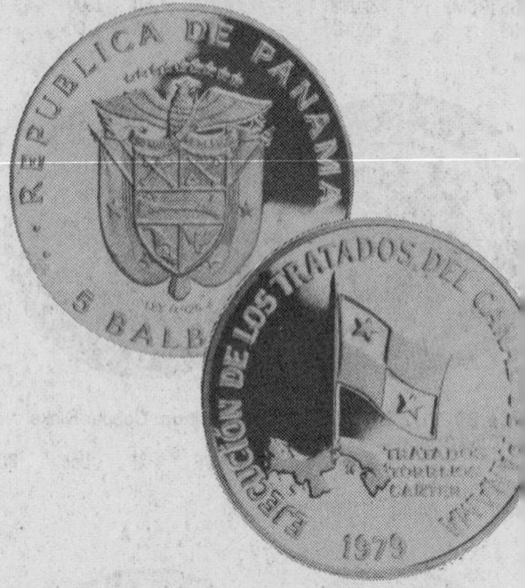

KM# 58 5 BALBOAS Weight: 35.1200 g. **Composition:** 0.9250 Silver 1.0466 oz. ASW **Subject:** Panama Canal Treaty Implementation

Date	Mintage	F	VF	XF	Unc
1979FM (P)	6,854	Value: 30.00			

KM# 63 5 BALBOAS Weight: 24.1100 g. **Composition:** 0.5000 Silver .3875 oz. ASW **Subject:** Champions of Boxing

Date	Mintage	F	VF	XF	Unc
1980 Proof	1,261	Value: 45.00			

KM# 77 5 BALBOAS Weight: 24.1600 g. **Composition:** 0.9250 Silver .7186 oz. ASW **Subject:** Chanpions of Soccer

Date	Mintage	F	VF	XF	Unc
1982 Proof	9,446	Value: 40.00			

KM# 105 20 BALBOAS **Weight:** 119.8800 g. **Composition:** 0.5000 Silver 1.9273 oz. ASW **Subject:** Discovery of the Pacific Ocean

Date	Mintage	F	VF	XF	Unc	BU
1985FM (P)	1,402	Value: 120				

KM# 73 50 BALBOAS **Weight:** 5.3700 g. **Composition:** 0.5000 Gold .0861 oz. AGW **Subject:** Christmas 1981

Date	Mintage	F	VF	XF	Unc	BU
1981FM (U)	154	—	—	—	200	—
1981FM (P)	1,940	Value: 75.00				

KM# 82 50 BALBOAS **Weight:** 5.3700 g. **Composition:** 0.5000 Gold .0861 oz. AGW **Subject:** Christmas 1982

Date	Mintage	F	VF	XF	Unc	BU
1982FM (U)	60	—	—	—	450	—
1982FM (P)	1,361	Value: 80.00				

KM# 94 50 BALBOAS **Weight:** 5.3700 g. **Composition:** 0.5000 Gold .0861 oz. AGW **Subject:** Christmas 1983

Date	Mintage	F	VF	XF	Unc	BU
1983FM (U)	—	—	—	—	175	—
1983FM (P)	1,283	Value: 80.00				

KM# 99 50 BALBOAS **Weight:** 5.3700 g. **Composition:** 0.5000 Gold .0861 oz. AGW **Subject:** Peace at Christmas

Date	F	VF	XF	Unc	BU
1984FM (P)	—	Value: 400			

KM# 55 75 BALBOAS **Weight:** 10.6000 g. **Composition:** 0.5000 Gold .1704 oz. AGW **Subject:** 75th Anniversary of Independence

Date	Mintage	F	VF	XF	Unc	BU
ND1978FM (U)	410	—	—	—	150	—
ND1978FM (P)	9,161	Value: 82.50				

KM# 41 100 BALBOAS **Weight:** 8.1600 g. **Composition:** 0.9000 Gold .2361 oz. AGW **Subject:** 500th Anniversary - Birth of Balboa

Date	Mintage	F	VF	XF	Unc	BU
1975FM (U)	44,000	—	—	—	105	—
1975FM (P)	75,000	Value: 110				
1976FM (M)	50	—	—	—	450	—
1976FM (U)	3,013	—	—	—	115	—
1976FM (P)	11,000	Value: 110				
1977FM (M)	50	—	—	—	350	—
1977FM (U)	324	—	—	—	200	—
1977FM (P)	5,092	Value: 125				

KM# 56 100 BALBOAS **Weight:** 8.1600 g. **Composition:** 0.9000 Gold .2361 oz. AGW **Subject:** Peace and progress

Date	Mintage	F	VF	XF	Unc	BU
1978FM (M)	50	—	—	—	350	—
1978FM (U)	300	—	—	—	220	—
1978FM (P)	6,086	Value: 125				

KM# 60 100 BALBOAS **Weight:** 8.1600 g. **Composition:** 0.9000 Gold .2361 oz. AGW **Subject:** Pre-Columbian Art - Golden Turtle

Date	Mintage	F	VF	XF	Unc	BU
1979FM (M)	50	—	—	—	350	—
1979FM (U)	240	—	—	—	250	—
1979FM (P)	4,829	Value: 150				

KM# 66 100 BALBOAS **Weight:** 8.1600 g. **Composition:** 0.9000 Gold .2361 oz. AGW **Subject:** Pre-Columbian Art - Golden Condor

Date	Mintage	F	VF	XF	Unc	BU
1980FM (U)	209	—	—	—	275	—
1980FM (P)	2,411	Value: 165				

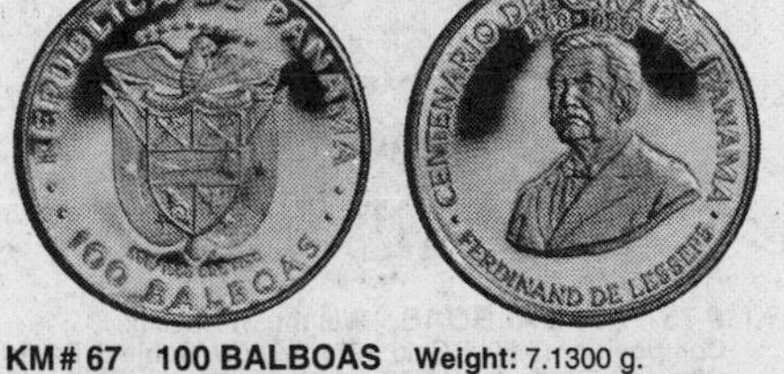

KM# 67 100 BALBOAS **Weight:** 7.1300 g. **Composition:** 0.5000 Gold .1146 oz. AGW **Subject:** Panama Canal Centennial

Date	Mintage	F	VF	XF	Unc	BU
ND (1980)FM (U)	77	—	—	—	475	—
ND (1980)FM (P)	2,468	Value: 125				

KM# 74 100 BALBOAS **Weight:** 7.1300 g. **Composition:** 0.5000 Gold .1146 oz. AGW **Subject:** Pre-Columbian Art **Reverse:** Cocle Peoples Ceremonial Mask

Date	Mintage	F	VF	XF	Unc	BU
1981FM (U)	174	—	—	—	300	—
1981FM (P)	1,841	Value: 150				

KM# 83 100 BALBOAS **Weight:** 7.1300 g. **Composition:** 0.5000 Gold .1146 oz. AGW **Subject:** Pre-Columbian Art **Reverse:** Native design

Date	Mintage	F	VF	XF	Unc	BU
1982FM (U)	26	—	—	—	600	—
1982FM (P)	578	Value: 185				

KM# 95 100 BALBOAS **Weight:** 7.1300 g. **Composition:** 0.5000 Gold .1146 oz. AGW **Subject:** Pre-Columbian Art **Reverse:** Cocle style birds

Date	Mintage	F	VF	XF	Unc	BU
1983FM (U)	—	—	—	—	300	—
1983FM (P)	1,308	Value: 150				

KM# 100 100 BALBOAS **Weight:** 7.1300 g. **Composition:** 0.5000 Gold .1146 oz. AGW **Subject:** Pre-Columbian Art **Reverse:** Native art

Date	F	VF	XF	Unc	BU
1984FM (U)	—	—	—	300	—
1984FM (P)	—	Value: 165			

KM# 131 100 BALBOAS **Weight:** 8.3000 g. **Composition:** 0.9000 Gold .2402 oz. AGW **Subject:** Panama Canal Transfer **Obverse:** Presidents; portrait **Reverse:** Ship in canal under Panamanian flag

Date	Mintage	F	VF	XF	Unc	BU
1999 Proof	1,000	Value: 300				

KM# 43 150 BALBOAS **Weight:** 9.3000 g. **Composition:** 0.9990 Platinum .2987 oz. APW **Subject:** 150th Anniversary - Panamanian Congress

Date	Mintage	F	VF	XF	Unc	BU
ND (1976)FM (M)	30	—	—	—	850	—
ND (1976)FM (U)	510	—	—	—	250	—
ND (1976)FM (P)	13,000	Value: 220				

KM# 68 150 BALBOAS **Weight:** 7.6700 g. **Composition:** 0.5000 Gold .1233 oz. AGW **Subject:** Sesquicentenarium - Death of Simon Bolivar

Date	Mintage	F	VF	XF	Unc	BU
ND (1980)FM (U)	169	—	—	—	350	—
ND (1980)FM (P)	1,837	Value: 180				

KM# 61 200 BALBOAS **Weight:** 9.5000 g. **Composition:** 0.9800 Platinum .2994 oz. APW **Subject:** Panal Canal Treaty Implementation

Date	Mintage	F	VF	XF	Unc	BU
1979FM (P)	2,178	Value: 285				

KM# 69 200 BALBOAS **Weight:** 9.9300 g. **Composition:** 0.9800 Platinum .2940 oz. APW **Subject:** Champions of Boxing

Date	Mintage	F	VF	XF	Unc	BU
1980 Proof	219	Value: 500				

KM# 42 500 BALBOAS **Weight:** 41.7000 g. **Composition:** 0.9000 Gold 1.2067 oz. AGW **Subject:** 500th Anniversary - Birth of Balboa

Date	Mintage	F	VF	XF	Unc	BU
1975FM (M)	10	—	—	—	2,000	—
1975FM (U)	1,496	—	—	—	600	—
1975FM (P)	9,824	Value: 500				
1976FM (M)	10	—	—	—	1,900	—
1976FM (U)	160	—	—	—	800	—
1976FM (P)	2,669	Value: 525				
1977FM (M)	10	—	—	—	1,800	—
1977FM (U)	59	—	—	—	1,250	—
1977FM (P)	1,980	Value: 575				

KM# 57 500 BALBOAS **Weight:** 41.7000 g. **Composition:** 0.9000 Gold 1.2067 oz. AGW **Subject:** 30th Anniversary - Organization of American States **Obverse:** Similar to KM#42

Date	Mintage	F	VF	XF	Unc	BU
NDFM (M)	10	—	—	—	1,800	—
NDFM (U)	106	—	—	—	900	—
NDFM (P)	2,009	Value: 575				

KM# 62 500 BALBOAS **Weight:** 41.7000 g. **Composition:** 0.9000 Gold 1.2067 oz. AGW **Subject:** Golden Jaguar **Obverse:** Similar to KM#42

Date	Mintage	F	VF	XF	Unc	BU
1979FM (U)	130	—	—	—	875	—
1979FM (P)	1,657	Value: 600				

KM# 70 500 BALBOAS **Weight:** 37.1800 g. **Composition:** 0.5000 Gold .5977 oz. AGW **Subject:** Great Egrets **Obverse:** Similar to KM#42

Date	Mintage	F	VF	XF	Unc	BU
1980FM (U)	54	—	—	—	1,350	—
1980FM (P)	612	Value: 675				

KM# 75 500 BALBOAS **Weight:** 37.1800 g. **Composition:** 0.5000 Gold .5977 oz. AGW **Subject:** Sailfish **Obverse:** Similar to KM#42

Date	Mintage	F	VF	XF	Unc	BU
1981FM (U)	41	—	—	—	1,500	—
1981FM (P)	487	Value: 765				

KM# 84 500 BALBOAS **Weight:** 37.1800 g. **Composition:** 0.5000 Gold .5977 oz. AGW **Subject:** Death of General Omar Torrijos **Obverse:** Similar to KM#42

Date	Mintage	F	VF	XF	Unc	BU
1982FM (U)	97	—	—	—	950	—
1982FM (P)	398	Value: 800				

KM# 96 500 BALBOAS **Weight:** 37.1800 g. **Composition:** 0.5000 Gold .5977 oz. AGW **Subject:** Owl Butterfly

Date	Mintage	F	VF	XF	Unc	BU
1983FM (U)	100	—	—	—	925	—
1983FM (P)	469	Value: 785				

KM# 101 500 BALBOAS **Weight:** 37.1200 g. **Composition:** 0.5000 Gold .5968 oz. AGW **Subject:** Golden Eagle

Date	Mintage	F	VF	XF	Unc	BU
1984FM (U)	10	—	—	—	5,000	—
1984FM (P)	156	Value: 1,400				

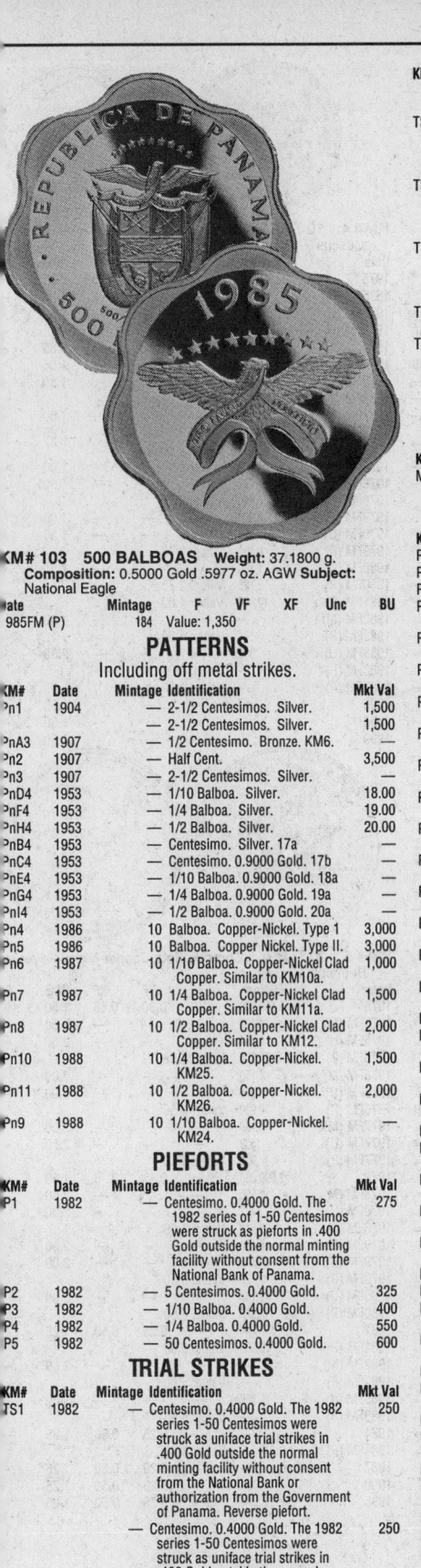

KM# 103 500 BALBOAS Weight: 37.1800 g. **Composition:** 0.5000 Gold .5977 oz. AGW **Subject:** National Eagle

Date	Mintage	F	VF	XF	Unc	BU
1985FM (P)	184	Value: 1,350				

PATTERNS

Including off metal strikes.

KM#	Date	Mintage	Identification	Mkt Val
Pn1	1904	—	2-1/2 Centesimos. Silver.	1,500
		—	2-1/2 Centesimos. Silver.	1,500
PnA3	1907	—	1/2 Centesimo. Bronze. KM6.	—
Pn2	1907	—	Half Cent.	3,500
Pn3	1907	—	2-1/2 Centesimos. Silver.	—
PnD4	1953	—	1/10 Balboa. Silver.	18.00
PnF4	1953	—	1/4 Balboa. Silver.	19.00
PnH4	1953	—	1/2 Balboa. Silver.	20.00
PnB4	1953	—	Centesimo. Silver. 17a	—
PnC4	1953	—	Centesimo. 0.9000 Gold. 17b	—
PnE4	1953	—	1/10 Balboa. 0.9000 Gold. 18a	—
PnG4	1953	—	1/4 Balboa. 0.9000 Gold. 19a	—
PnI4	1953	—	1/2 Balboa. 0.9000 Gold. 20a	—
Pn4	1986	10	Balboa. Copper-Nickel. Type 1	3,000
Pn5	1986	10	Balboa. Copper Nickel. Type II.	3,000
Pn6	1987	10	1/10 Balboa. Copper-Nickel Clad Copper. Similar to KM10a.	1,000
Pn7	1987	10	1/4 Balboa. Copper-Nickel Clad Copper. Similar to KM11a.	1,500
Pn8	1987	10	1/2 Balboa. Copper-Nickel Clad Copper. Similar to KM12.	2,000
Pn10	1988	10	1/4 Balboa. Copper-Nickel. KM25.	1,500
Pn11	1988	10	1/2 Balboa. Copper-Nickel. KM26.	2,000
Pn9	1988	10	1/10 Balboa. Copper-Nickel. KM24.	—

PIEFORTS

KM#	Date	Mintage	Identification	Mkt Val
P1	1982	—	Centesimo. 0.4000 Gold. The 1982 series of 1-50 Centesimos were struck as piefort in .400 Gold outside the normal minting facility without consent from the National Bank of Panama.	275
P2	1982	—	5 Centesimos. 0.4000 Gold.	325
P3	1982	—	1/10 Balboa. 0.4000 Gold.	400
P4	1982	—	1/4 Balboa. 0.4000 Gold.	550
P5	1982	—	50 Centesimos. 0.4000 Gold.	600

TRIAL STRIKES

KM#	Date	Mintage	Identification	Mkt Val
TS1	1982	—	Centesimo. 0.4000 Gold. The 1982 series 1-50 Centesimos were struck as uniface trial strikes in .400 Gold outside the normal minting facility without consent from the National Bank or authorization from the Government of Panama. Reverse piefort.	250
		—	Centesimo. 0.4000 Gold. The 1982 series 1-50 Centesimos were struck as uniface trial strikes in .400 Gold outside the normal minting facility without consent from the National Bank or authorization from the Government of Panama. Reverse piefort.	250
TS2	1982	—	Centesimo. 0.4000 Gold. Obverse piefort.	250
TS3	1982	—	5 Centesimos. 0.4000 Gold. Reverse piefort	300
TS4	1982	—	5 Centesimos. 0.4000 Gold. Obverse piefort	30,000
		—	5 Centesimos. 0.4000 Gold. Obverse piefort	300
TS5	1982	—	1/10 Balboa. 0.4000 Gold. Reverse piefort	375
		—	1/10 Balboa. 0.4000 Gold. Reverse piefort	375
TS6	1982	—	1/10 Balboa. 0.4000 Gold. Obverse piefort	375
		—	1/10 Balboa. 0.4000 Gold. Obverse piefort	375
TS7	1982	—	1/4 Balboa. 0.4000 Gold. Reverse piefort	500
		—	1/4 Balboa. 0.4000 Gold. Reverse piefort	500
TS8	1982	—	1/4 Balboa. 0.4000 Gold. Obverse piefort	500
		—	1/4 Balboa. 0.4000 Gold. Obverse piefort	500
TS9	1982	—	50 Centesimos. 0.4000 Gold. Reverse piefort	500
TS10	1982	—	50 Centesimos. 0.4000 Gold. Obverse piefort	500
		—	50 Centesimos. 0.4000 Gold. Obverse piefort	500

MINT SETS

KM#	Date	Mintage	Identification	Issue Price	Mkt Val
MS1	1975 (8)	1,410	KM33.1-40.1	25.00	75.00

PROOF SETS

KM#	Date	Mintage	Identification	Issue Price	Mkt Val
PS1	1904 (4)	12	KM2-5	—	9,000
PS2	1930 (3)	20	KM10.1-12.1	—	4,650
PS3	1962 (5)	25	KM10.2-12.2, 22, 23.2	—	2,850
PS4	1966 (6)	12,701	KM10a-11a, 12a.1, 22, 23.2, 27	15.25	20.00
PS5	1967 (6)	19,983	KM10a-11a, 12a.1, 22, 23.2, 27	15.25	16.50
PS6	1968 (6)	23,210	KM10a-11a, 12a.1, 22, 23.2, 27	15.25	16.50
PS7	1969 (6)	14,000	KM10a-11a, 12a.1, 22, 23.2, 27	15.25	16.50
PS13	1975 (9)	37,041	KM31, 33.1-38.1, 39.1a-40.1a	130	75.00
PS14	1975 (8)	4,057	KM31, 34.1-38.1, 39.1a-40.1a	50.00	40.00
PS8	1970 (6)	9,528	KM10a-11a, 12a.1, 22, 23.2, 27	15.25	20.00
PS27	1981 (9)	1,279	KM33.1-38.1, 39.1b-40.1b, 71	212	170
PS28	1981 (8)	694	KM33.1-38.1, 39.1b-40.1b	87.00	65.00
PS9	1971 (6)	10,696	KM10a-11a, 12a.1, 22, 23.2, 27	15.25	20.00
PS10	1972 (6)	13,322	KM10a-11a, 12a.1, 22, 23.2, 27	15.25	20.00
PS11	1973 (6)	16,946	KM10a-11a, 12b, 22, 23.2, 27	17.50	25.00
PS25	1980 (9)	1,686	KM33.2-38.2, 39.3-40.3, 65	287	150
PS26	1980 (8)	943	KM33.2-38.2, 39.3-40.3	87.00	65.00
PS12	1974 (6)	17,521	KM10a-11a, 12b, 22, 23.2, 27	17.50	25.00
PS15	1976 (9)	10,610	KM31, 33.1-38.1, 39.1a-40.1a	102	80.00
PS16	1976 (8)	1,792	KM33.1-38.1, 39.1a-40.1a	50.00	40.00
PS17	1976 (2)	11,479	KM31, 34.1	51.00	40.00
PS18	1977 (9)	8,093	KM33.1-38.1, 39.1a-40.1a, 44	100	90.00
PS19	1977 (8)	1,455	KM33.1-38.1, 39.1a-40.1a	50.00	40.00
PS30	1982 (9)	—	Error set; KM33-38, 39.1b, 40.4, 80	212	250
PS32	1982 (8)	—	Error set; KM33-38, 39.1b, 40.4	—	150
PS20	1978 (9)	9,667	KM45-50, 51a, 52a, 54	110	120
PS21	1978 (8)	1,122	KM45-50, 51a, 52a	—	40.00
PS22	1979 (9)	4,974	KM33.1-38.1, 39.1a-40.1a, 44	132	100
PS23	1979 (8)	975	KM33.1-38.1, 39.1a-40.1a	60.00	40.00
PS24	1979 (2)	1,775	KM58-59	125	65.00
PS29	1982 (9)	746	KM33.1-38.1, 39.1b-40.1b, 80	212	200
PS31	1982 (8)	734	KM33-38, 39.1b-40.1b	87.00	75.00
PS33	1983 (9)	—	KM22, 85-89, 90a, 91, 93	87.00	150
PS34	1983 (8)	—	KM22, 85-89, 90a, 91	—	80.00
PS35	1984 (9)	—	KM22, 85-89, 90a, 91, 98	—	200
PS36	1984 (8)	—	KM22, 85-89, 90a, 91	72.00	80.00
PS37	1985 (8)	765	KM22, 85-89, 90a, 104	72.00	180
PS39	1993 (4)	—	KM10a-11a, 12a.1, 23.2	—	1,350

PALO SECO

Palo Seco Leper Colony was established in Balboa, Canal Zone in 1907. It is known today as Palo Seco Hospital. The original issue of tokens totaled $1,800.00 of which $1,492.75 was destroyed on November 28, 1955. The issue was backed by United States Currency and was replaced by United States circulation coinage.

COLONY

LEPROSARIUM TOKEN COINAGE

KM# Tn1 CENT Composition: Copper

Date	VG	F	VF	XF	Unc
ND(1919)	35.00	65.00	125	—	—

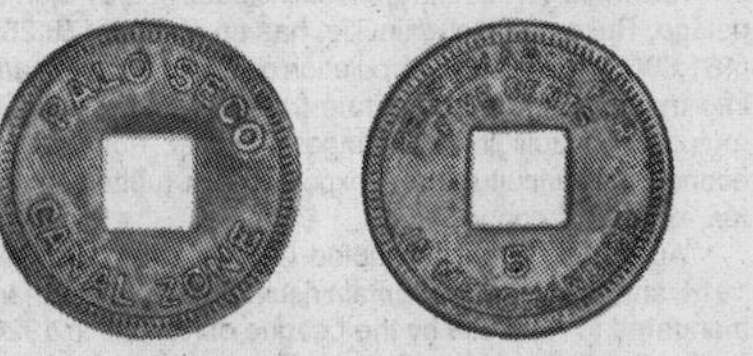

KM# Tn2 5 CENTS Composition: Brass

Date	VG	F	VF	XF	Unc
ND(1919)	50.00	75.00	150	—	—

KM# Tn3 10 CENTS Composition: Aluminum

Date	VG	F	VF	XF	Unc
ND(1919)	75.00	100	200	—	—

KM# Tn4 25 CENTS Composition: Aluminum

Date	VG	F	VF	XF	Unc
ND(1919)	100	200	300	—	—

KM# Tn5 50 CENTS Composition: Aluminum

Date	VG	F	VF	XF	Unc
ND(1919)	150	250	400	—	—

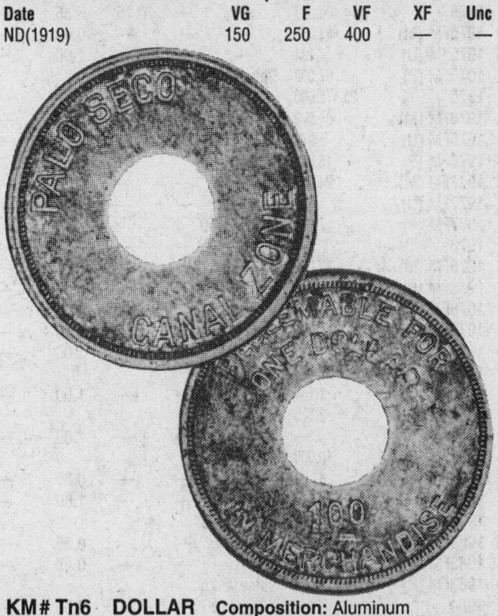

KM# Tn6 DOLLAR Composition: Aluminum

Date	VG	F	VF	XF	Unc
ND(1919)	200	300	500	—	—

PAPUA NEW GUINEA

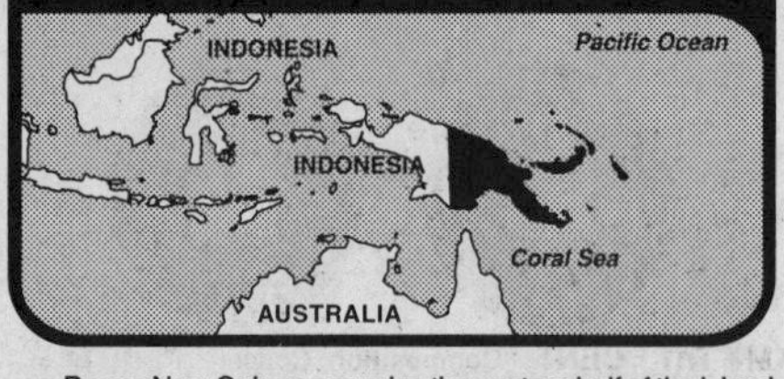

Papua New Guinea occupies the eastern half of the island of New Guinea. It lies north of Australia near the equator and borders on West Irian. The country, which includes nearby Bismark archipelago, Buka and Bougainville, has an area of 178,260 sq. mi. (461,690 sq. km.) and a population of *3.7 million who are divided into more than 1,000 separate tribes speaking more than 700 mutually unintelligible languages. Capital: Port Moresby. The economy is agricultural, and exports copra, rubber, cocoa, coffee, tea, gold and copper.

Australian troops occupied German New Guinea in Aug. 1914, shortly after Great Britain declared war on Germany. It was mandated to Australia by the League of Nations in 1920, known as the Territory of New Guinea. The territory was invaded and most of it was occupied by Japan in 1942. Following the Japanese surrender, it came under U.N. trusteeship, Dec. 13, 1946, with Australia as the administering power.

The Papua and New Guinea act, 1949, provided for the government of Papua and New Guinea as one administrative unit. On Dec. 1, 1973, Papua New Guinea became self-governing with Australia retaining responsibility for defense and foreign affairs. Full independence was achieved on Sept. 16, 1975. Papua New Guinea is a member of the Commonwealth of Nations. Elizabeth II is Head of State, as Queen of Papua New Guinea.

MINT MARKS

FM - Franklin Mint, U.S.A.*

***NOTE:** From 1975-1985 the Franklin Mint produced coinage in up to 3 different qualities. Qualities of issue are designated in ( ) after each date and are defined as follows:

(M) MATTE - Normal circulation strike or a dull finish produced by sandblasting special uncirculated (polish finish) or proof quality dies.

(U) SPECIAL UNCIRCULATED - Polished or proof-like in appearance without any frosted features.

(P) PROOF - The highest quality obtainable having mirror-like fields and frosted features.

MONETARY SYSTEM

100 Toea = 1 Kina

BRITISH ADMINISTRATION

STANDARD COINAGE

100 Toea = 1 Kina

KM# 1 TOEA Composition: Bronze **Obverse:** Paradise bird **Reverse:** Wing butterfly

Date	Mintage	F	VF	XF	Unc	BU
1975	14,400,000	—	—	0.15	0.35	—
1975FM (M)	83,000	—	—	—	0.45	—
1975FM (U)	4,134	—	—	—	1.00	—
1975FM (P)	67,000	Value: 1.00				
1976	25,175,000	—	—	—	0.35	—
1976FM (M)	84,000	—	—	—	0.35	—
1976FM (U)	976	—	—	—	1.00	—
1976FM (P)	16,000	Value: 1.00				
1977FM (M)	84,000	—	—	—	0.35	—
1977FM (U)	603	—	—	—	1.50	—
1977FM (P)	7,721	Value: 1.50				
1978	—	—	—	—	0.35	—
1978FM (M)	83,000	—	—	—	0.35	—
1978FM (U)	777	—	—	—	1.00	—
1978FM (P)	5,540	Value: 1.50				
1979FM (M)	84,000	—	—	—	0.35	—
1979FM (U)	1,366	—	—	—	1.00	—
1979FM (P)	2,728	Value: 1.50				
1980FM (U)	1,160	—	—	—	1.00	—
1980FM (P)	2,125	Value: 1.50				
1981	—	—	—	—	1.00	—
1981FM (P)	10,000	Value: 2.25				
1981FM (M)	—	—	—	—	0.35	—
1982FM (M)	—	—	—	—	1.00	—
1982FM (P)	—	Value: 2.25				
1983	—	—	—	—	0.35	—
1983FM (U)	360	—	—	—	0.45	—
1983FM (P)	—	Value: 2.25				
1984	—	—	—	—	0.35	—
1984FM (P)	—	Value: 2.25				
1987	—	—	—	—	0.35	—
1990	—	—	—	—	0.35	—
1995	—	—	—	—	0.35	—

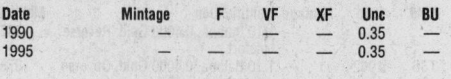

KM# 2 2 TOEA Composition: Bronze **Obverse:** Bird of Paradise **Reverse:** Zebra fish

Date	Mintage	F	VF	XF	Unc	BU
1975	11,400,000	—	—	0.10	0.60	—
1975FM (M)	42,000	—	—	—	0.65	—
1975FM (U)	4,134	—	—	—	1.00	—
1975FM (P)	67,000	Value: 1.00				
1976	15,175,000	—	—	0.10	0.50	—
1976FM (M)	42,000	—	—	—	0.50	—
1976FM (U)	976	—	—	—	1.00	—
1976FM (P)	16,000	Value: 1.00				
1977FM (M)	42,000	—	—	—	0.50	—
1977FM (U)	603	—	—	—	1.50	—
1977FM (P)	7,721	Value: 1.75				
1978	—	—	—	—	0.50	—
1978FM (M)	42,000	—	—	—	0.50	—
1978FM (U)	777	—	—	—	1.00	—
1978FM (P)	5,540	Value: 1.75				
1979FM (M)	42,000	—	—	—	0.50	—
1979FM (U)	1,366	—	—	—	1.00	—
1979FM (P)	2,728	Value: 1.75				
1980FM (U)	1,160	—	—	—	1.00	—
1980FM (P)	2,125	Value: 1.75				
1981	—	—	—	—	0.50	—
1981FM (P)	10,000	Value: 2.50				
1982FM (M)	—	—	—	—	1.00	—
1982FM (P)	—	Value: 2.50				
1983	—	—	—	—	0.50	—
1983FM (U)	360	—	—	—	1.50	—
1983FM (P)	—	Value: 2.50				
1984	—	—	—	—	0.50	—
1984 Proof	—	Value: 2.50				
1987	—	—	—	—	0.50	—
1990	—	—	—	—	0.50	—
1995	—	—	—	—	0.50	—
1996	—	—	—	—	0.50	—

KM# 3 5 TOEA Composition: Copper-Nickel **Reverse:** Plateless turtle

Date	Mintage	F	VF	XF	Unc	BU
1975	11,000,000	—	0.15	0.25	0.75	—
1975FM (M)	17,000	—	—	—	0.75	—
1975FM (U)	4,134	—	—	—	1.25	—
1975FM (P)	67,000	Value: 1.75				
1976	24,000,000	—	0.15	0.25	0.75	—
1976FM (M)	17,000	—	—	—	0.75	—
1976FM (U)	976	—	—	—	1.25	—
1976FM (P)	16,000	Value: 1.75				
1977FM (M)	17,000	—	—	—	0.75	—
1977FM (U)	603	—	—	—	1.75	—
1977FM (P)	7,721	Value: 2.25				
1978	2,000	—	—	—	2.50	—
1978FM (M)	17,000	—	—	—	0.75	—
1978FM (U)	777	—	—	—	1.25	—
1978FM (P)	5,540	Value: 2.25				
1979	—	—	—	—	0.75	—
1979FM (M)	17,000	—	—	—	0.75	—
1979FM (U)	1,366	—	—	—	1.25	—
1979FM (P)	2,728	Value: 2.25				
1980FM (U)	1,160	—	—	—	1.25	—
1980FM (P)	2,125	Value: 2.25				
1981FM (P)	10,000	Value: 3.50				
1982	—	—	—	—	0.75	—
1982FM (M)	—	—	—	—	1.25	—
1982FM (P)	—	Value: 3.50				
1983FM (U)	360	—	—	—	2.25	—
1983FM (P)	—	Value: 3.50				
1984	—	—	—	—	0.75	—
1984FM (P)	—	Value: 3.50				
1987	—	—	—	—	0.75	—
1990	—	—	—	—	0.75	—
1995	—	—	—	—	0.75	—
1996	—	—	—	—	0.75	—
1998	—	—	—	—	0.75	—

KM# 4 10 TOEA Composition: Copper-Nickel **Reverse:** Cuscus

Date	Mintage	F	VF	XF	Unc	BU
1975	8,600,000	—	0.20	0.35	0.65	—
1975FM (M)	8,300	—	—	—	1.00	—
1975FM (U)	4,134	—	—	—	1.50	—
1975FM (P)	67,000	Value: 1.75				
1976	—	—	0.20	0.35	0.65	—
1976FM (M)	8,300	—	—	—	1.00	—
1976FM (U)	976	—	—	—	1.50	—
1976FM (P)	16,000	Value: 1.75				
1977FM (M)	8,300	—	—	—	1.00	—
1977FM (U)	603	—	—	—	2.25	—
1977FM (P)	7,721	Value: 2.50				
1978FM (M)	8,300	—	—	—	1.00	—
1978FM (U)	777	—	—	—	1.50	—
1978FM (P)	5,540	Value: 2.75				
1979FM (M)	8,300	—	—	—	1.00	—
1979FM (U)	1,366	—	—	—	1.50	—
1979FM (P)	2,728	Value: 2.75				
1980FM (U)	1,160	—	—	—	1.50	—
1980FM (P)	2,125	Value: 2.75				
1981FM (P)	10,000	Value: 4.00				
1982FM (M)	—	—	—	—	1.50	—
1982FM (P)	—	Value: 4.00				
1983FM (U)	360	—	—	—	2.50	—
1983FM (P)	—	Value: 4.00				
1984FM (P)	—	Value: 4.00				
1995	—	—	—	—	1.50	—
1996	—	—	—	—	1.50	—
1999	—	—	—	—	1.50	—

KM# 5 20 TOEA Composition: Copper-Nickel **Reverse:** Bennett's Cassowary

Date	Mintage	F	VF	XF	Unc	BU
1975	15,500,000	—	0.30	0.65	1.50	—
1975FM (M)	4,150	—	—	—	2.00	—
1975FM (U)	4,134	—	—	—	2.00	—
1975FM (P)	67,000	Value: 2.50				
1976FM (M)	4,150	—	—	—	2.00	—
1976FM (U)	976	—	—	—	2.00	—
1976FM (P)	16,000	Value: 2.50				
1977FM (M)	4,150	—	—	—	2.00	—
1977FM (U)	603	—	—	—	2.50	—
1977FM (P)	7,721	Value: 3.50				
1978	2,500,000	—	0.45	0.75	1.50	—
1978FM (M)	4,150	—	—	—	2.00	—
1978FM (U)	777	—	—	—	2.00	—
1978FM (P)	5,540	Value: 3.50				
1979FM (M)	4,150	—	—	—	2.00	—
1979FM (U)	1,366	—	—	—	2.00	—
1979FM (P)	2,728	Value: 3.50				
1980FM (U)	1,160	—	—	—	2.00	—
1980FM (P)	2,125	Value: 3.50				
1981	—	—	0.25	0.50	1.25	—
1981FM (P)	10,000	Value: 5.00				
1982FM (M)	—	—	—	—	2.00	—
1982FM (P)	—	Value: 5.00				
1983FM (U)	360	—	—	—	3.00	—
1983FM (P)	—	Value: 5.00				
1984	—	—	0.25	0.50	1.25	—
1984FM (P)	—	Value: 5.00				
1987	—	—	0.25	0.50	1.25	—
1990	—	—	0.25	0.50	1.25	—
1995	—	—	0.25	0.50	1.25	—

KM# 15 50 TOEA Composition: Copper-Nickel **Subject:** South Pacific Festival of Arts

te	Mintage	F	VF	XF	Unc	BU
80	—	—	0.75	1.25	2.75	—
80FM (U)	1,160	—	—	—	12.50	—
80FM (P)	2,125	Value: 8.50				

M# 31 50 TOEA **Composition:** Copper-Nickel **Subject:** 9th South Pacific Games

ate	Mintage	F	VF	XF	Unc	BU
991	25,000	—	—	—	5.00	—

M# 41 50 TOEA **Weight:** 13.6300 g. **Composition:** Copper Nickel **Subject:** Silver Jubilee of Bank **Obverse:** National emblem. **Reverse:** Symbolic design. **Edge:** Reeded. **Shape:** Seven sided. **Size:** 30 mm.

ate	F	VF	XF	Unc	BU
998	—	—	—	5.50	—

M# 6 KINA **Composition:** Copper-Nickel **Reverse:** Sea and river crocodiles

ate	Mintage	F	VF	XF	Unc	BU
975	2,000,000	—	1.35	2.00	3.50	—
975FM (M)	829	—	—	—	8.50	—
975FM (U)	4,134	—	—	—	3.50	—
975FM (P)	67,000	Value: 3.75				
976FM (M)	829	—	—	—	8.50	—
976FM (U)	976	—	—	—	3.50	—
976FM (P)	16,000	Value: 3.75				
977FM (M)	829	—	—	—	8.50	—
977FM (U)	603	—	—	—	12.50	—
977FM (P)	7,721	Value: 4.50				
978FM (M)	829	—	—	—	8.50	—
978FM (U)	777	—	—	—	3.50	—
978FM (P)	5,540	Value: 4.00				
979FM (M)	829	—	—	—	8.50	—
979FM (U)	1,366	—	—	—	3.50	—
979FM (P)	2,728	Value: 6.00				
980FM (U)	1,160	—	—	—	3.50	—
980FM (P)	2,125	Value: 6.00				
981FM (P)	10,000	Value: 3.75				
982FM (M)	—	—	—	—	3.50	—
982FM (P)	—	Value: 7.50				
983FM (U)	360	—	—	—	14.50	—
983FM (P)	—	Value: 7.00				
984FM (P)	—	Value: 7.00				
995	—	—	—	—	3.50	—
996	—	—	—	—	3.50	—

KM# 7 5 KINA **Composition:** Copper-Nickel **Reverse:** New Guinea eagle

Date	Mintage	F	VF	XF	Unc	BU
1975FM (M)	166	—	—	—	35.00	—
1975FM (U)	4,134	—	—	—	6.00	—
1976FM (M)	166	—	—	—	35.00	—
1976FM (U)	976	—	—	—	10.00	—
1977FM (M)	166	—	—	—	35.00	—
1977FM (U)	603	—	—	—	20.00	—
1978FM (M)	166	—	—	—	35.00	—
1978FM (U)	777	—	—	—	10.00	—
1979FM (M)	166	—	—	—	35.00	—
1979FM (U)	1,366	—	—	—	7.50	—
1980FM (U)	1,160	—	—	—	7.50	—

KM# 7a 5 KINA **Weight:** 27.6000 g. **Composition:** 0.5000 Silver .4436 oz. ASW **Reverse:** New Guinea eagle

Date	Mintage	F	VF	XF	Unc	BU
1975FM (P)	67,000	Value: 6.00				
1976FM (P)	16,000	Value: 7.00				
1977FM (P)	7,721	Value: 7.50				
1978FM (P)	5,540	Value: 7.50				
1979FM (P)	2,728	Value: 10.00				
1980FM (P)	2,125	Value: 10.00				

KM# 18 5 KINA **Weight:** 28.2800 g. **Composition:** 0.5000 Silver .4656 oz. ASW **Series:** International Year of the Child

Date	Mintage	F	VF	XF	Unc	BU
1981	8,775	—	—	—	10.00	—

KM# 20 5 KINA **Composition:** Copper-Nickel **Subject:** Defense of the Kokoda Trail **Obverse:** Similar to 20 Toea, KM#5

Date	F	VF	XF	Unc	BU
1982FM (M)	—	—	—	7.50	—

KM# 20a 5 KINA **Weight:** 28.2800 g. **Composition:** 0.9250 Silver .8411 oz. ASW **Subject:** Defense of the Kokoda Trail **Obverse:** Similar to 20 Toea, KM#5

Date	Mintage	F	VF	XF	Unc	BU
1982FM (P)	1,795	Value: 22.50				

KM# 23 5 KINA **Composition:** Copper-Nickel **Subject:** 10th anniversary - Bank of Papua New Guinea **Obverse:** Similar to 20 Toea, KM#5

Date	Mintage	F	VF	XF	Unc	BU
1983FM (U)	360	—	—	—	7.50	—

KM# 23a 5 KINA **Weight:** 28.2800 g. **Composition:** 0.9250 Silver .8411 oz. ASW **Subject:** 10th anniversary - Bank of Papua New Guinea **Obverse:** Similar to 20 Toea, KM#5

Date	Mintage	F	VF	XF	Unc	BU
1983FM (P)	673	Value: 32.50				

KM# 25 (KM25a) 5 KINA **Weight:** 28.2800 g. **Composition:** 0.9250 Silver .8411 oz. ASW **Subject:** New Parliament building

Date	F	VF	XF	Unc	BU
1984FM (P) Proof	—	Value: 32.50			
1984FM (P) Proof	—	Value: 32.50			

KM# 28 5 KINA **Weight:** 28.2800 g. **Composition:** 0.9250 Silver .8411 oz. ASW **Series:** Decade for Women

Date	Mintage	F	VF	XF	Unc	BU
1984FM Proof	1,050	Value: 28.50				

KM# 34 5 KINA **Weight:** 23.3300 g. **Composition:** 0.9250 Silver .6938 oz. ASW **Reverse:** Queen Alexandra butterfly

Date	Mintage	F	VF	XF	Unc	BU
1992FM	500	—	—	—	85.00	—
1992FM (P)	—	—	—	—	—	—

KM# 37 5 KINA **Weight:** 27.7800 g. **Composition:** 0.9000 Silver .8038 oz. ASW **Subject:** Centennial of first coinage **Reverse:** Bird of paradise

Date	Mintage	F	VF	XF	Unc	BU
ND(1994) Proof	7,500	Value: 42.50				

KM# 39 5 KINA **Weight:** 31.4700 g. **Composition:** 0.9250 Silver .9359 oz. ASW **Series:** Endangered wildlife **Obverse:** National emblem **Reverse:** 2 ribbon sweetlips fish

Date	Mintage	F	VF	XF	Unc	BU
1997 Proof	10,000	Value: 32.50				

KM# 44 5 KINA **Weight:** 31.4300 g. **Composition:** 0.9250 Silver .9347 oz. ASW **Subject:** Green Tree Python **Obverse:** National arms **Reverse:** Snake in tree **Edge:** Reeded **Size:** 38.6 mm.

Date	F	VF	XF	Unc	BU
1997	—	—	—	—	—
1998 Proof	—	Value: 45.00			

KM# 43 5 KINA **Weight:** 31.5000 g. **Composition:** 0.9250 Silver .9368 oz. ASW **Obverse:** National emblem **Reverse:** Ship "La Recherche" and native sculpture **Edge:** Reeded **Size:** 38.6 mm.

Date	F	VF	XF	Unc	BU
1997 Proof	—	Value: 32.50			

KM# 40 5 KINA **Weight:** 20.0000 g. **Composition:** 0.9000 Silver .5787 oz. ASW **Series:** Olympic Games 2000 **Obverse:** National emblem **Reverse:** Sailboarder

Date	F	VF	XF	Unc	BU
1997 Proof	—	Value: 25.00			

KM# 45 5 KINA **Weight:** 31.8500 g. **Composition:** 0.9250 Silver 0.9472 oz. ASW **Subject:** Queen Mother **Obverse:** National arms. **Reverse:** Queen Mother and Queen Elizabeth II standing behind a crowned Prince Charles. **Edge:** Reeded. **Size:** 38.6 mm.

Date	F	VF	XF	Unc	BU
1998 Proof	—	Value: 37.50			

KM# 8 10 KINA **Composition:** Copper-Nickel **Reverse:** Bird of paradise

Date	Mintage	F	VF	XF	Unc	BU
1975FM (M)	82	—	—	—	65.00	
1975FM (U)	4,134	—	—	—	7.50	
1976FM (M)	82	—	—	—	65.00	
1976FM (U)	976	—	—	—	7.50	
1978FM (M)	168	—	—	—	55.00	
1978FM (U)	777	—	—	—	15.00	
1979FM (M)	82	—	—	—	65.00	
1979FM (U)	1,366	—	—	—	10.00	
1980FM (U)	776	—	—	—	12.50	
1983FM (U)	360	—	—	—	15.00	

KM# 8a 10 KINA **Weight:** 41.6000 g. **Composition:** 0.9250 Silver 1.2371 oz. ASW **Reverse:** Bird of paradise

Date	Mintage	F	VF	XF	Unc	BU
1975FM (P)	79,000	Value: 8.00				
1976FM (P)	21,000	Value: 9.00				
1978FM (P)	7,352	Value: 10.00				
1979FM (P)	4,147	Value: 12.50				
1980FM (P)	2,752	Value: 20.00				
1983FM (P)	1,025	Value: 22.50				

KM# 11 10 KINA **Composition:** Copper-Nickel **Subject:** Silver jubilee of Queen Elizabeth II

Date	Mintage	F	VF	XF	Unc	BU
1977FM (M)	82	—	—	—	70.00	—
1977FM (U)	603	—	—	—	25.00	—

KM# 11a 10 KINA **Weight:** 40.0000 g. **Composition:** 0.9250 Silver 1.2046 oz. ASW **Subject:** Silver jubilee of Queen Elizabeth II

Date	Mintage	F	VF	XF	Unc	BU
1977FM (P)	14,000	Value: 10.00				

KM# 21 10 KINA **Composition:** Copper-Nickel **Subject:** Royal visit **Obverse:** Similar to 5 Kina, KM#7

Date	F	VF	XF	Unc	BU
1982FM (M)	—	—	—	12.50	—

KM# 21a 10 KINA **Weight:** 40.5000 g. **Composition:** 0.9250 Silver 1.2046 oz. ASW **Subject:** Royal visit **Obverse:** Similar to 5 Kina, KM#7

Date	Mintage	F	VF	XF	Unc	BU
1982FM (P)	1,185	Value: 32.50				

KM# 26 (KM26a) 10 KINA **Weight:** 35.6000 g. **Composition:** 0.9250 Silver 1.0587 oz. ASW **Subject:** Papal visit **Obverse:** Similar to 5 Kina, KM#7

Date	Mintage	F	VF	XF	Unc	BU
1984FM (P)	597	Value: 40.00				
1984FM (P)	597	Value: 40.00				

KM# 30 10 KINA **Weight:** 42.1200 g. **Composition:** 0.9250 Silver 1.2528 oz. ASW **Subject:** 9th South Pacific Games

Date	Mintage	F	VF	XF	Unc	BU
1991 Proof	1,971	Value: 27.50				

KM# 33 10 KINA **Weight:** 1.5710 g. **Composition:** 0.9990 Gold .0504 oz. AGW **Reverse:** Butterfly

Date	F	VF	XF	Unc	BU
1992 Proof	—	Value: 60.00			

KM# 33a 10 KINA **Weight:** 1.5710 g. **Composition:** 0.9950 Platinum .0502 oz. APW **Reverse:** Butterfly

Date	F	VF	XF	Unc	BU
1992 Proof	—	Value: 70.00			

KM# 46 10 KINA **Weight:** 155.5000 g. **Composition:** 0.9990 Silver 4.9944 oz. ASW **Subject:** Queen Mother **Obverse:** National arms. **Reverse:** Queen Mother and her mother. **Edge:** Reeded. **Size:** 64.9 mm. **Note:** Illustration reduced.

Date	Mintage	F	VF	XF	Unc	BU
1998 Proof	3,000	Value: 150				

KM# 36 25 KINA **Weight:** 136.0000 g. **Composition:** 0.9250 Silver And Enamel 4.0445 oz. **Reverse:** Bird of paradise **Size:** 63 mm. **Note:** Illustration reduced.

Date	Mintage	F	VF	XF	Unc	BU
ND(1994) Proof	1,000	Value: 250				

KM# 42 50 KINA **Weight:** 6.2200 g. **Composition:** 0.9000 Gold .18 oz. AGW **Obverse:** Queen's head right **Reverse:** Golden butterfly and denomination **Edge:** Reeded **Size:** 21.9 mm.

Date	F	VF	XF	Unc	BU
1993 Proof	—	Value: 110			

KM# 38 50 KINA **Weight:** 7.9700 g. **Composition:** 0.9000 Gold .2306 oz. AGW **Subject:** Centennial of first coinage **Note:** Similar to 5 Kina, KM#37.

Date	Mintage	F	VF	XF	Unc	BU
1994 Proof	1,500	Value: 200				

KM# 9 100 KINA **Weight:** 9.5700 g. **Composition:** 0.9000 Gold .2769 oz. AGW **Subject:** Independence

Date	Mintage	F	VF	XF	Unc	BU
1975FM (M)	100	—	—	—	225	—
1975FM (U)	8,081	—	—	—	100	—
1975FM (P)	18,000	Value: 100				

KM# 10 100 KINA **Weight:** 9.5700 g. **Composition:** 0.9000 Gold .2769 oz. AGW **Subject:** 1st anniversary of independence

Date	Mintage	F	VF	XF	Unc	BU
1976FM (M)	100	—	—	—	225	—
1976FM (U)	250	—	—	—	150	—
1976FM (P)	8,020	Value: 120				

KM# 12 100 KINA **Weight:** 9.5700 g. **Composition:** 0.9000 Gold .2769 oz. AGW **Reverse:** Papuan hornbill

Date	Mintage	F	VF	XF	Unc	BU
1977FM (M)	100	—	—	—	200	—
1977FM (U)	362	—	—	—	145	—
1977FM (P)	3,460	Value: 125				

KM# 13 100 KINA **Weight:** 9.5700 g. **Composition:** 0.9000 Gold .2769 oz. AGW **Reverse:** Bird wing butterfly

Date	Mintage	F	VF	XF	Unc	BU
1978FM (U)	400	—	—	—	225	—
1978FM (P)	4,751	Value: 175				

KM# 14 100 KINA **Weight:** 9.5700 g. **Composition:** 0.9000 Gold .2769 oz. AGW **Subject:** 4 faces of the nation

Date	Mintage	F	VF	XF	Unc	BU
1979FM (M)	102	—	—	—	180	—
1979FM (U)	286	—	—	—	160	—
1979FM (P)	3,492	Value: 125				

KM# 16 100 KINA **Weight:** 7.8300 g. **Composition:** 0.5000 Gold .1258 oz. AGW **Subject:** South Pacific Festival of Arts

Date	Mintage	F	VF	XF	Unc	BU
1980 Proof	7,500	Value: 110				

KM# 17 100 KINA **Weight:** 9.5700 g. **Composition:** 0.9000 Gold .2769 oz. AGW **Subject:** 5th anniversary of independence

Date	Mintage	F	VF	XF	Unc	BU
1980FM (M)	30	—	—	—	350	—
1980FM (P)	1,118	Value: 175				

KM# 19 100 KINA **Weight:** 9.5700 g. **Composition:** 0.9000 Gold .2769 oz. AGW **Obverse:** Prime Minister Sir Julius Chan bust facing left

Date	Mintage	F	VF	XF	Unc	BU
1981FM (P)	685	Value: 175				

KM# 22 100 KINA **Weight:** 9.5700 g. **Composition:** 0.9000 Gold .2769 oz. AGW **Subject:** Royal Visit

Date	Mintage	F	VF	XF	Unc	BU
1982FM (P)	484	Value: 225				

KM# 24 100 KINA **Weight:** 9.5700 g. **Composition:** 0.9000 Gold .2769 oz. AGW **Subject:** 10th anniversary - Bank of Papua New Guinea

Date	Mintage	F	VF	XF	Unc	BU
1983FM (P)	378	Value: 260				

KM# 27 100 KINA **Weight:** 9.5700 g. **Composition:** 0.9000 Gold .2769 oz. AGW **Subject:** 100th anniversary - founding of British and German protectorates

Date	Mintage	F	VF	XF	Unc	BU
1984FM (P)	274	Value: 250				

KM# 29 100 KINA **Weight:** 9.5700 g. **Composition:** 0.9000 Gold .2769 oz. AGW **Reverse:** Queen Alexandra butterfly

Date	Mintage	F	VF	XF	Unc	BU
1990	—	—	—	—	225	—
1990 Proof	Est. 5,000	Value: 300				
1992 Proof	Est. 5,000	Value: 325				

KM# 29a 100 KINA **Weight:** 9.5700 g. **Composition:** 0.9950 Platinum .3061 oz. APW **Reverse:** Queen Alexandra butterfly

Date	Mintage	F	VF	XF	Unc	BU
1992	—	—	—	—	235	—
1992 Proof	Est. 5,000	Value: 285				

KM# 35 100 KINA **Weight:** 9.5700 g. **Composition:** 0.9000 Gold .2769 oz. AGW **Subject:** 9th South Pacific Games

Date	Mintage	F	VF	XF	Unc	BU
1991 Proof	5,000	Value: 150				

PIEFORTS

KM#	Date	Mintage	Identification	Mkt Val
P1	1982	39	5 Kina. KM18.	100

The Republic of Paraguay, a landlocked country in the heart of South America surrounded by Argentina, Bolivia and Brazil has an area of 157,048 sq. mi. (406,750 sq. km.) and a population of *4.5 million, 95 percent of whom are of mixed Spanish and Indian descent. Capital: Asuncion. The country is predominantly agrarian, with no important mineral deposits or oil reserves. Meat, timber, hides, oilseeds, tobacco and cotton account for 70 percent of Paraguay's export revenue.

Paraguay was first visited by a ship-wrecked Spaniard named Alejo Garcia, in 1524. The interior was explored by Sebastian Cabot in 1527 and 1528, when he sailed up the Parana and Paraguay rivers. Asuncion, which would become the center of a Spanish colonial province embracing much of southern South America, was established by the Spanish explorer Juan de Salazar on Aug. 15,1537. For 150 years the history of Paraguay was largely the history of the agricultural colonies established by the Jesuits in the south and east to Christianize the Indians. In 1811, following the outbreak of the South American wars of independence, Paraguayan patriots over-threw the local Spanish authorities and proclaimed their country's independence.

During the Triple Alliance War (1864-1870) in which Paraguay faced Argentina, Brazil and Uruguay, Asuncion's ladies gathered in an Assembly on Feb. 24, 1867 and decided to give up their jewelry in order to help the national defense. The President of the Republic, Francisco Solano Lopez accepted the offering and ordered one twentieth of it be used to mint the first Paraguayan gold coins according to the Decree of the 11th of Sept.,1867.

Two dies were made, one by Bouvet, and another by an American, Leonard Charles, while only the die made by Bouvet was eventually used.

MONETARY SYSTEM

100 Centavos (Centesimos) = 1 Peso

MINT MARKS

HF – LeLocle (Swiss)

REPUBLIC

DECIMAL COINAGE

100 Centavos (Centesimos) = Peso

KM# 6 5 CENTAVOS **Composition:** Copper-Nickel

Date	Mintage	F	VF	XF	Unc	BU
1903	600,000	2.00	6.00	20.00	50.00	—

KM# 9 5 CENTAVOS **Composition:** Copper-Nickel

Date	Mintage	F	VF	XF	Unc	BU
1908	400,000	2.50	8.00	30.00	75.00	—

KM# 7 10 CENTAVOS **Composition:** Copper-Nickel

Date	Mintage	F	VF	XF	Unc	BU
1903	1,200,000	1.50	4.00	15.00	35.00	—

KM# 10 10 CENTAVOS **Composition:** Copper-Nickel

Date	Mintage	F	VF	XF	Unc	BU
1908	800,000	2.50	6.50	25.00	75.00	—

KM# 8 20 CENTAVOS **Composition:** Copper-Nickel

Date	Mintage	F	VF	XF	Unc	BU
1903	750,000	1.50	4.00	15.00	45.00	—

KM# 11 20 CENTAVOS **Composition:** Copper-Nickel

Date	Mintage	F	VF	XF	Unc	BU
1908	1,000,000	2.50	7.00	35.00	80.00	—

KM# 12 50 CENTAVOS **Composition:** Copper-Nickel

Date	Mintage	F	VF	XF	Unc	BU
1925	4,000,000	0.50	1.50	5.00	15.00	—

KM# 15 50 CENTAVOS **Composition:** Aluminum

Date	Mintage	F	VF	XF	Unc	BU
1938	400,000	0.50	1.00	3.50	10.00	—

KM# 13 PESO **Composition:** Copper-Nickel

Date	Mintage	F	VF	XF	Unc	BU
1925	3,500,000	0.50	1.00	5.00	10.00	—

KM# 16 PESO **Composition:** Aluminum

Date	F	VF	XF	Unc	BU
1938	0.50	1.50	3.00	8.00	—

KM# 14 2 PESOS **Composition:** Copper-Nickel

Date	Mintage	F	VF	XF	Unc	BU
1925	2,500,000	0.50	1.00	6.00	12.00	—

KM# 17 2 PESOS **Composition:** Aluminum

Date	F	VF	XF	Unc	BU
1938	0.50	1.50	3.00	10.00	—

KM# 18 5 PESOS **Composition:** Copper-Nickel

Date	Mintage	F	VF	XF	Unc	BU
1939	4,000,000	1.00	3.50	10.00	20.00	—

KM# 19 10 PESOS **Composition:** Copper-Nickel

Date	Mintage	F	VF	XF	Unc	BU
1939	4,000,000	1.00	2.00	7.00	18.00	—

REFORM COINAGE

100 Centimos = 1 Guarani

KM# 20 CENTIMO **Composition:** Aluminum-Bronze **Obverse:** Flower

Date	Mintage	F	VF	XF	Unc	BU
1944	3,500,000	0.10	0.50	1.00	3.50	—
1948HF	2,000,000	0.10	0.50	1.00	3.50	—
1950HF	1,096,000	0.10	0.25	0.75	2.50	—

KM# 21 5 CENTIMOS **Composition:** Aluminum-Bronze **Obverse:** Passion flower

Date	Mintage	F	VF	XF	Unc	BU
1944	2,195,000	0.10	0.50	1.00	4.00	—
1947HF	13,111,000	0.10	0.20	0.50	2.00	—

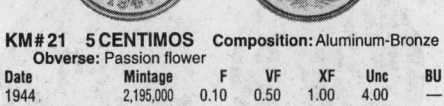

KM# 22 10 CENTIMOS **Composition:** Aluminum-Bronze **Obverse:** Orchid

Date	Mintage	F	VF	XF	Unc	BU
1944	975,000	0.25	0.75	2.50	5.00	—
1947	6,656,000	0.10	0.25	0.50	1.00	—
1947HF	—	0.10	0.25	0.50	1.00	—

KM# 25 10 CENTIMOS **Composition:** Aluminum-Bronze **Obverse:** Orchid

Date	Mintage	F	VF	XF	Unc	BU
1953	5,000,000	0.10	0.15	0.30	0.75	—
1953 Proof; 1 known	—	Value: 350				

Note: Medal die rotation

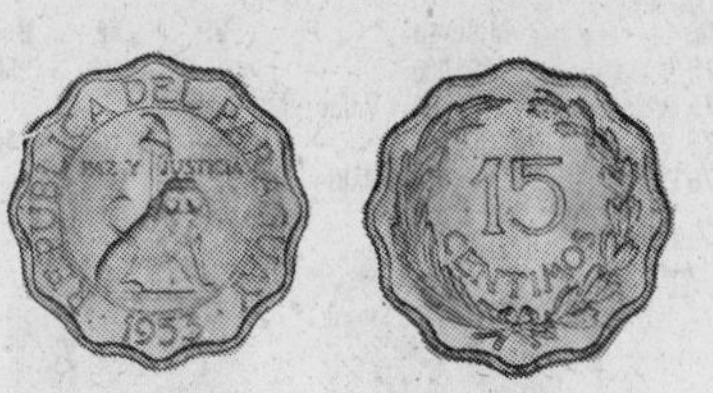

KM# 26 15 CENTIMOS **Composition:** Aluminum-Bronze

Date	Mintage	F	VF	XF	Unc	BU
1953	5,000,000	0.10	0.20	0.35	1.00	—
1953 Proof; 1 known	—	Value: 350				

Note: Medal die rotation

KM# 23 25 CENTIMOS **Composition:** Aluminum-Bronze **Obverse:** Orchid

Date	Mintage	F	VF	XF	Unc	BU
1944	700,000	0.25	1.00	3.00	12.00	—
1948HF	600,000	0.25	0.75	2.50	9.00	—
1951HF	1,000,000	0.25	0.75	1.25	3.50	—

KM# 27 25 CENTIMOS **Composition:** Aluminum-Bronze

Date	Mintage	F	VF	XF	Unc	BU
1953	2,000,000	0.10	0.15	0.30	1.00	—
1953 Proof; 1 known	—	Value: 400				

Note: Medal die rotation

KM# 24 50 CENTIMOS **Composition:** Aluminum-Bronze

Date	Mintage	F	VF	XF	Unc	BU
1944	2,485,000	0.25	1.00	2.00	7.00	—
1951	2,893,000	0.25	0.50	1.25	3.00	—

KM# 28 50 CENTIMOS **Composition:** Aluminum-Bronze

Date	Mintage	F	VF	XF	Unc	BU
1953	2,000,000	0.10	0.15	0.30	1.00	—
1953 Proof; 1 known	—	Value: 400				

Note: Medal die rotation

KM# 151 GUARANI **Composition:** Stainless Steel

Date	Mintage	F	VF	XF	Unc	BU
1975	10,000,000	—	—	0.15	0.50	—
1975 Proof	1,000	Value: 6.00				
1976	12,000,000	—	—	0.10	0.40	—
1976 Proof	1,000	Value: 8.00				

KM# 165 GUARANI **Composition:** Stainless Steel **Series:** F.A.O. **Note:** Varieties exist.

Date	Mintage	F	VF	XF	Unc	BU
1978	15,000,000	—	—	0.15	0.50	—
1980	13,000,000	—	—	0.15	0.50	—
1980 Proof	1,000	Value: 6.00				
1984	15,000,000	—	—	0.10	0.30	—
1986	15,000,000	—	—	0.10	0.30	—
1988	15,000,000	—	—	0.10	0.30	—

KM# 192 GUARANI **Composition:** Brass Plated Steel **Series:** F.A.O.

Date	Mintage	F	VF	XF	Unc	BU
1993	5,000,000	—	—	0.15	0.50	—

KM# 193 GUARANI **Weight:** 27.0000 g. **Composition:** 0.9250 Silver .8030 oz. ASW **Subject:** Encuentro De Dos Mundos **Obverse:** Paraguayan arms in circle of arms **Reverse:** Dancer

Date	F	VF	XF	Unc	BU
1997 Proof	—	Value: 45.00			

KM# 196 GUARANI **Weight:** 27.1000 g. **Composition:** 0.9250 Silver 0.8059 oz. ASW **Subject:** Ibero-America **Series Obverse:** National arms in circle of arms **Reverse:** Cowboy on horse **Edge:** Reeded **Size:** 40 mm.

Date	F	VF	XF	Unc	BU
2000 Proof	—	Value: 60.00			

KM# 152 5 GUARANIES **Composition:** Stainless Steel

Date	Mintage	F	VF	XF	Unc	BU
1975	7,500,000	—	—	0.15	0.50	—
1975 Proof	1,000	Value: 6.00				

KM# 166 5 GUARANIES **Composition:** Stainless Steel **Series:** F.A.O. **Note:** Varieties exist.

Date	Mintage	F	VF	XF	Unc	BU
1978	10,000,000	—	—	0.15	0.60	—
1980	12,000,000	—	—	0.15	0.60	—
1980 Proof	1,000	Value: 6.00				
1984	15,000,000	—	—	0.10	0.40	—
1986	15,000,000	—	—	0.10	0.40	—

KM# 166a 5 GUARANIES **Composition:** Nickel-Bronze **Series:** F.A.O.

Date	Mintage	F	VF	XF	Unc	BU
1992	15,000,000	—	—	0.10	0.30	—

KM# 153 10 GUARANIES **Composition:** Stainless Steel

Date	Mintage	F	VF	XF	Unc	BU
1975	10,000,000	—	0.10	0.20	0.75	—
1975 Proof	1,000	Value: 8.00				
1976	10,000,000	—	0.10	0.20	0.75	—
1976 Proof	1,000	Value: 10.00				

KM# 167 10 GUARANIES **Composition:** Stainless Steel **Series:** F.A.O. **Note:** Varieties exist.

Date	Mintage	F	VF	XF	Unc	BU
1978	15,000,000	—	0.10	0.20	0.75	—
1980	15,000,000	—	0.10	0.20	0.75	—
1980 Proof	1,000	Value: 8.00				
1984	20,000,000	—	0.10	0.15	0.50	—
1986	35,000,000	—	0.10	0.15	0.50	—
1988	40,000,000	—	0.10	0.15	0.50	—

KM# 178 10 GUARANIES **Composition:** Nickel-Bronze **Series:** F.A.O. **Reverse:** Cow

Date	Mintage	F	VF	XF	Unc	BU
1990	40,000,000	—	—	0.10	0.40	—
1996	—	—	—	0.10	0.40	—

KM# 154 50 GUARANIES **Composition:** Stainless Steel

Date	Mintage	F	VF	XF	Unc	BU
1975	9,500,000	0.20	0.40	0.60	1.25	—
1975 Proof	1,000	Value: 10.00				

KM# 169 50 GUARANIES **Composition:** Stainless Steel **Obverse:** General Estigarribia **Reverse:** Acaray River Dam **Note:** Varieties exist.

Date	Mintage	F	VF	XF	Unc	BU
1980	10,700,000	0.20	0.40	0.60	1.25	—
1980 Proof	1,000	Value: 10.00				
1986	15,000,000	0.20	0.40	0.60	1.25	—
1988	25,000,000	0.20	0.30	0.50	1.00	—

KM# 191 50 GUARANIES **Composition:** Copper-Zinc-Nickel **Obverse:** General Estigarribia **Reverse:** Acaray River Dam

Date	Mintage	F	VF	XF	Unc	BU
1992	35,000,000	—	—	—	0.75	—
1995	35,000,000	—	—	—	0.75	—

KM# 177 100 GUARANIES **Composition:** Copper-Zinc-Nickel

Date	Mintage	F	VF	XF	Unc	BU
1990	35,000,000	—	—	—	2.25	—

KM# 177a 100 GUARANIES **Composition:** Brass Plated Steel

Date	Mintage	F	VF	XF	Unc	BU
1993	35,000,000	—	—	—	1.50	—
1995	35,000,000	—	—	—	1.50	—
1996	—	—	—	—	1.50	—

KM# 31 150 GUARANIES **Weight:** 25.0000 g. **Composition:** 0.9990 Silver .8030 oz. ASW **Obverse:** Arms **Reverse:** Bust of General A. Stroessner facing

Date	Mintage	F	VF	XF	Unc	BU
1972 Proof	Est. 10,000	Value: 60.00				

KM# 32 150 GUARANIES **Weight:** 25.0000 g. **Composition:** 0.9990 Silver .8030 oz. ASW **Subject:** Munich Olympics **Obverse:** Arms **Reverse:** Runner

Date	Mintage	F	VF	XF	Unc	BU
1972 Proof	Est. 10,000	Value: 70.00				

KM# 33 150 GUARANIES **Weight:** 25.0000 g. **Composition:** 0.9990 Silver .8030 oz. ASW **Subject:** Munich Olympics **Obverse:** Arms **Reverse:** Broad jumper

Date	Mintage	F	VF	XF	Unc	BU
1972 Proof	Est. 10,000	Value: 70.00				

KM# 34 150 GUARANIES **Weight:** 25.0000 g. **Composition:** 0.9990 Silver .8030 oz. ASW **Subject:** Munich Olympics **Obverse:** Arms **Reverse:** Soccer

Date	Mintage	F	VF	XF	Unc	BU
1972 Proof	Est. 10,000	Value: 70.00				

KM# 35 150 GUARANIES **Weight:** 25.0000 g. **Composition:** 0.9990 Silver .8030 oz. ASW **Subject:** Munich Olympics **Obverse:** Arms **Reverse:** Hurdler

Date	Mintage	F	VF	XF	Unc	BU
1972 Proof	Est. 10,000	Value: 70.00				

KM# 36 150 GUARANIES **Weight:** 25.0000 g. **Composition:** 0.9990 Silver .8030 oz. ASW **Subject:** Munich Olympics **Obverse:** Arms **Reverse:** High jumper

Date	Mintage	F	VF	XF	Unc	BU
1972 Proof	Est. 10,000	Value: 70.00				

KM# 37 150 GUARANIES **Weight:** 25.0000 g. **Composition:** 0.9990 Silver .8030 oz. ASW **Subject:** Munich Olympics **Obverse:** Arms **Reverse:** Boxer

Date	Mintage	F	VF	XF	Unc	BU
1973 Proof	Est. 10,000	Value: 70.00				

KM# 59 150 GUARANIES **Weight:** 25.0000 g. **Composition:** 0.9990 Silver .8030 oz. ASW **Obverse:** Arms **Reverse:** Bust of Mariscal Jose F. Estigarribia facing

Date	Mintage	F	VF	XF	Unc	BU
1973 Proof	Est. 10,000	Value: 55.00				

KM# 60 150 GUARANIES **Weight:** 25.0000 g. **Composition:** 0.9990 Silver .8030 oz. ASW **Obverse:** Arms **Reverse:** Bust of Mariscal Francisco Solano Lopez facing

Date	Mintage	F	VF	XF	Unc	BU
1973 Proof	Est. 10,000	Value: 55.00				

KM# 61 150 GUARANIES **Weight:** 25.0000 g. **Composition:** 0.9990 Silver .8030 oz. ASW **Obverse:** Arms **Reverse:** Bust of General Jose E. Diaz facing

Date	Mintage	F	VF	XF	Unc	BU
1973 Proof	Est. 10,000	Value: 52.50				

KM# 62 150 GUARANIES **Weight:** 25.0000 g. **Composition:** 0.9990 Silver .8030 oz. ASW **Obverse:** Arms **Reverse:** Bust of General Bernardino Caballero facing

Date	Mintage	F	VF	XF	Unc	BU
1973 Proof	Est. 10,000	Value: 52.50				

KM# 63 150 GUARANIES **Weight:** 25.0000 g. **Composition:** 0.9990 Silver .8030 oz. ASW **Obverse:** Arms **Reverse:** Teotihucana Culture sculpture

Date	Mintage	F	VF	XF	Unc	BU
1973 Proof	Est. 10,000	Value: 52.50				

KM# 64 150 GUARANIES **Weight:** 25.0000 g. **Composition:** 0.9990 Silver .8030 oz. ASW **Obverse:** Arms **Reverse:** Huasteca Culture sculpture

Date	Mintage	F	VF	XF	Unc	BU
1973 Proof	Est. 10,000	Value: 52.50				

KM# 65 150 GUARANIES **Weight:** 25.0000 g. **Composition:** 0.9990 Silver .8030 oz. ASW **Obverse:** Arms **Reverse:** Mixteca Culture animal sculpture

Date	Mintage	F	VF	XF	Unc	BU
1973 Proof	Est. 10,000	Value: 52.50				

KM# 66 150 GUARANIES **Weight:** 25.0000 g. **Composition:** 0.9990 Silver .8030 oz. ASW **Obverse:** Arms **Reverse:** Veracruz Ceramica Vase

Date	Mintage	F	VF	XF	Unc	BU
1973 Proof	Est. 10,000	Value: 52.50				

KM# 67 150 GUARANIES **Weight:** 25.0000 g. **Composition:** 0.9990 Silver .8030 oz. ASW **Obverse:** Arms **Reverse:** Veracruz Culture sculpture

Date	Mintage	F	VF	XF	Unc	BU
1973 Proof	Est. 10,000	Value: 52.50				

KM# 68 150 GUARANIES **Weight:** 25.0000 g. **Composition:** 0.9990 Silver .8030 oz. ASW **Obverse:** Arms **Reverse:** Bust of Albrecht Durer facing

Date	Mintage	F	VF	XF	Unc	BU
1973 Proof	Est. 10,000	Value: 65.00				

KM# 69 150 GUARANIES **Weight:** 25.0000 g. **Composition:** 0.9990 Silver .8030 oz. ASW **Obverse:** Arms **Reverse:** Bust of Johann Wolfgang Goethe facing

Date	Mintage	F	VF	XF	Unc	BU
1973 Proof	Est. 10,000	Value: 65.00				

KM# 107 150 GUARANIES **Weight:** 25.0000 g. **Composition:** 0.9990 Silver .8030 oz. ASW **Obverse:** Arms **Reverse:** Bust of President Abraham Lincoln left

Date	Mintage	F	VF	XF	Unc	BU
1974 Proof	Est. 10,000	Value: 75.00				

KM# 108 150 GUARANIES **Weight:** 25.0000 g. **Composition:** 0.9990 Silver .8030 oz. ASW **Obverse:** Arms **Reverse:** Bust of Ludwig van Beethoven half left

Date	Mintage	F	VF	XF	Unc	BU
1974 Proof	Est. 10,000	Value: 75.00				

KM# 109 150 GUARANIES **Weight:** 25.0000 g. **Composition:** 0.9990 Silver .8030 oz. ASW **Obverse:** Arms **Reverse:** Bust of Otto von Bismarck right

Date	Mintage	F	VF	XF	Unc	BU
1974 Proof	Est. 10,000	Value: 75.00				

KM# 110 150 GUARANIES **Weight:** 25.0000 g. **Composition:** 0.9990 Silver .8030 oz. ASW **Obverse:** Arms **Reverse:** Bust of Albert Einstein left

Date	Mintage	F	VF	XF	Unc	BU
1974 Proof	Est. 10,000	Value: 85.00				

KM# 111 150 GUARANIES **Weight:** 25.0000 g. **Composition:** 0.9990 Silver .8030 oz. ASW **Obverse:** Arms **Reverse:** Bust of Giuseppe Garibaldi facing

Date	Mintage	F	VF	XF	Unc	BU
1974 Proof	Est. 10,000	Value: 65.00				

KM# 112 150 GUARANIES **Weight:** 25.0000 g. **Composition:** 0.9990 Silver .8030 oz. ASW **Obverse:** Arms **Reverse:** Bust of Alessandro Manzoni facing

Date	Mintage	F	VF	XF	Unc	BU
1974 Proof	Est. 10,000	Value: 57.50				

KM# 113 150 GUARANIES **Weight:** 25.0000 g. **Composition:** 0.9990 Silver .8030 oz. ASW **Obverse:** Arms **Reverse:** William Tell and son standing facing

Date	Mintage	F	VF	XF	Unc	BU
1974 Proof	Est. 10,000	Value: 57.50				

KM# 114 150 GUARANIES **Weight:** 25.0000 g. **Composition:** 0.9990 Silver .8030 oz. ASW **Obverse:** Arms **Reverse:** Bust of President John F. Kennedy left

Date	Mintage	F	VF	XF	Unc	BU
1974 Proof	Est. 10,000	Value: 55.00				

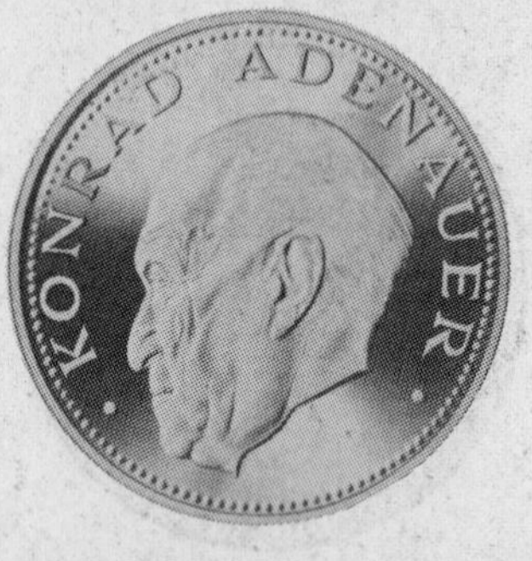

KM# 115 150 GUARANIES **Weight:** 25.0000 g. **Composition:** 0.9990 Silver .8030 oz. ASW **Obverse:** Arms **Reverse:** Bust of Konrad Adenauer left

Date	Mintage	F	VF	XF	Unc	BU
1974 Proof	Est. 10,000	Value: 65.00				

KM# 116 150 GUARANIES **Weight:** 25.0000 g. **Composition:** 0.9990 Silver .8030 oz. ASW **Obverse:** Arms **Reverse:** Bust of Winston Churchill left

Date	Mintage	F	VF	XF	Unc	BU
1974 Proof	Est. 10,000	Value: 55.00				

KM# 117 150 GUARANIES **Weight:** 25.0000 g. **Composition:** 0.9990 Silver .8030 oz. ASW **Obverse:** Arms **Reverse:** Bust of Pope John XXIII left

Date	Mintage	F	VF	XF	Unc	BU
1974 Proof	Est. 10,000	Value: 65.00				

KM# 118 150 GUARANIES **Weight:** 25.0000 g. **Composition:** 0.9990 Silver .8030 oz. ASW **Obverse:** Arms **Reverse:** Bust of Pope Paul VI left

Date	Mintage	F	VF	XF	Unc	BU
1974 Proof	Est. 10,000	Value: 65.00				

KM# 155 150 GUARANIES **Weight:** 25.0000 g. **Composition:** 0.9990 Silver .8030 oz. ASW **Obverse:** Arms **Reverse:** Parliament building of Paraguay

Date	Mintage	F	VF	XF	Unc	BU
1975 Proof	Est. 10,000	Value: 55.00				

KM# 156 150 GUARANIES **Weight:** 25.0000 g. **Composition:** 0.9990 Silver .8030 oz. ASW **Subject:** Apollo 11 Mission **Obverse:** Arms **Reverse:** Eagle landing on moon with earth at left

Date	Mintage	F	VF	XF	Unc	BU
1975 Proof	Est. 10,000	Value: 65.00				

KM# 157 150 GUARANIES **Weight:** 25.0000 g. **Composition:** 0.9990 Silver .8030 oz. ASW **Subject:** Apollo 15 Mission **Obverse:** Arms

Date	Mintage	F	VF	XF	Unc	BU
1975 Proof	Est. 10,000	Value: 65.00				

KM# 158 150 GUARANIES **Weight:** 25.0000 g. **Composition:** 0.9990 Silver .8030 oz. ASW **Obverse:** Arms **Reverse:** Friendship Bridge

Date	Mintage	F	VF	XF	Unc	BU
1975 Proof	Est. 10,000	Value: 57.50				

KM# 159 150 GUARANIES **Weight:** 25.0000 g. **Composition:** 0.9990 Silver .8030 oz. ASW **Obverse:** Arms **Reverse:** Holy Trinity Church

Date	Mintage	F	VF	XF	Unc	BU
1975 Proof	Est. 10,000	Value: 57.50				

KM# 160 150 GUARANIES **Weight:** 25.0000 g. **Composition:** 0.9990 Silver .8030 oz. ASW **Obverse:** Arms **Reverse:** Ruins of Humaita

Date	Mintage	F	VF	XF	Unc	BU
1975 Proof	Est. 10,000	Value: 57.50				

KM# 29 300 GUARANIES **Weight:** 26.6000 g. **Composition:** 0.7200 Silver .6157 oz. ASW **Subject:** 4th Term of President Stroessner **Obverse:** Lion arms **Reverse:** Bust of President A. Stroessner left

Date	Mintage	F	VF	XF	Unc	BU
1968	250,000	—	—	6.00	9.00	—

KM# 194 500 GUARANIES **Composition:** Brass **Obverse:** Bust of General Bernardino Caballero facing **Reverse:** Central Bank of Paraguay

Date	F	VF	XF	Unc	BU
1997	—	—	—	2.50	—

KM# 195 500 GUARANIES **Composition:** Brass **Obverse:** Bust of General Bernardino Caballero facing **Reverse:** Central Bank of Paraguay above denomination

Date	Mintage	F	VF	XF	Unc	BU
1998	15,000	—	—	—	2.50	—

KM# 38 1500 GUARANIES **Weight:** 10.7000 g. **Composition:** 0.9000 Gold .3096 oz. AGW **Obverse:** Arms **Reverse:** Bust of General A. Stroessner facing

Date	Mintage	F	VF	XF	Unc	BU
1972 Proof	Est. 1,500	Value: 300				

KM# 39 1500 GUARANIES **Weight:** 10.7000 g. **Composition:** 0.9000 Gold .3096 oz. AGW **Subject:** Munich Olympics **Obverse:** Arms **Reverse:** Runner

Date	Mintage	F	VF	XF	Unc	BU
1972 Proof	Est. 1,500	Value: 750				

KM# 40 1500 GUARANIES **Weight:** 10.7000 g. **Composition:** 0.9000 Gold .3096 oz. AGW **Subject:** Munich Olympics **Obverse:** Arms **Reverse:** Broad jumper

Date	Mintage	F	VF	XF	Unc	BU
1972 Proof	Est. 1,500	Value: 750				

KM# 41 1500 GUARANIES **Weight:** 10.7000 g. **Composition:** 0.9000 Gold .3096 oz. AGW **Subject:** Munich Olympics **Obverse:** Arms **Reverse:** Soccer

Date	Mintage	F	VF	XF	Unc	BU
1972 Proof	Est. 1,500	Value: 750				

KM# 42 1500 GUARANIES **Weight:** 10.7000 g. **Composition:** 0.9000 Gold .3096 oz. AGW **Subject:** Munich Olympics **Obverse:** Arms **Reverse:** Hurdler

Date	Mintage	F	VF	XF	Unc	BU
1972 Proof	Est. 1,500	Value: 750				

KM# 43 1500 GUARANIES **Weight:** 10.7000 g. **Composition:** 0.9000 Gold .3096 oz. AGW **Subject:** Munich Olympics **Obverse:** Arms **Reverse:** High Jumper

Date	Mintage	F	VF	XF	Unc	BU
1973 Proof	1,500	Value: 750				

KM# 44 1500 GUARANIES **Weight:** 10.7000 g. **Composition:** 0.9000 Gold .3096 oz. AGW **Subject:** Munich Olympics **Obverse:** Arms **Reverse:** Boxer

Date	Mintage	F	VF	XF	Unc	BU
1973 Proof	Est. 1,500	Value: 750				

KM# 70 1500 GUARANIES **Weight:** 10.7000 g. **Composition:** 0.9000 Gold .3096 oz. AGW **Obverse:** Arms **Reverse:** Bust of Jose F. Estigarribia facing

Date	Mintage	F	VF	XF	Unc	BU
1973 Proof	Est. 1,500	Value: 400				

KM# 71 1500 GUARANIES **Weight:** 10.7000 g. **Composition:** 0.9000 Gold .3096 oz. AGW **Obverse:** Arms **Reverse:** Bust of Mariscal Francisco Solano Lopez facing

Date	Mintage	F	VF	XF	Unc	BU
1973 Proof	Est. 1,500	Value: 400				

KM# 72 1500 GUARANIES **Weight:** 10.7000 g. **Composition:** 0.9000 Gold .3096 oz. AGW **Obverse:** Arms **Reverse:** Bust of General Jose E. Diaz facing

Date	Mintage	F	VF	XF	Unc	BU
1973 Proof	Est. 1,500	Value: 400				

KM# 73 1500 GUARANIES **Weight:** 10.7000 g. **Composition:** 0.9000 Gold .3096 oz. AGW **Obverse:** Arms **Reverse:** Busty of General Bernardino Caballero facing

Date	Mintage	F	VF	XF	Unc	BU
1973 Proof	Est. 1,500	Value: 400				

KM# 74 1500 GUARANIES **Weight:** 10.7000 g. **Composition:** 0.9000 Gold .3096 oz. AGW **Obverse:** Arms **Reverse:** Teotihucana Culture sculpture

Date	Mintage	F	VF	XF	Unc	BU
1973 Proof	Est. 1,500	Value: 400				

KM# 75 1500 GUARANIES **Weight:** 10.7000 g. **Composition:** 0.9000 Gold .3096 oz. AGW **Obverse:** Arms **Reverse:** Huasteca Culture sculpture

Date	Mintage	F	VF	XF	Unc	BU
1973 Proof	Est. 1,500	Value: 400				

KM# 76 1500 GUARANIES **Weight:** 10.7000 g. **Composition:** 0.9000 Gold .3096 oz. AGW **Obverse:** Arms **Reverse:** Mixteca Culture sculpture

Date	Mintage	F	VF	XF	Unc	BU
1973 Proof	Est. 1,500	Value: 400				

KM# 77 1500 GUARANIES **Weight:** 10.7000 g. **Composition:** 0.9000 Gold .3096 oz. AGW **Obverse:** Arms **Reverse:** Veracruz Ceramica vase

Date	Mintage	F	VF	XF	Unc	BU
1973 Proof	Est. 1,500	Value: 400				

KM# 78 1500 GUARANIES **Weight:** 10.7000 g. **Composition:** 0.9000 Gold .3096 oz. AGW **Obverse:** Arms **Reverse:** Veracruz Culture sculpture

Date	Mintage	F	VF	XF	Unc	BU
1973 Proof	Est. 1,500	Value: 400				

KM# 79 1500 GUARANIES **Weight:** 10.7000 g. **Composition:** 0.9000 Gold .3096 oz. AGW **Obverse:** Arms **Reverse:** Bust of Albrecht Durer facing

Date	Mintage	F	VF	XF	Unc	BU
1973 Proof	Est. 1,500	Value: 400				

KM# 80 1500 GUARANIES **Weight:** 10.7000 g. **Composition:** 0.9000 Gold .3096 oz. AGW **Obverse:** Arms **Reverse:** Bust of Johann Wolfgang Goethe facing

Date	Mintage	F	VF	XF	Unc	BU
1973 Proof	Est. 1,500	Value: 400				

KM# 119 1500 GUARANIES **Weight:** 10.7000 g. **Composition:** 0.9000 Gold .3096 oz. AGW **Obverse:** Arms **Reverse:** Bust of President Abraham Lincoln left

Date	Mintage	F	VF	XF	Unc	BU
1974 Proof	Est. 1,500	Value: 400				

KM# 120 1500 GUARANIES **Weight:** 10.7000 g. **Composition:** 0.9000 Gold .3096 oz. AGW **Obverse:** Arms **Reverse:** Bust of Ludwig van Beethoven half left

Date	Mintage	F	VF	XF	Unc	BU
1974 Proof	Est. 1,500	Value: 750				

KM# 121 1500 GUARANIES **Weight:** 10.7000 g. **Composition:** 0.9000 Gold .3096 oz. AGW **Obverse:** Arms **Reverse:** Bust of Otto von Bismarck right

Date	Mintage	F	VF	XF	Unc	BU
1974 Proof	Est. 1,500	Value: 400				

KM# 122 1500 GUARANIES **Weight:** 10.7000 g. **Composition:** 0.9000 Gold .3096 oz. AGW **Obverse:** Arms **Reverse:** Bust of Albert Einstein left

Date	Mintage	F	VF	XF	Unc	BU
1974 Proof	Est. 1,500	Value: 400				

KM# 123 1500 GUARANIES **Weight:** 10.7000 g. **Composition:** 0.9000 Gold .3096 oz. AGW **Obverse:** Arms **Reverse:** Bust of Giuseppe Garibaldi facing

Date	Mintage	F	VF	XF	Unc	BU
1974 Proof	Est. 1,500	Value: 400				

KM# 124 1500 GUARANIES **Weight:** 10.7000 g. **Composition:** 0.9000 Gold .3096 oz. AGW **Obverse:** Arms **Reverse:** Bust of Alessandro Manzoni facing

Date	Mintage	F	VF	XF	Unc	BU
1974 Proof	Est. 1,500	Value: 400				

KM# 125 1500 GUARANIES **Weight:** 10.7000 g. **Composition:** 0.9000 Gold .3096 oz. AGW **Obverse:** Arms **Reverse:** William Tell and son standing facing

Date	Mintage	F	VF	XF	Unc	BU
1974 Proof	Est. 1,500	Value: 400				

KM# 126 1500 GUARANIES **Weight:** 10.7000 g. **Composition:** 0.9000 Gold .3096 oz. AGW **Obverse:** Arms **Reverse:** Bust of President John F. Kennedy left

Date	Mintage	F	VF	XF	Unc	BU
1974 Proof	Est. 1,500	Value: 400				

KM# 127 1500 GUARANIES **Weight:** 10.7000 g. **Composition:** 0.9000 Gold .3096 oz. AGW **Obverse:** Arms **Reverse:** Bust of Konrad Adenauer left

Date	Mintage	F	VF	XF	Unc	BU
1974 Proof	Est. 1,500	Value: 400				

KM# 128 1500 GUARANIES **Weight:** 10.7000 g. **Composition:** 0.9000 Gold .3096 oz. AGW **Obverse:** Arms **Reverse:** Bust of Winston Churchill left

Date	Mintage	F	VF	XF	Unc	BU
1974 Proof	Est. 1,500	Value: 400				

KM# 129 1500 GUARANIES **Weight:** 10.7000 g. **Composition:** 0.9000 Gold .3096 oz. AGW **Obverse:** Arms **Reverse:** Bust of Pope John XXIII left

Date	Mintage	F	VF	XF	Unc	BU
1974 Proof	Est. 1,500	Value: 400				

KM# 130 1500 GUARANIES **Weight:** 10.7000 g. **Composition:** 0.9000 Gold .3096 oz. AGW **Obverse:** Arms **Reverse:** Bust of Pope Paul VI left

Date	Mintage	F	VF	XF	Unc	BU
1974 Proof	Est. 1,500	Value: 400				

KM# 179 1500 GUARANIES **Weight:** 10.7000 g. **Composition:** 0.9000 Gold .3096 oz. AGW **Obverse:** Arms **Reverse:** Parliament building of Paraguay

Date	Mintage	F	VF	XF	Unc	BU
1975 Proof	1,500	Value: 400				

KM# 180 1500 GUARANIES **Weight:** 10.7000 g. **Composition:** 0.9000 Gold **Subject:** Apollo 11 Mission **Obverse:** Arms **Reverse:** Eagle landing on moon with earth at left

Date	Mintage	F	VF	XF	Unc	BU
1975 Proof	1,500	Value: 500				

KM# 181 1500 GUARANIES **Weight:** 10.7000 g. **Composition:** 0.9000 Gold **Subject:** Apollo 15 Mission **Obverse:** Arms

Date	Mintage	F	VF	XF	Unc	BU
1975 Proof	1,500	Value: 500				

KM# 182 1500 GUARANIES **Weight:** 10.7000 g. **Composition:** 0.9000 Gold **Obverse:** Arms **Reverse:** Friendship Bridge

Date	Mintage	F	VF	XF	Unc	BU
1975 Proof	1,500	Value: 400				

KM# 183 1500 GUARANIES **Weight:** 10.7000 g. **Composition:** 0.9000 Gold **Obverse:** Arms **Reverse:** Holy Trinity Chruch

Date	Mintage	F	VF	XF	Unc	BU
1975 Proof	1,500	Value: 400				

KM# 184 1500 GUARANIES **Weight:** 10.7000 g. **Composition:** 0.9000 Gold **Obverse:** Arms **Reverse:** Ruins of Humaita

Date	Mintage	F	VF	XF	Unc	BU
1975 Proof	Est. 1,500	Value: 400				

KM# 45 3000 GUARANIES **Weight:** 21.3000 g. **Composition:** 0.9000 Gold .6164 oz. AGW **Obverse:** Arms **Reverse:** Bust of General A. Stroessner facing

Date	Mintage	F	VF	XF	Unc	BU
1972 Proof	Est. 1,500	Value: 450				

KM# 46 3000 GUARANIES **Weight:** 21.3000 g. **Composition:** 0.9000 Gold .6164 oz. AGW **Subject:** Munich Olympics **Obverse:** Arms **Reverse:** Runner

Date	Mintage	F	VF	XF	Unc	BU
1972 Proof	Est. 1,500	Value: 1,500				

KM# 47 3000 GUARANIES **Weight:** 21.3000 g. **Composition:** 0.9000 Gold .6164 oz. AGW **Subject:** Munich Olympics **Obverse:** Arms **Reverse:** Broad Jumper

Date	Mintage	F	VF	XF	Unc	BU
1972 Proof	Est. 1,500	Value: 1,500				

KM# 81 3000 GUARANIES **Weight:** 21.3000 g. **Composition:** 0.9000 Gold .6164 oz. AGW **Obverse:** Arms **Reverse:** Bust of Jose F. Estigarribia facing

Date	Mintage	F	VF	XF	Unc	BU
1973 Proof	Est. 1,500	Value: 700				

KM# 86 3000 GUARANIES **Weight:** 21.3000 g. **Composition:** 0.9000 Gold .6164 oz. AGW **Obverse:** Arms **Reverse:** Huasteca Culture sculpture

Date	Mintage	F	VF	XF	Unc	BU
1973 Proof	Est. 1,500	Value: 700				

KM# 48 3000 GUARANIES **Weight:** 21.3000 g. **Composition:** 0.9000 Gold .6164 oz. AGW **Subject:** Munich Olympics **Obverse:** Arms **Reverse:** Soccer

Date	Mintage	F	VF	XF	Unc	BU
1972 Proof	Est. 1,500	Value: 1,500				

KM# 82 3000 GUARANIES **Weight:** 21.3000 g. **Composition:** 0.9000 Gold .6164 oz. AGW **Obverse:** Arms **Reverse:** Bust of Mariscal Francisco Solano Lopez facing

Date	Mintage	F	VF	XF	Unc	BU
1973 Proof	Est. 1,500	Value: 700				

KM# 87 3000 GUARANIES **Weight:** 21.3000 g. **Composition:** 0.9000 Gold .6164 oz. AGW **Obverse:** Arms **Reverse:** Mixteca Culture sculpture

Date	Mintage	F	VF	XF	Unc	BU
1973 Proof	Est. 1,500	Value: 700				

KM# 49 3000 GUARANIES **Weight:** 21.3000 g. **Composition:** 0.9000 Gold .6164 oz. AGW **Subject:** Munich Olympics **Obverse:** Arms **Reverse:** Hurdler

Date	Mintage	F	VF	XF	Unc	BU
1972 Proof	Est. 1,500	Value: 1,500				

KM# 83 3000 GUARANIES **Weight:** 21.3000 g. **Composition:** 0.9000 Gold .6164 oz. AGW **Obverse:** Arms **Reverse:** Bust of General Jose E. Diaz facing

Date	Mintage	F	VF	XF	Unc	BU
1973 Proof	Est. 1,500	Value: 700				

KM# 88 3000 GUARANIES **Weight:** 21.3000 g. **Composition:** 0.9000 Gold .6164 oz. AGW **Obverse:** Arms **Reverse:** Veracruz Ceramica vase

Date	Mintage	F	VF	XF	Unc	BU
1973 Proof	Est. 1,500	Value: 700				

KM# 50 3000 GUARANIES **Weight:** 21.3000 g. **Composition:** 0.9000 Gold .6164 oz. AGW **Subject:** Munich Olympics **Obverse:** Arms **Reverse:** High jumper

Date	Mintage	F	VF	XF	Unc	BU
1972 Proof	Est. 1,500	Value: 1,500				

KM# 84 3000 GUARANIES **Weight:** 21.3000 g. **Composition:** 0.9000 Gold .6164 oz. AGW **Obverse:** Arms **Reverse:** Bust of General Bernardino Caballero facing

Date	Mintage	F	VF	XF	Unc	BU
1973 Proof	Est. 1,500	Value: 700				

KM# 89 3000 GUARANIES **Weight:** 21.3000 g. **Composition:** 0.9000 Gold .6164 oz. AGW **Obverse:** Arms **Reverse:** Veracruz Culture sculpture

Date	Mintage	F	VF	XF	Unc	BU
1973 Proof	Est. 1,500	Value: 700				

KM# 51 3000 GUARANIES **Weight:** 21.3000 g. **Composition:** 0.9000 Gold .6164 oz. AGW **Subject:** Munich Olympics **Obverse:** Arms **Reverse:** Boxer

Date	Mintage	F	VF	XF	Unc	BU
1973 Proof	Est. 1,500	Value: 1,500				

KM# 85 3000 GUARANIES **Weight:** 21.3000 g. **Composition:** 0.9000 Gold .6164 oz. AGW **Obverse:** Arms **Reverse:** Teotihucana Culture sculpture

Date	Mintage	F	VF	XF	Unc	BU
1973 Proof	Est. 1,500	Value: 700				

KM# 90 3000 GUARANIES **Weight:** 21.3000 g. **Composition:** 0.9000 Gold .6164 oz. AGW **Obverse:** Arms **Reverse:** Bust of Albrecht Durer facing

Date	Mintage	F	VF	XF	Unc	BU
1973 Proof	Est. 1,500	Value: 700				

KM# 91 3000 GUARANIES **Weight:** 21.3000 g. **Composition:** 0.9000 Gold .6164 oz. AGW **Obverse:** Arms **Reverse:** Bust of Johann Wolfgang von Goethe facing

Date	Mintage	F	VF	XF	Unc	BU
1973 Proof	Est. 1,500	Value: 700				

KM# 131 3000 GUARANIES **Weight:** 21.3000 g. **Composition:** 0.9000 Gold .6164 oz. AGW **Obverse:** Arms **Reverse:** Bust of President Abraham Lincoln left

Date	Mintage	F	VF	XF	Unc	BU
1974 Proof	Est. 1,500	Value: 700				

KM# 132 3000 GUARANIES **Weight:** 21.3000 g. **Composition:** 0.9000 Gold .6164 oz. AGW **Obverse:** Arms **Reverse:** Bust of Ludwig van Beethoven facing half left

Date	Mintage	F	VF	XF	Unc	BU
1974 Proof	Est. 1,500	Value: 1,350				

KM# 133 3000 GUARANIES **Weight:** 21.3000 g. **Composition:** 0.9000 Gold .6164 oz. AGW **Obverse:** Arms **Reverse:** Bust of Otto von Bismarck right

Date	Mintage	F	VF	XF	Unc	BU
1974 Proof	Est. 1,500	Value: 700				

KM# 134 3000 GUARANIES **Weight:** 21.3000 g. **Composition:** 0.9000 Gold .6164 oz. AGW **Obverse:** Arms **Reverse:** Bust of Albert Einstein left

Date	Mintage	F	VF	XF	Unc	BU
1974 Proof	Est. 1,500	Value: 700				

KM# 135 3000 GUARANIES **Weight:** 21.3000 g. **Composition:** 0.9000 Gold .6164 oz. AGW **Obverse:** Arms **Reverse:** Bust of Giuseppe Garibaldi facing

Date	Mintage	F	VF	XF	Unc	BU
1974 Proof	Est. 1,500	Value: 700				

KM# 136 3000 GUARANIES **Weight:** 21.3000 g. **Composition:** 0.9000 Gold .6164 oz. AGW **Obverse:** Arms **Reverse:** Bust of Alessandro Manzoni facing

Date	Mintage	F	VF	XF	Unc	BU
1974 Proof	Est. 1,500	Value: 700				

KM# 137 3000 GUARANIES **Weight:** 21.3000 g. **Composition:** 0.9000 Gold .6164 oz. AGW **Obverse:** Arms **Reverse:** William Tell and son standing facing

Date	Mintage	F	VF	XF	Unc	BU
1974 Proof	Est. 1,500	Value: 700				

KM# 138 3000 GUARANIES **Weight:** 21.3000 g. **Composition:** 0.9000 Gold .6164 oz. AGW **Obverse:** Arms **Reverse:** Bust of President John F. Kennedy left

Date	Mintage	F	VF	XF	Unc	BU
1974 Proof	Est. 1,500	Value: 700				

KM# 139 3000 GUARANIES **Weight:** 21.3000 g. **Composition:** 0.9000 Gold .6164 oz. AGW **Obverse:** Arms **Reverse:** Bust of Konrad Adenauer left

Date	Mintage	F	VF	XF	Unc	BU
1974 Proof	Est. 1,500	Value: 700				

KM# 140 3000 GUARANIES **Weight:** 21.3000 g. **Composition:** 0.9000 Gold .6164 oz. AGW **Obverse:** Arms **Reverse:** Bust of Sir Winston Churchill left

Date	Mintage	F	VF	XF	Unc	BU
1974 Proof	Est. 1,500	Value: 700				

KM# 141 3000 GUARANIES **Weight:** 21.3000 g. **Composition:** 0.9000 Gold .6164 oz. AGW **Obverse:** Arms **Reverse:** Bust of Pope John XXIII left

Date	Mintage	F	VF	XF	Unc	BU
1974 Proof	Est. 1,500	Value: 700				

KM# 142 3000 GUARANIES **Weight:** 21.3000 g. **Composition:** 0.9000 Gold .6164 oz. AGW **Obverse:** Arms **Reverse:** Bust of Pope Paul VI left

Date	Mintage	F	VF	XF	Unc	BU
1974 Proof	Est. 1,500	Value: 700				

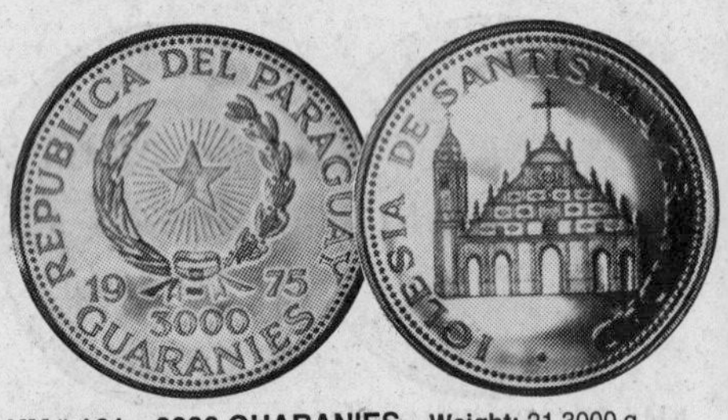

KM# 161 3000 GUARANIES **Weight:** 21.3000 g. **Composition:** 0.9000 Gold .6164 oz. AGW **Obverse:** Arms **Reverse:** Holy Trinity Chruch

Date	F	VF	XF	Unc	BU
1975 Proof	—	Value: 650			

KM# 162 3000 GUARANIES **Weight:** 21.3000 g. **Composition:** 0.9000 Gold .6164 oz. AGW **Obverse:** Arms **Reverse:** Parliament building of Paraguay

Date	F	VF	XF	Unc	BU
1975 Proof	—	Value: 650			

KM# 163 3000 GUARANIES **Weight:** 21.3000 g. **Composition:** 0.9000 Gold .6164 oz. AGW **Obverse:** Arms **Reverse:** Friendship bridge

Date	F	VF	XF	Unc	BU
1975 Proof	—	Value: 650			

KM# 164 3000 GUARANIES **Weight:** 21.3000 g. **Composition:** 0.9000 Gold .6164 oz. AGW **Obverse:** Arms **Reverse:** Humaita ruins

Date		F	VF	XF	Unc	BU
1975 Proof	—	Value: 650				

KM# 175 3000 GUARANIES **Weight:** 21.3000 g. **Composition:** 0.9000 Gold .6164 oz. AGW **Subject:** Apollo 11 Mission **Obverse:** Arms **Reverse:** Eagle landing on moon with earth at upper left

Date		F	VF	XF	Unc	BU
1975 Proof	—	Value: 1,000				

KM# 176 3000 GUARANIES **Weight:** 21.3000 g. **Composition:** 0.9000 Gold .6164 oz. AGW **Subject:** Apollo 15 Mission **Obverse:** Arms

Date		F	VF	XF	Unc	BU
1975 Proof	—	Value: 1,000				

KM# 52 4500 GUARANIES **Weight:** 31.9000 g. **Composition:** 0.9000 Gold .9231 oz. AGW **Obverse:** Arms **Reverse:** Bust of General A. Stroessner facing

Date	Mintage	F	VF	XF	Unc	BU
1972 Proof	Est. 1,500	Value: 750				

KM# 53 4500 GUARANIES **Weight:** 31.9000 g. **Composition:** 0.9000 Gold .9231 oz. AGW **Subject:** Munich Olympics **Obverse:** Arms **Reverse:** Runner

Date	Mintage	F	VF	XF	Unc	BU
1972 Proof	Est. 1,500	Value: 2,700				

KM# 54 4500 GUARANIES **Weight:** 31.9000 g. **Composition:** 0.9000 Gold .9231 oz. AGW **Subject:** Munich Olympics **Obverse:** Arms **Reverse:** Broad jumper

Date	Mintage	F	VF	XF	Unc	BU
1972 Proof	Est. 1,500	Value: 2,700				

KM# 55 4500 GUARANIES **Weight:** 31.9000 g. **Composition:** 0.9000 Gold .9231 oz. AGW **Subject:** Munich Olympics **Obverse:** Arms **Reverse:** Soccer

Date	Mintage	F	VF	XF	Unc	BU
1972 Proof	Est. 1,500	Value: 2,700				

KM# 56 4500 GUARANIES **Weight:** 31.9000 g. **Composition:** 0.9000 Gold .9231 oz. AGW **Subject:** Munich Olympics **Obverse:** Arms **Reverse:** Hurdler

Date	Mintage	F	VF	XF	Unc	BU
1972 Proof	Est. 1,500	Value: 2,700				

KM# 57 4500 GUARANIES **Weight:** 31.9000 g. **Composition:** 0.9000 Gold .9231 oz. AGW **Subject:** Munich Olympics **Obverse:** Arms **Reverse:** High jumper

Date	Mintage	F	VF	XF	Unc	BU
1972 Proof	Est. 1,500	Value: 2,700				

KM# 58 4500 GUARANIES **Weight:** 31.9000 g. **Composition:** 0.9000 Gold .9231 oz. AGW **Subject:** Munich Olympics **Obverse:** Arms **Reverse:** Boxer

Date	Mintage	F	VF	XF	Unc	BU
1973 Proof	Est. 1,500	Value: 2,700				

KM# 92 4500 GUARANIES **Weight:** 31.9000 g. **Composition:** 0.9000 Gold .9231 oz. AGW **Obverse:** Arms **Reverse:** Bust of Mariscal Jose F. Estigarribia facing

Date	Mintage	F	VF	XF	Unc	BU
1973 Proof	Est. 1,500	Value: 1,200				

KM# 93 4500 GUARANIES **Weight:** 31.9000 g. **Composition:** 0.9000 Gold .9231 oz. AGW **Obverse:** Arms **Reverse:** Bust of Mariscal Francisco Solano Lopez facing

Date	Mintage	F	VF	XF	Unc	BU
1973 Proof	Est. 1,500	Value: 1,200				

KM# 94 4500 GUARANIES **Weight:** 31.9000 g. **Composition:** 0.9000 Gold .9231 oz. AGW **Obverse:** Arms **Reverse:** Bust of General Jose E. Diaz facing

Date	Mintage	F	VF	XF	Unc	BU
1973 Proof	Est. 1,500	Value: 1,200				

KM# 95 4500 GUARANIES **Weight:** 31.9000 g. **Composition:** 0.9000 Gold .9231 oz. AGW **Obverse:** Arms **Reverse:** Bust of General Bernardino Caballero facing

Date	Mintage	F	VF	XF	Unc	BU
1973 Proof	Est. 1,500	Value: 1,200				

KM# 96 4500 GUARANIES **Weight:** 31.9000 g. **Composition:** 0.9000 Gold .9231 oz. AGW **Obverse:** Arms **Reverse:** Teotihucana Culture sculpture

Date	Mintage	F	VF	XF	Unc	BU
1973 Proof	Est. 1,500	Value: 1,200				

KM# 97 4500 GUARANIES **Weight:** 31.9000 g. **Composition:** 0.9000 Gold .9231 oz. AGW **Obverse:** Arms **Reverse:** Huasteca Culture sculpture

Date	Mintage	F	VF	XF	Unc	BU
1973 Proof	Est. 1,500	Value: 1,200				

KM# 98 4500 GUARANIES **Weight:** 31.9000 g. **Composition:** 0.9000 Gold .9231 oz. AGW **Obverse:** Arms **Reverse:** Mixteca Culture sculpture

Date	Mintage	F	VF	XF	Unc	BU
1973 Proof	Est. 1,500	Value: 1,200				

KM# 99 4500 GUARANIES **Weight:** 31.9000 g. **Composition:** 0.9000 Gold .9231 oz. AGW **Obverse:** Arms **Reverse:** Veracruz Ceramica sculpture

Date	Mintage	F	VF	XF	Unc	BU
1973 Proof	Est. 1,500	Value: 1,200				

KM# 100 4500 GUARANIES **Weight:** 31.9000 g. **Composition:** 0.9000 Gold .9231 oz. AGW **Obverse:** Arms **Reverse:** Veracruz Culture bust

Date	Mintage	F	VF	XF	Unc	BU
1973 Proof	Est. 1,500	Value: 1,200				

KM# 101 4500 GUARANIES **Weight:** 31.9000 g. **Composition:** 0.9000 Gold .9231 oz. AGW **Obverse:** Arms **Reverse:** Bust of Albrecht Durer facing

Date	Mintage	F	VF	XF	Unc	BU
1973 Proof	Est. 1,500	Value: 1,200				

KM# 102 4500 GUARANIES **Weight:** 31.9000 g. **Composition:** 0.9000 Gold .9231 oz. AGW **Obverse:** Arms **Reverse:** Bust of Johann Wolfgang von Goethe facing

Date	Mintage	F	VF	XF	Unc	BU
1973 Proof	Est. 1,500	Value: 1,200				

KM# 103 4500 GUARANIES **Weight:** 31.9000 g. **Composition:** 0.9000 Gold .9231 oz. AGW **Obverse:** Arms **Reverse:** Bust of Ludwig van Beethoven half left

Date	Mintage	F	VF	XF	Unc	BU
1974 Proof	Est. 1,500	Value: 2,100				

KM# 104 4500 GUARANIES **Weight:** 31.9000 g. **Composition:** 0.9000 Gold .9231 oz. AGW **Obverse:** Arms **Reverse:** Bust of Otto von Bismarck right

Date	Mintage	F	VF	XF	Unc	BU
1974 Proof	Est. 1,500	Value: 1,200				

KM# 105 4500 GUARANIES **Weight:** 31.9000 g. **Composition:** 0.9000 Gold .9231 oz. AGW **Obverse:** Arms **Reverse:** Bust of Giuseppe Garibaldi facing

Date	Mintage	F	VF	XF	Unc	BU
1974 Proof	Est. 1,500	Value: 1,200				

KM# 106 4500 GUARANIES **Weight:** 31.9000 g. **Composition:** 0.9000 Gold .9231 oz. AGW **Obverse:** Arms **Reverse:** Bust of Alessandro Manzoni facing

Date	Mintage	F	VF	XF	Unc	BU
1974 Proof	Est. 1,500	Value: 1,200				

KM# 143 4500 GUARANIES **Weight:** 31.9000 g. **Composition:** 0.9000 Gold .9231 oz. AGW **Obverse:** Arms **Reverse:** Bust of President Abraham Lincoln left

Date	Mintage	F	VF	XF	Unc	BU
1974 Proof	Est. 1,500	Value: 1,200				

KM# 144 4500 GUARANIES **Weight:** 31.9000 g. **Composition:** 0.9000 Gold .9231 oz. AGW **Obverse:** Arms **Reverse:** Bust of Albert Einstein left

Date	Mintage	F	VF	XF	Unc	BU
1974 Proof	Est. 1,500	Value: 1,200				

KM# 145 4500 GUARANIES **Weight:** 31.9000 g. **Composition:** 0.9000 Gold .9231 oz. AGW **Obverse:** Arms **Reverse:** William Tell and son standing facing

Date	Mintage	F	VF	XF	Unc	BU
1974 Proof	Est. 1,500	Value: 1,200				

KM# 146 4500 GUARANIES **Weight:** 31.9000 g. **Composition:** 0.9000 Gold .9231 oz. AGW **Obverse:** Arms **Reverse:** Bust of President John F. Kennedy left

Date	Mintage	F	VF	XF	Unc	BU
1974 Proof	Est. 1,500	Value: 1,200				

KM# 147 4500 GUARANIES **Weight:** 31.9000 g. **Composition:** 0.9000 Gold .9231 oz. AGW **Obverse:** Arms **Reverse:** Bust of Konrad Adenauer left

Date	Mintage	F	VF	XF	Unc	BU
1974 Proof	Est. 1,500	Value: 1,200				

KM# 148 4500 GUARANIES **Weight:** 31.9000 g. **Composition:** 0.9000 Gold .9231 oz. AGW **Obverse:** Arms **Reverse:** Bust of Winston Churchill left

Date	Mintage	F	VF	XF	Unc	BU
1974 Proof	Est. 1,500	Value: 1,200				

KM# 149 4500 GUARANIES **Weight:** 31.9000 g. **Composition:** 0.9000 Gold .9231 oz. AGW **Obverse:** Arms **Reverse:** Bust of Pope John XXIII left

Date	Mintage	F	VF	XF	Unc	BU
1974 Proof	Est. 1,500	Value: 1,200				

KM# 150 4500 GUARANIES **Weight:** 31.9000 g. **Composition:** 0.9000 Gold .9231 oz. AGW **Obverse:** Arms **Reverse:** Bust of Pope Paul VI left

Date	Mintage	F	VF	XF	Unc	BU
1974 Proof	Est. 1,500	Value: 1,200				

KM# 185 4500 GUARANIES **Weight:** 31.9000 g. **Composition:** 0.9000 Gold .9231 oz. AGW **Obverse:** Arms **Reverse:** Parliament building of Paraguay

Date	Mintage	F	VF	XF	Unc	BU
1975 Proof	Est. 1,500	Value: 1,200				

KM# 186 4500 GUARANIES **Weight:** 31.9000 g. **Composition:** 0.9000 Gold .9231 oz. AGW **Subject:** Apollo 11 Mission **Obverse:** Arms **Reverse:** Eagle landing on moon with earth at upper left

Date	Mintage	F	VF	XF	Unc	BU
1975 Proof	Est. 1,500	Value: 1,200				

KM# 187 4500 GUARANIES **Weight:** 31.9000 g. **Composition:** 0.9000 Gold .9231 oz. AGW **Subject:** Apollo 15 Mission **Obverse:** Arms

Date	Mintage	F	VF	XF	Unc	BU
1975 Proof	Est. 1,500	Value: 1,200				

KM# 188 4500 GUARANIES **Weight:** 31.9000 g. **Composition:** 0.9000 Gold .9231 oz. AGW **Obverse:** Arms **Reverse:** Friendship bridge

Date	Mintage	F	VF	XF	Unc	BU
1975 Proof	Est. 1,500	Value: 1,200				

KM# 189 4500 GUARANIES **Weight:** 31.9000 g. **Composition:** 0.9000 Gold .9231 oz. AGW **Obverse:** Arms **Reverse:** Holy Trinity Church

Date	Mintage	F	VF	XF	Unc	BU
1975 Proof	Est. 1,500	Value: 1,200				

KM# 190 4500 GUARANIES **Weight:** 31.9000 g. **Composition:** 0.9000 Gold .9231 oz. AGW **Obverse:** Arms **Reverse:** Ruins of Humaita

Date	Mintage	F	VF	XF	Unc	BU
1975 Proof	Est. 1,500	Value: 1,200				

KM# 30 10000 GUARANIES **Weight:** 46.0100 g. **Composition:** 0.9000 Gold 1.3315 oz. AGW **Subject:** 4th Term of President Stroessner **Obverse:** Lion arms **Reverse:** Bust of General A. Stroessner facing **Note:** Similar to 300 Guaranies KM#29.

Date	Mintage	F	VF	XF	Unc	BU
1968 Proof	Est. 50	Value: 4,500				

Note: KM#30 struck for presentation

KM# 171 10000 GUARANIES **Weight:** 28.7000 g. **Composition:** 0.9990 Silver .9219 oz. ASW **Obverse:** Central Bank building of Paraguay **Reverse:** Conjoined busts of Caballero and Stroessner left

Date	Mintage	F	VF	XF	Unc	BU
ND(1987) Proof	1,000	Value: 40.00				

KM# 173 10000 GUARANIES **Weight:** 28.7000 g. **Composition:** 0.9990 Silver .9219 oz. ASW **Subject:** 8th Term of President A. Stroessner **Obverse:** Lion arms **Reverse:** Bust of President A. Stroessner left

Date	Mintage	F	VF	XF	Unc	BU
ND(1988) Proof	1,000	Value: 40.00				

KM# 168 70000 GUARANIES **Weight:** 46.0000 g. **Composition:** 0.9000 Gold 1.3310 oz. AGW **Subject:** 6th Term of President A. Stroessner **Obverse:** Lion arms **Reverse:** Bust of President A. Stroessner left

Date	Mintage	F	VF	XF	Unc	BU
ND(1978) Proof	300	Value: 750				

KM# 170 100000 GUARANIES **Weight:** 46.0000 g. **Composition:** 0.9000 Gold 1.3310 oz. AGW **Subject:** 7th Term of President A. Stroessner **Obverse:** Lion arms **Reverse:** Bust of President A. Stroessner left

Date	Mintage	F	VF	XF	Unc	BU
ND(1983) Proof	300	Value: 750				

KM# 172 250000 GUARANIES **Weight:** 46.0000 g. **Composition:** 0.9170 Gold 1.3561 oz. AGW **Obverse:** Central Bank building of Paraguay **Reverse:** Conjoined busts of Caballero - Stroessner left

Date	Mintage	F	VF	XF	Unc	BU
ND(1987) Proof	Est. 500	Value: 750				

Note: 250 pieces remelted

KM# 174 300000 GUARANIES **Weight:** 46.0000 g. **Composition:** 0.9170 Gold 1.3561 oz. AGW **Subject:** 8th Term of President A. Stroessner **Obverse:** Lion arms **Reverse:** Bust of President A. Stroessner left

Date	Mintage	F	VF	XF	Unc	BU
ND(1988) Proof	Est. 500	Value: 750				

Note: 250 pieces remelted

PATTERNS

Including off metal strikes

KM#	Date	Mintage	Identification	Mkt Val
Pn40	1925	—	2 Pesos. Aluminum. Narrow flan, KM14.	100
Pn41	1925	—	2 Pesos. Aluminum. Broad flan, KM14.	125
Pn42	1939	—	5 Pesos. Brass. KM#8.	175
Pn43	1939	—	5 Pesos. Copper. KM18.	175
Pn44	1976	10	Guarani. Gold.	400
Pn45	1976	10	10 Guaranies. Gold.	700
Pn46	1978	10	Guarani. Gold.	400
Pn47	1978	10	5 Guaranies. Gold.	500
Pn48	1978	10	10 Guaranies. Gold.	700
Pn49	1980	10	Guarani. Gold.	400
Pn50	1980	10	5 Guaranies. Gold.	500
Pn51	1980	10	10 Guaranies. Gold.	700
Pn52	1980	10	50 Guaranies. Gold.	1,000

PROOF SETS

KM#	Date	Mintage	Identification	Issue Price	Mkt Val
PS2	1965 (5)	10	KM#237-240, 290	—	1,500
PS3	1965 (5)	—	KM#220.5, 221.2b, 222, 223.2, 224.2	—	300
PS4	1966 (5)	1,000	KM244.1-246.1, 247-248	—	100

PERU

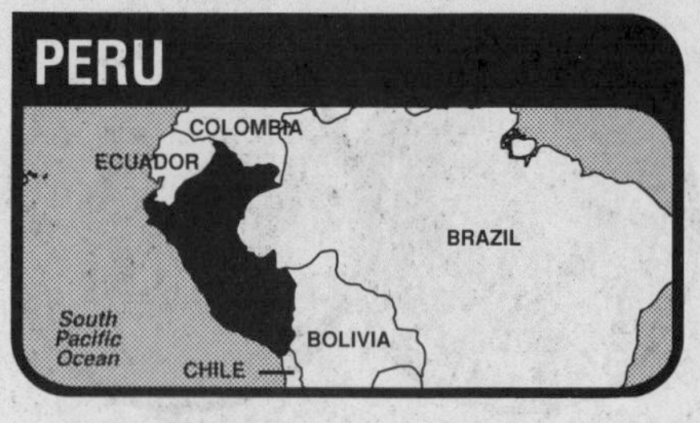

The Republic of Peru, located on the Pacific coast of South America, has an area of 496,225 sq. mi. (1,285,220sq. km.) and a population of *21.4 million. Capital: Lima. The diversified economy includes mining, fishing and agriculture. Fishmeal, copper, sugar, zinc and iron ore are exported.

Once part of the great Inca Empire that reached from northern Ecuador to central Chile, the conquest of Peru by Francisco Pizarro began in 1531. Desirable as the richest of the Spanish viceroyalties, it was torn by warfare between avaricious Spaniards until the arrival in 1569 of Francisco de Toledo, who initiated 2-1/2 centuries of efficient colonial rule, which made Lima the most aristocratic colonial capital and the stronghold of Spain's American possessions. Jose de San Martin of Argentina proclaimed Peru's independence on July 28, 1821; Simon Bolivar of Venezuela secured it in December, 1824 when he defeated the last Spanish army in South America. After several futile attempts to re-establish its South American Empire, Spain recognized Peru's independence in 1879.

Andres de Santa Cruz, whose mother was a high-ranking Inca, was the best of Bolivia's early presidents, and temporarily united Peru and Bolivia 1836-39, thus realizing his dream of a Peruvian/Bolivian confederation. This prompted the separate coinages of North and South Peru. Peruvian resistance and Chilean intervention finally broke up the confederation, sending Santa Cruz into exile. A succession of military strongman presidents ruled Peru until Marshall Castilla revitalized Peruvian politics in the mid-19th century and repulsed Spain's attempt to reclaim its one-time colony. Subsequent loss of southern territory to Chile in the War of the Pacific, 1879-81, and gradually increasing rejection of foreign economic domination, combined with recent serious inflation, affected the country numismatically.

As a result of the discovery of silver at Potosi in 1545, a mint was eventually authorized in 1565 with the first coinage taking place in 1568. The mint had an uneven life span during the Spanish Colonial period from 1568-72. It was closed from 1573-76, reopened from 1577-88. It remained closed until 1659-1660 when an unauthorized coinage in both silver and gold were struck. After being closed in 1660, it remained closed until 1684 when it struck cob style coins until 1752.

MINT MARKS

AREQUIPA, AREQ = Arequipa
AYACUCHO = Ayacucho
(B) = Brussels
CUZCO (monogram), Cuzco, Co. Cuzco
L, LIMAE (monogram), Lima
(monogram), LIMA = Lima
(L) = London
PASCO (monogram), Pasco, Paz, Po= Pasco
P, (P) = Philadelphia
S = San Francisco
(W) = Waterbury, CT, USA

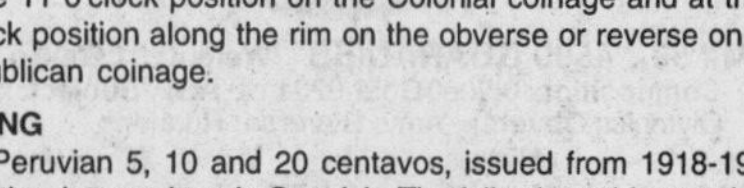

NOTE: The LIMAE monogram appears in three forms. The early LM monogram form looks like a dotted L with M. The later LIMAE monogram has all the letters of LIMAE more readily distinguishable. The third form appears as an M monogram during early Republican issues.

MINT ASSAYERS INITIALS

The letter(s) following the dates of Peruvian coins are the assayer's initials appearing on the coins. They generally appear at the 11 o'clock position on the Colonial coinage and at the 5 o'clock position along the rim on the obverse or reverse on the Republican coinage.

DATING

Peruvian 5, 10 and 20 centavos, issued from 1918-1944, bear the dates written in Spanish. The following table translates those written dates into numerals:

1918 - UN MIL NOVECIENTOS DIECIOCHO
1919 - UN MIL NOVECIENTOS DIECINUEVE
1920 - UN MIL NOVECIENTOS VEINTE
1921 - UN MIL NOVECIENTOS VEINTIUNO
1923 - UN MIL NOVECIENTOS VEINTITRES
1926 - UN MIL NOVECIENTOS VEINTISEIS
1934 - UN MIL NOVECIENTOS TREINTICUATRO
1935 - UN MIL NOVECIENTOS TREINTICINCO
1937 - UN MIL NOVECIENTOS TREINTISIETE
1939 - UN MIL NOVECIENTOS TREINTINUEVE
1940 - UN MIL NOVECIENTOS CUARENTA
1941 - UN MIL NOVECIENTOS CUARENTIUNO

U.S. Mints

1942 - MIL NOVECIENTOS CUARENTA Y DOS

Lima Mint

1942 - UN MIL NOVECIENTOS CUARENTIDOS

U.S. Mints

1943 - MIL NOVECIENTOS CUARENTA Y TRES
1944 - MIL NOVECIENTOS CUARENTA Y CUATRO

Lima Mint

1944 - MIL NOVECIENTOS CUARENTICUATRO

MONETARY SYSTEM

100 Centavos (10 Dineros) = 1 Sol
10 Soles = 1 Libra

REPUBLIC

DECIMAL COINAGE

100 Centavos (10 Dineros) = 1 Sol; 10 Soles = 1 Libra

KM# 208.1 CENTAVO **Composition:** Bronze **Obverse:** Small date at bottom and legend **Reverse:** Straight centavo **Note:** Thick planchet.

Date	Mintage	F	VF	XF	Unc	BU
1901	600,000	1.00	3.00	8.00	20.00	—
1904	1,000,000	8.00	15.00	30.00	60.00	—

KM# 208.2 CENTAVO **Composition:** Bronze **Obverse:** Large date and legend **Reverse:** Straight centavo **Note:** Thick planchet. Varieties exist.

Date	Mintage	F	VF	XF	Unc	BU
1933	275,000	1.50	3.00	8.00	20.00	—
1934	1,185,000	1.00	2.00	5.00	15.00	—
1935	1,105,000	1.00	2.00	5.00	15.00	—
1936	565,000	1.50	3.00	8.00	20.00	—
1937/6	735,000	1.00	2.00	4.00	20.00	—
1937	Inc. above	0.75	1.50	2.50	15.00	—
1938	340,000	0.75	1.50	2.50	15.00	—
1939	1,225,000	1.50	3.00	5.50	20.00	—
1940	1,250,000	1.50	3.00	5.50	20.00	—
1941	2,593,000	0.40	0.75	1.50	10.00	—

KM# 208a CENTAVO **Composition:** Bronze **Obverse:** Large date and legend **Reverse:** Straight centavo **Note:** Thin planchet.

Date	Mintage	F	VF	XF	Unc	BU
1941 Inc. KM#208.2	—	0.40	0.75	2.00	8.00	—
1942	2,865,000	0.50	1.00	2.50	10.00	—
1944	—	10.00	20.00	35.00	70.00	—

KM# 211 CENTAVO **Composition:** Bronze **Obverse:** Large date and legend **Note:** Thick planchet. Engravers initial R appears below ribbon on most or all new dies, but often became weak or filled. Most coins show at least a faint trace of an R. Date varieteis also exist.

Date	Mintage	F	VF	XF	Unc	BU
1909/999 R	Inc. above	10.00	20.00	35.00	70.00	—
1909 R	Inc. above	10.00	20.00	35.00	70.00	—
1909	252,000	10.00	20.00	35.00	70.00	—
1915	250,000	3.00	6.00	10.00	30.00	—
1916	360,000	1.00	2.00	7.00	20.00	—
1916 R	Inc. above	1.00	2.00	6.00	15.00	—
1917	830,000	1.00	2.00	6.00	15.00	—
1917 R	Inc. above	1.00	2.00	6.00	15.00	—
1918	1,060,000	1.00	2.00	5.00	14.00	—
1918 R	Inc. above	1.00	2.00	5.00	14.00	—
1920	360,000	1.00	2.50	7.00	20.00	—
1920 R	Inc. above	1.00	2.50	7.00	20.00	—
1933 R Inc. KM208.2	—	1.00	2.50	7.00	20.00	—
1934 Inc. KM#208.2	—	4.50	8.00	20.00	55.00	—
1935 R Inc. KM#208.2	—	4.00	7.00	20.00	50.00	—
1936 R Inc. KM#208.2	—	1.50	3.50	7.00	20.00	—
1937	—	—	—	—	—	—
1937 R Inc. KM#208.2	—	1.50	3.50	7.00	20.00	—
1939 R Inc. KM#208.2	—	4.50	8.00	20.00	55.00	—

KM# 211a CENTAVO **Composition:** Bronze **Obverse:** Large date and legend **Reverse:** Curved centavo **Note:** Thin planchet. Many varieties exist.

Date	Mintage	F	VF	XF	Unc	BU
1941 Inc. KM#208.2	—	1.00	2.00	5.00	15.00	—
1942 Inc. KM#208a	—	0.50	1.00	3.00	10.00	—
1943	—	2.50	5.00	15.00	35.00	—
1944	2,490,000	0.15	0.40	1.00	4.00	—
1945	2,157,000	0.15	0.40	1.00	4.00	—
1946	3,198,000	0.15	0.40	1.00	4.00	—
1947	2,976,000	0.15	0.40	1.00	4.00	—
1948	3,195,000	0.15	0.40	1.00	4.00	—
1949	1,104,000	0.25	0.65	2.00	6.00	—

KM# 227 CENTAVO **Composition:** Zinc **Note:** Varieties exist.

Date	Mintage	F	VF	XF	Unc	BU
1950	3,196,000	0.35	0.25	1.25	5.00	—
1951	3,289,000	0.25	0.40	0.65	3.00	—

Note: Copper-plated examples of type dated 1951 are known

Date	Mintage	F	VF	XF	Unc	BU
1952	3,050,000	0.25	0.40	0.65	3.00	—
1953	3,260,000	0.35	0.60	1.00	4.00	—
1954	3,215,000	0.75	1.50	2.50	10.00	—
1955	3,400,000	0.25	0.40	0.65	3.00	—
1956 Pointed 6	2,500,000	0.25	0.40	0.65	3.00	—
1956 Knobbed 6	Inc. above	0.25	0.40	0.65	3.00	—
1957	4,400,000	0.40	0.85	2.00	7.00	—
1958/7	—	0.35	0.60	1.00	4.00	—
1958	2,600,000	0.35	0.60	1.00	4.00	—
1958/8	3,200,000	0.50	1.00	2.00	7.00	—
1959	Inc. above	0.25	0.40	0.65	3.00	—
1960/50	3,060,000	0.35	0.60	1.00	4.00	—
1960	Inc. above	0.75	1.50	3.00	8.00	—
1961/51	2,600,000	0.25	0.40	1.00	3.00	—
1961	Inc. above	0.25	0.40	1.00	3.00	—
1962/52	2,600,000	0.25	0.40	1.00	3.00	—
1962	Inc. above	0.25	0.40	1.00	3.00	—
1963/53	2,400,000	0.25	0.40	1.00	3.00	—
1963	Inc. above	0.25	0.40	1.00	3.00	—
1965	360,000	0.75	1.50	3.00	10.00	—

KM# 187.2 CENTAVO **Composition:** Bronze **Obverse:** Date at top **Reverse:** Sharper die work **Note:** Earlier dates 1875-1878 listed as KM#187.1a in 19th Century book.

Date	Mintage	F	VF	XF	Unc	BU
1919(P)	4,000,000	0.50	1.00	2.50	10.00	—

KM# 212.1 2 CENTAVOS **Composition:** Copper Or Bronze **Obverse:** Date at bottom **Note:** Thick planchet. Engraver's initial C appeared below ribbon on most or all new dies, but often became weak or filled. Most coins show at least a faint trace of C. Other varieties also exist.

Date	Mintage	F	VF	XF	Unc	BU
1918/17	580,000	3.50	6.00	10.00	35.00	—
1918	Inc. above	3.50	6.00	15.00	40.00	—
1918 C	Inc. above	3.50	6.00	15.00	40.00	—
1918/17 C	Inc. above	4.00	10.00	20.00	50.00	—
1917 C	73,000	4.00	6.50	15.00	40.00	—
1920/7 C	328,000	2.00	4.00	10.00	30.00	—
1920	Inc. above	1.00	2.00	5.00	15.00	—
1920 C	Inc. above	1.00	2.00	5.00	15.00	—
1933	285,000	1.00	2.00	5.00	15.00	—
1933 C	Inc. above	1.00	2.00	5.00	15.00	—
1934	973,000	0.75	1.50	4.00	15.00	—
1934 C	Inc. above	0.75	1.50	4.00	15.00	—
1935	950,000	0.75	1.50	4.00	15.00	—
1935 C	Inc. above	0.75	1.50	4.00	15.00	—
1936	763,000	0.75	1.50	4.00	15.00	—
1936/5 C	Inc. above	1.50	2.50	8.00	20.00	—
1936 C	Inc. above	0.75	1.25	3.00	12.00	—
1937	963,000	0.75	1.50	4.00	15.00	—
1937 C	Inc. above	0.75	1.50	4.00	15.00	—
1938 C	428,000	1.00	1.75	4.00	15.00	—
1939/8 C	—	—	—	—	—	—

Note: Reported, not confirmed

Date	Mintage	F	VF	XF	Unc	BU
1939/8	—	1.50	2.50	8.00	20.00	—
1939 C Inverted A for V in CENTAVOS	783,000	0.75	1.50	4.00	15.00	—
1940	—	1.00	2.00	4.00	15.00	—
1940 C	565,000	1.00	1.75	4.00	15.00	—
1941/0	Inc. above	1.00	2.00	4.00	15.00	—
1941/0 C	Inc. above	1.00	2.00	4.00	15.00	—
1941/22	Inc. above	1.00	2.00	4.00	15.00	—
1941	Inc. above	1.00	2.00	4.00	15.00	—
1941 C	Inc. above	2.00	5.00	12.00	20.00	—

KM# 212.2 2 CENTAVOS **Composition:** Copper Or Bronze **Obverse:** Date at bottom **Note:** Thin planchet. Varieties exist.

Date	Mintage	F	VF	XF	Unc	BU
1941/32	870,000	1.00	2.00	3.50	10.00	—
1941/33 C	Inc. above	1.00	2.00	3.50	10.00	—
1941/33	Inc. above	1.00	2.00	3.50	10.00	—
1941/38	Inc. above	1.00	2.00	3.50	10.00	—
1941/38 C	Inc. above	1.00	2.00	3.50	10.00	—
1941/39 C	Inc. above	1.00	2.00	3.50	10.00	—
1941/0	Inc. above	1.00	2.00	3.50	10.00	—
1941	Inc. above	0.50	1.00	2.00	7.00	—
1942/22	4,418,000	—	0.50	1.00	5.00	—
1942/32	4,418,000	—	0.50	1.00	5.00	—
1942	Inc. above	0.25	0.50	1.00	5.00	—
1943/2	1,829,000	0.50	1.00	3.00	10.00	—
1943	Inc. above	0.50	1.00	3.00	10.00	—
1944	2,068,000	1.00	2.00	4.00	12.00	—
1945	2,288,000	1.00	2.00	4.00	12.00	—
1946	2,121,000	0.25	0.50	0.75	4.00	—
1947	1,280,000	0.25	0.50	0.75	4.00	—
1948	1,518,000	0.25	0.50	0.75	5.00	—
1949/8	938,000	0.25	0.60	4.00	7.00	—
1949	Inc. above	0.50	1.00	4.00	7.00	—

KM# 228 2 CENTAVOS **Composition:** Zinc

Date	Mintage	F	VF	XF	Unc	BU
1950	1,702,000	0.35	0.75	1.25	3.00	—
1951	3,289,000	0.35	0.75	1.25	3.00	—

Note: Copper-plated examples of type dated 1951 exist

Date	Mintage	F	VF	XF	Unc	BU
1952	1,155,000	0.35	0.75	1.25	3.00	—
1953	1,150,000	0.40	0.85	1.50	4.00	—
1954	—	2.00	4.00	8.00	25.00	—
1955	1,185,000	0.35	0.75	1.25	3.00	—
1956	400,000	0.50	1.00	2.00	5.00	—
1957	520,000	1.50	3.00	6.00	25.00	—
1958	200,000	1.25	2.50	4.50	15.00	—

KM# A212 2 CENTAVOS **Composition:** Copper Or Bronze **Note:** Sharper diework. Earlier date 1895 listed as KM#188.2 in 19th Century book.

Date	Mintage	F	VF	XF	Unc	BU
1919(P)	3,000,000	0.35	0.75	2.00	9.00	—

KM# 213.1 5 CENTAVOS **Composition:** Copper-Nickel **Obverse:** Date UN MIL NOVECIENTOS DIECIOCHO **Note:** Struck at Philadelphia.

Date	Mintage	F	VF	XF	Unc	BU
1918	4,000,000	0.50	1.25	2.50	10.00	—
1919	10,000,000	0.40	1.00	2.00	7.00	—
1923	2,000,000	1.00	2.00	3.50	12.50	—
1926	4,000,000	1.50	3.00	6.00	20.00	—

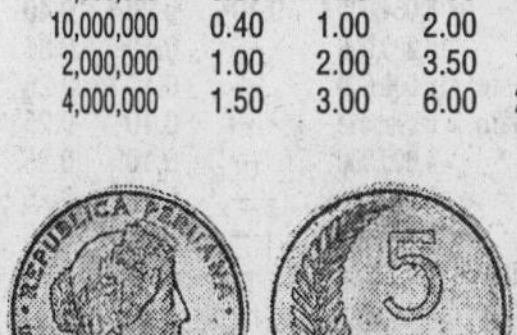

KM# 213.2 5 CENTAVOS **Composition:** Copper-Nickel **Obverse:** Date UN MIL NOVECIENTOS DIECIOCHO **Note:** Struck at London.

Date	Mintage	F	VF	XF	Unc	BU
1934	4,000,000	0.75	2.00	3.00	8.50	—
1934 Proof	—	Value: 175				
1935	4,000,000	0.50	1.25	2.00	6.00	—
1935 Proof	—	—	—	—	—	—
1937	2,000,000	0.75	2.00	3.00	8.50	—
1937 Proof	—	—	—	—	—	—
1939	2,000,000	0.50	1.25	2.00	6.00	—
1939 Proof	—	—	—	—	—	—
1940	2,000,000	0.50	1.25	2.00	6.00	—
1940 Proof	—	—	—	—	—	—
1941	2,000,000	0.50	1.25	2.00	6.00	—
1941 Proof	—	—	—	—	—	—

KM# 213.2a.1 5 CENTAVOS **Composition:** Brass **Obverse:** Date MIL NOVECIENTOS CUARENTA Y DOS **Note:** Struck at Philadelphia.

Date	Mintage	F	VF	XF	Unc	BU
1942	4,000,000	1.00	3.00	5.00	20.00	—
1943	4,000,000	1.00	3.00	5.00	20.00	—
1944	4,000,000	1.00	2.75	4.50	20.00	—

KM# 213.2a.2 5 CENTAVOS **Composition:** Brass **Obverse:** Date MIL NOVECIENTOS CUARENTA Y DOS

Date	Mintage	F	VF	XF	Unc	BU
1942S	4,000,000	2.50	4.50	9.00	45.00	—
1943S	4,000,000	2.50	4.50	8.00	40.00	—

KM# 213.2a.3 5 CENTAVOS **Composition:** Brass **Obverse:** Date MIL NOVECIENTOS CUARENTICUATRO **Note:** Struck at Lima.

Date	Mintage	F	VF	XF	Unc	BU
1944	1,106,000	1.50	3.50	6.00	15.00	—

KM# 223.1 5 CENTAVOS **Composition:** Brass **Obverse:** Short legend **Note:** Thick planchet.

Date	Mintage	F	VF	XF	Unc	BU
1945	2,768,000	0.35	0.75	1.50	4.00	—
1946/5	4,270,000	1.00	2.50	5.00	14.00	—
1946	Inc. above	0.25	0.50	1.00	3.50	—

KM# 223.3 5 CENTAVOS **Composition:** Brass **Obverse:** Long legend **Note:** Thick planchet.

Date	Mintage	F	VF	XF	Unc	BU
1947	7,683,000	0.25	0.50	1.00	3.00	—
1948	6,711,000	0.25	0.50	1.00	3.00	—
1949/8	5,550,000	1.00	2.00	4.00	10.00	—

KM# 223.4 5 CENTAVOS **Composition:** Brass **Obverse:** Different style legend **Note:** Thick planchet.

Date	Mintage	F	VF	XF	Unc	BU
1949	Inc. above	1.00	2.00	4.00	10.00	—
1950	7,933,000	0.25	0.50	1.00	3.00	—
195.1	8,064,000	0.25	0.50	1.00	3.00	—
1951	Inc. above	1.00	2.00	4.00	35.00	—

KM# 223.2 5 CENTAVOS **Composition:** Brass **Note:** Thin planchet. Varieties exist.

Date	Mintage	F	VF	XF	Unc	BU
1951	Inc. above	0.10	0.25	0.50	4.00	—
1952	7,840,000	0.10	0.25	0.50	4.00	—
1953	6,976,000	0.10	0.25	0.50	4.00	—
1954	6,244,000	0.10	0.20	0.40	1.00	—
1955	8,064,000	0.10	0.20	0.40	2.00	—
1956	16,200,000	—	0.10	0.35	1.50	—
1957 Small date	16,000,000	—	0.10	0.25	1.00	—
1957 Large date	Inc. above	—	0.10	0.25	1.00	—
1958	4,600,000	—	0.10	0.25	1.00	—
1959	8,300,000	—	0.10	0.25	1.00	—
1960/50	9,900,000	—	0.10	0.25	1.00	—
1960 Large date	Inc. above	—	0.10	0.25	1.00	—
1960 Small date	Inc. above	—	0.10	0.25	1.00	—
1961	10,200,000	—	0.10	0.20	1.00	—
1962 Curved 9	11,064,000	—	0.10	0.20	1.00	—
1962 Straight 9	Inc. above	—	0.10	0.20	1.00	—
1963	12,012,000	—	0.10	0.20	1.00	—
1964/3	12,304,000	—	0.10	0.35	1.50	—
1964	Inc. above	—	—	0.10	1.00	—
1965 Small date	12,500,000	—	—	0.10	1.00	—

Date	Mintage	F	VF	XF	Unc	BU
1965 Large date	Inc. above	—	0.10	0.20	1.00	—
1965 Proof	—	Value: 20.00				

KM# 232 5 CENTAVOS **Composition:** Brass **Obverse:** President Castilla

Date	Mintage	F	VF	XF	Unc	BU
1954	2,080,000	1.00	2.00	4.00	8.00	—

KM# 290 5 CENTAVOS **Composition:** Brass **Subject:** 400th Anniversary of Lima Mint **Obverse:** President Castilla

Date	Mintage	F	VF	XF	Unc	BU
1965	712,000	—	—	0.25	1.00	—
1965 Proof	—	Value: 100				

KM# 244.1 5 CENTAVOS **Composition:** Brass **Obverse:** Large arms

Date	Mintage	F	VF	XF	Unc	BU
1966	—	—	—	0.10	0.20	—

Note: PAREJA in field at lower left of arms

Date	Mintage	F	VF	XF	Unc	BU
1966 Proof	1,000	Value: 15.00				
1967	—	—	—	0.10	0.20	—
1968	—	—	—	0.10	0.20	—

KM# 244.1a 5 CENTAVOS **Composition:** Silver Plated Brass

Date	F	VF	XF	Unc	BU
1967	—	—	—	—	—

KM# 244.1b 5 CENTAVOS **Composition:** Silver

Date	F	VF	XF	Unc	BU
1967	—	—	—	—	—

KM# 244.2 5 CENTAVOS **Composition:** Brass **Edge:** Plain

Date	Mintage	F	VF	XF	Unc	BU
1969	17,880,000	—	—	—	0.10	—
1970	—	—	—	—	0.10	—
1971	24,320,000	—	—	—	0.10	—
1972	24,342,000	—	—	—	0.10	—
1973	25,074,000	—	—	—	0.10	—

KM# 244.3 5 CENTAVOS **Composition:** Brass **Obverse:** Small arms **Edge:** Plain

Date	F	VF	XF	Unc	BU
1973	—	—	—	0.10	—
1974	—	—	—	0.10	—
1975	—	—	—	0.10	—

KM# 214.1 10 CENTAVOS **Composition:** Copper-Nickel **Reverse:** UN MIL NOVECIENTOS DIECIOCHO **Note:** Struck at Philadelphia.

Date	Mintage	F	VF	XF	Unc	BU
1918	3,000,000	0.40	1.00	2.00	12.00	—
1919	2,500,000	0.40	1.00	2.00	12.00	—
1920	3,080,000	0.35	0.75	1.50	10.00	—
1921	6,920,000	0.35	0.75	1.50	10.00	—
1926	3,000,000	2.50	5.00	8.50	25.00	—

KM# 214.2 10 CENTAVOS **Composition:** Copper-Nickel **Note:** Struck at London.

Date	Mintage	F	VF	XF	Unc	BU
1935	1,000,000	0.75	1.50	3.00	12.00	—
1935 Proof	—	Value: 150				
1937	1,000,000	0.40	1.00	2.00	7.00	—
1937 Proof	—	—	—	—	—	—
1939	2,000,000	0.35	0.75	1.25	5.00	—
1939 Proof	—	—	—	—	—	—
1940	2,000,000	0.35	0.75	1.25	5.00	—
1940 Proof	—	Value: 125				
1941	2,000,000	0.35	0.75	1.25	5.00	—
1941 Proof	—	—	—	—	—	—

KM# 214a.3 10 CENTAVOS **Composition:** Brass **Obverse:** Date begins MIL..., spelled out with an "I" **Note:** Struck at Lima.

Date	F	VF	XF	Unc	BU
1942	5.00	9.00	15.00	40.00	—

KM# 214a.2 10 CENTAVOS **Composition:** Brass **Edge:** Plain

Date	Mintage	F	VF	XF	Unc	BU
1942S	2,000,000	6.00	12.00	20.00	50.00	—
1943S	2,000,000	1.50	3.00	6.00	20.00	—

KM# 214a.1 10 CENTAVOS **Composition:** Brass **Obverse:** Date begins MIL..., spelled out without "Y" **Note:** Struck at Philadelphia.

Date	Mintage	F	VF	XF	Unc	BU
1942	2,000,000	1.50	3.00	6.00	20.00	—
1943	2,000,000	1.50	3.00	6.00	20.00	—
1944	2,000,000	1.50	3.50	7.00	25.00	—

KM# 214a.4 10 CENTAVOS **Composition:** Brass **Obverse:** Date begins MIL..., spelled out with an "I" **Note:** Varieties exist.

Date	F	VF	XF	Unc	BU
1944	3.50	7.00	12.00	35.00	—

KM# 224.1 10 CENTAVOS **Composition:** Brass **Obverse:** Short legend **Note:** Thick planchet.

Date	Mintage	F	VF	XF	Unc	BU
1945	2,810,000	0.25	0.50	1.50	4.00	—
1946/5	4,863,000	0.50	1.00	2.50	8.00	—
1946	Inc. above	0.35	0.75	2.00	7.00	—

KM# 226.1 10 CENTAVOS **Composition:** Brass **Obverse:** Long legend **Note:** Thick planchet.

Date	Mintage	F	VF	XF	Unc	BU
1947	6,806,000	0.25	0.50	1.00	3.00	—
1948	5,771,000	0.25	0.50	1.25	4.00	—
1949/8	4,730,000	0.50	1.00	1.50	7.50	—

KM# 226.2 10 CENTAVOS **Composition:** Brass **Obverse:** Different legend style

Date	Mintage	F	VF	XF	Unc	BU
1949	Inc. above	0.25	0.50	1.00	5.00	—
1950	5,298,000	0.20	0.40	0.80	4.00	—
1950 AFP	Inc. above	0.25	0.50	1.25	8.00	—

Date	Mintage	F	VF	XF	Unc	BU
1951	7,324,000	6.00	10.00	15.00	40.00	—
1951/0 AFP	—	0.25	0.50	1.00	4.00	—
1951 AFP	—	0.20	0.40	0.80	3.00	—

KM# 224.2 10 CENTAVOS Composition: Brass
Obverse: Long legend **Note:** Thin planchet - 1.3 millimeters. Date varieties exist.

Date	Mintage	F	VF	XF	Unc	BU
1951	Inc. above	0.10	0.20	0.40	2.00	—
1951 AFP	—	0.10	0.20	0.40	2.00	—
1952	6,694,000	0.10	0.20	0.40	3.00	—
1952 AFP	—	0.10	0.20	0.40	3.00	—
1953	5,668,000	0.10	0.20	0.40	2.00	—
1953 AFP	—	0.10	0.20	0.40	2.00	—
1954	7,786,000	—	0.10	0.35	1.50	—
1954 AFP	—	—	0.10	0.35	1.50	—
1955	6,690,000	—	0.10	0.35	1.50	—
1955 AFP	—	—	0.10	0.35	1.50	—
1956/5	8,410,000	0.10	0.35	0.75	3.50	—
1956	Inc. above	—	0.10	0.25	1.00	—
1956 AFP	—	—	0.20	0.40	2.00	—
1957	8,420,000	—	0.10	0.25	1.00	—
1957 AFP	—	—	0.10	0.25	1.00	—
1958	10,380,000	—	0.10	0.25	1.00	—
1958 AFP	—	—	—	—	—	—
1959	8,300,000	—	0.10	0.25	1.00	—
1959 AFP	—	—	—	—	—	—
1960	12,600,000	—	0.10	0.25	1.00	—
1961	12,700,000	—	0.10	0.15	1.00	—
1962	14,598,000	—	0.10	0.15	1.00	—
1963	16,100,000	—	0.10	0.15	1.00	—
1964	16,504,000	—	0.10	0.15	1.00	—
1965	17,808,000	—	0.10	0.15	1.00	—
1965 Proof	—	Value: 25.00				

KM# 233 10 CENTAVOS Composition: Brass
Obverse: President Castilla

Date	Mintage	F	VF	XF	Unc	BU
1954	1,818,000	1.00	2.00	4.50	10.00	—

KM# 237 10 CENTAVOS Composition: Brass
Subject: 400th Anniversary of Lima Mint

Date	Mintage	F	VF	XF	Unc	BU
1965	572,000	—	—	0.35	1.00	—
1965 Proof	—	Value: 150				

KM# 245.1 10 CENTAVOS Composition: Brass
Obverse: Large arms **Edge:** Reeded **Note:** Date varieties exist.

Date	Mintage	F	VF	XF	Unc	BU
1966		—	—	0.10	0.75	—

Note: PAREJA in field at lower left of arms

Date	Mintage	F	VF	XF	Unc	BU
1966 Proof	1,000	Value: 15.00				
1967		—	—	0.10	0.75	—
1968		—	—	0.10	0.75	—

KM# 245.2 10 CENTAVOS Composition: Brass
Obverse: Vicuna arms **Edge:** Plain **Note:** Date varieties exist.

Date	Mintage	F	VF	XF	Unc	BU
1967	—	—	—	0.10	0.25	—
1969	24,390,000	—	—	0.10	0.25	—

Date	Mintage	F	VF	XF	Unc	BU
1970	29,110,000	—	—	0.10	0.20	—
1971	30,590,000	—	—	0.10	0.20	—
1972	34,442,000	—	—	0.10	0.20	—
1973	33,864,000	—	—	0.10	0.20	—

KM# 245.1a 10 CENTAVOS Composition: Silver Plated Brass

Date		F	VF	XF	Unc	BU
1967		—	—	—	—	—

KM# 245.3 10 CENTAVOS Composition: Brass
Obverse: Small arms **Edge:** Plain

Date	Mintage	F	VF	XF	Unc	BU
1973	Inc. above	—	—	0.10	0.15	—
1974	—	—	—	0.10	0.15	—
1975	10,430,000	—	—	0.10	0.15	—

KM# 263 10 CENTAVOS Composition: Brass

Date		F	VF	XF	Unc	BU
1975		—	—	0.10	0.15	—

KM# 215.1 20 CENTAVOS Composition: Copper-Nickel **Obverse:** Date UN NOVECIENTOS DIECIOCHO **Note:** Struck at Philadelphia.

Date	Mintage	F	VF	XF	Unc	BU
1918	2,500,000	0.40	1.00	2.50	15.00	—
1919	1,250,000	1.25	1.25	3.00	15.00	—
1920	1,464,000	1.25	1.25	3.00	18.00	—
1921	8,536,000	0.85	0.85	2.00	10.00	—
1926	2,500,000	2.50	2.50	6.00	25.00	—

KM# 215.2 20 CENTAVOS Composition: Copper-Nickel **Note:** Struck at London.

Date	Mintage	F	VF	XF	Unc	BU
1940	1,000,000	0.25	0.75	1.75	5.50	—
1940 Proof	—	Value: 150				
1941	1,000,000	0.35	1.00	2.50	7.50	—
1941 Proof	—	Value: 125				

KM# 215a.1 20 CENTAVOS Composition: Copper-Nickel **Obverse:** Date MIL NOVECIENTOS CUARENTA Y TRES **Note:** Struck at Philadelphia.

Date	Mintage	F	VF	XF	Unc	BU
1942	500,000	3.00	6.00	13.50	60.00	—
1943	500,000	3.00	6.00	13.50	60.00	—
1944	500,000	4.00	7.50	16.50	65.00	—

KM# 221.1 20 CENTAVOS Composition: Copper-Nickel **Obverse:** Divided legend **Note:** Thick planchet. Struck at Lima.

Date	Mintage	F	VF	XF	Unc	BU
1942	300,000	1.00	2.50	5.00	12.50	—
1943	1,900,000	0.75	1.50	2.50	7.50	—
1944	2,963,000	0.60	1.25	2.00	6.00	—

KM# 215a.2 20 CENTAVOS Composition: Copper-Nickel

Date	Mintage	F	VF	XF	Unc	BU
1942S	500,000	6.00	12.00	25.00	100	—
1943S	500,000	3.00	6.00	12.50	75.00	—

KM# 221.3 20 CENTAVOS Composition: Copper-Nickel **Obverse:** Continuous legend

Date	Mintage	F	VF	XF	Unc	BU
1945	3,043,000	0.25	—	0.75	1.50	—
1946/5	Inc. above	0.25	0.65	1.00	2.00	—
1946	Inc. above	0.25	0.50	0.75	1.50	—

KM# 221.2 20 CENTAVOS Composition: Copper-Nickel **Obverse:** AFP on truncation, continuous legend

Date	Mintage	F	VF	XF	Unc	BU
1946	3,410,000	0.25	0.50	0.85	3.00	—
1947	4,307,000	0.25	0.50	0.85	3.00	—
1948	3,578,000	0.25	0.50	0.85	3.00	—
1949/8	2,709,000	0.75	1.50	2.50	6.50	—

KM# 221.2a 20 CENTAVOS Composition: Copper

Date	Mintage	F	VF	XF	Unc	BU
1947	300	—	—	—	100	—

KM# 221.4 20 CENTAVOS Composition: Copper-Nickel **Obverse:** Different legend style

Date	Mintage	F	VF	XF	Unc	BU
1949	Inc. above	0.50	1.00	1.75	4.50	—
1950	2,427,000	1.00	1.75	3.00	8.00	—
1951	2,941,000	3.00	7.50	12.50	35.00	—

KM# 221.2b 20 CENTAVOS Composition: Brass
Note: Thin planchet - 1.3 millimeters. AFP. Date varieties exist.

Date	Mintage	F	VF	XF	Unc	BU
1951	Inc. above	0.20	0.40	0.75	2.00	—
1951 Without AFP	—	—	—	—	—	—
1952	4,410,000	0.20	0.40	0.75	2.50	—
1952 Without AFP	Inc. above	—	—	—	—	—
1953	2,615,000	0.20	0.40	1.50	8.00	—
1954	1,816,000	1.50	2.50	4.00	12.00	—
1955 Large date	4,050,000	0.10	0.15	0.30	1.50	—
1955 Small date	Inc. above	0.20	0.40	1.50	8.00	—
1956	3,760,000	0.10	0.15	0.30	1.50	—
1957	3,680,000	0.10	0.15	0.30	1.00	—
1958	3,100,000	0.10	0.15	0.30	1.00	—
1959	5,450,000	—	0.10	0.20	1.00	—
1959 Without AFP	—	—	—	—	—	—
1960/90 Without AFP	—	—	—	—	—	—
1960	6,750,000	—	0.10	0.20	1.00	—
1960 Without AFP	—	0.25	0.75	1.50	4.00	—
1961	6,800,000	—	0.10	0.20	1.00	—
1961 Without AFP	—	—	—	—	—	—
1962	7,357,000	—	0.10	0.20	1.00	—
1963/2	8,843,000	0.15	0.25	0.50	2.00	—
1963	Inc. above	—	0.10	0.20	1.00	—
1964	9,550,000	—	0.10	0.20	1.00	—
1965 With inverted V for A in AFP	—	—	0.10	0.20	1.00	—
1965 Without AFP	—	—	—	—	—	—

KM# 234 20 CENTAVOS Composition: Copper-Nickel **Subject:** President Castilla **Edge:** Reeded **Note:** Thin planchet - 1.3 millimeters. AFP.

Date	Mintage	F	VF	XF	Unc	BU
1954	799,000	2.00	4.00	8.00	15.00	—

KM# 221.2c 20 CENTAVOS Composition: Copper-Nickel **Edge:** Reeded **Note:** Thin planchet - 1.3 millimeters. AFP.

Date	F	VF	XF	Unc	BU
1958	—	—	—	150	—
1965 Proof	—	Value: 30.00			

KM# 264 20 CENTAVOS Composition: Copper-Nickel

Date	F	VF	XF	Unc	BU
1975	0.10	0.20	0.50	1.00	—

KM# 238 25 CENTAVOS Composition: Brass **Subject:** 400th Anniversary of Lima Mint

Date	Mintage	F	VF	XF	Unc	BU
1965	1,113,000	—	0.25	0.35	0.75	—
1965 Proof	—	Value: 200				

KM# 246.1 25 CENTAVOS Composition: Brass **Obverse:** Large arms **Edge:** Reeded

Date	Mintage	F	VF	XF	Unc	BU
1966 PAREJA in field at lower left of arms		—	0.15	0.25	0.50	—
1966 Proof	1,000	Value: 15.00				
1967		—	0.15	0.25	0.50	—
1968		—	0.15	0.25	0.50	—

KM# 246.1a 25 CENTAVOS Composition: Silver Plated Brass

Date	F	VF	XF	Unc	BU
1967	—	—	—	—	—

KM# 246.2 25 CENTAVOS Composition: Brass **Edge:** Plain

Date	Mintage	F	VF	XF	Unc	BU
1968 AP	Inc. above	—	0.15	0.25	0.50	—
1969 AP on reverse	7,440,000	—	0.20	0.40	1.00	—
1969 With inverted V for A in AP	Inc. above	—	0.20	0.40	1.00	—
1969 Without AP	Inc. above	—	0.15	0.25	0.50	—
1970	6,341,000	—	0.20	0.40	1.00	—
1971	3,196,000	—	0.20	0.40	1.00	—
1972	5,523,000	—	0.20	0.40	1.00	—
1973	7,492,000	—	0.15	0.25	0.50	—

KM# 259 25 CENTAVOS Composition: Brass **Obverse:** Small arms

Date	F	VF	XF	Unc	BU
1973	—	0.10	0.15	0.25	—
1974	—	0.10	0.15	0.25	—
1975	—	0.10	0.15	0.25	—

KM# 206.2 1/2 DINERO Weight: 1.2500 g. **Composition:** 0.9000 Silver .0362 oz. ASW **Obverse:** Without JR on stems **Reverse:** Denomination in straight line **Note:** Most coins 1900-06 show faint to strong traces of 9/8 or 90/89 in date. Non-overdates without such traces are scarce. Most coins of 1907-17 have engraver's initial R at left of shield tip on reverse. Many other varieties exist. Struck at Lima.

Date	Mintage	F	VF	XF	Unc	BU
1900/899 JF	Inc. above	1.00	2.00	5.00	14.00	—
1901/801 JF	500,000	0.60	1.25	2.50	6.00	—
1901/801/701 JF	Inc. above	0.60	1.25	2.50	6.00	—
1901/891/791	Inc. above	0.60	1.25	2.00	5.00	—
1901/891 JF	Inc. above	0.60	1.25	2.00	5.00	—
1901 JF	Inc. above	0.75	1.50	3.50	10.00	—
1902/802 JF	616,000	0.60	1.25	2.00	5.00	—
1902/892 JF	Inc. above	0.60	1.25	2.00	5.00	—
1902/92	Inc. above	0.60	1.25	2.00	5.00	—
1902 JF	Inc. above	0.75	1.50	3.50	10.00	—
1903/803 JF	1,798,000	0.50	1.50	3.00	9.00	—
1903/893 JF	Inc. above	0.50	1.50	3.00	9.00	—
1903/897 JF	Inc. above	0.50	1.00	2.50	7.00	—
1903 JF	Inc. above	0.75	1.50	3.00	10.00	—
1904/804 JF	723,000	0.60	1.25	2.00	5.00	—
1904/804 JF FFLIZ Error	Inc. above	3.00	6.00	12.00	25.00	—
1904/884 JF	Inc. above	0.60	1.25	2.00	6.00	—
1904/891 JF	Inc. above	0.60	1.25	2.00	6.00	—
1904/893 JF	Inc. above	0.60	1.25	2.00	5.00	—
1904/894 JF	Inc. above	0.60	1.25	2.00	5.00	—
1904/894 JF FFLIZ Error	Inc. above	2.00	4.50	8.00	12.00	—
1904 JF	Inc. above	0.75	1.50	3.50	10.00	—
1904 JF FFLIZ Error	Inc. above	2.00	4.50	8.00	12.00	—
1905/805 JF	1,400,000	0.75	1.50	3.50	8.00	—
1905/891 JF	Inc. above	1.00	2.00	4.50	12.00	—
1905/893 JF	Inc. above	1.00	2.00	4.50	12.00	—
1905/894	Inc. above	1.00	2.00	4.50	12.00	—
1905/895 JF	Inc. above	0.50	1.25	2.00	5.00	—
1905/3 JF	Inc. above	1.00	2.00	4.50	12.00	—
1905 JF	Inc. above	0.75	1.50	3.50	10.00	—
1906/806 JF	900,000	0.75	1.50	3.50	8.00	—
1906/886 JF	Inc. above	0.75	1.50	3.50	8.00	—
1906/895 JF	Inc. above	0.75	1.50	3.50	8.00	—
1906/896 JF	Inc. above	0.50	1.25	2.00	5.00	—
1906 JF	Inc. above	0.75	1.50	3.00	10.00	—
1907 FG	600,000	0.75	1.50	3.00	10.00	—
1908/7 FG	200,000	1.50	3.00	6.00	15.00	—
1908 FG	Inc. above	0.75	1.50	3.50	10.00	—
1909/7 FG	—	3.00	6.00	12.50	30.00	—
1909 FG	—	0.75	1.50	3.50	8.00	—
1910 FG	640,000	0.50	1.00	2.00	5.00	—
1911 FG	460,000	0.50	1.25	2.00	5.00	—
1912 FG	120,000	0.60	1.25	2.50	6.00	—
1913 FG	480,000	0.50	1.00	2.00	5.00	—
1914/3 FG	—	0.75	1.50	3.50	10.00	—
1914/03 FG	—	1.00	2.50	5.50	15.00	—
1914/04 FG	—	1.00	2.50	5.50	15.00	—
1914 FG	—	0.50	1.00	2.00	5.00	—
1916/3 FG	860,000	0.50	1.00	2.00	5.00	—
1916/3 FG FERUANA Error	—	1.00	2.00	4.50	12.00	—
1916 FG	Inc. above	0.35	0.75	1.75	4.50	—
1916/5 FG PERUANA Error	Inc. above	1.00	2.00	4.50	12.00	—
1916/5 FG FERUANA Error	Inc. above	1.00	2.00	4.50	12.00	—
1916/5 Without FERUANA	Inc. above	1.00	2.00	4.50	12.00	—
1916 FG FERUANA Error	Inc. above	1.00	2.00	4.50	15.00	—
1916 Matte	—	—	—	—	—	—
1917/87 FG	140,000	0.50	1.00	2.00	5.00	—
1917 FG	Inc. above	0.50	1.00	2.00	5.00	—

KM# 204.2 DINERO Weight: 2.5000 g. **Composition:** 0.9000 Silver .0723 oz. ASW **Obverse:** Large wreath **Reverse:** Denomination in curved line **Note:** Varieties exist. Struck at Lima.

Date	Mintage	F	VF	XF	Unc	BU
1902/1 JF	375,000	1.00	2.00	3.50	15.00	—
1902/891 JF	Inc. above	1.00	2.00	3.50	15.00	—
1902/892 JF	Inc. above	1.00	2.00	3.50	15.00	—
1902/897 JF	Inc. above	1.00	2.00	3.50	15.00	—
1902 JF	Inc. above	1.00	2.00	4.00	18.00	—
1903/803 JF	887,000	1.00	2.00	3.50	15.00	—
1903/807 JF	Inc. above	1.00	2.00	3.50	15.00	—
1903/892 JF	Inc. above	0.75	2.00	3.50	12.00	—
1903/893 JF	Inc. above	0.75	2.00	3.50	12.00	—
1903/92 JF	Inc. above	0.75	2.00	3.50	12.00	—
1903 JF	Inc. above	0.75	2.00	3.50	15.00	—
1904 JF	380,000	1.00	2.50	4.00	15.00	—
1905/1 JF	700,000	1.00	2.50	4.00	15.00	—
1905/3 JF	Inc. above	1.00	2.50	4.00	15.00	—
1905 JF	Inc. above	0.75	2.00	3.50	15.00	—
1906 JF	826,000	0.75	2.00	3.50	15.00	—
1907 JF Rare	500,000	—	—	—	—	—
1907 FG/JF	Inc. above	1.25	2.50	4.50	15.00	—
1907 FG	Inc. above	1.00	1.75	3.00	12.00	—
1908/6 FG/JF	Inc. above	1.00	2.25	4.00	15.00	—
1908 FG/JF	200,000	1.00	2.25	4.00	15.00	—
1908 FG/GF	Inc. above	1.00	2.25	4.00	15.00	—
1908 FG	Inc. above	1.00	1.75	3.00	15.00	—
1909 FG	—	2.00	4.00	8.00	20.00	—
1909 FG/FO	—	2.00	4.00	8.00	20.00	—
1909 FG/FF	—	2.00	4.00	8.00	20.00	—
1910 FG	210,000	0.60	1.25	3.00	15.00	—
1910 FG/JF	Inc. above	1.00	2.25	4.00	18.00	—
1910 FG/JG	Inc. above	1.00	2.25	4.00	18.00	—
1911 FG	200,000	0.75	1.50	3.00	15.00	—
1911 FG/JF	Inc. above	1.00	2.25	4.00	18.00	—
1911 FG/JG	—	1.00	2.25	4.00	18.00	—
1912 FG	400,000	0.60	1.25	3.00	15.00	—
1912/02 FG/JF	Inc. above	1.00	2.25	4.00	18.00	—
1912 FG/JF	Inc. above	1.00	2.25	4.00	18.00	—
1912 FG/JG	Inc. above	1.00	2.25	4.00	18.00	—
1913/1 FG/JF	Inc. above	1.00	2.25	4.00	18.00	—
1913/2 FG	360,000	1.00	2.25	4.00	18.00	—
1913/7 FG/G	Inc. above	1.00	2.25	4.00	18.00	—
1913 FG	Inc. above	0.60	1.25	3.00	15.00	—
1913 FG/G	Inc. above	0.60	1.25	2.50	12.00	—
1913 FG/JB	Inc. above	1.50	3.00	5.50	18.00	—
1916 FG Large date	430,000	1.25	2.50	4.50	15.00	—
1916 FG Small date	Inc. above	0.60	1.25	2.00	6.00	—
1916 FG/JG	Inc. above	2.00	5.00	7.50	20.00	—
1916 FG/FF	Inc. above	2.00	5.00	7.50	20.00	—

KM# 205.2 1/5 SOL Weight: 5.0000 g. **Composition:** 0.9000 Silver .1447 oz. ASW **Reverse:** Libertad incuse **Edge:** Plain **Note:** Die varieties exist. Some coins 1893-1900 have engraver's initials JR left of shield on reverse and some 1911-17 have R in same location. Struck at Lima.

Date	Mintage	F	VF	XF	Unc	BU
1901 JF	638,000	1.50	3.00	5.50	12.00	—
1903/1 JF	702,000	2.00	4.00	7.00	17.50	—
1903/13 JF	Inc. above	1.75	3.50	6.00	15.00	—
1903 JF	Inc. above	1.50	3.00	5.50	12.00	—
1906 JF	660,000	1.50	3.00	5.50	12.00	—
1907 JF	1,370,000	1.25	2.00	4.00	10.00	—
1907 FG	Inc. above	1.50	3.00	5.50	12.00	—
1908/7 FG	560,000	1.75	3.50	6.00	15.00	—
1908 FG	Inc. above	1.50	3.00	5.50	12.00	—
1909 FG	42,000	2.00	4.00	9.00	27.50	—
1910/00 FG	165,000	3.00	7.00	12.00	25.00	—
1910 FG	Inc. above	3.00	7.00	12.00	25.00	—
1911 FG	250,000	1.50	3.00	5.50	9.00	—
1911 FG-R	Inc. above	1.50	3.00	5.50	9.00	—
1912 FG	300,000	1.25	2.00	4.00	8.00	—
1912 FG-R	Inc. above	1.50	3.00	5.50	9.00	—
1913 FG	223,000	1.75	3.50	6.00	15.00	—
1913 FG-R	Inc. above	1.75	3.50	6.00	15.00	—
1914 FG	10,000	5.00	10.00	20.00	45.00	—
1915 FG	—	25.00	35.00	60.00	100	—
1916 FG	425,000	2.00	5.00	10.00	25.00	—
1916 FG-R	Inc. above	1.50	3.00	5.00	9.00	—
1917 FG-R	20,000	8.00	15.00	30.00	60.00	—

KM# 203 1/2 SOL Weight: 12.5000 g. **Composition:** 0.9000 Silver .3617 oz. ASW **Obverse:** Large wreath **Reverse:** Denomination in straight line **Note:** Mint mark: LIMA. Date varieties exist. Most coins have engraver's initials JR left of shield tip on reverse.

Date	Mintage	F	VF	XF	Unc	BU
1907 LIMA FG-JR	1,000,000	BV	4.00	10.00	20.00	—
1908/7 LIMA FG-JR	30,000	15.00	30.00	60.00	290	—
1908 LIMA FG-JR	Inc. above	12.00	25.00	50.00	150	—
1914 LIMA FG-JR	173,000	BV	4.50	15.00	35.00	—
1915 LIMA FG-JR	570,000	BV	3.50	6.50	15.00	—
1916 LIMA FG	384,000	BV	3.50	6.50	15.00	—
1916 LIMA FG-JR	—	BV	3.50	6.50	15.00	—
1917 LIMA FG-JR	178,000	BV	4.00	10.00	20.00	—

KM# 216 1/2 SOL Weight: 12.5000 g. **Composition:** 0.5000 Silver .2009 oz. ASW **Note:** Date varieties exist. Engraver's initials appear on stems of obverse wreath.

Date	Mintage	F	VF	XF	Unc	BU
1922 LIMA LIBERTAD incuse, J.R. on reverse	465,000	BV	4.50	18.50	70.00	—
1922 LIMA LIBERTAD in relief	Inc. above	BV	4.50	18.50	50.00	—
1923 LIMA GM LIBER/TAD, round-top 3	2,520,000	BV	2.50	6.00	20.00	—
1923/2 LIMA Flat-top 3	Inc. above	BV	2.50	5.50	20.00	—
1923 LIMA Flat-top 3	Inc. above	BV	2.50	5.50	20.00	—
1924 LIMA GM	238,000	BV	6.00	20.00	50.00	—
1926 LIMA GM	694,000	BV	3.50	7.50	25.00	—
1927 LIMA GM	2,640,000	BV	2.50	5.50	15.00	—
1928/7 LIMA GM	3,028,000	—	—	—	—	—
1928 LIMA GM	Inc. above	BV	2.50	5.50	15.00	—
1929 LIMA GM	3,068,000	BV	2.50	5.50	15.00	—
1935 LIMA AP	2,653,000	BV	2.50	5.00	14.00	—
1935 LIMA	—	—	—	—	—	—

KM# 220.1 1/2 SOL Composition: Brass **Obverse:** Five palm leaves point to llama on shield **Note:** Struck at London.

Date	Mintage	F	VF	XF	Unc	BU
1935 Proof	—	Value: 200				
1935	10,000,000	0.50	1.25	2.25	7.00	—
1941	4,000,000	0.50	1.25	2.25	7.00	—

KM# 220.2 1/2 SOL Composition: Brass **Note:** Struck at Philadelphia.

Date	Mintage	F	VF	XF	Unc	BU
1942	4,000,000	1.50	3.00	5.00	20.00	—
1943	4,000,000	3.00	6.50	12.50	35.00	—
1944	Inc. above	1.50	3.00	5.00	20.00	—

KM# 220.4 1/2 SOL Composition: Brass **Obverse:** Three palm leaves point to llama on shield **Note:** Dates 1941-44 have thick flat-top 4 without serifs. 1945 has narrow 4 like KM#220.5. Struck at Lima.

Date	Mintage	F	VF	XF	Unc	BU
1941	2,000,000	3.00	6.50	12.50	35.00	—
1942	Inc. above	1.50	3.00	5.00	15.00	—
1942 AP	—	—	—	—	—	—
1943	2,000,000	0.50	1.00	2.00	12.00	—
1944/2	4,000,000	—	—	—	—	—
1944	Inc. above	0.40	0.85	1.75	7.00	—
1944 AP	Inc. above	—	—	—	—	—
1945	4,000,000	0.75	1.50	3.00	10.00	—

KM# 220.5 1/2 SOL Composition: Brass **Obverse:** Three palm leaves point to llama on shield **Note:** 1942, 1944 AP, and all 1945-49 have narrow 4 without serif on crossbar. 1944 without AP has flat-top 4 like KM#220.4. Engraver's initials AP appear on wreath stems of some 1944-45, all 1946 and some 1947 coins. Varieties exist, including narrow and wide dates for 1956 and 1961 issues.

Date	Mintage	F	VF	XF	Unc	BU
1942 Long-top 2	Inc. above	1.50	3.00	5.00	15.00	—
1944	Inc. above	0.75	1.50	3.00	10.00	—
1944 AP	Inc. above	0.50	1.00	2.00	7.00	—
1945	Inc. above	0.75	1.50	3.00	10.00	—
1945 AP	Inc. above	0.75	1.50	3.00	10.00	—
1946/5 AP	3,744,000	2.00	3.50	6.50	17.50	—
1946 AP	Inc. above	0.40	0.75	1.25	4.00	—
1947 AP	6,066,000	0.40	0.75	1.25	5.00	—
1947	Inc. above	0.40	0.75	1.25	5.00	—
1948	3,324,000	0.40	0.75	1.25	4.00	—
1949/8	420,000	1.00	2.00	4.00	12.00	—
1949	Inc. above	1.50	3.00	6.00	18.00	—
1950	91,000	1.25	2.25	4.50	15.00	—
1951/8	930,000	0.50	1.00	2.00	7.00	—
1951	Inc. above	0.50	1.00	2.00	7.00	—
1952	935,000	0.75	1.50	3.00	10.00	—
1953	817,000	0.50	1.00	2.00	7.00	—
1954	637,000	0.75	1.50	3.00	10.00	—
1955	1,383,000	0.15	0.35	0.75	4.00	—
1956	2,309,000	0.10	0.25	0.40	1.50	—
1957	2,700,000	0.10	0.25	0.50	2.00	—
1958	2,691,000	0.10	0.25	0.40	1.50	—
1959	3,609,000	0.10	0.25	0.40	1.50	—
1960	5,600,000	0.10	0.20	0.35	0.75	—
1961	4,400,000	0.10	0.20	0.35	0.75	—
1962	3,540,000	0.10	0.20	0.35	1.00	—
1963	4,345,000	0.10	0.20	0.35	0.75	—
1964	5,315,000	0.10	0.20	0.35	1.50	—
1965	7,090,000	0.10	0.20	0.35	1.75	—
1965 Proof	—	Value: 50.00				

KM# 220.3 1/2 SOL Composition: Brass **Note:** The coins struck in Philadelphia and San Francisco have a serif on the "4" of the date; the Lima and London coins do not.

Date	Mintage	F	VF	XF	Unc	BU
1942S	1,668,000	1.50	3.00	5.00	15.00	—
1943S	6,332,000	1.50	3.00	5.00	15.00	—

KM# 239 1/2 SOL Composition: Brass **Subject:** 400th Anniversary of Lima Mint

Date	Mintage	F	VF	XF	Unc	BU
ND(1965)	10,971,000	BV	2.50	5.50	15.00	—
ND(1965) Proof	—	BV	2.50	5.00	14.00	—

KM# 247 1/2 SOL Composition: Brass **Obverse:** Large arms **Reverse:** Vicuna

Date	Mintage	F	VF	XF	Unc	BU
1966	—	0.10	0.20	0.50	—	
1966 Proof	1,000	Value: 20.00				
1967	—	0.10	0.20	0.50	—	
1967 PAREJA on obverse and reverse	—	0.10	0.20	0.50	—	
1968	3.00	7.00	15.00	30.00	—	
1968 JAS	—	0.10	0.20	0.50	—	
1969	—	0.10	0.20	0.50	—	
1970	—	0.10	0.20	0.50	—	

Note: Date varieties exist

Date	Mintage	F	VF	XF	Unc	BU
1971	—	0.15	0.20	0.50	—	
1972	—	0.10	0.20	0.50	—	
1973	—	0.10	0.20	0.50	—	

KM# 247a 1/2 SOL Composition: Silver Plated Brass

Date	F	VF	XF	Unc	BU
1967	—	—	—	—	—

KM# 247b 1/2 SOL Composition: Silver

Date	F	VF	XF	Unc	BU
1967	—	—	—	—	—

KM# 260 1/2 SOL Composition: Silver Plated Brass **Obverse:** Small arms

Date	Mintage	F	VF	XF	Unc	BU
1973	Inc. above	—	0.10	0.20	0.50	—
1974/1	—	—	0.10	0.20	0.50	—
1974	14,518,000	—	0.10	0.20	0.50	—
1975	14,039,000	—	0.10	0.20	0.50	—

KM# 265 1/2 SOL Composition: Silver **Obverse:** Small arms **Note:** Without mint mark.

Date	Mintage	F	VF	XF	Unc	BU
1975	62,682,000	—	0.10	0.20	0.30	—
1976	369,828,000	—	0.10	0.20	0.30	—
1977	18,943,000	—	0.10	0.20	0.30	—

KM# 268 1/2 SOL Weight: 9.3500 g. **Composition:** 0.9000 Silver .2706 oz. ASW **Subject:** 150th Anniversary - Battle of Ayacucho

Date	Mintage	F	VF	XF	Unc	BU
1976	10,000	—	—	—	150	—

KM# 196.26 SOL Weight: 25.0000 g. **Composition:** 0.9000 Silver .7234 oz. ASW **Reverse:** Libertad incuse **Note:** Type XII. Legends have smaller lettering. Varieties exist.

Date	Mintage	F	VF	XF	Unc	BU
1914 FG	620,000	6.00	7.00	9.00	22.00	—
1915 FG	Inc. above	6.00	7.00	9.00	20.00	—

KM# 196.28 SOL Weight: 25.0000 g. **Composition:** 0.9000 Silver .7234 oz. ASW **Reverse:** Libertad in relief **Note:** Type III.

Date	F	VF	XF	Unc	BU
1916 FG	6.00	7.00	8.00	20.00	—

KM# 196.27 SOL Weight: 25.0000 g. **Composition:** 0.9000 Silver .7234 oz. ASW **Reverse:** Libertad incuse

Date	Mintage	F	VF	XF	Unc	BU
1916 FG	1,927,000	6.00	7.00	8.00	20.00	—

KM# 217.1 SOL Weight: 25.0000 g. **Composition:** 0.5000 Silver .4019 oz. ASW **Obverse:** Finess omitted from legend **Reverse:** Libertad in relief

Date	Mintage	F	VF	XF	Unc	BU
1922 Rare	—	—	—	—	—	—
1923	3,600	15.00	30.00	70.00	275	—

KM# 217.2 SOL Weight: 25.0000 g. **Composition:** 0.5000 Silver .4019 oz. ASW **Reverse:** LIBERTAD incuse

Date	Mintage	F	VF	XF	Unc	BU
1923	1,400	35.00	75.00	165	475	—

KM# 218.1 SOL Weight: 25.0000 g. **Composition:** 0.5000 Silver .4019 oz. ASW **Note:** Small letters. The Philadelphia and Lima strikings may be distinguished by the fact that the letters in the legends are smaller on those pieces produced at Philadelphia. All bear the name of the Lima Mint.

Date	F	VF	XF	Unc	BU
1923	BV	5.50	8.50	15.00	—
1924/823	5.50	10.00	20.00	40.00	—
1924/824	5.50	10.00	20.00	40.00	—
1924	BV	5.50	8.50	15.00	—
1925	BV	5.50	10.00	20.00	—
1926	BV	5.50	8.50	15.00	—

KM# 218.2 SOL Weight: 25.0000 g. **Composition:** 0.5000 Silver .4019 oz. ASW **Obverse:** Engraver's initials GM on stems flanking date **Note:** Large letters. Struck at Lima.

Date	Mintage	F	VF	XF	Unc	BU
1924	96,000	5.50	9.00	20.00	65.00	—
1925	1,004,999	BV	5.50	8.50	15.00	—
1930	76,000	BV	5.50	10.00	20.00	—
1931	24,000	BV	5.50	10.00	22.00	—
1933	5,000	6.00	12.00	20.00	40.00	—
1934/3	2,855,000	BV	5.50	10.00	20.00	—
1934	Inc. above	BV	5.50	7.00	12.50	—
1935	695,000	BV	5.50	10.00	20.00	—

KM# 222 SOL **Composition:** Brass **Note:** Date varieties exist.

Date	Mintage	F	VF	XF	Unc	BU
1943	10,000,000	0.35	1.25	3.00	8.00	—
1944	Inc. above	0.35	1.25	3.00	7.00	—
1945	—	0.50	1.50	3.50	9.00	—
1946	1,752,000	0.50	1.50	3.00	8.00	—
1947	3,302,000	0.35	1.00	2.00	6.00	—
1948	1,992,000	0.35	1.00	2.00	6.00	—
1949/8	751,000	2.00	4.00	7.00	20.00	—
1949	Inc. above	3.50	7.50	12.00	25.00	—
1950	1,249,000	7.00	10.00	15.00	25.00	—
1951/0	2,093,999	0.25	0.50	1.50	6.00	—
1951	Inc. above	0.25	0.50	1.50	6.00	—
1952	2,037,000	0.25	0.50	1.50	6.00	—
1953	1,243,000	3.00	6.00	10.00	25.00	—
1954	1,220,000	0.35	0.75	1.75	6.00	—
1955	1,323,000	0.35	0.75	1.75	6.00	—
1956	3,450,000	0.15	0.35	0.75	3.00	—
1957	3,086,000	0.15	0.35	1.00	5.00	—
1958	3,390,000	0.15	0.35	0.75	3.00	—
1958 Wide date and narrow date	—	0.15	0.35	0.75	3.00	—
1959	4,975,000	0.15	0.35	1.00	5.00	—
1960	5,800,000	0.15	0.35	0.75	1.50	—
1961	5,200,000	0.15	0.35	0.75	2.00	—
1962	5,102,000	0.15	0.35	0.75	1.50	—
1963	5,499,000	0.15	0.35	0.75	2.00	—
1964	5,888,000	0.15	0.35	0.75	2.00	—
1964 Wide date and narrow date	—	0.15	0.35	0.75	3.00	—
1965	5,504,000	0.15	0.35	0.75	2.00	—
1965 Proof	—	Value: 75.00				

KM# 240 SOL **Composition:** Brass **Subject:** 400th Anniversary of the Lima Mint

Date	Mintage	F	VF	XF	Unc	BU
ND(1965)	3,103,000	—	0.35	0.75	1.50	—
ND(1965) Proof	—	Value: 500				

KM# 248 SOL **Composition:** Brass

Date	Mintage	F	VF	XF	Unc	BU
1966		—	0.10	0.25	0.75	—
1966 Proof	1,000	Value: 25.00				
1967		—	0.10	0.25	0.75	—
1968		—	0.10	0.25	0.75	—
1969		—	0.10	0.25	0.75	—
1970		—	0.10	0.25	0.75	—
1971		—	0.10	0.25	0.75	—
1972		—	0.10	0.25	0.75	—
1973		—	0.10	0.25	0.75	—
1974		—	0.10	0.25	0.75	—
1975		—	0.10	0.25	0.75	—

KM# 248a SOL **Composition:** Silver Plated Brass

Date	F	VF	XF	Unc	BU
1967	—	—	—	—	—

KM# 248b SOL **Composition:** Silver

Date	F	VF	XF	Unc	BU
1967	—	—	—	—	—

KM# 266.1 SOL **Composition:** Brass

Date	Mintage	F	VF	XF	Unc	BU
1975	354,485,000	—	—	0.10	0.25	—
1976	114,660,000	—	—	0.10	0.25	—

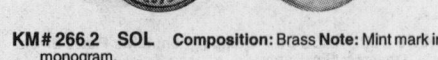

KM# 269 SOL Weight: 23.4000 g. **Composition:** 0.9000 Gold .6772 oz. AGW **Subject:** 150th Anniversary - Battle of Ayacucho **Note:** Mint mark in monogram.

Date	Mintage	F	VF	XF	Unc	BU
1976 LIMA	10,000	—	—	—	450	—

KM# 266.2 SOL **Composition:** Brass **Note:** Mint mark in monogram.

Date	Mintage	F	VF	XF	Unc	BU
1978 LIMA	9,000,000	—	—	0.15	0.35	—
1979 LIMA	4,842,000	—	—	0.15	0.35	—
1980 LIMA	28,826,000	—	—	0.15	0.35	—
1981 LIMA	51,630,000	—	—	0.15	0.35	—
1982 LIMA	4,155,000	—	—	0.15	0.35	—

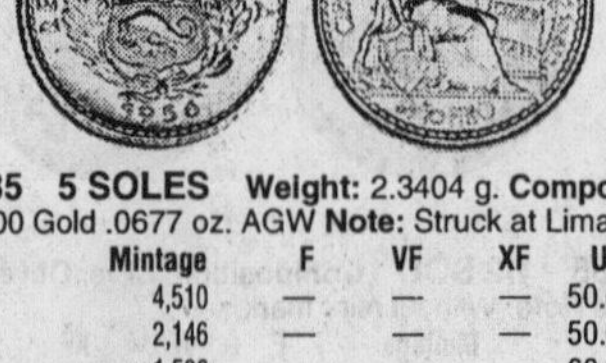

KM# 235 5 SOLES Weight: 2.3404 g. **Composition:** 0.9000 Gold .0677 oz. AGW **Note:** Struck at Lima.

Date	Mintage	F	VF	XF	Unc	BU
1956	4,510	—	—	—	50.00	—
1957	2,146	—	—	—	50.00	—
1959	1,536	—	—	—	60.00	—
1960	8,133	—	—	—	50.00	—
1961	1,154	—	—	—	60.00	—
1962	1,550	—	—	—	60.00	—
1963	3,945	—	—	—	50.00	—
1964	2,063	—	—	—	55.00	—

Date	Mintage	F	VF	XF	Unc	BU
1965	14,000	—	—	—	50.00	—
1966	4,738	—	—	—	50.00	—
1967	3,651	—	—	—	50.00	—
1969	127	—	—	—	175	—

KM# 252 5 SOLES **Composition:** Copper-Nickel **Note:** Struck at Paris.

Date	Mintage	F	VF	XF	Unc	BU
1969	10,000,000	0.20	0.40	0.60	1.50	—

KM# 254 5 SOLES **Composition:** Copper-Nickel **Subject:** 150th Anniversary of Independence **Note:** Mint mark in monogram.

Date	Mintage	F	VF	XF	Unc	BU
1971 LIMA	3,480,000	0.20	0.40	0.80	2.00	—

KM# 257 5 SOLES **Composition:** Copper-Nickel **Note:** Regular issue.

Date	Mintage	F	VF	XF	Unc	BU
1972	2,068,000	—	0.10	0.35	1.00	—
1973	475,000	—	0.10	0.35	1.00	—
1974	—	—	0.10	0.35	1.50	—
1975	—	—	0.10	0.35	1.50	—

KM# 267 5 SOLES **Composition:** Copper-Nickel

Date	Mintage	F	VF	XF	Unc	BU
1975	—	—	0.10	0.35	1.00	—
1976	17,016,000	—	0.10	0.35	1.00	—
1977	94,272,000	—	0.10	0.35	1.00	—

KM# 271 5 SOLES **Composition:** Brass

Date	Mintage	F	VF	XF	Unc	BU
1978	38,015,000	—	0.10	0.20	0.60	—
1979	64,524,000	—	0.10	0.20	0.60	—
1980	76,964,000	—	0.10	0.20	0.60	—
1981	31,632,000	—	0.10	0.20	0.60	—
1982	23,252,000	—	0.10	0.20	0.60	—
1983	650	20.00	30.00	40.00	60.00	—

KM# 236 10 SOLES Weight: 4.6070 g. **Composition:** 0.9000 Gold .1354 oz. AGW **Note:** Struck at Lima.

Date	Mintage	F	VF	XF	Unc	BU
1956	5,410	—	—	BV	75.00	—
1957	1,300	—	—	BV	85.00	—
1959	1,103	—	—	BV	85.00	—
1960	7,178	—	—	BV	75.00	—
1961	1,634	—	—	BV	85.00	—

Date	Mintage	F	VF	XF	Unc	BU
1962	1,676	—	—	BV	85.00	—
1963	3,372	—	—	BV	75.00	—
1964	1,554	—	—	BV	85.00	—
1965	14,000	—	—	BV	70.00	—
1966	2,601	—	—	BV	75.00	—
1967	3,002	—	—	BV	75.00	—
1968	100	—	BV	100	200	—
1969	100	—	BV	100	200	—

KM# 253 10 SOLES **Composition:** Copper-Nickel **Note:** Struck at Paris.

Date	Mintage	F	VF	XF	Unc	BU
1969	15,000,000	0.25	0.50	0.75	1.75	—

KM# 255 10 SOLES **Composition:** Copper-Nickel **Subject:** 150th Anniversary of Independence **Note:** Struck at Lima. Mint mark in monogram.

Date	Mintage	F	VF	XF	Unc	BU
1971 LIMA	2,460,000	0.25	0.50	1.00	2.50	—

KM# 258 10 SOLES **Composition:** Copper-Nickel

Date	Mintage	F	VF	XF	Unc	BU
1972	2,235	—	0.10	0.40	1.25	—
1973	1,765	—	0.10	0.40	1.25	—
1974	—	—	0.10	0.40	1.25	—
1975	—	—	0.10	0.40	1.25	—

KM# 272.1 10 SOLES **Composition:** Brass **Obverse:** Large arms, small letters; inner circle 18.1mm **Edge:** Plain

Date	Mintage	F	VF	XF	Unc	BU
1978	46,970,000	—	0.10	0.40	0.85	—

KM# 272.2 10 SOLES **Composition:** Brass **Obverse:** Small arms, small letters; inner circle 17.2mm

Date	Mintage	F	VF	XF	Unc	BU
1978	—	—	0.10	0.40	0.85	—
1979	82,220,000	—	0.10	0.40	0.85	—
1980	99,595,000	—	0.10	0.40	0.85	—
1981	25,660,000	—	0.10	0.40	0.85	—
1982	61,035,000	—	0.10	0.40	0.85	—
1983	15,820,000	—	0.10	0.40	0.85	—

KM# 287 10 SOLES **Composition:** Brass **Subject:** 150th Anniversary - Birth of Admiral Grau

Date	Mintage	F	VF	XF	Unc	BU
1984	30,000,000	—	—	0.20	0.50	—

KM# 229 20 SOLES **Weight:** 9.3614 g. **Composition:** 0.9000 Gold .2709 oz. AGW **Note:** Struck at Lima.

Date	Mintage	F	VF	XF	Unc	BU
1950	1,800	—	—	BV	200	—
1951	9,264	—	—	BV	150	—
1952	424	—	—	BV	225	—
1953	1,435	—	—	BV	200	—
1954	1,732	—	—	BV	200	—
1955	1,971	—	—	BV	200	—
1956	1,201	—	—	BV	200	—
1957	11,000	—	—	BV	150	—
1958	11,000	—	—	BV	150	—
1959	12,000	—	—	BV	150	—
1960	7,753	—	—	BV	150	—
1961	1,825	—	—	BV	200	—
1962	2,282	—	—	BV	175	—
1963	3,892	—	—	BV	165	—
1964	1,302	—	—	BV	200	—
1965	12,000	—	—	BV	150	—
1966	4,001	—	—	BV	150	—
1967	5,003	—	—	BV	150	—
1968	640	—	—	BV	200	—
1969	640	—	—	BV	200	—

KM# 241 20 SOLES **Weight:** 8.0000 g. **Composition:** 0.9000 Silver .2315 oz. ASW **Subject:** 400th Anniversary of Lima Mint.

Date	Mintage	F	VF	XF	Unc	BU
ND(1965)	150,000	—	—	—	7.00	—

KM# 249 20 SOLES **Weight:** 7.9700 g. **Composition:** 0.9000 Silver .2306 oz. ASW **Subject:** 100th Anniversary of Peru-Spain Naval Battle

Date	Mintage	F	VF	XF	Unc	BU
ND(1966)	4,001	—	—	—	16.50	—

KM# 219 50 SOLES **Weight:** 33.4363 g. **Composition:** 0.9000 Gold .9675 oz. AGW

Date	Mintage	F	VF	XF	Unc	BU
1930	5,584	475	625	950	1,600	—
1931	5,538	475	625	950	1,500	—
1967	10,000	—	—	—	500	—
1968	300	—	—	—	650	—
1969	403	—	—	—	650	—

KM# 230 50 SOLES **Weight:** 23.4056 g. **Composition:** 0.9000 Gold .6772 oz. AGW **Note:** Struck at Lima.

Date	Mintage	F	VF	XF	Unc	BU
1950	1,927	—	—	BV	350	—
1951	5,292	—	—	BV	350	—
1952	1,201	—	—	BV	450	—
1953	1,464	—	—	BV	400	—
1954	1,839	—	—	BV	375	—
1955	1,898	—	—	BV	375	—
1956	11,000	—	—	BV	325	—
1957	11,000	—	—	BV	325	—
1958	11,000	—	—	BV	325	—
1959	5,734	—	—	BV	325	—
1960	2,139	—	—	BV	365	—
1961	1,110	—	—	BV	450	—
1962	3,319	—	—	BV	350	—
1963	3,089	—	—	BV	350	—
1964/3	2,425	—	—	BV	350	—
1964	Inc. above	—	—	BV	360	—
1965	23,000	—	—	BV	325	—
1966	3,409	—	—	BV	350	—
1967	5,805	—	—	BV	350	—
1968	443	—	—	BV	450	—
1969	443	—	—	BV	450	—
1970	553	—	—	BV	450	—

KM# 242 50 SOLES **Weight:** 23.4056 g. **Composition:** 0.9000 Gold .6772 oz. AGW **Subject:** 400th Anniversary of Lima Mint

Date	Mintage	F	VF	XF	Unc	BU
ND(1965)	17,000	—	—	—	350	—

KM# 250 50 SOLES **Weight:** 23.4056 g. **Composition:** 0.9000 Gold .6772 oz. AGW **Subject:** 100th Anniversary of Peru-Spain Naval Battle

Date	Mintage	F	VF	XF	Unc	BU
ND(1966)	6,409	—	—	—	550	—

KM# 256 50 SOLES **Weight:** 21.4500 g. **Composition:** 0.8000 Silver .5517 oz. ASW **Subject:** 150th Anniversary of Independence **Note:** Struck at Lima. Mint mark in monogram.

Date	Mintage	F	VF	XF	Unc	BU
1971 LIMA	100,000	—	—	—	7.00	—

KM# 273 50 SOLES **Composition:** Aluminum-Bronze

Date	Mintage	F	VF	XF	Unc	BU
1979	1,323,000	—	0.15	0.35	1.00	—
1980	452,573,000	—	0.10	0.20	0.50	—
1981	19,923,000	—	0.10	0.20	0.50	—
1982 LIMA	18,471,000	—	0.10	0.20	0.50	—
1982 Without LIMA	Inc. above	—	0.15	0.35	1.00	—
1983	8,175,000	—	0.10	0.20	0.50	—

KM# 297 50 SOLES **Composition:** Brass **Subject:** 150th Anniversary - Birth of Admiral Grau

Date	Mintage	F	VF	XF	Unc	BU
1984	11,475,000	—	—	0.20	0.50	—
1985	8,525,000	—	—	0.20	0.50	—

KM# 321 50 SOLES **Composition:** Brass **Obverse:** Denomination **Reverse:** Admiral Grau portrait without dates below **Edge:** Plain **Size:** 17 mm.

Date	F	VF	XF	Unc	BU
1985LIMAE	—	—	—	0.50	—

KM# 231 100 SOLES **Weight:** 46.8071 g. **Composition:** 0.9000 Gold 1.3544 oz. AGW **Note:** Struck at Lima.

Date	Mintage	F	VF	XF	Unc	BU
1950	1,176	—	—	BV	700	—
1951	8,241	—	—	BV	650	—
1952	126	—	—	2,000	3,000	—
1953	498	—	—	BV	750	—
1954	1,808	—	—	BV	650	—
1955	901	—	—	BV	750	—
1956	1,159	—	—	BV	650	—
1957	550	—	—	BV	750	—
1958	101	—	—	3,000	4,000	—
1959	4,710	—	—	BV	625	—
1960	2,207	—	—	BV	625	—
1961	6,982	—	—	BV	600	—
1962	9,678	—	—	BV	600	—
1963	7,342	—	—	BV	600	—
1964	11,000	—	—	BV	600	—
1965	23,000	—	—	BV	600	—
1966	3,409	—	—	BV	625	—
1967	6,431	—	—	BV	625	—
1968	540	—	—	BV	750	—
1969	540	—	—	BV	750	—
1970	425	—	—	BV	750	—

KM# 243 100 SOLES **Weight:** 46.8071 g. **Composition:** 0.9000 Gold 1.3544 oz. AGW **Subject:** 400th Anniversary of Lima Mint

Date	Mintage	F	VF	XF	Unc	BU
ND(1965)	27,000	—	—	—	650	—

KM# 251 100 SOLES **Weight:** 46.8071 g. **Composition:** 0.9000 Gold 1.3544 oz. AGW **Subject:** 100th Anniversary of Peru-Spain Naval Battle

Date	Mintage	F	VF	XF	Unc	BU
ND(1966)	6,253	—	—	—	825	—

KM# 261 100 SOLES **Weight:** 22.4500 g. **Composition:** 0.8000 Silver .5774 oz. ASW **Subject:** Centennial Peru-Japan Trade Relations **Note:** Mint mark in monogram.

Date	Mintage	F	VF	XF	Unc	BU
1973 LIMA	375,000	—	—	—	12.50	—

KM# 283 100 SOLES **Composition:** Copper-Nickel **Note:** Without mint mark.

Date	Mintage	F	VF	XF	Unc	BU
1980	100,000,000	—	0.20	0.40	1.50	—
1982	—	—	0.20	0.40	1.50	—

KM# 288 100 SOLES **Composition:** Brass **Subject:** 150th Anniversary - Birth of Admiral Grau **Note:** Mint mark in monogram.

Date	Mintage	F	VF	XF	Unc	BU
1981 LIMA	20,000,000	—	0.15	0.35	1.00	—

KM# 262 200 SOLES **Weight:** 22.0000 g. **Composition:** 0.8000 Silver .5659 oz. ASW **Subject:** Aviation Heroes - Chavez and Guinones

Date	Mintage	F	VF	XF	Unc	BU
1974	25,000	—	—	—	15.00	—
1975	90,000	—	—	—	10.00	—
1976	25,000	—	—	—	20.00	—
1977	3,000	—	—	—	30.00	—
1978	3,000	—	—	—	30.00	—

KM# 270 400 SOLES **Weight:** 28.1000 g. **Composition:** 0.9000 Silver .8131 oz. ASW **Subject:** 150th Anniversary - Battle of Ayacucho **Obverse:** Similar to 200 Soles, KM#262 **Note:** Mint mark in monogram.

Date	Mintage	F	VF	XF	Unc	BU
1976 LIMA	350,000	—	—	—	15.00	—

KM# 289 500 SOLES **Composition:** Brass **Subject:** 150th Anniversary - Birth of Admiral Grau **Note:** Mint mark in monogram.

Date	Mintage	F	VF	XF	Unc	BU
1984 LIMA	16,962,000	—	0.20	0.50	2.00	—

KM# 310 500 SOLES **Composition:** Brass **Reverse:** Admiral Grau; without date **Note:** Mint mark in monogram.

Date	Mintage	F	VF	XF	Unc	BU
1985 LIMA	13,038,000	—	0.20	0.50	2.50	—

KM# 275 1000 SOLES **Weight:** 15.5500 g. **Composition:** 0.5000 Silver .2500 oz. ASW **Subject:** National Congress **Edge:** Smooth with incuse stars **Note:** Mint mark in monogram.

Date	Mintage	F	VF	XF	Unc	BU
1979 LIMA	200,000	—	—	—	5.00	—

KM# 276 5000 SOLES **Weight:** 31.1077 g. **Composition:** 0.9250 Silver .9251 oz. ASW **Subject:** 100th Anniversary - Battle of Iquique **Note:** Mint mark in monogram.

Date	Mintage	F	VF	XF	Unc	BU
1979 LIMA	100,000	—	—	12.50	20.00	—

KM# 284 5000 SOLES **Weight:** 23.3700 g. **Composition:** 0.9250 Silver .6951 oz. ASW **Subject:** Champions of Soccer **Note:** Mint mark in monogram.

Date	Mintage	F	VF	XF	Unc	BU
1982 LIMA Proof	8,250	Value: 26.50				

KM# 285 5000 SOLES **Composition:** Silver **Subject:** Champions of Soccer **Note:** Mint mark in monogram.

Date	Mintage	F	VF	XF	Unc	BU
1982 LIMA Proof	8,300	Value: 26.50				

KM# 286 10000 SOLES **Weight:** 16.8000 g. **Composition:** 0.9250 Silver .4997 oz. ASW **Subject:** Battle of La Brena **Reverse:** General Caceras **Note:** Mint mark in monogram.

Date	Mintage	F	VF	XF	Unc	BU
1982 LIMA	100,000	—	—	—	12.50	—

KM# 277 50000 SOLES **Weight:** 16.8600 g. **Composition:** 0.9170 Gold .5004 oz. AGW **Reverse:** Alfonso Urgarte **Note:** Mint mark in monogram.

Date	Mintage	F	VF	XF	Unc	BU
1979 LIMA	10,000	—	—	—	285	—

KM# 278 50000 SOLES **Weight:** 16.8600 g. **Composition:** 0.9170 Gold .5004 oz. AGW **Reverse:** Elias Aguirre **Note:** Mint mark in monogram.

Date	Mintage	F	VF	XF	Unc	BU
1979 LIMA	10,000	—	—	—	285	—

KM# 279 50000 SOLES **Weight:** 16.8600 g. **Composition:** 0.9170 Gold .5004 oz. AGW **Reverse:** Garcia Calderon **Note:** Mint mark in monogram.

Date	Mintage	F	VF	XF	Unc	BU
1979 LIMA	10,000	—	—	—	285	—

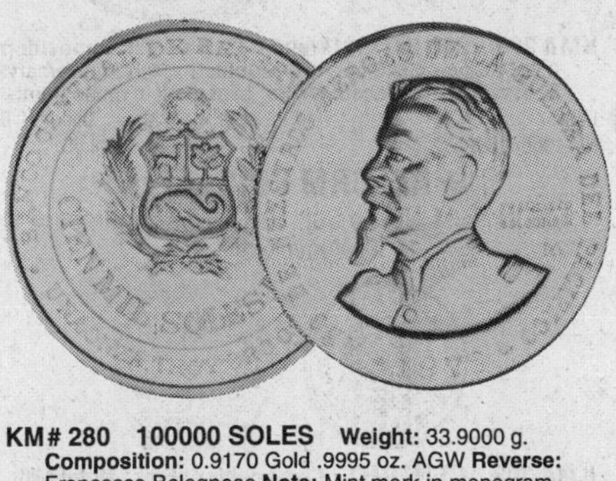

KM# 280 100000 SOLES **Weight:** 33.9000 g. **Composition:** 0.9170 Gold .9995 oz. AGW **Reverse:** Francesco Bolognese **Note:** Mint mark in monogram.

Date	Mintage	F	VF	XF	Unc	BU
1979 LIMA	10,000	—	—	—	500	—

KM# 281 100000 SOLES **Weight:** 33.9000 g. **Composition:** 0.9170 Gold .9995 oz. AGW **Reverse:** Andres A. Caceres **Note:** Mint mark in monogram.

Date	Mintage	F	VF	XF	Unc	BU
1979 LIMA	10,000	—	—	—	500	—

KM# 282 100000 SOLES **Weight:** 33.9000 g. **Composition:** 0.9170 Gold .9995 oz. AGW **Reverse:** Miguel Grau **Note:** Mint mark in monogram.

Date	Mintage	F	VF	XF	Unc	BU
1979 LIMA	10,000	—	—	—	500	—

KM# 313 2 NUEVOS SOLES **Ring Composition:** Steel **Center Weight:** 0.2306 g. **Center Composition:** Brass **Obverse:** National arms

Date	F	VF	XF	Unc	BU
1994	—	—	—	4.50	—
1995	—	—	—	4.50	—

KM# 316 5 NUEVOS SOLES **Ring Composition:** Steel **Center Weight:** 0.2306 g. **Center Composition:** Brass **Obverse:** National arms **Note:** Mint mark in monogram.

Date	F	VF	XF	Unc	BU
1994 LIMA	—	—	—	6.50	—
1995 LIMA	—	—	—	6.50	—

REFORM COINAGE

1000 Soles de Oro = 1 Inti

KM# 291 CENTIMO **Composition:** Brass **Note:** Mint mark in monogram.

Date	Mintage	F	VF	XF	Unc	BU
1985 LIMA	4,179,999	—	—	—	0.25	—
1986 LIMA	20,000	—	—	—	0.35	—
1987 LIMA	—	—	—	—	0.35	—
1988 LIMA	—	—	—	—	0.35	—

KM# 292 5 CENTIMOS **Composition:** Brass **Note:** Mint mark in monogram.

Date	Mintage	F	VF	XF	Unc	BU
1985 LIMA	20,000,000	—	—	—	0.35	—
1986 LIMA	—	—	—	—	0.45	—
1987 LIMA	—	—	—	—	0.45	—
1988	—	—	—	—	0.45	—

KM# 293 10 CENTIMOS **Composition:** Brass **Note:** Mint mark in monogram.

Date	Mintage	F	VF	XF	Unc	BU
1985 LIMA	143,900,000	—	—	—	1.00	—
1986 LIMA	48,730,000	—	—	—	0.65	—
1987 LIMA	42,370,000	—	—	—	0.65	—
1988 LIMA	—	—	—	—	0.65	—

KM# 294 20 CENTIMOS **Composition:** Brass **Note:** Mint mark in monogram.

Date	Mintage	F	VF	XF	Unc	BU
1985 LIMA	4,739,000	—	—	—	1.25	—
1986 LIMA	96,699,000	—	—	—	1.00	—
1987 LIMA	59,668,000	—	—	—	1.00	—
1988 LIMA	—	—	—	—	1.00	—

KM# 295 50 CENTIMOS **Composition:** Brass **Note:** Mint mark in monogram.

Date	Mintage	F	VF	XF	Unc	BU
1985 LIMA	43,320,000	—	—	—	1.25	—
1986 LIMA	72,802,000	—	—	—	1.25	—
1987 LIMA	63,878,000	—	—	—	1.25	—
1988 LIMA	80,000,000	—	—	—	1.25	—

KM# 301a 1/2 INTI **Composition:** Copper-Nickel

Date	F	VF	XF	Unc	BU
1989	—	—	—	—	—

KM# 301 1/2 INTI **Weight:** 16.8000 g. **Composition:** 0.9250 Silver .4997 oz. ASW **Subject:** Pachacutec **Note:** Mint mark in monogram.

Date	F	VF	XF	Unc	BU
1989 LIMA	—	—	—	20.00	—

KM# 296 INTI **Composition:** Copper-Nickel **Note:** Mint mark in monogram.

Date	Mintage	F	VF	XF	Unc	BU
1985 LIMA	15,760,000	—	—	—	1.75	—
1986 LIMA	87,240,000	—	—	—	1.25	—
1987 LIMA	120,000,000	—	—	—	1.00	—
1988 LIMA	17,304,000	—	—	—	1.75	—

KM# 300 5 INTIS **Composition:** Copper-Nickel **Reverse:** Admiral Grau **Note:** Mint mark in monogram.

Date	Mintage	F	VF	XF	Unc	BU
1985 LIMA	3,972	—	—	—	—	—
1986 LIMA	28,000	—	—	—	3.50	—
1987 LIMA	20,106,000	—	—	—	2.50	—
1988 LIMA	34,084,000	—	—	—	2.50	—

KM# 298 100 INTIS **Weight:** 11.1100 g. **Composition:** 0.9250 Silver .3271 oz. ASW **Subject:** 150th Anniversary - Birth of Marshal Caceres **Note:** Mint mark in monogram.

Date	Mintage	F	VF	XF	Unc	BU
ND(1986) LIMA	10,000	—	—	—	17.50	—

KM# 299 200 INTIS **Weight:** 22.0400 g. **Composition:** 0.9250 Silver .6543 oz. ASW **Subject:** 150th Anniversary - Birth of Marshal Caceres **Note:** Mint mark in monogram.

Date	F	VF	XF	Unc	BU
ND(1986) LIMA	—	—	—	32.50	—

REFORM COINAGE

1/M Intis = 1 Nuevo Sol; 100 (New) Centimos = 1 Nuevo Sol

KM# 303 CENTIMO **Composition:** Brass **Note:** Mint mark in monogram. Varieties exist.

Date	F	VF	XF	Unc	BU
1991 LIMA CHAVEZ	—	—	—	0.35	—
1992 LIMA CHAVEZ	—	—	—	0.45	—
1993 LIMA	—	—	—	0.35	—
1997	—	—	—	0.35	—

KM# 304 5 CENTIMOS **Composition:** Brass **Note:** Mint mark in monogram. Varieties exist.

Date	F	VF	XF	Unc	BU
1991 LIMA CHAVEZ	—	—	—	0.45	—
1992 LIMA CHAVEZ	—	—	—	0.50	—
1993 LIMA	—	—	—	0.45	—
1993 LIMA CHAVEZ	—	—	—	0.45	—
1994 LIMA	—	—	—	0.45	—
1995	—	—	—	0.45	—
1996 LIMA	—	—	—	0.45	—
1998	—	—	—	0.70	—

KM# 305 10 CENTIMOS **Composition:** Brass **Note:** Mint mark in monogram. Varieties exist.

Date	F	VF	XF	Unc	BU
1991 LIMA	—	—	—	0.65	—
1992 LIMA	—	—	—	0.70	—
1993 LIMA	—	—	—	0.65	—
1993 LIMA CHAVEZ	—	—	—	0.65	—
1994 LIMA	—	—	—	0.65	—
1995 LIMA	—	—	—	0.65	—
1996	—	—	—	0.65	—
1997 LIMA	—	—	—	0.65	—
1998	—	—	—	0.65	—
2000	—	—	—	0.70	—

KM# 305.1 10 CENTIMOS **Composition:** Brass **Obverse:** National arms **Reverse:** Denomination without Braille dots above

Date	F	VF	XF	Unc	BU
2001LM	—	—	—	0.65	—
2002LM	—	—	—	0.65	—

KM# 306 20 CENTIMOS **Composition:** Brass **Note:** Mint mark in monogram. Varieties exist.

Date	F	VF	XF	Unc	BU
1991 LIMA CHAVEZ	—	—	—	0.85	—
1992 LIMA	—	—	—	0.85	—
1993 LIMA	—	—	—	0.85	—
1994 LIMA	—	—	—	0.85	—
1996	—	—	—	0.85	—

KM# 307 50 CENTIMOS **Composition:** Copper-Nickel **Note:** Mint mark in monogram. Varieties exist.

Date	F	VF	XF	Unc	BU
1991 LIMA	—	—	—	1.50	—
1992 LIMA	—	—	—	1.75	—
1993 LIMA	—	—	—	1.50	—
1994 LIMA	—	—	—	1.50	—

KM# 302 NUEVO SOL **Weight:** 27.0000 g. **Composition:** 0.9250 Silver .8029 oz. ASW **Series:** Ibero - American

Date	Mintage	F	VF	XF	Unc	BU
1991 Proof	60,000	Value: 45.00				

KM# 308.2 NUEVO SOL Composition: Copper-Nickel **Reverse:** With F. Diaz below wreath

Date	F	VF	XF	Unc	BU
1991	2.00	5.00	15.00	35.00	—

KM# 327 NUEVO SOL Weight: 27.0000 g. **Composition:** 0.9250 Silver 0.803 oz. ASW **Series:** Ibero-American **Obverse:** Arms around, as KM302 but without date below denomination **Reverse:** Like KM302, but with Anniversary dates below Spaniards head **Size:** 39 mm.

Date	F	VF	XF	Unc	BU
ND(1991) Proof	—	Value: 50.00			

KM# 308.1 NUEVO SOL Composition: Copper-Nickel **Note:** Mint mark in monogram.

Date	F	VF	XF	Unc	BU
1991 LIMA	—	—	—	5.00	—
1992 LIMA	—	—	—	5.00	—
1993 LIMA	—	—	—	5.00	—
1994 LIMA	—	—	—	4.00	—
1995 LIMA	—	—	—	4.00	—
2000	—	—	—	4.00	—

KM# 312 NUEVO SOL Weight: 33.6250 g. **Composition:** 0.9170 Gold 1.0000 oz. AGW **Note:** Similar to KM#311.

Date	Mintage	F	VF	XF	Unc	BU
1994	—	—	—	—	—	—
1994 Proof	100	Value: 350				

KM# 325 NUEVO SOL Weight: 33.6250 g. **Composition:** 0.9250 Silver 1 oz. ASW **Obverse:** National arms **Reverse:** Bust of Jose Carlos Mariategui half right **Edge:** Reeded **Size:** 37.1 mm.

Date	F	VF	XF	Unc	BU
1994 Proof	—	Value: 100			

KM# 311 NUEVO SOL Weight: 33.6250 g. **Composition:** 0.9170 Gold 1.0000 oz. AGW **Subject:** Pre-Inca Moche Cultural Artifacts

Date	Mintage	F	VF	XF	Unc	BU
1994		—	—	—	—	—
1994 Proof	2,000	Value: 47.50				

KM# 314 NUEVO SOL Weight: 20.0000 g. **Composition:** 0.9990 Silver .6430 oz. ASW **Series:** Environmental Protection **Subject:** Two Young Vicunas

Date	F	VF	XF	Unc	BU
1994 Proof	—	—	—	—	—

KM# 317 NUEVO SOL Weight: 20.0000 g. **Composition:** 0.9990 Silver .6430 oz. ASW **Series:** Environmental Protection **Reverse:** Vicuna, yellow-tailed wooly monkey and American crocodile

Date	Mintage	F	VF	XF	Unc	BU
1994 Proof	20,000	Value: 47.50				

KM# 318 NUEVO SOL Weight: 33.6250 g. **Composition:** 0.9250 Silver 1.0000 oz. ASW **Subject:** Centennial of Victor Raul Haya de la Torre

Date	Mintage	F	VF	XF	Unc	BU
1995	883	—	—	—	100	—

KM# 319 NUEVO SOL Weight: 33.6250 g. **Composition:** 0.9250 Silver 1.0000 oz. ASW **Subject:** National Mineral and Petrolium Society Centennial **Reverse:** Miner, oil derrick and cart

Date	F	VF	XF	Unc	BU
1996	—	—	—	40.00	—

KM# 323 NUEVO SOL Weight: 33.4700 g. **Composition:** 0.9250 Silver .9954 oz. ASW **Subject:** Centennial of Chorrillos Military School **Obverse:** National arms **Reverse:** Monument and building **Edge:** Reeded **Size:** 37.1 mm.

Date	F	VF	XF	Unc	BU
1998 Proof	—	Value: 45.00			

KM# 322 NUEVO SOL Weight: 33.6250 g. **Composition:** 0.9250 Silver 1.0000 oz. ASW **Subject:** Centennial of Japanese Immigration **Obverse:** National arms **Reverse:** Radiant sun above maps

Date	F	VF	XF	Unc	BU
1999 Proof	—	Value: 45.00			

KM# 326 NUEVO SOL Weight: 26.9500 g. **Composition:** 0.9250 Silver 0.8015 oz. ASW **Series:** Ibero-American **Obverse:** National arms in circle of arms **Reverse:** Horse and rider in courtyard **Edge:** Reeded **Size:** 40 mm.

Date	F	VF	XF	Unc	BU
2000 Proof	—	Value: 60.00			

KM# 308.3 NUEVO SOL **Composition:** Copper-Nickel **Obverse:** National arms **Reverse:** Denomination without Braille dots above

Date	F	VF	XF	Unc	BU
2001LM	—	—	—	4.00	—

KM# 309 20 NUEVO SOLES **Weight:** 33.6250 g. **Composition:** 0.9250 Silver 1.0000 oz. ASW **Subject:** Rio De Janeiro Protocal

Date	Mintage	F	VF	XF	Unc	BU
1992	50,000	—	—	—	22.50	—

KM# 315 20 NUEVO SOLES **Weight:** 33.6250 g. **Composition:** 0.9250 Silver 1.0000 oz. ASW **Reverse:** Cesar Vallejo

Date	F	VF	XF	Unc	BU
1992 Proof	—	Value: 22.50			

KM# 320 50 NUEVOS SOLES **Weight:** 33.6250 g. **Composition:** 0.9250 Silver 1.0000 oz. ASW **Subject:** Peru-Japan Commercial Exchange **Obverse:** Peruvian arms **Reverse:** Stylized bird design

Date	F	VF	XF	Unc	BU
1993	—	—	—	40.00	—

TOKEN COINAGE

KM# Tn3 50 CENTAVOS **Composition:** Silver **Subject:** National Defense

Date	F	VF	XF	Unc	BU
1932	8.50	12.50	18.50	30.00	—

KM# Tn1 SOL **Composition:** 0.9000 Silver

Date	F	VF	XF	Unc	BU
1910	8.50	12.50	18.50	30.00	—

KM# Tn4 SOL **Composition:** Silver **Subject:** National Defense

Date	F	VF	XF	Unc	BU
1932	5.00	11.50	16.50	28.50	—

KM# Tn2 5 SOLES **Weight:** 2.3404 g. **Composition:** 0.9000 Gold .0677 oz. AGW

Date	F	VF	XF	Unc	BU
1910	60.00	80.00	110	150	—

KM# Tn5 5 SOLES **Composition:** Silver **Subject:** National Defense

Date	F	VF	XF	Unc	BU
1932	12.00	17.50	28.50	42.50	—

KM# Tn6 10 SOLES **Composition:** Gold Plated Silver **Subject:** National Defense

Date	F	VF	XF	Unc	BU
1932	15.00	20.00	38.50	55.00	—

TRADE COINAGE

KM# 210 1/5 LIBRA (Pound) **Weight:** 1.5976 g. **Composition:** 0.9170 Gold .0471 oz. AGW **Note:** Struck at Lima.

Date	Mintage	F	VF	XF	Unc	BU
1906 GOZF	106,000	—	BV	25.00	35.00	—
1907 GOZF	31,000	—	BV	25.00	35.00	—
1907 GOZG	—	—	BV	25.00	35.00	—
1909 GOZG	—	—	BV	25.00	35.00	—
1910 GOZG	—	—	BV	25.00	35.00	—
1911 GOZF	62,000	—	BV	25.00	35.00	—
1912 GOZG	—	—	BV	25.00	35.00	—
1912 POZG	—	—	BV	25.00	35.00	—
1913 POZG	60,000	—	BV	25.00	35.00	—
1914 POZG	25,000	—	BV	25.00	35.00	—
1914 PBLG	Inc. above	—	—	—	—	—
Note: Reported, not confirmed						
1915	10,000	—	BV	25.00	35.00	—
1916	13,000	—	—	—	—	—
Note: Reported, not confirmed						
1917	3,896	—	BV	25.00	35.00	—
1918	16,000	—	BV	25.00	35.00	—
1919	10,000	—	BV	25.00	35.00	—
1920	72,000	—	BV	25.00	35.00	—
1922	8,110	—	BV	25.00	35.00	—
1923	27,000	—	BV	25.00	35.00	—
1924	—	—	BV	25.00	35.00	—
1925	20,000	—	BV	25.00	35.00	—
1926	11,000	—	BV	25.00	35.00	—
1927	14,000	—	BV	25.00	35.00	—
1928	9,322	—	BV	25.00	35.00	—
1929	8,971	—	BV	25.00	35.00	—
1930	9,991	—	BV	35.00	50.00	—
1953 BBR	9,821	—	—	—	40.00	—
1955 ZBR	10,000	—	—	—	40.00	—
1958 ZBR	5,098	—	—	—	32.50	—
1959 ZBR	6,308	—	—	—	32.50	—
1960 ZBR	6,083	—	—	—	32.50	—
1961 ZBR	12,000	—	—	—	32.50	—
1962 ZBR	5,431	—	—	—	32.50	—
1963 ZBR	11,000	—	—	—	32.50	—
1964 ZBR	25,000	—	—	—	32.50	—
1965 ZBR	19,000	—	—	—	32.50	—
1966 ZBR	60,000	—	—	—	32.50	—
1967 BBR	9,914	—	—	—	32.50	—
1968 BBB	4,781	—	—	—	32.50	—
1969 BBB	15,000	—	—	—	32.50	—

KM# 209 1/2 LIBRA (Pound) **Weight:** 3.9940 g. **Composition:** 0.9170 Gold .1177 oz. AGW

Date	Mintage	F	VF	XF	Unc	BU
1902 ROZF	7,800	—	BV	50.00	75.00	—
1903 ROZF	7,245	—	BV	50.00	75.00	—
1904 ROZF	8,360	—	BV	50.00	75.00	—
1905 ROZF	8,010	—	BV	50.00	75.00	—
1905 GOZF	Inc. above	—	BV	50.00	75.00	—
1906 GOZF	9,176	—	BV	50.00	75.00	—
1907 GOZG	—	—	BV	50.00	75.00	—
1908 GOZG	8,180	—	BV	50.00	75.00	—
1953 BBR	9,210	—	BV	50.00	75.00	—
1955 ZBR	14,000	—	BV	50.00	70.00	—
1961 ZBR	752	—	—	BV	100	—
1962 ZBR	4,286	—	—	BV	75.00	—
1963 ZBR	908	—	—	BV	100	—
1964 ZBR	10,000	—	—	BV	65.00	—
1965 ZBR	5,490	—	—	BV	75.00	—
1966 ZBR	44,000	—	—	BV	65.00	—
1967 BBR	—	—	—	BV	65.00	—
1968 BBB	Inc. above	—	—	BV	65.00	—
1969 BBB	4,400	—	—	BV	75.00	—

KM# 207 LIBRA (Pound) **Weight:** 7.9881 g. **Composition:** 0.9170 Gold .2354 oz. AGW

Date	Mintage	F	VF	XF	Unc	BU
1901 ROZF	81,000	—	BV	100	145	—
1902 ROZF	89,000	—	BV	100	145	—
1903 ROZF	100,000	—	BV	100	145	—
1904 ROZF	33,000	—	BV	100	145	—
1905 ROZF	141,000	—	BV	100	160	—
1905 GOZF	—	—	BV	100	135	—
1906 GOZF	201,000	—	BV	100	135	—
1907 GOZG	Inc. above	—	BV	100	135	—
1908 GOZG	36,000	—	BV	100	160	—
1909 GOZG	52,000	—	BV	100	160	—
1910 GOZG	47,000	—	BV	100	160	—
1911 GOZG	42,000	—	BV	100	160	—
1912 GOZG	54,000	—	BV	100	160	—
1912 POZG	Inc. above	—	BV	100	175	—
1913 POZG	—	—	BV	100	160	—
1914 POZG	—	—	BV	100	175	—
1914 PBLG	119,000	—	BV	100	160	—
1915 PVG	91,000	—	BV	100	170	—
1915 PMGG	Inc. above	—	BV	115	200	—
1915	Inc. above	—	BV	100	150	—
1916	582,000	—	BV	100	135	—
1917	1,928,000	—	BV	100	135	—
1918	600,000	—	BV	100	135	—
1919	Inc. above	—	BV	100	145	—
1920	152,000	—	BV	100	160	—
1921	Inc. above	—	BV	100	165	—
1922	13,000	—	BV	110	175	—
1923	15,000	—	BV	110	175	—
1924	8,113	—	BV	110	175	—
1925	9,068	—	BV	100	165	—
1926	4,596	—	BV	100	160	—
1927	8,360	—	BV	100	160	—
1928	2,184	—	BV	100	160	—
1929	3,119	—	BV	100	160	—
1930	1,050	—	BV	100	145	—
1959 ZBR	605	—	BV	120	240	—
1961 ZBR	402	—	BV	120	240	—
1962 ZBR	6,203	—	BV	110	165	—
1963 ZBR	302	—	BV	120	250	—
1964 ZBR	13,000	—	BV	110	165	—

Date	Mintage	F	VF	XF	Unc	BU
1965 ZBR	9,917	—	BV	110	165	—
1966 ZBR	39,000	—	BV	110	165	—
1967 BBR	2,002	—	BV	110	165	—
1968 BBR	7,307	—	BV	115	175	—
1969 BBR	7,307	—	BV	115	175	—

PATTERNS

Including off metal strikes

KM#	Date	Mintage	Identification	Mkt Val
PnF26	1930	3	50 Soles. Native inscription.	—
Pn26	1932	—	Sol.	—
PnA28	1932	—	10 Soles.	—
PnG26	1932	—	50 Centavos.	—
Pn27	1932	—	5 Soles.	—
Pn28	1947	—	100 Soles. Gilt Bronze.	—
Pn29	1948	—	Sol. Aluminum.	—
PnA30	1949	—	Centavo. Zinc. KM#211.	75.00
PnB30	1949	—	2 Centavos. Zinc. KM#212.2.	50.00
Pn30	1952	—	1 Sol De Oro. Brass.	—
PnA31	1958	—	20 Centavos. Copper Nickel.	50.00
Pn31	1958	—	50 Soles. Silver. With PRUEBA.	900
Pn32	1964	—	50 Soles. Silver. With PRUEBA.	900
Pn33	1965	—	50 Soles. Silver. With PRUEBA.	900
PnA33	1965	—	5 Centavos. Copper-Nickel-Zinc. KM#290.	900
Pn34	1966	200	Sol. Silver. With PAREJA.	—
Pn35	1967	—	1/2 Sol. With PAREJA.	—
Pn36	1967	7	50 Soles. Silver.	—
Pn37	1988	—	Inti. Brass. KM#296.	—
Pn38	198x	—	5 Intis. Copper-Nickel-Zinc. KM#300.	—
Pn39	1988	—	5 Intis. Brass.	—

TRIAL STRIKES

KM#	Date	Mintage	Identification	Mkt Val
TS4	1935	—	Sol. KM#218.1. Alloy percentage: N. 3/25, PLT/0, NKL 10 ZNC/55 CRE.	—
TS5	1935	—	Sol. KM#218.1. Alloy percentage: N. 4/20, PLT/15, NKL 10 ZNC/55 CRE.	—

PROOF SETS

KM#	Date	Mintage	Identification	Issue Price	Mkt Val
PS2	1965 (5)	10	KM#237-240, 290	—	1,500
PS3	1965 (5)	—	KM#220.5, 221.2b, 222, 223.2, 224.2	—	300
PS4	1966 (5)	1,000	KM244.1-246.1, 247-248	—	100

SPECIMEN SETS (SS)

KM#	Date	Mintage	Identification	Issue Price	Mkt Val
SS1	1964 (5)	—	KM220.5, 221.2b, 222, 223.2, 224.2	—	200
SS3	1965 (5)	—	KM220.5, 221.2b, 222, 223.2, 224.2	—	150
SS2	1965 (5)	—	KM220.5, 221.2b, 222, 223.2, 224.2	—	150

PHILIPPINES

The Republic of the Philippines, an archipelago in the western Pacific 500 miles (805 km.) from the southeast coast of Asia, has an area of 115,830 sq. mi. (300,000 sq. km.) and a population of *64.9 million. Capital: Manila. The economy of the 7,000-island group is based on agriculture, forestry and fishing. Timber, coconut products, sugar and hemp are exported.

Migration to the Philippines began about 30,000 years ago when land bridges connected the islands with Borneo and Sumatra. Ferdinand Magellan claimed the islands for Spain in 1521. The first permanent settlement was established by Miguel de Legazpi at Cebu April 1565. Manila was established in 1572. A British expedition captured Manila and occupied the Spanish colony in October 1762, but returned it to Spain by the treaty of Paris, 1763. Spain held the Philippines despite growing Filipino nationalism until 1898 when they were ceded to the United States at the end of the Spanish-American War. The Philippines became a self-governing commonwealth under the United States in 1935, and attained independence as the Republic of the Philippines on July 4, 1946.

MINT MARKS

(b) Brussels, privy marks only
BSP - Bangko Sentral Pilipinas
D - Denver, 1944-1945
(Lt) - Llantrisant
M, MA - Manila
PM - Pobjoy Mint
S - San Francisco, 1903-1947
SGV - Madrid
(Sh) - Sherritt
(US) - United States
FM - Franklin Mint, U.S.A.*
(VDM) - Vereinigte Deutsche Metall Werks; Altona, Germany
Star - Manila (Spanish) = Manila

***NOTE:** From 1975-1977 the Franklin Mint produced coinage in up to 3 different qualities. Beginning in 1978only (U) and (P) were struck. Qualities of issue are designated in ( ) after each date and are defined as follows:

(M) MATTE - Normal circulation strike or a dull finish produced by sandblasting special uncirculated (polish-finish) or proof quality dies.

(U) SPECIAL UNCIRCULATED - Polished or prooflike in appearance without any frosted features.

(P) PROOF - The highest quality obtainable having mirror-like fields and frosted features.

MONETARY SYSTEM

4 Quartos = 1 Real
8 Reales = 1 Peso

UNITED STATES ADMINISTRATION

100 Centavos = 1 Peso

DECIMAL COINAGE

KM# 162 1/2 CENTAVO Composition: Bronze

Date	Mintage	F	VF	XF	Unc	BU
1903	12,084,000	0.50	1.00	2.00	15.00	18.00
1903 Proof	2,558	Value: 45.00				
1904	5,654,000	0.50	1.25	2.50	20.00	25.00
1904 Proof	1,355	Value: 60.00				
1905 Proof	471	Value: 120				
1906 Proof	500	Value: 100				
1908 Proof	500	Value: 100				

KM# 163 CENTAVO Composition: Bronze

Date	Mintage	F	VF	XF	Unc	BU
1903	10,790,000	0.50	1.00	2.50	20.00	—
1903 Proof	2,558	Value: 45.00				

Date	Mintage	F	VF	XF	Unc	BU
1904	17,040,000	0.50	1.00	2.50	18.00	—
1904 Proof	1,355	Value: 50.00				
1905	10,000,000	0.50	1.00	3.50	25.00	—
1905 Proof	471	Value: 125				
1906 Proof	500	Value: 100				
1908 Proof	500	Value: 100				
1908S	2,187,000	2.50	5.50	12.50	60.00	75.00
1909S	1,738,000	7.50	15.00	25.00	85.00	120
1910S	2,700,000	2.50	5.00	10.00	45.00	60.00
1911S	4,803,000	1.00	3.00	7.00	40.00	50.00
1912S	3,000,000	2.50	5.50	10.00	60.00	80.00
1913S	5,000,000	1.00	2.50	6.00	40.00	50.00
1914S	5,000,000	1.00	2.50	6.00	40.00	50.00
1914S Large S	Inc. above	—	—	—	—	—

Note: This variety has been questioned by leading authorities

Date	Mintage	F	VF	XF	Unc	BU
1915S	2,500,000	15.00	40.00	90.00	425	600
1916S	4,330,000	5.00	10.00	15.00	100	135
1917/6S	7,070,000	15.00	25.00	60.00	200	—
1917S	Inc. above	2.00	4.00	10.00	35.00	45.00
1918S	11,660,000	2.00	3.50	8.00	45.00	80.00
1918S Large S	Inc. above	80.00	150	250	900	1,500
1919S	4,540,000	0.75	2.00	6.00	45.00	—
1920S	2,500,000	6.00	12.00	18.00	125	—
1920	3,552,000	1.00	2.00	8.50	45.00	50.00
1921	7,283,000	0.75	1.50	6.50	45.00	70.00
1922	3,519,000	0.50	1.50	6.00	45.00	55.00
1925M	9,332,000	0.50	1.50	6.00	35.00	45.00
1926M	9,000,000	0.50	1.50	6.00	40.00	50.00
1927M	9,270,000	0.25	1.00	5.00	35.00	45.00
1928M	9,150,000	0.25	1.00	5.00	25.00	40.00
1929M	5,657,000	1.00	3.00	9.00	40.00	60.00
1930M	5,577,000	0.50	1.50	4.00	25.00	35.00
1931M	5,659,000	0.50	1.50	5.00	30.00	40.00
1932M	4,000,000	0.75	2.50	8.00	40.00	50.00
1933M	8,393,000	0.35	1.75	4.00	25.00	35.00
1934M	3,179,000	0.75	2.00	4.00	30.00	40.00
1936M	17,455,000	0.25	1.00	4.00	30.00	—

KM# 164 5 CENTAVOS Composition: Copper-Nickel

Date	Mintage	F	VF	XF	Unc	BU
1903	8,910,000	0.50	1.00	3.00	22.00	30.00
1903 Proof	2,558	Value: 50.00				
1904	1,075,000	0.75	1.75	4.00	27.00	35.00
1904 Proof	1,355	Value: 65.00				
1905 Proof	471	Value: 135				
1906 Proof	500	Value: 100				
1908 Proof	500	Value: 100				
1916S	300,000	25.00	60.00	90.00	500	650
1917S	2,300,000	2.00	4.00	12.00	100	125
1918S	2,780,000	1.50	3.00	8.00	75.00	100
1919S	1,220,000	2.00	6.00	12.00	100	135
1920	1,421,000	2.50	8.00	15.00	125	150
1921	2,132,000	2.50	6.00	12.50	100	125
1925M	1,000,000	5.00	15.00	30.00	125	175
1926M	1,200,000	3.00	8.00	15.00	60.00	85.00
1927M	1,000,000	2.00	5.00	12.00	50.00	75.00
1928M	1,000,000	3.00	8.00	15.00	50.00	75.00

KM# 173 5 CENTAVOS Composition: Copper-Nickel **Obverse:** KM#164 **Reverse:** 20 Centavos, KM#170 **Note:** Mule.

Date	F	VF	XF	Unc	BU
1918S	125	350	1,000	2,500	3,000

KM# 175 5 CENTAVOS Composition: Copper-Nickel

Date	Mintage	F	VF	XF	Unc	BU
1930M	2,905,000	1.00	2.50	5.00	50.00	65.00
1931M	3,477,000	1.00	2.50	6.00	50.00	65.00
1932M	3,956,000	1.00	2.50	5.00	45.00	55.00
1934M	2,154,000	1.00	3.00	8.00	75.00	90.00
1935M	2,754,000	1.00	2.00	8.00	65.00	85.00

KM# 165 10 CENTAVOS Weight: 2.6924 g. Composition: 0.9000 Silver .0779 oz. ASW

Date	Mintage	F	VF	XF	Unc	BU
1903	5,103,000	1.50	3.00	5.00	35.00	45.00
1903 Proof	2,558	Value: 60.00				
1903S	1,200,000	7.50	20.00	35.00	350	500
1904	11,000	10.00	18.00	35.00	120	—
1904 Proof	1,355	Value: 95.00				
1904S	5,040,000	1.50	2.50	5.00	35.00	45.00
1905 Proof	471	Value: 145				
1906 Proof	500	Value: 125				

KM# 169 10 CENTAVOS Weight: 2.0000 g. Composition: 0.7500 Silver .0482 oz. ASW

Date	Mintage	F	VF	XF	Unc	BU
1907	1,501,000	1.50	3.00	5.00	40.00	50.00
1907S	4,930,000	1.00	2.50	3.50	35.00	40.00
1908 Proof	500	Value: 120				
1908S	3,364,000	1.00	2.00	5.00	40.00	60.00
1909S	312,000	15.00	30.00	60.00	300	400
1910S	—	—	—	—	—	—

Note: Unknown in any collection. Counterfeits of the 1910S are commonly encountered.

Date	Mintage	F	VF	XF	Unc	BU
1911S	1,101,000	1.50	3.00	8.00	50.00	75.00
1912S	1,010,000	2.00	5.00	9.00	65.00	80.00
1913S	1,361,000	1.50	4.00	9.00	50.00	75.00
1914S	1,180,000	3.00	5.00	10.00	125	150
1915S	450,000	10.00	16.00	35.00	225	300
1917S	5,991,000	1.00	2.00	3.00	35.00	50.00
1918S	8,420,000	0.75	1.75	2.50	30.00	40.00
1919S	1,630,000	1.00	2.00	3.50	45.00	60.00
1920	520,000	4.00	6.00	12.00	65.00	80.00
1921	3,863,000	0.75	1.50	2.50	25.00	35.00
1929M	1,000,000	0.75	1.50	2.50	20.00	25.00
1935M	1,280,000	0.75	1.50	2.50	20.00	25.00

KM# 166 20 CENTAVOS Weight: 5.3849 g. Composition: 0.9000 Silver .1558 oz. ASW

Date	Mintage	F	VF	XF	Unc	BU
1903	5,353,000	2.50	3.00	5.00	40.00	—
1903 Proof	2,558	Value: 85.00				
1903S	150,000	10.00	20.00	60.00	325	—
1904	11,000	15.00	30.00	45.00	90.00	125
1904 Proof	1,355	Value: 100				
1904S	2,060,000	2.50	4.00	7.00	40.00	60.00
1905 Proof	471	Value: 225				
1905S	420,000	7.50	12.50	20.00	150	175
1906 Proof	500	Value: 185				

KM# 170 20 CENTAVOS Weight: 4.0000 g. Composition: 0.7500 Silver .0965 oz. ASW

Date	Mintage	F	VF	XF	Unc	BU
1907	1,251,000	2.00	4.00	10.00	50.00	75.00
1907S	3,165,000	2.00	3.00	7.50	40.00	60.00
1908 Proof	500	Value: 185				
1908S	1,535,000	2.00	3.00	6.00	45.00	65.00
1909S	450,000	8.00	15.00	45.00	275	400
1910S	500,000	8.00	15.00	45.00	325	500
1911S	505,000	6.00	12.00	30.00	175	225
1912S	750,000	4.00	8.00	20.00	150	170
1913S/S	949,000	12.50	22.50	40.00	175	250
1913S	Inc. above	3.00	6.00	14.00	140	165
1914S	795,000	2.50	4.00	20.00	125	145
1915S	655,000	4.50	12.00	35.00	200	300
1916S	1,435,000	3.00	6.00	15.00	85.00	120
1917S	3,151,000	1.50	3.00	5.00	50.00	65.00
1918S	5,560,000	1.00	2.50	4.00	50.00	60.00
1919S	850,000	1.50	5.00	8.00	55.00	70.00
1920	1,046,000	1.50	5.00	10.00	90.00	120

Date	Mintage	F	VF	XF	Unc	BU
1921	1,843,000	1.50	3.00	4.00	45.00	55.00
1929M	1,970,000	1.50	3.00	4.00	30.00	50.00

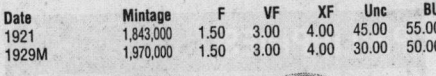

KM# 174 20 CENTAVOS Weight: 4.0000 g. Composition: 0.7500 Silver .0965 oz. ASW **Obverse:** KM#170 **Reverse:** 5 Centavos, KM#164 **Note:** Mule.

Date	Mintage	F	VF	XF	Unc	BU
1928/7M	100,000	4.50	10.00	35.00	400	700

KM# 167 50 CENTAVOS Weight: 13.4784 g. Composition: 0.9000 Silver .3900 oz. ASW

Date	Mintage	F	VF	XF	Unc	BU
1903	3,102,000	5.00	8.00	14.00	60.00	75.00
1903 Proof	2,558	Value: 125				
1903S	—	—	—	22,000	—	—
1904	11,000	25.00	32.00	45.00	85.00	—
1904 Proof	1,355	Value: 130				
1904S	2,160,000	5.00	10.00	20.00	75.00	110
1905 Proof	471	Value: 350				
1905S	852,000	8.00	15.00	40.00	400	1,000
1906 Proof	500	Value: 275				

KM# 171 50 CENTAVOS Weight: 10.0000 g. Composition: 0.7500 Silver .2411 oz. ASW

Date	Mintage	F	VF	XF	Unc	BU
1907	1,201,000	4.00	8.00	20.00	120	150
1907S	2,112,000	2.50	5.00	12.50	100	125
1908 Proof	500	Value: 285				
1908S	1,601,000	2.50	5.00	12.50	100	200
1909S	528,000	5.00	10.00	25.00	250	325
1917S	674,000	4.00	8.00	20.00	100	125
1918S	2,202,000	3.00	5.00	8.00	65.00	90.00
1919S	1,200,000	3.50	5.50	9.00	80.00	110
1920	420,000	3.00	4.00	7.00	25.00	50.00
1921	2,317,000	2.50	4.00	6.00	20.00	50.00

KM# 168 PESO Weight: 26.9568 g. Composition: 0.9000 Silver .7800 oz. ASW

Date	Mintage	F	VF	XF	Unc	BU
1903	2,791,000	12.00	18.00	30.00	150	200
1903 Proof	2,558	Value: 250				
1903S	11,361,000	9.00	16.00	25.00	95.00	150
1904	11,000	50.00	75.00	120	175	275
1904 Proof	1,355	Value: 300				
1904S	6,600,000	10.00	16.00	30.00	100	150
1905 Proof	471	Value: 750				
1905S straight serif on 1	—	20.00	30.00	50.00	225	325
1905S curved serif on 1	6,056,000	12.00	20.00	35.00	175	250
1906 Proof	500	Value: 575				
1906S	201,000	700	1,200	2,500	9,500	11,500

Note: Counterfeits of the 1906S exist

KM# 172 PESO Weight: 20.0000 g. Composition: 0.8000 Silver .5144 oz. ASW

Date	Mintage	F	VF	XF	Unc	BU
1907 Proof	—	—	—	—	—	—

Note: Two pieces known

Date	Mintage	F	VF	XF	Unc	BU
1907S	10,276,000	3.50	5.50	10.00	55.00	70.00
1908 Proof	500	Value: 575				
1908S	20,955,000	3.50	5.50	10.00	50.00	65.00
1909S	7,578,000	3.50	5.50	12.00	60.00	75.00
1910S	3,154,000	4.50	10.00	25.00	125	150
1911S	463,000	11.00	20.00	35.00	550	1,000
1912S	680,000	11.00	20.00	35.00	650	1,200

UNITED STATES ADMINISTRATION

Commonwealth

DECIMAL COINAGE

KM# 179 CENTAVO Composition: Bronze

Date	Mintage	F	VF	XF	Unc	BU
1937M	15,790,000	—	1.00	4.00	12.00	18.00
1938M	10,000,000	—	0.75	3.00	10.00	16.00
1939M	6,500,000	—	1.00	4.00	15.00	20.00
1940M	4,000,000	—	0.75	2.00	10.00	15.00
1941M	5,000,000	—	1.00	4.00	15.00	25.00
1944S	58,000,000	—	0.15	0.20	1.00	2.50

KM# 180 5 CENTAVOS Composition: Copper-Nickel

Date	Mintage	F	VF	XF	Unc	BU
1937M	2,494,000	—	2.00	5.00	35.00	50.00
1938M	4,000,000	—	1.25	2.50	15.00	25.00
1941M	2,750,000	—	2.50	7.50	30.00	50.00

KM# 180a 5 CENTAVOS Composition: Copper-Nickel-Zinc

Date	Mintage	F	VF	XF	Unc	BU
1944	21,198,000	—	0.15	0.50	1.25	2.25
1944S	14,040,000	—	0.15	0.25	0.75	1.25
1945S	72,796,000	—	0.15	0.20	0.50	1.00

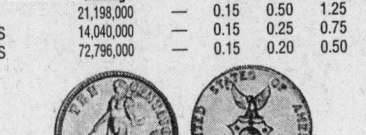

KM# 181 10 CENTAVOS Weight: 2.0000 g. Composition: 0.7500 Silver .0482 oz. ASW

Date	Mintage	F	VF	XF	Unc	BU
1937M	3,500,000	—	2.00	3.00	15.00	20.00
1938M	3,750,000	—	0.75	2.00	10.00	15.00
1941M	2,500,000	—	1.00	2.50	12.50	18.00
1944D	31,592,000	—	BV	0.50	1.00	1.50
1945D	137,208,000	—	BV	0.35	0.75	1.25

Note: 1937, 1938, and 1941 dated strikes have inverted W's for M's

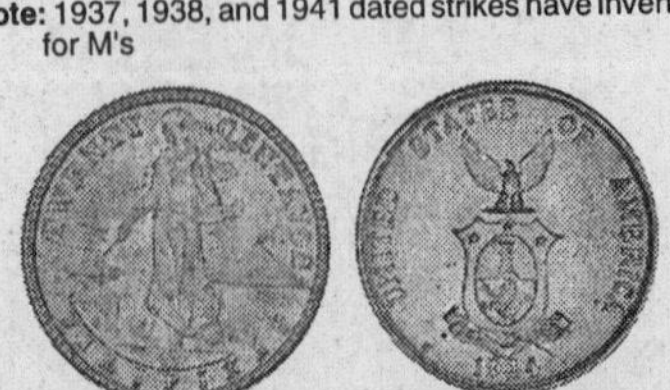

KM# 182 20 CENTAVOS Weight: 4.0000 g. Composition: 0.7500 Silver .0965 oz. ASW

Date	Mintage	F	VF	XF	Unc	BU
1937M	2,665,000	—	2.00	4.00	20.00	30.00
1938M	3,000,000	—	1.25	2.50	7.50	10.00
1941M	1,500,000	—	2.00	3.00	10.00	18.00
1944D	28,596,000	—	BV	0.75	1.25	2.00
1944D/S	—	—	—	25.00	45.00	65.00
1945D	82,804,000	—	BV	0.50	1.00	1.50

KM# 176 50 CENTAVOS Weight: 10.0000 g. **Composition:** 0.7500 Silver .2411 oz. ASW **Subject:** Establishment of the Commonwealth

Date	Mintage	F	VF	XF	Unc	BU
1936	20,000	—	25.00	45.00	65.00	85.00

KM# 183 50 CENTAVOS Weight: 10.0000 g. **Composition:** 0.7500 Silver .2411 oz. ASW

Date	Mintage	F	VF	XF	Unc	BU
1944S	19,187,000	—	BV	1.50	3.00	4.50
1945S	18,120,000	—	BV	1.50	3.00	4.50

KM# 177 PESO Weight: 20.0000 g. **Composition:** 0.9000 Silver .5787 oz. ASW **Subject:** Establishment of the Commonwealth **Obverse:** Conjoined busts of Presidents Roosevelt and Quezon facing left

Date	Mintage	F	VF	XF	Unc	BU
1936	10,000	—	50.00	65.00	135	160

KM# 178 PESO Weight: 20.0000 g. **Composition:** 0.9000 Silver .5787 oz. ASW **Subject:** Establishment of the Commonwealth **Obverse:** Conjoined busts of Governor General Murphy and President Quezon facing left **Reverse:** Similar to KM#177

Date	Mintage	F	VF	XF	Unc	BU
1936	10,000	—	50.00	65.00	135	160

REPUBLIC

DECIMAL COINAGE

KM# 186 CENTAVO Composition: Bronze

Date	Mintage	F	VF	XF	Unc	BU
1958	20,000,000	—	—	0.10	0.25	0.50
1960	40,000,000	—	—	0.10	0.15	0.35
1962	30,000,000	—	—	0.10	0.15	0.35
1963	130,000,000	—	—	0.10	0.15	0.35

KM# 187 5 CENTAVOS Composition: Brass

Date	Mintage	F	VF	XF	Unc	BU
1958	10,000,000	—	—	0.10	0.25	0.50
1959	10,000,000	—	—	0.10	0.20	0.50
1960	40,000,000	—	—	0.10	0.15	0.40
1962	40,000,000	—	—	0.10	0.15	0.40
1963	50,000,000	—	—	0.10	0.15	0.40
1964	100,000,000	—	—	—	0.10	0.40
1966	10,000,000	—	—	0.10	0.20	0.50

KM# 188 10 CENTAVOS Composition: Nickel-Brass

Date	Mintage	F	VF	XF	Unc	BU
1958	10,000,000	—	—	0.15	0.25	0.50
1960	70,000,000	—	—	0.15	0.20	0.40
1962	50,000,000	—	—	0.15	0.20	0.40
1963	50,000,000	—	—	0.15	0.20	0.40
1964	100,000,000	—	—	0.10	0.20	0.40
1966	110,000,000	—	—	0.10	0.20	0.45

KM# 189.1 25 CENTAVOS Composition: Nickel-Brass **Reverse:** Eight smoke rings from volcano

Date	Mintage	F	VF	XF	Unc	BU
1958	10,000,000	—	—	0.25	0.50	0.75
1960	10,000,000	—	—	0.30	0.50	0.75
1962	40,000,000	—	—	0.25	0.50	0.75
1964	49,800,000	—	—	0.20	0.35	0.75
1966	50,000,000	—	0.25	0.50	1.00	1.25

KM# 189.2 25 CENTAVOS Composition: Nickel-Brass **Reverse:** Six smoke rings from volcano

Date	Mintage	F	VF	XF	Unc	BU
1966	40,000,000	—	—	0.20	0.40	0.75
1966 Matte finish	Inc. above	—	—	—	—	—

KM# 184 50 CENTAVOS Weight: 10.0000 g. **Composition:** 0.7500 Silver .2411 oz. ASW **Note:** General Douglas MacArthur

Date	Mintage	F	VF	XF	Unc	BU
1947S	200,000	—	BV	2.50	6.00	7.00

KM# 190 50 CENTAVOS Composition: Nickel-Brass

Date	Mintage	F	VF	XF	Unc	BU
1958	5,000,000	—	0.30	0.45	1.00	1.25
1964	25,000,000	—	0.20	0.30	0.60	1.00

KM# 191 1/2 PESO Weight: 12.5000 g. **Composition:** 0.9000 Silver .3617 oz. ASW **Subject:** 100th Anniversary Birth of Dr. Jose Rizal

Date	Mintage	F	VF	XF	Unc	BU
ND1961	100,000	—	—	3.00	4.00	5.00
ND(1961)	100,000	—	—	3.00	4.00	5.00

KM# 185 PESO Weight: 20.0000 g. **Composition:** 0.9000 Silver .5787 oz. ASW **Obverse:** Bust of General Douglas MacArthur facing right

Date	Mintage	F	VF	XF	Unc	BU
1947S	100,000	—	BV	10.00	17.00	20.00

KM# 192 PESO Weight: 26.0000 g. **Composition:** 0.9000 Silver .7697 oz. ASW **Subject:** 100th Anniversary Birth of Dr. Jose Rizal

Date	Mintage	F	VF	XF	Unc	BU
ND(1961)	100,000	—	—	4.50	7.50	9.00

KM# 193 PESO Weight: 26.0000 g. **Composition:** 0.9000 Silver .7697 oz. ASW **Subject:** 100th Anniversary Birth of Andres Bonifacio

Date	Mintage	F	VF	XF	Unc	BU
ND(1963)	100,000	—	—	4.50	7.50	9.00

KM# 194 PESO **Weight:** 26.0000 g. **Composition:** 0.9000 Silver .7697 oz. ASW **Subject:** 100th Anniversary Birth of Apolinario Mabini

Date	Mintage	F	VF	XF	Unc	BU
ND(1964)	100,000	—	—	4.50	7.50	9.00

KM# 195 PESO **Weight:** 26.0000 g. **Composition:** 0.9000 Silver .7697 oz. ASW **Subject:** 25th Anniversary of Bataan Day

Date	Mintage	F	VF	XF	Unc	BU
ND(1967)	100,000	—	—	4.50	7.50	9.00

Note: KM#195 is a prooflike issue

REFORM COINAGE

100 Sentimos = 1 Piso

KM# 196 SENTIMO **Composition:** Aluminum **Obverse:** Bust of King Lapu-Lapu facing left

Date	Mintage	F	VF	XF	Unc	BU
1967	10,000,000	—	—	—	0.25	—
1968	27,940,000	—	—	—	0.10	—
1969/6	12,060,000	—	—	—	0.20	—
1970	130,000,000	—	—	—	0.10	—
1974 0	165,000,000	—	—	—	0.10	—
1974 1 Proof	10,000	Value: 3.50				

KM# 205 SENTIMO **Composition:** Aluminum **Shape:** Square

Date	Mintage	F	VF	XF	Unc	BU
1975FM (M)	108,000	—	—	—	0.50	—
1975FM (U)	5,875	—	—	—	2.00	—
1975FM (P)	37,000	Value: 1.50				
1975(Lt)	10,000,000	—	—	—	0.10	—
1975(US)	60,190,000	—	—	—	0.10	—
1976FM (M)	10,000	—	—	—	0.75	—
1976FM (U)	1,826	—	—	1.00	2.50	—
1976FM (P)	9,901	Value: 2.00				
1976(US)	60,000,000	—	—	—	0.10	—
1977	4,808,000	—	—	—	0.25	—
1977FM (M)	10,000	—	—	—	1.00	—
1977FM (U)	354	—	—	—	4.00	—
1977FM (P)	4,822	Value: 2.00				
1978	24,813,000	—	—	—	0.10	—
1978FM (U)	10,000	—	—	—	1.00	—
1978FM (P)	4,792	Value: 2.00				

KM# 224 SENTIMO **Composition:** Aluminum **Reverse:** Redesigned seal **Shape:** Square **Note:** Varieties exist in date.

Date	Mintage	F	VF	XF	Unc	BU
1979BSP		—	—	—	0.25	—
1979FM (U)		—	—	—	1.00	—
1979FM (P)	3,645	Value: 2.00				
1980BSP		—	—	—	0.25	—
1980FM (U)		—	—	—	1.00	—
1980FM (P)	3,133	Value: 2.00				
1981BSP		—	—	—	0.20	—
1981FM (U)		—	—	—	1.00	—
1981FM (P)	1,795	Value: 2.00				
1982BSP		—	—	—	0.10	—
1982FM (P)	—	Value: 2.00				

KM# 238 SENTIMO **Composition:** Aluminum **Obverse:** King Lapu-Lapu bust facing left **Reverse:** Sea shell

Date	Mintage	F	VF	XF	Unc	BU
1983	62,090,000	—	—	—	0.40	—
1983 Proof	—	Value: 2.00				
1984	320,000	—	—	—	0.75	—
1985	16,000	—	—	—	1.00	—
1986	80,000	—	—	—	1.00	—
1987	13,570,000	—	—	—	0.40	—
1988	26,861,000	—	—	—	0.40	—
1989	—	—	—	—	0.40	—
1990	—	—	—	—	0.40	—
1991	—	—	—	—	0.40	—
1992	—	—	—	—	0.40	—
1993	—	—	0.35	1.50	9.00	—

KM# 273 SENTIMO **Composition:** Copper Plated Steel **Obverse:** Denomination **Reverse:** Central bank seal

Date	F	VF	XF	Unc	BU
1995	—	—	—	0.35	—
1996	—	—	—	0.35	—
1997	—	—	—	0.35	—
1998	—	—	—	0.35	—
1999	—	—	—	0.35	—
2000	—	—	—	0.35	—

KM# 197 5 SENTIMOS **Composition:** Brass **Reverse:** Bust of Melchora Aquino facing right

Date	Mintage	F	VF	XF	Unc	BU
1967		—	—	—	0.30	—
1968		—	—	—	0.30	—
1970		—	—	1.00	3.50	—
1972		—	—	—	0.30	—
1974		—	—	—	0.30	—
1974 Proof	10,000	Value: 4.00				

KM# 206 5 SENTIMOS **Composition:** Brass

Date	Mintage	F	VF	XF	Unc	BU
1975FM (M)	104,000	—	—	—	0.50	—
1975FM (U)	5,875	—	—	—	2.50	—
1975FM (P)	37,000	Value: 2.00				
1975(US)	98,928,000	—	—	—	0.10	—
1975(Lt)	10,000,000	—	—	—	0.10	—
1976FM (M)	10,000	—	—	—	1.50	—
1976FM (U)	1,826	—	—	—	4.00	—
1976FM (P)	9,901	Value: 2.50				
1976(US)	98,000,000	—	—	—	0.20	—
1977	19,367,000	—	—	—	0.35	—
1977FM (M)	10,000	—	—	—	1.50	—
1977FM (U)	354	—	—	—	4.00	—
1977FM (P)	4,822	Value: 2.50				
1978	61,838,000	—	—	—	0.20	—
1978FM (U)	10,000	—	—	—	1.50	—
1978FM (P)	4,792	Value: 2.50				

KM# 225 5 SENTIMOS **Composition:** Brass **Reverse:** Redesigned seal **Shape:** Scalloped

Date	Mintage	F	VF	XF	Unc	BU
1979BSP		—	—	—	0.30	—
1979FM (U)		—	—	—	1.00	—
1979FM (P)	3,645	Value: 2.50				
1980BSP		—	—	—	0.10	—
1980FM (U)		—	—	—	1.00	—
1980FM (P)	3,133	Value: 2.50				
1981BSP		—	—	—	0.10	—
1981FM (U)		—	—	—	1.00	—
1981FM (P)	1,795	Value: 3.00				
1982BSP		—	—	—	0.10	—
1982FM (P)	—	Value: 3.00				

KM# 239 5 SENTIMOS **Composition:** Aluminum **Reverse:** Waling-Waling orchid

Date	Mintage	F	VF	XF	Unc	BU
1983	100,016,000	—	—	—	0.20	—
1983 Proof	—	Value: 2.00				
1984	141,744,000	—	—	—	0.40	—
1985	50,416,000	—	—	—	0.20	—
1986	11,664,000	—	—	—	0.35	—
1987	79,008,000	—	—	—	0.10	—
1988	90,487,000	—	—	—	0.10	—
1989	—	—	—	—	0.10	—
1990	—	—	—	—	0.10	—
1991	—	—	—	—	0.25	—
1992	—	—	—	—	0.10	—

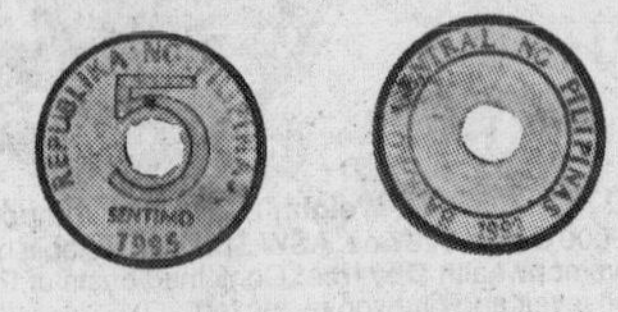

KM# 268 5 SENTIMOS **Composition:** Copper Plated Steel **Rev. Legend:** 1993 BANGKO CENTRAL NG PILIPINAS **Note:** Hole punched out of center.

Date	F	VF	XF	Unc	BU
1995	—	—	—	0.50	—
1996	—	—	—	0.50	—
1997	—	—	—	0.50	—
1998	—	—	—	0.50	—
1999	—	—	—	0.50	—
2000	—	—	—	0.50	—

KM# 198 10 SENTIMOS **Composition:** Copper-Nickel **Reverse:** Bust of Francisco Baltasar facing left

Date	Mintage	F	VF	XF	Unc	BU
1967	50,000,000	—	—	—	0.35	—
1968	60,000,000	—	—	—	0.35	—
1969	40,000,000	—	—	—	0.35	—
1970	50,000,000	—	—	—	0.35	—
1971	80,000,000	—	—	—	0.35	—
1972	121,390,000	—	—	—	0.35	—
1974	60,208,000	—	—	—	0.35	—
1974 Proof	10,000	Value: 4.00				

KM# 207 10 SENTIMOS **Composition:** Copper-Nickel

Date	Mintage	F	VF	XF	Unc	BU
1975FM (M)	104,000	—	—	—	0.50	—
1975FM (U)	5,875	—	—	—	2.50	—
1975FM (P)	37,000	Value: 2.00				
1975(VDM)	10,000,000	—	—	—	0.25	—

Date	Mintage	F	VF	XF	Unc	BU
1975(US)	50,000,000	—	—	—	0.20	—
1976FM (M)	10,000	—	—	—	0.50	—
1976FM (U)	1,826	—	—	—	5.00	—
1976FM (P)	9,901	Value: 3.00				
1976(US)	50,000,000	—	—	—	0.20	—
1977	29,314,000	—	—	—	0.25	—
1977FM (M)	10,000	—	—	—	1.50	—
1977FM (U)	354	—	—	—	6.50	—
1977FM (P)	4,822	Value: 3.00				
1978	60,042,000	—	—	—	0.10	—
1978FM (U)	10,000	—	—	—	3.00	—
1978FM (P)	4,792	Value: 3.00				

KM# 226 10 SENTIMOS **Composition:** Copper-Nickel **Reverse:** Redesigned seal **Note:** Varieties with thick and thin legends exist for coins with BSP mint mark.

Date	Mintage	F	VF	XF	Unc	BU
1979BSP	6,446,000	—	—	—	0.50	—
1979FM (U)	10,000	—	—	—	1.00	—
1979FM (P)	3,645	Value: 3.00				
1980BSP	—	—	—	—	0.30	—
1980FM (U)	10,000	—	—	—	1.50	—
1980FM (P)	3,133	Value: 3.25				
1981BSP	—	—	—	—	0.30	—
1981FM (U)	—	—	—	—	1.00	—
1981FM (P)	1,795	Value: 3.50				
1982BSP	—	—	—	—	0.30	—
1982FM (P)	—	Value: 3.50				

KM# 240.1 10 SENTIMOS **Composition:** Aluminum **Series:** F.A.O. **Subject:** World Conference on Fisheries **Reverse:** Fish's name in error: PANDAKA PYGMEA

Date	Mintage	F	VF	XF	Unc	BU
1983	95,640,000	—	—	—	8.00	—
1983 Proof	—	Value: 8.00				
1987	Inc. below	—	—	—	0.50	—

KM# 240.2 10 SENTIMOS **Composition:** Aluminum **Series:** F.A.O. **Subject:** World Conference on Fisheries **Reverse:** Fish's name: PANDAKA PYGMAEA

Date	Mintage	F	VF	XF	Unc	BU
1983	—	—	—	—	0.35	—
1984	235,900,000	—	—	—	0.35	—
1985	90,169,000	—	—	—	0.35	—
1986	4,270,000	—	—	—	0.50	—
1987	99,520,000	—	—	—	0.35	—
1988	117,166,000	—	—	—	0.35	—
1989	—	—	—	—	0.35	—
1990	—	—	—	—	0.35	—
1991	—	—	—	—	0.35	—
1992	—	—	—	—	0.35	—
1993	—	—	—	—	0.50	—
1994	—	—	—	—	0.50	—

KM# 270 10 SENTIMOS **Composition:** Bronze Plated Steel **Reverse:** Central Bank seal

Date	F	VF	XF	Unc	BU
1995	—	—	—	0.25	—
1996	—	—	—	0.50	—
1997	—	—	—	0.25	—
1998	—	—	—	0.25	—
1999	—	—	—	0.25	—

KM# 199 25 SENTIMOS **Composition:** Copper-Nickel **Reverse:** Bust of Juan Luna facing left

Date	Mintage	F	VF	XF	Unc	BU
1967	40,000,000	—	—	0.10	0.50	—
1968	10,000,000	—	—	0.10	0.50	—
1969	10,000,000	—	—	0.10	0.50	—
1970	40,000,000	—	—	0.10	0.40	—
1971	60,000,000	—	—	0.10	0.40	—
1972	90,000,000	—	—	0.10	0.40	—
1974	10,000,000	—	—	0.10	0.50	—
1974 Proof	10,000	Value: 12.00				

KM# 208 25 SENTIMOS **Composition:** Copper-Nickel

Date	Mintage	F	VF	XF	Unc	BU
1975FM (M)	104,000	—	—	—	0.80	—
1975FM (U)	5,875	—	—	—	5.00	—
1975FM (P)	37,000	Value: 3.00				
1975(US)	10,000,000	—	—	0.10	0.40	—
1975(VDM)	10,000,000	—	—	0.10	0.40	—
1976FM (M)	10,000	—	—	0.10	1.00	—
1976FM (U)	1,826	—	—	—	6.50	—
1976FM (P)	9,901	Value: 3.50				
1976(US)	10,000,000	—	—	0.10	0.25	—
1977	24,654,000	—	—	0.10	0.25	—
1977FM (M)	10,000	—	—	—	1.50	—
1977FM (U)	354	—	—	—	8.00	—
1977FM (P)	4,822	Value: 4.50				
1978	40,466,000	—	—	0.10	0.25	—
1978FM (U)	10,000	—	—	—	2.50	—
1978FM (P)	4,792	Value: 4.00				

KM# 227 25 SENTIMOS **Composition:** Copper-Nickel **Reverse:** Redesigned seal

Date	Mintage	F	VF	XF	Unc	BU
1979BSP	20,725,000	—	—	0.10	0.50	—
1979FM (U)	10,000	—	—	—	1.50	—
1979FM (P)	3,645	Value: 4.50				
1980BSP	—	—	—	0.10	0.75	—
1980FM (U)	10,000	—	—	—	2.00	—
1980FM (P)	3,133	Value: 4.50				
1981BSP	—	—	—	0.10	1.00	—
1981FM (U)	—	—	—	—	1.50	—
1981FM (P)	1,795	Value: 5.00				
1982BSP	—	—	—	0.10	0.50	—
1982FM (P)	—	Value: 5.00				

KM# 241.1 25 SENTIMOS **Composition:** Brass **Reverse:** Butterfly

Date	Mintage	F	VF	XF	Unc	BU
1983	92,944,000	—	—	0.15	0.75	—
1983 Proof	—	Value: 3.00				
1984	254,324,000	—	—	0.15	0.75	—
1985	84,922,000	—	—	0.15	0.75	—
1986	65,284,000	—	—	0.15	0.75	—
1987	1,680,000	—	—	0.50	1.75	—
1988	51,062,000	—	—	—	0.75	—
1989	—	—	—	—	0.75	—
1990	—	—	—	—	0.75	—

KM# 241.2 25 SENTIMOS **Composition:** Brass **Note:** Reduced size.

Date	F	VF	XF	Unc	BU
1991	—	—	—	0.75	—
1992	—	—	—	0.75	—
1993	—	—	—	1.00	—
1994	—	—	—	1.00	—

KM# 271 25 SENTIMOS **Composition:** Brass **Reverse:** Central Bank seal

Date	F	VF	XF	Unc	BU
1995	—	—	—	1.00	—
1996	—	—	—	0.75	—
1997	—	—	—	0.75	—
1998	—	—	—	0.75	—
1999	—	—	—	0.75	—
2000	—	—	—	0.75	—

KM# 200 50 SENTIMOS **Composition:** Copper-Nickel-Zinc **Reverse:** Bust of Marcelo H. del Pilar facing right

Date	Mintage	F	VF	XF	Unc	BU
1967	20,000,000	—	0.10	0.25	0.75	—
1971	10,000,000	—	0.10	0.50	1.00	—
1972 Serif on 2	30,000,000	—	0.10	1.25	2.00	—
1972 Plain 2	20,517,000	—	0.10	1.00	1.50	—
1974	5,004,000	—	0.10	0.75	1.25	—
1974 Proof	10,000	Value: 20.00				
1975	5,714,000	—	0.10	0.20	1.00	—

KM# 242.1 50 SENTIMOS **Composition:** Copper-Nickel **Reverse:** Monkey-eating eagle **Note:** Eagle's name: PITHECOPHAGA

Date	Mintage	F	VF	XF	Unc	BU
1983	27,644,000	—	0.10	0.50	1.25	—
1983 Proof	—	Value: 5.00				
1984	121,408,000	—	0.10	0.20	1.00	—
1985	107,048,000	—	0.10	0.20	1.00	—
1986	120,000,000	—	0.10	0.20	1.00	—
1987	1,078,000	—	0.10	1.00	1.50	—
1988	24,008,000	—	0.10	0.20	1.00	—
1989	—	—	0.10	0.20	1.00	—
1990	—	—	0.10	0.20	1.00	—

KM# 242.2 50 SENTIMOS **Composition:** Copper-Nickel **Reverse:** Monkey-eating eagle **Note:** Error eagle's name: PITHECOBHAGA

Date	F	VF	XF	Unc	BU
1983	—	3.00	5.00	10.00	—

KM# 242.3 50 SENTIMOS **Composition:** Brass **Note:** Reduced size.

Date	F	VF	XF	Unc	BU
1991	—	—	0.25	1.50	—
1992	—	—	0.25	1.50	—
1993	—	—	0.25	2.25	—
1994	—	—	0.25	2.25	—

KM# 201 PISO **Weight:** 26.4500 g. **Composition:** 0.9000 Silver .7653 oz. ASW **Subject:** Centennial - Birth of Aquinaldo

Date	Mintage	F	VF	XF	Unc	BU
1969 Prooflike	100,000	—	—	5.00	8.00	9.00

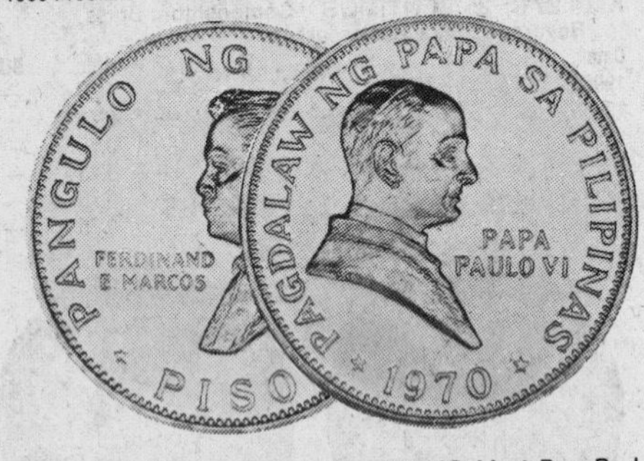

KM# 202 PISO **Composition:** Nickel **Subject:** Pope Paul VI visit

Date	Mintage	F	VF	XF	Unc	BU
1970	70,000	—	—	1.00	2.50	3.50

KM# 202a PISO **Weight:** 26.4500 g. **Composition:** 0.9000 Silver .7653 oz. ASW

Date	Mintage	F	VF	XF	Unc	BU
1970	30,000	—	—	7.00	10.00	12.00

KM# 202b PISO **Weight:** 19.3000 g. **Composition:** 0.9170 Gold .5691 oz. AGW **Subject:** Pope Paul VI visit

Date	Mintage	F	VF	XF	Unc	BU
1970	1,000	—	—	—	—	500

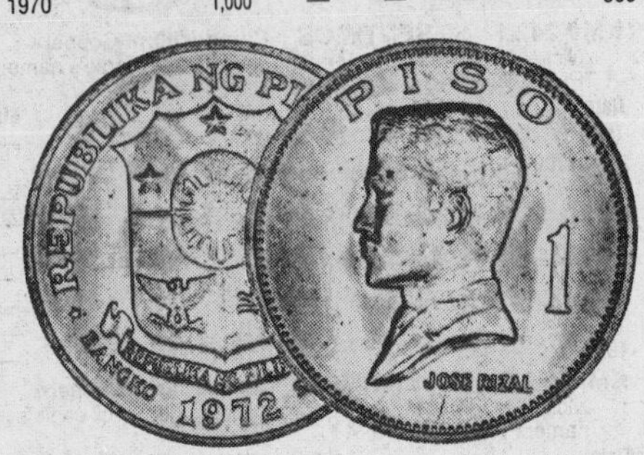

KM# 203 PISO **Composition:** Copper-Nickel **Reverse:** Bust of Jose Rizal facing left

Date	Mintage	F	VF	XF	Unc	BU
1972	121,821,000	—	0.25	0.50	1.25	—
1974	45,631,000	—	0.25	0.50	1.25	—
1974 Proof	10,000	Value: 30.00				

KM# 209.1 PISO **Composition:** Copper-Nickel

Date	Mintage	F	VF	XF	Unc	BU
1975FM (M)	104,000	—	—	—	2.00	—
1975FM (U)	5,877	—	—	—	5.50	—
1975FM (P)	37,000	Value: 2.50				
1975(VDM)	10,000,000	—	0.15	0.25	1.25	—
1975(US)	30,000,000	—	0.15	0.25	1.00	—
1976FM (M)	10,000	—	—	—	1.00	—
1976FM (U)	1,826	—	—	—	10.00	—
1976FM (P)	9,901	Value: 3.00				
1976(US)	30,000,000	—	0.15	0.25	0.75	—
1977	14,771,000	—	0.15	0.25	1.25	—
1977FM (M)	12,000	—	—	—	4.00	—
1977FM (U)	354	—	—	—	10.00	—
1977FM (P)	4,822	Value: 3.50				
1978	19,408,000	—	0.15	0.25	1.00	—
1978FM (U)	10,000	—	—	—	4.00	—
1978FM (P)	4,792	Value: 6.50				

KM# 209.2 PISO **Composition:** Copper-Nickel **Reverse:** Legend below shield **Rev. Legend:** ISANG BANSA ISANG DIWA

Date	Mintage	F	VF	XF	Unc	BU
1979BSP	321,000	—	0.15	0.25	1.00	—
1979FM (U)	10,000	—	—	—	2.50	—
1979FM (P)	3,645	Value: 3.50				
1980BSP	19,693,000	—	0.15	0.25	0.75	—
1980FM (U)	10,000	—	—	—	7.50	—
1980FM (P)	3,133	Value: 12.50				
1981BSP	7,944,000	—	0.15	0.25	1.00	—
1981FM (U)	—	—	—	—	3.00	—
1981FM (P)	1,795	Value: 6.00				
1982FM (P)	—	Value: 6.00				
1982BSP Large date	52,110,000	—	0.15	0.25	1.00	—
1982BSP Small date	Inc. above	—	0.15	0.25	1.00	—

KM# 243.1 PISO **Composition:** Copper-Nickel **Reverse:** Tamara bull **Note:** Large legends and design elements.

Date	Mintage	F	VF	XF	Unc	BU
1983	55,869,000	—	—	0.30	1.25	—
1983 Proof	—	Value: 6.50				
1984	4,997,000	—	—	1.00	2.50	—
1985	182,592,000	—	—	0.30	1.25	—
1986	19,072,000	—	—	0.30	1.25	—
1987	1,391,000	—	—	1.00	2.00	—
1988	54,636,000	—	—	0.30	1.25	—

KM# 243.2 PISO **Composition:** Stainless Steel **Note:** Reduced size.

Date	F	VF	XF	Unc	BU
1991	—	—	0.50	1.25	—
1992	—	—	0.50	1.25	—
1993	—	—	0.75	2.00	—
1994	—	—	0.75	2.00	—

KM# 243.3 PISO **Composition:** Copper-Nickel **Note:** Smaller legends and design elements.

Date	F	VF	XF	Unc	BU
1989	—	—	0.30	1.25	—
1990	—	—	0.30	1.25	—

KM# 251 PISO **Composition:** Copper-Nickel **Subject:** Philippine Cultures Decade

Date	F	VF	XF	Unc	BU
1989	—	—	—	2.50	—

KM# 257 PISO **Composition:** Copper-Nickel **Note:** Waterfall, ship, and flower.

Date	F	VF	XF	Unc	BU
1991	—	—	—	2.00	—
1991 Matte	—	—	—	10.00	—

Note: Special striking by CB

KM# 260 PISO **Composition:** Nickel Clad Steel **Subject:** 50th Anniversary - Battle of Kagitingan

Date	F	VF	XF	Unc	BU
ND(1992)	—	—	—	2.50	—

KM# 269 PISO **Composition:** Copper-Nickel **Obverse:** Jose Rizal **Reverse:** Bank seal, date 1993.

Date	F	VF	XF	Unc	BU
1995	—	—	—	2.00	—
1996	—	—	—	1.00	—
1997	—	—	—	1.00	—
1998	—	—	—	1.00	—
1999	—	—	—	1.00	—
2000	—	—	—	1.00	—

KM# 244 2 PISO **Composition:** Copper-Nickel **Obverse:** Bust of Andres Bonifacio facing left **Shape:** 10-sided

Date	Mintage	F	VF	XF	Unc	BU
1983	15,640,000	—	—	0.35	4.00	—
1983 Proof	—	Value: 10.00				
1984	121,111,000	—	—	0.35	1.25	—
1985	115,211,000	—	—	0.35	1.25	—
1986	25,260,000	—	—	0.35	1.25	—
1987	2,196,000	—	—	0.35	3.50	—
1988	16,094,000	—	—	—	1.50	—
1989	—	—	—	—	1.25	—
1990	—	—	—	—	1.25	—

KM# 253 2 PISO Composition: Copper-Nickel **Reverse:** Bust of Elpidio Quirino facing right **Shape:** 10-sided

Date	Mintage	F	VF	XF	Unc	BU
ND(1991)	10,000,000	—	—	—	3.00	—
ND(1991) Matte	—	—	—	—	10.00	—

Note: Special striking by CB

KM# 258 2 PISO Composition: Stainless Steel **Obverse:** Bust of Andres Bonifacio facing left

Date	F	VF	XF	Unc	BU
1991	—	—	—	2.50	—
1992	—	—	—	3.00	—
1993	—	—	—	3.00	—
1994	—	—	—	3.00	—

KM# 261 2 PISO Composition: Nickel Clad Steel **Reverse:** Bust of Manuel A. Roxas facing right

Date	F	VF	XF	Unc	BU
ND(1992)	—	—	—	3.50	—
ND(1992) Matte	—	—	—	15.00	—

Note: Special striking by CB

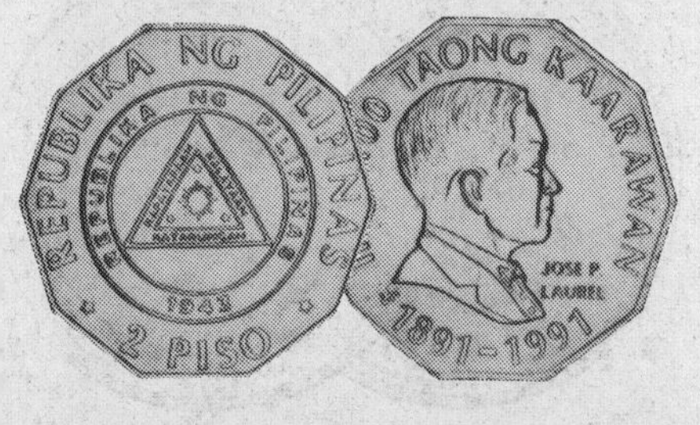

KM# 256 2 PISO Composition: Copper-Nickel **Reverse:** Bust of Jose Laurel facing right **Shape:** 10-sided

Date	F	VF	XF	Unc	BU
ND(1992)	—	—	1.75	3.50	—
ND(1992) Matte	—	—	—	10.00	—

Note: Special striking by CB

KM# 210.1 5 PISO Composition: Nickel **Reverse:** Bust of Ferdinand E. Marcos facing left

Date	Mintage	F	VF	XF	Unc	BU
1975FM (M)	3,850	—	—	—	10.00	—
1975FM (U)	7,875	—	—	—	8.00	—
1975FM (P)	39,000	Value: 5.00				
1975(Sh)	20,000,000	—	0.50	1.00	2.00	—
1976FM (M)	10,000	—	—	—	5.00	—
1976FM (U)	1,826	—	—	—	15.00	—
1976FM (P)	9,901	Value: 6.00				
1977FM (M)	10,000	—	—	—	5.00	—
1977FM (U)	354	—	—	—	15.00	—
1977FM (P)	4,822	Value: 7.50				
1978FM (U)	10,000	—	—	—	2.50	—
1978FM (P)	4,792	Value: 9.00				
1982	—	—	0.50	0.75	1.50	—

KM# 210.2 5 PISO Composition: Nickel **Obverse:** Legend below shield **Obv. Legend:** ISANG BANSA ISANG DIWA

Date	Mintage	F	VF	XF	Unc	BU
1979FM (U)	10,000	—	—	—	4.50	—
1979FM (P)	3,645	Value: 8.00				
1980FM (U)	10,000	—	—	—	4.50	—
1980FM (P)	3,133	Value: 10.00				
1981FM (U)	11,000	—	—	—	4.50	—
1981FM (P)	1,795	Value: 10.00				
1982FM (P)	—	Value: 10.00				
1982FM (U); Prooflike	—	—	—	—	9.00	—

KM# 259 5 PISO Composition: Nickel-Brass **Obverse:** Bust of Emilio Aguinaldo facing right; Pterocarpus Indicus flower

Date	F	VF	XF	Unc	BU
1991	—	—	—	5.00	—
1992	—	—	—	3.50	—
1993	—	—	—	5.00	—
1994	—	—	—	5.00	—

KM# 262 5 PISO Composition: Nickel-Brass **Subject:** 30th Chess Olympiad **Note:** Varieties exist.

Date	F	VF	XF	Unc	BU
1992	—	—	—	12.00	—

KM# 263 5 PISO Composition: Nickel-Brass **Subject:** Leyte Gulf Landings

Date	Mintage	F	VF	XF	Unc	BU
ND(1994)	7,800	—	—	—	7.50	—

KM# 272 5 PISO Composition: Nickel-Brass **Obverse:** Aguinaldo **Reverse:** Central Bank seal

Date	F	VF	XF	Unc	BU
1995	—	—	—	2.50	—
1996	—	—	—	1.50	—
1997	—	—	—	1.50	—
1997BSP	—	—	—	1.50	—
1998	—	—	—	1.50	—

KM# 250 10 PISO Composition: Nickel **Subject:** People Power Revolution

Date	F	VF	XF	Unc	BU
1988	—	—	—	4.00	—

KM# 278 10 PISO Ring Weight: 8.7000 g. **Ring Composition:** Copper-Nickel **Center Composition:** Brass **Obverse:** Conjoined busts of Mobini and Bonifacio facing right **Reverse:** Bank seal **Edge:** Plain and reeded sections **Size:** 26.5 mm.

Date	F	VF	XF	Unc	BU
2000	—	—	—	3.50	—
2001	—	—	—	3.00	—

KM# 204 25 PISO Weight: 26.4000 g. **Composition:** 0.9000 Silver .7639 oz. ASW **Subject:** 25th Anniversary of Bank

Date	Mintage	F	VF	XF	Unc	BU
ND(1974)	90,000	—	—	—	7.00	—

KM# 204a 25 PISO Weight: 26.4000 g. **Composition:** 0.9000 Silver .7639 oz. ASW

Date	Mintage	F	VF	XF	Unc	BU
ND(1974) Proof	10,000	Value: 12.00				

KM# 211 25 PISO Weight: 25.0000 g. **Composition:** 0.5000 Silver .4018 oz. ASW **Obverse:** Bust of Emilio Aguinaldo facing right

Date	Mintage	F	VF	XF	Unc	BU
1975FM (M)	10,000	—	—	—	8.00	—
1975FM (U)	5,875	—	—	—	15.00	—
1975FM (P)	37,000	Value: 10.00				

KM# 214 25 PISO **Weight:** 25.0000 g. **Composition:** 0.5000 Silver .4018 oz. ASW **Series:** F.A.O.

Date	Mintage	F	VF	XF	Unc	BU
1976FM (M)	22,000	—	—	—	12.50	—
1976FM (U)	1,826	—	—	—	20.00	—
1976FM (P)	9,901	Value: 12.50				

KM# 217 25 PISO **Weight:** 25.0000 g. **Composition:** 0.5000 Silver .4018 oz. ASW **Subject:** Banaue Rice Terraces

Date	Mintage	F	VF	XF	Unc	BU
1977FM (M)	10,000	—	—	—	12.50	—
1977FM (U)	354	—	—	—	30.00	—
1977FM (P)	4,822	Value: 20.00				

KM# 221 25 PISO **Weight:** 25.0000 g. **Composition:** 0.5000 Silver .4018 oz. ASW **Subject:** 100th Anniversary - Birth of Quezon

Date	Mintage	F	VF	XF	Unc	BU
ND(1978)FM (U)	10,000	—	—	—	15.00	—
ND(1978)FM (P)	9,930	Value: 20.00				

KM# 228 25 PISO **Weight:** 25.0000 g. **Composition:** 0.5000 Silver .4018 oz. ASW **Subject:** UN Conference on Trade and Development

Date	Mintage	F	VF	XF	Unc	BU
1979FM (U)	10,000	—	—	—	15.00	—
1979FM (P)	7,093	Value: 20.00				

KM# 230 25 PISO **Weight:** 25.0000 g. **Composition:** 0.5000 Silver .4018 oz. ASW **Subject:** 100th Anniversary - Birth of Gen. Douglas MacArthur **Reverse:** Bust of Gen. Douglas MacArthur turned left

Date	Mintage	F	VF	XF	Unc	BU
ND(1980)FM (U)	9,800	—	—	—	25.00	—
ND(1980)FM (P)	6,318	Value: 50.00				

KM# 232 25 PISO **Weight:** 25.0000 g. **Composition:** 0.5000 Silver .4018 oz. ASW **Subject:** World Food Day

Date	Mintage	F	VF	XF	Unc	BU
1981FM (U)	10,000	—	—	—	22.50	—
1981FM (P)	3,033	Value: 25.00				

KM# 235 25 PISO **Weight:** 25.0000 g. **Composition:** 0.5000 Silver .4018 oz. ASW **Reverse:** Presidents Marcos and Reagan profiles

Date	Mintage	F	VF	XF	Unc	BU
1982	8,000	—	—	—	35.00	—
1982 Proof	250	Value: 475				

KM# 246 25 PISO **Weight:** 18.4100 g. **Composition:** 0.9250 Silver .5475 oz. ASW **Subject:** President Aquino's visit in Washington

Date	Mintage	F	VF	XF	Unc	BU
1986 Proof	Est. 1,000	Value: 120				

KM# 212 50 PISO **Weight:** 27.4000 g. **Composition:** 0.9250 Silver .8148 oz. ASW **Subject:** 3rd Anniversary of the New Society

Date	Mintage	F	VF	XF	Unc	BU
1975FM (M)	10,000	—	—	—	10.00	—
1975FM (U)	7,875	—	—	—	15.00	—
1975FM (P)	54,000	Value: 10.00				

KM# 215 50 PISO **Weight:** 27.4000 g. **Composition:** 0.9250 Silver .8148 oz. ASW **Subject:** I.M.F. Meeting

Date	Mintage	F	VF	XF	Unc	BU
1976 Proof	5,477	Value: 20.00				
1976FM (M)	10,000	—	—	—	12.50	—
1976FM (U)	1,826	—	—	—	35.00	—
1976FM (P)	15,000	Value: 18.00				

KM# 218 50 PISO **Weight:** 27.4000 g. **Composition:** 0.9250 Silver .8148 oz. ASW **Subject:** Inauguration of new mint facilities

Date	Mintage	F	VF	XF	Unc	BU
1977FM (M)	10,000	—	—	—	15.00	—
1977FM (U)	354	—	—	—	50.00	—
1977FM (P)	6,704	Value: 20.00				

KM# 222 50 PISO **Weight:** 27.4000 g. **Composition:** 0.9250 Silver .8148 oz. ASW **Subject:** 100th Anniversary - Birth of Quezon

Date	Mintage	F	VF	XF	Unc	BU
ND(1978)FM (U)	10,000	—	—	—	12.50	—
ND(1978)FM (P)	9,969	Value: 20.00				

KM# 229 50 PISO Weight: 27.4000 g. **Composition:** 0.9250 Silver .8148 oz. ASW **Subject:** International Year of the Child

Date	Mintage	F	VF	XF	Unc	BU
1979FM (U)	10,000	—	—	—	10.00	—
1979FM (P)	27,000	Value: 12.50				

KM# 233 50 PISO Weight: 27.4000 g. **Composition:** 0.9250 Silver .8148 oz. ASW **Subject:** Pope John Paul II visit

Date	Mintage	F	VF	XF	Unc	BU
1981FM (U)	10,000	—	—	—	40.00	—
1981FM (P)	3,353	Value: 65.00				

KM# 236 50 PISO Weight: 27.4000 g. **Composition:** 0.9250 Silver .8148 oz. ASW **Subject:** 40th Anniversary of Bataan-Corregidor

Date	Mintage	F	VF	XF	Unc	BU
ND(1982)FM (U)	13,000	—	—	—	25.00	—
ND(1982)FM (P)	4,626	Value: 50.00				

KM# 245 100 PISO Weight: 25.0000 g. **Composition:** 0.5000 Silver .4019 oz. ASW **Subject:** 75th Anniversary - University of the Philippines

Date	Mintage	F	VF	XF	Unc	BU
ND(1983)	15,000	—	—	—	15.00	—
ND(1983) Proof	2,000	Value: 35.00				

KM# 264 100 PISO Weight: 10.0000 g. **Composition:** 0.9250 Silver .2974 oz. ASW **Subject:** Papal Visit 1995

Date	Mintage	F	VF	XF	Unc	BU
ND(1994) Proof	1,000	Value: 85.00				

KM# 279 100 PISO Weight: 16.7300 g. **Composition:** 0.8000 Silver .4303 oz. ASW **Subject:** Leyte Gulf Landing

Date	Mintage	F	VF	XF	Unc	BU
ND(1994) Proof	1,000	Value: 75.00				

KM# 254 150 PISO Weight: 16.8200 g. **Composition:** 0.9250 Silver .5002 oz. ASW **Subject:** Southeast Asian Games **Reverse:** Official logo

Date	Mintage	F	VF	XF	Unc	BU
1991 Proof	5,000	Value: 50.00				

KM# 248 200 PISO Weight: 25.0000 g. **Composition:** 0.9250 Silver .7436 oz. ASW **Subject:** World Wildlife Fund **Reverse:** Mindoro Buffalo

Date	Mintage	F	VF	XF	Unc	BU
1987 Proof	25,000	Value: 50.00				

KM# 252 200 PISO Weight: 25.0000 g. **Composition:** 0.9250 Silver .7436 oz. ASW **Subject:** Save the Children Fund

Date	Mintage	F	VF	XF	Unc	BU
1990 Proof	Est. 20,000	Value: 60.00				

KM# 265 200 PISO Weight: 15.5600 g. **Composition:** 0.9990 Silver .4998 oz. ASW **Subject:** Papal Visit 1995 **Note:** Similar to 100 Piso, KM#264.

Date	Mintage	F	VF	XF	Unc	BU
ND(1994) Proof	1,000	Value: 110				

KM# 249 500 PISO Weight: 28.0000 g. **Composition:** 0.9250 Silver .8328 oz. ASW **Subject:** People Power Revolution

Date	Mintage	F	VF	XF	Unc	BU
1988 Proof	Est. 7,500	Value: 50.00				

KM# 280 500 PISO Weight: 23.1000 g. **Composition:** 0.9250 Silver .6870 oz. ASW **Subject:** Leyte Gulf Landing

Date	Mintage	F	VF	XF	Unc	BU
ND(1994) Proof	1,000	Value: 125				

KM# 276 500 PISO Weight: 28.2800 g. **Composition:** 0.9250 Silver .8410 oz. ASW **Subject:** Centennial - Andres Bonifacio 1897-1997

Date		F	VF	XF	Unc	BU
ND(1997) Proof	—	Value: 75.00				

KM# 274 500 PISO Weight: 28.2800 g. **Composition:** 0.9250 Silver .8410 oz. ASW **Subject:** Carlos P. Romulo Centennial **Obverse:** National arms above denomination **Reverse:** Portrait, dates

Date	Mintage	F	VF	XF	Unc	BU
ND(1998) Proof	Est. 2,100	Value: 75.00				

KM# 277 500 PISO Weight: 28.2800 g. **Composition:** 0.9250 Silver .8410 oz. ASW **Subject:** Centennial - Emilio F. Aguinaldo 1898-1998

Date	Mintage	F	VF	XF	Unc	BU
ND(1998) Proof	2,100	Value: 75.00				

KM# 275 500 PISO Weight: 28.2800 g. **Composition:** 0.9250 Silver .8410 oz. ASW **Subject:** 50th Anniversary - Central Bank **Obverse:** Old and new bank buildings **Reverse:** Old and new bank seals

Date	Mintage	F	VF	XF	Unc	BU
ND(1999) Proof	Est. 5,000	Value: 50.00				

KM# 213 1000 PISO Weight: 9.9500 g. **Composition:** 0.9000 Gold .2879 oz. AGW **Subject:** 3rd Anniversary of the New Society

Date	Mintage	F	VF	XF	Unc	BU
1975	23,000	—	—	—	135	—
1975 Proof	13,000	Value: 150				

KM# 281 1000 PISO Weight: 31.1000 g. **Composition:** 0.9990 Silver .9989 oz. ASW **Subject:** Leyte Gulf Landing

Date	Mintage	F	VF	XF	Unc	BU
ND(1994) Proof	1,000	Value: 225				

KM# 216 1500 PISO Weight: 20.5500 g. **Composition:** 0.9000 Gold .5947 oz. AGW **Subject:** I.M.F. Meeting

Date	Mintage	F	VF	XF	Unc	BU
1976	5,500	—	—	—	260	—
1976 Proof	6,500	Value: 280				

KM# 219 1500 PISO Weight: 20.5500 g. **Composition:** 0.9000 Gold .5947 oz. AGW **Subject:** 5th Anniversary of the New Society

Date	Mintage	F	VF	XF	Unc	BU
ND(1977)	4,000	—	—	—	260	—
ND(1977) Proof	6,000	Value: 280				

KM# 223 1500 PISO Weight: 20.5500 g. **Composition:** 0.9000 Gold .5947 oz. AGW **Subject:** Inauguration of New Mint Facilities

Date	Mintage	F	VF	XF	Unc	BU
1978	3,000	—	—	—	275	—
1978 Proof	3,000	Value: 300				

KM# 234 1500 PISO Weight: 9.9500 g. **Composition:** 0.9000 Gold .2879 oz. AGW **Subject:** Pope John Paul II Visit

Date	Mintage	F	VF	XF	Unc	BU
1981 Proof	1,000	Value: 525				
1982 Proof	—	—	—	—	—	—

KM# 237 1500 PISO Weight: 9.7800 g. **Composition:** 0.9000 Gold .2830 oz. AGW **Subject:** 40th Anniversary of Bataan-Corregidor

Date	Mintage	F	VF	XF	Unc	BU
ND(1982)FM (U)	1,000	—	—	—	300	—
ND(1982)FM (P)	445	Value: 400				

KM# 231 2500 PISO Weight: 14.5700 g. **Composition:** 0.5000 Gold .2342 oz. AGW **Subject:** 100th Anniversary - Birth of General Douglas MacArthur

Date	Mintage	F	VF	XF	Unc	BU
ND(1980)FM (P)	3,073	Value: 300				

KM# 247 2500 PISO Weight: 15.0000 g. **Composition:** 0.5000 Gold .2414 oz. AGW **Subject:** President Aquino's Visit in Washington

Date	Mintage	F	VF	XF	Unc	BU
1986 Proof	Est. 250	Value: 450				

KM# 266 2500 PISO Weight: 7.9800 g. **Composition:** 0.9167 Gold .2352 oz. AGW **Subject:** Papal Visit 1995 **Note:** Similar to 100 Piso, KM#264.

Date	F	VF	XF	Unc	BU
ND(1994) Proof	—	Value: 400			

KM# 220 5000 PISO Weight: 68.7400 g. **Composition:** 0.9000 Gold 1.9893 oz. AGW **Subject:** 5th Anniversary of the New Society

Date	Mintage	F	VF	XF	Unc	BU
ND(1977)FM (U)	100	—	—	—	1,600	-
ND(1977)FM (P)	3,832	Value: 950				

KM# 267 5000 PISO Weight: 16.8100 g. **Composition:** 0.9250 Gold .4999 oz. AGW **Subject:** Papal Visit 1995 **Note:** Similar to 100 Piso, KM#264.

Date	F	VF	XF	Unc	BU
ND(1994) Proof	—	Value: 700			

KM# 255 10000 PESOS Weight: 33.5500 g. **Composition:** 0.9250 Gold 1 oz. AGW **Subject:** People Power

Date	Mintage	F	VF	XF	Unc	BU
ND(1992) Proof	1,600	Value: 650				

PATTERNS

Including off metal strikes

KM#	Date	Mintage	Identification	Mkt Val
Pn20	1922	—	Centavo. Silver. KM#163.	[illegible]
Pn21	ND(1965-66)	—	Peso. Silver. Marcos	[illegible]
Pn22	1966	—	Centavo. Copper. Central Bank	[illegible]
Pn23	1966	—	Brass.	[illegible]
Pn24	1966	—	Copper.	[illegible]
Pn25	1966	—	Silver.	[illegible]
Pn26	1966	—	Copper.	[illegible]
Pn27	1966	—	Brass.	[illegible]
PnA28	1966	—	Copper. Similar to Pn28. Conjoined busts of Ferdinand and Imelda Marcos.	[illegible]
PnB28	1966	—	Copper. As Pn28	[illegible]
Pn28	1966	—	Silver.	[illegible]
Pn29	1966	—	Piso. Silver.	[illegible]
Pn30	1966	—	Peso. Silver. Ferd and Imelda Marcos	[illegible]
PnA31	1966	—	Piso. Copper. Similar to Pn28. As Pn38.	[illegible]
PnB31	1966	—	Piso. Brass. Similar to Pn38 wtihout eagle and lion on arms.	[illegible]
pnB34	1967	—	10 Centavos. Bronze. Bust of Francisco Baltazar.	[illegible]
pnb35	1967	—	50 Sentimos. Bronze. Similar to Pn28. Bust of Juan Luna.	[illegible]
Pn31	1967	—	Copper.	[illegible]

KM#	Date	Mintage	Identification	Mkt Val
Pn32	1967	—		125
Pn33	1967	—	Copper. Similar to Pn32. Similar to Pn27.	125
PnA34	1967	—	25 Centavos. Copper. Design similar to Pn28, legend as Pn34. Similar to Pn27.	100
Pn34	1967	—	25 Sentimos. Silver.	125
PnA35	1967	—	Copper. As Pn36. Small conjoined busts of Ferdinand and Imelda Marcos.	125
Pn35	1967	—	50 Sentimos. Copper. Large conjoined busts of Ferdinand and Imelda Marcos.	150
Pn36	1967	—	50 Sentimos. Silver. Del Pilar left. Del Pilar	125
Pn37	1967	—	50 Sentimos. Copper. Del Pilar left. Del Pilar	125
PnA38	1967	—	Peso. Copper. Similar to KM#195	150
PnB38	1967	—	Peso. Brass. Similar to KM#195	150
Pn38	1968	—	Peso. Silver. Sower walking left.	225
Pn39	1968	—	Piso. Silver. Sower walking right.	225
PnA40	1969	—	Peso. Copper. Similar to KM#195. As Pn40.	150
Pn40	1969	—	Piso. Silver. Dated 1966. Aquinaldo	225
Pn41	ND(1970)	—	Peso. Copper. Similar to KM#195. Conjoined busts of Marcos and Pope Paul VI left.	150
Pn42	1970	—	Peso. Copper. Similar to KM#195. Bust of Pope Paul VI 3/4 right.	150

PIEFORTS

All standard metals unless otherwise indicated

KM#	Date	Mintage	Identification	Mkt Val
P1	1999	—	50 Pisa. KM#229	—

TRIAL STRIKES

KM#	Date	Mintage	Identification	Mkt Val
TS8	1967	—	Peso. Brass. KM#195. Bataan Day	75.00

CULION ISLAND

The Culion Leper Colony was established around 1903 on the island of Culion about 150 miles southeast of Manila by the Commission of Public Health. The first issue of coins valid only in the colony was produced by a private firm, Frank & Company. Later issues were struck at the Manila Mint.

MINT MARKS

PM = Philippine Mint at Manila

MONETARY SYSTEM

100 Centavos = 1 Peso

CULION LEPER COLONY

Philippine Commission of Public Health

LEPROSARIUM COINAGE

The Culion Leper Colony was established around 1903 on the island of Culion about 150 miles southeast of Manila by the Commission of Public Health. The first issue of coins valid only in the colony was produced by a private firm, Frank & Company. Later issues were struck at the Manila Mint.

KM# 1 1/2 CENTAVO **Composition:** Aluminum

Date	Mintage	F	VF	XF	Unc	BU
1913	17,000	1.00	2.00	4.00	5.00	6.00

Note: Some authorities doubt that this coin circulated

KM# 2 CENTAVO **Composition:** Aluminum

Date	Mintage	Good	VG	F	VF	XF
1913	33,000	70.00	100	250	550	—

Note: This coin exists with thick and thin planchets

KM# 3 CENTAVO **Composition:** Copper-Nickel **Note:** Similar to KM#4 but first die, better strike.

Date	Mintage	Good	VG	F	VF	XF
1927PM	30,000	10.00	15.00	25.00	50.00	110

Note: Type I - One-button coat, legible motto, "7" in date over "T" in Centavo

KM# 4 CENTAVO **Composition:** Copper-Nickel **Note:** Second die, poor strike. This coin exists with thick and thin planchets.

Date	Good	VG	F	VF	XF
1927PM	12.00	18.00	35.00	70.00	125

Note: Type II - One-button coat, illegible motto, end of ribbon two widths from shield edge, "7" over "N"

KM# A5 CENTAVO **Composition:** Copper Nickel

Date	Good	VG	F	VF	XF
1927PM	25.00	35.00	60.00	100	150

Note: Type III - Two-button coat, illegible motto, end of ribbon one width from shield edge,

KM# 5 CENTAVO **Composition:** Copper-Nickel **Obverse:** Bust of Rizal in circle **Reverse:** PHILIPPINE HEALTH SERVICE/LEPER COIN ONE CENTAVO

Date	Good	VG	F	VF	XF
1930	—	—	—	—	—

Note: Reported, not confirmed

KM# 6 5 CENTAVOS **Composition:** Aluminum

Date	Mintage	Good	VG	F	VF	XF
1913	6,600	35.00	65.00	225	400	—

KM# 7 5 CENTAVOS **Composition:** Copper-Nickel

Date	Mintage	Good	VG	F	VF	XF
1927	16,000	3.00	6.00	10.00	18.00	25.00

KM# 8 10 CENTAVOS **Composition:** Aluminum **Note:** Similar to 1/2 Centavo, KM#1.

Date	Mintage	Good	VG	F	VF	XF
1913	6,600	12.00	25.00	50.00	100	—

KM# 9 10 CENTAVOS **Composition:** Aluminum **Note:** Similar to 1 Peso, KM#14.

Date	Mintage	Good	VG	F	VF	XF
1920	20,000	4.00	10.00	20.00	50.00	—

KM# 10 10 CENTAVOS **Composition:** Copper-Nickel

Date	Mintage	VG	F	VF	XF	Unc
1930	17,000	2.00	4.00	7.50	15.00	25.00

Note: One pattern in copper, has been authenticated by ANACS

KM# 11 20 CENTAVOS **Composition:** Aluminum **Note:** Similar to 1/2 Centavo, KM#1.

Date	Mintage	Good	VG	F	VF	XF
1913	10,000	30.00	30.00	75.00	150	—

KM# 12 20 CENTAVOS **Composition:** Aluminum

Date	Mintage	Good	VG	F	VF	XF
1920	10,000	5.00	15.00	25.00	50.00	—

KM# 13 20 CENTAVOS **Composition:** Copper-Nickel

Date	Mintage	VG	F	VF	XF	Unc
1922PM	10,000	5.00	15.00	25.00	45.00	—

Note: This coin exists with thick and thin planchets

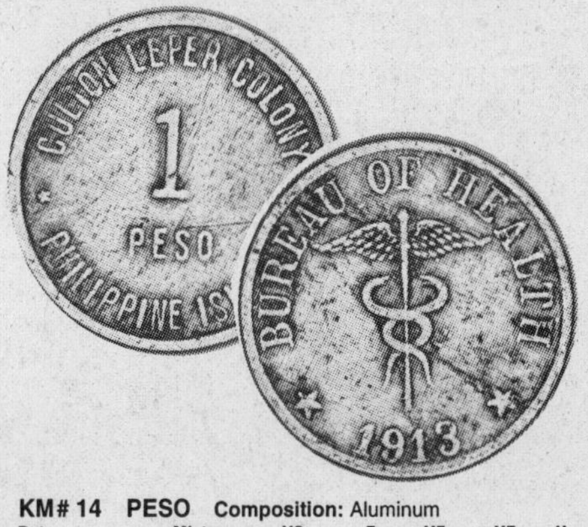

KM# 14 PESO **Composition:** Aluminum

Date	Mintage	VG	F	VF	XF	Unc
1913	8,600	7.00	12.00	25.00	40.00	—

Note: This coin exists with thick and thin planchets

KM# 15 PESO **Composition:** Aluminum

Date	Mintage	VG	F	VF	XF	Unc
1920	4,000	10.00	15.00	25.00	50.00	—

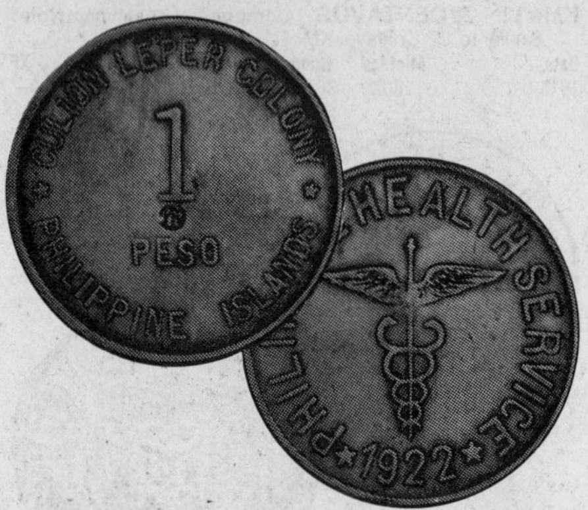

KM# 16 PESO **Composition:** Copper-Nickel **Note:** Varieties exist.

Date	Mintage	VG	F	VF	XF	Unc
1922	8,280	5.00	10.00	15.00	25.00	—

KM# 17 PESO **Composition:** Copper-Nickel **Note:** Similar to KM#16, but caduceus has curved wings.

Date	VG	F	VF	XF	Unc
1922PM	35.00	100	150	190	—

KM# 18 PESO **Composition:** Copper-Nickel

Date	Mintage	VG	F	VF	XF	Unc
1925	20,000	2.00	5.00	8.00	12.50	—

A small volcanic island, along with the uninhabited islands of Oeno, Henderson, and Ducie, constitute the British Colony of Pitcairn Islands. The main island has an area of about 2 sq. mi. (5 sq. km.) and a population of *68. It is located 1350 miles southeast of Tahiti. The islanders subsist on fishing, garden produce and crops. The sale of postage stamps and carved curios to passing ships brings cash income.

Discovered in 1767 by a British naval officer, Pitcairn was not occupied until 1790 when Fletcher Christian and nine mutineers from the British ship, *HMS Bounty*, along with some Tahitian men and women went ashore, and survived in obscurity until discovered by American whalers in 1808.

Adamstown is the chief settlement, located on the north coast, one of the few places that island-made longboats can land. The primary religion is Seventh-day Adventist and a public school provides basic education. In 1898 the settlement was placed under the jurisdiction of the Commissioner for the Western Pacific. Since 1970 this British settlement has been governed through a locally elected council under a governor.

New Zealand currency has been used since July 10, 1967.

BRITISH COLONY

REGULAR COINAGE

KM# 3 DOLLAR **Composition:** Copper Nickel **Subject:** Drafting of Constitution, 1838-1988 **Obverse:** Queen Elizabeth II **Reverse:** Ship with sails furled

Date	F	VF	XF	Unc	BU
ND(1988)	—	—	—	8.00	—

KM# 3a DOLLAR **Weight:** 28.2800 g. **Composition:** 0.9250 Silver .8411 oz. ASW **Subject:** Drafting of constitution, 1838-1988 **Obverse:** Queen Elizabeth II **Reverse:** Ship with sails furled

Date	F	VF	XF	Unc	BU
ND(1988) Proof	—	Value: 40.00			

KM# 4 DOLLAR **Composition:** Copper-Nickel **Subject:** HMAV Bounty, 1789-1989 **Obverse:** Queen Elizabeth II

Date	Mintage	F	VF	XF	Unc	BU
ND(1989)	50,000	—	—	—	8.00	—

KM# 4a DOLLAR **Weight:** 28.2800 g. **Composition:** 0.9250 Silver .8411 oz. ASW **Subject:** HMAV Bounty, 1789-1989 **Obverse:** Queen Elizabeth II

Date	Mintage	F	VF	XF	Unc	BU
ND(1989) Proof	20,000	Value: 40.00				

KM# 7 DOLLAR **Composition:** Copper-Nickel **Subject:** Establishment of settlement, 1790-1990 **Obverse:** Queen Elizabeth II **Reverse:** Ship in flames

Date	F	VF	XF	Unc	BU
ND(1990)	—	—	—	8.00	—

KM# 7a DOLLAR **Weight:** 28.2800 g. **Composition:** 0.9250 Silver .8411 oz. ASW **Subject:** Establishment of settlement, 1790-1990 **Obverse:** Queen Elizabeth II **Reverse:** Ship in flames

Date	Mintage	F	VF	XF	Unc	BU
ND(1990) Proof	10,000	Value: 45.00				

KM# 10 DOLLAR **Composition:** Copper-Nickel **Subject:** British Queen Mother **Obverse:** Queen's head right **Reverse:** Queen Mother and the Order of the Garter **Size:** 38.5 mm. **Note:** Struck at the British Royal Mint.

Date	F	VF	XF	Unc	BU
1997	—	—	—	10.00	—

KM# 1 50 DOLLARS **Weight:** 155.6000 g. **Composition:** 0.9990 Silver 5 oz. ASW **Subject:** Drafting of constitution, 1838-1988 **Obverse:** Queen Elizabeth II **Reverse:** Ship with sails furled **Size:** 65 mm. **Note:** Illustration reduced.

Date	Mintage	F	VF	XF	Unc	BU
ND(1988) Proof	10,000	Value: 125				

KM# 5 50 DOLLARS **Weight:** 155.6000 g. **Composition:** 0.9990 Silver 5 oz. ASW **Subject:** HMAV Bounty, 1789-1989 **Note:** Similar to 250 Dollars, KM#2.

Date	Mintage	F	VF	XF	Unc	BU
ND(1989) Proof	10,000	Value: 135				

KM# 8 50 DOLLARS **Weight:** 155.6000 g. **Composition:** 0.9990 Silver 5 oz. ASW **Subject:** Establishment of settlement, 1790-1990 **Note:** Similar to 250 Dollars, KM#9.

Date	Mintage	F	VF	XF	Unc	BU
ND(1990) Proof	2,500	Value: 165				

KM# 2 250 DOLLARS **Weight:** 15.9800 g. **Composition:** 0.9170 Gold .4708 oz. AGW **Subject:** Drafting of Constitution, 1838-1988 **Obverse:** Queen Elizabeth II **Reverse:** Ship with sails furled

Date	Mintage	F	VF	XF	Unc	BU
ND(1988) Proof	2,500	Value: 300				

KM# 6 250 DOLLARS **Weight:** 15.9800 g. **Composition:** 0.9170 Gold .4708 oz. AGW **Subject:** HMAV Bounty, 1789-1989 **Obverse:** Queen Elizabeth II

Date	Mintage	F	VF	XF	Unc	BU
ND(1989) Proof	2,500	Value: 300				

KM# 9 250 DOLLARS **Weight:** 15.9800 g. **Composition:** 0.9170 Gold .4708 oz. AGW **Subject:** Establishment of settlement, 1790-1990 **Obverse:** Queen Elizabeth II

Date	Mintage	F	VF	XF	Unc	BU
ND(1990) Proof	500	Value: 350				

POLAND

The Republic of Poland, located in central Europe, has an area of 120,725 sq. mi. (312,680 sq. km.) and a population of *38.2 million. Capital: Warszawa (Warsaw). The economy is essentially agricultural, but industrial activity provides the products for foreign trade. Machinery, coal, coke, iron, steel and transport equipment are exported.

Poland, which began as a Slavic duchy in the 10th century and reached its peak of power between the 14th and 16th centuries, has had a turbulent history of invasion, occupation or partition by Mongols, Turkey, Transylvania, Sweden, Austria, Prussia and Russia.

The first partition took place in 1772. Prussia took Polish Pomerania, Russia took part of the eastern provinces, and Austria occupied Galicia and its capital city Lwów. The second partition occurred in 1793 when Russia took another slice of the eastern provinces and Prussia took what remained of western Poland. The third partition, 1795, literally removed Poland from the map. Russia took what was left of the eastern provinces. Prussia seized most of central Poland, including Warsaw. Austria took what was left of the south. Napoleon restored to Poland much of the territory lost to Prussia and Austria, but after his defeat another partition returned the Duchy of Warsaw to Prussia, made Kraków into a tiny republic, and declared what remained to be the Kingdom of Poland under the czar and in permanent union with Russia.

Poland re-emerged as an independent state recognized by the Treaty of Versailles on June 28, 1919, and maintained its independence until 1939 when it was invaded by, and partitioned between, Germany and Russia. Poland's present boundaries were determined by the U.S.-British-Russian agreement of Aug. 16, 1945. The Government of National Unity was replaced when the Polish Communist-Socialist faction claimed victory at the polls in 1947 and established a Peoples Democratic Republic' of the Soviet type in 1952. On December 29, 1989 Poland was proclaimed as the Republic of Poland.

MINT MARKS

MV, MW, MW-monogram - Warsaw Mint, 1965-
FF - Stuttgart Germany 1916-1917
(w) - Warsaw 1923-39 (opened officially in 1924) arrow mintmark
CHI - Valcambi, Switzerland

Other letters appearing with date denote the Mintmaster at the time the coin was struck.

GERMAN-AUSTRIAN REGENCY

REGENCY COINAGE

100 Fenigow = 1 Marka

Y# 4 FENIG **Composition:** Iron

Date	Mintage	F	VF	XF	Unc	BU
1918FF	51,484,000	0.35	0.85	2.00	5.00	—
1918FF Proof	—	Value: 200				

Y# 5 5 FENIGOW **Composition:** Iron

Date	Mintage	F	VF	XF	Unc	BU
1917FF	18,700,000	0.25	0.75	1.50	3.50	—
1917FF Proof	—	Value: 100				
1918FF	22,690,000	0.25	0.75	1.50	3.50	—
1918FF Proof	—	Value: 200				

Y# 5.1 5 FENIGOW **Composition:** Iron **Obverse:** Poland Y#5 **Reverse:** German KM#15 **Note:** Mule.

Date	F	VF	XF	Unc	BU
1917FF	50.00	100	150	200	—

Y# 6 10 FENIGOW **Composition:** Iron

Date	Mintage	F	VF	XF	Unc	BU
1917FF	33,000,000	7.50	15.00	20.00	28.00	—
Note: Obverse legend touches edge						
1917FF Proof	—	Value: 100				
1917FF	Inc. above	0.25	0.75	1.25	3.50	—
Note: Obverse legend away from edge						
1918FF	—	0.50	1.00	2.00	5.00	—
Note: Obverse legend away from edge						
1918FF Proof	—	Value: 200				
Note: Obverse legend away from edge						

Y# 6a 10 FENIGOW **Composition:** Zinc **Note:** Error planchet.

Date	F	VF	XF	Unc	BU
1917FF	25.00	45.00	85.00	150	—

Y# 6.1 10 FENIGOW **Composition:** Zinc **Obverse:** Y#6 **Reverse:** German 10 Pfennig, KM#20 **Note:** Mule.

Date	F	VF	XF	Unc	BU
1917FF	50.00	100	150	200	—

Y# 7 20 FENIGOW **Composition:** Iron

Date	Mintage	F	VF	XF	Unc	BU
1917FF	1,900,000	2.00	4.00	6.00	11.50	—
1918FF	19,260,000	0.75	1.25	2.50	5.50	—

Y# 7a 20 FENIGOW **Composition:** Zinc **Note:** Error planchet.

Date	F	VF	XF	Unc	BU
1917FF	35.00	60.00	100	200	—

REPUBLIC

STANDARD COINAGE

100 Groszy = 1 Zloty

Y# 8 GROSZ **Composition:** Brass **Note:** Some authorities consider this strike a pattern.

Date	F	VF	XF	Unc	BU
1923	18.00	25.00	75.00	200	—

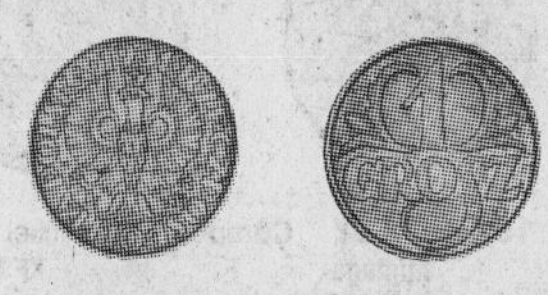

Y# 8a GROSZ **Composition:** Bronze

Date	Mintage	F	VF	XF	Unc	BU
1923	30,000,000	0.25	0.50	1.75	10.00	—
1925(w)	40,000,000	0.25	0.50	1.75	9.00	—
1927(w)	17,000,000	0.25	0.50	1.75	10.00	—
1928(w)	13,600,000	0.25	0.50	1.75	9.00	—
1930(w)	22,500,000	4.00	10.00	25.00	40.00	—
1931(w)	9,000,000	0.50	1.00	2.00	10.00	—
1932(w)	12,000,000	0.50	1.00	2.00	10.00	—
1933(w)	7,000,000	0.50	1.00	2.00	10.00	—
1934(w)	5,900,000	0.75	1.00	2.00	12.00	—
1935(w)	7,300,000	0.75	0.25	0.50	5.00	—
1936(w)	12,600,000	0.75	1.00	2.00	5.00	—
1937(w)	17,370,000	0.25	1.00	2.00	2.50	—
1938(w)	20,530,000	0.25	0.50	0.75	2.50	—
1939(w)	12,000,000	0.25	0.50	0.75	2.50	—

Y# 9 2 GROSZE **Composition:** Brass

Date	Mintage	F	VF	XF	Unc	BU
1923	20,500,000	3.50	15.00	35.00	50.00	—

Y# 9a 2 GROSZE **Composition:** Bronze

Date	Mintage	F	VF	XF	Unc	BU
1925(w)	39,000,000	0.50	2.00	4.50	10.00	—
1927(w)	15,300,000	0.50	2.00	4.50	10.00	—
1928(w)	13,400,000	0.50	2.00	4.50	10.00	—
1930(w)	20,000,000	0.50	2.00	4.50	10.00	—
1931(w)	9,500,000	1.75	2.50	5.50	12.75	—
1932(w)	6,500,000	2.00	4.00	6.00	15.00	—
1933(w)	7,000,000	2.00	4.00	6.00	15.00	—
1934(w)	9,350,000	1.75	3.00	7.50	17.50	—
1935(w)	5,800,000	0.20	0.75	2.00	5.00	—
1936(w)	5,800,000	0.20	0.75	2.00	5.00	—
1937(w)	17,360,000	0.20	0.40	0.60	2.50	—
1938(w)	20,530,000	0.20	0.40	0.60	2.50	—
1939(w)	12,000,000	0.20	0.40	0.60	2.50	—

Y# 10 5 GROSZY **Composition:** Brass

Date	Mintage	F	VF	XF	Unc	BU
1923	32,000,000	0.50	2.00	5.00	10.00	—

Y# 10a 5 GROSZY **Composition:** Bronze

Date	Mintage	F	VF	XF	Unc	BU
1923 Proof	350	Value: 150				
1925(w)	45,500,000	0.20	0.40	4.00	8.00	—
1928(w)	8,900,000	0.20	0.40	5.00	10.00	—
1930(w)	14,200,000	0.20	0.40	5.00	12.00	—
1931(w)	1,500,000	0.50	1.00	10.00	20.00	—
1934(w)	420,000	5.00	7.50	35.00	75.00	—
1935(w)	4,660,000	0.20	0.40	0.60	5.00	—
1936(w)	4,660,000	0.20	0.40	0.60	5.00	—
1937(w)	9,050,000	0.20	0.40	0.60	2.50	—
1938(w)	17,300,000	0.20	0.40	0.60	2.50	—
1939(w)	10,000,000	0.20	0.40	0.60	2.50	—

Y# 11 10 GROSZY **Composition:** Nickel

Date	Mintage	F	VF	XF	Unc	BU
1923	100,000,000	0.20	0.45	0.80	1.25	—

Y# 12 20 GROSZY **Composition:** Nickel

Date	Mintage	F	VF	XF	Unc	BU
1923	150,000,000	0.35	0.75	1.25	2.00	—
1923 Proof	10	Value: 300				

Y# 13 50 GROSZY **Composition:** Nickel

Date	Mintage	F	VF	XF	Unc	BU
1923	100,000,000	0.40	0.80	1.50	3.50	—
1923 Proof	10	Value: 350				

Y# 15 ZLOTY **Weight:** 5.0000 g. **Composition:** 0.7500 Silver .1206 oz. ASW

Date	Mintage	F	VF	XF	Unc	BU
1924 (Paris)	16,000,000	2.50	6.00	20.00	55.00	—
Note: Torch and cornucopia flank date						
1924 (Birmingham); Proof	8	Value: 600				
1925 (London)	24,000,000	2.50	5.00	12.00	30.00	—
Note: Dot after date						

Y# 14 ZLOTY **Composition:** Nickel

Date	Mintage	F	VF	XF	Unc	BU
1929(w)	32,000,000	0.75	1.50	2.50	7.00	—

Y# 16 2 ZLOTE **Weight:** 10.0000 g. **Composition:** 0.7500 Silver .2400 oz. ASW

Date	Mintage	F	VF	XF	Unc	BU
1924 (Paris)	—	5.00	10.00	20.00	85.00	—
Note: Torch and cornucopia flank date						
1924 H (Birmingham)	1,200,000	17.50	35.00	175	450	—
1924 (Birmingham); Proof	60	Value: 600				
1924 (Philadelphia)	800,000	10.00	20.00	60.00	125	—
Note: Without privy marks						
1925 (London)	11,000,000	4.00	8.00	17.50	47.50	—
Note: Dot after date						
1925 (Philadelphia)	5,200,000	6.00	12.00	40.00	75.00	—
Note: Without privy marks						

Y# 20 2 ZLOTE **Weight:** 4.4000 g. **Composition:** 0.7500 Silver .1061 oz. ASW

Date	Mintage	F	VF	XF	Unc	BU
1932(w)	15,700,000	2.00	4.00	7.00	13.50	16.50
1933(w)	9,250,000	2.00	4.00	7.00	13.50	16.50
1934(w)	250,000	4.00	7.00	12.00	27.50	—

Y# 27 2 ZLOTE **Weight:** 4.4000 g. **Composition:** 0.7500 Silver .1061 oz. ASW

Date	Mintage	F	VF	XF	Unc	BU
1934(w)	10,425,000	3.00	6.00	10.00	25.00	—
1936(w)	75,000	20.00	75.00	125	250	—

Y# 30 2 ZLOTE **Weight:** 4.4000 g. **Composition:** 0.7500 Silver .1061 oz. ASW **Subject:** 15th Anniversary of Gdynia Seaport

Date	Mintage	F	VF	XF	Unc	BU
1936(w)	3,918,000	3.00	6.00	12.00	30.00	—

Y# 17.1 5 ZLOTYCH **Weight:** 25.0000 g. **Composition:** 0.9000 Silver .7234 oz. ASW **Subject:** Adoption of the Constitution **Reverse:** 100 pearls in circle

Date	Mintage	F	VF	XF	Unc	BU
1925(w)	100	150	300	700	1,500	—

Y# 17.1a 5 ZLOTYCH **Composition:** Gold

Date	Mintage	F	VF	XF	Unc	BU
1925(w) Rare	2	—	—	—	—	—

Y# 17.2 5 ZLOTYCH **Weight:** 25.0000 g. **Composition:** 0.9000 Silver .7234 oz. ASW **Obverse:** Wthout monogram by date

Date	Mintage	F	VF	XF	Unc	BU
1925(w)	1,000	—	—	450	950	—

Y# 17.2a 5 ZLOTYCH **Composition:** Bronze

Date	Mintage	F	VF	XF	Unc	BU
1925(w)	100	—	—	200	300	—

Y# 17.2c 5 ZLOTYCH **Composition:** Gold **Obverse:** Without monogram by date

Date	Mintage	F	VF	XF	Unc	BU
1925(w) Rare	1	—	—	—	—	—

Y# 17.3 5 ZLOTYCH **Weight:** 25.0000 g. **Composition:** 0.9000 Silver .7234 oz. ASW **Obverse:** Monogram by date **Reverse:** 81 pearls in circle

Date	Mintage	F	VF	XF	Unc	BU
1925(w)	1,000	—	—	450	950	—

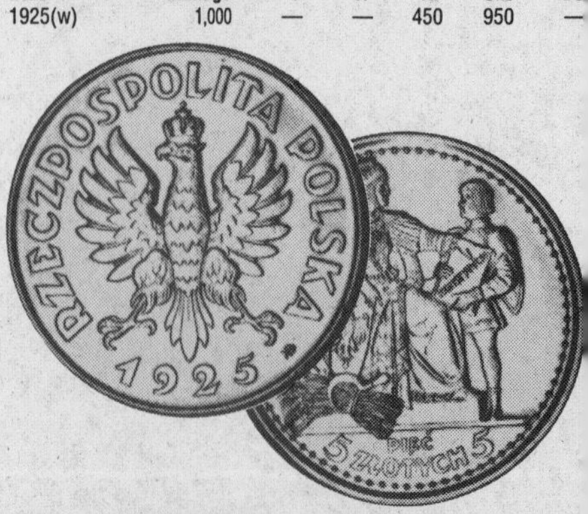

Y# 17.3a 5 ZLOTYCH **Weight:** 43.3300 g. **Composition:** 0.9000 Gold 1.3407 oz. AGW **Obverse:** Mint mark right of date **Edge Lettering:** "SALUS REIPUBLICAE SUPREMA LEX"

Date	Mintage	F	VF	XF	Unc	BU
1925(w) Rare	1	—	—	—	—	—

Y# 17.4 5 ZLOTYCH **Weight:** 43.3300 g. **Composition:** 0.9000 Gold 1.3407 oz. AGW **Obverse:** Without monogram by date, with mint mark

Date	Mintage	F	VF	XF	Unc	BU
1925(w)	1,000	—	—	450	950	—

Y# 17.4a 5 ZLOTYCH **Composition:** Tombac

Date	Mintage	F	VF	XF	Unc	BU
1925(w)	100	—	—	200	300	—

Y# 18 5 ZLOTYCH **Weight:** 18.0000 g. **Composition:** 0.7500 Silver .4340 oz. ASW

Date	Mintage	F	VF	XF	Unc	BU
1928(w)	7,500,000	15.00	30.00	55.00	120	—
Note: Conjoined arrow and K mint mark						
1928 Error	Inc. above	40.00	75.00	100	225	—
Note: "SUPRMA" edge inscription						
1928 Without mint mark	10,000,000	12.50	22.50	55.00	120	—
Note: 4,300,000 struck in London and 5,700,000 in Belgium						
1930(w)	5,900,000	60.00	120	275	450	—
1931(w)	2,200,000	75.00	150	200	500	—
1932(w)	3,100,000	90.00	175	350	—	—

Y# 19.1 5 ZLOTYCH **Weight:** 18.0000 g. **Composition:** 0.7500 Silver .4340 oz. ASW **Subject:** Centennial of 1830 Revolution

Date	Mintage	F	VF	XF	Unc	BU
1930(w)	1,000,000	7.00	16.50	35.00	90.00	—

Y# 19.2 5 ZLOTYCH **Weight:** 18.0000 g. **Composition:** 0.7500 Silver .4340 oz. ASW **Note:** High relief.

Date	Mintage	F	VF	XF	Unc	BU
1930(w)	200	70.00	175	375	750	—

Y# 21 5 ZLOTYCH **Weight:** 11.0000 g. **Composition:** 0.7500 Silver .2652 oz. ASW

Date	Mintage	F	VF	XF	Unc	BU
1932 (Warsaw)	1,000,000	15.00	50.00	200	475	—
1932 (London); without mint mark	3,000,000	1.20	2.50	6.00	15.00	20.00
1933(w)	11,000,000	1.20	2.00	5.00	12.50	17.50
1933(w) Proof	100	—	—	—	—	—
1934(w)	250,000	1.20	2.50	7.00	20.00	—

Y# 25 5 ZLOTYCH **Weight:** 11.0000 g. **Composition:** 0.7500 Silver .2652 oz. ASW **Subject:** Rifle Corps August 6, 1914 **Obverse:** Rifle Corps symbol below eagle **Reverse:** Jozef Pilsudski

Date	Mintage	F	VF	XF	Unc	BU
1934(w)	300,000	5.00	8.00	16.50	40.00	—

Y# 28 5 ZLOTYCH **Weight:** 11.0000 g. **Composition:** 0.7500 Silver .2652 oz. ASW **Reverse:** Bust of Jozef Pilsudski left

Date	Mintage	F	VF	XF	Unc	BU
1934(w)	6,510,000	2.50	4.00	9.00	20.00	25.00
1935(w)	1,800,000	3.00	4.50	10.00	22.00	28.00
1936(w)	1,800,000	3.00	4.50	10.00	22.00	28.00
1938(w)	289,000	5.00	7.50	15.00	30.00	—

Y# 31 5 ZLOTYCH **Weight:** 11.0000 g. **Composition:** 0.7500 Silver .2652 oz. ASW **Subject:** 15th Anniversary of Gdynia Seaport

Date	Mintage	F	VF	XF	Unc	BU
1936(w)	1,000,000	7.00	12.00	25.00	50.00	—

Y# 32 10 ZLOTYCH **Weight:** 3.2258 g. **Composition:** 0.9000 Gold .0933 oz. AGW **Reverse:** Boleslaw I **Note:** Never released into circulation.

Date	Mintage	F	VF	XF	Unc	BU
ND(1925)(w)	50,000	—	50.00	65.00	100	—

Y# 22 10 ZLOTYCH **Weight:** 22.0000 g. **Composition:** 0.7500 Silver .5305 oz. ASW

Date	Mintage	F	VF	XF	Unc	BU
1932(w)	3,100,000	5.00	8.00	12.50	30.00	38.00
1932 (London) without mint mark	6,000,000	5.00	8.00	12.50	30.00	38.00
1932(w) Proof	100	—	—	—	—	—
1933(w)	2,800,000	5.00	8.00	12.50	30.00	38.00
1933(w) Proof	100	—	—	—	—	—

Y# 23 10 ZLOTYCH **Weight:** 22.0000 g. **Composition:** 0.7500 Silver .5305 oz. ASW **Subject:** Jan III Sobieski's Victory Over the Turks **Obverse:** Similar to Y#22 **Reverse:** Bust of Sobieski right

Date	Mintage	F	VF	XF	Unc	BU
ND(1933)(w)	300,000	8.00	16.00	25.00	55.00	—
ND(1933)(w) Proof	100	—	—	—	—	—

Y# 24 10 ZLOTYCH **Weight:** 22.0000 g. **Composition:** 0.7500 Silver .5305 oz. ASW **Subject:** 70th Anniversary of 1863 Insurrection **Obverse:** Similar to Y#23 **Reverse:** Bust of Romuald Traugutt 1/4 right

Date	Mintage	F	VF	XF	Unc	BU
ND(1933)(w)	300,000	10.00	20.00	35.00	60.00	—
ND(1933)(w) Proof	100	—	—	—	—	—

Y# 26 10 ZLOTYCH **Weight:** 22.0000 g. **Composition:** 0.7500 Silver .5305 oz. ASW **Subject:** Rifle Corps August 6, 1914 **Obverse:** Rifle Corps symbol below eagle **Reverse:** Jozef Pilsudski

Date	Mintage	F	VF	XF	Unc	BU
1934(w)	300,000	9.00	17.50	25.00	50.00	—

Y# 29 10 ZLOTYCH **Weight:** 22.0000 g. **Composition:** 0.7500 Silver .5305 oz. ASW **Obverse:** Jozef Pilsudski

Date	Mintage	F	VF	XF	Unc	BU
1934(w)	200,000	12.00	18.00	25.00	55.00	—
1935(w)	1,670,000	4.00	7.00	14.00	30.00	40.00
1936(w)	2,130,000	4.00	7.00	14.00	30.00	40.00
1937(w)	908,000	4.00	7.00	16.00	40.00	—
1938(w)	234,000	6.00	9.00	20.00	50.00	—
1939(w)	—	4.00	7.00	16.00	40.00	—

Y# 33 20 ZLOTYCH **Weight:** 6.4516 g. **Composition:** 0.9000 Gold .1867 oz. AGW **Reverse:** Boleslaw I **Note:** Never released into circulation.

Date	Mintage	F	VF	XF	Unc	BU
ND(1925)(w)	27,000	—	90.00	100	185	—

WWII GERMAN OCCUPATION

OCCUPATION COINAGE

Y# 34 GROSZ **Composition:** Zinc

Date	Mintage	F	VF	XF	Unc	BU
1939(w)	33,909,000	0.50	1.00	1.75	3.50	—

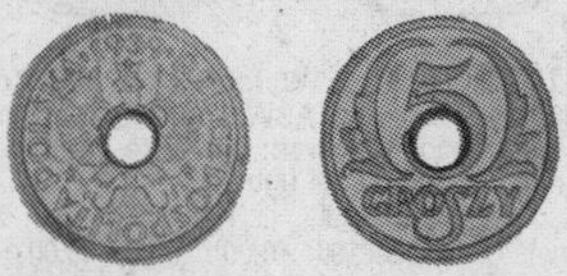

Y# 35 5 GROSZY **Composition:** Zinc

Date	Mintage	F	VF	XF	Unc	BU
1939(w)	15,324,000	0.50	1.50	2.00	5.00	—

Y# 36 10 GROSZY **Composition:** Zinc

Date	Mintage	F	VF	XF	Unc	BU
1923(w)	42,175,000	0.10	0.20	0.40	2.00	—

Note: Actually struck in 1941-44

Y# 37 20 GROSZY **Composition:** Zinc

Date	Mintage	F	VF	XF	Unc	BU
1923(w)	40,025,000	0.15	0.25	0.50	2.00	—

Note: Actually struck in 1941-44

Y# 38 50 GROSZY **Composition:** Nickel Plated Iron

Date	Mintage	F	VF	XF	Unc	BU
1938(w)	32,000,000	1.00	2.00	4.00	8.50	—

Y# 38a 50 GROSZY **Composition:** Iron

Date	F	VF	XF	Unc	BU
1938(w)	1.25	2.50	5.00	10.00	—

Note: Varieties exist

TOKEN COINAGE

Lodz Ghetto, 1942-1944

A major industrial city in western Poland before World War II and site of the first wartime ghetto under German occupation (May 1940). It was also the last ghetto to close during the war (August 1944). Token coinage was struck in 1942 and 1943, in the name of the Jewish Elders of Litzmannstadt. This series has seen very little circulation, but is commonly found in conditions from slightly to badly corroded. The badly corroded specimens have the appearance of zinc.

KM# Tn1 10 PFENNIG **Composition:** Aluminum-Magnesium

Date	VG	F	VF	XF	Unc
1942	60.00	125	200	—	—

Note: Most were destroyed or remelted as the design was too similar to regular German coinage

KM# Tn5 10 PFENNIG **Composition:** Aluminum-Magnesium

Date	Mintage	VG	F	VF	XF	Unc
1942	100,000	35.00	50.00	65.00	125	—

KM# Tn2 5 MARK **Composition:** Aluminum

Date	Mintage	VG	F	VF	XF	Unc
1943	600,000	5.00	10.00	25.00	45.00	—

KM# Tn2a 5 MARK **Composition:** Aluminum-Magnesium

Date	VG	F	VF	XF	Unc
1943	20.00	40.00	75.00	—	—

KM# Tn3 10 MARK **Composition:** Aluminum **Note:** Thick and thin planchets exist.

Date	Mintage	VG	F	VF	XF	Unc
1943	100,000	5.00	10.00	25.00	45.00	—

KM# Tn3a 10 MARK **Composition:** Aluminum-Magnesium

Date	VG	F	VF	XF	Unc
1943	25.00	45.00	85.00	—	—

KM# Tn4 20 MARK **Composition:** Aluminum **Note:** Beware of numerous counterfeits.

Date	VG	F	VF	XF	Unc
1943	75.00	110	150	250	—

REPUBLIC

Post War

STANDARD COINAGE

Y# 39 GROSZ **Composition:** Aluminum **Note:** 116,000 were struck at Warsaw, the remainder at Budapest.

Date	Mintage	F	VF	XF	Unc	BU
1949	400,116,000	0.10	0.20	0.30	0.75	—

Y# 40 2 GROSZE **Composition:** Aluminum **Note:** 106,000 were struck at Warsaw, the remainder at Budapest

Date	Mintage	F	VF	XF	Unc	BU
1949	300,106,000	0.10	0.25	0.50	1.00	—

Y# 41 5 GROSZY **Composition:** Bronze **Note:** Struck at Basel.

Date	Mintage	F	VF	XF	Unc	BU
1949	300,000,000	0.10	0.25	0.50	1.00	—

Y# 41a 5 GROSZY **Composition:** Aluminum **Note:** Struck at Kremnica.

Date	Mintage	F	VF	XF	Unc	BU
1949	200,000,000	0.10	0.25	0.75	1.50	—

Y# 42 10 GROSZY **Composition:** Copper-Nickel **Note:** Struck at Kremnica.

Date	Mintage	F	VF	XF	Unc	BU
1949	200,000,000	0.20	0.40	0.60	1.50	—

Y# 42a 10 GROSZY **Composition:** Aluminum **Note:** Struck at Warsaw.

Date	Mintage	F	VF	XF	Unc	BU
1949	31,047,000	0.10	0.25	0.75	2.50	—

Y# 43 20 GROSZY **Composition:** Copper-Nickel **Note:** Struck at Kremnica.

Date	Mintage	F	VF	XF	Unc	BU
1949	133,383,000	0.25	0.45	0.75	2.00	—

Y# 43a 20 GROSZY **Composition:** Aluminum

Date	Mintage	F	VF	XF	Unc	BU
1949	197,472,000	0.10	0.25	0.75	2.50	—

Y# 44 50 GROSZY **Composition:** Copper-Nickel **Note:** Struck at Kremnica.

Date	Mintage	F	VF	XF	Unc	BU
1949	109,000,000	0.35	0.65	1.00	2.50	—

Y# 44a 50 GROSZY **Composition:** Aluminum **Note:** Struck at Warsaw.

Date	Mintage	F	VF	XF	Unc	BU
1949	59,393,000	0.10	0.25	1.50	5.00	—

Y# 45 ZLOTY **Composition:** Copper-Nickel **Note:** Struck at Kremnica.

Date	Mintage	F	VF	XF	Unc	BU
1949	87,053,000	1.00	1.50	2.25	4.00	—

Y# 45a ZLOTY **Composition:** Aluminum **Note:** Struck at Warsaw.

Date	Mintage	F	VF	XF	Unc	BU
1949	43,000,000	0.10	0.25	2.50	6.00	—

58 **10 ZLOTYCH** **Composition:** Copper-Nickel
Subject: 20th Anniversary - Death of General Swierczewski

te	Mintage	F	VF	XF	Unc	BU
67MW	2,000,000	—	0.50	1.00	2.25	—

59 **10 ZLOTYCH** **Composition:** Copper-Nickel
Subject: Centennial - Birth of Marie Sklodowska Curie

te	Mintage	F	VF	XF	Unc	BU
67MW	2,000,000	—	0.50	1.00	2.25	—

60 **10 ZLOTYCH** **Composition:** Copper-Nickel
Subject: 25th Anniversary - Peoples Army

ate	Mintage	F	VF	XF	Unc	BU
968MW	2,000,000	—	0.50	1.00	2.25	—

61 **10 ZLOTYCH** **Composition:** Copper-Nickel
Subject: 25th Anniversary - Peoples Republic

ate	Mintage	F	VF	XF	Unc	BU
969MW	2,000,000	—	0.50	1.00	2.25	—

Y# 62 **10 ZLOTYCH** **Composition:** Copper-Nickel
Subject: 25th Anniversary - Provincial Annexations

ate	Mintage	F	VF	XF	Unc	BU
970MW	2,000,000	—	0.50	1.00	2.25	—

Y# 63 **10 ZLOTYCH** **Composition:** Copper-Nickel
Series: F.A.O.

Date	Mintage	F	VF	XF	Unc	BU
1971MW	2,000,000	—	0.75	1.50	4.50	—

Y# 64 **10 ZLOTYCH** **Composition:** Copper-Nickel
Subject: 50th Anniversary - Battle of Upper Silesia

Date	Mintage	F	VF	XF	Unc	BU
1971MW	2,000,000	—	0.50	1.00	2.25	—

Y# 65 **10 ZLOTYCH** **Composition:** Copper-Nickel
Subject: 50th Anniversary - Gdynia Seaport

Date	Mintage	F	VF	XF	Unc	BU
1972MW	2,000,000	—	0.50	1.00	2.25	—

Y# 73 **10 ZLOTYCH** **Composition:** Copper-Nickel
Reverse: Boleslaw Prus

Date	Mintage	F	VF	XF	Unc	BU
1975MW	35,000,000	—	0.25	0.65	1.25	—
1976MW	20,000,000	—	0.25	0.65	1.25	—
1977MW	25,000,000	—	0.25	0.65	1.25	—
1978MW	4,006,999	—	0.25	0.75	2.25	—
1981MW	2,655,000	—	0.25	1.00	3.75	—
1982MW	16,341,000	—	0.25	0.65	1.25	—
1983MW	14,248,000	—	0.25	0.65	1.25	—
1984MW	19,064,000	—	0.25	0.65	1.25	—

Y# 74 **10 ZLOTYCH** **Composition:** Copper-Nickel
Reverse: Adam Mickiewicz

Date	Mintage	F	VF	XF	Unc	BU
1975MW	35,000,000	—	0.25	0.65	1.25	—
1976MW	20,000,000	—	0.25	0.65	1.25	—

Y# 152.1 **10 ZLOTYCH** **Composition:** Copper-Nickel
Size: 25 mm.

Date	Mintage	F	VF	XF	Unc	BU
1984MW	15,756,000	—	0.20	0.50	1.00	—
1985MW	5,282,000	—	0.20	0.50	1.00	—
1986MW	31,043,000	—	0.20	0.50	1.00	—
1986MW Proof	5,000	Value: 4.00				
1987MW	69,636,000	—	0.20	0.50	1.00	—
1987MW Proof	5,000	Value: 4.00				
1988MW	102,493,000	—	0.20	0.50	1.00	—
1988MW Proof	5,000	Value: 4.00				

Y# 152.2 **10 ZLOTYCH** **Composition:** Brass **Size:** 21.8 mm.

Date	Mintage	F	VF	XF	Unc	BU
1989MW	80,800,000	—	0.20	0.40	0.80	—
1989MW Proof	5,000	Value: 4.00				
1990MW	106,892,000	—	0.20	0.40	0.80	—
1990MW Proof	5,000	Value: 4.00				

Y# 67 **20 ZLOTYCH** **Composition:** Copper-Nickel

Date	Mintage	F	VF	XF	Unc	BU
1973	25,000,000	—	0.25	1.00	2.50	—
Note: Struck at Kremnica Mint						
1974	12,000,000	—	0.25	0.75	1.50	—
Note: Struck at Kremnica Mint						
1976	20,000,000	—	0.25	0.75	1.50	—
Note: Struck at Warsaw Mint						

Y# 69 **20 ZLOTYCH** **Composition:** Copper-Nickel
Reverse: Marceli Nowotko

Date	Mintage	F	VF	XF	Unc	BU
1974MW	10,000,000	—	0.25	1.00	2.50	—
1975	10,000,000	—	0.25	1.00	2.00	—
Note: Struck at Kremnica Mint						
1976	20,000,000	—	0.25	0.75	1.50	—
Note: Struck at Kremnica Mint						
1976MW	30,000,000	—	0.25	0.75	1.50	—
1977MW	16,000,000	—	0.25	1.00	2.00	—
1983MW	152,000	—	0.25	5.00	12.50	—

Y# 70 **20 ZLOTYCH** **Composition:** Copper-Nickel
Subject: 25th Anniversary of the Comcon

Date	Mintage	F	VF	XF	Unc	BU
1974MW	2,000,000	—	0.75	1.25	2.50	—

Y# 75 **20 ZLOTYCH** **Composition:** Copper-Nickel
Subject: International Women's Year

Date	Mintage	F	VF	XF	Unc	BU
1975MW	2,000,000	—	0.75	1.25	2.50	—

Y# 95 20 ZLOTYCH Composition: Copper-Nickel
Reverse: Maria Konopnicka

Date	Mintage	F	VF	XF	Unc	BU
1978MW	2,010,000	—	0.75	1.25	2.75	—

Y# 97 20 ZLOTYCH Composition: Copper-Nickel
Subject: First Polish Cosmonaut

Date	Mintage	F	VF	XF	Unc	BU
1978MW	2,009,000	—	0.75	1.25	2.75	—

Y# 99 20 ZLOTYCH Composition: Copper-Nickel
Series: International Year of the Child

Date	Mintage	F	VF	XF	Unc	BU
1979MW	2,007,000	—	1.00	1.50	3.00	—

Y# 108 20 ZLOTYCH Composition: Copper-Nickel
Series: 1980 Olympics **Reverse:** Runner

Date	Mintage	F	VF	XF	Unc	BU
1980MW	2,012,000	—	1.00	1.75	5.00	—
1980MW Proof	100	Value: 28.00				

Y# 112 20 ZLOTYCH Composition: Copper-Nickel
Subject: 50th Anniversary - Training Ship Daru Pomorza

Date	Mintage	F	VF	XF	Unc	BU
1980MW	2,007,000	—	1.00	1.75	3.50	—

Y# 153.1 20 ZLOTYCH Composition: Copper-Nickel
Note: Circulation coinage.

Date	Mintage	F	VF	XF	Unc	BU
1984MW	12,703,000	—	0.25	0.60	1.25	—
1985MW	15,514,000	—	0.25	0.60	1.25	—
1986MW	37,959,000	—	0.25	0.60	1.25	—
1986MW Proof	5,000	Value: 4.00				
1987MW	22,213,000	—	0.25	0.60	1.25	—
1987MW Proof	5,000	Value: 4.00				
1988MW	14,994,000	—	0.25	0.60	1.25	—
1988MW Proof	5,000	Value: 4.00				

Y# 153.2 20 ZLOTYCH Composition: Copper-Nickel
Size: 23.9 mm. **Note:** Reduced size.

Date	Mintage	F	VF	XF	Unc	BU
1989MW	95,974,000	—	0.25	0.35	0.75	—
1989MW Proof	5,000	Value: 4.00				
1990MW	104,712,000	—	0.25	0.35	0.75	—
1990MW Proof	5,000	Value: 4.00				

Y# 66 50 ZLOTYCH Weight: 12.6400 g. **Composition:** 0.7500 Silver .3048 oz. ASW **Reverse:** Fryderyk Chopin

Date	Mintage	F	VF	XF	Unc	BU
1972MW Proof	50,000	Value: 11.50				
1974MW Proof	10,000	Value: 16.50				

Y# 100 50 ZLOTYCH Composition: Copper-Nickel
Reverse: Duke Mieszko I

Date	Mintage	F	VF	XF	Unc	BU
1979MW	2,640,000	—	1.00	2.00	5.00	—

Y# 114 50 ZLOTYCH Composition: Copper-Nickel
Reverse: King Boleslaw I Chrobry

Date	Mintage	F	VF	XF	Unc	BU
1980MW	2,564,000	—	1.00	2.00	5.00	—

Y# 117 50 ZLOTYCH Composition: Copper-Nickel
Reverse: Duke Kazimierz I Odnowiciel

Date	Mintage	F	VF	XF	Unc
1980MW	2,504,000	—	1.00	2.00	5.00

Y# 122 50 ZLOTYCH Composition: Copper-Nickel
Reverse: General Broni Wladyslaw Sikorski

Date	Mintage	F	VF	XF	Unc
1981MW	2,505,000	—	1.00	2.00	5.00

Y# 124 50 ZLOTYCH Composition: Copper-Nickel
Reverse: King Koleslaw II Smialy

Date	Mintage	F	VF	XF	Unc
1981MW	2,538,000	—	1.00	2.00	4.50

Y# 127 50 ZLOTYCH Composition: Copper-Nickel
Series: F.A.O. - World Food Day

Date	Mintage	F	VF	XF	Unc
1981MW	2,524,000	—	1.00	2.00	4.50

Y# 128 50 ZLOTYCH Composition: Copper-Nickel
Reverse: King Wladyslaw I Herman

Date	Mintage	F	VF	XF	Unc
1981MW	2,500,000	—	1.00	2.00	4.50

Y# 133 50 ZLOTYCH Composition: Copper-Nickel
Reverse: King Boleslaw III Krzywousty

te	Mintage	F	VF	XF	Unc	BU
82MW	2,616,000	—	1.00	2.00	4.50	—

 # 142 50 ZLOTYCH **Composition:** Copper-Nickel **Subject:** 150th Anniversary of Great Theater

ate	Mintage	F	VF	XF	Unc	BU
983MW	615,000	—	1.00	4.00	8.00	—

 # 145 50 ZLOTYCH **Composition:** Copper-Nickel **Reverse:** King Jan III Sobieski

ate	Mintage	F	VF	XF	Unc	BU
983MW	2,576,000	—	1.00	2.00	4.50	—

 # 146 50 ZLOTYCH **Composition:** Copper-Nickel **Reverse:** Ignacy Lukasiewicz

ate	Mintage	F	VF	XF	Unc	BU
983MW	612,000	—	1.00	4.00	8.00	—

Y# 57 100 ZLOTYCH **Weight:** 20.0000 g. **Composition:** 0.9000 Silver .5787 oz. ASW **Subject:** Polish Millennium

Date	Mintage	F	VF	XF	Unc	BU
1966MW	198,000	—	—	6.00	11.50	—

Y# 68 100 ZLOTYCH **Weight:** 16.5000 g. **Composition:** 0.6250 Silver .3316 oz. ASW **Subject:** 500th Anniversary - Birth of Mikolaj Kopernik

Date	Mintage	F	VF	XF	Unc	BU
1973MW Proof	51,000	Value: 9.00				
1974MW Proof	50,000	Value: 9.00				

Y# 71 100 ZLOTYCH **Weight:** 16.5000 g. **Composition:** 0.6250 Silver .3316 oz. ASW **Subject:** 40th Anniversary - Death of Maria Sklodowska Curie **Reverse:** Profile left of Curie

Date	Mintage	F	VF	XF	Unc	BU
1974MW Proof	50,000	Value: 7.50				

Y# 76 100 ZLOTYCH **Weight:** 16.5000 g. **Composition:** 0.6250 Silver .3316 oz. ASW **Reverse:** Royal castle in Warsaw

Date	Mintage	F	VF	XF	Unc	BU
1975MW Proof	50,000	Value: 7.50				

Y# 77 100 ZLOTYCH **Weight:** 16.5000 g. **Composition:** 0.6250 Silver .3316 oz. ASW **Reverse:** Ignacy Jan Paderewski left

Date	Mintage	F	VF	XF	Unc	BU
1975MW Proof	60,000	Value: 6.50				

Y# 78 100 ZLOTYCH **Weight:** 16.5000 g. **Composition:** 0.6250 Silver .3316 oz. ASW **Reverse:** Helena Modrzejewska right

Date	Mintage	F	VF	XF	Unc	BU
1975MW Proof	60,000	Value: 6.50				

Y# 82 100 ZLOTYCH **Weight:** 16.5000 g. **Composition:** 0.6250 Silver .3316 oz. ASW **Reverse:** Tadeusz Kosciuszko right

Date	Mintage	F	VF	XF	Unc	BU
1976MW Proof	100,000	Value: 6.50				

Y# 84 100 ZLOTYCH **Weight:** 16.5000 g. **Composition:** 0.6250 Silver .3316 oz. ASW **Reverse:** Kazimierz Pulaski left

Date	Mintage	F	VF	XF	Unc	BU
1976MW Proof	100,000	Value: 7.00				

Y# 87 100 ZLOTYCH **Weight:** 16.5000 g. **Composition:** 0.6250 Silver .3316 oz. ASW **Series:** Environment Protection **Reverse:** Aurchs

Date	Mintage	F	VF	XF	Unc	BU
1977MW Proof	30,000	Value: 20.00				

Y# 88 100 ZLOTYCH **Weight:** 16.5000 g. **Composition:** 0.6250 Silver .3316 oz. ASW **Reverse:** Henryk Sienkiewicz left

Date	Mintage	F	VF	XF	Unc	BU
1977MW Proof	20,000	Value: 8.50				

Y# 89 100 ZLOTYCH **Weight:** 16.5000 g. **Composition:** 0.6250 Silver .3316 oz. ASW **Reverse:** Wladyslaw Reymont half right

Date	Mintage	F	VF	XF	Unc	BU
1977MW Proof	20,000	Value: 8.50				

Y# 91 100 ZLOTYCH **Weight:** 16.5000 g. **Composition:** 0.6250 Silver .3316 oz. ASW **Reverse:** Wawel Castle in Krakow

Date	Mintage	F	VF	XF	Unc	BU
1977MW Proof	30,000	Value: 11.50				

Y# 92 100 ZLOTYCH **Weight:** 16.5000 g. **Composition:** 0.6250 Silver .3316 oz. ASW **Reverse:** Adam Mickiewicz facing

Date	Mintage	F	VF	XF	Unc	BU
1978MW Proof	30,000	Value: 11.50				

Y# 93 100 ZLOTYCH **Weight:** 16.5000 g. **Composition:** 0.6250 Silver .3316 oz. ASW **Series:** Environment Protection **Reverse:** Moose heading left

Date	Mintage	F	VF	XF	Unc	BU
1978MW Proof	30,000	Value: 22.00				

Y# 94 100 ZLOTYCH **Weight:** 16.5000 g. **Composition:** 0.6250 Silver .3316 oz. ASW **Subject:** 100th Anniversary - Birth of Janusz Korczak **Reverse:** Bust facing

Date	Mintage	F	VF	XF	Unc	BU
1978MW Proof	30,000	Value: 9.00				

Y# 96 100 ZLOTYCH **Weight:** 16.5000 g. **Composition:** 0.6250 Silver .3316 oz. ASW **Series:** Environment Protection **Reverse:** Beaver

Date	Mintage	F	VF	XF	Unc	BU
1978MW Proof	30,000	Value: 22.50				

Y# 98 100 ZLOTYCH **Weight:** 16.5000 g. **Composition:** 0.6250 Silver .3316 oz. ASW **Reverse:** Henryk Wieniawski

Date	Mintage	F	VF	XF	Unc	BU
1979MW Proof	30,000	Value: 9.00				

Y# 103 100 ZLOTYCH **Weight:** 16.5000 g. **Composition:** 0.6250 Silver .3316 oz. ASW **Reverse:** Ludwik Zamenhof left

Date	Mintage	F	VF	XF	Unc	BU
1979MW Proof	30,000	Value: 9.00				

Y# 104 100 ZLOTYCH **Weight:** 16.5000 g. **Composition:** 0.6250 Silver .3316 oz. ASW **Series:** Environment Protection **Reverse:** Lynx

Date	Mintage	F	VF	XF	Unc	BU
1979MW Proof	20,000	Value: 21.50				

Y# 105 100 ZLOTYCH **Weight:** 16.5000 g. **Composition:** 0.6250 Silver .3316 oz. ASW **Series:** Environment Protection **Reverse:** Chamois

Date	Mintage	F	VF	XF	Unc	BU
1979MW Proof	20,000	Value: 21.50				

Y# 120 100 ZLOTYCH **Weight:** 16.5000 g. **Composition:** 0.6250 Silver .3316 oz. ASW **Subject:** 450th Anniversary - Birth of Jan Kochanowski

Date	Mintage	F	VF	XF	Unc	BU
1980MW Proof	10,000	Value: 17.50				

Y# 109 100 ZLOTYCH **Weight:** 16.5000 g. **Composition:** 0.6250 Silver .3316 oz. ASW **Series:** 1980 Olympics **Reverse:** Olympic rings and runner

Date	Mintage	F	VF	XF	Unc	BU
1980MW Proof	10,000	Value: 32.50				

Y# 121 100 ZLOTYCH **Weight:** 16.5000 g. **Composition:** 0.6250 Silver .3316 oz. ASW **Series:** Environment Protection **Reverse:** Cappercaillie

Date	Mintage	F	VF	XF	Unc	BU
1980MW Proof	18,000	Value: 17.50				

Y# 123 100 ZLOTYCH **Weight:** 16.5000 g. **Composition:** 0.6250 Silver .3316 oz. ASW **Reverse:** General Broni Wladyslaw Sikorski left

Date	Mintage	F	VF	XF	Unc	BU
1981MW Proof	12,000	Value: 16.00				

Y# 126 100 ZLOTYCH **Weight:** 16.5000 g. **Composition:** 0.6250 Silver .3316 oz. ASW **Series:** Environment Protection **Reverse:** Horse right

Date	Mintage	F	VF	XF	Unc	BU
1981MW Proof	12,000	Value: 25.00				

 # 136 100 ZLOTYCH **Weight:** 14.1500 g. **Composition:** 0.7500 Silver .3412 oz. ASW **Subject:** Visit of Pope John Paul II **Reverse:** Bust left

te	Mintage	F	VF	XF	Unc	BU
82CHI	8,700	—	—	—	45.00	—
82CHI Proof	3,750	Value: 80.00				
85CHI	1	—	—	—	—	—
85CHI Proof	5	—	—	—	—	—
86CHI	80	—	—	—	400	—
86CHI Proof	128	Value: 450				

 # 141 100 ZLOTYCH **Weight:** 16.5000 g. **Composition:** 0.6250 Silver .3316 oz. ASW **Series:** Environment Protection **Reverse:** Stork walking right

ate	Mintage	F	VF	XF	Unc	BU
982MW Proof	12,000	Value: 25.00				

 # 147 100 ZLOTYCH **Weight:** 16.5000 g. **Composition:** 0.6250 Silver .3316 oz. ASW **Series:** Environment Protection **Reverse:** Bear half right

ate	Mintage	F	VF	XF	Unc	BU
983MW Proof	8,000	Value: 30.00				

Y# 148 100 ZLOTYCH **Composition:** Copper-Nickel **Reverse:** Wincenty Witos

ate	Mintage	F	VF	XF	Unc	BU
984MW	1,530,000	—	—	—	3.00	—

Y# 151 100 ZLOTYCH **Composition:** Copper-Nickel **Subject:** 40th Anniversary of Peoples Republic

ate	Mintage	F	VF	XF	Unc	BU
984MW	2,595,000	—	—	—	3.00	—

Y# 155 100 ZLOTYCH **Composition:** Copper-Nickel **Reverse:** King Przemyslaw II

Date	Mintage	F	VF	XF	Unc	BU
1985MW	2,924,000	—	—	—	3.00	—

Y# 157 100 ZLOTYCH **Composition:** Nickel Plated Steel **Reverse:** Woman and Child - Polish Women's Memorial Hospital Center

Date	Mintage	F	VF	XF	Unc	BU
1985MW	1,927,000	—	—	—	3.00	—

Y# 160 100 ZLOTYCH **Composition:** Copper-Nickel **Reverse:** King Wladyslaw I Lokietek half right

Date	Mintage	F	VF	XF	Unc	BU
1986MW	2,540,000	—	—	—	3.00	—
1986MW Proof	5,000	Value: 12.00				

Y# 167 100 ZLOTYCH **Composition:** Copper-Nickel **Reverse:** King Kazimierz III half left

Date	Mintage	F	VF	XF	Unc	BU
1987MW	2,479,000	—	—	—	4.00	—
1987MW Proof	5,000	Value: 12.00				

Y# 182 100 ZLOTYCH **Composition:** Copper-Nickel **Subject:** 70th Anniversary - Wielkopolskiego Insurrection

Date	Mintage	F	VF	XF	Unc	BU
1988MW	2,513,000	—	—	—	3.00	—
1988MW Proof	5,000	Value: 12.00				

Y# 183 100 ZLOTYCH **Composition:** Copper-Nickel **Reverse:** Queen Jadwiga 1384-1399

Date	Mintage	F	VF	XF	Unc	BU
1988MW	2,469,000	—	—	—	3.00	—
1988MW Proof	5,000	Value: 12.00				

Y# 72 200 ZLOTYCH **Weight:** 14.4700 g. **Composition:** 0.6250 Silver .2907 oz. ASW **Subject:** 30th Anniversary - Polish Peoples Republic

Date	Mintage	F	VF	XF	Unc	BU
1974MW	13,062,000	—	—	—	3.50	—
1974MW Proof	6,000	Value: 22.50				

Y# 79 200 ZLOTYCH **Weight:** 14.4700 g. **Composition:** 0.7500 Silver .3490 oz. ASW **Subject:** 30th Anniversary - Victory Over Fascism

Date	Mintage	F	VF	XF	Unc	BU
1975MW	1,826,000	—	—	—	4.50	—
1975MW Proof	2,600	Value: 25.00				

Y# 86 200 ZLOTYCH **Weight:** 14.4700 g. **Composition:** 0.6250 Silver .2907 oz. ASW **Series:** XXI Olympics **Reverse:** Rings and torch

Date	Mintage	F	VF	XF	Unc	BU
1976MW	2,072,000	—	—	—	8.50	—
1976MW Proof	11,000	Value: 22.50				

Y# 101 200 ZLOTYCH **Weight:** 17.6000 g. **Composition:** 0.7500 Silver .4244 oz. ASW **Reverse:** Duke Mieszko I half left

Date	Mintage	F	VF	XF	Unc	BU
1979MW Proof	12,000	Value: 25.00				

Y# 110 200 ZLOTYCH Weight: 17.6000 g. **Composition:** 0.7500 Silver .4244 oz. ASW **Series:** Winter Olympics **Reverse:** Torch below ski jumper

Date	Mintage	F	VF	XF	Unc	BU
1980MW Proof	32,000	Value: 16.50				

Y# 110a 200 ZLOTYCH Weight: 17.6000 g. **Composition:** 0.7500 Silver .4244 oz. ASW **Reverse:** Without torch below ski jumper

Date	Mintage	F	VF	XF	Unc	BU
1980MW Proof	28,000	Value: 10.00				

Y# 115 200 ZLOTYCH Weight: 17.6000 g. **Composition:** 0.7500 Silver .4244 oz. ASW **Reverse:** King Boleslaw I Chrobry

Date	Mintage	F	VF	XF	Unc	BU
1980MW Proof	12,000	Value: 25.00				

Y# 118 200 ZLOTYCH Weight: 17.6000 g. **Composition:** 0.7500 Silver .4244 oz. ASW **Reverse:** Duke Kazimierz I facing

Date	Mintage	F	VF	XF	Unc	BU
1980MW Proof	12,000	Value: 15.00				

Y# 125 200 ZLOTYCH Weight: 17.6000 g. **Composition:** 0.7500 Silver .4244 oz. ASW **Reverse:** King Bolaslaw II Smialy

Date	Mintage	F	VF	XF	Unc	BU
1981MW Proof	12,000	Value: 18.50				

Y# 129 200 ZLOTYCH Weight: 17.6000 g. **Composition:** 0.7500 Silver .4244 oz. ASW **Reverse:** King Wladyslaw I Herman

Date	Mintage	F	VF	XF	Unc	BU
1981MW Proof	12,000	Value: 20.00				

Y# 130 200 ZLOTYCH Weight: 17.6000 g. **Composition:** 0.7500 Silver .4244 oz. ASW **Subject:** World Soccer Championship Games in Spain

Date	Mintage	F	VF	XF	Unc	BU
1982MW Proof	21,000	Value: 16.50				

Y# 132 200 ZLOTYCH Weight: 17.6000 g. **Composition:** 0.7500 Silver .4244 oz. ASW **Reverse:** King Koleslaw III Krzywousty

Date	Mintage	F	VF	XF	Unc	BU
1982MW Proof	12,000	Value: 20.00				

Y# 137 200 ZLOTYCH Weight: 28.3000 g. **Composition:** 0.7500 Silver .6825 oz. ASW **Subject:** Visit of Pope John Paul II **Obverse:** Similar to Y#132 **Reverse:** Bust of Pope left

Date	Mintage	F	VF	XF	Unc	BU
1982CHI	3,000	—	—	—	100	—
1982CHI Proof	3,650	Value: 125				
1985CHI	1	—	—	—	—	—
1985CHI Proof	5	—	—	—	—	—
1986CHI	32	—	—	—	700	—
1986CHI Proof	75	Value: 750				

Y# 143 200 ZLOTYCH Weight: 17.6000 g. **Composition:** 0.7500 Silver .4244 oz. ASW **Reverse:** K Jan III Sobieski

Date	Mintage	F	VF	XF	Unc
1983MW Proof	11,000	Value: 25.00			

Y# 149 200 ZLOTYCH Weight: 17.6000 g. **Composition:** 0.7500 Silver .4244 oz. ASW **Series:** Wi Olympics **Reverse:** Ice Skater

Date	Mintage	F	VF	XF	Unc
1984MW Proof	15,000	Value: 22.50			

Y# 150 200 ZLOTYCH Weight: 17.6000 g. **Composition:** 0.7500 Silver .4244 oz. ASW **Series:** Summer Olympics **Reverse:** Hurdler

Date	Mintage	F	VF	XF	Unc
1984MW Proof	16,000	Value: 20.00			

Y# 83 500 ZLOTYCH Weight: 30.0000 g. **Composition:** 0.9000 Gold .8681 oz. AGW **Reverse:** Tadeusz Kosciuszko right

Date	Mintage	F	VF	XF	Unc
1976MW	2,318	—	—	—	425

Y# 85 500 ZLOTYCH Weight: 30.0000 g. **Composition:** 0.9000 Gold .8681 oz. AGW **Reverse:** Kazimierz Pulaski left

Date	Mintage	F	VF	XF	Unc
1976MW	2,315	—	—	—	425

Y# 154 500 ZLOTYCH **Weight:** 16.5000 g. **Composition:** 0.6250 Silver .3283 oz. ASW **Series:** Environment Protection **Reverse:** Mute Swan

Date	Mintage	F	VF	XF	Unc	BU
1984MW Proof	10,000	Value: 30.00				

Y# 156 500 ZLOTYCH **Weight:** 16.5000 g. **Composition:** 0.7500 Silver .3979 oz. ASW **Reverse:** King Przemyslaw II

Date	Mintage	F	VF	XF	Unc	BU
1985MW Proof	8,000	Value: 25.00				

Y# 158 500 ZLOTYCH **Weight:** 16.5000 g. **Composition:** 0.7500 Silver .3979 oz. ASW **Subject:** 40th Anniversary of United Nations

Date	Mintage	F	VF	XF	Unc	BU
1985MW Proof	10,000	Value: 22.50				

Y# 159 500 ZLOTYCH **Weight:** 16.5000 g. **Composition:** 0.7500 Silver .3979 oz. ASW **Series:** Environmental Protection **Reverse:** Red Squirrel

Date	Mintage	F	VF	XF	Unc	BU
1985MW Proof	8,000	Value: 27.50				

Y# 161 500 ZLOTYCH **Weight:** 16.5000 g. **Composition:** 0.7500 Silver .3979 oz. ASW **Reverse:** King Wladyslaw I Lokietek half right

Date	Mintage	F	VF	XF	Unc	BU
1986MW Proof	8,000	Value: 22.00				

Y# 162 500 ZLOTYCH **Weight:** 16.5000 g. **Composition:** 0.7500 Silver .3979 oz. ASW **Series:** Environment Protection **Reverse:** Eagle Owl

Date	Mintage	F	VF	XF	Unc	BU
1986MW Proof	12,000	Value: 30.00				

Y# 225 500 ZLOTYCH **Weight:** 16.5000 g. **Composition:** 0.7500 Silver .3979 oz. ASW **Reverse:** Soccer ball in net

Date	Mintage	F	VF	XF	Unc	BU
1986MW Proof	16,000	Value: 30.00				

Y# 165 500 ZLOTYCH **Weight:** 16.5000 g. **Composition:** 0.7500 Silver .3979 oz. ASW **Series:** Olympics **Reverse:** Equestrian

Date	Mintage	F	VF	XF	Unc	BU
1987MW Proof	15,000	Value: 25.00				

Y# 166 500 ZLOTYCH **Weight:** 16.5000 g. **Composition:** 0.7500 Silver .3979 oz. ASW **Subject:** European Championship Soccer Games

Date	Mintage	F	VF	XF	Unc	BU
1987MW Proof	12,000	Value: 30.00				

Y# 172 500 ZLOTYCH **Weight:** 16.5000 g. **Composition:** 0.7500 Silver .3979 oz. ASW **Series:** Winter Olympics **Reverse:** Ice hockey goalie

Date	Mintage	F	VF	XF	Unc	BU
1987MW Proof	15,000	Value: 18.50				

Y# 173 500 ZLOTYCH **Weight:** 16.5000 g. **Composition:** 0.7500 Silver .3979 oz. ASW **Reverse:** King Kazimierz III

Date	Mintage	F	VF	XF	Unc	BU
1987MW Proof	8,000	Value: 25.00				

Y# 181 500 ZLOTYCH **Weight:** 16.5000 g. **Composition:** 0.7500 Silver .3979 oz. ASW **Reverse:** Queen Jadwiga 1384-1399

Date	Mintage	F	VF	XF	Unc	BU
1988MW Proof	8,000	Value: 22.50				

Y# 184 500 ZLOTYCH **Weight:** 16.5000 g. **Composition:** 0.7500 Silver .3979 oz. ASW **Reverse:** Colosseum in Rome - Soccer 1990

Date	Mintage	F	VF	XF	Unc	BU
1988MW Proof	15,000	Value: 22.50				

Y# 185 500 ZLOTYCH **Composition:** Copper-Nickel **Subject:** 50th Anniversary - Beginning of WWII **Reverse:** Infantry soldiers advancing

Date	Mintage	F	VF	XF	Unc	BU
1989MW	10,135,000	—	—	—	2.50	—
1989MW Proof	5,000	Value: 10.00				

Y# 194 500 ZLOTYCH **Composition:** Copper-Nickel **Reverse:** King Wladyslaw II 1386-1434

Date	Mintage	F	VF	XF	Unc	BU
1989MW	2,544,000	—	—	—	3.00	—
1989MW Proof	5,000	Value: 10.00				

Y# 138 1000 ZLOTYCH **Weight:** 3.4000 g. **Composition:** 0.9000 Gold .0984 oz. AGW **Subject:** Visit of Pope John Paul II

Date	Mintage	F	VF	XF	Unc	BU
1982CHI	900	—	—	—	125	—
1982CHI Proof	1,700	Value: 150				
1985CHI	1	—	—	—	650	—
1985CHI Proof	2	Value: 850				
1986CHI	83	—	—	—	300	—
1986CHI Proof	53	Value: 350				

Y# 144 1000 ZLOTYCH **Weight:** 14.5000 g. **Composition:** 0.7500 Silver .3497 oz. ASW **Subject:** Visit of Pope John Paul II **Reverse:** Bust left

Date	Mintage	F	VF	XF	Unc	BU
1982MW	803,000	—	—	—	12.50	—
1983MW	1,530,000	—	—	—	9.00	—
1983MW Proof	10,000	Value: 27.50				

Y# 168 1000 ZLOTYCH **Weight:** 3.1100 g. **Composition:** 0.9990 Gold .1000 oz. AGW **Subject:** Papal Visit in America

Date	Mintage	F	VF	XF	Unc	BU
1987MW Proof	201	Value: 250				

Y# 174 1000 ZLOTYCH **Weight:** 3.1100 g. **Composition:** 0.9990 Gold .1000 oz. AGW **Subject:** 10th Anniversary of Pope John Paul II

Date	Mintage	F	VF	XF	Unc	BU
1988MW Proof	1,000	Value: 125				

Y# 186 1000 ZLOTYCH **Weight:** 3.1100 g. **Composition:** 0.9990 Gold .1000 oz. AGW **Subject:** Pope John Paul II **Obverse:** Similar to Y#174 **Reverse:** Similar to 200,000 Zlotych, Y#190

Date	F	VF	XF	Unc	BU
1989MW In sets only	—	—	—	125	—

Y# 90 2000 ZLOTYCH **Weight:** 8.0000 g. **Composition:** 0.9000 Gold .2315 oz. AGW **Reverse:** Fryderyk Chopin

Date	Mintage	F	VF	XF	Unc	BU
1977MW Proof	4,000	Value: 135				

Y# 102 2000 ZLOTYCH **Weight:** 8.0000 g. **Composition:** 0.9000 Gold .2315 oz. AGW **Reverse:** Duke Mieszko I

Date	Mintage	F	VF	XF	Unc	BU
1979MW Proof	3,000	Value: 135				

Y# 106 2000 ZLOTYCH **Weight:** 8.0000 g. **Composition:** 0.9000 Gold .2315 oz. AGW **Reverse:** Mikolaj Kopernik

Date	Mintage	F	VF	XF	Unc	BU
1979MW Proof	5,000	Value: 135				

Y# 107 2000 ZLOTYCH **Weight:** 8.0000 g. **Composition:** 0.9000 Gold .2315 oz. AGW **Reverse:** Maria Sklodowska Curie

Date	Mintage	F	VF	XF	Unc	BU
1979MW Proof	5,000	Value: 135				

Y# 111 2000 ZLOTYCH **Weight:** 8.0000 g. **Composition:** 0.9000 Gold .2315 oz. AGW **Series:** Winter Olympics **Obverse:** Similar to Y#107 **Reverse:** Ski jumper

Date	Mintage	F	VF	XF	Unc	BU
1980MW Proof	5,250	Value: 135				

Y# 116 2000 ZLOTYCH **Weight:** 8.0000 g. **Composition:** 0.9000 Gold .2315 oz. AGW **Reverse:** King Koleslaw I Chrobry

Date	Mintage	F	VF	XF	Unc	BU
1980MW Proof	2,500	Value: 150				

Y# 119 2000 ZLOTYCH **Weight:** 8.0000 g. **Composition:** 0.9000 Gold .2315 oz. AGW **Reverse:** Kazimierz I

Date	Mintage	F	VF	XF	Unc	BU
1980MW Proof	2,500	Value: 150				

Y# 131 2000 ZLOTYCH **Weight:** 8.0000 g. **Composition:** 0.9000 Gold .2315 oz. AGW **Reverse:** Wladyslaw I Herman **Note:** Similar to 200 Zlotych, Y#129.

Date	Mintage	F	VF	XF	Unc	BU
1981MW Proof	3,113	Value: 150				

Y# 135 2000 ZLOTYCH **Weight:** 8.0000 g. **Composition:** 0.9000 Gold .2315 oz. AGW **Reverse:** Boleslaw II

Date	F	VF	XF	Unc	BU
1981MW	—	—	—	—	—

Y# 139 2000 ZLOTYCH **Weight:** 6.8000 g. **Composition:** 0.9000 Gold .1968 oz. AGW **Subject:** Visit of Pope John Paul II

Date	Mintage	F	VF	XF	Unc	BU
1982CHI		—	—	—	250	—
1982CHI Proof	1,250	Value: 300				
1985CHI		—	—	—	900	—
1985CHI Proof	Est. 2	Value: 1,100				
1986CHI		—	—	—	450	—
1986CHI Proof	Est. 79	Value: 500				

Y# 169 2000 ZLOTYCH **Weight:** 7.7700 g. **Composition:** 0.9990 Gold .2500 oz. AGW **Subject:** Papal Visit in America

Date	Mintage	F	VF	XF	Unc	B
1987MW Proof	201	Value: 350				

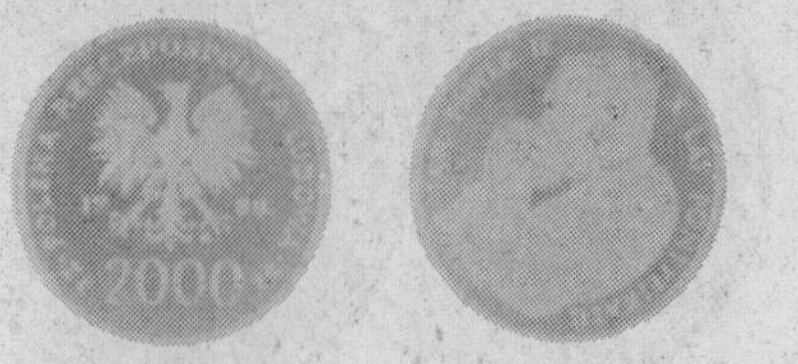

Y# 175 2000 ZLOTYCH **Weight:** 7.7700 g. **Composition:** 0.9990 Gold .2500 oz. AGW **Subject:** 10th Anniversary of Pope John Paul II

Date	Mintage	F	VF	XF	Unc	B
1988 Proof	1,000	Value: 200				

Y# 187 2000 ZLOTYCH **Weight:** 7.7700 g. **Composition:** 0.9990 Gold .2500 oz. AGW **Obverse:** Similar to Y#175 **Reverse:** Similar to 200,000 Zlotych, Y#19 **Note:** Pope John Paul II.

Date	F	VF	XF	Unc	B
1989MW In sets only	—	—	—	200	–

Y# 170 5000 ZLOTYCH **Weight:** 15.5500 g. **Composition:** 0.9990 Gold .5000 oz. AGW **Subject:** Papa Visit in America

Date	Mintage	F	VF	XF	Unc	B
1987MW Proof	201	Value: 550				

Y# 176 5000 ZLOTYCH **Weight:** 15.5500 g. **Composition:** 0.9990 Gold .5000 oz. AGW **Subject:** 10th Anniversary of Pope John Paul II

Date	Mintage	F	VF	XF	Unc	B
1988MW Proof	1,000	Value: 300				

Y# 188 5000 ZLOTYCH **Weight:** 15.5500 g. **Composition:** 0.9990 Gold .5000 oz. AGW **Obverse:** Similar to Y#176 **Reverse:** Similar to 200,000 Zlotych, Y#19 **Note:** Pope John Paul II.

Date	F	VF	XF	Unc	B
1989MW In sets only	—	—	—	300	–

Y# 191 5000 ZLOTYCH **Weight:** 16.5000 g. **Composition:** 0.7500 Silver .3978 oz. ASW **Reverse:** Toru - Kopernik

Date	Mintage	F	VF	XF	Unc	B
1989MW Proof	20,000	Value: 30.00				

Y# 192 5000 ZLOTYCH **Weight:** 16.5000 g. **Composition:** 0.7500 Silver .3978 oz. ASW **Reverse:** Torunia Town Hall

Date	Mintage	F	VF	XF	Unc	B
1989MW Proof	20,000	Value: 30.00				

Y# 193 5000 ZLOTYCH **Weight:** 16.5000 g. **Composition:** 0.7500 Silver .3978 oz. ASW **Reverse:** Henryk Sucharski

Date	Mintage	F	VF	XF	Unc	BU
1989MW Proof	25,000	Value: 27.50				

Y# 197 5000 ZLOTYCH **Weight:** 16.5000 g. **Composition:** 0.7500 Silver .3978 oz. ASW **Reverse:** Bust of King Wladyslaw II

Date	Mintage	F	VF	XF	Unc	BU
1989MW Proof	8,000	Value: 35.00				

Y# 198 5000 ZLOTYCH **Weight:** 16.5000 g. **Composition:** 0.7500 Silver .3978 oz. ASW **Reverse:** Half-length portrait of King Wladyslaw II

Date	Mintage	F	VF	XF	Unc	BU
1989MW Proof	2,500	Value: 45.00				

Y# 140 10000 ZLOTYCH **Weight:** 34.5000 g. **Composition:** 0.9000 Gold .9984 oz. AGW **Subject:** Visit of Pope John Paul II

Date	Mintage	F	VF	XF	Unc	BU
1982CHI		—	—	—	1,250	—
1982CHI Proof	700	Value: 1,500				
1985CHI Proof		—	—	—	—	—
1986CHI		—	—	—	1,750	—
1986CHI Proof	Est. 13	Value: 1,850				

Y# 399 10000 ZLOTYCH **Weight:** 28.3100 g. **Composition:** 0.9000 Silver .8192 oz. ASW **Subject:** Pope John Paul II **Obverse:** Eagle **Reverse:** Bust of Pope John Paul II left **Edge:** Plain **Size:** 40.2 mm.

Date	Mintage	F	VF	XF	Unc	BU
1986 Proof	9	Value: 1,900				

Y# 164 10000 ZLOTYCH **Weight:** 19.0600 g. **Composition:** 0.7500 Silver .4582 oz. ASW **Subject:** Papal Visit

Date	Mintage	F	VF	XF	Unc	BU
1987MW	908,000	—	—	—	25.00	—
1987MW Proof	15,000	Value: 42.50				

Y# 171 10000 ZLOTYCH **Weight:** 31.1030 g. **Composition:** 0.9990 Gold 1.0000 oz. AGW **Subject:** Papal Visit in America

Date	Mintage	F	VF	XF	Unc	BU
1987MW Proof	201	Value: 1,150				

Y# 177 10000 ZLOTYCH **Weight:** 31.1030 g. **Composition:** 0.9990 Gold 1.0000 oz. AGW **Subject:** 10th Anniversary of Pope John Paul II

Date	Mintage	F	VF	XF	Unc	BU
1988MW	1,000	—	—	—	550	—
1988MW Proof	1,000	Value: 600				

Y# 177a 10000 ZLOTYCH **Weight:** 31.1030 g. **Composition:** 0.9990 Silver 1.0000 oz. ASW **Subject:** 10th Anniversary of Pope John Paul II

Date	Mintage	F	VF	XF	Unc	BU
1988MW	5,000	—	—	—	40.00	—
1988MW Proof	—	Value: 50.00				

Y# 179 10000 ZLOTYCH **Weight:** 31.1030 g. **Composition:** 0.9990 Silver 1.0000 oz. ASW **Subject:** Pope John Paul - Christmas

Date	Mintage	F	VF	XF	Unc	BU
1988MW Proof	5,000	Value: 37.50				

Y# 189 10000 ZLOTYCH **Weight:** 31.1030 g. **Composition:** 0.9990 Gold 1.0000 oz. AGW **Reverse:** Pope John Paul II

Date	Mintage	F	VF	XF	Unc	BU
1989MW Proof	Est. 2,000	Value: 575				

Y# 189a 10000 ZLOTYCH **Weight:** 31.1000 g. **Composition:** 0.9990 Silver 1.0000 oz. ASW **Reverse:** Pope John Paul II

Date	Mintage	F	VF	XF	Unc	BU
1989MW		—	—	—	40.00	—
1989MW Proof	5,000	Value: 50.00				

Y# 237 10000 ZLOTYCH **Weight:** 31.1000 g. **Composition:** 0.9990 Silver 1.0000 oz. ASW **Reverse:** Pope John Paul II

Date		F	VF	XF	Unc	BU
1989MW Proof	—	Value: 40.00				

Y# 223 20000 ZLOTYCH **Weight:** 19.0000 g. **Composition:** 0.7500 Silver .4558 oz. ASW **Reverse:** Soccer ball, map, and globe

Date	Mintage	F	VF	XF	Unc	BU
1989 Proof	25,000	Value: 35.00				

Y# 224 20000 ZLOTYCH **Weight:** 19.0000 g. **Composition:** 0.7500 Silver .4558 oz. ASW **Reverse:** Soccer player behind vertical lines

Date	Mintage	F	VF	XF	Unc	BU
1989 Proof	25,000	Value: 35.00				

Y# 180 50000 ZLOTYCH Weight: 19.3000 g. **Composition:** 0.7500 Silver .4654 oz. ASW **Subject:** 70 Years of Polish Independence

Date	Mintage	F	VF	XF	Unc	BU
1988	1,000,000	—	—	—	10.00	—
1988 Proof	20,000	Value: 45.00				

Y# 163 200000 ZLOTYCH Weight: 373.2420 g. **Composition:** 0.9990 Gold 12.0000 oz. AGW **Subject:** Papal Visit in America **Size:** 70 mm. **Note:** Illustration reduced.

Date	Mintage	F	VF	XF	Unc	BU
1987 Proof	101	Value: 6,500				

Y# 178 200000 ZLOTYCH Weight: 373.2420 g. **Composition:** 0.9990 Gold 12.0000 oz. AGW **Subject:** 10th Anniversary of Pope John Paul II **Size:** 70 mm. **Note:** Illustration reduced.

Date	Mintage	F	VF	XF	Unc	BU
1988MW Proof	300	Value: 5,500				

Y# 190 200000 ZLOTYCH Weight: 373.2420 g. **Composition:** 0.9990 Gold 12.0000 oz. AGW **Obverse:** Similar to 10,000 Zlotych, Y#179 **Reverse:** Pope John Paul II **Note:** Illustration reduced.

Date	Mintage	F	VF	XF	Unc	BU
1989MW Proof	Est. 200	Value: 6,000				

REPUBLIC

Democratic

STANDARD COINAGE

Y# 216 50 ZLOTYCH Composition: (No Composition)

Date	Mintage	F	VF	XF	Unc	BU
1990MW	28,707,000	—	—	—	1.25	—
1990MW Proof	5,000	Value: 12.00				

Y# 214 100 ZLOTYCH Composition: (No Composition)

Date	Mintage	F	VF	XF	Unc	BU
1990MW	37,341,000	—	—	—	2.00	—
1990MW Proof	5,000	Value: 15.00				

Y# 195 10000 ZLOTYCH Composition: Copper-Nickel **Subject:** 10th Anniversary of Solidarity

Date	Mintage	F	VF	XF	Unc	BU
1990MW	15,164,000	—	—	—	4.50	—
1990MW Proof	5,000	Value: 16.50				

Y# 217 10000 ZLOTYCH Composition: Nickel Plated Steel **Subject:** 200th Anniversary of Polish Constitution

Date	Mintage	F	VF	XF	Unc	BU
1991MW	2,605,000	—	—	—	6.00	—

Y# 246 10000 ZLOTYCH Composition: Copper-Nickel **Reverse:** Wladyslaw III

Date	Mintage	F	VF	XF	Unc	BU
1992MW	2,500,000	—	—	—	3.50	—

Y# 219 20000 ZLOTYCH Weight: 3.1100 g. **Composition:** 0.9990 Gold .1 oz. AGW **Subject:** 10th Anniversary of Solidarity **Note:** Similar to 10000 Zlotych, Y#195.

Date	Mintage	F	VF	XF	Unc	BU
1990 Proof	1,004	Value: 120				

Y# 215 20000 ZLOTYCH Ring Composition: Brass **Center Composition:** Copper-Nickel **Subject:** 225th Anniversary of Warsaw Mint

Date	Mintage	F	VF	XF	Unc	BU
1991MW	100,000	—	—	—	18.00	

Y# 243 20000 ZLOTYCH Composition: Copper-Nickel **Reverse:** Barn swallows

Date	Mintage	F	VF	XF	Unc	BU
1993MW	500,000	—	—	—	5.00	

Y# 244 20000 ZLOTYCH Composition: Copper-Nickel **Reverse:** Lancut Castle

Date	Mintage	F	VF	XF	Unc	BU
1993MW	500,000	—	—	—	4.50	

Y# 256 20000 ZLOTYCH Composition: Copper-Nickel **Reverse:** Kazimierz IV

Date	Mintage	F	VF	XF	Unc	BU
1993	1,500,000	—	—	—	4.50	

Y# 261 20000 ZLOTYCH Composition: Copper-Nickel **Series:** Olympics **Reverse:** Slalom skier

Date	Mintage	F	VF	XF	Unc	BU
1993	988,000	—	—	—	7.50	

Y#265 20000 ZLOTYCH **Composition:** Copper-Nickel **Subject:** 75th Anniversary - Disabled Association

Date	Mintage	F	VF	XF	Unc	BU
1994	75,000	—	—	—	4.50	—

Y#270 20000 ZLOTYCH **Composition:** Copper-Nickel **Reverse:** New mint building

Date	Mintage	F	VF	XF	Unc	BU
1994	252,000	—	—	—	4.50	—

Y#271 20000 ZLOTYCH **Composition:** Copper-Nickel **Subject:** 200th Anniversary - Kosciuszko Insurrection

Date	Mintage	F	VF	XF	Unc	BU
1994	100,000	—	—	—	5.00	—

Y#272 20000 ZLOTYCH **Composition:** Copper-Nickel **Reverse:** Zygmunt I, 1506-1548

Date	Mintage	F	VF	XF	Unc	BU
1994	1,500,000	—	—	—	4.50	—

Y# 220 50000 ZLOTYCH **Weight:** 13.1000 g. **Composition:** 0.9990 Gold .4212 oz. AGW **Subject:** 10th Anniversary of Solidarity **Note:** Similar to 10000 Zlotych, Y#195.

Date	Mintage	F	VF	XF	Unc	BU
1990 Proof	1,001	Value: 265				

Y#229 50000 ZLOTYCH **Composition:** Copper-Nickel **Subject:** 200th Anniversary of Order Virtuti Militari

Date	Mintage	F	VF	XF	Unc	BU
1992 Proof	100,000	Value: 12.50				

Y# 196.1 100000 ZLOTYCH **Weight:** 31.1000 g. **Composition:** 0.9990 Silver 1.0000 oz. ASW **Subject:** 10th Anniversary of Solidarity

Date	Mintage	F	VF	XF	Unc	BU
1990	500,000	—	—	—	18.00	—
1990 Proof	—	Value: 85.00				

Y# 196.2 100000 ZLOTYCH **Weight:** 31.1000 g. **Composition:** 0.9990 Silver 1.0000 oz. ASW **Size:** 31.9 mm. **Note:** Reduced size.

Date		F	VF	XF	Unc	BU
1990 Proof	—	Value: 60.00				

Y# 199 100000 ZLOTYCH **Weight:** 31.1000 g. **Composition:** 0.9990 Silver 1.0000 oz. ASW **Reverse:** Fryderyk Chopin

Date	Mintage	F	VF	XF	Unc	BU
1990 Proof	10,000	Value: 25.00				

Y# 200 100000 ZLOTYCH **Weight:** 31.1000 g. **Composition:** 0.9990 Silver 1.0000 oz. ASW **Reverse:** Tadeusz Kosciuszko

Date	Mintage	F	VF	XF	Unc	BU
1990 Proof	10,000	Value: 25.00				

Y# 201 100000 ZLOTYCH **Weight:** 31.1000 g. **Composition:** 0.9990 Silver 1.0000 oz. ASW **Reverse:** Marszalek Pilsudski

Date	Mintage	F	VF	XF	Unc	BU
1990 Proof	10,000	Value: 25.00				

Y# 221 100000 ZLOTYCH **Weight:** 15.5500 g. **Composition:** 0.9990 Gold .5000 oz. AGW **Subject:** 10th Anniversary of Solidarity **Note:** Similar to 10000 Zlotych, Y#195.

Date	Mintage	F	VF	XF	Unc	BU
1990 Proof	Est. 1,000	Value: 280				

Y# 235 100000 ZLOTYCH **Weight:** 16.5000 g. **Composition:** 0.7500 Silver .3979 oz. ASW **Series:** WWII **Reverse:** Major Henrik Dobrzanski - Hubal - Cavalry

Date	Mintage	F	VF	XF	Unc	BU
1991 Proof	12,000	Value: 27.50				

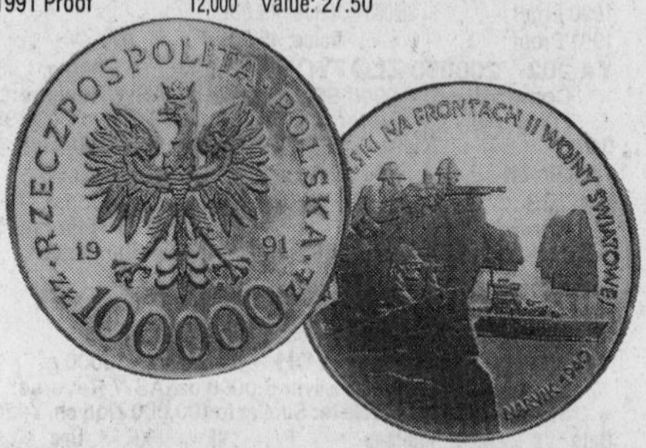

Y# 236 100000 ZLOTYCH **Weight:** 16.5000 g. **Composition:** 0.7500 Silver .3979 oz. ASW **Series:** WWII **Subject:** Defense of Narvik **Reverse:** Polish troops

Date	Mintage	F	VF	XF	Unc	BU
1991 Proof	12,000	Value: 27.50				

Y# 238 100000 ZLOTYCH **Weight:** 16.5000 g. **Composition:** 0.7500 Silver .3979 oz. ASW **Series:** WWII **Reverse:** Polish troops at Battle of Tobruk

Date	Mintage	F	VF	XF	Unc	BU
1991 Proof	12,000	Value: 27.50				

Y# 239 100000 ZLOTYCH **Weight:** 16.5000 g. **Composition:** 0.7500 Silver .3979 oz. ASW **Series:** WWII **Reverse:** Polish pilots in Battle of Britain

Date	Mintage	F	VF	XF	Unc	BU
1991 Proof	12,000	Value: 27.50				

Y# 227 100000 ZLOTYCH **Weight:** 16.5000 g. **Composition:** 0.7500 Silver .3979 oz. ASW **Subject:** Unification of Upper Silesia and Poland

Date	Mintage	F	VF	XF	Unc	BU
1992 Proof	30,000	Value: 27.50				

Y# 268 100000 ZLOTYCH **Weight:** 16.5000 g. **Composition:** 0.9000 Silver .4775 oz. ASW **Subject:** Warsaw Uprising

Date	Mintage	F	VF	XF	Unc	BU
1994	150,000	—	—	—	32.50	—

Y# 240 200000 ZLOTYCH **Weight:** 19.0600 g. **Composition:** 0.9990 Silver .6122 oz. ASW **Reverse:** General Dyw. Stefan Rowecki "Grot"

Date	Mintage	F	VF	XF	Unc	BU
1990 Proof	25,000	Value: 45.00				
1991 Proof	—	Value: 45.00				

Y# 202 200000 ZLOTYCH **Weight:** 155.5000 g. **Composition:** 0.9990 Silver 5.0000 oz. ASW **Reverse:** Fryderyk Chopin **Note:** Similar to 100,000 Zlotych, Y#199.

Date	Mintage	F	VF	XF	Unc	BU
1990 Proof	10,000	Value: 90.00				

Y# 203 200000 ZLOTYCH **Weight:** 155.5000 g. **Composition:** 0.9990 Silver 5.0000 oz. ASW **Reverse:** Tadeusz Kosciuszko **Note:** Similar to 100,000 Zlotych, Y#200.

Date	Mintage	F	VF	XF	Unc	BU
1990 Proof	10,000	Value: 90.00				

Y# 204 200000 ZLOTYCH **Weight:** 155.5000 g. **Composition:** 0.9990 Silver 5.0000 oz. ASW **Reverse:** Marszalck Pilsudski **Note:** Similar to 100,000 Zlotych, Y#201.

Date	Mintage	F	VF	XF	Unc	BU
1990 Proof	10,000	Value: 90.00				

Y# 205 200000 ZLOTYCH **Weight:** 31.1000 g. **Composition:** 0.9990 Gold 1.0000 oz. AGW **Reverse:** Fryderyk Chopin

Date	Mintage	F	VF	XF	Unc	BU
1990 Proof	10,000	Value: 475				

Y# 206 200000 ZLOTYCH **Weight:** 31.1000 g. **Composition:** 0.9990 Gold 1.0000 oz. AGW **Reverse:** Tadeusz Kosciuszko

Date	Mintage	F	VF	XF	Unc	BU
1990 Proof	10,000	Value: 475				

Y# 207 200000 ZLOTYCH **Weight:** 31.1000 g. **Composition:** 0.9990 Gold 1.0000 oz. AGW **Reverse:** Marszalck Pilsudski

Date	Mintage	F	VF	XF	Unc	BU
1990 Proof	10,000	Value: 475				

Y# 222 200000 ZLOTYCH **Weight:** 31.1000 g. **Composition:** 0.9990 Gold 1.0000 oz. AGW **Subject:** Solidarity **Reverse:** Solidarity monument with city view background

Date	Mintage	F	VF	XF	Unc	BU
1990 Proof	Est. 1,000	Value: 600				

Y# 250 200000 ZLOTYCH **Weight:** 19.2650 g. **Composition:** 0.9990 Silver .6188 oz. ASW **Reverse:** General Komorowski

Date	Mintage	F	VF	XF	Unc	BU
1990 Proof	25,000	Value: 27.50				

Y# 218 200000 ZLOTYCH **Weight:** 38.9000 g. **Composition:** 0.9990 Silver 1.2496 oz. ASW **Subject:** 200th Anniversary of Polish Constitution

Date	Mintage	F	VF	XF	Unc	BU
1991	100,000	—	—	—	20.00	—

Y# 226 200000 ZLOTYCH **Weight:** 31.1000 g. **Composition:** 0.9250 Silver .9250 oz. ASW **Series:** Albertville Olympics **Reverse:** Slalom skier

Date	Mintage	F	VF	XF	Unc	BU
1991 Proof	20,000	Value: 27.50				

Y# 228 200000 ZLOTYCH **Weight:** 31.1000 g. **Composition:** 0.9250 Silver .9250 oz. ASW **Series:** Barcelona Olympics **Reverse:** Weight lifter

Date	Mintage	F	VF	XF	Unc	BU
1991 Proof	20,000	Value: 27.50				

Y# 241 200000 ZLOTYCH **Weight:** 31.1600 g. **Composition:** 0.9250 Silver .9267 oz. ASW **Series:** Barcelona Olympics **Reverse:** Two sailboats

Date	Mintage	F	VF	XF	Unc	BU
1991 Proof	20,000	Value: 37.50				

Y# 242 200000 ZLOTYCH **Weight:** 19.3300 g. **Composition:** 0.7500 Silver .4661 oz. ASW **Subject:** 70th Anniversary of Poznan Fair

Date	Mintage	F	VF	XF	Unc	BU
1991 Proof	20,000	Value: 27.50				

Y# 251 200000 ZLOTYCH **Weight:** 19.3300 g. **Composition:** 0.7500 Silver .4661 oz. ASW **Reverse:** General Okulicki

Date	Mintage	F	VF	XF	Unc	BU
1991 Proof	25,000	Value: 27.50				

Y# 252 200000 ZLOTYCH **Weight:** 19.3300 g. **Composition:** 0.7500 Silver .4661 oz. ASW **Reverse:** General Tokarzewski - Karaszewicz

Date	Mintage	F	VF	XF	Unc	BU
1991 Proof	25,000	Value: 27.50				

Y# 230 200000 ZLOTYCH **Weight:** 31.1000 g. **Composition:** 0.9990 Silver 1.0000 oz. ASW **Subject:** Discovery of America **Reverse:** Portrait and ship

Date	Mintage	F	VF	XF	Unc	B
1992 Proof	20,000	Value: 40.00				

Y# 231 200000 ZLOTYCH **Weight:** 31.1000 g. **Composition:** 0.9990 Silver 1.0000 oz. ASW **Subject:** Seville Expo '92

Date	Mintage	F	VF	XF	Unc	BU
1992 Proof	45,000	Value: 25.00				

Y# 232 200000 ZLOTYCH **Weight:** 16.5000 g. **Composition:** 0.7500 Silver .3979 oz. ASW **Series:** WWII **Reverse:** Polish protection of WWII sea convoys

Date	Mintage	F	VF	XF	Unc	BU
1992 Proof	15,000	Value: 27.50				

Y# 233 200000 ZLOTYCH **Weight:** 16.5000 g. **Composition:** 0.7500 Silver .3979 oz. ASW **Reverse:** Stanislaw Staszic

Date	Mintage	F	VF	XF	Unc	BU
1992 Proof	20,000	Value: 27.50				

Y# 253 200000 ZLOTYCH **Weight:** 16.5000 g. **Composition:** 0.7500 Silver .3979 oz. ASW **Reverse:** Full bust Wladyslaw III

Date	Mintage	F	VF	XF	Unc	BU
1992 Proof	15,000	Value: 27.50				

Y# 254 200000 ZLOTYCH **Weight:** 16.5000 g. **Composition:** 0.7500 Silver .3979 oz. ASW **Reverse:** Half bust Wladyslaw III

Date	Mintage	F	VF	XF	Unc	BU
1992 Proof	5,000	Value: 30.00				

Y# 255 200000 ZLOTYCH **Weight:** 16.5000 g. **Composition:** 0.7500 Silver .3979 oz. ASW **Subject:** 750th Anniversary - City of Stettin

Date	Mintage	F	VF	XF	Unc	BU
1993 Proof	20,000	Value: 25.00				

Y# 257 200000 ZLOTYCH **Weight:** 16.5000 g. **Composition:** 0.7500 Silver .3979 oz. ASW **Reverse:** Kazimierz IV

Date	Mintage	F	VF	XF	Unc	BU
1993 Proof	15,000	Value: 25.00				

Y# 258 200000 ZLOTYCH **Weight:** 16.5000 g. **Composition:** 0.7500 Silver .3979 oz. ASW **Reverse:** Enthroned Kazimierz IV

Date	Mintage	F	VF	XF	Unc	BU
1993 Proof	5,000	Value: 32.50				

Y# 259 200000 ZLOTYCH **Weight:** 16.5000 g. **Composition:** 0.7500 Silver .3979 oz. ASW **Series:** WWII **Reverse:** Polish partisans sabotaging railways

Date	Mintage	F	VF	XF	Unc	BU
1993 Proof	10,000	Value: 27.50				

Y# 262 200000 ZLOTYCH **Weight:** 16.5000 g. **Composition:** 0.7500 Silver .3979 oz. ASW **Series:** WWII **Reverse:** Battle of Monte Cassino

Date	Mintage	F	VF	XF	Unc	BU
1994 Proof	15,000	Value: 37.50				

Y# 266 200000 ZLOTYCH **Weight:** 16.5000 g. **Composition:** 0.7500 Silver .3979 oz. ASW **Subject:** 75th Anniversary - Disabled Association

Date	Mintage	F	VF	XF	Unc	BU
1994 Proof	15,000	Value: 27.50				

Y# 273 200000 ZLOTYCH **Weight:** 16.5000 g. **Composition:** 0.7500 Silver .3979 oz. ASW **Reverse:** Sigismund I, 1506-1548

Date	Mintage	F	VF	XF	Unc	BU
1994 Proof	15,000	Value: 27.50				

Y# 274 200000 ZLOTYCH **Weight:** 16.5000 g. **Composition:** 0.7500 Silver .3979 oz. ASW **Reverse:** Half-length portrait of Sigismund I

Date	Mintage	F	VF	XF	Unc	BU
1994 Proof	5,000	Value: 32.50				

Y# 275 200000 ZLOTYCH **Weight:** 16.5000 g. **Composition:** 0.7500 Silver .3979 oz. ASW **Subject:** 200th Anniversary - Kosciuszko Insurrection

Date	Mintage	F	VF	XF	Unc	BU
1994 Proof	15,000	Value: 32.50				

Y# 245 300000 ZLOTYCH **Weight:** 31.1600 g. **Composition:** 0.9250 Silver .9267 oz. ASW **Subject:** 50th Anniversary of Warsaw Ghetto Uprising

Date	Mintage	F	VF	XF	Unc	BU
1993 Proof	30,000	Value: 37.50				

Y# 247 300000 ZLOTYCH **Weight:** 31.1600 g. **Composition:** 0.9250 Silver .9267 oz. ASW **Series:** 1994 Olympics **Reverse:** Lillehammer

Date	Mintage	F	VF	XF	Unc	BU
1993 Proof	20,000	Value: 27.50				

Y# 263 300000 ZLOTYCH **Weight:** 31.1600 g. **Composition:** 0.9250 Silver .9267 oz. ASW **Reverse:** St. Maksymilian Kolbe

Date	Mintage	F	VF	XF	Unc	BU
1994 Proof	15,000	Value: 37.50				

Y# 248 300000 ZLOTYCH **Weight:** 31.1450 g. **Composition:** 0.9990 Silver 1.0004 oz. ASW **Reverse:** Barn swallows

Date	Mintage	F	VF	XF	Unc	BU
1993 Proof	20,000	Value: 42.50				

Y# 264 300000 ZLOTYCH **Weight:** 31.1000 g. **Composition:** 0.9250 Silver .9250 oz. ASW **Subject:** 70th Anniversary - Polish National Bank **Shape:** 7-sided

Date	Mintage	F	VF	XF	Unc	BU
1994 Proof	20,000	Value: 45.00				

Y# 249 300000 ZLOTYCH **Weight:** 31.1450 g. **Composition:** 0.9990 Silver 1.0004 oz. ASW **Reverse:** Lancut Castle

Date	Mintage	F	VF	XF	Unc	BU
1993 Proof	20,000	Value: 37.50				

Y# 269 300000 ZLOTYCH **Weight:** 31.1035 g. **Composition:** 0.9990 Silver 1.0000 oz. ASW **Subject:** Warsaw Uprising

Date	Mintage	F	VF	XF	Unc	BU
1994 Proof	30,000	Value: 35.00				

Y# 208 500000 ZLOTYCH **Weight:** 62.2000 g. **Composition:** 0.9990 Gold 2.0000 oz. AGW **Reverse:** Fryderyk Chopin **Note:** Similar to 100,000 Zlotych, Y#199.

Date	Mintage	F	VF	XF	Unc	BU
1990 Proof	2,000	Value: 900				

Y# 209 500000 ZLOTYCH **Weight:** 62.2000 g. **Composition:** 0.9990 Gold 2.0000 oz. AGW **Reverse:** Tadeusz Kosciuszko **Note:** Similar to 100,000 Zlotych, Y#200.

Date	Mintage	F	VF	XF	Unc	BU
1990 Proof	2,000	Value: 900				

Y# 210 500000 ZLOTYCH **Weight:** 62.2000 g. **Composition:** 0.9990 Gold 2.0000 oz. AGW **Reverse:** Marszalek Pilsudski **Note:** Similar to 100,000 Zlotych, Y#201.

Date	Mintage	F	VF	XF	Unc	BU
1990 Proof	2,000	Value: 900				

Y# 211 1000000 ZLOTYCH **Weight:** 373.2000 g. **Composition:** 0.9990 Gold 12.0000 oz. AGW **Reverse:** Fryderyk Chopin **Note:** Similar to 100,000 Zlotych, Y#199.

Date	Mintage	F	VF	XF	Unc	BU
1990 Proof	250	Value: 6,250				

Y# 212 1000000 ZLOTYCH **Weight:** 373.2000 g. **Composition:** 0.9990 Gold 12.0000 oz. AGW **Reverse:** Tadeusz Kosciuszko **Note:** Similar to 100,000 Zlotych, Y#200.

Date	Mintage	F	VF	XF	Unc	BU
1990 Proof	250	Value: 6,250				

Y# 213 1000000 ZLOTYCH **Weight:** 373.2000 g. **Composition:** 0.9990 Gold 12.0000 oz. AGW **Reverse:** Marszalek Pilsudski **Note:** Similar to 100,000 Zlotych, Y#201.

Date	Mintage	F	VF	XF	Unc	BU
1990 Proof	250	Value: 6,250				

Y# 260 300000 ZLOTYCH **Weight:** 31.1000 g. **Composition:** 0.9990 Silver .9990 oz. ASW **Reverse:** Aerial view of Zamosc

Date	Mintage	F	VF	XF	Unc	BU
1993 Proof	20,000	Value: 32.50				

REFORM COINAGE

100 Old Zlotych = 1 Grosz; 10,000 Old Zlotych = 1 Zlot

As far back as 1990, production was initiated for th new 1 Grosz - 1 Zlotych coins for a forthcoming mon tary reform. It wasn't announced until the Act of July 1994 and was enacted on January 1, 1995.

Y# 276 GROSZ **Composition:** Brass

Date	F	VF	XF	Unc	B
1990	—	—	—	0.10	-
1991	—	—	—	0.10	-
1992	—	—	—	0.10	-
1993	—	—	—	0.10	-
1995	—	—	—	0.10	-
1997	—	—	—	0.10	-
1998	—	—	—	0.10	-
1999	—	—	—	0.10	-
2000	—	—	—	0.10	-
2001	—	—	—	0.10	-
2002	—	—	—	0.10	-

Y# 277 2 GROSZE **Composition:** Brass

Date	F	VF	XF	Unc	B
1990	—	—	—	0.15	-
1991	—	—	—	0.15	-
1992	—	—	—	0.15	-
1997	—	—	—	0.15	-
1998	—	—	—	0.15	-
1999	—	—	—	0.15	-
2000	—	—	—	0.15	-
2001	—	—	—	0.15	-

Y# 278 5 GROSZY **Composition:** Brass

Date	F	VF	XF	Unc	B
1990	—	—	—	0.25	-
1991	—	—	—	0.25	-
1992	—	—	—	0.25	-
1993	—	—	—	0.25	-
1998	—	—	—	0.25	-
1999	—	—	—	0.25	-
2000	—	—	—	0.25	-
2001	—	—	—	0.25	-

Y# 279 10 GROSZY **Composition:** Copper-Nickel

Date	F	VF	XF	Unc	B
1990	—	—	—	0.40	-
1991	—	—	—	0.40	-
1992	—	—	—	0.40	-
1993	—	—	—	0.40	-
1998	—	—	—	0.40	-
1999	—	—	—	0.40	-
2000	—	—	—	0.40	-

Y# 280 20 GROSZY **Composition:** Copper-Nickel

Date	F	VF	XF	Unc	B
1990	—	—	—	0.65	-
1991	—	—	—	0.65	-
1992	—	—	—	0.65	-
1996	—	—	—	0.65	-
1997	—	—	—	0.65	-
1998	—	—	—	0.65	-

Date	F	VF	XF	Unc	BU
1999	—	—	—	0.65	—
2000	—	—	—	0.65	—

Y# 281 50 GROSZY **Composition:** Copper-Nickel

Date	F	VF	XF	Unc	BU
1990	—	—	—	1.00	—
1991	—	—	—	1.00	—
1992	—	—	—	1.00	—
1995	—	—	—	1.00	—
1996	—	—	—	1.00	—
1997	—	—	—	1.00	—
1998	—	—	—	1.00	—

Y# 282 ZLOTY **Composition:** Copper-Nickel

Date	F	VF	XF	Unc	BU
1990	—	—	—	1.75	—
1991	—	—	—	1.75	—
1992	—	—	—	1.75	—
1993	—	—	—	1.75	—
1994	—	—	—	1.75	—
1995	—	—	—	1.75	—

Y# 283 2 ZLOTE **Ring Composition:** Brass **Center Composition:** Copper-Nickel

Date	F	VF	XF	Unc	BU
1994	—	—	—	4.00	—
1995	—	—	—	4.00	—
1998	—	—	—	4.00	—

Y# 285 2 ZLOTE **Composition:** Copper-Nickel **Subject:** 55th Anniversary - Katyn Forest Massacre

Date	Mintage	F	VF	XF	Unc	BU
1995	300,000	—	—	—	3.50	—

Y# 289 2 ZLOTE **Composition:** Copper-Nickel **Reverse:** European catfish

Date	Mintage	F	VF	XF	Unc	BU
1995	300,000	—	—	—	5.00	—

Y# 297 2 ZLOTE **Composition:** Copper-Nickel **Subject:** 75th Anniversary - Battle of Warsaw

Date	Mintage	F	VF	XF	Unc	BU
1995	300,000	—	—	—	3.50	—

Y# 300 2 ZLOTE **Composition:** Copper-Nickel **Series:** 1996 Olympic Games **Reverse:** Centennial

Date	F	VF	XF	Unc	BU
1995	—	—	—	3.50	—

Y# 303 2 ZLOTE **Composition:** Copper-Nickel **Series:** 1996 Olympics - Atlanta **Reverse:** Wrestling

Date	F	VF	XF	Unc	BU
1995	—	—	—	3.50	—

Y# 310 2 ZLOTE **Composition:** Copper-Nickel **Series:** 1996 Olympics - Atlanta **Reverse:** Lazienki Royal Palace

Date	Mintage	F	VF	XF	Unc	BU
1995	287,000	—	—	—	3.75	—

Y# 306 2 ZLOTE **Composition:** Brass **Reverse:** Bust of Zygmunt II

Date	Mintage	F	VF	XF	Unc	BU
1996	200,000	—	—	—	4.00	—

Y# 311 2 ZLOTE **Composition:** Copper-Zinc-Tin **Reverse:** Hedgehog with young

Date	F	VF	XF	Unc	BU
1996	—	—	—	9.00	—

Y# 313 2 ZLOTE **Composition:** Copper-Aluminum-Zinc-Tin **Reverse:** Ligzbark Warminski Castle, with Bishop's arms

Date	F	VF	XF	Unc	BU
1996	—	—	—	3.00	—

Y# 315 2 ZLOTE **Composition:** Copper-Aluminum-Zinc-Tin **Reverse:** Henryk Sienkiewicz

Date	F	VF	XF	Unc	BU
1996	—	—	—	3.00	—

Y# 325 2 ZLOTE **Composition:** Brass **Obverse:** Polish eagle **Reverse:** Stefan Batory

Date	F	VF	XF	Unc	BU
1997	—	—	—	3.50	—

Y# 329 2 ZLOTE **Composition:** Brass **Obverse:** Polish eagle **Reverse:** Stag beetle **Note:** Jelenek Rogacz - Lucanus cervus.

Date	F	VF	XF	Unc	BU
1997	—	—	—	5.00	—

Y# 331 2 ZLOTE **Composition:** Brass **Obverse:** Polish eagle **Reverse:** Zamek W Pieskowej Skale

Date	F	VF	XF	Unc	BU
1997	—	—	—	3.00	—

Y# 333 2 ZLOTE **Composition:** Copper-Aluminum-Zinc-Tin **Obverse:** Polish eagle **Reverse:** Pawel Edmund Strzelecki

Date	F	VF	XF	Unc	BU
1997	—	—	—	5.00	—

Y# 335 2 ZLOTE **Composition:** Brass **Series:** Nagano Olympics **Obverse:** Polish eagle **Reverse:** Snow boarder

Date	Mintage	F	VF	XF	Unc	BU
1998	400,000	—	—	—	3.00	—

Y# 336 2 ZLOTE **Composition:** Brass **Obverse:** Polish eagle **Reverse:** Sigismund III (1587-1632)

Date	Mintage	F	VF	XF	Unc	BU
1998	400,000	—	—	—	3.00	—

Y# 340 2 ZLOTE **Composition:** Brass **Obverse:** Polish eagle **Reverse:** Popucha Paskowka - Toad

Date	F	VF	XF	Unc	BU
1998	—	—	—	3.75	—

Y# 344 2 ZLOTE **Composition:** Brass **Subject:** Discovery of Radium and Polomium **Obverse:** Polish eagle

Date	F	VF	XF	Unc	BU
1998	—	—	—	3.00	—

Y# 347 2 ZLOTE **Composition:** Brass **Obverse:** Polish eagle **Reverse:** Zamek W. Korniku - Palace

Date	Mintage	F	VF	XF	Unc	BU
1998	400,000	—	—	—	3.50	—

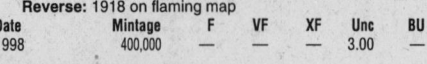

Y# 349 2 ZLOTE **Composition:** Brass **Subject:** 80th Anniversary - Polish Independence **Obverse:** Polish eagle **Reverse:** 1918 on flaming map

Date	Mintage	F	VF	XF	Unc	BU
1998	400,000	—	—	—	3.00	—

Y# 352 2 ZLOTE **Composition:** Brass **Subject:** 200th Birthday - Adam Mickiewicz **Obverse:** Polish eagle **Reverse:** Portrait, dates

Date	Mintage	F	VF	XF	Unc	BU
1998	400,000	—	—	—	3.00	—

Y# 355 2 ZLOTE **Composition:** Brass **Obverse:** Polish eagle **Reverse:** Gray wolves and cubs **Edge Lettering:** POLSKI NARODOWY BANK

Date	F	VF	XF	Unc	BU
1999	—	—	—	3.50	—

Y# 356 2 ZLOTE **Composition:** Brass **Obverse:** Polish eagle **Reverse:** Portrait Juliusz Slowacki, dates

Date	F	VF	XF	Unc	BU
1999	—	—	—	3.00	—

Y# 357 2 ZLOTE **Composition:** Brass **Obverse:** Polish eagle **Reverse:** NATO globe, soldiers rapelling from helicopter **Edge Lettering:** NARODOWY BANK POLSKI

Date	Mintage	F	VF	XF	Unc	BU
1999	450,000	—	—	—	3.00	—

Y# 358 2 ZLOTE **Composition:** Brass **Obverse:** Polish eagle **Reverse:** Portrait of Ernest Malinowsky above slanted text

Date	F	VF	XF	Unc	BU
1999	—	—	—	3.00	—

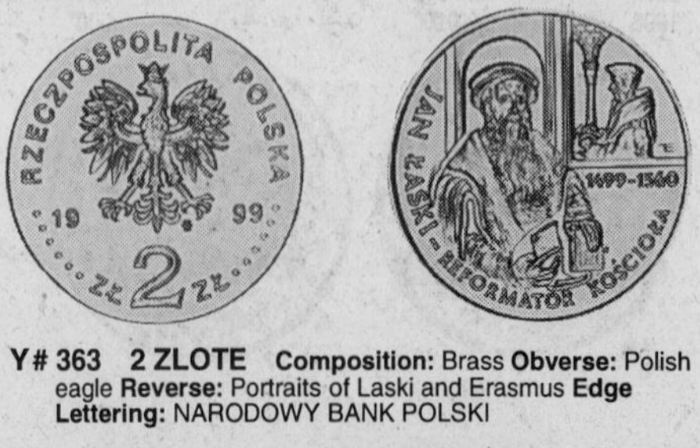

Y# 363 2 ZLOTE **Composition:** Brass **Obverse:** Polish eagle **Reverse:** Portraits of Laski and Erasmus **Edge Lettering:** NARODOWY BANK POLSKI

Date	Mintage	F	VF	XF	Unc	BU
1999	450,000	—	—	—	3.00	—

Y# 365 2 ZLOTE **Composition:** Brass **Obverse:** Polish eagle **Reverse:** Fryderyk Chopin with stylized piano and music score

Date	Mintage	F	VF	XF	Unc	BU
1999	420,000	—	—	—	3.00	—

Y# 368 2 ZLOTE **Composition:** Brass **Obverse:** Polish eagle **Reverse:** Portrait of Wladyslaw IV **Edge Lettering:** NARODOWY BANK POLSKI

Date	Mintage	F	VF	XF	Unc	BU
1999	500,000	—	—	—	3.00	—

Y# 372 2 ZLOTE **Composition:** Brass **Obverse:** Polish eagle **Reverse:** Radzyn Podlaski Palace behind sculpted arms

Date	Mintage	F	VF	XF	Unc	BU
1999	450,000	—	—	—	3.50	—

Y# 404 2 ZLOTE **Weight:** 8.1500 g. **Composition:** Brass **Subject:** Grudnia 1970 **Obverse:** Crowned eagle **Reverse:** Fist **Edge:** "NBP" repeatedly **Size:** 26.7 mm.

Date	Mintage	F	VF	XF	Unc	BU
2000	750,000	—	—	—	3.00	—

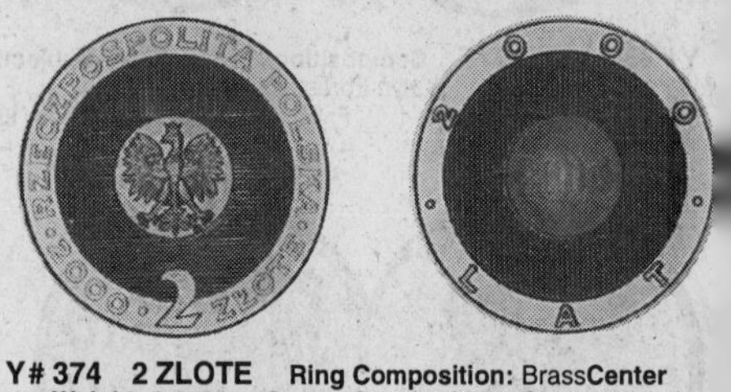

Y# 374 2 ZLOTE **Ring Composition:** BrassCenter **Weight:** 8.3100 g. **Center Composition:** Copper-Nickel **Subject:** Millennium **Obverse:** Crowned eagle in center **Reverse:** Latent image dates in center **Edge Lettering:** NARODOWY BANK POLSKI

Date	Mintage	F	VF	XF	Unc	BU
2000	2,000	—	—	—	3.00	—

Y#376 2 ZLOTE **Weight:** 8.1500 g. **Composition:** Brass **Subject:** Holy Year **Obverse:** Polish eagle **Reverse:** Cross with holy symbolic animals

Date	Mintage	F	VF	XF	Unc	BU
2000	1,500	—	—	—	5.00	—

Y#377 2 ZLOTE **Weight:** 8.1500 g. **Composition:** Brass **Subject:** 1000th Anniversary - Gniezno Convention **Reverse:** Denar coin design of Boleslaw Chrobry

Date	Mintage	F	VF	XF	Unc	BU
2000	450,000	—	—	—	5.00	—

Y#388 2 ZLOTE **Weight:** 8.1400 g. **Composition:** Brass **Subject:** "Dudek-Upupa epops" **Obverse:** Polish eagle **Reverse:** Long-billed Hoopoe **Edge Lettering:** NARODOWY BANK POLSKI **Size:** 26.8 mm.

Date	F	VF	XF	Unc	BU
2000	—	—	—	3.00	—

Y#389 2 ZLOTE **Weight:** 8.1400 g. **Composition:** Brass **Subject:** 1000th Anniversary - Wroclawia (Breslau) **Obverse:** Polish eagle **Reverse:** Jesus with city view in background

Date	F	VF	XF	Unc	BU
2000	—	—	—	3.00	—

Y#390 2 ZLOTE **Weight:** 8.1400 g. **Composition:** Brass **Reverse:** Wilanowie Palace

Date	F	VF	XF	Unc	BU
2000	—	—	—	3.00	—

Y#394 2 ZLOTE **Weight:** 8.2200 g. **Composition:** Brass **Subject:** Solidarity **Reverse:** Solidarity logo, map, children **Edge Lettering:** NARODOWY BANK POLSKI

Date	F	VF	XF	Unc	BU
2000	—	—	—	3.00	—

Y#398 2 ZLOTE **Weight:** 8.2200 g. **Composition:** Brass **Obverse:** Crowned eagle **Reverse:** Bust Jan II Kazimierz facing **Edge Lettering:** POLSKA NARODOWY BANK **Note:** Jan II Kazimierz - 1648-68.

Date	F	VF	XF	Unc	BU
2000	—	—	—	3.00	—

Y#421 2 ZLOTE **Weight:** 8.1000 g. **Composition:** Brass **Issuer:** Michal Siedlecki **Obverse:** Eagle **Reverse:** Portrait and art work **Edge:** "NBP" eight times **Size:** 26.8 mm.

Date	F	VF	XF	Unc	BU
2001	—	—	—	3.00	—

Y#422 2 ZLOTE **Composition:** Brass **Subject:** Koledicy **Obverse:** Eagle **Reverse:** Christmas celebration scene

Date	F	VF	XF	Unc	BU
2001	—	—	—	3.00	—

Y#408 2 ZLOTE **Weight:** 8.1500 g. **Composition:** Brass **Subject:** Wieliczka Salt Mine **Obverse:** Crowned eagle **Reverse:** Ancient salt miners

Date	Mintage	F	VF	XF	Unc	BU
2001	500,000	—	—	—	3.00	—

Y#410 2 ZLOTE **Weight:** 8.1500 g. **Composition:** Brass **Subject:** Amber Route **Obverse:** Crowned eagle **Reverse:** Ancient Roman coin and man with route marked in stars

Date	Mintage	F	VF	XF	Unc	BU
2001	500,000	—	—	—	3.00	—

Y#412 2 ZLOTE **Weight:** 8.1500 g. **Composition:** Brass **Subject:** 15th Constitutional Congress **Obverse:** Crowned eagle **Reverse:** Crowned eagle head and scale **Edge:** "*NBP*" eight times **Size:** 27 mm.

Date	Mintage	F	VF	XF	Unc	BU
2001	500,000	—	—	—	3.00	—

Y#414 2 ZLOTE **Weight:** 8.1500 g. **Composition:** Brass **Obverse:** Crowned eagle **Reverse:** Flying Swallowtail butterfly **Edge:** "*NBP*" eight times **Size:** 27 mm.

Date	Mintage	F	VF	XF	Unc	BU
2001	600,000	—	—	—	3.50	—

Y#418 2 ZLOTE **Weight:** 8.1500 g. **Composition:** Brass **Subject:** Cardinal Stefan Wyszynski **Obverse:** Polish eagle **Reverse:** Portrait wearing mitre **Edge:** "NBP" eight times **Size:** 27 mm.

Date	Mintage	F	VF	XF	Unc	BU
2001	1,200	—	—	—	3.00	—

Y#423 2 ZLOTE **Weight:** 8.1500 g. **Composition:** Brass **Subject:** Jan III Sobieski **Obverse:** Polish eagle **Reverse:** Half bust of Sobieski facing **Edge Lettering:** *NBP* repeated **Size:** 26.8 mm.

Date	F	VF	XF	Unc	BU
2001	—	—	—	3.00	—

Y#426 2 ZLOTE **Weight:** 8.1500 g. **Composition:** Brass **Subject:** Henryk Wieniawski **Obverse:** Polish eagle **Reverse:** Bust of Wieniawski facing right **Edge Lettering:** *NBP* repeated **Size:** 26.8 mm.

Date	Mintage	F	VF	XF	Unc	BU
2001	600,000	—	—	—	3.00	—

Y#427 2 ZLOTE **Weight:** 8.1000 g. **Composition:** Brass **Obverse:** Crowned eagle **Reverse:** Two pond turtles **Edge:** Lettered **Edge Lettering:** "NBP" repeatedly **Size:** 26.7 mm.

Date	Mintage	F	VF	XF	Unc	BU
2002	750,000	—	—	—	5.00	—

Y#431 2 ZLOTE **Weight:** 8.1500 g. **Composition:** Brass **Subject:** Bronislaw Malinowski **Obverse:** Crowned eagle **Reverse:** Portrait and Trobriand Islanders **Edge Lettering:** "NBP" eight times **Size:** 27 mm.

Date	Mintage	F	VF	XF	Unc	BU
2002	680,000	—	—	—	3.50	—

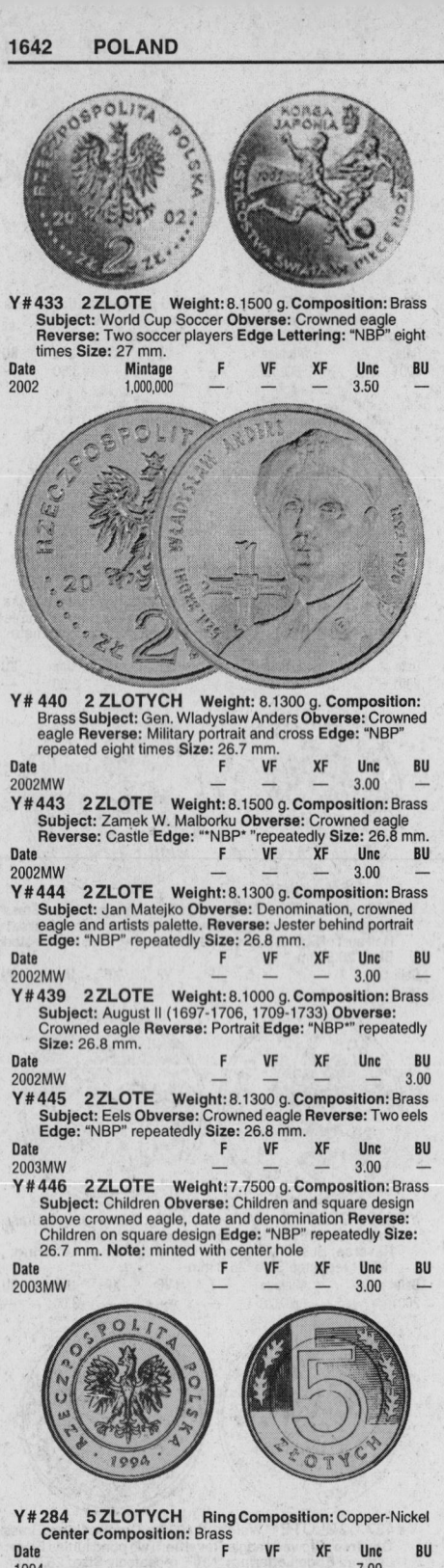

Y#433 2 ZLOTE **Weight:** 8.1500 g. **Composition:** Brass **Subject:** World Cup Soccer **Obverse:** Crowned eagle **Reverse:** Two soccer players **Edge Lettering:** "NBP" eight times **Size:** 27 mm.

Date	Mintage	F	VF	XF	Unc	BU
2002	1,000,000	—	—	—	3.50	—

Y# 440 2 ZLOTYCH **Weight:** 8.1300 g. **Composition:** Brass **Subject:** Gen. Wladyslaw Anders **Obverse:** Crowned eagle **Reverse:** Military portrait and cross **Edge:** "NBP" repeated eight times **Size:** 26.7 mm.

Date	F	VF	XF	Unc	BU
2002MW	—	—	—	3.00	—

Y#443 2 ZLOTE **Weight:** 8.1500 g. **Composition:** Brass **Subject:** Zamek W. Malborku **Obverse:** Crowned eagle **Reverse:** Castle **Edge:** "*NBP* "repeatedly **Size:** 26.8 mm.

Date	F	VF	XF	Unc	BU
2002MW	—	—	—	3.00	—

Y#444 2 ZLOTE **Weight:** 8.1300 g. **Composition:** Brass **Subject:** Jan Matejko **Obverse:** Denomination, crowned eagle and artists palette. **Reverse:** Jester behind portrait **Edge:** "NBP" repeatedly **Size:** 26.8 mm.

Date	F	VF	XF	Unc	BU
2002MW	—	—	—	3.00	—

Y#439 2 ZLOTE **Weight:** 8.1000 g. **Composition:** Brass **Subject:** August II (1697-1706, 1709-1733) **Obverse:** Crowned eagle **Reverse:** Portrait **Edge:** "NBP*" repeatedly **Size:** 26.8 mm.

Date	F	VF	XF	Unc	BU
2002MW	—	—	—	—	3.00

Y#445 2 ZLOTE **Weight:** 8.1300 g. **Composition:** Brass **Subject:** Eels **Obverse:** Crowned eagle **Reverse:** Two eels **Edge:** "NBP" repeatedly **Size:** 26.8 mm.

Date	F	VF	XF	Unc	BU
2003MW	—	—	—	3.00	—

Y#446 2 ZLOTE **Weight:** 7.7500 g. **Composition:** Brass **Subject:** Children **Obverse:** Children and square design above crowned eagle, date and denomination **Reverse:** Children on square design **Edge:** "NBP" repeatedly **Size:** 26.7 mm. **Note:** minted with center hole

Date	F	VF	XF	Unc	BU
2003MW	—	—	—	3.00	—

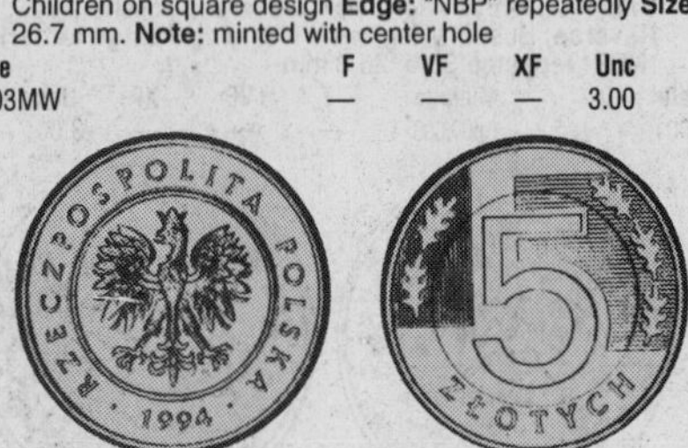

Y#284 5 ZLOTYCH **Ring Composition:** Copper-Nickel **Center Composition:** Brass

Date	F	VF	XF	Unc	BU
1994	—	—	—	7.00	—
1996	—	—	—	7.00	—

Y# 287 10 ZLOTYCH **Weight:** 16.5500 g. **Composition:** 0.7500 Silver .3979 oz. ASW **Reverse:** Capture of Berlin

Date	Mintage	F	VF	XF	Unc	BU
1995 Proof	12,000	Value: 22.50				

Y# 301 10 ZLOTYCH **Weight:** 16.4400 g. **Composition:** 0.9250 Silver .4889 oz. ASW **Series:** 1996 Olympics **Reverse:** Centennial - Atlanta

Date	Mintage	F	VF	XF	Unc	BU
1995 Proof	20,000	Value: 20.00				

Y# 305 10 ZLOTYCH **Weight:** 16.5000 g. **Composition:** 0.9250 Silver .4907 oz. ASW **Subject:** Centennial of Organized Peasant Movement **Reverse:** Wincenty Witos

Date	Mintage	F	VF	XF	Unc	BU
1995 Proof	20,000	Value: 25.00				

Y# 307 10 ZLOTYCH **Weight:** 16.5000 g. **Composition:** 0.9250 Silver .4907 oz. ASW **Reverse:** Bust of Zygmunt II August left

Date	Mintage	F	VF	XF	Unc	BU
1996 Proof	15,000	Value: 25.00				

Y# 308 10 ZLOTYCH **Weight:** 16.5000 g. **Composition:** 0.9250 Silver .4907 oz. ASW **Reverse:** Half-length figure of Zygmunt II August

Date	Mintage	F	VF	XF	Unc	BU
1996 Proof	5,000	Value: 28.00				

Y# 317 10 ZLOTYCH **Weight:** 16.5000 g. **Composition:** 0.9250 Silver .4907 oz. ASW **Reverse:** Stanislaw Mikolajczyk

Date	Mintage	F	VF	XF	Unc	BU
1996 Proof	15,000	Value: 25.00				

Y# 318 10 ZLOTYCH **Weight:** 16.5000 g. **Composition:** 0.9250 Silver .4907 oz. ASW **Reverse:** Mazurka of Dabrowski

Date	Mintage	F	VF	XF	Unc
1996 Proof	15,000	Value: 25.00			

Y# 324 10 ZLOTYCH **Weight:** 16.5000 g. **Composition:** 0.9250 Silver .4907 oz. ASW **Subject:** 40 Anniversary - Poznan Workers Protest **Obverse:** Polish eagle

Date	F	VF	XF	Unc
1996 Proof	—	Value: 25.00		

Y# 321 10 ZLOTYCH **Weight:** 14.1400 g. **Composition:** 0.9250 Silver .4205 oz. ASW **Subject:** St. Adalbert's Martyrdom **Obverse:** Polish eagle **Reverse:** Bi and funeral scenes

Date	Mintage	F	VF	XF	Unc
1997 Proof	25,000	Value: 25.00			

Y# 322 10 ZLOTYCH **Weight:** 14.1400 g. **Composition:** 0.9250 Silver .4205 oz. ASW **Subject:** 46 Eucharistic Congress **Obverse:** Polish eagle in design **Reverse:** Pope

Date	Mintage	F	VF	XF	Unc
1997 Proof	Est. 50,000	Value: 28.00			

Y# 326 10 ZLOTYCH **Weight:** 14.1400 g. **Composition:** 0.9250 Silver .4205 oz. ASW **Obverse:** Polish eagle **Reverse:** Stefan Batory

Date	Mintage	F	VF	XF	Unc
1997 Proof	5,000	Value: 32.50			

Y# 327 10 ZLOTYCH **Weight:** 14.1400 g. **Composition:** 0.9250 Silver .4205 oz. ASW **Obverse:** Polish eagle **Reverse:** Stefan Batory

Date	Mintage	F	VF	XF	Unc	BU
1997 Proof	15,000	Value: 22.50				

Y# 334 10 ZLOTYCH **Weight:** 14.1400 g. **Composition:** 0.9250 Silver .4205 oz. ASW **Obverse:** Polish eagle **Reverse:** Pawel Edmund Strzelecki **Edge Lettering:** 200 LECIE URODZIN

Date	Mintage	F	VF	XF	Unc	BU
1997 Proof	20,000	Value: 25.00				

Y# 337 10 ZLOTYCH **Weight:** 14.1400 g. **Composition:** 0.9250 Silver .4205 oz. ASW **Obverse:** Polish eagle **Reverse:** Sigismund III (1587-1632)

Date	Mintage	F	VF	XF	Unc	BU
1998 Proof	22,000	Value: 25.00				

Y# 338 10 ZLOTYCH **Weight:** 14.1400 g. **Composition:** 0.9250 Silver .4205 oz. ASW **Obverse:** Polish eagle **Reverse:** Sigismund III (1587-1632)

Date	Mintage	F	VF	XF	Unc	BU
1998 Proof	14,000	Value: 27.50				

Y# 341 10 ZLOTYCH **Weight:** 14.1400 g. **Composition:** 0.9250 Silver .4205 oz. ASW **Series:** 1998 Winter Olympics **Obverse:** Polish eagle **Reverse:** Snow boarder

Date	Mintage	F	VF	XF	Unc	BU
1998 Proof	30,000	Value: 17.50				

Y# 342 10 ZLOTYCH **Weight:** 14.1400 g. **Composition:** 0.9250 Silver .4205 oz. ASW **Obverse:** Polish eagle **Reverse:** Brigadier General August Emil Fieldorf

Date	F	VF	XF	Unc	BU
1998 Proof	—	Value: 32.50			

Y# 345 10 ZLOTYCH **Weight:** 14.1400 g. **Composition:** 0.9250 Silver .4205 oz. ASW **Obverse:** Denomination and eagles in cross design **Reverse:** Pope John Paul II

Date	Mintage	F	VF	XF	Unc	BU
1998 Proof	65,000	Value: 35.00				

Y# 350 10 ZLOTYCH **Weight:** 14.1400 g. **Composition:** 0.9250 Silver .4205 oz. ASW **Subject:** 80th Anniversary - Polish Independence **Obverse:** Polish eagle on stylized flames **Reverse:** Anniversary dates

Date	Mintage	F	VF	XF	Unc	BU
1998 Proof	20,000	Value: 27.50				

Y# 351 10 ZLOTYCH **Weight:** 14.1400 g. **Composition:** 0.9250 Silver .4205 oz. ASW **Subject:** Universal Declaration of Human Rights **Obverse:** Polish eagle **Reverse:** Human figure between two hands **Edge Lettering:** 50 ROCZNICA UCHWALENIA (three times)

Date	Mintage	F	VF	XF	Unc	BU
1998 Proof	14,000	Value: 27.50				

Y# 359 10 ZLOTYCH **Weight:** 14.1400 g. **Composition:** 0.9250 Silver .4205 oz. ASW **Subject:** NATO **Obverse:** Polish eagle **Reverse:** NATO globe, soldiers rapelling from helicopter

Date	Mintage	F	VF	XF	Unc	BU
1999 Proof	22,000	Value: 20.00				

Y# 360 10 ZLOTYCH **Weight:** 14.1400 g. **Composition:** 0.9250 Silver .4205 oz. ASW **Obverse:** Crucifix designs and Polish eagle **Reverse:** Portrait of Pope John Paul II and dove

Date	Mintage	F	VF	XF	Unc	BU
1999 Proof	70,000	Value: 30.00				

Y# 362 10 ZLOTYCH **Weight:** 14.1400 g. **Composition:** 0.9250 Silver .4205 oz. ASW **Obverse:** Polish eagle **Reverse:** Queen Jadwiga and coat of arms **Edge Lettering:** 1400-2000. (five times) **Note:** Cracow University.

Date	Mintage	F	VF	XF	Unc	BU
1999 Proof	22,000	Value: 21.50				

Y# 364 10 ZLOTYCH **Weight:** 14.1400 g. **Composition:** 0.9250 Silver .4205 oz. ASW **Obverse:** Polish eagle above windowed brick wall **Reverse:** Portrait of Laski with Erasmus in background **Note:** Jan Laski 1490-1560.

Date	Mintage	F	VF	XF	Unc	BU
1999 Proof	20,000	Value: 21.50				

Y# 366 10 ZLOTYCH **Weight:** 14.1400 g. **Composition:** 0.9250 Silver .4205 oz. ASW **Obverse:** Polish eagle over twisted chords **Reverse:** Portrait of Fryderyk Chopin with stylized design

Date	Mintage	F	VF	XF	Unc	BU
1999 Proof	27,000	Value: 21.50				

Y# 369 10 ZLOTYCH **Weight:** 14.1400 g. **Composition:** 0.9250 Silver .4205 oz. ASW **Obverse:** Polish eagle **Reverse:** Portrait of Wladyslaw IV, dates

Date	Mintage	F	VF	XF	Unc	BU
1999 Proof	20,000	Value: 21.50				

Y# 370 10 ZLOTYCH **Weight:** 14.1400 g. **Composition:** 0.9250 Silver .4205 oz. ASW **Obverse:** Polish eagle **Reverse:** Framed half-length portrait of Wladyslaw IV

Date	Mintage	F	VF	XF	Unc	BU
1999 Proof	13,000	Value: 25.00				

Y# 378 10 ZLOTYCH Weight: 14.1400 g. **Composition:** 0.9250 Silver .4205 oz. ASW **Obverse:** World globe and Polish eagle **Reverse:** Bust Ernest Malinowski facing, train in background **Edge Lettering:** 100-LECIE SMIERCI twice

Date		F	VF	XF	Unc	BU
1999 Proof	—	Value: 32.50				

Y# 379 10 ZLOTYCH Weight: 14.1400 g. **Composition:** 0.9250 Silver .4205 oz. ASW **Obverse:** Inscription and Polish eagle **Reverse:** Bust Juliusz Slowacki half right **Edge:** Plain

Date		F	VF	XF	Unc	BU
1999 Proof	—	Value: 27.50				

Y# 380 10 ZLOTYCH Weight: 14.1400 g. **Composition:** 0.9250 Silver .4205 oz. ASW **Subject:** Holy Year **Obverse:** Polish eagle in frame **Reverse:** Cross with symbols of the evangelists **Edge Lettering:** WIELKI JUBILEUSZ ROKU 2000

Date	Mintage	F	VF	XF	Unc	BU
2000 Proof	60,000	Value: 32.50				

Y# 381 10 ZLOTYCH Weight: 14.1400 g. **Composition:** 0.9250 Silver .4205 oz. ASW **Subject:** 1000th Anniversary - Gniezno Convention **Obverse:** Old coin designs in oxidized center **Reverse:** Seated figures of Boleslaw Chrobry and Otto III in oxidized center **Edge:** Plain

Date	Mintage	F	VF	XF	Unc	BU
2000 Proof	32,000	Value: 32.50				

Y# 392 10 ZLOTYCH Weight: 14.2000 g. **Composition:** 0.9250 Silver .4223 oz. ASW **Subject:** 1000 Years Wroclaw (Breslau) **Obverse:** Polish eagle in front of city view **Reverse:** City arms in arch **Edge:** Plain

Date		F	VF	XF	Unc	BU
2000 Proof	—	Value: 25.00				

Y# 395 10 ZLOTYCH Weight: 14.2200 g. **Composition:** 0.9250 Silver .4229 oz. ASW **Subject:** Solidarity **Obverse:** Polish eagle **Reverse:** Solidarity logo and two children **Edge:** Plain **Size:** 32 mm.

Date		F	VF	XF	Unc	BU
2000 Proof	—	Value: 27.50				

Y# 400 10 ZLOTYCH Subject: Jan Kazimierz II (1648-68) **Obverse:** Crowned eagle **Reverse:** Half-length portrait with crown **Edge:** Plain **Size:** 32 mm.

Date	Mintage	F	VF	XF	Unc	BU
2000 Proof	14,000	—	—	—	27.50	—

Y# 401 10 ZLOTYCH Weight: 14.1400 g. **Composition:** 0.9250 Silver .4205 oz. ASW **Subject:** Jan Kazimierz II (1648-68) **Obverse:** Crowned eagle **Reverse:** Portrait

Date	Mintage	F	VF	XF	Unc	BU
2000 Proof	20,000	—	—	—	27.50	—

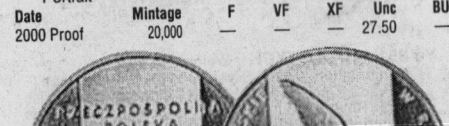

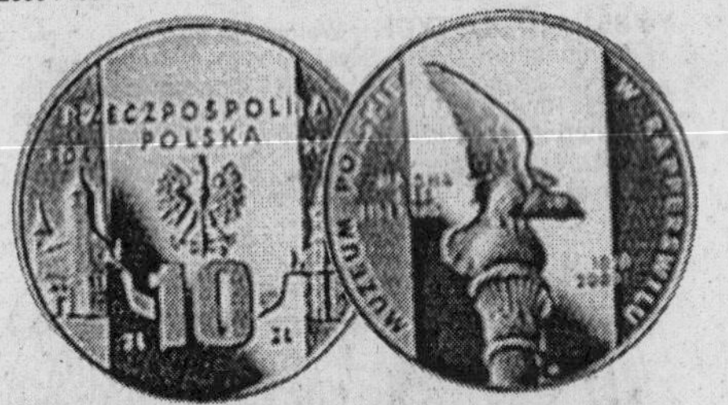

Y# 403 10 ZLOTYCH Weight: 14.1400 g. **Composition:** 0.9250 Silver .4205 oz. ASW **Subject:** Rapperswil Polish Museum **Obverse:** Crowned eagle and denomination between two buildings **Reverse:** Eagle-topped column

Date	Mintage	F	VF	XF	Unc	BU
2000 Proof	25,000	—	—	—	27.50	—

Y# 405 10 ZLOTYCH Weight: 14.1400 g. **Composition:** 0.9250 Silver .4205 oz. ASW **Subject:** Grudnia 1970 **Obverse:** Two crowned eagles **Reverse:** Shadow figures on pavement

Date	Mintage	F	VF	XF	Unc	BU
2000 Proof	37,000	—	—	—	27.50	—

Note: Antiqued finish

Y# 406 10 ZLOTYCH Weight: 14.1400 g. **Composition:** 0.9250 Silver .4205 oz. ASW **Subject:** Year 2001 **Obverse:** Crowned eagle **Reverse:** Printed circuit board

Date	Mintage	F	VF	XF	Unc	BU
2001 Proof	35,000	—	—	—	27.50	—

Y# 413 10 ZLOTYCH Weight: 14.1400 g. **Composition:** 0.9250 Silver .4205 oz. ASW **Subject:** 15th Constitutional Tribunal **Obverse:** Crowned eagle suspended from a judge's neck chain **Reverse:** Crowned eagle head and balance scale **Edge Lettering:** "TRYBUNAL KONSTYTUCYJNY W SLUZBIE PANSTWA PRAWA" **Size:** 32 mm.

Date	Mintage	F	VF	XF	Unc	BU
2001 Proof	25,000	—	—	—	22.50	—

Y# 419 10 ZLOTYCH Weight: 14.1400 g. **Composition:** 0.9250 Silver .4205 oz. ASW **Subject:** Cardinal Stefan Wyszynski **Obverse:** Polish eagle above ribbon **Reverse:** Portrait with raised hands **Edge Lettering:** "100.ROCZNIA URODZIN" **Size:** 32 mm.

Date	Mintage	F	VF	XF	Unc	BU
2001 Proof	60,000	Value: 27.50				

Y# 425 10 ZLOTYCH Weight: 14.2100 g. **Composition:** 0.9250 Silver 0.4226 oz. ASW **Subject:** Jan III Sobieski **Obverse:** Polish eagle above denomination **Reverse:** 3/4 bust Jan III Sobieski lower left, army in background **Edge:** Plain **Size:** 32 mm.

Date		F	VF	XF	Unc	BU
2001 Proof	—	Value: 30.00				

Y# 432 10 ZLOTYCH Weight: 14.1400 g. **Composition:** 0.9250 Silver 0.4205 oz. ASW **Subject:** Bronislaw Malinowski **Obverse:** Portrait and crowned eagle **Reverse:** Trobriand Islands village scene **Edge Lettering:** "etnolog, antropolog kultury" **Size:** 32 mm.

Date	Mintage	F	VF	XF	Unc	BU
2002 Proof	33,500	Value: 20.00				

Y# 434 10 ZLOTYCH **Weight:** 14.1400 g. **Composition:** 0.9250 Silver 0.4205 oz. ASW **Subject:** World Cup Soccer **Obverse:** Crowned eagle **Reverse:** Soccer player **Edge Lettering:** "etnolog, antropolog kultury" **Size:** 32 mm.

Date	Mintage	F	VF	XF	Unc	BU
2002 Proof	55,000	Value: 20.00				

Y# 435 10 ZLOTYCH **Weight:** 14.1400 g. **Composition:** 0.9250 Silver 0.4205 oz. ASW **Subject:** World Cup Soccer **Obverse:** Amber soccer ball inset entering goal net **Reverse:** Two soccer players with amber soccer ball inset **Edge Lettering:** "etnolog, antropolog kultury" **Size:** 32 mm.

Date	Mintage	F	VF	XF	Unc	BU
2002 Proof	65,000	Value: 25.00				

Y# 437 10 ZLOTYCH **Weight:** 14.1400 g. **Composition:** 0.9250 Silver 0.4205 oz. ASW **Subject:** Pope John Paul II **Obverse:** Polish eagle and two views of praying Pope **Reverse:** Pope facing radiant Holy Door **Edge:** Plain **Size:** 32 mm.

Date	Mintage	F	VF	XF	Unc	BU
2002 Proof	80,000	Value: 27.50				

Y# 441 10 ZLOTYCH **Weight:** 14.2000 g. **Composition:** 0.9250 Silver 0.4223 oz. ASW **Subject:** Gen. Wladyslaw Anders **Obverse:** Crowned eagle, cross and multicolor flowers **Reverse:** Military portrait **Edge:** Plain **Size:** 32 mm.

Date	F	VF	XF	Unc	BU
2002MW Proof	—	Value: 35.00			

Y# 286 20 ZLOTYCH **Weight:** 31.1100 g. **Composition:** 0.9990 Silver .9990 oz. ASW **Subject:** Katyn Forest Massacre

Date	Mintage	F	VF	XF	Unc	BU
1995 Proof	30,000	Value: 30.00				

Y# 288 20 ZLOTYCH **Weight:** 31.1100 g. **Composition:** 0.9990 Silver .9990 oz. ASW **Subject:** 500th Anniversary - Plock Province

Date	Mintage	F	VF	XF	Unc	BU
1995 Proof	15,000	Value: 35.00				

Y# 290 20 ZLOTYCH **Weight:** 31.1100 g. **Composition:** 0.9990 Silver .9990 oz. ASW **Reverse:** European catfish

Date	Mintage	F	VF	XF	Unc	BU
1995 Proof	20,000	Value: 32.50				

Y# 291 20 ZLOTYCH **Weight:** 31.1100 g. **Composition:** 0.9990 Silver .9990 oz. ASW **Subject:** 50th Anniversary - United Nations

Date	Mintage	F	VF	XF	Unc	BU
1995 Proof	20,000	Value: 32.50				

Y# 296 20 ZLOTYCH **Weight:** 31.1700 g. **Composition:** 0.9990 Silver 1.0011 oz. ASW **Reverse:** Lazienki Royal Palace

Date	Mintage	F	VF	XF	Unc	BU
1995 Prof	20,000	Value: 35.00				

Y# 298 20 ZLOTYCH **Weight:** 30.9200 g. **Composition:** 0.9250 Silver .9195 oz. ASW **Subject:** 75th Anniversary - Battle of Warsaw

Date	Mintage	F	VF	XF	Unc	BU
1995 Proof	20,000	Value: 32.50				

Y# 302 20 ZLOTYCH **Weight:** 31.0500 g. **Composition:** 0.9250 Silver .9234 oz. ASW **Reverse:** Copernicus and Ecu

Date	Mintage	F	VF	XF	Unc	BU
1995 Proof	15,000	Value: 37.50				

Y# 304 20 ZLOTYCH **Weight:** 31.1000 g. **Composition:** 0.9250 Silver .9240 oz. ASW **Series:** 1996 Olympics - Atlanta **Reverse:** Wrestlers

Date	F	VF	XF	Unc	BU
1995 Proof	—	Value: 37.50			

Y# 309 20 ZLOTYCH **Weight:** 31.1000 g. **Composition:** 0.9250 Silver .9240 oz. ASW **Subject:** 400th Anniversary - Warsaw as Capital City

Date	Mintage	F	VF	XF	Unc	BU
1996 Proof	Est. 20,000	Value: 27.50				

Y# 330 20 ZLOTYCH **Weight:** 28.5200 g. **Composition:** 0.9250 Silver .8482 oz. ASW **Obverse:** Polish eagle **Reverse:** Stag beetle **Note:** Jelonek Rogacz - Lucanus Cervus.

Date	F	VF	XF	Unc	BU
1997 Proof	—	Value: 32.50			

Y# 354 20 ZLOTYCH **Weight:** 28.1500 g. **Composition:** 0.9250 Silver .8372 oz. ASW **Subject:** Discovery of Radium and Polonium **Obverse:** Atom **Reverse:** Madame and Monsieur Curie and formulas

Date	F	VF	XF	Unc	BU
1998 Proof	—	Value: 32.50			

Y# 312 20 ZLOTYCH **Weight:** 31.1000 g. **Composition:** 0.9250 Silver .9240 oz. ASW **Reverse:** Hedgehog with young

Date	Mintage	F	VF	XF	Unc	BU
1996 Proof	Est. 20,000	Value: 40.00				

Y# 332 20 ZLOTYCH **Weight:** 28.5200 g. **Composition:** 0.9250 Silver .8482 oz. ASW **Obverse:** Polish eagle **Reverse:** Zemek W Pieskowej Skale

Date	F	VF	XF	Unc	BU
1997 Proof	—	Value: 27.50			

Y# 373 20 ZLOTYCH **Weight:** 28.2800 g. **Composition:** 0.9250 Silver .8410 oz. ASW **Obverse:** Polish eagle within inner circle **Reverse:** Radzyn Podlaski Palace behind sculpted arms

Date	Mintage	F	VF	XF	Unc	BU
1999 Proof	15,000	Value: 32.50				

Y# 314 20 ZLOTYCH **Weight:** 31.1000 g. **Composition:** 0.9250 Silver .9240 oz. ASW **Reverse:** Bishop's arms and Lidzibark Warminski castle

Date	Mintage	F	VF	XF	Unc	BU
1996 Proof	Est. 20,000	Value: 27.50				

Y# 343 20 ZLOTYCH **Weight:** 28.4700 g. **Composition:** 0.9250 Silver .8467 oz. ASW **Obverse:** Polish eagle **Reverse:** Ropucha Paskowka - Natterjack Toad

Date	F	VF	XF	Unc	BU
1998 Proof	—	Value: 37.50			

Y# 382 20 ZLOTYCH **Weight:** 28.3000 g. **Composition:** 0.9250 Silver .8416 oz. ASW **Reverse:** Wolf family

Date	F	VF	XF	Unc	BU
1999 Proof	—	Value: 40.00			

Y# 319 20 ZLOTYCH **Weight:** 31.1000 g. **Composition:** 0.9250 Silver .9240 oz. ASW **Subject:** Millennium of Gdansk (Danzig) **Edge Lettering:** MONUMENTUM MILLENNII CIVITATIS GEDANENSIS

Date	Mintage	F	VF	XF	Unc	BU
1996 Proof	20,000	Value: 37.50				

Y# 348 20 ZLOTYCH **Weight:** 28.2800 g. **Composition:** 0.9250 Silver .8410 oz. ASW **Obverse:** Polish eagle **Reverse:** Zamek W. Koniku - Palace

Date	Mintage	F	VF	XF	Unc	BU
1998 Proof	20,000	Value: 37.50				

Y# 387 20 ZLOTYCH **Weight:** 28.3700 g. **Composition:** 0.9250 Silver .8437 oz. ASW **Reverse:** Dudek - Upupa epops - Eurasian Hoopoe

Date	F	VF	XF	Unc	BU
2000 Proof	—	Value: 32.50			

Y# 391 20 ZLOTYCH **Weight:** 28.2400 g. **Composition:** 0.9250 Silver .8398 oz. ASW **Obverse:** Polish eagle **Reverse:** View of Wilanowie Palace through front gate **Edge:** Plain **Size:** 38.5 mm.

Date		F	VF	XF	Unc	BU
2000 Proof	—	Value: 35.00				

Y# 424 20 ZLOTYCH **Weight:** 28.7700 g. **Composition:** 0.9250 Silver 0.8556 oz. ASW **Subject:** Christmas **Obverse:** Ornate city view **Reverse:** Celebration scene including an attached zirconia star **Edge:** Plain **Size:** 38.6 mm. **Note:** Antiqued finish.

Date	F	VF	XF	Unc	BU
2001	—	—	—	35.00	—

Y# 409 20 ZLOTYCH **Weight:** 28.2800 g. **Composition:** 0.9250 Silver .8410 oz. ASW **Subject:** Wieliezce Salt Mine **Obverse:** Crowned eagle and rock **Reverse:** Ancient salt miners **Edge:** Plain **Size:** 38.6 mm.

Date	Mintage	F	VF	XF	Unc	BU
2001 Proof	25,000	—	—	—	40.00	—

Y# 411 20 ZLOTYCH **Weight:** 28.2800 g. **Composition:** 0.9250 Silver .8410 oz. ASW **Subject:** Amber Route **Obverse:** Crowned eagle and two ancient Roman silver cups **Reverse:** Piece of amber mounted above an ancient Roman coin design and map with the route marked with stars **Edge:** Plain **Size:** 38.6 mm.

Date	Mintage	F	VF	XF	Unc	BU
2001	30,000	—	—	—	45.00	—

Note: Antiqued finish

Y# 415 20 ZLOTYCH **Weight:** 28.2800 g. **Composition:** 0.9250 Silver .8410 oz. ASW **Obverse:** Crowned eagle between two flags **Reverse:** Flying Swallowtail butterfly **Edge:** Plain **Size:** 38.6 mm.

Date	Mintage	F	VF	XF	Unc	BU
2001 Proof	27,000	—	—	—	40.00	—

Y# 428 20 ZLOTYCH **Weight:** 28.2800 g. **Composition:** 0.9250 Silver 0.841 oz. ASW **Obverse:** Crowned eagle **Reverse:** Two pond turtles **Edge:** Plain **Size:** 38.6 mm.

Date	Mintage	F	VF	XF	Unc	BU
2002 Proof	35,000	Value: 35.00				

Y# 442 20 ZLOTYCH **Weight:** 28.0500 g. **Composition:** 0.9250 Silver 0.8342 oz. ASW **Subject:** Jan Matejko **Obverse:** Seated figure with crowned eagle at lower right **Reverse:** Portrait with multicolor artist's palette **Edge:** Plain **Shape:** Rectangular **Note:** Actual size 40 x 37.9 millimeters.

Date		F	VF	XF	Unc	BU
2002MW Proof	—	Value: 40.00				

Y# 292 50 ZLOTYCH **Weight:** 3.1000 g. **Composition:** 0.9999 Gold .1000 oz. AGW **Reverse:** Golden eagle

Date	Mintage	F	VF	XF	Unc	BU
1995	2,000	—	—	—	140	—

Y# 293 100 ZLOTYCH **Weight:** 7.7800 g. **Composition:** 0.9999 Gold .2500 oz. AGW **Reverse:** Golden eagle

Date	Mintage	F	VF	XF	Unc	BU
1995	1,500	—	—	—	245	—

Y# 328 100 ZLOTYCH **Weight:** 8.0000 g. **Composition:** 0.9000 Gold .2315 oz. AGW **Obverse:** Polish eagle **Reverse:** Stefan Batory

Date	Mintage	F	VF	XF	Unc	BU
1997 Proof	2,000	Value: 220				

Y# 339 100 ZLOTYCH **Weight:** 8.0000 g. **Composition:** 0.9000 Gold .2315 oz. AGW **Obverse:** Polish eagle **Reverse:** Sigismund III

Date	Mintage	F	VF	XF	Unc	BU
1998 Proof	2,500	Value: 220				

Y# 361 100 ZLOTYCH **Weight:** 8.0000 g. **Composition:** 0.9000 Gold .2315 oz. AGW **Obverse:** Polish eagle in inner circle **Reverse:** Pope John Paul II and crucifix

Date	Mintage	F	VF	XF	Unc	BU
1999 Proof	7,000	Value: 190				

Y# 371 100 ZLOTYCH **Weight:** 8.0000 g. **Composition:** 0.9000 Gold .2315 oz. AGW **Obverse:** Polish eagle **Reverse:** Framed portrait of Wladyslaw IV

Date	Mintage	F	VF	XF	Unc	BU
1999 Proof	2,300	Value: 220				

Y# 383 100 ZLOTYCH **Weight:** 8.0000 g. **Composition:** 0.9000 Gold .2315 oz. AGW **Obverse:** Polish eagle **Reverse:** Bust King Zygmunt II left

Date	Mintage	F	VF	XF	Unc	BU
1999 Proof	2,000	Value: 140				

Y# 384 100 ZLOTYCH **Weight:** 8.0000 g. **Composition:** 0.9000 Gold .2315 oz. AGW **Subject:** 100th Anniversary - Gniezno Convention **Obverse:** Old coin designs **Reverse:** Seated figures of Boleslaw Chrobry and Otto III

Date	Mintage	F	VF	XF	Unc	BU
2000 Proof	2,200	Value: 140				

Y# 396 100 ZLOTYCH **Weight:** 8.0000 g. **Composition:** 0.9000 Gold .2315 oz. AGW **Obverse:** Polish eagle **Reverse:** Half-length bust of Queen Jadwiga facing **Edge:** Plain

Date	Mintage	F	VF	XF	Unc	BU
2000 Proof	2,000	Value: 220				

Y# 402 100 ZLOTYCH **Weight:** 8.0000 g. **Composition:** 0.9000 Gold .2315 oz. AGW **Subject:** Jan Kazimierz II (1648-68) **Obverse:** Crowned eagle **Reverse:** Portrait with name and dates **Edge:** Plain **Size:** 21 mm.

Date	Mintage	F	VF	XF	Unc	BU
2000 Proof	2,000	Value: 225				

Y# 416 100 ZLOTYCH **Weight:** 8.0000 g. **Composition:** 0.9000 Gold .2315 oz. AGW **Subject:** Wladyslaw I (1320-33) **Obverse:** Crowned eagle **Reverse:** Crowned portrait **Edge:** Plain **Size:** 21 mm.

Date	Mintage	F	VF	XF	Unc	BU
2001 Proof	2,000	Value: 225				

Y# 417 100 ZLOTYCH **Weight:** 8.0000 g. **Composition:** 0.9000 Gold .2315 oz. AGW **Subject:** Boleslaw III (1102-1138) **Obverse:** Polish eagle **Reverse:** Portrait **Edge:** Plain **Size:** 21 mm.

Date	Mintage	F	VF	XF	Unc	BU
2001 Proof	2,000	Value: 220				

Y# 436 100 ZLOTYCH **Weight:** 8.0000 g. **Composition:** 0.9000 Gold 0.2315 oz. AGW **Subject:** World Cup Soccer **Obverse:** Crowned eagle with world background **Reverse:** Soccer player **Edge:** Plain **Size:** 21 mm.

Date	Mintage	F	VF	XF	Unc	BU
2002 Proof	4,500	Value: 225				

Y# 429 100 ZLOTYCH **Weight:** 8.0000 g. **Composition:** 0.9000 Gold 0.2315 oz. AGW **Obverse:** Crowned eagle **Reverse:** Bust of crowned King Kazimierz III (1333-1370) **Edge:** Plain **Size:** 21 mm.

Date	Mintage	F	VF	XF	Unc	BU
2002 Proof	2,400	Value: 225				

Y# 430 100 ZLOTYCH **Weight:** 8.0000 g. **Composition:** 0.9000 Silver 0.2315 oz. ASW **Obverse:** Crowned eagle **Reverse:** Bust of crowned King Wladyslaw II Jagiello (1386-1434) half left **Edge:** Plain **Size:** 21 mm.

Date	Mintage	F	VF	XF	Unc	BU
2002 Proof	2,200	Value: 225				

Y# 294 200 ZLOTYCH **Weight:** 15.5000 g. **Composition:** 0.9000 Gold .4485 oz. AGW **Reverse:** Golden eagle

Date	Mintage	F	VF	XF	Unc	BU
1995	1,000	—	—	—	485	—

Y# 299 200 ZLOTYCH **Weight:** 15.5000 g. **Composition:** 0.9000 Gold .4485 oz. AGW **Subject:** XII Chopin Piano Competition **Edge:** Lettered

Date	Mintage	F	VF	XF	Unc	BU
1995 Proof	500	Value: 420				

Y# 316 200 ZLOTYCH **Weight:** 15.5000 g. **Composition:** 0.9000 Gold .4485 oz. AGW **Reverse:** Henryk Sienkiewicz

Date	Mintage	F	VF	XF	Unc	B
1996 Proof	Est. 1,000	Value: 385				

Y# 320 200 ZLOTYCH **Weight:** 15.5000 g. **Composition:** 0.9000 Gold .4485 oz. AGW **Subject:** Millenium of Gdansk (Danzig) **Reverse:** City arms in old co style

Date	Mintage	F	VF	XF	Unc	B
1996	2,000	—	—	—	340	

Y# 323 200 ZLOTYCH **Weight:** 15.5000 g. **Composition:** 0.9000 Gold .4485 oz. AGW **Subject:** St. Adalbert's Martyrdom **Obverse:** Police eagle

Date	Mintage	F	VF	XF	Unc	B
1997 Proof	2,000	Value: 340				

Y# 346 200 ZLOTYCH **Weight:** 15.5000 g. **Composition:** 0.9000 Gold .4485 oz. AGW **Obverse:** Polis eagle **Reverse:** Pope John Paul II

Date	Mintage	F	VF	XF	Unc	B
1998 Proof	5,000	Value: 350				

Y# 353 200 ZLOTYCH **Weight:** 15.5000 g. **Composition:** 0.9000 Gold .4485 oz. AGW **Subject:** 200 Birthday - Adam Mickiewicz **Obverse:** Small Polish eagle quote **Reverse:** Portrait with silhouette

Date	Mintage	F	VF	XF	Unc	B
1998 Proof	3,000	Value: 340				

Y# 367 200 ZLOTYCH **Weight:** 15.5000 g. **Composition:** 0.9000 Gold .4485 oz. AGW **Obverse:** Polis eagle on sash, music **Reverse:** Portrait of Fryderyk Chopi with music background

Date	Mintage	F	VF	XF	Unc	B
1999 Proof	2,200	Value: 340				

Y# 385 200 ZLOTYCH Weight: 15.5000 g. **Composition:** 0.9000 Gold .4485 oz. AGW **Obverse:** Polish eagle **Reverse:** Head Juliusz Slowacki left

Date	Mintage	F	VF	XF	Unc	BU
1999 Proof	1,900	Value: 325				

Y# 386 200 ZLOTYCH Weight: 15.5000 g. **Composition:** 0.9000 Gold .4485 oz. AGW **Subject:** 1000th Anniversary - Gniezno Convention **Obverse:** Old coin designs **Reverse:** Seated figures of Boleslaw Chrobry and Otto III

Date	Mintage	F	VF	XF	Unc	BU
2000 Proof	1,250	Value: 340				

Y# 393 200 ZLOTYCH Weight: 15.5000 g. **Composition:** 0.9000 Gold .4485 oz. AGW **Subject:** 1000 Years - Wroclzaw (Breslau) **Obverse:** Polish eagle **Reverse:** Bust of Jesus holding city arms **Edge:** Plain **Size:** 27 mm.

Date	Mintage	F	VF	XF	Unc	BU
2000 Proof	2,500	Value: 340				

Y# 397 200 ZLOTYCH Weight: 23.3200 g. **Composition:** 0.9000 Gold .6748 oz. AGW **Subject:** Solidarity **Obverse:** Polish eagle **Reverse:** Multicolor Soldiarity logo, map and two children **Edge:** Plain

Date	Mintage	F	VF	XF	Unc	BU
2000 Proof	2,500	Value: 485				

Y# 375 200 ZLOTYCH Ring Weight: 0.9250 g. **Ring Composition:** 0.9000 Silver**Center Weight:** 13.6000 g. **Center Composition:** 0.9000 Gold **Subject:** Millennium **Obverse:** Crowned eagle and world globe **Reverse:** Various computer, DNA and atomic symbols **Note:** 13.6000 g, .900 Gold center in .925 Silver inner ring in a .900 Gold outer ring.

Date	Mintage	F	VF	XF	Unc	BU
2000 Proof	6,000	Value: 150				

Y# 407 200 ZLOTYCH Ring Composition: 0.9000 Gold With Silver **Center Composition:** 0.9000 Gold With Palladium .4398 oz. **Subject:** Year 2001 **Obverse:** Crowned eagle in a swirl **Reverse:** Couple looking into the future **Edge:** Plain **Size:** 27 mm.

Date		F	VF	XF	Unc	BU
2001 Proof	4,000	Value: 150				

Y# 420 200 ZLOTYCH Weight: 15.5000 g. **Composition:** 0.9000 Gold .4485 oz. AGW **Subject:** Cardinal Stefan Wyszynski **Obverse:** Pillar divides arms and eagle **Reverse:** Cardinal's portrait **Edge Lettering:** "100 ROCZNIA URODZIN" **Size:** 27 mm.

Date	Mintage	F	VF	XF	Unc	BU
2001 Proof	4,500	Value: 340				

Y# 438 200 ZLOTYCH Weight: 15.5000 g. **Composition:** 0.9000 Gold 0.4485 oz. AGW **Subject:** Pope John Paul II **Obverse:** Bust of Pope at right facing left, small eagle in background **Reverse:** Pope facing radiant Holy Door **Edge:** Plain **Size:** 27 mm.

Date	Mintage	F	VF	XF	Unc	BU
2002 Proof	5,000	Value: 340				

Y# 295 500 ZLOTYCH Weight: 31.1035 g. **Composition:** 0.9999 Gold 1.0000 oz. AGW

Date	Mintage	F	VF	XF	Unc	BU
1995	500	—	—	—	775	—

Y# 267 1000 ZLOTYCH Weight: 27.9500 g. **Composition:** 0.9250 Silver .8313 oz. ASW **Subject:** World Cup Soccer **Reverse:** Soccer stadium

Date	Mintage	F	VF	XF	Unc	BU
1994MW Proof	10,000	Value: 25.00				

TRIAL STRIKES

KM#	Date	Mintage	Identification	Mkt Val
TS1	1923	—	Grosz. Copper. Uniface.	75.00
TS2	1923	—	Grosz. Copper. Uniface.	75.00

PATTERNS

Including off metal strikes

KM#	Date	Mintage	Identification	Mkt Val
Pn232	1919	—	50 Groszy. Nickel. 7.5600 g. Small eagle.	—
Pn233	1919	—	50 Groszy. Nickel. Large eagle.	—
Pn234	1922	60	100 Marek. Copper. 8.8400 g.	175
Pn235	1922	100	100 Marek. Bronze. 8.8400 g.	80.00
Pn236	1922	10	100 Marek. Brass. 8.8400 g.	—
Pn237	1922	4	100 Marek. Tin. 4.5700 g.	—
Pn238	1922	50	100 Marek. Silver. 8.8000 g.	175
Pn239	1922	3	100 Marek. Gold.	—
Pn240	1923	120	50 Marek. Bronze. 5.1300 g.	80.00
Pn241	1923	12	50 Marek. Silver. 5.2500 g.	—
Pn242	1923	1	50 Marek. Gold.	—
Pn243	1923	30	Grosz. Bronze. 1.5000 g.	150
Pn244	1923	125	2 Grosze. Bronze. 1.5600 g.	160
Pn245	1923	—	2 Grosze. Gold.	—
Pn246	1923	10	5 Groszy. Brass. 3.0000 g.	—
Pn247	1923	100	5 Groszy. Silver. 3.2900 g.	80.00
Pn248	1923	3	5 Groszy. Brass. 3.0000 g.	125
Pn249	1923	30	20 Groszy. Brass. 4.5200 g.	60.00
Pn250	1923	30	50 Groszy. Brass. 4.5200 g.	—
Pn251	1923	—	50 Groszy. Nickel. HUGUENIN in 0 of 50.	—
Pn265	1924	105	50 Zlotych. Copper. 10.4200 g.	100
Pn252	1924	10	20 Groszy. Nickel. 3.0000 g.	—
Pn253	1924	15	Zloty. Silver. 5.0000 g. ESSAI.	—
Pn254	1924	40	Zloty. Silver. With torch.	400
Pn255	1924 H	8	Zloty. Silver.	—
Pn256	1924	40	2 Zlote. Brass. 9.6500 g.	175
Pn257	1924	100	2 Zlote. Brass. 10.0000 g. Rotated dies.	150
Pn258	1924	15	2 Zlote. Silver. 10.0000 g. ESSAI. Paris Mint.	—
Pn259	1924 H	60	2 Zlote. Silver. 10.0000 g.	400
Pn260	1924	10	2 Zlote. Silver. 10.0000 g.	—
Pn261	1924	3	2 Zlote. Silver. 10.0000 g. Larger eagle.	—
Pn262	1924	120	20 Zlotych. Bronze. 3.3500 g.	100
Pn263	1924	10	20 Zlotych. Silver. 5.6900 g.	225
Pn264	1924	10	20 Zlotych. Gold.	—
Pn266	1924	2	50 Zlotych. Lead. 7.8000 g.	—
Pn267	1924	2	50 Zlotych. Aluminum. 2.8000 g.	—
Pn268	1924	1	50 Zlotych. Gold.	—
Pn269	1925	15	5 Groszy. Brass. 3.0000 g.	—
Pn272	1925	100	10 Zlotych. Bronze. 3.3100 g.	100
Pn273	1925	50	10 Zlotych. Silver. 4.3700 g.	125
Pn274	1925	1	10 Zlotych. Gold.	—
Pn275	1925	105	20 Zlotych. Bronze. 5.3900 g.	100
Pn276	1925	10	20 Zlotych. Copper. 5.3900 g.	150
Pn277	1925	12	20 Zlotych. Silver. 4.3200 g.	200
Pn278	1925	5	20 Zlotych. Gold.	—
Pn279	1925	35	20 Zlotych. Brass. 3.2700 g. Boleslaus I, Y#33.	—
Pn280	1925	20	20 Zlotych. Nickel. 3.5000 g. Boleslaus I, Y#33.	—
Pn281	1925	2	100 Zlotych. Silver. 24.2000 g. Plain edge.	—
Pn282	1925	100	100 Zlotych. Silver. 24.5300 g. Edge lettering: SALUS REIPUBLICAE SUPREMA LEX.	—
Pn283	1925	100	100 Zlotych. Bronze. 3.5000 g. Kopernik Commemorative.	90.00
Pn284	1925	50	100 Zlotych. Silver. 4.1500 g.	175
Pn285	1925	1	100 Zlotych. Gold.	—
Pn286	1926	20	2 Grosze. Nickel. 2.4700 g.	—
Pn287	1926	100	2 Grosze. Silver. 2.2900 g.	80.00
Pn288	1927	100	Grosz. Silver. 5.2500 g.	—
Pn289	1927	6	Grosz. Gold.	—
Pn290	1927	100	2 Zlote. (No Composition). 10.0000 g.	65.00
Pn291	1927	10	2 Zlote. Bronze. 9.8600 g. With PROBA.	—
Pn292	1927	100	2 Zlote. Silver. 10.0000 g. Warsau Mint.	65.00
Pn293	1927	81	5 Zlotych. Silver. 18.4000 g. With MM, PROBA.	225
Pn294	1927	20	5 Zlotych. Silver. 18.4000 g. Without MM, without PROBA.	—
Pn295	1927	100	5 Zlotych. Silver. 16.0000 g. Without MM, with PROBA.	—
Pn296	1928	2	Zloty. Copper. 7.9000 g.	—
Pn297	1928	2	Zloty. Tombac. 6.0000 g.	—
Pn298	1928	25	Zloty. Nickel. 6.8400 g.	—
Pn300	1928	35	Zloty. Nickel. 7.0000 g. Mint mark.	—
Pn299	1928	110	Zloty. Nickel. 7.0000 g.	50.00
Pn301	1928	35	Zloty. Bronze. 7.0000 g.	—
Pn302	1928	15	Zloty. Nickel. 7.0700 g.	—
Pn303	1928	8	Zloty. Tombac. 6.0000 g.	—
Pn304	1928	2	Zloty. Copper. 6.9800 g.	—
Pn305	1928	125	Zloty. Bronze. 6.0000 g.	200
Pn306	1928	—	Zloty. Nickel. Madonna.	—
Pn307	1928	—	2 Zlotych. Aluminum. Madonna.	—
Pn308	1928	—	2 Zlotych. Copper. Madonna.	—
Pn309	1928	—	2 Zlotych. Silver. Madonna.	—
Pn310	1928	—	2 Zlotych. Gold. Madonna.	525
Pn311	1928	—	2 Zlotych. Platinum. Madonna.	700
Pn312	1928	—	5 Zlotych. Aluminum. Madonna.	—
Pn313	1928	—	5 Zlotych. Copper. Madonna.	—
Pn314	1928	—	5 Zlotych. Nickel. Madonna.	—
Pn315	1928	—	5 Zlotych. Silver. Madonna.	175
Pn316	1928	—	5 Zlotych. Gold. Madonna.	1,200
Pn317	1928	—	5 Zlotych. Platinum. Madonna.	1,485

KM#	Date	Mintage	Identification	Mkt Val
Pn318	1928	20	5 Zlotych. Silver. 18.4000 g. Nike.	—
Pn319	1928	—	5 Zlotych. Tombac. ESSAI/30.	275
Pn320	1928	20	5 Zlotych. Tombac. Denticals instead of dots.	450
Pn321	1929	10	Zloty. Aluminum. 2.2800 g.	—
Pn322	1929	12	Zloty. Bronze. 4.8700 g.	—
Pn323	1929	115	Zloty. Nickel. 6.8400 g. Without PROBA.	55.00
Pn324	1930	20	5 Zlotych. Bronze. 16.0000 g. PROBA.	150
Pn325	1930	200	5 Zlotych. Bronze. Without PROBA.	—
Pn326	1932	100	Zloty. Bronze. 2.0500 g.	60.00
Pn327	1932	120	Zloty. Silver. 2.0200 g.	75.00
Pn328	1932	100	2 Zlote. Bronze. 3.8700 g.	65.00
Pn329	1932	110	2 Zlote. Silver. 4.4000 g.	60.00
Pn330	1932	100	10 Zlotych. Silver. 22.0000 g.	165
Pn331	1932	10	10 Zlotych. Bronze. 19.2200 g.	—
Pn332	1932	100	10 Zlotych. Bronze. 19.7000 g.	125
PnA333	1933	—	2 Zlote. Silver. PROBA.	—
Pn333	1933	100	5 Zlotych. Bronze. 10.0700 g.	85.00
Pn334	1933	100	5 Zlotych. Silver. 11.0000 g.	100
Pn335	1933	100	10 Zlotych. Silver. 22.0000 g.	450
Pn336	1933	100	10 Zlotych. Silver. 22.0000 g. PROBA.	450
Pn337	1933	100	10 Zlotych. Silver. 30.0000 g. Klippe.	300
Pn338	1933	100	10 Zlotych. Silver. 30.0000 g. Klippe.	450
Pn339	1934	100	5 Zlotych. Bronze. 9.4700 g. PROBA.	85.00
Pn340	1934	100	5 Zlotych. Silver. 11.0000 g. PROBA.	100
Pn341	1934	100	5 Zlotych. Silver. 11.0000 g. Without PROBA.	—
PnA342	1934	—	10 Zlotych. Silver.	—
Pn342	1934	2	10 Zlotych. Aluminum.	250
Pn343	1934	130	10 Zlotych. Iron-Plated Nickel. 4.9700 g.	125
Pn344	1934	3	10 Zlotych. Tombac. 10.3000 g.	350
Pn345	1934	100	10 Zlotych. Silver. 22.0000 g. PROBA.	400
Pn346	1934	100	10 Zlotych. Silver. 22.0000 g. Without PROBA.	—
Pn347	1934	100	10 Zlotych. Bronze. 19.4000 g. PROBA.	—
Pn348	1934	3	10 Zlotych. Silver. 15.0000 g.	425
Pn349	1934	300	10 Zlotych. Silver. 42.0000 g. Klippe.	650
Pn351	1936	110	5 Zlotych. (No Composition). 11.0000 g.	150
Pn350	1936	100	2 Zlote. Silver. 4.4000 g. With PROBA.	90.00
PnA351	1936	100	2 Zlote. Silver. 4.4000 g. Without PROBA.	—
Pn352	1936	200	5 Zlotych. Bronze. 17.4600 g. Klippe.	300
Pn353	1936	200	5 Zlotych. Silver. 20.0000 g. Klippe.	600
PnA356	1938	100	20 Groszy. Nickeled Iron. Without PROBA.	—
Pn354	1938	100	10 Groszy. Bronze. 4.9000 g.	90.00
Pn355	1938	100	20 Groszy. Nickeled Iron. 3.4900 g. With PROBA.	60.00
Pn356	1938	120	50 Groszy. Iron.	50.00
Pn357	1938	10	50 Groszy. Aluminum.	—
Pn358	1938	100	50 Groszy. Iron. 4.5000 g.	50.00
Pn359	1938	1	50 Groszy. Bronze. 3.4000 g.	—
Pn360	1938	3	50 Groszy. Aluminum.	—
Pn361	1938	200	50 Groszy. Iron-Plated Nickel.	35.00
Pn362	1939	200	Grosz. Zinc. 14.7000 g.	35.00
Pn363	1939	200	2 Grosze. Zinc. 1.7500 g.	35.00
Pn364	1939	200	5 Groszy. Zinc. 1.7200 g. 2/hole.	35.00
Pn365	1981MW	3,000	2000 Zlotych. Gold. 8.0000 g. Boleslaw II.	—

PIEFORTS

KM#	Date	Mintage	Identification	Mkt Val
P1	1989	—	10000 Zlotych. (No Composition). Y#189.	—
P2	1989	—	10000 Zlotych. (No Composition). Y#237.	—

PROBAS

Standard metals unless otherwise stated

In Poland, rejected coin designs are often minted in large numbers for sale to collectors. These coins have the word PROBA on them, usually stamped incuse. The coins struck in nickel are not available to the general public. Of the 500 pieces struck, 250 pieces are distributed among the members of the Polish Numismatic Society and the other 250 pieces are distributed between various banks and museums.

KM#	Date	Mintage	Identification	Mkt Val
PrA1	1929	—	Zloty. Nickel.	—
Pr1	1949	—	Grosz. Aluminum.	—

KM#	Date	Mintage	Identification	Mkt Val
Pr2	1949	100	Grosz. Brass. Y#39.	65.00
Pr3	1949	500	Grosz. Nickel. Y#39.	40.00

KM#	Date	Mintage	Identification	Mkt Val
Pr4	1949	100	2 Grosze. Brass. Y#40.	65.00
Pr5	1949	500	2 Grosze. Nickel. Y#40.	45.00
Pr6	1949	—	2 Grosze. Aluminum.	—

KM#	Date	Mintage	Identification	Mkt Val
Pr7	1949	100	5 Groszy. Brass. Y#41.	75.00

KM#	Date	Mintage	Identification	Mkt Val
PrA7	1949	500	5 Groszy. Nickel. Y#41.	45.00
Pr8	1949	100	5 Groszy. Brass.	—
Pr9	1949	—	5 Groszy. Aluminum.	—
Pr10	1949	—	10 Groszy. Aluminum.	—

KM#	Date	Mintage	Identification	Mkt Val
Pr11	1949	100	10 Groszy. Brass. Y#42.	65.00
Pr12	1949	500	10 Groszy. Nickel. Y#42.	45.00

KM#	Date	Mintage	Identification	Mkt Val
Pr13	1949	100	20 Groszy. Brass. Y#43.	65.00
Pr14	1949	500	20 Groszy. Nickel. Y#43.	45.00
Pr15	1949	—	20 Groszy. Aluminum.	—

KM#	Date	Mintage	Identification	Mkt Val
Pr16	1949	100	50 Groszy. Brass. Y#44.	65.00
Pr17	1949	20	50 Groszy. Tombac. Y#44.	—
Pr18	1949	500	50 Groszy. Nickel. Y#44.	45.00
Pr19	1949	—	50 Groszy. Aluminum.	—

KM#	Date	Mintage	Identification	Mkt Val
Pr20	1949	100	Zloty. Brass. Y#45.	80.00
Pr21	1949	—	Zloty. Aluminum.	—

KM#	Date	Mintage	Identification	Mkt Val
Pr22	1949	500	Zloty. Nickel. Y#45.	45.00

KM#	Date	Mintage	Identification	Mkt Val
Pr23	1957	100	20 Groszy. Brass. Y#A47.	80.00

KM#	Date	Mintage	Identification	Mkt Val
Pr24	1957	100	50 Groszy. Brass. Y#48.1.	80.00
Pr25	1957	500	50 Groszy. Nickel. Y#48.1.	45.00

KM#	Date	Mintage	Identification	Mkt Val
Pr26	1957	100	Zloty. Brass. Y#49.1.	80.00
Pr27	1957	500	Zloty. Nickel. Y#49.1.	45.00
Pr28	1957	5	Zloty. Copper-Nickel-Zinc. Y#49.1 without PROBA.	—

KM#	Date	Mintage	Identification	Mkt Val
Pr29	1958	100	5 Groszy. Brass. Y#A46.	—
Pr30	1958	245	50 Groszy. Aluminum. Crossed hammers.	35.00
Pr31	1958	500	50 Groszy. Nickel. Crossed hammers.	35.00

KM#	Date	Mintage	Identification	Mkt Val
Pr32	1958	198	50 Groszy. Aluminum. Antenna below denomination.	35.0
Pr33	1958	500	50 Groszy. Nickel. Antenna below denomination.	35.0
Pr34	1958	212	50 Groszy. Aluminum. 50 above spears of grain.	35.0
Pr35	1958	500	50 Groszy. Nickel. 50 above spears of grain.	35.0

KM#	Date	Mintage	Identification	Mkt Val
Pr36	1958	234	Zloty. Aluminum. 1 between spears of grain.	30.00
Pr37	1958	500	Zloty. Nickel. 1 between spears of grain.	35.00

KM#	Date	Mintage	Identification	Mkt Val
Pr38	1958	235	Zloty. Aluminum. 1 within circle.	35.00
Pr39	1958	500	Zloty. Nickel. 1 within circle.	35.00

KM#	Date	Mintage	Identification	Mkt Val
Pr40	1958	211	Zloty. Aluminum. Acorns and oak leaves.	30.00
Pr41	1958	500	Zloty. Nickel. Acorns and oak leaves.	35.00

KM#	Date	Mintage	Identification	Mkt Val
Pr42	1958	210	Zloty. Aluminum. 1 between doves, low relief.	30.00
Pr43	1958	53	Zloty. Aluminum. 1 between doves, high relief.	125
Pr44	1958	500	Zloty. Nickel. 1 between birds.	35.00

KM#	Date	Mintage	Identification	Mkt Val
Pr45	1958	100	2 Zlote. Brass. Y#46.	55.00

KM#	Date	Mintage	Identification	Mkt Val
Pr46	1958	5	5 Zlotych. Aluminum. Hammer and shovel without PROBA.	—

KM#	Date	Mintage	Identification	Mkt Val
Pr47	1958	5	5 Zlotych. Brass. Ship.	—
Pr48	1958	20	5 Zlotych. Aluminum. Ship, without PROBA.	150

KM#	Date	Mintage	Identification	Mkt Val
Pr49	1958	500	5 Zlotych. Nickel. Ship.	35.00
Pr50	1958	10	5 Zlotych. Aluminum. Without PROBA, reverse of Pr49.	—

KM#	Date	Mintage	Identification	Mkt Val
Pr51	1958	5	10 Zlotych. Aluminum. Caliper and gear, without PROBA.	100

KM#	Date	Mintage	Identification	Mkt Val
Pr52	1958	10	10 Zlotych. Aluminum. Kosciuszko with ornaments, without PROBA.	—
Pr53	1958	10	10 Zlotych. Copper-Nickel. Kosciuszko with ornaments, without PROBA.	—
Pr54	1958	5	10 Zlotych. Aluminum. With ornaments and PROBA.	100
Pr55	1958	5	10 Zlotych. Brass. Kosciuszko with ornaments without PROBA.	—
Pr56	1958	5	10 Zlotych. Copper-Nickel. Kosciuszko with ornaments and PROBA.	—
Pr57	1958	10	10 Zlotych. Aluminum.	—

KM#	Date	Mintage	Identification	Mkt Val
Pr58	1958	5	10 Zlotych. Copper-Nickel. Without ornaments and PROBA, high relief.	—

KM#	Date	Mintage	Identification	Mkt Val
Pr59	1959	500	2 Zlote. Nickel. Y#46.	30.00

KM#	Date	Mintage	Identification	Mkt Val
Pr60	1959	100	5 Zlotych. Brass. Y#47.	65.00
Pr61	1959	500	5 Zlotych. Nickel. Y#47.	30.00
Pr62	1959	500	5 Zlotych. Nickel. Industrial collage.	30.00

KM#	Date	Mintage	Identification	Mkt Val
Pr63	1959	500	5 Zlotych. Nickel. Hammer and shovel.	30.00

KM#	Date	Mintage	Identification	Mkt Val
Pr64	1959	10	10 Zlotych. Aluminum. Y#51.	—
Pr65	1959	500	10 Zlotych. Nickel. Y#51.	30.00
Pr66	1960	196	5 Zlotych. Aluminum. Ship.	—

KM#	Date	Mintage	Identification	Mkt Val
Pr67	1960	500	5 Zlotych. Nickel. Ship.	32.50

KM#	Date	Mintage	Identification	Mkt Val
Pr68	1960	500	10 Zlotych. Nickel. Caliper and gear.	30.00

KM#	Date	Mintage	Identification	Mkt Val

Pr69	1960	500	10 Zlotych. Nickel. Kosciuszko with ornaments and PROBA.	30.00

Pr70	1960	500	10 Zlotych. Nickel. Kosciuszko with PROBA in front of neck.	30.00

Pr71	1960	10	100 Zlotych. Nickel. Y#57, with crosshatched field.	—
Pr72	1960	500	100 Zlotych. Nickel. Y#57, with crosshatched field.	35.00
Pr73	1960	50	100 Zlotych. 0.5000 Silver. Without PROBA, Y#57 with crosshatched field.	40.00
Pr74	1960	20	100 Zlotych. 0.7500 Silver. Y#57, with crosshatched field.	40.00
Pr75	1960	500	100 Zlotych. Nickel. Y#57.	35.00

Pr76	1960	12	100 Zlotych. 0.7500 Silver.	100
Pr77	1960	14	100 Zlotych. 0.7500 Silver.	100
Pr78	1960	4	100 Zlotych. 0.7000 Silver. High relief.	—
Pr79	1960	9	100 Zlotych. 0.7000 Silver. Flat relief.	—
Pr80	1960	20	100 Zlotych. 0.5000 Silver.	100

Pr81	1960	13	100 Zlotych. 0.7500 Silver.	100
Pr82	1960	500	100 Zlotych. Nickel.	30.00
Pr83	1960	5	100 Zlotych. 0.7500 Silver.	120

KM#	Date	Mintage	Identification	Mkt Val

Pr84	1960	500	100 Zlotych. Nickel.	30.00
Pr85	1960	29	100 Zlotych. 0.7000 Silver.	100

Pr86	1960	500	100 Zlotych. Nickel.	30.00
Pr87	1960	12	100 Zlotych. 0.7500 Silver.	100

Pr88	1960	500	100 Zlotych. Nickel.	30.00
Pr89	1960	6	100 Zlotych. 0.7500 Silver.	—

Pr90	1962	500	10 Groszy. Nickel. Y#AA47.	30.00

Pr91	1963	500	5 Groszy. Nickel. Y#A46.	30.00

Pr92	1963	500	20 Groszy. Nickel. Y#A47.	30.00

Pr93	1964	125	10 Zlotych. Copper-Nickel. Raised legend, Y#52.	50.00
Pr94	1964	500	10 Zlotych. Nickel. Y#52a.	25.00
Pr95	1964	125	10 Zlotych. Copper-Nickel. Incuse legend, Y#52a.	50.00

KM#	Date	Mintage	Identification	Mkt Val
Pr96	1964	5	10 Zlotych. Tombac. Y#52a.	90.00
Pr97	1964	500	10 Zlotych. Nickel. Y#52a.	25.00

Pr98	1964	30	10 Zlotych. Copper-Nickel-Zinc. Eagle without crown. PROBA raised.	7.00
Pr99	1964	30,000	10 Zlotych. Copper-Nickel. 12.9000 g. PROBA incuse.	7.00
Pr100	1964	I.A.	10 Zlotych. Copper-Nickel. Wthout PROBA. Without PROBA.	150
Pr101	1964	500	10 Zlotych. Nickel. PROBA raised. PROBA raised.	20.00

Pr102	1964	500	10 Zlotych. Nickel. Raised PROBA, crowned eagle. Raised PROBA.	25.00
Pr103	1964	10	10 Zlotych. Copper-Nickel.	—

Pr104	1964	10	10 Zlotych. Copper-Nickel.	—
Pr105	1964	500	10 Zlotych. Nickel.	25.00

Pr106	1964	10	10 Zlotych. Copper-Nickel.	—

Pr107	1964	10	10 Zlotych. Copper-Nickel.	—

KM#	Date	Mintage	Identification	Mkt Val

Pr108	1964	20	10 Zlotych. Copper-Nickel.	—
Pr109	1964	500	10 Zlotych. Nickel.	25.00

Pr110	1964	10	10 Zlotych. Copper-Nickel.	—

Pr111	1964	10	10 Zlotych. Copper-Nickel.	—
Pr112	1964	500	10 Zlotych. Nickel.	25.00

Pr113	1964	10	10 Zlotych. Copper-Nickel.	—

Pr114	1964	20	10 Zlotych. Copper-Nickel.	—
Pr115	1964	500	10 Zlotych. Nickel.	25.00

Pr116	1964	20	20 Zlotych. Copper-Nickel.	—
Pr117	1964	500	20 Zlotych. Nickel.	25.00

KM#	Date	Mintage	Identification	Mkt Val

Pr118	1964	20	20 Zlotych. Copper-Nickel.	—

Pr119	1964	10	20 Zlotych. Copper-Nickel.	—

Pr120	1964	20	20 Zlotych. Copper-Nickel.	—
Pr121	1964	500	20 Zlotych. Nickel.	25.00

Pr122	1964	20	20 Zlotych. Copper-Nickel.	—
Pr123	1964	500	20 Zlotych. Nickel.	25.00

Pr124	1964	20	20 Zlotych. Copper-Nickel.	—

Pr125	1964	20	20 Zlotych. Copper-Nickel.	—

KM#	Date	Mintage	Identification	Mkt Val
Pr126	1964	500	20 Zlotych. Nickel.	25.00
Pr127	1965	20	10 Zlotych. Copper-Nickel.	—
Pr128	1965	500	10 Zlotych. Nickel.	25.00

Pr129	1965	20	10 Zlotych. Copper-Nickel. Y#54.	—
Pr130	1965	500	10 Zlotych. Nickel. Y#54.	35.00

Pr131	1965	30,000	10 Zlotych. Copper-Nickel. 12.9000 g.	10.00
Pr132	1965	500	10 Zlotych. Nickel.	25.00

Pr133	1965	30,000	10 Zlotych. Copper-Nickel. 12.9000 g.	10.00
Pr134	1965	500	10 Zlotych. Nickel.	25.00

Pr135	1965	20	10 Zlotych. Copper-Nickel.	—
Pr136	1965	500	10 Zlotych. Nickel.	25.00

Pr137	1965	5	10 Zlotych. Aluminum. Kopernik.	—

Pr138	1966	25	10 Zlotych. Copper-Nickel.	—
Pr139	1966	500	10 Zlotych. Nickel.	25.00

KM#	Date	Mintage	Identification	Mkt Val
Pr140	1966	500	10 Zlotych. Nickel.	25.00
Pr141	1966	10	10 Zlotych. Copper-Nickel.	—
Pr142	1966	10	100 Zlotych. Copper-Nickel.	—
Pr143	1966	10	100 Zlotych. 0.7500 Silver.	—

KM#	Date	Mintage	Identification	Mkt Val
Pr144	1966	500	100 Zlotych. Nickel. Y#57.	25.00
Pr145	1966	500	100 Zlotych. Nickel.	25.00

KM#	Date	Mintage	Identification	Mkt Val
Pr146	1966	31,000	100 Zlotych. 0.9000 Silver. 20.0000 g. 2 busts.	22.50

KM#	Date	Mintage	Identification	Mkt Val
Pr147	1966	500	100 Zlotych. Nickel. 2 heads.	25.00
Pr148	1966	30,000	100 Zlotych. 0.9000 Silver. 2 heads.	22.50
Pr149	1967	10	10 Zlotych. Copper-Nickel. Plain edge. Y#59.	—
Pr150	1967	16	10 Zlotych. Copper-Nickel. Milled edge. Y#59.	—
Pr151	1967	500	10 Zlotych. Nickel. Y#59.	25.00

KM#	Date	Mintage	Identification	Mkt Val
Pr152	1967	20	10 Zlotych. Copper-Nickel.	—
Pr153	1967	500	10 Zlotych. Nickel.	25.00

KM#	Date	Mintage	Identification	Mkt Val
Pr154	1967	16	10 Zlotych. Copper-Nickel.	—
Pr155	1967	10	10 Zlotych. (No Composition). Plain edge.	—
Pr156	1967	500	10 Zlotych. Nickel.	25.00

KM#	Date	Mintage	Identification	Mkt Val
Pr157	1967	25	10 Zlotych. Copper-Nickel.	—
Pr158	1967	500	10 Zlotych. Nickel.	12.50
Pr159	1967	40	10 Zlotych. Copper-Nickel.	—
Pr160	1967	500	10 Zlotych. Nickel.	12.50

KM#	Date	Mintage	Identification	Mkt Val
Pr161	1967	17	10 Zlotych. Aluminum. Kopernik.	—
Pr162	1967	1	10 Zlotych. Copper-Nickel. Kopernik.	—
Pr163	1967	10	10 Zlotych. Aluminum. Kopernik.	—

KM#	Date	Mintage	Identification	Mkt Val
Pr164	1968	20	10 Zlotych. Copper-Nickel.	—
Pr165	1968	500	10 Zlotych. Nickel.	25.00

KM#	Date	Mintage	Identification	Mkt Val
Pr166	1969	20	10 Zlotych. Copper-Nickel. PROBA at lower right.	—
Pr167	1969	500	10 Zlotych. Nickel. PROBA at lower right.	—
Pr168	1969	5	10 Zlotych. Gold. PROBA at lower right.	—

KM#	Date	Mintage	Identification	Mkt Val
Pr169	1969	20	10 Zlotych. Copper-Nickel. PROBA at right.	—
Pr170	1969	500	10 Zlotych. Nickel. PROBA at right.	—
Pr171	1969	500	10 Zlotych. Nickel. Wthout PROBA.	25.00

KM#	Date	Mintage	Identification	Mkt Val
Pr172	1969	20	10 Zlotych. Copper-Nickel.	
Pr173	1969	500	10 Zlotych. Nickel.	25.

KM#	Date	Mintage	Identification	Mkt Val
Pr174	1969	20	10 Zlotych. Copper-Nickel.	
Pr175	1969	500	10 Zlotych. Nickel.	25.

KM#	Date	Mintage	Identification	Mkt Val
Pr176	1970	20	10 Zlotych. Copper-Nickel. 25th Anniversary of Provincial Annexation.	
Pr177	1970	500	10 Zlotych. Nickel. 25th Anniversary of Provincial Annexation.	20.
Pr178	1970	10	10 Zlotych. Copper-Nickel. Without PROBA.	
Pr179	1970	20	10 Zlotych. Copper-Nickel. Y#62.	
Pr180	1970	500	10 Zlotych. Nickel. Y#62.	20.
Pr181	1970	300	10 Zlotych. Silver. Y#62.	35.
Pr182	1970	5	10 Zlotych. Aluminum. Kopernik.	
Pr183	1971	20	10 Zlotych. Copper-Nickel. Y#63.	
Pr184	1971	500	10 Zlotych. Nickel. Y#63.	20.

KM#	Date	Mintage	Identification	Mkt Val
Pr185	1971	51,000	10 Zlotych. Copper-Nickel. FAO, baby nursing.	12.
Pr186	1971	500	10 Zlotych. Nickel. FAO, baby nursing.	20.

KM#	Date	Mintage	Identification	Mkt Val
Pr187	1971	52,000	10 Zlotych. Copper-Nickel. 9.5000 g. FAO, wheat.	12.
Pr188	1971	500	10 Zlotych. Nickel. FAO, wheat.	20.

KM#	Date	Mintage	Identification	Mkt Val
Pr189	1971	20	10 Zlotych. Copper-Nickel. Y#64.	—
Pr190	1971	500	10 Zlotych. Nickel. Y#64.	20.00

KM#	Date	Mintage	Identification	Mkt Val
Pr191	1971	20	10 Zlotych. Copper-Nickel. Medal.	—
Pr192	1971	500	10 Zlotych. Nickel. Medal.	20.00

KM#	Date	Mintage	Identification	Mkt Val
Pr193	1972	20	10 Zlotych. Copper-Nickel. Y#65 but date inside legend.	20.00
Pr194	1972	500	10 Zlotych. Nickel. Y#65 but date inside legend.	—

KM#	Date	Mintage	Identification	Mkt Val
Pr195	1972	20	10 Zlotych. Copper-Nickel. Y#65.	—
Pr196	1972	500	10 Zlotych. Nickel. Y#65.	20.00
Pr197	1972	—	50 Zlotych. Copper-Nickel.	—
Pr198	1972	20	50 Zlotych. 0.7500 Silver. Y#66, Chopin.	—
Pr199	1972	500	50 Zlotych. Nickel. Y#66.	18.00
Pr200	1972	—	50 Zlotych. Bronze. Chopin, without PROBA.	—
Pr201	1972	20	50 Zlotych. 0.7500 Silver. Chopin, without PROBA.	—
Pr202	1972	15,000	50 Zlotych. 0.7500 Silver. Chopin.	12.50
Pr203	1972	500	50 Zlotych. Nickel. Chopin.	20.00

KM#	Date	Mintage	Identification	Mkt Val
Pr204	1973	20	10 Zlotych. Copper-Nickel.	—
Pr205	1973	500	10 Zlotych. Nickel.	20.00

KM#	Date	Mintage	Identification	Mkt Val
Pr206	1973	20	10 Zlotych. Copper-Nickel.	—
Pr207	1973	500	10 Zlotych. Nickel.	20.00

KM#	Date	Mintage	Identification	Mkt Val
Pr208	1973	10	10 Zlotych. Copper-Nickel. Kopernik.	—
Pr209	1973	500	10 Zlotych. Nickel. Kopernik.	—
Pr210	1973	20	20 Zlotych. Copper-Nickel. Plain edge. Without PROBA, Y#67.	—

KM#	Date	Mintage	Identification	Mkt Val
Pr211	1973	20	20 Zlotych. Copper-Nickel. Ornamented edge.	20.00

KM#	Date	Mintage	Identification	Mkt Val
Pr212	1973	13,000	20 Zlotych. Copper-Nickel. 10.1500 g. Milled edge. Y#67.	—
Pr213	1973	500	20 Zlotych. Nickel. Y#67.	20.00

KM#	Date	Mintage	Identification	Mkt Val
Pr214	1973	16,000	20 Zlotych. Copper-Nickel. 10.1500 g. Tree.	—
Pr215	1973	500	20 Zlotych. Nickel. Tree.	20.00
Pr216	1973	—	100 Zlotych. Copper. Kopernik.	—
Pr217	1973	20	100 Zlotych. 0.6250 Silver. Kopernik.	—
Pr218	1973	500	100 Zlotych. Nickel. Kopernik.	20.00
Pr219	1973	500	100 Zlotych. Nickel. Y#68.	15.00

KM#	Date	Mintage	Identification	Mkt Val
Pr220	1973	5,000	100 Zlotych. 0.6250 Silver. Y#68.	12.50

KM#	Date	Mintage	Identification	Mkt Val
Pr221	1973	1,222	100 Zlotych. 0.6250 Silver. Kopernik.	25.00
Pr222	1973	500	100 Zlotych. Nickel. Kopernik.	20.00

KM#	Date	Mintage	Identification	Mkt Val
Pr223	1974	40	10 Zlotych. Copper-Nickel. Sienkiewicz.	—
Pr224	1974	500	10 Zlotych. Nickel. Sienkiewicz.	20.00

KM#	Date	Mintage	Identification	Mkt Val
Pr225	1974	40	10 Zlotych. Copper-Nickel. Y#74.	—
Pr226	1974	500	10 Zlotych. Nickel. Y#74.	20.00

KM#	Date	Mintage	Identification	Mkt Val
Pr227	1974	10,000	20 Zlotych. Copper-Nickel. Y#69.	—
Pr228	1974	500	20 Zlotych. Nickel. Y#69.	20.00

KM#	Date	Mintage	Identification	Mkt Val
Pr229	1974	20	20 Zlotych. Copper-Nickel. 4 laborers.	—
Pr230	1974	500	20 Zlotych. Nickel. 4 laborers.	20.00
Pr231	1974	20	20 Zlotych. Copper-Nickel.	—
Pr232	1974	500	20 Zlotych. Nickel.	—

KM#	Date	Mintage	Identification	Mkt Val
Pr233	1974	20	20 Zlotych. Copper-Nickel. XXX LAT PRL.	—
Pr234	1974	500	20 Zlotych. Nickel. XXX LAT PRL.	20.00

KM#	Date	Mintage	Identification	Mkt Val
Pr235	1974	20	20 Zlotych. Copper-Nickel. Y#70.	—
Pr236	1974	500	20 Zlotych. Nickel. Y#70.	—

KM#	Date	Mintage	Identification	Mkt Val
Pr237	1974	20	20 Zlotych. Copper-Nickel.	—
Pr238	1974	500	20 Zlotych. Nickel.	20.00

KM# Date Mintage Identification Mkt Val

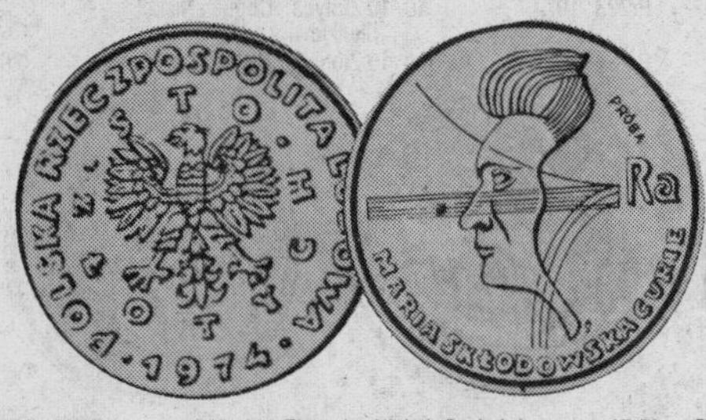

Pr239 1974 500 100 Zlotych. Nickel. Curie left. 17.50
Pr240 1974 10,000 100 Zlotych. 0.6250 Silver. Curie left. 7.50
Pr241 1974 500 100 Zlotych. Nickel. Y#71. 30.00
Pr242 1974 10 100 Zlotych. 0.6250 Silver. Y#71. 10.00

Pr243 1974 500 100 Zlotych. Nickel. Curie right. 12.50
Pr244 1974 10,000 100 Zlotych. 0.6250 Silver. Curie right. 12.50

Pr245 1974 500 100 Zlotych. Nickel. Royal Castle in Warsaw. —
Pr246 1974 20 100 Zlotych. 0.6250 Silver. Royal Castle in Warsaw. —

Pr247 1974 500 200 Zlotych. Nickel. 20.00
Pr248 1974 20 200 Zlotych. 0.6250 Silver. —
Pr249 1975 — 10 Zlotych. Aluminum. Boleslaw Prus. —
Pr250 1975 40 10 Zlotych. Copper-Nickel. Boleslaw Prus. —
Pr251 1975 500 10 Zlotych. Nickel. Boleslaw Prus. 20.00

Pr252 1975 20 20 Zlotych. Copper-Nickel. Year of the Woman. —
Pr253 1975 500 20 Zlotych. Nickel. Year of the Woman. 20.00

KM# Date Mintage Identification Mkt Val

Pr254 1975 20 20 Zlotych. Copper-Nickel. Globe. —
Pr255 1975 500 20 Zlotych. Nickel. Globe. 12.50
Pr256 1975 5,000 100 Zlotych. 0.6250 Silver. Y#76. 7.50

Pr257 1975 500 100 Zlotych. Nickel. Y#78. 17.50
Pr258 1975 20 100 Zlotych. 0.6250 Silver. Y#78. —

Pr259 1975 500 100 Zlotych. Nickel. Modrzeiewska. 17.50
Pr260 1975 20 100 Zlotych. 0.6250 Silver. Modrzeiewska. —
Pr261 1975 500 100 Zlotych. Nickel. Y#77. 17.50
Pr262 1975 20 100 Zlotych. 0.6250 Silver. Y#77. —

Pr263 1975 500 100 Zlotych. Nickel. Paderewski. 12.50
Pr264 1975 20 100 Zlotych. 0.6250 Silver. Paderewski. —

Pr265 1975 500 200 Zlotych. Nickel. 20.00
Pr266 1975 10,000 200 Zlotych. 0.7500 Silver. 17.50

Pr267 1975 500 200 Zlotych. Nickel. 20.00

KM# Date Mintage Identification Mkt Va
Pr268 1975 10,000 200 Zlotych. 0.7500 Silver. 10.0

Pr269 1975 500 200 Zlotych. Nickel. Y#79. 20.0
Pr270 1975 2,600 200 Zlotych. 0.7500 Silver. Y#79. —
Pr271 1976 20 20 Zlotych. Copper-Nickel. 30 Years of Budget Bill. —
Pr272 1976 500 20 Zlotych. Nickel. 30 Years of Budget Bill. —
Pr273 1976 20 20 Zlotych. Copper-Nickel. 30 Years of Budget Bill - PRL. —
Pr274 1976 500 20 Zlotych. Nickel. PRL. —

Pr275 1976 500 100 Zlotych. Nickel. Y#82. 20.00
Pr276 1976 20 100 Zlotych. 0.6250 Silver. Y#82. —

Pr277 1976 3,000 100 Zlotych. 0.6250 Silver. Kosciuszko. 30.00
Pr278 1976 500 100 Zlotych. Nickel. Kosciuszko. 20.00
Pr279 1976 20 100 Zlotych. (No Composition). —

Pr280 1976 500 100 Zlotych. Nickel. Pulaski. 20.0
Pr281 1976 3,000 100 Zlotych. 0.6250 Silver. Pulaski. 25.0

Pr282 1976 20 200 Zlotych. 0.6250 Silver. Olympics. —
Pr283 1976 — 200 Zlotych. Nickel. Olympic rings and torch. —

KM#	Date	Mintage	Identification	Mkt Val
Pr284	1976	500	200 Zlotych. Nickel. Y#86.	30.00
Pr285	1976	6,048	200 Zlotych. 0.7500 Silver. Y#86.	13.50

KM#	Date	Mintage	Identification	Mkt Val
Pr286	1976	500	200 Zlotych. Nickel.	25.00
Pr287	1976	6,050	200 Zlotych. 0.6250 Silver.	20.00

KM#	Date	Mintage	Identification	Mkt Val
Pr288	1976	500	500 Zlotych. Nickel. Y#83.	20.00
Pr289	1976	300	500 Zlotych. 0.9000 Gold. Y#83.	550

KM#	Date	Mintage	Identification	Mkt Val
Pr290	1976	500	500 Zlotych. Nickel. Kosciuszko.	20.00
Pr291	1976	500	500 Zlotych. Nickel. Y#85.	20.00
Pr292	1976	300	500 Zlotych. 0.9000 Gold. Y#85.	550

KM#	Date	Mintage	Identification	Mkt Val
Pr293	1976	500	500 Zlotych. Nickel. Pulaski facing.	20.00
Pr294	1977	100	20 Zlotych. Copper-Nickel. Y#96.	—
Pr295	1977	200	20 Zlotych. Nickel. Y#96.	—

KM#	Date	Mintage	Identification	Mkt Val
Pr296	1977	500	100 Zlotych. Nickel. Y#88.	—
Pr297	1977	3,000	100 Zlotych. 0.6250 Silver. Y#88.	7.50

KM#	Date	Mintage	Identification	Mkt Val
Pr298	1977	500	100 Zlotych. Nickel. Sienkiewicz facing.	12.50
Pr299	1977	3,000	100 Zlotych. 0.6250 Silver. Sienkiewicz facing.	22.50
Pr300	1977	500	100 Zlotych. Nickel. Y#89.	—
Pr301	1977	3,100	100 Zlotych. 0.6250 Silver. Y#89.	7.50

KM#	Date	Mintage	Identification	Mkt Val
Pr302	1977	500	100 Zlotych. Nickel. Reymont profile left.	—
Pr303	1977	3,100	100 Zlotych. 0.6250 Silver. Reymont profile left.	17.50

KM#	Date	Mintage	Identification	Mkt Val
Pr304	1977	500	100 Zlotych. Nickel. Fish.	30.00
Pr305	1977	5,100	100 Zlotych. 0.6250 Silver. Fish.	20.00

KM#	Date	Mintage	Identification	Mkt Val
Pr306	1977	500	100 Zlotych. Nickel. Y#91.	25.00
Pr307	1977	100	100 Zlotych. 0.6250 Silver. Y#91.	—

KM#	Date	Mintage	Identification	Mkt Val
Pr308	1977	500	100 Zlotych. Nickel. Distant Krakow castle.	—
Pr309	1977	3,100	100 Zlotych. 0.6250 Silver. Distant Krakow castle.	32.50

KM#	Date	Mintage	Identification	Mkt Val
Pr310	1977	500	100 Zlotych. Nickel. Bison.	35.00
Pr311	1977	5,400	100 Zlotych. 0.6250 Silver. Bison.	20.00

KM#	Date	Mintage	Identification	Mkt Val
Pr312	1977	6	2000 Zlotych. Gold. Chopin.	—
Pr313	1977	500	2000 Zlotych. Nickel. Chopin.	—
Pr314	1978	100	20 Zlotych. Copper-Nickel. Y#97.	—
Pr315	1978	500	20 Zlotych. Nickel. Y#97.	—
Pr316	1978	100	20 Zlotych. Copper-Nickel. Y#96.	—
Pr317	1978	500	20 Zlotych. Nickel. Y#96.	—

KM#	Date	Mintage	Identification	Mkt Val
Pr318	1978	100	100 Zlotych. 0.6250 Silver. Y#92.	—
Pr319	1978	500	100 Zlotych. Nickel. Y#92.	—
Pr320	1978	100	100 Zlotych. 0.6250 Silver. Similar to KM#PrM255 but with lock of hair at left of face.	—
Pr321	1978	500	100 Zlotych. Nickel. Similar to KM#PrK255.	—
Pr322	1978	500	100 Zlotych. Nickel. Mickiewicz profile.	—

KM#	Date	Mintage	Identification	Mkt Val
Pr323	1978	3,100	100 Zlotych. 0.6250 Silver. Mickiewicz profile.	28.50
Pr324	1978	100	100 Zlotych. 0.6250 Silver. Y#93.	—
Pr325	1978	500	100 Zlotych. Nickel. Y#93.	—
Pr326	1978	500	100 Zlotych. Nickel. Elk head.	—

KM#	Date	Mintage	Identification	Mkt Val
Pr327	1978	3,100	100 Zlotych. 0.6250 Silver. Moose head.	30.00
Pr328	1978	500	100 Zlotych. Nickel. Beaver on wood.	—
Pr329	1978	3,100	100 Zlotych. 0.6250 Silver. Beaver on wood.	—

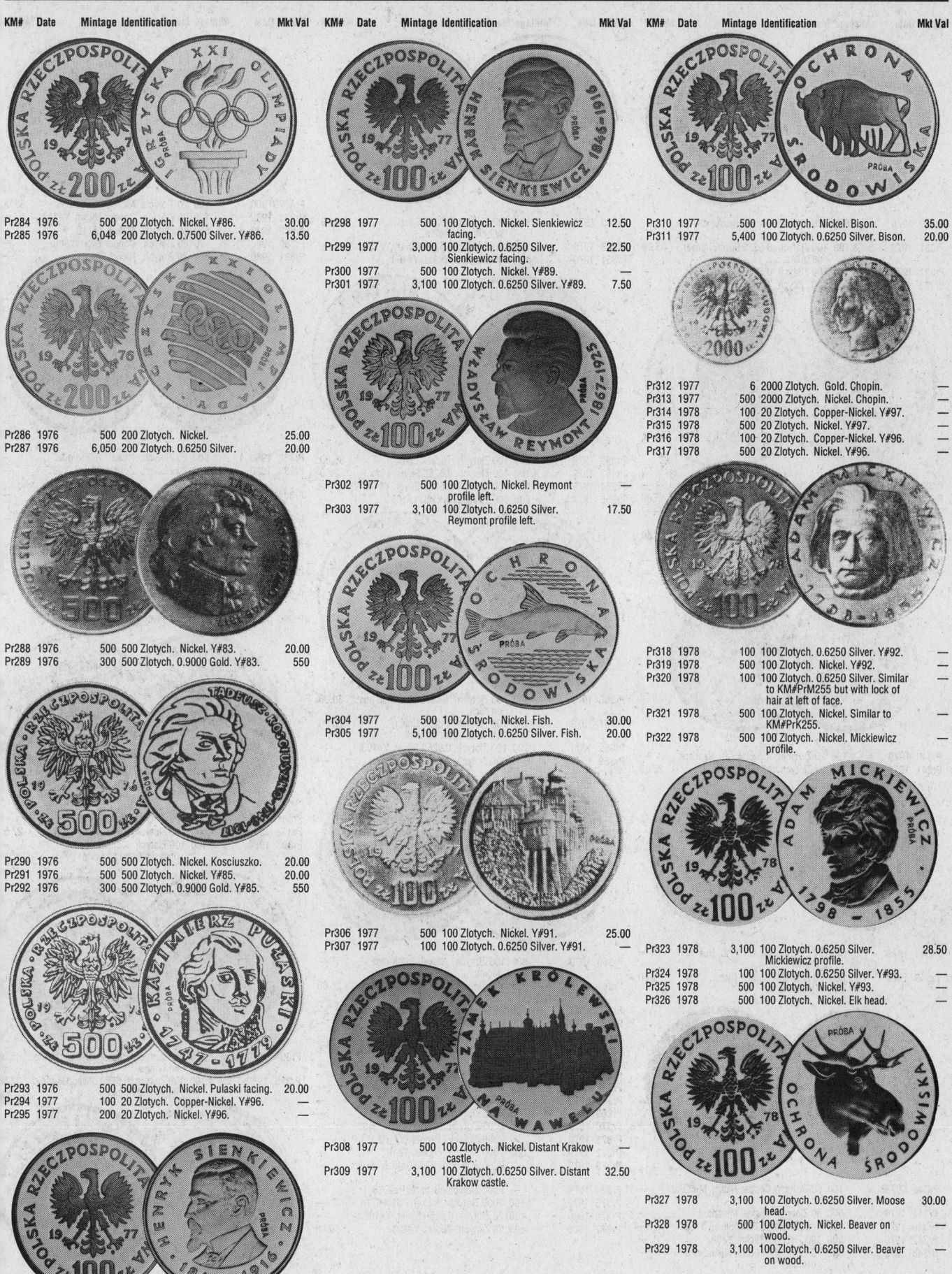

KM#	Date	Mintage	Identification	Mkt Val
Pr330	1978	500	100 Zlotych. Nickel. Beaver on grass.	—
Pr331	1978	3,100	100 Zlotych. 0.6250 Silver. Beaver on grass.	35.00
Pr332	1978	100	100 Zlotych. 0.6250 Silver. Y#94.	—
Pr333	1978	500	100 Zlotych. Nickel. Y#94.	—

KM#	Date	Mintage	Identification	Mkt Val
Pr334	1978	500	100 Zlotych. Nickel. Korczak.	—
Pr335	1978	3,100	100 Zlotych. 0.6250 Silver. Korczak.	15.00
Pr336	1978	500	100 Zlotych. Nickel. Globe in legend.	—
Pr337	1978	3,100	100 Zlotych. 0.6250 Silver. Globe in legend.	28.50
Pr338	1979	500	2 Zlotych. Nickel.	—
Pr339	1979	500	5 Zlotych. Nickel.	—

KM#	Date	Mintage	Identification	Mkt Val
Pr340	1979	500	20 Zlotych. Nickel. I.Y.C., dancers.	—
Pr341	1979	4,100	20 Zlotych. 0.6250 Silver. I.Y.C.	22.00

KM#	Date	Mintage	Identification	Mkt Val
Pr342	1979	500	20 Zlotych. Nickel. I.Y.C. Health Center.	—
Pr343	1979	30,000	20 Zlotych. Copper-Nickel. I.Y.C. Health Center.	5.00

KM#	Date	Mintage	Identification	Mkt Val
Pr344	1979	100	50 Zlotych. Copper-Nickel. Mieszko I.	—
Pr345	1979	500	50 Zlotych. Nickel. Mieszko I.	—
Pr346	1979	100	100 Zlotych. 0.6250 Silver. Y#98.	—
Pr347	1979	500	100 Zlotych. Nickel. Y#98.	—
Pr348	1979	500	100 Zlotych. Nickel. Wieniawski profile.	—

KM#	Date	Mintage	Identification	Mkt Val
Pr349	1979	3,100	100 Zlotych. 0.6250 Silver. Wieniawski profile.	10.00
Pr350	1979	100	100 Zlotych. 0.6250 Silver. Y#104.	—
Pr351	1979	500	100 Zlotych. Nickel. Y#104.	—

KM#	Date	Mintage	Identification	Mkt Val
Pr352	1979	500	100 Zlotych. Nickel. Lynx.	35.00
Pr353	1979	4,100	100 Zlotych. 0.6250 Silver. Lynx.	22.50
Pr354	1979	100	100 Zlotych. 0.6250 Silver. Y#105.	—
Pr355	1979	500	100 Zlotych. Nickel. Y#105.	—

KM#	Date	Mintage	Identification	Mkt Val
Pr356	1979	500	100 Zlotych. Nickel. Mountain goat on rock.	30.00
Pr357	1979	4,100	100 Zlotych. 0.6250 Silver. Mountain goat on rock.	25.00
Pr358	1979	100	100 Zlotych. 0.6250 Silver. Y#103.	—
Pr359	1979	500	100 Zlotych. Nickel. Y#103.	—

KM#	Date	Mintage	Identification	Mkt Val
Pr360	1979	500	100 Zlotych. Nickel. Zamenhof facing.	—
Pr361	1979	3,100	100 Zlotych. 0.6250 Silver. Zamenhof facing.	25.00
Pr362	1979	100	200 Zlotych. 0.7500 Silver. Y#101.	—
Pr363	1979	500	200 Zlotych. Nickel. Y#101.	—
Pr364	1979	500	200 Zlotych. Nickel. Mieszko.	—
Pr365	1979	4,100	200 Zlotych. 0.7500 Silver. Mieszko I.	12.50
Pr366	1979	5	2000 Zlotych. 0.9000 Gold. Y#106.	—
Pr367	1979	500	2000 Zlotych. Nickel. Y#106.	—
Pr368	1979	6	2000 Zlotych. 0.9000 Gold. Y#107.	—
Pr369	1979	500	2000 Zlotych. Nickel. Y#107.	—
Pr370	1979	4	2000 Zlotych. 0.9000 Gold. Y#102.	—
Pr371	1979	—	2000 Zlotych. Bronze. Y#102.	—
Pr372	1979	500	2000 Zlotych. Nickel. Y#102.	—
Pr373	1979	4	2000 Zlotych. 0.9000 Gold. Mieszko I, PrG266.	—
Pr374	1979	—	2000 Zlotych. Bronze. PrG266.	—
Pr375	1979	500	2000 Zlotych. Nickel. PrG266.	—
Pr376	1980	100	20 Zlotych. 0.6250 Silver. Y#108.	—
Pr377	1980	500	20 Zlotych. Nickel. Y#108.	70.00

KM#	Date	Mintage	Identification	Mkt Val
PrA378	1980	100	20 Zlotych. Nickel.	80.00
Pr378	1980	100	20 Zlotych. Copper-Nickel. Y#112.	—
Pr379	1980	500	20 Zlotych. Nickel. Y#112.	—
Pr380	1980	20	20 Zlotych. Copper-Nickel. Ship.	—
Pr381	1980	500	20 Zlotych. Nickel. Ship.	—

KM#	Date	Mintage	Identification	Mkt Val
Pr382	1980	500	20 Zlotych. Nickel. 1905-Lodz.	—
Pr383	1980	10,000	20 Zlotych. Copper-Nickel. 1905-Lodz.	—
Pr384	1980	20	20 Zlotych. Copper-Nickel. 75th Anniversary of Lodz riots.	—
Pr385	1980	500	20 Zlotych. Nickel. 75th Anniversary of Lodz riots.	—
Pr386	1980	20	50 Zlotych. Copper-Nickel. Y#114.	—
Pr387	1980	500	50 Zlotych. Nickel. Y#114.	—
Pr388	1980	20	50 Zlotych. Copper-Nickel. Boleslaw I inscription below.	—
Pr389	1980	500	50 Zlotych. Nickel. Boleslaw I, inscription below.	—
Pr390	1980	20	50 Zlotych. Copper-Nickel. Y#117.	—

KM#	Date	Mintage	Identification	Mkt Val
Pr391	1980	500	100 Zlotych. Nickel. Ship.	—
Pr392	1980	4,000	100 Zlotych. 0.6250 Silver. Ship.	27.50
Pr393	1980	100	100 Zlotych. Copper-Nickel. Olympic flame and rings.	—

KM#	Date	Mintage	Identification	Mkt Val
Pr394	1980	500	100 Zlotych. Nickel. Olympic flame and rings.	85.00
Pr395	1980	4,100	100 Zlotych. 0.6250 Silver. Olympic flame and rings.	32.50

KM#	Date	Mintage	Identification	Mkt Val
PrA396	1980	500	100 Zlotych. Nickel. Y#109.	85.0
Pr396	1980	20	100 Zlotych. 0.6250 Silver. Y#121.	–
Pr397	1980	500	100 Zlotych. Nickel. Y#121.	–

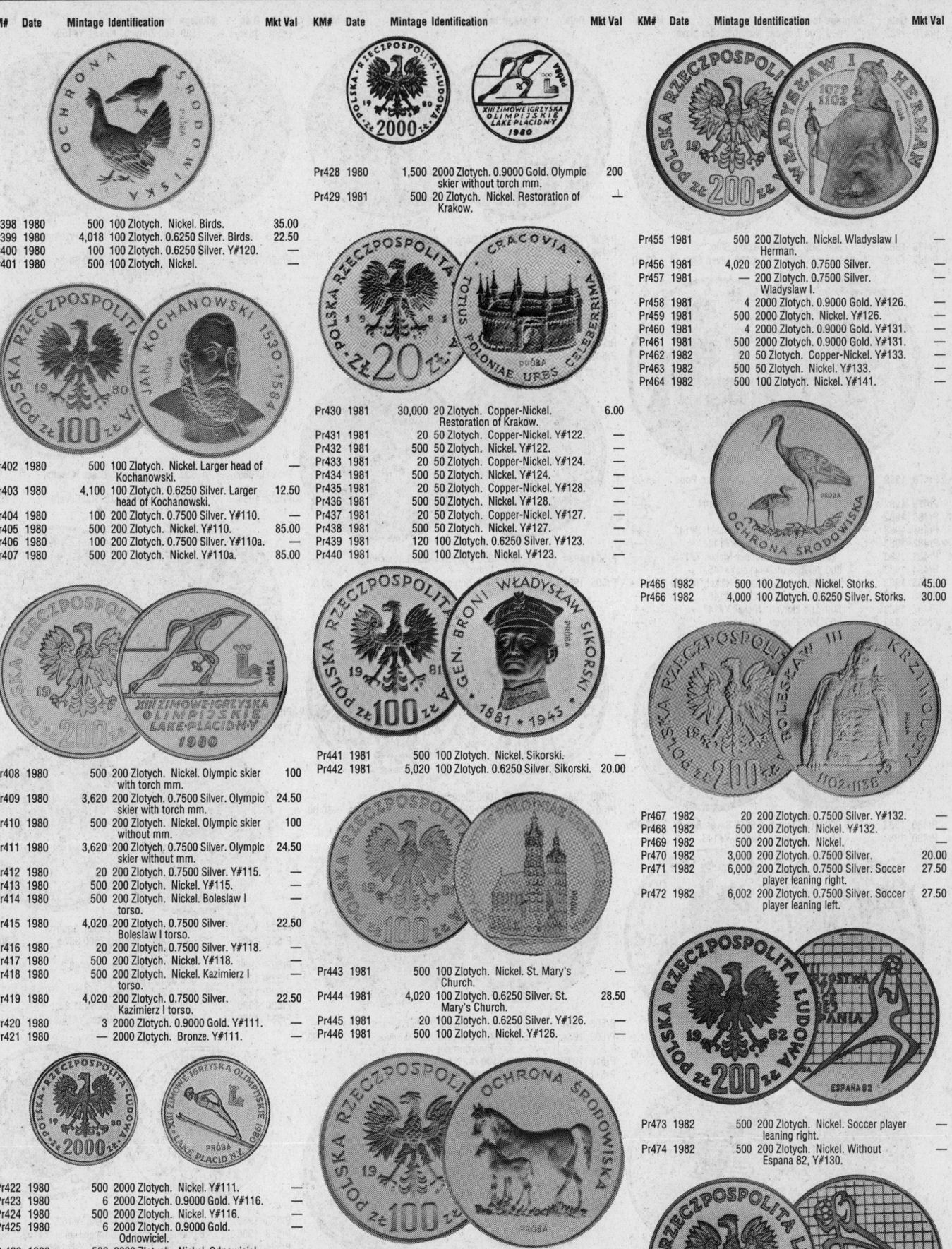

KM#	Date	Mintage	Identification	Mkt Val
Pr398	1980	500	100 Zlotych. Nickel. Birds.	35.00
Pr399	1980	4,018	100 Zlotych. 0.6250 Silver. Birds.	22.50
Pr400	1980	100	100 Zlotych. 0.6250 Silver. Y#120.	—
Pr401	1980	500	100 Zlotych. Nickel.	—

KM#	Date	Mintage	Identification	Mkt Val
Pr402	1980	500	100 Zlotych. Nickel. Larger head of Kochanowski.	—
Pr403	1980	4,100	100 Zlotych. 0.6250 Silver. Larger head of Kochanowski.	12.50
Pr404	1980	100	200 Zlotych. 0.7500 Silver. Y#110.	—
Pr405	1980	500	200 Zlotych. Nickel. Y#110.	85.00
Pr406	1980	100	200 Zlotych. 0.7500 Silver. Y#110a.	—
Pr407	1980	500	200 Zlotych. Nickel. Y#110a.	85.00

KM#	Date	Mintage	Identification	Mkt Val
Pr408	1980	500	200 Zlotych. Nickel. Olympic skier with torch mm.	100
Pr409	1980	3,620	200 Zlotych. 0.7500 Silver. Olympic skier with torch mm.	24.50
Pr410	1980	500	200 Zlotych. Nickel. Olympic skier without mm.	100
Pr411	1980	3,620	200 Zlotych. 0.7500 Silver. Olympic skier without mm.	24.50
Pr412	1980	20	200 Zlotych. 0.7500 Silver. Y#115.	—
Pr413	1980	500	200 Zlotych. Nickel. Y#115.	—
Pr414	1980	500	200 Zlotych. Nickel. Boleslaw I torso.	—
Pr415	1980	4,020	200 Zlotych. 0.7500 Silver. Boleslaw I torso.	22.50
Pr416	1980	20	200 Zlotych. 0.7500 Silver. Y#118.	—
Pr417	1980	500	200 Zlotych. Nickel. Y#118.	—
Pr418	1980	500	200 Zlotych. Nickel. Kazimierz I torso.	—
Pr419	1980	4,020	200 Zlotych. 0.7500 Silver. Kazimierz I torso.	22.50
Pr420	1980	3	2000 Zlotych. 0.9000 Gold. Y#111.	—
Pr421	1980	—	2000 Zlotych. Bronze. Y#111.	—

KM#	Date	Mintage	Identification	Mkt Val
Pr422	1980	500	2000 Zlotych. Nickel. Y#111.	—
Pr423	1980	6	2000 Zlotych. 0.9000 Gold. Y#116.	—
Pr424	1980	500	2000 Zlotych. Nickel. Y#116.	—
Pr425	1980	6	2000 Zlotych. 0.9000 Gold. Odnowiciel.	—
Pr426	1980	500	2000 Zlotych. Nickel. Odnowiciel.	—
Pr427	1980	500	2000 Zlotych. Nickel. Olympic skier without torch mm.	—

KM#	Date	Mintage	Identification	Mkt Val
Pr428	1980	1,500	2000 Zlotych. 0.9000 Gold. Olympic skier without torch mm.	200
Pr429	1981	500	20 Zlotych. Nickel. Restoration of Krakow.	—

KM#	Date	Mintage	Identification	Mkt Val
Pr430	1981	30,000	20 Zlotych. Copper-Nickel. Restoration of Krakow.	6.00
Pr431	1981	20	50 Zlotych. Copper-Nickel. Y#122.	—
Pr432	1981	500	50 Zlotych. Nickel. Y#122.	—
Pr433	1981	20	50 Zlotych. Copper-Nickel. Y#124.	—
Pr434	1981	500	50 Zlotych. Nickel. Y#124.	—
Pr435	1981	20	50 Zlotych. Copper-Nickel. Y#128.	—
Pr436	1981	500	50 Zlotych. Nickel. Y#128.	—
Pr437	1981	20	50 Zlotych. Copper-Nickel. Y#127.	—
Pr438	1981	500	50 Zlotych. Nickel. Y#127.	—
Pr439	1981	120	100 Zlotych. 0.6250 Silver. Y#123.	—
Pr440	1981	500	100 Zlotych. Nickel. Y#123.	—

KM#	Date	Mintage	Identification	Mkt Val
Pr441	1981	500	100 Zlotych. Nickel. Sikorski.	—
Pr442	1981	5,020	100 Zlotych. 0.6250 Silver. Sikorski.	20.00

KM#	Date	Mintage	Identification	Mkt Val
Pr443	1981	500	100 Zlotych. Nickel. St. Mary's Church.	—
Pr444	1981	4,020	100 Zlotych. 0.6250 Silver. St. Mary's Church.	28.50
Pr445	1981	20	100 Zlotych. 0.6250 Silver. Y#126.	—
Pr446	1981	500	100 Zlotych. Nickel. Y#126.	—

KM#	Date	Mintage	Identification	Mkt Val
Pr447	1981	500	100 Zlotych. Nickel.	40.00
Pr448	1981	4,020	100 Zlotych. 0.6250 Silver. Horses.	30.00
Pr449	1981	20	100 Zlotych. 0.7500 Silver. Y#125.	—
Pr450	1981	500	200 Zlotych. Nickel. Y#125.	—
Pr451	1981	500	200 Zlotych. Nickel. Boleslaw II.	—
Pr452	1981	4,020	200 Zlotych. 0.7500 Silver. Boleslaw II.	25.00
Pr453	1981	20	200 Zlotych. 0.7500 Silver. Y#129.	—
Pr454	1981	500	200 Zlotych. Nickel. Y#129.	—

KM#	Date	Mintage	Identification	Mkt Val
Pr455	1981	500	200 Zlotych. Nickel. Wladyslaw I Herman.	—
Pr456	1981	4,020	200 Zlotych. 0.7500 Silver.	—
Pr457	1981	—	200 Zlotych. 0.7500 Silver. Wladyslaw I.	—
Pr458	1981	4	2000 Zlotych. 0.9000 Gold. Y#126.	—
Pr459	1981	500	2000 Zlotych. Nickel. Y#126.	—
Pr460	1981	4	2000 Zlotych. 0.9000 Gold. Y#131.	—
Pr461	1981	500	2000 Zlotych. 0.9000 Gold. Y#131.	—
Pr462	1982	20	50 Zlotych. Copper-Nickel. Y#133.	—
Pr463	1982	500	50 Zlotych. Nickel. Y#133.	—
Pr464	1982	500	100 Zlotych. Nickel. Y#141.	—

KM#	Date	Mintage	Identification	Mkt Val
Pr465	1982	500	100 Zlotych. Nickel. Storks.	45.00
Pr466	1982	4,000	100 Zlotych. 0.6250 Silver. Storks.	30.00

KM#	Date	Mintage	Identification	Mkt Val
Pr467	1982	20	200 Zlotych. 0.7500 Silver. Y#132.	—
Pr468	1982	500	200 Zlotych. Nickel. Y#132.	—
Pr469	1982	500	200 Zlotych. Nickel.	—
Pr470	1982	3,000	200 Zlotych. 0.7500 Silver.	20.00
Pr471	1982	6,000	200 Zlotych. 0.7500 Silver. Soccer player leaning right.	27.50
Pr472	1982	6,002	200 Zlotych. 0.7500 Silver. Soccer player leaning left.	27.50

KM#	Date	Mintage	Identification	Mkt Val
Pr473	1982	500	200 Zlotych. Nickel. Soccer player leaning right.	—
Pr474	1982	500	200 Zlotych. Nickel. Without Espana 82, Y#130.	—

KM#	Date	Mintage	Identification	Mkt Val
Pr475	1982	500	200 Zlotych. Nickel. Soccer player leaning left.	—

KM#	Date	Mintage	Identification	Mkt Val
Pr476	1982	500	500 Zlotych. Nickel. Ship.	—
Pr477	1982	25,000	500 Zlotych. 0.6250 Silver. Ship.	22.50

KM#	Date	Mintage	Identification	Mkt Val
Pr478	1982	10,000	1000 Zlotych. 0.7500 Silver. Pope John Paul II.	25.00
Pr479	1982	500	1000 Zlotych. Nickel. Y#144.	—
Pr480	1982	500	1000 Zlotych. Nickel.	—
Pr481	1983	20	50 Zlotych. Copper-Nickel. Y#142.	—
Pr482	1983	500	50 Zlotych. Nickel. Y#142.	—
Pr483	1983	20	50 Zlotych. Copper-Nickel. Y#145.	—
Pr484	1983	500	50 Zlotych. Nickel. Y#145.	—
Pr485	1983	20	50 Zlotych. Copper-Nickel. Y#146.	—
Pr486	1983	500	50 Zlotych. Nickel. Y#146.	—
Pr487	1983	500	100 Zlotych. Nickel. Y#147.	—
Pr488	1983	500	100 Zlotych. Nickel.	—

KM#	Date	Mintage	Identification	Mkt Val
Pr489	1983	3,000	100 Zlotych. 0.6250 Silver. Bears.	35.00
Pr490	1983	500	200 Zlotych. Nickel. Y#143.	—

KM#	Date	Mintage	Identification	Mkt Val
Pr491	1983	500	200 Zlotych. Nickel.	—
Pr492	1983	4,000	200 Zlotych. 0.7500 Silver. Jan III Sobieski.	35.00

KM#	Date	Mintage	Identification	Mkt Val
Pr493	1983	500	500 Zlotych. Nickel.	—
Pr494	1983	7,000	500 Zlotych. 0.7500 Silver. Gymnast.	30.00

KM#	Date	Mintage	Identification	Mkt Val
Pr495	1983	500	500 Zlotych. Nickel.	—
Pr496	1983	6,000	500 Zlotych. 0.7500 Silver. Speed skater.	30.00
Pr497	1984	500	10 Zlotych. Nickel. Y#152.1.	—
Pr498	1984	500	20 Zlotych. Nickel. Y#153.1.	—
Pr499	1984	500	100 Zlotych. Nickel. Y#148.	—
Pr500	1984	500	100 Zlotych. Nickel. Y#151.	—
Pr501	1984	500	200 Zlotych. Nickel. Y#149.	—
Pr502	1984	500	200 Zlotych. Nickel. Y#150.	—
Pr503	1984	500	500 Zlotych. Nickel. Y#154.	—

KM#	Date	Mintage	Identification	Mkt Val
Pr504	1984	500	1000 Zlotych. Nickel. Wincenty Witos.	—
Pr505	1984	3,000	1000 Zlotych. 0.6250 Silver. Wincenty Witos.	30.00

KM#	Date	Mintage	Identification	Mkt Val
Pr506	1984	500	1000 Zlotych. Nickel. PRL.	—
Pr507	1984	2,004	1000 Zlotych. 0.6250 Silver. 40th Anniversary of Peoples Republic.	30.00

KM#	Date	Mintage	Identification	Mkt Val
Pr508	1984	500	1000 Zlotych. Nickel. Swans.	—
Pr509	1984	5,700	1000 Zlotych. 0.6250 Silver. Environment.	25.00
Pr510	1985	500	100 Zlotych. Nickel. Y#155.	—
Pr511	1985	500	100 Zlotych. Nickel. Y#157.	—

KM#	Date	Mintage	Identification	Mkt Val
Pr512	1985	500	200 Zlotych. Nickel.	—
Pr513	1985	15,000	200 Zlotych. Copper-Nickel.	7.50
Pr514	1985	500	200 Zlotych. Nickel. Hospital Center.	—
Pr515	1985	37,300	200 Zlotych. Nickel Plated Iron. Hospital Center, soccer.	12.50
Pr516	1985	500	500 Zlotych. Nickel. Y#156.	—
Pr517	1985	500	500 Zlotych. Nickel. Y#158.	—
Pr518	1985	500	500 Zlotych. Nickel. Y#159.	—

KM#	Date	Mintage	Identification	Mkt Val
Pr519	1985	500	1000 Zlotych. Nickel. Przemyslaw II.	—
Pr520	1985	2,500	1000 Zlotych. 0.7500 Silver. Przemyslaw II.	10.00

KM#	Date	Mintage	Identification	Mkt Val
Pr521	1985	500	1000 Zlotych. Nickel. Hospital Center.	—
Pr522	1985	2,500	1000 Zlotych. 0.7500 Silver. Hospital Center.	25.00

KM#	Date	Mintage	Identification	Mkt Val
Pr523	1985	500	1000 Zlotych. Nickel. U.N.	—
Pr524	1985	2,500	1000 Zlotych. 0.7500 Silver. U.N.	40.00

KM#	Date	Mintage	Identification	Mkt Val
Pr525	1985	500	1000 Zlotych. Nickel. Squirrel.	—
Pr526	1985	2,500	1000 Zlotych. 0.7500 Silver. Squirrel.	30.00
Pr527	1986	500	50 Groszy. Nickel. Y#48.2.	—
Pr528	1986	500	Zloty. Nickel. Y#49.2.	—
Pr529	1986	500	2 Zlote. Nickel. Y#80.2.	—
Pr530	1986	500	5 Zlotych. Nickel. Y#81.2.	—
Pr531	1986	500	100 Zlotych. Nickel. Y#160.	—

KM#	Date	Mintage	Identification	Mkt Val
Pr532	1986	500	200 Zlotych. Nickel. Y#162.	40.00
Pr533	1986	6,000	200 Zlotych. Copper-Nickel. Y#162.	30.00
Pr534	1986	500	200 Zlotych. Nickel. Wladyslaw.	—
Pr535	1986	10,000	200 Zlotych. Copper-Nickel. Wladyslaw.	15.00
Pr536	1986	500	500 Zlotych. Nickel. Y#161.	—
Pr537	1986	500	500 Zlotych. Nickel. Y#162.	—
Pr538	1986	500	500 Zlotych. Nickel. Y#166.	—

KM#	Date	Mintage	Identification	Mkt Val
Pr539	1986	—	500 Zlotych. Nickel. Y#225.	—
Pr540	1986	500	1000 Zlotych. Nickel. Soccer.	—

KM#	Date	Mintage	Identification	Mkt Val
Pr541	1986	9,000	1000 Zlotych. 0.7500 Silver. Soccer.	—
Pr542	1986	500	1000 Zlotych. Nickel. Education.	—
Pr543	1986	25,400	1000 Zlotych. 0.6250 Silver. Education.	—
Pr544	1986	22,000	1000 Zlotych. 0.7500 Silver. Hospital Center.	—

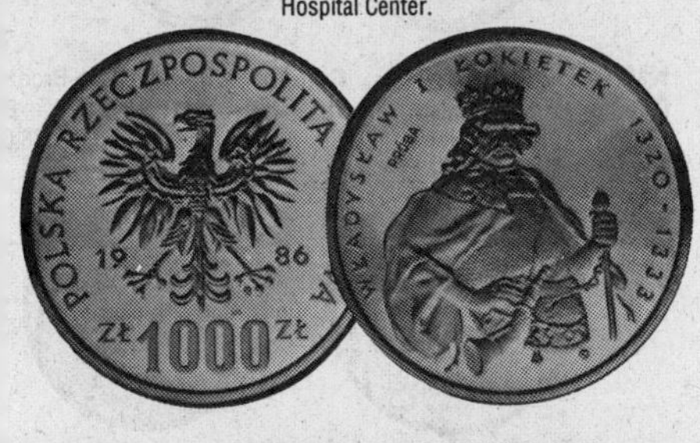

KM#	Date	Mintage	Identification	Mkt Val
Pr545	1986	500	1000 Zlotych. Nickel. Wladyslaw I.	—
Pr546	1986	2,500	1000 Zlotych. 0.7500 Silver. Wladyslaw I.	26.00

KM#	Date	Mintage	Identification	Mkt Val
Pr547	1986	500	1000 Zlotych. Nickel. Owl.	45.00
Pr548	1986	6,000	1000 Zlotych. 0.7500 Silver. Owl.	40.00
Pr549	1986	—	1000 Zlotych. Nickel.	—

KM#	Date	Mintage	Identification	Mkt Val
Pr550	1986	—	1000 Zlotych. 0.6250 Silver. School aid.	—
Pr551	1987	500	100 Zlotych. Nickel. Y#167.	—

KM#	Date	Mintage	Identification	Mkt Val
Pr552	1987	500	200 Zlotych. Nickel. Europe soccer.	—
Pr553	1987	15,000	200 Zlotych. Copper-Nickel. Europe soccer.	12.00
Pr554	1987	500	200 Zlotych. Nickel. Olympics - Tennis.	—
Pr555	1987	10,000	200 Zlotych. Copper-Nickel. Olympics - Tennis.	17.00
Pr556	1987	500	500 Zlotych. Nickel. Y#165.	—
Pr557	1987	500	500 Zlotych. Nickel. Y#166.	—
Pr558	1987	500	500 Zlotych. Nickel. Y#172.	—
Pr559	1987	500	500 Zlotych. Nickel. Y#173.	—

KM#	Date	Mintage	Identification	Mkt Val
Pr560	1987	500	1000 Zlotych. Nickel. Wratislavia.	—
Pr561	1987	24,000	1000 Zlotych. 0.7500 Silver. Wratislavia.	22.50

KM#	Date	Mintage	Identification	Mkt Val
Pr562	1987	500	1000 Zlotych. Nickel. Slaskie Museum.	—
Pr563	1987	11,500	1000 Zlotych. 0.7500 Silver. Slaskie Museum.	25.00

KM#	Date	Mintage	Identification	Mkt Val
Pr564	1987	500	1000 Zlotych. Nickel. Olympic cross country skier.	—
Pr565	1987	10,000	1000 Zlotych. 0.7500 Silver. Olympic cross country skier.	15.00

KM#	Date	Mintage	Identification	Mkt Val
Pr566	1987	500	1000 Zlotych. Nickel. Olympic archery.	—
Pr567	1987	10,000	1000 Zlotych. 0.7500 Silver. Olympic archery.	37.50

KM#	Date	Mintage	Identification	Mkt Val
Pr568	1987	500	1000 Zlotych. Nickel. Kazimierz III.	—
Pr569	1987	2,500	1000 Zlotych. 0.7500 Silver. Kazimierz III.	47.50

KM#	Date	Mintage	Identification	Mkt Val
Pr570	1987	9	1000 Zlotych. Gold. Y#168.	—

KM#	Date	Mintage	Identification	Mkt Val
Pr571	1987	9	2000 Zlotych. Gold. Y#169.	—

KM#	Date	Mintage	Identification	Mkt Val
Pr572	1987	9	5000 Zlotych. Gold. Y#170.	—

KM#	Date	Mintage	Identification	Mkt Val
Pr573	1987	9	10000 Zlotych. Gold. Y#171.	—

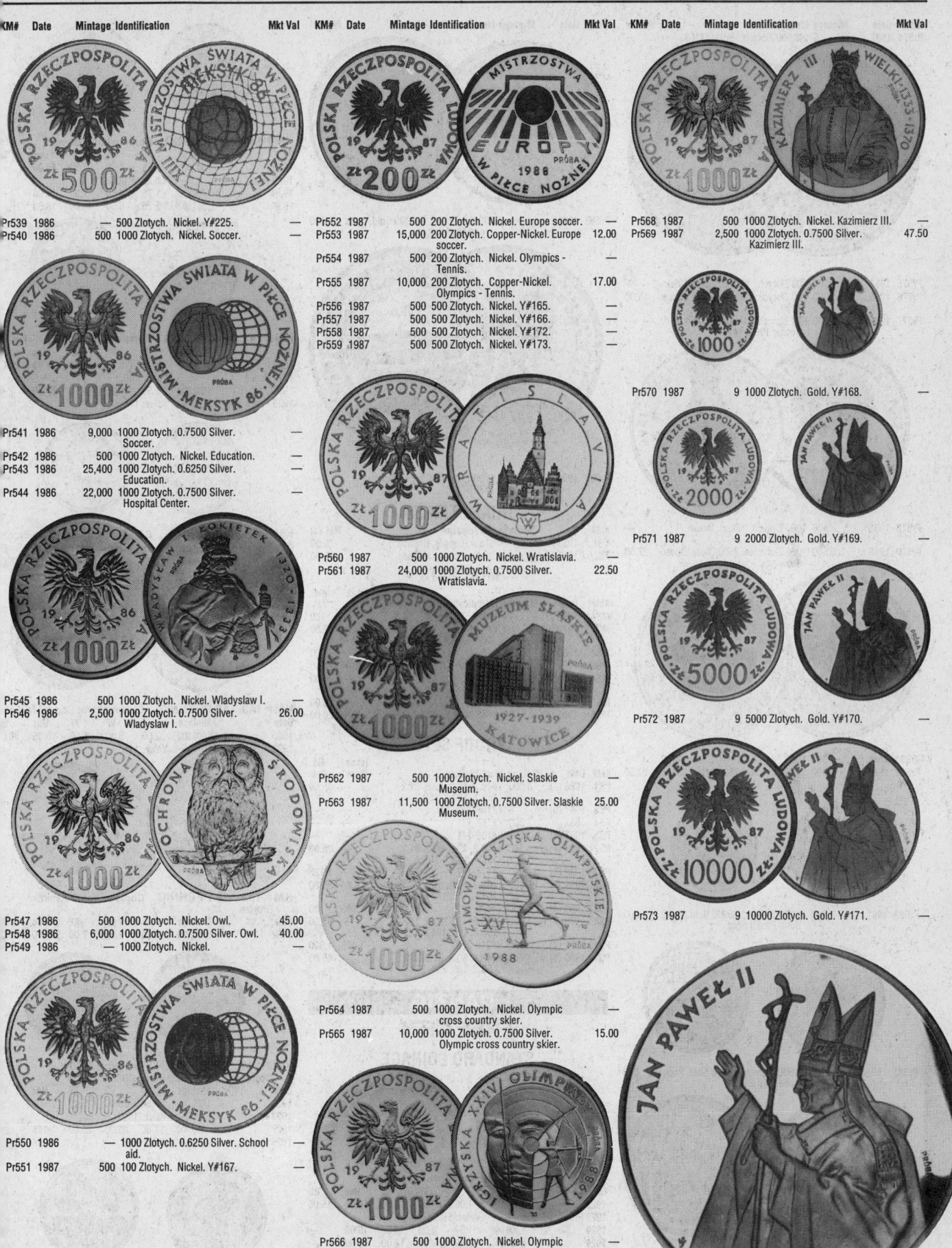

KM#	Date	Mintage	Identification	Mkt Val
Pr574	1987	5	200000 Zlotych. Gold. Y#163.	—

KM#	Date	Mintage	Identification	Mkt Val
Pr575	1988	500	200 Zlotych. Nickel. Soccer 1990.	—
Pr576	1988	10,000	200 Zlotych. Copper-Nickel. Soccer 1990.	15.00
Pr577	1988	7,000	500 Zlotych. (No Composition). Soccer 1990, Y#184.	—

KM#	Date	Mintage	Identification	Mkt Val
Pr578	1988	500	1000 Zlotych. Nickel. Queen Jadwiga.	—
Pr579	1988	2,500	1000 Zlotych. 0.7500 Silver. Queen Jadwiga.	37.50

KM#	Date	Mintage	Identification	Mkt Val
Pr580	1988	500	1000 Zlotych. Nickel. Soccer 1990.	—
Pr581	1988	7,000	1000 Zlotych. 0.7500 Silver. Soccer 1990.	27.50

KM#	Date	Mintage	Identification	Mkt Val
Pr582	1991	300	20000 Zlotych. 0.9990 Gold. Pope John Paul II right.	200

KM#	Date	Mintage	Identification	Mkt Val
Pr583	1991	—	50000 Zlotych. 0.9990 Gold. Pope John Paul II right.	300

KM#	Date	Mintage	Identification	Mkt Val
Pr584	1991	—	100000 Zlotych. 0.9990 Gold. Pope John Paul II right.	400

KM#	Date	Mintage	Identification	Mkt Val
Pr585	1991	—	200000 Zlotych. 0.9990 Gold. Pope John Paul II right.	500

KM#	Date	Mintage	Identification	Mkt Val
Pr586	1994	—	1000 Zlotych. Copper-Nickel. Y#267.	—

TRIAL STRIKES

KM#	Date	Mintage	Identification	Mkt Val
TS1	1923	—	Grosz. Copper. Uniface.	75.00
TS2	1923	—	Grosz. Copper. Uniface.	75.00

MINT SETS

KM#	Date	Mintage	Identification	Issue Price	Mkt Val
MSA1	1964 (3)	—	Y#52, 52A, Pr100	—	160
MS1	1979 (6)	5,000	Y#AA47, A47, 80.1-81.1, 99, 100	—	32.50
MS2	1980 (5)	5,000	Y#AA47, A47, 49.1, 80.1-81.1	—	20.00
MS3	1980 (4)	5,000	Y#108, 112, 114, 117	—	20.00
MS4	1981 (6)	5,000	Y#AA47, A47, 49.1, 73, 80.1-81.1	—	20.00
MS5	1981 (4)	5,000	Y#122, 124, 127-128	—	20.00
MS6	1982 (6)	5,000	Y#48.1-49.1, 73, 80.1-81.1, 133	—	20.00

PROOF SETS

KM#	Date	Mintage	Identification	Issue Price	Mkt Val
PS1	1986 (7)	5,000	Y#48.2, 49.2, 80.2, 81.2, 152.1, 153.1, 160	—	85.00
PS3	1987 (5)	6	Y#163, 168-171	—	—
PS4	1987	300	Y#168-171	—	—
PS5	1987 (4)	201	Y#168-171	—	—
PS2	1987 (7)	500	Y#48.2, 49.2, 80.2, 81.2, 152.1, 153.1, 167	—	85.00
PS7	1988 (4)	1,000	Y#174-177	—	1,125
PS6	1988 (7)	5,000	Y#49.2, 80.2, 81.2, 152.1, 153.1, 182, 183 Mint medal	—	85.00
PS9	1989 (4)	1,000	Y#186-189	1,595	1,100
PS8	1989 (7)	5,000	Y#49.3, 80.3, 81.3, 152.2, 153.2, 185, 194	—	85.00
PS10	1990 (4)	1,000	Y#219-222	1,495	1,300
PS11	1990 (8)	5,000	Y#49.3, 80.3, 81.3, 152.2, 153.2, 195, 214, 216	—	65.00

DANZIG

FREE CITY

STANDARD COINAGE

KM# 140 PFENNIG **Composition:** Bronze

Date	Mintage	F	VF	XF	Unc	BU
1923	4,000,000	1.00	3.00	5.00	10.00	15.00
1923 Proof	—	Value: 50.00				
1926	1,500,000	1.50	4.00	8.00	16.00	—
1929	1,000,000	2.50	7.50	12.00	20.00	—
1930	2,000,000	1.25	3.50	6.50	12.00	18.00
1937	3,000,000	1.25	3.50	6.50	12.00	18.00

KM# 141 2 PFENNIG **Composition:** Bronze

Date	Mintage	F	VF	XF	Unc	B
1923	1,000,000	1.75	4.50	7.50	15.00	–
1923 Proof	—	Value: 65.00				
1926	1,750,000	1.75	4.50	7.50	15.00	–
1937	500,000	2.75	6.50	11.00	18.50	–

KM# 142 5 PFENNIG **Composition:** Copper-Nickel

Date	Mintage	F	VF	XF	Unc	B
1923	3,000,000	1.25	2.75	6.00	12.00	20.0
1923 Proof	—	Value: 100				
1928	1,000,000	3.50	8.25	14.00	27.50	–
1928 Proof	—	Value: 175				

KM# 151 5 PFENNIG **Composition:** Aluminum-Bronz

Date	Mintage	F	VF	XF	Unc	B
1932	4,000,000	1.25	2.25	6.00	16.00	28.0

KM# 143 10 PFENNIG **Composition:** Copper-Nickel

Date	Mintage	F	VF	XF	Unc	B
1923	5,000,000	2.00	3.00	8.00	18.00	30.0
1923 Proof	—	Value: 115				

KM# 152 10 PFENNIG **Composition:** Aluminum-Bronze

Date	Mintage	F	VF	XF	Unc	B
1932	5,000,000	1.50	2.50	7.00	17.00	30.0

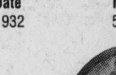

KM# 144 1/2 GULDEN **Weight:** 2.5000 g. **Composition:** 0.7500 Silver .0603 oz. ASW

Date	Mintage	F	VF	XF	Unc	B
1923	1,000,000	7.50	20.00	35.00	75.00	–
1923 Proof	—	Value: 150				
1927	400,000	17.50	35.00	70.00	125	–
1927 Proof	—	Value: 250				

KM# 153 1/2 GULDEN **Composition:** Nickel

Date	Mintage	F	VF	XF	Unc	B
1932	1,400,000	8.00	25.00	37.50	70.00	

M# 145 GULDEN **Weight:** 5.0000 g. **Composition:** 0.7500 Silver .1206 oz. ASW

ate	Mintage	F	VF	XF	Unc	BU
23	2,500,000	11.00	27.50	40.00	95.00	—
23 Proof	—	Value: 200				

M# 154 GULDEN **Composition:** Nickel

ate	Mintage	F	VF	XF	Unc	BU
932	2,500,000	8.00	25.00	35.00	60.00	90.00

:M# 146 2 GULDEN **Weight:** 10.0000 g. **Composition:** 0.7500 Silver .2411 oz. ASW

ate	Mintage	F	VF	XF	Unc	BU
923	1,250,000	25.00	65.00	120	225	—
923 Proof	—	Value: 300				

:M# 155 2 GULDEN **Weight:** 10.0000 g. **Composition:** 0.5000 Silver .1608 oz. ASW

ate	Mintage	F	VF	XF	Unc	BU
932	1,250,000	—	150	200	375	—

:M# 147 5 GULDEN **Weight:** 25.0000 g. **Composition:** 0.7500 Silver .6028 oz. ASW

ate	Mintage	F	VF	XF	Unc	BU
923	700,000	65.00	135	220	450	—
923 Proof	—	Value: 550				
927	160,000	150	250	375	650	—
927 Proof	—	Value: 1,000				

KM# 156 5 GULDEN **Weight:** 14.8200 g. **Composition:** 0.5000 Silver .2382 oz. ASW

Date	Mintage	F	VF	XF	Unc	BU
1932	430,000	125	225	350	950	—

KM# 157 5 GULDEN **Weight:** 14.8200 g. **Composition:** 0.5000 Silver .2382 oz. ASW

Date	Mintage	F	VF	XF	Unc	BU
1932	430,000	150	350	850	1,500	—

KM# 158 5 GULDEN **Composition:** Nickel

Date	Mintage	F	VF	XF	Unc	BU
1935	800,000	100	160	235	475	—

KM# 159 10 GULDEN **Composition:** Nickel

Date	Mintage	F	VF	XF	Unc	BU
1935	380,000	300	500	700	1,350	—

KM# 148 25 GULDEN **Weight:** 7.9881 g. **Composition:** 0.9170 Gold .2354 oz. AGW **Note:** Presented to senate members.

Date	Mintage	F	VF	XF	Unc	BU
1923	800	—	1,500	1,850	2,700	—
1923 Proof	200	Value: 3,500				

KM# 150 25 GULDEN **Weight:** 7.9881 g. **Composition:** 0.9170 Gold .2354 oz. AGW **Note:** Not released for circulation. A few were given Sept. 1, 1939, in VIP presentation cases.

Date	F	VF	XF	Unc	BU
1930	—	—	6,500	9,500	—

TOKEN COINAGE

KM# Tn1 10 PFENNIG **Composition:** Zinc

Date	Mintage	F	VF	XF	Unc	BU
1920	876,000	10.00	15.00	30.00	65.00	—

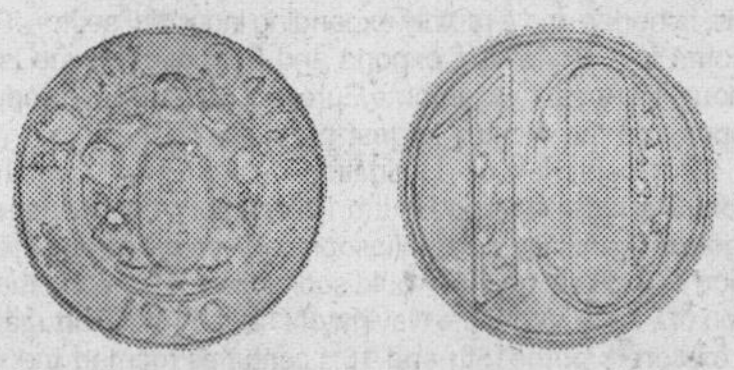

KM# Tn2 10 PFENNIG **Composition:** Zinc

Date	Mintage	F	VF	XF	Unc	BU
1920	124,000	100	150	225	350	—

PATTERNS

Including off metal strikes

KM#	Date	Mintage	Identification	Mkt Val
Pn43	1920	30	10 Pfennig. Silver.	3,250
Pn44	1920	30	10 Pfennig. Silver. Large 10.	3,250
Pn45	1923	—	5 Pfennig. Brass.	165
Pn46	1923	—	10 Pfennig. Brass.	170
Pn47	1923	10	Gulden. Gold. KM145.	7,500
Pn48	1927	—	2 Pfennig. Brass.	—
Pn49	1935	—	5 Gulden. Nickel. PROBE.	—
Pn50	1935	—	10 Gulden. Nickel. PROBE.	—
Pn51	1935	—	10 Gulden. Tin.	110

PROOF SETS

KM#	Date	Mintage	Identification	Issue Price	Mkt Val
PS1	1923 (8)	—	KM140-147	—	1,475

PORTUGAL

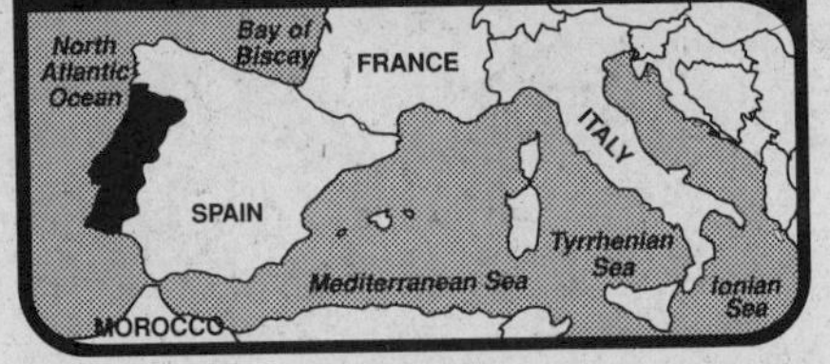

The Portuguese Republic, located in the western part of the Iberian Peninsula in southwestern Europe, has an area of 35,553 sq. mi. (92,080 sq. km.) and a population of *10.5 million. Capital: Lisbon. Portugal's economy is based on agriculture, tourism, minerals, fisheries and a rapidly expanding industrial sector. Textiles account for 33% of the exports and Portuguese wine is world famous. Portugal has become Europe's number one producer of copper and the world's largest producer of cork.

After centuries of domination by Romans, Visigoths and Moors, Portugal emerged in the 12th century as an independent kingdom financially and philosophically prepared for the great period of exploration that would soon follow. Attuned to the inspiration of Prince Henry the Navigator (1394-1460), Portugal's daring explorers of the15th and 16th centuries roamed the world's oceans from Brazil to Japan in an unprecedented burst of energy and endeavor that culminated in 1494 with Portugal laying claim to half the transoceanic world. Unfortunately for the fortunes of the tiny kingdom, the Portuguese population was too small to colonize this vast territory. Less than a century after Portugal laid claim to half the world, English, French and Dutch trading companies had seized the lion's share of the world's colonies and commerce, and Portugal's place as an imperial power was lost forever. The monarchy was overthrown in 1910 and a republic was established.

On April 25, 1974, the government of Portugal was seized by a military junta which reached agreements providing for independence for the Portuguese overseas provinces of Portuguese Guinea (*Guinea-Bissau*), Mozambique, Cape Verde Islands, Angola, and St. Thomas and Prince Islands (*Sao Tome and Principe*).

On January 1, 1986, Portugal became the eleventh member of the European Economic Community and in the first half of 1992 held its first EEC Presidency.

RULERS

Carlos I, 1889-1908
Manuel II, 1908-1910
Republic, 1910 to date

MONETARY SYSTEM

Beginning in 1836 all coins were expressed in terms of Reis and arranged in a decimal sequence (until 1910).

Commencing 1910

100 Centavos = 1 Escudo

KINGDOM

DECIMAL COINAGE

KM# 530 5 REIS Composition: Bronze **Obverse:** Bust of Carlos I right

Date	Mintage	F	VF	XF	Unc	BU
1901	1,070,000	2.50	12.50	40.00	90.00	—
1904	720,000	0.75	1.75	12.50	30.00	—
1905	1,340,000	0.50	1.00	4.50	12.50	—
1906/0	1,260	0.30	1.00	2.50	8.00	—
1906/9	Inc. above	0.25	0.75	2.00	7.00	—
1906	Inc. above	0.30	1.00	2.50	8.00	—

KM# 555 5 REIS Composition: Bronze **Obverse:** Bust of Emanuel II left

Date	Mintage	F	VF	XF	Unc	BU
1910	1,000,000	0.30	1.00	2.50	7.00	—

KM# 548 100 REIS Weight: 2.5000 g. **Composition:** 0.8350 Silver .0671 oz. ASW **Obverse:** Bust of Emanuel II left

Date	Mintage	F	VF	XF	Unc	BU
1909	6,363,000	1.50	3.50	6.50	22.00	—
1910	Inc. above	1.00	2.00	3.50	9.00	—

KM# 534 200 REIS Weight: 5.0000 g. **Composition:** 0.9170 Silver .1474 oz. ASW **Obverse:** Bust right **Obv. Legend:** CARLOS I..

Date	Mintage	VG	F	VF	XF	Unc
1901	205,000	30.00	75.00	125	300	—
1903	200,000	12.50	35.00	65.00	115	—

KM# 549 200 REIS Weight: 5.0000 g. **Composition:** 0.8350 Silver .1342 oz. ASW **Obverse:** Bust left **Obv. Legend:** EMANVEL II..

Date	Mintage	VG	F	VF	XF	Unc
1909	7,656,000	1.50	2.50	4.50	9.00	—

KM# 535 500 REIS Weight: 12.5000 g. **Composition:** 0.9170 Silver .3684 oz. ASW **Obverse:** Head right **Obv. Legend:** CARLOS I..

Date	Mintage	VG	F	VF	XF	Unc
1901	1,050,000	6.50	22.50	40.00	75.00	—
1903	680,000	4.00	9.00	15.00	30.00	—
1906/3	240,000	15.00	35.00	70.00	100	—
1906	Inc. above	12.00	30.00	60.00	90.00	—
1907	384,000	4.00	6.00	10.00	18.00	—
1908	1,840,000	4.00	6.00	10.00	16.00	—

KM# 547 500 REIS Weight: 12.5000 g. **Composition:** 0.9170 Silver .3684 oz. ASW **Obverse:** Bust left **Obv. Legend:** EMANVEL II..

Date	Mintage	VG	F	VF	XF	Unc
1908	2,500,000	3.50	6.00	10.00	18.00	—
1909/8	1,513,000	8.00	25.00	45.00	85.00	—
1909	Inc. above	8.00	25.00	45.00	85.00	—

KM# 556 500 REIS Weight: 12.5000 g. **Composition:** 0.9170 Silver .3684 oz. ASW **Subject:** Peninsular War Centennial **Obv. Legend:** EMANVEL II..

Date	Mintage	VG	F	VF	XF	Unc
1910	200,000	12.50	35.00	55.00	90.00	—

KM# 557 500 REIS Weight: 12.5000 g. **Composition:** 0.9170 Silver .3684 oz. ASW **Subject:** Marquis De Pombal **Obv. Legend:** EMANVEL II..

Date	Mintage	VG	F	VF	XF	Unc
1910	400,000	6.50	13.50	22.50	38.00	—
1910 Proof	—	Value: 600				

KM# 558 1000 REIS Weight: 25.0000 g. **Composition:** 0.9170 Silver .7368 oz. ASW **Subject:** Peninsular War Centennial **Obv. Legend:** EMANVEL II..

Date	Mintage	VG	F	VF	XF	Unc
1910	200,000	15.00	40.00	65.00	100	—
1910 Proof	—	Value: 900				

REPUBLIC

DECIMAL COINAGE

KM# 565 CENTAVO Composition: Bronze

Date	Mintage	F	VF	XF	Unc	BU
1917	2,250,000	0.25	0.50	1.00	3.50	—
1918	22,996,000	0.25	0.50	1.00	3.50	—
1920	12,535,000	0.50	1.00	2.50	7.50	—
1921	4,492,000	10.00	20.00	35.00	70.00	—
1922 Rare	Inc. above	—	—	—	—	—

KM# 567 2 CENTAVOS Composition: Iron

Date	Mintage	F	VF	XF	Unc	BU
1918	170,000	65.00	125	300	700	—

KM# 568 2 CENTAVOS Composition: Bronze

Date	Mintage	F	VF	XF	Unc	BU
1918	4,295,000	0.25	0.50	1.50	4.00	—
1920	10,109,000	0.50	1.50	3.00	6.50	—
1921	679,000	25.00	45.00	80.00	150	—

KM# 566 4 CENTAVOS Composition: Copper Nickel

Date	Mintage	F	VF	XF	Unc	BU
1917	4,961,000	0.25	0.50	1.50	4.00	—
1919	10,067,000	0.50	1.00	2.00	5.00	—

KM# 569 5 CENTAVOS Center Composition: Bronze

ate	Mintage	F	VF	XF	Unc	BU
920	114,000	35.00	70.00	120	200	—
921	5,916,000	0.50	1.50	3.50	7.00	—
922	Inc. above	125	250	400	700	—

KM# 572 5 CENTAVOS Composition: Bronze

ate	Mintage	F	VF	XF	Unc	BU
924	6,480,000	0.50	1.50	6.00	14.00	—
925	7,260,000	3.50	7.50	22.00	40.00	—
927	26,320,000	0.25	0.75	2.00	5.00	—

KM# 563 10 CENTAVOS Weight: 2.5000 g. Composition: 0.8350 Silver .0671 oz. ASW

ate	Mintage	F	VF	XF	Unc	BU
915	3,418,000	1.00	2.00	3.00	8.00	—

KM# 570 10 CENTAVOS Composition: Copper Nickel

Date	Mintage	F	VF	XF	Unc	BU
1920	1,120,000	3.00	6.00	12.00	20.00	—
1921	1,285,000	3.00	6.00	12.00	20.00	—

KM# 573 10 CENTAVOS Composition: Bronze

Date	Mintage	F	VF	XF	Unc	BU
1924	1,210,000	3.00	12.50	45.00	100	—
1925	9,090,000	0.50	1.00	12.50	30.00	—
1926	26,250,000	0.75	1.50	14.50	35.00	—
1930	1,730,000	55.00	125	250	650	—
1938	2,000,000	5.00	15.00	50.00	100	—
1940	3,384,000	1.50	4.00	12.50	30.00	—

KM# 583 10 CENTAVOS Composition: Bronze

Date	Mintage	F	VF	XF	Unc	BU
1942	1,035,000	2.00	6.00	22.50	45.00	—
1943	18,765,000	1.50	5.00	20.00	40.00	—
1944	5,090,000	1.50	3.50	15.00	30.00	—
1945	6,090,000	1.50	4.00	17.50	35.00	—
1946	7,740,000	1.00	2.50	12.50	25.00	—
1947	9,283,000	1.00	2.00	7.50	15.00	—
1948	5,900,000	10.00	30.00	100	275	—
1949	15,240,000	0.25	1.00	5.00	10.00	—
1950	8,860,000	1.50	3.00	35.00	100	—
1951	5,040,000	1.50	3.00	35.00	100	—
1952	4,960,000	2.50	12.00	90.00	225	—
1953	7,548,000	0.75	1.50	20.00	55.00	—
1954	2,452,000	1.50	4.00	17.50	35.00	—
1955	10,000,000	0.10	0.50	2.50	6.00	—
1956	3,336,000	0.10	0.50	2.00	5.00	—
1957	6,654,000	0.10	0.25	2.00	5.00	—

Date	Mintage	F	VF	XF	Unc	BU
1958	7,320,000	0.10	0.25	2.00	5.00	—
1959	7,140,000	0.10	0.25	2.00	5.00	—
1960	15,055,000	0.10	0.25	2.00	5.00	—
1961	5,020,000	—	0.10	1.50	4.00	—
1962	14,980,000	—	0.10	0.50	1.00	—
1963	5,393,000	—	0.10	1.25	3.50	—
1964	10,257,000	—	0.10	0.75	1.50	—
1965	15,550,000	—	0.10	1.00	2.50	—
1966	10,200,000	—	0.10	0.50	1.00	—
1967	18,592,000	—	0.10	0.50	1.00	—
1968	22,515,000	—	0.10	0.50	1.00	—
1969	3,871,000	0.10	0.25	1.25	2.50	—

KM# 594 10 CENTAVOS Composition: Aluminum

Date	Mintage	F	VF	XF	Unc	BU
1969	—	—	400	600	900	—
1970 Rare	—	—	—	—	—	—
1971	25,673,000	—	—	0.50	1.00	—
1972	10,558,000	—	—	0.50	1.00	—
1973	3,149,000	—	—	1.25	3.50	—
1974	17,043,000	—	—	0.50	1.00	—
1975	22,410,000	—	—	0.50	1.00	—
1976	19,907,000	—	—	0.50	1.00	—
1977	8,431,000	—	—	0.50	1.00	—
1978	2,205,000	—	—	0.50	1.00	—
1979	9,083,000	—	—	1.00	2.50	—

KM# 562 20 CENTAVOS Weight: 5.0000 g. Composition: 0.8350 Silver .1342 oz. ASW

Date	Mintage	F	VF	XF	Unc	BU
1913	540,000	5.00	20.00	40.00	175	—
1916	706,000	3.00	15.00	30.00	100	—

KM# 571 20 CENTAVOS Composition: Copper Nickel

Date	Mintage	F	VF	XF	Unc	BU
1920	1,568,000	3.50	7.00	12.00	20.00	—
1921	3,030,000	4.00	8.00	14.00	22.50	—
1922	580,000	500	900	1,500	3,000	—

KM# 574 20 CENTAVOS Composition: Bronze

Date	Mintage	F	VF	XF	Unc	BU
1924	6,220,000	0.75	3.00	20.00	45.00	—
1925	10,580,000	0.75	3.00	20.00	45.00	—

KM# 584 20 CENTAVOS Composition: Bronze

Date	Mintage	F	VF	XF	Unc	BU
1942	10,170,000	1.50	3.50	25.00	60.00	—
1943	Inc. above	1.00	2.00	25.00	60.00	—
1944	7,290,000	1.00	2.00	25.00	60.00	—
1945	7,552,000	1.00	2.00	25.00	60.00	—
1948	2,750,000	2.50	12.00	50.00	135	—
1949	12,250,000	0.10	0.50	6.00	12.50	—
1951	3,185,000	0.50	2.00	60.00	160	—
1952	1,815,000	2.00	12.00	100	250	—
1953	9,426,000	—	0.50	3.50	8.00	—
1955	5,574,000	—	0.50	3.50	8.00	—

Date	Mintage	F	VF	XF	Unc	BU
1956	6,450,000	—	0.50	3.50	8.00	—
1958	7,470,000	—	0.50	3.50	8.00	—
1959	4,780,000	—	0.50	3.50	8.00	—
1960	4,790,000	—	0.50	3.50	8.00	—
1961	5,180,000	—	0.50	3.50	8.00	—
1962	2,500,000	0.25	1.50	15.00	35.00	—
1963	7,990,000	—	0.25	2.00	5.00	—
1964	7,010,000	—	0.25	1.50	4.00	—
1965	7,365,000	—	0.25	1.00	2.50	—
1966	8,074,999	—	0.25	0.50	2.00	—
1967	9,220,000	—	0.25	0.50	2.00	—
1968	10,372,000	—	0.25	0.50	2.00	—
1969	8,657,000	—	0.25	1.00	3.00	—

KM# 595 20 CENTAVOS Composition: Bronze

Date	Mintage	F	VF	XF	Unc	BU
1969	10,891,000	—	0.25	0.75	2.50	—
1970	16,120,000	—	0.25	1.00	3.00	—
1971	1,933,000	—	1.00	2.50	7.50	—
1972	16,354,000	—	—	0.25	1.00	—
1973	4,900,000	—	—	0.25	1.00	—
1974	26,975,000	—	—	0.25	1.00	—

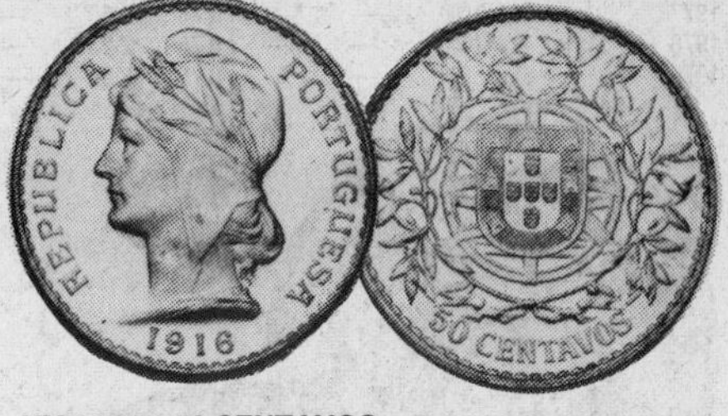

KM# 561 50 CENTAVOS Weight: 12.5000 g. Composition: 0.8350 Silver .3356 oz. ASW

Date	Mintage	F	VF	XF	Unc	BU
1912	1,695,000	4.00	8.00	15.00	30.00	—
1913	4,443,000	3.00	5.00	9.00	20.00	—
1914	4,992,000	4.00	8.00	15.00	30.00	—
1916	5,080,000	3.00	5.00	9.00	20.00	—

KM# 575 50 CENTAVOS Composition: Aluminum-Bronze

Date	Mintage	F	VF	XF	Unc	BU
1924	810,000	65.00	125	250	475	—
1925	—	1,000	2,000	4,500	8,500	—
1926	4,340,000	2.00	6.00	18.00	40.00	—

KM# 577 50 CENTAVOS Composition: Copper Nickel

Date	Mintage	F	VF	XF	Unc	BU
1927	2,330,000	2.50	12.50	75.00	165	—
1928	6,823,000	2.50	12.50	100	220	—
1929	9,779,000	2.50	12.50	75.00	165	—
1930	1,116,000	2.50	20.00	200	550	—
1931	7,127,000	4.00	20.00	200	550	—
1935	902,000	8.50	35.00	300	875	—
Note: For exclusive use in Azores						
1938	923,000	8.00	37.00	375	950	—
1940	2,000,000	1.00	5.00	50.00	125	—
1944	2,974,000	0.25	1.00	9.00	25.00	—
1945	5,700,000	0.25	1.00	8.00	25.00	—
1946	4,334,000	—	2.00	20.00	50.00	—
1947	6,998,000	0.10	1.00	9.00	25.00	—
1951	4,610,000	—	0.50	4.00	15.00	—
1952	2,421,000	0.10	1.00	12.00	30.00	—
1953	2,369,000	0.10	1.00	12.50	32.00	—
1955	3,057,000	0.10	0.50	3.00	9.00	—
1956	3,003,000	—	0.50	3.00	9.00	—
1957	3,940,000	—	0.50	3.00	9.00	—
1958	2,687,000	—	0.50	4.00	12.00	—
1959	4,027,000	—	0.50	3.00	9.00	—
1960	2,592,000	—	0.50	3.00	9.00	—

Date	Mintage	F	VF	XF	Unc	BU
1961	3,324,000	—	0.25	1.50	4.00	—
1962	6,678,000	—	0.25	1.00	2.50	—
1963	2,346,000	—	0.25	3.00	9.00	—
1964	7,654,000	—	0.25	1.00	2.50	—
1965	3,366,000	—	0.25	1.00	2.50	—
1966	6,085,000	—	0.25	1.00	2.50	—
1967	19,391,000	—	0.25	1.00	2.50	—
1968	11,448,000	—	0.25	1.00	2.50	—

KM# 596 50 CENTAVOS **Composition:** Bronze

Date	Mintage	F	VF	XF	Unc	BU
1969	3,481,000	—	—	1.00	3.50	—
1970	17,280,000	—	—	1.00	3.00	—
1971	9,139,000	—	—	1.00	3.00	—
1972	24,729,000	—	—	1.00	3.00	—
1973	35,588,000	—	—	0.75	2.50	—
1974	28,719,000	—	—	0.75	2.50	—
1975	17,793,000	—	—	0.75	2.50	—
1976	23,734,000	—	—	0.75	2.50	—
1977	16,340,000	—	—	0.75	2.50	—
1978	48,348,000	—	—	0.75	2.25	—
1979	61,652,000	—	—	0.75	2.00	—

KM# 560 ESCUDO **Weight:** 25.0000 g. **Composition:** 0.8350 Silver .6711 oz. ASW **Subject:** October 5, 1910, Birth of the Republic

Date	F	VF	XF	Unc	BU
1910	25.00	50.00	85.00	150	—

Note: Struck in 1914

KM# 564 ESCUDO **Weight:** 25.0000 g. **Composition:** 0.8350 Silver .6711 oz. ASW

Date	Mintage	F	VF	XF	Unc	BU
1915	1,818,000	10.00	20.00	30.00	60.00	—
1916	1,405,000	12.00	22.00	35.00	70.00	—

KM# 576 ESCUDO **Composition:** Aluminum-Bronze

Date	Mintage	F	VF	XF	Unc	BU
1924	2,709,000	5.00	10.00	25.00	60.00	—
1926	2,346,000	85.00	175	300	700	—

KM# 578 ESCUDO **Composition:** Copper Nickel

Date	Mintage	F	VF	XF	Unc	BU
1927	1,917,000	2.00	15.00	85.00	200	—
1928	7,462,000	1.00	15.00	100	225	—
1929	1,617,000	1.00	15.00	110	300	—
1930	1,911,000	6.00	25.00	350	1,000	—
1931	2,039,000	7.50	25.00	350	1,000	—
1935	—	125	325	2,750	6,000	—
Note: For exclusive use in Azores						
1939	304,000	10.00	30.00	250	700	—
1940	1,259,000	1.00	15.00	65.00	150	—
1944	993,000	10.00	30.00	200	400	—
1945	Inc. above	0.50	1.50	22.00	50.00	—
1946	2,507,000	0.50	1.50	20.00	50.00	—
1951	2,500,000	0.25	0.50	6.00	12.00	—
1952	2,500,000	0.75	2.50	40.00	90.00	—
1957	1,656,000	0.10	0.50	7.00	15.00	—
1958	1,447,000	0.10	0.50	7.00	15.00	—
1959	1,908,000	0.10	0.50	7.00	15.00	—
1961	2,505,000	0.10	0.25	2.50	6.50	—
1962	2,757,000	0.10	0.25	2.00	5.00	—
1964	1,611,000	0.10	0.25	2.00	5.00	—
1965	1,683,000	0.10	0.25	1.50	4.00	—
1966	2,607,000	0.10	0.20	1.50	4.00	—
1968	4,099,000	0.10	0.20	1.50	3.50	—

KM# 597 ESCUDO **Composition:** Bronze

Date	Mintage	F	VF	XF	Unc	BU
1969	3,020,000	—	0.10	1.50	5.00	—
1970	6,009,000	—	0.10	1.50	4.00	—
1971	7,860,000	—	0.10	1.50	4.00	—
1972	3,815,000	—	0.10	1.50	4.50	—
1973	20,467,000	—	0.10	1.00	3.00	—
1974	11,444,000	—	0.10	1.00	3.00	—
1975	8,473,000	—	0.10	1.00	3.00	—
1976	7,353,000	—	0.10	0.50	2.00	—
1977	6,218,000	—	0.10	0.50	2.00	—
1978	7,061,000	—	0.10	0.50	2.00	—
1979	14,241,000	—	0.10	0.25	1.50	—

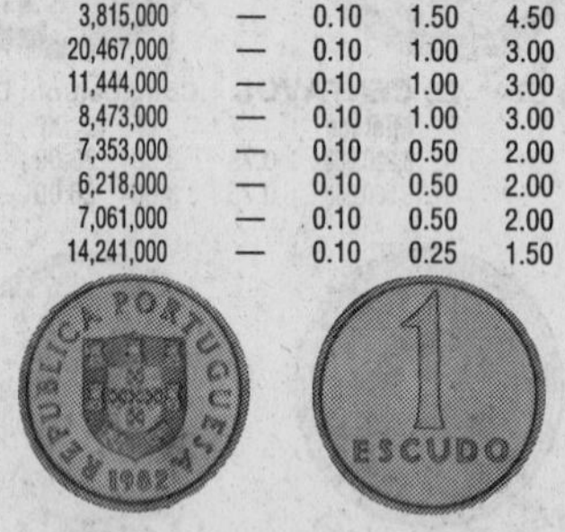

KM# 614 ESCUDO **Composition:** Nickel-Brass **Note:** Previously KM#611.

Date	Mintage	F	VF	XF	Unc	BU
1981	30,165,000	—	—	0.10	0.50	—
1982	53,018,000	—	—	0.10	0.50	—
1983	53,165,000	—	—	0.10	0.50	—
1984	59,463,000	—	—	0.10	0.50	—
1985	46,832,000	—	—	0.10	0.50	—
1986	8,029,999	—	—	0.10	2.00	—

KM# 612 ESCUDO **Composition:** Nickel-Brass **Subject:** World Roller Hockey Championship Games

Date	Mintage	F	VF	XF	Unc	BU
ND(1983)	1,990,000	—	0.10	0.25	0.75	—

KM# 631 ESCUDO **Composition:** Nickel-Brass

Date	Mintage	F	VF	XF	Unc	BU
1986	14,882,000	—	—	0.10	0.35	—
1987	21,922,000	—	—	0.10	0.35	—
1988	17,168,000	—	—	0.10	0.35	—
1989	17,194,000	—	—	0.10	0.35	—
1990	19,008,000	—	—	0.10	0.35	—
1991	21,500,000	—	—	—	0.35	—
1992	22,000,000	—	—	—	0.35	—
1993	10,505,000	—	—	—	0.35	—
1994	—	—	—	—	0.35	—
1995 In Mint sets only	—	—	—	—	0.50	—
1996	—	—	—	—	0.35	—
1996 Proof	7,000	Value: 0.50				
1997	—	—	—	—	0.35	—
1997 Proof	—	Value: 0.50				
1998	—	—	—	—	0.35	—
1998 Proof	—	Value: 2.00				
1999	—	—	—	—	0.35	—
2000	—	—	—	—	0.35	—

KM# 631a ESCUDO **Weight:** 4.6000 g. **Composition:** 0.9167 Gold 0.1356 oz. AGW **Subject:** Last Escudo **Obverse:** Similar to KM#631 but with addition of "Au" above top left shield corner **Reverse:** Same as KM#631 **Edge:** Plain **Size:** 16 mm.

Date	Mintage	F	VF	XF	Unc	BU
2001	50,000	—	—	—	106	—

KM# 580 2-1/2 ESCUDOS **Weight:** 3.5000 g. **Composition:** 0.6500 Silver .0731 oz. ASW

Date	Mintage	F	VF	XF	Unc	BU
1932	2,592,000	5.00	20.00	50.00	120	—
1933	2,457,000	20.00	50.00	100	200	—
1937	1,000,000	150	350	650	1,250	—
1940	2,763,000	3.00	12.00	30.00	70.00	—
1942	3,847,000	BV	3.00	9.00	20.00	—
1943	8,302,000	BV	1.75	4.00	10.00	—
1944	9,134,000	BV	1.50	2.50	7.00	—
1945	6,316,000	BV	3.50	12.00	28.00	—
1946	3,208,000	BV	3.00	10.00	22.00	—
1947	2,610,000	BV	3.00	10.00	22.00	—
1948	1,814,000	10.00	20.00	40.00	110	—
1951	4,000,000	BV	1.25	2.00	5.00	—

KM# 590 2-1/2 ESCUDOS **Composition:** Copper-Nickel

Date	Mintage	F	VF	XF	Unc	BU
1963	12,711,000	—	0.50	20.00	45.00	—
1964	17,948,000	—	0.50	20.00	45.00	—
1965	19,512,000	—	0.25	5.00	15.00	—
1966	3,828,000	—	2.00	35.00	85.00	—
1967	5,545,000	—	0.25	7.00	18.00	—
1968	6,087,000	—	0.25	2.75	6.00	—
1969	9,969,000	—	0.25	1.75	5.00	—
1970	2,400,000	—	0.25	2.25	6.00	—
1971	6,791,000	—	0.25	1.50	4.50	—
1972	6,713,000	—	0.25	1.75	5.00	—
1973	9,104,000	—	0.25	1.00	3.00	—
1974	22,743,000	—	0.10	0.75	2.50	—
1975	16,623,999	—	0.10	0.50	1.50	—
1976	21,516,000	—	0.10	0.50	1.50	—
1977	45,726,000	—	0.10	0.50	1.50	—
1978	27,375,000	—	0.10	0.25	1.00	—
1979	44,804,000	—	0.10	0.25	1.00	—
1980	22,319,000	—	0.10	0.25	1.00	—

ate	Mintage	F	VF	XF	Unc	BU
981	25,420,000	—	0.10	0.20	1.00	—
982	45,910,000	—	0.10	0.20	1.00	—
983	62,946,000	—	0.10	0.20	1.00	—
984	58,210,000	—	0.10	0.20	1.00	—
985	60,142,000	—	0.10	0.20	1.00	—

KM# 605 2-1/2 ESCUDOS **Composition:** Copper-Nickel **Subject:** 100th Anniversary - Death of Alexandre Herculano

ate	Mintage	F	VF	XF	Unc	BU
ND(1977)	5,990,000	—	0.20	0.75	2.00	—
ND(1977) Proof	13,000	Value: 3.50				

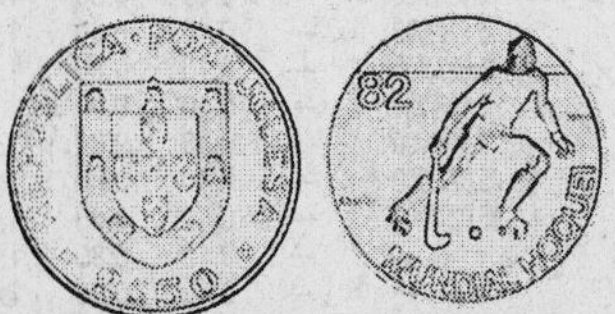

KM# 613 2-1/2 ESCUDOS **Composition:** Copper-Nickel **Subject:** World Roller Hockey Championship Games

ate	Mintage	F	VF	XF	Unc	BU
ND(1983)	1,990,000	—	0.10	0.25	1.00	—

KM# 617 2-1/2 ESCUDOS **Composition:** Copper-Nickel **Series:** F.A.O.

ate	Mintage	F	VF	XF	Unc	BU
1983	995,000	—	0.10	0.35	1.25	—

KM# 581 5 ESCUDOS **Weight:** 7.0000 g. **Composition:** 0.6500 Silver .1463 oz. ASW

Date	Mintage	F	VF	XF	Unc	BU
1932	800,000	10.00	65.00	200	450	—
1933	6,717,000	2.00	7.00	25.00	70.00	—
1934	1,012,000	4.00	15.00	30.00	120	—
1937	1,500,000	20.00	80.00	250	500	—
1940	1,500,000	4.00	15.00	50.00	120	—
1942	2,051,000	2.00	4.00	8.00	20.00	—
1943	1,354,000	6.00	20.00	60.00	140	—
1946	404,000	4.00	12.50	28.00	60.00	—
1947	2,420,000	2.00	3.00	5.00	12.00	—
1948	2,017,999	1.75	3.00	5.00	12.00	—
1951	966,000	1.50	2.50	4.00	10.00	—

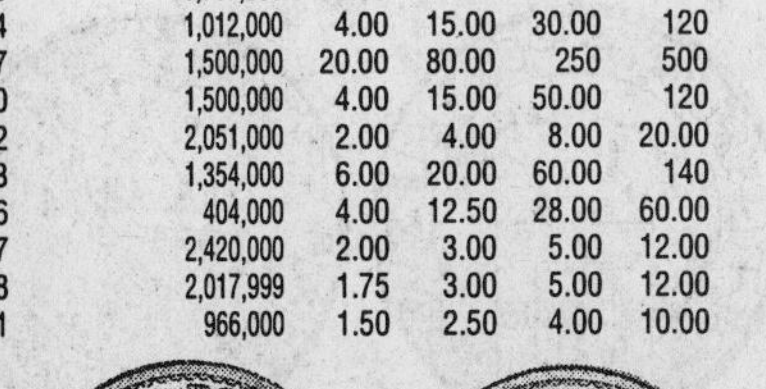

KM# 587 5 ESCUDOS **Weight:** 7.0000 g. **Composition:** 0.6500 Silver .1463 oz. ASW **Subject:** 500th Anniversary - Death of Prince Henry the Navigator

Date	Mintage	F	VF	XF	Unc	BU
1960	800,000	—	2.00	3.00	6.00	—
1960 Matte	—	—	—	—	20.00	—

Note: A small quantity of these coins were given a matte finish by the Lisbon Mint on private contract

KM# 591 5 ESCUDOS **Composition:** Copper-Nickel

Date	Mintage	F	VF	XF	Unc	BU
1963	2,200,000	—	0.50	15.00	40.00	—
1964	4,268,000	—	0.50	12.50	35.00	—
1965	7,294,000	—	0.35	12.50	35.00	—
1966	8,119,999	—	0.35	10.00	30.00	—
1967	8,128,000	—	0.25	7.00	20.00	—
1968	5,023,000	—	0.25	3.00	10.00	—
1969	3,571,000	—	0.10	2.00	6.00	—
1970	1,200,000	—	0.10	2.50	7.00	—
1971	2,721,000	—	0.10	2.00	6.00	—
1972	1,880,000	—	0.10	2.00	6.00	—
1973	2,836,000	—	0.10	1.25	4.00	—
1974	3,984,000	—	0.10	1.00	3.50	—
1975	7,496,000	—	0.10	1.00	3.50	—
1976	11,379,000	—	0.10	1.00	3.50	—
1977	29,058,000	—	0.10	0.50	1.50	—
1978	672,000	—	2.00	8.00	20.00	—
1979	19,546,000	—	0.10	0.50	1.50	—
1980	46,244,000	—	0.10	0.50	1.50	—
1981	15,267,000	—	0.10	0.50	1.50	—
1982	31,318,000	—	0.10	0.50	1.50	—
1983	51,056,000	—	0.10	0.50	1.50	—
1984	46,794,000	—	0.10	0.50	1.50	—
1985	45,441,000	—	0.10	0.50	1.50	—
1986	18,753,000	—	0.10	0.50	1.50	—

KM# 606 5 ESCUDOS **Composition:** Copper-Nickel **Subject:** 100th Anniversary - Death of Alexandre Herculano

Date	Mintage	F	VF	XF	Unc	BU
ND(1977)	9,176,000	—	0.35	1.00	3.00	—
ND(1977) Proof	10,000	Value: 4.00				

KM# 615 5 ESCUDOS **Composition:** Copper-Nickel **Subject:** World Roller Hockey Championship Games

Date	Mintage	F	VF	XF	Unc	BU
ND(1983)	1,990,000	—	0.25	0.50	1.50	—

KM# 618 5 ESCUDOS **Composition:** Copper-Nickel **Series:** F.A.O.

Date	Mintage	F	VF	XF	Unc	BU
ND(1983)	995,000	—	0.30	0.75	2.00	—

KM# 632 5 ESCUDOS **Composition:** Nickel-Brass

Date	Mintage	F	VF	XF	Unc	BU
1986	21,426,000	—	0.10	0.25	0.50	—
1987	40,548,000	—	0.10	0.25	0.50	—
1988	19,382,000	—	0.10	0.25	0.50	—
1989	27,641,000	—	0.10	0.25	0.50	—
1990	77,977,000	—	0.10	0.25	0.50	—
1991	32,000,000	—	—	—	0.50	—
1992	16,000,000	—	—	—	0.50	—
1993	8,300,000	—	—	—	0.50	—
1994	—	—	—	—	0.50	—
1995	—	—	—	—	0.50	—
1996	—	—	—	—	0.50	—
1996 Proof	7,000	Value: 0.75				
1997	—	—	—	—	0.50	—
1997 Proof	—	Value: 0.75				
1998	—	—	—	—	0.50	—
1998 Proof	—	Value: 0.75				
1999	—	—	—	—	0.50	—

KM# 579 10 ESCUDOS **Weight:** 12.5000 g. **Composition:** 0.8350 Silver .3356 oz. ASW

Date	Mintage	F	VF	XF	Unc	BU
1928	200,000	6.00	15.00	25.00	55.00	—

KM# 582 10 ESCUDOS **Weight:** 12.5000 g. **Composition:** 0.8350 Silver .3356 oz. ASW

Date	Mintage	F	VF	XF	Unc	BU
1932	3,220,000	4.00	10.00	22.00	58.00	—
1933	1,780,000	30.00	70.00	200	600	—
1934	400,000	15.00	30.00	70.00	150	—
1937	500,000	60.00	120	225	650	—
1940	1,200,000	7.00	16.00	30.00	60.00	—
1942	186,000	200	300	550	1,150	—
1948	507,000	30.00	60.00	100	220	—

KM# 586 10 ESCUDOS **Weight:** 12.5000 g. **Composition:** 0.6800 Silver .2732 oz. ASW

Date	Mintage	F	VF	XF	Unc	BU
1954	5,764,000	2.00	3.00	5.00	8.00	—
1955	4,056,000	2.00	3.00	5.00	8.00	—

KM# 588 10 ESCUDOS **Weight:** 12.5000 g. **Composition:** 0.6800 Silver .2732 oz. ASW **Subject:** 500th Anniversary - Death of Prince Henry the Navigator

Date	Mintage	F	VF	XF	Unc	BU
1960	200,000	—	10.00	18.00	30.00	—
1960 Matte	—	—	—	—	35.00	—

Note: A small quantity of these coins were given a matte finish by the Lisbon Mint on private contract

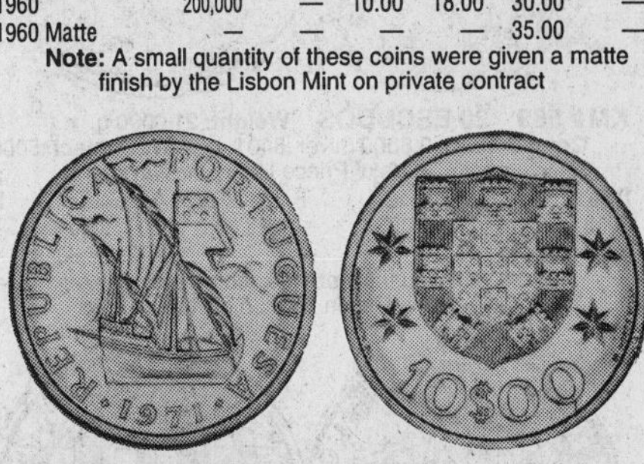

KM# 600 10 ESCUDOS **Composition:** Copper-Nickel Clad Nickel

Date	Mintage	F	VF	XF	Unc	BU
1971	3,876,000	—	0.25	0.75	2.50	—
1972	2,694,000	—	0.25	1.00	3.00	—
1973	5,418,000	—	0.25	0.75	2.50	—
1974	4,043,000	—	0.25	0.75	2.50	—

KM# 633 10 ESCUDOS **Composition:** Nickel-Brass

Date	Mintage	F	VF	XF	Unc	BU
1986	12,818,000	—	0.20	0.40	1.00	—
1987	32,814,999	—	0.20	0.40	1.00	—
1988	32,579,000	—	0.20	0.40	1.00	—
1989	12,788,000	—	0.20	0.40	1.00	—
1990	26,500,000	—	0.20	0.40	1.00	—
1991	9,500,000	—	—	—	1.00	—
1992	5,600,000	—	—	—	1.00	—
1993 In Mint sets only	20,000	—	—	—	10.00	—
1994 In Mint sets only	20,000	—	—	—	10.00	—
1995 In Mint sets only	—	—	—	—	10.00	—
1996	—	—	—	—	1.00	—
1996 Proof	7,000	Value: 2.50				
1997	—	—	—	—	1.00	—
1997 Proof	—	Value: 2.50				
1998	—	—	—	—	1.00	—
1998 Proof	—	Value: 3.00				
1999	—	—	—	—	1.00	—

KM# 638 10 ESCUDOS **Composition:** Nickel-Brass
Subject: Rural World

Date	Mintage	F	VF	XF	Unc	BU
1987	2,000,000	—	0.40	0.60	1.50	—

KM# 585 20 ESCUDOS **Weight:** 21.0000 g. **Composition:** 0.8000 Silver .5401 oz. ASW **Subject:** 25th Anniversary of Financial Reform

Date	Mintage	F	VF	XF	Unc	BU
1953	1,000,000	—	4.00	6.00	9.00	—
1953 Matte	—	—	—	—	—	—

Note: A small quantity of these coins were given a matte finish by the Lisbon Mint on private contract

KM# 589 20 ESCUDOS **Weight:** 21.0000 g. **Composition:** 0.8000 Silver .5401 oz. ASW **Subject:** 500th Anniversary - Death of Prince Henry the Navigator

Date	Mintage	F	VF	XF	Unc	BU
1960	200,000	—	12.00	18.00	30.00	—
1960 Matte	—	—	—	—	55.00	—

Note: A small quantity of these coins were given a matte finish by the Lisbon Mint on private contract

KM# 592 20 ESCUDOS **Weight:** 10.0000 g. **Composition:** 0.6500 Silver .2090 oz. ASW **Subject:** Opening of Salazar Bridge

Date	Mintage	F	VF	XF	Unc	BU
1966	2,000,000	—	2.00	3.00	5.00	—
1966 Matte	200	—	—	—	35.00	—

Note: A small quantity of these coins were given a matte finish by the Lisbon Mint on private contract

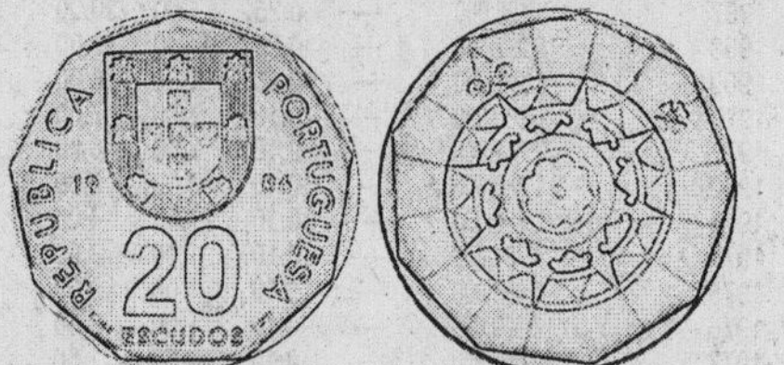

KM# 634 20 ESCUDOS **Composition:** Copper-Nickel

Date	Mintage	F	VF	XF	Unc	BU
1986	45,361,000	—	0.15	0.25	1.00	—
1987	68,216,000	—	0.15	0.25	1.00	—
1988	57,482,000	—	0.15	0.25	1.00	—
1989	25,060,000	—	0.15	0.25	1.00	—
1990 In Mint sets only	50,000	—	—	—	10.00	—
1991 In Mint sets only	50,000	—	—	—	10.00	—
1992 In Mint sets only	20,000	—	—	—	10.00	—
1993 In Mint sets only	20,000	—	—	—	10.00	—
1994 In Mint sets only	20,000	—	—	—	10.00	—
1995 In Mint sets only	—	—	—	—	10.00	—
1996 In Mint sets only	—	—	—	—	10.00	—
1996 Proof	7,000	Value: 2.50				
1997 In Mint sets only	—	—	—	—	10.00	—
1997 Proof	—	Value: 2.50				
1998	—	—	—	—	1.00	—
1998 Proof	—	Value: 4.00				
1999	—	—	—	—	1.00	—

KM# 607 25 ESCUDOS **Composition:** Copper-Nickel

Date	Mintage	F	VF	XF	Unc	BU
1977	7,657,000	—	0.40	1.00	2.00	—
1978	12,277,000	—	0.40	1.50	3.00	—

KM# 608 25 ESCUDOS **Composition:** Copper-Nickel
Subject: 100th Anniversary - Death of Alexandre Herculano

Date	Mintage	F	VF	XF	Unc	BU
ND(1977)	5,990,000	—	0.50	1.00	2.50	—
ND(1977) Proof	13,000	Value: 7.00				

KM# 609 25 ESCUDOS **Composition:** Copper-Nickel
Subject: International Year of the Child

Date	Mintage	F	VF	XF	Unc	BU
1979	990,000	—	0.50	1.00	2.50	—
1979 Prooflike	10,000	—	—	—	8.00	—

KM# 607a (KM610) 25 ESCUDOS **Composition:** Copper-Nickel **Size:** 28.5 mm. **Note:** Increased size.

Date	Mintage	F	VF	XF	Unc
1980	750,000	—	0.40	0.80	1.50
1980	750,000	—	0.40	0.80	1.50
1981	19,924,000	—	0.40	0.80	1.50
1981	19,924,000	—	0.40	0.80	1.50
1982	12,158,000	—	0.40	0.80	1.50
1982	12,158,000	—	0.40	0.80	1.50
1983	5,622,000	—	0.40	0.80	1.50
1983	5,622,000	—	0.40	0.80	1.50
1984	3,453,000	—	0.40	0.80	1.50
1984	3,453,000	—	0.40	0.80	1.50
1985	25,027,000	—	0.40	0.80	1.50
1985	25,027,000	—	0.40	0.80	1.50
1986	—	—	0.40	0.80	1.50
1986	—	—	0.40	0.80	1.50

KM# 616 25 ESCUDOS **Composition:** Copper-Nicke
Subject: World Roller Hockey Championship Games

Date	Mintage	F	VF	XF	Unc
ND(1983)	1,990,000	—	0.50	1.00	2.25

KM# 619 25 ESCUDOS **Composition:** Copper-Nicke
Series: F.A.O.

Date	Mintage	F	VF	XF	Unc
1983	995,000	—	0.60	1.25	3.00

KM# 623 25 ESCUDOS **Composition:** Copper-Nicke
Subject: 10th Anniversary of Revolution **Obverse:** Waves breaking over arms **Reverse:** Stylized 25

Date	Mintage	F	VF	XF	Unc
ND(1984)	1,980,000	—	0.40	1.00	2.00

KM# 624 25 ESCUDOS **Composition:** Copper-Nicke
Subject: International Year of Disabled Persons

Date	Mintage	F	VF	XF	Unc
ND(1984)	1,990,000	—	0.40	1.00	2.00

M# 627 25 ESCUDOS **Composition:** Copper-Nickel
Subject: 600th Anniversary - Battle of Aljubarrota

ate	Mintage	F	VF	XF	Unc	BU
)(1985)	500,000	—	0.50	1.00	2.75	—

⁽M# 627a 25 ESCUDOS **Weight:** 10.8300 g.
Composition: 0.9250 Silver .3270 oz. ASW

ate	Mintage	F	VF	XF	Unc	BU
)(1985) In Mint sets only	20,000	—	—	—	15.00	—
)(1985) In Proof sets only	5,000	Value: 40.00				

M# 635 25 ESCUDOS **Composition:** Copper-Nickel
Subject: Admission to European Common Market

ate	Mintage	F	VF	XF	Unc	BU
986	4,990,000	—	0.40	1.00	2.00	—

M# 635a 25 ESCUDOS **Weight:** 11.0000 g.
Composition: 0.9250 Silver .3272 oz. ASW

ate	Mintage	F	VF	XF	Unc	BU
986 Proof	5,000	Value: 85.00				

KM# 593 50 ESCUDOS **Weight:** 18.0000 g.
Composition: 0.6500 Silver .3761 oz. ASW **Subject:** 500th Anniversary - Birth of Pedro Alvares Cabral

Date	Mintage	F	VF	XF	Unc	BU
1968	1,000,000	—	—	—	6.00	—
1968 Matte	400	—	—	—	32.50	—

Note: A small quantity of these coins were given a matte finish by the Lisbon Mint on private contract

KM# 598 50 ESCUDOS **Weight:** 18.0000 g.
Composition: 0.6500 Silver .3761 oz. ASW **Subject:** 500th Anniversary - Birth of Vasco Da Gama

Date	Mintage	F	VF	XF	Unc	BU
ND(1969)	1,000,000	—	—	—	6.50	—
ND(1969) Matte	400	—	—	—	32.50	—

Note: A small quantity of these coins were given a matte finish by the Lisbon Mint on private contract

KM# 599 50 ESCUDOS **Weight:** 18.0000 g.
Composition: 0.6500 Silver .3761 oz. ASW **Subject:** 100th Anniversary - Birth of Marechal Carmona

Date	Mintage	F	VF	XF	Unc	BU
ND(1969)	500,000	—	—	—	7.50	—
ND(1969) Matte	400	—	—	—	32.50	—

Note: A small quantity of these coins were given a matte finish by the Lisbon Mint on private contract

KM# 601 50 ESCUDOS **Weight:** 18.0000 g.
Composition: 0.6500 Silver .3761 oz. ASW **Subject:** 125th Anniversary - Bank of Portugal

Date	Mintage	F	VF	XF	Unc	BU
ND(1971)	500,000	—	—	—	8.50	—
ND(1971) Matte	—	—	—	—	32.50	—

Note: A small quantity of these coins were given a matte finish by the Lisbon Mint on private contract

KM# 602 50 ESCUDOS **Weight:** 18.0000 g.
Composition: 0.6500 Silver .3761 oz. ASW **Subject:** 400th Anniversary of Heroic Epic 'Os Lusiadas'

Date	Mintage	F	VF	XF	Unc	BU
ND(1972)	1,000,000	—	—	—	6.50	—
ND(1972) Matte	—	—	—	—	32.50	—

Note: A small quantity of these coins were given a matte finish by the Lisbon Mint on private contract

KM# 636 50 ESCUDOS **Composition:** Copper-Nickel

Date	Mintage	F	VF	XF	Unc	BU
1986	51,110,000	—	—	—	2.25	—
1987	28,248,000	—	—	—	2.25	—
1988	41,905,000	—	—	—	2.25	—
1989	18,327,000	—	—	—	2.25	—
1990 In Mint sets only	50,000	—	—	—	15.00	—
1991	2,000,000	—	—	—	3.00	—
1992 In Mint sets only	20,000	—	—	—	15.00	—
1993 In Mint sets only	20,000	—	—	—	15.00	—
1994 In Mint sets only	20,000	—	—	—	15.00	—
1995 In Mint sets only	20,000	—	—	—	15.00	—
1996 In Mint sets only	—	—	—	—	8.00	—
1996 Proof	7,000	Value: 5.00				
1997 In Mint sets only	—	—	—	—	8.00	—
1997 Proof	—	Value: 5.00				
1998 In Mint sets only	—	—	—	—	8.00	—
1998 Proof	—	Value: 6.00				
1999	—	—	—	—	3.00	—

KM# 603 100 ESCUDOS **Weight:** 18.0000 g.
Composition: 0.6500 Silver .3762 oz. ASW **Subject:** 1974 Revolution

Date	Mintage	F	VF	XF	Unc	BU
ND(1976)	950,000	—	3.00	5.00	9.00	—
ND(1976) Proof	10,000	Value: 15.00				

KM# 625 100 ESCUDOS **Composition:** Copper-Nickel
Subject: International Year of Disabled Persons

Date	Mintage	F	VF	XF	Unc	BU
ND(1984)	990,000	—	0.75	1.50	3.00	—

KM# 628 100 ESCUDOS **Composition:** Copper-Nickel
Subject: 50th Anniversary - Death of Fernando Pessoa - Poet

Date	Mintage	F	VF	XF	Unc	BU
1985	480,000	—	0.75	2.00	4.00	—

KM# 628a 100 ESCUDOS **Weight:** 16.5000 g.
Composition: 0.9250 Silver .4907 oz. ASW

Date	Mintage	F	VF	XF	Unc	BU
1985 Proof	5,000	Value: 200				

KM# 629 100 ESCUDOS **Composition:** Copper-Nickel
Subject: 800th Anniversary - Death of King Alfonso Henriques

Date	Mintage	F	VF	XF	Unc	BU
1985	500,000	—	0.75	2.00	4.00	—

KM# 629a 100 ESCUDOS **Weight:** 16.5000 g.
Composition: 0.9250 Silver .4907 oz. ASW **Subject:** 800th Anniversary - Death of King Alfonso Henriques

Date	Mintage	F	VF	XF	Unc	BU
1985	20,000	—	—	—	27.00	—
1985 Proof	5,000	Value: 110				

KM# 630 100 ESCUDOS **Composition:** Copper-Nickel
Subject: 600th Anniversary - Battle of Aljubarrota

Date	Mintage	F	VF	XF	Unc	BU
ND(1985)	500,000	—	0.75	2.00	4.00	—

KM# 630a 100 ESCUDOS **Weight:** 16.5000 g.
Composition: 0.9250 Silver .4907 oz. ASW **Subject:** 600th Anniversary - Battle of Aljubarrota

Date	Mintage	F	VF	XF	Unc	BU
ND(1985)	20,000	—	—	—	22.00	—
ND(1985) Proof	5,000	Value: 80.00				

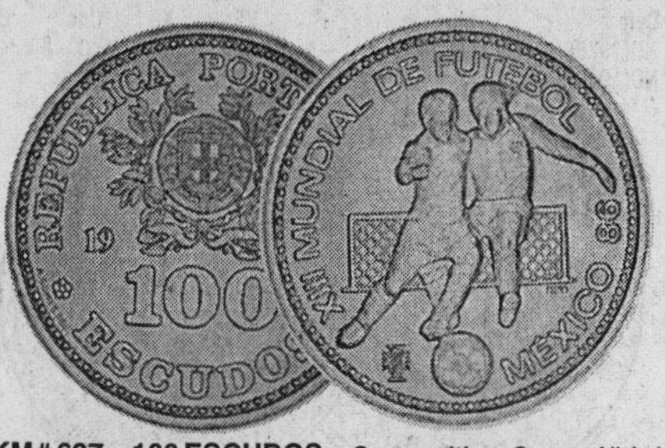

KM# 637 100 ESCUDOS Composition: Copper-Nickel **Subject:** World Cup Soccer - Mexico

Date	Mintage	F	VF	XF	Unc	BU
1986	500,000	—	0.75	2.00	4.00	—

KM# 637a 100 ESCUDOS Weight: 16.5000 g. **Composition:** 0.9250 Silver .4907 oz. ASW **Subject:** World Cup Soccer - Mexico

Date	Mintage	F	VF	XF	Unc	BU
1986	50,000	—	—	—	12.50	—
1986 Proof	20,000	Value: 27.50				

KM# 639 100 ESCUDOS Composition: Copper Nickel **Subject:** Golden Age of Portuguese Discoveries - Gil Eanes

Date	Mintage	F	VF	XF	Unc	BU
1987	1,000,000	—	0.75	1.00	2.50	—

KM# 639a 100 ESCUDOS Weight: 16.5000 g. **Composition:** 0.9250 Silver .4907 oz. ASW **Subject:** Golden Age of Portuguese Discoveries - Gil Eanes

Date	Mintage	F	VF	XF	Unc	BU
1987	50,000	—	—	—	12.50	—
1987 Proof	22,000	Value: 20.00				

KM# 639b 100 ESCUDOS Weight: 24.0000 g. **Composition:** 0.9170 Gold .7075 oz. AGW **Subject:** Golden Age of Portuguese Discoveries - Gil Eanes

Date	Mintage	F	VF	XF	Unc	BU
1987	5,772	—	—	—	500	—

KM# 640 100 ESCUDOS Composition: Copper-Nickel **Subject:** Golden Age of Portuguese Discoveries - Nuno Tristao

Date	Mintage	F	VF	XF	Unc	BU
1987	1,000,000	—	0.75	1.00	2.50	—

KM# 640a 100 ESCUDOS Weight: 16.5000 g. **Composition:** 0.9250 Silver .4907 oz. ASW **Subject:** Golden Age of Portuguese Discoveries - Nuno Tristao

Date	Mintage	F	VF	XF	Unc	BU
1987	50,000	—	—	—	12.50	—
1987 Proof	20,000	Value: 20.00				

KM# 640b 100 ESCUDOS Weight: 24.0000 g. **Composition:** 0.9170 Gold .7075 oz. AGW **Subject:** Golden Age of Portuguese Discoveries - Nuno Tristao

Date	Mintage	F	VF	XF	Unc	BU
1987	5,497	—	—	—	500	—

KM# 640c 100 ESCUDOS Weight: 31.1190 g. **Composition:** 0.9990 Palladium 1.0000 oz. **Subject:** Golden Age of Portuguese Discoveries - Nuno Tristao

Date	Mintage	F	VF	XF	Unc	BU
1987	323	—	—	—	765	—
1987 Proof	2,000	Value: 775				

KM# 641 100 ESCUDOS Composition: Copper-Nickel **Subject:** Golden Age of Portuguese Discoveries - Diogo Cao

Date	Mintage	F	VF	XF	Unc	BU
1987	1,000,000	—	0.75	1.00	2.50	—

KM# 641a 100 ESCUDOS Weight: 16.5000 g. **Composition:** 0.9250 Silver .4907 oz. ASW **Subject:** Golden Age of Portuguese Discoveries - Diogo Cao

Date	Mintage	F	VF	XF	Unc	BU
1987	50,000	—	—	—	12.50	—
1987 Proof	20,000	Value: 20.00				

KM# 641b 100 ESCUDOS Weight: 24.0000 g. **Composition:** 0.9170 Gold .7075 oz. AGW **Subject:** Golden Age of Portuguese Discoveries - Diogo Cao

Date	Mintage	F	VF	XF	Unc	BU
1987	5,256	—	—	—	450	—
1987 Proof	5,387	Value: 500				

KM# 644 100 ESCUDOS Composition: Copper-Nickel **Subject:** Amadeo De Souza Cardoso

Date	Mintage	F	VF	XF	Unc	BU
1987	800,000	—	0.75	1.25	3.00	—

KM# 644a 100 ESCUDOS Weight: 21.0000 g. **Composition:** 0.9250 Silver .6246 oz. ASW **Subject:** Amadeo De Souza Cardoso

Date	Mintage	F	VF	XF	Unc	BU
1987	30,000	—	—	—	18.50	—
1987 Proof	15,000	Value: 28.50				

KM# 642 100 ESCUDOS Composition: Copper-Nickel **Subject:** Golden Age of Portuguese Discoveries - Bartolomeu Dias

Date	Mintage	F	VF	XF	Unc	BU
ND(1988)	1,000,000	—	0.75	1.00	2.50	—

KM# 642a 100 ESCUDOS Weight: 16.5000 g. **Composition:** 0.9250 Silver .4907 oz. ASW **Subject:** Golden Age of Portuguese Discoveries - Bartolomeu Dias

Date	Mintage	F	VF	XF	Unc	BU
ND(1988)	50,000	—	—	—	12.50	—
ND(1988) Proof	20,000	Value: 20.00				

KM# 642b 100 ESCUDOS Weight: 24.0000 g. **Composition:** 0.9170 Gold .7077 oz. AGW **Subject:** Golden Age of Portuguese Discoveries - Bartolomeu Dias

Date	Mintage	F	VF	XF	Unc	BU
ND(1988)	5,503	—	—	—	450	—

KM# 642c 100 ESCUDOS Weight: 31.1190 g. **Composition:** 0.9990 Platinum 1.0000 oz. APW **Subject:** Golden Age of Portuguese Discoveries - Bartolomeu Dias

Date	Mintage	F	VF	XF	Unc	BU
ND(1988)	907	—	—	—	850	—
ND(1988) Proof	2,000	Value: 1,450				

KM# 645.1 100 ESCUDOS Ring Composition: Copper-Nickel **Center Composition:** Aluminum-Bronze **Reverse:** Pedro Nunes **Edge:** 5 reeded and 5 plain sectio

Date	Mintage	F	VF	XF	Unc
1989	20,000,000	—	—	1.00	2.50
1990	52,000,000	—	—	1.00	2.50
1991	45,500,000	—	—	1.00	2.50
1992	14,500,000	—	—	1.00	2.50
1993 In Mint sets only	20,000	—	—	—	15.00
1994 In Mint sets only	20,000	—	—	—	15.00
1996 In Mint sets only	—	—	—	—	15.00
1996 Proof	7,000	Value: 10.00			
1997	—	—	—	—	2.50
1997 Proof	—	Value: 2.50			
1998	—	—	—	—	2.50
1998 Proof	—	Value: 10.00			
1999	—	—	—	—	2.50

KM# 645.2 100 ESCUDOS Ring Composition: Copper-Nickel **Center Composition:** Aluminum-Bronze **Reverse:** Pedro Nunes **Edge:** Six reeded and six plain sections

Date	Mintage	F	VF	XF	Unc
1989	20	—	—	1.00	2.50
1990	Inc. above	—	—	1.50	2.50
1991	Inc. above	—	—	1.00	3.00

KM# 646 100 ESCUDOS Composition: Copper-Nick **Subject:** Discovery of the Canary Islands

Date	Mintage	F	VF	XF	Unc
1989	2,000,000	—	—	1.00	2.50

KM# 646a 100 ESCUDOS Weight: 21.0000 g. **Composition:** 0.9250 Silver .6246 oz. ASW **Subject:** Discovery of the Canary Islands

Date	Mintage	F	VF	XF	Unc
1989	50,000	—	—	—	12.50
1989 Proof	23,000	Value: 20.00			

KM# 646b 100 ESCUDOS Weight: 24.0000 g. **Composition:** 0.9170 Gold .7077 oz. AGW **Subject:** Discovery of the Canary Islands

Date	Mintage	F	VF	XF	Unc
1989 Proof	2,981	Value: 550			

KM# 647 100 ESCUDOS Composition: Copper-Nick **Subject:** Discovery of Madeira

Date	Mintage	F	VF	XF	Unc
1989	2,000,000	—	—	1.00	2.50

KM# 647a 100 ESCUDOS Weight: 21.0000 g. **Composition:** 0.9250 Silver .6246 oz. ASW **Subject:** Discovery of Madeira

Date	Mintage	F	VF	XF	Unc
1989	50,000	—	—	—	12.50
1989 Proof	20,000	Value: 20.00			

KM# 647b 100 ESCUDOS Weight: 24.0000 g. **Composition:** 0.9170 Gold .7077 oz. AGW **Subject:** Discovery of Madeira

Date	Mintage	F	VF	XF	Unc
1989 Proof	2,996	Value: 550			

KM# 647c 100 ESCUDOS Weight: 31.1190 g. **Composition:** 0.9990 Palladium 1.0000 oz. **Subject:** Discovery of Madeira

Date	Mintage	F	VF	XF	Unc
1989 Proof	2,500	Value: 775			

M# 648 100 ESCUDOS **Composition:** Copper-Nickel **Subject:** Discovery of the Azores

ate	Mintage	F	VF	XF	Unc	BU
D(1989)	2,000,000	—	—	1.00	2.50	—

M# 648a 100 ESCUDOS **Weight:** 21.0000 g. **Composition:** 0.9250 Silver .6246 oz. ASW **Subject:** Discovery of the Azores

ate	Mintage	F	VF	XF	Unc	BU
D(1989)	50,000	—	—	—	12.50	—
D(1989) Proof	20,000	Value: 20.00				

M# 648b 100 ESCUDOS **Weight:** 24.0000 g. **Composition:** 0.9170 Gold .7077 oz. AGW **Subject:** Discovery of the Avores

ate	Mintage	F	VF	XF	Unc	BU
D(1989) Proof	5,495	Value: 500				

KM# 649 100 ESCUDOS **Composition:** Copper-Nickel **Subject:** Celestial Navigation

ate	Mintage	F	VF	XF	Unc	BU
1990	2,000,000	—	—	1.00	2.50	—

KM# 649a 100 ESCUDOS **Weight:** 21.0000 g. **Composition:** 0.9250 Silver .6246 oz. ASW **Subject:** Celestial Navigation

Date	Mintage	F	VF	XF	Unc	BU
1990	50,000	—	—	—	12.50	—
1990 Proof	20,000	Value: 20.00				

KM# 649b 100 ESCUDOS **Weight:** 24.0000 g. **Composition:** 0.9170 Gold .7077 oz. AGW **Subject:** Celestial Navigation

Date	Mintage	F	VF	XF	Unc	BU
1990 Proof	2,958	Value: 550				

KM# 649c 100 ESCUDOS **Weight:** 31.1190 g. **Composition:** 0.9990 Platinum 1.0000 oz. APW **Subject:** Celestial Navigation

Date	Mintage	F	VF	XF	Unc	BU
1990 Proof	2,500	Value: 1,500				

KM# 651 100 ESCUDOS **Composition:** Copper-Nickel **Subject:** 350th Anniversary - Restoration of Portuguese Independence

Date	Mintage	F	VF	XF	Unc	BU
ND(1990)	1,000,000	—	—	1.00	2.50	—

KM# 651a 100 ESCUDOS **Weight:** 18.5000 g. **Composition:** 0.9250 Silver .5502 oz. ASW **Subject:** 350th Anniversary - Restoration of Portuguese

Date	Mintage	F	VF	XF	Unc	BU
ND(1990)	25,000	—	—	—	20.00	—
ND(1990) Proof	10,000	Value: 40.00				

KM# 656 100 ESCUDOS **Composition:** Copper-Nickel **Reverse:** Camilo Castelo Branco

Date	Mintage	F	VF	XF	Unc	BU
1990	1,000,000	—	—	1.00	2.50	—

KM# 656a 100 ESCUDOS **Weight:** 18.5000 g. **Composition:** 0.9250 Silver .5502 oz. ASW **Reverse:** Camilo Castelo Branco

Date	Mintage	F	VF	XF	Unc	BU
1990	25,000	—	—	—	18.50	—
1990 Proof	10,000	Value: 42.00				

KM# 678 100 ESCUDOS **Ring Composition:** Copper-Nickel **Center Composition:** Aluminum-Bronze **Subject:** 50th Anniversary - F.A.O.

Date	Mintage	F	VF	XF	Unc	BU
1995	500,000	—	—	1.50	4.00	—
1995 In Proof sets only	17,000	Value: 15.00				

KM# 680 100 ESCUDOS **Composition:** Copper-Nickel **Subject:** 400th Anniversary - Antonio Prior de Crato

Date	F	VF	XF	Unc	BU
ND(1995)	—	—	1.00	2.50	—

KM# 680a 100 ESCUDOS **Weight:** 18.5000 g. **Composition:** 0.9250 Silver .5502 oz. ASW **Subject:** 400th Anniversary - Antonio Prior de Crato

Date	Mintage	F	VF	XF	Unc	BU
ND(1995)	5,000	—	—	—	30.00	—
ND(1995) Proof	10,000	Value: 32.50				

KM# 693 100 ESCUDOS **Ring Composition:** Copper-Nickel **Center Composition:** Aluminum-Bronze **Subject:** Lisbon World Expo '98 **Obverse:** National arms and denomination **Reverse:** Sea Lion

Date	Mintage	F	VF	XF	Unc	BU
1997	—	—	—	1.50	4.00	—
1997 In Mint sets only	7,000	—	—	—	15.00	—

KM# 722.1 100 ESCUDOS **Ring Composition:** Copper-Nickel**Center Weight:** 8.3200 g. **Center Composition:** Brass **Obverse:** National arms, denomination and country name **Reverse:** UNICEF logo **Edge:** Reeded and plain sections **Size:** 25 mm.

Date	F	VF	XF	Unc	BU
1999	—	—	—	5.00	—

KM# 722.2 100 ESCUDOS **Ring Composition:** Copper-Nickel**Center Weight:** 8.3200 g. **Center Composition:** Brass **Obverse:** Country name as "PORTUGUSA" **Reverse:** UNICEF logo **Edge:** Reeded and plain sections **Size:** 25 mm.

Date	F	VF	XF	Unc	BU
1999	—	—	—	6.00	—

KM# 655 200 ESCUDOS **Ring Composition:** Aluminum-Bronze **Center Composition:** Copper-Nickel **Reverse:** Garcia De Orta

Date	Mintage	F	VF	XF	Unc	BU
1991	33,000,000	—	—	1.25	3.00	—
1992	11,000,000	—	—	1.50	4.00	—
1993 In Mint sets only	20,000	—	—	—	18.00	—
1996 In Mint sets only	—	—	—	—	18.00	—
1996 Proof	7,000	Value: 20.00				
1997	—	—	—	1.50	4.00	—
1997 Proof	—	Value: 20.00				
1998	—	—	—	1.50	4.00	—
1998 Proof	—	Value: 20.00				
1999	—	—	—	1.50	4.00	—

KM# 658 200 ESCUDOS **Composition:** Copper-Nickel **Subject:** Columbus and Portugal

Date	Mintage	F	VF	XF	Unc	BU
1991	1,500,000	—	—	1.50	4.50	—

KM# 658a 200 ESCUDOS **Weight:** 26.5000 g. **Composition:** 0.9250 Silver .788 oz. ASW **Subject:** Columbus and Portugal

Date	Mintage	F	VF	XF	Unc	BU
1991	10,000	—	—	—	15.00	—
1991 Proof	15,000	Value: 30.00				

KM# 658b 200 ESCUDOS **Weight:** 27.2000 g. **Composition:** 0.9170 Gold .8000 oz. AGW **Subject:** Columbus and Portugal

Date	Mintage	F	VF	XF	Unc	BU
1991 Proof	3,500	Value: 550				

KM# 658c 200 ESCUDOS **Weight:** 31.1190 g. **Composition:** 0.9990 Platinum 1.000 oz. APW **Subject:** Columbus and Portugal

Date	Mintage	F	VF	XF	Unc	BU
1991 Proof	2,500	Value: 850				

KM# 658d 200 ESCUDOS **Weight:** 31.1190 g. **Composition:** 0.9990 Palladium 1.0000 oz. **Subject:** Columbus and Portugal

Date	Mintage	F	VF	XF	Unc	BU
1991 Proof	2,500	Value: 775				

KM# 659 200 ESCUDOS **Composition:** Copper-Nickel **Subject:** Westward Navigation **Reverse:** Stylized ship

Date	Mintage	F	VF	XF	Unc	BU
1991	1,500,000	—	—	1.50	4.50	—

KM# 659a 200 ESCUDOS **Weight:** 26.5000 g. **Composition:** 0.9250 Silver .7880 oz. ASW **Subject:** Westward Navigation **Reverse:** Stylized ship

Date	Mintage	F	VF	XF	Unc	BU
1991	10,000	—	—	—	15.00	—
1991 Proof	15,000	Value: 25.00				

KM# 659b 200 ESCUDOS **Weight:** 27.2000 g. **Composition:** 0.9170 Gold .8000 oz. AGW **Subject:** Westward Navigation **Reverse:** Stylized ship

Date	Mintage	F	VF	XF	Unc	BU
1991 Proof	3,500	Value: 550				

KM# 659c 200 ESCUDOS **Weight:** 31.1190 g. **Composition:** 0.9990 Platinum 1.0000 oz. APW **Subject:** Westward Navigation **Reverse:** Stylized ship

Date	Mintage	F	VF	XF	Unc	BU
1991 Proof	2,500	Value: 850				

KM# 659d 200 ESCUDOS **Weight:** 31.1190 g. **Composition:** 0.9990 Palladium 1.0000 oz. **Subject:** Westward Navigation **Reverse:** Stylized ship

Date	Mintage	F	VF	XF	Unc	BU
1991 Proof	2,500	Value: 775				

KM# 660 200 ESCUDOS **Composition:** Copper-Nickel **Subject:** New World - America **Reverse:** Columbus and ships

Date	Mintage	F	VF	XF	Unc	BU
ND(1992)	1,300,000	—	—	1.50	4.50	—

KM# 660a 200 ESCUDOS **Weight:** 26.5000 g. **Composition:** 0.9250 Silver .7880 oz. ASW **Subject:** New World - America **Reverse:** Columbus and ships

Date	Mintage	F	VF	XF	Unc	BU
ND(1992)	10,000	—	—	—	15.00	—
ND(1992) Proof	15,000	Value: 25.00				

KM# 660b 200 ESCUDOS **Weight:** 27.2000 g. **Composition:** 0.9170 Gold .8000 oz. AGW **Subject:** New World - America **Reverse:** Columbus and ships

Date	Mintage	F	VF	XF	Unc	BU
ND(1992) Proof	6,000	Value: 550				

KM# 660c 200 ESCUDOS **Weight:** 31.1190 g. **Composition:** 0.9990 Platinum 1.0000 oz. APW **Subject:** New World - America **Reverse:** Columbus and ships

Date	Mintage	F	VF	XF	Unc	BU
ND(1992) Proof	2,500	Value: 850				

KM# 660d 200 ESCUDOS **Weight:** 31.1190 g. **Composition:** 0.9990 Palladium 1.0000 oz. **Subject:** New World - America **Reverse:** Columbus and ships

Date	Mintage	F	VF	XF	Unc	BU
ND(1992) Proof	2,500	Value: 775				

KM# 661 200 ESCUDOS **Composition:** Copper-Nickel **Reverse:** Joao Rodrigues Cabrilho, map

Date	Mintage	F	VF	XF	Unc	BU
ND(1992)	1,300,000	—	—	1.50	4.50	—

KM# 661a 200 ESCUDOS **Weight:** 26.5000 g. **Composition:** 0.9250 Silver .7880 oz. ASW **Reverse:** Joao Rodrigues Cabrilho, map

Date	Mintage	F	VF	XF	Unc	BU
ND(1992)	10,000	—	—	—	15.00	—
ND(1992) Proof	15,000	Value: 25.00				

KM# 661b 200 ESCUDOS **Weight:** 27.2000 g. **Composition:** 0.9170 Gold .8000 oz. AGW **Reverse:** Joao Rodrigues Cabrilho, map

Date	Mintage	F	VF	XF	Unc	BU
ND(1992) Proof	3,500	Value: 550				

KM# 661c 200 ESCUDOS **Weight:** 31.1190 g. **Composition:** 0.9990 Platinum 1.0000 oz. APW **Reverse:** Joao Rodrigues Cabrilho, map

Date	Mintage	F	VF	XF	Unc	BU
ND(1992) Proof	2,500	Value: 850				

KM# 661d 200 ESCUDOS **Weight:** 31.1190 g. **Composition:** 0.9990 Palladium 1.0000 oz. **Reverse:** Joao Rodrigues Cabrilho, map

Date	Mintage	F	VF	XF	Unc	BU
ND(1992) Proof	2,500	Value: 775				

KM# 662 200 ESCUDOS **Composition:** Copper-Nickel **Series:** Olympics **Reverse:** Stylized runner

Date	Mintage	F	VF	XF	Unc	BU
1992	1,000,000	—	—	1.50	4.50	—

KM# 662a 200 ESCUDOS **Weight:** 26.5000 g. **Composition:** 0.9250 Silver .7881 oz. ASW **Series:** Olympics **Reverse:** Stylized runner

Date	Mintage	F	VF	XF	Unc	BU
1992	20,000	—	—	—	17.50	—
1992 Proof	30,000	Value: 32.50				

KM# 663 200 ESCUDOS **Composition:** Copper-Nickel **Subject:** Portugal's Presidency of the European Community

Date	Mintage	F	VF	XF	Unc	BU
1992	1,000,000	—	—	1.50	4.50	—

KM# 663a 200 ESCUDOS **Weight:** 26.5000 g. **Composition:** 0.9250 Silver .7881 oz. ASW **Subject:** Portugal's Presidency of the European Community

Date	Mintage	F	VF	XF	Unc	BU
1992	20,000	—	—	—	20.00	—
1992 Proof	30,000	Value: 35.00				

KM# 665 200 ESCUDOS **Composition:** Copper-Nickel **Subject:** Tanegashima - Site 1st Portuguese Landing in Japan

Date	Mintage	F	VF	XF	Unc	BU
ND(1993)	1,000,000	—	—	1.50	4.50	—

KM# 665a 200 ESCUDOS **Weight:** 26.5000 g. **Composition:** 0.9250 Silver .7881 oz. ASW **Subject:** Tanegashima - Site 1st Portuguese Landing in Japan

Date	Mintage	F	VF	XF	Unc	BU
ND(1993)	30,000	—	—	—	18.50	—
ND(1993) Proof	22,000	Value: 30.00				

KM# 665b 200 ESCUDOS **Weight:** 27.2000 g. **Composition:** 0.9170 Gold .8020 oz. AGW **Subject:** Tanegashima - 1st Portuguese Ship to Japan

Date	Mintage	F	VF	XF	Unc	BU
ND(1993) Proof	7,000	Value: 600				

KM# 666 200 ESCUDOS **Composition:** Copper-Nickel **Subject:** Espingarda **Reverse:** Mounted cavalryman shooting rifle

Date	Mintage	F	VF	XF	Unc	BU
1993	1,000,000	—	—	1.50	4.50	—

KM# 666a 200 ESCUDOS **Weight:** 26.5000 g. **Composition:** 0.9250 Silver .7881 oz. ASW **Subject:** Espingarda **Reverse:** Mounted cavalryman shooting rifle

Date	Mintage	F	VF	XF	Unc
1993	30,000	—	—	—	18.50
1993 Proof	20,000	Value: 35.00			

KM# 666b 200 ESCUDOS **Weight:** 27.2000 g. **Composition:** 0.9170 Gold .8020 oz. AGW **Subject:** Espingarda **Reverse:** Mounted cavalryman shooting rifle

Date	Mintage	F	VF	XF	Unc
1993 Proof	7,000	Value: 600			

KM# 666c 200 ESCUDOS **Weight:** 31.1190 g. **Composition:** 0.9990 Palladium 1.0000 oz. **Subject:** Espingarda **Reverse:** Mounted cavalryman shooting rifle

Date	Mintage	F	VF	XF	Unc
1993 Proof	2,000	Value: 775			

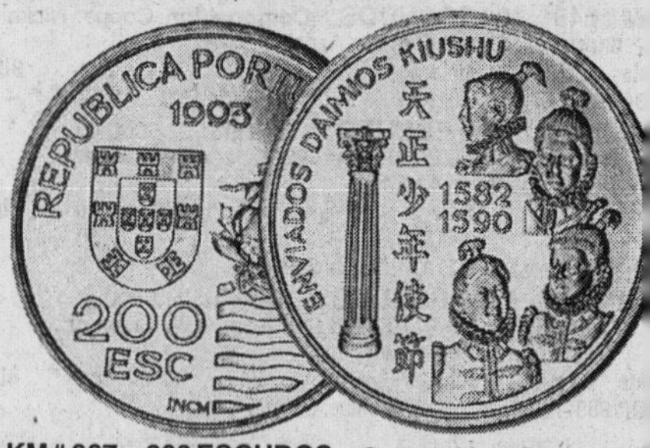

KM# 667 200 ESCUDOS **Composition:** Copper-Nick **Reverse:** Enviados Daimos Kiushu

Date	Mintage	F	VF	XF	Unc
1993	1,000,000	—	—	1.50	4.50

KM# 667a 200 ESCUDOS **Weight:** 26.5000 g. **Composition:** 0.9250 Silver .7881 oz. ASW **Reverse:** Enviados Daimos Kiushu

Date	Mintage	F	VF	XF	Unc
1993	30,000	—	—	—	18.50
1993 Proof	20,000	Value: 35.00			

KM# 667b 200 ESCUDOS **Weight:** 27.2000 g. **Composition:** 0.9170 Gold .8020 oz. AGW **Reverse:** Enviados Daimos Kiushu

Date	Mintage	F	VF	XF	Unc
1993 Proof	7,000	Value: 600			

KM# 668 200 ESCUDOS **Composition:** Copper-Nick **Reverse:** Arte Namban

Date	Mintage	F	VF	XF	Unc
1993	1,000,000	—	—	1.50	4.50

KM# 668a 200 ESCUDOS **Weight:** 26.5000 g. **Composition:** 0.9250 Silver .7881 oz. ASW **Reverse:** Ar Namban

Date	Mintage	F	VF	XF	Unc
1993	30,000	—	—	—	18.50
1993 Proof	22,000	Value: 35.00			

KM# 668b 200 ESCUDOS **Weight:** 27.2000 g. **Composition:** 0.9170 Gold .8020 oz. AGW **Reverse:** Art Namban

Date	Mintage	F	VF	XF	Unc
1993 Proof	7,000	Value: 600			

KM# 668c 200 ESCUDOS **Weight:** 31.1190 g. **Composition:** 0.9990 Platinum 1.000 oz. APW **Reverse:** Arte Namban

Date	Mintage	F	VF	XF	Unc
1993 Proof	2,000	Value: 850			

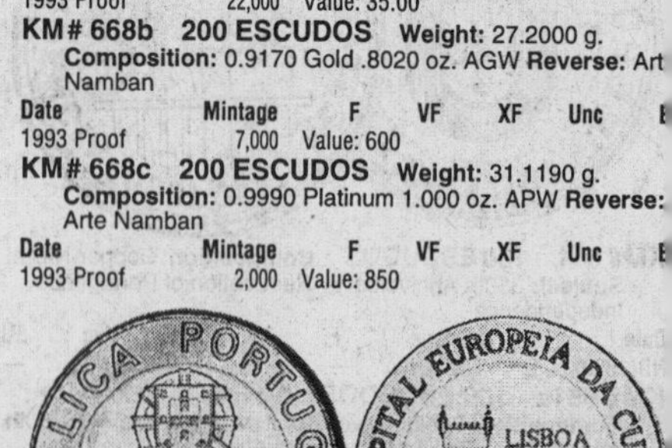

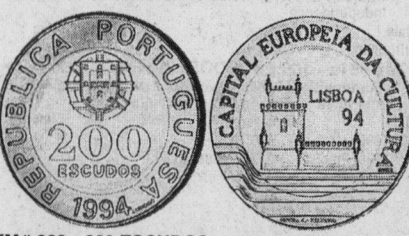

KM# 669 200 ESCUDOS **Ring Composition:** Aluminum-Bronze **Center Composition:** Copper-Nickel **Subject:** Lisbon - European Cultural Capital

Date	Mintage	F	VF	XF	Unc
1994	1,000,000	—	—	—	4.50
1994 Proof Sets	7,000	—	—	—	20.00

M# 670 200 ESCUDOS **Composition:** Copper-Nickel **Reverse:** Prince Henry the Navigator

te	Mintage	F	VF	XF	Unc	BU
)(1994)	750,000	—	—	—	5.50	—

M# 670a 200 ESCUDOS **Weight:** 26.5000 g. **Composition:** 0.9250 Silver .7881 oz. ASW **Reverse:** Prince Henry the Navigator

te	Mintage	F	VF	XF	Unc	BU
)(1994)	20,000	—	—	—	17.50	—
)(1994) Proof	13,000	Value: 27.50				

M# 670b 200 ESCUDOS **Weight:** 27.2000 g. **Composition:** 0.9170 Gold .8020 oz. AGW **Reverse:** Prince Henry the Navigator

te	Mintage	F	VF	XF	Unc	BU
)(1994) Proof	2,000	Value: 600				

M# 671 200 ESCUDOS **Composition:** Copper-Nickel **Subject:** Treaty of Tordesilhas

ate	Mintage	F	VF	XF	Unc	BU
)(1994)	750,000	—	—	—	5.50	—

M# 671a 200 ESCUDOS **Weight:** 26.5000 g. **Composition:** 0.9250 Silver .7881 oz. ASW **Subject:** Treaty of Tordesilhas.

ate	Mintage	F	VF	XF	Unc	BU
)(1994)	20,000	—	—	—	17.50	—
)(1994) Proof	13,000	Value: 27.50				

M# 671b 200 ESCUDOS **Weight:** 27.2000 g. **Composition:** 0.9170 Gold .8020 oz. AGW **Subject:** Treaty of Tordesilhas

ate	Mintage	F	VF	XF	Unc	BU
)(1994) Proof	2,000	Value: 600				

M# 671c 200 ESCUDOS **Weight:** 31.1190 g. **Composition:** 0.9990 Palladium 1.0000 oz. **Subject:** Treaty of Tordesilhas.

ate	Mintage	F	VF	XF	Unc	BU
)(1994) Proof	1,000	Value: 800				

M# 672 200 ESCUDOS **Composition:** Copper-Nickel **Subject:** Dividing Up The World

ate	Mintage	F	VF	XF	Unc	BU
994	750,000	—	—	—	5.50	—

M# 672a 200 ESCUDOS **Weight:** 26.5000 g. **Composition:** 0.9250 Silver .7881 oz. ASW **Subject:** Dividing up the World.

ate	Mintage	F	VF	XF	Unc	BU
994	20,000	—	—	—	17.50	—
994 Proof	12,000	Value: 27.50				

M# 672b 200 ESCUDOS **Weight:** 27.2000 g. **Composition:** 0.9170 Gold .8020 oz. AGW **Subject:** Dividing Up The World

ate	Mintage	F	VF	XF	Unc	BU
994 Proof	3,000	Value: 600				

KM# 673 200 ESCUDOS **Composition:** Copper-Nickel **Reverse:** King John II

Date	Mintage	F	VF	XF	Unc	BU
ND(1994)	750,000	—	—	—	5.50	—

KM# 673a 200 ESCUDOS **Weight:** 26.5000 g. **Composition:** 0.9250 Silver .7881 oz. ASW **Reverse:** King John II

Date	Mintage	F	VF	XF	Unc	BU
ND(1994)	20,000	—	—	—	18.50	—
ND(1994) Proof	13,000	Value: 37.50				

KM# 673b 200 ESCUDOS **Weight:** 27.2000 g. **Composition:** 0.9170 Gold .8020 oz. AGW **Reverse:** King John II

Date	Mintage	F	VF	XF	Unc	BU
ND(1994) Proof	2,000	Value: 600				

KM# 673c 200 ESCUDOS **Weight:** 31.1190 g. **Composition:** 0.9990 Platinum 1.0000 oz. APW **Reverse:** King John II

Date	Mintage	F	VF	XF	Unc	BU
ND(1994) Proof	1,000	Value: 850				

KM# 679 200 ESCUDOS **Ring Composition:** Aluminum-Bronze **Center Composition:** Copper Nickel **Subject:** 50th Anniversary - United Nations

Date	Mintage	F	VF	XF	Unc	BU
1995	500,000	—	—	—	5.50	—
1995 In proof sets only	17,000	Value: 20.00				

KM# 681 200 ESCUDOS **Composition:** Copper-Nickel **Reverse:** Afonso de Albuquerque

Date	Mintage	F	VF	XF	Unc	BU
1995	750,000	—	—	—	5.00	—

KM# 681a 200 ESCUDOS **Weight:** 26.5000 g. **Composition:** 0.9250 Silver .7881 oz. ASW **Reverse:** Afonso de Albuquerque

Date	Mintage	F	VF	XF	Unc	BU
1995	20,000	—	—	—	18.50	—
1995 Proof	13,000	Value: 32.50				

KM# 681b 200 ESCUDOS **Weight:** 27.2000 g. **Composition:** 0.9170 Gold .8016 oz. AGW **Reverse:** Afonso de Albuquerque

Date	Mintage	F	VF	XF	Unc	BU
1995 Proof	4,000	Value: 500				

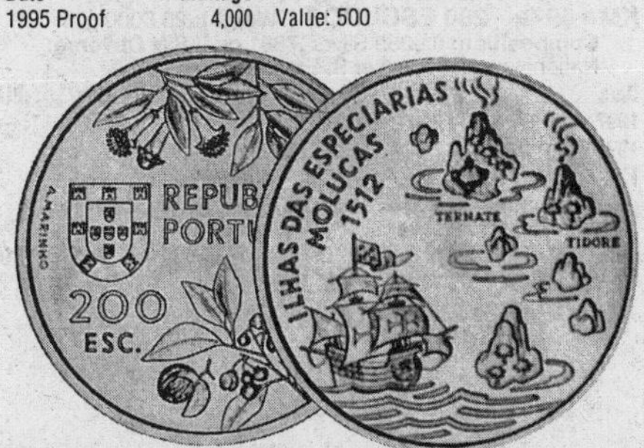

KM# 682 200 ESCUDOS **Composition:** Copper-Nickel **Reverse:** Moluca Islands

Date	Mintage	F	VF	XF	Unc	BU
1995	750,000	—	—	—	5.00	—

KM# 682a 200 ESCUDOS **Weight:** 26.5000 g. **Composition:** 0.9250 Silver .7881 oz. ASW **Reverse:** Moluca Islands

Date	Mintage	F	VF	XF	Unc	BU
1995	20,000	—	—	—	18.50	—
1995 Proof	13,000	Value: 35.00				

KM# 682b 200 ESCUDOS **Weight:** 27.2000 g. **Composition:** 0.9170 Gold .8016 oz. AGW **Reverse:** Moluca Islands

Date	Mintage	F	VF	XF	Unc	BU
1995 Proof	4,000	Value: 500				

KM# 682c 200 ESCUDOS **Weight:** 31.1190 g. **Composition:** 0.9995 Palladium 1.0000 oz. **Reverse:** Moluca Islands

Date	Mintage	F	VF	XF	Unc	BU
1995 In proof sets only	1,000	Value: 800				

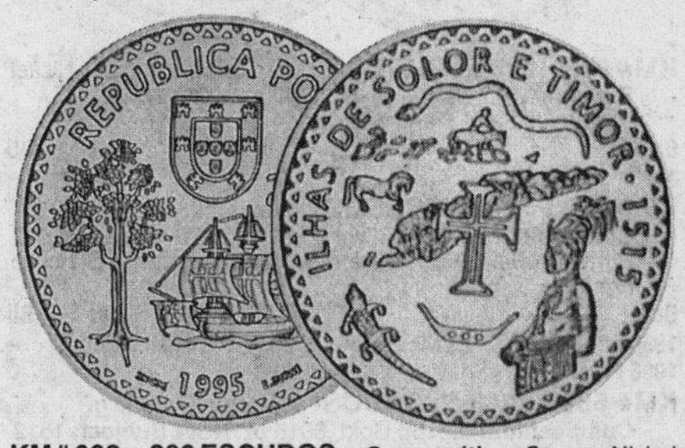

KM# 683 200 ESCUDOS **Composition:** Copper-Nickel **Reverse:** Solor and Timor Islands

Date	Mintage	F	VF	XF	Unc	BU
1995	750,000	—	—	—	5.00	—

KM# 683a 200 ESCUDOS **Weight:** 26.5000 g. **Composition:** 0.9250 Silver .7881 oz. ASW **Reverse:** Solor and Timor Islands

Date	Mintage	F	VF	XF	Unc	BU
1995	20,000	—	—	—	18.50	—
1995 Proof	13,000	Value: 35.00				

KM# 683b 200 ESCUDOS **Weight:** 27.2000 g. **Composition:** 0.9170 Gold .8016 oz. AGW **Reverse:** Solar and Timor Islands

Date	Mintage	F	VF	XF	Unc	BU
1995 Proof	4,000	Value: 500				

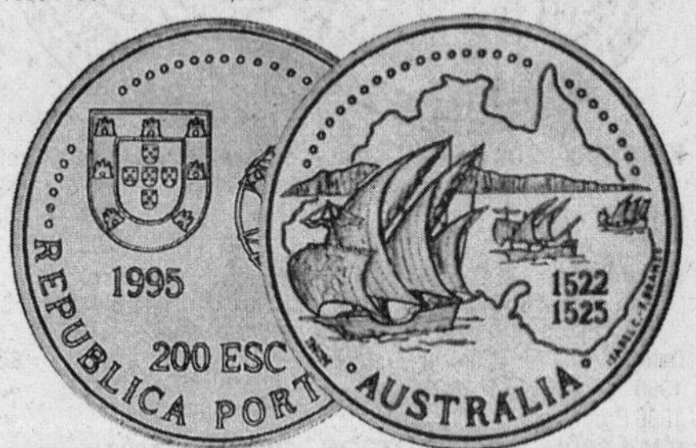

KM# 684 200 ESCUDOS **Composition:** Copper-Nickel **Reverse:** Australia

Date	Mintage	F	VF	XF	Unc	BU
1995	750,000	—	—	—	5.00	—

KM# 684a 200 ESCUDOS **Weight:** 26.5000 g. **Composition:** 0.9250 Silver .7881 oz. ASW **Reverse:** Australia

Date	Mintage	F	VF	XF	Unc	BU
1995	20,000	—	—	—	18.50	—
1995 Proof	13,000	Value: 35.00				

KM# 684b 200 ESCUDOS **Weight:** 27.2000 g. **Composition:** 0.9170 Gold .8016 oz. AGW **Reverse:** Australia

Date	Mintage	F	VF	XF	Unc	BU
1995 Proof	4,000	Value: 500				

KM# 684c 200 ESCUDOS **Weight:** 31.1190 g. **Composition:** 0.9995 Platinum 1.0000 oz. APW **Reverse:** Australia

Date	Mintage	F	VF	XF	Unc	BU
1995 In proof sets only	1,000	Value: 850				

KM# 687 200 ESCUDOS **Ring Composition:** Brass **Center Composition:** Copper-Nickel **Series:** Olympics **Reverse:** High jumper

Date	Mintage	F	VF	XF	Unc	BU
1996	7,000	—	—	—	5.00	—
1996 Proof	—	Value: 20.00				

KM# 687a 200 ESCUDOS **Weight:** 26.4500 g. **Composition:** 0.9250 Silver .7866 oz. ASW **Series:** Olympics **Reverse:** High jumper

Date	Mintage	F	VF	XF	Unc	BU
1996 Proof	20,000	Value: 50.00				

KM# 689 200 ESCUDOS **Composition:** Copper-Nickel **Subject:** 1512 Portugal - Siam Alliance **Reverse:** Portuguese and Siamese arms

Date	F	VF	XF	Unc	BU
1996	—	—	—	5.00	—

KM# 689a 200 ESCUDOS **Weight:** 26.5000 g. **Composition:** 0.9250 Silver .7881 oz. ASW **Subject:** 1512 Portugal - Siam Alliance **Reverse:** Portuguese and Siamese arms

Date	Mintage	F	VF	XF	Unc	BU
1996	20,000	—	—	—	17.50	—
1996 Proof	11,000	Value: 32.50				

KM# 689b 200 ESCUDOS **Weight:** 27.0000 g. **Composition:** 0.9166 Gold .8015 oz. AGW **Subject:** 1512 Portugal - Siam Alliance **Reverse:** Portuguese and Siamese arms

Date	Mintage	F	VF	XF	Unc	BU
1996 Proof	3,000	Value: 500				

KM# 690 200 ESCUDOS **Composition:** Copper-Nickel **Subject:** 1513 Portuguese Arrival in China

Date	F	VF	XF	Unc	BU
1996	—	—	—	6.00	—

KM# 690a 200 ESCUDOS **Weight:** 26.5000 g. **Composition:** 0.9250 Silver .7881 oz. ASW **Subject:** 1513 Portuguese Arrival in China

Date	Mintage	F	VF	XF	Unc	BU
1996	20,000	—	—	—	22.50	—
1996 Proof	10,000	Value: 40.00				

KM# 690b 200 ESCUDOS **Weight:** 27.2000 g. **Composition:** 0.9166 Gold .8015 oz. AGW **Subject:** 1513 Portuguese Arrival in China

Date	Mintage	F	VF	XF	Unc	BU
1996 Proof	3,000	Value: 500				

KM# 690c 200 ESCUDOS **Weight:** 31.1190 g. **Composition:** 0.9995 Palladium 1.0000 oz. **Subject:** 1513 Portuguese Arrival in China

Date	Mintage	F	VF	XF	Unc	BU
1996 Proof	1,000	Value: 800				

KM# 691 200 ESCUDOS **Composition:** Copper-Nickel **Subject:** 1557 Portuguese Establishment in Macau

Date	F	VF	XF	Unc	BU
1996	—	—	—	5.00	—

KM# 691a 200 ESCUDOS **Weight:** 26.5000 g. **Composition:** 0.9250 Silver .7881 oz. ASW **Subject:** 1557 Portuguese Establishment in Macau

Date	Mintage	F	VF	XF	Unc	BU
1996	20,000	—	—	—	17.50	—
1996 Proof	10,000	Value: 32.50				

KM# 691b 200 ESCUDOS **Weight:** 27.2000 g. **Composition:** 0.9166 Gold .8015 oz. AGW **Subject:** 1557 Portuguese Establishment in Macau

Date	Mintage	F	VF	XF	Unc	BU
1996 Proof	4,000	Value: 500				

KM# 692 200 ESCUDOS **Composition:** Copper-Nickel **Subject:** 1582 Portuguese Discovery of Taiwan

Date	F	VF	XF	Unc	BU
1996	—	—	—	5.00	—

KM# 692a 200 ESCUDOS **Weight:** 26.5000 g. **Composition:** 0.9250 Silver .7881 oz. ASW **Subject:** 1582 Portuguese Discovery of Taiwan

Date	Mintage	F	VF	XF	Unc	BU
1996	20,000	—	—	—	17.50	—
1996 Proof	10,000	Value: 32.50				

KM# 692b 200 ESCUDOS **Weight:** 27.2000 g. **Composition:** 0.9166 Gold .8015 oz. AGW **Subject:** 1582 Portuguese Discovery of Taiwan

Date	Mintage	F	VF	XF	Unc	BU
1996 Proof	3,000	Value: 500				

KM# 692c 200 ESCUDOS **Weight:** 31.1190 g. **Composition:** 0.9995 Platinum 1.0000 oz. APW **Subject:** 1582 Portuguese Discovery of Taiwan

Date	Mintage	F	VF	XF	Unc	BU
1996 Proof	1,000	Value: 850				

KM# 694 200 ESCUDOS **Ring Composition:** Copper-Aluminum **Center Composition:** Copper-Nickel **Subject:** Lisbon World Expo '98 **Obverse:** National arms and denomination **Reverse:** Dolphins

Date	Mintage	F	VF	XF	Unc	BU
1997	—	—	—	—	6.00	—
1997 In proof sets only	7,000	Value: 20.00				

KM# 697 200 ESCUDOS **Composition:** Copper-Nickel **Obverse:** National arms **Reverse:** S. Francisco Xavier

Date	F	VF	XF	Unc	BU
1997	—	—	—	5.00	—

KM# 697a 200 ESCUDOS **Weight:** 26.5000 g. **Composition:** 0.9250 Silver .7881 oz. ASW **Obverse:** National arms **Reverse:** S. Francisco Xavier

Date	Mintage	F	VF	XF	Unc	BU
1997	25,000	—	—	—	17.50	—
1997 Proof	25,000	Value: 30.00				

KM# 697b 200 ESCUDOS **Weight:** 27.2000 g. **Composition:** 0.9167 Gold .8017 oz. AGW **Obverse:** National arms **Reverse:** S. Francisco Xavier

Date	Mintage	F	VF	XF	Unc	BU
1997 Proof	4,000	Value: 500				

KM# 698 200 ESCUDOS **Composition:** Copper-Nick **Obverse:** National arms **Reverse:** Pe. Luis Frois, Japanes man

Date	F	VF	XF	Unc
1997	—	—	—	5.00

KM# 698a 200 ESCUDOS **Weight:** 26.5000 g. **Composition:** 0.9250 Silver .7881 oz. ASW **Obverse:** National arms **Reverse:** Pe. Luis Frois, Japanese man

Date	Mintage	F	VF	XF	Unc
1997	25,000	—	—	—	17.50
1997 Proof	24,000	Value: 32.50			

KM# 698b 200 ESCUDOS **Weight:** 27.2000 g. **Composition:** 0.9167 Gold .8017 oz. AGW **Obverse:** National arms **Reverse:** Pe. Luis Frois, Japanese man

Date	Mintage	F	VF	XF	Unc
1997 Proof	5,000	Value: 500			

KM# 699 200 ESCUDOS **Composition:** Copper-Nick **Obverse:** National arms and map of South America **Reverse:** Bto. Jose de Anchieta

Date	F	VF	XF	Unc
1997	—	—	—	5.00

KM# 699a 200 ESCUDOS **Weight:** 26.5000 g. **Composition:** 0.9250 Silver .7881 oz. ASW **Obverse:** National arms and map of South America **Reverse:** Bto. Jos de Anchieta

Date	Mintage	F	VF	XF	Unc
1997	25,000	—	—	—	17.50
1997 Proof	24,000	Value: 32.50			

KM# 699b 200 ESCUDOS **Weight:** 27.2000 g. **Composition:** 0.9167 Gold .8017 oz. AGW **Obverse:** National arms and map of South America **Reverse:** Bto. Jo de Anchieta

Date	Mintage	F	VF	XF	Unc
1997 Proof	4,000	Value: 500			

KM# 699c 200 ESCUDOS **Weight:** 31.1190 g. **Composition:** 0.9995 Palladium 1.0000 oz. **Obverse:** National arms and map of South America **Reverse:** Bto. Jo de Anchieta

Date	Mintage	F	VF	XF	Unc
1997 Proof	1,000	Value: 800			

KM# 700 200 ESCUDOS **Composition:** Copper-Nick **Obverse:** National cross and arms **Reverse:** Irmao Bent de Gois, map of China's coast

Date	F	VF	XF	Unc
1997	—	—	—	5.00

KM# 700a 200 ESCUDOS **Weight:** 26.5000 g. **Composition:** 0.9250 Silver .7881 oz. ASW **Obverse:** National cross and arms **Reverse:** Irmao Bento de Gois, ma of China's coast

Date	Mintage	F	VF	XF	Unc
1997	25,000	—	—	—	17.50
1997 Proof	24,000	Value: 32.50			

KM# 700b 200 ESCUDOS **Weight:** 27.2000 g. **Composition:** 0.9160 Gold .8017 oz. AGW **Obverse:** National cross and arms **Reverse:** Irmao Bento de Gois, ma of China's coast

Date	Mintage	F	VF	XF	Unc
1997 Proof	4,000	Value: 500			

KM# 700c 200 ESCUDOS **Weight:** 31.1190 g. **Composition:** 0.9995 Platinum 1.0000 oz. APW **Obverse:** National cross and arms **Reverse:** Irmao Bento de Gois, map of China's coast

Date	Mintage	F	VF	XF	Unc	BU
1997 Proof	1,000	Value: 900				

KM# 706 200 ESCUDOS **Ring Composition:** Aluminum-Bronze **Center Composition:** Copper-Nickel **Subject:** International Year of the Oceans Expo **Obverse:** Arms above denominations

Date	Mintage	F	VF	XF	Unc	BU
1998	—	—	—	—	4.50	—
1998 In proof sets only	Est. 20,000	Value: 12.00				

KM# 709 200 ESCUDOS **Composition:** Copper-Nickel **Obverse:** Three ships, arms, and denomination **Reverse:** Portrait of Vasco Da Gama, dates

Date	Mintage	F	VF	XF	Unc	BU
1998		—	—	—	5.00	—

KM# 709a 200 ESCUDOS **Weight:** 26.5000 g. **Composition:** 0.9250 Silver .7881 oz. ASW **Obverse:** Three ships, arms, and denomination **Reverse:** Bust of Vasco da Gama left, dates

Date	Mintage	F	VF	XF	Unc	BU
1998 Proof	25,000	Value: 32.50				

KM# 709b 200 ESCUDOS **Weight:** 27.2000 g. **Composition:** 0.9167 Gold .8017 oz. AGW **Obverse:** Three ships, arms, and denomination **Reverse:** Bust of Vasco Da Gama left, dates

Date	Mintage	F	VF	XF	Unc	BU
1998 Proof	5,000	Value: 500				

KM# 709c 200 ESCUDOS **Weight:** 31.1190 g. **Composition:** 0.9995 Platinum 1.0000 oz. APW **Obverse:** Three ships, arms, and denomination **Reverse:** Bust of Vasco da Gama, dates

Date	Mintage	F	VF	XF	Unc	BU
1998 Proof	1,000	Value: 900				

KM# 710 200 ESCUDOS **Composition:** Copper-Nickel **Subject:** Discovery of Africa **Obverse:** Arms, ship, and palm tree **Reverse:** Ship, map, and hunter

Date	Mintage	F	VF	XF	Unc	BU
1998		—	—	—	5.00	—

KM# 710a 200 ESCUDOS **Weight:** 26.5000 g. **Composition:** 0.9250 Silver .7881 oz. ASW **Subject:** Discovery of Africa **Obverse:** Arms, ship, and palm tree **Reverse:** Ship, map, and hunter

Date	Mintage	F	VF	XF	Unc	BU
1998	25,000	—	—	—	17.50	—
1998 Proof	26,000	Value: 30.00				

KM# 710b 200 ESCUDOS **Weight:** 27.2000 g. **Composition:** 0.9167 Gold .8017 oz. AGW **Subject:** Discovery of Africa **Obverse:** Arms, ship, and palm tree **Reverse:** Ship, map, and hunter

Date	Mintage	F	VF	XF	Unc	BU
1998 Proof	5,000	Value: 500				

KM# 711 200 ESCUDOS **Composition:** Copper-Nickel **Subject:** Mozambique **Obverse:** Arms above mermaid **Reverse:** Two ships and island map

Date	Mintage	F	VF	XF	Unc	BU
1998		—	—	—	5.00	—

KM# 711a 200 ESCUDOS **Weight:** 26.5000 g. **Composition:** 0.9250 Silver .7881 oz. ASW **Subject:** Mozambique **Obverse:** Arms above mermaid **Reverse:** Two ships and island map

Date	Mintage	F	VF	XF	Unc	BU
1998	25,000	—	—	—	17.50	—
1998 Proof	25,000	Value: 30.00				

KM# 711b 200 ESCUDOS **Weight:** 27.2000 g. **Composition:** 0.9167 Gold .8017 oz. AGW **Subject:** Mozambique **Obverse:** Arms above mermaid **Reverse:** Two ships and island map

Date	Mintage	F	VF	XF	Unc	BU
1998 Proof	6,000	Value: 500				

KM# 712 200 ESCUDOS **Composition:** Copper-Nickel **Subject:** India 1498 **Obverse:** Arms and sailing ship **Reverse:** Ship and coastal map of India

Date	Mintage	F	VF	XF	Unc	BU
1998		—	—	—	5.00	—

KM# 712a 200 ESCUDOS **Weight:** 26.5000 g. **Composition:** 0.9250 Silver .7881 oz. ASW **Subject:** India 1498 **Obverse:** Arms and sailing ship **Reverse:** Ship and coastal map of India

Date	Mintage	F	VF	XF	Unc	BU
1998	25,000	—	—	—	17.50	—
1998 Proof	25,000	Value: 32.50				

KM# 712b 200 ESCUDOS **Weight:** 27.2000 g. **Composition:** 0.9167 Gold .8017 oz. AGW **Subject:** India 1498 **Obverse:** Arms and sailing ship **Reverse:** Ship and coastal map of India

Date	Mintage	F	VF	XF	Unc	BU
1998 Proof	5,000	Value: 500				

KM# 712c 200 ESCUDOS **Weight:** 31.1190 g. **Composition:** 0.9995 Palladium 1.0000 oz. **Subject:** India 1498 **Obverse:** Arms and sailing ship **Reverse:** Ship and coastal map of India

Date	Mintage	F	VF	XF	Unc	BU
1998 Proof	1,000	Value: 800				

KM# 716 200 ESCUDOS **Composition:** Copper-Nickel 1.0000 oz. **Subject:** Death on the Sea **Obverse:** National arms and ropes **Reverse:** Stylized sinking ship **Edge:** Reeded **Size:** 36 mm.

Date	Mintage	F	VF	XF	Unc	BU
1999		—	—	—	4.00	—

KM# 716a 200 ESCUDOS **Weight:** 26.5000 g. **Composition:** 0.9250 Silver .7881 oz. ASW **Subject:** Death on the Sea **Obverse:** National arms and ropes **Reverse:** Stylized sinking ship **Edge:** Reeded **Size:** 36 mm.

Date	Mintage	F	VF	XF	Unc	BU
1999	10,000	—	—	—	20.00	—
1999 Proof	10,000	Value: 35.00				

KM# 716b 200 ESCUDOS **Weight:** 27.2000 g. **Composition:** 0.9167 Gold .8017 oz. AGW **Subject:** Death on the Sea **Obverse:** National arms and ropes **Reverse:** Stylized sinking ship **Edge:** Reeded **Size:** 36 mm.

Date	Mintage	F	VF	XF	Unc	BU
1999 Proof	1,000	Value: 450				

KM# 717 200 ESCUDOS **Composition:** Copper-Nickel **Subject:** Brasil 1500 **Obverse:** Fleet of sailing ships **Reverse:** Head of Pedro Alvares Cabral right

Date	Mintage	F	VF	XF	Unc	BU
1999		—	—	—	4.00	—

KM# 717a 200 ESCUDOS **Weight:** 26.5000 g. **Composition:** 0.9250 Silver .7881 oz. ASW **Subject:** Brasil 1500 **Obverse:** Fleet of sailing ships **Reverse:** Head of Pedro Alvares Cabral right

Date	Mintage	F	VF	XF	Unc	BU
1999	1,000	—	—	—	20.00	—
1999 Proof	1,000	Value: 35.00				

KM# 717b 200 ESCUDOS **Weight:** 27.2000 g. **Composition:** 0.9167 Gold .8017 oz. AGW **Subject:** Brasil 1500 **Obverse:** Fleet of sailing ships **Reverse:** Head of Pedro Alvares Cabral

Date	Mintage	F	VF	XF	Unc	BU
1999 Proof	1,000	Value: 450				

KM# 718 200 ESCUDOS **Composition:** Copper-Nickel **Subject:** Brasil **Obverse:** Natives, palm trees **Reverse:** Ship, native, and map

Date	Mintage	F	VF	XF	Unc	BU
1999		—	—	—	4.00	—

KM# 718a 200 ESCUDOS **Weight:** 26.5000 g. **Composition:** 0.9250 Silver .7881 oz. ASW **Subject:** Brasil **Obverse:** Natives, palm trees **Reverse:** Ship, native, and map

Date	Mintage	F	VF	XF	Unc	BU
1999		—	—	—	20.00	—
1999 Proof	Est. 10,000	Value: 35.00				

KM# 718b 200 ESCUDOS **Weight:** 27.2000 g. **Composition:** 0.9167 Gold .8017 oz. AGW **Subject:** Brasil **Obverse:** Natives and palm trees **Reverse:** Ship, native, and map

Date	Mintage	F	VF	XF	Unc	BU
1999 Proof	1,000	Value: 450				

KM# 719 200 ESCUDOS **Composition:** Copper-Nickel **Subject:** Duarte Pacheco Pereira **Reverse:** Armored half-length bust of Duarte Pacheco Pereira facing

Date	Mintage	F	VF	XF	Unc	BU
1999		—	—	—	4.00	—

KM# 719a 200 ESCUDOS **Weight:** 26.5000 g. **Composition:** 0.9250 Silver .7881 oz. ASW **Subject:** Duarte Pacheco Pereira **Reverse:** Armored half-length bust of Duarte Pacheco Pereira facing

Date	Mintage	F	VF	XF	Unc	BU
1999	1,000	—	—	—	20.00	—
1999 Proof	1,000	Value: 35.00				

KM# 719b 200 ESCUDOS **Weight:** 27.2000 g. **Composition:** 0.9167 Gold .8017 oz. AGW **Subject:** Duarte Pacheco Pereira **Reverse:** Armored half-length bust of Duarte Pacheco Pereira facing

Date	Mintage	F	VF	XF	Unc	BU
1999 Proof	1,000	Value: 450				

KM# 720 200 ESCUDOS **Ring Composition:** Brass **Center Composition:** Copper-Nickel **Obverse:** National arms above denominations **Reverse:** Push toy and logo **Edge:** Reeded and plain sections

Date	F	VF	XF	Unc	BU
1999	—	—	—	4.50	—

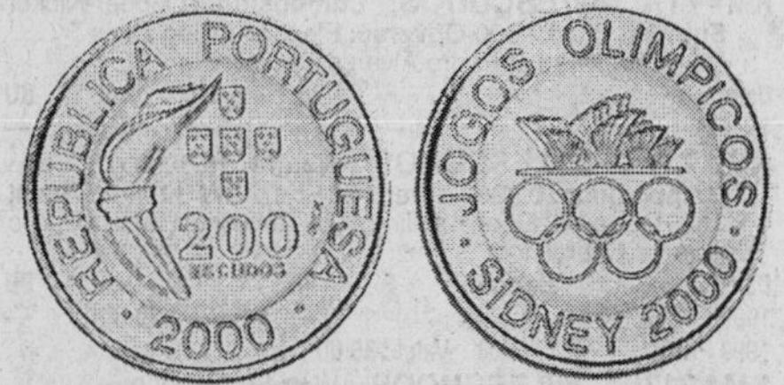

KM# 726 200 ESCUDOS **Ring Composition:** Nickel-Brass **Center Composition:** Copper-Nickel **Obverse:** Torch, arms and denomination **Reverse:** Olympic logo **Edge:** Reeded and plain sections

Date	Mintage	F	VF	XF	Unc	BU
2000	10,000	—	—	—	4.00	—
2000 Proof	5,000	Value: 7.50				

KM# 728 200 ESCUDOS **Weight:** 21.1000 g. **Composition:** Copper-Nickel **Subject:** Terra Do Lavrado **Obverse:** National arms, compass, etc. **Reverse:** Labrador coast and ship **Edge:** Reeded **Size:** 36 mm.

Date	F	VF	XF	Unc	BU
2000	—	—	—	4.00	—

KM# 728a 200 ESCUDOS **Weight:** 26.5000 g. **Composition:** 0.9250 Silver .7881 oz. ASW **Subject:** Terra do Lavrado **Obverse:** National arms, compass, etc. **Reverse:** Labrador coast and ship **Edge:** Reeded **Size:** 36 mm.

Date	Mintage	F	VF	XF	Unc	BU
2000	—	—	—	—	25.00	—
2000 Proof	Est. 10,000	Value: 37.50				

KM# 728b 200 ESCUDOS **Weight:** 27.2000 g. **Composition:** 0.9166 Gold .8016 oz. AGW **Subject:** Terra Do Lavrado **Obverse:** National arms, compass, etc. **Reverse:** Labrador coast and ship **Edge:** Reeded **Size:** 36 mm.

Date	Mintage	F	VF	XF	Unc	BU
2000 Proof	Est. 1,375	Value: 500				

KM# 729 200 ESCUDOS **Weight:** 21.1400 g. **Composition:** Copper-Nickel **Subject:** Terra Dos Corte-Real **Obverse:** Cross above national arms **Reverse:** Ship above 1501-1502 **Edge:** Reeded **Size:** 36 mm.

Date	F	VF	XF	Unc	BU
2000	—	—	—	4.00	—

KM# 729a 200 ESCUDOS **Weight:** 26.5000 g. **Composition:** 0.9250 Silver .7881 oz. ASW **Subject:** Terra Dos Corte-Real **Obverse:** Cross above national arms **Reverse:** Ship above 1501-1502 **Edge:** Reeded **Size:** 36 mm.

Date	Mintage	F	VF	XF	Unc	BU
2000	—	—	—	—	25.00	—
2000 Proof	Est. 10,000	Value: 37.50				

KM# 729b 200 ESCUDOS **Weight:** 27.2000 g. **Composition:** 0.9166 Gold .8016 oz. AGW **Subject:** Terra Dos Corte-Real **Obverse:** Cross above national arms **Reverse:** Ship above 1501-1502

Date	Mintage	F	VF	XF	Unc	BU
2000 Proof	Est. 1,375	Value: 500				

KM# 729c 200 ESCUDOS **Weight:** 31.1190 g. **Composition:** 0.9995 Palladium 1.0000 oz. **Subject:** Terra Dos Corte-Real **Obverse:** Cross above national arms **Reverse:** Ship above 1501-1502 **Edge:** Reeded

Date	Mintage	F	VF	XF	Unc	BU
2000 Proof	Est. 250	Value: 900				

KM# 730 200 ESCUDOS **Weight:** 21.1400 g. **Composition:** Copper-Nickel **Subject:** Terra Florida **Obverse:** National arms above compass **Reverse:** Ship and Florida coast **Edge:** Reeded **Size:** 36 mm.

Date	F	VF	XF	Unc	BU
2000	—	—	—	4.00	—

KM# 730a 200 ESCUDOS **Weight:** 26.5000 g. **Composition:** 0.9250 Silver .7881 oz. ASW **Subject:** Terra Florida **Obverse:** National arms above compass **Reverse:** Ship and Florida coast **Edge:** Reeded

Date	Mintage	F	VF	XF	Unc	BU
2000	—	—	—	—	25.00	—
2000 Proof	Est. 10,000	Value: 37.50				

KM# 730b 200 ESCUDOS **Weight:** 27.2000 g. **Composition:** 0.9166 Gold .8016 oz. AGW **Obverse:** National arms above compass **Reverse:** Ship and Florida coast **Edge:** Reeded **Edge Lettering:** Terra Florida

Date	Mintage	F	VF	XF	Unc	BU
2000 Proof	Est. 1,375	Value: 500				

KM# 731 200 ESCUDOS **Weight:** 21.1400 g. **Composition:** Copper-Nickel **Subject:** Fernao De Magalhaes **Obverse:** National arms, ship, and denomination **Reverse:** Bearded portrait **Edge:** Reeded **Size:** 36 mm.

Date	F	VF	XF	Unc	BU
2000	—	—	—	4.00	—

KM# 731a 200 ESCUDOS **Weight:** 26.5000 g. **Composition:** 0.9250 Silver .7881 oz. ASW **Subject:** Fernao de Magalhaes **Obverse:** National arms, ship, and denomination **Reverse:** Bearded portrait **Edge:** Reeded

Date	F	VF	XF	Unc	BU
2000	—	—	—	25.00	—

KM# 731b 200 ESCUDOS **Weight:** 27.2000 g. **Composition:** 0.9166 Gold .8016 oz. AGW **Subject:** Fernao de Magalhaes **Obverse:** National arms, ship, and denomination **Reverse:** Bearded portrait **Edge:** Reeded

Date	Mintage	F	VF	XF	Unc	BU
2000 Proof	Est. 1,375	Value: 500				

KM# 731c 200 ESCUDOS **Weight:** 31.1190 g. **Composition:** 0.9995 Platinum 1.0000 oz. APW **Subject:** Fernao de Magalhaes **Obverse:** National arms, ship, and denomination **Reverse:** Bearded portrait **Edge:** Reeded

Date	Mintage	F	VF	XF	Unc	BU
2000 Proof	Est. 250	Value: 1,000				

KM# 604 250 ESCUDOS **Weight:** 25.0000 g. **Composition:** 0.6800 Silver .5466 oz. ASW **Subject:** 1974 Revolution

Date	Mintage	F	VF	XF	Unc	BU
ND(1976)	950,000	—	—	6.00	10.00	—
ND(1976) Proof	10,000	Value: 18.50				

KM# 626 250 ESCUDOS **Composition:** Copper-Nickel **Subject:** World Fisheries Conference

Date	Mintage	F	VF	XF	Unc	BU
ND(1984)	24,000	—	—	30.00	65.00	—

KM# 626a 250 ESCUDOS **Weight:** 23.0000 g. **Composition:** 0.9250 Silver .6841 oz. ASW **Edge Lettering:** World Fisheries Conference

Date	Mintage	F	VF	XF	Unc	BU
ND(1984) Proof	8,000	Value: 120				

KM# 643 250 ESCUDOS **Composition:** Copper-Nickel **Subject:** Seoul Olympics **Reverse:** Runners

Date	Mintage	F	VF	XF	Unc	BU
1988	850,000	—	—	2.50	5.00	—

KM# 643a 250 ESCUDOS **Weight:** 28.0000 g. **Composition:** 0.9250 Silver .8327 oz. ASW **Subject:** Seoul Olympics **Reverse:** Runners

Date	Mintage	F	VF	XF	Unc	BU
1988	70,000	—	—	—	16.00	—
1988 Proof	30,000	Value: 27.50				

KM# 650 250 ESCUDOS **Composition:** Copper-Nick **Subject:** 850th Anniversary - Founding of Portugal

Date	Mintage	F	VF	XF	Unc
1989	750,000	—	—	2.50	5.00

KM# 650a 250 ESCUDOS **Weight:** 28.0000 g. **Composition:** 0.9250 Silver .8327 oz. ASW **Subject:** 850 Anniversary - Founding of Portugal

Date	Mintage	F	VF	XF	Unc
1989	15,000	—	—	—	22.50
1989 Proof	30,000	Value: 40.00			

KM# 620 500 ESCUDOS **Weight:** 7.0000 g. **Composition:** 0.8350 Silver .1879 oz. ASW **Subject:** XV European Art Exhibition

Date	Mintage	F	VF	XF	Unc
1983	200,000	—	—	6.00	12.00
1983 Proof	8,500	Value: 30.00			

KM# 686a 500 ESCUDOS **Weight:** 7.0000 g. **Composition:** 0.8350 Silver .1879 oz. ASW **Subject:** 800 Anniversary - Birth of Saint Anthony

Date	F	VF	XF	Unc
1995	—	—	—	8.50

KM# 686b 500 ESCUDOS **Weight:** 14.0000 g. **Composition:** 0.9250 Silver .4163 oz. ASW **Subject:** 800 Anniversary - Birth of Saint Anthony

Date	Mintage	F	VF	XF	Unc
1995 Proof	10,000	Value: 45.00			

KM# 686c 500 ESCUDOS **Weight:** 17.5000 g. **Composition:** 0.9177 Gold .5159 oz. AGW **Subject:** 800 Anniversary - Birth of Saint Anthony

Date	Mintage	F	VF	XF	Unc
1995 Proof	5,000	Value: 325			

KM# 702 500 ESCUDOS **Weight:** 13.8700 g. **Composition:** 0.5000 Silver .2230 oz. ASW **Obverse:** National arms **Reverse:** Bank seal - Banco de Portugal

Date	F	VF	XF	Unc
ND(1996)	—	—	—	8.50

M# 701 500 ESCUDOS **Composition:** Copper-Nickel **Obverse:** National arms superimposed on radiant sun **Reverse:** Head of Padre Antonio Vieira facing

e	F	VF	XF	Unc	BU
(1997)	—	—	—	5.50	—

M# 701a 500 ESCUDOS **Weight:** 14.0000 g. **Composition:** 0.9250 Silver .4051 oz. ASW **Obverse:** National arms superimposed on radiant sun **Reverse:** Head of Padre Antonio Vieira facing

e	F	VF	XF	Unc	BU
(1997) Proof	— Value: 37.50				

M# 701b 500 ESCUDOS **Composition:** Silver And Gold **Obverse:** National arms superimposed on radiant sun **Reverse:** Head of Padre Antonio Vieira facing **Note:** 14.0000 gram, .925 Silver, .4051 ounce with 3.1000 gram .9167 gold, .0914 ounce lamination on reverse.

e	Mintage	F	VF	XF	Unc	BU
(1997) Proof	15,000	Value: 125				

M# 705 500 ESCUDOS **Weight:** 14.0000 g. **Composition:** 0.9250 Silver .4164 oz. ASW **Obverse:** Arms and denomination **Reverse:** Vasco Da Gama Bridge

e	Mintage	F	VF	XF	Unc	BU
98	—	—	—	—	6.50	—
98 Proof	30,000	Value: 42.50				

M# 705a 500 ESCUDOS **Ring Composition:** Silver **Center Composition:** Gold **Obverse:** Arms and denomination **Reverse:** Vasco Da Gama Bridge **Note:** 14.000 gram, .925 Silver, .4164 ounce with 3.1000 gram .9167 gold, .0914 ounce lamination on reverse.

te	Mintage	F	VF	XF	Unc	BU
98 Proof	15,000	Value: 125				

M# 723 500 ESCUDOS **Weight:** 14.0000 g. **Composition:** 0.5000 Silver .2236 oz. ASW **Subject:** Macao's Return to China **Obverse:** Partial bridge above arms **Reverse:** Bridge above monument **Edge:** Reeded

ate	F	VF	XF	Unc	BU
99	—	—	—	5.50	—

M# 725 500 ESCUDOS **Weight:** 14.0000 g. **Composition:** 0.0925 Silver .4164 oz. ASW **Subject:** Eca de Queiroz **Obverse:** National arms and denomination **Reverse:** Stylized portrait of Eca de Gueiroz **Edge:** Reeded

ate	Mintage	F	VF	XF	Unc	BU
D(2000)	450,000	—	—	—	8.50	—
D(2000) Proof	10,000	Value: 45.00				

M# 725a 500 ESCUDOS **Weight:** 14.0000 g. **Composition:** 0.9250 Silver .4164 oz. ASW **Subject:** Eca de Queiroz **Obverse:** National arms above denomination **Reverse:** Stylized portrait of Eca de Queiroz **Edge:** Reeded **Note:** 14.000 gram, .925 Silver, .4164 ounce with 3.1000 gram .9167 gold, .1000 ounce lamination on reverse.

ate	Mintage	F	VF	XF	Unc	BU
D(2000) Proof	10,000	Value: 125				

M# 733 500 ESCUDOS **Weight:** 13.9600 g. **Composition:** 0.5000 Silver .2244 oz. ASW **Subject:** European Culture Capital **Obverse:** National arms and denomination **Reverse:** Stylized design **Edge:** Reeded **Size:** 30.1 mm.

Date	F	VF	XF	Unc	BU
2001	—	—	—	6.50	—

KM# 621 750 ESCUDOS **Weight:** 12.5000 g. **Composition:** 0.8350 Silver .3356 oz. ASW **Subject:** XVII European Art Exhibition

Date	Mintage	F	VF	XF	Unc	BU
1983	200,000	—	—	6.50	13.50	—
1983 Proof	8,500	Value: 35.00				

KM# 611 1000 ESCUDOS **Weight:** 17.0000 g. **Composition:** 0.9250 Silver .5056 oz. ASW **Subject:** 400th Anniversary - Death of Louis de Camoes

Date	Mintage	F	VF	XF	Unc	BU
ND(1983)	150,000	—	—	—	16.50	—
ND(1983) Proof	10,000	Value: 42.50				

KM# 622 1000 ESCUDOS **Weight:** 21.0000 g. **Composition:** 0.8350 Silver .5638 oz. ASW **Subject:** XVII European Art Exhibition

Date	Mintage	F	VF	XF	Unc	BU
1983	200,000	—	—	7.50	16.50	—
1983 Proof	8,500	Value: 40.00				

KM# 657 1000 ESCUDOS **Weight:** 27.0000 g. **Composition:** 0.5000 Silver .4340 oz. ASW **Series:** Ibero - American

Date	Mintage	F	VF	XF	Unc	BU
ND(1992)	326,000	—	—	—	17.50	—

KM# 657a 1000 ESCUDOS **Weight:** 27.0000 g. **Composition:** 0.9250 Silver .8029 oz. ASW **Series:** Ibero - American

Date	Mintage	F	VF	XF	Unc	BU
ND(1992) Proof	30,000	Value: 65.00				

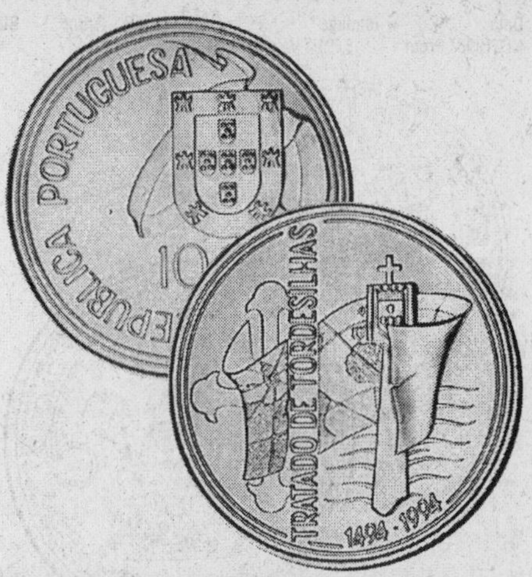

KM# 675 1000 ESCUDOS **Weight:** 28.0000 g. **Composition:** 0.5000 Silver .4501 oz. ASW **Subject:** Treaty of Tordesilhas

Date	F	VF	XF	Unc	BU
ND(1994)	—	—	—	14.50	—

KM# 675a 1000 ESCUDOS **Weight:** 28.0000 g. **Composition:** 0.9250 Silver .8327 oz. ASW **Subject:** Treaty of Tordesilhas

Date	Mintage	F	VF	XF	Unc	BU
ND(1994) Proof	10,000	Value: 45.00				

KM# 676 1000 ESCUDOS **Weight:** 28.0000 g. **Composition:** 0.5000 Silver .4501 oz. ASW **Subject:** Endangered Wildlife **Reverse:** Gray wolves

Date	Mintage	F	VF	XF	Unc	BU
1994	70,000	—	—	—	100	—

KM# 676a 1000 ESCUDOS **Weight:** 28.0000 g. **Composition:** 0.9250 Silver .8327 oz. ASW **Subject:** Endangered Wildlife

Date	Mintage	F	VF	XF	Unc	BU
1994 Proof	30,000	Value: 150				

KM# 685 1000 ESCUDOS **Weight:** 28.0000 g. **Composition:** 0.5000 Silver .4501 oz. ASW **Subject:** 500th Anniversary - Death of John II

Date	Mintage	F	VF	XF	Unc	BU
ND(1995)	650,000	—	—	—	13.50	—

KM# 685a 1000 ESCUDOS **Weight:** 28.0000 g. **Composition:** 0.9250 Silver .8327 oz. ASW **Subject:** 500th Anniversary - Death of John II

Date	Mintage	F	VF	XF	Unc	BU
ND(1995) Proof	15,000	Value: 40.00				

KM# 688 1000 ESCUDOS **Weight:** 28.0000 g. **Composition:** 0.5000 Silver .4501 oz. ASW **Subject:** Restoration of the Frigate Ferdinand II and Gloria **Obverse:** Arms, figure head, ship's hull

Date	F	VF	XF	Unc	BU
ND(1996)	—	—	—	14.50	—

KM# 688a 1000 ESCUDOS **Weight:** 28.0000 g. **Composition:** 0.9250 Silver .8327 oz. ASW **Subject:** Restoration of the Frigate Ferdinand II and Gloria **Obverse:** Arms, figure head, ship's hull

Date	Mintage	F	VF	XF	Unc	BU
ND(1996) Proof	15,000	Value: 45.00				

KM# 696 1000 ESCUDOS **Weight:** 28.0000 g. **Composition:** 0.5000 Silver .4501 oz. ASW **Subject:** N. S. Da Conceicao Padroeira de Portugal **Obverse:** National arms **Reverse:** Madonna and child

Date	F	VF	XF	Unc	BU
ND(1996)	—	—	—	13.50	—

KM# 696a 1000 ESCUDOS **Weight:** 28.0000 g. **Composition:** 0.9250 Silver .8327 oz. ASW **Subject:** N. S. Da Conceicao Padroeira de Portugal **Obverse:** National arms **Reverse:** Madonna and child

Date	F	VF	XF	Unc	BU
ND(1996) Proof	—	Value: 45.00			

KM# 695 1000 ESCUDOS **Weight:** 28.0000 g. **Composition:** 0.5000 Silver .4501 oz. ASW **Subject:** 100th Anniversary - Portuguese Oceanic Expedition **Obverse:** National arms and fish

Date	F	VF	XF	Unc	BU
1997	—	—	—	14.50	—

KM# 695a 1000 ESCUDOS **Weight:** 28.0000 g. **Composition:** 0.9250 Silver .8327 oz. ASW **Subject:** 100th Anniversary - Portuguese Oceanic Expedition **Obverse:** National arms and fish

Date	Mintage	F	VF	XF	Unc	BU
1997 Proof	Est. 15,000	Value: 45.00				

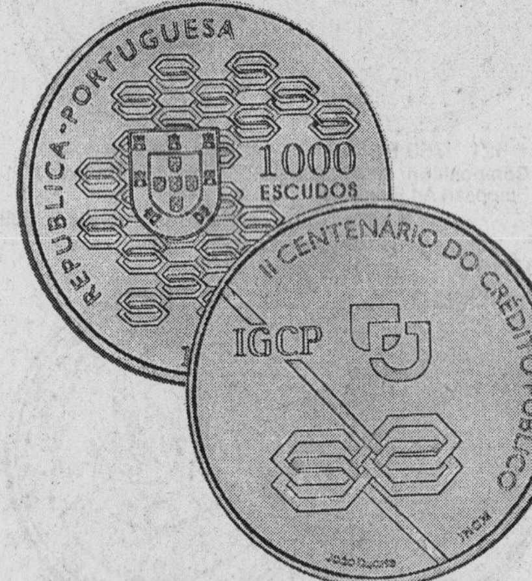

KM# 703 1000 ESCUDOS **Weight:** 28.0000 g. **Composition:** 0.5000 Silver .4501 oz. ASW **Subject:** Credito Publico **Obverse:** National arms and hexagonal design

Date	F	VF	XF	Unc	BU
1997	—	—	—	13.50	—

KM# 703a 1000 ESCUDOS **Weight:** 28.0000 g. **Composition:** 0.9250 Silver .8327 oz. ASW **Subject:** Credito Publico **Obverse:** National arms and hexagonal design

Date	Mintage	F	VF	XF	Unc	BU
1997 Proof	Est. 15,000	Value: 50.00				

KM# 704 1000 ESCUDOS **Weight:** 27.0000 g. **Composition:** 0.5000 Silver .4340 oz. ASW **Obverse:** National arms within circle of arms **Reverse:** Pauliteiros dancers

Date	F	VF	XF	Unc	BU
1997	—	—	—	13.50	—

KM# 704a 1000 ESCUDOS **Weight:** 27.0000 g. **Composition:** 0.9250 Silver .8327 oz. ASW **Obverse:** National arms within circle of arms **Reverse:** Pauliteiros dancers

Date	F	VF	XF	Unc	BU
1997 Proof	—	Value: 45.00			

KM# 707 1000 ESCUDOS **Weight:** 27.0000 g. **Composition:** 0.5000 Silver .4340 oz. ASW **Subject:** International Year of the Oceans Expo **Obverse:** Nation arms and logo

Date	F	VF	XF	Unc
1998	—	—	—	13.50

KM# 707a 1000 ESCUDOS **Weight:** 27.0000 g. **Composition:** 0.9250 Silver .8030 oz. ASW **Subject:** International Year of the Oceans Expo **Obverse:** Nation arms and logo

Date	Mintage	F	VF	XF	Unc
1998 Proof	Est. 20,000	Value: 45.00			

KM# 708 1000 ESCUDOS **Weight:** 27.0000 g. **Composition:** 0.5000 Silver .4340 oz. ASW **Subject:** 50 Anniversary - Misericordia Church **Obverse:** Basket des

Date	F	VF	XF	Unc
ND(1998)	—	—	—	13.50

KM# 708a 1000 ESCUDOS **Weight:** 27.0000 g. **Composition:** 0.9250 Silver .8030 oz. ASW **Subject:** 50 Anniversary - Misericordia Church **Obverse:** Basket des

Date	F	VF	XF	Unc
ND(1998) Proof	—	Value: 45.00		

KM# 713 1000 ESCUDOS **Weight:** 27.0000 g. **Composition:** 0.5000 Silver .4340 oz. ASW **Obverse:** T ships, crowned arms, armillary sphere **Reverse:** King D Manuel I with sword seated on throne

Date	F	VF	XF	Unc
1998	—	—	—	13.50

KM# 713a 1000 ESCUDOS **Weight:** 27.0000 g. **Composition:** 0.9250 Silver .8030 oz. ASW **Obverse:** T ships, crowned arms, armillary sphere **Reverse:** King D Manuel I with sword seated on throne

Date	Mintage	F	VF	XF	Unc
1998 Proof	Est. 15,000	Value: 45.00			

KM# 714 1000 ESCUDOS **Weight:** 27.0000 g. **Composition:** 0.5000 Silver .4340 oz. ASW **Subject:** 75th Anniversary - League of Combatants **Obverse:** Stylized arms **Reverse:** Sword and laurel branch

Date	F	VF	XF	Unc	BU
1998	—	—	—	13.50	—

KM# 714a 1000 ESCUDOS **Weight:** 27.0000 g. **Composition:** 0.9250 Silver .8030 oz. ASW **Subject:** 75th Anniversary - League of Combatants **Obverse:** Stylized arms **Reverse:** Sword and laurel branch

Date	F	VF	XF	Unc	BU
1998 Proof	—	Value: 45.00			

KM# 715 1000 ESCUDOS **Weight:** 27.0000 g. **Composition:** 0.5000 Silver .4340 oz. ASW **Subject:** 25th Anniversary - Revolution of April 25 **Obverse:** National arms and denomination **Reverse:** Date and anniversary number

Date	F	VF	XF	Unc	BU
1999	—	—	—	13.50	—

KM# 715a 1000 ESCUDOS **Weight:** 27.0000 g. **Composition:** 0.9250 Silver .8030 oz. ASW **Subject:** 25th Anniversary - Revolution of April 25 **Obverse:** National arms and denomination **Reverse:** Date and anniversary number

Date	Mintage	F	VF	XF	Unc	BU
1999 Proof	Est. 15,000	Value: 45.00				

KM# 721 1000 ESCUDOS **Weight:** 27.2000 g. **Composition:** 0.5000 Silver .4372 oz. ASW **Subject:** Millennium of Atlantic Sailing **Obverse:** National arms above logo **Reverse:** Ship on stormy waves **Edge:** Reeded

Date	F	VF	XF	Unc	BU
1999	—	—	—	18.50	—

KM# 721a 1000 ESCUDOS **Weight:** 27.0000 g. **Composition:** 0.9250 Silver .8030 oz. ASW **Subject:** Millennium of Atlantic Sailing **Obverse:** National arms above logo **Reverse:** Ship on stormy waves **Edge:** Reeded

Date	Mintage	F	VF	XF	Unc	BU
1999 Proof	15,000	Value: 45.00				

KM# 724 1000 ESCUDOS **Weight:** 27.0000 g. **Composition:** 0.5000 Silver .4340 oz. ASW **Subject:** Presidency of the European Union **Obverse:** National arms and cave drawings **Reverse:** Stylized design **Edge:** Reeded **Size:** 40.2 mm.

Date	Mintage	F	VF	XF	Unc	BU
2000	450,000	—	—	—	13.50	—

KM# 724a 1000 ESCUDOS

Date	Mintage	F	VF	XF	Unc	BU
2000 Proof	10,000	Value: 75.00				

KM# 727 1000 ESCUDOS **Weight:** 27.0000 g. **Composition:** 0.5000 Silver .4340 oz. ASW **Series:** Ibero-America **Obverse:** Portuguese arms within circle of foreign arms **Reverse:** Lusitano horses and rider **Edge:** Reeded **Size:** 40 mm.

Date	F	VF	XF	Unc	BU
2000	—	—	—	22.50	—

KM# 727a 1000 ESCUDOS **Weight:** 27.0000 g. **Composition:** 0.9250 Silver .8030 oz. ASW **Series:** Ibero-America **Obverse:** Portuguese arms within circle of foreign arms **Reverse:** Lusitano horses and rider **Edge:** Reeded **Size:** 40 mm.

Date	F	VF	XF	Unc	BU
2000 Proof	—	—	—	100	—

KM# 732 1000 ESCUDOS **Weight:** 27.0000 g. **Composition:** 0.5000 Silver .4340 oz. ASW **Subject:** D. Joso De Castro **Obverse:** Portuguese arms above denomination **Reverse:** Bearded portrait

Date	F	VF	XF	Unc	BU
2000	—	—	—	20.00	—

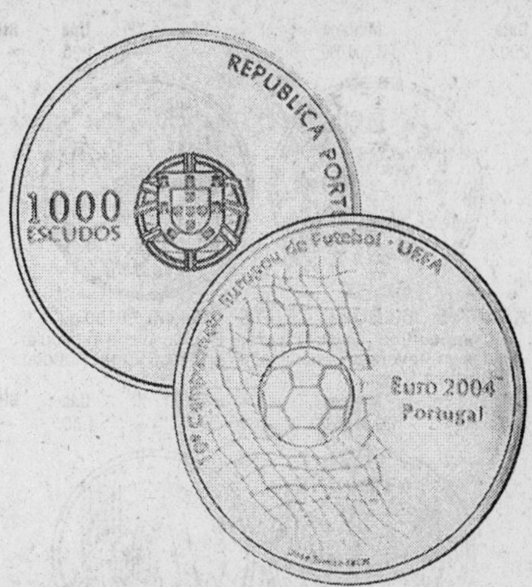

KM# 734 1000 ESCUDOS **Weight:** 26.9500 g. **Composition:** 0.5000 Silver .4332 oz. ASW **Obverse:** National arms and denomination **Reverse:** Soccer ball **Edge:** Reeded **Size:** 40 mm.

Date	F	VF	XF	Unc	BU
2001	—	—	—	13.50	—

EURO COINAGE

European Economic Community Issues

KM# 740 EURO CENT **Weight:** 2.2700 g. **Composition:** Copper Plated Steel **Obverse:** Country name in cross **Reverse:** Denomination and globe **Edge:** Plain **Size:** 16.2 mm.

Date	Mintage	F	VF	XF	Unc	BU
2002	290,000,000	—	—	—	0.35	—

KM# 741 2 EURO CENTS **Weight:** 3.0300 g. **Composition:** Copper Plated Steel **Obverse:** Country name in cross **Reverse:** Denomination and globe **Edge:** Grooved **Size:** 18.7 mm.

Date	Mintage	F	VF	XF	Unc	BU
2002	340,000,000	—	—	—	0.50	—

KM# 742 5 EURO CENTS **Weight:** 3.8600 g. **Composition:** Copper Plated Steel **Obverse:** Country name in cross **Reverse:** Denomination and globe **Edge:** Plain **Size:** 21.2 mm.

Date	Mintage	F	VF	XF	Unc	BU
2002	340,000,000	—	—	—	0.75	—

KM# 743 10 EURO CENTS **Weight:** 4.0700 g. **Composition:** Brass **Obverse:** Country name in circular design **Reverse:** Denomination and map **Edge:** Reeded **Size:** 19.7 mm.

Date	Mintage	F	VF	XF	Unc	BU
2002	275,000,000	—	—	—	0.75	—

KM# 744 20 EURO CENTS **Weight:** 5.7300 g. **Composition:** Brass **Obverse:** Country name in circular design **Reverse:** Denomination and map **Edge:** Notched **Size:** 22.1 mm.

Date	Mintage	F	VF	XF	Unc	BU
2002	145,000,000	—	—	—	1.25	—

KM# 745 50 EURO CENTS **Weight:** 7.8100 g. **Composition:** Brass **Obverse:** Country name in circular design **Reverse:** Denomination and map **Edge:** Reeded **Size:** 24.2 mm.

Date	Mintage	F	VF	XF	Unc	BU
2002	190,000,000	—	—	—	1.50	—

KM# 746 EURO **Ring Composition:** Brass**Center Weight:** 7.5000 g. **Center Composition:** Copper-Nickel **Obverse:** Country name in looped design **Reverse:** Denomination and map **Edge:** Reeded and plain sections **Size:** 23.2 mm.

Date	Mintage	F	VF	XF	Unc	BU
2002	85,000,000	—	—	—	2.75	—

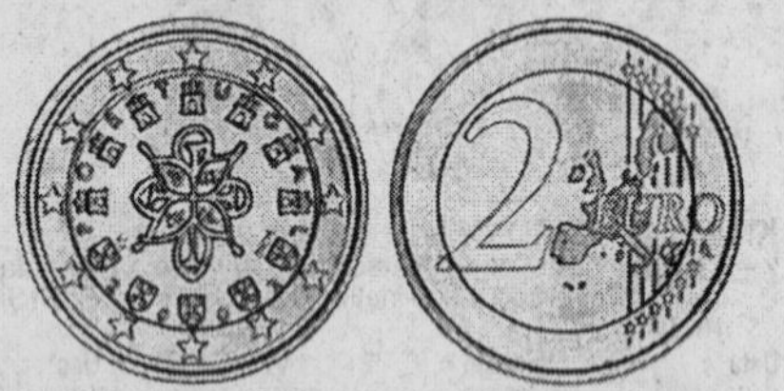

KM# 747 2 EUROS **Ring Composition:** Copper-Nickel**Center Weight:** 8.5200 g. **Center Composition:** Brass **Obverse:** Country name in looped design **Reverse:** Denomination and map **Edge:** Reeding over castles and shields **Size:** 25.7 mm.

Date	Mintage	F	VF	XF	Unc	BU
2002	50,000,000	—	—	—	4.50	—

ESSAIS

KM#	Date	Mintage	Identification	Mkt Val
E1	1986	30	100 Escudos. Copper Nickel. KM637	—
E2	1998	—	100 Escudos. Silver. "ENSAIO" on obverse and reverse.	—
E3	1998	—	100 Escudos. Silver. "ENSAIO" on reverse only.	—

PATTERNS

Including off metal strikes

KM#	Date	Mintage	Identification	Mkt Val
Pn200	1903	—	2 Reis. Nickel. Plain royal arms.	—
Pn201	1903	—	20 Reis. Nickel. Royal arms with wreath.	350
Pn202	1903	—	20 Reis. Nickel. Plain edge. Without wreath.	350
Pn203	1903	—	20 Reis. Nickel. Reeded edge. Value on reeded edge.	275
Pn204	1903	—	20 Reis. Nickel. Plain edge. Value on plain edge.	275
Pn205	1903	—	100 Reis. Silver. Crowned value.	1,500
Pn206	1903	—	200 Reis. Silver. Crowned value.	2,200
Pn207	ND	—	20 Centavos. Silver. Two reverses.	600
Pn208	1912	—	50 Centavos. Copper. Plain edge. Type as adopted.	750
Pn209	1912	—	50 Centavos. Silver. Reeded edge. Type as adopted.	1,000
Pn210	1912	—	Escudo. Gold. 'October 5, 1910'.	550
Pn211	1912	—	Escudo. Gold. Obverse variety.	550
Pn212	1912	—	Escudo. Gold.	550
Pn213	1919	—	4 Centavos. Copper Nickel. Plain edge. Wide border.	—
Pn214	1919	—	4 Centavos. Copper Nickel. Reeded edge. Wide border.	—
Pn215	1919	—	4 Centavos. Copper Nickel. Plain edge. Semi-wide border.	—
Pn216	1919	—	4 Centavos. Copper Nickel. Alternate edge. Narrow border.	—
Pn218	1920	—	10 Centavos. Brass. Plain edge. Larger type.	—
Pn217	1920	—	10 Centavos. Copper Nickel. Plain edge. Larger type.	1,500
Pn219	1920	—	5 Escudos. Copper. 'Abundance Through Labor'	1,000
Pn220	1920	—	5 Escudos. Copper Nickel. 'Abundance Through Labor'	1,000
Pn221	1920	—	5 Escudos. Gold. 'Abundance Through Labor'	—
Pn222	1921	—	10 Centavos. Bronze. Reeded edge. 19mm	500
Pn224	1927	—	50 Centavos. Silver. Obverse 1924 type.	500
Pn225	1927	—	Escudo. Silver. Reverse 1924 type.	—
Pn223	1927	—	50 Centavos. Silver. Reeded edge. Large type.	500
Pn226	1928	—	Escudo. Brass.	650
Pn227	1928	—	10 Escudos. Copper. 'Battle of Orique'.	750
Pn228	1929	—	10 Escudos. Brass. 'Battle of Orique'.	—
Pn229	1932	—	5 Escudos. Copper Nickel. Type adopted.	—
Pn230	1932	—	10 Escudos. Copper.	225
Pn231	1932	—	10 Escudos. Copper Nickel. Type adopted.	225
Pn232	1940	—	10 Escudos. Copper Nickel. Large type.	225
Pn233	1953	—	20 Escudos. Copper. 'National Revival'.	650
Pn235	1953	—	20 Escudos. Silver. Variety of type adopted.	1,250
Pn234	1953	—	20 Escudos. Gold. 'National Revival'.	—
Pn236	1961	—	2-1/2 Escudos. Nickel. Reeded edge.	—
Pn237	1961	—	2-1/2 Escudos. Nickel. Reeded edge.	—
Pn238	1961	—	2-1/2 Escudos. Copper Nickel.	—
Pn241	1961	—	10 Escudos. Silver.	—
Pn242	1961	—	10 Escudos. Copper Nickel. Legend in relief.	—
Pn243	ND	—	10 Centavos. Aluminum.	—
Pn246	ND	—	10 Escudos. Nickel. Reeded edge. Type adopted.	—
Pn247	ND	—	10 Escudos. Nickel. Plain edge. Type adopted.	—
Pn248	ND	—	10 Centavos. Bronze-Aluminum. Plain edge.	—
Pn239	1961	—	10 Escudos. Silver. Legend incuse.	600
Pn240	1961	—	10 Escudos. Copper Nickel.	350
Pn244	ND	—	20 Centavos. Brass.	225
Pn245	ND	—	5 Escudos. Brass. Type adopted.	225
Pn249	1966	—	Escudo. Bronze-Aluminum.	200
Pn250	1966	—	Escudo. Bronze-Aluminum. Reeded edge.	200
Pn251	1966	—	20 Escudos. Nickel. Reeded edge.	350
Pn252	1968	—	10 Centavos. Aluminum. Similar to 1942 type.	225
Pn253	1969	—	10 Centavos. Aluminum. Large type as adopted.	—
Pn254	1970	—	Escudo. Nickel. Type adopted.	100
Pn255	1970	—	20 Escudos. Nickel. Reeded edge.	200
Pn256	1970	—	20 Escudos. Nickel. Plain edge.	200
Pn257	1970	—	20 Escudos. Nickel. Reeded edge.	200
Pn258	1970	—	20 Escudos. Nickel. Plain edge.	200
Pn259	1979	—	50 Centavos. Reeded edge.	125
Pn260	1979	—	Escudo. Reeded edge.	125
Pn261	1979	—	5 Escudos. Aluminum.	150
Pn262	ND	—	250 Escudos. Copper Nickel. Decade of Women, United Nations.	—
Pn263	1989	—	100 Escudos.	1,650

PROVAS

Stamped

KM#	Date	Mintage	Identification	Mkt Val
PrA7	1942	—	10 Centavos. Bronze. KM583.	—
PrB7	1942	—	20 Centavos. Bronze. KM584.	55.00
Pr7	1943	—	5 Escudos. Silver. KM581.	35.00
Pr8	1943	—	10 Centavos. Bronze. KM583.	20.00
Pr9	1943	—	20 Centavos. Bronze. KM584.	20.00
Pr10	1960	—	5 Escudos. Silver. KM587.	15.00
Pr11	1960	—	10 Escudos. Silver. KM588.	20.00
Pr12	1960	—	20 Escudos.	30.00
PrA13	1962	—	10 Centavos. Bronze. KM583.	—
PrB13	1962	—	20 Centavos. Bronze. KM584.	—
PrC13	1962	—	50 Centavos. Copper Nickel. KM577.	—
PrD13	1962	—	Escudo. Copper Nickel. KM578.	—
Pr13	1964	—	Escudo. KM578.	—
Pr14	1964	—	2-1/2 Escudos. KM590.	—
Pr15	1966	—	20 Centavos. KM584.	—
Pr16	1966	—	Escudo. KM578.	—
Pr17	1966	—	2-1/2 Escudos. KM590.	17.50
Pr18	1966	—	5 Escudos. KM591.	15.00
Pr19	1966	—	20 Escudos. Silver. Salazar Bridge, KM592.	25.00
Pr20	1966	—	20 Escudos. Gold. Salazar Bridge, KM592.	2,500
Pr21	1968	—	50 Escudos. KM593.	30.00
Pr23	1969	—	50 Escudos. KM598, 'Prova' in relief.	35.00
Pr24	1969	—	50 Escudos. KM599.	30.00
Pr22	1969	—	50 Escudos. KM598, 'Prova' incuse.	30.00
Pr25	1971	—	50 Escudos. KM601.	30.00
Pr26	1972	—	50 Escudos. KM602.	30.00

KM#	Date	Mintage	Identification	Mkt Val
Pr27	ND(1984)	100	25 Escudos. KM623, Revolution.	15.00
Pr28	1985	5,000	100 Escudos. KM629, Henrique.	—

TRIAL STRIKES

KM#	Date	Mintage	Identification	Mkt Val
TS33	1910	—	1000 Reis. Nickel Alloy. KM558; ALP	400
TS34	1915	—	Escudo. Nickel Alloy. KM564; ALP.	400
TS35	1927	—	5 Centavos. Bronze. Reverse.	—
TS36	ND	—	20 Centavos. Brass. Reverse, Roman numeral.	—
TS37	ND	—	50 Centavos. Brass. Reverse.	—
TS38	ND (1927)	—	2 Escudos. Brass. Uniface, KM#591.	25.00
TS36	ND (1963)	—	20 Centavos. Brass. Reverse, Roman numeral.	—

MINT SETS

KM#	Date	Mintage	Identification	Issue Price	Mkt Val
MS1	1960 (3)	—	KM587-589	—	50.00
MS2	1982 (4)	10,000	KM612-613, 615-616	3.00	7.00
MS3	1983 (3)	50,000	KM620-622	30.00	30.00
MS4	1983 (3)	5,000	KM617-619	4.00	25.00
MS5	1984 (2)	10,000	KM624-625	3.00	25.00
MS6	1985 (2)	20,000	KM627a, 630a	20.00	37.50
MSA6	1985 (2)	—	KM627, 630	—	10.00
MS7	1986 (5)	50,000	KM631-634, 636	6.00	30.00
MS10	1987 (6)	5,000	KM631-634, 636, 638	10.00	30.00
MS8	1987/8 (4)	40,000	KM639a-642a	78.00	70.00
MS9	1987/8 (4)	5,000	KM639b-642b	2,080	2,200
MS11	1988 (5)	30,000	KM631-634, 636	10.00	200
MS12	1989 (6)	50,000	KM631-634, 636, 645.1	12.00	20.00
MS14	1989/90 (4)	30,000	KM646a-649a	79.50	80.00
MSA14	1989/90 (4)	—	KM646-649	—	15.00
MS13	1990 (6)	50,000	KM631-634, 636, 645.1	15.00	17.50
MS15	1991 (7)	—	KM631-634, 636, 645.1, 655	17.50	17.50
MS16	1992 (7)	—	KM631-634, 636, 645.1, 655	—	32.50
MS17	1993 (7)	—	KM631-634, 636, 645.1, 655	—	25.00
MS18	1993 (4)	30,000	KM665a-668a	79.50	75.00
MS19	1994 (7)	—	KM631-634, 636, 645.1, 669	—	32.50
MS20	1994 (4)	—	KM670a-673a	—	90.00
MS21	1995 (7)	—	KM631-634, 636, 678-679	—	20.00
MS23	1995 (2)	5,000	KM678-679	—	60.00
MS22	1995 (4)	20,000	KM681a-684a	77.50	70.00
MS24	1996 (8)	—	KM631-634, 636, 645.1, 655, 687	—	35.00
MS25	1996 (4)	10,000	KM689a, 690a, 691a, 692a	105	70.00
MS26	1997 (9)	20,000	KM631-634, 636, 645.1, 655, 693-694	32.50	30.00
MS27	1998 (8)	50,000	KM631-634, 636, 645.1, 655, 706	32.50	30.00
MS28	1998 (4)	25,000	KM709a-712a	95.00	95.00
MS29	1999 (9)	—	KM631-634, 636, 645.1, 655, 720, 722	—	30.00
MS30	1999 (4)	10,000	KM716a-719a	95.00	95.00
MS31	2000 (4)	10,000	KM#728a-731a	65.00	95.00

PROOF SETS

KM#	Date	Mintage	Identification	Issue Price	Mkt Val
PS1	1960 (3)	—	KM587-589; matte finish	—	—
PS2	1974 (2)	10,000	KM603-604	6.00	35.00
PS3	1977 (3)	10,000	KM605-606, 608	2.50	25.00
PS4	1983 (3)	8,500	KM620-622	60.00	100
PS5	1985 (2)	5,000	KM627a, 630a	40.00	150
PS6	1985 (2)	5,000	KM628, 628a	35.00	300
PS7	1987 (4)	20,000	KM639a-642a	128	150
PS8	1987/88 (4)	2,000	KM639a, 640c, 641b, 642c; Prestige	2,200	2,750
PS10	1989/90 (4)	5,000	KM646b-649b	2,425	2,450
PS11	1989/90 (4)	2,500	KM646a, 647c, 648b, 649c; Prestige	2,650	2,800
PS9	1989/90 (4)	20,000	KM646a-649a	137	150
PS12	1991/92 (4)	15,000	KM658a-661a	150	150
PS13	1991/92 (4)	3,500	KM658b-661b	2,350	2,350
PS14	1991/92 (4)	2,500	KM658c-661c; Prestige	2,400	3,000
PS15	1993 (7)	—	KM631-634, 636, 645.1, 655	—	100
PS16	1993 (4)	22,000	KM665a-668a	150	150
PS17	1993 (4)	5,000	KM665b-668b	1,980	2,500
PS18	1993 (4)	2,000	KM665a, 666c, 667b, 668c; Prestige	2,300	2,150
PS19	1994 (7)	—	KM631-634, 636, 645.1, 669	—	50.0

KM#	Date	Mintage	Identification	Issue Price	Mkt Val
PS20	1994 (4)	10,000	KM670a-673a	—	150
PS21	1994 (4)	—	KM670b-673b	—	2,400
PS22	1994 (4)	1,000	KM670a, 671c, 672b, 673c; Prestige	—	2,175
PS23	1995 (7)	7,000	KM631-634, 636, 678, 679	47.50	50.00
PS27	1995 (2)	10,000	KM678, 679	—	35.00
PS24	1995 (4)	13,000	KM681a-684a	150	150
PS26	1995 (4)	1,000	KM681a, 682c, 683b, 684c	1,800	2,100
PS25	1995 (4)	2,000	KM681b-684b	1,980	2,000
PS28	1996 (8)	7,000	KM631-634, 636, 645.1, 655, 687	—	50.00
PS29	1996 (4)	10,000	KM689a, 690a, 691a, 692a	160	150
PS30	1996 (4)	2,000	KM689b, 690b, 691b, 692b	—	2,000
PS31	1996 (4)	1,000	KM689a, 690c, 691b, 692c	—	2,100
PS32	1997 (9)	7,000	KM631-634, 636, 645.1, 655, 693-694	55.00	50.00
PS33	1997 (4)	24,000	KM697a-700a	145	150
PS35	1997 (4)	1,000	KM697a, 698b, 699c, 700c	2,000	2,250
PS34	1997 (4)	4,000	KM697b-700b	1,980	2,000
PS36	1998 (8)	20,000	KM631-634, 636, 645.1, 655, 706	52.50	50.00
PS37	1998 (4)	25,000	KM709a-712a	150	150
PS38	1998 (4)	5,000	KM709b-712b	1,980	1,980
PS39	1998 (4)	1,000	KM709c, 710a, 711b, 712c	2,000	2,250
PS40	1999 (4)	10,000	KM716a-719a	150	150
PS41	1999 (4)	1,000	KM716b-719b	1,800	1,800
PS43	2000 (4)	1,000	KM#728b-731b	1,405	1,850
PS44	2000 (4)	250	KM#728a, 729c, 730b, 731c	2,988	3,000
PS42	2000 (4)	10,000	KM#728a-731a	125	150

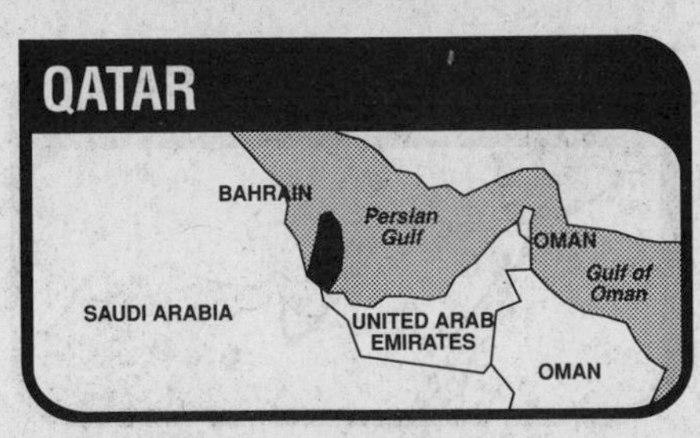

The State of Qatar, an emirate in the Persian Gulf between Bahrain and Trucial Oman, has an area of 4,247sq. mi. (11,000 sq. km.) and a population of *469,000. Capital: Doha. Oil is the chief industry and export.

Qatar was under Turkish control from 1872 until the beginning of World War I when the Ottoman Turks evacuated the Qatar Peninsula. In 1916 Sheikh Abdullah placed Qatar under the protection of Great Britain and gave Britain responsibility for its defense and foreign relations. Qatar joined with Dubai in a Monetary Union and issued coins and paper money in 1966 and 1969. When Britain announced in 1968 that it would end treaty relationships with the Persian Gulf sheikhdoms in 1971, this union was dissolved; Qatar joined Bahrain and the seven trucial sheikhdoms (called the United Arab Emirates) in an effort to form a union of Arab Emirates. However the nine sheikhdoms were unable to agree on terms of union, and Qatar declared its independence as the State of Qatar on Sept. 3, 1971.

TITLES

دولة قطر

Daulat Qatar

RULERS

Al-Thani Dynasty

Qasim Bin Muhammad, 1876-1913
Abdullah Bin Qasim, 1913-1948
Ali Bin Abdullah, 1948-1960
Ahmad Bin Ali, 1960-1972
Khalifah bin Hamad, 1972-1995
Hamad bin Khalifah, 1995-

MONETARY SYSTEM

100 Dirhem = 1 Riyal

REPUBLIC

STANDARD COINAGE

KM# 2 DIRHEM **Composition:** Bronze **Ruler:** Khalifah Bin Hamad

Date	Mintage	F	VF	XF	Unc	BU
AH1393 (1973)	500,000	—	0.10	0.25	0.60	—

KM# 3 5 DIRHEMS **Composition:** Bronze **Ruler:** Khalifah Bin Hamad

Date	Mintage	F	VF	XF	Unc	BU
AH1393 (1973)	1,000,000	—	0.10	0.25	0.75	—
AH1398 (1978)	1,000,000	—	0.10	0.25	0.75	—

KM# 1 10 DIRHEMS **Composition:** Bronze **Ruler:** Khalifah Bin Hamad

Date	Mintage	F	VF	XF	Unc	BU
AH1392 (1972)	1,500,000	—	0.50	1.00	2.50	—
AH1393 (1973)	1,500,000	—	0.20	0.50	1.50	—

KM# 4 25 DIRHEMS **Composition:** Copper-Nickel **Ruler:** Khalifah Bin Hamad

Date	Mintage	F	VF	XF	Unc	BU
AH1393 (1973)	1,500,000	—	0.25	0.65	1.50	—
AH1396 (1976)	2,000,000	—	0.25	0.65	1.75	—
AH1398 (1978)	—	—	0.25	0.65	1.75	—
AH1401 (1981)	—	—	0.25	0.65	1.75	—
AH1407 (1987)	—	—	0.25	0.65	1.75	—
AH1410 (1990)	—	—	0.25	0.65	1.75	—
AH1414 (1993)	—	—	0.25	0.65	1.75	—
AH1419 (1998)	—	—	0.25	0.65	1.75	—

KM# 8 25 DIRHEMS **Weight:** 3.5000 g. **Composition:** Copper-Nickel **Ruler:** Hamad bin Khalifah **Obverse:** Denomination. **Reverse:** Sailboat and palm trees. **Edge:** Reeded. **Size:** 19 mm.

Date	F	VF	XF	Unc	BU
AH1421 (2000)	—	—	—	1.50	—

KM# 5 50 DIRHEMS **Composition:** Copper-Nickel **Ruler:** Khalifah Bin Hamad

Date	Mintage	F	VF	XF	Unc	BU
AH1393 (1973)	1,500,000	—	0.40	0.85	2.00	—
AH1398 (1978)	2,000,000	—	0.40	0.85	2.25	—
AH1401 (1981)	—	—	0.40	0.85	2.25	—
AH1407 (1987)	—	—	0.40	0.85	2.25	—
AH1410 (1990)	—	—	0.40	0.85	2.25	—
AH1414 (1993)	—	—	0.40	0.85	2.25	—
AH1419 (1998)	—	—	0.40	0.85	2.25	—

KM# 9 50 DIRHEMS **Weight:** 6.5000 g. **Composition:** Copper-Nickel **Ruler:** Hamad bin Khalifah **Obverse:** Denomination. **Reverse:** Sailboat and palm trees. **Edge:** Reeded. **Size:** 24 mm.

Date	F	VF	XF	Unc	BU
AH1421 (2000)	—	—	—	2.00	—

KM# 6 100 RIYALS **Weight:** 22.2000 g. **Composition:** 0.9250 Silver .6602 oz. ASW **Ruler:** Hamad bin Khalifah **Subject:** Central Bank **Obverse:** National arms **Reverse:** Bank building **Edge:** Plain **Size:** 37 mm.

Date	Mintage	F	VF	XF	Unc	BU
ND(1998) Proof	400	Value: 250				

KM#10 200 RIYALS **Weight:** 22.2000 g. **Composition:** 0.9250 Silver 0.6602 oz. ASW **Ruler:** Hamad bin Khalifah **Subject:** Qatar University 25th Anniversary **Obverse:**

National arms **Reverse:** University logo, denomination and dates **Edge:** Plain **Size:** 37 mm.

Date	Mintage	F	VF	XF	Unc	BU
ND(1998) Proof	1,000	Value: 275				

KM# 7 500 RIYALS Weight: 17.0000 g. **Composition:** 0.9170 Gold .5012 oz. AGW **Ruler:** Hamad bin Khalifah **Subject:** Central Bank **Obverse:** National arms **Reverse:** Bank building **Edge:** Plain **Size:** 31 mm.

Date	Mintage	F	VF	XF	Unc	BU
ND(1998) Proof	100	Value: 600				

The State of Qatar, which occupies the Qatar Peninsula jutting into the Persian Gulf from eastern Saudi Arabia, has an area of 4,247 sq. mi. (11,000 sq. km.) and a population of *469,000. Capital: Doha. The traditional occupations of pearling, fishing, and herding have been replaced in economics by petroleum-related industries. Crude oil, petroleum products, and tomatoes are exported.

Dubai is one of the seven sheikhdoms comprising the United Arab Emirates (formerly Trucial States) located along the southern shore of the Persian Gulf. It has a population of about 60,000. Capital (of the United Arab Emirates): Abu Dhabi.

Qatar, which initiated protective treaty relations with Great Britain in 1916, achieved independence on Sept. 3,1971, upon withdrawal of the British military presence from the Persian Gulf, and replaced its special treaty arrangement with Britain with a treaty of general friendship. Dubai attained independence on Dec. 1, 1971, upon termination of Britain's protective treaty with the trucial Sheikhdoms, and on Dec. 2, 1971, entered into the union of the United Arab Emirates.

Despite the fact that the Emirate of Qatar and the Sheikhdom of Dubai were merged under a monetary union, the two territories were governed independently from each other. Qatar now uses its own currency while Dubai uses the United Arab Emirates currency and coins.

TITLES

قطرودبي

Qatar Wa Dubai

RULERS

Ahmad II, 1960-1972

MONETARY SYSTEM

100 Dirhem = 1 Riyal

BRITISH PROTECTORATES

STANDARD COINAGE

KM# 1 DIRHEM Composition: Bronze **Ruler:** Ahmad II **Obverse:** Denomination **Reverse:** Goitered gazelle

Date	Mintage	F	VF	XF	Unc	BU
AH1386 (1966)	1,000,000	—	0.10	0.30	0.75	—

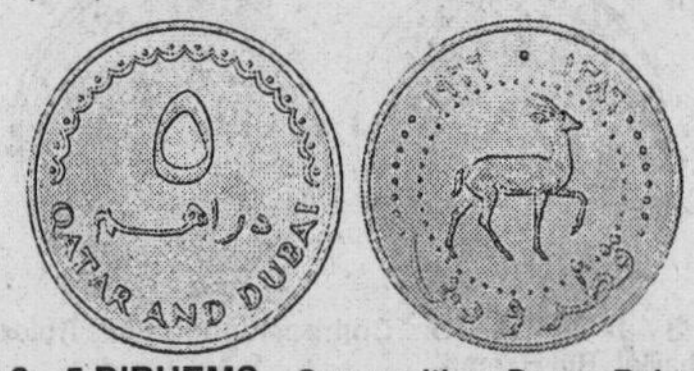

KM# 2 5 DIRHEMS Composition: Bronze **Ruler:** Ahmad II **Obverse:** Denomination **Reverse:** Goitered gazelle

Date	Mintage	F	VF	XF	Unc	BU
AH1386 (1966)	2,000,000	—	0.10	0.30	1.00	—
AH1389 (1969)	2,000,000	—	0.10	0.30	1.00	—

KM# 3 10 DIRHEMS Composition: Bronze **Ruler:** Ahmad II **Obverse:** Denomination **Reverse:** Goitered gazelle

Date	Mintage	F	VF	XF	Unc	BU
AH1386 (1966)	2,000,000	—	0.20	0.60	1.50	—
AH1391 (1971)	1,500	—	—	—	15.00	—

Note: Official mintage figure reported for Qatar by British Royal Mint.

KM# 4 25 DIRHEMS Composition: Copper-Nickel **Ruler:** Ahmad II **Obverse:** Denomination **Reverse:** Goitered gazelle

Date	Mintage	F	VF	XF	Unc	BU
AH1386 (1966)	2,000,000	—	0.30	0.75	2.00	—
AH1389 (1969)	2,000,000	—	0.30	0.75	2.00	—

KM# 5 50 DIRHEMS Composition: Copper-Nickel **Ruler:** Ahmad II **Obverse:** Denomination **Reverse:** Goitered gazelle

Date	Mintage	F	VF	XF	Unc	BU
AH1386 (1966)	2,000,000	—	0.50	1.00	2.50	—

QUAITI STATE OF HADHRAMAUT

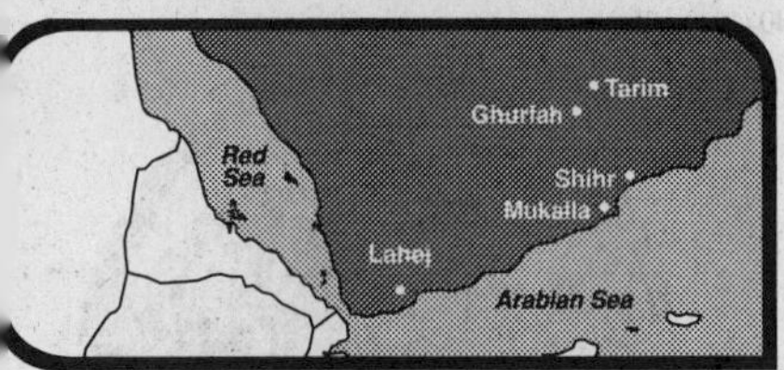

GHURFAH

A city sultanate of Eastern Aden Protectorate was an oasis set-
ement located in the Hadhramaut Wadi region of southern Arabia.

TLES

الغرفة

-Ghurfah

ULERS

aleh 'Ubayd bin Abdat, AH1339-1358/1920-1939AD
bayd bin Saleh bin Abdat, AH1358-1365/1939-1945AD

NOTE: The Arabic *129* in the obv. leg. is an anagram for Saleh.

EAST ADEN PROTECTORATE

Between 1200 B.C. and the 6th century A.D., what is now the eople's Democratic Republic of Yemen was part of the Minaean ingdom. In subsequent years it was controlled by Persians, Egyp- ans and Turks. Aden, one of the cities mentioned in the Bible, had een a port for trade between the East and West for 2,000 years. ritish rule began in 1839 when the British East India Co. seized ontrol to put an end to the piracy threatening trade with India. To rotect their foothold in Aden, the British found it necessary to xtend their control into the area known historically as the Hadhra- aut, and to sign protection treaties with the shaiks of the hinterland.

STANDARD COINAGE

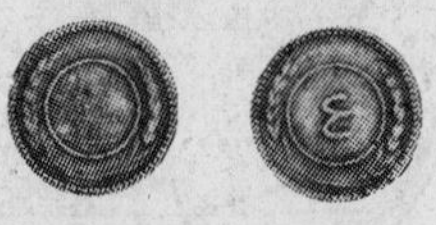

KM# 1 4 KHUMSI **Weight:** 0.6500 g. **Composition:** 0.9000 Silver .0188 oz. ASW **Ruler:** Saleh 'Ubayd bin Abdat AH1339-1358/1920-1939AD

ate	Mintage	F	VF	XF	Unc	BU
H1344	5,000	30.00	45.00	65.00	100	—

KM# 2 8 KHUMSI **Weight:** 1.1000 g. **Composition:** 0.9000 Silver .0318 oz. ASW **Ruler:** Saleh 'Ubayd bin Abdat AH1339-1358/1920-1939AD

ate	Mintage	F	VF	XF	Unc	BU
H1344	5,000	27.50	37.50	55.00	85.00	—

KM# 3 15 KHUMSI **Weight:** 2.0000 g. **Composition:** 0.9000 Silver .0578 oz. ASW **Ruler:** Saleh 'Ubayd bin Abdat AH1339-1358/1920-1939AD

ate	Mintage	F	VF	XF	Unc	BU
H1344	10,000	10.00	15.00	22.50	35.00	—

KM# 4 30 KHUMSI **Weight:** 3.9500 g. **Composition:** 0.9000 Silver .1142 oz. ASW **Ruler:** Saleh 'Ubayd bin Abdat AH1339-1358/1920-1939AD

ate	Mintage	F	VF	XF	Unc	BU
H1344	10,000	15.00	22.50	32.50	50.00	—

KM# 5 45 KHUMSI **Weight:** 5.9000 g. **Composition:** 0.9000 Silver .1707 oz. ASW **Ruler:** Saleh 'Ubayd bin Abdat AH1339-1358/1920-1939AD

Date	Mintage	F	VF	XF	Unc	BU
AH1344	10,000	175	275	425	600	—

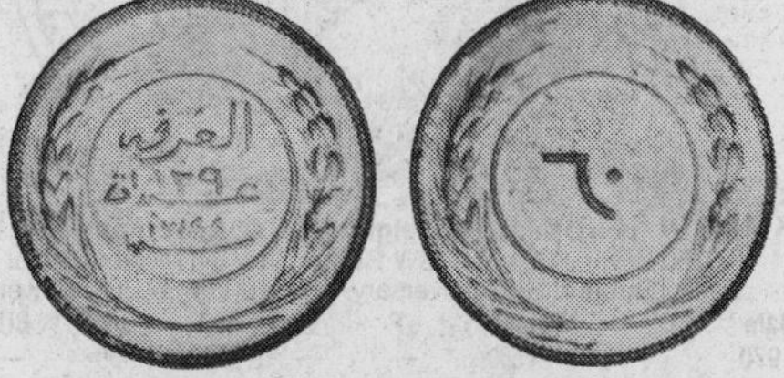

KM# 6 60 KHUMSI **Weight:** 7.8000 g. **Composition:** 0.9000 Silver .2257 oz. ASW **Ruler:** Saleh 'Ubayd bin Abdat AH1339-1358/1920-1939AD

Date	Mintage	F	VF	XF	Unc	BU
AH1344	10,000	37.50	55.00	80.00	125	—

RAS AL-KHAIMAH

Ras al-Khaimah is only one of the coin issuing emirates that was not one of the original members of the United Arab Emirates. It was a part of Sharjah. It has an estimated area of 650 sq. mi. (1700 sq. km.) and a population of 30,000. Ras al Khaimah is the only member of the United Arab Emirates that has agriculture as its principal industry.

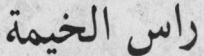

TITLES

راس الخيمة

Ras al-Khaimah(t)

RULERS

Sultan bin Salim al-Qasimi,/1921-1948
Saqr Bin Muhammad al-Qasimi,/1948—

MONETARY SYSTEM

100 Dirhams = 1 Rial

UNITED ARAB EMIRATE

NON-CIRCULATING LEGAL TENDER COINAGE

KM# 28 50 DIRHAMS **Composition:** Copper-Nickel **Ruler:** Saqr bin Muhammad al Qasimi **Reverse:** Barbary Falcon

Date	F	VF	XF	Unc	BU
AH1390 (1970)	—	—	—	20.00	—

KM# 1 RIAL **Weight:** 3.9500 g. **Composition:** 0.6400 Silver .0812 oz. ASW **Ruler:** Saqr bin Muhammad al Qasimi

Date	Mintage	F	VF	XF	Unc	BU
AH1389 (1969)	—	—	—	—	12.50	—
AH1389 (1969) Proof	1,500	Value: 25.00				

KM# 2 2 RIALS **Weight:** 6.4500 g. **Composition:** 0.8350 Silver .1731 oz. ASW **Ruler:** Saqr bin Muhammad al Qasimi

Date	Mintage	F	VF	XF	Unc	BU
AH1389 (1969)	—	—	—	—	17.50	—
AH1389 (1969) Proof	1,500	Value: 35.00				

KM# 29 2-1/2 RIALS **Weight:** 7.5000 g. **Composition:** 0.9250 Silver .2231 oz. ASW **Ruler:** Saqr bin Muhammad al Qasimi **Reverse:** Barbary Falcon

Date	F	VF	XF	Unc	BU
AH1390 (1970)	—	—	—	25.00	—

KM# 3 5 RIALS **Weight:** 15.0000 g. **Composition:** 0.8350 Silver .4027 oz. ASW **Ruler:** Saqr bin Muhammad al Qasimi

Date	Mintage	F	VF	XF	Unc	BU
AH1389 (1969)	—	—	—	—	25.00	—
AH1389 (1969) Proof	1,500	Value: 45.00				

KM#17 7-1/2 RIYALS **Weight:** 22.5000 g. **Composition:** 0.9250 Silver .6692 oz. ASW **Ruler:** Saqr bin Muhammad al Qasimi **Subject:** Centennial of Rome **Reverse:** Man plowing

Date	Mintage	F	VF	XF	Unc	BU
1970 Proof	Est. 2,000	Value: 120				

KM#32 7-1/2 RIYALS **Weight:** 22.5000 g. **Composition:** 0.9250 Silver .6692 oz. ASW **Ruler:** Saqr bin Muhammad al Qasimi **Subject:** World Championship Football **Reverse:** Jules Rimet Cup

Date	Mintage	F	VF	XF	Unc	BU
1970 Proof	Est. 2,000	Value: 235				

KM#30 7-1/2 RIYALS **Weight:** 22.5000 g. **Composition:** 0.9250 Silver .6692 oz. ASW **Ruler:** Saqr bin Muhammad al Qasimi **Reverse:** Barbary Falcon

Date	F	VF	XF	Unc	BU
AH1390 (1970)	—	—	—	65.00	—

KM#5 7-1/2 RIYALS **Weight:** 22.5000 g. **Composition:** 0.9250 Silver .6692 oz. ASW **Ruler:** Saqr bin Muhammad al Qasimi **Reverse:** Giacomo Agostini

Date	Mintage	F	VF	XF	Unc	BU
ND (1970) Proof	Est. 2,000	Value: 425				

KM# 31 10 RIYALS **Weight:** 30.0000 g. **Composition:** 0.9250 Silver .8921 oz. ASW **Ruler:** Saqr bin Muhammad al Qasimi **Subject:** 1st Anniversary - Death of Dwight Eisenhower

Date	Mintage	F	VF	XF	Unc	BU
1970	4,500	—	—	—	15.00	—
1970 Proof	1,400	Value: 30.00				

KM# 6 10 RIYALS **Weight:** 30.0000 g. **Composition:** 0.9250 Silver .8921 oz. ASW **Ruler:** Saqr bin Muhammad al Qasimi **Subject:** World Championship Football **Obverse:** Similar to KM#18 **Reverse:** Jules Rimet Cup

Date	Mintage	F	VF	XF	Unc	BU
1970 Proof	Est. 2,000	Value: 350				

KM# 18 10 RIYALS **Weight:** 30.0000 g. **Composition:** 0.9250 Silver .8921 oz. ASW **Ruler:** Saqr bin Muhammad al Qasimi **Subject:** Centennial of Rome **Reverse:** Emperor standing with charging horses

Date	Mintage	F	VF	XF	Unc	BU
1970 Proof	Est. 2,000	Value: 175				

KM# 7 10 RIYALS **Weight:** 30.0000 g. **Composition:** 0.9250 Silver .8921 oz. ASW **Ruler:** Saqr bin Muhammad al Qasimi **Subject:** Felice Gimondi **Obverse:** Similar to KM#18

Date	Mintage	F	VF	XF	Unc	BU
ND (1970) Proof	Est. 2,000	Value: 500				

KM# 8 15 RIYALS **Weight:** 45.0000 g. **Composition:** 0.9250 Silver 1.3384 oz. ASW **Ruler:** Saqr bin Muhammad al Qasimi **Subject:** Champions of Sport **Obverse:** Denomination

Date	Mintage	F	VF	XF	Unc	BU
ND(1970) Proof	Est. 2,000	Value: 675				

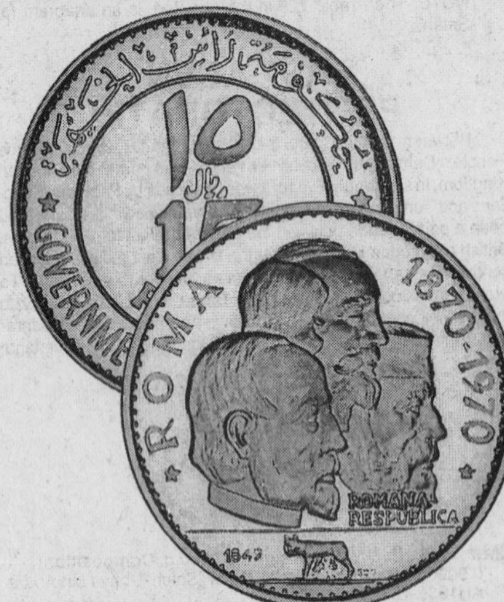

KM# 19 15 RIYALS **Weight:** 45.0000 g. **Composition:** 0.9250 Silver 1.3384 oz. ASW **Ruler:** Saqr bin Muhammad al Qasimi **Subject:** Centennial of Rome **Reverse:** Founders, three heads facing right

Date	Mintage	F	VF	XF	Unc	BU
1970 Proof	Est. 2,000	Value: 220				

KM# 33 15 RIYALS **Weight:** 45.0000 g. **Composition:** 0.9250 Silver 1.3384 oz. ASW **Ruler:** Saqr bin Muhamma[d] al Qasimi **Subject:** World Championship Football - Jules Rimet Cup

Date		F	VF	XF	Unc	B
1970 Proof	—	Value: 525				

M# 21 50 RIYALS **Weight:** 10.3500 g. **Composition:** 0.9000 Gold .2995 oz. AGW **Ruler:** Saqr bin Muhammad al Qasimi **Subject:** Centennial of Rome **Reverse:** Vittorio Emanuele II head left

ate	Mintage	F	VF	XF	Unc	BU
970 Proof	Est. 2,000	Value: 325				

KM# 10 50 RIYALS **Weight:** 10.3500 g. **Composition:** 0.9000 Gold .2995 oz. AGW **Ruler:** Saqr bin Muhammad al Qasimi **Subject:** Gigi Riva

ate	Mintage	F	VF	XF	Unc	BU
D (1970) Proof	Est. 2,000	Value: 350				

KM# 22 75 RIYALS **Weight:** 15.5300 g. **Composition:** 0.9000 Gold .4494 oz. AGW **Ruler:** Saqr bin Muhammad al Qasimi **Subject:** Centennial of Rome Capitol

ate	Mintage	F	VF	XF	Unc	BU
970 Proof	Est. 2,000	Value: 450				

KM# 11 75 RIYALS **Weight:** 15.5300 g. **Composition:** 0.9000 Gold .4494 oz. AGW **Ruler:** Saqr bin Muhammad al Qasimi **Subject:** Gianni Rivera

Date	Mintage	F	VF	XF	Unc	BU
ND (1970) Proof	Est. 2,000	Value: 425				

KM# 12 100 RIYALS **Weight:** 20.7000 g. **Composition:** 0.9000 Gold .5990 oz. AGW **Ruler:** Saqr bin Muhammad al Qasimi **Subject:** World Chmapionship Football - Jules Rimet Cup

Date	Mintage	F	VF	XF	Unc	BU
1970 Proof	Est. 2,000	Value: 625				

KM# 23 100 RIYALS **Weight:** 20.7000 g. **Composition:** 0.9000 Gold .5990 oz. AGW **Ruler:** Saqr bin Muhammad al Qasimi **Subject:** Centennial of Rome - WWI Victory

Date	Mintage	F	VF	XF	Unc	BU
1970 Proof	Est. 2,000	Value: 525				

KM# 24 100 RIYALS **Weight:** 31.0500 g. **Composition:** 0.9000 Gold .8985 oz. AGW **Ruler:** Saqr bin Muhammad al Qasimi **Subject:** Centennial of Rome **Reverse:** Standing Liberty

Date	Mintage	F	VF	XF	Unc	BU
1970 Proof	Est. 2,000	Value: 950				

KM# 13 150 RIYALS **Weight:** 31.0500 g. **Composition:** 0.9000 Gold .8985 oz. AGW **Ruler:** Saqr bin Muhammad al Qasimi **Series:** 1972 Munich Olympics

Date	Mintage	F	VF	XF	Unc	BU
ND (1970) Proof	3,060	Value: 1,800				

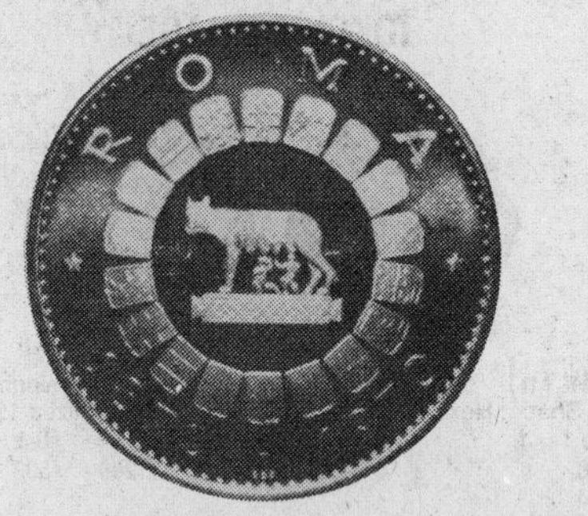

KM# 25 200 RIYALS **Weight:** 41.4000 g. **Composition:** 0.9000 Gold 1.1980 oz. AGW **Ruler:** Saqr bin Muhammad al Qasimi **Subject:** Centennial of Rome - Romulus and Remus

Date	Mintage	F	VF	XF	Unc	BU
1970 Proof	Est. 2,000	Value: 1,200				

KM# 14 200 RIYALS **Weight:** 41.4000 g. **Composition:** 0.9000 Gold 1.1980 oz. AGW **Ruler:** Saqr bin Muhammad al Qasimi **Subject:** Champions of Sport

Date	Mintage	F	VF	XF	Unc	BU
ND (1970) Proof	Est. 2,000	Value: 1,350				

ESSAIS

KM#	Date	Mintage	Identification	Issue Price	Mkt Val
E1	1969	—	Riyal. With ASSAY.	—	15.00
E2	1969	—	2 Riyals. (No Composition). With ASSAY.	—	22.50
E3	1969	—	5 Riyals. (No Composition). With ASSAY.	—	37.50
E4	1970	—	10 Riyals. (No Composition). With ASSAY.	—	45.00

MINT SETS

KM#	Date	Mintage	Identification	Issue Price	Mkt Val
MS1	1969 (3)	—	KM#1-3	—	55.00

PROOF SETS

KM#	Date	Mintage	Identification	Issue Price	Mkt Val
PS1	1969 (3)	1,500	KM#1-3	10.80	100
PS2	(1970) (9)	—	KM#5-8, 10-14	—	6,500
PS3	1970 (8)	—	KM#17-19, 21-25	—	4,000
PS4	(1970) (5)	—	KM#10-14	—	4,550
PS5	1970 (5)	—	KM#21-25	—	3,450
PS6	(1970) (4)	—	KM#5-8	41.50	1,950
PS7	1970 (3)	—	KM#17-19	—	500
PS8	1970 (4)	—	KM#6, 10-12	—	1,750

REUNION

The Department of Reunion, an overseas department of France located in the Indian Ocean 400 miles (640 km.) east of Madagascar, has an area of 969 sq. mi. (2,510 sq. km.) and a population of *566,000. Capital: Saint-Denis. The island's volcanic soil is extremely fertile. Sugar, vanilla, coffee and rum are exported.

Although first visited by Portuguese navigators in the 16th century, Reunion was uninhabited when claimed for France by Capt. Goubert in 1638. The French first colonized the Isle de Bourbon in 1662 as a layover station for ships rounding the Cape of Good Hope to India. It was renamed Reunion in 1793. The island remained in French possession except for the period of 1810-15, when the British occupied it. Reunion became an overseas department of France in 1946, and in 1958 voted to continue that status within the new French Union.

During the first half of the 19th century, Reunion was officially known as Isle de Bonaparte (1801-14) and Isle de Bourbon (1814-48). Reunion coinage of those periods is so designated.

Mint Marks

(a) – Paris, privy marks only

MONETARY SYSTEM

100 Centimes = 1 Franc

FRENCH DEPARTMENT

STANDARD COINAGE

KM# 6.1 FRANC **Composition:** Aluminum

Date	Mintage	F	VF	XF	Unc	BU
1948(a)	3,000,000	—	0.35	0.60	2.00	—
1964(a)	1,000,000	—	0.35	0.60	2.50	—
1968(a)	450,000	—	0.60	1.25	4.00	—
1969(a)	500,000	—	0.60	0.85	3.00	—
1971(a)	800,000	—	0.60	0.85	2.50	—
1973(a)	500,000	—	0.60	0.85	3.00	—

KM# 6.2 FRANC **Composition:** Aluminum **Note:** Thinner planchet.

Date	F	VF	XF	Unc	BU
1969(a)	—	0.75	1.50	4.50	—

KM# 7 FRANC **Composition:** Aluminum **Obverse:** French Equatorial Africa **Reverse:** KM#6.1 **Note:** Mule.

Date	F	VF	XF	Unc	BU
1948(a)	—	—	150	260	—

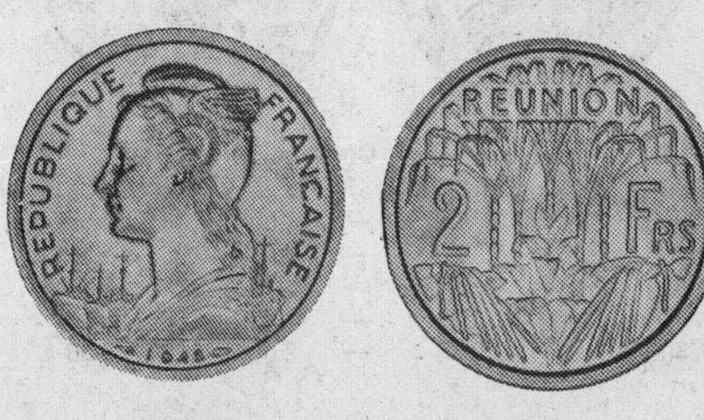

KM# 8 2 FRANCS **Composition:** Aluminum

Date	Mintage	F	VF	XF	Unc	BU
1948(a)	2,000,000	—	0.35	0.85	3.00	—
1968(a)	100,000	—	3.00	5.00	10.00	—
1969(a)	150,000	—	1.75	3.50	6.50	—
1970(a)	300,000	—	0.85	1.75	3.50	—
1971(a)	300,000	—	0.85	1.75	3.50	—
1973(a)	500,000	—	0.85	1.75	3.50	—

KM# 9 5 FRANCS Composition: Aluminum

Date	Mintage	F	VF	XF	Unc	BU
1955(a)	3,000,000	—	0.60	1.00	2.50	—
1969(a)	100,000	—	2.50	5.00	9.00	—
1970(a)	200,000	—	1.75	3.50	6.50	—
1971(a)	100,000	—	1.75	3.50	6.50	—
1972(a)	300,000	—	0.85	1.75	3.00	—
1973(a)	250,000	—	0.85	1.75	3.00	—

KM# 10 10 FRANCS Composition: Aluminum-Bronze

Date	Mintage	F	VF	XF	Unc	BU
1955(a)	1,500,000	—	0.45	0.75	2.50	—
1962(a)	700,000	—	1.75	3.50	6.50	—
1964(a)	1,000,000	—	0.45	0.75	2.50	—

KM# 10a 10 FRANCS Composition: Aluminum-Nickel-Bronze

Date	Mintage	VG	F	VF	XF	Unc
1964(a)	Inc. above	—	—	0.45	0.75	2.50
1969(a)	300,000	—	—	1.25	2.50	5.50
1970(a)	300,000	—	—	1.25	2.50	4.50
1971(a)	200,000	—	—	1.75	3.75	7.50
1972(a)	400,000	—	—	1.25	2.50	5.50
1973(a)	700,000	—	—	0.85	1.75	3.00

KM# 11 20 FRANCS Composition: Aluminum-Bronze

Date	Mintage	F	VF	XF	Unc	BU
1955(a)	1,250,000	—	0.75	1.50	3.50	—
1960(a)	100,000	—	3.00	6.00	12.00	—
1961(a)	300,000	—	2.50	4.75	8.00	—
1962(a)	190,000	—	2.75	5.50	9.00	—
1964(a)	750,000	—	0.75	1.50	3.00	—

KM# 11a 20 FRANCS Composition: Aluminum-Nickel-Bronze

Date	Mintage	F	VF	XF	Unc	BU
1969(a)	200,000	—	2.75	5.50	9.00	—
1970(a)	200,000	—	2.75	5.50	9.00	—
1971(a)	200,000	—	2.75	5.50	9.00	—
1972(a)	300,000	—	2.00	3.50	6.50	—
1973(a)	550,000	—	0.75	1.50	3.00	—

KM# 12 50 FRANCS Composition: Nickel

Date	Mintage	F	VF	XF	Unc	BU
1962(a)	1,000,000	—	1.50	2.50	4.50	—
1964(a)	500,000	—	2.00	3.00	5.50	—
1969(a)	100,000	—	2.75	5.00	8.50	—
1970(a)	100,000	—	2.75	5.00	8.50	—
1973(a)	350,000	—	2.00	3.50	6.00	—

KM# 13 100 FRANCS Composition: Nickel

Date	Mintage	F	VF	XF	Unc	BU
1964(a)	2,000,000	—	1.00	2.00	3.50	—
1969(a)	200,000	—	2.25	4.50	7.00	—
1970(a)	150,000	—	2.25	5.00	8.50	—
1971(a)	100,000	—	2.75	6.00	12.50	—
1972(a)	400,000	—	2.00	3.50	5.50	—
1973(a)	200,000	—	2.25	4.50	7.00	—

TOKEN COINAGE

KM# Tn1 5 CENTIMES Composition: Aluminum Shape: Hexagon Note: Bank token. Demonetized 1941.

Date	F	VF	XF	Unc	BU
1920	30.00	65.00	200	500	—

KM# Tn2 10 CENTIMES Composition: Aluminum Shape: Hexagon Note: Bank token. Demonetized 1941.

Date	F	VF	XF	Unc	BU
1920	35.00	75.00	200	500	—

KM# Tn3 25 CENTIMES Composition: Aluminum Shape: Hexagon Note: Bank token. Demonetized 1941.

Date	F	VF	XF	Unc	BU
1920	50.00	100	275	775	—

ESSAIS

Standard metals unless otherwise noted

KM#	Date	Mintage	Identification	Mkt Val
E3	1948(a)	2,000	Franc. Copper-Nickel. KM6.1.	30.00
E4	1948(a)	2,000	2 Francs. Copper-Nickel. KM8.	32.00
E5	1955(a)	1,200	5 Francs. KM9.	20.00
E6	1955(a)	1,200	10 Francs. KM10.	22.00
E7	1955(a)	1,200	20 Francs. KM11.	25.00
E8	1962(a)	1,200	50 Francs. KM12.	25.00
E9	1964(a)	2,000	50 Francs. KM12.	30.00
E10	1964(a)	2,000	100 Francs. KM13.	40.00

PIEFORTS WITH ESSAI

Double thickness; standard metals unless otherwise noted

KM#	Date	Mintage	Identification	Mkt Val
PE3	1948(a)	104	Franc. KM6.1.	75.00
PE4	1948(a)	104	2 Francs. KM8.	90.00

RHODESIA & NYASALAND

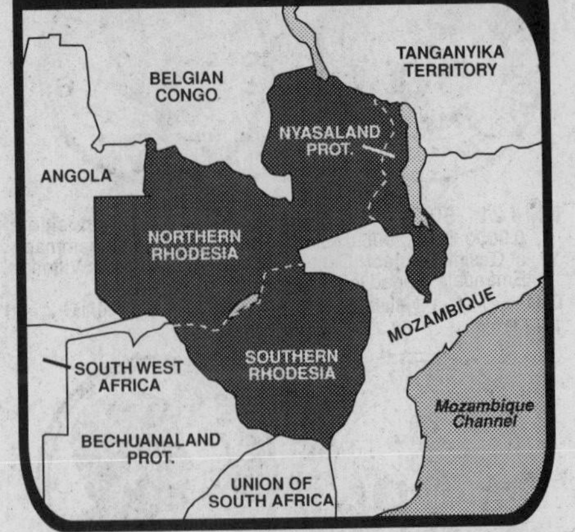

The Federation of Rhodesia and Nyasaland was located in the east-central part of southern Africa. The multiracial federation has an area of about 487,000 sq. mi. (1,261,330 sq. km.) and a population of 6.8 million. Capital: Salisbury, in Southern Rhodesia.

The geographical unity of the three British possessions suggested the desirability of political and economic union as early as 1924. Despite objections by the African constituency of Northern Rhodesia and Nyasaland, who feared that African self-determination would be retarded by the dominant influence of prosperous and self-governing Southern Rhodesia. The Central African Federation was established in Sept. of 1953. As feared by the European constituency, Southern Rhodesia despite the fact that the three component countries largely retained their pre-federation political structure effectively and profitably dominated the Federation. It was dissolved at the end of 1963, largely because of the effective opposition of the Nyasaland African Congress. Northern Rhodesia and Nyasaland became the independent states of Zambia and Malawi in 1964. Southern Rhodesia unilaterally declared its independence the following year, which was not recognized by the British Government.

For earlier coinage refer to Southern Rhodesia. For later coinage refer to Malawi, Zambia, Rhodesia and Zimbabwe.

RULERS

Elizabeth II, 1952-1964

MONETARY SYSTEM

12 Pence = 1 Shilling
5 Shillings = 1 Crown
20 Shillings = 1 Pound

FEDERATION

STANDARD COINAGE

KM# 1 1/2 PENNY Composition: Bronze Ruler: Elizabeth II Obverse: Giraffes

Date	Mintage	F	VF	XF	Unc	BU
1955	720,000	0.15	0.25	0.50	3.00	—
1955 Proof	2,010	Value: 5.00				
1956	480,000	0.20	0.50	1.00	3.50	—
1956 Proof	—	Value: 400				
1957	1,920,000	0.10	0.15	0.25	3.00	—
1957 Proof	—	Value: 400				
1958	2,400,000	0.10	0.15	0.25	3.00	—
1958 Proof	—	Value: 400				
1964	1,440,000	0.10	0.15	0.25	3.00	—

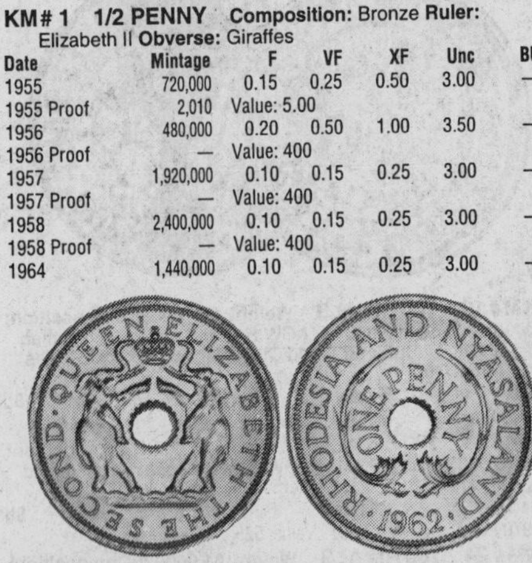

KM# 2 PENNY Composition: Bronze Ruler: Elizabeth II Obverse: Elephants

Date	Mintage	F	VF	XF	Unc	BU
1955	2,040,000	0.15	0.25	0.75	3.75	—
1955 Proof	2,010	Value: 5.00				
1956	4,800,000	0.15	0.25	0.50	3.50	—
1956 Proof	—	Value: 400				
1957	7,200,000	0.10	0.15	0.25	3.00	—

ate	Mintage	F	VF	XF	Unc	BU
957 Proof	—	—	—	—	—	—
958	2,880,000	0.10	0.15	0.25	3.00	—
958 Proof	—	Value: 400				
961	4,800,000	0.10	0.15	0.25	3.00	—
961 Proof	—	—	—	—	—	—
962	6,000,000	0.10	0.15	0.25	3.00	—
963	6,000,000	0.10	0.15	0.25	3.00	—
963 Proof	—	Value: 400				

KM# 3 3 PENCE Composition: Copper-Nickel **Ruler:** Elizabeth II **Obverse:** Flame lily

ate	Mintage	F	VF	XF	Unc	BU
955	1,200,000	0.20	0.50	1.00	4.00	—
955 Proof	10	Value: 400				
956	3,200,000	0.50	1.00	2.50	20.00	—
956 Proof	—	Value: 600				
957	6,000,000	0.20	0.50	0.75	3.00	—
957 Proof	—	Value: 600				
962	4,000,000	0.20	0.50	0.75	3.00	—
962 Proof	—	—	—	—	—	—
963	2,000,000	0.20	0.50	0.75	3.00	—
963 Proof	—	—	—	—	—	—
964	3,600,000	0.15	0.25	0.50	1.50	—

KM# 3a 3 PENCE Weight: 1.4100 g. **Composition:** 0.5000 Silver .0226 oz. ASW **Ruler:** Elizabeth II **Obverse:** Flame lily

Date	Mintage	F	VF	XF	Unc	BU
1955 Proof	2,000	Value: 7.50				

KM# 4 6 PENCE Composition: Copper-Nickel **Ruler:** Elizabeth II **Reverse:** Lion

Date	Mintage	F	VF	XF	Unc	BU
1955	400,000	0.50	1.00	2.50	7.50	—
1955 Proof	10	Value: 400				
1956	800,000	0.75	2.00	7.00	40.00	—
1956 Proof	—	—	—	—	—	—
1957	4,000,000	0.20	0.50	1.00	4.00	—
1957 Proof	—	—	—	—	—	—
1962	2,800,000	0.20	0.50	1.00	4.00	—
1962 Proof	—	—	—	—	—	—
1963	800,000	5.00	10.00	20.00	45.00	—
1963 Proof	—	—	—	—	—	—

KM# 4a 6 PENCE Weight: 2.8300 g. **Composition:** 0.5000 Silver .0454 oz. ASW **Ruler:** Elizabeth II **Reverse:** Lion

Date	Mintage	F	VF	XF	Unc	BU
1955 Proof	2,000	Value: 10.00				

KM# 5 SHILLING Composition: Copper-Nickel **Ruler:** Elizabeth II **Reverse:** Antelope

Date	Mintage	F	VF	XF	Unc	BU
1955	200,000	1.50	2.50	7.00	18.00	—
1955 Proof	10	Value: 400				
1956	1,700,000	0.75	1.50	3.50	30.00	—
1956 Proof	—	—	—	—	—	—
1957	3,500,000	0.50	1.00	2.50	8.00	—
1957 Proof	—	—	—	—	—	—

KM# 5a SHILLING Weight: 5.6600 g. **Composition:** 0.5000 Silver .0909 oz. ASW **Ruler:** Elizabeth II **Reverse:** Antelope

Date	Mintage	F	VF	XF	Unc	BU
1955 Proof	2,000	Value: 25.00				

KM# 6 2 SHILLINGS Composition: Copper-Nickel **Ruler:** Elizabeth II **Reverse:** African fish eagle

Date	Mintage	F	VF	XF	Unc	BU
1955	1,750,000	1.25	2.50	5.00	12.50	—
1955 Proof	10	Value: 400				
1956	1,850,000	1.25	2.50	4.50	12.00	—
1956 Proof	—	—	—	—	—	—
1957	1,500,000	1.25	2.50	4.50	12.00	—
1957 Proof	—	—	—	—	—	—

KM# 6a 2 SHILLINGS Weight: 11.3100 g. **Composition:** 0.5000 Silver .1818 oz. ASW **Ruler:** Elizabeth II **Reverse:** African fish eagle

Date	Mintage	F	VF	XF	Unc	BU
1955 Proof	2,000	Value: 30.00				

KM# 7 1/2 CROWN Composition: Copper-Nickel **Ruler:** Elizabeth II

Date	Mintage	F	VF	XF	Unc	BU
1955	1,600,000	1.50	3.00	6.00	15.00	—
1955 Proof	10	Value: 550				
1956	160,000	7.50	15.00	35.00	250	—
1956 Proof	—	—	—	—	—	—
1957	2,400,000	7.50	15.00	35.00	75.00	—
1957 Proof	—	—	—	—	—	—

KM# 7a 1/2 CROWN Weight: 14.1400 g. **Composition:** 0.5000 Silver .2273 oz. ASW **Ruler:** Elizabeth II

Date	Mintage	F	VF	XF	Unc	BU
1955 Proof	2,000	Value: 35.00				

PROOF SETS

KM#	Date	Mintage	Identification	Issue Price	Mkt Val
PS2	1955 (7)	2,000	KM1-2, 3a-7a	—	110
PS1	1955 (7)	10	KM1-7	—	2,200

RHODESIA

RULERS
British, until 1966

MONETARY SYSTEM
12 Pence = 1 Shilling = 10 Cents
10 Shillings = 1 Dollar
20 Shillings = 1 Pound

BRITISH PROTECTORATE

POUND COINAGE

KM# 8 3 PENCE = 2-1/2 CENTS Composition: Copper-Nickel

Date	Mintage	F	VF	XF	Unc	BU
1968	2,400,000	0.25	0.50	0.75	2.00	—
1968 Proof	10	Value: 1,000				

KM# 1 6 PENCE = 5 CENTS Composition: Copper-Nickel **Reverse:** Flame lily

Date	Mintage	F	VF	XF	Unc	BU
1964	13,500,000	0.15	0.25	0.40	1.25	—
1964 Proof	2,060	Value: 10.00				

KM# 2 SHILLING = 10 CENTS Composition: Copper-Nickel

Date	Mintage	F	VF	XF	Unc	BU
1964	15,500,000	0.15	0.25	0.65	1.50	—
1964 Proof	2,060	Value: 10.00				

KM# 3 2 SHILLINGS = 20 CENTS Composition: Copper-Nickel **Reverse:** Bird sculpture

Date	Mintage	F	VF	XF	Unc	BU
1964	10,500,000	0.25	0.50	1.25	3.00	—
1964 Proof	2,060	Value: 12.50				

KM# 4 2-1/2 SHILLINGS = 25 CENTS Composition: Copper-Nickel **Reverse:** Sable antelope

Date	Mintage	F	VF	XF	Unc	BU
1964	11,500,000	0.50	1.00	2.00	4.00	—
1964 Proof	2,060	Value: 17.50				

KM# 5 10 SHILLINGS **Weight:** 3.9940 g. **Composition:** 0.9160 Gold .1177 oz. AGW

Date	Mintage	F	VF	XF	Unc	BU
1966 Proof	6,000	Value: 100				

KM# 6 POUND **Weight:** 7.9881 g. **Composition:** 0.9160 Gold .2354 oz. AGW

Date	Mintage	F	VF	XF	Unc	BU
1966 Proof	5,000	Value: 175				

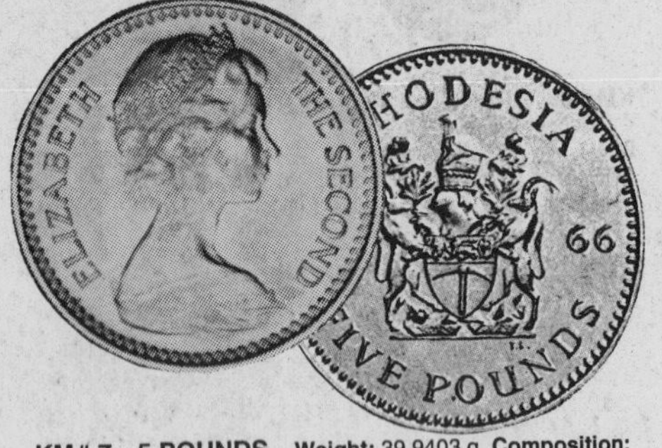

KM# 7 5 POUNDS **Weight:** 39.9403 g. **Composition:** 0.9160 Gold 1.1772 oz. AGW

Date	Mintage	F	VF	XF	Unc	BU
1966 Proof	3,000	Value: 550				

REPUBLIC

DECIMAL COINAGE

KM# 9 1/2 CENT **Composition:** Bronze

Date	Mintage	F	VF	XF	Unc	BU
1970	10,000,000	—	0.10	0.20	0.50	—
1970 Proof	12	Value: 750				
1971	2,000,000	—	0.10	0.25	1.00	—
1972	2,000,000	—	0.10	0.25	1.00	—
1972 Proof	12	Value: 750				
1975	10,001,000	—	0.10	0.20	0.50	—
1975 Proof	10	Value: 750				
1977	—	—	—	800	1,500	—

Note: Circulation mintage melted, less than 10 surviving specimens known

Date	Mintage	F	VF	XF	Unc	BU
1977 Proof	10	Value: 1,500				

KM# 10 CENT **Composition:** Bronze

Date	Mintage	F	VF	XF	Unc	BU
1970	25,000,000	—	0.10	0.20	0.50	—
1970 Proof	12	Value: 750				
1971	15,000,000	—	0.10	0.20	0.50	—
1972	10,000,000	—	0.10	0.20	0.50	—
1972 Proof	12	Value: 750				
1973	5,000,000	—	0.10	0.20	0.75	—
1973 Proof	10	Value: 750				
1974	—	—	0.10	0.20	0.50	—
1975	10,000,000	—	0.10	0.20	0.50	—
1975 Proof	10	Value: 750				
1976	20,000,000	—	0.10	0.20	0.50	—
1976 Proof	10	Value: 750				
1977	10,000,000	—	0.10	0.20	0.50	—

KM# 11 2-1/2 CENTS **Composition:** Copper-Nickel

Date	Mintage	F	VF	XF	Unc	BU
1970	4,000,000	0.15	0.25	0.40	1.00	—
1970 Proof	12	Value: 750				

KM# 12 5 CENTS **Composition:** Copper-Nickel

Date	Mintage	F	VF	XF	Unc	BU
1973	—	0.25	0.75	1.50	3.00	—
1973 Proof	10	Value: 750				

KM# 13 5 CENTS **Composition:** Copper-Nickel

Date	Mintage	F	VF	XF	Unc	BU
1975	3,500,000	0.15	0.25	0.40	0.75	—
1975 Proof	10	Value: 750				
1976	8,038,000	0.15	0.25	0.40	0.75	—
1977	3,015,000	0.25	0.75	1.50	3.00	—

KM# 14 10 CENTS **Composition:** Copper-Nickel

Date	Mintage	F	VF	XF	Unc	BU
1975	2,003,000	0.15	0.30	0.60	1.50	—
1975 Proof	10	Value: 750				

KM# 15 20 CENTS **Composition:** Copper-Nickel

Date	Mintage	F	VF	XF	Unc	BU
1975	1,937,000	0.50	0.75	1.00	3.00	—
1975 Proof	10	Value: 750				
1977	—	0.50	0.75	1.50	3.50	—

KM# 16 25 CENTS **Composition:** Copper-Nickel

Date	Mintage	F	VF	XF	Unc	BU
1975	1,011,000	0.50	1.00	2.00	5.00	—
1975 Proof	10	Value: 750				

PROOF SETS

KM#	Date	Mintage	Identification	Issue Price	Mkt Val
PS1	1964 (8)	10	KM#1-4 Double set	—	250
PS2	1964 (4)	2,060	KM#1-4	—	50.00
PS3	1966 (3)	2,000	KM#5-7	280	825
PS4	1968 (2)	3	KM#8 Double set	—	2,250
PS5	1970 (6)	3	KM#9-11 Double set	—	4,500
PS6	1973 (2)	2	KM#12 Double set	—	1,500
PS7	1975 (8)	1	KM#13-16 Double set	—	7,000
PS8	1975 (6)	4	KM#9, 10, 13-16	—	5,000
PS9	1975 (4)	4	KM#13-16	—	3,500

ROMANIA

Romania (formerly the Socialist Republic of Romania), a country in southeast Europe, has an area of 91,699 sq. mi. (237,500 sq. km.) and a population of 23.2 million. Capital: Bucharest. Machinery, foodstuffs, raw minerals and petroleum products are exported. Heavy industry and oil have become increasingly important to the economy since 1959.

In 1526, Hungary came under Turkish rule. With defeat in 1526, Hungary came under Turkish rule. Transylvania became a separate principality under the protection of the Sultan (1541).

In 1881, Carol I became king. In 1888, Romania became a constitutional monarchy with a bicameral legislature. Neutral during the First Balkan War (1912), Romania joined Serbia and Greece in the Second Balkan War (1913) against Bulgaria The intervention and deployment of Romanian troops into Bulgaria resulted in the acquisition of southern Dobruja.

When WW I began, the kingdom was neutral until 1916, when the Romanian army invaded Transylvania, but Austro-German, Turkish and Bulgarian forces occupied the south of the country. The Romanians, with the triumph of the Allies, persisted in keeping Moldavia. In March 1918, the Bessarabian legislature voted in favor of reunification with Romania. With the triumph of the Allies, the Romanian army liberated their southern region and reoccupied Transylvania. Bukovina (Oct. 28, 1918) and Transylvania (Dec. 1) proclaimed their reunification with Romania. In 1919, the Romanian army shattered the Bolshevik forces, which were installed in Hungary.

A new constitution was adopted in 1923. During this period in history, the Romanian government struggled with domestic problems, agrarian reform and economic reconstruction.

In the background of WW II, in 1940, after the defeat of France, following the Soviet-Nazi agreement of August1939, the Red army occupied Bessarabia and northern Bukovina (June). Later, northern Transylvania was annexed by Hungary (August) and southern Dobruja was returned to Bulgaria (September). In this context, King Carol II abdicated in favor of his son Mihai.

The government was reorganized along Fascist lines between September 14, 1940 & January 23, 1941. A military dictatorship followed when the German's Antonescu installed himself as chief of state. When the Germans invaded the Soviet Union, Romania also became involved in recovering the regions of Bessarabia and northern Bukovina annexed by Stalin in 1940.

On August 23, 1944, King Mihai I proclaimed an armistice with the Allied Forces. The Romanian army drove out the Germans and Hungarians in northern Transylvania, but the country was subsequently occupied by the Soviet army. That monarchy was abolished on December 30, 1947,and Romania became a "People's Republic" based on the Soviet regime. The process of sovietization included Soviet regime. The anti-Communist combative resistance movement developed frequent purges of dissidents: mainly political but also clerical, cultural and peasants. Romanian elite disappeared into the concentration camps. The anti-Communist combative resistance movement developed in spite of the Soviet army presence until 1956. The partisans remained in the mountains until 1964. With the accession of N. Ceausescu to power, Romania began to exercise a considerable degree of independence, refusing to participate in the invasion of Czechoslovakia (August 1968). In 1965, it was proclaimed a "Socialist Republic". After 1977, an oppressed and impoverished domestic scene worsened.

On December 17, 1989, an anti-Communist revolt in Timisoara. On December 22, 1989 the Communist government was overthrown. Ceausescu and his wife were arrested and later executed. The new government established a republic, the constitutional name being Romania.

RULERS

Carol I (as Prince), 1866-81 (as King), 1881-1914
Ferdinand I, 1914-1927
Mihai I, 1927-1930
Carol II, 1930-1940
Mihai I, 1940-1947

MINT MARKS

(a) - Paris, privy marks only
(b) - Brussels, privy marks only
angel head (1872-1876),
no marks (1894-1924)
B - Bucharest (1870-1900)
B - Hamburg, Germany
C - Candescu, chief engineer of the Bucharest Mint (1870-
FM - Franklin Mint, USA
H - Heaton, Birmingham, England
HF - Huguenin Freres & Co., Le Locle, Switzerland
J - Hamburg
KN - Kings Norton, Birmingham, England
(p) - Thunderbolt - Poissy, France
zig zag (1924)
V - Vienna, Austria
W - Watt (James Watt & Co.)
Huguenin - Le Locle, Switzerland
( ) - no marks, 1930 (10, 20 Lei),
1932 (100 Lei), Royal Mint – London

MONETARY SYSTEM

100 Bani = 1 Leu

KINGDOM

STANDARD COINAGE

M# 31 5 BANI **Weight:** 2.5000 g. **Composition:** Copper-Nickel **Ruler:** Carol I as King = Rege

ate	Mintage	F	VF	XF	Unc	BU
05	2,000,000	0.50	1.00	3.50	12.00	—
905 Proof	—	Value: 40.00				
906	48,000,000	0.25	0.50	2.00	9.00	—
906J	24,000,000	0.25	0.50	1.50	6.00	—

M# 32 10 BANI **Weight:** 4.0000 g. **Composition:** Copper-Nickel **Ruler:** Carol I as King = Rege

ate	Mintage	F	VF	XF	Unc	BU
905	10,820,000	0.50	1.00	4.00	16.00	—
906	24,180,000	0.25	0.75	2.50	10.00	—
906J	17,000,000	0.25	0.75	1.50	6.00	—

KM# 33 20 BANI **Weight:** 6.0000 g. **Composition:** Copper-Nickel **Ruler:** Carol I as King = Rege

ate	Mintage	F	VF	XF	Unc	BU
905	2,500,000	2.00	6.00	15.00	48.00	—
906	3,000,000	2.00	4.00	12.00	36.00	—
906J	2,500,000	2.00	4.00	12.00	35.00	—

KM# 44 25 BANI **Weight:** 0.8960 g. **Composition:** Aluminum **Ruler:** Ferdinand I **Note:** Center hole sizes vary from 4 to 4.5 millimeters. No engraver name.

ate	Mintage	F	VF	XF	Unc	BU
921Huguenin	20,000,000	0.50	1.00	2.50	7.50	—

KM# 23 50 BANI **Weight:** 2.5000 g. **Composition:** 0.8350 Silver .0671 oz. ASW **Ruler:** Carol I as King = Rege **Obv. Designer:** Tasset **Reverse:** Small letters **Rev. Designer:** I. Bassarab

ate	Mintage	F	VF	XF	Unc	BU
901	194,205	6.00	16.00	50.00	200	—

KM# 41 50 BANI **Weight:** 2.5000 g. **Composition:** 0.8350 Silver .0671 oz. ASW **Ruler:** Carol I as King = Rege

Date	Mintage	F	VF	XF	Unc	BU
1910	3,600,000	1.50	3.00	8.00	17.00	—

Note: Edge varieties (round or flat) exist

Date	Mintage	F	VF	XF	Unc	BU
1910 Proof	—	Value: 150				
1911	3,000,000	2.00	4.00	10.00	20.00	—
1912	1,800,000	1.50	3.00	8.00	18.00	—
1914	1,600,000	1.25	2.00	4.50	12.00	—

Note: Edge varieties (round or flat) exist

Date	Mintage	F	VF	XF	Unc	BU
1914 Proof	—	Value: 90.00				

KM# 45 50 BANI **Weight:** 1.2030 g. **Composition:** Aluminum **Ruler:** Ferdinand I **Note:** Center hole size varies from 4 to 4.5 millimeters.

Date	Mintage	F	VF	XF	Unc	BU
1921Huguenin	30,000,000	0.50	1.00	3.50	9.00	—

KM# 24 LEU **Weight:** 5.0000 g. **Composition:** 0.8350 Silver .1342 oz. ASW **Ruler:** Carol I as King = Rege

Date	Mintage	F	VF	XF	Unc	BU
1901	369,614	4.00	10.00	32.00	125	—
1901 Proof	—	Value: 250				

KM# 34 LEU **Weight:** 5.0000 g. **Composition:** 0.8350 Silver .1342 oz. ASW **Ruler:** Carol I as King = Rege **Subject:** 40th Anniversary - Reign of Carol I **Note:** Designer's name below truncation on reverse.

Date	Mintage	F	VF	XF	Unc	BU
ND(1906)	2,500,000	5.00	12.00	25.00	56.00	—
ND(1906) Proof	—	Value: 200				

KM# 42 LEU **Weight:** 5.0000 g. **Composition:** 0.8350 Silver .1342 oz. ASW **Ruler:** Carol I as King = Rege **Obverse:** Tasset **Rev. Designer:** I. Bassarab

Date	Mintage	F	VF	XF	Unc	BU
1910	4,600,000	3.00	6.00	9.00	25.00	—

Note: Edge varieties (round or flat) exist

Date	Mintage	F	VF	XF	Unc	BU
1910 Proof	—	Value: 350				
1911	2,573,000	4.00	8.00	12.00	30.00	—
1912	3,540,000	3.00	5.00	8.00	19.00	—
1914	4,282,935	2.00	3.00	6.00	15.00	—

Note: Edge varieties (round or flat) exist

Date	Mintage	F	VF	XF	Unc	BU
1914 Proof	—	Value: 100				

KM# 46 LEU **Weight:** 3.5000 g. **Composition:** Copper-Nickel **Ruler:** Ferdinand I **Edge:** Reeded

Date	Mintage	F	VF	XF	Unc	BU
1924(b) Thin	100,000,000	0.50	1.50	3.50	9.00	—
1924(p) Thick	100,006,000	0.50	1.50	4.00	10.00	—

KM# 56 LEU **Composition:** Nickel-Brass **Edge:** Plain **Note:** Without mint mark.

Date	Mintage	F	VF	XF	Unc	BU
1938	27,900,000	0.20	0.60	1.60	4.50	—
1939	72,200,000	0.20	0.50	1.50	3.00	—
1940	Inc. above	0.20	0.50	1.00	2.50	—
1941	Inc. above	0.20	0.50	1.50	3.50	—

KM# 25 2 LEI **Weight:** 10.0000 g. **Composition:** 0.8350 Silver .2684 oz. ASW **Obverse:** Tasset **Rev. Designer:** I. Bassarab **Edge:** Reeded

Date	Mintage	F	VF	XF	Unc	BU
1901	12,476	350	520	860	1,950	—

KM# 43 2 LEI **Weight:** 10.0000 g. **Composition:** 0.8350 Silver .2684 oz. ASW **Ruler:** Carol I as King = Rege

Date	Mintage	F	VF	XF	Unc	BU
1910	1,800,000	4.00	8.00	15.00	36.00	—

Note: Edge varieties (round and flat) exist

Date	Mintage	F	VF	XF	Unc	BU
1910 Proof	—	Value: 200				
1911	1,000,000	6.00	12.00	25.00	50.00	—
1912	1,500,000	4.00	7.00	12.00	30.00	—
1914	2,452,000	3.00	5.00	9.00	20.00	—

Note: Edge varieties (round and flat) exist

Date	Mintage	F	VF	XF	Unc	BU
1914 Proof	—	Value: 120				

KM# 47 2 LEI **Weight:** 7.0000 g. **Composition:** Copper-Nickel **Ruler:** Ferdinand I **Edge:** Reeded

Date	Mintage	F	VF	XF	Unc	BU
1924(b)	50,000,000	1.00	1.75	4.00	11.00	—
1924(p)	50,008,000	1.00	1.75	4.50	12.00	—

KM# 58 2 LEI **Weight:** 3.2000 g. **Composition:** Zinc **Ruler:** Mihai II

Date	Mintage	F	VF	XF	Unc	BU
1941	101,778,000	0.50	1.50	3.00	9.50	—

KM# 17.2 5 LEI **Weight:** 25.0000 g. **Composition:** 0.9000 Silver .7234 oz. ASW **Ruler:** Carol I as King = Rege **Edge:** Reeded

Date	Mintage	F	VF	XF	Unc	BU
1901B	460,000	45.00	70.00	160	350	—
1901B Proof	—	Value: 950				

KM# 35 5 LEI **Weight:** 25.0000 g. **Composition:** 0.9000 Silver .7234 oz. ASW **Ruler:** Carol I as King = Rege **Subject:** 40th Anniversary - Reign of Carol I

Date	Mintage	F	VF	XF	Unc	BU
ND(1906)	200,000	40.00	70.00	160	320	—
ND(1906) Proof	—	Value: 950				

KM# 48 5 LEI **Weight:** 3.5000 g. **Composition:** Nickel-Brass **Ruler:** Mihai I **Obverse:** Bust of King Mihai I **Edge:** Reeded

Date	Mintage	F	VF	XF	Unc	BU
1930H	15,000,000	1.50	2.50	6.50	19.00	—
1930KN	15,000,000	1.50	3.50	8.00	22.00	—
1930(a)	30,000,000	1.00	2.50	5.50	16.00	—

KM# 61 5 LEI **Weight:** 4.5000 g. **Composition:** Zinc **Ruler:** Mihai II

Date	Mintage	F	VF	XF	Unc	BU
1942	140,000,000	0.50	1.25	2.75	7.50	—

KM# 49 10 LEI **Weight:** 5.0000 g. **Composition:** Nickel-Brass **Ruler:** Carol II **Obverse:** Bust of King Carol II **Edge:** Reeded

Date	Mintage	F	VF	XF	Unc	BU
1930	15,000,000	1.00	3.00	8.00	24.00	—
1930 Proof	—	—	—	—	—	—
1930(a)	30,000,000	1.00	3.00	7.50	22.00	—
1930H	7,500,000	2.50	4.50	10.00	28.00	—
1930KN	7,500,000	3.00	7.00	15.00	36.00	—
1930(a) Proof	—	Value: 175				

KM# 36 12-1/2 LEI **Weight:** 4.0325 g. **Composition:** 0.9000 Gold .1167 oz. AGW **Ruler:** Carol I as King = Rege **Subject:** 40th Anniversary - Reign of Carol I

Date	Mintage	F	VF	XF	Unc	BU
1906	32,000	70.00	95.00	130	260	—

KM# 37 20 LEI **Weight:** 6.4516 g. **Composition:** 0.9000 Gold .1867 oz. AGW **Ruler:** Carol I as King = Rege **Subject:** 40th Anniversary - Reign of Carol I

Date	Mintage	F	VF	XF	Unc	BU
ND(1906)(b)	15,000	115	145	190	320	—

KM# 50 20 LEI **Weight:** 7.5000 g. **Composition:** Nickel-Brass **Ruler:** Mihai I **Obverse:** Bust of King Mihai I **Rev. Designer:** I. Bassarab **Edge:** Reeded

Date	Mintage	F	VF	XF	Unc	BU
1930 London	40,000,000	2.00	6.50	18.00	38.00	—
1930 Proof	—	—	—	—	—	—
1930H	5,000,000	3.00	8.00	25.00	50.00	—
1930KN	5,000,000	3.00	10.00	30.00	70.00	—

KM# 51 20 LEI **Composition:** Nickel-Brass **Ruler:** Carol II **Obverse:** Bust of King Carol II **Edge:** Reeded

Date	Mintage	F	VF	XF	Unc	BU
1930	6,750,000	1.50	3.00	12.00	23.00	—
1930 Proof	—	—	—	—	—	—
1930(a)	17,500,000	1.00	2.00	10.00	22.00	—
1930H	7,750,000	2.00	4.00	16.00	37.50	—
1930KN	7,750,000	2.50	6.00	25.00	55.00	—
1930(a) Proof	—	Value: 185				

KM# 62 20 LEI **Weight:** 6.0000 g. **Composition:** Zinc **Ruler:** Mihai II **Edge:** Reeded

Date	Mintage	F	VF	XF	Unc	BU
1942	44,000,000	0.75	1.50	3.00	8.00	—
1943	25,783,000	1.00	2.25	4.00	9.00	—
1944	5,034,000	1.50	3.00	5.00	12.00	—

KM# 38 25 LEI **Weight:** 8.0650 g. **Composition:** 0.9000 Gold .2333 oz. AGW **Ruler:** Carol I as King = Rege **Subject:** 40th Anniversary - Reign of Carol I

Date	Mintage	F	VF	XF	Unc	BU
ND(1906)(b)	24,000	145	185	300	460	—

KM# 39 50 LEI **Weight:** 16.1300 g. **Composition:** 0.9000 Gold .4667 oz. AGW **Ruler:** Carol I as King = Rege **Subject:** 40th Anniversary - Reign of Carol I

Date	Mintage	F	VF	XF	Unc	BU
ND(1906)(b)	28,000	240	360	520	920	—

KM# 55 50 LEI **Weight:** 5.8300 g. **Composition:** Nickel **Ruler:** Carol II **Edge:** Reeded **Note:** 16,731 melted.

Date	Mintage	F	VF	XF	Unc	BU
1937	12,000,000	1.25	2.50	4.50	11.00	—
1938	8,000,000	3.00	6.00	14.00	35.00	—

KM# 40 100 LEI **Weight:** 32.2600 g. **Composition:** 0.9000 Gold .9335 oz. AGW **Ruler:** Carol I as King = Rege **Subject:** 40th Anniversary - Reign of Carol I **Note:** Similar to KM#35.

Date	Mintage	F	VF	XF	Unc	BU
ND(1906)(b)	3,000	460	760	1,200	2,200	—

KM# 52 100 LEI **Weight:** 14.0000 g. **Composition:** 0.5000 Silver .1929 oz. ASW **Ruler:** Carol II **Edge:** Reeded

Date	Mintage	F	VF	XF	Unc	BU
1932(a)	2,000,000	10.00	20.00	45.00	145	—
1932	16,400,000	5.00	10.00	20.00	90.00	—
1932 Proof	—	Value: 250				

KM# 54 100 LEI **Weight:** 8.2000 g. **Composition:** Nickel **Ruler:** Carol II **Edge:** Reeded **Note:** 17,030 melted.

Date	Mintage	F	VF	XF	Unc	BU
1936	20,230,000	2.00	4.00	8.00	15.00	—
1938	3,250,000	3.00	7.00	12.50	40.00	—

KM# 64 100 LEI **Weight:** 8.5000 g. **Composition:** Nickel Clad Steel **Ruler:** Mihai II **Edge:** Incuse lettering **Edge Lettering:** NIHIL SINE DEO

Date	Mintage	F	VF	XF	Unc	BU
1943	40,590,000	0.25	0.50	1.20	4.00	—
Note: Portrait varieties exist.						
1944	21,289,000	0.25	0.50	1.40	5.00	—

KM# 63 200 LEI **Weight:** 6.0000 g. **Composition:** 0.8350 Silver .1611 oz. ASW **Ruler:** Mihai II **Edge:** Incuse lettering **Edge Lettering:** NIHIL SINE DEO

Date	Mintage	F	VF	XF	Unc	BU
1942	30,025,000	1.50	2.50	6.00	15.00	—

KM# 66 200 LEI **Weight:** 7.5000 g. **Composition:** Brass **Ruler:** Mihai II **Note:** Many were silver plated privately.

Date	Mintage	F	VF	XF	Unc	BU
1945	1,399,000	1.00	2.00	5.00	13.00	—

KM# 53 250 LEI **Weight:** 13.5000 g. **Composition:** 0.7500 Silver .3255 oz. ASW **Ruler:** Carol II

Date	Mintage	F	VF	XF	Unc	BU
1935	4,500,000	12.00	24.00	60.00	160	—

KM# 57 250 LEI **Weight:** 12.0000 g. **Composition:** 0.8350 Silver .3222 oz. ASW **Ruler:** Carol II **Edge:** Incuse lettering, line interrupted by two rhombs **Edge Lettering:** MUNCA CREDINTA REGE NATIUNE

Date	Mintage	F	VF	XF	Unc	BU
1939	10,000,000	6.00	12.00	30.00	75.00	—
1940	8,000,000	10.00	18.00	42.00	125	—

KM# 59.1 250 LEI **Weight:** 12.0000 g. **Composition:** 0.8350 Silver .3222 oz. ASW **Ruler:** Carol II **Reverse:** Date divided by portcullis **Edge:** Incuse lettering **Edge Lettering:** TOTUL PENTRU TARA **Note:** Mintage unissued and reportedly melted.

Date	F	VF	XF	Unc	BU
1940	—	—	—	3,500	—

KM# 59.2 250 LEI **Weight:** 12.0000 g. **Composition:** 0.8350 Silver .3222 oz. ASW **Ruler:** Mihai II **Reverse:** Date not divided **Edge:** Incuse lettering **Edge Lettering:** TOTUL PENTRU TARA

Date	Mintage	F	VF	XF	Unc	BU
1941	2,250,000	9.00	15.00	32.00	68.00	—

KM# 59.3 250 LEI **Weight:** 12.0000 g. **Composition:** 0.8350 Silver .3222 oz. ASW **Ruler:** Mihai II **Edge:** Lettered **Edge Lettering:** NIHIL SINE DEO

Date	Mintage	F	VF	XF	Unc	BU
1941B	13,750,000	6.00	9.00	15.00	28.00	—

KM# 60 500 LEI **Weight:** 25.0000 g. **Composition:** 0.8350 Silver .6711 oz. ASW **Ruler:** Mihai II **Subject:** Basarabia Reunion **Reverse:** On bended knee, King Stephen presents Putna Monastery to the Lord **Edge:** Incuse lettering **Edge Lettering:** PRIN STATORNICIE LA IZBANADA ✱

Date	Mintage	F	VF	XF	Unc	BU
1941	775,000	8.00	12.00	18.00	34.00	—

KM# 65 500 LEI **Weight:** 12.0000 g. **Composition:** 0.7000 Silver .2701 oz. ASW **Ruler:** Mihai II **Edge:** Incuse lettering **Edge Lettering:** NIHIL SINE DEO

Date	Mintage	F	VF	XF	Unc	BU
1944	9,731,000	2.50	3.50	5.00	10.00	—

KM# 67 500 LEI **Weight:** 10.0000 g. **Composition:** Brass **Ruler:** Mihai II **Edge:** Reeded **Note:** Many were silver plated privately.

Date	Mintage	F	VF	XF	Unc	BU
1945	3,422,000	1.00	2.00	4.00	8.00	—

KM# 68 500 LEI **Weight:** 1.5000 g. **Composition:** Aluminum **Ruler:** Mihai II **Edge:** Reeded **Note:** Without designer's name, the result of a filled die.

Date	Mintage	F	VF	XF	Unc	BU
1946	5,823,000	0.50	1.00	3.00	7.00	—

KM# 69 2000 LEI **Weight:** 5.1000 g. **Composition:** Brass **Ruler:** Mihai II **Edge:** Incuse lettering **Edge Lettering:** NIHIL SINE DEO **Note:** Many were silver plated privately.

Date	Mintage	F	VF	XF	Unc	BU
1946	24,619,000	0.50	1.00	3.00	7.50	—

KM# 76 10000 LEI **Weight:** 10.0000 g. **Composition:** Brass **Ruler:** Mihai II **Edge:** Incuse lettering **Edge Lettering:** NIHIL SINE DEO **Note:** Many were silver plated privately.

Date	Mintage	F	VF	XF	Unc	BU
1947	11,850,000	1.00	2.00	4.00	8.50	—

KM# 70 25000 LEI **Weight:** 12.5000 g. **Composition:** 0.7000 Silver .2813 oz. ASW **Ruler:** Mihai II **Edge:** Incuse lettering **Edge Lettering:** NIHIL SINE DEO

Date	Mintage	F	VF	XF	Unc	BU
1946	2,372,000	2.00	3.00	6.00	12.00	—

KM# 71 100000 LEI **Weight:** 25.0000 g. **Composition:** 0.7000 Silver .5626 oz. ASW **Ruler:** Mihai II **Edge:** Incuse lettering **Edge Lettering:** NIHIL SINE DEO

Date	Mintage	F	VF	XF	Unc	BU
1946	2,002,000	5.00	7.00	10.00	19.00	—

REFORM COINAGE

Aug. 15, 1947; 100 Bani = 1 Leu

KM# 72 50 BANI **Weight:** 1.7000 g. **Composition:** Brass **Ruler:** Mihai II **Edge:** Plain

Date	Mintage	F	VF	XF	Unc	BU
1947	13,266,000	1.00	2.00	3.00	9.50	—

KM# 73 LEU **Weight:** 2.5000 g. **Composition:** Brass **Ruler:** Mihai II **Edge:** Plain

Date	Mintage	F	VF	XF	Unc	BU
1947	88,341,000	1.00	2.25	4.00	10.00	—

KM# 74 2 LEI **Weight:** 3.5000 g. **Composition:** Bronze **Ruler:** Mihai II **Edge:** Plain

Date	Mintage	F	VF	XF	Unc	BU
1947	40,000,000	1.00	2.50	5.00	14.00	—

KM# 75 5 LEI **Weight:** 1.5000 g. **Composition:** Aluminum **Ruler:** Mihai II

Date	Mintage	F	VF	XF	Unc	BU
1947	56,026,000	1.50	2.50	6.50	18.00	—

PEOPLE'S REPUBLIC

STANDARD COINAGE

KM# 78 LEU Weight: 1.8300 g. **Composition:** Copper-Nickel-Zinc **Edge:** Plain

Date	F	VF	XF	Unc	BU
1949	0.75	1.50	3.00	8.50	—
1950	0.75	1.50	3.25	8.00	—
1951	1.00	2.00	4.50	10.00	—

KM# 78a LEU Weight: 0.6100 g. **Composition:** Aluminum

Date	F	VF	XF	Unc	BU
1951	1.00	2.00	5.00	11.50	—
1952	6.00	12.00	22.00	60.00	—

KM# 79 2 LEI Weight: 2.4400 g. **Composition:** Copper-Nickel-Zinc **Edge:** Plain

Date	F	VF	XF	Unc	BU
1950	1.00	2.50	5.00	10.00	—
1951	2.00	5.00	10.00	22.00	—

KM# 79a 2 LEI Weight: 0.8400 g. **Composition:** Aluminum

Date	F	VF	XF	Unc	BU
1951	0.75	2.00	4.00	10.00	—
1952	6.00	12.50	26.00	65.00	—

KM# 77 5 LEI Weight: 1.5000 g. **Composition:** Aluminum **Edge:** Plain

Date	F	VF	XF	Unc	BU
1948	1.50	2.50	4.50	18.00	—
1949	1.25	2.00	3.50	10.00	—
1950	1.25	2.00	3.50	10.00	—
1951	1.25	2.00	4.00	14.00	—

KM# 80 20 LEI Weight: 2.1200 g. **Composition:** Aluminum **Edge:** Plain

Date	F	VF	XF	Unc	BU
1951	2.00	6.00	16.00	45.00	—

REFORM COINAGE

Jan. 26, 1952; 100 Bani = 1 Leu

KM# 81.1 BAN Weight: 1.0000 g. **Composition:** Copper-Nickel-Zinc **Obverse:** Without star at top of arms **Edge:** Reeded

Date	F	VF	XF	Unc	BU
1952	0.20	0.50	1.00	2.00	—

KM# 81.2 BAN Weight: 1.0000 g. **Composition:** Copper-Nickel-Zinc **Obverse:** Star at top of arms

Date	F	VF	XF	Unc	BU
1953	1.00	2.00	6.00	15.00	—
1954	2.00	4.00	8.00	30.00	—

KM# 82.1 3 BANI Weight: 2.0000 g. **Composition:** Copper-Nickel-Zinc **Obverse:** Without star at top of arms **Edge:** Reeded

Date	F	VF	XF	Unc	BU
1952	1.00	2.00	4.00	10.00	—

KM# 82.2 3 BANI Weight: 2.0000 g. **Composition:** Copper-Nickel-Zinc **Obverse:** Star at top of arms

Date	F	VF	XF	Unc	BU
1953	0.50	1.00	2.00	7.00	—
1954	3.00	6.50	17.00	46.00	—

KM# 83.1 5 BANI Weight: 2.4000 g. **Composition:** Copper-Nickel-Zinc **Obverse:** Without star at top of arms **Edge:** Reeded

Date	F	VF	XF	Unc	BU
1952	0.50	1.00	2.50	7.00	—

KM# 83.2 5 BANI Weight: 2.4000 g. **Composition:** Copper-Nickel-Zinc **Obverse:** Star at top of arms

Date	F	VF	XF	Unc	BU
1953	0.25	0.50	1.50	5.00	—
1954	0.25	0.50	1.50	4.00	—
1955	0.25	0.50	1.50	4.00	—
1956	0.25	0.50	1.25	3.50	—
1957	0.25	0.50	1.75	5.00	—

KM# 89 5 BANI Weight: 1.7000 g. **Composition:** Nickel Clad Steel **Obverse:** RPR on ribbon in arms **Edge:** Plain

Date	F	VF	XF	Unc	BU
1963	0.20	0.50	1.00	2.00	—

KM# 84.1 10 BANI Weight: 1.8000 g. **Composition:** Copper-Nickel **Obverse:** Without star at top of arms **Edge:** Reeded

Date	F	VF	XF	Unc	BU
1952	1.50	2.50	7.50	18.00	—

KM# 84.2 10 BANI Weight: 1.8000 g. **Composition:** Copper-Nickel **Obverse:** Star at top of arms **Obv. Legend:** ROMANA

Date	F	VF	XF	Unc	BU
1954	0.30	1.50	3.00	7.00	—

KM# 84.3 10 BANI Weight: 1.8000 g. **Composition:** Copper-Nickel **Obv. Legend:** ROMINA

Date	F	VF	XF	Unc	BU
1955	0.10	0.20	0.75	3.00	—
1956	0.10	0.20	0.75	3.00	—

KM# 87 15 BANI Weight: 2.8800 g. **Composition:** Nickel Clad Steel **Edge:** Plain

Date	F	VF	XF	Unc	BU
1960	0.10	0.25	0.60	2.00	—

KM# 85.1 25 BANI Weight: 3.6000 g. **Composition:** Copper-Nickel **Obverse:** Without star at top of arms **Edge:** Reeded

Date	F	VF	XF	Unc	BU
1952	1.50	3.50	10.00	25.00	—

KM# 85.2 25 BANI Weight: 3.6000 g. **Composition:** Copper-Nickel **Obverse:** Star at top of arms **Obv. Legend:** ROMANA

Date	F	VF	XF	Unc	BU
1953	0.20	0.75	2.00	5.00	—
1954	0.20	0.60	1.50	4.00	—

KM# 85.3 25 BANI Weight: 3.6000 g. **Composition:** Copper-Nickel **Obv. Legend:** ROMINA

Date	F	VF	XF	Unc	BU
1955	0.15	0.35	0.80	3.00	—

KM# 88 25 BANI Weight: 3.3800 g. **Composition:** Nickel Clad Steel **Edge:** Plain

Date	F	VF	XF	Unc	BU
1960	0.15	0.30	0.60	2.00	—

KM# 86 50 BANI Weight: 4.5500 g. **Composition:** Copper-Nickel **Edge:** Reeded

Date	F	VF	XF	Unc	BU
1955	0.50	1.00	2.00	10.00	—
1956	0.50	1.00	2.00	10.00	—

KM# 90 LEU Weight: 5.0600 g. **Composition:** Nickel Clad Steel **Edge:** Plain

Date	F	VF	XF	Unc	BU
1963	0.25	0.50	0.75	2.00	—

KM# 91 3 LEI Weight: 5.8600 g. **Composition:** Nickel Clad Steel **Edge:** Plain

Date	F	VF	XF	Unc	BU
1963	0.25	0.50	1.20	3.00	—

SOCIALIST REPUBLIC

STANDARD COINAGE

KM# 92 5 BANI Weight: 1.7000 g. **Composition:** Nickel Clad Steel **Obverse:** ROMANIA on ribbon in arms **Edge:** Plain

Date	F	VF	XF	Unc	BU
1966	0.10	0.20	0.60	1.50	—

KM# 92a 5 BANI Composition: Aluminum **Edge:** Plain

Date	F	VF	XF	Unc	BU
1975	—	0.10	0.20	0.50	—

KM# 93 15 BANI Weight: 2.8800 g. **Composition:** Nickel Clad Steel **Edge:** Plain

Date	F	VF	XF	Unc	BU
1966	—	0.15	0.35	1.20	—

KM# 93a 15 BANI Composition: Aluminum **Edge:** Plain

Date	F	VF	XF	Unc	BU
1975	—	0.10	0.25	0.75	—

KM# 94 25 BANI Weight: 3.3800 g. **Composition:** Nickel Clad Steel **Edge:** Plain

Date	F	VF	XF	Unc	BU
1966	—	0.20	0.55	2.00	—

KM# 94a 25 BANI Composition: Aluminum **Edge:** Plain

Date	F	VF	XF	Unc	BU
1982	—	0.50	1.00	3.00	—

KM# 95 LEU Weight: 5.0600 g. **Composition:** Nickel Clad Steel

Date	F	VF	XF	Unc	BU
1966	0.10	0.25	0.60	2.20	—

KM# 96 3 LEI Weight: 5.8600 g. **Composition:** Nickel Clad Steel **Edge:** Plain

Date	F	VF	XF	Unc	BU
1966	0.25	0.50	1.20	3.00	—

KM# 97 5 LEI Composition: Aluminum **Reverse:** Large and small dot varieties exist **Edge:** Security

Date	F	VF	XF	Unc	BU
1978	—	0.50	1.00	3.50	—

KM# 100 50 LEI Weight: 13.8800 g. **Composition:** 0.9250 Silver .4128 oz. ASW **Subject:** 2,050th Anniversary of Airst Independent State **Obverse:** Similar to 100 Lei, KM#98

Date	Mintage	F	VF	XF	Unc	BU
1983FM Proof	7,000	Value: 75.00				
1983FM Proof	1,000	Value: 220				

Note: Serially numbered on edges

KM# 98 100 LEI Weight: 27.7500 g. **Composition:** 0.9250 Silver .8253 oz. ASW **Subject:** 2,050th Anniversary of First Independent State

Date		F	VF	XF	Unc	BU
1982FM Proof	7,500	Value: 90.00				
1983FM Proof	7,000	Value: 100				
1983FM Proof	1,000	Value: 320				

Note: Serially numbered on edge

KM# 99 500 LEI Weight: 7.2000 g. **Composition:** 0.9000 Gold .2038 oz. AGW **Subject:** 2,050th Anniversary of First Independent State

Date		F	VF	XF	Unc	BU
1982FM Proof	7,500	Value: 360				
1983FM Proof	7,000	Value: 380				
1983FM Proof	1,000	Value: 520				

Note: Serially numbered on edges

KM# 101 1000 LEI Weight: 14.4000 g. **Composition:** 0.9000 Gold .4167 oz. AGW **Subject:** 2,050th Anniversary of First Independent State **Obverse:** Similar to 500 Lei, KM#99

Date		F	VF	XF	Unc	BU
1983FM Proof	7,000	Value: 560				
1983FM Proof	1,000	Value: 900				

Note: Serially numbered on edges

REPUBLIC

STANDARD COINAGE

KM# 113 LEU Weight: 2.5000 g. **Composition:** Copper Clad Steel **Subject:** National Bank of Romania **Edge:** Plain

Date	F	VF	XF	Unc	BU
1992	0.10	0.40	0.80	3.00	—

KM# 115 LEU Composition: Copper Clad Steel **Reverse:** Coat of arms

Date	Mintage	F	VF	XF	Unc	BU
1993		—	0.10	0.25	1.50	—
1994		—	—	0.20	1.00	—
1995		—	—	0.10	1.00	—
1996		—	0.50	1.00	4.00	—
2000 In proof sets only	4,500	Value: 4.50				
2002 In proof sets only	1,500	Value: 5.00				

KM# 112 5 LEI Weight: 3.3500 g. **Composition:** Aluminum **Subject:** Prince Mahai Viteazul **Note:** Similar to 100 Lei, KM#111. Not released for circulation; majority were melted.

Date	F	VF	XF	Unc	BU
1991	—	—	—	95.00	—

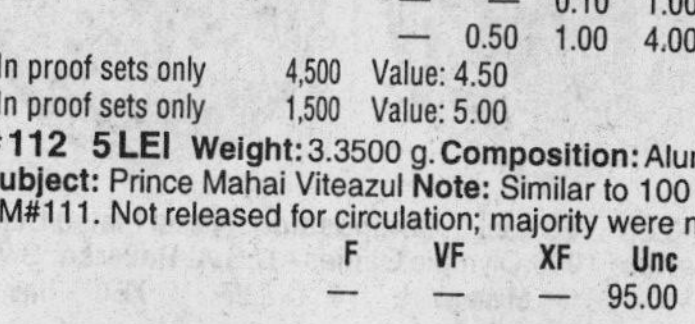

KM# 114 5 LEI Composition: Nickel Plated Steel **Edge:** Plain

Date	Mintage	F	VF	XF	Unc	BU
1992 CD VG		—	0.25	0.60	3.00	—
1993 CD		—	—	0.30	2.00	—
1994		—	—	0.20	1.00	—
1995		—	—	0.20	1.00	—
2000 In proof sets only	4,500	Value: 4.50				
2002 In proof sets only	1,500	Value: 5.00				

KM# 108 10 LEI Weight: 4.6500 g. **Composition:** Nickel-Clad Steel **Subject:** Revolution Anniversary **Note:** Rotated die varieties exist.

Date	Mintage	F	VF	XF	Unc	BU
1990	30,000,000	—	0.50	1.00	3.00	—
1991	31,303,000	—	0.25	0.60	2.00	—
1992	60,000,000	—	0.25	0.50	1.00	—

KM# 116 10 LEI Composition: Nickel-Clad Steel

Date	Mintage	F	VF	XF	Unc	BU
1993		—	0.75	1.50	3.50	—
1994		—	0.50	1.00	3.00	—
1995		—	—	0.30	1.00	—
1996		—	—	—	—	—
2000 In proof set only	4,500	Value: 4.50				
2002 In proof sets only	1,500	Value: 6.00				

KM# 117.1 10 LEI Composition: Nickel Plated Steel **Series:** F.A.O. **Subject:** 50 Years - F.A.O. **Edge:** Plain

Date	Mintage	F	VF	XF	Unc	BU
1995	200,000	—	—	2.00	5.00	—

KM# 117.2 10 LEI Composition: Nickel Plated Steel **Series:** F.A.O. **Subject:** 50 Years - F.A.O. **Obverse:** N in diamond at right for Numismatists

Date	Mintage	F	VF	XF	Unc	BU
1995	30,000	—	—	3.00	7.50	—

KM# 120 10 LEI Composition: Nickel Plated Steel **Series:** 1996 Olympic Games - U.S.A. **Reverse:** Swimmer

Date	Mintage	F	VF	XF	Unc	BU
1996	10,000	—	—	—	7.00	—

KM# 121 10 LEI Composition: Nickel Plated Steel **Series:** 1996 Olympic Games - U.S.A. **Reverse:** Four Olympic scenes

Date	Mintage	F	VF	XF	Unc	BU
1996	10,000	—	—	—	7.00	—

KM# 122 10 LEI Composition: Nickel Plated Steel **Series:** 1996 Olympic Games - U.S.A. **Reverse:** Windsurfer

Date	Mintage	F	VF	XF	Unc	BU
1996	10,000	—	—	—	7.00	—

KM# 123 10 LEI Composition: Nickel Plated Steel **Series:** 1996 Olympic Games - U.S.A. **Reverse:** Sailboat with two racers

Date	Mintage	F	VF	XF	Unc	BU
1996	10,000	—	—	—	7.00	—

KM# 124 10 LEI Composition: Nickel Plated Steel **Series:** 1996 Olympic Games - U.S.A. **Reverse:** Canoe with two racers

Date	Mintage	F	VF	XF	Unc	BU
1996	10,000	—	—	—	7.00	—

KM# 125 10 LEI Composition: Nickel Plated Steel **Series:** 1996 Olympic Games - U.S.A. **Reverse:** Scullcraft with racers

Date	Mintage	F	VF	XF	Unc	BU
1996	10,000	—	—	—	7.00	—

KM# 126 10 LEI Composition: Nickel Plated Steel **Subject:** World Food Summit - Rome

Date	Mintage	F	VF	XF	Unc	BU
1996	50,000	—	—	—	5.00	—

KM# 134 10 LEI Composition: Nickel Plated Steel **Subject:** Euro Soccer **Reverse:** Players

Date	Mintage	F	VF	XF	Unc	BU
1996	50,000	—	—	—	5.50	—

KM# 109 20 LEI Weight: 5.0000 g. **Composition:** Brass Clad Steel **Obverse:** Bust of King Stefan Cel Mare **Edge:** Plain **Note:** Date varieties exist.

Date	Mintage	F	VF	XF	Unc	BU
1991		—	—	1.00	2.50	—
1992		—	—	0.60	2.50	—
1993		—	—	0.50	2.25	—
1994		—	—	1.25	3.00	—
1995		—	—	0.75	3.00	—

Date	Mintage	F	VF	XF	Unc	BU
1996		—	0.75	1.50	6.00	—
2000 In proof sets only	4,500	Value: 6.00				
2002 In proof sets only	1,500	Value: 7.50				

KM# 110 50 LEI Weight: 5.9000 g. **Composition:** Brass Clad Steel **Obverse:** Bust of Prince Alexandru Ioan Cuza **Edge:** Plain

Date	Mintage	F	VF	XF	Unc	BU
1991		—	—	1.50	3.00	—
1992		—	—	1.00	1.85	—

Note: 1992 date varieties exist

Date	Mintage	F	VF	XF	Unc	BU
1993		—	—	1.00	1.85	—
1994		—	—	1.00	2.00	—
1995		—	—	1.00	2.00	—
1996		—	—	1.00	3.50	—
2000 In proof sets only	4,500	Value: 7.00				
2002 In proof sets only	1,500	Value: 8.00				

KM# 159 50 LEI Weight: 15.5510 g. **Composition:** 0.9990 Silver 0.4995 oz. ASW **Series:** Romanian Aviation **Obverse:** AVIONUL VUIA 1 - 1906 airplane **Reverse:** Portrait of Traian Vuia **Edge:** Plain **Shape:** Octagonal **Size:** 31.1 mm.

Date	Mintage	F	VF	XF	Unc	BU
2001 Proof	500	Value: 50.00				

KM# 160 50 LEI Weight: 15.5510 g. **Composition:** 0.9990 Silver 0.4995 oz. ASW **Series:** Romanian Aviation **Obverse:** Avionul Coanda 1910, world's first (?) jet airplane **Reverse:** Portrait of Henri Coanda **Edge:** Plain **Shape:** Octagonal **Size:** 31.1 mm.

Date	Mintage	F	VF	XF	Unc	BU
2001 Proof	500	Value: 50.00				

KM# 161 50 LEI Weight: 15.5510 g. **Composition:** 0.9990 Silver 0.4995 oz. ASW **Series:** Romanian Aviation **Obverse:** IAR CV-11 airplane **Reverse:** Elie Carafoli portrait **Edge:** Plain **Shape:** Octagonal **Size:** 31.1 mm.

Date	Mintage	F	VF	XF	Unc	BU
2001 Proof	500	Value: 50.00				

KM# 111 100 LEI Weight: 8.7500 g. **Composition:** Nickel Plated Steel **Obverse:** Bust of Prince Miahai Viteazul **Edge Lettering:** ROMANIA

Date	Mintage	F	VF	XF	Unc	BU
1991		—	—	2.50	6.00	—
1992		—	—	1.50	3.00	—

Note: Reported edge varieties for 1992 with TOTUL PENTRU TARA; without ROMANIA are presumed mint errors

Date	Mintage	F	VF	XF	Unc	BU
1993		—	—	1.50	3.00	—
1994		—	—	1.50	2.50	—
1995		—	—	1.50	3.00	—
1996		—	—	2.50	8.00	—
2000 In proof sets only	4,500	Value: 7.50				
2002 In proof sets only	1,500	Value: 8.00				

KM# 118 100 LEI Weight: 27.5000 g. **Composition:** 0.9250 Silver .8178 oz. ASW **Series:** F.A.O. **Subject:** 50 Years - F.A.O.

Date	Mintage	F	VF	XF	Unc	BU
1995	30,000	—	—	—	22.50	—

KM# 119 100 LEI Weight: 27.0000 g. **Composition:** 0.9250 Silver .8030 oz. ASW **Subject:** Euro Soccer **Reverse:** Players

Date	Mintage	F	VF	XF	Unc	BU
1996 Proof	12,000	Value: 25.00				

KM# 127 100 LEI Weight: 27.0000 g. **Composition:** 0.9250 Silver .8030 oz. ASW **Series:** 1996 Olympic Games - U.S.A. **Reverse:** Swimmer

Date	Mintage	F	VF	XF	Unc	BU
1996 Proof	10,000	Value: 25.00				

KM# 128 100 LEI Weight: 27.0000 g. **Composition:** 0.9250 Silver .8030 oz. ASW **Series:** 1996 Olympic Games - U.S.A. **Reverse:** Four Olympic scenes

Date	Mintage	F	VF	XF	Unc	BU
1996 Proof	10,000	Value: 27.50				

KM# 129 100 LEI Weight: 27.0000 g. **Composition:** 0.9250 Silver .8030 oz. ASW **Series:** 1996 Olympic Games - U.S.A. **Reverse:** Windsurfer

Date	Mintage	F	VF	XF	Unc	BU
1996 Proof	10,000	Value: 26.50				

KM# 130 100 LEI Weight: 27.0000 g. **Composition:** 0.9250 Silver .8030 oz. ASW **Series:** 1996 Olympic Games - U.S.A. **Reverse:** Sailboat with three crewmen

Date	Mintage	F	VF	XF	Unc	BU
1996 Proof	10,000	Value: 26.50				

KM# 131 100 LEI Weight: 27.0000 g. **Composition:** 0.9250 Silver .8030 oz. ASW **Series:** 1996 Olympic Games - U.S.A. **Reverse:** Canoe with two canoeists

Date	Mintage	F	VF	XF	Unc	BU
1996 Proof	10,000	Value: 27.50				

KM# 132 100 LEI Weight: 27.0000 g. **Composition:** 0.9250 Silver .8030 oz. ASW **Series:** 1996 Olympic Games - U.S.A. **Reverse:** Scullcraft with rowers

Date	Mintage	F	VF	XF	Unc	BU
1996 Proof	10,000	Value: 27.50				

KM# 133 100 LEI Weight: 27.5000 g. **Composition:** 0.9250 Silver .8178 oz. ASW **Subject:** World Food Summit - Rome

Date	Mintage	F	VF	XF	Unc	BU
1996 Proof	5,000	Value: 32.50				

KM# 135 100 LEI Weight: 27.0000 g. **Composition:** 0.9250 Silver .8030 oz. ASW **Subject:** 50th Anniversary - UNICEF

Date	Mintage	F	VF	XF	Unc	BU
1996 Proof	5,000	Value: 32.50				

KM# 138 100 LEI Weight: 27.0000 g. **Composition:** 0.9250 Silver .8030 oz. ASW **Subject:** 120th Anniversary of Independence **Obverse:** National arms above denomination **Reverse:** Three soldiers, flag, and cannon

Date	Mintage	F	VF	XF	Unc	BU
1998 Proof	Est. 5,000	Value: 37.50				

KM# 139 100 LEI Weight: 27.0000 g. **Composition:** 0.9250 Silver .8030 oz. ASW **Subject:** Andrei Saguna **Obverse:** National arms divide denomination **Reverse:** Portrait, church towers, and date

Date	Mintage	F	VF	XF	Unc	BU
1998 Proof	2,000	Value: 45.00				

KM# 140 100 LEI Weight: 27.0000 g. **Composition:** 0.9250 Silver .8030 oz. ASW **Series:** Olympic Games - Nagano 1998 **Reverse:** Bobsled

Date	Mintage	F	VF	XF	Unc	BU
1998 Proof	2,000	Value: 42.50				

KM# 141 100 LEI Weight: 27.0000 g. **Composition:** 0.9250 Silver .8030 oz. ASW **Series:** Olympic Games - Nagano 1998 **Reverse:** Figure skaters

Date	Mintage	F	VF	XF	Unc	BU
1998 Proof	2,000	Value: 42.50				

KM# 142 100 LEI Weight: 27.0000 g. **Composition:** 0.9250 Silver .8030 oz. ASW **Series:** Olympic Games - Nagano 1998 **Reverse:** Slalom

Date	Mintage	F	VF	XF	Unc	BU
1998 Proof	2,000	Value: 40.00				

KM# 143 100 LEI Weight: 27.0000 g. **Composition:** 0.9250 Silver .8030 oz. ASW **Subject:** World Cup Soccer - France 1998 **Reverse:** Eiffel Tower

Date	Mintage	F	VF	XF	Unc	BU
1998 Proof	5,000	Value: 37.50				

KM# 149 100 LEI Weight: 27.0000 g. **Composition:** 0.9250 Silver .8030 oz. ASW **Subject:** Visit of Pope John Paul II **Obverse:** National arms **Reverse:** Portraits of Pope and Patriarch Theoctist

Date	Mintage	F	VF	XF	Unc	BU
1999 Proof	2,000	Value: 47.50				

KM# 148 100 LEI Weight: 27.0000 g. **Composition:** 0.9250 Silver .8030 oz. ASW **Subject:** 100th Anniversary - Belgica Expedition **Obverse:** National arms **Reverse:** Silhouette of Belgica ship, bust of scientist Emil Racovita

Date	Mintage	F	VF	XF	Unc	BU
1999 Proof	20,000	Value: 32.50				

KM# 136 500 LEI Weight: 8.6400 g. **Composition:** 0.9000 Gold .25 oz. AGW **Subject:** Revolution of 1848

Date	Mintage	F	VF	XF	Unc	BU
1998 Proof	Est. 2,000	Value: 275				

KM# 145 500 LEI Weight: 3.7000 g. **Composition:** Aluminum **Obverse:** Denomination **Reverse:** National arms **Edge:** Lettered **Edge Lettering:** ROMANIA (three times)

Date	Mintage	F	VF	XF	Unc	BU
1998	—	—	—	—	2.00	—
1999	—	—	—	0.50	1.50	—
2000	—	—	—	0.50	1.50	—
2000 In proof sets only	4,500	Value: 6.00				
2001	—	—	—	0.50	1.50	—
2002 In proof sets only	1,500	Value: 7.00				

KM# 146 500 LEI Composition: Aluminum **Obverse:** National arms **Reverse:** Solar eclipse **Edge:** Lettered **Edge Lettering:** ROMANIA (three times)

Date	Mintage	VG	F	VF	XF	Unc
1999 Proof	3,000	Value: 15.00				

KM# 147 500 LEI Composition: Aluminum **Subject:** Solar eclipse **Obverse:** National arms, eclipse and observatory **Reverse:** Solar eclipse **Edge:** Lettered **Edge Lettering:** ROMANIA (3x) **Note:** This design never gained broad release and is considered to be a pattern by several authorities

Date	Mintage	VG	F	VF	XF	Unc
1999	4,000,000	—	—	—	—	3.00

KM# 154 500 LEI Weight: 27.0000 g. **Composition:** 0.9990 Silver .8030 oz. ASW **Subject:** Alexander the Good of Moldavia **Obverse:** Old seal design and denomination **Reverse:** Crowned portrait **Edge:** Plain **Size:** 37 mm.

Date	Mintage	F	VF	XF	Unc	BU
2000 Proof	Est. 1,000	Value: 60.00				

KM# 137 1000 LEI Weight: 31.1035 g. **Composition:** 0.9990 Gold 1 oz. AGW **Subject:** Revolution of 1848

Date	Mintage	F	VF	XF	Unc	BU
1998 Proof	Est. 1,000	Value: 675				

KM# 144 1000 LEI Weight: 31.1035 g. **Composition:** 0.9990 Gold 1 oz. AGW **Subject:** 80th Anniversary - Union of Transylvania **Obverse:** Arms of Wallachia, Moldova and Transylvania

Date	Mintage	F	VF	XF	Unc	BU
1998 Proof	2,000	Value: 650				

KM# 151 1000 LEI Weight: 31.1035 g. **Composition:** 0.9990 Gold 1 oz. AGW **Subject:** Visit of Pope John Paul II **Obverse:** National arms **Reverse:** Portraits of Pope and Patriarch Theoctist

Date	Mintage	F	VF	XF	Unc	BU
1999 Proof	1,000	Value: 700				

KM# 153 1000 LEI Weight: 2.0000 g. **Composition:** Aluminum **Subject:** Constantin Brancoveanu **Obverse:** Denomination above arms **Reverse:** Portrait **Edge:** Reeded and plain sections **Size:** 22.2 mm.

Date	Mintage	VG	F	VF	XF	Unc
2000	—	—	—	—	—	3.00
2000 In proof sets only	4,500	Value: 10.00				
2001	—	—	—	—	—	2.50
2002	—	—	—	—	—	2.50
2002 In proof sets only	1,500	Value: 12.00				

KM# 156 1000 LEI Weight: 15.5510 g. **Composition:** 0.9990 Gold .4995 oz. AGW **Subject:** 1900th Anniversary o the First Roman-Dacian War **Obverse:** Trojan's column **Reverse:** Monument and cameo portraits of Trajan and Kin Decebal **Edge:** Plain **Size:** 27 mm.

Date	Mintage	VG	F	VF	XF	Un
2001 Proof	500	Value: 400				

KM# 157 2000 LEI Weight: 31.1030 g. **Composition:** 0.9990 Gold .9990 oz. AGW **Obverse:** National arms and quill **Reverse:** Mihai Eminesu **Edge:** Plain **Size:** 35 mm.

Date	Mintage	VG	F	VF	XF	Ur
2000 Proof	1,500	Value: 675				

KM# 155 5000 LEI Weight: 31.1030 g. **Composition:** 0.9990 Gold .9990 oz. AGW **Subject:** Michael the Brave's Unification of Romania in 1600 **Obverse:** National arms an old seal **Reverse:** Mihai Viteazu **Edge:** Plain **Size:** 35 mm

Date	Mintage	F	VF	XF	Unc	B
2000 Proof	Est. 1,500	Value: 725				

KM# 158 5000 LEI Weight: 2.5200 g. **Composition:** Aluminum **Obverse:** Denomination and country name **Reverse:** National arms and date **Edge:** Plain **Shape:** 12-sided **Size:** 23.5 mm.

Date	Mintage	F	VF	XF	Unc	B
2001	—	—	—	—	0.25	–
2002	—	—	—	—	0.25	–
2002 Proof	1,500	Value: 15.00				

KM# 162 5000 LEI Weight: 31.1035 g. **Composition:** 0.9990 Gold 0.999 oz. AGW **Subject:** Constantin Brancus 125th Anniversary of Birth **Obverse:** National arms, denomination and sculpture **Reverse:** Bearded portrait **Edge:** Plain **Size:** 35 mm.

Date	Mintage	F	VF	XF	Unc	B
2001 Proof	500	Value: 750				

ESSAIS

KM#	Date	Mintage	Identification	Mkt Val
E1	1905	—	10 Bani. Copper-Nickel. KM29. With center hole.	200

KM#	Date	Mintage	Identification	Mkt Val
E2	1910	—	50 Bani. Silver.	300
E3	1910	—	Leu. Silver.	300
E4	1910	—	2 Lei. Silver.	300
E5	1914	—	50 Bani. Silver.	200
E6	1914	—	50 Bani. Silver. KM41	150
E7	1914	—	Leu. Silver.	250
E8	1914	—	Leu. Silver. KM42.	—

KM#	Date	Mintage	Identification	Mkt Val
E9	1914	—	2 Lei. Silver.	275
E10	1914	—	2 Lei. Silver. KM43.	—
E11	1924	—	2 Lei. Silver.	125

PATTERNS

Including off metal strikes

KM#	Date	Mintage	Identification	Mkt Val
Pn49	1905	—	5 Bani. White Metal. KM28.	100
Pn50	1905	—	5 Bani. Pewter. KM28.	—
Pn51	1905	—	5 Bani. Aluminum. KM28.	—
Pn52	1905	—	5 Bani. Zinc. KM28.	—
Pn53	1905	—	5 Bani. Bronze. KM28.	—
Pn54	1905	—	5 Bani. Brass. KM28.	125
Pn55	1905	—	5 Bani. Copper. KM28. With center hole.	125
Pn56	1905	—	5 Bani. Copper. KM28.	500
Pn57	1905	—	5 Bani. Gilt Copper. KM28.	—
Pn58	1905	—	5 Bani. Silver. KM31. Without center hole.	250
Pn59	1905	—	5 Bani. Bronze. KM31. Without center hole.	—
Pn60	1905	—	5 Bani. Pewter. KM31. Without center hole.	100
Pn61	1905	—	5 Bani. Aluminum. KM31. Without center hole.	—
Pn62	1905	—	5 Bani. Zinc. KM31. Without center hole.	—
Pn63	1905	—	5 Bani. Copper-Nickel. KM31. Without center hole.	—
Pn64	1905	—	5 Bani. Gold. Without center hole.	1,500
Pn65	1905	—	5 Bani. Gold. Without center hole.	1,200
PnA66	1905	—	10 Bani. White Metal. With center hole.	—
PnB66	1905	—	10 Bani. White Metal. Without center hole.	—
Pn66	1905	—	10 Bani. Pewter. KM29. With center hole.	125
Pn67	1905	—	10 Bani. Brass. KM29. With center hole.	125
Pn68	1905	—	10 Bani. Aluminum. KM29. With center hole.	75.00
PnA69	1905	—	10 Bani. Bronze. KM29. Red. With center hole.	—
Pn69	1905	—	10 Bani. Bronze. KM29. Red. Without center hole.	100
Pn70	1905	—	10 Bani. Bronze. KM29. Green. Without center hole.	100
Pn71	1905	—	10 Bani. Zinc. KM29.	160
PnA72	1905	—	10 Bani. Gilt Bronze. KM29. With center hole.	—
Pn72	1905	—	10 Bani. Gilt Bronze. KM29. Without center hole.	100
Pn73	1905	—	10 Bani. Copper-Nickel-Zinc. With center hole.	150
Pn74	1905	—	10 Bani. Nickel. KM29. With center hole.	—
Pn75	1905	—	10 Bani. Silver. KM29. Without center hole.	350
Pn76	1905	—	10 Bani. Silver. KM29. With center hole.	250
PnA77	1905	—	10 Bani. Gilt Copper. With branches and small date. Without center hole.	—
Pn77	1905	—	10 Bani. Copper. KM29. Without center hole.	100
Pn78	1905	—	10 Bani. Gold. Without branches. KM29. Without center hole.	1,650
Pn79	1905	—	10 Bani. Gold. KM29. With center hole.	1,400
Pn80	1905	—	10 Bani. Pewter. KM32. Without center hole.	150
Pn81	1905	—	10 Bani. Brass. KM32. Without center hole.	150
Pn82	1905	—	10 Bani. Aluminum. KM32. Without center hole.	100
Pn83	1905	—	10 Bani. Bronze. KM32. Without center hole.	125
Pn84	1905	—	10 Bani. Gold. KM32. Without center hole.	1,250
Pn85	1905	—	20 Bani. Lead. KM30.	100
Pn86	1905	—	20 Bani. Brass. KM30.	150
Pn87	1905	—	20 Bani. Copper. KM30.	125
Pn88	1905	—	20 Bani. Aluminum. KM30.	100
Pn89	1905	—	20 Bani. White Metal. KM30.	100
Pn90	1905	—	20 Bani. Zinc. KM30.	—
Pn91	1905	—	20 Bani. Pewter. KM30.	—
Pn92	1905	—	20 Bani. Gilt Bronze. KM30.	125
PnA93	1905	—	20 Bani. Bronze. KM30.	—
Pn93	1905	—	20 Bani. Silver. KM30.	250
Pn94	1905	—	20 Bani. Gold. Without center hole.	1,750
Pn95	1905	—	20 Bani. Gold. With center hole.	1,500
Pn96	1905	—	20 Bani. Brass. KM33. Without center hole.	—
Pn97	1905	—	20 Bani. Copper. KM33. Without center hole.	200
Pn98	1905	—	20 Bani. Aluminum. KM33. Without center hole.	—
Pn99	1905	—	20 Bani. Pewter. KM33. Without center hole.	200
Pn100	1905	—	20 Bani. Silver. KM33. Without center hole.	400
Pn101	1906	—	Leu. White Metal.	125
Pn102	1906	—	Leu. Brass.	150
Pn103	1906	—	Leu. Aluminum.	100
Pn104	1906	—	Leu. Copper.	125
Pn105	1906	—	Leu. Gilt Bronze.	125
Pn106	1906	—	Leu. Copper-Nickel.	—
Pn107	1906	—	Leu. Gilt Bronze.	125
Pn108	1906	—	Leu. Silver.	250
Pn109	1906	—	Leu. Gold.	—
Pn110	1906	—	5 Lei. Silver.	4,500
Pn111	1906	—	12-1/2 Lei. Lead.	250
Pn112	1906	—	12-1/2 Lei. White Metal.	250
Pn113	1906	—	12-1/2 Lei. Brass.	250
Pn114	1906	—	12-1/2 Lei. Pewter.	—
Pn115	1906	—	12-1/2 Lei. Gilt Bronze.	250
PnA116	1906	—	12-1/2 Lei. Bronze. Plain edge.	250
Pn116	1906	—	12-1/2 Lei. Aluminum.	250
Pn117	1906	—	12-1/2 Lei. Aluminum. Gilt.	250
Pn118	1906	—	12-1/2 Lei. Copper.	350
Pn119	1906	—	12-1/2 Lei. Copper-Nickel.	—
Pn120	1906	—	12-1/2 Lei. Silver.	550
Pn121	1906	—	12-1/2 Lei. Gold.	1,200
Pn122	1906	—	12-1/2 Lei. Gold. Pale.	2,150
Pn123	1906	—	20 Lei. Copper.	350
Pn124	1906	—	20 Lei. Bronze.	200
Pn125	1906	—	20 Lei. White Metal.	—
Pn126	1906	—	20 Lei. White Metal. Gilt.	—
Pn127	1906	—	20 Lei. Gold.	1,200
Pn128	1906	—	20 Lei. Gold. Pale.	2,150
Pn129	1906	—	25 Lei. Pewter.	250
Pn130	1906	—	25 Lei. Zinc.	400
Pn131	1906	—	25 Lei. Lead.	200
Pn132	1906	—	25 Lei. Copper.	175
Pn133	1906	—	25 Lei. Gilt Copper.	—
Pn134	1906	—	25 Lei. Aluminum.	175
Pn135	1906	—	25 Lei. Brass.	175
Pn136	1906	—	25 Lei. Bronze. Antique.	175
Pn137	1906	—	25 Lei. Gilt Bronze.	175
Pn138	1906	—	25 Lei. Silver.	800
Pn139	1906	—	25 Lei. Gold.	2,400
Pn140	1906	—	25 Lei. Gold. Pale.	4,000
Pn141	1906	—	50 Lei. Aluminum.	350
Pn142	1906	—	50 Lei. Bronze.	400
Pn143	1906	—	50 Lei. White Metal.	—
Pn144	1906	—	50 Lei. Pewter.	425
Pn145	1906	—	50 Lei. Brass.	400
Pn146	1906	—	50 Lei. Silver.	850
Pn147	1906	12	50 Lei. Gold.	12,500
Pn148	1906	—	100 Lei. Copper.	650
Pn149	1906	—	100 Lei. Bronze.	650
Pn150	1906	—	100 Lei. Silver.	—
Pn151	1906	—	100 Lei. Gold.	5,000
PnA152	1910	—	10 Bani. Zinc.	—
Pn152	1910	—	10 Bani. Copper.	—
Pn153	1910	—	50 Bani. Lead.	—
Pn154	1910	—	50 Bani. Tin.	—
PnA155	1910	—	50 Bani. Pewter. Plain edge.	—
Pn155	1910	—	50 Bani. Pewter. Milled edge.	100
Pn156	1910	—	50 Bani. White Metal.	75.00
Pn157	1910	—	50 Bani. Aluminum.	60.00
Pn158	1910	—	50 Bani. Zinc.	—
Pn159	1910	—	50 Bani. Copper.	—
Pn160	1910	—	50 Bani. Copper-Nickel.	—
Pn161	1910	—	50 Bani. Brass.	75.00
PnA162	1910	—	50 Bani. Bronze. Plain edge. Thin planchet.	—
PnB162	1910	—	50 Bani. Bronze. Plain edge. Thick planchet.	—
PnC162	1910	—	50 Bani. Bronze. Milled edge. Thin planchet.	—
PnD162	1910	—	50 Bani. Bronze. Milled edge. Thick planchet.	—
Pn162	1910	—	50 Bani. Nickel.	100
Pn163	1910	—	Leu. Lead.	100
Pn164	1910	—	Leu. Aluminum.	100
Pn165	1910	—	Leu. Bronze.	85.00
Pn166	1910	—	Leu. Gilt Bronze.	85.00
Pn167	1910	—	Leu. Pewter.	125
Pn168	1910	—	Leu. Zinc.	—
PnA169	1910	—	Leu. Gilt Copper.	—
Pn169	1910	—	Leu. Copper.	—
Pn170	1910	—	Leu. Copper-Nickel.	—
Pn171	1910	—	2 Lei. Lead.	100
Pn172	1910	—	2 Lei. Tin.	150
Pn173	1910	—	2 Lei. Pewter.	150
Pn174	1910	—	2 Lei. Aluminum.	100
Pn175	1910	—	2 Lei. Brass.	100
PnA176	1910	—	2 Lei. Gilt Copper.	—
Pn176	1910	—	2 Lei. Copper.	—
Pn177	1910	—	2 Lei. Gilt Bronze.	100
PnA178	1910	—	2 Lei. Bronze.	—
Pn178	1910	—	2 Lei. Nickel.	—
PnA179	1910	—	2 Lei. Silver.	—
Pn179	1921	—	25 Bani. Aluminum. HF at left of date.	125
PnA180	1921	—	25 Bani. Bronze. HF at left of date.	200
PnB180	1921	—	25 Bani. Copper-Nickel.	185
PnC180	1921	—	25 Bani. Bronze. Without hole.	185
PnD180	1921	—	25 Bani. Nickel.	200
Pn180	1921	—	50 Bani. Nickel.	200
PnA181	1921	—	50 Bani. Bronze.	200
Pn181	1921	—	1.25 Leu. Nickel.	325
PnA182	1921	—	5 Lei. Billon. Arms, cornucopia. Hand numbered 1-15. Struck at Paris.	—
Pn182	1921	—	5 Lei. Copper-Nickel.	450
Pn183	1921	—	5 Lei. Nickel.	—
Pn184	1922	—	25 Bani. Aluminum.	—
Pn185	1922	—	50 Bani. Aluminum.	175
Pn186	1922	—	Leu. Bronze.	220
Pn187	1922	—	Leu. Nickel.	250
Pn188	1922	—	Leu. Copper-Nickel.	210
Pn189	1922	—	2 Lei. Bronze.	250
Pn190	1922	—	2 Lei. Nickel.	250
Pn191	1922	—	2 Lei. Brass.	150
Pn192	1922	—	5 Lei. Bronze.	285
Pn193	1922	—	5 Lei. Copper-Nickel.	285
Pn194	1922	—	5 Lei. Nickel.	265
Pn195	1922	—	5 Lei. Brass.	265
Pn196	1922	—	5 Lei. Copper-Nickel.	265
Pn197	1922	—	20 Lei. Gold.	2,000
Pn198	1922	—	25 Lei. Gold.	2,500
Pn199	1922	—	50 Lei. Gold.	4,000
Pn200	1922	—	100 Lei. Gold.	5,500
PnA201	1923	—	Leu. Nickel.	275
Pn201	1924	—	Leu. Nickel.	65.00
Pn202	1924	—	Leu. Aluminum.	45.00
Pn203	1924	—	Leu. Tin.	45.00
Pn204	1924	—	Leu. Zinc.	—
Pn205	1924	—	Leu. Copper.	—
Pn206	1924	—	Leu. Brass.	110
Pn207	1924	—	Leu. Bronze.	60.00
Pn208	1924	—	Leu. Gilt Bronze.	50.00
Pn209	1924	—	Leu. Silver. Plain edge.	125
Pn210	1924	—	Leu. Silver. Reeded edge.	125
Pn211	1924	—	2 Lei. Zinc.	75.00
Pn212	1924	—	2 Lei. Aluminum.	50.00
Pn213	1924	—	2 Lei. Tin.	—
Pn214	1924	—	2 Lei. Bronze.	240
Pn215	1924	—	2 Lei. Brass.	100
Pn216	1924	—	2 Lei. Copper.	65.00
Pn217	1924	—	2 Lei. Nickel.	75.00
PnA217	1924	—	2 Lei. Copper-Nickel.	—
Pn218	1924	—	2 Lei. Silver. Plain edge. Thick planchet.	200
PnA219	1930	—	10 Lei. Copper-Nickel. KM49.	100
Pn219	1930	—	20 Lei. Gold. Plain.	—
Pn220	1930	—	20 Lei. Gold. Ornamented.	—
Pn221	1930	—	100 Lei. Gold. Plain.	—
Pn222	1930	—	100 Lei. Gold. Ornamented.	—
Pn223	1931	—	20 Lei. Gold. Plain.	—
Pn224	1931	—	20 Lei. Gold. Ornamented.	—
Pn225	1931	—	100 Lei. Gold. Plain.	—
Pn226	1931	—	100 Lei. Gold. Ornamented.	—
Pn227	1932	—	20 Lei. Gold. Plain.	—
Pn228	1932	—	20 Lei. Gold. Ornamented.	—
Pn229	1932	—	100 Lei. Silver. Y62.	75.00
Pn230	1932	—	100 Lei. Gold. Plain.	—
Pn231	1932	—	100 Lei. Gold. Ornamented.	—
Pn232	1933	—	20 Lei. Gold. Plain.	—
Pn233	1933	—	20 Lei. Gold. Ornamented.	—
Pn234	1933	—	100 Lei. Gold. Plain.	—
Pn235	1933	—	100 Lei. Gold. Ornamented.	—
Pn236	1934	—	20 Lei. Gold. Plain.	—
Pn237	1934	—	20 Lei. Gold. Ornamented.	—
Pn238	1934	—	100 Lei. Gold. Plain.	—
Pn239	1934	—	100 Lei. Gold. Ornamented.	—
Pn240	1935	—	20 Lei. Gold. Plain.	—
Pn241	1935	—	20 Lei. Gold. Ornamented.	—
Pn242	1935	—	50 Lei. Silver.	—
Pn243	1935	—	100 Lei. Gold. Plain.	—
Pn244	1935	—	100 Lei. Gold. Ornamented.	—
Pn245	1935	—	200 Lei. Silver.	450
PnA245	1935	—	250 Lei. Nickel.	—
PnB245	1935	—	250 Lei. Brass.	—

KM#	Date	Mintage	Identification	Mkt Val
Pn246	1936	—	20 Lei. Gold. Plain.	—
Pn247	1936	—	20 Lei. Gold. Ornamented.	—
Pn248	1936	—	50 Lei. Nickel.	—
Pn249	1936	—	100 Lei. Gold. Plain.	—
Pn250	1936	—	100 Lei. Gold. Ornamented.	—
PnA251	1937	—	50 Lei. Nickel. KM55.	12.00
Pn251	1937	—	Leu. Copper-Nickel-Zinc.	—
Pn252	ND 1937	—	Leu. Copper-Nickel-Zinc.	—
Pn253	1937	—	2 Lei. Copper-Nickel-Zinc.	—
Pn254	1937	—	20 Lei. Gold. Plain.	—
Pn255	1937	—	20 Lei. Gold. Ornamented.	—
Pn256	1937	—	50 Lei. Copper-Nickel-Zinc.	240
Pn257	1937	—	100 Lei. Gold. Plain.	—
Pn258	1937	—	100 Lei. Gold. Ornamented.	—
Pn259	1938	—	Leu. Copper-Nickel-Zinc.	—
Pn260	1938	—	20 Lei. Gold. Plain.	—
Pn261	1938	—	20 Lei. Gold. Ornamented.	—
Pn262	1938	—	100 Lei. Gold. Plain.	—
Pn263	1938	—	100 Lei. Gold. Ornamented.	—
Pn264	1939	—	20 Lei. Gold. Plain.	—
Pn265	1939	—	20 Lei. Gold. Ornamented.	—
Pn266	1939	—	20 Lei. Gold. Arms.	—
Pn267	1939	—	20 Lei. Gold. Eagle.	—
Pn268	1939	—	100 Lei. Gold. Plain.	—
Pn269	1939	—	100 Lei. Gold. Ornamented.	—
Pn270	1939	—	100 Lei. Gold. Bust.	—
Pn271	1940	—	20 Lei. Gold. Plain.	—
Pn272	1940	—	20 Lei. Gold. Ornamented.	—
Pn273	1940	—	100 Lei. Gold. Plain.	—
Pn274	1940	—	100 Lei. Gold. Ornamented.	—
Pn275	1940	—	250 Lei. 0.7500 Silver. Iron guard emblem.	9,000
Pn276	1941	—	Leu. Zinc.	—
Pn277	1941	—	Leu. Copper-Nickel-Zinc.	—
Pn278	1944	—	20 Lei. Copper-Nickel-Zinc.	—
PnA279	1944	—	500 Lei. Silver. Plain edge.	180
Pn279	1944	—	500 Lei. Aluminum.	115
Pn280	1945	—	100 Lei. Nickel Clad Steel.	125
PnA280	1945	—	200 Lei. Aluminum.	—
Pn281	1945	—	500 Lei. Brass. Nickel plated.	125
Pn282	1945	—	2000 Lei. Brass. Nickel plated.	—
PnA283	1946	—	1000 Lei. Aluminum.	—
PnB283	1946	—	500 Lei. Aluminum.	—
Pn283	1946	—	25000 Lei. Silver.	800
PnA284	1952	—	10 Bani. Copper-Nickel. With cogged wheel instead of wreath.	—
PnB284	1956	—	10 Bani. Aluminum.	100
PnC284	1956	—	50 Bani. Aluminum.	150
Pn284	1958	—	5 Bani. Copper-Nickel-Zinc.	100
PnD284	ND 1958	—	5 Bani. Aluminum-Bronze.	—
Pn285	1960	—	10 Bani. Nickel. 20 teeth to wheel.	100
PnA285	1960	—	10 Bani. Nickel. 12 teeth to wheel.	—
PnB285	1966	—	5 Bani. Aluminum.	—
PnC285	1966	—	15 Bani. Aluminum.	—
PnD285	1966	—	15 Bani. Brass.	—
PnE285	1966	—	15 Bani. Copper.	—
PnF285	1966	—	3 Lei. Silver.	—
PnG285	1966	—	5 Lei. Copper. Factory.	—
PnH285	1966	—	5 Lei. Copper.	—
PnI285	1966	—	5 Lei. Brass.	—
PnJ285	1984	—	100 Lei. Silver.	—
PnK285	ND (1984)	—	100 Lei.	—
PnL285	1987	—	2 Lei. Nickel Plated Steel.	180
Pn286	1987	—	10 Lei. Nickel. Steel plated.	75.00
Pn287	1987	—	10 Lei. Aluminum.	70.00
Pn288	1987	—	10 Lei. Aluminum.	70.00
Pn289	1987	—	10 Lei. Bronze.	80.00
Pn290	1987	—	10 Lei. Nickel. Steel plated.	75.00
PnA290	1987	—	10 Lei. Nickel Plated Steel.	—
PnB290	1987	—	10 Lei. Aluminum.	—
PnC290	1987	—	10 Lei. Brass.	—
Pn291	1988	—	10 Lei. Aluminum.	75.00
Pn292	1988	—	10 Lei. Aluminum.	75.00
PnA293	1990	—	10 Lei. Aluminum.	100
PnB293	1991	—	Leu. Copper-Nickel. 3 oak leaves.	60.00
Pn293	1991	—	5 Lei. Iron. Nickel clad. Similar to 100 Lei, KM#111.	70.00
Pn294	1991	—	5 Lei. Brass. Similar to 100 Lei, KM#111.	70.00
PnA296	1991	—	20 Lei. Aluminum.	70.00
PnB296	1991	—	20 Lei. Nickel Plated Steel. Similar to 100 Lei, KM#111.	95.00
PnC296	1991	—	50 Lei. Aluminum.	60.00
PnD296	1991	—	50 Lei. Copper-Nickel.	60.00
Pn296	1991	—	50 Lei. Silver. KM110.	150
PnA297	1991	—	100 Lei. Brass. King Stephen.	300
PnB297	1991	—	100 Lei. Brass. Prince M. Viteazul.	200
PnC297	1991	—	100 Lei. Aluminum. Prince M. Viteazul.	150
PnD297	1991	—	100 Lei. Nickel Plated Steel. Lettered edge.	—
PnE297	1991	—	100 Lei. Nickel Plated Steel. Sinus line edge.	90.00
PnF297	1991	—	100 Lei. Nickel Plated Steel. Lettered edge.	90.00
PnG297	1991	—	100 Lei. Nickel Plated Steel. Lettered edge.	90.00
PnH297	ND (1992)	—	Leu. Nickel.	—
Pn297	1992	—	Leu. Silver.	100
Pn298	ND (1992)	—	Leu. Nickel.	80.00
PnA299	1992	—	Leu. Silver.	—
PnB299	1992	—	5 Lei. Brass.	70.00
PnC299	1992	—	5 Lei. Copper-Nickel.	70.00
PnD299	1992	—	5 Lei. Nickel Plated Steel.	70.00
Pn299	1992	—	5 Lei. Aluminum.	50.00
PnA300	1993	—	Leu. Copper. Like KM#113.	80.00
pnB300	1995	—	100 Lei. Aluminum. KM#118.	40.00
PnA315.1	1996	125	100 Lei. Aluminum. National arms. Gymnast on balance beam. Plain with denomination edge. Piefort version.	35.00
Pn351.1	1996	125	100 Lei. Aluminum. 37 mm. National arms. Skier. Plain with denomination edge. Piefort version.	35.00
Pn351A1	1996	125	100 Lei. Aluminum. 37 mm. National arms. Skier. Plain with denomination edge. Piefort version.	35.00
Pn351B	1996	125	100 Lei. Copper. 37 mm. National arms. Skier. Plain with denomination edge.	30.00
Pn351B1	1996	125	100 Lei. Copper. 37 mm. National arms. Skier. Plain with denomination edge. Piefort version.	35.00
Pn351C	1996	125	100 Lei. Brass center. Copper-Nickel ring. 37 mm. National arms. Skier. Plain with denomination edge.	35.00
Pn351c1	1996	125	100 Lei. Brass center. Copper-Nickel ring. 37 mm. National arms. Skier. Plain with denomination edge. Piefort version.	40.00
Pn351D	1996	125	100 Lei. 0.9250 Silver. 27.2500 g. 37 mm. National arms. Skier. Plain with denomination edge.	75.00
Pn351D1	1996	125	100 Lei. 0.9250 Silver. 27.2500 g. 37 mm. National arms. Skier. Plain with denomination edge. Piefort version.	90.00
PnD315A	1996	125	100 Lei. Brass. 37 mm. National arms. Tennis player. Plain with denomination edge.	30.00
PnA326	1996	125	100 Lei. Aluminum. 37 mm. National arms. Shooter and target.	30.00
PnA326a	1996	125	100 Lei. Aluminum. Piefort version.	35.00
PnB326	1996	125	100 Lei. Bronze.	30.00
PnB326a	1996	125	100 Lei. Bronze. Piefort version.	35.00
PnC326	1996	125	100 Lei. Copper.	30.00
PnC326a	1996	125	100 Lei. Copper. Piefort version.	35.00
PnD326	1996	125	100 Lei. Bi-Metallic.	35.00
PnD326a	1996	125	100 Lei. Bi-Metallic. Piefort version.	40.00
PnE326	1996	125	100 Lei. 0.9250 Silver. 27.2500 g.	75.00
PnE326a	1996	126	100 Lei. 0.9250 Silver. 27.2500 g. Piefort version.	90.00
PnA315D1	1996	125	100 Lei. 0.9250 Silver. 27.2500 g. 37 mm. Nationl arms. Gymnast on balance beam. Plain with denomination edge. Piefort version.	90.00
PnA315B	1996	125	100 Lei. Copper. 37 mm. National arms. Gymnast on balance beam. Plain with denomination edge.	30.00
PnA315B1	1996	125	100 Lei. Copper. 37 mm. National arms. Gymnast on balance beam. Plain with denomination edge. Piefort version.	35.00
PnA315C	1996	125	100 Lei. Brass center. Copper-Nickel ring. 37 mm. National arms. Gymnast on balance beam. Plain with denomination edge.	35.00
PnA315D	1996	125	100 Lei. 0.9250 Silver. 27.2500 g. 37 mm. National arms. Gymnast on balance beam. Plain with denomination edge.	75.00
PnB315.1	1996	125	100 Lei. Aluminum. 37 mm. National arms. Horse and rider. Plain with denomination edge. Piefert version.	35.00
PnB315A	1996	125	100 Lei. Brass. 37 mm. National arms. Horse and rider. Plain with denomination edge.	30.00
PnB315A1	1996	125	100 Lei. Brass. 37 mm. National arms. Horse and rider. Plain with denomination edge. Piefort version.	35.00
PnB315B	1996	125	100 Lei. Copper. 37 mm. National arms. Horse and rider. Plain with denomination edge.	30.00
PnB315B1	1996	125	100 Lei. Copper. 37 mm. National arms. Horse and rider. Plain with denomination edge. Piefort version.	35.00
PnB315C	1996	125	100 Lei. Brass center. Copper-Nickel ring. 37 mm. National arms. Horse and rider. Plain with denomination edge.	35.00
PnB315C1	1996	125	100 Lei. Brass center. Copper-Nickel ring. 37 mm. National arms. Horse and rider. Plain with denomination edge. Piefort version.	40.00
PnB315E	1996	125	100 Lei. 0.9250 Silver. 27.2500 g. 37 mm. National arms. Horse and rider. Plain with denomination edge.	75.00
PnB315E1	1996	125	100 Lei. 0.9250 Silver. 27.2500 g. 37 mm. National arms. Horse and rider. Plain with denomination edge. Piefort version.	90.00
PnA315a	1996	125	100 Lei. Brass. 37 mm. National arms. Gymnast on balance beam. Plain with denomination edge.	30.00
PnC315.1	1996	125	100 Lei. Aluminum. 37 mm. National arms. Two basketbal players. Plain with denomination edge. Piefort version.	35.00
PnC315A	1996	125	100 Lei. Brass. 37 mm. National arms. Two basketball players. Plain with denomination edge.	30.00
PnC315A1	1996	125	100 Lei. Brass. 37 mm. National arms. Two basketball players. Plain with denomination edge. Piefort version.	35.00
PnC315B	1996	125	100 Lei. Copper. 37 mm. National arms. Two basketball players. Plain with denomination edge.	30.00
PnC315B1	1996	125	100 Lei. Copper. 37 mm. National arms. Two basketball players. Plain with denomination edge. Piefort version.	35.00
PnC315C	1996	125	100 Lei. Brass center. Copper-Nickel ring. 37 mm. National arms. Two basketball players. Plain with denomination edge.	35.00
PnC315C1	1996	125	100 Lei. Brass center. Copper-Nickel ring. 37 mm. National arms. Two basketball players. Plain with denomination edge. Piefort version.	40.00
PnC315D	1996	125	100 Lei. 0.9250 Silver. 27.2500 g. 37 mm. National arms. Two basketball players. Plain with denomination edge.	75.00
PnC315D1	1996	125	100 Lei. 0.9250 Silver. 27.2500 g. 37 mm. National arms. Two basketball players. Plain with denomination edge. Piefort version.	90.00
PnD315.1	1996	125	100 Lei. Aluminum. 37 mm. National arms. Tennis player. Plain with denomination edge. Piefort version.	35.00
	1996	125	100 Lei. Brass. 37 mm. National arms. Tennis player. Plain with denomination edge.	30.00
PnD315A1	1996	125	100 Lei. Brass. 37 mm. National arms. Tennis player. Plain with denomination edge. Piefort version.	35.00
PnD315B	1996	125	100 Lei. Copper. 37 mm. National arms. Tennis player. Plain with denomination edge.	30.00
PnD315B1	1996	125	100 Lei. Copper. 37 mm. National arms. Tennis player. Plain with denomination edge. Piefort version.	35.00
PnD315C	1996	125	100 Lei. Brass center. Copper-Nickel ring. 37 mm. National arms. Tennis player. Plain with denomination edge.	35.00
PnD315C1	1996	125	100 Lei. Brass center. Copper-Nickel ring. 37 mm. National arms. Tennis player. Plain with denomination edge. Piefort version.	40.00
PnD315D	1996	125	100 Lei. 0.9250 Silver. 27.2500 g. 37 mm. National arms. Tennis player. Plain with denomination edge.	75.00
PnD315D1	1996	125	100 Lei. 0.9250 Silver. 27.2500 g. 37 mm. National arms. Tennis player. Plain with denomination edge. Piefort version.	90.00
Pn300	1996	—	10 Lei. Nickel Plated Steel. Similar to KM#117. KM#134.	35.00
Pn301	1996	—	100 Lei. Aluminum. KM#119.	45.00
Pn302	1996	—	100 Lei. Brass. KM#119.	50.00
Pn303	1996	—	100 Lei. Copper-Nickel. KM#127. Brass plated.	45.00
Pn304	1996	—	100 Lei. Aluminum. KM#127.	40.00
Pn305	1996	—	100 Lei. Copper-Nickel. KM#128. Brass plated.	45.00
Pn306	1996	—	100 Lei. Aluminum. KM#128.	40.(
Pn307	1996	—	100 Lei. Copper-Nickel. KM#129. Brass plated.	45.(
Pn351A	1996	—	100 Lei. Brass. 37 mm. National arms. Skier. Plain with denomination edge.	30.(

KM#	Date	Mintage	Identification	Mkt Val
Pn308	1996	—	100 Lei. Aluminum. KM#129.	40.00
Pn309	1996	—	100 Lei. Copper-Nickel. KM#130. Brass plated.	45.00
Pn310	1996	—	100 Lei. Aluminum. KM#130.	40.00
Pn311	1996	—	100 Lei. Copper-Nickel. KM#131. Brass plated.	45.00
Pn312	1996	—	100 Lei. Aluminum. KM#131.	40.00
Pn313	1996	—	100 Lei. Copper-Nickel. KM#132. Brass plated.	45.00
	1996	125	100 Lei. 0.9250 Silver. 27.2500 g. Lettered edge. Piefort. Balance beam.	90.00
	1996	125	100 Lei. 0.9250 Silver. 27.2500 g. Lettered edge. Piefort. Balance beam.	90.00
Pn314	1996	—	100 Lei. Aluminum. KM#132.	40.00
PnA315	1996	125	100 Lei. Aluminum. 37 mm. National arms. Gymnast on balance beam. Plain with denomination edge.	30.00
PnB315	1996	125	100 Lei. Aluminum. 37 mm. National arms. Horse and rider. Plain with denomination edge.	30.00
PnC315	1996	125	100 Lei. Aluminum. 37 mm. National arms. Two basketball players. Plain with denomination edge.	30.00
PnD315	1996	125	100 Lei. Aluminum. 37 mm. National arms. Tennis player. Plain with denomination edge.	30.00
PnA315A1	1996	—	100 Lei. Brass. 37 mm. National arms. Gymnast on balance beam. Plain with denomination edge. Piefort version.	35.00
PnE315	1996	125	100 Lei. Aluminum. Lettered edge. Piefort. Balance beam.	35.00
Pn316	1996	—	100 Lei. Aluminum. KM#133.	45.00
Pn317	1996	—	100 Lei. Brass. KM#135.	50.00
Pn318	1996	—	500 Lei. Brass. KM#147. Arms without outline.	—
Pn319	1996	—	500 Lei. Aluminum. KM#147. Arms without outline.	—
Pn320	1996	—	500 Lei. Nickel. KM#147. Arms without outline.	—
Pn351	1996	125	100 Lei. Aluminum. 37 mm. National arms. Skier. Plain with denomination edge.	30.00
Pn321	1996	—	500 Lei. KM#147. Arms without outline. Bimetal.	—
Pn322	1996	—	3000 Lei. Copper. 1 ECU. Dracula.	—
Pn323	1996	—	3000 Lei. 1 ECU. Dracula. Golden brass.	—
Pn324	1996	—	3000 Lei. Silver. 1 ECU. Dracula.	—
Pn325	1996	—	3000 Lei. Aluminum. 1 ECU. Dracula.	—
Pn350.1	1998	125	100 Lei. Aluminum. 37 mm. National arms. Two hockey players. Plain with denomination edge. Piefort version.	35.00
Pn350A1	1998	125	100 Lei. Brass. 37 mm. National arms. Two hockey players. Plain with denomination edge. Piefort version.	35.00
Pn350B	1998	125	100 Lei. Copper. 37 mm. National arms. Two hockey players. Plain with denomination edge.	30.00
Pn350B1	1998	125	100 Lei. Copper. 37 mm. National arms. Two hockey players. Plain with denomination edge. Piefort version.	35.00
Pn350C	1998	125	100 Lei. Brass center. Copper-Nickel ring. 37 mm. National arms. Two hockey players. Plain with denomination edge.	35.00
Pn350C1	1998	125	100 Lei. Brass center. Copper-Nickel ring. 37 mm. National arms. Two hockey players. Plain with denomination edge. Piefort version.	40.00
Pn350D	1998	125	100 Lei. 0.9250 Silver. 27.2500 g. 37 mm. National arms. Two hockey players. Plain with denomination edge.	75.00
Pn350D1	1998	125	100 Lei. 0.9250 Silver. 27.2500 g. 37 mm. National arms. Two hockey players. Plain with denomination edge. Piefort version.	90.00
Pn353.1	1998	125	100 Lei. Aluminum. 37 mm. National arms. Two ice dancers. Plain with denomination edge. Piefort version.	35.00
Pn353A1	1998	125	100 Lei. Brass. 37 mm. National arms. Two ice dancers. Plain with denomination edge. Piefort version.	35.00
Pn353B	1998	125	100 Lei. Copper. 37 mm. National arms. Two ice dancers. Plain with denomination edge.	30.00
Pn353B1	1998	125	100 Lei. Copper. 37 mm. National arms. Two ice dancers. Plain with denomination edge. Piefort version.	35.00
Pn353C	1998	125	100 Lei. Brass center. Copper-Nickel ring. 37 mm. National arms. Two ice dancers. Plain with denomination edge.	35.00
Pn353C1	1998	125	100 Lei. Brass center. Copper-Nickel ring. 37 mm. National arms. Two ice dancers. Plain with denomination edge. Piefort version.	40.00
Pn353D	1998	125	100 Lei. 0.9250 Silver. 27.2500 g. 37 mm. National arms. Two ice dancers. Plain with denomination edge.	75.00
Pn353D1	1998	125	100 Lei. 0.9250 Silver. 27.2500 g. 37 mm. National arms. Two ice dancers. Plain with denomination edge. Piefort version.	90.00
Pn326	1998	—	100 Lei. KM#119. Eiffel Tower. Golden brass.	—
Pn327	1998	—	100 Lei. Aluminum. KM#119. Eiffel Tower.	—
Pn328	1998	—	100 Lei. Brass. One player.	—
Pn329	1998	—	100 Lei. One player. Bimetal.	—
Pn330	1998	—	100 Lei. Brass. Two players.	—
Pn331	1998	—	100 Lei. Two players. Bimetal.	—
Pn332	1998	—	100 Lei. Bimetal. Gaelic cock.	—
Pn350a	1998	—	100 Lei. Brass. Hockey.	35.00
Pn333	1998	—	500 Lei. Silver.	—
Pn334	1998	—	500 Lei. Golden brass.	—
Pn335	1998	—	500 Lei. Brass. KM#136.	25.00
Pn353A	1998	—	100 Lei. Brass. Ice dancing.	35.00
Pn336	1998	—	1000 Lei. Silver. Arms at 6.	—
Pn337	1998	—	1000 Lei. Brass. Arms at 6.	45.00
Pn338	1998	—	1000 Lei. Arms at 9. Golden brass.	50.00
Pn339	1998	—	500 Lei. Brass. KM#147. Arms without outline.	35.00
Pn340	1998	—	500 Lei. Nickel. KM#147. Arms without outline.	40.00
Pn341	1998	—	500 Lei. Aluminum. KM#147. Arms without outline.	30.00
Pn342	1998	—	500 Lei. KM#147. Arms without outline. Bimetal.	45.00
Pn343	1998	—	100 Lei. Brass.	—
Pn344	1998	—	100 Lei. KM#138. Bimetal.	—
Pn345	1998	—	100 Lei. Aluminum. KM#138.	—
Pn346	1998	—	100 Lei. Brass.	—
Pn347	1998	—	100 Lei. Silver.	—
Pn348	1998	—	100 Lei. Bimetal.	—
Pn349	1998	—	100 Lei. Aluminum.	—
Pn350	1998	125	100 Lei. Aluminum. 37 mm. National arms. Two hockey players. Plain with denomination edge.	30.00
Pn352	1998	—	100 Lei. Brass. Women single.	35.00
Pn353	1998	125	100 Lei. Aluminum. 37 mm. National arms. Two ice dancers. Plain with denomination edge.	30.00
Pn354	1998	—	100 Lei. Brass. Ice dancing, without inscription.	35.00
Pn355	1998	—	100 Lei. Brass. Bobsled, without inscription.	40.00
Pn356	1998	—	100 Lei. Brass. Slalom, without inscription.	40.00
Pn357	1998	—	1000 Lei. Brass. Large.	—
Pn358	1998	—	1000 Lei. Brass. Thin.	—
Pn359	1998	—	1000 Lei. Golden brass.	—
Pn360	1999	—	100 Lei. Brass. Young.	—
Pn361	1999	—	100 Lei. Brass. Old.	—
Pn362	1999	—	100 Lei. Brass.	—
Pn363	1999	—	100 Lei. Brass.	—
Pn364	1999	—	100 Lei. Aluminum. Plain edge. KM146.	100
Pn365	1999	—	100 Lei. Aluminum. Plain edge. KM147.	100

PIEFORTS

KM#	Date	Mintage	Identification	Mkt Val
P3	1905	—	20 Bani. Aluminum-Bronze.	200
P4	1905	—	20 Bani. Bronze.	200
P5	1906	—	12-1/2 Lei. Gold.	—
P6	1906	—	25 Lei. Gold.	—

KM#	Date	Mintage	Identification	Mkt Val
P7	1906	—	50 Lei. Lead.	325
P8	1906	—	50 Lei. Copper.	325
P9	1906	—	50 Lei. Silver.	1,200
P10	1906	—	50 Lei. Gold.	—

TRIAL COINAGE

KM#	Date	Mintage	Identification	Mkt Val
TS1	1906	—	5 Lei. Silver.	4,500
TS2	1906	—	100 Lei. Silver.	400
TS3	1910	—	Leu. Pewter. Milled edge. Thin planchet.	—
TS4	1910	—	Leu. Pewter. Milled edge. Thick planchet.	—
TS5	1996	—	10 Lei. Nickel Plated Steel. KM#134.	100

PROOF SETS

KM#	Date	Mintage	Identification	Issue Price	Mkt Val
PS1	1982 (2)	7,000	KM98-99	429	420
PS2	1983 (4)	1,000	KM98, 99, 101, 110 edge numbering	850	1,900
PS3	2000 (8)	—	KM109-111, 114-116, 145, 153	—	45.00
PS4	2001 (3)	500	KM#159,160,161	150	150

RUSSIA (U.S.S.R.)

EMPIRE

RULERS
Nicholas II, 1894-1917

MINT MARKS
Л – Leningrad, 1991
М – Moscow, 1990
СП – St. Petersburg, 1999
СПБ – St. Petersburg, 1724-1914
СПМД – St. Petersburg, 1999

(sp) (l) – LMD (ЛМД) monogram in oval, (Leningrad), (St. Petersburg) 1977-1997

(m) – MMD (ММД) monogram in oval, Moscow, 1977-

MINT OFFICIAL'S INITIALS

Leningrad Mint

Initials	Years	Mint Official
АГ	1921-22	A.F. Hartman
ПЛ	1922-27	P.V. Latishev

London Mint

T.P.	1924	Thomas Ross
ФР	1924	Thomas Ross

St. Petersburg Mint

ФЗ	1899-1901	Felix Zaleman
АР	1901-05	Alexander Redko
ЭБ	1906-13	Elikum Babayantz
ВС	1913-17	Victor Smirnov

NOTE: St. Petersburg Mint became Petrograd in 1914 and Leningrad in 1924. It was renamed St. Petersburg in 1991.

MONETARY SYSTEM
1/4 Kopek = Polushka ПОЛУШКА
1/2 Kopek = Denga, Denezhka ДЕНГА, ДЕНЕЖКА
Kopek = КОПѢЙКА
(2, 3 & 4) Kopeks КОПѢЙКИ
(5 and up) Kopeks КОПѢЕКЪ
(1924 – 5 and up) Kopeks КОПЕЕК
50 Kopeks = Poltina, Poltinnik ПОЛТИНА,…ПОЛРУБЛЪ
100 Kopeks = Rouble, Ruble РУБЛЪ
10 Roubles = Imperial ИМПЕРIАЛЪ
10 Roubles = Chervonetz ЧЕРВОНЕЦ

NOTE: Mintage figures for years after 1885 are for fiscal years and may or may not reflect actual rarity, the commemorative and 1917 silver figures being exceptions.

STANDARD COINAGE

Y# 47.1 POLUSHKA (1/4 Kopek) **Weight:** 3.0000 g. **Composition:** Copper

Date	Mintage	F	VF	XF	Unc	BU
1909	2,000,000	1.00	2.00	4.00	12.00	—
1910	8,000,000	4.00	8.00	15.00	30.00	—
1909-1910 Common date Proof	—	Value: 125				

Y# 47.2 POLUSHKA (1/4 Kopek) **Weight:** 3.0000 g. **Composition:** Copper

Date	Mintage	F	VF	XF	Unc	BU
1915	500,000	2.00	5.00	10.00	20.00	—
1916	1,200,000	40.00	80.00	150	300	—

Y# 48.1 1/2 KOPEK **Weight:** 4.0000 g. **Composition:** Copper

Date	Mintage	F	VF	XF	Unc	BU
Common date Proof	—	Value: 125				
1908СПБ	8,000,000	0.25	0.50	1.00	5.00	—
1909СПБ	49,500,000	0.25	0.50	1.00	4.00	—
1910СПБ	24,000,000	0.25	0.50	1.00	5.00	—
1911СПБ	35,800,000	0.25	0.50	1.00	5.00	—
1912СПБ	28,000,000	0.25	0.50	1.00	5.00	—
1913СПБ	50,000,000	0.25	0.50	1.00	5.00	—
1914СПБ	14,000,000	0.25	0.50	1.00	5.00	—
1908-14 Common date Proof	—	Value: 125				

Y# 48.2 1/2 KOPEK **Weight:** 4.0000 g. **Composition:** Copper **Note:** Struck at Petrograd without mint mark.

Date	Mintage	F	VF	XF	Unc	BU
1915	12,000,000	0.25	0.50	1.00	5.00	—
1916	9,400,000	0.25	0.50	1.00	5.00	—

Y# 9.2 KOPEK **Weight:** 4.0000 g. **Composition:** Copper

Date	Mintage	F	VF	XF	Unc	BU
1897СПБ	30,000,000	0.25	0.50	1.50	8.00	—
1901СПБ	30,000,000	0.25	0.50	1.50	8.00	—
1902СПБ	20,000,000	2.50	5.00	10.00	20.00	—
1903СПБ	74,400,000	0.25	0.50	1.50	8.00	—
1904СПБ	30,600,000	0.25	0.50	1.50	8.00	—
1905СПБ	23,000	0.25	0.50	1.50	8.00	—
1906СПБ	20,000,000	0.25	0.50	1.50	8.00	—
1907СПБ	20,000,000	0.25	0.50	1.50	8.00	—
1908СПБ	40,000,000	0.25	0.50	1.50	8.00	—
1909СПБ	27,500,000	0.25	0.50	1.50	8.00	—
1910СПБ	36,500,000	0.25	0.50	1.50	8.00	—
1911СПБ	38,150,000	0.25	0.50	1.50	8.00	—
1912СПБ	31,850,000	0.25	0.50	1.50	8.00	—
1913СПБ	61,500,000	0.25	0.50	1.50	8.00	—
1914СПБ	32,500,000	0.25	0.50	1.50	8.00	—
1901-14 Common date Proof	—	Value: 150				

Y# 9.3 KOPEK **Weight:** 4.0000 g. **Composition:** Copper **Note:** Struck at Petrograd without mint mark.

Date	Mintage	F	VF	XF	Unc	BU
1915	58,000,000	0.25	0.50	1.50	8.00	—
1916	46,500,000	0.25	0.50	1.50	8.00	—
1917 Unique	—	—	—	—	—	—

Y# 10.2 2 KOPEKS **Composition:** Copper

Date	Mintage	F	VF	XF	Unc	BU
1901СПБ	20,000,000	0.50	1.00	2.00	8.00	—
1902СПБ	10,000,000	0.50	1.00	2.00	8.00	—
1903СПБ	29,200,000	0.50	1.00	2.00	8.00	—
1904СПБ	13,300,000	0.50	1.00	2.00	8.00	—
1905СПБ	15,000,000	0.50	1.00	2.00	8.00	—
1906СПБ	6,250,000	0.50	1.00	2.00	8.00	—
1907СПБ	7,500,000	0.50	1.00	2.00	8.00	—
1908СПБ	19,000,000	0.50	1.00	2.00	8.00	—
1909СПБ	16,250,000	0.50	1.00	2.00	8.00	—
1910СПБ	12,000,000	0.50	1.00	2.00	8.00	—
1911СПБ	17,200,000	0.50	1.00	2.00	8.00	—
1912СПБ	17,050,000	0.50	1.00	2.00	8.00	—
1913СПБ	26,000,000	0.50	1.00	2.00	8.00	—
1914СПБ	20,000,000	0.50	1.00	2.00	8.00	—
1901-14 Common date proof	—	Value: 165				

Y# 10.3 2 KOPEKS **Composition:** Copper **Note:** Struck at Petrograd without mint mark.

Date	Mintage	F	VF	XF	Unc	BU
1915	33,750,000	0.50	1.00	2.00	5.00	—
1916	31,500,000	0.50	1.00	2.00	5.00	—

Y# 11.2 3 KOPEKS **Composition:** Copper

Date	Mintage	F	VF	XF	Unc	BU
1901СПБ	10,000,000	0.75	1.50	3.00	15.00	—
1902СПБ	3,333,000	0.75	1.50	3.00	15.00	—
1903СПБ	11,400,000	0.75	1.50	3.00	15.00	—
1904СПБ	6,934,000	0.75	1.50	3.00	15.00	—
1905СПБ	3,333,000	0.75	1.50	3.00	15.00	—
1906СПБ	5,667,000	0.75	1.50	3.00	15.00	—
1907СПБ	2,500,000	0.75	1.50	3.00	15.00	—
1908СПБ	12,667,000	0.75	1.50	3.00	15.00	—
1909СПБ	6,733,000	0.75	1.50	3.00	15.00	—
1910СПБ	6,667,000	0.75	1.50	3.00	15.00	—
1911СПБ	9,467,000	0.75	1.50	3.00	15.00	—
1912СПБ	8,533,000	0.75	1.50	3.00	15.00	—
1913СПБ	15,333,000	0.75	1.50	3.00	15.00	—
1914СПБ	8,167,000	0.75	1.50	3.00	15.00	—
1901-14СПБ Common date proof	—	Value: 175				

Y# 11.3 3 KOPEKS **Composition:** Copper **Note:** Struck at Petrograd without mint mark.

Date	Mintage	F	VF	XF	Unc	BU
1915	19,833,000	0.75	1.50	3.00	16.00	—
1916	25,667,000	0.75	1.50	3.00	16.00	—
1917 Rare	—	—	—	—	—	—

Y# 19a.1 5 KOPEKS **Weight:** 0.8998 g. **Composition:** 0.5000 Silver .0144 oz. ASW **Obverse:** Eagle **Edge:** Reeded

Date	Mintage	F	VF	XF	Unc	BU
1901СПБ ФЗ	5,790,000	1.00	2.00	4.00	15.00	—
1901СПБ АР	Inc. above	1.00	2.00	4.00	15.00	—
1902СПБ АР	6,000,000	1.00	2.00	4.00	15.00	—
1903СПБ АР	9,000,000	1.00	2.00	4.00	15.00	—
1904СПБ АР Rare	9	—	—	—	—	—
1905СПБ АР	10,000,000	1.00	2.00	4.00	15.00	—
1906СПБ ЭБ	4,000,000	1.00	2.00	4.00	15.00	—
1908СПБ ЭБ	400,000	1.00	2.00	4.00	15.00	—
1909СПБ ЭБ	3,100,000	1.00	2.00	4.00	15.00	—
1910СПБ ЭБ	2,500,000	1.00	2.00	4.00	15.00	—
1911СПБ ЭБ	2,700,000	1.00	2.00	4.00	15.00	—
1912СПБ ЭБ	3,000,000	1.00	2.00	4.00	15.00	—
1913СПБ ЭБ Proof	Inc. below	Value: 150				
1913СПБ ВС	1,300,000	1.00	2.00	4.00	15.00	—
1914СПБ ВС	4,200,000	1.00	2.00	4.00	15.00	—
1901-14 Common date proof	—	Value: 150				

Y# 12.2 5 KOPEKS **Composition:** Copper

Date	Mintage	F	VF	XF	Unc	BU
1911СПБ	3,800,000	6.00	12.50	25.00	50.00	—
1912СПБ	2,700,000	10.00	17.50	35.00	70.00	—

Y# 19a.2 5 KOPEKS **Weight:** 0.8998 g. **Composition:** 0.5000 Silver .0144 oz. ASW **Note:** Struck at Petrograd without mint mark.

Date	Mintage	F	VF	XF	Unc	BU
1915 ВС	3,000,000	1.00	2.00	4.00	15.00	—

Y# 12.3 5 KOPEKS **Composition:** Copper **Note:** Struck at Petrograd without mint mark.

Date	Mintage	F	VF	XF	Unc	BU
1916	8,000,000	40.00	80.00	150	250	—
1917 Rare	—	—	—	—	—	—

Y#20a.2 10 KOPEKS **Weight:** 1.7996 g. **Composition:** 0.5000 Silver .0289 oz. ASW **Edge:** Reeded

Date	Mintage	F	VF	XF	Unc	BU
1867СПБ НІ	6,445,000	0.50	1.00	3.00	25.00	—
1868СПБ НІ	4,740,000	0.50	1.00	3.00	25.00	—
1869СПБ НІ	3,710,000	0.50	1.00	3.00	25.00	—
1870СПБ НІ	3,310,000	0.50	1.00	3.00	25.00	—
1871СПБ НІ	4,195,000	0.50	1.00	3.00	25.00	—
1872СПБ НІ	2,130,000	0.50	1.00	3.00	25.00	—
1873СПБ НІ	2,620,000	0.50	1.00	3.00	25.00	—
1901СПБ ФЗ	15,000,000	0.50	1.00	2.00	15.00	—
1901СПБ АР	Inc. above	0.50	1.00	2.00	15.00	—
1902СПБ АР	17,000,000	0.50	1.00	2.00	15.00	—
1903СПБ АР	28,500,000	0.50	1.00	2.00	15.00	—
1904СПБ АР	20,000,000	0.50	1.00	2.00	15.00	—
1905СПБ АР	25,000,000	0.50	1.00	2.00	15.00	—
1906СПБ ЭБ	17,500,000	0.50	1.00	2.00	15.00	—
1908СПБ ЭБ	8,210,000	0.50	1.00	2.00	15.00	—
1909СПБ ЭБ	25,290,000	0.50	1.00	2.00	15.00	—
1910СПБ ЭБ	20,000,000	0.50	1.00	2.00	15.00	—
1911СПБ ЭБ	19,180,000	0.50	1.00	2.00	15.00	—
1912СПБ ЭБ	20,000,000	0.50	1.00	2.00	15.00	—
1913СПБ ЭБ Proof	Inc. below	Value: 265				
1913СПБ ВС	7,250,000	0.50	1.00	2.00	15.00	—
1914СПБ ВС	51,250,000	0.50	1.00	2.00	15.00	—
1901-14 Common date proof	—	Value: 265				

Y#20a.3 10 KOPEKS **Weight:** 1.7996 g. **Composition:** 0.5000 Silver .0289 oz. ASW **Note:** Struck at Petrograd without mint mark.

Date	Mintage	F	VF	XF	Unc	BU
1915 ВС	82,500,000	0.50	0.75	1.00	6.00	—
1916 ВС	121,500,000	0.50	0.75	1.00	6.00	—
1917 ВС	17,600,000	—	20.00	30.00	80.00	—

Y#20a.1 10 KOPEKS **Weight:** 1.7996 g. **Composition:** 0.5000 Silver .0289 oz. ASW **Note:** Struck at Osaka, Japan without mint mark.

Date	Mintage	F	VF	XF	Unc	BU
1916	70,001,000	BV	1.00	2.00	10.00	—

Y#21a.2 15 KOPEKS **Weight:** 2.6994 g. **Composition:** 0.5000 Silver .0434 oz. ASW **Edge:** Reticulated

Date	Mintage	F	VF	XF	Unc	BU
1901СПБ ФЗ	6,670,000	0.75	1.00	2.00	10.00	—
1901СПБ АР	Inc. above	0.75	1.00	2.00	10.00	—
1902СПБ АР	28,667,000	0.75	1.00	2.00	10.00	—
1903СПБ АР	16,667,000	0.75	1.00	2.00	10.00	—
1904СПБ АР	15,600,000	0.75	1.00	2.00	10.00	—
1905СПБ АР	24,000,000	0.75	1.00	2.00	10.00	—
1906СПБ ЭБ	23,333,000	0.75	1.00	2.00	10.00	—
1907СПБ ЭБ	30,000,000	0.75	1.00	2.00	10.00	—
1908СПБ ЭБ	29,000,000	0.75	1.00	2.00	10.00	—
1909СПБ ЭБ	21,667,000	0.75	1.00	2.00	10.00	—
1911СПБ ЭБ	6,313,000	0.75	1.00	2.00	10.00	—
1912СПБ ЭБ	13,333,000	0.75	1.00	2.00	10.00	—
1912СПБ ВС	Inc. above	2.00	5.00	12.50	40.00	—
1913СПБ ЭБ Proof	Inc. below	Value: 265				
1913СПБ ВС	5,300,000	0.75	1.00	2.00	10.00	—
1914СПБ ВС	43,367,000	0.75	1.00	2.00	10.00	—
1901-14 Common date proof	—	Value: 265				

Y#21a.3 15 KOPEKS **Weight:** 2.6994 g. **Composition:** 0.5000 Silver .0434 oz. ASW **Note:** Struck at Petrograd without mint mark.

Date	Mintage	F	VF	XF	Unc	BU
1915 ВС	59,333,000	0.75	1.50	2.00	10.00	—
1916 ВС	96,773,000	0.75	1.50	2.00	10.00	—
1917 ВС	14,320,000	—	20.00	30.00	80.00	—

Y#21a.1 15 KOPEKS **Weight:** 2.6994 g. **Composition:** 0.5000 Silver .0434 oz. ASW **Edge:** Reeded **Note:** Struck at Osaka, Japan without mint mark.

Date	Mintage	F	VF	XF	Unc	BU
1916	96,666,000	BV	1.00	2.00	10.00	—

Y#22a.1 20 KOPEKS **Weight:** 3.5992 g. **Composition:** 0.5000 Silver .0579 oz. ASW

Date	Mintage	F	VF	XF	Unc	BU
1901СПБ ФЗ	7,750,000	0.75	1.00	2.00	12.50	—
1901СПБ АР	Inc. above	0.75	1.00	2.00	12.50	—
1902СПБ АР	10,000,000	0.75	1.00	2.00	12.50	—
1903СПБ АР	Inc. above	0.75	1.00	2.00	12.50	—
1904СПБ АР	13,000,000	0.75	1.00	2.00	12.50	—
1905СПБ АР	11,000,000	0.75	1.00	2.00	12.50	—
1906СПБ ЭБ	15,000,000	0.75	1.00	2.00	12.50	—
1907СПБ ЭБ	20,000,000	0.75	1.00	2.00	12.50	—
1908СПБ ЭБ	5,000,000	0.75	1.00	2.00	12.50	—
1909СПБ ЭБ	18,875,000	0.75	1.00	2.00	12.50	—
1910СПБ ЭБ	11,000,000	0.75	1.00	2.00	12.50	—
1911СПБ ЭБ	7,100,000	0.75	1.00	2.00	12.50	—
1912СПБ ЭБ	15,000,000	0.75	1.00	2.00	12.50	—
1912СПБ ВС	Inc. above	5.00	10.00	20.00	60.00	—
1913СПБ ЭБ Proof	Inc. below	Value: 265				
1913СПБ ВС	4,250,000	0.75	1.00	2.00	12.50	—
1914СПБ ВС	52,750,000	0.75	1.00	2.00	12.50	—
1901-14 Common date proof	—	Value: 265				

Y#22a.2 20 KOPEKS **Weight:** 3.5992 g. **Composition:** 0.5000 Silver .0579 oz. ASW **Note:** Struck at Petrograd without mint mark.

Date	Mintage	F	VF	XF	Unc	BU
1915 ВС	105,500,000	BV	1.00	2.00	10.00	—
1916 ВС	131,670,000	BV	1.00	2.00	10.00	—
1917 ВС	3,500,000	—	25.00	35.00	100	—
1915-17 Common date proof	—	Value: 265				

Y# 57 25 KOPEKS **Weight:** 4.9990 g. **Composition:** 0.9000 Silver .1446 oz. ASW **Note:** Struck at St. Petersburg without mint mark.

Date	Mintage	F	VF	XF	Unc	BU
1901 Proof	Est. 150	Value: 1,250				

Y# 58.2 50 KOPEKS **Weight:** 9.9980 g. **Composition:** 0.9000 Silver .2893 oz. ASW **Note:** Struck at St. Petersburg without mint mark.

Date	Mintage	F	VF	XF	Unc	BU
1901 АР	412,000	5.00	12.50	35.00	80.00	—
1901 ФЗ	Inc. above	5.00	12.50	35.00	80.00	—
1902 АР	36,000	10.00	20.00	40.00	175	—
1903 АР Proof	—	Value: 2,000				
1904 АР	4,010,000	100	200	400	1,200	—
1906 ЭБ	—	25.00	50.00	100	300	—
1907 ЭБ	200,000	10.00	20.00	40.00	175	—
1908 ЭБ	40,000	10.00	20.00	40.00	175	—
1909 ЭБ	50,000	10.00	20.00	40.00	175	—
1910 ЭБ	150,000	10.00	20.00	40.00	175	—
1911 ЭБ	800,000	10.00	20.00	40.00	80.00	—
1912 ЭБ	7,085,000	5.00	8.00	15.00	45.00	—
1913 ЭБ	6,420,000	7.50	15.00	35.00	70.00	—
1913 ВС	Inc. above	5.00	10.00	20.00	45.00	—
1914 ВС	1,200,000	5.00	10.00	20.00	45.00	—
1901-14 Common date proof	—	Value: 500				

Y# 59.3 ROUBLE **Weight:** 19.9960 g. **Composition:** 0.9000 Silver .5786 oz. ASW **Note:** Struck at St. Petersburg without mint mark.

Date	Mintage	F	VF	XF	Unc	BU
1901 ФЗ	2,608,000	9.00	16.00	45.00	200	—
1901 АР	Inc. above	40.00	80.00	125	450	—
1902 АН	140,000	20.00	30.00	60.00	400	—
1903 АР	56,000	40.00	80.00	180	750	—
1904 АР	12,000	75.00	150	300	900	—
1905 АР	21,000	40.00	80.00	180	750	—
1906 ЭБ	46,000	40.00	80.00	180	750	—
1907 ЭБ	400,000	20.00	30.00	60.00	400	—
1908 ЭБ	130,000	75.00	150	300	900	—
1909 ЭБ	51,000	40.00	80.00	180	600	—
1910 ЭБ	75,000	25.00	40.00	80.00	450	—
1911 ЭБ	129,000	25.00	40.00	80.00	400	—
1912 ЭБ	2,111,000	9.00	15.00	40.00	180	—
1913 ЭБ	22,000	50.00	100	200	700	—
1913 ВС	Inc. above	50.00	100	200	700	—
1914 ВС	536,000	25.00	35.00	90.00	550	—
1915 ВС	5,000	30.00	60.00	125	350	—

Note: Varieties exist with plain edge, these are mint errors and rare

Date	Mintage	F	VF	XF	Unc	BU
1901-15 Common date proof	—	Value: 900				

Y# 68 ROUBLE **Weight:** 19.9960 g. **Composition:** 0.9000 Silver .5786 oz. ASW **Subject:** Centennial - Napolean's Defeat

Date	Mintage	F	VF	XF	Unc	BU
1912 ЭБ	46,000	60.00	110	225	400	—
1912 ЭБ Proof	—	Value: 2,000				

Y# 69 ROUBLE **Weight:** 19.9960 g. **Composition:** 0.9000 Silver .5786 oz. ASW **Subject:** Alexander III Memorial

Date	Mintage	F	VF	XF	Unc	BU
1912 ЭБ	2,100	200	400	1,000	1,600	—
1912 ЭБ Proof	—	Value: 2,250				

Y# 70 ROUBLE **Weight:** 19.9960 g. **Composition:** 0.9000 Silver .5786 oz. ASW **Subject:** 300th Anniversary - Romanov Dynasty **Note:** Struck at St. Petersburg without mint mark.

Date	Mintage	F	VF	XF	Unc	BU
1913 ВС	1,472,000	12.00	22.00	32.00	100	—

Y# 71 ROUBLE **Weight:** 19.9960 g. **Composition:** 0.9000 Silver .5786 oz. ASW **Subject:** 200th Anniversary - Battle of Gangut

Date	F	VF	XF	Unc	BU
1914 ВС	400	600	1,700	3,000	—

Note: Only 317 pieces were issued through 1917, but an unknown number of restrikes were made in the 1920's

Y# 62 5 ROUBLES **Weight:** 6.4516 g. **Composition:** 0.9000 Gold .1244 oz. AGW **Note:** Struck at St. Petersburg without mint mark.

Date	Mintage	F	VF	XF	Unc	BU
1901 ФЗ	7,500,000	—	BV	55.00	75.00	—
1901 АР	Inc. above	—	BV	70.00	100	—
1902 АР	6,240,000	—	BV	55.00	75.00	—
1903 АР	5,148,000	—	BV	55.00	75.00	—
1904 АР	2,016,000	—	BV	55.00	75.00	—
1906 ЭБ	10	—	—	7,000	10,000	—
1907 ЭБ	109	—	—	4,000	7,500	—
1909 ЭБ	—	BV	60.00	75.00	90.00	—
1910 ЭБ	200,000	BV	60.00	75.00	100	—
1911 ЭБ	100,000	BV	60.00	150	250	—
1901-11 Common date proof	—	Value: 1,500				

Y# 64 10 ROUBLES **Weight:** 8.6026 g. **Composition:** 0.9000 Gold .2489 oz. AGW **Note:** Struck at St. Petersburg without mint mark.

Date	Mintage	F	VF	XF	Unc	BU
1901 ФЗ	2,377,000	—	BV	100	150	—
1901 АР	Inc. above	—	BV	110	165	—
1902 АР	2,019,000	—	BV	100	150	—
1903 АР	2,817,000	—	BV	100	145	—
1904 АР	1,025,000	—	BV	100	145	—
1906 ЭБ Proof	10	Value: 8,500				
1909 ЭБ	50,000	BV	110	125	200	—
1910 ЭБ	100,000	BV	110	125	200	—
1911 ЭБ	50,000	BV	110	125	200	—
1901-11 Common date proof	—	Value: 2,500				

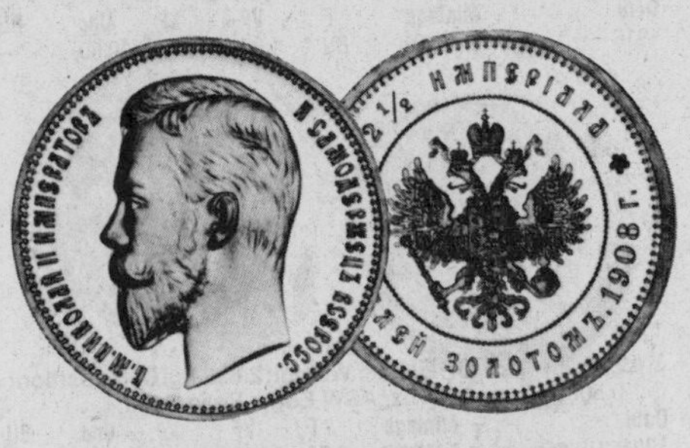

Y# A65 25 ROUBLES **Weight:** 32.2500 g. **Composition:** 0.9000 Gold .9332 oz. AGW **Rev. Legend:** 2-1/2 ИМПЕРІАЛА (IMPERIALS) **Note:** Struck at St. Petersburg without mint mark.

Date	Mintage	F	VF	XF	Unc	BU
1908		—	7,500	9,500	20,000	—
1908 Proof	25	Value: 23,000				

Y# B65a 37 ROUBLES 50 KOPEKS **Composition:** Copper-Nickel **Reverse:** Letter "P" after "1902 G" **Edge:** Plain

Date	F	VF	XF	Unc	BU
1902 (1991) P Restrike	—	—	—	12.50	—

Y# B65 37 ROUBLES 50 KOPEKS **Weight:** 32.2500 g. **Composition:** 0.9000 Gold .9335 oz. AGW **Rev. Legend:** 100 ФРАНКОВЪ **Note:** Struck at St. Petersburg without mint mark.

Date	Mintage	F	VF	XF	Unc	BU
1902	225	—	7,500	15,000	25,000	—
1902 Proof	—	Value: 25,000				

GOLD MINE INGOTS

During the late 19th and early 20th century, Russian law provided that gold mine owners who supplied gold to the mints should receive back whatever silver was recovered during refining of the gold. The silver was returned in the form of circular ingots of various weights which resembled coins. These pieces have often been erroneously described as Russian trade coins for use in Mongolia, China, and Turkestan.

Note: Both the Doyla and the Zolotnik are weights, not denominations.

KM# 1 24 DOLYA **Weight:** 1.0664 g. **Composition:** 0.9900 Silver .0343 oz. ASW **Ruler:** Nicholas II

Date	F	VF	XF	Unc	BU
ND(1901)	—	350	450	650	—

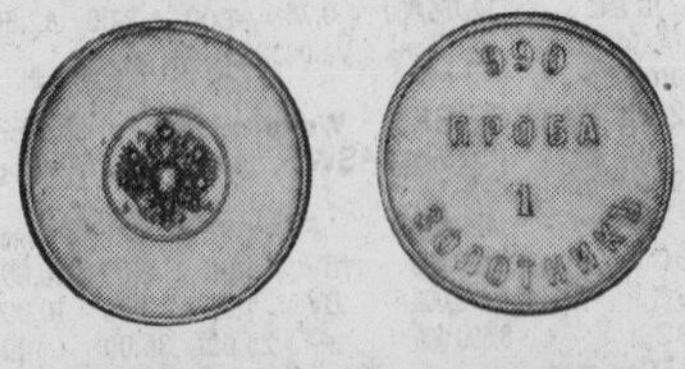

KM# 2 ZOLOTNIK **Weight:** 4.2656 g. **Composition:** 0.9900 Silver .1371 oz. ASW **Ruler:** Nicholas II

Date	F	VF	XF	Unc	BU
ND(1901)	—	225	325	475	—

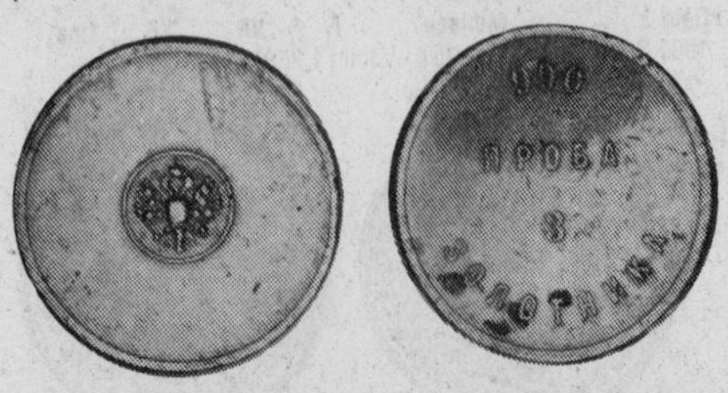

KM# 3 3 ZOLOTNIKS **Weight:** 12.7969 g. **Composition:** 0.9900 Silver .4114 oz. ASW **Ruler:** Nicholas II

Date	F	VF	XF	Unc	BU
ND(1901)	—	1,000	1,500	2,000	—

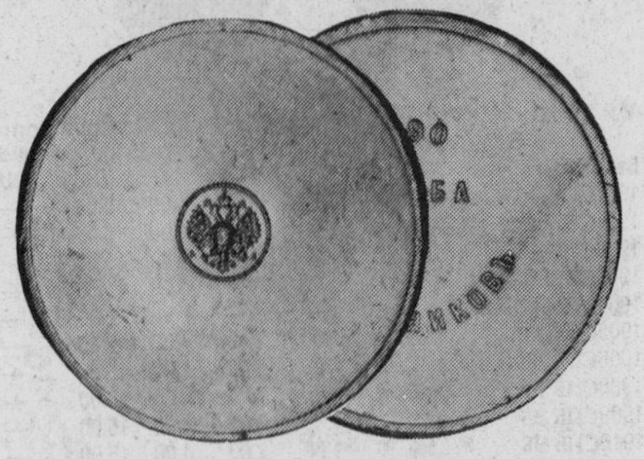

KM# 4 10 ZOLOTNIKS **Weight:** 42.6563 g. **Composition:** 0.9900 Silver 1.3714 oz. ASW **Ruler:** Nicholas II

Date	F	VF	XF	Unc	BU
ND(1901)	—	250	450	700	—

РСФСР (R.S.F.S.R.)
(Russian Soviet Federated Socialist Republic)

STANDARD COINAGE

Y# 80 10 KOPEKS **Weight:** 1.8000 g. **Composition:** 0.5000 Silver .0289 oz. ASW

Date	Mintage	F	VF	XF	Unc	BU
1921	950,000	5.00	10.00	25.00	50.00	—
1921 Proof	—	Value: 250				
1922	18,640,000	1.00	2.00	4.50	12.00	—
1922 Proof	—	Value: 115				
1923	33,424,000	1.00	2.00	4.00	10.00	—
1923 Proof	—	Value: 60.00				

Y# 81 15 KOPEKS **Weight:** 2.7000 g. **Composition:** 0.5000 Silver .0434 oz. ASW

Date	Mintage	F	VF	XF	Unc	BU
1921	933,000	6.00	12.00	30.00	60.00	—
1921 Proof	—	Value: 275				
1922	13,633,000	2.00	3.00	6.00	16.00	—
1922 Proof	—	Value: 140				
1923	28,504,000	1.50	2.50	4.50	12.00	—
1923 Proof	—	Value: 80.00				

Y# 82 20 KOPEKS **Weight:** 3.6000 g. **Composition:** 0.5000 Silver .0578 oz. ASW **Note:** Varieties exist.

Date	Mintage	F	VF	XF	Unc	BU
1921	825,000	6.00	12.00	30.00	60.00	—
1921 Proof	—	Value: 300				
1922	14,220,000	2.00	4.00	8.00	20.00	—
1922 Proof	—	Value: 165				
1923	27,580,000	2.00	3.50	7.00	15.00	—
1923 Proof	—	Value: 100				

Y# 83 50 KOPEKS Weight: 9.9980 g. **Composition:** 0.9000 Silver .2893 oz. ASW **Edge Lettering:** Mintmaster's initials

Date	Mintage	F	VF	XF	Unc	BU
1921 АГ	1,400,000	5.00	7.00	10.00	25.00	—
1921 АГ Proof	—	Value: 325				
1922 АГ	8,224,000	5.00	7.00	10.00	25.00	—
1922 АГ Proof	—	Value: 350				
1922 ПЛ	Inc. above	5.00	7.00	10.00	25.00	—
1922 ПЛ Proof	—	Value: 250				

Y# 84 ROUBLE Weight: 19.9960 g. **Composition:** 0.9000 Silver .5786 oz. ASW **Edge Lettering:** Mintmaster's initials **Note:** Varieties exist.

Date	Mintage	F	VF	XF	Unc	BU
1921 АГ	1,000,000	8.50	13.50	25.00	65.00	90.00
1921 АГ Proof	—	Value: 425				
1922 АГ	2,050,000	10.00	18.00	35.00	85.00	110
1922 АГ Proof	—	Value: 600				
1922 ПЛ	Inc. above	10.00	18.00	35.00	85.00	110
1922 ПЛ Proof	—	Value: 450				

TRADE COINAGE

Y# 85 CHERVONETZ (10 Roubles) Weight: 8.6026 g. **Composition:** 0.9000 Gold .2489 oz. AGW **Obverse:** РСФСР below arms **Edge Lettering:** Mintmaster's initials

Date	Mintage	F	VF	XF	Unc	BU
1923 ПЛ		130	160	200	250	—
1923 ПЛ Proof	—	Value: 1,350				
1975		—	—	—BV+10%		—
1976 ЛМД		—	—	—BV+10%		—
1977 ММД		—	—	—BV+10%		—
1977 ЛМД		—	—	—BV+10%		—
1978 ММД		—	—	—BV+10%		—
1979 ММД		—	—	—BV+10%		—
1980 ММД		—	—	—BV+10%		—
1980 ММД Proof	100,000	Value: 150				
1981		—	—	—BV+10%		—
1982		—	—	—BV+10%		—

Y# A86 CHERVONETZ (10 Roubles) Weight: 8.6026 g. **Composition:** 0.9000 Gold .2489 oz. AGW **Obverse:** CCCP below arms

Date	Mintage	F	VF	XF	Unc	BU
1925 Unique	600,000	—	—	—	—	—

Note: Chervonetz were first struck in 1923 under the R.S.F.S.R. government; in 1925 the U.S.S.R. government attempted a new issue of these coins, of which only one remaining coin is known; from 1975 to 1982 the U.S.S.R. government continued striking the original type with new dates

CCCP (U.S.S.R.)
(Union of Soviet Socialist Republics)

STANDARD COINAGE

Y# 75 1/2 KOPEK Composition: Copper

Date	Mintage	F	VF	XF	Unc	BU
1925	45,380,000	3.50	7.50	14.50	30.00	—
1927	45,380,000	3.50	7.50	14.50	30.00	—
1927 Proof	—	Value: 100				
1928	—	4.50	8.00	16.50	35.00	—

Y# 76 KOPEK Composition: Bronze

Date	Mintage	F	VF	XF	Unc	BU
1924	34,705,000	5.00	10.00	20.00	45.00	—
Note: Reeded edge						
1924 Proof	—	Value: 125				
Note: Reeded edge						
1924	Inc. above	30.00	60.00	120	250	—
Note: Plain edge						
1925	141,806,000	45.00	90.00	160	275	—

Y# 91 KOPEK Composition: Aluminum-Bronze **Note:** Varieties exist.

Date	Mintage	F	VF	XF	Unc	BU
1926	87,915,000	0.50	1.00	1.50	5.50	—
1926 Proof	—	Value: 60.00				
1927	—	0.50	1.00	1.50	5.00	—
1928	—	0.50	1.00	1.50	5.00	—
1929	95,950,000	0.50	1.00	1.50	5.00	—
1930	85,351,000	0.50	1.00	1.50	5.00	—
1931	106,100,000	0.50	1.00	1.50	5.00	—
1932	56,900,000	0.50	1.00	1.50	5.00	—
1933	111,257,000	0.50	1.00	1.50	5.00	—
1934	100,245	0.50	1.00	1.50	5.00	—
1935	66,405,000	0.50	1.00	2.00	6.00	—

Y# 98 KOPEK Composition: Aluminum-Bronze

Date	Mintage	F	VF	XF	Unc	BU
1935	—	0.50	1.00	2.50	9.00	—
Note: Mintage inc.Y91						
1936	132,204,000	0.50	1.00	2.00	7.50	—

Y# 105 KOPEK Composition: Aluminum-Bronze **Note:** Varieties exist.

Date	F	VF	XF	Unc	BU
1937	0.25	0.65	1.00	4.00	—
1938	0.25	0.65	1.00	4.00	—
1939	0.25	0.65	1.00	4.00	—
1940	0.25	0.65	1.00	4.00	—
1941	0.50	1.00	2.00	6.00	—
1945	0.50	1.00	2.00	6.00	—
1946	0.50	1.00	2.00	6.00	—

Y# 112 KOPEK Composition: Aluminum-Bronze **Obverse:** Eight and seven ribbons on wreath **Note:** Varieties exist.

Date	F	VF	XF	Unc	BU
1948	0.50	1.00	2.00	5.00	—
1949	0.50	1.00	2.00	5.00	—
1950	0.50	1.00	2.50	8.00	—
1951	0.50	1.00	2.50	8.00	—
1952	0.30	0.75	1.50	3.00	—
1953	0.30	0.75	1.50	3.00	—
1954	0.30	0.75	1.50	3.00	—
1955	0.30	0.75	1.50	3.00	—
1956	0.30	0.75	1.50	3.00	—

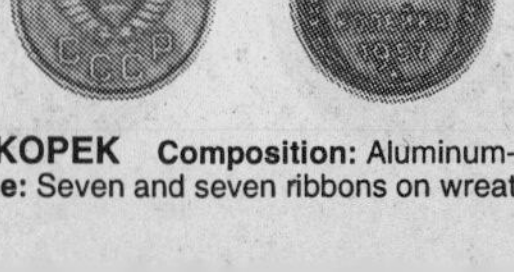

Y# 119 KOPEK Composition: Aluminum-Bronze **Obverse:** Seven and seven ribbons on wreath

Date	F	VF	XF	Unc	BU
1957	1.00	2.00	4.00	12.00	—

Y# 126 KOPEK Composition: Copper-Nickel

Date	Mintage	F	VF	XF	Unc	BU
1958	30,265,000	—	—	—	250	—

Note: Never officially released for circulation; majority of mintage remelted

Y# 126a KOPEK Composition: Brass **Note:** Varieties exist.

Date	F	VF	XF	Unc	BU
1961	0.10	0.15	0.25	1.00	—
1962	0.10	0.15	0.25	0.50	—
1963	0.10	0.15	0.25	0.50	—
1964	0.20	0.30	0.50	2.00	—
1965	0.10	0.15	0.25	0.50	—
1966	0.10	0.15	0.25	0.50	—
1967	0.10	0.15	0.25	0.50	—
1968	0.10	0.15	0.25	0.50	—
1969	0.10	0.15	0.25	0.50	—
1970	0.10	0.15	0.25	0.50	—
1971	0.10	0.15	0.25	0.50	—
1972	0.10	0.15	0.25	0.50	—
1973	0.10	0.15	0.25	0.50	—
1974	0.10	0.15	0.25	0.50	—
1975	0.10	0.15	0.25	0.50	—
1976	0.10	0.15	0.25	0.50	—
1977	0.10	0.15	0.25	0.50	—
1978	0.10	0.15	0.25	0.50	—
1979	0.10	0.15	0.25	0.50	—
1980	0.10	0.15	0.25	0.50	—
1981	0.10	0.15	0.25	0.50	—
1982	0.10	0.15	0.25	0.50	—
1983	0.10	0.15	0.25	0.50	—
1984	0.10	0.15	0.25	0.50	—
1985	0.10	0.15	0.25	0.50	—
1986	0.10	0.15	0.25	0.50	—
1987	0.10	0.15	0.25	0.50	—
1988	0.10	0.15	0.25	0.50	—
1989	0.10	0.15	0.20	0.30	—
1990	0.10	0.15	0.20	0.30	—
1991 (M)	0.10	0.15	0.20	0.30	—
1991 (l)	0.10	0.15	0.20	0.30	—

Y# 77 2 KOPEKS Composition: Bronze **Note:** Varieties exist.

Date	Mintage	F	VF	XF	Unc	BU
1924	119,996,000	5.00	12.00	22.00	50.00	—
Note: Reeded edge						
1924	Inc. above	30.00	60.00	120	250	—
Note: Plain edge						
1925 Rare	Inc. above	—	—	—	—	—

Y# 92 2 KOPEKS Composition: Aluminum-Bronze **Note:** Varieties exist.

Date	Mintage	F	VF	XF	Unc	BU
1926	105,053,000	0.25	0.50	1.00	4.00	—
1926 Proof	—	Value: 65.00				
1927 Rare	—	—	—	—	—	—
1928	—	0.25	0.50	1.00	4.00	—
1929	80,000,000	0.25	0.50	1.00	5.00	—
1930	134,186,000	0.25	0.50	1.00	4.00	—
1931	99,523,000	0.25	0.50	1.00	4.00	—
1932	39,573,000	0.35	0.65	1.25	4.50	—
1933	54,874,000	0.50	1.00	2.00	7.00	—
1934	61,574,000	0.35	0.65	1.25	4.50	—
1935	81,121,000	0.35	0.65	1.50	5.00	—

Y# 99 2 KOPEKS **Composition:** Aluminum-Bronze
Note: Varieties exist.

Date	Mintage	F	VF	XF	Unc	BU
1935	—	0.50	1.00	2.50	9.00	—
1936	94,354,000	0.25	0.50	2.00	7.00	—

Y# 106 2 KOPEKS **Composition:** Aluminum-Bronze

Date	F	VF	XF	Unc	BU
1937	0.25	0.65	1.00	3.00	—
1938	0.25	0.65	1.00	3.00	—
1939	0.25	0.65	1.00	3.00	—
1940	0.25	0.65	1.00	3.00	—
1941	0.25	0.65	1.00	3.00	—
1945	0.50	1.00	2.00	5.00	—
1946	0.25	0.65	1.00	4.00	—
1948	40.00	70.00	130	225	—

Y# 113 2 KOPEKS **Composition:** Aluminum-Bronze
Obverse: Eight and seven ribbons on wreath **Note:** Varieties exist.

Date	F	VF	XF	Unc	BU
1948	0.25	0.50	1.00	2.50	—
1949	0.25	0.50	1.00	2.50	—
1950	0.25	0.50	1.00	2.50	—
1951	0.50	1.00	2.00	6.00	—
1952	0.25	0.50	0.50	3.00	—
1953	0.20	0.50	0.50	2.00	—
1954	0.20	0.50	0.50	2.00	—
1955	0.20	0.50	0.50	2.00	—
1956	0.20	0.50	0.50	2.00	—

Y# 120 2 KOPEKS **Composition:** Aluminum-Bronze
Obverse: Seven and seven ribbons on wreath

Date	F	VF	XF	Unc	BU
1957	0.50	1.00	2.50	9.00	—

Y# 127 2 KOPEKS **Composition:** Copper-Nickel

Date	Mintage	F	VF	XF	Unc	BU
1958	39,591,000	—	—	—	250	—

Note: Never officially released for circulation; majority of mintage remelted

Y# 127a 2 KOPEKS **Composition:** Brass **Note:** Varieties exist.

Date	F	VF	XF	Unc	BU
1961	0.10	0.15	0.25	0.50	—
1962	0.10	0.15	0.25	0.50	—
1963	0.10	0.15	0.25	0.50	—
1964	0.15	0.25	0.50	1.00	—
1965	0.10	0.15	0.25	0.50	—
1966	0.10	0.15	0.25	0.50	—
1967	0.10	0.15	0.25	0.50	—
1968	0.10	0.15	0.25	0.50	—

Date	F	VF	XF	Unc	BU
1969	0.10	0.15	0.25	0.50	—
1970	0.10	0.15	0.25	0.50	—
1971	0.10	0.15	0.25	0.50	—
1972	0.10	0.15	0.25	0.50	—
1973	0.10	0.15	0.25	0.50	—
1974	0.10	0.15	0.25	0.50	—
1975	0.10	0.15	0.25	0.50	—
1976	0.10	0.15	0.25	0.50	—
1977	0.10	0.15	0.25	0.50	—
1978	0.10	0.15	0.25	0.50	—
1979	0.10	0.15	0.25	0.50	—
1980	0.10	0.15	0.25	0.50	—
1981	0.10	0.15	0.25	0.50	—
1982	0.10	0.15	0.25	0.50	—
1983	0.10	0.15	0.25	0.50	—
1984	0.10	0.15	0.25	0.50	—
1985	0.10	0.15	0.25	0.50	—
1986	0.10	0.15	0.25	0.50	—
1987	0.10	0.15	0.25	0.50	—
1988	0.10	0.15	0.25	0.50	—
1989	0.10	0.15	0.20	0.35	—
1990	0.10	0.15	0.20	0.35	—
1991 (M)	0.10	0.15	0.20	0.35	—
1991 (l)	0.10	0.15	0.20	0.35	—

Y# 78 3 KOPEKS **Composition:** Bronze **Note:** Varieties exist.

Date	Mintage	F	VF	XF	Unc	BU
1924	101,283,000	50.00	100	175	275	—
Note: Reeded edge						
1924	Inc. above	6.00	12.50	25.00	65.00	—
Note: Plain edge						

Y# 93 3 KOPEKS **Composition:** Aluminum-Bronze
Note: Varieties exist.

Date	Mintage	F	VF	XF	Unc	BU
1926	19,940,000	1.25	2.00	4.00	7.00	—
1926 Proof	—	Value: 75.00				
1926 Rare	—	—	—	—	—	—
Note: Obverse of Y#100						
1927	—	5.00	10.00	20.00	40.00	—
1928	—	1.00	2.00	4.00	7.00	—
1929	50,150,000	1.00	2.00	4.00	8.00	—
1930	74,159,000	0.50	0.75	1.50	5.00	—
1931	121,168,000	0.50	0.75	1.50	5.00	—
1931 Rare	—	—	—	—	—	—
Note: Without CCCP obverse						
1932	37,718,000	0.50	0.75	1.50	5.00	—
1933	44,764,000	0.50	0.75	2.00	6.00	—
1934	44,529,000	0.50	0.75	2.00	6.00	—
1935	58,303,000	0.50	0.75	2.50	7.00	—

Y# 100 3 KOPEKS **Composition:** Aluminum-Bronze
Note: Varieties exist.

Date	Mintage	F	VF	XF	Unc	BU
1935	—	0.50	2.00	5.00	14.00	—
1936	62,757,000	0.25	1.00	4.00	10.00	—

Y# 107 3 KOPEKS **Composition:** Aluminum-Bronze
Note: Varieties exist.

Date	F	VF	XF	Unc	BU
1937	0.25	0.50	1.00	4.00	—
1938	0.25	0.50	1.00	4.00	—
1939	0.25	0.50	1.00	4.00	—
1940	0.25	0.50	1.00	3.00	—
1941	0.25	0.50	1.00	4.00	—
1943	0.25	0.50	1.00	5.00	—
1945	0.50	1.00	3.00	9.00	—
1946	0.25	0.50	1.00	5.00	—
1948	40.00	70.00	130	225	—

Y# 114 3 KOPEKS **Composition:** Aluminum-Bronze
Obverse: Eight and seven ribbons on wreath **Note:** Varieties exist.

Date	F	VF	XF	Unc	BU
1948	0.25	0.50	1.00	5.00	—
1949	0.25	0.50	1.00	4.00	—
1950	0.25	0.50	1.00	4.00	—
1951	0.50	1.00	2.00	7.00	—
1952	0.25	0.50	1.00	4.00	—
1953	0.25	0.50	1.00	3.00	—
1954	0.25	0.50	1.00	3.00	—
1955	0.25	0.50	1.00	3.00	—
1956	0.25	0.50	1.00	3.00	—
1957	0.25	0.50	1.00	3.00	—

Y# 121 3 KOPEKS **Composition:** Aluminum-Bronze
Obverse: Seven and seven ribbons on wreath

Date	F	VF	XF	Unc	BU
1957	0.50	1.00	2.50	9.00	—

Y# 128 3 KOPEKS **Composition:** Copper-Zinc

Date	Mintage	F	VF	XF	Unc	BU
1958	26,676,000	—	—	—	250	—

Note: Never officially released for circulation; majority of mintage remelted

Y# 128a 3 KOPEKS **Composition:** Aluminum-Bronze
Note: Varieties exist.

Date	F	VF	XF	Unc	BU
1961	0.10	0.15	0.25	0.60	—
1962	0.10	0.15	0.25	0.60	—
1965	0.10	0.15	0.25	0.60	—
1966	0.10	0.15	0.25	0.60	—
1967	0.10	0.15	0.25	0.60	—
1968	0.10	0.15	0.25	0.60	—
1969	0.10	0.15	0.25	0.60	—
1970	0.10	0.15	0.25	0.60	—
1971	0.10	0.15	0.25	0.60	—
1972	0.10	0.15	0.25	0.60	—
1973	0.10	0.15	0.25	0.60	—
1974	0.10	0.15	0.25	0.60	—
1975	0.10	0.15	0.25	0.60	—
1976	0.10	0.15	0.25	0.60	—
1977	0.10	0.15	0.25	0.60	—
1978	0.10	0.15	0.25	0.60	—
1979	0.10	0.15	0.25	0.60	—
1980	0.10	0.15	0.25	0.60	—
1981	0.10	0.15	0.25	0.60	—
1982	0.10	0.15	0.25	0.60	—
1983	0.10	0.15	0.25	0.60	—
1984	0.10	0.15	0.25	0.60	—

Date	F	VF	XF	Unc	BU
1985	0.10	0.15	0.25	0.60	—
1986	0.10	0.15	0.25	0.60	—
1987	0.10	0.15	0.25	0.60	—
1988	0.10	0.15	0.25	0.60	—
1989	0.10	0.15	0.20	0.40	—
1990	0.10	0.15	0.20	0.40	—
1991 (M)	0.10	0.15	0.20	0.40	—
1991 (l)	0.10	0.15	0.20	0.40	—

Y# 79 5 KOPEKS **Composition:** Bronze **Note:** Varieties exist.

Date	Mintage	F	VF	XF	Unc	BU
1924	88,510,000	50.00	100	175	275	—
Note: Reeded edge						
1924	Inc. above	7.00	15.00	30.00	75.00	—
Note: Plain edge						

Y# 94 5 KOPEKS **Composition:** Aluminum-Bronze **Note:** Varieties exist.

Date	Mintage	F	VF	XF	Unc	BU
1926	14,697,000	1.00	2.00	6.00	10.00	—
1926 Proof	—	Value: 85.00				
1927	—	5.00	10.00	20.00	40.00	—
1928	—	0.75	1.25	3.00	7.00	—
1929	20,220,000	0.75	1.25	3.00	7.00	—
1930	44,490,000	0.75	1.25	2.00	6.00	—
1931	89,540,000	0.75	1.25	2.00	6.00	—
1932	65,100,000	0.75	1.25	2.00	6.00	—
1932	18,135,000	15.00	30.00	75.00	250	—
1934	5,354,000	2.00	4.00	12.00	30.00	—
1935	11,735,000	3.00	6.00	15.00	50.00	—

Y# 101 5 KOPEKS **Composition:** Aluminum-Bronze **Note:** Varieties exist.

Date	Mintage	F	VF	XF	Unc	BU
1935	—	2.00	4.00	9.00	26.00	—
1936	5,242,000	2.00	4.00	9.00	28.00	—

Y# 108 5 KOPEKS **Composition:** Aluminum-Bronze **Note:** Varieties exist.

Date	F	VF	XF	Unc	BU
1937	2.00	4.00	9.00	28.00	—
1938	0.25	0.50	1.00	4.50	—
1939	0.25	0.50	1.00	4.50	—
1940	0.25	0.50	1.00	4.00	—
1941	0.25	0.50	1.00	4.50	—
1943	0.25	0.50	1.00	4.50	—
1945	1.00	2.00	5.00	12.00	—
1946	0.25	0.50	1.00	6.00	—

Y# 115 5 KOPEKS **Composition:** Aluminum-Bronze **Obverse:** Eight and seven ribbons on wreath **Note:** Varieties exist.

Date	F	VF	XF	Unc	BU
1948	0.25	0.50	1.50	5.00	—
1949	0.25	0.50	1.00	4.00	—
1950	0.25	0.50	1.00	4.00	—
1951	0.50	1.00	2.00	5.00	—
1952	0.25	0.50	1.00	4.00	—
1953	0.25	0.50	1.00	4.00	—
1954	0.25	0.50	1.00	4.00	—
1955	0.25	0.50	1.00	4.00	—
1956	0.25	0.50	1.00	4.00	—

Y# 122 5 KOPEKS **Composition:** Aluminum-Bronze **Obverse:** Seven and seven ribbons on wreath **Note:** Varieties exist.

Date	F	VF	XF	Unc	BU
1957	1.00	2.00	3.00	9.00	—

Y# 129 5 KOPEKS **Composition:** Copper-Zinc

Date	Mintage	F	VF	XF	Unc	BU
1958	61,119,000	—	—	—	375	—

Note: Never officially released for circulation; majority of mintage remelted

Y# 129a 5 KOPEKS **Composition:** Aluminum-Bronze **Note:** Varieties exist.

Date	F	VF	XF	Unc	BU
1961	0.10	0.15	0.30	0.75	—
1962	0.10	0.15	0.30	0.75	—
1965	0.25	0.50	1.00	3.00	—
1966	0.20	0.30	0.70	2.00	—
1967	0.15	0.25	5.50	1.50	—
1968	0.15	0.25	0.50	1.50	—
1969	0.20	0.30	0.75	2.00	—
1970	0.50	1.00	2.00	5.00	—
1971	0.15	0.25	0.50	1.50	—
1972	0.15	0.25	0.50	1.50	—
1973	0.10	0.15	0.30	0.75	—
1974	0.10	0.15	0.30	0.75	—
1975	0.10	0.15	0.30	0.75	—
1976	0.10	0.15	0.30	0.75	—
1977	0.10	0.15	0.30	0.75	—
1978	0.10	0.15	0.30	0.75	—
1979	0.10	0.15	0.30	0.75	—
1980	0.10	0.15	0.30	0.75	—
1981	0.10	0.15	0.30	0.75	—
1982	0.10	0.15	0.30	0.70	—
1983	0.10	0.15	0.30	0.75	—
1984	0.10	0.15	0.30	0.75	—
1985	0.10	0.15	0.30	0.75	—
1986	0.10	0.15	0.30	0.75	—
1987	0.10	0.15	0.30	0.75	—
1988	0.10	0.15	0.30	0.75	—
1989	0.10	0.15	0.25	0.50	—
1990	0.15	0.25	0.45	1.25	—
1991 (M)	0.10	0.15	0.25	0.50	—
1991 (l)	0.10	0.15	0.25	0.50	—
1991 Л	0.10	0.15	0.25	0.50	—

Y# 86 10 KOPEKS **Weight:** 1.8000 g. **Composition:** 0.5000 Silver .0289 oz. ASW **Note:** Varieties exist.

Date	Mintage	F	VF	XF	Unc	BU
1924	67,351,000	0.50	1.00	3.00	9.00	—
1924 Proof	—	Value: 200				
1925	101,013,000	0.50	1.00	2.50	8.00	—
1925 Proof	—	Value: 75.00				
1927	—	0.50	1.00	3.00	9.00	—
1927 Proof	—	Value: 75.00				
1928	—	0.50	1.00	2.50	8.00	—
1929	64,900,000	0.50	1.00	3.00	9.00	—
1930	163,424,000	0.50	1.00	2.50	8.00	—
1931 Rare	8,791,000	—	—	—	—	—

Y# 95 10 KOPEKS **Composition:** Copper-Nickel **Note:** Varieties exist.

Date	Mintage	F	VF	XF	Unc	BU
1931	122,511,000	1.00	2.00	4.00	8.00	—
1932	171,641,000	0.25	0.50	1.00	4.00	—
1933	163,125,000	0.25	0.50	1.00	4.00	—
1934	104,059,000	0.25	0.50	1.00	5.00	—

Y# 102 10 KOPEKS **Composition:** Copper-Nickel

Date	Mintage	F	VF	XF	Unc	BU
1935	79,628,000	0.25	0.50	1.00	5.00	—
1936	122,260,000	0.25	0.50	1.00	4.00	—

Y# 109 10 KOPEKS **Composition:** Copper-Nickel **Note:** Varieties exist.

Date	F	VF	XF	Unc	BU
1937	0.50	1.00	2.50	6.00	—
1938	0.30	0.75	1.25	2.50	—
1939	0.30	0.60	1.00	2.00	—
1940	0.30	0.60	1.00	2.00	—
1941	0.30	0.60	1.00	3.00	—
1942	7.50	15.00	40.00	75.00	—
1943	0.30	0.60	1.00	2.00	—
1944	0.50	1.00	2.00	5.00	—
1945	0.30	0.75	1.25	3.00	—
1946	0.30	0.75	1.25	3.00	—

Y# A110 10 KOPEKS **Composition:** Copper-Nickel **Obverse:** Y#102. **Reverse:** Y#109. **Note:** Mule.

Date	F	VF	XF	Unc	BU
1946 Rare	—	—	—	—	—

Y# 116 10 KOPEKS **Composition:** Copper-Nickel **Obverse:** Eight and seven ribbons on wreath **Note:** Varieties exist.

Date	F	VF	XF	Unc	BU
1948	0.25	0.50	2.00	5.00	—
1949	0.25	0.50	1.00	3.00	—
1950	0.25	0.50	1.00	2.00	—
1951	0.25	0.50	1.00	5.00	—
1952	0.25	0.50	1.00	4.00	—
1953	0.25	0.50	1.00	2.00	—
1954	0.25	0.50	1.00	2.00	—
1955	0.25	0.50	1.00	2.00	—
1956	0.25	0.50	1.00	2.00	—
1956	50.00	75.00	150	250	—

Note: Reverse of Y#123

Y# 123 10 KOPEKS Composition: Copper-Nickel
Obverse: Seven and seven ribbons on wreath

Date	F	VF	XF	Unc	BU
1957	50.00	75.00	150	250	—

Note: Reverse of Y#116

Date	F	VF	XF	Unc	BU
1957	0.25	0.50	2.00	6.00	—

Y# A130 10 KOPEKS Composition: Copper-Nickel

Date	Mintage	F	VF	XF	Unc	BU
1958	108,023,000	—	—	—	350	—

Note: Never officially released for circulation; majority of mintage remelted

Y# 130 10 KOPEKS Composition: Copper-Nickel-Zinc

Date	F	VF	XF	Unc	BU
1961	0.10	0.20	0.35	0.75	—
1962	0.10	0.20	0.35	0.75	—
1965	0.10	0.20	0.35	0.75	—
1966	0.10	0.20	0.35	0.75	—
1967	0.10	0.20	0.35	0.75	—
1968	0.10	0.20	0.35	0.75	—
1969	0.10	0.20	0.35	0.75	—
1970	0.10	0.20	0.35	0.75	—
1971	0.10	0.20	0.35	0.75	—
1972	0.10	0.20	0.35	0.75	—
1973	0.10	0.20	0.35	0.75	—
1974	0.10	0.20	0.35	0.75	—
1975	0.10	0.20	0.35	0.75	—
1976	0.10	0.20	0.35	0.75	—
1977	0.10	0.20	0.35	0.75	—
1978	0.10	0.20	0.35	0.75	—
1979	0.10	0.20	0.35	0.75	—
1980	0.10	0.20	0.35	0.75	—
1981	0.10	0.20	0.35	0.75	—
1982	0.10	0.20	0.35	0.75	—
1983	0.10	0.20	0.35	0.75	—
1984	0.10	0.20	0.35	0.75	—
1985	0.10	0.20	0.35	0.75	—
1986	0.10	0.20	0.35	0.75	—
1987	0.10	0.20	0.35	0.75	—
1988	0.10	0.20	0.35	0.75	—
1989	0.10	0.20	0.30	0.50	—
1990	0.25	0.50	1.00	2.50	—
1990 Л	0.10	0.20	0.30	0.50	—
1991	0.15	0.25	0.50	1.25	—
1991 Л	0.10	0.20	0.30	0.50	—
1991 M	0.10	0.20	0.30	0.50	—
1991 (l)	0.10	0.20	0.30	0.50	—
1991 (m)	0.10	0.20	0.30	0.50	—

Y# 136 10 KOPEKS Composition: Copper-Nickel-Zinc **Subject:** 50th Anniversary of Revolution **Size:** 17 mm.

Date	Mintage	F	VF	XF	Unc	BU
1967	49,789,000	—	0.20	0.30	1.00	—
1967 Prooflike	211,000	—	—	—	—	—

Y# 87 15 KOPEKS Weight: 2.7000 g. **Composition:** 0.5000 Silver .0434 oz. ASW **Note:** Varieties exist.

Date	Mintage	F	VF	XF	Unc	BU
1924	72,426,000	0.75	1.25	3.50	10.00	—
1924 Proof	—	Value: 200				
1925	112,709,000	0.75	1.25	2.50	8.00	—
1925 Proof	—	Value: 75.00				
1927	—	0.75	1.25	2.50	8.00	—
1927 Proof	—	Value: 75.00				
1928	—	0.75	1.25	2.50	8.00	—
1929	46,400,000	0.75	1.25	2.50	8.00	—
1930	79,868,000	0.75	1.25	2.50	8.00	—
1931 Rare	5,099,000	—	—	—	—	—

Y# 96 15 KOPEKS Composition: Copper-Nickel **Note:** Varieties exist.

Date	Mintage	F	VF	XF	Unc	BU
1931	75,859,000	0.50	1.00	1.75	4.50	—
1932	136,046,000	0.50	1.00	1.75	4.00	—
1933	127,591,000	0.50	1.00	1.75	4.00	—
1934	58,367,000	0.50	1.00	2.00	5.50	—

Y# 103 15 KOPEKS Composition: Copper-Nickel

Date	Mintage	F	VF	XF	Unc	BU
1935	51,308,000	0.50	1.00	1.75	4.50	—
1936	52,183,000	0.35	0.75	1.50	4.00	—

Y#110 15 KOPEKS Composition: Copper-Nickel **Note:** Varieties exist.

Date	F	VF	XF	Unc	BU
1937	0.35	0.75	1.50	3.00	—
1938	0.30	0.50	1.00	2.00	—
1939	0.30	0.50	1.00	2.00	—
1940	0.30	0.50	1.00	2.00	—
1941	0.30	0.50	1.00	2.00	—
1942	7.50	15.00	40.00	75.00	—
1943	0.35	0.75	1.25	2.50	—
1944	1.00	1.00	5.00	10.00	—
1945	0.50	1.25	2.50	5.00	—
1946	0.35	0.75	2.00	4.00	—

Y# 117 15 KOPEKS Composition: Copper-Nickel
Obverse: Eight and seven ribbons on wreath **Note:** Varieties exist.

Date	F	VF	XF	Unc	BU
1948	0.35	0.75	2.00	4.00	—
1949	0.35	0.75	1.50	3.50	—
1950	0.30	0.50	1.00	2.00	—
1951	0.50	1.00	2.50	8.00	—
1952	0.30	0.50	1.00	2.00	—
1953	0.30	0.50	1.00	2.00	—
1954	0.30	0.50	1.00	2.00	—
1955	0.30	0.50	1.00	2.00	—
1956	0.30	0.50	1.00	2.00	—

Y# 124 15 KOPEKS Composition: Copper-Nickel
Obverse: Seven and seven ribbons on wreath

Date	F	VF	XF	Unc	BU
1957	0.30	0.50	1.00	5.00	—

Y# A131 15 KOPEKS Composition: Copper-Nickel

Date	Mintage	F	VF	XF	Unc	BU
1958	80,052,000	—	—	—	450	—

Note: Never officially released for circulation; majority of mintage remelted

Y# 131 15 KOPEKS Composition: Copper-Nickel-Zinc
Size: 19.5 mm.

Date	F	VF	XF	Unc	BU
1961	0.10	0.20	0.40	0.75	—
1962	0.10	0.20	0.40	1.00	—
1965	0.10	0.20	0.40	0.75	—
1966	0.10	0.20	0.40	0.75	—
1967	0.10	0.20	0.40	0.75	—
1968	0.10	0.20	0.40	0.75	—
1969	0.10	0.20	0.40	0.75	—
1970	0.10	0.20	0.40	0.75	—
1971	0.10	0.20	0.40	0.75	—
1972	0.10	0.20	0.40	0.75	—
1973	0.10	0.20	0.40	0.75	—
1974	0.10	0.20	0.40	0.75	—
1975	0.10	0.20	0.40	0.75	—
1976	0.10	0.20	0.40	0.75	—
1977	0.10	0.20	0.40	0.75	—
1978	0.10	0.20	0.40	0.75	—
1979	0.10	0.20	0.40	0.75	—
1980	0.10	0.20	0.40	0.75	—
1981	0.10	0.20	0.40	0.75	—
1982	0.10	0.20	0.40	0.75	—
1983	0.10	0.20	0.40	0.75	—
1984	0.10	0.20	0.40	0.75	—
1985	0.10	0.20	0.40	0.75	—
1986	0.10	0.20	0.40	0.75	—
1987	0.10	0.20	0.40	0.75	—
1988	0.10	0.20	0.30	0.50	—
1989	0.10	0.20	0.30	0.50	—
1990	0.10	0.20	0.30	0.50	—
1991L	0.10	0.20	0.30	0.50	—
1991M	0.10	0.20	0.30	0.50	—

Y# 137 15 KOPEKS Composition: Copper-Nickel-Zinc
Subject: 50th Anniversary of Revolution

Date	Mintage	F	VF	XF	Unc	BU
1967	49,789,000	0.15	0.30	0.50	1.50	—
1967 Prooflike	211,000	—	—	—	—	—

Y# 88 20 KOPEKS Weight: 3.6000 g. **Composition:** 0.5000 Silver .0578 oz. ASW

Date	Mintage	F	VF	XF	Unc	BU
1924	93,810,000	1.00	1.75	3.50	10.00	—
1924 Proof	—	Value: 225				
1925	135,188,000	1.00	1.75	3.00	9.00	—
1925 Proof	—	Value: 75.00				
1927	—	1.00	2.00	4.00	12.00	—
1928	—	1.00	1.75	3.00	9.00	—
1929	67,250,000	1.00	1.75	3.00	9.00	—
1930	125,658,000	1.00	1.75	3.00	9.00	—
1931 Rare	9,530,000	—	—	—	—	—

Y# 97 20 KOPEKS **Composition:** Copper-Nickel **Note:** Varieties exist.

Date	Mintage	F	VF	XF	Unc	BU
1931	82,200,000	0.50	1.00	2.00	5.00	—
1932	175,350,000	0.50	1.00	2.00	5.00	—
1933	143,927,000	0.50	1.00	2.00	5.00	—
1934	70,425,000	—	—	—	—	—

Y# 104 20 KOPEKS **Composition:** Copper-Nickel **Note:** Varieties exist.

Date	Mintage	F	VF	XF	Unc	BU
1935	125,165,000	0.50	1.00	2.00	4.50	—
1936	52,968,000	0.50	1.00	2.00	5.00	—

Y# 111 20 KOPEKS **Composition:** Copper-Nickel **Note:** Varieties exist.

Date	F	VF	XF	Unc	BU
1937	0.40	0.60	1.00	3.00	—
1938	0.40	0.60	1.00	3.00	—
1939	0.40	0.60	1.00	3.00	—
1940	0.40	0.60	1.00	3.00	—
1941	0.40	0.60	1.00	3.00	—
1942	0.50	0.75	1.50	4.00	—
1943	0.40	0.60	1.00	3.00	—
1944	0.60	1.25	2.50	6.00	—
1945	0.40	0.60	1.50	4.00	—
1946	0.45	0.75	2.50	5.00	—

Y# 118 20 KOPEKS **Composition:** Copper-Nickel **Obverse:** Eight and seven ribbons on wreath **Note:** Varieties exist.

Date	F	VF	XF	Unc	BU
1948	0.45	0.75	1.50	4.00	—
1949	0.45	0.75	1.50	4.00	—
1950	1.00	2.00	5.00	10.00	—
1951	0.50	1.00	2.50	7.00	—
1952	0.40	0.60	1.00	2.00	—
1953	0.40	0.60	1.00	2.00	—
1954	0.40	0.60	1.00	2.00	—
1955	0.40	0.60	1.00	2.00	—
1956	0.40	0.60	1.00	2.00	—

Y# 125 20 KOPEKS **Composition:** Copper-Nickel **Obverse:** Seven and seven ribbons on wreath

Date	F	VF	XF	Unc	BU
1957	0.40	0.60	1.00	4.00	—

Y# A132 20 KOPEKS **Composition:** Copper-Nickel

Date	Mintage	F	VF	XF	Unc	BU
1958	175,355,000	—	—	—	450	—

Note: Never officially released for circulation; majority of mintage remelted

Y# 132 20 KOPEKS **Composition:** Copper-Nickel-Zinc **Note:** Varieties exist.

Date	F	VF	XF	Unc	BU
1961	0.15	0.30	0.50	1.00	—
1962	0.15	0.35	0.75	1.50	—
1965	0.15	0.30	0.50	1.00	—
1966	0.15	0.30	0.50	1.00	—
1967	0.15	0.30	0.50	1.00	—
1968	0.15	0.30	0.50	1.00	—
1969	0.15	0.30	0.50	1.00	—
1970	0.15	0.30	0.50	1.00	—
1971	0.15	0.30	0.50	1.00	—
1972	0.15	0.30	0.50	1.00	—
1973	0.15	0.30	0.50	1.00	—
1974	0.15	0.30	0.50	1.00	—
1975	0.10	0.30	0.50	1.00	—
1976	2.00	2.00	4.00	7.50	—
1977	0.15	0.30	0.50	1.00	—
1978	0.15	0.30	0.50	1.00	—
1979	0.15	0.30	0.50	1.00	—
1980	0.15	0.30	0.50	1.00	—
1981	0.15	0.30	0.50	1.00	—
1982	0.15	0.30	0.50	1.00	—
1983	0.15	0.30	0.50	1.00	—
1984	0.15	0.30	0.50	1.00	—
1985	0.15	0.30	0.50	1.00	—
1986	0.15	0.30	0.50	1.00	—
1987	0.15	0.30	0.50	1.00	—
1988	0.15	0.30	0.50	1.00	—
1989	0.10	0.20	0.30	0.75	—
1990	0.10	0.20	0.30	0.75	—
1991	0.20	0.40	0.65	1.50	—
1991 Л	0.10	0.20	0.30	0.50	—
1991 M	0.10	0.20	0.30	0.50	—
1991 (l)	0.10	0.20	0.30	0.75	—
1991 (m)	0.10	0.20	0.30	0.75	—

Y# 138 20 KOPEKS **Composition:** Copper-Nickel-Zinc **Subject:** 50th Anniversary of Revolution

Date	Mintage	F	VF	XF	Unc	BU
1967	49,789,000	0.40	0.60	0.75	2.00	—
1967 Prooflike	211,000	—	—	—	—	—

Y# 89.1 50 KOPEKS **Weight:** 9.9980 g. **Composition:** 0.9000 Silver .2893 oz. ASW **Edge Lettering:** Weight shown in old Russian units

Date	Mintage	F	VF	XF	Unc	BU
1924 ПЛ	26,559,000	5.00	7.00	11.50	25.00	—
1924 ПЛ Proof	—	Value: 250				
1924 TP	40,000,000	5.00	7.00	11.50	25.00	—

Y# 89.2 50 KOPEKS **Weight:** 9.9980 g. **Composition:** 0.9000 Silver .2893 oz. ASW **Edge Lettering:** Weight shown in Грамм (grams) only **Note:** Varieties exist.

Date	Mintage	F	VF	XF	Unc	BU
1925 ПЛ	43,558,000	5.00	7.00	11.50	25.00	—
1925 ПЛ Proof	—	Value: 125				
1926 ПЛ	24,374,000	5.00	7.00	11.50	25.00	—
1926 ПЛ Proof	—	Value: 125				
1927 ПЛ	—	5.00	8.00	15.00	35.00	—
1927 ПЛ Proof	—	Value: 165				

Y# 133 50 KOPEKS **Composition:** Copper-Nickel

Date	Mintage	F	VF	XF	Unc	BU
1958	40,600,000	—	—	—	—	—

Note: Never officially released for circulation; majority of mintage remelted

Y# 133a.1 50 KOPEKS **Composition:** Copper-Nickel-Zinc **Edge:** Plain **Note:** Varieties exist.

Date	F	VF	XF	Unc	BU
1961	1.00	2.00	5.00	12.00	—

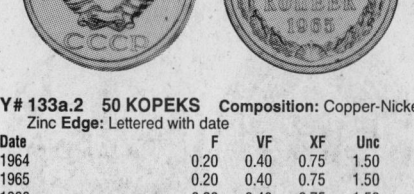

Y# 133a.2 50 KOPEKS **Composition:** Copper-Nickel-Zinc **Edge:** Lettered with date

Date	F	VF	XF	Unc	BU
1964	0.20	0.40	0.75	1.50	—
1965	0.20	0.40	0.75	1.50	—
1966	0.20	0.40	0.75	1.50	—
1967	0.20	0.40	0.75	1.50	—
1968	0.20	0.40	0.75	1.50	—
1969	0.20	0.40	0.75	1.50	—
1970	0.20	0.40	0.75	1.50	—
1971	0.20	0.40	0.75	1.50	—
1972	0.20	0.40	0.75	1.50	—
1973	0.20	0.40	0.75	1.50	—
1974	0.20	0.40	0.75	1.50	—
1975	0.20	0.40	0.75	1.50	—
1976	0.20	0.40	0.75	1.50	—
1977	0.20	0.40	0.75	1.50	—
1978	0.20	0.40	0.75	1.50	—
1979	0.20	0.40	0.75	1.50	—
1980	0.20	0.40	0.75	1.50	—
1981	0.20	0.40	0.75	1.50	—
1982	0.20	0.40	0.75	1.50	—
1983	0.20	0.40	0.75	1.50	—
1984	0.20	0.40	0.75	1.50	—
1985	0.20	0.40	0.75	1.50	—
1986	1.00	2.00	4.00	10.00	—
Note: With 1985 edge					
1986	0.20	0.40	0.75	1.50	—
1987	0.20	0.40	0.75	1.50	—
1988	1.00	2.00	4.00	10.00	—
Note: With 1987 edge					
1988	0.20	0.40	0.75	1.50	—
1989	0.15	0.25	0.50	1.00	—
1990	2.50	5.00	10.00	25.00	—
Note: With 1989 edge					
1990	0.15	0.25	0.50	1.00	—
1991 M	0.15	0.25	0.50	1.00	—
1991 L	0.15	0.25	0.50	1.00	—

Y# 139 50 KOPEKS **Composition:** Copper-Nickel-Zinc **Subject:** 50th Anniversary of Revolution

Date	Mintage	F	VF	XF	Unc	BU
ND(1967)	49,789,000	—	1.00	1.50	2.50	—
ND(1967) Prooflike	—	—	—	—	3.00	—

Y# 90.1 ROUBLE **Weight:** 19.9960 g. **Composition:** 0.9000 Silver .5786 oz. ASW **Edge Lettering:** 18 Грамм (grams) (43.21d) **Note:** Varieties exist.

Date	Mintage	F	VF	XF	Unc	BU
1924 ПЛ	12,998,000	7.50	12.50	22.50	50.00	75.00
1924 ПЛ Proof	—	Value: 750				

Y# 90.2 ROUBLE **Weight:** 19.9960 g. **Composition:** 0.9000 Silver .5786 oz. ASW **Edge:** 4 Zolotniks 21 Dolyas

Date	F	VF	XF	Unc	BU
1924 Rare	—	—	—	—	—

Y# 134 ROUBLE **Composition:** Copper-Nickel

Date	Mintage	F	VF	XF	Unc	BU
1958	30,700,000	—	—	—	—	—

Note: Never officially released for circulation; majority of mintage remelted

Y# 134a.1 ROUBLE **Composition:** Copper-Nickel-Zinc **Edge:** Plain

Date	F	VF	XF	Unc	BU
1961	2.00	3.50	6.00	15.00	—

Y# 134a.2 ROUBLE **Composition:** Copper-Nickel-Zinc **Edge:** Lettered with date

Date	F	VF	XF	Unc	BU
1964	0.40	0.75	1.50	2.50	—
1965	0.40	0.75	1.50	2.50	—
1966	0.40	0.75	1.50	2.50	—
1967	3.00	6.00	12.00	30.00	—
Note: With 1966 edge					
1967	0.40	0.75	1.50	2.50	—
1968	0.40	0.75	1.50	2.50	—
1969	0.40	0.75	1.50	2.50	—
1970	0.40	0.75	1.50	2.50	—
1971	0.40	0.75	1.50	2.50	—
1972	0.40	0.75	1.50	2.50	—
1973	0.40	0.75	1.50	2.50	—
1974	0.40	0.75	1.50	2.50	—
1975	0.40	0.75	1.50	2.50	—
1976	0.40	0.75	1.50	2.50	—
1977	0.40	0.75	1.50	2.50	—
1978	0.40	0.75	1.50	2.50	—
1979	0.40	0.75	1.50	2.50	—
1980	0.40	0.75	1.50	2.50	—
1981	0.40	0.75	1.50	2.50	—
1982	0.40	0.75	1.50	2.50	—
1983	0.40	0.75	1.50	2.50	—
1984	0.40	0.75	1.50	2.50	—
1985	0.40	0.75	1.50	2.50	—
1986	0.40	0.75	1.50	2.50	—
1987	0.40	0.75	1.50	2.50	—
1988	0.40	0.75	1.50	2.50	—
1989	0.25	0.50	1.00	2.50	—
1990	1.50	3.00	6.00	15.00	—
Note: With 1989 edge					
1990	0.25	0.50	1.00	2.50	—
1991 (m)	0.25	0.50	1.00	2.50	—
1991 (l)	0.25	0.50	1.00	2.50	—

Y# 135.1 ROUBLE **Composition:** Copper-Nickel-Zinc **Subject:** 20th Anniversary of World War II Victory

Date	Mintage	F	VF	XF	Unc	BU
1965	59,989,000	—	0.50	1.00	2.50	—
1965 Prooflike	—	—	—	—	3.00	—
1965 Proof	—	Value: 30.00				

Y# 135.2 ROUBLE **Composition:** Copper-Nickel-Zinc **Edge Lettering:** 1988.N.

Date	Mintage	F	VF	XF	Unc	BU
1965 Proof, restrike	55,000	Value: 3.50				

Y# 140.1 ROUBLE **Composition:** Copper-Nickel-Zinc **Subject:** 50th Anniversary of Revolution **Edge:** Lettered, with date

Date	Mintage	F	VF	XF	Unc	BU
1967	52,289,000	—	0.50	1.00	2.50	—
1967 Prooflike	—	—	—	—	3.00	—
1967 Proof	—	Value: 30.00				

Y# 140.2 ROUBLE **Composition:** Copper-Nickel-Zinc **Edge Lettering:** 1988.N.

Date	Mintage	F	VF	XF	Unc	BU
1967 Proof, restrike	55,000	Value: 4.00				

Y# 141 ROUBLE **Composition:** Copper-Nickel-Zinc **Subject:** Centennial of Lenin's Birth

Date	Mintage	F	VF	XF	Unc	BU
ND(1970)	99,889,000	—	0.50	1.00	2.50	—
ND(1970) Prooflike	—	—	—	—	3.00	—
ND(1970) Proof	—	Value: 50.00				

Y# 142.1 ROUBLE **Composition:** Copper-Nickel-Zinc **Subject:** 30th Anniversary of World War II Victory **Edge:** Date **Note:** Varieties exist.

Date	Mintage	F	VF	XF	Unc	BU
ND(1975)	14,989,000	—	0.50	1.00	2.50	—
ND(1975) Prooflike	—	—	—	—	3.00	—
ND(1975) Proof	—	Value: 25.00				

Y# 142.2 ROUBLE **Composition:** Copper-Nickel-Zinc **Edge Lettering:** 1988.N.

Date	Mintage	F	VF	XF	Unc	BU
ND(1975) Proof, restrike	55,000	Value: 3.50				

Y# 143.1 ROUBLE **Composition:** Copper-Nickel-Zinc **Subject:** 60th Anniversary of Bolshevik Revolution

Date	Mintage	F	VF	XF	Unc	BU
ND(1977)	4,987,000	—	0.50	1.00	2.50	—
ND(1977) Prooflike	—	—	—	—	3.00	—
ND(1977) Proof	—	Value: 25.00				

Y# 143.2 ROUBLE **Composition:** Copper-Nickel-Zinc **Edge Lettering:** 1988.N.

Date	Mintage	F	VF	XF	Unc	BU
ND(1977) Proof, restrike	55,000	Value: 3.50				

Y# A144 ROUBLE **Composition:** Copper-Nickel-Zinc **Obverse:** KM#143.1 **Reverse:** KM#144 **Note:** Mule

Date	F	VF	XF	Unc	BU
1977 Rare	—	—	—	—	—

Y# 144 ROUBLE **Composition:** Copper-Nickel-Zinc **Series:** 1980 Olympics **Reverse:** Emblem

Date	Mintage	F	VF	XF	Unc	BU
1977	8,665,000	—	0.50	1.00	2.50	—
1977 Prooflike	—	—	—	—	3.00	—
1977 Proof	—	Value: 25.00				

Y# 153.1 ROUBLE **Composition:** Copper-Nickel-Zinc **Series:** 1980 Olympics **Reverse:** Moscow Kremlin

Date	Mintage	F	VF	XF	Unc	BU
1978	6,490,000	—	0.50	1.00	2.50	—
1978 Prooflike	—	—	—	—	3.00	—
1978 Proof	—	Value: 50.00				

Y# 153.2 ROUBLE **Composition:** Copper-Nickel-Zinc **Reverse:** Clock on tower shows Roman 6 instead of 4

Date	F	VF	XF	Unc	BU
1978	—	8.00	16.00	25.00	—

Y# 165 ROUBLE **Composition:** Copper-Nickel-Zinc **Series:** 1980 Olympics **Reverse:** Monument, Sputnik, and Sojuz

Date	Mintage	F	VF	XF	Unc	BU
1979	4,665,000	—	0.50	1.00	2.50	—
1979 Prooflike	—	—	—	—	3.00	—
1979 Proof	—	Value: 25.00				

Y# 164 ROUBLE **Composition:** Copper-Nickel-Zinc **Series:** 1980 Olympics **Reverse:** Moscow University **Note:** Varieties in window arrangements exist.

Date	Mintage	F	VF	XF	Unc	BU
1979	4,665,000	—	0.50	1.00	2.50	—
1979 Prooflike	—	—	—	—	3.00	—
1979 Proof	—	Value: 25.00				

Y# 177 ROUBLE **Composition:** Copper-Nickel **Series:** 1980 Olympics **Reverse:** Dolgorukij Monument

Date	Mintage	F	VF	XF	Unc	BU
1980	4,490,000	—	0.50	1.00	2.50	—
1980 Prooflike	—	—	—	—	3.00	—
1980 Proof	—	Value: 25.00				

Y# 178 ROUBLE Composition: Copper-Nickel **Series:** 1980 Olympics **Reverse:** Torch

Date	Mintage	F	VF	XF	Unc	BU
1980	4,490,000	—	0.50	1.00	2.50	—
1980 Prooflike	—	—	—	—	3.00	—
1980 Proof	—	Value: 25.00				

Y# 188.1 ROUBLE Composition: Copper-Nickel **Subject:** 20th Anniversary of Manned Space Flights **Reverse:** Yuri Gagarin

Date	Mintage	F	VF	XF	Unc	BU
ND(1981)	3,962,000	—	0.50	1.00	3.00	—
ND(1981) Proof	—	Value: 7.50				

Y# 188.2 ROUBLE Composition: Copper-Nickel **Edge Lettering:** 1988.N.

Date	Mintage	F	VF	XF	Unc	BU
ND(1981) Proof; restrike	55,000	Value: 3.50				

Y# 189.1 ROUBLE Composition: Copper-Nickel **Subject:** Russian-Bulgarian Friendship

Date	Mintage	F	VF	XF	Unc	BU
1981	—	—	0.50	1.00	3.00	—
1981	16,000	Value: 20.00				

Y# 189.2 ROUBLE Composition: Copper-Nickel **Edge Lettering:** 1988.N.

Date	Mintage	F	VF	XF	Unc	BU
1981 Proof; restrike	55,000	Value: 3.50				

Note: The same reverse die was used for both Russia 1 Rouble KM#189 and Bulgaria 1 Lev KM#119

Y# 190.1 ROUBLE Composition: Copper-Nickel **Subject:** 60th Anniversary of the Soviet Union

Date	Mintage	F	VF	XF	Unc	BU
ND(1982)	—	—	0.50	1.50	3.50	—
ND(1982) Proof	79,000	Value: 6.00				

Y# 190.2 ROUBLE Composition: Copper-Nickel **Edge Lettering:** 1988.N.

Date	Mintage	F	VF	XF	Unc	BU
ND(1982) Proof; restrike	55,000	Value: 4.50				

Y# 191.1 ROUBLE Composition: Copper-Nickel **Subject:** Death of Karl Marx Centennial

Date	Mintage	F	VF	XF	Unc	BU
1983	—	—	0.50	1.50	3.50	—
1983 Proof	79,000	Value: 6.00				

Y# 191.2 ROUBLE Composition: Copper-Nickel **Edge Lettering:** 1988.N.

Date	Mintage	F	VF	XF	Unc	BU
1983 Proof; restrike	55,000	Value: 4.50				

Y# 192.1 ROUBLE Composition: Copper-Nickel **Subject:** 20th Anniversary of First Woman in Space **Reverse:** Valentina Tereshkova

Date	Mintage	F	VF	XF	Unc	BU
1983 Proof	55,000	Value: 6.00				
1983	—	—	0.50	1.00	3.00	—

Y# 192.2 ROUBLE Composition: Copper-Nickel **Edge Lettering:** 1988.N.

Date	Mintage	F	VF	XF	Unc	BU
1983 Proof; restrike	55,000	Value: 3.50				

Y# 193.1 ROUBLE Composition: Copper-Nickel **Subject:** First Russian Printer **Reverse:** Ivan Fedorov

Date	Mintage	F	VF	XF	Unc	BU
1983	—	—	0.50	1.00	3.00	—
1983 Proof	35,000	Value: 5.00				

Y# 193.2 ROUBLE Composition: Copper-Nickel **Edge Lettering:** 1988.N.

Date	Mintage	F	VF	XF	Unc	BU
1983 Proof; restrike	55,000	Value: 3.50				

Y# 194.1 ROUBLE Composition: Copper-Nickel **Subject:** 150th Anniversary - Birth of Dmitri Ivanovich Mendeleyev

Date	Mintage	F	VF	XF	Unc	BU
1984	—	—	0.50	1.00	3.00	—
1984 Proof	35,000	Value: 5.00				

Y# 194.2 ROUBLE Composition: Copper-Nickel **Edge Lettering:** 1988.N.

Date	Mintage	F	VF	XF	Unc	BU
1984 Proof; restrike	55,000	Value: 3.50				

Y# 195.1 ROUBLE Composition: Copper-Nickel **Subject:** 125th Anniversary - Birth of Alexander Popov

Date	Mintage	F	VF	XF	Unc	BU
1984	—	—	0.50	1.00	3.00	—
1984 Proof	35,000	Value: 5.00				

Y# 195.2 ROUBLE Composition: Copper-Nickel **Edge Lettering:** 1988.N.

Date	Mintage	F	VF	XF	Unc	BU
1984 Proof; restrike	55,000	Value: 3.50				

Y# 196.1 ROUBLE Composition: Copper-Nickel **Subject:** 185th Anniversary - Birth of Alexander Sergeevich Pushkin

Date	Mintage	F	VF	XF	Unc	BU
1984	—	—	0.50	1.00	3.00	—
1984 Proof	35,000	Value: 5.00				

Y# 196.2 ROUBLE Composition: Copper-Nickel **Edge Lettering:** 1988.N.

Date	Mintage	F	VF	XF	Unc	BU
1984 Proof; restrike	55,000	Value: 3.50				
1985 Error	—	—	—	—	—	—
1985 Proof; restrike	—	Value: 4.50				

Y# 197.1 ROUBLE Composition: Copper-Nickel **Subject:** 115th Anniversary - Birth of Vladimir Lenin

Date	Mintage	F	VF	XF	Unc	BU
1985	—	—	0.50	1.50	3.50	—
1985 Proof	40,000	Value: 6.00				

Y# 197.2 ROUBLE Composition: Copper-Nickel **Edge Lettering:** 1988.N.

Date	Mintage	F	VF	XF	Unc	BU
1985 Proof; restrike	55,000	Value: 4.50				
1988 Error	—	—	—	—	—	—

Y# 198.1 ROUBLE Composition: Copper-Nickel **Subject:** 40th Anniversary - World War II Victory

Date	Mintage	F	VF	XF	Unc	BU
1985	—	—	0.50	1.00	3.00	—
1985 Proof	40,000	Value: 6.00				

Y# 198.2 ROUBLE Composition: Copper-Nickel **Edge Lettering:** 1988.N.

Date	Mintage	F	VF	XF	Unc	BU
1985 Proof; restrike	55,000	Value: 3.50				

Y# 199.1 ROUBLE Composition: Copper-Nickel **Subject:** 12th World Youth Festival in Moscow

Date	Mintage	F	VF	XF	Unc	BU
1985	—	—	0.50	1.00	3.00	—
1985 Proof	40,000	Value: 6.00				

Y# 199.2 ROUBLE Composition: Copper-Nickel **Edge Lettering:** 1988.N.

Date	Mintage	F	VF	XF	Unc	BU
1985 Proof; restrike	55,000	Value: 3.50				

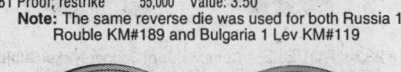

Y# 200.1 ROUBLE **Composition:** Copper-Nickel **Subject:** 165th Anniversary - Birth of Friedrich Engels

Date	Mintage	F	VF	XF	Unc	BU
1985	1,960,000	—	0.50	1.50	3.50	—
1985 Proof	—	Value: 6.00				

Y# 200.2 ROUBLE **Composition:** Copper-Nickel **Edge Lettering:** 1988.N.

Date	Mintage	F	VF	XF	Unc	BU
1983 Proof; restrike	—	Value: 55.00				
Note: Error date						
1985 Proof; restrike	55,000	Value: 4.50				

Y# 201.1 ROUBLE **Composition:** Copper-Nickel **Subject:** International Year of Peace **Note:** Rouble written with inverted "V" for Л.

Date	Mintage	F	VF	XF	Unc	BU
1986	—	—	0.50	1.00	3.00	—
1986 Proof	45,000	Value: 5.00				

Y# 201.2 ROUBLE **Composition:** Copper-Nickel **Edge Lettering:** 1988.N.

Date	Mintage	F	VF	XF	Unc	BU
1986 Proof; restrike	55,000	Value: 3.50				

Y# 201.3 ROUBLE **Composition:** Copper-Nickel **Note:** Rouble written **РУБЛЬ.**

Date	Mintage	F	VF	XF	Unc	BU
1986	—	—	0.50	1.00	3.00	—
1986 Proof	45,000	Value: 5.00				

Y# 201.4 ROUBLE **Composition:** Copper-Nickel **Edge Lettering:** 1988.N.

Date	Mintage	F	VF	XF	Unc	BU
1986	—	—	—	—	—	—

Y# 202.1 ROUBLE **Composition:** Copper-Nickel **Subject:** 275th Anniversary - Birth of Mikhail Lomonosov

Date	Mintage	F	VF	XF	Unc	BU
1986	—	—	0.50	1.00	3.00	—
1986 Proof	35,000	Value: 5.00				

Y# 202.2 ROUBLE **Composition:** Copper-Nickel **Edge Lettering:** 1988.N.

Date	Mintage	F	VF	XF	Unc	BU
1984 Error	—	—	—	—	—	—
1986 Proof; restrike	55,000	Value: 3.50				

Y#205 ROUBLE **Composition:** Copper-Nickel **Subject:** 130th Anniversary - Birth of Constantin Tsiolkovsky

Date	Mintage	F	VF	XF	Unc	BU
1987	—	—	0.50	1.00	3.00	—
1987 Proof	170,000	Value: 5.00				

Y#203 ROUBLE **Composition:** Copper-Nickel **Subject:** 175th Anniversary - Battle of Borodino - Soldiers **Note:** Varieties with wheat in coat of arms.

Date	Mintage	F	VF	XF	Unc	BU
1987	—	—	0.50	1.00	3.00	—
1987 Proof	220,000	Value: 5.00				

Y#204 ROUBLE **Composition:** Copper-Nickel **Subject:** 175th Anniversary - Battle of Borodino - Kutuzov Monument **Note:** Varieties with wheat in coat of arms.

Date	Mintage	F	VF	XF	Unc	BU
1987	—	—	0.50	1.00	3.00	—
1987 Proof	220,000	Value: 5.00				

Y#206 ROUBLE **Composition:** Copper-Nickel **Subject:** 70th Anniversary of Bolshevik Revolution **Note:** Varieties with wheat in coat of arms.

Date	Mintage	F	VF	XF	Unc	BU
1987	—	—	0.50	1.00	3.00	—
1987 Proof	200,000	Value: 6.00				

Y#216 ROUBLE **Composition:** Copper-Nickel **Subject:** 160th Anniversary - Birth of Leo Tolstoi

Date	Mintage	F	VF	XF	Unc	BU
1987 Error	—	—	—	—	—	—
1988	—	—	0.50	1.00	3.00	—
1988 Proof	225,000	Value: 5.00				

Y#209 ROUBLE **Composition:** Copper-Nickel **Subject:** 120th Anniversary - Birth of Maxin Gorky

Date	Mintage	F	VF	XF	Unc	BU
1988	—	—	0.50	1.00	3.00	—
1988 Proof	225,000	Value: 6.00				

Y#220 ROUBLE **Composition:** Copper-Nickel **Subject:** 150th Anniversary - Birth of Musorgsky

Date	Mintage	F	VF	XF	Unc	BU
1989	—	—	0.50	1.00	3.00	—
1989 Proof	300,000	Value: 5.50				

Y#228 ROUBLE **Composition:** Copper-Nickel **Subject:** 175th Anniversary - Birth of M.Y. Lermontov

Date	Mintage	F	VF	XF	Unc	BU
1989	—	—	0.50	1.00	3.00	—
1989 Proof	300,000	Value: 6.00				

Y#232 ROUBLE **Composition:** Copper-Nickel **Subject:** 100th Anniversary - Birth of Hamza Hakim-zade Niyazi

Date	Mintage	F	VF	XF	Unc	BU
1989	—	—	0.50	1.00	3.00	—
1989 Proof	200,000	Value: 6.00				

Y#233 ROUBLE **Composition:** Copper-Nickel **Subject:** 100th Anniversary - Death of Mihai Eminescu

Date	Mintage	F	VF	XF	Unc	BU
1989	—	—	0.50	1.00	3.00	—
1989 Proof	200,000	Value: 6.00				

Y#235 ROUBLE Composition: Copper-Nickel **Subject:** 175th Anniversary - Birth of T.G. Shevchenko

Date	Mintage	F	VF	XF	Unc	BU
1989	—	0.50	1.00	3.00	—	
1989 Proof	300,000	Value: 5.50				

Y#236 ROUBLE Composition: Copper-Nickel **Subject:** 100th Anniversary - Birth of Tschaikovsky - Composer

Date	Mintage	F	VF	XF	Unc	BU
1990	—	—	—	3.00	—	
1990 Proof	400,000	Value: 6.50				

Y#237 ROUBLE Composition: Copper-Nickel **Subject:** Anniversary - Marshal Zhukov

Date	Mintage	F	VF	XF	Unc	BU
1990	—	—	—	3.00	—	
1990 Proof	400,000	Value: 6.50				

Y#240 ROUBLE Composition: Copper-Nickel **Subject:** 130th Anniversary - Birth of Anton Chekhov

Date	Mintage	F	VF	XF	Unc	BU
1990	—	—	—	3.00	—	
1990 Proof	400,000	Value: 6.50				

Y#257 ROUBLE Composition: Copper-Nickel **Subject:** 125th Anniversary - Birth of Janis Rainis

Date	Mintage	F	VF	XF	Unc	BU
1990	—	—	—	3.00	—	
1990 Proof	400,000	Value: 6.50				

Y#258 ROUBLE Composition: Copper-Nickel **Subject:** 500th Anniversary - Birth of Francisk Scorina

Date	Mintage	F	VF	XF	Unc	BU
1990	—	—	—	3.00	—	
1990 Proof	400,000	Value: 6.50				

Y#260 ROUBLE Composition: Copper-Nickel **Subject:** 550th Anniversary - Birth of Alisher Navoi

Date	Mintage	F	VF	XF	Unc	BU
1990 Error	—	—	—	—	—	
1991	—	—	—	3.00	—	
1991 Proof	350,000	Value: 5.50				

Y#261 ROUBLE Composition: Copper-Nickel **Subject:** 125th Anniversary - Birth of P. N. Lebedev

Date	Mintage	F	VF	XF	Unc	BU
1991	—	—	—	3.00	—	
1991 Proof	350,000	Value: 5.50				

Y#263 ROUBLE Composition: Copper-Nickel **Subject:** 100th Birthday of Sergey Prokofiev

Date	Mintage	F	VF	XF	Unc	BU
1991	—	—	—	3.00	—	
1991 Proof	350,000	Value: 5.50				

Y#282 ROUBLE Composition: Copper-Nickel **Subject:** K. V. Ivanon **Reverse:** K.T. Ivanov.

Date	Mintage	F	VF	XF	Unc	BU
1991	—	—	—	3.00	—	
1991 Proof	350,000	Value: 5.50				

Y#283 ROUBLE Composition: Copper-Nickel **Reverse:** Turkman Poet Makhtumkuli.

Date	Mintage	F	VF	XF	Unc	BU
1991	—	—	—	3.00	—	
1991 Proof	350,000	Value: 5.50				

Y#284 ROUBLE Composition: Copper-Nickel **Subject:** 850th Anniversary - Birth of Nizami Gyanzhevi - Poet

Date	Mintage	F	VF	XF	Unc	BU
1991	—	—	—	3.00	—	
1991 Proof	300,000	Value: 5.50				

Y#289 ROUBLE Composition: Copper-Nickel **Series:** Olympics **Reverse:** Wrestlers

Date	Mintage	F	VF	XF	Unc	BU
1991 Proof	250,000	Value: 5.50				

Y#290 ROUBLE Composition: Copper-Nickel **Series:** Olympics **Reverse:** Javelin thrower

Date	Mintage	F	VF	XF	Unc	BU
1991 Proof	250,000	Value: 5.50				

Y#291 ROUBLE Composition: Copper-Nickel **Series:** Olympics **Reverse:** Cyclist and charioteer

Date	Mintage	F	VF	XF	Unc	BU
1991 Proof	250,000	Value: 5.50				

Y# 299 ROUBLE **Composition:** Copper-Nickel **Series:** Olympics **Reverse:** Weight lifters

Date	Mintage	F	VF	XF	Unc	BU
1991 Proof	250,000	Value: 5.50				

Y# 300 ROUBLE **Composition:** Copper-Nickel **Series:** Olympics **Reverse:** Broad jumpers

Date	Mintage	F	VF	XF	Unc	BU
1991 Proof	250,000	Value: 5.50				

Y# 302 ROUBLE **Composition:** Copper-Nickel **Series:** Olympics **Reverse:** Runners

Date	Mintage	F	VF	XF	Unc	BU
1991 Proof	250,000	Value: 5.50				

Y# A134 2 ROUBLES **Composition:** Copper-Nickel

Date	Mintage	F	VF	XF	Unc	BU
1958	20,976,000	—	—	—	250	—

Note: Never officially released for circulation; majority of mintage remelted

Y# B134 3 ROUBLES **Composition:** Copper-Nickel

Date	Mintage	F	VF	XF	Unc	BU
1958	4,050,000	—	—	—	—	—

Note: Never officially released for circulation; majority of mintage remelted

Y# 207 3 ROUBLES **Composition:** Copper-Nickel **Subject:** 70th Anniversary - Bolshevik Revolution

Date	Mintage	F	VF	XF	Unc	BU
1987	—	—	—	—	5.00	—
1987 Proof	200,000	Value: 7.50				

Y# 210 3 ROUBLES **Weight:** 34.5600 g. **Composition:** 0.9000 Silver 1.0000 oz. ASW **Subject:** 1000th Anniversary of Russian Architecture **Reverse:** Cathedral of St. Sophie in Kiev

Date	Mintage	F	VF	XF	Unc	BU
1988 (m) Proof	Est. 35,000	Value: 45.00				

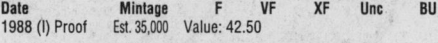

Y# 211 3 ROUBLES **Weight:** 34.5600 g. **Composition:** 0.9000 Silver 1.0000 oz. ASW **Subject:** 1000th Anniversary of Minting in Russian **Reverse:** Coin design of St. Vladimir, 977-1015

Date	Mintage	F	VF	XF	Unc	BU
1988 (l) Proof	Est. 35,000	Value: 42.50				

Y# 222 3 ROUBLES **Weight:** 34.5600 g. **Composition:** 0.9000 Silver 1.0000 oz. ASW **Subject:** 500th Anniversary United Russia **Obverse:** State emblem and denomination **Reverse:** Kremlin

Date	Mintage	F	VF	XF	Unc	BU
1989 (l) Proof	Est. 40,000	Value: 32.50				

Y# 223 3 ROUBLES **Weight:** 34.5600 g. **Composition:** 0.9000 Silver 1.0000 oz. ASW **Subject:** 500th Anniversary of the First All-Russian Coinage

Date	Mintage	F	VF	XF	Unc	BU
1989 (l) Proof	Est. 40,000	Value: 37.50				

Y# 234 3 ROUBLES **Composition:** Copper-Nickel **Subject:** Armenian Earthquake Relief

Date	Mintage	F	VF	XF	Unc	BU
1989	—	—	—	—	4.00	—
1989 Proof	300,000	Value: 6.50				

Y# 242 3 ROUBLES **Weight:** 34.5600 g. **Composition:** 0.9000 Silver 1.0000 oz. ASW **Reverse:** Capt. Cook on Unalaska Island

Date	Mintage	F	VF	XF	Unc	BU
1990 (l) Proof	25,000	Value: 47.50				

Y# 247 3 ROUBLES **Weight:** 34.5600 g. **Composition** 0.9000 Silver 1.0000 oz. ASW **Subject:** World Summit for Children

Date	Mintage	F	VF	XF	Unc	BU
1990 (l) Proof	20,000	Value: 37.50				

 # 248 3 ROUBLES **Weight:** 34.5600 g. **Composition:** 0.9000 Silver 1.0000 oz. ASW **Reverse:** Peter the Great's fleet

ate	Mintage	F	VF	XF	Unc	BU
990 (m) Proof	40,000	Value: 30.00				

 # 249 3 ROUBLES **Weight:** 34.5600 g. **Composition:** 0.9000 Silver 1.0000 oz. ASW **Reverse:** St. Peter and Paul Fortress in Leningrad

ate	Mintage	F	VF	XF	Unc	BU
990 (l) Proof	40,000	Value: 30.00				

 # 262 3 ROUBLES **Weight:** 34.5600 g. **Composition:** 0.9000 Silver 1.0000 oz. ASW **Reverse:** Yuri Gagarin Monument

ate	Mintage	F	VF	XF	Unc	BU
991 (l) Proof	35,000	Value: 32.50				

 # 264 3 ROUBLES **Weight:** 34.5600 g. **Composition:** 0.9000 Silver 1.0000 oz. ASW **Reverse:** Fort Ross in California

ate	Mintage	F	VF	XF	Unc	BU
991 (l) Proof	Est. 25,000	Value: 40.00				

Y# 274 3 ROUBLES **Weight:** 34.5600 g. **Composition:** 0.9000 Silver 1.0000 oz. ASW **Reverse:** Bolshoi Theater

Date	Mintage	F	VF	XF	Unc	BU
1991 (l) Proof	40,000	Value: 22.50				

Y# 275 3 ROUBLES **Weight:** 34.5600 g. **Composition:** 0.9000 Silver 1.0000 oz. ASW **Reverse:** Moscow's Arch of Triumph

Date	Mintage	F	VF	XF	Unc	BU
1991 (m) Proof	40,000	Value: 22.50				

Y# 301 3 ROUBLES **Composition:** Copper-Nickel **Subject:** 50th Anniversary - Defense of Moscow

Date	Mintage	F	VF	XF	Unc	BU
1991	2,150,000	—	—	—	4.50	—
1991 Proof	—	Value: 6.50				

Y# C134 5 ROUBLES **Composition:** Copper-Nickel

Date	Mintage	F	VF	XF	Unc	BU
1958	5,150,000	—	—	—	300	—

Note: Never officially released for circulation; majority of mintage remelted

Y# 145 5 ROUBLES **Weight:** 16.6700 g. **Composition:** 0.9000 Silver .4824 oz. ASW **Series:** 1980 Olympics **Reverse:** Scenes of Kiev

Date	Mintage	F	VF	XF	Unc	BU
1977 (l)		—	—	—	4.50	—
1977 (l) Frosted unc.		—	—	—	—	—
1977 (l) Proof	121,000	Value: 6.00				
1977 (m) Proof	—	Value: 6.00				

Y# 146 5 ROUBLES **Weight:** 16.6700 g. **Composition:** 0.9000 Silver .4824 oz. ASW **Series:** 1980 Olympics **Reverse:** Scenes of Leningrad

Date	Mintage	F	VF	XF	Unc	BU
1977 (l)		—	—	—	4.50	—
1977 (l) Frosted unc.		—	—	—	—	—
1977 (l) Proof	121,000	Value: 6.00				
1977 (m)		—	—	—	4.50	—
1977 (m) Proof	Inc. above	Value: 6.00				

Y# 147 5 ROUBLES **Weight:** 16.6700 g. **Composition:** 0.9000 Silver .4824 oz. ASW **Series:** 1980 Olympics **Reverse:** Scenes of Minsk

Date	Mintage	F	VF	XF	Unc	BU
1977(l)		—	—	—	4.50	—
1977(l) Proof	121,000	Value: 6.00				
1977(m) Proof	Inc. above	Value: 6.00				

Y# 148 5 ROUBLES **Weight:** 16.6700 g. **Composition:** 0.9000 Silver .4824 oz. ASW **Series:** 1980 Olympics **Reverse:** Scenes of Tallinn

Date	Mintage	F	VF	XF	Unc	BU
1977(l)		—	—	—	4.50	—
1977(l) Frosted		—	—	—	—	—
1977(l) Proof	122,000	Value: 6.00				
1977(m)		—	—	—	4.50	—
1977(m) Proof	Inc. above	Value: 6.00				

Y# 154 5 ROUBLES **Weight:** 16.6700 g. **Composition:** 0.9000 Silver .4824 oz. ASW **Series:** 1980 Olympics **Reverse:** Runner in front of stadium

Date	Mintage	F	VF	XF	Unc	BU
1978(l)	227,000	—	—	—	4.50	—
1978(m) Proof	118,000	Value: 6.00				
1978(l) Matte proof	—	Value: 25.00				

Y# 155 5 ROUBLES **Weight:** 16.6700 g. **Composition:** 0.9000 Silver .4824 oz. ASW **Series:** 1980 Olympics **Subject:** Swimming

Date	Mintage	F	VF	XF	Unc	BU
1978(l)	227,000	—	—	—	4.50	—
1978(l) Frosted	Inc. above	—	—	—	—	—
1978(l) Proof	118,000	Value: 6.00				
1978(l) Matte proof	—	Value: 25.00				

Y# 156 5 ROUBLES **Weight:** 16.6700 g. **Composition:** 0.9000 Silver .4824 oz. ASW **Series:** 1980 Olympics **Subject:** High jumping

Date	Mintage	F	VF	XF	Unc	BU
1978(l)		—	—	—	4.50	—
1978(l) Proof	119,000	Value: 6.00				
1978(m)		—	—	—	4.50	—
1978(m) Proof	Inc. above	Value: 6.00				

Y# 157 5 ROUBLES **Weight:** 16.6700 g. **Composition:** 0.9000 Silver .4824 oz. ASW **Series:** 1980 Olympics **Subject:** Equestrian show jumping

Date	Mintage	F	VF	XF	Unc	BU
1978(l)		—	—	—	4.50	—
1978(l) Proof	119,000	Value: 6.00				
1978(m)		—	—	—	4.50	—
1978(m) Proof	Inc. above	Value: 6.00				

Y# 166 5 ROUBLES **Weight:** 16.6700 g. **Composition:** 0.9000 Silver 0.4824 oz. ASW **Series:** 1980 Olympics **Subject:** Weightlifting

Date	Mintage	F	VF	XF	Unc	BU
1979(l)		—	—	—	4.50	—
1979(l) Proof	108,000	Value: 6.00				
1979(m)		—	—	—	4.50	—
1979(m) Proof	Inc. above	Value: 6.00				

Y# 167 5 ROUBLES **Weight:** 16.6700 g. **Composition:** 0.9000 Silver .4824 oz. ASW **Series:** 1980 Olympics **Subject:** Hammer throw

Date	Mintage	F	VF	XF	Unc	BU
1979(l)		—	—	—	4.50	—
1979(l) Proof	119,000	Value: 6.00				
1979(m)		—	—	—	4.50	—
1979(m) Proof	Inc. above	Value: 6.00				

Y# 179 5 ROUBLES **Weight:** 16.6700 g. **Composition:** 0.9000 Silver **Series:** 1980 Olympics **Subject:** Archery

Date	Mintage	F	VF	XF	Unc	BU
1980(l)		—	—	—	5.00	—
1980(l) Proof	95,000	Value: 7.00				
1980(m)		—	—	—	5.00	—
1980(m) Proof	Inc. above	Value: 7.00				

Y# 180 5 ROUBLES **Weight:** 16.6700 g. **Composition:** 0.9000 Silver **Series:** 1980 Olympics **Subject:** Gymnastics

Date	Mintage	F	VF	XF	Unc	BU
1980(l)		—	—	—	5.00	—
1980(l) Proof	95,000	Value: 7.00				
1980(m)		—	—	—	5.00	—
1980(m) Proof	Inc. above	Value: 7.00				

Y# 181 5 ROUBLES **Weight:** 16.6700 g. **Composition:** 0.9000 Silver **Series:** 1980 Olympics **Subject:** Equestrian - Isindi

Date	Mintage	F	VF	XF	Unc	BU
1980(l)		—	—	—	5.00	—
1980(l) Proof	96,000	Value: 7.00				

Y# 182 5 ROUBLES **Weight:** 16.6700 g. **Compositio**n: 0.9000 Silver **Series:** 1980 Olympics **Subject:** Gorodki - Stick Throwing

Date	Mintage	F	VF	XF	Unc
1980(l)		—	—	—	5.00
1980(l) Proof	96,000	Value: 7.00			

Y# 208 5 ROUBLES **Composition:** Copper-Nickel **Subject:** 70th Anniversary - Bolshevik Revolution

Date	Mintage	F	VF	XF	Unc
1987		—	—	—	5.00
1987 Proof	200,000	Value: 7.00			

Y# 217 5 ROUBLES **Composition:** Copper-Nickel **Reverse:** Peter the Great mounted on horse in Leningra

Date	Mintage	F	VF	XF	Unc
1988		—	—	—	5.00
1988 Proof	325,000	Value: 7.00			

Y# 218 5 ROUBLES **Composition:** Copper-Nickel **Reverse:** Novgorod Monument to the Russian millenniur

Date	Mintage	F	VF	XF	Unc
1988		—	—	—	5.00
1988 Proof	325,000	Value: 7.00			

Y# 219 5 ROUBLES **Composition:** Copper-Nickel **Reverse:** St. Sophia Cathedral in Kiev

Date	Mintage	F	VF	XF	Unc
1988		—	—	—	5.00
1988 Proof	325,000	Value: 7.00			

Y# 221 5 ROUBLES Composition: Copper-Nickel **Reverse:** Pokrowsky Cathedral in Moscow

Date	Mintage	F	VF	XF	Unc	BU
1989	—	—	—	—	5.00	—
1989 Proof	300,000	Value: 7.00				

Y# 229 5 ROUBLES Composition: Copper-Nickel **Reverse:** Samarkand

Date	Mintage	F	VF	XF	Unc	BU
1989	—	—	—	—	5.00	—
1989 Proof	300,000	Value: 7.00				

Y# 230 5 ROUBLES Composition: Copper-Nickel **Reverse:** Cathedral of the Annunciation in Moscow

Date	Mintage	F	VF	XF	Unc	BU
1989	—	—	—	—	5.00	—
1989 Proof	300,000	Value: 7.00				

Y# 241 5 ROUBLES Composition: Copper-Nickel **Reverse:** Petergoff Palace

Date	Mintage	F	VF	XF	Unc	BU
1990	—	—	—	—	5.00	—
1990 Proof	400,000	Value: 7.00				

Y# 246 5 ROUBLES Composition: Copper-Nickel **Reverse:** Uspenski Cathedral

Date	Mintage	F	VF	XF	Unc	BU
1990	—	—	—	—	5.00	
1990 Proof	400,000	Value: 7.00				

Y# 259 5 ROUBLES Composition: Copper-Nickel **Reverse:** Matenadarin Depository of Ancient Armenian Manuscripts

Date	Mintage	F	VF	XF	Unc	BU
1990	—	—	—	—	5.00	—
1990 Proof	350,000	Value: 7.00				

Y# 268 5 ROUBLES Weight: 7.7758 g. **Composition:** 0.9990 Palladium .2500 oz. **Series:** Ballet

Date	Mintage	F	VF	XF	Unc	BU
1991	9,000	—	—	—	225	—

Y# 271 5 ROUBLES Composition: Copper-Nickel **Reverse:** Cathedral of the Archangel Michael in Moscow

Date	Mintage	F	VF	XF	Unc	BU
1991	—	—	—	—	5.00	—
1991 Proof	350,000	Value: 7.00				

Y# 272 5 ROUBLES Composition: Copper-Nickel **Reverse:** State bank building in Moscow

Date	Mintage	F	VF	XF	Unc	BU
1991	—	—	—	—	5.00	—
1991 Proof	400,000	Value: 7.00				

Y# 273 5 ROUBLES Composition: Copper-Nickel **Reverse:** David Sasunsky Monument

Date	Mintage	F	VF	XF	Unc	BU
1991	—	—	—	—	5.00	—
1991 Proof	350,000	Value: 7.00				

Y# 149 10 ROUBLES Weight: 33.3000 g. **Composition:** 0.9000 Silver .9636 oz. ASW **Series:** 1980 Olympics **Reverse:** Scenes of Moscow

Date	Mintage	F	VF	XF	Unc	BU
1977(l)	—	—	—	—	10.00	—
1977(l) Proof	121,000	Value: 12.00				
1977(m)	—	—	—	—	10.00	—
1977(m) Proof	Inc. above	Value: 12.00				

Y# 150 10 ROUBLES Weight: 33.3000 g. **Composition:** 0.9000 Silver .9636 oz. ASW **Series:** 1980 Olympics **Obverse:** Similar to Y#149 **Reverse:** Map of U.S.S.R.

Date	Mintage	F	VF	XF	Unc	BU
1977(l)	—	—	—	—	10.00	—
1977(l) Proof	121,000	Value: 12.00				

Y# 158.1 10 ROUBLES Weight: 33.3000 g. **Composition:** 0.9000 Silver .9636 oz. ASW **Series:** 1980 Olympics **Subject:** Cycling **Obverse:** Similar to Y#149

Date	Mintage	F	VF	XF	Unc	BU
1978(l)	—	—	—	—	10.00	—
1978(l) Proof	118,000	Value: 12.00				

Y# 158.2 10 ROUBLES Weight: 33.3000 g. **Composition:** 0.9000 Silver .9636 oz. ASW **Series:** 1980 Olympics **Reverse:** Without mint mark **Note:** Struck at Leningrad without mint mark.

Date	Mintage	F	VF	XF	Unc	BU
1978	—	—	—	—	—	—
1978 Proof	100	Value: 120				

Y# 159 10 ROUBLES **Weight:** 33.3000 g. **Composition:** 0.9000 Silver .9636 oz. ASW **Series:** 1980 Olympics **Subject:** Canoeing **Obverse:** Similar to Y#149

Date	Mintage	F	VF	XF	Unc	BU
1978(l)		—	—	—	25.00	—
1978(m)		—	—	—	10.00	—
1978(m) Proof	118,000	Value: 12.00				

Y# 160 10 ROUBLES **Weight:** 33.3000 g. **Composition:** 0.9000 Silver .9636 oz. ASW **Series:** 1980 Olympics **Subject:** Equestrian Sport **Obverse:** Similar to Y#149

Date	Mintage	F	VF	XF	Unc	BU
1978(l)		—	—	—	25.00	—
1978(m)		—	—	—	10.00	—
1978(m) Proof	118,000	Value: 12.00				

Y# 161 10 ROUBLES **Weight:** 33.3000 g. **Composition:** 0.9000 Silver .9636 oz. ASW **Series:** 1980 Olympics **Subject:** Pole vaulting **Obverse:** Similar to Y#149

Date	Mintage	F	VF	XF	Unc	BU
1978(l)		—	—	—	10.00	—
1978(l) Proof	119,000	Value: 12.00				
1978(m)		—	—	—	10.00	—
1978(m) Proof	Inc. above	Value: 12.00				

Y# 168 10 ROUBLES **Weight:** 33.3000 g. **Composition:** 0.9000 Silver .9636 oz. ASW **Series:** 1980 Olympics **Subject:** Basketball **Obverse:** Similar to Y#149

Date	Mintage	F	VF	XF	Unc	BU
1979(l)		—	—	—	10.00	—
1979(l) Proof	119,000	Value: 12.00				
1979		—	—	—	120	—

Y# 169 10 ROUBLES **Weight:** 33.3000 g. **Composition:** 0.9000 Silver .9636 oz. ASW **Series:** 1980 Olympics **Subject:** Volleyball **Obverse:** Similar to Y#149

Date	Mintage	F	VF	XF	Unc	BU
1979(l)		—	—	—	10.00	—
1979(l) Proof	119,000	Value: 12.00				

Y# 170 10 ROUBLES **Weight:** 33.3000 g. **Composition:** 0.9000 Silver .9636 oz. ASW **Series:** 1980 Olympics **Subject:** Boxing **Obverse:** Similar to Y#149

Date	Mintage	F	VF	XF	Unc	BU
1979(l)		—	—	—	12.00	—
1979(l) Proof	108,000	Value: 15.00				

Y# 171 10 ROUBLES **Weight:** 33.3000 g. **Composition:** 0.9000 Silver .9636 oz. ASW **Series:** 1980 Olympics **Subject:** Judo **Obverse:** Similar to Y#149

Date	Mintage	F	VF	XF	Unc	BU
1979(l)		—	—	—	12.00	—
1979(l) Proof	108,000	Value: 15.00				
1979(m)		—	—	—	12.00	—
1979(m) Proof	Inc. above	Value: 15.00				

Y# 172 10 ROUBLES **Weight:** 33.3000 g. **Composition:** 0.9000 Silver .9636 oz. ASW **Series:** 1980 Olympics **Subject:** Lifting of the Weight **Obverse:** Similar to Y#149

Date	Mintage	F	VF	XF	Unc	BU
1979(l)		—	—	—	12.00	—
1979(l) Proof	108,000	Value: 15.00				

Y# 183 10 ROUBLES **Weight:** 33.3000 g. **Composition:** 0.9000 Silver .9636 oz. ASW **Series:** 1980 Olympics **Subject:** Wrestling **Obverse:** Similar to Y#149

Date	Mintage	F	VF	XF	Unc	BU
1980(l)		—	—	—	12.00	—
1980(l) Proof	95,000	Value: 15.00				
1980(m)		—	—	—	12.00	—
1980(m) Proof	Inc. above	Value: 15.00				

Y# 184 10 ROUBLES **Weight:** 33.3000 g. **Composition:** 0.9000 Silver .9636 oz. ASW **Series:** 1980 Olympics **Subject:** Tug of War **Obverse:** Similar to Y#149

Date	Mintage	F	VF	XF	Unc	BU
1980(l)		—	—	—	12.00	—
1980(l) Proof	95,000	Value: 15.00				

Y# 185 10 ROUBLES **Weight:** 33.3000 g. **Composition:** 0.9000 Silver .9636 oz. ASW **Series:** 1980 Olympics **Subject:** Reindeer Racing **Obverse:** Similar to Y#149

Date	Mintage	F	VF	XF	Unc	BU
1980(l)		—	—	—	12.00	—
1980(l) Proof	95,000	Value: 15.00				

Y# 238 10 ROUBLES **Weight:** 15.5500 g. **Composition:** 0.9990 Palladium .5000 oz. **Subject:** Ballet **Obverse:** Similar to Y#269 **Reverse:** Ballerina

Date	F	VF	XF	Unc	BU
1990	—	—	—	300	

Y# 269 10 ROUBLES **Weight:** 15.5500 g. **Composition:** 0.9990 Palladium .5000 oz. **Subject:** Ballet **Reverse:** Ballerina

Date	Mintage	F	VF	XF	Unc	BU
1991	15,000	—	—	—	300	—

Y# 285 10 ROUBLES **Weight:** 2.6600 g. **Composition:** 0.5850 Gold .0500 oz. AGW **Subject:** Bolshoi Ballet **Obverse:** Similar to 50 Roubles, Y#287 **Reverse:** Ballerina

Date	Mintage	F	VF	XF	Unc	BU
1991	6,000	—	—	—	50.00	—

Y# 212 25 ROUBLES **Weight:** 31.1000 g. **Composition:** 0.9990 Palladium 1.0000 oz. **Reverse:** Monument to Vladimir, Graand Duke of Kiev and to the Millennium of Christianity in Russia

Date	Mintage	F	VF	XF	Unc	BU
1988(l)	7,000	—	—	—	625	—

Y# 224 25 ROUBLES **Weight:** 31.1000 g. **Composition:** 0.9990 Palladium 1.0000 oz. **Subject:** 500th Anniversary of Russian State **Reverse:** Ivan III

Date	Mintage	F	VF	XF	Unc	BU
1989(l) Proof	Est. 12,000	Value: 650				

Y# 231 25 ROUBLES **Weight:** 31.1000 g. **Composition:** 0.9990 Palladium 1.0000 oz. **Subject:** Ballet **Reverse:** Ballerina

Date	Mintage	F	VF	XF	Unc	BU
1989	—	—	—	—	625	—
1989 Matte proof	—	Value: 650				
1989 Proof	3,000	Value: 650				

Y# 239 25 ROUBLES **Weight:** 31.1000 g. **Composition:** 0.9990 Palladium 1.0000 oz. **Subject:** Ballet **Reverse:** Ballerina

Date	Mintage	F	VF	XF	Unc	BU
1990	—	—	—	—	625	—
1990 Proof	3,000	Value: 650				

Y# 243 25 ROUBLES **Weight:** 31.1000 g. **Composition:** 0.9990 Palladium 1.0000 oz. **Subject:** 250th Anniversary - Discovery of Russian America - Ship - St. Peter

Date	Mintage	F	VF	XF	Unc	BU
1990(l) Proof	6,500	Value: 650				

Y# 244 25 ROUBLES **Weight:** 31.1000 g. **Composition:** 0.9990 Palladium 1.0000 oz. **Subject:** 250th Anniversary - Discovery of Russian America - Ship - St. Paul

Date	Mintage	F	VF	XF	Unc	BU
1990(l) Proof	6,500	Value: 650				

Y# 250 25 ROUBLES **Weight:** 31.1000 g. **Composition:** 0.9990 Palladium 1.0000 oz. **Subject:** 500th Anniversary of Russian State - Peter the Great

Date	Mintage	F	VF	XF	Unc	BU
1990(l) Proof	12,000	Value: 650				

Y# 265 25 ROUBLES **Weight:** 31.1000 g. **Composition:** 0.9990 Palladium 1.0000 oz. **Note:** Three Saints Harbor - Russian settlement in America

Date	Mintage	F	VF	XF	Unc	BU
1991 Proof	Est. 6,500	Value: 650				

Y# 266 25 ROUBLES **Weight:** 31.1000 g. **Composition:** 0.9990 Palladium 1.0000 oz. **Note:** Novo Archangelsk 1799 - three-masted ship

Date	Mintage	F	VF	XF	Unc	BU
1991(l) Proof	Est. 6,500	Value: 650				

Y# 270 25 ROUBLES **Weight:** 31.1000 g. **Composition:** 0.9990 Palladium 1.0000 oz. **Subject:** Ballet **Reverse:** Ballerina

Date	Mintage	F	VF	XF	Unc	BU
1991	—	—	—	—	625	—
1991 Proof	30,000	Value: 650				

Y# 276 25 ROUBLES **Weight:** 31.1000 g. **Composition:** 0.9990 Palladium 1.0000 oz. **Subject:** 500th Anniversary of Russian State - Abolition of Serfdom in Russia **Obverse:** State emblem

Date	Mintage	F	VF	XF	Unc	BU
1991(l) Proof	Est. 12,000	Value: 650				

Y# 286 25 ROUBLES **Weight:** 5.3200 g. **Composition:** 0.5850 Gold 1.0000 oz. AGW **Subject:** Bolshoi Ballet

Date	Mintage	F	VF	XF	Unc	BU
1991	5,000	—	—	—	100	—

Y# 286a 25 ROUBLES **Weight:** 3.1100 g. **Composition:** 0.9990 Gold 1.0000 oz. AGW

Date	Mintage	F	VF	XF	Unc	BU
1991 Proof	1,500	Value: 250				

Y# 213 50 ROUBLES **Weight:** 8.6397 g. **Composition:** 0.9000 Gold .2500 oz. AGW **Subject:** 1000th Anniversary of Russian Architecture **Obverse:** Similar to 100 Roubles, Y#A163 **Reverse:** Cathedral of St. Sophia in Novgorod

Date	Mintage	F	VF	XF	Unc	BU
1988(m)	25,000	—	—	—	125	—

Y# 225 50 ROUBLES **Weight:** 8.6397 g. **Composition:** 0.9000 Gold .2500 oz. AGW **Subject:** 500th Anniversary of Russian State **Obverse:** State emblem and denomination **Reverse:** Cathedral of the Ascension

Date	Mintage	F	VF	XF	Unc	BU
1989(m) Proof	Est. 25,000	Value: 140				

Y# 251 50 ROUBLES **Weight:** 8.6397 g. **Composition:** 0.9000 Gold .2500 oz. AGW **Subject:** 500th Anniversary of Russian State **Reverse:** Moscow Church of the Archangel

Date	Mintage	F	VF	XF	Unc	BU
1990(m) Proof	25,000	Value: 140				

Y# 277 50 ROUBLES **Weight:** 8.6440 g. **Composition:** 0.9000 Gold .2500 oz. AGW **Subject:** 500th Anniversary of Russian State **Reverse:** St. Isaac Cathedral in St. Petersburg

Date	Mintage	F	VF	XF	Unc	BU
1991(m) Proof	25,000	Value: 140				

Y# 287 50 ROUBLES **Weight:** 13.3000 g. **Composition:** 0.5850 Gold .2500 oz. AGW **Subject:** Bolshoi Ballet **Reverse:** Ballerina

Date	Mintage	F	VF	XF	Unc	BU
1991	2,400	—	—	—	250	—

Y# 287a 50 ROUBLES **Weight:** 7.7800 g. **Composition:** 0.9990 Gold .2500 oz. AGW **Reverse:** Ballerina **Edge Lettering:** Bolshoi Ballet

Date	Mintage	F	VF	XF	Unc	BU
1991 Proof	1,500	Value: 450				

Y# A163 100 ROUBLES **Weight:** 17.2800 g. **Composition:** 0.9000 Gold .5000 oz. AGW **Series:** 1980 Olympics **Reverse:** Symbols

Date	Mintage	F	VF	XF	Unc	BU
1977(l)	—	—	—	—	175	—
1977(l) Proof	38,000	Value: 200				
1977(m)	—	—	—	—	175	—
1977(m) Proof	Inc. above	Value: 200				

Y# 151 100 ROUBLES **Weight:** 17.2800 g. **Composition:** 0.9000 Gold .5000 oz. AGW **Series:** 1980 Olympics **Reverse:** Lenin Stadium

Date	Mintage	F	VF	XF	Unc	BU
1978(l)	—	—	—	—	175	—
1978(l) Proof	45,000	Value: 200				
1978(m)	—	—	—	—	175	—
1978(m) Proof	Inc. above	Value: 200				

Y# 162 100 ROUBLES **Weight:** 17.2800 g. **Composition:** 0.9000 Gold .5000 oz. AGW **Series:** 1980 Olympics **Reverse:** Waterside grandstand

Date	Mintage	F	VF	XF	Unc	BU
1978(l)	—	—	—	—	175	—
1978 Matte	—	—	—	—	—	—
1978(l) Proof	43,000	Value: 200				
1978(m)	—	—	—	—	175	—
1978(m) Proof	Inc. above	Value: 200				

Y# 173 100 ROUBLES **Weight:** 17.2800 g. **Composition:** 0.9000 Gold .5000 oz. AGW **Series:** 1980 Olympics **Reverse:** Velodrome building

Date	Mintage	F	VF	XF	Unc	BU
1979(l)	—	—	—	—	175	—
1979(l) Proof	42,000	Value: 200				
1979(m)	—	—	—	—	175	—
1979(m) Proof	Inc. above	Value: 200				

Y# 174 100 ROUBLES **Weight:** 17.2800 g. **Composition:** 0.9000 Gold .5000 oz. AGW **Series:** 1980 Olympics **Reverse:** Druzhba Sports Hall

Date	Mintage	F	VF	XF	Unc	BU
1979(m)	—	—	—	—	175	—
1979(l) Proof	38,000	Value: 200				

Y# 186 100 ROUBLES **Weight:** 17.2800 g. **Composition:** 0.9000 Gold .5000 oz. AGW **Series:** 1980 Olympics **Reverse:** Torch

Date	Mintage	F	VF	XF	Unc	BU
1980(m)	—	—	—	—	175	—
1980(l) Proof	28,000	Value: 200				

Y# 214 100 ROUBLES **Weight:** 17.2800 g. **Composition:** 0.9000 Gold .5000 oz. AGW **Series:** 1980 Olympics **Subject:** 1000th Anniversary of Minting in Russia - Coin design of St. Vladimir, 977-1015 **Obverse:** Similar to Y#186

Date	Mintage	F	VF	XF	Unc	BU
1988(m)	14,000	—	—	—	250	—

Y# 226 100 ROUBLES **Weight:** 17.2800 g. **Composition:** 0.9000 Gold .5000 oz. AGW **Series:** 1980 Olympics **Subject:** 500th Anniversary of Russian State **Obverse:** State emblem and denomination **Reverse:** Seal of Ivan III

Date	Mintage	F	VF	XF	Unc	BU
1989(m) Proof	Est. 14,000	Value: 265				

Y# 252 100 ROUBLES **Weight:** 17.2800 g. **Composition:** 0.9000 Gold .5000 oz. AGW **Series:** 1980 Olympics **Subject:** 500th Anniversary of Russian State **Reverse:** Peter the Great Monument

Date	Mintage	F	VF	XF	Unc	BU
1990(m) Proof	14,000	Value: 250				

Y# 278 100 ROUBLES **Weight:** 17.2800 g. **Composition:** 0.9000 Gold .5000 oz. AGW **Series:** 1980 Olympics **Subject:** 500th Anniversary of Russian State **Reverse:** Tolstoi Monument

Date	Mintage	F	VF	XF	Unc	BU
1991(m) Proof	14,000	Value: 250				

Y# 288 100 ROUBLES **Weight:** 26.5900 g. **Composition:** 0.5850 Gold .5000 oz. AGW **Subject:** Bolshoi Ballet **Reverse:** Ballerina

Date	Mintage	F	VF	XF	Unc	BU
1991	1,200	—	—	—	500	—

Y# 288a 100 ROUBLES **Weight:** 15.5500 g. **Composition:** 0.9990 Gold .5000 oz. AGW **Subject:** Bolshoi Ballet **Reverse:** Ballerina

Date	Mintage	F	VF	XF	Unc	BU
1991 Proof	1,500	Value: 750				

Y# 152 150 ROUBLES **Weight:** 15.5400 g. **Composition:** 0.9990 Platinum .4991 oz. APW **Series:** 1980 Olympics **Reverse:** Symbols over logo

Date	Mintage	F	VF	XF	Unc	BU
1977(l)	—	—	—	—	425	—
1977(m) Proof	24,000	Value: 450				

Y# 163 150 ROUBLES **Weight:** 15.5400 g. **Composition:** 0.9990 Platinum .4991 oz. APW **Series:** 1980 Olympics **Reverse:** Throwing discus

Date	Mintage	F	VF	XF	Unc	BU
1978(l)	—	—	—	—	425	—
1978(l) Proof	20,000	Value: 450				

Y# 175 150 ROUBLES **Weight:** 15.5400 g. **Composition:** 0.9990 Platinum .4991 oz. APW **Series:** 1980 Olympics **Reverse:** Greek wrestlers

Date	Mintage	F	VF	XF	Unc	BU
1979(l)	14,000	—	—	—	425	—
1979(l)	19,000	—	—	—	450	—

Y# 176 150 ROUBLES **Weight:** 15.5400 g. **Composition:** 0.9990 Platinum .4991 oz. APW **Series:** 1980 Olympics **Reverse:** Roman chariot race

Date	Mintage	F	VF	XF	Unc	BU
1979(l)	—	—	—	—	425	—
1979(l) Proof	17,000	Value: 450				

Y# 187 150 ROUBLES **Weight:** 15.5400 g. **Composition:** 0.9990 Platinum .4991 oz. APW **Series:** 1980 Olympics **Reverse:** Ancient Greek runners

Date	Mintage	F	VF	XF	Unc	BU
1980(I)		—	—	—	425	—
1980(I) Proof	13,000	Value: 450				

Y# 215 150 ROUBLES **Weight:** 15.5500 g. **Composition:** 0.9990 Platinum .5000 oz. APW **Subject:** 1000th Anniversary of Russian Literature **Obverse:** Similar to Y#187 **Reverse:** Chronicler writing epic about Grand Duke Igor

Date	Mintage	F	VF	XF	Unc	BU
1988(I)	16,000	—	—	—	435	—

Y# 227 150 ROUBLES **Weight:** 15.5500 g. **Composition:** 0.9990 Platinum .5000 oz. APW **Subject:** 500th Anniversary of Russian State **Obverse:** State emblem and denomination **Reverse:** Ugra River encounter

Date	Mintage	F	VF	XF	Unc	BU
1989(I) Proof	Est. 16,000	Value: 435				

Y# 245 150 ROUBLES **Weight:** 15.5500 g. **Composition:** 0.9990 Platinum .5000 oz. APW **Subject:** 250th Anniversary - Discovery of Russian America - Ship - St. Gavriil **Obverse:** Similar to Y#187

Date	Mintage	F	VF	XF	Unc	BU
1990(I) Proof	6,500	Value: 475				

Y# 253 150 ROUBLES **Weight:** 15.5500 g. **Composition:** 0.9990 Platinum .5000 oz. APW **Subject:** 500th Anniversary of Russian State **Reverse:** Battle of Poltava River

Date	Mintage	F	VF	XF	Unc	BU
1990(I) Proof	16,000	Value: 435				

Y# 267 150 ROUBLES **Weight:** 15.5500 g. **Composition:** 0.9990 Platinum .5000 oz. APW **Subject:** 250th Anniversary - Discovery of Russian America **Reverse:** Bishop Veniaminov

Date	Mintage	F	VF	XF	Unc	BU
1991(I) Proof	Est. 6,500	Value: 475				

Y# 279 150 ROUBLES **Weight:** 17.5000 g. **Composition:** 0.9990 Platinum .5000 oz. APW **Subject:** 500th Anniversary of Russian State - War of Liberation Against Napoleon

Date	Mintage	F	VF	XF	Unc	BU
1991(I) Proof	16,000	Value: 450				

GOVERNMENT BANK ISSUES

1991-1992

Y# 296 10 KOPEKS **Composition:** Copper Clad Steel **Obverse:** Kremlin tower and dome

Date	F	VF	XF	Unc	BU
1991 M	0.10	0.15	0.25	0.35	—

Y# 292 50 KOPEKS **Composition:** Copper-Nickel

Date	F	VF	XF	Unc	BU
1991Л	0.15	0.25	0.35	0.50	—

Y# 293 ROUBLE **Composition:** Copper-Nickel

Date	F	VF	XF	Unc	BU
1991(I)	—	—	—	0.75	—
1991(m)	—	—	—	1.25	—

Y# 280 5 ROUBLES **Ring Composition:** Copper-Nickel **Center Composition:** Brass **Series:** Wildlife **Reverse:** Owl

Date	Mintage	F	VF	XF	Unc	BU
1991(I)	500,000	—	—	—	1.50	—

Y# 281 5 ROUBLES **Ring Composition:** Copper-Nickel **Center Composition:** Brass **Series:** Wildlife **Reverse:** Mountain Goat

Date	Mintage	F	VF	XF	Unc	BU
1991(I)	500,000	—	—	—	1.50	—

Y# 294 5 ROUBLES **Composition:** Copper-Nickel

Date	F	VF	XF	Unc	BU
1991(I)	—	—	—	2.50	—
1991(m)	—	—	—	5.00	—

Y# 295 10 ROUBLES **Center Composition:** Aluminum-Bronze

Date	F	VF	XF	Unc	BU
1991(I)	0.25	0.50	1.00	3.00	—
1991(m)	4.50	3.00	5.00	10.00	—
1992(I) Error	—	30.00	50.00	80.00	—

COMMONWEALTH OF INDEPENDENT STATES

Issued by БАНК РОССИИ (Bank Russia)

STANDARD COINAGE

Y# 303 ROUBLE **Composition:** Copper-Nickel **Subject:** Rebirth of Russian Sovereignty and Democracy

Date	Mintage	F	VF	XF	Unc	BU
1992(I)		—	—	—	2.50	—
1992(I) Proof	300,000	Value: 5.00				

Y# 305 ROUBLE **Composition:** Copper-Nickel **Subject:** 110th Anniversary - Birth of Jacob Kolas

Date		F	VF	XF	Unc	BU
1992(I)		—	—	—	2.50	—
1992(I) Proof	—	Value: 5.00				

Y# 306 ROUBLE **Composition:** Copper-Nickel **Subject:** 190th Anniversary - Birth of Admiral Nakhimov

Date		F	VF	XF	Unc	BU
1992(I)		—	—	—	2.50	—
1992(I) Proof	—	Value: 5.00				

Y# 311 ROUBLE **Composition:** Brass Clad Steel
Obverse: Double-headed eagle

Date	F	VF	XF	Unc	BU
1992	2.00	5.00	10.00	20.00	—
1992Л	—	—	—	1.25	—
1992M	—	—	—	1.00	—
1992(m)	—	—	—	2.00	—
1992(l)	—	—	—	2.50	—

Y# 320 ROUBLE **Composition:** Copper-Nickel
Reverse: Yanka Kupala

Date	Mintage	F	VF	XF	Unc	BU
1992(l)		—	—	—	2.50	—
1992(l) Prooflike		—	—	—	—	—
1992(l) Proof	350,000	Value: 5.00				

Y# 321 ROUBLE **Composition:** Copper-Nickel
Obverse: Double-headed eagle **Reverse:** N. I. Lobachevsky

Date	Mintage	F	VF	XF	Unc	BU
1992(m)	1,000,000	—	—	—	2.50	—
1992(m) Prooflike	500,000	—	—	—	—	—
1992(m) Proof	—	Value: 5.00				

Y# 319.1 ROUBLE **Composition:** Copper-Nickel
Obverse: Double-headed eagle **Reverse:** Vladimir Ivanovich Vernadsky

Date	Mintage	F	VF	XF	Unc	BU
1993(l)		—	—	—	2.50	—
1993(l) Prooflike		—	—	—	—	—
1993(l) Proof	35,000	Value: 5.50				

Y# 319.2 ROUBLE **Composition:** Copper-Nickel
Obverse: Double-headed eagle, without mint mark below eagle's claw **Reverse:** Vladimir Ivanovich Vernadsky

Date	F	VF	XF	Unc	BU
1993	—	—	—	2.50	—
1993 Proof	—	—	—	5.00	—

Y# 325 ROUBLE **Composition:** Copper-Nickel
Obverse: Double-headed eagle **Reverse:** Gavrilla Romanovich Derzhavin

Date	F	VF	XF	Unc	BU
1993(l)	—	—	—	2.50	—
1993(l) Proof	—	Value: 5.00			

Y# 326 ROUBLE **Composition:** Copper-Nickel
Obverse: Double-headed eagle **Reverse:** K. A. Timiryazev

Date	F	VF	XF	Unc	BU
1993(m)	—	—	—	2.50	—
1993(m) Proof	—	Value: 5.00			

Y# 327 ROUBLE **Composition:** Copper-Nickel
Reverse: V. Maikovski

Date	F	VF	XF	Unc	BU
1993(m)	—	—	—	2.50	—
1993(m) Proof	—	Value: 5.00			

Y# 335 ROUBLE **Weight:** 15.5500 g. **Composition:** 0.9000 Silver .4500 oz. ASW **Series:** Red Book Wildlife
Reverse: Tiger

Date	F	VF	XF	Unc	BU
1993 Proof	—	Value: 22.00			

Y# 336 ROUBLE **Weight:** 15.5500 g. **Composition:** 0.9000 Silver .4500 oz. ASW **Series:** Red Book Wildlife
Reverse: Blackiston's Fish Owl

Date	F	VF	XF	Unc	BU
1993 Proof	—	Value: 24.00			

Y# 337 ROUBLE **Weight:** 15.5500 g. **Composition:** 0.9000 Silver .4500 oz. ASW **Series:** Red Book Wildlife
Reverse: Mountain goat (Markhor)

Date	F	VF	XF	Unc	B
1993 Proof	—	Value: 17.50			

Y# 347 ROUBLE **Composition:** Copper-Nickel
Reverse: A. P. Borodin

Date	F	VF	XF	Unc	B
1993(m)	—	—	—	2.50	-
1993(m) Proof	—	Value: 5.00			

Y# 348 ROUBLE **Composition:** Copper-Nickel
Reverse: I. S. Turgenev

Date	F	VF	XF	Unc	B
1993(l)	—	—	—	2.50	
1993(l) Proof	—	Value: 5.00			

Y# 372 ROUBLE **Weight:** 15.5500 g. **Composition:** 0.9000 Silver .4500 oz. ASW **Series:** Wildlife **Reverse:** Re
breasted Kazarka

Date	Mintage	F	VF	XF	Unc	B
1994 Proof	50,000	Value: 18.50				

Y# 373 ROUBLE **Weight:** 15.5500 g. **Composition:** 0.9000 Silver .4500 oz. ASW **Series:** Wildlife **Obverse:** Similar to KM#372 **Reverse:** Asiatic Cobra

Date	Mintage	F	VF	XF	Unc	B
1994 Proof	50,000	Value: 22.00				

Y# 374 ROUBLE **Weight:** 15.5500 g. **Composition:** 0.9000 Silver .4500 oz. ASW **Series:** Wildlife **Obverse:** Similar to KM#372 **Reverse:** Asiatic Bear

Date	Mintage	F	VF	XF	Unc	BU
1994 Proof	50,000	Value: 22.00				

Y# 399 ROUBLE **Composition:** Aluminum-Bronze **Subject:** WWII Victory **Reverse:** Mother Russia calling for volunteers

Date	Mintage	F	VF	XF	Unc	BU
1995	200,000	—	—	—	1.50	—

Note: In mint sets only

Y# 446 ROUBLE **Weight:** 17.4600 g. **Composition:** 0.9000 Silver .5052 oz. ASW **Series:** Wildlife **Reverse:** Oriental White Stork

Date	Mintage	F	VF	XF	Unc	BU
1995 Proof	20,000	Value: 18.50				

'# 447 ROUBLE **Weight:** 17.4600 g. **Composition:** 0.9000 Silver .5052 oz. ASW **Series:** Wildlife **Reverse:** Caucasian Black Grouse

ate	Mintage	F	VF	XF	Unc	BU
995 Proof	20,000	Value: 18.50				

 # 448 ROUBLE **Weight:** 17.4600 g. **Composition:** 0.9000 Silver .5052 oz. ASW **Series:** Wildlife **Reverse:** Black Sea Porpoise

ate	Mintage	F	VF	XF	Unc	BU
95 Proof	20,000	Value: 20.00				

Y# 492 ROUBLE **Weight:** 17.4600 g. **Composition:** 0.9000 Silver .5052 oz. ASW **Series:** Wildlife **Reverse:** Peregrine Falcon

Date	Mintage	F	VF	XF	Unc	BU
1996 Proof	50,000	Value: 20.00				

Y# 493 ROUBLE **Weight:** 17.4600 g. **Composition:** 0.9000 Silver .5052 oz. ASW **Series:** Wildlife **Reverse:** Turkmenian Gecko

Date	Mintage	F	VF	XF	Unc	BU
1996 Proof	50,000	Value: 25.00				

Y# 494 ROUBLE **Weight:** 17.4600 g. **Composition:** 0.9000 Silver .5052 oz. ASW **Series:** Wildlife **Reverse:** Ukrainian Blind Mole Rat

Date	Mintage	F	VF	XF	Unc	BU
1996 Proof	50,000	Value: 22.50				

Y# 504 ROUBLE **Composition:** Brass **Subject:** 300th Anniversary - Russian Fleet

Date	Mintage	F	VF	XF	Unc	BU
1996	100,000	—	—	—	1.50	—

Note: In sets only

Y# 561 ROUBLE **Weight:** 8.4150 g. **Composition:** 0.9250 Silver .2502 oz. ASW **Subject:** 850th Anniversary - Moscow **Obverse:** Double-headed eagle

Date	Mintage	F	VF	XF	Unc	BU
1997 Proof	25,000	Value: 14.50				

Y# 562 ROUBLE **Weight:** 8.4150 g. **Composition:** 0.9250 Silver .2502 oz. ASW **Subject:** 850th Anniversary - Moscow **Obverse:** Double-headed eagle **Reverse:** Cathedral of the Kazan Icon of the Holy Virgin

Date	Mintage	F	VF	XF	Unc	BU
1997 Proof	25,000	Value: 14.50				

Y# 563 ROUBLE **Weight:** 8.4150 g. **Composition:** 0.9250 Silver .2502 oz. ASW **Subject:** 850th Anniversary - Moscow **Obverse:** Double-headed eagle **Reverse:** State University

Date	Mintage	F	VF	XF	Unc	BU
1997 Proof	25,000	Value: 14.50				

Y# 564 ROUBLE **Weight:** 8.4150 g. **Composition:** 0.9250 Silver .2502 oz. ASW **Subject:** 850th Anniversary - Moscow **Obverse:** Double-headed eagle **Reverse:** Bolshoi Theatre

Date	Mintage	F	VF	XF	Unc	BU
1997 Proof	25,000	Value: 14.50				

Y# 565 ROUBLE **Weight:** 8.4150 g. **Composition:** 0.9250 Silver .2502 oz. ASW **Subject:** 850th Anniversary - Moscow **Obverse:** Double-headed eagle **Reverse:** Resurrection Gate on Red Square

Date	Mintage	F	VF	XF	Unc	BU
1997 Proof	25,000	Value: 14.50				

Y# 566 ROUBLE **Weight:** 8.4150 g. **Composition:** 0.9250 Silver .2502 oz. ASW **Subject:** 850th Anniversary - Moscow **Obverse:** Double-headed eagle **Reverse:** Temple of Christ the Savior

Date	Mintage	F	VF	XF	Unc	BU
1997 Proof	25,000	Value: 14.50				

Y# 576 ROUBLE **Weight:** 8.4150 g. **Composition:** 0.9250 Silver .2502 oz. ASW **Series:** World Soccer Championship **Subject:** Paris 1998 - Soccer players, Eiffel Tower, globe

Date	Mintage	F	VF	XF	Unc	BU
1997(l) Proof	20,000	Value: 17.50				

Y# 577 ROUBLE **Weight:** 8.4150 g. **Composition:** 0.9250 Silver .2502 oz. ASW **Series:** 1998 Winter Olympics **Subject:** Ice Hockey

Date	Mintage	F	VF	XF	Unc	BU
1997(m) Proof	20,000	Value: 17.50				

Y# 578 ROUBLE **Weight:** 8.4150 g. **Composition:** 0.9250 Silver .2502 oz. ASW **Series:** 1998 Winter Olympics **Subject:** Biathalon

Date	Mintage	F	VF	XF	Unc	BU
1997(m) Proof	20,000	Value: 17.50				

Y# 579 ROUBLE **Weight:** 8.4150 g. **Composition:** 0.9250 Silver .2502 oz. ASW **Subject:** 1897 Soccer **Reverse:** Three soccer players

Date	Mintage	F	VF	XF	Unc	BU
1997(l) Proof	25,000	Value: 17.50				

Y# 580 ROUBLE **Weight:** 8.4150 g. **Composition:** 0.9250 Silver .2502 oz. ASW **Subject:** 1945 Soccer **Reverse:** Goalie

Date	Mintage	F	VF	XF	Unc	BU
1997(l) Proof	25,000	Value: 17.50				

Y# 581 ROUBLE **Weight:** 8.4150 g. **Composition:** 0.9250 Silver .2502 oz. ASW **Subject:** 1956 Soccer **Reverse:** Players and kangaroo

Date	Mintage	F	VF	XF	Unc	BU
1997(l) Proof	25,000	Value: 17.50				

Y# 582 ROUBLE **Weight:** 8.4150 g. **Composition:** 0.9250 Silver .2502 oz. ASW **Subject:** 1960 Soccer **Reverse:** Players, Eiffel Tower

Date	Mintage	F	VF	XF	Unc	BU
1997(l) Proof	25,000	Value: 17.50				

Y# 583 ROUBLE **Weight:** 8.4150 g. **Composition:** 0.9250 Silver .2502 oz. ASW **Subject:** 1988 Soccer **Reverse:** Three players

Date	Mintage	F	VF	XF	Unc	BU
1997(l) Proof	25,000	Value: 17.50				

Y# 611 ROUBLE **Weight:** 17.5500 g. **Composition:** 0.9000 Silver .5078 oz. ASW **Series:** Wildlife **Reverse:** Two flamingos

Date	Mintage	F	VF	XF	Unc	BU
1997 Proof	15,000	Value: 22.50				

Y# 612 ROUBLE **Weight:** 17.5500 g. **Composition:** 0.9000 Silver .5078 oz. ASW **Series:** Wildlife **Reverse:** Goitered Gazelle

Date	Mintage	F	VF	XF	Unc	BU
1997 Proof	15,000	Value: 20.00				

Y# 613 ROUBLE **Weight:** 17.5500 g. **Composition:** 0.9000 Silver .5078 oz. ASW **Series:** Wildlife **Reverse:** European Bison

Date	Mintage	F	VF	XF	Unc	BU
1997 Proof	15,000	Value: 20.00				

Y# 342 2 ROUBLES **Weight:** 15.8700 g. **Composition:** 0.5000 Silver .2552 oz. ASW **Obverse:** Double-headed eagle **Reverse:** Pavel Bazhov - Author of Ural Tales

Date	Mintage	F	VF	XF	Unc	BU
1994 Proof	250,000	Value: 12.50				

Y# 343 2 ROUBLES **Weight:** 15.8700 g. **Compositi** 0.5000 Silver .2552 oz. ASW **Obverse:** Double-headed eagle **Reverse:** Ivan Krylov - author of Fables

Date	Mintage	F	VF	XF	Unc
1994 Proof	250,000	Value: 12.50			

Y# 344 2 ROUBLES **Weight:** 15.8700 g. **Compositi** 0.5000 Silver .2552 oz. ASW **Obverse:** Double-headed eagle **Reverse:** Nickolai Gogol - writer

Date	Mintage	F	VF	XF	Unc
1994 Proof	250,000	Value: 12.50			

Y# 363 2 ROUBLES **Weight:** 15.8700 g. **Compositi** 0.5000 Silver .2552 oz. ASW **Obverse:** Double-headed eagle **Reverse:** Admiral Ushakov

Date	Mintage	F	VF	XF	Unc
1994 Proof	250,000	Value: 12.50			

Y# 364 2 ROUBLES **Weight:** 15.8700 g. **Compositi** 0.5000 Silver .2552 oz. ASW **Obverse:** Double-headed eagle **Reverse:** Ilya Repin - painter

Date	Mintage	F	VF	XF	Unc
1994 Proof	250,000	Value: 12.50			

Y# 377 2 ROUBLES **Weight:** 15.8700 g. **Compositi** 0.5000 Silver .2552 oz. ASW **Obverse:** Double-headed eagle **Reverse:** A. S. Griboyedov

Date	Mintage	F	VF	XF	Unc
1995 Proof	200,000	Value: 14.50			

#391 2 ROUBLES **Weight:** 15.8700 g. **Composition:** 0.5000 Silver .2552 oz. ASW **Series:** WWII Victory **Subject:** Victory Parade **Obverse:** Kremlin

te	Mintage	F	VF	XF	Unc	BU
95 Proof	200,000	Value: 16.50				

#392 2 ROUBLES **Weight:** 15.8700 g. **Composition:** 0.5000 Silver .2552 oz. ASW **Series:** WWII **Obverse:** Kremlin **Reverse:** Marshal Zhukov on horseback

te	Mintage	F	VF	XF	Unc	BU
95 Proof	200,000	Value: 16.50				

#393 2 ROUBLES **Weight:** 15.8700 g. **Composition:** 0.5000 Silver .2552 oz. ASW **Series:** WWII **Obverse:** Kremlin **Reverse:** Nuremberg trial

te	Mintage	F	VF	XF	Unc	BU
95 Proof	200,000	Value: 16.50				

#414 2 ROUBLES **Weight:** 15.8700 g. **Composition:** 0.5000 Silver .2552 oz. ASW **Obverse:** Double-headed eagle **Reverse:** Sergei Esenin

te	Mintage	F	VF	XF	Unc	BU
95 Proof	200,000	Value: 14.50				

#415 2 ROUBLES **Weight:** 15.8700 g. **Composition:** 0.5000 Silver .2552 oz. ASW **Obverse:** Double-headed eagle **Reverse:** Field Marshal Kutozov

te	Mintage	F	VF	XF	Unc	BU
95 Proof	200,000	Value: 13.50				

Y# 449 2 ROUBLES **Weight:** 15.8700 g. **Composition:** 0.5000 Silver .2552 oz. ASW **Obverse:** Double-headed eagle **Reverse:** Ivan Bunin

Date	Mintage	F	VF	XF	Unc	BU
1995 Proof	200,000	Value: 14.50				

Y# 514 2 ROUBLES **Weight:** 15.8700 g. **Composition:** 0.5000 Silver .2552 oz. ASW **Obverse:** Double-headed eagle **Reverse:** Nikolai Nekrasov

Date	Mintage	F	VF	XF	Unc	BU
1996 Proof	50,000	Value: 13.50				

Y# 515 2 ROUBLES **Weight:** 15.8700 g. **Composition:** 0.5000 Silver .2552 oz. ASW **Obverse:** Double-headed eagle **Reverse:** Fyodor Dostoevsky

Date	Mintage	F	VF	XF	Unc	BU
1996 Proof	50,000	Value: 17.50				

Y# 549 2 ROUBLES **Weight:** 15.8700 g. **Composition:** 0.5000 Silver .2552 oz. ASW **Obverse:** Double-headed eagle **Reverse:** N. E. Zhukovsky

Date	Mintage	F	VF	XF	Unc	BU
1997 Proof	50,000	Value: 17.50				

Y# 550 2 ROUBLES **Weight:** 15.8700 g. **Composition:** 0.5000 Silver .2552 oz. ASW **Obverse:** Double-headed eagle **Reverse:** A. N. Skryabin - musician

Date	Mintage	F	VF	XF	Unc	BU
1997 Proof	50,000	Value: 18.50				

Y# 551 2 ROUBLES **Weight:** 15.8700 g. **Composition:** 0.5000 Silver .2552 oz. ASW **Obverse:** Double-headed eagle **Reverse:** A. L. Chizhevsky

Date	Mintage	F	VF	XF	Unc	BU
1997 Proof	10,000	Value: 20.00				

Y# 558 2 ROUBLES **Weight:** 15.8700 g. **Composition:** 0.5000 Silver .2552 oz. ASW **Obverse:** Double-headed eagle **Reverse:** Afanasi Nikitin - sailing ship

Date	Mintage	F	VF	XF	Unc	BU
1997 Proof	15,000	Value: 20.00				

Y# 559 2 ROUBLES **Weight:** 15.8700 g. **Composition:** 0.5000 Silver .2552 oz. ASW **Obverse:** Double-headed eagle **Reverse:** Afanasi Nikitin - indian scene

Date	Mintage	F	VF	XF	Unc	BU
1997 Proof	7,500	Value: 20.00				

Y# 584 2 ROUBLES **Weight:** 15.8700 g. **Composition:** 0.5000 Silver .2552 oz. ASW **Obverse:** Double-headed eagle **Reverse:** Cameo of A. K. Savrasov - church, trees

Date	Mintage	F	VF	XF	Unc	BU
1997 Proof	7,500	Value: 20.00				

Y# 297 3 ROUBLES **Composition:** Copper-Nickel **Subject:** International Space Year

Date	Mintage	F	VF	XF	Unc	BU
1992(m)	—	—	—	—	3.50	—
1992(m) Proof	400,000	Value: 5.50				

Y# 298 3 ROUBLES **Composition:** Copper-Nickel **Subject:** Battle of Chudskoye Lake

Date	Mintage	F	VF	XF	Unc	BU
1992(l)		—	—	—	3.50	—
1992(l) Proof	400,000	Value: 5.50				

Y# 304 3 ROUBLES **Composition:** Copper-Nickel **Series:** WWII **Reverse:** Allied supply convoys to Murmansk

Date	Mintage	F	VF	XF	Unc	BU
1992(l) Proof	400,000	Value: 5.50				

Y# 317 3 ROUBLES **Composition:** Copper-Nickel **Subject:** 1st Anniversary - Defeat of Communist Attempted Coup

Date		F	VF	XF	Unc	BU
1992(m)		—	—	—	3.50	—
1992(m) Prooflike		—	—	—	4.00	—
1992(m) Proof	—	Value: 5.50				

Y# 349 3 ROUBLES **Weight:** 34.5600 g. **Composition:** 0.9000 Silver 1.0000 oz. ASW **Reverse:** St. Petersburg Trinity Cathedral

Date	Mintage	F	VF	XF	Unc	BU
1992 Proof	40,000	Value: 18.50				

Y# 350 3 ROUBLES **Weight:** 34.5600 g. **Composition:** 0.9000 Silver 1.0000 oz. ASW **Reverse:** St. Petersburg Academy of Science

Date	Mintage	F	VF	XF	Unc	BU
1992 Proof	40,000	Value: 20.00				

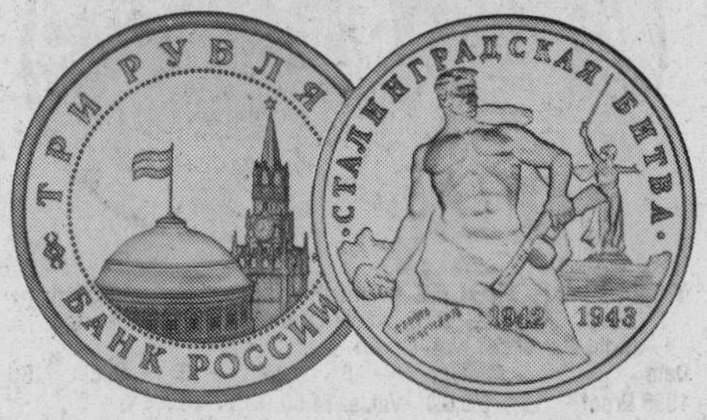

Y# 318 3 ROUBLES **Composition:** Copper-Nickel **Subject:** Battle of Stalingrad

Date	Mintage	F	VF	XF	Unc	BU
1993(m)		—	—	—	3.50	—
1993(m) Prooflike		—	—	—	4.00	—
1993(m) Proof	350,000	Value: 5.50				

Y# 323 3 ROUBLES **Weight:** 34.5600 g. **Composition:** 0.9000 Silver 1.0000 oz. ASW **Subject:** Bolshoi Ballet **Reverse:** Ballet couple **Note:** Struck at Moscow without mint mark.

Date	Mintage	F	VF	XF	Unc	BU
1993 Proof	40,000	Value: 15.00				
1993		—	—	—	12.00	—

Y# 328 3 ROUBLES **Composition:** Copper-Nickel **Subject:** 50th Anniversary - Battle of Kursk **Obverse:** Kremlin

Date		F	VF	XF	Unc	BU
1993(l)		—	—	—	3.50	—
1993(l) Proof	—	Value: 5.50				

Y# 340 3 ROUBLES **Composition:** Copper-Nickel **Subject:** 50th Anniversary - Kiev's Liberation from German Fascists **Obverse:** Kremlin

Date		F	VF	XF	Unc	BU
1993(m)		—	—	—	3.50	—
1993(m) Proof	—	Value: 5.50				

Y# 351 3 ROUBLES **Weight:** 34.5600 g. **Compositio** 0.9000 Silver 1.0000 oz. ASW **Series:** Olympics **Subjec** Soccer **Obverse:** Double-headed eagle

Date	Mintage	F	VF	XF	Unc
1993 Proof	40,000	Value: 27.50			

Y# 409 3 ROUBLES **Weight:** 34.5600 g. **Compositio** 0.9000 Silver 1.0000 oz. ASW **Series:** Wildlife **Obverse:** Similar to KM#323 **Reverse:** Bear

Date	Mintage	F	VF	XF	Unc
1993 Proof	5,000	Value: 75.00			

Y# 450 3 ROUBLES **Weight:** 34.5600 g. **Compositio** 0.9000 Silver 1.0000 oz. ASW **Subject:** Ballet **Reverse:** Ballerina - Anna Pavlova

Date	Mintage	F	VF	XF	Unc
1993 Proof	45,000	Value: 27.50			

Y# 451 3 ROUBLES **Weight:** 34.5600 g. **Compositic** 0.9000 Silver 1.0000 oz. ASW **Reverse:** Fedor Schalyap

Date	Mintage	F	VF	XF	Unc
1993 Proof	45,000	Value: 25.00			

Y# 456 3 ROUBLES **Weight:** 34.5600 g. **Composition:** 0.9000 Silver 1.0000 oz. ASW **Reverse:** Vasilyblazheny Cathedral, Moscow

Date	Mintage	F	VF	XF	Unc	BU
1993 Proof	30,000	Value: 23.50				

Y# 457 3 ROUBLES **Weight:** 34.5600 g. **Composition:** 0.9000 Silver 1.0000 oz. ASW **Reverse:** Ivan the Great Cathedral, Moscow

Date	Mintage	F	VF	XF	Unc	BU
1993 Proof	30,000	Value: 23.50				

Y# 464 3 ROUBLES **Weight:** 34.5600 g. **Composition:** 0.9000 Silver 1.0000 oz. ASW **Reverse:** Sailing ships "Nadezhda" and "Neva" on world voyage

Date		F	VF	XF	Unc	BU
1993 Proof	—	Value: 32.50				

Y# 465 3 ROUBLES **Weight:** 34.5600 g. **Composition:** 0.9000 Silver 1.0000 oz. ASW **Subject:** Russ-French Space Flight

Date	Mintage	F	VF	XF	Unc	BU
1993 Proof	40,000	Value: 32.50				

 # 341 3 ROUBLES **Composition:** Copper-Nickel **Subject:** 50th Anniversary - Battle of Leningrad **Obverse:** Kremlin

ate	Mintage	F	VF	XF	Unc	BU
94(l) Proof	250,000	Value: 5.50				

Y# 345 3 ROUBLES **Weight:** 34.5600 g. **Composition:** 0.9000 Silver 1.0000 oz. ASW **Obverse:** Double-headed eagle **Reverse:** Cathedral of the Nativity of the Mother of God

Date	Mintage	F	VF	XF	Unc	BU
1994 Proof	30,000	Value: 30.00				

Y# 346 3 ROUBLES **Composition:** Copper-Nickel **Subject:** 50th Anniversary - Liberation of Sevastopol from German Fascists **Obverse:** Kremlin

Date	Mintage	F	VF	XF	Unc	BU
1994(l) Proof	250,000	Value: 5.50				

Y# 362 3 ROUBLES **Composition:** Copper-Nickel **Subject:** Normandy invasion **Obverse:** Kremlin

Date	Mintage	F	VF	XF	Unc	BU
1994(m) Proof	250,000	Value: 5.50				

Y# 365 3 ROUBLES **Composition:** Copper-Nickel **Series:** WWII **Subject:** Partisans Activities **Obverse:** Kremlin

Date	Mintage	F	VF	XF	Unc	BU
1994(m) Proof	250,000	Value: 5.50				

Y# 366 3 ROUBLES **Composition:** Copper-Nickel **Series:** WWII **Subject:** Liberation of Belgrade **Obverse:** Kremlin

Date	Mintage	F	VF	XF	Unc	BU
1994(m) Proof	250,000	Value: 5.50				

Y# 405 3 ROUBLES **Weight:** 34.5600 g. **Composition:** 0.9000 Silver 1.0000 oz. ASW **Subject:** Ballet **Reverse:** Ballet couple

Date	Mintage	F	VF	XF	Unc	BU
1994 Proof	40,000	Value: 22.50				

Y# 458 3 ROUBLES **Weight:** 34.5600 g. **Composition:** 0.9000 Silver 1.0000 oz. ASW **Reverse:** Pocrov Church on the Nerl

Date	Mintage	F	VF	XF	Unc	BU
1994 Proof	30,000	Value: 20.00				

Y# 460 3 ROUBLES **Weight:** 34.5600 g. **Composition:** 0.9000 Silver 1.0000 oz. ASW **Series:** Wildlife **Reverse:** Sable

Date	Mintage	F	VF	XF	Unc	BU
1994 Proof	10,000	Value: 35.00				

Y# 466 3 ROUBLES **Weight:** 34.5600 g. **Composition:** 0.9000 Silver 1.0000 oz. ASW **Subject:** Discovery of Antarctica **Reverse:** Sailing ships Vostok and Mirny

Date	Mintage	F	VF	XF	Unc	BU
1994 Proof	25,000	Value: 30.00				

Y# 513 3 ROUBLES **Weight:** 34.6800 g. **Composition:** 0.9000 Silver 1.0034 oz. ASW **Reverse:** Building and churches

Date	Mintage	F	VF	XF	Unc	BU
1994 Proof	30,000	Value: 20.00				

Y# 520 3 ROUBLES **Weight:** 34.6800 g. **Composition:** 0.9000 Silver 1.0034 oz. ASW **Obverse:** Double-headed eagle **Reverse:** Ryazan Kremlin - city view

Date	Mintage	F	VF	XF	Unc	BU
1994 Proof	30,000	Value: 22.50				

Y# 528 3 ROUBLES **Weight:** 34.6800 g. **Composition:** 0.9000 Silver 1.0034 oz. ASW **Obverse:** Double-headed eagle **Reverse:** Vassili Ivanovich Surikov; Siberian sled scene

Date	Mintage	F	VF	XF	Unc	BU
1994 Proof	40,000	Value: 20.00				

Y# 529 3 ROUBLES **Weight:** 34.6800 g. **Composition:** 0.9000 Silver 1.0034 oz. ASW **Obverse:** Double-headed eagle **Reverse:** Alexander Andreyevich Ivannov

Date	Mintage	F	VF	XF	Unc	BU
1994 Proof	40,000	Value: 20.00				

Y# 389 (Y398) 3 ROUBLES **Weight:** 34.8800 g. **Composition:** 0.9000 Silver 1.0093 oz. ASW **Subject:** Trans-Siberian railway **Obverse:** Double-headed eagle

Date	Mintage	F	VF	XF	Unc	BU
1994 Proof	25,000	Value: 35.00				
1994 Proof	25,000	Value: 35.00				

Y# 382 3 ROUBLES **Composition:** Copper-Nickel **Series:** WWII **Reverse:** American and Russian soldiers in front of their country's respective flag **Note:** 50-star U.S.A. flag.

Date	Mintage	F	VF	XF	Unc	BU
1995(m) Proof	200,000	Value: 6.00				

Y# 461 3 ROUBLES **Weight:** 34.5600 g. **Composition:** 0.9000 Silver 1.0000 oz. ASW **Note:** Arctic Explorers 1733-43

Date	Mintage	F	VF	XF	Unc	BU
1995 Proof	25,000	Value: 32.50				

Y# 378 3 ROUBLES **Composition:** Copper-Nickel **Subject:** Liberation of Warsaw **Obverse:** Kremlin

Date	Mintage	F	VF	XF	Unc	BU
1995(l) Proof	200,000	Value: 6.00				

Y# 379 3 ROUBLES **Composition:** Copper-Nickel **Subject:** Liberation of Budapest **Obverse:** Kremlin

Date	Mintage	F	VF	XF	Unc	BU
1995(m) Proof	200,000	Value: 6.00				

Y# 380 3 ROUBLES **Composition:** Copper-Nickel **Series:** WWII **Subject:** Capture of Konigsberg **Obverse:** Kremlin

Date	Mintage	F	VF	XF	Unc	BU
1995(m) Proof	200,000	Value: 6.00				

Y# 381 3 ROUBLES **Composition:** Copper-Nickel **Series:** WWII **Subject:** Capture of Vienna **Obverse:** Kremlin

Date	Mintage	F	VF	XF	Unc	BU
1995(l) Proof	200,000	Value: 6.00				

Y# 383 3 ROUBLES **Composition:** Copper-Nickel **Series:** WWII **Subject:** Capture of Berlin **Obverse:** Kremlin

Date	Mintage	F	VF	XF	Unc	BU
1995(l) Proof	200,000	Value: 6.00				

Y# 384 3 ROUBLES **Composition:** Copper-Nickel **Series:** WWII **Subject:** German Surrender **Obverse:** Kremlin

Date	Mintage	F	VF	XF	Unc	BU
1995(l) Proof	200,000	Value: 6.00				

Y# 385 3 ROUBLES **Composition:** Copper-Nickel **Series:** WWII **Subject:** Liberation of Prague **Obverse:** Kremlin

Date	Mintage	F	VF	XF	Unc
1995(m) Proof	200,000	Value: 6.00			

Y# 386 3 ROUBLES **Composition:** Copper-Nickel **Series:** WWII **Subject:** Surrender of Japanese Army in Kwantung **Obverse:** Kremlin

Date	Mintage	F	VF	XF	Unc
1995(m) Proof	200,000	Value: 6.00			

Y# 387 3 ROUBLES **Composition:** Copper-Nickel **Series:** WWII **Subject:** Japanese Formal Surrender on Battleship U.S.S. Missouri **Obverse:** Kremlin

Date	Mintage	F	VF	XF	Unc	BU
1995 Proof	200,000	Value: 6.00				

Y# 388 3 ROUBLES **Weight:** 34.5600 g. **Composition:** 0.9000 Silver 1.0000 oz. ASW **Obverse:** Double-headed eagle **Reverse:** Vladimir's Golden Gate

Date	Mintage	F	VF	XF	Unc	BU
1995 Proof	30,000	Value: 32.50				

Y# 394 3 ROUBLES **Weight:** 34.5600 g. **Composition:** 0.9000 Silver 1.0000 oz. ASW **Subject:** Ballet - Sleeping Beauty

Date	Mintage	F	VF	XF	Unc	BU
1995 Proof	40,000	Value: 27.50				

Y# 407 3 ROUBLES **Weight:** 34.5600 g. **Composition:** 0.9000 Silver 1.0000 oz. ASW **Subject:** 50th Anniversary - United Nations

Date	Mintage	F	VF	XF	Unc	BU
1995 Proof	20,000	Value: 35.00				

Y# 445 3 ROUBLES **Weight:** 34.5600 g. **Composition:** 0.9000 Silver 1.0000 oz. ASW **Reverse:** Smolensk Kremlin

Date	Mintage	F	VF	XF	Unc	BU
1995 Proof	30,000	Value: 30.00				

Y# 459 3 ROUBLES **Weight:** 34.5600 g. **Composition:** 0.9000 Silver 1.0000 oz. ASW **Reverse:** Kizhi Church on Onega Lake

Date	Mintage	F	VF	XF	Unc	BU
1995 Proof	30,000	Value: 30.00				

Y# 462 3 ROUBLES **Weight:** 34.5600 g. **Composition:** 0.9000 Silver 1.0000 oz. ASW **Reverse:** Roald Amundsen - arctic explorer

Date	Mintage	F	VF	XF	Unc	BU
1995 Proof	25,000	Value: 32.50				

Y# 463 3 ROUBLES **Weight:** 34.5600 g. **Composition:** 0.9000 Silver 1.0000 oz. ASW **Subject:** 200th Anniversary - Russian National Library

Date	Mintage	F	VF	XF	Unc	BU
1995 Proof	15,000	Value: 32.50				

Y# 467 3 ROUBLES **Weight:** 34.5600 g. **Composition:** 0.9000 Silver 1.0000 oz. ASW **Subject:** Russian Millennium of Belgorod

Date	Mintage	F	VF	XF	Unc	BU
1995 Proof	30,000	Value: 25.00				

Y# 468 3 ROUBLES **Weight:** 34.5600 g. **Composition:** 0.9000 Silver 1.0000 oz. ASW **Subject:** Russian Millennium **Reverse:** Novgorod Kremlin

Date	F	VF	XF	Unc	BU
1995 Proof	—	Value: 25.00			

Y# 469 3 ROUBLES **Weight:** 34.5600 g. **Composition:** 0.9000 Silver 1.0000 oz. ASW **Subject:** Russian Millennium **Reverse:** Spaso - Preobrazhensky Cathedral

Date	Mintage	F	VF	XF	Unc	BU
1995 Proof	40,000	Value: 22.50				

Y# 473 3 ROUBLES **Weight:** 34.5600 g. **Composition:** 0.9000 Silver 1.0000 oz. ASW **Series:** Wildlife **Reverse:** Sable on branch

Date	Mintage	F	VF	XF	Unc	BU
1995(l) Matte	500,000	—	—	—	27.50	—
1995(m) Matte	500,000	—	—	—	27.50	—

Y# 474 3 ROUBLES **Weight:** 34.5600 g. **Composition:** 0.9000 Silver 1.0000 oz. ASW **Series:** Wildlife **Reverse:** Lynx

Date	Mintage	F	VF	XF	Unc	BU
1995(l)	25,000	—	—	—	35.00	—

Y# 470 3 ROUBLES **Weight:** 34.5600 g. **Composition:** 0.9000 Silver 1.0000 oz. ASW **Reverse:** Ilya the Prophet's Church in Yaroslavl

Date	Mintage	F	VF	XF	Unc	BU
1996 Proof	30,000	Value: 27.50				

Y# 477 3 ROUBLES **Weight:** 34.5600 g. **Composition:** 0.9000 Silver 1.0000 oz. ASW **Subject:** Combat Between Peresvet and Chelubey

Date	Mintage	F	VF	XF	Unc	BU
1996 Proof	40,000	Value: 25.00				

Y# 478 3 ROUBLES **Weight:** 34.5600 g. **Composition:** 0.9000 Silver 1.0000 oz. ASW **Reverse:** Old Testament Trinity icon

Date	Mintage	F	VF	XF	Unc	BU
1996 Proof	40,000	Value: 28.00				

Y# 482 3 ROUBLES **Weight:** 34.5600 g. **Composition:** 0.9000 Silver 1.0000 oz. ASW **Subject:** Nutcracker Ballet

Date	Mintage	F	VF	XF	Unc	BU
1996 Proof	25,000	Value: 30.00				

Y# 483 3 ROUBLES **Weight:** 34.5600 g. **Composition:** 0.9000 Silver 1.0000 oz. ASW **Subject:** Nutcracker Ballet - Duel with Mouse King

Date	Mintage	F	VF	XF	Unc	BU
1996 Proof	25,000	Value: 30.00				

Y# 490 3 ROUBLES **Weight:** 34.5600 g. **Composition:** 0.9000 Silver 1.0000 oz. ASW **Reverse:** Kremlin of Kazan

Date	Mintage	F	VF	XF	Unc	BU
1996 Proof	20,000	Value: 32.50				

Y# 491 3 ROUBLES **Weight:** 34.5600 g. **Composition:** 0.9000 Silver 1.0000 oz. ASW **Reverse:** Kremlin of Tobolsk - city view

Date	Mintage	F	VF	XF	Unc	BU
1996 Proof	50,000	Value: 30.00				

Y# 510 3 ROUBLES **Weight:** 34.5600 g. **Composition:** 0.9000 Silver 1.0000 oz. ASW **Reverse:** Alexander Column and Hermitage

Date	Mintage	F	VF	XF	Unc	BU
1996 Proof	20,000	Value: 32.50				

Y# 511 3 ROUBLES **Weight:** 34.5600 g. **Composition:** 0.9000 Silver 1.0000 oz. ASW **Subject:** 300th Anniversary - Russian Navy **Reverse:** Icebreaker

Date	Mintage	F	VF	XF	Unc	BU
1996 Proof	10,000	Value: 35.00				

Y# 512 3 ROUBLES **Weight:** 34.5600 g. **Compositio** 0.9000 Silver 1.0000 oz. ASW **Subject:** 300th Anniversary Russian Navy **Reverse:** Carrier ship

Date	Mintage	F	VF	XF	Unc
1996 Proof	10,000	Value: 27.50			

Y# 535 3 ROUBLES **Weight:** 34.5600 g. **Compositio** 0.9000 Silver 1.0000 oz. ASW **Series:** Wildlife **Reverse:** Amur tiger

Date	Mintage	F	VF	XF	Unc
1996 Proof	10,000	Value: 27.50			

Y# 552 3 ROUBLES **Weight:** 34.5600 g. **Compositio** 0.9000 Silver 1.0000 oz. ASW **Subject:** 850th Anniversary Moscow **Reverse:** Workers rebuilding original Moscow, modern skyline behind

Date	Mintage	F	VF	XF	Unc
1997 Proof	40,000	Value: 30.00			

Y# 553 3 ROUBLES **Weight:** 34.5600 g. **Compositio** 0.9000 Silver 1.0000 oz. ASW **Subject:** 850th Anniversar Moscow **Reverse:** Riverside city view

Date	Mintage	F	VF	XF	Unc
1997 Proof	40,000	Value: 30.00			

Y# 560 3 ROUBLES **Weight:** 34.5600 g. **Composition:** 0.9000 Silver 1.0000 oz. ASW **Reverse:** Monastery of the Saint Virgin in Yaroslavl

Date	Mintage	F	VF	XF	Unc	BU
1997 Proof	15,000	Value: 37.50				

Y# 567 3 ROUBLES **Weight:** 34.5600 g. **Composition:** 0.9000 Silver 1.0000 oz. ASW **Subject:** Ballet - Swan Lake **Reverse:** Four ballerinas

Date	Mintage	F	VF	XF	Unc	BU
1997 Proof	10,000	Value: 32.50				

Y# 568 3 ROUBLES **Weight:** 34.5600 g. **Composition:** 0.9000 Silver 1.0000 oz. ASW **Subject:** Ballet - Swan Lake **Reverse:** Between Rothbart and Prince Siegfried

Date	Mintage	F	VF	XF	Unc	BU
1997 Proof	10,000	Value: 32.50				

Y# 575 3 ROUBLES **Weight:** 34.5600 g. **Composition:** 0.9000 Silver 1.0000 oz. ASW **Subject:** First Anniversary - Russian-Belarus Treaty **Reverse:** Two city views

Date	Mintage	F	VF	XF	Unc	BU
1997 Proof	10,000	Value: 32.50				

Y# 585 3 ROUBLES **Weight:** 34.5600 g. **Composition:** 0.9000 Silver 1.0000 oz. ASW **Subject:** Underroot Nativity of the Virgin Hermitage Monastery of Kursk **Reverse:** Painting above monastery

Date	Mintage	F	VF	XF	Unc	BU
1997 Proof	15,000	Value: 37.50				

Y# 586 3 ROUBLES **Weight:** 34.5600 g. **Composition:** 0.9000 Silver 1.0000 oz. ASW **Reverse:** Sergy Julievich Witte

Date	Mintage	F	VF	XF	Unc	BU
1997 Proof	10,000	Value: 32.50				

Y# 587 3 ROUBLES **Weight:** 34.5600 g. **Composition:** 0.9000 Silver 1.0000 oz. ASW **Subject:** Year of Reconciliation

Date	Mintage	F	VF	XF	Unc	BU
1997 Proof	7,500	Value: 38.50				

Y# 591 3 ROUBLES **Weight:** 34.5600 g. **Composition:** 0.9000 Silver 1.0000 oz. ASW **Reverse:** Solovetski Monastery

Date	Mintage	F	VF	XF	Unc	BU
1997 Proof	15,000	Value: 37.50				

Y# 593 3 ROUBLES **Weight:** 34.5600 g. **Composition:** 0.9000 Silver 1.0000 oz. ASW **Series:** Wildlife **Reverse:** Polar bear watching walrus

Date	Mintage	F	VF	XF	Unc	BU
1997 Proof	10,000	Value: 35.00				

Y# 312 5 ROUBLES **Composition:** Brass Clad Steel **Obverse:** Double-headed eagle

Date	F	VF	XF	Unc	BU
1992Л	—	—	—	1.75	—
1992М	—	—	—	1.50	—
1992(m)	—	—	—	2.00	—
1992(l)	—	—	—	2.50	—

Y# 322 5 ROUBLES **Composition:** Brass Clad Steel **Subject:** Kazakhstan

Date	Mintage	F	VF	XF	Unc	BU
1992(l) Proof	200,000	Value: 10.00				

Y# 324 5 ROUBLES **Composition:** Brass Clad Steel **Subject:** Troitsk - Sergievsk Monastery

Date	Mintage	F	VF	XF	Unc	BU
1993(l)		—	—	—	6.00	—
1993(l) Proof	—	Value: 9.00				

Y# 339 5 ROUBLES **Composition:** Copper-Nickel **Subject:** 2500 Years of Merv Minaret, Turkmenistan

Date	Mintage	F	VF	XF	Unc	BU
1993(l)		—	—	—	4.00	—
1993(l) Proof	6	Value: 6.50				

Y# 420 5 ROUBLES **Weight:** 7.7758 g. **Composition:** 0.9990 Palladium .2500 oz. **Subject:** Ballet **Reverse:** Ballerina

Date	Mintage	F	VF	XF	Unc	BU
1993	6,000	—	—	—	175	—
1993 Proof	—	Value: 210				

Y# 431 5 ROUBLES **Weight:** 7.7758 g. **Composition:** 0.9990 Palladium .2500 oz. **Subject:** Ballet - Sleeping Beauty **Reverse:** Ballerina

Date		F	VF	XF	Unc	BU
1994		—	—	—	225	—
1994 Proof	5,000	Value: 250				

Y# 400 5 ROUBLES **Composition:** Aluminum-Bronze **Series:** WWII **Reverse:** Infantry officer leading attack

Date	Mintage	F	VF	XF	Unc	BU
1995	200,000	—	—	—	1.50	—

Note: In mint sets only

Y# 435 5 ROUBLES **Weight:** 7.7758 g. **Composition:** 0.9990 Palladium .2500 oz. **Reverse:** Ballerina

Date	Mintage	F	VF	XF	Unc	BU
1995 Proof	4,000	Value: 190				

Y# 505 5 ROUBLES **Composition:** Brass **Subject:** 300th Anniversary - Russian Fleet

Date	Mintage	F	VF	XF	Unc	BU
1996	100,000	—	—	—	2.50	—

Note: In mint sets only

Y# 606.1 5 ROUBLES **Composition:** Copper-Nickel Clad Copper **Reverse:** Denomination **Edge:** Reeded and plain sections

Date	F	VF	XF	Unc	BU
1997(m)	—	—	—	2.00	—
1997(sp)	—	—	—	2.00	—

Y# 606.2 5 ROUBLES **Composition:** Copper-Nickel Clad Copper **Edge:** Plain

Date	F	VF	XF	Unc	BU
1997(m)	—	—	—	2.00	—
1997(sp) Reported, not confirmed	—	—	—	—	—

Y# 307 10 ROUBLES **Ring Composition:** Copper-Nickel **Center Composition:** Aluminum-Bronze **Series:** Wildlife **Reverse:** Red-breasted Kazarka

Date	Mintage	F	VF	XF	Unc	BU
1992(l)	300,000	—	—	—	2.00	—

Y# 308 10 ROUBLES **Center Composition:** Aluminum-Bronze **Series:** Wildlife **Reverse:** Tiger

Date	Mintage	F	VF	XF	Unc	BU
1992(l)	300,000	—	—	—	2.50	—

Y# 309 10 ROUBLES **Center Composition:** Aluminum-Bronze **Series:** Wildlife **Reverse:** Cobra

Date	Mintage	F	VF	XF	Unc	BU
1992(l)	300,000	—	—	—	2.50	—

Y# 313 10 ROUBLES **Composition:** Copper-Nickel **Obverse:** Double-headed eagle **Reverse:** Denomination **Edge:** Reeded **Note:** St. Petersburg minted coins have a round-top 3 in date. Moscow minted coins have a flat-top 3 in date.

Date	F	VF	XF	Unc	BU
1992(l)	—	—	—	1.50	—
1992(m)	—	—	—	2.00	—
1993(l)	—	—	—	1.50	—
1993(m)	—	—	—	10.00	—

Y# 313a 10 ROUBLES **Composition:** Copper-Nickel Clad Steel **Edge:** Plain **Note:** St. Petersburg minted coins have a round-top 3 in date. Moscow minted coins have a flat-top 3 in date.

Date	F	VF	XF	Unc	BU
1992(m)	—	—	—	10.00	—
1993(l)	—	—	—	1.50	—
1993(m)	—	—	—	1.50	—

Y# 352 10 ROUBLES **Weight:** 15.5517 g. **Composition:** 0.9990 Palladium .5000 oz. **Series:** Olympics **Reverse:** Cubertin and Butovsky

Date	Mintage	F	VF	XF	Unc	BU
1993 Proof	7,500	Value: 475				

Y# 416 10 ROUBLES **Weight:** 1.5552 g. **Composition:** 0.9990 Gold .0500 oz. AGW **Subject:** Ballet **Reverse:** Ballerina

Date	Mintage	F	VF	XF	Unc	BU
1993	57,000	—	—	—	45.00	—
1993 Proof	—	Value: 60.00				

Y# 421 10 ROUBLES **Weight:** 15.5500 g. **Composition:** 0.9990 Palladium .5000 oz.

Date		F	VF	XF	Unc
1993		—	—	—	300
1993 Proof	2,000	Value: 350			

Y# 424 10 ROUBLES **Weight:** 1.5552 g. **Compositio** 0.9990 Gold .0500 oz. AGW

Date	Mintage	F	VF	XF	Unc
1994 Proof	7,000	Value: 60.00			

Y# 432 10 ROUBLES **Weight:** 15.5500 g. **Compositio** 0.9990 Palladium .5000 oz.

Date	Mintage	F	VF	XF	Unc
1994		—	—	—	300
1994 Proof	1,500	Value: 350			

Y# 401 10 ROUBLES **Composition:** Copper-Nickel **Series:** WWII **Reverse:** Munitions workers

Date	Mintage	F	VF	XF	Unc
1995	200,000	—	—	—	2.00

Note: In mint sets only

Y# 436 10 ROUBLES **Weight:** 15.5500 g. **Composition:** 0.9990 Palladium .5000 oz. **Subject:** Balle Sleeping Beauty **Reverse:** Ballerina

Date	Mintage	F	VF	XF	Unc
1995 Proof	1,500	Value: 350			

Y# 438 10 ROUBLES **Weight:** 1.5552 g. **Compositio** 0.9990 Gold .0500 oz. AGW

Date	Mintage	F	VF	XF	Unc
1995 Proof	7,000	Value: 60.00			

Y# 484 10 ROUBLES **Weight:** 1.5552 g. **Compositio** 0.9990 Gold .0500 oz. AGW **Subject:** Ballet **Reverse:** Nutcracker doll

Date	Mintage	F	VF	XF	Unc
1996 Proof	7,500	Value: 60.00			

 # 506 10 ROUBLES **Composition:** Copper-Nickel **Subject:** 300th Anniversary - Russian Fleet **Reverse:** Cargo ship

ate	Mintage	F	VF	XF	Unc	BU
996	100,000	—	—	—	3.00	—

Note: In mint sets only

 # 569 10 ROUBLES **Weight:** 1.5500 g. **Composition:** 0.9990 Gold .0498 oz. AGW **Subject:** Ballet - Swan Lake

ate	Mintage	F	VF	XF	Unc	BU
997 Proof	2,500	Value: 65.00				

 # 314 20 ROUBLES **Composition:** Copper-Nickel **Obverse:** Double-headed eagle **Reverse:** Denomination **Edge:** Reeded and plain sections

ate	F	VF	XF	Unc	BU
992(l)	—	—	—	2.00	—
992(m)	—	—	—	2.50	—
993(m)	—	—	—	20.00	—

 # 314a 20 ROUBLES **Composition:** Copper-Nickel Clad Steel **Edge:** Plain

ate	F	VF	XF	Unc	BU
993(l)	—	—	—	2.50	—
993(m)	—	—	—	2.50	—

 # 402 20 ROUBLES **Composition:** Copper-Nickel **Series:** WWII **Reverse:** Soldiers and tanks

ate	Mintage	F	VF	XF	Unc	BU
995	200,000	—	—	—	3.00	—

Note: In mint sets only

 # 507 20 ROUBLES **Composition:** Copper-Nickel **Subject:** 300th Anniversary - Russian Fleet **Reverse:** Scientific research ship

ate	Mintage	F	VF	XF	Unc	BU
996	100,000	—	—	—	4.50	—

Note: In mint sets only

 # 353 25 ROUBLES **Weight:** 31.1035 g. **Composition:** 0.9990 Palladium 1.0000 oz. **Reverse:** Catherine the Great

Date	Mintage	F	VF	XF	Unc	BU
1992 Proof	5,500	Value: 650				

Y# 395 25 ROUBLES **Weight:** 3.1104 g. **Composition:** 0.9990 Platinum .1000 oz. APW **Subject:** Ballet **Reverse:** Ballerina

Date	Mintage	F	VF	XF	Unc	BU
1993	750	—	—	—	150	—

Note: Proof sets only

Y# 410 25 ROUBLES **Weight:** 3.1100 g. **Composition:** 0.9990 Gold .1000 oz. AGW **Series:** Wildlife **Reverse:** Bear

Date	Mintage	F	VF	XF	Unc	BU
1993 Proof	2,000	Value: 120				

Y# 417 25 ROUBLES **Weight:** 3.1100 g. **Composition:** 0.9990 Gold .1000 oz. AGW **Subject:** Ballet **Reverse:** Ballerina

Date	Mintage	F	VF	XF	Unc	BU
1993		—	—	—	100	—
1993 Proof	6,000	Value: 120				

Y# 422 25 ROUBLES **Weight:** 31.1035 g. **Composition:** 0.9990 Palladium 1.0000 oz. **Reverse:** Ballerina

Date	Mintage	F	VF	XF	Unc	BU
1993	—	—	—	—	625	—
1993 Proof	2,000	Value: 650				

Y# 452 25 ROUBLES **Weight:** 31.1035 g. **Composition:** 0.9990 Palladium 1.0000 oz. **Reverse:** M. P. Musorgsky

Date	Mintage	F	VF	XF	Unc	BU
1993 Proof	5,500	Value: 650				

Y# 517 25 ROUBLES **Weight:** 31.1035 g. **Composition:** 0.9990 Palladium 1.0000 oz. **Subject:** First Russian Global Circumnavigation **Reverse:** Sloop "Nadyezhda"

Date	Mintage	F	VF	XF	Unc	BU
1993 Proof	25,000	Value: 650				

Y# 518 25 ROUBLES **Weight:** 31.1035 g. **Composition:** 0.9990 Palladium 1.0000 oz. **Reverse:** Sloop "Neva"

Date	Mintage	F	VF	XF	Unc	BU
1993 Proof	25,000	Value: 650				

Y# 406 25 ROUBLES **Weight:** 156.0400 g. **Composition:** 0.9990 Silver 5.0118 oz. ASW **Subject:** Ballet **Obverse:** Bolshoi ballet building **Reverse:** Ballet couple **Note:** Illustration reduced.

Date	Mintage	F	VF	XF	Unc	BU
1993(m) Proof	10,000	Value: 85.00				
1993(l) Proof	Inc. above	Value: 85.00				

Y# 390 25 ROUBLES **Weight:** 172.8300 g. **Composition:** 0.9000 Silver 5.0009 oz. ASW **Reverse:** Building of the Trans-Siberian railroad; Similar to Y#398

Date	Mintage	F	VF	XF	Unc	BU
1994 Proof	3,000	Value: 175				

Y# 423 25 ROUBLES **Weight:** 172.8300 g. **Composition:** 0.9000 Silver 5.0009 oz. ASW **Subject:** Ballet

Date	Mintage	F	VF	XF	Unc	BU
1994 Proof	7,500	Value: 150				

Y#425 25 ROUBLES **Weight:** 3.1100 g. **Composition:** 0.9990 Gold .1000 oz. AGW **Reverse:** Ballerina

Date	Mintage	F	VF	XF	Unc	BU
1994 Proof	5,000	Value: 110				

Y#428 25 ROUBLES **Weight:** 3.1104 g. **Composition:** 0.9990 Platinum .1000 oz. APW **Reverse:** Ballerina

Date	Mintage	F	VF	XF	Unc	BU
1994 Proof	900	Value: 175				

Y#433 25 ROUBLES **Weight:** 31.1035 g. **Composition:** 0.9990 Palladium 1.0000 oz. **Reverse:** Ballerina

Date	Mintage	F	VF	XF	Unc	BU
1994	—	—	—	—	650	—
1994 Proof	1,500	Value: 650				

Y#521 25 ROUBLES **Weight:** 31.1035 g. **Composition:** 0.9990 Palladium 1.0000 oz. **Reverse:** Sloop "Mirny"

Date	Mintage	F	VF	XF	Unc	BU
1994 Proof	4,000	Value: 650				

Y#522 25 ROUBLES **Weight:** 31.1035 g. **Composition:** 0.9990 Palladium 1.0000 oz. **Reverse:** Sloop "Vostok"

Date	Mintage	F	VF	XF	Unc	BU
1994 Proof	4,000	Value: 650				

Y#524 25 ROUBLES **Weight:** 3.1103 g. **Composition:** 0.9990 Gold .1000 oz. AGW **Series:** Wildlife **Reverse:** Sable's head

Date	Mintage	F	VF	XF	Unc	BU
1994 Proof	4,000	Value: 100				

Y#530 25 ROUBLES **Weight:** 31.1035 g. **Composition:** 0.9990 Palladium 1.0000 oz. **Reverse:** Andrei Rublev

Date	Mintage	F	VF	XF	Unc	BU
1994 Proof	6,000	Value: 650				

Y#534 25 ROUBLES **Weight:** 4.3198 g. **Composition:** 0.9000 Gold .1245 oz. AGW **Reverse:** Baikal railroad tunnel

Date	Mintage	F	VF	XF	Unc	BU
1994 Proof	3,000	Value: 115				

Y#437 25 ROUBLES **Weight:** 31.1035 g. **Composition:** 0.9990 Palladium 1.0000 oz. **Reverse:** Ballerina

Date	Mintage	F	VF	XF	Unc	BU
1995 Proof	1,500	Value: 650				

Y#439 25 ROUBLES **Weight:** 3.1100 g. **Composition:** 0.9990 Gold .1000 oz. AGW

Date	Mintage	F	VF	XF	Unc	BU
1995 Proof	5,000	Value: 120				

Y#442 25 ROUBLES **Weight:** 3.1104 g. **Composition:** 0.9990 Platinum .1000 oz. APW

Date	Mintage	F	VF	XF	Unc	BU
1995 Proof	900	Value: 175				

Y# 472 25 ROUBLES **Weight:** 155.5000 g. **Composition:** 0.9000 Silver 4.4995 oz. ASW **Subject:** Fi Station at North Pole **Reverse:** Men, ship, and airplane

Date	Mintage	F	VF	XF	Unc
1995 Proof	5,000	Value: 175			

Y#475 25 ROUBLES **Weight:** 31.1035 g. **Compositio** 0.9990 Palladium 1.0000 oz. **Reverse:** Alexander Nevsk

Date	Mintage	F	VF	XF	Unc
1995 Proof	5,425	Value: 650			

Y# 471 25 ROUBLES **Weight:** 155.5000 g. **Composition:** 0.9000 Silver 4.4995 oz. ASW **Series:** Wildlife **Reverse:** Lynx on log **Note:** Illustration reduced.

Date	Mintage	F	VF	XF	Unc
1995 Proof	5,000	Value: 110			

Y# 485 25 ROUBLES **Weight:** 155.5175 g. **Composition:** 0.9990 Silver 5.0000 oz. ASW **Subject:** Ballet - Nutcracker **Reverse:** Children dancing around tr **Note:** Illustration reduced.

Date	Mintage	F	VF	XF	Unc
1996 Proof	5,000	Value: 175			

Y# 479 25 ROUBLES **Weight:** 155.5000 g. **Composition:** 0.9000 Silver 4.4995 oz. ASW **Subject:** Battle of Kulikova Plains **Note:** Illustration reduced.

Date	Mintage	F	VF	XF	Unc	BU
1996 Proof	5,000	Value: 175				

Y# 536 25 ROUBLES **Weight:** 172.7972 g. **Composition:** 0.9000 Silver 5.0000 oz. ASW **Series:** Wildlife **Reverse:** Amur tiger **Note:** Illustration reduced.

Date	F	VF	XF	Unc	BU
1996 Proof	—	Value: 125			

Y# 542 25 ROUBLES **Weight:** 172.7972 g. **Composition:** 0.9000 Silver 5.0000 oz. ASW **Subject:** Battle of Gangut, 1714 **Note:** Illustration reduced.

Date	Mintage	F	VF	XF	Unc	BU
1996 Proof	3,000	Value: 175				

Y# 543 25 ROUBLES **Weight:** 172.7972 g. **Composition:** 0.9000 Silver 5.0000 oz. ASW **Subject:** Battle of Chesme, 1770 **Note:** Illustration reduced.

Date	Mintage	F	VF	XF	Unc	BU
1996 Proof	3,000	Value: 175				

Y# 544 25 ROUBLES **Weight:** 172.7972 g. **Composition:** 0.9000 Silver 5.0000 oz. ASW **Subject:** Battle of Corfu, 1799 **Note:** Illustration reduced.

Date	Mintage	F	VF	XF	Unc	BU
1996 Proof	3,000	Value: 175				

Y# 545 25 ROUBLES **Weight:** 172.7972 g. **Composition:** 0.9000 Silver 5.0000 oz. ASW **Subject:** Battle of Sinop, 1853 **Note:** Illustration reduced.

Date	Mintage	F	VF	XF	Unc	BU
1996 Proof	3,000	Value: 175				

Y# 486 25 ROUBLES **Weight:** 3.1103 g. **Composition:** 0.9990 Gold .1000 oz. AGW **Subject:** Ballet - Nutcracker **Reverse:** Marsha with nutcracker doll

Date	Mintage	F	VF	XF	Unc	BU
1996 Proof	5,000	Value: 125				

Y# 554 25 ROUBLES **Weight:** 172.7972 g. **Composition:** 0.9000 Silver 5.0000 oz. ASW **Subject:** 850th Anniversary - Moscow **Reverse:** Monument

Date	Mintage	F	VF	XF	Unc	BU
1997 Proof	5,000	Value: 155				

Y# 571 25 ROUBLES **Weight:** 3.1103 g. **Composition:** 0.9990 Gold .1000 oz. AGW **Subject:** Ballet - Swan Lake **Reverse:** Winged figure of Rothbart and swan

Date	Mintage	F	VF	XF	Unc	BU
1997 Proof	2,000	Value: 175				

Y# 594 25 ROUBLES **Weight:** 172.7972 g. **Composition:** 0.9000 Silver 5.0000 oz. ASW **Series:** Wildlife **Reverse:** Polar bear, caribou, seal

Date	Mintage	F	VF	XF	Unc	BU
1997 Proof	3,000	Value: 175				

Y# 570 25 ROUBLES **Weight:** 172.7972 g. **Composition:** 0.9000 Silver 5.0000 oz. ASW **Subject:** Ballet - Swan Lake **Reverse:** Prince Siegfried dancing with Odile **Note:** Illustration reduced.

Date	Mintage	F	VF	XF	Unc	BU
1997 Proof	3,000	Value: 145				

Y# 592 25 ROUBLES **Weight:** 172.7972 g. **Composition:** 0.9000 Silver 5.0000 oz. ASW **Series:** Wildlife **Reverse:** Bear with cub **Note:** Illustration reduced.

Date	Mintage	F	VF	XF	Unc	BU
1997 Proof	1,000	Value: 175				

Y# 622 25 ROUBLES **Weight:** 173.2900 g. **Composition:** 0.9000 Silver 5.0143 oz. ASW **Series:** Wildlife **Reverse:** Sable

Date	Mintage	F	VF	XF	Unc	BU
1997 Proof	1,000	Value: 185				

Y# 315 50 ROUBLES **Ring Composition:** Copper-Nickel **Center Composition:** Aluminum-Bronze **Obverse:** Double-headed eagle **Reverse:** Denomination

Date	F	VF	XF	Unc	BU
1992(l)	0.50	0.75	1.00	2.50	—
1992(m)	0.75	1.00	1.50	3.50	—

Y# 354 50 ROUBLES **Weight:** 8.6397 g. **Composition:** 0.9000 Gold .2500 oz. AGW **Obverse:** Double-headed eagle **Reverse:** Moscow's Pashkov Palace

Date	Mintage	F	VF	XF	Unc	BU
1992 Proof	7,500	Value: 150				

Y# 516 50 ROUBLES **Weight:** 8.6397 g. **Composition:** 0.9000 Gold .2500 oz. AGW **Obverse:** Double-headed eagle **Reverse:** Chubuku (snow ram) on map **Note:** Yakutia.

Date	Mintage	F	VF	XF	Unc	BU
1992 Proof	25,000	Value: 200				

Y# 329.1 50 ROUBLES **Composition:** Aluminum-Bronze **Obverse:** Double-headed eagle **Reverse:** Denomination **Edge:** Reeded and plain sections

Date	F	VF	XF	Unc	BU
1993(l)	—	—	—	2.50	—
1993(m)	—	—	—	2.50	—

Y# 329.2 50 ROUBLES **Composition:** Brass Clad Steel **Obverse:** Double-headed eagle **Reverse:** Denomination **Edge:** Plain

Date	F	VF	XF	Unc	BU
1993(l)	—	—	—	3.50	—
1993(m)	—	—	—	2.50	—

Y# 330 50 ROUBLES **Ring Composition:** Copper-Nickel **Center Composition:** Aluminum-Bronze **Series:** Wildlife **Reverse:** Bear

Date	Mintage	F	VF	XF	Unc	BU
1993(l)	300,000	—	—	—	2.50	—

Y# 331 50 ROUBLES **Ring Composition:** Copper-Nickel **Center Composition:** Aluminum-Bronze **Series:** Wildlife **Reverse:** Gecko

Date	Mintage	F	VF	XF	Unc	BU
1993(l)	300,000	—	—	—	2.50	—

Y# 332 50 ROUBLES **Ring Composition:** Copper-Nickel **Center Composition:** Aluminum-Bronze **Series:** Wildlife **Reverse:** Caucasian grouse

Date	Mintage	F	VF	XF	Unc	BU
1993(l)	300,000	—	—	—	2.00	—

Y# 333 50 ROUBLES **Ring Composition:** Copper-Nickel **Center Composition:** Aluminum-Bronze **Series:** Wildlife **Reverse:** Far Eastern stork

Date	Mintage	F	VF	XF	Unc	BU
1993(l)	300,000	—	—	—	2.00	—

Y# 334 50 ROUBLES **Ring Composition:** Copper-Nickel **Center Composition:** Aluminum-Bronze **Series:** Wildlife **Reverse:** Black sea porpoise

Date	Mintage	F	VF	XF	Unc	BU
1993(l)	300,000	—	—	—	2.25	—

Y# 355 50 ROUBLES **Weight:** 8.6397 g. **Composition:** 0.9000 Gold .2500 oz. AGW **Series:** Olympics **Reverse:** Figure skater

Date	Mintage	F	VF	XF	Unc	BU
1993 Proof	7,500	Value: 160				

Y# 356 50 ROUBLES **Weight:** 7.7758 g. **Composition** 0.9990 Platinum .2498 oz. APW **Series:** Olympics **Subject** Formal riding

Date	Mintage	F	VF	XF	Unc	B
1993 Proof	7,500	Value: 275				

Y# 396 50 ROUBLES **Weight:** 7.7758 g. **Composition** 0.9990 Platinum .2498 oz. APW **Subject:** Bolshoi Ballet **Reverse:** Ballerina

Date	Mintage	F	VF	XF	Unc	B
1993	750	—	—	—	285	-

Note: Proof sets only

Y# 411 50 ROUBLES **Weight:** 7.7800 g. **Composition** 0.9990 Gold .2500 oz. AGW **Series:** Wildlife **Reverse:** Be

Date	Mintage	F	VF	XF	Unc	B
1993 Proof	1,480	Value: 200				

Y# 418 50 ROUBLES **Weight:** 7.7800 g. **Composition** 0.9990 Gold .2500 oz. AGW **Subject:** Bolshoi Ballet **Reverse:** Ballerina

Date	Mintage	F	VF	XF	Unc	B
1993		—	—	—	300	
1993 Proof	1,500	Value: 350				

Y# 453 50 ROUBLES **Weight:** 7.7800 g. **Compositio** 0.9990 Gold .2500 oz. AGW **Reverse:** Sergei Rachmanin

Date	Mintage	F	VF	XF	Unc	
1993 Proof	7,500	Value: 175				

Y# 367 50 ROUBLES **Ring Composition:** Copper-Nickel **Center Composition:** Aluminum-Bronze **Series:** Wildlife **Reverse:** Spalax

Date	Mintage	F	VF	XF	Unc	
1994(l)	300,000	—	—	—	2.50	

Y# 368 50 ROUBLES Ring Composition: Copper-Nickel **Center Composition:** Aluminum-Bronze **Series:** Wildlife **Reverse:** Bison

ate	Mintage	F	VF	XF	Unc	BU
994(I)	300,000	—	—	—	2.50	—

Y# 369 50 ROUBLES Ring Composition: Copper-Nickel **Center Composition:** Aluminum-Bronze **Series:** Wildlife **Reverse:** Gazelle

ate	Mintage	F	VF	XF	Unc	BU
994(I)	300,000	—	—	—	2.50	—

Y# 370 50 ROUBLES Ring Composition: Copper-Nickel **Center Composition:** Aluminum-Bronze **Series:** Wildlife **Reverse:** Peregrine falcon

ate	Mintage	F	VF	XF	Unc	BU
994(I)	300,000	—	—	—	2.50	—

Y# 371 50 ROUBLES Ring Composition: Copper-Nickel **Center Composition:** Aluminum-Bronze **Series:** Wildlife **Reverse:** Two flamingos

ate	Mintage	F	VF	XF	Unc	BU
994(I)	300,000	—	—	—	2.50	—

Y# 426 50 ROUBLES Weight: 7.7759 g. **Composition:** 0.9990 Gold .2500 oz. AGW **Subject:** Bolshoi Ballet **Reverse:** Ballerina

ate	Mintage	F	VF	XF	Unc	BU
994 Proof	2,500	Value: 250				

Y# 429 50 ROUBLES Weight: 7.7759 g. **Composition:** 0.9990 Platinum .2500 oz. APW **Subject:** Bolshoi Ballet **Reverse:** Ballerina

ate	Mintage	F	VF	XF	Unc	BU
994 Proof	900	Value: 475				

Y# 525 50 ROUBLES Weight: 7.7759 g. **Composition:** 0.9990 Gold .2500 oz. AGW **Series:** Wildlife **Reverse:** Sable

Date	Mintage	F	VF	XF	Unc	BU
1994 Proof	2,500	Value: 185				

Y# 531 50 ROUBLES Weight: 7.7759 g. **Composition:** 0.9990 Gold .2500 oz. AGW **Reverse:** Dimitri Grigorievich Levitsky

Date	Mintage	F	VF	XF	Unc	BU
1994 Proof	8,000	Value: 225				

Y# 403 50 ROUBLES Composition: Aluminum-Bronze **Series:** WWII **Reverse:** Two sailors, ship, and plane

Date	Mintage	F	VF	XF	Unc	BU
1995	200,000	—	—	—	4.00	—

Note: In mint sets only

Y# 440 50 ROUBLES Weight: 7.7800 g. **Composition:** 0.9990 Gold .2499 oz. AGW **Subject:** Bolshoi Ballet - Sleeping Beauty **Reverse:** Ballerina

Date	Mintage	F	VF	XF	Unc	BU
1995 Proof	2,500	Value: 350				

Y# 443 50 ROUBLES Weight: 7.7759 g. **Composition:** 0.9990 Platinum .2500 oz. APW **Subject:** Bolshoi Ballet - Sleeping Beauty **Reverse:** Ballerina

Date	Mintage	F	VF	XF	Unc	BU
1995 Proof	900	Value: 475				

Y# A475 50 ROUBLES Weight: 7.7800 g. **Composition:** 0.9990 Gold .2499 oz. AGW **Series:** Wildlife **Reverse:** Lynx

Date	Mintage	F	VF	XF	Unc	BU
1995 Proof	5,000	Value: 185				

Y# 408 50 ROUBLES Weight: 7.7800 g. **Composition:** 0.9990 Gold .2499 oz. AGW **Subject:** 50th Anniversary - United Nations **Note:** Similar to 3 Roubles, Y#407.

Date	Mintage	F	VF	XF	Unc	BU
1995 Proof	5,000	Value: 200				

Y# 496 50 ROUBLES Weight: 8.6397 g. **Composition:** 0.9000 Gold .2500 oz. AGW **Subject:** F. Nansen and the "Fram"

Date	Mintage	F	VF	XF	Unc	BU
1995 Proof	5,000	Value: 175				

Y# 501 50 ROUBLES Weight: 8.6397 g. **Composition:** 0.9000 Gold .2500 oz. AGW **Reverse:** Church of the Savior on the Nereditza River

Date	Mintage	F	VF	XF	Unc	BU
1996 Proof	10,000	Value: 175				

Y# 508 50 ROUBLES Composition: Aluminum-Bronze **Subject:** 300th Anniversary - Russian Fleet **Reverse:** Submarine

Date	Mintage	F	VF	XF	Unc	BU
1996	100,000	—	—	—	6.00	—

Note: In mint sets only

Y# 537 50 ROUBLES Weight: 7.7759 g. **Composition:** 0.9990 Gold .2500 oz. AGW **Series:** Wildlife **Reverse:** Amur tiger

Date	Mintage	F	VF	XF	Unc	BU
1996 Proof	1,500	Value: 185				

Y# 546 50 ROUBLES Weight: 8.6397 g. **Composition:** 0.9000 Gold .2500 oz. AGW **Reverse:** Cruiser Varyag 1904

Date	Mintage	F	VF	XF	Unc	BU
1996 Proof	1,500	Value: 250				

Y# 480 50 ROUBLES Weight: 7.7800 g. **Composition:** 0.9990 Gold .2499 oz. AGW **Reverse:** Dmitri Donskoy Monument

Date	Mintage	F	VF	XF	Unc	BU
1996 Proof	10,000	Value: 200				

Y# 487 50 ROUBLES Weight: 7.7800 g. **Composition:** 0.9990 Gold .2499 oz. AGW **Subject:** Ballet - Nutcracker **Reverse:** Marsha and Drosselmeyer with broken doll

Date	Mintage	F	VF	XF	Unc	BU
1996 Proof	2,500	Value: 250				

Y# 555 50 ROUBLES **Weight:** 8.6397 g. **Composition:** 0.9000 Gold .2500 oz. AGW **Subject:** 850th Anniversary - Moscow

Date	Mintage	F	VF	XF	Unc	BU
1997 Proof	10,000	Value: 200				

Y# 572 50 ROUBLES **Weight:** 7.7759 g. **Composition:** 0.9990 Gold .2500 oz. AGW **Subject:** Ballet - Swan Lake **Reverse:** Prince Siegfried with crossbow and swan

Date	Mintage	F	VF	XF	Unc	BU
1997 Proof	1,500	Value: 225				

Y# 595 50 ROUBLES **Weight:** 7.7759 g. **Composition:** 0.9990 Gold .2500 oz. AGW **Series:** Wildlife **Reverse:** Polar bear

Date	Mintage	F	VF	XF	Unc	BU
1997 Proof	1,500	Value: 200				

Y# 316 100 ROUBLES **Ring Composition:** Aluminum-Bronze **Center Composition:** Copper-Nickel **Obverse:** Double-headed eagle **Reverse:** Denomination

Date	F	VF	XF	Unc	BU
1992(l)	0.50	0.75	1.00	3.00	—
1992(m)	0.75	1.00	1.50	4.50	—

Y# 357 100 ROUBLES **Weight:** 17.5000 g. **Composition:** 0.9000 Gold .5000 oz. AGW **Obverse:** Double-headed eagle **Reverse:** Michael Lomonosov

Date	Mintage	F	VF	XF	Unc	BU
1992 Proof	5,700	Value: 275				

Y# 375 100 ROUBLES **Weight:** 17.5000 g. **Composition:** 0.9000 Gold .5000 oz. AGW **Obverse:** Double-headed eagle **Reverse:** Wooly Mammoth **Note:** Yakutia

Date	Mintage	F	VF	XF	Unc	BU
1992	14,000	—	—	—	300	—

Y# 338 100 ROUBLES **Composition:** Copper-Nickel-Zinc

Date	F	VF	XF	Unc	BU
1993(l)	0.25	0.50	1.00	3.00	—
1993(m)	0.25	0.50	1.00	3.00	—

Y# 412 100 ROUBLES **Weight:** 15.5500 g. **Composition:** 0.9990 Gold .5000 oz. AGW **Series:** Wildlife **Reverse:** Bear

Date	Mintage	F	VF	XF	Unc	BU
1993 Proof	1,400	Value: 325				

Y# 419 100 ROUBLES **Weight:** 15.5500 g. **Composition:** 0.9990 Gold .5000 oz. AGW **Subject:** Bolshoi Ballet **Reverse:** Ballerina

Date	Mintage	F	VF	XF	Unc	BU
1993	—	—	—	—	500	—
1993 Proof	1,500	Value: 700				

Y# 454 100 ROUBLES **Weight:** 17.5000 g. **Composition:** 0.9000 Gold .5000 oz. AGW **Reverse:** Peter Tchaikovsky

Date	Mintage	F	VF	XF	Unc	BU
1993 Proof	5,700	Value: 275				

Y# 427 100 ROUBLES **Weight:** 15.5500 g. **Composition:** 0.9990 Gold .5000 oz. AGW **Subject:** Bolshoi Ballet **Reverse:** Ballerina

Date	Mintage	F	VF	XF	Unc	BU
1994 Proof	2,500	Value: 695				

Y# 526 100 ROUBLES **Weight:** 15.5500 g. **Composition:** 0.9990 Gold .5000 oz. AGW **Series:** Wildlif **Reverse:** Sable

Date	Mintage	F	VF	XF	Unc	B
1994 Proof	2,500	Value: 400				

Y# 532 100 ROUBLES **Weight:** 15.5500 g. **Composition:** 0.9990 Gold .5000 oz. AGW **Reverse:** Vass Vassilievich Kandinsky - The Blue Horse

Date	Mintage	F	VF	XF	Unc	B
1994 Proof	6,000	Value: 275				

Y# 404 100 ROUBLES **Composition:** Copper-Nickel **Series:** WWII **Reverse:** Berlin Soldier Monument

Date	Mintage	F	VF	XF	Unc
1995	200,000	—	—	—	5.00

Note: In mint sets only

Y# 497 100 ROUBLES **Weight:** 17.5000 g. **Composition:** 0.9000 Gold .5000 oz. AGW **Reverse:** Icebreaker "Krassin"

Date	Mintage	F	VF	XF	Unc
1995 Proof	2,500	Value: 300			

Y# 498 100 ROUBLES **Weight:** 912.3693 g. **Composition:** 0.9000 Silver 26.4000 oz. ASW **Series:** Wildlife **Reverse:** Lynx with two kits

Date	Mintage	F	VF	XF	Unc
1995 Proof	500	Value: 950			

Y# 499 100 ROUBLES **Weight:** 17.5000 g. **Composition:** 0.9000 Gold .5000 oz. AGW **Series:** Wildlife **Reverse:** Lynx

Date	Mintage	F	VF	XF	Unc	BU
1995 Proof	3,500	Value: 275				

Y# 502 100 ROUBLES **Weight:** 17.5000 g. **Composition:** 0.9000 Gold .5000 oz. AGW **Reverse:** Order of Alexander Nevsky

Date	Mintage	F	VF	XF	Unc	BU
1995 Proof	5,000	Value: 275				

Y# 441 100 ROUBLES **Weight:** 15.5500 g. **Composition:** 0.9990 Gold .5000 oz. AGW **Subject:** Ballet - Sleeping Beauty **Obverse:** Ballerina

Date	Mintage	F	VF	XF	Unc	BU
1995 Proof	2,500	Value: 695				

Y# 376 100 ROUBLES **Weight:** 1111.0861 g. **Composition:** 0.9000 Silver 32.1500 oz. ASW **Series:** Wildlife **Reverse:** Mother bear with cubs **Size:** 100 mm. **Note:** Illustration reduced.

Date	Mintage	F	VF	XF	Unc	BU
1995 Proof	500	Value: 950				

Y# A387 100 ROUBLES **Weight:** 1000.2108 g. **Composition:** 0.9000 Silver 28.9417 oz. ASW **Series:** WWII **Subject:** WWII Victory **Reverse:** Allied commanders **Size:** 103 mm. **Note:** Illustration reduced.

Date	Mintage	F	VF	XF	Unc	BU
1995 Proof	1,500	Value: 750				

Y# 434 100 ROUBLES **Weight:** 912.3693 g. **Composition:** 0.9000 Silver 26.4000 oz. ASW **Subject:** Ballet - Sleeping Beauty **Size:** 100 mm. **Note:** Illustration reduced.

Date	Mintage	F	VF	XF	Unc	BU
1995 Proof	1,000	Value: 600				

Y# 488 100 ROUBLES **Weight:** 1111.0861 g. **Composition:** 0.9990 Silver 32.1500 oz. ASW **Subject:** Ballet - Nutcracker **Reverse:** Marsha cradling nutcracker doll **Note:** Illustration reduced.

Date	Mintage	F	VF	XF	Unc	BU
1996 Proof	1,000	Value: 750				

Y# 538 100 ROUBLES **Weight:** 1111.0861 g. **Composition:** 0.9000 Silver 32.1500 oz. ASW **Series:** Wildlife **Reverse:** Amur tiger **Note:** Illustration reduced.

Date	Mintage	F	VF	XF	Unc	BU
1996 Proof	1,000	Value: 750				

Y# 547 100 ROUBLES **Weight:** 912.3693 g. **Composition:** 0.9000 Silver 26.4000 oz. ASW **Reverse:** Warship - Poltava, 1712 **Note:** Illustration reduced.

Date	Mintage	F	VF	XF	Unc	BU
1996 Proof	1,000	Value: 750				

Y# 481 100 ROUBLES **Weight:** 17.5000 g. **Composition:** 0.9000 Gold .5000 oz. AGW **Obverse:** Double-headed eagle **Reverse:** All Saints Church in Kulishki

Date	Mintage	F	VF	XF	Unc	BU
1996 Proof	5,000	Value: 275				

Y# 489 100 ROUBLES **Weight:** 15.5517 g. **Composition:** 0.9990 Gold .5000 oz. AGW **Subject:** Ballet - Nutcracker **Reverse:** Dancing prince

Date	Mintage	F	VF	XF	Unc	BU
1996 Proof	2,500	Value: 400				

Y# 495 100 ROUBLES **Weight:** 912.3693 g. **Composition:** 0.9000 Silver 26.4000 oz. ASW **Obverse:** Double-headed eagle **Reverse:** Sables around walled city

Date	Mintage	F	VF	XF	Unc	BU
1996 Proof	500	Value: 1,500				

Y# 509 100 ROUBLES Composition: Copper-Nickel **Subject:** 300th Anniversary - Russian Fleet **Reverse:** Nuclear icebreaker "Arctica"

Date	Mintage	F	VF	XF	Unc	BU
1996	100,000	—	—	—	7.00	—

Note: In mint sets only

Y# 539 100 ROUBLES Weight: 15.5517 g. **Composition:** 0.9990 Gold .5000 oz. AGW **Series:** Wildlife **Reverse:** Amur tiger

Date	Mintage	F	VF	XF	Unc	BU
1996 Proof	1,000	Value: 300				

Y# 548 100 ROUBLES Weight: 17.5000 g. **Composition:** 0.9000 Gold .5000 oz. AGW **Subject:** Battleships of WWII **Reverse:** Destroyers "Gremyashij" and "Soobrazitelny"

Date	Mintage	F	VF	XF	Unc	BU
1996 Proof	1,000	Value: 450				

Y# 557 100 ROUBLES Weight: 17.2890 g. **Composition:** 0.9000 Gold .5000 oz. AGW **Subject:** 850th Anniversary - Moscow **Reverse:** Yuri Dolgoruky monument

Date	Mintage	F	VF	XF	Unc	BU
1997 Proof	5,000	Value: 325				

Y# 574 100 ROUBLES Weight: 15.5517 g. **Composition:** 0.9990 Gold .5000 oz. AGW **Subject:** Ballet - Swan Lake **Reverse:** Prince Siegfried and Odette's duet

Date	Mintage	F	VF	XF	Unc	BU
1997 Proof	1,500	Value: 400				

Y# 596 100 ROUBLES Weight: 15.5517 g. **Composition:** 0.9990 Gold .5000 oz. AGW **Series:** Wildlife **Reverse:** Polar bear on ice floe

Date	Mintage	F	VF	XF	Unc	BU
1997 Proof	1,000	Value: 425				

Note: Notice the face on the bear's hind quarter

Y# 597 100 ROUBLES Weight: 1111.0861 g. **Composition:** 0.9000 Silver 32.1500 oz. ASW **Series:** Wildlife **Reverse:** Two polar bears

Date	Mintage	F	VF	XF	Unc	BU
1997 Proof	1,000	Value: 750				

Y# 556 100 ROUBLES Weight: 1111.0861 g. **Composition:** 0.9000 Silver 32.1500 oz. ASW **Subject:** 850th Anniversary - Moscow **Reverse:** Kuzma Minin and Dmitri Pozharsky monument **Note:** Illustration reduced.

Date	Mintage	F	VF	XF	Unc	BU
1997 Proof	1,000	Value: 750				

Y# 573 100 ROUBLES Weight: 1111.0861 g. **Composition:** 0.9000 Silver 32.1500 oz. ASW **Subject:** Ballet - Swan Lake **Reverse:** Prince Siegfried dancing with Odette **Note:** Illustration reduced.

Date	Mintage	F	VF	XF	Unc	BU
1997 Proof	1,000	Value: 750				

Y# 588 100 ROUBLES Weight: 1111.0861 g. **Composition:** 0.9000 Silver 32.1500 oz. ASW **Reverse:** The Bark "Krusenstern" 4-masted ship **Note:** Illustration reduced.

Date	Mintage	F	VF	XF	Unc	BU
1997 Proof	500	Value: 775				

Y# 623 100 ROUBLES Weight: 15.7200 g. **Composition:** 0.9990 Gold .5049 oz. AGW

Date	Mintage	F	VF	XF	Unc	BU
1997 Proof	1,000	Value: 400				

Y# 358 150 ROUBLES Weight: 15.5517 g. **Composition:** 0.9990 Platinum .5000 oz. APW **Subject:** Naval battle of Chesme

Date	Mintage	F	VF	XF	Unc	BU
1992 Proof	3,000	Value: 550				

Y# 397 150 ROUBLES Weight: 15.5517 g. **Composition:** 0.9990 Platinum .5000 oz. APW **Subject:** Ballet **Reverse:** Ballerina

Date	Mintage	F	VF	XF	Unc	BU
1993	750	—	—	—	600	—

Note: Proof sets only

Y# 455 150 ROUBLES Weight: 15.5517 g. **Composition:** 0.9990 Platinum .5000 oz. APW **Reverse:** Igor Stravinsky

Date	Mintage	F	VF	XF	Unc	BU
1993 Proof	3,000	Value: 550				

Y# 519 150 ROUBLES Weight: 15.5517 g. **Compositio[n]** 0.9990 Platinum .5000 oz. APW **Subject:** First Global Circumnavigation **Reverse:** Sloops - "Nadyezdha" and "Ne[va]"

Date	Mintage	F	VF	XF	Unc
1993 Proof	25,000	Value: 550			

Y# 430 150 ROUBLES Weight: 15.5517 g. **Composition:** 0.9990 Platinum .5000 oz. APW **Subject:** Bolshoi Ballet **Reverse:** Ballerina

Date	Mintage	F	VF	XF	Unc	BU
1994 Proof	900	Value: 900				

Y# 523 150 ROUBLES Weight: 15.5517 g. **Composition:** 0.9990 Platinum .5000 oz. APW **Subject:** First Global Circumnavigation **Reverse:** Sloops - "Mirny" and "Vostok"

Date	Mintage	F	VF	XF	Unc	BU
1994 Proof	4,000	Value: 550				

Y# 533 150 ROUBLES Weight: 15.5517 g. **Composition:** 0.9990 Platinum .5000 oz. APW **Subject:** Michail Alexandrowich Vrubel - The Demon

Date	Mintage	F	VF	XF	Unc	BU
1994 Proof	3,000	Value: 550				

Y# 444 150 ROUBLES Weight: 15.5517 g. **Composition:** 0.9990 Platinum .5000 oz. APW **Subject:** Ballet - Sleeping Beauty **Reverse:** Male dancer

Date	Mintage	F	VF	XF	Unc	BU
1995 Proof	900	Value: 795				

Y# 503 150 ROUBLES Weight: 15.5517 g. **Composition:** 0.9990 Platinum .5000 oz. APW **Subject:** Battle of the Neva River in 1240

Date	Mintage	F	VF	XF	Unc	BU
1995 Proof	3,000	Value: 550				

Y# 413 200 ROUBLES Weight: 31.1035 g. **Composition:** 0.9990 Gold 1.0000 oz. AGW **Series:** Wildlife **Reverse:** Bear with cub

Date	Mintage	F	VF	XF	Unc	BU
1993 Proof	1,000	Value: 600				

Y# 527 200 ROUBLES Weight: 31.1035 g. **Composition:** 0.9990 Gold 1.0000 oz. AGW **Series:** Wildlife **Reverse:** Two sables

Date	Mintage	F	VF	XF	Unc	BU
1994 Proof	2,000	Value: 500				

Y# 500 200 ROUBLES Weight: 31.1035 g. **Composition:** 0.9990 Gold 1.0000 oz. AGW **Series:** Wildlife **Reverse:** Seated lynx

Date	Mintage	F	VF	XF	Unc	BU
1995 Proof	1,750	Value: 500				

Y# 540 200 ROUBLES Weight: 31.1035 g. **Composition:** 0.9990 Gold 1.0000 oz. AGW **Series:** Wildlife **Reverse:** Amur tiger

Date	Mintage	F	VF	XF	Unc	BU
1996 Proof	1,000	Value: 550				

Y# 598 200 ROUBLES Weight: 31.1035 g. **Composition:** 0.9990 Gold 1.0000 oz. AGW **Series:** Wildlife **Reverse:** Seated polar bear

Date	Mintage	F	VF	XF	Unc	BU
1997 Proof	1,000	Value: 750				

Y# 589 1000 ROUBLES Weight: 155.5000 g. **Composition:** 0.9990 Gold 4.9944 oz. AGW **Reverse:** The Bark "Krusenstern" - 4-masted ship

Date	Mintage	F	VF	XF	Unc	BU
1997 Proof	250	Value: 3,250				

Y# 541 10000 ROUBLES Weight: 1111.0861 g. **Composition:** 0.9990 Gold 35.6865 oz. AGW **Series:** Wildlife **Obverse:** Double-headed eagle **Reverse:** Amur tiger with two cubs **Size:** 100 mm. **Note:** Illustration reduced.

Date	Mintage	F	VF	XF	Unc	BU
1996 Prooflike	100	—	—	—	—	—

Y# 599 10000 ROUBLES Weight: 1111.0861 g. **Composition:** 0.9990 Gold 35.6865 oz. AGW **Series:** Wildlife **Obverse:** Double-headed eagle **Reverse:** Polar bear with two cubs **Size:** 100 mm. **Note:** Illustration reduced.

Date	Mintage	F	VF	XF	Unc	BU
1997 Proof	100	Value: 16,500				

REFORM COINAGE

January 1, 1998

1,000 Old Roubles = 1 New Rouble

Y# 600 KOPEK Composition: Nickel Clad Steel **Obverse:** St. George **Reverse:** Denomination

Date	F	VF	XF	Unc	BU
1997 M	—	—	—	0.25	—
1997 SP	—	—	—	0.25	—
1998 M	—	—	—	0.25	—
1998 SP	—	—	—	0.25	—
1999 M	—	—	—	0.25	—
1999 SP	—	—	—	0.25	—

Date	F	VF	XF	Unc	BU
2000 M	—	—	—	0.25	—
2000 SP	—	—	—	0.25	—
2001 M	—	—	—	0.25	—
2001 SP	—	—	—	0.25	—
2002 M	—	—	—	0.25	—
2002 SP	—	—	—	0.25	—

Y# 601 5 KOPEKS **Composition:** Nickel Clad Steel **Obverse:** St. George **Reverse:** Denomination

Date	F	VF	XF	Unc	BU
1997 M	—	—	—	0.35	—
1997 SP	—	—	—	0.35	—
1998 M	—	—	—	0.35	—
1998 SP	—	—	—	0.35	—
1999 M	—	—	—	0.35	—
1999 SP	—	—	—	0.35	—
2000 M	—	—	—	0.35	—
2000 SP	—	—	—	0.35	—
2001 M	—	—	—	0.35	—
2001 SP	—	—	—	0.35	—
2002 M	—	—	—	0.35	—
2002 SP	—	—	—	0.35	—

Y# 602 10 KOPEKS **Composition:** Brass **Obverse:** St. George **Reverse:** Denomination

Date	F	VF	XF	Unc	BU
1997 M	—	—	—	0.50	—
1997 SP	—	—	—	0.50	—
1998 M	—	—	—	0.50	—
1998 SP	—	—	—	0.50	—
1999 M	—	—	—	0.50	—
1999 SP	—	—	—	0.50	—
2000 M	—	—	—	0.50	—
2000 SP	—	—	—	0.50	—
2001 M	—	—	—	0.50	—
2001 SP	—	—	—	0.50	—
2002 M	—	—	—	0.50	—
2002 SP	—	—	—	0.50	—

Y# 603 50 KOPEKS **Composition:** Brass **Obverse:** Stanislavski **Reverse:** Denomination

Date	F	VF	XF	Unc	BU
1997 M	—	—	—	0.75	—
1997 SP	—	—	—	0.75	—
1998 M	—	—	—	0.75	—
1998 (SP)	—	—	—	0.75	—
1999 M	—	—	—	0.75	—
2002 SP	—	—	—	0.75	—

Y# 604 ROUBLE **Composition:** Copper-Nickel-Zinc **Reverse:** Denomination

Date	F	VF	XF	Unc	BU
1997(m)	—	—	—	1.00	—
1997(sp)	—	—	—	1.00	—
1998 (m)	—	—	—	1.00	—

Y# 614 ROUBLE **Weight:** 8.5300 g. **Composition:** 0.9250 Silver .2357 oz. ASW **Series:** World Youth Games **Reverse:** Female tennis player

Date	Mintage	F	VF	XF	Unc	BU
1998 Proof	25,000	Value: 13.50				

Y# 615 ROUBLE **Weight:** 8.5300 g. **Composition:** 0.9250 Silver .2357 oz. ASW **Series:** World Youth Games **Reverse:** Female gymnast

Date	Mintage	F	VF	XF	Unc	BU
1998 Proof	25,000	Value: 13.50				

Y# 616 ROUBLE **Weight:** 8.5300 g. **Composition:** 0.9250 Silver .2357 oz. ASW **Series:** World Youth Games **Reverse:** Fencer

Date	Mintage	F	VF	XF	Unc	BU
1998 Proof	25,000	—	—	—	—	—

Y# 617 ROUBLE **Weight:** 8.5300 g. **Composition:** 0.9250 Silver .2357 oz. ASW **Series:** World Youth Games **Reverse:** Hammer thrower

Date	Mintage	F	VF	XF	Unc	BU
1998 Proof	25,000	Value: 13.50				

Y# 618 ROUBLE **Weight:** 8.5300 g. **Composition:** 0.9250 Silver .2357 oz. ASW **Series:** World Youth Games **Reverse:** Female gymnast

Date	Mintage	F	VF	XF	Unc	BU
1998 Proof	25,000	Value: 13.50				

Y# 619 ROUBLE **Weight:** 8.5300 g. **Composition:** 0.9250 Silver .2357 oz. ASW **Series:** World Youth Games **Reverse:** Volleyball player

Date	Mintage	F	VF	XF	Unc	BU
1998 Proof	25,000	Value: 13.50				

Y# 628 ROUBLE **Weight:** 17.5500 g. **Composition:** 0.9000 Silver .5078 oz. ASW **Series:** Wildlife **Reverse:** Far Eastern Skink

Date	Mintage	F	VF	XF	Unc	BU
1998 Proof	15,000	Value: 27.50				

Y# 629 ROUBLE **Weight:** 17.5500 g. **Composition:** 0.9000 Silver .5078 oz. ASW **Series:** Wildlife **Reverse:** Lavtev Walrus

Date	Mintage	F	VF	XF	Unc	BU
1998 Proof	15,000	Value: 27.50				

Y# 630 ROUBLE **Weight:** 17.5500 g. **Composition:** 0.9000 Silver .5078 oz. ASW **Series:** Wildlife **Reverse:** White-neck Goose

Date	Mintage	F	VF	XF	Unc	BU
1998 Proof	15,000	Value: 25.00				

Y# 640 ROUBLE **Composition:** Copper-Nickel-Zinc **Obverse:** Double-headed eagle **Reverse:** Alexander Pushkin portrait

Date	Mintage	F	VF	XF	Unc	BU
1999(m)	5,000,000	—	—	—	0.75	—
1999СП	5,000,000	—	—	—	0.75	—

Y# 641 ROUBLE **Weight:** 17.4400 g. **Composition:** 0.9000 Silver .5046 oz. ASW **Series:** Wildlife **Obverse:** Double-headed eagle **Reverse:** Hedgehogs

Date	Mintage	F	VF	XF	Unc	BU
1999 Proof	15,000	Value: 25.00				

Y# 642 ROUBLE **Weight:** 17.4400 g. **Composition:** 0.9000 Silver .5046 oz. ASW **Series:** Wildlife **Obverse:** Double-headed eagle **Reverse:** Caucasian viper

Date	Mintage	F	VF	XF	Unc	B
1999 Proof	15,000	Value: 27.50				

Y# 643 ROUBLE **Weight:** 17.4400 g. **Composition:** 0.9000 Silver .5046 oz. ASW **Series:** Wildlife **Obverse:** Double-headed eagle **Reverse:** Gull standing on shore

Date	Mintage	F	VF	XF	Unc	BU
1999 Proof	15,000	Value: 25.00				

Y# 719 ROUBLE **Weight:** 17.4400 g. **Composition:** 0.9000 Silver .5046 oz. ASW **Subject:** Queen Mother's 100th Birthday **Obverse:** Double-headed eagle **Reverse:** Two black-hooded cranes **Edge:** Reeded **Size:** 33 mm.

Date	Mintage	F	VF	XF	Unc	BU
2000 (SP) Proof	3,000	Value: 25.00				

Y# 720 ROUBLE **Weight:** 17.4400 g. **Composition:** 0.9000 Silver .5046 oz. ASW **Obverse:** Double-headed eagle **Reverse:** Leopard Runner snake

Date	Mintage	F	VF	XF	Unc	BU
2000 (SP) Proof	3,000	Value: 27.50				

Y# 721 ROUBLE **Weight:** 17.4400 g. **Composition:** 0.9000 Silver .5046 oz. ASW **Obverse:** Double-headed eagle **Reverse:** Russian Desman

Date	Mintage	F	VF	XF	Unc	BU
2000 (SP) Proof	3,000	Value: 25.00				

Y# 732 ROUBLE **Weight:** 17.4300 g. **Composition:** 0.9000 Silver 0.5043 oz. ASW **Subject:** Sturgeon **Obverse:** Double-headed eagle **Reverse:** Sakhalin sturgeon and other fish **Edge:** Reeded **Size:** 32.8 mm.

Date	Mintage	F	VF	XF	Unc	BU
2001 Proof	15,000	Value: 25.00				

Y# 745 ROUBLE **Weight:** 17.4000 g. **Composition:** 0.9000 Silver 0.5035 oz. ASW **Subject:** Altai Mountain Sheep **Obverse:** Double-headed eagle **Reverse:** Mountain sheep **Edge:** Reeded **Size:** 32.8 mm.

Date	Mintage	F	VF	XF	Unc	BU
2001(sp)	10,000	Value: 25.00				

Note: Proof

Y# 746 ROUBLE **Weight:** 17.4000 g. **Composition:** 0.9000 Silver 0.5035 oz. ASW **Subject:** Eurasian Beaver **Obverse:** Double-headed eagle **Reverse:** Two beavers **Edge:** Reeded **Size:** 32.8 mm.

Date	Mintage	F	VF	XF	Unc	BU
2001(sp) Proof	10,000	Value: 25.00				

Y# 731 ROUBLE **Weight:** 3.2100 g. **Composition:** Copper-Nickel **Obverse:** Double-headed eagle **Reverse:** Stylized design above hologram **Edge:** Reeded **Size:** 20.7 mm.

Date	Mintage	F	VF	XF	Unc	BU
2001	100,000,000	—	—	—	1.50	—

Y# 758 ROUBLE **Weight:** 17.4400 g. **Composition:** 0.9000 Silver 0.5046 oz. ASW **Subject:** Amur Goral **Obverse:** Double-headed eagle **Reverse:** Mountain goat **Edge:** Reeded **Size:** 33 mm.

Date	Mintage	F	VF	XF	Unc	BU
2002 (SP) Proof	10,000	Value: 25.00				

Y# 759 ROUBLE **Weight:** 17.4400 g. **Composition:** 0.9000 Silver 0.5046 oz. ASW **Subject:** The Seywal **Obverse:** Double-headed eagle **Reverse:** Wale **Edge:** Reeded **Size:** 33 mm.

Date	Mintage	F	VF	XF	Unc	BU
2002 (SP) Proof	10,000	Value: 25.00				

Y# 760 ROUBLE **Weight:** 17.4400 g. **Composition:** 0.9000 Silver 0.5046 oz. ASW **Subject:** Golden Eagle **Obverse:** Double-headed eagle **Reverse:** Eagle with nestling **Edge:** Reeded **Size:** 33 mm.

Date	Mintage	F	VF	XF	Unc	BU
2002 (SP) Proof	10,000	Value: 25.00				

Y# 770 ROUBLE **Weight:** 8.5300 g. **Composition:** 0.9250 Silver 0.2537 oz. ASW **Subject:** Ministry of Education **Obverse:** Double-headed eagle **Reverse:** Seedling and open book **Edge:** Reeded **Size:** 25 mm.

Date	Mintage	F	VF	XF	Unc	BU
2002(m) Proof	3,000	Value: 25.00				

Y# 771 ROUBLE **Weight:** 8.5300 g. **Composition:** 0.9250 Silver 0.2537 oz. ASW **Subject:** Ministry of Finances **Obverse:** Double-headed eagle **Reverse:** Caduceus in monogram **Edge:** Reeded **Size:** 25 mm.

Date	Mintage	F	VF	XF	Unc	BU
2002 (SP) Proof	3,000	Value: 25.00				

Y# 772 ROUBLE **Weight:** 8.5300 g. **Composition:** 0.9250 Silver 0.2537 oz. ASW **Subject:** Ministry of Economic Developement **Obverse:** Double-headed eagle **Reverse:** Crowned two headed eagle with cornucopia and caduceus **Edge:** Reeded **Size:** 25 mm.

Date	Mintage	F	VF	XF	Unc	BU
2002 (SP) Proof	3,000	Value: 25.00				

Y# 773 ROUBLE **Weight:** 8.5300 g. **Composition:** 0.9250 Silver 0.2537 oz. ASW **Subject:** Ministry of Foreign Affairs **Obverse:** Two headed eagle **Reverse:** Crowned two headed eagle above crossed palms **Edge:** Reeded **Size:** 25 mm.

Date	Mintage	F	VF	XF	Unc	BU
2002 (SP) Proof	3,000	Value: 25.00				

Y# 774 ROUBLE **Weight:** 8.5300 g. **Composition:** 0.9250 Silver 0.2537 oz. ASW **Subject:** Ministry of Internal Affairs **Obverse:** Double-headed eagle **Reverse:** Crowned two headed eagle with round breast shield **Edge:** Reeded **Size:** 25 mm.

Date	Mintage	F	VF	XF	Unc	BU
2002 (SP) Proof	3,000	Value: 25.00				

Y# 775 ROUBLE **Weight:** 8.5300 g. **Composition:** 0.9250 Silver 0.2537 oz. ASW **Subject:** Ministry of Justice **Obverse:** Double-headed eagle **Reverse:** Crowned double-headed eagle with column on breast shield **Edge:** Reeded **Size:** 25 mm.

Date	Mintage	F	VF	XF	Unc	BU
2002 (SP) Proof	3,000	Value: 25.00				

Y# 776 ROUBLE **Weight:** 8.5300 g. **Composition:** 0.9250 Silver 0.2537 oz. ASW **Subject:** Russian Armed Forces **Obverse:** Double-headed eagle **Reverse:** Double-headed eagle with crowned top pointed breast shield **Edge:** Reeded **Size:** 25 mm.

Date	Mintage	F	VF	XF	Unc	BU
2002(m) Proof	3,000	Value: 25.00				

Y# 797 ROUBLE **Weight:** 3.2500 g. **Composition:** Copper Nickel **Obverse:** Curved bank name below eagle

Date	F	VF	XF	Unc	BU
2002	—	—	—	1.00	—

Y# 605 2 ROUBLES **Composition:** Copper-Nickel-Zinc **Reverse:** Denomination

Date	F	VF	XF	Unc	BU
1997(m)	—	—	—	1.65	—
1997(sp)	—	—	—	1.65	—
1998	—	—	—	1.65	—
1998 (M)	—	—	—	—	—

Y# 607 2 ROUBLES **Weight:** 16.8108 g. **Composition:** 0.9250 Silver .4999 oz. ASW **Subject:** 100th Anniversary - Sergei Eisenstein **Obverse:** Double-headed eagle

Date	Mintage	F	VF	XF	Unc	BU
1998	15,000	—	—	—	16.50	—

Y# 608 2 ROUBLES **Weight:** 16.8108 g. **Composition:** 0.9250 Silver .4999 oz. ASW **Subject:** 100th Anniversary - Sergei Eisenstein **Obverse:** Double-headed eagle

Date	Mintage	F	VF	XF	Unc	BU
1998	15,000	—	—	—	17.50	—

Y# 609 2 ROUBLES **Weight:** 16.8108 g. **Composition:** 0.9250 Silver .4999 oz. ASW **Obverse:** Double-headed eagle **Reverse:** K. S. Stanslavski

Date	Mintage	F	VF	XF	Unc	BU
1998	15,000	—	—	—	17.50	—

Y# 610 2 ROUBLES **Weight:** 16.8108 g. **Composition:** 0.9250 Silver .4999 oz. ASW **Obverse:** Double-headed eagle **Reverse:** Maxim Gorky play - Stanislavsky method

Date	Mintage	F	VF	XF	Unc	BU
1998	15,000	—	—	—	17.50	—

Y# 620 2 ROUBLES **Weight:** 17.0000 g. **Composition:** 0.9250 Silver .5056 oz. ASW **Obverse:** Double-headed eagle **Reverse:** Victor Mikhailovich Vasnetsov - three ancient warriors

Date	Mintage	F	VF	XF	Unc	BU
1998	15,000	—	—	—	17.50	—

Y# 621 2 ROUBLES **Weight:** 17.0000 g. **Composition:** 0.9250 Silver .5056 oz. ASW **Obverse:** Double-headed eagle **Reverse:** Victor Mikhailovich Vasnetsov - three seated figures

Date	Mintage	F	VF	XF	Unc	BU
1998	15,000	—	—	—	17.50	—

Y# 649 2 ROUBLES **Weight:** 17.0000 g. **Composition:** 0.9250 Silver .5056 oz. ASW **Subject:** K. L. Khetagurov 1859-1906 **Obverse:** Double-headed eagle **Reverse:** Portrait with mountain tops and buildings

Date	Mintage	F	VF	XF	Unc	BU
1999 Proof	3,000	Value: 22.50				

Y# 650 2 ROUBLES **Weight:** 17.0000 g. **Composition:** 0.9250 Silver .5056 oz. ASW **Subject:** N. K. Rerikh 1874-1947 **Obverse:** Double-headed eagle **Reverse:** Painter with mountains in the background

Date	Mintage	F	VF	XF	Unc	BU
1999 Proof	15,000	Value: 17.50				

Y# 651 2 ROUBLES **Weight:** 17.0000 g. **Composition:** 0.9250 Silver .5056 oz. ASW **Subject:** The Human Acts by Rerikh. **Obverse:** Double-headed eagle **Reverse:** Detail from painting, artist's portrait above

Date	Mintage	F	VF	XF	Unc	BU
1999 Proof	15,000	Value: 17.50				

Y# 652 2 ROUBLES **Weight:** 17.0000 g. **Composition:** 0.9250 Silver .5056 oz. ASW **Subject:** K. P. Bryulbv 1799-1852 **Obverse:** Double-headed eagle **Reverse:** Portrait of painter

Date	Mintage	F	VF	XF	Unc	BU
1999 Proof	15,000	Value: 22.50				

Y# 653 2 ROUBLES **Weight:** 17.0000 g. **Composition:** 0.9250 Silver .5056 oz. ASW **Subject:** The Last Day of Pompei **Obverse:** Double-headed eagle **Reverse:** Detail from painting, portrait in exergue

Date	Mintage	F	VF	XF	Unc	BU
1999 Proof	15,000	Value: 17.50				

Y# 654 2 ROUBLES **Weight:** 17.0000 g. **Composition:** 0.9250 Silver .5056 oz. ASW **Obverse:** Double-headed eagle **Reverse:** Half bust of I.P. Pavlov, dog, books, cap, and gown

Date	Mintage	F	VF	XF	Unc	BU
1999 Proof	15,000	Value: 17.50				

Y# 655 2 ROUBLES **Weight:** 17.0000 g. **Composition:** 0.9250 Silver .5056 oz. ASW **Obverse:** Double-headed eagle **Reverse:** Portrait and silence tower

Date	Mintage	F	VF	XF	Unc	BU
1999 Proof	15,000	Value: 17.50				

Y# 659 2 ROUBLES **Weight:** 17.0000 g. **Composition:** 0.9250 Silver .5056 oz. ASW **Subject:** Eugeny Abramovich Baratynsky **Reverse:** Bust of Baratynsky at right, scenery at left **Edge:** Reeded

Date	Mintage	F	VF	XF	Unc	BU
2000 Proof	5,000	Value: 22.50				

Y# 660 2 ROUBLES **Weight:** 17.0000 g. **Composition:** 0.9250 Silver .5056 oz. ASW **Subject:** F. A. Vassiliyev **Reverse:** Cameo bust of Vassiliyev left, dates below, scenery at left

Date	Mintage	F	VF	XF	Unc	BU
2000 Proof	5,000	Value: 22.50				

Y# 662 2 ROUBLES **Weight:** 17.0000 g. **Composition:** 0.9250 Silver .5056 oz. ASW **Subject:** S. V. Kovaleuskaya **Reverse:** Cameo bust of Kovaleuskaya right at left, academic items at right

Date	Mintage	F	VF	XF	Unc	BU
2000 Proof	5,000	Value: 22.50				

Y# 663 2 ROUBLES **Weight:** 5.1000 g. **Composition:** Copper-Nickel-Zinc **Series:** World War II **Obverse:** Denomination **Reverse:** Infantry assault at Stalingrad **Edge:** Reeded and plain sections

Date	Mintage	F	VF	XF	Unc	BU
2000 (SP)	10,000,000	—	—	—	1.25	—

Y# 664 2 ROUBLES **Composition:** Copper-Nickel-Zinc **Reverse:** Cannon manufacturing scene in Tula

Date	Mintage	F	VF	XF	Unc	BU
2000 (M)	10,000,000	—	—	—	1.25	—

Y# 665 2 ROUBLES **Composition:** Copper-Nickel-Zinc **Reverse:** Truck-mounted rocket launchers in Smolensk

Date	Mintage	F	VF	XF	Unc	BU
2000 (M)	10,000,000	—	—	—	1.25	—

Y# 666 2 ROUBLES **Composition:** Copper-Nickel-Zinc **Reverse:** Murmansk ship convoy

Date	Mintage	F	VF	XF	Unc	BU
2000 (M)	10,000,000	—	—	—	1.25	—

Y# 667 2 ROUBLES **Composition:** Copper-Nickel-Zinc **Reverse:** Defense of Moscow scene

Date	Mintage	F	VF	XF	Unc	BU
2000 (M)	10,000,000	—	—	—	1.25	—

Y# 668 2 ROUBLES **Composition:** Copper-Nickel-Zinc **Reverse:** Marine landing scene in Novorusiisk

Date	Mintage	F	VF	XF	Unc	BU
2000 (SP)	10,000,000	—	—	—	1.25	—

Y# 669 2 ROUBLES **Composition:** Copper-Nickel-Zinc **Reverse:** Siege of Leningrad truck convoy scene

Date	Mintage	F	VF	XF	Unc	BU
2000 (SP)	10,000,000	—	—	—	1.25	—

Y# 704 2 ROUBLES **Weight:** 17.4400 g. **Composition:** 0.9250 Silver .5056 oz. ASW **Subject:** M.I. Chigorin **Obverse:** Double-headed eagle **Reverse:** Cameo portrait and chess pieces **Edge:** Reeded **Size:** 33 mm.

Date	Mintage	F	VF	XF	Unc	BU
2000 (SP) Proof	5,000	Value: 25.00				

Y# 730 2 ROUBLES **Weight:** 17.0000 g. **Composition:** 0.9250 Silver .5056 oz. ASW **Subject:** V.I. Dal **Obverse:** Double-headed eagle **Reverse:** Portrait, book, signature, figures **Edge:** Reeded **Size:** 33 mm.

Date	Mintage	F	VF	XF	Unc	BU
2001(m) Proof	7,500	Value: 22.50				

Y# 675 2 ROUBLES **Weight:** 5.2000 g. **Composition:** Copper-Nickel **Subject:** Yuri Gagarin **Obverse:** Denomination and date **Reverse:** Uniformed portrait **Edge:** Segmented reeding **Size:** 23 mm.

Date		F	VF	XF	Unc	BU
2001		—	—	—	2.00	—

Y# 742 2 ROUBLES **Weight:** 17.0000 g. **Composition:** 0.9250 Silver 0.5056 oz. ASW **Subject:** Zodiac Signs: Leo **Obverse:** Double-headed eagle **Reverse:** Lion and symbol **Edge:** Reeded **Size:** 33 mm.

Date	Mintage	F	VF	XF	Unc	BU
2002 Proof	20,000	Value: 20.00				

Y# 798 2 ROUBLES **Weight:** 5.1000 g. **Composition:** Copper Nickel **Obverse:** Curved bank name below eagle

Date		F	VF	XF	Unc	BU
2002		—	—	—	1.50	—

KM# 747 2 ROUBLES **Weight:** 17.0000 g. **Composition:** 0.9250 Silver 0.5056 oz. ASW **Subject:** Zodiac Signs **Obverse:** Double-headed eagle **Reverse:** Virgo **Edge:** Reeded **Size:** 33 mm.

Date	Mintage	F	VF	XF	Unc	BU
2002(m) Proof	20,000	Value: 25.00				

Y# 761 2 ROUBLES **Weight:** 17.0000 g. **Composition:** 0.9250 Silver 0.5056 oz. ASW **Subject:** Zodiac Signs **Obverse:** Double-headed eagle **Reverse:** Capricorn **Edge:** Reeded **Size:** 33 mm.

Date	Mintage	F	VF	XF	Unc	BU
2002 (SP) Proof	20,000	Value: 22.50				

Y# 762 2 ROUBLES **Weight:** 17.0000 g. **Composition:** 0.9250 Silver 0.5056 oz. ASW **Subject:** Zodiac Signs **Obverse:** Double-headed eagle **Reverse:** Sagittarius **Edge:** Reeded **Size:** 33 mm.

Date	Mintage	F	VF	XF	Unc	BU
2002 (SP) Proof	20,000	Value: 22.50				

Y# 766 2 ROUBLES **Weight:** 17.0000 g. **Composition:** 0.9250 Silver 0.5056 oz. ASW **Subject:** Zodiac Signs **Obverse:** Double-headed eagle **Reverse:** Scorpion **Edge:** Reeded **Size:** 33 mm.

Date	Mintage	F	VF	XF	Unc	BU
2002(m) Proof	20,000	Value: 22.50				

Y# 768 2 ROUBLES **Weight:** 17.0000 g. **Composition:** 0.9250 Silver 0.5056 oz. ASW **Subject:** Zodiac Signs **Obverse:** Double-headed eagle **Reverse:** Balance scale **Edge:** Reeded **Size:** 33 mm.

Date	Mintage	F	VF	XF	Unc	BU
2002 (SP) Proof	20,000	Value: 22.50				

Y# 793 2 ROUBLES **Weight:** 17.0000 g. **Composition:** 0.9250 Silver 0.5056 oz. ASW **Subject:** L.P. Orlova **Obverse:** Double-headed eagle **Reverse:** Actress' portrait **Edge:** Reeded **Size:** 33 mm.

Date	Mintage	F	VF	XF	Unc	BU
2002(m) Proof	10,000	Value: 25.00				

Y# 624 3 ROUBLES **Weight:** 34.5600 g. **Composition:** 0.9000 Silver 1.0000 oz. ASW **Reverse:** Officer Davydov

Date	Mintage	F	VF	XF	Unc	BU
1998 Proof	15,000	Value: 22.50				

Y# 625 3 ROUBLES **Weight:** 34.5600 g. **Composition:** 0.9000 Silver 1.0000 oz. ASW **Reverse:** "Russian Sosaveta" sculpture

Date	Mintage	F	VF	XF	Unc	BU
1998 Proof	15,000	Value: 22.50				

Y# 626 3 ROUBLES **Weight:** 34.5600 g. **Composition:** 0.9000 Silver 1.0000 oz. ASW **Reverse:** Archangel's head

Date	Mintage	F	VF	XF	Unc	BU
1998 Proof	15,000	Value: 22.50				

Y# 627 3 ROUBLES **Weight:** 34.5600 g. **Composition:** 0.9000 Silver 1.0000 oz. ASW **Reverse:** "Merchant Woman Drinking Tea"

Date	Mintage	F	VF	XF	Unc	BU
1998 Proof	15,000	Value: 22.50				

Y# 631 3 ROUBLES **Weight:** 34.5600 g. **Composition:** 0.9000 Silver 1.0000 oz. ASW **Subject:** Nilo Stolobenskaya Hermitage **Reverse:** Saint.

Date	Mintage	F	VF	XF	Unc	BU
1998 Proof	15,000	Value: 37.50				

Y# 632 3 ROUBLES **Weight:** 34.5600 g. **Composition:** 0.9000 Silver 1.0000 oz. ASW **Reverse:** Church, view from bell tower

Date	Mintage	F	VF	XF	Unc	BU
1998 Proof	5,000	Value: 35.00				

Y# 633 3 ROUBLES **Weight:** 34.8800 g. **Composition:** 0.9000 Silver 1.0093 oz. ASW **Subject:** Russian Human Rights Year **Reverse:** Document, people, and map **Edge:** Reeded

Date	Mintage	F	VF	XF	Unc	BU
1998 Proof	15,000	Value: 37.50				

Y# 634 3 ROUBLES **Weight:** 34.7700 g. **Composition:** 0.9000 Silver 1.0061 oz. ASW **Subject:** 275th Anniversary - St. Petersburg University **Obverse:** Double-headed eagle **Reverse:** Four portraits and building

Date	Mintage	F	VF	XF	Unc	BU
1999 Proof	15,000	Value: 40.00				

Y# 635 3 ROUBLES **Weight:** 34.7300 g. **Composition:** 0.9000 Silver 1.0049 oz. ASW **Obverse:** Double-headed eagle **Reverse:** Mardjany Mosque in Kazan

Date	Mintage	F	VF	XF	Unc	BU
1999 Proof	15,000	Value: 37.50				

Y# 636 3 ROUBLES **Weight:** 34.7300 g. **Composition** 0.9000 Silver 1.0049 oz. ASW **Subject:** 200th Birthday - A S. Pushkin **Obverse:** Double-headed eagle **Reverse:** Pushkin at his desk

Date	Mintage	F	VF	XF	Unc	B
1999 Proof	15,000	Value: 32.50				

Y# 637 3 ROUBLES **Weight:** 34.7300 g. **Compositio** 0.9000 Silver 1.0049 oz. ASW **Subject:** 200th Birthday - A S. Pushkin **Obverse:** Double-headed eagle **Reverse:** Pushkin standing

Date	Mintage	F	VF	XF	Unc	B
1999 Proof	15,000	Value: 32.50				

Y# 638 3 ROUBLES **Weight:** 34.7300 g. **Compositio** 0.9000 Silver 1.0049 oz. ASW **Subject:** First Tibet Exhibitic 1879-1880 **Obverse:** Double-headed eagle **Reverse:** Me on horseback

Date	Mintage	F	VF	XF	Unc	
1999 Proof	15,000	Value: 27.50				

Y# 639 3 ROUBLES **Weight:** 34.7300 g. **Compositio** 0.9000 Silver 1.0049 oz. ASW **Subject:** Second Tibet Exhibition 1883-1885 **Obverse:** Double-headed eagle **Reverse:** Camp scene

Date	Mintage	F	VF	XF	Unc
1999 Proof	15,000	Value: 27.50			

Y# 644 3 ROUBLES **Weight:** 34.7100 g. **Composition:** 0.9000 Silver 1.0044 oz. ASW **Subject:** Science Academy. **Obverse:** Double-headed eagle **Reverse:** Allegorical figure, building, portraits, imperial double eagle

Date	Mintage	F	VF	XF	Unc	BU
1999 Proof	5,000	Value: 40.00				

Y# 645 3 ROUBLES **Weight:** 34.7100 g. **Composition:** 0.9000 Silver 1.0044 oz. ASW **Subject:** Estada Kuskovo palace. **Obverse:** Double-headed eagle **Reverse:** Palace from three perspectives

Date	Mintage	F	VF	XF	Unc	BU
1999 Proof	15,000	Value: 37.50				

Y# 646 3 ROUBLES **Weight:** 34.7100 g. **Composition:** 0.9000 Silver 1.0044 oz. ASW **Subject:** Juryev Monastery, Movgorod **Obverse:** Double-headed eagle **Reverse:** Building view and detail from interior

Date	Mintage	F	VF	XF	Unc	BU
1999 Proof	15,000	Value: 37.50				

Y# 647 3 ROUBLES **Weight:** 34.8800 g. **Composition:** 0.9000 Silver 1.0093 oz. ASW **Subject:** 50th Anniversary - Diplomacy wtih China **Obverse:** Double-headed eagle **Reverse:** Moscow Kremlin and Tiananmen gate

Date	Mintage	F	VF	XF	Unc	BU
1999 Proof	3,000	Value: 250				

Y# 657 3 ROUBLES **Weight:** 34.7300 g. **Composition:** 0.9000 Silver 1.0049 oz. ASW **Subject:** Ballet **Obverse:** Double-headed eagle **Reverse:** Sword fight

Date	Mintage	F	VF	XF	Unc	BU
1999 Proof	10,000	Value: 45.00				

Y# 658 3 ROUBLES **Weight:** 34.7300 g. **Composition:** 0.9000 Silver 1.0049 oz. ASW **Subject:** Ballet **Obverse:** Double-headed eagle **Reverse:** Couple dancing, Arabic soldiers in background

Date	Mintage	F	VF	XF	Unc	BU
1999 Proof	10,000	Value: 45.00				

Y# 690 3 ROUBLES **Weight:** 34.7300 g. **Composition:** 0.9000 Silver 1.0049 oz. ASW **Subject:** Ufa Friendship Monument **Obverse:** Russian eagle **Reverse:** Five people and monument **Edge:** Reeded **Size:** 38.8 mm.

Date	Mintage	F	VF	XF	Unc	BU
1999 Proof	3,000	Value: 42.50				

Y# 661 3 ROUBLES **Weight:** 34.8800 g. **Composition:** 0.9000 Silver 1.0093 oz. ASW **Subject:** World Ice Hockey Championship **Reverse:** Two hockey players **Edge:** Reeded

Date	Mintage	F	VF	XF	Unc	BU
2000 Proof	3,000	Value: 40.00				

Y# 671 3 ROUBLES **Weight:** 34.7600 g. **Composition:** 0.9000 Silver 1.0058 oz. ASW **Series:** Olympics **Reverse:** 2000 Olympic design **Edge:** Reeded

Date	Mintage	F	VF	XF	Unc	BU
2000 Proof	5,000	Value: 45.00				

Y# 673 3 ROUBLES **Weight:** 34.6700 g. **Composition:** 0.9990 Silver 1.1135 oz. ASW **Subject:** Soccer **Obverse:** Double-headed eagle **Reverse:** Two soccer players, map, and net **Edge:** Reeded

Date	Mintage	F	VF	XF	Unc	BU
2000 Proof	3,000	Value: 40.00				

Y# 674 3 ROUBLES **Weight:** 34.9400 g. **Composition:** 0.9000 Silver 1.0110 oz. ASW **Series:** WWII **Subject:** 55th Anniversary - WWII **Obverse:** Seated soldier **Reverse:** Soviet Order of Glory **Edge:** Lettered **Edge Lettering:** BANK of RUSSIA THREE ROUBLES 2000

Date	Mintage	F	VF	XF	Unc	BU
2000 Proof	5,000	Value: 42.50				

Y# 705 3 ROUBLES **Weight:** 34.8800 g. **Composition:** 0.9000 Silver 1.0093 oz. ASW **Subject:** St. Nicholas Monastery **Obverse:** Double-headed eagle **Reverse:** Saint and buildings **Edge:** Reeded **Size:** 39 mm.

Date	Mintage	F	VF	XF	Unc	BU
2000(m) Proof	5,000	Value: 42.50				

Y# 706 3 ROUBLES **Weight:** 34.8800 g. **Composition:** 0.9000 Silver 1.0093 oz. ASW **Subject:** Novgorod Kremlin **Obverse:** Double-headed eagle **Reverse:** Buildings

Date	Mintage	F	VF	XF	Unc	BU
2000(m) Proof	5,000	Value: 42.50				

Y# 707 3 ROUBLES **Weight:** 34.8800 g. **Composition:** 0.9000 Silver 1.0093 oz. ASW **Subject:** City of Pushkin **Obverse:** Double-headed eagle **Reverse:** Park and city view

Date	Mintage	F	VF	XF	Unc	BU
2000(m) Proof	5,000	Value: 47.50				

Y# 708 3 ROUBLES **Weight:** 34.8800 g. **Composition:** 0.9000 Silver 1.0093 oz. ASW **Series:** Third Mellennium **Subject:** Science **Obverse:** Double-headed eagle **Reverse:** Astronaut, atomic elements chart, etc. **Edge:** Reeded **Size:** 39 mm.

Date	Mintage	F	VF	XF	Unc	BU
2000(m) Proof	5,000	Value: 42.50				

Y# 709 3 ROUBLES **Weight:** 34.8800 g. **Composition:** 0.9000 Silver 1.0093 oz. ASW **Series:** Third Millennium **Subject:** Human Role **Obverse:** Double-headed eagle **Reverse:** People between cog wheel and computer.

Date	Mintage	F	VF	XF	Unc	BU
2000(m) Proof	5,000	Value: 42.50				

Y# 714 3 ROUBLES **Weight:** 34.8800 g. **Composition:** 0.9000 Silver 1.0093 oz. ASW **Subject:** 140th Anniversary - State Bank of Russia **Obverse:** Double-headed eagle **Reverse:** Seated allegorical woman

Date	Mintage	F	VF	XF	Unc	BU
2000(m) Proof	3,000	Value: 45.00				

Y# 716 3 ROUBLES **Weight:** 34.8800 g. **Composition:** 1.0093 Silver **Subject:** Field Marshal Suvorov in Switzerland **Obverse:** Double-headed eagle **Reverse:** Battle scene

Date	Mintage	F	VF	XF	Unc	BU
2000(sp) Proof	5,000	Value: 42.50				

Y# 722 3 ROUBLES **Weight:** 34.8800 g. **Composition:** 0.9000 Silver 1.0093 oz. ASW **Subject:** Snow Leopard **Obverse:** Double-headed eagle **Reverse:** Leopard on log

Date	Mintage	F	VF	XF	Unc	BU
2000(m) Proof	5,000	Value: 45.00				

Y# 677 3 ROUBLES **Weight:** 34.8800 g. **Composition:** 0.9000 Silver 1.0093 oz. ASW **Subject:** 225 Years - Bolshoi Theater **Obverse:** Double-headed eagle **Reverse:** Five men, one with pole ax **Edge:** Reeded **Size:** 39 mm.

Date	Mintage	F	VF	XF	Unc	BU
2001 Proof	7,500	Value: 40.00				

Y# 680 3 ROUBLES **Weight:** 34.8800 g. **Compositio** 0.9000 Silver 1.0093 oz. ASW **Subject:** 40th Anniversary Manned Space Flight **Obverse:** Double-headed eagle **Reverse:** Uniformed portrait of Yuri Gagarin holding dove **Edge:** Reeded **Size:** 39 mm.

Date	Mintage	F	VF	XF	Unc
2001 Proof	7,500	Value: 40.00			

Y# 682 3 ROUBLES **Weight:** 34.8800 g. **Compositio** 0.9000 Silver 1.0093 oz. ASW **Subject:** Siberian Exploratic **Obverse:** Double-headed eagle **Reverse:** Men riding horses, deer and sleds **Edge:** Reeded **Size:** 39 mm.

Date	Mintage	F	VF	XF	Unc
2001 Proof	5,000	Value: 37.50			

Y# 733 3 ROUBLES **Weight:** 34.8800 g. **Compositio** 0.9000 Silver 1.0093 oz. ASW **Subject:** 200th Anniversa of Navigation School **Obverse:** Double-headed eagle **Reverse:** Navigational tools and building **Edge:** Reeded **Size:** 39 mm.

Date	Mintage	F	VF	XF	Unc
2001 Proof	5,000	Value: 40.00			

Y# 734 3 ROUBLES **Weight:** 34.8800 g. **Compositic** 0.9000 Silver 1.0093 oz. ASW **Subject:** First Moscow Savings Bank **Obverse:** Double-headed eagle **Reverse:** Beehive above building **Edge:** Reeded **Size:** 39 mm.

Date	Mintage	F	VF	XF	Unc
2001 Proof	17,500	Value: 40.00			

#735 3 ROUBLES **Weight:** 34.8800 g. **Composition:** 0.9000 Silver 1.0093 oz. ASW **Subject:** State Labor Savings Bank **Obverse:** Double-headed eagle **Reverse:** Dam, passbook and tractor **Edge:** Reeded **Size:** 39 mm.

ate	Mintage	F	VF	XF	Unc	BU
001 Proof	17,500	Value: 40.00				

#736 3 ROUBLES **Weight:** 34.8800 g. **Composition:** 0.9000 Silver 1.0093 oz. ASW **Subject:** Savings Bank of the Russian Federation **Obverse:** Double-headed eagle **Reverse:** Chevrons above building **Edge:** Reeded **Size:** 39 mm.

ate	Mintage	F	VF	XF	Unc	BU
001 Proof	17,500	Value: 40.00				

#737 3 ROUBLES **Weight:** 34.8800 g. **Composition:** 0.9000 Silver 1.0093 oz. ASW **Subject:** 10th Anniversary - Commonwealth of Independent States **Obverse:** Double-headed eagle **Reverse:** Hologram below logo **Edge:** Reeded **Size:** 39 mm.

ate	Mintage	F	VF	XF	Unc	BU
001 Proof	7,500	Value: 45.00				

#738 3 ROUBLES **Weight:** 34.8800 g. **Composition:** 0.9000 Silver 1.0093 oz. ASW **Subject:** Olympics **Obverse:** Double-headed eagle **Reverse:** Two cross country skiers **Edge:** Reeded **Size:** 39 mm.

ate	Mintage	F	VF	XF	Unc	BU
002 Proof	25,000	Value: 40.00				

Y#744 3 ROUBLES **Weight:** 34.8800 g. **Composition:** 0.9000 Silver 1.0093 oz. ASW **Subject:** St. John's Nunnery, St. Petersburg **Obverse:** Double-headed eagle **Reverse:** Nunnery and cameo portraits of John of Kronstadt **Edge:** Reeded **Size:** 39 mm.

Date	Mintage	F	VF	XF	Unc	BU
2002 Proof	5,000	Value: 35.00				

Y#778 3 ROUBLES **Weight:** 34.8800 g. **Composition:** 0.9000 Silver 1.0093 oz. ASW **Subject:** Kidekshа **Obverse:** Double-headed eagle **Reverse:** Three churches on river bank **Edge:** Reeded **Size:** 39 mm.

Date	Mintage	F	VF	XF	Unc	BU
2002 (SP) Proof	10,000	Value: 35.00				

Y#779 3 ROUBLES **Weight:** 34.8800 g. **Composition:** 0.9000 Silver 1.0093 oz. ASW **Subject:** Iversky Monastery, Valdaiy **Obverse:** Double-headed eagle **Reverse:** Building complex on an island in Lake Valdaiy **Edge:** Reeded **Size:** 39 mm.

Date	Mintage	F	VF	XF	Unc	BU
2002 (SP) Proof	10,000	Value: 35.00				

Y#780 3 ROUBLES **Weight:** 34.8800 g. **Composition:** 0.9000 Silver 1.0093 oz. ASW **Subject:** Miraculous Savior Church **Obverse:** Double-headed eagle **Reverse:** Church with separate bell tower **Edge:** Reeded **Size:** 39 mm.

Date	Mintage	F	VF	XF	Unc	BU
2002(m) Proof	5,000	Value: 35.00				

Y#781 3 ROUBLES **Weight:** 34.8800 g. **Composition:** 0.9000 Silver 1.0093 oz. ASW **Subject:** Works of Dionissy **Obverse:** Double-headed eagle **Reverse:** "The Crucifix" **Edge:** Reeded **Size:** 39 mm.

Date	Mintage	F	VF	XF	Unc	BU
2002 (SP) Proof	10,000	Value: 35.00				

Y#755 3 ROUBLES **Weight:** 34.8800 g. **Composition:** 0.9000 Silver 1.0093 oz. ASW **Subject:** Admiral Nakhimov **Obverse:** Double-headed eagle **Reverse:** Monument, Admiral with cannon and naval battle scene **Edge:** Reeded **Size:** 39 mm.

Date	Mintage	F	VF	XF	Unc	BU
2002 (SP) Proof	10,000	Value: 35.00				

Y#787 3 ROUBLES **Weight:** 34.8800 g. **Composition:** 0.9000 Silver 1.0093 oz. ASW **Subject:** World Cup Soccer **Obverse:** Double-headed eagle **Reverse:** Soccer ball center in circle of players **Edge:** Reeded **Size:** 39 mm.

Date	Mintage	F	VF	XF	Unc	BU
2002 (SP) Proof	25,000	Value: 25.00				

Y#756 3 ROUBLES **Weight:** 34.8800 g. **Composition:** 0.9000 Silver 1.0093 oz. ASW **Subject:** Hermitage **Obverse:** Double-headed eagle **Reverse:** Statues and arch **Edge:** Reeded **Size:** 39 mm.

Date	Mintage	F	VF	XF	Unc	BU
2002 (SP) Proof	10,000	Value: 35.00				

Y#799 5 ROUBLES **Weight:** 6.4500 g. **Composition:** Copper-Nickel Clad Copper **Obverse:** Curved bank name below eagle

Date	F	VF	XF	Unc	BU
2002	—	—	—	2.00	—

Y#695 10 ROUBLES **Weight:** 1.5500 g. **Composition:** 0.9990 Gold .0499 oz. AGW **Subject:** Russian Ballet

Obverse: Two headed eagle **Reverse:** Standing knight Jean de Brienne **Edge:** Reeded **Size:** 12 mm.

Date	Mintage	F	VF	XF	Unc	BU
1999(m) Proof	2,500	Value: 65.00				

Y# 670 10 ROUBLES Ring **Composition:** Brass Center **Weight:** 8.2600 g. **Center Composition:** Copper-Nickel **Series:** WWII **Subject:** 55th Anniversary - Victorious Conclusion of WWII **Obverse:** Denomination **Reverse:** Infantry officer leading an assault **Edge:** Reeded and lettered **Note:** Struck at St. Petersburg Mint.

Date	Mintage	F	VF	XF	Unc	BU
2000(sp)	10,000,000	—	—	—	3.00	—
2000(m)	10,000,000	—	—	—	3.00	—

Y# 686 10 ROUBLES Weight: 1.6100 g. **Composition:** 0.9990 Gold .0517 oz. AGW **Subject:** Bolshoi Theater 225 Years **Obverse:** Double-headed eagle **Reverse:** Building above number 225 **Edge:** Reeded **Size:** 12 mm.

Date	Mintage	F	VF	XF	Unc	BU
2001 Proof	3,000	Value: 50.00				

Y# 676 10 ROUBLES Ring **Weight:** 8.2200 g. Ring **Composition:** Brass **Center Composition:** Copper-Nickel **Subject:** Yuri Gagarin **Obverse:** Denomination with latent image in zero, and date **Reverse:** Helmeted portrait **Edge:** Reeding over denomination **Size:** 27 mm.

Date	F	VF	XF	Unc	BU
2001	—	—	—	3.00	—

Y# 739 10 ROUBLES Ring **Composition:** Brass Center **Weight:** 8.2200 g. **Center Composition:** Copper-Nickel **Subject:** Ancient Towns - Derbent **Obverse:** Denomination in wreath **Reverse:** City arms above walled city view **Edge:** Reeding over denomination **Size:** 27 mm.

Date	Mintage	F	VF	XF	Unc	BU
2002	5,000,000	—	—	—	3.00	—

Y# 740 10 ROUBLES Ring **Composition:** Brass Center **Weight:** 8.2200 g. **Center Composition:** Copper-Nickel **Subject:** Ancient Towns - Kostroma **Obverse:** Denomination in wreath **Reverse:** Cupola, city arms and river view **Edge:** Reeding over denomination **Size:** 27 mm.

Date	Mintage	F	VF	XF	Unc	BU
2002	5,000,000	—	—	—	3.00	—

Y# 741 10 ROUBLES Ring **Composition:** Brass Center **Weight:** 8.2200 g. **Center Composition:** Copper-Nickel **Subject:** Ancient Towns - Staraya Russa **Obverse:** Denomination in wreath **Reverse:** City arms and cathedral **Edge:** Reeding over denomination **Size:** 27 mm.

Date	Mintage	F	VF	XF	Unc	BU
2002	5,000,000	—	—	—	3.00	—

Y# 748 10 ROUBLES Weight: 8.2200 g. **Composition:** Copper-Nickel **Subject:** Ministry of Education **Obverse:** Denomination **Reverse:** Seedling and open book **Edge:** Reeding over denomination **Size:** 27 mm.

Date	Mintage	F	VF	XF	Unc	BU
2002(m)	5,000,000	—	—	—	—	3.00

Y# 749 10 ROUBLES Weight: 8.2200 g. **Composition:** Copper Nickel **Subject:** Ministry of Finance **Obverse:** Denomination **Reverse:** Caduceus in monogram **Edge:** Reeding over denomination **Size:** 27 mm.

Date	Mintage	F	VF	XF	Unc	BU
2002 (SP)	5,000,000	—	—	—	—	3.00

Y# 750 10 ROUBLES Weight: 8.2200 g. **Composition:** Copper Nickel **Subject:** Ministry of Economic Developement **Obverse:** Denomination **Reverse:** Crowned double-headed eagle with comucopia and Caduceus **Edge:** Reeding over denomination **Size:** 27 mm.

Date	Mintage	F	VF	XF	Unc	BU
2002 (SP)	5,000,000	—	—	—	—	3.00

Y# 751 10 ROUBLES Weight: 8.2200 g. **Composition:** Copper Nickel **Subject:** Ministry of Foreign Affairs **Obverse:** Denomination **Reverse:** Crowned double-headed eagle above crossed palms **Edge:** Reeding over denomination **Size:** 27 mm.

Date	Mintage	F	VF	XF	Unc	BU
2002 (SP)	5,000,000	—	—	—	—	3.00

Y# 752 10 ROUBLES Weight: 8.2200 g. **Composition:** Copper-Nickel **Subject:** Ministry of Internal Affairs **Obverse:** Denomination **Reverse:** Crowned double-headed eagle with round breast shield **Edge:** Reeding over denomination **Size:** 27 mm.

Date	Mintage	F	VF	XF	Unc	BU
2002 (SP)	5,000,000	—	—	—	—	3.00

Y# 753 10 ROUBLES Weight: 8.2200 g. **Composition:** Copper Nickel **Subject:** Ministry of Justice **Obverse:** Denomination **Reverse:** Crowned double-headed eagle with column on breast shield **Edge:** Reeding over denomination **Size:** 27 mm.

Date	Mintage	F	VF	XF	Unc	BU
2002 (SP)	5,000,000	—	—	—	—	3.00

Y# 754 10 ROUBLES Weight: 8.2200 g. **Composition:** Copper Nickel **Subject:** Russian Armed Forces **Obverse:** Denomination **Reverse:** Crowned double-headed eagle with crowned pointed top shield **Edge:** Reeding over denomination **Size:** 27 mm.

Date	Mintage	F	VF	XF	Unc	BU
2002(m)	5,000,000	—	—	—	—	3.00

Y# 697 25 ROUBLES Weight: 3.2000 g. **Composition:** 0.9990 Gold .1028 oz. AGW **Subject:** Russian Ballet **Obverse:** Double-headed eagle **Reverse:** Dancing Saracen **Edge:** Reeded **Size:** 16 mm.

Date	Mintage	F	VF	XF	Unc	BU
1999(sp) Proof	2,000	Value: 150				

Y# 691 25 ROUBLES Weight: 173.2900 g. **Composition:** 0.9000 Silver 5.0143 oz. ASW **Subject:** Alexander Pushkin **Obverse:** Double-headed eagle **Reverse:** Walking figure with hat and cane **Edge:** Reeded **Size:** 60 mm. **Note:** Illustration reduced.

Date	Mintage	F	VF	XF	Unc	BU
1999(m) Proof	3,000	Value: 165				

Y# 696 25 ROUBLES Weight: 173.2900 g. **Composition:** 0.9000 Silver 5.0143 oz. ASW **Subject:** Russian Ballet **Obverse:** Double-headed eagle **Reverse:** Raymonda and the knight dance scene **Edge:** Reeded **Size:** 60 mm. **Note:** Illustration reduced.

Date	Mintage	F	VF	XF	Unc	BU
1999(m) Proof	3,000	Value: 165				

Y# 701 25 ROUBLES **Weight:** 173.2900 g. **Composition:** 0.9000 Silver 5.0143 oz. ASW **Subject:** Russian Exploers: N.M. Przhevalsky **Obverse:** Double-headed eagle **Reverse:** Caravan in Central Asia **Edge:** Reeded **Size:** 60 mm. **Note:** Illustration reduced.

Date	Mintage	F	VF	XF	Unc	BU
1999(sp) Proof	3,000	Value: 165				

Y# 710 25 ROUBLES **Weight:** 173.2900 g. **Composition:** 0.9000 Silver 5.0143 oz. ASW **Series:** Third Millennium **Subject:** Education **Obverse:** Double-headed eagle **Reverse:** Ancient monk and modern student **Edge:** Reeded **Size:** 60 mm. **Note:** Illustration reduced.

Date	Mintage	F	VF	XF	Unc	BU
2000(m) Proof	1,000	Value: 185				

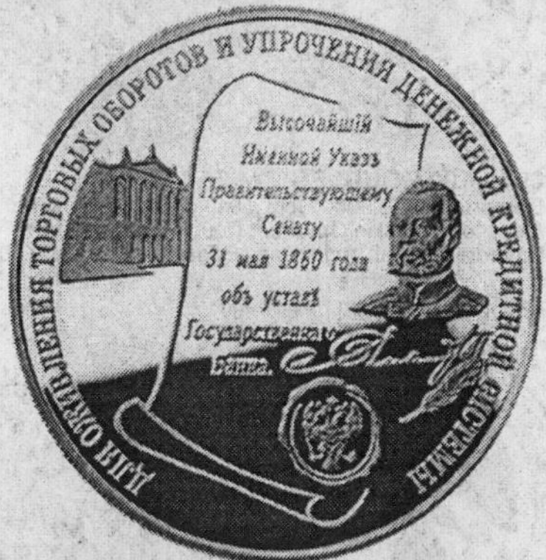

Y# 715 25 ROUBLES **Weight:** 173.2900 g. **Composition:** 0.9000 Silver 5.0143 oz. ASW **Subject:** State Bank of Russia 140th Anniversary **Obverse:** Double-headed eagle **Reverse:** Document, portrait and building **Edge:** Reeded **Size:** 60 mm. **Note:** Illustration reduced.

Date	Mintage	F	VF	XF	Unc	BU
2000(m) Proof	1,000	Value: 185				

Y# 717 25 ROUBLES **Weight:** 173.2900 g. **Composition:** 0.9000 Silver 5.0143 oz. ASW **Subject:** Field Marshal Suvorov **Obverse:** Double-headed eagle **Reverse:** Suvorov with maps and battle scene **Edge:** Reeded **Size:** 60 mm. **Note:** Illustration reduced.

Date	Mintage	F	VF	XF	Unc	BU
2000(m) Proof	1,000	Value: 185				

Y# 723 25 ROUBLES **Weight:** 173.2900 g. **Composition:** 0.9000 Silver 5.0143 oz. ASW **Subject:** Snow Leopard **Obverse:** Double-headed eagle **Reverse:** Leopard on branch **Edge:** Reeded **Size:** 60 mm. **Note:** Illustration reduced.

Date	Mintage	F	VF	XF	Unc	BU
2000(m) Proof	1,000	Value: 185				

Y# 678 25 ROUBLES **Weight:** 173.2900 g. **Composition:** 0.9000 Silver 5.0143 oz. ASW **Subject:** Bolshoi Theater 225 Years **Obverse:** Double-headed eagle **Reverse:** Dancing couple scene **Edge:** Reeded **Size:** 60 mm. **Note:** Illustration reduced.

Date	Mintage	F	VF	XF	Unc	BU
2001 Proof	2,000	Value: 125				

Y# 683 25 ROUBLES **Weight:** 173.2900 g. **Composition:** 0.9000 Silver 5.0143 oz. ASW **Subject:** Siberian Exploration **Obverse:** Double-headed eagle **Reverse:** Standing king and river boats **Edge:** Reeded **Size:** 60 mm. **Note:** Illustration reduced.

Date	Mintage	F	VF	XF	Unc	BU
2001 Proof	1,000	Value: 140				

Y# 687 25 ROUBLES **Weight:** 3.2000 g. **Composition:** 0.9990 Gold .1028 oz. AGW **Subject:** Bolshoi Theater 225 Years **Obverse:** Double-headed eagle **Reverse:** Ballerina **Edge:** Reeded **Size:** 16 mm.

Date	Mintage	F	VF	XF	Unc	BU
2001 Proof	2,500	Value: 125				

Y# 794 25 ROUBLES **Weight:** 173.1300 g. **Composition:** 0.9000 Silver 5.0096 oz. ASW **Subject:** Foundation of Russian Savings Banks **Obverse:** Double-headed eagle **Reverse:** Czar Nicholas I and document **Edge:** Reeded **Size:** 60.2 mm.

Date	Mintage	F	VF	XF	Unc	BU
2001(m) Proof	10,500	—	—	—	—	—

Y# 743 25 ROUBLES **Weight:** 3.2000 g. **Composition:** 0.9990 Gold 0.1028 oz. AGW **Subject:** Zodiac Signs: Leo **Obverse:** Double-headed eagle **Reverse:** Lion and symbol **Edge:** Reeded **Size:** 16 mm.

Date	Mintage	F	VF	XF	Unc	BU
2002 Proof	50,000	Value: 100				

Y# 763 25 ROUBLES **Weight:** 3.2000 g. **Composition:** 0.9990 Gold 0.1028 oz. AGW **Subject:** Zodiac Signs **Obverse:** Double-headed eagle **Reverse:** Capricorn **Edge:** Reeded **Size:** 16 mm.

Date	Mintage	F	VF	XF	Unc	BU
2002(m)	10,000	—	—	—	—	100

Y# 764 25 ROUBLES **Weight:** 3.2000 g. **Composition:** 0.9990 Gold 0.1028 oz. AGW **Subject:** Zodiac Signs **Obverse:** Double-headed eagle **Reverse:** Virgo, seated woman **Edge:** Reeded **Size:** 16 mm.

Date	Mintage	F	VF	XF	Unc	BU
2002 (SP)	50,000	—	—	—	—	100

Y# 765 25 ROUBLES **Weight:** 3.2000 g. **Composition:** 0.9990 Gold 0.1028 oz. AGW **Subject:** Zodiac Signs **Obverse:** Double-headed eagle **Reverse:** Sagittarius the archer **Edge:** Reeded **Size:** 16 mm.

Date	Mintage	F	VF	XF	Unc	BU
2002 (SP)	50,000	—	—	—	—	100

Y# 767 25 ROUBLES **Weight:** 3.2000 g. **Composition:** 0.9990 Gold 0.1028 oz. AGW **Subject:** Zodiac Signs **Obverse:** Double-headed eagle **Reverse:** Scorpion **Edge:** Reeded **Size:** 16 mm.

Date	Mintage	F	VF	XF	Unc	BU
2002(m)	50,000	—	—	—	—	100

Y# 769 25 ROUBLES **Subject:** Zodiac Signs **Obverse:** Double-headed eagle **Reverse:** Libra, balance scale **Edge:** Reeded

Date	Mintage	F	VF	XF	Unc	BU
2002 (SP)	50,000	—	—	—	—	—

Y# 777 25 ROUBLES **Weight:** 173.2900 g. **Composition:** 0.9000 Silver 5.0143 oz. ASW **Subject:** Czar Alexander I **Obverse:** Double-headed eagle **Reverse:** Portrait and Imperial eagle above document text establishing government ministries **Edge:** Reeded **Size:** 60 mm.

Date	Mintage	F	VF	XF	Unc	BU
2002(m) Proof	1,500	Value: 155				

Y# 785 25 ROUBLES **Weight:** 173.2900 g. **Composition:** 0.9000 Silver 5.0143 oz. ASW **Subject:** Admiral Nakhimov **Obverse:** Double-headed eagle **Reverse:** Admiral watching naval battle **Edge:** Reeded **Size:** 60 mm.

Date	Mintage	F	VF	XF	Unc	BU
2002 (SP) Proof	2,000	Value: 150				

Y# 790 25 ROUBLES **Weight:** 173.2900 g. **Composition:** 0.9000 Silver 5.0143 oz. ASW **Subject:** Hermitage **Obverse:** Double-headed eagle **Reverse:** Staircase viewed through door way **Edge:** Reeded **Size:** 60 mm.

Date	Mintage	F	VF	XF	Unc	BU
2002 (SP) Proof	2,000	Value: 150				

Y# 692 50 ROUBLES **Weight:** 8.7500 g. **Composition:** 0.9000 Gold .2532 oz. AGW **Subject:** Alexander Pushkin **Obverse:** Double-headed eagle **Reverse:** Portrait above quill and signature **Edge:** Reeded **Size:** 22.6 mm.

Date	Mintage	F	VF	XF	Unc	BU
1999(m) Proof	1,500	Value: 225				

Y# 698 50 ROUBLES **Weight:** 8.7500 g. **Composition:** 0.9990 Gold .2534 oz. AGW **Subject:** Russian Ballet **Obverse:** Double-headed eagle **Reverse:** Raymonda and Saracen dancing **Edge:** Reeded **Size:** 22.6 mm.

Date	Mintage	F	VF	XF	Unc	BU
1999(m) Proof	1,500	Value: 225				

Y# 702 50 ROUBLES **Weight:** 8.7500 g. **Composition:** 0.9000 Gold .2532 oz. AGW **Subject:** Russian Explorer N.M. Przhevalsky **Obverse:** Double-headed eagle **Reverse:** Portrait **Edge:** Reeded **Size:** 22.6 mm.

Date	Mintage	F	VF	XF	Unc	BU
1999(sp) Proof	1,500	Value: 225				

Y# 648 50 ROUBLES **Weight:** 8.7500 g. **Composition:** 0.9000 Gold .2532 oz. AGW **Subject:** 50th Anniversary - Diplomacy with China **Obverse:** Double-headed eagle **Reverse:** Moscow Kremllin and Tiananmen gate

Date	Mintage	F	VF	XF	Unc	BU
1999 Proof	1,000	Value: 265				

Y# 672 50 ROUBLES **Weight:** 8.7100 g. **Composition:** 0.9000 Gold .2520 oz. AGW **Series:** Olympics **Obverse:** Double-headed eagle **Reverse:** Torch runner on map

Date	Mintage	F	VF	XF	Unc	BU
2000 Proof	1,000	Value: 265				

Y# 718 50 ROUBLES **Weight:** 8.7500 g. **Composition:** 0.9000 Gold .2532 oz. AGW **Subject:** Field Marshal Suvorov **Obverse:** Double-headed eagle **Reverse:** Portrait above cannons **Edge:** Reeded **Size:** 22.6 mm.

Date	Mintage	F	VF	XF	Unc	BU
2000(sp) Proof	500	Value: 265				

Y# 725 50 ROUBLES **Weight:** 7.8900 g. **Composition:** 0.9990 Gold .2534 oz. AGW **Subject:** Snow Leopard **Obverse:** Double-headed eagle **Reverse:** Leopard head **Edge:** Reeded **Size:** 22.6 mm.

Date	Mintage	F	VF	XF	Unc	BU
2000(sp) Proof	1,000	Value: 250				

Y# 679 50 ROUBLES **Weight:** 8.7500 g. **Composition:** 0.9990 Gold .2532 oz. AGW **Subject:** Bolshoi Theater 225 Years **Obverse:** Double-headed eagle **Reverse:** Dueling figures **Edge:** Reeded **Size:** 22.6 mm.

Date	Mintage	F	VF	XF	Unc	BU
2001 Proof	2,000	Value: 150				

Y# 684 50 ROUBLES **Weight:** 8.7500 g. **Composition:** 0.9000 Gold .2532 oz. AGW **Subject:** Siberian Exploration **Obverse:** Double-headed eagle **Reverse:** Portrait and boat **Edge:** Reeded **Size:** 22.6 mm.

Date	Mintage	F	VF	XF	Unc	BU
2001 Proof	1,500	Value: 150				

Y# 757 50 ROUBLES **Weight:** 8.6444 g. **Composition:** 0.9000 Gold 0.2501 oz. AGW **Subject:** Olympics **Obverse:** Double-headed eagle **Reverse:** Figure skater and flying eagle **Edge:** Reeded **Size:** 22.6 mm.

Date	Mintage	F	VF	XF	Unc	BU
2002 Proof	3,000	Value: 250				

Y# 782 50 ROUBLES **Weight:** 7.8900 g. **Composition:** 0.9990 Gold 0.2534 oz. AGW **Subject:** Works of Dionissy **Obverse:** Double-headed eagle **Reverse:** Virgin of Odygitriya **Edge:** Reeded **Size:** 22.6 mm.

Date	Mintage	F	VF	XF	Unc	BU
2002(m) Proof	1,500	Value: 225				

Y# 786 50 ROUBLES **Weight:** 8.7500 g. **Composition:** 0.9000 Gold 0.2532 oz. AGW **Subject:** Admiral Nakhimov **Obverse:** Double-headed eagle **Reverse:** Portrait above flags and anchor **Edge:** Reeded **Size:** 22.6 mm.

Date	Mintage	F	VF	XF	Unc	BU
2002 (SP) Proof	1,500	Value: 225				

Y# 788 50 ROUBLES **Weight:** 8.7500 g. **Composition:** 0.9000 Gold 0.2532 oz. AGW **Subject:** World Cup Soccer **Obverse:** Double-headed eagle **Reverse:** Player kicking soccer ball **Edge:** Reeded **Size:** 22.6 mm.

Date	Mintage	F	VF	XF	Unc	BU
2002(m) Proof	3,000	Value: 200				

Y# 694 100 ROUBLES **Weight:** 17.4500 g. **Composition:** 0.9000 Gold .5049 oz. AGW **Subject:** Alexander Pushkin **Obverse:** Double-headed eagle **Reverse:** Portrait and scenes **Edge:** Reeded **Size:** 30 mm.

Date	Mintage	F	VF	XF	Unc	BU
1999 Proof	1,000	Value: 400				

Y# 700 100 ROUBLES **Weight:** 15.7200 g. **Composition:** 0.9990 Gold .5049 oz. AGW **Subject:** Russian Ballet **Obverse:** Double-headed eagle **Reverse:** Raymonda dancing alone **Edge:** Reeded **Size:** 30 mm.

Date	Mintage	F	VF	XF	Unc	BU
1999(sp) Proof	1,500	Value: 400				

Y# 703 100 ROUBLES **Weight:** 17.4500 g. **Composition:** 0.9000 Gold .5049 oz. AGW **Subject:** Russian Explorer N.M. Przhevalsky **Obverse:** Double-headed eagle **Reverse:** Two men viewing lake **Edge:** Reeded **Size:** 30 mm.

Date	Mintage	F	VF	XF	Unc	BU
1999(sp) Proof	1,000	Value: 400				

Y# 693 100 ROUBLES **Weight:** 1111.1200 g. **Composition:** 0.9000 Silver 32.1510 oz. ASW **Subject:** Alexander Pushkin **Obverse:** Double-headed eagle **Reverse:** Statue, monuments and buildings **Edge:** Reeded **Size:** 100 mm. **Note:** Illustration reduced.

Date	Mintage	F	VF	XF	Unc	BU
1999(m) Proof	1,000	Value: 775				

Y# 711 100 ROUBLES **Weight:** 1111.1200 g. **Composition:** 0.9000 Silver 32.1510 oz. ASW **Subject:** Russian State **Obverse:** Double-headed eagle **Reverse:** Mother Russia, mythological bird and map **Edge:** Reeded **Size:** 100 mm. **Note:** Illustration reduced.

Date	Mintage	F	VF	XF	Unc	BU
2000(m) Proof	500	Value: 775				

Y# 724 100 ROUBLES **Weight:** 1111.1200 g. **Composition:** 0.9000 Silver 32.1510 oz. ASW **Subject:** Snow Leopard **Obverse:** Double-headed eagle **Reverse:** Two leopards **Edge:** Reeded **Size:** 100 mm. **Note:** Illustration reduced.

Date	Mintage	F	VF	XF	Unc	BU
2000(sp) Proof	500	Value: 775				

Y# 729 100 ROUBLES **Weight:** 1111.1200 g. **Composition:** 0.9000 Silver 32.1510 oz. ASW **Subject:** WWII Victory 55th Anniversary **Obverse:** Russian soldier writing on Reichstag building pillar **Reverse:** Conference scene **Edge:** Reeded **Size:** 100 mm. **Note:** Illustration reduced.

Date	Mintage	F	VF	XF	Unc	BU
2000(sp) Proof	500	Value: 775				

Y# 713 100 ROUBLES **Weight:** 17.4500 g. **Composition:** 0.9000 Gold .5049 oz. AGW **Subject:** Department of Mining 300 Years **Obverse:** Double-headed eagle **Reverse:** Miner and equipment **Edge:** Reeded **Size:** 30 mm.

Date	Mintage	F	VF	XF	Unc	BU
2000(m) Proof	1,000	Value: 325				

Y# 726 100 ROUBLES **Weight:** 15.7200 g. **Composition:** 0.9990 Gold .5049 oz. AGW **Subject:** Snow Leopard **Obverse:** Double-headed eagle **Reverse:** Leopard on branch **Edge:** Reeded **Size:** 30 mm.

Date	Mintage	F	VF	XF	Unc	BU
2000(sp) Proof	1,000	Value: 400				

Y# 685 100 ROUBLES **Weight:** 17.4500 g. **Composition:** 0.9000 Gold .5049 oz. AGW **Subject:** Siberian Exploration **Obverse:** Double-headed eagle **Reverse:** Two portraits and sailboat **Edge:** Reeded **Size:** 30 mm.

Date	Mintage	F	VF	XF	Unc	BU
2001 Proof	1,000	Value: 275				

Y# 795 100 ROUBLES **Weight:** 1111.1200 g. **Composition:** 0.9000 Silver 32.151 oz. ASW **Subject:** The Bark Sedov **Obverse:** Double-headed eagle **Reverse:** Cameo portrait and sailing ship **Edge:** Reeded **Size:** 100 mm. **Note:** Illustration reduced.

Date	Mintage	F	VF	XF	Unc	BU
2001(m) Proof	500	Value: 800				

Y# 681 100 ROUBLES **Weight:** 1111.1000 g. **Composition:** 0.9000 Silver 32.1504 oz. ASW **Subject:** Yuri Gagarin **Obverse:** Double-headed eagle **Reverse:** Astronaut and rocket in space **Edge:** Reeded **Size:** 100 mm. **Note:** Illustration reduced.

Date	Mintage	F	VF	XF	Unc	BU
2001 Proof	750	Value: 800				

Y# 688 100 ROUBLES **Weight:** 15.7200 g. **Composition:** 0.9990 Gold .5049 oz. AGW **Subject:** Bolshoi Theater 225 Years **Obverse:** Double-headed eagle **Reverse:** Three dancers with swords **Edge:** Reeded **Size:** 30 mm.

Date	Mintage	F	VF	XF	Unc	BU
2001 Proof	1,500	Value: 275				

Y# 689 100 ROUBLES **Weight:** 1111.1000 g. **Composition:** 0.9000 Silver 32.1504 oz. ASW **Subject:** Bolshoi Theater 225 Years **Obverse:** Double-headed eagle **Reverse:** Casino gambling scene **Edge:** Reeded **Size:** 100 mm. **Note:** Illustration reduced.

Date	Mintage	F	VF	XF	Unc	BU
2001 Proof	500	Value: 1,000				

Y# 792 100 ROUBLES **Weight:** 17.4500 g. **Composition:** 0.9000 Gold 0.5049 oz. AGW **Subject:** Hermitage **Obverse:** Double-headed eagle **Reverse:** Ancient battle scene sculpted on comb **Edge:** Reeded **Size:** 30 mm.

Date	Mintage	F	VF	XF	Unc	BU
2002 (SP) Proof	1,000	Value: 300				

Y# 783 100 ROUBLES **Weight:** 1111.1200 g. **Composition:** 0.9000 Silver 32.151 oz. ASW **Subject:** Works of Dionissy **Obverse:** Double-headed eagle **Reverse:** St. Ferapont Monastery in the center of a fresco covered cross **Edge:** Reeded **Size:** 100 mm. **Note:** Illustration reduced.

Date	Mintage	F	VF	XF	Unc	BU
2002 (SP) Prooflike	500	—	—	—	—	—

Y# 789 100 ROUBLES **Weight:** 1111.1200 g. **Composition:** 0.9000 Silver 32.151 oz. ASW **Subject:** World Cup Soccer **Obverse:** Double-headed eagle **Reverse:** Soccer ball design with map and players **Edge:** Reeded **Size:** 100 mm. **Note:** Illustration reduced.

Date	Mintage	F	VF	XF	Unc	BU
2002 (SP) Proof	500	Value: 900				

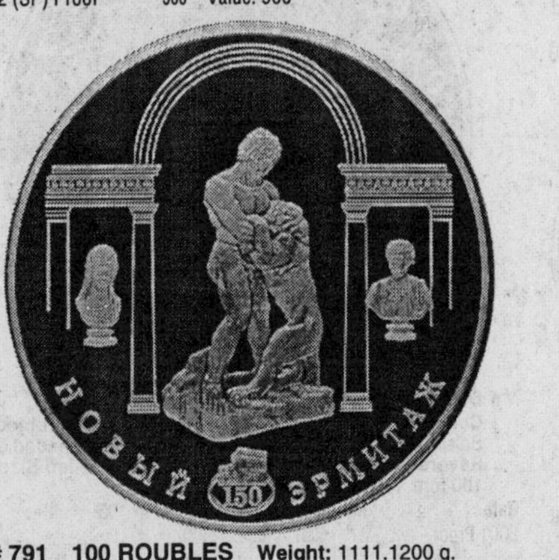

Y# 791 100 ROUBLES **Weight:** 1111.1200 g. **Composition:** 0.9000 Silver 32.151 oz. ASW **Subject:** Hermitage **Obverse:** Double-headed eagle **Reverse:** Staues and arches **Edge:** Reeded **Size:** 100 mm. **Note:** Illustration reduced.

Date	Mintage	F	VF	XF	Unc	BU
2002 (SP) Proof	1,000	—	—	—	—	—

Y# 656 200 ROUBLES **Weight:** 3342.3899 g. **Composition:** 0.9000 Silver 96.7142 oz. ASW **Subject:** 25th Anniversary - St. Petersburg Mint **Obverse:** Double-headed eagle **Reverse:** Peter the Great, mint view, coin designs, and medal of the Imperial Order **Note:** Illustration reduced.

Date	Mintage	F	VF	XF	Unc	BU
1999 Proof	150	—	—	—	—	—

Y# 727 200 ROUBLES **Weight:** 31.3700 g. **Composition:** 0.9990 Gold 1.0076 oz. AGW **Subject:** Snow Leopard **Obverse:** Double-headed eagle **Reverse:** Leopard on branch **Edge:** Reeded **Size:** 33 mm.

Date	Mintage	F	VF	XF	Unc	BU
2000(sp) Proof	500	Value: 600				

Y# 796 1000 ROUBLES **Subject:** The Bark Sedov **Obverse:** Double-headed eagle **Reverse:** Four masted ship sailing to the left **Edge:** Reeded **Size:** 50 mm.

Date	Mintage	F	VF	XF	Unc	BU
2001(m) Proof	250	—	—	—	—	—

Y# 728 10000 ROUBLES **Weight:** 822.8449 g. **Composition:** 0.9990 Gold 26.4551 oz. AGW **Subject:** Snow Leopard **Obverse:** Double-headed eagle **Reverse:** Leopard with two cubs **Edge:** Reeded **Size:** 100 mm. **Note:** Illustration reduced.

Date	Mintage	F	VF	XF	Unc	BU
2000(m) Proof	100	Value: 16,500				

Y# 784 10000 ROUBLES **Weight:** 1001.1000 g. **Composition:** 0.9990 Gold 32.1539 oz. AGW **Subject:** Works of Dionissy **Obverse:** Double-headed eagle **Reverse:** Interior view of the carved portal of the Virgin of the Nativity Church **Edge:** Reeded **Size:** 100 mm. **Note:** Illustration reduced.

Date	Mintage	F	VF	XF	Unc	BU
2002 (SP) Prooflike	100	—	—	—	—	—

PATTERNS

Including off metal strikes

KM#	Date	Mintage	Identification	Mkt Val
Pn160	1911	—	5 Kopeks. Nickel.	—
Pn161	1911	—	10 Kopeks. Nickel.	—
Pn162	1911	—	20 Kopeks. Nickel.	—
Pn163	1911	—	20 Kopeks. Nickel.	—
Pn164	1911	—	25 Kopeks. Nickel. Eagle, date below. 25 in circle.	—
Pn165	1916	—	Kopek. Copper. Dotted background in circle, date.	—
Pn166	1916	—	Kopek. Copper. Plain background.	—
Pn167	1916	—	Kopek. Copper. Value, date below.	—
Pn168	1916	—	2 Kopeks. Copper. Eagle in circle. 2 in circle, value, date below.	—
Pn169	1916	—	3 Kopeks. Copper. Eagle in circle. 3 in circle, value, date below.	—
Pn170	1916	—	5 Kopeks. Copper.	—
Pn171	1916	—	5 Roubles. Unknown Metal.	2,000
Pn172	1917	—	3 Kopeks. Copper. 8.2500 g. Plain edge. 1/2milimeter larger than 1916.	2,000
Pn173	1922	—	20 Kopeks. Bronze. Y#82	—
Pn174	1922	—	50 Kopeks. Silver. Plain edge. Y#89	—
Pn175	1923	—	20 Kopeks. Bronze. Y#82	150
Pn176	1923	—	20 Kopeks. Copper. Y#82	150
Pn202	1924	—	50 Kopeks. Copper-Nickel. Plain edge. Y#89; London Mint.	650
Pn203	1924	—	50 Kopeks. Copper-Nickel. Plain edge. Y#89	1,000
Pn177	1924	—	Kopek. Copper-Aluminum. Y#76	—
Pn178	1924	—	Kopek. Bronze. Y#76	—
Pn179	1924	—	Kopek. Aluminum. Y#76	—
Pn180	1924	—	Kopek. Copper-Nickel. Y#76	—
Pn181	1924	—	Kopek. Copper-Zinc. Y#76	—
Note: Additional metals exist				
Pn182	1924	—	2 Kopeks. Copper-Aluminum. Y#77	—
Pn183	1924	—	2 Kopeks. Bronze. Y#77	—
Pn184	1924	—	2 Kopeks. Aluminum. Y#77	—
Pn185	1924	—	2 Kopeks. Copper-Nickel. Y#77	—
Pn186	1924	—	2 Kopeks. Copper-Zinc. Y#77	—
Note: Additional metals exist				
Pn187	1924	—	3 Kopeks. Copper-Aluminum. Y#78	—
Pn188	1924	—	3 Kopeks. Bronze. Y#78	—
Pn189	1924	—	3 Kopeks. Aluminum. Y#78	—
Pn190	1924	—	3 Kopeks. Copper-Nickel. Y#78	—
Pn191	1924	—	3 Kopeks. Copper-Zinc. Y#78	—
Note: Additional metals exist				
Pn192	1924	—	5 Kopeks. Unknown Metal.	—
Pn193	1924	—	5 Kopeks. Copper-Zinc. 12.0000 g. Y#79	—
Pn194	1924	—	5 Kopeks. Copper-Zinc. 18.0000 g. Y#79	—
Pn195	1924	—	5 Kopeks. Copper-Zinc. 20.0000 g. Y#79	—
Pn196	1924	—	10 Kopeks. Bronze. Y#86	—
Pn197	1924	—	15 Kopeks. Bronze. Y#87	—
Pn198	1924	—	15 Kopeks. Copper. Y#87	—
Pn199	1924	—	20 Kopeks. Bronze. Y#88	—
Pn200	1924	—	50 Kopeks. Bronze. Y#89	—
Pn201	1924	—	50 Kopeks. Unknown Metal. Y#89	—
Pn204	1924	—	Rouble. Aluminum. Y#90	—
Note: There are additional 1924 patterns but information is sketchy at present				
Pn205	1925	—	1/2 Kopek. Copper-Aluminum. Y#75	—
Pn206	1925	—	1/2 Kopek. Aluminum. Y#75	—
Pn207	1925	—	1/2 Kopek. Copper-Nickel. Y#75	—
Pn208	1925	—	1/2 Kopek. Bronze. Y#75	—
Pn209	1925	—	1/2 Kopek. Copper-Zinc. Y#75	—
Note: Additional metals exist				
Pn210	1925	—	10 Kopeks. Nickel. Y#86	—
Pn211	1925	—	10 Kopeks. Aluminum-Bronze. Y#86	—
Pn212	1925	—	15 Kopeks. Nickel. Y#87	—
Pn213	1925	—	15 Kopeks. Copper. Y#87	—
Pn214	1925	—	15 Kopeks. Aluminum-Bronze. Y#87	—
Pn215	1925	—	20 Kopeks. Nickel. Y#88	—
Pn216	1925	—	20 Kopeks. Copper. Y#88	—

KM#	Date	Mintage	Identification	Mkt Val
Pn217	1925	—	20 Kopeks. Aluminum-Bronze. Y#88	—
Pn218	1925	—	50 Kopeks. Silver. Plain edge. Y#89.2	—
Pn219	1925	—	50 Kopeks. Bronze. Y#89.2	—
Pn221	1925	—	Chervonetz. Copper. Y#85	—
Pn220	1925	—	50 Kopeks. Lead. Y#89.2	175
Pn222	1926	—	3 Kopeks. Aluminum.	—
Pn223	1926	—	3 Kopeks. Aluminum.	—
Pn224	1926	—	3 Kopeks. Unknown Metal. Y#100	—
Pn225	1929	—	10 Kopeks. Nickel.	—
Pn226	1929	—	15 Kopeks. 35% Silver; Y#87	—
Pn227	1929	—	50 Kopeks. Unknown Metal.	—
Pn228	1931	—	2 Kopeks. Copper. Y#92	—
Pn229	1931	—	3 Kopeks. Copper. Y#93	—
Pn230	1931	—	10 Kopeks. Unknown Metal. Y#93	—
Pn231	1931	—	20 Kopeks. Bronze. Y#97	—
Pn232	1932	—	3 Kopeks. Copper. KM#93	—
Note: Additional metals exist				
Pn233	1932	—	15 Kopeks. Unknown Metal. Y#96	—
Pn234	1933	—	10 Kopeks. Unknown Metal. Similar to Y#95	—
Pn235	1934	—	2 Kopeks. Copper. Y#92	—
Pn236	1934	—	3 Kopeks. Copper. Y#93	—
Pn237	1936	—	20 Kopeks. Aluminum. Y#104	—
Pn238	1937	—	20 Kopeks. Aluminum. Y#111	—
Pn239	1938	—	5 Kopeks. Unknown Metal. Y#101	—
Pn240	1938	—	15 Kopeks. Aluminum. Plain edge. Y#110	—
Pn241	1941	—	3 Kopeks. Unknown Metal. Y#107	—
Pn242	1941	—	50 Kopeks. Unknown Metal. Similar to Y#109	—
Pn243	1943	—	Rouble. Unknown Metal. Portrait Stalin.	—
Pn244	1946	—	10 Kopeks. Unknown Metal. Y#102	—
Pn245	1946	—	20 Kopeks. Unknown Metal. Y#111	—
Pn246	1947	—	Kopek. Aluminum-Bronze. Similar to Y#112; 16 bands on wreath.	—
Pn247	1947	—	2 Kopeks. Aluminum-Bronze. Similar to Y#113; 16 bands on wreath.	—
Pn248	1947	—	3 Kopeks. Unknown Metal. Similar to Y#114; 16 bands on wreath.	—
Pn249	1947	—	5 Kopeks. Aluminum-Bronze. Similar to Y#115; 16 bands on wreath.	—
Pn250	1947	—	10 Kopeks. Nickel. Similar to Y#116; 16 bands on wreath.	—
Pn251	1947	—	15 Kopeks. Unknown Metal. Similar to Y#117; 16 bands on wreath.	—
Pn252	1947	—	20 Kopeks. Nickel. Similar to Y#118; 16 bands on wreath.	—
Pn253	1949	—	Chervonetz. Copper.	—
Pn255	1953	—	Kopek. Aluminum.	—
Pn256	1953	—	Kopek. Nickel.	—
Note: Additional metals exist				
Pn257	1953	—	Kopek. Copper-Nickel. With legend. Hammer and sickle, value above, date below.	—
Pn258	1953	—	Kopek. Aluminum.	—
Pn259	1953	—	Kopek. Nickel.	—
Note: Additonal metals exist				
Pn261	1953	—	2 Kopeks. Aluminum.	—
Pn262	1953	—	2 Kopeks. Nickel.	—
Note: Additional metals exist				
Pn264	1953	—	2 Kopeks. Aluminum.	—
Pn265	1953	—	2 Kopeks. Nickel.	—
Note: Additional metals exist				
Pn267	1953	—	3 Kopeks. Aluminum.	—
Pn268	1953	—	3 Kopeks. Nickel.	—
Note: Additional metals exist				
Pn270	1953	—	3 Kopeks. Aluminum.	—
Pn271	1953	—	3 Kopeks. Nickel.	—
Note: Additional metals exist				
Pn272	1953	—	5 Kopeks. Aluminum. With legend.	—
Pn273	1953	—	5 Kopeks. Nickel.	—
Note: Additional metals exist				
Pn274	1953	—	5 Kopeks. Aluminum. Without legend.	—
Pn275	1953	—	5 Kopeks. Nickel.	—
Note: Additional metals exist				
Pn276	1953	—	10 Kopeks. Aluminum. With legend. Value and date within wreath.	—
Pn277	1953	—	10 Kopeks. Aluminum. Value, star above, date below.	—
Pn278	1953	—	10 Kopeks. Aluminum. Value, date below.	—
Pn279	1953	—	10 Kopeks. Aluminum. Value in wreath, star above date.	—
Pn280	1953	—	10 Kopeks. Aluminum. Value in wreath, date incircle at bottom.	—
Pn281	1953	—	10 Kopeks. Aluminum. Value in wreath in pellet border, date in circle at bottom.	—
Pn282	1953	—	10 Kopeks. Aluminum. Oak leaves behind value.	—
Pn283	1953	—	10 Kopeks. Aluminum. Without legend. Similar to KM#Pn276.	—
Pn284	1953	—	10 Kopeks. Aluminum. Similar to KM#Pn277.	—
Pn285	1953	—	10 Kopeks. Aluminum. Similar to KM#Pn278.	—
Pn286	1953	—	10 Kopeks. Aluminum. Similar to KM#Pn279.	—
Pn287	1953	—	10 Kopeks. Aluminum. Similar to KM#Pn280.	—
Pn288	1953	—	10 Kopeks. Aluminum. Similar to KM#Pn281.	—
Pn289	1953	—	10 Kopeks. Aluminum. Similar to KM#Pn282.	—
Note: For Pn276-Pn289 at least four other base metal strikings exist of each				
Pn290	1953	—	15 Kopeks. Aluminum. With legend. Value and date within wreath.	—
Pn291	1953	—	15 Kopeks. Aluminum. Value, star above, date below.	—
Pn292	1953	—	15 Kopeks. Aluminum. Value, date below.	—
Pn293	1953	—	15 Kopeks. Aluminum. Value in wreath, star above date in circle at bottom.	—
Pn294	1953	—	15 Kopeks. Aluminum. Value in wreath, date in circle at bottom.	—
Pn295	1953	—	15 Kopeks. Aluminum. Value in wreath, pellet border, date in circle at bottom.	—
Pn296	1953	—	15 Kopeks. Aluminum. Oak leaves behind value, date below.	—
Pn297	1953	—	15 Kopeks. Aluminum. Legend. Similar to KM#Pn290.	—
Pn298	1953	—	15 Kopeks. Aluminum. Similar to KM#Pn291.	—
Pn299	1953	—	15 Kopeks. Aluminum. Similar to KM#Pn292.	—
Pn300	1953	—	15 Kopeks. Aluminum. Similar to KM#Pn293.	—
Pn301	1953	—	15 Kopeks. Aluminum. Similar to KM#Pn294.	—
Pn302	1953	—	15 Kopeks. Aluminum. Similar to KM#Pn295.	—
Pn303	1953	—	15 Kopeks. Aluminum. Similar to KM#Pn296.	—
Note: For Pn290-Pn303 at least four other base metal strikings exist of each				
Pn304	1953	—	20 Kopeks. Aluminum. With legend. Value and date within wreath.	—
Pn305	1953	—	20 Kopeks. Aluminum. Value, star above, date below.	—
Pn306	1953	—	20 Kopeks. Aluminum. Value, date below.	—
Pn307	1953	—	20 Kopeks. Aluminum. Value in wreath, star above date in circle at bottom.	—
Pn308	1953	—	20 Kopeks. Aluminum. Value in wreath, date in circle at bottom.	—
Pn309	1953	—	20 Kopeks. Aluminum. Value in wreath, pellet border, date in circle at bottom.	—
Pn310	1953	—	20 Kopeks. Aluminum. Oak leaves behind value, date below.	—
Pn311	1953	—	20 Kopeks. Aluminum. Without legend. Similar to KM#Pn304.	—
Pn312	1953	—	20 Kopeks. Aluminum. Similar to KM#Pn305.	—
Pn313	1953	—	20 Kopeks. Aluminum. Similar to KM#Pn306.	—
Pn314	1953	—	20 Kopeks. Aluminum. Similar to KM#Pn307.	—
Pn315	1953	—	20 Kopeks. Aluminum. Similar to KM#Pn308.	—
Pn316	1953	—	20 Kopeks. Aluminum. Similar to KM#Pn309.	—
Pn317	1953	—	20 Kopeks. Aluminum. Similar to KM#Pn310.	—
Note: Pn304-Pn317 exist in at least four additional metals				
Pn318	1953	—	50 Kopeks. Bronze.	—
Pn319	1953	—	50 Kopeks. Aluminum.	—
Pn320	1953	—	50 Kopeks. Bronze.	—
Pn321	1953	—	50 Kopeks. Aluminum.	—
Pn322	1953	—	50 Kopeks. Bronze.	—
Pn323	1953	—	50 Kopeks. Aluminum.	—
Pn324	1953	—	50 Kopeks. Bronze.	—
Pn325	1953	—	50 Kopeks. Aluminum.	—
Note: Pn318-Pn325 exist in at least one other metal				
Pn254	1953	—	Kopek. Copper-Nickel. With legend. Hammer and sickle, value above, date below.	350
Pn260	1953	—	2 Kopeks. Copper-Nickel. With legend.	350
Pn263	1953	—	2 Kopeks. Copper-Nickel. Without legend.	350
Pn266	1953	—	3 Kopeks. Copper-Nickel. With legend.	350
Pn269	1953	—	3 Kopeks. Copper-Nickel. Without legend.	350
Pn326	1955	—	25 Kopeks. Probably copper-nickel	—
Pn327	1956	—	10 Kopeks. Nickel.	—
Pn328	1956	—	10 Kopeks. Brass.	—
Pn329	1956	—	10 Kopeks. Copper.	—
Pn330	1956	—	10 Kopeks. Aluminum.	—
Pn331	1956	—	15 Kopeks. Nickel.	—
Pn332	1956	—	15 Kopeks. Brass.	—
Pn333	1956	—	15 Kopeks. Copper.	—
Pn334	1956	—	15 Kopeks. Aluminum.	—
Pn335	1956	—	20 Kopeks. Nickel.	—
Pn336	1956	—	20 Kopeks. Brass.	—
Pn337	1956	—	20 Kopeks. Copper.	—
Pn338	1956	—	20 Kopeks. Aluminum.	—
Pn339	1956	—	50 Kopeks. Nickel.	—
Pn340	1956	—	50 Kopeks. Brass.	—
Pn341	1956	—	50 Kopeks. Copper.	—
Pn342	1956	—	50 Kopeks. Aluminum.	—
Pn343	1956	—	Rouble. Nickel.	—
Pn344	1956	—	Rouble. Brass.	—
Pn345	1956	—	Rouble. Copper.	—
Pn346	1956	—	Rouble. Aluminum.	—
Pn347	1956	—	2 Roubles. Nickel.	—
Pn348	1956	—	2 Roubles. Brass.	—
Pn349	1956	—	2 Roubles. Copper.	—
Pn350	1956	—	2 Roubles. Aluminum.	—
Pn351	1956	—	3 Roubles. Nickel.	—
Pn352	1956	—	3 Roubles. Brass.	—
Pn353	1956	—	3 Roubles. Copper.	—
Pn354	1956	—	3 Roubles. Aluminum.	—
Pn355	1956	—	5 Roubles. Nickel.	—
Pn356	1956	—	5 Roubles. Brass.	—
Pn357	1956	—	5 Roubles. Copper.	—
Pn358	1956	—	5 Roubles. Aluminum.	—
Pn359	1957	—	10 Kopeks. Copper-Nickel. Y#123	—
Pn360	1957	—	10 Kopeks. Aluminum. Y#123	—
Pn361	1957	—	20 Kopeks. Copper-Nickel. Y#125	—
Pn362	1958	—	Kopek. Aluminum. Y#126	—
Pn363	1958	—	2 Kopeks. Aluminum. Y#127	—
Pn364	1958	—	3 Kopeks. Aluminum. Y#128	—
Pn365	1958	—	5 Kopeks. Aluminum. Y#129	—
Pn366	1958	—	10 Kopeks. Aluminum. Y#A130	—
Pn367	1958	—	15 Kopeks. Aluminum. Y#A131	—
Pn368	1958	—	20 Kopeks. Aluminum. Y#A132	—
Pn369	1958	—	50 Kopeks. Aluminum. Y#133	—
Pn370	1958	—	Rouble. Aluminum. Y#134	—
Pn371	1958	—	2 Roubles. Aluminum. Y#A134	—
Pn372	1958	—	3 Roubles. Aluminum. Y#B134	—
Pn373	1958	—	5 Roubles. Aluminum. Y#C134	—
Pn374	1959	—	10 Kopeks. Copper-Nickel.	—
Pn375	1959	—	15 Kopeks. Copper-Nickel.	—
Pn376	1959	—	20 Kopeks. Copper-Nickel.	—
Pn377	1961	—	1/2 Kopek. Copper.	—
Pn378	1961	—	Kopek. Copper. Y#126	—
Pn379	1961	—	2 Kopeks. Copper. Y#127	—
Pn380	1961	—	3 Kopeks. Copper. Y#128	—
Pn381	1961	—	5 Kopeks. Copper. Y#129	—
Pn382	1961	—	10 Kopeks. Copper. Y#130	—
Pn383	1961	—	15 Kopeks. Copper. Y#131	—
Pn384	1961	—	20 Kopeks. Copper. Y#132	—
Pn385	1962	—	50 Kopeks. Copper-Nickel. Y#133.1	—
Pn386	1962	—	50 Kopeks. Copper-Nickel.	—
Pn387	1962	—	Rouble. Copper-Nickel. Y#134.1	—
Pn388	1962	—	Rouble. Copper-Nickel.	—
Pn389	1963	—	50 Kopeks. Copper-Nickel.	—
Pn390	1963	—	Rouble. Copper-Nickel.	—
Pn393	1967	—	15 Kopeks. Unknown Metal. Uncertain 1917-67 commemorative disign	—
Pn395	1967	—	50 Kopeks. Unknown Metal. Uncertain 1917-67 commemorative disign	—
Pn391	1967	—	10 Kopeks. Copper-Nickel-Zinc. Arms. Ship.	150
Pn392	1967	—	10 Kopeks. Copper-Nickel-Zinc. Arms. Worker and soldier.	150
Pn396	ND	—	100 Roubles. 0.9000 Gold. Y#162	—
Note: Pn390-Pn396 minor varieties exist				
PN397	1993	—	3 Roubles. Copper-Nickel. 34.0000 g. 38.8 mm. Same as Y-323 including silver content statement.. Same as Y-323 including silver content statement.. Reeded. edge.	—

TRIAL STRIKES

KM#	Date	Mintage	Identification	Mkt Val
TS1	1924	—	5 Kopeks. Copper. Y#79.	300
TS2	1924	—	5 Kopeks. Copper. Y#79.	300

MINT SETS

KM#	Date	Mintage	Identification	Issue Price	Mkt Val
MS1	1957 (4)	—	Y#122-125	2.25	35.00
MS8	1967 (5)	211,250	Y#136-140	6.00	8.00
MSA27	1986 (9)	—	Y#126a-129a, 130-132, 133a.2, 134a.2	—	14.00
MS32	1990 (9)	—	Y#126a-129a, 130-132, 133a.2, 134a.2	—	12.00
MSA32	1990 (9)	—	Y#126a-129a, 130-132, 133a.2, 134a.2	—	12.00
MS33	1991 (3)	—	Y#268-270	245	1,950
MSA33	1991 (9)	—	Y#126a-129a, 130-132, 133a.2, 134a.2	—	10.00
MS35	1993 (4)	2,700	Y#416-419	—	960
MS36	1993 (3)	3,000	Y#420-422	—	1,950
MS37	1994 (3)	2,000	Y#431-433	—	1,950
MS38	1995 (6)	200,000	Y#399-404 and medal	—	17.00
MS39	1996 (6)	100,000	Y#504-509 and medal	—	25.00
MS40	1997(SP) (7)	—	Y#600-606	—	12.50
MS44	2002 (7)	—	Y#600-603, 797-799, plus mint medal	7.50	—

PROOF SETS

KM#	Date	Mintage	Identification	Issue Price	Mkt Val
PS2	1987 (3)	—	Y#206-208	—	37.50
PS3	1990 (9)	—	Y#126a-129a, 130-132, 133a.2, 134a.2	—	15.00
PS5	1991 (3)	1,500	Y#286a-288a	—	1,450
PS4	1991(L) (9)	—	Y#126a-129a, 130-132, 133a.2, 134a.2	—	15.00
PS7	1993 (3)	750	Y#395-397	—	725
PS9	1993 (2)	10,000	Y#323, 406	—	150
PS6	1993 (4)	1,500	Y#416-419	—	1,230
PS8	1993 (3)	2,000	Y#420-422	—	2,050
PS10	1994 (4)	2,500	Y#424-427	—	1,255
PS11	1994 (3)	900	Y#428-430	—	1,360
PS13	1994 (2)	7,500	Y#405, 423	—	180
PS12	1994 (3)	1,500	Y#431-433	—	2,050
PS14	1995 (4)	2,500	Y#438-441	1,250	1,250
PS15	1995 (3)	1,500	Y#435-437	875	875
PS16	1995 (3)	900	Y#442-444	1,350	1,350

RUSSIAN CAUCASIA

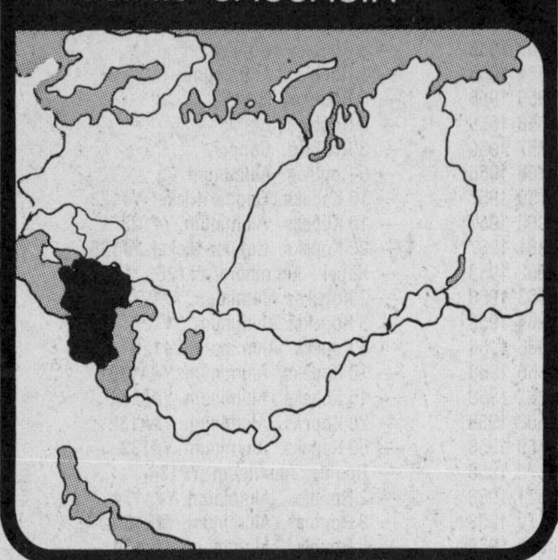

Russian Caucasia, a natural area in Russia located between the Black and Caspian Seas, was a region of mystery and myth to the Ancient Greeks. It was there that Prometheus was bound for the eagle's torment and the Argonauts sought the Golden Fleece. For more than a thousand years Caucasia was the refuge for wave after wave of migrating peoples. Greeks, Romans, Persians, Turks, Huns, Mongols and finally the Russians invaded the treeless steppes and wooded highlands of this range-flanked granite bridge between Europe and Asia. Russian aggression, heroically resisted by the independent mountain races, began early in the 18th century and continued until the last opposition was stifled. The several states of Caucasia made a futile attempt to establish an independent federated republic during the Russian February Revolution of 1917, but were quickly reconquered after the triumph of Bolshevism over the Kerensky administration.

The following areas of Russian Caucasia were coin-issuing entities of interest to numismatists.

ARMAVIR

Armavir is a city located in Krasnodar Territory, Southern Russia north of the Caucasus.

LOCAL CURRENCY UNDER THE WHITE RUSSIANS

CITY

LOCAL COINAGE

Under the White Russians

KM# 1 ROUBLE Composition: Copper **Obverse:** Monogram below tail **Edge:** Reeded **Note:** Thin planchet.

Date	VG	F	VF	XF	Unc
1918	100	150	250	400	—

KM# 2.1 3 ROUBLES Composition: Copper **Obverse:** Monogram below tail **Edge:** Reeded **Note:** Varieties exist.

Date	VG	F	VF	XF	Unc
1918	60.00	80.00	150	250	—

KM# 2.2 3 ROUBLES Composition: Copper **Note:** Monogram below claw.

Date	VG	F	VF	XF	Unc
1918	75.00	100	175	275	—

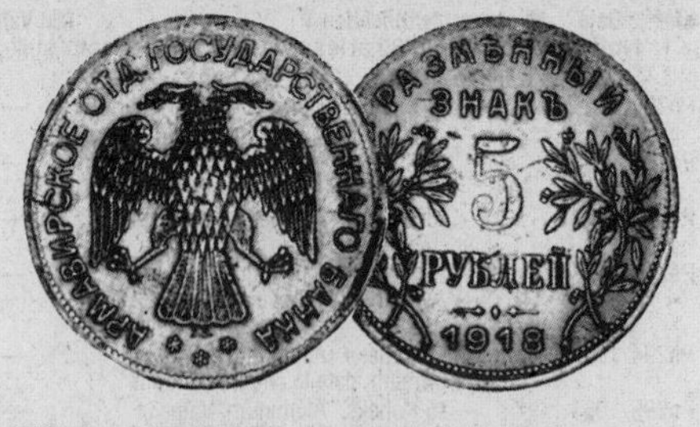

KM# 3 5 ROUBLES Composition: Copper

Date	VG	F	VF	XF	Unc
1918	150	225	400	550	—

PATTERNS

Including off metal strikes

KM#	Date	Mintage	Identification	Mkt Val
Pn1	1918	—	Rouble. Copper. 28 mm. Reeded edge. Thin planchet. Y1.	—
Pn2	1918	—	Rouble. Copper. 28 mm. Plain edge. Thin planchet. Y1.	—
Pn3	1918	—	Rouble. Copper. 28 mm. Plain edge. Thick planchet. Y1.	—
Pn3a	1918	—	Rouble. Brass.	—
Pn4	1918	—	3 Roubles. Copper. 31 mm. Monogram under tail. Y2.1.	350
Pn5	1918	—	3 Roubles. Silver. Y2.1.	650
Pn6	1918	—	5 Roubles. Aluminum. Y3.	—

CHECHNYA

The North Caucasian Emirate

Chechnya is a mountainous republic bounded on the north and the east by Daghestan, on the south by Georgia and on the west by Ingushetia. During a short period in 1919-1920 a considerable part of Chechen highlands comprised most of the self-proclaimed Moslem state with a capital in Vedeno village under the government of Emir Uzun Khayr. The emirate had its own flag, arms and currency (coins and paper money). The Chechen Republic of Ichkeria is now part of the Russian Federation.

RULERS

Emir Uzun Khayir (Khayr Uzun Haji, Uzun Khayr Ghazi Khan, Uzun Haji),
AH1338-1339 / 1919-1920AD

MINTNAME

Vidan (The aul or village of Vedeno)

MONETARY SYSTEM

10 Som (Kurush Sum, Manat, Roubles) = 1 Toman

REPUBLIC

STANDARD COINAGE

KM# 1 25 SOM (2-1/2 Toman) Composition: Copper **Note:** Quite recently one specimen has been reported from Russia.

Date	F	VF	XF	Unc	BU
AH1338(1919) Rare	—	—	—	—	—

KM# 2 5 TOMAN Composition: Brass

Date	F	VF	XF	Unc	BU
AH1338(1919)	—	—	—	—	—

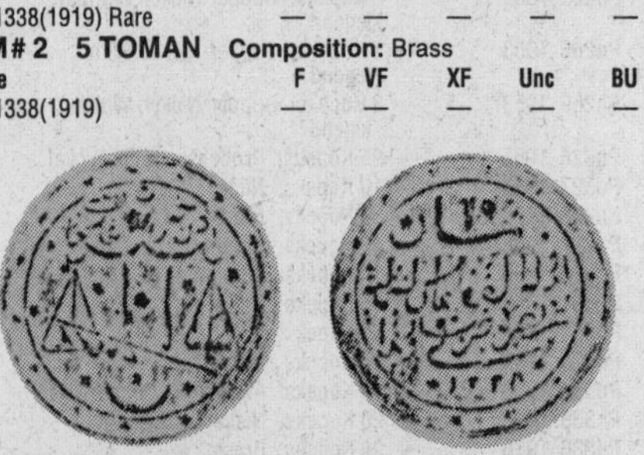

KM# 3 10 TOMAN Composition: Brass **Obverse:** Crowned balance scale, banner, rifle and sabre, crescent below **Reverse:** Arabian inscription **Note:** According to reliable sources, all 10 Toman coins were released to circulation.

Date	F	VF	XF	Unc	BU
AH1338(1919)	100	250	—	—	—

KM# 4 10 TOMAN Composition: Copper **Obverse:** Crowned balance scale, crescent below **Reverse:** Arabian denomination and date **Note:** Struck over Russia 2 Kopek, Y#10. Modern forgeries exist.

Date	F	VF	XF	Unc	BU
AH1338(1919)	—	—	—	—	—

RWANDA

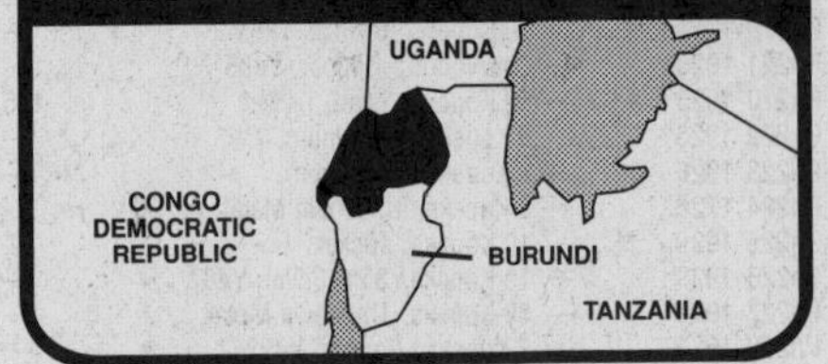

The Republic of Rwanda, located in central Africa between the Republic of the Congo and Tanzania, has an area of 10,169 sq. mi. (26,340 sq. km.) and a population of 7.3 million. Capital: Kigali. The economy is based on agriculture and mining. Coffee and tin are exported.

German Lieutenant Count von Goetzen was the first European to visit Rwanda, 1894. Four years later the court of the Mwami (the Tutsi king of Rwanda) willingly permitted the kingdom to become a protectorate of Germany. In 1916, during the African campaigns of World War I, Belgian troops from Congo occupied Rwanda. After the war it, together with Burundi, became a Belgian League of Nations mandate under the name of the Territory of Ruanda-Urundi. Following World War II, Ruanda-Urundi became a Belgian administered U.N. trust territory. The Tutsi monarchy was deposed by the U.N. supervised election of 1961, after which Belgium granted Rwanda internal autonomy. On July 1, 1962, the U.N. terminated the Belgian trusteeship and granted full independence to both Rwanda and Burundi.

For earlier coinage see Belgian Congo, and Rwanda and Burundi.

MINT MARKS

(a) - Paris, privy marks only
(b) - Brussels, privy marks only

MONETARY SYSTEM

100 Centimes = 1 Franc

REPUBLIC

STANDARD COINAGE

KM# 9 1/2 FRANC Composition: Aluminum

Date	Mintage	F	VF	XF	Unc	BU
1970	5,000,000	—	0.50	0.85	1.75	—

KM# 5 FRANC Composition: Copper-Nickel

Date	Mintage	F	VF	XF	Unc	BU
1964(b)	3,000,000	—	5.00	10.00	20.00	—
1965(b)	4,500,000	—	0.50	0.85	1.75	—

KM# 8 FRANC Composition: Aluminum

Date	Mintage	F	VF	XF	Unc	BU
1969	5,000,000	—	0.50	1.50	3.50	—

KM# 12 FRANC Composition: Aluminum

Date	Mintage	F	VF	XF	Unc	BU
1974	13,000,000	—	0.20	0.50	1.00	
1977	15,000,000	—	0.15	0.25	0.75	
1985	—	—	0.10	0.15	0.65	

KM# 10 2 FRANCS **Composition:** Aluminum **Series:** F.A.O. **Shape:** Scalloped

Date	Mintage	F	VF	XF	Unc	BU
1970	5,000,000	—	0.10	0.20	0.50	—

KM# 6 5 FRANCS **Composition:** Bronze

Date	Mintage	F	VF	XF	Unc	BU
1964(b)	4,000,000	—	0.25	0.50	1.75	—
1965(b)	3,000,000	—	5.00	10.00	20.00	—

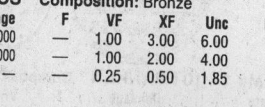

KM# 13 5 FRANCS **Composition:** Bronze

Date	Mintage	F	VF	XF	Unc	BU
1974	7,000,000	—	1.00	3.00	6.00	—
1977	7,002,000	—	1.00	2.00	4.00	—
1987	—	—	0.25	0.50	1.85	—

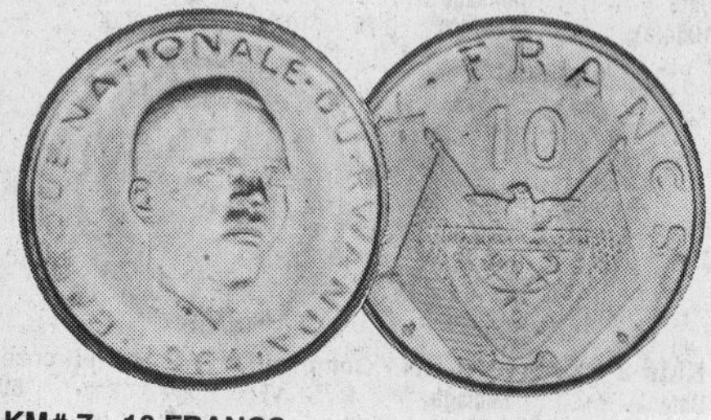

KM# 7 10 FRANCS **Composition:** Copper-Nickel

Date	Mintage	F	VF	XF	Unc	BU
1964(b)	6,000,000	—	1.00	2.00	4.50	—

KM# 1 10 FRANCS **Weight:** 3.0000 g. **Composition:** 0.9000 Gold .1085 oz. AGW **Obverse:** Arms **Reverse:** Bust right

Date	Mintage	VG	F	VF	XF	Unc
1965	10,000	—	—	—	—	60.00
1965 Proof	—	Value: 65.00				

KM# 14.1 10 FRANCS **Composition:** Copper-Nickel

Date	Mintage	F	VF	XF	Unc	BU
1974	6,000,000	—	3.00	5.00	10.00	—

KM# 14.2 10 FRANCS **Composition:** Copper-Nickel **Note:** Reduced size.

Date	F	VF	XF	Unc	BU
1985	—	0.50	0.85	1.85	—

KM# 15 20 FRANCS **Composition:** Brass

Date	Mintage	F	VF	XF	Unc	BU
1977(a)	22,000,000	—	1.00	2.00	4.00	—

KM# 2 25 FRANCS **Weight:** 7.5000 g. **Composition:** 0.9000 Gold .2170 oz. AGW **Note:** Similar to 10 Francs, KM#1.

Date	Mintage	F	VF	XF	Unc	BU
1965 Proof	4,000	Value: 100				

KM# 3 50 FRANCS **Weight:** 15.0000 g. **Composition:** 0.9000 Gold .4340 oz. AGW **Note:** Similar to 10 Francs, KM#1.

Date	Mintage	F	VF	XF	Unc	BU
1965 Proof	3,000	Value: 175				

KM# 16 50 FRANCS **Composition:** Brass

Date	Mintage	F	VF	XF	Unc	BU
1977(a)	9,000,000	—	2.50	3.50	7.00	—

KM# 4 100 FRANCS **Weight:** 30.0000 g. **Composition:** 0.9000 Gold .8681 oz. AGW

Date	Mintage	F	VF	XF	Unc	BU
1965 Proof	3,000	Value: 360				

KM# 18 100 FRANCS **Weight:** 31.2300 g. **Composition:** 0.9990 Silver 1.0041 oz. ASW **Subject:** Nelson Mandela

Date	Mintage	F	VF	XF	Unc	BU
1990	—	—	—	—	30.00	—
1990 Proof	Est. 50,000	Value: 40.00				

KM# 21 100 FRANCS **Weight:** 31.1035 g. **Composition:** 0.9990 Silver 1 oz. ASW **Subject:** Environmental Protection **Reverse:** Gorilla

Date	Mintage	F	VF	XF	Unc	BU
1993 Proof	Est. 20,000	Value: 45.00				

KM# 11 200 FRANCS **Weight:** 18.0000 g. **Composition:** 0.8000 Silver .4630 oz. ASW **Series:** F.A.O. **Subject:** 10th Anniversray of Independence and F.A.O. Issue

Date	Mintage	F	VF	XF	Unc	BU
1972	30,000	—	—	6.00	11.50	—

KM# 17 1000 FRANCS **Weight:** 31.6400 g. **Composition:** 0.9990 Silver 1.0173 oz. ASW **Subject:** 25th Anniversary of National Bank

Date	F	VF	XF	Unc	BU
1989	—	—	—	42.50	—

KM# 19 2000 FRANCS **Weight:** 7.8000 g. **Composition:** 0.9990 Gold .25 oz. AGW **Subject:** Nelson Mandela **Note:** Similar to 5,000 Francs, KM#20.

Date	Mintage	F	VF	XF	Unc	BU
1990 Proof	Est. 50,000	Value: 200				

KM# 20 5000 FRANCS **Weight:** 15.5300 g. **Composition:** 0.9990 Gold .5 oz. AGW **Subject:** Nelson Mandela

Date	Mintage	F	VF	XF	Unc	BU
1990 Proof	3,000	Value: 400				

ESSAIS

KM#	Date	Mintage	Identification	Issue Price	Mkt Val
E1	1964(b)	—	Franc. Aluminum.	—	35.00

KM#	Date	Mintage	Identification	Issue Price	Mkt Val

KM#	Date	Mintage	Identification	Issue Price	Mkt Val
E2	1964(b)	—	5 Francs. Bronze.	—	55.00
E3	1964(b)	—	10 Francs. Copper-Nickel.	—	70.00
E4	1977(a)	—	Franc. Aluminum.	—	20.00
E5	1977(a)	—	5 Francs. Bronze.	—	25.00
E6	1977(a)	—	20 Francs. Brass.	—	30.00
E7	1977(a)	—	50 Francs. Brass.	—	35.00

PROOF SETS

KM#	Date	Mintage	Identification	Issue Price	Mkt Val
PS1	1965(a) (4)	3,000	KM1-4	—	700

RWANDA-BURUNDI

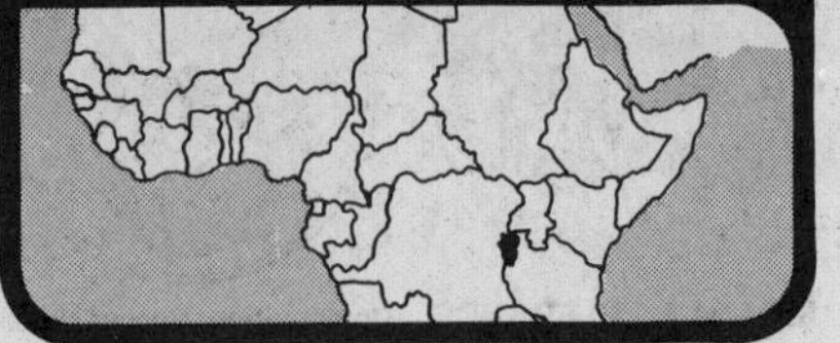

Rwanda-Burundi, a Belgian League of Nations mandate and United Nations trust territory comprising the provinces of Ruanda-Urundi of the former colony of German East Africa, was located in central Africa between the present Democratic Republic of the Congo, Uganda and mainland Tanzania. The mandate-trust territory had an area of 20,916 sq. mi. (54,272 sq. km.) and a population of 4.3 million.

For specific statistics and history of Ruanda and of Urundi see individual entries.

When Rwanda and Burundi were formed into a mandate for administration by Belgium, their names were combined as Ruanda-Urundi and they were organized as an integral part of the Belgian Congo. During the mandate-trust territory period, they utilized the coinage of the Belgian Congo, which from 1954 through 1960carried the appropriate dual identification. After the Belgian Congo acquired independence as the Democratic Republic of the Congo, the provinces of Ruanda and Urundi reverted to their former names of Rwanda and Burundi and utilized a common currency issued by a Central Bank (B.E.R.B.) established for that purpose until the time when, as independent republics, each issued its own national coinage.

For earlier coinage see Belgian Congo.

MONETARY SYSTEM
100 Centimes = 1 Franc

PROVINCES

STANDARD COINAGE

KM# 1 FRANC Composition: Brass

Date	Mintage	F	VF	XF	Unc	BU
1960	2,000,000	—	3.50	7.50	17.50	—
1961	16,000,000	—	0.50	1.00	3.00	—
1964	3,000,000	—	3.00	6.50	15.00	—

KM# 2 FRANC Composition: Copper-Nickel **Obverse:** Rwanda-Burundi KM#1 **Reverse:** Belgium Franc, KM#142 or KM#143 **Note:** Mule.

Date	Mintage	F	VF	XF	Unc	BU
1961 Rare	50	—	—	—	—	—

ESSAIS

KM#	Date	Mintage	Identification	Issue Price	Mkt Val

KM#	Date	Mintage	Identification	Issue Price	Mkt Val
E1	1960	—	Franc. Bronze.	—	160

KM#	Date	Mintage	Identification	Issue Price	Mkt Val
E2	1960	—	Franc. Brass. KM1.	—	70.00
E3	1960	—	Franc. Silver. KM1.	—	150

SAARLAND

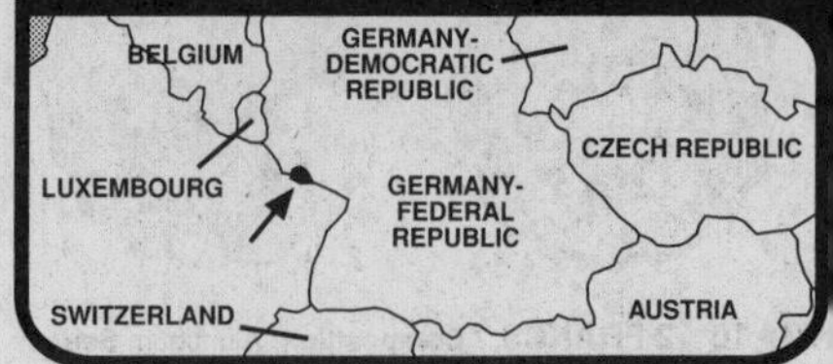

The Saar, the 10th state of the German Federal Republic, i located in the coal-rich Saar basin on the Franco-German frontie and has an area of 991 sq. mi. and a population of 1.2 million. Cap ital: Saarbrucken. It is an important center of mining and heav industry.

From the late 14th century until the fall of Napoleon, the cit of Saarbrucken was ruled by the counts of Nassau-Saarbrucken but the surrounding territory was subject to the political and cu tural domination of France. At the close of the Napoleonic era, th Saarland came under the control of Prussia. France was awarde the Saar coal mines following World War I, and the Saarland wa made an autonomous territory of the League of Nations, its futur political affiliation to be determined by referendum. The plebiscite 1935, chose re-incorporation into Germany. France reoccupie the Saarland, 1945, establishing strong economic ties an assuming the obligation of defense and foreign affairs. After sus tained agitation by West Germany, France agreed, 1955, to the r turn of the Saar to Germany by Jan. 1957.

MINT MARKS
(a) - Paris - privy marks only

GERMAN REPUBLIC STATE

STANDARD COINAGE

KM# 1 10 FRANKEN Composition: Aluminum-Bronz

Date	Mintage	F	VF	XF	Unc	B
1954(a)	11,000,000	0.75	1.50	3.00	7.00	–

KM# 2 20 FRANKEN Composition: Aluminum-Bronz

Date	Mintage	F	VF	XF	Unc	B
1954(a)	12,950,000	0.75	1.50	3.50	9.00	–

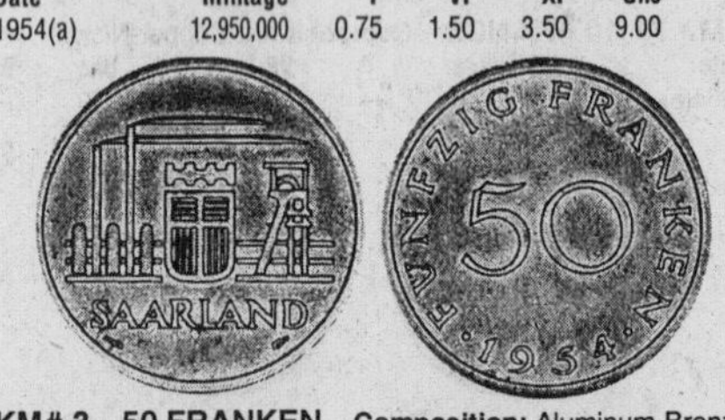

KM# 3 50 FRANKEN Composition: Aluminum-Bronz

Date	Mintage	F	VF	XF	Unc	B
1954(a)	5,300,000	3.00	6.00	12.00	25.00	–

KM# 4 100 FRANKEN Composition: Copper-Nickel

Date	Mintage	F	VF	XF	Unc	B
1955(a)	11,000,000	2.00	4.00	8.00	18.00	-

ESSAIS

Standard metals unless otherwise noted

KM#	Date	Mintage	Identification	Issue Price	Mk Va
E1	1954(a)	1,100	10 Franken. KM1.	—	30.0
E3	1954(a)	1,100	20 Franken. KM2.	—	40.0
E5	1954(a)	1,100	50 Franken. KM3.	—	50.0
E4	1954(a)	50	20 Franken. Gold. KM2.	—	1,85
E7	1955(a)	50	100 Franken. Gold. KM4.	—	2,25

SAHARAWI ARAB D.R.

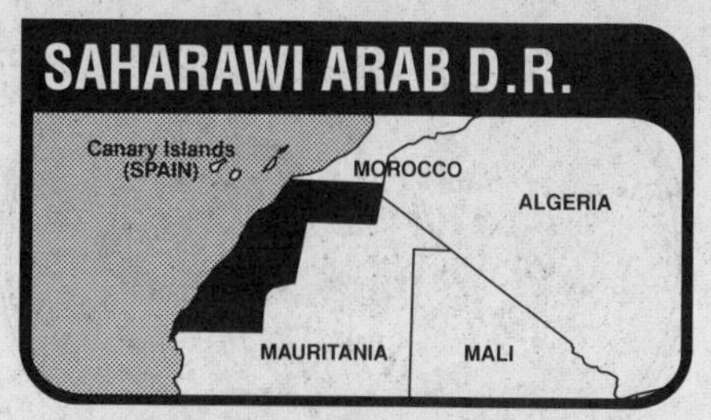

The Saharawi Arab Democratic Republic, located in northwest Africa has an area of 102,703 sq. mi. and a population (census taken 1974) of 76,425. Formerly known as Spanish Sahara, the area is bounded on the north by Morocco, on the east and southeast by Mauritania, on the northeast by Algeria, and on the west by the Atlantic Ocean. Capital: El Aaium. Agriculture, fishing and mining are the two main industries. Exports are barley, livestock and phosphates.

A Spanish trading post was established in 1476 but was abandoned in 1524. A Spanish protectorate for the region was proclaimed in 1884. The status of the Spanish Sahara changed from a colony to an overseas province in 1958. Spain relinquished its holdings in 1975 and it was divided between Mauritania, which gave up its claim in August 1979 and Morocco, which subsequently occupied the entire territory. The official languages are Spanish and an Arab dialect: The Hassaniya.

DEMOCRATIC REPUBLIC

NON-CIRCULATING COLLECTOR COINAGE

KM# 14 PESETA Composition: Copper-Nickel **Reverse:** Arab and camel

Date	F	VF	XF	Unc	BU
1992	—	—	—	0.75	—

KM# 15 2 PESETAS Composition: Copper-Nickel **Reverse:** Arab and camel

Date	F	VF	XF	Unc	BU
1992	—	—	—	1.25	—

KM# 16 5 PESETAS Composition: Copper-Nickel **Reverse:** Arab and camel

Date	F	VF	XF	Unc	BU
1992	—	—	—	2.00	—

KM# 1 50 PESETAS Composition: Copper-Nickel **Reverse:** Arab and camel

Date	F	VF	XF	Unc	BU
1990	—	—	—	5.00	—

KM# 18 100 PESETAS Composition: Copper-Nickel **Reverse:** Arab and sailing ship

Date	F	VF	XF	Unc	BU
1990	—	—	—	10.00	—

KM# 20 100 PESETAS Composition: Copper **Reverse:** Arab and camel

Date	F	VF	XF	Unc	BU
1990	—	—	—	9.50	—

KM# 25 100 PESETAS Composition: Copper **Reverse:** Arab and sailboat

Date	F	VF	XF	Unc	BU
1990	—	—	—	8.00	—
1990 Proof	—	Value: 60.00			

KM# 7 100 PESETAS Composition: Nickel Plated Steel **Series:** Olympics **Subject:** Equestrian event

Date	Mintage	F	VF	XF	Unc	BU
1991	5,000	—	—	—	10.00	—

KM# 26 100 PESETAS Composition: Nickel Plated Steel **Reverse:** Ship above Canary Islands map

Date	F	VF	XF	Unc	BU
1992	—	—	—	12.00	—

KM# 40 100 PESETAS Composition: Copper **Subject:** Columbus' ship - Santa Maria **Obverse:** National emblem

Date	Mintage	F	VF	XF	Unc	BU
1992 Proof	78	Value: 60.00				

KM# 13 100 PESETAS Composition: Copper-Nickel **Series:** Prehistoric Animals **Subject:** Brontosaurus

Date	F	VF	XF	Unc	BU
1992	—	—	—	24.00	—

KM# 19 100 PESETAS Composition: Copper **Series:** Prehistoric Animals **Subject:** Tarbosaurus Bataar

Date	F	VF	XF	Unc	BU
1993	—	—	—	22.50	—

KM# 17 100 PESETAS Composition: Nickel Clad Steel **Series:** Prehistoric Animals **Subject:** Triceratops

Date	F	VF	XF	Unc	BU
1994	—	—	—	24.00	—

KM# 41 100 PESETAS Composition: Nickel Clad Steel **Series:** Prehistoric Animals **Subject:** Camaarasaurus **Obverse:** National emblem

Date	Mintage	F	VF	XF	Unc	BU
1994 Proof	100	Value: 60.00				

KM# 23 100 PESETAS **Composition:** Nickel Clad Steel And Enamel **Reverse:** WWII British Spitfire MK II

Date	F	VF	XF	Unc	BU
1995	—	—	—	20.00	—

KM# 22 100 PESETAS **Composition:** Copper **Series:** Olympics **Reverse:** Wrestlers

Date	F	VF	XF	Unc	BU
1996	—	—	—	8.00	—

KM# 31 200 PESETAS **Composition:** Copper **Subject:** 20th Anniversary - Proclamation of Republic **Obverse:** Republic emblem

Date	F	VF	XF	Unc	BU
1996 Proof	—	Value: 7.50			

KM# 2 500 PESETAS **Weight:** 16.0000 g. **Composition:** 0.9990 Silver .5145 oz. ASW **Series:** Transportation **Reverse:** Arab walking camel

Date	F	VF	XF	Unc	BU
1990	—	—	—	27.50	—

KM# 3 500 PESETAS **Weight:** 16.0000 g. **Composition:** 0.9990 Silver .5145 oz. ASW **Reverse:** Arab and sailing ship

Date	F	VF	XF	Unc	BU
1990	—	—	—	30.00	—

KM# 42 500 PESETAS **Composition:** Copper **Obverse:** National arms **Reverse:** Antique sailing ship

Date	Mintage	F	VF	XF	Unc	BU
1990 Proof	13	Value: 1,450				

KM# 4 500 PESETAS **Weight:** 6.0000 g. **Composition:** 0.9990 Silver .1929 oz. ASW **Series:** Olympics **Reverse:** Tennis player, skier

Date	F	VF	XF	Unc	BU
1991	—	—	—	20.00	—

KM# 5 500 PESETAS **Weight:** 12.0000 g. **Composition:** 0.9990 Silver .3858 oz. ASW **Subject:** Soccer **Reverse:** Player kicking ball

Date	F	VF	XF	Unc	BU
1991	—	—	—	32.50	—

KM# 8 500 PESETAS **Weight:** 15.8400 g. **Composition:** 0.9990 Silver .5093 oz. ASW **Subject:** Soccer **Reverse:** Ball divided by inscription

Date	Mintage	F	VF	XF	Unc	BU
1991	15,000	—	—	—	35.00	—

KM# 9.1 500 PESETAS **Weight:** 20.0000 g. **Composition:** 0.9990 Silver .6430 oz. ASW **Subject:** Meeting of Two Worlds **Reverse:** Sailing ship above Canary Islands map **Note:** Thick letters.

Date	F	VF	XF	Unc	BU
1992	—	—	—	27.50	—

KM# 9.1a 500 PESETAS **Composition:** Copper **Subject:** Meeting of Two Worlds **Reverse:** Sailing ship above Canary Islands map

Date	Mintage	F	VF	XF	Unc	BU
1992 Proof	22	Value: 1,250				
1992 Proof	—	Value: 32.50				

KM# 9.2 500 PESETAS **Composition:** Copper **Subject:** Meeting of Two Worlds **Reverse:** Sailing ship above Canary Islands map **Note:** Thin letters.

Date	F	VF	XF	Unc	BU
1992 Proof	—	Value: 35.00			

KM# 11 500 PESETAS **Composition:** Copper **Subject:** Defense of Nature **Reverse:** Elephant

Date	F	VF	XF	Unc	BU
1993	—	—	—	35.00	—

KM# 12 500 PESETAS **Weight:** 16.0000 g. **Composition:** 0.9990 Silver .5140 oz. ASW **Series:** Prehistoric Animals **Subject:** Tarbosaurus Bataar

Date	F	VF	XF	Unc	BU
1993	—	—	—	32.50	—

KM# 27 500 PESETAS **Weight:** 16.0000 g. **Composition:** 0.9990 Silver .5140 oz. ASW **Series:** Prehistoric Animals **Subject:** Camarasaurus

Date	F	VF	XF	Unc	BU
1994	—	—	—	30.00	—

M# 21 500 PESETAS **Weight:** 20.0000 g. **Composition:** 0.9990 Silver .6430 oz. ASW **Series:** 1996 Olympics **Reverse:** Wrestlers

te	Mintage	F	VF	XF	Unc	BU
95 Proof	15,000	—	—	—	22.50	—

M# 24 500 PESETAS **Weight:** 20.0000 g. **Composition:** 0.9990 Silver .6430 oz. ASW **Reverse:** WWII British Spitfire MK II

te	Mintage	F	VF	XF	Unc	BU
95 Proof	15,000	Value: 32.50				

M# 28 500 PESETAS **Weight:** 16.0000 g. **Composition:** 0.9990 Silver .5140 oz. ASW **Series:** Prehistoric Animals **Subject:** Plateosaurus

te	F	VF	XF	Unc	BU
95 Proof	—	Value: 37.50			

M# 29 500 PESETAS **Weight:** 20.0000 g. **Composition:** 0.9990 Silver .6424 oz. ASW **Reverse:** Multicolored leopard

te	F	VF	XF	Unc	BU
96 Proof	—	Value: 45.00			

M# 32 500 PESETAS **Weight:** 20.0000 g. **Composition:** 0.9990 Silver .6430 oz. ASW **Subject:** XVI Copa Mundial - Francia 1998 - Soccer **Reverse:** Player kicking ball

te	F	VF	XF	Unc	BU
96 Proof	—	Value: 50.00			

KM# 33 500 PESETAS **Weight:** 20.0000 g. **Composition:** 0.9990 Silver .6430 oz. ASW **Subject:** XVI Copa Mundial - Francia 1998 - Soccer **Reverse:** Multicolored player kicking ball

Date	F	VF	XF	Unc	BU
1996 Proof	—	Value: 50.00			

KM# 34 500 PESETAS **Weight:** 20.0000 g. **Composition:** 0.9990 Silver .6430 oz. ASW **Series:** XXVII Olimpiada - Sydney 2000 **Reverse:** Muticolored kayaker

Date	F	VF	XF	Unc	BU
1996 Proof	—	Value: 32.50			

KM# 30 500 PESETAS **Weight:** 16.0000 g. **Composition:** 0.9990 Silver .6424 oz. ASW **Series:** Sydney Olympics **Reverse:** Muticolored weight lifter

Date	F	VF	XF	Unc	BU
1997 Proof	—	Value: 32.50			

KM# 6 1000 PESETAS **Weight:** 3.1000 g. **Composition:** 0.9990 Gold .1000 oz. AGW **Series:** Transportation **Reverse:** Arab walking with camel **Note:** Similar to 500 Pesetas, KM#2.

Date	Mintage	F	VF	XF	Unc	BU
1991	508	—	—	—	125	—

KM# 44 1000 PESETAS **Weight:** 30.5000 g. **Composition:** 0.9990 Silver .9796 oz. ASW **Subject:** Thor Heyerdahl **Obverse:** National arms **Reverse:** Muticolored reed boats **Edge:** Plain

Date	F	VF	XF	Unc	BU
1996	—	Value: 32.50			

KM# 45 1000 PESETAS **Weight:** 30.5000 g. **Composition:** 0.9990 Silver .9796 oz. ASW **Subject:** Horudsch Chaireddin **Obverse:** National arms **Reverse:** Multicolored pirates sailing vessels in background

Date	F	VF	XF	Unc	BU
1996 Proof	—	Value: 32.50			

KM# 37 1000 PESETAS **Weight:** 31.5000 g. **Composition:** 0.9990 Silver 1.0117 oz. ASW **Subject:** 15th Anniversary - Diplomacy between Venezuela and Arabic Sahara **Obverse:** Pillar between national emblems **Reverse:** Bolivar and El Vali standing by canon

Date	Mintage	F	VF	XF	Unc	BU
1997	200	—	—	—	65.00	—
1997 Proof	800	Value: 55.00				

KM# 43 1000 PESETAS **Composition:** Silver **Obverse:** National emblem **Reverse:** Viking ship

Date	Mintage	F	VF	XF	Unc	BU
1998 Proof	100	Value: 110				

KM# 10 1000 PESETAS - 10 ECU **Weight:** 31.0000 g. **Composition:** 0.9990 Silver .9957 oz. ASW **Subject:** European Community

Date	Mintage	F	VF	XF	Unc	BU
ND(1992) Proof	15,000	Value: 40.00				

KM# 35 5000 PESETAS **Weight:** 33.5400 g. **Composition:** 0.9200 Silver .9975 oz. ASW **Subject:** 20th Anniversary - Proclamation of Republic **Obverse:** Republican emblem **Reverse:** Female guerilla with rifle

Date	F	VF	XF	Unc	BU
1996 Proof	—	Value: 65.00			

KM# 36 5000 PESETAS **Weight:** 33.5400 g. **Composition:** 0.9200 Silver .9975 oz. ASW **Subject:** 20th Anniversary - Proclamation of Republic **Reverse:** Land Rover with armed guerillas

Date	F	VF	XF	Unc	BU
1996 Proof	—	Value: 65.00			

KM# 38 40000 PESETAS **Weight:** 15.5200 g. **Composition:** 0.9000 Gold .4491 oz. AGW **Subject:** 20th Anniversary - Diplomacy between Venezuela and Saharawi Arab Democratic Republic **Reverse:** Bolivar and El Vali

Date	Mintage	F	VF	XF	Unc	BU
1997 Proof	90	Value: 1,000				

KM# 38a 40000 PESETAS **Weight:** 15.5000 g. **Composition:** 0.9990 Gold .4978 oz. AGW

Date	Mintage	F	VF	XF	Unc	BU
1997 Proof, rare	10	—	—	—	—	—

ESSAIS

KM#	Date	Mintage	Identification	Mkt Val
E1	1997	8	1000 Pesetas. Copper. KM#37.	3,000

PATTERNS

KM#	Date	Mintage	Identification	Mkt Val
Pn2	1997	8	40000 Pesetas. Copper. KM#38.	3,000
Pn3	1997	8	40000 Pesetas. Silver. KM#38.	3,000

PIEFORTS

KM#	Date	Mintage	Identification	Mkt Val
P1	1990	110	500 Pesetas. KM#3.	80.00
P2	1997	8	40000 Pesetas. KM#38.	6,000

SAINT HELENA & ASCENSION

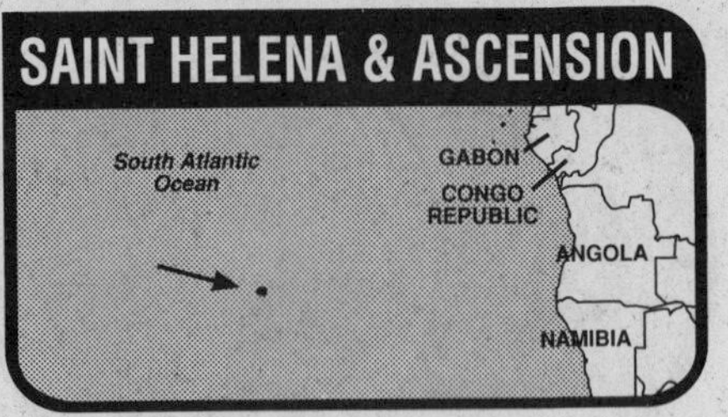

Saint Helena, a British colony located about 1,150 miles (1,850 km.) from the west coast of Africa, has an area of 47 sq. mi. (410 sq. km.) and a population of *7,000. Capital: Jamestown. Flax, lace, and rope are produced for export. Ascension and Tristan da Cunha are dependencies of Saint Helena.

The island was discovered and named by the Portuguese navigator Joao de Nova Castella in 1502. The Portuguese imported livestock, fruit trees, and vegetables but established no permanent settlement. The Dutch occupied the island temporarily, 1645-51. The original European settlement was founded by representatives of the British East India Company sent to annex the island after the departure of the Dutch. The Dutch returned and captured Saint Helena from the British on New Year's Day, 1673, but were in turn ejected by a British force under Sir Richard Munden. Thereafter Saint Helena was the undisputed possession of Great Britain. The island served as the place of exile for Napoleon, several Zulu chiefs, and an ex-sultan of Zanzibar.

RULERS
British

MINT MARKS
PM - Pobjoy Mint

MONETARY SYSTEM
12 Pence = 1 Shilling
100 Pence = 1 Pound

BRITISH COLONY

SAINT HELENA

STANDARD COINAGE

KM# 5 25 PENCE (Crown) **Composition:** Copper-Nickel **Subject:** St. Helena Tercentenary

Date	Mintage	VG	F	VF	XF	Unc
ND(1973)	100,000	—	—	—	—	4.00

KM# 5a 25 PENCE (Crown) **Weight:** 28.2800 g. **Composition:** 0.9250 Silver .8411 oz. ASW **Subject:** St. Helena Tercentenary

Date	Mintage	VG	F	VF	XF	Unc
ND(1973) Proof	10,000	Value: 20.00				

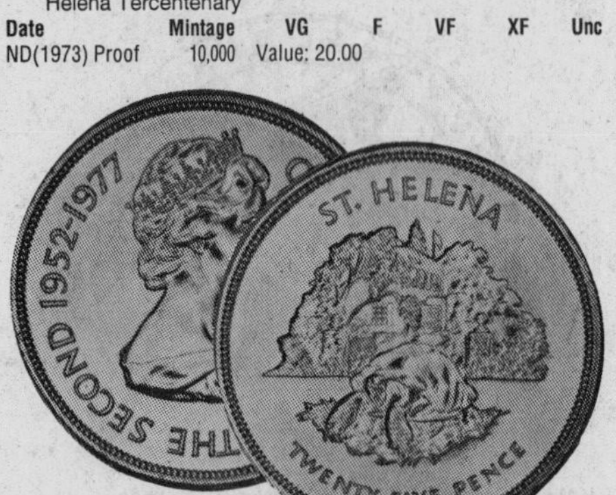

KM# 6 25 PENCE (Crown) **Composition:** Copper-Nickel **Subject:** Queen Elizabeth II Silver Jubilee

Date	Mintage	VG	F	VF	XF	Unc
ND(1977)	50,000	—	—	—	—	6.00

KM# 6a 25 PENCE (Crown) **Weight:** 28.2800 g. **Composition:** 0.9250 Silver .8411 oz. ASW **Subject:** Queen Elizabeth II Silver Jubilee

Date	Mintage	VG	F	VF	XF	Unc
ND(1977) Proof	25,000	Value: 13.50				

KM# 7 25 PENCE (Crown) **Composition:** Copper-Nickel **Subject:** 25th Anniversary of Coronation

Date	VG	F	VF	XF	
1978PM	—	—	—	—	3

KM# 7a 25 PENCE (Crown) **Weight:** 28.2800 g. **Composition:** 0.9250 Silver .8411 oz. ASW **Subject:** 25 Anniversary of Coronation

Date	Mintage	VG	F	VF	XF	
1978PM	—	—	—	—	—	11
1978PM Proof	25,000	Value: 16.50				

KM# 8 25 PENCE (Crown) **Composition:** Copper-Nickel **Subject:** Queen Mother's 80th Birthday

Date	Mintage	VG	F	VF	XF	
1980	100,000	—	—	—	—	3

KM# 8a 25 PENCE (Crown) **Weight:** 28.2800 g. **Composition:** 0.9250 Silver **Subject:** Queen Mother's 80 Birthday

Date	Mintage	VG	F	VF	XF
1980 Proof	25,000	Value: 13.50			

KM# 9 25 PENCE (Crown) **Composition:** Copper-Nickel **Subject:** Wedding of Prince Charles and Lady Dia

Date	Mintage	VG	F	VF	XF	
ND(1981)	50,000	—	—	—	—	3

KM# 9a 25 PENCE (Crown) **Weight:** 28.2800 g. **Composition:** 0.9250 Silver .8411 oz. ASW **Subject:** Wedding of Prince Charles and Lady Diana

Date	Mintage	VG	F	VF	XF
ND(1981) Proof	30,000	Value: 20.00			

KM# 10 25 PENCE (Crown) **Weight:** 28.2800 g. **Composition:** 0.9250 Silver .8411 oz. ASW **Series:** International Year of the Scout **Obverse:** Queen Elizabet

e	Mintage	VG	F	VF	XF	Unc
(1983)		—	—	—	—	30.00
(1983) Proof	10,000	Value: 42.50				

M# 12 50 PENCE **Composition:** Copper-Nickel
Subject: 150th Anniversary - Saint Helena Colony

te	Mintage	VG	F	VF	XF	Unc
(1984)	10,000	—	—	—	—	4.00

M# 12a 50 PENCE **Weight:** 28.2800 g. **Composition:** 0.9250 Silver .8411 oz. ASW **Subject:** 150th Anniversary - Saint Helena Colony

te	Mintage	VG	F	VF	XF	Unc
(1984) Proof	5,000	Value: 28.00				

M# 12b 50 PENCE **Weight:** 47.5400 g. **Composition:** 0.9170 Gold 1.4017 oz. AGW **Subject:** 150th Anniversary - Saint Helena Colony

te	Mintage	VG	F	VF	XF	Unc
(1984) Proof	150	Value: 775				

M# 13 50 PENCE **Composition:** Copper-Nickel
Subject: Royal Visit of Prince Andrew **Reverse:** Bust left

te	Mintage	VG	F	VF	XF	Unc
84	125,000	—	—	—	—	3.00

M# 13a 50 PENCE **Weight:** 28.2800 g. **Composition:** 0.9250 Silver .8411 oz. ASW **Subject:** Royal Visit of Prince Andrew **Reverse:** Bust left

te	Mintage	VG	F	VF	XF	Unc
84 Proof	5,000	Value: 30.00				

M# 14 50 PENCE **Composition:** Copper-Nickel
Subject: Queen Mother

ate	VG	F	VF	XF	Unc
95	—	—	—	—	6.00

M# 14a 50 PENCE **Weight:** 28.2800 g. **Composition:** 0.9250 Silver .8411 oz. ASW **Subject:** Queen Mother

ate	Mintage	VG	F	VF	XF	Unc
95 Proof	10,000	Value: 35.00				

M# 14b 50 PENCE **Weight:** 47.5400 g. **Composition:** 0.9160 Gold 1.4011 oz. AGW **Subject:** Queen Mother

ate	Mintage	VG	F	VF	XF	Unc
995 Proof	150	Value: 950				

KM# 15 50 PENCE **Composition:** Copper-Nickel
Subject: Queen Elizabeth II's 70th Birthday **Reverse:** Mounted guardsman

Date	VG	F	VF	XF	Unc
1996	—	—	—	—	6.00

KM# 15a 50 PENCE **Weight:** 28.2800 g. **Composition:** 0.9250 Silver .8411 oz. ASW **Subject:** Queen Elizabeth II's 70th Birthday **Reverse:** Mounted guardsman

Date	Mintage	VG	F	VF	XF	Unc
1996 Proof	5,000	Value: 50.00				

KM# 18 50 PENCE **Composition:** Copper-Nickel
Subject: Elizabeth and Philip **Obverse:** Queen's portrait **Reverse:** Royal couple reviewing troops

Date	VG	F	VF	XF	Unc
ND(1997)	—	—	—	—	6.50

KM# 16 50 PENCE **Composition:** Copper-Nickel
Series: World Wildlife Fund **Subject:** Conserving Nature **Reverse:** Three blue whales

Date	VG	F	VF	XF	Unc
1998	—	—	—	—	8.50

KM# 17 50 PENCE **Composition:** Copper-Nickel
Series: World Wildlife Fund **Subject:** Conserving Nature **Obverse:** Queen's portrait **Reverse:** Rain piper bird, shoreline, lily

Date	VG	F	VF	XF	Unc
1998	—	—	—	—	8.00

KM# 19 50 PENCE **Weight:** 38.6000 g. **Composition:** Copper Nickel **Subject:** Queen's 75th Birthday **Obverse:** Queen's crowned portrait **Reverse:** Queen's uncrowned portrait **Edge:** Reeded **Size:** 38.6 mm.

Date	VG	F	VF	XF	Unc
2001	—	—	—	—	8.00

KM# 20 50 PENCE **Weight:** 28.5500 g. **Composition:** Copper Nickel **Subject:** Queen Victoria's Death **Obverse:** Queen's crowned portrait **Reverse:** Queen Victoria and ship **Edge:** Reeded **Size:** 38.6 mm.

Date	VG	F	VF	XF	Unc
2001	—	—	—	—	8.00

KM# 21 POUND **Weight:** 4.2000 g. **Composition:** Brass Plated Steel **Subject:** Pattern? **Obverse:** Queen's portrait **Reverse:** Coat of arms and denomination **Edge:** Reeded and plain sections **Size:** 22 mm.

Date	F	VF	XF	Unc	BU
1980PM	—	—	—	—	—

KM# 11 2 POUNDS **Weight:** 15.9800 g. **Composition:** 0.9170 Gold .4712 oz. AGW **Series:** International Year of the Scout

Date	Mintage	VG	F	VF	XF	Unc
ND(1983)		—	—	—	—	450
ND(1983) Proof	2,000	Value: 500				

PIEFORTS

KM#	Date	Mintage	Identification	Mkt Val
P1	1984	500	50 Pence. Silver. KM13a.	50.00
P2	1995	500	50 Pence. Silver. KM14a.	90.00

SAINT HELENA & ASCENSION

STANDARD COINAGE

100 Pence = 1 Pound

KM# 1 PENNY **Composition:** Bronze **Reverse:** Tuna

Date	Mintage	F	VF	XF	Unc	BU
1984	—	—	—	0.15	0.35	—
1984 Proof	10,000	Value: 1.25				

KM# 13 PENNY **Composition:** Bronze **Obverse:** Queen's portrait by dePedery-Hunt

Date	F	VF	XF	Unc	BU
1991	—	—	0.15	0.35	—

KM# 13a PENNY **Composition:** Chrome Plated Steel

Date	F	VF	XF	Unc	BU
1997	—	—	0.15	0.35	—

KM# 2 2 PENCE **Composition:** Bronze **Reverse:** Donkey with Fire Wood

Date	Mintage	F	VF	XF	Unc	BU
1984	—	—	—	0.20	0.50	—
1984 Proof	10,000	Value: 1.50				

KM# 12 2 PENCE **Composition:** Bronze **Obverse:** Queen's portrait by dePedery-Hunt

Date	F	VF	XF	Unc	BU
1991	—	—	0.20	0.50	—

KM# 3 5 PENCE **Composition:** Copper-Nickel **Reverse:** Rain Piper

Date	F	VF	XF	Unc	BU
1984	—	—	0.20	0.50	—
1984 Proof	—	Value: 1.75			

KM# 14 5 PENCE **Composition:** Copper-Nickel **Obverse:** Queen's portrait by dePedery-Hunt

Date	F	VF	XF	Unc	BU
1991	—	—	0.20	0.50	—

KM# 22 5 PENCE **Composition:** Copper-Nickel **Subject:** The Giant Tortoise **Obverse:** Queen's portrait **Reverse:** Giant tortoise

Date	F	VF	XF	Unc	BU
1998	—	—	—	0.75	—

KM# 4 10 PENCE **Composition:** Copper-Nickel **Reverse:** Arum Lily

Date	F	VF	XF	Unc	BU
1984	—	—	0.30	1.00	—
1984 Proof	—	Value: 2.00			

KM# 15 10 PENCE **Composition:** Copper-Nickel **Obverse:** Queen's portrait by dePedery-Hunt

Date	F	VF	XF	Unc	BU
1991	—	—	0.30	1.00	—

KM# 23 10 PENCE **Composition:** Copper-Nickel **Obverse:** Queen's portrait **Reverse:** Dolphins

Date	F	VF	XF	Unc	BU
1998	—	—	—	1.25	—

KM# 21 20 PENCE **Composition:** Copper-Nickel **Obverse:** Queen's portrait **Reverse:** Flower

Date	F	VF	XF	Unc	BU
1998	—	—	—	1.25	—

KM# 5 50 PENCE **Composition:** Copper-Nickel **Reverse:** Sea Turtle

Date	F	VF	XF	Unc	BU
1984	—	—	1.50	3.50	—
1984 Proof	—	Value: 4.00			

KM# 7 50 PENCE **Composition:** Copper-Nickel **Subject:** Wedding of Prince Andrew and Sarah Ferguson

Date	Mintage	F	VF	XF	Unc	BU
ND(1986)	13,000	—	—	—	4.00	—

KM# 7a 50 PENCE **Weight:** 28.2800 g. **Composition:** 0.9250 Silver .8411 oz. ASW

Date	Mintage	F	VF	XF	Unc	BU
ND(1986) Proof	2,500	Value: 27.50				

KM# 7b 50 PENCE **Weight:** 47.5400 g. **Composition:** 0.9170 Gold 1.4017 oz. AGW **Subject:** Wedding of Prince Andrew and Sarah Ferguson

Date	Mintage	F	VF	XF	Unc	BU
ND(1986) Proof	50	Value: 1,150				

KM# 8 50 PENCE **Composition:** Copper-Nickel **Subject:** 165th Anniversary of Napoleon's Death

Date	Mintage	F	VF	XF	Unc
1986	50,000	—	—	—	5.00

KM# 16 50 PENCE **Composition:** Copper-Nickel **Subject:** 165th Anniversary of Napoleon's Death **Obve** Elizabeth II DePedery-Hunt portrait **Reverse:** Napoleo standing, facing right, sailing ship behind him

Date	F	VF	XF	Unc
1991	—	—	—	5.00

KM# 19 50 PENCE **Composition:** Copper-Nickel **Subject:** Normandy Invasion

Date	F	VF	XF	Unc
ND(1994)	—	—	—	6.00

KM# 19a 50 PENCE **Weight:** 28.2800 g. **Composit** 0.9250 Silver .8411 oz. ASW

Date	Mintage	F	VF	XF	Unc
ND(1994) Proof	5,000	Value: 40.00			

KM# 6 POUND **Composition:** Nickel-Brass **Revers** Sooty Terns

Date	F	VF	XF	Unc
1984	—	—	2.25	5.00
1984 Proof	—	Value: 5.00		

KM# 6a POUND **Weight:** 9.5000 g. **Composition:** 0.9250 Silver .2826 oz. ASW

Date	Mintage	F	VF	XF	Unc
1984 Proof	10,000	Value: 18.00			

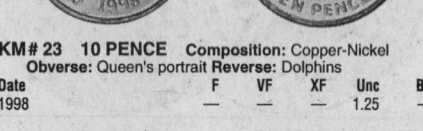

KM# 17 POUND **Composition:** Nickel-Brass **Obverse:** Bust of Queen Elizabeth II right. **Reverse:** Two birds in flight left.

Date	F	VF	XF	Unc	BU
1991	—	—	2.25	5.00	—

KM# 11 2 POUNDS **Composition:** Copper-Nickel **Subject:** Queen Mother

Date	F	VF	XF	Unc	BU
ND(1990)	—	—	—	12.00	—

KM#11a 2 POUNDS **Weight:** 28.2800 g. **Composition:** 0.9250 Silver .8411 oz. ASW

Date	Mintage	F	VF	XF	Unc	BU
ND(1990) Proof	50,000	Value: 50.00				

KM# 18 2 POUNDS **Weight:** 28.2800 g. **Composition:** 0.9250 Silver .8411 oz. ASW **Subject:** 40th Anniversary - Coronation of Elizabeth II

Date	Mintage	F	VF	XF	Unc	BU
ND(1993) Proof	10,000	Value: 55.00				

KM#9 25 POUNDS **Weight:** 155.0000 g. **Composition:** 0.9990 Silver 4.9839 oz. ASW **Subject:** 165th Anniversary of Napoleon's Death **Obverse:** Similar to 50 Pence, KM#7 **Note:** Illustration reduced.

Date	Mintage	F	VF	XF	Unc	BU
1986 Proof	15,000	Value: 110				

KM# 20 25 POUNDS **Weight:** 155.5175 g. **Composition:** 0.9990 Silver 5.0000 oz. ASW **Subject:** 70th Birthday - Queen Elizabeth II **Reverse:** Mounted drummer **Note:** Illustration reduced.

Date	Mintage	F	VF	XF	Unc	BU
1996 Proof	1,000	Value: 200				

KM#10 50 POUNDS **Weight:** 32.2600 g. **Composition:** 0.9990 Platinum 1.0051 oz. APW **Subject:** 165th Anniversary of Napoleon's Death

Date	Mintage	F	VF	XF	Unc	BU
1986 Proof	5,000	Value: 650				

PIEFORTS

KM#	Date	Mintage	Identification	Issue Price	Mkt Val
P1	1984	2,500	Pound. KM#6a.	49.75	28.00
P2	1986	250	50 Pence. KM#7a.	74.00	75.00
P3	1994	500	50 Pence. KM#19.	—	60.00

MINT SETS

KM#	Date	Mintage	Identification	Issue Price	Mkt Val
MS1	1984 (6)	—	KM#1-6	—	5.50

PROOF SETS

KM#	Date	Mintage	Identification	Issue Price	Mkt Val
PS1	1984 (6)	—	KM#1-6	—	25.00

SAINT KITTS & NEVIS

Saint Kitts (Saint Christopher), a West Indian island located in the Leeward Islands southeast of Puerto Rico, is the principal component of a British associated state com-posed of the islands of Saint Kitts, Nevis, and Anguilla. The associated state has an area of 104 sq. mi. (360 sq. km.) and a population of *40,000. Capital: Basseterre, on Saint Kitts. The islands export sugar, molasses, rum, cotton, and coconuts.

Saint Kitts was discovered by Columbus in 1493 and was settled by Thomas Warner, an Englishman, in 1623. The island was ceded to the British by the Treaty of Utrecht, 1713. France protested British occupancy, and on three occasions between 1616 and 1782 seized the island and held it for short periods. Saint Kitts used the coins and currency of the British Caribbean Territories (Eastern Group).

In early 1967 Saint Kitts was united politically with Nevis and Anguilla to form a self-governing British associated state. In June 1967 Anguilla declared its independence of the federated state, and in Feb. 1969 unilaterally severed all ties with Britain and established the Republic of Anguilla. Britain refused to accept the unilateral movement and installed a commissioner to govern Anguilla, which would remain a nominal part of the associated state. Currently, Elizabeth II is Head of State, as Queen of Saint Christopher & Nevis.

From approximately 1750-1830, billon 2 sous of the French colony of Cayenne were countermarked SK' and used on Saint Kitts. They were valued at 1-1/3 Pence.

RULERS
British

MONETARY SYSTEM
100 Cents = 1 Dollar

NOTE: The grades shown describe the condition of the raised countermarks, not the host coin itself, which is typically well worn.

BRITISH ASSOCIATED STATE

STANDARD COINAGE

100 Cents = 1 Dollar

KM# 1 4 DOLLARS **Composition:** Copper-Nickel **Series:** F.A.O

Date	Mintage	F	VF	XF	Unc	BU
1970	13,000	—	3.50	7.00	12.50	—
1970 Proof	2,000	Value: 22.50				

KM# 3 10 DOLLARS **Composition:** Copper-Nickel
Subject: Royal Visit

Date	Mintage	F	VF	XF	Unc	BU
1985	100,000	—	—	—	8.00	—

KM# 3a 10 DOLLARS **Weight:** 28.2800 g.
Composition: 0.9250 Silver .8411 oz. ASW

Date	Mintage	F	VF	XF	Unc	BU
1985 Proof	5,000	Value: 40.00				

KM# 3b 10 DOLLARS **Weight:** 47.5400 g. **Composition:** 0.9170 Gold 1.4013 oz. AGW **Subject:** Royal Visit

Date	Mintage	F	VF	XF	Unc	BU
1985 Proof	250	Value: 1,100				

KM# 4 20 DOLLARS **Composition:** Copper-Nickel
Subject: 200th Anniversary - Battle of the Saints

Date	F	VF	XF	Unc	BU
ND(1982)	—	—	—	12.50	—

KM# 4a 20 DOLLARS **Weight:** 28.2800 g.
Composition: 0.9250 Silver .8411 oz. ASW

Date	Mintage	F	VF	XF	Unc	BU
ND(1982) Proof	2,500	Value: 42.50				

KM# 2 20 DOLLARS **Composition:** Copper-Nickel
Subject: Attainment of Independence

Date	F	VF	XF	Unc	BU
1983	—	—	—	15.00	—

KM# 2a 20 DOLLARS **Weight:** 28.2800 g.
Composition: 0.9250 Silver .8411 oz. ASW

Date	Mintage	F	VF	XF	Unc	BU
1983 Proof	5,000	Value: 40.00				

KM# 5 100 DOLLARS **Weight:** 7.9900 g. **Composition:** 0.9170 Gold .2356 oz. AGW **Subject:** 200th Anniversary - Siege of Brimstone Hill

Date	Mintage	F	VF	XF	Unc	BU
ND(1982)	—	—	—	—	200	—
ND(1982) Proof	15	Value: 675				

KM# 6 100 DOLLARS **Weight:** 129.5900 g.
Composition: 0.9250 Silver 3.8543 oz. ASW **Subject:** Tropical birds **Reverse:** Green-throated Carib Hummingbird **Size:** 63 mm. **Note:** Illustration reduced.

Date	Mintage	F	VF	XF	Unc	BU
1988 Proof	Est. 10,000	Value: 125				

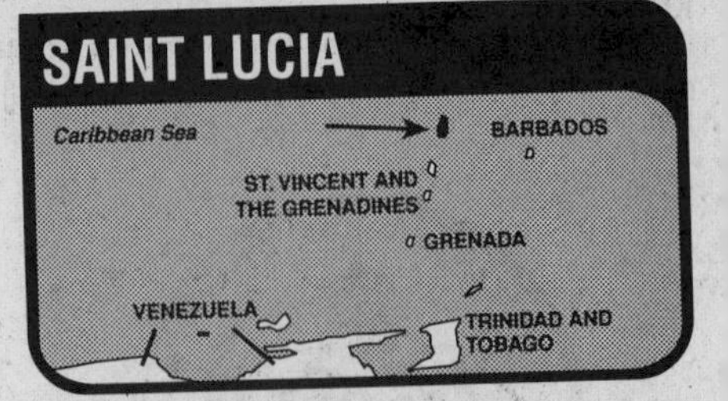

Saint Lucia, an independent island nation located in the Windward Islands of the West Indies between Saint Vincent and Martinique, has an area of 238 sq. mi. (620 sq. km.) and a population of *150,000. Capital: Castries. The economy is agricultural. Bananas, copra, cocoa, sugar and logwood are exported.

Columbus discovered Saint Lucia in 1502. The first attempts at settlement undertaken by the British in1605 and 1638 were frustrated by sickness and the determined hostility of the fierce Carib inhabitants. The French settled it in 1650 and made a treaty with the natives. Until 1814, when the island became a definite British possession, it was the scene of a continuous conflict between the British and French, which saw the island change, hands on at least 14 occasions. In 1967,under the West Indies Act, Saint Lucia was established as a British associated state, self-governing in internal affairs. Complete independence was attained on February 22,1979. Saint Lucia is a member of the Commonwealth of Nations. Elizabeth II is Head of State as Queen of Saint Lucia.

Prior to 1950, the island used sterling, which was superseded by the currency of the British Caribbean Territories (Eastern Group) and the East Caribbean State.

RULERS
British

MONETARY SYSTEM
100 Cents = 1 Dollar

BRITISH ASSOCIATED STATE

MODERN COINAGE

100 Cents = 1 Dollar

KM# 11 4 DOLLARS **Composition:** Copper-Nickel
Series: F.A.O

Date	Mintage	F	VF	XF	Unc
1970	13,000	—	3.50	7.00	12.50
1970 Proof	2,000	Value: 22.50			

KM# 14 5 DOLLARS Composition: Copper-Nickel **Subject:** Papal Visit **Obverse:** Similar to 10 Dollars, KM#12

Date	F	VF	XF	Unc	BU
1986	—	—	—	8.50	—

KM# 14a 5 DOLLARS Weight: 28.2800 g. **Composition:** 0.9250 Silver .8411 oz. ASW

Date	Mintage	F	VF	XF	Unc	BU
1986 Proof	2,120	Value: 42.50				

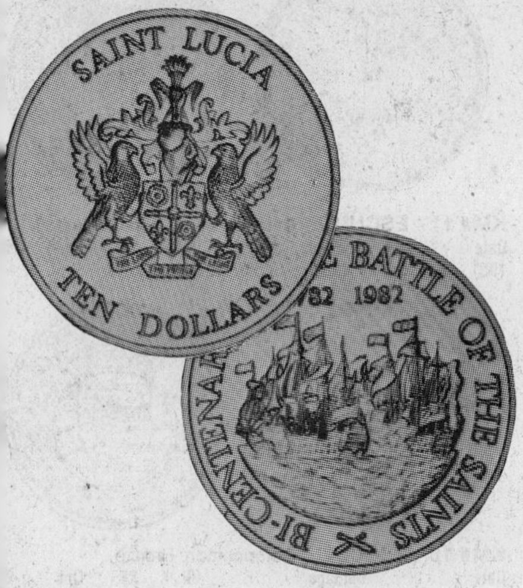

KM# 12 10 DOLLARS Composition: Copper-Nickel **Subject:** 200th Anniversary - Battle of the Saints

Date	F	VF	XF	Unc	BU
1982	—	—	—	12.50	—

KM# 12a 10 DOLLARS Weight: 28.2800 g. **Composition:** 0.9250 Silver .8411 oz. ASW

Date	Mintage	F	VF	XF	Unc	BU
1982 Proof	2,500	Value: 42.50				

KM# 13 10 DOLLARS Composition: Copper-Nickel **Subject:** Royal Visit - Queen Elizabeth II

Date	Mintage	F	VF	XF	Unc	BU
1985	100,000	—	—	—	8.50	—

KM# 13a 10 DOLLARS Weight: 28.2800 g. **Composition:** 0.9250 Silver .8411 oz. ASW

Date	Mintage	F	VF	XF	Unc	BU
1985 Proof	5,000	Value: 40.00				

KM# 13b 10 DOLLARS Weight: 47.5400 g. **Composition:** 0.9170 Gold 1.4013 oz. AGW **Subject:** Royal Visit

Date	Mintage	F	VF	XF	Unc	BU
1985 Proof	250	Value: 1,100				

KM# 16 10 DOLLARS Weight: 28.2800 g. **Composition:** 0.9250 Silver .8411 oz. ASW **Subject:** Commonwealth Finance Ministers Meeting

Date	Mintage	F	VF	XF	Unc	BU
1986 Proof	1,000	Value: 55.00				

KM# 17 100 DOLLARS Weight: 129.5900 g. **Composition:** 0.9250 Silver 3.8543 oz. ASW **Subject:** Tropical Birds **Reverse:** Two St. Lucia Amazon Parrots **Size:** 63 mm. **Note:** Illustration reduced.

Date	Mintage	F	VF	XF	Unc	BU
1988 Proof	Est. 10,000	Value: 125				

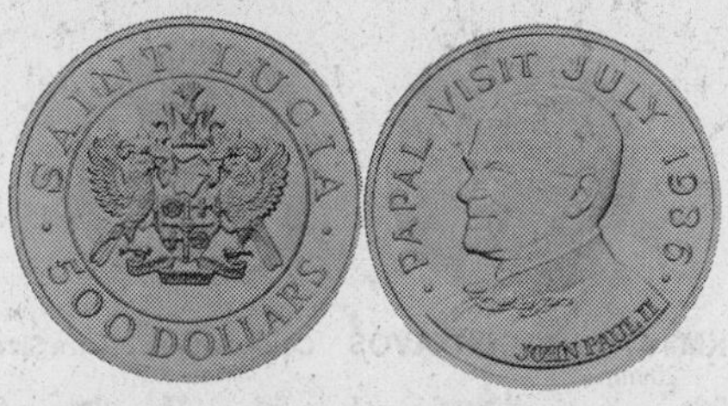

KM# 15 500 DOLLARS Weight: 15.9800 g. **Composition:** 0.9170 Gold .4709 oz. AGW **Subject:** Papal Visit

Date	Mintage	F	VF	XF	Unc	BU
1986 Proof	100	Value: 850				

SAINT PIERRE & MIQUELON

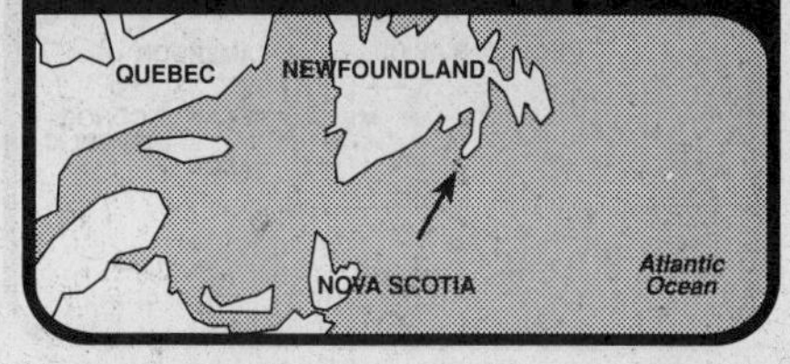

The Territorial Collectivity of Saint Pierre and Miquelon, a French overseas territory located 10 miles (16 km.) off the south coast of Newfoundland, has an area of 93 sq. mi. (242 sq. km.) and a population of *6,000. Capital: Saint Pierre. The economy of the barren archipelago is based on cod fishing and fur farming. Fish and fish products, and mink and silver fox pelts are exported.

The islands were occupied by the French in 1604, then were captured by the British in 1702 and held until 1763, at which time they were returned to the possession of France and employed as a fishing station. They passed between France and England on six more occasions between 1778 and 1814 when the Treaty of Paris awarded them permanently to France. The rugged, soil-poor granite islands, which will support only evergreen shrubs, are all that remain of France's extensive North American colonies. In 1958 Saint Pierre and Miquelon voted in favor of the new constitution of the Fifth Republic of France, thereby choosing to remain within the new French Community.

RULERS
French

MINT MARKS
(a) - Paris, privy marks only

MONETARY SYSTEM
100 Centimes = 1 Franc

FRENCH TERRITORY

STANDARD COINAGE

100 Centimes = 1 Franc

KM# 1 FRANC Composition: Aluminum

Date	Mintage	F	VF	XF	Unc	BU
1948(a)	600,000	0.50	0.75	1.50	5.50	—

KM# 2 2 FRANCS Composition: Aluminum

Date	Mintage	F	VF	XF	Unc	BU
1948(a)	300,000	0.75	1.00	2.00	6.50	—

ESSAIS

Standard metals unless otherwise noted

KM#	Date	Mintage	Identification	Issue Price	Mkt Val
E1a	1948(a)	2,000	Franc. Copper-Nickel.	—	40.00
E2a	1948(a)	2,000	2 Francs. Copper-Nickel.	—	45.00

PIEFORTS WITH ESSAIS

Double thickness, standard metals unless otherwise noted

KM#	Date	Mintage	Identification	Issue Price	Mkt Val
PE1	1948(a)	104	Franc.	—	120
PE2	1948(a)	104	2 Francs.	—	150

SAINT THOMAS & PRINCE

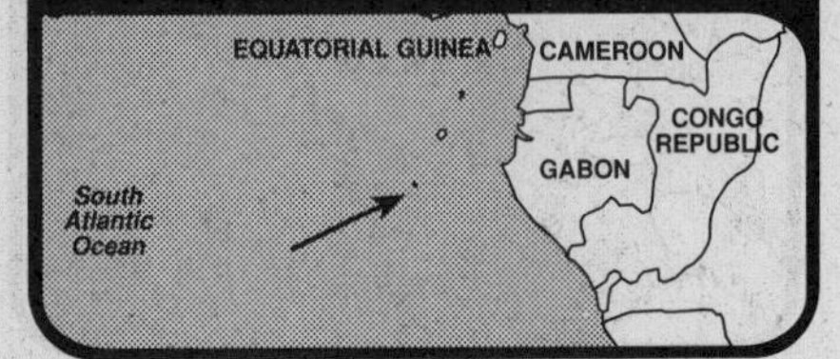

The Democratic Republic of Sao Tome and Principe (formerly the Portuguese overseas province of Saint Thomas and Prince Islands) is located in the Gulf of Guinea 150 miles (241 km.) off the western coast of Africa. It has an area of 372 sq. mi. (960 sq. km.) and a population of *121,000. Capital: Sao Tome. The economy of the islands is based on cocoa, copra and coffee.

Saint Thomas and Saint Prince were uninhabited when discovered by Portuguese navigators Joao de Santarem and Pedro de Escobar in 1470. After the failure of their initial settlement of 1485, the Portuguese successfully colonized St. Thomas with a colony of prisoners and exiled Jews in 1493. An initial prosperity based on the sugar trade gave way to a time of misfortune, 1567-1709, that saw the colony attacked and occupied or plundered by the French and Dutch, ravaged by the slave revolt of 1595; and finally rendered destitute by the transfer of the world sugar trade to Brazil. In the late 1800s, the colony turned from the production of sugar to cocoa, the basis of its present economy

The islands were designated a Portuguese overseas province in 1951. On April 25, 1974, the government of Portugal was seized by a military junta, which reached agreements providing for independence for the Portuguese overseas provinces of Portuguese Guinea (Guinea-Bissau), Mozambique, Cape Verde Islands, Angola, and Saint Thomas and Prince Islands. The Democratic Republic of Sao Tome and Principe was declared on July 12, 1975.

RULERS
Portuguese, until 1975

MINT MARKS
R - Rio

MONETARY SYSTEM
100 Centavos = 1 Escudo

POTUGUESE COLONY

REFORM COINAGE

100 Centavos = 1 Escudo

KM# 2 10 CENTAVOS **Composition:** Nickel-Bronze

Date	Mintage	F	VF	XF	Unc	BU
1929	500,000	1.50	5.50	20.00	50.00	—

KM# 15 10 CENTAVOS **Composition:** Bronze

Date	Mintage	F	VF	XF	Unc	BU
1962	500,000	0.50	1.25	4.50	12.00	—

KM# 15a 10 CENTAVOS **Composition:** Aluminum

Date	Mintage	F	VF	XF	Unc	BU
1971	1,000,000	0.35	0.65	1.25	3.50	—

KM# 3 20 CENTAVOS **Composition:** Nickel-Bronze

Date	Mintage	F	VF	XF	Unc	BU
1929	250,000	1.50	5.50	20.00	50.00	—

KM# 16.1 20 CENTAVOS **Composition:** Bronze **Size:** 18 mm.

Date	Mintage	F	VF	XF	Unc	BU
1962	250,000	0.50	1.25	5.50	15.00	—

KM# 16.2 20 CENTAVOS **Composition:** Bronze **Size:** 16 mm.

Date	Mintage	F	VF	XF	Unc	BU
1971	750,000	0.35	0.75	1.50	4.00	—

KM# 1 50 CENTAVOS **Composition:** Nickel-Bronze

Date	Mintage	F	VF	XF	Unc	BU
1928	—	30.00	90.00	350	900	—
1929	400,000	3.50	12.00	50.00	150	—

KM# 8 50 CENTAVOS **Composition:** Nickel-Bronze

Date	Mintage	F	VF	XF	Unc	BU
1948	80,000	10.00	30.00	100	265	—

KM# 10 50 CENTAVOS **Composition:** Copper-Nickel

Date	Mintage	F	VF	XF	Unc	BU
1951	48,000	1.75	3.50	25.00	70.00	—

KM# 17.1 50 CENTAVOS **Composition:** Bronze **Size:** 20 mm.

Date	Mintage	F	VF	XF	Unc	BU
1962	480,000	0.25	0.50	2.50	5.00	—

KM# 17.2 50 CENTAVOS **Composition:** Bronze **Size:** 22 mm.

Date	Mintage	F	VF	XF	Unc	BU
1971	600,000	0.20	0.35	1.50	3.00	—

KM# 4 ESCUDO **Composition:** Copper-Nickel

Date	Mintage	F	VF	XF	Unc
1939	100,000	9.00	25.00	100	285

KM# 9 ESCUDO **Composition:** Nickel-Bronze

Date	Mintage	F	VF	XF	Unc
1948	60,000	12.50	40.00	120	300

KM# 11 ESCUDO **Composition:** Copper-Nickel

Date	Mintage	F	VF	XF	Unc
1951	18,000	3.50	12.00	60.00	175

KM# 18 ESCUDO **Composition:** Bronze

Date	Mintage	F	VF	XF	Unc
1962	160,000	0.75	2.50	15.00	35.00
1971	350,000	0.35	0.75	1.50	3.50

KM# 5 2-1/2 ESCUDOS **Weight:** 3.5000 g. **Composition:** 0.6500 Silver .0732 oz. ASW

Date	Mintage	F	VF	XF	Unc
1939	80,000	10.00	30.00	100	300
1948	120,000	15.00	35.00	100	300

KM# 12 2-1/2 ESCUDOS **Weight:** 3.5000 g. **Composition:** 0.6500 Silver .0732 oz. ASW

Date	Mintage	F	VF	XF	Unc
1951	64,000	2.50	6.00	30.00	100

M# 19 2-1/2 ESCUDOS **Composition:** Copper-Nickel

e	Mintage	F	VF	XF	Unc	BU
2	140,000	0.75	1.50	5.00	15.00	—
'1	250,000	0.50	1.00	2.50	7.00	—

1# 6 5 ESCUDOS **Weight:** 7.0000 g. **Composition:** 0.6500 Silver .1462 oz. ASW

te	Mintage	F	VF	XF	Unc	BU
39	60,000	12.50	35.00	100	300	—
48	100,000	18.00	45.00	110	300	—

M# 13 5 ESCUDOS **Weight:** 7.0000 g. **Composition:** 0.6500 Silver .1462 oz. ASW **Size:** 25 mm.

te	Mintage	F	VF	XF	Unc	BU
51	72,000	2.50	6.00	20.00	45.00	—

M# 20 5 ESCUDOS **Weight:** 4.0000 g. **Composition:** 0.6000 Silver .0771 oz. ASW **Size:** 22 mm.

ate	Mintage	F	VF	XF	Unc	BU
962	88,000	1.00	2.00	5.50	12.00	—

(M# 22 5 ESCUDOS **Composition:** Copper-Nickel

ate	Mintage	F	VF	XF	Unc	BU
971	100,000	0.75	1.50	3.50	8.00	—

KM# 7 10 ESCUDOS **Weight:** 12.5000 g. **Composition:** 0.8350 Silver .3356 oz. ASW

ate	Mintage	F	VF	XF	Unc	BU
939	40,000	12.00	25.00	65.00	250	—

KM# 14 10 ESCUDOS **Weight:** 12.5000 g. **Composition:** 0.7200 Silver .2894 oz. ASW

Date	Mintage	F	VF	XF	Unc	BU
1951	40,000	3.00	7.00	15.00	35.00	—

KM# 23 10 ESCUDOS **Composition:** Copper-Nickel

Date	Mintage	F	VF	XF	Unc	BU
1971	100,000	1.25	2.50	5.50	12.50	—

KM# 24 20 ESCUDOS **Composition:** Nickel

Date	Mintage	F	VF	XF	Unc	BU
1971	75,000	1.50	3.00	6.00	13.50	—

KM# 21 50 ESCUDOS **Weight:** 18.0000 g. **Composition:** 0.6500 Silver .3762 oz. ASW **Subject:** 500th anniversary of discovery

Date	F	VF	XF	Unc	BU
1970	—	—	—	8.00	—
1970 Matte proof	—	—	—	—	—

Note: Produced at the Lisbon Mint on private contract.

DEMOCRATIC REPUBLIC

STANDARD COINAGE

100 Centimos = 1 Dobra

KM# 25 50 CENTIMOS **Composition:** Brass **Series:** F.A.O.

Date	Mintage	F	VF	XF	Unc	BU
1977	2,000,000	—	0.10	0.20	0.75	—
1977 Proof	2,500	Value: 3.00				

KM# 26 DOBRA **Composition:** Brass **Series:** F.A.O.

Date	Mintage	F	VF	XF	Unc	BU
1977	1,500,000	—	0.15	0.25	1.00	—
1977 Proof	2,500	Value: 3.00				

KM# 27 2 DOBRAS **Composition:** Copper-Nickel **Series:** F.A.O.

Date	Mintage	F	VF	XF	Unc	BU
1977	1,000,000	—	0.25	0.40	1.50	—
1977 Proof	2,500	Value: 3.50				

KM# 28 5 DOBRAS **Composition:** Copper-Nickel **Series:** F.A.O.

Date	Mintage	F	VF	XF	Unc	BU
1977	750,000	—	0.35	0.65	2.00	—
1977 Proof	2,500	Value: 5.00				

KM# 29 10 DOBRAS **Composition:** Copper-Nickel **Series:** F.A.O.

Date	Mintage	F	VF	XF	Unc	BU
1977	300,000	—	0.60	1.25	4.00	—
1977 Proof	2,500	Value: 7.00				

KM# 29a 10 DOBRAS **Composition:** Copper-Nickel Clad Steel **Series:** F.A.O.

Date	F	VF	XF	Unc	BU
1990	—	0.60	1.25	4.00	—

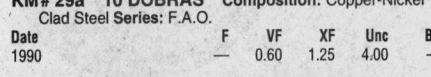

KM# 30 20 DOBRAS **Composition:** Copper-Nickel Clad Steel **Series:** F.A.O.

Date	Mintage	F	VF	XF	Unc	BU
1977	500,000	—	1.00	2.00	6.00	—
1977 Proof	2,500	Value: 10.00				

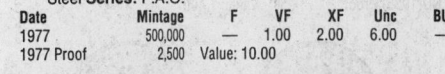

KM# 52 50 DOBRAS **Composition:** Copper-Nickel Clad Steel **Series:** F.A.O.

Date	F	VF	XF	Unc	BU
1990	—	—	—	6.00	—

KM# 41 100 DOBRAS **Composition:** Copper-Nickel **Subject:** World Fisheries Conference

Date	Mintage	F	VF	XF	Unc	BU
ND(1984)	1,000,000	—	—	—	9.00	—

KM# 41a 100 DOBRAS **Weight:** 28.2800 g. **Composition:** 0.9250 Silver .8411 oz. ASW **Subject:** World Fisheries Conference

Date	Mintage	F	VF	XF	Unc	BU
ND(1984) Proof	20,000	Value: 40.00				

KM# 41b 100 DOBRAS **Weight:** 47.5400 g. **Composition:** 0.9170 Gold 1.4017 oz. AGW **Subject:** World Fisheries Conference

Date	Mintage	F	VF	XF	Unc	BU
ND(1984) Proof	100	Value: 1,250				

KM# 42 100 DOBRAS **Composition:** Copper-Nickel **Subject:** 10th anniversary of independence

Date	F	VF	XF	Unc	BU
ND(1985)	—	—	—	6.50	—

KM# 42a 100 DOBRAS **Weight:** 28.2800 g. **Composition:** 0.9250 Silver .8411 oz. ASW **Subject:** 10th anniversary of independence

Date	Mintage	F	VF	XF	Unc	BU
ND(1985) Proof	1,000	Value: 42.50				

KM# 42b 100 DOBRAS **Weight:** 47.5400 g. **Composition:** 0.9170 Gold 1.4017 oz. AGW **Subject:** 10th anniversary of independence

Date	Mintage	F	VF	XF	Unc	BU
ND(1985) Proof	50	Value: 1,400				

KM# 87 100 DOBRAS **Composition:** Chrome Clad Steel **Obverse:** National arms **Reverse:** Denomination below bird

Date	F	VF	XF	Unc	BU
1997	—	—	—	1.25	—

KM# 31 250 DOBRAS **Weight:** 17.4000 g. **Composition:** 0.9250 Silver .5175 oz. ASW **Obverse:** Independence - world population

Date	Mintage	F	VF	XF	Unc	BU
1977	450	—	—	—	42.50	—
1977 Proof	750	Value: 40.00				

KM# 32 250 DOBRAS **Weight:** 17.4000 g. **Composition:** 0.9250 Silver .5175 oz. ASW **Obverse:** Independence - world friendship

Date	Mintage	F	VF	XF	Unc	BU
1977	450	—	—	—	42.50	—
1977 Proof	800	Value: 40.00				

KM# 33 250 DOBRAS **Weight:** 17.4000 g. **Composition:** 0.9250 Silver .5175 oz. ASW **Obverse:** Independence - folklore

Date	Mintage	F	VF	XF	Unc	BU
1977	300	—	—	—	42.50	—
1977 Proof	600	Value: 40.00				

KM# 34 250 DOBRAS **Weight:** 17.4000 g. **Composition:** 0.9250 Silver .5175 oz. ASW **Obverse:** Independence - world unity

Date	Mintage	F	VF	XF	Unc	BU
1977	400	—	—	—	42.50	—
1977 Proof	700	Value: 40.00				

KM# 35 250 DOBRAS **Weight:** 17.4000 g. **Composition:** 0.9250 Silver .5175 oz. ASW **Obverse:** Independence - mother and child

Date	Mintage	F	VF	XF	Unc	BU
1977	350	—	—	—	42.50	—
1977 Proof	700	Value: 40.00				

KM# 88 250 DOBRAS **Composition:** Chrome Cla Steel **Obverse:** National arms **Reverse:** Denominatio above bird

Date	F	VF	XF	Unc
1997	—	—	—	1.50

KM# 70 500 DOBRAS **Composition:** Copper-Nick **Reverse:** Elvis Presley

Date	F	VF	XF	Unc
1993	—	—	—	12.50

KM# 89 500 DOBRAS **Composition:** Chrome Clac Steel **Reverse:** Monkey

Date	F	VF	XF	Unc
1997	—	—	—	2.00

KM# 44 1000 DOBRAS **Weight:** 23.3300 g. **Composition:** 0.9250 Silver .6938 oz. ASW **Subject:** Soccer **Reverse:** 2 players

Date	Mintage	F	VF	XF	Unc
1990 Proof	15,000	Value: 30.00			

KM# 45 1000 DOBRAS **Weight:** 23.3300 g. **Composition:** 0.9250 Silver .6938 oz. ASW **Subject:** Soccer **Reverse:** 2 players running

Date	Mintage	F	VF	XF	Unc
1990 Proof	15,000	Value: 30.00			

M# 47 1000 DOBRAS **Weight:** 25.9600 g. **Composition:** 0.9990 Silver .8347 oz. ASW **Subject:** Soccer **Obverse:** Similar to KM#45 **Reverse:** 1 player

e		F	VF	XF	Unc	BU
0 Proof	—	Value: 45.00				

M# 48 1000 DOBRAS **Weight:** 25.9600 g. **Composition:** 0.9990 Silver .8347 oz. ASW **Subject:** Soccer **Reverse:** 2 players and ball

e		F	VF	XF	Unc	BU
90 Proof	—	Value: 45.00				

M# 49 1000 DOBRAS **Weight:** 20.0000 g. **Composition:** 0.9990 Silver .6431 oz. ASW **Subject:** National independence

ate		F	VF	XF	Unc	BU
90 Proof	—	Value: 37.50				

KM# 50 1000 DOBRAS **Weight:** 20.0000 g. **Composition:** 0.9990 Silver .6431 oz. ASW **Subject:** Vasco de Gama

ate		F	VF	XF	Unc	BU
990 Proof	—	Value: 37.50				

KM# 53 1000 DOBRAS **Weight:** 20.0000 g. **Composition:** 0.9990 Silver .6431 oz. ASW **Subject:** Olympics and discovery of America

Date		F	VF	XF	Unc	BU
1990 Proof	—	Value: 35.00				

KM# 73 1000 DOBRAS **Weight:** 23.7400 g. **Composition:** 0.9250 Silver .7060 oz. ASW **Series:** 1992 Olympics **Reverse:** Flame

Date	Mintage	F	VF	XF	Unc	BU
1990 Proof	10,000	Value: 32.50				

KM# 74 1000 DOBRAS **Weight:** 23.7400 g. **Composition:** 0.9250 Silver .7060 oz. ASW **Series:** 1992 Olympics **Reverse:** Diver

Date	Mintage	F	VF	XF	Unc	BU
1990 Proof	10,000	Value: 27.50				

KM# 54 1000 DOBRAS **Composition:** Copper-Nickel **Series:** Atlanta Olympics **Reverse:** Wrestling

Date		F	VF	XF	Unc	BU
ND(1993) Proof	—	Value: 28.50				

KM# 63 1000 DOBRAS **Composition:** Copper-Nickel **Series:** Atlanta Olympics **Reverse:** Swimmers

Date		F	VF	XF	Unc	BU
ND(1993) Proof	—	Value: 28.50				

KM# 55 1000 DOBRAS **Composition:** Copper-Nickel **Series:** Atlanta Olympics **Reverse:** Soccer players

Date		F	VF	XF	Unc	BU
ND(1993) Proof	—	Value: 28.50				

KM# 56 1000 DOBRAS **Composition:** Copper-Nickel **Series:** Atlanta Olympics **Reverse:** Boxer

Date		F	VF	XF	Unc	BU
ND(1993) Proof	—	Value: 28.50				

KM# 57 1000 DOBRAS **Composition:** Copper-Nickel **Series:** Atlanta Olympics **Reverse:** Bicyclist

Date		F	VF	XF	Unc	BU
ND(1993) Proof	—	Value: 28.50				

KM# 58 1000 DOBRAS **Composition:** Copper-Nickel **Series:** Atlanta Olympics **Reverse:** Karate competition

Date		F	VF	XF	Unc	BU
ND(1993) Proof	—	Value: 28.50				

KM# 59 1000 DOBRAS **Composition:** Copper-Nickel **Series:** Atlanta Olympics **Reverse:** Runner

Date		F	VF	XF	Unc	BU
ND(1993) Proof	—	Value: 28.50				

KM# 60 1000 DOBRAS **Composition:** Copper-Nickel **Series:** Atlanta Olympics **Reverse:** Field hockey players

Date		F	VF	XF	Unc	BU
ND(1993) Proof	—	Value: 28.50				

KM# 61 1000 DOBRAS **Composition:** Copper-Nickel **Series:** Atlanta Olympics **Reverse:** 4 track and field events

Date		F	VF	XF	Unc	BU
ND(1993) Proof	—	Value: 28.50				

KM# 62 1000 DOBRAS **Composition:** Copper-Nic **Series:** Atlanta Olympics **Reverse:** Surfer

Date		F	VF	XF	Unc
ND(1993) Proof	—	Value: 28.50			

KM# 64 1000 DOBRAS **Composition:** Copper-Nic **Series:** Atlanta Olympics **Reverse:** 3 gymnastic events

Date		F	VF	XF	Unc
ND(1993) Proof	—	Value: 28.50			

KM# 65 1000 DOBRAS **Composition:** Copper-Nick **Series:** Atlanta Olympics **Reverse:** Tennis players

Date		F	VF	XF	Unc
ND(1993) Proof	—	Value: 28.50			

M# 71 1000 DOBRAS **Weight:** 25.0000 g. **Composition:** 0.9250 Silver .7242 oz. ASW **Reverse:** Elvis Presley

ate	F	VF	XF	Unc	BU
993 Proof	—	Value: 30.00			

(M# 76 1000 DOBRAS **Weight:** 25.0000 g. **Composition:** 0.9250 Silver .7242 oz. ASW **Reverse:** Arms & falcon **Note:** Enamel.

ate	Mintage	F	VF	XF	Unc	BU
995 Proof	15,000	Value: 32.50				

KM# 77 1000 DOBRAS **Weight:** 25.0000 g. **Composition:** 0.9250 Silver .7242 oz. ASW **Reverse:** Porcelain rose **Note:** Enamel.

Date	Mintage	F	VF	XF	Unc	BU
1995 Proof	15,000	Value: 32.50				

KM# 78 1000 DOBRAS **Weight:** 25.0000 g. **Composition:** 0.9250 Silver .7242 oz. ASW **Reverse:** Seahorse and crab **Note:** Enamel.

Date	Mintage	F	VF	XF	Unc	BU
1995 Proof	15,000	Value: 35.00				

KM# 85a (KM85.1) 1000 DOBRAS **Weight:** 31.1035 g. **Composition:** 0.9990 Silver 1 oz. ASW **Subject:** Diana - Queen of the Hearts

Date	Mintage	F	VF	XF	Unc	BU
1997 Proof	5,000	Value: 32.50				
1997 Proof	5,000	Value: 32.50				

KM# 102 (KM85.2) 1000 DOBRAS **Weight:** 1.2500 g. **Composition:** 0.9990 Gold .0402 oz. AGW **Subject:** Diana - Queen of the Hearts **Obverse:** National arms **Reverse:** Profile of Lady Diana, crowds

Date	Mintage	F	VF	XF	Unc	BU
1997 Proof	3,000	Value: 60.00				
1997 Proof	3,000	Value: 60.00				

KM# 90 1000 DOBRAS **Composition:** Chrome Clad Steel **Reverse:** Flowers and denomination

Date	F	VF	XF	Unc	BU
1997	—	—	—	2.75	—

KM# 92 1000 DOBRAS **Composition:** Copper-Nickel **Reverse:** Heidiland - girl with goats

Date	Mintage	F	VF	XF	Unc	BU
1998	15,000	—	—	—	10.00	—

KM# 93 1000 DOBRAS **Weight:** 25.0000 g. **Composition:** 0.9250 Silver .7435 oz. ASW **Reverse:** Heidiland

Date	Mintage	F	VF	XF	Unc	BU
1998 Proof	10,000	Value: 32.50				

KM# 79 1000 DOBRAS Weight: 31.1035 g. Composition: 0.9990 Silver 1 oz. ASW Reverse: Peacock hologram

Date	Mintage	F	VF	XF	Unc	BU
1998(1997) Prooflike	10,000	—	—	—	42.50	—

KM# 80 1000 DOBRAS Weight: 31.1035 g. Composition: 0.9990 Silver 1 oz. ASW Reverse: Hummingbird hologram

Date	Mintage	F	VF	XF	Unc	BU
1998(1997) Prooflike	10,000	—	—	—	45.00	—

KM# 94 1000 DOBRAS Weight: 25.1400 g. Composition: 0.9250 Silver .7476 oz. ASW Subject: World Cup soccer - France 1998

Date	Mintage	F	VF	XF	Unc	BU
1998 Proof	10,000	Value: 35.00				

KM# 82 1000 DOBRAS Weight: 31.1035 g. Composition: 0.9990 Silver 1 oz. ASW Reverse: Butterfly hologram

Date	Mintage	F	VF	XF	Unc	BU
1998(1997) Prooflike	10,000	—	—	—	45.00	—

KM# 81 1000 DOBRAS Weight: 31.1035 g. Composition: 0.9990 Silver 1 oz. ASW Reverse: Fish hologram

Date	Mintage	F	VF	XF	Unc	BU
1998(1997) Prooflike	10,000	—	—	—	45.00	—

KM# 99 1000 DOBRAS Weight: 36.5500 g. Subject: Millennium Obverse: National arms Reverse: Perforated gold insert exposing digital clock Edge: Reeded Size: 34.9 mm. Note: Silver shell with gold insert encased digital clock. 8.1 millimeters thick.

Date		F	VF	XF	Unc	BU
1999 Proof	—	Value: 32.50				

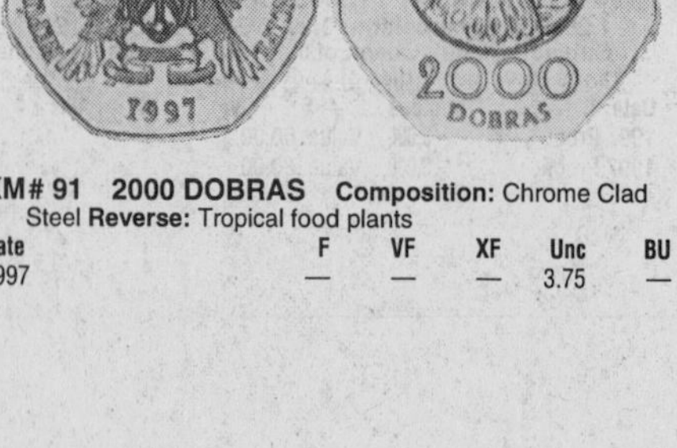

KM# 91 2000 DOBRAS Composition: Chrome Clad Steel Reverse: Tropical food plants

Date	F	VF	XF	Unc	BU
1997	—	—	—	3.75	—

KM# 86 2000 DOBRAS Weight: 25.0000 g. Composition: 0.9250 Silver .7435 oz. ASW Subject: Th Christian millennium Reverse: Year 2000 CE calendar

Date	Mintage	F	VF	XF	Unc
1998 Proof	5,000	Value: 28.00			

KM# 86a 2000 DOBRAS Composition: Copper-Nic Subject: Third Christian millennium Reverse: Year 2000 calendar

Date	F	VF	XF	Unc
1998 Prooflike	—	—	—	10.00

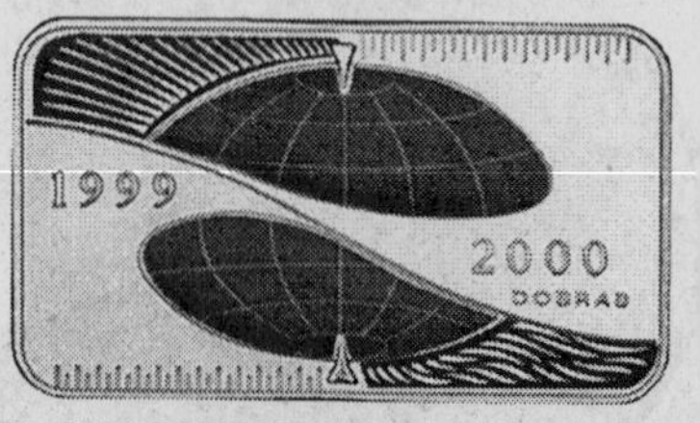

KM# 98 2000 DOBRAS Weight: 31.1600 g. Composition: 0.9990 Silver 1 oz. ASW Subject: Pseud millennium Obverse: National arms Reverse: Multicolor world and year split Edge: Plain Note: 27.1 x 47.2 millimete

Date		VG	F	VF	XF
1998 Proof	—	Value: 47.50			

KM# 36 2500 DOBRAS Weight: 6.4800 g. Composition: 0.9000 Gold .1875 oz. AGW Subject: Independence - world friendship

Date	Mintage	F	VF	XF	Unc
1977	100	—	—	—	240
1977 Proof	170	Value: 190			

M# 37 2500 DOBRAS **Weight:** 6.4800 g. **Composition:** 0.9000 Gold .1875 oz. AGW **Subject:** Independence - world population

te	Mintage	F	VF	XF	Unc	BU
77	100	—	—	—	240	—
7 Proof	170	Value: 190				

M# 38 2500 DOBRAS **Weight:** 6.4800 g. **Composition:** 0.9000 Gold .1875 oz. AGW **Subject:** Independence - folklore

te	Mintage	F	VF	XF	Unc	BU
77	100	—	—	—	240	—
7 Proof	170	Value: 190				

M# 39 2500 DOBRAS **Weight:** 6.4800 g. **Composition:** 0.9000 Gold .1875 oz. AGW **Subject:** Independence - world unity

ate	Mintage	F	VF	XF	Unc	BU
77	100	—	—	—	240	—
77 Proof	170	Value: 190				

M# 40 2500 DOBRAS **Weight:** 6.4800 g. **Composition:** 0.9000 Gold .1875 oz. AGW **Subject:** Independence - mother and child

ate	Mintage	F	VF	XF	Unc	BU
977	100	—	—	—	240	—
977 Proof	170	Value: 190				

M# 83 2500 DOBRAS **Weight:** 6.2207 g. **Composition:** 0.9999 Gold .2000 oz. AGW **Reverse:** Hummingbird hologram **Note:** Similar to 1,000 Dobras, KM#80.

ate	Mintage	F	VF	XF	Unc	BU
998(1997) Proof	2,500	Value: 250				

M# 84 2500 DOBRAS **Weight:** 6.2207 g. **Composition:** 0.9999 Gold .2000 oz. AGW **Reverse:** Butterfly hologram **Note:** Similar to 1,000 Dobras, KM#82.

ate	Mintage	F	VF	XF	Unc	BU
998(1997) Proof	2,500	Value: 250				

KM# 46 3500 DOBRAS **Weight:** 136.0800 g. **Composition:** 0.9250 Silver 4.3755 oz. ASW **Subject:** Wildlife protection **Reverse:** Sea turtle **Size:** 63 mm. **Note:** Illustration reduced.

Date	Mintage	F	VF	XF	Unc	BU
1990 Proof	750	Value: 150				

KM# 100 5000 DOBRAS **Weight:** 168.5600 g. **Subject:** Millennium **Obverse:** National arms **Reverse:** Perforated silver insert exposing digital clock **Edge:** Reeded **Note:** Silver shell with encased digital clock. 9 millimeters thick.

Date	F	VF	XF	Unc	BU
1999 Proof	—	Value: 70.00			

KM# 51 10000 DOBRAS **Weight:** 7.7750 g. **Composition:** 0.9000 Gold .2250 oz. AGW **Reverse:** Sea turtle

Date	Mintage	F	VF	XF	Unc	BU
1992 Proof	500	Value: 320				

KM# 72 25000 DOBRAS **Weight:** 15.5500 g. **Composition:** 0.9990 Gold .5 oz. AGW **Obverse:** National emblem **Reverse:** Elvis Presley

Date		F	VF	XF	Unc	BU
1993 Proof	—	Value: 550				

DUAL DENOMINATED COINAGE

KM# 67 500 DOBRAS - 1 ECU **Composition:** Copper-Nickel **Subject:** 15th anniversary of association with European Common Market

Date	Mintage	F	VF	XF	Unc	BU
1993	20,000	—	—	—	11.50	—

KM# 68 2500 DOBRAS - 5 ECU **Weight:** 25.0000 g. **Composition:** 0.9250 Silver .7434 oz. ASW **Subject:** 15th anniversary of association with European Common Market

Date	Mintage	F	VF	XF	Unc	BU
1993 Proof	12,000	Value: 32.50				

KM# 69 25000 DOBRAS - 50 ECU **Weight:** 6.7200 g. **Composition:** 0.9000 Gold .1944 oz. AGW **Subject:** 15th anniversary of association with European Common Market **Obverse:** National arms **Reverse:** Old harbor scene **Note:** Similar to 2500 Dobras, 5 Ecu, KM#68.

Date	Mintage	F	VF	XF	Unc	BU
1993 Proof	1,000	Value: 200				

KM# 95 2000 DOBRAS - 1 EURO **Composition:** Copper-Nickel **Obverse:** National arms **Reverse:** Helvetia portrait and multicolored Swiss flag in circle of stars applique, denomination

Date	Mintage	F	VF	XF	Unc	BU
1997 Proof	5,000	Value: 12.50				

KM# 96 10000 DOBRAS - 5 EURO **Weight:** 25.0000 g. **Composition:** 0.9250 Silver .7435 oz. ASW **Obverse:** National arms **Reverse:** Helvetia portrait and Swiss flag in star circle, denomination

Date	Mintage	F	VF	XF	Unc	BU
1998 Proof	5,000	Value: 35.00				

KM# 101 15000 DOBRAS - 7.5 EUROS **Weight:** 25.0000 g. **Composition:** Silver **Subject:** Switzerland and the European Union **Obverse:** National arms. **Reverse:** Helvetia viewing a Swiss flag within a circle of stars. **Edge:** Reeded. **Size:** 38.55 mm.

Date	F	VF	XF	Unc	BU
1997 Proof	—	Value: 40.00			

PATTERNS

KM#	Date	Mintage	Identification	Mkt Val
Pn1	ND(1994)	—	1000 Dobras. Copper-Nickel. 1 player.	55.00
Pn2	ND(1994)	—	1000 Dobras. Copper-Nickel. With denticles.	55.00
Pn3	ND(1994)	—	1000 Dobras. 0.9990 Silver. 19.7100 g. With 999 CuNi in error.	65.00
Pn4	ND(1994)	—	1000 Dobras. Copper-Nickel. 2 soccer players and E.P. 999.	55.00
Pn5	ND(1994)	—	1000 Dobras. 0.9990 Silver. 21.0000 g. E.P. 999.	65.00

PIEFORTS

KM#	Date	Mintage	Identification	Mkt Val
P1	1984	500	100 Dobras. Silver.	65.00

PROVAS

Standard metals; stamped "PROVA"; in field

KM#	Date	Mintage	Identification	Mkt Val
Pr1	1928	—	50 Centavos. KM1.	200
Pr2	1929	—	10 Centavos. KM2.	50.00
Pr3	1929	—	20 Centavos. KM3.	50.00
Pr4	1929	—	50 Centavos. KM1.	125
Pr5	1939	—	Escudo. KM5.	200
Pr6	1939	—	2-1/2 Escudos. KM5.	150
Pr7	1939	—	5 Escudos. KM6.	150
Pr8	1939	—	10 Escudos. KM7.	300
Pr9	1948	—	50 Centavos. KM8.	65.00
Pr10	1948	—	Escudo. KM9.	65.00
Pr11	1948	—	2-1/2 Escudos. KM5.	65.00
Pr12	1948	—	5 Escudos. KM6.	70.00
Pr13	1951	—	50 Centavos. KM10.	85.00
Pr14	1951	—	Escudo. KM11.	125
Pr15	1951	—	2-1/2 Escudos. KM12.	40.00
Pr16	1951	—	5 Escudos. KM13.	60.00
Pr17	1951	—	10 Escudos. KM14.	100
Pr18	1962	—	10 Centavos. KM15.	20.00
Pr19	1962	—	20 Centavos. KM16.	22.50
Pr20	1962	—	50 Centavos. KM17.	22.50
Pr21	1962	—	Escudo. KM18.	25.00
Pr22	1962	—	2-1/2 Escudos. KM19.	27.50
Pr23	1962	—	5 Escudos. KM20.	40.00
Pr24	1970	—	50 Escudos. KM21.	65.00
Pr25	1971	—	10 Centavos. KM15a.	20.00
Pr26	1971	—	20 Centavos. KM16.2.	20.00
Pr27	1971	—	50 Centavos. KM17.2.	20.00
Pr28	1971	—	Escudo. KM18.	20.00
Pr29	1971	—	2-1/2 Escudos. KM19.	22.50
Pr30	1971	—	5 Escudos. KM22.	25.00
Pr31	1971	—	10 Escudos. KM23.	27.50
Pr32	1971	—	20 Escudos. KM24.	30.00

MINT SETS

KM#	Date	Mintage	Identification	Issue Price	Mkt Val
MS1	1977 (5)	—	KM31-35	71.00	215
MS2	1977 (5)	100	KM36-40	655	1,200

PROOF SETS

KM#	Date	Mintage	Identification	Issue Price	Mkt Val
PS1	1977 (5)	—	KM31-35	93.50	200
PS2	1977 (5)	170	KM36-40	805	950

SAINT VINCENT

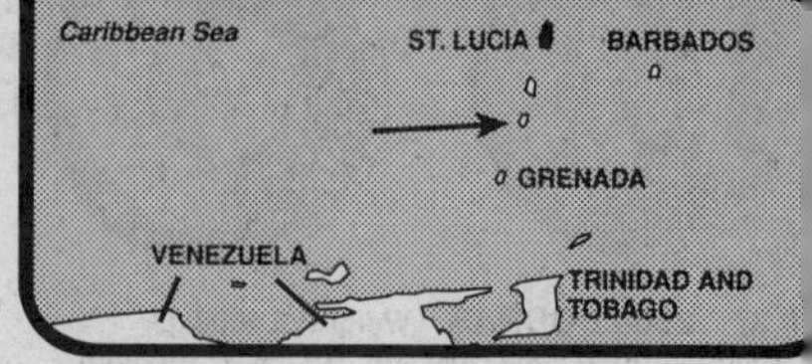

Saint Vincent and the Grenadines, consisting of the isla Saint Vincent and the northern Grenadines (a string of i stretching southward from Saint Vincent), is located in the W ward Islands of the West Indies, West of Barbados and sou Saint Lucia. The tiny nation has an area of 150sq. mi. (340 sq. and a population of *105,000.Capital: Kingstown. Arrowroot, ton, sugar, molasses, rum and cocoa are exported. Tourism principal industry.

Saint Vincent was discovered by Columbus on Jan. 22, 1 but was left undisturbed for more than a century. The B began colonization early in the 18th century against bitter and longed Carib resistance. The island was taken by the Frenc 1779, but was restored to the British in 1783, at the end o American Revolution. Saint Vincent and the northern Grenad became a British associated state in Oct. 1969. Independe under the name of Saint Vincent and the Grenadines was atta at midnight of Oct. 26, 1979. The new nation chose to becor member of the Commonwealth of Nations with Elizabeth I Head of State and Queen of Saint Vincent.

A local coinage was introduced in 1797, with the gold w drawn in 1818 and the silver in 1823. This was replaced by s ling. From the mid-1950's, Saint Vincent used the currency o British Caribbean Territories (Eastern Group), then that of East Caribbean States.

RULERS

British

MONETARY SYSTEM

Commencing 1979

100 Cents = 1 Dollar

BRITISH ADMINISTRATION

MODERN COINAGE

KM# 13 4 DOLLARS **Composition:** Copper-Nickel **Series:** F.A.O

Date	Mintage	F	VF	XF	Unc
1970	13,000	—	4.00	8.00	12.50
1970 Proof	2,000	Value: 22.50			

KM# 14 **10 DOLLARS** **Composition:** Copper-Nickel **Subject:** Royal Visit

Date	Mintage	F	VF	XF	Unc	BU
1985	100,000	—	—	—	10.00	—

KM# 14a **10 DOLLARS** **Weight:** 28.2800 g. **Composition:** 0.9250 Silver .8411 oz. ASW

Date	Mintage	F	VF	XF	Unc	BU
1985 Proof	5,000	Value: 55.00				

KM# 14b **10 DOLLARS** **Weight:** 47.5400 g. **Composition:** 0.9170 Gold 1.4013 oz. AGW **Subject:** Royal Visit

Date	Mintage	F	VF	XF	Unc	BU
1985 Proof	250	Value: 875				

KM# 15 **100 DOLLARS** **Weight:** 129.5900 g. **Composition:** 0.9250 Silver 3.8543 oz. ASW **Subject:** Tropical Birds - Pelican **Obverse:** Coat of arms **Size:** 63 mm. **Note:** Illustration reduced.

Date	Mintage	F	VF	XF	Unc	BU
1988 Proof	Est. 10,000	Value: 135				

SAN MARINO

The Republic of San Marino, the oldest and smallest republic in the world is located in north central Italy entirely surrounded by the Province of Emilia-Romagna. It has an area of 24 sq. mi. (60 sq. km.) and a population of *23,000. Capital: San Marino. The principal economic activities are farming, livestock raising, cheese making, tourism and light manufacturing. Building stone, lime, wheat, hides and baked goods are exported. The government derives most of its revenue from the sale of postage stamps for philatelic purposes.

According to tradition, San Marino was founded about350AD by a Christian stonecutter as a refuge against religious persecution. While gradually acquiring the institutions of an independent state, it avoided the factional fights of the Middle Ages and, except for a brief period in fief to Cesare Borgia, retained its freedom despite attacks on its sovereignty by the Papacy, the Lords of Rimini, Napoleon and Mussolini. In 1862 San Marino established a customs union with, and put itself under the protection of, Italy. A Communist-Socialist coalition controlled the Government for 12 years after World War II. The Christian Democratic Party has been the core of government since1957. In 1978 a Communist-Socialist coalition again came into power and remained in control until 1991.

San Marino has its own coinage, but Italian and Vatican City coins and currency are also in circulation.

MINT MARKS

M - Milan

R – Rome

MONETARY SYSTEM

100 Centesimi = 1 Lira

REPUBLIC

STANDARD COINAGE

100 Centesimi = 1 Lira

KM# 12 **5 CENTESIMI** **Composition:** Bronze

Date	Mintage	F	VF	XF	Unc	BU
1935R	400,000	1.25	2.00	3.00	5.50	—
1936R	400,000	1.25	2.00	3.00	5.50	—
1937R	400,000	1.25	2.00	3.00	5.50	—
1938R	200,000	1.50	2.25	3.50	6.50	—

KM# 13 **10 CENTESIMI** **Composition:** Bronze

Date	Mintage	F	VF	XF	Unc	BU
1935R	300,000	1.50	2.25	3.50	7.00	—
1936R	300,000	1.50	2.25	3.50	7.00	—
1937R	300,000	1.50	2.25	3.50	7.00	—
1938R	400,000	1.50	2.25	3.50	7.00	—

KM# 4 **LIRA** **Weight:** 5.0000 g. **Composition:** 0.8350 Silver .1342 oz. ASW

Date	Mintage	F	VF	XF	Unc	BU
1906R	30,000	15.00	22.50	40.00	75.00	—

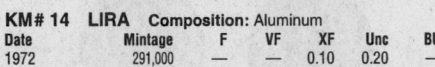

KM# 14 **LIRA** **Composition:** Aluminum

Date	Mintage	F	VF	XF	Unc	BU
1972	291,000	—	—	0.10	0.20	—

KM# 22 **LIRA** **Composition:** Aluminum

Date	Mintage	F	VF	XF	Unc	BU
1973	291,000	—	—	0.10	0.20	—

KM# 30 **LIRA** **Composition:** Aluminum

Date	Mintage	F	VF	XF	Unc	BU
1974	276,000	—	—	0.25	1.25	—

KM# 40 **LIRA** **Composition:** Aluminum

Date	Mintage	F	VF	XF	Unc	BU
1975	291,000	—	—	0.25	1.25	—

KM# 51 **LIRA** **Composition:** Aluminum

Date	Mintage	F	VF	XF	Unc	BU
1976	195,000	—	—	0.10	0.20	—

KM# 63 **LIRA** **Composition:** Aluminum **Series:** F.A.O.

Date	Mintage	F	VF	XF	Unc	BU
1977	1,180,000	—	—	0.10	0.20	—

KM# 76 **LIRA** **Composition:** Aluminum

Date	Mintage	F	VF	XF	Unc	BU
1978	130,000	—	—	0.15	0.30	—

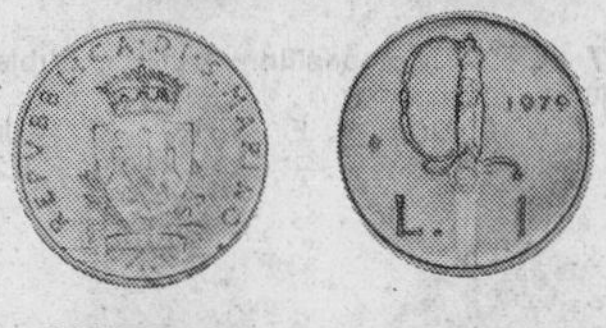

KM# 89 **LIRA** **Composition:** Aluminum

Date	Mintage	F	VF	XF	Unc	BU
1979	125,000	—	—	0.15	0.30	—

KM# 102 **LIRA** **Composition:** Aluminum **Series:** 1980 Olympics

Date	Mintage	F	VF	XF	Unc	BU
1980	125,000	—	—	0.15	0.30	—

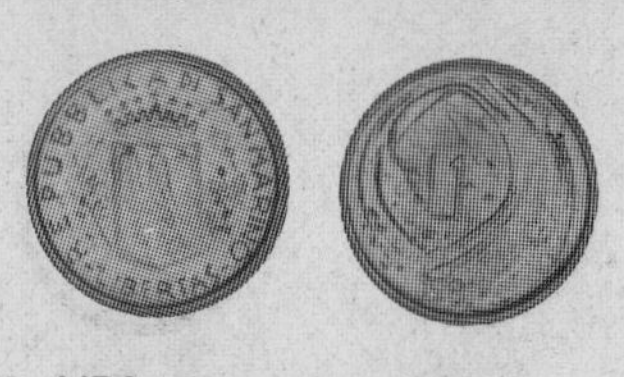

KM# 116 LIRA **Composition:** Aluminum

Date	Mintage	F	VF	XF	Unc	BU
1981	100,000	—	—	0.15	0.30	—

KM# 131 LIRA **Composition:** Aluminum **Subject:** Social conquest

Date	Mintage	F	VF	XF	Unc	BU
1982R	78,000	—	—	0.15	0.30	—

KM# 145 LIRA **Composition:** Aluminum **Subject:** Nuclear war threat **Reverse:** Beast of war

Date	Mintage	F	VF	XF	Unc	BU
1983R	72,000	—	—	0.20	0.40	—

KM# 159 LIRA **Composition:** Aluminum **Reverse:** Hippocrates

Date	Mintage	F	VF	XF	Unc	BU
1984R	65,000	—	—	0.20	0.40	—

KM# 173 LIRA **Composition:** Aluminum **Subject:** War on drugs **Reverse:** Male figure

Date	Mintage	F	VF	XF	Unc	BU
1985R	60,000	—	—	0.10	0.25	—

KM# 187 LIRA **Composition:** Aluminum **Subject:** Revolution of technology

Date	Mintage	F	VF	XF	Unc	BU
1986R	50,000	—	—	0.10	0.25	—

KM# 201 LIRA **Composition:** Aluminum **Subject:** 15th Anniversary - Resumption of Coinage

Date	Mintage	F	VF	XF	Unc	BU
1987R	83,000	—	—	0.10	0.25	—

KM# 218 LIRA **Composition:** Aluminum **Subject:** Fortifications **Reverse:** Corner Tower

Date	Mintage	F	VF	XF	Unc	BU
1988R	38,000	—	—	0.10	0.25	—

KM# 231 LIRA **Composition:** Aluminum **Subject:** History **Reverse:** Stone Age tool

Date	Mintage	F	VF	XF	Unc	BU
1989R	37,000	—	—	0.10	0.25	—

KM# 248 LIRA **Composition:** Aluminum **Subject:** 1,600 years of history **Reverse:** Saint

Date	Mintage	F	VF	XF	Unc	BU
1990R	36,000	—	—	0.10	0.25	—

KM# 261 LIRA **Composition:** Aluminum **Reverse:** Hands holding hammer and chisel

Date	F	VF	XF	Unc	BU
1991R	—	—	0.10	0.25	—

KM# 278 LIRA **Composition:** Aluminum **Subject:** Columbus **Reverse:** Potato plant and potatoes

Date	F	VF	XF	Unc	BU
ND(1992)R	—	—	0.10	0.25	—

KM# 293 LIRA **Composition:** Aluminum **Reverse:** Seedling

Date	F	VF	XF	Unc	BU
1993R	—	—	0.10	0.25	—

KM# 306 LIRA **Composition:** Aluminum **Reverse:** Mother and child

Date	Mintage	F	VF	XF	Unc	BU
1994R	40,000	—	—	0.10	0.25	—

KM# 322 LIRA **Composition:** Aluminum **Reverse:** Child on broken sword

Date	F	VF	XF	Unc	BU
1995R	—	—	0.10	0.25	—

KM# 349 LIRA **Composition:** Aluminum **Subject:** Talete - Child of the Universe

Date	Mintage	F	VF	XF	Unc	BU
1996	32,000	—	—	0.10	0.25	—

KM# 359 LIRA **Composition:** Aluminum **Subject:** The arts - prehistoric

Date	Mintage	F	VF	XF	Unc	BU
1997	28,000	—	—	0.10	0.25	—

KM# 5 2 LIRE **Weight:** 10.0000 g. **Composition:** 0.8350 Silver .2684 oz. ASW

Date	Mintage	F	VF	XF	Unc	BU
1906R	15,000	25.00	40.00	80.00	165	—

KM# 15 2 LIRE **Composition:** Aluminum

Date	Mintage	F	VF	XF	Unc	BU
1972	291,000	—	—	0.10	0.30	—

KM# 23 2 LIRE **Composition:** Aluminum

Date	Mintage	F	VF	XF	Unc	BU
1973	291,000	—	—	0.20	1.00	—

KM# 31 2 LIRE **Composition:** Aluminum

Date	Mintage	F	VF	XF	Unc	BU
1974	276,000	—	—	0.25	1.25	—

KM# 41 2 LIRE **Composition:** Aluminum

Date	Mintage	F	VF	XF	Unc	B
1975	291,000	—	—	0.25	1.25	—

KM# 52 2 LIRE **Composition:** Aluminum

Date	Mintage	F	VF	XF	Unc
1976	195,000	—	—	0.10	0.30

KM# 64 2 LIRE **Composition:** Aluminum

Date	Mintage	F	VF	XF	Unc
1977	180,000	—	—	0.10	0.30

I# 77 2 LIRE Composition: Aluminum

e	Mintage	F	VF	XF	Unc	BU
'8	130,000	—	—	0.10	0.30	—

M# 90 2 LIRE Composition: Aluminum

te	Mintage	F	VF	XF	Unc	BU
79	125,000	—	—	0.10	0.30	—

M# 103 2 LIRE Composition: Aluminum **Series:** 1980 Olympics **Reverse:** Soccer player

te	Mintage	F	VF	XF	Unc	BU
30	125,000	—	—	0.25	0.75	—

M# 117 2 LIRE Composition: Aluminum

ate	Mintage	F	VF	XF	Unc	BU
81	100,000	—	—	0.10	0.30	—

M# 132 2 LIRE Composition: Aluminum **Subject:** Social conquests

ate	Mintage	F	VF	XF	Unc	BU
982R	78,000	—	—	0.10	0.30	—

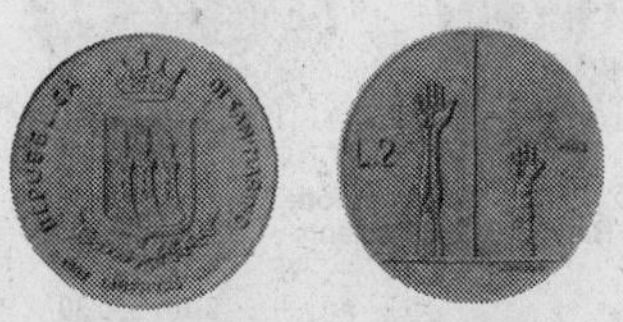

M# 146 2 LIRE Composition: Aluminum **Subject:** Nuclear war threat **Reverse:** 2 arms

ate	Mintage	F	VF	XF	Unc	BU
983R	72,000	—	—	0.20	0.40	—

M# 160 2 LIRE Composition: Aluminum **Reverse:** Leonardo da Vinci

ate	Mintage	F	VF	XF	Unc	BU
984R	65,000	—	—	0.20	0.40	—

M# 174 2 LIRE Composition: Aluminum **Subject:** War on drugs **Reverse:** Clenched fist

ate	Mintage	F	VF	XF	Unc	BU
985R	60,000	—	—	0.10	0.25	—

KM# 188 2 LIRE Composition: Aluminum **Subject:** Revolution of technology

Date	Mintage	F	VF	XF	Unc	BU
1986R	50,000	—	—	0.10	0.25	—

KM# 202 2 LIRE Composition: Aluminum **Subject:** 15th anniversary - resumption of coinage

Date	Mintage	F	VF	XF	Unc	BU
1987R	83,000	—	—	0.10	0.25	—

KM# 219 2 LIRE Composition: Aluminum **Subject:** Fortifications **Reverse:** Fortified archway

Date	Mintage	F	VF	XF	Unc	BU
1988R	38,000	—	—	0.10	0.25	—

KM# 232 2 LIRE Composition: Aluminum **Subject:** History **Reverse:** Wheat stalk and olive branch

Date	Mintage	F	VF	XF	Unc	BU
1989R	37,000	—	—	0.10	0.25	—

KM# 249 2 LIRE Composition: Aluminum **Subject:** 1,600 years of history **Reverse:** Figure with spear

Date	Mintage	F	VF	XF	Unc	BU
1990R	36,000	—	—	0.10	0.25	—

KM# 262 2 LIRE Composition: Aluminum **Reverse:** Hands with interlocked fingers

Date	F	VF	XF	Unc	BU
1991R	—	—	0.10	0.25	—

KM# 279 2 LIRE Composition: Aluminum **Subject:** Columbus **Reverse:** Ear of corn

Date	F	VF	XF	Unc	BU
ND(1992)R	—	—	0.10	0.25	—

KM# 294 2 LIRE Composition: Aluminum **Reverse:** Rose

Date	F	VF	XF	Unc	BU
1993R	—	—	0.10	0.25	—

KM# 307 2 LIRE Composition: Aluminum **Reverse:** Stonecutter at work

Date	Mintage	F	VF	XF	Unc	BU
1994R	40,000	—	—	0.10	0.25	—

KM# 323 2 LIRE Composition: Aluminum **Reverse:** Child with toy castle

Date	F	VF	XF	Unc	BU
1995R	—	—	0.10	0.25	—

KM# 350 2 LIRE Composition: Aluminum **Reverse:** Socrates

Date	Mintage	F	VF	XF	Unc	BU
1996	32,000	—	—	0.10	0.25	—

KM# 360 2 LIRE Composition: Aluminum **Subject:** The arts - literature **Reverse:** Dante holding Divine Comedy

Date	Mintage	F	VF	XF	Unc	BU
1997	28,000	—	—	0.10	0.25	—

KM# 9 5 LIRE Weight: 5.0000 g. **Composition:** 0.8350 Silver .1342 oz. ASW

Date	Mintage	F	VF	XF	Unc	BU
1931R	50,000	3.50	5.50	10.00	25.00	—
1932R	50,000	3.50	5.50	10.00	25.00	—
1933R	50,000	3.50	5.50	8.50	20.00	—
1935R	200,000	3.50	5.50	8.50	20.00	—
1936R	Inc. above	3.50	5.50	8.50	20.00	—
1937R	100,000	3.50	5.50	8.50	20.00	—
1938R	120,000	3.50	5.50	8.50	20.00	—

KM# 16 5 LIRE Composition: Aluminum

Date	Mintage	F	VF	XF	Unc	BU
1972	291,000	—	—	0.10	0.35	—

KM# 24 5 LIRE Composition: Aluminum

Date	Mintage	F	VF	XF	Unc	BU
1973	291,000	—	—	0.10	0.35	—

KM# 32 5 LIRE **Composition:** Aluminum **Reverse:** Porcupine

Date	Mintage	F	VF	XF	Unc	BU
1974	276,000	—	—	0.25	1.25	—

KM# 42 5 LIRE **Composition:** Aluminum

Date	Mintage	F	VF	XF	Unc	BU
1975	291,000	—	—	0.20	1.00	—

KM# 53 5 LIRE **Composition:** Aluminum **Series:** F.A.O.

Date	Mintage	F	VF	XF	Unc	BU
1976	695,000	—	—	0.10	0.25	—

KM# 65 5 LIRE **Composition:** Aluminum

Date	Mintage	F	VF	XF	Unc	BU
1977	180,000	—	—	0.10	0.35	—

KM# 78 5 LIRE **Composition:** Aluminum

Date	Mintage	F	VF	XF	Unc	BU
1978	130,000	—	—	0.10	0.35	—

KM# 91 5 LIRE **Composition:** Aluminum

Date	Mintage	F	VF	XF	Unc	BU
1979	125,000	—	—	0.10	0.35	—

KM# 104 5 LIRE **Composition:** Aluminum **Series:** 1980 Olympics

Date	Mintage	F	VF	XF	Unc	BU
1980	125,000	—	—	0.25	0.75	—

KM# 118 5 LIRE **Composition:** Aluminum

Date	Mintage	F	VF	XF	Unc	BU
1981	100,000	—	—	0.25	0.75	—

KM# 133 5 LIRE **Composition:** Aluminum **Subject:** Social conquests

Date	Mintage	F	VF	XF	Unc	BU
1982R	78,000	—	—	0.10	0.30	—

KM# 147 5 LIRE **Composition:** Aluminum **Subject:** Nuclear war threat **Reverse:** Arm in window

Date	Mintage	F	VF	XF	Unc	BU
1983R	72,000	—	—	0.20	0.40	—

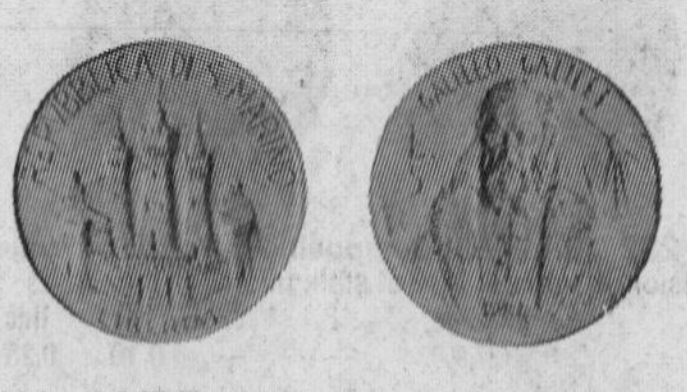

KM# 161 5 LIRE **Composition:** Aluminum **Reverse:** Galileo

Date	Mintage	F	VF	XF	Unc	BU
1984R	65,000	—	—	0.20	0.40	—

KM# 175 5 LIRE **Composition:** Aluminum **Subject:** War on drugs **Reverse:** Face of addict

Date	Mintage	F	VF	XF	Unc	BU
1985R	60,000	—	—	0.10	0.30	—

KM# 189 5 LIRE **Composition:** Aluminum **Subject:** Revolution of technology

Date	Mintage	F	VF	XF	Unc	BU
1986R	50,000	—	—	0.10	0.30	—

KM# 203 5 LIRE **Composition:** Aluminum **Subject:** 15th Anniversary - Resumption of Coinage

Date	Mintage	F	VF	XF	Unc	BU
1987R	83,000	—	—	0.10	0.30	—

KM# 220 5 LIRE **Composition:** Aluminum **Subject:** Fortification **Reverse:** Round corner tower

Date	Mintage	F	VF	XF	Unc
1988R	38,000	—	—	0.10	0.30

KM# 233 5 LIRE **Composition:** Aluminum **Subject:** History **Reverse:** Bunch of grapes

Date	Mintage	F	VF	XF	Unc
1989R	37,000	—	—	0.10	0.30

KM# 250 5 LIRE **Composition:** Aluminum **Subject:** 1,600 years of history **Reverse:** 2 facing figures

Date	Mintage	F	VF	XF	Unc
1990R	36,000	—	—	0.10	0.30

KM# 263 5 LIRE **Composition:** Aluminum **Reverse:** Hand holding quill

Date	F	VF	XF	Unc
1991R	—	—	0.10	0.30

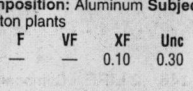

KM# 280 5 LIRE **Composition:** Aluminum **Subject:** Columbus **Reverse:** Cotton plants

Date	F	VF	XF	Unc
ND(1992)R	—	—	0.10	0.30

KM# 295 5 LIRE **Composition:** Aluminum **Reverse:** Spade and hoe

Date	F	VF	XF	Unc
1993R	—	—	0.10	0.30

KM# 308 5 LIRE **Composition:** Aluminum **Reverse:** Marino and Leo with tools

Date	Mintage	F	VF	XF	Unc
1994R	40,000	—	—	0.10	0.30

KM# 324 5 LIRE **Composition:** Aluminum **Reverse:** Child with 2 deer

Date	F	VF	XF	Unc	BU
1995R	—	—	0.10	0.30	—

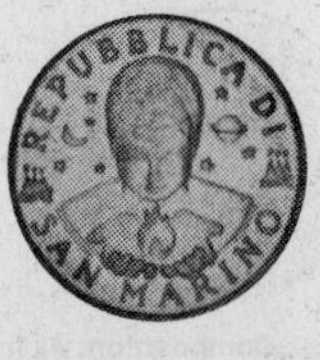

KM# 351 5 LIRE **Composition:** Aluminum **Reverse:** Plato

Date	Mintage	F	VF	XF	Unc	BU
1996	32,000	—	—	0.10	0.30	—

KM# 361 5 LIRE **Composition:** Aluminum **Subject:** The arts - theater **Reverse:** Hamlet, skull

Date	Mintage	F	VF	XF	Unc	BU
1997	28,000	—	—	0.10	0.30	—

KM# 7 10 LIRE **Weight:** 3.2258 g. **Composition:** 0.9000 Gold .0933 oz. AGW **Note:** 16,000 coins melted at the mint.

Date	Mintage	F	VF	XF	Unc	BU
1925R	20,000	175	325	450	750	—

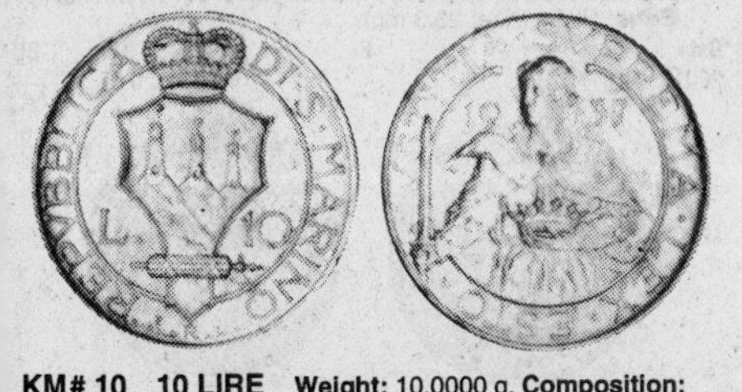

KM# 10 10 LIRE **Weight:** 10.0000 g. **Composition:** 0.8350 Silver .2684 oz. ASW

Date	Mintage	F	VF	XF	Unc	BU
1931R	25,000	8.50	15.00	35.00	75.00	—
1932R	25,000	8.50	15.00	35.00	75.00	—
1933R	25,000	8.50	15.00	35.00	75.00	—
1935R	30,000	6.50	10.00	25.00	60.00	—
1936R	Inc. above	10.00	18.00	40.00	85.00	—
1937R	15,000	6.50	10.00	25.00	60.00	—
1938R	10,000	12.00	20.00	50.00	100	—

KM# 17 10 LIRE **Composition:** Aluminum

Date	Mintage	F	VF	XF	Unc	BU
1972	291,000	—	0.10	0.20	0.50	—

KM# 25 10 LIRE **Composition:** Aluminum

Date	Mintage	F	VF	XF	Unc	BU
1973	291,000	—	0.10	0.15	0.40	—

KM# 33 10 LIRE **Composition:** Aluminum **Series:** F.A.O.

Date	Mintage	F	VF	XF	Unc	BU
1974	1,276,000	—	—	0.15	0.45	—

KM# 43 10 LIRE **Composition:** Aluminum

Date	Mintage	F	VF	XF	Unc	BU
1975	291,000	—	0.10	0.25	1.00	—

KM# 54 10 LIRE **Composition:** Aluminum

Date	Mintage	F	VF	XF	Unc	BU
1976	195,000	—	0.10	0.15	0.40	—

KM# 66 10 LIRE **Composition:** Aluminum

Date	Mintage	F	VF	XF	Unc	BU
1977	180,000	—	0.10	0.15	0.40	—

KM# 79 10 LIRE **Composition:** Aluminum

Date	Mintage	F	VF	XF	Unc	BU
1978	130,000	—	0.10	0.15	0.40	—

KM# 92 10 LIRE **Composition:** Aluminum

Date	Mintage	F	VF	XF	Unc	BU
1979	125,000	—	0.10	0.15	0.40	—

KM# 105 10 LIRE **Composition:** Aluminum **Series:** 1980 Olympics

Date	Mintage	F	VF	XF	Unc	BU
1980	125,000	—	0.25	0.50	0.80	—

KM# 119 10 LIRE **Composition:** Aluminum

Date	Mintage	F	VF	XF	Unc	BU
1981	100,000	—	0.10	0.20	0.50	—

KM# 134 10 LIRE **Composition:** Aluminum **Subject:** Social conquests

Date	Mintage	F	VF	XF	Unc	BU
1982R	78,000	—	0.10	0.20	0.50	—

KM# 148 10 LIRE **Composition:** Aluminum **Subject:** Nuclear war threat **Reverse:** 2 arms in frame

Date	Mintage	F	VF	XF	Unc	BU
1983R	72,000	—	0.10	0.25	0.75	—

KM# 162 10 LIRE **Composition:** Aluminum **Reverse:** Alessandro Volta

Date	Mintage	F	VF	XF	Unc	BU
1984R	65,000	—	0.10	0.25	0.75	—

KM# 176 10 LIRE **Composition:** Aluminum **Subject:** War on drugs **Reverse:** Mother lecturing son

Date	Mintage	F	VF	XF	Unc	BU
1985R	60,000	—	—	0.10	0.35	—

KM# 190 10 LIRE Composition: Aluminum **Subject:** Revolution of technology

Date	Mintage	F	VF	XF	Unc	BU
1986R	50,000	—	—	0.10	0.35	—

KM# 204 10 LIRE Composition: Aluminum **Subject:** 15th Anniversary - Resumption of Coinage

Date	Mintage	F	VF	XF	Unc	BU
1987R	83,000	—	—	0.10	0.35	—

KM# 221 10 LIRE Composition: Aluminum **Subject:** Fortifications **Reverse:** Sloping fortress wall

Date	Mintage	F	VF	XF	Unc	BU
1988R	38,000	—	—	0.10	0.35	—

KM# 234 10 LIRE Composition: Aluminum **Subject:** History **Reverse:** Ancient pottery

Date	Mintage	F	VF	XF	Unc	BU
1989R	37,000	—	—	0.10	0.35	—

KM# 251 10 LIRE Composition: Aluminum **Subject:** 1,600 years of history **Reverse:** Soldier

Date	Mintage	F	VF	XF	Unc	BU
1990R	36,000	—	—	0.10	0.35	—

KM# 264 10 LIRE Composition: Aluminum **Reverse:** Hand holding castle tower

Date	F	VF	XF	Unc	BU
1991R	—	—	0.10	0.35	—

KM# 281 10 LIRE Composition: Aluminum **Subject:** Columbus **Reverse:** Dolphin and ship

Date	F	VF	XF	Unc	BU
ND(1992)R	—	—	0.20	0.75	—

KM# 296 10 LIRE Composition: Aluminum **Reverse:** Corinthian column

Date	F	VF	XF	Unc	BU
1993R	—	—	0.10	0.35	—

KM# 309 10 LIRE Composition: Aluminum **Reverse:** Marino and Leo working

Date	Mintage	F	VF	XF	Unc	BU
1994R	40,000	—	—	0.10	0.35	—

KM# 325 10 LIRE Composition: Aluminum **Reverse:** Child with 2 urns

Date	F	VF	XF	Unc	BU
1995R	—	—	0.10	0.35	—

KM# 352 10 LIRE Composition: Aluminum **Reverse:** Aristotle

Date	Mintage	F	VF	XF	Unc	BU
1996	28,000	—	—	0.10	0.35	—

KM# 362 10 LIRE Composition: Aluminum **Subject:** The Arts - Architecture

Date	Mintage	F	VF	XF	Unc	BU
1997	28,000	—	—	0.10	0.35	—

KM# 378 10 LIRE Composition: Aluminum **Subject:** Mathematics **Reverse:** Hand and geometric shape

Date	F	VF	XF	Unc	BU
1998	—	—	0.10	0.35	—

KM# 389 10 LIRE Composition: Aluminum **Subject:** Exploration **Obverse:** Crowned arms **Reverse:** Earth flat, as once envisioned

Date	F	VF	XF	Unc	BU
1999	—	—	0.10	0.35	—

KM# 399 10 LIRE Weight: 1.6000 g. **Composition:** Aluminum **Subject:** Love **Obverse:** Child of the Universe **Reverse:** Child on flower on star **Edge:** Plain **Size:** 23.3 mm. **Note:** Struck at Rome.

Date	F	VF	XF	Unc	BU
2000	—	—	—	0.35	—

KM# 424 10 LIRE Weight: 1.6000 g. **Composition:** Aluminum **Obverse:** Three towers. **Reverse:** Wheat stalks. **Edge:** Plain. **Size:** 23.3 mm.

Date	F	VF	XF	Unc	BU
2001	—	—	—	0.35	—

KM# 8 20 LIRE Weight: 6.4516 g. **Composition:** 0.9000 Gold .1867 oz. AGW **Note:** 7,334 coins were melted at the mint.

Date	Mintage	F	VF	XF	Unc	BU
1925R	9,334	400	700	1,150	2,200	—

KM# 11 20 LIRE Weight: 15.0000 g. **Composition:** 0.8000 Silver .3858 oz. ASW

Date	Mintage	F	VF	XF	Unc	BU
1931R	10,000	25.00	45.00	90.00	185	—
1932R	10,000	35.00	60.00	110	220	—
1933R	10,000	30.00	50.00	100	200	—
1935R	10,000	30.00	50.00	100	200	—
1936R	Inc. above	60.00	125	200	400	—

KM# 11a 20 LIRE Weight: 20.0000 g. **Composition:** 0.8000 Silver .5145 oz. ASW

Date	Mintage	F	VF	XF	Unc	BU
1935R Rare	—	—	—	—	—	—
1937R	5,100	100	200	400	725	—
1938R	2,500	200	400	800	1,250	—

KM# 18 20 LIRE Composition: Aluminum-Bronze

Date	Mintage	F	VF	XF	Unc	BU
1972	291,000	—	0.10	0.25	0.60	—

KM# 26 20 LIRE Composition: Aluminum-Bronze

Date	Mintage	F	VF	XF	Unc	BU
1973	291,000	—	0.10	0.25	0.60	—

KM# 34 20 LIRE Composition: Aluminum-Bronze

Date	Mintage	F	VF	XF	Unc	BU
1974	276,000	—	0.10	0.30	1.00	—

KM# 44 20 LIRE Composition: Aluminum-Bronze
Series: F.A.O.

Date	Mintage	F	VF	XF	Unc	BU
1975	291,000	—	0.10	0.30	0.75	—

KM# 55 20 LIRE Composition: Aluminum-Bronze

Date	Mintage	F	VF	XF	Unc	BU
1976	195,000	—	0.10	0.25	0.60	—

KM# 67 20 LIRE Composition: Aluminum-Bronze

Date	Mintage	F	VF	XF	Unc	BU
1977	180,000	—	0.10	0.25	0.60	—

KM# 80 20 LIRE Composition: Aluminum-Bronze

Date	Mintage	F	VF	XF	Unc	BU
1978	130,000	—	0.10	0.25	0.60	—

KM# 93 20 LIRE Composition: Aluminum-Bronze

Date	Mintage	F	VF	XF	Unc	BU
1979	125,000	—	0.10	0.30	0.60	—

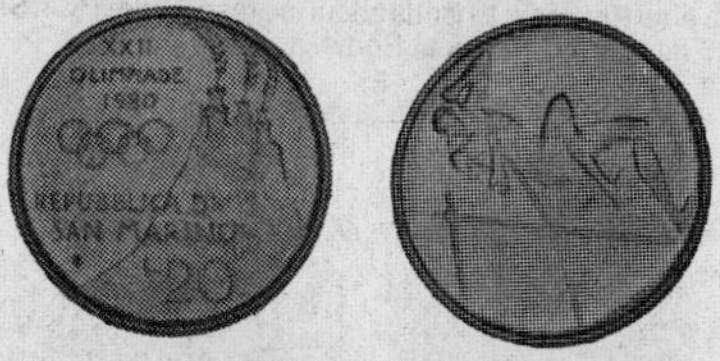

KM# 106 20 LIRE Composition: Aluminum-Bronze
Series: 1980 Olympics

Date	Mintage	F	VF	XF	Unc	BU
1980	125,000	—	0.25	0.50	1.00	—

KM# 120 20 LIRE Composition: Aluminum-Bronze

Date	Mintage	F	VF	XF	Unc	BU
1981	100,000	—	0.10	0.30	0.65	—

KM# 135 20 LIRE Composition: Aluminum-Bronze
Subject: Social conquests

Date	Mintage	F	VF	XF	Unc	BU
1982R	78,000	—	0.10	0.25	0.60	—

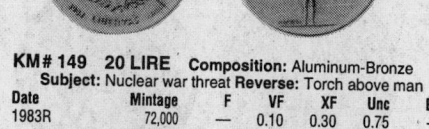

KM# 149 20 LIRE Composition: Aluminum-Bronze
Subject: Nuclear war threat **Reverse:** Torch above man

Date	Mintage	F	VF	XF	Unc	BU
1983R	72,000	—	0.10	0.30	0.75	—

KM# 163 20 LIRE Composition: Aluminum-Bronze
Reverse: Louis Pasteur

Date	Mintage	F	VF	XF	Unc	BU
1984R	65,000	—	0.10	0.30	0.75	—

KM# 177 20 LIRE Composition: Aluminum-Bronze
Subject: War on drugs **Reverse:** Open hand

Date	Mintage	F	VF	XF	Unc	BU
1985R	60,000	—	—	0.15	0.55	—

KM# 191 20 LIRE Composition: Aluminum-Bronze
Subject: Revolution of technology

Date	Mintage	F	VF	XF	Unc	BU
1986R	50,000	—	—	0.15	0.55	—

KM# 205 20 LIRE Composition: Aluminum-Bronze
Subject: 15th anniversary - resumption of coinage

Date	Mintage	F	VF	XF	Unc	BU
1987R	83,000	—	—	0.15	0.55	—

KM# 222 20 LIRE Composition: Aluminum-Bronze
Subject: Fortifications **Reverse:** Small fortified gate

Date	Mintage	F	VF	XF	Unc	BU
1988R	38,000	—	—	0.15	0.55	—

KM# 235 20 LIRE Composition: Aluminum-Bronze
Subject: History **Reverse:** Sword and flag

Date	Mintage	F	VF	XF	Unc	BU
1989R	37,000	—	—	0.15	0.55	—

KM# 252 20 LIRE Composition: Aluminum-Bronze
Subject: 1,600 years of history **Reverse:** Figure straddling denomination

Date	Mintage	F	VF	XF	Unc	BU
1990R	96,000	—	—	0.15	0.55	—

KM# 265 20 LIRE Composition: Aluminum-Bronze
Reverse: Gloved hand rejecting cardinal ring

Date	Mintage	F	VF	XF	Unc	BU
1991R		—	—	0.15	0.55	—

KM# 282 20 LIRE Composition: Aluminum-Bronze **Reverse:** Columbus landing on Hispaniola

Date	F	VF	XF	Unc	BU
1992R	—	—	0.10	0.55	—

KM# 297 20 LIRE Composition: Aluminum-Bronze **Reverse:** Scroll and arch

Date	F	VF	XF	Unc	BU
1993R	—	—	0.10	0.55	—

KM# 310 20 LIRE Composition: Aluminum-Bronze **Reverse:** Workers pulling stone

Date	Mintage	F	VF	XF	Unc	BU
1994R	40,000	—	—	0.10	0.55	—

KM# 326 20 LIRE Composition: Aluminum-Bronze **Reverse:** Child straddling cornucopia

Date	F	VF	XF	Unc	BU
1995R	—	—	0.10	0.55	—

KM# 353 20 LIRE Composition: Aluminum-Bronze **Obverse:** St. Thomas

Date	Mintage	F	VF	XF	Unc	BU
1996	32,000	—	—	0.10	0.55	—

KM# 363 20 LIRE Composition: Aluminum-Bronze **Subject:** The arts - cinema **Reverse:** Film strips

Date	Mintage	F	VF	XF	Unc	BU
1997	28,000	—	—	0.10	0.55	—

KM# 379 20 LIRE Composition: Aluminum-Bronze **Subject:** Communications **Reverse:** Two profiles in silhouette

Date	F	VF	XF	Unc	BU
1998	—	—	0.10	0.55	—

KM# 390 20 LIRE Composition: Aluminum-Bronze **Subject:** Exploration **Obverse:** Crowned arms **Reverse:** Earth as known today

Date	F	VF	XF	Unc	BU
1999	—	—	0.10	0.55	—

KM# 400 20 LIRE Weight: 3.6000 g. **Composition:** Aluminum-Bronze **Subject:** Solidarity **Obverse:** Child of the Universe **Reverse:** 2 hands about to grasp **Edge:** Plain **Size:** 21.8 mm. **Note:** Struck at Rome.

Date	F	VF	XF	Unc	BU
2000	—	—	0.10	0.55	—

KM# 425 20 LIRE Weight: 3.6000 g. **Composition:** Aluminum-Bronze **Obverse:** Three towers. **Reverse:** Two dolphins. **Edge:** Plain. **Size:** 21.8 mm.

Date	F	VF	XF	Unc	BU
2001	—	—	—	0.35	—

KM# 19 50 LIRE Composition: Steel

Date	Mintage	F	VF	XF	Unc	BU
1972	291,000	0.15	0.25	0.50	1.00	—

KM# 27 50 LIRE Composition: Steel

Date	Mintage	F	VF	XF	Unc	BU
1973	291,000	0.15	0.25	0.50	1.00	—

KM# 35 50 LIRE Composition: Steel

Date	Mintage	F	VF	XF	Unc	BU
1974	276,000	0.15	0.25	0.60	1.25	—

KM# 45 50 LIRE Composition: Steel

Date	Mintage	F	VF	XF	Unc	BU
1975	831,000	0.15	0.25	0.60	1.25	—

KM# 56 50 LIRE Composition: Steel

Date	Mintage	F	VF	XF	Unc	BU
1976	195,000	0.15	0.25	0.50	1.00	—

KM# 68 50 LIRE Composition: Steel

Date	Mintage	F	VF	XF	Unc	BU
1977	180,000	0.15	0.25	0.50	1.00	—

KM# 81 50 LIRE Composition: Steel

Date	Mintage	F	VF	XF	Unc	BU
1978	130,000	0.15	0.25	0.50	1.00	—

KM# 94 50 LIRE Composition: Steel

Date	Mintage	F	VF	XF	Unc	BU
1979	125,000	0.15	0.25	0.50	1.00	—

KM# 107 50 LIRE Composition: Steel **Series:** 1980 Olympics **Reverse:** Downhill skier

Date	Mintage	F	VF	XF	Unc	BU
1980	125,000	0.25	0.50	1.00	2.00	-

KM# 121 50 LIRE Composition: Steel

Date	Mintage	F	VF	XF	Unc
1981	100,000	0.15	0.25	0.50	1.00

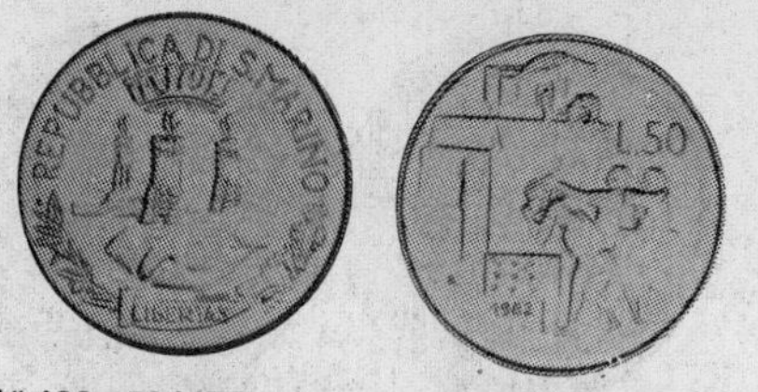

KM# 136 50 LIRE **Composition:** Steel **Subject:** Social conquests

Date	Mintage	F	VF	XF	Unc	BU
1982R	78,000	0.15	0.25	0.50	1.00	—

KM# 150 50 LIRE **Composition:** Steel **Subject:** Nuclear war threat **Reverse:** Beast above woman

Date	Mintage	F	VF	XF	Unc	BU
1983R	72,000	0.20	0.40	0.80	1.50	—

KM# 164 50 LIRE **Composition:** Steel **Reverse:** Pierre and Marie Curie

Date	Mintage	F	VF	XF	Unc	BU
1984R	65,000	0.20	0.40	0.80	1.50	—

KM# 178 50 LIRE **Composition:** Steel **Subject:** War on drugs **Reverse:** Stylized figures

Date	Mintage	F	VF	XF	Unc	BU
1985R	110,000	—	0.10	0.20	0.85	—

KM# 192 50 LIRE **Composition:** Steel **Subject:** Revolution of technology

Date	Mintage	F	VF	XF	Unc	BU
1986R	50,000	—	0.10	0.20	0.85	—

KM# 206 50 LIRE **Composition:** Steel **Subject:** 15th Anniversary -Resumption of Coinage

Date	Mintage	F	VF	XF	Unc	BU
1987R	93,000	—	0.10	0.20	0.85	—

KM# 223 50 LIRE **Composition:** Steel **Subject:** Fortifications **Reverse:** Ramp leading to gate house

Date	Mintage	F	VF	XF	Unc	BU
1988R	38,000	—	0.10	0.20	0.85	—

KM# 236 50 LIRE **Composition:** Steel **Subject:** History **Reverse:** Cross bow

Date	Mintage	VG	F	VF	XF	Unc
1989R	87,000	—	—	0.10	0.20	0.85

KM# 253 50 LIRE **Composition:** Steel **Subject:** 1,600 years of history **Reverse:** Bird

Date	Mintage	F	VF	XF	Unc	BU
1990R	52,000	—	0.10	0.20	0.85	—

KM# 266 50 LIRE **Composition:** Steel **Reverse:** Hand holding cannon barrels and wheat stalks

Date	F	VF	XF	Unc	BU
1991R	—	0.10	0.20	0.85	—

KM# 283 50 LIRE **Composition:** Steel **Subject:** Columbus **Reverse:** Seagulls flying over radiant seascape

Date	F	VF	XF	Unc	BU
1992R	—	0.10	0.20	0.85	—

KM# 298 50 LIRE **Composition:** Steel **Reverse:** Wheat growing through barbed wire

Date	F	VF	XF	Unc	BU
1993R	—	0.10	0.20	0.85	—

KM# 311 50 LIRE **Composition:** Stainless Steel **Reverse:** Two stonecutters

Date	Mintage	F	VF	XF	Unc	BU
1994R	40,000	—	0.10	0.20	0.85	—

KM# 327 50 LIRE **Composition:** Stainless Steel **Reverse:** Child hugging bird

Date	F	VF	XF	Unc	BU
1995R	—	0.10	0.20	0.85	—

KM# 354 50 LIRE **Composition:** Stainless Steel **Reverse:** Descartes

Date	Mintage	F	VF	XF	Unc	BU
1996	32,000	—	0.10	0.20	0.85	—

KM# 364 50 LIRE **Composition:** Stainless Steel **Subject:** The arts - sculpture **Reverse:** Han Dynasty horse statue

Date	Mintage	F	VF	XF	Unc	BU
1997	28,000	—	0.10	0.20	0.85	—

KM# 380 50 LIRE **Composition:** Copper-Nickel **Subject:** Engineering **Reverse:** Cogwheel mind

Date	F	VF	XF	Unc	BU
1998	—	0.10	0.20	0.85	—

KM# 391 50 LIRE **Composition:** Copper-Nickel **Subject:** Exploration **Obverse:** Crowned arms **Reverse:** Ship sail, sun and waves

Date	F	VF	XF	Unc	BU
1999	—	0.10	0.20	0.85	—

KM# 401 50 LIRE **Weight:** 4.5000 g. **Composition:** Copper-Nickel **Subject:** Equality **Obverse:** Child of the Universe **Reverse:** 5 different plant leaves on 1 stem **Edge:** Plain **Size:** 19.2 mm. **Note:** Struck at Rome.

Date	F	VF	XF	Unc	BU
2000	—	0.10	0.20	0.85	—

KM# 426 50 LIRE **Weight:** 4.5000 g. **Composition:** Stainless Steel **Obverse:** Three towers. **Reverse:** Tree. **Edge:** Plain. **Size:** 19.2 mm.

Date	F	VF	XF	Unc	BU
2001	—	—	—	0.85	—

KM# 20 100 LIRE **Composition:** Steel

Date	Mintage	F	VF	XF	Unc	BU
1972	291,000	0.15	0.30	0.60	1.50	—

KM# 28 100 LIRE **Composition:** Steel

Date	Mintage	F	VF	XF	Unc	BU
1973	291,000	0.15	0.30	0.60	1.50	—

KM# 36 100 LIRE **Composition:** Steel

Date	Mintage	F	VF	XF	Unc	BU
1974	276,000	0.15	0.30	0.65	1.65	—

KM# 46 100 LIRE **Composition:** Steel

Date	Mintage	F	VF	XF	Unc	BU
1975	821,000	0.15	0.30	0.65	1.85	—

KM# 57 100 LIRE **Composition:** Steel

Date	Mintage	F	VF	XF	Unc	BU
1976	1,853,000	0.15	0.30	0.60	1.50	—

KM# 69 100 LIRE **Composition:** Steel

Date	Mintage	F	VF	XF	Unc	BU
1977	565,000	0.15	0.30	0.60	1.50	—

KM# 70 100 LIRE **Composition:** Steel

Date	Mintage	F	VF	XF	Unc	BU
1977	565,000	0.15	0.30	0.60	1.50	—

KM# 82 100 LIRE **Composition:** Steel **Series:** F.A.O.

Date	Mintage	F	VF	XF	Unc	BU
1978	875,000	0.15	0.30	0.60	1.50	—

KM# 95 100 LIRE **Composition:** Steel

Date	Mintage	F	VF	XF	Unc	BU
1979	665,000	0.15	0.30	0.60	1.50	—

KM# 108 100 LIRE **Composition:** Steel **Series:** 1980 Olympics **Subject:** Archery

Date	Mintage	F	VF	XF	Unc	BU
1980	350,000	0.25	0.50	1.00	2.00	—

KM# 122 100 LIRE **Composition:** Steel

Date	Mintage	F	VF	XF	Unc	BU
1981	512,000	0.15	0.30	0.60	1.50	—

KM# 137 100 LIRE **Composition:** Steel **Subject:** Social conquests

Date	Mintage	F	VF	XF	Unc	BU
1982R	178,000	0.15	0.30	0.60	1.50	—

KM# 151 100 LIRE **Composition:** Steel **Subject:** Nuclear war threat **Reverse:** Beast above man and woman

Date	Mintage	F	VF	XF	Unc	BU
1983R	172,000	0.15	0.30	0.60	1.50	—

KM# 165 100 LIRE **Composition:** Steel **Reverse:** Guglielmo Marconi

Date	Mintage	F	VF	XF	Unc
1984R	165,000	0.15	0.30	0.60	1.50

KM# 179 100 LIRE **Composition:** Steel **Subject:** Wa on drugs **Reverse:** 3 figures in discussion

Date	Mintage	F	VF	XF	Unc
1985R	210,000	—	—	0.35	1.25

KM# 193 100 LIRE **Composition:** Steel **Subject:** Revolution of technology

Date	Mintage	F	VF	XF	Unc
1986R	150,000	—	—	0.35	1.25

KM# 207 100 LIRE **Composition:** Steel **Subject:** 15t Anniversary - Resumption of Coinage

Date	Mintage	F	VF	XF	Unc
1987R	143,000	—	—	0.35	1.25

KM# 224 100 LIRE **Composition:** Steel **Subject:** Fortifications **Reverse:** Gate tower

Date	Mintage	F	VF	XF	Unc
1988R	38,000	—	—	0.35	1.25

KM#237 100 LIRE **Composition:** Steel **Subject:** Histo **Reverse:** Teacher and student

Date	Mintage	F	VF	XF	Unc
1989R	37,000	—	—	0.35	1.25

KM# 254 100 LIRE Composition: Steel **Subject:** 1,600 Years of History **Reverse:** Balance scale

Date	Mintage	F	VF	XF	Unc	BU
1990R	1,086,000	—	—	0.35	1.25	—

KM# 267 100 LIRE Composition: Steel **Reverse:** Clasped hands

Date	F	VF	XF	Unc	BU
1991R	—	—	0.35	1.25	—

KM# 284 100 LIRE Composition: Steel **Subject:** Columbus **Reverse:** Three sailing ships

Date	F	VF	XF	Unc	BU
1992R	—	—	0.35	1.25	—

KM# 299 100 LIRE Composition: Copper-Nickel **Reverse:** Pan swallow above western Europe

Date	F	VF	XF	Unc	BU
1993R	—	—	0.35	1.25	—

KM# 312 100 LIRE Composition: Copper-Nickel **Reverse:** 2 stonecutters

Date	Mintage	F	VF	XF	Unc	BU
1994R	40,000	—	—	0.35	1.25	—

KM# 328 100 LIRE Composition: Copper-Nickel **Reverse:** 3 children

Date	F	VF	XF	Unc	BU
1995R	—	—	0.35	1.25	—

KM# 355 100 LIRE Composition: Copper-Nickel **Reverse:** Rousseau

Date	Mintage	F	VF	XF	Unc	BU
1996	32,000	—	—	0.35	1.25	—

KM# 365 100 LIRE Composition: Copper-Nickel **Subject:** The Arts - Dance **Reverse:** Ballet

Date	Mintage	F	VF	XF	Unc	BU
1997	28,000	—	—	0.35	1.25	—

KM# 381 100 LIRE Composition: Copper-Nickel **Subject:** Physics **Reverse:** Human, crossbow

Date	F	VF	XF	Unc	BU
1998	—	—	0.35	1.25	—

KM# 392 100 LIRE Composition: Copper-Nickel **Subject:** Exploration **Obverse:** Crowned arms **Reverse:** Submarine below Arctic ice-cap

Date	F	VF	XF	Unc	BU
1999	—	—	0.35	1.25	—

KM# 402 100 LIRE Weight: 4.5000 g. **Composition:** Copper-Nickel **Subject:** Ecology **Obverse:** Child of the Universe **Reverse:** Leaf on house on leaf **Edge:** Reeded and plain sectioned **Size:** 22 mm.

Date	F	VF	XF	Unc	BU
2000	—	—	0.35	1.25	—

KM# 427 100 LIRE Weight: 4.5000 g. **Composition:** Copper-Nickel **Obverse:** Three towers **Reverse:** Two hands **Edge:** Plain and reeded sections **Size:** 22 mm.

Date	F	VF	XF	Unc	BU
2001	—	—	—	1.25	—

KM# 83 200 LIRE Composition: Aluminum-Bronze

Date	Mintage	F	VF	XF	Unc	BU
1978	530,000	—	0.25	0.75	1.75	—

KM# 96 200 LIRE Composition: Aluminum-Bronze **Series:** F.A.O.

Date	Mintage	F	VF	XF	Unc	BU
1979	675,000	—	0.25	0.75	1.75	—

KM# 109 200 LIRE Composition: Aluminum-Bronze **Series:** 1980 Olympics **Reverse:** Wrestling

Date	Mintage	F	VF	XF	Unc	BU
1980	675,000	—	0.50	1.00	2.50	—

KM# 123 200 LIRE Composition: Aluminum-Bronze **Series:** F.A.O.

Date	Mintage	F	VF	XF	Unc	BU
1981	700,000	—	0.25	0.75	1.75	—

KM# 138 200 LIRE Composition: Aluminum-Bronze **Subject:** Social conquests

Date	Mintage	F	VF	XF	Unc	BU
1982R	178,000	—	0.25	0.75	1.75	—

KM# 152 200 LIRE Composition: Aluminum-Bronze **Subject:** Nuclear war threat **Reverse:** Rider spearing victim

Date	Mintage	F	VF	XF	Unc	BU
1983	172,000	—	0.25	0.75	1.75	—

KM# 166 200 LIRE Composition: Aluminum-Bronze **Reverse:** Enrico Fermi

Date	Mintage	F	VF	XF	Unc	BU
1984R	165,000	—	0.25	0.75	1.75	—

KM# 180 200 LIRE Composition: Aluminum-Bronze **Subject:** War on drugs **Reverse:** Family group

Date	Mintage	F	VF	XF	Unc	BU
1985R	210,000	—	—	0.40	1.50	—

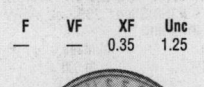

KM# 194 200 LIRE **Composition:** Aluminum-Bronze **Subject:** Revolution of technology

Date	Mintage	F	VF	XF	Unc	BU
1986R	150,000	—	—	0.40	1.50	—

KM# 208 200 LIRE **Composition:** Aluminum-Bronze **Subject:** 15th Anniversary - Resumption of Coinage

Date	Mintage	F	VF	XF	Unc	BU
1987R	143,000	—	—	0.40	1.50	—

KM# 225 200 LIRE **Composition:** Aluminum-Bronze **Subject:** Fortifications **Reverse:** Tower

Date	Mintage	F	VF	XF	Unc	BU
1988R	38,000	—	—	0.40	1.50	—

KM# 238 200 LIRE **Composition:** Aluminum-Bronze **Subject:** History **Reverse:** Stylized view of San Marino

Date	Mintage	F	VF	XF	Unc	BU
1989R	1,037,000	—	—	0.40	1.50	—

KM# 255 200 LIRE **Composition:** Aluminum-Bronze **Subject:** 1,600 years of history **Reverse:** Female portrait

Date	Mintage	F	VF	XF	Unc	BU
1990R	36,000	—	—	0.40	1.50	—

KM# 268 200 LIRE **Composition:** Aluminum-Bronze **Reverse:** Hand holding coin die

Date	F	VF	XF	Unc	BU
1991R	—	—	0.40	1.50	—

KM# 285 200 LIRE **Composition:** Aluminum-Bronze **Reverse:** Columbus navigating by the stars

Date	F	VF	XF	Unc	BU
ND(1992)R	—	—	0.40	1.50	—

KM# 300 200 LIRE **Composition:** Aluminum-Bronze **Reverse:** Door and arches

Date	F	VF	XF	Unc	BU
1993R	—	—	0.40	1.50	—

KM# 313 200 LIRE **Composition:** Aluminum-Bronze **Reverse:** Man and tame bear

Date	Mintage	F	VF	XF	Unc	BU
1994R	40,000	—	—	0.40	1.50	—

KM# 329 200 LIRE **Composition:** Aluminum-Bronze **Reverse:** 2 children

Date	F	VF	XF	Unc	BU
1995R	—	—	0.40	1.50	—

KM# 356 200 LIRE **Composition:** Aluminum-Bronze **Subject:** Kant

Date	Mintage	F	VF	XF	Unc	BU
1996	32,000	—	—	0.40	1.50	—

KM# 366 200 LIRE **Composition:** Aluminum-Bronze **Subject:** The Arts - Painting

Date	Mintage	F	VF	XF	Unc	BU
1997	28,000	—	—	0.40	1.50	—

KM# 382 200 LIRE **Composition:** Aluminum-Bronze **Subject:** Zoology **Reverse:** 2 dolphins

Date	F	VF	XF	Unc	BU
1998	—	—	0.40	1.50	—

KM# 393 200 LIRE **Composition:** Aluminum-Bronze **Subject:** Exploration **Obverse:** Crowned arms **Reverse:** Stonehenge beneath the sun and stars

Date	F	VF	XF	Unc	BU
1999	—	—	0.40	1.50	—

KM# 403 200 LIRE **Weight:** 5.0000 g. **Composition:** Aluminum-Bronze **Subject:** Knowledge **Obverse:** Child of the Universe **Reverse:** Allegorical female portrait **Edge:** Reeded **Size:** 24 mm. **Note:** Struck at Rome.

Date	VG	F	VF	XF	Unc
2000	—	—	—	0.40	1.50

KM# 428 200 LIRE **Weight:** 5.0000 g. **Composition:** Aluminum-Bronze **Obverse:** Three towers. **Reverse:** Broken chain, leaves and vines. **Edge:** Reeded. **Size:** 24 mm.

Date	F	VF	XF	Unc	BU
2001	—	—	—	1.50	—

KM# 21 500 LIRE **Weight:** 11.0000 g. **Composition:** 0.8350 Silver .2953 oz. ASW **Note:** 22,374 coins melted at the mint.

Date	Mintage	F	VF	XF	Unc	BU
1972	291,000	—	—	6.00	10.00	—

KM# 29 500 LIRE **Weight:** 11.0000 g. **Composition:** 0.8350 Silver .2953 oz. ASW **Note:** 6,544 coins melted at the mint.

Date	Mintage	F	VF	XF	Unc	B
1973	291,000	—	—	6.00	10.00	-

KM# 37 500 LIRE **Weight:** 11.0000 g. **Composition:** 0.8350 Silver .2953 oz. ASW **Reverse:** Two pigeons **Note:** 6,295 coins melted at the mint.

Date	Mintage	F	VF	XF	Unc	BU
1974	276,000	—	—	6.50	12.50	—

KM# 47 500 LIRE **Weight:** 11.0000 g. **Composition:** 0.8350 Silver .2953 oz. ASW **Note:** 119,743 coins melted at the mint.

Date	Mintage	F	VF	XF	Unc	BU
1975	291,000	—	—	7.00	12.50	—

KM# 48 500 LIRE **Weight:** 11.0000 g. **Composition:** 0.8350 Silver .2953 oz. ASW **Subject:** Numismatic Agency opening **Note:** 47,495 coins melted at the mint.

Date	Mintage	F	VF	XF	Unc	BU
1975	200,000	—	—	6.50	11.50	—

KM# 58 500 LIRE **Weight:** 11.0000 g. **Composition:** 0.8350 Silver .2953 oz. ASW **Note:** 40,509 coins melted at the mint.

Date	Mintage	F	VF	XF	Unc	BU
1976	195,000	—	—	6.50	11.50	—

KM# 59 500 LIRE **Weight:** 11.0000 g. **Composition:** 0.8350 Silver .2953 oz. ASW **Subject:** Social Security **Note:** 106,604 coins melted at the mint.

Date	Mintage	F	VF	XF	Unc	BU
1976	195,000	—	—	6.50	11.50	—

KM# 71 500 LIRE **Weight:** 11.0000 g. **Composition:** 0.8350 Silver .2953 oz. ASW **Note:** 45,483 coins melted at the mint.

Date	Mintage	F	VF	XF	Unc	BU
1977	180,000	—	—	6.50	11.50	—

KM# 84 500 LIRE **Weight:** 11.0000 g. **Composition:** 0.8350 Silver .2953 oz. ASW **Note:** 16,297 coins melted at the mint.

Date	Mintage	F	VF	XF	Unc	BU
1978	130,000	—	—	6.50	11.50	—

KM# 97 500 LIRE **Weight:** 11.0000 g. **Composition:** 0.8350 Silver .2953 oz. ASW **Note:** 33,278 coins melted at the mint.

Date	Mintage	F	VF	XF	Unc	BU
1979	125,000	—	—	7.00	12.50	—

KM# 110 500 LIRE **Weight:** 11.0000 g. **Composition:** 0.8350 Silver .2953 oz. ASW **Series:** 1980 Olympics **Note:** 47,724 coins melted at the mint.

Date	Mintage	F	VF	XF	Unc	BU
1980	125,000	—	—	7.00	12.50	—

KM# 124 500 LIRE **Weight:** 11.0000 g. **Composition:** 0.8350 Silver .2953 oz. ASW **Subject:** 2,000th anniversary - Virgil's death **Note:** 9,122 coins melted at the mint.

Date	Mintage	F	VF	XF	Unc	BU
1981	75,000	—	—	7.00	12.50	—

KM# 125 500 LIRE **Weight:** 11.0000 g. **Composition:** 0.8350 Silver .2953 oz. ASW **Subject:** 2,000th anniversary - Virgil's death **Note:** 9,122 coins melted at the mint.

Date	Mintage	F	VF	XF	Unc	BU
1981	75,000	—	—	7.00	12.50	—

KM# 126 500 LIRE **Weight:** 11.0000 g. **Composition:** 0.8350 Silver .2953 oz. ASW **Note:** 21,124 coins melted at the mint.

Date	Mintage	F	VF	XF	Unc	BU
1981	100,000	—	—	7.00	12.50	—

KM# 139 500 LIRE **Weight:** 11.0000 g. **Composition:** 0.8350 Silver .2953 oz. ASW **Subject:** Centennial - death of Garibaldi **Note:** 112 uncirculated and 369 proof coins melted at the mint.

Date	Mintage	F	VF	XF	Unc	BU
ND(1982)R	48,000	—	—	7.00	12.50	—
ND(1982)R Proof	13,000	Value: 22.50				

KM# 140 500 LIRE **Ring Composition:** Steel **Center Composition:** Aluminum-Bronze **Subject:** Social conquests

Date	Mintage	F	VF	XF	Unc	BU
1982R	1,900,000	—	—	1.00	3.00	—

KM# 153 500 LIRE **Ring Composition:** Steel **Center Composition:** Aluminum-Bronze **Subject:** Nuclear war threat **Reverse:** 3 horses above 2 people

Date	Mintage	F	VF	XF	Unc	BU
1983R	1,922,000	—	—	1.00	3.00	—

KM# 154 500 LIRE **Weight:** 11.0000 g. **Composition:** 0.8350 Silver .2953 oz. ASW **Subject:** 500th anniversary - birth of artist Raphael **Note:** 80 uncirculated and 1,939 proof coins melted at the mint.

Date	Mintage	F	VF	XF	Unc	BU
1983R	42,000	—	—	7.00	12.50	—
1983R Proof	12,000	Value: 22.50				

KM# 167 500 LIRE **Ring Composition:** Steel **Center Composition:** Aluminum-Bronze **Reverse:** Albert Einstein

Date	Mintage	F	VF	XF	Unc	BU
1984R	2,633,000	—	—	1.00	3.00	—

KM# 168 500 LIRE **Weight:** 11.0000 g. **Composition:** 0.8350 Silver .2953 oz. ASW **Series:** 1984 Summer Olympics **Note:** 2,920 uncirculated and 20 proof coins melted at the mint.

Date	Mintage	F	VF	XF	Unc	BU
1984	52,000	—	—	6.50	10.00	—
1984 Proof	15,000	Value: 12.50				

KM# 181 500 LIRE **Ring Composition:** Steel **Center Composition:** Aluminum-Bronze **Subject:** War on drugs **Reverse:** Cured addict

Date	Mintage	F	VF	XF	Unc	BU
1985R	2,647,000	—	—	1.00	3.00	—

KM# 182 500 LIRE **Weight:** 11.0000 g. **Composition:** 0.8350 Silver .2953 oz. ASW **Subject:** European Music Year **Note:** 6,704 uncirculated and 122 proof coins melted at the mint.

Date	Mintage	F	VF	XF	Unc	BU
1985	40,000	—	—	7.00	12.50	—
1985 Proof	12,000	Value: 15.00				

KM# 195 500 LIRE **Ring Composition:** Steel **Center Composition:** Aluminum-Bronze **Subject:** Revolution of technology

Date	Mintage	F	VF	XF	Unc	BU
1986R	3,111,000	—	—	1.00	3.00	—

KM# 196 500 LIRE **Weight:** 11.0000 g. **Composition:** 0.8350 Silver .2953 oz. ASW **Subject:** Soccer **Reverse:** Field **Note:** 5,212 uncirculated and 60 proof coins melted at the mint.

Date	Mintage	F	VF	XF	Unc	BU
1986R	45,000	—	—	—	12.50	—
1986R Proof	12,000	Value: 15.00				

KM# 209 500 LIRE **Ring Composition:** Steel **Center Composition:** Aluminum-Bronze **Subject:** 15th anniversary - resumption of coinage

Date	Mintage	F	VF	XF	Unc	BU
1987R	3,063,000	—	—	1.00	3.00	—

KM# 213 500 LIRE **Weight:** 11.0000 g. **Composition:** 0.8350 Silver .2953 oz. ASW **Subject:** Zagreb University Games **Reverse:** Runner **Note:** 9,208 uncirculated and 1,206 proof coins melted at the mint.

Date	Mintage	F	VF	XF	Unc	BU
1987R	35,000	—	—	—	12.50	—
1987R Proof	10,000	Value: 15.00				

KM# 216 500 LIRE **Weight:** 11.0000 g. **Composition:** 0.8350 Silver .2953 oz. ASW **Series:** Winter Olympics **Reverse:** Downhill skier **Note:** 146 uncirculated and 3 proof coins melted at the mint.

Date	Mintage	F	VF	XF	Unc	BU
1988R	32,000	—	—	—	9.00	—
1988R Proof	9,600	Value: 15.00				

KM# 226 500 LIRE **Ring Composition:** Steel **Center Composition:** Aluminum-Bronze **Subject:** Fortifications **Reverse:** Hilltop fortification

Date	Mintage	F	VF	XF	Unc	BU
1988R	3,526,000	—	—	1.00	3.00	—

KM# 239 500 LIRE **Ring Composition:** Steel **Center Composition:** Aluminum-Bronze **Subject:** History **Reverse:** Stone carver

Date	Mintage	F	VF	XF	Unc	BU
1989R	3,145,000	—	—	1.00	3.00	—

KM# 243 500 LIRE **Weight:** 11.0000 g. **Composition:** 0.8350 Silver .2953 oz. ASW **Subject:** San Marino Grand Prix **Note:** 5,180 coins melted at the mint.

Date	Mintage	F	VF	XF	Unc	BU
1989R	30,000	—	—	—	10.00	—
1989R Proof	8,000	Value: 25.00				

KM# 246 500 LIRE **Weight:** 11.0000 g. **Composition:** 0.8350 Silver .2953 oz. ASW **Subject:** World Cup soccer championship game

Date	Mintage	F	VF	XF	Unc	B
1990R	40,000	—	—	—	10.00	[illegible]
1990R Proof	19,000	Value: 20.00				

KM# 256 500 LIRE **Ring Composition:** Steel **Center Composition:** Aluminum-Bronze **Subject:** 1,600 years of history **Reverse:** Birds and stamp

Date	F	VF	XF	Unc	[illegible]
1990R	—	—	1.00	3.00	[illegible]

KM# 269 500 LIRE **Ring Composition:** Steel **Cente Composition:** Aluminum-Bronze **Reverse:** Hand holding flowers

Date	Mintage	F	VF	XF	Unc
1991R	3,580,563	—	—	1.00	3.00

KM# 271 500 LIRE **Weight:** 11.0000 g. **Compositio** 0.8350 Silver .2953 oz. ASW **Series:** Barcelona Olympi **Reverse:** Priestess lighting fire with sun beam

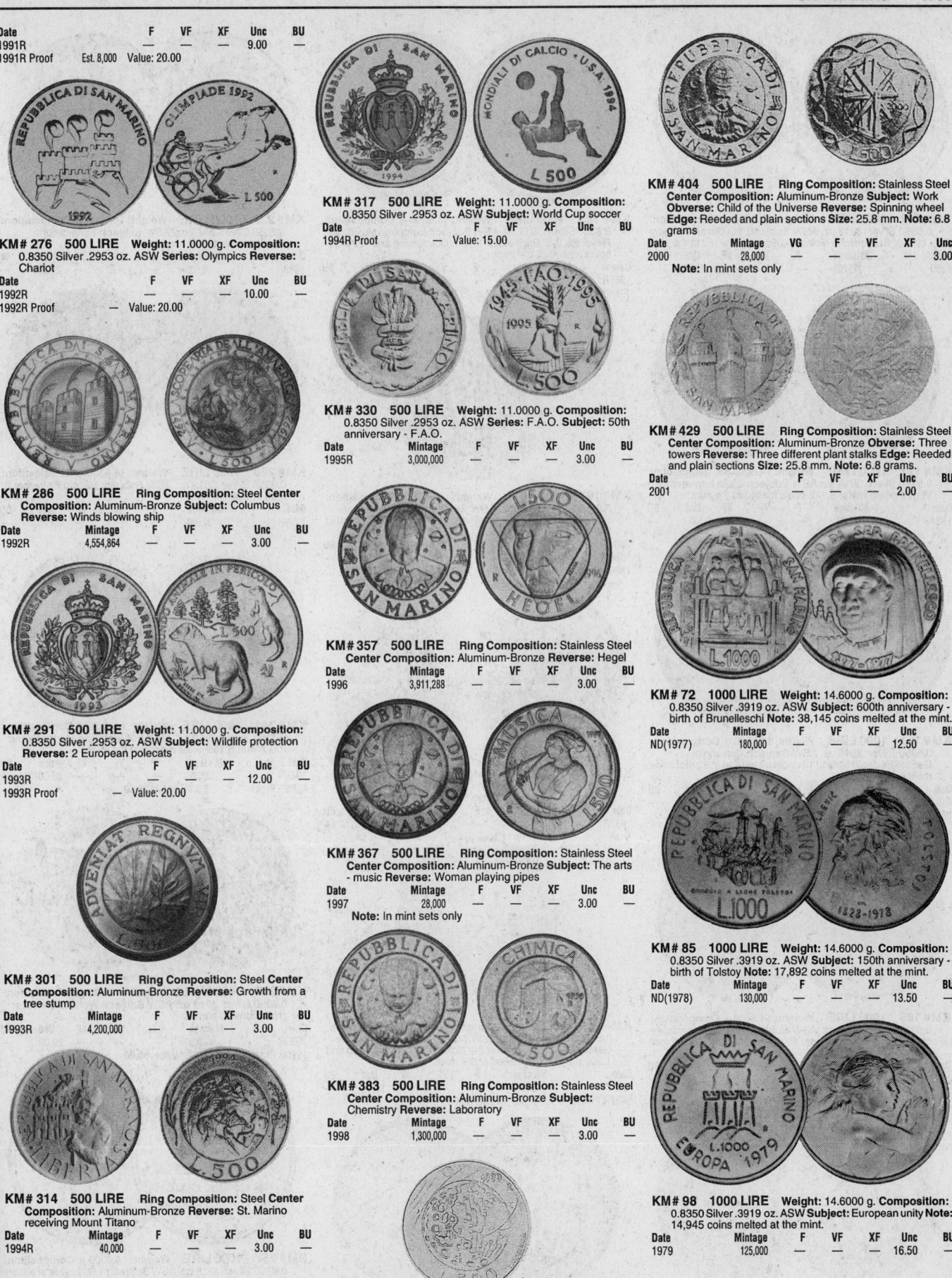

Date		F	VF	XF	Unc	BU
1991R		—	—	—	9.00	—
1991R Proof	Est. 8,000	Value: 20.00				

KM# 276 500 LIRE **Weight:** 11.0000 g. **Composition:** 0.8350 Silver .2953 oz. ASW **Series:** Olympics **Reverse:** Chariot

Date		F	VF	XF	Unc	BU
1992R		—	—	—	10.00	—
1992R Proof	—	Value: 20.00				

KM# 286 500 LIRE **Ring Composition:** Steel **Center Composition:** Aluminum-Bronze **Subject:** Columbus **Reverse:** Winds blowing ship

Date	Mintage	F	VF	XF	Unc	BU
1992R	4,554,864	—	—	—	3.00	—

KM# 291 500 LIRE **Weight:** 11.0000 g. **Composition:** 0.8350 Silver .2953 oz. ASW **Subject:** Wildlife protection **Reverse:** 2 European polecats

Date		F	VF	XF	Unc	BU
1993R		—	—	—	12.00	—
1993R Proof	—	Value: 20.00				

KM# 301 500 LIRE **Ring Composition:** Steel **Center Composition:** Aluminum-Bronze **Reverse:** Growth from a tree stump

Date	Mintage	F	VF	XF	Unc	BU
1993R	4,200,000	—	—	—	3.00	—

KM# 314 500 LIRE **Ring Composition:** Steel **Center Composition:** Aluminum-Bronze **Reverse:** St. Marino receiving Mount Titano

Date	Mintage	F	VF	XF	Unc	BU
1994R	40,000	—	—	—	3.00	—

KM# 317 500 LIRE **Weight:** 11.0000 g. **Composition:** 0.8350 Silver .2953 oz. ASW **Subject:** World Cup soccer

Date		F	VF	XF	Unc	BU
1994R Proof	—	Value: 15.00				

KM# 330 500 LIRE **Weight:** 11.0000 g. **Composition:** 0.8350 Silver .2953 oz. ASW **Series:** F.A.O. **Subject:** 50th anniversary - F.A.O.

Date	Mintage	F	VF	XF	Unc	BU
1995R	3,000,000	—	—	—	3.00	—

KM# 357 500 LIRE **Ring Composition:** Stainless Steel **Center Composition:** Aluminum-Bronze **Reverse:** Hegel

Date	Mintage	F	VF	XF	Unc	BU
1996	3,911,288	—	—	—	3.00	—

KM# 367 500 LIRE **Ring Composition:** Stainless Steel **Center Composition:** Aluminum-Bronze **Subject:** The arts - music **Reverse:** Woman playing pipes

Date	Mintage	F	VF	XF	Unc	BU
1997	28,000	—	—	—	3.00	—

Note: In mint sets only

KM# 383 500 LIRE **Ring Composition:** Stainless Steel **Center Composition:** Aluminum-Bronze **Subject:** Chemistry **Reverse:** Laboratory

Date	Mintage	F	VF	XF	Unc	BU
1998	1,300,000	—	—	—	3.00	—

KM# 394 500 LIRE **Ring Composition:** Stainless Steel **Center Composition:** Aluminum-Bronze **Subject:** Exploration **Obverse:** Crowned arms **Reverse:** Moon's surface, radio waves and Saturn

Date	Mintage	F	VF	XF	Unc	BU
1999	2,000,000	—	—	—	3.00	—

KM# 404 500 LIRE **Ring Composition:** Stainless Steel **Center Composition:** Aluminum-Bronze **Subject:** Work **Obverse:** Child of the Universe **Reverse:** Spinning wheel **Edge:** Reeded and plain sections **Size:** 25.8 mm. **Note:** 6.8 grams

Date	Mintage	VG	F	VF	XF	Unc
2000	28,000	—	—	—	—	3.00

Note: In mint sets only

KM# 429 500 LIRE **Ring Composition:** Stainless Steel **Center Composition:** Aluminum-Bronze **Obverse:** Three towers **Reverse:** Three different plant stalks **Edge:** Reeded and plain sections **Size:** 25.8 mm. **Note:** 6.8 grams.

Date	F	VF	XF	Unc	BU
2001	—	—	—	2.00	—

KM# 72 1000 LIRE **Weight:** 14.6000 g. **Composition:** 0.8350 Silver .3919 oz. ASW **Subject:** 600th anniversary - birth of Brunelleschi **Note:** 38,145 coins melted at the mint.

Date	Mintage	F	VF	XF	Unc	BU
ND(1977)	180,000	—	—	—	12.50	—

KM# 85 1000 LIRE **Weight:** 14.6000 g. **Composition:** 0.8350 Silver .3919 oz. ASW **Subject:** 150th anniversary - birth of Tolstoy **Note:** 17,892 coins melted at the mint.

Date	Mintage	F	VF	XF	Unc	BU
ND(1978)	130,000	—	—	—	13.50	—

KM# 98 1000 LIRE **Weight:** 14.6000 g. **Composition:** 0.8350 Silver .3919 oz. ASW **Subject:** European unity **Note:** 14,945 coins melted at the mint.

Date	Mintage	F	VF	XF	Unc	BU
1979	125,000	—	—	—	16.50	—

KM# 112 1000 LIRE **Weight:** 14.6000 g. **Composition:** 0.8350 Silver .3919 oz. ASW **Subject:** 1,500th anniversary - birth of St. Benedict **Note:** 49,095 coins melted at the mint.

Date	Mintage	F	VF	XF	Unc	BU
1980	125,000	—	—	—	15.00	—

KM# 127 1000 LIRE **Weight:** 14.6000 g. **Composition:** 0.8350 Silver .3919 oz. ASW **Subject:** 200th anniversary - Virgil's death **Note:** 9,122 coins melted at the mint.

Date	Mintage	F	VF	XF	Unc	BU
1981	75,000	—	—	—	15.00	—

KM# 141 1000 LIRE **Weight:** 14.6000 g. **Composition:** 0.8350 Silver .3919 oz. ASW **Subject:** Centennial - Garibaldi's death **Note:** 112 uncirculated and 369 proof coins melted at the mint.

Date	Mintage	F	VF	XF	Unc	BU
ND(1982)R	48,000	—	—	—	15.00	—
ND(1982)R Proof	13,000	Value: 25.00				

KM# 155 1000 LIRE **Weight:** 14.6000 g. **Composition:** 0.8350 Silver .3919 oz. ASW **Subject:** 500th anniversary - birth of artist Raphael **Note:** 80 uncirculated and 1,939 proof coins melted at the mint.

Date	Mintage	F	VF	XF	Unc	BU
1983R	42,000	—	—	—	15.00	—
1983R Proof	12,000	Value: 25.00				

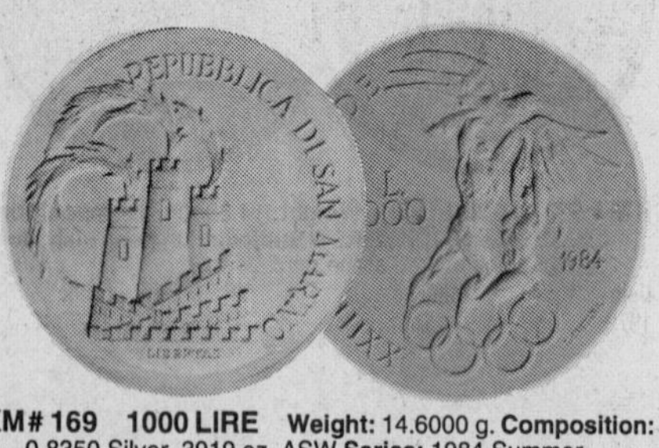

KM# 169 1000 LIRE **Weight:** 14.6000 g. **Composition:** 0.8350 Silver .3919 oz. ASW **Series:** 1984 Summer Olympics **Note:** 2,920 uncirculated and 20 proof coins melted at the mint.

Date	Mintage	F	VF	XF	Unc	BU
1984R	52,000	—	—	—	12.50	—
1984R Proof	15,000	Value: 22.50				

KM# 183 1000 LIRE **Weight:** 14.6000 g. **Composition:** 0.8350 Silver .3919 oz. ASW **Subject:** European Music Year **Reverse:** J.S. Bach **Note:** 6,704 uncirculated and 122 proof coins melted at the mint.

Date	Mintage	F	VF	XF	Unc	BU
1985R	40,000	—	—	—	15.00	—
1985R Proof	12,000	Value: 25.00				

KM# 197 1000 LIRE **Weight:** 14.6000 g. **Composition:** 0.8350 Silver .3919 oz. ASW **Subject:** Soccer **Reverse:** Flags **Note:** 5,212 uncirculated and 60 proof coins melted at the mint.

Date	Mintage	F	VF	XF	Unc	BU
1986R	45,000	—	—	—	16.00	—
1986R Proof	12,000	Value: 30.00				

KM# 210 1000 LIRE **Weight:** 14.6000 g. **Composition:** 0.8350 Silver .3919 oz. ASW **Subject:** 15th anniversary - resumption of coinage **Note:** 13 coins melted at the mint.

Date	Mintage	F	VF	XF	Unc	BU
1987R	43,000	—	—	—	18.00	—

KM# 214 1000 LIRE **Weight:** 14.6000 g. **Composition:** 0.8350 Silver .3919 oz. ASW **Subject:** Zagreb University Games **Reverse:** Pole vaulter **Note:** 9,207 uncirculated and 1,206 proof coins melted at the mint.

Date	Mintage	F	VF	XF	Unc	BU
1987R	35,000	—	—	—	16.00	—
1987R Proof	10,000	Value: 30.00				

KM# 217 1000 LIRE **Weight:** 14.6000 g. **Composition:** 0.8350 Silver .3919 oz. ASW **Series:** Summer Olympics **Reverse:** Diver **Note:** 146 uncirculated and 3 proof coins melted at the mint.

Date	Mintage	F	VF	XF	Unc	BU
1988R	32,000	—	—	—	17.50	—
1988R Proof	9,600	Value: 30.00				

KM# 227 1000 LIRE **Weight:** 14.6000 g. **Composition:** 0.8350 Silver .3919 oz. ASW **Subject:** Fortifications **Reverse:** Walls and towers

Date	Mintage	F	VF	XF	Unc	BU
1988R	38,000	—	—	—	20.00	—

KM# 240 1000 LIRE **Weight:** 14.6000 g. **Composition:** 0.8350 Silver .3919 oz. ASW **Subject:** History **Reverse:** 2 men in boat

Date	Mintage	F	VF	XF	Unc	BU
1989R	32,000	—	—	—	20.00	—

KM# 244 1000 LIRE **Weight:** 14.6000 g. **Composition:** 0.8350 Silver .3919 oz. ASW **Subject:** San Marino Grand Prix **Note:** 5,180 coins melted at the mint.

Date	Mintage	F	VF	XF	Unc	BU
1989R	30,000	—	—	—	20.00	—
1989R Proof	8,000	Value: 35.00				

KM# 247 1000 LIRE **Weight:** 14.6000 g. **Composition:** 0.8350 Silver .3919 oz. ASW **Subject:** World Cup soccer championship games

Date	Mintage	F	VF	XF	Unc	BU
1990R	40,000	—	—	—	20.00	—
1990R Proof	19,000	Value: 30.00				

KM# 257 1000 LIRE **Weight:** 14.6000 g. **Composition:** 0.8350 Silver .3919 oz. ASW **Subject:** 1,600 years of history **Reverse:** Hand and 2 figures

Date	Mintage	F	VF	XF	Unc	BU
1990R	36,000	—	—	—	20.00	—

KM# 270 1000 LIRE Weight: 14.6000 g. **Composition:** 0.8350 Silver .3919 oz. ASW **Reverse:** Hand holding dove

Date	F	VF	XF	Unc	BU
1991R	—	—	—	20.00	—

KM# 272 1000 LIRE Weight: 14.6000 g. **Composition:** 0.8350 Silver .3919 oz. ASW **Series:** Barcelona Olympics

Date	Mintage	F	VF	XF	Unc	BU
1991R		—	—	—	20.00	—
1991R Proof	Est. 8,000	Value: 32.50				

KM# 277 1000 LIRE Weight: 14.6000 g. **Composition:** 0.8350 Silver .3919 oz. ASW **Series:** Olympics **Reverse:** 3 athletes

Date	F	VF	XF	Unc	BU
1992R	—	—	—	20.00	—
1992R Proof	— Value: 32.50				

KM# 287 1000 LIRE Weight: 14.6000 g. **Composition:** 0.8350 Silver .3919 oz. ASW **Reverse:** Columbus studying chart

Date	F	VF	XF	Unc	BU
ND(1992)R	—	—	—	22.50	—

KM# 292 1000 LIRE Weight: 14.6000 g. **Composition:** 0.8350 Silver .3919 oz. ASW **Series:** Wildlife Protection **Reverse:** Falcon and woodpecker

Date	F	VF	XF	Unc	BU
1993R	—	—	—	20.00	—
1993R Proof	— Value: 30.00				

KM# 302 1000 LIRE Weight: 14.6000 g. **Composition:** 0.8350 Silver .3919 oz. ASW **Reverse:** Wing above globe

Date	F	VF	XF	Unc	BU
1993R	—	—	—	22.50	—

KM# 315 1000 LIRE Weight: 14.6000 g. **Composition:** 0.8350 Silver .3919 oz. ASW **Subject:** Founder building first San Marino church

Date	Mintage	F	VF	XF	Unc	BU
1994R	40,000	—	—	—	22.50	—

KM# 316 1000 LIRE Weight: 14.6000 g. **Composition:** 0.8350 Silver .3919 oz. ASW **Series:** Olympics **Reverse:** Ski jumper

Date	F	VF	XF	Unc	BU
1994R Proof	— Value: 18.50				

KM# 318 1000 LIRE Weight: 14.6000 g. **Composition:** 0.8350 Silver .3919 oz. ASW **Subject:** World Cup soccer

Date	F	VF	XF	Unc	BU
1994R Proof	— Value: 27.50				

KM# 331 1000 LIRE Weight: 14.6000 g. **Composition:** 0.8350 Silver .3919 oz. ASW **Subject:** Pyramid of children

Date	F	VF	XF	Unc	BU
1995R	—	—	—	22.50	—

KM# 332 1000 LIRE Weight: 14.6000 g. **Composition:** 0.8350 Silver .3919 oz. ASW **Series:** 1996 Olympics **Reverse:** Pole vaulting and discus

Date	Mintage	F	VF	XF	Unc	BU
1995R Proof	50,000	Value: 20.00				

KM# 358 1000 LIRE Weight: 14.6000 g. **Composition:** 0.8350 Silver .3919 oz. ASW **Reverse:** Popper

Date	Mintage	F	VF	XF	Unc	BU
1996	32,000	—	—	—	20.00	—

KM# 368 1000 LIRE Ring Composition: Aluminum-Bronze **Center Composition:** Copper-Nickel **Obverse:** Heraldic lion **Reverse:** Statue, building and denomination

Date	Mintage	F	VF	XF	Unc	BU
1997	2,232,541	—	—	—	8.00	—

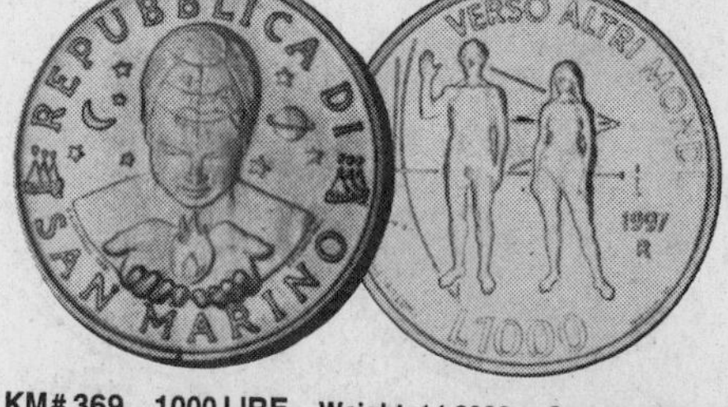

KM# 369 1000 LIRE Weight: 14.6000 g. **Composition:** 0.8350 Silver .3919 oz. ASW **Subject:** The arts - interplanetary communication **Reverse:** Nude couple from Pioneer 10 space probe plaque

Date	Mintage	F	VF	XF	Unc	BU
1997	28,000	—	—	—	25.00	—

KM# 384 1000 LIRE Ring Composition: Aluminum-Bronze **Center Composition:** Copper-Nickel **Subject:** Geology **Reverse:** Family standing on earth

Date	Mintage	F	VF	XF	Unc	BU
1998	2,061,275	—	—	—	8.00	—

KM# 395 1000 LIRE **Ring Composition:** Aluminum-Bronze **Center Composition:** Copper-Nickel **Subject:** Exploration **Obverse:** Crowned arms **Reverse:** Radiant north star design

Date	Mintage	F	VF	XF	Unc	BU
1999	1,836,495	—	—	—	8.00	—

KM# 405 1000 LIRE **Ring Composition:** Aluminum-Bronze **Center Composition:** Stainless Steel **Subject:** Liberty **Obverse:** Child of the Universe **Reverse:** Swallow flying over world globe **Edge:** Reeded and plain sectioned **Size:** 27 mm. **Note:** 8.8 grams. Struck at Rome.

Date	Mintage	VG	F	VF	XF	Unc
2000	2,898,805	—	—	—	—	9.00

KM# 430 1000 LIRE **Ring Composition:** Aluminum-Bronze **Center Composition:** Stainless Steel **Obverse:** Three towers **Reverse:** Circle of birds **Edge:** Reeded and plain sections **Size:** 27 mm. **Note:** 8.8 grams.

Date	F	VF	XF	Unc	BU
2001	—	—	—	7.50	—

KM# 333 5000 LIRE **Weight:** 18.0000 g. **Composition:** 0.8350 Silver .4832 oz. ASW **Subject:** Sail training ship "Amerigo Vespucci"

Date	Mintage	F	VF	XF	Unc	BU
1995R Proof	Est. 35,000	Value: 17.50				

KM# 340 5000 LIRE **Weight:** 18.0000 g. **Composition:** 0.8350 Silver .4832 oz. ASW **Series:** Wildlife Protection **Reverse:** Falcons

Date	Mintage	F	VF	XF	Unc	BU
1996 Proof	Est. 35,000	Value: 22.50				

KM# 370 5000 LIRE **Weight:** 18.0000 g. **Composition:** 0.8350 Silver .4832 oz. ASW **Reverse:** Sailing ship & map of Africa **Rev. Legend:** VASCO DA GAMA 1497

Date	F	VF	XF	Unc	BU
1997 Proof	—	Value: 17.50			

KM# 385 5000 LIRE **Weight:** 18.0000 g. **Composition:** 0.8350 Silver .4832 oz. ASW **Subject:** Medicine **Reverse:** Emblem

Date	F	VF	XF	Unc	BU
1998	—	—	—	18.00	—

KM# 386 5000 LIRE **Weight:** 18.0000 g. **Composition:** 0.8350 Silver .4832 oz. ASW **Subject:** Europe in the new millennium **Reverse:** Euro bridge with ivy, olive and oak trees **Edge:** Lettered **Edge Lettering:** RELINQUO VOS LIBEROS **Size:** 32 mm. **Note:** Struck at Rome.

Date	VG	F	VF	XF	Unc
1998 Proof	—	Value: 20.00			

KM# 396 5000 LIRE **Weight:** 18.0000 g. **Composition:** 0.8350 Silver .4832 oz. ASW **Subject:** Exploration **Obverse:** Crowned arms **Reverse:** Solar system, European map and dish in human mind

Date	F	VF	XF	Unc	BU
1999	—	—	—	18.00	—

KM# 410 5000 LIRE **Weight:** 18.0000 g. **Composition:** 0.8350 Silver .4832 oz. ASW **Subject:** European Union **Reverse:** Denomination above flags **Edge:** Lettered **Edge Lettering:** RELINQUO VOS LIBEROS

Date	VG	F	VF	XF	Unc
1999 Proof	—	Value: 30.00			

KM# 406 5000 LIRE **Weight:** 18.0000 g. **Composition:** 0.8350 Silver .4832 oz. ASW **Subject:** Peace **Obverse:** Child of the Universe **Reverse:** Hawk and dove with same olive branch in their beaks **Edge:** Reeded and plain sectioned **Size:** 32 mm. **Note:** Struck at Rome.

Date	VG	F	VF	XF	Unc
2000	—	—	—	—	18.00

KM# 421 5000 LIRE **Weight:** 18.0000 g. **Composition:** 0.8350 Silver .4832 oz. ASW **Subject:** First holy year jubilee **Reverse:** Pope Boniface VIII with 2 aides **Edge:** Lettered **Edge Lettering:** RELINQUO VOS LIBEROS

Date	VG	F	VF	XF	Unc
2000 Proof	—	Value: 20.00			

KM# 436 5000 LIRE **Weight:** 18.0000 g. **Composition:** 0.8350 Silver .4832 oz. ASW **Subject:** Last Lire Coinage **Obverse:** National arms. **Reverse:** Six old coin designs. **Edge:** Lettered. **Size:** 32 mm.

Date	Mintage	VG	F	VF	XF	Unc
2001 Proof	20,000	Value: 20.00				

KM# 431 5000 LIRE **Weight:** 18.0000 g. **Composition:** 0.8350 Silver .4832 oz. ASW **Obverse:** Three towers. **Reverse:** Dove on laurel branch. **Edge:** Reeded and plain sections. **Size:** 32 mm.

Date	F	VF	XF	Unc	BU
2001	—	—	—	15.00	—

KM# 334 10000 LIRE **Weight:** 22.0000 g. **Composition:** 0.8350 Silver .5907 oz. ASW **Subject:** Amerigo Vespucci

Date	Mintage	F	VF	XF	Unc	B
1995R Proof	Est. 35,000	Value: 22.50				

KM# 341 10000 LIRE **Weight:** 22.0000 g. **Composition:** 0.8350 Silver .5907 oz. ASW **Series:** Wildlife Protection **Reverse:** Wolves

ate	Mintage	F	VF	XF	Unc	BU
996 Proof	Est. 35,000	Value: 37.50				

KM# 342 10000 LIRE **Weight:** 22.0000 g. **Composition:** 0.8350 Silver .5907 oz. ASW **Subject:** Euro **Reverse:** Parliament building and map

ate	F	VF	XF	Unc	BU
996 Proof	—	Value: 30.00			

KM# 371 10000 LIRE **Weight:** 22.0000 g. **Composition:** 0.8350 Silver .5907 oz. ASW **Subject:** Giovanni Caboto 1497 **Reverse:** Ship, Atlantic map

ate	F	VF	XF	Unc	BU
997 Proof	—	Value: 28.00			

KM# 372 10000 LIRE **Weight:** 22.0000 g. **Composition:** 0.8350 Silver .5907 oz. ASW **Subject:** Euro - "Libertas" **Obverse:** National arms above the 9 Casteli arms

ate	F	VF	XF	Unc	BU
997 Proof	—	Value: 32.00			

KM# 376 10000 LIRE **Weight:** 22.0000 g. **Composition:** 0.8350 Silver .5907 oz. ASW **Subject:** Soccer World Championship **Reverse:** 3 soccer players

ate	F	VF	XF	Unc	BU
98 Proof	—	Value: 30.00			

KM# 377 10000 LIRE **Weight:** 22.0000 g. **Composition:** 0.8350 Silver .5907 oz. ASW **Subject:** 50th anniversary - Ferrari **Obverse:** Crowned arms **Reverse:** 2 racing Ferraris above denomination **Edge:** Reeded and plain sectioned **Size:** 34 mm. **Note:** Struck at Rome.

Date	Mintage	VG	F	VF	XF	Unc
1998 Proof	30,000	Value: 27.50				

KM# 387 10000 LIRE **Weight:** 22.0000 g. **Composition:** 0.8350 Silver .5907 oz. ASW **Subject:** Europe in the new millennium **Obverse:** Crowned arms **Reverse:** Child with flags

Date	F	VF	XF	Unc	BU
1998 Proof	—	Value: 27.50			

KM# 397 10000 LIRE **Weight:** 22.0000 g. **Composition:** 0.8350 Silver .5907 oz. ASW **Subject:** III millennium **Obverse:** Crowned arms **Reverse:** Allegorical portrait of DNA unraveling from human mind

Date	Mintage	F	VF	XF	Unc	BU
1999 Proof	Est. 25,000	Value: 30.00				

KM# 398 10000 LIRE **Weight:** 22.0000 g. **Composition:** 0.8350 Silver .5907 oz. ASW **Series:** 2000 Olympics **Obverse:** Crowned arms **Reverse:** Prone shooter

Date	Mintage	F	VF	XF	Unc	BU
1999 Proof	Est. 35,000	Value: 27.50				

KM# 411 10000 LIRE **Weight:** 22.0000 g. **Composition:** 0.8350 Silver .5907 oz. ASW **Subject:** European Union **Reverse:** Circle of paper dolls above denomination

Date	VG	F	VF	XF	Unc
1999 Proof	—	Value: 35.00			

KM# 419 10000 LIRE **Weight:** 22.0000 g. **Composition:** 0.8350 Silver .5907 oz. ASW **Subject:** 17th centennial of the republic **Reverse:** St. Marino's portrait

Date	Mintage	VG	F	VF	XF	Unc
2000 Proof	18,000	Value: 22.50				

KM# 422 10000 LIRE **Weight:** 22.0000 g. **Composition:** 0.8350 Silver .5907 oz. ASW **Subject:** Holy Year **Obverse:** Crowned arms **Reverse:** Pope kneeling before an open door **Edge:** Reeded and plain sections **Size:** 34 mm.

Date	VG	F	VF	XF	Unc
2000 Proof	—	Value: 30.00			

KM# 423 10000 LIRE **Weight:** 22.0000 g. **Composition:** 0.8350 Silver .5907 oz. ASW **Subject:** Michelangelo's Sacred Family painting **Obverse:** Crowned arms **Reverse:** Painting detail **Edge:** Reeded and plain sections **Size:** 34 mm.

Date	VG	F	VF	XF	Unc
2000 Proof	—	Value: 30.00			

KM# 437 10000 LIRE **Weight:** 22.0000 g. **Composition:** 0.8350 Silver .5906 oz. ASW **Subject:** Last Lire Coinage **Obverse:** National arms. **Reverse:** Six old coin designs. **Edge:** Reeded and plain sections. **Size:** 34 mm.

Date	Mintage	VG	F	VF	XF	Unc
2001 Proof	20,000	Value: 30.00				

KM# 438 10000 LIRE **Weight:** 22.0000 g. **Composition:** 0.8350 Silver .5906 oz. ASW **Subject:** 2nd International Chambers of Commerce Convention **Obverse:** National arms. **Reverse:** Mercury running by a computer. **Edge:** Reeded and plain sections. **Size:** 34 mm.

Date	Mintage	VG	F	VF	XF	Unc
2001 Proof	20,000	Value: 20.00				

KM# 432 10000 LIRE **Weight:** 22.0000 g. **Composition:** 0.8350 Silver .5906 oz. ASW **Subject:** Ferrari **Obverse:** Three towers. **Reverse:** Race car with "FERRARI" background. **Edge:** Reeded and plain sections. **Size:** 34 mm.

Date	Mintage	F	VF	XF	Unc	BU
2001 Proof	20,000	Value: 25.00				

KM# 416 1/2 SCUDO **Weight:** 1.6100 g. **Composition:** 0.9000 Gold .0466 oz. AGW **Subject:** Ilcenacolo **Obverse:** Crowned arms **Reverse:** Bearded portrait **Edge:** Reeded **Size:** 14 mm. **Note:** Struck at Rome. 1,915 coins melted at the mint.

Date	Mintage	F	VF	XF	Unc	BU
1998	8,000	—	—	—	37.50	—

KM# 413 1/2 SCUDO **Weight:** 1.6100 g. **Composition:** 0.9000 Gold .0466 oz. AGW **Subject:** Ritratto di Agnolo Doni **Obverse:** Crowned arms **Reverse:** Portrait

Date	Mintage	VG	F	VF	XF	Unc
1999 Proof	8,000	Value: 35.00				

KM# 407 1/2 SCUDO **Weight:** 1.6100 g. **Composition:** 0.9000 Gold .0466 oz. AGW **Subject:** Ritratto di Agnolo Doni **Obverse:** Crowned arms **Reverse:** Portrait

Date	F	VF	XF	Unc	BU
2000 Proof	—	—	—	35.00	—

KM# 433 1/2 SCUDO **Weight:** 1.6100 g. **Composition:** 0.9000 Gold .0466 oz. AGW **Subject:** Cavaliere **Obverse:** National arms. **Reverse:** Horse and rider. **Edge:** Reeded. **Size:** 13.8 mm.

Date	Mintage	F	VF	XF	Unc	BU
2001 Proof	4,500	Value: 26.00				

KM# 38 SCUDO **Weight:** 3.0000 g. **Composition:** 0.9170 Gold .0883 oz. AGW **Note:** 2,491 coins melted at the mint.

Date	Mintage	F	VF	XF	Unc	BU
1974	87,000	—	—	—	55.00	—

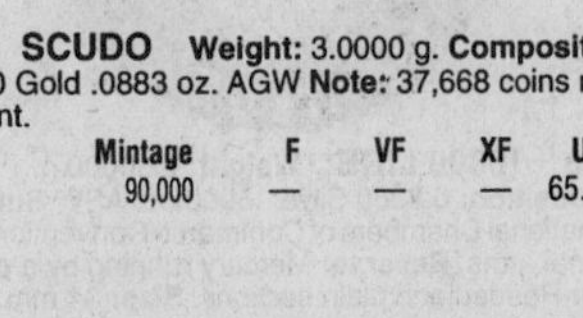

KM# 49 SCUDO **Weight:** 3.0000 g. **Composition:** 0.9170 Gold .0883 oz. AGW **Note:** 37,668 coins melted at the mint.

Date	Mintage	F	VF	XF	Unc	BU
1975	90,000	—	—	—	65.00	—

KM# 60 SCUDO **Weight:** 3.0000 g. **Composition:** 0.9170 Gold .0883 oz. AGW **Note:** 30,026 coins melted at the mint.

Date	Mintage	F	VF	XF	Unc	BU
1976	65,000	—	—	—	55.00	—

KM# 73 SCUDO **Weight:** 3.0000 g. **Composition:** 0.9170 Gold .0883 oz. AGW **Subject:** Democrazia **Note:** 1,839 coins melted at the mint.

Date	Mintage	F	VF	XF	Unc	BU
1977	35,000	—	—	—	60.00	—

KM# 86 SCUDO **Weight:** 3.0000 g. **Composition:** 0.9170 Gold .0883 oz. AGW **Subject:** Miss Liberta **Note:** 9,021 coins melted at the mint.

Date	Mintage	F	VF	XF	Unc	BU
1978	38,000	—	—	—	60.00	—

KM# 99 SCUDO **Weight:** 3.0000 g. **Composition:** 0.9170 Gold .0883 oz. AGW **Subject:** Peace **Note:** 4,152 coins melted at the mint.

Date	Mintage	F	VF	XF	Unc	BU
1979	38,000	—	—	—	60.00	—

KM# 113 SCUDO **Weight:** 3.0000 g. **Composition:** 0.9170 Gold .0883 oz. AGW **Note:** 10,309 coins melted at the mint.

Date	Mintage	F	VF	XF	Unc	BU
1980	38,000	—	—	—	60.00	—

KM# 128 SCUDO **Weight:** 3.0000 g. **Composition:** 0.9170 Gold .0883 oz. AGW **Series:** World Food Day **Note:** 196 coins melted at the mint.

Date	Mintage	F	VF	XF	Unc	BU
1981	31,000	—	—	—	60.00	—

KM# 142 SCUDO **Weight:** 3.0000 g. **Composition:** 0.9170 Gold .0883 oz. AGW **Note:** 1,192 coins melted at the mint.

Date	Mintage	F	VF	XF	Unc	BU
1982R	17,000	—	—	—	60.00	—

KM# 156 SCUDO **Weight:** 2.0000 g. **Composition:** 0.9170 Gold .059 oz. AGW **Subject:** Perpetual liberty **No** 917 coins melted at the mint.

Date	Mintage	F	VF	XF	Unc
1983R	14,000	—	—	—	65.00

KM# 170 SCUDO **Weight:** 2.0000 g. **Composition:** 0.9170 Gold .059 oz. AGW **Subject:** Peace **Obverse:** Similar to 2 Scudi, KM#171 **Note:** 979 coins melted at th mint.

Date	Mintage	F	VF	XF	Unc
1984R	11,000	—	—	—	65.00

KM# 184 SCUDO **Weight:** 2.0000 g. **Composition:** 0.9170 Gold .059 oz. AGW **Subject:** International Year Youth **Note:** 1,162 coins melted at the mint.

Date	Mintage	F	VF	XF	Unc
1985R	10,000	—	—	—	90.00

KM# 198 SCUDO **Weight:** 3.3920 g. **Composition:** 0.9170 Gold .1 oz. AGW **Subject:** Insects at work **Note:** 1,308 coins melted at the mint.

Date	Mintage	F	VF	XF	Unc
1986R	9,000	—	—	—	70.00

KM# 211 SCUDO **Weight:** 3.3920 g. **Composition:** 0.9170 Gold .1 oz. AGW **Subject:** European Year for Environment **Note:** 962 coins melted at the mint.

Date	Mintage	F	VF	XF	Unc
1987R	8,000	—	—	—	70.00

KM# 228 SCUDO **Weight:** 3.3920 g. **Composition:** 0.9170 Gold .1 oz. AGW **Subject:** Disarmament **Note:** 8 coins melted at the mint.

Date	Mintage	F	VF	XF	Unc
1988R	7,000	—	—	—	70.00

KM# 241 SCUDO **Weight:** 3.2258 g. **Composition:** 0.9000 Gold .0933 oz. AGW **Subject:** French Revolutio **Note:** 731 coins melted at the mint.

Date	Mintage	F	VF	XF	Unc
1989R	7,500	—	—	—	65.00

KM# 258 SCUDO **Weight:** 3.2258 g. **Composition:** 0.9000 Gold .0933 oz. AGW **Subject:** San Marino's presidency of the European Council

Date	Mintage	F	VF	XF	Unc	BU
1990R	7,300	—	—	—	65.00	—

KM# 273 SCUDO Weight: 3.2258 g. **Composition:** 0.9000 Gold .0933 oz. AGW **Subject:** Peace **Reverse:** Child fleeing

Date	Mintage	F	VF	XF	Unc	BU
1991R Proof	Est. 7,500	Value: 65.00				

KM# 288 SCUDO Weight: 3.2258 g. **Composition:** 0.9000 Gold .0933 oz. AGW **Subject:** San Marino's entry into the United Nations

Date	Mintage	F	VF	XF	Unc	BU
1992R	8,500	Value: 65.00				

KM# 303 SCUDO Weight: 3.2258 g. **Composition:** 0.9000 Gold .0933 oz. AGW **Series:** International Monetary Fund **Reverse:** 3 figures **Note:** 455 coins melted at the mint.

Date	Mintage	F	VF	XF	Unc	BU
1993R	7,500	—	—	—	60.00	—
1993R Proof	—	Value: 70.00				

KM# 319 SCUDO Weight: 3.2258 g. **Composition:** 0.9000 Gold .0933 oz. AGW **Series:** International Year of the Family **Note:** Sets only. 648 coins melted at the mint.

Date	Mintage	F	VF	XF	Unc	BU
1994R Proof	7,500	Value: 75.00				

KM# 335 SCUDO Weight: 3.2258 g. **Composition:** 0.9000 Gold .0933 oz. AGW **Series:** 50th anniversary - United Nations **Note:** Sets only. 494 coins melted at the mint.

Date	Mintage	F	VF	XF	Unc	BU
1995R Proof	6,500	Value: 65.00				

KM# 338 SCUDO Weight: 3.2258 g. **Composition:** 0.9000 Gold .0933 oz. AGW **Series:** 1996 Olympics **Reverse:** Boxers **Note:** 664 coins melted at the mint.

Date	Mintage	F	VF	XF	Unc	BU
1996 Proof	7,000	Value: 65.00				

KM# 373 SCUDO Weight: 3.2258 g. **Composition:** 0.9000 Gold .0933 oz. AGW **Subject:** Michelangelo's "Kneeling Angel" **Note:** 412 coins melted at the mint.

Date	Mintage	F	VF	XF	Unc	BU
1997 Proof	6,500	Value: 65.00				

KM# 417 SCUDO Weight: 3.2258 g. **Composition:** 0.9000 Gold .0933 oz. AGW **Subject:** Canone Delle Proporzioni **Obverse:** Crowned arms **Reverse:** Anatomical drawing **Edge:** Reeded **Size:** 15.9 mm. **Note:** Struck at Rome. 312 coins melted at the mint.

Date	Mintage	F	VF	XF	Unc	BU
1998 Proof	6,000	Value: 65.00				

KM# 414 SCUDO Weight: 3.2258 g. **Composition:** 0.9000 Gold .0933 oz. AGW **Subject:** La Velata **Obverse:** Crowned arms **Reverse:** Woman's portrait

Date	Mintage	VG	F	VF	XF	Unc
1999 Proof	8,000	Value: 60.00				

KM# 408 SCUDO Weight: 3.2258 g. **Composition:** 0.9000 Gold .0933 oz. AGW **Subject:** La Primavera **Obverse:** Crowned arms **Reverse:** 3 allegorical female figures

Date	VG	F	VF	XF	Unc
2000 Proof	—	Value: 60.00			

KM# 434 SCUDO Weight: 3.2200 g. **Composition:** 0.9000 Gold .0932 oz. AGW **Subject:** Tiziano **Obverse:** National arms. **Reverse:** Bearded male portrait. **Edge:** Reeded. **Size:** 16 mm.

Date	Mintage	F	VF	XF	Unc	BU
2001 Proof	4,500	Value: 51.00				

KM# 39 2 SCUDI Weight: 6.0000 g. **Composition:** 0.9170 Gold .1769 oz. AGW **Note:** 1,637 coins melted at the mint.

Date	Mintage	F	VF	XF	Unc	BU
1974	77,000	—	—	—	90.00	—

KM# 50 2 SCUDI Weight: 6.0000 g. **Composition:** 0.9170 Gold .1769 oz. AGW **Note:** 3,373 coins melted at the mint.

Date	Mintage	F	VF	XF	Unc	BU
1975	80,000	—	—	—	90.00	—

KM# 61 2 SCUDI Weight: 6.0000 g. **Composition:** 0.9170 Gold .1769 oz. AGW **Note:** 20,246 coins melted at the mint.

Date	Mintage	F	VF	XF	Unc	BU
1976	55,000	—	—	—	90.00	—

KM# 74 2 SCUDI Weight: 6.0000 g. **Composition:** 0.9170 Gold .1769 oz. AGW **Subject:** Democrazia **Note:** 912 coins melted at the mint.

Date	Mintage	F	VF	XF	Unc	BU
1977	34,000	—	—	—	100	—

KM# 87 2 SCUDI Weight: 6.0000 g. **Composition:** 0.9170 Gold .1769 oz. AGW **Subject:** Libertas **Note:** 8,120 coins melted at the mint.

Date	Mintage	F	VF	XF	Unc	BU
1978	37,000	—	—	—	100	—

KM# 100 2 SCUDI Weight: 6.0000 g. **Composition:** 0.9170 Gold .1769 oz. AGW **Subject:** Peace **Note:** 3,238 coins melted at the mint.

Date	Mintage	F	VF	XF	Unc	BU
1979	37,000	—	—	—	100	—

KM# 114 2 SCUDI Weight: 6.0000 g. **Composition:** 0.9170 Gold .1769 oz. AGW **Subject:** Justice **Note:** 9,340 coins melted at the mint.

Date	Mintage	F	VF	XF	Unc	BU
1980	37,000	—	—	—	100	—

KM# 129 2 SCUDI Weight: 6.0000 g. **Composition:** 0.9170 Gold .1769 oz. AGW **Series:** World Food Day **Note:** 196 coins melted at the mint.

Date	Mintage	F	VF	XF	Unc	BU
1981	30,000	—	—	—	100	—

KM# 143 2 SCUDI Weight: 6.0000 g. **Composition:** 0.9170 Gold .1769 oz. AGW **Note:** 244 coins melted at the mint.

Date	Mintage	F	VF	XF	Unc	BU
1982R	16,000	—	—	—	110	—

KM# 157 2 SCUDI Weight: 4.0000 g. **Composition:** 0.9170 Gold .1179 oz. AGW **Subject:** Perpetual liberty **Note:** 17 coins melted at the mint.

Date	Mintage	F	VF	XF	Unc	BU
1983R	13,000	—	—	—	110	—

KM# 171 2 SCUDI **Weight:** 4.0000 g. **Composition:** 0.9170 Gold .1179 oz. AGW **Subject:** Liberty **Note:** 12 coins melted at the mint.

Date	Mintage	F	VF	XF	Unc	BU
1984R	10,000	—	—	—	110	—

KM# 185 2 SCUDI **Weight:** 4.0000 g. **Composition:** 0.9170 Gold .1179 oz. AGW **Series:** International Year for Youth **Note:** 200 coins melted at the mint.

Date	Mintage	F	VF	XF	Unc	BU
1985R	9,000	—	—	—	110	—

KM# 199 2 SCUDI **Weight:** 6.7840 g. **Composition:** 0.9170 Gold .2 oz. AGW **Subject:** Spider at work **Note:** 329 coins melted at the mint.

Date	Mintage	F	VF	XF	Unc	BU
1986R	8,000	—	—	—	150	—

KM# 212 2 SCUDI **Weight:** 6.7840 g. **Composition:** 0.9170 Gold .2 oz. AGW **Subject:** European Year for Envrionment **Note:** 14 coins melted at the mint.

Date	Mintage	F	VF	XF	Unc	BU
1987R	7,000	—	—	—	120	—

KM# 229 2 SCUDI **Weight:** 6.7840 g. **Composition:** 0.9170 Gold .2 oz. AGW **Subject:** Disarmament **Note:** 7 coins melted at the mint.

Date	Mintage	F	VF	XF	Unc	BU
1988R	6,000	—	—	—	120	—

KM# 242 2 SCUDI **Weight:** 6.4516 g. **Composition:** 0.9000 Gold .1867 oz. AGW **Subject:** French Revolution

Date	Mintage	F	VF	XF	Unc	BU
1989R	6,500	—	—	—	110	—

KM# 259 2 SCUDI **Weight:** 6.4516 g. **Composition:** 0.9000 Gold .1867 oz. AGW **Subject:** San Marino's presidency of the European Council

Date	Mintage	F	VF	XF	Unc	BU
1990R	6,800	—	—	—	110	—

KM# 274 2 SCUDI **Weight:** 6.4516 g. **Composition:** 0.9000 Gold .1867 oz. AGW **Subject:** Peace **Reverse:** New shoots growing from stump

Date	Mintage	F	VF	XF	Unc	BU
1991R Proof	Est. 6,500	Value: 110				

KM# 289 2 SCUDI **Weight:** 6.4516 g. **Composition:** 0.9000 Gold .1867 oz. AGW **Subject:** San Marino's entry into the United Nations

Date	Mintage	F	VF	XF	Unc	BU
1992R Proof	7,500	Value: 110				

KM# 304 2 SCUDI **Weight:** 6.4516 g. **Composition:** 0.9000 Gold .1867 oz. AGW **Series:** International Monetary Fund **Reverse:** 2 figures **Note:** 106 coins melted at the mint.

Date	Mintage	F	VF	XF	Unc	BU
1993R	6,500	—	—	—	100	—
1993R Proof	—	Value: 120				

KM# 320 2 SCUDI **Weight:** 6.4516 g. **Composition:** 0.9000 Gold .1867 oz. AGW **Series:** International Year of the Family **Note:** Sets only. 252 coins melted at the mint.

Date	Mintage	F	VF	XF	Unc	BU
1994R Proof	6,500	Value: 125				

KM# 336 2 SCUDI **Weight:** 6.4516 g. **Composition:** 0.9000 Gold .1867 oz. AGW **Series:** 50th Anniversary - United Nations **Note:** Sets only.

Date	Mintage	F	VF	XF	Unc	BU
1995R Proof	Est. 7,000	Value: 125				

KM# 339 2 SCUDI **Weight:** 6.4516 g. **Composition:** 0.9000 Gold .1867 oz. AGW **Series:** 1996 Olympics **Subject:** Track and field **Note:** 1 coin melted at the mint.

Date	Mintage	F	VF	XF	Unc	BU
1996 Proof	6,000	Value: 125				

KM# 374 2 SCUDI **Weight:** 6.4516 g. **Composition:** 0.9000 Gold .1867 oz. AGW **Subject:** Michelangelo's "David" **Note:** 124 coins melted at the mint.

Date	Mintage	F	VF	XF	Unc	BU
1997 Proof	5,800	Value: 125				

KM# 418 2 SCUDI **Weight:** 6.4516 g. **Composition:** 0.9000 Gold .1867 oz. AGW **Subject:** Vergine Delle Rocce **Obverse:** Crowned arms **Reverse:** Hallowed portrait **Edge:** Reeded **Size:** 21 mm. **Note:** Struck at Rome. 334 coins melted at the mint.

Date	Mintage	F	VF	XF	Unc	BU
1998 Proof	5,500	Value: 125				

KM# 415 2 SCUDI **Weight:** 6.4516 g. **Composition:** 0.9000 Gold .1867 oz. AGW **Subject:** Sposalizio Della Vergine **Obverse:** Crowned arms **Reverse:** Wedding scene

Date	Mintage	VG	F	VF	XF	Unc
1999 Proof	8,000	Value: 115				

KM# 409 2 SCUDI **Weight:** 6.4516 g. **Composition:** 0.9000 Gold .1867 oz. AGW **Subject:** Madonna Della Melagrna **Obverse:** Crowned arms **Reverse:** Madonna and child

Date	Mintage	VG	F	VF	XF	Unc
2000 Proof	6,000	Value: 115				

KM# 435 2 SCUDI **Weight:** 6.4400 g. **Composition:** 0.9000 Gold .1863 oz. AGW **Subject:** "Flora" **Obverse:** National arms. **Reverse:** Portrait. **Edge:** Reeded. **Size:** 21 mm.

Date	Mintage	F	VF	XF	Unc	BU
2001 Proof	4,500	Value: 102				

KM# 62 5 SCUDI **Weight:** 15.0000 g. **Composition:** 0.9170 Gold .4422 oz. AGW **Note:** 25 coins melted at mint.

Date	Mintage	F	VF	XF	Unc	BU
1976	8,000	—	—	—	625	—

KM# 75 5 SCUDI **Weight:** 15.0000 g. **Composition:** 0.9170 Gold .4422 oz. AGW **Subject:** Democrazia **Note:** 2[illegible] coins melted at mint.

Date	Mintage	F	VF	XF	Unc	B
1977	16,000	—	—	—	240	-

KM# 101 5 SCUDI **Weight:** 15.0000 g. **Composition:** 0.9170 Gold .4422 oz. AGW **Subject:** Peace **Note:** 161 coins melted at mint.

Date	Mintage	F	VF	XF	Unc	BU
1979	24,000	—	—	—	240	—

KM# 115 5 SCUDI **Weight:** 15.0000 g. **Composition:** 0.9170 Gold .4422 oz. AGW **Subject:** Justice **Note:** 1,428 coins melted at mint.

Date	Mintage	F	VF	XF	Unc	BU
1980	24,000	—	—	—	240	—

KM# 130 5 SCUDI **Weight:** 15.0000 g. **Composition:** 0.9170 Gold .4422 oz. AGW **Series:** World Food Day **Note:** 33 coins melted at mint.

Date	Mintage	F	VF	XF	Unc	BU
1981	24,000	—	—	—	240	—

KM# 144 5 SCUDI **Weight:** 15.0000 g. **Composition:** 0.9170 Gold .4422 oz. AGW **Subject:** Defense of liberty **Note:** 19 coins melted at mint.

Date	Mintage	F	VF	XF	Unc	BU
1982R	15,000	—	—	—	240	—

KM# 158 5 SCUDI **Weight:** 10.0000 g. **Composition:** 0.9170 Gold .2949 oz. AGW **Subject:** Perpetual liberty **Note:** 25 coins melted at mint.

Date	Mintage	F	VF	XF	Unc	BU
1983R	11,000	—	—	—	250	—

KM# 172 5 SCUDI **Weight:** 10.0000 g. **Composition:** 0.9170 Gold .2949 oz. AGW **Subject:** Justice **Note:** 28 coins melted at mint.

Date	Mintage	F	VF	XF	Unc	BU
1984R	9,000	—	—	—	300	—

KM# 186 5 SCUDI **Weight:** 10.0000 g. **Composition:** 0.9170 Gold .2949 oz. AGW **Subject:** Libertas **Note:** 13 coins melted at mint.

Date	Mintage	F	VF	XF	Unc	BU
1985R	7,400	—	—	—	400	—

KM# 200 5 SCUDI **Weight:** 16.9500 g. **Composition:** 0.9170 Gold .5 oz. AGW **Subject:** Work **Reverse:** Bees **Note:** 14 coins melted at mint.

Date	Mintage	F	VF	XF	Unc	BU
1986R	7,000	—	—	—	320	—

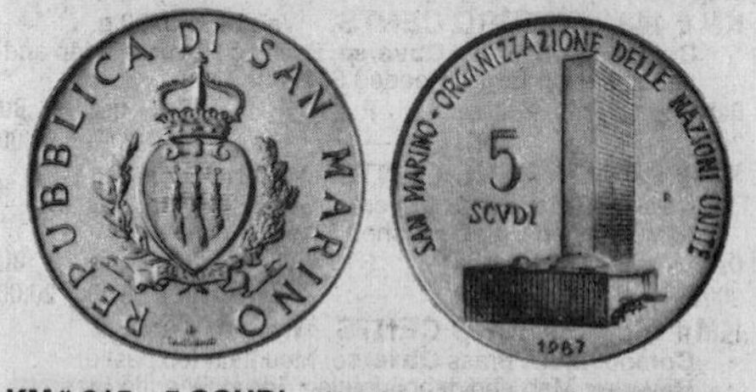

KM# 215 5 SCUDI **Weight:** 16.9500 g. **Composition:** 0.9170 Gold .5 oz. AGW **Subject:** United Nations **Note:** 49 coins melted at mint.

Date	Mintage	F	VF	XF	Unc	BU
1987R	6,000	—	—	—	320	—

KM# 230 5 SCUDI **Weight:** 16.9500 g. **Composition:** 0.9170 Gold .5 oz. AGW **Subject:** Human rights **Note:** 11 coins melted at mint.

Date	Mintage	F	VF	XF	Unc	BU
1988R	5,000	—	—	—	320	—

KM# 245 5 SCUDI **Weight:** 16.9500 g. **Composition:** 0.9170 Gold .5 oz. AGW **Subject:** Entrance of San Marino in Common Market

Date	Mintage	F	VF	XF	Unc	BU
1989R	6,000	—	—	—	320	—

KM# 260 5 SCUDI **Weight:** 16.9500 g. **Composition:** 0.9170 Gold .5 oz. AGW **Subject:** Founding of the republic

Date	Mintage	F	VF	XF	Unc	BU
1990R Proof	6,500	Value: 300				

KM# 275 5 SCUDI **Weight:** 16.9500 g. **Composition:** 0.9170 Gold .5 oz. AGW **Subject:** Peace and freedom **Reverse:** Family

Date	Mintage	F	VF	XF	Unc	BU
1991R Proof	7,000	Value: 300				

KM# 290 5 SCUDI **Weight:** 16.9500 g. **Composition:** 0.9170 Gold .5 oz. AGW **Subject:** Customer agreement with European Economic Community

Date	Mintage	F	VF	XF	Unc	BU
1992R Proof	Est. 6,500	Value: 300				

KM# 305 5 SCUDI **Weight:** 16.9500 g. **Composition:** 0.9170 Gold .5 oz. AGW **Series:** International Monetary Fund **Reverse:** Figure holding scale **Note:** 68 coins melted at the mint.

Date	Mintage	F	VF	XF	Unc	BU
1993R Proof	5,500	Value: 300				

KM# 321 5 SCUDI **Weight:** 16.9500 g. **Composition:** 0.9170 Gold .5 oz. AGW **Series:** International Year of the Family **Note:** 207 coins melted at the mint.

Date	Mintage	F	VF	XF	Unc	BU
1994R Proof	5,500	Value: 300				

KM# 337 5 SCUDI **Weight:** 16.9500 g. **Composition:** 0.9170 Gold .5 oz. AGW **Series:** 50th Anniversary - United Nations **Note:** 65 coins melted at the mint.

Date	Mintage	F	VF	XF	Unc	BU
1995R Proof	5,000	Value: 300				

KM# 343 5 SCUDI **Weight:** 16.9500 g. **Composition:** 0.9170 Gold .5 oz. AGW **Subject:** Pieta **Reverse:** Mary receives Jesus' body **Note:** 19 coins melted at the mint.

Date	Mintage	F	VF	XF	Unc	BU
1996 Proof	5,840	Value: 300				

KM# 375 5 SCUDI **Weight:** 16.9500 g. **Composition:** 0.9170 Gold .5 oz. AGW **Subject:** The Annunciation **Reverse:** Angel **Note:** 469 coins melted at the mint.

Date	Mintage	F	VF	XF	Unc	BU
1997 Proof	5,500	Value: 300				

KM# 412 5 SCUDI **Weight:** 16.9590 g. **Composition:** 0.9170 Gold .5 oz. AGW **Subject:** Madonna Della Seggiola **Reverse:** Woman with 2 children **Note:** 1,151 coins melted at the mint.

Date	Mintage	F	VF	XF	Unc	BU
1998 Proof	5,000	Value: 300				

KM# 388 5 SCUDI **Weight:** 16.9590 g. **Composition:** 0.9170 Gold .5 oz. AGW **Subject:** Birth of Venus **Obverse:** Crowned arms **Reverse:** Venus standing in shell

Date	Mintage	F	VF	XF	Unc	BU
1999 Proof	Est. 5,500	Value: 300				

KM# 420 5 SCUDI **Weight:** 16.9590 g. **Composition:** 0.9170 Gold .5 oz. AGW **Subject:** Tiziano's painting "Rape of Europa" **Reverse:** Europa on a bull's (Zeus) back

Date	VG	F	VF	XF	Unc
2000 Proof	—	—	—	—	285

KM# 439 5 SCUDI **Weight:** 16.9655 g. **Composition:** 0.9166 Gold .5000 oz. AGW **Subject:** San Marino's World Bank Membership **Obverse:** National arms. **Reverse:** Orchid and bee. **Edge:** Reeded. **Size:** 28 mm.

Date	Mintage	VG	F	VF	XF	Unc
2001 Proof	4,000	Value: 226				

KM# 88 10 SCUDI **Weight:** 30.0000 g. **Composition:** 0.9170 Gold .8844 oz. AGW **Note:** 54 coins melted at the mint.

Date	Mintage	F	VF	XF	Unc	BU
1978	20,000	—	—	—	450	—

EURO COINAGE

KM# 440 EURO CENT **Weight:** 2.2700 g. **Composition:** Copper Plated Steel **Obverse:** Tower **Reverse:** Denomination and globe **Edge:** Plain **Size:** 16.2 mm.

Date	Mintage	F	VF	XF	Unc	BU
2002	120,000	—	—	—	—	50.00

KM# 441 2 EURO CENTS **Weight:** 3.0300 g. **Composition:** Copper Plated Steel **Obverse:** Statue **Reverse:** Denomination and globe **Edge:** Grooved **Size:** 18.7 mm.

Date	Mintage	F	VF	XF	Unc	BU
2002	120,000	—	—	—	—	50.00

KM# 442 5 EURO CENTS **Weight:** 3.8600 g. **Composition:** Copper Plated Steel **Obverse:** Castle towers **Reverse:** Denomination and globe **Edge:** Plain **Size:** 21.2 mm.

Date	Mintage	F	VF	XF	Unc	BU
2002	120,000	—	—	—	—	50.00

KM# 443 10 EURO CENTS **Weight:** 4.0700 g. **Composition:** Brass **Obverse:** Building **Reverse:** Map and denomination **Edge:** Reeded **Size:** 19.7 mm.

Date	Mintage	F	VF	XF	Unc	BU
2002	120,000	—	—	—	—	50.00

KM# 444 20 EURO CENTS **Weight:** 5.7300 g. **Composition:** Brass **Obverse:** Saint **Reverse:** Map and denomination **Edge:** Notched **Size:** 22.1 mm.

Date	Mintage	F	VF	XF	Unc	BU
2002	302,400	—	—	—	18.00	20.00

KM# 445 50 EURO CENTS **Weight:** 7.8100 g. **Composition:** Brass **Obverse:** Mountain top castle **Reverse:** Map and denomination **Edge:** Reeded **Size:** 24.2 mm.

Date	Mintage	F	VF	XF	Unc	BU
2002	230,400	—	—	—	20.00	22.50

KM# 446 EURO **Weight:** 7.5000 g. **Composition:** Bi-Metallic **Obverse:** Crowned arms **Reverse:** Denomination and map **Edge:** Reeded and plain sections **Size:** 23.2 mm.

Date	Mintage	F	VF	XF	Unc	BU
2002	360,800	—	—	—	22.00	25.00

KM# 447 2 EURO **Weight:** 8.5200 g. **Composition:** Bi-Metallic **Obverse:** Towered building **Reverse:** Denomination and map **Edge:** Reeded with "2's" and stars **Size:** 25.7 mm.

Date	Mintage	F	VF	XF	Unc	BU
2002	255,760	—	—	—	25.00	28.00

KM# 448 5 EURO **Weight:** 18.0000 g. **Composition:** 0.9250 Silver 0.5353 oz. ASW **Subject:** Welcome Euro **Obverse:** Three plumed towers **Reverse:** Circle of roses **Size:** 32 mm.

Date	Mintage	F	VF	XF	Unc	BU
2002	37,000	—	—	—	—	75.00

KM# 449 10 EURO **Weight:** 22.0000 g. **Composition:** 0.9250 Silver 0.6543 oz. ASW **Subject:** Welcome Euro **Obverse:** Three plumed towers **Reverse:** Infant sleeping in flower **Size:** 34 mm.

Date	Mintage	F	VF	XF	Unc	BU
2002	37,000	—	—	—	—	100

PROVAS

KM#	Date	Mintage	Identification	Mkt Val
Pr1	1925R	75	20 Lire. KM8.	3,200

KM#	Date	Mintage	Identification	Mkt Val
Pr2	1931R	—	5 Lire. KM9.	250
Pr3	1931R	—	10 Lire. KM10.	225
Pr4	1931R	—	20 Lire. KM11.	500

KM#	Date	Mintage	Identification	Mkt Val
Pr5	1932R	—	5 Lire. KM9.	850

KM#	Date	Mintage	Identification	Mkt Val
Pr6	1932R	—	10 Lire. KM10.	500
Pr7	1933	—	5 Lire. KM9.	175
Pr8	1933	—	10 Lire. KM10.	185
Pr9	1933	—	20 Lire. KM11.	200

KM#	Date	Mintage	Identification	Mkt Val
Pr10	1935R	—	5 Lire. KM9.	500
Pr11	1935R	—	20 Lire. KM11.	550

KM#	Date	Mintage	Identification	Mkt Val
Pr12	1937R	—	10 Lire. KM10.	400

MINT SETS

KM#	Date	Mintage	Identification	Issue Price	Mkt Val
MS1	1972 (8)	—	KM14-21	5.00	12.50
MS2	1973 (8)	—	KM22-29	6.00	12.50
MS3	1974 (8)	60,000	KM30-37	9.00	15.00

KM#	Date	Mintage	Identification	Issue Price	Mkt Val
MS4	1974 (2)	60,000	KM38-39	—	175
MS5	1975 (8)	—	KM40-47	6.50	15.00
MS6	1975 (5)	—	KM40-44	—	—
MS7	1975 (2)	90,000	KM49-50	—	175
MS8	1976 (8)	—	KM51-58	6.00	12.50
MS9	1976 (2)	40,000	KM60-61	—	175
MS10	1977 (9)	—	KM63-71	—	15.00
MS11	1977 (2)	30,000	KM73-74	—	175
MS12	1978 (9)	—	KM76-84	—	15.00
MS13	1978 (2)	—	KM86-87	—	160
MS14	1979 (9)	—	KM89-98	—	15.00
MS15	1979 (2)	—	KM99-100	—	160
MS16	1980 (9)	—	KM102-110	—	15.00
MS17	1980 (2)	—	KM113-114	—	160
MS18	1981 (9)	—	KM116-123, 126	—	15.00
MS19	1981 (3)	—	KM124-125, 127	—	—
MS20	1981 (2)	—	KM128-129	—	160
MS21	1982 (9)	—	KM131-138, 140	6.00	8.50
MS22	1982 (2)	—	KM139, 141	—	27.50
MS23	1982 (2)	—	KM142-143	—	170
MS24	1983 (9)	—	KM145-153	5.50	8.50
MS25	1983 (2)	—	KM154-155	—	27.50
MS26	1983 (2)	—	KM156-157	—	175
MS27	1984 (9)	—	KM159-167	—	—
MS28	1984 (2)	—	KM168-169	—	22.00
MS29	1984 (2)	—	KM170-171	—	175
KM30	1985 (9)	—	KM173-181	—	8.50
KM31	1985 (2)	—	KM182-183	—	22.00
MS32	1985 (2)	—	KM184-185	—	200
MS33	1986 (9)	—	KM187-195	7.00	8.50
MS34	1986 (2)	—	KM196-197	—	30.00
MS35	1986 (2)	—	KM198-199	—	190
MS36	1987 (10)	43,000	KM201-210	—	25.00
MS38	1987 (2)	—	KM211-212	—	190
MS37	1987 (2)	—	KM213-214	—	30.00
MS39	1988 (10)	80,000	KM218-227	22.00	26.00
MS40	1988 (2)	—	KM216-217	—	30.00
MS41	1988 (2)	—	KM228-229	—	190
MS42	1989 (10)	32,000	KM231-240	—	28.00
MS44	1989 (2)	6,500	KM241-242	—	170
MS43	1989 (2)	30,000	KM243-244	—	30.00
MS45	1990 (10)	36,000	KM248-257	—	35.00
MS46	1990 (2)	40,000	KM246-247	—	175
MS47	1990 (2)	6,800	KM258-259	—	175
MS48	1991 (10)	36,000	KM261-270	—	32.00
MS49	1991 (2)	25,000	KM271-272	—	32.00
MS50	1992 (10)	45,000	KM278-287	—	32.00
MS51	1992 (2)	—	KM276-277	34.00	40.00
MS52	1993 (10)	—	KM293-302	18.00	28.00
MS53	1993 (2)	35,000	KM291-292	26.00	30.00
MS54	1994 (10)	40,000	KM307-315	18.00	30.00
MS55	1995 (10)	—	KM322-331	—	30.00
MS56	1996 (10)	32,000	KM344, 349-357	18.00	30.00
MS57	1997 (10)	28,000	KM358-367	18.00	30.00
MS58	1998 (8)	—	KM378-385	18.00	25.00
MS59	1999 (8)	—	KM389-396	18.00	25.00
MS60	2000 (8)	28,000	KM399-406	18.00	25.00
MS61	2001 (8)	2,000	KM424-431	18.00	25.00

PROOF SETS

KM#	Date	Mintage	Identification	Issue Price	Mkt Val
PS1	1989 (2)	8,000	KM243-244	55.00	60.00
PS2	1990 (2)	18,800	KM246-247	55.00	60.00
PS4	1991 (2)	6,800	KM273-274	—	175
PS3	1991 (2)	8,000	KM271-272	55.00	60.00
PS5	1993 (2)	—	KM303-304	158	160
PS6	1994 (2)	7,500	KM319-320	—	200
PS7	1995 (2)	—	KM333-334	31.00	45.00
PS8	1995 (2)	7,000	KM335-336	161	175
PS9	1996 (2)	—	KM340-341	35.00	45.00
PS12	1999 (3)	8,000	KM413-415	179	180
PS11	1999 (2)	—	KM410-411	—	60.00
PS13	2000 (3)	6,000	KM407-409	179	180
PS14	2001 (3)	4,500	KM433-435	179	180

SARAWAK

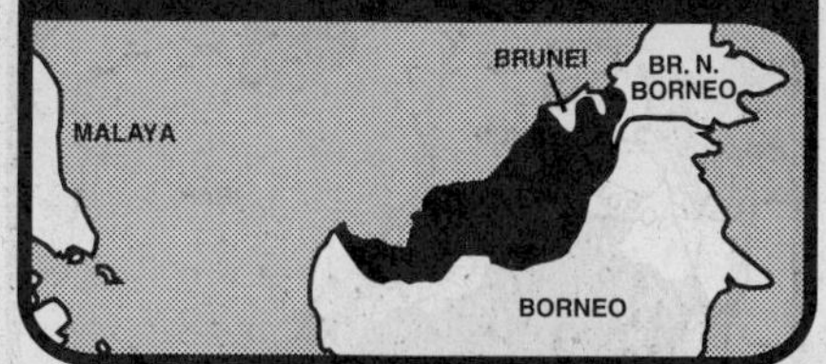

Sarawak is a former British colony located on the north-west coast of Borneo. The Japanese occupation during World War II so thoroughly devastated the economy that Rajah Sir Charles Vyner Brooke ceded it to Great Britain on July 1, 1946. In September, 1963 the colony joined the Federation of Malaysia.

RULERS
Charles J. Brooke, Rajah, 1868-1917
Charles V. Brooke, Rajah, 1917-1946

MINT MARKS
H - Heaton, Birmingham

MONETARY SYSTEM
100 Cents = 1 Dollar

BRITISH COLONY

STANDARD COINAGE

100 Cents = 1 Dollar

KM# 20 1/2 CENT Composition: Bronze **Ruler:** Charles V. Brooke Rajah

Date	Mintage	F	VF	XF	Unc	BU
1933H	2,000,000	1.00	2.00	4.00	9.00	—
1933H Proof	—	Value: 240				

KM# 12 CENT Composition: Copper-Nickel **Ruler:** Charles V. Brooke Rajah

Date	Mintage	F	VF	XF	Unc	BU
1920H	5,000,000	3.00	7.50	18.00	55.00	—

KM# 18 CENT Composition: Bronze **Ruler:** Charles V. Brooke Rajah

Date	Mintage	F	VF	XF	Unc	BU
1927H	5,000,000	1.25	2.25	4.50	9.00	—
1927H Proof	—	Value: 210				
1929H	2,000,000	1.25	2.50	5.00	10.00	—
1930H	3,000,000	1.25	2.50	5.00	10.00	—
1930H Proof	—	Value: 210				
1937H	3,000,000	1.25	2.25	4.50	9.00	—
1941H	3,000,000	250	350	525	900	—

Note: Estimate 50 pieces exist

KM# 8 5 CENTS Weight: 1.3500 g. **Composition:** 0.8000 Silver .0347 oz. ASW **Ruler:** Charles J. Brooke Rajah

Date	Mintage	F	VF	XF	Unc	BU
1908H	40,000	30.00	50.00	90.00	140	—
1908H Proof	—	Value: 350				
1911H	40,000	30.00	50.00	90.00	140	—
1913H	100,000	20.00	40.00	70.00	120	—
1913H Proof	—	Value: 350				
1915H	100,000	20.00	40.00	75.00	130	—
1915H Proof	—	Value: 350				

KM# 13 5 CENTS Weight: 1.3500 g. **Composition:** 0.4000 Silver .0174 oz. ASW **Ruler:** Charles V. Brooke Rajah

Date	Mintage	F	VF	XF	Unc	BU
1920H	100,000	40.00	60.00	100	180	—
1920H Proof	—	Value: 400				

KM# 14 5 CENTS Composition: Copper-Nickel **Ruler:** Charles V. Brooke Rajah

Date	Mintage	F	VF	XF	Unc	BU
1920H	400,000	2.00	4.00	8.00	20.00	—
1927H	600,000	2.00	4.00	8.00	20.00	—
1927H Proof	—	Value: 275				

KM# 9 10 CENTS Weight: 2.7100 g. **Composition:** 0.8000 Silver .0697 oz. ASW **Ruler:** Charles J. Brooke Rajah

Date	Mintage	F	VF	XF	Unc	BU
1906H	50,000	20.00	30.00	55.00	100	—
1906H Proof	—	Value: 350				
1910H	50,000	20.00	30.00	55.00	100	—
1910H Proof	—	Value: 350				
1911/10H	100,000	20.00	30.00	60.00	120	—
1911H	Inc. above	15.00	20.00	40.00	90.00	—
1913H	100,000	15.00	20.00	40.00	90.00	—
1913H Proof	—	Value: 350				
1915H	100,000	30.00	45.00	75.00	185	—
1915H Proof	—	Value: 350				

KM# 15 10 CENTS Weight: 2.7100 g. **Composition:** 0.4000 Silver .0349 oz. ASW **Ruler:** Charles V. Brooke Rajah

Date	Mintage	F	VF	XF	Unc	BU
1920H	150,000	18.00	27.50	50.00	90.00	—
1920H Proof	—	Value: 350				

KM# 16 10 CENTS Composition: Copper-Nickel **Ruler:** Charles V. Brooke Rajah

Date	Mintage	F	VF	XF	Unc	BU
1920H	800,000	2.00	4.00	8.00	17.50	—
1927H	1,000,000	2.00	3.00	6.00	17.50	—
1927H Proof	—	Value: 300				
1934H	2,000,000	2.00	3.00	6.00	17.50	—
1934H Proof	—	Value: 300				

KM# 10 20 CENTS Weight: 5.4300 g. **Composition:** 0.8000 Silver .1396 oz. ASW **Ruler:** Charles J. Brooke Rajah

Date	Mintage	F	VF	XF	Unc	BU
1906H	25,000	30.00	60.00	100	215	—
1906H Proof	—	Value: 550				
1910H	25,000	30.00	60.00	100	215	—
1910H Proof	—	Value: 550				
1911H	15,000	30.00	60.00	100	215	—
1913H	25,000	30.00	60.00	100	215	—
1913H Proof	—	Value: 550				
1915H	25,000	125	175	300	500	—
1915H Proof	—	Value: 725				

KM# 17 20 CENTS Weight: 5.4300 g. **Composition:** 0.4000 Silver .0699 oz. ASW **Ruler:** Charles V. Brooke Rajah

Date	Mintage	F	VF	XF	Unc	BU
1920	25,000	65.00	120	220	400	—
1920 Proof	—	Value: 600				

KM# 17a 20 CENTS Weight: 5.0800 g. **Composition:** 0.4000 Silver .0653 oz. ASW **Ruler:** Charles V. Brooke Rajah

Date	Mintage	F	VF	XF	Unc	BU
1927H	250,000	5.00	10.00	22.50	50.00	—
1927H Proof	—	Value: 400				

KM# 11 50 CENTS Weight: 13.5700 g. **Composition:** 0.8000 Silver .349 oz. ASW **Ruler:** Charles V. Brooke Rajah

Date	Mintage	F	VF	XF	Unc	BU
1906H	10,000	225	325	500	950	—
1906H Proof	—	Value: 1,350				

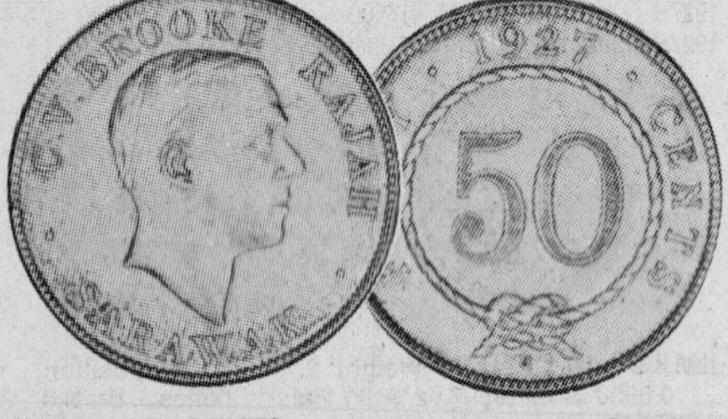

KM# 19 50 CENTS Weight: 10.3000 g. **Composition:** 0.5000 Silver .1656 oz. ASW **Ruler:** Charles V. Brooke Rajah

Date	Mintage	F	VF	XF	Unc	BU
1927H	200,000	12.00	20.00	38.00	90.00	—
1927H Proof	—	Value: 400				

SAUDI ARABIA

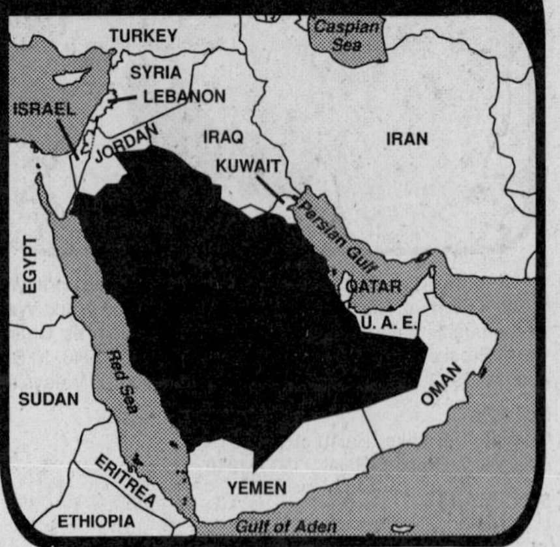

The Kingdom of Saudi Arabia, an independent and absolute hereditary monarchy comprising the former sultanate of Nejd, the old kingdom of Hejaz, Asir and Al Hasa, occupies four-fifths of the Arabian peninsula. The kingdom has an area of 830,000 sq. mi. (2,149,690 sq. km.) and a population of *16.1 million. Capital: Riyadh. The economy is based on oil, which provides 85 percent of Saudi Arabia's revenue.

Mohammed united the Arabs in the 7th century and his followers founded a great empire with its capital at Medina. The Turks established nominal rule over much of Arabia in the 16th and 17th centuries, and in the 18thcentury divided it into principalities.

The Kingdom of Saudi Arabia was created by King Abd Al-Aziz Bin Saud (1882-1953), a descendant of earlier Wahhabi rulers of the Arabian peninsula. In 1901 he seized Riyadh, capital of the Sultanate of Nejd, and in 1905 established himself as Sultan. In 1913 he captured the Turkish province of Al Hasa; took the Hejaz in 1925 and by 1926 most of Asir. In1932 he combined Nejd and Hejaz into the single kingdom of Saudi Arabia. Asir was incorporated into the kingdom a year later.

TITLES

العربية السعودية

Al-Arabiya(t) as-Sa'udiya(t)

المملكة العربية السعودية

Al-Mamlaka(t) al-'Arabiya(t) as-Sa'udiya(t)

RULERS

al Sa'ud Dynasty

Abd Al-Aziz Bin Sa'ud, (Ibn Sa'ud), AH1344-1373/1926-1953AD
Sa'ud Bin Abd Al-Aziz, AH1373-1383/1953-1964AD
Faisal Bin Abd Al-Aziz, AH1383-1395/1964-1975AD
Khalid Bin Abd Al-Aziz, AH1395-1403/1975-1982AD
Fahad Bin Abd Al-Aziz, AH1403-/1982-AD

MONETARY SYSTEM

Until 1960

20-22 Ghirsh = 1 Riyal
40 Riyals = 1 Guinea

NOTE: Copper-nickel, reeded-edge coins dated AH1356 and silver coins dated AH1354 were struck at the U. S. Mint in Philadelphia between 1944-1949.

KINGDOM

STANDARD COINAGE

KM# 19.1 1/4 GHIRSH Composition: Copper-Nickel **Edge:** Plain

Date	Mintage	VG	F	VF	XF	Unc
AH1356 (1937)	1,000,000	1.00	2.00	6.00	15.00	—

KM# 19.2 1/4 GHIRSH Composition: Copper-Nickel **Edge:** Reeded

Date	Mintage	VG	F	VF	XF	Unc
AH1356 (1937)	21,500,000	0.25	0.50	1.00	2.50	—

Note: Struck in 1947 (AH1366-67) at Philadelphia

KM# 20.1 1/2 GHIRSH Composition: Copper-Nickel **Edge:** Plain

Date	Mintage	VG	F	VF	XF	Unc
AH1356 (1937)	1,000,000	1.25	3.00	8.00	20.00	—

KM# 20.2 1/2 GHIRSH Composition: Copper-Nickel **Edge:** Reeded

Date	Mintage	VG	F	VF	XF	Unc
AH1356 (1937)	10,850,000	0.20	0.50	1.50	3.00	—

Note: Struck in 1947 (AH1366-67) at Philadelphia

KM# 21.2 GHIRSH Composition: Copper-Nickel **Edge:** Reeded

Date	Mintage	VG	F	VF	XF	Unc
AH1356 (1937)	7,150,000	0.50	1.00	2.50	5.00	—

Note: Struck in 1947 (AH1366-67) at Philadelphia

KM# 21.1 GHIRSH Composition: Copper-Nickel **Edge:** Plain

Date	Mintage	VG	F	VF	XF	Unc
AH1356 (1937)	4,000,000	1.00	2.00	6.00	15.00	—

KM# 40 GHIRSH Composition: Copper-Nickel

Date	Mintage	F	VF	XF	Unc	BU
AH1376 (1957)	10,000,000	0.15	0.25	0.50	3.00	—
AH1378 (1958)	50,000,000	0.15	0.25	0.50	2.00	—

KM# 41 2 GHIRSH Composition: Copper-Nickel

Date	Mintage	F	VF	XF	Unc	BU
AH1376 (1957)	50,000,000	0.10	0.35	0.75	5.00	—
AH1379 (1959)	28,110,000	0.10	0.35	0.70	3.50	—

KM# 42 4 GHIRSH Composition: Copper-Nickel

Date	Mintage	F	VF	XF	Unc	BU
AH1376 (1956)	49,100,000	0.25	0.50	1.00	6.00	—
AH1378 (1958)	10,000,000	0.25	0.50	1.00	5.00	—

KM# 16 1/4 RIYAL Weight: 3.1000 g. Composition: 0.9170 Silver .0913 oz. ASW

Date	Mintage	F	VF	XF	Unc	BU
AH1354 (1935)	900,000	1.75	2.50	3.00	5.50	—
AH1354 (1935) Proof	—	Value: 150				

KM# 37 1/4 RIYAL Weight: 2.9500 g. Composition: 0.9170 Silver .0869 oz. ASW

Date	Mintage	F	VF	XF	Unc	BU
AH1374 (1954)	4,000,000	BV	1.00	3.00	5.50	—

KM# 17 1/2 RIYAL Weight: 5.8500 g. Composition: 0.9170 Silver .1724 oz. ASW

Date	Mintage	F	VF	XF	Unc	BU
AH1354 (1935)	950,000	1.50	4.00	6.00	12.50	—

KM# 38 1/2 RIYAL Weight: 5.9500 g. Composition: 0.9170 Silver .1754 oz. ASW

Date	Mintage	F	VF	XF	Unc	BU
AH1374 (1954)	2,000,000	1.50	3.00	4.50	10.00	—

KM# 18 RIYAL Weight: 11.6000 g. Composition: 0.9170 Silver .3419 oz. ASW

Date	Mintage	F	VF	XF	Unc	BU
AH1354 (1935)	60,000,000	BV	2.50	5.50	12.50	—
AH1354 (1935) Proof	20,000,000	—	—	—	—	—
AH1367 (1947)	Inc. above	BV	2.50	5.50	15.00	—
AH1370 (1950)	—	BV	2.50	5.50	17.50	—

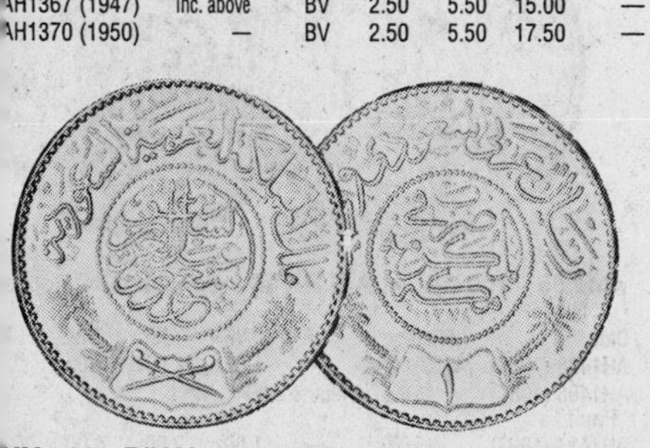

KM# 39 RIYAL Weight: 11.6000 g. Composition: 0.9170 Silver .3419 oz. ASW

Date	Mintage	F	VF	XF	Unc	BU
AH1374 (1954)	48,000,000	BV	2.50	6.00	17.50	—

COUNTERMARKED COINAGE

70 = 65 Countermark

The following pieces are countermarked examples of earlier types bearing the Arabic numerals 65. They were countermarked in a move to break money changers' monopoly on small coins in AH1365 (1946AD). These countermarks vary in size and are found with the Arabic numbers raised in a circle. Incuse countermarks are considered a recent fabrication.

KM# 24 1/4 GHIRSH Countermark: "65" Note: Countermark in Arabic numerals on 1/4 Ghirsh, KM#13.

CM Date	Host Date	Good	VG	F	VF	XF
AH1365	AH1348	6.00	12.00	30.00	65.00	—

KM# 25 1/4 GHIRSH Countermark: "65" Edge: Plain Note: Countermark in Arabic numerals on 1/4 Ghirsh, KM#19.

CM Date	Host Date	Good	VG	F	VF	XF
AH1365	AH1356	2.50	4.00	8.00	15.00	—

KM# 22 1/4 GHIRSH Countermark: "65" Note: Countermark in Arabic numerals on 1/4 Ghirsh, KM#4.

CM Date	Host Date	Good	VG	F	VF	XF
AH1365	AH1344	6.00	12.00	30.00	65.00	—

KM# 23 1/4 GHIRSH Countermark: "65" Note: Countermark in Arabic numerals on 1/4 Ghirsh, KM#7.

CM Date	Host Date	Good	VG	F	VF	XF
AH1365	AH1346	6.00	12.00	30.00	65.00	—

KM# 28 1/2 GHIRSH Countermark: "65" Note: Countermark in Arabic numerals on 1/2 Ghirsh, KM#14.

CM Date	Host Date	Good	VG	F	VF	XF
AH1365	AH1348	6.00	12.00	25.00	60.00	—

KM# 29 1/2 GHIRSH Countermark: "65" Edge: Plain Note: Countermark in Arabic numerals on 1/2 Ghirsh, KM#20.1.

CM Date	Host Date	Good	VG	F	VF	XF
AH1365	AH1356	1.25	2.25	5.00	12.00	—

KM# 26 1/2 GHIRSH Countermark: "65" Note: Countermark in Arabic numerals on 1/2 Ghirsh, KM#5.

CM Date	Host Date	Good	VG	F	VF	XF
AH1365	AH1344	6.00	12.00	25.00	60.00	—

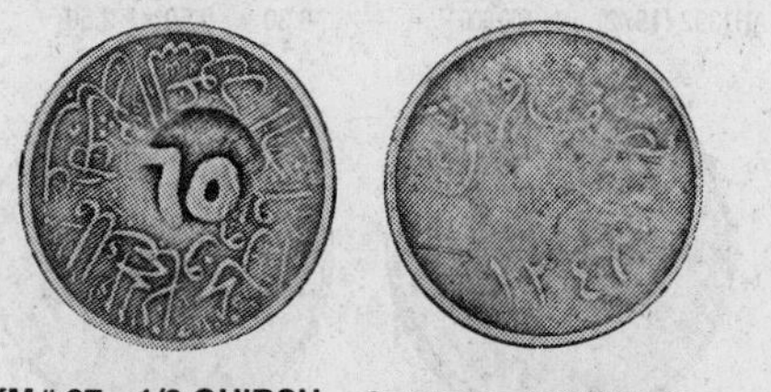

KM# 27 1/2 GHIRSH Countermark: "65" Note: Countermark in Arabic numerals on 1/2 Ghirsh, KM#8.

CM Date	Host Date	Good	VG	F	VF	XF
AH1365	AH1346	6.00	12.00	25.00	60.00	—

KM# 32 GHIRSH Countermark: "65" Note: Countermark in Arabic numerals on 1 Ghirsh, KM#15.

CM Date	Host Date	Good	VG	F	VF	XF
AH1365	AH1348	10.00	20.00	50.00	90.00	—

KM# 33 GHIRSH Countermark: "65" Edge: Plain Note: Countermark in Arabic numerals on 1 Ghirsh, KM#21.

CM Date	Host Date	Good	VG	F	VF	XF
AH1365	AH1356	2.00	3.00	8.00	20.00	—

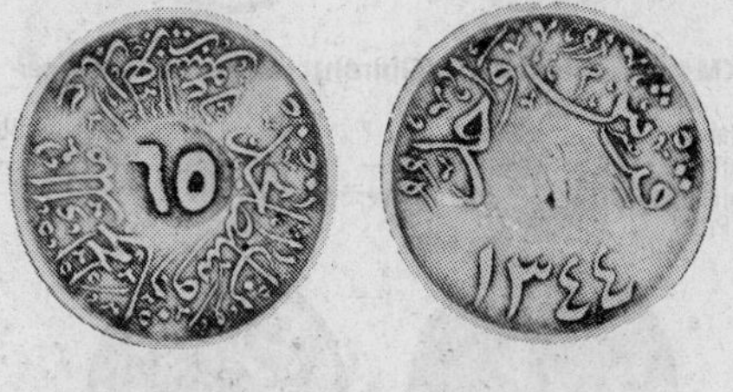

KM# 30 GHIRSH Countermark: "65" Note: Countermark in Arabic numerals on 1 Ghirsh, KM#6.

CM Date	Host Date	Good	VG	F	VF	XF
AH1365	AH1344	6.00	12.00	45.00	80.00	—

KM# 31 GHIRSH Countermark: "65" Note: Countermark in Arabic numerals on 1 Ghirsh, KM#9.

CM Date	Host Date	Good	VG	F	VF	XF
AH1365	AH1346	6.00	12.00	30.00	65.00	—

REFORM COINAGE

5 Halala = 1 Ghirsh; 100 Halala = 1 Riyal

KM# 44 HALALA Composition: Bronze

Date	Mintage	F	VF	XF	Unc	BU
AH1383 (1963)	5,000,000	0.50	0.60	0.85	3.00	—

KM# 60 HALALA Composition: Bronze Obverse: Different inscription

Date	F	VF	XF	Unc	BU
AH1397 (1979) Rare	—	—	—	—	—

Note: Not released for circulation

KM# 45 5 HALALA (Ghirsh) Composition: Copper-Nickel

Date	Mintage	F	VF	XF	Unc	BU
AH1392 (1972)	130,000,000	0.10	0.15	0.30	0.50	—

KM# 53 5 HALALA (Ghirsh) Composition: Copper-Nickel

Date	Mintage	F	VF	XF	Unc	BU
AH1397 (1976)	20,000,000	0.15	0.25	0.60	2.00	—
AH1400 (1979)	—	0.15	0.25	0.60	2.00	—

KM# 57 5 HALALA (Ghirsh) Composition: Copper-Nickel **Series:** F.A.O.

Date	Mintage	F	VF	XF	Unc	BU
AH1398 (1977)	1,500,000	—	0.30	0.50	1.00	—

KM# 61 5 HALALA (Ghirsh) Composition: Copper-Nickel

Date	Mintage	F	VF	XF	Unc	BU
AH1408 (1987)	80,000,000	—	0.30	0.50	1.00	—
AH1408 (1987) Proof	5,000	Value: 5.00				

KM# 46 10 HALALA (2 Ghirsh) Composition: Copper-Nickel

Date	Mintage	F	VF	XF	Unc	BU
AH1392 (1972)	55,000,000	0.10	0.20	0.35	0.50	—

KM# 54 10 HALALA (2 Ghirsh) Composition: Copper-Nickel

Date	Mintage	F	VF	XF	Unc	BU
AH1397 (1976)	50,000,000	0.15	0.25	1.00	2.50	—
AH1400 (1979)	29,500,000	0.25	0.75	1.00	3.00	—

KM# 58 10 HALALA (2 Ghirsh) Composition: Copper-Nickel **Series:** F.A.O.

Date	Mintage	F	VF	XF	Unc	BU
AH1398 (1977)	1,000,000	—	0.25	0.50	1.00	—

KM# 62 10 HALALA (2 Ghirsh) Composition: Copper-Nickel

Date	Mintage	F	VF	XF	Unc	BU
AH1408 (1987)	100,000,000	—	0.30	0.60	1.25	—
AH1408 (1987) Proof	5,000	Value: 6.00				
AH1423 (2002)	—	—	0.30	0.60	1.25	—

KM# 49 25 HALALA (1/4 Riyal) Composition: Copper-Nickel **Series:** F.A.O.

Date	Mintage	F	VF	XF	Unc	BU
AH1392 (1972)	200,000	—	0.20	0.50	1.00	—

KM# 48 25 HALALA (1/4 Riyal) Composition: Copper-Nickel **Note:** Corrected denomination; feminine gender.

Date	F	VF	XF	Unc	BU
AH1392 (1972)	0.25	0.50	1.00	2.00	—

KM# 47 25 HALALA (1/4 Riyal) Composition: Copper-Nickel **Note:** Error. Denomination in masculine gender.

Date	Mintage	F	VF	XF	Unc	BU
AH1392 (1972)	48,465,000	1.00	2.00	6.00	15.00	—

KM# 55 25 HALALA (1/4 Riyal) Composition: Copper-Nickel

Date	Mintage	F	VF	XF	Unc	BU
AH1397 (1976)	20,000,000	0.35	0.50	1.00	3.00	—
AH1400 (1979)	57,000,000	0.35	0.50	0.85	2.50	—

KM# 63 25 HALALA (1/4 Riyal) Composition: Copper-Nickel

Date	Mintage	F	VF	XF	Unc	BU
AH1408 (1987)	100,000,000	—	0.40	0.70	1.50	—
AH1408 (1987) Proof	5,000	Value: 7.50				
AH1423 (2002)	—	—	0.40	0.70	1.50	—

KM# 50 50 HALALA (1/2 Riyal) Composition: Copper-Nickel **Series:** F.A.O.

Date	Mintage	F	VF	XF	Unc	BU
AH1392 (1972)	500,000	—	0.30	0.60	2.50	—

KM# 51 50 HALALA (1/2 Riyal) Composition: Copper-Nickel

Date	Mintage	F	VF	XF	Unc	BU
AH1392 (1972)	16,000,000	0.20	0.35	0.60	2.00	—

KM# 56 50 HALALA (1/2 Riyal) Composition: Copper-Nickel

Date	Mintage	F	VF	XF	Unc	BU
AH1397 (1976)	20,000,000	0.50	0.75	1.00	3.00	—
AH1400 (1979)	21,600,000	0.75	1.00	1.50	3.50	—

KM# 64 50 HALALA (1/2 Riyal) Composition: Copper-Nickel

Date	Mintage	F	VF	XF	Unc	BU
AH1408 (1987)	70,000,000	0.20	0.50	2.25	3.50	—
AH1408 (1987) Proof	5,000	Value: 15.00				
AH1423 (2002)	—	0.20	0.50	2.25	3.50	—

KM# 52 100 HALALA (1 Riyal) Composition: Copper-Nickel

Date	Mintage	F	VF	XF	Unc	BU
AH1396 (1976)	250,000	—	0.65	1.00	3.50	—
AH1400 (1980)	30,000,000	—	0.65	1.00	3.00	—

KM# 59 100 HALALA (1 Riyal) Composition: Copper-Nickel **Series:** F.A.O.

Date	Mintage	F	VF	XF	Unc	BU
AH1397 (1977)	—	—	—	125	225	
AH1398 (1978)	10,000,000	—	0.75	1.50	3.50	

Note: AH1397 date was struck as samples for the Saudi Arabia government by the British Royal Mint

KM# 65 100 HALALA (1 Riyal) Composition: Copper-Nickel

Date	Mintage	F	VF	XF	Unc	BU
AH1408 (1987)	40,000,000	—	1.00	2.00	3.00	
AH1408 (1987) Proof	5,000	Value: 22.00				
AH1414 (1993)	5,000	—	1.00	2.00	4.00	

KM# 66 100 HALALA (1 Riyal) **Ring Composition:** Copper-Nickel **Center Composition:** Brass **Obverse:** Palm tree above crossed swords **Reverse:** Inscription, denomination, and date

Date	F	VF	XF	Unc	BU
AH1419 (1999)	—	1.00	2.50	5.00	—

KM# 67 100 HALALA (1 Riyal) **Ring Composition:** Copper-Nickel **Center Composition:** Brass **Subject:** Centennial of Kingdom **Obverse:** Palm tree design and inscription **Reverse:** Inscription, denomination, and date

Date	F	VF	XF	Unc	BU
AH1419 (1999)	—	1.50	3.50	7.00	—
AH1419 (1999) Proof	—	Value: 15.00			

TRADE COINAGE

KM# 36 GUINEA **Weight:** 7.9881 g. **Composition:** 0.9170 Gold .2354 oz. AGW

Date	Mintage	F	VF	XF	Unc	BU
AH1370 (1950)	2,000,000	—	BV	95.00	125	—

KM# 43 GUINEA **Weight:** 7.9881 g. **Composition:** 0.9170 Gold .2354 oz. AGW

Date	Mintage	F	VF	XF	Unc	BU
AH1377 (1957)	1,579,000	—	BV	100	145	—

BULLION COINAGE

KM# 35 SOVEREIGN (Pound) **Weight:** 7.9881 g. **Composition:** 0.9170 Gold .2354 oz. AGW

Date	Mintage	F	VF	XF	Unc	BU
ND(1947) (1947)	123,000	—	300	500	750	—

KM# 34 4 POUNDS **Weight:** 31.9500 g. **Composition:** 0.9170 Gold .9420 oz. AGW

Date	Mintage	F	VF	XF	Unc	BU
ND(1945-46) (1945)	91,000	—	—	600	800	—

Note: KM#35 and KM#34 were struck at the Philadelphia Mint for a concession payment for oil to the Saudi Government; most were melted into bullion

SENEGAL

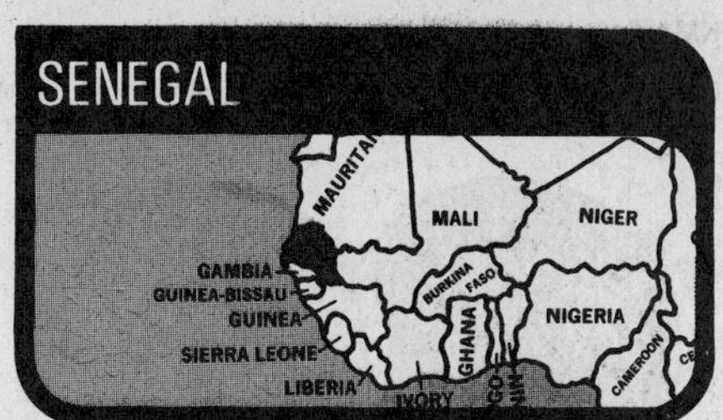

The Republic of Senegal, located on the bulge of West Africa between Mauritania and Guinea-Bissau, has an area of 75,750 sq. mi. (196,190 sq. km.) and a population of *7.5 million. Capital: Dakar. The economy is primarily agricultural. Peanuts and products, phosphates, and canned fish are exported.

An abundance of megalithic remains indicates that Senegal was inhabited in prehistoric times. The Portuguese had some trading stations on the banks of the Senegal River in the 15th century. French commercial establishments date from the 17th century. The French gradually acquired control over the interior regions, which were administered as a protectorate until 1920, and as a colony thereafter. After the 1958 French constitutional referendum, Senegal became a member of the French Community with virtual autonomy. In 1959 Senegal and the French Soudan merged to form the Mali Federation, which became fully independent on June 20, 1960. (April 4, the date the transfer of power agreement was signed with France, is celebrated as Senegal's independence day). The Federation broke up on Aug. 20, 1960, when Senegal seceded and proclaimed the Republic of Senegal. Soudan became the Republic of Mali a month later.

Senegal is a member of a monetary union of autonomous republics called the Monetary Union of West African States (*Union Monetaire Ouest-Africaine*). The other members are Ivory Coast, Benin, Burkina Faso (Upper Volta), Niger, Mauritania and Togo. Mali was a member, but seceded in1962. Some of the member countries have issued coinage in addition to the common currency issued by the Monetary Union of West African States.

REPUBLIC

STANDARD COINAGE

KM# 1 10 FRANCS **Weight:** 3.2000 g. **Composition:** 0.9000 Gold .0926 oz. AGW **Subject:** 8th Anniversary of Independence

Date	F	VF	XF	Unc	BU
1968 Proof	—	Value: 65.00			

KM# 2 25 FRANCS **Weight:** 8.0000 g. **Composition:** 0.9000 Gold .2315 oz. AGW **Subject:** 8th Anniversary of Independence

Date	F	VF	XF	Unc	BU
1968 Proof	—	Value: 125			

KM# 3 50 FRANCS **Weight:** 16.0000 g. **Composition:** 0.9000 Gold .463 oz. AGW **Subject:** 8th Anniversary of Independence

Date	F	VF	XF	Unc	BU
1968 Proof	—	Value: 250			

KM# 5 50 FRANCS **Weight:** 28.2800 g. **Composition:** 0.9250 Silver .8411 oz. ASW **Subject:** 25th Anniversary of Eurafrique Program

Date	Mintage	F	VF	XF	Unc	BU
1975	1,968	—	—	—	110	—
1975 Proof	10,000	Value: 125				

KM# 4 100 FRANCS **Weight:** 32.0000 g. **Composition:** 0.9000 Gold .926 oz. AGW **Subject:** 8th Anniversary of Independence

Date	F	VF	XF	Unc	BU
1968 Proof	—	Value: 450			

KM# 6 150 FRANCS **Weight:** 79.9700 g. **Composition:** 0.9250 Silver 2.3776 oz. ASW **Subject:** 25th Anniversary of Eurafrique Program **Reverse:** Similar to 50 Francs, KM#5.

Date	Mintage	F	VF	XF	Unc	BU
1975	1,075	—	—	—	170	—
1975 Proof	10,000	Value: 175				

KM# 7 250 FRANCS **Weight:** 3.9800 g. **Composition:** 0.9170 Gold .1172 oz. AGW **Subject:** 25th Anniversary of Eurafrique Program

Date	Mintage	F	VF	XF	Unc	BU
1975	1,000	—	—	—	75.00	—
1975 Proof	1,250	Value: 75.00				

KM# 8 500 FRANCS **Weight:** 7.9600 g. **Composition:** 0.9170 Gold .2344 oz. AGW **Subject:** 25th Anniversary of Eurafrique Program

Date	Mintage	F	VF	XF	Unc	BU
1975	500	—	—	—	150	—
1975 Proof	1,250	Value: 125				

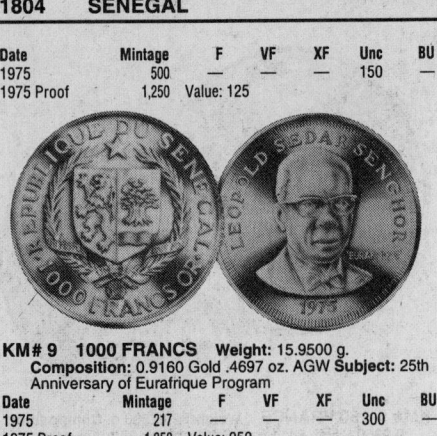

KM# 9 1000 FRANCS **Weight:** 15.9500 g. **Composition:** 0.9160 Gold .4697 oz. AGW **Subject:** 25th Anniversary of Eurafrique Program

Date	Mintage	F	VF	XF	Unc	BU
1975	217	—	—	—	300	—
1975 Proof	1,250	Value: 250				

KM# 10 2500 FRANCS **Weight:** 39.9300 g. **Composition:** 0.9160 Gold 1.176 oz. AGW **Subject:** 25th Anniversary of Eurafrique Program

Date	Mintage	F	VF	XF	Unc	BU
1975	195	—	—	—	700	—
1975 Proof	1,250	Value: 650				

KM# 11 2 AFRICA - 3000 CFA FRANCS **Weight:** 9.9300 g. **Composition:** Brass **Subject:** West African Development Institute **Obverse:** Bush baby **Reverse:** Elephant on map **Edge:** Plain **Size:** 27.6 mm.

Date	F	VF	XF	Unc	BU
2003	—	—	—	30.00	—

TOKEN COINAGE

KM# Tn2 5 CENTIMES **Composition:** Aluminum **Issuer:** Dakar, Chamber of Commerce

Date	VG	F	VF	XF	Unc
1920	9.00	18.00	40.00	120	—

KM# Tn7 5 CENTIMES **Composition:** Aluminum **Issuer:** Kayes, Upper Senegal-Niger Chamber of Commerce

Date	VG	F	VF	XF	Unc
1920	12.00	22.00	45.00	125	—

KM# Tn12 5 CENTIMES **Composition:** Aluminum **Issuer:** Rufisque, Chamber of Commerce

Date	VG	F	VF	XF	Unc
1920	9.00	18.00	40.00	120	—

KM# Tn3 10 CENTIMES **Composition:** Aluminum **Issuer:** Dakar, Chamber of Commerce

Date	VG	F	VF	XF	Unc
1920	6.00	12.00	30.00	90.00	—

KM# Tn4 10 CENTIMES **Composition:** Brass **Issuer:** Dakar, Chamber of Commerce

Date	VG	F	VF	XF	Unc
1920	9.00	18.00	40.00	120	—

KM# Tn8 10 CENTIMES **Composition:** Aluminum **Issuer:** Kayes, Upper Senegal-Niger Chamber of Commerce

Date	VG	F	VF	XF	Unc
1920	14.00	28.00	60.00	150	—

KM# Tn13 10 CENTIMES **Composition:** Aluminum **Issuer:** Rufisque, Chamber of Commerce

Date	VG	F	VF	XF	Unc
1920	6.00	12.00	30.00	100	—

KM# Tn5 25 CENTIMES **Composition:** Aluminum **Issuer:** Dakar, Chamber of Commerce

Date	VG	F	VF	XF	Unc
1920	7.00	15.00	35.00	100	—

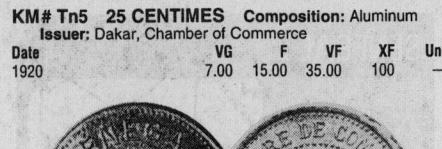

KM# Tn9 25 CENTIMES **Composition:** Aluminum **Issuer:** Kayes, Upper Senegal-Niger Chamber of Commerce

Date	VG	F	VF	XF	Unc
1920	15.00	30.00	65.00	180	—

KM# Tn10 25 CENTIMES **Composition:** Copper-Nickel **Issuer:** Kayes, Upper Senegal-Niger Chamber of Commerce

Date	VG	F	VF	XF	Unc
1920	18.00	35.00	75.00	220	—

KM# Tn14 25 CENTIMES **Composition:** Aluminum **Issuer:** Rufisque, Chamber of Commerce

Date	VG	F	VF	XF	Unc
1920	12.00	25.00	50.00	150	—

KM# Tn6 50 CENTIMES **Composition:** Aluminum **Issuer:** Dakar, Chamber of Commerce **Shape:** Octagon

Date	VG	F	VF	XF	Unc
1920	12.00	25.00	50.00	150	—

KM# Tn11 50 CENTIMES **Composition:** Aluminum **Issuer:** Kayes, Upper Senegal-Niger Chamber of Commerce

Date	VG	F	VF	XF	Unc
1920	20.00	40.00	85.00	200	—

KM# Tn15 50 CENTIMES **Composition:** Aluminum **Issuer:** Rufisque, Chamber of Commerce

Date	VG	F	VF	XF	Unc
1920	18.00	30.00	60.00	160	—

KM# Tn16 50 CENTIMES **Composition:** Brass **Issuer:** Rufisque, Chamber of Commerce

Date	VG	F	VF	XF	Unc
1920	20.00	35.00	70.00	175	—

KM# Tn17 50 CENTIMES **Composition:** Brass **Issuer:** Ziguinchor, Chamber of Commerce

Date	VG	F	VF	XF	Unc
1921	22.00	40.00	80.00	180	—

KM# Tn18 FRANC **Composition:** Brass **Issuer:** Ziguinchor, Chamber of Commerce

Date	VG	F	VF	XF	Unc
1921	30.00	45.00	90.00	200	—

KM# Tn19 FRANC **Composition:** Aluminum **Issuer:** Ziguinchor, Chamber of Commerce

Date	VG	F	VF	XF	Unc
1921	40.00	80.00	175	350	—

ESSAIS

Standard metals unless otherwise noted

KM#	Date	Mintage	Identification	Mkt Val
E1	1920	—	25 Centimes. Kayes. KM-Tn10.	250
E2	1921	—	50 Centimes. Zinguinchor. KMTn17.	300
E3	1921	—	Franc. Zinguinchor. KMTn18.	320

MINT SETS

KM#	Date	Mintage	Identification	Issue Price	Mkt Val
MS1	1975 (4)	195	KM7-10	—	1,150

PROOF SETS

KM#	Date	Mintage	Identification	Issue Price	Mkt Val
PS1	1968 (4)	—	KM1-4	—	900
PS2	1975 (2)	—	KM5-6	—	300

SERBIA

Serbia, a former inland Balkan kingdom has an area of 34,116 sq. mi. (88,361 sq. km.). Capital: Belgrade.

Serbia emerged as a separate kingdom in the 12th century and attained its greatest expansion and political influence in the mid-14th century. After the Battle of Kosovo, 1389, Serbia became a vassal principality of Turkey and remained under Turkish suzerainty until it was re-established as an independent kingdom by the 1878 Treaty of Berlin. Following World War I, which had its immediate cause in the assassination of Austrian Archduke Francis Ferdinand by a Serbian nationalist, Serbia joined with the Croats and Slovenes to form the new Kingdom of the South Slavs with Peter I of Serbia as King. The name of the kingdom was later changed to Yugoslavia. Invaded by Germany during World War II, Serbia emerged as a constituent republic of the Socialist Federal Republic of Yugoslavia.

RULERS

Alexander I, 1889-1902
Peter I, 1903-1918

MINT MARKS

A - Paris
(a) - Paris, privy mark only
(g) - Gorham Mfg. Co., Providence, R.I.
H - Birmingham
V - Vienna
ÁÏ - (BP) Budapest

MONETARY SYSTEM

100 Para = 1 Dinara

DENOMINATIONS

ÏÀÐÀ = Para
ÏÀÐÅ = Pare
ÄÈÍÀÐ = Dinar
ÄÈÍÀÐÀ = Dinara

KINGDOM

STANDARD COINAGE

KM# 23 2 PARE **Composition:** Bronze **Ruler:** Peter I **Note:** Medallic die alignment.

Date	Mintage	F	VF	XF	Unc	BU
1904	12,500,000	2.00	5.00	15.00	38.00	—

KM# 18 5 PARA **Composition:** Copper-Nickel **Ruler:** Peter I **Note:** Medallic die alignment.

Date	Mintage	F	VF	XF	Unc	BU
1904	8,000,000	1.00	2.50	6.00	16.00	—
1904 Proof	Inc. above	Value: 200				
1912	10,000,000	0.75	1.50	3.50	12.00	—
1912 Proof	—	Value: 120				
1917(g)	5,000,000	5.00	10.00	20.00	35.00	—

KM# 19 10 PARA **Composition:** Copper-Nickel **Ruler:** Peter I **Note:** Medallic die alignment.

Date	Mintage	F	VF	XF	Unc
1904 Proof	—	Value: 350			
1912	7,700,000	0.75	1.25	3.50	11.00
1912 Proof	—	Value: 120			
1917(g)	5,000,000	1.00	2.50	8.00	24.00
1917(g) Proof	—	Value: 200			

KM# 20 20 PARA Composition: Copper-Nickel **Ruler:** Peter I **Note:** Medallic die alignment.

Date	Mintage	F	VF	XF	Unc	BU
1904 Proof	—	Value: 400				
1912	5,650,000	0.75	2.00	4.50	12.00	—
1912 Proof	—	Value: 125				
1917(g)	5,000,000	1.00	3.00	9.00	25.00	—

KM# 24.1 50 PARA Weight: 2.5000 g. **Composition:** 0.8350 Silver .0671 oz. ASW **Ruler:** Peter I **Note:** Medallic die alignment.

Date	Mintage	F	VF	XF	Unc	BU
1904	1,400,000	2.00	5.00	12.50	32.00	—
1904 Proof	—	Value: 200				
1912	800,000	2.50	6.00	15.00	34.00	—
1915(a)	12,138,000	1.00	2.00	4.50	12.00	—

Note: Not medal turn

KM# 24.2 50 PARA Weight: 2.5000 g. **Composition:** 0.8350 Silver .0671 oz. ASW **Ruler:** Peter I **Obverse:** Without designer's signature

Date	Mintage	F	VF	XF	Unc	BU
1915(a)	1,862,000	6.00	12.00	32.00	95.00	—

KM# 24.3 50 PARA Composition: Silver **Ruler:** Peter I **Note:** Coin die alignment.

Date	F	VF	XF	Unc	BU
1915	—	—	—	—	—

KM# 25.1 DINAR Weight: 5.0000 g. **Composition:** 0.8350 Silver .1342 oz. ASW **Ruler:** Peter I **Obverse:** Designer's signature below neck

Date	Mintage	F	VF	XF	Unc	BU
1904	994,000	4.50	12.00	25.00	75.00	—
1904 Proof	—	Value: 250				
1912	8,000,000	3.00	6.00	15.00	35.00	—
1915(a)	10,688,000	2.00	4.00	8.00	18.00	—

KM# 25.2 DINAR Weight: 5.0000 g. **Composition:** 0.8350 Silver .1342 oz. ASW **Ruler:** Peter I **Obverse:** Without designer's signature **Note:** Medallic die alignment.

Date	Mintage	F	VF	XF	Unc	BU
1915(a)	2,322,000	5.00	14.00	32.00	90.00	—

KM# 26.1 2 DINARA Weight: 10.0000 g. **Composition:** 0.8350 Silver .2684 oz. ASW **Ruler:** Peter I **Obverse:** Designer's signature below neck

Date	Mintage	F	VF	XF	Unc	BU
1904	1,150,000	7.50	15.00	32.00	85.00	—
1904 Proof	—	Value: 325				
1912	800,000	8.00	16.00	35.00	85.00	—
1915(a)	4,174,000	5.00	10.00	18.00	35.00	—

KM# 26.2 2 DINARA Weight: 10.0000 g. **Composition:** 0.8350 Silver .2684 oz. ASW **Ruler:** Peter I **Obverse:** Without designer's signature **Note:** Medallic die alignment.

Date	Mintage	F	VF	XF	Unc	BU
1915(a)	826,000	8.00	20.00	42.00	115	—

KM# 26.3 2 DINARA Weight: 10.0000 g. **Composition:** 0.8350 Silver .2684 oz. ASW **Ruler:** Peter I **Note:** Coin die alignment.

Date	VG	F	VF	XF	Unc
1915(a)	—	5.00	10.00	18.00	35.00

KM# 27 5 DINARA Weight: 25.0000 g. **Composition:** 0.9000 Silver .7234 oz. ASW **Ruler:** Peter I **Subject:** 100th Anniversary - Karageorgevich Dynasty **Edge:** Lettered, Type I

Date	Mintage	F	VF	XF	Unc	BU
1904	200,000	35.00	75.00	180	650	—
1904 Proof	—	Value: 2,000				

KM# 28 5 DINARA Weight: 25.0000 g. **Composition:** 0.9000 Silver .7234 oz. ASW **Ruler:** Peter I **Subject:** 100th Anniversary - Karageorgevich Dynasty **Edge:** Lettered, Type II

Date	F	VF	XF	Unc	BU
1904	150	250	425	1,600	—

GERMAN OCCUPATION

World War II

OCCUPATION COINAGE

KM# 30 50 PARA Composition: Zinc

Date	F	VF	XF	Unc	BU
1942(BP)	2.00	4.50	10.00	18.00	—

KM# 31 DINAR Composition: Zinc

Date	F	VF	XF	Unc	BU
1942(BP)	0.50	1.50	5.00	14.00	—

KM# 32 2 DINARA Composition: Zinc

Date	F	VF	XF	Unc	BU
1942(BP)	0.50	1.50	6.00	16.00	—

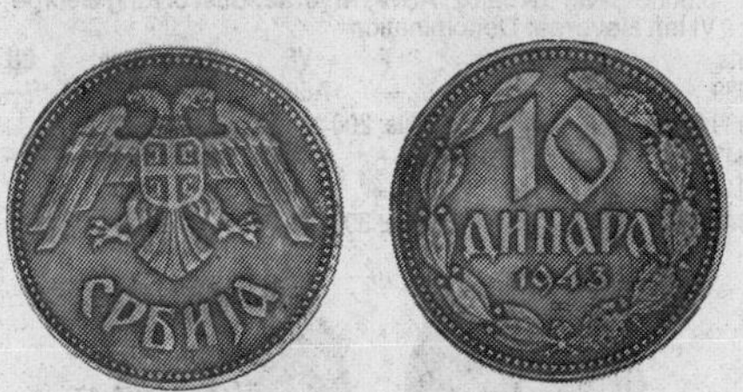

KM# 33 10 DINARA Composition: Zinc

Date	Mintage	F	VF	XF	Unc	BU
1943(BP)	1,750,000	1.00	2.50	7.50	18.00	—

PATTERNS

KM#	Date	Mintage	Identification	Mkt Val
PnD6	1904	4	5 Dinara. Gold. 44.5000 g.	—
PnC6	1904	—	2 Dinara. Bronze.	1,500
Pn6	1917	—	5 Para. Gold.	—
Pn7	1917	—	10 Para. Gold.	—
Pn8	1917	—	20 Para. Gold.	—
Pn9	1917	—	20 Dinara. Gold.	—

SEYCHELLES

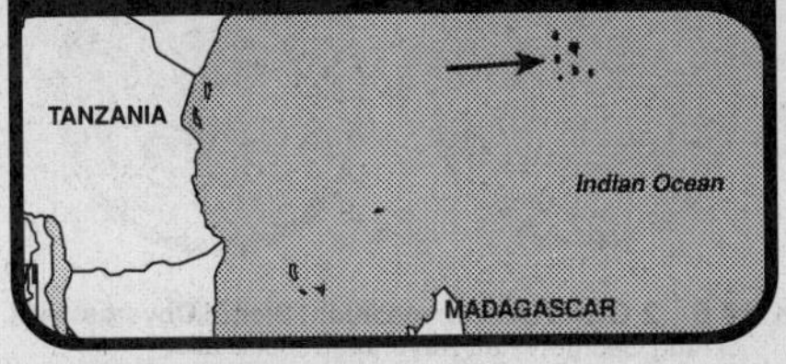

The Republic of Seychelles, an archipelago of 85 granite and coral islands situated in the Indian Ocean 600 miles (965 km.) northeast of Madagascar, has an area of 156sq. mi. (455 sq. km.) and a population of *70,000. Among these islands are the Aldabra Islands, the Farquhar Group, and Ile Desroches, which the United Kingdom ceded to the Seychelles upon its independence. Capital: Victoria, on Mahe. The economy is based on fishing, a plantation system of agriculture, and tourism. Copra, cinnamon and vanilla are exported.

Although the Seychelles is marked on Portuguese charts of the early 16th century, the first recorded visit to the islands, by an English ship, occurred in 1609. The Seychelles were annexed to France by Captain Lazare Picault in 1743 and permanently settled in 1768, with the intention of establishing spice plantations to compete with the Dutch monopoly of the spice trade. British troops seized the islands in 1810, during the Napoleonic Wars; the Treaty of Paris, 1814, formally ceded them to Britain. The Seychelles was a dependency of Mauritius until Aug. 31, 1903, when they became a separate British Crown Colony. The colony was granted limited internal self-government in 1970, and attained independence on June 28, 1976, becoming Britain's last African possession to do so. Seychelles is a member of the Commonwealth of Nations. The president is the Head of State and of Government.

RULERS
British, until 1976

MINT MARKS
PM - Pobjoy Mint
None - British Royal Mint

MONETARY SYSTEM
100 Cents = 1 Rupee

BRITISH CROWN COLONY

STANDARD COINAGE

100 Cents = 1 Rupee

KM# 5 CENT Composition: Bronze **Obverse:** Bust of King George VI left **Reverse:** Denomination

Date	Mintage	F	VF	XF	Unc	BU
1948	300,000	—	0.25	0.50	1.25	—
1948 Proof	—	Value: 50.00				

KM# 14 CENT Composition: Bronze **Obverse:** Bust of Queen Elizabeth II right

Date	F	VF	XF	Unc	BU
1959	—	0.75	1.50	3.00	—
1959 Proof	—	—	—	—	—
1961	—	0.50	1.00	2.25	—
1961 Proof	—	—	—	—	—
1963	—	0.50	1.00	1.50	—
1963 Proof	—	—	—	—	—
1965	—	2.00	3.00	5.00	—
1969	—	15.00	25.00	60.00	—

Note: Latest reports indicate only 5,000 circulation strikes have been releasesd to date in addition to proof issues

Date	F	VF	XF	Unc	BU
1969 Proof	—	Value: 5.00			

KM# 17 CENT Composition: Aluminum **Series:** F.A.O. **Obverse:** Bust of Queen Elizabeth II right **Reverse:** Cow

Date	Mintage	F	VF	XF	Unc	BU
1972	2,350,000	—	—	0.10	0.25	—

KM# 6 2 CENTS Composition: Bronze **Obverse:** Bust of King George VI left **Reverse:** Denomination

Date	Mintage	F	VF	XF	Unc	BU
1948	350,000	—	0.35	0.60	1.50	—
1948 Proof	—	Value: 75.00				

KM# 15 2 CENTS Composition: Bronze **Obverse:** Bust of Queen Elizabeth II right

Date	Mintage	F	VF	XF	Unc	BU
1959	30,000	—	0.50	1.00	2.50	—
1959 Proof	—	—	—	—	—	—
1961	30,000	—	0.50	1.00	2.75	—
1961 Proof	—	—	—	—	—	—
1963	40,000	—	0.75	1.25	2.50	—
1963 Proof	—	—	—	—	—	—
1965	20,000	—	2.00	3.00	4.00	—
1968	20,000	—	2.00	3.00	5.50	—
1969 Proof	5,000	Value: 4.00				

KM# 7 5 CENTS Composition: Bronze **Obverse:** Crowned King George VI left

Date	Mintage	F	VF	XF	Unc	BU
1948	300,000	—	0.40	0.80	2.00	—
1948 Proof	—	Value: 100				

KM# 16 5 CENTS Composition: Bronze **Obverse:** Bust of Queen Elizabeth II right

Date	Mintage	F	VF	XF	Unc	BU
1964	20,000	—	1.00	2.00	4.50	—
1964 Proof	—	—	—	—	—	—
1965	40,000	—	1.50	2.50	5.50	—
1967	20,000	—	1.50	3.00	8.00	—
1968	40,000	—	1.00	2.00	7.00	—
1969	100,000	—	0.50	1.00	5.00	—
1969 Proof	—	Value: 4.00				
1971	25,000	—	0.50	1.50	2.50	—

KM# 18 5 CENTS Composition: Aluminum **Series:** F.A.O. **Obverse:** Bust of Queen Elizabeth II right **Reverse:** Cabbage **Shape:** Scalloped

Date	Mintage	F	VF	XF	Unc	BU
1972	2,200,000	—	—	0.10	0.25	—
1975	1,200,000	—	—	0.10	0.25	—

KM# 1 10 CENTS Composition: Copper-Nickel **Obverse:** Bust of King George VI left **Reverse:** Denomination **Shape:** Scalloped

Date	Mintage	F	VF	XF	Unc	BU
1939	36,000	—	8.00	20.00	70.00	—
1939 Proof	—	Value: 150				
1943	36,000	—	6.00	12.00	40.00	—
1944	36,000	—	6.00	12.00	40.00	—
1944 Proof	—	Value: 175				

KM# 8 10 CENTS Composition: Copper-Nickel **Obverse:** Bust of King George VI left **Reverse:** Denomination **Shape:** Scalloped

Date	Mintage	F	VF	XF	Unc	BU
1951	36,000	—	2.00	5.00	9.00	—
1951 Proof	—	Value: 135				

KM# 10 10 CENTS Composition: Nickel-Brass **Obverse:** Bust of Queen Elizabeth II right **Shape:** 12-sided

Date	Mintage	F	VF	XF	Unc	BU
1953	130,000	—	0.50	1.00	3.00	—
1953 Proof	—	Value: 100				
1965	40,000	—	1.00	1.50	5.00	—
1967	20,000	—	4.00	7.50	15.00	—
1968	50,000	—	1.00	4.00	12.50	—
1969	60,000	—	1.00	2.00	7.00	—
1969 Proof	—	Value: 2.00				
1970	75,000	—	0.50	1.00	4.50	—
1971	100,000	—	0.50	1.00	1.75	—
1972	120,000	—	0.30	0.50	1.00	—
1973	100,000	—	0.15	0.25	1.00	—
1974	100,000	—	0.15	0.25	0.75	—

KM# 2 25 CENTS Weight: 2.9200 g. **Composition:** 0.5000 Silver .0469 oz. ASW **Obverse:** Bust of King George VI left **Reverse:** Denomination

Date	Mintage	F	VF	XF	Unc	BU
1939	36,000	—	7.50	35.00	125	—
1939 Proof	—	Value: 200				
1943	36,000	—	5.00	25.00	100	—
1944	36,000	—	3.50	20.00	85.00	—
1944 Proof	—	Value: 300				

KM# 9 25 CENTS Composition: Copper-Nickel **Obverse:** Bust of King George VI left **Reverse:** Denomination

Date	Mintage	F	VF	XF	Unc	BU
1951	36,000	—	2.00	7.50	35.00	—
1951 Proof	—	Value: 160				

KM# 11 25 CENTS Composition: Copper-Nickel **Obverse:** Bust of Queen Elizabeth II right

Date	Mintage	F	VF	XF	Unc	BU
1954	124,000	—	0.75	1.25	4.00	—
1954 Proof	—	Value: 120				
1960	40,000	—	0.75	1.25	2.00	—
1960 Proof	—	—	—	—	—	—
1964	40,000	—	1.00	2.00	5.00	—
1965	40,000	—	1.00	2.00	5.00	—
1966	10,000	—	3.50	10.00	22.50	—
1967	20,000	—	2.50	4.00	15.00	—
1968	20,000	—	2.50	4.00	15.00	—
1969	100,000	—	1.00	2.00	4.00	—
1969 Proof	—	Value: 3.00				
1970	40,000	—	1.50	3.00	10.00	—
1972	120,000	—	0.50	0.75	1.50	—
1973	100,000	—	0.50	0.75	1.50	—
1974	100,000	—	0.50	0.75	1.50	—

KM# 3 1/2 RUPEE Weight: 5.8300 g. **Composition:** 0.5000 Silver .0937 oz. ASW **Obverse:** Bust of King George VI left

Date	Mintage	F	VF	XF	Unc	BU
1939	36,000	—	12.00	50.00	175	—
1939 Proof	—	Value: 250				

KM# 12 1/2 RUPEE Composition: Copper-Nickel **Obverse:** Bust of crowned Queen Elizabeth II right

Date	Mintage	F	VF	XF	Unc	BU
1954	72,000	—	0.50	1.25	3.75	—
1954 Proof	—	Value: 150				
1960	60,000	—	0.50	1.00	3.00	—
1960 Proof	—	Value: 150				
1966	15,000	—	1.50	5.00	20.00	—
1967	20,000	—	3.00	8.00	25.00	—
1968	20,000	—	3.00	8.00	30.00	—
1969	60,000	—	0.75	1.00	12.00	—
1969 Proof	—	Value: 3.00				
1970	50,000	—	0.75	1.00	8.00	—
1971	100,000	—	0.75	1.00	3.00	—
1972	120,000	—	0.50	0.75	1.00	—
1974	100,000	—	0.50	0.75	1.00	—

KM# 4 RUPEE Weight: 11.6600 g. **Composition:** 0.5000 Silver .1874 oz. ASW **Obverse:** Bust of King Georg VI left

Date	Mintage	F	VF	XF	Unc	B
1939	90,000	—	15.00	60.00	165	-
1939 Proof	—	Value: 400				

KM# 13 RUPEE **Composition:** Copper-Nickel **Obverse:** Bust of crowned Queen Elizabeth II right

Date	Mintage	F	VF	XF	Unc	BU
1954	150,000	—	0.50	1.00	3.00	—
1954 Proof	—	Value: 200				
1960	60,000	—	0.75	1.25	3.50	—
1960 Proof	—	—	—	—	—	—
1966	45,000	—	1.25	2.25	8.50	—
1967	10,000	—	3.50	7.50	27.50	—
1968	40,000	—	2.50	5.00	20.00	—
1969	50,000	—	1.50	3.00	12.50	—
1969 Proof	—	Value: 5.00				
1970	50,000	—	1.50	2.50	10.00	—
1971	100,000	—	0.75	1.50	5.00	—
1972	120,000	—	0.75	1.50	2.00	—
1974	100,000	—	—	—	1.50	—

KM# 19 5 RUPEES **Composition:** Copper-Nickel **Obverse:** Bust of Queen Elizabeth II right **Reverse:** Palm tree left, harbor with sailing boats to right

Date	Mintage	F	VF	XF	Unc	BU
1972	220,000	—	1.50	2.50	5.00	—

KM# 19a 5 RUPEES **Weight:** 15.5000 g. **Composition:** 0.9250 Silver .4609 oz. ASW **Obverse:** Bust of Queen Elizabeth II right **Reverse:** Palm tree left, harbor with sailing boats to right

Date	Mintage	F	VF	XF	Unc	BU
1972 Proof	2,500	Value: 16.50				
1974 Proof	5,000	Value: 14.50				

KM# 20 10 RUPEES **Composition:** Copper-Nickel **Obverse:** Bust of Queen Elizabeth II right **Reverse:** Sea turtle

Date	F	VF	XF	Unc	BU
1974	—	2.00	4.00	9.00	—

KM# 20a 10 RUPEES **Weight:** 28.2800 g. **Composition:** 0.9250 Silver .8411 oz. ASW

Date	Mintage	F	VF	XF	Unc	BU
1974 Proof	25,000	Value: 14.00				

REPUBLIC

STANDARD COINAGE

100 Cents = 1 Rupee

KM# 21 CENT **Composition:** Aluminum **Subject:** Declaration of Independence **Obverse:** Bust **Reverse:** Boaeteur fish left

ate	Mintage	F	VF	XF	Unc	BU
976	109,000	—	0.10	0.20	0.75	—
976 Proof	8,500	Value: 1.50				

KM# 30 CENT **Composition:** Aluminum **Reverse:** Boueteur fish left

Date	F	VF	XF	Unc	BU
1977	—	—	0.15	0.75	—

KM# 46.1 CENT **Composition:** Brass **Obverse:** Coat of arms **Reverse:** Crab

Date	Mintage	F	VF	XF	Unc	BU
1982	500,000	—	—	0.15	0.50	—
1982 Proof	—	Value: 2.25				

KM# 46.2 CENT **Composition:** Brass **Obverse:** Altered coat of arms

Date	F	VF	XF	Unc	BU
1990 PM	—	—	0.15	0.45	—
1992 PM	—	—	0.15	0.45	—
1992 PM Proof	—	Value: 2.25			

KM# 22 5 CENTS **Composition:** Aluminum **Subject:** Declaration of Independence **Reverse:** Bourgeois fish **Shape:** Scalloped **Note:** Varieties exist.

Date	Mintage	F	VF	XF	Unc	BU
1976	209,000	—	0.10	0.20	0.75	—
1976 Proof	8,500	Value: 1.50				

KM# 31 5 CENTS **Composition:** Aluminum **Series:** F.A.O. **Reverse:** Bourgeois Fish **Shape:** Scalloped

Date	Mintage	F	VF	XF	Unc	BU
1977	300,000	—	—	0.15	0.75	—

KM# 43 5 CENTS **Composition:** Brass **Series:** World Food Day

Date	Mintage	F	VF	XF	Unc	BU
1981	720,000	—	—	0.15	0.45	—

KM# 47.1 5 CENTS **Composition:** Brass

Date	Mintage	F	VF	XF	Unc	BU
1982	1,500,000	—	—	0.10	0.30	—
1982 Proof	Inc. above	Value: 2.50				

KM# 47.2 5 CENTS **Composition:** Brass **Obverse:** Altered coat of arms

Date	F	VF	XF	Unc	BU
1990 PM	—	—	0.10	0.30	—
1992 PM	—	—	0.10	0.30	—
1992 PM Proof	—	Value: 2.50			
1995 PM	—	—	0.10	0.30	—
1997 PM	—	—	0.10	0.30	—
1997 PM Proof	—	Value: 2.50			
2000 PM	—	—	0.10	0.30	—

KM# 23 10 CENTS **Composition:** Nickel-Brass **Subject:** Declaration of Independence **Shape:** 12-sided

Date	Mintage	F	VF	XF	Unc	BU
1976	209,000	—	0.20	0.50	1.50	—
1976 Proof	8,500	Value: 2.50				

KM# 32 10 CENTS **Composition:** Nickel-Brass **Series:** F.A.O. **Reverse:** Swordfish

Date	Mintage	F	VF	XF	Unc	BU
1977	125,000	—	0.10	0.35	1.50	—

KM# 44 10 CENTS **Composition:** Brass **Series:** World Food Day

Date	Mintage	F	VF	XF	Unc	BU
1981	145,000	—	0.10	0.25	1.00	1.25

KM# 48.1 10 CENTS **Composition:** Brass

Date	Mintage	F	VF	XF	Unc	BU
1982	1,000,000	—	0.10	0.25	1.00	1.25
1982 Proof	Inc. above	Value: 2.75				

KM# 48.2 10 CENTS **Composition:** Brass **Obverse:** Altered coat of arms

Date	F	VF	XF	Unc	BU
1990	—	0.10	0.25	1.00	1.25
1992	—	0.10	0.25	1.00	1.25
1992 Proof	—	Value: 2.75			
1994	—	0.10	0.25	1.00	1.25
1997	—	0.10	0.25	1.00	1.25

KM# 24 25 CENTS **Composition:** Copper-Nickel **Subject:** Declaration of Independence

Date	Mintage	F	VF	XF	Unc	BU
1976	209,000	—	0.50	1.00	3.00	—
1976 Proof	8,500	Value: 3.50				

KM# 33 25 CENTS **Composition:** Copper-Nickel **Reverse:** Black Parrot

Date	F	VF	XF	Unc	BU
1977	—	0.25	0.75	2.50	—

KM# 49.1 25 CENTS **Composition:** Copper-Nickel

Date	Mintage	F	VF	XF	Unc	BU
1982	375,000	—	0.25	0.75	2.50	—
1982 Proof	Inc. above	Value: 3.00				

KM# 49.2 25 CENTS **Composition:** Copper-Nickel **Obverse:** Altered coat of arms

Date	Mintage	F	VF	XF	Unc	BU
1989	1,500,000	—	0.25	0.75	2.50	—
1992 PM	—	—	0.25	0.75	2.50	—
1992 PM Proof	—	Value: 3.00				
1997 PM	—	—	0.25	0.75	2.50	—

KM# 49.3 25 CENTS **Composition:** Nickel Clad Steel

Date	F	VF	XF	Unc	BU
1993 PM	—	0.25	0.75	2.50	—

KM# 25 50 CENTS **Composition:** Copper-Nickel **Subject:** Declaration of Independence **Reverse:** Vanilla Orchid

Date	Mintage	F	VF	XF	Unc	BU
1976	209,000	—	0.50	1.00	2.50	—
1976 Proof	8,500	Value: 3.50				

KM# 34 50 CENTS **Composition:** Copper-Nickel **Reverse:** Vanilla Orchid

Date	F	VF	XF	Unc	BU
1977	—	0.20	0.45	1.00	—

KM# 26 RUPEE **Composition:** Copper-Nickel **Subject:** Declaration of Independence **Reverse:** Triton Conch shell

Date	Mintage	F	VF	XF	Unc	BU
1976	259,000	—	0.75	1.00	1.75	—
1976 Proof	8,500	Value: 2.50				

KM# 35 RUPEE **Composition:** Copper-Nickel **Reverse:** Triton Conch Shell

Date	F	VF	XF	Unc	BU
1977	—	0.50	0.75	1.50	—

KM# 50.1 RUPEE **Composition:** Copper-Nickel **Reverse:** Triton Conch shell

Date	Mintage	F	VF	XF	Unc	BU
1982	2,000,000	—	0.25	0.50	1.25	—
1982 Proof	Inc. above	Value: 5.00				
1983	—	—	0.50	1.00	2.00	—

KM# 50.2 RUPEE **Composition:** Copper-Nickel **Obverse:** Altered coat of arms

Date	F	VF	XF	Unc	BU
1992 PM	—	0.25	0.50	1.25	—
1992 PM Proof	—	Value: 5.00			
1995 PM	—	0.25	0.50	1.25	—
1997 PM	—	0.25	0.50	1.25	—

KM# 85 RUPEE **Composition:** Copper-Nickel **Reverse:** British Queen Mother wedding portrait

Date	F	VF	XF	Unc	BU
1995	—	—	—	10.00	—

KM# 27 5 RUPEES **Composition:** Copper-Nickel **Subject:** Declaration of Independence **Shape:** 7-sided

Date	Mintage	F	VF	XF	Unc	BU
1976	50,000	—	1.25	1.75	3.00	—

KM# 27a 5 RUPEES **Weight:** 15.5000 g. **Composition:** 0.9250 Silver .4609 oz. ASW

Date	Mintage	F	VF	XF	Unc	BU
1976 Proof	8,500	Value: 10.00				

KM# 36 5 RUPEES **Composition:** Copper-Nickel **Reverse:** Coco-de-mer Palm Tree **Shape:** 7-sided

Date	F	VF	XF	Unc	BU
1977	—	1.00	1.50	2.25	—

KM# 51.1 5 RUPEES **Composition:** Copper-Nickel

Date	Mintage	F	VF	XF	Unc	BU
1982	300,000	—	1.00	1.50	2.00	—
1982 Proof	Inc. above	Value: 5.00				

KM# 51.2 5 RUPEES **Composition:** Copper-Nickel **Obverse:** Altered coat of arms

Date	F	VF	XF	Unc	BU
1992 PM	—	1.00	1.50	2.00	—
1992 PM Proof	—	Value: 5.00			
1997 PM	—	1.00	1.50	2.00	—

KM# 89 5 RUPEES **Composition:** Copper-Nickel **Series:** 50th Anniversary United Nations

Date	F	VF	XF	Unc	BU
1995	—	—	—	9.00	—

KM# 109 5 RUPEES **Composition:** Copper-Nickel **Subject:** Marriage of Prince Edward **Obverse:** National arms **Reverse:** Tied initials and birds **Note:** Similar to 25 Rupees, KM#110.

Date	F	VF	XF	Unc	BU
1999	—	—	—	9.00	—

KM# 112 5 RUPEES **Composition:** Copper-Nickel **Subject:** Millennium **Obverse:** National arms **Reverse:** Latent image 1999-2000 dates **Note:** Similar to 25 Rupees, KM#113.

Date	F	VF	XF	Unc	BU
2000	—	—	—	9.00	—

KM# 114 5 RUPEES **Composition:** Copper-Nickel **Subject:** British Queen Mother **Obverse:** National arms **Reverse:** Queen Mother's portrait **Edge:** Reeded

Date	F	VF	XF	Unc	B
2000	—	—	—	9.00	

KM# 28 10 RUPEES **Composition:** Copper-Nickel **Subject:** Declaration of Independence **Reverse:** Sea turtle

Date	Mintage	F	VF	XF	Unc	BU
1976	50,000	—	2.00	2.75	6.00	—

KM# 28a 10 RUPEES **Weight:** 28.2800 g. **Composition:** 0.9250 Silver .8411 oz. ASW **Subject:** Declaration of Independence

Date	Mintage	F	VF	XF	Unc	BU
1976 Proof	29,000	Value: 12.50				

KM# 37 10 RUPEES **Composition:** Copper-Nickel **Series:** F.A.O. **Reverse:** Sea turtle

Date	F	VF	XF	Unc	BU
1977	—	2.00	3.00	6.00	—
1977 Proof	— Value: 8.00				

KM# 64 10 RUPEES **Weight:** 10.0000 g. **Composition:** 0.9250 Silver .2974 oz. ASW **Series:** Endagered Wildlife **Reverse:** Magpie Robin **Note:** Similar to 25 Rupees, KM#65.

Date	Mintage	F	VF	XF	Unc	BU
1993 Proof	Est. 20,000	Value: 17.50				

KM# 87 10 RUPEES **Weight:** 10.0000 g. **Composition:** 0.5000 Silver .1607 oz. ASW **Series:** 1996 Olympics **Reverse:** Cyclist

Date	F	VF	XF	Unc	BU
1996	—	—	—	30.00	—

KM# 52 20 RUPEES **Composition:** Copper-Nickel **Subject:** 5th Anniversary of Central Bank

Date	F	VF	XF	Unc	BU
1983	—	4.00	5.00	6.00	—

KM# 52a 20 RUPEES **Weight:** 19.4400 g. **Composition:** 0.9250 Silver .5781 oz. ASW **Subject:** 5th Anniversary of Central Bank

Date	Mintage	F	VF	XF	Unc	BU
1983 Proof	5,000	Value: 50.00				

KM# 52b 20 RUPEES **Weight:** 33.9000 g. **Composition:** 0.9170 Gold .9994 oz. AGW **Subject:** 5th Anniversary of Central Bank

Date	Mintage	F	VF	XF	Unc	BU
1983 Proof	50	Value: 950				

KM# 38 25 RUPEES **Weight:** 28.2800 g. **Composition:** 0.5000 Silver .4546 oz. ASW **Subject:** Queen's Silver Jubilee

Date	Mintage	F	VF	XF	Unc	BU
ND(1977)	17,000	—	—	—	8.00	—

KM# 38a 25 RUPEES **Weight:** 28.2800 g. **Composition:** 0.9250 Silver .8411 oz. ASW **Subject:** Queen's Silver Jubilee

Date	Mintage	F	VF	XF	Unc	BU
ND(1977) Proof	15,000	Value: 12.50				

KM# 53 25 RUPEES **Composition:** Copper-Nickel **Subject:** World Fisheries Conference

Date	Mintage	F	VF	XF	Unc	BU
1983	100,000	—	5.00	6.00	9.00	—

KM# 53a 25 RUPEES **Weight:** 28.2800 g. **Composition:** 0.9250 Silver .8411 oz. ASW **Subject:** World Fisheries Conference

Date	Mintage	F	VF	XF	Unc	BU
1983 Proof	20,000	Value: 37.50				

KM# 53b 25 RUPEES **Weight:** 47.5400 g. **Composition:** 0.9170 Gold 1.4015 oz. AGW **Subject:** World Fisheries Conference

Date	Mintage	F	VF	XF	Unc	BU
1983 Proof	100	Value: 1,000				

KM# 63 25 RUPEES **Weight:** 31.4700 g. **Composition:** 0.9250 Silver .9359 oz. ASW **Subject:** 40th Anniversary of Queen Elizabeth's Coronation **Reverse:** Royal carriage

Date	Mintage	F	VF	XF	Unc	BU
1993 Proof	Est. 10,000	Value: 45.00				

KM# 65 25 RUPEES **Weight:** 28.2800 g. **Composition:** 0.9250 Silver .8411 oz. ASW **Series:** Endangered Wildlife **Reverse:** Magpie Robin

Date		F	VF	XF	Unc	BU
1993 Proof	Est. 20,000	Value: 30.00				

KM# 67 25 RUPEES **Weight:** 31.4600 g. **Composition:** 0.9250 Silver .9359 oz. ASW **Subject:** World Cup Soccer **Reverse:** Goalie at net

Date	Mintage	F	VF	XF	Unc	BU
1993 Proof	Est. 15,000	Value: 28.00				

KM# 68 25 RUPEES **Weight:** 31.4600 g. **Composition:** 0.9250 Silver .9359 oz. ASW **Obverse:** Coat of arms **Reverse:** Space shuttle

Date	Mintage	F	VF	XF	Unc	BU
1993 Proof	Est. 10,000	Value: 25.00				

KM# 69 25 RUPEES **Weight:** 31.4600 g. **Composition:** 0.9250 Silver .9359 oz. ASW **Subject:** First French Landing

Date	Mintage	F	VF	XF	Unc	BU
1993 Proof	Est. 10,000	Value: 22.50				

KM# 70 25 RUPEES **Weight:** 31.4600 g. **Composition:** 0.9250 Silver .9359 oz. ASW **Series:** 1992 Olympics **Reverse:** Balance beam gymnasts

Date	Mintage	F	VF	XF	Unc	BU
1993 Proof	Est. 40,000	Value: 12.50				

KM# 71 25 RUPEES **Weight:** 31.4600 g. **Composition:** 0.9250 Silver .9359 oz. ASW **Series:** Protect Our World **Reverse:** Fish and coral

Date	Mintage	F	VF	XF	Unc	BU
1993 Proof	Est. 10,000	Value: 35.00				

KM# 78 25 RUPEES **Weight:** 28.2800 g. **Composition:** 0.9250 Silver .8411 oz. ASW **Series:** Endangered Wildlife **Reverse:** Kestrel

Date	Mintage	F	VF	XF	Unc	BU
1995 Proof	Est. 20,000	Value: 27.50				

KM# 83 25 RUPEES **Weight:** 28.2800 g. **Composition:** 0.9250 Silver .8411 oz. ASW **Series:** Endangered Wildlife **Reverse:** Paradise Flycatcher Bird

Date	Mintage	F	VF	XF	Unc	BU
1996 Proof	Est. 20,000	Value: 40.00				

KM# 72 25 RUPEES **Weight:** 19.4400 g. **Composition:** 0.9250 Silver .5782 oz. ASW **Subject:** 15th Anniversary - Central Bank

Date	Mintage	F	VF	XF	Unc	BU
1993 Proof	Est. 1,000	Value: 65.00				

KM# 80 25 RUPEES **Weight:** 28.2800 g. **Composition:** 0.9250 Silver .8411 oz. ASW **Series:** Olympics **Reverse:** Sailing

Date	Mintage	F	VF	XF	Unc	BU
1995 Proof	Est. 30,000	Value: 25.00				

KM# 81 25 RUPEES **Weight:** 28.2800 g. **Composition:** 0.9250 Silver .8411 oz. ASW **Subject:** Vasco Da Gama

Date	Mintage	F	VF	XF	Unc	BU
1995 Proof	Est. 10,000	Value: 37.50				

KM# 108 25 RUPEES **Weight:** 28.2800 g. **Composition:** 0.9250 Silver .8411 oz. ASW **Series:** 50th Anniversary U.N.

Date		F	VF	XF	Unc	BU
1995 Proof	—	Value: 37.50				

KM# 117 25 RUPEES **Weight:** 19.4400 g. **Composition:** 0.9250 Silver 0.5781 oz. ASW **Subject:** UNICEF **Obverse:** National arms **Reverse:** Boy fishing **Edge:** Reeded **Size:** 36 mm.

Date	Mintage	F	VF	XF	Unc	BU
1997 Proof	25,000	Value: 25.00				

KM# 74 25 RUPEES **Weight:** 19.4400 g. **Composition:** 0.9250 Silver .5782 oz. ASW **Series:** Endangered Wildlife **Reverse:** Milkweed Butterfly

Date	Mintage	F	VF	XF	Unc	BU
1994PM Proof	20,000	Value: 35.00				

KM# 97 25 RUPEES **Weight:** 31.4700 g. **Composition:** 0.9250 Silver .9359 oz. ASW **Series:** 1996 Olympic Games **Obverse:** National arms **Reverse:** Cyclist

Date		F	VF	XF	Unc	BU
1995 Proof	—	Value: 25.00				

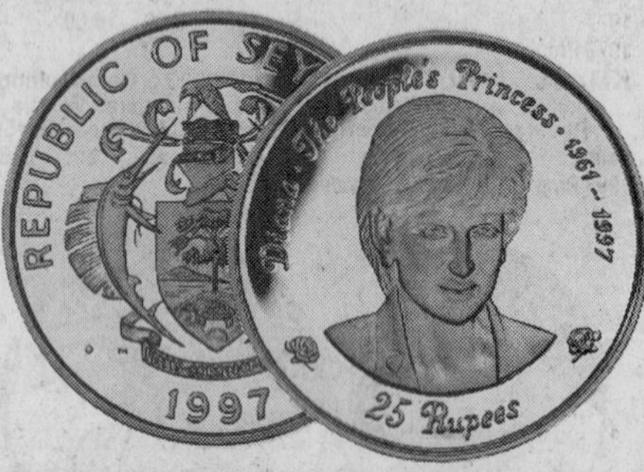

KM# 91 25 RUPEES **Weight:** 28.2800 g. **Composition:** 0.9250 Silver .8410 oz. ASW **Subject:** Diana - The People's Princess

Date	Mintage	F	VF	XF	Unc	BU
1997 Proof	Est. 10,000	Value: 40.00				

KM# 79 25 RUPEES **Weight:** 31.4700 g. **Composition:** 0.9250 Silver .9359 oz. ASW **Reverse:** British Queen Mother's wedding portrait

Date	Mintage	F	VF	XF	Unc	BU
1994 Proof	50,000	Value: 28.00				

KM# 88 25 RUPEES **Weight:** 31.4700 g. **Composition:** 0.9250 Silver .9359 oz. ASW **Subject:** Foundation of the Commonwealth **Reverse:** Crown and flags

Date	Mintage	F	VF	XF	Unc	BU
1996	40,000	—	—	—	42.00	—

KM# 95 25 RUPEES **Weight:** 28.2800 g. **Composition:** 0.9250 Silver .8410 oz. ASW **Subject:** Diana - The People's Princess **Reverse:** Holding baby Prince William

Date	Mintage	F	VF	XF	Unc	BU
1997 Proof	Est. 10,000	Value: 30.00				

KM# 99 25 RUPEES **Weight:** 28.2800 g. **Composition:** 0.9250 Silver .8410 oz. ASW **Subject:** Diana - The People's Princess **Reverse:** Holding young cancer patient

Date	Mintage	F	VF	XF	Unc	BU
1997 Proof	Est. 10,000	Value: 40.00				

KM# 92 25 RUPEES **Weight:** 1.2400 g. **Composition:** 0.9990 Gold .0398 oz. AGW **Subject:** Diana - The People's Princess **Note:** Similar to KM#91.

Date	Mintage	F	VF	XF	Unc	BU
1997 Proof	Est. 10,000	Value: 45.00				

KM# 96 25 RUPEES **Weight:** 1.2400 g. **Composition:** 0.9990 Gold .0398 oz. AGW **Subject:** Diana - The People's Princess **Note:** Similar to KM#95.

Date	Mintage	F	VF	XF	Unc	BU
1997 Proof	Est. 10,000	Value: 50.00				

KM# 100 25 RUPEES **Weight:** 1.2400 g. **Composition:** 0.9990 Gold .0398 oz. AGW **Subject:** Diana - The People's Princess **Note:** Similar to KM#99.

Date	Mintage	F	VF	XF	Unc	BU
1997 Proof	Est. 10,000	Value: 50.00				

KM# 103 25 RUPEES **Weight:** 28.2800 g. **Composition:** 0.9250 Silver .8410 oz. ASW **Subject:** Diana - The People's Princess **Reverse:** In summer clothes

Date	Mintage	F	VF	XF	Unc	BU
1998 Proof	Est. 10,000	Value: 42.50				

KM# 104 25 RUPEES **Weight:** 1.2441 g. **Composition:** 0.9999 Gold .0400 oz. AGW **Subject:** Diana - The People's Princess **Note:** Similar to KM#103.

Date	Mintage	F	VF	XF	Unc	BU
1998 Proof	Est. 10,000	Value: 55.00				

KM# 110 25 RUPEES **Weight:** 28.2800 g. **Composition:** 0.9250 Silver .8410 oz. ASW **Subject:** Marriage of Prince Edward **Obverse:** National arms **Reverse:** Tied letters and birds

Date	Mintage	F	VF	XF	Unc	BU
1999 Proof	Est. 10,000	Value: 47.50				

KM# 113 25 RUPEES **Weight:** 1.2441 g. **Composition:** 0.9999 Gold .0400 oz. AGW **Subject:** Millennium **Obverse:** National arms **Reverse:** Latent image of 1999-2000 dates

Date	Mintage	F	VF	XF	Unc	BU
2000 Proof	Est. 10,000	Value: 47.50				

KM# 115 25 RUPEES **Weight:** 1.2441 g. **Composition:** 0.9999 Gold .0400 oz. AGW **Subject:** 100th Birthday - British Queen Mother **Obverse:** National arms **Reverse:** Queen Mother's portrait **Edge:** Reeded

Date	Mintage	F	VF	XF	Unc	BU
2000 Proof	Est. 10,000	Value: 47.50				

KM# 39 50 RUPEES **Weight:** 28.2800 g. **Composition:** 0.9250 Silver .8411 oz. ASW **Subject:** Conservation **Reverse:** Squirrel Fish

Date	Mintage	F	VF	XF	Unc	BU
1978	4,453	—	—	—	16.50	—
1978 Proof	4,281	Value: 20.00				

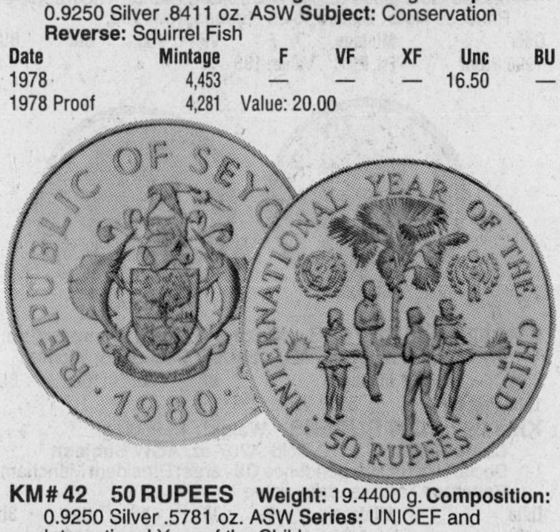

KM# 42 50 RUPEES **Weight:** 19.4400 g. **Composition:** 0.9250 Silver .5781 oz. ASW **Series:** UNICEF and International Year of the Child

Date	Mintage	F	VF	XF	Unc	BU
1980 Proof	10,000	Value: 17.50				

KM# 54 50 RUPEES **Weight:** 19.4400 g. **Composition:** 0.9250 Silver .5781 oz. ASW **Series:** Decade for Women

Date	Mintage	F	VF	XF	Unc	BU
1985 Proof	500	Value: 28.00				

KM# 75 50 RUPEES **Weight:** 1.2440 g. **Composition:** 0.9999 Gold .0497 oz. AGW **Series:** Endangered Wildlife **Obverse:** Coat of arms **Reverse:** Milkweed Butterfly **Note:** Similar to 25 Rupees, KM#74.

Date	F	VF	XF	Unc	BU
1994 PM Prooflike	—	—	—	—	—

KM# 107 50 RUPEES **Weight:** 3.1100 g. **Composition:** 0.5833 Gold .0583 oz. AGW **Series:** Olympics Games 2000 **Obverse:** National arms **Reverse:** Two divers

Date	Mintage	F	VF	XF	Unc	BU
1997 Proof	5,000	Value: 50.00				

KM# 40 100 RUPEES **Weight:** 31.6500 g. **Composition:** 0.9250 Silver .9413 oz. ASW **Subject:** Consservation **Reverse:** White-tailed Tropicbird

Date	Mintage	F	VF	XF	Unc	BU
1978	4,453	—	—	—	20.00	—
1978 Proof	4,075	Value: 25.00				

KM# 45 100 RUPEES **Weight:** 31.6500 g. **Composition:** 0.9250 Silver .9413 oz. ASW **Series:** World Food Day

Date	Mintage	F	VF	XF	Unc	BU
1981	6,000	—	—	—	22.50	—
1981 Proof	5,000	Value: 37.50				

KM# 45a 100 RUPEES **Weight:** 35.0000 g. **Composition:** 0.5000 Silver .5627 oz. ASW **Subject:** World Food Day

Date	Mintage	F	VF	XF	Unc	BU
1981 Proof	10,000	Value: 25.00				

KM# 55 100 RUPEES **Weight:** 19.4400 g. **Composition:** 0.9250 Silver .5781 oz. ASW **Subject:** 10th Anniversary of Independence

Date	Mintage	F	VF	XF	Unc	BU
ND(1986) Proof	1,000	Value: 45.00				

KM# 57 100 RUPEES **Weight:** 19.4400 g. **Composition:** 0.9250 Silver .5781 oz. ASW **Subject:** 10th Anniversary of Liberation

Date	Mintage	F	VF	XF	Unc	BU
ND(1987) PM Proof	1,000	Value: 40.00				

KM# 59 100 RUPEES **Weight:** 19.4000 g. **Composition:** 0.9170 Silver .5720 oz. ASW **Subject:** 10th Anniversary of Central Bank

Date	F	VF	XF	Unc	BU
ND(1988) PM Proof	—	Value: 75.00			

KM# 60 100 RUPEES **Weight:** 1.7000 g. **Composition:** 0.9170 Gold .0501 oz. AGW **Subject:** 10th Anniversary of Central Bank **Obverse:** Arms **Reverse:** Sea turtle **Note:** Similar to KM#59.

Date	F	VF	XF	Unc	BU
ND(1988) PM Proof	—	Value: 75.00			

KM# 76 100 RUPEES **Weight:** 3.1103 g. **Composition:** 0.9999 Gold .1000 oz. AGW **Series:** Endangered Wildlife **Obverse:** Coat of arms **Reverse:** Milkweed Butterfly **Note:** Similar to 25 Rupees, KM#74.

Date	F	VF	XF	Unc	BU
1994 PM Prooflike	—	—	—	—	—

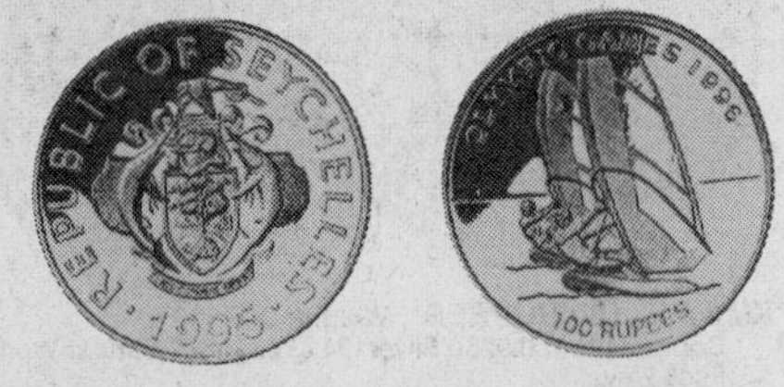

KM# 82 100 RUPEES **Weight:** 7.7760 g. **Composition:** 0.5830 Gold .1458 oz. AGW **Series:** Olympics **Reverse:** Sailboats

Date	Mintage	F	VF	XF	Unc	BU
1995 Proof	Est. 3,000	Value: 120				

KM# 86 100 RUPEES **Weight:** 7.7760 g. **Composition:** 0.5830 Gold .1458 oz. AGW **Subject:** British Queen Mother **Reverse:** Wedding portrait

Date	F	VF	XF	Unc	BU
1995	—	—	—	125	—

KM# 93 100 RUPEES **Weight:** 7.7760 g. **Composition:** 0.5830 Gold .1458 oz. AGW **Subject:** Diana - The People's Princess **Note:** Similar to 25 Rupees, KM#91.

Date	Mintage	F	VF	XF	Unc	BU
1997 Proof	Est. 7,500	Value: 110				

KM# A97 100 RUPEES **Weight:** 7.7760 g. **Composition:** 0.5830 Gold .1458 oz. AGW **Subject:** Diana - The People's Princess **Note:** Similar to 25 Rupees, KM#95.

Date	Mintage	F	VF	XF	Unc	BU
1997	7,500	Value: 110				

KM# 101 100 RUPEES **Weight:** 7.7760 g. **Composition:** 0.5830 Gold .1458 oz. AGW **Subject:** Diana - The People's Princess **Note:** Similar to 25 Rupees, KM#99.

Date	Mintage	F	VF	XF	Unc	BU
1997 Proof	Est. 7,500	Value: 110				

KM# 105 100 RUPEES **Weight:** 7.7760 g. **Composition:** 0.5830 Gold .1458 oz. AGW **Subject:** Diana - The People's Princess **Note:** Similar to 25 Rupees, KM#103.

Date	Mintage	F	VF	XF	Unc	BU
1998 Proof	Est. 7,500	Value: 110				

KM# 111 100 RUPEES **Weight:** 6.2200 g. **Composition:** 0.9999 Gold .2000 oz. AGW **Subject:** Marriage of Prince Edward **Obverse:** National arms **Reverse:** Tied initials and birds **Note:** Similar to 25 Rupees, KM#110.

Date	Mintage	F	VF	XF	Unc	BU
1999 Proof	Est. 2,000	Value: 185				

KM# 116 100 RUPEES **Weight:** 6.2200 g. **Composition:** 0.9999 Gold .2000 oz. AGW **Subject:** 100th Birthday Queen Mother **Obverse:** National arms **Reverse:** Queen Mother's portrait **Edge:** Reeded **Size:** 22 mm.

Date	Mintage	F	VF	XF	Unc	BU
2000 Proof	2,000	Value: 175				

KM# 66 250 RUPEES **Weight:** 6.2200 g. **Composition:** 0.9990 Gold .2000 oz. AGW **Series:** Endangered Wildlife **Reverse:** Magpie Robin **Note:** Similar to 25 Rupees, KM#65.

Date	F	VF	XF	Unc	BU
1993 Proof	—	Value: 145			

KM# 77 250 RUPEES **Weight:** 6.2200 g. **Composition:** 0.9990 Gold .2000 oz. AGW **Series:** Endangered Wildlife **Obverse:** Coat of arms **Reverse:** Milkweed Butterfly **Note:** Similar to 25 Rupees, KM#74.

Date	Mintage	F	VF	XF	Unc	BU
1993 Proof	—	Value: 190				
1994 PM Prooflike	—	—	—	—	—	—
1996PM Proof	5,000	—	—	—	—	—

KM# 84 250 RUPEES **Weight:** 6.2200 g. **Composition:** 0.9990 Gold .2000 oz. AGW **Series:** Endangered Wildlife **Reverse:** Paradise Flycatcher Bird **Note:** Similar to 25 Rupees, KM#83.

Date	Mintage	F	VF	XF	Unc	BU
1996 Proof	Est. 5,000	Value: 185				

KM# 94 250 RUPEES **Weight:** 6.2200 g. **Composition:** 0.9990 Gold .2000 oz. AGW **Subject:** Diana - The People's Princess **Note:** Similar to 25 Rupees, KM#91.

Date	Mintage	F	VF	XF	Unc	BU
1997 Proof	Est. 5,000	Value: 185				

KM# 98 250 RUPEES **Weight:** 6.2200 g. **Composition:** 0.9990 Gold .2000 oz. AGW **Subject:** Diana - The People's Princess **Note:** Similar to 25 Rupees, KM#95.

Date	Mintage	F	VF	XF	Unc	BU
1997 Proof	Est. 5,000	Value: 185				

KM# 102 250 RUPEES **Weight:** 6.2200 g. **Composition:** 0.9990 Gold .2000 oz. AGW **Subject:** Diana - The People's Princess **Note:** Similar to 25 Rupees, KM#99.

Date	Mintage	F	VF	XF	Unc	BU
1997 Proof	Est. 5,000	Value: 185				

KM# 106 250 RUPEES **Weight:** 6.2200 g. **Composition:** 0.9990 Gold .2000 oz. AGW **Subject:** Diana - The People's Princess **Note:** Similar to 25 Rupees, KM#103.

Date	Mintage	F	VF	XF	Unc	BU
1998 Proof	Est. 5,000	Value: 185				

KM# 62 500 RUPEES **Weight:** 7.1300 g. **Composition:** 0.9000 Gold .2036 oz. AGW **Series:** Decade for Women

Date	Mintage	F	VF	XF	Unc	BU
1985 Proof	500	Value: 135				

KM# 29 1000 RUPEES **Weight:** 15.9800 g. **Composition:** 0.9170 Gold .4707 oz. AGW **Subject:** Declaration of Independence **Obverse:** President Mancham **Reverse:** Tortoise, date, value

Date	Mintage	F	VF	XF	Unc	BU
1976	5,000	—	—	—	200	—
1976 Proof	1,000	Value: 300				

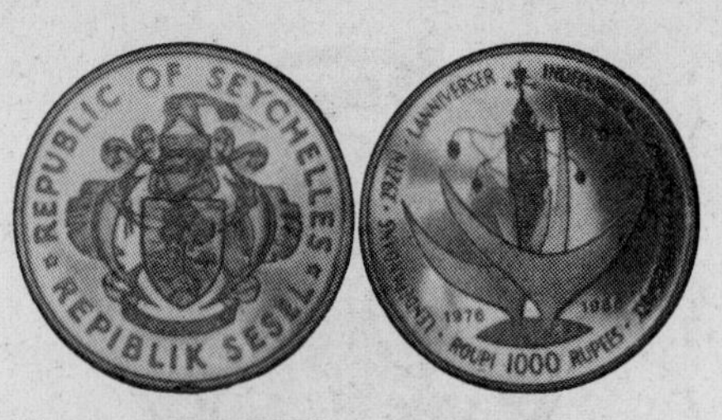

KM# 56 1000 RUPEES **Weight:** 15.9800 g. **Composition:** 0.9170 Gold .4707 oz. AGW **Subject:** 10th Anniversary of Independence

Date	Mintage	F	VF	XF	Unc	BU
ND(1986) Proof	100	Value: 385				

KM# 58 1000 RUPEES **Weight:** 15.9800 g. **Composition:** 0.9170 Gold .4707 oz. AGW **Subject:** 10th Anniversary of Liberation

Date	Mintage	F	VF	XF	Unc	BU
ND(1987) PM Proof	100	Value: 375				

KM# 61 1000 RUPEES **Weight:** 15.9400 g. **Composition:** 0.9170 Gold .4698 oz. AGW **Subject:** 100th Anniversary of Central Bank **Obverse:** Arms **Reverse:** Sea turtle **Note:** Similar to 100 Rupees, KM#59.

Date	Mintage	F	VF	XF	Unc	BU
ND(1988) PM Proof	Est. 5,000	Value: 235				

KM# 73 1000 RUPEES **Weight:** 15.9800 g. **Composition:** 0.9170 Gold .4710 oz. AGW **Subject:** Central Banking

Date	Mintage	F	VF	XF	Unc	BU
1993 Proof	Est. 200	Value: 350				

KM# 41 1500 RUPEES **Weight:** 33.4370 g. **Composition:** 0.9000 Gold .9676 oz. AGW **Subject:** Conservation **Reverse:** Black Paradise Flycatcher

Date	Mintage	F	VF	XF	Unc	BU
1978	683	—	—	—	475	—
1978 Proof	201	Value: 850				

PATTERNS

Including off metal strikes

KM#	Date	Mintage	Identification	Mkt Va
Pn1	1974	—	10 Rupees. Brass. KM#20.	–
Pn2	1974	—	10 Rupees. Bronze. KM#20.	–
Pn3	1974	—	10 Rupees. Copper-Nickel. KM#20.	–
Pn4	1974	—	10 Rupees. Silver. KM#20.	–
Pn6	1976	—	1000 Rupees. Bronze. KM#29.	–
Pn5	1976	—	10 Cents. Silver. KM#23, thick planchet.	25

PIEFORTS

KM#	Date	Mintage	Identification	Mkt Va
P1	1980	78	50 Rupees. KM#42.	85.0
P2	1983	500	50 Rupees.	65.0
P3	1984	500	50 Rupees. 0.9250 Silver.	65.0
P4	1984	100	50 Rupees. 0.9000 Gold.	1,50

MINT SETS

KM#	Date	Mintage	Identification	Issue Price	Mk Va
MS1	1972 (7)	—	KM#10-13, 17-19	—	8.5
MS2	1974 (5)	—	KM#10-13, 20	—	8.5
MS3	1976 (8)	—	KM#21-28	—	16.
MS4	1977 (8)	—	KM#30-37	—	11.5
MS7	Mixed dates (6)	—	KM#46.2 (1990), 47.2-51.2 (1997)	—	8.5

PROOF SETS

KM#	Date	Mintage	Identification	Issue Price	Mk Va
PS1	1939 (4)	—	KM#1-4	—	1,0
PS2	1969 (7)	5,000	KM#10-16	8.40	20.
PS3	1974 (2)	5,000	KM#19-a, 20a	37.00	32.
PS4	1976 (9)	1,000	KM#21-26 , 27a, 28a, 29	375	3
PS5	1976 (8)	7,500	KM#21-26, 27a, 28a	42.50	42.
PS6	1982 (6)	5,000	KM#46.1-51.1	29.95	20.
PS7	1992 (6)	—	KM#46.2-51.2	—	20

SHARJAH

Sharjah is the only one of the emirates that shares boundaries with all of the others plus Oman. It has an area of 1,000 sq. mi. (2,600 sq. km.) and a population of 40,000. Sharjah was an important pirate base in the 18th and early 19th centuries. Most of the treaties and diplomatic relations were with Great Britain.

TITLES

Ash-Sharqa(t) الشارقة

RULERS

Saqr Bin Khalid al-Qasimi, 1883-1914
Khalid Bin Ahmad al-Qasimi, 1914-1924
Sultan Bin Saqr al-Qasimi, 1924-1951
Saqr Bin Sultan al-Qasimi, 1951-1965
Khalid Bin Muhammad al-Qasimi, 1965-1972
Sultan Bin Muhammad al-Qasimi,1972-

EMIRATE

NON-CIRCULATING LEGAL TENDER COINAGE

KM# 1 5 RUPEE Weight: 25.0000 g. **Composition:** 0.7200 Silver .5787 oz. ASW **Ruler:** Khalid bin Muhammad al-Qasimi **Subject:** President John F. Kennedy Memorial **Obverse:** National arms

Date	F	VF	XF	Unc	BU
1964	—	—	—	15.00	—
1964 "PROOF" below flags on obverse	—	Value: 25.00			

Note: KM#1 was ordered by the Sheik, who according to the British has no authority to issue it

KM# 2 RIYAL Weight: 3.0000 g. **Composition:** 1.0000 Silver .0965 oz. ASW **Ruler:** Khalid bin Muhammad al-Qasimi **Subject:** Mona Lisa **Obverse:** National arms

Date	Mintage	F	VF	XF	Unc	BU
AH1389 (1969) Proof	3,850	Value: 17.50				

KM# 3 2 RIYALS Weight: 6.0000 g. **Composition:** 1.0000 Silver .1929 oz. ASW **Ruler:** Khalid bin Muhammad al-Qasimi **Subject:** Mexico World Soccer Cup **Obverse:** National arms

Date	Mintage	F	VF	XF	Unc	BU
AH1389 (1969) Proof	4,500	Value: 27.50				

KM# 4 5 RIYALS Weight: 15.0000 g. **Composition:** 1.0000 Silver .4823 oz. ASW **Ruler:** Khalid bin Muhammad al-Qasimi **Subject:** Napoleon **Obverse:** National arms

Date	Mintage	F	VF	XF	Unc	BU
AH1389 (1969) Proof	2,500	Value: 37.50				

KM# 5 10 RIYALS Weight: 30.0000 g. **Composition:** 1.0000 Silver .9646 oz. ASW **Ruler:** Khalid bin Muhammad al-Qasimi **Subject:** Bolivar **Obverse:** National arms

Date	Mintage	F	VF	XF	Unc	BU
AH1389 (1969) Proof	3,200	Value: 60.00				

KM# 7 25 RIYALS Weight: 5.1800 g. **Composition:** 0.9000 Gold .1499 oz. AGW **Ruler:** Khalid bin Muhammad al-Qasimi **Subject:** Mona Lisa **Obverse:** National arms

Date	Mintage	F	VF	XF	Unc	BU
AH1389 (1969) Proof	6,775	Value: 175				

KM# 8 50 RIYALS Weight: 10.3600 g. **Composition:** 0.9000 Gold .2998 oz. AGW **Ruler:** Khalid bin Muhammad al-Qasimi **Subject:** Mexico World Soccer Cup **Obverse:** National arms

Date	Mintage	F	VF	XF	Unc	BU
AH1389 (1969) Proof	1,815	Value: 250				

KM# 9 100 RIYALS Weight: 20.7300 g. **Composition:** 0.9000 Gold .5999 oz. AGW **Ruler:** Khalid bin Muhammad al-Qasimi **Subject:** Napoleon **Obverse:** National arms

Date	F	VF	XF	Unc	BU
AH1389 (1969) Proof	—	Value: 450			

KM# 10 100 RIYALS Weight: 20.7300 g. **Composition:** 0.9000 Gold .5999 oz. AGW **Ruler:** Khalid bin Muhammad al-Qasimi **Subject:** Bolivar **Obverse:** National arms

Date	F	VF	XF	Unc	BU
AH1389 (1969) Proof	—	Value: 375			

KM# 11 200 RIYALS Weight: 41.4600 g. **Composition:** 0.9000 Gold 1.1998 oz. AGW **Ruler:** Khalid bin Muhammad al-Qasimi **Subject:** Khalid III **Obverse:** National arms

Date	Mintage	F	VF	XF	Unc	BU
AH1389 (1969) Proof	435	Value: 750				

The Republic of Sierra Leone is located in western Africa between Guinea and Liberia, has an area of 27,699 sq. mi. (71,740 sq. km.) and a population of *4.1 million. Capital: Freetown. The economy is predominantly agricultural but mining contributes significantly to export revenues. Diamonds, iron ore, palm kernels, cocoa, and coffee are exported.

The coast of Sierra Leone was first visited by Portuguese and British slavers in the 15th and 16thcenturies. The first settlement, at Freetown, 1787, was established as a refuge for freed slaves within the British Empire, runaway slaves from the United States and Negroes discharged from the British armed forces. The first settlers were virtually wiped out by tribal attacks and disease. The colony was re-established under the auspices of the Sierra Leone Company and transferred to the British Crown in 1807. The interior region was secured and established as a protectorate in 1896. Sierra Leone became independent on April 27, 1961, and adopted a republican constitution ten years later. It is a member of the Commonwealth of Nations. The president is Chief of State and Head of Government.

For similar coinage refer to British West Africa.

RULERS
British, until 1971

MONETARY SYSTEM

Until 1906
100 Cents = 1 Dollar

Commencing 1964
100 Cents = 1 Leone = 1 Dollar

NOTE: Sierra Leone's official currency is the Leone.

REPUBLIC

STANDARD COINAGE

KM# 16 1/2 CENT Composition: Bronze **Obverse:** Bonga Fish

Date	Mintage	F	VF	XF	Unc	BU
1964	600,000	—	—	0.15	0.25	—
1964 Proof	10,000	Value: 1.00				

KM# 16a 1/2 CENT Weight: 2.8300 g. **Composition:** 0.9250 Silver .0841 oz. ASW **Obverse:** Bonga fish

Date	Mintage	F	VF	XF	Unc	BU
1964 Proof	22	Value: 650				

KM# 31 1/2 CENT Composition: Bronze

Date	Mintage	F	VF	XF	Unc	BU
1980	—	—	0.15	0.30	1.00	—
1980 Proof	10,000	Value: 1.50				

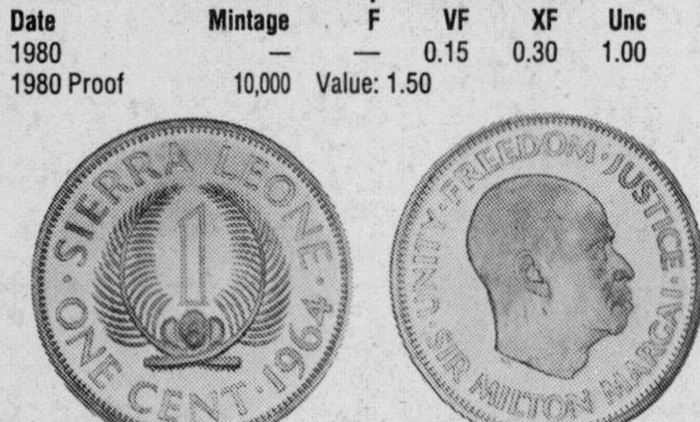

KM# 17 CENT Composition: Bronze **Obverse:** Palm branches and fruit stalks

Date	Mintage	F	VF	XF	Unc	BU
1964	35,000,000	—	—	0.15	0.25	—
1964 Proof	10,000	Value: 1.25				

KM# 17a CENT Weight: 5.6700 g. **Composition:** 0.9250 Silver .1686 oz. ASW **Obverse:** Palm branches and fruit stalks

Date	Mintage	F	VF	XF	Unc	BU
1964 Proof	22	Value: 650				

KM# 32 CENT Composition: Bronze **Reverse:** Dr. Siaka Stevens right

Date	Mintage	F	VF	XF	Unc	BU
1980	—	—	0.15	0.30	1.00	—
1980 Proof	10,000	Value: 1.50				

KM# 18 5 CENTS Composition: Copper-Nickel **Obverse:** Kapok tree

Date	Mintage	F	VF	XF	Unc	BU
1964	900,000	—	0.15	0.25	0.50	—
1964 Proof	10,000	Value: 1.50				

KM# 18a 5 CENTS Weight: 2.4900 g. **Composition:** 0.9250 Silver .0740 oz. ASW **Obverse:** Kapok tree

Date	Mintage	F	VF	XF	Unc	BU
1964 Proof	22	Value: 650				

KM# 33 5 CENTS Composition: Copper-Nickel **Reverse:** Dr. Siaka Stevens right

Date	Mintage	F	VF	XF	Unc	BU
1980	—	—	0.15	0.30	0.75	—
1980 Proof	10,000	Value: 2.50				
1984	—	—	0.15	0.30	0.75	—

KM# 19 10 CENTS Composition: Copper-Nickel **Obverse:** Cocoa beans **Reverse:** Sir Milton Margai right

Date	Mintage	F	VF	XF	Unc	BU
1964	24,000,000	—	0.25	0.40	0.65	—
1964 Proof	10,000	Value: 1.25				

KM# 19a 10 CENTS Weight: 4.9200 g. **Composition:** 0.9250 Silver .1463 oz. ASW **Reverse:** Sir Milton Margai right

Date	Mintage	F	VF	XF	Unc	BU
1964 Proof	22	Value: 650				

KM# 34 10 CENTS Composition: Copper-Nickel **Reverse:** Dr. Siaka Stevens right

Date	Mintage	F	VF	XF	Unc	BU
1978	200,000	—	0.25	0.50	1.00	—
1980	—	—	0.20	0.40	0.75	—
1980 Proof	10,000	Value: 5.00				
1984	—	—	0.20	0.40	0.75	—

KM# 20 20 CENTS Composition: Copper-Nickel **Reverse:** Sir Milton Margai right

Date	Mintage	F	VF	XF	Unc
1964	11,000,000	—	0.35	0.60	1.25
1964 Proof	10,000	Value: 2.00			

KM# 20a 20 CENTS Weight: 8.2200 g. **Compositior** 0.9250 Silver .2444 oz. ASW **Reverse:** Sir Milton Margai rig

Date	Mintage	F	VF	XF	Unc
1964 Proof	22	Value: 650			

KM# 30 20 CENTS Composition: Copper-Nickel **Reverse:** Dr. Siaka Stevens right

Date	Mintage	F	VF	XF	Unc
1978	2,375,000	—	0.35	0.65	1.50
1980	—	—	0.35	0.60	1.25
1980 Proof	10,000	Value: 7.00			
1984	—	—	0.35	0.60	1.25

KM# 25 50 CENTS Composition: Copper-Nickel **Reverse:** Dr. Siaka Stevens right

Date	Mintage	F	VF	XF	Unc
1972	1,000,000	—	1.00	1.75	3.00
1972 Proof	2,000	Value: 5.00			
1980	—	—	1.00	1.50	2.75
1980 Proof	10,000	Value: 10.00			
1984	—	—	1.00	1.50	2.75

KM# 21 LEONE Composition: Copper-Nickel **Revers** Sir Milton Margai head facing right

Date	Mintage	F	VF	XF	Unc
1964 Proof	10,000	Value: 10.00			

KM# 21a LEONE Weight: 22.6220 g. **Composition:** 0.9250 Silver .6738 oz. ASW **Reverse:** Sir Milton Margai head facing right

Date	Mintage	F	VF	XF	Unc
1964 Proof	12	Value: 1,000			

KM# 21b LEONE Composition: 0.9170 Gold **Revers** Sir Milton Marcai head facing right

Date	Mintage	F	VF	XF	Unc
1964 Proof	10	Value: 2,500			

KM# 26 LEONE Composition: Copper-Nickel **Subjec** 10 Anniversary of Bank **Reverse:** Dr. Siaka Stevens righ

Date	Mintage	F	VF	XF	Unc
ND(1974)	103,000	—	1.50	2.50	5.50

KM# 26a LEONE Weight: 28.2800 g. **Composition:** 0.9250 Silver .8411 oz. ASW **Reverse:** Dr. Siaka Stevens ri

Date	Mintage	F	VF	XF	Unc
1974 Proof	22,000	Value: 12.50			

M# 26b LEONE **Composition:** Gold **Subject:** 10 Anniversary of Bank **Reverse:** Dr. Siaka Stevens right

ate	Mintage	F	VF	XF	Unc	BU
974	100	—	—	—	1,200	—

M# 36 LEONE **Composition:** Copper-Nickel **Subject:** O.A.U. Summit Conference **Obverse:** Map of Africa in inner ring **Reverse:** Dr. Siaka Stevens right

ate	Mintage	F	VF	XF	Unc	BU
980	75,000	—	1.75	2.75	6.00	—

M# 36a LEONE **Weight:** 28.2800 g. **Composition:** 0.9250 Silver .8411 oz. ASW **Obverse:** Map of Africa in inner ring **Reverse:** Dr. Siaka Stevens right

ate	Mintage	F	VF	XF	Unc	BU
980 Proof	15,000	Value: 20.00				

M# 40 LEONE **Weight:** 9.5000 g. **Composition:** 0.9250 Silver .2825 oz. ASW **Subject:** Freetown Bicentennial **Reverse:** Dr. Joseph Saido Momoh left **Shape:** Octagon

ate	Mintage	F	VF	XF	Unc	BU
987 Proof	3,000	Value: 25.00				

M# 40a LEONE **Weight:** 16.0000 g. **Composition:** 0.9170 Gold .4716 oz. AGW **Subject:** Freetown Bicentennial **Reverse:** Dr. Joseph Saido Momoh left **Shape:** Octagon

ate	Mintage	F	VF	XF	Unc	BU
987 Proof	1,250	Value: 275				

M# 43 LEONE **Composition:** Nickel-Bronze **Reverse:** Dr. Joseph Saido Momoh left **Shape:** Octagon

ate	F	VF	XF	Unc	BU
987	—	0.50	0.75	1.50	—
988	—	0.50	0.75	1.50	—

M# 47 DOLLAR **Composition:** Copper-Nickel **Obverse:** Crowned lion **Note:** Similar to 10 Dollars, KM#49.

ate	F	VF	XF	Unc	BU
997	—	—	—	7.50	—

M# 48 DOLLAR **Composition:** Copper-Nickel **Obverse:** Unicorn **Note:** Similar to 10 Dollars, KM#50.

ate	F	VF	XF	Unc	BU
997	—	—	—	7.50	—

M# 53 DOLLAR **Composition:** Copper-Nickel **Subject:** Golden Wedding Anniversary **Reverse:** E and P monogram **Note:** Similar to 10 Dollars, KM#54.

ate	F	VF	XF	Unc	BU
997	—	—	—	10.00	—

M# 56 DOLLAR **Composition:** Copper-Nickel **Subject:** Golden Wedding Anniversary **Reverse:** Yacht **Note:** Similar to 10 Dollars, KM#57.

ate	F	VF	XF	Unc	BU
997	—	—	—	7.00	—

M# 59 DOLLAR **Composition:** Copper-Nickel **Subject:** Golden Wedding Anniversary **Reverse:** Royal couple **Note:** Similar to 10 Dollars, KM#60.

ate	F	VF	XF	Unc	BU
997	—	—	—	7.00	—

M# 62 DOLLAR **Composition:** Copper-Nickel **Subject:** Golden Wedding Anniversary **Reverse:** Fireworks above palace **Note:** Similar to 10 Dollars, KM#63.

ate	F	VF	XF	Unc	BU
997	—	—	—	7.00	—

M# 65 DOLLAR **Composition:** Copper-Nickel **Subject:** Golden Wedding Anniversary **Reverse:** Queen with two children **Note:** Similar to 10 Dollars, KM#66.

ate	F	VF	XF	Unc	BU
997	—	—	—	7.00	—

KM# 68 DOLLAR **Composition:** Copper-Nickel **Subject:** Golden Wedding Anniversary **Reverse:** Royal couple with two children **Note:** Similar to 10 Dollars, KM#69.

Date	F	VF	XF	Unc	BU
1997	—	—	—	7.00	—

KM# 71 DOLLAR **Composition:** Copper-Nickel **Subject:** Diana - The Peoples' Princess **Reverse:** Portrait of Lady Diana

Date	F	VF	XF	Unc	BU
1997	—	—	—	8.00	—

KM# 77 DOLLAR **Composition:** Copper-Nickel **Subject:** Diana - The Peoples' Princess **Reverse:** Lady Diana and Mother Theresa

Date	F	VF	XF	Unc	BU
1997	—	—	—	8.00	—

KM# 83 DOLLAR **Composition:** Copper-Nickel **Subject:** Diana - The Peoples' Princess **Reverse:** Lady Diana and AIDS patient

Date	F	VF	XF	Unc	BU
1997	—	—	—	8.00	—

KM# 89 DOLLAR **Composition:** Copper-Nickel **Subject:** Diana - The Peoples' Princess **Reverse:** Lady Diana with sons William and Harry

Date	F	VF	XF	Unc	BU
1997	—	—	—	8.00	—

KM# 95 DOLLAR **Composition:** Copper-Nickel **Subject:** Jurassic Park **Reverse:** Velociraptor **Note:** Similar to 10 Dollars, KM#96.

Date	F	VF	XF	Unc	BU
1997	—	—	—	9.00	—

KM# 103 DOLLAR **Composition:** Copper-Nickel **Subject:** In Memoriam, Diana - The Peoples' Princess **Reverse:** Head of Lady Diana half left **Note:** Similar to 10 Dollars, KM#104.

Date	F	VF	XF	Unc	BU
1998	—	—	—	8.00	—

KM# 109 DOLLAR **Composition:** Copper-Nickel **Subject:** Dr. Livingston **Note:** Similar to 10 Dollars, KM#110.

Date	F	VF	XF	Unc	BU
1998	—	—	—	8.00	—

KM# 118 DOLLAR **Composition:** Copper-Nickel **Subject:** China 2000 Series **Obverse:** National arms **Reverse:** Kneeling Terracotta warrior **Note:** Similar to 10 Dollars, KM#119.

Date	F	VF	XF	Unc	BU
1999	—	—	—	8.50	—

KM# 112 DOLLAR **Composition:** Copper-Nickel **Subject:** Amerigo Vespucci **Obverse:** National arms **Reverse:** Ship and portrait **Note:** Similar to 10 Dollars, KM#113.

Date	F	VF	XF	Unc	BU
1999	—	—	—	8.00	—

KM# 115 DOLLAR **Composition:** Copper-Nickel **Subject:** Charles Darwin **Obverse:** National arms **Reverse:** Ship and portrait **Note:** Similar to 10 Dollars, KM#116.

Date	F	VF	XF	Unc	BU
1999	—	—	—	8.00	—

KM# 121 DOLLAR **Composition:** Copper-Nickel **Subject:** China 2000 Series - Ming Dynasty **Obverse:** National arms **Reverse:** Temple of Heaven **Note:** Similar to 10 Dollars, KM#122.

Date	F	VF	XF	Unc	BU
1999	—	—	—	8.50	—

KM# 124 DOLLAR **Composition:** Copper-Nickel **Subject:** China 2000 Series **Obverse:** National arms **Reverse:** Portion of the Great Wall **Note:** Similar to 10 Dollars, KM#125.

Date	F	VF	XF	Unc	BU
1999	—	—	—	8.50	—

KM# 127 DOLLAR **Composition:** Copper-Nickel **Subject:** China 2000 Series **Obverse:** National arms **Reverse:** Bronze chariot **Note:** Similar to 10 Dollars, KM#128.

Date	F	VF	XF	Unc	BU
1999	—	—	—	8.50	—

KM# 130 DOLLAR **Composition:** Copper-Nickel **Subject:** China 2000 Series **Obverse:** National arms **Reverse:** First century armillary sphere **Note:** Similar to 10 Dollars, KM#131.

Date	F	VF	XF	Unc	BU
1999	—	—	—	8.50	—

KM# 133 DOLLAR **Composition:** Copper-Nickel **Subject:** China 2000 Series **Obverse:** National arms **Reverse:** Tang Dynasty Royal Horse **Note:** Similar to 10 Dollars, KM#134.

Date	F	VF	XF	Unc	BU
1999	—	—	—	8.50	—

KM# 136 DOLLAR **Composition:** Copper-Nickel **Subject:** Macau returns to China **Obverse:** National arms **Reverse:** Church, car, roulette wheel, and hands shaking **Note:** Similar to 10 Dollars, KM#137.

Date	F	VF	XF	Unc	BU
1999	—	—	—	8.00	—

KM# 139 DOLLAR **Composition:** Copper-Nickel **Subject:** Prince Edward's Wedding **Obverse:** National arms **Reverse:** Symbolic wedding design **Note:** Similar to 10 Dollars, KM#140.

Date	F	VF	XF	Unc	BU
1999	—	—	—	8.50	—

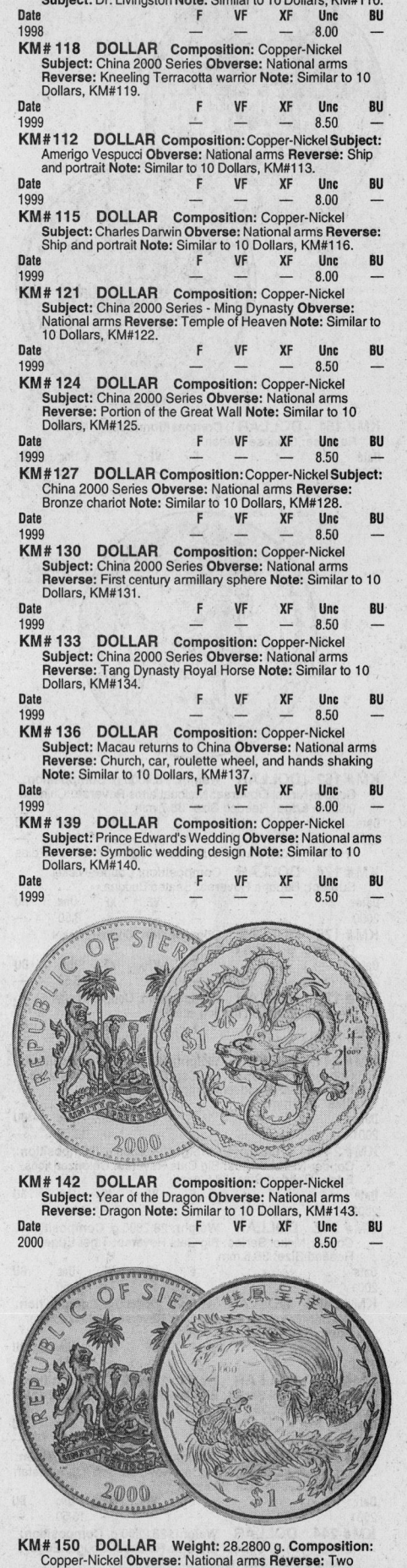

KM# 142 DOLLAR **Composition:** Copper-Nickel **Subject:** Year of the Dragon **Obverse:** National arms **Reverse:** Dragon **Note:** Similar to 10 Dollars, KM#143.

Date	F	VF	XF	Unc	BU
2000	—	—	—	8.50	—

KM# 150 DOLLAR **Weight:** 28.2800 g. **Composition:** Copper-Nickel **Obverse:** National arms **Reverse:** Two Phoenix birds **Edge:** Reeded **Note:** Struck at Pobjoy Mint.

Date	F	VF	XF	Unc	BU
2000	—	—	—	8.50	—

KM# 151 DOLLAR **Composition:** Copper-Nickel **Reverse:** Chinese dragon

Date	F	VF	XF	Unc	BU
2000	—	—	—	8.50	—

KM# 152 DOLLAR **Weight:** 28.4300 g. **Composition:** Copper-Nickel **Obverse:** National arms **Reverse:** Chinese unicorn **Edge:** Reeded **Size:** 38.7 mm.

Date	F	VF	XF	Unc	BU
2000	—	—	—	8.50	—

Note: Reported as an error date resulting from muled dies

KM# 174 DOLLAR **Composition:** Copper-Nickel **Subject:** Buddha **Reverse:** Seated Buddha

Date	F	VF	XF	Unc	BU
2000	—	—	—	8.50	—

KM# 175 DOLLAR **Composition:** Copper-Nickel **Reverse:** Goddess of Mercy

Date	F	VF	XF	Unc	BU
2000	—	—	—	8.50	—

KM# 176 DOLLAR **Composition:** Copper-Nickel **Reverse:** Tzai-yen holding scroll

Date	F	VF	XF	Unc	BU
2000	—	—	—	10.00	—

KM# 241 DOLLAR **Weight:** 28.2800 g. **Composition:** Copper-Nickel **Series:** Big Cats **Obverse:** National arms **Reverse:** Male and female lions **Edge:** Reeded **Size:** 38.6 mm.

Date	F	VF	XF	Unc	BU
2001	—	—	—	12.00	—

KM# 241a DOLLAR **Weight:** 28.2800 g. **Composition:** Copper-Nickel **Series:** Big Cats **Reverse:** Colorized lions **Edge:** Reeded **Size:** 38.6 mm.

Date	F	VF	XF	Unc	BU
2001	—	—	—	14.50	—

KM# 242 DOLLAR **Weight:** 28.2800 g. **Composition:** Copper-Nickel **Series:** Big Cats **Reverse:** Tiger **Edge:** Reeded **Size:** 38.6 mm.

Date	F	VF	XF	Unc	BU
2001	—	—	—	9.50	—

KM# 242a DOLLAR **Weight:** 28.2800 g. **Composition:** Copper-Nickel **Series:** Big Cats **Reverse:** Colorized tiger **Edge:** Reeded **Size:** 38.6 mm.

Date	F	VF	XF	Unc	BU
2001	—	—	—	13.50	—

KM# 243 DOLLAR **Weight:** 28.2800 g. **Composition:** Copper-Nickel **Series:** Big Cats **Reverse:** Cheetah **Edge:** Reeded **Size:** 38.6 mm.

Date	F	VF	XF	Unc	BU
2001	—	—	—	9.50	—

KM# 243a DOLLAR **Weight:** 28.2800 g. **Composition:** Copper-Nickel **Series:** Big Cats **Reverse:** Colorized cheetah **Edge:** Reeded **Size:** 38.6 mm.

Date	F	VF	XF	Unc	BU
2001	—	—	—	13.50	—

KM# 244 DOLLAR **Weight:** 28.2800 g. **Composition:** Copper-Nickel **Series:** Big Cats **Reverse:** Cougar **Edge:** Reeded **Size:** 38.6 mm.

Date	F	VF	XF	Unc	BU
2001	—	—	—	9.50	—

KM# 244a DOLLAR **Weight:** 28.2800 g. **Composition:** Copper-Nickel **Series:** Big Cats **Reverse:** Colorized cougar **Edge:** Reeded **Size:** 38.6 mm.

Date	F	VF	XF	Unc	BU
2001	—	—	—	13.50	—

KM# 245 DOLLAR **Weight:** 28.2800 g. **Composition:** Copper-Nickel **Series:** Big Cats **Reverse:** Black panther **Edge:** Reeded **Size:** 38.6 mm.

Date	F	VF	XF	Unc	BU
2001	—	—	—	9.50	—

KM# 245a DOLLAR **Weight:** 28.2800 g. **Composition:** Copper-Nickel **Series:** Big Cats **Reverse:** Colorized black panther **Edge:** Reeded **Size:** 38.6 mm.

Date	F	VF	XF	Unc	BU
2001	—	—	—	13.50	—

KM# 198 DOLLAR **Weight:** 28.2800 g. **Composition:** Copper-Nickel **Subject:** Year of the Snake **Obverse:** National arms **Reverse:** Snake **Edge:** Reeded **Size:** 38.6 mm.

Date	F	VF	XF	Unc	BU
2001	—	—	—	9.00	—

KM# 206 DOLLAR **Composition:** Copper-Nickel **Subject:** P'an Ku **Obverse:** National arms **Reverse:** Dragon

Date	F	VF	XF	Unc	BU
2001	—	—	—	9.00	—

KM# 214 DOLLAR **Composition:** Copper-Nickel **Subject:** P'an Ku **Obverse:** National arms **Reverse:** Dragon and three animals

Date	F	VF	XF	Unc	BU
2001	—	—	—	9.00	—

KM# 222 DOLLAR **Weight:** 28.2800 g. **Composition:** Copper-Nickel **Series:** The Big Five **Obverse:** National arms **Reverse:** Rhino **Edge:** Reeded **Size:** 38.6 mm.

Date	F	VF	XF	Unc	BU
2001	—	—	—	9.00	—

KM# 225 DOLLAR **Weight:** 28.2800 g. **Composition:** Copper-Nickel **Series:** The Big Five **Obverse:** National arms **Reverse:** Lion

Date	F	VF	XF	Unc	BU
2001	—	—	—	9.00	—

KM# 228 DOLLAR **Weight:** 28.2800 g. **Composition:** Copper-Nickel **Series:** The Big Five **Obverse:** National arms **Reverse:** Leopard

Date	F	VF	XF	Unc	BU
2001	—	—	—	9.00	—

KM# 231 DOLLAR **Weight:** 28.2800 g. **Composition:** Copper-Nickel **Series:** The Big Five **Obverse:** National arms **Reverse:** Elephants

Date	F	VF	XF	Unc	BU
2001	—	—	—	9.00	—

KM# 234 DOLLAR **Weight:** 28.2800 g. **Composition:** Copper-Nickel **Series:** The Big Five **Obverse:** National arms **Reverse:** Buffalo

Date	F	VF	XF	Unc	BU
2001	—	—	—	9.00	—

KM# 237 DOLLAR **Weight:** 28.2800 g. **Composition:** Copper-Nickel **Series:** The Big Five **Obverse:** National arms **Reverse:** All five animals

Date	F	VF	XF	Unc	BU
2001	—	—	—	9.00	—

KM# 264 DOLLAR **Weight:** 28.2800 g. **Composition:** Copper Nickel **Subject:** RMS Titanic **Obverse:** National arms **Reverse:** Titanic at dock **Edge:** Reeded **Size:** 38.6 mm.

Date	F	VF	XF	Unc	BU
2002	—	—	—	10.00	—

KM# 268 DOLLAR **Weight:** 28.2800 g. **Composition:** Copper Nickel **Subject:** Queen's Golden Jubilee **Obverse:** National arms **Reverse:** Queen Elizabeth II and Prince Philip visiting blacksmiths in Sierra Leone **Edge:** Reeded **Size:** 38.6 mm.

Date	F	VF	XF	Unc	BU
2002	—	—	—	10.00	—

KM# 269 DOLLAR **Weight:** 28.2800 g. **Composition:** Copper Nickel **Subject:** Queen's Golden Jubilee **Obverse:** National arms **Reverse:** Queen Elizabeth II with her two sons **Edge:** Reeded **Size:** 38.6 mm.

Date	F	VF	XF	Unc	BU
2002	—	—	—	10.00	—

KM# 282 DOLLAR **Weight:** 28.2800 g. **Composition:** Copper Nickel **Subject:** Queen Elizabeth's Golden Jubilee **Obverse:** National arms **Reverse:** The Queen and a young Prince Charles **Edge:** Reeded **Size:** 38.6 mm.

Date	F	VF	XF	Unc	BU
2002	—	—	—	10.00	—

KM# 285 DOLLAR **Weight:** 28.2800 g. **Composition:** Copper-Nickel **Subject:** Queen Elizabeth's Golden Jubilee **Obverse:** National arms **Reverse:** Queen and Prince Philip **Edge:** Reeded **Size:** 38.6 mm.

Date	F	VF	XF	Unc	BU
2002	—	—	—	10.00	—

KM# 276 DOLLAR **Weight:** 28.2800 g. **Composition:** Copper Nickel **Subject:** British Queen Mother **Obverse:** National arms **Reverse:** Queen Mother with dog in garden **Edge:** Reeded **Size:** 38.6 mm.

Date	F	VF	XF	Unc	BU
2002	—	—	—	10.00	—

KM# 279 DOLLAR **Weight:** 28.2800 g. **Composition:** Copper Nickel **Subject:** British Queen Mother **Obverse:** National arms **Reverse:** Queen Mother with daughters **Edge:** Reeded **Size:** 38.6 mm.

Date	F	VF	XF	Unc	BU
2002	—	—	—	10.00	—

KM# 256 DOLLAR **Weight:** 28.2800 g. **Composition:** Copper Nickel **Subject:** Year of the Horse **Obverse:** National arms **Reverse:** Horse **Edge:** Reeded **Size:** 38.6 mm.

Date	F	VF	XF	Unc	BU
2002	—	—	—	9.50	—

KM# 29 2 LEONES **Composition:** Copper-Nickel **Series:** F.A.O. **Subject:** Regional Conference for Africa **Obverse:** Farmer tilling field **Reverse:** Dr. Siaka Stevens right **Shape:** 7-sided

Date	Mintage	F	VF	XF	Unc
1976	20,000	—	1.00	2.50	5.50

KM# 98 5 DOLLARS **Weight:** 15.5517 g. **Compositio** 0.9990 Silver .5000 oz. ASW **Subject:** Shanghai Coin ar Stamp Exposition **Obverse:** National arms **Reverse:** Crowned lion

Date	Mintage	F	VF	XF	Unc
1997 Proof	Est. 10,000	Value: 30.00			

KM# 99 5 DOLLARS **Weight:** 15.5517 g. **Compositio** 0.9990 Silver .5000 oz. ASW **Subject:** Shanghai Coin ar Stamp Exposition **Reverse:** Unicorn

Date	Mintage	F	VF	XF	Unc
1997 Proof	Est. 10,000	Value: 30.00			

KM# 101 5 DOLLARS **Weight:** 15.5517 g. **Composition:** 0.9990 Silver .5000 oz. ASW **Subject:** Vis of President Clinton to China

Date	Mintage	F	VF	XF	Unc
1998 Proof	Est. 10,000	Value: 30.00			

KM# 102 5 DOLLARS **Weight:** 15.5517 g. **Composition:** 0.9990 Silver .5000 oz. ASW **Subject:** Vis of President Clinton to Beijing **Reverse:** Great Wall

Date	Mintage	F	VF	XF	Unc
1998 Proof	Est. 10,000	Value: 30.00			

/I# 38 10 LEONES **Weight:** 28.2800 g. **Composition:** 0.9250 Silver .8411 oz. ASW **Series:** Year of the Scout

te	Mintage	F	VF	XF	Unc	BU
(1983)	10,000	—	—	—	35.00	—
(1983) Proof	10,000	Value: 47.50				

M# 41 10 LEONES **Weight:** 28.2800 g. **Composition:** 0.9250 Silver .8411 oz. ASW **Series:** World Wildlife Fund **Obverse:** Pygmy Hippopotamus **Reverse:** Dr. Joseph Saidu Momoh left

te	Mintage	F	VF	XF	Unc	BU
87 Proof	25,000	Value: 25.00				

M# 44 10 LEONES **Composition:** Nickel Clad Steel **Obverse:** Denomination **Reverse:** Bust of Mammy Yoko facing within inner ring

ate	F	VF	XF	Unc	BU
96	—	—	—	0.75	—

KM# 49 10 DOLLARS **Weight:** 28.2800 g. **Composition:** 0.9250 Silver .8411 oz. ASW **Obverse:** National arms **Reverse:** Crowned lion

ate	Mintage	F	VF	XF	Unc	BU
997 Proof	Est. 10,000	Value: 47.50				

KM# 50 10 DOLLARS **Weight:** 28.2800 g. **Composition:** 0.9250 Silver .8411 oz. ASW **Reverse:** Unicorn

Date	Mintage	F	VF	XF	Unc	BU
1997 Proof	Est. 10,000	Value: 47.50				

KM# 54 10 DOLLARS **Weight:** 28.2800 g. **Composition:** 0.9250 Silver .8411 oz. ASW **Subject:** Golden Wedding Anniversary **Reverse:** E and P monogram within flower circle

Date	Mintage	F	VF	XF	Unc	BU
1997 Proof	Est. 10,000	Value: 47.50				

KM# 57 10 DOLLARS **Weight:** 28.2800 g. **Composition:** 0.9250 Silver .8411 oz. ASW **Subject:** Golden Wedding Anniversary **Reverse:** Royal Yacht "Britannia"

Date	Mintage	F	VF	XF	Unc	BU
1997 Proof	Est. 10,000	Value: 47.50				

KM# 60 10 DOLLARS **Weight:** 28.2800 g. **Composition:** 0.9250 Silver .8411 oz. ASW **Subject:** Golden Wedding Anniversary **Reverse:** Royal couple

Date	Mintage	F	VF	XF	Unc	BU
1997 Proof	Est. 10,000	Value: 47.50				

KM# 63 10 DOLLARS **Weight:** 28.2800 g. **Composition:** 0.9250 Silver .8411 oz. ASW **Subject:** Golden Wedding Anniversary **Reverse:** Fireworks above palace

Date	Mintage	F	VF	XF	Unc	BU
1997 Proof	Est. 10,000	Value: 47.50				

KM# 66 10 DOLLARS **Weight:** 28.2800 g. **Composition:** 0.9250 Silver .8411 oz. ASW **Subject:** Golden Wedding Anniversary **Reverse:** Queen with two children

Date	Mintage	F	VF	XF	Unc	BU
1997 Proof	Est. 10,000	Value: 47.50				

KM# 69 10 DOLLARS **Weight:** 28.2800 g. **Composition:** 0.9250 Silver .8411 oz. ASW **Subject:** Golden Wedding Anniversary **Reverse:** Royal couple with two children

Date	Mintage	F	VF	XF	Unc	BU
1997 Proof	Est. 10,000	Value: 47.50				

KM# 72 10 DOLLARS **Weight:** 28.2800 g. **Composition:** 0.9250 Silver .8411 oz. ASW **Subject:** Diana - The Peoples' Princess **Reverse:** Portrait of Lady Diana

Date	Mintage	F	VF	XF	Unc	BU
1997 Proof	Est. 10,000	Value: 30.00				

KM# 78 10 DOLLARS **Weight:** 28.2800 g. **Composition:** 0.9250 Silver .8411 oz. ASW **Subject:** Diana - The Peoples' Princess **Reverse:** Lady Diana and Mother Theresa

Date	Mintage	F	VF	XF	Unc	BU
1997	Est. 10,000	Value: 42.50				

KM# 84 10 DOLLARS **Weight:** 28.2800 g. **Composition:** 0.9250 Silver .8411 oz. ASW **Subject:** Diana - The Peoples' Princess **Reverse:** Lady Diana and AIDS patient

Date		F	VF	XF	Unc	BU
1997 Proof	Est. 10,000	Value: 22.50				

KM# 90 10 DOLLARS **Weight:** 28.2800 g. **Composition:** 0.9250 Silver .8411 oz. ASW **Subject:** Diana - The Peoples' Princess **Reverse:** Lady Diana with sons William and Harry

Date	Mintage	F	VF	XF	Unc	BU
1997 Proof	Est. 10,000	Value: 27.50				

KM# 96 10 DOLLARS **Weight:** 28.2800 g. **Composition:** 0.9250 Silver .8411 oz. ASW **Subject:** Jurassic Park **Reverse:** Velociraptor

Date	Mintage	F	VF	XF	Unc	BU
1997 Proof	Est. 10,000	Value: 47.50				

KM# 104 10 DOLLARS **Weight:** 28.2800 g. **Composition:** 0.9250 Silver .8411 oz. ASW **Subject:** In Memoriam, Diana - The Peoples' Princess **Reverse:** Lady Diana portrait

Date	Mintage	F	VF	XF	Unc	BU
1998 Proof	Est. 10,000	Value: 37.50				

KM# A110 10 DOLLARS **Weight:** 28.2800 g. **Composition:** 0.9250 Silver .8411 oz. ASW **Subject:** Dr. Livingstone **Note:** Previously KM#110.

Date	Mintage	F	VF	XF	Unc	BU
1998 Proof	Est. 10,000	Value: 50.00				

KM# 113 10 DOLLARS **Weight:** 28.2800 g. **Composition:** 0.9250 Silver .8411 oz. ASW **Subject:** Amerigo Vespucci **Obverse:** National arms **Reverse:** Ship and Vespucci portrait

Date	Mintage	F	VF	XF	Unc	BU
1999 Proof	Est. 10,000	Value: 50.00				

KM# 116 10 DOLLARS **Weight:** 28.2800 g. **Composition:** 0.9250 Silver .8411 oz. ASW **Subject:** Charles Darwin **Obverse:** National arms **Reverse:** Ship and portrait

Date	Mintage	F	VF	XF	Unc	BU
1999 Proof	Est. 10,000	Value: 50.00				

KM# 119 10 DOLLARS **Weight:** 28.2800 g. **Composition:** 0.9250 Silver .8411 oz. ASW **Subject:** China 2000 Series **Obverse:** National arms **Reverse:** Kneeling Terracotta warrior

Date	Mintage	F	VF	XF	Unc	BU
1999 Proof	Est. 10,000	Value: 47.50				

KM# 122 10 DOLLARS **Weight:** 28.2800 g. **Composition:** 0.9250 Silver .8411 oz. ASW **Subject:** China 2000 Series - Ming Dynasty **Obverse:** National arms **Reverse:** Temple of Heaven

Date	Mintage	F	VF	XF	Unc	BU
1999 Proof	Est. 10,000	Value: 47.50				

KM# 125 10 DOLLARS **Weight:** 28.2800 g. **Composition:** 0.9250 Silver .8411 oz. ASW **Subject:** China 2000 Series - The Great Wall **Obverse:** National arms **Reverse:** Portion of the Great Wall

Date		F	VF	XF	Unc	BU
1999 Proof	Est. 10,000	Value: 47.50				

KM# 128 10 DOLLARS **Weight:** 28.2800 g. **Composition:** 0.9250 Silver .8411 oz. ASW **Subject:** China 2000 Series **Obverse:** National arms **Reverse:** Bronze chariot

Date	Mintage	F	VF	XF	Unc	BU
1999 Proof	Est. 10,000	Value: 47.50				

KM# 131 10 DOLLARS **Weight:** 28.2800 g. **Composition:** 0.9250 Silver .8411 oz. ASW **Subject:** Ch 2000 Series - Armillary Sphere **Obverse:** National arms **Reverse:** First century armillary sphere

Date	Mintage	F	VF	XF	Unc
1999 Proof	Est. 10,000	Value: 47.50			

KM# 134 10 DOLLARS **Weight:** 28.2800 g. **Composition:** 0.9250 Silver .8411 oz. ASW **Subject:** Ch 2000 Series - Tang Dynasty **Obverse:** National arms **Reverse:** Tang Dynasty royal horse

Date	Mintage	F	VF	XF	Unc
1999 Proof	Est. 10,000	Value: 47.50			

KM# 137 10 DOLLARS **Weight:** 28.2800 g. **Composition:** 0.9250 Silver .8411 oz. ASW **Subject:** Ma Return to China **Obverse:** National arms **Reverse:** Chur car, roulette wheel; clasped hands below

Date	Mintage	F	VF	XF	Unc
1999 Proof	Est. 10,000	Value: 50.00			

KM# 140 10 DOLLARS **Weight:** 28.2800 g. **Composition:** 0.9250 Silver .8411 oz. ASW **Subject:** Prir Edward's Wedding **Obverse:** National arms **Reverse:** Symbolic wedding design

Date	Mintage	F	VF	XF	Unc
1999 Proof	Est. 10,000	Value: 50.00			

M# 143 10 DOLLARS **Weight:** 28.2800 g. **Composition:** 0.9250 Silver .8411 oz. ASW **Subject:** Year of the Dragon **Obverse:** National arms **Reverse:** Dragon

e	Mintage	F	VF	XF	Unc	BU
0 Proof	Est. 25,000	Value: 47.50				

M# 153 10 DOLLARS **Weight:** 28.2800 g. **Composition:** 0.9250 Silver .8411 oz. ASW **Obverse:** National arms **Reverse:** Two Phoenix birds **Note:** Struck at Pobjoy Mint.

te	Mintage	F	VF	XF	Unc	BU
0 Proof	Est. 10,000	Value: 47.50				

M# 154 10 DOLLARS **Weight:** 28.2800 g. **Composition:** 0.9250 Silver .8411 oz. ASW **Reverse:** Chinese dragon

te	Mintage	F	VF	XF	Unc	BU
00 Proof	Est. 10,000	Value: 47.50				

M# 155 10 DOLLARS **Weight:** 28.2800 g. **Composition:** 0.9250 Silver .8411 oz. ASW **Reverse:** Chinese unicorn

te	Mintage	F	VF	XF	Unc	BU
00 Proof	Est. 10,000	Value: 47.50				

KM# 177 10 DOLLARS **Weight:** 28.2800 g. **Composition:** 0.9250 Silver .8411 oz. ASW **Reverse:** Seated Buddha

Date	Mintage	F	VF	XF	Unc	BU
2000 Proof	Est. 25,000	Value: 47.50				

KM# 178 10 DOLLARS **Weight:** 28.2800 g. **Composition:** 0.9250 Silver .8411 oz. ASW **Reverse:** Goddess of Mercy

Date	Mintage	F	VF	XF	Unc	BU
2000 Proof	Est. 25,000	Value: 47.50				

KM# 179 10 DOLLARS **Weight:** 28.2800 g. **Composition:** 0.9250 Silver .8411 oz. ASW **Reverse:** Tzai-yen holding scroll

Date	Mintage	F	VF	XF	Unc	BU
2000 Proof	Est. 25,000	Value: 47.50				

KM# 199 10 DOLLARS **Weight:** 28.2800 g. **Composition:** 0.9250 Silver .8410 oz. ASW **Subject:** Year of the Snake **Obverse:** National arms **Reverse:** Snake on bamboo **Edge:** Reeded **Size:** 38.6 mm.

Date	Mintage	F	VF	XF	Unc	BU
2001 Proof	Est. 25,000	Value: 47.50				

KM# 207 10 DOLLARS **Weight:** 28.2800 g. **Composition:** 0.9250 Silver .8410 oz. ASW **Subject:** P'an Ku **Obverse:** National arms **Reverse:** Dragon

Date	Mintage	F	VF	XF	Unc	BU
2001	Est. 5,000	Value: 47.50				

KM# 215 10 DOLLARS **Weight:** 28.2800 g. **Composition:** 0.9250 Silver .8410 oz. ASW **Subject:** P'an Ku **Obverse:** National arms **Reverse:** Dragon and three animals

Date	Mintage	F	VF	XF	Unc	BU
2001 Proof	Est. 5,000	Value: 47.50				

KM# 223 10 DOLLARS **Weight:** 28.2800 g. **Composition:** 0.9250 Silver .8410 oz. ASW **Series:** The Big Five **Obverse:** National arms **Reverse:** Rhino **Edge:** Reeded **Size:** 38.6 mm.

Date	F	VF	XF	Unc	BU
2001	—	—	—	47.50	—

KM# 226 10 DOLLARS **Weight:** 28.2800 g. **Composition:** 0.9250 Silver .8410 oz. ASW **Series:** The Big Five **Obverse:** National arms **Reverse:** Lion

Date	Mintage	F	VF	XF	Unc	BU
2001 Proof	Est. 10,000	Value: 42.50				

KM# 229 10 DOLLARS **Weight:** 28.2800 g. **Composition:** 0.9250 Silver .8410 oz. ASW **Series:** The Big Five **Obverse:** National arms **Reverse:** Leopard

Date	Mintage	F	VF	XF	Unc	BU
2001 Proof	Est. 10,000	Value: 42.50				

KM# 232 10 DOLLARS **Weight:** 28.2800 g. **Composition:** 0.9250 Silver .8410 oz. ASW **Series:** The Big Five **Obverse:** National arms **Reverse:** Elephants

Date	Mintage	F	VF	XF	Unc	BU
2001 Proof	Est. 10,000	Value: 42.50				

KM# 235 10 DOLLARS **Weight:** 28.2800 g. **Composition:** 0.9250 Silver .8410 oz. ASW **Series:** The Big Five **Obverse:** National arms **Reverse:** Buffalo

Date	Mintage	F	VF	XF	Unc	BU
2001 Proof	Est. 10,000	Value: 47.50				

KM# 238 10 DOLLARS **Weight:** 28.2800 g. **Composition:** 0.9250 Silver .8410 oz. ASW **Series:** The Big Five **Obverse:** National arms **Reverse:** All five animals

Date	Mintage	F	VF	XF	Unc	BU
2001 Proof	Est. 10,000	Value: 47.50				

KM# 246 10 DOLLARS **Weight:** 28.2800 g. **Composition:** 0.9250 Silver .8410 oz. ASW **Series:** Big Cats **Obverse:** National arms **Reverse:** Male and female lions **Edge:** Reeded **Size:** 38.6 mm.

Date	Mintage	F	VF	XF	Unc	BU
2001 Proof	10,000	Value: 45.00				

KM# 246a 10 DOLLARS **Weight:** 28.2800 g. **Composition:** 0.9250 Silver .8410 oz. ASW **Series:** Big Cats **Obverse:** Natioanl arms **Reverse:** Male and female lions **Edge:** Reeded **Size:** 38.6 mm.

Date	F	VF	XF	Unc	BU
2001 Proof	—	Value: 50.00			

KM# 247 10 DOLLARS **Weight:** 28.2800 g. **Composition:** 0.9250 Silver .8410 oz. ASW **Series:** Big Cats **Reverse:** Tiger **Edge:** Reeded **Size:** 38.6 mm.

Date	F	VF	XF	Unc	BU
2001 Proof	—	Value: 47.50			

KM# 247a 10 DOLLARS **Weight:** 28.2800 g. **Composition:** 0.9250 Silver .8410 oz. ASW **Series:** Big Cats **Reverse:** Multicolored tiger **Edge:** Reeded **Size:** 38.6 mm.

Date	F	VF	XF	Unc	BU
2001 Proof	—	Value: 50.00			

KM# 248 10 DOLLARS **Weight:** 28.2800 g. **Composition:** 0.9250 Silver .8410 oz. ASW **Series:** Big Cats **Reverse:** Cheetah head facing **Edge:** Reeded **Size:** 38.6 mm.

Date	Mintage	F	VF	XF	Unc	BU
2001 Proof	10,000	Value: 47.50				

KM# 248a 10 DOLLARS **Weight:** 28.2800 g. **Composition:** 0.9250 Silver .8410 oz. ASW **Series:** Big Cats **Reverse:** Multicolored cheetah **Edge:** Reeded **Size:** 38.6 mm.

Date	F	VF	XF	Unc	BU
2001 Proof	—	Value: 50.00			

KM# 249 10 DOLLARS **Weight:** 28.2800 g. **Composition:** 0.9250 Silver .8410 oz. ASW **Series:** Big Cats **Reverse:** Cougar **Edge:** Reeded **Size:** 38.6 mm.

Date	Mintage	F	VF	XF	Unc	BU
2001 Proof	10,000	Value: 47.50				

KM# 249a 10 DOLLARS **Weight:** 28.2800 g. **Composition:** 0.9250 Silver .8410 oz. ASW **Series:** Big Cats **Reverse:** Multicolored cougar **Edge:** Reeded **Size:** 38.6 mm.

Date	F	VF	XF	Unc	BU
2001 Proof	—	Value: 50.00			

KM# 250 10 DOLLARS **Weight:** 28.2800 g. **Composition:** 0.9250 Silver .8410 oz. ASW **Series:** Big Cats **Reverse:** Black panther **Edge:** Reeded **Size:** 38.6 mm.

Date	Mintage	F	VF	XF	Unc	BU
2001 Proof	10,000	Value: 47.50				

KM# 250a 10 DOLLARS **Weight:** 28.2800 g. **Compositi** 0.9250 Silver .8410 oz. ASW **Series:** Big Cats **Reverse:** Multicolored black panther **Edge:** Reeded **Size:** 38.6 mm

Date	F	VF	XF	Unc
2001 Proof	—	Value: 50.00		

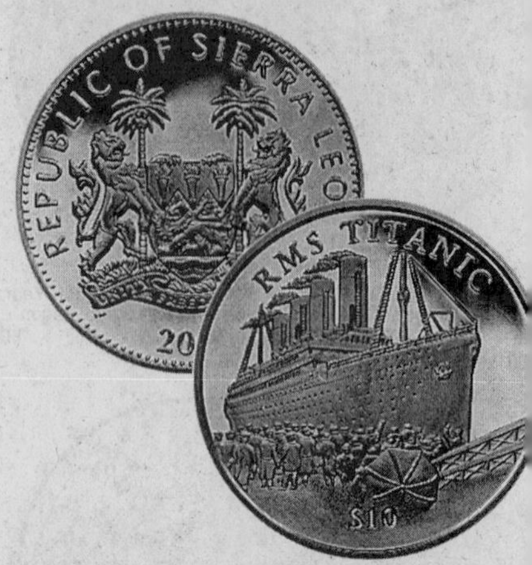

KM# 265 10 DOLLARS **Weight:** 28.2800 g. **Composition:** 0.9250 Silver 0.841 oz. ASW **Subject:** RM Titanic **Obverse:** National arms. **Reverse:** Titanic at doc **Edge:** Reeded. **Size:** 38.6 mm.

Date	Mintage	F	VF	XF	Unc
2002 Proof	10,000	Value: 47.50			

KM# 270 10 DOLLARS **Weight:** 28.2800 g. **Composition:** 0.9250 Gold Clad Silver 0.841 oz. **Subjec** Queen's Golden Jubilee **Obverse:** National arms **Revers** Queen Elizabeth II and Prince Philip visiting blacksmiths Sierra Leone **Edge:** Reeded **Size:** 38.6 mm.

Date	Mintage	F	VF	XF	Unc
2002 Proof	10,000	Value: 50.00			

KM# 271 10 DOLLARS **Weight:** 28.2800 g. **Compositio** 0.9250 Gold Clad Silver 0.841 oz. **Subject:** Queen's Golde Jubilee **Obverse:** National arms **Reverse:** Queen Elizabe II with her two sons **Edge:** Reeded **Size:** 38.6 mm.

Date	Mintage	F	VF	XF	Unc
2002 Proof	10,000	Value: 50.00			

 # 283 10 DOLLARS **Weight:** 28.2800 g. **Composition:** 0.9250 Gold Clad Silver 0.841 oz. **Subject:** Queen Elizabeth's Golden Jubilee **Obverse:** National arms **Reverse:** Queen and young Prince Charles **Edge:** Reeded **Size:** 38.6 mm.

e	Mintage	F	VF	XF	Unc	BU
2 Proof	10,000	Value: 47.50				

#286 10 DOLLARS **Weight:** 28.2800 g. **Composition:** 0.9250 Gold Clad Silver 0.841 oz. **Subject:** Queen Elizabeth's Golden Jubilee **Obverse:** National arms **Reverse:** Queen and Prince Philip **Edge:** Reeded **Size:** 38.6 mm.

e	Mintage	F	VF	XF	Unc	BU
2 Proof	10,000	Value: 47.50				

#277 10 DOLLARS **Weight:** 28.2800 g. **Composition:** 0.9250 Gold Clad Silver 0.841 oz. **Subject:** British Queen Mother **Obverse:** National arms **Reverse:** Queen Mother in garden with dog **Edge:** Reeded **Size:** 38.6 mm.

e	Mintage	F	VF	XF	Unc	BU
2 Proof	10,000	Value: 47.50				

 # 280 10 DOLLARS **Weight:** 28.2800 g. **Composition:** 0.9250 Gold Clad Silver 0.841 oz. **Subject:** British Queen Mother **Obverse:** National arms **Reverse:** Queen Mother and daughters **Edge:** Reeded **Size:** 38.6 mm.

e	Mintage	F	VF	XF	Unc	BU
2 Proof	10,000	Value: 47.50				

 # 257 10 DOLLARS **Weight:** 28.2800 g. **Composition:** 0.9250 Silver .8410 oz. ASW **Subject:** Year of the Horse **Obverse:** National arms **Reverse:** Horse **Edge:** Reeded **Size:** 38.6 mm.

te	Mintage	F	VF	XF	Unc	BU
02 Proof	5,000	Value: 47.50				

#73 20 DOLLARS **Weight:** 1.2441 g. **Composition:** 0.9990 Gold .0400 oz. AGW **Subject:** Diana - The Peoples' Princess **Note:** Similar to 1 Dollar, KM#71.

te	Mintage	F	VF	XF	Unc	BU
97 Proof	Est. 101,000	Value: 45.00				

#79 20 DOLLARS **Weight:** 1.2441 g. **Composition:** 0.9990 Gold .0400 oz. AGW **Subject:** Diana - The Peoples' Princess **Reverse:** Lady Diana and Mother Theresa **Note:** Similar to 1 Dollar, KM#77.

te	Mintage	F	VF	XF	Unc	BU
97 Proof	Est. 101,000	Value: 45.00				

KM# 85 20 DOLLARS **Weight:** 1.2441 g. **Composition:** 0.9990 Gold .0400 oz. AGW **Subject:** Diana - The Peoples' Princess **Reverse:** Lady Diana and AIDS patient **Note:** Similar to 1 Dollar, KM#83.

Date	Mintage	F	VF	XF	Unc	BU
1997 Proof	Est. 101,000	Value: 45.00				

KM# 91 20 DOLLARS **Weight:** 1.2441 g. **Composition:** 0.9990 Gold .0400 oz. AGW **Subject:** Diana - The Peoples' Princess **Reverse:** With sons William and Harry **Note:** Similar to 1 Dollar, KM#89.

Date	Mintage	F	VF	XF	Unc	BU
1997 Proof	Est. 101,000	Value: 45.00				

KM# 105 20 DOLLARS **Weight:** 1.2441 g. **Composition:** 0.9990 Gold .0400 oz. AGW **Subject:** In Memorium **Reverse:** Lady Diana portrait

Date	Mintage	F	VF	XF	Unc	BU
1998 Proof	Est. 10,000	Value: 50.00				

KM# 144 20 DOLLARS **Weight:** 1.2441 g. **Composition:** 0.9990 Gold .0400 oz. AGW **Subject:** Year of the Dragon **Obverse:** National arms **Reverse:** Dragon **Note:** Similar to 1 Dollar, KM#143.

Date	Mintage	F	VF	XF	Unc	BU
2000 Proof	Est. 15,000	Value: 55.00				

KM# 180 20 DOLLARS **Weight:** 1.2400 g. **Composition:** 0.9990 Gold .0399 oz. AGW **Subject:** Buddha **Obverse:** National arms **Reverse:** Seated Buddha **Edge:** Reeded **Note:** Struck at Pobjoy Mint.

Date	Mintage	F	VF	XF	Unc	BU
2000 Proof	Est. 5,000	Value: 55.00				

KM# 181 20 DOLLARS **Weight:** 1.2400 g. **Composition:** 0.9990 Gold .0399 oz. AGW **Reverse:** Goddess of Mercy

Date	Mintage	F	VF	XF	Unc	BU
2000 Proof	Est. 5,000	Value: 55.00				

KM# 182 20 DOLLARS **Weight:** 1.2400 g. **Composition:** 0.9990 Gold .0399 oz. AGW **Reverse:** Tzai-yen holding scroll

Date	Mintage	F	VF	XF	Unc	BU
2000 Proof	Est. 5,000	Value: 55.00				

KM# 200 20 DOLLARS **Weight:** 1.2441 g. **Composition:** 0.9990 Gold .0400 oz. AGW **Subject:** Year of the Snake **Obverse:** National arms **Reverse:** Snake **Edge:** Reeded **Size:** 13.9 mm.

Date	Mintage	F	VF	XF	Unc	BU
2001 Proof	Est. 50,000	Value: 58.00				

KM# 208 20 DOLLARS **Weight:** 1.2441 g. **Composition:** 0.9990 Gold .0400 oz. AGW **Subject:** P'an Ku **Obverse:** National arms **Reverse:** Dragon

Date	Mintage	F	VF	XF	Unc	BU
2001 Proof	Est. 5,000	Value: 58.00				

KM# 216 20 DOLLARS **Weight:** 1.2441 g. **Composition:** 0.9990 Gold .0400 oz. AGW **Subject:** P'an Ku **Obverse:** National arms **Reverse:** Dragon and three animals

Date	Mintage	F	VF	XF	Unc	BU
2001 Proof	Est. 5,000	Value: 58.00				

KM# 258 20 DOLLARS **Weight:** 1.2400 g. **Composition:** 0.9990 Gold .0398 oz. AGW **Subject:** Year of the Horse **Obverse:** National arms **Reverse:** Horse **Edge:** Reeded **Size:** 13.92 mm.

Date	Mintage	F	VF	XF	Unc	BU
2002 Proof	5,000	Value: 49.50				

KM# 272 30 DOLLARS **Weight:** 6.2200 g. **Composition:** 0.3750 Gold 0.075 oz. AGW **Subject:** Queen's Golden Jubilee **Obverse:** National arms **Reverse:** Queen Elizabeth II and Prince Philip **Edge:** Reeded **Size:** 22 mm.

Date	Mintage	F	VF	XF	Unc	BU
2002 Proof	5,000	Value: 95.00				

KM# 273 30 DOLLARS **Weight:** 6.2200 g. **Composition:** 0.3750 Gold 0.075 oz. AGW **Subject:** Queen's Golden Jubilee **Obverse:** National arms **Reverse:** Queen Elizabeth II and two sons **Edge:** Reeded **Size:** 22 mm.

Date	Mintage	F	VF	XF	Unc	BU
2002 Proof	5,000	Value: 95.00				

KM# 45 50 LEONES **Composition:** Nickel Clad Steel **Obverse:** Building above denomination **Reverse:** Sir Henry Lightfoot bust **Shape:** Octagon

Date	F	VF	XF	Unc	BU
1996	—	—	—	1.25	—

KM# 74 50 DOLLARS **Weight:** 3.1100 g. **Composition:** 0.9990 Gold .1000 oz. AGW **Subject:** Diana - The Peoples' Princess **Reverse:** Portrait of Lady Diana

Date	Mintage	F	VF	XF	Unc	BU
1997 Proof	Est. 7,500	Value: 85.00				

KM# 80 50 DOLLARS **Weight:** 3.1100 g. **Composition:** 0.9990 Gold .1000 oz. AGW **Subject:** Diana - The Peoples' Princess **Reverse:** Lady Diana and Mother Theresa **Note:** Similar to 1 Dollar, KM#77.

Date	Mintage	F	VF	XF	Unc	BU
1997 Proof	Est. 7,500	Value: 85.00				

KM# 86 50 DOLLARS **Weight:** 3.1100 g. **Composition:** 0.9990 Gold .1000 oz. AGW **Subject:** Diana - The Peoples' Princess **Reverse:** Lady Diana and AIDS patient **Note:** Similar to 1 Dollar, KM#83.

Date	Mintage	F	VF	XF	Unc	BU
1997 Proof	Est. 7,500	Value: 85.00				

KM# 92 50 DOLLARS **Weight:** 3.1100 g. **Composition:** 0.9990 Gold .1000 oz. AGW **Subject:** Diana - The Peoples' Princess **Reverse:** With sons William and Harry **Note:** Similar to 1 Dollar, KM#89.

Date	Mintage	F	VF	XF	Unc	BU
1997 Proof	Est. 7,500	Value: 85.00				

KM# 106 50 DOLLARS **Weight:** 3.1100 g. **Composition:** 0.9990 Gold .1000 oz. AGW **Subject:** Diana - The Peoples' Princess **Reverse:** Portrait of Lady Diana **Note:** Similar to 1 Dollar, KM#104.

Date	Mintage	F	VF	XF	Unc	BU
1998 Proof	Est. 7,500	Value: 85.00				

KM# 184 50 DOLLARS **Weight:** 3.1100 g. **Composition:** 0.9990 Gold .1000 oz. AGW **Reverse:** Goddess of Mercy

Date	Mintage	F	VF	XF	Unc	BU
2000 Proof	Est. 5,000	Value: 95.00				

KM# 145 50 DOLLARS **Weight:** 3.1100 g. **Composition:** 0.9990 Gold .1000 oz. AGW **Subject:** Year of the Dragon **Obverse:** National arms **Reverse:** Dragon **Note:** Similar to 1 Dollar, KM#143.

Date	Mintage	F	VF	XF	Unc	BU
2000 Proof	Est. 20,000	Value: 90.00				

KM# 183 50 DOLLARS **Weight:** 3.1100 g. **Composition:** 0.9990 Gold .1000 oz. AGW **Subject:** Buddha **Obverse:** National arms **Reverse:** Seated Buddha **Edge:** Reeded **Note:** Similar to 1 Dollar, KM#143. Struck at Pobjoy Mint.

Date	Mintage	F	VF	XF	Unc	BU
2000 Proof	Est. 5,000	Value: 95.00				

KM# 185 50 DOLLARS **Weight:** 3.1100 g. **Composition:** 0.9990 Gold .1000 oz. AGW **Reverse:** Tzai-yen holding scroll

Date	Mintage	F	VF	XF	Unc	BU
2000 Proof	Est. 5,000	Value: 95.00				

KM# 201 50 DOLLARS **Weight:** 3.1103 g. **Composition:** 0.9990 Gold .1000 oz. AGW **Subject:** Year of the Snake **Obverse:** National arms **Reverse:** Snake **Edge:** Reeded **Size:** 18 mm.

Date	Mintage	F	VF	XF	Unc	BU
2001 Proof	Est. 10,000	Value: 95.00				

KM# 209 50 DOLLARS **Weight:** 3.1103 g. **Composition:** 0.9990 Gold .1000 oz. AGW **Subject:** P'an Ku **Obverse:** National arms **Reverse:** Dragon

Date	Mintage	F	VF	XF	Unc	BU
2001 Proof	Est. 5,000	Value: 95.00				

KM# 217 50 DOLLARS **Weight:** 3.1103 g. **Composition:** 0.9990 Gold .1000 oz. AGW **Subject:** P'an Ku **Obverse:** National arms **Reverse:** Dragon and three animals

Date	Mintage	F	VF	XF	Unc	BU
2001 Proof	Est. 5,000	Value: 95.00				

KM# 266 50 DOLLARS **Weight:** 155.5500 g. **Composition:** 0.9999 Silver 5.0005 oz. ASW **Subject:** RMS Titanic **Obverse:** National arms **Reverse:** Titanic at dock **Edge:** Reeded **Size:** 65 mm.

Date	Mintage	F	VF	XF	Unc	BU
2002 Proof	2,000	Value: 150				

KM# 259 50 DOLLARS **Weight:** 3.1100 g. **Composition:** 0.9990 Gold .0999 oz. AGW **Subject:** Year of the Horse **Obverse:** National arms **Reverse:** Horse **Edge:** Reeded **Size:** 17.95 mm.

Date	Mintage	F	VF	XF	Unc	BU
2002 Proof	5,000	Value: 95.00				

KM# 39 100 LEONES **Weight:** 15.9800 g. **Composition:** 0.9170 Gold .4711 oz. AGW **Series:** Year of the Scout

Date	Mintage	F	VF	XF	Unc	BU
ND(1983)	2,000	—	—	—	275	—
ND(1983) Proof	2,000	Value: 350				

KM# 46 100 LEONES **Composition:** Nickel Clad Steel **Obverse:** Cocoa pods **Reverse:** Naimbana bust

Date	F	VF	XF	Unc	BU
1996	—	—	—	1.75	—

KM# 51 100 DOLLARS **Weight:** 6.2200 g. **Composition:** 0.9999 Gold .2000 oz. AGW **Subject:** Shanghai Coin and Stamp Exposition **Reverse:** Crowned lion **Note:** Similar to 5 Dollars, KM#98.

Date	Mintage	F	VF	XF	Unc	BU
1997 Proof	Est. 5,000	Value: 175				

KM# 52 100 DOLLARS **Weight:** 6.2200 g. **Composition:** 0.9999 Gold .2000 oz. AGW **Subject:** Shanghai Coin and Stamp Exposition **Reverse:** Crowned lion **Note:** Similar to 5 Dollars, KM#99.

Date	Mintage	F	VF	XF	Unc	BU
1997 Proof	Est. 5,000	Value: 175				

KM# 55 100 DOLLARS **Weight:** 6.2200 g. **Composition:** 0.9999 Gold .2000 oz. AGW **Subject:** Golden Wedding Anniversary **Reverse:** E and P monogram **Note:** Similar to 10 Dollars, KM#54.

Date	Mintage	F	VF	XF	Unc	BU
1997 Proof	Est. 3,500	Value: 175				

KM# 58 100 DOLLARS **Weight:** 6.2200 g. **Composition:** 0.9999 Gold .2000 oz. AGW **Subject:** Golden Wedding Anniversary **Reverse:** Yacht **Note:** Similar to 10 Dollars, KM#57.

Date	Mintage	F	VF	XF	Unc	BU
1997 Proof	Est. 3,500	Value: 175				

KM# 61 100 DOLLARS **Weight:** 6.2200 g. **Composition:** 0.9999 Gold .2000 oz. AGW **Subject:** Golden Wedding Anniversary **Reverse:** Royal couple **Note:** Similar to 10 Dollars, KM#60.

Date	Mintage	F	VF	XF	Unc	BU
1997 Proof	Est. 10,000	Value: 175				

KM# 64 100 DOLLARS **Weight:** 6.2200 g. **Composition:** 0.9999 Gold .2000 oz. AGW **Subject:** Golden Wedding Anniversary **Reverse:** Fireworks above palace **Note:** Similar to 10 Dollars, KM#63.

Date	Mintage	F	VF	XF	Unc	BU
1997 Proof	Est. 3,500	Value: 175				

KM# 67 100 DOLLARS **Weight:** 6.2200 g. **Composition:** 0.9999 Gold .2000 oz. AGW **Subject:** Golden Wedding Anniversary **Reverse:** Queen with two children **Note:** Similar to 10 Dollars, KM#66.

Date	Mintage	F	VF	XF	Unc	BU
1997 Proof	Est. 3,500	Value: 175				

KM# 70 100 DOLLARS **Weight:** 6.2200 g. **Composition:** 0.9999 Gold .2000 oz. AGW **Subject:** Golden Wedding Anniversary **Reverse:** Royal couple with two children **Note:** Similar to 10 Dollars, KM#69.

Date	Mintage	F	VF	XF	Unc	BU
1997 Proof	Est. 3,500	Value: 175				

KM# 75 100 DOLLARS **Weight:** 6.2200 g. **Composition:** 0.9999 Gold .2000 oz. AGW **Subject:** Diana - The Peoples' Princess **Reverse:** Portrait of Lady Diana **Note:** Similar to 1 Dollar, KM#71.

Date	Mintage	F	VF	XF	Unc	BU
1997 Proof	Est. 5,000	Value: 160				

KM#81 100 DOLLARS **Weight:** 6.2200 g. **Composition:** 0.9999 Gold .2000 oz. AGW **Subject:** Diana - The Peoples' Princess **Reverse:** Lady Diana and Mother Theresa

Date	Mintage	F	VF	XF	Unc	BU
1997 Proof	Est. 5,000	Value: 160				

KM# 87 100 DOLLARS **Weight:** 6.2200 g. **Composition:** 0.9999 Gold .2000 oz. AGW **Subject:** Diana - The Peoples' Princess **Reverse:** Lady Diana and AIDS patient **Note:** Similar to 1 Dollar, KM#83.

Date	Mintage	F	VF	XF	Unc	BU
1997 Proof	Est. 5,000	Value: 160				

KM# 93 100 DOLLARS **Weight:** 6.2200 g. **Composition:** 0.9999 Gold .2000 oz. AGW **Subject:** Diana - The Peoples' Princess **Reverse:** With sons William and Harry **Note:** Similar to 1 Dollar, KM#89.

Date	Mintage	F	VF	XF	Unc	BU
1997 Proof	Est. 5,000	Value: 160				

KM# 97 100 DOLLARS **Weight:** 6.2200 g. **Composition:** 0.9999 Gold .2000 oz. AGW **Subject:** Jurassic Park **Reverse:** Velociraptor **Note:** Similar to 10 Dollars, KM#96.

Date	Mintage	F	VF	XF	Unc	BU
1997 Proof	Est. 5,000	Value: 175				

KM# 100 100 DOLLARS **Weight:** 6.2200 g. **Composition:** 0.9999 Gold .2000 oz. AGW **Subject:** Queen Victoria's Diamond Jubilee Centennial **Obverse:** National arms **Reverse:** Youthful portrait of Queen with .06 carat diamond mounted in gown

Date	Mintage	F	VF	XF	Unc	BU
1997 Proof	Est. 3,500	Value: 200				

KM# 107 100 DOLLARS **Weight:** 6.2200 g. **Composition:** 0.9999 Gold .2000 oz. AGW **Subject:** Diana - The People's Princess **Note:** Similar to 10 Dollars, KM#104.

Date	Mintage	F	VF	XF	Unc	BU
1998 Proof	Est. 5,000	Value: 160				

KM# 111 100 DOLLARS **Weight:** 6.2200 g. **Composition:** 0.9999 Gold .2000 oz. AGW **Subject:** Dr. Livingstone **Obverse:** National arms **Note:** Similar to 10 Dollars, KM#110.

Date	Mintage	F	VF	XF	Unc	BU
1998 Proof	Est. 5,000	Value: 165				

KM# 114 100 DOLLARS **Weight:** 6.2200 g. **Composition:** 0.9999 Gold .2000 oz. AGW **Subject:** Amerigo Vespucci **Obverse:** National arms **Reverse:** Ship and mountainous portrait **Note:** Similar to 10 Dollars, KM#113.

Date	Mintage	F	VF	XF	Unc	BU
1999 Proof	Est. 5,000	Value: 175				

KM# 117 100 DOLLARS **Weight:** 6.2200 g. **Composition:** 0.9999 Gold .2000 oz. AGW **Subject:** Charles Darwin **Obverse:** National arms **Reverse:** Ship and portrait **Note:** Similar to 10 Dollars, KM#116.

Date	Mintage	F	VF	XF	Unc	BU
1999 Proof	Est. 5,000	Value: 175				

KM# 120 100 DOLLARS **Weight:** 6.2200 g. **Composition:** 0.9999 Gold .2000 oz. AGW **Subject:** China 2000 Series **Obverse:** National arms **Reverse:** Kneeling terra cotta warrior **Note:** Similar to 10 Dollars, KM#119.

Date	Mintage	F	VF	XF	Unc	BU
1999 Proof	Est. 5,000	Value: 165				

KM# 123 100 DOLLARS **Weight:** 6.2200 g. **Composition:** 0.9999 Gold .2000 oz. AGW **Subject:** China 2000 Series - Ming Dynasty **Obverse:** National arms **Reverse:** Temple of Heaven **Note:** Similar to 10 Dollars, KM#122.

Date	Mintage	F	VF	XF	Unc	BU
1999 Proof	Est. 5,000	Value: 165				

KM# 126 100 DOLLARS **Weight:** 6.2200 g. **Composition:** 0.9999 Gold .2000 oz. AGW **Subject:** China 2000 Series - The Great Wall **Obverse:** National arms **Reverse:** Portion of the Great Wall **Note:** Similar to 10 Dollars, KM#125.

Date	Mintage	F	VF	XF	Unc	BU
1999 Proof	Est. 5,000	Value: 165				

KM# 129 100 DOLLARS **Weight:** 6.2200 g. **Composition:** 0.9999 Gold .2000 oz. AGW **Series:** China 2000 **Obverse:** National arms **Reverse:** Bronze chariot **Note:** Similar to 10 Dollars, KM#128.

Date	Mintage	F	VF	XF	Unc	BU
1999 Proof	Est. 5,000	Value: 165				

KM# 132 100 DOLLARS **Weight:** 6.2200 g. **Composition:** 0.9999 Gold .2000 oz. AGW **Series:** China 2000 **Obverse:** National arms **Reverse:** First century armillary sphere **Note:** Similar to 10 Dollars, KM#131.

Date	Mintage	F	VF	XF	Unc	BU
1999 Proof	Est. 5,000	Value: 165				

KM# 135 100 DOLLARS **Weight:** 6.2200 g. **Composition:** 0.9999 Gold .2000 oz. AGW **Series:** China 2000 **Obverse:** National arms **Reverse:** Tang Dynasty royal horse **Note:** Similar to 10 Dollars, KM#134.

Date	Mintage	F	VF	XF	Unc	BU
1999 Proof	Est. 5,000	Value: 165				

KM# 138 100 DOLLARS **Weight:** 6.2200 g. **Composition:** 0.9999 Gold .2000 oz. AGW **Subject:** Macau Return to China **Obverse:** National arms **Reverse:** Church, car, roulette wheel, and hands shaking **Note:** Similar to 10 Dollars, KM#137.

Date	Mintage	F	VF	XF	Unc	BU
1999 Proof	Est. 5,000	Value: 175				

KM# 141 100 DOLLARS **Weight:** 6.2200 g. **Composition:** 0.9999 Gold .2000 oz. AGW **Subject:** Prince Edward's Wedding **Obverse:** National arms **Reverse:** Symbolic wedding design **Note:** Similar to 10 Dollars, KM#140.

Date	Mintage	F	VF	XF	Unc	BU
1999 Proof	Est. 5,000	Value: 175				

KM# 146 100 DOLLARS **Weight:** 6.2200 g. **Composition:** 0.9999 Gold .2000 oz. AGW **Subject:** Year of the Dragon **Obverse:** National arms **Reverse:** Dragon **Note:** Similar to 10 Dollars, KM#143.

Date	Mintage	F	VF	XF	Unc	BU
2000 Proof	Est. 20,000	Value: 165				

KM# 186 100 DOLLARS **Weight:** 6.2200 g. **Composition:** 0.9999 Gold .2000 oz. AGW **Subject:** Buddha **Obverse:** National arms **Reverse:** Seated Buddha **Edge:** Reeded **Note:** Struck at Pobjoy Mint.

Date	Mintage	F	VF	XF	Unc	BU
2000	Est. 5,000	Value: 175				

KM# 187 100 DOLLARS **Weight:** 6.2200 g. **Composition:** 0.9999 Gold .2000 oz. AGW **Subject:** Buddha **Obverse:** National arms **Reverse:** Goddess of Mercy

Date	Mintage	F	VF	XF	Unc	BU
2000 Proof	Est. 5,000	Value: 175				

KM# 188 100 DOLLARS **Weight:** 6.2200 g. **Composition:** 0.9999 Gold .2000 oz. AGW **Reverse:** Tzai-yen holding scroll

Date	Mintage	F	VF	XF	Unc	BU
2000 Proof	Est. 5,000	Value: 175				

KM# 251 100 DOLLARS **Weight:** 6.2200 g. **Composition:** 0.9990 Gold .1998 oz. AGW **Series:** Big Cats **Obverse:** National arms **Reverse:** Male and female lions **Edge:** Reeded **Size:** 22 mm.

Date	Mintage	F	VF	XF	Unc	BU
2001 Proof	5,000	Value: 175				

KM# 252 100 DOLLARS **Weight:** 6.2200 g. **Composition:** 0.9990 Gold .1998 oz. AGW **Series:** Big Cats **Reverse:** Tiger **Edge:** Reeded **Size:** 22 mm.

Date	Mintage	F	VF	XF	Unc	BU
2001 Proof	5,000	Value: 175				

KM# 253 100 DOLLARS **Weight:** 6.2200 g. **Composition:** 0.9990 Gold .1998 oz. AGW **Series:** Big Cats **Reverse:** Cheetah **Edge:** Reeded **Size:** 22 mm.

Date	Mintage	F	VF	XF	Unc	BU
2001 Proof	5,000	Value: 175				

KM# 254 100 DOLLARS **Weight:** 6.2200 g. **Composition:** 0.9990 Gold .1998 oz. AGW **Series:** Big Cats **Reverse:** Cougar **Edge:** Reeded **Size:** 22 mm.

Date	Mintage	F	VF	XF	Unc	BU
2001 Proof	5,000	Value: 175				

KM# 255 100 DOLLARS **Weight:** 6.2200 g. **Composition:** 0.9990 Gold .1998 oz. AGW **Series:** Big Cats **Reverse:** Black panther **Edge:** Reeded **Size:** 22 mm.

Date	Mintage	F	VF	XF	Unc	BU
2001 Proof	5,000	Value: 175				

KM# 202 100 DOLLARS **Weight:** 6.2200 g. **Composition:** 0.9990 Gold .2000 oz. AGW **Subject:** Y of the Snake **Obverse:** National arms **Reverse:** Snake **Edge:** Reeded **Size:** 22 mm.

Date	F	VF	XF	Unc
2001 Proof	—	Value: 175		

KM# 210 100 DOLLARS **Weight:** 6.2200 g. **Composition:** 0.9990 Gold .2000 oz. AGW **Subject:** P Ku **Obverse:** National arms **Reverse:** Dragon

Date		F	VF	XF	Unc
2001 Proof	Est. 10,000	Value: 175			

KM# 218 100 DOLLARS **Weight:** 6.2200 g. **Composition:** 0.9990 Gold .2000 oz. AGW **Subject:** P Ku **Obverse:** National arms **Reverse:** Dragon and thre animals

Date		F	VF	XF	Unc
2001 Proof	Est. 10,000	Value: 175			

KM# 224 100 DOLLARS **Weight:** 6.2200 g. **Composition:** 0.9990 Gold .2000 oz. AGW **Series:** The Five **Obverse:** National arms **Reverse:** Rhino **Edge:** Ree **Size:** 22 mm.

Date	Mintage	F	VF	XF	Unc
2001 Proof	Est. 5,000	Value: 175			

KM# 227 100 DOLLARS **Weight:** 6.2200 g. **Composition:** 0.9990 Gold .2000 oz. AGW **Series:** The Five **Obverse:** National arms **Reverse:** Lion

Date	Mintage	F	VF	XF	Unc
2001 Proof	Est. 5,000	Value: 175			

KM# 230 100 DOLLARS **Weight:** 6.2200 g. **Composition:** 0.9990 Gold .2000 oz. AGW **Series:** The Five **Obverse:** National arms **Reverse:** Leopard

Date	Mintage	F	VF	XF	Unc
2001 Proof	Est. 5,000	Value: 175			

KM# 233 100 DOLLARS **Weight:** 6.2200 g. **Composition:** 0.9990 Gold .2000 oz. AGW **Series:** The Five **Obverse:** National arms **Reverse:** Elephants

Date	Mintage	F	VF	XF	Unc
2001 Proof	Est. 5,000	Value: 175			

KM# 236 100 DOLLARS **Weight:** 6.2200 g. **Composition:** 0.9990 Gold .2000 oz. AGW **Series:** The Five **Obverse:** National arms **Reverse:** Buffalo

Date	Mintage	F	VF	XF	Unc
2001 Proof	Est. 5,000	Value: 175			

KM# 239 100 DOLLARS **Weight:** 6.2200 g. **Composition:** 0.9990 Gold .2000 oz. AGW **Series:** The Five **Obverse:** National arms **Reverse:** All five animals

Date	Mintage	F	VF	XF	Unc
2001 Proof	Est. 5,000	Value: 175			

KM# 274 100 DOLLARS **Weight:** 6.2200 g. **Composition:** 0.9999 Gold 0.2 oz. AGW **Subject:** Quee Golden Jubilee **Obverse:** National arms. **Reverse:** Que Elizabeth II and Prince Philip. **Edge:** Reeded. **Size:** 22

Date	Mintage	F	VF	XF	Unc
2002 Proof	2,002	Value: 175			

KM# 275 100 DOLLARS **Weight:** 6.2200 g. **Composition:** 0.9999 Gold 0.2 oz. AGW **Subject:** Quee Golden Jubilee **Obverse:** National arms **Reverse:** Que Elizabeth II and two sons **Edge:** Reeded **Size:** 22 mm.

Date	Mintage	F	VF	XF	Unc
2002 Proof	5,000	Value: 175			

KM# 284 100 DOLLARS **Weight:** 6.2200 g. **Composition:** 0.9999 Gold 0.2 oz. AGW **Subject:** Quee Elizabeth's Golden Jubilee **Obverse:** National arms **Reve** Queen and young Prince Charles **Edge:** Reeded **Size:** 22

Date	Mintage	F	VF	XF	Unc
2002 Proof	2,002	Value: 175			

KM# 287 100 DOLLARS **Weight:** 6.2200 g. **Composition:** 0.9999 Gold 0.2 oz. AGW **Subject:** Quee Elizabeth's Golden Jubilee **Obverse:** National arms **Reve** Queen and Prince Philip **Edge:** Reeded **Size:** 22 mm.

Date	Mintage	F	VF	XF	Unc
2002 Proof	2,002	Value: 175			

KM# 278 100 DOLLARS **Weight:** 6.2200 g. **Composition:** 0.9999 Gold 0.2 oz. AGW **Subject:** Britis Queen Mother **Obverse:** National arms **Reverse:** Que Mother in garden with dog **Edge:** Reeded **Size:** 22 mm.

Date	Mintage	F	VF	XF	Unc
2002 Proof	2,000	Value: 175			

KM# 281 100 DOLLARS **Weight:** 6.2200 g. **Composition:** 0.9999 Gold 0.2 oz. AGW **Subject:** Britis Queen Mother **Obverse:** National arms **Reverse:** Quee Mother with daughters **Edge:** Reeded **Size:** 22 mm.

Date	Mintage	F	VF	XF	Unc
2002 Proof	2,000	Value: 175			

KM# 260 100 DOLLARS **Weight:** 6.2200 g. **Composition:** 0.9990 Gold .1998 oz. AGW **Subject:** Ye of the Horse **Obverse:** National arms **Reverse:** Horse **Ed** Reeded **Size:** 22 mm.

Date	Mintage	F	VF	XF	Unc
2002 Proof	2,000	Value: 175			

KM# 267 150 DOLLARS **Weight:** 1000.0000 g. **Composition:** 0.9999 Silver 32.1475 oz. ASW **Subject** RMS Titanic **Obverse:** National arms **Reverse:** Titanic dock **Edge:** Reeded **Size:** 85 mm.

Date	Mintage	F	VF	XF	Unc
2002 Proof	500	Value: 450			

M# 240 250 DOLLARS **Weight:** 15.5500 g. **Composition:** 0.9999 Gold .4999 oz. AGW **Subject:** Centennial of Queen Victoria's Diamond Jubilee **Obverse:** National arms **Reverse:** Young portrait of Queen Victoria with a .06 carat diamond mounted on her gown **Edge:** Reeded **Size:** 29.9 mm. **Note:** This denomination was never offered to the public. The entire issue is reported to have been commissioned by and sold to a single purchaser.

te		F	VF	XF	Unc	BU
97 Proof		—	—	—	300	—

M# 76 250 DOLLARS **Weight:** 15.5000 g. **Composition:** 0.9990 Gold .5000 oz. AGW **Subject:** Diana - The Peoples' Princess **Reverse:** Portrait of Lady Diana **Note:** Similar to 1 Dollar, KM#71.

te	Mintage	F	VF	XF	Unc	BU
97 Proof	Est. 3,000	Value: 320				

M# 82 250 DOLLARS **Weight:** 15.5000 g. **Composition:** 0.9990 Gold .5000 oz. AGW **Subject:** Diana - The Peoples' Princess **Reverse:** Mother Theresa and Lady Diana **Note:** Similar to 1 Dollar, KM#77.

te	Mintage	F	VF	XF	Unc	BU
97 Proof	Est. 3,000	Value: 320				

M# 88 250 DOLLARS **Weight:** 15.5000 g. **Composition:** 0.9990 Gold .5000 oz. AGW **Subject:** Diana - The Peoples' Princess **Reverse:** Lady Diana with AIDS patient **Note:** Similar to 1 Dollar, KM#83.

te	Mintage	F	VF	XF	Unc	BU
97 Proof	Est. 3,000	Value: 320				

M# 94 250 DOLLARS **Weight:** 15.5000 g. **Composition:** 0.9990 Gold .5000 oz. AGW **Subject:** Diana - The Peoples' Princess **Reverse:** Lady Diana with sons William and Harry **Note:** Similar to 1 Dollar, KM#89.

te	Mintage	F	VF	XF	Unc	BU
97 Proof	Est. 3,000	Value: 320				

M# 108 250 DOLLARS **Weight:** 15.5000 g. **Composition:** 0.9990 Gold .5000 oz. AGW **Subject:** Diana - The Peoples' Princess **Note:** Similar to 10 Dollars, KM#104.

te	Mintage	F	VF	XF	Unc	BU
98 Proof	Est. 3,000	Value: 320				

M# 147 250 DOLLARS **Weight:** 15.5000 g. **Composition:** 0.9990 Gold .5000 oz. AGW **Subject:** Year of the Dragon **Obverse:** National arms **Reverse:** Dragon **Note:** Similar to 10 Dollars, KM#143

te	Mintage	F	VF	XF	Unc	BU
00 Proof	Est. 5,000	Value: 300				

M# 189 250 DOLLARS **Weight:** 15.5000 g. **Composition:** 0.9990 Gold .5000 oz. AGW **Subject:** Buddha **Obverse:** National arms **Reverse:** Seated Buddha

ate	Mintage	F	VF	XF	Unc	BU
00 Proof	Est. 5,000	Value: 340				

M# 190 250 DOLLARS **Weight:** 15.5500 g. **Composition:** 0.9990 Gold .5000 oz. AGW **Reverse:** Goddess of Mercy

ate	Mintage	F	VF	XF	Unc	BU
00 Proof	Est. 5,000	Value: 340				

M# 191 250 DOLLARS **Weight:** 15.5500 g. **Composition:** 0.9990 Gold .5000 oz. AGW **Reverse:** Tzai-yen holding scroll

ate	Mintage	F	VF	XF	Unc	BU
00 Proof	Est. 5,000	Value: 340				

M# 203 250 DOLLARS **Weight:** 15.5118 g. **Composition:** 0.9990 Gold .5000 oz. AGW **Subject:** Year of the Snake **Obverse:** National arms **Reverse:** Snake **Edge:** Reeded **Size:** 30 mm.

ate	Mintage	F	VF	XF	Unc	BU
01 Proof	Est. 5,000	Value: 340				

M# 211 250 DOLLARS **Weight:** 15.5518 g. **Composition:** 0.9990 Gold .5000 oz. AGW **Subject:** P'an Ku **Obverse:** National arms **Reverse:** Dragon

ate	Mintage	F	VF	XF	Unc	BU
01 Proof	Est. 2,000	Value: 340				

M# 219 250 DOLLARS **Weight:** 15.5518 g. **Composition:** 0.9990 Gold .5000 oz. AGW **Subject:** P'an Ku **Obverse:** National arms **Reverse:** Dragon and three animals

ate	Mintage	F	VF	XF	Unc	BU
01 Proof	Est. 2,000	Value: 340				

M# 261 250 DOLLARS **Weight:** 15.5500 g. **Composition:** 0.9990 Gold .4994 oz. AGW **Subject:** Year of the Horse **Obverse:** National arms **Reverse:** Horse **Edge:** Reeded **Size:** 30 mm.

ate	Mintage	F	VF	XF	Unc	BU
002 Proof	2,000	Value: 340				

KM# 148 500 DOLLARS **Weight:** 31.1035 g. **Composition:** 0.9990 Gold 1.0000 oz. AGW **Subject:** Year of the Dragon **Obverse:** National arms **Reverse:** Dragon **Note:** Similar to 10 Dollars, KM#143.

ate	Mintage	F	VF	XF	Unc	BU
000 Proof	Est. 1,000	Value: 650				

KM# 192 500 DOLLARS **Weight:** 31.1035 g. **Composition:** 0.9990 Gold 1.0000 oz. AGW **Subject:** Buddha **Obverse:** National arms **Reverse:** Seated Buddha **Edge:** Reeded **Note:** Struck at Pobjoy Mint.

ate	Mintage	F	VF	XF	Unc	BU
000 Proof	Est. 5,000	Value: 650				

KM# 193 500 DOLLARS **Weight:** 31.1035 g. **Composition:** 0.9990 Gold 1.0000 oz. AGW **Reverse:** Goddess of Mercy

Date	Mintage	F	VF	XF	Unc	BU
2000 Proof	Est. 5,000	Value: 650				

KM# 194 500 DOLLARS **Weight:** 31.1035 g. **Composition:** 0.9990 Gold 1.0000 oz. AGW **Reverse:** Tzai-yen holding scroll

Date	Mintage	F	VF	XF	Unc	BU
2000 Proof	Est. 5,000	Value: 650				

KM# 204 500 DOLLARS **Weight:** 31.1035 g. **Composition:** 0.9990 Gold 1.000 oz. AGW **Subject:** Year of the Snake **Obverse:** National arms **Reverse:** Snake **Edge:** Reeded **Size:** 32.7 mm.

Date	Mintage	F	VF	XF	Unc	BU
2001 Proof	Est. 1,000	Value: 650				

KM# 212 500 DOLLARS **Weight:** 31.1035 g. **Composition:** 0.9990 Gold 1.0000 oz. AGW **Subject:** P'an Ku **Obverse:** National arms **Reverse:** Dragon

Date	Mintage	F	VF	XF	Unc	BU
2001 Proof	Est. 1,000	Value: 650				

KM# 220 500 DOLLARS **Weight:** 31.1035 g. **Composition:** 0.9990 Gold 1.0000 oz. AGW **Subject:** P'an Ku **Obverse:** National arms **Reverse:** Dragon and three animals

Date	Mintage	F	VF	XF	Unc	BU
2001 Proof	Est. 1,000	Value: 650				

KM# 262 500 DOLLARS **Weight:** 31.1000 g. **Composition:** 0.9990 Gold .9989 oz. AGW **Subject:** Year of the Horse **Obverse:** National arms **Reverse:** Horse **Edge:** Reeded **Size:** 32.7 mm.

Date	Mintage	F	VF	XF	Unc	BU
2002 Proof	1,000	Value: 650				

KM# 149 2500 DOLLARS **Weight:** 155.5175 g. **Composition:** 0.9990 Gold 5.0000 oz. AGW **Subject:** Year of the Dragon **Obverse:** National arms **Reverse:** Dragon **Note:** Similar to 10 Dollars, KM#143.

Date	Mintage	F	VF	XF	Unc	BU
2000 Proof	250	Value: 3,250				

KM# 195 2500 DOLLARS **Weight:** 155.5175 g. **Composition:** 0.9990 Gold 5.0000 oz. AGW **Subject:** Buddha **Obverse:** National arms **Reverse:** Seated Buddha **Edge:** Reeded **Note:** Struck at Pobjoy Mint.

Date	Mintage	F	VF	XF	Unc	BU
2000 Proof	Est. 250	Value: 3,250				

KM# 196 2500 DOLLARS **Weight:** 155.5175 g. **Composition:** 0.9990 Gold 5.0000 oz. AGW **Reverse:** Goddess of Mercy

Date	Mintage	F	VF	XF	Unc	BU
2000 Proof	Est. 250	Value: 3,250				

KM# 197 2500 DOLLARS **Weight:** 155.5175 g. **Composition:** 0.9990 Gold 5.0000 oz. AGW **Reverse:** Tzai-yen holding scroll

Date	Mintage	F	VF	XF	Unc	BU
2000 Proof	Est. 250	Value: 3,250				

KM# 205 2500 DOLLARS **Weight:** 155.5175 g. **Composition:** 0.9990 Gold 5.0000 oz. AGW **Subject:** Year of the Snake **Obverse:** National arms **Reverse:** Snake **Edge:** Reeded **Size:** 50 mm.

Date	Mintage	F	VF	XF	Unc	BU
2001 Proof	Est. 250	Value: 3,000				

KM# 213 2500 DOLLARS **Weight:** 155.5175 g. **Composition:** 0.9990 Gold 5.0000 oz. AGW **Subject:** P'an Ku **Obverse:** National arms **Reverse:** Dragon

Date	Mintage	F	VF	XF	Unc	BU
2001 Proof	Est. 250	Value: 3,000				

KM# 263 2500 DOLLARS **Weight:** 155.5100 g. **Composition:** 0.9990 Gold 4.9948 oz. AGW **Subject:** Year of the Horse **Obverse:** National arms **Reverse:** Horse **Edge:** Reeded **Size:** 50 mm.

Date	Mintage	F	VF	XF	Unc	BU
2002 Proof	250	Value: 3,000				

KM# 22 1/4 GOLDE **Weight:** 13.6360 g. **Composition:** 0.9000 Gold .3946 oz. AGW **Subject:** 5th Anniversary of Independence

Date	Mintage	F	VF	XF	Unc	BU
ND(1966)	5,000	—	—	—	180	—

KM# 22a 1/4 GOLDE **Weight:** 15.0000 g. **Composition:** 0.9160 Gold .4418 oz. AGW

Date	Mintage	F	VF	XF	Unc	BU
ND(1966) Proof	600	Value: 300				

KM# 22b 1/4 GOLDE **Weight:** 10.3150 g. **Composition:** Palladium

Date	Mintage	F	VF	XF	Unc	BU
ND(1966) Proof	100	Value: 350				

KM# 23a 1/4 GOLDE **Weight:** 30.0000 g. **Composition:** 0.9160 Gold .8836 oz. AGW

Date	Mintage	F	VF	XF	Unc	BU
ND(1966) Proof	600	Value: 450				

KM# 23b 1/4 GOLDE **Weight:** 20.6290 g. **Composition:** Palladium

Date	Mintage	F	VF	XF	Unc	BU
ND(1966) Proof	100	Value: 550				

KM# 23 1/2 GOLDE **Weight:** 27.2730 g. **Composition:** 0.9000 Gold .7891 oz. AGW **Subject:** 5th Anniversary of Independence

Date	Mintage	F	VF	XF	Unc	BU
ND(1966)	2,500	—	—	—	350	—

KM# 24 GOLDE **Weight:** 54.5450 g. **Composition:** 0.9000 Gold 1.5783 oz. AGW **Subject:** 5th Anniversary of Independence

Date	Mintage	F	VF	XF	Unc	BU
ND(1966)	1,500	—	—	—	800	—
ND(1966)	1,500	—	—	—	800	—

KM# 24a GOLDE **Weight:** 60.0000 g. **Composition:** 0.9160 Gold 1.7672 oz. AGW

Date	Mintage	F	VF	XF	Unc	BU
ND(1966) Proof	400	Value: 1,000				

KM# 24b GOLDE **Weight:** 41.2590 g. **Composition:** Palladium

Date	Mintage	F	VF	XF	Unc	BU
ND(1966) Proof	100	Value: 1,150				

KM# 24c GOLDE **Weight:** 41.2590 g. **Composition:** Platinum APW

Date		F	VF	XF	Unc	BU
ND(1966) Proof	—	Value: 1,350				

KM# 37 5 GOLDE **Weight:** 15.9800 g. **Composition:** 0.9170 Gold .4711 oz. AGW **Subject:** O.A.U. Summit Conference

Date	Mintage	F	VF	XF	Unc	BU
1980	457	—	—	—	245	—
1980 Proof	325	Value: 285				

KM# 42 5 GOLDE **Weight:** 15.9980 g. **Composition:** 0.9170 Gold .4711 oz. AGW **Series:** World Wildlife Fund **Reverse:** Duiker Zebra

Date	Mintage	F	VF	XF	Unc	BU
1987 Proof	5,000	Value: 250				

KM# 28 10 GOLDE **Weight:** 57.6000 g. **Composition:** 0.9160 Gold 1.6965 oz. AGW **Subject:** 70th Birthday - Dr. Siaka Stevens

Date	Mintage	F	VF	XF	Unc	BU
ND(1975)	727	—	—	—	850	—
ND(1975) Proof	307	Value: 1,000				

TRIAL STRIKES

KM#	Date	Mintage	Identification	Mkt Val
TS1	ND	—	5 Centesimos. Steel. Portrait of Milton Margai, Prime Minster (1967-67). Uruguay 5 Centavos design with MBLAT top, HA in number 5. Reeded edge.	65.00

KM#	Date	Mintage	Identification	Mkt Val
TS2	ND(1964)	—	10 Cents. Brass. Reverse of KM#19. Uruguay 10 Centesimos.	65.00

KM#	Date	Mintage	Identification	Mkt Val
TS3	ND(1964)	—	10 Cents. Aluminum. Reverse of KM#19. Uruguay 10 Centesimos.	65.00

MINT SETS

KM#	Date	Mintage	Identification	Issue Price	Mkt Val
MS1	1966 (3)	—	KM#22-24	—	1,400

PROOF SETS

KM#	Date	Mintage	Identification	Issue Price	Mkt Val
PS1	1964 (6)	10,000	KM#16-21	—	16.50
PS2	1964 (6)	12	KM#16a-20a, 21b	—	5,750
PS3	1964 (6)	10	KM#16a-21a	—	4,250
PS4	1966 (3)	400	KM#22a-24a	—	1,750
PS5	1972 (2)	1,000	KM25 (2 pieces with 50 cent bank note (0 serial#) in plush case	—	20.00
PS6	1980 (6)	10,000	KM25, 30-34	34.00	28.00

SINGAPORE

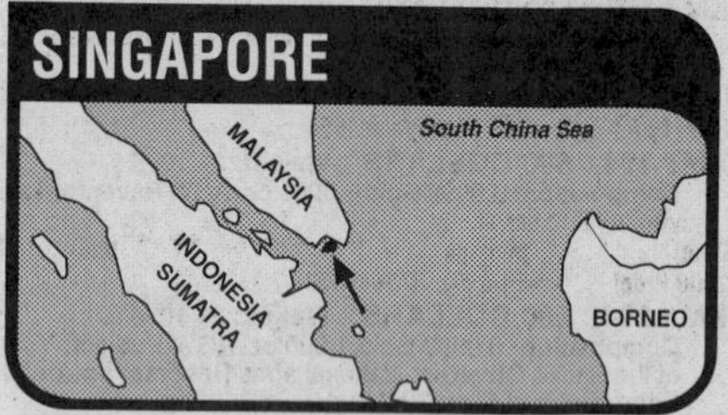

The Republic of Singapore, a member of the Commonwealth of Nations situated off the southern tip of the Malay peninsula, has an area of 224 sq. mi. (633 sq. km.) and a population of *2.7 million. Capital: Singapore. The economy is based on entrepot trade, manufacturing and oil. Rubber, petroleum products, machinery and spices are exported.

Singapore's modern history - it was an important shipping center in the 14th century before the rise of Malacca and Penang - began in 1819 when Sir Thomas Stamford Raffles, an agent for the British East India Company, founded the town of Singapore. By 1825 its trade exceeded that of Malacca and Penang combined. The opening of the Suez Canal (1869) and the demand for rubber and tin created by the automobile and packaging industries combined to make Singapore one of the major ports of the world. In 1826 Singapore, Penang and Malacca were combined to form the Straits Settlements, which was made a Crown Colony in 1867. Singapore became a separate Crown Colony in 1946 when the Straits Settlements was dissolved. It joined in the formation of Malaysia in 1963, but broke away on Aug. 9, 1965, to become an independent republic. The President is Chief of State. The prime minister is Head of Government.

For earlier coinage see Straits Settlements, Malaya, Malaya and British Borneo.

MINT MARKS

sm = "*sm*" - Singapore Mint monogram

MONETARY SYSTEM

100 Cents = 1 Dollar

REPUBLIC

STANDARD COINAGE

100 Cents = 1 Dollar

KM# 1 CENT **Composition:** Bronze **Reverse:** Apartment Building

Date	Mintage	F	VF	XF	Unc	BU
1967	7,500,000	—	—	0.20	0.40	—
1967 Proof	2,000	Value: 2.25				
1968	2,969,000	—	—	0.25	0.50	—
1968 Proof	5,000	Value: 2.00				
1969	7,220,000	—	—	0.20	0.30	—
1969 Proof	3,000	Value: 10.00				
1970	1,402,000	—	—	0.40	0.80	—
1971	9,731,000	—	—	0.20	0.25	—
1972	1,665,000	—	—	0.20	0.70	—
1972 Proof	749	Value: 40.00				
1973	6,377,000	—	—	0.10	0.20	—
1973 Proof	1,000	Value: 5.00				
1974	9,421,000	—	—	—	0.20	—
1974 Proof	1,500	Value: 4.00				
1975	24,226,000	—	—	—	0.20	—
1975 Proof	3,000	Value: 1.50				
1976	2,500,000	—	—	0.10	0.60	—
1976sm Proof	3,500	Value: 1.25				
1977sm Proof	3,500	Value: 1.25				
1978sm Proof	4,000	Value: 1.25				
1979sm Proof	3,500	Value: 1.25				
1980sm Proof	14,000	Value: 1.00				
1982sm Proof	20,000	Value: 1.00				
1983sm Proof	15,000	Value: 1.00				
1984sm Proof	15,000	Value: 1.00				

KM# 1a CENT **Composition:** Copper Clad Steel

Date	Mintage	F	VF	XF	Unc	BU
1976	13,665,000	—	—	—	0.25	—
1977	13,940,000	—	—	—	0.25	—
1978	5,931,000	—	—	—	0.25	—
1979	11,986,000	—	—	—	0.15	—
1980	19,922,000	—	—	—	0.15	—
1981	38,084,000	—	—	—	0.10	—
1982	24,105,000	—	—	—	0.10	—
1983	2,204,000	—	—	—	0.10	—
1984	5,695,000	—	—	—	0.10	—
1985	148,000	—	—	0.15	0.35	—

KM# 1b CENT **Weight:** 2.9200 g. **Composition:** 0.9250 Silver .0869 oz. ASW

Date	Mintage	F	VF	XF	Unc	BU
1981sm Proof	30,000	Value: 5.00				

KM# 49 CENT **Composition:** Bronze **Reverse:** Vanda Miss Joaquim Plants

Date	Mintage	F	VF	XF	Unc
1986	20,000,000	—	—	—	0.10
1987	—	—	—	—	0.10
1988	—	—	—	—	0.10
1989	20,080,000	—	—	—	0.10
1990	10,000,000	—	—	—	0.10

KM# 49a CENT **Weight:** 1.8100 g. **Composition:** 0.925 Silver .0538 oz. ASW

Date	Mintage	F	VF	XF	Unc
1985sm Proof	20,000	Value: 2.25			
1986sm Proof	15,000	Value: 2.25			
1987sm Proof	15,000	Value: 2.25			
1988 Proof	15,000	Value: 2.25			
1989 Proof	15,000	Value: 2.25			
1990 Proof	15,000	Value: 2.25			
1991 Proof	15,000	Value: 2.25			

KM# 49b CENT **Composition:** Copper Plated Zinc

Date	F	VF	XF	Unc
1991	—	—	—	0.10

KM# 98 CENT **Composition:** Copper Plated Zinc **Note:** Similar to KM#49 but motto ribbon on arms curves down center.

Date	Mintage	F	VF	XF	Unc
1992	20,000,000	—	—	—	0.10
1993	39,920,000	—	—	—	0.10
1994	130,810,000	—	—	—	0.10
1995	220,000,000	—	—	—	0.10
1996	—	—	—	—	0.10
1997	—	—	—	—	0.10
1998	—	—	—	—	0.10
1999	—	—	—	—	0.10
2000	—	—	—	—	0.10

KM# 98a CENT **Weight:** 1.8100 g. **Composition:** 0.925 Silver .0538 oz. ASW

Date	Mintage	F	VF	XF	Unc
1992 Proof	15,000	Value: 2.25			
1993 Proof	15,000	Value: 2.25			
1994 Proof	10,000	Value: 2.25			
1995 Proof	10,000	Value: 2.25			
1996 Proof	17,000	Value: 2.25			
1997 Proof	20,000	Value: 2.25			
1998 Proof	—	Value: 2.25			
1999 Proof	—	Value: 2.25			
2000 Proof	17,000	Value: 2.25			

KM# 2 5 CENTS **Composition:** Copper-Nickel **Reverse:** Great White Egret

Date	Mintage	F	VF	XF	Unc
1967	28,000,000	—	—	0.15	0.35
1967 Proof	2,000	Value: 3.25			
1968	4,217,000	—	—	0.20	0.40
1968 Proof	5,000	Value: 3.00			
1969	14,778,000	—	—	0.10	0.35
1969 Proof	3,000	Value: 15.00			
1970	4,065,000	—	—	0.20	0.40
1971	13,202,000	—	—	0.10	0.35
1972	9,817,000	—	—	0.10	0.35
1972 Proof	749	Value: 50.00			
1973	2,980,000	—	—	0.30	0.50
1973 Proof	1,000	Value: 7.50			
1974	10,868,000	—	—	0.10	0.35
1974 Proof	1,500	Value: 6.50			
1975	1,729,000	—	—	0.40	1.00
1975 Proof	3,000	Value: 2.50			
1976	15,541,000	—	—	0.10	0.35
1976sm Proof	3,500	Value: 2.25			
1977	9,956,000	—	—	0.10	0.35
1977sm Proof	3,500	Value: 2.25			
1978	5,956,000	—	—	0.10	0.35
1978sm Proof	4,000	Value: 2.25			
1979	9,974,000	—	—	—	0.35
1979sm Proof	3,500	Value: 2.25			
1980	20,534,000	—	—	—	0.35
1980sm Proof	14,000	Value: 2.00			
1981	110,000	—	—	—	0.35
1982	160,000	—	—	—	0.35
1982sm Proof	20,000	Value: 2.00			
1983	40,000	—	—	—	0.35

Date	Mintage	F	VF	XF	Unc	BU
1983sm Proof	15,000	Value: 2.00				
1984	18,880,000	—	—	—	0.35	—
1984sm Proof	15,000	Value: 2.00				
1985	148,000	—	—	—	0.35	—

KM# 2a 5 CENTS Composition: Copper-Nickel Clad Steel

Date	Mintage	F	VF	XF	Unc	BU
1980	12,001,000	—	—	—	0.35	—
1981	23,866,000	—	—	—	0.35	—
1982	24,413,000	—	—	—	0.35	—
1983	4,016,000	—	—	—	0.35	—
1984	18,880,000	—	—	—	0.35	—

KM# 2b 5 CENTS Weight: 1.6500 g. **Composition:** 0.9250 Silver .0491 oz. ASW

Date	Mintage	F	VF	XF	Unc	BU
1981 Proof	30,000	Value: 5.00				

KM# 8 5 CENTS Composition: Aluminum **Series:** F.A.O.

Date	Mintage	F	VF	XF	Unc	BU
1971	3,049,000	—	—	0.10	0.50	—

KM# 50 5 CENTS Composition: Aluminum-Bronze **Reverse:** Fruit Salad Plant

Date	Mintage	F	VF	XF	Unc	BU
1985	14,840,000	—	—	—	0.10	—
1986	15,480,000	—	—	—	0.10	—
1987	31,040,000	—	—	—	0.10	—
1988	45,180,000	—	—	—	0.10	—
1989	69,988,000	—	—	—	0.10	—
1990	26,052,000	—	—	—	0.10	—
1991	—	—	—	—	0.10	

KM# 50a 5 CENTS Weight: 2.0000 g. **Composition:** 0.9250 Silver .0595 oz. ASW

Date	Mintage	F	VF	XF	Unc	BU
1985sm Proof	20,000	Value: 2.50				
1986sm Proof	15,000	Value: 2.50				
1987sm Proof	15,000	Value: 2.50				
1988 Proof	15,000	Value: 2.50				
1989 Proof	15,000	Value: 2.50				
1990 Proof	15,000	Value: 2.50				
1991 Proof	15,000	Value: 2.50				

KM# 99a 5 CENTS Weight: 2.0000 g. **Composition:** 0.9250 Silver .0595 oz. ASW

Date	Mintage	F	VF	XF	Unc	BU
1992 Proof	15,000	Value: 2.50				
1993 Proof	15,000	Value: 2.50				
1994 Proof	10,000	Value: 2.50				
1995 Proof	10,000	Value: 2.50				
1996 Proof	17,000	Value: 2.50				
1997 Proof	20,000	Value: 2.50				
1998 Proof	—	Value: 2.50				
1999 Proof	—	Value: 2.50				
2000 Proof	17,000	Value: 2.50				

KM# 99 5 CENTS Composition: Aluminum-Bronze **Note:** Similar to KM#50 but motto ribbon on arms curves down at center.

Date	Mintage	F	VF	XF	Unc	BU
1992	—	—	—	—	0.10	—
1993	7,296,000	—	—	—	0.10	—
1994	—	—	—	—	0.10	—
1995	90,000,000	—	—	—	0.10	—
1996	—	—	—	—	0.10	—
1997	—	—	—	—	0.10	—
1998	—	—	—	—	0.10	—
1999	—	—	—	—	0.10	—
2000	—	—	—	—	0.10	—

KM# 3 10 CENTS Composition: Copper-Nickel **Reverse:** Stylized Great Crowned Seahorse

Date	Mintage	F	VF	XF	Unc	BU
1967	40,000,000	—	—	0.15	0.50	—
1967 Proof	2,000	Value: 4.50				
1968	36,261,000	—	—	0.20	0.50	—
1968 Proof	5,000	Value: 4.25				
1969	25,000,000	—	—	0.10	0.65	—
1969 Proof	3,000	Value: 20.00				
1970	21,304,000	—	—	0.20	0.65	—
1971	33,040,999	—	—	0.10	0.50	—
1972	2,675,000	—	—	0.10	0.50	—
1972 Proof	749	Value: 60.00				
1973	14,290,000	—	—	0.10	0.35	—
1973 Proof	1,000	Value: 10.00				
1974	13,450,000	—	—	0.10	0.35	—
1974 Proof	1,500	Value: 7.50				
1975	828,000	—	0.10	0.60	1.25	—
1975 Proof	3,000	Value: 4.00				
1976	29,718,000	—	—	0.10	0.35	—
1976sm Proof	3,500	Value: 3.50				
1977	11,776,000	—	—	0.10	0.35	—
1977sm Proof	3,500	Value: 3.50				
1978	5,936,000	—	—	0.10	0.35	—
1978sm Proof	4,000	Value: 3.50				
1979	12,001,000	—	—	0.10	0.35	—
1979sm Proof	3,500	Value: 3.50				
1980	40,299,000	—	—	0.10	0.35	—
1980sm Proof	14,000	Value: 3.00				
1981	58,600,000	—	—	0.10	0.35	—
1982	48,514,000	—	—	0.10	0.35	—
1982sm Proof	20,000	Value: 3.00				
1983	10,415,000	—	—	0.10	0.35	—
1983sm Proof	15,000	Value: 3.00				
1984	29,700,000	—	—	0.10	0.35	—
1984sm Proof	15,000	Value: 3.00				
1985	148,000	—	—	0.10	0.35	—

KM# 3a 10 CENTS Weight: 3.3500 g. **Composition:** 0.9250 Silver .0996 oz. ASW

Date	Mintage	F	VF	XF	Unc	BU
1981sm Proof	30,000	Value: 7.50				

KM# 51 10 CENTS Composition: Copper-Nickel **Reverse:** Star Jasmine Plant

Date	Mintage	F	VF	XF	Unc	BU
1985	45,040,000	—	—	—	0.20	—
1986	113,000,000	—	—	—	0.20	—
1987	90,000,000	—	—	—	0.20	—
1988	54,455,000	—	—	—	0.20	—
1989	134,190,000	—	—	—	0.20	—
1990	51,720,000	—	—	—	0.20	—
1991	159,770,000	—	—	—	0.20	—

KM# 51a 10 CENTS Weight: 3.0500 g. **Composition:** 0.9250 Silver .0907 oz. ASW

Date	Mintage	F	VF	XF	Unc	BU
1985sm Proof	20,000	Value: 4.00				
1986sm Proof	15,000	Value: 4.00				
1987sm Proof	15,000	Value: 4.00				
1988 Proof	15,000	Value: 4.00				
1989 Proof	15,000	Value: 4.00				
1990 Proof	15,000	Value: 4.00				
1991 Proof	15,000	Value: 4.00				

KM# 100a 10 CENTS Weight: 3.0500 g. **Composition:** 0.9250 Silver .0907 oz. ASW

Date	Mintage	F	VF	XF	Unc	BU
1992 Proof	15,000	Value: 4.00				
1993 Proof	15,000	Value: 4.00				
1994 Proof	10,000	Value: 4.00				
1995 Proof	10,000	Value: 4.00				
1996 Proof	17,000	Value: 4.00				
1997 Proof	20,000	Value: 4.00				
1998 Proof	—	Value: 4.00				
1999 Proof	—	Value: 4.00				
2000 Proof	17,000	Value: 4.00				

KM# 100 10 CENTS Composition: Copper-Nickel **Note:** Similar to KM#51 but motto ribbon on arms curves down at center.

Date	Mintage	F	VF	XF	Unc	BU
1992	—	—	—	—	0.20	—
1993	89,855,000	—	—	—	0.20	—
1994	—	—	—	—	0.20	—
1995	—	—	—	—	0.20	—
1996	—	—	—	—	0.20	—
1997	—	—	—	—	0.20	—
1998	—	—	—	—	0.20	—
1999	—	—	—	—	0.20	—
2000	—	—	—	—	0.20	—

KM# 4 20 CENTS Composition: Copper-Nickel **Reverse:** Swordfish

Date	Mintage	F	VF	XF	Unc	BU
1967	36,500,000	—	0.15	0.30	0.75	—
1967 Proof	2,000	Value: 7.00				
1968	10,934,000	—	0.15	0.30	0.75	—
1968 Proof	5,000	Value: 6.00				
1969	8,460,000	—	0.15	0.30	0.75	—
1969 Proof	3,000	Value: 30.00				
1970	3,250,000	—	0.15	0.30	0.75	—
1971	1,732,000	—	0.15	0.70	2.00	—
1972	9,107,000	—	0.15	0.30	0.75	—
1972 Proof	749	Value: 70.00				
1973	8,838,000	—	0.15	0.30	0.75	—
1973 Proof	1,000	Value: 17.50				
1974	4,567,000	—	0.15	0.30	0.75	—
1974 Proof	1,500	Value: 12.50				
1975	1,546,000	—	0.15	0.50	1.00	—
1975 Proof	3,000	Value: 6.50				
1976	19,760,000	—	0.15	0.25	0.70	—
1976sm Proof	3,500	Value: 6.00				
1977	7,074,000	—	0.15	0.30	0.75	—
1977sm Proof	3,500	Value: 6.00				
1978	4,450,000	—	0.15	0.30	0.75	—
1978sm Proof	4,000	Value: 6.00				
1979	14,865,000	—	—	0.15	0.45	—
1979sm Proof	3,500	Value: 6.00				
1980	27,903,000	—	—	0.15	0.45	—
1980sm Proof	14,000	Value: 5.00				
1981	46,997,000	—	—	0.15	0.45	—
1982	25,234,000	—	—	0.15	0.45	—
1982sm Proof	20,000	Value: 4.00				
1983	6,424,000	—	—	0.15	0.45	—
1983sm Proof	15,000	Value: 4.00				
1984	9,290,000	—	—	0.15	0.45	—
1984sm Proof	15,000	Value: 4.00				
1985	148,000	—	—	0.15	0.45	—

KM# 4a 20 CENTS Weight: 6.5100 g. **Composition:** 0.9250 Silver .1936 oz. ASW

Date	Mintage	F	VF	XF	Unc	BU
1981sm Proof	30,000	Value: 12.50				

KM# 52 20 CENTS Composition: Copper-Nickel **Reverse:** Powder-puff Plant

Date	Mintage	F	VF	XF	Unc	BU
1985	25,980,000	—	—	0.15	0.30	—
1986	47,560,000	—	—	0.15	0.30	—
1987	80,010,000	—	—	0.15	0.30	—
1988	35,783,000	—	—	0.15	0.30	—
1989	51,890,000	—	—	0.15	0.30	—
1990	49,958,000	—	—	0.15	0.30	—
1991	60,000,000	—	—	0.15	0.30	—

KM# 52a 20 CENTS Weight: 5.2400 g. **Composition:** 0.9250 Silver .1559 oz. ASW

Date	Mintage	F	VF	XF	Unc	BU
1985sm Proof	20,000	Value: 6.50				
1986sm Proof	15,000	Value: 6.50				
1987sm Proof	15,000	Value: 6.50				
1988 Proof	15,000	Value: 6.50				
1989 Proof	15,000	Value: 6.50				
1990 Proof	15,000	Value: 6.50				
1991 Proof	15,000	Value: 6.50				

KM# 101 20 CENTS Composition: Copper-Nickel **Note:** Similar to KM#52 but motto ribbon on arms curves down at center.

Date	Mintage	F	VF	XF	Unc	BU
1992	—	—	—	—	0.30	—
1993	24,998,000	—	—	—	0.30	—
1994	—	—	—	—	0.30	—
1995	—	—	—	—	0.30	—
1996	—	—	—	—	0.30	—
1997	—	—	—	—	0.30	—
1998	—	—	—	—	0.30	—
1999	—	—	—	—	0.30	—
2000	—	—	—	—	0.30	—

KM# 101a 20 CENTS Weight: 5.2400 g. **Composition:** 0.9250 Silver .1936 oz. ASW

Date	Mintage	F	VF	XF	Unc	BU
1992 Proof	15,000	Value: 6.50				
1993 Proof	15,000	Value: 6.50				
1994 Proof	10,000	Value: 6.50				
1995 Proof	10,000	Value: 6.50				
1996 Proof	17,000	Value: 6.50				
1997 Proof	20,000	Value: 6.50				
1998 Proof	—	Value: 6.50				
1999 Proof	—	Value: 6.50				
2000 Proof	17,000	Value: 6.50				

KM# 5 50 CENTS **Composition:** Copper-Nickel
Reverse: Zebra Fish

Date	Mintage	F	VF	XF	Unc	BU
1967	11,000,000	—	0.30	0.40	1.00	—
1967 Proof	2,000	Value: 10.00				
1968	3,189,000	—	0.30	0.60	1.50	—
1968 Proof	5,000	Value: 8.50				
1969	2,008,000	—	0.30	0.60	1.50	—
1969 Proof	3,000	Value: 35.00				
1970	3,102,000	—	0.30	0.60	1.50	—
1971	3,933,000	—	0.30	0.60	1.50	—
1972	5,427,000	—	0.30	0.50	1.00	—
1972 Proof	749	Value: 90.00				
1973	4,474,000	—	0.30	0.50	1.00	—
1973 Proof	1,000	Value: 30.00				
1974	11,550,000	—	—	0.40	1.00	—
1974 Proof	1,500	Value: 22.50				
1975	1,432,000	—	0.35	0.75	2.00	—
1975 Proof	3,000	Value: 10.00				
1976	5,728,000	—	0.30	0.50	1.00	—
1976sm Proof	3,500	Value: 8.50				
1977	6,953,000	—	—	0.40	1.00	—
1977sm Proof	3,500	Value: 8.50				
1978	3,934,000	—	—	0.40	1.00	—
1978sm Proof	4,000	Value: 8.50				
1979	8,461,000	—	—	0.40	1.00	—
1979sm Proof	3,500	Value: 8.50				
1980	14,717,000	—	—	0.35	0.85	—
1980sm Proof	14,000	Value: 7.00				
1981	29,542,000	—	—	0.35	0.85	—
1982	13,756,000	—	—	0.35	0.85	—
1982sm Proof	20,000	Value: 5.00				
1983	4,482,000	—	—	0.35	0.85	—
1983sm Proof	15,000	Value: 5.00				
1984	3,658,000	—	—	0.35	0.85	—
1984sm Proof	15,000	Value: 5.00				
1985	148,000	—	—	0.35	0.85	—

KM# 5a 50 CENTS **Weight:** 10.8200 g. **Composition:** 0.9250 Silver .3218 oz. ASW

Date	Mintage	F	VF	XF	Unc	BU
1981sm Proof	30,000	Value: 15.00				

KM# 53.1 50 CENTS **Composition:** Copper-Nickel
Reverse: Yellow Allamanda Plant **Edge:** Reeded

Date	Mintage	F	VF	XF	Unc	BU
1985	14,960,000	—	—	0.35	0.60	—
1986	15,022,000	—	—	0.35	0.60	—
1987	30,000,000	—	—	0.35	0.60	—
1988	25,000,000	—	—	0.35	0.60	—

KM# 53.1a 50 CENTS **Weight:** 8.5600 g. **Composition:** 0.9250 Silver .2546 oz. ASW

Date	Mintage	F	VF	XF	Unc	BU
1985sm Proof	20,000	Value: 12.00				
1986sm Proof	15,000	Value: 12.00				
1987sm Proof	15,000	Value: 12.00				
1988 Proof	15,000	Value: 12.00				

KM# 53.2 50 CENTS **Composition:** Copper-Nickel
Edge: Lettered

Date	Mintage	F	VF	XF	Unc	BU
1989	20,046,000	—	—	0.35	0.60	—
1990	472,000,000	—	—	0.35	0.60	—
1991	508,000,000	—	—	0.35	0.60	—

KM# 53.2a 50 CENTS **Weight:** 8.5600 g. **Composition:** 0.9250 Silver .2546 oz. ASW

Date	Mintage	F	VF	XF	Unc	BU
1989 Proof	15,000	Value: 12.00				
1990 Proof	—	Value: 12.00				
1991 Proof	—	Value: 12.00				

KM# 102 50 CENTS **Composition:** Copper-Nickel
Note: Similar to KM#53 but motto ribbon on arms curves down at center.

Date	Mintage	F	VF	XF	Unc	BU
1992	—	—	—	—	0.60	—
1993	4,878,000	—	—	—	0.60	—
1994	—	—	—	—	0.60	—
1995	49,440,000	—	—	—	0.60	—
1996	—	—	—	—	0.60	—
1997	—	—	—	—	0.60	—
1998	—	—	—	—	0.60	—
1999	—	—	—	—	0.60	—
2000	—	—	—	—	0.60	—

KM# 102a 50 CENTS **Weight:** 8.5600 g. **Composition:** 0.9250 Silver .2546 oz. ASW

Date	Mintage	F	VF	XF	Unc	BU
1992 Proof	15,000	Value: 12.00				
1993 Proof	15,000	Value: 12.00				
1994 Proof	10,000	Value: 12.00				
1995 Proof	10,000	Value: 12.00				
1996 Proof	17,000	Value: 12.00				
1997 Proof	20,000	Value: 12.00				
1998 Proof	—	Value: 12.00				
1999 Proof	—	Value: 12.00				
2000 Proof	17,000	Value: 12.00				

KM# 6 DOLLAR **Composition:** Copper-Nickel

Date	Mintage	F	VF	XF	Unc	BU
1967	3,000,000	—	0.65	1.00	2.00	—
1967 Proof	2,000	Value: 22.50				
1968	2,194,000	—	0.65	1.00	2.00	—
1968 Proof	5,000	Value: 20.00				
1969	1,871,000	—	0.65	1.00	2.00	—
1969 Proof	3,000	Value: 75.00				
1970	560,000	—	0.65	1.25	2.50	—
1971	900,000	—	0.65	1.00	2.00	—
1972	458,000	—	0.75	2.00	4.00	—
1972 Proof	749	Value: 150				
1973	341,000	—	0.75	1.50	3.00	—
1973 Proof	1,000	Value: 50.00				
1974	352,000	—	0.75	1.50	3.00	—
1974 Proof	1,500	Value: 40.00				
1975	430,000	—	0.75	1.50	3.00	—
1975 Proof	3,000	Value: 20.00				
1976	165,000	—	0.75	2.00	4.00	—
1976sm Proof	3,500	Value: 13.50				
1977	132,000	—	0.75	3.00	6.00	—
1977sm Proof	3,500	Value: 13.50				
1978	37,000	—	1.00	6.00	12.00	—
1978sm Proof	4,000	Value: 13.50				
1979	100,000	—	—	2.00	4.00	—
1979sm Proof	3,500	Value: 13.50				
1980	166,000	—	—	2.00	4.00	—
1980sm Proof	14,000	Value; 11.50				
1981	1,230,000	—	—	1.00	2.00	—
1982	1,080,000	—	—	1.00	2.00	—
1983	101,000	—	—	1.25	3.00	—
1984	170,000	—	—	1.00	2.00	—
1985	148,000	—	—	0.65	1.25	—

KM# 6a DOLLAR **Weight:** 18.0500 g. **Composition:** 0.9250 Silver .5368 oz. ASW

Date	Mintage	F	VF	XF	Unc	BU
1975 Proof	3,000	Value: 50.00				
1976sm Proof	10,000	Value: 16.50				
1977sm Proof	10,000	Value: 16.50				
1978sm Proof	10,000	Value: 16.50				
1979sm Proof	8,000	Value: 18.50				
1980sm Proof	15,000	Value: 16.50				
1981sm Proof	30,000	Value: 12.50				
1982sm Proof	20,000	Value: 15.00				
1983sm Proof	15,000	Value: 12.50				
1984sm Proof	15,000	Value: 12.50				

KM# 28 DOLLAR **Weight:** 3.1100 g. **Composition:** 0.9990 Gold .1000 oz. AGW **Reverse:** Carp and lotus flower

Date	Mintage	F	VF	XF	Unc	BU
1983	20,000	—	—	—	BV+15%	—
1984	10,000	—	—	—	BV+15%	—

KM# 54 DOLLAR **Composition:** Copper-Nickel
Reverse: Periwinkle

Date	Mintage	F	VF	XF	Unc	BU
1985	120,000	—	—	—	1.75	—
1986	120,000	—	—	—	1.75	—
1987	120,000	—	—	—	1.75	—

KM# 54a DOLLAR **Weight:** 9.9700 g. **Composition:** 0.9250 Silver .2965 oz. ASW

Date	Mintage	F	VF	XF	Unc	BU
1985sm Proof	20,000	Value: 15.00				
1986sm Proof	15,000	Value: 15.00				

KM# 54b DOLLAR **Composition:** Aluminum-Bronze

Date	Mintage	F	VF	XF	Unc	BU
1987	21,772,000	—	—	0.75	1.50	—
1988	59,332,000	—	—	0.75	1.50	—
1989	62,586,000	—	—	0.75	1.50	—
1990	37,608,000	—	—	0.75	1.50	—
1991	—	—	—	0.75	1.50	—

KM# 54c DOLLAR **Weight:** 8.4273 g. **Composition:** 0.9250 Silver .2507 oz. ASW

Date	Mintage	F	VF	XF	Unc	BU
1987sm Proof	15,000	Value: 15.00				
1988 Proof	15,000	Value: 15.00				
1989 Proof	15,000	Value: 15.00				
1990	15,000	—	—	—	—	—
1991	15,000	—	—	—	—	—

KM# 103 DOLLAR **Composition:** Aluminum-Bronze
Note: Similar to KM#54 but motto ribbon on arms curves down at center.

Date	Mintage	F	VF	XF	Unc	BU
1992	—	—	—	—	1.50	—
1993	—	—	—	—	1.50	—
1994	—	—	—	—	1.50	—
1995	65,000,000	—	—	—	1.50	—
1996	—	—	—	—	1.50	—
1997	—	—	—	—	1.50	—
1998	—	—	—	—	1.50	—
1999	—	—	—	—	1.50	—
2000	—	—	—	—	1.50	—

KM# 103a DOLLAR **Weight:** 8.4273 g. **Composition:** 0.9250 Silver .2507 oz. ASW

Date	Mintage	F	VF	XF	Unc	BU
1992 Proof	15,000	Value: 15.00				
1993 Proof	15,000	Value: 15.00				
1994 Proof	10,000	Value: 15.00				
1995 Proof	10,000	Value: 15.00				
1996 Proof	17,000	Value: 15.00				
1997 Proof	20,000	Value: 15.00				
1998 Proof	—	Value: 15.00				
1999 Proof	—	Value: 15.00				
2000 Proof	17,000	Value: 15.00				

KM# 144 DOLLAR **Weight:** 1.5552 g. **Composition:** 0.9990 Gold .0400 oz. AGW **Subject:** Year of the Rat
Reverse: Lion

Date	Mintage	F	VF	XF	Unc	BU
1996 Proof	2,688	Value: 30.00				

KM# 158 DOLLAR **Weight:** 1.5552 g. **Composition:** 0.9990 Gold .0400 oz. AGW **Subject:** Year of the Ox
Reverse: Lion **Note:** Similar to 20 DOllars, KM#161.

Date		F	VF	XF	Unc	BU
1997 Proof	Est. 2,200	Value: 40.00				

KM# 29 2 DOLLARS **Weight:** 7.7750 g. **Composition:** 0.9990 Gold .2500 oz. AGW **Reverse:** Qilin

Date	Mintage	F	VF	XF	Unc	BU
1983	20,000	—	—	—	BV+12%	
1984	10,000	—	—	—	BV+12%	

M# 156 2 DOLLARS **Weight:** 20.0000 g. **Composition:** 0.9250 Silver .5948 oz. ASW **Series:** UNICEF **Obverse:** National arms **Reverse:** Children Using Computer

te	Mintage	F	VF	XF	Unc	BU
97 Proof	25,000	Value: 90.00				

M# 10 5 DOLLARS **Weight:** 25.0000 g. **Composition:** 0.5000 Silver .4019 oz. ASW **Subject:** 7th Southeast Asia Peninsular Games

ate	Mintage	F	VF	XF	Unc	BU
73	250,000	—	—	—	8.00	—
73 Proof	5,000	Value: 35.00				

M# 19 5 DOLLARS **Composition:** Copper-Nickel **Reverse:** Changi Airport

ate	Mintage	F	VF	XF	Unc	BU
981	220,000	—	—	3.50	6.50	—

M# 19a 5 DOLLARS **Weight:** 18.0500 g. **Composition:** 0.9250 Silver .5368 oz. ASW

ate	Mintage	F	VF	XF	Unc	BU
981sm Proof	20,000	Value: 18.50				

KM# 22 5 DOLLARS **Composition:** Copper-Nickel **Reverse:** Benjamin Shears Bridge

Date	Mintage	F	VF	XF	Unc	BU
1982	260,000	—	—	3.50	6.50	—

KM# 22a 5 DOLLARS **Weight:** 18.0500 g. **Composition:** 0.9250 Silver .5368 oz. ASW

Date	Mintage	F	VF	XF	Unc	BU
1982sm Proof	20,000	Value: 18.50				

KM# 25 5 DOLLARS **Composition:** Copper-Nickel **Subject:** 12th SEA Games

Date	Mintage	F	VF	XF	Unc	BU
1983	270,000	—	—	3.50	6.50	—

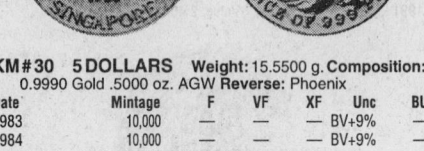

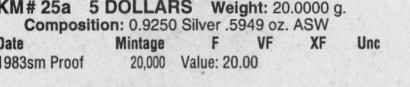

KM# 30 5 DOLLARS **Weight:** 15.5500 g. **Composition:** 0.9990 Gold .5000 oz. AGW **Reverse:** Phoenix

Date	Mintage	F	VF	XF	Unc	BU
1983	10,000	—	—	—	BV+9%	—
1984	10,000	—	—	—	BV+9%	—

KM# 25a 5 DOLLARS **Weight:** 20.0000 g. **Composition:** 0.9250 Silver .5949 oz. ASW

Date	Mintage	F	VF	XF	Unc	BU
1983sm Proof	20,000	Value: 20.00				

KM# 32 5 DOLLARS **Composition:** Copper-Nickel **Subject:** 25 Years of Nation Building

Date	Mintage	F	VF	XF	Unc	BU
ND(1984)	270,000	—	—	3.50	6.50	—

KM# 32a 5 DOLLARS **Weight:** 20.0000 g. **Composition:** 0.9250 Silver .5949 oz. ASW

Date	Mintage	F	VF	XF	Unc	BU
ND(1984)sm Proof	20,000	Value: 18.50				

KM# 48 5 DOLLARS **Composition:** Copper-Nickel **Subject:** 25 Years of Public Housing **Obverse:** Coat of arms and legend

Date	Mintage	F	VF	XF	Unc	BU
1985	117,000	—	—	3.50	6.50	—

KM# 48a 5 DOLLARS **Weight:** 20.0000 g. **Composition:** 0.9250 Silver .5949 oz. ASW

Date	Mintage	F	VF	XF	Unc	BU
1985sm Proof	20,000	Value: 18.50				

KM# 68 5 DOLLARS **Composition:** Copper-Nickel **Subject:** 100th Anniversary of National Museum

Date	Mintage	F	VF	XF	Unc	BU
ND(1987)	70,000	—	—	—	7.50	—

KM# 68a 5 DOLLARS **Weight:** 20.0000 g. **Composition:** 0.9250 Silver .5949 oz. ASW

Date	Mintage	F	VF	XF	Unc	BU
ND(1987)sm Proof	25,000	Value: 18.00				

KM# 70 5 DOLLARS **Composition:** Copper-Nickel **Subject:** 100th Anniversary of Singapore Fire Brigade

Date	Mintage	F	VF	XF	Unc	BU
ND(1988)	50,000	—	—	—	15.00	—

KM# 70a 5 DOLLARS **Weight:** 20.0000 g. **Composition:** 0.9250 Silver .5949 oz. ASW

Date	Mintage	F	VF	XF	Unc	BU
ND(1988)sm Proof	25,000	Value: 27.50				

KM# 74 5 DOLLARS **Composition:** Copper-Nickel **Subject:** Rapid Transit System

Date	Mintage	F	VF	XF	Unc	BU
1989	60,000	—	—	—	12.00	—

KM# 74a 5 DOLLARS **Weight:** 20.0000 g. **Composition:** 0.9250 Silver .5949 oz. ASW

Date	Mintage	F	VF	XF	Unc	BU
1989 Proof	30,000	Value: 20.00				

KM#77 5 DOLLARS **Weight:** 20.0000 g. **Composition:** 0.9250 Silver .5949 oz. ASW **Series:** Save the Children Fund

Date	Mintage	F	VF	XF	Unc	BU
1989 Proof	20,000	Value: 25.00				

KM# 79 5 DOLLARS **Weight:** 1.5550 g. **Composition:** 0.9990 Gold .0500 oz. AGW

Date	Mintage	F	VF	XF	Unc	BU
1990		—	—	—BV+20%		—
1990 Proof	Est. 2,000	Value: 30.00				

KM# 94 5 DOLLARS **Composition:** Copper-Aluminum-Nickel **Subject:** 25th Anniversary of Independence

Date	Mintage	F	VF	XF	Unc	BU
1990	1,000,000	—	—	—	8.00	—

KM# 86 5 DOLLARS **Composition:** Copper-Nickel **Subject:** Civil Defense

Date	Mintage	F	VF	XF	Unc	BU
1991	55,000	—	—	—	8.00	—
1991 Proof	10,000	Value: 16.50				

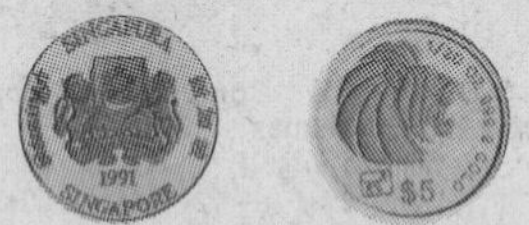

KM# 87 5 DOLLARS **Weight:** 1.5550 g. **Composition:** 0.9990 Gold .0500 oz. AGW **Subject:** Year of the Goat

Date	Mintage	F	VF	XF	Unc	BU
1991	8,000	—	—	—BV+20%		—
1991 Proof	2,500	Value: 30.00				

KM# 86a 5 DOLLARS **Weight:** 20.0000 g. **Composition:** 0.9250 Silver .4949 oz. ASW

Date	Mintage	F	VF	XF	Unc	BU
1991 Proof	15,000	Value: 25.00				

KM# 104 5 DOLLARS **Ring Composition:** Copper-Nickel **Center Composition:** Aluminum-Bronze **Subject:** Vanda Miss Joaquim

Date	F	VF	XF	Unc	BU
1992 In mint sets only	—	—	—	14.00	—
1993 In mint sets only	—	—	—	15.00	—
1994 In mint sets only	—	—	—	15.00	—
1995 In mint sets only	—	—	—	15.00	—
1996 In mint sets only	—	—	—	14.00	—
1997 In mint sets only	—	—	—	14.00	—
1998 In mint sets only	—	—	—	14.00	—
1999 In mint sets only	—	—	—	14.00	—
2000 In mint sets only	—	—	—	14.00	—

KM# 104a 5 DOLLARS **Weight:** 20.0000 g. **Composition:** 0.9250 Silver .4949 oz. ASW

Date	Mintage	F	VF	XF	Unc	BU
1992 Proof	15,000	Value: 25.00				
1994 Proof	10,000	Value: 25.00				
1995 Proof	10,000	Value: 25.00				
1996 Proof	17,000	Value: 25.00				
1997 Proof	20,000	Value: 25.00				
1998 Proof	—	Value: 25.00				
1999 Proof	—	Value: 25.00				
2000 Proof	17,000	Value: 25.00				

KM#108 5 DOLLARS **Weight:** 1.5550 g. **Composition:** 0.9990 Gold .0500 oz. AGW **Subject:** Year of the Monkey

Date	Mintage	F	VF	XF	Unc	BU
1992	6,500	—	—	—BV+20%		—
1992 Proof	2,000	Value: 30.00				

KM# 115 5 DOLLARS **Composition:** Copper-Nickel **Subject:** XVII Sea Games - Martial Arts

Date	Mintage	F	VF	XF	Unc
1993	23,000	—	—	—	9.00
1993 Proof	2,000	Value: 30.00			

KM# 115a 5 DOLLARS **Weight:** 20.0000 g. **Composition:** 0.9250 Silver .5949 oz. ASW

Date	Mintage	F	VF	XF	Unc
1993 Proof	10,000	Value: 32.50			

KM#117 5 DOLLARS **Weight:** 1.5550 g. **Compositio** 0.9990 Gold .0500 oz. AGW **Subject:** Year of the Rooste

Date	F	VF	XF	Unc
1993 In proof sets only	—	—	—	35.00
1993	—	—	—BV+20%	

KM# 124 5 DOLLARS **Composition:** Copper-Nickel **Subject:** Year of the Family

Date	Mintage	F	VF	XF	Unc
1994	20,000	—	—	—	8.00

KM# 124a 5 DOLLARS **Weight:** 20.0000 g. **Composition:** 0.9250 Silver .4949 oz. ASW

Date	Mintage	F	VF	XF	Unc
1994 Proof	8,000	Value: 30.00			

KM#128 5 DOLLARS **Weight:** 1.5550 g. **Compositio** 0.9990 Gold .0500 oz. AGW **Subject:** Year of the Dog

Date	F	VF	XF	Unc
1994 In proof sets only	—	—	—	35.00
1994	—	—	—BV+20%	

KM#133 5 DOLLARS **Weight:** 1.5550 g. **Compositio** 0.9990 Gold .0500 oz. AGW **Subject:** Year of the Pig

Date	Mintage	F	VF	XF	Unc
1995	—	—	—	—BV+20%	
1995 Proof	1,500	Value: 35.00			

KM# 138 5 DOLLARS **Ring Composition:** Copper-Nickel **Center Composition:** Aluminum-Bronze **Series:** 50th Anniversary - United Nations

Date	Mintage	F	VF	XF	Unc
1995	500,000	—	—	—	10.00

KM# 139 5 DOLLARS **Weight:** 20.0000 g. **Composition:** 0.9250 Silver .4949 oz. ASW **Series:** 50th Anniversary - United Nations

Date	Mintage	F	VF	XF	Unc	BU
1995 Proof	9,000	Value: 60.00				

KM# 150 5 DOLLARS **Composition:** Copper-Nickel **Subject:** 30th Anniversary - Singapore's Independence

Date	Mintage	F	VF	XF	Unc	BU
1995	20,000	—	—	—	8.00	—

KM# 150a 5 DOLLARS **Weight:** 20.0000 g. **Composition:** 0.9250 Silver .4949 oz. ASW

Date	Mintage	F	VF	XF	Unc	BU
1995 Proof	8,000	Value: 30.00				

KM# 149 5 DOLLARS **Composition:** Copper-Nickel **Subject:** World Trade Organization Conference

Date	F	VF	XF	Unc	BU
1996	—	—	—	12.00	—

KM# 149a 5 DOLLARS **Weight:** 20.0000 g. **Composition:** 0.9250 Silver .4949 oz. ASW **Obverse:** Mintmark

Date	Mintage	F	VF	XF	Unc	BU
1996 Proof	17,000	Value: 40.00				

KM# 145 5 DOLLARS **Weight:** 3.1103 g. **Composition:** 0.9990 Gold .1000 oz. AGW **Subject:** Year of the Rat

Date	Mintage	F	VF	XF	Unc	BU
1996 Proof	2,688	Value: 55.00				

KM# 151 5 DOLLARS **Composition:** Copper-Nickel **Subject:** 50th Anniversary - Singapore Airlines **Obverse:** National arms, no mint mark

Date	F	VF	XF	Unc	BU
1997	—	—	—	12.00	—

KM# 151a 5 DOLLARS **Weight:** 20.0000 g. **Composition:** 0.9250 Silver .4949 oz. ASW **Obverse:** With mint mark

Date	Mintage	F	VF	XF	Unc	BU
1997 Proof	23,000	Value: 40.00				

KM# 157 5 DOLLARS **Weight:** 7.7760 g. **Composition:** 0.9999 Gold .2500 oz. AGW **Series:** UNICEF **Reverse:** Children Using Computer **Note:** Similar to 2 Dollars, KM#156.

Date	Mintage	F	VF	XF	Unc	BU
1997 Proof	10,000	Value: 665				

KM# 159 5 DOLLARS **Weight:** 3.1103 g. **Composition:** 0.9999 Gold .1000 oz. AGW **Subject:** Year of the Ox **Reverse:** Lion **Note:** Similar to 20 Dollars, KM#161.

Date	Mintage	F	VF	XF	Unc	BU
1997 Proof	Est. 2,200	Value: 65.00				

KM# 163 5 DOLLARS **Composition:** Copper-Nickel **Subject:** Charity Work in Singapore **Obverse:** National arms **Reverse:** Two hands holding heart-shaped fruit

Date	F	VF	XF	Unc	BU
1998	—	—	—	12.00	—

KM# 163a 5 DOLLARS **Weight:** 20.0000 g. **Composition:** 0.9250 Silver .5948 oz. ASW **Subject:** Charity Work in Singapore **Obverse:** National arms **Reverse:** Two hands holding golden heart-shaped fruit

Date	Mintage	F	VF	XF	Unc	BU
1998 Proof	12,000	Value: 50.00				

KM# 173 5 DOLLARS **Weight:** 20.0000 g. **Composition:** Copper-Nickel **Subject:** Parliament **Obverse:** National arms **Reverse:** Parliament building **Edge:** Reeded

Date	F	VF	XF	Unc	BU
1999	—	—	—	12.00	—

KM# 173a 5 DOLLARS **Weight:** 20.0000 g. **Composition:** 0.9250 Silver .5948 oz. ASW

Date	Mintage	F	VF	XF	Unc	BU
1999 Proof	10,000	Value: 55.00				

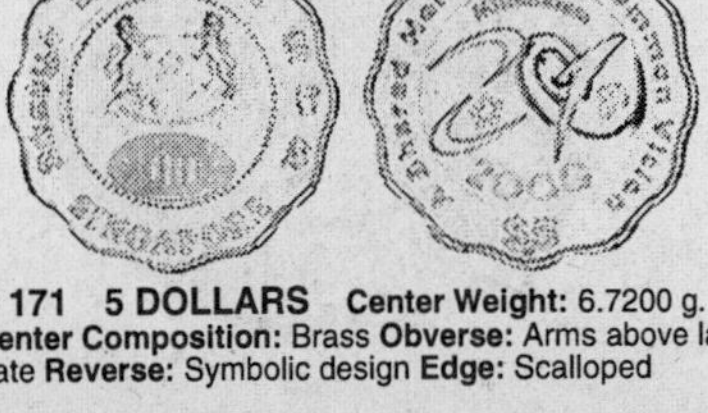

KM# 171 5 DOLLARS **Center Weight:** 6.7200 g. **Center Composition:** Brass **Obverse:** Arms above latent date **Reverse:** Symbolic design **Edge:** Scalloped

Date	F	VF	XF	Unc	BU
2000	—	—	—	11.50	—

KM# 172 5 DOLLARS **Center Weight:** 31.1030 g. **Center Composition:** 0.9990 Gold 1.0000 oz. AGW **Subject:** Millennium **Obverse:** Multicolor holographic national arms **Reverse:** Millennium design **Edge:** Scalloped

Date	Mintage	F	VF	XF	Unc	BU
2000 Proof	3,000	Value: 1,250				

KM# 177 5 DOLLARS **Weight:** 20.0000 g. **Composition:** Copper-Nickel **Subject:** Productivity Movement **Obverse:** National arms **Reverse:** Spiral design **Edge:** Reeded **Size:** 38.6 mm.

Date	Mintage	F	VF	XF	Unc	BU
2001 Proof	10,000	Value: 32.50				

KM# 177a 5 DOLLARS **Subject:** Productivity Movement **Obverse:** National arms **Reverse:** Spiral design **Edge:** Reeded **Size:** 38.6 mm.

Date	F	VF	XF	Unc	BU
2001	—	—	—	—	—

KM# 9.1 10 DOLLARS **Weight:** 31.1000 g. **Composition:** 0.9000 Silver .8999 oz. ASW **Obv. Legend:** SINGAPORE inverted

Date	Mintage	F	VF	XF	Unc	BU
1972	80,000	—	—	—	17.50	—
1972 Proof	3,000	Value: 37.50				

KM# 9.2 10 DOLLARS **Weight:** 31.1000 g. **Composition:** 0.9000 Silver .8999 oz. ASW

Date	Mintage	F	VF	XF	Unc	BU
1973	80,000	—	—	—	16.50	—
1973 Proof	5,000	Value: 32.50				

KM# 9.2a 10 DOLLARS **Weight:** 31.1000 g. **Composition:** 0.5000 Silver .5000 oz. ASW

Date	Mintage	F	VF	XF	Unc	BU
1974	100,000	—	—	—	12.50	—
1974 Proof	6,000	Value: 22.50				

KM# 11 10 DOLLARS **Weight:** 31.1000 g. **Composition:** 0.5000 Silver .5000 oz. ASW **Subject:** 10th Anniversary of Independence

Date	Mintage	F	VF	XF	Unc	BU
ND(1975)	200,000	—	—	—	6.00	—
ND(1975) Proof	10,000	Value: 17.50				

KM# 15 10 DOLLARS **Weight:** 31.1000 g. **Composition:** 0.5000 Silver .5000 oz. ASW

Date	Mintage	F	VF	XF	Unc	BU
1976	150,000	—	—	—	6.00	—
1976sm Proof	10,000	Value: 18.50				
1977	150,000	—	—	—	6.00	—
1977sm Proof	10,000	Value: 18.50				

KM# 16 10 DOLLARS **Weight:** 31.1000 g. **Composition:** 0.5000 Silver .5000 oz. ASW **Subject:** ASEAN 10th Anniversary

Date	Mintage	F	VF	XF	Unc	BU
ND(1977)	200,000	—	—	—	7.00	—
ND(1977)sm Proof	10,000	Value: 20.00				

KM# 17.1 10 DOLLARS **Weight:** 31.1000 g. **Composition:** 0.5000 Silver .5000 oz. ASW **Subject:** Communications Satellites

Date	Mintage	F	VF	XF	Unc	BU
1978	167,000	—	—	—	7.50	—
1978sm Proof	10,000	Value: 14.50				
1979	168,000	—	—	—	7.50	—
1979sm Proof	9,000	Value: 14.50				

KM# 17.1a 10 DOLLARS **Composition:** Copper-Nickel

Date	Mintage	F	VF	XF	Unc	BU
1980	120,000	—	—	—	8.00	—

KM# 17.2 10 DOLLARS **Composition:** Copper-Nickel **Obverse:** Raised stars and moon in arms

Date	Mintage	F	VF	XF	Unc	BU
1980sm Proof	15,000	Value: 15.00				

KM# 20 10 DOLLARS **Composition:** Copper-Nickel **Subject:** Year of the Rooster

Date	Mintage	F	VF	XF	Unc	BU
1981	180,000	—	—	—	18.50	—

KM# 20a 10 DOLLARS **Weight:** 31.1000 g. **Composition:** 0.5000 Silver .5000 oz. ASW

Date	Mintage	F	VF	XF	Unc	BU
1981sm Proof	20,000	Value: 65.00				

KM# 23 10 DOLLARS **Composition:** Nickel **Subject:** Year of the Dog

Date	Mintage	F	VF	XF	Unc	BU
1982	210,000	—	—	—	25.00	—

KM# 23a 10 DOLLARS **Weight:** 31.1000 g. **Composition:** 0.5000 Silver .5000 oz. ASW

Date	Mintage	F	VF	XF	Unc	BU
1982sm Proof	20,000	Value: 47.50				

KM# 31 10 DOLLARS **Weight:** 31.1000 g. **Composition:** 0.9990 Gold 1.0000 oz. AGW **Subject:** Year of the Dragon

Date	Mintage	F	VF	XF	Unc	BU
1983	10,000	—	—	—	BV+7%	—
1984 Proof	10,000	—	—	—	BV+7%	—

KM# 26 10 DOLLARS **Composition:** Nickel **Subject:** Year of the Pig

Date	Mintage	F	VF	XF	Unc	BU
1983	307,000	—	—	—	17.50	—

KM# 26a 10 DOLLARS **Weight:** 31.1000 g. **Composition:** 0.5000 Silver .5000 oz. ASW

Date	Mintage	F	VF	XF	Unc	BU
1983sm Proof	20,000	Value: 40.00				

KM# 33 10 DOLLARS **Composition:** Nickel **Subject:** Year of the Rat

Date	Mintage	F	VF	XF	Unc	BU
1984	300,000	—	—	—	15.00	—

KM# 33a 10 DOLLARS **Weight:** 31.1000 g. **Composition:** 0.5000 Silver .5000 oz. ASW

Date	Mintage	F	VF	XF	Unc	BU
1984sm Proof	20,000	Value: 40.00				

KM# 44 10 DOLLARS **Composition:** Nickel **Subject:** Year of the Ox

Date	Mintage	F	VF	XF	Unc	BU
1985	307,000	—	—	—	15.00	—

KM# 44a 10 DOLLARS **Weight:** 31.1000 g. **Composition:** 0.5000 Silver .5000 oz. ASW

Date	Mintage	F	VF	XF	Unc	BU
1985sm Proof	20,000	Value: 40.00				

KM# 59 10 DOLLARS **Composition:** Nickel **Subject:** Year of the Tiger

Date	Mintage	F	VF	XF	Unc	BU
1986	300,000	—	—	—	15.00	—

KM# 59a 10 DOLLARS **Weight:** 31.1000 g. **Composition:** 0.5000 Silver .5000 oz. ASW

Date	Mintage	F	VF	XF	Unc	BU
1986 Proof	20,000	Value: 42.50				

KM# 66 10 DOLLARS **Composition:** Nickel **Subject:** Year of the Rabbit

Date	Mintage	F	VF	XF	Unc	BU
1987	300,000	—	—	—	15.00	—

KM# 66a 10 DOLLARS **Weight:** 31.1000 g. **Composition:** 0.5000 Silver .5000 oz. ASW

Date	Mintage	F	VF	XF	Unc	BU
1987sm Proof	25,000	Value: 32.50				

KM# 67 10 DOLLARS **Composition:** Copper-Nickel **Subject:** Association of Southeast Asian Nations **Obverse:** Coat of arms above 1967-1987 **Reverse:** ASEAN logo within legend, value below

Date	Mintage	F	VF	XF	Unc	BU
1987	80,000	—	—	—	8.50	—

KM# 67a 10 DOLLARS **Weight:** 31.1030 g. **Composition:** 0.5000 Silver .5000 oz. ASW

Date	Mintage	F	VF	XF	Unc	BU
1987sm Proof	25,000	Value: 20.00				

KM# 69 10 DOLLARS **Composition:** Nickel **Subject:** Year of the Dragon

Date	Mintage	F	VF	XF	Unc	BU
1988	300,000	—	—	—	15.00	—

KM# 69a 10 DOLLARS **Weight:** 31.1030 g. **Composition:** 0.5000 Silver .5000 oz. ASW

Date	Mintage	F	VF	XF	Unc	BU
1988 Proof	25,000	Value: 42.50				

KM# 71 10 DOLLARS **Composition:** Nickel **Subject:** Year of the Snake

Date	Mintage	F	VF	XF	Unc	BU
1989	250,000	—	—	—	15.00	—

KM# 71a 10 DOLLARS **Weight:** 31.1030 g. **Composition:** 0.9250 Silver .9250 oz. ASW

Date	Mintage	F	VF	XF	Unc	BU
1989 Proof	25,000	Value: 37.50				

KM# 75 10 DOLLARS **Composition:** Nickel **Subject:** Year of the Horse

Date	Mintage	F	VF	XF	Unc	BU
1990	330,000	—	—	—	15.00	—

KM# 80 10 DOLLARS **Weight:** 3.1103 g. **Composition:** 0.9990 Gold .1000 oz. AGW

Date	F	VF	XF	Unc	BU
1990 Proof	Est. 2,000	Value: 50.00			
1990	—	—	—BV+15%		—

KM# 75a 10 DOLLARS **Weight:** 31.1030 g. **Composition:** 0.9250 Silver .9250 oz. ASW

Date	Mintage	F	VF	XF	Unc	BU
1990sm Proof	30,000	Value: 32.50				

KM# 95 10 DOLLARS **Weight:** 31.1030 g. **Composition:** 0.9250 Silver **Subject:** 25th Anniversary of Independence

Date	Mintage	F	VF	XF	Unc	BU
1990 Proof	50,000	Value: 25.00				

KM# 84 10 DOLLARS **Composition:** Nickel

Date	Mintage	F	VF	XF	Unc	BU
1991	300,000	—	—	—	15.00	—

KM# 84a 10 DOLLARS **Weight:** 31.1030 g. **Composition:** 0.9250 Silver .9250 oz. ASW

Date	Mintage	F	VF	XF	Unc	BU
1991sm Proof	30,000	Value: 32.50				

KM# 88 10 DOLLARS **Weight:** 3.1103 g. **Composition:** 0.9990 Gold .1000 oz. AGW **Subject:** Year of the Goat

Date	Mintage	F	VF	XF	Unc	BU
1991 Proof	2,500	Value: 50.00				
1991	5,500	—	—	—BV+15%		—

KM# 92 10 DOLLARS **Composition:** Nickel **Subject:** Year of the Monkey **Note:** Similar to 500 Dollars, KM#93.

Date	Mintage	F	VF	XF	Unc	BU
1992	300,000	—	—	—	10.00	—

KM# 109 10 DOLLARS **Weight:** 3.1103 g. **Composition:** 0.9990 Gold .1000 oz. AGW **Reverse:** Similar to KM#88 **Note:** Year of the Monkey Privy Mark.

Date	Mintage	F	VF	XF	Unc	BU
1992 Proof	2,000	Value: 50.00				
1992	4,000	—	—	—BV+15%		—

KM# 92a 10 DOLLARS **Weight:** 31.1030 g. **Composition:** 0.9250 Silver .9250 oz. ASW

Date	Mintage	F	VF	XF	Unc	BU
1992 Proof	30,000	Value: 30.00				

KM# 105 10 DOLLARS **Composition:** 0.9250 Silver .0550 oz. ASW **Subject:** 25th Anniversary - Board of Commissioners of Currency

Date	Mintage	F	VF	XF	Unc	BU
1992 Proof	15,000	Value: 65.00				

KM# 113 10 DOLLARS **Composition:** Copper-Nickel **Subject:** Year of the Rooster **Obverse:** Similar to 250 Dollars, KM#114

Date	Mintage	F	VF	XF	Unc	BU
1993 Prooflike	209,000	—	—	—	25.00	—

KM# 118 10 DOLLARS **Weight:** 3.1103 g. **Composition:** 0.9990 Gold .1000 oz. AGW **Note:** Lion/Year of the Rooster Privy Mark.

Date	Mintage	F	VF	XF	Unc	BU
1993		—	—	—BV+15%		—
1993 In proof sets only	Est. 1,500	Value: 55.00				

KM# 113a 10 DOLLARS **Weight:** 62.2070 g. **Composition:** 0.9990 Silver 2.0000 oz. ASW

Date	Mintage	F	VF	XF	Unc	BU
1993 Proof	40,000	Value: 50.00				

KM# 122 10 DOLLARS **Composition:** Copper-Nickel **Subject:** Year of the Dog

Date	Mintage	F	VF	XF	Unc	BU
1994 Prooflike	215,000	—	—	—	28.00	—

KM# 129 10 DOLLARS **Weight:** 3.1103 g. **Composition:** 0.9990 Gold .1000 oz. AGW **Note:** Lion/Year of the Dog Privy Mark.

Date	Mintage	F	VF	XF	Unc	BU
1994		—	—	—BV+15%		—
1994 In proof sets only	Est. 1,500	Value: 55.00				

KM# 122a 10 DOLLARS **Weight:** 62.2070 g. **Composition:** 0.9990 Silver 2.0000 oz. ASW **Reverse:** Silver content at bottom

Date	Mintage	F	VF	XF	Unc	BU
1994 Proof	35,000	Value: 55.00				

KM# 125 10 DOLLARS **Composition:** Copper-Nickel **Subject:** Year of the Pig

Date	Mintage	F	VF	XF	Unc	BU
1995 Prooflike	210,000	—	—	—	17.50	—

KM# 125a 10 DOLLARS **Weight:** 62.2070 g. **Composition:** 0.9990 Silver 2.0000 oz. ASW **Reverse:** Silver content at bottom

Date	Mintage	F	VF	XF	Unc	BU
1995 Proof	35,000	Value: 70.00				

KM# 134 10 DOLLARS **Weight:** 3.1103 g. **Composition:** 0.9990 Gold .1000 oz. AGW **Note:** Lion/Year of the Pig Privy Mark.

Date		F	VF	XF	Unc	BU
1995 Proof	—	Value: 55.00				
1995		—	—	—BV+15%		—

KM# 141 10 DOLLARS **Composition:** Copper-Nickel **Subject:** Year of the Rat

Date	Mintage	F	VF	XF	Unc	BU
1996 Prooflike	245,000	—	—	—	16.00	—

KM# 141a 10 DOLLARS **Weight:** 62.2070 g. **Composition:** 0.9990 Silver 2.0000 oz. ASW **Reverse:** Silver content at bottom

Date	Mintage	F	VF	XF	Unc	BU
1996 Proof	35,000	Value: 70.00				

KM# 146 10 DOLLARS **Weight:** 7.7759 g. **Composition:** 0.9990 Gold .2500 oz. AGW **Note:** Year of the Rat Privy Mark.

Date	Mintage	F	VF	XF	Unc	BU
1996 Proof	2,688	Value: 115				

KM# 160 10 DOLLARS **Weight:** 7.7759 g. **Composition:** 0.9999 Gold .2500 oz. AGW **Note:** Lion/Year of the Ox Privy Mark. Similar to KM#154.

Date	Mintage	F	VF	XF	Unc	BU
1997 Proof	Est. 2,200	Value: 125				

KM# 153 10 DOLLARS **Composition:** Copper-Nickel **Subject:** Year of the Ox **Note:** Similar to KM#154.

Date		F	VF	XF	Unc	BU
1997 Prooflike		—	—	—	15.00	—

KM# 154 10 DOLLARS **Weight:** 62.2070 g. **Composition:** 0.9990 Silver 2.0000 oz. ASW **Subject:** Year of the Ox

Date	Mintage	F	VF	XF	Unc	BU
1997 Proof	38,000	Value: 70.00				

KM# 165 10 DOLLARS **Weight:** 62.2070 g. **Composition:** 0.9990 Silver 1.9980 oz. ASW **Subject:** Year of the Tiger **Obverse:** National arms **Reverse:** Stylized tiger

Date	Mintage	F	VF	XF	Unc	BU
1998 Proof	38,000	Value: 70.00				

KM# 164 10 DOLLARS **Composition:** Copper-Nickel **Subject:** Year of the Tiger **Obverse:** National emblem **Reverse:** Stylized tiger **Note:** Similar to KM#165.

Date		F	VF	XF	Unc	BU
1998 Prooflike		—	—	—	15.00	—

KM# 167 10 DOLLARS **Weight:** 28.0000 g. **Composition:** Copper-Nickel **Subject:** Year of the Rabbit **Obverse:** National arms **Reverse:** Stylized rabbit **Edge:** Reeded

Date		F	VF	XF	Unc	BU
1999		—	—	—	15.00	—

KM# 168 10 DOLLARS **Weight:** 62.2070 g. **Composition:** 0.9990 Silver 1.9980 oz. ASW

Date	Mintage	F	VF	XF	Unc	BU
1999 Proof	38,000	Value: 70.00				

KM# 174 10 DOLLARS **Composition:** Copper-Nickel **Subject:** Year of the Dragon **Obverse:** National arms **Reverse:** Dragon **Edge:** Reeded

Date		F	VF	XF	Unc	BU
2000 Prooflike		—	—	—	15.00	—

KM# 175 10 DOLLARS **Weight:** 62.2060 g. **Composition:** 0.9990 Silver 1.9980 oz. ASW **Subject:** Year of the Dragon **Obverse:** National arms **Reverse:** Dragon **Edge:** Reeded **Size:** 40.7 mm. **Note:** Size: 40.7 millimeters, piefort thickness.

Date	Mintage	F	VF	XF	Unc	BU
2000 Proof	38,000	Value: 70.00				

KM# 179 10 DOLLARS **Weight:** 28.0000 g. **Composition:** Copper-Nickel **Subject:** Year of the Snake **Obverse:** National arms. **Reverse:** Snake. **Edge:** Reeded. **Size:** 40.7 mm.

Date		F	VF	XF	Unc	BU
2001		—	—	—	15.00	—

KM# 180 10 DOLLARS **Weight:** 62.2060 g. **Composition:** 0.9990 Silver 1.998 oz. ASW **Subject:** Year of the Snake **Obverse:** National arms. **Reverse:** Snake. **Edge:** Reeded. **Size:** 40.7 mm.

Date	Mintage	F	VF	XF	Unc	BU
2001 Proof	38,000	—	—	—	70.00	—

KM# 147 20 DOLLARS **Weight:** 15.5517 g. **Composition:** 0.9990 Gold .5000 oz. AGW **Note:** Lion/Year of the Rat Privy Mark.

Date	Mintage	F	VF	XF	Unc	BU
1996 Proof	2,688	Value: 200				

KM# 161 20 DOLLARS **Weight:** 15.5517 g. **Composition:** 0.9999 Gold .5000 oz. AGW **Note:** Lion/Year of the Ox Privy Mark.

Date	Mintage	F	VF	XF	Unc	BU
1997 Proof	Est. 2,200	Value: 220				

KM# 81 25 DOLLARS **Weight:** 7.7757 g. **Composition:** 0.9990 Gold .2500 oz. AGW

Date	Mintage	F	VF	XF	Unc	BU
1990	—	—	—	—BV+12%		—
1990 Proof	Est. 2,000	Value: 90.00				

KM# 89 25 DOLLARS **Weight:** 7.7757 g. **Composition:** 0.9990 Gold .2500 oz. AGW **Note:** Year of the Goat Privy Mark.

Date	Mintage	F	VF	XF	Unc	BU
1991	5,500	—	—	—BV+12%		—
1991 Proof	2,500	Value: 90.00				

KM# 110 25 DOLLARS **Weight:** 7.7757 g. **Composition:** 0.9990 Gold .2500 oz. AGW **Note:** Year of the Monkey Privy Mark.

Date	Mintage	F	VF	XF	Unc	BU
1992	4,000	—	—	—BV+12%		—
1992 Proof	2,000	Value: 90.00				

KM# 119 25 DOLLARS **Weight:** 7.7757 g. **Composition:** 0.9990 Gold .2500 oz. AGW **Note:** Year of the Rooster Privy Mark.

Date	Mintage	F	VF	XF	Unc	BU
1993		—	—	— BV+12%		—
1993 In proof sets only	Est. 1,500	Value: 95.00				

KM# 130 25 DOLLARS **Weight:** 7.7757 g. **Composition:** 0.9990 Gold .2500 oz. AGW **Note:** Year of the Dog Privy Mark.

Date	Mintage	F	VF	XF	Unc	B
1994		—	—	— BV+12%		-
1994 In proof sets only	Est. 1,500	Value: 95.00				

KM# 135 25 DOLLARS **Weight:** 7.7757 g. **Composition:** 0.9990 Gold .2500 oz. AGW **Note:** Year of the Pig Privy Mark.

Date	Mintage	F	VF	XF	Unc	B
1995	—	—	—	—BV+12%		-
1995 Proof	1,500	Value: 95.00				

M# 18 50 DOLLARS Weight: 31.1000 g. **Composition:** 0.5000 Silver .5000 oz. ASW **Subject:** International Financial Center

te	Mintage	F	VF	XF	Unc	BU
30	25,000	—	—	—	35.00	—
30sm Proof	15,000	Value: 45.00				
31	50,000	—	—	—	30.00	—
31sm Proof	20,000	Value: 35.00				

M# 78 50 DOLLARS Weight: 10.0000 g. **Composition:** 0.9160 Gold .2945 oz. AGW **Series:** Save the Children Fund

te	Mintage	F	VF	XF	Unc	BU
89 Proof	3,000	Value: 150				

M# 82 50 DOLLARS Weight: 15.5500 g. **Composition:** 0.9990 Gold .5000 oz. AGW

te	Mintage	F	VF	XF	Unc	BU
90	—	—	—	—	BV	—
90 Proof	Est. 2,000	Value: 185				

M# 90 50 DOLLARS Weight: 15.5500 g. **Composition:** 0.9990 Gold .5000 oz. AGW **Note:** Year of the Goat Privy Mark.

te	Mintage	F	VF	XF	Unc	BU
91	5,500	—	—	—BV+10%		—
91 Proof	2,500	Value: 185				

M# 111 50 DOLLARS Weight: 15.5500 g. **Composition:** 0.9990 Gold .5000 oz. AGW **Note:** Year of the Monkey Privy Mark.

te	Mintage	F	VF	XF	Unc	BU
92	4,000	—	—	—BV+10%		—
92 Proof	2,000	Value: 185				

M# 120 50 DOLLARS Weight: 15.5500 g. **Composition:** 0.9990 Gold .5000 oz. AGW **Note:** Year of the Rooster Privy Mark.

ate	Mintage	F	VF	XF	Unc	BU
993	—	—	—	—BV+10%		—
993 In proof sets only	Est. 1,500	Value: 190				

KM# 131 50 DOLLARS Weight: 15.5500 g. **Composition:** 0.9990 Gold .5000 oz. AGW **Note:** Year of the Dog Privy Mark.

Date	Mintage	F	VF	XF	Unc	BU
1994	—	—	—	—BV+10%		—
1994 In proof sets only	Est. 1,500	Value: 190				

KM# 136 50 DOLLARS Weight: 15.5500 g. **Composition:** 0.9990 Gold .5000 oz. AGW **Note:** Year of the Pig Privy Mark.

Date	Mintage	F	VF	XF	Unc	BU
1995	—	—	—	—BV+10%		—
1995 Proof	1,500	Value: 190				

KM# 140 50 DOLLARS Weight: 31.1035 g. **Composition:** 0.9999 Gold 1.0000 oz. AGW **Series:** 50th Anniversary - United Nations

Date	Mintage	F	VF	XF	Unc	BU
1995 Proof	1,000	Value: 750				

KM# 148 50 DOLLARS Weight: 31.1035 g. **Composition:** 0.9999 Gold 1.0000 oz. AGW **Note:** Lion/Year of the Rat Privy Mark.

Date	Mintage	F	VF	XF	Unc	BU
1996 Proof	2,688	Value: 420				

KM# 162 50 DOLLARS Weight: 31.1035 g. **Composition:** 0.9999 Gold 1.0000 oz. AGW **Note:** Lion/Year of the Ox Privy Mark.

Date	Mintage	F	VF	XF	Unc	BU
1997 Proof	Est. 2,200	Value: 435				

KM# 152 50 DOLLARS Weight: 31.1035 g. **Composition:** 0.9999 Gold 1.0000 oz. AGW **Subject:** 50th Anniversary - Singapore Airlines

Date	Mintage	F	VF	XF	Unc	BU
1997 Proof	3,576	Value: 500				

KM# 170 50 DOLLARS Weight: 31.1035 g. **Composition:** 0.9999 Gold 1.0000 oz. AGW **Subject:** Parliament **Obverse:** National arms **Reverse:** Parliament House buildings

Date	Mintage	F	VF	XF	Unc	BU
1999 Proof	1,000	Value: 750				

KM# 12 100 DOLLARS Weight: 6.9119 g. **Composition:** 0.9000 Gold .2000 oz. AGW **Subject:** 10th Anniversary of Independence

Date	Mintage	F	VF	XF	Unc	BU
1975	100,000	—	—	—	75.00	—
1975 Proof	3,000	Value: 125				

KM# 83 100 DOLLARS Weight: 31.1000 g. **Composition:** 0.9990 Gold 1.0000 oz. AGW

Date	Mintage	F	VF	XF	Unc	BU
1990	—	—	—	—	BV+7%	—
1990 Proof	Est. 2,000	Value: 375				

KM# 91 100 DOLLARS Weight: 31.1000 g. **Composition:** 0.9990 Gold 1.0000 oz. AGW **Note:** Year of the Goat Privy Mark.

Date	Mintage	F	VF	XF	Unc	BU
1991	13,000	—	—	—	BV+7%	—
1991 Proof	2,500	Value: 375				

KM# 112 100 DOLLARS Weight: 31.1000 g. **Composition:** 0.9990 Gold 1.0000 oz. AGW **Note:** Year of the Monkey Privy Mark.

Date	Mintage	F	VF	XF	Unc	BU
1992	4,000	—	—	—	BV+7%	—
1992 Proof	2,000	Value: 375				

KM# 106 100 DOLLARS Weight: 31.1000 g. **Composition:** 0.9990 Gold 1.0000 oz. AGW **Subject:** 25th Anniversary - Board of Commissioners of Currency

Date	Mintage	F	VF	XF	Unc	BU
1992 Proof	800	Value: 485				

KM# 121 100 DOLLARS **Weight:** 31.1000 g. **Composition:** 0.9990 Gold 1.0000 oz. AGW **Note:** Year of the Rooster Privy Mark.

Date	Mintage	F	VF	XF	Unc	BU
1993	—	—	—	—	BV+7%	—
1993 In proof sets only	Est. 1,500	Value: 385				

KM# 132 100 DOLLARS **Weight:** 31.1000 g. **Composition:** 0.9990 Gold 1.0000 oz. AGW **Note:** Year of the Dog Privy Mark.

Date	Mintage	F	VF	XF	Unc	BU
1994	—	—	—	—	BV+7%	—
1994 In proof sets only	Est. 1,500	Value: 385				

KM# 137 100 DOLLARS **Weight:** 31.1000 g. **Composition:** 0.9990 Gold 1.0000 oz. AGW **Note:** Year of the Pig Privy Mark.

Date	Mintage	F	VF	XF	Unc	BU
1995	—	—	—	—	BV+7%	—
1995 Proof	1,500	Value: 385				

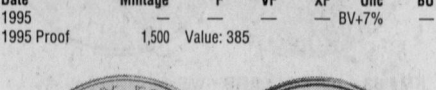

KM# 7 150 DOLLARS **Weight:** 24.8830 g. **Composition:** 0.9160 Gold .7360 oz. AGW **Subject:** 150th Anniversary - Founding of Singapore

Date	Mintage	F	VF	XF	Unc	BU
ND(1969)	198,000	—	—	—	265	—
ND(1969) Proof	500	Value: 1,350				

KM# 107 200 DOLLARS **Weight:** 31.1035 g. **Composition:** 0.9990 Platinum 1.0000 oz. APW **Subject:** 25th Anniversary - Board of Commissioners of Currency **Note:** Similar to KM#106.

Date	Mintage	F	VF	XF	Unc	BU
1992 Proof	300	Value: 975				

KM# 13 250 DOLLARS **Weight:** 17.2797 g. **Composition:** 0.9000 Gold .5000 oz. AGW **Subject:** 10th Anniversary of Independence

Date	Mintage	F	VF	XF	Unc	BU
ND(1975)	30,000	—	—	—	175	—
ND(1975) Proof	2,000	Value: 275				

KM# 96 250 DOLLARS **Weight:** 31.1040 g. **Composition:** 0.9990 Gold 1.0000 oz. AGW **Subject:** 25th Anniversary of Independence

Date	Mintage	F	VF	XF	Unc	BU
1990 Proof	6,000	Value: 500				

KM# 114 250 DOLLARS **Weight:** 31.1035 g. **Composition:** 0.9990 Gold 1.0000 oz. AGW **Subject:** Year of the Rooster

Date	Mintage	F	VF	XF	Unc	BU
1993 Proof	10,000	Value: 425				

KM# 123 250 DOLLARS **Weight:** 31.1035 g. **Composition:** 0.9990 Gold 1.0000 oz. AGW **Subject:** Year of the Dog

Date	Mintage	F	VF	XF	Unc	BU
1994 Proof	7,500	Value: 450				

KM# 127 250 DOLLARS **Weight:** 31.1035 g. **Composition:** 0.9990 Gold 1.0000 oz. AGW **Subject:** Year of the Pig

Date	Mintage	F	VF	XF	Unc	BU
1995 Proof	7,500	Value: 485				

KM# 143 250 DOLLARS **Weight:** 31.1035 g. **Composition:** 0.9990 Gold 1.0000 oz. AGW **Subject:** Year of the Rat

Date	Mintage	F	VF	XF	Unc	BU
1996 Proof	7,500	Value: 485				

KM# 155 250 DOLLARS **Weight:** 31.1035 g. **Composition:** 0.9990 Gold 1.0000 oz. AGW **Subject:** Ye of the Ox

Date	Mintage	F	VF	XF	Unc
1997 Proof	7,800	Value: 520			

KM# 166 250 DOLLARS **Weight:** 31.1035 g. **Composition:** 0.9990 Gold 1.0000 oz. AGW **Subject:** Ye of the Tiger **Obverse:** National arms **Reverse:** Stylized ti

Date	Mintage	F	VF	XF	Unc
1998 Proof	7,600	Value: 520			

KM# 169 250 DOLLARS **Weight:** 31.1035 g. **Composition:** 0.9990 Gold 1.0000 oz. AGW **Obverse:** National arms **Reverse:** Stylized rabbit **Edge:** Reeded

Date	Mintage	F	VF	XF	Unc
1999 Proof	7,600	Value: 520			

KM# 176 250 DOLLARS **Weight:** 31.1035 g. **Composition:** 0.9990 Gold 1.0000 oz. AGW **Subject:** Ye of the Dragon **Obverse:** National arms **Reverse:** Dragon **Edge:** Reeded **Size:** 32.12 mm.

Date	Mintage	F	VF	XF	Unc
2000 Proof	7,600	Value: 520			

KM# 178 250 DOLLARS **Weight:** 31.1035 g. **Composition:** 0.9990 Gold 0.999 oz. AGW **Subject:** Yea of the Snake **Obverse:** National arms. **Reverse:** Stylized snake. **Edge:** Reeded. **Size:** 32.1 mm.

Date	Mintage	F	VF	XF	Unc
2001 Proof	7,000	Value: 663			

KM# 14 500 DOLLARS **Weight:** 34.5594 g. **Composition:** 0.9000 Gold 1.0000 oz. AGW **Subject:** 10 Anniversary of Independence

Date	Mintage	F	VF	XF	Unc
ND(1975)	30,000	—	—	—	365
ND(1975) Proof	2,000	Value: 625			

KM# 21 500 DOLLARS **Weight:** 16.9650 g. **Composition:** 0.9160 Gold .5000 oz. AGW **Subject:** Year of the Rooster

Date	Mintage	F	VF	XF	Unc	BU
1981sm Proof	12,000	Value: 360				

KM# 24 500 DOLLARS **Weight:** 16.9650 g. **Composition:** 0.9160 Gold .5000 oz. AGW **Subject:** Year of the Dog

Date	Mintage	F	VF	XF	Unc	BU
1982sm Proof	5,500	Value: 400				

KM# 27 500 DOLLARS **Weight:** 16.9650 g. **Composition:** 0.9160 Gold .5000 oz. AGW **Subject:** Year of the Pig

Date	Mintage	F	VF	XF	Unc	BU
1983sm Proof	5,000	Value: 400				

KM# 34 500 DOLLARS **Weight:** 16.9650 g. **Composition:** 0.9160 Gold .5000 oz. AGW **Subject:** Year of the Rat

Date	Mintage	F	VF	XF	Unc	BU
1984sm Proof	4,000	Value: 415				

KM# 45 500 DOLLARS **Weight:** 16.9650 g. **Composition:** 0.9160 Gold .5000 oz. AGW **Subject:** Year of the Ox

Date	Mintage	F	VF	XF	Unc	BU
1985sm Proof	4,000	Value: 415				

KM# 60 500 DOLLARS **Weight:** 16.9650 g. **Composition:** 0.9160 Gold .5000 oz. AGW **Subject:** Year of the Tiger

Date	Mintage	F	VF	XF	Unc	BU
1986sm Proof	3,000	Value: 500				

KM# 64 500 DOLLARS **Weight:** 16.9650 g. **Composition:** 0.9160 Gold .5000 oz. AGW **Subject:** Year of the Rabbit

Date	Mintage	F	VF	XF	Unc	BU
1987sm Proof	2,400	Value: 725				

KM# 73 500 DOLLARS **Weight:** 16.9650 g. **Composition:** 0.9160 Gold .5000 oz. AGW **Subject:** Year of the Dragon

Date	Mintage	F	VF	XF	Unc	BU
1988sm Proof	4,000	Value: 420				

KM# 72 500 DOLLARS **Weight:** 16.9650 g. **Composition:** 0.9160 Gold .5000 oz. AGW **Subject:** Year of the Snake

Date	Mintage	F	VF	XF	Unc	BU
1989sm Proof	2,500	Value: 700				

KM# 76 500 DOLLARS **Weight:** 16.9650 g. **Composition:** 0.9160 Gold .5000 oz. AGW **Subject:** Year of the Horse

Date	Mintage	F	VF	XF	Unc	BU
1990sm Proof	5,000	Value: 385				

KM# 97 500 DOLLARS **Weight:** 31.1040 g. **Composition:** 0.9990 Platinum 1.0000 oz. APW **Subject:** 25th Anniversary of Independence

Date	Mintage	F	VF	XF	Unc	BU
1990 Proof	2,000	Value: 850				

KM# 85 500 DOLLARS **Weight:** 16.9650 g. **Composition:** 0.9160 Gold .5000 oz. AGW **Subject:** Year of the Goat

Date	Mintage	F	VF	XF	Unc	BU
1991sm Proof	5,000	Value: 385				

KM# 93 500 DOLLARS **Weight:** 16.9650 g. **Composition:** 0.9160 Gold .5000 oz. AGW **Subject:** Year of the Monkey

Date	Mintage	F	VF	XF	Unc	BU
1992sm Proof	5,000	Value: 385				

MINT SETS

KM#	Date	Mintage	Identification	Issue Price	Mkt Val
MS1	1967 (6)	8,000	KM#1-6	1.50	20.00
MS2	1968 (6)	16,000	KM#1-6	1.50	20.00
MS3	1969 (6)	14,000	KM#1-6	1.50	25.00
MS4	1970 (6)	13,000	KM#1-6	1.50	60.00
MS5	1970 (6)	27,000	KM#1-6	1.75	60.00
MS7	1972 (6)	13,000	KM#1-6	3.00	35.00
MS8	1973 (6)	15,000	KM#1-6	2.00	18.00
MS9	1974 (6)	20,000	KM#1-6	2.00	15.00
MS10	1975 (6)	30,000	KM#1-6	12.00	15.00
MS11	1975 (3)	30,000	KM#12-14	—	875
MS12	1976 (6)	35,000	KM#1-6	2.00	12.00
MS13	1977 (6)	40,000	KM#1a, 2-6	2.00	12.00
MS14	1978 (6)	55,000	KM#1a, 2-6	—	25.00
MS15	1979 (6)	65,000	KM#1a, 2-6	—	10.00
MS16	1980 (6)	70,000	kM#1a, 2-6	—	8.00
MS17	1981 (6)	110,000	KM#1a, 2-6	5.00	6.50
MS18	1982 (6)	160,000	KM#1a, 2-6	5.00	6.50
MS19	1983 (6)	40,000	KM#1a, 2-6 with Medallion, I.A.P.N.	—	9.00
MS20	1983 (6)	150,000	KM#1a, 2-6	5.00	8.00
MS21	1984 (6)	160,000	KM#1a, 2-6	3.75	7.50
MS22	1985 (6)	148,424	KM#1a, 2-6	—	15.00
MS23	1986 (6)	120,000	KM#49-52, 53.1, 54	—	7.00
MS24	1987 (6)	120,000	KM#49-52, 53.1, 54	—	7.00
MS25	1988 (6)	120,000	KM#49-52, 53.1, 54b	—	5.50
MS26	1989 (6)	100,000	KM#49-52, 53.2, 54b	—	5.50
MS27	1990 (6)	100,000	KM#49-52, 53.2, 54b	—	5.50
MS28	1990 (5)	5,000	KM#79-83	—	700
MS29	1991 (7)	70,000	KM#49b, 50-52, 53.2, 54b (1991), 94 (1990)	—	20.00
MS30	1992 (7)	55,000	KM#98-104	—	20.00
MS31	1993 (7)	—	KM#98-104	—	20.00
MS32	1994 (7)	100,000	KM#98-104	—	20.00
MS33	1995 (7)	124,000	KM#98-104	—	20.00
MS34	1996 (7)	180,000	KM#98-104	—	20.00
MS35	1997 (7)	—	KM#98-104	—	20.00
MS36	1998 (7)	—	KM#98-104	—	20.00
MS37	1999 (7)	—	KM#98-104	—	20.00
MS38	2000 (7)	—	KM#98-104	—	20.00

PROOF SETS

KM#	Date	Mintage	Identification	Issue Price	Mkt Val
PS1	1967 (6)	2,000	KM#1-6	25.00	60.00
PS2	1968 (6)	5,000	KM#1-6	25.00	55.00
PS3	1969 (6)	3,000	KM#1-6	25.00	275
PS4	1972 (6)	749	KM#1-6	25.00	475
PS5	1973 (6)	1,000	KM#1-6	32.00	175
PS6	1974 (6)	1,500	KM#1-6	34.00	130
PS7	1975 (6)	3,000	KM#1-6	35.00	60.00
PS8	1975 (3)	2,000	KM#12-14	—	1,400
PS9	1976 (6)	3,500	KM#1-6	37.00	50.00
PS10	1977 (6)	3,500	kM#1-6	—	50.00
PS11	1978 (6)	4,000	KM#1-6	—	60.00
PS12	1979 (7)	3,500	KM#1-6, 17.1	—	120
PS13	1980 (7)	14,000	KM#1-6, 17.2	64.00	90.00
PS14	1981 (6)	30,000	KM#1b-2b, 3a-6a, .925 Silver	82.00	100
PS15	1982 (6)	20,000	KM#1-5, 6a	52.00	50.00
PS16	1983 (6)	15,000	KM#1-5, 6a	52.00	50.00
PS17	1984 (6)	15,000	KM#1-5, 6a	52.00	50.00
PS18	1985 (6)	20,000	KM#49a-52a, 53.1a, 54a	40.00	50.00
PS19	1986 (6)	15,000	KM#49a-52a, 53.1a, 54a	—	48.00
PS20	1987 (6)	15,000	KM#49a-52a, 53.1a, 54c	42.00	48.00

KM#	Date	Mintage	Identification	Issue Price	Mkt Val
PS22	1988 (6)	15,000	KM#49a-52a, 53.1a, 54c	—	45.00
PS24	1989 (6)	15,000	KM#49a-52a, 53.2a, 54c	—	45.00
PS26	1990 (6)	15,000	KM#49a-52a, 53.2a, 54c	—	45.00
PS27	1990 (5)	2,000	KM#79-83	—	750
PSA28	1990 (3)	1,000	KM#95-97	—	1,700
PS28	1991 (7)	15,000	KM#49a-52a, 53.2a, 54c, 86a	—	70.00
PS29	1991 (5)	2,500	KM#87-91	—	750
PS30	1991 (2)	5,000	KM#86, 86a	—	40.00
PS33	1992 (3)	200	KM#105-107	—	1,490
PS31	1992 (7)	15,000	KM#98a-104a	—	75.00
PS32	1992 (5)	2,000	KM#108-112 Ingot	—	750
PS34	1993 (7)	15,000	KM#98a-104a	—	75.00
PS35	1993 (5)	1,500	KM#117-121 Ingot	—	775
PS36	1993 (2)	2,000	KM#115, 115a	—	50.00
PS37	1994 (7)	10,000	KM#98a-104a	—	75.00
PS38	1994 (5)	1,500	KM#128-132 Ingot	—	775
PS39	1995 (7)	10,000	KM#98a-104a	—	75.00
PS42	1995 (3)	2,689	KM#138-140	1,052	650
PS41	1995 (5)	1,500	KM#133-137 Ingot	1,718	775
PS43	1996 (7)	17,000	KM#98a-104a Ingot	—	75.00
PS44	1996 (5)	2,688	KM#144-148 Ingot	—	820
PS45	1996 (2)	2,800	KM#149, 149a	66.00	66.00
PS46	1997 (7)	20,000	KM#98a-104a Ingot	90.00	100
PS47	1997 (2)	3,800	KM#151, 151a Ingot	—	60.00
PS48	1997 (3)	888	KM#151, 151a, 152 Ingot	—	550
PS49	1997 (5)	2,200	KM#158-162	—	885
PS50	1998 (3)	1,998	KM#164-166 Ingot	—	600
PS51	1998 (7)	—	KM#98a-104a	—	100
PS52	1999 (7)	—	KM#98a-104a	—	100
PS53	2000 (7)	17,000	KM#98a-104a	74.25	100
PS54	2000 (3)	2,000	KM#174-176 Plus Ingot	—	605
PS55	2001 (2)	3,000	KM#179-180 plus copper-nickel ingot	—	85.00
PS56	2001 (3)	2,000	KM#178-180 plus copper-nickel ingot	—	605

SLOVAKIA

The Republic of Slovakia has an area of 18,923 sq. mi. (49,035 sq. km.) and a population of 4.9 million. Capital: Bratislava. Textiles, steel, and wood products are exported.

The Slovak lands were united with the Czechs and the Czechoslovak State came into existence on Oct. 28, 1918 upon the dissolution of Austro-Hungarian Empire at the close of World War I. In March 1939, the German-influenced Slovak government proclaimed Slovakia independent and Germany incorporated the Czech lands into the Third Reich as the "Protectorate of Bohemia and Moravia". A Czechoslovak government-in-exile was setup in London in July 1940. The Soviet and USA forces liberated the area by May, 1945. At the close of World War II, Communist influence increased steadily while pressure for liberalization culminated in the overthrow of the Stalinist leader Antonin Novotn'y and his associates in 1968.The Communist Party then introduced far reaching reforms which received warnings from Moscow, followed by occupation by Warsaw Pact forces resulting in stationing of Soviet forces. Mass civilian demonstrations for reform began in Nov.1989 and the Federal Assembly abolished the Communist Party's sole right to govern. New governments followed on Dec. 3 and Dec. 10 and the Czech and Slovak Federal Republic was formed. The Movement for Democratic Slovakia was apparent in the June 1992 elections with the Slovak National Council adopting a declaration of sovereignty. Later, a constitution for an independent Slovakia with the Federal Assembly voting for the dissolution of the Republic came into effect on Dec. 31, 1992, and two new republics came into being on Jan. 1, 1993.

MINT MARK

Kremnica Mint

AUTONOMOUS REPUBLIC

STANDARD COINAGE

100 Halierov = 1 Koruna Slovenska (Ks)

KM# 8 5 HALIEROV Weight: 0.9400 g. **Composition:** Zinc **Obverse:** Slovak shield **Obv. Designer:** Anton Ham **Reverse:** Large value **Rev. Designer:** S. Grosch **Edge:** Plain **Size:** 14 mm.

Date	Mintage	F	VF	XF	Unc	BU
1942	1,000,000	1.50	3.00	7.50	20.00	—

KM# 1 10 HALIEROV Weight: 1.6600 g. **Composition:** Bronze **Obverse:** Slovak shield, wreath. **Reverse:** Bratislava castle above Danube (Dunaj) and large value **Rev. Designer:** A. Peter **Size:** 16 mm.

Date	Mintage	F	VF	XF	Unc	BU
1939	15,000,000	1.50	2.00	4.00	8.00	—
1942	7,000,000	1.50	2.00	4.00	8.00	—

KM# 4 20 HALIEROV Weight: 2.5000 g. **Composition:** Bronze **Obverse:** Slovak shield, wreath. **Obv. Designer:** A. Ham **Reverse:** Nitra Castle, large value **Rev. Designer:** A. Peter **Edge:** Plain **Size:** 18 mm.

Date	Mintage	F	VF	XF	Unc	BU
1940	10,972,000	1.25	2.00	3.00	6.00	—
1941	4,028,000	1.25	2.00	3.00	6.00	—
1942	6,474,000	1.25	3.00	5.00	9.00	—

KM# 4a 20 HALIEROV Weight: 0.6500 g. **Composition:** Aluminum **Edge:** Plain **Size:** 18 mm. **Note:** Varieties exist.

Date	Mintage	F	VF	XF	Unc	BU
1942	Inc. above	1.00	1.50	2.00	4.50	—
1943	15,000,000	1.00	1.50	2.00	4.50	—

KM# 5 50 HALIEROV Weight: 3.3300 g. **Composition:** Copper-Nickel **Obverse:** Slovak shield, wreath and date below **Reverse:** Value above plow **Edge:** Plain **Size:** 20 mm.

Date	Mintage	F	VF	XF	Unc	BU
1940	Inc. above	30.00	45.00	60.00	125	—
1941	8,000,000	1.00	2.00	3.00	6.00	—

KM# 5a 50 HALIEROV Weight: 1.0000 g. **Composition:** Aluminum **Edge:** Milled **Size:** 20 mm.

Date	Mintage	F	VF	XF	Unc	BU
1943	4,400,000	1.00	1.50	2.50	5.00	—
1944	2,621,000	1.25	2.00	4.00	7.00	—

KM# 6 KORUNA Weight: 5.0000 g. **Composition:** Copper-Nickel **Obverse:** Slovak shield, wreath and date below **Reverse:** Value above plow **Edge:** Milled **Size:** 22 mm.

Date	Mintage	F	VF	XF	Unc	BU
1940	2,350,000	0.75	1.25	2.25	6.00	—
1941	11,650,000	0.50	1.00	2.00	5.00	—
1942	6,000,000	0.50	1.00	2.00	5.00	—
Note: Varieties exist of 1942, in the numeral 4						
1944	884,000	1.50	2.50	4.50	10.00	—
1945	3,321,000	0.75	1.25	2.25	6.00	—

KM# 2 5 KORUN Composition: Nickel **Obverse:** Slovak shield, wheat ears flanking, date below **Reverse:** Bust of Andrej Hlinka **Edge:** Milled **Size:** 27 mm. **Note:** Two varieties exist in the letter A in NAROD.

Date	Mintage	F	VF	XF	Unc	BU
1939	5,101,000	1.50	2.00	3.50	12.50	—

Note: Approximately 2,000,000 pieces were melted down by the Czechoslovak National Bank in 1947

KM# 9.1 10 KORUN Weight: 7.0000 g. **Composition:** 0.5000 Silver .1125 oz. ASW **Obverse:** Slovak shield within rays **Reverse:** Prince Pribina standing, flanked by bishop with church building and knight **Edge:** Plain **Size:** 29 mm. **Note:** Variety 1 - Cross atop church held by left figure.

Date	Mintage	F	VF	XF	Unc	BU
1944	1,381,000	2.00	4.00	5.00	8.00	—

KM# 9.2 10 KORUN Weight: 7.0000 g. **Composition:** 0.5000 Silver .1125 oz. ASW **Note:** Variety 2 - Without cross atop church held by left figure.

Date	F	VF	XF	Unc	BU
1944	2.50	5.00	7.00	10.00	—

KM# 3 20 KORUN Weight: 15.0000 g. **Composition:** 0.5000 Silver .2411 oz. ASW **Obverse:** State emblem, date

Reverse: Dr. Joseph Tiso bust facing right **Edge:** Milled **Size:** 31 mm.

Date	Mintage	F	VF	XF	Unc	BU
1939	200,000	5.00	10.00	15.00	30.00	—

KM# 7.1 20 KORUN Weight: 15.0000 g. **Composition:** 0.5000 Silver .2411 oz. ASW **Subject:** St. Kyrill and St. Methodius **Obverse:** State emblem, date **Reverse:** Variety 1 - Single bar cross in church at lower right **Edge:** Milled **Size:** 31 mm.

Date	Mintage	F	VF	XF	Unc	BU
1941	2,500,000	2.00	3.50	5.00	10.00	—

KM# 7.2 20 KORUN Weight: 15.0000 g. **Composition:** 0.5000 Silver .2411 oz. ASW **Reverse:** Variety 2 - Double bar cross

Date	F	VF	XF	Unc	BU
1941	4.00	6.50	9.00	15.00	—

KM# 10 50 KORUN Weight: 16.5000 g. **Composition:** 0.7000 Silver .3713 oz. ASW **Subject:** 5th Anniversary of Independence **Obverse:** Slovak shiled within wreath **Reverse:** Dr. Josef Tiso bust right **Edge:** Milled **Size:** 34 mm.

Date	Mintage	F	VF	XF	Unc	BU
1944	2,000,000	3.00	5.00	7.50	12.50	—

REPUBLIC

STANDARD COINAGE

100 Halierov = 1 Slovak Koruna (Sk)

KM# 17 10 HALIEROV Composition: Aluminum **Obverse:** Slovak shield **Reverse:** 19th century Wooden belfry from Zeuplen **Edge:** Plain **Size:** 17 mm.

Date	F	VF	XF	Unc	BU
1993	—	—	—	0.35	—
Note: Varieties of cross on state emblem					
1994	—	—	—	0.35	—
1995 In sets only	—	—	—	1.00	—
1996	—	—	—	0.35	—
1997	—	—	—	0.35	—
1998	—	—	—	0.35	—
1999	—	—	—	0.35	—
1999 Proof	—	—	—	—	—
2000	—	—	—	0.35	—
Note: In 1999 and 2000, 11,500 proofs were struck for mint sets					
2000 Proof	—	—	—	—	—
2001	—	—	—	0.35	—

KM# 18 20 HALIEROV Composition: Aluminum **Obverse:** Slovak shield **Reverse:** Tatra Mountain peak of Krivan **Edge:** Plain **Size:** 19.5 mm.

Date	Mintage	F	VF	XF	Unc	BU
1993	—	—	—	—	0.45	—
1994	—	—	—	—	0.45	—
1995 In sets only	—	—	—	—	1.00	—
1996	—	—	—	—	0.45	—
1997	—	—	—	—	0.45	—
1998	—	—	—	—	0.45	—
1999	15,710,000	—	—	—	0.45	—
2000	31,120,000	—	—	—	0.45	—
Note: In 1999 (11,500) and in 2000 (12,500) proofs were struck for proof sets						
2002	—	—	—	—	0.45	—

KM# 15 50 HALIEROV Composition: Aluminum **Obverse:** Slovak shield **Reverse:** Watch tower of Denin castle **Edge:** Plain **Size:** 22 mm.

Date	Mintage	F	VF	XF	Unc	BU
1993	—	—	—	—	0.55	—
1994 In sets only	19,900	—	—	—	1.50	—
1995 In sets only	—	—	—	—	1.50	—

KM# 35 50 HALIEROV Weight: 2.8000 g. **Composition:** Copper Plated Steel **Obverse:** Slovak shield **Reverse:** Watch tower of Denin castle **Edge:** Milled and plain **Size:** 18.7 mm.

Date	Mintage	F	VF	XF	Unc	BU
1996	—	—	—	—	0.60	—
1997 In sets only	—	—	—	—	1.50	—
1998	—	—	—	—	0.60	—
1999 In sets only	115,000	—	—	—	1.50	—
2000	20,212,000	—	—	—	0.60	—
Note: In 2000, 12,500 were struck for sets only						
2001	—	—	—	—	0.60	—

KM# 12 KORUNA Composition: Bronze Clad Steel **Obverse:** Slovak shield **Reverse:** 15th century of Madonna and Child **Edge:** Milled **Size:** 21 mm.

Date	Mintage	F	VF	XF	Unc	BU
1993	—	—	—	—	0.75	—
1994	—	—	—	—	0.75	—
1995	—	—	—	—	0.75	—
1996 In sets only	—	—	—	—	1.50	—
1997 In sets only	—	—	—	—	1.50	—
1998 In sets only	—	—	—	—	1.50	—
1999 In sets only	11,500	—	—	—	1.50	—
2000 In sets only	12,500	—	—	—	1.50	—

KM# 13 2 KORUNA Weight: 4.4000 g. **Composition:** Nickel Clad Steel **Obverse:** Slovak shield **Reverse:** 4th century B.C. Venus statue **Size:** 21.5 mm.

Date	Mintage	F	VF	XF	Unc	BU
1994	—	—	—	—	0.85	—
1995	—	—	—	—	0.85	—
1996 In sets only	—	—	—	—	2.00	—
1997 In sets only	—	—	—	—	2.00	—
1998 In sets only	—	—	—	—	2.00	—
1999 In sets only	11,500	—	—	—	2.00	—
2000 In sets only	12,500	—	—	—	2.00	—

KM# 14 5 KORUNA Weight: 5.4000 g. **Composition:** Nickel Clad Steel **Obverse:** Slovak shield **Reverse:** 1st century Celtic coin of BIATEC **Edge:** Milled **Size:** 24.75 mm.

Date	Mintage	F	VF	XF	Unc	BU
1993	—	—	—	—	1.25	—
Note: Varieties of sign artist						
1994	—	—	—	—	1.25	—
1995	—	—	—	—	1.25	—
1996 In sets only	—	—	—	—	2.00	—
1997 In sets only	—	—	—	—	2.00	—
1998 In sets only	—	—	—	—	2.00	—
1999 In sets only	11,500	—	—	—	2.00	—
2000 In sets only	—	—	—	—	2.00	—

KM# 11.1 10 KORUNA Weight: 6.6000 g. **Composition:** Brass **Obverse:** Slovak shield **Reverse:** 11th century bronze cross **Size:** 26.5 mm.

Date	Mintage	F	VF	XF	Unc	BU
1993	—	—	—	—	2.50	—
1994	—	—	—	—	2.50	—
1995	—	—	—	—	2.50	—
1996 In sets only	—	—	—	—	4.00	—
1997 In sets only	—	—	—	—	4.00	—
1998 In sets only	—	—	—	—	4.00	—
1999 In sets only	11,500	—	—	—	4.00	—
2000 In sets only	12,500	—	—	—	4.00	—

KM# 11.2 10 KORUNA Weight: 8.5000 g. **Composition:** 0.7500 Silver .2527 oz. ASW

Date		F	VF	XF	Unc	BU
1993 Proof	1,000	Value: 350				
Note: These coins are numbered and punched with an R						

KM# 16 100 KORUN Weight: 13.0000 g. **Composition:** 0.7500 Silver .3135 oz. ASW **Subject:** National Independence **Obverse:** Slovak shield **Reverse:** Map of Slovakia and three doves **Edge:** Milled **Size:** 29 mm. **Note:** Mint mark: MK.

Date	Mintage	F	VF	XF	Unc	BU
1993	65,000	—	—	—	9.00	—
1993 Proof	5,000	Value: 18.00				

KM# 19 200 KORUN Weight: 20.0000 g. **Composition:** 0.7500 Silver .4823 oz. ASW **Subject:** 150th Anniversary of Slovak Language **Obverse:** Slovak shield **Reverse:** Creators of Slovak language: Hurban, Stur, and Hodza **Edge:** Plain with ornament **Size:** 34 mm. **Note:** Mint mark: MK.

Date	Mintage	F	VF	XF	Unc	BU
1993	35,000	—	—	—	15.00	—
1993 Proof	2,000	Value: 30.00				

KM# 20 200 KORUN **Weight:** 20.0000 g. **Composition:** 0.7500 Silver .4823 oz. ASW **Subject:** 200th Anniversary - Birth of Jan Kollar **Obverse:** State emblem, value, date **Reverse:** Windswept theatre mask **Edge Lettering:** SLAVME SLAVNE SLAVU SLAVOV SLAVNYCH **Size:** 34 mm. **Note:** Mint mark: MK.

Date	Mintage	F	VF	XF	Unc	BU
1993	35,000	—	—	—	15.00	—
1993 Proof	2,000	Value: 35.00				

KM# 23 200 KORUN **Weight:** 20.0000 g. **Composition:** 0.7500 Silver .4823 oz. ASW **Subject:** 50th Anniversary - D-Day **Obverse:** State emblem, value, date, stylized linden leaves **Reverse:** Emblem of 312th Czechoslovak squadron **Edge Lettering:** SLOVACI PROTI FASISMU **Size:** 34 mm.

Date	Mintage	F	VF	XF	Unc	BU
1994	35,000	—	—	—	20.00	—
1994 Proof	2,600	Value: 45.00				

KM# 21 200 KORUN **Weight:** 20.0000 g. **Composition:** 0.7500 Silver .4823 oz. ASW **Subject:** 100th Anniversary - Olympic Committee **Obverse:** Olympic rings, state emblem **Reverse:** Value, hockey player **Edge:** Snowflakes **Size:** 34 mm.

Date	Mintage	F	VF	XF	Unc	BU
1994	45,000	—	—	—	15.00	—
1994 Proof	3,000	Value: 32.50				

KM# 22 200 KORUN **Weight:** 20.0000 g. **Composition:** 0.7500 Silver .4823 oz. ASW **Subject:** 100th Anniversary - Birth of poet and painter Janko Alexy **Obverse:** State emblem, value, head of young girl in winter **Reverse:** Bust of Janko Alexy **Edge:** Plain with ornament **Size:** 34 mm. **Note:** Mint mark: MK.

Date	Mintage	F	VF	XF	Unc	BU
1994	31,500	—	—	—	15.00	—
1994 Proof	2,500	Value: 35.00				

KM# 24 200 KORUN **Weight:** 20.0000 g. **Composition:** 0.7500 Silver .4823 oz. ASW **Subject:** 200th Anniversary - Birth of Pavol Jozef Safarik **Obverse:** State emblem, date **Reverse:** bust of Slovak scientist, Pavol Jozef Safarik **Edge Lettering:** ZAKLADATEL VEDECKEJ SLAVISTIKY **Size:** 34 mm. **Note:** Mint mark: MK.

Date	Mintage	F	VF	XF	Unc	BU
1995	23,500	—	—	—	15.00	—
1995 Proof	1,500	Value: 37.50				

KM# 25 200 KORUN **Weight:** 20.0000 g. **Composition:** 0.7500 Silver .4823 oz. ASW **Subject:** 100th Anniversary - Birth of Mikulas Galanda **Obverse:** State emblem, mother with child **Reverse:** Head of Mikulas Galanda **Edge Lettering:** MIKULAS GALANDA - MALIAR A GRAFIK **Size:** 34 mm.

Date	Mintage	F	VF	XF	Unc	BU
1995	23,500	—	—	—	15.00	—
1995 Proof	1,500	Value: 30.00				

KM# 26 200 KORUN **Weight:** 20.0000 g. **Composition:** 0.7500 Silver .4823 oz. ASW **Subject:** European Environmental Protection **Obverse:** State emblem, woodpecker feeding young **Reverse:** Two storks and a swallow, value **Edge Lettering:** ENCY 1995 (3 fish) **Size:** 34 mm.

Date	Mintage	F	VF	XF	Unc	BU
1995	28,000	—	—	—	15.00	—
1995 Proof	2,000	Value: 40.00				

KM# 27 200 KORUN **Weight:** 20.0000 g. **Composition:** 0.7500 Silver .4823 oz. ASW **Subject:** Centennial of Bratislava Electric Tram **Obverse:** State emblem, value **Reverse:** Two tram cars **Edge Lettering:** HLAVNE NADRAZIE TEREZIANSKA STVRT **Size:** 34 mm.

Date	Mintage	F	VF	XF	Unc	BU
1995	27,500	—	—	—	15.00	—
1995 Proof	1,600	Value: 40.00				

KM# 33 200 KORUN **Weight:** 20.0000 g. **Composition:** 0.7500 Silver .4823 oz. ASW **Subject:** Centennial - Mountain Railway to Strba Lake **Obverse:** State emblem, value, date **Reverse:** Locomotive and passenger car at foot of Tatra mountain **Edge Lettering:** VYSOKE TATRY VYSOKE TATRY **Size:** 34 mm.

Date	Mintage	F	VF	XF	Unc	BU
1996	22,000	—	—	—	15.00	—
1996 Proof	1,500	Value: 32.50				

KM# 34 200 KORUN **Weight:** 20.0000 g. **Composition:** 0.7500 Silver .4823 oz. ASW **Subject:** 200th Anniversary - Birth of Moric Benovsky **Obverse:** State emblem, clipper ship **Reverse:** Portrait of Benovsky, value **Edge Lettering:** IN ADVERSIS ET PROSPERIS **Size:** 34 mm.

Date	Mintage	F	VF	XF	Unc	BU
1996	21,400	—	—	—	15.00	—
1996 Proof	2,000	Value: 40.00				

KM# 30 200 KORUN **Weight:** 20.0000 g. **Composition:** 0.7500 Silver .4823 oz. ASW **Subject:** 200th Anniversary - Birth of Samuel Jurkovic **Obverse:** State emblem, date **Reverse:** Head of Samuel Jurkovic **Edge Lettering:** V SLUZBACH NARODA **Size:** 34 mm. **Note:** Mint mark: MK.

Date	Mintage	F	VF	XF	Unc	BU
1996	26,000	—	—	—	15.00	—
1996 Proof	1,600	Value: 37.50				

KM# 31 200 KORUN **Weight:** 20.0000 g. **Composition:** 0.7500 Silver .4823 oz. ASW **Subject:** Olympic Games **Obverse:** State emblem, Olympic rings, date **Reverse:** Oval track and greek column **Edge Lettering:** V DUCHU ODKAZU PIERRA DE COUBERTINA **Size:** 34 mm. **Note:** Mint mark: MK.

Date	Mintage	F	VF	XF	Unc	BU
1996	23,000	—	—	—	16.50	—
1996 Proof	1,700	Value: 35.00				

KM# 32 200 KORUN **Weight:** 20.0000 g. **Composition:** 0.7500 Silver .4823 oz. ASW **Subject:** 100th Anniversary - Birth of Jozef Ciger Hronsky **Obverse:** State emblem, value **Reverse:** Half face of Ciger and sun **Edge Lettering:** NIET KRAJSICH SLOV AKO SKUTKY **Size:** 34 mm. **Note:** Mint mark: MK.

Date	Mintage	F	VF	XF	Unc	BU
1996	21,000	—	—	—	15.00	—
1996 Proof	1,500	Value: 32.50				

KM# 37 200 KORUN **Weight:** 20.0000 g. **Composition:** 0.7500 Silver .4823 oz. ASW **Subject:** 150th Anniversary - Birth of Svetozar Hurban Vajansky 1847-1916 **Obverse:** State emblem, value, date **Reverse:** Head of Svetozar Hurban Vajansky **Edge Lettering:** POLITIK SPISOVATEL KRITIK NOVINAR **Size:** 34 mm.

Date	Mintage	F	VF	XF	Unc	BU
1997	17,400	—	—	—	15.00	—
1997 Proof	1,800	Value: 35.00				

KM# 38 200 KORUN **Weight:** 20.0000 g. **Composition:** 0.7500 Silver .4823 oz. ASW **Subject:** Banska Stiavnica - UNESCO **Obverse:** State emblem, value, head gear tower **Reverse:** Baroque building in Banska Stiavnica **Edge Lettering:** PATRIMOINE MODIAL **Size:** 34 mm.

Date	Mintage	F	VF	XF	Unc	BU
1997	15,000	—	—	—	15.00	—
1997 Proof	1,500	Value: 37.50				

KM# 40 200 KORUN **Weight:** 20.0000 g. **Composition:** 0.7500 Silver .4823 oz. ASW **Subject:** 200th Anniversary - Birth of Stefan Moyzes, 1797-1997 **Obverse:** Stylized national emblem in tree form **Reverse:** Face of Moyzes, book, value **Edge Lettering:** PRVY PREDSEDA MATICE SLOVENSKEJ **Size:** 34 mm.

Date	Mintage	F	VF	XF	Unc	BU
1997	—	—	—	—	15.00	—
1997 Proof	1,500	Value: 35.00				

KM# 41 200 KORUN **Weight:** 20.0000 g. **Composition:** 0.7500 Silver .4823 oz. ASW **Subject:** 50th Anniversary - Slovak National Gallery **Obverse:** Madonna and child **Reverse:** Daughters of King Lycomed **Edge Lettering:** GOTIKA A BAROK V ZBIERKACH SNG **Size:** 34 mm.

Date	Mintage	F	VF	XF	Unc	BU
1998	15,000	—	—	—	15.00	—
1998 Proof	1,600	Value: 30.00				

KM# 42 200 KORUN **Weight:** 20.0000 g. **Composition:** 0.7500 Silver .4823 oz. ASW **Subject:** 150th Anniversary - 1st Railroad in Slovakia **Obverse:** State emblem, value, train emerging from tunnel **Reverse:** Bratislava Castle and locomotive **Edge Lettering:** 150 ROKOV ZELEZNIC NA SLOVENSKU

Date	Mintage	F	VF	XF	Unc	BU
1998	14,000	—	—	—	15.00	—
1998 Proof	1,800	Value: 32.50				

KM# 43 200 KORUN **Weight:** 20.0000 g. **Composition:** 0.7500 Silver .4823 oz. ASW **Subject:** 150th Anniversary - Slovak Revolt of 1848 **Obverse:** State emblem, value, date, seal of Slovenska Narodni Rada **Reverse:** Slovak warrior **Edge Lettering:** ZA NARODNU SLOBODU

Date	Mintage	F	VF	XF	Unc	BU
1998	12,000	—	—	—	15.00	—
1998 Proof	1,500	Value: 37.50				

KM# 44 200 KORUN **Weight:** 20.0000 g. **Composition:** 0.7500 Silver .4823 oz. ASW **Subject:** UNESCO World Heritage site **Obverse:** St. Martin's Cathedral towers **Reverse:** Spis Castle and gothic window arch **Edge Lettering:** PATRIMONIE MONDIAL WORLD HERITAGE **Size:** 34 mm.

Date	Mintage	F	VF	XF	Unc	BU
1998	13,500	—	—	—	15.00	—
1998 Proof	1,500	Value: 35.00				

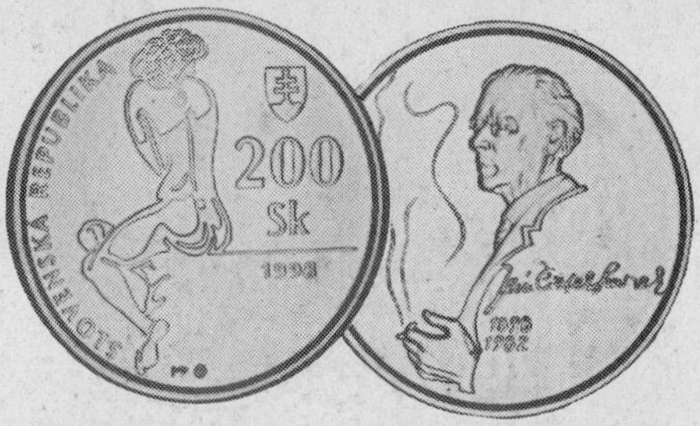

KM# 45 200 KORUN **Weight:** 20.0000 g. **Composition:** 0.7500 Silver .4823 oz. ASW **Subject:** Centennial - Birth of Jan Smrek **Obverse:** Seated female figure **Reverse:** Bust of Jan Smrek **Edge Lettering:** BASNIK JAN SMREK 100 VYROCIE NARODENIA **Size:** 34 mm.

Date	Mintage	F	VF	XF	Unc	BU
1998	13,400	—	—	—	15.00	—
1998 Proof	1,500	Value: 35.00				

KM# 48 200 KORUN **Weight:** 20.0000 g. **Composition:** 0.7500 Silver .4823 oz. ASW **Subject:** 150th Anniversary - Birth of Pavol Orszagh Hviezdoslav **Obverse:** Portrait of face made with treetops **Reverse:** Portrait of the artist **Edge Lettering:** HEROLD SVITAJUCICH CASOV **Size:** 34 mm.

Date	Mintage	F	VF	XF	Unc	BU
1999	12,700	—	—	—	15.00	—
1999 Proof	1,400	Value: 35.00				

KM# 49 200 KORUN **Weight:** 20.0000 g. **Composition:** 0.7500 Silver .4823 oz. ASW **Subject:** 50th Anniversary - Slovac Philharmonic **Obverse:** Pipe organ above national arms **Reverse:** Reduta building bay window **Edge Lettering:** HUDBA-UNIVERZALNA REC LUDSTVA **Size:** 34 mm. **Note:** Mint mark: MK.

Date	Mintage	F	VF	XF	Unc	BU
1999	12,700	—	—	—	15.00	—
1999 Proof	1,400	Value: 35.00				

KM# 55 200 KORUN **Weight:** 20.0000 g. **Composition:** 0.7500 Silver .4823 oz. ASW **Subject:** Juraj Fandly **Obverse:** Radiant book above arms **Reverse:** Portrait writing **Edge Lettering:** NIE SILOU ANI MOCOU, ALE MOJIM DUCHM **Size:** 33.9 mm.

Date	Mintage	F	VF	XF	Unc	BU
2000	—	—	—	—	15.00	—
2000 Proof	1,600	Value: 35.00				

KM# 59 200 KORUN **Weight:** 20.0000 g. **Composition:** 0.7500 Silver .4823 oz. ASW **Subject:** Alexander Dubeck **Obverse:** National arms and tree **Reverse:** Portrait **Edge Lettering:** "BUDSKOST SLOBODA DEMOKRACIA" **Size:** 34 mm.

Date	Mintage	F	VF	XF	Unc	BU
2001	12,800	—	—	—	15.00	—
2001 Proof	3,000	Value: 30.00				

KM# 62 200 KORUN **Weight:** 20.3500 g. **Composition:** 0.7500 Silver 0.4907 oz. ASW **Subject:** UNESCO World Heritage site **Obverse:** Log building **Reverse:** Wooden tower and denomination **Edge Lettering:** WORLD HERITAGE PATRIMONE MONDIAL **Size:** 34 mm.

Date	Mintage	F	VF	XF	Unc	BU
2002 Proof	2,800	Value: 35.00				

KM# 28 500 KORUN **Weight:** 33.6300 g. **Composition:** 0.9250 Silver 1.0001 oz. ASW **Subject:** Slovensky Raj National Park **Obverse:** State emblem, date, value, flowers **Reverse:** Machovy waterfall in gorge Vysny Kysel **Edge Lettering:** OCHRANA PRIRODY A. KRAJINY **Size:** 40 mm.

Date	Mintage	F	VF	XF	Unc	BU
1994	28,000	—	—	—	35.00	—
1994 Proof	2,400	Value: 45.00				

KM# 39 500 KORUN **Weight:** 33.6300 g. **Composition:** 0.9250 Silver 1.0001 oz. ASW **Subject:** Pieninsky National Park **Obverse:** Swallowtail butterfly **Edge Lettering:** OCHRANA PRIRODY A KRAJINY **Size:** 40 mm.

Date	Mintage	F	VF	XF	Unc	BU
1997	14,500	—	—	—	45.00	—
1997 Proof	1,700	Value: 65.00				

KM# 47 500 KORUN **Weight:** 33.6300 g. **Composition:** 0.9250 Silver 1.0001 oz. ASW **Subject:** Tatransky National Park **Obverse:** Two tatran chamois and Leontopodium flowers **Reverse:** Value, flower gentian **Edge Lettering:** OCHRANA PRIRODY A KRAJINY **Size:** 40 mm.

Date	Mintage	F	VF	XF	Unc	BU
1999	12,000	—	—	—	40.00	—
1999 Proof	1,400	Value: 60.00				

KM# 50 500 KORUN **Weight:** 33.6300 g. **Composition:** 0.9250 Silver 1.0001 oz. ASW **Subject:** 500th Anniversary - First Thalers of Kremnica **Obverse:** Mining scene **Reverse:** Old coin designs and city view **Edge Lettering:** GULDINER-PREDCHODCA TOLIARA **Size:** 40 mm.

Date	Mintage	F	VF	XF	Unc	BU
1999	12,400	—	—	—	40.00	—
1999 Proof	1,400	Value: 60.00				

KM# 53 500 KORUN **Weight:** 33.6300 g. **Composition:** 0.9250 Silver 1.0001 oz. ASW **Subject:** 250th Anniversary - Dealth of Samuel Mikovini **Obverse:** Allegorical scene and map **Reverse:** Portrait and cartographic instruments **Edge Lettering:** KARTOGRAF - MATEMATIK - STAVITEL **Size:** 40 mm.

Date	Mintage	F	VF	XF	Unc	BU
2000	—	—	—	—	37.50	—
2000 Proof	1,500	Value: 60.00				

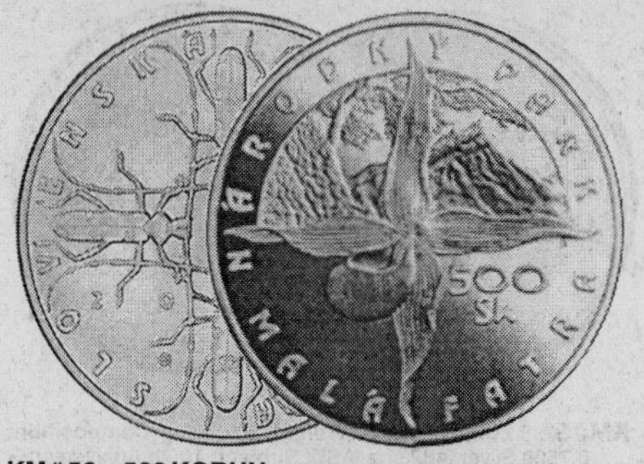

KM# 56 500 KORUN **Weight:** 33.6300 g. **Composition:** 0.9250 Silver 1.0001 oz. ASW **Subject:** Mala Fatra National Park **Obverse:** National arms center of insect cross. **Reverse:** Orchid with mountain background. **Edge Lettering:** OCHRANA PRIRODY A KRAJINY. **Size:** 40 mm.

Date	Mintage	F	VF	XF	Unc	BU
2001	—	—	—	—	37.50	—
2001 Proof	1,800	Value: 60.00				

KM# 57 500 KORUN **Weight:** 31.1035 g. **Composition:** 0.9990 Silver 1.0000 oz. ASW **Subject:** Third Millennium **Obverse:** "The Universe" **Reverse:** Three hands **Edge:** Plain, triangular shape **Shape:** Triangular **Size:** 45 mm.

Date	Mintage	F	VF	XF	Unc	BU
2001	13,000	—	—	—	40.00	—
2001 Proof	4,000	Value: 60.00				

KM# 58 500 KORUN **Series:** Third Millennium **Obverse:** "The Universe" **Reverse:** Three hands **Edge:** Plain, triangula shape **Shape:** Triangular **Size:** 50 mm. **Note:** 31.1035, .999 Silver, 1.0000 oz ASW with 6,2200, .999 Gold, .1998 oz AGV and .3100, .999 Platinum, .0100 oz APW inserts.

Date	Mintage	F	VF	XF	Unc	B
2001 Proof	8,000	Value: 400				

KM# 63 1000 KORUN **Weight:** 62.2070 g. **Composition:** 0.9990 Silver 1.998 oz. ASW **Subject:** 10th Anniversary of Republic **Obverse:** National arms between hands **Reverse:** Denomination above map **Edge:** Interrupted reeding, square **Shape:** Square **Size:** 43.6 mm.

Date	Mintage	F	VF	XF	Unc	BU
2003 Proof	12,000	Value: 60.00				

KM#51 2000 KORUN **Weight:** 124.4140 g. **Composition:** 0.9990 Silver 3.9960 oz. ASW **Subject:** 2000 Bi-millennium **Obverse:** National arms, denomination, historical scenes **Reverse:** Jesus with churches **Edge:** Plain **Size:** 65 mm.

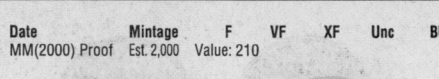

Date	Mintage	F	VF	XF	Unc	BU
MM(2000) Proof	Est. 2,000	Value: 210				

KM#29 5000 KORUN **Weight:** 7.0000 g. **Composition:** 0.9000 Gold .2025 oz. AGW **Subject:** 1100th Anniversary - Death of Great Moravian King Svatopluk **Obverse:** State emblem, value, date **Reverse:** Head of Svatopluk and ruin of castle Devin **Edge:** Milled **Size:** 24 mm.

Date	Mintage	F	VF	XF	Unc	BU
1994 Proof	5,000	Value: 500				

KM#36 5000 KORUN **Weight:** 9.5000 g. **Composition:** 0.9000 Gold .2749 oz. AGW **Subject:** Banska Stiavnica Historical Mines - UNESCO **Obverse:** State emblem, value, date **Edge:** Milled **Size:** 26 mm.

Date	Mintage	F	VF	XF	Unc	BU
1997 Proof	8,000	Value: 325				

KM#46 5000 KORUN **Weight:** 9.5000 g. **Composition:** 0.9000 Gold .2749 oz. AGW **Subject:** Spissky Castle - UNESCO **Obverse:** State emblem, lion, date **Edge:** Milled **Size:** 26 mm.

Date	Mintage	F	VF	XF	Unc	BU
1998 Proof	6,000	Value: 300				

KM#54 5000 KORUN **Weight:** 9.5000 g. **Composition:** 0.9000 Gold .2749 oz. AGW **Subject:** 500th Anniversary - Kremnica Mint **Obverse:** Hungarian coin design **Reverse:** Hungarian coin design **Edge:** Reeded **Size:** 26 mm.

Date	Mintage	F	VF	XF	Unc	BU
ND(1999) Proof	5,500	Value: 325				

KM#61 5000 KORUN **Weight:** 9.5000 g. **Composition:** 0.9000 Gold 0.2749 oz. AGW **Subject:** Vikolinec Village **Obverse:** Enclosed communal well. **Reverse:** Window and fence. **Edge:** Reeded. **Size:** 26 mm.

Date	Mintage	F	VF	XF	Unc	BU
2002 Proof	7,200	Value: 325				

KM# 52 10000 KORUN **Weight:** 19.0000 g. **Composition:** 0.9000 Gold .5498 oz. AGW **Subject:** 2000 Bi-millennium **Obverse:** National arms, denomination, historical scenes **Reverse:** Jesus with churches **Edge:** Milled **Size:** 34 mm. **Note:** Similar to 2000 Korun, KM#51.

Date	Mintage	F	VF	XF	Unc	BU
MM(2000) Proof	Est. 3,500	Value: 600				

KM# 64 10000 KORUN **Weight:** 18.8350 g. **Composition:** Bi-Metallic **Subject:** 10th Anniversary of the Republic **Obverse:** Girls portrait above national arms **Reverse:** Bratislava castle above denomination **Edge:** Interrupted reeding **Shape:** Square **Size:** 29.5 mm.

Date	Mintage	F	VF	XF	Unc	BU
2003 Proof	6,000	Value: 750				

ESSAIS

KM#	Date	Mintage	Identification	Mkt Val
E1	1939	—	20 Korun. 0.5000 Silver. KM#7	—
E2	1941	—	10 Korun. 0.5000 Silver. KM#9.1	—

MINT SETS

KM#	Date	Mintage	Identification	Issue Price	Mkt Val
MS1	1993 (7)	—	KM#11.1-15, 17-18, plus medal	—	12.00
MS2	1994 (7)	—	KM#11.1-15, 17-18, plus medal	—	12.00
MS3	1995 (7)	—	KM#11.1-15, 17-18, plus medal	—	12.00

SLOVENIA

The Republic of Slovenia is located northwest of Yugoslavia in the valleys of the Danube River. It has an area of 7,819 sq. mi. and a population of *1.9 million. Capital: Ljubljana. Agriculture is the main industry with large amounts of hops and fodder crops grown as well as many varieties of fruit trees. Sheep raising, timber production and the mining of mercury from one of the country's oldest mines are also very important to the economy.

Slovenia was important as a land route between Europe and the eastern Mediterranean region. The Roman Catholic Austro-Hungarian Empire gained control of the area during the 14th century and retained its dominance until World War I. The United Kingdom of the Serbs, Croats and Slovenes (Yugoslavia) was founded in 1918 and consisted of various groups of South Slavs.

In 1929, King Alexander declared his assumption of power temporarily, however he was assassinated in 1934.His son Peter's regent, Prince Paul tried to settle internal problems, however, the Slovenes denounced the agreement he made. He resigned in 1941 and Peter assumed the throne. Peter was forced to flee when Yugoslavia was occupied. Slovenia was divided between Germany and Italy. Even though Yugoslavia attempted to remain neutral, the Nazis occupied the country and were resisted by guerilla armies, most notably Marshal Josif Broz Tito.

Under Marshal Tito, the Constitution of 1946 established6 constituent republics which made up Yugoslavia. Each republic was permitted Liberties under supervision of the Communist Party.

In Oct. 1989 the Slovene Assembly voted a constitutional amendment giving it the right to secede from Yugoslavia. A referendum on Dec. 23, 1990 resulted in a majority vote for independence, which was formally declared on Dec. 26.

On June 25 Slovenia declared independence, but agreed to suspend this for3 months at peace talks sponsored by the EC. Federal troops moved into Slovenia on June 27 to secure Yugoslavia's external borders, but after some fighting withdrew by the end of July. The 3-month moratorium agreed at the EC having expired, Slovenia (and Croatia) declared their complete independence of the Yugoslav federation on Oct.8, 1991.

MINT MARKS

Based on last digit in date.
(K) - Kremnitz (Slovakia): open 4, upturned 5
(BP) - Budapest (Hungary): closed 4, downturned 5

MONETARY SYSTEM

100 Stotinov = 1 Tolar

REPUBLIC

STANDARD COINAGE

100 Stotinow = 1 Tolar

KM# 7 10 STOTINOV **Composition:** Aluminum **Reverse:** Salamandar - larval stage **Note:** Varieties exist.

Date	Mintage	F	VF	XF	Unc	BU
1992	—	—	—	0.35	—	
1992 Proof	1,000	Value: 3.00				
1993	—	—	—	0.35	—	
1993 Proof	1,000	Value: 3.00				
1994 In sets only	—	—	—	—	3.00	
1994 Proof	1,000	Value: 3.00				
1995 In sets only	—	—	—	—	3.00	
1995 Proof	1,000	Value: 3.00				

KM# 8 20 STOTINOV **Composition:** Aluminum **Obverse:** Similar to 10 Stotinov, KM#7 **Reverse:** Long-eared owl

Date	Mintage	F	VF	XF	Unc	BU
1992 Minor reverse varieties exist	—	—	—	0.40	—	
1992 Proof	1,000	Value: 4.00				
1993 Minor reverse varieties exist	—	—	—	0.40	—	
1993 Proof	1,000	Value: 4.00				
1994 In sets only	—	—	—	—	4.00	
1994 Proof	1,000	Value: 4.00				
1995 In sets only	—	—	—	—	4.00	
1995 Proof	1,000	Value: 4.00				

KM# 3 50 STOTINOV **Composition:** Aluminum **Reverse:** Bee

Date	Mintage	F	VF	XF	Unc	BU
1992 Minor reverse varieties exist	—	—	0.10	0.50	—	
1992 Proof	1,000	Value: 6.00				
1993	—	—	0.10	0.50	—	
1993 Proof	1,000	Value: 6.00				
1994 In sets only	—	—	—	—	6.00	
1994 Proof	1,000	Value: 6.00				
1995	—	—	0.10	0.50	—	
1995 In sets only	—	—	—	—	6.00	
1995 Proof	1,000	Value: 6.00				
1996	—	—	0.10	0.50	—	
1996 Proof	Est. 3,000	Value: 6.00				

KM# 4 TOLAR **Composition:** Brass **Reverse:** 3 brown trout **Note:** Varieties exist.

Date	Mintage	F	VF	XF	Unc	BU
1992	—	—	0.20	0.85	—	
1992 Proof	1,000	Value: 5.00				
1993	—	—	0.20	0.85	—	
1993 Proof	1,000	Value: 5.00				
1994 (K)	—	—	—	0.75	—	
Note: 4 open to the top						
1994 (K) In sets only	—	—	—	—	5.00	
Note: 4 open to right						
1994 (K) Proof	1,000	Value: 5.00				
Note: 4 open to right						
1994 (BP)	—	—	—	0.75	—	
1995 (K)	—	—	—	0.75	—	
1995 (K) In sets only	—	—	—	—	5.00	
1995 (K) Proof	1,000	Value: 5.00				
1995 (BP)	—	—	—	0.75	—	
1996	—	—	—	0.75	—	
1996 Proof	Est. 3,000	Value: 5.00				
1997	—	—	—	0.75	—	
1998	—	—	—	0.75	—	
1999	—	—	—	0.75	—	
2000	—	—	—	0.75	—	

KM#5 2 TOLARJA **Composition:** Brass **Reverse:** Barn swallow in flight **Note:** Minor varieties exist for each date after 1998.

Date	Mintage	F	VF	XF	Unc	BU
1992	—	—	0.25	0.85	—	
1992 Proof	1,000	Value: 7.00				
1993	—	—	0.25	0.85	—	
1993 Proof	1,000	Value: 7.00				
1994 (K)	—	—	—	0.75	—	
Note: 4 open to the top						
1994 (K) In sets only	—	—	—	—	7.00	
Note: 4 open to right						
1994 (K) Proof	1,000	Value: 7.00				
Note: 4 open to right						
1994 (BP)	—	—	—	0.75	—	
1995 (K)	—	—	—	0.75	—	
1995 (K) In sets only	—	—	—	—	7.00	
1995 (K) Proof	1,000	Value: 7.00				
1995 (BP)	—	—	—	0.75	—	
1996	—	—	—	0.75	—	
1996 Proof	1,000	Value: 7.00				
1997	—	—	—	0.75	—	
1998	—	—	—	0.75	—	
1999	—	—	—	0.75	—	
2000	—	—	—	0.75	—	

KM# 6 5 TOLARJEV **Composition:** Brass **Reverse:** Head and horns of ibex **Note:** Varieties exist.

Date	Mintage	F	VF	XF	Unc	BU
1992	—	—	0.35	1.00	—	
1992 Proof	1,000	Value: 8.00				
1993	—	—	0.35	1.00	—	
1993 Proof	1,000	Value: 8.00				
1994 (K)	—	—	—	0.85	—	
Note: 4 open to the top						
1994 (K) In sets only	—	—	—	—	8.00	
Note: 4 open to right						
1994 (K) Proof	1,000	Value: 8.00				
Note: 4 open to right						
1994 (BP)	—	—	—	0.85	—	
1995	—	—	—	0.85	—	
1995 2 tip	—	—	—	0.85	—	
1996	—	—	—	0.85	—	
1996 Proof	Est. 3,000	Value: 8.00				
1997	—	—	—	0.85	—	
1998	—	—	—	0.85	—	
1999	—	—	—	0.85	—	

KM# 9 5 TOLARJEV **Weight:** 6.4000 g. **Composition:** Brass **Subject:** 400th Anniversary - Battle of Sisek **Obverse:** Value, date **Reverse:** City view, arms, 1593, Andrej G. Turjaski **Size:** 26 mm.

Date	Mintage	F	VF	XF	Unc	BU
1993	100,000	—	—	—	1.65	—

KM# 12 5 TOLARJEV **Weight:** 6.4000 g. **Composition:** Brass **Subject:** 300th Anniversary - Establishment of Operosorum Labacensium Academy **Obverse:** Value, date **Reverse:** Beehive and bees, 1693-1993 **Size:** 26 mm.

Date	Mintage	F	VF	XF	Unc	BU
1993	100,000	—	—	—	1.75	—

KM# 15 5 TOLARJEV **Composition:** Brass **Subject:** 50th Anniversary - Slovenian Bank **Reverse:** Linden leaf an seed pod

Date	Mintage	F	VF	XF	Unc	B
1994	100,000	—	—	—	1.65	-

KM# 16 5 TOLARJEV **Composition:** Brass **Subject** 1,000th Anniversary - Glagolitic Alphabet **Reverse:** Feath

Date	Mintage	F	VF	XF	Unc	BU
1994	200,000	—	—	—	1.65	—

KM# 21 5 TOLARJEV Composition: Brass **Series:** F.A.O. **Subject:** 50th Anniversary - F.A.O.

Date	Mintage	F	VF	XF	Unc	BU
1995	500,000	—	—	—	1.65	—

KM# 22 5 TOLARJEV Composition: Brass **Subject:** 50th Anniversary - Defeat of Fascism

Date	Mintage	F	VF	XF	Unc	BU
1995	200,000	—	—	—	1.65	—

KM# 26 5 TOLARJEV Composition: Brass **Subject:** Aljazev Stolp

Date	Mintage	F	VF	XF	Unc	BU
1995	200,000	—	—	—	1.65	—

KM# 29 5 TOLARJEV Composition: Brass **Subject:** 100th Anniversary - First Railway in Slovenia

Date	Mintage	F	VF	XF	Unc	BU
1996	—	—	—	—	1.65	—
1996 Proof	Inc. above	Value: 8.00				

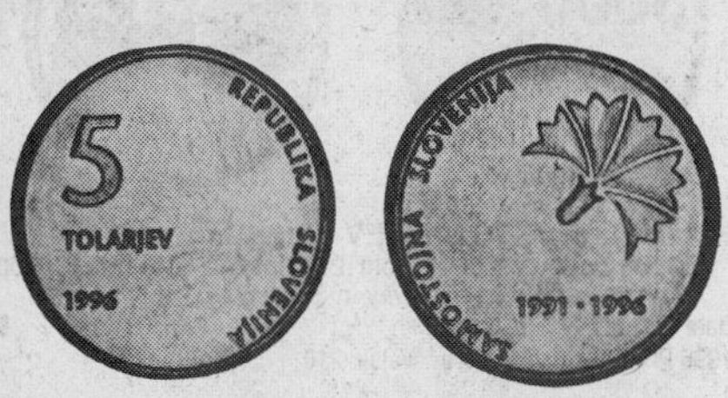

KM# 32 5 TOLARJEV Composition: Brass **Subject:** 5th Anniversary of Independence **Reverse:** Stylized flower

Date	Mintage	F	VF	XF	Unc	BU
1996	200,000	—	—	—	1.65	—
1996 Proof	—	Value: 8.00				

KM# 33 5 TOLARJEV Composition: Brass **Series:** Olympics **Subject:** Olympics Centennial **Reverse:** Gymnast

Date	Mintage	F	VF	XF	Unc	BU
1996	—	—	—	—	1.65	—
1996 Proof	Est. 3,000	Value: 8.00				

KM# 38 5 TOLARJEV Composition: Brass **Subject:** Ziga Zois **Obverse:** Denomination

Date	Mintage	F	VF	XF	Unc	BU
1997	200,000	—	—	—	1.65	—

KM# 41 10 TOLARJEV Weight: 5.7500 g. **Composition:** Copper Nickel

Date	F	VF	XF	Unc	BU
2000	—	—	—	3.00	—
2001	—	—	—	3.00	—
2002	—	—	—	3.00	—

KM# 42 100 TOLARJEV Weight: 9.1000 g. **Composition:** Copper-Nickel **Subject:** 10th Anniversary of Slovenia and the Tolar **Obverse:** Denomination **Reverse:** Tree rings and inscription **Edge:** Reeded **Size:** 28 mm.

Date	Mintage	F	VF	XF	Unc	BU
2001	500,000	—	—	—	3.00	—

KM# 1 500 TOLARJEV Weight: 15.0000 g. **Composition:** 0.9250 Silver .4461 oz. ASW **Subject:** 1st Anniversary of Independence **Note:** Eight minor obverse and reverse varieties exist.

Date	Mintage	F	VF	XF	Unc	BU
1991 Proof	50,000	Value: 35.00				

KM# 10 500 TOLARJEV Weight: 15.0000 g. **Composition:** 0.9250 Silver .4461 oz. ASW **Subject:** Battle of Sisek

Date	Mintage	F	VF	XF	Unc	BU
1993 Proof	Est. 5,000	Value: 28.50				

KM# 13 500 TOLARJEV Weight: 15.0000 g. **Composition:** 0.9250 Silver .4461 oz. ASW **Subject:** 300th Anniversary - Establishment of Operasorum Labacensium Academy

Date	Mintage	F	VF	XF	Unc	BU
1993 Proof	5,000	Value: 28.50				

KM# 17 500 TOLARJEV Weight: 15.0000 g. **Composition:** 0.9250 Silver .4461 oz. ASW **Subject:** 50th Anniversary - Slovenian Bank

Date	Mintage	F	VF	XF	Unc	BU
1994 Proof	5,000	Value: 28.50				

KM# 19 500 TOLARJEV Weight: 15.0000 g. **Composition:** 0.9250 Silver .4461 oz. ASW **Subject:** 1000th Anniversary - Bishop Abraham - Glagolistic Alphabet

Date	Mintage	F	VF	XF	Unc	BU
1994 Proof	3,000	Value: 28.50				

KM# 23 500 TOLARJEV Weight: 15.0000 g. **Composition:** 0.9250 Silver .4461 oz. ASW **Subject:** 50th Anniversary - Defeat of Fascism

Date	Mintage	F	VF	XF	Unc	BU
1995 Proof	3,000	Value: 28.50				

KM# 25 500 TOLARJEV Weight: 15.0000 g. **Composition:** 0.9250 Silver .4461 oz. ASW **Series:** F.A.O. **Subject:** 50th Anniversary - F.A.O.

Date	Mintage	F	VF	XF	Unc	BU
1995 Proof	3,000	Value: 28.50				

KM# 27 500 TOLARJEV Weight: 15.0000 g. **Composition:** 0.9250 Silver .4461 oz. ASW **Subject:** 100th Anniversary - Aljazev Stolp

Date	Mintage	F	VF	XF	Unc	BU
1995 Proof	3,000	Value: 28.50				

KM# 30 500 TOLARJEV Weight: 15.0000 g. **Composition:** 0.9250 Silver .4461 oz. ASW **Subject:** 100th Anniversary - First Railway in Slovenia

Date	Mintage	F	VF	XF	Unc	BU
1996 Proof	3,000	Value: 28.50				

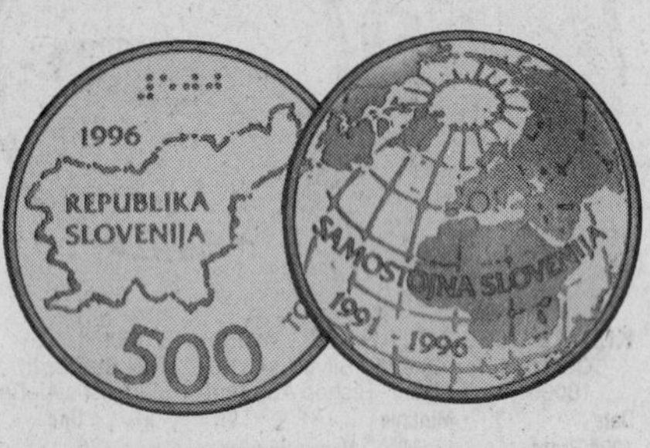

KM# 34 500 TOLARJEV Weight: 15.0000 g. **Composition:** 0.9250 Silver .4461 oz. ASW **Subject:** 5th Anniversary of Independence **Obverse:** Map of Slovenia **Reverse:** Globe

Date	Mintage	F	VF	XF	Unc	BU
1996 Proof	3,000	Value: 28.50				

KM# 36 500 TOLARJEV Weight: 15.0000 g. **Composition:** 0.9250 Silver .4461 oz. ASW **Series:** Olympics **Reverse:** Gymnast

Date	Mintage	F	VF	XF	Unc	BU
1996 Proof	3,000	Value: 27.50				

KM# 39 500 TOLARJEV Weight: 15.0000 g. **Composition:** 0.9250 Silver .4461 oz. ASW **Subject:** Zois Ziga

Date	Mintage	F	VF	XF	Unc	BU
1997 Proof	3,000	Value: 28.50				

KM# 45 500 TOLARJEV Weight: 8.5400 g. **Composition:** Copper-Nickel **Subject:** Soccer **Obverse:** Denomination **Reverse:** Soccer player and radiant sun **Edge:** Reeded **Size:** 28.1 mm.

Date	F	VF	XF	Unc	BU
2002	—	—	—	5.50	—

KM# 43 2000 TOLARJEV Weight: 15.0000 g. **Composition:** 0.9250 Silver 0.4461 oz. ASW **Subject:** 10th Anniversary of Slovenia and the Tolar **Obverse:** Denomination **Reverse:** Tree rings and inscription **Edge:** Reeded **Size:** 32 mm.

Date	Mintage	F	VF	XF	Unc	BU
2001	3,000	—	—	—	35.00	—

KM# 46 2500 TOLARJEV Weight: 15.0000 g. **Composition:** 0.9250 Silver 0.4461 oz. ASW **Subject:** Soccer **Obverse:** Denomination **Reverse:** Soccer player and radiant sun **Edge:** Reeded **Size:** 32 mm.

Date		F	VF	XF	Unc	BU
2002 Proof	—	Value: 35.00				

KM# 2.1 5000 TOLARJEV Weight: 7.0000 g. **Composition:** 0.9000 Gold .2025 oz. AGW **Subject:** 1st Anniversary of Independence **Reverse:** Bird's beak at center of spiral

Date	Mintage	F	VF	XF	Unc	BU
1991 Proof	4,000	Value: 225				

KM# 2.2 5000 TOLARJEV Weight: 7.0000 g. **Composition:** 0.9000 Gold .2025 oz. AGW **Reverse:** Bird's beak lower than center of spiral

Date	Mintage	F	VF	XF	Unc	BU
1991 Proof	Inc. above	Value: 200				

KM# 11 5000 TOLARJEV Weight: 7.0000 g. **Composition:** 0.9000 Gold .2025 oz. AGW **Subject:** Battle of Sisek

Date	Mintage	F	VF	XF	Unc	BU
1993 Proof	Est. 2,000	Value: 200				

KM# 14 5000 TOLARJEV Weight: 7.0000 g. **Composition:** 0.9000 Gold .2025 oz. AGW **Subject:** 300th Anniversary - Establishment of Operosorum Labacensium Academy

Date	Mintage	F	VF	XF	Unc	BU
1993 Proof	2,000	Value: 210				

KM# 18 5000 TOLARJEV Weight: 7.0000 g. **Composition:** 0.9000 Gold .2025 oz. AGW **Subject:** 50th Anniversary - Slovenian Bank

Date	Mintage	F	VF	XF	Unc	BU
1994 Proof	2,000	Value: 200				

KM# 20 5000 TOLARJEV Weight: 7.0000 g. **Composition:** 0.9000 Gold .2025 oz. AGW **Subject:** 1000th Anniversary - Bishop Abraham - Glagolitic Alphabet

Date	Mintage	F	VF	XF	Unc	BU
1994 Proof	1,000	Value: 200				

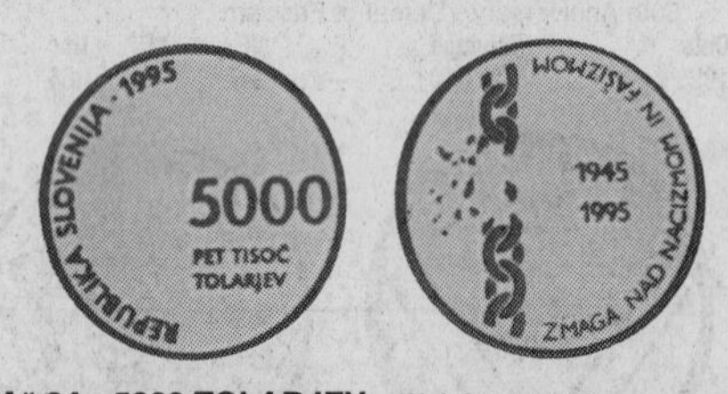

KM# 24 5000 TOLARJEV Weight: 7.0000 g. **Composition:** 0.9000 Gold .2025 oz. AGW **Subject:** 50th Anniversary - Defeat of Fascism

Date	Mintage	F	VF	XF	Unc	BU
1995 Proof	1,000	Value: 200				

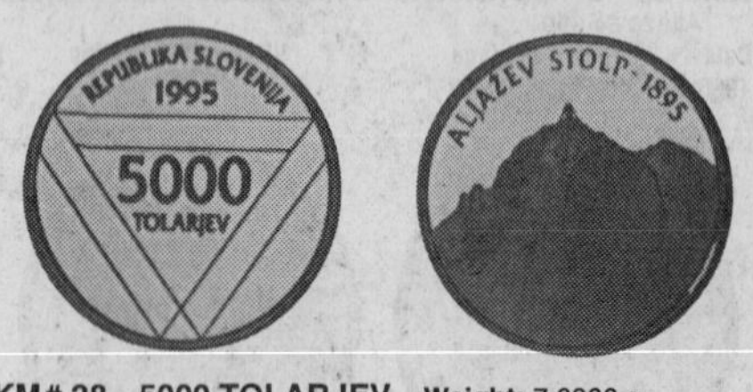

KM# 28 5000 TOLARJEV Weight: 7.0000 g. **Composition:** 0.9000 Gold .2025 oz. AGW **Subject:** Aljazev Stolp and Mountain Summit

Date	Mintage	F	VF	XF	Unc	BU
1995 Proof	1,000	Value: 200				

KM# 31 5000 TOLARJEV Weight: 7.0000 g. **Composition:** 0.9000 Gold .2025 oz. AGW **Subject:** 100th Anniversary - First Railway in Slovenia

Date	Mintage	F	VF	XF	Unc	B
1996 Proof	1,000	Value: 210				

KM# 35 5000 TOLARJEV Weight: 7.0000 g. **Composition:** 0.9000 Gold .2025 oz. AGW **Subject:** 5th Anniversary of Independence **Reverse:** 5-petal flower

Date	Mintage	F	VF	XF	Unc
1996 Proof	1,000	Value: 200			

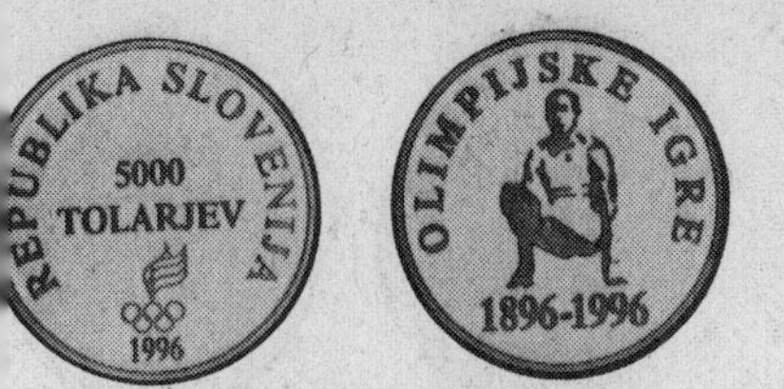

1# 37 5000 TOLARJEV **Weight:** 7.0000 g. **Composition:** 0.9000 Gold .2025 oz. AGW **Series:** Olympics **Reverse:** Gymnast

e	Mintage	F	VF	XF	Unc	BU
6 Proof	1,000	Value: 225				

1# 40 5000 TOLARJEV **Weight:** 7.0000 g. **Composition:** 0.9000 Gold .2025 oz. AGW **Subject:** Zois Ziga

e	Mintage	F	VF	XF	Unc	BU
7 Proof	1,000	Value: 200				

1# 44 20000 TOLARJE **Weight:** 7.0000 g. **Composition:** 0.9000 Gold 0.2025 oz. AGW **Subject:** 10th Anniversary of Slovenia and the Tolar **Obverse:** Denomination **Reverse:** Tree rings and inscription **Edge:** Reeded **Size:** 24 mm.

te	Mintage	F	VF	XF	Unc	BU
)1 Proof	1,000	Value: 275				

TOKEN COINAGE

100 Vinar = 1 Lipa

M# Tn1 VINAR **Composition:** Copper-Zinc

te	Mintage	F	VF	XF	Unc	BU
90	6,000	—	—	—	20.00	—

M# Tn4 2/1000 LIPE **Composition:** Copper-Zinc

te	F	VF	XF	Unc	BU
91	—	—	—	—	—

Note: Fewer than five known

M# Tn11 0.02 LIPE **Composition:** Brass

te	F	VF	XF	Unc	BU
92	—	—	—	4.00	—

M# Tn5 0.02 LIPE **Composition:** Brass **Note:** Some examples of KM#Tn5 have been found struck over Yugoslavian 10 Para 1990, KM#139.

te	F	VF	XF	Unc	BU
92	—	—	—	2.00	—

KM# Tn6 0.05 LIPE **Composition:** Brass

Date	Mintage	F	VF	XF	Unc	BU
1991	5,000	—	—	—	4.00	—

KM# Tn7 0.10 LIPE **Composition:** Brass

Date	Mintage	F	VF	XF	Unc	BU
1991	5,000	—	—	—	5.00	—

KM# Tn8 0.20 LIPE **Composition:** Copper-Nickel

Date	Mintage	F	VF	XF	Unc	BU
1991	5,000	—	—	—	7.00	—

KM# Tn9 0.50 LIPE **Composition:** Copper-Nickel

Date	F	VF	XF	Unc	BU
1991	—	—	—	—	—

KM# Tn2 LIPA **Weight:** 11.0000 g. **Composition:** 0.9250 Silver .3272 oz. ASW **Subject:** Dr. France Preseren

Date	Mintage	F	VF	XF	Unc	BU
1990 Proof	10,000	Value: 50.00				

KM# Tn10 10 LIP **Weight:** 6.7500 g. **Composition:** 0.9000 Gold .1953 oz. AGW **Reverse:** Ivan Cankar bust facing left

Date	Mintage	F	VF	XF	Unc	BU
1991 Proof	273	Value: 325				

KM# Tn3 50 LIP **Weight:** 11.0000 g. **Composition:** 0.9000 Gold .3183 oz. AGW **Reverse:** Ivan Cankar bust facing forward

Date	Mintage	F	VF	XF	Unc	BU
1990 Proof	400	Value: 400				

MINT SETS

KM#	Date	Mintage	Identification	Issue Price	Mkt Val
MS1	1992 (6)	—	KM3-8	—	8.00
MS2	1992 (5)	15,000	KM4-8	—	7.00
MS3	1993 (6)	—	KM3-8	—	8.00
MS4	1993 (5)	15,000	KM4-8	—	7.00
MS6	1994	1,000	KM3-8	—	35.00
MS7	1995	1,000	KM3-8	—	35.00
MS5	1996 (9)	300	KM4-6, 29-30, 32-34, 36	—	45.00

PROOF SETS

KM#	Date	Mintage	Identification	Issue Price	Mkt Val
PS1	1991 (2)	—	KM1, 2.2	—	325
PS2	1992 (6)	1,000	KM3-8	—	35.00
PS3	1992 (5)	1,000	KM4-8	—	30.00
PS4	1993 (6)	1,000	KM3-8	—	35.00
PS5	1993 (5)	1,000	KM4-8	—	30.00
PS7	1994	1,000	KM3-8	—	35.00
PS8	1995	1,000	KM3-8	—	35.00
PS6	1996 (9)	3,000	KM4-6, 29-30, 32-34, 36	—	125

SOLOMON ISLANDS

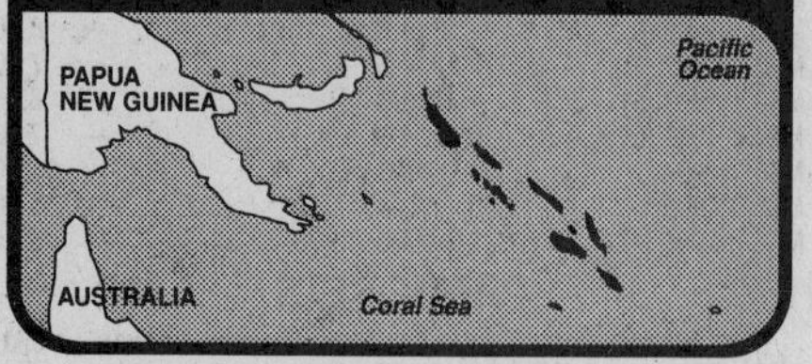

The Solomon Islands, located in the southwest Pacific east of Papua New Guinea, has an area of 10,983 sq. mi. (28,450 sq. km.) and a population of *324,000. Capital: Honiara. The most important islands of the Solomon chain are Guadalcanal (scene of some of the fiercest fighting of World War II), Malaitia, New Georgia, Florida, Vella Lavella, Choiseul, Rendova, San Cristobal, the Lord Howe group, the Santa Cruz islands, and the Duff group. Copra is the only important cash crop but it is hoped that timber will become an economic factor.

The Solomon Islands were discovered by Spanish navigator Alvaro de Mendana in 1567, and in 1569 he made an unsuccessful attempt to colonize them. European know-ledge of the group would not be completed until the end of the 18th century. Germany declared a protectorate over the northern Solomons in 1885. The British protectorate over the southern Solomons was established in 1893. In1899 Germany transferred its claim to all Solomon Islands except Buka and Bougainville to Great Britain in exchange for recognition of German claims in Western Samoa. Australia occupied the two German islands in 1914, and administered them after1920.

The Japanese invaded the Solomons during 1942-43,but were driven out by an American counteroffensive after a series of bloody clashes.

Following World War II, the islands returned to the status of a British protectorate. In 1976 the protectorate was abolished, and the Solomons became a self-governing dependency. Full independence was achieved on July 7,1978. Solomon Islands is a member of the Common-wealth of Nations. Queen Elizabeth II is Head of State, as Queen of the Solomon Islands.

RULERS

British, until 1978

MINT MARKS

FM - Franklin Mint, U.S.A.*

NOTE: From 1977-1985 the Franklin Mint produced coinage in up to 3 different qualities. Qualities of issue are designated in ( ) after each date and are defined as follows:

(M) MATTE - Normal circulation strike or a dull finish produced by sandblasting special uncirculated (polish finish) or proof quality dies.

(U) - SPECIAL UNCIRCULATED - Polished or proof-like in appearance without any frosted features.

(P) PROOF - The highest quality obtainable having mirror-like fields and frosted features.

MONETARY SYSTEM

100 Cents = 1 Dollar

COMMONWEALTH NATION

STANDARD COINAGE

100 Cents = 1 Dollar

KM# 1 CENT **Composition:** Bronze **Series:** F.A.O. **Reverse:** Food bowl

Date	Mintage	F	VF	XF	Unc	BU
1977	1,828,000	—	—	0.10	0.20	—
1977FM (M)	6,000	—	—	—	0.50	—
1977FM (U)	—	—	—	—	2.00	—
1977FM (P)	14,000	Value: 1.00				
1978FM (M)	6,000	—	—	—	0.50	—
1978FM (U)	544	—	—	—	2.00	—
1978FM (P)	5,122	Value: 1.00				
1979FM (M)	6,000	—	—	—	0.50	—
1979FM (U)	677	—	—	—	2.00	—
1979FM (P)	2,845	Value: 1.50				
1980FM (M)	6,000	—	—	—	0.50	—
1980FM (U)	624	—	—	—	2.00	—
1980FM (P)	1,031	Value: 1.50				
1981	—	—	—	—	0.50	—
1981FM (M)	6,000	—	—	—	0.50	—
1981FM (U)	212	—	—	—	2.00	—
1981FM (P)	448	Value: 1.50				
1982FM (U)	—	—	—	—	2.00	—
1982FM (P)	—	Value: 1.50				
1983FM (M)	—	—	—	—	0.50	—
1983FM (U)	200	—	—	—	3.00	—
1983FM (P)	—	Value: 1.50				

KM# 1a CENT **Composition:** Bronze Plated Steel **Series:** F.A.O. **Reverse:** Food bowl

Date	F	VF	XF	Unc	BU
1985	—	—	—	0.35	—

KM# 24 CENT **Composition:** Bronze Plated Steel **Series:** F.A.O. **Reverse:** Food bowl

Date	F	VF	XF	Unc	BU
1987	—	—	—	0.35	—
1996	—	—	—	0.35	—

KM# 2 2 CENTS **Composition:** Bronze **Subject:** Eagle Spirit of Malaita

Date		F	VF	XF	Unc	BU
1977		—	—	0.10	0.25	—
1977FM (M)		—	—	—	0.75	—
1977FM (U)		—	—	—	3.00	—
1977FM (P)	14,000	Value: 1.50				
1978FM (M)		—	—	—	0.75	—
1978FM (U)		—	—	—	3.00	—
1978FM (P)	5,122	Value: 1.50				
1979FM (M)		—	—	—	0.75	—
1979FM (U)		—	—	—	3.00	—
1979FM (P)	2,845	Value: 2.00				
1980FM (M)		—	—	—	0.75	—
1980FM (U)		—	—	—	3.00	—
1980FM (P)		—	—	—	2.00	—
1981FM (M)		—	—	—	0.75	—
1981FM (U)		—	—	—	3.00	—
1981FM (P)	448	Value: 2.00				
1982FM (U)		—	—	—	3.00	—
1982FM (P)	—	Value: 2.00				
1983FM (M)		—	—	—	0.75	—
1983FM (U)		—	—	—	3.00	—
1983FM (P)	—	Value: 2.00				

KM# 2a 2 CENTS **Composition:** Bronze Plated Steel **Subject:** Eagle Spirit of Malaita

Date	F	VF	XF	Unc	BU
1985	—	—	—	0.35	—

KM# 25 2 CENTS **Composition:** Bronze Plated Steel **Obverse:** Similar to Cent, KM#24

Date	F	VF	XF	Unc	BU
1987	—	—	—	0.35	—
1996	—	—	—	0.35	—

KM# 3 5 CENTS **Composition:** Copper-Nickel **Subject:** Santa Ysabel - native mask

Date	Mintage	F	VF	XF	Unc	BU
1977	1,200,000	—	0.10	0.20	0.40	—
1977FM (U)	—	—	—	—	3.00	—
1977FM (M)	6,000	—	—	—	1.50	—
1977FM (P)	14,000	Value: 2.00				
1978FM (M)	6,000	—	—	—	1.50	—
1978FM (U)	544	—	—	—	3.00	—
1978FM (P)	5,122	Value: 2.00				
1979FM (M)	6,000	—	—	—	1.50	—
1979FM (U)	677	—	—	—	3.00	—
1979FM (P)	2,845	Value: 2.50				
1980FM (M)	6,000	—	—	—	1.50	—
1980FM (U)	624	—	—	—	3.00	—
1980FM (P)	1,031	Value: 2.50				
1981	—	—	—	—	—	—
1981FM (M)	6,000	—	—	—	1.50	—
1981FM (U)	212	—	—	—	3.00	—
1981FM (P)	448	Value: 2.50				
1982FM (U)	—	—	—	—	3.00	—
1982FM (P)	—	Value: 2.50				
1983FM (M)	—	—	—	—	1.50	—
1983FM (U)	200	—	—	—	4.00	—
1983FM (P)	—	Value: 2.50				
1985	—	—	—	—	0.30	—

KM# 26 5 CENTS **Composition:** Copper-Nickel **Obverse:** Similar to Cent, KM#24

Date	F	VF	XF	Unc	BU
1988	—	—	—	0.40	—
1993	—	—	—	0.40	—
1996	—	—	—	0.40	—

KM# 4 10 CENTS **Composition:** Copper-Nickel **Subject:** Ngorieru - sea spirit

Date	Mintage	F	VF	XF	Unc
1977	3,600,000	—	0.15	0.25	0.50
1977FM (M)	6,000	—	—	—	2.00
1977FM (U)	—	—	—	—	5.00
1977FM (P)	14,000	Value: 3.00			
1978FM (M)	6,000	—	—	—	2.00
1978FM (U)	544	—	—	—	5.00
1978FM (P)	5,122	Value: 3.00			
1979FM (M)	6,000	—	—	—	2.00
1979FM (U)	677	—	—	—	5.00
1979FM (P)	2,845	Value: 4.00			
1980FM (M)	6,000	—	—	—	2.00
1980FM (U)	624	—	—	—	5.00
1980FM (P)	1,031	Value: 4.00			
1981FM (M)	6,000	—	—	—	2.00
1981FM (U)	212	—	—	—	5.00
1981FM (P)	448	Value: 4.00			
1982FM (U)	—	—	—	—	5.00
1982FM (P)	—	Value: 4.00			
1983FM (M)	—	—	—	—	2.00
1983FM (U)	200	—	—	—	6.00
1983FM (P)	—	Value: 4.00			

KM# 27 10 CENTS **Composition:** Copper-Nickel **Subject:** Ngorieru - sea spirit

Date	F	VF	XF	Unc
1988	—	—	—	0.65

KM# 27a 10 CENTS **Composition:** Nickel Plated Ste **Subject:** Ngorieru - sea spirit

Date	F	VF	XF	Unc
1990	—	—	—	0.65
1993	—	—	—	0.65
1996	—	—	—	0.65

KM# 5 20 CENTS **Composition:** Copper-Nickel **Subject:** Malaita pendant design

Date	Mintage	F	VF	XF	Unc
1977	3,000,000	—	0.20	0.35	0.80
1977FM (M)	5,000	—	—	—	3.00
1977FM (P)	14,000	Value: 4.00			
1978	293,000	—	0.25	0.50	1.00
1978FM (M)	5,000	—	—	—	3.00
1978FM (U)	544	—	—	—	5.50
1978FM (P)	5,122	Value: 4.00			
1979FM (M)	5,000	—	—	—	3.00
1979FM (U)	677	—	—	—	5.00
1979FM (P)	2,845	Value: 4.00			
1980FM (M)	5,000	—	—	—	3.00
1980FM (U)	624	—	—	—	5.00
1980FM (P)	1,031	Value: 4.00			
1981FM (M)	5,000	—	—	—	3.00
1981FM (U)	212	—	—	—	6.00
1981FM (P)	448	Value: 4.00			
1982FM (U)	—	—	—	—	6.00
1982FM (P)	—	Value: 4.00			
1983FM (M)	—	—	—	—	3.00
1983FM (U)	200	—	—	—	7.00
1983FM (P)	—	Value: 4.00			

 # 28 20 CENTS **Composition:** Nickel Plated Steel
Subject: Malaita pendant design

te	F	VF	XF	Unc	BU
89	—	—	—	0.85	—
96	—	—	—	0.85	—
97	—	—	—	0.85	—

M# 23 50 CENTS **Composition:** Copper-Nickel
Subject: 10th anniversary of independence

te	F	VF	XF	Unc	BU
88	—	—	—	2.50	—

M# 29 50 CENTS **Composition:** Copper-Nickel **Note:** Circulation type.

te	F	VF	XF	Unc	BU
90	—	—	—	2.50	—
96	—	—	—	2.50	—
97	—	—	—	2.50	—

M# 6 DOLLAR **Composition:** Copper-Nickel **Subject:** Nusu-Nusu head - sea spirit

te	Mintage	F	VF	XF	Unc	BU
77	1,500,000	—	1.00	1.50	2.50	—
77FM (M)	3,000	—	—	—	5.00	—
77FM (P)	14,000	Value: 6.50				
78FM (M)	3,000	—	—	—	5.00	—
78FM (U)	544	—	—	—	9.00	—
78FM (P)	5,122	Value: 6.50				
79FM (M)	3,000	—	—	—	5.00	—
79FM (U)	677	—	—	—	9.00	—
79FM (P)	2,845	Value: 7.50				
80FM (M)	3,000	—	—	—	5.00	—
80FM (U)	624	—	—	—	9.00	—
80FM (P)	1,031	Value: 8.50				
81FM (M)	3,000	—	—	—	5.00	—
81FM (U)	212	—	—	—	10.00	—
81FM (P)	448	Value: 8.50				
82FM (U)	—	—	—	—	10.00	—
82FM (P)	—	Value: 8.50				
83FM (M)	—	—	—	—	5.00	—
83FM (U)	200	—	—	—	12.00	—
83FM (P)	—	Value: 8.50				

KM# 19 DOLLAR **Composition:** Copper-Nickel **Series:** 1984 Olympics **Reverse:** Runners

Date	Mintage	F	VF	XF	Unc	BU
1984	5,000	—	—	—	18.00	—

KM# 30 DOLLAR **Composition:** Copper-Nickel
Subject: 50th anniversary of Pearl Harbor

Date	F	VF	XF	Unc	BU
1991	—	—	—	7.00	—

KM# 30a DOLLAR **Weight:** 28.2800 g. **Composition:** 0.9250 Silver .8411 oz. ASW **Subject:** 50th anniversary of Pearl Harbor

Date	Mintage	F	VF	XF	Unc	BU
1991 Proof	Est. 25,000	Value: 27.50				

KM# 35 DOLLAR **Composition:** Copper-Nickel
Subject: 50th anniversary - Battle of the Coral Sea

Date	F	VF	XF	Unc	BU
1992	—	—	—	7.00	—

KM# 35a DOLLAR **Weight:** 28.2800 g. **Composition:** 0.9250 Silver .8411 oz. ASW **Subject:** 50th anniversary - Battle of the Coral Sea

Date	Mintage	F	VF	XF	Unc	BU
1992 Proof	Est. 25,000	Value: 35.00				

KM# 41 DOLLAR **Composition:** Copper-Nickel
Subject: 50th anniversary - Battle of Guadalcanal

Date	F	VF	XF	Unc	BU
1992	—	—	—	7.00	—

KM# 41a DOLLAR **Weight:** 28.2800 g. **Composition:** 0.9250 Silver .8411 oz. ASW **Subject:** 50th anniversary - Battle of Guadalcanal

Date	Mintage	F	VF	XF	Unc	BU
1992 Proof	Est. 25,000	Value: 30.00				

KM# 72 DOLLAR **Weight:** 13.4500 g. **Composition:** Copper-Nickel **Obverse:** Queen's portrait by Maklouf **Reverse:** Depiction of "Nusu-Nusu" **Edge:** Plain, seven sided **Size:** 30 mm.

Date	F	VF	XF	Unc	BU
1996	—	—	—	2.50	—

KM# 64 DOLLAR **Composition:** Copper-Nickel
Subject: World Wildlife Fund - conserving nature **Obverse:** Queen's portrait **Reverse:** Fish eagle descending on prey

Date	F	VF	XF	Unc	BU
1998	—	—	—	7.50	—

KM# 64a DOLLAR **Weight:** 28.2800 g. **Composition:** 0.9250 Silver .8411 oz. ASW **Subject:** World Wildlife Fund - conserving nature **Obverse:** Queen's portrait **Reverse:** Fish eagle descending on prey

Date	F	VF	XF	Unc	BU
1998 Proof	—	Value: 35.00			

KM# 65 DOLLAR **Weight:** 32.3200 g. **Composition:** Silver **Series:** Olympics 2000 **Obverse:** Queen's head right **Reverse:** Multicolored koala swimming **Edge:** Reeded **Size:** 38.6 mm. **Note:** Struck at Valcambi.

Date	Mintage	F	VF	XF	Unc	BU
2000 Proof	50,000	Value: 15.00				

KM# 66 DOLLAR **Weight:** 32.3200 g. **Composition:** Silver **Series:** Olympics 2000 **Obverse:** Queen's head right **Reverse:** Multicolored kangaroo sail boarding

Date	Mintage	F	VF	XF	Unc	BU
2000 Proof	50,000	Value: 15.00				

KM# 7 5 DOLLARS **Weight:** 28.2800 g. **Composition:** 0.9250 Silver .8411 oz. ASW **Obverse:** Bokolo - fossilized clam shell

Date	Mintage	F	VF	XF	Unc	BU
1977FM (U)	200	—	—	—	50.00	—
1977FM (P)	15,000	Value: 12.50				
1978FM (P)	5,148	Value: 15.00				
1979FM (P)	2,845	Value: 20.00				
1980FM (P)	1,031	Value: 22.50				
1981FM (P)	448	Value: 30.00				
1983FM (P)	339	Value: 30.00				

KM# 7a 5 DOLLARS **Composition:** Copper-Nickel **Obverse:** Bokolo - fossilized clam shell

Date	Mintage	F	VF	XF	Unc	BU
1978FM (M)	200	—	—	—	40.00	—
1978FM (U)	544	—	—	—	18.00	—
1979FM (M)	200	—	—	—	40.00	—
1979FM (U)	677	—	—	—	18.00	—
1980FM (M)	200	—	—	—	40.00	—
1980FM (U)	624	—	—	—	18.00	—
1981FM (M)	200	—	—	—	40.00	—
1981FM (U)	212	—	—	—	35.00	—
1983FM (U)	202	—	—	—	35.00	—

KM# 8 5 DOLLARS **Weight:** 28.2800 g. **Composition:** 0.9250 Silver .8411 oz. ASW **Subject:** Coronation jubilee **Obverse:** Similar to 20 Cents, KM#5

Date	Mintage	F	VF	XF	Unc	BU
1978	8,886	Value: 15.00				

KM# 13 5 DOLLARS **Composition:** Copper-Nickel **Subject:** Battle of Guadalcanal **Obverse:** Similar to 20 Cents, KM#5

Date	F	VF	XF	Unc	BU
1982FM (U)	—	—	—	25.00	—

KM# 13a 5 DOLLARS **Weight:** 28.2800 g. **Composition:** 0.9250 Silver .8411 oz. ASW **Subject:** Battle of Guadalcanal **Obverse:** Similar to 20 Cents, KM#5

Date	Mintage	F	VF	XF	Unc	BU
1982FM (P)	1,368	Value: 42.50				

KM# 15 5 DOLLARS **Weight:** 30.2800 g. **Composition:** 0.5000 Silver .4868 oz. ASW **Subject:** 30th anniversary of coronation

Date	Mintage	F	VF	XF	Unc	BU
1983FM (P)	2,944	Value: 16.50				

KM# 16 5 DOLLARS **Weight:** 28.2800 g. **Composition:** 0.9250 Silver .8411 oz. ASW **Series:** International Year of the Child

Date	Mintage	F	VF	XF	Unc	BU
1983 Proof	5,775	Value: 16.50				

KM# 22 5 DOLLARS **Weight:** 28.2800 g. **Compositi** 0.9250 Silver .8589 oz. ASW **Series:** Decade for Wome

Date	Mintage	F	VF	XF	Unc
1985 Proof	1,050	Value: 30.00			

KM# 63 5 DOLLARS **Weight:** 10.0000 g. **Compositi** 0.5000 Silver .1607 oz. ASW **Subject:** Alvaro Mendana Neyra

Date	Mintage	F	VF	XF	Unc
1994 Proof	Est. 20,000	Value: 17.50			

KM# 54 5 DOLLARS **Composition:** Copper-Nickel **Subject:** MacArthur accepting Japanese surrender

Date	F	VF	XF	Unc
1995	—	—	—	8.50

KM# 54a 5 DOLLARS **Weight:** 28.2800 g. **Composition:** 0.9250 Silver .8411 oz. ASW **Subject:** MacArthur accepting Japanese surrender **Note:** Similar 50 Dollars, KM#57.

Date	Mintage	F	VF	XF	Unc
1995 Proof	Est. 10,000	Value: 50.00			

KM# 69 5 DOLLARS **Weight:** 20.1000 g. **Compositic** 0.8000 Silver .5170 oz. ASW **Subject:** Ship of Death **Obverse:** Portrait of Queen Elizabeth II **Reverse:** Sailing ship circa 1596 **Edge:** Reeded **Size:** 33.9 mm.

Date	Mintage	F	VF	XF	Unc
1999 Proof	Est. 20,000	Value: 30.00			

KM# 67 5 DOLLARS **Weight:** 24.9100 g. **Composition:** 0.9250 Silver .7408 oz. ASW **Series:** Olympics 2000 **Obverse:** Queen's head right **Reverse:** Multicolored koala tennis player **Edge:** Reeded **Size:** 38.7 mm. **Note:** Struck at Valcambi.

Date	Mintage	F	VF	XF	Unc	BU
2000 Proof	15,000	Value: 37.50				

KM# 68 5 DOLLARS **Weight:** 24.9100 g. **Composition:** 0.9250 Silver .7408 oz. ASW **Series:** Olympics 2000 **Obverse:** Queen's head right **Reverse:** Multicolored kangaroo bicyclist

Date	Mintage	F	VF	XF	Unc	BU
2000 Proof	15,000	Value: 37.50				

KM# 10 10 DOLLARS **Composition:** Copper-Nickel **Subject:** Frigate bird **Obverse:** Similar to 20 Cents, KM#5

Date	Mintage	F	VF	XF	Unc	BU
1979FM (M)	100	—	—	—	65.00	—
1979FM (U)	777	—	—	—	20.00	—
1980FM (M)	100	—	—	—	65.00	—
1980FM (U)	624	—	—	—	20.00	—
1981FM (M)	100	—	—	—	65.00	—
1981FM (U)	212	—	—	—	25.00	—
1982FM (U)	—	—	—	—	20.00	—

KM# 10a 10 DOLLARS **Weight:** 42.2700 g. **Composition:** 0.9250 Silver 1.2571 oz. ASW **Subject:** Frigate bird **Obverse:** Similar to 20 Cents, KM#5

Date	Mintage	F	VF	XF	Unc	BU
1979FM (P)	4,670	Value: 20.00				
1980FM (P)	1,569	Value: 27.50				
1981FM (P)	593	Value: 40.00				
1982FM (P)	579	Value: 40.00				

KM# 17 10 DOLLARS **Composition:** Copper-Nickel **Subject:** 5th anniversary of independence

Date	Mintage	F	VF	XF	Unc	BU
1983FM (U)	202	—	—	—	28.00	—

KM# 17a 10 DOLLARS **Weight:** 40.5000 g. **Composition:** 0.9250 Silver 1.2045 oz. ASW **Subject:** 5th anniversary of independence

Date	Mintage	F	VF	XF	Unc	BU
1983FM (P)	425	Value: 65.00				

KM# 20 10 DOLLARS **Weight:** 33.4400 g. **Composition:** 0.9250 Silver .9946 oz. ASW **Series:** 1984 Olympics **Reverse:** Runners

Date	Mintage	F	VF	XF	Unc	BU
1984 Proof	2,500	Value: 40.00				

KM# 47 10 DOLLARS **Weight:** 31.8000 g. **Composition:** 0.9250 Silver .9457 oz. ASW **Subject:** Alvaro de Neyra

Date	F	VF	XF	Unc	BU
1991 Proof	—	Value: 22.50			

KM# 31 10 DOLLARS **Weight:** 3.1300 g. **Composition:** 0.9990 Gold .1006 oz. AGW **Subject:** 50th anniversary of Pearl Harbor

Date	Mintage	F	VF	XF	Unc	BU
1991 Proof	Est. 500	Value: 85.00				

KM# 48 10 DOLLARS **Weight:** 31.4200 g. **Composition:** 0.9250 Silver .9359 oz. ASW **Series:** 1992 Olympics **Reverse:** Runners

Date	Mintage	F	VF	XF	Unc	BU
1991 Proof	Est. 40,000	Value: 13.50				

KM# 36 10 DOLLARS **Weight:** 3.1300 g. **Composition:** 0.9990 Gold .1006 oz. AGW **Subject:** 50th anniversary - Battle of the Coral Sea

Date	Mintage	F	VF	XF	Unc	BU
1992 Proof	500	Value: 85.00				

KM# 40 10 DOLLARS **Weight:** 31.4700 g. **Composition:** 0.9250 Silver .9359 oz. ASW **Subject:** First lunar vehicle

Date	Mintage	F	VF	XF	Unc	BU
1992 Proof	Est. 10,000	Value: 28.00				

KM# 42 10 DOLLARS **Weight:** 3.1300 g. **Composition:** 0.9990 Gold .1006 oz. AGW **Subject:** 50th anniversary - Battle of Guadalcanal

Date	Mintage	F	VF	XF	Unc	BU
1992 Proof	500	Value: 85.00				

KM# 46 10 DOLLARS **Weight:** 31.4700 g. **Composition:** 0.9250 Silver .9359 oz. ASW **Subject:** 40th anniversary - Queen Elizabeth's coronation

Date	Mintage	F	VF	XF	Unc	BU
1992 Proof	Est. 50,000	Value: 22.50				

KM# 50 10 DOLLARS **Weight:** 31.4700 g. **Composition:** 0.9250 Silver .9359 oz. ASW **Series:** 1992 Olympics **Reverse:** Boxer

Date	Mintage	F	VF	XF	Unc	BU
1992 Proof	40,000	Value: 15.00				

KM# 51 10 DOLLARS **Weight:** 31.4700 g. **Composition:** 0.9250 Silver .9359 oz. ASW **Series:** Endangered Wildlife **Reverse:** Saltwater crocodile

Date	Mintage	F	VF	XF	Unc	BU
1992 Proof	Est. 10,000	Value: 35.00				

KM# 49 10 DOLLARS **Weight:** 28.2800 g. **Composition:** 0.9250 Silver .8411 oz. ASW **Subject:** 100 years as British protectorate

Date	Mintage	F	VF	XF	Unc	BU
1993 Proof	5,000	Value: 50.00				

KM# 59 10 DOLLARS **Weight:** 31.4700 g. **Composition:** 0.9250 Silver .9359 oz. ASW **Subject:** Protect Our World **Reverse:** Orchid and butterfly

Date	Mintage	F	VF	XF	Unc	BU
1993 Proof	Est. 10,000	Value: 37.50				

KM# 52 10 DOLLARS **Weight:** 28.2800 g. **Composition:** 0.9250 Silver .8411 oz. ASW **Subject:** Sailing ship "Swallow"

Date	Mintage	F	VF	XF	Unc	BU
1994 Proof	Est. 15,000	Value: 27.50				

KM# 53 10 DOLLARS **Weight:** 28.2800 g. **Composition:** 0.9250 Silver .8411 oz. ASW **Series:** 1996 Olympics **Reverse:** Relay runners

Date	Mintage	F	VF	XF	Unc	BU
1994 Proof	Est. 30,000	Value: 20.00				

KM# 55 10 DOLLARS **Weight:** 31.1300 g. **Composition:** 0.9990 Gold .1006 oz. AGW **Reverse:** Marine and armored vehicle

Date	Mintage	F	VF	XF	Unc	BU
1995 Proof	Est. 500	Value: 90.00				

KM# 71 10 DOLLARS **Weight:** 31.4400 g. **Composition:** 0.9250 Silver 0.935 oz. ASW **Subject:** Queen Mother **Obverse:** Bust of Queen Elizabeth II right. **Reverse:** Queen Mother's 1937 coronation scene. **Edge:** Reeded. **Size:** 38.5 mm.

Date		F	VF	XF	Unc	BU
1995 Proof	—	Value: 40.00				

KM# 73 10 DOLLARS **Weight:** 28.3200 g. **Composition:** 0.9250 Silver 0.8422 oz. ASW **Subject:** Queen Mother **Obverse:** Queen's portrait **Reverse:** Queen Mother and Churchill viewing bomb damge to Buckingham Palace **Edge:** Reeded **Size:** 38.5 mm.

Date		F	VF	XF	Unc	BU
2000 Proof	—	Value: 50.00				

KM# 32 25 DOLLARS **Weight:** 7.8100 g. **Composition:** 0.9990 Gold .2514 oz. AGW **Subject:** 50th anniversary - Pearl Harbor

Date	Mintage	F	VF	XF	Unc	BU
1991 Proof	Est. 3,000	Value: 175				

KM# 37 25 DOLLARS **Weight:** 7.8100 g. **Composition:** 0.9990 Gold .2514 oz. AGW **Subject:** 50th anniversary - Battle of the Coral Sea

Date	Mintage	F	VF	XF	Unc	BU
1992 Proof	Est. 3,000	Value: 175				

KM# 43 25 DOLLARS **Weight:** 7.8100 g. **Composition:** 0.9990 Gold .2514 oz. AGW **Subject:** 50th anniversary - Battle of Guadalcanal

Date	Mintage	F	VF	XF	Unc	BU
1992 Proof	Est. 3,000	Value: 175				

KM# 56 25 DOLLARS **Weight:** 7.8100 g. **Composition:** 0.9990 Gold .2514 oz. AGW **Subject:** 50th anniversary - Iwo Jima flag raising

Date	Mintage	F	VF	XF	Unc	BU
1995 Proof	Est. 2,500	Value: 220				

KM# 33 50 DOLLARS **Weight:** 15.6000 g. **Composition:** 0.9990 Gold .5016 oz. AGW **Subject:** 50th anniversary - Pearl Harbor

Date	Mintage	F	VF	XF	Unc	BU
1991 Proof	Est. 500	Value: 390				

KM# 38 50 DOLLARS **Weight:** 15.6000 g. **Composition:** 0.9990 Gold .5016 oz. AGW **Subject:** 50th anniversary - Battle of the Coral Sea

Date	Mintage	F	VF	XF	Unc	B
1992 Proof	Est. 500	Value: 390				

KM# 44 50 DOLLARS **Weight:** 15.6000 g. **Composition:** 0.9990 Gold .5016 oz. AGW **Subject:** 50t anniversary - Battle of Guadalcanal

Date	Mintage	F	VF	XF	Unc
1992 Proof	Est. 500	Value: 390			

KM# 60 50 DOLLARS **Weight:** 7.7600 g. **Compositic** 0.5830 Gold .1458 oz. AGW **Series:** Endangered Wildlif **Reverse:** Sanford's eagle

Date	Mintage	F	VF	XF	Unc
1993 Proof	Est. 3,000	Value: 150			

M# 61 50 DOLLARS **Weight:** 155.5175 g. **Composition:** 0.9990 Silver 5 oz. ASW **Subject:** Johannes Kepler **Size:** 65 mm. **Note:** Illustration reduced.

te	Mintage	F	VF	XF	Unc	BU
94 Proof	Est. 2,000	Value: 200				

M# 62 50 DOLLARS **Weight:** 31.4700 g. **Composition:** 0.9250 Silver .9359 oz. ASW **Subject:** MacArthur accepting Japanese surrender **Note:** Similar to 5 Dollars, KM#54.

te		F	VF	XF	Unc	BU
95 Proof	—	Value: 65.00				

M# 57 50 DOLLARS **Weight:** 15.6100 g. **Composition:** 0.9990 Gold .5016 oz. AGW **Subject:** MacArthur accepting Japanese surrender **Note:** In proof sets only.

te	Mintage	F	VF	XF	Unc	BU
95 Proof	500	Value: 425				

M# 9 100 DOLLARS **Weight:** 9.3700 g. **Composition:** 0.9000 Gold .2711 oz. AGW **Subject:** Attainment of sovereignty

ate	Mintage	F	VF	XF	Unc	BU
978FM (M)	50	—	—	—	275	—
978FM (U)	213	—	—	—	225	—
978FM (P)	3,159	Value: 185				

M# 11 100 DOLLARS **Weight:** 7.6400 g. **Composition:** 0.5000 Gold .1228 oz. AGW **Subject:** Native art

Date	Mintage	F	VF	XF	Unc	BU
1980FM (U)	50	—	—	—	200	—
1980FM (P) Proof	7,500	Value: 100				

KM# 12 100 DOLLARS **Weight:** 7.6400 g. **Composition:** 0.5000 Gold .1228 oz. AGW **Reverse:** Shark

Date	Mintage	F	VF	XF	Unc	BU
1981 Proof	675	Value: 245				

KM# 14 100 DOLLARS **Weight:** 9.3700 g. **Composition:** 0.9000 Gold .2711 oz. AGW **Subject:** Battle of Guadalcanal

Date	Mintage	F	VF	XF	Unc	BU
1982FM (P)	311	Value: 325				

KM# 18 100 DOLLARS **Weight:** 9.3700 g. **Composition:** 0.9000 Gold .2711 oz. AGW **Subject:** 5th anniversary of independence

Date	Mintage	F	VF	XF	Unc	BU
1983FM (P)	268	Value: 275				

KM# 21 100 DOLLARS **Weight:** 7.5000 g. **Composition:** 0.9170 Gold .2211 oz. AGW **Series:** 1984 Olympics **Reverse:** Weightlifter

Date	Mintage	F	VF	XF	Unc	BU
1984 Proof	500	Value: 225				

KM# 34 100 DOLLARS **Weight:** 31.2100 g. **Composition:** 0.9990 Gold 1.0035 oz. AGW **Subject:** 50th anniversary of Pearl Harbor

Date	Mintage	F	VF	XF	Unc	BU
1991 Proof	Est. 500	Value: 590				

KM# 39 100 DOLLARS **Weight:** 31.2100 g. **Composition:** 0.9990 Gold 1.0035 oz. AGW **Subject:** 50th anniversary - Battle of Coral Sea

Date	Mintage	F	VF	XF	Unc	BU
1992 Proof	Est. 500	Value: 590				

KM# 45 100 DOLLARS **Weight:** 31.2100 g. **Composition:** 0.9990 Gold 1.0035 oz. AGW **Subject:** 50th anniversary - Battle of Guadalcanal

Date	Mintage	F	VF	XF	Unc	BU
1992 Proof	Est. 500	Value: 590				

KM# 58 100 DOLLARS **Weight:** 31.2100 g. **Composition:** 0.9990 Gold 1.0035 oz. AGW **Reverse:** B-25 bomber and mushroom cloud **Note:** In proof sets only.

Date	Mintage	F	VF	XF	Unc	BU
1995 Proof	Est. 500	Value: 850				

PIEFORTS

KM# Pn1 DOLLAR **Weight:** 32.3000 g. **Composition:** Copper Nickel **Subject:** Olympics - Sailing **Obverse:** Queen's portrait with italic legends **Reverse:** Cartoon kangaroo on sailboard **Edge:** Reeded **Size:** 38.6 mm.

Date	Mintage	F	VF	XF	Unc	BU
2000 Matte	1	—	—	—	—	—

KM# Pn2 DOLLAR **Weight:** 32.3000 g. **Composition:** Copper-Nickel **Subject:** Olympics - Sailing **Obverse:** Queen's portrait with italic legends **Reverse:** Cartoon kangaroo on sailboard **Edge:** Reeded **Size:** 38.6 mm.

Date	Mintage	F	VF	XF	Unc	BU
2000 Proof	30	—	—	—	—	—

KM# Pn3 DOLLAR **Weight:** 32.3000 g. **Composition:** Copper Nickel **Subject:** Olympic - Sailing **Obverse:** Queen's portrait with italic legend **Reverse:** Multicolor cartoon kangaroo on sailboard **Edge:** Reeded **Size:** 38.6 mm.

Date	F	VF	XF	Unc	BU
2000 Proof	—	—	—	—	—

Note: Mintage included in Pn2

PIEFORTS

KM#	Date	Mintage	Identification	Mkt Val
P1	1983	62	5 Dollars. KM16.	100

MINT SETS

KM#	Date	Mintage	Identification	Issue Price	Mkt Val
MS1	1978 (7)	544	KM1-6, 7a	22.00	32.50
MS2	1979 (8)	677	KM1-6, 7a, 10	31.00	42.50
MS3	1980 (8)	624	KM1-6, 7a, 10	35.00	50.00
MS4	1981 (8)	212	KM1-6, 7a, 10	36.00	60.00
MS5	1982 (8)	—	KM1-6, 10, 13	36.00	65.00
MS6	1983 (8)	192	KM1-6, 7a, 17	36.00	72.00

PROOF SETS

KM#	Date	Mintage	Identification	Issue Price	Mkt Val
PS1	1977 (7)	72,748	KM1-7	40.00	28.00
PSA2	1977 (6)	—	KM1-6	—	16.50
PS2	1978 (7)	5,122	KM1-7	45.00	32.50
PS3	1979 (8)	2,845	KM1-7, 10a	77.00	65.00
PS4	1980 (8)	1,031	KM1-7, 10a	135	70.00
PS5	1981 (8)	448	KM1-7, 10a	137	80.00
PS6	1982 (8)	—	KM1-6, 10a, 13a	87.00	100
PS7	1983 (8)	334	KM1-7, 17a	137	90.00
PS8	1991 (4)	500	KM31-34	1,650	1,250
PS9	1991 (2)	—	KM30a, 32	—	250
PS10	1992 (4)	500	KM36-39	1,595	1,250
PS11	1992 (4)	500	KM42-45	1,595	1,250
PS12	1995 (4)	500	KM55-58	1,595	1,595

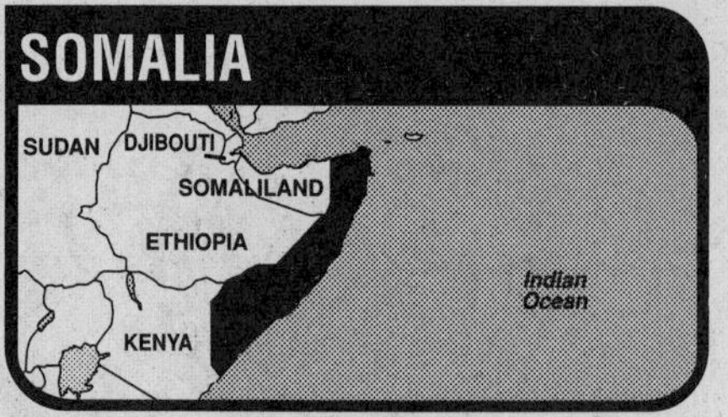

The Somali Democratic Republic, comprised of the former Italian Somaliland, is located on the coast of the eastern projection of the African continent commonly referred to as the "Horn". It has an area of 178,201 sq. mi. (461,657 sq. km.) and a population of *8.2 million. Capital: Mogadishu. The economy is pastoral and agricultural. Livestock, bananas and hides are exported.

The area of the British Somaliland Protectorate was known to the Egyptians at least 1,500 years B.C., and was occupied by the Arabs and Portuguese before British sea captains obtained trading and anchorage rights in 1827. The land of sandy clay and sporadic rainfall acquired a strategic importance with the opening of the Suez Canal in 1869. After negotiating treaties with the tribes, Britain declared the area a protectorate in 1888. Italy acquired Italian Somaliland in 1895 by purchase from the Sultan of Zanzibar. Britain occupied Italian Somaliland in 1941 and administered it until April 1, 1950, when it was returned to Italy as a U.N. trusteeship. The British Somaliland protectorate became independent on June 26, 1960. Five days later it joined with Italian Somaliland to form the Somali Republic. The country was under a revolutionary military regime installed Oct. 21, 1969. After eleven years of civil war rebel forces fought their way into the capital. A.M. Muhammad became president in Aug. 1991, but inter-factional fighting continued. A UN-sponsored truce was signed in March 1992 and a peace plan and pact was signed Jan. 15, 1993.

The Northern Somali National Movement (SNM) declared a secession of the northwestern Somaliland Republic on May 17, 1991, which is not recognized by the Somali Democratic Republic.

TITLES

Al-Jumhuriya(t)as - Somaliya(t)

RULERS

Italian, until 1941
British, until 1950

MINT MARKS

Az - Arezzo (Italy)
R – Rome

MONETARY SYSTEM

100 Centesimi = 1 Somalo

U. N. TRUSTEESHIP UNDER ITALY

STANDARD COINAGE

100 Centesimi = 1 Somalo

KM# 1 CENTESIMO **Composition:** Copper

Date	Mintage	F	VF	XF	Unc	BU
AH1369 (1950)	4,000,000	—	0.20	0.50	2.00	3.00

KM# 2 5 CENTESIMI **Composition:** Copper

Date	Mintage	F	VF	XF	Unc	BU
AH1369 (1950)	6,800,000	—	0.30	1.00	3.50	4.50

KM# 3 10 CENTESIMI **Composition:** Copper

Date	Mintage	F	VF	XF	Unc	BU
AH1369 (1950)	7,400,000	—	0.50	2.00	6.00	7.50

KM# 4 50 CENTESIMI **Weight:** 3.8000 g. **Composition:** 0.2500 Silver .0305 oz. ASW

Date	Mintage	F	VF	XF	Unc	BU
AH1369 (1950)	1,800,000	—	1.25	3.75	9.00	—

KM# 5 SOMALO **Weight:** 7.6000 g. **Composition:** 0.2500 Silver .0610 oz. ASW

Date	Mintage	F	VF	XF	Unc	BU
AH1369 (1950)	11,480,000	—	2.25	4.75	12.50	—

SOMALI REPUBLIC

STANDARD COINAGE

100 Centesimi = 1 Somalo

KM# 6 5 CENTESIMI **Composition:** Brass

Date	Mintage	F	VF	XF	Unc	BU
1967	10,000,000	—	—	0.20	0.60	—

KM# 7 10 CENTESIMI **Composition:** Brass

Date	Mintage	F	VF	XF	Unc	BU
1967	15,000,000	—	0.15	0.25	0.70	—

KM# 8 50 CENTESIMI **Composition:** Copper-Nickel

Date	Mintage	F	VF	XF	Unc	BU
1967	5,100,000	—	0.50	1.00	2.50	—

KM# 9 SCELLINO (Schilling) **Composition:** Copper-Nickel

Date	Mintage	F	VF	XF	Unc	BU
1967	8,150,000	—	1.00	3.00	6.00	—

KM# 10 20 SHILLINGS (Scellini) **Weight:** 2.8000 **Composition:** 0.9000 Gold .0810 oz. AGW **Subject:** 5t anniversary of independence

Date	Mintage	F	VF	XF	Unc
1965Az Proof	6,325	Value: 50.00			
1966Az Proof	—	Value: 50.00			

KM# 11 50 SHILLINGS **Weight:** 7.0000 g. **Composition:** 0.9000 Gold .2025 oz. AGW **Subject:** 5t anniversary of independence

Date	Mintage	F	VF	XF	Unc
1965Az Proof	6,325	Value: 100			
1966Az Proof	—	Value: 100			

KM# 12 100 SHILLINGS **Weight:** 14.0000 g. **Composition:** 0.9000 Gold .4051 oz. AGW **Subject:** 5t anniversary of independence

Date	Mintage	F	VF	XF	Unc
1965Az Proof	6,325	Value: 185			
1966Az Proof	—	Value: 185			

KM# 13 200 SHILLINGS **Weight:** 28.0000 g. **Composition:** 0.9000 Gold .8102 oz. AGW **Subject:** 5t anniversary of independence

Date	Mintage	F	VF	XF	Unc
1965Az Proof	6,325	Value: 375			
1966Az Proof	—	Value: 375			

KM# 14 500 SHILLINGS **Weight:** 70.0000 g. **Composition:** 0.9000 Gold 2.0257 oz. AGW **Subject:** 5 anniversary of independence **Obverse:** Similar to 20 Shillings, KM#10

Date	Mintage	F	VF	XF	Unc
1965Az Proof	6,325	Value: 875			
1966Az Proof	—	Value: 875			

DEMOCRATIC REPUBLIC

STANDARD COINAGE

100 Centesimi = 1 Somalo

KM# 15 5 SHILLINGS Composition: Copper-Nickel **Subject:** 2nd F.A.O. Conference

Date	Mintage	F	VF	XF	Unc	BU
1970	100,000	—	1.50	2.50	6.00	—
1970 Proof	1,000	Value: 16.50				

KM# 16 20 SHILLINGS Weight: 2.8000 g. **Composition:** 0.9000 Gold .0810 oz. AGW **Subject:** 10th anniversary of independence

Date	Mintage	F	VF	XF	Unc	BU
ND(1970) Proof	8,000	Value: 85.00				

KM# 17 50 SHILLINGS Weight: 7.0000 g. **Composition:** 0.9000 Gold .2025 oz. AGW **Subject:** 10th anniversary of independence

Date	Mintage	F	VF	XF	Unc	BU
ND(1970) Proof	8,000	Value: 165				

KM# 18 50 SHILLINGS Weight: 7.0000 g. **Composition:** 0.9000 Gold .2025 oz. AGW **Subject:** 1st anniversary of 1969 revolution

Date	F	VF	XF	Unc	BU
ND(1970) Proof	—	Value: 165			

KM# 19 100 SHILLINGS Weight: 14.0000 g. **Composition:** 0.9000 Gold .4051 oz. AGW **Subject:** 10th anniversary of independence

Date	Mintage	F	VF	XF	Unc	BU
ND(1970) Proof	8,000	Value: 300				

KM# 20 100 SHILLINGS Weight: 14.0000 g. **Composition:** 0.9000 Gold .4051 oz. AGW **Subject:** 1st anniversary of the 1969 revolution

Date	F	VF	XF	Unc	BU
ND(1970) Proof	—	Value: 285			

KM# 21 200 SHILLINGS Weight: 28.0000 g. **Composition:** 0.9000 Gold .8102 oz. AGW **Subject:** 10th anniversary of independence

Date	Mintage	F	VF	XF	Unc	BU
ND(1970) Proof	8,000	Value: 625				

KM# 22 200 SHILLINGS Weight: 28.0000 g. **Composition:** 0.9000 Gold .8102 oz. AGW **Subject:** 1st anniversary of 1969 revolution

Date	F	VF	XF	Unc	BU
ND(1970) Proof	—	Value: 600			

KM# 23 500 SHILLINGS Weight: 70.0000 g. **Composition:** 0.9000 Gold 2.0257 oz. AGW **Subject:** 10th anniversary of independence **Obverse:** Similar to 200 Shillings, KM#22

Date	Mintage	F	VF	XF	Unc	BU
ND(1970) Proof	8,000	Value: 1,100				

REFORM COINAGE

100 Senti = 1 Shilling

KM# A24 5 SENTI Composition: Aluminum **Series:** F.A.O. **Shape:** Round

Date	F	VF	XF	Unc	BU
1976	—	—	—	200	—

KM# 24 5 SENTI Composition: Aluminum **Series:** F.A.O. **Shape:** Multi-sided

Date	Mintage	F	VF	XF	Unc	BU
1976	18,500,000	—	0.10	0.20	0.35	—

KM# 25 10 SENTI Composition: Aluminum **Series:** F.A.O.

Date	Mintage	F	VF	XF	Unc	BU
1976	40,500,000	—	0.10	0.20	0.50	—

KM# 26 50 SENTI Composition: Copper-Nickel **Series:** F.A.O.

Date	Mintage	F	VF	XF	Unc	BU
1976	10,080,000	—	0.15	0.25	0.75	—

KM# 26a 50 SENTI Composition: Nickel Plated Steel **Series:** F.A.O.

Date	F	VF	XF	Unc	BU
1984	—	1.00	2.00	5.00	—

KM# 27 SHILLING Composition: Copper-Nickel **Series:** F.A.O.

Date	Mintage	F	VF	XF	Unc	BU
1976	20,040,000	—	0.35	0.65	2.25	—

KM# 27a SHILLING Composition: Nickel Plated Steel **Series:** F.A.O.

Date	F	VF	XF	Unc	BU
1984	—	2.00	4.00	10.00	—

KM# 28 10 SHILLINGS Composition: Copper-Nickel **Subject:** 10th anniversary of republic **Reverse:** Workers

Date	F	VF	XF	Unc	BU
ND(1979)	—	—	—	7.00	—

KM# 28a 10 SHILLINGS **Weight:** 28.2800 g. **Composition:** 0.9250 Silver .8411 oz. ASW **Subject:** 10th anniversary of republic **Reverse:** Workers

Date	Mintage	F	VF	XF	Unc	BU
ND(1979) Proof	Est. 5,000	Value: 37.50				

KM# 29 10 SHILLINGS **Composition:** Copper-Nickel **Subject:** 10th anniversary of republic **Reverse:** Camp scene

Date	F	VF	XF	Unc	BU
ND(1979)	—	—	—	7.00	—

KM# 29a 10 SHILLINGS **Weight:** 28.2800 g. **Composition:** 0.9250 Silver .8411 oz. ASW **Subject:** 10th anniversary of republic **Reverse:** Camp scene

Date	Mintage	F	VF	XF	Unc	BU
ND(1979) Proof	Est. 5,000	Value: 38.50				

KM# 30 10 SHILLINGS **Composition:** Copper-Nickel **Subject:** 10th anniversary of republic **Reverse:** Lab workers

Date	F	VF	XF	Unc	BU
ND(1979)	—	—	—	7.00	—

KM# 30a 10 SHILLINGS **Weight:** 28.2800 g. **Composition:** 0.9250 Silver .8411 oz. ASW **Subject:** 10th anniversary of republic **Reverse:** Lab workers

Date	Mintage	F	VF	XF	Unc	BU
ND(1979) Proof	Est. 5,000	Value: 36.50				

KM# 31 10 SHILLINGS **Composition:** Copper-Nickel **Subject:** 10th anniversary of republic **Reverse:** Dancers

Date	F	VF	XF	Unc	BU
ND(1979)	—	—	—	7.00	—

KM# 31a 10 SHILLINGS **Weight:** 28.2800 g. **Composition:** 0.9250 Silver .8411 oz. ASW **Subject:** 10th anniversary of republic **Reverse:** Dancers

Date	Mintage	F	VF	XF	Unc	BU
ND(1979) Proof	Est. 5,000	Value: 37.50				

KM# 32 10 SHILLINGS **Composition:** Copper-Nickel **Subject:** 10th anniversary of republic **Reverse:** Man and woman

Date	F	VF	XF	Unc	BU
ND(1979)	—	—	—	7.00	—

KM# 32a 10 SHILLINGS **Weight:** 28.2800 g. **Composition:** 0.9250 Silver .8411 oz. ASW **Subject:** 10th anniversary of republic **Reverse:** Man and woman

Date	Mintage	F	VF	XF	Unc	BU
ND(1979) Proof	Est. 5,000	Value: 37.50				

KM# 40 25 SHILLINGS **Composition:** Copper-Nickel **Subject:** World Fisheries Conference

Date	Mintage	F	VF	XF	Unc	BU
ND(1984)	100,000	—	—	12.00	30.00	—

KM# 40a 25 SHILLINGS **Weight:** 28.2800 g. **Composition:** 0.9250 Silver .8411 oz. ASW **Subject:** World Fisheries Conference

Date	Mintage	F	VF	XF	Unc	BU
ND(1984) Proof	20,000	Value: 65.00				

KM# 40b 25 SHILLINGS **Weight:** 47.5400 g. **Composition:** 0.9170 Gold 1.4011 oz. AGW **Subject:** World Fisheries Conference

Date	Mintage	F	VF	XF	Unc	BU
ND(1984) Proof	200	Value: 1,000				

KM# 38 150 SHILLINGS **Weight:** 28.2800 g. **Composition:** 0.9250 Silver .8411 oz. ASW **Series:** International Year of Disabled Persons **Obverse:** Cost of arms, date

Date	Mintage	F	VF	XF	Unc	BU
1983	5,500	—	—	—	40.00	—
1983 Proof	5,500	Value: 45.00				

KM# 33 1500 SHILLINGS **Weight:** 15.9800 g. **Composition:** 0.9170 Gold .4711 oz. AGW **Subject:** 10th anniversary of republic **Obverse:** Similar to KM#35

Date	Mintage	F	VF	XF	Unc	BU
ND(1979)	500	—	—	—	225	—
ND(1979) Proof	500	Value: 250				

KM# 34 1500 SHILLINGS **Weight:** 15.9800 g. **Composition:** 0.9170 Gold .4711 oz. AGW **Subject:** 10th anniversary of republic **Obverse:** Similar to KM#35

Date	Mintage	F	VF	XF	Unc	BU
ND(1979)	500	—	—	—	225	—
ND(1979) Proof	500	Value: 250				

KM# 35 1500 SHILLINGS **Weight:** 15.9800 g. **Composition:** 0.9170 Gold .4711 oz. AGW **Subject:** 10th anniversary of republic

Date	Mintage	F	VF	XF	Unc	BU
ND(1979)	500	—	—	—	225	—
ND(1979) Proof	500	Value: 250				

KM# 36 1500 SHILLINGS **Weight:** 15.9800 g. **Composition:** 0.9170 Gold .4711 oz. AGW **Subject:** 10th anniversary of republic

Date	Mintage	F	VF	XF	Unc	BU
ND(1979)	500	—	—	—	225	—
ND(1979) Proof	500	Value: 250				

KM# 37 1500 SHILLINGS **Weight:** 15.9800 g. **Composition:** 0.9170 Gold .4711 oz. AGW **Subject:** 10th anniversary of republic **Obverse:** Similar to KM#35

Date	Mintage	F	VF	XF	Unc
1979	500	—	—	—	225
1979 Proof	500	Value: 250			

l# 39 1500 SHILLINGS Weight: 15.9800 g. **Composition:** 0.9170 Gold .4711 oz. AGW **Series:** International Year of Disabled Persons

e	F	VF	XF	Unc	BU
3	—	—	—	350	—
3 Proof	—	Value: 400			

REPUBLIC OF SOMALIA

STANDARD COINAGE

100 Centesimi = 1 Somalo

l# 45 5 SHILLING / SCELLINI Composition: Aluminum **Series:** F.A.O. **Obverse:** National arms **Reverse:** Elephant

e	F	VF	XF	Unc	BU
0(1999)	—	—	—	1.50	—

l# 90 10 SHILLINGS Weight: 4.8200 g. **Composition:** Nickel Clad Steel **Series:** Asian Astrology **Obverse:** National arms **Reverse:** Rat **Edge:** Plain **Size:** 24.9 mm.

e	F	VF	XF	Unc	BU
0	—	—	—	1.25	—

/# 91 10 SHILLINGS Weight: 4.8200 g. **Composition:** Nickel Clad Steel **Series:** Asian Astrology **Obverse:** National arms **Reverse:** Ox

te	F	VF	XF	Unc	BU
0	—	—	—	1.25	—

/l# 92 10 SHILLINGS Weight: 4.8200 g. **Composition:** Nickel Clad Steel **Series:** Asian Astrology **Obverse:** National arms **Reverse:** Tiger

te	F	VF	XF	Unc	BU
0	—	—	—	1.25	—

/l# 93 10 SHILLINGS Weight: 4.8200 g. **Composition:** Nickel Clad Steel **Series:** Asian astrology **Obverse:** National arms **Reverse:** Rabbit

te	F	VF	XF	Unc	BU
00	—	—	—	1.25	—

KM# 94 10 SHILLINGS Weight: 4.8200 g. **Composition:** Nickel Clad Steel **Series:** Asian astrology **Obverse:** National arms **Reverse:** Dragon

Date	F	VF	XF	Unc	BU
2000	—	—	—	1.25	—

KM# 95 10 SHILLINGS Weight: 4.8200 g. **Composition:** Nickel Clad Steel **Series:** Asian astrology **Obverse:** National arms **Reverse:** Snake

Date	F	VF	XF	Unc	BU
2000	—	—	—	1.25	—

KM# 96 10 SHILLINGS Weight: 4.8200 g. **Composition:** Nickel Clad Steel **Series:** Asian astrology **Obverse:** National arms **Reverse:** Horse

Date	F	VF	XF	Unc	BU
2000	—	—	—	1.25	—

KM# 97 10 SHILLINGS Weight: 4.8200 g. **Composition:** Nickel Clad Steel **Series:** Asian astrology **Obverse:** National arms **Reverse:** Goat

Date	F	VF	XF	Unc	BU
2000	—	—	—	1.25	—

KM# 98 10 SHILLINGS Weight: 4.8200 g. **Composition:** Nickel Clad Steel **Series:** Asian astrology **Obverse:** National arms **Reverse:** Monkey

Date	F	VF	XF	Unc	BU
2000	—	—	—	1.25	—

KM# 99 10 SHILLINGS Weight: 4.8200 g. **Composition:** Nickel Clad Steel **Series:** Asian astrology **Obverse:** National arms **Reverse:** Rooster

Date	F	VF	XF	Unc	BU
2000	—	—	—	1.25	—

KM# 100 10 SHILLINGS Weight: 4.8200 g. **Composition:** Nickel Clad Steel **Series:** Asian astrology **Obverse:** National arms **Reverse:** Dog

Date	F	VF	XF	Unc	BU
2000	—	—	—	1.25	—

KM# 101 10 SHILLINGS Weight: 4.8200 g. **Composition:** Nickel Clad Steel **Series:** Asian astrology **Obverse:** National arms **Reverse:** Pig

Date	F	VF	XF	Unc	BU
2000	—	—	—	1.25	—

KM# 107 10 SHILLINGS / SCELLINI Composition: Silver **Obverse:** Multi-colored dragon

Date	F	VF	XF	Unc	BU
2000 Proof	—	Value: 36.00			

KM# 46 10 SHILLINGS / SCELLINI Composition: Aluminum **Series:** F.A.O. **Obverse:** National arms **Reverse:** Camel

Date	F	VF	XF	Unc	BU
2000(1999)	—	—	—	2.00	—

KM# 41 25 SHILLINGS Composition: Copper-Nickel **Subject:** History of world shipping - sinking of Titanic **Obverse:** National arms

Date	F	VF	XF	Unc	BU
1998 Proof	—	Value: 10.00			

KM# 47 25 SHILLINGS Weight: 2.0000 g. **Composition:** Copper-Nickel **Subject:** Wildlife of Somalia **Reverse:** Multicolored hippopotamus **Edge:** Plain **Size:** 37.9 mm.

Date	F	VF	XF	Unc	BU
1998	—	—	—	15.00	—

KM# 50 25 SHILLINGS **Composition:** Copper-Nickel **Subject:** History of world shipping - Cutty Sark **Obverse:** National arms **Reverse:** Multicolor clipper ship "Cutty Sark" **Edge:** Plain **Note:** Weight varies 18.42-20.2g.

Date	F	VF	XF	Unc	BU
1998 Proof	—	Value: 10.00			

KM# 51 25 SHILLINGS **Composition:** Copper-Nickel **Subject:** History of world shipping - Caravel Nina **Obverse:** National arms

Date	F	VF	XF	Unc	BU
1998 Proof	—	Value: 10.00			

KM# 52 25 SHILLINGS **Composition:** Copper-Nickel **Subject:** History of world shipping **Reverse:** Greek trireme **Note:** Multicolored. Weight varies 18.42-20.2g.

Date	VG	F	VF	XF	Unc
1998 Proof	—	Value: 10.00			

KM# 53 25 SHILLINGS **Composition:** Copper-Nickel **Subject:** History of world shipping **Reverse:** Roman merchant ship **Note:** Multicolored. Weight varies 18.42-20.2g.

Date	F	VF	XF	Unc	BU
1998 Proof	—	Value: 10.00			

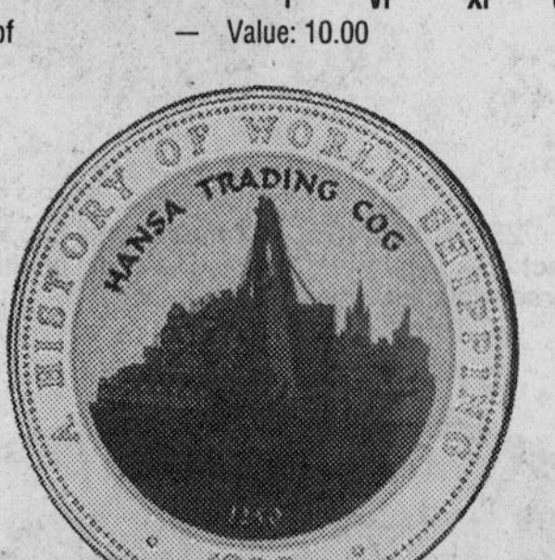

KM# 54 25 SHILLINGS **Composition:** Copper-Nickel **Subject:** History of world shipping **Reverse:** Hansa trading cog **Note:** Multicolored. Weight varies 18.42-20.2g.

Date	F	VF	XF	Unc	BU
1998 Proof	—	Value: 10.00			

KM# 55 25 SHILLINGS **Composition:** Copper-Nickel **Subject:** History of world shipping **Reverse:** Titanic **Note:** Multicolored. Weight varies 18.42-20.2g.

Date	F	VF	XF	Unc	BU
1998 Proof	—	Value: 10.00			

KM# 56 25 SHILLINGS **Composition:** Copper-Nickel **Subject:** Wildlife of Somalia **Obverse:** National arms **Reverse:** Ostrich **Note:** Multicolored. Weight varies 18.42-20.2g.

Date	F	VF	XF	Unc	BU
1998	—	—	—	13.50	—

KM# 57 25 SHILLINGS **Composition:** Copper-Nickel **Subject:** Wildlife of Somalia **Reverse:** Running Eland **Note:** Multicolored. Weight varies 18.42-20.2g.

Date	F	VF	XF	Unc	BU
1998	—	—	—	15.00	—

KM# 58 25 SHILLINGS **Composition:** Copper-Nickel **Subject:** Wildlife of Somalia **Reverse:** Yellow-necked Spurfowl in grass **Note:** Multicolored. Weight varies 18.42-20.2g.

Date	F	VF	XF	Unc	BU
1998	—	—	—	15.00	—

KM# 59 25 SHILLINGS **Composition:** Copper-Nick **Subject:** Wildlife of Somalia **Reverse:** Leopard **Note:** Multicolored. Weight varies 18.42-20.2g.

Date	F	VF	XF	Unc
1998	—	—	—	15.00

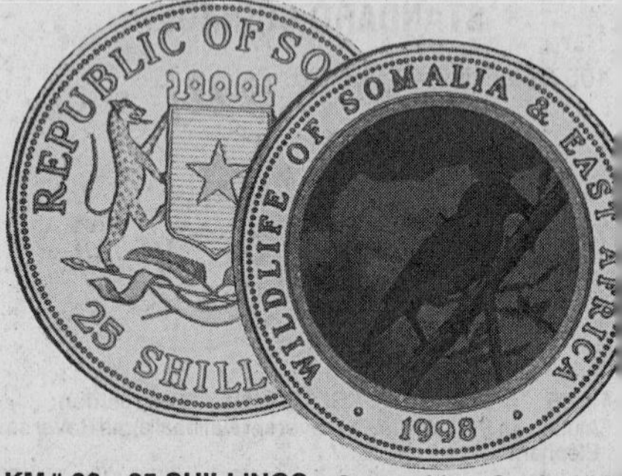

KM# 60 25 SHILLINGS **Composition:** Copper-Nick **Subject:** Wildlife of Somalia **Reverse:** Golden Palm Wea on branch **Note:** Multicolored. Weight varies 18.42-20.2

Date	F	VF	XF	Unc
1998	—	—	—	13.50

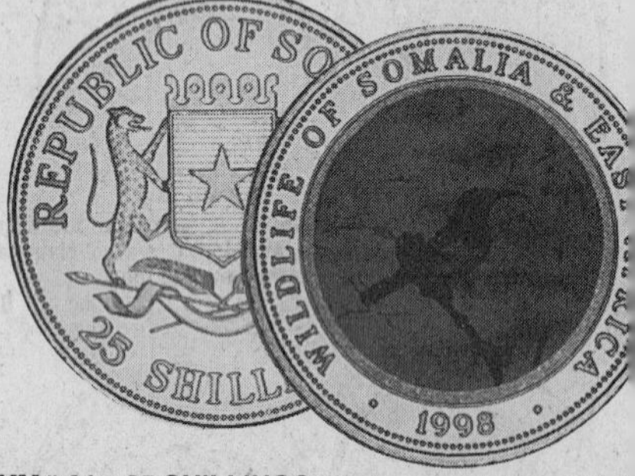

KM# 61 25 SHILLINGS **Composition:** Copper-Nick **Subject:** Wildlife of Somalia **Reverse:** Variable Sunbird a thin branch **Note:** Multicolored. Weight varies 18.42-20

Date	F	VF	XF	Unc
1998	—	—	—	13.50

KM# 62 25 SHILLINGS **Composition:** Copper-Nick **Subject:** Wildlife of Somalia **Reverse:** Superb Starling o broken branch **Note:** Multicolored. Weight varies 18.42-20.

Date	F	VF	XF	Unc
1998	—	—	—	13.50

KM# 106 25 SHILLINGS **Composition:** Copper-Nic **Subject:** Fall of Berlin Wall

Date	F	VF	XF	Unc
1999	—	—	—	8.00

KM# 108 25 SHILLINGS **Composition:** Silver **Obverse:** Multi-colored penguins

Date	F	VF	XF	Unc
2000 Proof	—	Value: 25.00		

KM# 70 25 SHILLINGS **Composition:** Copper-Nickel **Subject:** Winston Churchill **Obverse:** National arms **Reverse:** Portrait **Edge:** Plain **Size:** 38 mm.

Date	F	VF	XF	Unc	BU
2000	—	—	—	5.00	—

KM# 71 25 SHILLINGS **Composition:** Copper-Nickel **Subject:** Pope John Paul II **Obverse:** National arms **Reverse:** Portrait **Edge:** Plain **Size:** 38 mm.

Date	F	VF	XF	Unc	BU
2000	—	—	—	5.00	—

M# 72 25 SHILLINGS **Weight:** 20.0000 g. **Composition:** Copper-Nickel **Subject:** Nelson Mandela **Obverse:** National arms **Reverse:** Portrait **Edge:** Reeded **Size:** 38 mm.

ate	F	VF	XF	Unc	BU
000	—	—	—	5.00	—

M# 73 25 SHILLINGS **Composition:** Copper-Nickel **Subject:** Che Guevara **Obverse:** National arms **Reverse:** Portrait

te	F	VF	XF	Unc	BU
00	—	—	—	5.00	—

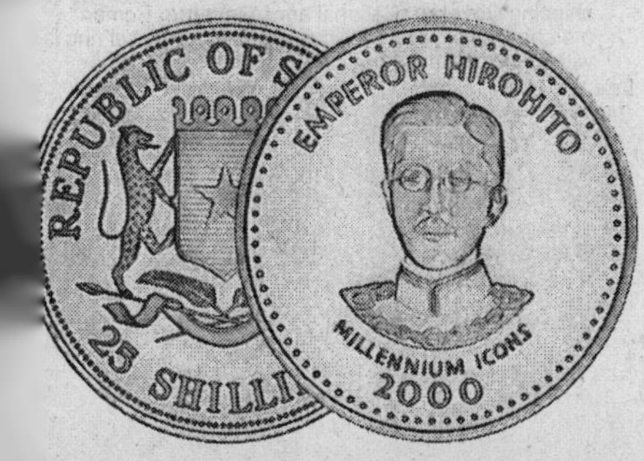

KM# 74 25 SHILLINGS **Composition:** Copper-Nickel **Subject:** Emperor Hirohito **Obverse:** National arms **Reverse:** Portrait **Edge:** Plain **Size:** 37.9 mm.

Date	F	VF	XF	Unc	BU
2000 Prooflike	—	—	—	7.00	—

KM# 75 25 SHILLINGS **Composition:** Copper-Nickel **Subject:** Mao Tse-Tung **Obverse:** National arms **Reverse:** Portrait

Date	F	VF	XF	Unc	BU
2000 Prooflike	—	—	—	7.00	—

KM# 76 25 SHILLINGS **Composition:** Copper-Nickel **Subject:** Berlin **Obverse:** National arms **Reverse:** Berlin wall destruction scene

Date	F	VF	XF	Unc	BU
ND(2000) Prooflike	—	—	—	7.00	—

KM# 103 25 SHILLINGS **Weight:** 4.3700 g. **Composition:** Brass **Subject:** Soccer **Obverse:** National arms. **Reverse:** Soccer player. **Edge:** Plain. **Size:** 21.8 mm.

Date	F	VF	XF	Unc	BU
2001	—	—	—	1.25	—

KM# 77 150 SHILLINGS **Weight:** 14.8100 g. **Composition:** 0.9990 Silver .4757 oz. ASW **Subject:** Christopher Columbus **Obverse:** National arms **Reverse:** Cameo above 3 ships **Edge:** Reeded **Size:** 34.25 mm.

Date	F	VF	XF	Unc	BU
2000 Proof	—	Value: 25.00			

KM# 42 250 SHILLINGS **Weight:** 23.5000 g. **Composition:** 0.9250 Silver .6989 oz. ASW **Subject:** History of world shipping - sinking of Titanic **Obverse:** National arms

Date	Mintage	F	VF	XF	Unc	BU
1998 Proof	20,000	Value: 35.00				

KM# 42a 250 SHILLINGS **Ring Composition:** Copper-Nickel **Center Composition:** Brass **Subject:** Historic Ships **Obverse:** National arms **Reverse:** Multicolor sinking Titanic **Note:** Copper-nickel ring is within another brass ring.

Date	F	VF	XF	Unc	BU
1998	—	—	—	22.50	—

KM# 48 250 SHILLINGS **Weight:** 23.7000 g. **Composition:** 0.9250 Silver .7048 oz. ASW **Subject:** Wildlife of Somalia **Reverse:** Hippopotamus **Edge:** Reeded **Size:** 38.1 mm. **Note:** Multicolored.

Date	F	VF	XF	Unc	BU
1998 Proof	—	Value: 30.00			

KM# 48a 250 SHILLINGS **Ring Composition:** Copper-Nickel **Center Composition:** Brass **Subject:** Wildlife of Somalia **Obverse:** National arms **Reverse:** Hippopotamus **Edge:** Reeded **Note:** Multicolored. Copper-nickel ring is within another brass ring.

Date	F	VF	XF	Unc	BU
1998	—	—	—	20.00	—

KM# 49 250 SHILLINGS **Weight:** 23.7000 g. **Composition:** 0.9250 Silver .7048 oz. ASW **Subject:** Wildlife of Somalia **Reverse:** Ostrich **Note:** Multicolored.

Date	F	VF	XF	Unc	BU
1998 Proof	—	Value: 35.00			

KM# 49a 250 SHILLINGS **Ring Composition:** Copper-Nickel **Center Composition:** Brass **Subject:** Wildlife of Somalia **Obverse:** National arms **Reverse:** Ostrich **Note:** Multicolored. Copper-nickel ring is within another brass ring.

Date	F	VF	XF	Unc	BU
1998	—	—	—	20.00	—

KM# 64 250 SHILLINGS **Weight:** 24.8300 g. **Composition:** 0.9000 Silver .7185 oz. ASW **Subject:** Wildlife of Somalia **Obverse:** National arms **Reverse:** Yellow-necked Spurfowl in grass **Edge:** Reeded **Size:** 37.2 mm. **Note:** Multicolored.

Date	F	VF	XF	Unc	BU
1998 Proof	—	Value: 32.50			

KM# 64a 250 SHILLINGS **Ring Composition:** Copper-Nickel **Center Composition:** Brass **Subject:** Wildlife of Somalia **Obverse:** National arms **Reverse:** Yellow-necked Spurfowl in grass **Note:** Multicolored. Copper-nickel ring is within another brass ring.

Date	F	VF	XF	Unc	BU
1998	—	—	—	20.00	—

KM# 65 250 SHILLINGS **Weight:** 24.8300 g. **Composition:** 0.9000 Silver .7185 oz. ASW **Subject:** Wildlife of Somalia **Reverse:** Running Eland **Note:** Multicolored.

Date	F	VF	XF	Unc	BU
1998 Proof	—	Value: 32.50			

KM# 66 250 SHILLINGS **Weight:** 24.8300 g. **Composition:** 0.9000 Silver .7185 oz. ASW **Subject:** Wildlife of Somalia **Reverse:** Leopard **Note:** Multicolored.

Date	F	VF	XF	Unc	BU
1998 Proof	—	Value: 35.00			

KM# 66a 250 SHILLINGS **Ring Composition:** Copper-Nickel **Center Composition:** Brass **Subject:** Wildlife of Somalia **Obverse:** National arms **Reverse:** Leopard **Note:** Multicolored. Copper-nickel ring is within a brass ring.

Date	F	VF	XF	Unc	BU
1998	—	—	—	20.00	—

KM# 67 250 SHILLINGS **Weight:** 24.8300 g. **Composition:** 0.9000 Silver .7185 oz. ASW **Subject:** Wildlife of Somalia **Reverse:** Golden Palm Weaver on branch **Note:** Multicolored.

Date	F	VF	XF	Unc	BU
1998 Proof	—	Value: 32.50			

KM# 67a 250 SHILLINGS **Ring Composition:** Copper-Nickel **Center Composition:** Brass **Subject:** Wildlife of Somalia **Obverse:** National arms **Reverse:** Golden Palm Weaver on branch **Note:** Multicolored. Copper-nickel ring is within another brass ring.

Date	F	VF	XF	Unc	BU
1998	—	—	—	20.00	—

KM# 68 250 SHILLINGS **Weight:** 24.8300 g. **Composition:** 0.9000 Silver .7185 oz. ASW **Subject:** Wildlife of Somalia **Reverse:** Variable Sunbird on branch **Note:** Multicolored.

Date	F	VF	XF	Unc	BU
1998 Proof	—	Value: 32.50			

KM# 68a 250 SHILLINGS **Ring Composition:** Copper-Nickel **Center Composition:** Brass **Subject:** Wildlife of Somalia **Obverse:** National arms **Reverse:** Variable Sunbird on branch **Note:** Multicolored. Copper-nickel ring is within another brass ring.

Date	F	VF	XF	Unc	BU
1998	—	—	—	20.00	—

KM# 69 250 SHILLINGS **Weight:** 24.8300 g. **Composition:** 0.9000 Silver .7185 oz. ASW **Subject:** Wildlife of Somalia **Reverse:** Superb Starling on broken tree limb **Note:** Multicolored.

Date	F	VF	XF	Unc	BU
1998 Proof	—	Value: 32.50			

KM# 69a 250 SHILLINGS **Ring Composition:** Copper-Nickel **Center Composition:** Brass **Subject:** Wildlife of Somalia **Obverse:** National arms **Reverse:** Superb Starling on broken tree limb **Note:** Multicolored. Copper-nickel ring is within another brass ring.

Date	F	VF	XF	Unc	BU
1998	—	—	—	20.00	—

KM# 78a 250 SHILLINGS **Ring Composition:** Copper-Nickel **Center Composition:** Brass **Subject:** History of world shipping **Obverse:** National arms **Reverse:** Titanic **Note:** Multicolored. Copper-nickel ring is within another brass ring.

Date	F	VF	XF	Unc	BU
1998	—	—	—	22.50	—

KM# 79a 250 SHILLINGS **Ring Composition:** Coppe Nickel **Center Composition:** Brass **Subject:** History of wor shipping **Obverse:** National arms **Reverse:** Greek trirema **Note:** Multicolored. Copper-nickel ring is within another brass ring.

Date	F	VF	XF	Unc	
1998	—	—	—	22.50	

KM# 80a 250 SHILLINGS **Ring Composition:** Copp Nickel **Center Composition:** Brass **Subject:** History of wo shipping **Obverse:** National arms **Reverse:** Roman merchant ship **Note:** Multicolored. Copper-nickel ring is within another brass ring.

Date	F	VF	XF	Unc
1998	—	—	—	22.50

M# 81a 250 SHILLINGS **Ring Composition:** Copper-Nickel **Center Composition:** Brass **Subject:** History of world shipping **Obverse:** National arms **Reverse:** Hanseatic trading cog **Note:** Multicolored. Copper-nickel ring is within another brass ring.

e	F	VF	XF	Unc	BU
98	—	—	—	22.50	—

M# 82a 250 SHILLINGS **Ring Composition:** Copper-Nickel **Center Composition:** Brass **Subject:** History of world shipping **Obverse:** National arms **Reverse:** Caravel "Nina" **Note:** Multicolored. Copper-nickel ring is within another brass ring.

te	F	VF	XF	Unc	BU
98	—	—	—	22.50	—

M# 83a 250 SHILLINGS **Ring Composition:** Copper-Nickel **Center Composition:** Brass **Subject:** History of world shipping **Obverse:** National arms **Reverse:** Clipper "Cutty Sark" **Note:** Multicolored. Copper-nickel ring is within another brass ring.

te	F	VF	XF	Unc	BU
98	—	—	—	22.50	—

M# 102 250 SHILLINGS **Weight:** 24.0000 g. **Composition:** 0.9000 Silver .6945 oz. ASW **Subject:** Olympics **Obverse:** National arms. **Reverse:** Multicolor skier. **Edge:** Reeded. **Size:** 38.1 mm.

te	F	VF	XF	Unc	BU
98 Proof	—	Value: 40.00			

KM# 105 250 SHILLINGS **Weight:** 28.2800 g. **Composition:** 0.9250 Silver 0.841 oz. ASW **Obverse:** National arms. **Reverse:** Two giraffes. **Edge:** Reeded. **Size:** 38.6 mm.

Date	F	VF	XF	Unc	BU
1999 Proof	—	Value: 80.00			

KM# 104 250 SHILLINGS **Ring Composition:** Copper-Nickel **Center Weight:** 22.1000 g. **Center Composition:** Brass **Obverse:** National arms. **Reverse:** Facing bust of Che Guevara. **Edge:** Reeded. **Size:** 38 mm.

Date	F	VF	XF	Unc	BU
2000	—	—	—	30.00	—

KM# 63 250 SHILLINGS **Weight:** 24.8300 g. **Composition:** 0.9000 Silver .7185 oz. ASW **Subject:** Marine life protection **Obverse:** National arms **Reverse:** 2 multicolor penguins **Edge:** Reeded **Size:** 37.2 mm. **ote:** Multicolored.

Date	F	VF	XF	Unc	BU
2000 Proof	—	Value: 45.00			

KM# 84 5000 SHILLINGS **Weight:** 7.0600 g. **Composition:** 0.9990 Silver .2268 oz. ASW **Subject:** Tall Ship Series: Amerigo Vespucci **Obverse:** National arms **Reverse:** Sailing ship **Edge:** Plain **Size:** 29.7 mm.

Date	F	VF	XF	Unc	BU
1998 Proof	—	Value: 25.00			

KM# 85 5000 SHILLINGS **Weight:** 7.0600 g. **Composition:** 0.9990 Silver .2268 oz. ASW **Subject:** Tall Ships Series: Sedov **Obverse:** National arms **Reverse:** Sailing ship

Date	F	VF	XF	Unc	BU
1998 Proof	—	Value: 25.00			

KM# 86 5000 SHILLINGS **Weight:** 7.0600 g. **Composition:** 0.9990 Silver .2268 oz. ASW **Subject:** Tall Ships Series: Gorch Fock **Obverse:** National arms **Reverse:** Sailing ship

Date	F	VF	XF	Unc	BU
1998 Proof	—	Value: 25.00			

KM# 87 5000 SHILLINGS **Weight:** 7.0600 g. **Composition:** 0.9990 Silver .2268 oz. ASW **Subject:** Tall Ships Series: Libertad **Obverse:** National arms **Reverse:** Sailing ship

Date	F	VF	XF	Unc	BU
1998 Proof	—	Value: 25.00			

KM# 88 5000 SHILLINGS **Weight:** 7.0600 g. **Composition:** 0.9990 Silver .2268 oz. ASW **Subject:** Tall Ships Series: Alexander von Humboldt **Obverse:** National arms **Reverse:** Sailing ship

Date	F	VF	XF	Unc	BU
1998 Proof	—	Value: 25.00			

KM# 89 5000 SHILLINGS **Weight:** 7.0600 g. **Composition:** 0.9990 Silver .2268 oz. ASW **Subject:** Tall Ship Series: Eagle **Obverse:** National arms **Reverse:** Sailing ship

Date	F	VF	XF	Unc	BU
1998 Proof	—	Value: 25.00			

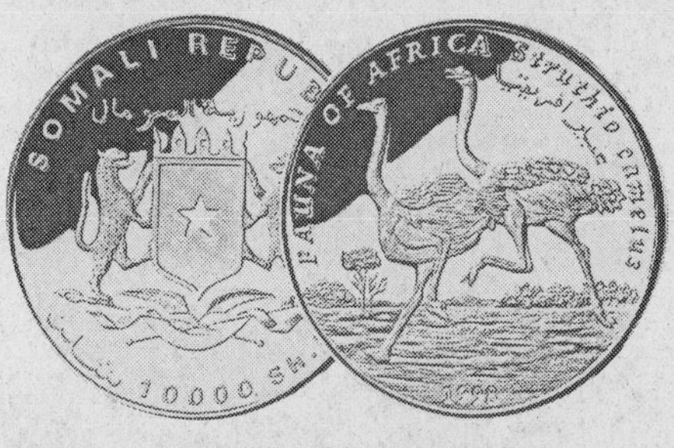

KM# 43 10000 SHILLINGS **Weight:** 15.0000 g. **Composition:** 0.9990 Silver .4818 oz. ASW **Subject:** Fauna of Africa **Obverse:** National arms **Reverse:** 2 ostriches

Date	F	VF	XF	Unc	BU
1998 Proof	—	Value: 40.00			

KM# 44 10000 SHILLINGS **Weight:** 15.0000 g. **Composition:** 0.9990 Silver .4818 oz. ASW **Subject:** Fauna of Africa **Obverse:** National arms **Reverse:** Scimitar-horned Oryx

Date	F	VF	XF	Unc	BU
1998 Proof	—	Value: 40.00			

PIEFORTS

KM#	Date	Mintage	Identification	Mkt Val
P2	1983	—	1500 Shillings. KM39.	850
P1	1983	500	150 Shillings. 0.9250 Silver.	115
P3	ND(1984)	500	25 Shillings. 0.9250 Silver.	100
P4	1998	2,500	250 Shillings. 0.9250 Silver. 47.5400 g. Skier.	135
P6	1998	—	250 Shillings. 0.9250 Silver. Ostrich. KM49.	50.00
P5	1998	—	250 Shillings. Titanic. KM42.	70.00

PROVAS

KM#	Date	Mintage	Identification	Mkt Val
Pr2	1950	—	5 Centesimi.	50.00
Pr3	1950	—	10 Centesimi.	50.00
Pr1	1950	—	Centesimo.	50.00
Pr4	1950	—	50 Centesimi.	75.00
Pr5	1950	—	Somalo.	100

MINT SETS

KM#	Date	Mintage	Identification	Issue Price	Mkt Val
MS1	1979 (5)	—	KM33-37	2,375	1,125

PROOF SETS

KM#	Date	Mintage	Identification	Issue Price	Mkt Val
PS1	1965 (5)	6,325	KM10-14	—	1,575
PS2	1965 (5)	—	KM10-14. Gillt copper nickel.	—	—
PS3	1970 (5)	8,000	KM16, 17, 19, 21, 23	335	2,500
PS4	1970 (3)	14,500	KM18, 20, 22	—	1,075
PS5	1979 (5)	5,000	KM28a-32a	325	150
PS6	1979 (5)	—	KM33-37	3,125	1,250

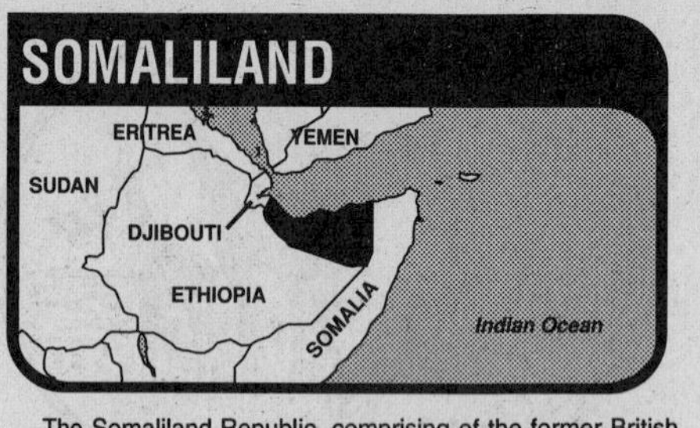

The Somaliland Republic, comprising of the former British Somaliland Protectorate is located on the coast of the north-eastern projection of the African continent commonly referred to as the "Horn" on the southwestern end of the Gulf of Aden.

Bordered by Eritrea to the west, Ethiopia to west and south and Somalia to the east. It has an area of 68,000* sq. mi. (176,000* sq. km). Capital: Hargeysa. It is mostly arid and mountainous except for the gulf shoreline.

The Protectorate of British Somaliland was established in 1888 and from 1905 a commissioner under the British Colonial Office administered the territory. Italian Somaliland was administered as a colony from1893 to 1941, when British forces occupied the territory. In 1950 the United Nations allowed Italy to resume control of Italian Somaliland under a trusteeship. In 1960 British and Italian Somaliland were united as Somalia, an independent republic outside the Commonwealth.

Civil war erupted in the late 1970's and continued until the capital of Somalia was taken in 1990. The United Nations provided aid and peacekeeping. A UN sponsored truce was signed in March 1992 and a peace plan and pact was signed Jan. 15, 1993. The northern Somali National Movement (SNM) declared a secession of the Somaliland Republic on May 17, 1991, which is not recognized by the Somali Democratic Republic.

The currency issued by the East African Currency Board was used in British Somaliland from 1945 to 1961; Somali currency was used later until 1995.

REPUBLIC

STANDARD COINAGE

KM# 1 SHILLING **Composition:** Aluminum **Obverse:** Bird **Reverse:** Denomination

Date	F	VF	XF	Unc	BU
1994	—	—	1.50	3.00	4.50

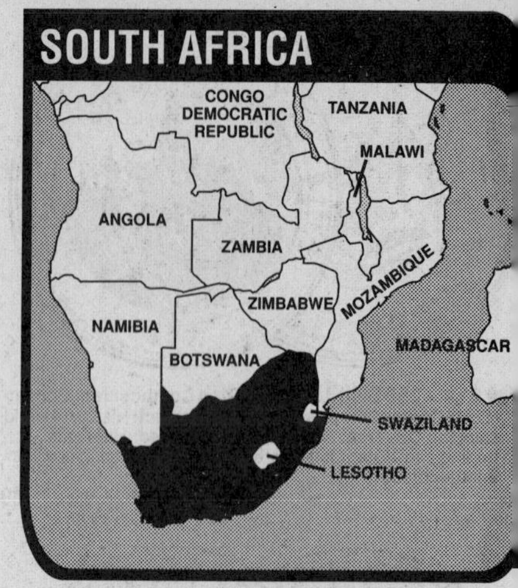

The Republic of South Africa, located at the southern ti Africa, has an area, including the enclave of Walvis Bay 472,359 sq. mi. (1,221,040 sq. km.) and a population of *38.5 lion. Capitals: Administrative, Pretoria; Legislative, Cape To Judicial, Bloemfontein. Manufacturing, mining and agriculture the principal industries. Exports include wool, diamonds, g and metallic ores.

Portuguese navigator Bartholomew Diaz became the European to sight the region of South Africa when he rounded Cape of Good Hope in 1488, but throughout the 16th century only white men to come ashore were the survivors of sh wrecked while attempting the stormy Cape passage. Jan van R beeck of the Dutch East India Company established the first p manent settlement in 1652. In subsequent decades additic Dutch, German and Huguenot refugees from France settled in Cape area to form the Afrikaner segment of today's populat

Great Britain captured the Cape colony in 1795, and ag in 1806, receiving permanent title in 1814. To escape British p ical rule and cultural dominance, many Afrikaner farmers (Bo migrated northward (the Great Trek) beginning in 1836, established the independent Boer Republics of the Transvaal South African Republic, Zuid Afrikaansche Republic) in 1852, the Orange Free State in 1854. British political intrigues aga the two republics, coupled with the discovery of diamonds gold in the Boer-settled regions, led to the bitter Boer Wars (18 81, 1899-1902) and the incorporation of the Boer republics the British Empire.

On May 31, 1910, the two former Boer Republics (Trans and Orange Free State) were joined with the British colonie Cape of Good Hope and Natal to form the Union of South Afr a dominion of the British Empire. In 1934 the Union achieved tus as a sovereign state within the British Empire.

Political integration of the various colonies did not still the c flict between the Afrikaners and the English-speaking groups, w continued to have a significant impact on political development resurgence of Afrikaner nationalism in the 1940s and 1950s le a referendum in the white community authorizing the relinquishn of dominion status and the establishment of a republic. The deci took effect on May 31, 1961. The Republic of South Africa withd from the British Commonwealth in Oct. 1961.

The apartheid era ended April 27, 1994 with the first d ocratic election for all people of South Africa. Nelson Mandela inaugurated President May 10, 1994, and South Africa was re mitted into the Commonwealth of Nations.

South African coins and currency bear inscriptions in t languages, Afrikaans and English.

RULERS

British, until 1934

MONETARY SYSTEM

Until 1961

12 Pence = 1 Shilling
2 Shillings = 1 Florin
20 Shillings = 1 Pound (Pond)

Commencing 1961

100 Cents = 1 Rand

ZUID-AFRIKAANSCHE REPUBLIEK

STANDARD COINAGE

12 Pence = 1 Shilling; 20 Shillings = 1 Pond

KM# 11 1/2 POND **Composition:** 0.9990 Gold **Subj** Veld-Boer War Siege Issue

Date	Mintage	F	VF	XF	Unc
1902	986	600	1,200	2,000	3,500

UNION OF SOUTH AFRICA

STANDARD COINAGE

12 Pence = 1 Shilling; 2 Shillings = 1 Florin; 20 Shillings 1 Pound

 # 12.1 1/4 PENNY (Farthing) Composition: Bronze **Obverse:** Bust of King George V left **Reverse:** Denomination: 1/4 PENNY 1/4; Cape Sparrow

	Mintage	F	VF	XF	Unc	BU
3	33,000	2.00	5.00	10.00	20.00	—
3 Proof	1,402	Value: 30.00				
4	95,000	1.50	2.50	5.00	10.00	—

 # 12.2 1/4 PENNY (Farthing) Composition: Bronze **Obverse:** Bust of King George V left **Reverse:** Denomination: 1/4 PENNY; Cape Sparrow

e	Mintage	F	VF	XF	Unc	BU
6 Proof	16	Value: 6,000				
8	64,000	1.50	3.00	5.00	12.50	—
0	6,560	30.00	60.00	120	200	—
0 Proof	14	Value: 1,200				
1	154,000	1.00	1.50	4.00	6.00	—

 # 12.3 1/4 PENNY (Farthing) Composition: Bronze **Obverse:** Bust of King George V left **Reverse:** Denomination: 1/4 D; Cape Sparrow

e	Mintage	F	VF	XF	Unc	BU
1	Inc. above	5.00	10.00	15.00	35.00	—
1 Proof	62	Value: 200				
2	105,000	1.00	1.50	3.50	7.00	—
2 Proof	12	Value: 375				
3	76	750	1,450	2,200	3,250	—
3 Proof	20	Value: 4,000				
4	52	750	1,450	2,200	3,250	—
4 Proof	24	Value: 3,750				
5	61,000	1.00	1.50	3.50	8.00	—
5 Proof	20	Value: 3,000				
6	43	350	750	1,100	2,000	—
6 Proof	40	Value: 3,000				

 # 23 1/4 PENNY (Farthing) Composition: Bronze **Obverse:** Bust of King George VI left **Reverse:** Cape Sparrow

e	Mintage	F	VF	XF	Unc	BU
7	38,000	1.50	3.00	6.00	12.50	—
7 Proof	116	Value: 40.00				
8	51,000	1.00	2.00	4.00	8.00	—
8 Proof	44	Value: 100				
9	102,000	0.50	1.50	3.00	7.50	—
9 Proof	30	Value: 125				
1	91,000	0.50	1.50	3.00	7.50	—
2	3,756,000	0.25	0.50	1.00	2.00	—
3	9,918,000	0.25	0.50	0.75	1.50	—
3 Proof	104	Value: 40.00				
4	4,468,000	0.25	0.50	0.75	2.00	—
4 Proof	150	Value: 35.00				
5	5,297,000	0.25	0.50	1.50	3.00	—
5 Proof	150	Value: 35.00				
6	4,378,000	0.25	0.50	1.50	4.00	—
6 Proof	150	Value: 35.00				
7	3,895,000	0.25	0.50	1.50	4.00	—
7 Proof	2,600	Value: 4.00				

KM# 32.1 1/4 PENNY (Farthing) Composition: Bronze **Obverse:** Bust of King George VI left **Reverse:** Cape Sparrow

Date	Mintage	F	VF	XF	Unc	BU
1948	2,415,000	0.25	0.50	1.00	2.00	—
1948 Proof	1,120	Value: 3.00				
1949	3,568,000	0.25	0.50	1.00	2.50	—
1949 Proof	800	Value: 5.00				
1950	8,694,000	0.25	0.50	0.75	1.50	—
1950 Proof	500	Value: 8.00				

KM# 32.2 1/4 PENNY (Farthing) Composition: Bronze **Obverse:** Bust of King George VI left **Reverse:** Reversed legend; Cape Sparrow **Rev. Legend:** SUID AFRIKA-SOUTH AFRICA

Date	Mintage	F	VF	XF	Unc	BU
1951	3,511,000	0.15	0.35	0.75	2.50	—
1951 Proof	2,000	Value: 2.00				
1952	2,805,000	0.15	0.35	0.75	2.00	—
1952 Proof	16,000	Value: 2.00				

KM# 44 1/4 PENNY (Farthing) Composition: Bronze **Obverse:** Bust of Queen Elizabeth II right **Reverse:** Two Cape Sparrows facing

Date	Mintage	F	VF	XF	Unc	BU
1953	7,193,000	0.15	0.25	0.50	1.50	—
1953 Proof	5,000	Value: 2.00				
1954	6,568,000	0.15	0.25	0.50	1.50	—
1954 Proof	3,150	Value: 2.00				
1955	11,798,000	0.15	0.25	0.50	1.50	—
1955 Proof	2,850	Value: 2.00				
1956	1,287,000	0.15	0.25	0.50	2.50	—
1956 Proof	1,700	Value: 3.00				
1957	3,065,000	0.15	0.25	0.50	1.50	—
1957 Proof	1,130	Value: 4.00				
1958	5,452,000	0.15	0.25	0.50	1.50	—
1958 Proof	985	Value: 5.00				
1959	1,567,000	0.15	0.25	0.50	1.50	—
1959 Proof	900	Value: 6.00				
1960	1,022,999	0.15	0.25	0.50	2.00	—
1960 Proof	3,360	Value: 1.50				

KM# 13.1 1/2 PENNY Composition: Bronze **Obverse:** Bust of King George V left **Reverse:** Denomination: 1/2 PENNY 1/2; ship under full sail

Date	Mintage	F	VF	XF	Unc	BU
1923	12,000	25.00	40.00	70.00	100	—
1923 Proof	1,402	Value: 100				
1924	64,000	7.50	12.50	30.00	60.00	—
1925	69,000	7.50	12.50	30.00	80.00	—
1926	65,000	10.00	15.00	35.00	100	—

KM# 13.2 1/2 PENNY Composition: Bronze **Obverse:** Bust of King George V left **Reverse:** Denomination: 1/2 PENNY; ship under full sail

Date	Mintage	F	VF	XF	Unc	BU
1928	105,000	5.00	12.50	35.00	75.00	—
1929	272,000	2.50	5.00	15.00	35.00	—
1930	147,000	3.50	7.00	20.00	40.00	—
1930 Proof	14	Value: 400				
1930	Inc. above	4.00	8.00	25.00	50.00	—
Note: Without star after date						
1931	145,000	3.50	7.00	25.00	50.00	—

KM# 13.3 1/2 PENNY Composition: Bronze **Obverse:** Bust of King George V left **Reverse:** Denomination: 1/2 D; ship under full sail

Date	Mintage	F	VF	XF	Unc	BU
1931 Proof	62	Value: 1,000				
1932	106,000	5.00	10.00	30.00	75.00	—
1932 Proof	12	Value: 1,000				
1933	63,000	8.00	25.00	55.00	100	—
1933 Proof	20	Value: 500				
1934	326,000	1.50	5.00	15.00	45.00	—
1934 Proof	24	Value: 500				
1935	405,000	1.50	5.00	15.00	40.00	—
1935 Proof	20	Value: 500				
1936	407,000	1.50	5.00	15.00	30.00	—
1936 Proof	40	Value: 200				

KM# 24 1/2 PENNY Composition: Bronze **Obverse:** Bust of King George VI left **Reverse:** Ship under full sail

Date	Mintage	F	VF	XF	Unc	BU
1937	638,000	1.00	2.00	9.00	15.00	—
1937 Proof	116	Value: 50.00				
1938	560,000	1.00	2.00	6.00	15.00	—
1938 Proof	44	Value: 125				
1939	271,000	2.50	5.00	10.00	20.00	—
1939 Proof	30	Value: 175				
1940	1,535,000	0.30	0.75	3.00	8.00	—
1941	2,053,000	0.30	0.75	3.00	8.00	—
1942	8,382,000	0.25	0.60	2.00	6.00	—
1943	5,135,000	0.25	0.60	2.00	6.00	—
1943 Proof	104	Value: 45.00				
1944	3,920,000	0.25	0.75	3.00	8.00	—
1944 Proof	150	Value: 35.00				
1945	2,357,000	0.25	0.60	2.50	7.00	—
1945 Proof	150	Value: 35.00				
1946	1,022,000	0.25	0.75	3.00	9.00	—
1946 Proof	150	Value: 35.00				
1947	258,000	1.00	3.00	6.00	17.50	—
1947 Proof	2,600	Value: 10.00				

KM# 33 1/2 PENNY Composition: Bronze **Obverse:** Bust of King George V left **Reverse:** Ship under full sail

Date	Mintage	F	VF	XF	Unc	BU
1948	685,000	0.50	1.00	4.00	9.00	—
1948 Proof	1,120	Value: 15.00				
1949	1,850,000	0.25	0.50	1.75	4.00	—
1949 Proof	800	Value: 15.00				
1950	2,186,000	0.25	0.50	1.50	3.00	—
1950 Proof	500	Value: 6.00				
1951	3,746,000	0.25	0.50	1.25	3.00	—
1951 Proof	2,000	Value: 5.00				
1952	4,174,000	0.25	0.50	1.00	2.50	—
1952 Proof	1,550	Value: 4.00				

KM# 45 1/2 PENNY **Composition:** Bronze **Obverse:** Bust of young Queen Elizabeth II right **Reverse:** Ship under full sail

Date	Mintage	F	VF	XF	Unc	BU
1953	5,572,000	0.15	0.35	1.00	3.00	—
1953 Proof	5,000	Value: 4.00				
1954	101,000	2.00	4.00	7.50	12.50	—
1954 Proof	3,150	Value: 15.00				
1955	3,774,000	0.15	0.35	1.00	3.00	—
1955 Proof	2,850	Value: 4.00				
1956	1,305,000	0.15	0.35	1.00	3.00	—
1956 Proof	1,700	Value: 4.00				
1957	2,025,000	0.15	0.35	1.00	3.00	—
1957 Proof	1,130	Value: 4.00				
1958	2,171,000	0.15	0.35	1.00	2.50	—
1958 Proof	985	Value: 5.00				
1959	2,397,000	0.15	0.25	0.75	2.00	—
1959 Proof	900	Value: 6.00				
1960	2,552,000	0.15	0.25	0.75	2.00	—
1960 Proof	3,360	Value: 1.50				

KM# 14.1 PENNY **Composition:** Bronze **Obverse:** Bust of King George V left **Reverse:** Denomination: 1 PENNY 1; ship under full sail

Date	Mintage	F	VF	XF	Unc	BU
1923	91,000	3.00	7.00	17.50	35.00	—
1923 Proof	1,402	Value: 50.00				
1924	134,000	4.00	10.00	25.00	50.00	—

KM# 14.2 PENNY **Composition:** Bronze **Obverse:** Bust of King George V left **Reverse:** Denomination: PENNY; ship under full sail

Date	Mintage	F	VF	XF	Unc	BU
1926	393,000	3.00	10.00	40.00	100	—
1926 Proof	16	Value: 600				
1927	285,000	3.00	10.00	40.00	90.00	—
1928	386,000	3.00	10.00	40.00	90.00	—
1929	1,093,000	1.00	5.00	15.00	35.00	—
1930	754,000	1.00	5.00	20.00	40.00	—
1930 Proof	14	Value: 600				

KM# 14.3 PENNY **Composition:** Bronze **Obverse:** Bust of King George V left **Reverse:** Denomination: 1 D; ship under full sail

Date	Mintage	F	VF	XF	Unc	BU
1931	284,000	1.00	5.00	17.50	40.00	—
1931 Proof	62	Value: 400				
1932	260,000	1.00	5.00	20.00	50.00	—
1932 Proof	12	Value: 800				
1933	225,000	2.00	10.00	30.00	45.00	—
1933 Proof	20	Value: 500				
1933	Inc. above	4.00	10.00	30.00	50.00	—
Note: Without star after date						
1934	2,089,999	0.50	1.50	8.00	22.50	—
1934 Proof	24	Value: 600				
1935	2,295,000	0.50	1.50	8.00	22.50	—
1935 Proof	20	Value: 600				
1936	1,819,000	0.35	1.00	5.00	20.00	—
1936 Proof	40	Value: 300				

KM# 25 PENNY **Composition:** Bronze **Obverse:** Bust of King George VI left **Reverse:** Ship under full sail

Date	Mintage	F	VF	XF	Unc	BU
1937	3,281,000	0.50	1.50	10.00	25.00	—
1937 Proof	116	Value: 75.00				
1938	1,840,000	0.50	1.50	8.00	30.00	—
1938 Proof	44	Value: 100				
1939	1,506,000	0.50	1.50	10.00	25.00	—
1939 Proof	30	Value: 175				
1940	3,592,000	0.35	1.00	4.00	10.00	—
1940	Inc. above	1.50	3.00	6.00	15.00	—
Note: Without star after date						
1941	7,871,000	0.25	0.75	2.50	7.00	—
1942	14,428,000	0.25	0.75	2.00	6.00	—
1942	Inc. above	3.00	6.00	12.50	30.00	—
Note: Without star after date						
1943	4,010,000	0.25	0.75	2.50	6.00	—
1943 Proof	104	Value: 55.00				
1944	6,425,000	0.25	0.75	2.50	7.00	—
1944 Proof	150	Value: 45.00				
1945	4,810,000	0.25	0.75	2.50	7.00	—
1945 Proof	150	Value: 45.00				
1946	2,605,000	0.25	0.75	3.00	8.00	—
1946 Proof	150	Value: 45.00				
1947	135,000	2.50	4.00	7.50	17.50	—
1947 Proof	2,600	Value: 7.00				

KM# 34.1 PENNY **Composition:** Bronze **Obverse:** Bust of King George VI left **Reverse:** Ship under full sail

Date	Mintage	F	VF	XF	Unc	BU
1948	2,398,000	0.25	0.75	2.50	6.00	—
1948 Proof	1,120	Value: 5.00				
1948	Inc. above	1.00	2.00	5.00	10.00	—
Note: Without star after date						
1949	3,634,000	0.25	0.75	2.00	6.00	—
1949 Proof	800	Value: 12.00				
1950	4,890,000	0.25	0.75	2.00	5.00	—
1950 Proof	500	Value: 10.00				

KM# 34.2 PENNY **Composition:** Bronze **Obverse:** Bust of King George VI left **Reverse:** Ship under full sail **Rev. Legend:** SUID AFRIKA-SOUTH AFRICA

Date	Mintage	F	VF	XF	Unc	BU
1951	3,787,000	0.25	0.75	1.50	4.00	—
1951 Proof	2,000	Value: 5.00				
1952	12,674,000	0.25	0.50	1.00	2.50	—
1952 Proof	16,000	Value: 4.00				

KM# 46 PENNY **Composition:** Bronze **Obverse:** Bus Queen Elizabeth II right **Reverse:** Ship under full sail

Date	Mintage	F	VF	XF	Unc
1953	5,491,000	0.20	0.35	0.75	2.00
1953 Proof	5,000	Value: 2.00			
1954	6,665,000	1.00	2.00	5.00	10.00
1954 Proof	3,150	Value: 15.00			
1955	6,508,000	0.20	0.35	0.75	3.00
1955 Proof	2,850	Value: 2.00			
1956	4,390,000	0.20	0.35	1.00	4.00
1956 Proof	1,700	Value: 3.00			
1957	3,973,000	0.20	0.35	0.75	3.00
1957 Proof	1,130	Value: 5.00			
1958	5,311,000	0.20	0.35	0.75	3.00
1958 Proof	985	Value: 6.00			
1959	5,066,000	0.20	0.35	0.75	2.00
1959 Proof	900	Value: 7.00			
1960	5,106,000	0.20	0.35	0.75	2.00
1960 Proof	3,360	Value: 2.00			

KM# 15.1 3 PENCE **Weight:** 1.4100 g. **Compositio** 0.8000 Silver .0362 oz. ASW **Obverse:** Bust of King Geo V left

Date	Mintage	F	VF	XF	Unc
1923	302,000	4.00	8.00	20.00	45.00
1923 Proof	1,402	Value: 50.00			
1924	501,000	4.00	10.00	25.00	50.00
1925	—	10.00	35.00	200	475

KM# 15.2 3 PENCE **Weight:** 1.4100 g. **Compositio** 0.8000 Silver .0362 oz. ASW **Obverse:** Bust of King Geo V left **Reverse:** Denomination: 3 PENCE

Date	Mintage	F	VF	XF	Unc
1925	358,000	5.00	25.00	90.00	175
1926	1,572,000	1.00	3.50	20.00	50.00
1926 Proof	16	Value: 2,000			
1927	2,285,000	1.00	2.50	15.00	45.00
1928	919,000	1.50	3.50	20.00	50.00
1929	1,948,000	1.00	2.50	15.00	45.00
1930	981,000	1.00	3.50	20.00	50.00
1930 Proof	14	Value: 800			

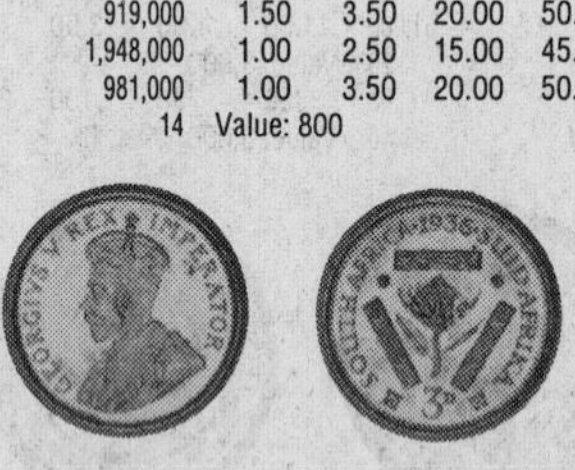

KM# 15.3 3 PENCE **Weight:** 1.4100 g. **Compositio** 0.8000 Silver .0362 oz. ASW **Obverse:** Bust of King Geo V left **Reverse:** Denomination: 3D

Date	Mintage	F	VF	XF	Unc
1931	66	750	1,000	1,750	3,500
1931 Proof	62	Value: 3,500			
1932	2,622,000	1.00	2.50	15.00	30.00
1932 Proof	12	Value: 1,000			
1933	5,135,000	1.00	2.50	15.00	30.00
1933 Proof	20	Value: 1,000			
1934	2,357,000	1.00	2.50	15.00	30.00
1934 Proof	24	Value: 1,000			
1935	1,655,000	1.00	2.50	15.00	30.00
1935 Proof	20	Value: 1,000			
1936	1,095,000	1.00	2.50	15.00	35.00
1936 Proof	40	Value: 250			

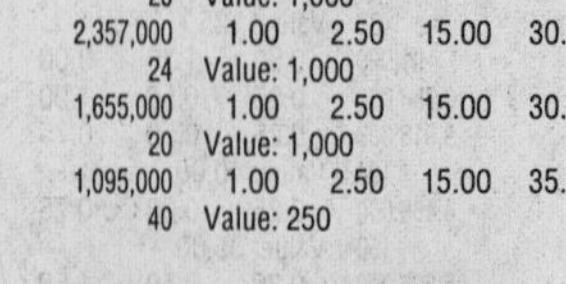

KM# 26 3 PENCE **Weight:** 1.4100 g. **Composition:** 0.8000 Silver .0362 oz. ASW **Obverse:** Bust of King George VI left

Date	Mintage	F	VF	XF	Unc	BU
1937	3,576,000	0.50	1.00	3.00	10.00	—
1937 Proof	116	Value: 80.00				
1938	2,394,000	0.50	1.50	7.00	20.00	—
1938 Proof	44	Value: 100				
1939	3,224,000	0.50	1.50	5.00	12.50	—
1939 Proof	30	Value: 250				
1940	4,887,000	0.50	1.00	3.00	12.50	—
1941	8,968,000	0.50	1.00	3.00	9.00	—
1942	8,055,999	0.50	1.00	3.00	9.00	—
1943	14,827,000	0.50	1.00	2.50	6.00	—
1943 Proof	104	Value: 70.00				
1944	3,331,000	0.50	1.00	3.00	9.00	—
1944 Proof	150	Value: 60.00				
1945/3	4,094,000	1.00	3.00	10.00	20.00	—
1945	Inc. above	0.50	1.00	3.00	9.00	—
1945 Proof	150	Value: 60.00				
1946	2,219,000	0.50	1.00	3.00	10.00	—
1946 Proof	150	Value: 65.00				
1947	1,127,000	0.50	1.00	2.50	8.00	—
1947 Proof	2,600	Value: 8.00				

KM# 35.1 3 PENCE **Weight:** 1.4100 g. **Composition:** 0.8000 Silver .0362 oz. ASW **Obverse:** Bust of King George VI left

Date	Mintage	F	VF	XF	Unc	BU
1948	2,720,000	0.50	1.00	3.00	7.00	—
1948 Proof	1,120	Value: 5.00				
1949	1,904,000	0.50	1.00	3.00	7.00	—
1949 Proof	800	Value: 5.00				
1950	4,096,000	0.50	1.00	2.50	5.00	—
1950 Proof	500	Value: 7.00				

‹M# 35.2 3 PENCE **Weight:** 1.4100 g. **Composition:** 0.5000 Silver .0226 oz. ASW **Obverse:** Bust of King George VI left **Reverse:** Modified design **Note:** Many varieties exist of George VI 3 Pence.

ate	Mintage	F	VF	XF	Unc	BU
951	6,323,000	0.25	0.50	1.00	3.00	—
951 Proof	2,000	Value: 4.00				
952	13,057,000	0.25	0.50	1.00	2.00	—
952 Proof	16,000	Value: 2.00				

M# 47 3 PENCE **Weight:** 1.4100 g. **Composition:** 0.5000 Silver .0226 oz. ASW **Obverse:** Bust of Queen Elizabeth II right

ate	Mintage	F	VF	XF	Unc	BU
953	5,483,000	0.25	0.50	1.00	3.00	—
953 Proof	5,000	Value: 3.00				
954	3,898,000	0.25	0.50	1.00	3.50	—
954 Proof	3,150	Value: 4.00				
55	4,720,000	0.25	0.50	1.00	3.00	—
55 Proof	2,850	Value: 3.00				
56	6,189,000	0.25	0.50	1.00	3.00	—
56 Proof	1,700	Value: 4.00				
57	1,893,000	0.25	0.50	1.00	3.00	—
57 Proof	1,130	Value: 5.00				
58	3,227,000	0.25	0.50	1.00	3.00	—
58 Proof	985	Value: 6.00				
59	2,552,000	0.25	0.50	1.00	2.00	—
59 No K-G on everse	Inc. above	2.00	3.00	5.00	10.00	—
59 Proof	900	Value: 7.00				
60	18,000	1.00	2.50	4.00	7.00	—
60 Proof	3,360	Value: 3.00				

1# 16.1 6 PENCE **Weight:** 2.8300 g. **Composition:** 0.8000 Silver .0727 oz. ASW **Obverse:** Bust of King George V left

e	Mintage	F	VF	XF	Unc	BU
3	208,000	4.00	15.00	35.00	80.00	—
3 Proof	1,402	Value: 80.00				
4	326,000	3.50	12.50	30.00	70.00	—

KM# 16.2 6 PENCE **Weight:** 2.8300 g. **Composition:** 0.8000 Silver .0727 oz. ASW **Obverse:** Bust of King George V left **Reverse:** Denomination: 6 PENCE

Date	Mintage	F	VF	XF	Unc	BU
1925	79,000	5.00	15.00	55.00	125	—
1926	722,000	2.00	10.00	45.00	100	—
1926 Proof	16	Value: 3,000				
1927	1,548,000	1.50	4.00	25.00	50.00	—
1929	784,000	2.00	8.00	30.00	60.00	—
1930	448,000	2.00	8.00	35.00	70.00	—
1930 Proof	14	Value: 1,000				

KM# 16.3 6 PENCE **Weight:** 2.8300 g. **Composition:** 0.8000 Silver .0727 oz. ASW **Obverse:** Bust of King George V left **Reverse:** Denomination: 6 D **Rev. Legend:** 6 D

Date	Mintage	F	VF	XF	Unc	BU
1931	4,743	75.00	150	250	550	—
1931 Proof	62	Value: 1,000				
1932	1,525,000	1.00	5.00	17.50	35.00	—
1932 Proof	12	Value: 1,200				
1933	2,819,000	1.00	5.00	17.50	35.00	—
1933 Proof	20	Value: 1,200				
1934	1,519,000	1.00	7.00	20.00	40.00	—
1934 Proof	24	Value: 1,200				
1935	573,000	2.00	8.00	30.00	100	—
1935 Proof	20	Value: 1,200				
1936	627,000	1.00	7.00	20.00	40.00	—
1936 Proof	40	Value: 275				

KM# 27 6 PENCE **Weight:** 2.8300 g. **Composition:** 0.8000 Silver .0727 oz. ASW **Obverse:** Bust of King George VI left

Date	Mintage	F	VF	XF	Unc	BU
1937	1,696,000	1.00	2.00	7.00	17.50	—
1937 Proof	116	Value: 90.00				
1938	1,725,000	1.00	2.00	7.00	17.50	—
1938 Proof	44	Value: 125				
1939 Proof	30	Value: 3,750				
1940	1,629,000	1.00	1.50	5.00	10.00	—
1941	2,263,000	1.00	1.50	5.00	10.00	—
1942	4,936,000	0.75	1.25	3.00	8.00	—
1943	3,776,000	0.75	1.25	3.00	8.00	—
1943 Proof	104	Value: 85.00				
1944	228,000	2.00	7.00	15.00	30.00	—
1944 Proof	150	Value: 75.00				
1945	420,000	1.00	5.00	15.00	35.00	—
1945 Proof	150	Value: 75.00				
1946	290,000	1.00	6.00	15.00	30.00	—
1946 Proof	150	Value: 80.00				
1947	577,000	1.00	1.50	5.00	10.00	—
1947 Proof	2,600	Value: 10.00				

KM# 36.1 6 PENCE **Weight:** 2.8300 g. **Composition:** 0.8000 Silver .0727 oz. ASW **Obverse:** Bust of King George VI left

Date	Mintage	F	VF	XF	Unc	BU
1948	2,266,000	0.75	1.25	2.50	6.00	—
1948 Proof	1,120	Value: 10.00				
1949	196,000	3.00	7.50	15.00	30.00	—
1949 Proof	800	Value: 15.00				
1950	2,122,000	0.75	1.00	2.00	5.00	—
1950 Proof	500	Value: 15.00				

KM# 36.2 6 PENCE **Weight:** 2.8300 g. **Composition:** 0.5000 Silver .0454 oz. ASW **Obverse:** Bust of King George VI left

Date	Mintage	F	VF	XF	Unc	BU
1951	2,602,000	0.50	1.00	2.00	4.00	—
1951 Proof	2,000	Value: 4.00				
1952	4,265,000	0.50	0.75	1.25	3.00	—
1952 Proof	16,000	Value: 2.00				

KM# 48 6 PENCE **Weight:** 2.8300 g. **Composition:** 0.5000 Silver .0454 oz. ASW **Obverse:** Bust of Queen Elizabeth II right

Date	Mintage	F	VF	XF	Unc	BU
1953	2,496,000	0.50	0.75	1.75	4.50	—
1953 Proof	5,000	Value: 3.00				
1954	2,196,000	0.50	1.00	2.00	4.50	—
1954 Proof	3,150	Value: 4.00				
1955	1,969,000	0.50	1.00	2.00	4.50	—
1955 Proof	2,850	Value: 3.00				
1956	1,772,000	0.50	1.00	2.00	5.00	—
1956 Proof	1,700	Value: 4.00				
1957	3,288,000	0.50	0.75	1.75	4.50	—
1957 Proof	1,130	Value: 6.00				
1958	1,172,000	0.50	1.00	2.00	4.50	—
1958 Proof	985	Value: 6.00				
1959	261,000	1.00	2.00	4.00	12.00	—
1959 Proof	900	Value: 8.00				
1960	1,587,000	0.50	0.75	1.25	2.50	—
1960 Proof	3,360	Value: 2.50				

KM# 17.1 SHILLING **Weight:** 5.6600 g. **Composition:** 0.8000 Silver .1455 oz. ASW **Obverse:** Bust of King George V left **Reverse:** Denomination: 1 SHILLING 1

Date	Mintage	F	VF	XF	Unc	BU
1923	808,000	4.00	15.00	35.00	75.00	—
1923 Proof	1,402	Value: 80.00				
1924	1,269,000	3.50	12.50	30.00	75.00	—

KM# 17.2 SHILLING **Weight:** 5.6600 g. **Composition:** 0.8000 Silver .1455 oz. ASW **Obverse:** Bust of King George V left **Reverse:** Denomination: SHILLING

Date	Mintage	F	VF	XF	Unc	BU
1926	238,000	15.00	75.00	400	1,150	—
1926 Proof	16	Value: 3,000				
1927	488,000	10.00	25.00	150	375	—
1928	889,000	8.00	25.00	100	250	—
1929	926,000	5.00	10.00	30.00	175	—
1930	422,000	6.00	15.00	60.00	150	—
1930 Proof	14	Value: 1,000				

KM# 17.3 SHILLING **Weight:** 5.6600 g. **Composition:** 0.8000 Silver .1455 oz. ASW **Obverse:** Bust of King George V left

Date	Mintage	F	VF	XF	Unc	BU
1931	6,541	80.00	165	375	600	—
1931 Proof	62	Value: 1,200				
1932	2,537,000	2.50	5.00	15.00	50.00	—
1932 Proof	12	Value: 1,400				
1933	1,463,000	3.50	7.00	30.00	70.00	—
1933 Proof	20	Value: 1,400				
1934	821,000	3.50	7.00	35.00	80.00	—
1934 Proof	24	Value: 1,400				
1935	685,000	4.00	8.50	45.00	90.00	—
1935 Proof	20	Value: 1,400				
1936	693,000	3.50	7.00	25.00	60.00	—
1936 Proof	40	Value: 500				

KM# 28 SHILLING **Weight:** 5.6600 g. **Composition:** 0.8000 Silver .1455 oz. ASW **Obverse:** Bust of King George VI left

Date	Mintage	F	VF	XF	Unc	BU
1937	1,194,000	1.50	3.00	10.00	25.00	—
1937 Proof	116	Value: 120				
1938	1,160,000	1.50	3.00	10.00	25.00	—
1938 Proof	44	Value: 250				
1939 Proof	30	Value: 4,000				
1940	1,365,000	1.50	2.50	7.50	17.50	—
1941	1,826,000	1.50	2.50	7.50	17.50	—
1942	3,867,000	1.50	2.50	7.50	17.50	—
1943	4,187,999	1.00	2.00	5.00	10.00	—
1943 Proof	104	Value: 165				
1944	48,000	8.00	20.00	40.00	70.00	—
1944 Proof	160	Value: 150				
1945	54,000	8.00	20.00	40.00	70.00	—
1945 Proof	150	Value: 150				
1946	27,000	10.00	30.00	60.00	120	—
1946 Proof	150	Value: 165				
1947	7,184	10.00	20.00	35.00	65.00	—
1947 Proof	2,600	Value: 70.00				

KM# 37.1 SHILLING **Weight:** 5.6600 g. **Composition:** 0.8000 Silver .1455 oz. ASW **Obverse:** Bust of King George VI left

Date	Mintage	F	VF	XF	Unc	BU
1948	4,974	10.00	20.00	35.00	65.00	—
1948 Proof	1,120	Value: 70.00				
1949 Proof	800	Value: 225				
1950	1,704,000	1.50	2.50	4.00	8.00	—
1950 Proof	500	Value: 40.00				

KM# 37.2 SHILLING **Weight:** 5.6600 g. **Composition:** 0.5000 Silver .0909 oz. ASW **Obverse:** Bust of King George VI left **Reverse:** Denomination: 1 S

Date	Mintage	F	VF	XF	Unc	BU
1951	2,405,000	1.00	1.50	4.00	8.00	—
1951 Proof	2,000	Value: 4.00				
1952	1,934,000	1.00	1.50	3.50	7.00	—
1952 Proof	1,550	Value: 3.00				

KM# 49 SHILLING **Weight:** 5.6600 g. **Composition:** 0.5000 Silver .0909 oz. ASW **Obverse:** Bust of Queen Elizabeth II right

Date	Mintage	F	VF	XF	Unc	BU
1953	2,672,000	0.75	1.25	2.50	5.50	—
1953 Proof	5,000	Value: 4.00				

Date	Mintage	F	VF	XF	Unc	BU
1954	3,576,000	0.75	1.25	2.00	5.50	—
1954 Proof	3,150	Value: 4.00				
1955	2,206,000	0.75	1.25	2.50	5.50	—
1955 Proof	2,850	Value: 5.50				
1956	2,142,000	0.75	1.25	2.50	6.00	—
1956 Proof	1,700	Value: 6.00				
1957	791,000	1.00	2.00	5.00	10.00	—
1957 Proof	1,130	Value: 6.00				
1958	4,067,000	0.75	1.25	2.00	5.50	—
1958 Proof	985	Value: 8.00				
1959	205,000	1.50	3.00	5.00	10.00	—
1959 Proof	900	Value: 10.00				
1960	2,187,000	0.75	1.25	2.00	5.50	—
1960 Proof	3,360	Value: 3.00				

KM# 18 FLORIN **Weight:** 11.3100 g. **Composition:** 0.8000 Silver .2909 oz. ASW **Obverse:** Bust of King George V left

Date	Mintage	F	VF	XF	Unc	BU
1923	695,000	5.00	20.00	40.00	80.00	—
1923 Proof	1,402	Value: 120				
1924	1,513,000	4.00	15.00	40.00	150	—
1925	50,000	125	350	1,000	2,200	—
1926	324,000	7.50	40.00	250	650	—
1927	399,000	7.50	35.00	200	600	—
1928	1,092,000	4.00	10.00	100	200	—
1929	648,000	5.00	15.00	120	225	—
1930	267,000	5.00	15.00	75.00	150	—
1930 Proof	14	Value: 1,200				

KM# 22 2 SHILLINGS **Weight:** 11.3100 g. **Composition:** 0.8000 Silver .2909 oz. ASW **Obverse:** Bust of King George V left **Reverse:** Denomination: 2 SHILLINGS

Date	Mintage	F	VF	XF	Unc	BU
1931	383	250	450	700	1,200	—
1931 Proof	62	Value: 1,500				
1932	1,315,000	3.00	6.00	18.00	75.00	—
1932 Proof	12	Value: 2,000				
1933	891,000	4.00	8.00	25.00	85.00	—
1933 Proof	20	Value: 2,000				
1934	559,000	4.00	8.00	25.00	60.00	—
1934 Proof	24	Value: 1,650				
1935	554,000	5.00	9.00	25.00	90.00	—
1935 Proof	20	Value: 1,650				
1936	669,000	4.00	8.00	25.00	65.00	—
1936 Proof	40	Value: 650				

KM# 29 2 SHILLINGS **Weight:** 11.3100 g. **Composition:** 0.8000 Silver .2909 oz. ASW **Obverse:** Bust of King George VI left

Date	Mintage	F	VF	XF	Unc	BU
1937	1,495,000	2.50	5.00	10.00	30.00	—
1937 Proof	116	Value: 150				
1938	214,000	5.00	10.00	20.00	50.00	—
1938 Proof	44	Value: 325				
1939	279,000	5.00	10.00	20.00	50.00	—
1939 Proof	30	Value: 1,000				
1940	2,600,000	2.50	3.50	8.00	20.00	—
1941	1,764,000	2.50	3.50	8.00	20.00	—
1942	2,847,000	2.00	3.00	5.00	10.00	—
1943	3,125,000	2.00	3.00	5.00	10.00	—
1943 Proof	104	Value: 135				
1944	225,000	3.50	7.00	17.50	40.00	—
1945	473,000	3.00	6.00	15.00	35.00	—
1945 Proof	150	Value: 120				
1946	14,000	7.50	20.00	40.00	90.00	—

Date	Mintage	F	VF	XF	Unc	BU
1946 Proof	150	Value: 135				
1947	2,892	15.00	25.00	40.00	85.00	—
1947 Proof	2,600	Value: 70.00				

KM# 38.1 2 SHILLINGS **Weight:** 11.3100 g. **Composition:** 0.8000 Silver .2909 oz. ASW **Obverse:** Bust of King George VI left

Date	Mintage	F	VF	XF	Unc	BU
1948	6,773	10.00	15.00	30.00	70.00	—
1948 Proof	1,120	Value: 70.00				
1949	203,000	5.00	10.00	15.00	35.00	—
1949 Proof	800	Value: 60.00				
1950	4,945	20.00	40.00	80.00	140	—
1950 Proof	500	Value: 160				

KM# 38.2 2 SHILLINGS **Weight:** 11.3100 g. **Composition:** 0.5000 Silver .1818 oz. ASW **Obverse:** Bust of King George VI left **Reverse:** Denomination: 2 S

Date	Mintage	F	VF	XF	Unc	BU
1951	730,000	2.00	3.00	5.00	10.00	—
1951 Proof	2,000	Value: 15.00				
1952	3,570,000	1.50	2.00	3.00	6.50	—
1952 Proof	16,000	Value: 8.00				

KM# 50 2 SHILLINGS **Weight:** 11.3100 g. **Composition:** 0.5000 Silver .1818 oz. ASW **Obverse:** Bu of Queen Elizabeth II right

Date	Mintage	F	VF	XF	Unc	BU
1953	3,274,000	1.50	2.25	4.00	8.50	
1953 Proof	5,000	Value: 6.50				
1954	5,866,000	1.50	2.25	3.00	7.00	
1954 Proof	3,150	Value: 6.50				
1955	3,745,000	1.50	2.25	3.00	7.50	
1955 Proof	2,850	Value: 6.50				
1956	2,549,000	1.50	2.25	4.00	9.00	
1956 Proof	1,700	Value: 7.50				
1957	2,507,000	1.50	2.25	4.00	10.00	
1957 Proof	1,130	Value: 7.50				
1958	2,821,000	1.50	2.25	4.00	10.00	
1958 Proof	985	Value: 15.00				
1959	1,219,000	1.50	2.25	4.00	10.00	
1959 Proof	900	Value: 20.00				
1960	1,951,000	1.50	2.25	3.00	5.00	
1960 Proof	3,360	Value: 4.00				

KM# 19.1 2-1/2 SHILLINGS **Weight:** 14.1400 g. **Composition:** 0.8000 Silver .3637 oz. ASW **Obverse:** B of King George V left **Reverse:** Denomination: 2-1/2 SHILLINGS 2-1/2 **Rev. Legend:** ZUID-AFRIKA

Date	Mintage	F	VF	XF	Unc
1923	1,227,000	4.00	15.00	35.00	70.00
1923 Proof	1,402	Value: 125			

Date	Mintage	F	VF	XF	Unc	BU
	2,556,000	3.50	10.00	50.00	120	—
	460,000	8.00	30.00	180	600	—

19.2 2-1/2 SHILLINGS **Weight:** 14.1400 g. **omposition:** 0.8000 Silver .3637 oz. ASW **Obverse:** Bust f King George V left **Reverse:** Denomination: 2-1/2 HILLINGS

Date	Mintage	F	VF	XF	Unc	BU
	205,000	10.00	40.00	250	650	—
Proof	16	Value: 4,000				
	194,000	10.00	40.00	350	850	—
	984,000	5.00	25.00	125	325	—
	617,000	5.00	25.00	175	350	—
	324,000	5.00	15.00	100	250	—
Proof	14	Value: 1,650				

 # 19.3 2-1/2 SHILLINGS **Weight:** 14.1400 g. **omposition:** 0.8000 Silver .3637 oz. ASW **Obverse:** Bust f King George V left **Rev. Legend:** SUID. AFRIKA

Date	Mintage	F	VF	XF	Unc	BU
	790	225	450	700	1,300	—
Proof	62	Value: 1,800				
	1,028,999	4.00	6.00	22.50	85.00	—
Proof	12	Value: 2,400				
	136,000	8.00	40.00	185	300	—
Proof	20	Value: 2,400				
	416,000	4.00	8.00	30.00	100	—
Proof	24	Value: 1,650				
	345,000	5.00	12.50	32.50	125	—
Proof	20	Value: 1,650				
	553,000	4.00	8.00	25.00	90.00	—
Proof	40	Value: 800				

 # 30 2-1/2 SHILLINGS **Weight:** 14.1400 g. **Composition:** 0.8000 Silver .3637 oz. ASW **Obverse:** Bust of King George VI left

Date	Mintage	F	VF	XF	Unc	BU
	1,154,000	3.00	5.00	15.00	32.50	—
Proof	116	Value: 175				
	534,000	4.00	8.00	20.00	60.00	—
Proof	44	Value: 400				
	133,000	6.00	15.00	40.00	80.00	—
Proof	30	Value: 800				
	2,976,000	3.00	4.50	8.00	20.00	—
	1,988,000	3.00	4.50	8.00	20.00	—
	3,180,000	3.00	4.50	8.00	20.00	—
	2,098,000	3.00	4.50	8.00	20.00	—
3 Proof	104	Value: 150				
4	1,360,000	3.00	5.00	10.00	25.00	—
4 Proof	150	Value: 130				
5	183,000	3.50	7.00	25.00	60.00	—
5 Proof	150	Value: 130				
6	11,000	15.00	30.00	50.00	90.00	—
6 Proof	150	Value: 150				
7	3,582	20.00	35.00	60.00	100	—
7 Proof	2,600	Value: 110				

KM# 39.1 2-1/2 SHILLINGS **Weight:** 14.1400 g. **Composition:** 0.8000 Silver .3637 oz. ASW **Obverse:** Bust of King George VI left

Date	Mintage	F	VF	XF	Unc	BU
1948	1,600	25.00	45.00	75.00	100	—
1948 Proof	1,120	Value: 110				
1949	1,891	25.00	45.00	75.00	110	—
1949 Proof	800	Value: 120				
1950	5,076	25.00	45.00	75.00	140	—
1950 Proof	500	Value: 200				

KM# 39.2 2-1/2 SHILLINGS **Weight:** 14.1400 g. **Composition:** 0.5000 Silver .2273 oz. ASW **Obverse:** Bust of King George VI left **Reverse:** Denomination: 2-1/2 S

Date	Mintage	F	VF	XF	Unc	BU
1951	783,000	3.00	4.50	6.00	15.00	—
1951 Proof	2,000	Value: 9.00				
1952	1,996,000	2.00	3.00	4.00	8.50	—
1952 Proof	16,000	Value: 5.00				

KM# 51 2-1/2 SHILLINGS **Weight:** 14.1400 g. **Composition:** 0.5000 Silver .2273 oz. ASW **Obverse:** Bust of Queen Elizabeth II right

Date	Mintage	F	VF	XF	Unc	BU
1953	2,513,000	2.00	3.00	4.00	8.50	—
1953 Proof	6,000	Value: 6.00				
1954	4,249,000	2.00	3.00	4.00	8.50	—
1954 Proof	3,150	Value: 7.50				
1955	3,863,000	2.00	3.00	4.00	8.50	—
1955 Proof	2,850	Value: 7.50				
1956	2,437,000	2.00	3.00	4.00	8.50	—
1956 Proof	1,700	Value: 8.50				
1957	2,137,000	2.00	3.00	4.00	8.50	—
1957 Proof	1,130	Value: 8.50				
1958	2,260,000	2.00	3.00	4.50	9.00	—
1958 Proof	985	Value: 14.00				
1959	46,000	2.50	4.00	6.00	12.00	—
1959 Proof	900	Value: 18.00				
1960	12,000	3.00	5.00	7.50	12.50	—
1960 Proof	3,360	Value: 5.00				

KM# 31 5 SHILLINGS **Weight:** 28.2800 g. **Composition:** 0.8000 Silver .7274 oz. ASW **Subject:** Royal Visit **Obverse:** Bust of King George VI left **Reverse:** Springbok

Date	Mintage	F	VF	XF	Unc	BU
1947	300,000	BV	7.00	7.50	15.00	—
1947 Proof	5,600	Value: 45.00				

KM# 40.1 5 SHILLINGS **Weight:** 28.2800 g. **Composition:** 0.8000 Silver .7274 oz. ASW **Obverse:** Bust of King George VI left **Reverse:** Springbok

Date	Mintage	F	VF	XF	Unc	BU
1948	780,000	BV	6.00	7.50	15.00	—
1948 Prooflike	1,000	—	—	—	20.00	—
1948 Proof	1,120	Value: 25.00				
1949	535,000	BV	6.00	7.50	15.00	—
1949 Prooflike	2,000	—	—	—	35.00	—
1949 Proof	800	Value: 50.00				
1950	83,000	BV	10.00	12.50	25.00	—
1950 Prooflike	1,200	—	—	—	60.00	—
1950 Proof	500	Value: 75.00				

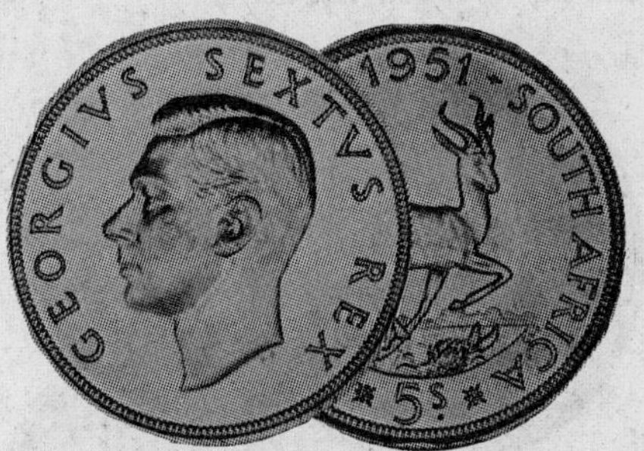

KM# 40.2 5 SHILLINGS **Weight:** 28.2800 g. **Composition:** 0.5000 Silver .4546 oz. ASW **Obverse:** Bust of King George VI left **Reverse:** Springbok

Date	Mintage	F	VF	XF	Unc	BU
1951	363,000	BV	5.00	7.00	15.00	—
1951 Prooflike	1,483	—	—	—	25.00	—
1951 Proof	2,000	Value: 35.00				

KM# 41 5 SHILLINGS **Weight:** 28.2800 g. **Composition:** 0.5000 Silver .4546 oz. ASW **Subject:** 300th Anniversary - Founding of Capetown **Obverse:** Bust of King George VI left **Reverse:** Schooner in harbor

Date	Mintage	F	VF	XF	Unc	BU
ND(1952)	1,698,000	BV	4.50	5.50	8.50	—
ND(1952) Prooflike	12,000	—	—	—	12.50	—
ND(1952) Proof	16,000	Value: 15.00				

KM# 52 5 SHILLINGS **Weight:** 28.2800 g. **Composition:** 0.5000 Silver .4546 oz. ASW **Obverse:** Bust of Queen Elizabeth II right **Reverse:** Springbok

Date	Mintage	F	VF	XF	Unc	BU
1953	250,000	BV	5.00	7.00	12.00	—
1953 Prooflike	8,000	—	—	—	15.00	—
1953 Proof	5,000	Value: 20.00				
1953 Matte Proof	—	Value: 700				
1954	10,000	BV	8.50	12.50	20.00	—
1954 Prooflike	3,890	—	—	—	22.00	—
1954 Proof	3,150	Value: 25.00				
1955	40,000	BV	7.50	10.00	15.00	—
1955 Prooflike	2,230	—	—	—	20.00	—
1955 Proof	2,850	Value: 22.50				
1956	100,000	BV	5.00	7.00	12.00	—
1956 Prooflike	2,200	—	—	—	20.00	—
1956 Proof	1,700	Value: 25.00				
1957	154,000	BV	5.00	7.00	12.00	—
1957 Prooflike	1,600	—	—	—	25.00	—
1957 Proof	1,130	Value: 30.00				
1958	233,000	BV	5.00	7.00	12.00	—
1958 Prooflike	1,500	—	—	—	25.00	—
1958 Proof	985	Value: 30.00				
1959	2,989	20.00	35.00	65.00	100	—
1959 Prooflike	2,200	—	—	—	110	—
1959 Proof	950	Value: 120				

KM# 55 5 SHILLINGS **Weight:** 28.2800 g. **Composition:** 0.5000 Silver .4546 oz. ASW **Subject:** 50th Anniversary - South African Union **Note:** Many varieties exist of letters HM below building.

Date	Mintage	F	VF	XF	Unc	BU
1960	396,000	BV	4.50	5.50	7.50	—
1960 Prooflike	22,000	—	—	—	11.50	—
1960 Proof	3,360	Value: 15.00				

KM# 20 1/2 SOVEREIGN **Weight:** 3.9940 g. **Composition:** 0.9170 Gold .1177 oz. AGW **Note:** British type with Pretoria mint mark: SA.

Date	Mintage	F	VF	XF	Unc	BU
1923 Proof	655	Value: 425				
1925	947,000	55.00	65.00	75.00	100	—
1926	809,000	55.00	65.00	75.00	100	—

KM# 42 1/2 POUND **Weight:** 3.9940 g. **Composition:** 0.9170 Gold .1177 oz. AGW **Reverse:** Springbok **Note:** Similar to 1 Pound, KM#43.

Date	Mintage	F	VF	XF	Unc	BU
1952	4,002	—	—	—	65.00	—
1952 Proof	12,000	Value: 75.00				

KM# 53 1/2 POUND **Weight:** 3.9940 g. **Composition:** 0.9170 Gold .1177 oz. AGW **Obverse:** Elizabeth II

Date	Mintage	F	VF	XF	Unc	BU
1953 Proof	4,000	Value: 75.00				
1954 Proof	1,275	Value: 85.00				
1955 Proof	900	Value: 100				
1956 Proof	508	Value: 180				
1957 Proof	560	Value: 150				
1958 Proof	515	Value: 175				
1959	500	—	—	—	90.00	—
1959 Proof	630	Value: 135				
1960	1,052	—	—	—	65.00	—
1960 Proof	1,950	Value: 75.00				

KM# 21 SOVEREIGN **Weight:** 7.9881 g. **Composition:** 0.9170 Gold .2354 oz. AGW **Note:** British type with Pretoria mint mark: SA.

Date	Mintage	F	VF	XF	Unc	BU
1923	64	200	300	400	500	—
1923 Proof	655	Value: 550				
1924	3,184	700	1,350	2,250	4,500	—
1925	6,086,000	—	BV	100	125	—
1926	11,108,000	—	BV	100	125	—
1927	16,379,999	—	BV	100	125	—
1928	18,235,000	—	BV	100	125	—

KM# A22 SOVEREIGN **Weight:** 7.9881 g. **Composition:** 0.9170 Gold .2354 oz. AGW **Obverse:** Modified effigy, slightly smaller bust

Date	Mintage	F	VF	XF	Unc	BU
1929	12,024,000	—	BV	100	125	—
1930	10,028,000	—	BV	100	125	—
1931	8,512,000	—	BV	100	125	—
1932	1,067,000	—	BV	110	145	—

KM# 43 POUND **Weight:** 7.9881 g. **Composition:** 0.9170 Gold .2354 oz. AGW **Reverse:** Springbok

Date	Mintage	F	VF	XF	Unc	BU
1952	4,508	—	—	—	125	—
1952 Proof	12,000	Value: 135				

KM# 54 POUND **Weight:** 7.9881 g. **Composition:** 0.9170 Gold .2354 oz. AGW **Reverse:** Springbok

Date	Mintage	F	VF	XF	Unc	BU
1953 Proof	4,000	Value: 125				
1954 Proof	1,275	Value: 135				

Date	Mintage	F	VF	XF	Unc
1955 Proof	900	Value: 150			
1956 Proof	508	Value: 245			
1957 Proof	560	Value: 235			
1958 Proof	515	Value: 235			
1959	502	—	—	—	145
1959 Proof	630	Value: 200			
1960	1,161	—	—	—	110
1960 Proof	1,950	Value: 135			

REPUBLIC

STANDARD COINAGE

100 Cents = 1 Rand

KM# 56 1/2 CENT **Composition:** Brass

Date	Mintage	F	VF	XF	Unc
1961	39,189,000	—	0.15	0.25	1.25
1961 Proof	7,530	Value: 1.00			
1962	17,895,000	—	0.15	0.25	1.25
1962 Proof	3,844	Value: 1.00			
1963	11,611,000	—	0.15	0.25	2.00
1963 Proof	4,025	Value: 1.00			
1964	9,258,000	—	0.15	0.25	1.25
1964 Proof	16,000	Value: 1.00			

KM# 81 1/2 CENT **Composition:** Bronze **Reverse:** Sparrows **Note:** Bilingual.

Date	F	VF	XF	Unc
1970	—	0.10	0.25	0.50

Note: Coins dated 1970 were also struck for circulation 1971, 1972 and 1973

Date	Mintage	F	VF	XF	Unc
1970 Proof	10,000	Value: 2.50			
1971	—	—	—	—	2.50
1971 Proof	12,000	Value: 2.50			
1972	—	—	—	—	2.50
1972 Proof	12,000	Value: 2.50			
1973	—	—	0.10	0.20	2.50
1973 Proof	11,000	Value: 2.50			
1974	—	—	0.20	0.40	2.50
1974 Proof	15,000	Value: 2.50			
1975	—	—	0.10	0.20	2.50
1975 Proof	18,000	Value: 2.50			
1977	—	—	0.10	0.20	2.50
1977 Proof	19,000	Value: 2.50			
1978	—	—	0.10	0.20	2.50
1978 Proof	19,000	Value: 2.50			
1980 Proof	15,000	Value: 2.50			
1981 Proof	10,000	Value: 2.50			
1983 Proof	14,000	Value: 2.50			

KM# 90 1/2 CENT **Composition:** Bronze **Obverse:** President Fouche **Note:** Similar to 1 Cent, KM#91.

Date	Mintage	F	VF	XF	Unc
1976	20,000	—	—	—	1.00
1976 Proof	21,000	Value: 1.50			

KM# 97 1/2 CENT **Composition:** Bronze **Obverse:** President Diederichs

Date	Mintage	F	VF	XF	Unc
1979	18,000	—	—	—	1.00
1979 Proof	17,000	Value: 1.50			

KM# 108 1/2 CENT **Composition:** Bronze **Obverse:** President Vorster

Date	Mintage	F	VF	XF	Unc
1982 Proof	12,000	Value: 1.50			

KM# 57 CENT **Composition:** Brass **Obverse:** Covered wagon

Date	Mintage	F	VF	XF	Unc	BU
1961	52,266,000	—	0.15	0.40	1.50	—
1961 Proof	7,530	Value: 0.75				
1962	21,929,000	—	0.15	0.40	1.50	—
1962 Proof	3,844	Value: 1.00				
1963	9,081,000	—	0.15	0.50	3.00	—
1963 Proof	4,025	Value: 1.00				
1964	14,265,000	—	0.15	0.40	1.50	—
1964 Proof	16,000	Value: 2.00				

KM# 65.1 CENT **Composition:** Bronze **Obverse:** English legend **Reverse:** Sparrows

Date	Mintage	F	VF	XF	Unc	BU
1965	26,000	—	—	—	2.00	—
1965 Proof	25,000	Value: 2.50				
966	50,157,000	—	—	0.10	0.50	—
967	21,114,000	—	—	0.10	0.50	—
969	10,196,000	—	—	0.10	0.50	—

KM# 65.2 CENT **Composition:** Bronze **Obverse:** Afrikaans legend

ate	Mintage	F	VF	XF	Unc	BU
965	846	—	100	200	300	—
965 Proof	185	Value: 350				
966	50,157,000	—	—	0.10	0.50	—
966 Proof	25,000	Value: 1.00				
967	21,114,000	—	—	0.10	0.50	—
967 Proof	25,000	Value: 1.00				
969	10,196,000	—	—	0.10	0.50	—
969 Proof	12,000	Value: 1.50				

M# 74.1 CENT **Composition:** Bronze **Subject:** President Charles Swart **Obverse:** English legend

ate	Mintage	F	VF	XF	Unc	BU
68	6,000,000	—	—	0.10	0.30	—
68 Proof	25,000	Value: 1.00				

M# 74.2 CENT **Composition:** Bronze **Obverse:** Afrikaans legend

	Mintage	F	VF	XF	Unc	BU
68	6,000,000	—	—	0.10	0.30	—

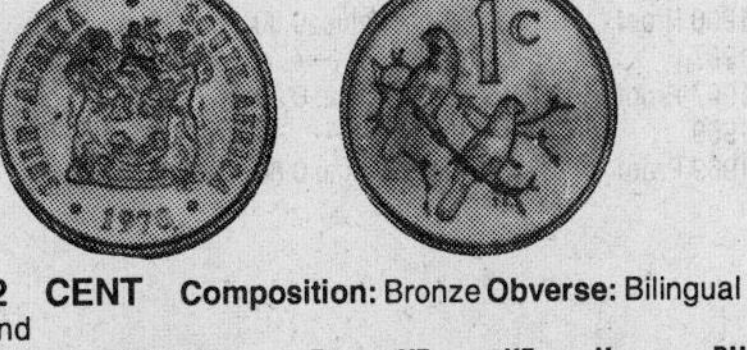

1# 82 CENT **Composition:** Bronze **Obverse:** Bilingual legend

	Mintage	F	VF	XF	Unc	BU
0	37,072,000	—	—	—	0.30	—
0 Proof	10,000	Value: 1.00				

Date	Mintage	F	VF	XF	Unc	BU
1971	34,053,000	—	—	—	0.30	—
1971 Proof	12,000	Value: 1.00				
1972	35,662,000	—	—	—	0.30	—
1972 Proof	10,000	Value: 1.00				
1973	35,898,000	—	0.10	0.20	0.40	—
1973 Proof	11,000	Value: 1.00				
1974	54,940,000	—	—	—	0.25	—
1974 Proof	15,000	Value: 1.00				
1975	62,982,000	—	—	—	0.25	—
1975 Proof	18,000	Value: 1.00				
1977	72,444,000	—	—	—	0.25	—
1977 Proof	19,000	Value: 1.00				
1978	70,152,000	—	—	—	0.20	—
1978 Proof	17,000	Value: 0.50				
1980	63,432,000	—	—	—	0.20	—
1980 Proof	15,000	Value: 0.50				
1981	63,444,000	—	—	—	0.20	—
1981 Proof	10,000	Value: 0.50				
1983	182,131,000	—	—	—	0.20	—
1983 Proof	14,000	Value: 0.50				
1984	107,155,000	—	—	—	0.20	—
1984 Proof	11,000	Value: 0.50				
1985	186,042,000	—	—	—	0.20	—
1985 Proof	9,859	Value: 0.50				
1986	169,734,000	—	—	—	0.20	—
1986 Proof	7,000	Value: 0.50				
1987	120,674,000	—	—	—	0.20	—
1987 Proof	6,781	Value: 0.50				
1988	240,272,000	—	—	—	0.20	—
1988 Proof	7,250	Value: 0.50				
1989	—	—	—	—	0.20	—
1989 Proof	—	Value: 0.50				

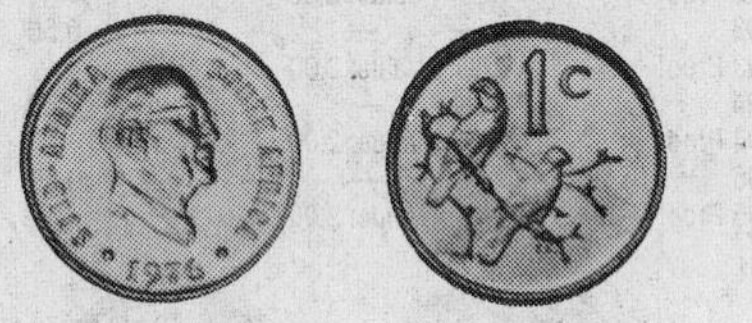

KM# 91 CENT **Composition:** Bronze **Obverse:** President Fouche

Date	Mintage	F	VF	XF	Unc	BU
1976	91,860,000	—	—	0.30	0.50	—
1976 Proof	21,000	Value: 0.75				

KM# 98 CENT **Composition:** Bronze **Obverse:** President Diederichs

Date	Mintage	F	VF	XF	Unc	BU
1979	63,432,000	—	—	0.30	0.50	—
1979 Proof	15,000	Value: 0.75				

KM# 109 CENT **Composition:** Bronze **Obverse:** President Vorster

Date	Mintage	F	VF	XF	Unc	BU
1982	145,954,000	—	—	0.30	0.50	—
1982 Proof	12,000	Value: 0.75				

KM# 132 CENT **Composition:** Copper-Plated-Steel

Date	Mintage	F	VF	XF	Unc	BU
1990	—	—	—	—	0.25	—
1990 Proof	—	Value: 0.50				
1991	—	—	—	—	0.25	—
1991 Proof	—	Value: 0.50				
1992	—	—	—	—	0.25	—
1992 Proof	—	Value: 0.50				
1993	—	—	—	—	0.25	—
1993 Proof	7,790	Value: 0.50				
1994	—	—	—	—	0.25	—
1994 Proof	5,804	Value: 0.50				
1995	—	—	—	—	0.25	—
1995 Proof	—	Value: 0.50				

KM# 158 CENT **Composition:** Copper-Plated-Steel **Obverse:** Zulu legend **Reverse:** Two Cape Sparrows

Date	Mintage	F	VF	XF	Unc	BU
1996	—	—	—	—	0.25	—
1996 Proof	10,000	Value: 0.50				

KM# 170 CENT **Composition:** Copper Plated Steel **Obverse:** Ndebele legend **Reverse:** Two Cape Sparrows

Date	Mintage	F	VF	XF	Unc	BU
1997	—	—	—	—	0.25	—
1997 Proof	3,596	Value: 0.50				
1998	—	—	—	—	0.25	—
1998 Proof	—	Value: 0.50				
1999	—	—	—	—	0.25	—
1999 Proof	—	Value: 0.50				
2000	—	Value: 0.25				

KM# 221 CENT **Weight:** 1.5100 g. **Composition:** Copper Plated Steel **Obverse:** National arms **Reverse:** Two Cape Sparrows **Edge:** Plain **Size:** 14.9 mm.

Date	F	VF	XF	Unc	BU
2000	—	—	—	0.35	—
2001	—	—	—	0.35	—

KM# 66.1 2 CENTS **Composition:** Bronze **Obverse:** English legend **Reverse:** Black Wildebeest

Date	Mintage	F	VF	XF	Unc	BU
1965	29,887,000	—	—	0.10	0.35	—
1966	9,267,000	—	—	0.10	0.40	—
1966 Proof	25,000	Value: 0.50				
1967	11,862,000	—	—	0.10	0.35	—
1967 Proof	25,000	Value: 0.50				
1969	5,817,000	—	—	0.10	0.40	—
1969 Proof	12,000	Value: 0.50				

KM# 66.2 2 CENTS **Composition:** Bronze **Obverse:** Afrikaans legend **Reverse:** Black Wildebeest

Date	Mintage	F	VF	XF	Unc	BU
1965	29,887,000	—	—	0.10	0.35	—
1965 Proof	25,000	Value: 0.50				
1966	9,267,000	—	—	0.10	0.35	—
1967	11,862,000	—	—	0.10	0.35	—
1969	5,817,000	—	—	0.10	0.40	—

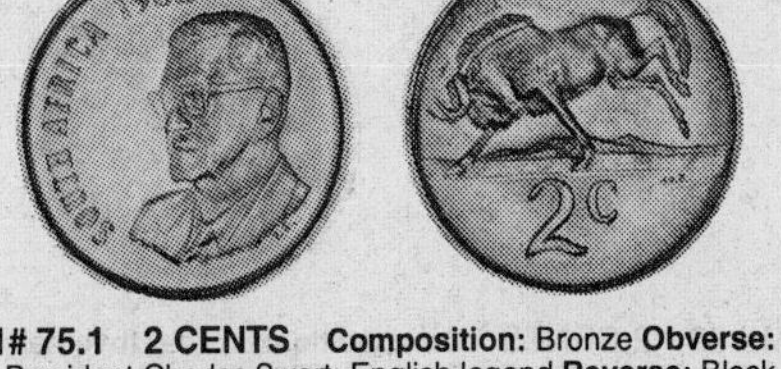

KM# 75.1 2 CENTS **Composition:** Bronze **Obverse:** President Charles Swart; English legend **Reverse:** Black Wildebeest

Date	Mintage	F	VF	XF	Unc	BU
1968	5,500,000	—	—	0.20	0.50	—

KM# 75.2 2 CENTS **Composition:** Bronze **Obverse:** Afrikaans legend **Reverse:** Black Wildebeest

Date	Mintage	F	VF	XF	Unc	BU
1968	5,525,000	—	—	0.20	0.50	—
1968 Proof	25,000	Value: 1.00				

KM# 83 2 CENTS **Composition:** Bronze **Obverse:** Bilingual legend **Reverse:** Black Wildebeest

Date	Mintage	F	VF	XF	Unc	BU
1970	35,217,000	—	—	0.15	0.50	—
1970 Proof	10,000	Value: 0.65				
1971	24,093,000	—	—	0.15	0.50	—
1971 Proof	12,000	Value: 0.65				
1972	7,304,000	—	—	0.15	0.50	—
1972 Proof	10,000	Value: 0.65				
1973	18,685,000	—	—	0.15	0.50	—
1973 Proof	11,000	Value: 0.65				
1974	25,301,000	—	—	0.15	0.50	—
1974 Proof	15,000	Value: 0.65				
1975	24,982,000	—	—	0.15	0.50	—
1975 Proof	18,000	Value: 0.65				
1977	45,116,000	—	—	0.15	0.50	—
1977 Proof	19,000	Value: 0.65				
1978	50,527,000	—	—	0.15	0.50	—
1978 Proof	17,000	Value: 0.65				
1980	37,795,000	—	—	0.15	0.50	—
1980 Proof	15,000	Value: 0.65				
1981	79,350,000	—	—	0.15	0.50	—
1981 Proof	10,000	Value: 0.65				
1983	112,575,000	—	—	0.15	0.50	—
1983 Proof	14,000	Value: 0.65				
1984	101,497,000	—	—	0.15	0.50	—
1984 Proof	11,000	Value: 0.65				
1985	102,708,000	—	—	0.15	0.50	—
1985 Proof	9,859	Value: 0.65				
1986	683,294,000	—	—	0.15	0.50	—
1986 Proof	7,100	Value: 0.65				
1987	104,981,000	—	—	0.15	0.50	—
1987 Proof	6,781	Value: 0.65				
1988	182,036,000	—	—	0.15	0.50	—
1988 Proof	7,250	Value: 0.65				
1989	—	—	—	0.15	0.50	—
1989 Proof	—	Value: 0.65				
1990	215,192,000	—	—	0.15	0.50	—

KM# 92 2 CENTS **Composition:** Bronze **Obverse:** President Fouche **Reverse:** Black Wildebeest

Date	Mintage	F	VF	XF	Unc	BU
1976	51,474,000	—	—	0.25	0.50	—
1976 Proof	21,000	Value: 0.75				

KM# 99 2 CENTS **Composition:** Bronze **Obverse:** President Diederichs **Reverse:** Black Wildebeest

Date	Mintage	F	VF	XF	Unc	BU
1979	40,043,000	—	—	0.25	0.50	—
1979 Proof	15,000	Value: 0.75				

KM# 110 2 CENTS **Composition:** Bronze **Obverse:** President Vorster **Reverse:** Black Wildebeest

Date	Mintage	F	VF	XF	Unc	BU
1982	53,962,000	—	—	0.25	0.50	—
1982 Proof	12,000	Value: 0.75				

KM# 133 2 CENTS **Composition:** Copper-Plated-Steel **Reverse:** African Fish Eagle

Date	Mintage	F	VF	XF	Unc	BU
1990	—	—	—	—	1.50	—
1990 Proof	—	Value: 2.00				
1991	—	—	—	—	1.50	—
1991 Proof	12,000	Value: 2.00				
1992	—	—	—	—	0.50	—
1992 Proof	—	Value: 2.00				
1993	—	—	—	—	0.50	—
1993 Proof	7,790	Value: 2.00				
1994	—	—	—	—	0.50	—
1994 Proof	5,804	Value: 2.00				
1995	—	—	—	—	0.50	—
1995 Proof	—	Value: 2.00				

KM# 159 2 CENTS **Composition:** Copper-Plated-Steel **Obverse:** Venda legend **Reverse:** African Fish Eagle

Date	Mintage	F	VF	XF	Unc	BU
1996	—	—	—	—	0.50	—
1996 Proof	—	Value: 1.00				
1997	—	—	—	—	0.50	—
1997 Proof	3,596	Value: 1.00				
1998	—	—	—	—	0.50	—
1998 Proof	—	Value: 1.00				
1999	—	—	—	—	0.50	—
1999 Proof	—	Value: 1.00				
2000	—	—	—	—	0.50	—

KM# 222 2 CENTS **Weight:** 3.0000 g. **Composition:** Copper Plated Steel **Obverse:** National arms **Reverse:** African Fish Eagle catching fish **Edge:** Plain **Size:** 17.9 mm.

Date	F	VF	XF	Unc	BU
2000	—	—	—	0.50	—
2001	—	—	—	0.50	—

KM# 58 2-1/2 CENTS **Weight:** 1.4100 g. **Composition:** 0.5000 Silver .0226 oz. ASW

Date	Mintage	F	VF	XF	Unc	BU
1961	292,000	—	0.50	1.00	2.00	—
1961 Proof	7,530	Value: 4.00				
1962	8,745	—	2.00	4.00	8.00	—
1962 Proof	3,844	Value: 8.00				
1963	33,000	—	1.50	2.50	4.00	—
1963 Proof	4,025	Value: 6.00				
1964	14,000	—	2.00	4.00	6.00	—
1964 Proof	16,000	Value: 4.00				

KM# 174 2-1/2 CENTS **Weight:** 1.4140 g. **Composition:** 0.9250 Silver .0420 oz. ASW **Obverse:** Protea flower **Reverse:** Knysna seahorse

Date	Mintage	F	VF	XF	Unc	BU
1997 Proof	Est. 2,627	Value: 18.50				

KM# 176 2-1/2 CENTS **Weight:** 1.4140 g. **Composition:** 0.9250 Silver .0420 oz. ASW **Reverse:** Jackass penguin

Date	Mintage	F	VF	XF	Unc	BU
1998 Proof	Est. 5,000	Value: 17.50				

KM# 217 2-1/2 CENTS **Weight:** 1.4100 g. **Composition:** 0.9250 Silver .0419 oz. ASW **Obverse:** Protea flower **Reverse:** Great white shark

Date	Mintage	F	VF	XF	Unc	BU
1999 Proof	5,000	Value: 17.50				

KM# 233 2-1/2 CENTS **Weight:** 1.4140 g. **Composition:** 0.9250 Silver 0.0421 oz. ASW **Obverse:** Protea flower. **Reverse:** Octopus. **Edge:** Reeded. **Size:** 16.3 mm.

Date		
2000 Proof	—	Value: 15.00

KM# 242 2-1/2 CENTS **Weight:** 1.4140 g. **Composition:** 0.9250 Silver 0.0421 oz. ASW **Obverse:** National arms. **Reverse:** Dolphin. **Edge:** Reeded. **Size:** 16.3 mm.

Date		
2001 Proof	—	Value: 18.00

KM# 59 5 CENTS **Weight:** 2.8300 g. **Composition:** 0.5000 Silver .0454 oz. ASW

Date	Mintage	F	VF	XF	Unc	BU
1961	1,479,000	—	BV	0.85	2.00	—
1961 Proof	7,530	Value: 2.50				
1962	4,187,999	—	BV	0.75	1.50	—
1962 Proof	3,844	Value: 3.00				
1963	8,054,000	—	BV	0.65	1.25	—
1963 Proof	4,025	Value: 3.00				
1964	3,567,000	—	BV	0.65	1.25	—
1964 Proof	16,000	Value: 1.50				

KM# 67.1 5 CENTS **Composition:** Nickel **Obverse:** English legend **Reverse:** Blue Crane

Date	Mintage	F	VF	XF	Unc	BU
1965	32,689,999	—	—	0.15	0.75	—
1965 Proof	25,000	Value: 0.80				
1966	4,101,000	—	—	0.15	0.75	—
1967	4,590,000	—	—	0.15	0.75	—
1969	5,020,000	—	—	0.15	0.75	—

KM# 67.2 5 CENTS **Composition:** Nickel **Obverse:** Afrikaans legend **Reverse:** Blue Crane

Date	Mintage	F	VF	XF	Unc
1965	32,689,999	—	—	0.15	0.75
1966	4,101,000	—	—	0.15	0.75
1966 Proof	25,000	Value: 0.80			
1967	4,590,000	—	—	0.15	0.75
1967 Proof	25,000	Value: 0.80			
1969	5,020,000	—	—	0.15	0.75
1969 Proof	12,000	Value: 0.80			

 # 76.1 5 CENTS Composition: Nickel **Subject:** President Charles Swart **Obverse:** English legend **Reverse:** Blue Crane

	Mintage	F	VF	XF	Unc	BU
	6,000,000	—	—	0.15	0.75	—
Proof	25,000	Value: 0.80				

 # 76.2 5 CENTS Composition: Nickel **Obverse:** Afrikaans legend **Reverse:** Blue Crane

	Mintage	F	VF	XF	Unc	BU
3	6,000,000	—	—	0.15	0.75	—

 # 84 5 CENTS Composition: Nickel **Obverse:** Bilingual legend **Reverse:** Blue Crane

	Mintage	F	VF	XF	Unc	BU
0	6,652,000	—	—	0.15	0.75	—
0 Proof	10,000	Value: 0.80				
1	20,329,000	—	—	0.15	0.75	—
1 Proof	12,000	Value: 0.80				
2	3,117,000	—	—	0.15	0.75	—
2 Proof	9,000	Value: 0.80				
3	17,092,000	—	—	0.15	0.75	—
3 Proof	11,000	Value: 0.80				
4	19,978,000	—	—	0.15	0.75	—
4 Proof	15,000	Value: 0.80				
5	21,982,000	—	—	0.15	0.75	—
5 Proof	18,000	Value: 0.80				
7	51,729,000	—	—	0.15	0.75	—
7 Proof	19,000	Value: 0.80				
8	30,050,000	—	—	0.15	0.75	—
8 Proof	19,000	Value: 0.80				
0	46,665,000	—	—	0.15	0.75	—
0 Proof	15,000	Value: 0.80				
1	40,351,000	—	—	0.15	0.75	—
1 Proof	10,000	Value: 0.80				
3	57,487,000	—	—	0.15	0.75	—
3 Proof	14,000	Value: 0.80				
4	67,345,000	—	—	0.15	0.75	—
4 Proof	11,000	Value: 0.80				
5	57,167,000	—	—	0.15	0.75	—
5 Proof	9,859	Value: 0.80				
6	54,226,000	—	—	0.15	0.75	—
6 Proof	7,100	Value: 0.80				
7	42,786,000	—	—	0.15	0.75	—
7 Proof	5,297	Value: 0.80				
8	110,164,000	—	—	0.15	0.75	—
8 Proof	7,250	Value: 0.80				
39	35,540,000	—	—	0.15	0.75	—
39 Proof	Inc. above	Value: 1.50				

 # 93 5 CENTS Composition: Nickel **Obverse:** President Fouche **Reverse:** Blue Crane

e	Mintage	F	VF	XF	Unc	BU
76	48,972,000	—	—	0.30	0.75	—
76 Proof	19,000	Value: 1.50				

 # 100 5 CENTS Composition: Nickel **Obverse:** President Diederichs **Reverse:** Blue Crane

e	Mintage	F	VF	XF	Unc	BU
79	17,533,000	—	—	0.30	0.75	—
79 Proof	17,000	Value: 1.50				

KM# 111 5 CENTS Composition: Nickel **Obverse:** President Vorster **Reverse:** Blue Crane

Date	Mintage	F	VF	XF	Unc	BU
1982	47,236,000	—	—	0.30	0.75	—
1982 Proof	12,000	Value: 1.50				

KM# 134 5 CENTS Composition: Copper-Plated-Steel

Date	Mintage	F	VF	XF	Unc	BU
1990	—	—	—	0.15	0.75	—
1990 Proof	—	Value: 0.80				
1991	—	—	—	0.15	0.75	—
1991 Proof	12,000	Value: 0.80				
1992	—	—	—	0.15	0.75	—
1992 Proof	—	Value: 0.80				
1993	—	—	—	0.15	0.75	—
1993 Proof	7,790	Value: 0.80				
1994	—	—	—	0.15	0.75	—
1994 Proof	5,804	Value: 0.80				
1995	—	—	—	0.15	0.75	—
1995 Proof	—	Value: 0.80				

KM# 160 5 CENTS Composition: Copper Plated Steel **Obverse:** Tsonga legend

Date	Mintage	F	VF	XF	Unc	BU
1996	—	—	—	0.15	0.75	—
1996 Proof	—	Value: 0.80				
1997	—	—	—	0.15	0.75	—
1997 Proof	3,596	Value: 0.80				
1998	—	—	—	0.15	0.75	—
1998 Proof	—	Value: 1.25				
1999	—	—	—	0.15	0.75	—
1999 Proof	—	Value: 1.25				
2000	—	—	—	0.15	0.75	—

KM# 223 5 CENTS Weight: 4.4300 g. **Composition:** Copper Plated Steel **Obverse:** National arms **Reverse:** Crane standing on shore **Edge:** Plain **Size:** 21 mm.

Date	F	VF	XF	Unc	BU
2000	—	—	—	0.50	—
2001	—	—	—	0.50	—

KM# 234 5 CENTS Weight: 8.4560 g. **Composition:** 0.9250 Silver 0.2515 oz. ASW **Obverse:** Lion and country name. **Reverse:** Lions and denomination. **Edge:** Reeded. **Size:** 26.7 mm.

Date		
2000 Proof	—	Value: 20.00

KM# 243 5 CENTS Weight: 8.4560 g. **Composition:** 0.9250 Silver 0.2515 oz. ASW **Obverse:** Water buffalo head. **Reverse:** Two buffalo drinking water. **Edge:** Reeded. **Size:** 26.7 mm.

Date		
2001 Proof	—	Value: 20.00

KM# 268 5 CENTS Weight: 4.5000 g. **Composition:** Copper Plated Steel **Subject:** Legend change **Obverse:** National arms **Reverse:** Blue Crane **Edge:** Plain **Size:** 21 mm.

Date	F	VF	XF	Unc	BU
2002	—	—	—	0.50	—
2002 Proof	—	Value: 1.25			

KM# 60 10 CENTS Weight: 5.6600 g. **Composition:** 0.5000 Silver .0909 oz. ASW

Date	Mintage	F	VF	XF	Unc	BU
1961	1,136,000	—	BV	1.25	2.50	—
1961 Proof	7,530	Value: 2.50				
1962	2,447,000	—	BV	1.25	2.50	—
1962 Proof	3,844	Value: 3.50				
1963	3,327,000	—	BV	1.25	2.50	—
1963 Proof	4,025	Value: 3.50				
1964	4,152,999	—	BV	1.25	2.00	—
1964 Proof	16,000	Value: 2.50				

KM# 68.1 10 CENTS Composition: Nickel **Obverse:** English legend **Reverse:** Aloe plant

Date	Mintage	F	VF	XF	Unc	BU
1965	29,210,000	—	—	0.10	0.35	—
1966	3,685,000	—	—	0.10	0.45	—
1966 Proof	25,000	Value: 0.60				
1967	50,000	—	—	—	1.00	—
1967 Proof	25,000	Value: 0.60				
1969	558,000	—	—	0.10	0.50	—
1969 Proof	12,000	Value: 1.00				

KM# 68.2 10 CENTS Composition: Nickel **Obverse:** Afrikaans legend

Date	Mintage	F	VF	XF	Unc	BU
1965	29,210,000	—	—	0.10	0.35	—
1965 Proof	25,000	Value: 0.60				
1966	3,685,000	—	—	0.10	0.45	—
1967	50,000	—	—	—	1.00	—
1969	558,000	—	0.10	0.20	2.50	—

KM# 77.1 10 CENTS Composition: Nickel **Obverse:** President Charles Swart

Date	Mintage	F	VF	XF	Unc	BU
1968	50,000	—	—	—	2.00	—

KM# 77.2 10 CENTS **Composition:** Nickel **Obverse:** Afrikaans legend

Date	Mintage	F	VF	XF	Unc	BU
1968	50,000	—	—	—	1.50	—
1968 Proof	25,000	Value: 0.60				

KM# 85 10 CENTS **Composition:** Nickel **Obverse:** Bilingual legend

Date	Mintage	F	VF	XF	Unc	BU
1970	7,598,000	—	—	0.10	0.35	—
1970 Proof	10,000	Value: 0.60				
1971	6,440,000	—	—	0.10	0.35	—
1971 Proof	12,000	Value: 0.60				
1972	10,028,000	—	—	0.10	0.35	—
1972 Proof	10,000	Value: 0.60				
1973	1,760,000	—	—	0.10	0.35	—
1973 Proof	11,000	Value: 0.60				
1974	9,897,000	—	—	0.10	0.35	—
1974 Proof	15,000	Value: 0.60				
1975	12,982,000	—	—	0.10	0.35	—
1975 Proof	18,000	Value: 0.60				
1977	28,851,000	—	—	0.10	0.35	—
1977 Proof	19,000	Value: 0.60				
1978	25,008,000	—	—	0.10	0.35	—
1978 Proof	19,000	Value: 0.60				
1980	5,040,000	—	—	0.10	0.35	—
1980 Proof	15,000	Value: 0.60				
1981	9,604,000	—	—	0.10	0.35	—
1981 Proof	10,000	Value: 0.60				
1983	26,495,000	—	—	0.10	0.35	—
1983 Proof	14,000	Value: 0.60				
1984	35,465,000	—	—	0.10	0.35	—
1984 Proof	11,000	Value: 0.60				
1985	29,270,000	—	—	0.10	0.35	—
1985 Proof	9,859	Value: 0.60				
1986	24,480,000	—	—	0.10	0.35	—
1986 Proof	7,100	Value: 0.60				
1987	43,234,000	—	—	0.10	0.35	—
1987 Proof	6,781	Value: 0.60				
1988	48,267,000	—	—	0.10	0.35	—
1988 Proof	7,250	Value: 0.60				
1989	—	—	—	—	0.35	—
1989 Proof	—	Value: 0.60				

KM# 94 10 CENTS **Composition:** Nickel **Obverse:** President Fouche

Date	Mintage	F	VF	XF	Unc	BU
1976	30,986,000	—	—	0.40	1.00	—
1976 Proof	21,000	Value: 1.50				

KM# 101 10 CENTS **Composition:** Nickel **Obverse:** President Diederichs

Date	Mintage	F	VF	XF	Unc	BU
1979	5,042,000	—	—	0.40	1.00	—
1979 Proof	17,000	Value: 1.50				

KM# 112 10 CENTS **Composition:** Nickel **Obverse:** President Vorster

Date	Mintage	F	VF	XF	Unc	BU
1982	15,806,000	—	—	0.40	1.00	—
1982 Proof	12,000	Value: 1.50				

KM# 135 10 CENTS **Composition:** Brass Plated Steel

Date	Mintage	F	VF	XF	Unc	BU
1990	—	—	—	—	0.40	—
1990 Proof	—	Value: 0.60				
1991	—	—	—	—	0.40	—
1991 Proof	12,000	Value: 0.60				
1992	—	—	—	—	0.40	—
1992 Proof	—	Value: 0.60				
1993	—	—	—	—	0.40	—
1993 Proof	7,790	Value: 0.60				
1994	—	—	—	—	0.40	—
1994 Proof	5,804	Value: 0.60				
1995	—	—	—	—	0.40	—
1995 Proof	—	Value: 0.60				

KM# 161 10 CENTS **Composition:** Brass Plated Steel **Obverse:** English legend above arms

Date	Mintage	F	VF	XF	Unc	BU
1996	—	—	—	—	0.40	—
1996 Proof	—	Value: 0.75				
1997	—	—	—	—	0.40	—
1997 Proof	3,596	Value: 0.75				
1998	—	—	—	—	0.40	—
1998 Proof	—	Value: 1.75				
1999	—	—	—	—	0.40	—
1999 Proof	—	Value: 1.75				
2000	—	—	—	—	0.40	—

KM# 224 10 CENTS **Weight:** 2.0000 g. **Composition:** Brass Plated Steel **Obverse:** National arms **Reverse:** Flower and denomination **Edge:** Reeded **Size:** 15.9 mm.

Date	F	VF	XF	Unc	BU
2000	—	—	—	0.60	—
2001	—	—	—	0.60	—

KM# 235 10 CENTS **Weight:** 16.8630 g. **Composition:** 0.9250 Silver 0.5015 oz. ASW **Obverse:** Lion and country name. **Edge:** Reeded. **Size:** 32.7 mm.

Date	F	VF	XF	Unc	BU
2000 Proof	— Value: 25.00				

KM# 244 10 CENTS **Weight:** 16.8630 g. **Composition:** 0.9250 Silver 0.5015 oz. ASW **Obverse:** Water buffalo and country name **Reverse:** Two water buffalo bulls facing off. **Edge:** Reeded. **Size:** 32.7 mm.

Date	F	VF	XF	Unc	BU
2001 Proof	— Value: 25.00				

KM# 269 10 CENTS **Weight:** 2.0000 g. **Composition:** Copper Plated Steel **Subject:** Legend change **Obverse:** National arms **Reverse:** Arum Lily **Edge:** Reeded **Size:** 16 mm.

Date	F	VF	XF	Unc	BU
2002	—	—	—	0.60	—
2002 Proof	— Value: 1.75				

KM# 61 20 CENTS **Weight:** 11.3100 g. **Compositio** 0.5000 Silver .1818 oz. ASW

Date	Mintage	F	VF	XF	Unc
1961	2,954,000	—	BV	1.50	2.50
1961 Proof	7,530	Value: 3.50			
1962 Small 2	3,568,000	—	BV	1.50	2.50
1962 Large 2	Inc. above	—	—	—	—
1962 Small 2; Proof	3,844	Value: 4.00			
1963	4,380,000	—	BV	1.50	2.50
1963 Proof	4,025	Value: 4.00			
1964	4,335,000	—	BV	1.50	2.50
1964 Proof	16,000	Value: 2.50			

KM# 69.1 20 CENTS **Composition:** Nickel **Obverse** English legend **Reverse:** Protea Cynaroides and Protea Repens

Date	Mintage	F	VF	XF	Unc
1965	29,210,000	—	0.15	0.20	0.40
1965 Proof	25,000	Value: 0.60			
1966	4,049,000	—	0.15	0.20	0.50
1967	58,000	—	—	—	1.00
1969	9,952	—	—	—	10.00

KM# 69.2 20 CENTS **Composition:** Nickel **Obverse:** Afrikaans legend

Date	Mintage	F	VF	XF	Unc
1965	29,210,000	—	0.15	0.20	0.40
1966	4,049,000	—	0.15	0.20	0.50
1966 Proof	25,000	Value: 0.60			
1967	58,000	—	—	—	1.00
1967 Proof	25,000	Value: 0.60			
1969	9,952	—	—	—	6.00
1969 Proof	12,000	Value: 4.00			

KM# 78.1 20 CENTS **Composition:** Nickel **Obverse:** President Vorster; English legend

Date	Mintage	F	VF	XF	Unc	B
1968	50,000	—	—	—	3.00	-
1968 Proof	25,000	Value: 0.60				

KM# 78.2 20 CENTS **Composition:** Nickel **Obverse:** Afrikaans legend

Date	Mintage	F	VF	XF	Unc
1968	50,000	—	—	—	3.50

 # 86 20 CENTS **Composition:** Nickel **Obverse:** Bilingual legend **Note:** Varieties exist.

e	Mintage	F	VF	XF	Unc	BU
0	14,000	—	—	—	10.00	—
0 Proof	10,000	Value: 1.50				
1	5,893,000	—	0.15	0.25	0.60	—
1 Proof	12,000	Value: 1.50				
2	9,069,000	—	0.15	0.25	0.60	—
2 Proof	10,000	Value: 1.50				
3	20,000	—	—	—	5.00	—
3 Proof	11,000	Value: 1.50				
4	2,436,000	—	0.15	0.35	0.75	—
4 Proof	15,000	Value: 1.50				
5	12,982,000	—	—	0.20	0.60	—
5 Proof	18,000	Value: 1.00				
7	30,650,000	—	—	0.20	0.60	—
7 Proof	19,000	Value: 0.75				
8	10,049,000	—	—	0.20	0.60	—
8 Proof	19,000	Value: 0.75				
30	13,335,000	—	—	0.20	0.60	—
30 Proof	15,000	Value: 0.75				
31	8,534,000	—	—	0.20	0.60	—
31 Proof	10,000	Value: 0.75				
33	25,667,000	—	—	0.20	0.60	—
33 Proof	14,000	Value: 0.75				
34	31,607,000	—	—	0.20	0.60	—
34 Proof	11,000	Value: 0.75				
35	29,329,000	—	—	0.20	0.60	—
35 Proof	9,859	Value: 0.75				
36	11,408,000	—	—	0.20	0.60	—
36 Proof	7,100	Value: 0.75				
37	36,904,000	—	—	0.20	0.60	—
37 Proof	6,781	Value: 0.75				
38	43,115,000	—	—	0.20	0.60	—
38 Proof	7,250	Value: 0.75				
39	—	—	—	0.20	0.60	—
39 Proof	—	Value: 0.75				
90	98,512,000	—	—	0.20	0.60	—

M# 95 20 CENTS **Composition:** Nickel **Obverse:** President Fouche

te	Mintage	F	VF	XF	Unc	BU
76	18,826,000	—	—	0.70	1.50	—
76 Proof	21,000	Value: 2.50				

M# 102 20 CENTS **Composition:** Nickel **Obverse:** President Diederichs

te	Mintage	F	VF	XF	Unc	BU
979	5,032,000	—	—	0.70	1.50	—
979 Proof	15,000	Value: 2.50				

M# 113 20 CENTS **Composition:** Nickel **Obverse:** President Vorster

te	Mintage	F	VF	XF	Unc	BU
982	18,083,000	—	—	0.70	1.50	—
982 Proof	12,000	Value: 2.50				

KM# 136 20 CENTS **Composition:** Brass Plated Steel

Date	Mintage	F	VF	XF	Unc	BU
1990	—	—	—	—	4.00	—
1990 Proof	—	Value: 8.00				
1991	—	—	—	—	4.00	—
1991 Proof	11,800	Value: 8.00				
1992	—	—	—	—	0.60	—
1992 Proof	—	Value: 8.00				
1993	—	—	—	—	0.60	—
1993 Proof	7,790	Value: 8.00				
1994	—	—	—	—	0.60	—
1994 Proof	5,804	Value: 8.00				
1995	—	—	—	—	0.60	—
1995 Proof	—	Value: 8.00				

KM# 162 20 CENTS **Composition:** Brass Plated Steel **Obverse:** Tswana legend above arms

Date	Mintage	F	VF	XF	Unc	BU
1996	—	—	—	—	0.60	—
1996 Proof	—	Value: 4.00				
1997	—	—	—	—	0.60	—
1997 Proof	3,596	Value: 4.00				
1998	—	—	—	—	0.60	—
1998 Proof	—	Value: 4.00				
1999	—	—	—	—	0.60	—
1999 Proof	—	Value: 4.00				
2000	—	—	—	—	0.60	—

KM# 225 20 CENTS **Weight:** 3.4500 g. **Composition:** Brass Plated Steel **Obverse:** National arms **Reverse:** Protea flower and denomination **Edge:** Reeded **Size:** 19 mm.

Date	F	VF	XF	Unc	BU
2000	—	—	—	0.75	—
2001	—	—	—	0.75	—

KM# 236 20 CENTS **Weight:** 33.7260 g. **Composition:** 0.9250 Silver 1.003 oz. ASW **Obverse:** Lion and country name. **Reverse:** Lions and denomination. **Edge:** Reeded. **Size:** 38.3 mm.

Date	F	VF	XF	Unc	BU
2000 Proof	—	Value: 35.00			

KM# 245 20 CENTS **Weight:** 33.7260 g. **Composition:** 0.9250 Silver 1.003 oz. ASW **Obverse:** Water buffalo and country name. **Reverse:** Two water buffalo facing viewer. **Edge:** Reeded. **Size:** 38.3 mm.

Date	F	VF	XF	Unc
2001 Proof	—	Value: 35.00		

KM# 270 20 CENTS **Weight:** 3.5000 g. **Composition:** Bronze Plated Steel **Subject:** Legend change **Obverse:** National arms **Reverse:** Protea flower **Edge:** Reeded **Size:** 19 mm.

Date	F	VF	XF	Unc	BU
2002	—	—	—	0.75	—
2002 Proof	—	Value: 4.00			

KM# 62 50 CENTS **Weight:** 28.2800 g. **Composition:** 0.5000 Silver .4546 oz. ASW **Note:** Varieties exist with narrow, high relief and wide, low letters.

Date	Mintage	F	VF	XF	Unc	BU
1961	26,000	—	BV	6.00	10.00	—
1961 Prooflike	20,000	—	—	—	10.00	—
1961 Proof	8,530	Value: 18.00				
1962	15,000	—	BV	6.00	10.00	—
1962 Prooflike	6,024	—	—	—	12.50	—
1962 Proof	3,844	Value: 20.00				
1963	143,000	—	BV	5.00	9.00	—
1963 Prooflike	10,000	—	—	—	12.50	—
1963 Proof	4,025	Value: 20.00				
1964	86,000	—	BV	5.00	9.00	—
1964 Prooflike	25,000	—	—	—	10.00	—
1964 Proof	16,000	Value: 10.00				

KM# 70.1 50 CENTS **Composition:** Nickel **Obverse:** English legend **Reverse:** Zantedeschia Elliottiana

Date	Mintage	F	VF	XF	Unc	BU
1965 Proof	—	Value: 3,500				
1966	8,055,999	—	—	0.50	2.50	—
1966 Proof	25,000	Value: 4.00				
1967 In sets only	52,000	—	—	—	1.50	—
1967 Proof	25,000	Value: 4.00				
1969 In sets only	7,968	—	—	—	10.00	—
1969 Proof	12,000	Value: 10.00				

KM# 70.2 50 CENTS **Composition:** Nickel **Obverse:** Afrikaans legend

Date	Mintage	F	VF	XF	Unc	BU
1965	28,000	—	—	—	6.00	—
1965 Proof	25,000	Value: 6.00				
1966	8,055,999	—	—	0.50	2.50	—
1967 In sets only	52,000	—	—	—	3.50	—
1969 In sets only	7,968	—	—	—	15.00	—

KM# 79.1 50 CENTS **Composition:** Nickel **Obverse:** English legend; President Charles Swart

Date	Mintage	F	VF	XF	Unc	BU
1968	750,000	—	—	0.50	1.50	—

KM# 79.2 50 CENTS **Composition:** Nickel **Obverse:** Afrikaans legend

Date	Mintage	F	VF	XF	Unc	BU
1968	750,000	—	—	0.50	2.00	—
1968 Proof	25,000	Value: 3.50				

KM# 87 50 CENTS **Composition:** Nickel **Obverse:** Bilingual legend **Note:** Varieties exist.

Date	Mintage	F	VF	XF	Unc	BU
1970	4,098,000	—	—	0.50	1.50	—
1970 Proof	10,000	Value: 2.00				
1971	5,062,000	—	—	0.50	1.50	—
1971 Proof	12,000	Value: 2.00				
1972	771,000	—	—	0.50	1.50	—
1972 Proof	10,000	Value: 2.00				
1973	1,042,999	—	—	0.50	1.50	—
1973 Proof	11,000	Value: 2.00				
1974	1,942,000	—	—	0.50	1.50	—
1974 Proof	15,000	Value: 2.00				
1975	4,888,000	—	—	0.50	1.50	—
1975 Proof	18,000	Value: 2.00				
1977	10,196,000	—	—	0.50	1.50	—
1977 Proof	19,000	Value: 2.00				
1978	5,071,000	—	—	0.50	1.50	—
1978 Proof	17,000	Value: 2.00				
1980	4,268,000	—	—	0.50	1.50	—
1980 Proof	15,000	Value: 2.00				
1981	5,681,000	—	—	0.50	1.50	—
1981 Proof	10,000	Value: 2.00				
1983	5,150,000	—	—	0.40	1.00	—
1983 Proof	14,000	Value: 1.50				
1984	9,687,000	—	—	0.40	1.00	—
1984 Proof	11,000	Value: 1.50				
1985	13,339,000	—	—	0.40	1.00	—
1985 Proof	9,859	Value: 1.50				
1986	2,294,000	—	—	0.40	1.00	—
1986 Proof	7,100	Value: 1.50				
1987	19,071,000	—	—	0.40	1.00	—
1987 Proof	6,781	Value: 1.50				
1988	27,698,000	—	—	0.40	1.00	—
1988 Proof	7,250	Value: 1.50				
1989	—	—	—	0.40	1.00	—
1989 Proof	—	Value: 1.50				
1990	29,442,000	—	—	0.40	1.00	—

KM# 96 50 CENTS **Composition:** Nickel **Obverse:** President Fouche

Date	Mintage	F	VF	XF	Unc	BU
1976	9,632,000	—	0.75	1.50	3.00	—
1976 Proof	21,000	Value: 5.00				

KM# 103 50 CENTS **Composition:** Nickel **Obverse:** President Diederichs

Date	Mintage	F	VF	XF	Unc	BU
1979	5,051,000	—	0.75	1.50	3.50	—
1979 Proof	15,000	Value: 5.00				

KM# 114 50 CENTS **Composition:** Nickel **Obverse:** President Vorster

Date	Mintage	F	VF	XF	Unc	BU
1982	2,069,999	—	0.75	1.50	3.50	—
1982 Proof	12,000	Value: 5.00				

KM# 137 50 CENTS **Composition:** Brass Plated Steel

Date	Mintage	F	VF	XF	Unc	BU
1990	—	—	—	—	5.00	—
1990 Proof	—	Value: 10.00				
1991	—	—	—	—	5.00	—
1991 Proof	12,000	Value: 10.00				
1992	—	—	—	—	1.00	—
1992 Proof	—	Value: 10.00				
1993	—	—	—	—	1.00	—
1993 Proof	7,790	Value: 10.00				
1994	—	—	—	—	1.00	—
1994 Proof	5,804	Value: 10.00				
1995	—	—	—	—	1.00	—
1995 Proof	—	Value: 10.00				

KM# 163 50 CENTS **Composition:** Bronze Plated Steel **Obverse:** Sotho legend

Date		F	VF	XF	Unc	BU
1996		—	—	—	1.00	—
1996 Proof	—	Value: 5.00				
1997		—	—	—	1.00	—
1997 Proof	—	Value: 5.00				
1998		—	—	—	1.00	—
1998 Proof	—	Value: 5.00				
1999		—	—	—	1.00	—
1999 Proof	—	Value: 5.00				
2000		—	—	—	1.00	—

KM# 237 50 CENTS **Weight:** 76.4020 g. **Composition:** 0.9250 Silver 2.2722 oz. ASW **Obverse:** Lion and country name. **Reverse:** Lion and denomination. **Edge:** Reeded. **Size:** 50 mm.

Date		F	VF	XF	Unc	BU
2000 Proof	—	Value: 50.00				

KM# 246 50 CENTS **Weight:** 76.4020 g. **Composition:** 0.9250 Silver 2.2722 oz. ASW **Obverse:** Water buffalo and country name. **Reverse:** Water buffalo head and denomination. **Edge:** Reeded. **Size:** 50 mm.

Date		F	VF	XF	Unc	BU
2001 Proof	—	Value: 50.00				

KM# 226 50 CENTS **Weight:** 4.9000 g. **Composition** Brass Plated Steel **Obverse:** National arms **Reverse:** Gras like plant and denomination **Edge:** Reeded **Size:** 22 mm.

Date	F	VF	XF	Unc
2001	—	—	—	1.00

KM# 271 50 CENTS **Weight:** 5.0000 g. **Composition** Bronze Plated Steel **Subject:** Legend change **Obverse:** National arms **Reverse:** Strelitzia plant **Edge:** Reeded **Size:** 22 mm.

Date		F	VF	XF	Unc	B
2002		—	—	—	1.00	—
2002 Proof	—	Value: 5.00				

KM# 63 RAND **Weight:** 3.9940 g. **Composition:** 0.917 Gold .1177 oz. AGW

Date	Mintage	F	VF	XF	Unc	B
1961	4,246	—	—	—	BV+15%	—
1961 Proof	4,932	—	—	—	BV+20%	—
1962	3,955	—	—	—	BV+15%	—
1962 Proof	2,344	—	—	—	BV+20%	—
1963	4,023	—	—	—	BV+15%	—
1963 Proof	2,508	—	—	—	BV+20%	—
1964	5,866	—	—	—	BV+15%	—
1964 Proof	4,000	—	—	—	BV+20%	—
1965	10,000	—	—	—	BV+15%	—
1965 Proof	6,024	—	—	—	BV+20%	—
1966	10,000	—	—	—	BV+15%	—
1966 Proof	11,000	—	—	—	BV+20%	—
1967	10,000	—	—	—	BV+15%	—
1967 Proof	11,000	—	—	—	BV+20%	—
1968	10,000	—	—	—	BV+15%	—
1968 Proof	11,000	—	—	—	BV+20%	—
1969	10,000	—	—	—	BV+15%	—
1969 Proof	8,000	—	—	—	BV+20%	—
1970	10,000	—	—	—	BV+15%	—
1970 Proof	7,000	—	—	—	BV+20%	—
1971	10,000	—	—	—	BV+15%	—
1971 Proof	7,650	—	—	—	BV+20%	—
1972	12,000	—	—	—	BV+15%	—
1972 Proof	7,500	—	—	—	BV+20%	—
1973	15,000	—	—	—	BV+15%	—
1973 Proof	12,000	—	—	—	BV+20%	—
1974	23,000	—	—	—	BV+15%	—
1974 Proof	17,000	—	—	—	BV+20%	—
1975	12,000	—	—	—	BV+15%	—
1975 Proof	18,000	—	—	—	BV+20%	—
1976	12,000	—	—	—	BV+15%	—
1976 Proof	21,000	—	—	—	BV+20%	—
1977	27,000	—	—	—	BV+15%	—
1977 Proof	20,000	—	—	—	BV+20%	—
1978	13,000	—	—	—	BV+15%	—
1978 Proof	19,000	—	—	—	BV+20%	—
1979	17,000	—	—	—	BV+15%	—
1979 Proof	17,000	—	—	—	BV+20%	—
1980	14,000	—	—	—	BV+15%	—
1980 Proof	18,000	—	—	—	BV+20%	—
1981	9,274	—	—	—	BV+15%	—
1981 Proof	10,000	—	—	—	BV+20%	—
1982	14,000	—	—	—	BV+20%	—
1983	15,000	—	—	—	BV+20%	—

 # 71.1 RAND **Weight:** 15.0000 g. **Composition:** 0.8000 Silver .3858 oz. ASW **Obverse:** English legend

	Mintage	F	VF	XF	Unc	BU
5	—	—	—	BV	5.00	—
5 Proof	25,000	Value: 20.00				
6	1,434,000	—	—	BV	4.00	—
6 Proof	20	Value: 1,250				
8 In sets only	50,000	—	—	—	4.00	—
8 Proof	25,000	Value: 5.00				

 # 71.2 RAND **Weight:** 15.0000 g. **Composition:** 0.8000 Silver .3858 oz. ASW **Obverse:** Afrikaans legend

e	Mintage	F	VF	XF	Unc	BU
5 V.I.P. Proof		—	—	—	1,000	—
6		—	—	BV	4.50	—
6 Proof	25,000	Value: 6.00				
8 In sets only		—	—	—	7.50	—
8 Proof	Est. 20	Value: 1,250				

 # 72.1 RAND **Weight:** 15.0000 g. **Composition:** 0.8000 Silver .3858 oz. ASW **Subject:** 1st Anniversary - Death of Dr. Verwoerd **Obverse:** English legend

te	Mintage	F	VF	XF	Unc	BU
67		—	—	BV	4.00	—
67 Proof	Est. 20	Value: 1,250				

 # 72.2 RAND **Weight:** 15.0000 g. **Composition:** 0.8000 Silver .3858 oz. ASW **Obverse:** Afrikaans legend

te	Mintage	F	VF	XF	Unc	BU
67	1,544,000	—	—	BV	4.50	—
67 Proof	25,000	Value: 6.00				

 # 80.1 RAND **Weight:** 15.0000 g. **Composition:** 0.8000 Silver .3858 oz. ASW **Subject:** Dr. T.E. Donges **Obverse:** English legend **Note:** The South African mint does not acknowledge the existence of these 1 Rand pieces struck in proof.

ate	Mintage	F	VF	XF	Unc	BU
969		—	—	BV	4.50	—
969 Proof	Est. 20	Value: 1,250				

KM# 80.2 RAND **Weight:** 15.0000 g. **Composition:** 0.8000 Silver .3858 oz. ASW **Obverse:** Afrikaans legend

Date	Mintage	F	VF	XF	Unc	BU
1969	506,000	—	—	BV	4.50	—
1969 Proof	12,000	Value: 6.00				

KM# 89 RAND **Weight:** 15.0000 g. **Composition:** 0.8000 Silver .3858 oz. ASW **Subject:** 50th Anniversary of Pretoria Mint

Date	Mintage	F	VF	XF	Unc	BU
1974	20,000	—	—	—	12.50	—
1974 Proof	15,000	Value: 15.00				

KM# 88 RAND **Weight:** 15.0000 g. **Composition:** 0.8000 Silver .3858 oz. ASW **Obverse:** Bilingual legend

Date	Mintage	F	VF	XF	Unc	BU
1970	14,000	—	—	BV	6.00	—
1970 Proof	10,000	Value: 8.00				
1971	20,000	—	—	BV	6.00	—
1971 Proof	12,000	Value: 8.00				
1972	20,000	—	—	BV	6.00	—
1972 Proof	10,000	Value: 8.00				
1973	20,000	—	—	BV	6.00	—
1973 Proof	11,000	Value: 8.00				
1975	20,000	—	—	BV	6.00	—
1975 Proof	18,000	Value: 8.00				
1976	20,000	—	—	BV	6.00	—
1976 Proof	21,000	Value: 8.00				
1977 Proof	19,000	Value: 9.00				
1978 Proof	17,000	Value: 9.00				
1979 Proof	15,000	Value: 9.00				
1980 Proof	15,000	Value: 9.00				
1981 Proof	12,000	Value: 12.50				
1982 Proof	10,000	Value: 12.50				
1983 Proof	14,000	Value: 12.50				
1984 Proof	11,000	Value: 12.50				
1987	4,526	—	—	BV	15.00	—
1987 Proof	13,000	Value: 12.50				
1988	21	—	—	—	—	—
1988 Proof	7,250	Value: 15.00				
1989	3,684	—	—	BV	15.00	—
1989 Proof	15,000	Value: 12.50				
1990 Proof	—	Value: 25.00				

KM# 88a RAND **Composition:** Nickel

Date	Mintage	F	VF	XF	Unc	BU
1977	29,871,000	—	—	0.75	2.00	—
1977 Proof	10	Value: 1,500				
1978	12,021,000	—	—	0.75	2.00	—
1978 Proof	10	Value: 1,500				
1980	2,690,000	—	—	0.75	2.00	—
1981	2,035,000	—	—	0.75	2.00	—
1983	7,182,000	—	—	0.75	2.00	—
1983 Proof	10	Value: 1,500				
1984	5,736,000	—	—	0.75	2.00	—
1984 Proof	11,000	Value: 5.00				
1986	1,570,000	—	—	0.75	2.00	—
1986 Proof	7,000	Value: 5.00				
1987	12,152,000	—	—	0.75	2.00	—
1987 Proof	6,781	Value: 5.00				
1988	21,335,000	—	—	0.75	2.00	—
1988 Proof	7,250	Value: 5.00				
1989	—	—	—	—	2.00	—
1989 Proof	—	Value: 5.00				

KM# 104 RAND **Composition:** Nickel **Obverse:** President Diederichs

Date	Mintage	F	VF	XF	Unc	BU
1979	13,466,000	—	2.00	4.00	10.00	—
1979 Proof	5	Value: 2,000				

KM# 115 RAND **Composition:** Nickel .3858 oz. **Obverse:** President Vorster

Date	Mintage	F	VF	XF	Unc	BU
1982	7,685,000	—	2.50	5.00	10.00	—
1982 Proof	15	Value: 1,500				

KM# 116 RAND **Weight:** 15.0000 g. **Composition:** 0.8000 Silver .3858 oz. ASW **Subject:** 75th Anniversary of Parliament **Reverse:** Parliament building

Date	Mintage	F	VF	XF	Unc	BU
1985	8,731	—	—	—	11.50	—
1985 Proof	26,000	Value: 18.50				

KM# 117 RAND **Composition:** Nickel **Obverse:** President Marais Viljoen

Date	Mintage	F	VF	XF	Unc	BU
1985	3,983,000	—	2.50	5.00	10.00	—
1985 Proof	9,859	Value: 5.00				

KM# 119 RAND **Weight:** 15.0000 g. **Composition:** 0.8000 Silver .3858 oz. ASW **Subject:** 100th Anniversary of Johannesburg **Reverse:** View of city

Date	Mintage	F	VF	XF	Unc	BU
1986	7,501	—	—	—	13.50	—
1986 Proof	5,683	Value: 22.50				

KM# 120 RAND **Weight:** 15.0000 g. **Composition:** 0.8000 Silver .3858 oz. ASW **Series:** Year of the Disabled

Date	Mintage	F	VF	XF	Unc	BU
1986	1,005	—	—	—	40.00	—
1986 Proof	5,150	Value: 22.50				

KM# 122 RAND **Weight:** 15.0000 g. **Composition:** 0.8000 Silver .3858 oz. ASW **Subject:** Bartolomeu Dias

Date	Mintage	F	VF	XF	Unc	BU
1988	7,091	—	—	—	12.50	—
1988 Proof	9,640	Value: 16.50				

KM# 125 RAND **Weight:** 15.0000 g. **Composition:** 0.8000 Silver .3858 oz. ASW **Subject:** Huguenots

Date	Mintage	F	VF	XF	Unc	BU
1988	5,497	—	—	—	12.50	—
1988 Proof	9,028	Value: 16.50				

KM# 128 RAND **Weight:** 15.0000 g. **Composition:** 0.8000 Silver .3858 oz. ASW **Subject:** The Great Trek

Date	Mintage	F	VF	XF	Unc	BU
1988	6,555	—	—	—	12.50	—
1988 Proof	7,941	Value: 17.50				

KM# 141 RAND **Composition:** Nickel **Obverse:** President Botha

Date	Mintage	F	VF	XF	Unc	BU
1990	25,323,000	—	—	1.75	3.50	—
1990 Proof	15,000	Value: 10.00				

KM# 148 RAND **Composition:** Nickel Plated Copper

Date	Mintage	F	VF	XF	Unc	BU
1990	12,000	—	—	—	10.00	—
1990 Proof	10,000	Value: 15.00				

KM# 138 RAND **Composition:** Nickel Plated Copper

Date	Mintage	F	VF	XF	Unc	BU
1991	20,765,000	—	—	—	2.50	—
1991 Proof	12,000	Value: 15.00				
1992	59,571,000	—	—	—	2.50	—
1992 Proof	10,000	Value: 15.00				
1993	37,977,000	—	—	—	2.50	—
1993 Proof	7,790	Value: 20.00				
1994	54,633,000	—	—	—	2.50	—
1994 Proof	5,804	Value: 20.00				
1995	28,012,000	—	—	—	2.50	—
1995 Proof	5,816	Value: 20.00				

KM# 142 RAND **Weight:** 14.9700 g. **Composition:** 0.9250 Silver .4452 oz. ASW **Subject:** South African Nursing Schools

Date	Mintage	F	VF	XF	Unc	BU
1991	4,901	—	—	—	12.50	—
1991 Proof	8,675	Value: 17.50				

KM# 143 RAND **Weight:** 14.9700 g. **Composition:** 0.9250 Silver .4452 oz. ASW **Subject:** Coinage Centennial

Date	Mintage	F	VF	XF	Unc	BU
1992	5,826	—	—	—	12.50	—
1992 Proof	8,094	Value: 17.50				

KM# 168 RAND **Weight:** 14.9700 g. **Composition:** 0.9250 Silver .4452 oz. ASW **Subject:** 200 Years of Bankir

Date	Mintage	F	VF	XF	Unc	E
1993	3,677	—	—	—	17.50	
1993 Proof	3,907	Value: 27.50				

KM#149 RAND **Weight:** 14.9700 g. **Composition:** 0.800 Silver .3858 oz. ASW **Subject:** Presidential Inauguration

Date	Mintage	F	VF	XF	Unc	B
1994 Proof	6,269	Value: 22.50				

KM# 167 RAND **Weight:** 15.0000 g. **Composition:** 0.9250 Silver .4461 oz. ASW **Subject:** Conservation

Date	Mintage	F	VF	XF	Unc	BI
1994	6,404	—	—	—	12.50	
1994 Proof	4,706	Value: 17.50				

KM#152 RAND **Weight:** 15.0000 g. **Composition:** 0.9250 Silver .4461 oz. ASW **Subject:** Protea/Railway Centennial

Date	Mintage	F	VF	XF	Unc	BL
1995	3,515	—	—	—	15.00	
1995 Proof	4,491	Value: 22.50				

KM# 164 RAND **Composition:** Nickel Plated Copper **Subject:** Afrikaans Legend

Date	Mintage	F	VF	XF	Unc	B
1996	12,199,000	—	—	—	1.75	
1996 Proof	4,827	Value: 6.00				
1997	38,876,000	—	—	—	1.75	
1997 Proof	3,596	Value: 6.00				
1998	—	—	—	—	1.75	
1998 Proof	—	Value: 6.00				
1999	—	—	—	—	1.75	

Date	Mintage	F	VF	XF	Unc	BU
1999 Proof	—	Value: 6.00				
2000	—	—	—	—	1.75	—

KM# 169 RAND **Weight:** 15.0000 g. **Composition:** 0.9250 Silver .4461 oz. ASW **Subject:** Constitution

Date	Mintage	F	VF	XF	Unc	BU
1996	2,585	—	—	—	15.00	—
1996 Proof	2,474	Value: 25.00				

KM# 181 RAND **Weight:** 15.0000 g. **Composition:** 0.9250 Silver .4461 oz. ASW **Subject:** Women of South Africa

Date	Mintage	F	VF	XF	Unc	BU
1997	1,983	—	—	—	16.50	—
1997 Proof	2,329	Value: 28.00				

KM# 182 RAND **Weight:** 3.1103 g. **Composition:** 0.9999 Gold .1000 oz. AGW **Subject:** 30th Anniversary - First Heart Transplant

ate	Mintage	F	VF	XF	Unc	BU
997 Proof	1,000	Value: 100				

M# 177 RAND **Weight:** 15.0000 g. **Composition:** 0.9250 Silver .4461 oz. ASW **Obverse:** Protea flower **Reverse:** Divided into 16 sections

te	F	VF	XF	Unc	BU
98	—	—	—	15.00	—
98 Proof	Value: 27.50				

M# 178 RAND **Weight:** 3.1103 g. **Composition:** 0.9999 Gold .1000 oz. AGW **Subject:** San Tribe **Reverse:** Tribesman Hunting

te	F	VF	XF	Unc	BU
98	—	—	—	100	—

M# 219 RAND **Weight:** 3.1103 g. **Composition:** 0.9999 Gold .1000 oz. AGW **Obverse:** National arms **Reverse:** Zulu warrior **Edge:** Reeded **Size:** 16.5 mm.

e	Mintage	F	VF	XF	Unc	BU
9 Proof	1,000	Value: 100				

KM# 232 RAND **Weight:** 15.0000 g. **Composition:** 0.9250 Silver 0.4461 oz. ASW **Obverse:** Protea flower. **Reverse:** Mine tower. **Edge:** Reeded. **Size:** 32.7 mm.

Date		
1999 Proof	—	Value: 22.50

KM# 238 RAND **Weight:** 15.0000 g. **Composition:** 0.9250 Silver 0.4461 oz. ASW **Obverse:** Protea flower. **Reverse:** Wine barrels. **Edge:** Reeded. **Size:** 32.7 mm.

Date		
2000 Proof	—	Value: 22.50

KM# 239 RAND **Weight:** 3.1103 g. **Composition:** 0.9999 Gold 0.1 oz. AGW **Obverse:** National arms. **Reverse:** Three Xhosa tribe members. **Edge:** Reeded. **Size:** 16.5 mm.

Date	F	VF	XF	Unc	BU
2000 Proof	— Value: 100				

KM# 247 RAND **Weight:** 3.1103 g. **Composition:** 0.9999 Gold 0.1 oz. AGW **Obverse:** National arms. **Reverse:** Sotho "healer". **Edge:** Reeded. **Size:** 16.5 mm.

Date		
2001 Proof	—	Value: 100

KM# 227 RAND **Weight:** 4.0000 g. **Composition:** Nickel Plated Steel **Obverse:** National arms **Reverse:** Springbok and denomination **Edge:** Reeded and plain sections **Size:** 20 mm.

Date	F	VF	XF	Unc	BU
2001	—	—	—	1.75	—

KM# 231 RAND **Weight:** 15.0000 g. **Composition:** 0.9250 Silver 0.4461 oz. ASW **Subject:** Tourism **Obverse:** Protea flower. **Reverse:** Steam locomotive and flower. **Edge:** Reeded. **Size:** 32.7 mm.

Date	Mintage	F	VF	XF	Unc	BU
2001 Proof	3,000	Value: 30.00				

KM# 272 RAND **Weight:** 4.0000 g. **Composition:** Nickel Plated Copper **Subject:** Legend change **Obverse:** National arms **Reverse:** Springbok **Edge:** Reeded **Size:** 20 mm.

Date	F	VF	XF	Unc	BU
2002	—	—	—	1.75	—
2002 Proof	— Value: 6.00				

KM# 64 2 RAND **Weight:** 7.9881 g. **Composition:** 0.9170 Gold .2354 oz. AGW

Date	Mintage	F	VF	XF	Unc	BU
1961	3,014	—	—	—	BV+10%	—
1961 Proof	3,932	—	—	—	BV+15%	—
1962	10,000	—	—	—	BV+10%	—
1962 Proof	2,344	—	—	—	BV+15%	—
1963	3,179	—	—	—	BV+10%	—
1963 Proof	2,508	—	—	—	BV+15%	—
1964	3,994	—	—	—	BV+10%	—
1964 Proof	4,000	—	—	—	BV+15%	—
1965	10,000	—	—	—	BV+10%	—
1965 Proof	6,024	—	—	—	BV+15%	—
1966	10,000	—	—	—	BV+10%	—
1966 Proof	11,000	—	—	—	BV+15%	—
1967	10,000	—	—	—	BV+10%	—
1967 Proof	11,000	—	—	—	BV+15%	—
1968	10,000	—	—	—	BV+10%	—
1968 Proof	11,000	—	—	—	BV+15%	—
1969	10,000	—	—	—	BV+10%	—
1969 Proof	8,000	—	—	—	BV+15%	—
1970	10,000	—	—	—	BV+10%	—
1970 Proof	7,000	—	—	—	BV+15%	—
1971	10,000	—	—	—	BV+10%	—
1971 Proof	7,650	—	—	—	BV+15%	—
1972	18,000	—	—	—	BV+10%	—
1972 Proof	7,500	—	—	—	BV+15%	—
1973	14,000	—	—	—	BV+10%	—
1973 Proof	13,000	—	—	—	BV+15%	—
1974	13,000	—	—	—	BV+10%	—
1974 Proof	17,000	—	—	—	BV+15%	—
1975	12,000	—	—	—	BV+10%	—
1975 Proof	18,000	—	—	—	BV+15%	—
1976	12,000	—	—	—	BV+10%	—
1976 Proof	21,000	—	—	—	BV+15%	—
1977	12,000	—	—	—	BV+10%	—
1977 Proof	20,000	—	—	—	BV+15%	—
1978	11,000	—	—	—	BV+10%	—
1978 Proof	19,000	—	—	—	BV+15%	—
1979	12,000	—	—	—	BV+10%	—
1979 Proof	20,000	—	—	—	BV+15%	—
1980	12,000	—	—	—	BV+10%	—
1980 Proof	18,000	—	—	—	BV+15%	—
1981	8,538	—	—	—	BV+10%	—
1981 Proof	10,000	—	—	—	BV+15%	—
1982	2,030	—	—	—	BV+10%	—
1982 Proof	12,000	—	—	—	BV+15%	—
1983	15,000	—	—	—	BV+15%	—

KM# 139 2 RAND **Composition:** Nickel Plated Copper **Reverse:** Greater Kudu

Date	Mintage	F	VF	XF	Unc	BU
1989	65,233,000	—	—	—	2.00	—
1989 Proof	13,000	Value: 10.00				
1990	70,655,000	—	—	—	2.00	—
1990 Proof	10,000	Value: 7.50				
1991	39,243,000	—	—	—	2.00	—
1991 Proof	12,000	Value: 7.50				
1992	2,115,000	—	—	—	2.00	—
1992 Proof	10,000	Value: 7.50				
1993	92,000	—	—	—	2.00	—
1993 Proof	7,790	Value: 7.50				
1994	994,000	—	—	—	2.00	—
1994 Proof	5,804	Value: 7.50				
1995	13,213,000	—	—	—	2.00	—
1995 Proof	5,816	Value: 7.50				

KM# 145 2 RAND **Weight:** 33.4700 g. **Composition:** 0.9250 Silver .9954 oz. ASW **Subject:** Coin Minting

Date	Mintage	F	VF	XF	Unc	BU
1992	50	—	—	—	—	—
1992 Proof	6,688	Value: 32.50				

KM# 147 2 RAND **Weight:** 33.4700 g. **Composition:** 0.9250 Silver .9954 oz. ASW **Series:** Barcelona Olympics **Reverse:** 3 event athletes

Date	Mintage	F	VF	XF	Unc	BU
1992	1,670	—	—	—	—	—
1992 Proof	15,000	Value: 27.50				

KM# 151 2 RAND **Weight:** 33.4700 g. **Composition:** 0.9250 Silver .9954 oz. ASW **Subject:** Peace

Date	Mintage	F	VF	XF	Unc	BU
1993	828	—	—	—	—	—
1993 Proof	4,800	Value: 42.50				

KM# 156 2 RAND **Weight:** 33.6750 g. **Composition:** 0.9250 Silver 1.0014 oz. ASW **Subject:** World Cup Soccer **Reverse:** Ball and North American Map

Date	Mintage	F	VF	XF	Unc	BU
1994	288	—	—	—	—	—
1994 Proof	3,210	Value: 40.00				

KM# 153 2 RAND **Weight:** 33.6260 g. **Composition:** 0.9250 Silver 1.0000 oz. ASW **Subject:** Rugby World Cup

Date	Mintage	F	VF	XF	Unc	BU
1995 Proof	3,981	Value: 40.00				

KM# 154 2 RAND **Weight:** 33.6260 g. **Composition:** 0.9250 Silver 1.0000 oz. ASW **Series:** 50th Anniversary - F.A.O. **Reverse:** Cape Sparrow

Date	Mintage	F	VF	XF	Unc	BU
1995 Proof	1,743	Value: 45.00				

KM# 155 2 RAND **Weight:** 33.6260 g. **Composition:** 0.9250 Silver 1.0000 oz. ASW **Series:** 50th Anniversary - United Nations

Date	Mintage	F	VF	XF	Unc	BU
1995 Proof	1,412	Value: 35.00				

KM# 157 2 RAND **Weight:** 33.6260 g. **Composition:** 0.9250 Silver 1.0000 oz. ASW **Reverse:** Soccer Player

Date	Mintage	F	VF	XF	Unc	BU
1996 Proof	2,690	Value: 40.00				

KM# 165 2 RAND **Composition:** Nickel Plated Copper **Obverse:** Xhosa legend **Reverse:** Greater Kudu

Date	Mintage	F	VF	XF	Unc	BU
1996	123,000	—	—	—	2.00	—
1996 Proof	4,827	Value: 8.00				
1997	1,804,000	—	—	—	2.00	—
1997 Proof	3,596	Value: 8.00				
1998	—	—	—	—	2.00	—
1998 Proof	—	Value: 8.00				
1999	—	—	—	—	2.00	—
1999 Proof	—	Value: 8.00				
2000	—	—	—	—	2.00	—

KM# 175 2 RAND **Weight:** 33.6260 g. **Composition:** 0.9250 Silver 1.0000 oz. ASW **Reverse:** Knysna seahorse

Date	Mintage	F	VF	XF	Unc	BU
1997 Proof	3,000	Value: 45.00				

KM# 183 2 RAND **Weight:** 7.7700 g. **Composition:** 0.9999 Gold .2500 oz. AGW **Subject:** Early Man **Reverse:** Australopithecus Africanus

Date	Mintage	F	VF	XF	Unc	BU
1997 Proof	1,000	Value: 165				

KM# 179 2 RAND **Weight:** 33.6200 g. **Composition:** 0.9250 Silver 1.0000 oz. ASW **Reverse:** Jackass penguin

Date	F	VF	XF	Unc	BU
1998 Proof	Est. 3,000	Value: 42.50			

KM# 180 2 RAND **Weight:** 7.7770 g. **Composition:** 0.9999 Gold .2500 oz. AGW **Reverse:** Coelacanth Fish and Fossil

Date	F	VF	XF	Unc	BU
1998 Proof	—	Value: 175			

KM# 220 2 RAND **Weight:** 7.7759 g. **Composition:** 0.9999 Gold .2500 oz. AGW **Obverse:** National arms **Reverse:** Thrinaxodon dinosaur

Date	Mintage	F	VF	XF	Unc	BU
1999 Proof	1,000	Value: 200				

KM# 218 2 RAND **Weight:** 33.6000 g. **Composition:** 0.9250 Silver .9992 oz. ASW **Obverse:** National arms **Reverse:** Great white shark **Edge:** Reeded **Size:** 38.7 mm. **Note:** Struck at Pretoria.

Date	Mintage	F	VF	XF	Unc	BU
1999 Proof	3,000	Value: 37.50				

KM# 240 2 RAND **Weight:** 33.6260 g. **Composition:** 0.9250 Silver 1 oz. ASW **Obverse:** Protea flower. **Reverse:** Octopus. **Edge:** Reeded. **Size:** 38.7 mm.

Date	F	VF	XF	Unc	BU
2000 Proof	—	Value: 35.00			

KM# 241 2 RAND **Weight:** 7.7770 g. **Composition:** 0.9999 Gold 0.25 oz. AGW **Obverse:** National arms. **Reverse:** "Little Foot" skeleton find. **Edge:** Reeded. **Size:** 22 mm.

Date	F	VF	XF	Unc	BU
2000 Proof	—	Value: 175			

KM# 248 2 RAND **Weight:** 33.6260 g. **Composition:** 0.9250 Silver 1 oz. ASW **Obverse:** National arms. **Reverse:** Dolphins. **Edge:** Reeded. **Size:** 38.7 mm.

Date	F	VF	XF	Unc	BU
2001 Proof	—	Value: 35.00			

KM# 249 2 RAND **Weight:** 7.7770 g. **Composition:** 0.9999 Gold 0.25 oz. AGW **Obverse:** National arms. **Reverse:** Gondwana theoretical landmass and dinosaur. **Edge:** Reeded. **Size:** 22 mm.

Date	F	VF	XF	Unc	BU
2001 Proof	—	Value: 175			

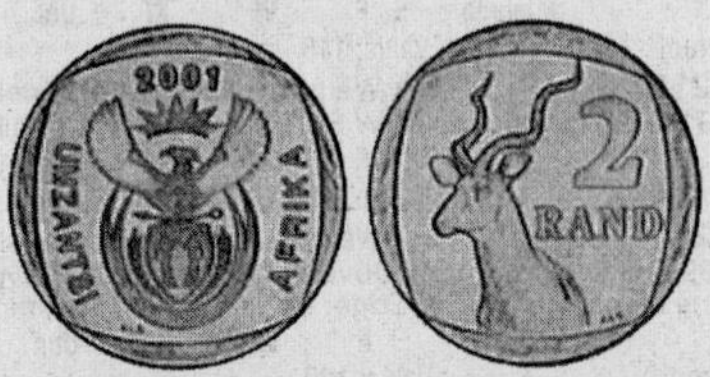

KM# 228 2 RAND **Weight:** 5.4300 g. **Composition:** Nickel Plated Steel **Obverse:** National arms **Reverse:** Greater Kudu and denomination **Edge:** Reeded and plain sections **Size:** 23 mm.

Date	F	VF	XF	Unc	BU
2001	—	—	—	2.00	—

KM# 273 2 RAND **Weight:** 5.5000 g. **Composition:** Nickel Plated Copper **Subject:** Legend change **Obverse:** National arms **Reverse:** Kudu **Edge:** Reeded and plain sections **Size:** 23 mm.

Date	F	VF	XF	Unc	BU
2002	—	—	—	2.00	—
2002 Proof	—	Value: 8.00			

KM# 140 5 RAND **Composition:** Nickel Plated Copper **Reverse:** Black Wildebeest

Date	Mintage	F	VF	XF	Unc	BU
1994	45,212,000	—	—	—	4.50	—
1994 Proof	5,804	Value: 10.00				
1995	41,238,000	—	—	—	4.50	—
1995 Proof	5,816	Value: 10.00				

KM# 150 5 RAND **Composition:** Nickel Plated Copper **Subject:** Presidential Inauguration

Date	Mintage	F	VF	XF	Unc	BU
1994	10,095,000	—	—	—	5.50	—
1994 Proof	10,000	Value: 8.50				

KM# 166 5 RAND **Composition:** Nickel Plated Copper **Obverse:** Zulu/Swati legend above arms

Date	Mintage	F	VF	XF	Unc	BU
1996	15,435,000	—	—	—	4.50	—
1996 Proof	4,827	Value: 10.00				
1997	1,276,000	—	—	—	4.50	—
1997 Proof	3,596	Value: 10.00				
1998	—	—	—	—	4.50	—
1998 Proof	—	Value: 10.00				
1999	—	—	—	—	4.50	—
1999 Proof	—	Value: 10.00				
2000	—	—	—	—	4.50	—

KM# 230 5 RAND **Weight:** 6.9400 g. **Composition:** Nickel Plated Steel **Subject:** Nelson Mandela **Obverse:** Portrait **Reverse:** Wildebeest and denomination **Edge:** Reeded and plain sections **Size:** 25.9 mm.

Date	F	VF	XF	Unc	BU
2000	—	—	—	4.50	—
2000 Proof	—	Value: 10.00			

KM# 229 5 RAND **Weight:** 6.9400 g. **Composition:** Nickel Plated Steel **Obverse:** National arms **Reverse:** Black Wildebeest and denomination **Edge:** Reeded and plain sections **Size:** 26 mm.

Date	F	VF	XF	Unc	BU
2001	—	—	—	4.50	—

KM# 274 5 RAND **Weight:** 7.0000 g. **Composition:** Nickel Plated Copper **Subject:** Legend change **Obverse:** National arms **Reverse:** Black Wildebeest **Edge:** Reeded and plain sections **Size:** 26 mm.

Date	F	VF	XF	Unc	BU
2002	—	—	—	4.50	—
2002 Proof	—	Value: 10.00			

BULLION COINAGE

Mint mark: GRC - Gold Reef City

KM# 105 1/10 KRUGERRAND **Weight:** 3.3900 g. **Composition:** 0.9170 Gold .1000 oz. AGW

Date	Mintage	F	VF	XF	Unc	BU
1980	857,000	—	—	—	BV+15%	—
1980 Proof	60	Value: 2,500				
1981	1,321,000	—	—	—	BV+15%	—
1981 Proof	7,500	Value: 90.00				
1982	1,065,000	—	—	—	BV+15%	—
1982 Proof	11,000	Value: 85.00				
1983	508,000	—	—	—	BV+15%	—
1983 Proof	12,000	Value: 85.00				
1984	898,000	—	—	—	BV+15%	—
1984 Proof	13,000	Value: 85.00				
1985	282,000	—	—	—	BV+15%	—
1985 Proof	6,700	Value: 85.00				
1986	87,000	—	—	—	BV+15%	—
1986 Proof	8,001	Value: 85.00				
1987	53,000	—	—	—	BV+15%	—
1987 Proof	6,065	Value: 85.00				
1987 GRC Proof	1,126	Value: 400				
1988	87,000	—	—	—	BV+15%	—
1988 Proof	2,056	Value: 90.00				
1988 GRC Proof	949	Value: 400				
1989	—	—	—	—	BV+15%	—
1989 Proof	3,316	Value: 90.00				
1989 GRC Proof	377	Value: 1,000				
1990	—	—	—	—	BV+15%	—
1990 Proof	3,459	Value: 90.00				
1990 GRC Proof	1,096	Value: 275				
1991 Proof	3,524	Value: 90.00				
1991 GRC Proof	426	Value: 275				
1992 Proof	1,789	Value: 90.00				
1993	54,000	—	—	—	BV+15%	—
1993 Proof	3,811	Value: 90.00				
1994	86,000	—	—	—	BV+15%	—
1994 Proof	—	Value: 90.00				
1995	25,000	—	—	—	BV+15%	—
1995 Proof	750	Value: 120				
1996 Proof	4,000	Value: 90.00				
1997 Proof	3,410	Value: 90.00				
1997 Proof	30	Value: 300				

Note: 30th Anniversary of Krugerrand privy mark

Date	Mintage	F	VF	XF	Unc	BU
1998 Proof	—	Value: 90.00				
1999 Proof	—	Value: 90.00				

KM# 106 1/4 KRUGERRAND **Weight:** 8.4800 g. **Composition:** 0.9170 Gold .2500 oz. AGW

Date	Mintage	F	VF	XF	Unc	BU
1980	534,000	—	—	—	BV+10%	—
1980 Proof	60	Value: 3,000				
1981	726,000	—	—	—	BV+10%	—
1981 Proof	7,500	Value: 165				
1982	1,269,000	—	—	—	BV+10%	—
1982 Proof	11,000	Value: 165				
1983	64,000	—	—	—	BV+10%	—
1983 Proof	12,000	Value: 165				
1984	503,000	—	—	—	BV+10%	—
1984 Proof	13,000	Value: 165				
1985	594,000	—	—	—	BV+10%	—
1985 Proof	6,700	Value: 165				
1986 Proof	8,001	Value: 165				
1987 Proof	6,050	Value: 165				
1987 GRC Proof	1,121	Value: 500				
1988	5,946	—	—	—	BV+10%	—
1988 Proof	2,056	Value: 175				
1988 GRC Proof	835	Value: 500				
1989	5,943	—	—	—	BV+10%	—
1989 Proof	3,316	Value: 175				
1989 GRC Proof	318	Value: 1,400				
1990 Proof	2,750	Value: 175				
1990 GRC Proof	1,066	Value: 400				
1991 Proof	1,626	Value: 175				
1991 GRC Proof	426	Value: 400				
1992 Proof	1,629	Value: 175				
1993 Proof	3,061	Value: 175				
1994	39,000	—	—	—	BV+10%	—
1994 Proof	1,874	Value: 175				
1995	13,000	—	—	—	BV+10%	—
1995 Proof	1,095	Value: 200				
1996 Proof	1,853	Value: 175				
1997 Proof	1,440	Value: 175				
1997 Proof	30	Value: 450				

Note: 30th Anniversary of Krugerrand privy mark

Date	Mintage	F	VF	XF	Unc	BU
1998 Proof	—	Value: 175				
1999 Proof	—	Value: 175				

KM# 107 1/2 KRUGERRAND **Weight:** 16.9700 g. **Composition:** 0.9170 Gold .5000 oz. AGW

Date	Mintage	F	VF	XF	Unc	BU
1980	374,000	—	—	—	BV+8%	—
1980 Proof	60	Value: 3,500				
1981	178,000	—	—	—	BV+8%	—
1981 Proof	9,000	Value: 285				
1982	429,000	—	—	—	BV+8%	—
1982 Proof	13,000	Value: 285				
1983	60,000	—	—	—	BV+8%	—
1983 Proof	14,000	Value: 285				
1984	187,000	—	—	—	BV+8%	—
1984 Proof	9,900	Value: 285				
1985	104,000	—	—	—	BV+8%	—
1985 Proof	5,945	Value: 285				
1986 Proof	8,002	Value: 285				
1987 Proof	5,389	Value: 285				
1987 GRC Proof	1,186	Value: 800				
1988	5,454	—	—	—	BV+8%	—
1988 Proof	2,282	Value: 300				
1988 GRC Proof	1,026	Value: 800				
1989	4,980	—	—	—	BV+8%	—
1989 Proof	3,727	Value: 300				
1989 GRC Proof	399	Value: 1,500				
1990 Proof	2,850	Value: 300				
1990 GRC Proof	1,066	Value: 500				
1991 Proof	3,459	Value: 300				
1991 GRC Proof	426	Value: 500				
1992 Proof	1,501	Value: 300				
1993	11,000	—	—	—	BV+8%	—

Date	Mintage	F	VF	XF	Unc	BU
1993 Proof	2,439	Value: 300				
1994	16,000	—	—	—	BV+8%	—
1994 Proof	2,146	Value: 300				
1995	10,000	—	—	—	BV+8%	—
1995 Proof	1,012	Value: 300				
1996 Proof	1,788	Value: 300				
1997 Proof	2,000	Value: 300				
1997 Proof	30	Value: 550				
Note: 30th Anniversary of Krugerrand privy mark						
1998 Proof	—	Value: 275				
1999 Proof	—	Value: 300				

KM# 73 KRUGERRAND **Weight:** 33.9305 g. **Composition:** 0.9170 Gold 1.0000 oz. AGW

Date	Mintage	F	VF	XF	Unc	BU
1967	40,000	—	—	—	BV+5%	—
1967 Proof	10,000	Value: 525				
1968	20,000	—	—	—	BV+5%	—
1968 Proof	5,000	Value: 1,000				
Note: Frosted bust and frosted reverse						
1968 Proof	8,956	Value: 550				
1969	20,000	—	—	—	BV+5%	—
1969 Proof	10,000	Value: 525				
1970	211,000	—	—	—	BV+5%	—
1970 Proof	10,000	Value: 485				
1971	550,000	—	—	—	BV+5%	—
1971 Proof	6,000	Value: 485				
1972	544,000	—	—	—	BV+5%	—
1972 Proof	6,625	Value: 485				
1973	859,000	—	—	—	BV+5%	—
1973 Proof	10,000	Value: 485				
1974	3,204,000	—	—	—	BV+5%	—
1974 Proof	6,352	Value: 485				
1975	4,804,000	—	—	—	BV+5%	—
1975 Proof	5,600	Value: 485				
1976	3,005,000	—	—	—	BV+5%	—
1976 Proof	6,600	Value: 485				
1977	3,331,000	—	—	—	BV+5%	—
Note: 188 serrations on edge						
1977 Proof	8,500	Value: 485				
Note: 188 serrations on edge						
1977	Inc. above	—	—	—	BV+5%	—
Note: 220 serrations on edge						
1977 Proof	Inc. above	Value: 485				
Note: 220 serrations on edge						
1978	6,012,000	—	—	—	BV+5%	—
1978 Proof	10,000	Value: 485				
1979	4,941,000	—	—	—	BV+5%	—
1979 Proof	12,000	Value: 485				
1980	3,143,000	—	—	—	BV+5%	—
1980 Proof	12,000	Value: 485				
1981	3,560,000	—	—	—	BV+5%	—
1981 Proof	13,000	Value: 485				
1982	2,566,000	—	—	—	BV+5%	—
1982 Proof	17,000	Value: 485				
1983	3,368,000	—	—	—	BV+5%	—
1983 Proof	19,000	Value: 485				
1984	2,070,000	—	—	—	BV+5%	—
1984 Proof	14,000	Value: 485				
1985	875,000	—	—	—	BV+5%	—
1985 Proof	10,000	Value: 485				
1986 Proof	20,000	Value: 485				
1987	11,000	—	—	—	BV+5%	—
1987 Proof	11,000	Value: 485				
1987 GRC Proof	1,160	Value: 1,200				
1988	615,000	—	—	—	BV+5%	—
1988 Proof	4,268	Value: 500				
1988 GRC Proof	1,220	Value: 1,200				
1989	194,000	—	—	—	BV+5%	—
1989 Proof	5,070	Value: 500				
1989 GRC Proof	987	Value: 1,600				
1990	391,000	—	—	—	BV+5%	—
1990 Proof	3,032	Value: 500				
1990 GRC Proof	1,066	Value: 1,600				
1991	283,000	—	—	—	BV+5%	—
1991 Proof	2,181	Value: 500				
1991 GRC Proof	426	Value: 1,600				
1992	1,803	—	—	—	BV+5%	—
1992 Proof	2,067	Value: 500				
1993	162,000	—	—	—	BV+5%	—
1993 Proof	3,963	Value: 500				
1994	130,000	—	—	—	BV+5%	—
1994 Proof	1,761	Value: 500				
1995	59,000	—	—	—	BV+5%	—
1995 Proof	1,678	Value: 500				
1996 Proof	2,188	Value: 500				
1997 Proof	1,663	Value: 500				
1997 SS Proof	72	Value: 850				

Date	Mintage	F	VF	XF	Unc	BU
1997 Proof	30	Value: 1,250				
Note: 30th Anniversary of Krugerrand privy mark						
1998 Proof	—	Value: 500				
1999 Proof	—	Value: 500				

KM# 118 OUNCE **Weight:** 33.9305 g. **Composition:** 0.9170 Gold 1.0000 oz. AGW **Subject:** 75th Anniversary of Parliament

Date	Mintage	F	VF	XF	Unc	BU
1985 Proof	3,019	Value: 1,200				

KM# 184 OUNCE **Weight:** 31.1070 g. **Composition:** 0.9999 Gold 1.0000 oz. AGW **Subject:** Presidential Inauguration

Date	Mintage	F	VF	XF	Unc	BU
1994 Proof	1,742	Value: 600				

KM# 185 OUNCE **Weight:** 31.1070 g. **Composition:** 0.9999 Gold 1.0000 oz. AGW **Subject:** Rugby

Date	Mintage	F	VF	XF	Unc	BU
1995 Proof	406	Value: 625				

KM# 131 1/10 PROTEA **Weight:** 3.3900 g. **Composition:** 0.9170 Gold .1000 oz. AGW **Subject:** 100th Anniversary of Johannesburg

Date	Mintage	F	VF	XF	Unc	BU
1986 Proof	5,212	Value: 100				

KM# 123 1/10 PROTEA **Weight:** 3.3900 g. **Composition:** 0.9170 Gold .1000 oz. AGW **Subject:** Bartolomeu Dias

Date	Mintage	F	VF	XF	Unc	BU
1988 Proof	2,199	Value: 100				

KM# 126 1/10 PROTEA **Weight:** 3.3900 g. **Composition:** 0.9170 Gold .1000 oz. AGW **Subject:** Huguenots

Date	Mintage	F	VF	XF	Unc	BU
1988 Proof	2,060	Value: 100				

KM# 129 1/10 PROTEA **Weight:** 3.3900 g. **Composition:** 0.9170 Gold .1000 oz. AGW **Subject:** The Great Trek

Date	Mintage	F	VF	XF	Unc	BU
1988 Proof	2,999	Value: 100				

KM# 171 1/10 PROTEA **Weight:** 3.3900 g. **Composition:** 0.9170 Gold .1000 oz. AGW **Subject:** South African Nursing Schools **Note:** Similar to 1 Rand, KM#142.

Date	Mintage	F	VF	XF	Unc	BU
1991 Proof	3,950	Value: 100				

KM# 144 1/10 PROTEA **Weight:** 3.3900 g. **Composition:** 0.9170 Gold .1000 oz. AGW **Subject:** Coinage Centennial

Date	Mintage	F	VF	XF	Unc	BU
1992 Proof	2,503	Value: 100				

KM# 172 1/10 PROTEA **Weight:** 3.3900 g. **Composition:** 0.9170 Gold .1000 oz. AGW **Subject:** 200 Years of Banking **Note:** Similar to 1 Rand, KM#168.

Date	Mintage	F	VF	XF	Unc	BU
1993 Proof	5,064	Value: 100				
1993 Proof	5,064	Value: 100				

KM# 187 1/10 PROTEA **Weight:** 3.3900 g. **Composition:** 0.9170 Gold .1000 oz. AGW **Subject:** Conservation

Date	Mintage	F	VF	XF	Unc	BU
1994 Proof	1,485	Value: 110				

KM# 193 1/10 PROTEA **Weight:** 3.3900 g. **Composition:** 0.9170 Gold .1000 oz. AGW **Subject:** Railways

Date	Mintage	F	VF	XF	Unc	BU
1995 Proof	1,217	Value: 110				

KM# 199 1/10 PROTEA **Weight:** 3.3900 g. **Composition:** 0.9170 Gold .1000 oz. AGW **Subject:** Constitution

Date	Mintage	F	VF	XF	Unc	BU
1996 Proof	946	Value: 110				

KM# 205 1/10 PROTEA **Weight:** 3.3900 g. **Composition:** 0.9170 Gold .1000 oz. AGW **Subject:** Women of South Africa

Date	Mintage	F	VF	XF	Unc	BU
1997 Proof	648	Value: 115				

KM# 211 1/10 PROTEA **Weight:** 3.3900 g. **Composition:** 0.9170 Gold .1000 oz. AGW **Subject:** Year of the Child

Date	F	VF	XF	Unc	BU
1998 Proof	—	Value: 115			

KM# 250 1/10 PROTEA **Weight:** 3.1103 g. **Composition:** 0.9999 Gold 0.1 oz. AGW **Obverse:** Protea flower. **Reverse:** Mine cart and entrance. **Edge:** Reeded. **Size:** 16.5 mm.

Date	F	VF	XF	Unc	BU
1999 Proof	—	Value: 100			

KM# 256 1/10 PROTEA **Weight:** 3.1103 g. **Composition:** 0.9999 Gold 0.1 oz. AGW **Obverse:** Protea flower. **Reverse:** Grape vines and building. **Edge:** Reeded. **Size:** 16.5 mm.

Date	F	VF	XF	Unc	BU
2000 Proof	—	Value: 100			

KM# 262 1/10 PROTEA **Weight:** 3.1103 g. **Composition:** 0.9999 Gold 0.1 oz. AGW **Obverse:** Protea flower. **Reverse:** Lion and partial shield. **Edge:** Reeded. **Size:** 16.5 mm.

Date	F	VF	XF	Unc	BU
2001 Proof	—	Value: 100			

KM# 121 PROTEA **Weight:** 33.9300 g. **Composition:** 0.9170 Gold 1.0000 oz. AGW **Subject:** 100th Anniversary of Johannesburg

Date	Mintage	F	VF	XF	Unc	BU
1986 Proof	4,701	Value: 600				

KM# 124 PROTEA **Weight:** 33.9300 g. **Composition:** 0.9170 Gold 1.0000 oz. AGW **Subject:** Bartolomeu Dias

Date	Mintage	F	VF	XF	Unc	BL
1988 Proof	3,776	Value: 600				

KM# 127 PROTEA **Weight:** 33.9300 g. **Composition:** 0.9170 Gold 1.0000 oz. AGW **Subject:** Huguenots

Date	Mintage	F	VF	XF	Unc	B
1988 Proof	3,391	Value: 600				

1# 130 **PROTEA** **Weight:** 33.9300 g. **Composition:** 0.9170 Gold 1.0000 oz. AGW **Subject:** The Great Trek

e	Mintage	F	VF	XF	Unc	BU
8 Proof	2,956	Value: 600				

/I# 186 **PROTEA** **Weight:** 33.9300 g. **Composition:** 0.9170 Gold 1.0000 oz. AGW **Subject:** Nursing

e	Mintage	F	VF	XF	Unc	BU
1 Proof	3,004	Value: 600				

/I# 146 **PROTEA** **Weight:** 33.9300 g. **Composition:** 0.9170 Gold 1.0000 oz. AGW **Subject:** Coinage Centennial

e	Mintage	F	VF	XF	Unc	BU
2 Proof	1,752	Value: 600				

/I# 173 **PROTEA** **Weight:** 33.9300 g. **Composition:** 0.9170 Gold 1.0000 oz. AGW **Subject:** 200 Years of Banking **Note:** Similar to 1 Rand, KM#168.

e	Mintage	F	VF	XF	Unc	BU
3 Proof	2,032	Value: 600				
3 GRC Proof	500	Value: 620				

/I# 188 **PROTEA** **Weight:** 33.9300 g. **Composition:** 0.9170 Gold 1.0000 oz. AGW **Subject:** Conservation

e	Mintage	F	VF	XF	Unc	BU
4 Proof	1,187	Value: 600				
4 Proof	600	Value: 620				

Note: PTA.ZOO

/I# 194 **PROTEA** **Weight:** 33.9300 g. **Composition:** 0.9170 Gold 1.0000 oz. AGW **Subject:** Railway

te	Mintage	F	VF	XF	Unc	BU
95 Proof	694	Value: 620				

M# 200 **PROTEA** **Weight:** 33.9300 g. **Composition:** 0.9170 Gold 1.0000 oz. AGW **Subject:** Constitution

te	Mintage	F	VF	XF	Unc	BU
96 Proof	641	Value: 620				

M# 206 **PROTEA** **Weight:** 33.9300 g. **Composition:** 0.9170 Gold 1.0000 oz. AGW **Subject:** Women of South Africa

te	Mintage	F	VF	XF	Unc	BU
97 Proof	207	Value: 635				

M# 212 **PROTEA** **Weight:** 33.9300 g. **Composition:** 0.9170 Gold 1.0000 oz. AGW **Subject:** Year of the Child

te		F	VF	XF	Unc	BU
98 Proof	—	Value: 635				

M# 251 **PROTEA** **Weight:** 31.1035 g. **Composition:** 0.9999 Gold 0.9999 oz. AGW **Obverse:** Protea flower. **Reverse:** Miner. **Edge:** Reeded. **Size:** 32.7 mm.

te		F	VF	XF	Unc	BU
99 Proof	—	Value: 600				

M# 257 **PROTEA** **Weight:** 31.1035 g. **Composition:** 0.9999 Gold 0.9999 oz. AGW **Obverse:** Protea flower. **Reverse:** Worker holding basket. **Edge:** Reeded. **Size:** 32.7 mm.

te		F	VF	XF	Unc	BU
00 Proof	—	Value: 600				

M# 263 **PROTEA** **Weight:** 31.1035 g. **Composition:** 0.9999 Gold 0.9999 oz. AGW **Obverse:** Protea flower. **Reverse:** Child on sandy beach and partial sun. **Edge:** Reeded. **Size:** 32.7 mm.

te		F	VF	XF	Unc	BU
01 Proof	—	Value: 600				

NATURA GOLD BULLION COINAGE

KM# 189 1/10 OUNCE **Weight:** 3.1104 g. **Composition:** 0.9990 Gold .1000 oz. AGW **Reverse:** Lions drinking

Date	Mintage	F	VF	XF	Unc	BU
1994 Proof	6,660	Value: 100				

KM# 195 1/10 OUNCE **Weight:** 3.1104 g. **Composition:** 0.9990 Gold .1000 oz. AGW **Reverse:** Rhinocerous drinking

Date	Mintage	F	VF	XF	Unc	BU
1995 Proof	2,703	Value: 100				

KM# 201 1/10 OUNCE **Weight:** 3.1104 g. **Composition:** 0.9990 Gold .1000 oz. AGW **Reverse:** Elephant

Date	Mintage	F	VF	XF	Unc	BU
1996 Proof	9,014	Value: 100				

KM# 207 1/10 OUNCE eight: 3.1104 g. **Composition:** 0.9990 Gold .1000 oz. AGW **Reverse:** Buffalo

Date	Mintage	F	VF	XF	Unc	BU
1997 Proof	3,590	Value: 100				

KM# 213 1/10 OUNCE **Weight:** 3.1104 g. **Composition:** 0.9990 Gold .1000 oz. AGW **Reverse:** Leopard

Date		F	VF	XF	Unc	BU
1998 Proof	—	Value: 100				

KM# 252 1/10 OUNCE **Weight:** 3.1103 g. **Composition:** 0.9999 Gold 0.1 oz. AGW **Obverse:** Greater Koodoo head. **Reverse:** Koodoo herd drinking. **Edge:** Reeded. **Size:** 16.5 mm.

Date		F	VF	XF	Unc	BU
1999 Proof	—	Value: 100				

KM# 258 1/10 OUNCE **Weight:** 3.1103 g. **Composition:** 0.9999 Gold 0.1 oz. AGW **Obverse:** Ibex head. **Reverse:** Ibex drinking. **Edge:** Reeded. **Size:** 16.5 mm.

Date		F	VF	XF	Unc	BU
2000 Proof	—	Value: 100				

KM# 264 1/10 OUNCE **Weight:** 3.1103 g. **Composition:** 0.9999 Gold 0.1 oz. AGW **Obverse:** Gemsbok head. **Reverse:** Gemsbok drinking. **Edge:** Reeded. **Size:** 16.5 mm.

Date		F	VF	XF	Unc	BU
2001 Proof	—	Value: 100				

KM# 190 1/4 OUNCE **Weight:** 7.7770 g. **Composition:** 0.9999 Gold .2500 oz. AGW **Reverse:** Lions

Date	Mintage	F	VF	XF	Unc	BU
1994 Proof	4,159	Value: 185				

KM# 196 1/4 OUNCE **Weight:** 7.7770 g. **Composition:** 0.9999 Gold .2500 oz. AGW **Reverse:** Rhinocerous

Date	Mintage	F	VF	XF	Unc	BU
1995 Proof	1,752	Value: 185				

KM# 202 1/4 OUNCE **Weight:** 7.7770 g. **Composition:** 0.9999 Gold .2500 oz. AGW **Reverse:** Elephant

Date	Mintage	F	VF	XF	Unc	BU
1996 Proof	3,740	Value: 185				

KM# 208 1/4 OUNCE **Weight:** 7.7770 g. **Composition:** 0.9999 Gold .2500 oz. AGW **Reverse:** Buffalo

Date	Mintage	F	VF	XF	Unc	BU
1997 Proof	2,164	Value: 185				

KM# 214 1/4 OUNCE **Weight:** 7.7770 g. **Composition:** 0.9999 Gold .2500 oz. AGW **Reverse:** Leopard

Date		F	VF	XF	Unc	BU
1998 Proof	—	Value: 185				

KM# 253 1/4 OUNCE **Weight:** 7.7770 g. **Composition:** 0.9999 Gold 0.25 oz. AGW **Obverse:** Greater Koodoo head. **Reverse:** Two Koodoos fighting. **Edge:** Reeded. **Size:** 22 mm.

Date		F	VF	XF	Unc	BU
1999 Proof	—	Value: 185				

KM# 259 1/4 OUNCE **Weight:** 7.7770 g. **Composition:** 0.9999 Gold 0.25 oz. AGW **Obverse:** Ibex head. **Reverse:** Two Ibexe males facing off. **Edge:** Reeded. **Size:** 22 mm.

Date		F	VF	XF	Unc	BU
2000 Proof	—	Value: 185				

KM# 265 1/4 OUNCE **Weight:** 7.7770 g. **Composition:** 0.9999 Gold 0.25 oz. AGW **Obverse:** Gemsbok head. **Reverse:** Two Gemsbok males facing off. **Edge:** Reeded. **Size:** 22 mm.

Date		F	VF	XF	Unc	BU
2001 Proof	—	Value: 185				

KM# 191 1/2 OUNCE **Weight:** 15.5530 g. **Composition:** 0.9999 Gold .5000 oz. AGW **Reverse:** Lions

Date	Mintage	F	VF	XF	Unc	BU
1994 Proof	3,999	Value: 300				

KM# 197 1/2 OUNCE **Weight:** 15.5530 g. **Composition:** 0.9999 Gold .5000 oz. AGW **Reverse:** Rhinocerous

Date	Mintage	F	VF	XF	Unc	BU
1995 Proof	1,551	Value: 300				

KM# 203 1/2 OUNCE **Weight:** 15.5530 g. **Composition:** 0.9999 Gold .5000 oz. AGW **Reverse:** Elephant

Date	Mintage	F	VF	XF	Unc	BU
1996 Proof	3,457	Value: 300				

KM# 209 1/2 OUNCE **Weight:** 15.5530 g. **Composition:** 0.9999 Gold .5000 oz. AGW **Reverse:** Buffalo

Date	Mintage	F	VF	XF	Unc	BU
1997 Proof	1,912	Value: 300				

KM# 215 1/2 OUNCE **Weight:** 15.5530 g. **Composition:** 0.9999 Gold .5000 oz. AGW **Reverse:** Leopard

Date		F	VF	XF	Unc	BU
1998 Proof	—	Value: 300				

KM# 254 1/2 OUNCE **Weight:** 15.5518 g. **Composition:** 0.9990 Gold 0.4995 oz. AGW **Obverse:** Greater Koodoo head. **Reverse:** Koodoo attacked by lion. **Edge:** Reeded. **Size:** 27 mm.

Date		F	VF	XF	Unc	BU
1999 Proof	—	Value: 300				

KM# 260 1/2 OUNCE **Weight:** 15.5518 g. **Composition:** 0.9990 Gold 0.4995 oz. AGW **Obverse:** Ibex head. **Reverse:** Ibex head. **Edge:** Reeded. **Size:** 27 mm.

Date		F	VF	XF	Unc	BU
2000 Proof	—	Value: 300				

KM# 266 1/2 OUNCE **Weight:** 15.5518 g. **Composition:** 0.9990 Gold 0.4995 oz. AGW **Obverse:** Gemsbok head. **Reverse:** Gemsbok grazing. **Edge:** Reeded. **Size:** 27 mm.

Date		F	VF	XF	Unc	BU
2001 Proof	—	Value: 300				

KM# 192 OUNCE **Weight:** 31.1070 g. **Composition:** 0.9999 Gold 1.0000 oz. AGW **Reverse:** Lions

Date	Mintage	F	VF	XF	Unc	BU
1994 Proof	2,902	Value: 600				
1994 Pre.Zoo Proof	775	Value: 620				

KM# 198 OUNCE **Weight:** 31.1070 g. **Composition:** 0.9999 Gold 1.0000 oz. AGW **Reverse:** Rhinocerous

Date	Mintage	F	VF	XF	Unc	BU
1995 Proof	1,800	Value: 600				
1995 Hluhuwe Proof	350	Value: 620				

KM# 204 OUNCE **Weight:** 31.1070 g. **Composition:** 0.9999 Gold 1.0000 oz. AGW **Reverse:** Elephant

Date	Mintage	F	VF	XF	Unc	BU
1996 Proof	4,472	Value: 600				
1996 Mandleve Proof	—	Value: 620				

KM# 210 OUNCE **Weight:** 31.1070 g. **Composition:** 0.9999 Gold 1.0000 oz. AGW **Reverse:** Buffalo

Date	Mintage	F	VF	XF	Unc	BU
1997 Proof	2,472	Value: 600				
1997 SS Proof	220	Value: 620				

KM# 216 OUNCE **Weight:** 31.1070 g. **Composition:** 0.9999 Gold 1.0000 oz. AGW **Reverse:** Leopard

Date		F	VF	XF	Unc	BU
1998 Proof	—	Value: 600				

KM# 255 OUNCE **Weight:** 31.1035 g. **Composition:** 0.9990 Gold 0.999 oz. AGW **Obverse:** Greater Koodoo head. **Reverse:** Koodoo eating tree leaves. **Edge:** Reeded. **Size:** 32.7 mm.

Date		F	VF	XF	Unc	BU
1999 Proof	—	Value: 600				

KM# 261 OUNCE **Weight:** 31.1035 g. **Composition:** 0.9990 Gold 0.999 oz. AGW **Obverse:** Ibex head. **Reverse:** Ibex head. **Edge:** Reeded. **Size:** 32.7 mm.

Date		F	VF	XF	Unc	BU
2000 Proof	—	Value: 600				

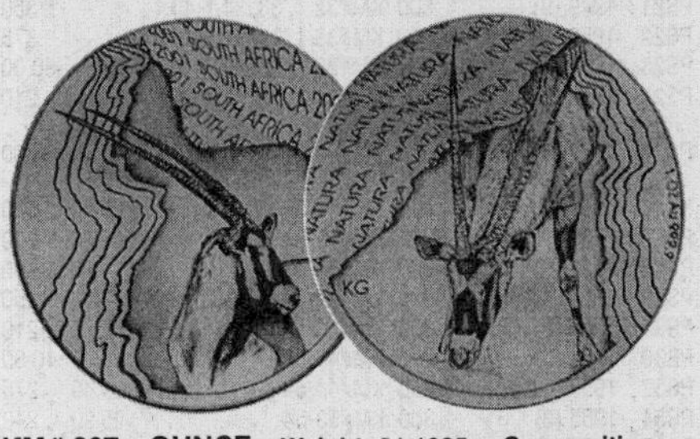

KM# 267 OUNCE **Weight:** 31.1035 g. **Composition:** 0.9990 Gold 0.999 oz. AGW **Obverse:** Gemsbok head. **Reverse:** Gemsbok grazing. **Edge:** Reeded. **Size:** 32.7 mm.

Date		F	VF	XF	Unc	BU
2001 Proof	—	Value: 600				

PATTERNS

Including off metal strikes

KM#	Date	Mintage	Identification	Mkt Val
Pn1	1925	—	1/4 Penny. Lead.	—
Pn3	1942	—	1/4 Penny. Bronze. Smaller head of George VI.	—

TRIAL STRIKES

KM#	Date	Mintage	Identification	Mkt Val
TS1	1925	—	2 Shilling 6 Pence. Lead. Uniface. 2s6d.	—

MINT SETS

KM#	Date	Mintage	Identification	Issue Price	Mkt Val
MS1	1967 (7)	50,000	KM#65.1-70.1, 72.1	7.50	10.00

KM#	Date	Mintage	Identification	Issue Price	Mkt Val
MS2	1967 (7)	50,000	KM#65.2-70.2, 72.2	7.50	10.00
MS3	1968 (7)	50,000	KM#71.1, 74.1-79.1	7.50	12.00
MS4	1968 (7)	50,000	KM#71.2, 74.2-79.2	7.50	12.00
MS5	1969 (7)	7,500	KM#65.1-70.1, 80.1	7.50	50.00
MS6	1969 (7)	7,500	KM#65.2-70.2, 80.2	7.50	50.00
MS7	1970 (8)	16,000	KM#81-88	7.50	12.00
MS8	1971 (8)	20,000	KM#81-88	7.50	8.00
MS9	1972 (8)	20,000	KM#81-88	7.50	8.00
MS10	1973 (8)	20,000	KM#81-88	7.50	8.00
MS11	1974 (8)	20,000	KM#81-87, 89	7.50	17.50
MS12	1975 (8)	20,000	KM#81-88	7.50	8.00
MS13	1976 (8)	20,000	KM#88, 90-96	5.65	8.00
MS14	1977 (8)	20,000	KM#81-87, 88a	—	8.00
MS15	1978 (8)	20,000	KM#81-87, 88a	—	8.00
MS16	1979 (8)	20,000	KM#97-104	—	25.00
MS17	1980 (7)	20,000	KM#82-87, 88a	—	8.00
MS18	1981 (7)	10,000	KM#82-87, 88a	—	10.00
MS19	1982 (7)	10,000	KM#109-115	—	25.00
MS20	1983 (7)	23,000	KM#82-87, 88a	—	8.00
MS21	1984 (7)	13,875	KM#82-87, 88a	—	10.00
MS22	1985 (7)	10,200	KM#82-87, 117	—	17.50
MS23	1986 (7)	9,100	KM#82-87, 88a	—	12.00
MS24	1987 (7)	7,642	KM#82-87, 88a	—	12.00
MS25	1988 (7)	6,250	KM#82-87, 88a	—	25.00
MS26	1989 (7)	13,000	KM#82-87, 88a	—	15.00
MS27	1990 (8)	12,000	KM#132-137, 139, 148	—	30.00
MS28	1991 (8)	15,000	KM#132-139	—	30.00
MSA29	1992 (8)	15,000	KM#132-139	—	30.00
MS29	1993 (8)	11,000	KM#132-139	—	30.00
MS30	1994 (9)	6,786	KM#132-140	—	35.00
MS31	1995 (9)	8,477	KM#132-140 Plastic holder	—	35.00
MS32	1995 (9)	—	KM#132-140 Cardboard holder	—	30.00
MS33	1996 (9)	12,000	KM#158-166	12.50	15.00
MS34	1997 (9)	7,515	KM#159-166, 170	—	30.00
MS35	1998 (9)	—	KM#159-166, 170	—	30.00
MS36	1999 (9)	10,000	KM#159-166, 170	19.50	30.00
MS37	2000 (9)	—	KM#159-166, 170	—	30.00

PROOF SETS

KM#	Date	Mintage	Identification	Issue Price	Mkt Val
PS1	1923 (10)	655	KM#12.1-17.1, 18, 19.1, 20-21	—	1,500
PS2	1923 (8)	747	KM#12.1-17.1, 18, 19.1	—	600
PS3	1926 (6)	3	KM#12.2, 14-2-17.2, 19.2	—	20,000
PS5	1930 (8)	—	KM#12.2 (dated 1928), 13.2-17.2, 18, 19.2	—	15,000
PS4	1930 (8)	14	KM#12.2-17.2, 18, 19.2	—	7,500
PS6	1931 (8)	62	KM#12.3-17.3, 19.3, 22	—	9,000
PS7	1932 (8)	12	KM#12.3-17.3, 19.3, 22	—	7,500
PS8	1933 (8)	20	KM#12.3-17.3, 19.3, 22	—	9,000
PS9	1934 (8)	24	KM#12.3-17.3, 19.3, 22	—	7,500
PS10	1935 (8)	20	KM#12.3-17.3, 19.3, 22	—	6,500
PS11	1936 (8)	40	KM#12.3-17.3, 19.3, 22	—	3,500
PS12	1937 (8)	116	KM#23-30	—	750
PS13	1938 (8)	44	KM#23-30	—	1,500
PS14	1939 (8)	30	KM#23-30	—	8,000
PS15	1943 (8)	104	KM#23-30	—	700
PS16	1944 (8)	150	KM#23-30	—	600
PS17	1945 (8)	150	KM#23-30	—	600
PS18	1946 (8)	150	KM#23-30	—	700
PS19	1947 (8)	2,600	KM#23-30	—	225
PS20	1948 (9)	1,120	KM#32.1, 33, 34.1-40.1	—	250
PS21	1949 (9)	800	KM#32.1, 33, 34.1-40.1	—	350
PS22	1950 (9)	500	KM#32.1, 33, 34.1-40.1	—	375
PS23	1951 (9)	2,000	KM#32.2, 33, 34.2-40.2	—	60.00
PS24	1952 (11)	12,000	KM#32.2, 33, 34.2-39.2, 41-43	—	210
PS25	1952 (9)	3,500	KM#32.2, 33, 34.2-39.2, 41	—	35.00
PS26	1953 (11)	3,000	KM#44-54	29.40	220
PS28	1953 (2)	1,000	KM#53-54	25.20	200
PS27	1953 (9)	2,000	KM#44-52	4.35	35.00
PS29	1954 (11)	875	KM#44-54	29.40	250
PS31	1954 (2)	350	KM#53-54	25.20	210
PS30	1954 (9)	2,275	KM#44-52	4.35	40.00
PS32	1955 (11)	600	KM#44-54	29.40	275
PS34	1955 (2)	300	KM#53-54	25.20	240
PS33	1955 (9)	2,250	KM#44-52	4.35	30.00
PS35	1956 (11)	350	KM#44-54	29.40	350
PS37	1956 (2)	158	KM#53-54	25.20	300
PS36	1956 (9)	1,350	KM#44-52	4.35	45.00
PS38	1957 (11)	380	KM#44-54	29.40	340
PS40	1957 (2)	180	KM#53-54	25.20	280
PS39	1957 (9)	750	KM#44-52	4.35	70.00
PS41	1958 (11)	360	KM#44-54	29.40	350
PS43	1958 (2)	155	KM#53-54	25.20	300
PS42	1958 (9)	625	KM#44-52	4.35	80.00
PS44	1959 (11)	390	KM#44-54	29.40	425
PS45	1959 (9)	560	KM#44-52	4.35	175
PS46	1959 (2)	240	KM#53-54	25.20	250
PS47	1960 (11)	1,500	KM#44-51, 53-55	29.40	220
PS48	1960 (9)	1,860	KM#44-51, 55	4.35	20.00
PS49	1960 (2)	450	KM#53-54	25.20	180
PS50	1961 (9)	3,139	KM#56-64	—	200
PS51	1961 (7)	4,391	KM#56-62	—	20.00
PS52	1961 (2)	793	KM#63-64 BV + 20%	—	—
PS53	1962 (9)	1,544	KM#56-64	—	210
PS54	1962 (7)	2,300	KM#56-62	—	15.00
PS55	1962 (2)	800	KM#63-64 BV+20%	—	—
PS56	1963 (9)	1,500	KM#56-64	—	200
PS57	1963 (7)	2,525	KM#56-62	—	12.00
PS58	1963 (2)	1,008	KM#63-64 BV+20%	—	—
PS59	1964 (9)	3,000	KM#56-64	—	190
PS60	1964 (7)	13,000	KM#56-62	—	10.00
PS61	1964 (2)	1,000	KM#63-64 BV+20%	—	—
PS63	1965 (9)	85	KM#63-64, 65.1-66.2, 67.1, 68.2, 69.1, 70.2, 71.2 V.I.P.	—	1,200
PS62	1965 (9)	5,099	KM#63-64, 65.1, 66.2, 67.1, 68.2, 69.1, 70.2, 71.1	23.50	185
PS64	1965 (7)	19,889	KM#65.1, 66.2, 67.1, 68.2, 69.1, 70.2, 71.1	5.00	12.00
PS65	1965 (2)	925	KM#63-64 BV+20%	18.15	—
PS66	1966 (9)	10,000	KM#63-64, 65.2, 66.1, 67.2, 68.1, 69.2, 70.1, 71.2	24.10	185
PS67	1966 (7)	15,000	KM#65.2, 66.1, 67.2, 68.1, 69.2, 70.1, 71.2	5.00	8.00
PS68	1966 (2)	1,000	KM#63-64 BV+20%	18.15	—
PS69	1967 (9)	10,000	KM#63-64, 65.2, 66.1, 67.2, 68.1, 69.2, 70.1, 72.2	24.10	185
PS70	1967 (7)	15,000	KM#65.2, 66.1, 67.2, 68.1, 69.2, 70.1, 72.2	5.00	8.00
PS71	1967 (2)	1,000	KM#63-64 BV+20%	18.15	—
PS72	1968 (9)	10,000	KM#63-64, 71.1, 74.1, 75.2, 76.1, 77.2, 78.1, 79.2	35.00	185
PS73	1968 (7)	15,000	KM#71.1, 74.1, 75.2, 76.1, 77.2, 78.1, 79.2	16.00	8.00
PS74	1968 (2)	1,000	KM#63-64 BV+20%	28.00	—
PS75	1969 (9)	7,000	KM#63-64, 65.2, 66.1, 67.2, 68.1, 69.2, 70.1, 80.2	34.85	185
PS76	1969 (7)	5,000	KM#65.2, 66.1, 67.2, 68.1, 69.2, 70.1, 80.2	13.95	8.00
PS77	1969 (2)	1,000	KM#63-64 BV+20%	27.85	—
PS78	1970 (10)	6,000	KM#63-64, 81-88	35.05	185
PS79	1970 (8)	4,000	KM#81-88	14.00	9.00
PS80	1970 (2)	1,000	KM#63-64 BV+20%	28.05	—
PS81	1971 (10)	7,000	KM#63-64, 81-88	35.00	185
PS82	1971 (8)	5,000	KM#81-88	14.00	9.00
PS83	1971 (2)	650	KM#63-64 BV+20%	28.00	—
PS84	1972 (10)	6,000	KM#63-64, 81-88	32.80	185
PS85	1972 (8)	4,000	KM#81-88	13.10	9.00
PS86	1972 (2)	1,500	KM#63-64 BV+20%	26.25	—
PS87	1973 (10)	6,850	KM#63-64, 81-88	32.00	185
PS88	1973 (8)	4,000	KM#81-88	12.80	9.00
PS89	1973 (2)	6,088	KM#63-64 BV+20%	25.60	—
PS90	1974 (10)	11,000	KM#63-64, 81-87, 89	52.50	185
PS91	1974 (8)	4,000	KM#81-87, 89	15.00	9.00
PS92	1974 (2)	5,600	KM#63-64 BV+20%	45.00	—
PS93	1975 (10)	12,500	KM#63-64, 81-87, 88	116	185
PS94	1975 (8)	5,500	KM#81-88	14.55	9.00
PS95	1975 (2)	7,000	KM#63-64 BV+20%	102	—
PS96	1976 (10)	14,000	KM#63-64, 88, 90-96	92.00	185
PS97	1976 (8)	7,000	KM#88, 90-96	11.50	9.00
PS98	1976 (2)	8,000	KM#63-64 BV+20%	80.50	—
PS100	1977 (8)	7,000	KM#81-88	11.50	12.00
PS99	1977 (10)	12,000	KM#63-64, 81-88	92.00	185
PS101	1977 (2)	8,000	KM#63-64 BV+20%	80.50	—
PS102	1978 (10)	10,000	KM#63-64, 81-88	—	185
PS103	1978 (8)	7,000	KM#81-88	—	12.00
PS104	1978 (2)	9,000	KM#63-64 BV+20%	—	—
PS106	1979 (8)	5,000	KM#88, 97-103	—	22.00
PS105	1979 (10)	10,000	KM#63-64, 97-103, 104a	—	185
PS107	1979 (2)	10,000	KM#63-64 BV+20%	—	—
PS108	1980 (10)	10,000	KM#63-64, 81-88	—	185
PS109	1980 (8)	5,000	KM#81-88	—	22.00
PS110	1980 (2)	8,000	kM#63-64 BV+20%	—	—
PS111	1980 (2)	8,000	KM#63-64	—	—
PS112	1980 (3)	60	KM#105-107	—	9,000
PS113	1981 (10)	6,000	KM#63-64, 81-88	—	185
PS114	1981 (8)	4,900	KM#81-88	—	22.00
PS115	1981 (2)	6,238	KM#63-64 BV+20%	—	—
PS116	1982 (10)	7,100	KM#63-64, 108-115	—	190
PS117	1982 (8)	4,900	KM#88, 108-114	—	22.00
PS118	1982 (2)	6,930	KM#63-64 BV+20%	—	—
PS119	1983 (10)	7,300	KM#63-64, 81-88	—	185
PS120	1983 (8)	6,835	KM#81-88	—	22.00
PS121	1983 (2)	7,300	KM#63-64 BV+20%	—	—
PS122	1984 (8)	11,250	KM#82-88, 88a	—	15.00
PS123	1985 (8)	9,859	KM#82-87, 116, 117	—	25.00
PS125	1986 (2)	428	KM#73, 121 Plus large gold plated Silver #1	—	1,400
PS126	1986 (2)	750	KM#121, 131	—	700
PS127	1986 (3)	500	KM#119, 121, 131	—	725
PS124	1986 (8)	7,000	KM#82-87, 88a, 119	—	25.00
PS129	1987 (4)	750	KM#73, 105-107	—	1,050
PS130	1987 GRC (4)	1,121	KM#73, 105-107	—	2,900
PS128	1987 (8)	6,781	KM#82-88, 88a	—	25.00
PS135	1988 (3)	600	KM#124, 127, 130	—	2,750
PS132	1988 (4)	806	KM#73, 105-107	—	1,050
PS133	1988 GRC (4)	835	KM#73, 105-107	—	2,900
PS131	1988 (8)	7,250	KM#82-88, 88a	—	50.00
PS134	1988 (3)	3,388	KM#122, 125, 128	—	70.00
PS136	1989 (8)	9,571	KM#82-88, 88a	—	50.00
PS137	1989 (4)	—	KM#73, 105-107	—	1,050
PS138	1989 GRC (4)	318	KM#73, 105-107	—	5,500
PS139	1990 (8)	10,000	KM#132-137, 139, 148	—	70.00
PS140	1990 (4)	—	KM#73, 105-107	—	1,050
PS141	1990 GRC (4)	1,066	KM#73, 105-107	—	2,
PS142	1991 (8)	12,000	KM#132-139	—	70
PSA143	1991 GRC (4)	426	KM#73, 105-107	—	2,
PS143	1992 (8)	10,000	KM#132-139	—	50
PS144	1993 (8)	—	KM#132-139	—	50
PS146	1994 (4)	168	KM#189-192 Wood case	—	1,
PS147	1994 (4)	1,750	KM#189-192 Velvet case	—	1,
PS148	1994 (3)	420	KM#167, 187-188	—	7
PS145	1994 (9)	5,804	KM#132-140	—	60
PS152	1995 (4)	89	KM#195-198 Wood case	—	1,
PS153	1995 (4)	925	KM#195-198 Velvet case	—	1,
PS154	1995 (3)	210	KM#152, 193-194	—	7
PS150	1995 (4)	750	KM#73, 105-107	—	1,4
PS151	1995	—	KM#73, 105-107 Wooden box	—	1,4
PS149	1995 (9)	5,816	KM#132-140	—	65.
PS156	1996 (4)	368	KM#201-402 Wood case	—	1,
PS157	1996 (4)	1,677	KM#201-204 Velvet case	—	1,1
PS158	1996 (3)	346	KM#169, 199-200	—	7
PS155	1996 (9)	4,827	KM#158-166	30.00	36.
PS160	1997 (4)	500	KM#207-210 Wood case	—	1,2
PS161	1997 (4)	1,015	KM#207-210 Velvet case	—	1,
PS162	1997 (3)	144	KM#181, 205-206	—	7
PS159	1997 (4)	500	KM#73, 105-107	—	1,
PS163	1997 (4)	30	KM#73, 105-107, 30 Year Wine set with privy marks	—	2,5
PS164	1997 (9)	3,596	KM#159-166, 170	—	40
PS165	1998 (9)	—	KM#159-166, 170	—	40.
PS166	1998 (4)	—	KM#213-216 Wood case	—	1,2
PS167	1998 (4)	—	KM#213-216 Velvet case	—	1,1
PS168	1998 (3)	—	KM#177, 211-212	—	7
PS169	1999 (9)	6,000	KM#159-166, 170	39.50	40.

SPECIMEN SETS (SS)

KM#	Date	Mintage	Identification	Issue Price	Mkt Val
SS1	1994 (9)	5,508	KM#132-140	—	25.
SS2	1995 (9)	4,956	KM#132-140	—	25.
SS3	1996 (9)	5,766	KM#158-166	19.50	25.
SS4	1997 (9)	4,236	KM#159-166, 170	—	25.
SS5	1998 (9)	—	KM#159-166, 170	—	25.
SS6	1999 (9)	—	KM#159-166, 170	—	25.

SOUTH ARABIA

Fifteen of the sixteen Western Protectorate States, the Wahidi State of the Eastern Protectorate, and Aden Colony joined to form the Federation of South Arabia.

In 1959, Britain agreed to prepare South Arabia for full independence, which was achieved on Nov. 30, 1967, at which time South Arabia, including Aden, changed its name to the Peoples Republic of Southern Yemen. On Dec. 1, 1970, following the overthrow of the new government by the National Liberation Front, Southern Yemen changed its name to the Peoples Democratic Republic of Yemen.

TITLES

Al-Junubiya(t) al-Arabiya(t)

MONETARY SYSTEM

1000 Fils = 1 Dinar

FEDERATION

STANDARD COINAGE

KM# 1 FILS Composition: Aluminum

Date	Mintage	F	VF	XF	Unc	BU
1964	10,000,000	—	—	0.10	0.15	0.25
1964 Proof	—	Value: 1.50				

KM# 2 5 FILS Composition: Bronze

Date	Mintage	F	VF	XF	Unc	BU
1964	10,000,000	—	0.15	0.25	0.50	0.65
1964 Proof	—	Value: 2.00				

KM# 3 25 FILS Composition: Copper-Nickel

Date	Mintage	F	VF	XF	Unc	BU
1964	4,000,000	—	0.25	0.45	0.85	1.00
1964 Proof	—	Value: 2.75				

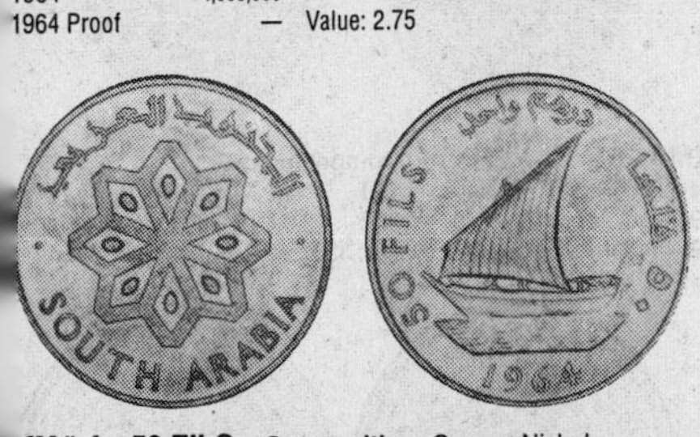

KM# 4 50 FILS Composition: Copper-Nickel

Date	Mintage	F	VF	XF	Unc	BU
964	6,000,000	—	0.45	0.65	1.25	1.50
964 Proof	—	Value: 3.75				

PROOF SETS

KM#	Date	Mintage	Identification	Issue Price	Mkt Val
S1	1964 (4)	10,500	KM1-4	9.90	10.00

S. GEORGIA & THE S. SANDWICH IS.

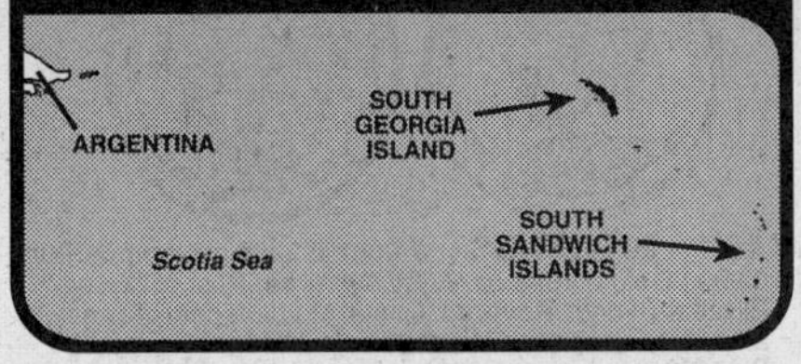

South Georgia and the South Sandwich Islands are a dependency of the Falkland Islands, and located about 800 miles east of them. South Georgia is 1,450 sq. mi. (1,770 sq. km.), South Sandwich Islands is 120 sq. mi. (311 sq. km.) Fishing and Antarctic research are the main industries. The islands were claimed for Great Britain in 1775 by Captain James Cook.

RULERS

British since 1775

BRITISH ADMINISTRATION

STANDARD COINAGE

KM# 1 2 POUNDS Weight: 28.2800 g. **Composition:** Copper-Nickel **Subject:** 100th Birthday - Queen Mother **Obverse:** Queen Elizabeth's head right **Reverse:** Queen Mother's coat of arms **Edge:** Reeded **Size:** 38.7 mm. **Note:** Struck at the Pobjoy Mint.

Date	F	VF	XF	Unc	BU
2000	—	—	—	10.00	—

KM# 1a 2 POUNDS Weight: 28.2800 g. **Composition:** 0.9250 Silver .841 oz. ASW **Subject:** 100th Birthday - Queen Mother **Obverse:** Queen Elizabeth's head right **Reverse:** Queen Mother's coat of arms **Edge:** Reeded **Note:** Struck at the Pobjoy Mint.

Date	F	VF	XF	Unc	BU
2000 Proof	—	Value: 50.00			

KM# 3 2 POUNDS Weight: 28.2800 g. **Composition:** Copper-Nickel **Obverse:** Queen Elizabeth's head right **Reverse:** Antoine de la Roche standing on the deck of the ship Discovery **Edge:** Reeded **Size:** 38.6 mm. **Note:** Struck at the Pobjoy Mint.

Date	F	VF	XF	Unc	BU
2000	—	—	—	8.50	—

KM# 3a 2 POUNDS Weight: 28.2800 g. **Composition:** 0.9250 Silver .841 oz. ASW **Obverse:** Queen Elizabeth's head right **Reverse:** Antoine de la Roche standing on the deck of the ship Discovery **Edge:** Reeded **Size:** 38.7 mm. **Note:** Struck at the Pobjoy Mint.

Date	F	VF	XF	Unc	BU
2000 Proof	—	Value: 47.50			

KM# 4 2 POUNDS Weight: 28.2800 g. **Composition:** Copper-Nickel **Subject:** 225th Anniversary - Possession by Captain Cook **Obverse:** Queen Elizabeth's head right **Reverse:** 1/3-length bust of Captain Cook right **Note:** Struck at the Pobjoy Mint.

Date	F	VF	XF	Unc	BU
2000	—	—	—	8.50	—

KM# 4a 2 POUNDS Weight: 28.2800 g. **Composition:** 0.9250 Silver .841 oz. ASW **Subject:** 225th Anniversary - Possession by Captain Cook **Obverse:** Queen Elizabeth's head right **Reverse:** 1/3-length bust of Captain Cook right **Note:** Struck at the Pobjoy Mint.

Date	F	VF	XF	Unc	BU
2000 Proof	—	Value: 47.50			

KM# 1a.1 2 POUNDS Weight: 28.2800 g. **Composition:** 0.9250 Silver 0.841 oz. ASW **Subject:** Queen Mother **Obverse:** Bust of Queen Elizabeth II right. **Reverse:** Queen Mother's coat of arms with a tiny black sapphire mounted below. **Edge:** Reeded. **Size:** 38.6 mm.

Date	Mintage	F	VF	XF	Unc	BU
2000 Proof	1,000	Value: 55.00				

KM# 7 2 POUNDS Weight: 28.2800 g. **Composition:** Copper-Nickel **Subject:** Sir Ernest H. Shackleton **Obverse:** Queen's portrait **Reverse:** Portrait and ship **Edge:** Reeded **Size:** 38.6 mm.

Date	F	VF	XF	Unc	BU
2001	—	—	—	9.00	—

KM# 7a 2 POUNDS Weight: 28.2800 g. **Composition:** 0.9250 Silver .8410 oz. ASW

Date	F	VF	XF	Unc	BU
2001 Proof	—	—	—	47.50	—

KM# 9 2 POUNDS Composition: Copper-Nickel **Subject:** Sir Joseph Banks **Obverse:** Queen's portrait **Reverse:** Cameo portrait and ship

Date	F	VF	XF	Unc	BU
2001	—	—	—	9.00	—

KM# 11 2 POUNDS **Weight:** 28.2800 g. **Composition:** Copper-Nickel **Subject:** Queen Elizabeth II's Golden Jubilee **Obverse:** Bust of Queen Elizabeth II right. **Reverse:** Young crowned portrait. **Edge:** Reeded. **Size:** 38.6 mm.

Date	F	VF	XF	Unc	BU
2002	—	—	—	10.00	—

KM# 11a 2 POUNDS **Weight:** 28.2800 g. **Composition:** 0.9250 Gold Clad Silver 0.841 oz. **Subject:** Queen Elizabeth II's Golden Jubilee **Obverse:** Bust of Queen Elizabeth II right. **Reverse:** Young crowned portrait. **Edge:** Reeded. **Size:** 38.6 mm.

Date	Mintage	F	VF	XF	Unc	BU
2002 Proof	10,000	Value: 47.50				

KM# 13 2 POUNDS **Weight:** 28.2800 g. **Composition:** Copper-Nickel **Subject:** Queen Elizabeth II's Golden Jubilee **Obverse:** Bust of Queen Elizabeth II right. **Reverse:** National arms. **Edge:** Reeded. **Size:** 38.6 mm.

Date	F	VF	XF	Unc	BU
2002	—	—	—	10.00	—

KM# 13a 2 POUNDS **Weight:** 28.2800 g. **Composition:** 0.9250 Gold Clad Silver 0.841 oz. **Subject:** Queen Elizabeth II's Golden Jubilee **Obverse:** Bust of Queen Elizabeth II right. **Reverse:** National arms. **Edge:** Reeded. **Size:** 38.6 mm.

Date	Mintage	F	VF	XF	Unc	BU
2002 Proof	10,000	—	—	—	47.50	—

KM# 15 2 POUNDS **Weight:** 28.2800 g. **Composition:** Copper-Nickel **Subject:** Princess Diana **Obverse:** Queen's portrait **Reverse:** Diana's portrait **Edge:** Reeded **Size:** 38.6 mm.

Date	VG	F	VF	XF	Unc
2002	—	—	—	—	10.00
2002	—	—	—	—	10.00

KM# 2.1 20 POUNDS **Weight:** 6.2200 g. **Composition:** 0.9990 Gold 0.1998 oz. AGW **Obverse:** Bust of Queen Elizabeth II right. **Reverse:** Queen Mother's coat of arms with a tiny black sapphire mounted below. **Edge:** Reeded. **Size:** 22 mm.

Date	Mintage	F	VF	XF	Unc	BU
2000 Proof	1,000	Value: 190				

KM# 2 20 POUNDS **Weight:** 6.2200 g. **Composition:** 0.9999 Gold .2 oz. AGW **Subject:** 100th Birthday - Queen Mother **Obverse:** Queen Elizabeth's head right **Reverse:** Queen Mother's coat of arms **Edge:** Reeded **Note:** Struck at the Pobjoy Mint.

Date		F	VF	XF	Unc	BU
2000 Proof	—	Value: 185				

KM# 5 20 POUNDS **Weight:** 6.2200 g. **Composition:** 0.9999 Gold .2 oz. AGW **Obverse:** Queen Elizabeth's head right **Reverse:** Antoine de la Roche standing on the deck of the ship Discovery **Edge:** Reeded **Size:** 22 mm. **Note:** Struck at the Pobjoy Mint.

Date		F	VF	XF	Unc	BU
2000 Proof	—	Value: 175				

KM# 6 20 POUNDS **Weight:** 6.2200 g. **Composition:** 0.9999 Gold .2 oz. AGW **Subject:** 225th Anniversary - Possession by Captain Cook **Obverse:** Queen Elizabeth's head right **Reverse:** 1/3-length bust of Captain Cook right **Note:** Struck at the Pobjoy Mint.

Date		F	VF	XF	Unc	BU
2000 Proof	—	Value: 175				

KM# 8 20 POUNDS **Weight:** 6.2200 g. **Composition:** 0.9999 Gold .2000 oz. AGW **Obverse:** Queen's portrait **Reverse:** Sir Ernest H. Shackleton and ship **Edge:** Reeded **Size:** 22 mm.

Date	Mintage	F	VF	XF	Unc	BU
2001 Proof	Est. 2,000	Value: 175				

KM# 10 20 POUNDS **Weight:** 6.2200 g. **Composition:** 0.9999 Gold .2000 oz. AGW **Obverse:** Queen's portrait **Reverse:** Sir Joseph Banks cameo and ship

Date	Mintage	F	VF	XF	Unc	BU
2001 Proof	Est. 2,000	Value: 175				

KM# 12 20 POUNDS **Weight:** 6.2200 g. **Composition:** 0.9990 Gold 0.1998 oz. AGW **Subject:** Queen Elizabeth II's Golden Jubilee **Obverse:** Bust of Queen Elizabeth II right. **Reverse:** Young crowned portrait of the Queen. **Edge:** Reeded. **Size:** 22 mm.

Date	Mintage	F	VF	XF	Unc	BU
2002 Proof	2,002	Value: 175				

KM# 14 20 POUNDS **Weight:** 6.2200 g. **Composition:** 0.9990 Gold 0.1998 oz. AGW **Subject:** Queen Elizabeth II's Golden Jubilee **Obverse:** Bust of Queen Elizabeth II right. **Reverse:** National arms. **Edge:** Reeded. **Size:** 22 mm.

Date	Mintage	F	VF	XF	Unc	BU
2002 Proof	2,002	Value: 175				

KM# 16 20 POUNDS **Weight:** 6.2200 g. **Composition:** 0.9999 Gold 0.2 oz. AGW **Subject:** Princess Diana **Obverse:** Queen's portrait **Reverse:** Diana's portrait **Edge:** reeded **Size:** 22 mm.

Date	Mintage	F	VF	XF	Unc	BU
2002PM	5	Value: 175				

SOUTHERN RHODESIA

RULERS
British, until 1966

MONETARY SYSTEM
12 Pence = 1 Shilling
2 Shillings = 1 Florin
5 Shillings = 1 Crown
20 Shillings = 1 Pound

BRITISH COLONY

POUND COINAGE

KM# 6 1/2 PENNY **Composition:** Copper-Nickel

Date	Mintage	F	VF	XF	Unc	BU
1934	240,000	1.00	2.00	8.00	22.50	—
1934 Proof	—	Value: 125				
1936	240,000	3.50	7.00	20.00	150	—
1936 Proof	—	—	—	—	—	—

KM# 14 1/2 PENNY **Composition:** Copper-Nickel

Date	Mintage	F	VF	XF	Unc	BU
1938	240,000	0.75	1.75	6.50	20.00	—
1938 Proof	—	—	—	—	—	—
1939	480,000	1.00	2.00	9.00	60.00	—
1939 Proof	—	—	—	—	—	—

KM# 14a 1/2 PENNY **Composition:** Bronze

Date	Mintage	F	VF	XF	Unc	BU
1942	480,000	0.60	1.50	3.50	25.00	—
1942 Proof	—	—	—	—	—	—
1943	960,000	0.35	0.75	2.25	6.50	—
1944	960,000	0.35	0.75	2.50	8.00	—
1944 Proof	—	—	—	—	—	—

KM# 26 1/2 PENNY **Composition:** Bronze **Obv. Legend:** KING GEORGE THE SIXTH

Date	Mintage	F	VF	XF	Unc	BU
1951	480,000	0.75	1.25	2.25	6.50	—
1951 Proof	—	—	—	—	—	—
1952	480,000	0.75	1.25	2.50	10.00	—
1952 Proof	—	—	—	—	—	—

KM# 28 1/2 PENNY **Composition:** Bronze

Date	Mintage	F	VF	XF	Unc	BU
1954	960,000	0.75	2.00	10.00	65.00	—
1954 Proof	20	Value: 350				

KM# 7 PENNY **Composition:** Copper-Nickel

Date	Mintage	F	VF	XF	Unc	BU
1934	360,000	0.75	1.50	3.50	25.00	—
1934 Proof	—	Value: 125				

Date	Mintage	F	VF	XF	Unc	BU
1935	492,000	0.75	2.50	12.00	125	—
1935 Proof	—	—	—	—	—	—
1936	1,044,000	0.60	1.25	3.50	30.00	—
1936 Proof	—	—	—	—	—	—

KM# 8 PENNY Composition: Copper-Nickel

Date	Mintage	F	VF	XF	Unc	BU
1937	908,000	0.60	1.25	3.50	25.00	—
1937 Proof	—	Value: 300				
1938	240,000	1.50	3.00	7.50	50.00	—
1938 Proof	—	—	—	—	—	—
1939	1,284,000	0.45	1.00	3.50	37.50	—
1939 Proof	—	—	—	—	—	—
1940	1,080,000	0.45	1.00	3.50	37.50	—
1940 Proof	—	—	—	—	—	—
1941	720,000	0.50	1.25	4.50	40.00	—
1941 Proof	—	—	—	—	—	—
1942	960,000	0.50	1.25	4.50	65.00	—
1942	—	—	—	—	—	—

KM# 8a PENNY Composition: Bronze

Date	Mintage	F	VF	XF	Unc	BU
1942	480,000	4.00	6.50	22.50	100	—
1942 Proof	—	Value: 400				
1943	3,120,000	0.50	0.80	2.50	15.00	—
1944	2,400,000	0.50	0.80	2.50	20.00	—
1944 Proof	—	—	—	—	—	—
1947	3,600,000	0.75	1.25	3.50	20.00	—
1947 Proof	—	—	—	—	—	—

KM# 25 PENNY Composition: Bronze

Date	Mintage	F	VF	XF	Unc	BU
1949	1,440,000	0.50	1.00	2.00	25.00	—
1949 Proof	—	Value: 125				
1950	720,000	1.00	1.75	5.00	40.00	—
1950 Proof	—	Value: 125				
1951	4,896,000	0.50	0.75	1.25	10.00	—
1951 Proof	—	Value: 125				
1952	2,400,000	0.50	0.75	1.75	12.50	—
1952 Proof	—	—	—	—	—	—

KM# 29 PENNY Composition: Bronze

Date	Mintage	F	VF	XF	Unc	BU
1954	960,000	4.00	8.00	45.00	250	—
1954 Proof	20	Value: 450				

KM# 1 3 PENCE Weight: 1.4100 g. **Composition:** 0.9250 Silver .0419 oz. ASW **Obverse:** Bust of crowned King George V left

Date	Mintage	F	VF	XF	Unc	BU
1932	688,000	0.75	1.50	6.50	32.00	—
1932 Proof	—	Value: 60.00				
1934	628,000	0.75	2.00	10.00	60.00	—
1934 Proof	—	—	—	—	—	—
1935	840,000	0.75	2.00	7.00	45.00	—
1935 Proof	—	—	—	—	—	—
1936	1,052,000	0.75	2.00	7.00	45.00	—
1936 Proof	—	—	—	—	—	—

KM# 9 3 PENCE Weight: 1.4100 g. **Composition:** 0.9250 Silver .0419 oz. ASW **Obverse:** Bust of King George VI left

Date	Mintage	F	VF	XF	Unc	BU
1937	1,228,000	0.75	2.00	6.00	40.00	—
1937 Proof	—	Value: 225				

KM# 16 3 PENCE Weight: 1.4100 g. **Composition:** 0.9250 Silver .0419 oz. ASW **Obverse:** Bust of King George VI left

Date	Mintage	F	VF	XF	Unc	BU
1939	160,000	6.00	10.00	22.00	150	—
1939 Proof	—	Value: 300				
1940	1,200,000	0.75	2.00	7.00	40.00	—
1940 Proof	—	—	—	—	—	—
1941	600,000	2.50	5.00	10.00	50.00	—
1941 Proof	—	—	—	—	—	—
1942	2,000,000	0.50	1.50	6.50	30.00	—
1942 Proof	—	—	—	—	—	—

KM# 16a 3 PENCE Weight: 1.4100 g. **Composition:** 0.5000 Silver .0226 oz. ASW **Obverse:** Bust of King George VI left

Date	Mintage	F	VF	XF	Unc	BU
1944	1,600,000	0.50	1.50	10.00	60.00	—
1945	800,000	1.00	3.00	12.00	60.00	—
1945 Proof	—	—	—	—	—	—
1946	2,400,000	0.50	1.50	7.00	35.00	—
1946 Proof	—	—	—	—	—	—

KM# 16b 3 PENCE Composition: Copper-Nickel **Obverse:** Bust of King George VI left

Date	Mintage	F	VF	XF	Unc	BU
1947	8,000,000	0.40	0.80	2.50	20.00	—
1947 Proof	—	Value: 250				

KM# 20 3 PENCE Composition: Copper-Nickel **Obverse:** Bust of King George VI left

Date	Mintage	F	VF	XF	Unc	BU
1948	2,000,000	0.40	0.80	3.50	30.00	—
1948 Proof	—	—	—	—	—	—
1949	4,000,000	0.40	0.80	3.00	25.00	—
1949 Proof	—	Value: 150				
1951	5,600,000	0.40	0.80	2.50	20.00	—
1951 Proof	—	—	—	—	—	—
1952	4,800,000	0.40	0.80	2.50	30.00	—
1952 Proof	—	Value: 150				

KM# 2 6 PENCE Weight: 2.8300 g. **Composition:** 0.9250 Silver .0841 oz. ASW **Obverse:** Bust of King George V

Date	Mintage	F	VF	XF	Unc	BU
1932	544,000	2.00	3.50	10.00	55.00	—
1932 Proof	—	Value: 65.00				
1934	214,000	3.00	7.00	30.00	90.00	—
1935	380,000	2.00	6.00	25.00	75.00	—
1935 Proof	—	—	—	—	—	—
1936	675,000	1.50	3.50	15.00	60.00	—
1936 Proof	—	—	—	—	—	—

KM# 10 6 PENCE Weight: 2.8300 g. **Composition:** 0.9250 Silver .0841 oz. ASW **Obverse:** Bust of King George VI

Date	Mintage	F	VF	XF	Unc	BU
1937	823,000	2.50	5.00	15.00	55.00	—
1937 Proof	—	Value: 300				

KM# 17 6 PENCE Weight: 2.8300 g. **Composition:** 0.9250 Silver .0841 oz. ASW **Obverse:** Bust of King George VI; "KING" moved behind head

Date	Mintage	F	VF	XF	Unc	BU
1939	200,000	3.00	7.00	45.00	200	—
1939 Proof	—	Value: 450				
1940	600,000	1.50	3.00	20.00	75.00	—
1940 Proof	—	—	—	—	—	—
1941	300,000	2.00	4.00	15.00	65.00	—
1941 Proof	—	—	—	—	—	—
1942	1,200,000	1.00	2.00	7.50	55.00	—
1942 Proof	—	Value: 200				

KM# 17a 6 PENCE Weight: 2.8300 g. **Composition:** 0.5000 Silver .0454 oz. ASW **Obverse:** Bust of King George VI

Date	Mintage	F	VF	XF	Unc	BU
1944	800,000	1.25	2.50	15.00	90.00	—
1945	400,000	15.00	25.00	45.00	150	—
1945 Proof	—	—	—	—	—	—
1946	1,600,000	1.25	2.50	15.00	60.00	—
1946 Proof	—	—	—	—	—	—

KM# 17b 6 PENCE Composition: Copper-Nickel **Obverse:** Bust of King George VI

Date	Mintage	F	VF	XF	Unc	BU
1947	5,000,000	0.50	1.00	4.00	20.00	—
1947 Proof	—	Value: 250				

KM# 21 6 PENCE Composition: Copper-Nickel **Obverse:** Bust of King George VI

Date	Mintage	F	VF	XF	Unc	BU
1948	1,000,000	0.50	1.25	4.50	27.50	—
1948 Proof	—	—	—	—	—	—
1949	2,000,000	0.50	1.00	3.50	30.00	—
1949 Proof	—	Value: 250				
1950	2,000,000	0.50	1.00	4.50	45.00	—
1950 Proof	—	Value: 250				
1951	2,800,000	0.50	1.00	2.50	22.50	—
1951 Proof	—	—	—	—	—	—
1952	1,200,000	0.50	1.50	3.50	45.00	—
1952 Proof	—	—	—	—	—	—

KM# 3 SHILLING Weight: 5.6600 g. **Composition:** 0.9250 Silver .1683 oz. ASW **Obverse:** Bust of King George V **Reverse:** Bird sculpture

Date	Mintage	F	VF	XF	Unc	BU
1932	896,000	2.00	4.00	12.00	80.00	—
1932 Proof	—	Value: 90.00				
1934	333,000	4.00	8.00	35.00	175	—
1935	830,000	2.00	4.00	12.00	120	—
1935 Proof	—	Value: 220				
1936	1,663,000	1.50	3.50	10.00	115	—
1936 Proof	—	—	—	—	—	—

KM# 11 SHILLING Weight: 5.6600 g. **Composition:** 0.9250 Silver .1683 oz. ASW **Obverse:** Bust of King George VI

Date	Mintage	F	VF	XF	Unc	BU
1937	1,700,000	2.00	4.00	12.00	90.00	—
1937 Proof	—	Value: 300				

KM# 18 SHILLING **Weight:** 5.6600 g. **Composition:** 0.9250 Silver .1683 oz. ASW **Obverse:** Bust of King George VI; "KING" moved behind head

Date	Mintage	F	VF	XF	Unc	BU
1939	420,000	7.00	15.00	70.00	275	—
1939 Proof	—	Value: 500				
1940	750,000	5.50	12.00	50.00	165	—
1940 Proof	—	—	—	—	—	—
1941	800,000	6.50	12.00	45.00	140	—
1941 Proof	—	—	—	—	—	—
1942	2,100,000	2.00	4.00	15.00	55.00	—
1942 Proof	—	—	—	—	—	—

KM# 18a SHILLING **Weight:** 5.6600 g. **Composition:** 0.5000 Silver .0909 oz. ASW **Obverse:** Bust of King George VI

Date	Mintage	F	VF	XF	Unc	BU
1944	1,600,000	2.00	4.00	12.50	80.00	—
1946	1,700,000	3.50	8.00	40.00	120	—
1946 Proof	—	—	—	—	—	—

KM# 18b SHILLING **Composition:** Copper-Nickel **Obverse:** Bust of King George VI

Date	Mintage	F	VF	XF	Unc	BU
1947	8,000,000	0.75	1.50	4.50	40.00	—
1947 Proof	—	Value: 300				

KM# 22 SHILLING **Composition:** Copper-Nickel **Obverse:** Bust of King George VI

Date	Mintage	F	VF	XF	Unc	BU
1948	1,500,000	0.75	1.50	6.50	30.00	—
1948 Proof	—	—	—	—	—	—
1949	4,000,000	0.75	1.25	4.50	35.00	—
1949 Proof	—	Value: 250				
1950	2,000,000	1.00	3.00	10.00	55.00	—
1950 Proof	—	Value: 225				
1951	3,000,000	0.75	1.25	4.50	20.00	—
1951 Proof	—	—	—	—	—	—
1952	2,600,000	0.75	1.50	4.50	55.00	—
1952 Proof	—	—	—	—	—	—

KM# 4 2 SHILLINGS **Weight:** 11.3100 g. **Composition:** 0.9250 Silver .3363 oz. ASW **Obverse:** Bust of King George V **Reverse:** Sable antelope

Date	Mintage	F	VF	XF	Unc	BU
1932	498,000	4.00	10.00	30.00	110	—
1932 Proof	—	Value: 125				
1934	154,000	12.50	20.00	60.00	225	—
1935	365,000	5.00	10.00	40.00	120	—
1935 Proof	—	—	—	—	—	—
1936	683,000	4.00	9.00	35.00	120	—
1936 Proof	—	—	—	—	—	—

KM# 12 2 SHILLINGS **Weight:** 11.3100 g. **Composition:** 0.9250 Silver .3363 oz. ASW **Obverse:** Bust of King George VI

Date	Mintage	F	VF	XF	Unc	BU
1937	552,000	7.50	20.00	45.00	135	—
1937 Proof	—	Value: 400				

KM# 19 2 SHILLINGS **Weight:** 11.3100 g. **Composition:** 0.9250 Silver .3363 oz. ASW **Obverse:** Bust of King George VI; "KING" moved behind head

Date	Mintage	F	VF	XF	Unc	BU
1939	120,000	50.00	125	350	650	—
1939 Proof	—	Value: 750				
1940	525,000	8.00	16.00	75.00	250	—
1940 Proof	—	—	—	—	—	—
1941	400,000	8.00	16.00	100	300	—
1941 Proof	—	—	—	—	—	—
1942	850,000	4.00	8.00	25.00	90.00	—

KM# 19a 2 SHILLINGS **Weight:** 11.3100 g. **Composition:** 0.5000 Silver .1818 oz. ASW **Obverse:** Bust of King George VI

Date	Mintage	F	VF	XF	Unc	BU
1944	1,300,000	6.00	12.00	35.00	135	—
1946	700,000	100	200	300	650	—
1946 Proof	—	—	—	—	—	—

KM# 19b 2 SHILLINGS **Composition:** Copper-Nickel **Obverse:** Bust of King George VI

Date	Mintage	F	VF	XF	Unc	BU
1947	3,750,000	1.75	4.00	12.50	45.00	—
1947 Proof	—	Value: 300				

KM# 23 2 SHILLINGS **Composition:** Copper-Nickel **Obverse:** Bust of King George VI

Date	Mintage	F	VF	XF	Unc	BU
1948	750,000	1.00	3.00	10.00	40.00	—
1948 Proof	—	—	—	—	—	—
1949	2,000,000	1.00	3.00	10.00	50.00	—
1949 Proof	—	Value: 350				
1950	1,000,000	1.00	4.00	15.00	75.00	—
1950 Proof	—	Value: 350				
1951	2,600,000	1.00	3.00	6.00	27.50	—
1951 Proof	—	—	—	—	—	—
1952	1,800,000	1.00	3.00	10.00	75.00	—
1952 Proof	—	—	—	—	—	—

KM# 30 2 SHILLINGS **Composition:** Copper-Nickel **Obverse:** Bust of Queen Elizabeth II right

Date	Mintage	F	VF	XF	Unc	BU
1954	300,000	25.00	55.00	175	900	—
1954 Proof	20	Value: 1,250				

KM# 5 1/2 CROWN **Weight:** 14.1400 g. **Composition:** 0.9250 Silver .4205 oz. ASW **Obverse:** Bust of King George V

Date	Mintage	F	VF	XF	Unc	BU
1932	634,000	5.00	8.00	30.00	95.00	—
1932 Proof	—	Value: 125				
1934	419,000	6.00	10.00	45.00	240	—
1934 Proof	—	—	—	—	—	—
1935	512,000	5.00	8.00	32.50	175	—
1935 Proof	—	—	—	—	—	—

Date	Mintage	F	VF	XF	Unc	BU
1936	518,000	5.00	8.00	30.00	145	—
1936 Proof	—	—	—	—	—	—

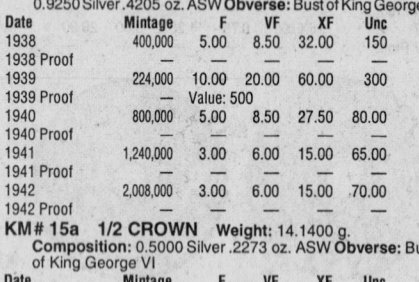

KM# 13 1/2 CROWN **Weight:** 14.1400 g. **Composition:** 0.9250 Silver .4205 oz. ASW **Obverse:** Bust of King George VI

Date	Mintage	F	VF	XF	Unc	BU
1937	1,174,000	4.50	8.00	30.00	130	—
1937 Proof	—	Value: 350				

KM# 15 1/2 CROWN **Weight:** 14.1400 g. **Composition:** 0.9250 Silver .4205 oz. ASW **Obverse:** Bust of King George VI

Date	Mintage	F	VF	XF	Unc	BU
1938	400,000	5.00	8.50	32.00	150	—
1938 Proof	—	—	—	—	—	—
1939	224,000	10.00	20.00	60.00	300	—
1939 Proof	—	Value: 500				
1940	800,000	5.00	8.50	27.50	80.00	—
1940 Proof	—	—	—	—	—	—
1941	1,240,000	3.00	6.00	15.00	65.00	—
1941 Proof	—	—	—	—	—	—
1942	2,008,000	3.00	6.00	15.00	70.00	—
1942 Proof	—	—	—	—	—	—

KM# 15a 1/2 CROWN **Weight:** 14.1400 g. **Composition:** 0.5000 Silver .2273 oz. ASW **Obverse:** Bust of King George VI

Date	Mintage	F	VF	XF	Unc	BU
1944	800,000	3.50	7.00	20.00	75.00	—
1946	1,400,000	4.00	10.00	27.50	135	—
1946 Proof	—	—	—	—	—	—

KM# 15b 1/2 CROWN **Composition:** Copper-Nickel **Obverse:** Bust of King George VI

Date	Mintage	F	VF	XF	Unc	BU
1947	6,000,000	1.25	2.50	5.00	20.00	—
1947 Proof	—	Value: 300				

KM# 24 1/2 CROWN **Composition:** Copper-Nickel **Obverse:** Bust of King George VI

Date	Mintage	F	VF	XF	Unc	BU
1948	800,000	1.25	2.50	10.00	50.00	—
1948 Proof	—	—	—	—	—	—
1949	1,600,000	1.25	2.50	9.00	45.00	—
1949 Proof	—	Value: 450				
1950	1,200,000	1.25	2.50	10.00	65.00	—
1950 Proof	—	Value: 450				
1951	3,200,000	1.25	2.50	7.00	30.00	—
1951 Proof	—	Value: 350				
1952	2,800,000	1.25	2.50	8.00	60.00	—
1952 Proof	—	Value: 350				

KM# 31 1/2 CROWN Composition: Copper-Nickel **Obverse:** Bust of Queen Elizabeth II

Date	Mintage	F	VF	XF	Unc	BU
1954	1,200,000	8.00	16.00	35.00	75.00	—
1954 Proof	20	Value: 450				

KM# 27 CROWN Weight: 28.2800 g. **Composition:** 0.5000 Silver .4546 oz. ASW **Subject:** Birth of Cecil Rhodes Centennial **Obverse:** Bust of Queen Elizabeth II **Edge Lettering:** 1853 OUT OF VISION CAME REALITY 1953 **Note:** Both upright and inverted edge varieties exist.

Date	Mintage	F	VF	XF	Unc	BU
1953	124,000	4.00	5.50	9.00	20.00	35.00
1953 Proof	1,500	Value: 85.00				
1953 Matte Proof	—	Value: 350				

PROOF SETS

KM#	Date	Mintage	Identification	Issue Price	Mkt Val
PS1	1932 (5)	496	KM#1-5	—	450
PS2	1937 (6)	40	KM#8-13	—	2,000
PS3	1939 (5)	10	KM#15-19	—	2,500
PS6	1947 (5)	10	KM#15b-19b	—	1,500
PS4	1953 (2)	3	KM#27 Double set; Rare	—	—
PS5	1954 (4)	20	KM#28-31	—	2,500

SPAIN

The Spanish State, forming the greater part of the Iberian Peninsula of southwest Europe, has an area of 195,988 sq. mi. (504,714 sq. km.) and a population of 39.4 million including the Balearic and the Canary Islands. Capital: Madrid. The economy is based on agriculture, industry and tourism. Machinery, fruit, vegetables and chemicals are exported.

It isn't known when man first came to the Iberian Peninsula - the Altamira caves off the Cantabrian coast approximately 50 miles west of Santander were fashioned in Paleolithic times. Spain was a battleground for centuries before it became a united nation, fought for by Phoenicians, Carthaginians, Greeks, Celts, Romans, Vandals, Visigoths and Moors. Ferdinand and Isabella destroyed the last Moorish stronghold in 1492, freeing the national energy and resources for the era of discovery and colonization that would make Spain the most powerful country in Europe during the 16th century. After the destruction of the Spanish Armada, 1588, Spain never again played a major role in European politics. Forcing Ferdinand to give up his throne and placing him under military guard at Valencay in 1808, Napoleonic France ruled Spain until 1814. When the monarchy was restored in 1814 it continued, only interrupted by the short-lived republic of 1873-74, until the exile of Alfonso XIII in 1931 when the Second Republic was established.

Discontent against the mother country increased after1808 as colonists faced new imperialist policies from Napoleon or Spanish liberals. The revolutionary movement was established which resulted in the eventual independence of the Vice-royalties of New Spain, New Granada and Rio de la Plata within 2 decades.

The doomed republic was trapped in a tug-of-war between the right and left wing forces inevitably resulting in the Spanish Civil War of 1936-38. The leftist Republicans were supported by the U.S.S.R. and the International Brigade, which consisted of mainly communist volunteers from all over the western world. The right wing Nationalists were supported by the Fascist governments of Italy and Germany. Under the leadership of Gen. Francisco Franco, the Nationalists emerged victorious and immediately embarked on a program of reconstruction and neutrality as dictated by the new "Caudillo"(leader) Franco.

The monarchy was reconstituted in 1947 under the regency of General Francisco Franco; the king designate to be crowned after Franco's death. Franco died on Nov. 20, 1975. Two days after his passing, Juan Carlos de Borbon, the grandson of Alfonso XIII, was proclaimed King of Spain.

RULERS

Alfonso XIII, 1886-1931
2nd Republic and Civil War, 1931-1939
Francisco Franco, 1939-1947
as Caudillo and regent, 1947-1975
Juan Carlos I, 1975-

NOTE: From 1868 to 1982, two dates may be found on most Spanish coinage. The larger date is the year of authorization and the smaller date incused on the two 6-pointed-stars found on most types is the year of issue. The latter appears in parentheses in these listings.

MINT MARKS

Until 1980

6-pointed star - Madrid

NOTE: Letters after date are initials of mint officials.

After 1982

Crowned M – Madrid

KINGDOM, PRE-1931

DECIMAL COINAGE

Peseta System

100 Centimos = 1 Peseta

KM# 726 CENTIMO Composition: Bronze **Obverse:** Alfonso XIII left **Note:** Mint mark: 6-pointed star.

Date	Mintage	F	VF	XF	Unc	BU
1906 (6) SL-V	7,500,000	0.25	0.65	1.25	2.25	3.50
1906 (6) SM-V	Inc. above	200	300	400	600	750

KM# 731 CENTIMO Composition: Bronze **Obverse:** Alfonso XIII right **Note:** Mint mark: 6-pointed star.

Date	Mintage	F	VF	XF	Unc	BU
1911 (1) PC-V	1,462,000	30.00	50.00	70.00	85.00	100
1912 (2) PC-V	2,109,000	2.00	3.50	6.00	10.00	15.00
1913 (3) PC-V	1,429,000	3.50	6.50	12.00	18.00	22.00

KM# 722 2 CENTIMOS Composition: Copper **Obverse:** Alfonso XIII left **Note:** Mint mark: 6-pointed star.

Date	Mintage	F	VF	XF	Unc	BU
1904 (04) SM-V	10,000,000	0.65	1.75	4.00	9.00	13.50
1905 (05) SM-V	5,000,000	0.65	2.25	5.00	12.00	16.50

KM# 732 2 CENTIMOS Composition: Copper **Obverse:** Alfonso XIII left **Note:** Mint mark: 6-pointed star.

Date	Mintage	F	VF	XF	Unc	BU
1911 (11) PC-V	2,284,000	0.65	1.75	3.50	10.00	16.00
1912 (12) PC-V	5,216,000	0.65	1.75	3.00	8.00	12.50

KM# 740 25 CENTIMOS Composition: Copper-Nickel **Obverse:** Ship under full sail **Reverse:** Crowned value

Date	Mintage	F	VF	XF	Unc	BU
1925 PC-S	8,001,000	0.65	1.75	10.00	30.00	40.00

KM# 742 25 CENTIMOS Composition: Copper-Nickel

Date	Mintage	F	VF	XF	Unc	BU
1927 PC-S	12,000,000	0.45	1.00	9.00	28.00	40.00

KM# 723 50 CENTIMOS Weight: 2.5000 g. **Composition:** 0.8350 Silver .0671 oz. ASW **Obverse:** Alfonso XIII left **Note:** Mint mark: 6-pointed star.

Date	Mintage	F	VF	XF	Unc	BU
1904 (04) SM-V	4,851,000	1.25	2.25	3.25	13.50	15.00
1904 (10) PC-V	1,303,000	1.25	2.50	3.75	15.00	18.00

KM# 730 50 CENTIMOS **Weight:** 2.5000 g. **Composition:** 0.8350 Silver .0671 oz. ASW **Obverse:** Alfonso XIII **Note:** Mint mark: 6-pointed star.

Date	Mintage	F	VF	XF	Unc	BU
1910 (10) PC-V	4,526,000	1.25	2.50	5.00	18.00	24.00

KM# 741 50 CENTIMOS **Weight:** 2.5000 g. **Composition:** 0.8350 Silver .0671 oz. ASW **Obverse:** Alfonso XIII

Date	Mintage	VG	F	VF	XF	Unc
1926 PC-S	4,000,000	—	1.25	2.50	3.25	6.50

KM# 721 PESETA **Weight:** 5.0000 g. **Composition:** 0.8350 Silver .1342 oz. ASW **Obverse:** Alfonso XIII **Note:** Mint mark 6 pointed star

Date	Mintage	VG	F	VF	XF	Unc
1903 //03 SM-V	10,602,000	—	2.00	5.00	20.00	50.00
1904 //04 SM-V	5,294,000	—	2.00	8.50	27.50	65.00
1905 //05 SM-V	492,000	—	40.00	125	450	850

KM# 725 2 PESETAS **Weight:** 10.0000 g. **Composition:** 0.8350 Silver .2685 oz. ASW **Obverse:** Alfonso XIII **Note:** Mint mark: 6-pointed star.

Date	Mintage	F	VF	XF	Unc	BU
1905 (05) SM-V	3,589,000	4.50	7.00	15.00	24.00	30.00

REPUBLIC
1931 - 1939
DECIMAL COINAGE
Peseta System

100 Centimos = 1 Peseta

KM# 752 5 CENTIMOS **Composition:** Iron

Date	Mintage	F	VF	XF	Unc	BU
1937	10,000,000	0.35	1.00	2.00	5.00	9.00

KM# 756 10 CENTIMOS **Composition:** Iron

Date	Mintage	F	VF	XF	Unc	BU
1938	1,000	—	—	—	1,800	—

Note: This coin was never released into circulation

KM# 751 25 CENTIMOS **Composition:** Copper-Nickel

Date	Mintage	F	VF	XF	Unc	BU
1934	12,272,000	0.20	0.50	3.50	15.00	20.00

KM# 753 25 CENTIMOS **Composition:** Copper-Nickel **Note:** Struck at the Vienna mint

Date	Mintage	F	VF	XF	Unc	BU
1937	42,000,000	0.20	0.40	1.00	3.00	5.00

Note: This coin was issued by way of decree April 5, 1938, by the Governmant in Burgos. Franco and the Nationalist forces controlled the majority of Spain by this point in time

KM# 757 25 CENTIMOS **Composition:** Copper

Date	Mintage	F	VF	XF	Unc	BU
1938	45,500,000	1.00	2.00	4.00	6.00	9.00

KM# 754.1 50 CENTIMOS **Composition:** Copper **Reverse:** Border of dots **Note:** Mint mark: 6-pointed star. Several varieties exist.

Date	Mintage	F	VF	XF	Unc	BU
1937 (34)	50,000,000	0.65	1.50	4.50	10.00	13.50
1937 (36)	1,000,000	0.65	1.50	5.00	11.50	15.00

KM# 754.2 50 CENTIMOS **Composition:** Copper **Obverse:** Seated allegorical figure left **Reverse:** Border of rectangles **Note:** Mint mark: 6-pointed star.

Date	Mintage	F	VF	XF	Unc	BU
1937 (36)		1.50	3.00	6.00	16.00	22.00

KM# 750 PESETA **Weight:** 5.0000 g. **Composition:** 0.8350 Silver .1342 oz. ASW **Note:** Mint mark: 6-pointed star.

Date	Mintage	F	VF	XF	Unc	BU
1933 (3-4)	2,000,000	4.00	9.00	15.00	20.00	25.00

Note: Rotated reverse varieties exist, with values increasing by the degree of rotation.

KM# 755 PESETA **Composition:** Brass

Date	Mintage	F	VF	XF	Unc	BU
1937	50,000,000	0.35	0.85	2.00	5.00	7.00

NATIONALIST GOVERNMENT
1939 - 1947
DECIMAL COINAGE
Peseta System

100 Centimos = 1 Peseta

KM# 765 5 CENTIMOS **Composition:** Aluminum **Note:** Mint mark: 6-pointed star. To realize the values below all Unc. and BU coins must have full strike including letters.

Date	Mintage	F	VF	XF	Unc	BU
1940 PLUS	175,000,000	—	2.00	7.00	24.00	30.00
1940 PLVS	Inc. above	—	7.00	15.00	40.00	65.00
1941	202,107,000	—	0.50	2.00	8.00	12.00
1945	221,500,000	—	0.25	1.00	4.00	8.00
1953	31,573,000	—	10.00	20.00	50.00	75.00

KM# 766 10 CENTIMOS **Composition:** Aluminum **Note:** Mint mark: 6-pointed star. Varieties exist. To realize the values below all Unc. and BU coins must have full strike including letters.

Date	Mintage	F	VF	XF	Unc	BU
1940 PLUS	225,000,000	—	2.00	6.00	28.00	40.00
1940 PLVS	Inc. above	—	15.00	50.00	100	175
1941 PLUS	247,981,000	—	0.75	3.50	8.00	12.00
1941 PLVS	Inc. above	—	10.00	25.00	50.00	100
1945	250,000,000	—	0.60	2.50	6.00	8.00
1953	865,850,000	—	0.35	1.25	4.50	5.50

KM# 767 PESETA **Composition:** Aluminum-Bronze **Note:** Mint mark: 6-pointed star. To realize the values below all Unc. and BU coins must have full strike including letters.

Date	Mintage	F	VF	XF	Unc	BU
1944	150,000,000	—	0.25	5.00	18.00	25.00

KINGDOM, 1949-PRESENT
DECIMAL COINAGE
Peseta System

100 Centimos = 1 Peseta

KM# 790 10 CENTIMOS **Composition:** Aluminum **Note:** Mint mark: 6-pointed star.

Date	Mintage	F	VF	XF	Unc	BU
1959		—	—	—	0.10	0.15
1959 Proof	101,000	Value: 1.50				

KM# 776 50 CENTIMOS **Composition:** Copper-Nickel **Reverse:** Arrows pointing down **Note:** Mint mark: 6-pointed star.

e	Mintage	F	VF	XF	Unc	BU
9 (51)	990,000	3.00	5.00	8.00	20.00	28.00

/I# 777 50 CENTIMOS Composition: Copper-Nickel **Reverse:** Arrows pointing up **Note:** Mint mark: 6-pointed star.

te	F	VF	XF	Unc	BU
49 (51)	—	0.25	3.00	12.00	20.00
49 (E51)	—	—	—	350	550

Note: Issued to commemorate a numismatic exposition December 2, 1951. An E replaces the 19 on the lower star

49 (52)	—	0.15	1.50	9.00	16.00
49 (53)	—	0.15	3.00	22.00	30.00
49 (54)	—	0.15	2.50	8.00	16.00
49 (56)	—	0.15	2.00	7.00	15.00
49 (62)	—	0.15	1.00	5.00	10.00
63 (63)	—	0.15	5.00	24.00	32.00
63 (64)	—	0.10	0.25	1.50	3.50
63 (65)	—	0.10	0.25	1.50	2.50

M# 795 50 CENTIMOS Composition: Aluminum **Note:** Mint mark: 6-pointed star.

te	Mintage	F	VF	XF	Unc	BU
66 //67		—	—	0.10	0.50	0.75
66 //68		—	—	0.10	0.25	0.45
66 //69		—	—	0.25	1.00	2.00
66 //70 rooflike	Est. 6,000	Value: 135				
66 //71		—	—	0.10	0.25	0.50
66 //72		—	—	0.25	1.25	2.00
66 //72 Proof	23,000	Value: 4.00				
66 //73		—	—	0.10	0.25	0.50
66 //73 Proof	28,000	Value: 1.50				
66 //74 Proof	25,000	Value: 45.00				
66 //75 Proof	75,000	Value: 6.50				

M# 805 50 CENTIMOS Composition: Copper-Nickel **Note:** Mint mark: 6-pointed star.

ate	Mintage	F	VF	XF	Unc	BU
975 //76	4,060,000	—	—	0.10	0.25	0.45
975 //76	—	Value: 0.85				

:M# 815 50 CENTIMOS Center Composition: Aluminum **Subject:** World Cup Soccer Games **Note:** Mint mark: 6-pointed star.

ate	Mintage	F	VF	XF	Unc	BU
980 //80	15,000,000	—	—	0.10	0.20	0.35

M# 775 PESETA Composition: Aluminum-Bronze **Note:** Mint mark: 6-pointed star.

ate	F	VF	XF	Unc	BU
946 (48)	600	900	1,800	—	—
947 (48)	—	1.00	15.00	100	135
947 (49)	—	0.75	15.00	95.00	125
947 (50)	—	5.00	24.00	225	425
947 (51)	—	4.00	20.00	100	300
947 (E51)	—	—	—	500	650

Note: Issued to commemorate the Second National Numismatic Exposition December 2, 1951. An E replaces the 19 on the lower star.

Date	F	VF	XF	Unc	BU
1947 (52)	—	1.00	7.00	50.00	100
1947 (53)	—	0.75	6.00	35.00	70.00
1947 (54)	—	0.75	6.50	40.00	75.00
1947 (56)	—	20.00	50.00	250	475
1953 (54)	—	4.00	15.00	150	250
1953 (56)	—	0.10	0.75	3.50	6.00
1953 (60)	—	0.75	8.00	60.00	100
1953 (61)	—	0.60	6.00	45.00	75.00
1953 (62)	—	0.10	0.50	1.75	5.00
1953 (63)	—	0.25	1.50	6.00	20.00
1963 (63)	—	0.25	1.50	8.00	20.00
1963 (64)	—	0.10	0.50	1.75	3.00
1963 (65)	—	0.10	0.50	1.75	3.00
1963 (66)	—	0.10	0.50	3.00	6.00
1963 (67)	—	2.00	10.00	40.00	65.00

KM# 796 PESETA Composition: Aluminum-Bronze **Note:** Mint mark: 6-pointed star.

Date	Mintage	F	VF	XF	Unc	BU
1966 //67	59,000,000	—	0.10	0.20	1.00	2.00
1966 //67 Proof	25,000	Value: 1.00				
1966 //68	120,000,000	—	0.10	0.20	1.00	1.50
1966 //69	120,000,000	—	0.10	0.20	1.00	1.50
1966 //70	75,000,000	—	0.10	0.20	2.00	3.00
1966 //71	115,270,000	—	0.10	0.20	1.00	1.50
1966 //72	106,000,000	—	—	0.10	0.50	0.75
1966 //72 Proof	23,000	Value: 1.50				
1966 //73	152,000,000	—	—	0.10	0.35	0.65
1966 //73 Proof	28,000,000	Value: 1.00				
1966 //74	181,000,000	—	—	0.10	0.35	0.65
1966 //75	227,580,000	—	—	0.10	0.25	0.35
1966 //75 Proof	25,000	Value: 0.50				

KM# 806 PESETA Composition: Aluminum-Bronze **Note:** Two varieties of tilde size for the n in Espana exist of this date. Large is Madrid mint, small is Santiago de Chile.

Date	Mintage	F	VF	XF	Unc	BU
1975 //76		—	—	0.10	0.25	0.35
1975 //76 Proof	177,080,000	Value: 0.75				
1975 //77		—	—	0.10	0.25	0.35
1975 //77 Proof	Inc. above	Value: 0.75				
1975 //78		—	—	0.10	0.25	0.35
1975 //79		—	—	0.10	0.25	0.35

Note: Two varieties of tilde size for the n in Espana exist of this date. Large is Madrid mint, small is Santiago de Chile.

1975 //79 Proof	—	Value: 0.75				
1975 //80		—	—	0.10	0.25	0.35

KM# 816 PESETA Composition: Aluminum-Bronze **Subject:** World Cup Soccer Games

Date	Mintage	F	VF	XF	Unc	BU
1980 //80	Inc. above	—	—	0.10	0.20	0.30
1980 //81	385,000,000	—	—	0.10	0.25	0.35
1980 //82	333,000,000	—	—	0.10	0.25	0.35

KM# 821 PESETA Composition: Aluminum

Date	Mintage	F	VF	XF	Unc	BU
1982		—	—	0.10	0.20	0.35

Note: Mintage included in KM#816, 1980 (82)

1983		—	—	0.10	0.60	1.00
1984		—	—	0.10	0.20	0.35
1985		—	—	0.10	0.20	0.35
1986		—	—	0.10	0.20	0.35

Date	Mintage	F	VF	XF	Unc	BU
1987		—	—	0.10	0.20	0.35
1987 Proof	60,000	Value: 40.00				
1988		—	—	0.10	0.20	0.35
1989		—	—	0.10	0.60	1.00

Note: Mintage included in KM#832, 1989

KM# 832 PESETA Composition: Aluminum

Date	Mintage	F	VF	XF	Unc	BU
1989	198,415,000	—	—	0.10	0.30	0.50
1990	197,700,000	—	—	0.10	0.25	0.40
1991	173,780,000	—	—	0.10	0.30	0.50
1992	168,870,000	—	—	0.10	0.20	0.25
1993	300,013,000	—	—	0.10	0.20	0.25
1994	162,860,000	—	—	0.10	0.20	0.25
1995	183,175,000	—	—	0.10	0.20	0.25
1996	101,885,000	—	—	0.10	0.20	0.25
1997	342,620,000	—	—	0.10	0.20	0.25
1998	411,614,000	—	—	0.10	0.20	0.25
1999	84,946,000	—	—	0.10	0.20	0.25
2000	—	—	—	0.10	0.20	0.25
2001	—	—	—	0.10	0.30	0.50

KM# 822 2 PESETAS Composition: Aluminum

Date	Mintage	F	VF	XF	Unc	BU
1982	21,500,000	—	—	0.10	0.35	0.60
1984	47,650,000	—	—	0.10	0.30	0.50

KM# 785 2-1/2 PESETAS Composition: Aluminum-Bronze

Date	Mintage	F	VF	XF	Unc	BU
1953 //54	22,729,000	—	0.25	1.00	3.00	5.00
1953 //56	30,322,000	—	0.25	1.00	3.00	5.00
1953 //68 In sets only	1,000	—	—	—	—	650
1953 //69 In sets only	2,000	—	—	—	—	750
1953 //70 In sets only	6,000	—	—	—	—	100
1953 //71 In sets only	10,000	—	—	—	—	100

KM# 778 5 PESETAS Composition: Nickel

Date	F	VF	XF	Unc	BU
1949 (49)	—	2.00	6.50	15.00	25.00
1949 (50)	—	1.25	3.00	7.00	11.50
1949 (E51)	—	—	—	900	1,200

Note: Issued to commemorate the Second National Numismatic Exposition December 2, 1951. An E replaces the 19 on the lower star

1949 (51)	—	—	—	—	3,500
1949 (52)	—	—	—	—	6,000

KM# 786 5 PESETAS Composition: Copper-Nickel
Note: Values in uncirculated drop by 50% or more when the PLUS in legend is not readable. This defect is most often seen on coins struck before 1968.

Date	Mintage	F	VF	XF	Unc	BU
1957 (58)		—	0.75	4.00	30.00	60.00
1957 BA		—	40.00	75.00	125	175

Note: Issued to commemorate the 1958 2nd Ibero-American Numismatic Exposition in Barcelona with BA replacing the star on left side of reverse

Date	Mintage	F	VF	XF	Unc	BU
1957 (59)		—	0.10	1.00	15.00	20.00
1957 (60)		—	0.10	0.75	7.50	15.00
1957 (61)		—	0.10	2.00	20.00	30.00
1957 (62)		—	0.10	1.00	3.50	12.50
1957 (63)		—	2.00	15.00	80.00	150
1957 (64)		—	0.10	0.75	8.00	16.00
1957 (65)		—	0.10	0.25	5.00	10.00
1957 (66)		—	0.10	1.00	18.00	25.00
1957 (67)		—	0.10	0.25	2.00	5.00
1957 (68)		—	0.10	0.25	1.75	3.00
1957 (69)		—	0.10	0.25	2.25	4.00
1957 (70)		—	0.10	0.25	3.00	7.00
1957 (71)		—	0.10	0.25	1.50	3.00
1957 (72)		—	—	0.10	1.50	3.00
1957 (72) Proof	23,000	Value: 5.00				
1957 (73)		—	—	0.10	0.75	1.00
1957 (73) Proof	28,000	Value: 2.00				
1957 (74)		—	—	0.10	0.45	0.75
1957 (74) Proof	25,000	Value: 2.00				
1957 (75)		—	—	0.10	0.25	0.45
1957 (75) Proof	25,000	Value: 1.00				

KM# 811 5 PESETAS Composition: Copper-Nickel
Obverse: KM#807 **Reverse:** KM#817 with (80) star **Note:** Mule.

Date	F	VF	XF	Unc	BU
1975 (80)	—	—	150	225	250

KM# 807 5 PESETAS Composition: Copper-Nickel

Date	Mintage	F	VF	XF	Unc	BU
1975 (76)	150,560,000	—	—	0.10	0.25	0.35
1975 (76) Proof	—	Value: 1.00				
1975 (77)	154,982,000	—	—	0.10	0.25	0.35
1975 (77) Proof	Inc. above	Value: 1.00				
1975 (78)	412,610,000	—	—	0.10	0.50	1.00
1975 (79)	436,000,000	—	—	0.10	0.25	0.35
1975 (79) Proof	—	Value: 1.00				
1975 (80)	322,000,000	—	—	0.10	0.50	1.00

KM# 817 5 PESETAS Composition: Copper-Nickel
Subject: World Cup Soccer Games

Date	Mintage	F	VF	XF	Unc	BU
1980 (80)	75,000,000	—	—	0.10	0.25	0.35
1980 (81)	294,000,000	—	—	0.10	0.25	0.50
1980 (82)	291,000,000	—	—	0.10	0.25	0.50

KM# 823 5 PESETAS Composition: Copper-Nickel
Note: Mint mark: Crowned M.

Date	Mintage	F	VF	XF	Unc	BU
1982	—	—	—	0.10	1.00	1.50

Note: Mintage included in KM#817, 1980 (82)

Date	Mintage	F	VF	XF	Unc	BU
1983	200,000,000	—	—	0.10	0.50	0.65
1984	169,000,000	—	—	0.10	0.60	0.80
1989	—	—	—	0.10	0.75	1.00

KM# 833 5 PESETAS Composition: Aluminum-Bronze

Date	Mintage	F	VF	XF	Unc	BU
1989	109,270,000	—	—	0.15	0.40	0.50
1990	191,740,000	—	—	0.15	0.80	1.00
1991	313,820,000	—	—	0.15	0.70	0.85
1992	493,224,000	—	—	0.10	0.35	0.50
1998	923,978,000	—	—	0.10	0.25	0.35
2000	—	—	—	0.10	0.25	0.35
2001	—	—	—	0.10	0.25	0.35

KM# 919 5 PESETAS Composition: Nickel-Brass
Subject: Jacobeo **Note:** Coins with extra metal in the denomination 5 sell for a premium.

Date	Mintage	F	VF	XF	Unc	BU
1993	372,746,000	—	—	—	0.25	0.35

KM# 931 5 PESETAS Composition: Nickel-Brass
Subject: Aragon **Note:** Wide rim variety exists.

Date	Mintage	F	VF	XF	Unc	BU
1994	199,678,000	—	—	—	0.30	0.40

KM# 946 5 PESETAS Composition: Aluminum-Bronze
Subject: Asturias

Date	Mintage	F	VF	XF	Unc	BU
1995	301,756,000	—	—	—	0.30	0.40

KM# 960 5 PESETAS Composition: Aluminum-Bronze
Subject: La Rioja

Date	Mintage	F	VF	XF	Unc	BU
1996	674,168,000	—	—	—	0.15	0.25

KM# 981 5 PESETAS Composition: Brass **Subject:** Balearic Islands **Obverse:** Stone monument **Reverse:** Horse and rider

Date	Mintage	F	VF	XF	Unc	BU
1997	709,006,000	—	—	—	0.15	0.25

KM# 1008 5 PESETAS Composition: Brass **Reverse:** Murcia Waterwheel

Date	Mintage	F	VF	XF	Unc	BU
1999	216,230,000	—	—	—	0.25	0.45

KM# 827 10 PESETAS Composition: Copper-Nickel
Note: Denomination DIEZ

Date	Mintage	F	VF	XF	Unc	BU
1983	149,000,000	—	—	0.25	0.35	0.40
1984	66,000,000	—	—	0.25	0.40	0.50
1985	45,706,000	—	—	0.25	0.50	0.60

KM# 903 10 PESETAS Composition: Copper-Nickel

Date	Mintage	F	VF	XF	Unc	B
1992	51,820,000	—	—	0.25	0.40	0.
1998	—	—	—	0.25	0.85	1.
1999	2,125,000	—	—	0.35	0.70	0.

KM# 918 10 PESETAS Composition: Copper-Nickel
Subject: Juan Miro

Date	Mintage	F	VF	XF	Unc	B
1993	53,845,000	—	—	0.35	0.85	1.0

KM# 932 10 PESETAS Composition: Copper-Nickel
Subject: Musician P. Sarasate

Date	Mintage	F	VF	XF	Unc	B
1994	3,050,000	—	—	0.50	2.00	2.5

KM# 947 10 PESETAS Composition: Copper-Nickel
Subject: Don Francisco de Quevedo

Date	Mintage	F	VF	XF	Unc	B
1995	1,050,000	—	—	1.00	3.50	4.5

KM# 961 10 PESETAS Composition: Copper-Nickel
Subject: Emilia Pardo Bazan

Date	Mintage	F	VF	XF	Unc	B
1996	1,060,000	—	—	0.50	2.00	2.5

KM# 982 10 PESETAS Composition: Copper-Nickel
Subject: Seneca **Obverse:** Portrait **Reverse:** Castle gate

Date	F	VF	XF	Unc	BU
1997	—	—	0.25	0.50	0.65

KM# 1012 10 PESETAS Composition: Copper-Nickel
Note: Older portrait.

Date	Mintage	F	VF	XF	Unc	BU
1998	14,965,000	—	—	0.25	0.40	0.50
1999	2,125,000	—	—	0.25	0.75	1.50
2000	—	—	—	0.25	0.75	1.50

KM# 787 25 PESETAS Composition: Copper-Nickel
Note: Values in uncirculated drop by 50% or more when the PLUS in legend is not readable. This defect is most often seen on coins struck before 1968.

ate	Mintage	F	VF	XF	Unc	BU
957 (58)		—	0.50	7.00	50.00	85.00
957 BA		—	20.00	40.00	60.00	90.00

Note: Issued to commemorate the 1958 Barcelona Exposition with BA replacing the star on left isde of reverse

957 (59)		—	0.20	1.00	22.00	35.00
957 (61)		—	3.00	20.00	100	125
957 (64)		—	0.20	1.00	15.00	25.00
957 (65)		—	0.20	0.75	3.50	10.00
957 (66)		—	0.20	1.00	5.00	10.00
957 (67)		—	0.20	1.75	12.00	20.00
957 (68)		—	0.20	0.65	2.50	5.00
957 (69)		—	0.20	0.50	1.50	3.00
957 (70)		—	0.20	0.30	3.00	5.50
957 (71)		—	0.75	3.50	25.00	40.00
957 (72)		—	0.20	0.75	3.50	6.50
957 (72) Proof	23,000	Value: 10.00				
957 (73) Proof	28,000	Value: 75.00				
957 (74)		—	0.20	0.30	4.00	5.50
957 (74) Proof	25,000	Value: 10.00				
957 (75)		—	0.20	0.30	1.50	2.00
957 (75) Proof	25,000	Value: 3.50				

KM# 808 25 PESETAS Composition: Copper-Nickel **Edge:** Lettered

ate	Mintage	F	VF	XF	Unc	BU
975 (76)	35,707,000	—	0.20	0.25	0.75	1.00
975 (76) Proof	—	Value: 1.00				
975 (77)	46,690,000	—	0.20	0.25	0.75	1.00
975 (77) Proof	Inc. above	Value: 1.00				
975 (78)	97,555,000	—	0.20	0.25	2.00	3.00
975 (79)	172,000,000	—	0.20	0.25	0.75	1.00
975 (79) Proof	—	Value: 1.00				
975 (80)	136,000,000	—	0.20	0.25	2.50	4.00

KM# 818 25 PESETAS Composition: Copper-Nickel **Subject:** World Cup Soccer Games

ate	Mintage	F	VF	XF	Unc	BU
980 (80)	35,000,000	—	0.20	0.30	0.60	0.75
980 (81)	117,000,000	—	0.20	0.30	0.75	1.00
980 (82)	100,000,000	—	0.20	0.30	1.00	2.00

KM# 824 25 PESETAS Composition: Copper-Nickel **Edge:** Reeded **Note:** Mint mark: Crowned M; Similar to KM#808.

ate	Mintage	F	VF	XF	Unc	BU
982	146,000,000	—	0.20	0.30	2.00	3.00
983	248,000,000	—	0.20	0.30	1.00	1.50
984	242,000,000	—	0.20	0.30	2.50	4.00

KM# 850 25 PESETAS Composition: Nickel-Bronze **Subject:** 1992 Olympics **Obvverse:** Discus thrower

ate	Mintage	F	VF	XF	Unc	BU
990	150,000,000	—	0.25	0.30	1.25	1.50
991	Inc. above	—	0.25	0.35	5.00	6.50

KM# 851 25 PESETAS Composition: Nickel-Bronze **Subject:** 1992 Olympics **Reverse:** High jumper

ate	Mintage	F	VF	XF	Unc	BU
990	Inc. above	—	—	—	1.25	1.50
991	87,000,000	—	—	—	1.25	1.50

KM# 904 25 PESETAS Composition: Nickel-Bronze **Subject:** Giralda Tower of Sevilla

Date	Mintage	F	VF	XF	Unc	BU
1992	179,833,000	—	—	—	2.50	3.00

KM# 905 25 PESETAS Composition: Nickel-Bronze **Subject:** Tower of Gold in Seville **Obverse:** Globe

Date	F	VF	XF	Unc	BU
1992	—	—	—	1.00	1.25

KM# 920 25 PESETAS Composition: Nickel-Bronze **Subject:** Vasc Country

Date	Mintage	F	VF	XF	Unc	BU
1993	150,012,000	—	—	—	0.80	1.00

KM# 933 25 PESETAS Composition: Nickel-Bronze **Subject:** Canary Islands

Date	Mintage	F	VF	XF	Unc	BU
1994	242,566,000	—	—	—	0.60	0.75

KM# 948 25 PESETAS Composition: Brass **Subject:** Castilla and Leon

Date	Mintage	F	VF	XF	Unc	BU
1995	221,963,000	—	—	—	0.50	0.60
1995 without Y	Inc. above	—	—	45.00	65.00	80.00

KM# 962 25 PESETAS Composition: Copper-Zinc-Nickel **Subject:** Castilla - La Mancha - Don Quiote

Date	Mintage	F	VF	XF	Unc	BU
1996	37,403,000	—	—	—	0.60	0.70

KM# 983 25 PESETAS Composition: Brass **Subject:** Melilla **Obverse:** Two towered buildings **Reverse:** Ancient amphora, dates

Date	Mintage	F	VF	XF	Unc	BU
1997	461,688,000	—	—	—	0.60	0.70

KM# 990 25 PESETAS Composition: Copper-Zinc-Nickel **Subject:** Ceuta **Obverse:** Ornamented building corner **Reverse:** Statue on wall shelf

Date	Mintage	F	VF	XF	Unc	BU
1998	184,360,000	—	—	—	0.70	0.80

KM# 1007 25 PESETAS Composition: Nickel-Brass **Subject:** Navarra **Reverse:** Running of the bulls in Pamplona

Date	Mintage	F	VF	XF	Unc	BU
1999	2,130,000	—	—	—	2.25	3.00

KM# 1013 25 PESETAS Composition: Nickel-Brass **Subject:** Navarra **Obverse:** King's portrait **Reverse:** Crown, denomination and order **Edge:** Plain **Size:** 19.5 mm.

Date	F	VF	XF	Unc	BU
2000	—	—	—	1.20	1.35
2001	—	—	—	2.00	2.25

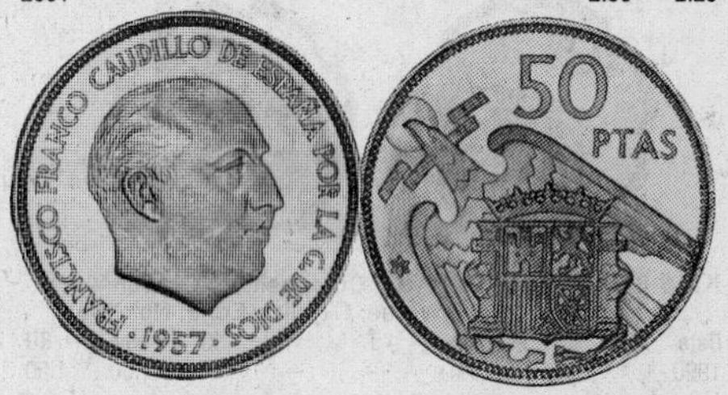

KM# 788 50 PESETAS Composition: Copper-Nickel

Date	Mintage	F	VF	XF	Unc	BU
1957 (58)		—	0.50	0.75	2.50	3.50
1957 (58) BA		—	18.00	35.00	55.00	75.00

Note: Issued to commemorate the 1958 Barcelona Exposition with BA replacing the star on left side of reverse

1957 (59)		—	0.50	0.75	2.50	3.50
1957 (60)		—	0.50	0.75	2.50	3.50
1957 (67)		—	0.75	1.50	5.00	7.00
1957 (68) In sets only		—	—	—	—	800
1957 (69) In sets only		—	—	—	—	700
1957 (70) In sets only		—	—	—	—	180
1957 (71)		—	1.00	4.00	20.00	25.00
1957 (72) Proof	23,000	Value: 25.00				
1957 (73) Proof	28,000	Value: 50.00				
1957 (74) Proof	25,000	Value: 50.00				
1957 (75) Proof	75,000	Value: 8.50				

Note: Edge varieties exist

KM# 809 50 PESETAS Composition: Copper-Nickel

Date	Mintage	F	VF	XF	Unc	BU
1975 (76)	4,400,000	—	0.50	0.65	1.20	1.50
1975 (76) Proof	—	Value: 2.00				
1975 (78)	17,555,000	—	0.50	0.75	2.50	3.00
1975 (79)	33,000,000	—	0.50	0.60	1.00	1.50
1975 (79) Proof	—	Value: 2.00				
1975 (80)	34,000,000	—	0.50	0.60	3.50	4.50

KM# 819 50 PESETAS **Composition:** Copper-Nickel
Subject: World Cup Soccer Games

Date	Mintage	F	VF	XF	Unc	BU
1980 (80)	15,000,000	—	0.50	0.60	0.75	0.85
1980 (81)	38,300,000	—	0.50	0.60	1.35	1.50
1980 (82)	30,950,000	—	0.50	0.60	2.00	2.50

KM# 825 50 PESETAS **Composition:** Copper-Nickel
Note: Mint mark: Crowned M.

Date	Mintage	F	VF	XF	Unc	BU
1982	27,000,000	—	0.50	1.00	2.50	4.50
1983	93,000,000	—	0.50	1.00	2.00	2.75
1984	17,500,000	7.00	15.00	25.00	45.00	60.00

KM# 852 50 PESETAS **Composition:** Copper-Nickel
Subject: Expo '92 **Obverse:** Juan Carlos I **Edge:** Notched

Date	Mintage	F	VF	XF	Unc	BU
1990	25,234,000	—	—	—	1.00	1.35

KM# 853 50 PESETAS **Composition:** Copper-Nickel
Subject: Expo '92 **Obverse:** City view **Edge:** Notched

Date	Mintage	F	VF	XF	Unc	BU
1990	7,916,000	—	—	—	1.00	1.50

KM# 906 50 PESETAS **Composition:** Copper-Nickel
Subject: 1992 Olympics **Obverse:** "La Pedrera" building (Gaudi) **Edge:** Notched

Date	Mintage	F	VF	XF	Unc	BU
1992	40,370,000	—	—	—	1.00	1.25

KM# 907 50 PESETAS **Composition:** Copper-Nickel
Subject: 1992 Olympics **Obverse:** Cathedral Sagrada Familia (Gaudi) **Edge:** Notched

Date	F	VF	XF	Unc	BU
1992	—	—	—	1.00	1.50

KM# 921 50 PESETAS **Composition:** Copper-Nickel
Subject: Extremadura **Reverse:** Roman bridge in Alcantara **Edge:** Notched

Date	Mintage	F	VF	XF	Unc	BU
1993	24,314,000	—	—	—	1.00	1.50

KM# 934 50 PESETAS **Composition:** Copper-Nickel
Subject: Altamira Cave Paintings **Edge:** Notched

Date	Mintage	F	VF	XF	Unc	BU
1994	3,002,000	—	—	—	2.25	2.75

KM# 949 50 PESETAS **Composition:** Copper-Nickel
Subject: Alcala Gate **Edge:** Notched

Date	Mintage	F	VF	XF	Unc	BU
1995	1,001,000	—	—	—	3.50	4.50

KM# 963 50 PESETAS **Composition:** Copper-Nickel
Subject: Philip V **Edge:** Notched

Date	Mintage	F	VF	XF	Unc	BU
1996	11,047,000	—	—	—	1.00	1.50

KM# 985 50 PESETAS **Composition:** Copper-Nickel
Obverse: Juan De Herrera **Reverse:** Escorial Monastery **Edge:** Notched

Date	Mintage	F	VF	XF	Unc	BU
1997	17,496,000	—	—	—	1.00	1.50

KM# 991 50 PESETAS **Composition:** Copper-Nickel
Obverse: King Juan Carlos **Reverse:** National arms and denomination **Edge:** Notched

Date	Mintage	F	VF	XF	Unc	BU
1998	17,496,000	—	—	—	1.00	1.50
1999	2,100,000	—	—	—	2.25	2.50
2000	—	—	—	—	2.00	2.25

KM# 797 100 PESETAS **Weight:** 19.0000 g.
Composition: 0.8000 Silver .4887 oz. ASW

Date	Mintage	F	VF	XF	Unc	BU
1966 (66)	35,000,000	—	—	3.00	5.00	6.00
1966 (67)	15,000,000	—	—	3.00	6.00	7.00
1966 (68)	24,000,000	—	—	3.00	5.00	6.00
1966 (69)	1,000,000	—	—	150	250	350
Note: 69 with straight 9 in star						
1966 (69)	Inc. above	—	—	50.00	110	135
Note: 69 with curved 9 in star						
1966 (70)	995,000	—	4.00	7.50	15.00	18.00

Note: 1966(69) coins heavily altered; authentication recommended

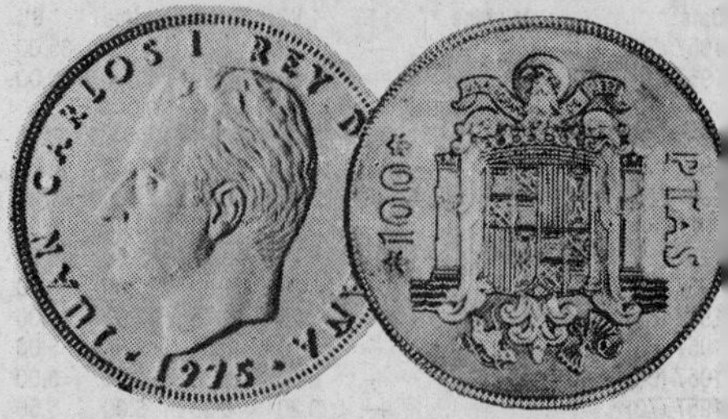

KM# 810 100 PESETAS **Composition:** Copper-Nickel
Obverse: Head of King Juan Carlos I left

Date	Mintage	F	VF	XF	Unc	BU
1975 (76)	4,400,000	—	—	0.75	1.00	1.50
1975 (76) Proof	—	Value: 3.00				

KM# 820 100 PESETAS **Composition:** Copper-Nickel
Subject: World Cup Soccer Games - Spain '82 **Obverse:** Head of King Juan Carlos I left

Date	Mintage	F	VF	XF	Unc	BU
1980 (80)	20,000,000	—	—	0.75	1.00	1.50

KM# 826 100 PESETAS **Composition:** Aluminum-Bronze **Obverse:** Head of King Juan Carlos I left

Date	Mintage	F	VF	XF	Unc	BU
1982	117,600,000	—	0.75	1.25	3.50	5.00
1982 Proof	—	Value: 5.00				
1983	—	—	0.75	1.25	25.00	40.00
1984	208,000,000	—	0.75	1.25	6.00	10.00
1985	118,000,000	—	0.75	1.25	10.00	15.00
1986	160,000,000	—	0.75	1.25	3.00	4.00
1988	125,674,000	—	0.75	1.25	4.00	5.00
1989	80,877,000	—	0.75	1.25	2.50	3.00
1990	25,636,000	—	0.75	1.25	4.00	5.00

Note: Varieties exist

KM# 834 100 PESETAS **Weight:** 1.6800 g.
Composition: 0.9250 Silver .0500 oz. ASW **Subject:** Discovery of America **Reverse:** Mayan pyramid

Date	Mintage	F	VF	XF	Unc	BU
1989	43,000	—	—	—	—	5.00
1989 Proof	57,000	Value: 6.00				

KM# 854 100 PESETAS **Weight:** 1.6800 g.
Composition: 0.9250 Silver .0500 oz. ASW **Obverse:** Brother Juniper Serra **Reverse:** Mission ruins within legend

Date	Mintage	F	VF	XF	Unc	BU
1990	24,000	—	—	—	—	6.00
1990 Proof	27,000	Value: 6.00				

KM# 882 100 PESETAS **Weight:** 1.6800 g.
Composition: 0.9250 Silver .0500 oz. ASW **Obverse:** Celestino Mutis **Reverse:** Flower plant within legend

Date	Mintage	F	VF	XF	Unc	BU
1991	14,000	—	—	—	—	8.00
1991 Proof	—	Value: 8.50				

KM# 908 100 PESETAS **Composition:** Aluminum-Bronze

Date	Mintage	F	VF	XF	Unc	BU
1992	22,661,000	—	—	—	2.50	3.00

Note: Edge varieties exist with positioning of fleur-de-lis

KM# 993 100 PESETAS **Weight:** 1.6800 g. **Composition:** 0.9250 Silver .0500 oz. ASW **Subject:** Seville Expo '92 **Obverse:** Bridge

Date	Mintage	F	VF	XF	Unc	BU
1992	16,000	—	—	—	—	9.50
1992 Proof	16,000	Value: 10.00				

KM# 922 100 PESETAS **Composition:** Nickel-Brass **Subject:** European unity **Obverse:** Jacobean track to Santiago de Compostela

Date	Mintage	F	VF	XF	Unc	BU
1993	39,723,000	—	—	—	3.00	4.00

KM# 935 100 PESETAS **Composition:** Nickel-Brass **Subject:** Museo del Prado **Obverse:** Head of King Juan Carlos I left

Date	Mintage	F	VF	XF	Unc	BU
1994	24,853,000	—	—	—	2.50	3.50

KM# 950 100 PESETAS **Composition:** Copper-Nickel **Series:** F.A.O. **Obverse:** Head of King Juan Carlos I left

Date	Mintage	F	VF	XF	Unc	BU
1995	71,957,000	—	—	—	2.00	3.00

KM# 964 100 PESETAS **Composition:** Copper-Zinc-Nickel **Obverse:** Head of King Juan Carlos I left **Reverse:** National Library

Date	Mintage	F	VF	XF	Unc	BU
1996	21,466,000	—	—	—	2.50	3.50

KM# 984 100 PESETAS **Composition:** Copper-Zinc-Nickel **Subject:** Royal Theatre **Obverse:** King Juan Carlos

Date	Mintage	F	VF	XF	Unc	BU
1997	29,480,000	—	—	—	2.00	3.00

KM# 989 100 PESETAS **Composition:** Aluminum-Bronze **Obverse:** Head of King Juan Carlos I left

Date		F	VF	XF	Unc	BU
1998		—	—	—	1.50	2.25
2000		—	—	—	1.50	2.25

KM# 1006 100 PESETAS **Composition:** Brass **Obverse:** Head of King Juan Carlos I left **Reverse:** Denomination

Date	Mintage	F	VF	XF	Unc	BU
1999	60,332,000	—	—	—	1.75	2.50

KM# 1016 100 PESETAS **Weight:** 9.8000 g. **Composition:** Aluminum-Bronze **Ruler:** Juan Carlos I **Subject:** 132nd Anniversary of the Peseta **Obverse:** Head of King Juan Carlos I left **Reverse:** Seated allegorical figure from an old coin design **Edge:** Ornamented **Size:** 24.4 mm.

Date	F	VF	XF	Unc	BU
2001	—	—	—	2.00	2.75

KM# 829 200 PESETAS **Composition:** Copper-Nickel **Obverse:** Head of King Juan Carlos I left

Date	Mintage	F	VF	XF	Unc	BU
1986	43,576,000	—	—	2.00	6.00	8.00
1987	66,718,000	—	—	2.00	12.00	16.00
1988	37,190,000	—	—	2.00	9.50	12.50

KM# 830 200 PESETAS **Composition:** Copper-Nickel **Subject:** Madrid Numismatic Exposition **Obverse:** Head of King Juan Carlos I left

Date	Mintage	F	VF	XF	Unc	BU
1987 (E87) Proof	60,000	Value: 45.00				

KM# 835 200 PESETAS **Weight:** 3.3700 g. **Composition:** 0.9250 Silver .1000 oz. ASW **Subject:** Discovery of America **Reverse:** Astrolobe

Date	Mintage	F	VF	XF	Unc	BU
1989	43,000	—	—	—	—	7.00
1989 Proof	57,000	Value: 8.00				

KM# 855 200 PESETAS **Composition:** Copper-Nickel

Date	Mintage	F	VF	XF	Unc	BU
1990	8,000,000	—	—	—	4.00	5.00

KM# 856 200 PESETAS **Weight:** 3.3700 g. **Composition:** 0.9250 Silver .1000 oz. ASW **Subject:** History in Common **Reverse:** Hand writing in a book within legend

Date	Mintage	F	VF	XF	Unc	BU
1990	24,000	—	—	—	—	8.00
1990 Proof	27,000	Value: 8.00				

KM# 883 200 PESETAS **Weight:** 3.3700 g. **Composition:** 0.9250 Silver .1000 oz. ASW **Subject:** Las Casas **Reverse:** 3 indian figures

Date	Mintage	F	VF	XF	Unc	BU
1991	14,000	—	—	—	—	9.50
1991 Proof	14,000	Value: 10.00				

KM# 884 200 PESETAS **Composition:** Copper-Nickel **Subject:** Madrid - European Culture Capital **Obverse:** Conjoined busts of King Juan Carlos I and Crown Prince right

Date	Mintage	F	VF	XF	Unc	BU
1991	11,400,000	—	—	—	2.00	3.00

KM# 884a 200 PESETAS **Weight:** 12.2500 g. **Composition:** 0.9250 Silver .3643 oz. ASW **Subject:** Madrid - European Culture Capital **Obverse:** Conjoined busts of King Juan Carlos I and Crown Prince right

Date	Mintage	F	VF	XF	Unc	BU
1992 Proof	38,000	Value: 125				

KM# 909 200 PESETAS **Composition:** Copper-Nickel **Subject:** Madrid - European Culture Capital **Obverse:** Conjoined busts of King Juan Carlos I and Crown Prince right **Reverse:** Equestrian

Date	F	VF	XF	Unc	BU
1992	—	—	—	2.50	3.00

KM# 910 200 PESETAS Composition: Copper-Nickel **Subject:** Madrid - European Culture Capital **Obverse:** Conjoined busts of King Juan Carlos I and Crown Prince right **Reverse:** Bear by tree

Date	F	VF	XF	Unc	BU
1992	—	—	—	2.00	2.50

KM# 994 200 PESETAS Weight: 3.3700 g. **Composition:** 0.9250 Silver .1000 oz. ASW **Subject:** Seville Expo '92 **Obverse:** Hydro-electric dam **Reverse:** Tower of Seville

Date	Mintage	F	VF	XF	Unc	BU
1992	—	—	—	—	—	12.00
1992	16,000	Value: 12.50				

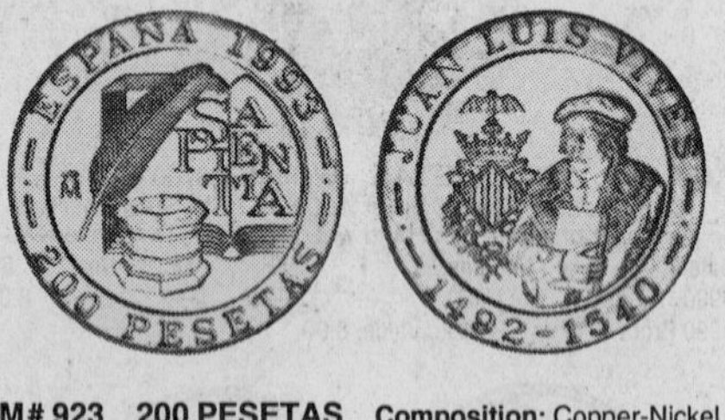

KM# 923 200 PESETAS Composition: Copper-Nickel **Subject:** Juan Luis Vives

Date	Mintage	F	VF	XF	Unc	BU
1993	2,811,000	—	—	—	5.00	6.00

KM# 936 200 PESETAS Composition: Copper-Nickel **Subject:** Velasquez and Goya Paintings

Date	Mintage	F	VF	XF	Unc	BU
1994	2,997,000	—	—	—	3.50	4.50

KM# 951 200 PESETAS Composition: Copper-Nickel **Subject:** Murillo and El Greco paintings

Date	Mintage	F	VF	XF	Unc	BU
1995	1,022,000	—	—	—	20.00	25.00

KM# 965 200 PESETAS Composition: Copper-Nickel **Subject:** Fortuny and Balleau paintings

Date	Mintage	F	VF	XF	Unc	BU
1996	9,206,000	—	—	—	2.00	3.00

KM# 986 200 PESETAS Composition: Copper-Nickel **Subject:** Jacinto Benavente **Obverse:** Stylized books **Reverse:** Potrait in inner circle

Date	Mintage	F	VF	XF	Unc	BU
1997	6,845,000	—	—	—	3.00	4.00

KM# 992 200 PESETAS Composition: Copper-Nickel **Obverse:** Conjoined busts of King Juan Carlos I and Crown Prince right **Reverse:** Denomination

Date	Mintage	F	VF	XF	Unc	BU
1998	5,008,000	—	—	—	2.00	3.50
1999	—	—	—	—	3.00	4.50
2000	—	—	—	—	3.00	4.50

KM# 831 500 PESETAS Composition: Copper-Aluminum-Nickel **Obverse:** Conjoined busts of King Juan Carlos I and Sofia facing left

Date	Mintage	F	VF	XF	Unc	BU
1987	400,000,000	—	—	3.50	10.00	12.00
1987 Proof	Inc. above	Value: 10.00				
1988	81,309,000	—	—	3.50	9.00	11.00
1989	103,861,000	—	—	3.50	5.00	6.00
1990	28,372,000	—	—	3.50	10.00	12.00

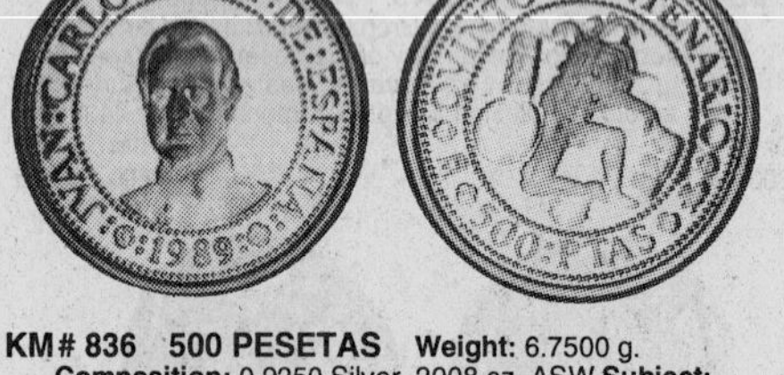

KM# 836 500 PESETAS Weight: 6.7500 g. **Composition:** 0.9250 Silver .2008 oz. ASW **Subject:** Discovery of America - Juego De Pelota Game **Obverse:** Bust of King Juan Carlos I facing

Date	Mintage	F	VF	XF	Unc	BU
1989	43,000	—	—	—	—	10.00
1989 Proof	57,000	Value: 10.00				

KM# 857 500 PESETAS Weight: 6.7500 g. **Composition:** 0.9250 Silver .2008 oz. ASW **Obverse:** Juan de la Cosa **Reverse:** Ocean navigation map within legend

Date	Mintage	F	VF	XF	Unc	BU
1990	24,000	—	—	—	—	12.00
1990 Proof	27,000	Value: 12.00				

KM# 885 500 PESETAS Weight: 6.7500 g. **Composition:** 0.9250 Silver .2008 oz. ASW **Obverse:** Jorge Juan **Reverse:** World globe map within legend

Date	Mintage	F	VF	XF	Unc	BU
1991	14,000	—	—	—	—	16.00
1991 Proof	14,000	Value: 16.00				

KM# 995 500 PESETAS Weight: 6.7500 g. **Composition:** 0.9250 Silver .2008 oz. ASW **Subject:** Seville Expo '92 **Obverse:** Church **Reverse:** Palace Portal

Date	Mintage	F	VF	XF	Unc	BU
1992	17,000	—	—	—	—	20.00
1992 Proof	16,000	Value: 20.00				

KM# 924 500 PESETAS Composition: Copper-Aluminum-Nickel **Obverse:** Conjoined busts of King Juan Carlos I and Sofia facing left

Date	Mintage	F	VF	XF	Unc	BU
1993	3,059,000	—	—	—	20.00	25.00
1994	3,041,000	—	—	—	25.00	35.00
1995	1,015,000	—	—	—	20.00	25.00
1996	1,031,000	—	—	—	12.00	16.00
1997	4,881,000	—	—	—	7.00	9.00
1998	5,161,000	—	—	—	8.00	10.00
1999	2,030,000	—	—	—	7.00	9.00
2000	—	—	—	—	7.00	9.00
2001	—	—	—	—	6.00	8.00

KM# 837 1000 PESETAS Weight: 13.5000 g. **Composition:** 0.9250 Silver .4015 oz. ASW **Subject:** Discovery of America - Capture of Granada

Date	Mintage	F	VF	XF	Unc	BU
1989	43,000	—	—	—	—	12.50
1989 Proof	57,000	Value: 12.50				

KM# 858 1000 PESETAS Weight: 13.5000 g. **Composition:** 0.9250 Silver .4015 oz. ASW **Subject:** Magallanes and Elcano **Reverse:** Primitive global world map within legend

te	Mintage	F	VF	XF	Unc	BU
90	24,000	—	—	—	—	15.00
90 Proof	27,000	Value: 15.00				

M# 886 1000 PESETAS **Weight:** 13.5000 g. **Composition:** 0.9250 Silver .4015 oz. ASW **Subject:** Simon Bolivar and San Martin **Reverse:** Portrait within legend

te	Mintage	F	VF	XF	Unc	BU
91	14,000	—	—	—	—	20.00
91 Proof	14,000	Value: 20.00				

M# 996 1000 PESETAS **Weight:** 13.5000 g. **Composition:** 0.9250 Silver .4015 oz. ASW **Subject:** Seville Expo '92 **Obverse:** Expo buildings **Reverse:** India's Archives Building

te	Mintage	F	VF	XF	Unc	BU
92	17,000	—	—	—	—	25.00
92 Proof	16,000	Value: 25.00				

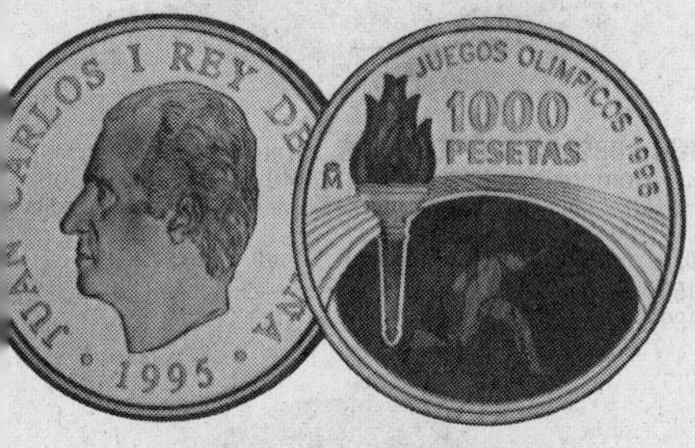

M# 952 1000 PESETAS **Weight:** 13.6600 g. **Composition:** 0.9250 Silver .4062 oz. ASW **Subject:** 1996 Olympics **Obverse:** Head of King Juan Carlos I left

te	Mintage	F	VF	XF	Unc	BU
95 Proof	67,743	Value: 25.00				

M# 973 1000 PESETAS **Weight:** 13.6600 g. **Composition:** 0.9250 Silver .4062 oz. ASW **Subject:** Olympics **Obverse:** Head of King Juan Carlos I left **Reverse:** 3 divers

te	Mintage	F	VF	XF	Unc	BU
96 Proof	30,000	Value: 25.00				

KM# 988 1000 PESETAS **Weight:** 13.5000 g. **Composition:** 0.9250 Silver .4015 oz. ASW **Subject:** Soccer World Championship - France '98 **Obverse:** Head of King Juan Carlos I left **Reverse:** 2 soccer players

Date	Mintage	F	VF	XF	Unc	BU
1998 Proof	30,000	Value: 40.00				

KM# 1000 1000 PESETAS **Weight:** 13.5000 g. **Composition:** 0.9250 Silver .4015 oz. ASW **Subject:** Expo '98 Lisbon **Obverse:** Head of King Juan Carlos I left **Reverse:** Sailing ship

Date	Mintage	F	VF	XF	Unc	BU
1998 Proof	50,000	Value: 22.50				

KM# 1034 1000 PESETAS **Weight:** 13.5000 g. **Composition:** 0.9250 Silver 0.4015 oz. ASW **Ruler:** Juan Carlos I **Subject:** Constitution **Obverse:** King's portrait **Reverse:** Building **Edge:** Reeded **Size:** 32.9 mm.

Date	Mintage	F	VF	XF	Unc	BU
1998Crowned M Proof	75,000	Value: 25.00				

KM# 1009 1000 PESETAS **Weight:** 13.5000 g. **Composition:** 0.9250 Silver .4015 oz. ASW **Subject:** Olympics - Sidney 2000 **Obverse:** Head of King Juan Carlos I left **Reverse:** Water polo players

Date	Mintage	F	VF	XF	Unc	BU
1999 Proof	50,000	Value: 22.50				

KM# 1010 1500 PESETAS **Weight:** 19.8300 g. **Composition:** 0.9250 Silver .5897 oz. ASW **Subject:** Millennium **Obverse:** Head of King Juan Carlos I left **Reverse:** Space walking astronaut above Columbus' ships **Shape:** Octagonal

Date	Mintage	F	VF	XF	Unc	BU
1999 Proof	50,000	Value: 25.00				

KM# 1035 1500 PESETAS **Ruler:** Juan Carlos I **Subject:** Printing **Obverse:** King's portrait **Reverse:** Antique printing press **Edge:** Plain, eight sided **Size:** 30.5 mm.

Date	Mintage	F	VF	XF	Unc	BU
2000Crowned M Proof	30,000	Value: 27.50				

KM# 838 2000 PESETAS **Weight:** 27.0000 g. **Composition:** 0.9250 Silver .8031 oz. ASW **Subject:** Discovery of America **Reverse:** Columbus

Date	Mintage	F	VF	XF	Unc	BU
1989	43,000	—	—	—	—	20.00
1989 Proof	57,000	Value: 20.00				

KM# 859 2000 PESETAS **Weight:** 27.0000 g. **Composition:** 0.9250 Silver .8031 oz. ASW **Subject:** 1992 Olympics **Obverse:** Similar to KM#861 **Reverse:** Symbols

Date	Mintage	F	VF	XF	Unc	BU
1990	52,524	—	—	—	—	20.00
1990 Proof	130,993	Value: 20.00				

Note: See note below KM#914

KM# 861 2000 PESETAS **Weight:** 26.7000 g. **Composition:** 0.9250 Silver .7940 oz. ASW **Subject:** 1992 Olympics **Reverse:** Archer

Date	Mintage	F	VF	XF	Unc	BU
1990	26,843	—	—	—	—	20.00
1990 Proof	87,655	Value: 20.00				

Note: Unccirculated strikes have medallic die alignment and edges with reeded and plain sections; Proof strikes have coin die alignment and reeded edges

KM# 862 2000 PESETAS **Weight:** 26.7000 g. **Composition:** 0.9250 Silver .7940 oz. ASW **Subject:** 1992 Olympics **Reverse:** Soccer player

Date	Mintage	F	VF	XF	Unc	BU
1990	—	—	—	—	—	20.00
1990 Proof	Est. 104,351	Value: 20.00				

Note: Uncirculated strikes have medallic die alignment and edges with reeded and plain sections; Proof strikes have coin die alignment and reeded edges

KM# 863 2000 PESETAS **Weight:** 26.7000 g. **Composition:** 0.9250 Silver .7940 oz. ASW **Subject:** 1992 Olympics **Reverse:** Human pyramid

Date	Mintage	F	VF	XF	Unc	BU
1990		—	—	—	—	22.50
1990 Proof	Est. 73,510	Value: 22.50				

Note: Uncirculated strikes have medallic die alignment and edges with reeded and plain sections; Proof strikes have coin die alignment and reeded edges

KM# 864 2000 PESETAS **Weight:** 26.7000 g. **Composition:** 0.9250 Silver .7940 oz. ASW **Subject:** 1992 Olympics **Obverse:** Similar to KM#859 **Reverse:** Greek runner

Date	Mintage	F	VF	XF	Unc	BU
1990		—	—	—	—	25.00
1990 Proof	Est. 73,469	Value: 25.00				

Note: Uncirculated strikes have medallic die alignment and edges with reeded and plain sections; Proof strikes have coin die alignment and reeded edges

KM# 865 2000 PESETAS **Weight:** 26.7000 g. **Composition:** 0.9250 Silver .7940 oz. ASW **Subject:** 1992 Olympics **Obverse:** Similar to KM#859 **Reverse:** Ancient boat

Date	Mintage	F	VF	XF	Unc	BU
1990		—	—	—	—	25.00
1990 Proof	Est. 53,835	Value: 25.00				

Note: Uncirculated strikes have medallic die alignment and edges with reeded and plain sections; Proof strikes have coin die alignment and reeded edges

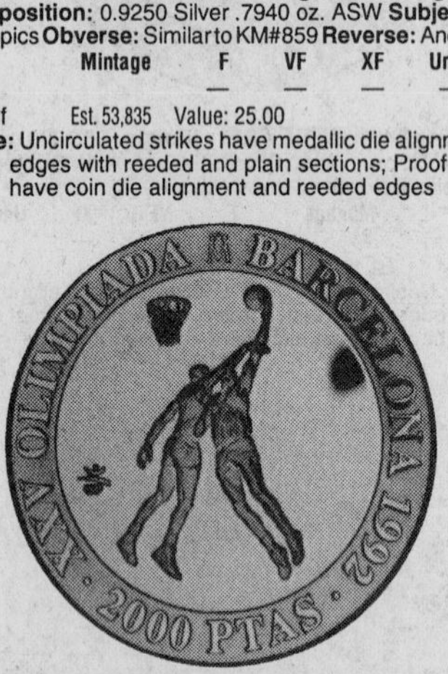

KM# 866 2000 PESETAS **Weight:** 26.7000 g. **Composition:** 0.9250 Silver .7940 oz. ASW **Subject:** 1992 Olympics **Obverse:** Similar to KM#859 **Reverse:** Basketball players

Date	Mintage	F	VF	XF	Unc	BU
1990		—	—	—	—	25.00
1990 Proof	Est. 56,356	Value: 25.00				

Note: Uncirculated strikes have medallic die alignment and edges with reeded and plain sections; Proof strikes have coin die alignment and reeded edges

KM# 867 2000 PESETAS **Weight:** 26.7000 g. **Composition:** 0.9250 Silver .7940 oz. ASW **Subject:** 1992 Olympics **Obverse:** Conjoined busts of King Juan Carlos I and Sofia facing left **Reverse:** Pelota player

Date	Mintage	F	VF	XF	Unc	BU
1990		—	—	—	—	25.00
1990 Proof	Est. 45,219	Value: 25.00				

Note: Uncirculated strikes have medallic die alignment and edges with reeded and plain sections; Proof strikes have coin die alignment and reeded edges

KM# 868 2000 PESETAS **Weight:** 26.7000 g. **Composition:** 0.9250 Silver .7940 oz. ASW **Subject:** Hidalgo, Morelos and Juarez **Reverse:** Aztec pictorial design within legend

Date	Mintage	F	VF	XF	Unc	BU
1990	24,000	—	—	—	—	27.50
1990 Proof	27,000	Value: 27.50				

KM# 860 2000 PESETAS **Weight:** 26.7000 g. **Composition:** 0.9250 Silver .7940 oz. ASW **Counterstamp:** INUTILIZACION/OCTOBRE 1992 **Note:** Counterstamp on reverse below Olympic rings

Date	F	VF	XF	Unc	BU
1990 1992; Proof	—	Value: 35.00			

Note: Uncirculated strikes have medallic die alignment and edges with reeded and plain sections; Proof strikes have coin die alignment and reeded edges

KM# 887 2000 PESETAS **Weight:** 26.7000 g. **Composition:** 0.9250 Silver .7940 oz. ASW **Subject:** Olympics **Reverse:** Torch and flag

Date	Mintage	F	VF	XF	Unc	BU
1991	18,545	—	—	—	—	40.00
1991 Proof	78,192	Value: 40.00				

KM# 888 2000 PESETAS **Weight:** 26.7000 g. **Composition:** 0.9250 Silver .7940 oz. ASW **Subject:** Olympics **Obverse:** Similar to KM#887 **Reverse:** Tennis player

Date	Mintage	F	VF	XF	Unc	BU
1991	12,350	—	—	—	—	40.00
1991 Proof	38,905	Value: 40.00				

Note: Medal rotation

KM# 889 2000 PESETAS **Weight:** 26.7000 g. **Composition:** 0.9250 Silver .7940 oz. ASW **Subject:** Olympics **Obverse:** Similar to KM#887 **Reverse:** Medieval rider

Date	Mintage	F	VF	XF	Unc	BU
1991	15,056	—	—	—	—	40.00
1991 Proof	31,317	Value: 40.00				

Note: Medal rotation

KM# 890 2000 PESETAS **Weight:** 26.7000 g. **Composition:** 0.9250 Silver .7940 oz. ASW **Subject:** Olympics **Obverse:** Similar to KM#887 **Reverse:** Bowling

Date	Mintage	F	VF	XF	Unc	BU
1991	10,561	—	—	—	—	40.00
1991 Proof	35,447	Value: 40.00				

Note: Medal rotation

KM# 891 2000 PESETAS **Weight:** 26.7000 g. **Composition:** 0.9250 Silver .7940 oz. ASW **Subject:** Ibero - American Series

Date	Mintage	F	VF	XF	Unc	BU
(19)91 Proof	20,000	Value: 90.00				

KM# 892 2000 PESETAS **Weight:** 26.7000 g. **Composition:** 0.9250 Silver .7940 oz. ASW **Subject:** Federman, Quesada and Benalcazar

Date	Mintage	F	VF	XF	Unc	BU
1991	14,000	—	—	—	—	25.00
1991 Proof	14,000	Value: 25.00				

KM# 911 2000 PESETAS **Weight:** 26.7000 g. **Composition:** 0.9250 Silver .7940 oz. ASW **Subject:** Olympics **Obverse:** Conjoined busts of King Juan Carlos I and Sofia facing left **Reverse:** Tug-of-war

Date	Mintage	F	VF	XF	Unc	BU
1992	9,043	—	—	—	—	50.00
1992 Proof	33,980	Value: 50.00				

Note: Uncirculated strikes have medallic die alignment and edges with reeded and plain sections; Proof strikes have coin die alignment and reeded edges

KM# 912 2000 PESETAS **Weight:** 26.7000 g. **Composition:** 0.9250 Silver .7940 oz. ASW **Subject:** Olympics **Reverse:** Wheelchair basketball

Date	Mintage	F	VF	XF	Unc	BU
1992	8,997	—	—	—	—	50.00
1992 Proof	27,886	Value: 50.00				

Note: Uncirculated strikes have medallic die alignment and edges with reeded and plain sections; Proof strikes have coin die alignment and reeded edges

KM# 913 2000 PESETAS **Weight:** 26.7000 g. **Composition:** 0.9250 Silver .7940 oz. ASW **Subject:** Olympics **Reverse:** Sprinters

Date	Mintage	F	VF	XF	Unc	BU
1992	16,000	—	—	—	—	40.00
1992 Proof	42,000	Value: 40.00				

Note: Uncirculated strikes have medallic die alignment and edges with reeded and plain sections; Proof strikes have coin die alignment and reeded edges

KM# 914 2000 PESETAS **Weight:** 26.7000 g. **Composition:** 0.9250 Silver .7940 oz. ASW **Subject:** Olympics **Reverse:** Chariot racing

Date	Mintage	F	VF	XF	Unc	BU
1992	13,000	—	—	—	—	50.00
1992 Proof	37,000	Value: 50.00				

Note: Uncirculated strikes have medallic die alignment and edges with reeded and plain sections; Proof strikes have coin die alignment and reeded edges

KM# 980 2000 PESETAS **Weight:** 26.7000 g. **Composition:** 0.9250 Silver .7940 oz. ASW **Subject:** Seville Expo '92 **Obverse:** Exposition Building, date **Reverse:** Tower of Seville

Date	Mintage	F	VF	XF	Unc	BU
1992	17,000	—	—	—	—	35.00
1992 Proof	16,000	Value: 35.00				

KM# 925 2000 PESETAS **Weight:** 26.7000 g. **Composition:** 0.9250 Silver .7940 oz. ASW **Subject:** Holy Jacobean Year **Obverse:** Head of King Juan Carlos I left **Reverse:** German Jacobean Pilgrims

Date	Mintage	F	VF	XF	Unc	BU
1993 Proof	10,000	Value: 75.00				

KM# 926 2000 PESETAS **Weight:** 26.7000 g. **Composition:** 0.9250 Silver .7940 oz. ASW **Subject:** Holy Jacobean Year **Reverse:** Santiago cross and scallop shell

Date	Mintage	F	VF	XF	Unc	BU
1993 Proof	17,000	Value: 75.00				

KM# 937 2000 PESETAS **Weight:** 18.0000 g. **Composition:** 0.9250 Silver .5353 oz. ASW **Subject:** International Monetary Fund and Bank **Obverse:** Head of King Juan Carlos I left

Date	Mintage	F	VF	XF	Unc	BU
1994	8,669,000	—	—	—	15.00	20.00

KM# 938 2000 PESETAS **Weight:** 27.0000 g. **Composition:** 0.9250 Silver .8031 oz. ASW **Subject:** Courtyard of the Lions

Date	Mintage	F	VF	XF	Unc	BU
1994 Proof	7,312	Value: 40.00				

KM# 939 2000 PESETAS **Weight:** 27.0000 g. **Composition:** 0.9250 Silver .8031 oz. ASW **Subject:** Environmental Protection **Reverse:** Spanish lynx

Date	Mintage	F	VF	XF	Unc	BU
1994 Proof	20,000	Value: 100				

KM# 940 2000 PESETAS **Weight:** 27.0000 g. **Composition:** 0.9250 Silver .8031 oz. ASW **Reverse:** Purple herons in swamp

Date	Mintage	F	VF	XF	Unc	BU
1994 Proof	6,555	Value: 45.00				

KM# 941 2000 PESETAS **Weight:** 27.0000 g. **Composition:** 0.9250 Silver .8031 oz. ASW **Subject:** 2 bulls

Date	Mintage	F	VF	XF	Unc	BU
1994 Proof	10,388	Value: 45.00				

KM# 953 2000 PESETAS **Weight:** 27.0000 g. **Composition:** 0.9250 Silver .8031 oz. ASW **Reverse:** Capercaillie bird

Date	Mintage	F	VF	XF	Unc	BU
1995 Proof	13,859	Value: 45.00				

KM# 954 2000 PESETAS **Weight:** 27.0000 g. **Composition:** 0.9250 Silver .8031 oz. ASW **Subject:** Presidential Council - V.E

Date	F	VF	XF	Unc	BU
1995	—	—	—	15.00	20.00

KM# 955 2000 PESETAS **Weight:** 27.0000 g. **Composition:** 0.9250 Silver .8031 oz. ASW **Subject:** 50th Anniversary - United Nations

Date	Mintage	F	VF	XF	Unc	BU
1995 Proof	26,049	Value: 100				

KM# 966 2000 PESETAS **Weight:** 27.0000 g. **Composition:** 0.9250 Silver .8031 oz. ASW **Reverse:** Wolves

Date	Mintage	F	VF	XF	Unc	BU
1996 Proof	35,000	Value: 70.00				

KM# 967 2000 PESETAS **Weight:** 27.0000 g. **Composition:** 0.9250 Silver .8031 oz. ASW **Reverse:** Bears

Date	Mintage	F	VF	XF	Unc	BU
1996 Proof	35,000	Value: 40.00				

KM# 968 2000 PESETAS **Weight:** 18.0000 g. **Composition:** 0.9250 Silver .5353 oz. ASW **Reverse:** Francisco de Goya

Date	F	VF	XF	Unc	BU
1996	—	—	—	15.00	20.00

KM# 974 2000 PESETAS **Weight:** 27.0000 g. **Composition:** 0.9250 Silver .8031 oz. ASW **Series:** Patrimonio de la Humanidad **Obverse:** UNESCO logo **Reverse:** Taj Mahal, India

Date	Mintage	F	VF	XF	Unc	BU
1996 Proof	30,000	Value: 35.00				

KM# 975 2000 PESETAS **Weight:** 27.0000 g. **Composition:** 0.9250 Silver .8031 oz. ASW **Series:** Patrimonio de la Humanidad **Obverse:** Similar to KM#293 **Reverse:** Djenne, Mali

Date	Mintage	F	VF	XF	Unc	BU
1996 Proof	30,000	Value: 35.00				

KM# 976 2000 PESETAS **Weight:** 27.0000 g. **Composition:** 0.9250 Silver .8031 oz. ASW **Series:** Patrimonio de la Humanidad **Obverse:** Similar to KM#293 **Reverse:** Abu Simbel, Egypt

Date	Mintage	F	VF	XF	Unc	BU
1996 Proof	30,000	Value: 35.00				

KM# 977 2000 PESETAS **Weight:** 27.0000 g. **Composition:** 0.9250 Silver .8031 oz. ASW **Series:** Patrimonio de la Humanidad **Obverse:** Similar to KM#293 **Reverse:** Palenque, Mexico

Date	Mintage	F	VF	XF	Unc	BU
1996 Proof	30,000	Value: 35.00				

KM# 978 2000 PESETAS **Weight:** 27.0000 g. **Composition:** 0.9250 Silver .8031 oz. ASW **Series:** Patrimonio de la Humanidad **Obverse:** Similar to KM#293 **Reverse:** Merida, Spain

Date	Mintage	F	VF	XF	Unc	B
1996 Proof	30,000	Value: 35.00				

M# 999 **2000 PESETAS** **Weight:** 18.0000 g. **Composition:** 0.9250 Silver .5353 oz. ASW **Subject:** Don Quixote **Obverse:** King Juan Carlos **Reverse:** Quixote and Sancho plus cameo of Cervantes

te	F	VF	XF	Unc	BU
97	—	—	—	15.00	20.00

M# 1018 **2000 PESETAS** **Weight:** 27.0000 g. **Composition:** 0.9250 Silver .8031 oz. ASW **Ruler:** Juan Carlos I **Series:** "Patrimono de la Humanidad" UNESCO **Obverse:** UNESCO logo **Reverse:** Abomey lion **Edge:** Reeded **Size:** 40 mm.

te	Mintage	F	VF	XF	Unc	BU
97 Proof	30,000	Value: 30.00				

M# 1019 **2000 PESETAS** **Weight:** 27.0000 g. **Composition:** 0.9250 Silver .8031 oz. ASW **Ruler:** Juan Carlos I **Series:** "Patrimono de la Humanidad" UNESCO **Obverse:** UNESCO logo **Reverse:** Easter Island statues

te	Mintage	F	VF	XF	Unc	BU
97 Proof	30,000	Value: 30.00				

M# 1020 **2000 PESETAS** **Weight:** 27.0000 g. **Composition:** 0.9250 Silver .8031 oz. ASW **Ruler:** Juan Carlos I **Series:** "Patrimono de la Humanidad" UNESCO **Obverse:** UNESCO logo **Reverse:** Temple at Petra

te	Mintage	F	VF	XF	Unc	BU
97 Proof	30,000	Value: 30.00				

KM# 1021 **2000 PESETAS** **Weight:** 27.0000 g. **Composition:** 0.9250 Silver .8031 oz. ASW **Ruler:** Juan Carlos I **Series:** "Patrimono de la Humanidad" UNESCO **Obverse:** UNESCO logo **Reverse:** Acropolis

Date	Mintage	F	VF	XF	Unc	BU
1997 Proof	30,000	Value: 30.00				

KM# 1022 **2000 PESETAS** **Weight:** 27.0000 g. **Composition:** 0.9250 Silver .8031 oz. ASW **Ruler:** Juan Carlos I **Series:** "Patrimono de la Humanidad" UNESCO **Obverse:** UNESCO logo **Reverse:** Horyu-Ji pagoda

Date	Mintage	F	VF	XF	Unc	BU
1997 Proof	30,000	Value: 30.00				

KM# 1024 **2000 PESETAS** **Weight:** 27.0000 g. **Composition:** 0.9250 Silver .0831 oz. ASW **Ruler:** Juan Carlos I **Subject:** House of Borbon - Philip V **Obverse:** Portrait of Philip V **Reverse:** Figural sculpture **Edge:** Reeded **Size:** 40 mm.

Date	F	VF	XF	Unc	BU
1997 Proof	—	Value: 30.00			

KM# 1025 **2000 PESETAS** **Weight:** 27.0000 g. **Composition:** 0.9250 Silver .8031 oz. ASW **Ruler:** Juan Carlos I **Subject:** House of Borbon - Louis I **Obverse:** Portrait of Louis I **Reverse:** Crowned arms in order chain

Date	F	VF	XF	Unc	BU
1997 Proof	—	Value: 30.00			

KM# 1026 **2000 PESETAS** **Weight:** 27.0000 g. **Composition:** 0.9250 Silver .8031 oz. ASW **Ruler:** Juan Carlos I **Subject:** House of Borbon - Ferdinand VI **Obverse:** Portrait of Ferdinand VI **Reverse:** Spanish galleon

Date	F	VF	XF	Unc	BU
1997 Proof	—	Value: 30.00			

KM# 1036 **2000 PESETAS** **Weight:** 27.3000 g. **Composition:** 0.9250 Silver 0.8119 oz. ASW **Ruler:** Juan Carlos I **Subject:** House of Borbon **Obverse:** Ferdinand VII portrait **Reverse:** Prado Museum **Edge:** Reeded **Size:** 39.9 mm.

Date	Mintage	F	VF	XF	Unc	BU
1998Crowned M Proof	30,000	Value: 30.00				

KM# 987 **2000 PESETAS** **Weight:** 18.0000 g. **Composition:** 0.9250 Silver **Subject:** Philip II **Obverse:** King Juan Carlos

Date	F	VF	XF	Unc	BU
1998	—	—	—	15.00	20.00

KM# 1011 **2000 PESETAS** **Weight:** 18.0000 g. **Composition:** 0.9250 Silver **Subject:** St. Jacob **Obverse:** King Juan Carlos **Reverse:** St. Jacob, denomination and dagger

Date	F	VF	XF	Unc	BU
1999	—	—	—	15.00	20.00

KM# 1029 **2000 PESETAS** **Weight:** 27.0000 g. **Composition:** 0.9250 Silver .8031 oz. ASW **Ruler:** Juan Carlos I **Subject:** Barcelona City Government 750 Years **Obverse:** Portrait of the King **Reverse:** Stylized city arms

Date	Mintage	F	VF	XF	Unc	BU
1999 Proof	30,000	Value: 30.00				

KM# 1030 2000 PESETAS **Weight:** 27.0000 g. **Composition:** 0.9250 Silver .8031 oz. ASW **Ruler:** Juan Carlos I **Subject:** House of Borbon - Isabel II **Obverse:** Portrait of Isabel II

Date		F	VF	XF	Unc	BU
1999 Proof	—	Value: 30.00				

KM# 1031 2000 PESETAS **Weight:** 27.0000 g. **Composition:** 0.9250 Silver .8031 oz. ASW **Ruler:** Juan Carlos I **Subject:** House of Borbon - Alfonso XII **Obverse:** Portrait of Alfonso XII

Date		F	VF	XF	Unc	BU
1999 Proof	—	Value: 30.00				

KM# 1032 2000 PESETAS **Weight:** 27.0000 g. **Composition:** 0.9250 Silver .8031 oz. ASW **Ruler:** Juan Carlos I **Subject:** House of Borbon - Alfonso XIII **Obverse:** Childhood portrait of Alfonso XIII

Date		F	VF	XF	Unc	BU
1999 Proof	—	Value: 30.00				

KM# 1033 2000 PESETAS **Weight:** 27.0000 g. **Composition:** 0.9250 Silver .8031 oz. ASW **Ruler:** Juan Carlos I **Subject:** House of Borbon - Alfonso XIII **Obverse:** Adult portrait of Alfonso XIII

Date		F	VF	XF	Unc	BU
1999 Proof	—	Value: 30.00				

KM# 1015 2000 PESETAS **Weight:** 18.0000 g. **Composition:** 0.9250 Silver .5353 oz. ASW **Subject:** Charles V **Obverse:** King's portrait **Reverse:** Portrait of Charles V **Edge:** Plain **Size:** 33 mm.

Date	F	VF	XF	Unc	BU
2000	—	—	—	25.00	30.00

KM# 1017 2000 PESETAS **Weight:** 18.0000 g. **Composition:** 0.9250 Silver .5353 oz. ASW **Subject:** 132nd Anniversary of the Peseta **Obverse:** Portraits of King and Queen **Reverse:** Seated allegorical design from the 1869 Spanish coin series **Edge:** Plain **Size:** 32.9 mm.

Date	F	VF	XF	Unc	BU
2001	—	—	—	15.00	20.00

KM# 839 5000 PESETAS **Weight:** 54.0000 g. **Composition:** 0.9250 Silver 1.6059 oz. ASW **Subject:** Discovery of America **Reverse:** Santa Maria

Date	Mintage	F	VF	XF	Unc	BU
1989	24,000	—	—	—	—	45.00
1989 Proof	33,000	Value: 45.00				

KM# 840 5000 PESETAS **Weight:** 1.6800 g. **Composition:** 0.9990 Gold .0540 oz. AGW **Subject:** Discovery of America **Reverse:** Compass face

Date	Mintage	F	VF	XF	Unc	BU
1989	6,000	—	—	—	—	60.00
1989 Proof	8,000	Value: 60.00				

KM# 869 5000 PESETAS **Weight:** 54.0000 g. **Composition:** 0.9250 Silver 1.6059 oz. ASW **Obverse:** Cortes, Montezuma, and Marina **Reverse:** Scene from Azte mythology within legend

Date	Mintage	F	VF	XF	Unc	B
1990	11,000	—	—	—	—	60.0
1990 Proof	13,000	Value: 60.00				

KM# 870 5000 PESETAS **Composition:** 0.9990 Gold .0540 oz. AGW **Obverse:** Phili V **Reverse:** Similar to KM#840

Date	Mintage	F	VF	XF	Unc	B
1990	3,000	—	—	—	—	65.0
1990 Proof	4,000	Value: 65.00				

KM# 893 5000 PESETAS **Weight:** 54.0000 g. **Composition:** 0.9250 Silver 1.6059 oz. ASW **Obverse:** Pizarro and Atahualpa **Reverse:** Incan ruins in mountains within legend

Date	Mintage	F	VF	XF	Unc	B
1991	8,000	—	—	—	—	85.0
1991 Proof	8,145	Value: 85.00				

KM# 894 5000 PESETAS **Weight:** 1.6800 g. **Composition:** 0.9990 Gold .0540 oz. AGW **Obverse:** Ferdinando VI **Reverse:** Similar to KM#840

Date	Mintage	F	VF	XF	Unc	B
1991	1,000	—	—	—	—	90.0
1991 Proof	2,000	Value: 90.00				

M# 997 5000 PESETAS **Weight:** 54.0000 g. **Composition:** 0.9250 Silver 1.6059 oz. ASW **Subject:** Seville Expo '92 **Obverse:** Mint building **Reverse:** Old coin press

ate	Mintage	F	VF	XF	Unc	BU
992	8,000	—	—	—	—	100
992 Proof	7,000	Value: 100				

M# 1001 5000 PESETAS **Weight:** 54.0000 g. **Composition:** 0.9250 Silver 1.6059 oz. ASW **Obverse:** Similar to KM#840 **Reverse:** Screw press

ate	Mintage	F	VF	XF	Unc	BU
992	1,000	—	—	—	—	110
992 Proof	—	Value: 110				

M# 942 5000 PESETAS **Weight:** 54.0000 g. **Composition:** 0.9250 Silver 1.6059 oz. ASW **Reverse:** Imperial Eagle

ate	Mintage	F	VF	XF	Unc	BU
994 Proof	30,000	Value: 70.00				

M# 956 5000 PESETAS **Weight:** 54.0000 g. **Composition:** 0.9250 Silver 1.6059 oz. ASW **Reverse:** Spanish Ibex

ate	Mintage	F	VF	XF	Unc	BU
995 Proof	25,000	Value: 70.00				

M# 969 5000 PESETAS **Weight:** 54.0000 g. **Composition:** 0.9250 Silver 1.6059 oz. ASW **Reverse:** Gaudi sculpture

ate	Mintage	F	VF	XF	Unc	BU
996 Proof	Est. 20,000	Value: 65.00				

M# 842 10000 PESETAS **Weight:** 3.3700 g. **Composition:** 0.9990 Gold .1084 oz. AGW **Subject:** Discovery of America **Reverse:** Armillary sphere

ate	Mintage	F	VF	XF	Unc	BU
989	5,000	—	—	—	—	90.00
989 Proof	7,000	Value: 90.00				

KM# 841 10000 PESETAS **Weight:** 168.7500 g. **Composition:** 0.9250 Silver 5.0191 oz. ASW **Subject:** Regional Autonomy **Reverse:** Crowned Provincial arms **Note:** Illustration reduced, actual size 73mm

Date	Mintage	F	VF	XF	Unc	BU
1989	47,000	—	—	—	—	120
1989 Proof	—	Value: 120				

KM# 873 10000 PESETAS **Weight:** 168.7500 g. **Composition:** 0.9250 Silver 5.0191 oz. ASW **Subject:** Spanish Royal Family **Reverse:** Similar to KM#896 **Note:** Illustration reduced, actual size 73mm

Date	Mintage	F	VF	XF	Unc	BU
1990	26,000	—	—	—	—	140
1990 Proof	—	Value: 140				

KM# 871 10000 PESETAS **Weight:** 3.3700 g. **Composition:** 0.9990 Gold .1084 oz. AGW **Series:** 1992 Olympics **Reverse:** Stylized field hockey player

Date	Mintage	F	VF	XF	Unc	BU
1990	3,000	—	—	—	—	90.00
1990 Proof	5,000	Value: 90.00				

Note: Uncirculated strikes have medallic die alignment and edges with reeded and plain sections; Proof strikes have coin die alignment and reeded edges

KM# 872 10000 PESETAS **Weight:** 3.3700 g. **Composition:** 0.9990 Gold .1084 oz. AGW **Series:** 1992 Olympics **Reverse:** Stylized gymnast

Date	Mintage	F	VF	XF	Unc	BU
1990	2,000	—	—	—	—	95.00
1990 Proof	3,000	Value: 95.00				

Note: Uncirculated strikes have medallic die alignment and edges with reeded and plain sections; Proof strikes have coin die alignment and reeded edges

KM# 874 10000 PESETAS **Weight:** 3.3700 g. **Composition:** 0.9990 Gold .1084 oz. AGW **Obverse:** Quauchtemoc **Reverse:** Similar to 5,000 Pesetas, KM#840

Date	Mintage	F	VF	XF	Unc	BU
1990	9,000	—	—	—	—	95.00
1990 Proof	2,000	Value: 95.00				

KM# 895 10000 PESETAS **Weight:** 3.3700 g. **Composition:** 0.9990 Gold .1084 oz. AGW **Series:** Olympics **Reverse:** Karate participant

Date	Mintage	F	VF	XF	Unc	BU
1991	2,000	—	—	—	—	180
1991 Proof	3,000	Value: 180				

Note: See note below KM#915

KM# 897 10000 PESETAS **Weight:** 3.3700 g. **Composition:** 0.9990 Gold .1084 oz. AGW **Obverse:** Tupac Amaru II **Reverse:** Similar to KM#842

Date	Mintage	F	VF	XF	Unc	BU
1991	1,000	—	—	—	—	150
1991 Proof	2,000	Value: 150				

KM# 896 10000 PESETAS **Weight:** 168.7500 g. **Composition:** 0.9250 Silver 5.0191 oz. ASW **Subject:** Discoverers and Liberators **Reverse:** Similar to KM#873 **Size:** 73 mm. **Note:** Illustration reduced.

Date	Mintage	F	VF	XF	Unc	BU
1991	17,000	—	—	—	—	175
1991 Proof	—	Value: 175				

KM# 1002 10000 PESETAS **Weight:** 3.3700 g. **Composition:** 0.9990 Gold .1084 oz. AGW **Ruler:** Juan Carlos I **Obverse:** Similar to KM#842 **Reverse:** Worker operating screw press

Date	Mintage	F	VF	XF	Unc	BU
1992	1,000	—	—	—	—	180
1992 Proof	—	Value: 180				

KM# 915 10000 PESETAS **Weight:** 3.3700 g. **Composition:** 0.9990 Gold .1084 oz. AGW **Series:** Olympics **Reverse:** Baseball player

Date	Mintage	F	VF	XF	Unc	BU
1992	1,000	—	—	—	—	180
1992 Proof	6,000	Value: 180				

Note: Uncirculated strikes have medallic die alignment and edges with reeded and plain sections; Proof strikes have coin die alignment and reeded edges

KM# 998 10000 PESETAS **Weight:** 168.7500 g. **Composition:** 0.9250 Silver 5.0191 oz. ASW **Series:** Seville Expo '92 - Nobel Prize winners **Reverse:** Royal Family portraits

Date	Mintage	F	VF	XF	Unc	BU
1992 Proof	14,000	Value: 235				

KM# 928 10000 PESETAS **Weight:** 168.7500 g. **Composition:** 0.9250 Silver 5.0191 oz. ASW **Subject:** Holy Jacobean Year **Reverse:** Cathedral and Pilgrims of the Middle Ages **Size:** 75 mm. **Note:** Illustration reduced.

Date	Mintage	F	VF	XF	Unc	BU
1993 Proof	7,000	Value: 265				

KM# 943 10000 PESETAS **Weight:** 167.7500 g. **Composition:** 0.9250 Silver 4.9888 oz. ASW **Subject:** Goya's paintings **Reverse:** Bull fighting scene **Size:** 73 mm. **Note:** Illustration reduced.

Date	Mintage	F	VF	XF	Unc	BU
1994 Proof	15,000	Value: 200				

KM# 957 10000 PESETAS **Weight:** 168.7500 g. **Composition:** 0.9250 Silver 5.0018 oz. ASW **Subject:** Velaguez's paintings **Size:** 73 mm. **Note:** Illustration reduced.

Date	Mintage	F	VF	XF	Unc	BU
1995 Proof	5,368	Value: 180				

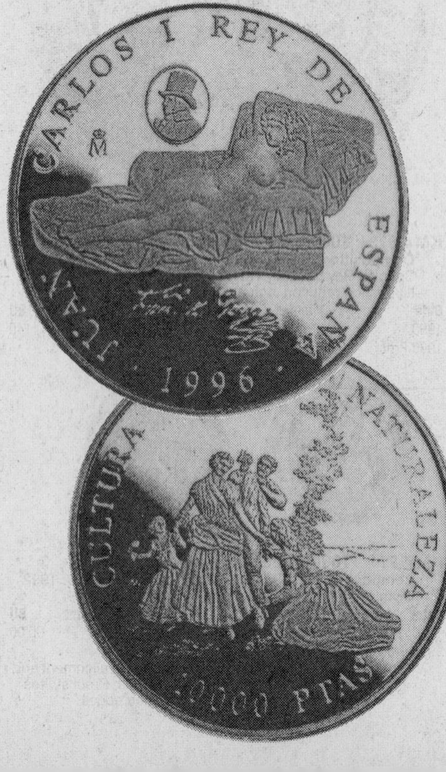

KM# 970 10000 PESETAS **Weight:** 168.7500 g. **Composition:** 0.9250 Silver 5.0018 oz. ASW **Subject:** Velaguez's paintings **Reverse:** Family picking flowers

Date	Mintage	F	VF	XF	Unc	BU
1996 Proof	15,000	Value: 150				

KM# 1027 10000 PESETAS **Weight:** 168.7500 g. **Composition:** 0.9250 Silver 5.0185 oz. ASW **Ruler:** Juan Carlos I **Subject:** House of Borbon - Juan Carlos I **Obverse:** King standing and Queen seated **Reverse:** Spanish arms in circle of portraits **Edge:** Reeded **Size:** 73 mm. **Note:** Illustration reduced.

Date	Mintage	F	VF	XF	Unc	BU
1997 Proof	10,000	Value: 150				

KM# 843 20000 PESETAS **Weight:** 6.7500 g. **Composition:** 0.9990 Gold .2170 oz. AGW **Subject:** Discovery of America **Reverse:** Pinzon Brother

Date	Mintage	F	VF	XF	Unc	BU
1989	5,000	—	—	—	—	150
1989 Proof	6,500	Value: 150				

KM# 875 20000 PESETAS **Weight:** 6.7500 g. **Composition:** 0.9990 Gold .2170 oz. AGW **Subject:** 1992 Olympics - La Sagrada Familia **Reverse:** Cathedral towers

Date	Mintage	F	VF	XF	Unc	BU
1990	4,000	—	—	—	—	180
1990 Proof	10,000	Value: 180				

Note: Uncirculated strikes have medallic die alignment and edges with reeded and plain sections; Proof strikes have coin die alignment and reeded edges

KM# 876 20000 PESETAS **Weight:** 6.7500 g. **Composition:** 0.9990 Gold .2170 oz. AGW **Series:** 1992 Olympics **Reverse:** Ruins of Empuries

Date	Mintage	F	VF	XF	Unc	BU
1990	2,000	—	—	—	—	180
1990 Proof	4,000	Value: 180				

Note: Uncirculated strikes have medallic die alignment and edges with reeded and plain sections; Proof strikes have coin die alignment and reeded edges

KM# 877 20000 PESETAS **Weight:** 6.7500 g. **Composition:** 0.9990 Gold .2170 oz. AGW **Subject:** Tupac Amaru I **Obverse:** Similar to KM#843

Date	Mintage	F	VF	XF	Unc	BU
1990	2,000	—	—	—	—	180
1990 Proof	3,000	Value: 180				

KM# 898 20000 PESETAS **Weight:** 6.7500 g. **Composition:** 0.9990 Gold .2170 oz. AGW **Series:** Olympics **Reverse:** Montjuic Stadium

Date	Mintage	F	VF	XF	Unc	BU
1991	2,000	—	—	—	—	270
1991 Proof	3,000	Value: 270				

Note: Uncirculated strikes have medallic die alignment and edges with reeded and plain sections; Proof strikes have coin die alignment and reeded edges

KM# 899 20000 PESETAS **Weight:** 6.7500 g. **Composition:** 0.9990 Gold .2170 oz. AGW **Obverse:** Portrait of Juan Carlos **Reverse:** Huascar

Date	Mintage	F	VF	XF	Unc	BU
1991	1,000	—	—	—	—	240
1991 Proof	2,000	Value: 240				

KM# 916 20000 PESETAS **Weight:** 6.7500 g. **Composition:** 0.9990 Gold .2170 oz. AGW **Series:** Olympics **Reverse:** Dome building

Date	Mintage	F	VF	XF	Unc	BU
1992	1,000	—	—	—	—	270
1992 Proof	3,000	Value: 270				

Note: Uncirculated strikes have medallic die alignment and edges with reeded and plain sections; Proof strikes have coin die alignment and reeded edges

KM# 1003 20000 PESETAS **Weight:** 6.7500 g. **Composition:** 0.9990 Gold .2170 oz. AGW **Obverse:** Similar to KM#843 **Reverse:** Worker feeding screw press

Date	Mintage	F	VF	XF	Unc	BU
1992	1,000	—	—	—	—	270
1992 Proof	—	Value: 270				

KM# 929 20000 PESETAS **Weight:** 6.7500 g. **Composition:** 0.9990 Gold .2170 oz. AGW **Subject:** Holy Jacobean Year - Conveyance of Santiago's body

Date	Mintage	F	VF	XF	Unc	BU
1993 Proof	2,000	Value: 240				

KM# 944 20000 PESETAS **Weight:** 6.7500 g. **Composition:** 0.9990 Gold .2170 oz. AGW **Subject:** Paleolithic Cave Painting

Date	Mintage	F	VF	XF	Unc	BU
1994 Proof	8,000	Value: 260				

KM# 958 20000 PESETAS **Weight:** 6.7500 g. **Composition:** 0.9990 Gold .2170 oz. AGW **Subject:** Ancient Sculpture - Dama de Elche

Date	Mintage	F	VF	XF	Unc	BU
1995 Proof	8,000	Value: 220				

KM# 971 20000 PESETAS **Weight:** 6.7500 g. **Composition:** 0.9990 Gold .2170 oz. AGW **Reverse:** Pillars and arches

Date	Mintage	F	VF	XF	Unc	BU
1996 Proof	Est. 6,000	Value: 220				

KM# 844 40000 PESETAS **Weight:** 13.5000 g. **Composition:** 0.9990 Gold .4341 oz. AGW **Subject:** Discovery of America **Reverse:** Sea monster attacking ship

Date	Mintage	F	VF	XF	Unc	BU
1989	4,500	—	—	—	—	320
1989 Proof	6,000	Value: 320				

KM# 878 40000 PESETAS **Weight:** 13.5000 g. **Composition:** 0.9990 Gold .4341 oz. AGW **Subject:** Felipe II **Obverse:** Similar to KM#844

Date	Mintage	F	VF	XF	Unc	BU
1990	2,000	—	—	—	—	350
1990 Proof	3,000	Value: 350				

KM# 900 40000 PESETAS **Weight:** 13.5000 g. **Composition:** 0.9990 Gold .4341 oz. AGW **Obverse:** Similar to KM#844 **Reverse:** Imperial double eagle

Date	Mintage	F	VF	XF	Unc	BU
1991	1,000	—	—	—	—	450
1991 Proof	2,000	Value: 450				

KM# 1004 40000 PESETAS **Weight:** 13.5000 g. **Composition:** 0.9990 Gold .4341 oz. AGW **Obverse:** Similar to KM#844 **Reverse:** Horse-powered coin press

Date	Mintage	F	VF	XF	Unc	BU
1992	1,000	—	—	—	—	500
1992 Proof	—	Value: 500				

KM# 979 40000 PESETAS **Weight:** 13.5000 g. **Composition:** 0.9990 Gold .4341 oz. AGW **Subject:** Patrimonio de la Humanidad **Obverse:** UNESCO logo **Reverse:** Statues at Abu Simbel

Date	Mintage	F	VF	XF	Unc	BU
1996 Proof	4,000	Value: 425				

KM# 1023 40000 PESETAS **Weight:** 13.5000 g. **Composition:** 0.9990 Gold .4341 oz. AGW **Ruler:** Juan Carlos I **Series:** "Patrimonio de la Humanidad - UNESCO" **Obverse:** UNESCO logo **Reverse:** Horyu-Ji pagoda **Edge:** Reeded **Size:** 30 mm.

Date	Mintage	F	VF	XF	Unc	BU
1997 Proof	4,000	Value: 425				

KM# 845 80000 PESETAS **Weight:** 27.0000 g. **Composition:** 0.9990 Gold .8682 oz. AGW **Subject:** Discovery of America **Reverse:** Ferdinand and Isabella

Date	Mintage	F	VF	XF	Unc	BU
1989	6,000	—	—	—	—	625
1989 Proof	7,000	Value: 625				

KM# 879 80000 PESETAS **Weight:** 27.0000 g. **Composition:** 0.9990 Gold .8682 oz. AGW **Series:** 1992 Olympics **Reverse:** Discus thrower

Date	Mintage	F	VF	XF	Unc	BU
1990	3,000	—	—	—	—	625
1990 Proof	5,000	Value: 625				

Note: Uncirculated strikes have medallic die alignment and edges with reeded and plain sections; Proof strikes have coin die alignment and reeded edges

KM# 880 80000 PESETAS **Weight:** 27.0000 g. **Composition:** 0.9990 Gold .8682 oz. AGW **Series:** 1992 Olympics **Reverse:** Prince Balthasar Carlos on horseback

Date	Mintage	F	VF	XF	Unc	BU
1990	1,000	—	—	—	—	675
1990 Proof	4,000	Value: 675				

Note: Uncirculated strikes have medallic die alignment and edges with reeded and plain sections; Proof strikes have coin die alignment and reeded edges

KM# 881 80000 PESETAS **Weight:** 27.0000 g. **Composition:** 0.9990 Gold .8682 oz. AGW **Subject:** Carlos V **Obverse:** Similar to KM#845

Date	Mintage	F	VF	XF	Unc	BU
1990	2,000	—	—	—	—	675
1990 Proof	3,000	Value: 675				

KM# 901 80000 PESETAS **Weight:** 27.0000 g. **Composition:** 0.9990 Gold .8682 oz. AGW **Series:** Olympics **Reverse:** Women tossing man

Date	Mintage	F	VF	XF	Unc	BU
1991	1,000	—	—	—	—	1,000
1991 Proof	2,000	Value: 1,000				

Note: Uncirculated strikes have medallic die alignment and edges with reeded and plain sections; Proof strikes have coin die alignment and reeded edges

KM# 902 80000 PESETAS **Weight:** 27.0000 g. **Composition:** 0.9990 Gold .8682 oz. AGW **Subject:** Carlos III **Obverse:** Similar to KM#845

Date	Mintage	F	VF	XF	Unc	BU
1991	1,000	—	—	—	—	925
1991 Proof	2,000	Value: 925				

KM# 917 80000 PESETAS **Weight:** 27.0000 g. **Composition:** 0.9990 Gold .8682 oz. AGW **Series:** Olympics **Reverse:** Two children playing

Date	Mintage	F	VF	XF	Unc	BU
1992	1,000	—	—	—	—	1,000
1992 Proof	2,000	Value: 1,000				

Note: Uncirculated strikes have medallic die alignment and edges with reeded and plain sections; Proof strikes have coin die alignment and reeded edges

KM# 1005 80000 PESETAS **Weight:** 27.0000 g. **Composition:** 0.9990 Gold .8682 oz. AGW **Obverse:** Similar to KM#845 **Reverse:** Hammer minting scene

Date	Mintage	F	VF	XF	Unc	BU
1992	1,000	—	—	—	—	1,000
1992 Proof	—	Value: 1,000				

KM# 930 80000 PESETAS **Weight:** 27.0000 g. **Composition:** 0.9990 Gold .8682 oz. AGW **Subject:** Holy Jacobean Year **Reverse:** French Fraternity of Santiago Medallion

Date	Mintage	F	VF	XF	Unc	BU
1993 Proof	1,500	Value: 850				

KM# 945 80000 PESETAS **Weight:** 27.0000 g. **Composition:** 0.9990 Gold .8682 oz. AGW **Reverse:** Iberian Lynx

Date	Mintage	F	VF	XF	Unc	BU
1994 Proof	5,000	Value: 750				

KM# 959 80000 PESETAS **Weight:** 27.0000 g. **Composition:** 0.9990 Gold .8682 oz. AGW **Subject:** Leda and the Swan

Date	Mintage	F	VF	XF	Unc	BU
1995 Proof	5,000	Value: 800				

KM# 972 80000 PESETAS **Weight:** 27.0000 g. **Composition:** 0.9990 Gold .8682 oz. AGW **Reverse:** Folk dancers

Date		F	VF	XF	Unc	BU
1996 Proof	Est. 3,500	Value: 800				

KM# 1028 80000 PESETAS **Weight:** 27.0000 g. **Composition:** 0.9990 Gold .8672 oz. AGW **Ruler:** Juan Carlos I **Subject:** House of Borbon **Obverse:** 8 Escudo obverse design of 1752 within legend **Reverse:** 8 Escudo reverse design of 1752 within legend **Edge:** Reeded **Size:** 38 mm.

Date	Mintage	F	VF	XF	Unc	BU
1997 Proof	4,000	Value: 800				

EURO COINAGE

European Economic Community Issues

KM# 1040 EURO CENT **Weight:** 2.2700 g. **Composition:** Copper Plated Steel **Obverse:** Cathedral **Reverse:** Denomination and globe **Edge:** Plain **Size:** 16.2 mm. **Note:** Mint mark: Crowned M.

Date	Mintage	F	VF	XF	Unc	BU
1999	721,000,000	—	—	—	0.35	—
2000	83,400,000	—	—	—	0.35	—
2001	130,900,000	—	—	—	0.35	—
2002	127,600,000	—	—	—	0.35	—

KM# 1041 2 EURO CENTS **Weight:** 3.0300 g. **Composition:** Copper Plated Steel **Obverse:** Cathedral **Reverse:** Denomination and globe **Edge:** Grooved **Size:** 18.7 mm. **Note:** Mint mark: Crowned M.

Date	Mintage	F	VF	XF	Unc	BU
2001	463,100,000	—	—	—	0.50	—
2002	2,900,000	—	—	—	4.50	—

KM# 1042 5 EURO CENTS **Weight:** 3.8600 g. **Composition:** Copper Plated Steel **Obverse:** Cathedral **Reverse:** Denomination and globe **Edge:** Plain **Size:** 21.2 mm. **Note:** Mint mark: Crowned M.

Date	Mintage	F	VF	XF	Unc	BU
1999	483,500,000	—	—	—	0.75	—
2000	399,900,000	—	—	—	0.75	—

e	Mintage	F	VF	XF	Unc	BU
1	216,100,000	—	—	—	0.75	—
2	8,300,000	—	—	—	3.50	—

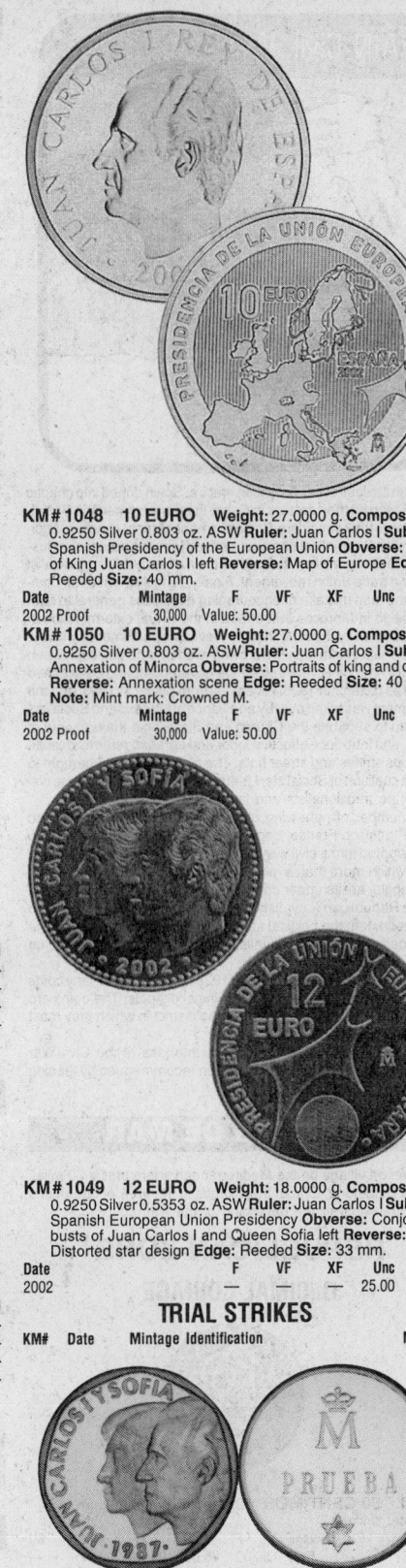

1# 1043 10 EURO CENTS **Weight:** 4.0700 g. **Composition:** Brass **Obverse:** Cervantes **Reverse:** Denomination and map **Edge:** Reeded **Size:** 19.7 mm. **Note:** Mint mark: Crowned M.

e	Mintage	F	VF	XF	Unc	BU
0	243,900,000	—	—	—	0.75	—
1	160,100,000	—	—	—	0.75	—
2	93,100,000	—	—	—	0.75	—

1# 1044 20 EURO CENTS **Weight:** 5.7300 g. **Composition:** Brass **Obverse:** Cervantes **Reverse:** Denomination and map **Edge:** Notched **Size:** 22.1 mm. **Note:** Mint mark: Crowned M.

e	Mintage	F	VF	XF	Unc	BU
9	762,300,000	—	—	—	1.00	—
0	29,300,000	—	—	—	1.00	—
1	146,600,000	—	—	—	1.00	—
2	84,000,000	—	—	—	1.00	—

1# 1045 50 EURO CENTS **Weight:** 7.8100 g. **Composition:** Brass **Obverse:** Cervantes **Reverse:** Denomination and map **Edge:** Reeded **Size:** 24.2 mm. **Note:** Mint mark: Crowned M.

te	Mintage	F	VF	XF	Unc	BU
99	371,000,000	—	—	—	1.25	—
00	519,600,000	—	—	—	1.25	—
01	351,100,000	—	—	—	1.25	—
02	9,700,000	—	—	—	3.50	—

1# 1046 EURO **Ring Composition:** BrassCenter **Weight:** 7.5000 g. **Center Composition:** Copper-Nickel **Obverse:** King's portrait **Reverse:** Denomination and map **Edge:** Reeded and plain sections **Size:** 23.2 mm. **Note:** Mint mark: Crowned M.

te	Mintage	F	VF	XF	Unc	BU
99	100,200,000	—	—	—	2.50	—
00	89,300,000	—	—	—	2.50	—
01	259,100,000	—	—	—	2.50	—
02	294,500,000	—	—	—	2.50	—

1# 1047 2 EUROS **Center Weight:** 8.5200 g. **Center Composition:** Brass **Obverse:** King's portrait **Reverse:** Denomination and stars **Edge:** Reeded **Edge Lettering:** 2's and stars **Size:** 25.7 mm. **Note:** Mint mark: Crowned M.

te	Mintage	F	VF	XF	Unc	BU
99	60,500,000	—	—	—	3.75	—
00	36,600,000	—	—	—	3.75	—
01	140,200,000	—	—	—	3.75	—
02	143,300,000	—	—	—	3.75	—

KM# 1048 10 EURO **Weight:** 27.0000 g. **Composition:** 0.9250 Silver 0.803 oz. ASW **Ruler:** Juan Carlos I **Subject:** Spanish Presidency of the European Union **Obverse:** Head of King Juan Carlos I left **Reverse:** Map of Europe **Edge:** Reeded **Size:** 40 mm.

Date	Mintage	F	VF	XF	Unc	BU
2002 Proof	30,000	Value: 50.00				

KM# 1050 10 EURO **Weight:** 27.0000 g. **Composition:** 0.9250 Silver 0.803 oz. ASW **Ruler:** Juan Carlos I **Subject:** Annexation of Minorca **Obverse:** Portraits of king and queen **Reverse:** Annexation scene **Edge:** Reeded **Size:** 40 mm. **Note:** Mint mark: Crowned M.

Date	Mintage	F	VF	XF	Unc	BU
2002 Proof	30,000	Value: 50.00				

KM# 1049 12 EURO **Weight:** 18.0000 g. **Composition:** 0.9250 Silver 0.5353 oz. ASW **Ruler:** Juan Carlos I **Subject:** Spanish European Union Presidency **Obverse:** Conjoined busts of Juan Carlos I and Queen Sofia left **Reverse:** Distorted star design **Edge:** Reeded **Size:** 33 mm.

Date	F	VF	XF	Unc	BU
2002	—	—	—	25.00	—

TRIAL STRIKES

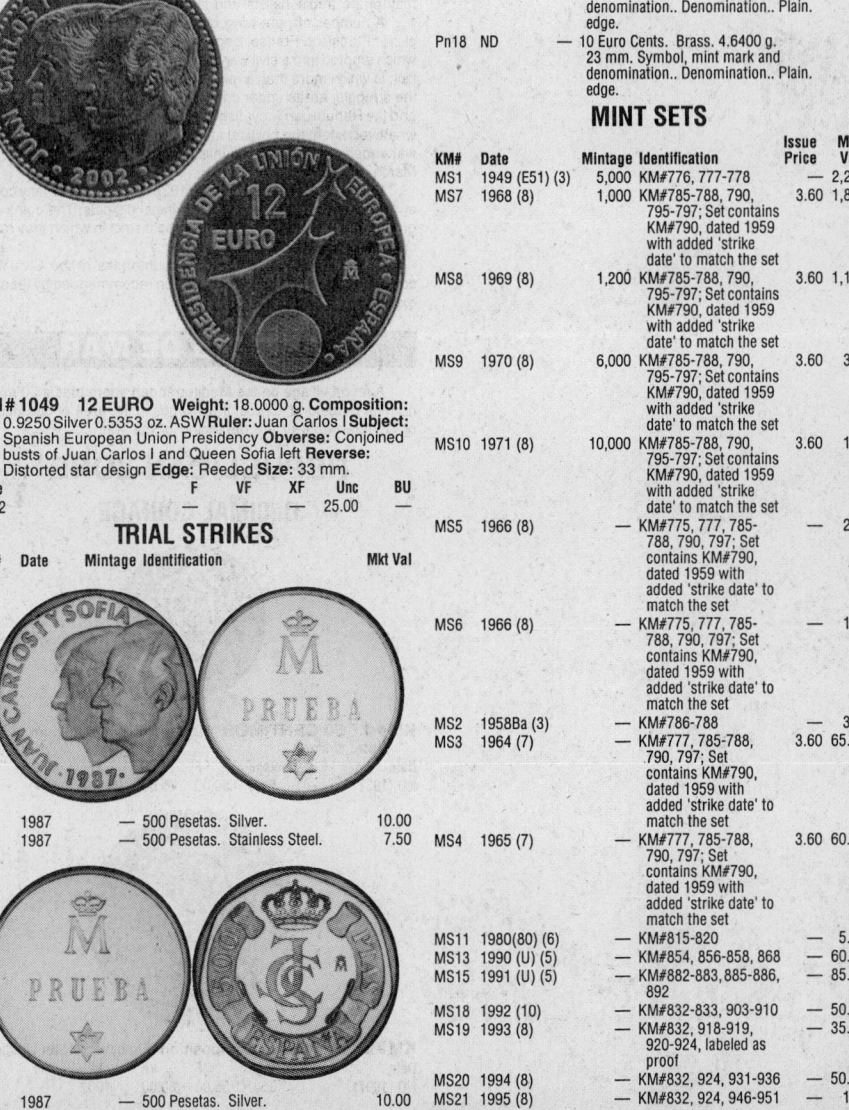

KM#	Date	Mintage	Identification	Mkt Val

TS1	1987	—	500 Pesetas. Silver.	10.00
TS2	1987	—	500 Pesetas. Stainless Steel.	7.50

TS3	1987	—	500 Pesetas. Silver.	10.00

TS4	1987	—	500 Pesetas. Stainless Steel.	7.50

TS5	ND	—	2000 Pesetas. (No Composition). Mint mark. Same as KM#859.	—

PATTERNS

Including off metal strikes

KM#	Date	Mintage	Identification	Mkt Val
Pn16	1937	—	10 Centimos. Zinc. Denomination. Crowned arms on eagle. III Año Triunfal.	2,000
Pn17	ND	—	5 Euro Cents. Bronze. 4.7200 g. 23.4 mm. Sumpol, mint mark and denomination.. Denomination.. Plain. edge.	—
Pn18	ND	—	10 Euro Cents. Brass. 4.6400 g. 23 mm. Symbol, mint mark and denomination.. Denomination.. Plain. edge.	—

MINT SETS

KM#	Date	Mintage	Identification	Issue Price	Mkt Val
MS1	1949 (E51) (3)	5,000	KM#776, 777-778	—	2,250
MS7	1968 (8)	1,000	KM#785-788, 790, 795-797; Set contains KM#790, dated 1959 with added 'strike date' to match the set	3.60	1,800
MS8	1969 (8)	1,200	KM#785-788, 790, 795-797; Set contains KM#790, dated 1959 with added 'strike date' to match the set	3.60	1,150
MS9	1970 (8)	6,000	KM#785-788, 790, 795-797; Set contains KM#790, dated 1959 with added 'strike date' to match the set	3.60	350
MS10	1971 (8)	10,000	KM#785-788, 790, 795-797; Set contains KM#790, dated 1959 with added 'strike date' to match the set	3.60	175
MS5	1966 (8)	—	KM#775, 777, 785-788, 790, 797; Set contains KM#790, dated 1959 with added 'strike date' to match the set	—	200
MS6	1966 (8)	—	KM#775, 777, 785-788, 790, 797; Set contains KM#790, dated 1959 with added 'strike date' to match the set	—	175
MS2	1958Ba (3)	—	KM#786-788	—	300
MS3	1964 (7)	—	KM#777, 785-788, 790, 797; Set contains KM#790, dated 1959 with added 'strike date' to match the set	3.60	65.00
MS4	1965 (7)	—	KM#777, 785-788, 790, 797; Set contains KM#790, dated 1959 with added 'strike date' to match the set	3.60	60.00
MS11	1980(80) (6)	—	KM#815-820	—	5.00
MS13	1990 (U) (5)	—	KM#854, 856-858, 868	—	60.00
MS15	1991 (U) (5)	—	KM#882-883, 885-886, 892	—	85.00
MS18	1992 (10)	—	KM#832-833, 903-910	—	50.00
MS19	1993 (8)	—	KM#832, 918-919, 920-924, labeled as proof	—	35.00
MS20	1994 (8)	—	KM#832, 924, 931-936	—	50.00
MS21	1995 (8)	—	KM#832, 924, 946-951	—	100

KM#	Date	Mintage	Identification	Issue Price	Mkt Val
MS22	1996 (8)	—	KM#832, 924, 960-965	—	45.00
MS23	1997 (8)	—	KM#832, 924, 981-986	—	15.00
MS24	1998 (8)	—	KM#832-833, 924, 989-992, 1012	—	15.00
MS25	1999 (8)	—	KM#832, 924, 991-992, 1006-1008, 1012	—	30.00
MSA25	1999 (8)	—	KM#832-833, 924, 989-992, 1012	—	30.00
MS26	2000 (8)	—	KM#832-833, 924, 989, 991-992, 1012-1013	—	30.00
MS27	2000-2001 (8)	—	KM#832-833, 924, 991-992 (both dated 2000), 1012-1013, 1016	—	20.00
MSA26	2000 (8)	—	KM#832-833, 924, 989-992, 1012	—	35.00

PROOF SETS

KM#	Date	Mintage	Identification	Issue Price	Mkt Val
PS3	1974 (6)	23,000	KM#786-788, 790, 795-796	10.00	90.00
PS1	1972 (6)	30,000	KM#786-788, 790, 795-796	10.00	40.00
PS2	1973 (6)	25,000	KM#786-788, 790, 795-796	10.00	100
PS4	1975 (6)	75,000	KM#786-788, 790, 795-796	10.00	15.00
PS5	1976 (6)	400,000	KM#805-810	7.50	5.00
PS6	1977 (3)	300,000	KM#806-808	—	2.00
PS7	1979 (4)	300,000	KM#806-809	—	3.00
PS8	1987 (6)	—	KM#831, Pn4, Pn4a, Pn5-6	55.00	35.00
PS10	1989 (7)	—	KM#834-839, 841	—	250
PS12	1989 (5)	—	KM#840, 842-845	3,177	1,775
PS13	1990 (7)	—	KM#854, 856-858, 868-869, 873	—	250
PS14	1991 (7)	—	KM#882-883, 885-886, 892-893, 896	—	375
PS15	1992 (7)	—	KM#980, 993-998	—	450
PS16	1995 (6)	I.A.	KM#938, 953, 956-959	—	1,350
PS17	1995 (4)	25,000	KM#938, 953, 956-959	—	300
PS18	1996 (6)	—	KM#966-967, 969-972	1,675	1,300
PS19	1996 (6)	—	KM#966-967, 969-972	1,650	1,300
PS20	1996 (4)	—	KM#966-967, 969-972	—	240
PS21	1996 (4)	—	KM#966-967, 969-970	—	240
PS22	1996 (5)	—	KM#973-978	198	160
PS23	1996 (6)	—	KM#973-979	702	600

With the loss of her American empire, Spain drifted into chaotic times. Stung by their defeats in Cuba, the army blamed the Socialists for what they considered to be mismanagement at home. Additional political complications were derived from the successful Russian Revolution which gave impetus to an already thriving Socialist party and trade union movement. Finally, King Alphonso XIII committed the fatal mistake of encouraging a reckless general to start a campaign in Morocco that ended in the virtual extermination of the Spanish army. Fearing that the inevitable parliamentary investigation would incriminate the crown, he offered no objection when General Primo de Rivera seized the government and established himself as dictator in 1926. Rivera fell from power in 1930, and the government was taken over by an alliance of Liberals and Socialists who tried to separate the Church and State, take the army out of politics, and introduce effective labor and agrarian reforms despite numerous strikes and street riots. The election of 1936 brought to power a coalition of Socialists, Liberals and Communists, to the dismay of the traditionalists and landowners.

A number of right-wing generals, including the young and clever Francisco Franco, began preparations for a military coup which erupted into a civil war in July of 1936.The destructive conflict, in which more than a million died, lasted three years. During the struggle, areas under control of both the Nationalist (rebels) and the Republican (Loyalists) issued coinages that circulated to whatever extent the political and military situation permitted. The war ended defeat for the Loyalists when Madrid fell to Franco on March 28, 1939.

During the Spanish Civil War (1936-1939) a great many coins and tokens were minted in the provincial districts. The coins are grouped here under the heading of the district in which they most commonly circulated.

CAUTIONARY NOTE: Many counterfeits of the Civil War coinage exist. Authentication has been recommended by leading experts in this field.

ARENYS DE MAR

A resort village on the Mediterranean shore that is 20 miles north of Barcelona. One of the villages in the area of operations of General Mola at the beginning of the war.

REPUBLICAN ZONE

DECIMAL COINAGE

KM# 1 50 CENTIMOS **Composition:** Aluminum
Note: Uniface.

Date	Mintage	F	VF	XF	Unc	BU
ND (1937)	6,000	50.00	75.00	90.00	—	—

KM# 2 PESETA **Composition:** Aluminum **Note:** Uniface.

Date	Mintage	F	VF	XF	Unc	BU
ND (1937)	3,500	55.00	80.00	100	—	—

ASTURIAS AND LEON

Asturias is a province on the northern coast of Spain with th province of Leon just to its south. The councils of these adjoinin provinces decided to mint coins in1937 for use in the area due lack of other circulating coins in the north.

REPUBLICAN ZONE

DECIMAL COINAGE

KM# 1 50 CENTIMOS **Composition:** Copper-Nickel
Note: Struck at Gijon.

Date	Mintage	F	VF	XF	Unc	B
1937	200,000	15.00	20.00	30.00	35.00	-

KM# 2 PESETA **Composition:** Copper **Note:** Struck a Guernica.

Date	Mintage	F	VF	XF	Unc	B
1937	100,000	15.00	25.00	35.00	55.00	-

KM# 3 2 PESETAS **Composition:** Copper-Nickel **Note** Struck at Gijon. Varieties exist with differences in the leave

Date	Mintage	F	VF	XF	Unc	B
1937	400,000	5.00	7.50	10.00	15.00	-

Note: Varieties exist with differences in the leaves

CAZALLA DE SIERRA

A town 43 miles north of Seville that issued a 10 Centimo in brass in 1936 (undated).

NATIONALIST ZONE

DECIMAL COINAGE

KM# 1 10 CENTIMOS **Composition:** Brass

Date	Mintage	F	VF	XF	Unc	B
ND (1936)	10,000	25.00	40.00	80.00	—	-

EL ARAHAL

A town 30 miles east of Seville. Issued 3 undated types c coins in 1936.

NATIONALIST ZONE

DECIMAL COINAGE

KM# 1 50 CENTIMOS **Composition:** Brass **Note:** Uniface

	Mintage	F	VF	XF	Unc	BU
1936)	3,000	50.00	100	150	200	—

 # 2 PESETA **Composition:** Brass **Note:** Uniface.

	Mintage	F	VF	XF	Unc	BU
(1936)	10,000	20.00	30.00	50.00	75.00	—

 # 3 2 PESETAS **Composition:** Brass **Note:** Uniface.

e	Mintage	F	VF	XF	Unc	BU
(1936)	10,000	20.00	30.00	50.00	75.00	—

EUZKADI

Euzkadi or the Viscayan Republic was located in north cen-Spain adjoining the southeast corner of France. It was made of 4 provinces - Bilbao, Guipuzcoa, Navarre, and Victoria. ese Basque provinces declared autonomy on October 8, 1936. e 2 nickel coins were made in Brussels, Belgium and saw some culation before the end of the Republic on June 18, 1937.

REPUBLICAN ZONE
Viscayan Republic
DECIMAL COINAGE

 # 1 PESETA **Composition:** Nickel **Note:** Struck at Brussels.

e	Mintage	F	VF	XF	Unc	BU
37	7,000,000	2.00	4.00	5.00	9.00	—

 # 2 2 PESETAS **Composition:** Nickel **Note:** Struck at Brussels.

te	Mintage	F	VF	XF	Unc	BU
37	6,000,000	2.00	4.00	5.00	10.00	—

IBI

A village north and west of Alicante on the east coast of Spain. e isolation of the area in comparison with other contending areas de the maintaining of this area during the war very difficult.

REPUBLICAN ZONE
DECIMAL COINAGE

KM# 1.1 25 CENTIMOS **Composition:** Copper **Note:** Varieties exist.

Date	Mintage	F	VF	XF	Unc	BU
1937	30,000	20.00	30.00	40.00	50.00	—

KM# 1.2 25 CENTIMOS **Composition:** Copper **Obverse:** Map of Spain in field

Date	Mintage	F	VF	XF	Unc	BU
1937	7,000	75.00	125	150	200	—

KM# 2 PESETA **Composition:** Nickel-Brass

Date	Mintage	F	VF	XF	Unc	BU
1937	5,000	75.00	125	175	250	—

L'AMETLLA DEL VALLES

A town in the province of Tarragona in northeastern Spain. The town adopted the name L'Ametlla del Valles in 1933. Before that the name was La Ametlla.

REPUBLICAN ZONE
DECIMAL COINAGE

KM# 1 25 CENTIMOS **Composition:** Brass

Date	Mintage	F	VF	XF	Unc	BU
ND (1937)	50,000	10.00	15.00	20.00	35.00	—

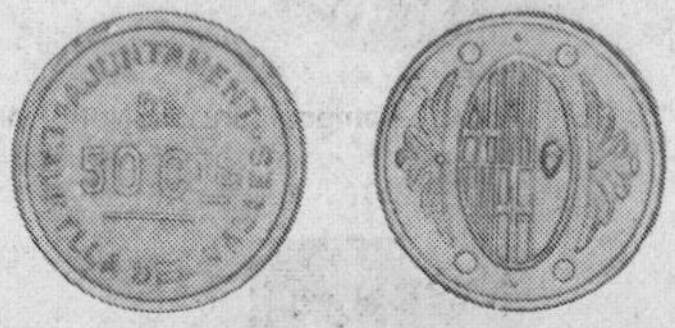

KM# 2.1 50 CENTIMOS **Composition:** Aluminum

Date	Mintage	F	VF	XF	Unc	BU
ND (1937)	3,000	100	200	250	300	—

KM# 2.2 50 CENTIMOS **Composition:** Aluminum **Obverse:** Without legend

Date	Mintage	F	VF	XF	Unc	BU
ND (1937)	30,000	25.00	50.00	70.00	100	—

KM# 3.1 PESETA **Composition:** Aluminum

Date	Mintage	F	VF	XF	Unc	BU
ND (1937)	3,000	75.00	100	125	150	—

KM# 3.2 PESETA **Composition:** Aluminum **Obverse:** Without legend

Date	Mintage	F	VF	XF	Unc	BU
ND (1937)	30,000	15.00	30.00	40.00	50.00	—

LA PUEBLA DE CAZALLA

A village only a few miles east of El Arahal and some 40 miles from Sevilla. Undated coins of 2 values were issued in 1936.

NATIONALIST ZONE
DECIMAL COINAGE

KM# 1 10 CENTIMOS **Composition:** Brass **Size:** 23 mm. **Note:** Counterstamped varieties exist.

Date	Mintage	F	VF	XF	Unc	BU
ND (1936)	1,500	100	175	225	300	—

KM# 2 25 CENTIMOS **Composition:** Brass **Note:** Counterstamped varieties exist.

Date	Mintage	F	VF	XF	Unc	BU
ND (1936)	5,000	75.00	100	150	200	—

LORA DEL RIO

A town 35 miles northeast of Seville. Issued an undated 25 Centimos in 1936.

NATIONALIST ZONE
DECIMAL COINAGE

KM# 1 25 CENTIMOS **Composition:** Brass **Obverse:** Crowned arms of Lora del Rio on cross **Reverse:** 5-line inscription, wheat ear right

Date	Mintage	F	VF	XF	Unc	BU
ND (1936)	1,500	200	275	325	450	—

MARCHENA

A village 30 miles east of Seville. It was the last issuer in Seville province. Two varieties of undated coins were produced in 1936.

NATIONALIST ZONE

DECIMAL COINAGE

KM# 1.1 25 CENTIMOS **Composition:** Brass **Note:** Uniface; denomination: 25C.

Date	Mintage	F	VF	XF	Unc	BU
ND (1936)	5,000	30.00	75.00	100	150	—

KM# 1.2 25 CENTIMOS **Composition:** Brass **Note:** Uniface; denomination: 025C.

Date	Mintage	F	VF	XF	Unc	BU
ND (1936)	500	400	600	800	1,000	—

MENORCA

Menorca is the smaller of the 2 major islands in the Balearic Islands. A serious coin and supply shortage developed during the war because of the isolation of the island from the mainland.

REPUBLICAN ZONE

DECIMAL COINAGE

KM# 1 5 CENTIMOS **Composition:** Brass **Note:** Varieties exist.

Date	Mintage	F	VF	XF	Unc	BU
1937	42,000	—	40.00	50.00	60.00	—

KM# 2 10 CENTIMOS **Composition:** Brass **Note:** Varieties exist.

Date	Mintage	F	VF	XF	Unc	BU
1937	32,000	—	25.00	35.00	45.00	—

KM# 3 25 CENTIMOS **Composition:** Brass

Date	Mintage	F	VF	XF	Unc	BU
1937	38,000	—	20.00	25.00	30.00	—

KM# 4 PESETA **Composition:** Brass

Date	Mintage	F	VF	XF	Unc	BU
1937	37,000	—	20.00	25.00	30.00	—

KM# 5 2-1/2 PESETAS **Composition:** Brass

Date	Mintage	F	VF	XF	Unc	BU
1937	24,000	—	40.00	50.00	60.00	—

NULLES

Nulles is a mountain village in the province of Tarragona. The mountainous terrain of the area isolated the village from friendly forces and normal commerce. Therefore, in 1937, an undated series of 5 denominations were issued.

REPUBLICAN ZONE

DECIMAL COINAGE

KM# 1 5 CENTIMOS **Composition:** Zinc **Shape:** Octagonal **Note:** Uniface, legends similar to 10 Centimos, KM#2.

Date	Mintage	F	VF	XF	Unc	BU
ND (1937)	5,000	200	350	450	—	—

KM# 2 10 CENTIMOS **Composition:** Zinc **Note:** Uniface.

Date	Mintage	F	VF	XF	Unc	BU
ND (1937)	3,000	250	400	500	—	—

KM# 3 25 CENTIMOS **Composition:** Brass **Shape:** Square **Note:** Uniface. Legends similar to 10 Centimos, KM#2.

Date	Mintage	F	VF	XF	Unc	BU
ND (1937)	5,000	200	350	450	—	—

KM# 4 50 CENTIMOS **Composition:** Brass **Shape:** Octagonal **Note:** Uniface, legends similar to 10 Centimos, KM#2.

Date	Mintage	F	VF	XF	Unc	BU
ND (1937)	1,000	250	400	500	—	—

KM# 5 PESETA **Composition:** Brass **Note:** Uniface.

Date	Mintage	F	VF	XF	Unc
ND (1937)	5,000	150	200	250	—

OLOT

A village in the province of Gerona in northeastern Spain ne the French border. The village council authorized 2 deno nations of coins on September 24, 1937.

REPUBLICAN ZONE

DECIMAL COINAGE

KM# 1 10 CENTIMOS **Composition:** Iron

Date	Mintage	F	VF	XF	Unc
1937	25,000	40.00	60.00	125	—

KM# 2 15 CENTIMOS **Composition:** Iron

Date	Mintage	F	VF	XF	Unc
1937	100	1,500	1,800	2,000	—

Note: The above is considered a pattern

SANTANDER, PALENCIA & BURGOS

REPUBLICAN ZONE

DECIMAL COINAGE

KM# 1.1 50 CENTIMOS **Composition:** Copper-Nicke **Size:** 20 mm.

Date	Mintage	F	VF	XF	Unc
1937	100,000	—	25.00	35.00	45.00

KM# 1.2 50 CENTIMOS **Composition:** Copper-Nicke **Reverse:** Letters PR or PJR below CTS

Date	Mintage	F	VF	XF	Unc
1937	10,000	15.00	30.00	40.00	50.00

KM# 2 PESETA **Composition:** Copper-Nickel

Date	Mintage	F	VF	XF	Unc
1937	300,000	—	10.00	15.00	20.00

SEGARRA DE GAIA

A village in the southern part of the province of Tarragona. A single denomination of coin was authorized in 1937.

REPUBLICAN ZONE

DECIMAL COINAGE

KM# 1 PESETA Composition: Copper-Nickel

Date	Mintage	F	VF	XF	Unc	BU
ND (1937)	5,000	15.00	25.00	30.00	35.00	—

KM# 1a PESETA Composition: Copper **Size:** 23 mm. **Note:** Uniface. Value over bars of Aragon in circle.

Date	Mintage	F	VF	XF	Unc	BU
ND (1937)	20,000	75.00	125	150	200	—

KM# 2 PESETA Composition: Aluminum

Date	Mintage	F	VF	XF	Unc	BU
ND (1937)	30,000	—	—	—	—	—

Note: Reported, not confirmed

KM# 2a PESETA Composition: Brass **Note:** Numbered, uniface, 5-line inscription.

Date	F	VF	XF	Unc	BU
ND (1937)	75.00	125	150	200	—

SPITZBERGEN

Spitzbergen (Svalbard), a Norwegian territory, is a group of mountainous islands in the Arctic Ocean 360 miles (579 km.) north of Norway. The islands have an area of 23,957 sq. mi. (62,050 sq. km.) and a population of about 4,000. West Spitzbergen, the largest island, is the seat of administration. Sealing and fishing are economically important. Despite rich carboniferous and tertiary coal deposits, coal mining, which was started on a commercial scale by the Arctic Coal Co. of Boston, Mass. in 1904, produces only small quantities.

Spitzbergen was probably discovered in 1194, but modern knowledge of it dates from its discovery by William Barents in 1596. Quarrels among the various nationalities involved in the whaling industry, which was set up in 1611, resulted in a de facto division of the coast, but despite diverse interests in, and claims to the islands by British, Dutch, Norwegians, Swedes, Danes, Russians and Americans, the question of sovereignty was not resolved until 1920, when a treaty agreed to by the claimants awarded the islands to Norway.

In 1932, the Russian mining company Arktikugol began operations in the islands. The tokens listed here were minted in Leningrad for use by the company in Spitzbergen.

RULERS
Norwegian, 1920-

NORWEGIAN TERRITORY

TOKEN COINAGE

Arktikugol

KM# Tn1 10 KOPEKS Composition: Aluminum-Bronze

Date	F	VF	XF	Unc	BU
1946	15.00	25.00	45.00	115	—

KM# Tn15 10 KOPEKS Weight: 11.9000 g. **Composition:** Copper-Nickel **Subject:** "9-11" Terrorist attack on New York **Obverse:** Large number 10 without denomination above date in center **Obv. Legend:** Translation; "Island Spitzbergen" at top. "Arctic coal" on bottom. **Reverse:** Twin towers attack scene **Rev. Legend:** Translation: "Anti Terrorism" at top. "New York 11 September" below **Edge:** Segmented reeding **Size:** 30 mm.

Date	F	VF	XF	Unc	BU
2001 Proof	—	—	—	—	—

KM# Tn2 15 KOPEKS Composition: Aluminum-Bronze

Date	F	VF	XF	Unc	BU
1946	20.00	30.00	50.00	120	—

KM# Tn3 20 KOPEKS Composition: Copper-Nickel

Date	F	VF	XF	Unc	BU
1946	22.00	38.00	60.00	135	—

KM# Tn4.1 50 KOPEKS Composition: Copper-Nickel **Obverse:** Large star

Date	F	VF	XF	Unc	BU
1946	25.00	40.00	65.00	140	—

KM# Tn4.2 50 KOPEKS Composition: Copper-Nickel **Obverse:** Small star

Date	F	VF	XF	Unc	BU
1946	25.00	40.00	65.00	140	—

KM# Tn5 10 ROUBLES Composition: Copper-Nickel Clad Steel

Date	F	VF	XF	Unc	BU
1993	—	—	—	3.50	—

KM# Tn6 25 ROUBLES Composition: Copper-Nickel Clad Steel

Date	F	VF	XF	Unc	BU
1993	—	—	—	4.50	—

KM# Tn7 50 ROUBLES Composition: Copper-Nickel Clad Steel

Date	F	VF	XF	Unc	BU
1993	—	—	—	6.50	—

KM# Tn8 100 ROUBLES Composition: Aluminum-Bronze

Date	F	VF	XF	Unc	BU
1993	—	—	—	9.00	—

REFORM COINAGE

KM# 9 10 KOPEKS (0.1 Rouble) Composition: Aluminum **Obverse:** 2 walruses above world globe **Reverse:** Numeric value

Date	Mintage	F	VF	XF	Unc	BU
1998	6,000	—	—	—	3.00	—

KM# 10 25 KOPEKS (0.25 Rouble) **Composition:** Aluminum **Obverse:** 2 walruses above world globe **Reverse:** Numeric value

Date	Mintage	F	VF	XF	Unc	BU
1998	6,000	—	—	—	3.50	—

KM# 11 50 KOPEKS (0.5 Rouble) **Composition:** Aluminum **Obverse:** 2 walruses above world globe **Reverse:** Numeric value

Date	Mintage	F	VF	XF	Unc	BU
1998	6,000	—	—	—	4.00	—

KM# 12 ROUBLE **Composition:** Brass **Obverse:** Polar bear above world globe **Reverse:** Numeric value

Date	Mintage	F	VF	XF	Unc	BU
1998	4,000	—	—	—	5.00	—

KM# 13 2 ROUBLES **Composition:** Brass **Obverse:** Polar bear above world globe **Reverse:** Numeric value

Date	Mintage	F	VF	XF	Unc	BU
1998	4,000	—	—	—	5.50	—

KM# 14 5 ROUBLES **Composition:** Copper-Nickel **Obverse:** Whale above world globe **Reverse:** Numeric value

Date	Mintage	F	VF	XF	Unc	BU
1998	4,000	—	—	—	6.50	—

SRI (SHRI) LANKA

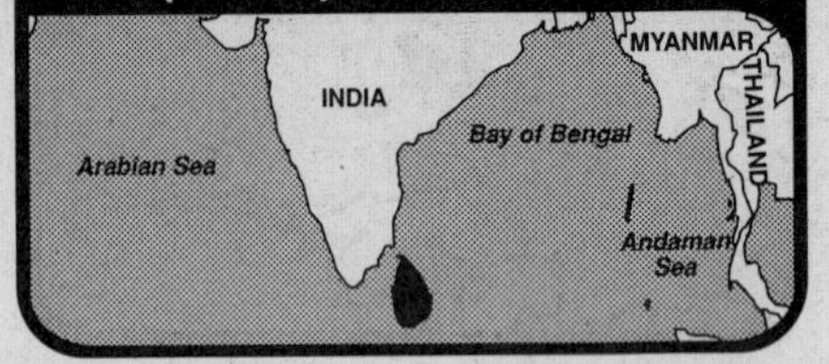

The Democratic Socialist Republic of Sri Lanka (formerly Ceylon) situated in the Indian Ocean 18 miles (29 km.) southeast of India, has an area of 25,332 sq. mi.(65,610 sq. km.) and a population of *16.9 million. Capital: Colombo. The economy is chiefly agricultural. Tea, coconut products and rubber are exported.

Sri Lanka remains a member of the Commonwealth of Nations. The president is Chief of State. The prime minister is Head of Government. The present leaders of the country have reverted the country name back to Sri Lanka.

RULERS
British, 1796-1948

DEMOCRATIC SOCIALIST REPUBLIC

DECIMAL COINAGE

100 Cents = 1 Rupee

KM# 137 CENT **Composition:** Aluminum

Date	Mintage	F	VF	XF	Unc	BU
1975	—	—		0.10	0.25	—
1975 Proof	1,431	Value: 2.50				
1978	—	—		0.10	0.25	—
1978 Proof	20,000	Value: 2.50				
1989	—	—		0.10	0.25	—
1994	—	—		0.10	0.25	—

KM# 138 2 CENTS **Composition:** Aluminum

Date	Mintage	F	VF	XF	Unc	BU
1975	—	—		0.10	0.25	—
1975 Proof	1,431	Value: 2.50				
1978	—	—		0.10	0.25	—
1978 Proof	20,000	Value: 3.00				

KM# 139 5 CENTS **Composition:** Nickel-Brass

Date	Mintage	F	VF	XF	Unc	BU
1975	19,584,000	—	—	0.10	0.25	—
1975 Proof	1,431	Value: 2.50				

KM# 139a 5 CENTS **Composition:** Aluminum

Date	Mintage	F	VF	XF	Unc	BU
1978	—	—		0.10	0.25	—
1978 Proof	20,000	Value: 3.00				
1988	—	—		0.10	0.25	—
1991	—	—		0.10	0.25	—

KM# 140 10 CENTS **Composition:** Nickel-Brass

Date	Mintage	F	VF	XF	Unc	BU
1975	10,800,000	—	—	0.10	0.25	—
1975 Proof	1,431	Value: 4.25				

KM# 140a 10 CENTS **Composition:** Aluminum

Date	Mintage	F	VF	XF	Unc	BU
1978	—	—		0.10	0.25	—
1978 Proof	20,000	Value: 3.50				

Date	Mintage	F	VF	XF	Unc	BU
1988	—	—		0.10	0.25	—
1991	—	—		0.10	0.25	—

KM# 141.1 25 CENTS **Composition:** Copper-Nickel **Edge:** Security

Date	Mintage	F	VF	XF	Unc	BU
1975	—	—		0.10	0.25	—
1975 Proof	1,431	Value: 4.00				
1978	—	—		0.10	0.25	—
1978 Proof	20,000	Value: 3.50				

KM# 141.2 25 CENTS **Composition:** Copper-Nickel **Edge:** Reeded

Date	Mintage	F	VF	XF	Unc	BU
1982	90,000,000	—	—	0.10	0.25	—
1989	45,000,000	—	—	0.10	0.25	—
1991	50,000,000	—	—	0.10	0.25	—
1994	50,000,000	—	—	0.10	0.25	—

KM#141.2a 25 CENTS **Composition:** Nickel Clad Steel **Edge:** Reeded

Date	Mintage	VG	F	VF	XF	Unc
1996	50,000,000	—	—	—	0.10	0.25
2001	10,000,000	—	—	—	0.10	0.25

KM# 135.1 50 CENTS **Composition:** Copper-Nickel **Edge:** Security

Date	Mintage	F	VF	XF	Unc	BU
1972	—	—	0.15	0.30	0.75	—
1975	—	—	0.15	0.30	0.75	—
1975 Proof	1,431	Value: 5.00				
1978	—	—	0.15	0.30	0.75	—
1978 Proof	20,000	Value: 4.50				

KM# 135.2 50 CENTS **Composition:** Copper-Nickel **Edge:** Reeded

Date	Mintage	F	VF	XF	Unc	BU
1982	65,000,000	—	0.10	0.25	0.65	—
1991	40,000,000	—	0.10	0.25	0.65	—
1994	40,000,000	—	0.10	0.25	0.65	—

KM#135.2a 50 CENTS **Composition:** Nickel Clad Steel **Edge:** Reeded

Date	Mintage	VG	F	VF	XF	Unc
1996	50,000,000	—	—	0.10	0.25	0.65
2001	30,000,000	—	—	0.10	0.25	0.65

KM# 136.1 RUPEE **Composition:** Copper-Nickel **Edge:** Security

Date	Mintage	F	VF	XF	Unc	BU
1972	—	—	0.30	0.60	1.25	—
1975	—	—	0.25	0.50	1.00	—
1975 Proof	1,431	Value: 6.50				
1978	—	—	0.25	0.50	1.00	—
1978 Proof	20,000	Value: 6.50				

KM# 136.2 RUPEE **Composition:** Copper-Nickel **Edge** Reeded

Date	Mintage	F	VF	XF	Unc	BU
1982	75,000,000	—	0.25	0.50	1.00	—
1994	50,000,000	—	0.25	0.50	1.00	—

KM# 136.2a RUPEE **Composition:** Nickel Clad Steel **Edge:** Reeded

Date	Mintage	VG	F	VF	XF	Ur
1996	50,000,000	—	—	0.25	0.50	1.0
2000	30,000,000	—	—	0.25	0.50	1.0

KM# 144.1 RUPEE **Composition:** Copper Nickel **Obverse:** Portrait with truncation line.

Date	Mintage	F	VF	XF	Unc	B
1978	2,600	—	—	—	—	—

KM# 144 RUPEE Composition: Copper-Nickel **Subject:** Inauguration of President Jayewardene **Note:** Right shoulder curves upward

Date	Mintage	F	VF	XF	Unc	BU
1978		—	0.30	0.60	1.25	—
1978 Right shoulder straight		—	—	—	—	50.00
1978 Proof	20,000	Value: 6.50				

Note: In sets only.

KM# 144a RUPEE Composition: Gold **Subject:** Inauguration of President Jayawardene

Date	F	VF	XF	Unc	BU
1978 Proof	—	—	—	—	—

KM# 151 RUPEE Composition: Copper-Nickel **Subject:** 2nd Executive President Premadusa

Date	Mintage	F	VF	XF	Unc	BU
1992	25,000,000	—	0.30	0.65	1.75	—
1992 Proof	—	Value: 6.50				

KM# 151a RUPEE Composition: 0.9250 Silver **Subject:** 3rd anniversary - induction of president

Date	VG	F	VF	XF	Unc
1992 Brilliant Proof	—	—	—	—	—
1992 Frosted Proof	—	—	—	—	—

KM# 151b RUPEE Composition: 0.9167 Gold **Subject:** 3rd anniversary - induction of president

Date	VG	F	VF	XF	Unc
1992 Proof	—	—	—	—	—

KM# 157 RUPEE Composition: Copper-Nickel **Series:** UNICEF **Subject:** UNICEF 50th anniversary **Obverse:** Denomination

Date	Mintage	F	VF	XF	Unc	BU
1996	5,000,000	—	—	—	1.75	—

KM# 162 RUPEE Weight: 7.1300 g. **Composition:** Nickel Plated Steel **Subject:** Army's 50th Anniversary **Obverse:** National arms on crossed swords above dates. **Reverse:** Soldier giving dove to boy. **Edge:** Reeded. **Size:** 25.4 mm.

Date	Mintage	F	VF	XF	Unc	BU
1999		—	—	—	2.00	—
1999 Proof	8,000	Value: 6.00				

KM# 164 RUPEE Weight: 7.1300 g. **Composition:** Nickel Plated Steel **Subject:** Sri Lankan Navy 50 Years **Obverse:** Patrol boat **Reverse:** Navy emblem **Edge:** Reeded **Size:** 25.4 mm. **Note:** Struck at Paris Mint.

Date	Mintage	F	VF	XF	Unc	BU
2000	20,000	—	—	—	2.00	—

KM# 164a RUPEE Composition: Copper Nickel **Subject:** Sri Lankan Navy 50 Years **Obverse:** Patrol boat. **Reverse:** Navy emblem. **Edge:** Reeded. **Size:** 25.4 mm.

Date	Mintage	F	VF	XF	Unc	BU
2000 Proof	2,000	Value: 6.00				

KM# 166 RUPEE Weight: 7.1300 g. **Composition:** Copper Nickel **Subject:** Air Force's 50th Anniversary **Obverse:** National arms on air force insignia. **Reverse:** Two jets above propeller plane. **Edge:** Reeded. **Size:** 25.4 mm. **Note:** Struck at British Royal Mint.

Date	Mintage	F	VF	XF	Unc	BU
2001 Proof	2,000	Value: 8.00				

KM# 142 2 RUPEES Composition: Copper-Nickel **Subject:** Non-Aligned Nations Conference

Date	Mintage	F	VF	XF	Unc	BU
1976		—	0.50	1.50	2.25	—
1976 Proof	500	Value: 10.00				

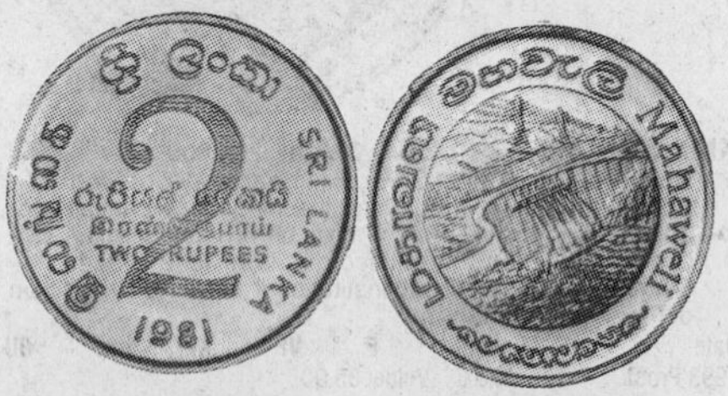

KM# 145 2 RUPEES Composition: Copper-Nickel **Subject:** Mahaweli Dam

Date	Mintage	F	VF	XF	Unc	BU
1981	45,000,000	—	0.35	0.75	2.50	—

KM# 147 2 RUPEES Composition: Copper-Nickel

Date	Mintage	F	VF	XF	Unc	BU
1984	25,000,000	—	0.25	0.50	1.00	—
1993	40,000,000	—	0.30	0.60	1.35	—
1996	50,000,000	—	0.30	0.60	1.35	—
2001	10,000,000	—	0.30	0.60	1.35	—

KM# 155 2 RUPEES Composition: Copper-Nickel **Series:** F.A.O. **Subject:** F.A.O. 50th anniversary

Date	Mintage	F	VF	XF	Unc	BU
1995	40,000,000	—	—	—	2.25	—

KM# 167 2 RUPEES Weight: 8.2500 g. **Composition:** Copper Nickel **Subject:** Colombo Plan's 50th Anniversary **Obverse:** Denomination. **Reverse:** Gear wheel. **Edge:** Reeded. **Size:** 28.5 mm. **Note:** Struck at British Royal Mint.

Date	Mintage	F	VF	XF	Unc	BU
2001	10,000,000	—	—	—	2.00	—

KM# 143 5 RUPEES Composition: Nickel **Subject:** Non-aligned Nations Conference

Date	Mintage	F	VF	XF	Unc	BU
1976		—	0.75	1.50	3.50	—
1976 Proof	500	Value: 12.00				

KM# 146 5 RUPEES Composition: Copper-Nickel **Subject:** 50th Anniversary - Universal Adult Franchise

Date	Mintage	F	VF	XF	Unc	BU
1981	2,000,000	—	0.75	1.50	3.50	—

KM# 148.1 5 RUPEES Composition: Aluminum-Bronze **Edge:** Lettered **Edge Lettering:** CBC - Central Bank of Ceylon

Date	Mintage	F	VF	XF	Unc	BU
1984	25,000,000	—	0.35	0.75	2.50	—

KM# 148.2 5 RUPEES Composition: Aluminum-Bronze **Edge:** Lettered **Edge Lettering:** CBSL - Central Bank of Sri Lanka

Date	Mintage	F	VF	XF	Unc	BU
1986	60,000,000	—	0.35	0.75	2.50	—
1991	40,000,000	—	0.35	0.75	2.50	—
1994	50,000,000	—	0.35	0.65	2.25	—

KM# 156 5 RUPEES Composition: Aluminum-Bronze **Subject:** 50th anniversary - United Nations **Obverse:** Denomination

Date	F	VF	XF	Unc	BU
1995	—	—	—	3.00	—
1995 Proof	—	—	—	—	—

KM# 161 5 RUPEES Composition: Aluminum-Bronze **Subject:** World cricket champions **Obverse:** Trophy **Reverse:** Batsman

Date	Mintage	F	VF	XF	Unc	BU
1999	50,000,000	—	—	—	3.50	—

KM# 149 10 RUPEES Composition: Copper-Nickel **Subject:** International Year of Shelter for Homeless

Date	F	VF	XF	Unc	BU
1987	—	—	—	4.00	—
1987 Proof	—	—	—	—	—

KM# 158 10 RUPEES Ring Composition: Copper-Nickel **Center Composition:** Brass **Subject:** 50th anniversary of independence **Edge:** CBSL, (4 times) reeded

Date	Mintage	F	VF	XF	Unc	BU
1998	50,000,000	—	—	—	4.50	—

KM# 152 100 RUPEES Weight: 10.2000 g. **Composition:** 0.9250 Silver .3033 oz. ASW **Subject:** 5th South Asian Federation Games

Date	Mintage	F	VF	XF	Unc	BU
1991 Proof	20,000	Value: 32.00				

KM# 150 500 RUPEES Weight: 28.1600 g. **Composition:** Copper-Nickel **Subject:** Central Bank 40th Anniversary **Obverse:** National arms **Reverse:** Building **Edge:** Reeded **Size:** 38.6 mm. **Note:** Struck at British Royal Mint.

Date	F	VF	XF	Unc	BU
ND(1990)	—	—	—	100	—

KM# 150a (KM150) 500 RUPEES Weight: 28.2800 g. **Composition:** 0.9250 Silver .8411 oz. ASW **Subject:** 40th anniversary of central bank

Date	F	VF	XF	Unc	BU
1990	—	—	—	—	60.00
1990	—	—	—	—	60.00
1990 frosted Proof	—	—	—	—	—
1990 frosted Proof	—	—	—	—	—

KM# 153 500 RUPEES Weight: 1.6000 g. **Composition:** 0.5000 Gold .0257 oz. AGW **Subject:** 5th South Asian Federation Games

Date	Mintage	F	VF	XF	Unc	BU
1991 Proof	8,000	Value: 30.00				

KM# 154 500 RUPEES Weight: 28.2800 g. **Composition:** 0.9250 Silver .8411 oz. ASW **Subject:** 2,300th anniversary - Buddha's teachings in Sri Lanka **Note:** This is the only coin on which the country name SHRI LANKA appears. Shri Lanka was used only from June 1992 to December 1993, without constitutional authority, by decision of President Premadasa.

Date	Mintage	F	VF	XF	Unc	BU
1993 Proof	30,000	Value: 55.00				

KM# 159 1000 RUPEES Weight: 28.2800 g. **Composition:** 0.9250 Silver .841 oz. ASW **Subject:** 50 years of independence **Obverse:** Flag and denomination in wreath **Reverse:** Lion statue

Date	Mintage	F	VF	XF	Unc	BU
1998 Proof	25,000	Value: 55.00				

KM# 163 1000 RUPEES Weight: 28.2800 g. **Composition:** 0.9250 Silver 8410 oz. ASW **Subject:** 1996 Cricket Champions **Obverse:** Trophy. **Reverse:** Two players. **Edge:** Reeded. **Size:** 38.6 mm. **Note:** Struck at British Royal Mint.

Date	Mintage	F	VF	XF	Unc	BU
1999 Proof	25,000	Value: 45.00				

KM# 165 1000 RUPEES Weight: 28.2800 g. **Composition:** 0.9250 Silver .8410 oz. ASW **Subject:** Central Bank 50 Years **Obverse:** Sun face. **Reverse:** Building. **Edge:** Milled. **Size:** 38.6 mm. **Note:** Struck at British Royal Mint.

Date	Mintage	F	VF	XF	Unc	BU
2000 Proof	10,000	Value: 50.00				

KM# 160 5000 RUPEES Weight: 7.9800 g. **Composition:** 0.9167 Gold .2352 oz. AGW **Subject:** 50 years of independence **Obverse:** Flag and denomination in wreath **Reverse:** Dancer statue

Date	Mintage	F	VF	XF	Unc	BU
1998 Proof	5,000	Value: 235				

PATTERNS

Including off metal strikes

KM#	Date	Mintage	Identification	Mkt Val
Pn1	1971	—	5 Cents. Nickel-Brass Plated Steel. similar to KM#129,with TRIAL in raised letters on obverse	—
Pn2	1971	—	5 Cents. Steel. similar to KM#129, with TRIAL in raised letters on obverse	—
Pn3	1971	—	5 Cents. Aluminum. similar to #KM129, with TRIAL in raised letters on obverse	—
Pn4	1971	—	10 Cents. Nickel-Brass Plated Steel. similar to KM#130, with TRIAL in raised letters on obverse	—
Pn5	1971	—	10 Cents. Steel. similar to KM#130, with TRIAL in raised letters on obverse	—
Pn6	1971	—	10 Cents. Aluminum. similar to KM#130, with TRIAL in raised letters on obverse	—
Pn7	1975	—	5 Cents. Aluminum. KM#139a	—
	1975	—	5 Cents. Aluminum. KM#139a	—
Pn8	1975	—	10 Cents. Aluminum. KM#140a	—
	1975	—	10 Cents. Aluminum. KM#140a	—

PROOF SETS

KM#	Date	Mintage	Identification	Issue Price	Mkt Val
PS1	1978 (8)	20,000	KM135.1, 136.1, 137, 138, 139a, 140a, 141.1, 144	26.00	35.00

STRAITS SETTLEMENTS

Straits Settlements, a former British crown colony situated on e Malay Peninsula of Asia, was formed in 1826 by combining e territories of Singapore, Penang and Malacca. The colony was ministered by the East India Company until its abolition in 1853. raits Settlements was a part of British India from 1858 to 1867 which time it became a Crown Colony. This name was changed Malaya in 1939.

ILERS
itish

INT MARKS
- Heaton, Birmingham
- Soho Mint
- Bombay

ONETARY SYSTEM
0 Cents = 1 Dollar

BRITISH COLONY
1867-1939
STANDARD COINAGE

M# 14 1/4 CENT Composition: Bronze **Obverse:** Head of Queen Victoria left **Edge:** Reeded

ate	Mintage	F	VF	XF	Unc	BU
01	2,000,000	2.00	4.00	20.00	50.00	—

M# 17 1/4 CENT Composition: Bronze **Obverse:** Bust of King Edward VII right

ate	Mintage	F	VF	XF	Unc	BU
04 Proof	—	Value: 500				
Note: Plain edge						
04 Proof	—	Value: 500				
Note: Milled edge						
05	2,008,000	1.25	6.00	15.00	40.00	—
05 Proof	—	Value: 250				
08	1,200,000	1.25	6.00	17.50	45.00	—

M# 27 1/4 CENT Composition: Bronze **Obverse:** Bust of King George V left

ate	Mintage	F	VF	XF	Unc	BU
16	4,000,000	1.00	2.00	4.50	12.00	—
16 Proof	—	Value: 220				

KM# 18 1/2 CENT Composition: Bronze **Obverse:** Bust of King Edward VII right

Date	Mintage	F	VF	XF	Unc	BU
1904 Proof	—	Value: 350				
1908	2,000,000	2.50	5.00	15.00	45.00	—

KM# 28 1/2 CENT Composition: Bronze **Obverse:** Bust of King George V left

Date	Mintage	F	VF	XF	Unc	BU
1916	3,000,000	1.00	2.50	7.50	17.50	—
1916 Proof	—	Value: 300				

KM# 37 1/2 CENT Composition: Bronze **Edge:** Bust of King George V left **Shape:** Square

Date	Mintage	F	VF	XF	Unc	BU
1932	5,000,000	0.75	1.00	3.00	12.50	—
1932 Proof	—	Value: 240				

KM# 16 CENT Composition: Bronze **Obverse:** Bust of Queen Victoria left **Edge:** Reeded

Date	Mintage	F	VF	XF	Unc	BU
1901	15,230,000	1.25	4.00	13.50	42.00	—

KM# 19 CENT Composition: Bronze **Obverse:** Bust of King Edward VII right

Date	Mintage	F	VF	XF	Unc	BU
1903	7,053,000	1.50	4.50	13.50	37.50	—
1903 Proof	—	Value: 200				
1904	6,647,000	1.50	4.50	13.50	37.50	—
1904 Proof	—	Value: 200				
1906	7,504,000	3.50	8.00	22.50	60.00	—
1907	5,015,000	1.00	4.00	15.00	40.00	—
1908	Inc. above	1.00	2.50	10.00	30.00	—
1908 Proof	—	Value: 200				

KM# 32 CENT Composition: Bronze **Obverse:** Bust of King George V left **Shape:** Square

Date	Mintage	F	VF	XF	Unc	BU
1919	20,165,000	0.50	0.75	6.00	20.00	—
1919 Proof	—	Value: 175				
1920	55,000,000	0.50	0.75	3.00	12.50	—
1920 Proof	—	Value: 150				
1926/0	5,000,000	2.00	5.00	10.00	25.00	—
1926	Inc. above	0.50	0.75	7.50	25.00	—

KM# 10 5 CENTS Weight: 1.3600 g. **Composition:** 0.8000 Silver .0349 oz. ASW **Obverse:** Bust of Queen Victoria left

Date	Mintage	F	VF	XF	Unc	BU
1901	3,000,000	1.50	2.50	12.50	45.00	—

KM# 20 5 CENTS Weight: 1.3600 g. **Composition:** 0.8000 Silver .0349 oz. ASW **Obverse:** Bust of King Edward VII right

Date	Mintage	F	VF	XF	Unc	BU
1902	1,920,000	5.00	12.00	50.00	90.00	—
1902 Proof	—	Value: 350				
1903	2,270,000	5.00	12.00	50.00	90.00	—
1903 Proof	—	Value: 350				

KM# 20a 5 CENTS Weight: 1.3600 g. **Composition:** 0.6000 Silver .0262 oz. ASW

Date	Mintage	F	VF	XF	Unc	BU
1910B	13,012,000	1.25	2.25	5.50	12.00	—
1910B Proof	—	Value: 350				

KM# 31 5 CENTS Weight: 1.3600 g. **Composition:** 0.4000 Silver .0174 oz. ASW **Obverse:** Bust of King George V left

Date	Mintage	F	VF	XF	Unc	BU
1918	3,100,000	0.50	1.25	5.00	12.00	—
1919	6,900,000	0.50	1.25	5.00	12.00	—
1920	4,000,000	120	250	600	1,200	—

KM# 34 5 CENTS Composition: Copper-Nickel **Obverse:** Bust of King George V left

Date	Mintage	F	VF	XF	Unc	BU
1920	20,000,000	1.00	12.00	50.00	100	—
1920 Proof	—	Value: 525				

KM# 36 5 CENTS Weight: 1.3600 g. **Composition:** 0.6000 Silver .0262 oz. ASW **Obverse:** Bust of King George V left **Note:** Similar to KM#31, smaller bust, broader rim.

Date	Mintage	F	VF	XF	Unc	BU
1926 Proof	—	Value: 240				
1926	10,000,000	0.50	0.75	4.00	12.00	—
1935	3,000,000	0.50	0.75	4.00	9.00	—
1935 Proof	—	Value: 240				

KM# 11 10 CENTS Weight: 2.7100 g. **Composition:** 0.8000 Silver .0697 oz. ASW

Date	Mintage	F	VF	XF	Unc	BU
1901	2,700,000	1.75	2.75	7.00	25.00	—

KM# 21 10 CENTS Weight: 2.7100 g. **Composition:** 0.8000 Silver .0697 oz. ASW **Obverse:** Bust of King Edward VII right

Date	Mintage	F	VF	XF	Unc	BU
1902	6,118,000	2.50	10.00	25.00	60.00	—
1902 Proof	—	Value: 250				
1903	1,401,000	3.00	12.00	32.50	80.00	—
1903 Proof	—	Value: 250				

KM# 21a 10 CENTS Weight: 2.7100 g. **Composition:** 0.6000 Silver .0522 oz. ASW

Date	Mintage	F	VF	XF	Unc	BU
1909B	11,088,000	5.00	20.00	40.00	90.00	—
1910B	1,657,000	1.00	2.00	3.00	10.00	—
1910B Proof	—	Value: 250				

KM# 29 10 CENTS Weight: 2.7100 g. **Composition:** 0.6000 Silver .0522 oz. ASW **Obverse:** Dot below bust

Date	Mintage	F	VF	XF	Unc	BU
1916	600,000	3.00	7.00	20.00	35.00	—
1917	5,600,000	1.00	2.00	7.00	22.00	—

KM# 29a 10 CENTS Weight: 2.7100 g. **Composition:** 0.4000 Silver .0348 oz. ASW **Obverse:** Cross below bust

Date	Mintage	F	VF	XF	Unc	BU
1918	7,500,000	1.00	2.50	8.00	22.00	—
1919	11,500,000	1.00	2.50	8.00	22.00	—
1920	4,000,000	5.00	15.00	40.00	115	—

KM# 29b 10 CENTS Weight: 2.7100 g. **Composition:** 0.6000 Silver .0522 oz. ASW **Obverse:** Plain field below bust

Date	Mintage	F	VF	XF	Unc	BU
1926	20,000,000	1.00	1.50	5.00	15.00	—
1926 Proof	—	Value: 225				
1927	23,000,000	0.50	0.75	1.00	3.25	—
1927 Proof	—	Value: 225				

KM# 12 20 CENTS Weight: 5.4300 g. **Composition:** 0.8000 Silver .1396 oz. ASW

Date	Mintage	F	VF	XF	Unc	BU
1901	600,000	3.00	4.50	12.50	40.00	—

KM# 22 20 CENTS Weight: 5.4300 g. **Composition:** 0.8000 Silver .1396 oz. ASW **Obverse:** Bust of King Edward VII right

Date	Mintage	F	VF	XF	Unc	BU
1902	1,105,000	6.00	15.00	50.00	120	—
1902 Proof	—	Value: 300				
1903	1,150,000	6.00	15.00	50.00	120	—
1903 Proof	—	Value: 300				

KM# 22a 20 CENTS Weight: 5.4300 g. **Composition:** 0.6000 Silver .1047 oz. ASW

Date	Mintage	F	VF	XF	Unc	BU
1910B	3,276,000	2.00	3.50	10.00	25.00	—
1910B Proof	—	Value: 300				

KM# 30 20 CENTS Weight: 5.4300 g. **Composition:** 0.6000 Silver .1047 oz. ASW **Obverse:** Dot below bust

Date	Mintage	F	VF	XF	Unc	BU
1916B	545,000	4.00	10.00	30.00	70.00	—
1916B Proof	—	Value: 250				
1917B	652,000	2.50	4.50	25.00	55.00	—

KM# 30a 20 CENTS Weight: 5.4300 g. **Composition:** 0.4000 Silver .0698 oz. ASW **Obverse:** Cross below bust

Date	Mintage	F	VF	XF	Unc	BU
1919B	2,500,000	2.50	4.50	12.00	35.00	—
1919B Proof	—	Value: 250				

KM# 30b 20 CENTS Weight: 5.4300 g. **Composition:** 0.6000 Silver .1047 oz. ASW **Obverse:** Plain field below bust

Date	Mintage	F	VF	XF	Unc	BU
1926	2,500,000	1.50	3.00	12.00	35.00	—
1926 Proof	—	Value: 250				
1927	3,000,000	1.50	2.50	6.00	12.00	—
1927 Proof	—	Value: 250				
1935 Round-top 3	1,000,000	1.50	2.50	3.50	7.00	—
1935 Flat-top 3	Inc. above	1.50	2.50	3.50	7.00	—

KM# 13 50 CENTS Weight: 13.5769 g. **Composition:** 0.8000 Silver .3492 oz. ASW

Date	Mintage	F	VF	XF	Unc	BU
1901	120,000	25.00	50.00	120	280	—

KM# 23 50 CENTS Weight: 13.5769 g. **Composition:** 0.8000 Silver .3492 oz. ASW **Obverse:** Bust of King Edward VII right

Date	Mintage	F	VF	XF	Unc	BU
1902	148,000	50.00	80.00	175	280	—
1902 Proof	—	Value: 900				
1903	193,000	50.00	80.00	175	280	—
1903 Proof	—	Value: 900				
1904 Proof	—	Value: 1,000				
1905B Raised	498,000	35.00	65.00	135	260	—
1905B Proof, raised	—	Value: 950				
1905B Incuse	—	Value: 950				

KM# 24 50 CENTS Weight: 10.1000 g. **Composition:** 0.9000 Silver .2922 oz. ASW **Obverse:** Bust of King Edward VII right

Date	Mintage	F	VF	XF	Unc	BU
1907	464,000	5.50	10.00	22.00	60.00	—
1907H	2,667,000	5.50	10.00	22.00	60.00	—
1907H Proof	—	Value: 200				
1908	2,869,000	7.00	12.50	27.50	80.00	—
1908H	Inc. above	7.00	10.00	22.00	60.00	—

Note: Mintage included with 1907H

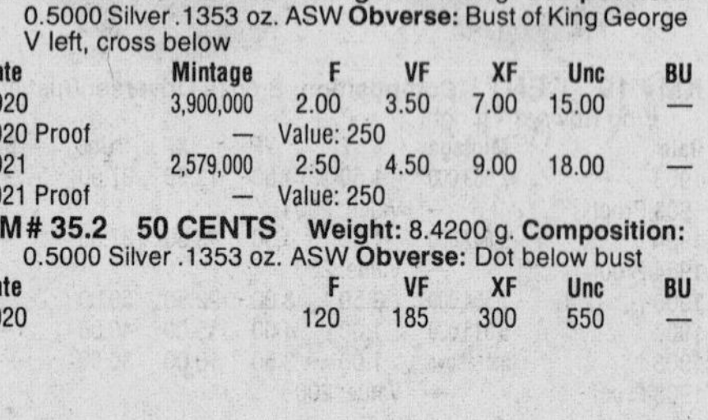

KM# 35.1 50 CENTS Weight: 8.4200 g. **Composition:** 0.5000 Silver .1353 oz. ASW **Obverse:** Bust of King George V left, cross below

Date	Mintage	F	VF	XF	Unc	BU
1920	3,900,000	2.00	3.50	7.00	15.00	—
1920 Proof	—	Value: 250				
1921	2,579,000	2.50	4.50	9.00	18.00	—
1921 Proof	—	Value: 250				

KM# 35.2 50 CENTS Weight: 8.4200 g. **Composition:** 0.5000 Silver .1353 oz. ASW **Obverse:** Dot below bust

Date	F	VF	XF	Unc	BU
1920	120	185	300	550	—

KM# 25 DOLLAR Weight: 26.9500 g. **Composition:** 0.9000 Silver .7799 oz. ASW **Obverse:** Bust of crowned King Edward VII right

Date	Mintage	F	VF	XF	Unc	BU
1903 Proof	—	Value: 1,000				
1903B Incuse	15,010,000	15.00	25.00	50.00	100	—
1903B Raised	Inc. above	70.00	120	250	600	—
1903B Proof, raised	—	Value: 1,100				
1904B	20,365,000	12.50	20.00	35.00	85.00	—
1904B Proof	—	Value: 1,000				

KM# 26 DOLLAR Weight: 20.2100 g. **Composition:** 0.9000 Silver .5848 oz. ASW **Size:** 34.5 mm. **Note:** Reduced size.

Date	Mintage	F	VF	XF	Unc	BU
1907	6,842,000	7.50	10.00	20.00	60.00	—
1907H	4,000,000	7.50	10.00	20.00	60.00	—
1907H Proof	—	Value: 550				
1908	4,152,000	7.50	10.00	20.00	60.00	—
1908 Proof	—	Value: 550				
1909	1,014,000	10.00	15.00	25.00	80.00	—
1909 Proof	—	Value: 550				

KM# 33 DOLLAR Weight: 16.8500 g. **Composition:** 0.5000 Silver .2709 oz. ASW **Obverse:** Bust of crowned King George V left

Date	Mintage	F	VF	XF	Unc	BU
1919	6,000,000	15.00	30.00	90.00	140	—
1919 Proof, restrike	—	Value: 70.00				
1920	8,164,000	10.00	20.00	30.00	65.00	—
1920 Proof, restrike	—	Value: 70.00				
1925	—	450	850	1,250	—	—
1925 Proof	—	Value: 3,500				
1925 Proof, restrike	—	Value: 600				
1926	—	450	850	1,250	—	—
1926 Proof	—	Value: 3,500				
1926 Proof	—	Value: 600				

SUDAN

The Democratic Republic of the Sudan, located in northeast Africa on the Red Sea between Egypt and Ethiopia, has an area of 967,500 sq. mi. (2,505,810 sq. km.) and a population of *24.5 million. Capital: Khartoum. Agriculture and livestock raising are the chief occupations. Cotton, gum arabic and peanuts are exported.

The Sudan, site of the powerful Nubian kingdom of Roman times, was a collection of small independent states from the 14th century until 1820-22 when it was conquered and united by Mohammed Ali, Pasha of Egypt. Egyptian forces were driven from the area during the Mahdist revolt, 1881-98, but the Sudan was retaken by Anglo-Egyptian expeditions, 1896-98, and established as an Anglo-Egyptian condominium in 1899. Britain supplied the administrative apparatus and personnel, but the appearance of joint Anglo-Egyptian administration was continued until Jan. 9, 1954, when the first Sudanese self-government parliament was inaugurated. The Sudan achieved independence on Jan. 1, 1956 with the consent of the British and Egyptian government.

TITLES

جمهورية السودان

umhuriya(t) as-Sudan

الجمهورية السودان
الديمقراطية

-Jumhuriya(t) as-Sudan ad-Dimiqratiya(t)

MINTNAME

ام درمان

ndurman

REPUBLIC

STANDARD COINAGE

KM# 29.1 MILLIM **Composition:** Bronze **Obverse:** Large legend and written denomination **Reverse:** Camel and rider running left

Date	Mintage	F	VF	XF	Unc	BU
1376 (1956)	5,000,000	—	—	0.15	0.30	0.50
1379 (1960)	1,300,000	—	—	0.15	0.35	0.60
1386 (1966) Proof	—	—	—	—	—	—
1387 (1967)	—	—	—	0.15	0.30	0.50
1388 (1968)	—	—	—	0.15	0.30	0.50
1389 (1969)	—	—	—	0.15	0.30	0.50

KM# 29.2 MILLIM **Composition:** Bronze **Obverse:** Small legend and written denomination **Reverse:** Camel and rider running left **Note:** Except for proof sets, mintage figures have generally not been released since 1967.

Date	Mintage	F	VF	XF	Unc	BU
1387 (1967) Proof	7,834	Value: 0.50				
1388 (1968) Proof	5,251	Value: 0.50				
1389 (1969) Proof	2,149	Value: 0.75				

KM# 39 MILLIM **Composition:** Bronze **Obverse:** New Arabic legend **Reverse:** Camel and rider running left

Date	Mintage	F	VF	XF	Unc	BU
AH1390 (1970)	—	—	—	—	—	—
AH1390 (1970) Proof	1,646	Value: 1.00				
AH1391 (1971) Proof	1,772	Value: 1.00				

KM# 30.1 2 MILLIM **Composition:** Bronze **Obverse:** Large written denomination **Reverse:** Camel and rider running left **Shape:** Scalloped

Date	Mintage	F	VF	XF	Unc	BU
AH1376 (1956)	5,000,000	—	—	0.15	0.50	0.65
AH1386 (1966) Proof	—	Value: 1.00				
AH1387 (1967)	—	—	—	0.15	0.50	0.65
AH1388 (1968)	—	—	—	0.15	0.50	0.65
AH1389 (1969)	—	—	—	0.15	0.50	0.65

KM# 30.2 2 MILLIM **Composition:** Bronze **Obverse:** Small written denomination **Reverse:** Camel and rider running left **Shape:** Scalloped

Date	Mintage	F	VF	XF	Unc	BU
AH1387 (1967) Proof	7,834	Value: 0.50				
AH1388 (1968) Proof	5,251	Value: 0.75				
AH1389 (1969) Proof	2,149	Value: 1.00				

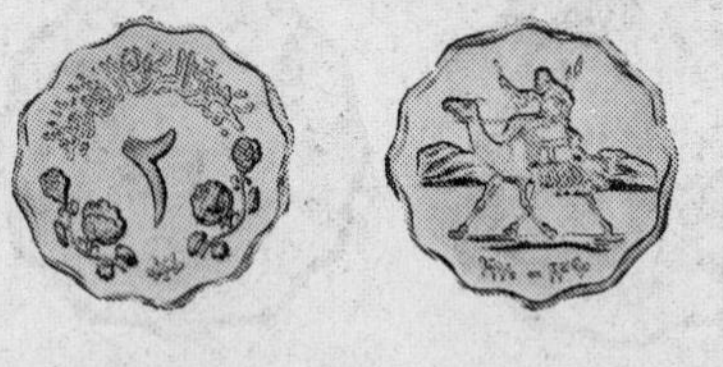

KM# 40 2 MILLIM **Composition:** Bronze **Obverse:** New Arabic legend **Reverse:** Camel and rider running left **Shape:** Scalloped **Note:** Existence of circulation strikes is uncertain.

Date	Mintage	F	VF	XF	Unc	BU
AH1390 (1970) Proof	1,646	Value: 1.25				
AH1391 (1971) Proof	1,772	Value: 1.25				

KM# 31.1 5 MILLIM **Composition:** Bronze **Obverse:** Thin legend and large denomination **Reverse:** Camel and rider running left **Shape:** Scalloped **Note:** Camel and rider size varieties exist.

Date	Mintage	F	VF	XF	Unc	BU
AH1376 (1956)	30,000,000	—	0.10	0.20	0.50	0.75
AH1382 (1962)	6,000,000	—	0.10	0.20	0.50	0.75
AH1386 (1966)	4,000,000	—	0.10	0.15	0.50	0.75
AH1386 (1966) Proof	—	—	—	—	—	—
AH1387 (1967)	4,000,000	—	0.10	0.15	0.35	0.70
AH1388 (1968)	—	—	0.10	0.15	0.35	0.70
AH1389 (1969)	—	—	0.10	0.15	0.35	0.70

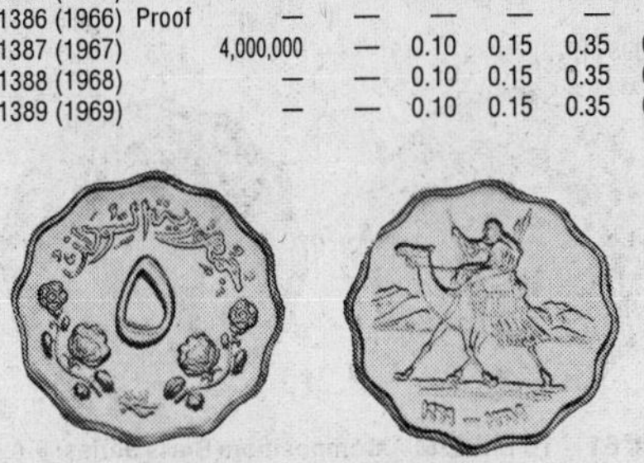

KM# 31.2 5 MILLIM **Composition:** Bronze **Obverse:** Thick legend and small denomination **Reverse:** Camel and rider running left **Shape:** Scalloped

Date	Mintage	F	VF	XF	Unc	BU
AH1387 (1967) Proof	7,834	Value: 0.75				
AH1388 (1968) Proof	5,251	Value: 1.00				
AH1389 (1969) Proof	2,149	Value: 1.25				

KM# 41.1 5 MILLIM **Composition:** Bronze **Obverse:** New large Arabic legend and denomination **Reverse:** Camel and rider running left **Shape:** Scalloped

Date	Mintage	F	VF	XF	Unc	BU
AH1390 (1970)	—	—	0.20	0.45	1.25	—
AH1391 (1971)	3,000,000	—	0.20	0.45	1.25	—

KM# 41.2 5 MILLIM **Composition:** Bronze **Obverse:** Small legend and denomination **Reverse:** Camel and rider running left **Shape:** Scalloped

Date	Mintage	F	VF	XF	Unc	BU
AH1390 (1970) Proof	1,646	Value: 2.00				
AH1391 (1971) Proof	1,772	Value: 2.00				

KM# 47 5 MILLIM **Composition:** Bronze **Subject:** 2nd Anniversary of Revolution **Reverse:** Eagle divides AH and CE dates

Date	Mintage	F	VF	XF	Unc	BU
AH1391 (1971)	500,000	—	0.15	0.25	0.50	—

KM# 53 5 MILLIM **Composition:** Bronze **Series:** F.A.O. **Reverse:** Eagle divides AH and CE dates

Date	Mintage	F	VF	XF	Unc	BU
AH1392 (1972)	6,000,000	—	—	0.15	0.35	—
AH1393 (1973)	9,000,000	—	—	0.15	0.35	—

KM# 54a.1 5 MILLIM **Composition:** Brass **Obverse:** Thick legend and written denomination **Reverse:** Ribbon with 3 equal sections, eagle divides AH and CE dates

Date	Mintage	F	VF	XF	Unc	BU
AH1395 (1972)	4,132,000	—	—	0.20	0.40	—
AH1398 (1978)	—	—	—	0.20	0.40	—

KM# 54 5 MILLIM **Composition:** Bronze **Reverse:** Eagle divides AH and CE dates **Note:** Similar to 10 Millim, KM#55, but round.

Date	F	VF	XF	Unc	BU
AH1392 (1972)	—	—	0.20	0.45	—

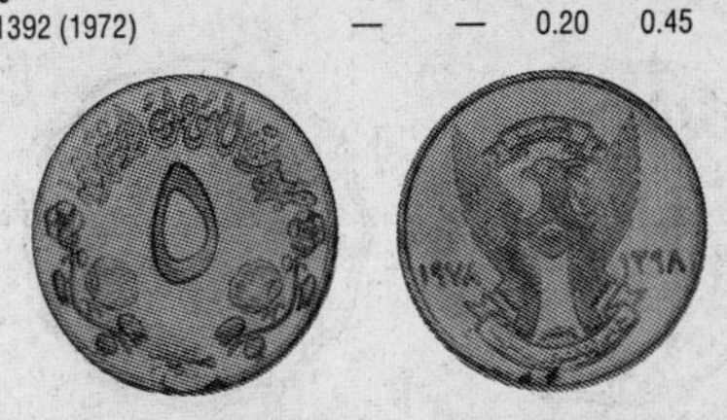

KM# 54a.2 5 MILLIM **Composition:** Brass **Reverse:** Ribbon with long center section, eagle divides AH and CE dates

Date	F	VF	XF	Unc	BU
AH1398 (1972)	—	—	0.20	0.40	—

KM# 54a.3 5 MILLIM **Composition:** Brass **Obverse:** Thin legend and written denomination, different style **Reverse:** Ribbon with 3 equal sections, eagle divides AH and CE dates

Date	F	VF	XF	Unc	BU
AH1400 (1972) Proof	—	Value: 1.00			

KM# 54a.4 5 MILLIM Composition: Brass **Obverse:** Small 5, crude lettering **Reverse:** Large eagle, ribbon with long center section, eagle divides AH and CE dates

Date	F	VF	XF	Unc	BU
AH1403 (1972)	—	—	—	—	—

KM# 60 5 MILLIM Composition: Brass **Series:** F.A.O.

Date	Mintage	F	VF	XF	Unc	BU
AH1396 (1976)	7,868,000	—	—	0.10	0.20	—
AH1398 (1978)	7,000,000	—	—	0.10	0.20	—

KM# 94 5 MILLIM Composition: Brass **Subject:** 20th Anniversary of Independence

Date	F	VF	XF	Unc	BU
AH1396 (1976)	—	0.15	0.20	0.25	—

KM# 32.1 10 MILLIM Composition: Bronze **Obverse:** Large written denomination **Shape:** Scalloped **Note:** Camel and rider size varieties exist.

Date	Mintage	F	VF	XF	Unc	BU
AH1376 (1956)	15,000,000	—	0.15	0.25	0.80	—
AH1380 (1960)	12,250,000	—	0.15	0.20	0.75	—
AH1381 (1962) High date	—	—	0.15	0.20	0.75	—
AH1381 (1962) Low date	—	—	0.15	0.20	0.75	—
AH1386 (1966)	1,000,000	—	0.15	0.25	0.80	—
AH1386 (1966) Proof	—	—	—	—	—	—
AH1387 (1967)	1,000,000	—	0.15	0.20	0.75	—
AH1388 (1968)	—	—	0.15	0.20	0.75	—
AH1389 (1969)	—	—	0.15	0.20	0.75	—

KM# 32.2 10 MILLIM Composition: Bronze **Obverse:** Small written denomination **Reverse:** Camel and rider running left **Shape:** Scalloped

Date	Mintage	F	VF	XF	Unc	BU
AH1387 (1967) Proof	7,834	Value: 1.00				
AH1388 (1968) Proof	5,251	Value: 1.25				
AH1389 (1969) Proof	2,149	Value: 1.50				

KM# 42.1 10 MILLIM Composition: Bronze **Obverse:** New large Arabic legend and written denomination **Reverse:** Camel and rider running left **Shape:** Scalloped

Date	Mintage	F	VF	XF	Unc	BU
AH1390 (1970)	—	—	0.20	0.40	1.00	—
AH1391 (1971)	3,000,000	—	0.20	0.40	1.00	—

KM# 42.2 10 MILLIM Composition: Bronze **Obverse:** Small legend and written denomination **Reverse:** Camel and rider running left **Shape:** Scalloped

Date	Mintage	F	VF	XF	Unc	BU
AH1390 (1970) Proof	1,646	Value: 1.25				
AH1391 (1971) Proof	1,772	Value: 1.25				

KM# 48 10 MILLIM Composition: Bronze **Subject:** 2nd Anniversary of the Revolution

Date	Mintage	F	VF	XF	Unc	BU
AH1391 (1971)	500,000	—	10.00	15.00	25.00	—

KM# 55a.1 10 MILLIM Composition: Brass **Obverse:** Thick legend and written denomination **Reverse:** Ribbon with 3 equal sections **Shape:** Scalloped

Date	Mintage	F	VF	XF	Unc	BU
AH1395 (1972)	12,000,000	—	0.25	0.35	0.75	—
AH1398 (1978)	9,410,000	—	0.25	0.45	1.00	—

KM# 55a.3 10 MILLIM Composition: Brass **Obverse:** Thin legend and written denomination, different style **Reverse:** Ribbon with 3 equal sections, eagle divides AH and AD dates **Shape:** Scalloped

Date	Mintage	F	VF	XF	Unc	BU
AH1400 (1972)	2,490,000	—	0.25	0.45	1.00	—
AH1400 (1980) Proof	—	Value: 2.50				

KM# 55 10 MILLIM Composition: Bronze **Shape:** Scalloped

Date	Mintage	F	VF	XF	Unc	BU
AH1392 (1972)	6,500,000	—	0.15	0.25	0.50	—

KM# 55a.2 10 MILLIM Composition: Brass **Reverse:** Ribbon with long center section, eagle divides AH and AD dates **Shape:** Scalloped

Date	F	VF	XF	Unc	BU
AH1398 (1972)	—	0.75	1.75	4.25	—

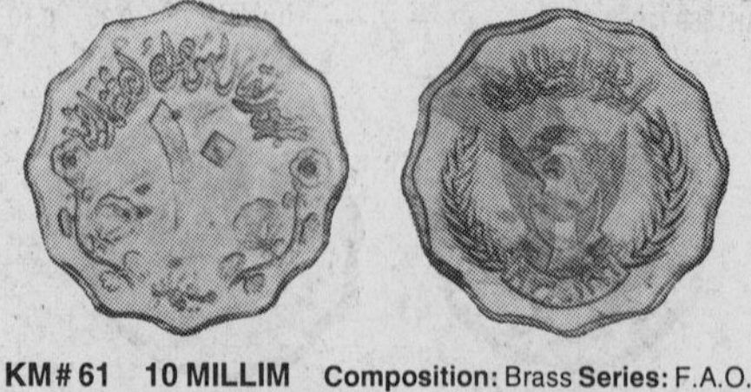

KM# 61 10 MILLIM Composition: Brass **Series:** F.A.O. **Reverse:** Eagle divides AH and AD dates **Shape:** Scalloped

Date	Mintage	F	VF	XF	Unc	BU
AH1396 (1976)	3,000,000	—	0.10	0.15	0.25	—
AH1398 (1978)	—	—	0.10	0.15	0.25	—

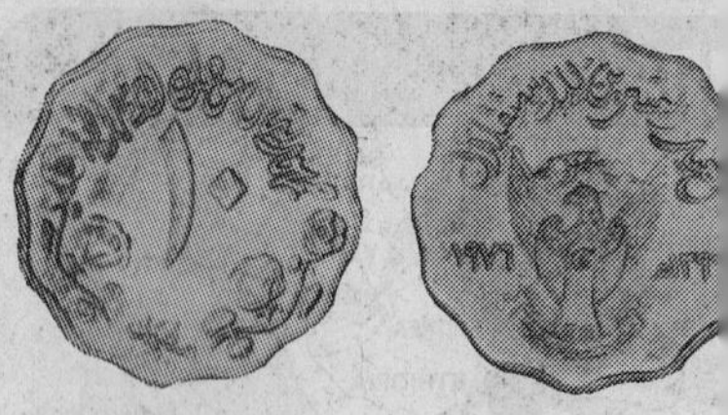

KM# 62 10 MILLIM Composition: Brass **Subject** Anniversary of Independence **Reverse:** Eagle divides and AD dates **Shape:** Scalloped

Date	Mintage	F	VF	XF	Unc
AH1396 (1976)	3,610,000	—	0.10	0.20	0.40

KM# 111 10 MILLIM Composition: Brass **Revers** Ribbon with long center section, eagle divides AH and AD

Date	F	VF	XF	Unc
AH1400 (1980)	—	1.25	3.75	7.50

KM# 97 GHIRSH Composition: Brass **Reverse:** R with 3 equal sections, eagle divides AH and AD dates

Date	Mintage	F	VF	XF	Unc
AH1403 (1983)	1,140,000	—	0.25	0.65	2.00

KM# 99 GHIRSH Composition: Aluminum-Bronze

Date	F	VF	XF	Unc
AH1408 (1987)	—	0.30	0.80	3.00

KM# 33 2 GHIRSH Composition: Copper-Nickel **Reverse:** Camel and rider running left

Date	Mintage	F	VF	XF	Unc
AH1376 (1956)	5,000,000	—	0.15	0.35	0.50
AH1381 (1962)	—	—	0.15	0.35	0.50

KM# 36 2 GHIRSH Composition: Copper-Nickel **Reverse:** Camel and rider running left

Date	Mintage	F	VF	XF	Unc
AH1382 (1963)		—	0.15	0.35	0.75
AH1386 (1966) Proof		—	—	—	—
AH1387 (1967)		—	0.15	0.35	0.75
AH1387 (1967) Proof	7,834	Value: 1.50			
AH1388 (1968)		—	0.15	0.35	0.75
AH1388 (1968) Proof	5,251	Value: 1.50			
AH1389 (1969)		—	0.15	0.35	0.75
AH1389 (1969) Proof	2,149	Value: 1.75			

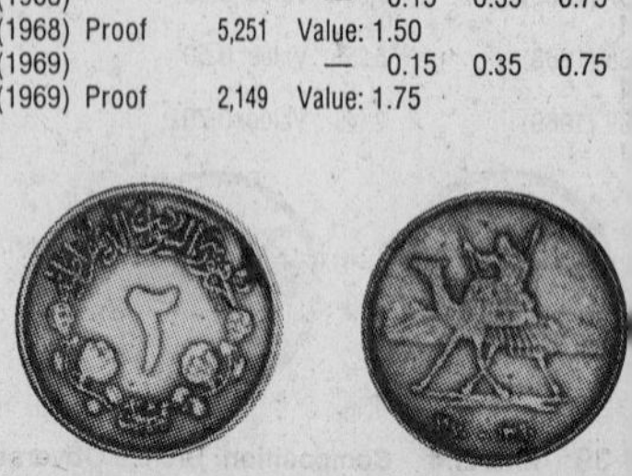

KM# 43.1 2 GHIRSH Composition: Copper-Nickel **Obverse:** New large Arabic legend and written denomination **Reverse:** Camel and rider running left

Date	F	VF	XF	Unc	BU
AH1390 (1970)	—	0.30	0.60	1.25	—

KM# 43.2 2 GHIRSH Composition: Copper-Nickel **Obverse:** Small legend and written denomination **Reverse:** Camel and rider running left

Date	Mintage	F	VF	XF	Unc	BU
AH1390 (1970) Proof	1,646	Value: 1.25				
AH1391 (1971) Proof	1,772	Value: 1.25				

KM# 49 2 GHIRSH Composition: Copper-Nickel **Subject:** 2nd Anniversary of Revolution **Reverse:** Eagle divides AH and AD dates

Date	Mintage	F	VF	XF	Unc	BU
AH1391 (1971)	500,000	—	0.25	0.45	0.80	—

M# 57.1 2 GHIRSH Composition: Copper-Nickel **Obverse:** Thick legend and denomination **Reverse:** Ribbon with 3 equal sections, eagle divides AH and AD dates

ate	Mintage	F	VF	XF	Unc	BU
H1395 (1975)	1,000,000	—	0.20	0.35	0.75	—
H1398 (1978)	1,250,000	—	0.20	0.35	0.75	—

M# 57.2 2 GHIRSH Composition: Copper-Nickel **Reverse:** Ribbon with long center section, eagle divides AH and AD dates

ate	F	VF	XF	Unc	BU
H1398 (1975)	—	0.20	0.35	0.75	—
H1400 (1980)	—	0.20	0.35	0.75	—

M# 57.3 2 GHIRSH Composition: Copper-Nickel **Obverse:** Thin legend and denomination **Reverse:** Ribbon with 3 equal sections, eagle divides AH and AD dates

te	Mintage	F	VF	XF	Unc	BU
1399 (1975)	2,000,000	—	0.20	0.35	0.75	—
1400 (1980)	6,825,000	—	0.20	0.35	0.75	—
1400 (1980) Proof	Inc. above	Value: 2.00				

 # 57.2a 2 GHIRSH Composition: Brass **Obverse:** Legend with different style **Reverse:** Eagle divides AH and AD dates

e	Mintage	F	VF	XF	Unc	BU
403 (1975)	100,000	—	0.75	1.50	3.50	—

 # 63.1 2 GHIRSH Composition: Copper-Nickel **Series:** F.A.O. **Obverse:** Thick denomination **Reverse:** Eagle divides AH and AD dates

e	Mintage	F	VF	XF	Unc	BU
396 (1976)	500,000	—	0.20	0.35	0.75	—
398 (1978)	Inc. above	—	0.20	0.35	0.75	—

KM# 64 2 GHIRSH Composition: Copper-Nickel **Subject:** 20th Anniversary of Independence **Reverse:** Eagle divides AH and AD dates

Date	Mintage	F	VF	XF	Unc	BU
AH1396 (1976)	1,750,000	—	0.20	0.30	0.60	—

KM# 63.2 2 GHIRSH Composition: Copper-Nickel **Series:** F.A.O. **Obverse:** Thin denomination **Reverse:** Eagle divides AH and AD dates

Date	F	VF	XF	Unc	BU
AH1398 (1978)	—	5.00	7.00	10.00	—

KM# 34.1 5 GHIRSH Composition: Copper-Nickel **Obverse:** Large written denomination **Reverse:** Camel and rider running left

Date	Mintage	F	VF	XF	Unc	BU
AH1376 (1956)	40,000,000	—	0.20	0.40	1.00	—
AH1386 (1966) Proof	—	Value: 1.50				
AH1387 (1967)	—	—	0.20	0.30	0.75	—
AH1388 (1968)	—	—	0.20	0.30	0.75	—
AH1389 (1969)	—	—	0.20	0.30	0.75	—

KM# 34.2 5 GHIRSH Composition: Copper-Nickel **Obverse:** Small written denomination **Reverse:** Camel and rider running left

Date	Mintage	F	VF	XF	Unc	BU
AH1387 (1956) Proof	7,834	Value: 1.50				
AH1388 (1968) Proof	5,251	Value: 1.75				
AH1389 (1969) Proof	2,149	Value: 2.50				

KM# 44 5 GHIRSH Composition: Copper-Nickel **Obverse:** New Arabic legend **Reverse:** Camel and rider running left **Note:** Existence of circulation strikes is uncertain.

Date	Mintage	F	VF	XF	Unc	BU
AH1390 (1970) Proof	1,646	Value: 2.50				
AH1391 (1971) Proof	1,772	Value: 2.50				

KM# 51 5 GHIRSH Composition: Copper-Nickel **Subject:** 2nd Anniversary of Revolution **Reverse:** Eagle divides AH and AD dates

Date	Mintage	F	VF	XF	Unc	BU
AH1391 (1971)	500,000	—	0.30	0.60	1.20	—

KM# 58.3 5 GHIRSH Composition: Copper-Nickel **Obverse:** Small legend, different style **Reverse:** Eagle divides AH and AD dates

Date	Mintage	F	VF	XF	Unc	BU
AH1397 (1975)	2,000,000	—	0.25	0.45	0.85	—
AH1398 (1978)	1,000,000	—	0.25	0.45	0.85	—
AH1400 (1980)	1,000,000	—	0.25	0.45	0.85	—
AH1400 (1980) Proof	Inc. above	Value: 3.00				

KM# 58.1 5 GHIRSH Composition: Copper-Nickel **Obverse:** Large legend and denomination **Reverse:** Ribbon with 3 equal sections, eagle divides AH and AD dates

Date	Mintage	F	VF	XF	Unc	BU
AH1395 (1975)	1,600,000	—	0.25	0.45	0.85	—

KM# 58.2 5 GHIRSH Composition: Copper-Nickel **Obverse:** Large legend style change, small denomination **Reverse:** Ribbon with long center section, eagle divides AH and AD dates **Note:** Edge varieties exist.

Date	F	VF	XF	Unc	BU
AH1400 (1975)	—	0.25	0.45	0.85	—

Note: Mintage included with KM#58.1.

KM# 58.4 5 GHIRSH Composition: Copper-Nickel **Obverse:** Large legend and small denomination, style similar to KM#58.1 **Reverse:** Eagle divides AH and AD dates **Note:** Edge varieties exist.

Date	F	VF	XF	Unc	BU
AH1400 (1975)	—	0.25	0.45	0.85	—

Note: Mintage included with KM#58.1.

KM# 65 5 GHIRSH Composition: Copper-Nickel **Series:** F.A.O. **Reverse:** Eagle divides AH and AD dates

Date	Mintage	F	VF	XF	Unc	BU
AH1396 (1976)	500,000	—	0.20	0.30	0.65	—
AH1398 (1978)	—	—	0.20	0.30	0.65	—

KM# 66 5 GHIRSH Composition: Copper-Nickel **Subject:** 20th Anniversary of Independence **Reverse:** Eagle divides AH and AD dates

Date	Mintage	F	VF	XF	Unc	BU
AH1396 (1976)	3,940,000	—	0.25	0.50	1.00	—

KM# 74 5 GHIRSH Composition: Copper-Nickel **Subject:** Council of Arab Economic Unity **Obverse:** Clasped hands **Reverse:** Eagle divides AH and AD dates **Note:** Edge varieties exist.

Date	Mintage	F	VF	XF	Unc	BU
AH1398 (1978)	5,040,000	—	0.15	0.25	0.50	—

KM# 84 5 GHIRSH **Composition:** Copper-Nickel **Series:** F.A.O. **Reverse:** Eagle divides AH and AD dates **Note:** Edge varieties exist.

Date	Mintage	F	VF	XF	Unc	BU
AH1401 (1981)	1,000,000	—	0.20	0.40	0.75	—

KM# 110.1 5 GHIRSH **Composition:** Brass **Obverse:** Large denomination **Reverse:** Ribbon with 3 equal sections, eagle divides AH and AD dates

Date	F	VF	XF	Unc	BU
AH1403 (1983)	—	0.25	0.60	1.55	—

KM# 110.2 5 GHIRSH **Composition:** Brass **Reverse:** Ribbon with long center section, eagle divides AH and AD dates

Date	F	VF	XF	Unc	BU
AH1403 (1983)	—	0.50	1.25	2.25	—

KM# 110.3 5 GHIRSH **Composition:** Brass **Obverse:** Small denomination, legend different style **Reverse:** Eagle divides AH and AD dates

Date	F	VF	XF	Unc	BU
AH1403 (1983)	—	5.00	7.00	10.00	—

KM# 110.4 5 GHIRSH **Composition:** Brass **Obverse:** Large denomination and legend, similar to KM#110.1 **Reverse:** Eagle divides AH and AD dates

Date	F	VF	XF	Unc	BU
AH1403 (1983)	—	1.50	4.50	7.50	—

KM# 100 5 GHIRSH **Composition:** Aluminum-Bronze **Obverse:** Denomination **Reverse:** Central bank building

Date	F	VF	XF	Unc	BU
AH1408 (1987)	—	0.40	1.00	2.00	—

KM# 35.1 10 GHIRSH **Composition:** Copper-Nickel **Obverse:** Large written denomination **Reverse:** Camel and rider running left

Date	Mintage	F	VF	XF	Unc	BU
AH1376 (1956)	15,000,000	—	0.35	0.75	2.00	—
AH1386 (1966) Proof	—	—	—	—	—	—
AH1387 (1967)	—	—	0.30	0.60	1.50	—
AH1388 (1968)	—	—	0.30	0.60	1.50	—
AH1389 (1969)	—	—	0.30	0.60	1.50	—

KM# 35.2 10 GHIRSH **Composition:** Copper-Nickel **Obverse:** Small written denomination **Reverse:** Camel and rider running left

Date	Mintage	F	VF	XF	Unc	BU
AH1387 (1967) Proof	7,834	Value: 2.00				
AH1388 (1968) Proof	5,251	Value: 2.00				
AH1389 (1969) Proof	2,149	Value: 2.25				

KM# 45.1 10 GHIRSH **Composition:** Copper-Nickel **Obverse:** New large Arabic legend and written denomination **Reverse:** Camel and rider running left

Date	Mintage	F	VF	XF	Unc	BU
AH1390 (1970)	—	—	0.60	1.25	2.50	—
AH1391 (1971)	385,000	—	0.60	1.25	2.50	—

KM# 45.2 10 GHIRSH **Composition:** Copper-Nickel **Obverse:** Small legend and written denomination **Reverse:** Camel and rider running left

Date	Mintage	F	VF	XF	Unc	BU
AH1390 (1970) Proof	1,646	Value: 3.00				
AH1391 (1971) Proof	1,772	Value: 3.00				

KM# 52 10 GHIRSH **Composition:** Copper-Nickel **Subject:** 2nd Anniversary of Revolution **Reverse:** Eagle divides AH and AD dates

Date	Mintage	F	VF	XF	Unc	BU
AH1391 (1971)	500,000	—	0.60	1.25	3.00	—

KM# 59.5 10 GHIRSH **Composition:** Copper-Nickel **Obverse:** Thin legend, different style **Reverse:** Eagle divides AH and AD dates

Date	Mintage	F	VF	XF	Unc	BU
AH1397 (1975)	1,000,000	—	0.50	1.00	2.75	—
AH1400 (1980)	2,965,000	—	0.50	1.00	2.75	—
AH1400 (1980) Proof	—	Value: 4.50				

KM# 59.1 10 GHIRSH **Composition:** Copper-Nickel **Obverse:** Thick legend **Reverse:** Ribbon with equal sections, eagle divides AH and AD dates

Date	Mintage	F	VF	XF	Unc	BU
AH1395 (1975)	1,000,000	—	0.50	1.00	2.50	—

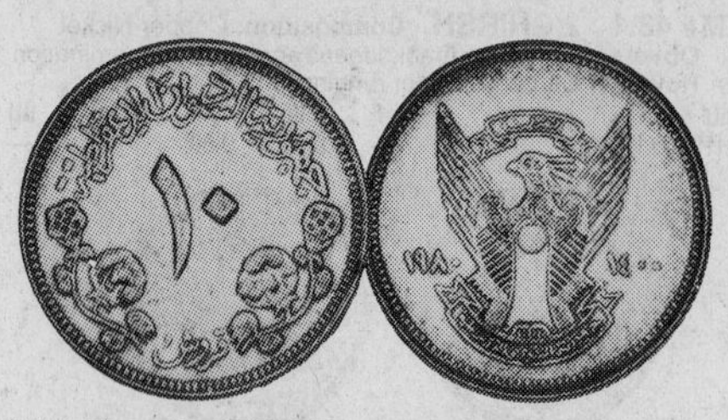

KM# 59.2 10 GHIRSH **Composition:** Copper-Nickel **Reverse:** Ribbon with long center section, eagle divides AH and AD dates **Note:** Edge varieties exist.

Date	F	VF	XF	Unc	BU
AH1400 (1975)	—	0.50	1.00	2.50	—

KM# 59.3 10 GHIRSH **Composition:** Copper-Nickel **Reverse:** Eagle divides AH and AD dates **Note:** Reduced size. Edge varieties exist.

Date	F	VF	XF	Unc	BU
AH1403 (1975)	—	0.50	1.00	2.50	—

KM# 59.4 10 GHIRSH **Composition:** Copper-Nickel **Obverse:** Similar to KM#59.3 **Reverse:** Ribbon with 3 equal sections, eagle divides AH and AD dates

Date	Mintage	F	VF	XF	Unc	BU
AH1403 (1975)	1,100,000	—	7.00	10.00	20.00	—

KM# 67 10 GHIRSH **Composition:** Copper-Nickel **Series:** F.A.O. **Reverse:** Eagle divides AH and AD dates

Date	Mintage	F	VF	XF	Unc	BU
AH1396 (1976)	500,000	—	0.30	0.65	1.50	—
AH1398 (1978)	—	—	0.30	0.65	1.50	—

KM# 68 10 GHIRSH **Composition:** Copper-Nickel **Subject:** 20th Anniversary of Independence **Reverse:** Eagle divides AH and AD dates **Note:** Edge varieties exist.

Date	Mintage	F	VF	XF	Unc
AH1396 (1976)	5,540,000	—	0.25	0.60	1.25

KM# 95 10 GHIRSH **Composition:** Copper-Nickel **Subject:** Council of Arab Economic Unity **Reverse:** Eagle divides AH and AD dates **Note:** Edge varieties exist.

Date	Mintage	F	VF	XF	Unc
AH1398 (1978)	1,000,000	—	0.60	1.25	2.50

 # 85 10 GHIRSH Composition: Copper-Nickel
;eries: F.A.O. **Reverse:** Eagle divides AH and AD dates
lote: Edge varieties exist.

	Mintage	F	VF	XF	Unc	BU
01 (1981)	1,000,000	—	0.60	1.25	2.50	—

 # 107 10 GHIRSH Composition: Aluminum-Bronze
)bverse: Denomination **Reverse:** Central bank building

	F	VF	XF	Unc	BU
08 (1987)	—	0.75	1.50	3.00	—

 # 37 20 GHIRSH Composition: Copper-Nickel
leverse: Camel and rider running left

	Mintage	F	VF	XF	Unc	BU
87 (1967) Proof	7,834	Value: 2.50				
88 (1968) Proof	5,251	Value: 3.00				
89 (1969) Proof	2,149	Value: 6.00				

 # 46 20 GHIRSH Composition: Copper-Nickel
)bverse: New Arabic legend **Reverse:** Camel and rider running left

	Mintage	F	VF	XF	Unc	BU
90 (1970) Proof	1,646	Value: 8.50				
91 (1971) Proof	1,772	Value: 8.50				

 # 98 20 GHIRSH Composition: Copper-Nickel
Reverse: Eagle divides AH and AD dates

	Mintage	F	VF	XF	Unc	BU
03 (1983)	72,000	—	—	—	5.00	—

KM# 96 20 GHIRSH Composition: Copper-Nickel
Series: F.A.O. **Reverse:** Eagle divides AH and AD dates

Date	F	VF	XF	Unc	BU
AH1405 (1985)	—	—	—	3.00	—

KM# 101.1 20 GHIRSH Composition: Aluminum-Bronze **Obverse:** Small denomination **Reverse:** Central bank building

Date	F	VF	XF	Unc	BU
AH1408 (1987)	—	0.60	1.25	2.50	—

KM# 101.2 20 GHIRSH Composition: Aluminum-Bronze **Obverse:** Large denomination

Date	F	VF	XF	Unc	BU
AH1408 (1987)	—	0.60	1.25	2.50	—

KM# 38 25 GHIRSH Composition: Copper-Nickel
Series: F.A.O. **Reverse:** Camel and rider running left

Date	Mintage	F	VF	XF	Unc	BU
AH1388 (1968) Prooflike	224,000	—	—	—	15.00	—

KM# 102 25 GHIRSH Composition: Aluminum-Bronze
Obverse: Denomination **Reverse:** Central bank building
Shape: Square

Date	F	VF	XF	Unc	BU
AH1408 (1987)	—	0.85	1.75	3.50	—

KM# 108 25 GHIRSH Composition: Stainless Steel
Obverse: Denomination **Reverse:** Central bank building

Date	F	VF	XF	Unc	BU
AH1409 (1989)	—	0.50	1.00	2.25	—

KM# 56.1 50 GHIRSH Composition: Copper-Nickel
Series: F.A.O. **Reverse:** Large design

Date	Mintage	F	VF	XF	Unc	BU
AH1392 (1972)	1,000,000	—	1.50	3.00	7.50	—

KM# 56.2 50 GHIRSH Composition: Copper-Nickel
Series: F.A.O. **Reverse:** Small design **Note:** Struck in 1976.

Date	Mintage	F	VF	XF	Unc	BU
AH1392 (1972)	30,000	—	5.00	10.00	20.00	—

KM# 69 50 GHIRSH Composition: Copper-Nickel
Subject: Establishment of Arab Cooperative

Date	F	VF	XF	Unc	BU
AH1396 (1976)	—	1.00	2.25	4.50	—

KM# 73 50 GHIRSH Composition: Copper-Nickel
Subject: 8th Anniversary of 1969 Revolt

Date	Mintage	F	VF	XF	Unc	BU
AH1397 (1977)	100,000	—	1.00	2.25	4.50	—

KM# 103 50 GHIRSH Composition: Aluminum-Bronze
Obverse: Denomination **Reverse:** Central bank building
Shape: Octagonal

Date	F	VF	XF	Unc	BU
AH1408 (1987)	—	0.75	1.75	3.75	—

KM# 105 50 GHIRSH Composition: Aluminum-Bronze
Subject: 33rd Anniversary of Independence **Shape:** Octagonal

Date	F	VF	XF	Unc	BU
AH1409 (1989)	—	0.75	1.75	3.75	—

KM# 109 50 GHIRSH **Composition:** Stainless Steel **Obverse:** Denomination **Reverse:** Central Bank building

Date	F	VF	XF	Unc	BU
AH1409 (1989)	—	0.65	1.25	2.75	—

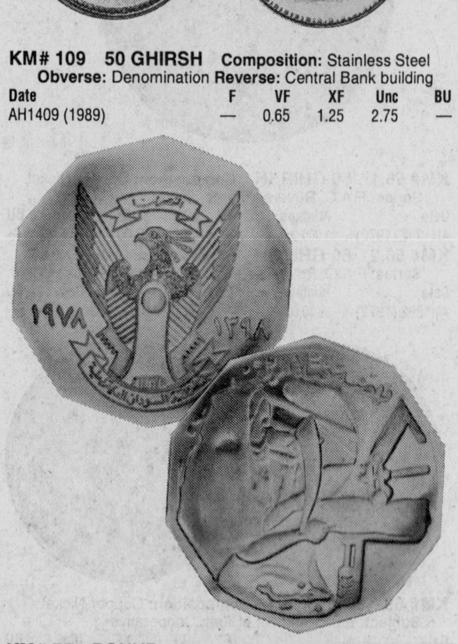

KM# 75 POUND **Composition:** Copper-Nickel **Series:** F.A.O. **Subject:** Rural women **Shape:** 10-sided

Date	Mintage	F	VF	XF	Unc	BU
AH1398 (1978)	456,000	—	2.50	4.00	8.00	—

KM# 104 POUND **Composition:** Aluminum-Bronze **Obverse:** Denomination **Reverse:** Central Bank building

Date	F	VF	XF	Unc	BU
AH1408 (1987)	—	2.00	3.00	7.00	—

KM# 106 POUND **Composition:** Stainless Steel **Obverse:** Denomination **Reverse:** Central Bank building

Date	F	VF	XF	Unc	BU
AH1409 (1989)	—	0.75	1.50	3.75	—

KM# 70 2-1/2 POUNDS **Weight:** 28.2800 g. **Composition:** 0.9250 Silver .841 oz. ASW **Subject:** Conservation **Reverse:** Shoebill stork

Date	Mintage	F	VF	XF	Unc	BU
AH1396 (1976)	5,183	—	—	—	17.50	—
AH1396 (1976) Proof	5,590	Value: 20.00				

KM# 71 5 POUNDS **Weight:** 35.0000 g. **Composition:** 0.9250 Silver 1.0409 oz. ASW **Subject:** Conservation **Reverse:** Hippopotamus with young one

Date	Mintage	F	VF	XF	Unc	BU
AH1396 (1976)	5,087	—	—	—	22.50	—
AH1396 (1976) Proof	5,393	Value: 30.00				

KM# 76 5 POUNDS **Weight:** 17.5000 g. **Composition:** 0.9250 Silver .5205 oz. ASW **Subject:** Khartoum meeting of O.A.U.

Date	Mintage	F	VF	XF	Unc	BU
AH1398 (1978)	21	—	—	—	—	—
AH1398 (1978) Proof	1,423	Value: 22.50				

Note: Without countermarks

Date	Mintage	F	VF	XF	Unc	BU
AH1398 (1978) Proof	2,000	Value: 15.00				

Note: AH1398 with countermarks of B23 in hexagon and bell between dates

KM# 80 5 POUNDS **Weight:** 17.5000 g. **Composition:** 0.9250 Silver .5205 oz. ASW **Subject:** 1,400th Anniversary of Islam

Date	Mintage	F	VF	XF	Unc	BU
AH1400 (1980)	7,500	—	—	—	17.50	—
AH1400 (1980) Proof	5,500	Value: 22.50				

KM# 86 5 POUNDS **Weight:** 28.2800 g. **Composition:** 0.9250 Silver .841 oz. ASW **Subject:** 25th Anniversary of Independence **Shape:** Hexagonal

Date	F	VF	XF	Unc	BU
AH1401 (1981)	—	—	—	40.00	—
AH1401 (1981) Proof 20,000	Value: 50.00				

KM# 87 5 POUNDS **Weight:** 19.4400 g. **Composit** 0.9250 Silver .5781 oz. ASW **Series:** UNICEF, Internat Year of the Child

Date	Mintage	F	VF	XF	Unc
AH1401 (1981) Proof	35,000	Value: 13.50			

KM# 92 5 POUNDS **Weight:** 19.4400 g. **Composit** 0.9250 Silver .5781 oz. ASW **Series:** Decade for Wom

Date	Mintage	F	VF	XF	Unc
AH1404 (1984) Proof	20,000	Value: 22.50			

KM#77 10 POUNDS **Weight:** 35.0000 g. **Composit** 0.9250 Silver 1.0409 oz. ASW **Subject:** Khartoum Mee of O.A.U.

Date	Mintage	F	VF	XF	Unc
AH1398 (1978)	21	—	—	—	—
AH1398 (1978) Proof	1,417	Value: 40.00			

Note: Without countermarks

Date	Mintage	F	VF	XF	Unc
AH1398 (1978) Proof	2,000	Value: 35.00			

Note: AH1398 with countermarks of B23 in hexagon a bell between dates

KM#81 10 POUNDS **Weight:** 35.0000 g. **Compositi** 0.9250 Silver 1.0409 oz. ASW **Subject:** 1,400th Annivers of Islam

Date	Mintage	F	VF	XF	Unc
AH1400 (1980)	3,000	—	—	—	32.50
AH1400 (1980) Proof	2,000	Value: 40.00			

#88 10 POUNDS **Weight:** 28.2800 g. **Composition:** 0.9250 Silver .8411 oz. ASW **Series:** Year of the Disabled Person

	Mintage	F	VF	XF	Unc	BU
401 (1981)		—	—	—	37.50	—
401 (1981) Proof	10,000	Value: 42.50				

#78 25 POUNDS **Weight:** 8.2500 g. **Composition:** 0.9170 Gold .2432 oz. AGW **Subject:** Khartoum Meeting of O.A.U.

	Mintage	F	VF	XF	Unc	BU
398 (1978)	15	—	—	—	600	—
398 (1978) Proof	467	Value: 200				

Note: Without countermarks

	Mintage	F	VF	XF	Unc	BU
398 (1978) Proof	350	Value: 150				

Note: With countermarks of B23 in hexagon and bell between dates

#82 25 POUNDS **Weight:** 8.2500 g. **Composition:** 0.9170 Gold .2432 oz. AGW **Subject:** 1,400th Anniversary of Islam

	Mintage	F	VF	XF	Unc	BU
400 (1980)	7,500	—	—	—	120	—
400 (1980) Proof	5,500	Value: 135				

#79 50 POUNDS **Weight:** 17.5000 g. **Composition:** 0.9170 Gold .5160 oz. AGW **Subject:** Khartoum Meeting of O.A.U.

	Mintage	F	VF	XF	Unc	BU
398 (1978)	11	—	—	—	1,500	—
398 (1978) Proof	211	Value: 300				

Note: Without countermarks

	Mintage	F	VF	XF	Unc	BU
398 (1978) Proof	350	Value: 265				

Note: With countermarks of B23 in hexagon and bell between dates

KM# 83 50 POUNDS **Weight:** 17.5000 g. **Composition:** 0.9170 Gold .5160 oz. AGW **Subject:** 1,400th Anniversary of Islam

Date	Mintage	F	VF	XF	Unc	BU
AH1400 (1979)	3,000	—	—	—	240	—
AH1400 (1979) Proof	2,000	Value: 260				

KM# 89 50 POUNDS **Weight:** 7.9900 g. **Composition:** 0.9170 Gold .2353 oz. AGW **Subject:** 25th Anniversary of Independence

Date	Mintage	F	VF	XF	Unc	BU
AH1401 (1981)		—	—	—	115	—
AH1401 (1981) Proof	5,000	Value: 125				

KM# 72 100 POUNDS **Weight:** 33.4370 g. **Composition:** 0.9000 Gold .9676 oz. AGW **Subject:** Conservation **Reverse:** Scimitar-horned oryx

Date	Mintage	F	VF	XF	Unc	BU
AH1396 (1976)	872	—	—	—	500	—
AH1396 (1976) Proof	251	Value: 725				

KM# 90 100 POUNDS **Weight:** 15.9800 g. **Composition:** 0.9170 Gold .4706 oz. AGW **Subject:** 25th Anniversary of Independence

Date	Mintage	F	VF	XF	Unc	BU
AH1401 (1981)		—	—	—	250	—
AH1401 (1981) Proof	2,500	Value: 275				

KM# 91 100 POUNDS **Weight:** 15.9800 g. **Composition:** 0.9170 Gold .4706 oz. AGW **Series:** Year of the Disabled Person

Date	Mintage	F	VF	XF	Unc	BU
AH1401 (1981)		—	—	—	325	—
AH1401 (1981) Proof	2,000	Value: 425				

KM# 93 100 POUNDS **Weight:** 8.1000 g. **Composition:** 0.9170 Gold .2388 oz. AGW **Series:** Decade for Women

Date	Mintage	F	VF	XF	Unc	BU
AH1404 (1984) Proof	513	Value: 200				

REFORM COINAGE

100 Dirhams = 1 Dinar

10 Pounds = 1 Dinar

KM# 112 DINAR **Composition:** Brass **Obverse:** Denomination **Reverse:** Central Bank building

Date	F	VF	XF	Unc	BU
AH1415 (1994)	—	0.35	0.75	1.50	—

KM# 113 2 DINAR **Composition:** Brass Plated Steel **Obverse:** Denomination **Reverse:** Central Bank building

Date	F	VF	XF	Unc	BU
AH1415 (1994)	—	0.75	1.50	3.00	—

KM# 114 5 DINARS **Composition:** Brass **Obverse:** Denomination **Reverse:** Central Bank building

Date	F	VF	XF	Unc	BU
AH1417 (1996)	—	1.00	2.00	4.50	—

KM# 115.1 10 DINARS **Composition:** Brass **Reverse:** Central bank building, thin inscription below

Date	VG	F	VF	XF	Unc
AH1417	—	—	1.50	3.00	6.50

KM# 115.2 10 DINARS **Composition:** Brass **Reverse:** Central bank building, thick inscription below

Date	VG	F	VF	XF	Unc
AH1417	—	—	1.50	3.00	6.50

KM# 116 20 DINARS **Composition:** Copper-Nickel **Reverse:** Central Bank building

Date	VG	F	VF	XF	Unc
AH1417	—	—	1.75	3.50	7.50

ESSAIS

KM#	Date	Mintage	Identification	Mkt Val
E1	1978	25	5 Pounds. Aluminum.	40.00
E3	1978	25	10 Pounds. Aluminum.	40.00
E5	1978	25	25 Pounds. Aluminum.	40.00
E7	1978	25	50 Pounds. Aluminum.	40.00
E2	1978	15	5 Pounds. Copper.	85.00
E4	1978	21	10 Pounds. Copper. KM77.	125
E6	1978	21	25 Pounds. Copper.	75.00
E8	1978	21	50 Pounds. Copper.	85.00
E9	1979	15	5 Pounds. Copper. KM817.	85.00
E10	1979	40	10 Pounds. Aluminum. KM81.	40.00
E12	1979	21	50 Pounds. Copper. KM83.	85.00
E11	1979	21	10 Pounds. Copper. KM81.	125
E13	1980	25	5 Pounds. Aluminum.	40.00
E15	1980	25	10 Pounds. Aluminum.	40.00
E17	1980	25	25 Pounds. Aluminum.	40.00
E19	1980	25	50 Pounds. Aluminum.	40.00
E14	1980	15	5 Pounds. Copper.	85.00
E18	1980	20	25 Pounds. Copper.	75.00
E20	1980	21	50 Pounds. Copper.	85.00
E16	1980	21	10 Pounds. Copper.	125

PIEFORTS

KM#	Date	Mintage	Identification	Mkt Val
P1	1978	5	5 Pounds. Copper. KM76.	185
P2	1978	10	5 Pounds. 0.9250 Silver. KM76.	—
P3	1978	5	10 Pounds. Copper.	225
P4	1978	10	10 Pounds. 0.9250 Silver. KM77.	—
P5	1978	5	25 Pounds. Copper.	185
P6	1979	5	5 Pounds. Copper. KM80.	185
P7	1979	10	5 Pounds. 0.9250 Silver. KM80.	—
P8	1979	5	10 Pounds. Copper. KM81.	225
P9	1979	10	10 Pounds. 0.9250 Silver. KM81.	—
P10	1979	—	25 Pounds. Brass. KM83.	185

KM#	Date	Mintage	Identification	Mkt Val
P11	1979	10	25 Pounds. Silver. KM83.	185
P12	1979	—	50 Pounds. Copper. KM83. Gold plated.	—
P16	1979	—	50 Pounds. Gold. KM83.	—
P13	1980	5	5 Pounds. Copper.	185
P14	1980	5	10 Pounds. Copper.	225
P15	1980	5	25 Pounds. Copper.	185
P17	1981	2,587	5 Pounds. KM87.	40.00
P18	1981	1,000	10 Pounds. KM88.	75.00
P19	1981	—	100 Pounds. KM91.	1,250

MINT SETS

KM#	Date	Mintage	Identification	Issue Price	Mkt Val
MS1	1976 (2)	—	KM70-71	—	40.00

PROOF SETS

KM#	Date	Mintage	Identification	Issue Price	Mkt Val
PS1	1967 (8)	7,834	KM29-32, 34-37	12.25	7.50
PS2	1968 (8)	5,251	KM29-32, 34-37	15.25	8.00
PS3	1969 (8)	2,149	KM29-32, 34-37	15.25	10.00
PS4	1970 (8)	1,646	KM39-46	15.25	15.00
PS5	1971 (8)	1,772	KM39-46	15.25	15.00
PS8	1980 (5)	—	KM54, 55a, 57-59	12.00	—
PS6	1976 (2)	—	KM70-71	—	50.00
PS7	1978 (4)	—	KM76-79	—	600
PS9	1980 (4)	—	KM80-83	—	535

DARFUR

The province of Darfur makes up most of the western border of the Republic of Sudan. Darfur had been an independent kingdom until taken over by Egypt in 1874.While the British were involved in subduing the eastern Sudan, Ali Dinar established the sultanate of Darfur in1898. His coins copied the Ottoman coins of Egypt. The mint was located at Al Fasher (the capital of the province) and was active from 1909 to 1914.

TITLES

الفشير

al-Fasher

RULERS

Ali Dinar, AH1316-1335/1898-1916AD

KINGDOM

HAMMERED COINAGE

KM# 4 1/2 PIASTRE **Composition:** Billon **Obverse:** Toughra **Note:** Struck at al-Fasher mint.

Date	Good	VG	F	VF	XF
AH1328/8 Rare	—	—	—	—	—

Note: Due to the low denomination and little demand, this coin was only struck for a very short time, though varieties do exist

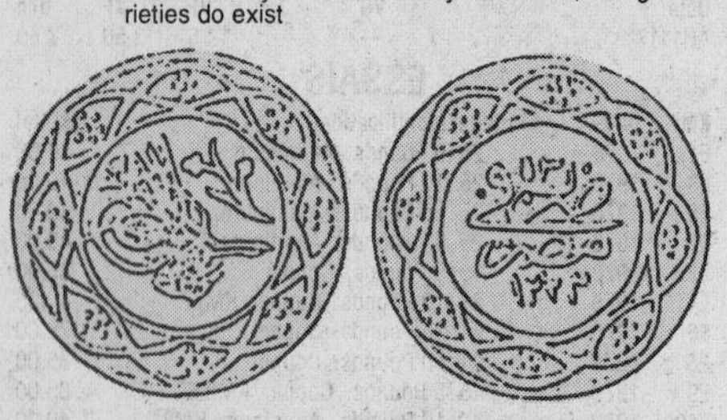

KM# 1 PIASTRE **Composition:** Copper-Nickel-Zinc **Note:** Struck at al-Fasher mint.

Date	Good	VG	F	VF	XF
AH1213 (sic)/13 Rare	—	—	—	—	—
AH1223 (sic)/13 Rare	—	—	—	—	—

Note: Due to a shortage of small change, thin, unmilled imitations of Egyptian Qirsh (Piastre) KM#181, which had been produced outside of Sudan were brought into circulation in Darfur from AH1323-1325/1905-1907AD in agreement with the Sultan

KM# 2 PIASTRE **Composition:** Billon **Obverse:** Toughra **Note:** Struck at al-Fasher mint. Struck from 1908-1914. Most are crudely struck and flan size varies and usually bear the date AH1327, regnal year 71, probably the sultan's approved type. Other year and date couplings may exist. All Hejira years and some regnal years are thought to have been copied from specimens of the Egyptian prototypes.

Date	Good	VG	F	VF	XF
AH1227(sic)/5	—	—	—	—	—
AH1237(sic)/71	—	—	—	—	—
Note: With retrograde 3					
AH1321(sic)/71	—	—	—	—	—
AH1323(sic)/65	—	—	—	—	—
AH1327(sic)/17	30.00	80.00	160	190	—
AH1327(sic)/26	—	—	—	—	—
AH1327(sic)/71	15.00	30.00	45.00	60.00	—
AH1327(sic)/71	—	—	—	—	—
Note: Retrograde 3					
AH1327(sic)/76	—	—	—	—	—
AHx321(sic)/17	—	—	—	—	—
AH1387(sic)/17	—	—	—	—	—
AH7132(sic)/x	—	—	—	—	—

KM# 5 5 PIASTRES (1/4 Rial) **Composition:** Copper-Nickel-Zinc **Obverse:** Toughra **Note:** Struck at al-Fasher mint.

Date	Good	VG	F	VF	XF
AH1328 Rare	—	—	—	—	—

Note: Copied from Ottoman Mejidiye coinage; about 800 are reported having been put into circulation; further striking was discontinued as the coin was unpopular due to low silver content and uncommon denomination

COUNTERMARKED COINAGE

KM# 3 PIASTRE **Composition:** Copper-Nickel-Zinc **Countermark:** "Ali" 1312 **Note:** Countermark on KM#1.

CM Date	Host Date	Good	VG	F	VF	XF
AH	AH1213/13 Rare	—	—	—	—	—
AH	AH1223/13 Rare	—	—	—	—	—

Note: In a move to control import and circulation of KM#1, the Sultan ordered the countermarking; AH1312 is probably an error for AH1316/1898AD, the year of Ali Dinar's accession

SURINAME

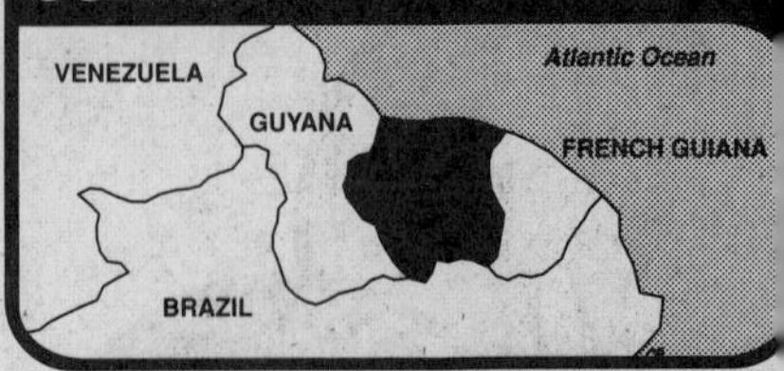

The Republic of Suriname also known as Dutch Guia located on the north central coast of South America between G ana and French Guiana has an area of 63,037 sq. mi. (163,2 sq. km.) and a population of *433,000.Capital: Paramaribo. T country is rich in minerals and forests, and self-sufficient in ri the staple food crop. The mining, processing and exporting bauxite is the principal economic activity.

Lieutenants of Amerigo Vespucci sighted the Guiana co in 1499. Spanish explorers of the 16th century, disappointed finding no gold, departed leaving the area to be settled by the E ish in 1652. The colony prospered and the Netherlands acqui it in 1667 in exchange for the Dutch rights in Nieuw Nederla (state of New York). During the European wars of the 18th a 19th centuries, which were fought in part in the new world, S name was occupied by the British from 1781-1784 and 17 1814.Suriname became an autonomous part of the Kingdom the Netherlands on Dec. 15, 1954. Full independence w achieved on Nov. 25, 1975. In 1980, a coup installed a milit government, which has since been dissolved.

RULERS

Dutch, until 1975

MINT MARKS

(B) - British Royal Mint, no mint mark
FM - Franklin Mint, U.S.A.**
P - Philadelphia, U.S.A.
S - Sydney
(u) - Utrecht (privy marks only)

**NOTE: From 1975-1985 the Franklin Mint produced co age in up to 3 different qualities. Qualities of issue are designa in ( ) after each date and are defined as follows:

(M) MATTE - Normal circulation strike or a dull finish p duced by sandblasting special uncirculated (polish finish) or pr quality dies.

(U) SPECIAL UNCIRCULATED - Polished or prooflike appearance without any frosted features.

(P) PROOF - The highest quality obtainable having mirr like fields and frosted features.

MONETARY SYSTEM

100 Cents = 1 Gulden (Guilders)

DUTCH ADMINISTRATION

WORLD WAR II COINAGE

The 1942-1943 issues that follow are homela coinage types of the Netherlands. KM#152, KM#1 and KM#164 were executed expressly for use in Su name. Related issues produced for use in Curacao a Suriname are listed under Curacao. They are disti guished by a palm tree (acorn on homeland issue and a mint mark (P-Philadelphia, D-Denver, S-S Francisco) flanking the date. See the Netherlands f similar issues. See Curacao for similar coins date 1941-P, 1942-P and 1943-P.

KM# 10 CENT **Weight:** 2.5000 g. **Composition:** Brass **Obverse:** Lion **Reverse:** Orange wreath

Date	Mintage	F	VF	XF	Unc
1943P Palm	4,000,000	1.75	3.50	7.00	14.00

KM# 10a CENT **Weight:** 2.5000 g. **Composition:** Bronze **Obverse:** Lion **Reverse:** Orange wreath

Date	Mintage	F	VF	XF	Unc
1957(u)	1,200,000	—	0.85	1.75	3.75
1957(u) Proof	—	Value: 28.00			
1959(u)	1,800,000	—	0.85	1.75	3.75
1959(u) Proof	—	Value: 28.00			
1960(u)	1,200,000	—	0.85	1.75	3.75
1960(u) Proof	—	Value: 28.00			

9 10 CENTS **Weight:** 1.4000 g. **Composition:** .6400 Silver .0288 oz. ASW **Obverse:** Queen Wilhelmina **Obv. Legend:** Orange wreath

Date	Mintage	F	VF	XF	Unc	BU
Palm	1,500,000	3.00	6.00	12.00	25.00	—

REPUBLIC

MODERN COINAGE

 # 11 CENT **Weight:** 2.5000 g. **Composition:** Bronze **Obverse:** Arms **Reverse:** Geometric design

Date	Mintage	F	VF	XF	Unc	BU
(u) Fish	6,000,000	—	0.25	0.50	1.00	—
(u) S Proof	650	Value: 28.00				
(u)	6,500,000	—	0.25	0.50	1.00	—
(u) Proof	—	Value: 42.00				
(u) Cock	5,000,000	—	0.25	0.50	1.00	—
(u)	6,000,000	—	0.25	0.50	1.00	—

 # 11a CENT **Composition:** Aluminum **Obverse:** Arms **Reverse:** Geometric design

Date	Mintage	F	VF	XF	Unc	BU
Proof	—	Value: 450				
(u)		—	0.10	0.25	0.45	—
(u)		—	0.10	0.25	0.45	—
(u)		—	0.10	0.25	0.45	—
Proof	Est. 10	Value: 55.00				
(u)		—	—	0.25	0.45	—
(u)		—	—	0.25	0.45	—
(u)		—	—	0.25	0.45	—
(u)		—	—	0.25	0.45	—

Note: Cock and star privy marks.

Date	Mintage	F	VF	XF	Unc	BU
(u) Anvil		—	—	0.25	0.45	—
		—	—	0.25	0.45	—
		—	—	0.25	0.45	—
		—	—	0.25	0.45	—

 # 11b CENT **Composition:** Copper Plated Steel **Obverse:** Arms **Reverse:** Geometric design

Date	Mintage	F	VF	XF	Unc	BU
(B)		—	—	—	0.45	—
(B) Proof	Est. 1,500	Value: 2.00				
(B)		—	—	—	0.45	—

 # 12.1 5 CENTS **Weight:** 4.0000 g. **Composition:** Nickel-Brass **Obverse:** Arms **Reverse:** Geometric design

Date	Mintage	F	VF	XF	Unc	BU
2(u) Fish	2,200,000	—	0.50	1.00	2.00	—
2(u) S Proof	650	Value: 20.00				
6(u)	2,300,000	—	0.50	1.00	2.00	—

Note: With mint mark and mintmaster's mark

Date	Mintage	F	VF	XF	Unc	BU
6(u) Proof	—	Value: 50.00				
6(u)	400,000	—	1.50	3.00	6.00	—

Note: Without mint mark and mint master's mark.

Date	Mintage	F	VF	XF	Unc	BU
(u) Cock	500,000	—	1.50	3.00	6.00	—
2(u)	1,500,000	—	0.50	1.00	2.00	—

 # 12.1a 5 CENTS **Composition:** Aluminum **Obverse:** Arms **Reverse:** Geometric design

Date	Mintage	F	VF	XF	Unc	BU
6(u) Proof	—	Value: 450				
6(u)		—	0.10	0.20	0.50	—
6 Proof	Est. 10	Value: 75.00				
8(u)		—	0.10	0.20	0.50	—
9(u)		—	0.10	0.20	0.50	—
0(u)		—	0.10	0.20	0.50	—

Note: Cock and star privy marks.

Date	Mintage	F	VF	XF	Unc	BU
2(u) Anvil		—	0.10	0.20	0.50	—
5(u)		—	0.10	0.20	0.50	—
6(u)		—	0.10	0.20	0.50	—

 # 12.1b 5 CENTS **Composition:** Copper Plated Steel **Obverse:** Arms **Reverse:** Geometric design

Date	Mintage	F	VF	XF	Unc	BU
7(B)		—	—	0.20	0.50	—
8(B)		—	—	0.20	0.50	—
8(B) Proof	Est. 1,500	Value: 2.00				
9(B)		—	—	0.20	0.50	—

 # 12.2 5 CENTS **Weight:** 4.0000 g. **Composition:** Nickel-Brass **Obverse:** Arms **Reverse:** Geometric design **Note:** Medal turn.

Date	F	VF	XF	Unc	BU
6(u)	—	6.25	12.50	25.00	30.00

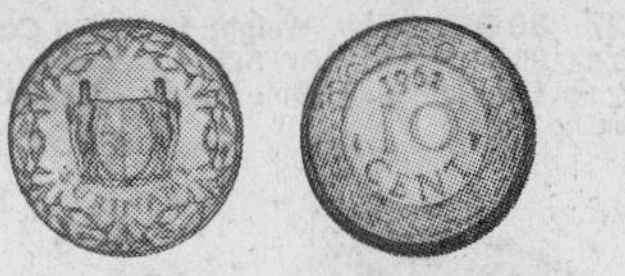

KM# 13 10 CENTS **Weight:** 2.0000 g. **Composition:** Copper-Nickel **Obverse:** Arms **Reverse:** Geometric design

Date	Mintage	F	VF	XF	Unc	BU
1962(u) Fish		—	0.25	0.50	1.00	—
1962(u) S Proof	650	Value: 20.00				
1966(u)		—	0.25	0.50	1.00	—
1966(u) Proof	—	Value: 50.00				
1971(u) Cock		0.40	0.80	1.75	3.00	—
1972(u)		—	0.25	0.50	1.00	—
1974(u)		—	0.25	0.50	1.00	—
1976(u)		—	0.10	0.25	0.50	—
1976 Proof	Est. 10	Value: 100				
1978(u)		—	0.10	0.25	0.50	—
1979(u)		—	0.10	0.25	0.50	—
1982(u) Anvil		—	0.10	0.25	0.50	—
1985(u)		—	0.10	0.25	0.50	—
1986(u)		—	0.10	0.25	0.50	—

KM# 13a 10 CENTS **Composition:** Nickel Plated Steel **Obverse:** Arms **Reverse:** Geometric design

Date	Mintage	F	VF	XF	Unc	BU
1987(B)		—	0.15	0.25	0.50	—
1988(B) Proof	Est. 1,500	Value: 3.00				
1989(B)		—	0.15	0.25	0.50	—

KM# 14 25 CENTS **Weight:** 3.5000 g. **Composition:** Copper-Nickel **Obverse:** Arms **Reverse:** Geometric design

Date	Mintage	F	VF	XF	Unc	BU
1962(u) Fish		0.25	0.30	0.50	1.00	—
1962(u) S Proof	650	Value: 20.00				
1966(u)		0.25	0.30	0.50	1.00	—
1966(u) Proof	—	Value: 50.00				
1972(u) Cock		0.25	0.30	0.50	1.00	—
1974(u)		0.30	0.30	0.50	1.00	—
1976(u)		0.20	0.30	0.50	1.00	—
1976 Proof	Est. 10	Value: 125				
1979(u)		0.20	0.30	0.50	1.00	—
1982(u) Anvil		0.20	0.30	0.50	1.00	—
1985(u)		0.20	0.35	0.65	1.25	—
1986(u)		0.20	0.35	0.65	1.25	—

KM# 14a 25 CENTS **Composition:** Nickel Plated Steel **Obverse:** Arms **Reverse:** Geometric design

Date	Mintage	F	VF	XF	Unc	BU
1987(B)		0.20	0.30	0.60	1.20	—
1988(B)		0.20	0.30	0.60	1.20	—
1988(B) Proof	Est. 1,500	Value: 5.00				

Note: Never officially released to circulation.

Date	Mintage	F	VF	XF	Unc	BU
1989(B)		0.20	0.30	0.60	1.20	—

KM# 23 100 CENTS **Composition:** Copper-Nickel **Obverse:** Arms **Reverse:** Geometric design

Date	Mintage	F	VF	XF	Unc	BU
1987(B)		—	0.50	0.85	2.00	—
1988(B)		—	0.50	0.85	2.00	—
1988(B) Proof	Est. 1,500	Value: 12.00				

Note: Never officially released to circulation.

Date	Mintage	F	VF	XF	Unc	BU
1989(B)		—	0.50	0.85	2.00	—

KM# 24 250 CENTS **Composition:** Copper-Nickel **Obverse:** Arms **Reverse:** Geometric design

Date	Mintage	F	VF	XF	Unc	BU
1987(B)		—	0.75	1.50	3.00	—
1988(B)		—	0.75	1.50	3.00	—
1988(B) Proof	Est. 1,500	Value: 17.50				

Date	Mintage	F	VF	XF	Unc	BU

Note: Never officially released to circulation.

Date	Mintage	F	VF	XF	Unc	BU
1989(B)		—	0.75	1.50	3.00	—

KM# 15 GULDEN **Weight:** 10.0000 g. **Composition:** 0.7200 Silver .2315 oz. ASW **Obverse:** Queen Juliana **Reverse:** Arms

Date	Mintage	F	VF	XF	Unc	BU
1962(u)		—	2.50	5.00	10.00	—
1962(u) S Proof	650	Value: 40.00				
1966(u)		—	—	—	120	—

Note: Never officially released to circulation.

Date	Mintage	F	VF	XF	Unc	BU
1966(u) Proof	—	Value: 150				

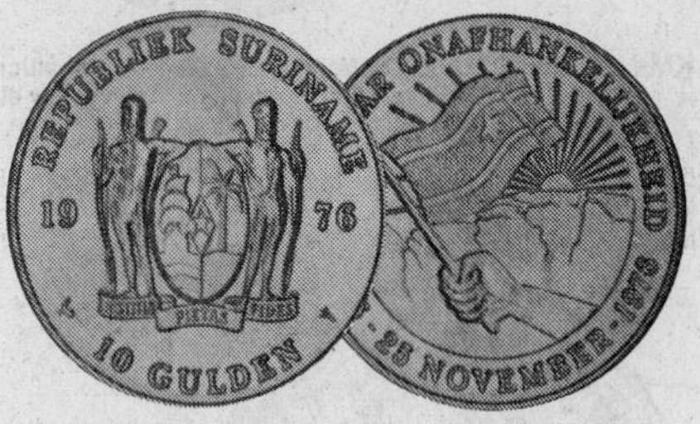

KM# 16 10 GULDEN **Weight:** 15.9500 g. **Composition:** 0.9250 Silver .4743 oz. ASW **Subject:** 1st Anniversary of Independence **Obverse:** Flag, Surinam map, rising sun **Reverse:** Arms

Date	Mintage	F	VF	XF	Unc	BU
1976(u)	100,000	—	—	—	10.00	—
1976(u) Proof	5,711	Value: 13.50				

KM# 17 25 GULDEN **Weight:** 26.2000 g. **Composition:** 0.9250 Silver .779 oz. ASW **Subject:** 1st Anniversary of Independence **Obverse:** Flag, Surinam map, rising sun **Reverse:** Arms

Date	Mintage	F	VF	XF	Unc	BU
1976(u)	75,000	—	—	—	15.00	—
1976(u) F Proof	5,503	Value: 20.00				

KM# 19 25 GULDEN **Weight:** 15.5000 g. **Composition:** 0.9250 Silver .461 oz. ASW **Subject:** 1st Anniversary of Independence **Obverse:** Revolution monument **Reverse:** Allegorical group of revolutionaries

Date	Mintage	F	VF	XF	Unc	BU
1981FM (U)	10,000	—	—	—	28.00	—
1981FM (P)	800	Value: 70.00				

KM# 21 25 GULDEN **Weight:** 25.1000 g. **Composition:** 0.9250 Silver .7435 oz. ASW **Subject:** 5th Anniversary of Revolution **Obverse:** Peace dove, flag superimposed on Surinam map **Reverse:** Fist with 5, star

Date	Mintage	F	VF	XF	Unc	BU
ND(1985)(u)	4,800	—	—	—	55.00	—
ND(1985)(u) Proof	200	Value: 90.00				

KM# 32 25 GUILDER **Weight:** 28.2800 g. **Composition:** 0.9250 Silver .8411 oz. ASW **Subject:** World Cup soccer **Obverse:** Arms **Reverse:** Player, stadium, half-globe

Date	Mintage	F	VF	XF	Unc	BU
1990(B) Proof	50,000	Value: 22.50				

KM# 36 25 GUILDER **Weight:** 28.2800 g. **Composition:** 0.9250 Silver .8411 oz. ASW **Series:** Save the Children **Obverse:** Arms **Reverse:** Children

Date	Mintage	F	VF	XF	Unc	BU
1991(B) Proof	30,000	Value: 37.50				

KM# 27 30 GULDEN **Weight:** 14.3000 g. **Composition:** 0.9250 Silver .425 oz. ASW **Subject:** 30th Anniversary of Central Bank **Obverse:** Arms **Reverse:** Central Bank building

Date	Mintage	F	VF	XF	Unc	BU
1987(u)	7,000	—	—	—	35.00	45.00

KM# 28 50 GUILDER **Weight:** 28.2800 g. **Composition:** 0.9250 Silver .8411 oz. ASW **Series:** Seoul Olympics **Subject:** Swimming **Obverse:** Arms **Reverse:** Swimmer Antony Nesty

Date	Mintage	F	VF	XF	Unc	BU
1988(B) Proof	Est. 25,000	Value: 30.00				

KM# 30 50 GUILDER **Weight:** 28.2800 g. **Composition:** 0.9250 Silver .8411 oz. ASW **Subject:** 35th Anniversary of the Suriname Bank **Obverse:** Arms **Reverse:** Geometric design

Date	Mintage	F	VF	XF	Unc	BU
ND(1990)(B) Proof	Est. 7,500	Value: 40.00				

KM# 34 50 GUILDER **Weight:** 26.0000 g. **Composition:** 0.9250 Silver .7733 oz. ASW **Subject:** 15th Anniversary of Independence **Obverse:** Arms **Reverse:** Floral design **Note:** Similar to 500 Guilders, KM#35.

Date	Mintage	F	VF	XF	Unc	BU
ND(1990)(B) Proof	Est. 5,000	Value: 35.00				

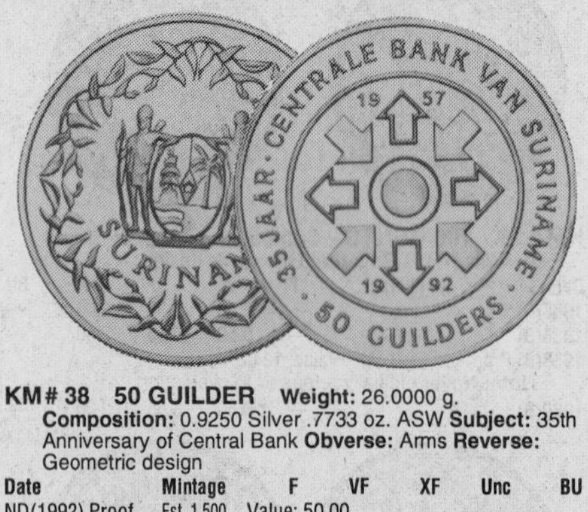

KM# 38 50 GUILDER **Weight:** 26.0000 g. **Composition:** 0.9250 Silver .7733 oz. ASW **Subject:** 35th Anniversary of Central Bank **Obverse:** Arms **Reverse:** Geometric design

Date	Mintage	F	VF	XF	Unc	BU
ND(1992) Proof	Est. 1,500	Value: 50.00				

KM# 18 100 GULDEN **Weight:** 6.7200 g. **Composition:** 0.9000 Gold .1945 oz. AGW **Subject:** 1st Anniversary of Independence **Obverse:** Arms **Reverse:** Flag, Surinam map, rising sun **Note:** Uncirculated pieces struck in "rose" gold have been reported. They are valued at $150-$200.

Date	Mintage	F	VF	XF	Unc	BU
1976(u)	20,000	—	—	—	80.00	
1976(u) Proof	4,749	Value: 90.00				

KM# 40 100 GUILDER **Weight:** 20.0000 g. **Composition:** 0.9990 Silver .642 oz. ASW **Series:** Barcel Olympics **Subject:** Basketball **Obverse:** Arms **Reverse** Basketball players **Note:** Struck at Nova Mint, Barcelona

Date	Mintage	F	VF	XF	Unc
1992 Proof	Est. 15,000	Value: 27.50			

KM# 41 100 GUILDER **Weight:** 20.0000 g. **Composition:** 0.9990 Silver .642 oz. ASW **Series:** Barcelona Olympics **Subject:** Cyclists **Obverse:** Arms **Reverse:** 3 Cyclists **Note:** Struck at Nova Mint, Barcelo

Date	Mintage	F	VF	XF	Unc
1992 Proof	Est. 15,000	Value: 28.50			

KM# 42.1 100 GUILDER **Weight:** 20.0000 g. **Composition:** 0.9990 Silver .642 oz. ASW **Series:** Barcel Olympics **Obverse:** Arms **Reverse:** Swimmer Antony Ne **Note:** Struck at Kaapstad (Capetown, South Africa).

Date	Mintage	F	VF	XF	Unc
ND(1992) Proof	2,500	Value: 50.00			

KM# 42.2 100 GUILDER **Weight:** 20.0000 g. **Compositi** 0.9990 Silver **Series:** Barcelona Olympics **Obverse:** Ar **Reverse:** Swimmer Antony Nesty, "200 M" above swimr **Note:** Struck at Kaapstad (Capetown, South Africa).

Date	F	VF	XF	Unc
ND(1992) Proof	—	Value: 65.00		

1# 43.1 100 GUILDER Weight: 19.7000 g. **Composition:** 0.9990 Silver .642 oz. ASW **Subject:** World Cup soccer **Obverse:** Arms **Reverse:** 2 soccer players, "999 E.P." at right

e		F	VF	XF	Unc	BU
1994) Proof	—	Value: 45.00				

1# 43.2 100 GUILDER Weight: 19.7000 g. **Composition:** 0.9990 Silver .6330 oz. ASW **Subject:** World Cup soccer **Obverse:** Arms **Reverse:** 2 soccer players, "999 E.P." at left

e		F	VF	XF	Unc	BU
(1994) Proof	—	Value: 50.00				

1# 44 100 GUILDER Weight: 20.0000 g. **Composition:** 0.9990 Silver .6430 oz. ASW **Subject:** World Cup soccer **Obverse:** Arms **Reverse:** Soccer player in stadium, Brazil winner **Note:** Struck at Capetown.

e		F	VF	XF	Unc	BU
(1994) Proof	—	Value: 37.50				

M# 46 100 GUILDER Composition: Copper-Nickel **Obverse:** Arms **Reverse:** 1956 Ford Thunderbird

te	Mintage	F	VF	XF	Unc	BU
96 Proof	500	Value: 50.00				

M# 47 100 GUILDER Composition: Copper-Nickel **Obverse:** Arms **Reverse:** 1957 Ford Thunderbird

te	Mintage	F	VF	XF	Unc	BU
96 Proof	500	Value: 50.00				

KM# 49 100 GUILDER Composition: Copper-Nickel **Series:** Olympics **Obverse:** Arms **Reverse:** Discus thrower

Date		F	VF	XF	Unc	BU
1996 Proof	—	Value: 125				

KM# 20 200 GULDEN Weight: 7.1200 g. **Composition:** 0.5000 Gold .1144 oz. AGW **Subject:** 1st Anniversary of Revolution **Obverse:** Revolution Monument **Reverse:** Player, stadium, half-globe

Date	Mintage	F	VF	XF	Unc	BU
1981FM (U)	11,000	—	—	—	100	—
1981FM (P) Proof	1,363	Value: 175				

KM# 22 250 GUILDER Weight: 6.7200 g. **Composition:** 0.9000 Gold .1945 oz. AGW **Subject:** 5th anniversary of revolution **Obverse:** Dove and 10 on map-shaped flag **Reverse:** Stylized fist on star design **Note:** Similar to 25 Gulden, KM#13.

Date	Mintage	F	VF	XF	Unc	BU
1985(u)	5,000	—	—	—	135	—
1985(u) Proof	200	Value: 225				

KM# 33 250 GUILDER Weight: 7.9800 g. **Composition:** 0.9170 Gold .2353 oz. AGW **Subject:** World Cup soccer **Obverse:** Arms **Reverse:** Player, stadium, half-globe

Date	Mintage	F	VF	XF	Unc	BU
1990(B) Proof	1,000	Value: 200				

KM# 37 250 GUILDER Weight: 7.9800 g. **Composition:** 0.9170 Gold .2353 oz. AGW **Series:** Save the Children **Obverse:** Arms **Reverse:** Children

Date	Mintage	F	VF	XF	Unc	BU
1991 Proof	3,000	Value: 160				
1992	—	—	—	—	125	—

KM# 25 500 GUILDER Weight: 7.9800 g. **Composition:** 0.9170 Gold .2353 oz. AGW **Subject:** 43rd general assembly, Military Sports Organization CISM **Obverse:** Arms **Reverse:** Globe, laurel wreath, rings and sword

Date	Mintage	F	VF	XF	Unc	BU
ND(1988)(B) Proof	2,500	Value: 220				

KM# 29 500 GUILDER Weight: 7.9800 g. **Composition:** 0.9170 Gold .2353 oz. AGW **Series:** Seoul Olympics **Subject:** Swimming **Obverse:** Arms **Reverse:** Swimmer Antony Nesty

Date	Mintage	F	VF	XF	Unc	BU
1988(B) Proof	Est. 2,000	Value: 220				

KM# 31 500 GUILDER Weight: 7.9800 g. **Composition:** 0.9170 Gold .2353 oz. AGW **Subject:** 125th Anniversary - Suriname Bank **Obverse:** Arms **Reverse:** Abstract design **Note:** Similar to 50 Guilders, KM#22.

Date	Mintage	F	VF	XF	Unc	BU
1990(B) Proof	Est. 2,000	Value: 275				

KM# 35 500 GUILDER Weight: 7.9800 g. **Composition:** 0.9170 Gold .2353 oz. AGW **Subject:** 15th anniversary of independence **Obverse:** Arms **Reverse:** Floral design

Date	Mintage	F	VF	XF	Unc	BU
ND(1990)(B) Proof	Est. 1,250	Value: 300				

KM# 39 500 GUILDER Weight: 7.9800 g. **Composition:** 0.9170 Gold .2353 oz. AGW **Subject:** 35th anniversary of central bank **Obverse:** Arms **Reverse:** Symetric arrow design and dates within circle and legend **Note:** Similar to 50 Guilders, KM#30.

Date	Mintage	F	VF	XF	Unc	BU
1992(B) Proof	Est. 300	Value: 300				

KM# 26 1000 GUILDER Weight: 15.9800 g. **Composition:** 0.9170 Gold .4708 oz. AGW **Subject:** 43rd anniversary - Military Sports Organization CISM **Obverse:** Arms **Reverse:** Globe, laurel wreath, rings and sword **Note:** Similar to 500 Guilders, KM#25.

Date	Mintage	F	VF	XF	Unc	BU
ND(1988)(B) Proof	1,250	Value: 400				

KM# 48 1000 GUILDER Weight: 4.8000 g. **Composition:** Gold Plated Brass .4708 oz. **Series:** Olympics **Obverse:** Arms **Reverse:** 3 Cyclists **Edge:** Plain **Note:** Similar to 100 Guilders, KM#41. Struck at Capetown.

Date	F	VF	XF	Unc	BU
1992	—	—	—	—	—

KM# 48a 1000 GUILDER Weight: 7.9800 g. **Composition:** 0.9160 Gold .2355 oz. AGW **Series:** Olympics **Obverse:** Arms **Reverse:** 3 Cyclists **Edge:** Reeded **Note:** Similar to 100 Guilders, KM#41. Struck at Capetown.

Date	Mintage	F	VF	XF	Unc	BU
1992 Proof	400	Value: 250				

KM# 50 12500 GULDEN Weight: 28.2800 g. **Composition:** 0.9250 Silver .8410 oz. ASW **Subject:** Hindu immigration **Obverse:** Arms **Reverse:** Hindu couple with ship in background

Date	Mintage	F	VF	XF	Unc	BU
ND(1999) Proof	Est. 1,000	Value: 70.00				

KM# 51 50000 GULDEN Weight: 7.9800 g. **Composition:** 0.9170 Gold .2353 oz. AGW **Subject:** Hindu immigration **Obverse:** Arms **Reverse:** Hindu couple with ship in background **Note:** Similar to 12,500 Gulden, KM#50.

Date	Mintage	F	VF	XF	Unc	BU
ND(1999) Proof	Est. 1,000	Value: 270				

KM# 53 75000 GULDEN Weight: 7.9800 g. **Composition:** 0.9170 Gold .2353 oz. AGW **Subject:** Coppename Bridge

Date	Mintage	F	VF	XF	Unc	BU
1999 Proof	—	Value: 700				

PATTERNS

Including off metal strikes

KM#	Date	Mintage	Identification	Mkt Val
Pn1	1962	—	Gulden. Bronze. KM#15. Nickel coated.	—
Pn2	ND(1994)	—	100 Guilder. Copper-Nickel. KM#44.	40.00
Pn3	ND(1994)	—	100 Guilder. Silver. KM#44.	—

TRIAL COINAGE

KM#	Date	Mintage	Identification	Mkt Val
TS1	1984	—	10 Guilders. Silver.	—

PROOF SETS

KM#	Date	Mintage	Identification	Issue Price	Mkt Val
PS1	1962 (5)	650	KM11-15	—	130
PS2	1966 (5)	—	KM11-15	—	250
PS3	1976 (4)	10	KM11a, 12.1a, 13, 14	—	300
PS4	1976 (3)	—	KM16-18	145	120
PS5	1976 (2)	—	KM16-17	50.00	50.00
PS6	1988 (6)	1,500	KM11b, 12.1b, 13a, 14a, 23, 24	42.00	50.00

SWAZILAND

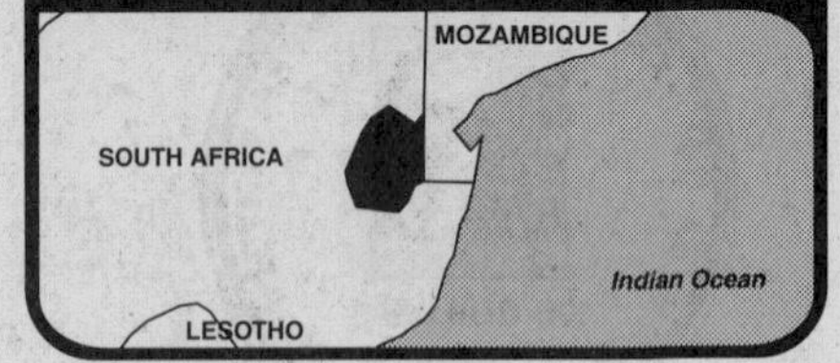

The Kingdom of Swaziland, located in southeastern Africa, has an area of 6,704 sq. mi. (17,360 sq. km.) and a population of *756,000. Capital: Mbabane (administrative); Lobamba (legislative). The diversified economy includes mining, agriculture, and light industry. Asbestos, iron ore, wood pulp, and sugar are exported.

The people of the present Swazi nation established themselves in an area including what is now Swaziland in the early 1800s. The first Swazi contact with the British came early in the reign of the extremely able Swazi leader Mswati when he asked the British for aid against Zulu raids into Swaziland. The British and Transvaal responded by guaranteeing the independence of Swaziland, 1881. South Africa assumed the power of protection and administration in 1894 and Swaziland continued under this administration until the conquest of the Transvaal during the Anglo-Boer War, when administration was transferred to the British government. After World War II, Britain began to prepare Swaziland for independence, which was achieved on Sept. 6, 1968. The Kingdom is a member of the Commonwealth of Nations. King Mswati III is Head of State. The prime minister is Head of Government.

RULERS

Sobhuza II, 1968-1982
Queen Dzeliwe, Regent for Prince Makhosetive, 1982-1986
King Msawati III, 1986-

MONETARY SYSTEM

100 Cents = 1 Luhlanga
25 Luhlanga = 1 Lilangeni
(plural - Emalangeni)

KINGDOM

STANDARD COINAGE

100 Cents = 1 Luhlanga; 25 Luhlanga = 1 Lilangeni

KM# 1 5 CENTS Weight: 2.7500 g. **Composition:** 0.8000 Silver .0707 oz. ASW **Subject:** Independence commemorative

Date	Mintage	F	VF	XF	Unc	BU
1968 Proof	10,000	Value: 5.00				

KM# 2 10 CENTS Weight: 4.3800 g. **Composition:** 0.8000 Silver .1126 oz. ASW **Subject:** Independence commemorative

Date	Mintage	F	VF	XF	Unc	BU
1968 Proof	10,000	Value: 7.00				

KM# 3 20 CENTS Weight: 6.6300 g. **Composition:** 0.8000 Silver .1705 oz. ASW **Subject:** Independence commemorative

Date	Mintage	F	VF	XF	Unc	BU
1968 Proof	10,000	Value: 8.00				

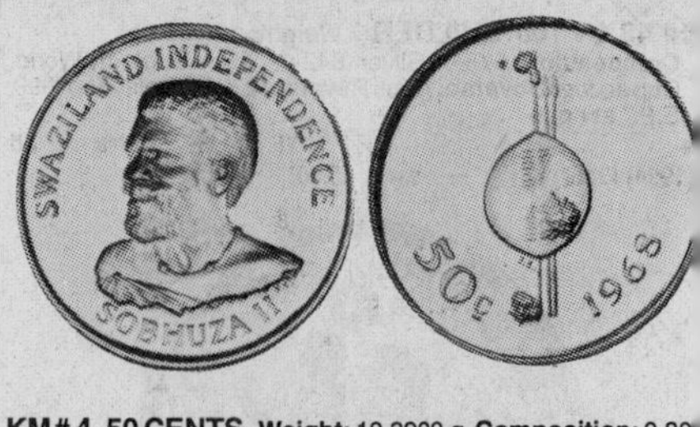

KM# 4 50 CENTS Weight: 10.3900 g. **Composition:** 0.80 Silver .2672 oz. ASW **Subject:** Independence commemorat

Date	Mintage	F	VF	XF	Unc
1968 Proof	10,000	Value: 9.00			

KM# 5 LUHLANGA Weight: 15.0000 g. **Compositio** 0.8000 Silver .3858 oz. ASW **Subject:** Independence commemorative

Date		VG	F	VF	XF	U
1968 Proof	10,000	Value: 12.00				

KM# 6 LILANGENI Weight: 33.9305 g. **Compositio** 0.9170 Gold 1 oz. AGW **Subject:** Independence commemorative **Note:** Approximately 1,450 melted.

Date	Mintage	F	VF	XF	Unc
1968 Proof	2,000	Value: 550			

DECIMAL COINAGE

100 Cents = 1 Lilangeni (plural emelangeni)

KM# 7 CENT **Composition:** Bronze **Subject:** Ananas

Date	Mintage	F	VF	XF	Unc
1974	6,002,000	—	—	0.10	0.20
1974 Proof	13,000	Value: 0.75			
1979	500,000	—	—	0.10	0.25
1979 Proof	10,000	Value: 0.75			
1982	—	—	—	0.10	0.25
1983	1,100,000	—	—	0.10	0.25

KM# 21 CENT **Composition:** Bronze **Series:** F.A.O.

Date	Mintage	F	VF	XF	Unc
1975	2,500,000	—	—	0.10	0.25

KM# 39 CENT **Composition:** Copper Plated Steel

Date	Mintage	F	VF	XF	Unc
1986	2,000,000	—	—	0.10	0.25
1987	10,000,000	—	—	0.10	0.25

KM# 39a CENT **Composition:** Bronze

Date	F	VF	XF	Unc
1986	—	—	—	—

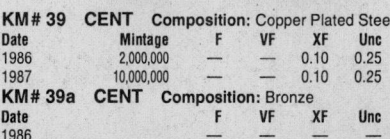

 # 51 CENT **Composition:** Bronze **Obverse:** King's bust **Reverse:** Pineapple

	F	VF	XF	Unc	BU
	—	—	—	0.25	—

 # 8 2 CENTS **Composition:** Bronze

	Mintage	F	VF	XF	Unc	BU
4	2,252,000	—	—	0.15	0.30	—
4 Proof	13,000	Value: 0.75				
9	1,000,000	—	—	0.15	0.30	—
9 Proof	10,000	Value: 1.00				
2	500,000	—	—	0.15	0.30	—

 # 22 2 CENTS **Composition:** Bronze **Series:** F.A.O.

	Mintage	F	VF	XF	Unc	BU
5	1,500,000	—	—	0.15	0.30	—

 # 9 5 CENTS **Composition:** Copper-Nickel **Reverse:** Arum lily

	Mintage	F	VF	XF	Unc	BU
4	1,252,000	—	0.10	0.20	0.40	—
4 Proof	13,000	Value: 1.00				
5	1,500,000	—	0.10	0.20	0.40	—
9	1,680,000	—	0.10	0.20	0.40	—
9 Proof	10,000	Value: 1.75				

 # 40.1 5 CENTS **Composition:** Copper-Nickel **Reverse:** Arum lily

	F	VF	XF	Unc	BU
6	—	0.15	0.25	0.50	—

 # 40.2 5 CENTS **Composition:** Nickel Plated Steel **Reverse:** Arum lily

	F	VF	XF	Unc	BU
2	—	0.15	0.25	0.50	—

 # 48 5 CENTS **Composition:** Nickel Plated Steel **Obverse:** King Msawati III

e	F	VF	XF	Unc	BU
5	—	—	—	0.50	—
6	—	—	—	0.50	—
8	—	—	—	0.50	—

KM# 10 10 CENTS **Composition:** Copper-Nickel **Reverse:** Sugar cane

Date	Mintage	F	VF	XF	Unc	BU
1974	752,000	—	0.15	0.25	0.50	—
1974 Proof	13,000	Value: 1.00				
1979	500,000	—	0.15	0.25	0.50	—
1979 Proof	4,231	Value: 2.50				

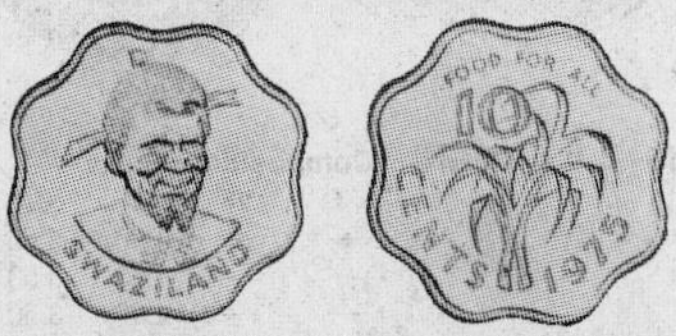

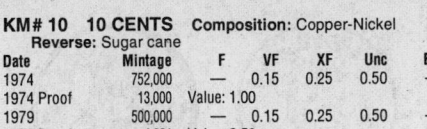

KM# 23 10 CENTS **Composition:** Copper-Nickel **Series:** F.A.O. **Reverse:** Sugar cane

Date	Mintage	F	VF	XF	Unc	BU
1975	1,500,000	—	0.15	0.25	0.50	—

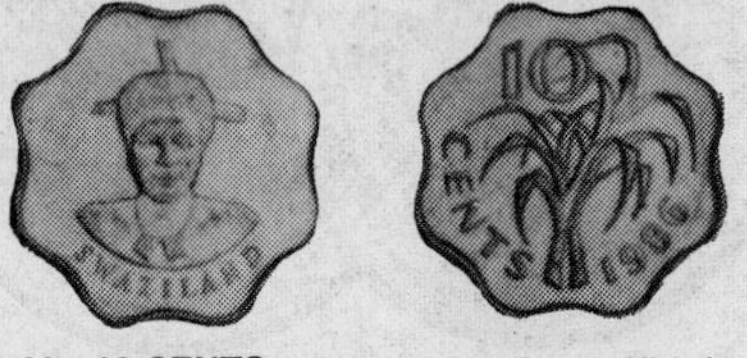

KM# 41 10 CENTS **Composition:** Copper-Nickel **Reverse:** Sugar cane

Date	F	VF	XF	Unc	BU
1986	—	0.15	0.25	0.50	—
1992	—	0.15	0.25	0.50	—

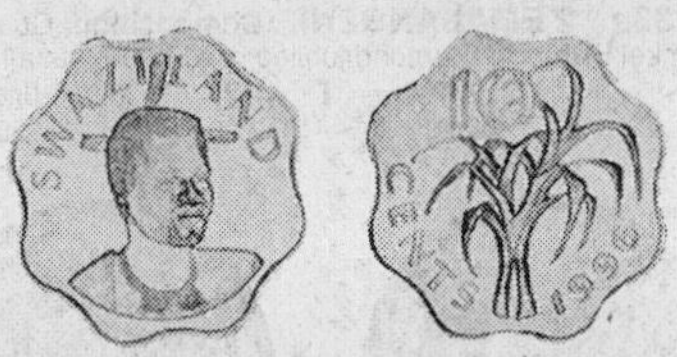

KM# 49 10 CENTS **Composition:** Copper-Nickel **Obverse:** King Msawati III **Reverse:** Sugar cane

Date	F	VF	XF	Unc	BU
1995	—	—	—	0.50	—
1996	—	—	—	0.50	—
1998	—	—	—	0.50	—

KM# 11 20 CENTS **Composition:** Copper-Nickel

Date	Mintage	F	VF	XF	Unc	BU
1974	502,000	—	0.35	0.75	2.00	—
1974 Proof	13,000	Value: 3.00				
1975	1,000,000	—	0.35	0.75	2.00	—
1979	—	—	0.35	0.75	2.00	—
1979 Proof	—	Value: 4.00				

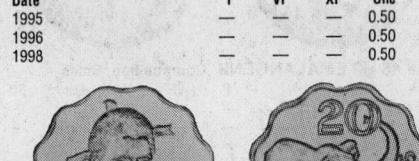

KM# 31 20 CENTS **Composition:** Copper-Nickel **Series:** F.A.O.

Date	Mintage	F	VF	XF	Unc	BU
1981	150,000	—	0.40	0.80	1.75	—

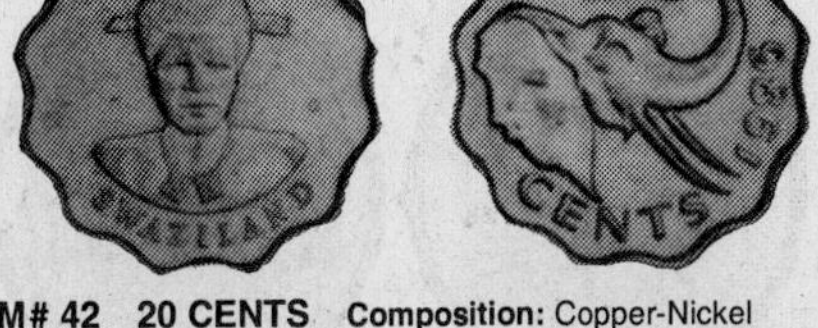

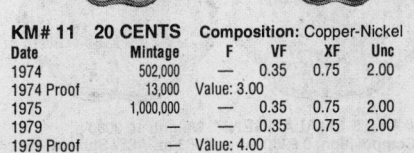

KM# 42 20 CENTS **Composition:** Copper-Nickel

Date	F	VF	XF	Unc	BU
1986	—	0.40	0.80	2.50	—

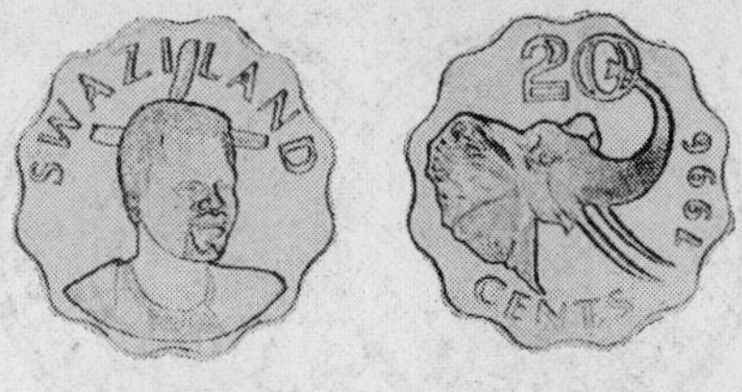

KM# 50 20 CENTS **Composition:** Copper-Nickel **Obverse:** King Msawati III

Date	F	VF	XF	Unc	BU
1996	—	0.40	0.80	2.50	—
1998	—	0.40	0.80	2.50	—

KM# 12 50 CENTS **Composition:** Copper-Nickel

Date	Mintage	F	VF	XF	Unc	BU
1974	252,000	—	1.00	1.50	2.75	—
1974 Proof	13,000	Value: 3.00				
1975	500,000	—	1.00	1.50	2.75	—
1979	—	—	0.50	1.00	2.50	—
1979 Proof	10,000	Value: 5.00				
1981	1,150,000	—	0.50	1.00	2.50	—

KM# 43 50 CENTS **Composition:** Copper-Nickel

Date	Mintage	F	VF	XF	Unc	BU
1986	1,000,000	—	0.50	1.50	3.50	—
1993	—	—	0.50	1.50	3.50	—

KM# 52 50 CENTS **Composition:** Copper-Nickel **Obverse:** King Msawati III

Date	F	VF	XF	Unc	BU
1996	—	—	—	3.75	—
1998	—	—	—	3.75	—

KM# 13 LILANGENI **Composition:** Copper-Nickel

Date	Mintage	F	VF	XF	Unc	BU
1974	127,000	—	1.50	2.50	4.50	—
1974 Proof	13,000	Value: 6.00				
1979	—	—	1.00	2.00	4.50	—
1979 Proof	110,000	Value: 7.50				

KM# 24 LILANGENI **Composition:** Copper-Nickel **Series:** F.A.O., International Women's Year

Date	Mintage	F	VF	XF	Unc	BU
1975	100,000	—	1.50	2.75	6.50	—

KM# 28 LILANGENI **Composition:** Copper-Nickel **Series:** F.A.O.

Date	Mintage	F	VF	XF	Unc	BU
1976	100,000	—	1.50	2.75	6.50	—

KM# 29.1 LILANGENI **Weight:** 15.5500 g. **Composition:** 0.9990 Gold .5 oz. AGW **Subject:** 80th Anniversary - Birth of King Sobhuza II **Reverse:** Dates 1921-1979 above arms

Date	Mintage	F	VF	XF	Unc	BU
ND(1979)	1,250	—	—	—	250	—
ND(1979) Proof	Inc. above	Value: 275				

KM# 29.2 LILANGENI **Weight:** 15.5500 g. **Composition:** 0.9990 Gold .5 oz. AGW **Subject:** 80th anniversary - birth of King Sobhuza II **Reverse:** Dates 1923-1979 above arms

Date	F	VF	XF	Unc	BU
ND(1979)	—	—	—	300	—

KM# 32 LILANGENI **Composition:** Copper-Nickel **Series:** F.A.O.

Date	Mintage	F	VF	XF	Unc	BU
1981	871,000	—	1.50	3.00	7.00	—

KM# 32a LILANGENI **Weight:** 11.6600 g. **Composition:** 0.9250 Silver .3468 oz. ASW

Date	Mintage	F	VF	XF	Unc	BU
1981	5,000	—	—	—	22.50	—
1981 Proof	5,000	Value: 32.50				

KM# 44.1 LILANGENI **Composition:** Nickel-Brass

Date	Mintage	F	VF	XF	Unc	BU
1986	1,025,000	—	—	2.00	4.00	—

KM# 44.2 LILANGENI **Composition:** Nickel-Brass Plated Steel

Date	F	VF	XF	Unc	BU
1992	—	—	1.50	3.50	—

KM# 45 LILANGENI **Composition:** Brass

Date	F	VF	XF	Unc	BU
1995	—	—	1.50	3.50	—
1996	—	—	1.50	3.50	—
1998	—	—	1.50	3.50	—

KM# 33 2 EMALANGENI **Weight:** 17.0000 g. **Composition:** 0.9250 Silver .5056 oz. ASW **Subject:** Diamond jubilee of King Sobhuza II

Date	F	VF	XF	Unc	BU
1981 Proof	—	Value: 32.50			

KM# 33a 2 EMALANGENI **Composition:** Copper-Nickel **Subject:** Diamond jubilee of King Sobhuza II

Date	Mintage	F	VF	XF	Unc	BU
1981	50,000	—	2.00	3.50	7.50	—

KM# 46 2 EMALANGENI **Composition:** Brass

Date	F	VF	XF	Unc	BU
1995	—	—	—	3.75	—
1996	—	—	—	3.75	—

KM# 14 5 EMALANGENI **Weight:** 10.3000 g. **Composition:** 0.9250 Silver .3063 oz. ASW **Subject:** 75th anniversary - birth of King Sobhuza II

Date	F	VF	XF	Unc	BU
1974 Proof	—	Value: 50.00			

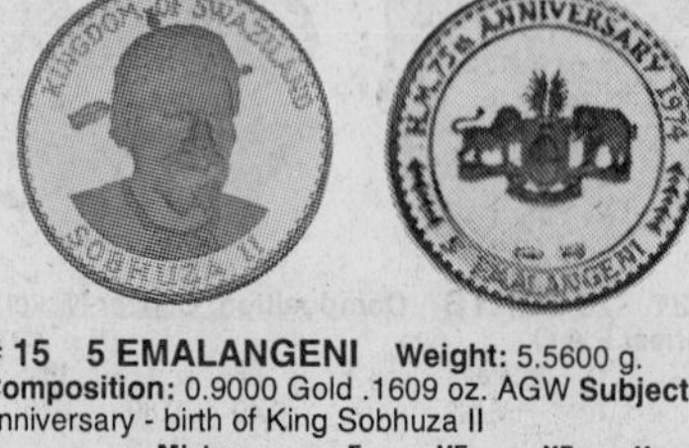

KM# 15 5 EMALANGENI **Weight:** 5.5600 g. **Composition:** 0.9000 Gold .1609 oz. AGW **Subject:** 75th anniversary - birth of King Sobhuza II

Date	Mintage	F	VF	XF	Unc	BU
1974 Proof	60,000	Value: 85.00				

KM# 47 5 EMALANGENI **Composition:** Brass

Date	F	VF	XF	Unc
1996	—	—	—	6.00
1998	—	—	—	6.00

KM# 53 5 EMALANGENI **Composition:** Brass **Subject:** Central bank's 25th anniversary **Obverse:** Kir portrait **Reverse:** Bank seal

Date	F	VF	XF	Unc
ND(1999)	—	—	—	5.50

KM# 16 7-1/2 EMALANGENI **Weight:** 16.2000 g. **Composition:** 0.9250 Silver .4818 oz. ASW **Subject:** 7 anniversary - birth of King Sobhuza II

Date	F	VF	XF	Unc
1974 Proof	—	Value: 65.00		

KM# 17 10 EMALANGENI **Weight:** 11.1200 g. **Composition:** 0.9000 Gold .3218 oz. AGW **Subject:** 75 anniversary - birth of King Sobhuza II

Date	Mintage	F	VF	XF	Unc
1974 Proof	Est. 40,000	Value: 250			

KM# 25 10 EMALANGENI **Weight:** 25.5000 g. **Composition:** 0.9250 Silver .7584 oz. ASW **Subject:** 7 anniversary - birth of King Sobhuza II

Date	Mintage	F	VF	XF	Unc
1975	—	—	—	—	40.00
1975 Proof	Est. 1,500	Value: 55.00			

KM# 18 15 EMALANGENI **Weight:** 32.6000 g. **Composition:** 0.9250 Silver .9696 oz. ASW **Subject:** 75th anniversary - birth of King Sobhuza II **Obverse:** Similar to 25 Emalangeni, KM#20 **Reverse:** Stamped serial number

Date	F	VF	XF	Unc	BU
1974 Proof	—	Value: 95.00			

KM# 19 20 EMALANGENI **Weight:** 22.2300 g. **Composition:** 0.9000 Gold .6433 oz. AGW **Subject:** 75th anniversary - birth of King Sobhuza II

Date	Mintage	F	VF	XF	Unc	BU
1974 Proof	Est. 25,000	Value: 350				

KM# 20 25 EMALANGENI **Weight:** 27.7800 g. **Composition:** 0.9000 Gold .8039 oz. AGW **Subject:** 75th anniversary - birth of King Sobhuza II

Date	F	VF	XF	Unc	BU
1974	—	—	—	375	—

KM# 34 25 EMALANGENI **Weight:** 28.2800 g. **Composition:** 0.9250 Silver .8411 oz. ASW **Subject:** Diamond jubilee of King Sobhuza II

Date	Mintage	F	VF	XF	Unc	BU
1981	—	—	—	—	37.50	—
1981 Proof	Est. 10,000	Value: 55.00				

KM# 37 25 EMALANGENI **Weight:** 28.2800 g. **Composition:** 0.9250 Silver .8411 oz. ASW **Subject:** Accession of King Makhosetive

Date	Mintage	F	VF	XF	Unc	BU
1986 Proof	Est. 2,500	Value: 45.00				

KM# 26 50 EMALANGENI **Weight:** 4.3100 g. **Composition:** 0.9000 Gold .1247 oz. AGW **Subject:** 75th anniversary - birth of King Sobhuza II

Date	Mintage	F	VF	XF	Unc	BU
1975	3,510	—	—	—	70.00	—
1975 Proof	3,262	Value: 85.00				

KM# 27 100 EMALANGENI **Weight:** 8.6400 g. **Composition:** 0.9000 Gold .25 oz. AGW **Subject:** 75th anniversary - birth of King Sobhuza II

Date	Mintage	F	VF	XF	Unc	BU
1975	1,000	—	—	—	165	—
1975 Proof	1,000	Value: 200				

KM# 35 250 EMALANGENI **Weight:** 15.9800 g. **Composition:** 0.9170 Gold .4711 oz. AGW **Subject:** Diamond jubilee of King Sobhuza II

Date	Mintage	F	VF	XF	Unc	BU
1981	2,000	—	—	—	225	—
1981 Proof	2,000	Value: 325				

KM# 38 250 EMALANGENI **Weight:** 15.9800 g. **Composition:** 0.9170 Gold .4711 oz. AGW **Subject:** Accession of King Makhosetive

Date	Mintage	F	VF	XF	Unc	BU
ND(1986)	250	—	—	—	275	—
ND(1986) Proof	250	Value: 375				

GOLD BULLION COINAGE

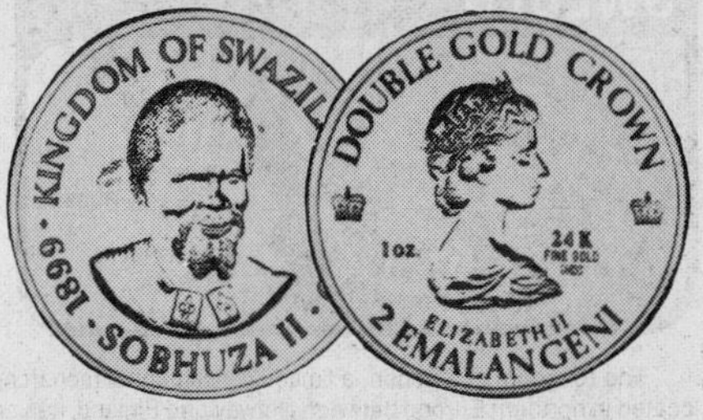

KM# 30 2 EMALANGENI **Weight:** 31.1000 g. **Composition:** 0.9990 Gold 1 oz. AGW **Subject:** 80th anniversary - birth of King Sobhuza II

Date	Mintage	F	VF	XF	Unc	BU
ND(1979)	1,250	—	—	—	450	—
ND(1979) Proof	Inc. above	Value: 550				

KM# 36 5 EMALANGENI **Weight:** 31.1000 g. **Composition:** 0.9990 Gold 1 oz. AGW **Subject:** Queen Elizabeth II's silver jubilee

Date	F	VF	XF	Unc	BU
ND(1978) Proof	—	Value: 550			

MINT SETS

KM#	Date	Mintage	Identification	Issue Price	Mkt Val
MS1	1974 (7)	—	KM7-13	10.00	10.00
MS2	1975 (3)	1,000	KM25-27	—	280
MS3	1986 (6)	—	KM39, 40.1, 41-43, 44.1	—	8.00

PROOF SETS

KM#	Date	Mintage	Identification	Issue Price	Mkt Val
PS1	1968 (5)	10,000	KM1-5	25.80	40.00
PS3	1974 (4)	—	KM15, 17, 19, 20	745	965
PS4	1974 (3)	—	KM14, 16, 17	70.00	335
PS2	1974 (7)	20,000	KM7-13	18.00	15.00
PS5	1975 (3)	—	KM25-27	—	340
PS6	1975 (2)	—	KM26-27	252	285
PS7	1979 (7)	3,231	KM7-13	34.00	22.50
PS8	1979 (2)	—	KM29.1, 30	1,172	825

SWEDEN

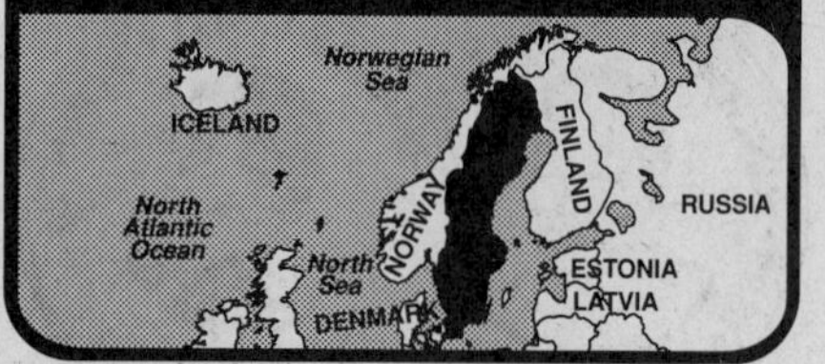

The Kingdom of Sweden, a limited constitutional monarchy located in northern Europe between Norway and Finland, has an area of 173,732 sq. mi. (449,960 sq. km.) and a population of *8.5 million. Capital: Stockholm. Mining, lumbering and a specialized machine industry dominate the economy. Machinery, paper, iron and steel, motor vehicles and wood pulp are exported.

Olaf Skottkonung founded Sweden as a Christian stronghold late in the 10th century. After conquering Finland late in the 13th century, Sweden, together with Norway, came under the rule of Denmark, 1397-1523, in an association known as the Union of Kalmar. Modern Sweden had its beginning in 1523 when Gustaf Vasa drove the Danes out of Sweden and was himself chosen king. Under Gustaf Adolphus II and Charles XII, Sweden was one of the great powers of 17th century Europe – until Charles invaded Russia in 1708, and was defeated at the Battle of Pultowa in June, 1709. Early in the 18th century, a coalition of Russia, Poland and Denmark took away Sweden's Baltic empire and in 1809 Sweden was forced to cede Finland to Russia. The Treaty of Kiel ceded Norway to Sweden in January 1814. The Norwegians resisted for a time but later signed the Act of Union at the Convention of Moss in August 1814,The Union was dissolved in 1905 and Norway became independent. A new constitution that took effect on Jan. 1, 1975, restricts the function of the king largely to a ceremonial role.

RULERS

Oscar II, 1872-1907
Gustaf V, 1907-1950
Gustaf VI, 1950-1973
Carl XVI Gustaf, 1973-

MINT OFFICIALS INITIALS

Letter	Date	Name
AL	1898-1916	Adolf Lindberg, engraver
D	1986-	Bengt Dennis
EB	1876-1908	Emil Brusewitz
EL	1916-1944	Erik Lindberg, engraver
G	1927-1945	Alf Grabe
LH	1944-1974	Leo Holmberg, engraver
TS	1945-1961	Torsten Swensson
U	1961-1986	Benkt Ulvfot
W	1908-1927	Karl-August Wallroth

MONETARY SYSTEM

100 Ore = 1 Krona

KINGDOM

REFORM COINAGE

1901 -

100 Ore = 1 Krona

KM# 750 ORE Composition: Bronze **Obverse:** Legend lengthened

Date	Mintage	F	VF	XF	Unc	BU
1901	3,074,700	1.00	3.00	8.00	22.50	—
1902	2,685,400	1.00	3.00	8.00	23.50	—
1903	2,695,600	1.00	3.00	8.00	25.00	—
1904	2,032,700	1.00	2.50	8.00	22.50	—
1905	3,556,000	1.00	2.50	6.00	18.00	—

KM# 768 ORE Composition: Bronze

Date	Mintage	F	VF	XF	Unc	BU
1906	1,783,300	3.00	8.00	14.50	67.50	—
1907	8,250,500	0.20	0.50	2.25	14.50	—

KM# 777.1 ORE Composition: Bronze **Obverse:** Small cross

Date	Mintage	F	VF	XF	Unc	BU
1909	3,805,600	6.00	9.00	20.00	110	—

KM# 777.2 ORE Composition: Bronze **Obverse:** Large cross

Date	Mintage	F	VF	XF	Unc	BU
1909	Inc. above	2.00	3.50	9.00	32.50	—
1910	1,582,600	3.00	6.50	12.00	52.00	—
1911	3,149,000	0.75	1.50	3.50	16.00	—
1912/1	3,170,000	8.50	22.00	50.00	260	—
1912	Inc. above	0.75	1.50	3.50	16.00	—
1913/12	3,197,300	4.00	12.00	25.00	130	—
1913	Inc. above	0.75	1.50	3.50	16.00	—
1914 Open 4	2,214,050	35.00	65.00	130	450	—
1914 Closed 4	Inc. above	0.75	1.50	5.50	32.50	—
1915/3	4,471,300	2.25	6.50	12.00	40.00	—
1915	Inc. above	0.25	0.50	1.75	8.00	—

Date	Mintage	F	VF	XF	Unc	BU
1916 Short 6	7,615,500	0.25	0.50	1.75	8.00	—

Date	Mintage	F	VF	XF	Unc	BU
1916 Long 6	Inc. above	0.30	0.75	2.50	12.00	—
1919 Unique	—	—	—	—	—	—
1920	5,547,600	0.25	0.50	1.25	5.75	—
1921	7,441,510	0.25	0.50	1.25	5.75	—
1922	1,165,700	2.00	4.00	7.00	32.50	—
1923	4,511,800	0.35	0.75	1.75	8.00	—
1924	2,578,900	0.25	0.75	1.75	9.00	—
1925	4,714,900	0.15	0.35	0.60	4.00	—
1926	7,739,300	0.15	0.35	0.60	4.00	—
1927	3,601,600	0.15	0.35	0.60	4.00	—
1928	2,380,800	0.25	0.75	2.50	12.00	—
1929 Curved 2	6,090,500	0.20	0.35	0.85	4.50	—
1929 Straight 2	Inc. above	0.40	0.60	2.00	10.00	—
1930	5,477,300	0.20	0.35	0.85	4.50	—
1931	5,678,500	0.20	0.35	0.85	4.50	—
1932	3,339,000	—	0.45	1.75	8.00	—
1933	3,426,800	—	0.45	0.85	6.50	—
1934	6,120,500	—	0.30	0.60	4.00	—
1935	4,599,800	—	0.30	0.60	4.00	—

Date	Mintage	F	VF	XF	Unc	BU
1936 Long 6	6,166,100	0.20	0.45	1.25	4.50	—

Date	Mintage	F	VF	XF	Unc	BU
1936 Short 6	Inc. above	0.10	0.30	0.60	3.25	—
1937	7,738,200	0.10	0.25	0.60	1.75	—
1938	6,992,900	0.10	0.25	0.60	1.75	—
1939	6,562,300	0.10	0.25	0.60	1.75	—
1940	4,059,900	0.10	0.25	0.50	1.50	—
1941	11,599,090	0.10	0.25	0.50	1.50	—
1942	3,992,000	0.10	0.25	0.60	1.75	—
1950	22,421,200	0.10	0.25	0.50	1.50	—

KM# 789 ORE Composition: Iron **Note:** World War I issues.

Date	Mintage	F	VF	XF	Unc	BU
1917	8,127,700	0.50	1.50	4.50	20.00	—
1918	9,706,100	1.00	2.50	7.00	27.50	—
1919	7,169,500	1.50	3.25	8.50	40.00	—

KM# 810 ORE Composition: Iron **Note:** World War II issues. Similar to KM#777.

Date	Mintage	F	VF	XF	Unc	BU
1942	10,053,000	0.10	0.25	0.75	4.00	—
1943	10,714,000	0.10	0.25	0.85	5.00	—
1944	8,648,500	0.10	0.25	0.75	5.00	—
1945	9,527,000	0.10	0.25	0.75	5.00	—
1945 Serif 4	Inc. above	3.50	6.50	15.00	30.00	—
1946	6,611,000	—	0.25	1.00	5.00	—
1947	14,244,500	—	0.20	0.40	2.00	—
1948	15,442,000	—	0.20	0.40	2.00	—
1949	11,778,900	—	0.20	0.40	2.00	—
1950	14,431,500	—	0.20	0.40	2.00	—

KM# 820 ORE Composition: Bronze **Note:** Varieties exist.

Date	Mintage	F	VF	XF	Unc	BU
1952 TS	3,819,000	—	0.20	0.85	4.00	—
1953 TS	22,635,800	—	—	0.30	2.50	—
1954 TS	15,492,000	—	—	0.30	2.50	—
1955 TS	24,008,000	—	—	0.30	2.50	—
1956 TS	20,792,000	—	—	0.30	2.50	—
1957 TS	21,018,500	—	—	0.30	2.50	—
1958 TS	20,220,000	—	—	0.30	2.50	—
1959 TS	14,027,500	—	—	0.30	2.50	—
1960 TS	21,840,000	—	—	0.25	2.50	—
1961 TS	11,457,500	—	—	0.35	2.75	—
1961 U	4,927,500	—	0.20	0.50	4.00	—
1962 U	19,692,500	—	—	0.30	2.50	—
1963 U	26,070,000	—	—	0.15	0.70	—
1964 U	19,290,000	—	—	0.15	0.70	—
1965 U	22,335,000	—	—	0.15	0.70	—
1966 U	24,092,500	—	—	0.15	0.30	—
1967 U	30,420,000	—	—	0.10	0.30	—
1968 U	20,760,000	—	—	0.10	0.30	—
1969 U	20,197,500	—	—	0.10	0.30	—
1970 U	44,400,000	—	—	0.10	0.30	—
1971 U	16,490,000	—	—	0.10	0.30	—

KM# 746 2 ORE Composition: Bronze **Obverse:** Large lettering

Date	Mintage	F	VF	XF	Unc	BU
1901	1,415,200	0.50	1.25	3.75	25.00	—
1902	2,035,550	0.50	1.25	3.75	25.00	—
1904	698,050	0.50	1.25	4.75	32.50	—
1905	1,429,900	0.50	1.25	3.75	25.00	—

KM# 769 2 ORE Composition: Bronze

Date	Mintage	F	VF	XF	Unc	BU
1906/5	994,250	100	200	420	885	—
1906	Inc. above	2.75	8.00	27.50	95.00	—
1907	3,807,350	0.30	0.60	2.50	16.50	—

KM# 778 2 ORE Composition: Bronze

Date	Mintage	F	VF	XF	Unc
1909	1,584,550	0.50	2.25	9.00	50.00
1910	809,400	2.25	9.00	25.00	95.00
1912	445,750	2.50	12.50	35.00	110
1913	805,650	0.30	2.25	12.00	50.00
1914	1,196,900	0.30	2.25	12.00	50.00
1915/4	813,850	4.50	13.50	40.00	110
1915	Inc. above	0.30	2.25	12.00	50.00
1916/5	2,815,450	2.75	10.00	30.00	95.00
1916 Short 6	Inc. above	0.25	0.60	6.00	32.50
1916 Long 6	Inc. above	0.25	0.60	6.00	32.50
1919	1,202,700	0.25	0.60	5.00	25.00
1920	3,464,750	0.30	0.50	2.50	12.50
1921	2,958,250	0.30	0.50	2.50	12.50
1922	521,600	0.75	1.75	7.00	40.00
1923	769,200	1.00	2.50	7.50	50.00
1924	1,283,000	0.30	0.75	3.75	30.00
1925	3,903,350	0.20	0.50	1.75	16.00
1926	3,573,950	0.20	0.50	1.75	16.00
1927	2,190,250	0.20	0.50	1.75	16.00
1928	832,250	0.40	1.00	5.00	32.50
1929	2,384,350	0.20	0.30	1.75	12.50
1930	2,589,850	0.20	0.30	1.75	12.50
1931	2,295,200	0.20	0.30	1.75	12.50

e	Mintage	F	VF	XF	Unc	BU
2	1,179,150	0.35	0.85	5.00	32.50	—
3	1,721,300	0.20	0.35	1.75	12.50	—
4	1,794,950	0.20	0.35	1.75	12.50	—
5	3,677,750	0.20	0.30	1.25	8.00	—
6 Short 6	2,244,100	0.20	0.30	1.00	6.50	—
6 Long 6	Inc. above	0.65	1.25	3.75	20.00	—
7	2,980,950	0.10	0.25	1.25	6.50	—
8	3,224,800	0.10	0.25	0.75	6.50	—
9	4,014,200	0.10	0.25	0.75	5.00	—
0	3,304,750	0.10	0.25	0.75	5.00	—
1	7,337,198	0.10	0.25	0.75	5.00	—
2	1,614,000	0.30	0.75	1.50	12.50	—
0	5,823,000	0.10	0.25	0.65	5.00	—

 # 790 2 ORE **Composition:** Iron **Note:** World War I issues. Similar to KM#553.

e	Mintage	F	VF	XF	Unc	BU
7	4,576,200	2.00	3.75	9.50	45.00	—
8	4,981,750	2.50	6.00	15.00	60.00	—
9	2,923,100	8.00	13.50	30.00	95.00	—
20	1	—	—	—	—	—

 # 811 2 ORE **Composition:** Iron **Note:** World War II issues.

e	Mintage	F	VF	XF	Unc	BU
42	9,343,350	0.15	0.30	1.75	11.50	—
43	6,999,300	0.15	0.30	1.75	11.50	—
44	6,125,900	0.15	0.30	1.75	11.50	—
45	4,773,400	0.20	0.40	1.75	12.50	—
46	5,854,000	0.15	0.30	1.75	11.50	—
47	9,535,750	0.15	0.30	0.85	8.00	—
48	11,424,250	0.15	0.30	0.85	8.00	—
49 Long 9	10,599,750	0.15	0.30	0.85	8.00	—
49 Short 9	Inc. above	0.15	0.30	0.85	8.00	—
50	13,323,000	0.15	0.30	0.85	8.00	—

M# 821 2 ORE **Composition:** Bronze **Note:** Varieties exist.

te	Mintage	F	VF	XF	Unc	BU
52 TS	3,011,000	0.20	0.50	0.85	6.50	—
53 TS	15,619,900	0.10	0.20	0.85	5.00	—
54 TS	10,086,000	0.10	0.20	0.85	5.00	—
55 TS	12,963,400	0.10	0.20	0.85	5.00	—
56 TS	13,890,250	0.10	0.20	0.85	5.00	—
57 TS	9,991,300	0.10	0.20	0.85	5.00	—
58 TS	10,105,500	0.10	0.20	0.85	5.00	—
59 TS	11,571,750	0.10	0.20	0.85	5.00	—
60 TS	11,092,500	0.10	0.20	0.85	5.00	—
61 TS	9,672,500	0.10	0.20	0.85	5.00	—
61 U	1,075,000	0.75	1.50	3.50	16.00	—
62 U	9,568,750	—	0.10	0.50	2.25	—
63 U	13,337,500	—	0.10	0.50	2.25	—
64 U	19,346,250	—	0.10	0.20	2.25	—
64 U O in crown	Inc. above	0.60	1.25	2.75	11.50	—
65 U	23,356,000	—	0.10	0.20	1.00	—
66 U	18,278,000	—	0.10	0.20	1.00	—
67 U	23,931,000	—	—	0.10	0.50	—
68 U	26,238,000	—	—	0.10	0.50	—
69 U	16,843,000	—	—	0.10	0.50	—
70 U	31,254,000	—	—	0.10	0.50	—
71 U	19,179,000	—	—	0.10	0.50	—

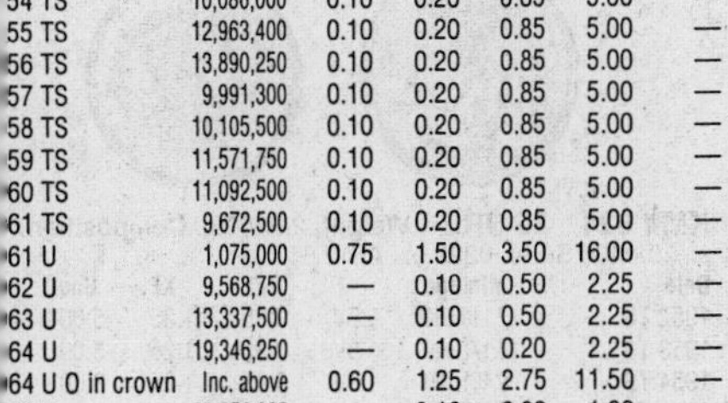

M# 757 5 ORE **Composition:** Bronze **Obverse:** Large lettering

te	Mintage	F	VF	XF	Unc	BU
01	441,660	1.00	5.00	13.50	65.00	—
02	652,420	1.00	5.00	13.50	65.00	—

Date	Mintage	F	VF	XF	Unc	BU
1903	243,000	1.75	6.00	20.00	75.00	—
1904	414,240	1.00	5.00	13.50	55.00	—
1905	545,080	1.00	5.00	16.00	60.00	—

KM# 770 5 ORE **Composition:** Bronze

Date	Mintage	F	VF	XF	Unc	BU
1906	565,280	0.75	3.75	13.50	50.00	—
1907	1,953,260	0.50	2.25	7.00	27.50	—

KM# 779.1 5 ORE **Composition:** Bronze **Obverse:** Small cross

Date	Mintage	F	VF	XF	Unc	BU
1909	917,230	2.00	6.50	32.00	175	—

KM# 779.2 5 ORE **Composition:** Bronze **Obverse:** Large cross **Note:** Varieties exist.

Date	Mintage	F	VF	XF	Unc	BU
1909	Inc. above	7.00	50.00	275	885	—
1910	30,630	120	275	550	1,350	—
1911 narrow base mint mark	778,000	0.85	4.00	27.50	150	—
1911 wide base mint mark	Inc. above	3.00	12.00	55.00	210	—
1912	547,480	1.00	4.00	37.50	200	—
1913	761,780	0.85	2.50	25.00	140	—
1914	400,100	2.50	6.00	45.00	245	—
1915	1,122,820	0.50	3.00	20.00	70.00	—
1916/5	955,440	10.00	22.00	42.00	175	—
1916 Short 6	Inc. above	0.50	3.00	17.50	75.00	—
1916 Long 6	Inc. above	0.50	3.00	17.50	75.00	—
1917	1	—	—	—	—	—
1919	1,129,380	0.25	1.00	15.00	70.00	—
1920	2,360,920	0.25	1.00	9.00	40.00	—
1921	1,878,500	0.20	0.75	12.00	55.00	—
1922	763,420	0.25	2.75	30.00	130	—
1923	505,580	0.85	5.00	70.00	250	—
1924	899,500	0.25	1.50	20.00	100	—
1925	1,943,500	0.20	0.75	10.00	55.00	—
1926	1,742,100	0.20	0.75	10.00	55.00	—
1927	36,380	80.00	190	550	1,225	—
1928	987,900	0.20	1.00	12.00	70.00	—
1929	1,668,560	0.20	0.50	10.00	55.00	—
1930	1,716,040	0.20	0.50	10.00	55.00	—
1931	1,130,960	0.20	0.50	10.00	55.00	—
1932	1,165,220	0.20	0.50	10.00	55.00	—
1933	574,340	0.65	2.75	30.00	145	—
1934	1,710,260	0.20	0.40	6.00	40.00	—
1935	1,682,020	0.20	0.40	6.00	40.00	—
1936 Short 6	1,625,700	0.20	0.40	7.00	40.00	—
1936	Inc. above	0.25	0.75	8.00	50.00	—
1937	2,637,260	—	0.30	5.00	28.00	—
1938	2,354,240	—	0.30	5.00	28.00	—
1939	2,591,500	—	0.45	7.00	32.50	—
1940	2,729,580	—	0.35	3.75	20.00	—
1940 Serif 4	Inc. above	—	0.45	5.00	28.00	—
1941	2,054,540	—	0.35	3.00	20.00	—
1942	395,400	2.00	4.00	25.00	100	—
1950	12,559,100	—	0.25	0.75	6.50	—

KM# 791 5 ORE **Composition:** Iron **Note:** World War I issues. Similar to KM#554.

Date	Mintage	F	VF	XF	Unc	BU
1917	2,953,320	4.50	9.00	20.00	75.00	—
1918	2,457,840	10.00	22.00	35.00	135	—
1919	2,302,480	10.00	22.00	35.00	130	—

KM# 812 5 ORE **Composition:** Iron **Note:** World War II issues.

Date	Mintage	F	VF	XF	Unc	BU
1942	4,343,420	0.20	0.75	5.00	32.50	—
1943	5,570,180	0.20	0.75	5.00	32.50	—
1944	4,561,980	0.20	0.75	5.00	32.50	—
1945	3,771,100	0.20	0.75	5.00	32.50	—
1946	2,375,080	—	0.50	3.50	20.00	—
1947	6,034,840	—	0.50	3.50	20.00	—
1948	6,246,000	—	0.50	3.50	20.00	—
1949	7,839,640	—	0.50	2.50	18.00	—
1950	5,289,500	—	0.50	2.50	18.00	—

KM# 822 5 ORE **Composition:** Bronze

Date	Mintage	F	VF	XF	Unc	BU
1952 TS	3,065,400	0.20	0.50	1.75	9.50	—
1953 TS	12,329,320	0.20	0.50	1.75	9.50	—
1954 TS	7,232,100	0.20	0.50	1.75	9.50	—
1955 TS	8,464,620	0.20	0.50	1.75	9.50	—
1956 TS	7,997,120	0.20	0.50	2.00	10.00	—
1957 TS	6,275,600	0.20	0.50	1.75	9.50	—
1958 TS	9,498,400	0.20	0.50	2.00	10.00	—
1959 TS	8,370,500	0.20	0.50	2.00	10.00	—
1960 TS	10,542,300	0.20	0.40	1.25	8.50	—
1961 TS	3,909,000	0.20	0.40	1.25	8.50	—
1961 U	2,451,500	0.20	0.50	1.25	9.50	—
1962 U	22,305,500	—	0.10	0.50	4.00	—
1963 U	17,156,500	—	0.10	0.50	4.00	—
1964 U	10,922,500	—	0.10	0.75	8.00	—
1964 U 50 in crown	Inc. above	2.75	5.50	12.00	32.50	—
1965 U	22,635,000	—	0.10	0.20	1.00	—
1966 U	18,213,000	—	0.10	0.20	1.00	—
1967 U	20,776,000	—	0.10	0.20	1.00	—
1968 U	27,093,500	—	0.10	0.20	1.00	—
1969 U	26,886,500	—	0.10	0.20	1.00	—
1970 U	29,419,500	—	0.10	0.20	1.00	—
1971 U	15,749,000	—	0.10	0.20	1.00	—

KM# 845 5 ORE **Composition:** Bronze

Date	Mintage	F	VF	XF	Unc	BU
1972 U	107,894,000	—	—	0.10	0.25	0.60
1973 U	193,037,580	—	—	0.10	0.25	0.60

KM# 849 5 ORE **Composition:** Copper-Tin-Zinc

Date	Mintage	F	VF	XF	Unc	BU
1976 U	4,672,350	—	—	0.10	0.40	0.60
1977 U	31,037,129	—	—	0.10	0.30	0.60
1978 U	46,021,707	—	—	0.10	0.30	0.60
1979 U	65,833,193	—	—	0.10	0.30	0.60
1980 U	60,996,699	—	—	0.10	0.25	0.60
1981 U	19,791,000	—	—	0.10	0.25	0.60

KM# 849a 5 ORE **Composition:** Copper-Zinc

Date	Mintage	F	VF	XF	Unc	BU
1981	34,960,593	—	—	0.10	0.20	0.60
1982	40,471,115	—	—	0.10	0.20	0.60
1983	36,304,042	—	—	0.10	0.20	0.60
1984	13,449,245	—	—	0.10	0.20	0.60

KM# 755 10 ORE Weight: 1.4500 g. Composition: 0.4000 Silver .0186 oz. ASW Obverse: Large lettering Note: Varieties exist.

Date	Mintage	F	VF	XF	Unc	BU
1902 EB	1,945,600	1.00	3.75	14.00	32.50	—
1903 EB	1,508,930	1.00	3.75	14.00	32.50	—
1904 EB	3,279,520	0.75	1.75	9.50	25.00	—

KM# 774 10 ORE Weight: 1.4500 g. Composition: 0.4000 Silver .0186 oz. ASW

Date	Mintage	F	VF	XF	Unc	BU
1907 EB	7,319,040	0.45	1.25	5.50	21.50	—

KM# 780 10 ORE Weight: 1.4500 g. Composition: 0.4000 Silver .0186 oz. ASW

Date	Mintage	F	VF	XF	Unc	BU
1909 W	1,610,400	1.25	4.50	15.00	70.00	—
1911 W	3,180,650	0.35	2.25	9.50	32.50	—
1913 W	1,580,910	1.00	2.75	12.00	50.00	—
1914 W	1,571,330	0.75	3.50	9.50	32.50	—
1914 Serif 4	Inc. above	0.75	2.75	12.00	50.00	—
1915 W	1,546,950	0.50	2.75	9.00	47.50	—
1916/5 W	3,034,880	2.50	8.00	25.00	110	—
1916 W	Inc. above	0.75	2.00	7.00	32.50	—
1917 W	4,996,139	0.35	0.75	3.00	18.50	—
1918 W	4,114,180	0.35	0.75	3.00	18.50	—
1919 W	5,737,020	0.35	0.75	3.00	18.50	—
1927 W	2,509,590	0.25	0.60	3.00	22.50	—
1928 G	2,901,150	0.25	0.60	3.00	22.50	—
1929 G	5,505,200	0.25	0.60	2.00	11.50	—
1930 G	3,222,710	0.25	0.60	2.00	11.50	—
1931 G	4,272,073	0.25	0.60	2.00	11.50	—
1933 G	1,948,090	0.85	2.00	3.50	25.00	—
1934 G	4,059,293	0.25	0.50	1.25	7.00	—
1935 G	2,426,283	0.25	0.50	1.25	7.00	—
1936 G Short 6	5,099,270	1.75	4.50	20.00	60.00	—
1936 G Long 6	Inc. above	0.25	0.45	1.50	9.50	—
1937 G	5,116,920	0.25	0.40	1.00	7.00	—
1938 G	7,428,140	0.25	0.40	1.00	7.00	—
1938 G Proof	—	Value: 12.50				
1939/29 G	2,020,670	3.75	8.00	22.00	55.00	—
1939 G	Inc. above	0.25	0.60	2.25	15.00	—
1939 G Proof	—	Value: 17.50				
1940 G	3,017,320	0.25	0.50	1.25	7.00	—
1941 G	9,106,380	0.25	0.50	1.25	6.50	—
1942 G	3,691,640	0.25	0.50	1.25	7.00	—

KM# 795 10 ORE Composition: Nickel-Bronze

Date	Mintage	F	VF	XF	Unc	BU
1920 W	3,612,250	0.50	1.25	6.00	42.00	—
1920 W Large W	Inc. above	13.50	28.00	60.00	300	—
1921 W	2,269,950	0.50	1.50	7.00	42.00	—
1923 W	2,143,560	0.50	1.50	9.00	52.00	—
1924 W	1,600,000	0.50	2.00	9.50	72.00	—
1925 W	1,472,340	0.75	3.75	18.00	90.00	—
1940 G	3,373,200	0.20	0.50	2.25	18.00	—
1941	815,880	0.75	1.50	4.50	32.50	—
1946 TS	4,115,940	0.10	0.30	0.85	7.00	—
1947 TS	4,132,950	0.10	0.30	0.85	7.00	—

KM# 813 10 ORE Weight: 1.4400 g. Composition: 0.4000 Silver .0185 oz. ASW Note: Varieties exist.

Date	Mintage	F	VF	XF	Unc	BU
1942 G	1,600,000	0.25	0.40	1.25	7.00	—
1942 G Proof	—	Value: 35.00				
1943 G	7,661,100	0.25	0.40	1.25	7.00	—
1944 G	12,276,900	0.20	0.35	0.85	5.50	—
1945 G	11,702,510	0.20	0.35	0.85	5.50	—
1945 TS	Inc. above	0.20	0.35	0.85	5.50	—
1945 TS/G	Inc. above	0.20	0.35	1.25	7.00	—
1946/5 TS Open 6	3,575,500	5.50	14.00	25.00	72.00	—
1946 TS Open 6	Inc. above	0.25	0.75	2.50	25.00	—
1946 TS Closed 6	Inc. above	0.20	0.35	1.75	15.00	—
1947 TS	7,293,250	0.20	0.30	0.85	5.50	—
1948 TS	10,418,650	0.20	0.30	0.75	5.50	—
1949 TS	12,044,000	0.20	0.30	0.75	5.50	—
1950 TS	31,823,870	0.20	0.30	0.75	4.50	—

KM# 823 10 ORE Weight: 1.4400 g. Composition: 0.4000 Silver .0185 oz. ASW

Date	Mintage	F	VF	XF	Unc	BU
1952 TS	4,659,700	BV	0.40	0.85	5.00	—
1953 TS	28,484,040	BV	0.20	0.85	5.00	—
1954 TS	15,913,250	BV	0.20	0.85	5.00	—
1955 TS	16,687,200	BV	0.20	0.85	5.00	—
1956 TS	21,985,600	BV	0.20	0.60	4.00	—
1957 TS	21,294,400	BV	0.20	0.60	4.00	—
1958 TS	19,605,400	BV	0.20	0.60	4.00	—
1959 TS	18,523,000	BV	0.20	0.60	4.00	—
1960 TS	16,605,000	BV	0.20	0.60	4.00	—
1961 TS	8,283,000	BV	0.20	0.60	4.00	—
1961 U	7,843,000	BV	0.20	0.60	4.00	—
1962 U	8,619,000	BV	0.20	0.60	4.00	—

KM# 835 10 ORE Composition: Copper-Nickel

Date	Mintage	F	VF	XF	Unc	BU
1962 U	8,814,000	0.10	0.25	0.60	4.00	8.00
1963 U	28,170,000	—	—	0.15	0.60	4.00
1964 U	36,895,000	—	—	0.15	0.60	4.00
1965 U	29,870,000	—	—	0.15	0.60	4.00
1966 U	20,435,000	—	—	0.15	0.60	4.00
1967 U	18,245,000	—	—	0.15	0.60	4.00
1968 U	51,490,000	—	—	0.15	0.50	4.00
1969 U	55,880,000	—	—	0.15	0.50	1.75
1970 U	60,910,000	—	—	0.15	0.50	1.75
1971 U	27,075,000	—	—	0.15	0.50	1.75
1972 U	36,766,500	—	—	0.15	0.25	1.00
1973 U	160,740,000	—	—	0.15	0.25	1.00

KM# 850 10 ORE Composition: Copper-Nickel

Date	Mintage	F	VF	XF	Unc	BU
1976 U	4,172,790	—	—	0.15	0.50	1.00
1977 U	44,517,287	—	—	0.10	0.35	0.75
1978 U	74,341,720	—	—	0.10	0.35	0.75
1979 U	75,305,608	—	—	0.10	0.20	0.40
1980 U	108,293,811	—	—	0.10	0.20	0.40
1981 U	102,453,931	—	—	0.10	0.15	0.30
1982 U	103,905,592	—	—	0.10	0.15	0.30
1983 U	773,149,400	—	—	0.10	0.20	0.40
1984 U	122,128,092	—	—	0.10	0.15	0.30
1985 U	79,154,951	—	—	0.10	0.20	0.40
1986 U	48,945,396	—	—	0.10	0.20	0.40
1986 D	48,945,220	—	—	0.10	0.20	0.40
1987 D	146,877,318	—	—	0.10	0.20	0.40
1988 D	194,986,479	—	—	0.10	0.15	0.30
1989 D	245,180,644	—	—	0.10	0.15	0.30
1990 D	139,298,404	—	—	0.10	0.15	0.30
1991 D	5,176,842	—	—	0.15	0.50	1.00

KM# 739 25 ORE Weight: 2.4200 g. Composition: 0.6000 Silver 0.0467 oz. ASW Obverse: Large lettering

Date	Mintage	F	VF	XF	Unc	BU
1902 EB	1,259,039	2.00	8.00	25.00	82.00	—
1904 EB	691,888	2.00	8.00	25.00	85.00	—
1905 EB	732,000	2.00	6.50	20.00	72.00	—

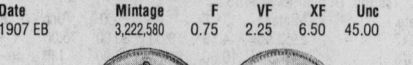

KM# 775 25 ORE Weight: 2.4200 g. Composition: 0.6000 Silver 0.0467 oz. ASW

Date	Mintage	F	VF	XF	Unc	BU
1907 EB	3,222,580	0.75	2.25	6.50	45.00	—

KM# 785 25 ORE Weight: 2.4200 g. Composition: 0.6000 Silver 0.0467 oz. ASW

Date	Mintage	F	VF	XF	Unc
1910 W Large cross	2,043,936	0.65	2.00	6.00	52.00
1910 W Small cross	Inc. above	7.00	27.50	75.00	480
1912 W	1,013,740	0.65	2.75	15.00	72.00
1914 W	3,719,232	0.65	2.75	15.00	42.00
1916 W	1,269,120	0.65	2.75	15.00	72.00
1917 W	1,657,312	0.65	2.25	5.50	42.00
1918 W Small 8	2,364,784	0.65	2.25	7.50	52.00
1918 W Wide 8	Inc. above	0.65	2.25	9.50	60.00
1919 W	3,205,164	0.65	1.50	5.00	37.50
1927 W	1,687,984	0.65	1.75	5.00	37.50
1928 G	836,899	0.65	2.00	9.50	60.00
1929 G	1,124,932	0.65	1.75	6.00	42.00
1930 G	3,489,628	0.50	1.50	3.00	20.00
1931 G	1,391,938	0.50	1.50	3.00	20.00
1932 G	1,133,344	0.50	1.50	3.00	20.00
1933 G	964,340	0.50	1.50	8.00	37.50
1934 G	1,403,648	0.50	1.50	3.00	12.50
1936 G	1,852,000	0.50	1.50	3.00	12.50
1937 G Small G	3,258,956	0.50	1.75	4.50	13.50
1937 G Proof	Inc. above	Value: 20.00			
1937 G Large G	Inc. above	0.75	2.00	4.50	20.00
1938	3,678,876	0.45	1.25	2.75	8.50
1939	2,136,600	0.35	1.25	2.75	8.50
1940	2,301,788	0.35	1.25	2.50	8.00
1941	1,995,200	0.35	1.25	2.50	8.00

KM# 798 25 ORE Composition: Nickel-Bronze

Date	Mintage	F	VF	XF	Unc
1921 W	1,354,656	1.50	3.50	15.00	90.00
1940 G	2,333,040	0.15	0.50	3.50	20.00
1941 G	1,056,680	0.15	0.50	3.50	28.50
1946 TS	2,066,048	0.15	0.30	1.25	9.50
1947 TS	1,594,200	0.15	0.30	1.25	9.50

KM# 816 25 ORE Weight: 2.3200 g. Composition: 0.4000 Silver .0298 oz. ASW

Date	Mintage	F	VF	XF	Unc
1943 G	9,854,640	BV	0.50	1.25	8.50
1944 G	9,532,148	BV	0.50	1.25	8.50
1945 G	5,362,800	BV	0.50	1.25	8.50
1945 TS	Inc. above	0.35	0.75	2.50	12.50
1945 G/TS	Inc. above	BV	0.60	3.50	17.50
1946 TS	2,249,600	BV	0.35	2.50	12.50
1946 TS serif 6	Inc. above	2.00	4.00	14.50	45.00
1947 TS	5,332,800	BV	0.35	1.25	5.50
1948 TS	3,191,000	BV	0.35	1.25	5.50
1949 TS	5,812,180	BV	0.35	1.25	5.50
1950 TS	12,059,144	BV	0.35	1.25	4.50

KM# 824 25 ORE Weight: 2.3200 g. Composition: 0.4000 Silver .0298 oz. ASW

Date	Mintage	F	VF	XF	Unc
1952 TS	2,113,890	BV	0.35	1.25	5.00
1953 TS	18,177,420	BV	0.35	1.25	3.00
1954 TS	9,491,740	BV	0.35	1.25	3.00
1955 TS	7,663,100	BV	0.35	1.25	4.50
1956 TS	10,930,800	BV	0.35	1.00	4.00
1957 TS	12,497,200	BV	0.35	1.00	4.00
1958 TS	6,883,940	BV	0.35	1.00	4.00
1959 TS	4,772,000	BV	0.35	1.00	4.00
1960 TS	4,374,000	BV	0.50	2.25	11.50
1961 TS	8,380,800	BV	0.35	1.00	4.00

KM# 836 25 ORE Composition: Copper-Nickel

Date	Mintage	F	VF	XF	Unc
1962 U	4,426,000	—	0.25	1.00	3.25
1963 U	26,710,000	—	0.20	0.50	2.50
1964 U	17,300,000	—	0.20	0.50	2.50
1965 U	6,884,000	—	0.20	0.50	2.50
1966 U	12,932,000	—	—	0.25	1.25
1967 U	28,038,000	—	—	0.20	0.65
1968 U	14,366,000	—	—	0.20	0.65

te	Mintage	F	VF	XF	Unc	BU
69 U	20,214,000	—	—	0.20	0.65	—
70 U	23,780,000	—	—	0.20	0.65	—
71 U	8,606,000	—	—	0.20	0.65	—
72 U	1,323,200	—	—	0.20	0.65	—
73 U	76,993,000	—	—	0.15	0.45	—

M# 851 25 ORE Composition: Copper-Nickel

te	Mintage	F	VF	XF	Unc	BU
76 U	2,515,285	—	—	0.15	0.65	—
77 U	5,509,491	—	—	0.15	0.50	—
78 U	54,593,293	—	—	0.10	0.35	—
79 U	48,423,422	—	—	0.10	0.35	—
80 U	38,889,325	—	—	0.10	0.35	—
81 U	46,371,204	—	—	0.10	0.35	—
82 U	43,212,638	—	—	0.10	0.35	—
83 U	28,954,257	—	—	0.10	0.35	—
84 U	7,293,722	—	—	0.10	0.35	—

M# 771 50 ORE Weight: 5.0000 g. **Composition:** 0.6000 Silver .0965 oz. ASW

te	Mintage	F	VF	XF	Unc	BU
06 EB	319,452	2.75	9.00	37.50	195	—
07 EB	803,340	2.00	6.00	35.00	130	—

M# 788 50 ORE Weight: 5.0000 g. **Composition:** 0.6000 Silver .0965 oz. ASW

ate	Mintage	F	VF	XF	Unc	BU
11 W	472,534	3.25	8.00	30.00	145	—
12 W	483,062	4.50	9.50	32.50	170	—
14 W	378,448	4.50	9.50	32.50	170	—
16 W	536,718	3.25	8.00	28.00	140	—
19 W	458,296	3.25	8.00	30.00	125	—
27 W	671,596	1.50	3.00	16.00	85.00	—
28 G	1,135,054	1.25	2.00	8.00	50.00	—
29 G	470,990	1.50	3.00	16.00	85.00	—
30 G	547,920	1.50	3.00	16.00	80.00	—
31 G	671,457	BV	2.00	13.50	60.00	—
33 G	547,606	BV	2.00	13.50	60.00	—
34 G	613,124	BV	2.00	8.00	42.00	—
35 G	690,792	BV	2.00	8.00	42.00	—
36 G Short 6	823,176	BV	2.00	8.00	42.00	—
36 G Long 6	Inc. above	BV	3.50	13.50	72.00	—
38 G	441,546	BV	1.25	5.50	28.00	—
39 G	921,750	BV	1.00	3.50	20.00	—
39 G Proof	—	Value: 35.00				

M# 796 50 ORE Composition: Nickel-Bronze **Note:** Varieties exist.

ate	Mintage	F	VF	XF	Unc	BU
20 W Oval 0	479,500	1.75	10.00	45.00	210	—
20 W Round 0	Inc. above	35.00	75.00	240	650	—
21 W	214,922	2.75	22.00	115	400	—
24 W	645,368	1.25	11.50	50.00	285	—
40 G	1,340,750	0.25	1.00	5.50	40.00	—
40 G large G	Inc. above	5.50	16.50	45.00	100	—
46 TS	1,425,990	0.25	1.00	4.25	25.00	—
47 TS	1,031,800	0.25	1.00	4.25	25.00	—

KM# 817 50 ORE Weight: 4.8000 g. **Composition:** 0.4000 Silver .0617 oz. ASW

Date	Mintage	F	VF	XF	Unc	BU
1943 G	784,700	1.50	3.50	11.50	60.00	—
1944 G	1,540,296	BV	1.00	2.25	15.00	—
1945 G	2,584,800	BV	1.00	2.25	15.00	—
1946 TS	1,091,000	BV	1.00	2.25	15.00	—
1947 TS	1,770,500	BV	1.00	2.25	15.00	—
1948 TS	1,731,400	BV	1.00	2.25	15.00	—
1949 TS	1,883,100	BV	1.00	2.25	15.00	—
1950 TS	3,353,620	BV	1.00	1.75	12.50	—

KM# 825 50 ORE Weight: 4.8000 g. **Composition:** 0.4000 Silver .0617 oz. ASW

Date	Mintage	F	VF	XF	Unc	BU
1952 TS	1,197,760	BV	0.85	3.50	23.50	—
1953 TS	4,395,620	BV	0.85	3.00	21.50	—
1954 TS	5,778,850	BV	0.85	3.00	21.50	—
1955 TS	2,699,700	BV	0.85	4.25	20.00	—
1956 TS	7,056,670	BV	0.65	2.00	10.00	—
1957 TS	2,404,700	BV	0.65	3.00	20.00	—
1958 TS	1,659,800	BV	0.65	3.00	20.00	—
1961 TS	2,775,000	BV	0.65	2.00	12.50	—

KM# 837 50 ORE Composition: Copper-Nickel

Date	Mintage	F	VF	XF	Unc	BU
1962 U	1,400,000	0.50	0.80	3.25	22.50	—
1963 U	5,808,000	0.15	0.25	1.25	12.50	—
1964 U	5,325,000	0.15	0.25	1.25	12.50	—
1965 U	6,453,000	0.15	0.25	0.60	8.00	—
1966 U	6,309,000	0.15	0.25	0.50	6.50	—
1967 U	7,890,000	0.15	0.25	0.50	6.50	—
1968 U	9,198,000	—	0.15	0.25	1.25	—
1969 U	7,265,000	—	0.15	0.25	1.25	—
1970 U	9,426,000	—	0.15	0.25	1.25	—
1971 U	7,218,000	—	0.15	0.25	1.25	—
1972 U	7,388,000	—	0.15	0.25	1.25	—
1973 U	52,467,000	—	0.15	0.20	0.60	—

KM# 855 50 ORE Composition: Copper-Nickel

Date	Mintage	F	VF	XF	Unc	BU
1976 U	2,588,575	—	0.15	0.25	1.00	—
1977 U	10,359,708	—	—	0.15	0.40	—
1978 U	33,282,476	—	—	0.15	0.40	—
1979 U	30,723,730	—	—	0.15	0.40	—
1980 U	28,665,662	—	—	0.15	0.40	—
1981 U	15,516,559	—	—	0.15	0.40	—
1982 U	14,778,358	—	—	0.15	0.40	—
1983 U	17,528,777	—	—	0.15	0.40	—
1984 U	27,527,534	—	—	0.15	0.40	—
1985 U	14,078,477	—	—	0.15	0.40	—
1986 U	937,214	—	—	0.20	0.75	—
1987 D	1,077,317	—	—	0.20	0.75	—
1988 D	531,669	—	—	0.20	0.75	—
1989 D	605,780	—	—	0.20	0.75	—
1990 D	31,934,675	—	—	0.10	0.20	—
1991 D	16,315,160	—	—	0.10	0.20	—

KM# 878 50 ORE Composition: Bronze

Date	Mintage	F	VF	XF	Unc	BU
1992 B	39,531,000	—	—	0.15	0.40	—
1992 B	39,530,810	—	—	0.15	0.40	—
1993 B	643,520	—	—	0.20	0.65	—
1994 B	517,575	—	—	0.20	0.65	—
1995 B	486,538	—	—	0.10	0.25	—
1996 B	247,620	—	—	0.10	0.25	—
1997 B	69,995	—	—	0.10	0.25	—
1998 B	5,064,956	—	—	0.10	0.20	—
1999 B	22,076,128	—	—	0.10	0.20	—
2000 B	33,060,252	—	—	0.10	0.20	—
2001 B	30,120,532	—	—	0.10	0.20	—

KM# 760 KRONA Weight: 7.5000 g. **Composition:** 0.8000 Silver .1929 oz. ASW **Obverse:** Without initials below bust

Date	Mintage	F	VF	XF	Unc	BU
1901/898 EB	270,960	9.00	35.00	160	575	—
1901 EB	Inc. above	7.00	32.50	145	565	—
1903 EB	473,386	6.00	30.00	100	385	—
1904 EB	563,586	9.00	20.00	100	350	—

KM# 772 KRONA Weight: 7.5000 g. **Composition:** 0.8000 Silver .1929 oz. ASW

Date	Mintage	F	VF	XF	Unc	BU
1906 EB	426,939	5.50	22.00	90.00	285	—
1907 EB	1,058,286	4.00	16.00	65.00	250	—

KM# 786.1 KRONA Weight: 7.5000 g. **Composition:** 0.8000 Silver .1929 oz. ASW **Obverse:** With dots in date

Date	Mintage	F	VF	XF	Unc	BU
1.9.1.0 W	643,065	3.00	13.50	47.50	180	—
1.9.1.2 W	303,420	7.50	25.00	115	445	—
1.9.1.3 W	353,051	3.50	13.50	47.50	195	—
1.9.1.4 W	622,217	3.00	12.50	42.00	182	—
1.9.1.5 W	1,415,956	3.00	8.00	30.00	150	—
1.9.1.6/5 W	1,139,245	4.00	15.00	60.00	235	—
1.9.1.6 W	Inc. above	3.00	12.50	42.00	195	—
1.9.1.8 W	258,091	3.25	9.00	32.00	210	—
1.9.2.3 W	746,277	2.50	9.00	30.00	145	—
1.9.2.4 W	2,066,155	2.00	7.00	20.00	110	—

KM# 786.2 KRONA Weight: 7.5000 g. **Composition:** 0.8000 Silver .1929 oz. ASW **Obverse:** Without dots in date

Date	Mintage	F	VF	XF	Unc	BU
1924 W	Inc. above	1.50	5.00	25.00	100	—
1925 W	369,919	3.00	9.00	47.50	210	—
1926 W	465,467	2.50	8.00	30.00	145	—
1927 G	401,167	2.75	8.50	42.00	190	—
1928 G	739,189	1.50	4.00	25.00	90.00	—
1929 G	1,345,647	1.25	3.00	14.50	52.00	—
1930 G	1,743,783	1.25	2.50	7.00	40.00	—
1931 G	1,007,523	1.25	2.50	7.00	40.00	—
1932 G	1,035,877	1.25	2.50	7.00	40.00	—
1933 G	1,044,634	1.25	2.50	7.00	40.00	—
1934 G	585,673	1.25	2.50	14.50	65.00	—
1935 G	1,604,343	1.00	2.00	3.50	15.00	—
1936 G	3,222,312	1.00	2.00	3.50	12.50	—
1937 G	2,666,998	1.00	2.00	3.50	12.50	—
1938 G	1,911,464	0.75	1.75	3.50	12.50	—
1938 G Proof	—	Value: 25.00				
1939 G	7,589,316	0.75	1.75	3.50	6.50	—
1940 G	6,917,460	0.75	1.75	3.50	6.50	—
1941/4 G	2,183,338	2.25	6.00	20.00	50.00	—
1941 G	Inc. above	0.75	1.75	4.00	12.50	—
1942 G	240,000	22.00	45.00	100	350	—

KM# 814 KRONA **Weight:** 7.0000 g. **Composition:** 0.4000 Silver .0900 oz. ASW

Date	Mintage	F	VF	XF	Unc	BU
1942 G	5,644,990	BV	1.00	3.50	20.00	—
1943 G Plain 4	7,915,850	BV	1.00	3.50	20.00	—
1943 G Crosslet 4	Inc. above	BV	1.00	3.50	20.00	—
1944 G	7,423,463	BV	1.00	2.50	9.00	—
1945 G	7,359,360	BV	1.00	2.50	9.00	—
1945 TS	Inc. above	BV	1.25	3.25	16.00	—
1945 TS/G	Inc. above	BV	1.50	3.50	22.50	—
1946 TS	19,170,454	BV	1.00	2.00	6.50	—
1947 TS	9,124,335	BV	1.00	2.00	6.50	—
1948 TS	10,430,588	BV	1.00	2.00	6.50	—
1949 TS	7,981,162	BV	1.00	2.00	6.50	—
1950 TS	5,310,141	BV	1.00	1.75	9.00	—

KM# 826 KRONA **Weight:** 7.0000 g. **Composition:** 0.4000 Silver .0900 oz. ASW

Date	Mintage	F	VF	XF	Unc	BU
1952 TS	1,101,625	BV	1.00	3.00	25.00	—
1953/2 TS	Inc. above	BV	1.50	4.50	22.50	—
1953 TS	3,305,843	BV	1.00	3.00	22.50	—
1954 TS	6,460,770	BV	1.00	3.00	16.00	—
1955 TS	4,140,904	BV	1.00	3.00	16.00	—
1956 TS	6,226,705	BV	1.00	3.00	9.00	—
1957 TS	3,544,268	BV	1.00	3.00	10.00	—
1958 TS	1,438,940	BV	1.50	4.50	22.50	—
1959 TS	1,187,000	1.25	2.75	7.50	40.00	—
1960 TS	4,085,250	BV	1.00	2.00	6.50	—
1961 TS	4,283,000	BV	1.00	2.00	6.50	—
1961 U	2,973,275	BV	1.25	3.00	22.50	—
1962 U	6,838,550	BV	1.00	2.00	6.50	—
1963 U	14,227,500	BV	BV	1.50	4.00	—
1964 U	15,972,500	BV	BV	1.25	3.50	—
1965 U	18,638,500	BV	BV	1.25	3.50	—
1966 U	22,396,500	BV	BV	1.25	2.50	—
1967 U	17,234,500	BV	BV	1.25	2.50	—
1968 U	12,325,500	BV	BV	1.25	2.50	—

KM# 826a KRONA **Composition:** Copper-Nickel Clad Copper

Date	Mintage	F	VF	XF	Unc	BU
1968 U	5,177,000	—	0.30	1.00	4.00	—
1969 U	30,855,500	—	0.30	0.40	1.50	—
1970 U	25,314,500	—	0.30	0.40	1.50	—
1971 U	18,342,000	—	0.30	0.40	1.50	—
1972 U	21,941,000	—	0.30	0.40	1.50	—
1973 U	142,000,000	—	0.30	0.40	1.50	—

KM# 852 KRONA **Composition:** Copper-Nickel Clad Copper

Date	Mintage	F	VF	XF	Unc	BU
1976 U	4,320,811	—	0.30	0.50	1.25	—
1977 U	80,477,822	—	0.30	0.40	0.75	—
1978 U	81,407,892	—	0.30	0.40	0.75	—
1979 U	47,450,148	—	0.30	0.40	0.75	—
1980 U	51,694,323	—	0.30	0.40	0.75	—
1981 U	62,078,991	—	0.30	0.40	0.75	—

KM# 852a KRONA **Composition:** Copper-Nickel

Date	Mintage	F	VF	XF	Unc	BU
1982 U	24,836,789	—	—	0.30	0.65	—
1983 U	23,530,222	—	—	0.30	0.65	—
1984 U	37,811,592	—	—	0.30	0.65	—
1985 U	4,909,279	—	—	0.30	0.70	—
1986 U	901,095	—	—	0.50	1.25	—
1987 B	21,543,317	—	—	0.30	0.65	—
1988 B	30,341,842	—	—	0.30	0.50	—
1989 B	55,963,148	—	—	—	0.30	—
1990 B	54,469,545	—	—	—	0.30	—
1991 B	34,249,994	—	—	—	0.30	—
1992 B	16,770,810	—	—	—	0.30	—
1993 B	407,208	—	0.30	0.50	1.00	—
1994 B	567,137	—	0.30	0.50	1.00	—
1995 B	499,758	—	0.30	0.50	1.00	—
1996 B	323,656	—	—	1.00	2.00	—
1997 B	25,042,398	—	—	—	0.25	—
1998 B	39,747,941	—	—	—	0.25	—
1999 B	55,018,508	—	—	—	0.25	—
2000 B	104,213,074	—	—	—	0.25	—

KM# 897 KRONA **Weight:** 6.9800 g. **Composition:** Copper-Nickel **Ruler:** Carl XVI Gustaf **Subject:** Millennium **Obverse:** Head of King Carl Gustav XVI left **Reverse:** Crowned monogram **Edge:** Reeded **Size:** 24.9 mm.

Date	Mintage	F	VF	XF	Unc	BU
2000	2,978,113	—	—	—	2.00	—

KM# 894 KRONA **Weight:** 6.9800 g. **Composition:** Copper-Nickel **Ruler:** Carl XVI Gustaf **Obverse:** King's new portrait **Reverse:** Crown and denomination **Edge:** Reeded **Size:** 24.9 mm.

Date	Mintage	F	VF	XF	Unc	BU
2001 B	23,905,454	—	—	—	0.65	—

KM# 761 2 KRONOR **Weight:** 15.0000 g. **Composition:** 0.8000 Silver .3858 oz. ASW **Obverse:** Without initials below bust

Date	Mintage	F	VF	XF	Unc	BU
1903 EB	64,308	25.00	90.00	250	885	—
1904 EB	175,029	12.00	45.00	150	475	—

KM# 773 2 KRONOR **Weight:** 15.0000 g. **Composition:** 0.8000 Silver .3858 oz. ASW

Date	Mintage	F	VF	XF	Unc	BU
1906 EB	112,468	9.00	25.00	100	345	—
1907 EB	300,573	6.50	20.00	85.00	325	—

KM# 776 2 KRONOR **Weight:** 15.0000 g. **Compositio** 0.8000 Silver .3858 oz. ASW **Subject:** Golden Wedding Anniversary

Date	Mintage	F	VF	XF	Unc	B
1907	251,000	2.75	6.75	12.00	25.00	-

KM# 787 2 KRONOR **Weight:** 15.0000 g. **Composition:** 0.8000 Silver .3858 oz. ASW

Date	Mintage	F	VF	XF	Unc	B
1910 W Initial far from date	374,725	5.50	16.50	72.00	225	-
1910 W	Inc. above	37.50	110	375	1,000	-
1912 W	156,912	5.00	27.50	100	325	-
1913 W	304,616	3.25	11.50	60.00	225	-
1914 W	191,905	4.50	15.00	72.00	245	-
1915 W	155,965	5.00	20.00	75.00	250	-
1922 W	201,821	2.75	8.00	35.00	115	-
1924 W	199,314	3.25	9.00	35.00	125	-
1926 W	221,577	2.25	7.00	30.00	110	-
1928 G	160,319	3.25	8.00	35.00	180	-
1929 G	184,458	2.25	7.00	30.00	115	-
1930 G	178,387	2.25	5.50	22.00	100	-
1931 G	210,576	2.25	4.00	12.00	32.50	-
1934 G	273,419	2.25	4.00	12.00	32.50	-
1935 G	211,059	2.25	4.00	12.00	32.50	-
1936 G	491,296	2.25	3.00	10.00	21.50	-
1937 G	129,760	2.25	4.50	18.00	75.00	-
1937 G Proof	—	Value: 200				
1938 G	638,970	BV	2.75	8.00	20.00	-
1938 G Proof	—	Value: 30.00				
1939 G	1,200,329	BV	2.25	6.00	15.00	-
1939 G Proof	—	Value: 30.00				
1940 G	517,740	BV	2.25	8.00	15.00	-
1940 G Serif 4	Inc. above	2.25	5.50	10.00	32.50	-

KM# 799 2 KRONOR **Weight:** 15.0000 g. **Composition:** 0.8000 Silver .3858 oz. ASW **Subject:** 400th Anniversary of Political Liberty

Date	Mintage	F	VF	XF	Unc	B
1921 W	265,943	2.25	4.00	9.00	22.00	-

KM# 805 2 KRONOR **Weight:** 15.0000 g. **Composition:** 0.8000 Silver .3858 oz. ASW **Subject:** 300th Anniversary - Death of Gustaf II Adolf

Date	Mintage	F	VF	XF	Unc	BU
1932 G	253,770	2.50	4.50	11.50	28.00	—

KM# 807 2 KRONOR **Weight:** 15.0000 g. **Composition:** 0.8000 Silver .3858 oz. ASW **Subject:** 300th Anniversary - Settlement of Delaware

Date	Mintage	F	VF	XF	Unc	B
ND(1938) G	508,815	2.25	4.00	10.00	22.50	-

KM# 815 2 KRONOR **Weight:** 14.0000 g. **Composition:** 0.4000 Silver .1800 oz. ASW

Date	Mintage	F	VF	XF	Unc	BU
1942 G	200,000	1.75	3.75	7.00	35.00	—
1943 G	271,824	2.75	5.50	15.00	75.00	—
1944 G	627,200	BV	2.25	5.00	22.00	—
1945 G	969,675	BV	2.25	4.50	16.00	—
1945 G	Inc. above	6.50	13.50	30.00	95.00	—
Note: Without dots in motto						
1945 TS	Inc. above	BV	2.25	5.00	22.00	—
1945 TS/G	Inc. above	2.00	4.00	8.00	30.00	—
1946 TS	978,000	BV	1.50	3.50	15.00	—
1947 TS	1,465,975	BV	1.50	3.25	15.00	—
1948 TS	281,660	BV	2.25	4.75	22.00	—
1949 TS	331,715	BV	2.25	4.75	22.00	—
1950/1 TS	3,727,465	BV	1.50	3.50	15.00	—
1950 TS	Inc. above	BV	1.50	3.00	9.00	—

KM# 827 2 KRONOR **Weight:** 14.0000 g. **Composition:** 0.4000 Silver .1800 oz. ASW

Date	Mintage	F	VF	XF	Unc	BU
1952 TS	315,325	1.25	2.00	4.00	18.00	—
1953 TS	1,009,380	BV	1.25	2.25	10.00	—
1954 TS	2,300,835	BV	1.25	2.25	8.00	—
1955 TS	1,137,734	BV	1.25	2.75	10.00	—
1956 TS	1,709,468	BV	1.25	2.25	8.00	—
1957 TS	688,900	BV	1.25	2.75	16.50	—
1958 TS	1,104,555	BV	1.25	2.25	8.00	—
1959 TS	581,330	BV	1.50	2.75	16.50	—
1961 TS	533,220	BV	1.50	2.75	15.00	—
1963 U	1,468,750	BV	BV	1.75	5.75	—
1964 U	1,212,750	BV	BV	1.75	5.25	—
1965 U	1,189,500	BV	BV	1.75	5.25	—
1966 U	989,250	BV	BV	1.75	5.75	—

KM# 827a 2 KRONOR **Composition:** Copper-Nickel

Date	Mintage	F	VF	XF	Unc	BU
1968 U	1,170,750	0.45	0.55	1.25	4.50	—
1969 U	1,148,250	0.45	0.55	0.70	2.25	—
1970 U	1,159,000	0.45	0.55	0.70	2.25	—
1971 U	1,213,250	0.45	0.55	0.85	3.25	—

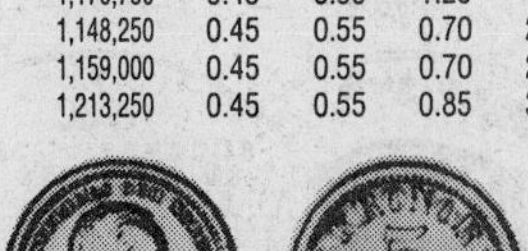

KM# 766 5 KRONOR **Weight:** 2.2402 g. **Composition:** 0.9000 Gold .0648 oz. AGW

Date	Mintage	F	VF	XF	Unc	BU
1901 EB	109,186	30.00	45.00	65.00	100	—

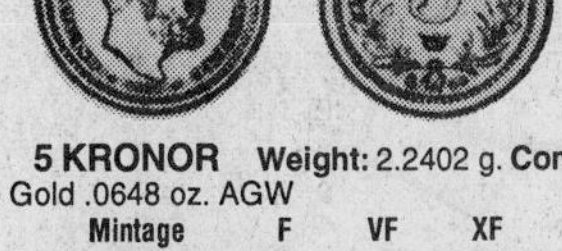

KM# 797 5 KRONOR **Weight:** 2.2402 g. **Composition:** 0.9000 Gold .0648 oz. AGW

Date	Mintage	F	VF	XF	Unc	BU
1920 W	103,000	30.00	45.00	65.00	100	—

KM# 806 5 KRONOR **Weight:** 25.0000 g. **Composition:** 0.9000 Silver .7234 oz. ASW **Subject:** 500th Anniversary of Riksdag

Date	Mintage	F	VF	XF	Unc	BU
ND(1935) G	663,819	4.00	7.00	11.50	25.00	—

KM# 828 5 KRONOR **Weight:** 22.7000 g. **Composition:** 0.4000 Silver .2920 oz. ASW **Subject:** 70th Birthday of Gustaf VI Adolf

Date	Mintage	F	VF	XF	Unc	BU
ND(1952) TS	219,237	3.50	8.50	14.50	32.50	—

KM# 829 5 KRONOR **Weight:** 18.0000 g. **Composition:** 0.4000 Silver .2315 oz. ASW **Note:** Regular issue.

Date	Mintage	F	VF	XF	Unc	BU
1954 TS	1,510,316	—	BV	3.50	7.50	—
1955 TS	3,568,985	—	BV	2.75	6.50	—
1971 U	712,500	—	BV	2.75	6.50	—

KM# 830 5 KRONOR **Weight:** 18.0000 g. **Composition:** 0.4000 Silver .2315 oz. ASW **Subject:** Constitution Sesquicentennial

Date	Mintage	F	VF	XF	Unc	BU
1959 TS	504,150	—	BV	5.00	9.00	—

KM# 838 5 KRONOR **Weight:** 18.0000 g. **Composition:** 0.4000 Silver .2315 oz. ASW **Subject:** 80th Birthday of Gustaf VI Adolf

Date	Mintage	F	VF	XF	Unc	BU
ND(1962) U	159,575	3.75	8.50	15.00	37.50	—

Note: An additional 596,525 melted

KM# 839 5 KRONOR **Weight:** 18.0000 g. **Composition:** 0.4000 Silver .2315 oz. ASW **Subject:** 100th Anniversary of Constitution Reform

Date	Mintage	F	VF	XF	Unc	BU
1966 U	1,023,500	—	BV	2.75	5.50	—

KM# 846 5 KRONOR **Composition:** Copper-Nickel Clad Nickel

Date	Mintage	F	VF	XF	Unc	BU
1972 U	21,736,000	—	—	1.25	2.00	—
1973 U	1,139,000	—	1.25	1.50	3.00	—

KM# 853 5 KRONOR **Composition:** Copper-Nickel

Date	F	VF	XF	Unc	BU
1976 U	—	—	1.00	1.75	—
1977 U	—	—	1.00	1.75	—
1978 U	—	—	1.00	1.75	—
1979 U	—	—	1.00	1.75	—
1980 U	—	—	1.00	1.75	—
1981 U	—	—	1.00	1.75	—
1982 U	—	—	0.75	1.25	—
1983 U	—	—	0.85	1.50	—
1984 U	—	—	0.85	1.50	—
1985 U	—	—	0.75	1.25	—
1986 U	—	—	1.25	4.00	—
1987 D	—	—	0.75	1.25	—
1988 D	—	—	0.85	1.50	—
1989 D	—	—	1.25	4.00	—
1990 D	—	—	0.75	1.25	—
1991 D	—	—	0.75	1.25	—
1991 U	16.50	27.50	55.00	110	—
1992 D	—	—	1.00	1.65	—

KM# 853a 5 KRONOR **Composition:** Copper-Nickel Clad Nickel

Date	Mintage	F	VF	XF	Unc	BU
1993 B	274,932	—	—	—	2.00	—
1994 B	173,438	—	—	—	2.00	—
1995 B	186,687	—	—	—	1.00	—
1996 B	180,405	—	—	—	1.00	—
1997 B	174,455	—	—	—	1.00	—
1998 B	84,991	—	—	—	1.00	—
1999 B	96,035	—	—	—	1.00	—
2000 B	3,851,326	—	—	—	1.00	—
2001 B	6,001,481	—	—	—	1.00	—

KM# 885 5 KRONOR **Composition:** Copper-Nickel Clad Nickel **Subject:** 50th Anniversary - United Nations

Date	Mintage	F	VF	XF	Unc	BU
ND(1995) B	300,000	—	—	1.00	4.00	—

KM# 767 10 KRONOR Weight: 4.4803 g. **Composition:** 0.9000 Gold .1296 oz. AGW **Obverse:** Large head

Date	Mintage	F	VF	XF	Unc	BU
1901 EB	213,286	BV	55.00	85.00	125	—
1901 EB Proof	Inc. above	Value: 525				

KM# 847 10 KRONOR Weight: 18.0000 g. **Composition:** 0.8300 Silver .4803 oz. ASW **Subject:** 90th Birthday of Gustaf VI Adolf

Date	Mintage	F	VF	XF	Unc	BU
1972 U	2,000,000	—	BV	5.00	9.00	—

Note: 652,907 were returned to the mint.

KM# 877 10 KRONOR Composition: Copper-Aluminum-Zinc

Date	Mintage	F	VF	XF	Unc	BU
1991 B Medal	106,548,000	—	—	2.00	3.00	—
1991 B Coin	Inc. above	22.50	35.00	45.00	65.00	—
1992 B	42,506,792	—	—	—	1.75	—
1993 B	20,107,110	—	—	—	1.75	—
1994 B	573,243	—	—	—	2.25	—
1995 B	523,685	—	—	—	2.25	—
1996 B	295,053	—	—	—	2.25	—
1997 B	332,450	—	—	—	2.25	—
1999 B	81,430	—	—	—	2.25	—
2000 B	8,520,983	—	—	—	1.75	—
2001 B	4,171,757	—	—	—	1.75	—

KM# 895 10 KRONOR Weight: 6.5700 g. **Composition:** Copper-Aluminum-Zinc **Ruler:** Carl XVI Gustaf **Obverse:** King's new portrait **Reverse:** Three crowns and denomination **Edge:** Reeded and plain sections **Size:** 20.4 mm.

Date	F	VF	XF	Unc	BU
2001B	—	—	—	1.75	—

KM# 765 20 KRONOR Weight: 8.9606 g. **Composition:** 0.9000 Gold .2593 oz. AGW **Obverse:** Large head

Date	Mintage	F	VF	XF	Unc	BU
1901 EB	226,679	95.00	120	160	245	—
1902 EB	113,810	95.00	125	175	265	—

KM# 800 20 KRONOR Weight: 8.9606 g. **Composition:** 0.9000 Gold .2593 oz. AGW

Date	Mintage	F	VF	XF	Unc	BU
1925 W	387,257	175	325	475	775	—

KM# 848 50 KRONOR Weight: 27.0000 g. **Composition:** 0.9250 Silver .8029 oz. ASW **Subject:** Constitutional Reform

Date	Mintage	F	VF	XF	Unc	BU
1975 U	500,000	—	5.50	8.50	12.00	—

KM# 854 50 KRONOR Weight: 27.0000 g. **Composition:** 0.9250 Silver .8029 oz. ASW **Subject:** Wedding of King Carl XVI Gustaf and Queen Silvia

Date	Mintage	F	VF	XF	Unc	BU
ND(1976) U	2,000,000	—	5.50	7.50	11.50	—

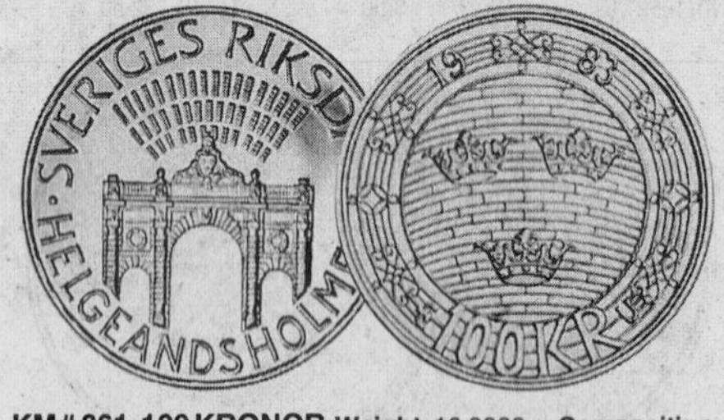

KM# 861 100 KRONOR Weight: 16.0000 g. **Composition:** 0.9250 Silver .4759 oz. ASW **Subject:** Parliament

Date	Mintage	F	VF	XF	Unc	BU
1983	400,000	—	—	—	18.50	—

KM# 863 100 KRONOR Weight: 16.0000 g. **Composition:** 0.9250 Silver .4759 oz. ASW **Subject:** Stockholm Conference

Date	Mintage	F	VF	XF	Unc	BU
1984	300,000	—	—	—	18.50	—

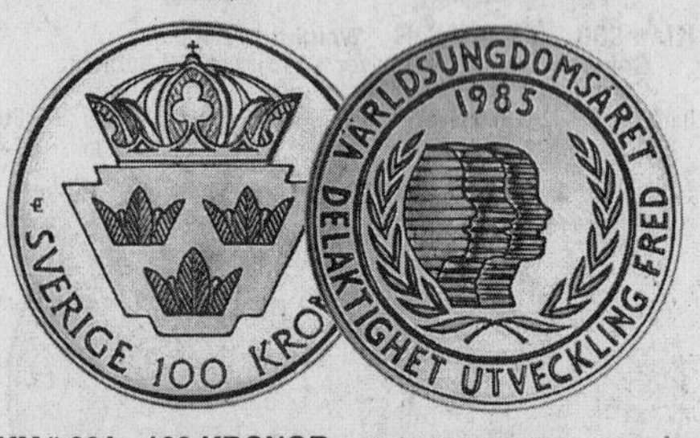

KM# 864 100 KRONOR Weight: 16.0000 g. **Composition:** 0.9250 Silver .4759 oz. ASW **Subject:** International Youth Year

Date	Mintage	F	VF	XF	Unc	BU
1985	120,000	—	—	—	20.00	—

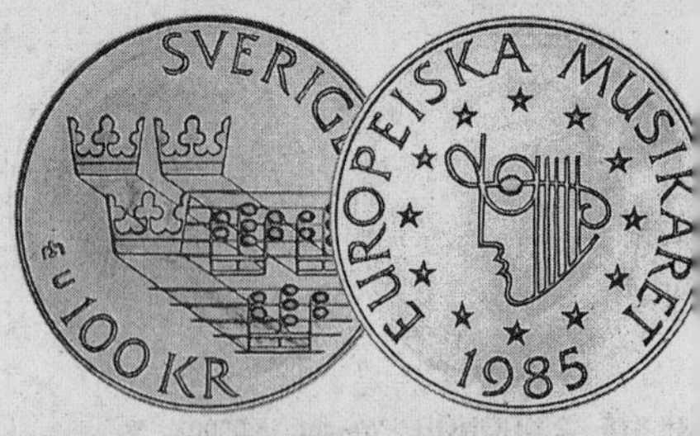

KM# 865 100 KRONOR Weight: 16.0000 g. **Composition:** 0.9250 Silver .4759 oz. ASW **Subject:** European Music Year

Date	Mintage	F	VF	XF	Unc
1985	120,000	—	—	—	20.00

KM# 866 100 KRONOR Weight: 16.0000 g. **Composition:** 0.9250 Silver .4759 oz. ASW **Subject:** International Year of the Forest

Date	Mintage	F	VF	XF	Unc
1985	120,000	—	—	—	22.50

KM# 867.1 100 KRONOR Weight: 16.0000 g. **Composition:** 0.9250 Silver .4759 oz. ASW **Subject:** 350 Anniversary of Swedish Colony in Delaware **Obverse:** Large head

Date	Mntage	F	VF	XF	Unc
ND(1988)	32,000	—	—	—	27.50

KM# 867.2 100 KRONOR Weight: 16.0000 g. **Composition:** 0.9250 Silver .4759 oz. ASW **Obverse:** Small head

Date	Mintage	F	VF	XF	Unc
ND(1988)	118,000	—	—	—	22.50

KM# 860 200 KRONOR Weight: 27.0000 g. **Composition:** 0.9250 Silver .8029 oz. ASW **Subject:** Swedish Royal Succession Law

Date	Mintage	F	VF	XF	Unc
1980 U Prooflike	500,000	—	—	—	35.00

KM# 862 200 KRONOR **Weight:** 27.0000 g. **Composition:** 0.9250 Silver .8029 oz. ASW **Subject:** 10th Anniversary of Reign

Date	Mintage	F	VF	XF	Unc	BU
1983	100,000	—	—	—	35.00	42.50

KM# 869 200 KRONOR **Weight:** 27.0000 g. **Composition:** 0.9250 Silver .8029 oz. ASW **Subject:** Ice Hockey

Date	F	VF	XF	Unc	BU
1989	—	—	—	35.00	40.00

KM# 875 200 KRONOR **Weight:** 27.0000 g. **Composition:** 0.9250 Silver .8029 oz. ASW **Subject:** Warship - Vasa

Date	Mintage	F	VF	XF	Unc	BU
1990	50,000	—	—	—	35.00	40.00

KM# 879 200 KRONOR **Weight:** 27.0000 g. **Composition:** 0.9250 Silver .8029 oz. ASW **Subject:** 200th Anniversary - Death of Gustaf III

Date	Mintage	F	VF	XF	Unc	BU
ND(1992)	50,000	—	—	—	35.00	40.00

KM# 881 200 KRONOR **Weight:** 27.0000 g. **Composition:** 0.9250 Silver .8029 oz. ASW **Subject:** 20th Anniversary of Reign

Date	Mintage	F	VF	XF	Unc	BU
1993	50,000	—	—	—	35.00	40.00

KM# 882 200 KRONOR **Weight:** 27.0000 g. **Composition:** 0.9250 Silver .8029 oz. ASW **Subject:** 50th Birthday of Queen Silvia

Date	Mintage	F	VF	XF	Unc	BU
ND(1993)	49,000	—	—	—	35.00	40.00
ND(1993) Prooflike	1,000	—	—	—	—	75.00

KM# 886 200 KRONOR **Weight:** 27.0000 g. **Composition:** 0.9250 Silver .8029 oz. ASW **Subject:** 1000th Anniversary - Swedish Mint

Date	Mintage	F	VF	XF	Unc	BU
ND(1995)	49,000	—	—	—	35.00	40.00
ND(1995) Prooflike	1,000	—	—	—	—	75.00

KM# 888 200 KRONOR **Weight:** 27.0000 g. **Composition:** 0.9250 Silver .8029 oz. ASW **Subject:** 50th Birthday - King Carl XVI Gustaf

Date	Mintage	F	VF	XF	Unc	BU
ND(1996)	49,000	—	—	—	35.00	40.00
ND(1996) Prooflike	1,000	—	—	—	—	75.00

KM# 890 200 KRONOR **Weight:** 27.0000 g. **Composition:** 0.9250 Silver .8029 oz. ASW **Subject:** Kalmar Union **Obverse:** King's portrait **Reverse:** Queen Margareta's portrait and castle

Date	F	VF	XF	Unc	BU
1997	—	—	—	35.00	45.00

KM# 892 200 KRONOR **Weight:** 27.0000 g. **Composition:** 0.9250 Silver .8029 oz. ASW **Subject:** 25th Anniversary - Reign of Carl XVI **Obverse:** King Carl XVI Gustaf

Date	Mintage	F	VF	XF	Unc	BU
1998	50,000	—	—	—	35.00	40.00

KM# 898 200 KRONOR **Weight:** 27.0300 g. **Composition:** 0.9250 Silver 0.8039 oz. ASW **Ruler:** Carl XVI Gustaf **Subject:** Millennium **Obverse:** Conjoined busts of the King Gustaf and Crown Princess Victoria **Reverse:** Arms **Edge:** Plain **Size:** 36 mm.

Date	Mintage	F	VF	XF	Unc	BU
2000	98,000	—	—	—	30.00	—
2000 Prooflike	2,000	—	—	—	—	40.00

KM# 896 200 KRONOR **Weight:** 27.2500 g. **Composition:** 0.9250 Silver .8104 oz. ASW **Ruler:** Carl XVI Gustaf **Subject:** 25th Wedding Anniversary **Obverse:** Conjoined busts of King Carl Gustaf XVI and Queen Silvia **Reverse:** National arms **Edge:** Plain **Size:** 36 mm.

Date	Mintage	F	VF	XF	Unc	BU
ND(2001)	50,000	—	—	—	35.00	45.00

KM# 868 1000 KRONOR **Weight:** 5.8000 g. **Composition:** 0.9000 Gold .1678 oz. AGW **Subject:** 350th Anniversary of Swedish Colony in Delaware

Date	Mintage	F	VF	XF	Unc	BU
ND(1988)	10,000	—	—	—	225	285

KM# 870 1000 KRONOR **Weight:** 5.8000 g. **Composition:** 0.9000 Gold .1678 oz. AGW **Subject:** Ice Hockey

Date	Mintage	F	VF	XF	Unc	BU
1989	20,000	—	—	—	175	225

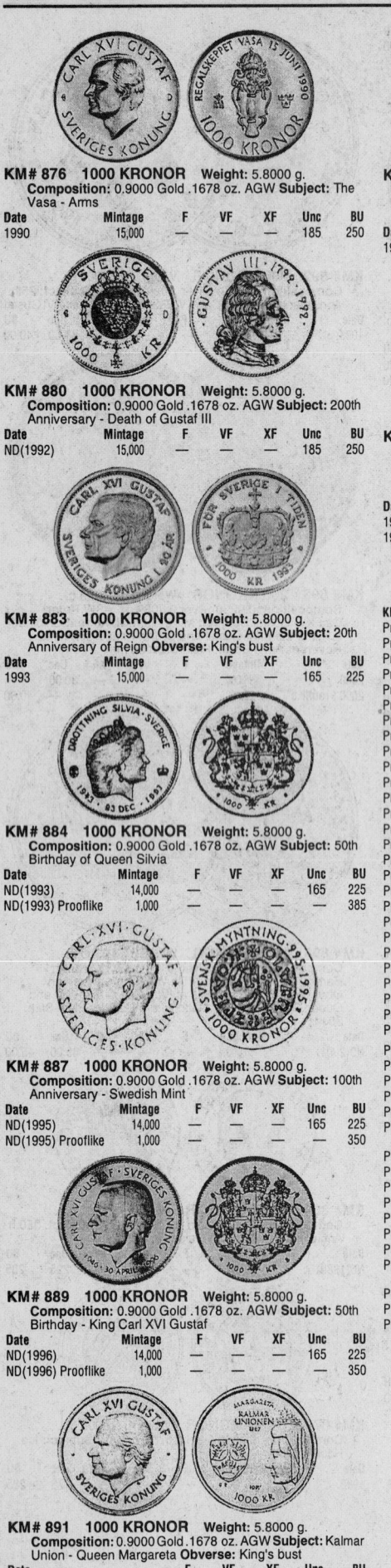

KM# 876 1000 KRONOR Weight: 5.8000 g. **Composition:** 0.9000 Gold .1678 oz. AGW **Subject:** The Vasa - Arms

Date	Mintage	F	VF	XF	Unc	BU
1990	15,000	—	—	—	185	250

KM# 880 1000 KRONOR Weight: 5.8000 g. **Composition:** 0.9000 Gold .1678 oz. AGW **Subject:** 200th Anniversary - Death of Gustaf III

Date	Mintage	F	VF	XF	Unc	BU
ND(1992)	15,000	—	—	—	185	250

KM# 883 1000 KRONOR Weight: 5.8000 g. **Composition:** 0.9000 Gold .1678 oz. AGW **Subject:** 20th Anniversary of Reign **Obverse:** King's bust

Date	Mintage	F	VF	XF	Unc	BU
1993	15,000	—	—	—	165	225

KM# 884 1000 KRONOR Weight: 5.8000 g. **Composition:** 0.9000 Gold .1678 oz. AGW **Subject:** 50th Birthday of Queen Silvia

Date	Mintage	F	VF	XF	Unc	BU
ND(1993)	14,000	—	—	—	165	225
ND(1993) Prooflike	1,000	—	—	—	—	385

KM# 887 1000 KRONOR Weight: 5.8000 g. **Composition:** 0.9000 Gold .1678 oz. AGW **Subject:** 100th Anniversary - Swedish Mint

Date	Mintage	F	VF	XF	Unc	BU
ND(1995)	14,000	—	—	—	165	225
ND(1995) Prooflike	1,000	—	—	—	—	350

KM# 889 1000 KRONOR Weight: 5.8000 g. **Composition:** 0.9000 Gold .1678 oz. AGW **Subject:** 50th Birthday - King Carl XVI Gustaf

Date	Mintage	F	VF	XF	Unc	BU
ND(1996)	14,000	—	—	—	165	225
ND(1996) Prooflike	1,000	—	—	—	—	350

KM# 891 1000 KRONOR Weight: 5.8000 g. **Composition:** 0.9000 Gold .1678 oz. AGW **Subject:** Kalmar Union - Queen Margareta **Obverse:** King's bust

Date	F	VF	XF	Unc	BU
1997	—	—	—	145	185

KM# 893 1000 KRONOR Weight: 5.8000 g. **Composition:** 0.9000 Gold .1678 oz. AGW **Subject:** 25th Anniversary - Reign of King Carl XVI **Obverse:** King Carl XVI Gustaf

Date	Mintage	F	VF	XF	Unc	BU
1998	15,000	—	—	—	145	185

KM# 899 2000 KRONOR Weight: 13.0000 g. **Composition:** 0.9000 Gold 0.3762 oz. AGW **Ruler:** Carl XVI Gustaf **Subject:** Millennium **Obverse:** Conjoined busts of the King Gustaf and Crown Princess Victoria. **Reverse:** Arms. **Edge:** Plain. **Size:** 26 mm.

Date	Mintage	F	VF	XF	Unc	BU
1999	30,000	—	—	—	225	—
1999 Prooflike	2,000	—	—	—	—	—

PATTERNS

Including off metal strikes

KM#	Date	Mintage	Identification	Mkt Val
Pn99	1901	—	2 Ore. Iron. KM#716	—
Pn100	1901	—	5 Kronor. Bronze. KM#766	—
Pn101	1909	—	2 Ore. Bronze. Flat-based 2	—
Pn102	1909	—	5 Ore. Bronze. Flat-based 5	—
Pn103	1913	—	2 Kronor. Bronze. KM#787	—
Pn104	1916	—	Ore. Iron. KM#777.2	—
Pn105	1916	—	2 Ore. Iron. KM#778	—
Pn106	1916	—	5 Ore. Iron. KM#779.2	—
Pn107	1918 W	—	10 Ore. Iron. Center hole	—
Pn108	1918 W	—	25 Ore. Iron. Center hole	—
Pn109	1918 W	—	25 Ore. Silver. Center hole	—
Pn110	1918 W	—	50 Ore. Iron. Center hole	—
Pn111	1918 W	—	50 Ore. Silver. Center hole	—
Pn112	1918 W	—	Krona. Iron. Center hole	—
Pn113	1918 W	—	Krona. Nickel. Center hole	—
Pn114	1918 W	—	Krona. Silver. Center hole	—
Pn115	1918	—	5 Kronor. Nickel. KM#797	—
Pn116	1919	—	Ore. Bronze. Center hole	—
Pn117	1919	—	5 Ore. Iron. Center hole	—
Pn118	1919	—	5 Ore. Bronze. Center hole	—
Pn119	1919	—	10 Ore. Nickel. KM#780	—
Pn120	1919	—	2 Kronor. Bronze. KM#787	—
Pn121	1920	—	2 Ore. Bronze. Copper hole	—
Pn122	1920	—	5 Ore. Bronze. Center hole	—
Pn123	1920 W	—	50 Ore. Silver.	—
Pn124	1921	—	2 Kronor. Bronze. KM#787	—
Pn125	1949	—	5 Ore. Bronze. "PROV"	—
PnA126	1949	—	50 Ore. Aluminum. "PROV"	—
Pn126	1950	—	Ore. Copper Plated Iron. KM#810	—
Pn127	1950	—	Ore. Copper Plated Iron. "PROV"	—
Pn128	1950	—	2 Ore. Copper Plated Iron. KM#811	—
Pn129	1950	—	2 Ore. Copper Plated Iron. "PROV"	—
Pn130	1950	—	5 Ore. Tombac Plated Iron. KM#812	—
Pn131	1950	—	5 Ore. Copper Plated Iron. "PROV"	—
Pn132	1950	—	10 Ore. Nickel Plated Iron. "PROV"	—
Pn133	1950	—	25 Ore. Nickel Plated Iron. "PROV"	—
Pn134	1951	—	2 Ore. Bronze. "PROV"	—
Pn135	1951	—	2 Ore. Iron. "PROV"	—
Pn136	1951	—	50 Ore. Silver. "PROV"	—
Pn137	1951	—	Krona. Silver. Plain edge. "PROV"	—
Pn138	1951	—	Krona. Silver. Reeded edge. "PROV"	—
Pn139	1951 TS	—	Krona. Silver. "PROV"	—
Pn140	1951 TS	—	5 Kronor. Silver. "PROV"	—
Pn141	1952 TS	—	5 Ore. Bronze. "PROV"	—
Pn142	1952 TS	—	10 Ore. Silver. "PROV"	
Pn143	1952 TS	—	10 Ore. Copper-Nickel. "PROV"	
Pn144	1952 TS	—	10 Ore. Silver. "PROV"	
Pn145	1952 TS	—	25 Ore. Silver. "PROV"	
Pn146	1952 TS	—	50 Ore. Silver. "PROV", high relief	
Pn147	1952 TS	—	50 Ore. Silver. "PROV", low relief	
Pn148	1952 TS	—	Krona. Silver. "PROV"	
Pn149	1952 TS	—	Krona. Silver. "PROV"; different head	
Pn150	1952 TS	—	5 Kronor. Silver. Plain edge. "PROV"	
Pn151	1952 TS	—	5 Kronor. Silver. Reeded edge. "PROV"	
Pn152	1953 TS	—	5 Kronor. Silver. Plain edge. "PROV"	
Pn153	1953 TS	—	5 Kronor. Silver. Reeded edge. "PROV"	
Pn154	1953 TS	—	5 Kronor. Silver. "PROV"; small value	
Pn155	1953 TS	—	5 Kronor. Silver. "PROV"; large value	
Pn156	1954 TS	—	5 Kronor. Silver. "PROV"	
Pn157	1970 U	—	Ore. Iron. 1.5000 g. KM#820	1

MINT SETS

KM#	Date	Mintage	Identification	Issue Price	Mkt Val
MS1	1973 (6)	20,000	KM#826a, 835-837, 845, 846	5.00	22.
MS2	1976 (6)	61,234	KM#849-853, 855 Swedish - soft plastic case	5.00	12.
MS3	1976 (6)	10,000	KM#849-853, 855 English - soft plastic case	5.00	12.
MS4	1977 (6)	43,346	KM#849-853, 855 Swedish - soft plastic case	5.00	12.
MS5	1977 (6)	5,800	KM#849-853, 855 English - soft plastic case	5.00	13.
MS6	1978 (6)	20,115	KM#849-853, 855 Swedish - soft plastic case	5.00	20.
MS7	1978 (6)	1,500	KM#849-853, 855 English - soft plastic case	5.00	22.
MS8	1978 (6)	31,245	KM#849-853, 855 Swedish - soft plastic case	5.00	27.
MS10	1979 (6)	1,900	KM#849-853, 855 English - soft plastic case	5.00	17.
MS11	1979 (6)	38,957	KM#849-853, 855 Swedish - soft plastic case	5.00	16.
MS12	1979 (6)	9,871	KM#849-853, 855 English - soft plastic case	5.00	25.
MS9	1979 (6)	10,200	KM#849-853, 855 Swedish - soft plastic case	5.00	12.
MS13	1980 (6)	10,140	KM#849-853, 855 Swedish - soft plastic case	5.00	12.
MS14	1980 (6)	2,000	KM#849-853, 855 English - soft plastic case	5.00	17.
MS15	1980 (6)	45,495	KM#849-853, 855 Swedish - soft plastic case	5.50	15.
MS16	1980 (6)	9,880	KM#849-853, 855 English - soft plastic case	5.50	25.
MS17	1981 (6)	11,927	KM#849a, 850-853, 855 Swedish - soft plastic case	5.50	12.
MS18	1981 (6)	2,000	KM#849a, 850-853, 855 English - soft plastic case	5.50	17.
MS19	1981 (6)	65,338	KM#849a, 850-853, 855 Swedish - hard plastic case	5.50	10.
MS20	1981 (6)	5,000	KM#849a, 850-853, 855 English - hard plastic case	5.50	30.
MS21	1982 (5)	9,463	KM#849a, 850-851, 852a, 853 Swedish - soft plastic case	5.50	12.
MS22	1982 (5)	2,300	KM#849a, 850-851, 852a, 853 English - soft plastic case	5.50	13.
MS23	1982 (5)	58,772	KM#849a, 850-851, 852a, 853 Swedish - hard plastic case	5.50	10.
MS24	1982 (5)	4,978	KM#849a, 850-851, 852a, 853 Swedish - hard plastic case	5.50	30.
MS25	1983 (5)	10,300	KM#849a, 850-851, 852a, 853 Swedish - soft plastic case	6.00	12.
MS26	1983 (6)	2,750	KM#849a, 850-851, 852a, 853 English - soft plastic case	6.00	13.
MS27	1983 (6)	57,205	KM#849a, 850-851, 852a, 853 Swedish - hard plastic case	6.00	10.
MS28	1983 (6)	5,017	KM#849a, 850-851, 852a, 853 English - hard plastic case	6.00	30.
MS29	1984 (5)	10,100	KM#849a, 850-851, 852a, 853 Swedish - soft plastic case	6.00	10.
MS30	1984 (5)	1,600	KM#849a, 850-851, 852a, 853 English - soft plastic case	6.00	22.
MS31	1984 (5)	70,849	KM#849a, 850-851, 852a, 853 Swedish - hard plastic case	6.00	10.
MS32	1984 (5)	4,271	KM#849a, 850-851, 852a, 853 English - hard plastic case	6.00	35.
MS33	1985 (4)	8,000	KM#850, 852a, 853, 855 Swedish - soft plastic case	6.50	11.
MS34	1985 (4)	1,445	KM#850, 852a, 853, 855 English - soft plastic case	6.50	22.
MS35	1985 (4)	52,462	KM#850, 852a, 853, 855 Swedish - hard plastic case	6.50	10.

KM#	Date	Mintage	Identification	Issue Price	Mkt Val
36	1985 (4)	2,717	KM#850, 852a, 853, 855 English - hard plastic case	6.50	45.00
37	1986 (4)	16,265	KM#850, 852a, 853, 855 Swedish - soft plastic case	6.50	16.50
38	1986 (4)	1,880	KM#850, 852a, 853, 855 English - soft plastic case	6.50	22.50
39	1986 (4)	54,890	KM#850, 852a, 853, 855 Swedish - hard plastic case	6.50	20.00
40	1986 (4)	967	KM#850, 852a, 853, 855 English - hard plastic case	6.50	100
35	1996 (4)	5,481	KM#852a, 853a, 877, 878 Souvenir folder	11.05	14.50
41	1987 (4)	5,600	KM#850, 852a, 853, 855 Swedish - soft plastic case	6.50	10.00
42	1987 (4)	1,100	KM#850, 852a, 853, 855 English - soft plastic case	6.55	25.00
43	1987 (4)	70,060	KM#850, 852a, 853, 855 Swedish - hard plastic case	6.50	10.00
44	1987 (4)	557	KM#850, 852a, 853, 855 Swedish and English - hard plastic case	6.50	200
45	1988 (4)	4,815	KM#850, 852a, 853, 855 Swedish - soft plastic case	6.50	15.00
46	1988 (4)	2,456	KM#850, 852a, 853, 855 English - soft plastic case	6.50	16.50
47	1988 (4)	56,753	KM#850, 852a, 853, 855 Swedish - hard plastic case	6.50	15.00
48	1988 (4)	1,777	KM#850, 852a, 853, 855 English - hard plastic case	6.50	47.50
49	1989 (4)	7,170	KM#850, 852a, 853, 855 Swedish - soft plastic case	6.50	16.00
50	1989 (4)	56,895	KM#850, 852a, 853, 855 Swedish - hard plastic case	6.50	15.00
51	1989 (4)	2,780	KM#850, 852a, 853, 855 English - hard plastic case	—	17.50
52	1989 (4)	1,000	KM#850, 852a, 853, 855 English - hard plastic case	—	32.50
53	1990 (4)	6,503	KM#850, 852a, 853, 855 Swedish - soft plastic case	6.50	12.50
54	1990 (4)	55,265	KM#850, 852a, 853, 855 Swedish - hard plastic case	6.50	13.50
55	1990 (4)	2,440	KM#850, 852a, 853, 855 English - hard plastic case	—	13.50
56	1990 (4)	2,492	KM#850, 852a, 853, 855 English - hard plastic case	—	11.50
57	1991 (5)	8,079	KM#850, 852a, 853, 855, 877 Swedish - soft plastic case	—	17.50
58	1991 (5)	1,680	KM#850, 852a, 853, 855, 877 English - soft plastic case	—	17.50
59	1991 (5)	62,517	KM#850, 852a, 853, 855, 877 Swedish - hard plastic case	—	18.50
60	1991 (5)	2,884	KM#850, 852a, 853, 855, 877 English - hard plastic case	—	20.00
61	1991 (5)	5,000	KM#850 (3), 855 (2), medal	—	12.00
62	1992 (4)	5,600	KM#852a, 853, 877-878 Swedish - soft plastic case	6.50	11.50
63	1992 (4)	1,840	KM#852a, 853, 877-878 English - soft plastic case	6.50	11.50
64	1992 (4)	61,183	KM#852a, 853, 877-878 Swedish - hard plastic case	6.50	11.00
65	1992 (4)	2,187	KM#852a, 853, 877-878 English - hard plastic case	6.50	13.50
66	1993 (4)	4,784	KM#852a, 853a, 877, 878 Swedish - soft plastic case	6.50	16.50
67	1993 (4)	2,016	KM#852a, 853a, 877, 878 English - soft plastic case	6.50	11.00
68	1993 (4)	57,700	KM#852a, 853a, 877, 878 Swedish - hard plastic case	6.50	16.50
69	1993 (4)	2,164	KM#852a, 853a, 877, 878 English - hard plastic case	6.50	17.50
S70	1993 (4)	4,956	KM#852a, 853a, 877, 878 Souvenir folder	—	22.50
S71	1994 (4)	5,360	KM#852a, 853a, 877, 878 Swedish - soft plastic case	—	16.50
S72	1994 (4)	2,240	KM#852a, 853a, 877, 878 English - soft plastic case	—	15.00
S73	1994 (4)	48,881	KM#852a, 853a, 877, 878, mint medal Swedish - hard plastic case	—	16.50
S74	1994 (4)	1,966	KM#852a, 853a, 877, 878, mint medal English - hard plastic case	—	17.50
S75	1994 (4)	9,950	KM#852a, 853a, 877, 878, mint medal Souvenir folder	—	13.50
S76	1995 (5)	10,000	KM#852a, 853a, 877, 878, 885 Swedish - soft plastic case	14.00	32.50
S77	1995 (4)	45,836	KM#852a, 877, 878, 885, medal Swedish - hard plastic case	20.00	16.50
S78	1995 (5)	4,650	KM#852a, 853a, 877, 878, 885 English - soft plastic case	—	15.00
S79	1995 (4)	2,479	KM#852a, 853a, 877, 878, 885, medal English - hard plastic case	—	18.50
S80	1995 (4)	5,000	KM#852a, 877, 878, 885, medal Souvenir folder	—	32.50
S81	1996 (4)	42,729	KM#852a, 853a, 877, 878 Swedish - hard plastic case	11.05	13.50
S82	1996 (4)	2,000	KM#852a, 853a, 877, 878 English - hard plastic case	11.05	16.50
S83	1996 (4)	7,100	KM#852a, 853a, 877, 878 Swedish - soft plastic case	7.55	11.50
S84	1996 (4)	2,500	KM#852a, 853a, 877, 878 English - soft plastic case	7.55	12.50

KM#	Date	Mintage	Identification	Issue Price	Mkt Val
MS86	1997 (4)	39,470	KM#852a, 853a, 877, 878 Swedish - hard plastic case	11.05	18.50
MS87	1997 (4)	1,997	KM#852a, 853a, 877, 878 English - hard plastic case	11.05	22.50
MS88	1997 (4)	5,100	KM#852a, 853a, 877, 878 Swedish - soft plastic case	7.55	15.00
MS89	1997 (4)	2,200	KM#852a, 853a, 877, 878 English - soft plastic case	7.55	16.50
MS90	1997 (4)	4,954	KM#852a, 853a, 877, 878 Souvenir folder	11.05	16.50
MS91	1998 (4)	7,067	KM#852a, 853a, 877, 878 Souvenir folder	13.34	13.50
MS92	1998 (4)	5,170	KM#852a, 853a, 877, 878 Swedish - soft plastic case	—	15.00
MS93	1998 (4)	2,000	KM#852a, 853a, 877, 878 English - soft plastic case	—	16.50
MS94	1998 (4)	34,750	KM#852a, 853a, 877, 878 Swedish - hard plastic case	—	18.50
MS95	1998 (4)	1,980	KM#852a, 853a, 877, 878 English - hard plastic case	—	20.00
MS100	1999 (4)	8,045	KM#852a, 853a, 877, 878 Souvenir folder	—	13.50
MS96	1999 (4)	4,480	KM#852a, 853a, 877, 878 Swedish - hard plastic case	—	11.50
MS97	1999 (4)	2,080	KM#852a, 853a, 877, 878 English - soft plastic case	—	12.50
MS98	1999 (4)	33,334	KM#852a, 853a, 877, 878 Swedish - hard plastic case	—	16.50
MS99	1999 (4)	1,970	KM#852a, 853a, 877, 878 English - hard plastic case	—	17.50
MS101	2000 (4)	5,000	KM#852a, 853a, 877, 878 Swedish - hard plastic case	—	8.00
MS102	2000 (4)	1,000	KM#852a, 853a, 877, 878 English - soft plastic case	—	8.00
MS103	2000 (4)	30,912	KM#852a, 853a, 877, 878 Swedish - hard plastic case	—	13.50
MS104	2000 (4)	1,801	KM#852a, 853a, 877, 878 English - hard plastic case	—	13.50
MS105	2000 (4)	7,209	KM#852a, 853a, 877, 878 Souvenir folder	—	13.50
MS106	2000 (4)	14,300	KM#852a, 853a, 877, 878 Special Millennium set	—	20.00

PROOF-LIKE SETS (PL)

KM#	Date	Mintage	Identification	Issue Price	Mkt Val
PL1	1993 (2)	1,000	KM#882, 884	—	460
PL2	1995 (2)	1,000	KM#886, 887	—	425
PL3	ND(1996) (2)	1,000	KM#888, 889	—	425
PL4	1999 (2)	2,000	KM#898-899	—	250

SWITZERLAND

The Swiss Confederation, located in central Europe north of Italy and south of Germany, has an area of 15,941 sq. mi. (41,290 sq. km.) and a population of *6.6 million. Capital: Bern. The economy centers about a well developed manufacturing industry. Machinery, chemicals, watches and clocks, and textiles are exported.

Switzerland, the habitat of lake dwellers in prehistoric times, was peopled by the Celtic Helvetians when Julius Caesar made it a part of the Roman Empire in 58 B.C. After the decline of Rome, Switzerland was invaded by Teutonic tribes, who established small temporal holdings which in the Middle Ages, became a federation of fiefs of the Holy Roman Empire. As a nation, Switzerland originated in 1291 when the districts of Nidwalden, Schwyz and Uri united to defeat Austria and attain independence as the Swiss Confederation. After acquiring new cantons in the 14th century, Switzerland was made independent from the Holy Roman Empire by the 1648 Treaty of Westphalia. The revolutionary armies of Napoleonic France occupied Switzerland and set up the Helvetian Republic, 1798-1803. After the fall of Napoleon, the Congress of Vienna, 1815, recognized the independence of Switzerland and guaranteed its neutrality. The Swiss Constitutions of 1848 and 1874 established a union modeled upon that of the United States.

MINT MARKS

B - Bern
BA - Basel
BB - Strasbourg
S – Solothurn

NOTE: The coinage of Switzerland has been struck at the Bern Mint since 1853 with but a few exceptions. All coins minted there carry a B mint mark through 1969, except for the 2-Centime and 2-Franc values where the mint mark was discontinued after 1968. In 1968 and 1969 some issues were struck at both Bern (B) and in London (no mint mark).

MONETARY SYSTEM

100 Rappen (Centimes) = 1 Franc

CONFEDERATION

DECIMAL COINAGE

100 Rappen (Centimes) = 1 Franc

KM# 3.2 RAPPEN **Composition:** Bronze **Obverse:** Thin cross in shield

Date	Mintage	F	VF	XF	Unc	BU
1902B	950,000	—	50.00	80.00	150	250
1903B	1,000,000	—	25.00	35.00	65.00	90.00
1904B	1,000,000	—	25.00	35.00	60.00	85.00
1905B	2,000,000	—	8.00	12.00	16.00	24.00
1906B	1,000,000	—	17.50	30.00	40.00	75.00
1907B	2,000,000	—	8.00	15.00	18.00	25.00
1908B	3,000,000	—	2.50	6.00	12.00	18.00
1909B	1,000,000	—	15.00	20.00	35.00	54.00
1910B	500,000	—	8.00	14.00	18.00	25.00
1911B	500,000	—	8.00	14.00	20.00	25.00
1912B	2,000,000	—	2.50	5.00	14.00	21.50
1913B	3,000,000	—	1.00	2.00	4.00	7.00
1914B	3,500,000	—	1.50	3.50	7.00	12.00
1915B	3,000,000	—	1.50	3.50	7.00	12.00
1917B	2,000,000	—	3.50	6.00	18.00	30.00
1918B	3,000,000	—	1.50	3.00	6.00	10.00
1919B	3,000,000	—	1.50	3.00	6.00	110
1920B	1,000,000	—	3.00	7.00	10.00	15.00
1921B	3,000,000	—	1.50	3.00	5.00	8.00
1924B	2,000,000	—	4.00	8.00	15.00	20.00
1925/4B	2,500,000	—	4.50	10.00	20.00	30.00
1925B	Inc. above	—	2.00	4.00	6.00	10.00
1926B	2,000,000	—	2.00	4.00	6.50	10.00
1927B	1,500,000	—	3.00	6.00	11.00	15.00
1928B	2,000,000	—	1.50	3.00	8.50	13.00
1929B	4,000,000	—	0.50	1.00	3.00	5.00
1930B	2,500,000	—	1.50	3.50	5.00	8.00
1931B	5,000,000	—	0.50	1.25	3.00	6.00
1932B	5,000,000	—	0.50	1.00	3.00	6.00
1933B	3,000,000	—	0.75	1.50	3.00	6.00
1934B	3,000,000	—	0.50	1.00	3.00	6.00
1936B	2,000,000	—	1.50	2.50	6.00	12.00
1937B	2,400,000	—	0.50	1.00	3.00	5.00
1938B	5,300,000	—	0.50	1.00	3.00	5.00
1939B	10,000	—	35.00	50.00	70.00	110

Date	Mintage	F	VF	XF	Unc	BU
1940B	3,027,000	—	1.00	1.50	6.00	9.00
1941B	12,794,000	—	0.25	0.50	1.50	2.50

KM# 3a RAPPEN Composition: Zinc

Date	Mintage	F	VF	XF	Unc	BU
1942B	17,969,000	—	0.50	1.00	3.50	6.00
1943B	8,647,000	—	0.75	1.25	3.50	6.00
1944B	11,825,000	—	0.50	1.00	3.50	6.00
1945B	2,800,000	—	6.00	9.00	17.50	27.50
1946B	12,063,000	—	0.50	1.00	3.50	6.00

KM# 46 RAPPEN Composition: Bronze

Date	Mintage	F	VF	XF	Unc	BU
1948B		—	0.10	0.50	2.00	5.00
1949B		—	0.10	0.50	2.00	5.00
1950B		—	1.00	2.50	4.00	7.00
1951B		—	0.10	0.30	2.00	4.00
1952B		—	0.10	0.30	2.00	4.00
1953B		—	0.10	0.30	2.00	4.00
1954B		—	0.10	0.30	2.00	4.00
1955B		—	0.10	0.60	2.00	4.00
1956B		—	0.10	0.30	2.00	4.00
1957B		—	0.10	0.15	0.35	0.50
1958B		—	0.10	0.15	0.35	0.50
1959B		—	0.10	0.15	0.35	0.50
1962B		—	0.10	0.15	0.35	0.50
1963B		—	—	0.10	0.25	0.35
1966B		—	—	0.10	0.25	0.35
1967B		—	—	0.10	0.25	0.35
1968B		—	—	0.10	0.25	0.35
1969B		—	—	0.10	0.25	0.35
1970		—	—	0.10	0.25	0.35
1971		—	—	0.10	0.25	0.35
1973		—	—	0.10	0.25	0.35
1974		—	—	0.10	0.25	0.35
1974 Proof	2,400	Value: 10.00				
1975		—	—	0.10	0.25	0.35
1975 Proof	10,000	Value: 1.25				
1976		—	—	0.10	0.25	0.35
1976 Proof	5,130	Value: 1.50				
1977		—	—	0.10	0.25	0.35
1977 Proof	7,030	Value: 1.00				
1978		—	—	0.10	0.25	0.35
1978 Proof	10,000	Value: 1.00				
1979		—	—	0.10	0.35	0.50
1979 Proof	10,000	Value: 1.00				
1980		—	—	0.10	0.35	0.50
1980 Proof	10,000	Value: 1.00				
1981		—	—	0.10	0.25	0.35
1981 Proof	10,000	Value: 1.00				
1982		—	—	0.10	0.20	0.30
1982 Proof	10,000	Value: 2.00				
1983		—	—	0.10	0.25	0.35
1983 Proof	11,000	Value: 1.00				
1984		—	—	0.10	0.25	0.35
1984 Proof	14,000	Value: 1.00				
1985		—	—	0.10	0.25	0.35
1985 Proof	12,000	Value: 1.00				
1986B		—	—	0.10	0.50	1.00
1986B Proof	10,000	Value: 1.00				
1987B		—	—	0.10	0.50	1.00
1987B Proof	8,800	Value: 1.25				
1988B		—	—	0.10	0.35	0.50
1988B Proof	9,000	Value: 1.25				
1989B		—	—	0.10	0.35	0.50
1989B Proof	8,800	Value: 1.25				
1990B		—	—	—	0.50	1.00
1990B Proof	8,900	Value: 1.25				
1991B		—	—	—	1.50	2.50
1991B Proof	9,900	Value: 5.00				
1992B		—	—	—	1.50	2.50
1992B Proof	7,450	Value: 3.50				
1993B		—	—	—	3.00	4.00
1993B Proof	6,200	Value: 5.00				
1994B		—	—	—	0.25	0.50
1994B Proof	6,100	Value: 1.00				
1995B		—	—	—	0.25	0.50
1995B Proof	6,100	Value: 1.00				
1996B		—	—	—	0.50	1.00
1996B Proof	6,100	Value: 2.00				
1997B		—	—	—	0.50	1.00
1997B Proof	5,500	Value: 2.00				
1998B		—	—	—	0.50	1.00
1998B Proof	4,800	Value: 2.00				
1999B		—	—	—	0.50	1.00
1999B Proof	5,000	Value: 2.00				
2000B		—	—	—	0.50	1.00
2000B Proof	5,500	Value: 2.00				
2001B		—	—	—	0.50	1.00
2001B Proof	6,000	Value: 2.00				
2002B		—	—	—	0.50	1.00
2002B Proof	—	Value: 2.00				

KM# 4 2 RAPPEN Composition: Bronze

Date	Mintage	F	VF	XF	Unc	BU
1902B	500,000	—	24.00	45.00	85.00	150
1903B	500,000	—	24.00	30.00	50.00	95.00
1904B	500,000	—	22.00	30.00	50.00	90.00
1906B	500,000	—	22.00	30.00	50.00	95.00
1907B	1,000,000	—	4.00	8.00	20.00	30.00
1908B	100,000	—	3.00	5.00	12.00	18.00
1909B	100,000	—	4.00	8.00	12.00	18.00
1910B	500,000	—	20.00	27.50	45.00	75.00
1912B	100,000	—	4.50	7.00	17.50	30.00
1913B	1,000,000	—	5.50	8.00	20.00	30.00
1914B	1,000,000	—	5.50	8.00	20.00	30.00
1915B	1,000,000	—	4.50	8.00	20.00	30.00
1918B	1,000,000	—	4.00	5.00	12.50	20.00
1919B	2,000,000	—	1.50	3.00	8.00	12.00
1920B	500,000	—	25.00	40.00	70.00	110
1925B	1,250,000	—	1.00	3.00	8.00	12.00
1926B	750,000	—	17.50	30.00	40.00	70.00
1927B	500,000	—	25.00	35.00	50.00	80.00
1928B	500,000	—	25.00	35.00	50.00	75.00
1929B	750,000	—	7.50	12.00	18.00	25.00
1930B	1,000,000	—	2.00	4.00	10.00	15.00
1931B	1,288,000	—	3.00	6.00	10.00	15.00
1932B	1,500,000	—	1.00	2.00	6.00	9.00
1933B	1,000,000	—	3.00	6.00	10.00	15.00
1934B	500,000	—	12.50	22.50	35.00	50.00
1936B	500,000	—	5.00	9.00	15.00	24.00
1937B	1,200,000	—	2.00	3.00	5.00	8.00
1938B	1,369,000	—	2.00	4.00	8.00	12.00
1941B	3,448,000	—	0.75	1.50	3.00	6.00

KM# 4a 2 RAPPEN Composition: Zinc

Date	Mintage	F	VF	XF	Unc	BU
1942B	8,954,000	—	0.50	1.50	4.00	7.00
1943B	4,499,000	—	0.75	3.00	8.00	12.00
1944B	8,086,000	—	0.50	1.50	4.00	7.00
1945B	3,640,000	—	2.00	6.00	16.00	22.50
1946B	1,393,000	—	10.00	20.00	30.00	45.00

KM# 47 2 RAPPEN Composition: Bronze

Date	Mintage	F	VF	XF	Unc	BU
1948B	10,197,000	—	0.25	0.50	4.00	6.00
1951B	9,622,000	—	0.25	0.50	3.00	5.00
1952B	1,915,000	—	0.50	1.00	3.00	7.00
1953B	2,006,000	—	0.50	1.00	2.50	4.00
1954B	2,539,000	—	0.50	1.00	2.50	4.00
1955B	2,493,000	—	0.25	1.00	2.50	3.50
1957B	8,099,000	—	0.15	0.25	1.25	2.00
1958B	6,078,000	—	0.15	0.25	1.25	2.00
1963B	10,065,000	—	0.10	0.15	0.45	0.75
1966B	2,510,000	—	0.10	0.20	0.45	0.75
1967B	1,510,000	—	0.10	0.20	0.50	0.75
1968B	2,860,000	—	0.10	0.20	0.45	0.75
1969	6,200,000	—	0.10	0.15	0.45	0.75
1970	3,115,000	—	0.10	0.15	0.45	0.75
1974	3,540,000	—	0.10	0.15	0.45	0.75
1974 Proof	2,400	Value: 25.00				

KM# 26 5 RAPPEN Composition: Copper-Nickel

Date	Mintage	F	VF	XF	Unc	BU
1901B	3,000,000	—	1.50	10.00	27.50	42.00
1902B	1,000,000	—	15.00	50.00	90.00	130
1902B T over L in HELVETICA	Inc. above	—	20.00	60.00	100	150
1903B	2,000,000	—	2.50	15.00	40.00	80.00
1904B	1,000,000	—	14.00	40.00	95.00	165
1905B	1,000,000	—	12.00	22.50	75.00	110
1906B	3,000,000	—	1.50	7.00	20.00	30.00
1907B	5,000,000	—	1.00	4.00	10.00	15.00
1908B	3,000,000	—	1.25	7.00	15.00	22.00
1909B	2,000,000	—	1.50	8.00	20.00	27.00
1910B	1,000,000	—	8.00	15.00	45.00	75.00
1911B	2,000,000	—	1.50	6.00	12.50	18.00
1912B	3,000,000	—	1.00	6.00	12.50	18.00
1913B	3,000,000	—	1.00	6.00	14.00	20.00
1914B	3,000,000	—	1.00	6.00	48.00	70.00
1915B	3,000,000	—	1.00	10.00	120	175
1917B	1,000,000	—	4.00	10.00	75.00	125

Date	Mintage	F	VF	XF	Unc	
1919B	6,000,000	—	0.25	5.00	16.00	24
1920B	5,000,000	—	0.25	5.00	16.00	24
1921B	3,000,000	—	0.25	5.00	16.00	24
1922B	4,000,000	—	0.25	4.00	12.50	20
1925B	3,000,000	—	0.25	4.00	12.50	20
1926B	3,000,000	—	0.25	4.00	12.50	20
1927B	2,000,000	—	0.25	4.00	17.50	25
1928B	2,000,000	—	0.25	4.00	15.00	22
1929B	2,000,000	—	0.25	2.50	12.50	20
1930B	3,000,000	—	0.25	2.50	12.00	17
1931B	5,037,000	—	0.25	2.00	8.00	12
1940B	1,416,000	—	0.40	1.50	50.00	1
1942B	5,078,000	—	0.25	1.00	10.00	17
1943B	6,591,000	—	0.25	1.00	10.00	17
1944B	9,981,000	—	0.25	1.00	10.00	17
1945B	985,000	—	1.00	9.00	75.00	1
1946B	6,179,000	—	0.25	1.00	5.00	8
1947B	5,125,000	—	0.25	1.00	8.00	12
1948B	4,710,000	—	0.25	1.00	3.00	4
1949B	4,589,000	—	0.25	1.00	3.00	4
1950B	920,000	—	0.50	1.00	2.00	3
1951B	2,141,000	—	0.50	1.00	20.00	35
1952B	4,690,000	—	0.20	0.35	3.00	4
1953B	9,131,000	—	0.20	0.35	2.00	3
1954B	8,038,000	—	0.20	0.35	2.00	3
1955B	19,943,000	—	0.20	0.35	1.50	2
1957B	10,147,000	—	0.20	0.35	1.50	2
1958B	10,217,000	—	0.20	0.35	1.50	2
1959B	11,086,000	—	0.20	0.35	1.50	2
1962B	23,840,000	—	0.10	0.20	0.50	2
1963B	29,730,000	—	0.10	0.20	0.50	1
1964B	17,080,000	—	0.10	0.20	0.50	1
1965B	1,430,000	—	0.10	0.20	0.75	1
1966B	10,010,000	—	—	0.15	0.35	0
1967B	13,010,000	—	—	0.15	0.35	0
1968B	10,020,000	—	—	0.15	0.40	0
1969B	32,990,000	—	—	0.10	0.35	0
1970	34,800,000	—	—	0.10	0.30	0.
1971	40,020,000	—	—	0.10	0.30	0.
1974	30,002,000	—	—	0.10	0.30	0.
1974 Proof	2,400	Value: 20.00				
1975	34,005,000	—	—	0.10	0.30	0.
1975 Proof	10,000	Value: 2.00				
1976	12,005,000	—	—	0.10	0.30	0.
1976 Proof	5,130	Value: 2.25				
1977	14,012,000	—	—	0.10	0.30	0.
1977 Proof	7,030	Value: 1.75				
1978	16,415,000	—	—	0.10	0.30	0.
1978 Proof	10,000	Value: 1.00				
1979	27,010,000	—	—	0.10	0.30	0.
1979 Proof	10,000	Value: 1.00				
1980	15,500,000	—	—	0.10	0.30	0.
1980 Proof	10,000	Value: 1.00				

KM# 26a 5 RAPPEN Composition: Brass

Date	Mintage	F	VF	XF	Unc	
1918B	6,000,000	—	12.50	20.00	25.00	40.

KM# 26b 5 RAPPEN Composition: Nickel

Date	Mintage	F	VF	XF	Unc	
1932B	6,000,000	—	0.25	1.00	3.50	6.
1933B	3,000,000	—	0.25	1.00	6.00	9.
1934B	4,000,000	—	0.25	1.00	5.00	7.
1936B	1,000,000	—	0.25	1.50	7.00	11.
1937B	2,000,000	—	0.25	1.25	8.00	12.
1938B	1,000,000	—	0.25	1.50	6.00	9.
1939B	10,048,000	—	0.25	1.00	3.00	5.
1941B	3,030,000	—	2.00	4.00	25.00	50.

KM# 26c 5 RAPPEN Composition: Aluminum-Brass

Date	Mintage	F	VF	XF	Unc	
1981		—	—	—	0.20	0.3
1981 Proof	10,000	Value: 1.00				
1982		—	—	—	0.20	0.3
1982 Proof	10,000	Value: 1.50				
1983		—	—	—	0.20	0.3
1983 Proof	11,000	Value: 1.00				
1984		—	—	—	0.20	0.3
1984 Proof	14,000	Value: 1.00				
1985		—	—	—	0.20	0.
1985 Proof	12,000	Value: 1.00				
1986B		—	—	—	0.20	0.
1986B Proof	10,000	Value: 1.00				
1987B		—	—	—	0.20	0.
1987B Proof	8,800	Value: 1.25				
1988B		—	—	—	0.20	0.
1988B Proof	9,000	Value: 1.25				
1989B		—	—	—	0.20	0,
1989B Proof	8,800	Value: 1.25				

	Mintage	F	VF	XF	Unc	BU
0B		—	—	—	0.20	0.30
0B Proof	8,900	Value: 1.25				
1B		—	—	—	0.20	0.30
1B Proof	9,900	Value: 1.25				
2B		—	—	—	0.20	0.30
2B Proof	7,450	Value: 1.00				
3B		—	—	—	0.20	0.30
3B Proof	6,200	Value: 1.25				
4B		—	—	—	0.20	0.30
4B Proof	6,100	Value: 1.25				
5B		—	—	—	0.20	0.30
5B Proof	6,100	Value: 1.25				
6B		—	—	—	0.20	0.30
6B Proof	6,100	Value: 1.25				
7B		—	—	—	0.20	0.30
7B Proof	5,500	Value: 1.25				
8B		—	—	—	0.20	0.30
8B Proof	4,800	Value: 1.25				
9B		—	—	—	0.20	0.30
9B Proof	5,000	Value: 1.25				
0B		—	—	—	0.20	0.30
0B Proof	5,500	Value: 1.25				
1B		—	—	—	0.20	0.30
1B Proof	6,000	Value: 1.25				

1# 27 10 RAPPEN **Composition:** Copper-Nickel

e	Mintage	F	VF	XF	Unc	BU
1B		—	3.50	15.00	50.00	85.00
2B		—	3.50	12.00	50.00	85.00
3B		—	3.50	12.00	60.00	85.00
4B		—	3.50	10.00	100	150
6B		—	3.50	15.00	45.00	65.00
7B		—	1.50	7.00	25.00	36.00
8B		—	1.50	6.00	20.00	30.00
9B		—	1.50	7.00	20.00	30.00
1B		—	3.00	12.00	30.00	42.00
2B		—	1.00	5.00	40.00	55.00
3B		—	1.00	5.00	40.00	60.00
4B		—	1.00	7.00	50.00	70.00
5B		—	2.00	12.00	200	300
9B		—	0.25	5.00	17.50	30.00
0B		—	0.25	3.00	17.50	24.00
1B		—	0.25	3.00	12.50	18.00
2B		—	0.25	3.00	22.50	35.00
4B		—	0.25	3.00	22.50	35.00
5B		—	0.25	2.00	18.00	24.00
6B		—	0.25	2.00	16.00	22.50
7B		—	0.25	2.00	14.00	21.00
8B		—	0.25	2.00	14.00	21.00
9B		—	0.25	2.00	14.00	21.00
0B		—	0.25	1.50	27.50	40.00
1B		—	0.25	1.50	25.00	36.00
0B		—	0.25	5.00	55.00	125
2B		—	0.25	5.00	32.00	50.00
3B		—	0.25	5.00	30.00	40.00
4B		—	0.25	1.50	6.00	9.00
5B		—	0.75	5.00	80.00	150
6B		—	0.25	1.50	25.00	36.00
7B		—	0.25	1.50	25.00	40.00
8B		—	0.50	3.00	100	175
9B		—	0.25	1.00	20.00	30.00
0B		—	0.25	1.00	2.50	4.00
1B		—	0.25	0.75	6.00	10.00
2B		—	0.25	0.75	6.00	8.00
3B		—	0.25	0.75	4.00	8.00
4B		—	0.25	1.00	15.00	25.00
5B		—	0.20	0.50	4.00	10.00
7B		—	0.20	0.50	4.00	10.00
8B		—	0.20	0.50	4.00	10.00
9B		—	0.20	0.50	3.00	6.00
0B		—	0.20	0.50	3.00	5.00
1B		—	0.20	0.35	1.25	2.00
2B		—	—	0.20	0.75	1.50
4B		—	—	0.20	0.75	1.50
5B		—	—	0.20	0.75	1.50
6B		—	—	0.20	0.75	1.50
7B		—	—	0.20	0.75	1.50
8B		—	—	0.15	0.50	0.75
9B		—	—	0.15	0.50	0.75
0		—	—	0.15	0.40	0.75
2		—	—	0.15	0.30	0.50
73		—	—	0.15	0.30	0.50
74		—	—	0.15	0.30	0.50
74 Proof	2,400	Value: 20.00				
75		—	—	—	0.30	0.50
75 Proof	10,000	Value: 2.00				
76		—	—	—	0.30	0.50
76 Proof	5,130	Value: 2.50				
77		—	—	—	0.30	0.50
77 Proof	7,030	Value: 1.50				
78		—	—	—	0.30	0.50
78 Proof	10,000	Value: 1.25				
79		—	—	—	0.30	0.50
79 Proof	10,000	Value: 1.25				
Date	Mintage	F	VF	XF	Unc	BU
1980		—	—	—	0.30	0.50
1980 Proof	10,000	Value: 1.50				
1981		—	—	—	0.30	0.50
1981 Proof	10,000	Value: 1.50				
1982		—	—	—	0.30	0.50
1982 Proof	10,000	Value: 2.50				
1983		—	—	—	0.30	0.50
1983 Proof	11,000	Value: 1.50				
1984		—	—	—	0.30	0.50
1984 Proof	14,000	Value: 1.50				
1985		—	—	—	0.50	0.75
1985 Proof	12,000	Value: 1.50				
1986B		—	—	—	0.50	0.75
1986B Proof	10,000	Value: 1.65				
1987B		—	—	—	0.50	0.75
1987B Proof	8,800	Value: 2.00				
1988B		—	—	—	0.50	0.75
1988B Proof	9,000	Value: 2.00				
1989B		—	—	—	0.30	0.50
1989B Proof	8,800	Value: 2.25				
1990B		—	—	—	0.20	0.50
1990B Proof	8,900	Value: 2.00				
1991B		—	—	—	0.20	0.40
1991B Proof	9,900	Value: 2.00				
1992B		—	—	—	0.20	0.40
1992B Proof	7,450	Value: 1.50				
1993B		—	—	—	0.20	0.40
1993B Proof	6,200	Value: 1.50				
1994B		—	—	—	0.20	0.40
1994B Proof	6,100	Value: 1.50				
1995B		—	—	—	0.20	0.40
1995B Proof	6,100	Value: 1.50				
1996B		—	—	—	0.20	0.40
1996B Proof	6,100	Value: 1.50				
1997B		—	—	—	0.20	0.40
1997B Proof	5,500	Value: 1.50				
1998B		—	—	—	0.20	0.40
1998B Proof	4,800	Value: 1.50				
1999B		—	—	—	0.20	0.40
1999B Proof	5,000	Value: 1.50				
2000B		—	—	—	0.20	0.40
2000B Proof	5,500	Value: 1.50				
2001B		—	—	—	0.20	0.40
2001B Proof	6,000	Value: 1.50				

KM# 27a 10 RAPPEN **Composition:** Brass

Date	Mintage	F	VF	XF	Unc	BU
1918B	6,000,000	—	15.00	25.00	35.00	50.00
1919B	3,000,000	—	60.00	45.00	110	175

KM# 27b 10 RAPPEN **Composition:** Nickel

Date	Mintage	F	VF	XF	Unc	BU
1932B	3,500,000	—	0.25	1.00	6.00	9.00
1933B	2,000,000	—	0.25	1.00	8.00	12.00
1934B	3,000,000	—	0.25	1.00	10.00	15.00
1936B	1,500,000	—	0.25	1.00	10.00	15.00
1937B	1,000,000	—	0.35	1.50	10.00	20.00
1938B	1,000,000	—	0.25	1.50	8.00	12.00
1939B	10,022,000	—	0.25	1.00	6.00	9.00

KM# 29 20 RAPPEN **Composition:** Nickel

Date	Mintage	F	VF	XF	Unc	BU
1901B	1,000,000	—	1.50	10.00	100	175
1902B	1,000,000	—	1.50	10.00	45.00	75.00
1903B	1,000,000	—	1.50	10.00	45.00	85.00
1906B	1,000,000	—	1.50	10.00	45.00	75.00
1907B	1,000,000	—	1.50	10.00	25.00	40.00
1908B	1,500,000	—	0.50	8.00	27.50	40.00
1909B	2,000,000	—	0.50	8.00	27.50	40.00
1911B	1,000,000	—	1.00	8.00	60.00	90.00
1912B	2,000,000	—	0.50	8.00	30.00	65.00
1913B	1,500,000	—	0.50	8.00	30.00	65.00
1919B	1,500,000	—	0.50	6.00	25.00	40.00
1920B	3,100,000	—	0.35	4.00	16.00	25.00
1921B	2,500,000	—	0.35	4.00	16.00	25.00
1924B	1,100,000	—	1.00	4.00	32.00	55.00
1925B	1,500,000	—	0.35	3.00	12.50	25.00
1926B	1,500,000	—	0.35	3.00	12.50	25.00
1927B	500,000	—	3.00	15.00	85.00	125
1929B	2,000,000	—	0.30	1.00	13.00	20.00
1930B	2,000,000	—	0.30	1.00	13.00	20.00
1931B	2,250,000	—	0.30	1.00	13.00	20.00
1932B	2,000,000	—	0.30	1.00	13.00	20.00
1933B	1,500,000	—	0.30	1.00	20.00	35.00
1934B	2,000,000	—	0.30	0.50	15.00	25.00
1936B	1,000,000	—	1.00	1.60	20.00	35.00
1938B	2,805,000	—	0.30	0.60	20.00	35.00

KM# 29a 20 RAPPEN **Composition:** Copper-Nickel

Date	Mintage	F	VF	XF	Unc	BU
1939B		—	0.25	3.00	125	200
1943B		—	0.25	1.00	20.00	30.00
1944B		—	0.25	1.00	8.00	12.00
1945B		—	0.50	2.50	40.00	100
1947B		—	0.25	0.50	15.00	30.00
1947B Dot over 4 in date		—	0.50	1.00	20.00	40.00
1950B		—	0.25	0.50	2.50	4.00
1951B		—	0.25	0.50	7.00	12.00
1952B		—	0.25	0.50	7.00	12.00
1953B		—	0.25	0.50	4.00	6.00
1954B		—	0.50	1.00	30.00	75.00
1955B		—	0.25	0.50	4.00	10.00
1956B		—	0.25	0.50	3.00	6.00
1957B		—	0.35	2.50	30.00	90.00
1958B		—	0.25	0.50	4.00	10.00
1959B		—	—	0.35	3.00	5.00
1960B		—	—	0.35	3.00	5.00
1961B		—	—	0.35	2.00	5.00
1962B		—	—	0.35	2.00	5.00
1963B		—	—	0.35	2.00	3.00
1964B		—	—	0.25	2.00	3.00
1965B		—	—	0.25	2.00	3.00
1966B		—	—	0.25	1.00	1.50
1967B		—	—	0.30	1.25	1.75
1968B		—	—	0.25	0.50	1.00
1969B		—	—	—	0.40	0.60
1970		—	—	—	0.40	0.60
1971		—	—	—	0.40	0.60
1974		—	—	—	0.40	0.60
1974 Proof	2,400	Value: 25.00				
1975		—	—	—	0.40	0.60
1975 Proof	10,000	Value: 2.50				
1976		—	—	—	0.40	0.60
1976 Proof	5,130	Value: 3.50				
1977		—	—	—	0.40	0.60
1977 Proof	7,030	Value: 2.25				
1978		—	—	—	0.40	0.60
1978 Proof	10,000	Value: 2.00				
1979		—	—	—	0.40	0.60
1979 Proof	10,000	Value: 2.00				
1980		—	—	—	0.40	0.60
1980 Proof	10,000	Value: 2.50				
1981		—	—	—	0.40	0.60
1981 Proof	10,000	Value: 2.50				
1982		—	—	—	0.40	0.60
1982 Proof	10,000	Value: 3.00				
1983		—	—	—	0.40	0.60
1983 Proof	11,000	Value: 2.00				
1984		—	—	—	0.40	0.60
1984 Proof	14,000	Value: 2.00				
1985		—	—	—	0.40	0.60
1985 Proof	12,000	Value: 2.00				
1986B		—	—	—	0.40	0.60
1986B Proof	10,000	Value: 2.00				
1987B		—	—	—	0.40	0.60
1987B Proof	8,800	Value: 2.25				
1988B		—	—	—	0.40	0.60
1988B Proof	9,000	Value: 2.50				
1989B		—	—	—	0.40	0.60
1989B Proof	8,800	Value: 2.50				
1990B		—	—	—	0.35	0.50
1990B Proof	8,900	Value: 2.50				
1991B		—	—	—	0.35	0.50
1991B Proof	9,900	Value: 2.50				
1992B		—	—	—	0.35	0.50
1992B Proof	7,450	Value: 2.25				
1993B		—	—	—	0.35	0.50
1993B Proof	6,200	Value: 3.50				
1994B		—	—	—	0.30	0.40
1994B Proof	6,100	Value: 2.25				
1995B		—	—	—	0.30	0.40
1995B Proof	6,100	Value: 2.25				
1996B		—	—	—	0.30	0.40
1996B Proof	6,100	Value: 2.25				
1997B		—	—	—	0.30	0.40
1997B Proof	5,500	Value: 2.25				
1998B		—	—	—	0.30	0.40
1998B Proof	4,800	Value: 2.25				
1999B		—	—	—	0.30	0.40
1999B Proof	5,000	Value: 2.25				
2000B		—	—	—	0.30	0.40
2000B Proof	5,500	Value: 2.25				
2001B		—	—	—	0.30	0.40
2001B Proof	6,000	Value: 2.25				
2002B		—	—	—	0.30	0.40
2002B Proof	—	Value: 2.25				

KM# 23 1/2 FRANC **Weight:** 2.5000 g. **Composition:** 0.8350 Silver .0671 oz. ASW

Date	Mintage	F	VF	XF	Unc	BU
1901B	200,000	—	40.00	250	825	1,300
1901B Specimen	—	—	—	—	—	3,000
1903B	800,000	—	3.00	25.00	80.00	125
1903B Specimen	—	—	—	—	—	1,000
1904B	400,000	—	10.00	125	800	1,250
1904B Specimen	—	—	—	—	—	3,000
1905B	600,000	—	3.50	40.00	110	175
1905B Specimen	—	—	—	—	—	900
1906B	1,000,000	—	2.00	40.00	140	210
1906B Specimen	—	—	—	—	—	900
1907B	1,200,000	—	2.00	30.00	100	150
1907B Specimen	—	—	—	—	—	750
1908B	800,000	—	2.00	35.00	100	150
1908B Specimen	—	—	—	—	—	750
1909B	1,000,000	—	2.00	25.00	80.00	120
1909B Specimen	—	—	—	—	—	750
1910B	1,000,000	—	2.00	20.00	75.00	110
1910B Specimen	—	—	—	—	—	750
1913B	800,000	—	2.00	15.00	75.00	110
1913B Specimen	—	—	—	—	—	600
1914B	2,000,000	—	2.00	7.50	30.00	45.00
1914B Specimen	—	—	—	—	—	360
1916B	800,000	—	2.00	8.00	75.00	110
1916B Specimen	—	—	—	—	—	450
1920B	5,400,000	—	1.50	7.00	14.00	21.00
1920B Specimen	—	—	—	—	—	150
1921B	6,000,000	—	1.50	7.00	14.00	21.00
1921B Specimen	—	—	—	—	—	150
1928B	1,000,000	—	2.00	12.50	75.00	110
1928B Specimen	—	—	—	—	—	300
1929B	2,000,000	—	1.50	7.00	16.00	24.00
1929B Specimen	—	—	—	—	—	180
1931B	1,000,000	—	1.50	10.00	40.00	65.00
1931B Specimen	—	—	—	—	—	240
1932B	1,000,000	—	1.50	8.00	20.00	30.00
1932B Specimen	—	—	—	—	—	240
1934B	2,000,000	—	1.50	5.00	14.00	21.00
1934B Specimen	—	—	—	—	—	120
1936B	400,000	—	2.00	10.00	40.00	100
1936B Specimen	—	—	—	—	—	240
1937B	1,000,000	—	1.25	5.00	14.00	21.00
1937B Specimen	—	—	—	—	—	180
1939B	1,000,999	—	1.25	5.00	14.00	21.00
1939B Specimen	—	—	—	—	—	120
1940B	2,001,999	—	1.25	4.00	12.00	18.00
1940B Specimen	—	—	—	—	—	120
1941B	200,000	—	1.50	5.00	16.00	22.00
1941B Specimen	—	—	—	—	—	90.00
1942B	2,969,000	—	1.25	3.00	6.00	9.00
1942B Specimen	—	—	—	—	—	90.00
1943B	4,572,000	—	1.00	3.00	6.00	9.00
1943B Specimen	—	—	—	—	—	90.00
1944B	7,456,000	—	1.00	2.50	4.00	6.00
1944B Specimen	—	—	—	—	—	90.00
1945B	4,928,000	—	1.00	2.50	4.00	6.00
1945B Specimen	—	—	—	—	—	90.00
1946B	6,817,000	—	1.00	2.50	4.00	6.00
1946B Medal alignment	Inc. above	—	60.00	100	200	400
1946B Specimen	—	—	—	—	—	90.00
1948B	6,113,000	—	0.75	1.50	2.50	4.00
1948B Specimen	—	—	—	—	—	90.00
1950B	7,148,000	—	0.75	1.50	2.25	3.50
1950B Specimen	—	—	—	—	—	90.00
1951B	8,530,000	—	0.65	1.50	2.25	3.50
1951B Specimen	—	—	—	—	—	90.00
1952B	14,023,000	—	0.60	1.25	2.00	3.00
1952B Specimen	—	—	—	—	—	75.00
1953B	3,567,000	—	0.65	1.25	3.00	4.25
1953B Specimen	—	—	—	—	—	90.00
1955B	1,320,000	—	0.71	1.50	6.00	9.00
1955B Specimen	—	—	—	—	—	110
1956B	4,250,000	—	0.60	1.00	2.25	3.25
1956B Specimen	—	—	—	—	—	60.00
1957B	12,085,000	—	0.50	0.85	2.00	3.00
1957B Specimen	—	—	—	—	—	30.00
1958B	11,558,000	—	0.50	0.85	2.00	3.00
1958B Specimen	—	—	—	—	—	30.00
1959B	12,581,000	—	0.50	0.85	2.00	3.00
1959B Specimen	—	—	—	—	—	30.00
1960B	14,528,000	—	0.50	0.85	2.00	3.00
1960B Specimen	—	—	—	—	—	30.00
1961B	6,906,000	—	0.50	0.85	2.00	3.00
1961B Specimen	—	—	—	—	—	30.00
1962B	18,272,000	—	0.50	0.75	1.50	2.25
1962B Specimen	—	—	—	—	—	30.00
1963B	25,168,000	—	0.50	0.75	1.50	2.25
1963B Specimen	—	—	—	—	—	30.00
1964B	22,720,000	—	0.50	0.75	1.50	2.25
1964B Specimen	—	—	—	—	—	30.00
1965B	17,920,000	—	0.50	0.75	1.50	2.25
1965B Specimen	—	—	—	—	—	30.00
1966B	10,008,000	—	0.50	0.75	1.50	2.25
1966B Specimen	—	—	—	—	—	30.00
1967B	16,096,000	—	0.50	0.75	1.50	2.25
1967B Specimen	—	—	—	—	—	30.00

KM# 23a.1 1/2 FRANC **Composition:** Copper-Nickel

Date	Mintage	F	VF	XF	Unc	BU
1968	20,000,000	—	—	—	1.50	3.00
1968B	44,920,000	—	—	—	1.50	3.00
1969	31,400,000	—	—	—	1.50	3.00
1969B	51,704,000	—	—	—	1.50	3.00
1970	52,620,000	—	—	—	1.00	2.00
1971	34,472,000	—	—	—	1.00	2.00
1972	9,996,000	—	—	—	1.00	2.00
1973	5,000,000	—	—	—	1.50	3.00
1974	45,006,000	—	—	—	1.00	2.00
1974 Proof	2,400	Value: 35.00				
1975	27,234,000	—	—	—	1.00	2.00
1975 Proof	10,000	Value: 3.50				
1976	10,009,000	—	—	—	1.00	2.00
1976 Proof	5,130	Value: 4.00				
1977	19,011,000	—	—	—	1.00	2.00
1977 Proof	7,030	Value: 3.00				
1978	20,818,000	—	—	—	1.00	2.00
1978 Proof	10,000	Value: 2.50				
1979	27,010,000	—	—	—	1.00	2.00
1979 Proof	10,000	Value: 2.50				
1980	31,064,000	—	—	—	1.00	2.00
1980 Proof	10,000	Value: 3.00				
1981	30,155,000	—	—	—	1.00	2.00
1981 Proof	10,000	Value: 3.00				

KM# 23a.2 1/2 FRANC **Composition:** Copper-Nickel **Obverse:** 22 stars around figure **Note:** Medal alignment.

Date	Mintage	F	VF	XF	Unc	BU
1982	30,151,000	—	—	—	1.00	2.00
1982 Proof	10,000	Value: 6.00				

KM# 23a.3 1/2 FRANC **Composition:** Copper-Nickel **Obverse:** 23 stars

Date		F	VF	XF	Unc	BU
1983		—	—	—	1.00	1.50
1983 Proof	11,000	Value: 3.00				
1984		—	—	—	1.00	1.50
1984 Proof	14,000	Value: 2.75				
1985		—	—	—	1.00	1.50
1985 Proof	12,000	Value: 2.75				
1986B		—	—	—	1.00	1.50
1986B Proof	10,000	Value: 3.00				
1987B		—	—	—	1.00	1.50
1987B Proof	8,800	Value: 3.25				
1988B		—	—	—	1.00	1.50
1988B Proof	9,000	Value: 3.25				
1989B		—	—	—	1.00	1.50
1989B Proof	8,800	Value: 3.25				
1990B		—	—	—	1.00	1.50
1990B Proof	8,900	Value: 3.25				
1991B		—	—	—	1.00	1.50
1991B Proof	9,900	Value: 3.25				
1992B		—	—	—	1.00	1.50
1992B Proof	7,450	Value: 3.00				
1993B		—	—	—	1.00	1.50
1993B Proof	6,200	Value: 3.00				
1994B		—	—	—	1.00	1.50
1994B Proof	6,100	Value: 3.50				
1995B		—	—	—	1.00	1.50
1995B Proof	6,000	Value: 3.50				
1996B		—	—	—	1.00	1.50
1996B Proof	6,100	Value: 3.50				
1997B		—	—	—	1.00	1.50
1997B Proof	5,500	Value: 3.50				
1998B		—	—	—	1.00	1.50
1998B Proof	4,800	Value: 3.50				
1999B		—	—	—	1.00	1.50
1999B Proof	5,000	Value: 3.50				
2000B		—	—	—	1.00	1.50
2000B Proof	5,500	Value: 3.50				
2001B		—	—	—	1.00	1.50
2001B Proof	6,000	Value: 3.50				

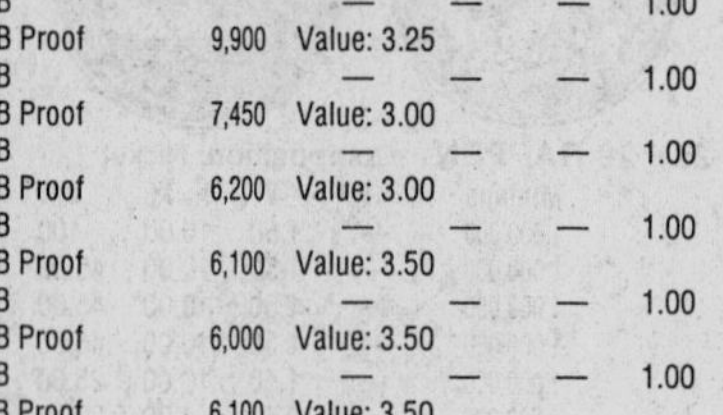

KM# 24 FRANC **Weight:** 5.0000 g. **Composition:** 0.8350 Silver .1342 oz. ASW

Date	Mintage	F	VF	XF	Unc	BU
1901B	400,000	—	12.00	250	575	850
1901B Specimen	—	—	—	—	—	2,400
1903B	1,000,000	—	5.00	40.00	140	210
1903B Specimen	—	—	—	—	—	1,200
1904B	400,000	—	15.00	300	1,000	2
1904B Specimen	—	—	—	—	—	4
1905B	700,000	—	5.00	45.00	200	
1905B Specimen	—	—	—	—	—	1,
1906B	700,000	—	5.00	75.00	350	
1906B Specimen	—	—	—	—	—	1,
1907B	800,000	—	5.00	75.00	300	
1907B Specimen	—	—	—	—	—	1,
1908B	1,200,000	—	5.00	40.00	125	
1908B Specimen	—	—	—	—	—	1,
1909B	900,000	—	5.00	25.00	125	
1909B Specimen	—	—	—	—	—	1,
1910B	1,000,000	—	5.00	30.00	100	
1910B Specimen	—	—	—	—	—	1,
1911B	1,200,000	—	5.00	25.00	100	
1911B Specimen	—	—	—	—	—	
1912B	1,200,000	—	5.00	20.00	70.00	
1912B Specimen	—	—	—	—	—	
1913B	1,200,000	—	5.00	20.00	75.00	
1913B Specimen	—	—	—	—	—	
1914B	4,200,000	—	4.00	10.00	35.00	55
1914B Specimen	—	—	—	—	—	
1916B	1,000,000	—	5.00	15.00	85.00	
1916B Specimen	—	—	—	—	—	1,
1920B	3,300,000	—	3.00	6.00	25.00	35
1920B Specimen	—	—	—	—	—	
1921B	3,800,000	—	3.00	6.00	25.00	35
1921B Specimen	—	—	—	—	—	
1928B	1,500,000	—	3.00	7.50	22.50	35
1928B Specimen	—	—	—	—	—	
1931B	1,000,000	—	3.50	7.50	32.50	48
1931B Specimen	—	—	—	—	—	
1932B	500,000	—	4.00	15.00	75.00	
1932B Specimen	—	—	—	—	—	
1934B	500,000	—	4.00	20.00	65.00	
1934B Specimen	—	—	—	—	—	
1936B	500,000	—	4.00	15.00	60.00	
1936B Specimen	—	—	—	—	—	
1937B	1,000,000	—	3.00	5.00	25.00	36
1937B Specimen	—	—	—	—	—	
1939B	2,106,000	—	2.00	3.00	10.00	15
1939B Specimen	—	—	—	—	—	
1940B	2,003,000	—	2.00	3.00	9.00	12
1940B Specimen	—	—	—	—	—	
1943B	3,526,000	—	1.50	3.00	6.00	9
1943B Specimen	—	—	—	—	—	
1944B	6,225,000	—	1.50	3.00	4.50	6
1944B Specimen	—	—	—	—	—	
1945B	7,794,000	—	1.50	3.00	5.00	7
1945B Specimen	—	—	—	—	—	
1946B	2,539,000	—	1.50	3.00	7.00	10
1946B Specimen	—	—	—	—	—	
1947B	624,000	—	2.50	5.00	16.00	22
1947B Specimen	—	—	—	—	—	
1952B	2,853,000	—	1.50	2.50	4.50	6.
1952B Specimen	—	—	—	—	—	
1953B	786,000	—	3.00	5.00	17.50	24
1953B Specimen	—	—	—	—	—	
1955B	194,000	—	5.00	8.00	22.00	32
1955B Specimen	—	—	—	—	—	
1956B	2,500,000	—	1.50	2.50	5.00	7
1956B Specimen	—	—	—	—	—	90
1957B	6,420,000	—	1.25	2.00	4.50	6
1957B Specimen	—	—	—	—	—	45
1958B	3,580,000	—	1.25	2.00	4.50	6.
1958B Specimen	—	—	—	—	—	45
1959B	1,859,000	—	1.25	2.00	4.50	6.
1959B Specimen	—	—	—	—	—	45.
1960B	3,523,000	—	—	1.50	3.00	5.
1960B Specimen	—	—	—	—	—	45.
1961B	6,549,000	—	—	1.50	3.00	5.
1961B Specimen	—	—	—	—	—	45.
1962B	6,220,000	—	—	1.50	3.00	5.
1962B Specimen	—	—	—	—	—	45.
1963B	13,476,000	—	—	1.25	3.00	4.
1963B Specimen	—	—	—	—	—	45.
1964B	12,560,000	—	—	1.25	3.00	4.
1964B Specimen	—	—	—	—	—	45.
1965B	5,032,000	—	—	1.25	3.00	5.
1965B Specimen	—	—	—	—	—	45.
1966B	3,032,000	—	—	1.25	3.50	5.
1966B Specimen	—	—	—	—	—	45.
1967B	2,088,000	—	—	1.00	3.50	5.
1967B Specimen	—	—	—	—	—	45.

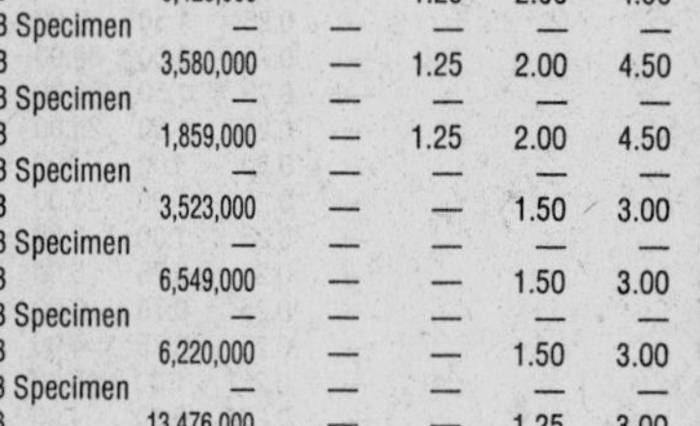

KM# 24a.1 FRANC **Composition:** Copper-Nickel

Date	Mintage	F	VF	XF	Unc	BU
1968	15,000,000	—	—	—	2.00	4.
1968B	40,864,000	—	—	—	2.00	4.
1969B	37,598,000	—	—	—	2.00	4.
1970	24,240,000	—	—	—	2.00	4.
1971	11,496,000	—	—	—	2.00	4.

	Mintage	F	VF	XF	Unc	BU
3	5,000,000	—	—	—	3.00	6.00
4	15,012,000	—	—	—	2.00	3.00
4 Proof	2,400	Value: 65.00				
5	13,012,000	—	—	—	2.00	3.00
5 Proof	10,000	Value: 5.00				
6	5,009,000	—	—	—	2.00	3.00
6 Proof	5,130	Value: 6.50				
7	6,019,000	—	—	—	2.00	3.00
7 Proof	7,030	Value: 4.00				
8	13,548,000	—	—	—	2.00	3.00
8 Proof	10,000	Value: 3.50				
9	10,800,000	—	—	—	2.00	3.00
9 Proof	10,000	Value: 3.50				
0	11,002,000	—	—	—	2.00	3.00
0 Proof	10,000	Value: 4.00				
1	18,013,000	—	—	—	2.00	3.00
1 Proof	10,000	Value: 4.00				

 # 24a.2 FRANC **Composition:** Copper-Nickel
Obverse: 22 stars around figure **Note:** Medal alignment.

	Mintage	F	VF	XF	Unc	BU
2	15,039,000	—	—	—	2.00	3.00
2 Proof	10,000	Value: 12.00				

 # 24a.3 FRANC **Composition:** Copper-Nickel
Obverse: 23 stars

	Mintage	F	VF	XF	Unc	BU
3		—	—	—	2.00	3.00
3 Proof	11,000	Value: 4.00				
4		—	—	—	2.00	3.00
4 Proof	14,000	Value: 3.50				
5		—	—	—	2.00	3.00
5 Proof	12,000	Value: 3.50				
6B		—	—	—	2.00	3.00
6B Proof	10,000	Value: 3.50				
7B		—	—	—	2.00	3.00
7B Proof	8,800	Value: 4.00				
8B		—	—	—	2.00	3.00
8B Proof	9,000	Value: 4.00				
9B		—	—	—	2.00	3.00
9B Proof	8,800	Value: 4.25				
0B		—	—	—	2.00	3.00
0B Proof	8,900	Value: 4.00				
1B		—	—	—	2.00	3.00
1B Proof	9,900	Value: 4.00				
2B		—	—	—	2.00	3.00
2B Proof	7,450	Value: 3.50				
3B		—	—	—	2.00	3.00
3B Proof	6,200	Value: 3.50				
4B		—	—	—	2.00	3.00
4B Proof	6,100	Value: 4.00				
5B		—	—	—	2.00	3.00
5B Proof	6,100	Value: 4.00				
6B		—	—	—	2.00	3.00
6B Proof	6,100	Value: 4.00				
7B		—	—	—	2.00	3.00
7B Proof	5,500	Value: 4.00				
8B		—	—	—	2.00	3.00
8B Proof	4,800	Value: 4.00				
9B		—	—	—	2.00	3.00
9B Proof	5,000	Value: 4.00				
0B		—	—	—	2.00	3.00
0B Proof	5,500	Value: 4.00				
1B		—	—	—	2.00	3.00
1B Proof	6,000	Value: 4.00				

M# 21 2 FRANCS **Weight:** 10.0000 g. **Composition:** 0.8350 Silver .2685 oz. ASW

te	Mintage	F	VF	XF	Unc	BU
1B	50,000	—	200	1,250	6,500	9,000
1B ecimen; Rare	—	—	—	—	—	—
3B	300,000	—	10.00	80.00	600	1,000
3B Specimen	—	—	—	—	—	2,700
4B	200,000	—	20.00	350	1,200	2,000
4B Specimen	—	—	—	—	—	5,700
5B	300,000	—	10.00	75.00	600	1,000
5B Specimen	—	—	—	—	—	2,700
6B	400,000	—	10.00	85.00	500	850
6B Specimen	—	—	—	—	—	3,000
7B	300,000	—	12.50	145	750	1,500
7B Specimen	—	—	—	—	—	3,000
8B	200,000	—	20.00	350	850	1,600

Date	Mintage	F	VF	XF	Unc	BU
1908B Specimen	—	—	—	—	—	5,400
1909B	300,000	—	9.00	75.00	350	700
1909B Specimen	—	—	—	—	—	3,900
1910B	250,000	—	9.00	175	800	1,200
1910B Specimen	—	—	—	—	—	4,200
1911B	400,000	—	7.50	40.00	180	300
1911B Specimen	—	—	—	—	—	1,800
1912B	400,000	—	7.50	40.00	125	200
1912B Specimen	—	—	—	—	—	1,500
1913B	300,000	—	7.50	40.00	160	275
1913B Specimen	—	—	—	—	—	2,100
1914B	1,000,000	—	5.00	25.00	100	175
1914B Specimen	—	—	—	—	—	1,200
1916B	250,000	—	7.50	130	500	800
1916B Specimen	—	—	—	—	—	2,400
1920B	2,300,000	—	3.00	10.00	27.50	50.00
1920B Specimen	—	—	—	—	—	450
1921B	2,000,000	—	3.00	10.00	25.00	50.00
1921B Specimen	—	—	—	—	—	450
1922B	400,000	—	3.00	35.00	160	225
1922B Specimen	—	—	—	—	—	1,200
1928B	750,000	—	3.00	12.50	30.00	50.00
1928B Specimen	—	—	—	—	—	450
1931B	500,000	—	3.00	12.50	40.00	70.00
1931B Specimen	—	—	—	—	—	450
1932B	250,000	—	4.00	40.00	220	300
1932B Specimen	—	—	—	—	—	1,050
1936B	250,000	—	4.00	35.00	110	165
1936B Specimen	—	—	—	—	—	600
1937B	250,000	—	4.00	22.50	70.00	100
1937B Specimen	—	—	—	—	—	450
1939B	1,455,000	—	2.25	5.00	8.00	12.00
1939B Specimen	—	—	—	—	—	600
1940B	2,502,000	—	2.25	5.00	8.00	12.00
1940B Specimen	—	—	—	—	—	180
1941B	1,192,000	—	2.25	5.00	8.00	12.00
1941B Specimen	—	—	—	—	—	180
1943B	2,089,000	—	2.25	4.00	8.00	12.00
1943B Specimen	—	—	—	—	—	180
1944B	6,276,000	—	2.25	4.00	8.00	12.00
1944B Specimen	—	—	—	—	—	180
1945B	1,134,000	—	2.50	7.00	15.00	22.50
1945B Specimen	—	—	—	—	—	180
1946B	1,629,000	—	2.50	4.00	10.00	15.00
1946B Specimen	—	—	—	—	—	180
1947B	500,000	—	4.00	8.00	22.00	32.00
1947B Specimen	—	—	—	—	—	180
1948B	920,000	—	2.50	4.00	10.00	15.00
1948B Specimen	—	—	—	—	—	180
1953B	438,000	—	3.00	6.00	20.00	35.00
1953B Specimen	—	—	—	—	—	180
1955B	1,032,000	—	2.50	3.50	8.00	12.00
1955B Specimen	—	—	—	—	—	150
1957B	2,298,000	—	2.00	3.00	5.00	8.00
1957B Specimen	—	—	—	—	—	60.00
1958B	650,000	—	2.50	3.50	5.00	8.00
1958B Specimen	—	—	—	—	—	60.00
1959B	2,905,000	—	2.00	3.00	5.00	10.00
1959B Specimen	—	—	—	—	—	60.00
1960B	1,980,000	—	2.00	3.00	5.00	10.00
1960B Specimen	—	—	—	—	—	60.00
1961B	4,653,000	—	—	2.50	4.00	7.00
1961B Specimen	—	—	—	—	—	60.00
1963B	8,029,999	—	—	2.00	4.00	7.00
1963B Specimen	—	—	—	—	—	60.00
1964B	4,558,000	—	—	2.00	4.00	7.00
1964B Specimen	—	—	—	—	—	60.00
1965B	8,526,000	—	—	2.00	4.00	7.00
1965B Specimen	—	—	—	—	—	60.00
1967B	4,131,999	—	—	2.00	4.00	7.00
1967B Specimen	—	—	—	—	—	60.00

KM# 21a.1 2 FRANCS **Composition:** Copper-Nickel

Date	Mintage	F	VF	XF	Unc	BU
1968	10,000,000	—	—	—	4.00	8.00
1968B	31,588,000	—	—	—	4.00	7.00
1969B	17,296,000	—	—	—	4.00	8.00
1970	10,350,000	—	—	—	4.00	7.00
1972	5,003,000	—	—	—	4.00	7.00
1973	5,996,000	—	—	—	4.00	7.00
1974	15,009,000	—	—	—	4.00	7.00
1974 Proof	2,400	Value: 65.00				
1975	7,061,000	—	—	—	4.00	6.00
1975 Proof	10,000	Value: 9.00				
1976	5,011,000	—	—	—	4.00	6.00
1976 Proof	5,130	Value: 10.00				
1977	2,009,999	—	—	—	4.00	6.00
1977 Proof	7,030	Value: 9.00				
1978	12,812,000	—	—	—	3.00	6.00
1978 Proof	10,000	Value: 7.00				
1979	10,990,000	—	—	—	3.00	6.00
1979 Proof	10,000	Value: 7.00				
1980	10,001,000	—	—	—	3.00	6.00
1980 Proof	10,000	Value: 7.00				
1981	13,852,000	—	—	—	3.00	6.00
1981 Proof	10,000	Value: 7.00				

KM# 21a.2 2 FRANCS **Composition:** Copper-Nickel
Obverse: 22 stars around figure **Note:** Medal alignment.

Date	Mintage	F	VF	XF	Unc	BU
1982	5,912,000	—	—	—	4.00	6.00
1982 Proof	10,000	Value: 15.00				

KM# 21a.3 2 FRANCS **Composition:** Copper-Nickel
Obverse: 23 stars

Date		F	VF	XF	Unc	BU
1983		—	—	—	3.00	4.00
1983 Proof	11,000	Value: 8.00				
1984		—	—	—	3.00	4.00
1984 Proof	14,000	Value: 8.00				
1985		—	—	—	3.00	4.00
1985 Proof	12,000	Value: 8.00				
1986B		—	—	—	3.00	4.00
1986B Proof	10,000	Value: 8.00				
1987B		—	—	—	3.00	4.00
1987B Proof	8,800	Value: 7.50				
1988B		—	—	—	3.00	4.00
1988B Proof	9,000	Value: 7.50				
1989B		—	—	—	3.00	4.00
1989B Proof	8,800	Value: 7.50				
1990B		—	—	—	3.00	4.00
1990B Proof	8,900	Value: 7.50				
1991B		—	—	—	3.00	4.00
1991B Proof	9,900	Value: 7.50				
1992B		—	—	—	3.00	4.00
1992B Proof	7,450	Value: 7.00				
1993B		—	—	—	3.00	4.00
1993B Proof	6,200	Value: 7.00				
1994B		—	—	—	3.00	4.00
1994B Proof	6,100	Value: 7.00				
1995B		—	—	—	3.00	4.00
1995B Proof	6,100	Value: 7.00				
1996B		—	—	—	3.00	4.00
1996B Proof	6,100	Value: 7.00				
1997B		—	—	—	3.00	4.00
1997B Proof	5,500	Value: 7.00				
1998B		—	—	—	2.50	3.50
1998B Proof	4,800	Value: 7.00				
1999B		—	—	—	2.50	3.50
1999B Proof	5,000	Value: 7.00				
2000B		—	—	—	2.50	3.50
2000B Proof	5,500	Value: 7.00				
2001B		—	—	—	2.50	3.50
2001B Proof	6,000	Value: 7.00				

KM# 34 5 FRANCS **Weight:** 25.0000 g. **Composition:** 0.9000 Silver .7234 oz. ASW

Date	Mintage	F	VF	XF	Unc	BU
1904B	40,000	—	600	1,000	2,000	3,500
1904B Specimen	—	—	—	—	—	7,800
1907B	277,000	—	125	300	600	1,100
1907B Specimen	—	—	—	—	—	3,600
1908B	200,000	—	135	325	650	1,100
1908B Specimen	—	—	—	—	—	3,600
1909B	120,000	—	175	350	650	1,100
1909B Specimen	—	—	—	—	—	3,600
1912B	11,000	—	2,750	3,500	4,500	7,000
1912B Specimen	—	—	—	—	—	12,000
1916B	22,000	—	1,000	1,500	2,000	3,000
1916B Specimen	—	—	—	—	—	6,000

KM# 37 5 FRANCS **Weight:** 25.0000 g. **Composition:** 0.9000 Silver .7234 oz. ASW

Date	Mintage	F	VF	XF	Unc	BU
1922B	2,400,000	—	50.00	125	200	300
1922B Specimen	—	—	—	—	—	1,800
1923B	11,300,000	—	40.00	70.00	175	250
1923B Specimen	—	—	—	—	—	3,000

KM# 38 5 FRANCS **Weight:** 25.0000 g. **Composition:** 0.9000 Silver .7234 oz. ASW

Date	Mintage	F	VF	XF	Unc	BU
1924B	182,000	—	375	550	850	1,250
1924B Specimen	—	—	—	—	—	2,400
1925B	2,830,000	—	75.00	150	225	325
1925B Specimen	—	—	—	—	—	1,500
1926B	2,000,000	—	80.00	150	250	350
1926B Specimen	—	—	—	—	—	1,500
1928B	24,000	—	7,000	9,000	12,500	16,000
1928B Specimen; Rare	—	—	—	—	—	—

KM# 40 5 FRANCS **Weight:** 15.0000 g. **Composition:** 0.8350 Silver .4027 oz. ASW **Note:** Raised edge lettering.

Date	Mintage	F	VF	XF	Unc	BU
1931B	3,520,000	—	5.00	12.00	50.00	90.00
Note: Edge lettering PROVIDEBIT ********** *** DOMINUS						
1931B Specimen	Inc. above	—	—	—	—	900
Note: Edge lettering PROVIDEBIT ********** *** DOMINUS						
1931B	Inc. above	—	12.50	25.00	70.00	115
Note: Common variety edge lettering ********** *** DOMINUS PROVIDEBIT						
1931B	Inc. above	—	35.00	90.00	200	325
Note: Somewhat rarer ********** PROVIDEBIT *** DOMINUS						
1931B	Inc. above	—	600	1,000	1,400	2,100
Note: *** DOMINUS ********** PROVIDEBIT						
1932B	10,580,000	—	4.00	7.50	12.00	25.00
1932B Specimen	—	—	—	—	—	450
1933B	5,900,000	—	6.00	10.00	20.00	35.00
1933B Specimen	—	—	—	—	—	450
1935B	3,000,000	—	6.00	10.00	25.00	45.00
1935B Specimen	—	—	—	—	—	450
1937B	645,000	—	6.50	12.50	32.50	65.00
1937B Specimen	—	—	—	—	—	900
1939B	2,197,000	—	5.00	7.50	12.50	20.00
1939B Specimen	—	—	—	—	—	450
1940B	1,601,000	—	6.00	10.00	25.00	45.00
1940B Specimen	—	—	—	—	—	600
1948B	416,000	—	6.50	13.00	30.00	50.00
1948B Specimen	—	—	—	—	—	600
1949B	407,000	—	6.50	15.00	35.00	60.00
1949B Specimen	—	—	—	—	—	600
1950B	482,000	—	6.50	10.00	30.00	45.00
1950B Specimen	—	—	—	—	—	600
1951B	1,196,000	—	5.00	10.00	20.00	30.00
1951B Specimen	—	—	—	—	—	300
1952B	155,000	—	30.00	60.00	125	225
1952B Specimen	—	—	—	—	—	750
1953B	3,403,000	—	—	6.00	9.00	15.00
1953B Specimen	—	—	—	—	—	150
1954B	6,600,000	—	—	6.00	8.00	12.00
1954B Specimen	—	—	—	—	—	150
1965B	5,021,000	—	—	4.00	8.00	12.00
1965B Specimen	—	—	—	—	—	120
1966B	9,016,000	—	—	4.00	7.00	10.00
1966B Specimen	—	—	—	—	—	120
1967B	13,817,000	—	—	4.00	7.00	10.00
Note: Edge lettering PROVIDEBIT ********** *** DOMINUS						
1967B Specimen	—	—	—	—	—	120
Note: Edge lettering PROVIDEBIT ********** *** DOMINUS						
1967B	—	—	45.00	80.00	110	155
Note: Common variety edge lettering ********** *** DOMINUS PROVIDEBIT						
1967B	—	—	400	750	1,100	1,550
Note: *** DOMINUS ********** PROVIDEBIT						
1969B	8,637,000	—	—	4.00	7.00	10.00
1969B Specimen	—	—	—	—	—	120

KM# 40a.1 5 FRANCS **Composition:** Copper-Nickel

Date	Mintage	F	VF	XF	Unc	BU
1968B	33,871,000	—	—	—	6.00	10.00
1970	6,306,000	—	—	—	6.00	10.00
1973	5,002,000	—	—	—	6.00	10.00
1974	6,007,000	—	—	—	6.00	10.00
1974 Proof	2,400	Value: 125				
1975	4,015,000	—	—	—	5.00	10.00
1975 Proof	10,000	Value: 12.00				
1976	3,007,000	—	—	—	5.00	8.00
1976 Proof	5,130	Value: 14.00				
1977	2,009,000	—	—	—	5.00	8.00
1977 Proof	7,030	Value: 12.00				
1978	4,411,000	—	—	—	5.00	8.00
1978 Proof	10,000	Value: 12.00				
1979	4,011,000	—	—	—	5.00	8.00
1979 Proof	10,000	Value: 12.00				
1980	4,026,000	—	—	—	5.00	8.00
1980 Proof	10,000	Value: 12.00				
1981	6,018,000	—	—	—	5.00	8.00
1981 Proof	10,000	Value: 12.00				

KM# 40a.2 5 FRANCS **Composition:** Copper-Nickel **Note:** Medal alignment.

Date	Mintage	F	VF	XF	Unc	BU
1982	5,050,000	—	—	—	5.00	8.00
1982 Proof	10,000	Value: 18.00				
1983	4,033,000	—	—	—	5.00	8.00
1983 Proof	11,000	Value: 12.00				
1984	3,953,000	—	—	—	5.00	8.00
1984 Proof	14,000	Value: 11.00				

KM# 40a.3 5 FRANCS **Composition:** Copper-Nickel **Note:** Incuse edge lettering.

Date	Mintage	F	VF	XF	Unc	BU
1985	4,050,000	—	—	—	5.00	8.00
1985 Proof	12,000	Value: 10.00				
1986B	7,083,000	—	—	—	5.00	8.00
1986B Proof	10,000	Value: 11.00				
1987B	7,028,000	—	—	—	5.00	8.00
1987B Proof	8,800	Value: 12.00				
1988B	7,029,000	—	—	—	5.00	8.00
1988B Proof	9,000	Value: 12.00				
1989B	5,031,000	—	—	—	5.00	8.00
1989B Proof	8,800	Value: 12.00				
1990B	1,049,000	—	—	—	5.00	8.00
1990B Proof	8,900	Value: 12.00				
1991B Mint sets only	26,000	—	—	—	—	125
1991B Proof	9,900	Value: 120				
1992B	5,034,000	—	—	—	5.00	8.00
1992B Proof	7,450	Value: 12.00				
1993B Mint sets only	16,000	—	—	—	—	115
1993B Proof	6,200	Value: 125				

KM# 40a.4 5 FRANCS **Composition:** Copper-Nickel **Note:** Raised edge lettering.

Date		F	VF	XF	Unc	BU
1994B		—	—	—	5.00	7.00
1994B Proof	6,100	Value: 15.00				
1995B		—	—	—	5.00	7.00
1995B Proof	6,100	Value: 15.00				
1996B		—	—	—	5.00	7.00
1996B Proof	6,100	Value: 12.00				
1997B		—	—	—	5.00	7.00
1997B Proof	5,500	Value: 12.00				
1998B		—	—	—	5.00	7.00
1998B Proof	4,800	Value: 12.00				
1999B		—	—	—	5.00	7.00
1999B Proof	5,000	Value: 12.00				
2000B		—	—	—	5.00	7.00
2000B Proof	5,500	Value: 12.00				
2001B		—	—	—	5.00	
2001B Proof	6,000	Value: 12.00				

KM# 36 10 FRANCS **Weight:** 3.2258 g. **Compositic** 0.9000 Gold .0933 oz. AGW

Date	Mintage	F	VF	XF	Unc	
1911B	100,000	—	100	160	300	
1912B	200,000	—	50.00	75.00	100	
1913B	600,000	—	40.00	60.00	90.00	
1914B	200,000	—	45.00	65.00	100	
1915B	400,000	—	40.00	60.00	90.00	
1916B	130,000	—	50.00	70.00	100	
1922B	1,020,000	—	BV	45.00	55.00	80

KM# 35.1 20 FRANCS **Weight:** 6.4516 g. **Composition:** 0.9000 Gold .1867 oz. AGW

Date	Mintage	F	VF	XF	Unc	
1901B	500,000	—	70.00	85.00	110	
1902B	600,000	—	65.00	75.00	105	
1903B	200,000	—	85.00	95.00	135	
1904B	100,000	—	105	125	155	
1905B	100,000	—	90.00	110	145	
1906B	100,000	—	90.00	110	130	
1907B	150,000	—	70.00	85.00	110	
1908B	355,000	—	60.00	70.00	85.00	
1909B	400,000	—	60.00	70.00	85.00	
1910B	375,000	—	60.00	70.00	85.00	
1911B	350,000	—	60.00	70.00	85.00	
1912B	450,000	—	60.00	70.00	85.00	
1913B	700,000	—	60.00	70.00	85.00	
1914B	700,000	—	60.00	70.00	85.00	
1915B	750,000	—	60.00	70.00	85.00	
1916B	300,000	—	60.00	70.00	85.00	
1922B	2,784,000	—	BV	60.00	75.00	90
1925B	400,000	—	BV	65.00	85.00	
1926B	50,000	—	75.00	100	125	
1927B	5,015,000	—	BV	60.00	75.00	90
1930B	3,372,000	—	BV	60.00	75.00	90
1935B	175,000	—	60.00	75.00	90.00	
1935L-B	20,009,000	—	BV	55.00	70.00	85

Note: The 1935L-B issue was struck in 1945, 1946 and 19

KM# 35.2 20 FRANCS **Weight:** 6.4516 g. **Composition:** 0.9000 Gold .1867 oz. AGW **Edge Letterin** AD LEGEM ANNI MCMXXXI

Date	Mintage	F	VF	XF	Unc	
1947B	9,200,000	—	BV	60.00	75.00	90.
1949B	10,000,000	—	BV	60.00	75.00	90.

KM# 49 25 FRANCS **Weight:** 5.6450 g. **Compositio** 0.9000 Gold .1634 oz. AGW **Note:** Not available in commercial channels.

Date	Mintage	F	VF	XF	Unc
1955B	5,000,000	—	—	—	—
1958B	5,000,000	—	—	—	—
1959B	5,000,000	—	—	—	—

KM# 50 50 FRANCS **Weight:** 11.2900 g. **Compositio** 0.9000 Gold .3267 oz. AGW **Note:** Not available in commercial channels.

Date	Mintage	F	VF	XF	Unc
1955B	2,000,000	—	—	—	—
1958B	2,000,000	—	—	—	—
1959B	2,000,000	—	—	—	—

 # 39 100 FRANCS **Weight:** 32.2581 g. **Composition:** 0.9000 Gold .9334 oz. AGW

	Mintage	F	VF	XF	Unc	BU
5B	5,000	—	3,500	4,000	5,250	6,500

COMMEMORATIVE COINAGE

 # 41 5 FRANCS **Weight:** 15.0000 g. **Composition:** 0.8350 Silver .4027 oz. ASW **Subject:** Confederation Armament Fund

e	Mintage	F	VF	XF	Unc	BU
6B	200,000	—	10.00	15.00	30.00	50.00
6B Specimen	—	—	—	—	—	300

 # 42 5 FRANCS **Weight:** 15.0000 g. **Composition:** 0.8350 Silver .4027 oz. ASW **Subject:** 600th Anniversary - Battle of Laupen

e	Mintage	F	VF	XF	Unc	BU
9B	31,000	—	150	250	350	500

 # 43 5 FRANCS **Weight:** 15.0000 g. **Composition:** 0.8350 Silver .4027 oz. ASW **Subject:** Zurich Exposition

e	Mintage	F	VF	XF	Unc	BU
9	60,000	—	30.00	50.00	70.00	100

Note: Minted at Huguenin, Le Locle

9 Specimen	—	—	—	—	—	900
9 Matte	—	—	—	—	—	1,500

 # 44 5 FRANCS **Weight:** 15.0000 g. **Composition:** 0.8350 Silver .4027 oz. ASW **Subject:** 650th Anniversary of Confederation

e	Mintage	F	VF	XF	Unc	BU
(1941)B	100,000	—	20.00	30.00	45.00	75.00
(1941)B Specimen	—	—	—	—	—	360

KM# 45 5 FRANCS **Weight:** 15.0000 g. **Composition:** 0.8350 Silver .4027 oz. ASW **Subject:** 500th Anniversary - Battle of St. Jakob An Der Birs

Date	Mintage	F	VF	XF	Unc	BU
1944B	102,000	—	12.00	20.00	35.00	50.00
1944B Specimen	—	—	—	—	—	360

KM# 48 5 FRANCS **Weight:** 15.0000 g. **Composition:** 0.8350 Silver .4027 oz. ASW **Subject:** Swiss Constitution Centennial

Date	Mintage	F	VF	XF	Unc	BU
1948B	500,000	—	5.00	6.00	10.00	15.00
1948B Specimen	—	—	—	—	—	150

KM# A48 5 FRANCS **Composition:** Gold

Date		F	VF	XF	Unc	BU
1948B		—	—	—	15,000	—

KM# 51 5 FRANCS **Composition:** Silver **Subject:** Red Cross Centennial

Date	Mintage	F	VF	XF	Unc	BU
ND(1963)B	623,000	—	4.50	6.00	9.00	15.00
ND(1963)B Specimen	—	—	—	—	—	120

KM# 52 5 FRANCS **Composition:** Copper-Nickel **Subject:** 100th Anniversary - Revision of Constitution

Date	Mintage	F	VF	XF	Unc	BU
ND(1974)	3,700,000	—	—	—	5.00	7.00
ND(1974) Proof	130,000	Value: 12.00				

KM# 53 5 FRANCS **Composition:** Copper-Nickel **Subject:** European Monument Protection Year

Date	Mintage	F	VF	XF	Unc	BU
1975	2,500,000	—	—	—	5.00	7.00
1975 Proof	60,000	Value: 22.00				

KM# 54 5 FRANCS **Composition:** Copper-Nickel **Subject:** 500th Anniversary - Battle of Murten

Date	Mintage	F	VF	XF	Unc	BU
1976	1,500,000	—	—	—	6.00	8.00
1976 Proof	100,000	Value: 14.00				

KM# 55 5 FRANCS **Composition:** Copper-Nickel **Subject:** 150th Anniversary - Death of Johann Pestalozzi

Date	Mintage	F	VF	XF	Unc	BU
1977	800,000	—	—	—	6.00	9.00
1977 Proof	50,000	Value: 18.00				

KM# 56 5 FRANCS **Composition:** Copper-Nickel **Subject:** 150th Anniversary - Birth of Henry Dunant

Date	Mintage	F	VF	XF	Unc	BU
1978	900,000	—	—	—	6.00	9.00
1978 Proof	60,000	Value: 14.00				

KM# 57 5 FRANCS **Composition:** Copper-Nickel **Subject:** Centennial - Birth of Albert Einstein

Date	Mintage	F	VF	XF	Unc	BU
1979	900,000	—	—	—	9.00	12.00
1979 Proof	35,000	Value: 55.00				

KM# 58 5 FRANCS **Composition:** Copper-Nickel **Subject:** Centennial - Birth of Albert Einstein

Date	Mintage	F	VF	XF	Unc	BU
1979	900,000	—	—	—	9.00	12.00
1979 Proof	35,000	Value: 55.00				

KM# 59 5 FRANCS **Composition:** Copper-Nickel **Subject:** Ferdinand Hodler - Painter

Date	Mintage	F	VF	XF	Unc	BU
1980	950,000	—	—	—	6.00	9.00
1980 Proof	50,000	Value: 18.00				

KM# 60 5 FRANCS **Composition:** Copper-Nickel **Subject:** 500th Anniversary - Stans Convention of 1481

Date	Mintage	F	VF	XF	Unc	BU
1981	900,000	—	—	—	6.00	8.00
1981 Proof	50,000	Value: 16.00				

KM# 61 5 FRANCS **Composition:** Copper-Nickel **Subject:** 100th Anniversary - Gotthard Railway

Date	Mintage	F	VF	XF	Unc	BU
1982	1,100,000	—	—	—	8.00	10.00
1982 Proof	65,000	Value: 18.00				

KM# 62 5 FRANCS **Composition:** Copper-Nickel **Subject:** 100th Anniversary - Birth of Ernest Ansermet

Date	Mintage	F	VF	XF	Unc	BU
1983	951,000	—	—	—	6.00	8.00
1983 Proof	60,000	Value: 16.00				

KM# 63 5 FRANCS **Composition:** Copper-Nickel **Subject:** Centennial - Birth of Auguste Piccard

Date	Mintage	F	VF	XF	Unc	BU
1984	1,000,000	—	—	—	6.00	8.00
1984 Proof	75,000	Value: 12.00				

KM# 64 5 FRANCS **Composition:** Copper-Nickel **Subject:** European Year of Music

Date	Mintage	F	VF	XF	Unc	BU
1985	1,156,000	—	—	—	5.00	6.50
1985 Proof	84,000	Value: 9.00				

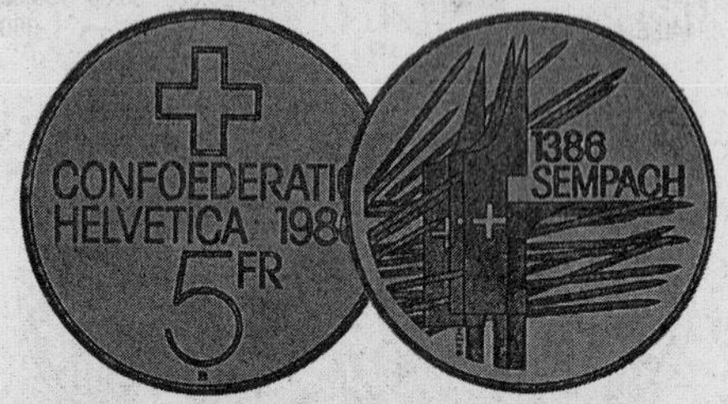

KM# 65 5 FRANCS **Composition:** Copper-Nickel **Subject:** 500th Anniversary - Battle of Sempach

Date	Mintage	F	VF	XF	Unc	BU
1986B	1,080,000	—	—	—	5.00	7.00
1986B Proof	76,000	Value: 10.00				

KM# 66 5 FRANCS **Composition:** Copper-Nickel **Subject:** 100th Anniversary - Birth of Le Corbusier

Date	Mintage	F	VF	XF	Unc	BU
1987B	960,000	—	—	—	5.00	8.00
1987B Proof	62,000	Value: 15.00				

KM# 67 5 FRANCS **Composition:** Copper-Nickel **Subject:** Olympics - Dove and Rings

Date	Mintage	F	VF	XF	Unc	BU
1988B	1,026,000	—	—	—	5.00	8.00
1988B Proof	69,000	Value: 18.00				

KM# 68 5 FRANCS **Composition:** Copper-Nickel **Subject:** General Guisan - 1939 Mobilization

Date	Mintage	F	VF	XF	Unc	BU
1989B	1,270,000	—	—	—	5.00	8.00
1989B Proof	69,000	Value: 18.00				

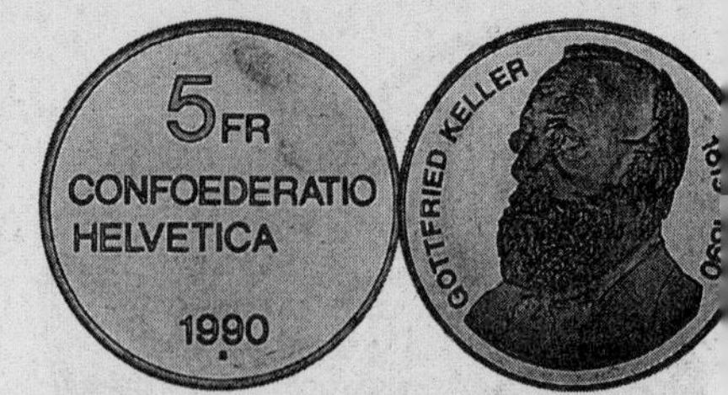

KM# 69 5 FRANCS **Composition:** Copper-Nickel **Subject:** Gottfried Keller

Date	Mintage	F	VF	XF	Unc
1990B	1,100,000	—	—	—	5.00
1990B Proof	69,000	Value: 10.00			

KM# 86 5 FRANCS **Ring Composition:** Copper-Nic **Center Composition:** Brass **Subject:** Wine Festival **Obverse:** Denomination **Reverse:** Grapes

Date	Mintage	F	VF	XF	Unc
1999	160,000	—	—	—	6.00
1999 Proof	16,000	Value: 18.00			

KM# 89 5 FRANCS **Ring Weight:** 14.9100 g. **Ring Composition:** Copper-Nickel **Center Composition:** Bra **Subject:** Basler Fasnacht **Obverse:** Denomination **Reverse:** Costumed flutists **Edge:** Reeded **Size:** 32.9 m

Date	Mintage	F	VF	XF	Unc
2000	170,000	—	—	—	6.00
2000 Proof	20,000	Value: 18.00			

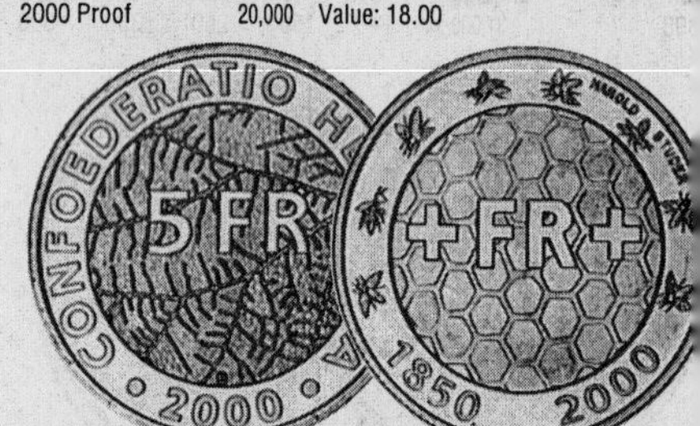

KM# 91 5 FRANCS **Ring Weight:** 15.0000 g. **Ring Composition:** Copper-Nickel **Center Composition:** Bra **Subject:** Swiss National Coinage, 150 Years **Obverse:** Detailed leaf surface showing vein structure **Reverse:** Honeycomb design **Edge:** Reeded **Size:** 32.9 mm.

Date	Mintage	F	VF	XF	Unc
2000	150,000	—	—	—	6.00

KM# 92 5 FRANCS **Ring Weight:** 14.8000 g. **Ring Composition:** Copper-Nickel **Center Composition:** Bra. **Subject:** Zurcher Sechselauten **Obverse:** Denomination **Reverse:** Burning strawman **Edge:** Reeded **Size:** 32.9 m

Date	Mintage	F	VF	XF	Unc
2001	170,000	—	—	—	6.00

M# 98 5 FRANCS **Ring Composition:** Copper-Nickel**Center Weight:** 19.0000 g. **Center Composition:** Brass **Subject:** Escalade 1602-2002 **Obverse:** Denomination **Reverse:** Swirling ladders design **Edge:** Reeded **Size:** 33 mm.

e	Mintage	F	VF	XF	Unc	BU
2	160,000	—	—	—	6.00	8.00
2 Proof	15,000	Value: 18.00				

M# 103 5 FRANCS **Weight:** 14.8000 g. **Composition:** Bi-Metallic **Subject:** Chalandamarz **Obverse:** Denomination **Reverse:** Boys inverting pots **Edge:** Reeded **Size:** 32.9 mm.

e	Mintage	F	VF	XF	Unc	BU
3B	—	—	—	—	8.50	—
3B	12,000	Value: 35.00				

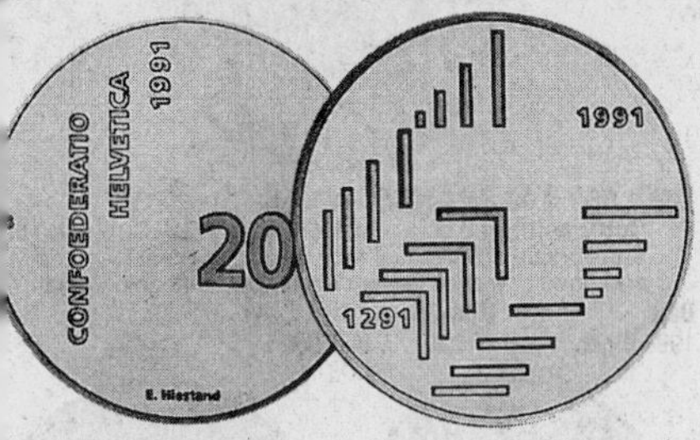

M# 70 20 FRANCS **Weight:** 20.0000 g. **Composition:** 0.8350 Silver .5369 oz. ASW **Subject:** 700 Years of Confederation

te	Mintage	F	VF	XF	Unc	BU
91B	2,440,000	—	—	—	18.00	22.50
91B Proof	100,000	Value: 25.00				

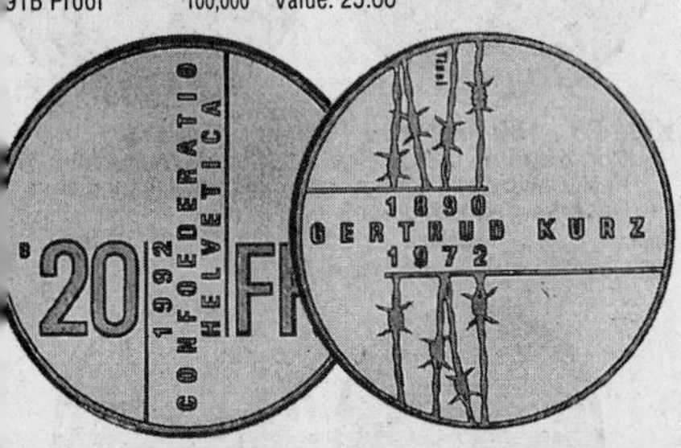

M# 72 20 FRANCS **Weight:** 20.0000 g. **Composition:** 0.8350 Silver .5369 oz. ASW **Subject:** Gertrud Kurz

te	Mintage	F	VF	XF	Unc	BU
92B	325,000	—	—	—	18.00	25.00
92B Proof	36,000	Value: 25.00				

M# 73 20 FRANCS **Weight:** 20.0000 g. **Composition:** 0.8350 Silver .5369 oz. ASW **Subject:** 500th Anniversary - Birth of Paracelsus

te	Mintage	F	VF	XF	Unc	BU
93B	260,000	—	—	—	18.00	25.00
93B Proof	30,000	Value: 32.00				

KM# 74 20 FRANCS **Weight:** 20.0000 g. **Composition:** 0.8350 Silver .5369 oz. ASW **Subject:** Devil's Bridge - Teufelsbrucke **Edge Lettering:** DOMINUS PROVIDEBEIT

Date	Mintage	F	VF	XF	Unc	BU
1994B	240,000	—	—	—	18.00	25.00
1994B Proof	32,000	Value: 32.00				

KM# 75 20 FRANCS **Weight:** 20.0000 g. **Composition:** 0.8350 Silver .5369 oz. ASW **Subject:** Mythological White Snake Queen **Edge Lettering:** DOMINUS PROVIDEBIT (13 stars)

Date	Mintage	F	VF	XF	Unc	BU
1995B	235,000	—	—	—	18.00	25.00
1995B Proof	26,000	Value: 32.00				

KM# 76 20 FRANCS **Weight:** 20.0000 g. **Composition:** 0.8350 Silver .5369 oz. ASW **Subject:** Mythological Giant Boy

Date	Mintage	F	VF	XF	Unc	BU
1996B	206,000	—	—	—	18.00	25.00
1996B Proof	30,000	Value: 32.00				

KM# 77 20 FRANCS **Weight:** 20.0000 g. **Composition:** 0.8350 Silver .5369 oz. ASW **Subject:** Mythological Dragon of Breno

Date	Mintage	F	VF	XF	Unc	BU
1996B	190,000	—	—	—	18.00	25.00
1996B Proof	27,000	Value: 32.00				

KM# 78 20 FRANCS **Weight:** 20.0000 g. **Composition:** 0.8350 Silver .5369 oz. ASW **Subject:** 150th Anniversary - Swiss Railway

Date	Mintage	F	VF	XF	Unc	BU
1997	215,000	—	—	—	18.00	25.00
1997 Proof	19,000	Value: 40.00				

KM# 79 20 FRANCS **Weight:** 20.0000 g. **Composition:** 0.8350 Silver .5369 oz. ASW **Subject:** 200th Anniversary - Birth of Jeremias Gotthelf

Date	Mintage	F	VF	XF	Unc	BU
1997	160,000	—	—	—	18.00	25.00
1997 Proof	20,000	Value: 40.00				

KM# 80 20 FRANCS **Weight:** 20.0000 g. **Composition:** 0.8350 Silver .5369 oz. ASW **Subject:** 200th Anniversary - Helvetian Republic **Obverse:** Denomination and boxed crosses design **Reverse:** 1798 coin design

Date	Mintage	F	VF	XF	Unc	BU
1998	108,000	—	—	—	18.00	25.00
1998 Proof	16,000	Value: 50.00				

KM# 82 20 FRANCS **Weight:** 20.0000 g. **Composition:** 0.8350 Silver .5369 oz. ASW **Subject:** 150th Anniversary - Confederation **Obverse:** Similar to KM#80 **Reverse:** 1848 coin design

Date	Mintage	F	VF	XF	Unc	BU
1998	109,000	—	—	—	18.00	25.00
1998 Proof	16,000	Value: 50.00				

KM# 84 20 FRANCS **Weight:** 20.0000 g. **Composition:** 0.8350 Silver .5369 oz. ASW **Subject:** Death of C.F. Meyer **Obverse:** Denomination, date and "Helvetia" **Reverse:** Portrait, signature

Date	Mintage	F	VF	XF	Unc	BU
1998	108,000	—	—	—	18.00	25.00
1998 Proof	15,000	Value: 40.00				

KM# 85 20 FRANCS **Weight:** 20.0000 g. **Composition:** 0.8350 Silver .5369 oz. ASW **Subject:** 150th Anniversary Swiss Postal Service **Obverse:** Denomination, date, country name in wreath **Reverse:** Cartoon-like postal carrier

Date	Mintage	F	VF	XF	Unc	BU
1999	91,000	—	—	—	18.00	25.00
1999 Proof	12,000	Value: 45.00				

KM# 87 20 FRANCS Weight: 20.0000 g. **Composition:** 0.8350 Silver .5369 oz. ASW **Subject:** Battle of Dornach **Obverse:** Denomination and cross design **Reverse:** Sword splitting and eagle **Edge Lettering:** DOMINUS PROVIDEBIT (13 stars)

Date	Mintage	F	VF	XF	Unc	BU
1999	85,000	—	—	—	18.00	25.00
1999 Proof	11,000	Value: 45.00				

KM# 90 20 FRANCS Weight: 20.0000 g. **Composition:** 0.8350 Silver .5369 oz. ASW **Subject:** Year 2000 - Peace on Earth **Obverse:** Olive branch **Reverse:** Angel floating above people **Size:** 32.7 mm.

Date	Mintage	F	VF	XF	Unc	BU
2000	100,000	—	—	—	18.00	25.00
2000 Proof	15,000	Value: 40.00				

KM# 97 20 FRANCS Weight: 20.0000 g. **Composition:** 0.8350 Silver .5369 oz. ASW **Subject:** Lumen Christi **Obverse:** Six line inscription above denomination **Reverse:** Jesus preaching **Size:** 32.7 mm.

Date	Mintage	F	VF	XF	Unc	BU
2000	85,000	—	—	—	18.00	25.00
2000 Proof	14,000	Value: 40.00				

KM# 93 20 FRANCS Weight: 20.0000 g. **Composition:** 0.9250 Silver .5369 oz. ASW **Subject:** Mustair Cloister **Obverse:** Church floor plan **Reverse:** Walled cloister **Edge:** "DOMINUS PROVIDEBIT" and 13 stars **Size:** 32.6 mm.

Date	Mintage	F	VF	XF	Unc	BU
2001	100,000	—	—	—	18.00	25.00

KM# 94 20 FRANCS Weight: 20.0000 g. **Composition:** 0.8350 Silver .5369 oz. ASW **Subject:** Johanna Spyri **Obverse:** Denomination and handwritten background **Reverse:** Portrait

Date	Mintage	F	VF	XF	Unc	BU
2001	100,000	—	—	—	18.00	25.00

KM# 99 20 FRANCS Weight: 20.0000 g. **Composition:** 0.8350 Silver 0.5369 oz. ASW **Obverse:** St. Gall and bear cub **Reverse:** St. Gall Cloister **Edge:** Lettered **Size:** 33 mm.

Date	Mintage	F	VF	XF	Unc	BU
2002	75,000	—	—	—	—	28.00
2002 Proof	12,000	Value: 50.00				

KM# 100 20 FRANCS Weight: 20.0000 g. **Composition:** 0.8350 Silver 0.5369 oz. ASW **Subject:** REGA **Obverse:** Denomination, inscription and cross above rotating propeller **Reverse:** Rescue helicopter in flight **Edge:** Lettered **Size:** 33 mm.

Date	Mintage	F	VF	XF	Unc	BU
2002	80,000	—	—	—	—	28.00
2002 Proof	12,000	Value: 50.00				

KM# 101 20 FRANCS Weight: 20.0000 g. **Composition:** 0.8350 Silver 0.5369 oz. ASW **Subject:** Expo '02 **Obverse:** Denomination and date in center **Reverse:** Child at waters edge **Edge:** Lettered **Size:** 33 mm.

Date	Mintage	F	VF	XF	Unc	BU
2002	100,000	—	—	—	—	28.00
2002 Proof	15,000	Value: 50.00				

KM# 104 20 FRANCS Weight: 19.9700 g. **Composition:** 0.8350 Silver 0.5361 oz. ASW **Subject:** St. Moritz Ski Championships **Obverse:** Denomination in snow storm **Reverse:** Skier in snow storm **Edge:** "DOMINUS PROVIDEBIT" and 13 stars **Size:** 32.5 mm.

Date	Mintage	F	VF	XF	Unc	BU
2003B	80,000	—	—	—	17.50	—
2003B Proof	10,000	—	—	—	—	—

KM# 95 50 FRANCS Weight: 11.2900 g. **Composition:** 0.9000 Gold .3267 oz. AGW **Subject:** Heidi **Obverse:** Landscape and denomination **Reverse:** Heidi and goat running **Edge:** Lettered **Size:** 25 mm.

Date	Mintage	F	VF	XF	Unc	BU
2001	7,000	Value: 250				

KM# 102 50 FRANCS Weight: 11.2900 g. **Composition:** 0.9000 Gold 0.3267 oz. AGW **Subject:** Expo '02 **Obverse:** Denomination **Reverse:** Aerial view of landscape **Edge:** Lettered **Size:** 25 mm.

Date	Mintage	F	VF	XF	Unc
2002 Proof	6,000	Value: 250			

KM# 81 100 FRANCS Weight: 22.5800 g. **Composition:** 0.9000 Gold .6534 oz. AGW **Subject:** 200 Anniversary of Helvetian Republic **Obverse:** Denominati and boxed crosses design **Reverse:** 1798 coin design

Date	Mintage	F	VF	XF	Unc
1998 Proof	2,500	Value: 600			

KM# 83 100 FRANCS Weight: 22.5800 g. **Composition:** 0.9000 Gold .6534 oz. AGW **Subject:** 150 Anniversary of Swiss Confederation **Obverse:** Denominati and boxed crosses design **Reverse:** 1848 coin design

Date	Mintage	F	VF	XF	Unc
1998 Proof	2,500	Value: 600			

KM# 88 100 FRANCS Weight: 22.5800 g. **Composition:** 0.9000 Gold .6534 oz. AGW **Subject:** Wir Festival **Obverse:** Denomination, fox looking at grapes **Reverse:** Fox with grapes

Date	Mintage	F	VF	XF	Unc
1999 Proof	3,000	Value: 400			

KM# 71.1 250 FRANCS Weight: 8.0000 g. **Composition:** 0.9000 Gold .2315 oz. AGW **Subject:** 700 Years of Confederation **Edge:** Plus sign between dates

Date	Mintage	F	VF	XF	Unc	B
1991B	297,000	—	—	—	—	2

Note: 200,000 recalled and melted due to poor quality

KM# 71.2 250 FRANCS Weight: 8.0000 g. **Composition:** 0.9000 Gold .2315 oz. AGW **Subject:** 700 Years of Confederation **Edge:** Elongated plus sign betwee dates

Date	Mintage	F	VF	XF	Unc	B
1991B	193,000	—	—	—	—	2

COMMEMORATIVE COINAGE

Shooting Festival

KM# S18 5 FRANCS Composition: 0.8350 Silver **Issuer:** Fribourg

Date	Mintage	F	VF	XF	Unc	B
1934B	40,000	—	15.00	35.00	55.00	80.
1934B Specimen	—	—	—	—	—	1
1934B Matte	650	—	—	—	—	6

M# S20 5 FRANCS **Composition:** 0.8350 Silver **Issuer:** Lucerne

te	Mintage	F	VF	XF	Unc	BU
39B	40,000	—	15.00	30.00	50.00	75.00
39B Specimen	—	—	—	—	—	180

M# S54 5 FRANCS **Composition:** Copper-Nickel **Issuer:** Albisgutli

te	Mintage	F	VF	XF	Unc	BU
98 Proof	2,500	Value: 40.00				

M# S55 20 FRANCS **Weight:** 25.0000 g. **Composition:** 0.9990 Silver .0803 oz. ASW **Issuer:** Albisgutli

ate	Mintage	F	VF	XF	Unc	BU
998 Proof	1,000	Value: 115				

M# S22 50 FRANCS **Weight:** 25.0000 g. **Composition:** 0.9000 Silver .7235 oz. ASW **Issuer:** Oberhasli

ate	Mintage	F	VF	XF	Unc	BU
984	6,000	—	—	—	40.00	50.00
984 Proof	200	Value: 600				

M# S24 50 FRANCS **Weight:** 25.0000 g. **Composition:** 0.9000 Silver .7235 oz. ASW **Issuer:** Altdorf

ate	Mintage	F	VF	XF	Unc	BU
985 Proof	3,500	Value: 150				

KM# S26 50 FRANCS **Weight:** 25.0000 g. **Composition:** 0.9000 Silver .7235 oz. ASW **Issuer:** Appenzell

Date	Mintage	F	VF	XF	Unc	BU
1986 Proof	3,700	Value: 85.00				

KM# S28 50 FRANCS **Weight:** 25.0000 g. **Composition:** 0.9000 Silver .7235 oz. ASW **Issuer:** Glarus

Date	Mintage	F	VF	XF	Unc	BU
1987 Proof	3,200	Value: 85.00				

KM# S30 50 FRANCS **Weight:** 25.0000 g. **Composition:** 0.9000 Silver .7235 oz. ASW **Issuer:** Aargau

Date	Mintage	F	VF	XF	Unc	BU
1988 Proof	3,000	Value: 145				

KM# S32 50 FRANCS **Weight:** 25.0000 g. **Composition:** 0.9000 Silver .7235 oz. ASW **Issuer:** Zug

Date	Mintage	F	VF	XF	Unc	BU
1989 Proof	2,200	Value: 155				

KM# S34 50 FRANCS **Weight:** 25.0000 g. **Composition:** 0.9000 Silver .7235 oz. ASW **Issuer:** Winterthur

Date	Mintage	F	VF	XF	Unc	BU
1990 Proof	5,000	Value: 70.00				

KM# S38 50 FRANCS **Weight:** 25.0000 g. **Composition:** 0.9000 Silver .7235 oz. ASW **Issuer:** Bern **Reverse:** William Tell with rifle and flag

Date	Mintage	F	VF	XF	Unc	BU
1991 Proof	4,000	Value: 95.00				

KM# S40 50 FRANCS **Weight:** 25.0000 g. **Composition:** 0.9000 Silver .7235 oz. ASW **Issuer:** Zurich

Date	Mintage	F	VF	XF	Unc	BU
1992 Proof	1,750	Value: 120				

KM# S42 50 FRANCS **Weight:** 25.0000 g. **Composition:** 0.9000 Silver .7235 oz. ASW **Issuer:** Thurgau

Date	Mintage	F	VF	XF	Unc	BU
1993 Proof	2,000	Value: 100				

KM# S44 50 FRANCS **Weight:** 25.0000 g. **Composition:** 0.9000 Silver .7235 oz. ASW **Issuer:** St. Gall

Date	Mintage	F	VF	XF	Unc	BU
1994 Proof	2,200	Value: 70.00				

KM# S46 50 FRANCS **Weight:** 25.0000 g. **Composition:** 0.9000 Silver .7235 oz. ASW **Issuer:** Thun in Bern

Date	Mintage	F	VF	XF	Unc	BU
1995 Proof	Est. 5,000	Value: 90.00				

KM# S48 50 FRANCS **Weight:** 25.0000 g. **Composition:** 0.9000 Silver .7235 oz. ASW **Issuer:** Sempach

Date	Mintage	F	VF	XF	Unc	BU
1996 Proof	1,500	Value: 80.00				

KM# S50 50 FRANCS **Weight:** 25.0000 g. **Composition:** 0.9000 Silver .7235 oz. ASW **Issuer:** Schaffhausen

Date	Mintage	F	VF	XF	Unc	BU
1997 Proof	1,500	Value: 80.00				

KM# S52 50 FRANCS **Weight:** 25.0000 g. **Composition:** 0.9000 Silver .7235 oz. ASW **Issuer:** Schwyz

Date	Mintage	F	VF	XF	Unc	BU
1998 Proof	1,500	Value: 100				

KM# S57 50 FRANCS **Weight:** 25.0000 g. **Composition:** 0.9000 Silver .7235 oz. ASW **Issuer:** Sion

Date	Mintage	F	VF	XF	Unc	BU
1999 Proof	1,500	Value: 75.00				

KM# S59 50 FRANCS **Weight:** 25.0000 g. **Composition:** 0.9000 Silver .7235 oz. ASW **Issuer:** Biere

Date	Mintage	F	VF	XF	Unc	BU
2000 Proof	3,000	Value: 65.00				

KM# S61 50 FRANCS **Weight:** 25.0000 g. **Composition:** 0.9000 Silver .7235 oz. ASW **Issuer:** Uri

Date	Mintage	F	VF	XF	Unc	BU
2001 Proof	1,500	Value: 65.00				

KM# S63 50 FRANCS **Weight:** 25.0000 g. **Composition:** 0.9000 Silver .7235 oz. ASW **Issuer:** Zurich

Date	Mintage	F	VF	XF	Unc	BU
2002 Proof	1,500	Value: 65.00				

KM# S19 100 FRANCS **Weight:** 25.9000 g. **Composition:** 0.9000 Gold .7494 oz. AGW **Issuer:** Fribourg

Date	Mintage	F	VF	XF	Unc	BU
1934B	2,000	—	1,000	1,500	2,000	2,250

KM# S21 100 FRANCS **Weight:** 17.5000 g. **Composition:** 0.9000 Gold .5064 oz. AGW **Issuer:** Lucerne

Date	Mintage	F	VF	XF	Unc	BU
1939B	6,000	—	400	475	550	700

KM# S36 100 FRANCS **Weight:** 31.1030 g. **Composition:** 0.9990 Platinum 1.0000 oz. APW **Subject:** William Tell and Son

Date	Mintage	F	VF	XF	Unc	BU
1986HF	60,000	—	—	—	—	—
1986HF Proof	10,000	Value: 650				
1987HF	—	—	—	—	—	—
1987HF Proof	15,000	Value: 650				

KM# S37 100 FRANCS **Weight:** 31.1030 g. **Composition:** 0.9990 Platinum 1.0000 oz. APW **Subject:** William Tell

Date	Mintage	F	VF	XF	Unc	BU
1988HF Proof	10,000	Value: 650				

KM# S37a 100 FRANCS **Composition:** Brass

Date	Mintage	F	VF	XF	Unc	BU
1988HF Proof	1,000	Value: 50.00				

KM# S56 200 FRANCS **Weight:** 13.9600 g. **Composition:** 0.9860 Gold .4426 oz. AGW **Issuer:** Albisgutli

Date	Mintage	F	VF	XF	Unc	BU
1998 Matte Proof	100	Value: 850				

KM# S47 500 FRANCS **Weight:** 13.0000 g. **Compositio** 0.9000 Gold .3762 oz. AGW **Issuer:** Thun in Bern

Date	Mintage	F	VF	XF	Unc
1995 Proof	500	Value: 500			

KM# S49 500 FRANCS **Weight:** 13.0000 g. **Compositio** 0.9000 Gold .3762 oz. AGW **Issuer:** Sempach

Date	Mintage	F	VF	XF	Unc
1996 Proof	96	Value: 700			

KM# S51 500 FRANCS **Weight:** 13.0000 g. **Compositio** 0.9000 Gold .3762 oz. AGW **Issuer:** Schaffhausen

Date	Mintage	F	VF	XF	Unc	B
1997 Proof	97	Value: 700				

KM# S53 500 FRANCS **Weight:** 13.0000 g. **Composition:** 0.9000 Gold .3762 oz. AGW **Issuer:** Schwy

Date	Mintage	F	VF	XF	Unc	B
1998 Proof	98	Value: 700				

KM# S58 500 FRANCS **Composition:** Gold **Issuer:** Sion

Date	Mintage	F	VF	XF	Unc	B
1999 Proof	99	Value: 600				

KM# S60 500 FRANCS **Composition:** Gold **Issuer:** Biere

Date	Mintage	F	VF	XF	Unc	B
2000 Proof	300	Value: 600				

KM# S64 500 FRANCS **Weight:** 13.0000 g. **Composition:** 0.9000 Gold .3762 oz. AGW **Issuer:** Zurich

Date	Mintage	F	VF	XF	Unc	B
2002 Proof	125	Value: 600				

KM# S35 1000 FRANCS **Weight:** 26.0000 g. **Composition:** 0.9000 Gold .7524 oz. AGW **Issuer:** Winterthur

Date	Mintage	F	VF	XF	Unc	B
1990 Proof	400	Value: 1,200				

KM# S39 1000 FRANCS **Weight:** 26.0000 g. **Composition:** 0.9000 Gold .7524 oz. AGW **Issuer:** Bern **Reverse:** William Tell with rifle and flag

Date	Mintage	F	VF	XF	Unc	B
1991 Proof	400	Value: 950				

KM# S41 1000 FRANCS **Weight:** 26.0000 g. **Composition:** 0.9000 Gold .7524 oz. AGW **Issuer:** Zurich **Note:** Similar to 50 Francs, KM#S40.

Date	Mintage	F	VF	XF	Unc	B
1992 Proof	175	Value: 1,100				

KM# S43 1000 FRANCS **Weight:** 26.0000 g. **Composition:** 0.9000 Gold .7524 oz. AGW **Issuer:** Thurgau **Note:** Similar to 50 Francs, KM#S42.

Date	Mintage	F	VF	XF	Unc	B
1993 Proof	200	Value: 1,000				

KM# S45 1000 FRANCS **Weight:** 26.0000 g. **Composition:** 0.9000 Gold .7524 oz. AGW **Issuer:** St. Gal **Note:** Similar to 50 Francs, KM#S44.

Date	Mintage	F	VF	XF	Unc	B
1994 Proof	200	Value: 1,000				

ESSAIS

KM#	Date	Mintage	Identification	Mkt V
E4	1911	—	10 Francs. Gold.	12,50
E5	1928B	—	100 Francs. Brass. Plain edge.	6,20
E6	1930B	—	100 Francs. Brass. Lettered edge.	7,50
E8	1930	—	Franc. Nickel.	5,00
EA8	1930B	—	5 Francs. Silver. Formerly Pn63.	12,00
E7	1998	250	5 Francs. Silver.	5,50

KM#	Date	Mintage	Identification	Mkt Val
E9	1998	250	20 Francs. Silver. KM#80.	425
E10	1998	250	20 Francs. Silver. KM#82.	425
E11	1998	500	20 Francs. Silver. KM#84.	320
E12	2000	—	20 Francs. Silver. KM#97	185

PATTERNS

KM#	Date	Mintage	Identification	Mkt Val
Pn40	1910	56	10 Francs. Gold. Reeded edge.	15,000
Pn41	1910	I.A.	10 Francs. Gold. Plain edge.	22,500
Pn42	1917	6	5 Rappen. Brass.	3,000
Pn43	1918	—	10 Rappen. Nickel.	—
Pn44	1922B	—	5 Francs. Silver.	3,500
Pn45	1924B	—	5 Francs. (No Composition).	20,000
Pn46	1925B	—	10 Francs. Silver.	6,000
Pn47	1925B	—	100 Francs. Copper.	5,000
Pn48	1927B	—	20 Rappen. Nickel.	4,500
Pn49	1928B	—	20 Rappen. Nickel.	4,500
Pn50	1928B	—	Franc. Nickel.	3,200
Pn51	1928B	—	2 Francs. Nickel.	3,200
Pn52	1928B	—	5 Francs. Silver.	10,000
Pn53	1928B	—	5 Francs. Nickel.	10,000
Pn54	1929B	—	5 Rappen. Bronze.	—
Pn55	1929B	—	50 Rappen. Nickel.	3,500
Pn56	1929	—	5 Francs. Silver.	20,000
Pn57	1930B	—	10 Rappen. Nickel.	2,500
Pn58	1930B	—	20 Rappen. Nickel.	2,500
Pn59	1930B	—	50 Rappen. Nickel.	3,500
Pn60	1930	—	50 Rappen. Nickel. Triangle.	3,000
Pn61	19xxB	—	Franc. Nickel.	—
Pn62	19xxB	—	5 Francs. Silver.	20,000
Pn64	1931	—	5 Rappen. Copper-Nickel.	—
Pn65	1931	—	50 Rappen. Nickel.	2,000
Pn66	1935	—	20 Francs. Copper.	—
Pn67	1937B	—	Franc. Copper-Nickel.	5,000
Pn68	1937B	—	2 Francs. Copper-Nickel.	5,000
Pn69	1937	—	5 Francs. Aluminum.	4,000
Pn70	1938B	—	20 Rappen. Zinc.	2,500
Pn71	1938B	—	Franc. Copper-Nickel.	2,150
Pn72	1938B	—	2 Francs. Copper-Nickel.	3,350
Pn73	1939B	—	5 Rappen. Zinc. KM#26.	1,600
Pn74	1939	—	5 Francs. Silver.	6,000
Pn75	1940B	—	5 Rappen. Aluminum. KM#26.	3,500
PnA76	1940B	—	20 Rappen. (No Composition). KM#29a.	2,850
Pn76	1940B	—	10 Rappen. Zinc. KM#27.	2,000
Pn77	1940B	—	10 Rappen. Aluminum. KM#27.	4,200
Pn78	1941B	—	2 Francs. Silver-Zinc.	2,500
Pn79	1941B	—	Rappen. Aluminum. KM#3.	2,500
Pn80	1941B	—	2 Rappen. Aluminum. KM#4.	3,000
Pn81	1947	—	20 Francs. Gold.	—
n82	1948B	—	5 Francs. Copper Gilt.	3,500
n83	1955B	—	25 Francs. Silver. KM#49.	14,000
n84	1955B	—	50 Francs. Silver. KM#50.	14,000
n85	1979	—	5 Rappen. Aluminum-Bronze.	2,000

TRIAL STRIKES

KM#	Date	Mintage	Identification	Mkt Val
S1	ND	3	20 Francs. Nickel. Uniface.	—

MINT SETS

KM#	Date	Mintage	Identification	Issue Price	Mkt Val
S36	2002 (9)	22,000	KM#21a.3, 23a.3, 24a.3, 26c, 27, 29a, 40a.3, 46, 89	20.00	—
S37	2002	2,000	KM#21a.3, 23a.3, 24a.3, 26c, 27, 29a, 40a.3, 46, 91 Includes a medal and different cover (intended at a birth year set for 2002 from the mint)	65.00	—

PROOF SETS

KM#	Date	Mintage	Identification	Issue Price	Mkt Val
PS31	2002 (9)	6,000	KM#21a.3, 23a.3, 24a.3, 26c, 27, 29a, 40a.4, 46, 92	45.00	—

SYRIA

The Syrian Arab Republic, located in the Near East at the eastern end of the Mediterranean Sea, has an area of 71,498 sq. mi. (185,180 sq. km.) and a population of *12 million. Capital: Greater Damascus. Agriculture and animal breeding are the chief industries. Cotton, crude oil and livestock are exported.

Ancient Syria, a land bridge connecting Europe, Africa and Asia, has spent much of its history in thrall to the conqueror's whim. Its subjection by Egypt about 1500 B.C. was followed by successive conquests by the Hebrews, Phoenicians, Babylonians, Assyrians, Persians, Macedonians, Romans, Byzantines and finally, in 636 A.D., by the Moslems. The Arabs made Damascus, one of the oldest continuously inhabited cities of the world, the trade center and capital of an empire stretching from India to Spain. In 1516, following the total destruction of Damascus by the Mongols of Tamerlane, Syria fell to the Ottoman Turks and remained a part of Turkey until the end of World War I. The League of Nations gave France a mandate to the Levant states of Syria and Lebanon in 1920. In 1930, following a series of uprisings, France recognized Syria as an independent republic, but still subject to the mandate. Lebanon became fully independent on Nov. 22, 1943, and Syria on Jan. 1,1944.

TITLES

الجمهورية السورية

al-Jumhuriya(t) al-Suriya(t)

الجمهورية لعربية السورية

al-Jumhuriya(t) al-Arabiya(t) as-Suriya(t)

RULERS

Ottoman, until 1918

Faysal, 1918-1920

MINT MARKS

(a)- Paris, privy marks only

MINTNAME

Damascus (Dimask) دمشق

Haleb (Aleppo) حلب

KINGDOM

STANDARD COINAGE

KM# 67 DINAR Weight: 6.7000 g. Composition: Gold

Date	F	VF	XF	Unc	BU
AH1338 (1919)	—	—	—	8,000	—

FRENCH PROTECTORATE

STANDARD COINAGE

KM# 68 1/2 PIASTRE Composition: Copper-Nickel

Date	Mintage	F	VF	XF	Unc	BU
1921(a)	4,000,000	0.50	2.00	5.00	15.00	—

KM# 75 1/2 PIASTRE Composition: Nickel-Brass

Date	Mintage	F	VF	XF	Unc	BU
1935(a)	600,000	1.00	4.00	12.00	42.50	—
1936(a)	800,000	1.00	4.00	9.00	30.00	—

KM# 71 PIASTRE Composition: Nickel-Brass

Date	Mintage	F	VF	XF	Unc	BU
1929(a)	750,000	1.00	3.00	7.00	32.50	—
1933(a)	600,000	1.50	4.00	10.00	40.00	—
1935(a)	1,950,000	0.75	2.50	5.00	22.50	—
1936(a)	1,400,000	0.75	2.50	7.00	25.00	—

KM# 71a PIASTRE Composition: Zinc

Date	Mintage	F	VF	XF	Unc	BU
1940(a)	2,060,000	2.00	5.00	15.00	60.00	—

KM# 69 2 PIASTRES Composition: Aluminum-Bronze

Date	Mintage	F	VF	XF	Unc	BU
1926(a)	600,000	5.00	10.00	25.00	75.00	—
1926	Inc. above	5.00	10.00	25.00	75.00	—

Note: Without privy marks by date

KM# 76 2-1/2 PIASTRES Composition: Aluminum-Bronze

Date	Mintage	F	VF	XF	Unc	BU
1940(a)	2,000,000	1.25	4.00	8.00	27.50	—

KM# 70 5 PIASTRES Composition: Aluminum-Bronze

Date	Mintage	F	VF	XF	Unc	BU
1926(a)	300,000	0.75	2.00	8.00	25.00	—
1926	400,000	0.75	3.00	12.00	35.00	—
1933(a)	1,200,000	0.40	2.00	12.50	40.00	—
1935(a)	2,000,000	0.30	1.50	8.00	25.00	—
1936(a)	900,000	0.50	2.00	10.00	30.00	—
1940(a)	500,000	0.50	1.50	4.00	15.00	—

KM# 72 10 PIASTRES Weight: 2.0000 g. Composition: 0.6800 Silver .0437 oz. ASW

Date	Mintage	F	VF	XF	Unc	BU
1929	1,000,000	4.00	12.00	28.00	90.00	—

KM# 73 25 PIASTRES **Weight:** 5.0000 g. **Composition:** 0.6800 Silver .1093 oz. ASW

Date	Mintage	F	VF	XF	Unc	BU
1929	1,000,000	3.00	5.00	27.50	85.00	—
1933(a)	500,000	4.00	12.00	40.00	160	—
1936(a)	897,000	3.50	7.00	30.00	100	—
1937(a)	393,000	5.00	10.00	35.00	140	—

KM# 74 50 PIASTRES **Weight:** 10.0000 g. **Composition:** 0.6800 Silver .2186 oz. ASW

Date	Mintage	F	VF	XF	Unc	BU
1929	880,000	4.00	8.00	35.00	140	—
1933(a)	250,000	6.00	10.00	45.00	190	—
1936(a)	400,000	5.00	10.00	40.00	160	—
1937(a)	Inc. above	7.00	12.00	50.00	200	—

WORLD WAR II EMERGENCY COINAGE

KM# 77 PIASTRE **Composition:** Brass

Date	F	VF	XF	Unc	BU
ND	2.50	5.00	10.00	20.00	—

KM# 78 2-1/2 PIASTRES **Composition:** Aluminum

Date	F	VF	XF	Unc	BU
ND	10.00	20.00	35.00	65.00	—

REPUBLIC

STANDARD COINAGE

KM# 81 2-1/2 PIASTRES **Composition:** Copper-Nickel

Date	Mintage	F	VF	XF	Unc	BU
AH1367 (1948)	2,500,000	0.75	1.50	3.00	6.00	—
AH1375 (1956)	5,000,000	0.75	1.50	3.00	6.00	—

KM# 82 5 PIASTRES **Composition:** Copper-Nickel

Date	Mintage	F	VF	XF	Unc	BU
AH1367 (1948)	8,000,000	0.75	1.50	3.00	6.00	—
AH1375 (1956)	4,000,000	0.75	1.50	3.00	6.00	—

KM# 83 10 PIASTRES **Composition:** Copper-Nickel

Date	Mintage	F	VF	XF	Unc	BU
AH1367 (1948)	—	0.75	1.50	3.00	6.00	—
AH1375 (1956)	4,000,000	0.75	1.50	3.00	6.00	—

KM# 79 25 PIASTRES **Weight:** 2.5000 g. **Composition:** 0.6000 Silver .0482 oz. ASW

Date	Mintage	F	VF	XF	Unc	BU
AH1366 (1947)	6,300,000	1.50	2.50	6.00	20.00	—

KM# 80 50 PIASTRES **Weight:** 5.0000 g. **Composition:** 0.6000 Silver .0965 oz. ASW

Date	Mintage	F	VF	XF	Unc	BU
AH1366 (1947)	4,500,000	2.50	5.00	10.00	25.00	—

KM# 84 1/2 POUND **Weight:** 3.3793 g. **Composition:** 0.9000 Gold .0978 oz. AGW

Date	Mintage	F	VF	XF	Unc	BU
AH1369 (1950)	100,000	45.00	55.00	65.00	100	—

KM# 85 LIRA **Weight:** 10.0000 g. **Composition:** 0.6800 Silver .2186 oz. ASW

Date	Mintage	F	VF	XF	Unc	BU
AH1369 (1950)	7,000,000	2.50	5.00	10.00	25.00	—

KM# 86 POUND **Weight:** 6.7586 g. **Composition:** 0.9000 Gold .1956 oz. AGW

Date	Mintage	F	VF	XF	Unc	BU
AH1369 (1950)	250,000	70.00	90.00	110	160	—

UNITED ARAB REPUBLIC

STANDARD COINAGE

KM# 90 2-1/2 PIASTRES **Composition:** Aluminum-Bro

Date	Mintage	F	VF	XF	Unc
AH1380 (1960)	1,100,000	0.10	0.20	0.35	0.75

KM# 91 5 PIASTRES **Composition:** Aluminum-Bro

Date	Mintage	F	VF	XF	Unc
AH1380 (1960)	4,240,000	0.10	0.20	0.35	0.75

KM# 92 10 PIASTRES **Composition:** Aluminum-Bro

Date	Mintage	F	VF	XF	Unc
AH1380 (1960)	2,800,000	0.10	0.20	0.40	1.00

KM# 87 25 PIASTRES **Weight:** 2.5000 g. **Composition:** 0.6000 Silver .0482 oz. ASW

Date	Mintage	F	VF	XF	Unc
AH1377 (1958)	2,300,000	0.75	1.50	2.00	6.00

KM# 88 50 PIASTRES **Weight:** 5.0000 g. **Composition:** 0.6000 Silver .0965 oz. ASW

Date	Mintage	F	VF	XF	Unc
AH1377 (1958)	120,000	2.00	3.00	6.50	18.00

KM# 89 50 PIASTRES **Weight:** 5.0000 g. **Composition:** 0.6000 Silver .0965 oz. ASW **Subject:** 1 anniversary - founding of United Arab Republic

Date	Mintage	F	VF	XF	Unc
AH1378 (1959)	1,500,000	1.50	2.50	4.50	12.00

SYRIAN ARAB REPUBLIC

STANDARD COINAGE

KM# 93 2-1/2 PIASTRES **Composition:** Aluminum-Bro

Date	Mintage	F	VF	XF	Unc
AH1382/1962	8,000,000	—	0.10	0.20	0.50
AH1385/1965	8,000,000	—	0.10	0.20	0.50

KM# 104 2-1/2 PIASTRES **Composition:** Aluminum-Bronze

Date	Mintage	F	VF	XF	Unc	BU
AH1393/1973	10,000,000	—	0.10	0.15	0.25	—

KM# 94 5 PIASTRES **Composition:** Aluminum-Bronze

Date	Mintage	F	VF	XF	Unc	BU
AH1382/1962	7,000,000	—	0.10	0.15	0.35	—
AH1385/1965	18,000,000	—	0.10	0.15	0.35	—

KM# 100 5 PIASTRES **Composition:** Aluminum-Bronze **Series:** F.A.O.

Date	Mintage	F	VF	XF	Unc	BU
AH1391/1971	15,000,000	—	0.10	0.15	0.25	—

KM# 105 5 PIASTRES **Composition:** Aluminum-Bronze

Date	F	VF	XF	Unc	BU
AH1394/1974	—	0.10	0.15	0.25	—

KM# 110 5 PIASTRES **Composition:** Aluminum-Bronze **Series:** F.A.O.

Date	Mintage	F	VF	XF	Unc	BU
AH1396/1976	2,000,000	—	0.10	0.15	0.25	—

KM# 116 5 PIASTRES **Composition:** Aluminum-Bronze **Note:** Similar to KM#94 but heavier neck feathers.

Date	F	VF	XF	Unc	BU
AH1399/1979	—	0.10	0.15	0.25	—

KM# 95 10 PIASTRES **Composition:** Aluminum-Bronze

Date	Mintage	F	VF	XF	Unc	BU
1382/1962	6,000,000	—	0.10	0.20	0.45	—
1385/1965	22,000,000	—	0.10	0.20	0.45	—

KM# 106 10 PIASTRES **Composition:** Aluminum-Bronze

Date	F	VF	XF	Unc	BU
1394/1974	—	0.10	0.15	0.30	—

KM# 111 10 PIASTRES **Composition:** Brass **Series:** F.A.O. **Note:** Similar to 5 Piastres, KM#110.

Date	Mintage	F	VF	XF	Unc	BU
1396/1976	500,000	—	0.10	0.15	0.25	—

KM# 117 10 PIASTRES **Composition:** Aluminum-Bronze

Date	F	VF	XF	Unc	BU
AH1399/1979	—	0.10	0.15	0.30	—

KM# 96 25 PIASTRES **Composition:** Nickel

Date	Mintage	F	VF	XF	Unc	BU
AH1387/1968	15,000,000	—	0.20	0.30	0.60	—

KM# 101 25 PIASTRES **Composition:** Nickel **Subject:** 25th Anniversary - Al-Ba'ath Party

Date	F	VF	XF	Unc	BU
AH1392/1972	—	0.15	0.25	0.60	—

KM# 107 25 PIASTRES **Composition:** Nickel

Date	F	VF	XF	Unc	BU
AH1394/1974	—	0.10	0.25	0.50	—

KM# 112 25 PIASTRES **Composition:** Nickel **Series:** F.A.O.

Date	Mintage	F	VF	XF	Unc	BU
AH1396/1976	1,000,000	—	0.10	0.25	0.50	—

KM# 118 25 PIASTRES **Composition:** Copper-Nickel

Date	F	VF	XF	Unc	BU
AH1399/1979	—	0.10	0.25	0.50	—

KM# 97 50 PIASTRES **Composition:** Nickel

Date	Mintage	F	VF	XF	Unc	BU
AH1387/1968	10,000,000	—	0.25	0.50	0.85	—

KM# 102 50 PIASTRES **Composition:** Nickel **Subject:** 25th Anniversary - Al-Ba'ath Party

Date	F	VF	XF	Unc	BU
AH1392/1972	—	0.50	1.00	2.00	—

KM# 108 50 PIASTRES **Composition:** Nickel

Date	F	VF	XF	Unc	BU
AH1394/1974	—	0.20	0.30	0.75	—

KM# 113 50 PIASTRES **Composition:** Nickel **Series:** F.A.O.

Date	Mintage	F	VF	XF	Unc	BU
AH1396/1976	1,000,000	—	0.20	0.50	1.00	—

KM# 119 50 PIASTRES **Composition:** Copper-Nickel

Date	F	VF	XF	Unc	BU
AH1399/1979	—	0.20	0.30	0.75	—

KM# 98 POUND **Composition:** Nickel

Date	Mintage	F	VF	XF	Unc	BU
AH1387/1968	10,000,000	—	0.30	0.75	1.25	—
AH1391/1971	10,000,000	—	0.30	0.75	1.25	—

KM# 99 POUND **Composition:** Nickel **Series:** F.A.O.

Date	Mintage	F	VF	XF	Unc	BU
AH1388/1968	500,000	—	1.00	2.00	3.50	—

KM# 103 POUND **Composition:** Nickel **Subject:** 25th Anniversary - Al-Ba'ath Party

Date	Mintage	F	VF	XF	Unc	BU
AH1392/1972	10,000,000	—	0.50	1.00	2.50	—

KM# 109 POUND **Composition:** Nickel

Date	F	VF	XF	Unc	BU
AH1394/1974	—	0.30	0.75	2.00	—

KM# 114 POUND **Composition:** Nickel **Series:** F.A.O.

Date	Mintage	F	VF	XF	Unc	BU
AH1396/1976	500,000	—	0.50	1.00	2.50	—

KM# 115 POUND **Composition:** Nickel **Subject:** Re-election of President

Date	F	VF	XF	Unc	BU
AH1398/1978	—	1.50	2.50	5.00	—

KM# 120.1 POUND **Composition:** Copper-Nickel

Date	F	VF	XF	Unc	BU
AH1399/1979	—	0.30	0.70	1.50	—

KM# 120.2 POUND **Composition:** Stainless Steel

Date	F	VF	XF	Unc	BU
AH1412/1991	—	0.30	0.70	1.50	—

KM# 121 POUND **Composition:** Stainless Steel

Date	F	VF	XF	Unc	BU
AH1414/1994	—	0.30	0.70	1.50	—

KM# 125 2 POUNDS **Composition:** Stainless Steel **Obverse:** National emblem **Reverse:** Ancient ruins

Date	F	VF	XF	Unc	BU
AH1416/1996	—	—	0.85	1.75	—

KM# 123 5 POUNDS **Composition:** Copper-Nickel **Reverse:** Palace

Date	F	VF	XF	Unc	BU
AH1416/1996	—	—	1.00	2.00	—

KM# 124 10 POUNDS **Composition:** Copper-Nickel **Reverse:** Ancient ruins

Date	F	VF	XF	Unc	BU
AH1416/1996	—	—	1.25	2.50	—
AH1417/1997(a)	—	—	1.25	2.50	—

KM# 128 10 POUNDS **Weight:** 7.0000 g. **Composition:** Copper-Nickel **Subject:** 50th Anniversary of Al Ba'ath Party **Obverse:** National arms **Reverse:** Map and flag **Edge:** Reeded **Size:** 26.5 mm.

Date	Mintage	F	VF	XF	Unc	BU
AH1417/1997	100,000	—	—	1.25	2.50	—

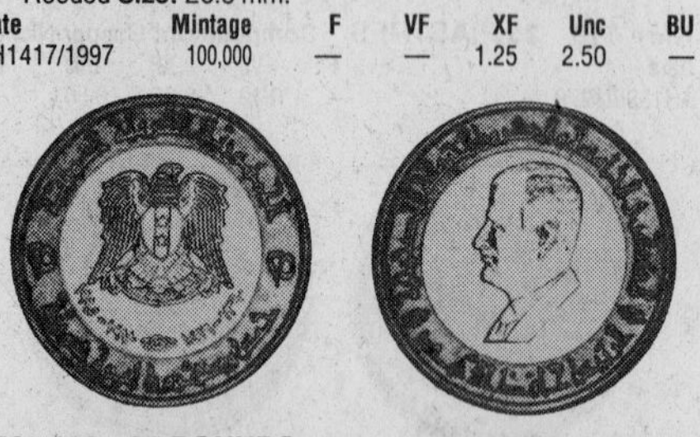

KM# 122 25 POUNDS **Ring Composition:** Bronze **Center Composition:** Stainless Steel **Obverse:** Heraldic eagle **Reverse:** President

Date	F	VF	XF	Unc	BU
ND(1995)	—	—	2.50	7.00	—

KM# 126 25 POUNDS **Ring Composition:** Bronze **Center Composition:** Stainless Steel **Obverse:** National emblem **Reverse:** Large modern building

Date	F	VF	XF	Unc	BU
AH1416/1996	—	—	2.00	6.00	—

ESSAIS

KM#	Date	Mintage	Identification	Issue Price	Mkt Val
E1	1926(a)	—	2 Piastres. KM69.	—	200
E2	1926(a)	—	5 Piastres. KM70.	—	220

KM#	Date	Mintage	Identification	Issue Price	Mkt Val
E3	1929(a)	—	Piastre. KM71.	—	115
E4	1929(a)	—	10 Piastres. KM72.	—	200
E5	1929(a)	—	25 Piastres. KM73.	—	250

KM#	Date	Mintage	Identification	Issue Price	Mkt Val
E6	1929(a)	—	50 Piastres. KM74.	—	265
E7	AH1350(a)	—	50 Piastres.	—	350
E8	1935(a)	—	1/2 Piastre. KM75.	—	60.0

MINT SETS

KM#	Date	Mintage	Identification	Issue Price	Mkt Val
MS1	1968 (3)	—	KM96-98	—	5.5
MS2	1978-79 (6)	—	KM115 (1978), 116-120.1 (1979)	—	8.5

AJIKISTAN

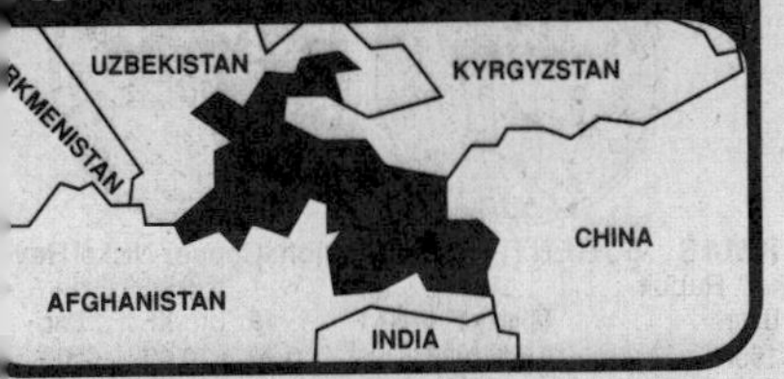

The Republic of Tajikistan (Tadjiquistan), was formed from regions of Bukhara and Turkestan where the population sted mainly of Tajiks. Is bordered in the north and west by kistan and Kyrgyzstan, in the east by China and in the south ghanistan. It has an area of 55,240 sq. miles (143,100 sq. and a population of 5.95 million. It includes 2 provinces of zand and Khatlon together with the Gorno-Badakhshan nomous Region with a population of 5,092,603. Capital: Dus-e. Tajikistan was admitted as a constituent republic of the t Union on Dec. 5, 1929. In August 1990 the Tajik Supreme t adopted a declaration of republican sovereignty, and in 1991 the republic became a member of the CIS.

After demonstrations and fighting, the Communist govern- was replaced by a Revolutionary Coalition Council on May 92. Following further demonstrations President Nabiev was d on Sept. 7, 1992. Civil war broke out, and the government ned on Nov. 10, 1992. On Nov. 30, 1992 it was announced CIS peacekeeping force would be sent to Tajikistan. A state ergency was imposed in Jan. 1993. A ceasefire was signed 96 and a peace agreement signed in June 1997.

ETARY SYSTEM
ble = 100 Tanga

REPUBLIC

DECIMAL COINAGE

 # 2 5 DRAMS **Weight:** 2.0500 g. **Composition:** Brass Clad Steel **Obverse:** Crown **Reverse:** Denomination **Edge:** Plain **Size:** 16.5 mm.

F	VF	XF	Unc	BU
—	—	—	0.50	—

 # 3 10 DRAMS **Weight:** 2.4700 g. **Composition:** Brass Clad Steel **Obverse:** Crown **Reverse:** Denomination **Edge:** Plain **Size:** 17.5 mm.

F	VF	XF	Unc	BU
—	—	—	0.75	—

 # 4 20 DRAMS **Weight:** 2.7300 g. **Composition:** Brass Clad Steel **Obverse:** Crown **Reverse:** Denomination **Edge:** Plain **Size:** 18.5 mm.

F	VF	XF	Unc	BU
—	—	—	1.00	—

 # 5 25 DRAMS **Weight:** 2.8000 g. **Composition:** Brass **Obverse:** Crown **Reverse:** Denomination **Edge:** Plain **Size:** 19.1 mm.

F	VF	XF	Unc	BU
—	—	—	1.25	—

KM# 6 50 DRAMS **Weight:** 3.5500 g. **Composition:** Brass **Obverse:** Crown **Reverse:** Denomination **Edge:** Plain **Size:** 21 mm.

Date	F	VF	XF	Unc	BU
2001	—	—	—	1.75	—

KM# 1 20 ROUBLES **Weight:** 20.0000 g. **Composition:** 0.9250 Silver .5948 oz. ASW **Obverse:** Royal device. **Reverse:** Crowned portrait. **Edge:** Reeded. **Size:** 35.1 mm.

Date	F	VF	XF	Unc	BU
1999 Proof	— Value: 65.00				

KM# 7 SOMONI **Weight:** 5.1500 g. **Composition:** Copper-Nickel-Zinc **Obverse:** King's bust 1/2 right. **Reverse:** Denomination. **Edge:** Reeded and plain sections. **Size:** 23.9 mm.

Date	F	VF	XF	Unc	BU
2001	—	—	—	4.00	—

KM# 8 3 SOMONI **Weight:** 6.3200 g. **Composition:** Copper-Nickel-Zinc **Obverse:** National arms. **Reverse:** Denomination. **Edge:** Lettered. **Size:** 25.5 mm.

Date	F	VF	XF	Unc	BU
2001	—	—	—	5.00	—

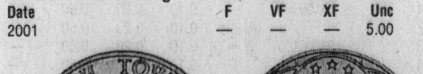

KM# 9 5 SOMONI **Weight:** 7.1000 g. **Composition:** Copper-Nickel-Zinc **Obverse:** Turbaned portrait. **Reverse:** Denomination. **Edge:** Reeded and plain sections with a star. **Size:** 26.4 mm.

Date	F	VF	XF	Unc	BU
2001	—	—	—	6.00	—

TANNU TUVA

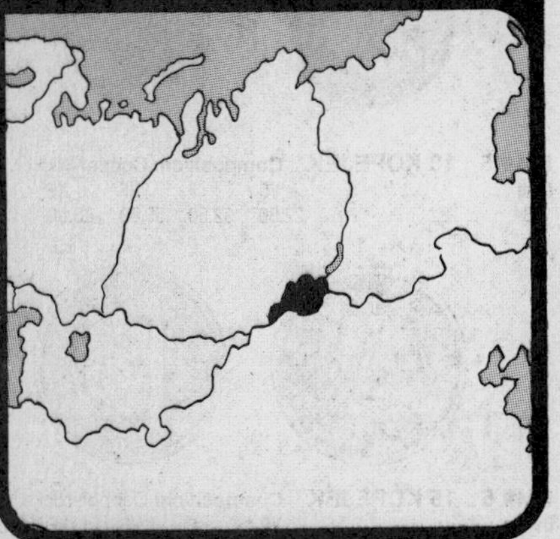

The Tannu-Tuva Peoples Republic (Tuva), an autonomous part of Russia located in central Asia on the northwest border of Outer Mongolia, has an area of 64,000 sq. mi. (165,760 sq. km.) and a population of about 175,000. Capital: Kyzyl. The economy is based on herding, forestry and mining.

As Urianghi, Tuva was part of Outer Mongolia of the Chinese Empire when tsarist Russia, after fomenting a separatist movement, extended its protection to the mountainous country in 1914. Tuva declared its independence as the Tannu-Tuva Peoples Republic in 1921 under the auspices of the Tuva Peoples Revolutionary Party. In 1926, following Russia's successful mediation of the resultant Tuvinian-Mongolian territorial dispute, Tannu-Tuva and Outer Mongolia formally recognized each other's independence. The Tannu-Tuva Peoples Republic became an autonomous region of the U.S.S.R. on Oct. 13, 1944.

MONETARY SYSTEM
100 Kopejek (Kopeks) = 1 Aksha

REPUBLIC

STANDARD COINAGE

KM# 1 KOPEJEK **Composition:** Aluminum-Bronze

Date	VG	F	VF	XF	Unc
1934	20.00	30.00	45.00	75.00	—

KM# 2 2 KOPEJEK **Composition:** Aluminum-Bronze

Date	VG	F	VF	XF	Unc
1933	—	—	—	—	—
1934	22.50	32.50	55.00	85.00	—

KM# 3 3 KOPEJEK **Composition:** Aluminum-Bronze

Date	VG	F	VF	XF	Unc
1933	—	—	—	—	—
1934	20.00	30.00	45.00	75.00	—

KM# 4 5 KOPEJEK **Composition:** Aluminum-Bronze

Date	VG	F	VF	XF	Unc
1934	22.50	32.50	55.00	85.00	—

KM# 5 10 KOPEJEK **Composition:** Copper-Nickel

Date	VG	F	VF	XF	Unc
1934	22.50	32.50	55.00	85.00	—

KM# 6 15 KOPEJEK **Composition:** Copper-Nickel

Date	VG	F	VF	XF	Unc
1934	22.50	32.50	55.00	85.00	—

KM# 7 20 KOPEJEK **Composition:** Copper-Nickel

Date	VG	F	VF	XF	Unc
1934	22.50	32.50	55.00	85.00	—

TANZANIA

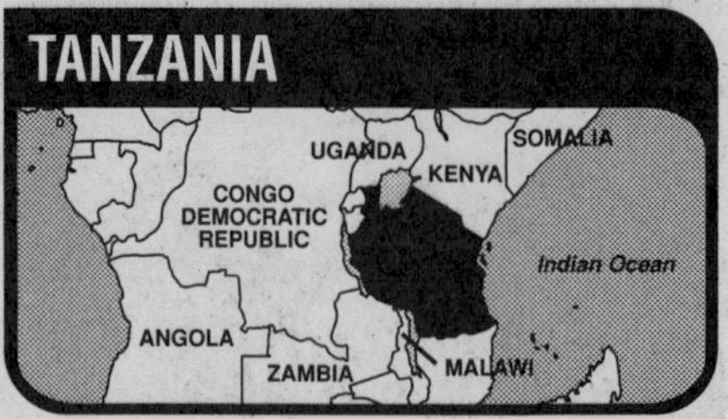

The United Republic of Tanzania, located on the east coast of Africa between Kenya and Mozambique, consists of Tanganyika and the islands of Zanzibar and Pemba. It has an area of 364,900 sq. mi. (945,090 sq. km.) and a population of *25.2 million. Capital: Dar es Salaam (Haven of Peace). The chief exports are cotton, coffee, diamonds, sisal, cloves, petroleum products, and cashew nuts.

Tanzania is a member of the Commonwealth of Nations. The President is Chief of State.

NOTE: For earlier coinage see East Africa.

REPUBLIC

STANDARD COINAGE

100 Senti = 1 Shilingi

KM# 1 5 SENTI **Composition:** Bronze

Date	Mintage	F	VF	XF	Unc	BU
1966	55,250,000	—	0.10	0.20	0.50	—
1966 Proof	5,500	Value: 1.00				
1971	5,000,000	—	0.10	0.20	0.50	—
1972	—	—	0.10	0.20	0.50	—
1973	20,000,000	—	0.10	0.20	0.50	—
1974	12,500,000	—	0.10	0.20	0.50	—
1975	—	—	0.10	0.20	0.50	—
1976	37,500,000	—	0.10	0.20	0.50	—
1977	10,000,000	—	0.10	0.20	0.50	—
1979	7,200,000	—	0.10	0.20	0.50	—
1980	10,000,000	—	0.10	0.20	0.50	—
1981	13,650,000	—	0.10	0.20	0.50	—
1982	—	—	0.10	0.20	0.50	—
1983	18,000	—	0.10	0.20	0.50	—
1984	—	—	0.10	0.20	0.50	—

KM# 11 10 SENTI **Composition:** Nickel-Brass **Reverse:** Zebra running right **Shape:** Scalloped

Date	Mintage	F	VF	XF	Unc	BU
1977	19,505,000	—	0.75	1.50	4.00	—
1979	8,000,000	—	0.75	1.50	4.00	—
1980	10,000,000	—	0.75	1.50	4.00	—
1981	10,000,000	—	0.75	1.50	4.00	—
1984	—	—	0.75	1.50	4.00	—

KM# 2 20 SENTI **Composition:** Nickel-Brass **Reverse:** Ostrich running left

Date	Mintage	F	VF	XF	Unc	BU
1966	26,500,000	—	0.20	0.40	1.50	—
1966 Proof	5,500	Value: 1.50				
1970	5,000,000	—	0.20	0.40	1.50	—
1973	20,100,000	—	0.20	0.40	1.50	—
1975	—	—	0.20	0.40	1.50	—
1976	10,000,000	—	0.20	0.40	1.50	—
1977	10,000,000	—	0.20	0.40	1.50	—
1979	10,000,000	—	0.20	0.40	1.50	—
1980	10,000,000	—	0.20	0.40	1.50	—
1981	10,000,000	—	0.20	0.40	1.50	—
1982	—	—	0.20	0.40	1.50	—
1983	50,000	—	0.20	0.40	1.50	—
1984	—	—	0.20	0.40	1.50	—

KM# 3 50 SENTI **Composition:** Copper-Nickel **Reve** Rabbit

Date	Mintage	F	VF	XF	Unc
1966	6,250,000	—	0.20	0.40	2.00
1966 Proof	5,500	Value: 3.00			
1970	10,000,000	—	0.20	0.40	2.00
1973	10,000,000	—	0.25	0.50	2.00
1980	10,000,000	—	0.25	0.50	2.00
1981	—	—	0.25	0.50	2.00
1982	10,000,000	—	0.25	0.50	2.00
1983	—	—	0.25	0.50	2.00
1984	10,000,000	—	0.25	0.50	2.00

KM# 26 50 SENTI **Composition:** Nickel Clad Steel **Reverse:** Rabbit

Date	Mintage	F	VF	XF	Unc
1988	10,000,000	—	0.25	0.75	1.50
1989	—	—	0.25	0.75	1.50
1990	—	—	0.25	0.75	1.50

KM# 4 SHILINGI **Composition:** Copper-Nickel **Reverse:** Hand holding torch

Date	Mintage	F	VF	XF	Unc
1966	48,000,000	—	0.25	0.50	1.50
1966 Proof	5,500	Value: 5.00			
1972	10,000,000	—	0.25	0.50	1.50
1974	15,000,000	—	0.30	0.60	1.75
1975	—	—	0.30	0.60	1.75
1977	5,000,000	—	0.30	0.60	1.75
1980	10,000,000	—	0.25	0.50	1.50
1981	—	—	0.30	0.60	1.75
1982	10,000,000	—	0.30	0.60	1.75
1983	10,000,000	—	0.30	0.60	1.75
1984	10,000,000	—	0.30	0.60	1.75

KM# 22 SHILINGI **Composition:** Nickel Clad Steel **Reverse:** Hand holding torch

Date	Mintage	F	VF	XF	Unc
1987	5,000,000	—	0.40	0.80	2.00
1988	10,000,000	—	0.40	0.80	2.00
1989	—	—	0.40	0.80	2.00
1990	—	—	0.20	0.40	1.25
1991	—	—	0.20	0.40	1.25
1992	—	—	0.20	0.40	1.25

KM# 5 5 SHILINGI **Composition:** Copper-Nickel **Seri** F.A.O. **Subject:** 10th Anniversary of Independence **Sha** 10-sided

Date	Mintage	F	VF	XF	Unc
ND(1971)	1,000,000	—	0.75	1.50	3.50

#6 **5 SHILINGI Composition:** Copper-Nickel **Series:** F.A.O. **Shape:** 10-sided

Date	Mintage	F	VF	XF	Unc	BU
	8,000,000	—	0.75	1.50	3.50	—
	5,000,000	—	0.75	1.75	4.00	—
	5,000,000	—	0.75	1.75	4.00	—

10 **5 SHILINGI Composition:** Copper-Nickel **Subject:** 10th Anniversary - Bank of Tanzania **Reverse:** Bank building **Shape:** 10-sided

Date	Mintage	F	VF	XF	Unc	BU
976)	1,000,000	—	0.75	1.50	3.50	—
976) Proof	200	Value: 40.00				

12 **5 SHILINGI Composition:** Copper-Nickel **Series:** F.A.O. **Subject:** Regional Conference for Africa **Reverse:** Farmer working with tractor **Shape:** 10-sided

Date	Mintage	F	VF	XF	Unc	BU
3	50,000	—	0.75	1.50	2.75	—
3 Proof	2,000	Value: 11.50				

23 **5 SHILINGI Composition:** Copper-Nickel **Obverse:** Small head (17mm) **Shape:** 10-sided

Date	Mintage	F	VF	XF	Unc	BU
7	5,000,000	—	0.75	1.50	3.00	—
3	10,000,000	—	0.75	1.50	3.00	—
9	—	—	0.75	1.50	3.00	—

23a.1 **5 SHILINGI Composition:** Nickel Clad Steel **Obverse:** Small (17mm) head **Edge:** Milled

Date	F	VF	XF	Unc	BU
0	—	0.60	1.20	1.85	—

23a.2 (KM23a) **5 SHILINGI Composition:** Nickel Clad Steel **Obverse:** Large (18mm) head

Date	F	VF	XF	Unc	BU
1	—	0.60	1.20	1.85	—
1	—	0.60	1.20	1.85	—
2	—	0.50	1.00	1.50	—
2	—	0.50	1.00	1.50	—
3	—	0.50	1.00	1.50	—
3	—	0.50	1.00	1.50	—

20a.1 **5 SHILINGI Composition:** Nickel Clad Steel **Reverse:** 4 millimeter "10"; inscription near edge

Date	F	VF	XF	Unc	BU
0	—	0.60	1.20	1.85	—

20a.2 **5 SHILINGI Composition:** Nickel Clad Steel **Reverse:** 3 millimeter "10"; inscription away from edge

Date	F	VF	XF	Unc	BU
1	—	0.60	1.20	1.85	—
2	—	0.60	1.20	1.85	—
3	—	0.60	1.20	1.85	—

KM# 20 **10 SHILINGI Composition:** Copper-Nickel **Reverse:** 4 millimeter "10"; inscription near edge

Date	Mintage	F	VF	XF	Unc	BU
1987	10,000,000	—	1.00	1.50	3.25	—
1988	10,000,000	—	1.00	1.50	3.25	—
1989	—	—	1.00	1.50	3.25	—

KM# 20a **10 SHILINGI Composition:** Nickel Clad Steel

Date	F	VF	XF	Unc	BU
1990	—	1.00	1.50	2.25	—
1991	—	1.00	1.50	2.25	—
1992	—	0.85	1.25	2.00	—
1993	—	0.85	1.25	2.00	—

KM# 13 **20 SHILINGI Composition:** Copper-Nickel **Subject:** 20th Anniversary of Independence

Date	Mintage	F	VF	XF	Unc	BU
ND(1981)	997,000	—	2.50	4.50	10.00	—

KM# 13a **20 SHILINGI Weight:** 16.0000 g. **Composition:** 0.9250 Silver .4759 oz. ASW

Date	Mintage	F	VF	XF	Unc	BU
ND(1981) Proof	20,000	Value: 42.50				

KM# 21 **20 SHILINGI Composition:** Copper-Nickel **Subject:** 20th Anniversary of Central Bank

Date	F	VF	XF	Unc	BU
ND(1986)	—	4.00	10.00	20.00	—

KM# 21a **20 SHILINGI Weight:** 16.0000 g. **Composition:** 0.9250 Silver .4759 oz. ASW

Date	Mintage	F	VF	XF	Unc	BU
ND(1986) Proof	5,000	Value: 110				

KM# 27.1 **20 SHILINGI Composition:** Nickel Bonded Steel **Reverse:** Elephants

Date	F	VF	XF	Unc	BU
1990	—	1.50	2.00	3.50	—
1991	—	1.50	2.00	3.50	—

KM# 27.2 **20 SHILINGI Composition:** Nickel Bonded Steel **Reverse:** Elephant with calf **Shape:** 7-sided **Note:** Reduced size.

Date	F	VF	XF	Unc	BU
1992	—	1.25	1.75	3.25	—

KM# 7 **25 SHILINGI Weight:** 25.4000 g. **Composition:** 0.5000 Silver .4083 oz. ASW **Subject:** Conservation **Obverse:** Similar to 1500 Shilingi, KM#9 **Reverse:** Three Southern Giraffes running right

Date	Mintage	F	VF	XF	Unc	BU
1974	8,848	—	—	—	17.50	—

KM# 7a **25 SHILINGI Weight:** 28.2800 g. **Composition:** 0.9250 Silver .8411 oz. ASW

Date	Mintage	F	VF	XF	Unc	BU
1974 Proof	13,000	Value: 22.50				

KM# 30 **25 SHILINGI Composition:** Copper-Nickel **Subject:** 25 Years of Independence

Date	Mintage	F	VF	XF	Unc	BU
ND(1985) Proof	—	Value: 100				

KM# 28 **25 SHILINGI Composition:** Nickel Bonded Steel **Subject:** 25th Anniversary of Central Bank

Date	F	VF	XF	Unc	BU
ND(1991)	—	—	—	3.00	—

KM# 28a **25 SHILINGI Weight:** 13.0400 g. **Composition:** 0.9250 Silver .3878 oz. ASW

Date	Mintage	F	VF	XF	Unc	BU
ND(1991) Proof	Est. 2,000	Value: 65.00				

KM# 8 **50 SHILINGI Weight:** 31.8500 g. **Composition:** 0.5000 Silver .5120 oz. ASW **Subject:** Conservation **Obverse:** Similar to 1500 Shilingi, KM#9 **Reverse:** Black Rhinoceros

Date	Mintage	F	VF	XF	Unc	BU
1974	8,826	—	—	—	21.50	—

KM# 8a **50 SHILINGI Weight:** 35.0000 g. **Composition:** 0.9250 Silver 1.0409 oz. ASW

Date	Mintage	F	VF	XF	Unc	BU
1974 Proof	12,000	Value: 27.50				

KM# 33 50 SHILINGI **Composition:** Brass Plated Steel **Subject:** Conservation **Reverse:** Mother rhino and calf **Shape:** 7-sided

Date	F	VF	XF	Unc	BU
1996	—	—	—	3.75	—

KM# 16 100 SHILINGI **Weight:** 23.3300 g. **Composition:** 0.9250 Silver .6938 oz. ASW **Series:** Decade for Women **Reverse:** Kneeling nurse holding baby in air

Date	Mintage	F	VF	XF	Unc	BU
1984 Proof	1,000	Value: 42.50				

KM# 18 100 SHILINGI **Composition:** Copper-Nickel **Subject:** Conservation **Reverse:** Elephant mother and calf

Date	F	VF	XF	Unc	BU
1986	—	—	—	6.50	—

KM# 18a 100 SHILINGI **Weight:** 19.4400 g. **Composition:** 0.9250 Silver .5782 oz. ASW **Reverse:** Elephant mother and calf

Date	Mintage	F	VF	XF	Unc	BU
1986 Proof	25,000	Value: 27.50				

KM# 24 100 SHILINGI **Weight:** 19.4400 g. **Composition:** 0.9250 Silver .5782 oz. ASW **Series:** Save the Children Fund **Reverse:** Two girls with clubs mashing grain in pail

Date	Mintage	F	VF	XF	Unc	BU
1990 Proof	Est. 20,000	Value: 22.50				

KM# 32 100 SHILINGI **Composition:** Brass Plated Steel **Subject:** Conservation **Reverse:** Four impalas running right

Date	F	VF	XF	Unc	BU
1993	—	—	—	4.00	—
1994	—	—	—	4.00	—

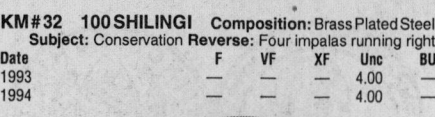

KM# 14 200 SHILINGI **Weight:** 28.2800 g. **Composition:** 0.9250 Silver .8411 oz. ASW **Subject:** 20th Anniversary of Independence **Obverse:** Similar to 20 Shilingi, KM#13

Date	Mintage	F	VF	XF	Unc	BU
ND(1981)	110	—	—	—	135	—
ND(1981) Proof	Inc. above	Value: 150				

KM# 41 200 SHILINGI **Weight:** 20.0000 g. **Composition:** 0.5000 Silver .3214 oz. ASW **Subject:** Wildlife of Africa **Obverse:** National arms **Reverse:** Adult and juvenile rhinos **Edge:** Reeded **Size:** 34 mm.

Date	F	VF	XF	Unc	BU
1997 Proof	—	Value: 22.50			

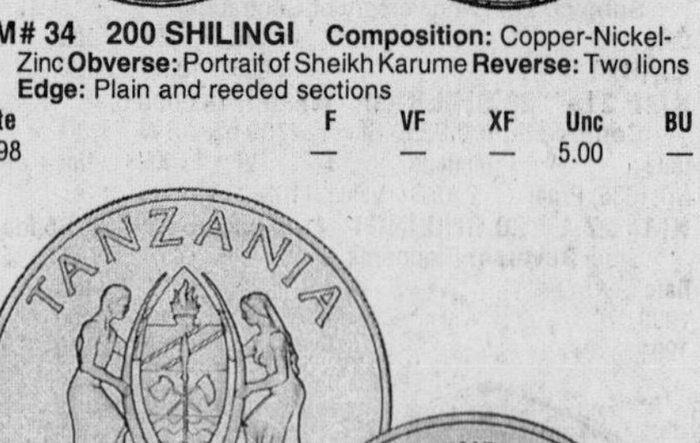

KM# 34 200 SHILINGI **Composition:** Copper-Nickel-Zinc **Obverse:** Portrait of Sheikh Karume **Reverse:** Two lions **Edge:** Plain and reeded sections

Date	F	VF	XF	Unc	BU
1998	—	—	—	5.00	—

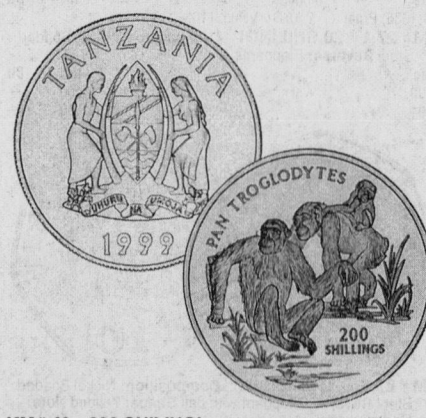

KM# 40 200 SHILINGI **Weight:** 15.4000 g. **Composition:** 0.9250 Silver .4580 oz. ASW **Subject:** Pan Troglodytes **Obverse:** National arms **Reverse:** Chimpanzee family **Edge:** Reeded **Size:** 33.9 mm.

Date	F	VF	XF	Unc	BU
1999 Proof	—	Value: 30.00			

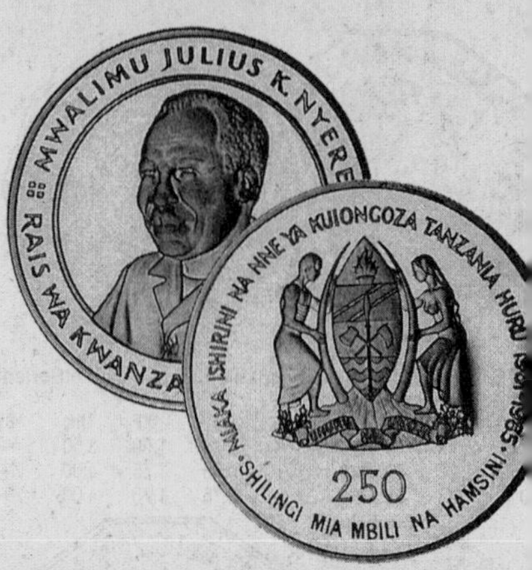

KM# 29 250 SHILINGI **Weight:** 28.1600 g. **Composit** 0.9250 Silver .8374 oz. ASW **Subject:** 25th Anniversary Independence

Date	F	VF	XF	Unc
ND(1985) Proof	—	Value: 250		

KM# 44 500 SHILINGI **Weight:** 20.0000 g. **Compositi** 0.9990 Silver .6424 oz. ASW **Subject:** Visit of Richard v Weizsacker **Obverse:** Arms **Reverse:** Weizsacker and elephant

Date	Mintage	F	VF	XF	Unc
1992 Proof	Est. 20,000	Value: 35.00			

KM# 43 500 SHILINGI **Weight:** 33.8000 g. **Composition:** 0.9250 Silver 1.0052 oz. ASW **Subject:** Serengeti Wildlife **Obverse:** National arms **Reverse:** Lic **Edge:** Reeded **Size:** 38.5 mm.

Date	F	VF	XF	Unc
1998 Proof	—	Value: 40.00		

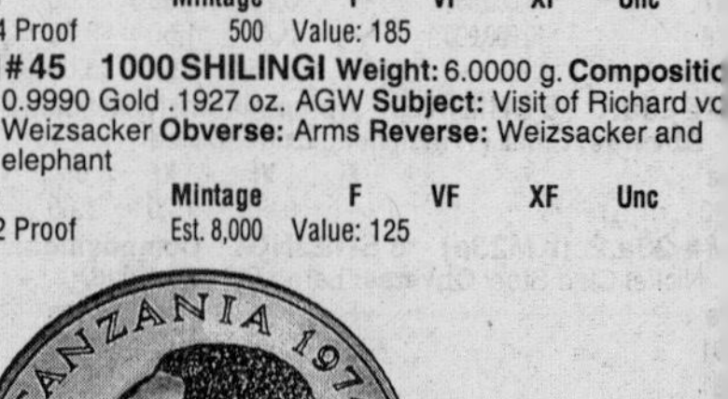

KM# 17 1000 SHILINGI **Weight:** 8.1000 g. **Compositic** 0.9000 Gold .2344 oz. AGW **Series:** Decade for Women

Date	Mintage	F	VF	XF	Unc
1984 Proof	500	Value: 185			

KM# 45 1000 SHILINGI **Weight:** 6.0000 g. **Compositic** 0.9990 Gold .1927 oz. AGW **Subject:** Visit of Richard vo Weizsacker **Obverse:** Arms **Reverse:** Weizsacker and elephant

Date	Mintage	F	VF	XF	Unc
1992 Proof	Est. 8,000	Value: 125			

 # 9 1500 SHILINGI **Weight:** 33.4370 g. **Composition:** 0.9000 Gold .9676 oz. AGW **Subject:** Conservation **Reverse:** Cheetah

	Mintage	F	VF	XF	Unc	BU
	2,779	—	—	—	420	—
Proof	866	Value: 650				

 # 15 2000 SHILINGI **Weight:** 15.9800 g. **Composition:** 0.9170 Gold .4712 oz. AGW **Subject:** 20th Anniversary of Independence **Reverse:** National arms

	Mintage	F	VF	XF	Unc	BU
1981)	110	—	—	—	375	—
1981) Proof	Inc. above	Value: 425				

 # 19 2000 SHILINGI **Weight:** 15.9800 g. **Composition:** 0.9170 Gold .4712 oz. AGW **Subject:** Conservation **Reverse:** Banded Green Sunbird

	Mintage	F	VF	XF	Unc	BU
6 Proof	5,000	Value: 275				

 # 25 2000 SHILINGI **Weight:** 10.0000 g. **Composition:** 0.9170 Gold .2948 oz. AGW **Series:** Save the Children Fund

		F	VF	XF	Unc	BU
0 Proof	Est. 3,000	Value: 225				

 # 46 2000 SHILINGI **Weight:** 10.0000 g. **Composition:** 0.9990 Gold .3212 oz. AGW **Subject:** Visit of Richard von Weizsacker **Obverse:** Arms **Reverse:** Weizsacker and elephant

		F	VF	XF	Unc	BU
2 Proof	Est. 5,000	Value: 200				

 # 31 2500 SHILINGI **Weight:** 46.8500 g. **Composition:** 0.9170 Gold 1.3808 oz. AGW **Subject:** 25 Years of Independence

		F	VF	XF	Unc	BU
(1985) Proof	—	Value: 850				

KM# 35 2500 SHILINGI **Weight:** 155.3600 g. **Composition:** 0.9990 Silver 4.9899 oz. ASW **Subject:** Serengeti Wildlife **Obverse:** National arms **Reverse:** Zebra head and full body portraits **Edge:** Reeded **Size:** 65 mm. **Note:** Illustration reduced.

Date		F	VF	XF	Unc	BU
1998 Proof	—	Value: 95.00				

KM# 36 2500 SHILINGI **Weight:** 155.3600 g. **Composition:** 0.9990 Silver 4.9899 oz. ASW **Subject:** Serengeti Wildlife **Reverse:** Giraffe head and full body portrait **Size:** 65 mm. **Note:** Illustration reduced.

Date		F	VF	XF	Unc	BU
1998 Proof	—	Value: 95.00				

KM# 37 2500 SHILINGI **Weight:** 155.3600 g. **Composition:** 0.9990 Silver 4.9899 oz. ASW **Subject:** Serengeti Wildlife **Reverse:** Cheetah head and full body portrait **Size:** 65 mm. **Note:** Illustration reduced.

Date		F	VF	XF	Unc	BU
1998 Proof	—	Value: 115				

KM# 38 2500 SHILINGI **Weight:** 155.3600 g. **Composition:** 0.9990 Silver 4.9899 oz. ASW **Subject:** Serengeti Wildlife **Reverse:** Wildebeest herd **Size:** 65 mm. **Note:** Illustration reduced.

Date		F	VF	XF	Unc	BU
1998 Proof	—	Value: 80.00				

KM# 39 2500 SHILINGI **Weight:** 155.3600 g. **Composition:** 0.9990 Silver 4.9899 oz. ASW **Subject:** Serengeti Wildlife **Reverse:** Gazelle head right, full body left **Size:** 65 mm. **Note:** Illustration reduced.

Date		F	VF	XF	Unc	BU
1998 Proof	—	Value: 80.00				

KM# 42 10000 SHILINGI **Weight:** 31.1035 g. **Composition:** 0.9999 Gold 1.0000 oz. AGW **Subject:** Serengeti Wildlife **Obverse:** National arms **Reverse:** Lion, cheetah, and zebra **Edge:** Reeded **Size:** 32.5 mm.

Date	Mintage	F	VF	XF	Unc	BU
1998 Proof	Est. 1,000	Value: 600				

PROOF SETS

KM#	Date	Mintage	Identification	Issue Price	Mkt Val
PS1	1966 (4)	5,500	KM#1-4	10.20	10.00
PS2	1974 (2)	30,000	KM#7a-8a	50.00	50.00
PS3	1985 (3)	—	KM#29-31	—	12.00

TATARSTAN

Tatarstan, an autonomous republic in the Russian Federation, is situated between the middle of the Volga river and its tributary Kama, extends east to the Ural mountains, covering 26,500 sq. mi. (68,000 sq. km.) and as of the 1970 census, has a population of 3,743,600. Capital: Kazan. Tatarstan's economy combines its ancient traditions in the craftmanship of wood, leather, cloth, and ceramics with modern engineering, chemical, and food industries.

Colonized by the Bulgars in the 5th century, the territory of the Volga-Kama Bulgar State was inhabited by Turks. In the 13th century, Ghengis Khan conquered the area and established control until the 15th century, when residual Mongol influence left Tatarstan as the Tatar Khanate, seat of the Kazan (Tatar) Khans. In 1552, under Ivan IV (The Terrible), Russia conquered, absorbed and controlled Tatarstan until the dissolution of the U.S.S.R. in the late 20th century.

Constituted as an autonomous republic on May 27,1990, and as a sovereign state equal with Russia April, 1992, Tatarstan, with Russia's president, signed a treaty in Feb. 1994 defining Tatarstan as a state united with Russia (Commonwealth of Independent States).

RULERS
President Mintimir Shaimiev

RUSSIAN STATE

TOKEN COINAGE

KM# Tn1 KILO (Bread) **Composition:** Bronze **Ruler:** President Mintimir Shaimiev **Obverse:** Arms **Reverse:** Wheat stalks **Edge:** Reeded

Date	F	VF	XF	Unc	BU
ND (1993)	1.25	2.50	5.00	9.00	—

KM# Tn2 10 LITRES (Petrol) **Composition:** Bronze **Ruler:** President Mintimir Shaimiev **Obverse:** Arms **Reverse:** Oil well pump **Edge:** Reeded **Note:** The bronze 10 Litres token was withdrawn from circulation because it was nickel plated in large numbers and passed off as the higher valued copper-nickel version KM-Tn3.

Date	F	VF	XF	Unc	BU
ND (1993)	2.00	3.50	8.50	13.50	—

KM# Tn3 20 LITRES (Petrol) **Composition:** Copper Nickel **Ruler:** President Mintimir Shaimiev **Obverse:** Arms **Reverse:** Oil well pump **Edge:** Reeded **Note:** The copper-nickel Tn3 are often found with test file notches, because of the nickel plating problems of the bronze Tn2.

Date	F	VF	XF	Unc	BU
ND (1993)	2.50	4.00	10.00	16.50	—

THAILAND

The Kingdom of Thailand (formerly Siam), a constitutional monarchy located in the center of mainland Southeast Asia between Burma and Laos, has an area of 198,457 mi. (514,000 sq. km.) and a population of *55.5 million. Capital: Bangkok. The economy is based on agriculture and mining. Rubber, rice, teakwood, tin and tungsten are exported.

The history of The Kingdom of Siam, the only country in south and Southeast Asia that was never colonized by an European power, dates from the 6th century A.D. when Thai people started to migrate into the area a process that accelerated with the Mongol invasion of China in the 13th century. After 400 years of sporadic warfare with the neighboring Burmese, King Taskin won the last battle in 1767. He founded a new capital, Dhonburi, on the west bank of the Chao Praya River. King Rama I moved the capital to Bangkok in 1782, thus initiating the so-called Bangkok Period of Siamese coinage characterized by Pot Duang money (bullet coins) stamped with regal symbols.

The Portuguese, who were followed by the Dutch, British and French, introduced the Thai to the Western world. Rama III of the present ruling dynasty negotiated a treaty of friendship and commerce with Britain in 1826, and in 1896 the independence of the kingdom was guaranteed by an Anglo-French accord.

In 1909 Siam ceded to Great Britain its suzerain rights over the dependencies of Kedah, Kelantan, Trengganu and Perlis, Malay states situated in southern Siam just north of British Malaya, which eliminated any British jurisdiction in Siam proper.

The absolute monarchy was changed into a constitutional monarchy in 1932.

On Dec. 8, 1941, after five hours of fighting, Thailand agreed to permit Japanese troops passage through the country to invade Northern British Malaysia. This eventually led to increased Japanese intervention and finally occupation of the country. On Jan. 25, 1942, Thailand declared war on Great Britain and the United States. A free Thai guerilla movement was soon organized to counteract the Japanese. In July 1943 Japan transferred the four northern Malay States back to Thailand. These were returned to Great Britain after peace treaties were signed in 1946.

RULERS
Rama V (Phra Maha Chulalongkorn), 1868-1910
Rama VI (Phra Maha Vajiravudh), 1910-1925
Rama VII (Phra Maha Prajadhipok), 1925-1935
Rama VIII (Phra Maha Ananda Mahidol), 1935-1946
Rama IX (Phra Maha Bhumifhol Adulyadej), 1946-

MONETARY SYSTEM

Old currency system

2 Solos = 1 Att
2 Att = 1 Sio (Pai)
2 Sio = 1 Sik
2 Sik = 1 Fuang
2 Fuang = 1 Salung (not Sal'ung)
4 Salung = 1 Baht
4 Baht = 1 Tamlung
20 Tamlung = 1 Chang

UNITS OF OLD THAI CURRENCY

Chang -	ชั่ง	Sik -	ซีก
Tamlung -	ตำลึง	Sio (Pai) -	เสี้ยว
Baht -	บาท	Att -	อัฐ
Salung -	สลึง	Solos -	โสพส
Fuang -	เฟื้อง		

MINT MARKS
H-Heaton Birmingham

Typical BE Dating

1 2 3 8   1 2 4 4

Typical CS Dating

NOTE: Sometimes the era designator *BE* or *CS* will actu appear on the coin itself.

Denomination

2 ½

2-1/2 (Satang)

RS Dating

DATE CONVERSION TABLES
B.E. date - 543 = A.D. date
Ex: 2516 - 543 = 1973
R.S. date + 1781 = A.D. date
Ex: 127 + 1781 = 1908
C.S. date + 638 = A.D. date
Ex 1238 + 638 = 1876

Primary denominations used were 1 Baht, 1/4 and 1/8 Baht to the reign of Rama IV. Other denominations are much scarc

KINGDOM

STANDARD COINAGE

Y# 21 1/2 ATT (1 Solot) **Composition:** Bronze **Rul** Rama V Phra Maha Chulalongkorn

Date	F	VF	XF	Unc	BU
RS124 (1905)	1.50	3.00	15.00	85.00	—

Note: These coins were also minted in RS114, RS115, RS121 ad RS122. The last year had a mintage of 5,120,000. Coins with these dates have not been observed and were probably additional mintings of coins dated RS109 and RS118. A nickel pattern dated RS114 does exist. Varieties in numeral size and rotated dies exist

Y# 22 ATT (1/64 Baht) **Composition:** Bronze **Ruler:** Rama V Phra Maha Chulalongkorn **Note:** Full red uncirculated coins of this type carry a substantial premium.

Date	Mintage	F	VF	XF	Unc	BU
RS121 (1902)	11,251,000	1.50	2.50	8.50	80.00	—
RS122 (1903)	4,109,000	1.50	3.00	10.00	90.00	—

Note: Exists with large (greater than 1mm) and small (less than 1mm) numerals

RS124	—	1.50	3.00	10.00	90.00	—

Y# 23 2 ATT **Composition:** Bronze **Ruler:** Rama V Phra Maha Chulalongkorn **Note:** Varieties in numeral size and rotated dies exist. Full red uncirculated coins of this type carry a substantial premium.

Date	Mintage	F	VF	XF	Unc	BU
RS107(1888)	—	1.50	3.00	12.00	110	—
RS108(1889)	—	1.50	3.00	12.00	110	—
RS121 (1902)	2,797,000	1.50	3.00	12.00	125	—
RS122 (1903)	2,323,000	1.50	3.00	12.00	125	—
RS124 (1905)	—	1.50	3.00	12.00	125	—

Y# 32a FUANG (1/8 Baht) **Weight:** 1.8900 g. **Composition:** Silver **Ruler:** Rama V Phra Maha Chulalongkorn

Date	Mintage	F	VF	XF	Unc	BU
RS120 (1901)	—	3.00	7.00	20.00	100	—
RS121 (1902)	380,000	3.00	7.00	20.00	100	—
RS122 (1903)	460,000	3.00	7.00	20.00	100	—
RS123 (1904)	310,000	3.00	7.00	20.00	100	—
RS124 (1905)	410,000	3.00	7.00	20.00	100	—
RS125 (1906)	—	3.00	7.00	20.00	100	—
RS126 (1907)	—	3.00	7.00	20.00	100	—
RS127 (1908)	480,000	3.00	7.00	20.00	100	—

Y# 32c FUANG (1/8 Baht) **Composition:** Gold **Ruler:** Rama V Phra Maha Chulalongkorn

Date	F	VF	XF	Unc	BU
RS122 (1903)	300	600	1,250	2,000	—
RS123 (1904)	300	600	1,250	2,000	—
RS124 (1905)	300	600	1,250	2,000	—
RS125 (1906)	300	600	1,250	2,000	—
RS126 (1907)	300	600	1,250	2,000	—
RS127 (1908)	300	600	1,250	2,000	—
RS128 (1909)	300	600	1,250	2,000	—
RS129 (1910)	300	600	1,250	2,000	—

 # 33a SALUNG = 1/4 BAHT **Weight:** 3.8200 g. **Composition:** Silver **Ruler:** Rama V Phra Maha Chulalongkorn

ate	Mintage	F	VF	XF	Unc	BU
S120 (1901)	—	5.00	12.00	35.00	275	—
S121 (1902)	560,000	3.50	9.00	27.50	170	—
S122 (1903)	340,000	3.50	9.00	27.50	170	—
S123 (1904)	190,000	3.50	9.00	27.50	170	—
S125 (1905)	—	3.50	9.00	27.50	170	—
S126 (1906)	—	3.50	9.00	27.50	170	—
S127 (1907)	270,000	3.50	9.00	27.50	170	—

Y# 34a BAHT **Composition:** Silver **Ruler:** Rama V Phra Maha Chulalongkorn

Date	Mintage	F	VF	XF	Unc	BU
RS120 (1901)	—	75.00	165	350	1,400	—
RS121 (1902)	4,070,000	7.50	25.00	80.00	300	—

Note: Because of a faulty die used the second 1 appears to be a 0 in some examples of this date

RS122 (1903)	19,150,000	6.50	22.00	65.00	275	—
RS123 (1904)	4,790,000	6.50	22.00	55.00	275	—
RS124 (1905)	6,770,000	6.50	22.00	55.00	275	—
RS125 (1906)	—	6.50	22.00	55.00	275	—
RS126 (1907)	—	15.00	35.00	100	375	—

DECIMAL COINAGE

25 Satang = 1 Salung; 100 Satang = 1 Baht

Y# 50 1/2 SATANG **Composition:** Bronze **Ruler:** Rama VIII Phra Maha Ananda Mahidol

Date	F	VF	XF	Unc	BU
BE2480 (1937)	—	0.75	1.75	3.50	—

Y# 35 SATANG **Composition:** Bronze **Note:** Variations in lettering exist.

Date	Mintage	F	VF	XF	Unc	BU
RS127 (1908)	17,000,000	—	2.50	5.00	18.00	—
RS128 (1909)	150,000	—	3.50	10.00	28.00	—
RS129 (1910)	9,000,000	—	1.50	3.50	18.00	—
RS130 (1911)	30,000,000	—	1.50	3.50	12.50	—
RS132 (1913) Rare	—	—	—	—	—	—
BE2456 (1913)	10,000,000	—	1.00	1.50	4.00	—
BE2457 (1914)	1,000,000	—	2.00	4.00	12.50	—
BE2458 (1915)	5,000,000	—	0.75	1.00	2.75	—
BE2461 (1918)	18,880,000	—	0.65	1.25	3.00	—
BE2462 (1919)	6,400,000	—	0.65	1.00	2.75	—
BE2463 (1920)	17,240,000	—	1.00	1.50	3.50	—
BE2464 (1921)	6,360,000	—	15.00	25.00	40.00	—
BE2466 (1923)	14,000,000	—	0.75	1.00	2.75	—
BE2467 (1924)	Inc. above	—	1.00	1.50	3.50	—
BE2469 (1926)	20,000,000	—	0.50	0.75	2.50	—
BE2470 (1927)	—	—	0.50	0.75	2.50	—
BE2472 (1929)	—	—	0.50	1.00	2.75	—
BE2478 (1935)	—	—	0.50	0.70	2.00	—
BE2480 (1937)	—	—	0.50	0.70	2.00	—

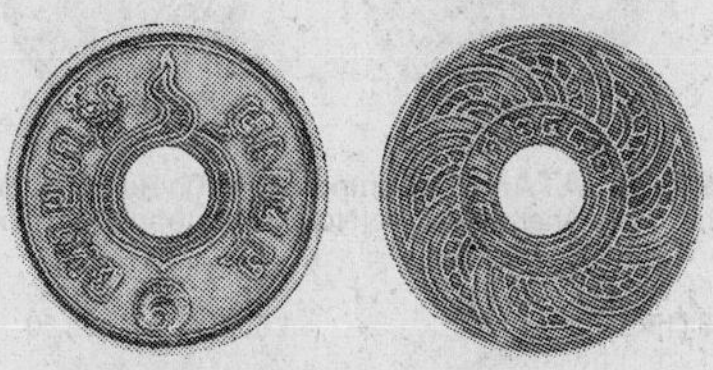

Y# 51 SATANG **Composition:** Bronze

Date	Mintage	F	VF	XF	Unc	BU
BE2482 (1939)	24,400,000	—	1.50	3.00	6.00	—

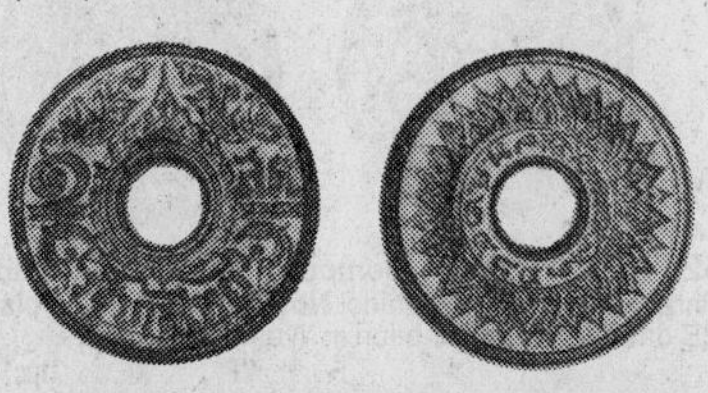

Y# 54 SATANG **Composition:** Bronze **Ruler:** Rama VIII Phra Maha Ananda Mahidol

Date	F	VF	XF	Unc	BU
BE2484 (1941)	—	0.50	1.50	3.00	—

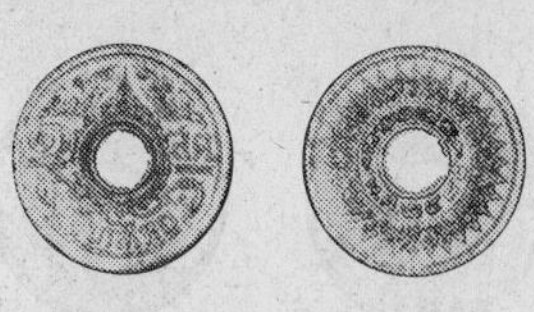

Y# 57 SATANG **Composition:** Tin **Ruler:** Rama VIII Phra Maha Ananda Mahidol **Note:** BE date and denomination in Thai numerals, without hole.

Date	Mintage	F	VF	XF	Unc	BU
BE2485 (1942)	20,700,000	—	0.30	0.50	1.00	—

Note: Approximately 790,000 coins were struck for circulation 1967-73

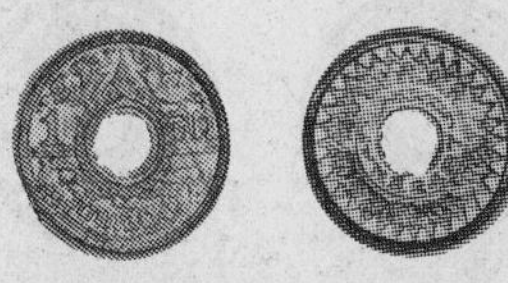

Y# 60 SATANG **Composition:** Tin **Ruler:** Rama VIII Phra Maha Ananda Mahidol **Note:** BE date and denomination in Western numerals.

Date	Mintage	F	VF	XF	Unc	BU
BE2487 (1944)	500,000	—	0.10	0.20	0.50	—

Y# 186 SATANG **Composition:** Aluminum **Ruler:** Rama IX Phra Maha Bhumithol Adulyadej

Date	Mintage	F	VF	XF	Unc	BU
BE2530 (1987)	93,000	—	—	—	0.10	—
BE2531 (1988)	200,000	—	—	—	0.10	—
BE2533 (1990)	—	—	—	—	0.10	—
BE2534 (1991)	—	—	—	—	0.10	—
BE2535 (1992)	—	—	—	—	0.10	—
BE2536 (1993)	—	—	—	—	0.10	—
BE2537 (1994)	—	—	—	—	0.10	—

Y# 342 SATANG **Composition:** Aluminum **Ruler:** Rama IX Phra Maha Bhumithol Adulyadej **Subject:** 50th Anniversary - Reign of King Rama IX **Obverse:** King Rama IX

Date	F	VF	XF	Unc	BU
BE2539 (1996)	—	—	—	0.15	—

Y# 36 5 SATANG **Composition:** Nickel

Date	Mintage	F	VF	XF	Unc	BU
RS127 (1908)	7,000,000	—	3.00	4.00	8.00	—
RS128 (1909)	4,000,000	—	3.50	4.50	10.00	—
RS129 (1910)	4,000,000	—	1.50	2.00	7.00	—
RS131 (1912)	2,000,000	—	1.50	2.50	8.00	—
RS132 (1913) Rare	—	—	—	—	—	—
BE2456 (1913)	2,000,000	—	1.50	2.50	6.00	—
BE2457 (1914)	2,000,000	—	1.50	2.50	6.00	—
BE2461 (1918)	2,000,000	—	1.50	2.50	6.00	—
BE2462 (1919)	2,000,000	—	1.00	2.00	6.00	—
BE2463 (1920)	9,900,000	—	1.00	1.50	4.50	—
BE2464 (1921)	13,000,000	—	0.60	1.25	3.00	—
BE2469 (1926)	20,000,000	—	0.60	1.25	3.00	—
BE2478 (1935)	10,000,000	—	0.60	1.25	3.00	—
BE2480 (1937)	20,000,000	—	0.60	1.25	3.00	—

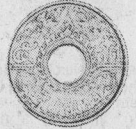

Y# 55 5 SATANG **Weight:** 1.5000 g. **Composition:** 0.6500 Silver .0313 oz. ASW **Ruler:** Rama VIII Phra Maha Ananda Mahidol

Date	F	VF	XF	Unc	BU
BE2484 (1941)	—	1.50	3.00	4.50	—

Y# 58 5 SATANG **Composition:** Tin **Ruler:** Rama VIII Phra Maha Ananda Mahidol **Note:** BE date and denomination in Thai numerals.

Date	F	VF	XF	Unc	BU
BE2485 (1942)	—	0.50	1.50	3.00	—

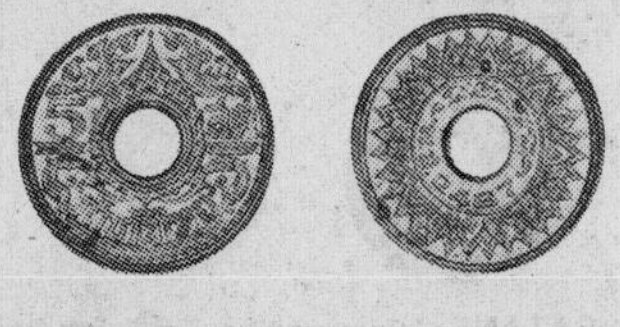

Y# 61 5 SATANG **Composition:** Tin **Ruler:** Rama VIII Phra Maha Ananda Mahidol **Note:** Thick (2.2mm) planchet. BE date and denomination in Western numerals.

Date	F	VF	XF	Unc	BU
BE2487 (1944)	—	0.50	1.25	3.00	—
BE2488 (1945)	—	0.50	1.25	3.00	—

Y# 61a 5 SATANG **Composition:** Tin **Ruler:** Rama VIII Phra Maha Ananda Mahidol **Note:** Thin (2.0mm) planchet.

Date	F	VF	XF	Unc	BU
BE2488 (1945)	—	0.50	1.25	3.00	—

Y# 61b 5 SATANG **Composition:** Tin **Ruler:** Rama VIII Phra Maha Ananda Mahidol **Note:** Medium planchet.

Date	F	VF	XF	Unc	BU
BE2488 (1945)	—	0.50	1.25	3.00	—

Y# 64 5 SATANG **Composition:** Tin **Ruler:** Rama VIII Phra Maha Ananda Mahidol **Obverse:** King Ananda, child head

Date	F	VF	XF	Unc	BU
BE2489 (1946)	—	0.50	1.00	2.00	—

Y# 68 5 SATANG **Composition:** Tin **Ruler:** Rama VIII Phra Maha Ananda Mahidol **Obverse:** King Ananda, youth head

Date	Mintage	F	VF	XF	Unc	BU
BE2489 (1946)	24,480,000	—	0.15	0.50	1.00	—

Y# 72 5 SATANG **Composition:** Tin **Ruler:** Rama IX Phra Maha Bhumithol Adulyadej **Obverse:** King Rama IX, 1 medal on uniform

Date	F	VF	XF	Unc	BU
BE2493 (1950)	—	0.50	0.75	1.25	—

Note: Coins bearing this date were also struck in 1954, 58, 59, and 73. Mintages are included here

Y# 72a 5 SATANG **Composition:** Aluminum-Bronze **Ruler:** Rama IX Phra Maha Bhumithol Adulyadej

Date	Mintage	F	VF	XF	Unc	BU
BE2493 (1950)	15,500,000	—	0.25	1.00	2.00	—

Y# 78 5 SATANG **Composition:** Aluminum-Bronze **Ruler:** Rama IX Phra Maha Bhumithol Adulyadej **Obverse:** Small head, 3 medals on uniform

Date	F	VF	XF	Unc	BU
BE2500 (1957)	—	—	0.10	0.25	—

Note: Current issues are minted without date change

Y# 78a 5 SATANG **Composition:** Bronze **Ruler:** Rama IX Phra Maha Bhumithol Adulyadej

Date	F	VF	XF	Unc	BU
BE2500 (1957)	—	0.50	1.50	2.00	—

Y# 78b 5 SATANG **Composition:** Tin **Ruler:** Rama IX Phra Maha Bhumithol Adulyadej

Date	F	VF	XF	Unc	BU
BE2500 (1957)	—	1.75	3.00	5.00	—

Note: The above coins were struck to replace Y#72 in mint sets

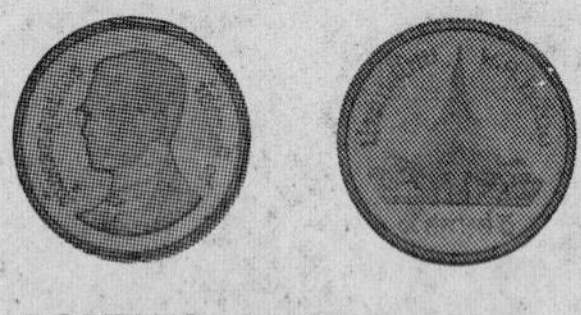

Y# 208 5 SATANG **Composition:** Aluminum **Ruler:** Rama IX Phra Maha Bhumithol Adulyadej

Date	Mintage	F	VF	XF	Unc	BU
BE2530 (1987)	—	—	—	—	20.00	—
BE2531 (1988)	704,000	—	—	—	0.10	—
BE2533 (1990)	—	—	—	—	0.10	—
BE2534 (1991)	—	—	—	—	0.10	—
BE2535 (1992)	—	—	—	—	0.10	—
BE2536 (1993)	—	—	—	—	0.10	—
BE2537 (1994)	—	—	—	—	0.10	—

Y# 343 5 SATANG **Composition:** Aluminum **Ruler:** Rama IX Phra Maha Bhumithol Adulyadej **Subject:** 50th Anniversary - Reign of King Rama IX **Obverse:** King Rama IX

Date	F	VF	XF	Unc	BU
BE2539 (1996)	—	—	—	0.25	—

Y# 37 10 SATANG **Composition:** Nickel **Note:** Variations in lettering exist.

Date	Mintage	F	VF	XF	Unc	BU
RS127 (1908)	7,000,000	—	1.50	3.00	8.50	—
RS129 (1910)	5,000,000	—	1.50	3.00	8.50	—
RS130 (1911)	500,000	—	2.00	5.00	12.00	—
RS131 (1912)	1,500,000	—	1.50	3.00	10.00	—
BE2456 (1913)	1,000,000	—	1.25	2.00	6.00	—
BE2457 (1914)	1,000,000	—	1.25	2.00	6.00	—
BE2461 (1918)	770,000	—	2.50	3.50	9.00	—
BE2462 (1919)	774,000	—	1.25	1.50	3.50	—
BE2463 (1920)	Inc. above	—	1.25	1.50	3.50	—
BE2464 (1921)	21,727,000	—	1.00	1.25	3.00	—
BE2478 (1935)	5,000,000	—	1.00	1.25	3.00	—
BE2480 (1937)	5,000,000	—	0.75	1.00	2.50	—

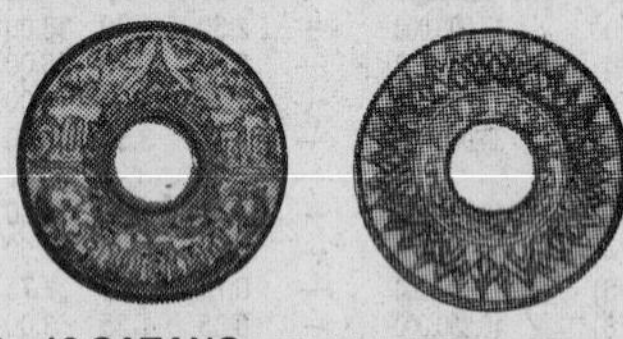

Y# 56 10 SATANG **Weight:** 2.5000 g. **Composition:** 0.6500 Silver .0522 oz. ASW **Ruler:** Rama VIII Phra Maha Ananda Mahidol

Date	F	VF	XF	Unc	BU
BE2484 (1941)	—	2.00	4.00	8.00	—

Y# 59 10 SATANG **Composition:** Tin **Ruler:** Rama VIII Phra Maha Ananda Mahidol **Note:** BE date and denomination in Thai numerals.

Date	Mintage	F	VF	XF	Unc	BU
BE2485 (1942)	230,000	—	1.00	2.00	3.50	—

Y# 62 10 SATANG **Composition:** Tin **Ruler:** Rama VIII Phra Maha Ananda Mahidol **Note:** Thick (2.5mm) planchet. BE date and denomination in Western numerals.

Date	F	VF	XF	Unc	BU
BE2487 (1944)	—	1.00	2.00	3.50	—
BE2488 (1945)	—	3.50	7.00	15.00	—

Y# 62a 10 SATANG **Composition:** Tin **Ruler:** Rama IX Phra Maha Bhumithol Adulyadej **Note:** Thin (2.0mm) planchet.

Date	F	VF	XF	Unc
BE2488 (1945)	—	1.00	2.50	4.00

Y# 65 10 SATANG **Composition:** Tin **Ruler:** Rama Phra Maha Bhumithol Adulyadej **Obverse:** King Ananda child head

Date	F	VF	XF	Unc
BE2489 (1946)	—	0.50	1.25	2.25

Y# 69 10 SATANG **Composition:** Tin **Ruler:** Rama Phra Maha Bhumithol Adulyadej **Obverse:** Youth head

Date	Mintage	F	VF	XF	Unc
BE2489 (1946)	40,470,000	—	0.50	1.25	2.00

Y# 73 10 SATANG **Composition:** Tin **Ruler:** Rama Phra Maha Bhumithol Adulyadej **Obverse:** King Bhumiph 1 medal on uniform

Date	Mintage	F	VF	XF	Unc
BE2493 (1950)	139,695,000	—	0.40	1.00	1.50

Note: These coins were also struck in 1954-1973 and t mintages are also included here

Y# 73a 10 SATANG **Composition:** Aluminum-Bronz **Ruler:** Rama IX Phra Maha Bhumithol Adulyadej

Date	Mintage	F	VF	XF	Unc
BE2493 (1950)	4,060,000	—	0.75	1.50	2.50

Y# 79 10 SATANG **Composition:** Aluminum-Bronze **Ruler:** Rama IX Phra Maha Bhumithol Adulyadej **Obvers** Smaller head. 3 medals on uniform **Rev. Legend:** THIN STY

Date	F	VF	XF	Unc
BE2500 (1957)	—	0.10	0.25	0.50

Note: Current issues are melted without date change

Y# 79a 10 SATANG **Composition:** Bronze **Ruler:** Rama IX Phra Maha Bhumithol Adulyadej **Rev. Legend:** THICK STYLE

Date	Mintage	F	VF	XF	Unc
BE2500 (1957)	13,365,000	—	0.25	0.75	1.25
BE2501 (1958)	—	—	0.25	0.75	1.25

Y# 79b 10 SATANG **Composition:** Tin **Ruler:** Rama Phra Maha Bhumithol Adulyadej

Date	F	VF	XF	Unc
BE2500 (1957)	—	7.00	15.00	45.00

Y# 79c 10 SATANG **Composition:** Bronze **Ruler:** Rama IX Phra Maha Bhumithol Adulyadej **Rev. Legend:** THIN STYLE

Date	F	VF	XF	Unc
BE2500 (1957)	—	2.50	5.00	10.00

Y# 79d 10 SATANG **Composition:** Aluminum-Bronze **Ruler:** Rama IX Phra Maha Bhumithol Adulyadej **Rev. Legend:** THICK STYLE

Date	F	VF	XF	Unc	BU
BE2500 (1957)	—	0.10	0.25	0.50	—

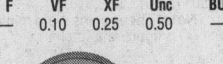

Y# 209 10 SATANG **Composition:** Aluminum **Ruler:** Rama IX Phra Maha Bhumithol Adulyadej

Date	Mintage	F	VF	XF	Unc	BU
BE2530 (1987)	—	—	—	—	20.00	—
BE2531 (1988)	900,000	—	—	—	0.10	—
BE2533 (1990)	—	—	—	—	0.10	—
BE2534 (1991)	—	—	—	—	0.10	—
BE2535 (1992)	—	—	—	—	0.10	—
BE2536 (1993)	—	—	—	—	0.10	—
BE2537 (1994)	—	—	—	—	0.10	—

Y# 344 10 SATANG **Composition:** Aluminum **Ruler:** Rama IX Phra Maha Bhumithol Adulyadej **Subject:** 50th Anniversary - Reign of King Rama IX

Date	F	VF	XF	Unc	BU
BE2539 (1996)	—	—	—	0.35	—

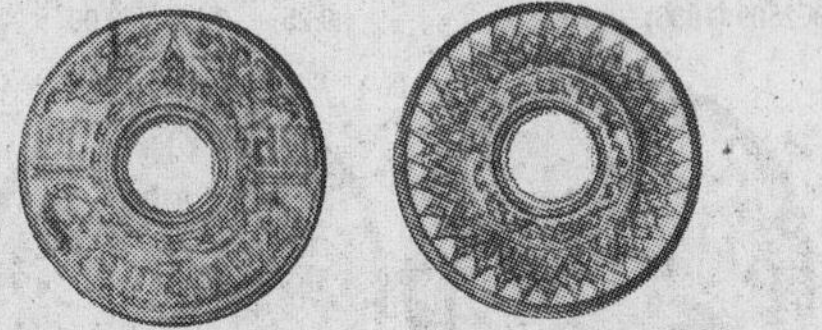

Y# A56 20 SATANG **Weight:** 3.0000 g. **Composition:** 0.6500 Silver .0627 oz. ASW **Ruler:** Rama VIII Phra Maha Ananda Mahidol **Note:** BE date and denomination in Thai numerals

ate	F	VF	XF	Unc	BU
E2485 (1942)	—	3.00	6.00	12.00	—

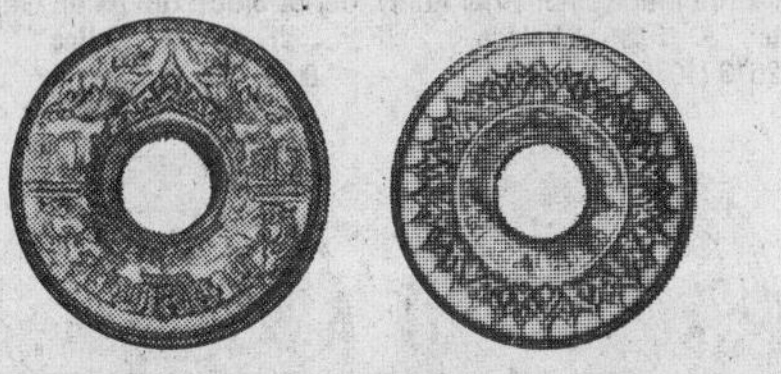

Y# 63 20 SATANG **Composition:** Tin **Ruler:** Rama VIII Phra Maha Ananda Mahidol **Note:** BE date and denomination in Western numerals.

ate	F	VF	XF	Unc	BU
:2488 (1945)	—	1.00	2.50	4.00	—

 # 43 SALUNG = 1/4 BAHT **Weight:** 3.7500 g. **Composition:** 0.8000 Silver .0965 oz. ASW **Ruler:** Rama VI Phra Maha Vajirajudh

te	Mintage	F	VF	XF	Unc	BU
2458 (1915)	2,040,000	—	5.00	10.00	20.00	—

 # 43a SALUNG = 1/4 BAHT **Weight:** 3.7500 g. **Composition:** 0.6500 Silver .0784 oz. ASW **Ruler:** Rama VI Phra Maha Vajirajudh

te	Mintage	F	VF	XF	Unc	BU
2460 (1917)	1,100,000	—	4.00	8.00	18.50	—
2461 (1918)	2,170,000	—	4.00	8.00	18.50	—
2462 (1919)	7,860,000	—	3.00	6.50	15.00	—
2467 (1924)	2,100,000	—	4.00	8.00	18.50	—
2468 (1925)	—	—	4.00	8.00	18.50	—

 # 43b SALUNG = 1/4 BAHT **Weight:** 3.7500 g. **Composition:** 0.5000 Silver .0603 oz. ASW **Ruler:** Rama VI Phra Maha Vajirajudh

te	F	VF	XF	Unc	BU
2462 (1919) Dot after gend	—	40.00	65.00	120	—

Y# 48 25 SATANG = 1/4 BAHT **Weight:** 3.7500 g. **Composition:** 0.6500 Silver .0784 oz. ASW **Ruler:** Rama VII Phra Maha Prajadhipok

Date	F	VF	XF	Unc	BU
BE2472 (1929)	—	4.50	9.00	22.50	—

Y# 66 25 SATANG = 1/4 BAHT **Composition:** Tin **Ruler:** Rama VIII Phra Maha Ananda Mahidol **Obverse:** King Ananda, child's head

Date	F	VF	XF	Unc	BU
BE2489 (1946)	—	2.50	4.50	12.50	—

Y# 70 25 SATANG = 1/4 BAHT **Composition:** Tin **Ruler:** Rama VIII Phra Maha Ananda Mahidol **Obverse:** Youth's head

Date	F	VF	XF	Unc	BU
BE2489 (1946)	—	0.20	0.40	0.75	—

Note: These coins were also struck 1954-64 and mintage figure is a total

Y# 76 25 SATANG = 1/4 BAHT **Composition:** Aluminum-Bronze **Ruler:** Rama IX Phra Maha Bhumithol Adulyadej **Obverse:** King Rama IX, 1 medal on uniform

Date	Mintage	F	VF	XF	Unc	BU
BE2493 (1950)	23,170,000	—	0.75	1.75	4.00	—

Y# 80 25 SATANG = 1/4 BAHT **Composition:** Aluminum-Bronze **Ruler:** Rama IX Phra Maha Bhumithol Adulyadej **Obverse:** Smaller head; 3 medals on uniform

Date	Mintage	F	VF	XF	Unc	BU
BE2500 (1957)	620,480,000	—	0.10	0.15	0.25	—

Note: Current issues are minted without date change and with and without reeded edges

Y# 109 25 SATANG = 1/4 BAHT **Composition:** Brass **Ruler:** Rama IX Phra Maha Bhumithol Adulyadej **Note:** Date varieties exist.

Date	Mintage	F	VF	XF	Unc	BU
BE2520 (1977)	183,356,000	—	—	0.10	0.15	—

Y# 187 25 SATANG = 1/4 BAHT **Composition:** Aluminum-Bronze **Ruler:** Rama IX Phra Maha Bhumithol Adulyadej

Date	Mintage	F	VF	XF	Unc	BU
BE2530 (1987)	5,108,000	—	—	—	0.20	—
BE2531 (1988)	42,096,000	—	—	—	0.10	—
BE2532 (1989)	—	—	—	—	0.10	—
BE2533 (1990)	—	—	—	—	0.10	—
BE2534 (1991)	—	—	—	—	0.10	—
BE2535 (1992)	—	—	—	—	0.10	—
BE2536 (1993)	—	—	—	—	0.10	—
BE2537 (1994)	—	—	—	—	0.10	—
BE2538 (1995)	—	—	—	—	0.10	—
BE2541 (1998)	—	—	—	—	0.10	—

Y# 345 25 SATANG = 1/4 BAHT **Composition:** Brass **Ruler:** Rama IX Phra Maha Bhumithol Adulyadej **Subject:** Golden Jubilee - Reign of King Rama IX

Date	F	VF	XF	Unc	BU
BE2539 (1996)	—	—	—	0.50	—

Y# 49 50 SATANG = 1/2 BAHT **Weight:** 7.5000 g. **Composition:** 0.6500 Silver .1567 oz. ASW **Ruler:** Rama VII Phra Maha Prajadhipok

Date	Mintage	F	VF	XF	Unc	BU
BE2472 (1929)	17,008,000	—	7.00	16.50	35.00	—

Y# 67 50 SATANG = 1/2 BAHT **Composition:** Tin **Ruler:** Rama VIII Phra Maha Ananda Mahidol **Obverse:** King Ananda, child's head

Date	F	VF	XF	Unc	BU
BE2489 (1946)	—	40.00	75.00	180	—

Y# 71 50 SATANG = 1/2 BAHT **Composition:** Tin **Ruler:** Rama VIII Phra Maha Ananda Mahidol **Obverse:** Youth's head

Date	Mintage	F	VF	XF	Unc	BU
BE2489 (1946)	17,008,000	—	0.75	1.50	3.00	—

Note: These coins were minted from 1954-1957 and mintage figure is a total

Y# 77 50 SATANG = 1/2 BAHT **Composition:** Aluminum-Bronze **Ruler:** Rama IX Phra Maha Bhumithol Adulyadej **Obverse:** King Rama IX, 1 medal on uniform

Date	Mintage	F	VF	XF	Unc	BU
BE2493 (1950)	20,710,000	—	0.75	1.75	5.00	—

Y# 81 50 SATANG = 1/2 BAHT Composition: Aluminum-Bronze **Ruler:** Rama IX Phra Maha Bhumithol Adulyadej **Obverse:** Smaller head; 3 medals on uniform

Date	Mintage	F	VF	XF	Unc	BU
BE2500 (1957)	439,874,000	—	0.10	0.15	0.25	—

Note: Current issues are minted without date change

Y# 168 50 SATANG = 1/2 BAHT Composition: Aluminum-Bronze **Ruler:** Rama IX Phra Maha Bhumithol Adulyadej

Date	Mintage	F	VF	XF	Unc	BU
BE2523 (1980)	122,260,000	—	0.10	0.15	0.25	—

Y# 203 50 SATANG = 1/2 BAHT Composition: Brass **Ruler:** Rama IX Phra Maha Bhumithol Adulyadej

Date	Mintage	F	VF	XF	Unc	BU
BE2530 (1987)	—	—	—	—	0.10	—
BE2531 (1988)	23,776,000	—	—	—	0.10	—
BE2532 (1989)	—	—	0.20	0.30	1.00	—
BE2533 (1990)	—	—	—	—	0.10	—
BE2534 (1991)	—	—	—	—	0.10	—
BE2535 (1992)	—	—	—	—	0.10	—
BE2536 (1993)	—	—	—	—	0.10	—
BE2537 (1994)	—	—	—	—	0.10	—
BE2538 (1995)	—	—	—	—	0.10	—
BE2539 (1996)	—	—	—	—	0.10	—
BE2545 (2000)	—	—	—	—	0.10	—

Y# 329 50 SATANG = 1/2 BAHT Composition: Aluminum-Bronze **Ruler:** Rama IX Phra Maha Bhumithol Adulyadej **Subject:** 50th Year of Reign - King Rama IX

Date	F	VF	XF	Unc	BU
BE2539 (1996)	—	—	—	0.35	—

Y# 44 2 SALUNG = 1/2 BAHT Weight: 7.5000 g. **Composition:** 0.8000 Silver .1929 oz. ASW **Ruler:** Rama VI Phra Maha Vajirajudh

Date	Mintage	F	VF	XF	Unc	BU
BE2458 (1915)	2,740,000	—	7.50	18.50	40.00	—

Y# 44b 2 SALUNG = 1/2 BAHT Weight: 7.5000 g. **Composition:** 0.5000 Silver .1206 oz. ASW **Ruler:** Rama VI Phra Maha Vajirajudh

Date	F	VF	XF	Unc	BU
BE2462 (1919) Large dot after legend	—	7.50	16.50	32.50	—
BE2462 (1919) Small dot after legend	—	7.50	16.50	32.50	—

Y# 44a 2 SALUNG = 1/2 BAHT Weight: 7.5000 g. **Composition:** 0.6500 Silver .1568 oz. ASW **Ruler:** Rama VI Phra Maha Vajirajudh **Note:** Date varieties exist.

Date	Mintage	F	VF	XF	Unc	BU
BE2462 (1919)	3,230,000	—	6.00	14.00	30.00	—
BE2463 (1920)	4,970,000	—	6.00	14.00	30.00	—
BE2464 (1921)	—	—	6.00	14.00	30.00	—

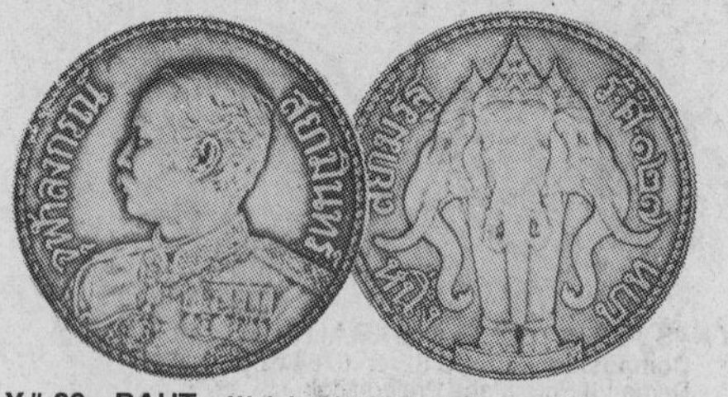

Y# 39 BAHT Weight: 15.0000 g. **Composition:** 0.9000 Silver .4340 oz. ASW **Ruler:** Rama V Phra Maha Chulalongkorn

Date	Mintage	F	VF	XF	Unc	BU
RS127 (1908)	1,037,000	—	2,500	3,750	7,000	—

Y# 45 BAHT Weight: 15.0000 g. **Composition:** 0.9000 Silver .4340 oz. ASW **Ruler:** Rama VI Phra Maha Vajirajudh

Date	Mintage	F	VF	XF	Unc	BU
BE2456 (1913)	2,690,000	—	10.00	17.50	40.00	—

Note: BE2456 is often found weakly struck so it does appear similar to a counterfeit

Date	Mintage	F	VF	XF	Unc	BU
BE2457 (1914)	490,000	—	12.50	25.00	50.00	—
BE2458 (1915)	5,000,000	—	10.00	17.50	40.00	—
BE2459 (1916)	9,080,000	—	10.00	17.50	32.00	—
BE2460 (1917)	14,340,000	—	10.00	17.50	32.00	—
BE2461 (1918)	3,840,000	—	10.00	17.50	45.00	—

Y# 82.1 BAHT Composition: Copper-Nickel-Silver-Zinc **Ruler:** Rama IX Phra Maha Bhumithol Adulyadej **Obverse:** King Rama IX, three medals on uniform **Reverse:** National arms

Date	Mintage	F	VF	XF	Unc	BU
BE2500 (1957)	3,143,000	—	0.75	1.50	6.00	—

Note: These coins were minted from 1958-60 and mintage figure is a total

Y# 82.2 BAHT Composition: Copper-Nickel **Ruler:** Rama IX Phra Maha Bhumithol Adulyadej **Obverse:** King Rama IX, one medal on uniform **Reverse:** National arms

Date	F	VF	XF	Unc	BU
BE2493 (1957)	—	0.75	1.50	6.00	—

Y# 82a BAHT Composition: Silver **Ruler:** Rama IX Phra Maha Bhumithol Adulyadej

Date	F	VF	XF	Unc	BU
BE2500 (1957)	—	—	—	30.00	—

Y# 83 BAHT Composition: Copper-Nickel **Ruler:** Rama IX Phra Maha Bhumithol Adulyadej **Subject:** King Rama IX and Queen Sirikit

Date	Mintage	F	VF	XF	Unc	BU
BE2504 (1961)	4,430,000	—	0.40	0.75	2.00	—

Y# 84 BAHT Composition: Copper-Nickel **Ruler:** Rama IX Phra Maha Bhumithol Adulyadej

Date	Mintage	F	VF	XF	Unc	BU
BE2505 (1962)	883,086,000	—	0.10	0.15	0.50	—

Note: These coins were minted from 1962-82 and mintage figure is a total

Y# 85 BAHT Composition: Copper-Nickel **Ruler:** Rama IX Phra Maha Bhumithol Adulyadej **Subject:** 36th Birthday - King Rama IX

Date	Mintage	F	VF	XF	Unc	BU
ND(1963) (1963)	3,000,000	—	0.25	0.75	2.00	—

Y# 87 BAHT Composition: Copper-Nickel **Ruler:** Rama IX Phra Maha Bhumithol Adulyadej **Subject:** 5th Asian Games

Date	Mintage	F	VF	XF	Unc	BU
BE2509 (1966)	9,000,000	—	0.25	0.75	3.00	—

Y# 91 BAHT Composition: Copper-Nickel **Ruler:** Rama IX Phra Maha Bhumithol Adulyadej **Subject:** 6th Asian Games

Date	Mintage	F	VF	XF	Unc	BU
BE2513 (1970)	9,000,000	—	0.25	0.75	1.50	—

Y# 96 BAHT Composition: Copper-Nickel **Ruler:** Rama IX Phra Maha Bhumithol Adulyadej **Series:** F.A.O.

Date	Mintage	F	VF	XF	Unc	BU
BE2515 (1972)	9,000,000	—	0.10	0.25	0.75	—

Y# 97 BAHT Composition: Copper-Nickel **Ruler:** Rama IX Phra Maha Bhumithol Adulyadej **Subject:** Prince Vajiralongkorn Investiture

Date	Mintage	F	VF	XF	Unc	BU
BE2515 (1972)	9,000,000	—	0.15	0.40	1.00	—

Y# 99 BAHT Composition: Copper-Nickel **Ruler:** Rama IX Phra Maha Bhumithol Adulyadej **Subject:** 25th Anniversary - World Health Organization

Date	Mintage	F	VF	XF	Unc	BU
BE2516 (1973)	1,000,000	—	0.25	0.65	1.25	—

Y# 100 BAHT Composition: Copper-Nickel **Ruler:** Rama IX Phra Maha Bhumithol Adulyadej

Date	Mintage	F	VF	XF	Unc	BU
BE2517 (1974)	248,978,000	—	0.15	0.40	1.00	—

 # 105 BAHT Composition: Copper-Nickel **Ruler:** Rama IX Phra Maha Bhumithol Adulyadej **Subject:** 8th SEAP Games

ate	Mintage	F	VF	XF	Unc	BU
E2518 (1975)	3,000,000	—	0.25	0.65	1.25	—

 # 107 BAHT Composition: Copper-Nickel **Ruler:** Rama IX Phra Maha Bhumithol Adulyadej **Subject:** 75th Birthday of Princess Mother

ate	Mintage	F	VF	XF	Unc	BU
E2518 (1975)	9,000,000	—	0.15	0.40	1.00	—

 # 110 BAHT Composition: Copper-Nickel **Ruler:** Rama IX Phra Maha Bhumithol Adulyadej

te	Mintage	F	VF	XF	Unc	BU
2520 (1977)	506,460,000	—	0.10	0.20	0.50	—

 # 112 BAHT Composition: Copper-Nickel **Ruler:** Rama IX Phra Maha Bhumithol Adulyadej **Series:** F.A.O.

e	Mintage	F	VF	XF	Unc	BU
2520 (1977)	2,000,000	—	0.15	0.40	1.00	—

Y# 114 BAHT Composition: Copper-Nickel **Ruler:** Rama IX Phra Maha Bhumithol Adulyadej **Subject:** Graduation of Princess Sirindhorn

Date	Mintage	F	VF	XF	Unc	BU
BE2520 (1977)	8,998,000	—	0.15	0.40	1.00	—

Y# 114a BAHT Composition: Bronze **Ruler:** Rama IX Phra Maha Bhumithol Adulyadej

Date	F	VF	XF	Unc	BU
BE2520 (1977)	—	—	—	—	—

Y# 124 BAHT Composition: Copper-Nickel **Ruler:** Rama IX Phra Maha Bhumithol Adulyadej **Subject:** Investiture of Princess Sirindhorn

Date	Mintage	F	VF	XF	Unc	BU
BE2520 (1977)	5,000,000	—	0.15	0.40	1.00	—

Y# 127 BAHT Composition: Copper-Nickel **Ruler:** Rama IX Phra Maha Bhumithol Adulyadej **Subject:** Graduation of Crown Prince Vijiralongkorn

Date	Mintage	F	VF	XF	Unc	BU
BE2521 (1978)	5,000,000	—	0.10	0.20	0.50	—

Y# 130 BAHT Composition: Copper-Nickel **Ruler:** Rama IX Phra Maha Bhumithol Adulyadej **Subject:** 8th Asian Games

Date	Mintage	F	VF	XF	Unc	BU
BE2521 (1978)	5,000,000	—	0.10	0.20	0.50	—

Y# 157 BAHT Composition: Copper-Nickel **Ruler:** Rama IX Phra Maha Bhumithol Adulyadej **Series:** World Food Day

Date	Mintage	F	VF	XF	Unc	BU
BE2525 (1982)	1,500,000	—	0.10	0.20	0.50	—

Y# 159.2 BAHT Composition: Copper-Nickel **Ruler:** Rama IX Phra Maha Bhumithol Adulyadej **Obverse:** Small portrait with space between collar and lower hairline

Date	F	VF	XF	Unc	BU
BE2525 (1982)	—	2.50	5.00	10.00	—

Y# 159.1 BAHT Composition: Copper-Nickel **Ruler:** Rama IX Phra Maha Bhumithol Adulyadej **Obverse:** Large portrait with collar touching hairline **Note:** 2527 and 2528 are frozen dates, with the Thai numerals for 27 and 28 in the Finance Ministry decal at the bottom of the reverse.

Date	Mintage	F	VF	XF	Unc	BU
BE2525 (1982)	123,585,000	—	0.10	0.20	0.50	—
BE2525 (1984)	—	—	0.10	0.20	0.50	—
BE2525 (1985)	—	—	0.10	0.20	0.50	—

Y# 183 BAHT Composition: Copper-Nickel **Ruler:** Rama IX Phra Maha Bhumithol Adulyadej **Note:** Circulation coinage. Varieties exist.

Date	Mintage	F	VF	XF	Unc	BU
BE2529 (1986)	—	—	0.20	0.30	1.00	—
BE2530 (1987)	325,271,000	—	—	—	0.10	—
BE2531 (1988)	391,442,000	—	—	—	0.10	—
BE2532 (1989)	—	—	—	—	0.10	—
BE2533 (1990)	—	—	—	—	0.10	—
BE2534 (1991)	—	—	—	—	0.10	—
BE2535 (1992)	—	—	—	—	0.10	—
BE2536 (1993)	—	—	—	—	0.10	—
BE2537 (1994)	—	—	—	—	0.10	—
BE2538 (1995)	—	—	—	—	0.10	—
BE2539 (1996)	—	—	—	—	0.10	—
BE2540 (1997)	—	—	—	—	0.10	—
BE2541 (1998)	—	—	—	—	0.10	—
BE2542 (1999)	—	—	—	—	0.10	—
BE2543 (2000)	—	—	—	—	0.10	—

Y# 330 BAHT Composition: Copper-Nickel **Ruler:** Rama IX Phra Maha Bhumithol Adulyadej **Subject:** 50th Anniversary - Reign of King Rama IX

Date	F	VF	XF	Unc	BU
BE2539 (1996)	—	—	—	0.35	—

Y# 134 2 BAHT Composition: Copper-Nickel **Ruler:** Rama IX Phra Maha Bhumithol Adulyadej **Subject:** Graduation of Princess Chulabhorn **Obverse:** Bust of Princess half left

Date	Mintage	F	VF	XF	Unc	BU
BE2522 (1979)	5,000,000	—	0.20	0.40	1.00	—

Y# 176 2 BAHT Composition: Copper-Nickel Clad Copper **Ruler:** Rama IX Phra Maha Bhumithol Adulyadej **Subject:** International Youth Year

Date	Mintage	F	VF	XF	Unc	BU
BE2528 (1985)	10,000,000	—	0.20	0.40	1.00	—

Y# 177 2 BAHT Composition: Copper-Nickel Clad Copper **Ruler:** Rama IX Phra Maha Bhumithol Adulyadej **Subject:** XII SEA Games

Date	Mintage	F	VF	XF	Unc	BU
BE2528 (1985)	5,000,000	—	0.20	0.40	1.00	—

Y# 178 2 BAHT Composition: Copper-Nickel Clad Copper **Ruler:** Rama IX Phra Maha Bhumithol Adulyadej **Subject:** National YEars of the Trees

Date	Mintage	F	VF	XF	Unc	BU
ND(1986) (1986)	3,000,000	—	0.50	1.00	3.50	—

Y# 180 2 BAHT Composition: Copper-Nickel Clad Copper **Ruler:** Rama IX Phra Maha Bhumithol Adulyadej **Subject:** Year of Peace

Date	Mintage	F	VF	XF	Unc	BU
BE2529 (1986)	5,000,000	—	—	—	0.50	—

Y# 191 2 BAHT Composition: Copper-Nickel Clad Copper **Ruler:** Rama IX Phra Maha Bhumithol Adulyadej **Subject:** Princess Chulabhorn Awarded Einstein Medal **Obverse:** Bust of princess in cap and gown half left

Date	Mintage	F	VF	XF	Unc	BU
BE2529 (1986)	3,000,000	—	—	—	0.50	—

Y# 194 2 BAHT Composition: Copper-Nickel Clad Copper **Ruler:** Rama IX Phra Maha Bhumithol Adulyadej **Subject:** 60th Birthday - King Rama IX

Date	Mintage	F	VF	XF	Unc	BU
BE2530 (1987)	10,000	—	—	—	0.50	—

Y# 188 2 BAHT Composition: Copper-Nickel Clad Copper **Ruler:** Rama IX Phra Maha Bhumithol Adulyadej **Subject:** Chulachomklao Royal Military Academy

Date	Mintage	F	VF	XF	Unc	BU
BE2530 (1987)	3,000,000	—	—	—	0.50	—

Y# 204 2 BAHT Composition: Copper-Nickel Clad Copper **Ruler:** Rama IX Phra Maha Bhumithol Adulyadej **Subject:** 72nd Anniversary of Thai Cooperatives

Date	Mintage	F	VF	XF	Unc	BU
BE2531 (1988)	3,000,000	—	—	—	0.50	—

Y# 210 2 BAHT Composition: Copper-Nickel Clad Copper **Ruler:** Rama IX Phra Maha Bhumithol Adulyadej **Subject:** 42nd Anniversary - Reign of King Rama IX

Date	Mintage	F	VF	XF	Unc	BU
BE2531 (1988)	5,000,000	—	—	—	0.50	—

Y# 220 2 BAHT Composition: Copper-Nickel Clad Copper **Ruler:** Rama IX Phra Maha Bhumithol Adulyadej **Subject:** 100th Anniversary of Siriraj Hospital

Date	Mintage	F	VF	XF	Unc	BU
BE2531 (1988)	3,412,000	—	—	—	0.50	—

Y# 222 2 BAHT Composition: Copper-Nickel Clad Copper **Ruler:** Rama IX Phra Maha Bhumithol Adulyadej **Subject:** Crown Prince's Birthday

Date	Mintage	F	VF	XF	Unc	BU
BE2531 (1988)	2,000,000	—	—	—	0.50	—

Y# 225 2 BAHT Composition: Copper-Nickel Clad Copper **Ruler:** Rama IX Phra Maha Bhumithol Adulyadej **Subject:** 72nd Anniversary of Chulalongkorn University

Date	Mintage	F	VF	XF	Unc	BU
BE2532 (1989)	3,000,000	—	—	—	0.50	—

Y# 230 2 BAHT Composition: Copper-Nickel Clad Copper **Ruler:** Rama IX Phra Maha Bhumithol Adulyadej **Subject:** Centennial of First Medical College

Date	Mintage	F	VF	XF	Unc	BU
BE2533 (1990)	1,000,000	—	—	—	0.50	—

Y# 232 2 BAHT Composition: Copper-Nickel Clad Copper **Ruler:** Rama IX Phra Maha Bhumithol Adulyadej **Subject:** 90th Birthday of Queen Mother

Date	Mintage	F	VF	XF	Unc	BU
BE2533 (1990)	2,000,000	—	—	—	0.50	—

Y# 235 2 BAHT Composition: Copper-Nickel Clad Copper **Ruler:** Rama IX Phra Maha Bhumithol Adulyadej **Subject:** 100th Anniversary - Office of the Comptroller General

Date	Mintage	F	VF	XF	Unc	BU
BE2533 (1990)	1,000,000	—	—	—	0.50	—

Y# 243 2 BAHT Composition: Copper-Nickel Clad Copper **Ruler:** Rama IX Phra Maha Bhumithol Adulyadej **Subject:** World Health Organization

Date	Mintage	F	VF	XF	Unc	BU
BE2533 (1990)	2,000,000	—	—	—	1.00	—

Y# 237 2 BAHT Composition: Copper-Nickel Clad Copper **Ruler:** Rama IX Phra Maha Bhumithol Adulyadej **Subject:** 36th Birthday of Princess Sirindhorn

Date	Mintage	F	VF	XF	Unc	BU
BE2534 (1991)	2,300,000	—	—	—	0.50	—

Y# 240 2 BAHT Composition: Copper-Nickel Clad Copper **Ruler:** Rama IX Phra Maha Bhumithol Adulyadej **Subject:** 80th Anniversary of Thai Boy Scouts

Date	Mintage	F	VF	XF	Unc	BU
BE2534 (1991)	2,000,000	—	—	—	1.50	—

Y# 255 2 BAHT Composition: Copper-Nickel Clad Copper **Ruler:** Rama IX Phra Maha Bhumithol Adulyadej **Subject:** Princess Sirindhorn's Magsaysay Foundation Award

Date	Mintage	F	VF	XF	Unc	BU
BE2534 (1991)	12,000,000	—	—	—	0.50	—

Y# 248 2 BAHT Composition: Copper-Nickel Clad Copper **Ruler:** Rama IX Phra Maha Bhumithol Adulyadej **Subject:** Centenary Celebration - Father of King Rama IX

Date	Mintage	F	VF	XF	Unc	BU
BE2535 (1992)	2,308,000	—	—	—	0.50	—

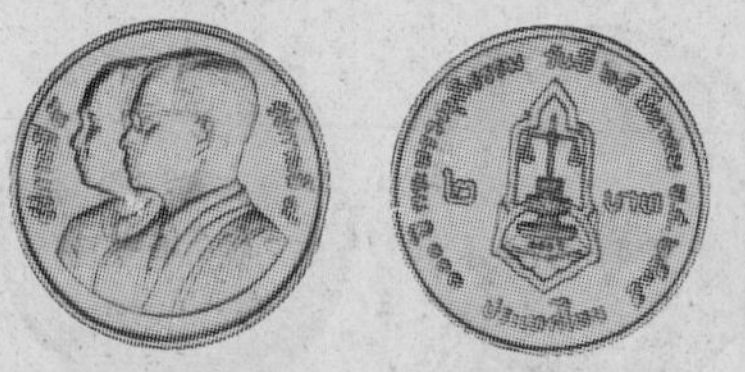

Y# 251 2 BAHT Composition: Copper-Nickel Clad Copper **Ruler:** Rama IX Phra Maha Bhumithol Adulyadej **Subject:** Ministry of Justice Centennial

Date	Mintage	F	VF	XF	Unc	BU
BE2535 (1992)	1,500,000	—	—	—	0.50	—

253 2 BAHT Composition: Copper-Nickel Clad Copper **Ruler:** Rama IX Phra Maha Bhumithol Adulyadej
Subject: Ministry of Interior Centennial

Date	Mintage	F	VF	XF	Unc	BU
(1992)	1,500,000	—	—	—	0.50	—

259 2 BAHT Composition: Copper-Nickel Clad Copper **Ruler:** Rama IX Phra Maha Bhumithol Adulyadej
Subject: Queen's 60th Birthday

Date	Mintage	F	VF	XF	Unc	BU
535 (1992)	1,700,000	—	—	—	0.50	—

268 2 BAHT Composition: Copper-Nickel Clad Copper **Ruler:** Rama IX Phra Maha Bhumithol Adulyadej
Subject: 60th Anniversary of the National Assembly - Anatasamakhom Throne Hall

e	Mintage	F	VF	XF	Unc	BU
535 (1992)	1,000,000	—	—	—	0.50	—

270 2 BAHT Composition: Copper-Nickel Clad Copper **Ruler:** Rama IX Phra Maha Bhumithol Adulyadej
Subject: Ministry of Agriculture

e	Mintage	F	VF	XF	Unc	BU
535 (1992)	1,000,000	—	—	—	0.50	—

272 2 BAHT Composition: Copper-Nickel Clad Copper **Ruler:** Rama IX Phra Maha Bhumithol Adulyadej
Subject: King's 64th Birthday

e	Mintage	F	VF	XF	Unc	BU
2535 (1992)	1,000,000	—	—	—	0.50	—

 # 276 2 BAHT Composition: Copper-Nickel Clad Copper **Ruler:** Rama IX Phra Maha Bhumithol Adulyadej
Subject: Centennial of Thai Teacher Training - Emblem

te	Mintage	F	VF	XF	Unc	BU
2535 (1992)	1,200,000	—	—	—	0.50	—

Y# 277 2 BAHT Composition: Copper-Nickel Clad Copper **Ruler:** Rama IX Phra Maha Bhumithol Adulyadej
Subject: Centennial of Thai National Bank - Seated Figure

Date	Mintage	F	VF	XF	Unc	BU
BE2535 (1992)	1,000,000	—	—	—	0.50	—

Y# 278 2 BAHT Composition: Copper-Nickel Clad Copper **Ruler:** Rama IX Phra Maha Bhumithol Adulyadej
Subject: Centennial of Attorney General's Office - Scale

Date	Mintage	F	VF	XF	Unc	BU
BE2536 (1993)	1,000,000	—	—	—	0.50	—

Y# 279 2 BAHT Composition: Copper-Nickel Clad Copper **Ruler:** Rama IX Phra Maha Bhumithol Adulyadej
Subject: Centennial of Thai Red Cross **Reverse:** Symbols

Date	Mintage	F	VF	XF	Unc	BU
BE2536 (1993)	1,200,000	—	—	—	0.50	—

Y# 282 2 BAHT Composition: Copper-Nickel Clad Copper **Ruler:** Rama IX Phra Maha Bhumithol Adulyadej
Subject: Treasury Department

Date	Mintage	F	VF	XF	Unc	BU
BE2536 (1993)	1,200,000	—	—	—	0.50	—

Y# 288 2 BAHT Composition: Copper-Nickel Clad Copper **Ruler:** Rama IX Phra Maha Bhumithol Adulyadej
Subject: 100th Anniversary of Rama VII

Date	Mintage	F	VF	XF	Unc	BU
BE2536 (1993)	1,500,000	—	—	—	0.50	—

Y# 292 2 BAHT Composition: Copper-Nickel Clad Copper **Ruler:** Rama IX Phra Maha Bhumithol Adulyadej
Subject: 60th Anniversary - Royal Institute

Date	Mintage	F	VF	XF	Unc	BU
BE2537 (1994)	1,200,000	—	—	—	0.50	—

Y# 294 2 BAHT Composition: Copper-Nickel Clad Copper **Ruler:** Rama IX Phra Maha Bhumithol Adulyadej
Subject: 120th Anniversary - Juridical Council

Date	Mintage	F	VF	XF	Unc	BU
BE2537 (1994)	1,200,000	—	—	—	0.50	—

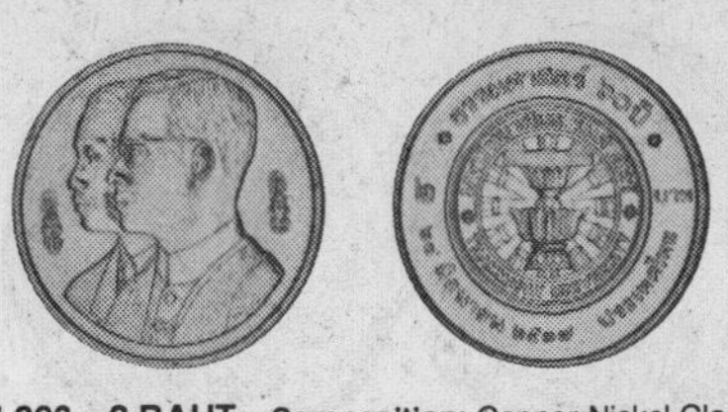

Y# 296 2 BAHT Composition: Copper-Nickel Clad Copper **Ruler:** Rama IX Phra Maha Bhumithol Adulyadej
Subject: 60th Anniversary - Thammasat University

Date	Mintage	F	VF	XF	Unc	BU
BE2537 (1994)	1,250,000	—	—	—	0.50	—

Y# 307 2 BAHT Composition: Copper-Nickel Clad Copper **Ruler:** Rama IX Phra Maha Bhumithol Adulyadej
Series: F.A.O.

Date	F	VF	XF	Unc	BU
BE2538 (1995)	—	—	—	0.65	—

Y# 313 2 BAHT Composition: Copper-Nickel Clad Copper **Ruler:** Rama IX Phra Maha Bhumithol Adulyadej
Subject: Information Technology Year

Date	F	VF	XF	Unc	BU
BE2538 (1995)	—	—	—	0.50	—

Y# 315 2 BAHT Composition: Copper-Nickel Clad Copper **Ruler:** Rama IX Phra Maha Bhumithol Adulyadej
Subject: Asian Environment Year

Date	F	VF	XF	Unc	BU
BE2538 (1995)	—	—	—	0.50	—

Y# 317 2 BAHT Composition: Copper-Nickel Clad Copper **Ruler:** Rama IX Phra Maha Bhumithol Adulyadej
Subject: Siriraj Nursing and Midwifery School Centennial

Date	F	VF	XF	Unc	BU
BE2539 (1996)	—	—	—	0.65	—

Y# 319 2 BAHT Composition: Copper-Nickel Clad Copper **Ruler:** Rama IX Phra Maha Bhumithol Adulyadej
Subject: King's 50th Year of Reign

Date	F	VF	XF	Unc	BU
BE2539 (1996)	—	—	—	1.25	—

Y# 98 5 BAHT Composition: Copper-Nickel **Ruler:** Rama IX Phra Maha Bhumithol Adulyadej **Shape:** 9-sided

Date	Mintage	F	VF	XF	Unc	BU
BE2515 (1972)	30,016,000	—	0.30	0.60	1.20	—

Y# 111 5 BAHT Composition: Copper-Nickel Clad Copper **Ruler:** Rama IX Phra Maha Bhumithol Adulyadej

Date	Mintage	F	VF	XF	Unc	BU
BE2520 (1977)	27,257,000	—	0.30	0.60	1.20	—
BE2522 (1979)	72,740,000	—	0.30	0.60	1.20	—

Y# 120 5 BAHT Composition: Copper-Nickel Clad Copper **Ruler:** Rama IX Phra Maha Bhumithol Adulyadej **Subject:** 50th Birthday - King Rama IX **Obv. Legend:** PRATHET THAI

Date	Mintage	F	VF	XF	Unc	BU
BE2520 (1977)	500,000	—	0.35	0.75	1.50	—

Y# 121 5 BAHT Composition: Copper-Nickel Clad Copper **Ruler:** Rama IX Phra Maha Bhumithol Adulyadej **Obverse:** Error **Obv. Legend:** "SIAM MINTA"

Date	F	VF	XF	Unc	BU
BE2520 (1977)	—	7.00	15.00	30.00	—

Y# 131 5 BAHT Composition: Copper-Nickel Clad Copper **Ruler:** Rama IX Phra Maha Bhumithol Adulyadej **Subject:** 8th Asian Games

Date	Mintage	F	VF	XF	Unc	BU
BE2521 (1978)	500,000	—	1.50	3.50	6.50	—

Y# 132 5 BAHT Composition: Copper-Nickel Clad Copper **Ruler:** Rama IX Phra Maha Bhumithol Adulyadej **Subject:** Royal Cradle Ceremony

Date	Mintage	F	VF	XF	Unc	BU
BE2522 (1979)	1,000,000	—	0.50	1.00	2.00	—

Y# 137 5 BAHT Composition: Copper-Nickel Clad Copper **Ruler:** Rama IX Phra Maha Bhumithol Adulyadej **Subject:** Queen's Anniversary and F.A.O. Ceres Medal

Date	Mintage	F	VF	XF	Unc	BU
BE2523 (1980)	9,000,000	—	0.25	0.50	1.50	—

Y# 140 5 BAHT Composition: Copper-Nickel Clad Copper **Ruler:** Rama IX Phra Maha Bhumithol Adulyadej **Subject:** 80th Birthday of King's Mother

Date	Mintage	F	VF	XF	Unc	BU
BE2523 (1980)	3,504,000	—	0.25	0.50	1.50	—

Y# 144 5 BAHT Composition: Copper-Nickel Clad Copper **Ruler:** Rama IX Phra Maha Bhumithol Adulyadej **Subject:** Rama VII Constitutional Monarchy

Date	Mintage	F	VF	XF	Unc	BU
BE2523 (1980)	2,113,000	—	0.25	0.50	1.50	—

Y# 142 5 BAHT Composition: Copper-Nickel Clad Copper **Ruler:** Rama IX Phra Maha Bhumithol Adulyadej **Subject:** Centennial - Birth of King Rama VI

Date	Mintage	F	VF	XF	Unc	BU
BE2524 (1981)	2,222,000	—	0.25	0.50	1.50	—

Y# 149 5 BAHT Composition: Copper-Nickel Clad Copper **Ruler:** Rama IX Phra Maha Bhumithol Adulyadej **Subject:** Bicentennial of Bangkok

Date	Mintage	F	VF	XF	Unc
BE2525 (1982)	5,000,000	—	0.25	0.50	1.50

Y# 158 5 BAHT Composition: Copper-Nickel Clad Copper **Ruler:** Rama IX Phra Maha Bhumithol Adulyadej **Series:** World Food Day

Date	Mintage	F	VF	XF	Unc
BE2525 (1982)	400,000	—	0.35	0.75	1.50

Y# 161 5 BAHT Composition: Copper-Nickel Clad Copper **Ruler:** Rama IX Phra Maha Bhumithol Adulyadej **Subject:** 75th Anniversary of Boy Scouts

Date	Mintage	F	VF	XF	Unc	B
BE2525 (1982)	206,000	—	1.50	3.50	6.50	-

Y# 160 5 BAHT Composition: Copper-Nickel Clad Copper **Ruler:** Rama IX Phra Maha Bhumithol Adulyadej **Note:** 2525 is a frozen date, with the Thai numerals for the first 2 digits of the actual year (25, 28, 29) in the Finance Minstry decal at the bottom of the reverse.

Date	Mintage	F	VF	XF	Unc	B
BE2525 (25) (1982)	200,000	—	0.50	1.00	2.00	-
BE2526 (1983)	—	—	0.60	1.25	2.25	-
BE2527 (1984)	—	—	0.60	1.25	2.25	-
BE2525 (1985)	—	—	5.00	10.00	25.00	-
BE2528 (1985)	—	—	1.00	2.00	5.00	-
BE2525 (1986)	—	—	0.20	0.50	1.00	-
BE2529 (1986)	—	—	0.20	0.50	1.00	-

Y# 171 5 BAHT Composition: Copper-Nickel Clad Copper **Ruler:** Rama IX Phra Maha Bhumithol Adulyadej **Subject:** 84th Birthday of Princess Mother

Date	Mintage	F	VF	XF	Unc
BE2527 (1984)	600,000	—	1.00	2.00	4.50

Y# 184 5 BAHT **Composition:** Copper-Nickel Clad Copper **Ruler:** Rama IX Phra Maha Bhumithol Adulyadej **Subject:** 200th Anniversary - Birth of Rama III

Date	Mintage	F	VF	XF	Unc	BU
BE2530 (1987)	2,000,000	—	—	—	0.75	—

Y# 195 5 BAHT **Composition:** Copper-Nickel Clad Copper **Ruler:** Rama IX Phra Maha Bhumithol Adulyadej **Subject:** 60th Birthday - King Rama IX

Date	Mintage	F	VF	XF	Unc	BU
BE2530 (1987)	1,500,000	—	—	—	2.00	—

Y# 185 5 BAHT **Composition:** Copper-Nickel Clad Copper **Ruler:** Rama IX Phra Maha Bhumithol Adulyadej **Note:** Circulation coinage.

Date	Mintage	F	VF	XF	Unc	BU
BE2530 (1987)	14,000,000	—	—	—	0.75	—
BE2531 (1988)	—	—	—	—	0.75	—

Y# 219 5 BAHT **Composition:** Copper-Nickel Clad Copper **Ruler:** Rama IX Phra Maha Bhumithol Adulyadej **Note:** Circulation coinage.

Date	F	VF	XF	Unc	BU
BE2531 (1988)	—	—	—	0.50	—
BE2532 (1989)	—	—	—	0.50	—
BE2533 (1990)	—	—	—	0.50	—
BE2534 (1991)	—	—	—	0.50	—
BE2535 (1992)	—	—	—	0.50	—
BE2536 (1993)	—	—	—	0.50	—
BE2537 (1994)	—	—	—	0.50	—
BE2538 (1995)	—	—	—	0.50	—
BE2539 (1996)	—	—	—	0.50	—
BE2540 (1997)	—	—	—	0.50	—
BE2541 (1998)	—	—	—	0.50	—
BE2542 (1999)	—	—	—	0.50	—
BE2543 (2000)	—	—	—	0.50	—

Y# 211 5 BAHT **Composition:** Copper-Nickel Clad Copper **Ruler:** Rama IX Phra Maha Bhumithol Adulyadej **Subject:** 42nd Anniversary - Reign of King Rama IX

Date	Mintage	F	VF	XF	Unc	BU
BE2531 (1988)	1,500,000	—	—	—	2.00	—

Y# 260 5 BAHT **Composition:** Copper-Nickel Clad Copper **Ruler:** Rama IX Phra Maha Bhumithol Adulyadej **Subject:** Queen's 60th Birthday

Date	Mintage	F	VF	XF	Unc	BU
BE2535 (1992)	1,000,000	—	—	—	1.25	—

Y# 306 5 BAHT **Composition:** Copper-Nickel Clad Copper **Ruler:** Rama IX Phra Maha Bhumithol Adulyadej **Subject:** 18th SEA Games

Date	F	VF	XF	Unc	BU
BE2538 (1995)	—	—	—	1.25	—

Y# 320 5 BAHT **Composition:** Copper-Nickel Clad Copper **Ruler:** Rama IX Phra Maha Bhumithol Adulyadej **Subject:** King's 50th Year of Reign

Date	F	VF	XF	Unc	BU
BE2539 (1996)	—	—	—	1.50	—

Y# 92 10 BAHT **Weight:** 5.0000 g. **Composition:** 0.8000 Silver .1286 oz. ASW **Ruler:** Rama IX Phra Maha Bhumithol Adulyadej **Subject:** 25th Anniversary - Reign of King Rama IX

Date	Mintage	F	VF	XF	Unc	BU
BE2514 (1971)	2,000,000	—	BV	2.00	4.50	—

Y# 115 10 BAHT **Composition:** Nickel **Ruler:** Rama IX Phra Maha Bhumithol Adulyadej **Subject:** Graduation of Princess Sirindhorn

Date	Mintage	F	VF	XF	Unc	BU
BE2520 (1977)	2,097,000	—	0.50	1.00	2.50	—

Y# 115a 10 BAHT **Composition:** Bronze **Ruler:** Rama IX Phra Maha Bhumithol Adulyadej

Date	F	VF	XF	Unc	BU
BE2520 (1977)	—	—	—	20.00	—

Y# 117 10 BAHT **Composition:** Nickel **Ruler:** Rama IX Phra Maha Bhumithol Adulyadej **Subject:** Crown Prince Vajiralongkorn and Princess Soamsawali Wedding

Date	Mintage	F	VF	XF	Unc	BU
BE2520 (1977)	1,890,000	—	0.50	1.00	2.50	—

Y# 135 10 BAHT **Composition:** Nickel **Ruler:** Rama IX Phra Maha Bhumithol Adulyadej **Subject:** Graduation of Princess Chulabhorn

Date	Mintage	F	VF	XF	Unc	BU
BE2522 (1979)	1,196,000	—	0.50	1.00	2.50	—

Y# 141 10 BAHT **Composition:** Nickel **Ruler:** Rama IX Phra Maha Bhumithol Adulyadej **Subject:** 80th Birthday of King's Mother

Date	Mintage	F	VF	XF	Unc	BU
BE2523 (1980)	1,288,000	—	0.50	1.00	2.50	—

Y# 145 10 BAHT **Composition:** Nickel **Ruler:** Rama IX Phra Maha Bhumithol Adulyadej **Subject:** 30th Anniversary of Buddhist Fellowship

Date	Mintage	F	VF	XF	Unc	BU
BE2523 (1980)	1,035,000	—	0.50	1.00	2.50	—

Y# 146 10 BAHT **Composition:** Nickel **Ruler:** Rama IX Phra Maha Bhumithol Adulyadej **Subject:** King Rama IX Anniversary of Reign

Date	Mintage	F	VF	XF	Unc	BU
BE2524 (1981)	2,039,000	—	0.50	1.00	2.50	—

Y# 154 10 BAHT **Composition:** Nickel **Ruler:** Rama IX Phra Maha Bhumithol Adulyadej **Subject:** 50th Birthday of Queen Sirikit

Date	Mintage	F	VF	XF	Unc	BU
BE2525 (1982)	500,000	—	0.75	1.50	3.50	—
BE2525 (1982) Proof	9,999	Value: 22.50				

Y# 162 10 BAHT **Composition:** Nickel **Ruler:** Rama IX Phra Maha Bhumithol Adulyadej **Subject:** 75th Anniversary of Boy Scouts **Note:** Similar to 5 Baht, Y#161.

Date	Mintage	F	VF	XF	Unc	BU
BE2525 (1982)	100,000	—	1.25	2.50	5.00	—
BE2525 (1982) Proof	1,500	Value: 45.00				

Y# 163 10 BAHT **Composition:** Nickel **Ruler:** Rama IX Phra Maha Bhumithol Adulyadej **Subject:** 100th Anniversary of Postal Service

Date	Mintage	F	VF	XF	Unc	BU
BE2526 (1983)	300,000	—	0.75	1.50	3.50	—
BE2526 (1983) Proof	5,000	Value: 25.00				

Y# 165 10 BAHT **Composition:** Nickel **Ruler:** Rama IX Phra Maha Bhumithol Adulyadej **Subject:** 700th Anniversary of Thai Alphabet **Reverse:** Six-line inscription

Date	Mintage	F	VF	XF	Unc	BU
BE2526 (1983)	500,000	—	0.75	1.50	3.50	—
BE2526 (1983) Proof	5,167	Value: 22.50				

Y# 172 10 BAHT **Composition:** Nickel **Ruler:** Rama IX Phra Maha Bhumithol Adulyadej **Subject:** 84th Birthday of Princess Mother **Note:** Similar to 5 Baht, Y#171.

Date	Mintage	F	VF	XF	Unc	BU
BE2527 (1984)	200,000	—	1.25	2.50	5.50	—
BE2527 (1984) Proof	3,492	Value: 37.50				

Y# 175 10 BAHT **Composition:** Nickel **Ruler:** Rama IX Phra Maha Bhumithol Adulyadej **Subject:** 72nd Anniversary of Government Savings Bank

Date	Mintage	F	VF	XF	Unc	BU
BE2528 (1985)	500,000	—	0.50	1.00	2.50	—
BE2528 (1985) Proof	3,000	Value: 37.50				

Y# 179 10 BAHT **Composition:** Nickel **Ruler:** Rama IX Phra Maha Bhumithol Adulyadej **Subject:** National Years of the Trees

Date	Mintage	F	VF	XF	Unc	BU
ND(1986) (1986)	100,000	—	1.50	3.00	6.50	—
ND(1986) (1986) Proof	2,100	Value: 45.00				

Y# 181 10 BAHT **Composition:** Nickel **Ruler:** Rama IX Phra Maha Bhumithol Adulyadej **Subject:** 6th ASEAN Orchid Congress

Date	Mintage	F	VF	XF	Unc	BU
BE2529 (1986)	200,000	—	—	—	2.50	—
BE2529 (1986) Proof	3,000	Value: 37.50				

Y# 192 10 BAHT **Composition:** Nickel **Ruler:** Rama IX Phra Maha Bhumithol Adulyadej **Subject:** Princess Chulabhorn Awarded Einstein Medal **Obverse:** Hexagon with bust of Albert Einstein within inner circle **Reverse:** Bust of princess in cap and gown facing half left

Date	Mintage	F	VF	XF	Unc	BU
BE2529 (1986)	200,000	—	—	—	2.50	—
BE2529 (1986) Proof	1,080	Value: 50.00				

Y# 196 10 BAHT **Composition:** Nickel **Ruler:** Rama IX Phra Maha Bhumithol Adulyadej **Subject:** 60th Birthday of King Rama IX

Date	Mintage	F	VF	XF	Unc	BU
BE2530 (1987)	500,000	—	—	—	2.50	—
BE2530 (1987) Proof	5,000	Value: 27.50				

Y# 189 10 BAHT **Composition:** Nickel **Ruler:** Rama IX Phra Maha Bhumithol Adulyadej **Subject:** Chulachomklao Royal Military Academy

Date	Mintage	F	VF	XF	Unc	BU
BE2530 (1987)	300,000	—	—	—	2.50	—
BE2530 (1987) Proof	2,060	Value: 45.00				

Y# 190 10 BAHT **Composition:** Nickel **Ruler:** Rama IX Phra Maha Bhumithol Adulyadej **Subject:** Asian Institute of Technology

Date	Mintage	F	VF	XF	Unc	BU
BE2530 (1987)	300,000	—	—	—	2.50	—
BE2530 (1987) Proof	2,100	Value: 45.00				

Y# 205 10 BAHT **Composition:** Nickel **Ruler:** Rama IX Phra Maha Bhumithol Adulyadej **Subject:** 72nd Anniversary of Thai Cooperatives

Date	Mintage	F	VF	XF	Unc	BU
BE2531 (1988)	143,000	—	—	—	2.50	—
BE2530 (1988) Proof	3,000	Value: 27.50				

Y# 212 10 BAHT **Composition:** Nickel **Ruler:** Rama IX Phra Maha Bhumithol Adulyadej **Subject:** 42nd Anniversary - Reign of King Rama IX

Date	Mintage	F	VF	XF	Unc	BU
BE2531 (1988)	500,000	—	—	—	2.50	—
BE2531 (1988) Proof	8,110	Value: 18.50				

Y# 221 10 BAHT **Composition:** Nickel **Ruler:** Rama IX Phra Maha Bhumithol Adulyadej **Subject:** 100th Anniversary of Siriraj Hospital

Date	Mintage	F	VF	XF	Unc	BU
BE2531 (1988)	290,000	—	—	—	2.50	—
BE2531 (1988) Proof	5,000	Value: 18.50				

Y# 223 10 BAHT **Composition:** Nickel **Ruler:** Rama IX Phra Maha Bhumithol Adulyadej **Subject:** Crown Prince's Birthday

Date	Mintage	F	VF	XF	Unc	BU
BE2531 (1988)	200,000	—	—	—	2.50	—
BE2531 (1988) Proof	3,000	Value: 18.50				

Y# 227 10 BAHT **Ring Composition:** Stainless Steel **Center Composition:** Aluminum-Bronze **Ruler:** Rama IX Phra Maha Bhumithol Adulyadej **Note:** Varieties exist.

Date	Mintage	F	VF	XF	Unc	BU
BE2531 (1988) Prooflike; Rare	100,000	—	—	—	—	—

Note: The BE2531 (1988) pieces were not released to general circulation and are very scarce in the numismatic community

Date	Mintage	F	VF	XF	Unc	BU
BE2532 (1989)	200,000,000	—	—	—	2.50	—
BE2534 (1991)	—	—	—	—	2.50	—

	Mintage	F	VF	XF	Unc	BU
535 (1992)	—	—	—	—	2.50	—
536 (1993)	—	—	—	—	2.50	—
537 (1994)	—	—	—	—	3.00	—
538 (1995)	—	—	—	—	3.00	—
539 (1996)	—	—	—	—	3.00	—

228 10 BAHT Composition: Nickel **Ruler:** Rama IX Phra Maha Bhumithol Adulyadej **Subject:** Chulalongkorn University

e	Mintage	F	VF	XF	Unc	BU
532 (1989)	500,000	—	—	—	2.50	—

231 10 BAHT Composition: Copper-Nickel **Ruler:** Rama IX Phra Maha Bhumithol Adulyadej **Subject:** Centennial of First Medical College

e	Mintage	F	VF	XF	Unc	BU
533 (1990)	300,000	—	—	—	2.50	—
533 (1990) Proof	3,772	Value: 32.50				

233 10 BAHT Composition: Copper-Nickel **Ruler:** Rama IX Phra Maha Bhumithol Adulyadej **Subject:** 90th Birthday of the Princess Mother

e	Mintage	F	VF	XF	Unc	BU
2533 (1990)	500,000	—	—	—	2.50	—
2533 (1991) Proof	6,076	Value: 32.50				

236 10 BAHT Composition: Copper-Nickel **Ruler:** Rama IX Phra Maha Bhumithol Adulyadej **Subject:** 100th Anniversary - Office of Comptroller General

te	Mintage	F	VF	XF	Unc	BU
2533 (1990)	300,000	—	—	—	2.50	—

244 10 BAHT Composition: Copper-Nickel **Ruler:** Rama IX Phra Maha Bhumithol Adulyadej **Subject:** World Health Organization

Date	Mintage	F	VF	XF	Unc	BU
BE2533 (1990)	800,000	—	—	—	3.00	—
BE2533 (1990) Proof	34,000	Value: 18.50				

Y# 238 10 BAHT Composition: Copper-Nickel **Ruler:** Rama IX Phra Maha Bhumithol Adulyadej **Subject:** 36th Birthday of Princess Sirindhorn

Date	Mintage	F	VF	XF	Unc	BU
BE2534 (1991)	1,100,000	—	—	—	2.50	—
BE2534 (1991) Proof	3,300	Value: 30.00				

Y# 241 10 BAHT Composition: Copper-Nickel **Ruler:** Rama IX Phra Maha Bhumithol Adulyadej **Subject:** 80th Anniversary of Thai Boy Scouts

Date	Mintage	F	VF	XF	Unc	BU
BE2534 (1991)	650,000	—	—	—	3.00	—
BE2534 (1991) Proof	3,237	Value: 30.00				

Y# 256 10 BAHT Composition: Copper-Nickel **Ruler:** Rama IX Phra Maha Bhumithol Adulyadej **Subject:** Princess Sirindhorn's Magsaysay Foundation Award

Date	Mintage	F	VF	XF	Unc	BU
BE2534 (1991)	800,000	—	—	—	2.50	—
BE2534 (1991) Proof	2,111	Value: 37.50				

Y# 249 10 BAHT Composition: Copper-Nickel **Ruler:** Rama IX Phra Maha Bhumithol Adulyadej **Subject:** Centenary Celebration - Father of King Rama IX

Date	Mintage	F	VF	XF	Unc	BU
BE2535 (1992)	800,000	—	—	—	2.50	—
BE2535 (1992) Proof	5,314	Value: 22.50				

Y# 252 10 BAHT Composition: Copper-Nickel **Ruler:** Rama IX Phra Maha Bhumithol Adulyadej **Subject:** Ministry of Justice Centennial

Date	Mintage	F	VF	XF	Unc	BU
BE2535 (1992)	800,000	—	—	—	2.50	—
BE2535 (1992) Proof	—	Value: 18.50				

Y# 254 10 BAHT Composition: Copper-Nickel **Ruler:** Rama IX Phra Maha Bhumithol Adulyadej **Subject:** Ministry of Interior Centennial

Date	Mintage	F	VF	XF	Unc	BU
BE2535 (1992)	800,000	—	—	—	2.50	—
BE2535 (1992) Proof	10,000	Value: 17.50				

Y# 261 10 BAHT Composition: Copper-Nickel **Ruler:** Rama IX Phra Maha Bhumithol Adulyadej **Subject:** Queen's 60th Birthday

Date	Mintage	F	VF	XF	Unc	BU
BE2535 (1992)	1,100,000	—	—	—	3.00	—
BE2535 (1992) Proof	18,000	Value: 17.50				

Y# 269 10 BAHT Composition: Copper-Nickel **Ruler:** Rama IX Phra Maha Bhumithol Adulyadej **Subject:** 60th Anniversary of National Assembly

Date	Mintage	F	VF	XF	Unc	BU
BE2535 (1992)	44,000	—	—	—	2.50	—

Y# 271 10 BAHT Composition: Copper-Nickel **Ruler:** Rama IX Phra Maha Bhumithol Adulyadej **Subject:** Ministry of Agriculture

Date	Mintage	F	VF	XF	Unc	BU
BE2535 (1992)	550,000	—	—	—	2.50	—
BE2535 (1992) Proof	—	Value: 22.50				

Y# 273 10 BAHT Composition: Copper-Nickel **Ruler:** Rama IX Phra Maha Bhumithol Adulyadej **Subject:** King's 64th Birthday

Date	Mintage	F	VF	XF	Unc	BU
BE2535 (1992)	550,000	—	—	—	2.50	—
BE2535 (1992) Proof	3,711	Value: 25.00				

Y# 284 10 BAHT Composition: Copper-Nickel **Ruler:** Rama IX Phra Maha Bhumithol Adulyadej **Subject:** Centennial of Thai Teacher Training **Reverse:** Emblem

Date	Mintage	F	VF	XF	Unc	BU
BE2535 (1992)	700,000	—	—	—	2.50	—

Y# 285 10 BAHT Composition: Copper-Nickel **Ruler:** Rama IX Phra Maha Bhumithol Adulyadej **Subject:** Centennial of Thai National Bank **Reverse:** Seated figure

Date	Mintage	F	VF	XF	Unc	BU
BE2535 (1992)	700,000	—	—	—	2.50	—
BE2535 (1992) Proof	6,927	Value: 18.50				

Y# 280 10 BAHT Composition: Copper-Nickel **Ruler:** Rama IX Phra Maha Bhumithol Adulyadej **Subject:** Centennial of Thai Red Cross **Reverse:** Symbols

Date	Mintage	F	VF	XF	Unc	BU
BE2536 (1993)	700,000	—	—	—	2.50	—
BE2535 (1993) Proof	14,000	Value: 17.50				

Y# 283 10 BAHT Composition: Copper-Nickel **Ruler:** Rama IX Phra Maha Bhumithol Adulyadej **Subject:** Treasury Department

Date	Mintage	F	VF	XF	Unc	BU
BE2536 (1993)	600,000	—	—	—	2.50	—
BE2535 (1993) Proof	10,000	Value: 17.50				

Y# 286 10 BAHT Composition: Copper-Nickel **Ruler:** Rama IX Phra Maha Bhumithol Adulyadej **Subject:** Centennial of Attorney General's Office

Date	Mintage	F	VF	XF	Unc	BU
BE2536 (1993)	700,000	—	—	—	2.50	—

Y# 289 10 BAHT Composition: Copper-Nickel **Ruler:** Rama IX Phra Maha Bhumithol Adulyadej **Subject:** 100th Anniversary of Rama VII

Date	Mintage	F	VF	XF	Unc	BU
BE2536 (1993)	800,000	—	—	—	2.50	—
BE2536 (1993) Proof	10,000	Value: 17.50				

Y# 293 10 BAHT Composition: Copper-Nickel **Ruler:** Rama IX Phra Maha Bhumithol Adulyadej **Subject:** 60th Anniversary - Royal Institute

Date	Mintage	F	VF	XF	Unc	BU
BE2537 (1994)	700,000	—	—	—	2.50	—
BE2537 (1994) Proof	10,000	Value: 17.50				

Y# 295 10 BAHT Composition: Copper-Nickel **Ruler:** Rama IX Phra Maha Bhumithol Adulyadej **Subject:** 120th Anniversary - Juridical Council

Date	Mintage	F	VF	XF	Unc	BU
BE2537 (1994)	800,000	—	—	—	2.50	—
BE2537 (1994) Proof	12,000	Value: 17.50				

Y# 297 10 BAHT Composition: Copper-Nickel **Ruler:** Rama IX Phra Maha Bhumithol Adulyadej **Subject:** 60th Anniversary - Thammasat University

Date	Mintage	F	VF	XF	Unc	BU
BE2537 (1994)	800,000	—	—	—	2.50	—
BE2537 (1994) Proof	12,000	Value: 17.50				

Y# 339 10 BAHT Composition: Copper-Nickel **Ruler:** Rama IX Phra Maha Bhumithol Adulyadej **Subject:** International Rice Award **Obverse:** King with camera **Reverse:** Rice plant

Date	F	VF	XF	Unc	BU
BE2535 (1996)	—	—	—	3.50	—

Y# 328.1 10 BAHT Composition: Copper-Nickel **Rul** Rama IX Phra Maha Bhumithol Adulyadej **Subject:** 50th Anniversary - Reign of King Rama IX **Obverse:** Small port does not contact inner ring

Date	F	VF	XF	Unc
BE2539 (1996)	—	—	—	3.00

Y# 328.2 10 BAHT Composition: Copper-Nickel **Rule** Rama IX Phra Maha Bhumithol Adulyadej **Subject:** 50th Anniversary - Reign of King Rama IX **Obverse:** Large portr contacts inner ring

Date	F	VF	XF	Unc
BE2539 (1996)	—	—	—	3.00

Y# 334 10 BAHT Composition: Copper-Nickel **Ruler:** Rama IX Phra Maha Bhumithol Adulyadej **Subject:** 50th Anniversary - Reign of King Rama IX and F.A.O. World Sum

Date	F	VF	XF	Unc
BE2539 (1996)	—	—	—	3.50

Y# 347 10 BAHT Composition: Copper-Nickel **Ruler:** Rama IX Phra Maha Bhumithol Adulyadej **Subject:** 100th Anniversary of Chulalongkorn's European Tour

Date	F	VF	XF	Unc
BE2540 (1997)	—	—	—	2.50

Y# 346 10 BAHT Composition: Copper-Nickel **Ruler:** Rama IX Phra Maha Bhumithol Adulyadej **Subject:** 100th Anniversary - Central General Hospital - Medication Offic

Date	F	VF	XF	Unc
BE2541 (1998)	—	—	—	3.00

Y# 348 10 BAHT Composition: Copper-Nickel **Ruler:** Rama IX Phra Maha Bhumithol Adulyadej **Subject:** 13th Asian Games **Reverse:** Symbols

Date	Mintage	F	VF	XF	Unc
BE2541 (1998)	10,000,000	—	—	—	2.50

352 10 BAHT **Composition:** Bi-Metallic **Ruler:** Rama IX Phra Maha Bhumithol Adulyadej **Edge:** Plain. **Size:** 26 mm.

e	F	VF	XF	Unc	BU
2541 (1998)	—	—	—	2.50	—

 # 349 10 BAHT **Composition:** Bi-Metallic **Ruler:** Rama IX Phra Maha Bhumithol Adulyadej **Edge:** Reeded and plain sections. **Size:** 26 mm.

te	F	VF	XF	Unc	BU
2542 (1999)	—	—	—	2.50	—

 # 350 10 BAHT **Composition:** Bi-Metallic **Ruler:** Rama IX Phra Maha Bhumithol Adulyadej **Edge:** Reeded and plain sections. **Size:** 26 mm.

te	Mintage	F	VF	XF	Unc	BU
2542 (1999)	10,000,000	—	—	—	1.75	—

 # 371 10 BAHT **Ring Weight:** 8.4500 g. **Ring Composition:** Copper-Nickel **Center Composition:** Brass **Ruler:** Rama IX Phra Maha Bhumithol Adulyadej **Subject:** National Economic and Social Development Board **Obverse:** King's portrait **Reverse:** Three seated figures **Edge:** Plain and reeded sections **Size:** 25.9 mm.

ate	F	VF	XF	Unc	BU
E2543(2000)	—	—	—	2.00	—

 # 354 10 BAHT **Ring Composition:** Copper-Nickel **Center Composition:** Brass **Ruler:** Rama IX Phra Maha Bhumithol Adulyadej **Subject:** 100th Anniversary Army Medical Department **Obverse:** Two portraits **Reverse:** Departmental emblem

ate	F	VF	XF	Unc	BU
D (2000)	—	—	—	2.00	—

 # 358 10 BAHT **Ring Composition:** Copper-Nickel **Center Composition:** Brass **Ruler:** Rama IX Phra Maha Bhumithol Adulyadej **Subject:** 80th Anniversary - Commerce Ministry **Obverse:** King's portrait **Reverse:** Ministry logo **Edge:** Reeded and plain sections **Size:** 25.9 mm.

Date	F	VF	XF	Unc	BU
BE2543 (2000)	—	—	—	2.00	—

Y# 361 10 BAHT **Ring Composition:** Copper-Nickel **Center Composition:** Brass **Ruler:** Rama IX Phra Maha Bhumithol Adulyadej **Subject:** 100th Birthday - Princess Mother **Obverse:** Princess Mother's portrait **Reverse:** Emblem divides date **Edge:** Reeded and plain sections **Size:** 26 mm.

Date	F	VF	XF	Unc	BU
BE2543 (2000)	—	—	—	2.00	—

Y# 373 10 BAHT **Ring Weight:** 8.5000 g. **Ring Composition:** Copper-Nickel **Center Composition:** Brass **Ruler:** Rama IX Phra Maha Bhumithol Adulyadej **Subject:** Department of Lands Centennial **Obverse:** Portraits of Kings Chulalongkorn and Bhumibol Adulyadej **Reverse:** Department seal **Edge:** Reeded and plain sections **Size:** 25.6 mm.

Date	F	VF	XF	Unc	BU
BE2544(2001)	—	—	—	2.50	—

Y# 381 10 BAHT **Weight:** 8.5500 g. **Composition:** Bi-Metallic **Ruler:** Rama IX Phra Maha Bhumithol Adulyadej **Subject:** Centennial of Irrigation Department **Obverse:** Portraits of Kings Rama V and Rama IX **Reverse:** Department logo **Edge:** Reeded and plain sections **Size:** 25.8 mm.

Date	F	VF	XF	Unc	BU
BE2545(2002)	—	—	—	2.00	—

Y# 382 10 BAHT **Weight:** 8.5500 g. **Composition:** Bi-Metallic **Ruler:** Rama IX Phra Maha Bhumithol Adulyadej **Subject:** Department of Internal Trade 60th Anniversary **Obverse:** King's portrait **Reverse:** Department logo **Edge:** Reeded and plain sections **Size:** 25.8 mm.

Date	F	VF	XF	Unc	BU
BE2545(2002)	—	—	—	2.00	—

Y# 383 10 BAHT **Weight:** 8.5500 g. **Composition:** Bi-Metallic **Ruler:** Rama IX Phra Maha Bhumithol Adulyadej **Subject:** State Highway Department 90th Anniversary **Obverse:** Portraits of Kings Rama VI and Rama IX **Reverse:** Department logo **Edge:** Reeded and Plain sections **Size:** 25.8 mm.

Date	F	VF	XF	Unc	BU
BE2545(2002)	—	—	—	2.00	—

Y# 384 10 BAHT **Weight:** 8.5500 g. **Composition:** Bi-Metallic **Ruler:** Rama IX Phra Maha Bhumithol Adulyadej **Subject:** Vajira Hospital 90th Anniversary **Obverse:** Portraits of Kings Rama VI and Rama IX **Reverse:** Hospital logo **Edge:** Reeded and plain sections **Size:** 25.8 mm.

Date	F	VF	XF	Unc	BU
BE2545(2002)	—	—	—	2.00	—

Y# 385 10 BAHT **Weight:** 8.5500 g. **Composition:** Bi-Metallic **Ruler:** Rama IX Phra Maha Bhumithol Adulyadej **Subject:** 20th World Scouting Jamboree **Obverse:** King's portrait wearing a scouting uniform **Reverse:** Jamboree logo **Edge:** Reeded and plain sections **Size:** 25.8 mm.

Date	F	VF	XF	Unc	BU
BE2545(2002)	—	—	—	2.00	—

Y# 387 10 BAHT **Weight:** 8.5500 g. **Composition:** Bi-Metallic **Ruler:** Rama IX Phra Maha Bhumithol Adulyadej **Subject:** King's 75th Birthday **Obverse:** King's portrait **Reverse:** Royal crown in radiant oval **Edge:** Reeded and plain sections **Size:** 25.8 mm.

Date	F	VF	XF	Unc	BU
BE2545(2002)	—	—	—	2.00	—

Y# 86 20 BAHT **Weight:** 19.6000 g. **Composition:** 0.7500 Silver .4726 oz. ASW **Ruler:** Rama IX Phra Maha Bhumithol Adulyadej **Subject:** 36th Birthday - King Rama IX

Date	Mintage	F	VF	XF	Unc	BU
ND (1963)	1,000,000	—	—	4.50	8.50	12.50

Y# 298 20 BAHT **Composition:** Copper-Nickel **Ruler:** Rama IX Phra Maha Bhumithol Adulyadej **Subject:** 120th Anniversary - Ministry of Finance

Date	Mintage	F	VF	XF	Unc	BU
BE2538 (1994)	800,000	—	—	—	3.50	—
BE2538 (1994) Proof	1,920	Value: 28.00				

Y# 300 20 BAHT **Composition:** Copper-Nickel **Ruler:** Rama IX Phra Maha Bhumithol Adulyadej **Subject:** 108th Anniversary - Minstry of Defense

Date	Mintage	F	VF	XF	Unc	BU
BE2538 (1994)	800,000	—	—	—	3.50	—
BE2538 (1994) Proof	2,000	Value: 28.00				

Y# 302 20 BAHT **Composition:** Copper-Nickel **Ruler:** Rama IX Phra Maha Bhumithol Adulyadej **Subject:** 120th Anniversary - Ministry of Foreign Affairs

Date	Mintage	F	VF	XF	Unc	BU
BE2538 (1994)	800,000	—	—	—	3.50	—
BE2538 (1994) Proof	740	Value: 55.00				

Y# 308 20 BAHT **Composition:** Copper-Nickel **Ruler:** Rama IX Phra Maha Bhumithol Adulyadej **Series:** F.A.O.

Date	Mintage	F	VF	XF	Unc	BU
BE2538 (1995)	400,000	—	—	—	3.50	—
BE2538 (1995) Proof	—	Value: 18.50				

Y# 309 20 BAHT **Composition:** Copper-Nickel **Ruler:** Rama IX Phra Maha Bhumithol Adulyadej **Subject:** 80th Anniversary - Department of Revenue

Date	Mintage	F	VF	XF	Unc	BU
BE2538 (1995)	800,000	—	—	—	3.50	—
BE2538 (1995) Proof	—	Value: 18.50				

Y# 311 20 BAHT **Composition:** Copper-Nickel **Ruler:** Rama IX Phra Maha Bhumithol Adulyadej **Subject:** 120th Anniversary - Audit Council

Date	Mintage	F	VF	XF	Unc	BU
BE2538 (1995)	800,000	—	—	—	3.50	—
BE2538 (1995) Proof	—	Value: 18.50				

Y# 314 20 BAHT **Composition:** Copper-Nickel **Ruler:** Rama IX Phra Maha Bhumithol Adulyadej **Subject:** Information Technology Year

Date	Mintage	F	VF	XF	Unc	BU
BE2538 (1995)		—	—	—	3.50	—
BE2538 (1995) Proof	—	Value: 18.50				

Y# 316 20 BAHT **Composition:** Copper-Nickel **Ruler:** Rama IX Phra Maha Bhumithol Adulyadej **Subject:** Asean Environment Year

Date	Mintage	F	VF	XF	Unc	BU
BE2538 (1995)		—	—	—	3.50	—
BE2538 (1995) Proof	—	Value: 18.50				

Y# 331 20 BAHT **Composition:** Copper-Nickel **Ruler:** Rama IX Phra Maha Bhumithol Adulyadej **Subject:** Ministry of Commerce **Reverse:** Seal

Date	F	VF	XF	Unc	BU
BE2538 (1995)	—	—	—	4.00	—

Y# 338 20 BAHT **Composition:** Copper-Nickel **Ruler:** Rama IX Phra Maha Bhumithol Adulyadej **Subject:** 50 Years of Peace

Date	F	VF	XF	Unc	BU
ND(BE2538) (1995)	—	—	—	3.50	—

Y# 304 20 BAHT **Composition:** Copper-Nickel **Ruler:** Rama IX Phra Maha Bhumithol Adulyadej **Subject:** 72nd Birthday of Princess **Note:** Similar to 600 Baht, Y#305.

Date	Mintage	F	VF	XF	Unc	BU
BE2538 (1995)	800,000	—	—	—	3.50	—
BE2538 (1995) Proof	1,560	Value: 22.50				

Y# 318 20 BAHT **Composition:** Copper-Nickel **Ruler:** Rama IX Phra Maha Bhumithol Adulyadej **Subject:** Siriraj Nursing and Midwife School Centennial

Date	F	VF	XF	Unc	BU
BE2539 (1996)	—	—	—	3.50	—

Y# 321.1 20 BAHT **Composition:** Copper-Nickel **Ruler:** Rama IX Phra Maha Bhumithol Adulyadej **Subject:** 50th Anniversary - Reign of King Rama IX

Date	F	VF	XF	Unc	BU
BE2539 (1996)	—	—	—	4.00	—
BE2539 (1996) Proof	—	Value: 25.00			

Y# 321.2 20 BAHT **Composition:** Copper-Nickel **Ruler:** Rama IX Phra Maha Bhumithol Adulyadej **Reverse:** Incomplete - missing the "Unalom" in center

Date	F	VF	XF	Unc	BU
BE2539 (1996)	—	—	—	4.00	—
BE2539 (1996) Proof	—	Value: 25.00			

Y# 335 20 BAHT **Composition:** Copper-Nickel **Ruler:** Rama IX Phra Maha Bhumithol Adulyadej **Subject:** 50th Anniversary - Reign of King Rama IX and F.A.O. World Food Summit

Date	F	VF	XF	Unc	BU
BE2539 (1996)	—	—	—	3.50	—

Y# 340 20 BAHT **Composition:** Copper-Nickel **Ruler:** Rama IX Phra Maha Bhumithol Adulyadej **Subject:** International Rice Award

Date	F	VF	XF	Unc	BU
BE2539 (1996)	—	—	—	3.50	—

Y# 332 20 BAHT **Composition:** Copper-Nickel **Ruler:** Rama IX Phra Maha Bhumithol Adulyadej **Subject:** 100th Anniversary - Thai Railway

Date	F	VF	XF	Unc	BU
BE2540 (1997)	—	—	—	3.50	
BE2540 (1997) Proof	—	Value: 30.00			

Y# 333 20 BAHT **Composition:** Copper-Nickel **Ruler:** Rama IX Phra Maha Bhumithol Adulyadej **Subject:** 84th Anniversary - Thai Savings Bank

Date	F	VF	XF	Unc	BU
BE2540 (1997)	—	—	—	3.50	—
BE2540 (1997) Proof	—	Value: 28.00			

Y# 341 20 BAHT **Composition:** Copper-Nickel **Ruler:** Rama IX Phra Maha Bhumithol Adulyadej **Subject:** 50th Anniversary - Thai Veterans Organization

Date	F	VF	XF	Unc	BU
BE2541 (1998)	—	—	—	3.50	—
BE2541 (1998) Proof	—	Value: 12.50			

Y# 351 20 BAHT **Composition:** Bi-Metallic **Ruler:** Rama IX Phra Maha Bhumithol Adulyadej **Edge:** Reeded. **Size:** 32 mm.

Date	Mintage	F	VF	XF	Unc	BU
BE2542 (1999)	—	—	—	—	1.00	—
BE2542 (1999) Proof	5,000	Value: 5.00				

Y# 355 20 BAHT **Weight:** 14.9100 g. **Composition:** Copper Nickel **Ruler:** Rama IX Phra Maha Bhumithol Adulyadej **Subject:** 84th Anniversary - Audit Council Bureau **Obverse:** King's portrait. **Reverse:** Balance scale. **Edge:** Reeded. **Size:** 31.9 mm.

Date	F	VF	XF	Unc	BU
BE2542 (1999)	—	—	—	3.50	—

357 20 BAHT Composition: Copper-Nickel **Ruler:** Rama IX Phra Maha Bhumithol Adulyadej **Subject:** Asian Development Bank Board Meeting **Obverse:** King's portrait **Reverse:** Chieng money illustration **Edge:** Reeded **Size:** 32 mm.

	F	VF	XF	Unc	BU
(2000)	—	—	—	4.00	—

362 20 BAHT Composition: Copper-Nickel **Ruler:** Rama IX Phra Maha Bhumithol Adulyadej **Subject:** 100th Birthday - Princess Mother **Obverse:** Princess Mother's portrait **Reverse:** Emblem divides date **Edge:** Reeded **Size:** 32 mm.

e	F	VF	XF	Unc	BU
.543 (2000)	—	—	—	3.50	—
:543 (2000) Proof	—	Value: 12.50			

376 20 BAHT Weight: 15.0000 g. **Composition:** Copper-Nickel **Ruler:** Rama IX Phra Maha Bhumithol Adulyadej **Subject:** King's 72nd Birthday **Obverse:** Busts of King and Rama I facing **Reverse:** Two royal symbols **Edge:** Reeded **Size:** 31.9 mm.

e	F	VF	XF	Unc	BU
2543(2000)	—	—	—	3.50	—

374 20 BAHT Weight: 15.1000 g. **Composition:** Copper-Nickel **Ruler:** Rama IX Phra Maha Bhumithol Adulyadej **Subject:** Chulalongkorn University 84th Anniversary **Obverse:** Portraits of Kings Chulalongkorn, Vjiravudh, and Bhumibol Adulyadej **Reverse:** University emblem dividing denomination **Edge:** Reeded **Size:** 31.9 mm.

e	F	VF	XF	Unc	BU
2544(2001)	—	—	—	3.50	—

Y# 375 20 BAHT Weight: 15.1000 g. **Composition:** Copper-Nickel **Ruler:** Rama IX Phra Maha Bhumithol Adulyadej **Subject:** Civil Service Comission 72nd Anniversary **Obverse:** Conjoined busts of Kings Prajadhipok and Bhumibol Adulyadej left **Reverse:** Civil service emblem dividing denomination

Date	F	VF	XF	Unc	BU
BE2544(2001)	—	—	—	3.50	—

Y# 386 20 BAHT Weight: 15.0000 g. **Composition:** Copper Nickel **Ruler:** Rama IX Phra Maha Bhumithol Adulyadej **Subject:** Centennial of Thai Banknotes **Obverse:** Portraits of Kings Rama V and Rama IX **Reverse:** Coat of arms in center of seal **Edge:** Reeded **Size:** 32 mm.

Date	F	VF	XF	Unc	BU
2545(2002)	—	—	—	3.50	—
2545(2002) Proof	—	Value: 12.00			

Y# 388 20 BAHT Weight: 15.0000 g. **Composition:** Copper-Nickel **Ruler:** Rama IX Phra Maha Bhumithol Adulyadej **Subject:** King's 75th Birthday **Reverse:** Royal crown in radiant oval **Edge:** Reeded **Size:** 32 mm.

Date	F	VF	XF	Unc	BU
2545(2002)	—	—	—	3.50	—
2545(2002) Proof	—	Value: 12.00			

Y# 95 50 BAHT Weight: 24.7000 g. **Composition:** 0.9000 Silver .7147 oz. ASW **Ruler:** Rama IX Phra Maha Bhumithol Adulyadej **Subject:** 20th Year Buddhist Fellowship

Date	Mintage	F	VF	XF	Unc	BU
BE2514 (1971)	200,000	—	—	7.50	14.00	—
BE2514 (1971) Prooflike	60,000	—	—	—	20.00	—

Y# 101 50 BAHT Weight: 24.8500 g. **Composition:** 0.4000 Silver .3195 oz. ASW **Ruler:** Rama IX Phra Maha Bhumithol Adulyadej **Subject:** National Museum Centennial

Date	Mintage	F	VF	XF	Unc	BU
BE2517 (1974)	200,000	—	—	6.50	13.50	—

Y# 102 50 BAHT Weight: 25.5500 g. **Composition:** 0.5000 Silver .4173 oz. ASW **Ruler:** Rama IX Phra Maha Bhumithol Adulyadej **Series:** Conservation **Reverse:** Sumatran Rhinoceros

Date	Mintage	F	VF	XF	Unc	BU
BE2517 (1974)	20,000	—	—	—	30.00	—

Y# 102a 50 BAHT Weight: 28.2800 g. **Composition:** 0.9250 Silver .8411 oz. ASW **Ruler:** Rama IX Phra Maha Bhumithol Adulyadej **Series:** Conservation

Date	Mintage	F	VF	XF	Unc	BU
BE2517 (1974) Proof	9,885	Value: 60.00				

Y# 336 50 BAHT Composition: Nickel **Ruler:** Rama IX Phra Maha Bhumithol Adulyadej **Subject:** 50th Anniversary - Reign of King Rama IX and F.A.O. World Food Summit **Note:** Similar to 20 Baht, Y#335.

Date	F	VF	XF	Unc	BU
BE2538 (1995)	—	—	—	11.50	—

Y# 363 50 BAHT Weight: 20.0000 g. **Composition:** 0.9250 Silver .5948 oz. ASW **Ruler:** Rama IX Phra Maha Bhumithol Adulyadej **Subject:** Year of the Dragon **Obverse:** King's portrait **Reverse:** Dragon and latent image date pearl **Edge:** Reeded **Size:** 38.7 mm.

Date	Mintage	F	VF	XF	Unc	BU
BE2543 (2000) Proof	8,500	Value: 55.00				

Y# 364 50 BAHT Weight: 20.0000 g. **Composition:** 0.9250 Silver .5948 oz. ASW **Ruler:** Rama IX Phra Maha Bhumithol Adulyadej **Subject:** Year of the Dragon **Obverse:** King's portrait **Reverse:** 2 dragons with pearl hologram

Date	Mintage	F	VF	XF	Unc	BU
BE2543 (2000) Proof	8,500	Value: 150				

Y# 365 50 BAHT Weight: 20.0000 g. **Composition:** 0.9250 Silver .5948 oz. ASW **Ruler:** Rama IX Phra Maha Bhumithol Adulyadej **Subject:** Year of the Dragon **Obverse:** King's portrait **Reverse:** Dragon with gold plated pearl

Date	Mintage	F	VF	XF	Unc	BU
BE2543 (2000) Proof	8,500	Value: 55.00				

Y# 103 100 BAHT **Weight:** 31.9000 g. **Composition:** 0.5000 Silver .5128 oz. ASW **Ruler:** Rama IX Phra Maha Bhumithol Adulyadej **Series:** Conservation **Reverse:** Brown-antlered deer

Date	Mintage	F	VF	XF	Unc	BU
BE2517 (1974)	20,000	—	—	—	37.50	—

Y# 103a 100 BAHT **Weight:** 35.0000 g. **Composition:** 0.9250 Silver 1.0409 oz. ASW **Ruler:** Rama IX Phra Maha Bhumithol Adulyadej **Reverse:** Brown-antlered deer

Date	Mintage	F	VF	XF	Unc	BU
BE2517 (1974) Proof	9,294	Value: 70.00				

Y# 106 100 BAHT **Weight:** 25.0000 g. **Composition:** 0.9000 Silver .7234 oz. ASW **Ruler:** Rama IX Phra Maha Bhumithol Adulyadej **Subject:** 100th Anniversary - Ministry of Finance

Date	Mintage	F	VF	XF	Unc	BU
BE2518 (1975)	30,000	—	—	9.00	18.50	—

Y# 242 100 BAHT **Composition:** Copper-Nickel **Ruler:** Rama IX Phra Maha Bhumithol Adulyadej **Subject:** World Bank - International Monetary Fund

Date	Mintage	F	VF	XF	Unc	BU
BE2534 (1991)	500,000	—	—	—	12.50	—
BE2534 (1991) Proof	60,000	Value: 32.50				

Y# 287 100 BAHT **Composition:** Copper-Nickel **Ruler:** Rama IX Phra Maha Bhumithol Adulyadej **Subject:** King and Prince in Scouting **Reverse:** Emblem

Date	Mintage	F	VF	XF	Unc	BU
BE2536 (1993)	200,000	—	—	—	17.50	—
BE2536 (1993) Proof	30,000	Value: 37.50				

Y# 359 100 BAHT **Weight:** 15.0000 g. **Composition:** 0.9250 Silver .4461 oz. ASW **Ruler:** Rama IX Phra Maha Bhumithol Adulyadej **Series:** World Wildlife Fund **Obverse:** King's portrait **Reverse:** Tiger head, denomination **Size:** 30 mm. **Note:** Thickness of coin is 4.7mm.

Date	Mintage	F	VF	XF	Unc	BU
BE2540 (1997) Proof	50,000	Value: 30.00				

Y# 366 100 BAHT **Weight:** 7.7759 g. **Composition:** 0.9999 Gold .2500 oz. AGW **Ruler:** Rama IX Phra Maha Bhumithol Adulyadej **Subject:** Year of the Dragon **Obverse:** King's portrait **Reverse:** Dragon with Golden Pearl **Edge:** Reeded **Size:** 22 mm.

Date	Mintage	F	VF	XF	Unc	BU
BE2543 (2000) Proof	1,800	Value: 150				

Y# 88 150 BAHT **Weight:** 3.7500 g. **Composition:** 0.9000 Gold .1085 oz. AGW **Ruler:** Rama IX Phra Maha Bhumithol Adulyadej **Subject:** Queen Sirikit 36th Birthday

Date	Mintage	F	VF	XF	Unc	BU
BE2511 (1968)	202,000	—	—	—	55.00	—

Y# 108 150 BAHT **Weight:** 22.0000 g. **Composition:** 0.9250 Silver .6543 oz. ASW **Ruler:** Rama IX Phra Maha Bhumithol Adulyadej **Subject:** 75th Birthday of Princess Mother

Date	Mintage	F	VF	XF	Unc	BU
BE2518 (1975)	200,000	—	—	9.00	17.50	—

Y# 113 150 BAHT **Weight:** 22.0000 g. **Composition:** 0.9250 Silver .6543 oz. ASW **Ruler:** Rama IX Phra Maha Bhumithol Adulyadej **Series:** F.A.O.

Date	Mintage	F	VF	XF	Unc	BU
BE2520 (1977)	50,000	—	—	9.00	17.50	—

Y# 118 150 BAHT **Weight:** 22.0000 g. **Composition.** 0.9250 Silver .6543 oz. ASW **Ruler:** Rama IX Phra Maha Bhumithol Adulyadej **Subject:** Crown Prince Vajiralongko and Princess Soamsawali Wedding

Date	Mintage	F	VF	XF	Unc
BE2520 (1977)	200,000	—	—	8.50	14.50

Y# 116 150 BAHT **Weight:** 22.0000 g. **Composition:** 0.9250 Silver .6543 oz. ASW **Ruler:** Rama IX Phra Maha Bhumithol Adulyadej **Subject:** Graduation of Princess Sirindhorn

Date	Mintage	F	VF	XF	Unc
BE2520 (1977)	100,000	—	—	8.50	14.50

Y# 125 150 BAHT **Weight:** 22.0000 g. **Composition:** 0.9250 Silver .6543 oz. ASW **Ruler:** Rama IX Phra Maha Bhumithol Adulyadej **Subject:** Investiture of Princess Sirindhorn

Date	Mintage	F	VF	XF	Unc
BE2520 (1977)	50,000	—	—	12.50	27.50

Y# 123 150 BAHT **Weight:** 22.0000 g. **Composition:** 0.9250 Silver .6543 oz. ASW **Ruler:** Rama IX Phra Maha Bhumithol Adulyadej **Subject:** 9th World Orchid Conferenc

Date	Mintage	F	VF	XF	Unc
BE2521 (1978)	30,000	—	—	10.00	22.50

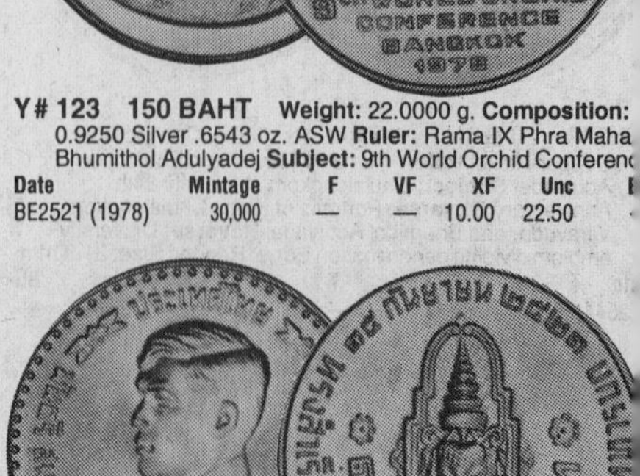

Y# 128 150 BAHT **Weight:** 22.0000 g. **Composition:** 0.9250 Silver .6543 oz. ASW **Ruler:** Rama IX Phra Maha Bhumithol Adulyadej **Subject:** Graduation of Crown Princ Vijiralongkorn

Date	Mintage	F	VF	XF	Unc	BU
BE2521 (1978)	50,000	—	—	9.00	17.50	—

Y# 197 150 BAHT **Weight:** 7.5000 g. **Composition:** 0.9250 Silver .2230 oz. ASW **Ruler:** Rama IX Phra Maha Bhumithol Adulyadej **Subject:** 60th Birthday - King Rama IX **Note:** Similar to 6000 Baht, Y#202.

Date	Mintage	F	VF	XF	Unc	BU
BE2530 (1987)	12,000	—	—	—	25.00	—
BE2530 (1987) Proof	1,100	Value: 125				

Y# 213 150 BAHT **Weight:** 7.5000 g. **Composition:** 0.9250 Silver .2230 oz. ASW **Ruler:** Rama IX Phra Maha Bhumithol Adulyadej **Subject:** 42nd Anniversary - Reign of King Rama IX **Note:** Similar to 10 Baht, Y#212.

Date	Mintage	F	VF	XF	Unc	BU
BE2531 (1988)	20,000	—	—	—	25.00	—
BE2531 (1988) Proof	2,454	Value: 135				

Y# 262 150 BAHT **Weight:** 7.5000 g. **Composition:** 0.9250 Silver .2230 oz. ASW **Ruler:** Rama IX Phra Maha Bhumithol Adulyadej **Subject:** Queen's 60th Birthday **Note:** Similar to 10 Baht, Y#261.

Date	Mintage	F	VF	XF	Unc	BU
BE2535 (1992)	25,000	—	—	—	25.00	—
BE2535 (1992) Proof	5,600	Value: 45.00				

Y# 322 150 BAHT **Weight:** 7.5000 g. **Composition:** 0.9250 Silver .2230 oz. ASW **Ruler:** Rama IX Phra Maha Bhumithol Adulyadej **Subject:** 50th Anniversary - Reign of King Rama IX **Note:** Similar to 20 Baht, Y#321.1.

Date	F	VF	XF	Unc	BU
BE2539 (1996)	—	—	—	17.50	—
BE2539 (1996) Proof	—	Value: 45.00			

Y# 133 200 BAHT **Weight:** 22.0000 g. **Composition:** 0.9250 Silver .6544 oz. ASW **Ruler:** Rama IX Phra Maha Bhumithol Adulyadej **Subject:** Royal Cradle Ceremony

Date	Mintage	F	VF	XF	Unc	BU
BE2522 (1979)	50,000	—	—	9.00	16.50	—

Y# 152 200 BAHT **Weight:** 23.3200 g. **Composition:** 0.9250 Silver .6935 oz. ASW **Ruler:** Rama IX Phra Maha Bhumithol Adulyadej **Series:** International Year of the Child

Date	Mintage	F	VF	XF	Unc	BU
BE2524 (1981) Proof	9,525	Value: 65.00				

Y# 206 200 BAHT **Weight:** 23.1800 g. **Composition:** 0.9250 Silver .6894 oz. ASW **Ruler:** Rama IX Phra Maha Bhumithol Adulyadej **Series:** 25th Anniversary of World Wildlife Fund **Reverse:** Siamese Fireback Pheasant

Date	Mintage	F	VF	XF	Unc	BU
BE2530 (1987) Proof	25,000	Value: 40.00				

Y# 379 200 BAHT **Weight:** 23.3300 g. **Composition:** 0.9250 Silver 0.6938 oz. ASW **Subject:** UNICEF **Obverse:** King's portrait. **Reverse:** Three seated children. **Edge:** Reeded. **Size:** 38.6 mm.

Date	Mintage	F	VF	XF	Unc	BU
BE2540 (1997) Proof	25,000	Value: 25.00				

Y# 360 200 BAHT **Weight:** 23.1800 g. **Composition:** 0.9250 Silver .6894 oz. ASW **Ruler:** Rama IX Phra Maha Bhumithol Adulyadej **Series:** World Wildlife Fund **Obverse:** King's portrait **Reverse:** Two tigers above denomination **Edge:** Reeded **Size:** 38.5 mm. **Note:** Thickness of coin is 4.7mm.

Date	Mintage	F	VF	XF	Unc	BU
BE2541 (1998) Proof	15,000	Value: 47.50				

Y# 367 200 BAHT **Weight:** 155.5175 g. **Composition:** 0.9250 Silver 4.625 oz. ASW **Ruler:** Rama IX Phra Maha Bhumithol Adulyadej **Subject:** Year of the Dragon **Obverse:** King's portrait **Reverse:** 2 dragons around silver pearl in orange circle **Edge:** Reeded **Size:** 65 mm.

Date	Mintage	F	VF	XF	Unc	BU
BE2543 (2000) Proof	2,000	Value: 175				

Y# 169 250 BAHT **Weight:** 28.2800 g. **Composition:** 0.9250 Silver .8411 oz. ASW **Ruler:** Rama IX Phra Maha Bhumithol Adulyadej **Series:** International Year of Disabled Persons

Date	Mintage	F	VF	XF	Unc	BU
BE2526 (1983)	307	—	—	—	275	—
BE2526 (1983) Proof	233	Value: 550				

Y# 368 250 BAHT **Weight:** 15.5510 g. **Composition:** 0.9999 Gold .5000 oz. AGW **Ruler:** Rama IX Phra Maha Bhumithol Adulyadej **Subject:** Year of the Dragon **Obverse:** King's portrait **Reverse:** Dragon with latent image pearl **Edge:** Reeded **Size:** 27 mm.

Date	Mintage	F	VF	XF	Unc	BU
BE2543 (2000) Proof	2,800	Value: 350				

Y# 89 300 BAHT **Weight:** 7.5000 g. **Composition:** 0.9000 Gold .2170 oz. AGW **Ruler:** Rama IX Phra Maha Bhumithol Adulyadej **Subject:** Queen Sirikit 36th Birthday

Date	Mintage	F	VF	XF	Unc	BU
BE2511 (1968)	101,000	—	—	—	110	—

Y# 136 300 BAHT **Weight:** 22.0000 g. **Composition:** 0.9250 Silver .6543 oz. ASW **Ruler:** Rama IX Phra Maha Bhumithol Adulyadej **Subject:** Graduation of Princess Chulabhorn **Note:** Similar to 10 Baht, Y#135.

Date	Mintage	F	VF	XF	Unc	BU
BE2522 (1979)	20,000	—	—	15.00	20.00	—

Y# 198 300 BAHT **Weight:** 15.0000 g. **Composition:** 0.9250 Silver .4461 oz. ASW **Ruler:** Rama IX Phra Maha Bhumithol Adulyadej **Subject:** 60th Birthday - King Rama IX **Note:** Similar to 6000 Baht, Y#202.

Date	Mintage	F	VF	XF	Unc	BU
BE2530 (1987)	6,680	—	—	—	25.00	—
BE2530 (1987) Proof	800	Value: 50.00				

Y# 214 300 BAHT **Weight:** 15.0000 g. **Composition:** 0.9250 Silver .4461 oz. ASW **Ruler:** Rama IX Phra Maha Bhumithol Adulyadej **Subject:** 42nd Anniversary - Reign of King Rama IX **Note:** Similar to 10 Baht, Y#212.

Date	Mintage	F	VF	XF	Unc	BU
BE2531 (1988)	11,000	—	—	—	20.00	—
BE2531 (1988) Proof	2,391	Value: 50.00				

Y# 263 300 BAHT **Weight:** 15.0000 g. **Composition:** 0.9250 Silver .4461 oz. ASW **Ruler:** Rama IX Phra Maha Bhumithol Adulyadej **Subject:** Queen's 60th Birthday **Note:** Similar to 10 Baht, Y#261.

Date	Mintage	F	VF	XF	Unc	BU
BE2535 (1992)	25,000	—	—	—	35.00	—
BE2535 (1992) Proof	4,000	Value: 45.00				

Y# 323 300 BAHT **Weight:** 15.0000 g. **Composition:** 0.9250 Silver .4461 oz. ASW **Ruler:** Rama IX Phra Maha Bhumithol Adulyadej **Subject:** 50th Anniversary - Reign of King Rama IX **Note:** Similar to 20 Baht, Y#321.1.

Date	F	VF	XF	Unc	BU
BE2539 (1996)	—	—	—	22.50	—
BE2539 (1996) Proof	—	Value: 50.00			

Y# 93 400 BAHT **Weight:** 10.0000 g. **Composition:** 0.9000 Gold .2893 oz. AGW **Ruler:** Rama IX Phra Maha Bhumithol Adulyadej **Subject:** 25th Anniversary - Reign of King Rama IX

Date	Mintage	F	VF	XF	Unc	BU
BE2514 (1971)	47,000	—	—	—	125	—

Y# 90 600 BAHT **Weight:** 15.0000 g. **Composition:** 0.9000 Gold .4340 oz. AGW **Ruler:** Rama IX Phra Maha Bhumithol Adulyadej **Subject:** Queen Sirikit 36th Birthday

Date	Mintage	F	VF	XF	Unc	BU
BE2511 (1968)	46,000	—	—	—	190	—

Y# 138 600 BAHT **Weight:** 14.9000 g. **Composition:** 0.9250 Silver .4432 oz. ASW **Ruler:** Rama IX Phra Maha Bhumithol Adulyadej **Subject:** Queen's Anniversary and F.A.O. Ceres Medal

Date	Mintage	F	VF	XF	Unc	BU
BE2523 (1980)	23,000	—	—	18.00	28.00	—

Y# 143 600 BAHT **Weight:** 14.9000 g. **Composition:** 0.9250 Silver .4432 oz. ASW **Ruler:** Rama IX Phra Maha Bhumithol Adulyadej **Subject:** Centennial - Birth of Rama VI

Date	Mintage	F	VF	XF	Unc	BU
BE2524 (1981)	19,000	—	—	15.00	25.00	—

Y# 147 600 BAHT **Weight:** 22.0000 g. **Composition:** 0.9250 Silver .6543 oz. ASW **Ruler:** Rama IX Phra Maha Bhumithol Adulyadej **Subject:** 35th Anniversary - Reign of King Rama IX

Date	Mintage	F	VF	XF	Unc	BU
BE2524 (1981)	15,000	—	—	20.00	30.00	—

Y# 150 600 BAHT **Weight:** 22.0000 g. **Composition:** 0.9250 Silver .6543 oz. ASW **Ruler:** Rama IX Phra Maha Bhumithol Adulyadej **Subject:** Bicentennial of Bangkok

Date	Mintage	F	VF	XF	Unc	BU
BE2525 (1982)	15,000	—	—	20.00	30.00	—

Y# 155 600 BAHT **Weight:** 22.0000 g. **Composition:** 0.9250 Silver .6543 oz. ASW **Ruler:** Rama IX Phra Maha Bhumithol Adulyadej **Subject:** 50th Birthday of Queen Sirikit

Date	Mintage	F	VF	XF	Unc	BU
BE2525 (1982)	3,895	—	—	28.00	55.00	—
BE2525 (1982) Proof	1,011	Value: 225				

Y# 164 600 BAHT **Weight:** 22.0000 g. **Composition:** 0.9250 Silver .6543 oz. ASW **Ruler:** Rama IX Phra Maha Bhumithol Adulyadej **Subject:** 100th Anniversary of Postage Stamps

Date	Mintage	F	VF	XF	Unc	BU
BE2526 (1983)	5,000	—	—	28.00	55.00	—
BE2526 (1983) Proof	1,400	Value: 165				

Y# 166 600 BAHT **Weight:** 22.0000 g. **Composition:** 0.9250 Silver .6543 oz. ASW **Ruler:** Rama IX Phra Maha Bhumithol Adulyadej **Subject:** 700th Anniversary of Thai Alphabet

Date	Mintage	F	VF	XF	Unc	BU
BE2526 (1983)	4,300	—	—	28.00	55.00	—
BE2526 (1983) Proof	1,000	Value: 200				

Y# 173 600 BAHT **Weight:** 22.0000 g. **Composition:** 0.9250 Silver .6543 oz. ASW **Ruler:** Rama IX Phra Maha Bhumithol Adulyadej **Subject:** 84th Birthday of Princess Mother

Date	Mintage	F	VF	XF	Unc	BU
BE2527 (1984)	3,530	—	—	28.00	45.00	—
BE2527 (1984) Proof	520	Value: 260				

Y# 193 600 BAHT **Weight:** 22.0000 g. **Composition:** 0.9250 Silver .6543 oz. ASW **Ruler:** Rama IX Phra Maha Bhumithol Adulyadej **Subject:** Princess Chulabhorn Awarded Einstein Medal **Note:** Similar to 10 Baht, Y#192.

Date	Mintage	F	VF	XF	Unc	BU
BE2529 (1986)	2,400	—	—	—	55.00	—
BE2529 (1986) Proof	212	Value: 225				

Y# 182 600 BAHT **Weight:** 22.0000 g. **Composition:** 0.9250 Silver .6543 oz. ASW **Ruler:** Rama IX Phra Maha Bhumithol Adulyadej **Subject:** 6th ASEAN Orchid Congress **Note:** Similar to 10 Baht, Y#181.

Date	Mintage	F	VF	XF	Unc	BU
BE2529 (1986)	5,000	—	—	—	45.00	—
BE2529 (1986) Proof	300	Value: 200				

Y# 229 600 BAHT **Weight:** 30.0000 g. **Composition:** 0.9250 Silver .8922 oz. ASW **Ruler:** Rama IX Phra Maha Bhumithol Adulyadej **Subject:** Asian Institute of Technology **Note:** Similar to 10 Baht, Y#190.

Date	Mintage	F	VF	XF	Unc	BU
BE2530 (1987)	2,700	—	—	—	40.00	—
BE2530 (1987) Proof	400	Value: 175				

Y# 199 600 BAHT **Weight:** 30.0000 g. **Composition:** 0.9250 Silver .8922 oz. ASW **Ruler:** Rama IX Phra Maha Bhumithol Adulyadej **Subject:** 60th Birthday - King Rama IX **Note:** Similar to 6000 Baht, Y#202.

Date	Mintage	F	VF	XF	Unc	BU
BE2530 (1987)	5,000	—	—	—	100	—
BE2530 (1987) Proof	750	Value: 350				

Y# 215 600 BAHT **Weight:** 30.0000 g. **Composition:** 0.9250 Silver .8922 oz. ASW **Ruler:** Rama IX Phra Maha Bhumithol Adulyadej **Subject:** 42nd Anniversary - Reign of King Rama IX **Note:** Similar to 10 Baht, Y#212.

Date	Mintage	F	VF	XF	Unc	BU
BE2531 (1988)	8,840	—	—	—	45.00	—
BE2531 (1988) Proof	1,110	Value: 175				

Y# 224 600 BAHT **Weight:** 30.0000 g. **Composition:** 0.9250 Silver .8922 oz. ASW **Ruler:** Rama IX Phra Maha Bhumithol Adulyadej **Subject:** Crown Prince's Birthday

Date	Mintage	F	VF	XF	Unc	BU
BE2531 (1988)	5,000	—	—	—	45.00	—
BE2531 (1988) Proof	1,000	Value: 180				

Y# 226 600 BAHT **Weight:** 30.0000 g. **Composition:** 0.9000 Silver .8682 oz. ASW **Ruler:** Rama IX Phra Maha Bhumithol Adulyadej **Subject:** 72nd Anniversary of Chulalongkorn University

Date	Mintage	F	VF	XF	Unc	BU
BE2532 (1989)	10,000	—	—	—	50.00	—

Y# 234 600 BAHT **Weight:** 30.0000 g. **Composition:** 0.9250 Silver .8922 oz. ASW **Ruler:** Rama IX Phra Maha Bhumithol Adulyadej **Subject:** 90th Birthday of Princess Mother

Date	Mintage	F	VF	XF	Unc	BU
BE2533 (1990)	20,000	—	—	—	32.50	—
BE2533 (1990) Proof	2,000	Value: 150				

Y# 245 600 BAHT **Weight:** 30.0000 g. **Composition:** 0.9250 Silver .8922 oz. ASW **Ruler:** Rama IX Phra Maha Bhumithol Adulyadej **Subject:** World Health Organization **Note:** Similar to 10 Baht, Y#244.

Date	Mintage	F	VF	XF	Unc	BU
BE2533 (1990)	25,000	—	—	—	32.50	—
BE2533 (1990) Proof	596	Value: 275				

Y# 239 600 BAHT **Weight:** 30.0000 g. **Composition:** 0.9000 Silver .8682 oz. ASW **Ruler:** Rama IX Phra Maha Bhumithol Adulyadej **Subject:** 36th Birthday of Princess Sirindhorn

Date	Mintage	F	VF	XF	Unc	BU
BE2534 (1991)	30,000	—	—	—	32.50	—
BE2534 (1991) Proof	2,583	Value: 135				

257 600 BAHT **Weight:** 30.0000 g. **Composition:**).9250 Silver .8922 oz. ASW **Ruler:** Rama IX Phra Maha 3humithol Adulyadej **Subject:** Princess Sirindhorn's Magsaysay Foundation Award

	Mintage	F	VF	XF	Unc	BU
534 (1991)	15,000	—	—	—	32.50	—
534 (1991) Proof	10,000	Value: 130				

250 600 BAHT **Weight:** 30.0000 g. **Composition:**).9250 Silver .8922 oz. ASW **Ruler:** Rama IX Phra Maha Bhumithol Adulyadej **Subject:** Centenary Celebration - Father of King Rama IX **Note:** Similar to 10 Baht, Y#249.

	Mintage	F	VF	XF	Unc	BU
535 (1992)	19,000	—	—	—	32.50	—
535 (1992) Proof	11,000	Value: 130				

264 600 BAHT **Weight:** 30.0000 g. **Composition:** 0.9250 Silver .8922 oz. ASW **Ruler:** Rama IX Phra Maha Bhumithol Adulyadej **Subject:** Queen's 60th Birthday **Note:** Similar to 10 Baht, Y#261.

	Mintage	F	VF	XF	Unc	BU
535 (1992)	25,000	—	—	—	32.50	—
535 (1992) Proof	3,500	Value: 125				

274 600 BAHT **Weight:** 30.0000 g. **Composition:** 0.9250 Silver .8922 oz. ASW **Ruler:** Rama IX Phra Maha Bhumithol Adulyadej **Subject:** 64th Birthday - King Rama IX **Note:** Similar to 10 Baht, Y#273.

	Mintage	F	VF	XF	Unc	BU
535 (1992)	10,000	—	—	—	35.00	—
535 (1992) Proof	511	Value: 320				

290 600 BAHT **Weight:** 30.0000 g. **Composition:** 0.9250 Silver .8922 oz. ASW **Ruler:** Rama IX Phra Maha Bhumithol Adulyadej **Subject:** 100th Anniversary of Rama VII **Note:** Similar to 10 Baht, Y#289.

	Mintage	F	VF	XF	Unc	BU
536 (1993)	12,000	—	—	—	35.00	—
536 (1993) Proof	1,000	Value: 185				

281 600 BAHT **Weight:** 30.0000 g. **Composition:** 0.9250 Silver .8922 oz. ASW **Ruler:** Rama IX Phra Maha Bhumithol Adulyadej **Subject:** Centennial of Thai Red Cross **Reverse:** Emblems

	Mintage	F	VF	XF	Unc	BU
536 (1993)	13,000	—	—	—	32.50	—

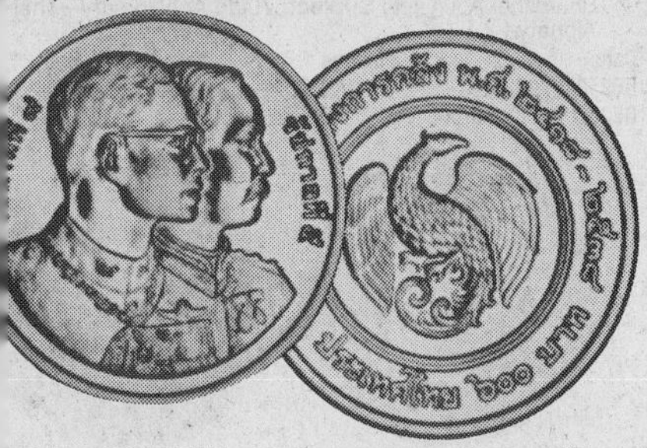

299 600 BAHT **Weight:** 22.1500 g. **Composition:** 0.9250 Silver .6587 oz. ASW **Ruler:** Rama IX Phra Maha Bhumithol Adulyadej **Subject:** 120th Anniversary - Ministry of Finance

	Mintage	F	VF	XF	Unc	B
538 (1995)	17,000	—	—	—	32.50	-
538 (1995) Proof	480	Value: 170				

Y# 301 600 BAHT **Weight:** 22.1500 g. **Composition:** 0.9250 Silver .6587 oz. ASW **Ruler:** Rama IX Phra Maha Bhumithol Adulyadej **Subject:** Ministry of Defense

Date	Mintage	F	VF	XF	Unc	BU
BE2538 (1995)	18,000	—	—	—	32.50	—
BE2538 (1995) Proof	2,960	Value: 125				

Y# 303 600 BAHT **Weight:** 22.1500 g. **Composition:** 0.9250 Silver .6587 oz. ASW **Ruler:** Rama IX Phra Maha Bhumithol Adulyadej **Subject:** Ministry of Foreign Affairs

Date	Mintage	F	VF	XF	Unc	BU
BE2538 (1995)	14,000	—	—	—	32.50	—
BE2538 (1995) Proof	16	—	—	—	—	—

Y# 305 600 BAHT **Weight:** 22.1500 g. **Composition:** 0.9250 Silver .6587 oz. ASW **Ruler:** Rama IX Phra Maha Bhumithol Adulyadej **Subject:** 72nd Birthday of Princess

Date	Mintage	F	VF	XF	Unc	BU
BE2538 (1995)	12,000	—	—	—	35.00	—
BE2538 (1995) Proof	600	Value: 165				

Y# 310 600 BAHT **Weight:** 22.0000 g. **Composition:** 0.9250 Silver .6543 oz. ASW **Ruler:** Rama IX Phra Maha Bhumithol Adulyadej **Subject:** 80th Anniversary - Department of Revenue

Date	F	VF	XF	Unc	BU
BE2538 (1995)	—	—	—	32.50	—

Y# 312 600 BAHT **Weight:** 22.0000 g. **Composition:** 0.9250 Silver .6543 oz. ASW **Ruler:** Rama IX Phra Maha Bhumithol Adulyadej **Subject:** 120th Anniversary - Audit Council

Date	F	VF	XF	Unc	BU
BE2538 (1995)	—	—	—	32.50	—

Y# 324 600 BAHT **Weight:** 30.0000 g. **Composition:** 0.9250 Silver .8922 oz. ASW **Ruler:** Rama IX Phra Maha Bhumithol Adulyadej **Subject:** 50th Anniversary - Reign of King Rama IX **Note:** Similar to 20 Baht, Y#321.1.

Date	F	VF	XF	Unc	BU
BE2539 (1996)	—	—	—	32.50	—
BE2539 (1996) Proof	—	Value: 125			

Y# 356 600 BAHT **Weight:** 22.1500 g. **Composition:** 0.9250 Silver .6587 oz. ASW **Ruler:** Rama IX Phra Maha Bhumithol Adulyadej **Subject:** King's 6th Cycle Birthday Anniversary **Obverse:** Portrait **Reverse:** Radiant arms **Edge:** Reeded **Size:** 35 mm.

Date	Mintage	F	VF	XF	Unc	BU
BE2542 (1999)	100,000	—	—	—	15.00	—
BE2542 (1999) Proof	30,000	Value: 30.00				

Y# 377 600 BAHT **Weight:** 22.1500 g. **Composition:** 0.9250 Silver .6587 oz. ASW **Ruler:** Rama IX Phra Maha Bhumithol Adulyadej **Subject:** King's 72nd Birthday **Obverse:** King and Rama I portraits **Reverse:** Two royal symbols **Edge:** Reeded **Size:** 35 mm.

Date	F	VF	XF	Unc	BU
BE2543(2000) Proof	—	Value: 125			

Y# 389 600 BAHT **Weight:** 22.1500 g. **Composition:** 0.9250 Silver 0.6587 oz. ASW **Ruler:** Rama IX Phra Maha Bhumithol Adulyadej **Subject:** King's 75th Birthday **Obverse:** King's portrait **Reverse:** Royal crown in radiant oval **Edge:** Reeded **Size:** 35 mm.

Date	F	VF	XF	Unc	BU
2545(2002)	—	—	—	25.00	—
2545(2002) Proof	—	Value: 35.00			

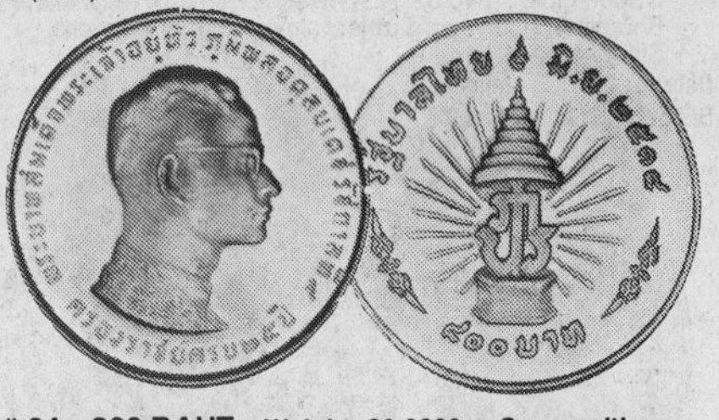

Y# 94 800 BAHT **Weight:** 20.0000 g. **Composition:** 0.9000 Gold .5787 oz. AGW **Ruler:** Rama IX Phra Maha Bhumithol Adulyadej **Subject:** 25th Anniversary - Reign of King Rama IX

Date	Mintage	F	VF	XF	Unc	BU
BE2514 (1971)	22,000	—	—	—	250	—

Y# 200 1500 BAHT **Weight:** 3.7500 g. **Composition:** 0.9000 Gold .1085 oz. AGW **Ruler:** Rama IX Phra Maha Bhumithol Adulyadej **Subject:** 60th Birthday - King Rama IX

Date	Mintage	F	VF	XF	Unc	BU
BE2530 (1987)	5,000	—	—	—	80.00	—
BE2530 (1987) Proof	400	Value: 170				

Y# 216 1500 BAHT **Weight:** 3.7500 g. **Composition:** 0.9000 Gold .1085 oz. AGW **Ruler:** Rama IX Phra Maha Bhumithol Adulyadej **Subject:** 42nd Anniversary - Reign of King Rama IX

Date	Mintage	F	VF	XF	Unc	BU
BE2531 (1988)	11,000	—	—	—	75.00	—
BE2531 (1988) Proof	995	Value: 150				

Y# 265 1500 BAHT **Weight:** 3.7500 g. **Composition:** 0.9000 Gold .1085 oz. AGW **Ruler:** Rama IX Phra Maha Bhumithol Adulyadej **Subject:** Queen's 60th Birthday **Obverse:** Queen's portrait **Reverse:** Crowned monogram **Note:** Similar to 10 Baht, Y#261.

Date	Mintage	F	VF	XF	Unc	BU
BE2535 (1992)	10,000	—	—	—	75.00	—
BE2535 (1992) Proof	1,500	Value: 140				

Y# 380 2000 BAHT **Weight:** 6.2200 g. **Composition:** 0.9990 Gold 0.1998 oz. AGW **Subject:** UNICEF **Obverse:** Bust of King facing half left **Reverse:** Girl with Thai desk **Edge:** Reeded **Size:** 22 mm.

Date	Mintage	F	VF	XF	Unc	BU
BE2540 (1997) Proof	10,000	Value: 125				

Y# 119 2500 BAHT **Weight:** 15.0000 g. **Composition:** 0.9000 Gold .4340 oz. AGW **Ruler:** Rama IX Phra Maha Bhumithol Adulyadej **Subject:** Crown Prince Vajiralongkorn and Princess Soamsawali Wedding

Date	Mintage	F	VF	XF	Unc	BU
BE2520 (1977)	20,000	—	—	—	225	—

Y# 126 2500 BAHT **Weight:** 15.0000 g. **Composition:** 0.9000 Gold .4340 oz. AGW **Ruler:** Rama IX Phra Maha Bhumithol Adulyadej **Subject:** Investiture of Princess Sirindhorn

Date	Mintage	F	VF	XF	Unc	BU
BE2520 (1977)	5,000	—	—	—	300	—

Y# 170 2500 BAHT **Weight:** 15.0000 g. **Composition:** 0.9000 Gold .4340 oz. AGW **Ruler:** Rama IX Phra Maha Bhumithol Adulyadej **Series:** International Year of Disabled Persons

Date	Mintage	F	VF	XF	Unc	BU
BE2526 (1983)	92	—	—	—	1,400	—
BE2526 (1983) Proof	793	Value: 1,250				

Y# 207 2500 BAHT **Weight:** 15.9800 g. **Composition:** 0.9000 Gold .4625 oz. AGW **Ruler:** Rama IX Phra Maha Bhumithol Adulyadej **Series:** 25th Anniversary of World Wildlife Fund **Reverse:** Asian Elephant

Date	Mintage	F	VF	XF	Unc	BU
BE2530 (1987) Proof	Est. 5,000	Value: 350				

Y# 325 2500 BAHT **Weight:** 3.7500 g. **Composition:** 0.9000 Gold .1085 oz. AGW **Ruler:** Rama IX Phra Maha Bhumithol Adulyadej **Subject:** 50th Anniversary - Reign of King Rama IX **Obverse:** King's portrait **Reverse:** King's emblem supported by elephants **Note:** Similar to 20 Baht, Y#321.1.

Date	F	VF	XF	Unc	BU
BE2539 (1996)	—	—	—	75.00	—
BE2539 (1996) Proof	— Value: 135				

Y# 369 2500 BAHT **Weight:** 155.5175 g. **Composition:** 0.9999 Gold 5.0000 oz. AGW **Ruler:** Rama IX Phra Maha Bhumithol Adulyadej **Subject:** Year of the Dragon **Obverse:** King's portrait **Reverse:** 2 dragons with multicolor hologram pearl **Edge:** Reeded **Size:** 55 mm.

Date	Mintage	F	VF	XF	Unc	BU
BE2543 (2000)	500	—	—	—	3,300	—
In sets only						

Y# 129 3000 BAHT **Weight:** 15.0000 g. **Composition:** 0.9000 Gold .4340 oz. AGW **Ruler:** Rama IX Phra Maha Bhumithol Adulyadej **Subject:** Graduation of Crown Prince Vijiralongkorn

Date	Mintage	F	VF	XF	Unc	BU
BE2521 (1978)	10,000	—	—	—	200	—

Y# 201 3000 BAHT **Weight:** 7.5000 g. **Composition:** 0.9000 Gold .2170 oz. AGW **Ruler:** Rama IX Phra Maha Bhumithol Adulyadej **Subject:** 60th Birthday - King Rama IX

Date	Mintage	F	VF	XF	Unc	BU
BE2530 (1987)	3,000	—	—	—	150	—
BE2530 (1987) Proof	400	Value: 260				

Y# 217 3000 BAHT **Weight:** 7.5000 g. **Composition:** 0.9000 Gold .2170 oz. AGW **Ruler:** Rama IX Phra Maha Bhumithol Adulyadej **Subject:** 42nd Anniversary - Reign of King Rama IX

Date	Mintage	F	VF	XF	Unc	BU
BE2531 (1988)	7,904	—	—	—	175	—
BE2531 (1988) Proof	780	Value: 320				

Y# 266 3000 BAHT **Weight:** 7.5000 g. **Composition:** 0.9000 Gold .2170 oz. AGW **Ruler:** Rama IX Phra Maha Bhumithol Adulyadej **Subject:** Queen's 60th Birthday **Obverse:** Queen's portrait **Reverse:** Crowned monogram **Note:** Similar to 10 Baht, Y#261.

Date	Mintage	F	VF	XF	Unc	BU
BE2535 (1992)	7,000	—	—	—	175	—
BE2535 (1992) Proof	1,100	Value: 330				

Y# 326 3000 BAHT **Weight:** 7.5000 g. **Composition:** 0.9000 Gold .2170 oz. AGW **Ruler:** Rama IX Phra Maha Bhumithol Adulyadej **Subject:** 50th Anniversary - Reign of King Rama IX **Obverse:** King's portrait **Reverse:** King's emblem supported by elephants **Note:** Similar to 20 Baht, Y#321.1.

Date	F	VF	XF	Unc	BU
BE2539 (1996)	—	—	—	185	—
BE2539 (1996) Proof	— Value: 325				

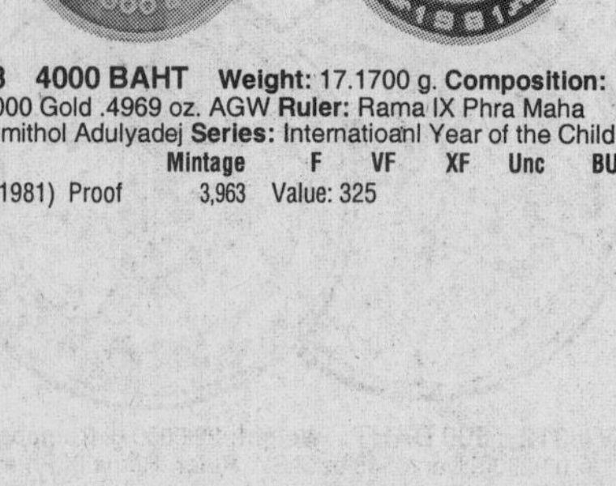

Y# 153 4000 BAHT **Weight:** 17.1700 g. **Composition:** 0.9000 Gold .4969 oz. AGW **Ruler:** Rama IX Phra Maha Bhumithol Adulyadej **Series:** Internatioanl Year of the Child

Date	Mintage	F	VF	XF	Unc	BU
BE2524 (1981) Proof	3,963	Value: 325				

Y# 104 5000 BAHT **Weight:** 33.4370 g. **Composition:** 0.9000 Gold .9676 oz. AGW **Ruler:** Rama IX Phra Maha Bhumithol Adulyadej **Series:** Conservation **Subject:** White-eyed River Martin

Date	Mintage	F	VF	XF	Unc	BU
BE2517 (1974)	2,602	—	—	—	650	—
BE2517 (1974) Proof	623	Value: 1,500				

Y# 122 5000 BAHT **Weight:** 30.0000 g. **Composition:** 0.9000 Gold .8681 oz. AGW **Ruler:** Rama IX Phra Maha Bhumithol Adulyadej **Subject:** 50th Birthday - King Rama IX

Date	Mintage	F	VF	XF	Unc	BU
BE2520 (1977)	6,400	—	—	—	400	—

Y# 156 6000 BAHT **Weight:** 15.0000 g. **Composition:** 0.9000 Gold .4341 oz. AGW **Ruler:** Rama IX Phra Maha Bhumithol Adulyadej **Subject:** 50th Birthday - Queen Sirikit

Date	Mintage	F	VF	XF	Unc	Bu
BE2525 (1982)	1,471	—	—	—	425	—
BE2525 (1982) Proof	99	Value: 4,000				

Y# 167 6000 BAHT **Weight:** 15.0000 g. **Composition:** 0.9000 Gold .4341 oz. AGW **Ruler:** Rama IX Phra Maha Bhumithol Adulyadej **Subject:** 700th Anniversary - Thai Alphabet

Date	Mintage	F	VF	XF	Unc	Bi
BE2526 (1983)	700	—	—	—	325	—
BE2526 (1983) Proof	235	Value: 600				

Y# 174 6000 BAHT **Weight:** 15.0000 g. **Compositio** 0.9000 Gold .4341 oz. AGW **Ruler:** Rama IX Phra Maha Bhumithol Adulyadej **Subject:** 84th Birthday - Princess Mother

Date	Mintage	F	VF	XF	Unc
BE2527 (1984)	835	—	—	—	350
BE2527 (1984) Proof	246	Value: 650			

02 6000 BAHT **Weight:** 15.0000 g. **Composition:** .9000 Gold .4341 oz. AGW **Ruler:** Rama IX Phra Maha humithol Adulyadej **Subject:** 60th Birthday - King Rama IX

Date	Mintage	F	VF	XF	Unc	BU
30 (1987)	2,000	—	—	—	275	—
30 (1987) Proof	350	Value: 425				

47 6000 BAHT **Weight:** 15.0000 g. **Composition:** .9000 Gold .4341 oz. AGW **Ruler:** Rama IX Phra Maha Bhumithol Adulyadej **Subject:** Asian Institute of Technology

Date	Mintage	F	VF	XF	Unc	BU
30 (1987)	700	—	—	—	350	—
30 (1987) Proof	100	Value: 650				

218 6000 BAHT **Weight:** 15.0000 g. **Composition:** 0.9000 Gold .4341 oz. AGW **Ruler:** Rama IX Phra Maha Bhumithol Adulyadej **Subject:** 42nd Anniversary - Reign of King Rama IX

Date	Mintage	F	VF	XF	Unc	BU
31 (1988)	6,067	—	—	—	300	—
31 (1988) Proof	670	Value: 500				

246 6000 BAHT **Weight:** 15.0000 g. **Composition:** 0.9000 Gold .4341 oz. AGW **Ruler:** Rama IX Phra Maha Bhumithol Adulyadej **Subject:** World Health Organization

Date	Mintage	F	VF	XF	Unc	BU
34 (1991)	5,000	—	—	—	350	—
34 (1991) Proof	591	Value: 600				

258 6000 BAHT **Weight:** 15.0000 g. **Composition:** 0.9000 Gold .4341 oz. AGW **Ruler:** Rama IX Phra Maha Bhumithol Adulyadej **Subject:** Princess Sirindhorn's Magsaysay Foundation Award **Obverse:** Princess seated with children **Reverse:** Obverse of medal above larger reverse with inscription

Date	Mintage	F	VF	XF	Unc	BU
535 (1992)	1,600	—	—	—	300	—
535 (1992) Proof	500	Value: 600				

267 6000 BAHT **Weight:** 15.0000 g. **Composition:** 0.9000 Gold .4341 oz. AGW **Ruler:** Rama IX Phra Maha Bhumithol Adulyadej **Subject:** Queen's 60th Birthday **Obverse:** Queen's portrait **Reverse:** Crowned monogram **Note:** Similar to 10 Baht, Y#261.

Date	Mintage	F	VF	XF	Unc	BU
535 (1992)	7,000	—	—	—	300	—
535 (1992) Proof	1,200	Value: 450				

275 6000 BAHT **Weight:** 15.0000 g. **Composition:** 0.9000 Gold .4341 oz. AGW **Ruler:** Rama IX Phra Maha Bhumithol Adulyadej **Subject:** 64th Birthday - King Rama IX **Obverse:** Portrait of Rama IX and Rama IV left **Reverse:** Crowned monograms of Rama IX and Rama IV **Note:** Similar to 10 Baht, Y#273.

Date	Mintage	F	VF	XF	Unc	BU
535 (1992)	3,000	—	—	—	300	—
535 (1992) Proof	500	Value: 600				

291 6000 BAHT **Weight:** 15.0000 g. **Composition:** 0.9000 Gold .4341 oz. AGW **Ruler:** Rama IX Phra Maha Bhumithol Adulyadej **Subject:** 100th Anniversary of Rama VII **Obverse:** Portrait left **Reverse:** Royal crown and accouterments

Date	Mintage	F	VF	XF	Unc	BU
536 (1993)	2,484	—	—	—	300	—
536 (1993) Proof	300	Value: 600				

327 6000 BAHT **Weight:** 15.0000 g. **Composition:** 0.9000 Gold .4341 oz. AGW **Ruler:** Rama IX Phra Maha Bhumithol Adulyadej **Subject:** King's 50th Year of Reign **Obverse:** King's portrait **Reverse:** King's emblem supported by elephants **Note:** Similar to 20 Baht, Y#321.1.

Date	F	VF	XF	Unc	BU
539 (1996)	—	—	—	300	—
539 (1996) Proof	—	Value: 550			

Y# 337 6000 BAHT **Weight:** 15.0000 g. **Composition:** 0.9000 Gold .4341 oz. AGW **Ruler:** Rama IX Phra Maha Bhumithol Adulyadej **Series:** F.A.O. **Subject:** 50th Anniversary - Reign of King Rama IX and World Food Summit **Obverse:** King's portrait **Reverse:** King planting seedlings before adoring crowd **Note:** Similar to 20 Baht, Y#335.

Date	F	VF	XF	Unc	BU
BE2539 (1996)	—	—	—	300	—
BE2539 (1996) Proof	—	Value: 550			

Y# 370 6000 BAHT **Weight:** 15.0000 g. **Composition:** 0.9000 Gold .4341 oz. AGW **Ruler:** Rama IX Phra Maha Bhumithol Adulyadej **Subject:** King's 72nd Birthday **Obverse:** King's portrait **Reverse:** Crowned emblem

Date	Mintage	F	VF	XF	Unc	BU
BE2542 (1999)	20,000	—	—	—	150	—
BE2542 (1999) Proof	10,000	Value: 300				

Y# 378 6000 BAHT **Weight:** 15.0000 g. **Composition:** 0.9000 Gold .4340 oz. AGW **Ruler:** Rama IX Phra Maha Bhumithol Adulyadej **Subject:** King's 72nd Birthday **Obverse:** King and Rama I portraits **Reverse:** Two royal symbols **Edge:** Reeded **Size:** 26 mm.

Date	F	VF	XF	Unc	BU
BE2543(2000) Proof	—	Value: 300			

Y# 390 7500 BAHT **Weight:** 15.0000 g. **Composition:** 0.9000 Gold 0.434 oz. AGW **Ruler:** Rama IX Phra Maha Bhumithol Adulyadej **Subject:** King's 75th Birthday **Obverse:** King's portrait **Reverse:** Royal crown in radiant oval **Edge:** Reeded **Size:** 26 mm.

Date	F	VF	XF	Unc	BU
2545(2002)	—	—	—	200	—
2545(2002) Proof	—	Value: 300			

Y# 139 9000 BAHT **Weight:** 12.0000 g. **Composition:** 0.9000 Gold .3472 oz. AGW **Ruler:** Rama IX Phra Maha Bhumithol Adulyadej **Series:** F.A.O. Ceres Medal **Subject:** Queen's Anniversary **Note:** Similar to 5 Baht, Y#137.

Date	Mintage	F	VF	XF	Unc	BU
BE2523 (1980)	3,900	—	—	—	375	—

Y# A143 9000 BAHT **Weight:** 12.0000 g. **Composition:** 0.9000 Gold .3472 oz. AGW **Ruler:** Rama IX Phra Maha Bhumithol Adulyadej **Subject:** Centennial - Birth of King Rama VI

Date	Mintage	F	VF	XF	Unc	BU
BE2524 (1981)	2,600	—	—	—	375	—

Y# 148 9000 BAHT **Weight:** 15.0000 g. **Composition:** 0.9000 Gold .4340 oz. AGW **Ruler:** Rama IX Phra Maha Bhumithol Adulyadej **Subject:** King Rama IX Anniversary of Reign

Date	Mintage	F	VF	XF	Unc	BU
BE2524 (1981)	4,000	—	—	—	375	—

Y# 151 9000 BAHT **Weight:** 15.0000 g. **Composition:** 0.9000 Gold .4340 oz. AGW **Ruler:** Rama IX Phra Maha Bhumithol Adulyadej **Subject:** Bicentennial of Bangkok

Date	Mintage	F	VF	XF	Unc	BU
BE2525 (1982)	3,290	—	—	—	375	—

OCCUPATION COINAGE

These coins were to be circulated in the four occupied provinces of Malaya during World War II. They were not put into circulation there but were later used in Japanese military service clubs in Bangkok before Japan's surrender in 1945.

KM# 5 SEN **Composition:** Tin **Ruler:** Rama IX Phra Maha Bhumithol Adulyadej

Date	F	VF	XF	Unc	BU
BE2486	—	—	—	2,250	—

KM# 10 5 SEN **Composition:** Tin **Ruler:** Rama IX Phra Maha Bhumithol Adulyadej

Date	F	VF	XF	Unc	BU
BE2486	—	—	—	2,250	—

KM# 15 10 SEN **Composition:** Tin **Ruler:** Rama IX Phra Maha Bhumithol Adulyadej

Date	F	VF	XF	Unc	BU
BE2486	—	—	1,000	1,500	—

BULLION COINAGE

In 1943, the government of Thailand made an internal loan by virtue of the Royal Act of Internal Loan related regulation of the Ministry of Finance, both dated 17th May, 1943.

Eight years later another Regulation of the Ministry of Finance dated 11th June, 1951 related to the actual redemption of the loan above mentioned was proclaimed with the following effect: Bond holders have the choice to be paid either in gold coins or gold bars or in other forms, all of which should bear the Garuda emblem and the specific inscription as to its weight and gold purity.

KM# 1 50 BAHT **Weight:** 8.6930 g. **Composition:** 0.9950 Gold .2781 oz. AGW **Ruler:** Rama IX Phra Maha Bhumithol Adulyadej

Date	F	VF	XF	Unc	BU
ND(1951)	—	175	210	275	—

KM# 2 100 BAHT **Weight:** 17.3870 g. **Composition:** 0.9950 Gold .5562 oz. AGW **Ruler:** Rama IX Phra Maha Bhumithol Adulyadej

Date	F	VF	XF	Unc	BU
ND(1951)	—	350	420	575	—

KM# 3 1000 BAHT **Weight:** 173.8790 g. **Composition:** 0.9950 Gold 5.5620 oz. AGW **Ruler:** Rama IX Phra Maha Bhumithol Adulyadej

Date	F	VF	XF	Unc	BU
ND(1951)	—	6,000	9,000	14,000	—

ESSAIS

KM#	Date	Mintage	Identification	Mkt Val
E1	RS127	—	Baht. Silver. Y#39.	23,000

KM#	Date	Mintage	Identification	Mkt Val

KM#	Date	Mintage	Identification	Mkt Val
E2	RS128	—	1/4 Baht. Silver.	10,000
E3	RS129	—	1/2 Baht. Silver.	—

Note: Struck at the Paris MInt. Taisei-Baldwin-Gillio Hong Kong sale 25 9-97 BU realized $23,000. Spink-Taisei Singapore Auction 14 3-93 Unc set of E 1, 2 and 2 realized $190,000

PATTERNS

Including off metal strikes

KM#	Date	Mintage	Identification	Mkt Val
Pn47	RS124	—	2 Att. Copper. Facing bust.	300
Pn48	RS126	—	Baht. Silver. Y#39. Vishnu and Garuda.	6,000
Pn49	RS127	—	Satang. Nickel. Y#35.	—
Pn50	RS127	—	Satang. Gold. Y#35a.	6,000
Pn51	RS127	—	5 Satang. Gold. Y#36a.	7,000
Pn52	RS127	—	10 Satang. Gold. Y#37a.	8,000
Pn53	RS129	—	Baht. Silver. Y#39.	—
PnA54	BE2488	—	Baht. Tin. 10.0000 g. 30 mm. "Child's head" of King Rama VIII (Ananda Mahidol) facing left.. National arms..	—
Pn54	BE2489	—	Baht. Tin. Y#67.	—
Pn55	BE2505	—	Baht. Copper-Nickel. Y#84.	—
Pn56	BE2515	—	5 Baht. Copper-Nickel. Small bust, Y#28.	—
Pn57	BE2515	—	5 Baht. Copper-Nickel. Royal parasol.	—
Pn58	BE2515	—	5 Baht. Copper-Nickel. Different bust.	—

PIEFORTS

KM#	Date	Mintage	Identification	Mkt Val
P1	BE2524	126	200 Baht. (No Composition). I.Y.O.C.	850
P2	BE2524	61	4000 Baht. (No Composition). I.Y.O.C.	2,200
P3	BE2526	500	250 Baht. 0.9250 Silver. I.Y.D.P.	1,250
P4	BE2526	—	2500 Baht. Gold. I.Y.D.P.	6,500
P5	BE2540	—	100 Baht. 0.9250 Silver. 30.0000 g. WWF Tiger.	75.00
P6	BE2541	—	200 Baht. 0.9250 Silver. 46.3600 g. WWF Tigers.	110
P7	BE2541	—	200 Baht. 0.9250 Silver. 46.3600 g. WWF Elephants.	125

MINT SETS

KM#	Date	Mintage	Identification	Issue Price	Mkt Val
MS13	Mixed (34)	—	Two each Y#57, 70, 72-73, 78, 78a, 79, 79a, 80-87, 91	—	60.00
MS14	Mixed (29)	—	Y#86 plus two each Y#57, 68, 73, 78, 78a, 79, 79a, 80-85, 87	—	35.00
MS2	Mixed (32)	—	Two each Y#57, 70, 72, 73, 78a, 78-87, 91	22.00	45.00
MS3	Mixed (30)	100,000	Two each Y#60, 70, 72, 73, 78, 78a, 79, 79a, 80-86	20.00	30.00
MS4	Mixed (10)	—	Y#70, 72, 73, 78, 78a, 79, 79a, 80-82	—	12.00
MS5	Mixed (10)	—	Y#70, 78, 78a, 78b, 79a, 79b, 79d, 80, 81, 82	—	12.00
MS6	Mixed (8)	—	Y#83, 85-87, 91, 92, 95, 97	11.00	35.00
MS7	1975 (2)	—	Y#102-103	32.50	70.00
MS8	1988 (7)	—	Y#183, 185-187, 203, 208-209	—	3.50
MS9	1991 (8)	—	Y#183, 186-187, 203, 208-209, 219, 227	4.00	10.00
MS10	1992 (8)	—	Y#183, 186-187, 203, 208-209, 219, 227	—	10.00
MS11	1993 (8)	—	Y#183, 186-187, 203, 208-209, 219, 227	—	10.00
MS12	1994 (8)	—	Y#183, 186-187, 203, 208-209, 219, 227	—	10.00

PROOF SETS

KM#	Date	Mintage	Identification	Issue Price	Mkt Val
PS1	1974 (2)	—	Y#102a-103a	50.00	160
PS2	2000 (3)	3,500	Y#363-365	115	115
PS3	2000 (5)	500	Y#363-365, 367, 369	3,480	3,650
PS4	2000 (2)	1,800	Y#366, 368	446	450

TIBET

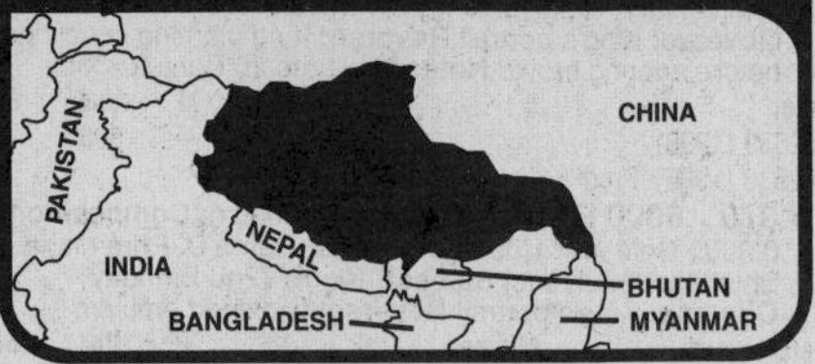

Tibet, an autonomous region of China located in central Asia between the Himalayan and Kunlun Mts. has an area of 471,660 sq. mi. (1,221,599 sq. km.) and a population of*1.9 million. Capital: Lhasa. The economy is based on agriculture and livestock raising. Wool, livestock, salt and hides are exported.

Lamaism, a form of Buddhism, developed in Tibet in the 8th century. From that time until the 1900s, the Tibetan rulers virtually isolated the country from the outside world. The British in India achieved some influence in the early 20th century. British troops were sent with the Young Husband mission to extend trade in the north of India in December 1903; leaving during September 1904. The 13th Dalai Lama had fled to Urga where he remained until 1907. In April 1905 a revolt broke out and spread through southwestern Szechuan and northwestern Yunnan. Chao Erh-feng was appointed to subdue this rebellion and entered Lhasa in January 1910 with 2,000 troops. The Dalai Lama fled to India until he returned in June 1912., The British encouraged Tibet to declare its independence from China in 1913. The Communist revolution in China marked a new era in Tibetan history. Chinese Communist troops invaded Tibet in Oct., 1950. After a token resistance, Tibet signed an agreement with China in which China recognized the spiritual and temporal leadership of the Dalai Lama, and Tibet recognized the suzeraInty of China. In 1959, a nationwide revolt triggered by Communist-initiated land reform broke out. The revolt was ruthlessly crushed. The dalai lama fled to India, and on Sept. 1,1965, the Chinese made Tibet an autonomous region of China.

The first coins to circulate in Tibet were those of neighboring Nepal from about 1570. Shortly after 1720, the Nepalese government began striking specific issues for use in Tibet. These coins had a lower silver content than those struck for use in Nepal and were exchanged with the Tibetans for an equal weight in silver bullion. Around 1763 the Tibetans struck their own coins for the first time in history. The number of coins struck at that time must have been very small. Larger quantities of coins were struck by the Tibetan government mint, which opened in 1791 with the permission of the Chinese. Operations of this mint however were suspended two years later. The Chinese opened a second mint in Lhasa in 1792. It produced a coinage until 1836. Shortly thereafter, the Tibetan mint was reopened and the government of Tibet continued to strike coins until 1953.

DATING

Based on the Tibetan calendar, Tibetan coins are dated by the cycle which contains 60 years. To calculate the western date use the following formula: Number of cycles -1, x 60 + number of years + 1026.Example 15th cycle 25th year = 1891 AD. Example: 15th cycle, 25th year 15 - 1 x 60 + 25 + 1026 = 1891AD.

13/30 = 1776	14/30 = 1836	15/30 = 1896
13/40 = 1786	14/40 = 1846	15/40 = 1906
13/50 = 1796	14/50 = 1856	15/50 = 1916
13/60 = 1806	14/60 = 1866	15/60 = 1926
14/10 = 1816	15/10 = 1876	16/10 = 1936
14/20 = 1826	15/20 = 1886	16/20 = 1946

Certain Sino-Tibetan issues are dated in the year of reign of the Emperor of China.

MONETARY SYSTEM

15 Skar = 1-1/2 Sho = 1 Tangka

10 Sho = 1 Srang

TANGKA

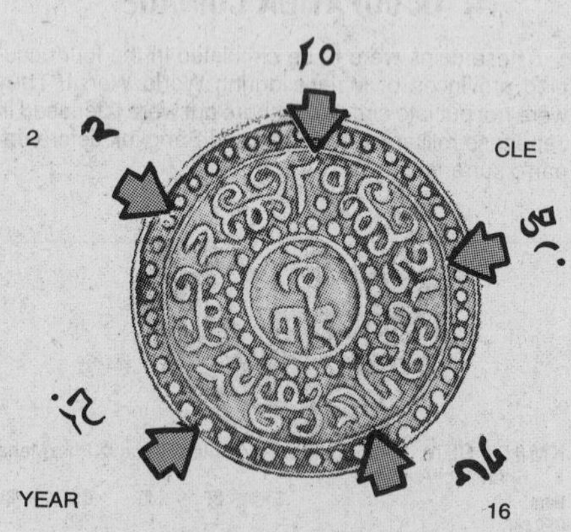

16(th)CYCLE 2(nd)YEAR = 1928AD

16(th) CYCLE 7(th) YEAR = 1933AD

NUMERALS

1	༡	གཅིག		
2	༢	གཉིས		
3	༣	གསུམ		
4	༤	བཞི		
5	༥	ལྔ		
6	༦	དྲུག		
7	༧	བདུན		
8	༨	བརྒྱད		
9	༩	དགུ		
10	༡༠	བཅུ	or	བཅུ་ཐམ་པ
11	༡༡	བཅུག	or	བཅུ་གཅིག
12	༡༢	བཅུས	or	བཅུ་གཉིས
13	༡༣	བཅུ་མ	or	བཅུ་གསུམ
14	༡༤	བཅུ་བཞི		
15	༡༥	བཅོ་ལྔ		
16	༡༦	བཅུ་དྲུག		
17	༡༧	བཅུ་བདུན		
18	༡༨	བཅོ་བརྒྱད		
19	༡༩	བཅུ་དགུ		
20	༢༠	ཉི་ཤུ		
21	༢༡	ཉི་ཤུ་རྩ་གཅིག	or	ཉེར་གཅིག
22	༢༢	ཉེར་གཉིས		
23	༢༣	ཉེར་གསུམ		
24	༢༤	ཉེར་བཞི		
25	༢༥	ཉེར་ལྔ		
26	༢༦	ཉེར་དྲུག		
27	༢༧	ཉེར་བདུན		
28	༢༨	ཉེར་བརྒྱད		

KINGDOM

SINO-TIBETAN COINAGE

Y# A4 1/2 SKAR Composition: Copper **Ruler:** Hsüan-t'ung **Note:** Weight varies. 3.10-3.60 grams.

Date	Good	VG	F	VF	XF
ND(1910)	300	400	500	600	—

Y# 4 SKAR Composition: Copper **Ruler:** Hsüan-t'ung **Rev. Inscription:** Hsüan-t'ung.... **Note:** Weight varies. 5.40-6.60 grams. Varieties exist. Modern counterfeits exist.

Date	Good	VG	F	VF	XF
ND(1910)	90.00	150	250	400	—

Y# 5 SHO Composition: Silver **Ruler:** Hsüan-t'ung **Rev. Inscription:** Hsüan-t'ung.... **Note:** 3.30-4.10 grams. Varieties exist, one having the inner circle of dots, on the Chinese side, connected by lines. Modern counterfeits exist.

Date	Good	VG	F	VF	XF
ND(1910)	20.00	30.00	50.00	80.00	—

Y# 6 2 SHO Composition: Silver **Ruler:** Hsüan-t'ung **Rev. Inscription:** Hsüan-t'ung.... **Note:** Weight varies. 5.20-8.40 grams. Varieties with different dragon claws and lotus exist. Modern counterfeits exist.

Date	Good	VG	F	VF	XF
ND(1910)	25.00	40.00	80.00	150	—

TANGKA COINAGE

Kong-par Tangka

The legend of this so called Rajana Tangka appears to be in ornamental Lansa script and has yet to be deciphered. The type is a copy of the Nepalese debased tangka of Pretap Simha. Struck unofficially by Nepalese traders in Tibet between 1880 and 1912, it was legal tender, due to an edict issued in 1881 ordering that no distinction be made between false and genuine coins. The Tangka, C#27 was cut in parts of 3, 4, and 5 petals to make change and the resulting fractions are occasionally encountered.

C# 27.1 TANGKA Composition: Silver **Obverse:** Crescent and moon at top. **Note:** Weight varies 4.60-5.40 grams. Previous #C27.

Date	Good	VG	F	VF	XF
BE15-40 (1906)	8.00	15.00	25.00	40.00	—

Note: In addition to the meaningful dated, the following meaningless ones exist: 13-16, 13-31, 13-92, 16-16, 16-61, 16-64, 16-69, 16-92, 16-93, 92-34, 92-39, 96-61 (sixes may be reversed threes and nines reversed ones). These are of billon, varying from 3.9 to 4.7 grams.

C# 27.2 TANGKA Composition: Silver **Obverse:** Crescent and swastika at top. **Note:** Weight varies 4.60-5.40 grams.

Date	Good	VG	F	VF	XF
BE15-46 (1912)	28.00	40.00	60.00	90.00	—

GA-DEN TANGKA COINAGE

The Ga-den Tangkas are among the most common and perhaps most beautiful of all Tibetan coins. The obverse shows a stylized Lotus flower within a circle surrounded by the 8 Buddhist lucky symbols in radiating petals. The reverse shows an 8-petalled wheel (flower) within a star surrounded by a Tibetan inscription (reading Ga-den Palace, happy and victorious in all directions), which is broken up into 8 oval frames. Compass directions indicate the location of the Buddhist emblems.

Numbers for Obverse Types A & B

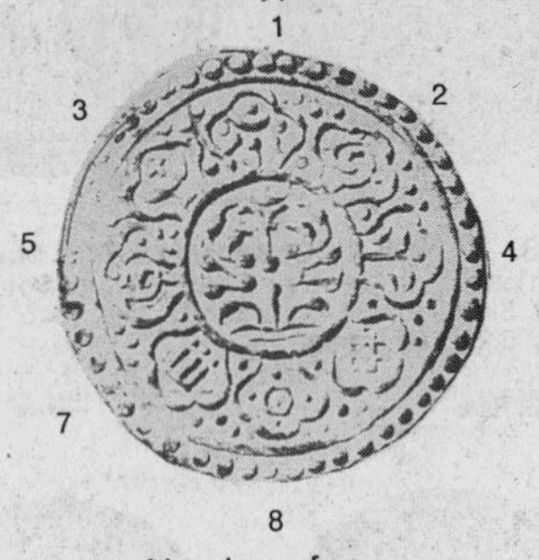

Numbers for Obverse Types C thru H

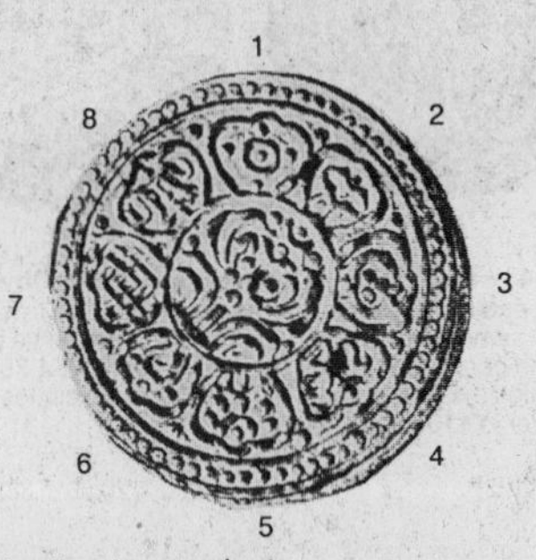

1. Umbrella of sovereignty.
2. Two golden fish of good fortune.
3. Amphora of ambrosia.
4. Lotus.
5. Conch shell.
6. Emblem of endless birth.
7. Banner of victory.
8. Wheel of empire.

Reverse - All Types

དགའ་	dGa'	"Ga-"
ལྡན་	lDan	"den"
ཕོ་	Pho	Po-
བྲང་	Braṅ	dang
ཕྱོགས་	Phyogs	Tschog-
ལས་	Las	le
རྣམ་	rNam	Nam-
རྒྱལ་	rGyal	gyel

Based on the ornamentation in the outer angles between the petals on both sides of the coin, the Ga-Den Tangkas can be differentiated in the following 8 types, A-H.

Type	Outer Obv.	Water-line	Outer Rev.	Rev. Ctr.
A	∵	None	〰	Pellet
B	∵	2 lines	〰	3 Crescents
C	∵	1 line	〰	2 Crescents
D	∵	1 line	∵	2 Crescents
E	〰	1 line	∵	2 Crescents
F	•	1 line	∵	2 Crescents
G	None	1 line	None	2 Crescents
H	•	1 line	•	3 Crescents

Within these types, changes in the order, design, and style of the 8 lucky signs or significant errors constitute subtypes. The sutypes appearing in this catalog are not the only ones. Some subtypes show a wide range of styles and die varieties. Weights given include 95 percent of the indicated types.

Error strikes with muled reverses exist. Specimens of Types D, E, and F with lumps are known, reportedly containing gold, probably used by high lamas in their offerings.

Type E

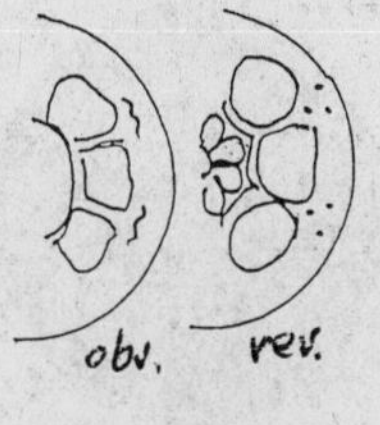

Obverse has wavy water-line in outer angles. New style lotus without three small leaves to left and right. Reverse has three dots in outer angles, wheel with spokes.

Y# E13.1 TANGKA Composition: Silver **Obverse:** Dot to left and right of lotus. **Note:** Weight varies 4.60-4.80 grams. Previous Y#13.4.

Date	VG	F	VF	XF	Unc
ND(ca.1899-1907)	3.00	4.00	7.00	12.00	—

Y# E13.2 TANGKA Composition: Silver **Obverse:** Similar to Y#E13.1, but machine struck

Date	Good	VG	F	VF	XF
ND(ca.1899-1907)	150	250	400	600	—

Y# E13.3 TANGKA Composition: Silver **Obverse:** Four dots (NE), one dot (E) **Note:** Weight varies: 3.80-5.70 grams. Similar to Y#E13.1 but obverse emblems rotated by one position clockwise (error).

Date	Good	VG	F	VF	XF
ND(ca.1899-1907)	75.00	100	150	200	—

Y# E13.4 TANGKA Weight: 3.8000 g. **Composition:** Silver **Obverse:** 7.5-8.0 millimeter lotus circle, no dot at left and right of lotus. **Note:** Previous (Y#13.5).

Date	VG	F	VF	XF	Unc
ND(ca.1904)	60.00	85.00	120	180	—

Type F

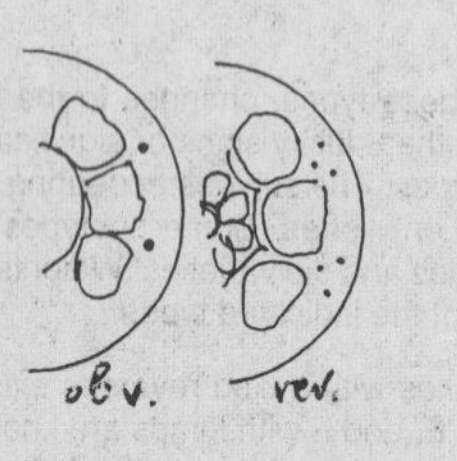

Obverse Reverse

Obverse has one dot in outer angles.
The reverse has three dots in outer angles.

Y# F13.1 TANGKA Composition: Billon **Obverse:** Nine dots within lotus circle **Reverse:** Flower buds full or outlined. **Note:** Struck at Dode Mint. Six varieties exist. Weight varies 4.10-4.70 grams. Previous Y#13.6.

Date	VG	F	VF	XF	Unc
ND(ca.1907-09)	4.00	6.00	10.00	16.00	—

Y# F13.2 TANGKA Composition: Billon **Obverse:** Northwest symbol circle with dots. No dot at left and right of lotus. Lotus circle varies 10-12mm. **Reverse:** Central lotus buds hollow **Note:** Weight varies 4.10-4.70. Struck at Dode Mint. Four varieties exist.

Date	Good	VG	F	VF	XF
ND(1910-15)	6.00	9.00	15.00	25.00	—

Y# F13.3 TANGKA Composition: Billon **Obverse:** 11mm lotus circle. **Reverse:** Solid lotus buds **Note:** Machine struck. Similar to Y#F13.2 and 2 Tangka, Y#15. Weight varies: 5.20-5.60 grams.

Date	Good	VG	F	VF	XF
ND(ca.1912) Rare	—	—	—	—	—

Y# F13.4 TANGKA Composition: Billon **Obverse:** Dot to left and right of lotus. Northeast symbol two fish with dots. South symbol with 3 dots. Northwest symbol circle with 4 dots around center dot. **Note:** Weight varies 4.10-4.70 grams. Varieties exist including 34-78 dots for outer circles. Previous number: Y#13.7.

Date	VG	F	VF	XF	Unc
ND(ca.1912-22)	8.00	12.00	20.00	32.00	—

Y# F13.5 TANGKA Composition: Billon **Obverse:** Dot to left and right of lotus. Northeast symbol double hook between two fish and dots. Northwest symbol circle with two hooks, dots south symbol has three dots. **Note:** Weight varies 4.10-4.70 grams. Varieties exist including 34-78 dots for outer circle. Previous number: Y13.8.

Date	Good	VG	F	VF	XF
ND(1912-22)	8.00	12.00	20.00	32.00	—

Y# F13.6 TANGKA Composition: Billon **Obverse:** Dots to left and right of base of lotus in the water line. Northwest symbol a circle with dots. Northeast symbol two fish with dots. South symbol very ornate with two side hooks and a dot **Size:** 27 mm. **Note:** Weight varies: 4.10-4.70 grams.

Date	Good	VG	F	VF	XF
ND(ca.1909)	8.00	12.00	18.00	30.00	—

Y# F13.7 TANGKA Composition: Billon **Size:** 31 mm. **Note:** Similar to Y#F13.6.

Date	Good	VG	F	VF	XF
ND(ca.1924-25) Rare	—	—	—	—	—

Type G

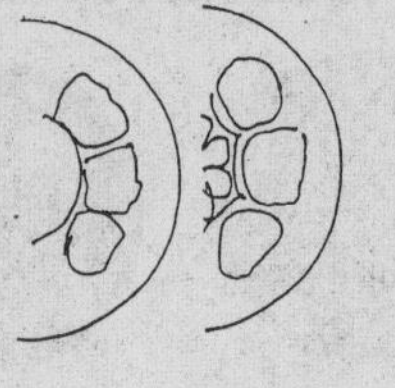

Obverse Reverse

The obverse and reverse have no outer angle symbols.
The petals are joined on the obverse.

Y# G13 TANGKA Composition: Billon **Reverse:** No outer angles at inner circle **Note:** Weight varies: 3.30-4.60 grams. Struck at Serkhang Mint. Previous Y#13.9.

Date	VG	F	VF	XF	Unc
ND(ca.1921)	4.00	6.00	9.00	15.00	—

Type H

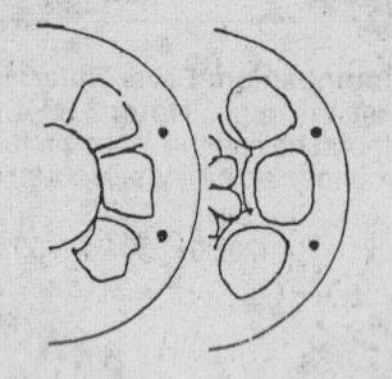

Obverse Reverse

The obverse and reverse have one dot in outer angles.
The obverse petals are joined.

Y# H13.1 TANGKA Composition: Billon **Obverse:** Dot between symbols at inner circle, lotus petals joined **Reverse** Dot between characters at inner circle **Note:** Weight varies 4.00-4.20 grams. Machine struck at Dode Mint. Two minor die varieties exist. Previous Y#13.10.

Date	VG	F	VF	XF	Un
ND(1929)	10.00	14.00	20.00	30.00	–

Y# H13.2 TANGKA Composition: Billon **Obverse:** Similar to Y#H13.1 **Reverse:** Similar to Y#H13.1 but Northeast character in retrograde **Note:** Weight varies: 4.0 4.20 grams. Machine struck.

Date	VG	F	VF	XF	U
ND(ca.1929-30)	60.00	90.00	120	150	-

Y# 15 2 TANGKA **Composition:** Billon **Note:** Weight varies 7.80-10.50 grams. Struck at Dode Mint. Machine struck. Varieties exist.

Date	VG	F	VF	XF	Unc
ND(ca.1912)	125	175	300	450	—

PRESENTATION TANGKA COINAGE

Struck for presentation to Monks. Circulated later but briefly with value of 5 and then 10 Srang.

Y# 14 TANGKA **Composition:** Silver **Note:** Weight varies: 2.70-5.00 grams. Obverse varieties exist without or up to two dots inside trapezoids enclosing the legend.

Date	Mintage	VG	F	VF	XF	Unc
ND(1910)	600,000	10.00	15.00	20.00	35.00	—

Y# 31 TANGKA **Composition:** Silver **Note:** Weight varies: 3.10-5.30 grams. Struck at Tapchi Mint.

ate	VG	F	VF	XF	Unc
D(1953)	7.00	10.00	15.00	22.00	—
D(ca.1953)	7.00	10.00	15.00	22.00	—

SHO-SRANG COINAGE

 # A7 1/8 SHO **Composition:** Copper **Note:** Struck at Dode Mint. Varieties exist.

ate	Good	VG	F	VF	XF
1 (1909)	85.00	150	225	350	—

Note: A silver striking of this type exists (rare), possibly a pattern

 # B7 1/4 SHO **Composition:** Copper

e	Good	VG	F	VF	XF
1 (1909)	85.00	150	225	350	—

Note: This coin struck in silver is a forgery; Modern forgeries struck in copper and copper-nickel exist

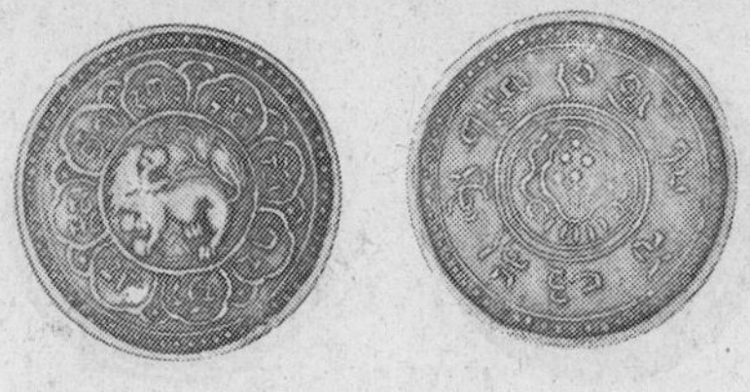

Y# 10 2-1/2 SKAR **Composition:** Copper **Obverse:** Lion standing left, looking backwards **Note:** Struck at Dode Mint. Lion varieties exist.

Date	Good	VG	F	VF	XF
BE15-43 (1909)	150	250	350	500	—

Y# 16.1 2-1/2 SKAR **Composition:** Copper **Obverse:** Lion crouching and looking upwards **Note:** Weight varies: 3.70-6.00 grams. Varieties exist.

Date	Good	VG	F	VF	XF
BE15-47 (1913)	5.00	12.00	20.00	50.00	—
BE15-48 (1914)	5.00	12.00	20.00	50.00	—
BE15-49 (1915)	15.00	30.00	60.00	120	—
BE15-50 (1916)	8.00	16.00	30.00	70.00	—
BE15-51 (1917)	15.00	30.00	60.00	120	—
BE15-52 (1918)	6.50	14.00	25.00	60.00	—

Y# 16.2 2-1/2 SKAR **Composition:** Copper **Obverse:** Lion standing left looking backwards **Note:** Struck at Mekyi Mint. Weight varies: 3.70-6.00 grams. Varieties exist, one with erroneous vowel, retrograde syllables on reverse top (error). With and without rays from sun.

Date	Good	VG	F	VF	XF
BE15-48 (1914)	8.00	16.00	30.00	70.00	—

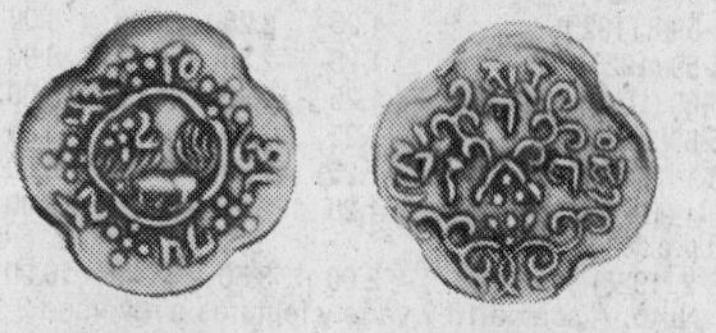

Y# A19 2-1/2 SKAR **Composition:** Copper **Obverse:** Lion standing left, looking back and upwards **Shape:** Scalloped **Note:** Struck at Dode Mint.

Date	Good	VG	F	VF	XF
BE15-52 (1918)	50.00	85.00	110	150	—
BE15-53 (1918)	50.00	90.00	120	165	—
BE15-55 (1921)	50.00	90.00	120	165	—

Y# A10 5 SKAR **Composition:** Copper **Obverse:** Lion standing left, looking back and upwards **Note:** Struck at Dode Mint.

Date	Good	VG	F	VF	XF
BE15-43 (1909)	150	250	350	500	—

Y# 17 5 SKAR **Composition:** Copper **Obverse:** Lion standing left.

Date	Good	VG	F	VF	XF
BE15-47 (1913)	6.00	10.00	25.00	55.00	—
BE15-48 (1914)	4.00	7.00	15.00	35.00	—
BE15-49 (1915)	5.00	8.00	18.00	40.00	—
BE15-50 (1916)	5.00	8.00	18.00	40.00	—
BE15-51 (1917)	3.50	6.00	12.00	30.00	—
BE15-52 (1918)	25.00	55.00	120	250	—

Y# 17.1 5 SKAR **Composition:** Copper **Obverse:** Lion standing left, looking back and upwards **Note:** Struck at Mekyi Mint. Size of obverse circle and weight of coin vary considerably.

Date	Good	VG	F	VF	XF
BE15-49 (1914)	4.00	7.00	15.00	32.00	—
BE15-50 (1916)	4.00	7.00	15.00	32.00	—
BE15-51 (1917)	4.00	7.00	15.00	32.00	—
BE15-52 (1918)	5.00	8.00	18.00	40.00	—

Y# 17.2 5 SKAR **Composition:** Copper **Obverse:** Lion standing left looking back and upwards

Date	Good	VG	F	VF	XF
BE15-48 (1914)	5.00	9.00	20.00	45.00	—
BE15-49 (1915)	8.00	14.00	35.00	70.00	—

Y# 17.3 5 SKAR **Composition:** Copper **Obverse:** Lion standing left looking back and upwards **Reverse:** Flower with eight petals rather than wheel with eight spokes

Date	Good	VG	F	VF	XF
BE15-48 (1914)	6.00	10.00	25.00	55.00	—

Y# 19 5 SKAR **Composition:** Copper **Obverse:** Lion standing left **Note:** Struck at Lower Dode Mint. Varieties exist.

Date	Good	VG	F	VF	XF
BE15-52 (1918)	2.25	3.50	6.00	12.00	—
BE15-53 (1919)	2.00	3.00	5.50	11.00	—
BE15-54 (1920)	1.50	2.50	5.00	10.00	—
BE15-55 (1921)	5.00	10.00	20.00	40.00	—
BE15-56 (1922)	1.50	2.50	5.00	10.00	—
BE56-15 (1922) Error	25.00	40.00	70.00	110	—

Note: Reverse inscription reads counterclockwise on error date coin

Y# 19.1 5 SKAR **Composition:** Copper **Obverse:** Lion standing left **Reverse:** Dot added above center **Note:** Struck at Upper Dode Mint.

Date	Good	VG	F	VF	XF
BE15-55 (1921)	10.00	20.00	35.00	65.00	—
BE15-56 (1922)	4.00	8.00	15.00	25.00	—

Y# 11 7-1/2 SKAR Composition: Copper **Obverse:** Lion standing left, looking back and upwards **Note:** Struck at Dode Mint.

Date	Good	VG	F	VF	XF
BE15-43 (1909)	150	250	350	500	—

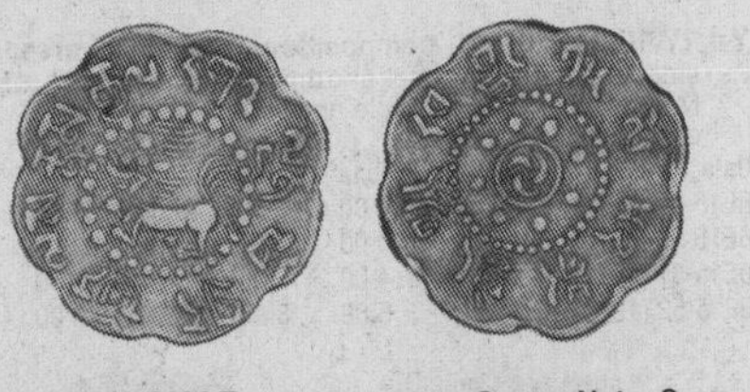

Y# 20 7-1/2 SKAR Composition: Copper **Note:** Some 15-52, 15-53, and 15-55 specimens have the reverse central "whirlwind" in a counterclockwise direction. Many varieties exist with size of inner circle on reverse.

Date	Good	VG	F	VF	XF
BE15-52 (1918)	2.00	3.00	5.00	8.50	—
BE15-53 (1919)	1.50	2.50	4.00	7.00	—
BE15-54 (1920)	1.50	2.50	4.00	7.00	—
BE15-55 (1921)	1.50	2.50	4.00	7.00	—
BE15-56 (1922)	1.50	2.50	4.00	7.00	—
BE15-60 (1926)	15.00	25.00	40.00	75.00	—

Y# 21 SHO Composition: Copper **Obverse:** Lion standing left, looking upwards **Reverse:** Central legend horizontal **Note:** Struck at Dode Mint.

Date	Good	VG	F	VF	XF
BE15-52 (1918)	30.00	45.00	75.00	120	—

Y# 21.1 SHO Composition: Copper **Obverse:** Lion standing left, looking upwards, without dot in reverse (NE), arabesque **Size:** 24 mm. **Note:** Weight varies: 3.95-7.13 grams. Struck at Mekyi Mint. Varieties exist.

Date	Good	VG	F	VF	XF
BE15-52 (1918)	1.50	2.00	3.25	7.00	—
BE15-53/52 (1919)	—	—	—	—	—
BE15-53 (1919)	1.00	1.50	2.50	5.00	—
BE15-54 (1920)	1.00	1.50	2.50	5.00	—
BE15-55 (1921)	1.00	1.50	2.50	5.00	—
BE15-56 (1922)	1.00	1.50	2.50	5.00	—
BE15-57 (1923)	1.50	2.00	3.25	7.00	—
BE15-57 (1923) Without dots (obverse)	5.00	10.00	20.00	30.00	—
BE15-58 (1924)	1.00	1.50	2.50	5.00	—
BE58-15 (1924) (error) year and cycle transposed	—	—	—	—	—
BE15-59 (1925)	1.00	1.50	2.50	5.00	—
BE15-59 (1925) Without dots (obverse)	5.00	10.00	20.00	30.00	—
BE15-60 (1926)	1.00	1.50	2.50	5.00	—
BE15-6 (1926) (error) for 15-60	—	—	—	—	—
BE16-1 (1927)	1.00	1.50	2.50	5.00	—
BE16-2 (1928)	1.00	1.50	2.50	5.00	—

Y# 21.2 SHO Composition: Copper **Obverse:** Lion looking upwards, with dot in reverse (NE) arabesque. **Note:** Struck at Ser-Khang Mint. Varieties exist.

Date	Good	VG	F	VF	XF
BE15-54 (1920)	2.00	3.00	5.00	9.00	—

Note: Specimens dated 15-54 may all be contemporary forgeries

Date	Good	VG	F	VF	XF
BE54-15 (1920) (Error) year and cycle transposed	25.00	40.00	65.00	100	—
BE15/51-54 (1920) (error) cycle transposed	25.00	40.00	65.00	100	—
BE15-55 (1921)	1.50	2.50	4.50	7.00	—
BE55-15 (1921) Error; "year" and "cycle" transposed	25.00	40.00	65.00	100	—
BE15-56/5 (1921)	1.00	1.50	2.50	5.00	—
BE15-56 (1922)	1.00	1.50	2.50	5.00	—
BE15-57 (1923)	1.25	1.75	3.25	7.00	—
BE15-58 (1924)	1.00	1.50	2.50	5.00	—
BE15-59 (1925)	1.00	1.50	2.50	5.00	—
BE15-60 (1926)	1.00	1.50	2.50	5.00	—
BE16-1/15-60 (1927)	15.00	25.00	40.00	65.00	—
BE16-1 (1927)	1.00	1.50	2.50	5.00	—
BE16-2/1 (1928)	1.00	1.50	2.50	5.00	—
BE16-2 (1928)	1.00	1.50	2.50	5.00	—

Y# 21a SHO Composition: Copper **Reverse:** Central legend vertical **Note:** Struck at Dode Mint. Two varieties (lion) exist for each of the following dates: 15-56, 15-57, 15-58, and 16-2. Overstrikes on 5 Skar, Y#17 exist.

Date	VG	F	VF	XF	Unc
BE15-56 (1922)	8.00	13.50	20.00	30.00	—
BE15-57 (1923)	2.00	3.50	6.00	10.00	—
BE57-15 (1923) Error; year and cycle transposed	25.00	40.00	65.00	100	—
BE15-58 (1924)	2.00	3.50	6.00	10.00	—
BE15-59/8 (1925)	1.25	2.25	4.00	8.00	—
BE15-59 (1925)	1.25	2.25	4.00	8.00	—
BE15-60 (1925)	1.25	2.25	4.00	8.00	—
BE15-60/59 (1926)	1.25	2.25	4.00	8.00	—
BE16-1 (1927)	1.25	2.25	4.00	8.00	—
BE16-1 (1927) Dot below O above denomination	1.25	2.25	4.00	8.00	—
BE16-2 (1928)	2.00	3.50	6.00	10.00	—

Note: A scarce 16-2 variety features a reversed 2

Date	VG	F	VF	XF	Unc
BE16-2 (1928) dot below rab	—	—	—	—	—

Y# 21b SHO Composition: Copper **Obverse:** Lion looking backwards

Date	Good	VG	F	VF	XF
BE15-52 (1923)	30.00	45.00	75.00	120	—

Y# 23 SHO Composition: Copper **Note:** Weight varies: 4.02-6.09 grams. Struck at Tapchi Mint. Dates 16-10, 16-11, 16-12, and 16-16 exist struck on thick and thin planchets and many lion obverse varieties.

Date	VG	F	VF	XF	Unc
BE16-6 (1932) (a)	2.00	3.00	6.00	10.00	—
BE16-7 (1933) (a)	2.25	3.50	6.50	11.00	—
BE16-8 (1934) (a)	2.50	4.00	9.00	15.00	—
BE16-9 (1935) (a)	2.00	3.50	6.00	11.00	—
BE16-9 (1935) (b)	1.50	3.00	5.00	10.00	—

Note: A scarce 16-9 variety features a hook ("bird") on the Sengi's (lion's) back

Date	VG	F	VF	XF	Unc
BE16-10 (1936) (a)	5.00	10.00	15.00	25.00	—
BE16-10 (1936) (b)	5.00	10.00	15.00	25.00	—
BE16-10 (1936) (c)	1.50	3.00	5.00	10.00	—
BE16-11 (1937) (a)	2.50	4.00	9.00	15.00	—
BE16-11 (1937) (b)	5.00	10.00	15.00	25.00	—
BE16-11 (1937) (c)	2.50	4.00	9.00	15.00	—
BE16-11 (1937) (d)	2.50	4.00	9.00	15.00	—
BE16-11 (1937) (e)	1.50	3.00	5.00	10.00	—
BE16-11 (1937) (f)	5.00	10.00	15.00	25.00	—
BE16-11 (1937) (g)	5.00	10.00	15.00	25.00	—
BE16-12 (1938) (d)	5.00	10.00	15.00	25.00	—
BE16-12 (1938) (f)	4.00	8.00	12.00	20.00	—
BE16-12 (1938) (g)	4.00	8.00	12.00	20.00	—
BE16-16 (1942) (f) Rare	—	—	—	—	—

Y# 27.1 3 SHO Composition: Copper **Note:** Single cloud line. Four varieties of conch shell on reverse.

Date	VG	F	VF	XF	Unc
BE16-20 (1946)	8.00	15.00	25.00	40.00	—

Y# 27.2 3 SHO Composition: Copper **Note:** Double cloud line.

Date	VG	F	VF	XF	Unc
BE16-20 (1946)	15.00	30.00	50.00	85.00	—

Y# 8 5 SHO Composition: Silver **Ruler:** Hsüan-t'ung **Note:** 9.4 - 9.7 grams

Date	VG	F	VF	XF	Unc
BE1 (1909)	600	1,200	2,000	2,500	-

Note: A forgery exists with some of the stars blundered an letters inaccurate

Y# 18 5 SHO Composition: Silver **Obverse:** Lion lookir upwards **Note:** Struck at Dode Mint. 8.4 - 11.4 grams.

Date	VG	F	VF	XF	Unc
BE15-47 (1913)	50.00	70.00	100	150	
BE15-48 (1914)	35.00	50.00	80.00	125	
BE15-49 (1915)	35.00	50.00	80.00	125	
BE15-50 (1916)	35.00	50.00	80.00	125	

Note: Two BE15-50 varieties exist; small and large lions or 13.5mm vs. 14.5mm obverse circle, short or lon flowers on reverse

Date	VG	F	VF	XF	Unc
BE15-58 (1924)	500	650	800	1,000	
BE15-59 (1925)	150	250	350	500	
BE15-60 (1926)	125	240	400	600	

8.1 5 SHO **Composition:** Silver **Obverse:** Lion ooking backwards **Note:** Struck at Mekyi Mint. Weight varies: .40-9.80 grams. Varieties exist.

	VG	F	VF	XF	Unc
49 (1915)	35.00	50.00	80.00	125	—
-50 (1916)	35.00	50.00	80.00	125	—
51 (1917)	35.00	50.00	80.00	125	—
52 (1918)	35.00	50.00	80.00	125	—
-53 (1919)	100	175	275	400	—
56 (1922)	100	175	275	400	—
59 (1925)	350	450	600	800	—
60 (1926)	200	350	500	700	—
-1 (1927)	125	225	350	500	—

8.1a 5 SHO **Composition:** Copper

	VG	F	VF	XF	Unc
-53 (1919)	225	300	400	500	—

8.2 5 SHO **Composition:** Silver **Note:** Struck at Dode Mint. Weight varies: 8.00-9.70 grams.

	VG	F	VF	XF	Unc
-52 (1920)	125	175	250	350	—

32 5 SHO **Composition:** Silver **Note:** Weight varies: .43-6.55 grams. Considered a pattern by some authorities.

	VG	F	VF	XF	Unc
928-29)	400	600	900	1,200	—

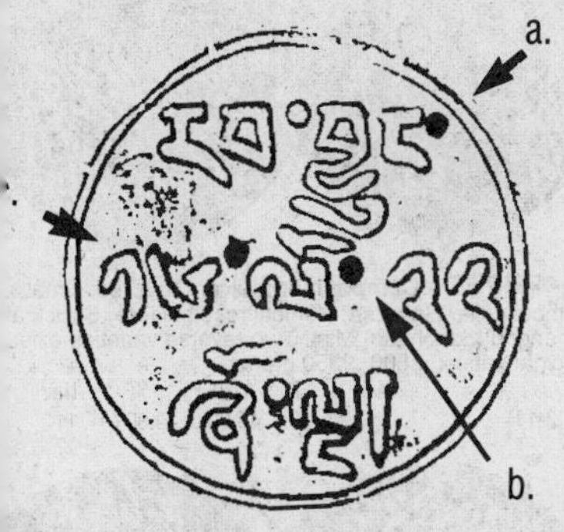

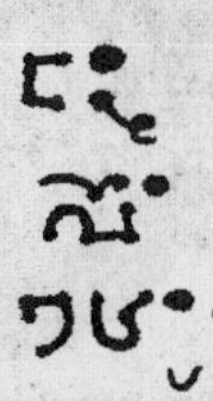

a. "CYCLE"

b. "YEAR"

c. "16"

Y# 28 5 SHO **Composition:** Copper **Obverse:** Two mountains with two suns **Note:** Struck at Tapchi Mint. Three lion die varieties exist.

Date	VG	F	VF	XF	Unc
BE16-21 (1947)	4.00	7.50	10.00	20.00	—

Y# 28.1 5 SHO **Composition:** Copper **Obverse:** Three mountains with two suns **Note:** Die varieties involving tail hairs (5 to 8), leg hairs (2 to 5) and yin-yang features (S, reversed S or the incuse of either) include 5 of 16-21, 38 of 16-22 and 30 of 16-23.

Date	VG	F	VF	XF	Unc
BE16-21 (1947)	2.00	3.50	6.00	10.00	—

Note: A modern medallic series dated 16-21 (1947) exists struck in copper, silver, and gold which were authorized by the Dalai Lama while in exile. Refer to Unusual World Coins, 3rd edition, Krause Publications, 1992.

Date	VG	F	VF	XF	Unc
BE16-22 (1948) dots a & c	2.50	4.00	7.50	12.50	—
BE16-22 (1948) Without dot after "16"	23.00	30.00	40.00	50.00	—
BE16-23 (1949) With 8 sun rays	5.00	8.00	14.00	25.00	—
BE16-23 (1949) With dot after 16	1.50	3.00	5.00	8.50	—

Note: Unclear overdates and varieties of BE16-23 exist

Date	VG	F	VF	XF	Unc
BE16-24 (1950)	30.00	40.00	50.00	65.00	—
BE16-24/3 (1950)	50.00	75.00	100	130	—

Y# 28.2 5 SHO **Composition:** Copper **Obverse:** Cloud above middle mountain missing

Date	VG	F	VF	XF	Unc
BE16-22 (1948)	35.00	60.00	95.00	150	—

Y# 28a 5 SHO **Composition:** Copper **Obverse:** Moon and sun above 3 mountains **Note:** Lion and edge varieties exist.

Date	VG	F	VF	XF	Unc
BE16-23 (1949)	20.00	28.00	38.00	50.00	—
BE16-24 (1950)	2.00	3.50	6.50	11.00	—
BE16-24 (1950) mountain as in illustration	10.00	15.00	22.00	30.00	—
BE16-24 (1950) Moon engraved over sun	15.00	22.00	30.00	40.00	—

Note: Unclear overdates exist for BE16-24

Date	VG	F	VF	XF	Unc
BE16-25/24 (1951)	4.00	7.00	12.50	20.00	—
BE16-25 (1951) moon over engraved sun	2.00	3.50	6.50	11.00	—

Note: Unclear overdates exist for BE16-25

Date	VG	F	VF	XF	Unc
BE16-26 (1952) Without dot after "26"	4.00	7.00	12.00	20.00	—
BE16-26 (1952)	4.00	7.00	12.00	20.00	—
BE16-27 (1953)	6.00	10.00	18.00	30.00	—
BE16-27 (1953) without dot after "27" or after "Cycle"	23.00	30.00	40.00	50.00	—

Y# 9 SRANG **Composition:** Silver **Note:** 17.2-19.9 g. Obverse varieties exist. Struck at Dode Mint.

Date	VG	F	VF	XF	Unc
BE1 (1909)	125	185	275	400	—

Y# 12 SRANG **Composition:** Silver **Obverse:** Lion standing left, looking backwards **Edge:** Plain **Note:** Weight varies: 18.00-18.30 grams. Varieties exist.

Date	VG	F	VF	XF	Unc
BE15-43 (1909)	140	225	325	450	—

Y# A18 SRANG **Weight:** 18.1000 g. **Composition:** Silver **Obverse:** Lion standing left looking back and upwards **Edge:** Reeded **Note:** Varieties exist.

Date	VG	F	VF	XF	Unc
BE15-48 (1914)	400	700	1,200	1,750	—

Y# A18.1 SRANG **Composition:** Silver **Obverse:** Lion looking backwards **Note:** Weight varies: 17.80-18.30 grams. Struck at Mekyi mint.

Date	VG	F	VF	XF	Unc
BE15-52 (1918)	350	650	850	1,200	—
BE15-53 (1919)	275	450	700	1,000	—

Y# 24 1-1/2 SRANG **Weight:** 5.0000 g. **Composition:** Silver **Note:** Struck at Tapchi Mint. Dates are written in words, not numerals. Obverse varieties exist.

Date	F	VF	XF	Unc	BU
BE16-10 (1936)	3.00	6.00	10.00	20.00	—
BE16-11 (1937)	2.50	5.00	9.00	17.00	—
BE16-12 (1938)	3.00	6.00	10.00	20.00	—
BE16-20 (1946)	20.00	40.00	70.00	90.00	—

Y# 25 3 SRANG **Weight:** 11.3000 g. **Composition:** Silver **Note:** Struck at Tapchi Mint. Dates are written in words, not numerals. Varieties exist in lion.

Date	F	VF	XF	Unc	BU
BE16-7 (1933)	8.00	12.00	20.00	35.00	—
BE16-8 (1934)	8.00	12.00	20.00	35.00	—

Y# 26 3 SRANG **Composition:** Silver **Note:** Dates are written in words, not numerals. Varieties in circular obverse and reverse legends exist.

Date	F	VF	XF	Unc	BU
BE16-9 (1935)	7.00	10.00	18.00	30.00	—
BE16-10 (1936)	6.00	9.00	15.00	25.00	—
BE16-10/9 (1936)	7.00	10.00	18.00	30.00	—
BE16-11 (1937)	6.00	9.00	15.00	25.00	—
BE16-12 (1938)	6.00	9.00	15.00	25.00	—
BE16-20 (1946)	20.00	40.00	70.00	110	—

Y# 29 10 SRANG **Composition:** Billon **Obverse:** Two suns **Reverse:** Numerals for denomination at center right **Note:** Struck at Tapchi Mint.

Date	F	VF	XF	Unc	BU
BE16-22 (1948)	4.50	9.00	18.00	40.00	—

Y# 29a 10 SRANG **Composition:** Billon **Obverse:** Moon and sun **Note:** The "dot" is after the denomination. A modern medallic series dated 16-24 (1950) exists struck in copper-nickel, silver, and gold which were authorized by the Dalai Lama while in exile. Refer to "Unusual World Coins", 3rd edition, Krause Publications, 1992.

Date	F	VF	XF	Unc	BU
BE16-23 (1949) With dot	20.00	45.00	100	175	—
BE16-24/23 (1950) With dot	7.00	15.00	30.00	60.00	—
BE16-24/23 (1950) with dot and moon cut over sun	20.00	40.00	80.00	140	—
BE16-24/22 (1950)	9.00	18.00	35.00	70.00	—
BE16-24 (1950) Moon cut over sun, denomination in words	10.00	20.00	40.00	70.00	—
BE16-24 (1950) With dot	12.00	22.00	50.00	90.00	—
BE16-25/24 (1951) With dot	7.00	15.00	30.00	60.00	—
BE16-25/24 (1951) Without dot	10.00	20.00	40.00	70.00	—
BE16-25 (1951) With dot	7.00	15.00	30.00	60.00	—
BE16-26/25 (1952) Without dot	7.00	15.00	30.00	60.00	—
BE16-26 (1952) With dot	7.00	15.00	30.00	60.00	—

Y# 29.1 10 SRANG **Composition:** Billon **Reverse:** Words for denomination at center right

Date	F	VF	XF	Unc	BU
BE16-23 (1949) With dot before and after ten	6.00	10.00	20.00	40.00	—
BE16-23 (1949) Without dot after ten	6.00	10.00	20.00	40.00	—
BE16-23/22 (1949)	12.00	20.00	35.00	70.00	—

Y# 30 10 SRANG **Composition:** Billon **Reverse:** Cycle and year in words **Note:** Struck at Dogu Mint.

Date	F	VF	XF	Unc	BU
BE16-24 (1950) Without dot after year	6.00	12.00	25.00	55.00	—
BE16-24 (1950)	7.00	15.00	30.00	65.00	—
BE16-25/4 (1951)	5.00	10.00	20.00	45.00	—
BE16-25 (1951)	5.00	10.00	20.00	45.00	—

Y# 22 20 SRANG **Composition:** Gold **Obverse:** Eight Buddhist lucky symbols in outer circle **Note:** Struck at Ser-Khang Mint.

Date	F	VF	XF	Unc	BU
BE15-52 (1918) with dot in reverse center	425	575	800	1,100	—
BE15-53 (1919) with large circle in reverse center	425	575	800	1,100	—

Note: Silver and copper strikings for 15-53 exist and are believed to be forgeries

Date	F	VF	XF	Unc	BU
BE15-53 (1919) with small circle in reverse center	425	575	800	1,100	—
BE15-54 (1920) with dot in reverse center	425	575	800	1,000	—
BE15-54 (1920) without dot in reverse center	425	575	800	1,100	—

Note: Silver and copper strikings for 15-54 exist and are believed to be forgeries

Date	F	VF	XF	Unc	BU
BE15-55 (1921)	700	1,000	1,500	2,000	—

TRADE COINAGE

1 Rupee = 3 Tangka

Total mintage of the 1 Rupee between 1902 and 1942 was between 25.5 and 27.5 million according to Chinese sources. In addition to the types illustrated above, large quantities of the following coins also circulated in Tibet: China Dollars, Y#318a, 329, and 345 plus Szechuan issues Y#449 and 459, and Indian Rupees, KM#473, 492, and 508.

Rupees exist with local merchant countermarks in Chinese, Tibetan, and other scripts. Examples of crown-size rupees struck in silver (26.30-27.50 grams) and gold (36.30 grams) are considered fantasies.

Y# 1 1/4 RUPEE **Weight:** 2.8000 g. **Composition:** 0.9350 Silver **Note:** Struck at Chengdu (Szechuan) Mi Varieties exist.

Date	Mintage	F	VF	XF	Unc
ND(1904-05)	120,000	40.00	60.00	90.00	150
ND(1904-05, 1912)	120,000	40.00	60.00	90.00	150

Y# 1a 1/4 RUPEE **Weight:** 5.4500 g. **Composition:** **Note:** Struck at Chengdu (Szechuan) Mint.

Date	F	VF	XF	Unc
ND(1905)	1,150	1,900	2,650	3,450

Y# 2 1/2 RUPEE **Weight:** 5.6000 g. **Composition:** 0.9350 Silver **Note:** Struck at Chengdu (Szechuan) Mi Varieties exist.

Date	Mintage	F	VF	XF	Unc
ND(1904-05, 1907, 1912)	130,000	50.00	75.00	125	200

Y# 2a 1/2 RUPEE **Weight:** 9.3800 g. **Composition:** **Note:** Struck at Chengdu (Szechuan) Mint.

Date	F	VF	XF	Unc
ND(1905)	1,250	2,000	2,750	3,500

Y# A1.1 RUPEE **Weight:** 11.5000 g. **Composition:** Silver **Ruler:** Hsüan-t'ung **Note:** Previous number: C2

Date	Good	VG	F	VF
ND(1902-03)	750	1,000	1,500	2,250

Note: Struck in or near Tachienlu (today Kang Ting) a known as Lu Kuan Rupee. It was meant to replace Indian Rupee which was used in eastern Tibet a western Szechuan (Sichuan) in the 19th century is considered the forerunner of the Szechuan Ru (Y#3). Varieties exist.

Y# A1.2 RUPEE **Composition:** Silver **Ruler:** Hsüan-t'ung **Note:** Obverse and reverse inscriptions deviating style. Kann#1285.

Date	Good	VG	F	VF
ND(1902-03)	750	1,000	1,500	2,250

Y# 3 RUPEE **Composition:** Silver **Obverse:** Small without collar **Reverse:** Vertical rosette **Note:** Struck at Chengdu (Szechuan) Mint. Two reverse varieties exist. Weight varies: .8800-.9350 grams.

Date	F	VF	XF	Unc
ND(1902-11)	25.00	45.00	70.00	110

Y# 3.1 RUPEE **Composition:** Silver **Reverse:** Horizo rosette **Note:** Two reverse varieties exist. Weight varie .8800-.9350 grams.

Date	F	VF	XF	Unc
ND(1902-11)	20.00	35.00	50.00	85.00

Y# 3.2a RUPEE **Weight:** 20.6700 g. **Composition:** **Note:** Previous number: Y#3b.

Date	F	VF	XF	Unc
ND(ca. 1903-05)	900	1,200	1,750	—

Note: An example with two obverses exists (20.40 gra

3.2 **RUPEE** **Composition:** 0.0700 Silver **Obverse:** Small bust with collar **Reverse:** Vertical rosette **Note:** Struck at Chengdu (Szechuan) Mint before 1930, then at Kangding Tachienlu) Mint after 1930. Two reverse varieties exist.

	F	VF	XF	Unc	BU
911-16, 1930-33)	12.00	20.00	35.00	60.00	—

Note: An example with two obverses exists

3.3 **RUPEE** **Composition:** Silver **Obverse:** Large bust **Reverse:** Vertical rosette **Note:** Finenesses vary .4200-.5000. Struck at Kangding (Tachienlu) Mint. Varieties exist.

	F	VF	XF	Unc	BU
939-42)	20.00	32.50	50.00	90.00	—

3.4 **RUPEE** **Composition:** Silver **Obverse:** Small bust with flat nose, revised non-floral gown. **Reverse:** Vertical rosette **Note:** .650-.500 silver

e	F	VF	XF	Unc	BU
1933-39)	20.00	32.50	50.00	90.00	—

3.5 **RUPEE** **Composition:** Silver **Obverse:** Small bust similar to Y#3.4 **Reverse:** Horizontal rosette **Note:** .650-.500 silver.

e	F	VF	XF	Unc	BU
(1933-39)	30.00	50.00	80.00	150	—

3a **RUPEE** **Composition:** Debased Silver/Billon

e	F	VF	XF	Unc	BU
(1939-42)	8.00	15.00	30.00	60.00	—

Note: Coins with copper base and silver wash exist

CUT COINAGE

Tibetan Rupees (Y3) due to their inscriptions also lled Szechuan Rupees, have been cut in half and arter for use as small change. The process of cutting e rupee frequently allowed customers to chip away om the coin's middle. In 1934 the treasury made cut-g of the rupee illegal. To enforce this decree, all offi-al payments had to be made with uncut coins; pay-ent of smaller values was to be made with copper ins. However, the shortage of coinage made this de-ee impractical.

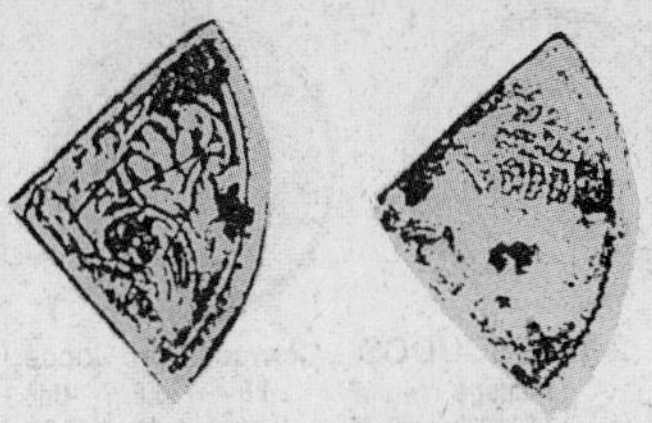

Y# A5 1/4 RUPEE **Note:** 1/4 segment of 1 Rupee, Y#3.

Date	VG	F	VF	XF	Unc
ND (1902-42)	—	—	—	—	—

Y# B5 1/2 RUPEE **Note:** 1/2 segment of 1 Rupee, Y#3.

Date	VG	F	VF	XF	Unc
ND (1902-42)	15.00	20.00	35.00	50.00	—

TOKEN COINAGE

KM# Tn1 4 SHO **Composition:** Copper **Note:** 8.23-8.98 grams. Struck over 3 Sho, Y#27 and 5 Sho, Y#28a

Date	VG	F	VF	XF	Unc
ND(1959-60) Rare	—	—	—	—	—

KM# Tn2 4 SHO **Composition:** Copper **Note:** Struck over 5 Sho, Y#28a and Y#28.1

Date	VG	F	VF	XF	Unc
ND	75.00	100	130	160	220

PATTERNS

Including off metal strikes

KM#	Date	Mintage	Identification	Mkt Val
Pn1	ND (1908)	—	1/2 Sho. Silver. Hsien Feng	—
Pn2	ND (1908)	—	Sho. Silver. Hsien Feng	—
Pn3	ND (1909)	—	10 Tam. Silver. 27.6700 g.	—
Pn4	ND (1910)	—	Shokang. Silver. 3.6000 g. Y5	—
Pn8	BE15-57 (1923)	—	20 Srang. Brass. 7.2300 g.	—
Pn5	BE15-57 (1923)	—	Sho. Copper.	—
Pn6	BE15-57 (1923)	—	Sho. Brass.	—
Pn9	BE16-1 (1928)	—	Sho. Brass. 5.2600 g.	—
Pn10	ND (1928)	—	Srang. Silver.	—
	ND (1928)	—	Srang. Silver.	—
Pn11	ND (1928)	—	10 Tam. Silver. 12.6100 g.	—
Pn12	ND (1929-30)	—	10 Tam. Silver. 8.3000 g.	—
Pn13	BE16-4 (1931)	—	5 Sho. Silver. 5.0000 g.	—
Pn17	Yr.925 (1951)	—	50 Srang. Silver. 26.0000 g.	—
Pn18	ND (1951)	—	50 Srang. Silver. 25.1000 g.	—
Pn14	Yr.925 (1951)	—	25 Srang. Silver. 13.5200 g.	—
Pn15	Yr.925 (1951)	—	50 Srang. Copper. 17.3000 g.	—
Pn17	Yr.925 (1951)	—	50 Srang. Silver. 26.0000 g.	—
Pn16	Yr.925 (1951)	—	50 Srang. Silver. 26.0000 g.	—
Pn20	Yr.927 (1953)	—	5 Srang. Copper. 6.2000 g.	—
Pn21	Yr. 927 (1953)	—	5 Srang. Silver. 5.0000 g.	—

TIMOR

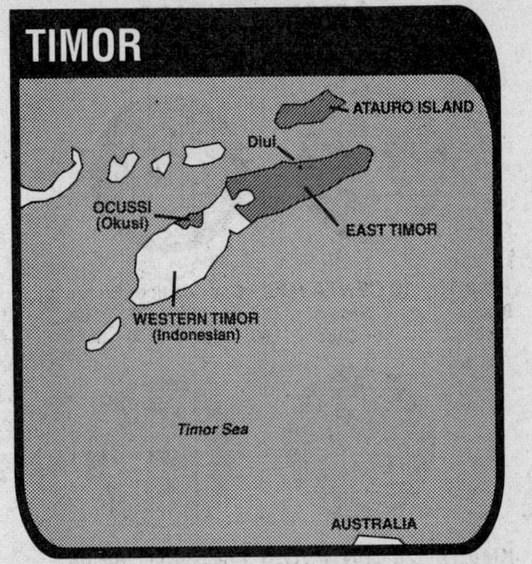

East Timor)

An island in the Lesser Sunda group, presently part of Indonesia but a treaty of 1859 fixed the division between Portugal and the Netherlands. Portugal discovered and owned the eastern half of the island including the Island of Atauro, located to its north, and the enclave of Ocussi situated on the northeastern portion of the island since 1524 and made coins for this colony. From 1865-1896, Timor was under the jurisdiction of Macao but was made a province in 1896 and became a colony in 1926. All of Timor fell under Japanese occupation from 1942-1945. In 1951 they became an overseas province.

MONETARY SYSTEM

100 Avos = 1 Pataca

COLONY

DECIMAL COINAGE

KM# 5 10 AVOS **Composition:** Bronze

Date	Mintage	F	VF	XF	Unc	BU
1945	50,000	120	220	400	1,000	—
1948	500,000	3.50	8.00	17.00	35.00	—
1951	6,250,000	1.50	3.50	7.50	15.00	—

KM# 6 20 AVOS **Composition:** Nickel-Bronze

Date	Mintage	F	VF	XF	Unc	BU
1945	50,000	16.00	35.00	70.00	175	—

KM# 7 50 AVOS **Weight:** 3.5000 g. **Composition:** 0.6500 Silver .0731 oz. ASW

Date	Mintage	F	VF	XF	Unc	BU
1945	100,000	45.00	90.00	135	275	—
1948	500,000	3.00	5.50	12.00	30.00	—
1951	6,250,000	2.00	3.75	8.50	18.00	—

REFORM COINAGE

100 Centavos = 1 Escudo

KM# 10 10 CENTAVOS **Composition:** Bronze

Date	Mintage	F	VF	XF	Unc	BU
1958	1,000,000	1.00	3.00	15.00	35.00	—

KM# 17 20 CENTAVOS **Composition:** Bronze

Date	Mintage	F	VF	XF	Unc	BU
1970	1,000,000	0.45	1.00	2.50	5.00	—

KM# 11 30 CENTAVOS **Composition:** Bronze

Date	Mintage	F	VF	XF	Unc	BU
1958	2,000,000	0.75	1.50	12.00	30.00	—

KM# 18 50 CENTAVOS **Composition:** Bronze

Date	Mintage	F	VF	XF	Unc	BU
1970	1,000,000	0.45	1.00	2.00	4.50	—

KM# 12 60 CENTAVOS **Composition:** Copper-Nickel-Zinc

Date	Mintage	F	VF	XF	Unc	BU
1958	1,000,000	1.25	2.75	12.00	30.00	—

KM# 13 ESCUDO **Composition:** Copper-Nickel-Zinc

Date	Mintage	F	VF	XF	Unc	BU
1958	1,200,000	2.00	4.00	40.00	80.00	—

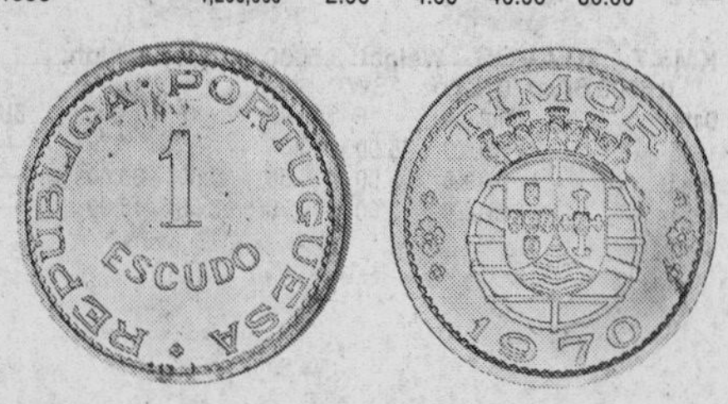

KM# 19 ESCUDO **Composition:** Bronze

Date	Mintage	F	VF	XF	Unc	BU
1970	1,200,000	1.50	3.50	9.00	18.00	—

KM# 20 2-1/2 ESCUDOS **Composition:** Copper-Nickel

Date	Mintage	F	VF	XF	Unc	BU
1970	1,000,000	0.75	1.50	3.50	7.50	—

KM# 14 3 ESCUDOS **Weight:** 3.5000 g. **Composition:** 0.6500 Silver .0731 oz. ASW

Date	Mintage	F	VF	XF	Unc	BU
1958	1,000,000	3.00	5.00	10.00	25.00	—

KM# 21 5 ESCUDOS **Composition:** Copper-Nickel

Date	Mintage	F	VF	XF	Unc	BU
1970	1,200,000	1.50	3.50	8.00	16.00	—

KM# 15 6 ESCUDOS **Weight:** 7.0000 g. **Composition:** 0.6500 Silver .1463 oz. ASW

Date	Mintage	F	VF	XF	Unc	BU
1958	1,000,000	3.50	6.00	12.50	25.00	—

KM# 16 10 ESCUDOS **Weight:** 7.0000 g. **Composition:** 0.6500 Silver .1463 oz. ASW

Date	Mintage	F	VF	XF	Unc	BU
1964	600,000	3.50	6.00	12.50	25.00	—

KM# 22 10 ESCUDOS **Composition:** Copper-Nickel

Date	Mintage	F	VF	XF	Unc	BU
1970	700,000	3.00	5.50	12.00	24.00	—

TOGO

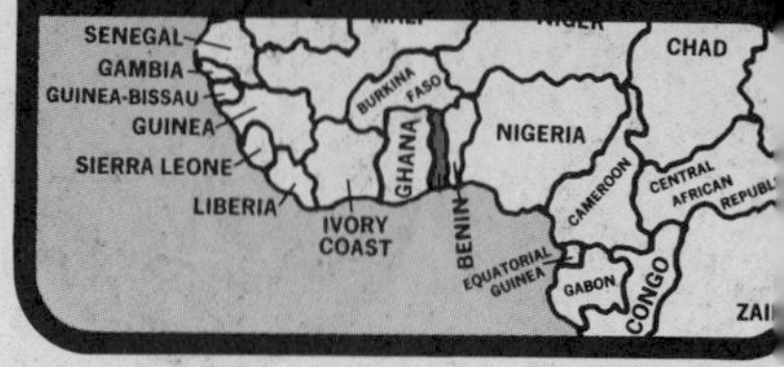

The Republic of Togo (formerly part of German Togol situated on the Gulf of Guinea in West Africa between Ghana Dahomey, has an area of 21,622 sq.mi. (56,790 sq. km.) a population of *3.4 million. Capital: Lome. Agriculture and her the production of dyewoods, and the mining of phosphates iron ore are the chief industries. Copra, phosphates and coffe exported.

Although Brazilians were the first traders to settle in T Germany achieved possession, in 1884, by inducing co chiefs to place their territories under German protection. The man protectorate was extended international recognition a Berlin conference of 1885 and its ultimate boundaries delin by treaties with France in 1897 and with Britain in 1904. Ar French forces occupied Togoland in 1914, subsequently bec ing a League of Nations mandate and a U.N. trusteeship divi for administrative purpose, between Great Britain and Fra The British portion voted in 1957 for incorporation with Gh The French portion became the independent Republic of Tog April 27, 1960.

RULERS

German, 1884-1914
Anglo - French, 1914-1957
French, 1957-1960

MINT MARKS

(a) - Paris, privy marks only

MONETARY SYSTEM

100 Centimes = 1 Franc

FRENCH COLONIAL

U.N. Trusteeship

STANDARD COINAGE

100 Centimes = 1 Franc

KM# 1 50 CENTIMES **Composition:** Aluminum-Bro

Date	Mintage	F	VF	XF	Unc
1924(a)	3,691,000	2.50	7.00	20.00	80.00
1925(a)	2,064,000	3.00	8.00	22.00	90.00
1926(a)	445,000	9.00	25.00	85.00	275

KM# 2 FRANC **Composition:** Aluminum-Bronze

Date	Mintage	F	VF	XF	Unc
1924(a)	3,472,000	3.50	7.50	40.00	125
1925(a)	2,768,000	4.00	9.00	45.00	140

KM# 4 FRANC **Composition:** Aluminum

Date	Mintage	F	VF	XF	Unc
1948(a)	5,000,000	2.50	7.00	22.00	55.00

 # 3 2 FRANCS **Composition:** Aluminum-Bronze

e	Mintage	F	VF	XF	Unc	BU
4(a)	750,000	6.00	15.00	60.00	250	—
5(a)	580,000	7.00	18.00	80.00	275	—

 # 5 2 FRANCS **Composition:** Aluminum **Note:** Similar to 1 Franc, KM#4.

e	Mintage	F	VF	XF	Unc	BU
8(a)	5,000,000	3.50	9.00	28.00	60.00	—

 # 6 5 FRANCS **Composition:** Aluminum-Bronze

te	Mintage	F	VF	XF	Unc	BU
56(a)	10,000,000	1.50	3.00	6.00	12.50	—

FRENCH WEST AFRICA - TOGO

STANDARD COINAGE

100 Centimes = 1 Franc

 # A8 10 FRANCS **Composition:** Aluminum-Bronze **Note:** Issued for circulation in French West Africa, including Togo.

te	Mintage	F	VF	XF	Unc	BU
57(a)	30,000,000	0.50	1.00	1.50	3.00	—

 # A9 25 FRANCS **Composition:** Aluminum-Bronze **Note:** Issued for circulation in French West Africa, including Togo.

te	Mintage	F	VF	XF	Unc	BU
57(a)	30,000,000	0.50	1.00	2.00	5.00	—

REPUBLIC

STANDARD COINAGE

100 Centimes = 1 Franc

M# 13 500 FRANCS **Weight:** 7.0000 g. **Composition:** 0.9990 Silver 0.2248 oz. ASW **Obverse:** National arms **Reverse:** Apollo 11 launch scene **Edge:** Plain **Size:** 30 mm.

ate	F	VF	XF	Unc	BU
D(1999) Proof	—	Value: 35.00			

KM# 14 500 FRANCS **Weight:** 7.0000 g. **Composition:** 0.9990 Silver 0.2248 oz. ASW **Obverse:** Three astronauts, moon and space capsule

Date	F	VF	XF	Unc	BU
ND(1999) Proof	—	Value: 35.00			

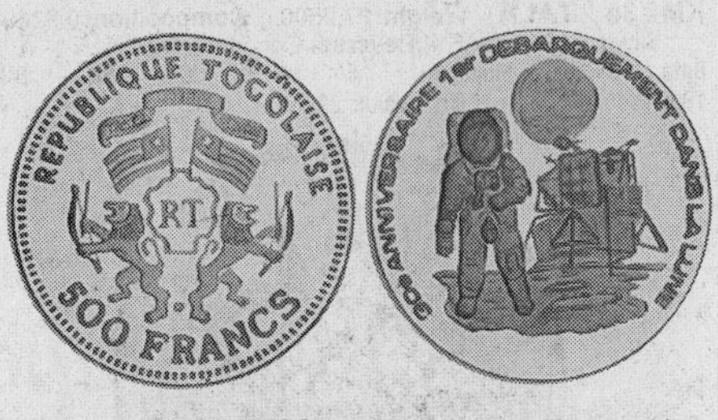

KM# 15 500 FRANCS **Weight:** 7.0000 g. **Composition:** 0.9990 Silver 0.2248 oz. ASW **Obverse:** National arms **Reverse:** Moon-walking astronaut

Date	F	VF	XF	Unc	BU
ND(1999) Proof	—	Value: 35.00			

KM# 16 1000 FRANCS **Weight:** 14.9700 g. **Composition:** 0.9990 Silver 0.4808 oz. ASW **Obverse:** National arms. **Reverse:** Bust of Martin Luther half right. **Edge:** Plain. **Size:** 35 mm.

Date	F	VF	XF	Unc	BU
1999 Proof	—	Value: 50.00			

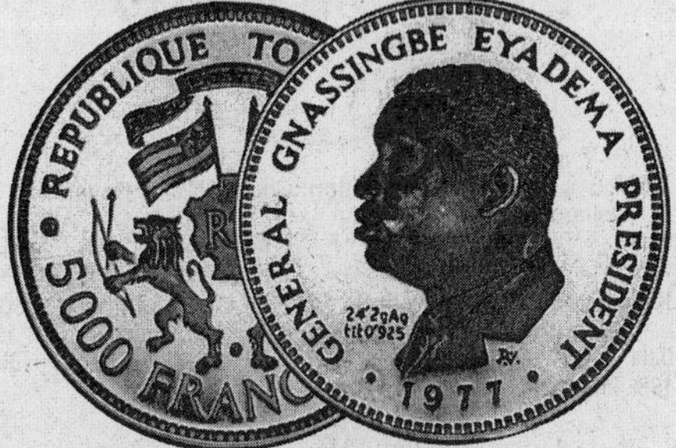

KM# 8 5000 FRANCS **Weight:** 24.3600 g. **Composition:** 0.9250 Silver .7245 oz. ASW **Subject:** 10th Year of General Eyadema as President

Date	F	VF	XF	Unc	BU
1977 Proof	—	Value: 65.00			

KM# 9 10000 FRANCS **Weight:** 49.3200 g. **Composition:** 0.9250 Silver 1.4669 oz. ASW **Subject:** 10th Year of General Eyadema as President

Date	F	VF	XF	Unc	BU
1977 Proof	—	Value: 80.00			

KM# 10 15000 FRANCS **Weight:** 4.4800 g. **Composition:** 0.9170 Gold .1320 oz. AGW **Subject:** 10th Year of General Eyadema as President

Date	F	VF	XF	Unc	BU
1977 Proof	—	Value: 125			

KM# 11 25000 FRANCS **Weight:** 9.0000 g. **Composition:** 0.9170 Gold .2653 oz. AGW **Subject:** 10th Year of General Eyadema as President

Date	F	VF	XF	Unc	BU
1977 Proof	—	Value: 250			

KM# 12 50000 FRANCS **Weight:** 18.0000 g. **Composition:** 0.9170 Gold .5306 oz. AGW **Subject:** 10th Year of General Eyadema as President **Note:** Similar to 25,000 Francs, KM#11.

Date	F	VF	XF	Unc	BU
1977 Proof	—	Value: 500			

ESSAIS

KM#	Date	Mintage	Identification	Mkt Val
E1	1924(a)	—	50 Centimes. KM#1.	110
E2	1924(a)	—	Franc. KM#2.	150
E3	1924(a)	—	2 Francs. KM#3.	200
E4	1948(a)	2,000	Franc. Copper-Nickel. KM#4.	30.00
E5	1948(a)	2,000	2 Francs. Copper-Nickel. KM#5.	37.50
E6	1956(a)	2,300	5 Francs. KM#6.	15.00
E7	1956(a)	2,300	10 Francs. KM#7.	37.50
E8	1956(a)	2,300	25 Francs.	45.00
EA8	1957	2,300	10 Francs. Aluminum-Bronze. KM#A8.	25.00
EB8	1957	2,300	25 Francs. Aluminum-Bronze. KM#A9.	30.00
E9	1977	25	5000 Francs. Aluminum. KM#8.	35.00
E10	1977	20	5000 Francs. Copper. KM#8.	45.00
E11	1977	25	10000 Francs. Aluminum. KM#9.	35.00
E12	1977	20	10000 Francs. Copper. KM#9.	60.00
E13	1977	25	15000 Francs. Aluminum. KM#10.	35.00
E14	1977	20	15000 Francs. Copper. KM#10.	70.00
E15	1977	25	25000 Francs. Aluminum. KM#11.	35.00
E16	1977	20	25000 Francs. Copper. KM#11.	75.00

PIEFORTS

KM#	Date	Mintage	Identification	Mkt Val
P1	1977	5	5000 Francs. Copper. KM#8.	120
P2	1977	5	5000 Francs. Silver. 48.7200 g. KM#8.	200
P3	1977	5	10000 Francs. Copper. KM#9.	130
P3a	1977	5	10000 Francs. Silver. KM#9.	225
P4	1977	5	15000 Francs. Copper. KM#10.	95.00
P5	1977	5	25000 Francs. Copper. KM#11.	100
P6	1977	—	25000 Francs. Gold. KM#11.	900

PIEFORTS WITH ESSAIS

KM#	Date	Mintage	Identification	Mkt Val
PE1	1948(a)	104	Franc. KM#4.	85.00
PE2	1948(a)	104	2 Francs. KM#5.	95.00

TOKELAU ISLANDS

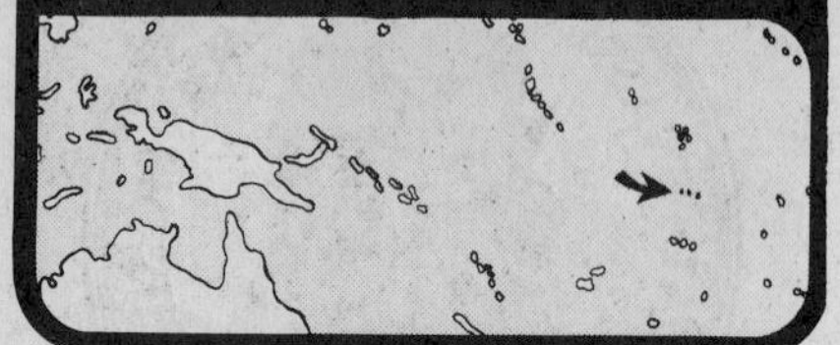

Tokelau or Union Islands, a New Zealand Territory located in the South Pacific 2,100 miles (3,379 km.) northeast of New Zealand and 300 miles (483 km.) north of Samoa, has an area of 4 sq. mi. (10 sq. km.) and a population of *2,000. Geographically, the group consists of four atolls - Atafu, Nukunono, Fakaofo and Swains – but the last belongs to American Samoa (and the United States claims the other three). The people are of Polynesian origin; Samoan is the official language. The New Zealand Minister for Foreign Affairs governs the islands; councils of family elders handle local government at the village level. The chief settlement is Fenuafala, on Fakaofo. It is connected by wireless with the offices of the New Zealand Administrative Center, located at Apia, Western Samoa. Subsistence farming and the production of copra for export are the main occupations. Revenue is also derived from the sale of postage stamps and, since 1978,coins.

Great Britain annexed the group of islands in 1889. They were added to the Gilbert and Ellice Islands colony in 1916. In 1926, they were brought under the jurisdiction of Western Samoa, which was held as a mandate of the League of Nations by New Zealand. They were declared a part of New Zealand in 1948.

Tokelau Islands issued its first coin in 1978, a "$1 TahiTala," Tokelauan for "One Dollar." The coin has a number of unusual features. The edge is inscribed, "Tokelau's First Coin." The obverse portrait of Queen Elizabeth II is identified by neither name nor title. The three dots of each such group comprising the obverse border symbolize the three principal atolls.

RULERS
British

MINT MARKS
PM - Pobjoy

NEW ZEALAND TERRITORY

STANDARD COINAGE

KM# 1 TALA **Composition:** Copper-Nickel

Date	Mintage	F	VF	XF	Unc	BU
1978	10,000	—	1.00	2.00	7.50	—

KM# 1a TALA **Weight:** 27.2500 g. **Composition:** 0.9250 Silver .8104 oz. ASW

Date	Mintage	F	VF	XF	Unc	BU
1978 Proof	5,000	Value: 22.50				

KM# 2 TALA **Composition:** Copper-Nickel

Date	F	VF	XF	Unc	BU
1979	—	1.00	2.00	6.50	—

KM# 2a TALA **Weight:** 27.2500 g. **Composition:** 0.9250 Silver .8104 oz. ASW

Date	F	VF	XF	Unc	BU
1979 Proof	—	Value: 20.00			

KM# 3 TALA **Composition:** Copper-Nickel **Reverse:** Coconut Crab

Date	Mintage	F	VF	XF	Unc	BU
1980	10,000	—	1.00	2.50	6.00	—

KM# 3a TALA **Weight:** 27.2500 g. **Composition:** 0.9250 Silver .8104 oz. ASW **Reverse:** Coconut Crab

Date	Mintage	F	VF	XF	Unc	BU
1980 Proof	6,004	Value: 22.50				

KM# 4 TALA **Composition:** Copper-Nickel **Reverse:** Frigate Bird

Date	Mintage	F	VF	XF	Unc	BU
1981	6,500	—	1.00	2.50	6.50	—

KM# 4a TALA **Weight:** 27.2500 g. **Composition:** 0.9250 Silver .8104 oz. ASW **Reverse:** Frigate Bird

Date	Mintage	F	VF	XF	Unc	BU
1981 Proof	6,500	Value: 23.50				

KM# 5 TALA **Composition:** Copper-Nickel **Reverse:** Outrigger Canoe

Date	Mintage	F	VF	XF	Unc	BU
1982	10,000	—	1.00	2.00	3.50	—

KM# 5a TALA **Weight:** 27.2500 g. **Composition:** 0.9250 Silver .8104 oz. ASW **Reverse:** Outrigger Canoe

Date	Mintage	F	VF	XF	Unc	BU
1982 Proof	5,000	Value: 25.00				

KM# 6 TALA **Composition:** Copper-Nickel

Date	Mintage	F	VF	XF	Unc	BU
1983	2,000	—	1.00	2.50	6.00	—

KM# 7 5 TALA **Weight:** 28.2800 g. **Composition:** 0.92 Silver .8411 oz. ASW **Subject:** Water Conservation **Not** Similar to 1 Tala, KM#6.

Date	Mintage	F	VF	XF	Unc
1983 Proof	1,000	Value: 55.00			

KM# 8.1 5 TALA **Weight:** 27.0500 g. **Composition:** 0.9250 Silver .8045 oz. ASW **Reverse:** Fishermen in sailbo **Edge:** Plain

Date	Mintage	F	VF	XF	Unc
1984	1,500	—	—	—	30.00

KM# 8.2 5 TALA **Weight:** 27.0500 g. **Composition:** 0.9250 Silver .8045 oz. ASW **Reverse:** Fishermen in sailbo **Edge:** Reeded

Date	Mintage	F	VF	XF	Unc
1984 Proof	500	Value: 45.00			

KM# 10 5 TALA **Weight:** 27.0500 g. **Composition:** 0.9250 Silver .8045 oz. ASW **Series:** Olympics **Reverse:** Javelin Thrower

Date	Mintage	F	VF	XF	Unc
1988	20,000	—	—	—	20.00

KM# 9 5 TALA **Weight:** 27.2100 g. **Composition:** 0.925 Silver .8093 oz. ASW **Reverse:** Captain John Byron and HMS Dolphin **Edge:** Reeded

Date	Mintage	F	VF	XF	Unc
1989 Proof	500	Value: 35.00			

11 **5 TALA** **Composition:** Copper-Nickel **Reverse:** 0th Anniversary of Attack on Pearl Harbor scene

Date	F	VF	XF	Unc	BU
Prooflike	—	—	—	8.50	—

13 **5 TALA** **Composition:** Copper-Nickel **Reverse:** Battle of Guadal canal scene

Date	F	VF	XF	Unc	BU
Proof-like	—	—	—	8.00	—

14 **5 TALA** **Composition:** Copper-Nickel **Reverse:** Bust of General Dwight Eisenhower half left saluting

Date	F	VF	XF	Unc	BU
Proof-like	—	—	—	8.00	—

15 **5 TALA** **Composition:** Copper-Nickel **Reverse:** Raising the flag on Iwo Jima scene

Date	F	VF	XF	Unc	BU
1 Proof-like	—	—	—	8.00	—

16 **5 TALA** **Weight:** 31.4700 g. **Composition:** 0.9250 Silver .9359 oz. ASW **Reverse:** Scene of first lunar orbit

Date	Mintage	F	VF	XF	Unc	BU
1993 Proof	10,000	Value: 32.50				

KM# 17 **5 TALA** **Weight:** 31.4700 g. **Composition:** 0.9250 Silver .9359 oz. ASW **Series:** Endangered Wildlife **Reverse:** Iguana

Date	Mintage	F	VF	XF	Unc	BU
1993 Proof	15,000	Value: 42.50				

KM# 18 **5 TALA** **Weight:** 31.4700 g. **Composition:** 0.9250 Silver .9359 oz. ASW **Reverse:** H.M.S. Pandora

Date	Mintage	F	VF	XF	Unc	BU
1993 Proof	15,000	Value: 32.50				

KM# 19 **5 TALA** **Weight:** 31.4700 g. **Composition:** 0.9250 Silver .9359 oz. ASW **Series:** Olympics **Reverse:** Swimming meet

Date	Mintage	F	VF	XF	Unc	BU
1994 Proof	40,000	Value: 25.00				

KM# 20 **5 TALA** **Weight:** 31.4700 g. **Composition:** 0.9250 Silver .9359 oz. ASW **Subject:** World Cup Soccer

Date	Mintage	F	VF	XF	Unc	BU
1994 Proof	25,000	Value: 28.00				

KM# 21 **5 TALA** **Weight:** 31.4700 g. **Composition:** 0.9250 Silver .9359 oz. ASW **Series:** Protect Our World **Reverse:** Swamp scene

Date	Mintage	F	VF	XF	Unc	BU
1994 Proof	10,000	Value: 37.50				

KM# 22 **5 TALA** **Weight:** 31.4700 g. **Composition:** 0.9250 Silver .9359 oz. ASW **Series:** Olympics **Reverse:** Sailboarding scene

Date	Mintage	F	VF	XF	Unc	BU
1994 Proof	50,000	Value: 35.00				

KM# 23 **5 TALA** **Weight:** 31.4700 g. **Composition:** 0.9250 Silver .9359 oz. ASW **Reverse:** Queen Mother and daughter seated, holding infant Prince Charles

Date	Mintage	F	VF	XF	Unc	BU
1995 Proof	30,000	Value: 40.00				

KM# 25 **5 TALA** **Weight:** 31.4700 g. **Composition:** 0.9250 Silver .9359 oz. ASW **Obverse:** Bust of Queen Elizabeth II right **Reverse:** H.M.S. Dolphin **Edge:** Reeded **Size:** 38.5 mm.

Date	Mintage	F	VF	XF	Unc	BU
1998 Proof	—	Value: 40.00				

KM# 26 **5 TALA** **Weight:** 28.1200 g. **Composition:** 0.9250 Silver 0.8363 oz. ASW **Subject:** Queen Mother **Obverse:** Queen's portrait **Reverse:** Queen Mother celebrating "VE" day **Edge:** Reeded **Size:** 38.4 mm.

Date	Mintage	F	VF	XF	Unc	BU
2000 Proof	10,000	Value: 40.00				

Note: With gold gilt outer ring

KM# 12 50 TALA **Weight:** 31.1030 g. **Composition:** 0.9990 Silver 1 oz. ASW **Reverse:** 50th anniversary of attack on Pearl Harbor scene

Date	Mintage	F	VF	XF	Unc	BU
1991 Proof	50,000	Value: 55.00				

KM# 24 100 TALA **Weight:** 32.1480 g. **Composition:** 0.9990 Silver 1 oz. ASW **Reverse:** Three sailing warships **Size:** 100 mm. **Note:** Illustration reduced.

Date	Mintage	F	VF	XF	Unc	BU
1996 Proof	1,500	Value: 375				

TONGA

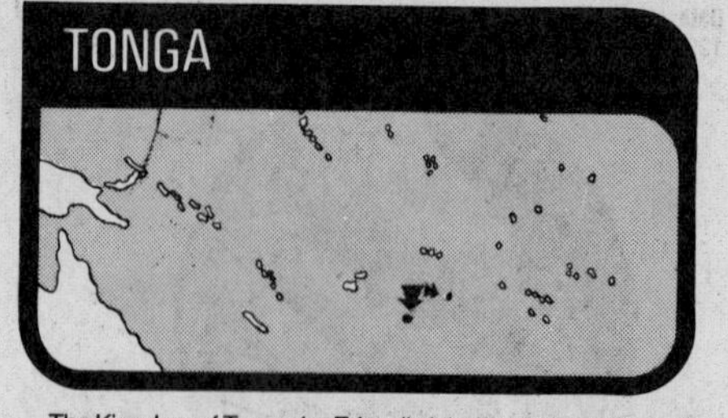

The Kingdom of Tonga (or Friendly Islands) is an archipelago situated in the southern Pacific Ocean south of Western Samoa and east of Fiji comprising 150 islands. Tonga has an area of 270 sq. mi. (748 sq. km.) and a population of *100,000.Capital: Nuku'alofa. Primarily agricultural, the kingdom exports bananas and copra.

Dutch navigators Willem Schouten and Jacob Lemaire were the first Europeans to visit Tonga in 1616. The noted Dutch explorer Abel Tasman who visited the Tongatapu group in 1643 followed them. No further European contact was made until 1773 when British navigator Capt. James Cook arrived and, impressed by the peaceful deportment of the natives, named the islands the Friendly Islands. Within a few years of Cook's visit, Tonga was embroiled in a civil war that lasted until the great chief Taufa'ahau, who reigned as Siasoi Tupou I (1845-93), was converted to Christianity and brought unity and peace to the islands. Tonga became a self-governing protectorate of Great Britain in 1900 and a fully independent state on June 4, 1970. The monarchy is a member of the Commonwealth of Nations. King Taufa'ahau is Head of State and Government.

RULERS

Queen Salote, 1918-1965
King Taufa'ahau IV, 1967—

MONETARY SYSTEM

12 Pence = 1 Shilling
20 Shillings = 1 Pound

KINGDOM

STANDARD COINAGE

16 Pounds = 1 Koula

KM# 1 1/4 KOULA **Weight:** 8.1250 g. **Composition:** 0.9160 Gold .2395 oz. AGW

Date	Mintage	F	VF	XF	Unc	BU
1962	—	—	—	—	110	—
1962 Proof	6,300	Value: 125				

KM# 1a 1/4 KOULA **Composition:** Platinum APW

Date		F	VF	XF	Unc	BU
1962 Proof	—	Value: 500				

KM# 2 1/2 KOULA **Weight:** 16.2500 g. **Composition:** 0.9160 Gold .4789 oz. AGW

Date	Mintage	F	VF	XF	Unc	BU
1962	—	—	—	—	210	—
1962 Proof	3,000	Value: 240				

KM# 2a 1/2 KOULA **Composition:** Platinum APW

Date		F	VF	XF	Unc	BU
1962 Proof	—	Value: 750				

KM# 3 KOULA **Weight:** 32.5000 g. **Composition:** 0.9160 Gold .9278 oz. AGW

Date		F	VF	XF	Unc
1962		—	—	—	435
1962 Proof	—	Value: 575			

KM# 3a KOULA **Composition:** Platinum APW

Date		F	VF	XF	Unc
1962 Proof	—	Value: 1,000			

DECIMAL COINAGE

100 Senti = 1 Pa'anga; 100 Pa'anga = 1 Hau

KM# 4 SENITI **Composition:** Bronze **Reverse:** Giant Tortoise

Date	Mintage	F	VF	XF	Unc
1967	500,000	—	0.10	0.15	1.00
1967 Proof	—	Value: 2.00			

KM# 27 SENITI **Composition:** Bronze **Reverse:** Gian tortoise

Date	Mintage	F	VF	XF	Unc
1968	500,000	—	0.10	0.15	1.00
1968 Proof	—	Value: 2.00			

KM# 27a SENITI **Composition:** Brass **Reverse:** Gian tortoise

Date	Mintage	F	VF	XF	Unc
1974	500,000	—	0.10	0.15	0.75

KM# 42 SENITI **Composition:** Bronze **Series:** F.A.O. **Reverse:** Pig

Date	Mintage	F	VF	XF	Unc
1975	1,000,000	—	—	0.10	0.35
1979	1,000,000	—	—	0.10	0.35

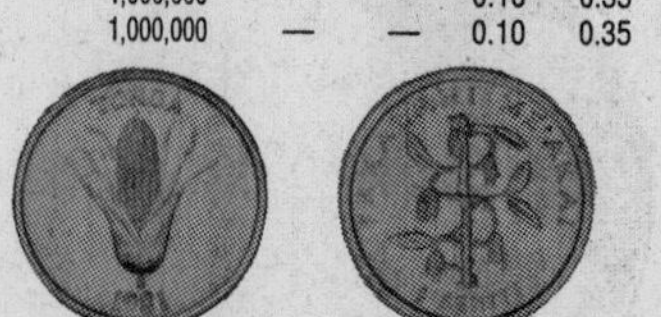

KM# 66 SENITI **Composition:** Bronze **Series:** World Food Day

Date	Mintage	F	VF	XF	Unc
1981	1,544,000	—	—	0.10	0.50
1990	—	—	—	0.10	0.35
1991	—	—	—	0.10	0.35

Mintage	F	VF	XF	Unc	BU
500,000	—	—	0.10	0.35	—
—	—	—	0.10	0.35	—

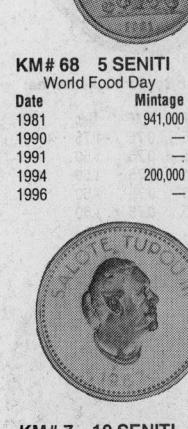

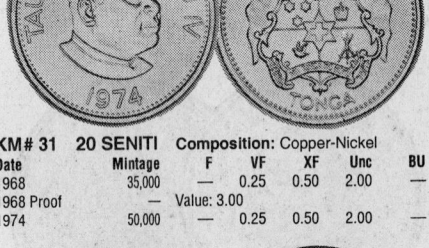

 # 5 2 SENITI Composition: Bronze **Reverse:** Giant 'ortoise

	Mintage	F	VF	XF	Unc	BU
	500,000	—	0.10	0.20	1.50	2.50
Proof	—	Value: 2.50				

 # 28 2 SENITI Composition: Bronze **Reverse:** Giant 'ortoise

	Mintage	F	VF	XF	Unc	BU
	200,000	—	0.10	0.20	1.75	2.75
Proof	—	Value: 2.50				
	25,000	—	0.10	0.20	1.75	2.75

 # 43 2 SENITI Composition: Bronze **Series:** F.A.O.

Mintage	F	VF	XF	Unc	BU
400,000	—	—	0.15	0.65	—
500,000	—	—	0.15	0.65	—

 # 67 2 SENITI Composition: Bronze **Series:** World Food Day

	Mintage	F	VF	XF	Unc	BU
1	1,102,000	—	—	0.15	0.65	—
)	—	—	—	0.15	0.50	—
	—	—	—	0.15	0.50	—
4	250,000	—	—	0.15	0.50	—
6	—	—	—	0.15	0.50	—

 # 6 5 SENITI Composition: Copper-Nickel

	Mintage	F	VF	XF	Unc	BU
7	300,000	—	0.10	0.25	1.75	—
7 Proof	—	Value: 2.50				

 # 29 5 SENITI Composition: Copper-Nickel

	Mintage	F	VF	XF	Unc	BU
8	100,000	—	0.10	0.25	1.50	—
8 Proof	—	Value: 2.50				
4	75,000	—	0.10	0.25	1.50	—

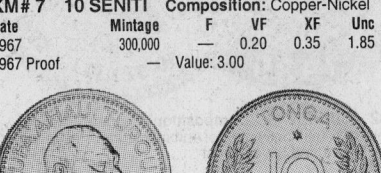

 # 44 5 SENITI Composition: Copper-Nickel **Series:** F.A.O. **Obverse:** Hen with chicks **Reverse:** Bunch of bananas

Date	Mintage	F	VF	XF	Unc	BU
1975	100,000	—	0.10	0.25	0.85	—
1977	110,000	—	0.10	0.25	0.85	—
1979	100,000	—	0.10	0.25	0.85	—

KM# 68 5 SENITI Composition: Copper-Nickel **Series:** World Food Day

Date	Mintage	F	VF	XF	Unc	BU
1981	941,000	—	0.10	0.25	1.00	—
1990	—	—	0.10	0.25	1.00	—
1991	—	—	—	0.25	1.00	—
1994	200,000	—	0.10	0.25	1.00	—
1996	—	—	0.10	0.25	1.00	—

KM# 7 10 SENITI Composition: Copper-Nickel

Date	Mintage	F	VF	XF	Unc	BU
1967	300,000	—	0.20	0.35	1.85	—
1967 Proof	—	Value: 3.00				

KM# 30 10 SENITI Composition: Copper-Nickel

Date	Mintage	F	VF	XF	Unc	BU
1968	100,000	—	0.20	0.40	1.75	—
1968 Proof	—	Value: 3.00				
1974	50,000	—	0.25	0.50	1.75	—

KM# 45 10 SENITI Composition: Copper-Nickel **Series:** F.A.O.

Date	Mintage	F	VF	XF	Unc	BU
1975	75,000	—	0.20	0.30	1.00	—
1977	25,000	—	0.20	0.30	1.00	—
1979	100,000	—	0.20	0.30	1.00	—

KM# 69 10 SENITI Composition: Copper-Nickel **Series:** World Food Day

Date	Mintage	F	VF	XF	Unc	BU
1981	712,000	—	0.20	0.30	1.25	—
1990	—	—	0.20	0.30	1.00	—
1991	—	—	0.20	0.30	1.00	—
1994	140,000	—	0.20	0.30	1.00	—
1996	—	—	0.20	0.30	1.00	—

KM# 8 20 SENITI Composition: Copper-Nickel

Date	Mintage	F	VF	XF	Unc	BU
1967	150,000	—	0.25	0.50	2.00	—
1967 Proof	—	Value: 3.50				

KM# 13 20 SENITI Composition: Copper-Nickel **Subject:** Coronation of Taufa'ahau Tupou IV

Date	Mintage	F	VF	XF	Unc	BU
ND(1967)	15,000	—	0.75	1.25	2.25	—
ND(1967) Proof	—	Value: 3.50				

KM# 31 20 SENITI Composition: Copper-Nickel

Date	Mintage	F	VF	XF	Unc	BU
1968	35,000	—	0.25	0.50	2.00	—
1968 Proof	—	Value: 3.00				
1974	50,000	—	0.25	0.50	2.00	—

KM# 46 20 SENITI Composition: Copper-Nickel **Series:** F.A.O.

Date	Mintage	F	VF	XF	Unc	BU
1975	75,000	—	0.25	0.60	1.50	—
1977	25,000	—	0.25	0.60	1.50	—
1979	50,000	—	0.25	0.60	1.50	—

KM# 70 20 SENITI Composition: Copper-Nickel **Series:** World Food Day

Date	Mintage	F	VF	XF	Unc	BU
1981	610,000	—	0.25	0.50	1.50	—
1990	610,000	—	0.25	0.50	1.25	—
1991	—	—	0.25	0.50	1.25	—
1994	680,000	—	0.25	0.50	1.25	—
1996	—	—	0.25	0.50	1.25	—

KM# 9 50 SENITI Composition: Copper-Nickel

Date	Mintage	F	VF	XF	Unc	BU
1967	75,000	—	0.75	1.25	2.50	—
1967 Proof	—	Value: 4.00				

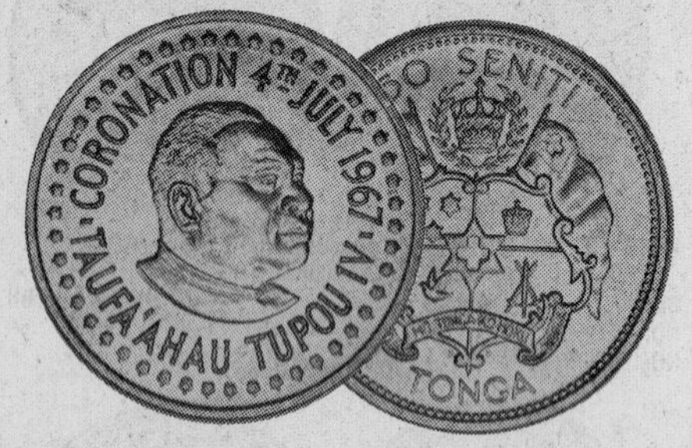

KM# 15 50 SENITI Composition: Copper-Nickel
Subject: Coronation of Taufa'ahau Tupou IV

Date	Mintage	F	VF	XF	Unc	BU
ND(1967)	15,000	—	1.00	2.00	3.50	—
ND(1967) Proof	—	Value: 6.00				

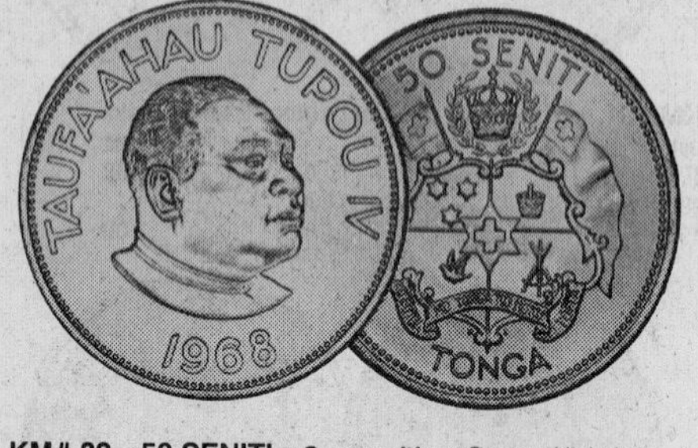

KM# 32 50 SENITI Composition: Copper-Nickel

Date	Mintage	F	VF	XF	Unc	BU
1968	25,000	—	0.75	1.25	2.25	—
1968 Proof	—	Value: 4.00				

KM# 41 50 SENITI Composition: Copper-Nickel **Shape:** 12-sided

Date	Mintage	F	VF	XF	Unc	BU
1974	50,000	—	0.75	1.25	2.00	—

KM# 47 50 SENITI Composition: Copper-Nickel **Series:** F.A.O. **Reverse:** Many fish swimming in circle formation

Date	Mintage	F	VF	XF	Unc	BU
1975	40,000	—	0.50	1.00	2.50	—
1977	20,000	—	0.75	1.25	2.75	—
1978	60,000	—	0.50	1.00	2.50	—

KM# 71 50 SENITI Composition: Copper-Nickel **Series:** World Food Day

Date	Mintage	F	VF	XF	Unc	BU
1981	555,000	—	0.45	0.75	1.75	—
1990	—	—	0.45	0.75	1.50	—
1991	—	—	0.45	0.75	1.50	—
1994	41,000	—	0.45	0.75	1.50	—
1996	—	—	0.45	0.75	1.50	—

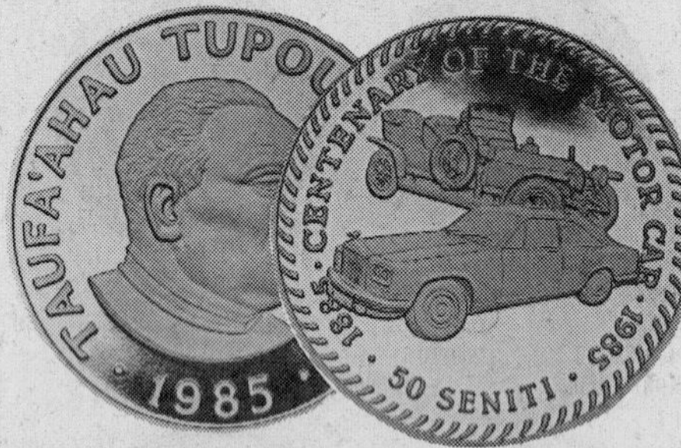

KM# 82 50 SENITI Composition: Copper-Nickel
Subject: 100th Anniversary of Automobile Industry **Reverse:** Rolls-Royce and Silver Ghost

Date	F	VF	XF	Unc	BU
1985	—	—	—	5.50	—

KM# 83 50 SENITI Composition: Copper-Nickel
Subject: 100th Anniversary of Automobile Industry **Reverse:** Range Rover and Land Rover

Date	F	VF	XF	Unc	BU
1985	—	—	—	6.00	—

KM# 84 50 SENITI Composition: Copper-Nickel
Subject: 100th Anniversary of Automobile Industry **Reverse:** Mini Morris Cowley and Touring Car

Date	F	VF	XF	Unc	BU
1985	—	—	—	5.50	—

KM# 85 50 SENITI Composition: Copper-Nickel
Subject: 100th Anniversary of Automobile Industry **Rever**
MGB GT and MGTA

Date	F	VF	XF	Unc
1985	—	—	—	5.50

KM# 98 50 SENITI Composition: Copper-Nickel
Subject: 85th Birthday of Queen Mother **Reverse:** Half b
of Queen Mother as a young girl facing

Date	F	VF	XF	Unc
1985	—	—	—	4.00

KM# 99 50 SENITI Composition: Copper-Nickel **Subje**
85th Birthday of Queen Mother **Reverse:** Wedding scene
3/4-length busts of King George VI and Elizabeth facing

Date	F	VF	XF	Unc
1985	—	—	—	4.00

KM# 100 50 SENITI Composition: Copper-Nickel
Subject: 85th Birthday of Queen Mother **Reverse:** Busts o
King George VI right and Elizabeth at left facing

Date	F	VF	XF	Unc	B
1985	—	—	—	4.00	

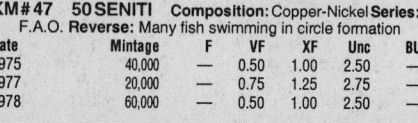

101 50 SENITI **Composition:** Copper-Nickel
ıbject: 85th Birthday of Queen Mother **Reverse:** Queen
ıther holding infant Elizabeth

F	VF	XF	Unc	BU
—	—	—	4.00	—

102 50 SENITI **Composition:** Copper-Nickel
ıbject: 85th Birthday of Queen Mother **Reverse:** Bust of
ueen Mother facing

F	VF	XF	Unc	BU
—	—	—	4.00	—

171 50 SENITI **Weight:** 20.0000 g. **Composition:** .9250 Silver .5948 oz. ASW **Subject:** Olympics - Boxing **bverse:** National arms **Reverse:** Boxer **Edge:** Reeded **ize:** 34 mm.

	Mintage	F	VF	XF	Unc	BU
Proof	50,000	Value: 27.50				

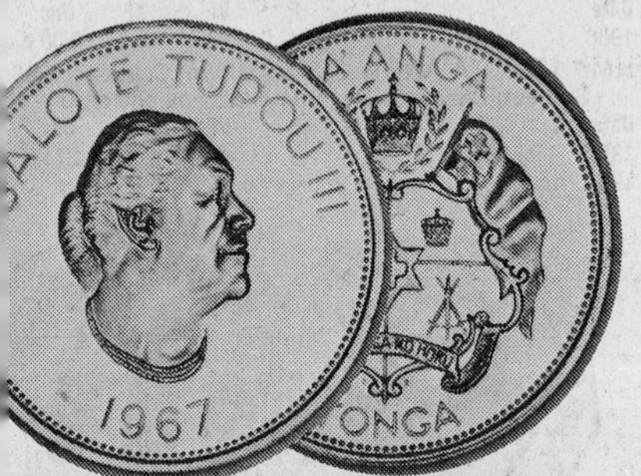

 # 11 PA'ANGA **Composition:** Copper-Nickel

	Mintage	F	VF	XF	Unc	BU
	78,000	—	1.00	2.00	4.50	—
Proof	—	Value: 5.50				

 # 17 PA'ANGA **Composition:** Copper-Nickel
Subject: Coronation of Taufa'ahau Tupou IV

	Mintage	F	VF	XF	Unc	BU
967)	13,000	—	1.00	2.00	4.00	—
967) Proof	1,923	Value: 5.50				

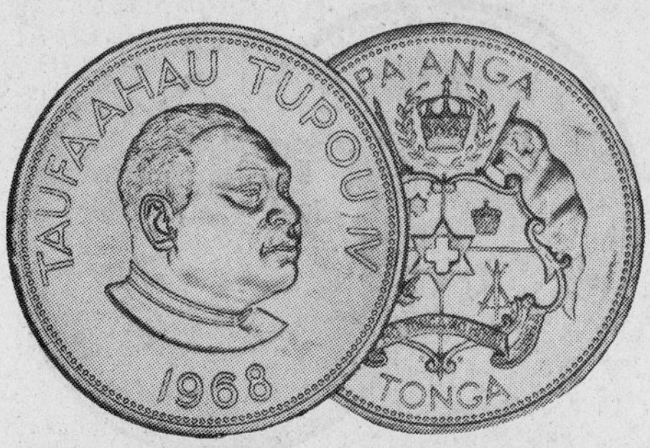

KM# 33 PA'ANGA **Composition:** Copper-Nickel

Date	Mintage	F	VF	XF	Unc	BU
1968	14,000	—	1.00	2.00	4.00	—
1968 Proof	—	Value: 6.50				
1974	10,000	—	1.00	2.00	4.50	—

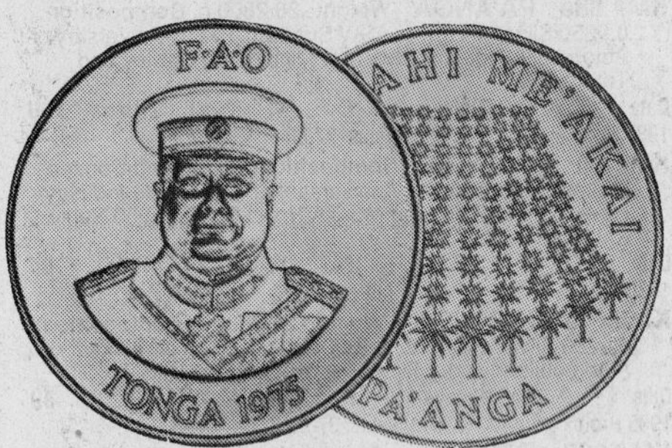

KM# 48 PA'ANGA **Composition:** Copper-Nickel
Series: F.A.O. **Reverse:** Forest of trees

Date	Mintage	F	VF	XF	Unc	BU
1975	13,000	—	1.25	2.50	5.50	10.00

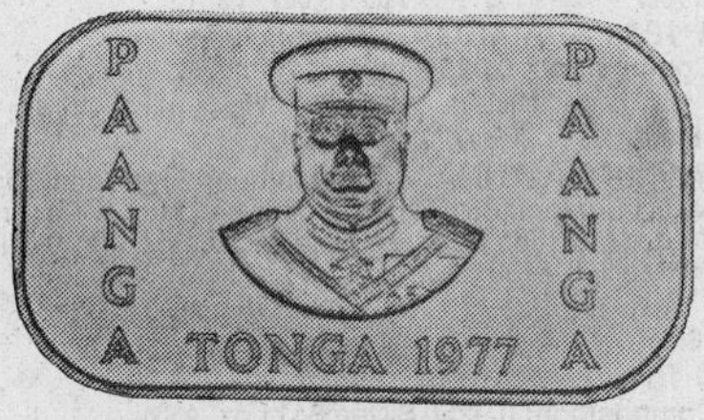

KM# 57 PA'ANGA **Composition:** Copper-Nickel
Series: F.A.O **Shape:** Rectangular

Date	Mintage	F	VF	XF	Unc	BU
1977	25,000	—	1.50	3.50	8.00	15.00

KM# 58 PA'ANGA **Composition:** Copper-Nickel
Series: F.A.O. **Subject:** 60th Birthday **Reverse:** Similar to KM#57 **Shape:** Rectangular

Date	Mintage	F	VF	XF	Unc	BU
1978	10,000	—	1.50	3.50	8.00	15.00

KM# 58a PA'ANGA **Weight:** 24.5000 g. **Composition:** 0.9990 Silver .7869 oz. ASW **Shape:** Rectangular

Date	Mintage	F	VF	XF	Unc	BU
1978 Proof	750	Value: 45.00				

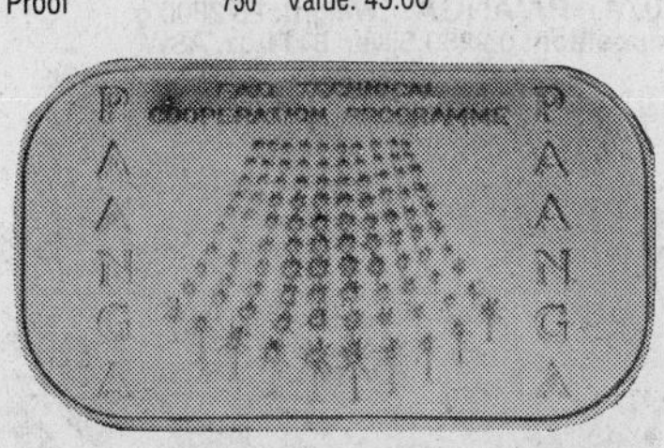

KM# 60 PA'ANGA **Composition:** Copper-Nickel
Series: F.A.O. **Subject:** Technical Cooperation Program **Shape:** Rectangular

Date	Mintage	F	VF	XF	Unc	BU
1979	26,000	—	1.50	3.50	8.00	15.00

KM# 60a PA'ANGA **Weight:** 24.5000 g. **Composition:** 0.9990 Silver .7869 oz. ASW **Shape:** Rectangular

Date	Mintage	F	VF	XF	Unc	BU
1979 Proof	850	Value: 42.50				

KM# 62 PA'ANGA **Composition:** Copper-Nickel
Series: F.A.O. **Subject:** Rural Women's Advancement **Shape:** Rectangular

Date	Mintage	F	VF	XF	Unc	BU
1980	8,000	—	1.50	3.50	8.00	15.00

KM# 62a PA'ANGA **Weight:** 24.5000 g. **Composition:** 0.9990 Silver .7869 oz. ASW **Shape:** Rectangular

Date	Mintage	F	VF	XF	Unc	BU
1980 Proof	2,200	Value: 40.00				

KM# 72 PA'ANGA **Composition:** Copper-Nickel
Series: World Food Day **Obverse:** Similar to KM#57 **Reverse:** Sailboat **Shape:** Rectangular

Date	Mintage	F	VF	XF	Unc	BU
1981	485,000	—	1.50	3.50	8.00	15.00

KM# 72a PA'ANGA **Weight:** 24.5000 g. **Composition:** 0.9990 Silver .7869 oz. ASW **Reverse:** Sailboat **Shape:** Rectangular

Date	Mintage	F	VF	XF	Unc	BU
1981 Proof	3,500	Value: 40.00				

KM# 77 PA'ANGA **Composition:** Copper-Nickel
Subject: Christmas **Reverse:** Two hands in praying position **Shape:** 7-sided

Date	Mintage	F	VF	XF	Unc	BU
1982	5,000	—	0.75	1.00	3.50	—
1982 Proof	—	Value: 5.50				

KM# 77a PA'ANGA **Weight:** 15.5000 g. **Composition:** 0.9250 Silver .4610 oz. ASW **Reverse:** Two hands in praying position **Shape:** 7-sided

Date	Mintage	F	VF	XF	Unc	BU
1982 Proof	2,500	Value: 12.50				

KM# 77b PA'ANGA **Weight:** 26.0000 g. **Composition:** 0.9170 Gold .7666 oz. AGW **Subject:** Christmas **Reverse:** Two hands in praying position **Shape:** 7-sided

Date	Mintage	F	VF	XF	Unc	BU
1982 Proof	250	Value: 500				

KM# 77c PA'ANGA **Weight:** 30.4000 g. **Composition:** 0.9500 Platinum .9286 oz. APW **Reverse:** Two hands in praying position **Shape:** 7-sided

Date	Mintage	F	VF	XF	Unc	BU
1982 Proof	25	Value: 850				

KM# 80 PA'ANGA **Composition:** Copper-Nickel **Subject:** Christmas **Reverse:** Kneeling Joseph and Mary **Shape:** 7-sided

Date	Mintage	F	VF	XF	Unc	BU
1983	5,000	—	0.75	1.00	3.50	—

KM# 80a PA'ANGA **Weight:** 15.5000 g. **Composition:** 0.9250 Silver .4610 oz. ASW **Reverse:** Kneeling Joseph and Mary **Shape:** 7-sided

Date	Mintage	F	VF	XF	Unc	BU
1983 Proof	2,500	Value: 12.50				

KM# 80b PA'ANGA **Weight:** 26.0000 g. **Composition:** 0.9170 Gold .7666 oz. AGW **Subject:** Christmas **Reverse:** Kneeling Joseph and Mary **Shape:** 7-sided

Date	Mintage	F	VF	XF	Unc	BU
1983 Proof	250	Value: 500				

KM# 80c PA'ANGA **Weight:** 30.4000 g. **Composition:** 0.9500 Platinum .9286 oz. APW **Reverse:** Kneeling Joseph and Mary **Shape:** 7-sided

Date	Mintage	F	VF	XF	Unc	BU
1983 Proof	25	Value: 850				

KM# 81 PA'ANGA **Composition:** Copper-Nickel **Subject:** Christmas **Reverse:** Mary holding infant Jesus **Shape:** 7-sided

Date	Mintage	F	VF	XF	Unc	BU
1984	5,000	—	0.75	1.00	3.50	—

KM# 81a PA'ANGA **Weight:** 15.5000 g. **Composition:** 0.9250 Silver .4610 oz. ASW **Reverse:** Kneeling Joseph and Mary **Shape:** 7-sided

Date	Mintage	F	VF	XF	Unc	BU
1984 Proof	2,500	Value: 12.50				

KM# 81b PA'ANGA **Weight:** 26.0000 g. **Composition:** 0.9170 Gold .7666 oz. AGW **Subject:** Christmas **Reverse:** Kneeling Joseph and Mary **Shape:** 7-sided

Date	Mintage	F	VF	XF	Unc	BU
1984 Proof	250	Value: 500				

KM# 81c PA'ANGA **Weight:** 30.4000 g. **Composition:** 0.9500 Platinum .9286 oz. APW **Reverse:** Kneeling Joseph and Mary **Shape:** 7-sided

Date	Mintage	F	VF	XF	Unc	BU
1984 Proof	25	Value: 850				

KM# 86 PA'ANGA **Composition:** Silver Clad Copper-Nickel **Subject:** 100th Anniversary of Automobile Industry **Reverse:** Rolls-Royce and Silver Ghost

Date	F	VF	XF	Unc	BU
1985 Proof	—	Value: 6.50			

KM# 86a PA'ANGA **Weight:** 28.2800 g. **Composition:** 0.9250 Silver .8411 oz. ASW **Subject:** 100th Anniversary of Automobile Industry **Reverse:** Rolls Royce and Silver Ghost

Date	Mintage	F	VF	XF	Unc	BU
1985 Proof	5,000	Value: 37.50				

KM# 87 PA'ANGA **Composition:** Silver Clad Copper-Nickel **Subject:** 100th Anniversary of Automobile Industry **Reverse:** Range Rover and Land Rover

Date	F	VF	XF	Unc	BU
1985 Proof	—	Value: 6.50			

KM# 87a PA'ANGA **Weight:** 28.2800 g. **Composition:** 0.9250 Silver .8411 oz. ASW **Subject:** 100th Anniversary of Automobile Industry **Reverse:** Range Rover and Land Rover

Date	Mintage	F	VF	XF	Unc	BU
1985 Proof	5,000	Value: 37.50				

KM# 88 PA'ANGA **Composition:** Silver Clad Copper-Nickel **Subject:** 100th Anniversary of Automobile Industry **Reverse:** Mini Morris Cowley and Touring Car

Date	F	VF	XF	Unc	BU
1985 Proof	—	Value: 6.50			

KM# 88a PA'ANGA **Weight:** 28.2800 g. **Composition:** 0.9250 Silver .8411 oz. ASW **Subject:** 100th Anniversary of Automobile Industry **Reverse:** Mini Morris Cowley and Touring Car

Date	Mintage	F	VF	XF	Unc	BU
1985 Proof	5,000	Value: 37.50				

KM# 89 PA'ANGA **Composition:** Silver Clad Copper-Nickel **Subject:** 100th Anniversary of Automobile Industry **Reverse:** MGB GT and MG TA **Note:** Similar to 50 Seniti, KM#85.

Date	F	VF	XF	Unc	BU
1985 Proof	—	Value: 6.50			

KM# 89a PA'ANGA **Weight:** 28.2800 g. **Composition:** 0.9250 Silver .8411 oz. ASW **Subject:** 100th Anniversary of Automobile Industry **Reverse:** MGB GT and MG TA

Date	Mintage	F	VF	XF	Unc	BU
1985 Proof	5,000	Value: 37.50				

KM# 103 PA'ANGA **Composition:** Silver Clad Copper-Nickel **Subject:** 85th Birthday of Queen Mother **Reverse:** Queen Mother as a young girl **Note:** Similar to 50 Seniti, KM#98.

Date	F	VF	XF	Unc	BU
1985 Proof	—	Value: 5.00			

KM# 103a PA'ANGA **Weight:** 28.2800 g. **Composition:** 0.9250 Silver .8411 oz. ASW

Date	Mintage	F	VF	XF	Unc	BU
1985 Proof	5,000	Value: 25.00				

KM# 104 PA'ANGA **Composition:** Silver Clad Copper-Nickel **Subject:** 85th Birthday of Queen Mother **Reverse:** Wedding of King George VI and Ellizabeth **Note:** Similar to 50 Seniti, KM#99.

Date	F	VF	XF	Unc	BU
1985 Proof	—	Value: 5.00			

KM# 104a PA'ANGA **Weight:** 28.2800 g. **Composition:** 0.9250 Silver .8411 oz. ASW

Date	Mintage	F	VF	XF	Unc	BU
1985 Proof	5,000	Value: 25.00				

KM# 105 PA'ANGA **Composition:** Silver Clad Copper-Nickel **Subject:** 85th Birthday of Queen Mother **Reverse:** King George VI and Ellizabeth **Note:** Similar to 50 Seniti, KM#100.

Date	F	VF	XF	Unc	BU
1985 Proof	—	Value: 5.50			

KM# 105a PA'ANGA **Weight:** 28.2800 g. **Composition:** 0.9250 Silver .8411 oz. ASW

Date	Mintage	F	VF	XF	Unc	BU
1985 Proof	5,000	Value: 30.00				

KM# 106 PA'ANGA **Composition:** Silver Clad Copper-Nickel **Subject:** 85th Birthday of Queen Mother **Reverse:** Queen Mother holding Queen Elizabeth **Note:** Similar to 50 Seniti, KM#101.

Date	F	VF	XF	Unc	BU
1985 Proof	—	Value: 5.50			

KM# 106a PA'ANGA **Weight:** 28.2800 g. **Composition:** 0.9250 Silver .8411 oz. ASW

Date	Mintage	F	VF	XF	Unc	BU
1985 Proof	5,000	Value: 30.00				

KM# 107 PA'ANGA **Composition:** Silver Clad Copper-Nickel **Subject:** 85th Birthday of Queen Mother **Note:** Similar to 50 Seniti, KM#102.

Date	F	VF	XF	Unc	BU
1985 Proof	—	Value: 5.50			

KM# 107a PA'ANGA **Weight:** 28.2800 g. **Composition:** 0.9250 Silver .8411 oz. ASW

Date	Mintage	F	VF	XF	Unc	BU
1985 Proof	5,000	Value: 30.00				

KM# 118 PA'ANGA **Composition:** Copper-Nickel **Subject:** Christmas

Date	F	VF	XF	Unc	BU
1985	—	—	1.00	3.00	—

KM# 118a PA'ANGA **Weight:** 15.5000 g. **Composition:** 0.9250 Silver .4610 oz. ASW

Date	Mintage	F	VF	XF	Unc
1985 Proof	250	Value: 35.00			

KM# 118b PA'ANGA **Weight:** 26.0000 g. **Composi** 0.9170 Gold .7666 oz. AGW **Subject:** Christmas

Date	Mintage	F	VF	XF	Unc
1985 Proof	250	Value: 500			

KM# 118c PA'ANGA **Weight:** 30.4000 g. **Composition:** 0.9500 Platinum .9286 oz. APW

Date	F	VF	XF	Unc
1985 Proof	—	Value: 950		

KM# 123 PA'ANGA **Composition:** Copper-Nickel **Subject:** Christmas **Reverse:** Three Wise Men

Date	F	VF	XF	Unc
1986	—	—	1.00	3.00

KM# 123a PA'ANGA **Weight:** 15.5000 g. **Composition:** 0.9250 Silver .4610 oz. ASW

Date	F	VF	XF	Unc
1986	—	—	—	35.00

KM# 123b PA'ANGA **Weight:** 26.0000 g. **Composi** 0.9170 Gold .7666 oz. AGW **Subject:** Christmas

Date	F	VF	XF	Unc
1986	—	—	—	500

KM# 123c PA'ANGA **Weight:** 30.4000 g. **Composition:** 0.9500 Platinum .9286 oz. APW

Date	F	VF	XF	Unc
1986	—	—	—	950

KM# 128 PA'ANGA **Composition:** Copper-Nickel **Series:** 25th Anniversary of World Wildlife Fund **Rever** Humpback whales - cow and calf

Date	F	VF	XF	Unc
1986	—	—	—	6.00

KM# 139 PA'ANGA **Composition:** Copper-Nickel **Subject:** Christmas **Reverse:** Madonna and child

Date	F	VF	XF	Unc
1987	—	—	—	2.75
1987 Proof	—	Value: 4.50		

KM# 127 PA'ANGA **Composition:** Copper-Nickel **Subject:** Christmas **Shape:** 7-sided

Date	F	VF	XF	Unc
1988	—	—	—	2.75
1988 Proof	—	Value: 4.50		

KM# 127a PA'ANGA **Weight:** 15.5000 g. **Composition:** 0.9250 Silver .4610 oz. ASW

Date	F	VF	XF	Unc
1988 Proof	—	Value: 27.50		

KM# 127b PA'ANGA **Weight:** 26.0000 g. **Compositi** 0.9170 Gold .7666 oz. AGW **Subject:** Christmas

Date	F	VF	XF	Unc
1988 Proof	—	Value: 500		

KM# 127c PA'ANGA **Weight:** 30.4000 g. **Composition:** 0.9500 Platinum .9286 oz. APW

Date	F	VF	XF	Unc
1988 Proof	—	Value: 850		

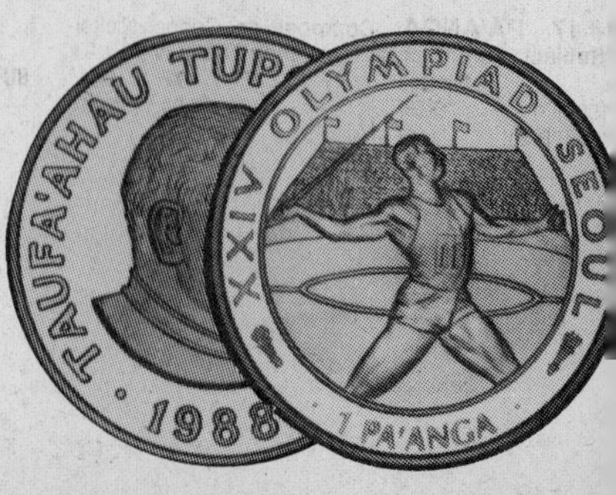

133 PA'ANGA **Weight:** 31.7300 g. **Composition:** .9250 Silver .9437 oz. ASW **Series:** Olympics **Reverse:** avelin thrower

	F	VF	XF	Unc	BU
Proof	—	Value: 27.50			

 # 134 PA'ANGA **Weight:** 31.7300 g. **Composition:** .9250 Silver .9437 oz. ASW **Series:** Olympics **Reverse:** Swimmers

	F	VF	XF	Unc	BU
Proof	—	Value: 27.50			

 # 135 PA'ANGA **Weight:** 31.7300 g. **Composition:** 0.9250 Silver .9437 oz. ASW **Series:** Olympics **Reverse:** Boxers

	F	VF	XF	Unc	BU
Proof	—	Value: 27.50			

 # 136 PA'ANGA **Weight:** 31.7300 g. **Composition:** 0.9250 Silver .9437 oz. ASW **Series:** Olympics **Reverse:** Discus thrower

	F	VF	XF	Unc	BU
3 Proof	—	Value: 27.50			

 # 137 PA'ANGA **Weight:** 31.7300 g. **Composition:** 0.9250 Silver .9437 oz. ASW **Series:** Olympics **Reverse:** Shotput thrower

	F	VF	XF	Unc	BU
3 Proof	—	Value: 27.50			

KM# 138 PA'ANGA **Weight:** 31.7300 g. **Composition:** 0.9250 Silver .9437 oz. ASW **Series:** Olympics **Reverse:** Runners

Date	F	VF	XF	Unc	BU
1988 Proof	—	Value: 27.50			

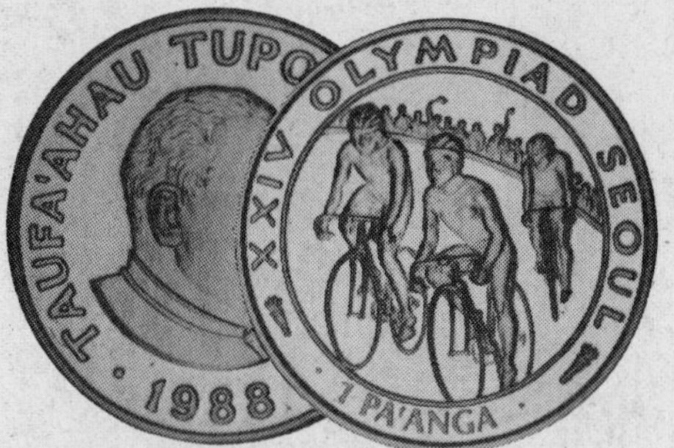

KM# 145 PA'ANGA **Weight:** 31.7300 g. **Composition:** 0.9250 Silver .9437 oz. ASW **Series:** Olympics **Reverse:** Bicycling

Date	F	VF	XF	Unc	BU
1988 Proof	—	Value: 27.50			

KM# 146 PA'ANGA **Weight:** 31.7300 g. **Composition:** 0.9250 Silver .9437 oz. ASW **Series:** Olympics **Reverse:** Gymnast on rings

Date	F	VF	XF	Unc	BU
1988 Proof	—	Value: 27.50			

KM# 147 PA'ANGA **Weight:** 31.7300 g. **Composition:** 0.9250 Silver .9437 oz. ASW **Series:** Olympics **Reverse:** Diver

Date	F	VF	XF	Unc	BU
1988 Proof	—	Value: 27.50			

KM# 148 PA'ANGA **Weight:** 31.7300 g. **Composition:** 0.9250 Silver .9437 oz. ASW **Series:** Olympics **Reverse:** Judo

Date	F	VF	XF	Unc	BU
1988 Proof	—	Value: 27.50			

KM# 149 PA'ANGA **Weight:** 31.7300 g. **Composition:** 0.9250 Silver .9437 oz. ASW **Series:** Olympics **Reverse:** Broad jump

Date	F	VF	XF	Unc	BU
1988 Proof	—	Value: 27.50			

KM# 150 PA'ANGA **Weight:** 31.7300 g. **Composition:** 0.9250 Silver .9437 oz. ASW **Series:** Olympics **Reverse:** Weight lifter

Date	F	VF	XF	Unc	BU
1988 Proof	—	Value: 27.50			

KM# 175 PA'ANGA **Weight:** 31.8000 g. **Composition:** 0.9250 Silver .9457 oz. ASW **Subject:** 25th Anniversary of Reign **Obverse:** National arms **Reverse:** Radiant sun rising through stone structure

Date	F	VF	XF	Unc	BU
ND(1990) Proof	—	Value: 30.00			

KM# 140 PA'ANGA **Weight:** 31.6000 g. **Composition:** 0.9250 Silver .9398 oz. ASW **Series:** Olympics **Reverse:** Diver

Date	Mintage	F	VF	XF	Unc	BU
1991 Proof	Est. 40,000	Value: 16.50				

KM# 141 PA'ANGA **Weight:** 31.6000 g. **Composition:** 0.9250 Silver .9398 oz. ASW **Subject:** Explorers **Reverse:** Busts of Schouten and LeMaire at left, ship at right

Date	Mintage	F	VF	XF	Unc	BU
1991 Proof	Est. 10,000	Value: 21.50				

KM# 143 PA'ANGA **Weight:** 31.6000 g. **Composition:** 0.9250 Silver .9398 oz. ASW **Subject:** Endangered Wildlife **Reverse:** Pritchard's Megapode Birds

Date	Mintage	F	VF	XF	Unc	BU
1991 Proof	—	Value: 24.00				

KM# 156 PA'ANGA **Weight:** 31.6000 g. **Composition:** 0.9250 Silver .9398 oz. ASW **Series:** 1996 Olympics **Reverse:** Sailing

Date	Mintage	F	VF	XF	Unc	BU
1992 Proof	40,000	Value: 16.50				

KM# 157 PA'ANGA **Weight:** 31.6000 g. **Composition:** 0.9250 Silver .9398 oz. ASW **Subject:** Soccer **Reverse:** Players

Date	Mintage	F	VF	XF	Unc	BU
1992 Proof	10,000	Value: 20.00				

KM# 158 PA'ANGA **Weight:** 31.6000 g. **Composition:** 0.9250 Silver .9398 oz. ASW **Subject:** Space Flight **Reverse:** Saturn on launchpad at right, US map at left

Date	Mintage	F	VF	XF	Unc	BU
1992 Proof	10,000	Value: 21.50				

KM# 168 PA'ANGA **Weight:** 31.6000 g. **Composition:** 0.9250 Silver .9398 oz. ASW **Subject:** 25th Anniversary - Coronation of Tupou IV

Date	Mintage	F	VF	XF	Unc	BU
1992 Proof	Est. 5,000	Value: 25.00				

KM# 144 PA'ANGA **Weight:** 31.4700 g. **Composition:** 0.9250 Silver .9359 oz. ASW **Subject:** 40th Anniversary of Queen Elizabeth's Coronation

Date	Mintage	F	VF	XF	Unc	BU
1993 Proof	Est. 10,000	Value: 16.50				

KM# 151 PA'ANGA **Weight:** 31.4700 g. **Composition:** 0.9250 Silver .9359 oz. ASW **Reverse:** Bust of Herman Orbeth at right facing left

Date	Mintage	F	VF	XF	Unc	BU
1993 Proof	Est. 10,000	Value: 20.00				

KM# 152 PA'ANGA **Weight:** 31.4700 g. **Composos** 0.9250 Silver .9359 oz. ASW **Reverse:** Half-length bu Johannes Gutenberg at left, stack of printed pages at press upper right

Date	Mintage	F	VF	XF	Unc
1993 Proof	Est. 10,000	Value: 20.00			

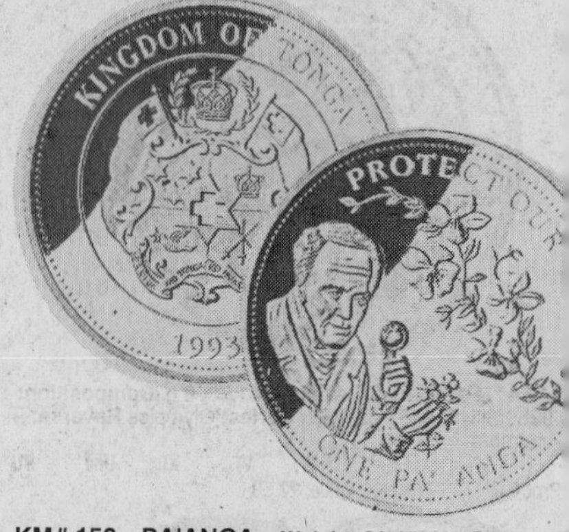

KM# 153 PA'ANGA **Weight:** 31.4700 g. **Composi** 0.9250 Silver .9359 oz. ASW **Subject:** Protect Our W **Reverse:** Alexander von Humboldt

Date	Mintage	F	VF	XF	Unc
1993 Proof	Est. 10,000	Value: 20.00			

KM# 154 PA'ANGA **Weight:** 31.4700 g. **Composi** 0.9250 Silver .9359 oz. ASW **Reverse:** Sailing ship - " Princesa"

Date	Mintage	F	VF	XF	Unc
1993 Proof	Est. 15,000	Value: 20.00			
1994 Proof	—	Value: 20.00			

KM# 160 PA'ANGA **Weight:** 31.4700 g. **Composit** 0.9250 Silver .9359 oz. ASW **Reverse:** Bust of Richard Wagner at right, dancers at upper left

Date	Mintage	F	VF	XF	Unc
1993 Proof	Est. 10,000	Value: 20.00			

KM# 169 PA'ANGA **Weight:** 31.4700 g. **Composit** 0.9250 Silver .9359 oz. ASW **Subject:** 75th Birthday **Obverse:** King Tupou IV **Reverse:** Siu'a'alo rowers

Date	Mintage	F	VF	XF	Unc
1993 Proof	Est. 2,000	Value: 25.00			

 # 159 PA'ANGA Weight: 31.5500 g. **Composition:** 0.9250 Silver .9383 oz. ASW **Series:** 1996 Olympics **Reverse:** Javelin thrower

	Mintage	F	VF	XF	Unc	BU
4 Proof	40,000	Value: 15.00				

 # 161 PA'ANGA Weight: 31.4700 g. **Composition:** 0.9250 Silver .9359 oz. ASW **Subject:** World Cup Soccer **Reverse:** Two players

e	Mintage	F	VF	XF	Unc	BU
94 Proof	Est. 10,000	Value: 16.50				

 # 162 PA'ANGA Weight: 31.4700 g. **Composition:** 0.9250 Silver .9359 oz. ASW **Series:** Endangered Wildlife **Reverse:** Humpback whales - cow and calf

te	Mintage	F	VF	XF	Unc	BU
94 Proof	Est. 10,000	Value: 28.00				

 # 166 PA'ANGA Weight: 31.4700 g. **Composition:** 0.9250 Silver .9359 oz. ASW **Reverse:** Queen Mothers's crown

ate	F	VF	XF	Unc	BU
96	—	—	—	13.50	—

KM# 170 PA'ANGA Weight: 31.4700 g. **Composition:** 0.9250 Silver .9359 oz. ASW **Subject:** 70th Birthday - Queen Mata'aho

Date	Mintage	F	VF	XF	Unc	BU
1996 Proof	Est. 5,000	Value: 27.50				

KM# 174 PA'ANGA Weight: 31.4700 g. **Composition:** 0.9250 Silver .9359 oz. ASW **Obverse:** National arms **Reverse:** Polynesian sailing catamaran

Date	Mintage	F	VF	XF	Unc	BU
1998 Proof	20,000	Value: 20.00				

KM# 176 PA'ANGA Weight: 31.1100 g. **Composition:** 0.9250 Silver .9252 oz. ASW **Subject:** Millennium 2000 **Obverse:** National arms **Reverse:** Stone archway **Edge:** Reeded **Shape:** Scalloped **Size:** 35.5 mm.

Date	F	VF	XF	Unc	BU
1999 Proof	—	Value: 40.00			

KM# 19 2 PA'ANGA Composition: Copper-Nickel **Subject:** Coronation of Taufa'ahau Tupou IV

Date	Mintage	F	VF	XF	Unc	BU
ND(1967)	10,000	—	1.25	2.75	5.00	—
ND(1967) Proof	—	Value: 10.00				

KM# 37 2 PA'ANGA Composition: Copper-Nickel

Date	Mintage	F	VF	XF	Unc	BU
1968	14,000	—	1.25	2.25	4.50	—
1968 Proof	—	Value: 8.00				
1974	10,000	—	1.25	3.00	6.00	—

KM# 49 2 PA'ANGA Composition: Copper-Nickel **Series:** F.A.O.

Date	Mintage	F	VF	XF	Unc	BU
1975	13,000	—	1.25	3.00	7.50	12.00
1977	12,000	—	1.25	3.00	7.50	12.00

KM# 59 2 PA'ANGA Composition: Copper-Nickel **Series:** F.A.O. **Subject:** 60th Birthday **Reverse:** Similar to KM#49

Date	Mintage	F	VF	XF	Unc	BU
1978	10,000	—	2.00	3.50	9.00	13.50

KM# 59a 2 PA'ANGA Weight: 42.1000 g. **Composition:** 0.9990 Silver 1.3523 oz. ASW

Date	Mintage	F	VF	XF	Unc	BU
1978 Proof	750	Value: 32.50				

KM# 61 2 PA'ANGA Composition: Copper-Nickel **Series:** F.A.O. **Subject:** SEA Resource Management **Reverse:** Humpback whale - bull in breach

Date	Mintage	F	VF	XF	Unc	BU
1979	8,000	—	1.25	3.00	7.50	12.00

KM# 61a 2 PA'ANGA Weight: 42.1000 g. **Composition:** 0.9990 Silver 1.3523 oz. ASW **Series:** F.A.O. **Subject:** SEA Resource Management **Reverse:** Humpback whale - bull in breach

Date	Mintage	F	VF	XF	Unc	BU
1979 Proof	850	Value: 47.50				

KM# 63 2 PA'ANGA **Composition:** Copper-Nickel **Series:** F.A.O. **Subject:** SEA Resource Management **Reverse:** Humpback whale - bull in breach

Date	Mintage	F	VF	XF	Unc	BU
1980	8,000	—	1.25	3.00	7.50	12.00

KM# 63a 2 PA'ANGA **Weight:** 42.1000 g. **Composition:** 0.9990 Silver 1.3523 oz. ASW **Series:** F.A.O. **Subject:** SEA Resource Management **Reverse:** Humpback whale - bull in breach

Date	Mintage	F	VF	XF	Unc	BU
1980 Proof	2,200	Value: 32.50				

KM# 73 2 PA'ANGA **Composition:** Copper-Nickel **Series:** World Food Day **Obverse:** Similar to KM#63 **Reverse:** Pigs, chickens, and nursing cow

Date	Mintage	F	VF	XF	Unc	BU
1981	485,000	—	—	2.50	6.50	11.50

KM# 73a 2 PA'ANGA **Weight:** 42.1000 g. **Composition:** 0.9990 Silver 1.3523 oz. ASW

Date	Mintage	F	VF	XF	Unc	BU
1981 Proof	3,500	Value: 22.50				

KM# 120 2 PA'ANGA **Weight:** 28.2800 g. **Composition:** 0.5000 Silver .4546 oz. ASW **Subject:** Commonwealth Games **Reverse:** Boxing match

Date	Mintage	F	VF	XF	Unc	BU
1986	50,000	—	—	—	11.50	—

KM# 120a 2 PA'ANGA **Weight:** 28.2800 g. **Composition:** 0.9250 Silver .8411 oz. ASW **Subject:** Commonwealth Games **Reverse:** Boxing match

Date	Mintage	F	VF	XF	Unc	BU
1986 Proof	20,000	Value: 22.50				

KM# 121 2 PA'ANGA **Weight:** 28.2800 g. **Composition:** 0.9250 Silver .8411 oz. ASW **Subject:** Wildlife **Reverse:** Humpback whales - cow and calf

Date	Mintage	F	VF	XF	Unc	BU
1986 Proof	25,000	Value: 22.50				

KM# 124 2 PA'ANGA **Weight:** 155.5200 g. **Composition:** 0.9990 Silver 5.0000 oz. ASW **Subject:** America's Cup **Size:** 65 mm. **Note:** Illustration reduced

Date	Mintage	F	VF	XF	Unc	BU
1987 Proof	7,500	Value: 45.00				

KM# 129 2 PA'ANGA **Weight:** 155.5200 g. **Composition:** 0.9990 Silver 5.0000 oz. ASW **Series:** Olympics **Obverse:** Similar to 10 Pa'anga, KM#130 **Reverse:** Swimmers **Size:** 65 mm. **Note:** Illustration reduced.

Date	Mintage	F	VF	XF	Unc	BU
1988 Proof	2,000	Value: 45.00				

KM# 50 5 PA'ANGA **Weight:** 31.0000 g. **Composition:** 0.9990 Silver .9957 oz. ASW **Subject:** Constitution Centennial

Date	Mintage	F	VF	XF	Unc	BU
ND(1975)	2,118	—	—	—	15.00	—
ND(1975) Proof	418	Value: 27.50				

KM# 51 10 PA'ANGA **Weight:** 62.0000 g. **Composition:** 0.9990 Silver 1.9915 oz. ASW **Subject:** Constitution Centennial **Reverse:** Similar to 5 Pa'anga, KM#50

Date	Mintage	F	VF	XF	Unc	BU
ND(1975)	1,116	—	—	—	20.00	—
ND(1975) Proof	420	Value: 32.50				

KM# 64 10 PA'ANGA **Weight:** 4.0000 g. **Composition:** 0.9170 Gold .0117 oz. AGW **Series:** F.A.O. **Subject:** Rural Women's Advancement **Obverse:** Queen Salote **Reverse:** Female symbol on dove

Date	Mintage	F	VF	XF	Unc	BU
1980	750	—	—	—	16.50	—
1980 Proof	2,000	Value: 17.50				

KM# 78 10 PA'ANGA **Weight:** 28.2800 g. **Composition:** 0.9250 Silver .8411 oz. ASW **Subject:** Commonwealth Games **Reverse:** Two runners at finish line

Date	Mintage	F	VF	XF	Unc	BU
1982	500	—	—	—	20.00	—
1982 Proof	1,000	Value: 25.00				

KM# 90 10 PA'ANGA **Weight:** 5.1000 g. **Composition:** 0.3750 Gold .0615 oz. AGW **Subject:** 100th Anniversary of Automobile Industry **Reverse:** Rolls-Royce and Silver Ghost **Note:** Similar to 50 Seniti, KM#82

Date	Mintage	F	VF	XF	Unc	BU
1985 Proof	1,000	Value: 32.50				

KM# 90a 10 PA'ANGA **Weight:** 7.9600 g. **Composition:** 0.9170 Gold .2347 oz. AGW **Subject:** 100th Anniversary of Automobile Industry **Reverse:** Rolls Royce and Silver Ghos

Date	Mintage	F	VF	XF	Unc	BU
1985 Proof	500	Value: 95.00				

KM# 91 10 PA'ANGA **Weight:** 5.1000 g. **Composition:** 0.3750 Gold .0615 oz. AGW **Subject:** 100th Anniversary of Automobile Industry **Reverse:** Range Rover and Land Rover **Note:** Similar to 50 Seniti, KM#83.2

Date	Mintage	F	VF	XF	Unc	BU
1985 Proof	1,000	Value: 32.50				

KM# 91a 10 PA'ANGA **Weight:** 7.9600 g. **Composition:** 0.9170 Gold .2347 oz. AGW **Subject:** 100th Anniversary of Automobile Industry **Reverse:** Range Rover and Land Rove

Date	Mintage	F	VF	XF	Unc	BU
1985 Proof	500	Value: 95.00				

KM# 92 10 PA'ANGA **Weight:** 5.1000 g. **Composition** 0.3750 Gold .0615 oz. AGW **Subject:** 100th Anniversary of Automobile Industry **Reverse:** Mini Morris Cowley and Touring Car **Note:** Similar to 50 Seniti, KM#84.

Date	Mintage	F	VF	XF	Unc	BU
1985 Proof	1,000	Value: 32.50				

KM# 92a 10 PA'ANGA **Weight:** 7.9600 g. **Composition:** 0.9170 Gold .2347 oz. AGW **Subject:** 100th

Anniversary of Automobile Industry **Reverse:** Mini Morris Cowley and Touring Car

Date	Mintage	F	VF	XF	Unc	BU
1985 Proof	500	Value: 95.00				

KM# 93 10 PA'ANGA Weight: 5.1000 g. **Composition:** 0.3750 Gold .0615 oz. AGW **Subject:** 100th Anniversary of Automobile Industry **Reverse:** MGB GT and MG TA **Note:** Similar to 50 Seniti, KM#85.

Date	Mintage	F	VF	XF	Unc	BU
1985 Proof	1,000	Value: 32.50				

KM# 93a 10 PA'ANGA Weight: 7.9600 g. **Composition:** 0.9170 Gold .2347 oz. AGW **Subject:** 100th Anniversary of Automobile Industry **Reverse:** MGB GT and MG TA

Date	Mintage	F	VF	XF	Unc	BU
1985 Proof	500	Value: 95.00				

KM# 108 10 PA'ANGA Weight: 5.1000 g. **Composition:** 0.3750 Gold .0615 oz. AGW **Subject:** 85th Birthday of Queen Mother **Reverse:** Queen Mother as a young girl **Note:** Similar to 50 Seniti, KM#98.

Date	Mintage	F	VF	XF	Unc	BU
1985 Proof	1,000	Value: 32.50				

KM# 108a 10 PA'ANGA Weight: 7.9600 g. **Composition:** 0.9170 Gold .2347 oz. AGW **Subject:** 85th Birthday of Queen Mother **Reverse:** Queen Mother as a young girl

Date	Mintage	F	VF	XF	Unc	BU
1985 Proof	500	Value: 95.00				

KM# 109 10 PA'ANGA Weight: 5.1000 g. **Composition:** 0.3750 Gold .0615 oz. AGW **Subject:** 85th Birthday of Queen Mother **Reverse:** Wedding of King George VI and Elizabeth **Note:** Similar to 50 Seniti, KM#99.

Date	Mintage	F	VF	XF	Unc	BU
1985 Proof	1,000	Value: 32.50				

KM# 109a 10 PA'ANGA Weight: 7.9600 g. **Composition:** 0.9170 Gold .2347 oz. AGW **Subject:** 85th Birthday of Queen Mother **Reverse:** Wedding of King George VI and Elizabeth

Date	Mintage	F	VF	XF	Unc	BU
1985 Proof	500	Value: 95.00				

KM# 110 10 PA'ANGA Weight: 5.1000 g. **Composition:** 0.3750 Gold .0615 oz. AGW **Subject:** 85th Birthday of Queen Mother **Reverse:** King George VI and Elizabeth **Note:** Similar to 50 Seniti, KM#100.

Date	Mintage	F	VF	XF	Unc	BU
1985 Proof	1,000	Value: 32.50				

KM# 110a 10 PA'ANGA Weight: 7.9600 g. **Composition:** 0.9170 Gold .2347 oz. AGW **Subject:** 85th Birthday of Queen Mother **Reverse:** King George VI and Elizabeth

Date	Mintage	F	VF	XF	Unc	BU
1985 Proof	500	Value: 95.00				

KM# 111 10 PA'ANGA Weight: 5.1000 g. **Composition:** 0.3750 Gold .0615 oz. AGW **Subject:** 85th Birthday of Queen Mother **Reverse:** Queen Mother holding Queen Elizabeth II **Note:** Similar to 50 Seniti, KM#101.

Date	Mintage	F	VF	XF	Unc	BU
1985 Proof	1,000	Value: 32.50				

KM# 111a 10 PA'ANGA Weight: 7.9600 g. **Composition:** 0.9170 Gold .2347 oz. AGW **Subject:** 85th Birthday of Queen Mother **Reverse:** Queen Mother holding Queen Elizabeth II

Date	Mintage	F	VF	XF	Unc	BU
1985 Proof	500	Value: 95.00				

KM# 112 10 PA'ANGA Weight: 5.1000 g. **Composition:** 0.3750 Gold .0615 oz. AGW **Subject:** 85th Birthday of Queen Mother **Note:** Similar to 50 Seniti, KM#102.

Date	Mintage	F	VF	XF	Unc	BU
1985 Proof	1,000	Value: 32.50				

KM# 112a 10 PA'ANGA Weight: 7.9600 g. **Composition:** 0.9170 Gold .2347 oz. AGW **Subject:** 85th Birthday of Queen Mother

Date	Mintage	F	VF	XF	Unc	BU
1985 Proof	500	Value: 95.00				

KM# 126 10 PA'ANGA Composition: Copper-Nickel **Subject:** America's Cup **Obverse:** Taufa'ahau Tupou IV **Reverse:** National flags

Date	F	VF	XF	Unc	BU
1987	—	—	—	6.00	—

KM# 126a 10 PA'ANGA Weight: 31.1030 g. **Composition:** 0.9990 Palladium 1.0000 oz. **Subject:** America's Cup **Obverse:** Taufa'ahau Tupou IV **Reverse:** National flags

Date	Mintage	F	VF	XF	Unc	BU
1987 Proof	25,000	Value: 375				

KM# 125 10 PA'ANGA Weight: 311.0400 g. **Composition:** 0.9990 Silver 10.0000 oz. ASW **Subject:** America's Cup **Obverse:** Taufa'ahau Tupou IV **Reverse:** Sailboat and map **Size:** 75 mm. **Note:** Illustration reduced.

Date	Mintage	F	VF	XF	Unc	BU
1987 Proof	5,000	Value: 185				

KM# 130 10 PA'ANGA Weight: 15.5500 g. **Composition:** 0.9990 Gold .5000 oz. AGW **Series:** Summer Olympics **Subject:** Boxing Match

Date	Mintage	F	VF	XF	Unc	BU
1988 Proof	Est. 2,000	Value: 175				

KM# 131 10 PA'ANGA Weight: 31.1000 g. **Composition:** 0.9990 Palladium 1.0000 oz. **Series:** Summer Olympics **Reverse:** Shot putter

Date	Mintage	F	VF	XF	Unc	BU
1988 Proof	Est. 2,000	Value: 850				

KM# 132 10 PA'ANGA Weight: 15.6300 g. **Composition:** 0.9500 Palladium .5000 oz. **Series:** Summer Olympics **Reverse:** Discus thrower

Date	Mintage	F	VF	XF	Unc	BU
1988 Proof	Est. 2,000	Value: 325				

KM# 173 10 PA'ANGA Weight: 1.2441 g. **Composition:** 0.9999 Gold .0400 oz. AGW **Subject:** Destruction of the English Privateer "Post-au-Prince" **Obverse:** National arms **Reverse:** Looted shipwreck and native **Edge:** Reeded **Size:** 13.92 mm.

Date		F	VF	XF	Unc	BU
1998 Proof	—	Value: 40.00				

KM# 172 10 PA'ANGA Weight: 1.2441 g. **Composition:** 0.9999 Gold .0400 oz. AGW **Subject:** King's 80th Birthday **Obverse:** National arms **Reverse:** King's portrait **Edge:** Reeded **Size:** 13.92 mm. **Note:** Struck at Valcambi Mint.

Date		F	VF	XF	Unc	BU
1998 Proof	—	Value: 40.00				

KM# 52 20 PA'ANGA Weight: 140.0000 g. **Composition:** 0.9990 Silver 4.4971 oz. ASW **Subject:** Constitution Centennial **Reverse:** Similar to 5 Pa'anga, KM#50

Date	Mintage	F	VF	XF	Unc	BU
1975	1,170	—	—	—	32.50	—
1975 Proof	800	Value: 50.00				

KM# 65 20 PA'ANGA Weight: 0.8000 g. **Composition:** 0.9170 Gold .0235 oz. AGW **Series:** F.A.O. **Subject:** Rural Women's Advancenment **Obverse:** Queen Salote **Reverse:** Female figure on dove

Date	Mintage	F	VF	XF	Unc	BU
1980	750	—	—	—	27.50	—
1980 Proof	2,000	Value: 27.50				

KM# 53 25 PA'ANGA Weight: 5.0000 g. **Composition:** 0.9170 Gold .1474 oz. AGW **Subject:** Constitution Centennial **Obverse:** King George Tupou I **Reverse:** Arms

Date	Mintage	F	VF	XF	Unc	BU
1975	405	—	—	—	55.00	—
1975 Proof	105	Value: 65.00				

KM# 54 50 PA'ANGA **Weight:** 10.0000 g. **Composition:** 0.9170 Gold .2948 oz. AGW **Subject:** Constitution Centennial **Obverse:** King George Tupou II **Reverse:** Arms

Date	Mintage	F	VF	XF	Unc	BU
1975	205	—	—	—	110	—
1975 Proof	105	Value: 125				

KM# 55 75 PA'ANGA **Weight:** 15.0000 g. **Composition:** 0.9170 Gold .4423 oz. AGW **Subject:** Constitution Centennial **Obverse:** Queen Salote Tupou III **Reverse:** Arms

Date	Mintage	F	VF	XF	Unc	BU
1975	204	—	—	—	160	—
1975 Proof	105	Value: 175				

KM# 56 100 PA'ANGA **Weight:** 20.0000 g. **Composition:** 0.9170 Gold .5897 oz. AGW **Subject:** Constitution Centennial

Date	Mintage	F	VF	XF	Unc	BU
ND(1975)	205	—	—	—	215	—
ND(1975) Proof	105	Value: 225				

KM# 167 100 PA'ANGA **Weight:** 17.7000 g. **Composition:** 0.5833 Gold .3319 oz. AGW **Subject:** 25th Jubilee of Accession

Date	Mintage	F	VF	XF	Unc	BU
ND(1990) Proof	Est. 5,000	Value: 120				

KM# 155 100 PA'ANGA **Weight:** 17.7000 g. **Composition:** 0.5833 Gold .3319 oz. AGW **Series:** Olympics **Reverse:** Gymnast on rings

Date	Mintage	F	VF	XF	Unc	BU
1993 Proof	3,000	Value: 120				

KM# 163 100 PA'ANGA **Weight:** 17.7000 g. **Composition:** 0.5833 Gold .3319 oz. AGW **Subject:** World Cup Soccer **Reverse:** Goalie

Date	Mintage	F	VF	XF	Unc	BU
1994 Proof	Est. 3,000	Value: 120				

KM# 164 100 PA'ANGA **Weight:** 17.7000 g. **Composition:** 0.5833 Gold .3319 oz. AGW **Series:** 1996 Olympic Games **Reverse:** High jumper

Date	Mintage	F	VF	XF	Unc	BU
1994 Proof	Est. 3,000	Value: 120				

KM# 165 100 PA'ANGA **Weight:** 17.7000 g. **Composition:** 0.5833 Gold .3319 oz. AGW **Series:** Endangered Wildlife **Reverse:** Banded Iguana Lizard

Date	Mintage	F	VF	XF	Unc	BU
1994 Proof	Est. 2,000	Value: 120				

KM# 21 1/4 HAU **Weight:** 16.0000 g. **Composition:** 0.9800 Palladium .5041 oz. **Subject:** Coronation of Taufa'ahau Tupou IV

Date	Mintage	F	VF	XF	Unc	BU
1967	1,700	—	—	—	350	—

KM# 23 1/2 HAU **Weight:** 32.0000 g. **Composition:** 0.9800 Palladium 1.0082 oz. **Subject:** Coronation of Taufa'ahau Tupou IV

Date	Mintage	F	VF	XF	Unc	BU
1967	1,650	—	—	—	750	—

KM# 74 1/2 HAU **Weight:** 28.2800 g. **Composition:** 0.9250 Silver .8411 oz. ASW **Subject:** Wedding and Treaty of Friendship

Date	Mintage	F	VF	XF	Unc	BU
1981	1,000	—	—	—	32.50	—
1981 Proof	15,000	Value: 27.50				

KM# 122 1/2 HAU **Weight:** 10.0000 g. **Composition:** 0.9170 Gold .2948 oz. AGW **Subject:** Wildlife **Reverse:** Pritchard's Megapode birds

Date	Mintage	F	VF	XF	Unc	BU
1986 Proof	5,000	Value: 150				

KM# 25 HAU **Weight:** 64.0000 g. **Composition:** 0.9800 Palladium 2.0164 oz. **Subject:** Coronation of Taufa'ahau Tupou IV

Date	Mintage	F	VF	XF	Unc	BU
1967	1,500	—	—	—	1,500	—

KM# 75 HAU **Weight:** 7.9900 g. **Composition:** 0.9170 Gold .2356 oz. AGW **Subject:** Wedding and Treaty of Friendship

Date	Mintage	F	VF	XF	Unc	BU
1981	500	—	—	—	115	—
1981 Proof	2,500	Value: 100				

KM# 79 HAU **Weight:** 7.9900 g. **Composition:** 0.9170 Gold .2356 oz. AGW **Subject:** Commonwealth Games **Obverse:** King Taufa'ahau Tupou IV **Reverse:** Runners

Date	Mintage	F	VF	XF	Unc	BU
1982	500	—	—	—	115	—
1982 Proof	500	Value: 115				

KM# 94 HAU **Weight:** 52.0000 g. **Composition:** 0.9500 Platinum 1.5884 oz. APW **Subject:** 100th Anniversary of Automobile Industry **Reverse:** Rolls-Royce and Silver Ghost **Note:** Similar to 50 Seniti, KM#82.

Date		F	VF	XF	Unc	BU
1985 Proof	—	Value: 1,200				

KM# 95 HAU **Weight:** 52.0000 g. **Composition:** 0.9500 Platinum 1.5884 oz. APW **Subject:** 100th Anniversary of Automobile Industry **Reverse:** Range Rover and Land Rover **Note:** Similar to 50 Seniti, KM#83.

Date		F	VF	XF	Unc	BU
1985 Proof	—	Value: 1,200				

KM# 96 HAU **Weight:** 52.0000 g. **Composition:** 0.9500 Platinum 1.5884 oz. APW **Subject:** 100th Anniversary of Automobile Industry **Reverse:** Mini Morris Cowley and Touring Car **Note:** Similar to 50 Seniti, KM#84.

Date		F	VF	XF	Unc	BU
1985 Proof	—	Value: 1,200				

KM# 97 HAU **Weight:** 52.0000 g. **Composition:** 0.9500 Platinum 1.5884 oz. APW **Subject:** 100th Anniversary of Automobile Industry **Reverse:** MGB GT and MG TA **Note:** Similar to 50 Seniti, KM#85.

Date		F	VF	XF	Unc	BU
1985 Proof	—	Value: 1,200				

KM# 113 HAU **Weight:** 52.0000 g. **Composition:** 0.9500 Platinum 1.5884 oz. APW **Subject:** 85th Birthday of Queen Mother **Reverse:** Queen Mother as a young girl **Note:** Similar to 50 Seniti, KM#98.

Date		F	VF	XF	Unc	BU
1985 Proof	—	Value: 1,200				

KM# 114 HAU **Weight:** 52.0000 g. **Composition:** 0.9500 Platinum 1.5884 oz. APW **Subject:** 85th Birthday of Queen Mother **Reverse:** Wedding of King George VI and Elizabeth **Note:** Similar to 50 Seniti, KM#99.

Date		F	VF	XF	Unc	BU
1985 Proof	—	Value: 1,200				

#115 HAU **Weight:** 52.0000 g. **Composition:** 0.9500 Platinum 1.5884 oz. APW **Subject:** 85th Birthday of Queen Mother **Reverse:** King George VI and Elizabeth **Note:** Similar to 50 Seniti, KM#100.

	F	VF	XF	Unc	BU
Proof	— Value: 1,200				

#116 HAU **Weight:** 52.0000 g. **Composition:** 0.9500 Platinum 1.5884 oz. APW **Subject:** 85th Birthday of Queen Mother **Reverse:** Queen Mother holding Queen Elizabeth **Note:** Similar to 50 Seniti, KM#101.

	F	VF	XF	Unc	BU
Proof	— Value: 1,200				

#117 HAU **Weight:** 52.0000 g. **Composition:** 0.9500 Platinum 1.5884 oz. APW **Subject:** 85th Birthday of Queen Mother **Note:** Similar to 50 Seniti, KM#102.

	F	VF	XF	Unc	BU
Proof	— Value: 1,200				

#76 5 HAU **Weight:** 15.9800 g. **Composition:** 0.9170 Gold .4711 oz. AGW **Subject:** Wedding and Treaty of Friendship

	Mintage	F	VF	XF	Unc	BU
	250	—	—	—	230	—
Proof	1,000	Value: 225				

COUNTERMARKED COMMEMORATIVE COINAGE

Commemorative coins which contain a countermark ating a new commemorative representation. The te listed refers to the original date the coin was struck.

#10 20 SENITI **Composition:** Gold Plated Copper-Nickel **Countermark:** IN MEMORIAM/1965 +1970 **Note:** Countermark on KM#9.

	F	VF	XF	Unc	BU
7	—	—	—	6.00	—

#14 20 SENITI **Composition:** Copper-Nickel **Countermark:** 1918/TTIV/1968 **Note:** Countermark on KM#13.

	Mintage	F	VF	XF	Unc	BU
(1967) Proof	1,577	Value: 7.00				

#16 20 SENITI **Composition:** Copper-Nickel **Countermark:** 1918/TTIV/1968 **Note:** Countermark on KM#15.

	Mintage	F	VF	XF	Unc	BU
(1967) Proof	1,577	Value: 8.00				

KM# 12 PA'ANGA **Composition:** Gold Plated Copper-Nickel **Countermark:** IN MEMORIAM/1965 + 1970 **Note:** Countermark on KM#11.

Date	F	VF	XF	Unc	BU
1967	—	—	—	7.50	—

KM# 18 PA'ANGA **Composition:** Copper-Nickel **Countermark:** 1918/TTIV/1968 **Note:** Countermark on KM# 17.

Date	Mintage	F	VF	XF	Unc	BU
1967 Proof	1,577	Value: 8.00				

KM# 34 PA'ANGA **Composition:** Gold Plated Copper-Nickel **Countermark:** Oil rig 1969 OIL SEARCH **Note:** Countermark on KM#17.

Date	Mintage	F	VF	XF	Unc	BU
1968	5,017	—	1.50	3.50	6.50	—

KM# 35 PA'ANGA **Composition:** Gold Plated Copper-Nickel **Countermark:** COMMONWEALTH MEMBER/1970 **Note:** Countermark on KM#17.

Date	Mintage	F	VF	XF	Unc	BU
1968	3,000	—	2.00	3.00	7.00	—

KM# 36 PA'ANGA **Composition:** Gold Plated Copper-Nickel **Countermark:** INVESTITURE/1971 **Note:** Countermark on KM#17.

Date	Mintage	F	VF	XF	Unc	BU
1968	3,000	—	2.00	3.00	7.00	—
1968 Proof	1,000	Value: 9.00				

KM# 20 2 PA'ANGA **Composition:** Copper-Nickel **Countermark:** 1918/TTIV/1968 **Note:** Countermark on KM#19.

Date	Mintage	F	VF	XF	Unc	BU
ND(1967) Proof	1,577	Value: 11.50				

KM# 38 2 PA'ANGA **Composition:** Gold Plated Copper-Nickel **Countermark:** Oil rig 1969 OIL SEARCH **Note:** Countermark on KM#37.

Date	Mintage	F	VF	XF	Unc	BU
1968	5,039	—	2.00	4.00	9.00	—

KM# 39 2 PA'ANGA **Composition:** Gold Plated Copper-Nickel **Countermark:** COMMONWEALTH MEMBER/1970 **Note:** Countermark on KM#37.

Date	Mintage	F	VF	XF	Unc	BU
1968	3,006	—	2.50	5.00	10.00	—

KM# 40 2 PA'ANGA **Composition:** Gold Plated Copper-Nickel **Countermark:** INVESTITURE/1971 **Note:** Countermark on KM#37.

Date	Mintage	F	VF	XF	Unc	BU
1968	3,000	—	2.50	5.00	10.00	—
1968 Proof	1,000	Value: 15.00				

KM# 22 1/4 HAU **Weight:** 16.0000 g. **Composition:** 0.9800 Palladium .5040 oz. **Countermark:** 1918/TTIV/1968 **Note:** Countermark on KM#21.

Date	Mintage	F	VF	XF	Unc	BU
1967	400	—	—	—	400	—

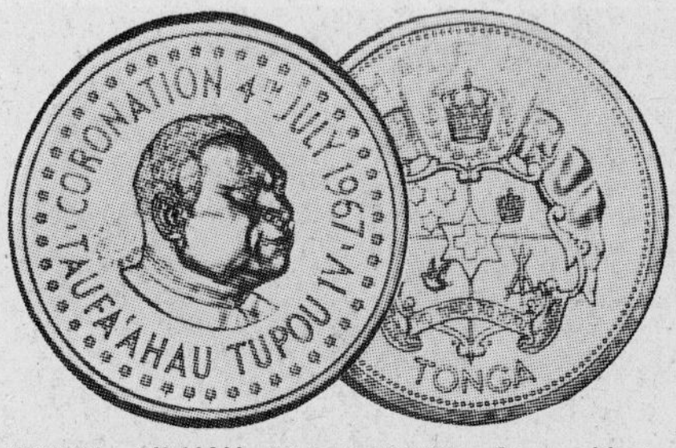

KM# 24 1/2 HAU **Weight:** 32.0000 g. **Composition:** 0.9800 Palladium 1.0082 oz. **Countermark:** 1918/TTIV/1968 **Note:** Countermark on KM#23.

Date	Mintage	F	VF	XF	Unc	BU
ND(1967)	513	—	—	—	800	—

KM# 26 HAU **Weight:** 64.0000 g. **Composition:** 0.9800 Palladium 2.0164 oz. **Countermark:** 1918/TTIV/1968 **Note:** Countermark on KM#25.

Date	Mintage	F	VF	XF	Unc	BU
ND(1967)	400	—	—	—	1,600	—

MINT SETS

KM#	Date	Mintage	Identification	Issue Price	Mkt Val
MS1	1962 (3)	—	KM#1-3	—	750
MS2	1967 (3)	1,500	KM#21, 23, 25	207	3,050
MS3	1968 (3)	400	KM#22, 24, 26	—	3,275
MS4	1970 (2)	10,000	KM#10, 12	2.30	14.50
MS5	1969 (2)	10,000	KM#34, 38	13.68	16.50
MS6	1970 (2)	3,000	KM#35, 39	13.68	20.00
MS7	1971 (2)	3,000	KM#36, 40	4.80	20.00
MS8	1974 (8)	10,000	KM#27-33, 37	7.60	22.50
MS10	1975 (4)	—	KM#53-56	384	535
MS11	1975 (3)	—	KM#50-52	59.60	75.00
MS9	1975 (8)	—	KM#42-49	7.75	25.00
MS12	1977 (5)	—	KM#44-47	0.85	8.00
MS13	1977 (2)	—	KM#49, 57	3.00	20.00
MS14	1978 (2)	—	KM#58-59	3.00	21.50

KM#	Date	Mintage	Identification	Issue Price	Mkt Val
MS16	1979 (2)	8,008	KM#60-61	3.00	20.00
MS17	1980 (2)	8,000	KM#62-63	3.00	20.00
MS18	1980 (2)	750	KM#64-65, Gold	30.00	50.00
MS19	1981 (8)	15,000	KM#66-73	5.38	25.00
MS20	1985 (5)	20,000	KM#98-102	25.25	22.50
MS21	1985 (4)	20,000	KM#82-85. Auto Industry.	21.00	25.00
MS22	1991 (6)	—	KM#66-71	—	6.00

PROOF SETS

KM#	Date	Mintage	Identification	Issue Price	Mkt Val
PS2	1962 (3)	25	KM#1a-3a. Platinum.	—	2,250
PS1	1962 (3)	250	KM#1-3	—	950
PS6	1968 (4)	1,577	KM#14, 16, 18, 20	22.80	37.50
PS3	1967 (7)	5,000	KM#4-9, 11	15.00	22.50
PS4	1967 (4)	1,923	KM#13, 15, 17, 19	17.25	27.50
PS5	1968 (8)	2,500	KM#27-33, 37	22.50	32.00
PS8	1971 (2)	1,000	KM#36, 40	13.40	25.00
PS10	1975 (4)	105	KM#53-56	538	600
PS9	1975 (3)	418	KM#50-52	82.00	120
PS11	1978 (2)	750	KM#58a-59a	—	82.50
PS12	1979 (2)	854	KM#60a-61a	45.00	90.00
PS13	1980 (2)	400	KM#62a-63a	80.00	70.00
PS14	1980 (2)	200	KM#64-65	60.00	55.00
PS15	1981 (2)	3,500	KM#72a-73a	88.00	62.50
PSA15	1981 (3)	—	KM#74-76	—	385
PS16	1985 (5)	20,000	KM#98-102, Copper-nickel	26.25	20.00
PS22	1985 (4)	10,000	KM#86-89	44.00	30.00
PS26	1985 (4)	50	KM#94-97, .950 Platinum. BV+15%.	4,680	—
PS23	1985 (4)	5,000	KM#86a-89a, .925 Silver	144	185
PS24	1985 (4)	1,000	KM#90-93, .374 Gold	252	140
PS25	1985 (4)	500	KM#90a-93a, .917 Gold	620	400
PS21	1985 (5)	50	KM#113-117, .950 Platinum. BV+15%.	5,850	—
PS17	1985 (5)	10,000	KM#103-107, Silver clad copper-nickel	55.00	30.00
PS18	1985 (5)	5,000	KM#103a-107a, .925 Silver	180	150
PS19	1985 (5)	1,000	KM#108-112, .374 Gold	315	175
PS20	1985 (5)	500	KM#108a-112a, .917 Gold	775	500
PS28	1988 (4)	2,000	KM#129-132	—	1,400

TONKIN

Tonkin (North Viet Nam), a former French protectorate in North Indo-China, comprises the greater part of present North Viet Nam. It had an area of 44,672 sq. mi. (75,700 sq. km.) and a population of about 4 million. Capital: Hanoi. The initial value of Tonkin to France was contained in the access it afforded to the trade of China's Yunnan province.

France established a protectorate over Annam and Tonkin by the treaties of Tientsin and Hue negotiated in1884. Tonkin was incorporated in the independent state of Viet Nam (within the French Union) and upon the defeat of France by the Viet Minh became the body of ***North Viet Nam***.

MINT MARKS

(a) - Paris, privy marks only

FRENCH PROTECTORATE

MILLED COINAGE

KM# 1 1/600 PIASTRE Weight: 2.1000 g. **Composition:** Zinc **Obv. Legend:** PROTECTORAT DU TONKIN **Reverse:** Value above and below, "Thong-bao" at left and right **Note:** 0.9 mm thick planchet.

Date	Mintage	F	VF	XF	Unc	BU
1905(a)	60,000,000	3.00	7.00	15.00	40.00	—

ESSAIS

KM#	Date	Mintage	Identification	Mkt Val
E1	1905(a)	—	1/600 Piastre. Zinc. 2.1000 g. PROTECTORAT DU TONKIN. Value above and below, "Thong-bao" at left and right. 0.9 mm thick planchet.	300

PIEFORTS

KM#	Date	Mintage	Identification	Mkt Val
P1	1905(a)	—	1/600 Piastre. Zinc. 4.8000 g. PROTECTORAT DU TONKIN. Value above and below, "Thong-bao" at left and right. 1.5 mm thick planchet.	700

TRANSNISTRIA

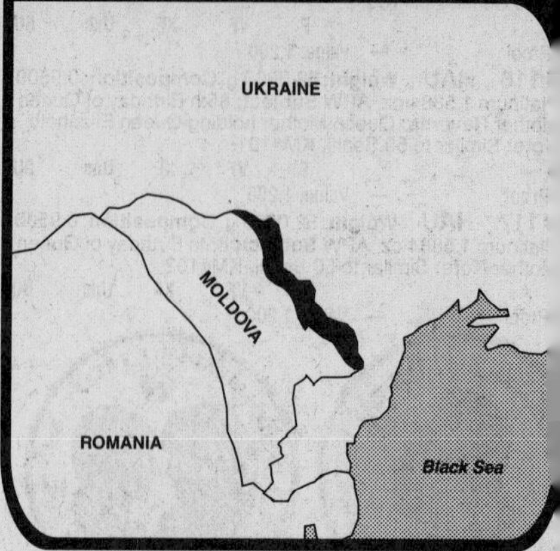

The Transnistria Moldavian Republic was formed in 1
even before the separation of Moldavia from Russia. It has
area of 11,544 sq. mi. (29,900 sq. km.) and a populatio
700,000. Capital: Tiraspol.

The area was conquered from the Turks in the last half of
18th century, and in 1792 the capital city of Bessarabia (pres
Moldova and part of the Ukraine) became part of the Russ
Empire. During the Russian Revolution, in 1918, the area
taken by Romanian troops, and in 1924 the Moldavian Au
omous SSR was formed on the left bank of the Dniester River.
June 22, 1941, Romania declared war on the U.S.S.R. and Ro
nian troops fought alongside the Germans up to Stalingra
Romanian occupation area between the Dniester and Bug Riv
called Transnistria was established in October 1941. Its ce
was the port of Odessa.

Once the Moldavian SSR declared independence in Au
1991, Transnistria did not want to be part of Moldavia. In 1
Moldova tried to solve the issue militarily with battles in Benc
and Doubossary. The conflict was ended with Russian media
and Russian peacekeeping forces were stationed there.

Transnistria has a president, parliament, army and po
forces, but as yet it is lacking international recognition.

MOLDAVIAN REPUBLIC

STANDARD COINAGE

KM# 1 KOPEEK Weight: 0.6200 g. **Composition:** Aluminum **Obverse:** State arms **Reverse:** Denominatio between wheat stalks **Edge:** Plain **Size:** 15.9 mm.

Date	F	VF	XF	Unc
2000	—	—	—	0.25

KM# 2 5 KOPEEK Weight: 0.7000 g. **Composition:** Aluminum **Obverse:** State arms **Reverse:** Denominatio between wheat stalks **Edge:** Plain **Size:** 17.9 mm.

Date	F	VF	XF	Unc
2000	—	—	—	0.50

KM# 3 10 KOPEEK Weight: 1.0000 g. **Composition** Aluminum **Obverse:** State arms **Reverse:** Denomination between wheat stalks **Edge:** Plain **Size:** 20 mm.

Date	F	VF	XF	Unc
2000	—	—	—	0.75

KM# 5a 25 KOPEEK Weight: 2.1400 g. **Compositio** Brass **Obverse:** State arms. **Reverse:** Denomination. **Edg** Plain. **Size:** 17 mm.

Date	F	VF	XF	Unc
2002	—	—	—	0.75

KM# 5 25 KOPEEK Composition: Aluminum-Bronze **Obverse:** State arms **Reverse:** Denomination between wheat stalks **Edge:** Plain **Size:** 17 mm.

Date	F	VF	XF	Unc
2002	—	—	—	1.00

 # 4 50 KOPEEK **Weight:** 2.7500 g. **Composition:** Brass **Obverse:** State arms **Reverse:** Denomination between wheat stalks **Edge:** Plain **Size:** 19 mm.

	F	VF	XF	Unc	BU
)	—	—	—	1.25	—

⁄l# 6 50 RUBLEI **Weight:** 14.3700 g. **Composition:** Copper-Nickel **Subject:** 10th Anniversary **Obverse:** State arms **Reverse:** Statue **Edge:** Plain **Size:** 32.75 mm.

e	F	VF	XF	Unc	BU
)2000 Proof	—	Value: 35.00			

M# 7 100 RUBLEI **Weight:** 14.1600 g. **Composition:** 0.9250 Silver - Billon 0.4211 oz. ASW **Subject:** City of Tiraspol **Obverse:** State arms **Reverse:** Statue and buildings **Edge:** Plain **Size:** 32 mm.

ıte	F	VF	XF	Unc	BU
02 Proof	—	Value: 45.00			

KM# 8 100 RUBLEI **Weight:** 14.1600 g. **Composition:** 0.9250 Silver 0.4211 oz. ASW **Subject:** City of Tiraspol **Obverse:** State arms **Reverse:** Cameo portrait above fortress **Edge:** Plain **Size:** 32 mm.

Date	F	VF	XF	Unc	BU
2002 Proof	—	Value: 45.00			

KM# 9 100 RUBLEI **Weight:** 14.1600 g. **Composition:** 0.9250 Silver 0.4211 oz. ASW **Subject:** K. K. Gedroets **Obverse:** State arms **Reverse:** Portrait with plants, beaker and book **Edge:** Plain **Size:** 32 mm.

Date	F	VF	XF	Unc	BU
2002 Proof	—	Value: 45.00			

KM#10 100 RUBLEI **Weight:** 14.0400 g. **Composition:** 0.9250 Silver 0.4175 oz. ASW **Subject:** Trans-Dniester Republican Bank 10th Anniversary **Obverse:** State arms **Reverse:** Colorized monogram in wreath with "1992" at top **Edge:** Plain **Size:** 32 mm.

Date	F	VF	XF	Unc	BU
2002 Proof	—	Value: 45.00			

TRINIDAD & TOBAGO

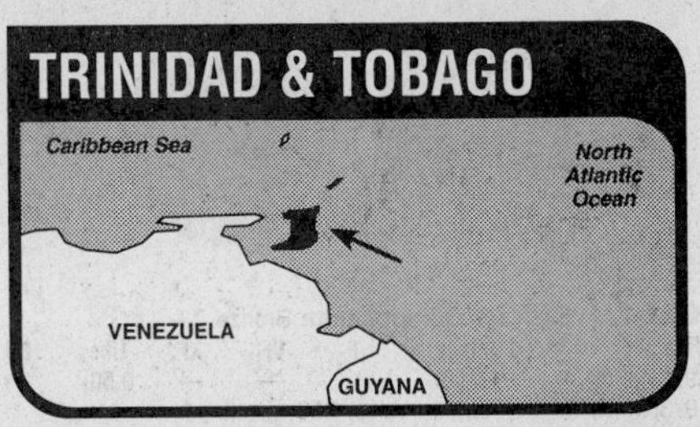

The Republic of Trinidad and Tobago is situated 7 miles (11 km.) off the coast of Venezuela, has an area of 1,981 sq. mi. (5,130 sq. km.) and a population of *1.2 million. Capital: Port-of-Spain. The island of Trinidad contains the world's largest natural asphalt bog. Birds of Paradise live on little Tobago, the only place outside of their native New Guinea where they can be found in a wild state. Petroleum and petroleum products are the mainstay of the economy. Petroleum products, crude oil and sugar are exported.

Columbus discovered Trinidad and Tobago in 1498. Trinidad remained under Spanish rule from the time of its settlement in 1592 until its capture by the British in 1797. It was ceded to the British in 1802. Tobago was occupied at various times by the French, Dutch and English before being ceded to Britain in 1814. Trinidad and Tobago were merged into a single colony in 1888. The colony was part of the Federation of the West Indies until Aug. 31, 1962, when it became independent. A new constitution establishing a republican form of government was adopted on Aug. 1, 1976. Trinidad and Tobago is a member of the Commonwealth of Nations. The President is Chief of State. The Prime Minister is Head of Government.

RULERS
British, until 1976

MINT MARKS
FM - Franklin Mint, U.S.A.*

*NOTE: From 1975-1985 the Franklin Mint produced coinage in up to 3 different qualities. Qualities of issue are designated in ( ) after each date and are defined as follows:

(M) MATTE - Normal circulation strike or a dull finish produced by sandblasting special uncirculated (polish finish) or proof quality dies.

(U) SPECIAL UNCIRCULATED - Polished or proof-like in appearance without any frosted features.

(P) PROOF - The highest quality obtainable having mirror-like fields and frosted features.

MONETARY SYSTEM
100 Cents = 1 Dollar

COLONIAL

STANDARD COINAGE

100 Cents = 1 Dollar

KM# 1 CENT **Composition:** Bronze

Date	Mintage	F	VF	XF	Unc	BU
1966	24,500,000	—	—	—	0.15	—
1966 Proof	8,000	Value: 1.00				
1967	4,000,000	—	—	—	0.15	—
1968	5,000,000	—	—	—	0.15	—
1970	5,000,000	—	—	—	0.15	—
1970 Proof	2,104	Value: 1.50				
1971	10,600,000	—	—	—	0.15	—
1971FM (M)	286,000	—	—	—	0.20	—
1971FM (P)	12,000	Value: 0.50				
1972	16,500,000	—	—	—	0.15	—
1973	10,000,000	—	—	—	0.15	—

KM# 9 CENT **Composition:** Bronze **Subject:** 10th Anniversary of Independence

Date	Mintage	F	VF	XF	Unc	BU
1972	5,000,000	—	—	0.10	0.15	—
1972FM (M)	125,000	—	—	—	0.25	—
1972FM (P)	16,000	Value: 0.50				

KM# 17 CENT **Composition:** Bronze

Date	Mintage	F	VF	XF	Unc	BU
1973FM (M)	127,000	—	—	—	0.50	—
1973FM (P)	20,000	Value: 1.50				

KM# 25 CENT **Composition:** Bronze **Reverse:** Balisier Hummingbird

Date	Mintage	F	VF	XF	Unc	BU
1974FM (M)	128,000	—	—	—	0.30	—
1974FM (P)	14,000	Value: 0.50				
1975	10,000,000	—	—	—	0.25	—
1975FM (M)	125,000	—	—	—	0.25	—
1975FM (U)	1,111	—	—	—	1.25	—
1975FM (P)	24,000	Value: 0.50				
1976	15,050,000	—	—	—	0.25	—

KM# 2 5 CENTS **Composition:** Bronze

Date		F	VF	XF	Unc	BU
1966		—	—	0.10	0.25	—
1966 Proof	8,000	Value: 1.25				
1967		—	—	0.10	0.25	—
1970 Proof	2,104	Value: 1.75				
1971		—	—	0.10	0.25	—
1971FM (M)		—	—	—	0.15	—
1971FM (P)	12,000	Value: 0.75				
1972		—	—	0.10	0.20	—

KM# 10 5 CENTS **Composition:** Bronze **Subject:** 10th Anniversary of Independence

Date	Mintage	F	VF	XF	Unc	BU
1972	15,000	—	—	—	0.35	—
1972FM (M)	25,000	—	—	—	0.25	—
1972FM (P)	16,000	Value: 0.75				

KM# 57 5 CENTS **Composition:** Bronze

Date	Mintage	F	VF	XF	Unc	BU
1973FM (M)	27,000	—	—	—	0.50	—
1973FM (P)	20,000	Value: 1.50				

KM# 26 5 CENTS **Composition:** Bronze **Reverse:** Bird of Paradise

Date	Mintage	F	VF	XF	Unc	BU
1974FM (M)	28,000	—	—	—	0.50	—
1974FM (P)	14,000	Value: 0.75				
1975	1,500,000	—	—	0.10	0.30	—
1975FM (M)	25,000	—	—	—	0.30	—
1975FM (U)	1,111	—	—	—	1.50	—
1975FM (P)	24,000	Value: 0.75				
1976	7,500,000	—	—	0.10	0.30	—

KM# 3 10 CENTS **Composition:** Copper-Nickel

Date	Mintage	F	VF	XF	Unc	BU
1966	7,800,000	—	—	0.10	0.30	—
1966 Proof	8,000	Value: 1.50				
1967	4,000,000	—	—	0.10	0.30	—
1970 Proof	2,104	Value: 2.00				
1971	—	—	—	0.10	0.30	—
1971FM (M)	29,000	—	—	—	0.35	—
1971FM (P)	12,000	Value: 1.00				
1972	4,000,000	—	—	0.10	0.30	—

KM# 11 10 CENTS **Composition:** Copper-Nickel **Subject:** 10th Anniversary of Independence

Date	Mintage	F	VF	XF	Unc	BU
1972	41,000	—	—	—	0.40	—
1972FM (M)	13,000	—	—	—	0.60	—
1972FM (P)	16,000	Value: 1.00				

KM# 58 10 CENTS **Composition:** Copper-Nickel

Date	Mintage	F	VF	XF	Unc	BU
1973FM (M)	14,000	—	—	—	1.00	—
1973FM (P)	20,000	Value: 2.50				

KM# 27 10 CENTS **Composition:** Copper-Nickel **Reverse:** Flaming Hibiscus

Date	Mintage	F	VF	XF	Unc	BU
1974FM (M)	16,000	—	—	—	1.00	—
1974FM (P)	14,000	Value: 1.00				
1975	4,000,000	—	—	0.10	0.25	—
1975FM (M)	13,000	—	—	—	0.50	—
1975FM (U)	1,111	—	—	—	1.75	—
1975FM (P)	24,000	Value: 1.00				
1976	14,720,000	—	—	0.10	0.20	—

KM# 4 25 CENTS **Composition:** Copper-Nickel

Date	Mintage	F	VF	XF	Unc	BU
1966	7,200,000	—	0.10	0.15	0.35	—
1966 Proof	8,000	Value: 1.75				
1967	1,800,000	—	0.10	0.15	0.50	—
1970 Proof	2,014	Value: 2.25				
1971	1,500,000	—	0.10	0.15	0.50	—
1971FM (M)	11,000	—	—	—	0.65	—
1971FM (P)	12,000	Value: 1.25				
1972	3,000,000	—	0.10	0.15	0.35	—

KM# 12 25 CENTS **Composition:** Copper-Nickel **Subject:** 10th Anniversary of Independence

Date	Mintage	F	VF	XF	Unc	BU
1972	14,000	—	—	—	0.60	—
1972FM (M)	5,000	—	—	—	1.50	—
1972FM (P)	16,000	Value: 1.25				

KM# 59 25 CENTS **Composition:** Copper-Nickel

Date	Mintage	F	VF	XF	Unc	BU
1973FM (M)	6,575	—	—	—	2.25	—
1973FM (P)	20,000	Value: 3.00				

KM# 28 25 CENTS **Composition:** Copper-Nickel **Reverse:** Chaconia

Date	Mintage	F	VF	XF	Unc	BU
1974FM (M)	8,258	—	—	—	1.75	—
1974FM (P)	14,000	Value: 1.25				
1975	3,000,000	—	0.10	0.15	0.30	—
1975FM (M)	5,000	—	—	—	1.50	—
1975FM (U)	1,111	—	—	—	2.00	—
1975FM (P)	24,000	Value: 1.25				
1976	9,000,000	—	0.10	0.15	0.30	—

KM# 5 50 CENTS **Composition:** Copper-Nickel

Date	Mintage	F	VF	XF	Unc	BU
1966	975,000	—	0.25	0.50	1.25	—
1966 Proof	8,000	Value: 2.50				
1967	750,000	—	0.25	0.50	1.25	—
1970 Proof	2,104	Value: 3.00				
1971FM (M)	5,714	—	—	—	2.00	—
1971FM (P)	12,000	Value: 1.75				

KM# 13 50 CENTS **Composition:** Copper-Nickel **Subject:** 10th Anniversary of Independence

Date	Mintage	F	VF	XF	Unc	BU
1972	375,000	—	0.50	0.75	1.50	—
1972FM (M)	2,500	—	—	—	5.00	—
1972FM (P)	16,000	Value: 1.75				

KM# 22 50 CENTS **Composition:** Copper-Nickel **Reverse:** Steel drum with hands of player

Date	Mintage	F	VF	XF	Unc	B
1973FM (M)	4,075	—	—	—	2.50	—
1973FM (P)	20,000	Value: 2.25				
1974FM (M)	5,758	—	—	—	2.00	—
1974FM (P)	14,000	Value: 2.25				
1975FM (M)	2,500	—	—	—	3.75	—
1975FM (U)	1,111	—	—	—	2.25	—
1975FM (P)	24,000	Value: 2.00				
1976	750,000	—	0.50	0.75	1.50	—

KM# 6 DOLLAR **Composition:** Nickel **Series:** F.A.O

Date	Mintage	F	VF	XF	Unc	BU
1969	250,000	—	0.75	1.50	3.50	—

KM# 7 DOLLAR **Composition:** Copper-Nickel

Date	Mintage	F	VF	XF	Unc	BU
1971FM (M)	2,857	—	—	—	4.00	—
1971FM (P)	12,000	Value: 2.00				

KM# 7a DOLLAR **Composition:** Nickel

ate	Mintage	F	VF	XF	Unc	BU
970 Proof	2,014	Value: 5.00				

M# 14 DOLLAR **Composition:** Copper-Nickel **Subject:** 10th Anniversary of Independence

te	Mintage	F	VF	XF	Unc	BU
72	9,700	—	—	—	4.00	—
72FM (M)	1,250	—	—	—	12.50	—
72FM (P)	16,000	Value: 3.00				

KM# 23 DOLLAR **Composition:** Copper-Nickel **Reverse:** Coerico

Date	Mintage	F	VF	XF	Unc	BU
1973FM (M)	2,825	—	—	—	4.00	—
1973FM (P)	20,000	Value: 3.00				
1974FM (M)	4,508	—	—	—	4.00	—
1974FM (P)	14,000	Value: 3.00				
1975FM (M)	1,250	—	—	—	6.00	—
1975FM (U)	1,111	—	—	—	5.00	—
1975FM (P)	24,000	Value: 3.00				

KM# 8 5 DOLLARS **Weight:** 29.7000 g. **Composition:** 0.9250 Silver .8833 oz. ASW **Reverse:** Scarlet Ibis

Date	Mintage	F	VF	XF	Unc	BU
1971FM (M)	571	—	—	—	25.00	—
1971FM (P)	11,000	Value: 10.00				
1973FM (M)	1,825	—	—	—	20.00	—
1973FM (P)	25,000	Value: 9.00				
1974FM (P)	16,000	Value: 12.00				
1975FM (P)	26,000	Value: 9.00				

KM# 8a 5 DOLLARS **Composition:** Copper-Nickel

Date	Mintage	F	VF	XF	Unc	BU
1974FM (M)	3,508	—	—	—	6.00	—
1975FM (M)	250	—	—	—	20.00	—
1975FM (U)	1,111	—	—	—	8.00	—

KM# 15 5 DOLLARS **Weight:** 29.7000 g. **Composition:** 0.9250 Silver .8833 oz. ASW **Subject:** 10th Anniversary of Independence

Date	Mintage	F	VF	XF	Unc	BU
1972	10,000	—	—	—	10.00	—
1972FM	250	—	—	—	40.00	—
1972FM Proof	19,000	Value: 10.00				

KM# 16 10 DOLLARS **Weight:** 35.0000 g. **Composition:** 0.9250 Silver 1.0409 oz. ASW **Subject:** 10th Anniversary of Independence

Date	Mintage	F	VF	XF	Unc	BU
1972	—	—	—	—	11.00	—
1972FM (M)	125	—	—	—	125	—
1972FM (P)	26,000	Value: 12.00				

KM# 24a 10 DOLLARS **Weight:** 35.0000 g. **Composition:** 0.9250 Silver 1.0409 oz. ASW **Reverse:** Antique mariner's map

Date	Mintage	F	VF	XF	Unc	BU
1973FM (M)	1,700	—	—	—	17.50	—
1973FM (U)	—	—	—	—	16.50	—
1973FM (P)	24,000	Value: 12.50				
1974FM (P)	21,000	Value: 12.50				
1975FM (P)	28,000	Value: 13.50				

KM# 24 10 DOLLARS **Composition:** Copper-Nickel

Date	Mintage	F	VF	XF	Unc	BU
1974FM (M)	3,632	—	—	—	10.00	—
1975FM (M)	125	—	—	—	50.00	—
1975FM (U)	1,111	—	—	—	12.00	—

REPUBLIC

STANDARD COINAGE

100 Cents = 1 Dollar

KM# 29 CENT **Composition:** Bronze

Date		F	VF	XF	Unc	BU
1976FM (M)		—	—	—	0.35	—
1976FM (U)		—	—	—	1.50	—
1976FM (P)	10,000	Value: 0.50				
1977		—	—	—	0.35	—
1977FM (M)		—	—	—	0.35	—
1977FM (U)		—	—	—	1.50	—
1977FM (P)	5,337	Value: 0.50				
1978		—	—	—	0.35	—
1978FM (M)		—	—	—	0.35	—
1978FM (U)		—	—	—	1.50	—
1978FM (P)	4,845	Value: 1.00				
1979		—	—	—	0.35	—
1979FM (M)		—	—	—	0.35	—
1979FM (U)		—	—	—	1.50	—
1979FM (P)	3,270	Value: 1.00				
1980		—	—	—	0.35	—
1980FM (M)		—	—	—	0.35	—
1980FM (U)		—	—	—	1.50	—
1980FM (P)	2,393	Value: 1.00				
1981		—	—	—	0.35	—
1981FM (M)		—	—	—	0.35	—
1981FM (U)		—	—	—	1.50	—
1981FM (P)	—	Value: 1.00				
1982		—	—	—	0.35	—
1983		—	—	—	0.35	—
1984		—	—	—	0.35	—
1985		—	—	—	0.35	—
1986		—	—	—	0.35	—
1987		—	—	—	0.35	—
1988		—	—	—	0.35	—
1989		—	—	—	0.35	—
1990		—	—	—	0.35	—
1991		—	—	—	0.35	—
1993		—	—	—	0.35	—
1994		—	—	—	0.35	—
1995		—	—	—	0.35	—
1996		—	—	—	0.35	—
1997		—	—	—	0.35	—
1998		—	—	—	0.35	—
1999		—	—	—	0.35	—
1999 Proof	3,000	Value: 0.50				
2000		—	—	—	0.35	—

KM# 29a CENT **Weight:** 2.0000 g. **Composition:** 0.9250 Silver .0594 oz. ASW

Date	Mintage	F	VF	XF	Unc	BU
1981FM (P)	898	Value: 10.00				

KM# 42 CENT **Composition:** Bronze **Subject:** 20th Anniversary of Independence

Date		F	VF	XF	Unc	BU
1982FM (M)		—	—	—	0.15	—
1982FM (U)		—	—	—	1.50	—
1982FM (P)	—	Value: 1.00				

KM# 42a CENT **Weight:** 2.0000 g. **Composition:** 0.9250 Silver .0594 oz. ASW

Date	Mintage	F	VF	XF	Unc	BU
1982FM (P)	699	Value: 10.00				

KM# 51 CENT **Composition:** Bronze

Date		F	VF	XF	Unc	BU
1983FM (M)		—	—	—	1.50	—
1983FM (P)	—	Value: 1.00				
1984FM (P)	—	Value: 1.00				

KM# 51a CENT **Weight:** 2.0000 g. **Composition:** 0.9250 Silver .0594 oz. ASW

Date	Mintage	F	VF	XF	Unc	BU
1983FM (P)	1,344	Value: 10.00				
1984FM (P)	—	Value: 10.00				

KM# 30 5 CENTS **Composition:** Bronze

Date		F	VF	XF	Unc	BU
1976FM (M)		—	—	—	0.25	—
1976FM (U)		—	—	—	1.75	—
1976FM (P)	10,000	Value: 0.75				
1977		—	—	0.10	0.25	—
1977FM (M)		—	—	—	0.25	—
1977FM (U)		—	—	—	1.75	—
1977FM (P)	5,337	Value: 0.75				
1978		—	—	0.10	0.25	—
1978FM (M)		—	—	—	0.25	—
1978FM (U)		—	—	—	1.75	—
1978FM (P)	4,845	Value: 1.25				
1979		—	—	0.10	0.25	—
1979FM (M)		—	—	—	0.25	—
1979FM (U)		—	—	—	1.75	—
1979FM (P)	3,270	Value: 1.25				
1980		—	—	0.10	0.25	—
1980FM (M)		—	—	—	0.25	—
1980FM (U)		—	—	—	5.00	—
1980FM (P)	2,393	Value: 1.25				
1981		—	—	0.10	0.25	—
1981FM (M)		—	—	—	0.25	—
1981FM (U)		—	—	—	1.75	—
1981FM (P)	—	Value: 1.25				
1983		—	—	0.10	0.25	—
1984		—	—	0.10	1.00	—
1988		—	—	0.10	0.25	—
1990		—	—	0.10	0.25	—
1992		—	—	0.10	0.25	—
1995		—	—	0.10	0.25	—
1996		—	—	0.10	0.25	—
1997		—	—	0.10	0.25	—
1998		—	—	0.10	0.25	—
1999 Proof	3,000	Value: 1.00				
1999		—	—	0.10	0.25	—
2000		—	—	0.10	0.25	—
2001		—	—	0.10	0.25	—

KM# 30a 5 CENTS **Weight:** 3.5000 g. **Composition:** 0.9250 Silver .1040 oz. ASW

Date	Mintage	F	VF	XF	Unc	BU
1981FM (P)	898	Value: 15.00				

KM# 43 5 CENTS **Composition:** Bronze **Subject:** 20th Anniversary of Independence **Obverse:** Coat of arms

Date		F	VF	XF	Unc	BU
1982FM (M)		—	—	—	1.00	—
1982FM (U)		—	—	—	2.00	—
1982FM (P)	—	Value: 1.50				

KM# 43a 5 CENTS **Weight:** 3.5000 g. **Composition:** 0.9250 Silver .1040 oz. ASW

Date	Mintage	F	VF	XF	Unc	BU
1982FM (P)	699	Value: 15.00				

KM# 52 5 CENTS **Composition:** Bronze **Obverse:** Coat of arms

Date		F	VF	XF	Unc	BU
1983FM (M)		—	—	—	2.50	—
1983FM (P)	—	Value: 1.75				
1984FM (P)	—	Value: 1.75				

KM# 52a 5 CENTS **Weight:** 3.5000 g. **Composition:** 0.9250 Silver .1040 oz. ASW

Date	Mintage	F	VF	XF	Unc	BU
1983FM (P)	1,324	Value: 15.00				
1984FM (P)	—	Value: 15.00				

KM# 31 10 CENTS **Composition:** Copper-Nickel

Date	Mintage	F	VF	XF	Unc	BU
1976FM (M)	15,000	—	—	—	0.50	—
1976FM (U)	582	—	—	—	5.00	—
1976FM (P)	10,000	Value: 1.00				
1977	17,280,000	—	—	0.10	0.20	—
1977FM (M)	15,000	—	—	—	0.50	—
1977FM (U)	633	—	—	—	5.00	—
1977FM (P)	5,337	Value: 1.00				
1978	10,000,000	—	—	0.10	0.20	—
1978FM (M)	15,000	—	—	—	0.50	—
1978FM (U)	472	—	—	—	5.00	—
1978FM (P)	4,845	Value: 1.50				
1979	1,970,000	—	—	0.10	0.30	—
1979FM (M)	15,000	—	—	—	0.50	—
1979FM (U)	518	—	—	—	5.00	—
1979FM (P)	3,270	Value: 1.50				
1980	20,000,000	—	—	0.10	0.30	—
1980FM (M)	7,500	—	—	—	0.50	—
1980FM (U)	796	—	—	—	5.00	—
1980FM (P)	2,393	Value: 1.50				
1981	—	—	—	0.10	0.30	—
1981FM (M)	—	—	—	—	0.50	—
1981FM (U)	—	—	—	—	5.00	—
1981FM (P)	—	Value: 1.50				
1990	—	—	—	0.10	0.30	—
1997	—	—	—	—	0.50	—
1998	—	—	—	—	0.50	—
1999	—	—	—	—	0.50	—
1999 Proof	—	Value: 2.00				
2000	—	—	—	—	0.50	—

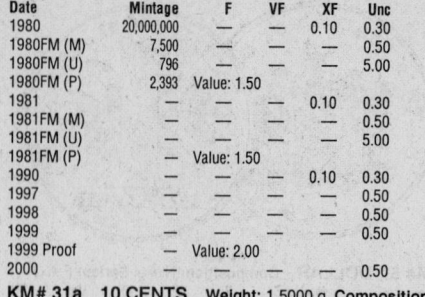

KM# 31a 10 CENTS **Weight:** 1.5000 g. **Composition:** 0.9250 Silver .0446 oz. ASW

Date	Mintage	F	VF	XF	Unc	BU
1981FM (P)	898	Value: 15.00				

KM# 44 10 CENTS **Composition:** Copper-Nickel **Subject:** 20th Anniversary of Independence **Obverse:** Coat of arms

Date		F	VF	XF	Unc	BU
1982FM (M)		—	—	—	1.50	—
1982FM (U)		—	—	—	3.00	—
1982FM (P)	—	Value: 2.50				

KM# 44a 10 CENTS **Weight:** 1.5000 g. **Composition:** 0.9250 Silver .0446 oz. ASW

Date	Mintage	F	VF	XF	Unc	BU
1982FM (P)	699	Value: 15.00				

KM# 53 10 CENTS **Composition:** Copper-Nickel **Obverse:** Coat of arms

Date		F	VF	XF	Unc	BU
1983FM (M)		—	—	—	2.50	—
1983FM (P)	—	Value: 2.00				
1984FM (P)	—	Value: 2.00				

KM# 53a 10 CENTS **Weight:** 1.5000 g. **Composition:** 0.9250 Silver .0446 oz. ASW

Date		F	VF	XF	Unc	BU
1983FM (P)	—	Value: 10.00				
1984FM (P)	—	Value: 10.00				

KM# 32 25 CENTS **Composition:** Copper-Nickel

Date	Mintage	F	VF	XF	Unc	BU
1976FM (M)	6,000	—	—	—	1.00	
1976FM (U)	582	—	—	—	5.00	
1976FM (P)	10,000	Value: 1.25				
1977	9,000,000	—	0.10	0.15	0.30	
1977FM (M)	6,000	—	—	—	1.00	
1977FM (U)	633	—	—	—	5.00	
1977FM (P)	5,337	Value: 1.25				
1978	5,470,000	—	0.10	0.15	0.30	
1978FM (M)	6,000	—	—	—	1.00	
1978FM (U)	472	—	—	—	5.00	
1978FM (P)	4,845	Value: 1.75				
1979	—	—	0.10	0.15	0.40	
1979FM (M)	6,000	—	—	—	1.00	
1979FM (U)	518	—	—	—	5.00	
1979FM (P)	3,270	Value: 1.75				
1980	15,000,000	—	0.10	0.15	0.40	
1980FM (M)	3,000	—	—	—	1.00	
1980FM (U)	796	—	—	—	5.00	
1980FM (P)	2,393	Value: 1.75				
1981	—	—	0.10	0.15	0.40	
1981FM (M)	—	—	—	—	1.00	
1981FM (U)	—	—	—	—	5.00	
1981FM (P)	—	Value: 1.75				
1983	—	—	0.10	0.15	0.40	
1983FM (M)	—	—	—	—	2.00	
1983FM (P)	—	Value: 1.75				
1984	—	—	0.10	0.15	0.40	
1984	—	Value: 1.75				
1993	—	—	—	0.15	0.40	
1997	—	—	—	0.15	0.40	
1998	—	—	—	0.15	0.40	
1999	—	—	—	0.15	0.40	
1999 Proof	—	Value: 3.00				

KM# 32a 25 CENTS **Weight:** 3.6000 g. **Compositio** 0.9250 Silver .1070 oz. ASW

Date	Mintage	F	VF	XF	Unc	BU
1981FM (P)	898	Value: 10.00				
1983FM (P)	—	Value: 10.00				
1984FM (P)	—	Value: 10.00				

KM# 45 25 CENTS **Composition:** Copper-Nickel **Subject:** 20th Anniversary of Independence **Obverse:** Coat of arms

Date	F	VF	XF	Unc	BU
1982FM (M)	—	—	—	1.00	—
1982FM (U)	—	—	—	2.25	—
1982FM (P)	— Value: 1.75				

KM# 45a 25 CENTS **Weight:** 3.6000 g. **Composition:** 0.9250 Silver .1070 oz. ASW

Date	Mintage	F	VF	XF	Unc	BU
1982FM (P)	699	Value: 15.00				

KM# 33 50 CENTS **Composition:** Copper-Nickel

Date	Mintage	F	VF	XF	Unc	BU
1976FM (M)		—	—	—	3.25	—
1976FM (U)		—	—	—	5.00	—
1976FM (P)	10,000	Value: 1.50				
1977		—	0.25	0.50	1.00	—
1977FM (M)		—	—	—	3.00	—
1977FM (U)		—	—	—	5.00	—
1977FM (P)	5,337	Value: 1.50				
1978		—	0.50	0.75	1.50	—
1978FM (M)		—	—	—	3.00	—
1978FM (U)		—	—	—	5.00	—
1978FM (P)	4,845	Value: 2.00				
1979		—	0.50	0.75	1.50	—
1979FM (M)		—	—	—	3.25	—
1979FM (U)		—	—	—	5.00	—
1979FM (P)	3,270	Value: 2.00				
1980		—	0.25	0.50	1.00	—
1980FM (M)		—	—	—	3.00	—
1980FM (U)		—	—	—	5.00	—
1980FM (P)	2,393	Value: 2.00				
1981FM (M)		—	—	—	3.00	—
1981FM (U)		—	—	—	5.00	—
1981FM (P)	—	Value: 2.00				
1999		—	—	—	2.00	—
1999 Proof	3,000	Value: 4.00				

KM# 33a 50 CENTS **Weight:** 7.2500 g. **Composition:** 0.9250 Silver .2156 oz. ASW

Date	Mintage	F	VF	XF	Unc	BU
1981FM (P)	898	Value: 15.00				

KM# 46 50 CENTS **Composition:** Copper-Nickel **Subject:** 20th Anniversary of Independence **Obverse:** Coat of arms

Date	F	VF	XF	Unc	BU
1982FM (M)	—	—	—	3.00	—
1982FM (U)	—	—	—	2.50	—
1982FM (P)	— Value: 2.00				

KM# 46a 50 CENTS **Weight:** 7.2500 g. **Composition:** 0.9250 Silver .2156 oz. ASW

Date	Mintage	F	VF	XF	Unc	BU
1982FM (P)	699	Value: 20.00				

KM# 54 50 CENTS **Composition:** Copper-Nickel **Obverse:** Coat of arms

Date	F	VF	XF	Unc	BU
1983FM (M)	—	—	—	4.00	—
1983FM (P)	— Value: 2.00				
1984FM (P)	— Value: 2.00				

KM# 54a 50 CENTS **Weight:** 7.2500 g. **Composition:** 0.9250 Silver .2156 oz. ASW

Date	Mintage	F	VF	XF	Unc	BU
1983FM (P)	1,325	Value: 15.00				
1984FM (P)	—	Value: 15.00				

KM# 34 DOLLAR **Composition:** Copper-Nickel

Date	Mintage	F	VF	XF	Unc	BU
1976FM (M)	1,500	—	—	—	5.00	—
1976FM (U)	582	—	—	—	8.00	—
1976FM (P)	10,000	Value: 2.00				
1977FM (M)	1,500	—	—	—	6.00	—
1977FM (U)	633	—	—	—	8.00	—
1977FM (P)	5,337	Value: 2.00				
1978FM (M)	1,500	—	—	—	6.00	—
1978FM (U)	472	—	—	—	8.00	—
1978FM (P)	4,845	Value: 3.00				
1979FM (M)	1,500	—	—	—	6.00	—
1979FM (U)	518	—	—	—	8.00	—
1979FM (P)	3,270	Value: 3.00				
1980FM (M)	750	—	—	—	8.00	—
1980FM (U)	796	—	—	—	8.00	—
1980FM (P)	2,393	Value: 5.00				
1981FM (M)	—	—	—	—	5.00	—
1981FM (U)	—	—	—	—	3.00	—
1981FM (P)	—	Value: 2.50				
1983FM (M)	—	—	—	—	5.00	—
1983FM (P)	—	Value: 2.50				
1984FM (P)	—	Value: 2.50				

KM# 38 DOLLAR **Weight:** 18.6000 g. **Composition:** 0.9250 Silver .5532 oz. ASW **Series:** F.A.O.

Date	F	VF	XF	Unc	BU
1979	—	0.75	1.50	3.50	—

KM# 34a DOLLAR **Weight:** 18.6000 g. **Composition:** 0.9250 Silver .5532 oz. ASW

Date	Mintage	F	VF	XF	Unc	BU
1981FM (P)	898	Value: 20.00				
1983FM (P)	2,544	Value: 16.50				
1984FM (P)	—	Value: 16.50				

KM# 47 DOLLAR **Composition:** Copper-Nickel **Subject:** 20th Anniversary of Independence **Obverse:** Coat of arms

Date	F	VF	XF	Unc	BU
1982FM (M)	—	—	—	8.00	—
1982FM (U)	—	—	—	5.00	—
1982FM (P)	— Value: 5.00				

KM# 47a DOLLAR **Weight:** 18.6000 g. **Composition:** 0.9250 Silver .5532 oz. ASW

Date	Mintage	F	VF	XF	Unc	BU
1982FM (P)	699	Value: 20.00				

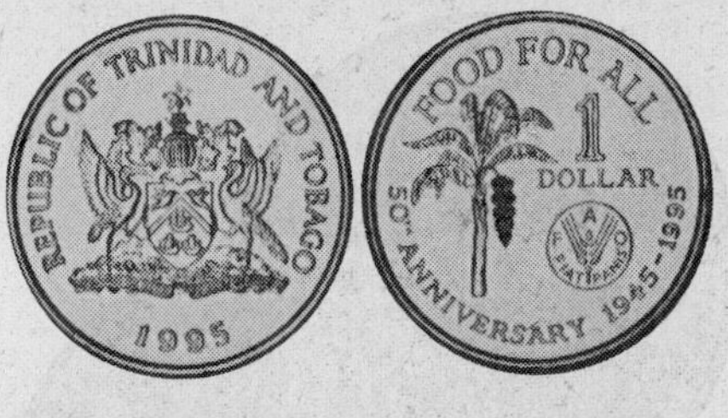

KM# 61 DOLLAR **Composition:** Copper-Nickel **Subject:** 50th Anniversary - F.A.O.

Date	Mintage	F	VF	XF	Unc	BU
1995		—	—	—	1.75	—
1999		—	—	—	1.75	—
1999 Proof	3,000	Value: 5.00				

KM# 35a 5 DOLLARS **Weight:** 29.7000 g. **Composition:** 0.9250 Silver .8833 oz. ASW

Date	Mintage	F	VF	XF	Unc	BU
1976FM (P)	11,000	Value: 10.00				
1977FM (P)	6,107	Value: 12.00				
1978FM (P)	5,460	Value: 15.00				
1979FM (P)	3,755	Value: 18.00				
1980FM (P)	2,393	Value: 20.00				
1981FM (P)	—	Value: 30.00				
1983FM (P)	—	Value: 30.00				
1984FM (P)	—	Value: 30.00				

KM# 35 5 DOLLARS **Composition:** Copper-Nickel

Date	Mintage	F	VF	XF	Unc	BU
1976FM (M)	300	—	—	—	20.00	—
1976FM (U)	582	—	—	—	25.00	—
1977FM (M)	300	—	—	—	20.00	—
1977FM (U)	633	—	—	—	17.00	—
1978FM (M)	300	—	—	—	20.00	—
1978FM (U)	472	—	—	—	17.00	—
1979FM (M)	300	—	—	—	20.00	—
1979FM (U)	518	—	—	—	17.00	—
1980FM (M)	150	—	—	—	25.00	—
1980FM (U)	796	—	—	—	17.00	—
1981FM (M)	—	—	—	—	20.00	—
1981FM (U)	—	—	—	—	17.00	—
1981FM (P)	—	Value: 20.00				
1983FM (U)	—	—	—	—	20.00	—
1983FM (P)	1,312	Value: 20.00				
1984FM (P)	—	Value: 20.00				

KM# 35a.1 5 DOLLARS **Weight:** 11.0000 g. **Composition:** Copper Nickel **Size:** 30 mm. **Note:** Reduced size.

Date	F	VF	XF	Unc	BU
1999 Proof	— Value: 20.00				

KM# 48 5 DOLLARS **Composition:** Copper-Nickel **Subject:** 20th Anniversary of Independence

Date		F	VF	XF	Unc	BU
1982FM (M)		—	—	—	20.00	—
1982FM (U)		—	—	—	12.50	—
1982FM (P)	—	Value: 17.00				

KM# 48a 5 DOLLARS **Weight:** 30.0000 g. **Composition:** 0.9250 Silver .8922 oz. ASW

Date	Mintage	F	VF	XF	Unc	BU
1982FM (P)	699	Value: 30.00				

KM# 36a 10 DOLLARS **Weight:** 35.0000 g. **Composition:** 0.9250 Silver 1.0409 oz. ASW **Reverse:** Similar to KM#16

Date	Mintage	F	VF	XF	Unc	BU
1976FM (P)	13,000	Value: 10.00				
1977FM (P)	6,643	Value: 15.00				
1978FM (P)	7,449	Value: 15.00				
1979FM (P)	4,994	Value: 20.00				
1980FM (P)	3,726	Value: 25.00				

KM# 36 10 DOLLARS **Composition:** Copper-Nickel

Date	Mintage	F	VF	XF	Unc	BU
1976FM (M)	150	—	—	—	40.00	—
1976FM (U)	582	—	—	—	30.00	—
1977FM (M)	150	—	—	—	40.00	—
1977FM (U)	633	—	—	—	30.00	—
1978FM (M)	150	—	—	—	40.00	—
1978FM (U)	472	—	—	—	30.00	—
1979FM (M)	150	—	—	—	40.00	—
1979FM (U)	518	—	—	—	30.00	—
1980FM (M)	796	—	—	—	40.00	—
1980FM (U)	—	—	—	—	30.00	—

KM# 40 10 DOLLARS **Composition:** Copper-Nickel **Subject:** 5th Anniversary of the Republic **Obverse:** Coat of arms

Date	F	VF	XF	Unc	BU
1981FM (U)	—	—	—	20.00	—

KM# 40a 10 DOLLARS **Weight:** 35.0000 g. **Composition:** 0.9250 Silver 1.0409 oz. ASW

Date	Mintage	F	VF	XF	Unc	BU
1981FM (P)	2,374	Value: 25.00				

KM# 49 10 DOLLARS **Composition:** Copper-Nickel **Subject:** 20th Anniversary of Independence **Obverse:** Coat of arms

Date		F	VF	XF	Unc	BU
1982FM (M)		—	—	—	20.00	—
1982FM (U)		—	—	—	20.00	—
1982FM (P)	—	Value: 20.00				

KM# 49a 10 DOLLARS **Weight:** 35.0000 g. **Composition:** 0.9250 Silver 1.0409 oz. ASW

Date	Mintage	F	VF	XF	Unc	BU
1982FM (P)	1,682	Value: 27.50				

KM# 55 10 DOLLARS **Composition:** Copper-Nickel **Obverse:** Coat of arms

Date	Mintage	F	VF	XF	Unc	BU
1983FM (U)	288	—	—	—	55.00	—

KM# 55a 10 DOLLARS **Weight:** 35.0000 g. **Composition:** 0.9250 Silver 1.0409 oz. ASW

Date	Mintage	F	VF	XF	Unc	BU
1983FM (P)	1,565	Value: 40.00				
1984FM (P)	—	Value: 40.00				

KM# 60 10 DOLLARS **Weight:** 28.2800 g. **Composition:** 0.9250 Silver .8411 oz. ASW **Subject:** 30th Anniversary - Central Bank

Date	Mintage	F	VF	XF	Unc	BU
1994 Proof	Est. 5,000	Value: 47.50				

KM# 62 10 DOLLARS **Ring Composition:** Gold Plated**Center Weight:** 12.0000 g. **Center Composition:** 0.9250 Silver .3569 oz. ASW **Subject:** Central Bank 35 Years **Obverse:** National arms **Reverse:** Bank building **Edge:** Reeded **Shape:** Octagonal **Size:** 28.4 mm.

Date	Mintage	F	VF	XF	Unc	BU
1999 Proof	6,500	Value: 55.00				

KM# 39 25 DOLLARS **Weight:** 30.2800 g. **Composition:** 0.5000 Silver .4868 oz. ASW **Subject:** 10th Anniversary of Caribbean Development Bank

Date	Mintage	F	VF	XF	Unc	BU
ND(1980)FM (P)	3,039	Value: 20.00				

KM# 37 100 DOLLARS **Weight:** 6.2100 g. **Composition:** 0.5000 Gold .0998 oz. AGW

Date	Mintage	F	VF	XF	Unc	BU
1976FM (M)	200	—	—	—	100	—
1976FM (P)	29,000	Value: 50.00				

KM# 41 100 DOLLARS **Weight:** 6.2100 g. **Composition:** 0.5000 Gold .0998 oz. AGW **Subject:** 5th Anniversary of the Republic

Date	Mintage	F	VF	XF	Unc	BU
1981FM (U)	100	—	—	—	175	—
1981FM (P)	400	Value: 130				

KM# 50 100 DOLLARS **Weight:** 6.2100 g. **Composition:** 0.5000 Gold .0998 oz. AGW **Subject:** 20th Anniversary of Independence

e	Mintage	F	VF	XF	Unc	BU
2FM (P)	1,380	Value: 90.00				

1# 56 **200 DOLLARS** **Weight:** 11.1700 g. **Composition:** 0.5000 Gold .1796 oz. AGW **Subject:** 20th Anniversary of Central Bank

e	Mintage	F	VF	XF	Unc	BU
4FM (P)	1,200	Value: 100				

MINT SETS

#	Date	Mintage	Identification	Issue Price	Mkt Val
2	1974 (8)	3,258	KM#8a, 22-23, 24a, 25-28	25.00	15.00
3	1975 (8)	1,111	KM#8a, 22-23, 24a, 25-28	27.50	20.00
4	1976 (8)	582	KM#29-34, 35a-36a	27.50	30.00
5	1977 (8)	632	KM#29-34, 35a-36a	27.50	30.00
6	1978 (8)	472	KM#29-34, 35a-36a	27.50	30.00
7	1979 (8)	518	KM#29-34, 35a-36a	28.50	40.00
8	1980 (8)	796	KM#29-34, 35a-36a	28.50	30.00
9	1981 (8)	—	KM#29-34, 35a, 40	28.50	45.00
10	1982 (8)	—	KM#42-49	28.50	45.00
11	1983 (8)	281	KM#32, 34, 35a, 51-55	37.00	80.00

PROOF SETS

#	Date	Mintage	Identification	Issue Price	Mkt Val
1	1966 (5)	8,000	KM#1-5	12.50	10.00
2	1970 (6)	2,104	KM#1-5, 7	15.25	12.50
3	1971 (7)	11,039	KM#1-5, 7a, 8	21.00	15.00
5	1972 (8)	13,874	KM#9-16	35.00	20.00
6	1972 (7)	15,957	KM#9-15	22.00	12.50
9	1974 (8)	13,991	KM#8, 22-28	50.00	20.00
10	1975 (8)	24,472	KM#8, 22-28	55.00	22.00
24	1999 (8)	3,000	KM#29-33, 35a.1, 61-62	90.00	95.00
11	1976 (8)	10,099	KM#29-36	55.00	25.00
12	1977 (8)	5,337	KM#29-36	55.00	35.00
13	1978 (8)	4,845	KM#29-36	55.00	35.00
14	1979 (8)	3,270	KM#29-36	57.00	40.00
15	1980 (8)	2,393	KM#29-36	66.00	55.00
16	1981 (8)	—	KM#29-34, 35a, 40a	87.00	65.00
17	1981 (8)	—	KM#29a-34a, 35, 40a	222	125
9	1982 (8)	—	KM#42a-49a	222	135
18	1982 (8)	—	KM#42-49	87.00	65.00
20	1983 (8)	461	KM#32, 34, 35a, 51-54, 55a	87.00	85.00
21	1983 (8)	753	KM#32a, 34a, 35, 51a-55a	197	100
22	1984 (8)	—	KM#32, 34, 35a, 51-54, 55a	87.00	75.00
23	1984 (8)	—	KM#32a, 34a, 35, 51a-55a	197	100

TRISTAN DA CUNHA

Tristan da Cunha is the principal island and group name of a small cluster of volcanic islands located in the South Atlantic midway between the Cape of Good Hope and South America, and 1,500 miles (2,414 km.) south-southwest of the British colony of St. Helena. The other islands are Inaccessible, Gough, and the three Nightingale Islands. The group, which comprises a dependency of St. Helena, has a total area of 40 sq. mi. (104 sq. km.) and a population of less than 300. There is a village of 60 houses called Edinburgh. Potatoes are the staple subsistence crop.

Portuguese admiral Tristao da Cunha discovered Tristan da Cunha in 1506. Unsuccessful attempts to colonize the islands were made by the Dutch in 1656, but the first permanent inhabitant didn't arrive until 1810.During the exile of Napoleon on St. Helena, Britain placed a temporary garrison on Tristan da Cunha to prevent any attempt to rescue Napoleon from his island prison. The islands were formally annexed to Britain in 1816 and became a dependency of St. Helena in 1938.

RULERS
British

MINT MARKS
PM - Pobjoy Mint

MONETARY SYSTEM
25 Pence = 1 Crown
4 Crowns = 1 Pound

ST. HELENA DEPENDENCY

STANDARD COINAGE

25 Pence = 1 Crown; 4 Crowns = 1 Pound

KM# 1 **25 PENCE** **Composition:** Copper-Nickel **Subject:** Queen's Silver Jubilee

Date	Mintage	F	VF	XF	Unc	BU
ND(1977)	50,000	—	1.00	2.00	5.00	—

KM# 1a **25 PENCE** **Weight:** 28.2800 g. **Composition:** 0.9250 Silver .8411 oz. ASW

Date	Mintage	F	VF	XF	Unc	BU
ND(1977) Proof	25,000	Value: 13.50				

KM# 3 **25 PENCE** **Composition:** Copper-Nickel **Subject:** 80th Birthday of Queen Mother

Date	Mintage	F	VF	XF	Unc	BU
ND(1980)	65,000	—	1.00	1.75	3.50	—

KM# 3a **25 PENCE** **Weight:** 28.2800 g. **Composition:** 0.9250 Silver .8411 oz. ASW

Date	Mintage	F	VF	XF	Unc	BU
ND(1980) Proof	25,000	Value: 13.50				

KM# 4 **25 PENCE** **Composition:** Copper-Nickel **Subject:** Wedding of Prince Charles and Lady Diana

Date	F	VF	XF	Unc	BU
ND(1981)PM	—	1.00	1.75	3.50	—

KM# 4a **25 PENCE** **Weight:** 28.2800 g. **Composition:** 0.9250 Silver .8411 oz. ASW

Date	Mintage	F	VF	XF	Unc	BU
ND(1981)PM Proof	30,000	Value: 20.00				

KM# 7 **50 PENCE** **Weight:** 28.2800 g. **Composition:** 0.9250 Silver .8411 oz. ASW **Subject:** 40th Wedding Anniversary of Queen Elizabeth and Prince Philip

Date	Mintage	F	VF	XF	Unc	BU
ND(1987) Proof	2,000	Value: 25.00				

KM# 7a **50 PENCE** **Weight:** 47.5400 g. **Composition:** 0.9170 Gold 1.4001 oz. AGW **Subject:** 40th Wedding Anniversary of Queen Elizabeth and Prince Philip

Date	Mintage	F	VF	XF	Unc	BU
ND(1987) Proof	75	Value: 950				

KM# 7b **50 PENCE** **Composition:** Copper-Nickel

Date	F	VF	XF	Unc	BU
ND(1987)	—	—	—	4.50	—

KM# 9 **50 PENCE** **Weight:** 28.2800 g. **Composition:** Copper-Nickel **Subject:** Winston Churchill **Obverse:** Queen's

portrait **Reverse:** Churchill and two fighter planes **Edge:** Reeded **Size:** 38.6 mm. **Note:** Struck at British Royal Mint.

Date	F	VF	XF	Unc	BU
1999	—	—	—	6.50	—

KM# 9a 50 PENCE **Weight:** 28.2800 g. **Composition:** 0.9250 Silver .8411 oz. ASW **Subject:** Winston Churchill

Date	Mintage	F	VF	XF	Unc	BU
1999 Proof	2,500	Value: 42.50				

KM# 9b 50 PENCE **Weight:** 47.5400 g. **Composition:** 0.9170 Gold 1.4001 oz. AGW **Subject:** Winston Churchill

Date	Mintage	F	VF	XF	Unc	BU
1999	Est. 100	Value: 950				

KM# 11 50 PENCE **Weight:** 28.6400 g. **Composition:** Copper-Nickel **Subject:** Princess Anne's 50th Birthday **Obverse:** Queen Elizabeth's portrait **Reverse:** Anne's portrait **Edge:** Reeded **Size:** 38.6 mm.

Date	F	VF	XF	Unc	BU
ND(2000)	—	—	—	6.50	—

KM# 10a 50 PENCE **Weight:** 28.4000 g. **Composition:** 0.9250 Silver 0.8446 oz. ASW

Date	Mintage	F	VF	XF	Unc	BU
ND(2000)		—	—	—	—	—
ND(2000) Proof	—	Value: 50.00				

KM# 10 50 PENCE **Weight:** 28.6400 g. **Composition:** Copper-Nickel **Subject:** Queen Mother's Centennial Birthday **Obverse:** Queen Elizabeth's portrait **Reverse:** Queen Mother's portrait **Edge:** Reeded **Size:** 38.6 mm.

Date	F	VF	XF	Unc	BU
ND(2001)	—	—	—	6.50	—

KM# 12 50 PENCE **Weight:** 29.1000 g. **Composition:** Copper-Nickel **Subject:** Queen Elizabeth's 75th Birthday **Obverse:** Queen's portrait in profile **Reverse:** Queen's portrait facing viewer **Edge:** Reeded **Size:** 38.6 mm.

Date	F	VF	XF	Unc	BU
2001	—	—	—	7.00	—

KM# 13 50 PENCE **Weight:** 29.6000 g. **Composition:** Copper-Nickel **Subject:** Centennial of Queen Victoria's Death **Obverse:** Queen Elizabeth's portrait. **Reverse:** Queen Victoria's portrait. **Edge:** Reeded. **Size:** 38.7 mm.

Date	F	VF	XF	Unc	BU
2001	—	—	—	8.00	—

KM# 2 CROWN **Composition:** Copper-Nickel **Subject:** 25th Anniversary of Coronation

Date	F	VF	XF	Unc	BU
1978PM	—	1.00	1.75	3.50	—

KM# 2a CROWN **Weight:** 28.2800 g. **Composition:** 0.9250 Silver .8411 oz. ASW

Date	Mintage	F	VF	XF	Unc	BU
1978PM	70,000	—	—	—	12.50	—
1978PM Proof	25,000	Value: 18.50				

KM# 5 CROWN **Weight:** 28.2800 g. **Composition:** 0.9250 Silver .8411 oz. ASW **Series:** International Year of the Scout **Obverse:** Queen Elizabeth II

Date	Mintage	F	VF	XF	Unc	BU
ND(1983)	10,000	—	—	—	32.50	—
ND(1983) Proof	10,000	Value: 47.50				

KM# 6 2 POUNDS **Weight:** 15.9800 g. **Composition:** 0.9170 Gold .4712 oz. AGW **Series:** International Year of the Scout **Obverse:** Queen Elizabeth II **Reverse:** Sail boat

Date	Mintage	F	VF	XF	Unc	BU
1983	2,000	—	—	—	350	—
1983 Proof	2,000	Value: 500				

KM# 8 2 POUNDS **Composition:** Copper-Nickel **Subject:** 90th Anniversary of Queen Mother

Date	F	VF	XF	Unc	BU
ND(1990)	—	—	—	12.50	—

KM# 8a 2 POUNDS **Weight:** 28.2800 g. **Composition:** 0.9250 Silver .8411 oz. ASW

Date	Mintage	F	VF	XF	Unc	BU
ND(1990) Proof	Est. 10,000	Value: 55.00				

TUNISIA

The Republic of Tunisia, located on the northern coast of ica between Algeria and Libya, has an area of 63,170sq. mi. 3,610 sq. km.) and a population of *7.9 million. Capital: Tunis. riculture is the backbone of the economy. Crude oil, phos- ates, olive oil, and wine are exported.

Tunisia, settled by the Phoenicians in the 12th century B.C., s the center of the seafaring Carthaginian Empire. After the al destruction of Carthage, Tunisia became part of Rome's Afri- n province. It remained a part of the Roman Empire (except for 439-533 interval of Vandal conquest) until taken by the Arabs, 3, who administered it until the Turkish invasion of 1570. Under kish control, the public revenue was heavily dependent upon piracy of Mediterranean shipping, an endeavor that wasn't andoned until 1819 when a coalition of powers threatened propriate reprisal. Deprived of its major source of income, Tuni- underwent a financial regression that ended in bankruptcy, abling France to establish a protectorate over the country in 31. National agitation and guerrilla fighting forced France to nt Tunisia internal autonomy in 1955 and to recognize Tuni- n independence on March20, 1956. Tunisia abolished the narchy and established a republic on July 25, 1957.

LES

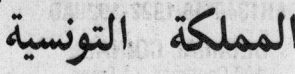

المملكة التونسية

Mamlaka(t) al-Tunisiya(t)

الجمهورية التونسية

Jumhuriya(t) al-Tunisiya(t)

NT MARKS

- Paris, AH1308/1891-AH1348/1928
- Paris, privy marks, H1349/1929-AH1376/1957
- Franklin Mint, Franklin Center, PA
  Numismatic Italiana, Arezzo, Italy

TUNIS

Tunis, the capital and major seaport of Tunisia, existed in the rthaginian era, but its importance dates only from the Moslem nquest, following which it became a major center of Arab power d prosperity. Spain seized it in 1535, lost it in 1564, retook it in 73 and ceded it to the Turks in 1574. Thereafter the history of nis merged with that of Tunisia.

cal Rulers

Bey, AH1299-1320/1882-1902AD
hammad Al-Hadi Bey, AH1320-1324/1902-1906AD
hammad Al-Nasir Bey, AH1324-1340/1906-1922AD
hammad Al-Habib Bey, AH1340-1348/1922-1929AD
mad Pasha Bey, AH1348-1361/1929-1942AD
hammad Al-Munsif Bey, AH1361-1362/1942-1943AD
hammad Al-Amin Bey, AH1362-1376/1943-1957AD

NOTE: All coins struck until AH1298/1881AD bear the name the Ottoman Sultan; the name of the Bey of Tunis was added AH1272/1855AD. After AH1298, when the French established ir protectorate, only the Bey's name appears on the coin until 1376/1956AD.

TUNISIA

FRENCH PROTECTORATE

ANONYMOUS COINAGE

AH1340-64/1921-45AD

Struck in the name of the Tunisian Bey.

M# 246 50 CENTIMES **Composition:** Aluminum-Bronze

e	Mintage	F	VF	XF	Unc
1340/1921(a)	4,000,000	—	1.00	7.00	20.00
1345/1926(a)	1,000,000	—	3.00	10.00	25.00
1352/1933(a)	500,000	—	6.00	17.00	50.00
1360/1941(a)	4,646,000	—	0.35	1.50	10.00
1364/1945(a)	11,180,000	—	0.25	1.00	10.00

KM# 247 FRANC **Composition:** Aluminum-Bronze

Date	Mintage	F	VF	XF	Unc
AH1340/1921(a)	5,000,000	—	1.00	7.00	20.00
AH1344/1926(a)	1,000,000	—	2.00	15.00	35.00
AH1345/1926(a)	1,000,000	—	4.00	17.00	40.00
AH1360/1941(a)	6,612,000	—	0.50	2.00	10.00
AH1364/1945(a)	10,699,000	—	0.35	1.75	10.00

KM# 248 2 FRANCS **Composition:** Aluminum-Bronze

Date	Mintage	F	VF	XF	Unc
AH1340/1921(a)	1,500,000	—	3.00	15.00	35.00
AH1343/1924(a)	500,000	—	8.00	20.00	50.00
AH1345/1926(a)	500,000	—	8.00	20.00	50.00
AH1360/1941(a)	1,976,000	—	1.50	6.00	15.00
AH1364/1945(a)	6,464,000	—	1.00	5.00	15.00

Ali Bey

AH1299-1320/1882-1902AD

DECIMAL COINAGE

100 Centimes = 1 Franc

The following coins all bear French inscriptions on one side, Arabic on the other, and usually have both AH and AD dates. Except for KM#246-48, they are struck in the name of the Tunisian Bey.

KM# 223 50 CENTIMES **Weight:** 2.5000 g. **Composition:** 0.8350 Silver .0671 oz. ASW **Obv. Legend:** ALI

Date	Mintage	F	VF	XF	Unc
AH1319/1901A	1,000	—	—	100	175
AH1320/1902A	1,000	—	—	100	175

KM# 224 FRANC **Weight:** 5.0000 g. **Composition:** 0.8350 Silver .1342 oz. ASW **Obv. Legend:** ALI

Date	Mintage	F	VF	XF	Unc
AH1319/1901A	700	—	—	135	225
AH1320/1902A	703	—	—	135	225

KM# 225 2 FRANCS **Weight:** 10.0000 g. **Composition:** 0.8350 Silver .2685 oz. ASW **Obv. Legend:** ALI

Date	Mintage	F	VF	XF	Unc
AH1319/1901A	300	—	—	150	250
AH1320/1902A	300	—	—	150	250

KM# 226 10 FRANCS **Weight:** 3.2258 g. **Composition:** 0.9000 Gold .0933 oz. AGW **Obv. Legend:** ALI

Date	Mintage	F	VF	XF	Unc
AH1319/1901A	80	—	—	450	850
AH1319/1901A	80	—	—	450	850
AH1320/1902A	83	—	—	450	850

KM# 233 10 FRANCS **Weight:** 3.2258 g. **Composition:** 0.9000 Gold .0933 oz. AGW **Obv. Legend:** MUHAMMAD AL-HADI

Date	Mintage	F	VF	XF	Unc
AH1321/1903A	83	—	—	450	900
AH1322/1904A	83	—	—	450	900
AH1323/1905A	83	—	—	450	900
AH1324/1906A	83	—	—	450	900

KM# 227 20 FRANCS **Weight:** 6.4516 g. **Composition:** 0.9000 Gold .1867 oz. AGW **Obv. Legend:** ALI

Date	Mintage	F	VF	XF	Unc
AH1319/1901A	150,000	—	BV	75.00	110
AH1319/1901A	150,000	—	BV	75.00	110
AH1320/1902A	20	—	—	550	1,000

Muhammad al-Hadi Bey

AH1320-24/1902-1906AD

DECIMAL COINAGE

100 Centimes = 1 Franc

The following coins all bear French inscriptions on one side, Arabic on the other, and usually have both AH and AD dates. Except for KM#246-48, they are struck in the name of the Tunisian Bey.

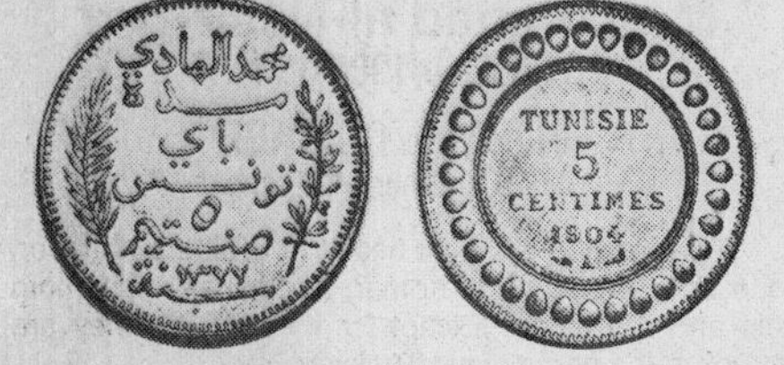

KM# 228 5 CENTIMES **Composition:** Bronze **Obv. Legend:** MUHAMMAD AL-HADI

Date	Mintage	F	VF	XF	Unc
AH1321/1903A	500,000	—	8.00	12.00	25.00
AH1322/1904A	1,000,000	—	8.00	12.00	25.00

KM# 235 5 CENTIMES **Composition:** Bronze **Obv. Legend:** MUHAMMAD AL-NASIR

Date	Mintage	F	VF	XF	Unc
AH1325/1907A	1,000,000	—	2.00	4.00	17.00
AH1326/1908A	1,000,000	—	2.00	4.00	17.00
AH1330/1912A	1,000,000	—	2.00	4.00	17.00
AH1332/1914A	1,000,000	—	2.00	4.00	17.00
AH1334/1916A	2,000,000	—	2.00	4.00	12.00
AH1336/1917A	2,021,000	—	2.00	4.00	12.00

KM# 229 10 CENTIMES **Composition:** Bronze **Obv. Legend:** MUHAMMAD AL-HADI

Date	Mintage	F	VF	XF	Unc
AH1321/1903A	250,000	—	10.00	20.00	30.00
AH1322/1904A	500,000	—	10.00	20.00	30.00

KM# 230 50 CENTIMES **Weight:** 2.5000 g. **Composition:** 0.8350 Silver .0671 oz. ASW **Obv. Legend:** MUHAMMAD AL-HADI

Date	Mintage	F	VF	XF	Unc
AH1321/1903A	1,002,999	—	—	150	250
AH1322/1904A	1,003	—	—	150	250
AH1323/1905A	1,003	—	—	150	250
AH1324/1906A	1,003	—	—	150	250

KM# 231 FRANC **Weight:** 5.0000 g. **Composition:** 0.8350 Silver .1342 oz. ASW **Obv. Legend:** MUHAMMAD AL-HADI

Date	Mintage	F	VF	XF	Unc
AH1321/1903A	703	—	—	135	225
AH1322/1904A	500,000	—	50.00	80.00	150
AH1323/1905A	703	—	—	135	225
AH1324/1906A	703	—	—	135	225

KM# 232 2 FRANCS **Weight:** 10.0000 g. **Composition:** 0.8350 Silver .2685 oz. ASW **Obv. Legend:** MUHAMMAD AL-HADI

Date	Mintage	F	VF	XF	Unc
AH1321/1903A	303	—	—	150	250
AH1322/1904A	150,000	—	70.00	110	200
AH1323/1905A	303	—	—	150	250
AH1324/1906A	303	—	—	150	250

KM# 234 20 FRANCS **Weight:** 6.4516 g. **Composition:** 0.9000 Gold .1867 oz. AGW **Obv. Legend:** MUHAMMAD AL-HADI

Date	Mintage	F	VF	XF	Unc
AH1321/1903A	300,000	—	BV	80.00	120
AH1321/1904A	600,000	—	BV	80.00	120
AH1322/1904A	Inc. above	—	BV	80.00	120
AH1323/1905A	23	—	—	550	1,000
AH1324/1906A	23	—	—	550	1,000

Muhammad al-Nasir Bey

AH1324-40/1906-1922AD

DECIMAL COINAGE

100 Centimes = 1 Franc

The following coins all bear French inscriptions on one side, Arabic on the other, and usually have both AH and AD dates. Except for KM#246-48, they are struck in the name of the Tunisian Bey.

KM# 242 5 CENTIMES Composition: Nickel-Bronze **Obv. Legend:** MOHAMMED AL-NASIR

Date	Mintage	F	VF	XF	Unc
AH1337/1918(a)	1,549,000	—	4.00	10.00	25.00
AH1337/1919(a)	4,451,000	—	3.00	8.00	20.00
AH1338/6/1920(a)	2,206,000	—	4.00	10.00	25.00
AH1338/7/1920(a)	Inc. above	—	4.00	10.00	25.00
AH1338/1920(a)	Inc. above	—	3.00	8.00	20.00
AH1339/1920(a)	Inc. above	—	3.00	8.00	20.00

KM# 245 5 CENTIMES Composition: Nickel-Bronze **Note:** Reduced size.

Date	Mintage	F	VF	XF	Unc
AH1339/1920(a)	1,794,000	—	20.00	40.00	75.00

KM# 236 10 CENTIMES Composition: Bronze **Obv. Legend:** MUHAMMAD AL-NASIR

Date	Mintage	F	VF	XF	Unc
AH1325/1907A	500,000	—	3.00	6.00	20.00
AH1326/1908A	500,000	—	3.00	6.00	20.00
AH1329/1911A	500,000	—	3.00	6.00	20.00
AH1330/1912A	500,000	—	3.00	6.00	20.00
AH1332/1914A	500,000	—	3.00	6.00	20.00
AH1334/1916A	1,000,000	—	3.00	6.00	20.00
AH1336/1917A	1,050,000	—	3.00	6.00	20.00

KM# 243 10 CENTIMES Composition: Nickel-Bronze **Obv. Legend:** MUHAMMAD AL-NASIR

Date	Mintage	F	VF	XF	Unc
AH1337/1918(a)	1,288,000	—	3.00	8.00	25.00
AH1337/1919(a)	2,712,000	—	3.00	8.00	20.00
AH1338/1920(a)	3,000,000	—	3.00	8.00	20.00

KM# 244 25 CENTIMES Composition: Nickel-Bronze **Obv. Legend:** MUHAMMAD AL-NASIR

Date	Mintage	F	VF	XF	Unc
AH1337/1918(a)	—	—	4.00	12.00	35.00
AH1337/1919(a)	2,000,000	—	3.00	10.00	25.00
AH1338/1920(a)	2,000,000	—	3.00	10.00	25.00

KM# 237 50 CENTIMES Weight: 2.5000 g. **Composition:** 0.8350 Silver .0671 oz. ASW **Obv. Legend:** MUHAMMAD AL-NASIR

Date	Mintage	F	VF	XF	Unc
AH1325/1907A	201,000	—	10.00	20.00	40.00
AH1326/1908A	2,006	—	—	75.00	135
AH1327/1909A	1,003	—	—	100	175
AH1328/1910A	1,003	—	—	100	175
AH1329/1911A	1,003	—	—	100	175
AH1330/1912A	201,000	—	10.00	20.00	40.00
AH1331/1913A	1,003	—	—	100	175
AH1332/1914A	201,000	—	10.00	20.00	40.00
AH1334/1915A	707,000	—	8.00	15.00	30.00
AH1334/1916A	3,614,000	—	7.00	12.00	25.00
AH1335/1916A	Inc. above	—	7.00	12.00	25.00
AH1335/1917A	2,139,000	—	7.00	12.00	25.00
AH1336/1917A	Inc. above	—	7.00	12.00	25.00
AH1337/1918A	1,003	—	—	100	175
AH1338/1919A	1,003	—	—	100	175
AH1339/1920A	1,003	—	—	100	175
AH1340/1921A	1,003	—	—	100	175

KM# 238 FRANC Weight: 5.0000 g. **Composition:** 0.8350 Silver .1342 oz. ASW **Obv. Legend:** MUHAMMAD AL-NASIR

Date	Mintage	F	VF	XF	Unc
AH1325/1907A	301,000	—	10.00	20.00	35.00
AH1326/1908A	401,000	—	10.00	15.00	35.00
AH1327/1909A	703	—	—	135	225
AH1328/1910A	703	—	—	135	225
AH1329/1911A	1,051,000	—	7.00	12.00	30.00
AH1330/1912A	501,000	—	8.00	15.00	30.00
AH1331/1913A	703	—	—	135	225
AH1332/1914A	201,000	—	8.00	15.00	25.00
AH1333/1914A	Inc. above	—	8.00	15.00	25.00
AH1334/1915A	1,060,000	—	7.00	12.00	20.00
AH1334/1916A	3,270,000	—	7.00	12.00	20.00
AH1335/1916A	Inc. above	—	7.00	12.00	20.00
AH1335/1917A	1,628,000	—	7.00	12.00	20.00
AH1336/1918A	804,000	—	7.00	12.00	18.00
AH1337/1918A	Inc. above	—	7.00	12.00	18.00
AH1338/1919A	703	—	—	135	225
AH1339/1920A	703	—	—	135	225
AH1340/1921A	703	—	—	135	225

KM# 239 2 FRANCS Weight: 10.0000 g. **Composition:** 0.8350 Silver .2685 oz. ASW **Obv. Legend:** MUHAMMAD AL-NASIR

Date	Mintage	F	VF	XF	Unc
AH1325/1907A	306	—	—	150	250
AH1326/1908A	101,000	—	20.00	40.00	85.00
AH1327/1909A	303	—	—	150	250
AH1328/1910A	303	—	—	150	250
AH1329/1911A	475,000	—	15.00	25.00	40.00
AH1330/1912A	200,000	—	15.00	25.00	45.00
AH1331/1913A	303	—	—	150	250
AH1332/1914A	100,000	—	15.00	25.00	35.00
AH1333/1914A	Inc. above	—	15.00	25.00	35.00
AH1334/1915A	408,000	—	15.00	25.00	35.00
AH1334/1916A	1,000,000	—	15.00	25.00	35.00
AH1335/1916A	Inc. above	—	15.00	25.00	35.00
AH1336/1917A	303	—	—	150	250
AH1337/1918A	303	—	—	150	250
AH1338/1919A	303	—	—	150	250
AH1339/1920A	303	—	—	150	250
AH1340/1921A	303	—	—	150	250

KM# 240 10 FRANCS Weight: 3.2258 g. **Composition:** 0.9000 Gold .0933 oz. AGW **Obv. Legend:** MUHAMMAD AL-NASIR

Date	Mintage	F	VF	XF	Unc
AH1325/1907A	36	—	—	500	900
AH1326/1908A	166	—	—	300	500
AH1327/1909A	83	—	—	450	850
AH1328/1910A	83	—	—	450	850
AH1329/1911A	83	—	—	450	850
AH1330/1912A	83	—	—	450	850
AH1331/1913A	83	—	—	450	850
AH1332/1914A	83	—	—	450	850
AH1334/1915A	83	—	—	450	850
AH1334/1916A	83	—	—	450	850
AH1336/1917A	83	—	—	450	850
AH1337/1918A	83	—	—	450	850
AH1338/1919A	83	—	—	450	850
AH1339/1920A	83	—	—	450	850
AH1340/1921A	83	—	—	450	850

KM# 241 20 FRANCS Weight: 6.4516 g. **Composition:** 0.9000 Gold .1867 oz. AGW **Obv. Legend:** MUHAMMAD AL-NASIR

Date	Mintage	F	VF	XF	Unc
AH1325/1907A	26	—	—	550	1,000
AH1326/1908A	46	—	—	450	850
AH1327/1909A	23	—	—	550	1,000
AH1328/1910A	23	—	—	550	1,000
AH1329/1911A	23	—	—	550	1,000
AH1330/1912A	23	—	—	550	1,000
AH1331/1913A	23	—	—	550	1,000
AH1332/1914A	23	—	—	550	1,000
AH1334/1915A	23	—	—	550	1,000
AH1334/1916A	23	—	—	550	1,000
AH1336/1917A	23	—	—	550	1,000
AH1337/1918A	23	—	—	550	1,000
AH1338/1919A	23	—	—	550	1,000
AH1339/1920A	23	—	—	550	1,000
AH1340/1921A	23	—	—	550	1,000

Muhammad al-Habib Bey

AH1340-48/1922-1929AD

DECIMAL COINAGE

100 Centimes = 1 Franc

The following coins all bear French inscriptions on one side, Arabic on the other, and usually have both AH and AD dates. Except for KM#246-48, they are struck in the name of the Tunisian Bey.

KM# 254 10 CENTIMES Composition: Nickel-Bronze **Obv. Legend:** MUHAMMAD AL-HABIB

Date	Mintage	F	VF	XF	Unc
AH1345/1926(a)	1,000,000	—	20.00	50.00	100

KM# 249 50 CENTIMES Weight: 2.5000 g. **Composition:** 0.8350 Silver .0671 oz. ASW **Obv. Legend:** MUHAMMAD AL-HABIB

Date	Mintage	F	VF	XF	Un
AH1341/1922A	1,003	—	—	100	20
AH1342/1923A	2,009	—	—	100	20
AH1343/1924A	1,003	—	—	100	20
AH1344/1925A	1,003	—	—	100	20
AH1345/1926A	1,003	—	—	100	20
AH1346/1927A	1,003	—	—	100	20
AH1347/1928A	1,003	—	—	100	20

KM# 250 FRANC Weight: 5.0000 g. **Composition:** 0.8350 Silver .1342 oz. ASW **Obv. Legend:** MUHAMMAD AL-HABIB

Date	Mintage	F	VF	XF	U
AH1341/1922A	703	—	—	135	27
AH1342/1923A	1,409	—	—	100	25
AH1343/1924A	703	—	—	135	27
AH1344/1925A	703	—	—	135	27
AH1345/1926A	703	—	—	135	27
AH1346/1927A	703	—	—	135	27
AH1347/1928A	703	—	—	135	27

KM# 250a FRANC Weight: 5.5000 g. **Composition:** 0.8350 Silver .1476 oz. ASW

Date	F	VF	XF	U
AH1347/1928A	—	—	135	2

KM# 251 2 FRANCS Weight: 10.0000 g. **Composition:** 0.8350 Silver .2685 oz. ASW **Obv. Legend:** MUHAMMAD AL-HABIB

Date	Mintage	F	VF	XF	U
AH1341/1922A	303	—	—	150	3
AH1342/1923A	690	—	—	135	2
AH1343/1924A	303	—	—	150	3
AH1344/1925A	303	—	—	150	3

	Mintage	F	VF	XF	Unc
5/1926A	303	—	—	150	325
6/1927A	303	—	—	150	325

251a 2 FRANCS Weight: 8.6000 g. **Composition:** .8350 Silver 0.2309 oz. ASW

	Mintage	F	VF	XF	Unc
7/1928A	303	—	—	150	325

252 10 FRANCS Weight: 3.2258 g. **Composition:** .9000 Gold .0933 oz. AGW **Obv. Legend:** MUHAMMAD L-HABIB BEY

	Mintage	F	VF	XF	Unc
1/1922A	83	—	—	450	850
2/1923A	169	—	—	300	500
3/1924A	83	—	—	450	850
4/1925A	83	—	—	450	850
5/1926A	83	—	—	450	850
6/1927A	83	—	—	450	850
7/1928A	83	—	—	450	850

253 20 FRANCS Weight: 6.4516 g. **Composition:** .9000 Gold .1867 oz. AGW **Obv. Legend:** MUHAMMAD L-HABIB

	Mintage	F	VF	XF	Unc
1/1922A	23	—	—	550	1,000
2/1923A	49	—	—	450	850
3/1924A	23	—	—	550	1,000
4/1925A	23	—	—	550	1,000
5/1926A	23	—	—	550	1,000
6/1927A	23	—	—	550	1,000
7/1928A	23	—	—	550	1,000

Ahmad Pasha Bey
AH1348-61/1929-1942AD

DECIMAL COINAGE
100 Centimes = 1 Franc

he following coins all bear French inscriptions on side, Arabic on the other, and usually have both and AD dates. Except for KM#246-48, they are k in the name of the Tunisian Bey.

 # 258 5 CENTIMES Composition: Nickel-Bronze **bv. Legend:** AHMAD

	Mintage	F	VF	XF	Unc
50/1931(a)	2,000,000	—	4.00	10.00	25.00
52/1933(a)	1,000,000	—	5.00	12.00	30.00
57/1938(a)	1,200,000	—	4.00	10.00	25.00

 # 259 10 CENTIMES Composition: Nickel-Bronze **bv. Legend:** AHMAD

	Mintage	F	VF	XF	Unc
50/1931(a)	750,000	—	6.00	15.00	35.00
52/1933(a)	1,000,000	—	6.00	15.00	35.00
57/1938(a)	1,200,000	—	5.00	12.00	25.00

 # 267 10 CENTIMES Composition: Zinc **Obv. egend:** AHMAD

	Mintage	F	VF	XF	Unc
60/1941(a)	5,000,000	—	2.50	6.00	25.00
61/1942(a)	10,000,000	—	1.50	4.00	20.00

 # 268 20 CENTIMES Composition: Zinc **Obv. egend:** AHMAD

	Mintage	F	VF	XF	Unc
61/1942A	5,000,000	—	20.00	35.00	50.00

KM# 260 25 CENTIMES Composition: Nickel-Aluminum-Bronze **Obv. Legend:** AHMAD

Date	Mintage	F	VF	XF	Unc
AH1350/1931(a)	300,000	—	8.00	15.00	35.00
AH1352/1933(a)	400,000	—	8.00	15.00	35.00
AH1357/1938(a)	480,000	—	4.00	10.00	25.00

KM# 261 5 FRANCS Weight: 5.0000 g. **Composition:** 0.6800 Silver .1093 oz. ASW **Obv. Legend:** AHMAD

Date	Mintage	F	VF	XF	Unc
AH1353/1934(a)	2,000,000	—	10.00	18.00	25.00
AH1355/1936(a)	2,000,000	—	10.00	18.00	25.00

KM# 264 5 FRANCS Weight: 5.0000 g. **Composition:** 0.6800 Silver .1093 oz. ASW **Obv. Legend:** AHMAD

Date	Mintage	F	VF	XF	Unc
AH1358/1939(a)	1,600,000	—	15.00	25.00	40.00

KM# 255 10 FRANCS Weight: 10.0000 g. **Composition:** 0.6800 Silver .2186 oz. ASW **Obv. Legend:** AHMAD

Date	Mintage	F	VF	XF	Unc
AH1349/1930(a)	60,000	—	45.00	70.00	110
AH1350/1931(a)	1,103	—	150	250	350
AH1351/1932(a)	60,000	—	60.00	100	200
AH1352/1933(a)	1,103	—	150	250	350
AH1353/1934(a)	30,000	—	45.00	70.00	110

KM# 262 10 FRANCS Weight: 10.0000 g. **Composition:** 0.6800 Silver .2186 oz. ASW

Date	Mintage	F	VF	XF	Unc
AH1353/1934(a)	1,501,000	—	10.00	20.00	35.00
AH1354/1935(a)	1,103	—	—	225	350
AH1355/1936(a)	2,006	—	—	225	350
AH1356/1937(a)	1,103	—	—	225	350
AH1357/1938	—	—	—	400	600
AH1358/1939	—	—	—	400	600

KM# 265 10 FRANCS Weight: 10.0000 g. **Composition:** 0.6800 Silver .2186 oz. ASW

Date	Mintage	F	VF	XF	Unc
AH1358/1939(a)	501,000	—	6.00	15.00	35.00
AH1359/1940(a)	—	—	—	225	350
AH1360/1941(a)	1,103	—	—	225	350
AH1361/1942(a)	1,103	—	—	225	350

KM# 256 20 FRANCS Weight: 20.0000 g. **Composition:** 0.6800 Silver .4372 oz. ASW **Obv. Legend:** AHMAD

Date	Mintage	F	VF	XF	Unc
AH1349/1930(a)	20,000	—	60.00	100	175
AH1350/1931(a)	53	—	200	300	500
AH1351/1932(a)	20,000	—	75.00	150	275
AH1352/1933(a)	53	—	200	300	500
AH1353/1934(a)	9,500	—	60.00	100	175

Note: It is believed that an additional number of coins dated AH1353/1934(a) were struck and included in mintage figures of KM#263 of the same date

KM# 263 20 FRANCS Weight: 20.0000 g. **Composition:** 0.6800 Silver .4372 oz. ASW

Date	Mintage	F	VF	XF	Unc
AH1353/1934(a)	1,250,000	—	12.00	25.00	60.00
AH1354/1935(a)	53	—	—	275	450
AH1355/1936(a)	106	—	—	225	375
AH1356/1937(a)	53	—	—	275	450

KM# 266 20 FRANCS Weight: 20.0000 g. **Composition:** 0.6800 Silver .4372 oz. ASW

Date	Mintage	F	VF	XF	Unc
AH1358/1939(a)	100,000	—	20.00	40.00	90.00
AH1359/1940(a)	—	—	—	—	—

Note: Reported, not confirmed.

Date	Mintage	F	VF	XF	Unc
AH1360/1941(a)	53	—	—	275	450
AH1361/1942(a)	53	—	—	275	450

KM# 257 100 FRANCS **Weight:** 6.5500 g. **Composition:** 0.9000 Gold .1895 oz. AGW **Obv. Legend:** AHMAD

Date	Mintage	F	VF	XF	Unc
AH1349/1930(a)	3,000	—	80.00	100	135
AH1350/1931(a)	33	—	—	500	900
AH1351/1932(a)	3,000	—	80.00	100	135
AH1352/1933(a)	33	—	—	500	900
AH1353/1934(a)	133	—	—	300	400
AH1354/1935(a)	3,000	—	80.00	100	135
AH1355/1936(a)	33	—	—	500	900
AH1356/1937(a)	33	—	—	500	900

Muhammad al-Amin Bey

AH1362-76/1943-1957AD

DECIMAL COINAGE

100 Centimes = 1 Franc

The following coins all bear French inscriptions on one side, Arabic on the other, and usually have both AH and AD dates. Except for KM#246-48, they are struck in the name of the Tunisian Bey.

KM# 271 10 CENTIMES **Composition:** Nickel-Aluminum-Bronze **Obv. Legend:** MUHAMMAD AL AMIN

Date	Mintage	F	VF	XF	Unc
AH1364/1945(a)	10,000,000	—	20.00	40.00	70.00

Note: Most were probably melted

KM# 272 20 CENTIMES **Composition:** Zinc **Obv. Legend:** MUHAMMAD AL-AMIN

Date	Mintage	F	VF	XF	Unc
AH1364/1945(a)	5,205,000	—	40.00	70.00	100

Note: A large quantity was remelted

KM# 273 5 FRANCS **Composition:** Aluminum-Bronze **Obv. Legend:** MUHAMMAD AL-AMIN

Date	Mintage	F	VF	XF	Unc
AH1365/1946(a)	10,000,000	—	1.50	5.00	10.00

KM# 277 5 FRANCS **Composition:** Copper-Nickel

Date	Mintage	F	VF	XF	Unc
AH1373/1954(a)	18,000,000	—	1.00	2.50	5.00
AH1376/1957(a)	4,000,000	—	2.00	4.00	7.00

KM# 269 10 FRANCS **Weight:** 10.0000 g. **Composition:** 0.6800 Silver .2186 oz. ASW

Date	Mintage	F	VF	XF	Unc
AH1363/1943(a)	1,503	—	—	225	350
AH1364/1944(a)	2,206	—	—	200	300

KM# 270 20 FRANCS **Weight:** 20.0000 g. **Composition:** 0.6800 Silver .4372 oz. ASW **Obv. Legend:** MUHAMMAD AL-AMIN

Date	Mintage	F	VF	XF	Unc
AH1363/1943(a)	103	—	—	300	500
AH1364/1944(a)	106	—	—	300	500

KM# 274 20 FRANCS **Composition:** Copper-Nickel

Date	Mintage	F	VF	XF	Unc
AH1370/1950(a)	10,000,000	—	0.60	2.25	6.50
AH1376/1957(a)	4,000,000	—	0.45	1.25	4.50

KM# 275 50 FRANCS **Composition:** Copper-Nickel **Obv. Legend:** MUHAMMAD AL-AMIN

Date	Mintage	F	VF	XF	Unc
AH1370/1950(a)	5,000,000	—	0.60	2.25	6.50
AH1376/1957(a)	600,000	—	1.25	2.75	6.50

KM# 276 100 FRANCS **Composition:** Copper-Nickel **Obv. Legend:** MUHAMMAD AL-AMIN

Date	Mintage	F	VF	XF	Unc
AH1370/1950(a)	8,000,000	—	2.25	5.50	11.50
AH1376/1957(a)	1,000,000	—	2.25	4.50	10.00

REPUBLIC

DECIMAL COINAGE

1000 Millim = 1 Dinar

KM# 280 MILLIM **Composition:** Aluminum

Date	F	VF	XF	Unc
1960	—	—	0.10	0.25
1983	—	—	0.10	0.25

KM# 349 MILLIM **Composition:** Aluminum **Series:** F.A.O. **Obverse:** Tree, date **Reverse:** Denomination

Date	F	VF	XF	Unc
2000(1999)	—	—	—	1.00

KM# 281 2 MILLIM **Composition:** Aluminum

Date	F	VF	XF	Unc
1960	—	—	0.10	0.25
1983	—	—	0.10	0.25

KM# 282 5 MILLIM **Composition:** Aluminum

Date	F	VF	XF	Unc
1960	—	—	0.10	0.25
1983	—	—	0.10	0.25
1993	—	—	0.10	0.25
1996	—	—	0.10	0.25

KM# 348 5 MILLIM **Composition:** Aluminum **Obverse:** Tree above dates **Reverse:** Denomination

Date	F	VF	XF	Un
AH1418 (1997)	—	—	—	0.5

KM# 306 10 MILLIM **Composition:** Brass

Date	F	VF	XF	U
AH1380 (1960)	—	0.15	0.25	0.5
AH1403 (1983)	—	0.15	0.25	0.5
AH1414 (1993)	—	0.15	0.25	0.5
AH1416 (1996)	—	0.15	0.25	0.5
AH1418 (1997)	—	0.15	0.50	0.8

KM# 307 20 MILLIM **Composition:** Brass

Date	F	VF	XF	
AH1380 (1960)	—	0.30	0.50	0
AH1403 (1983)	—	0.30	0.50	0
AH1414 (1993)	—	0.30	0.50	0
AH1416 (1996)	—	0.30	0.50	0
AH1418 (1997)	—	0.30	0.50	0

KM# 308 50 MILLIM **Composition:** Brass

Date	F	VF	XF
AH1380 (1960)	—	0.65	0.85
AH1403 (1983)	—	0.65	0.85
AH1414 (1993)	—	0.65	0.85
AH1416 (1996)	—	0.65	0.85
AH1417 (1997)	—	0.65	0.85
AH1418 (1997)	—	0.65	0.85

KM# 309 100 MILLIM **Composition:** Brass

Date	F	VF	XF
AH1380 (1960)	—	1.25	1.50
AH1403 (1983)	—	1.25	1.50

Date	F	VF	XF	Unc
AH1414 (1993)	—	1.25	1.50	2.00
AH1416 (1996)	—	1.25	1.50	2.00
AH1418 (1997)	—	1.25	1.50	2.00
AH1421 (2000)	—	1.25	1.50	2.00

KM# 291 1/2 DINAR Composition: Nickel

Date	Mintage	F	VF	XF	Unc
1968(a)	500,000	—	1.00	2.00	4.50

KM# 303 1/2 DINAR Composition: Copper-Nickel **Series:** F.A.O. **Note:** Varieties exist.

Date	F	VF	XF	Unc
1976	—	1.50	3.50	6.50
983	—	1.50	3.50	6.50

M# 318 1/2 DINAR Composition: Copper-Nickel **Series:** F.A.O.

ate	F	VF	XF	Unc
988	—	1.00	3.00	5.50
990	—	1.00	3.00	5.50

M# 346 1/2 DINAR Composition: Copper-Nickel **Obverse:** National arms **Reverse:** 2 hands with fruit and wheat stalk

te	F	VF	XF	Unc
1416 (1996)	—	1.00	2.50	4.50
1418 (1998)	—	1.00	2.50	4.50

M# 292 DINAR Weight: 20.0000 g. **Composition:** 0.9250 Silver .5949 oz. ASW **Reverse:** Hannibal

Date	Mintage	F	VF	XF	Unc
1969FM NI Proof	15,000	Value: 10.00			
1969 NI Proof	5,000	Value: 47.50			

KM# 293 DINAR Weight: 20.0000 g. **Composition:** 0.9250 Silver .5949 oz. ASW **Obverse:** Similar to KM#292 **Reverse:** Masinissa

Date	Mintage	F	VF	XF	Unc
1969FM NI Proof	15,000	Value: 10.00			
1969 NI Proof	5,000	Value: 45.00			

KM# 294 DINAR Weight: 20.0000 g. **Composition:** 0.9250 Silver .5949 oz. ASW **Obverse:** Similar to KM#292 **Reverse:** Jugurtha

Date	Mintage	F	VF	XF	Unc
1969FM NI Proof	15,000	Value: 10.00			
1969 NI Proof	5,000	Value: 45.00			

KM# 295 DINAR Weight: 20.0000 g. **Composition:** 0.9250 Silver .5949 oz. ASW **Obverse:** Similar to KM#292 **Reverse:** Virgil

Date	Mintage	F	VF	XF	Unc
1969FM NI Proof	15,000	Value: 10.00			
1969 NI Proof	5,000	Value: 45.00			

KM# 296 DINAR Weight: 20.0000 g. **Composition:** 0.9250 Silver .5949 oz. ASW **Obverse:** Similar to KM#292 **Reverse:** St. Augustine

Date	Mintage	F	VF	XF	Unc
1969FM NI Proof	15,000	Value: 10.00			
1969 NI Proof	5,000	Value: 45.00			

KM# 297 DINAR Weight: 20.0000 g. **Composition:** 0.9250 Silver .5949 oz. ASW **Obverse:** Similar to KM#292 **Reverse:** Phoenician Ship

Date	Mintage	F	VF	XF	Unc
1969FM NI Proof	15,000	Value: 18.50			
1969 NI Proof	5,000	Value: 55.00			

KM# 298 DINAR Weight: 20.0000 g. **Composition:** 0.9250 Silver .5949 oz. ASW **Obverse:** Similar to KM#292 **Reverse:** Neptune

Date	Mintage	F	VF	XF	Unc
1969FM NI Proof	15,000	Value: 10.00			
1969 NI Proof	5,000	Value: 45.00			

KM# 299 DINAR Weight: 20.0000 g. **Composition:** 0.9250 Silver .5949 oz. ASW **Obverse:** Similar to KM#292 **Reverse:** Venus

Date	Mintage	F	VF	XF	Unc
1969FM NI Proof	15,000	Value: 18.50			
1969 NI Proof	5,000	Value: 55.00			

KM# 300 DINAR Weight: 20.0000 g. **Composition:** 0.9250 Silver .5949 oz. ASW **Obverse:** Similar to KM#292 **Reverse:** Thysdrus-El Djem

Date	Mintage	F	VF	XF	Unc
1969FM NI Proof	15,000	Value: 10.00			
1969 NI Proof	5,000	Value: 45.00			

KM# 301 DINAR **Weight:** 20.0000 g. **Composition:** 0.9250 Silver .5949 oz. ASW **Obverse:** Similar to KM#292 **Reverse:** Sbeitla-Sufetula

Date	Mintage	F	VF	XF	Unc
1969FM NI Proof	15,000	Value: 10.00			
1969 NI Proof	5,000	Value: 45.00			

KM# 302 DINAR **Weight:** 18.0000 g. **Composition:** 0.6800 Silver .3935 oz. ASW **Series:** F.A.O.

Date	Mintage	F	VF	XF	Unc
1970(a)	100,000	—	3.00	5.50	10.00
1970(a) Proof	1,250	Value: 40.00			

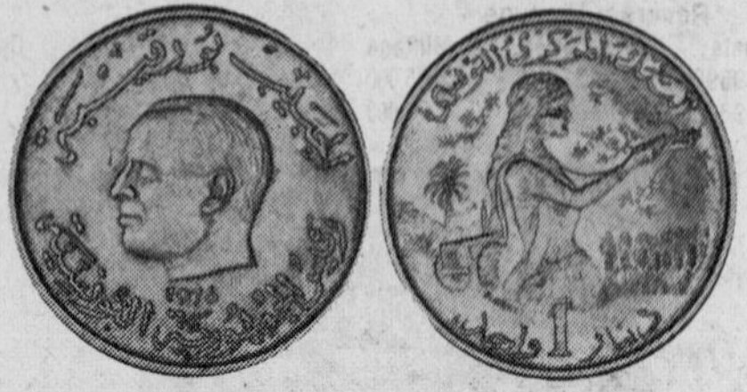

KM# 304 DINAR **Composition:** Copper-Nickel **Series:** F.A.O. **Note:** Varieties exist. Coins dated 1976 exist with or without dots (error) below iy of Tunisiya.

Date	F	VF	XF	Unc
1976	—	2.00	5.00	9.00
1983	—	2.00	5.00	9.00

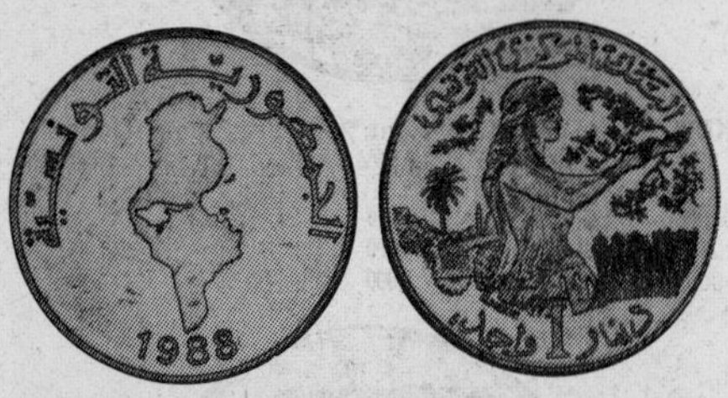

KM# 319 DINAR **Composition:** Copper-Nickel **Series:** F.A.O.

Date	F	VF	XF	Unc
1988	—	2.00	4.50	8.50
1989	—	2.00	4.50	8.50
1990	—	2.00	4.50	8.50

KM# 347 DINAR **Composition:** Copper-Nickel **Series:** F.A.O.

Date	F	VF	XF	Unc
AH1416 (1996)	—	2.00	4.00	7.50
AH1417 (1997)	—	2.00	4.00	7.50
AH1418 (1997)	—	2.00	4.00	7.50

KM# 286 2 DINARS **Weight:** 3.8000 g. **Composition:** 0.9000 Gold .1099 oz. AGW **Subject:** 10th Anniversary of Republic

Date	Mintage	F	VF	XF	Unc
ND(1967) NI Proof	7,259	Value: 60.00			

KM# 283 5 DINARS **Weight:** 11.7900 g. **Composition:** 0.9000 Gold .3412 oz. AGW **Obverse:** French legends **Reverse:** French legends

Date	F	VF	XF	Unc
1962 Proof	—	Value: 550		

KM# 320 5 DINARS **Weight:** 11.7900 g. **Composition:** 0.9000 Gold .3412 oz. AGW **Obverse:** Arabic legends **Reverse:** Arabic legends

Date	F	VF	XF	Unc
1962 Proof	—	Value: 550		

KM# 284 5 DINARS **Weight:** 11.7900 g. **Composition:** 0.9000 Gold .3412 oz. AGW **Obverse:** French legends **Reverse:** French legends

Date	F	VF	XF	Unc
1963 Proof	—	Value: 550		

KM# 321 5 DINARS **Weight:** 9.3600 g. **Composition:** 0.9000 Gold .2708 oz. AGW **Obverse:** Arabic legends **Reverse:** Arabic legends

Date	F	VF	XF	Unc
1963 Proof	—	Value: 550		

KM# 287 5 DINARS **Weight:** 9.5000 g. **Composition:** 0.9000 Gold .2749 oz. AGW **Subject:** 10th Anniversary of Republic

Date	Mintage	F	VF	XF	Unc
ND(1967) NI Proof	7,259	Value: 125			

KM# 305 5 DINARS **Weight:** 24.0000 g. **Composition:** 0.6800 Silver .5247 oz. ASW **Subject:** 20th Anniversary of Independence

Date	Mintage	F	VF	XF	Unc
1976	200,000	—	—	—	17.50
1976 Proof	1,000	Value: 40.00			

KM# 284a 5 DINARS **Weight:** 9.3600 g. **Composition:** 0.9000 Gold .2708 oz. AGW

Date	F	VF	XF	Unc
1976 Proof	—	Value: 500		

KM# 310 5 DINARS **Weight:** 9.4120 g. **Composition:** 0.9000 Gold .2723 oz. AGW **Obverse:** Habib Bourguiba **Reverse:** President's return

Date	Mintage	F	VF	XF	Unc
1981 Proof	1,450	Value: 175			

KM# 313 5 DINARS **Weight:** 27.2200 g. **Composition:** 0.9250 Silver .8096 oz. ASW **Series:** International Year of the Child **Obverse:** Similar to 1 Dinar, KM#302

Date	Mintage	F	VF	XF	Unc
1982	7,575	—	—	—	15.00
1982 Proof	1,108	Value: 20.00			

KM# 326 5 DINARS **Weight:** 9.4120 g. **Composition:** 0.9000 Gold .2723 oz. AGW **Reverse:** Arabic legends

Date	Mintage	F	VF	XF	Unc
AH1402 Proof	725	Value: 220			

KM# 325 5 DINARS **Weight:** 9.4120 g. **Composition:** 0.9000 Gold .2723 oz. AGW **Obverse:** President **Reverse:** Coat of arms **Note:** French legends.

Date	Mintage	F	VF	XF	Unc
1982 Proof	725	Value: 220			

KM# 327 5 DINARS **Weight:** 9.4120 g. **Composition:** 0.9000 Gold .2723 oz. AGW **Subject:** 25th Anniversary of Republic **Note:** French legends.

Date	F	VF	XF	Unc
1983-85 Proof	—	Value: 220		

KM# 328 5 DINARS **Weight:** 9.4120 g. **Composition:** 0.9000 Gold .2723 oz. AGW **Note:** Arabic legends.

Date	F	VF	XF	Unc
AH1403-05 Proof	—	Value: 220		

KM# 330 5 DINARS **Weight:** 9.4120 g. **Composition:** 0.9000 Gold .2723 oz. AGW **Note:** Arabic legends.

Date	Mintage	F	VF	XF	Unc
AH1408	375	—	—	—	25
AH1409	Inc. above	—	—	—	25

KM# 329 5 DINARS **Weight:** 9.4120 g. **Composition:** 0.9000 Gold .2723 oz. AGW **Obverse:** Map **Reverse:** Allegorical design **Note:** French legends.

Date	Mintage	F	VF	XF	Unc
1988	375	—	—	—	25
1989	Inc. above	—	—	—	25

KM# 322 10 DINARS **Weight:** 23.4800 g. **Composition:** 0.9000 Gold .6795 oz. AGW **Obverse:** French legends **Reverse:** French legends

Date	F	VF	XF	Unc
1962 Proof	—	Value: 850		

KM# 285 10 DINARS **Weight:** 23.4800 g. **Composition:** 0.9000 Gold .6795 oz. AGW **Obverse:** Arabic legends **Reverse:** Arabic legends

Date	F	VF	XF	Unc
AH1382 (1962) Proof	—	Value: 850		
AH1384 (1964) Proof	—	Value: 850		

KM# 288 10 DINARS **Weight:** 19.0000 g. **Composition:** 0.9000 Gold .5498 oz. AGW **Subject:** 10th Anniversary of Republic

Date	Mintage	F	VF	XF
ND(1967) NI Proof	6,480	Value: 245		

KM# 324 10 DINARS **Composition:** 0.9000 Gold **Subject:** 20th Anniversary of Independence

Date	F	VF	XF	Unc
1976	—	—	—	750

KM# 345 10 DINARS **Weight:** 18.8080 g. **Composition:** 0.9000 Gold .5442 oz. AGW **Subject:** 20th Anniversary - Central Bank

Date	Mintage	F	VF	XF	Unc
1978	2,000	—	—	—	700

KM# 344 10 DINARS **Weight:** 38.0000 g. **Composition:** 0.9000 Silver 1.0995 oz. ASW **Subject:** 20th Anniversary - Central Bank **Obverse:** President's portrait left **Reverse:** Large old style bank building

Date	F	VF	XF	Unc
1978	—	—	—	35.00

KM# 343 10 DINARS **Weight:** 18.7700 g. **Composition:** 0.9000 Gold .5431 oz. AGW **Obverse:** Arabic legends **Reverse:** Arabic legends

Date	F	VF	XF	Unc
AH1399 (1979)	—	—	—	900

KM# 342 10 DINARS **Weight:** 18.7700 g. **Composition:** 0.9000 Gold .5431 oz. AGW **Obverse:** French legends **Reverse:** French legends

Date	F	VF	XF	Unc
1979	—	—	—	900

KM# 311 10 DINARS **Weight:** 18.8240 g. **Composition:** 0.9000 Gold .5447 oz. AGW **Obverse:** Habib Bourguiba **Reverse:** President's return

Date	Mintage	F	VF	XF	Unc
1981 Proof	2,000	Value: 550			

KM# 312 10 DINARS **Weight:** 18.8080 g. **Composition:** 0.9000 Gold .5442 oz. AGW **Subject:** 25th Anniversary of Independence **Obverse:** Habib Bourguiba **Reverse:** Silhouette of girl

Date	Mintage	F	VF	XF	Unc
1981 Proof	2,000	Value: 550			

KM# 314 10 DINARS **Weight:** 38.0000 g. **Composition:** 0.9000 Silver 1.0995 oz. ASW **Subject:** Gabes Bank **Obverse:** President's portrait left **Reverse:** Gabes branch bank building

Date	Mintage	F	VF	XF	Unc
1982 Proof	2,500	Value: 35.00			

KM# 315 10 DINARS **Weight:** 38.0000 g. **Composition:** 0.9000 Silver 1.0995 oz. ASW **Subject:** Central Bank of Nabeul **Obverse:** President's portrait left **Reverse:** Nabeul bank building

Date	Mintage	F	VF	XF	Unc
1982 Proof	1,000	Value: 45.00			

KM# 316 10 DINARS **Weight:** 38.0000 g. **Composition:** 0.9000 Silver 1.0995 oz. ASW **Subject:** Sfax Branch Office **Obverse:** President's portrait left **Reverse:** Sfax branch bank building

Date	Mintage	F	VF	XF	Unc
1982 Proof	1,000	Value: 45.00			

KM# 333 10 DINARS **Weight:** 38.0000 g. **Composition:** 0.9000 Silver 1.0995 oz. ASW **Note:** Tunisian girl.

Date	Mintage	F	VF	XF	Unc
1982 Proof	2,000	Value: 40.00			

KM# 332 10 DINARS **Weight:** 38.0000 g. **Composition:** 0.9000 Silver 1.0995 oz. ASW **Note:** Arabic legends.

Date	Mintage	F	VF	XF	Unc
AH1402 Proof	700	Value: 55.00			

KM# 331 10 DINARS **Weight:** 38.0000 g. **Composition:** 0.9000 Silver 1.0995 oz. ASW **Obverse:** President **Reverse:** Coat of arms **Note:** French legends.

Date	Mintage	F	VF	XF	Unc
1982 Proof	700	Value: 55.00			

KM# 334 10 DINARS **Weight:** 38.0000 g. **Composition:** 0.9000 Silver 1.0995 oz. ASW **Subject:** 25th Anniversary of Republic **Note:** French legends.

Date	F	VF	XF	Unc
1983-85 Proof	—	Value: 45.00		

KM# 335 10 DINARS **Weight:** 38.0000 g. **Composition:** 0.9000 Silver 1.0995 oz. ASW **Note:** Arabic legends.

Date	F	VF	XF	Unc
AH1403-05 Proof	—	Value: 45.00		

KM# 336 10 DINARS **Weight:** 38.0000 g. **Composition:** 0.9000 Silver 1.0995 oz. ASW **Subject:** 50th Anniversary of the Socialist Party

Date	F	VF	XF	Unc
1984 Proof	—	Value: 45.00		

KM# 323 10 DINARS **Weight:** 18.8080 g. **Composition:** 0.9000 Gold .5442 oz. AGW **Obverse:** Portrait left **Reverse:** Statue of Burgiba

Date	Mintage	F	VF	XF	Unc
AH1405 (1985) Proof	2,000	Value: 550			

KM# 337 10 DINARS **Weight:** 18.8080 g. **Composition:** 0.9000 Gold .5442 oz. AGW **Subject:** 30th Anniversary of Independence

Date	F	VF	XF	Unc
1986 Proof	—	Value: 550		

KM# 338 10 DINARS **Weight:** 18.8080 g. **Composition:** 0.9000 Gold .5442 oz. AGW **Subject:** 30th Anniversary of Republic

Date	Mintage	F	VF	XF	Unc
1987 Proof	2,000	Value: 550			

KM# 339 10 DINARS **Weight:** 38.0000 g. **Composition:** 0.9000 Silver 1.0995 oz. ASW

Date	Mintage	F	VF	XF	Unc
1988 Proof	4,000	Value: 35.00			

KM# 341 10 DINARS **Weight:** 18.8080 g. **Composition:** 0.9000 Gold .5442 oz. AGW **Note:** Arabic legends.

Date	Mintage	F	VF	XF	Unc
AH1408	375	—	—	—	650
AH1409	Inc. above	—	—	—	650

KM# 340 10 DINARS **Weight:** 18.8080 g. **Composition:** 0.9000 Gold .5442 oz. AGW **Obverse:** Map **Reverse:** Allegorical design **Note:** French legends.

Date	Mintage	F	VF	XF	Unc
1988	375	—	—	—	650
1989	Inc. above	—	—	—	650

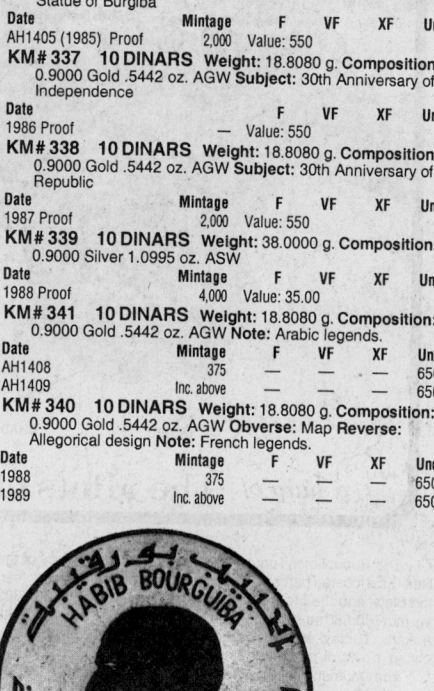

KM# 289 20 DINARS **Weight:** 38.0000 g. **Composition:** 0.9000 Gold 1.0996 oz. AGW **Subject:** 10th Anniversary of Republic

Date	Mintage	F	VF	XF	Unc
ND(1967) NI	3,536	—	—	—	475

KM# 290 40 DINARS **Weight:** 76.0000 g. **Composition:** 0.9000 Gold 2.1991 oz. AGW **Subject:** 10th Anniversary of Republic **Obverse:** Similar to 10 Dinars, KM#288

Date	Mintage	F	VF	XF	Unc
ND(1967) NI Proof	3,031	Value: 950			

KM# 317 75 DINARS **Weight:** 15.5500 g. **Composition:** 0.9000 Gold .4500 oz. AGW **Series:** International Year of the Child

Date	Mintage	F	VF	XF	Unc
1982 Proof	4,518	Value: 225			

ESSAIS

Standard metals unless otherwise noted

KM#	Date	Mintage	Identification	Mkt Val
E1	1918	—	5 Centimes. KM#242.	75.00
E2	1918	—	10 Centimes. KM#243.	80.00
E3	1918	—	25 Centimes. KM#244.	85.00
E4	1920	—	5 Centimes. KM#245.	125
E5	1921	—	50 Centimes. KM#246.	90.00
E6	1921	—	Franc. KM#247.	120
E7	1921	—	Franc. Aluminum. KM#247.	130
E8	1928	—	Franc. Nickel-Bronze. KM#250a.	260
E9	1928	—	2 Francs. Silver-Bronze. KM#251.	260
E10	1930	—	10 Francs. KM#255, uniface.	170
E11	1930	—	20 Francs. KM#256, uniface.	350
E12	1930	—	100 Francs. KM#257, uniface.	350
E13	1931	—	5 Centimes. KM#258.	75.00
E14	1931	—	10 Centimes. KM#259.	80.00
E15	1931	—	25 Centimes. KM#260.	85.00
E16	1353	—	5 Francs. KM#261.	90.00
E17	1353	—	10 Francs. KM#255.	100
E18	1353	—	20 Francs. KM#256.	175

KM#	Date	Mintage	Identification	Mkt Val
E-A19	1354	—	100 Francs. Gilt Bronze. KM#257.	—
E19	1938	—	100 Francs. Gilt Bronze. KM-M1.	110
E20	1938	—	100 Francs. Gold. KM-M1.	875
E21	1939	—	5 Francs. KM#264.	60.00
E22	1939	—	10 Francs. KM#265.	80.00
E23	1939	—	20 Francs. KM#266.	150
E24	1942	—	20 Centimes. KM#268.	50.00
E25	1945	1,100	10 Centimes. KM#271.	50.00
E26	1945	1,100	20 Centimes. KM#272.	60.00

KM#	Date	Mintage	Identification	Mkt Val
E27	1946	1,100	5 Francs. KM#273.	35.00
E28	1950	1,100	20 Francs. KM#274.	35.00
E29	1950	1,100	50 Francs. KM#275.	35.00

KM#	Date	Mintage	Identification	Mkt Val
E30	1950	1,100	100 Francs. KM#276.	35.00
E31	1954	1,100	5 Francs. KM#277.	20.00
E32	1968	1,260	1/2 Dinar. KM#291.	35.00
E33	1968	70	1/2 Dinar. Gold.	—
E34	1970	1,250	Dinar. KM#302.	45.00
E35	1976	2,050	1/2 Dinar. KM#303.	30.00
E36	1976	2,050	Dinar. KM#304.	40.00

PIEFORTS

Double thickness; standard metals unless otherwise noted

KM#	Date	Mintage	Identification	Issue Price	Mkt Val
P1	1968	500	1/2 Dinar. (No Composition). KM#291	—	35.00
P2	1982	96	5 Dinars. (No Composition). KM#313.	—	165
P3	1982	55	75 Dinars. (No Composition). KM#317.	—	1,250

PIEFORTS WITH ESSAI

Double thickness

KM#	Date	Mintage	Identification	Mkt Val
PE1	1945	104	20 Centimes. (No Composition). KM#272.	100

KM#	Date	Mintage	Identification	Mkt Val
PE2	1945	104	50 Centimes. (No Composition). KM#246.	100
PE3	1945	104	Franc. (No Composition). KM#247.	100

KM#	Date	Mintage	Identification	Mkt Val
PE4	1945	104	2 Francs. (No Composition). KM#248.	100
PE5	1946	104	5 Francs. (No Composition). KM#273.	120
PE6	1954	104	5 Francs. (No Composition). KM#277.	90.00

MINT SETS

KM#	Date	Mintage	Identification	Issue Price	Mkt Val
MS1	1960 (7)	—	KM#280-282, 306-309	—	5.50
MS2	1996 (7)	—	KM#282, 306-309, 346-347	—	16.50

PROOF SETS

KM#	Date	Mintage	Identification	Issue Price	Mkt Val
PS2	1967 (5)	3,031	KM#286-290	—	1,850
PS3	1969FM-NI (10)	15,202	KM#292-301	77.00	120
PS4	1969NI (10)	5,000	KM#292-301	—	475

Many sets were ruined while in storage.

TURKEY

The Republic of Turkey, a parliamentary democracy of the Near East located partially in Europe and partially in Asia between the Black and the Mediterranean Seas, has an area of 301,382 sq. mi. (780,580 sq. km.) and a population of *55.4 million. Capital: Ankara. Turkey exports cotton, hazelnuts, and tobacco, and enjoys a virtual monopoly in meerschaum.

The Ottoman Turks, a tribe from Central Asia, first appeared in the early 13th century, and by the 17th century had established the Ottoman Empire which stretched from the Persian Gulf to the southern frontier of Poland, and from the Caspian Sea to the Algerian plateau. The defeat of the Turkish navy by the Holy League in 1571, and of the Turkish forces besieging Vienna in 1683, began the steady decline of the Ottoman Empire which, accelerated by the rise of nationalism, contracted its European border, and by the end of World War I deprived it of its Arab lands. The present Turkish boundaries were largely fixed by the Treaty of Lausanne in 1923. The sultanate and caliphate, the political and spiritual ruling institutions of the old empire, were separated and the sultanate abolished in 1922. On Oct. 29, 1923, Turkey formally became a republic.

RULERS

Abdul Hamid II, AH1293-1327/1876-1909AD
Muhammad V, AH1327-1336/1909-1918AD
Muhammad VI, AH1336-1341/1918-1923AD
Republic, AH1341/AD1923-

MINTNAMES

Constantinople (Qustantiniyah) قسطنطنية

Misr
See Egypt مصر

MONETARY EQUIVALENTS

3 Akche = 1 Para
5 Para = Beshlik (Beshparalik)
10 Para = Onluk
20 Para = Yirmilik
30 Para = Zolota
40 Para = Kurush (Piastre)
1-1/2 Kurush (Piastres) = Altmishlik

MONETARY SYSTEM

Silver Coinage

40 Para = 1 Kurush (Piastre)
2 Kurush (Piastres) = 1 Ikilik
2-1/2 Kurush (Piastres) = Yuzluk
3 Kurush (Piastres) = Uechlik
5 Kurush (Piastres) = Beshlik
6 Kurush (Piastres) = Altilik

Gold Coinage

100 Kurush (Piastres) = 1 Turkish Pound (Lira)

This system has remained essentially unchanged since its introduction by Ahmad III in 1688, except that the Asper and Para have long since ceased to be coined. The Piastre, established as a crown-sized silver coin approximately equal to the French Ecu of Louis XIV, has shrunk to a tiny copper coin, worth about 1/15 of a U.S. cent. Since the establishment of the Republic in 1923, the Turkish terms, Kurus and Lira, have replaced the European names Piastres and Turkish Pounds.

MINT VISIT ISSUES

From time to time, certain cities of the Ottoman Empire, such as Bursa, Edirne, Kosova, Manistir and Salonika were honored by having special coins struck at Istanbul, but with inscriptions stating that they were struck in the city of honor. These were produced on the occasion of the Sultan's visit to that city. The coins were struck in limited, but not small quantities, and were probably intended for distribution to the notables of the city and the Sultan's own followers. Because they were of the same size and type as the regular circulation issues struck at Istanbul, many specimens found their way into circulation and worn or mounted specimens are found today, although some have been preserved in XF or better condition. Mintage statistics are not known.

MONNAIE DE LUXE

In the 23rd year of the reign of Abdul Hamid II, two parallel series of gold coins were produced, regular mint issues and monnaies de luxe', which were intended primarily for presentation and jewelry purposes. The Monnaie de Luxe' were struck to a slightly less weight and the same fineness as regular issues, but were broader and thinner, and from more ornate dies.

Coins are listed by type, followed by a list of reported years. Most of the reported years have never been confirmed and other years may also exist. Mintage figures are known for the AH1293 and 1327 series, but are unreliable and of little utility.

Although some years are undoubtedly much rarer than others, there is at present no date collecting of Ottoman gold and therefore little justification for higher prices for rare dates.

There is no change in design in the regular series. Only the toughra, accessional date and regnal year vary. The deluxe series show ornamental changes. The standard coins generally do not bear the denomination.

HONORIFIC TITLES

El Ghazi

Reshat

The first coinage of Abdul Hamid II has a flower right of the toughra while the second coinage has *el Ghazi* (The Victorious). The first coinage of Mohammad Reshat Vhas *Reshat* right of the toughra while his second coinage has *el Ghazi.*

SULTANATE

Abdul Hamid II
AH1293-1327/1876-1909AD

STANDARD COINAGE

√# 743 5 PARA **Weight:** 1.0023 g. **Composition:** 0.1000 Silver .0032 oz. ASW **Obverse:** Toughra; "el-Ghazi" to right **Note:** Struck at Qustantiniyah.

te	VG	F	VF	XF	Unc
1293//26 (1900)	0.25	0.50	1.25	4.00	—
1293//27 (1901)	0.25	0.50	1.25	4.00	—
1293//28 (1902)	0.50	1.00	3.00	12.00	—
1293//30 (1904)	6.00	12.00	20.00	40.00	—

√# 744 10 PARA **Weight:** 2.0046 g. **Composition:** 0.1000 Silver .0064 oz. ASW **Obverse:** Toughra; "el-Ghazi" to right **Note:** Struck at Qustantiniyah.

te	VG	F	VF	XF	Unc
1293//26 (1900)	0.25	0.50	1.00	4.00	—
1293//27 (1901)	0.25	0.50	1.00	4.00	—
Note: Varieties exist in size of regnal year 27					
1293//28 (1902)	0.25	0.50	1.50	6.00	—
1293//30 (1904)	1.00	2.00	5.00	15.00	—

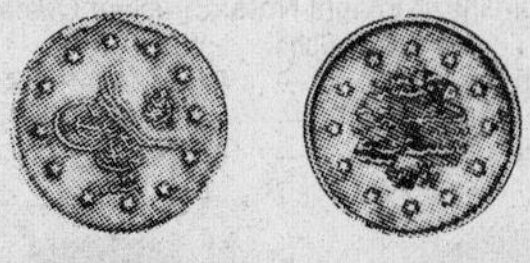

√# 735 KURUS **Weight:** 1.2027 g. **Composition:** 0.8300 Silver .0321 oz. ASW **Obverse:** Toughra; "el-Ghazi" to right **Note:** Varieties exist in the size of year and inscription. Struck at Qustantiniyah.

te	Mintage	VG	F	VF	XF	Unc
1293//26 (1900)	55,000	3.00	7.50	15.00	30.00	—
1293//27 (1901)	9,945,000	1.00	2.00	3.00	5.00	—
1293//28 (1902)	16,139,000	1.00	2.00	3.00	5.00	—
1293//29 (1903)	7,076,000	1.00	2.00	3.00	5.00	—
1293//30 (1904)	707,000	2.00	4.00	8.00	15.00	—
1293//31 (1905)	1,366,000	1.00	2.00	3.00	5.00	—
1293//32 (1906)	1,140,000	1.00	2.00	3.00	5.00	—
1293//33 (1907)	1,700,000	1.00	2.00	3.00	5.00	—
1293//34 (1908)	—	40.00	60.00	115	225	—

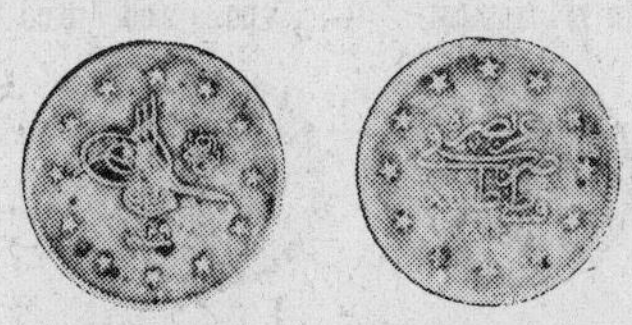

√# 736 2 KURUS **Weight:** 2.4055 g. **Composition:** 0.8300 Silver .0642 oz. ASW **Obverse:** Toughra; "el-Ghazi" to right **Note:** Varieties exist in the size of toughra and year. Struck at Qustantiniyah.

te	Mintage	VG	F	VF	XF	Unc
1293//26 (1900)	17,000	15.00	25.00	35.00	75.00	—
1293//27 (1901)	4,689,000	1.50	2.00	4.00	7.00	—
1293//28 (1902)	7,567,000	1.50	2.00	4.00	7.00	—
1293//29 (1903)	7,775,000	1.50	2.00	4.00	7.00	—
1293//30 (1904)	1,366,000	1.50	2.00	4.00	7.00	—
1293//31 (1905)	3,014,000	1.50	2.00	4.00	7.00	—
1293//32 (1906)	1,625,000	1.50	2.00	4.00	7.00	—
1293//33 (1907)	2,173,000	1.50	2.00	4.00	7.00	—
1293//34 (1908)	—	45.00	90.00	140	200	—

√# 737 5 KURUS **Weight:** 6.0130 g. **Composition:** 0.8300 Silver .1605 oz. ASW **Obverse:** Toughra; "el-Ghazi" to right **Note:** Varieties exist in the size of toughra, inscription, and date. Struck at Qustantiniyah.

Date	Mintage	VG	F	VF	XF	Unc
AH1293//26 (1900)	8,000	15.00	30.00	45.00	75.00	—
AH1293//27 (1901)	16,000	15.00	30.00	45.00	75.00	—
AH1293//28 (1902)	6,000	15.00	30.00	45.00	75.00	—
AH1293//29 (1903)	7,000	15.00	30.00	45.00	75.00	—
AH1293//30 (1904)	38,000	5.00	10.00	15.00	30.00	—
AH1293//31 (1905)	Inc. above	3.50	4.50	7.00	15.00	—
AH1293//31/0 (1905)	3,175,000	6.00	13.00	25.00	35.00	—
AH1293//32 (1906)	3,334,000	2.00	3.25	4.50	9.50	—
AH1293//33 (1907)	907,000	3.00	5.00	9.00	16.00	—
AH1293//34 (1908)	—	50.00	80.00	110	200	—

KM# 738 10 KURUS **Weight:** 12.0270 g. **Composition:** 0.8300 Silver .3210 oz. ASW **Obverse:** Toughra; "el-Ghazi" to right **Note:** Struck at Qustantiniyah.

Date	Mintage	VG	F	VF	XF	Unc
AH1293//31 (1905)	51,000	20.00	40.00	75.00	125	—
AH1293//32 (1906)	575,000	7.50	12.50	18.00	30.00	—
AH1293//33 (1907)	273,000	6.00	10.00	20.00	35.00	—

KM# 745 12-1/2 KURUS **Weight:** 0.8770 g. **Composition:** 0.9170 Gold .0258 oz. AGW **Series:** Monnaie de Luxe **Obverse:** Toughra **Note:** Struck at Qustantiniyah.

Date	Mintage	VG	F	VF	XF	Unc
AH1293//28 (1902)	800	40.00	70.00	100	180	—
AH1293//29 (1903)	12,000	20.00	30.00	45.00	75.00	—
AH1293//30 (1904)	13,000	20.00	30.00	45.00	75.00	—
AH1293//31 (1905)	24,000	20.00	30.00	45.00	75.00	—
AH1293//32 (1906)	14,000	20.00	30.00	45.00	75.00	—
AH1293//33 (1907)	13,000	20.00	30.00	45.00	75.00	—
AH1293//34 (1908)	—	20.00	30.00	45.00	75.00	—

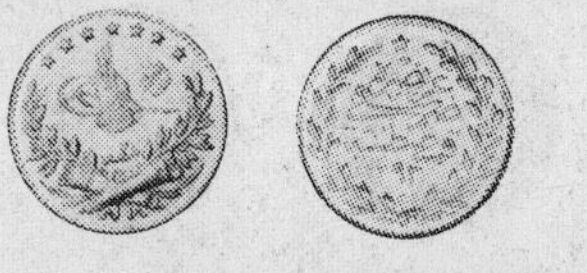

KM# 729 25 KURUS **Weight:** 1.8040 g. **Composition:** 0.9170 Gold .0532 oz. AGW **Obverse:** Toughra; "el-Ghazi" to right **Note:** Struck at Qustantiniyah.

Date	Mintage	VG	F	VF	XF	Unc
AH1293//26 (1900)	48,000	BV	25.00	32.00	45.00	—
AH1293//27 (1901)	99,000	BV	25.00	32.00	45.00	—
AH1293//28 (1902)	77,000	BV	25.00	32.00	45.00	—
AH1293//29 (1903)	102,000	BV	25.00	32.00	45.00	—
AH1293//30 (1904)	156,000	BV	25.00	32.00	45.00	—
AH1293//31 (1905)	58,000	BV	25.00	32.00	45.00	—
AH1293//32 (1906)	112,000	BV	25.00	32.00	45.00	—
AH1293//33 (1907)	16,000	BV	25.00	32.00	45.00	—
AH1293//34 (1908)	—	BV	25.00	32.00	45.00	—

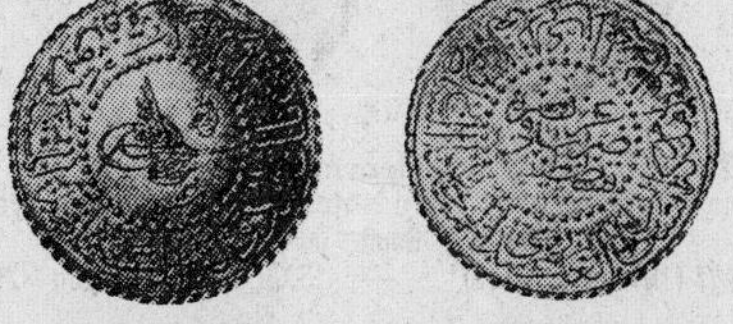

KM# 739 25 KURUS **Weight:** 1.7540 g. **Composition:** 0.9170 Gold .0517 oz. AGW **Series:** Monnaie de Luxe **Obverse:** Toughra; "el-Ghazi" to right **Note:** Struck at Qustantiniyah.

Date	Mintage	VG	F	VF	XF	Unc
AH1293//26 (1900)	4,300	50.00	65.00	75.00	95.00	—
AH1293//27 (1901)	7,620	50.00	65.00	75.00	95.00	—
AH1293//28 (1902)	9,268	50.00	65.00	75.00	95.00	—
AH1293//29 (1903)	7,600	50.00	65.00	75.00	95.00	—
AH1293//30 (1904)	26,056	50.00	65.00	75.00	95.00	—
AH1293//31 (1905)	27,964	50.00	65.00	75.00	95.00	—
AH1293//32 (1906)	39,192	50.00	65.00	75.00	95.00	—
AH1293//33 (1907)	41,696	50.00	65.00	75.00	95.00	—
AH1293//34 (1908)	17,728	50.00	65.00	75.00	95.00	—

KM# 731 50 KURUS **Weight:** 3.6080 g. **Composition:** 0.9170 Gold .1064 oz. AGW **Obverse:** Toughra; "el-Ghazi" to right **Note:** Struck at Qustantiniyah.

Date	Mintage	VG	F	VF	XF	Unc
AH1293//26 (1900)	14,000	BV	50.00	60.00	90.00	—
AH1293//27 (1901)	14,000	BV	50.00	60.00	90.00	—
AH1293//28 (1902)	33,000	BV	50.00	60.00	90.00	—
AH1293//29 (1903)	24,000	BV	50.00	60.00	90.00	—
AH1293//30 (1904)	66,000	BV	50.00	60.00	90.00	—
AH1293//31 (1905)	59,000	BV	50.00	60.00	90.00	—
AH1293//32 (1906)	48,000	BV	50.00	60.00	90.00	—
AH1293//33 (1907)	16,000	BV	50.00	60.00	90.00	—
AH1293//34 (1908)	—	BV	50.00	60.00	90.00	—

KM# 740 50 KURUS **Weight:** 3.5080 g. **Composition:** 0.9170 Gold .1034 oz. AGW **Series:** Monnaie de Luxe **Obverse:** Toughra; "el-Ghazi" to right **Note:** Struck at Qustantiniyah.

Date	Mintage	VG	F	VF	XF	Unc
AH1293//26 (1900)	4,820	50.00	75.00	90.00	140	—
AH1293//27 (1901)	5,436	50.00	75.00	90.00	140	—
AH1293//28 (1902)	6,630	50.00	75.00	90.00	140	—
AH1293//29 (1903)	8,660	50.00	75.00	90.00	140	—
AH1293//30 (1904)	14,924	50.00	75.00	90.00	140	—
AH1293//31 (1905)	18,813	50.00	75.00	90.00	140	—
AH1293//32 (1906)	22,460	50.00	75.00	90.00	140	—
AH1293//33 (1907)	27,542	50.00	75.00	90.00	140	—
AH1293//34 (1908)	12,886	50.00	75.00	90.00	140	—

KM# 730 100 KURUS **Weight:** 7.2160 g. **Composition:** 0.9170 Gold .2128 oz. AGW **Obverse:** Toughra; "el-Ghazi" to right **Note:** Struck at Qustantiniyah.

Date	Mintage	VG	F	VF	XF	Unc
AH1293//26 (1900)	2,000	—	BV	100	115	—
AH1293//27 (1901)	48,000	—	BV	100	115	—
AH1293//28 (1902)	865,000	—	BV	100	115	—
AH1293//29 (1903)	1,026,000	—	BV	100	115	—
AH1293//30 (1904)	1,644,000	—	BV	100	115	—
AH1293//31 (1905)	2,748,000	—	BV	100	115	—
AH1293//32 (1906)	1,952,000	—	BV	100	115	—
AH1293//33 (1907)	963,000	—	BV	100	115	—
AH1293//34 (1908)	—	—	BV	100	115	—

KM# 741 100 KURUS **Weight:** 7.0160 g. **Composition:** 0.9170 Gold .2068 oz. AGW **Series:** Monnaie de Luxe **Obverse:** Toughra; "el-Ghazi" to right **Note:** Struck at Qustantiniyah.

Date	Mintage	VG	F	VF	XF	Unc
AH1293//26 (1900)	3,635	BV	100	135	190	—
AH1293//27 (1901)	5,590	BV	100	135	190	—
AH1293//28 (1902)	9,870	BV	100	135	190	—
AH1293//29 (1903)	13,638	BV	100	135	190	—
AH1293//30 (1904)	18,129	BV	100	135	190	—
AH1293//31 (1905)	22,796	BV	100	135	190	—
AH1293//32 (1906)	31,126	BV	100	135	190	—
AH1293//33 (1907)	42,667	BV	100	135	190	—
AH1293//34 (1908)	18,716	BV	100	135	190	—

KM# 732 250 KURUS **Weight:** 18.0400 g. **Composition:** 0.9170 Gold .5319 oz. AGW **Obverse:** Toughra; "el-Ghazi" to right **Note:** Struck at Qustantiniyah.

Date	Mintage	VG	F	VF	XF	Unc
AH1293//26 (1900)	1,428	BV	250	300	450	—
AH1293//27 (1901)	1,450	BV	250	300	450	—
AH1293//28 (1902)	7,027	BV	250	300	450	—
AH1293//29 (1903)	7,522	BV	250	300	450	—
AH1293//30 (1904)	7,522	BV	250	300	450	—
AH1293//31 (1905)	4,900	BV	250	300	450	—
AH1293//32 (1906)	8,729	BV	250	300	450	—
AH1293//33 (1907)	2,669	BV	225	275	450	—

KM# 742 250 KURUS **Weight:** 17.5400 g. **Composition:** 0.9170 Gold .5169 oz. AGW **Series:** Monnaie de Luxe **Obverse:** Toughra; "el-Ghazi" to right **Note:** Struck at Qustantiniyah.

Date	Mintage	VG	F	VF	XF	Unc
AH1293//26 (1900)	1,544	BV	275	400	600	—
AH1293//27 (1901)	1,538	BV	275	400	600	—
AH1293//28 (1902)	1,770	BV	275	400	600	—
AH1293//29 (1903)	1,520	BV	275	400	600	—
AH1293//30 (1904)	1,631	BV	275	400	600	—
AH1293//31 (1905)	1,922	BV	275	400	600	—
AH1293//32 (1906)	1,778	BV	275	400	600	—
AH1293//33 (1907)	2,650	BV	275	400	600	—
AH1293//34 (1908) Rare	931	—	—	—	—	—

KM# 733 500 KURUS **Weight:** 36.0800 g. **Composition:** 0.9170 Gold 1.0638 oz. AGW **Obverse:** Toughra; "el-Ghazi" to right **Note:** Struck at Qustantiniyah.

Date	Mintage	VG	F	VF	XF	Unc
AH1293//26 (1900)	8,765	BV	500	550	750	—
AH1293//27 (1901)	22,000	BV	500	550	750	—
AH1293//28 (1902)	36,000	BV	500	550	750	—
AH1293//29 (1903)	17,000	BV	500	550	750	—
AH1293//30 (1904)	33,000	BV	500	550	750	—
AH1293//31 (1905)	41,000	BV	500	550	750	—
AH1293//32 (1906)	33,000	BV	500	550	750	—
AH1293//33 (1907)	16,000	BV	500	550	750	—
AH1293//34 (1908)	—	BV	500	550	750	—

KM# 746 500 KURUS **Weight:** 35.0800 g. **Composition:** 0.9170 Gold 1.0338 oz. AGW **Series:** Monnaie de Luxe **Obverse:** Toughra above crossed flags, ornamental base **Note:** Struck at Qustantiniyah.

Date	Mintage	Good	VG	F	VF	XF
AH1293//26 (1900)	—	—	600	750	900	1,200
AH1293//27 (1901)	550	—	600	750	900	1,200
AH1293//28 (1902)	1,428	—	600	750	900	1,200
AH1293//29 (1903)	858	—	600	750	900	1,200
AH1293//30 (1904)	804	—	600	750	900	1,200
AH1293//31 (1905)	1,204	—	600	750	900	1,200
AH1293//32 (1906)	1,021	—	600	750	900	1,200
AH1293//33 (1907)	1,234	—	600	750	900	1,200
AH1293//34 (1908)	812	—	600	750	900	1,200

Muhammad V
AH1327-36/1909-18AD
STANDARD COINAGE

KM# 759 5 PARA **Composition:** Nickel **Obverse:** Toughra; "Reshat" to right **Note:** Struck at Qustantiniyah.

Date	Mintage	Good	VG	F	VF	XF
AH1327//2 (1910)	1,664,000	—	1.00	2.00	4.00	8.00
AH1327//3 (1911)	21,760,000	—	0.50	1.00	2.00	4.00
AH1327//4 (1912)	21,392,000	—	0.50	1.00	2.00	4.00
AH1327//5 (1913)	30,579,000	—	0.50	1.00	2.00	4.00
AH1327//6 (1914)	15,751,000	—	0.50	1.00	2.00	4.00
AH1327//7 (1915)	2,512,000	—	15.00	35.00	60.00	100

KM# 767 5 PARA **Composition:** Nickel **Obverse:** Toughra; "el-Ghazi" to right **Note:** Struck at Qustantiniyah.

Date	Mintage	Good	VG	F	VF	XF
AH1327//7 (1915)	740,000	—	15.00	30.00	45.00	70.00

KM# 760 10 PARA **Composition:** Nickel **Obverse:** Toughra; "el-Ghazi" to right **Note:** Struck at Qustantiniyah.

Date	Mintage	Good	VG	F	VF	XF
AH1327//2 (1910)	2,576,000	—	0.25	0.50	2.00	5.00
AH1327//3 (1911)	18,992,000	—	0.15	0.25	1.00	3.00
AH1327//4 (1912)	18,576,000	—	0.15	0.25	1.00	3.00
AH1327//5 (1913)	31,799,000	—	0.15	0.25	1.00	3.00
AH1327//6 (1914)	17,024,000	—	0.15	0.25	1.00	3.00
AH1327//7 (1915)	21,680,000	—	0.30	0.65	1.50	4.00

KM# 768 10 PARA **Composition:** Nickel **Obverse:** Toughra; "el-Ghazi" to right **Note:** Struck at Qustantiniyah.

Date	Mintage	Good	VG	F	VF	XF
AH1327//7 (1915)	—	—	0.30	0.60	1.50	4.00
Note: Mintage included in KM760						
AH1327//8 (1916)	7,590,000	—	0.50	1.00	4.00	10.00

KM# 761 20 PARA **Composition:** Nickel **Obverse:** Toughra; "Reshat" to right **Note:** Struck at Qustantiniyah.

Date	Mintage	Good	VG	F	VF	XF
AH1327 (1909) No regnal year	—	—	5.00	8.50	15.00	25.00
AH1327//2 (1910)	1,524,000	—	0.25	0.50	2.00	8.00
AH1327//3 (1911)	11,418,000	—	0.15	0.35	1.50	6.00
AH1327//4 (1912)	10,848,000	—	0.15	0.25	1.00	5.00
AH1327//5 (1913)	24,350,000	—	0.15	0.25	1.00	5.00
AH1327//6 (1914)	20,663,000	—	0.15	0.25	1.00	5.00
AH1327//7 (1915) Rare	—	—	—	—	—	—

KM# 769 20 PARA **Composition:** Nickel **Obverse:** Toughra; "el-Ghazi" to right **Note:** Struck at Qustantiniyah.

Date	Good	VG	F	VF	XF
AH1327//7 (1915) Rare	—	—	—	—	—

KM# 766 40 PARA **Composition:** Nickel **Obverse:** Toughra; "el-Ghazi" to right **Note:** Struck at Qustantiniyah.

Date	Mintage	Good	VG	F	VF	XF
AH1327//3 (1910)	1,992,000	—	0.50	1.00	3.00	10.00
AH1327//4 (1911)	8,716,000	—	0.15	0.30	2.00	5.00
AH1327//5 (1912)	9,248,000	—	0.15	0.30	2.00	5.00

KM# 779 40 PARA **Composition:** Copper-Nickel **Obverse:** Toughra; "el-Ghazi" to right **Note:** Struck at Qustantiniyah.

Date	Mintage	Good	VG	F	VF	XF
AH1327//8 (1916)	16,339,000	—	0.15	0.30	2.00	5.00
AH1327//9 (1917)	3,034,000	—	1.00	2.00	10.00	25.00

KM# 748 KURUS **Weight:** 1.2027 g. **Composition:** 0.8300 Silver .0321 oz. ASW **Obverse:** Toughra **Note:** Struck at Qustantiniyah.

Date	Mintage	Good	VG	F	VF	XF
AH1327//1 (1909)	1,270,000	—	1.25	2.50	3.50	6.00
AH1327//2 (1910)	8,770,000	—	1.00	2.00	3.00	5.00
AH1327//3 (1911)	840,000	—	1.50	3.00	6.00	12.50

KM# 749 2 KURUS **Weight:** 2.4055 g. **Composition:** 0.8300 Silver .0642 oz. ASW **Obverse:** Toughra; "Reshat" to right **Note:** Struck at Qustantiniyah. Varieties exist in the size of date.

Date	Mintage	Good	VG	F	VF	XF
AH1327//1 (1909)	5,157,000	—	1.75	2.25	3.50	7.5
AH1327//2 (1910)	11,120,000	—	1.50	2.00	3.00	6.5
AH1327//3 (1911)	6,110,000	—	1.50	2.00	3.00	6.5
AH1327//4 (1912)	4,031,000	—	1.50	2.00	3.00	6.5
AH1327//5 (1913)	301,000	—	2.50	5.00	10.00	20.0
AH1327//6 (1914)	1,884,000	—	2.00	2.50	4.00	8.0
AH1327//6/2 (1914)	Inc. above	—	2.00	2.50	4.00	8.0

 # 770 2 KURUS **Weight:** 2.4055 g. **Composition:**).8300 Silver .0642 oz. ASW **Obverse:** Toughra; "el-Ghazi" :o right **Note:** Struck at Qustantiniyah. Varieties exist in the size of date.

	Mintage	Good	VG	F	VF	XF
27//7 (1915)	17,000	—	12.50	25.00	40.00	75.00
27//8 (1916)	398,000	—	20.00	30.00	50.00	100
27//9 (1917)	8,000	—	60.00	100	200	350

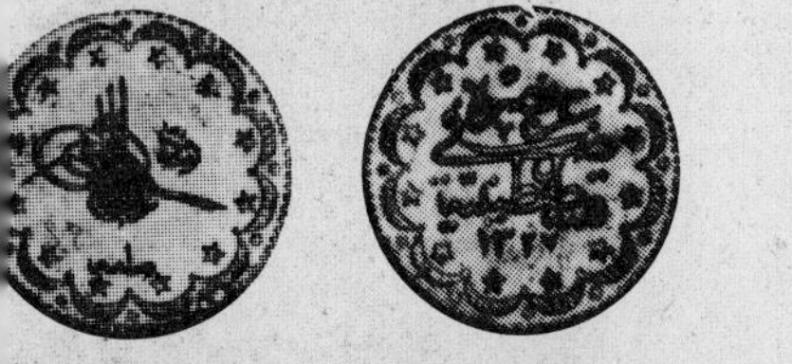

 # 750 5 KURUS **Weight:** 6.0130 g. **Composition:** 0.8300 Silver 1605 oz. ASW **Obverse:** Toughra; "Reshat" to right **Note:** Struck at Qustantiniyah.

	Mintage	Good	VG	F	VF	XF
327//1 (1909)	1,558,000	—	BV	3.50	6.00	10.00
327//2 (1910)	1,886,000	—	BV	3.50	6.00	10.00
327//3 (1911)	1,273,000	—	BV	3.50	6.00	10.00
327//4 (1912)	1,635,000	—	BV	3.50	6.00	10.00
327//5 (1913)	194,000	—	6.00	9.00	15.00	28.00
327//6 (1914)	664,000	—	3.25	3.50	5.00	9.00
327//7 (1915)	834,000	—	3.25	3.50	5.00	9.00

 # 771 5 KURUS **Weight:** 6.0130 g. **Composition:** 0.8300 Silver 1605 oz. ASW **Obverse:** Toughra; "el-Ghazi" to right **Note:** Struck at Qustantiniyah.

	Mintage	Good	VG	F	VF	XF
327//7 (1915)	—	—	3.50	4.50	7.00	10.00
ntage included KM750						
327//8 (1916)	648,000	—	4.00	7.00	10.00	20.00
327//9 (1917)	3,938	—	50.00	100	200	350

 # 751 10 KURUS **Weight:** 12.0270 g. **Composition:** 0.8300 Silver .3210 oz. ASW **Obverse:** Toughra; "Reshat" to right **Note:** Struck at Qustantiniyah.

	Mintage	Good	VG	F	VF	XF
327//1 (1909)	110,000	—	12.50	25.00	50.00	100
327//2 (1910)	Inc. above	—	10.00	20.00	50.00	100
327//3 (1911)	8,000	—	150	250	500	1,000
327//4 (1912)	96,000	—	3.50	7.50	15.00	25.00
327//5 (1913)	34,000	—	10.00	20.00	50.00	100
327//6 (1914)	81,000	—	7.50	12.50	17.50	30.00
327//7 (1915)	582,000	—	5.00	10.00	16.50	32.00

 # 772 10 KURUS **Weight:** 12.0270 g. **Composition:** 0.8300 Silver .3210 oz. ASW **Obverse:** Toughra; "el-Ghazi" to right **Note:** Struck at Qustantiniyah.

	Mintage	Good	VG	F	VF	XF
327//7 (1915)	—	—	3.50	7.50	15.00	28.00
Note: Mintage included in KM751						
327//8 (1916)	408,000	—	7.00	9.00	17.50	32.00

Date	Mintage	Good	VG	F	VF	XF
AH1327//9 (1917)	299,000	—	10.00	20.00	35.00	50.00
AH1327//10 (1918)	666,000	—	12.50	25.00	50.00	85.00

KM# 762 12-1/2 KURUS **Weight:** 0.9020 g. **Composition:** 0.9170 Gold .0266 oz. AGW **Series:** Monnaie de Luxe **Obverse:** Toughra; "Reshat" right of toughra **Note:** Struck at Qustantiniyah.

Date	Mintage	Good	VG	F	VF	XF
AH1327//2 (1910)	43,568	—	20.00	30.00	50.00	90.00
AH1327//3 (1911)	50,368	—	20.00	30.00	50.00	90.00
AH1327//4 (1912)	19,344	—	20.00	30.00	50.00	90.00
AH1327//5 (1913)	9,160	—	20.00	30.00	50.00	90.00
AH1327//6 (1914)	11,880	—	20.00	30.00	50.00	90.00

KM# 780 20 KURUS **Weight:** 24.0550 g. **Composition:** 0.8300 Silver .6419 oz. ASW **Obverse:** Toughra **Note:** Struck at Qustantiniyah.

Date	Mintage	Good	VG	F	VF	XF
AH1327//8 (1916)	713,000	—	9.00	12.00	20.00	35.00
AH1327//9 (1917)	5,962,000	—	8.00	10.00	15.00	30.00
AH1327//10 (1918)	11,025,000	—	9.00	12.00	20.00	35.00

KM# 752 25 KURUS **Weight:** 1.8040 g. **Composition:** 0.9170 Gold .0532 oz. AGW **Obverse:** Toughra; "Reshat" to right **Note:** Struck at Qustantiniyah.

Date	Mintage	Good	VG	F	VF	XF
AH1327//1 (1909)	115,484	—	BV	30.00	40.00	50.00
AH1327//2 (1910)	194,740	—	BV	30.00	40.00	50.00
AH1327//3 (1911)	249,416	—	BV	30.00	40.00	50.00
AH1327//4 (1912)	338,172	—	BV	30.00	40.00	50.00
AH1327//5 (1913)	167,598	—	BV	30.00	40.00	50.00
AH1327//6 (1914)	72,872	—	BV	30.00	40.00	50.00

KM# 763 25 KURUS **Weight:** 1.7540 g. **Composition:** 0.9170 Gold .0517 oz. AGW **Series:** Monnaie de Luxe **Obverse:** Toughra **Note:** Struck at Qustantiniyah.

Date	Mintage	Good	VG	F	VF	XF
AH1327//2 (1910)	47,788	—	35.00	50.00	60.00	70.00
AH1327//3 (1911)	70,775	—	35.00	50.00	60.00	70.00
AH1327//4 (1912)	47,088	—	35.00	50.00	60.00	70.00
AH1327//5 (1913)	25,964	—	50.00	60.00	75.00	100
AH1327//6 (1914)	23,348	—	50.00	60.00	75.00	100

KM# 773 25 KURUS **Weight:** 1.8040 g. **Composition:** 0.9170 Gold .0532 oz. AGW **Obverse:** Toughra; "el-Ghazi" to right **Note:** Struck at Qustantiniyah.

Date	Mintage	Good	VG	F	VF	XF
AH1327//7 (1915)	22,420	—	BV	35.00	45.00	55.00
AH1327//8 (1916)	5,926	—	BV	35.00	45.00	55.00
AH1327//9 (1917)	4,060	—	BV	35.00	45.00	55.00
AH1327//10 (1918)	—	—	1,000	1,500	2,000	3,000

KM# 774 25 KURUS **Weight:** 1.7540 g. **Composition:** 0.9170 Gold .0517 oz. AGW **Series:** Monnaie de Luxe **Obverse:** Toughra **Note:** Struck at Qustantiniyah.

Date	Mintage	Good	VG	F	VF	XF
AH1327//8 (1916)	10,612	—	1,750	2,500	3,500	5,000

KM# 753 50 KURUS **Weight:** 3.6080 g. **Composition:** 0.9170 Gold .1064 oz. AGW **Obverse:** Toughra; "Reshat" to right **Note:** Struck at Qustantiniyah.

Date	Mintage	Good	VG	F	VF	XF
AH1327//1 (1909)	6,276	—	1,000	1,500	2,000	3,000
AH1327//2 (1910)	89,712	—	BV	55.00	65.00	80.00
AH1327//3 (1911)	75,442	—	BV	55.00	65.00	80.00
AH1327//4 (1912)	96,030	—	BV	55.00	65.00	80.00
AH1327//5 (1913)	40,618	—	BV	55.00	65.00	80.00
AH1327//6 (1914)	26,408	—	BV	55.00	65.00	80.00

KM# 764 50 KURUS **Weight:** 3.5080 g. **Composition:** 0.9170 Gold .1034 oz. AGW **Series:** Monnaie de Luxe **Obverse:** Toughra **Note:** Struck at Qustantiniyah.

Date	Mintage	Good	VG	F	VF	XF
AH1327//2 (1910)	25,224	—	60.00	70.00	90.00	120
AH1327//3 (1911)	23,971	—	60.00	70.00	90.00	120
AH1327//4 (1912)	15,716	—	60.00	70.00	90.00	120
AH1327//5 (1913)	17,118	—	60.00	70.00	90.00	120
AH1327//6 (1914)	8,706	—	60.00	70.00	90.00	120

KM# 775 50 KURUS **Weight:** 3.6080 g. **Composition:** 0.9170 Gold .1064 oz. AGW **Obverse:** Toughra; "el-Ghazi" to right **Note:** Struck at Qustantiniyah.

Date	Mintage	Good	VG	F	VF	XF
AH1327//7 (1915)	9,175	—	60.00	75.00	150	250
AH1327//8 (1916)	7,330	—	60.00	75.00	150	250
AH1327//9 (1917)	2,000	—	60.00	75.00	150	250
AH1327//10 (1918)	—	—	1,000	1,500	2,000	3,000

KM# 781 50 KURUS **Weight:** 3.5080 g. **Composition:** 0.9170 Gold .1034 oz. AGW **Series:** Monnaie de Luxe **Obverse:** Toughra **Note:** Struck at Qustantiniyah.

Date	Mintage	Good	VG	F	VF	XF
AH1327//8 (1916)	3,291	—	250	400	600	1,000

KM# 755 100 KURUS **Weight:** 7.0160 g. **Composition:** 0.9170 Gold .2068 oz. AGW **Series:** Monnaie de Luxe **Obverse:** Toughra

Date	Mintage	Good	VG	F	VF	XF
AH1327//1 (1909)	—	—	BV	100	135	200
AH1327//2 (1910)	37,110	—	BV	100	135	200
AH1327//3 (1911)	53,738	—	BV	100	135	200
AH1327//4 (1912)	41,507	—	BV	100	135	200
AH1327//5 (1913)	58,819	—	BV	100	135	200
AH1327//6 (1914)	19,768	—	BV	100	135	200

KM# 754 100 KURUS **Weight:** 7.2160 g. **Composition:** 0.9170 Gold .2125 oz. AGW **Obverse:** Toughra; "Reshat" to right **Note:** Struck at Qustantiniyah.

Date	Mintage	Good	VG	F	VF	XF
AH1327//1 (1909)	1,715,274	—	—	BV	100	135
AH1327//2 (1910)	3,376,679	—	—	BV	100	135
AH1327//3 (1911)	4,627,115	—	—	BV	100	135
AH1327//4 (1912)	3,591,676	—	—	BV	100	135
AH1327//5 (1913)	881,895	—	—	BV	100	135
AH1327//6 (1914)	3,769,100	—	—	BV	100	135
AH1327//7 (1915)	—	—	—	BV	100	135

KM# 776 100 KURUS **Weight:** 7.2160 g. **Composition:** 0.9170 Gold .2128 oz. AGW **Obverse:** Toughra; "el-Ghazi" to right **Note:** Struck at Qustantiniyah.

Date	Mintage	Good	VG	F	VF	XF
AH1327//7 (1915)	1,232,090	—	—	BV	110	150
AH1327//8 (1916)	Inc. above	—	—	BV	110	150
AH1327//9 (1917)	3,582,005	—	—	BV	110	150
AH1327//10 (1918)	—	—	—	BV	110	150

KM# 782 100 KURUS **Weight:** 7.0160 g. **Composition:** 0.9170 Gold .2068 oz. AGW **Series:** Monnaie de Luxe **Obverse:** Toughra **Note:** Struck at Qustantiniyah.

Date	Mintage	Good	VG	F	VF	XF
AH1327//8 (1916)	13,250	—	250	400	600	1,000

KM# 756 250 KURUS **Weight:** 18.0400 g. **Composition:** 0.9170 Gold .5319 oz. AGW **Obverse:** Toughra; "Reshat" to right **Note:** Struck at Qustantiniyah.

Date	Mintage	Good	VG	F	VF	XF
AH1327//1 (1909)	6,878	—	—	BV	350	425
AH1327//2 (1910)	9,207	—	—	BV	350	425
AH1327//3 (1911)	9,990	—	—	BV	350	425
AH1327//4 (1912)	13,400	—	—	BV	350	425
AH1327//5 (1913)	18,143	—	—	BV	350	425
AH1327//6 (1914)	6,155	—	—	BV	350	425

KM# 757 250 KURUS **Weight:** 17.5400 g. **Composition:** 0.9170 Gold .5619 oz. AGW **Series:** Monnaie de Luxe **Obverse:** Toughra **Note:** Struck at Qustantiniyah.

Date	Mintage	Good	VG	F	VF	XF
AH1327//1 (1909)	—	—	BV	350	450	625
AH1327//2 (1910)	6,998	—	BV	350	450	625
AH1327//3 (1911)	12,084	—	BV	350	450	625
AH1327//4 (1912)	10,250	—	BV	350	450	625
AH1327//5 (1913)	16,879	—	BV	350	450	625
AH1327//6 (1914)	9,036	—	BV	350	450	625

KM# 777 250 KURUS **Weight:** 18.0400 g. **Composition:** 0.9170 Gold .5319 oz. AGW **Obverse:** Toughra; "el-Ghazi" to right **Note:** Struck at Qustantiniyah.

Date	Mintage	Good	VG	F	VF	XF
AH1327//7 (1915)	30	—	1,250	1,750	2,800	4,000
AH1327//8 (1916)	21	—	1,750	2,500	3,500	5,000
AH1327//9 (1917)	28	—	1,750	2,500	3,500	5,000

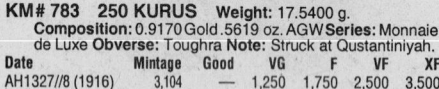

KM# 783 250 KURUS **Weight:** 17.5400 g. **Composition:** 0.9170 Gold .5619 oz. AGW **Series:** Monnaie de Luxe **Obverse:** Toughra **Note:** Struck at Qustantiniyah.

Date	Mintage	Good	VG	F	VF	XF
AH1327//8 (1916)	3,104	—	1,250	1,750	2,500	3,500

KM# 758 500 KURUS **Weight:** 17.5400 g. **Composition:** 0.9170 Gold .5619 oz. AGW **Obverse:** Toughra; "Reshat" to right **Note:** Struck at Qustantiniyah.

Date	Mintage	Good	VG	F	VF	XF
AH1327//1 (1909)	39,028	—	—	BV	525	650
AH1327//2 (1910)	37,478	—	—	BV	525	650
AH1327//3 (1911)	53,900	—	—	BV	525	650
AH1327//4 (1912)	41,863	—	—	BV	525	650
AH1327//5 (1913)	36,996	—	—	BV	525	650
AH1327//6 (1914)	17,692	—	—	BV	525	650

KM# 765 500 KURUS **Weight:** 35.0800 g. **Composition:** 0.9170 Gold 1.0338 oz. AGW **Series:** Monnaie de Luxe **Obverse:** Toughra above crossed flags, ornamental base **Note:** Struck at Qustantiniyah.

Date	Mintage	Good	VG	F	VF	XF
AH1327//2 (1910)	1,748	—	600	750	900	1,350
AH1327//3 (1911)	4,631	—	600	750	900	1,350
AH1327//4 (1912)	3,887	—	600	750	900	1,350
AH1327//5 (1913)	5,145	—	600	750	900	1,350
AH1327//6 (1914)	2,401	—	600	750	900	1,350

KM# 784 500 KURUS **Weight:** 36.0800 g. **Composition:** 0.9170 Gold 1.0638 oz. AGW **Obverse:** Toughra; "el-Ghazi" to right **Note:** Struck at Qustantiniyah.

Date	Mintage	Good	VG	F	VF	X
AH1327//7 (1915)	484	—	1,750	2,500	3,500	5,00
AH1327//8 (1916)	19	—	1,750	2,750	4,250	6,00
AH1327//9 (1917)	22	—	1,750	2,750	4,250	6,00
AH1327//10 (1918)	—	—	1,750	2,500	3,500	5,00

 # 778 500 KURUS Weight: 35.0800 g. Composition: 0.9170 Gold 1.0338 oz. AGW Series: Monnaie de Luxe Obverse: Toughra above crossed flags, ornamental base Note: Struck at Qustantiniyah.

Date	Mintage	Good	VG	F	VF	XF
27//7 (1915)	295	—	1,200	1,750	2,500	3,500
27//8 (1916)	1,216	—	1,000	1,500	2,200	3,000

MINT VISIT COINAGE

 # 785 2 KURUS Weight: 2.4055 g. Composition: 0.8300 Silver .0642 oz. ASW Obverse: Toughra Note: Struck at Bursa.

Date	F	VF	XF	Unc
27//1 (1909)	15.00	30.00	75.00	125

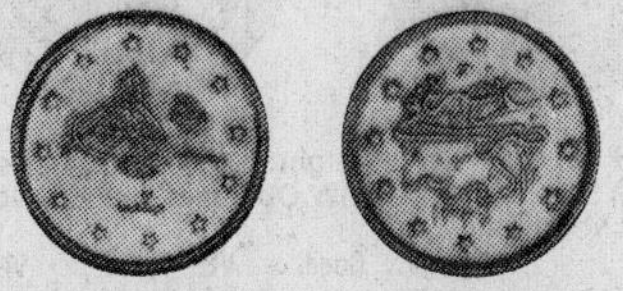

 # 790 2 KURUS Weight: 2.4055 g. Composition: 0.8300 Silver .0642 oz. ASW Obverse: Toughra Note: Struck at Edirne.

Date	F	VF	XF	Unc
327//2 (1910)	15.00	30.00	75.00	125

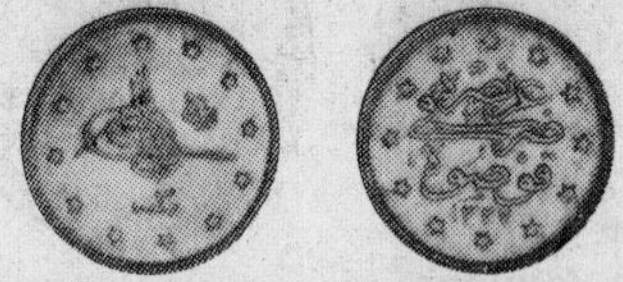

 # 796 2 KURUS Weight: 2.4055 g. Composition: 0.8300 Silver .0642 oz. ASW Obverse: Toughra Note: Struck at Kosova.

Date	Mintage	F	VF	XF	Unc
327//3 (1911)	13,000	15.00	30.00	100	150

 # 802 2 KURUS Weight: 2.4055 g. Composition: 0.8300 Silver .0642 oz. ASW Obverse: Toughra Note: Struck at Manastir.

Date	Mintage	F	VF	XF	Unc
327//3 (1911)	13,000	15.00	30.00	100	150

 # 808 2 KURUS Weight: 2.4055 g. Composition: 0.8300 Silver .0642 oz. ASW Obverse: Toughra Note: Struck at Salonika.

Date	Mintage	F	VF	XF	Unc
327//3 (1911)	13,000	15.00	30.00	100	150

 # 786 5 KURUS Weight: 6.0130 g. Composition: 0.8300 Silver .1605 oz. ASW Obverse: Toughra Note: Struck at Bursa.

Date	F	VF	XF	Unc
327//1 (1909)	20.00	40.00	90.00	165

KM# 791 5 KURUS Weight: 6.0130 g. Composition: 0.8300 Silver .1605 oz. ASW Obverse: Toughra Note: Struck at Edirne.

Date	F	VF	XF	Unc
AH1327//2 (1910)	20.00	40.00	90.00	165

KM# 797 5 KURUS Weight: 6.0130 g. Composition: 0.8300 Silver .1605 oz. ASW Obverse: Toughra Note: Struck at Kosova.

Date	Mintage	F	VF	XF	Unc
AH1327//3 (1911)	3,000	20.00	40.00	125	185

KM# 803 5 KURUS Weight: 6.0130 g. Composition: 0.8300 Silver .1605 oz. ASW Obverse: Toughra Note: Struck at Manastir.

Date	Mintage	F	VF	XF	Unc
AH1327//3 (1911)	3,000	20.00	40.00	125	185

KM# 809 5 KURUS Weight: 6.0130 g. Composition: 0.8300 Silver .1605 oz. ASW Obverse: Toughra Note: Struck at Salonika.

Date	Mintage	F	VF	XF	Unc
AH1327//3 (1911)	3,000	20.00	40.00	125	185

KM# 792 10 KURUS Weight: 12.0270 g. Composition: 0.8300 Silver .3210 oz. ASW Obverse: Toughra Note: Struck at Edirne.

Date	F	VF	XF	Unc
AH1327//2 (1910)	90.00	150	250	455

KM# 798 10 KURUS Weight: 12.0270 g. Composition: 0.8300 Silver .3210 oz. ASW Obverse: Toughra Note: Struck at Kosova.

Date	Mintage	F	VF	XF	Unc
AH1327//3 (1911)	1,500	100	175	300	525

KM# 804 10 KURUS Weight: 12.0270 g. Composition: 0.8300 Silver .3210 oz. ASW Obverse: Toughra Note: Struck at Manastir.

Date	Mintage	F	VF	XF	Unc
AH1327//3 (1911)	1,500	100	200	350	550

KM# 810 10 KURUS Weight: 12.0270 g. Composition: 0.8300 Silver .3210 oz. ASW Obverse: Toughra Note: Struck at Salonika.

Date	Mintage	F	VF	XF	Unc
AH1327//3 (1911)	1,500	100	200	350	550

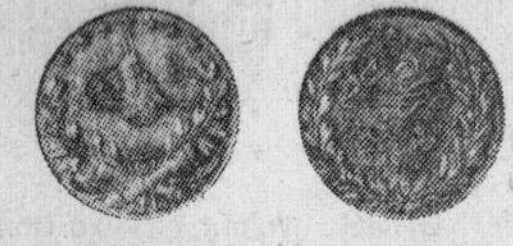

KM# 787 25 KURUS Weight: 1.8040 g. Composition: 0.9170 Gold .0532 oz. AGW Obverse: Toughra Note: Struck at Bursa.

Date	F	VF	XF	Unc
AH1327//1 (1909)	185	275	400	800

KM# 788 50 KURUS Weight: 3.6080 g. Composition: 0.9170 Gold .1064 oz. AGW Obverse: Toughra Note: Struck at Bursa.

Date	F	VF	XF	Unc
AH1327//1 (1909)	165	275	350	650

KM# 793 50 KURUS Weight: 3.6080 g. Composition: 0.9170 Gold .1064 oz. AGW Obverse: Toughra Note: Struck at Edirne.

Date	F	VF	XF	Unc
AH1327//2 (1910)	200	275	350	600

KM# 799 50 KURUS Weight: 3.6080 g. Composition: 0.9170 Gold .1064 oz. AGW Obverse: Toughra Note: Struck at Kosova.

Date	Mintage	F	VF	XF	Unc
AH1327//3 (1911)	1,200	225	275	400	700

KM# 805 50 KURUS Weight: 3.6080 g. Composition: 0.9170 Gold .1064 oz. AGW Obverse: Toughra Note: Struck at Manastir.

Date	Mintage	F	VF	XF	Unc
AH1327//3 (1911)	1,200	200	325	450	700

KM# 811 50 KURUS Weight: 3.6080 g. **Composition:** 0.9170 Gold .1064 oz. AGW **Obverse:** Toughra **Note:** Struck at Salonika.

Date	Mintage	F	VF	XF	Unc
AH1327//3 (1911)	1,200	200	325	400	700

KM# 789 100 KURUS Weight: 7.2160 g. **Composition:** 0.9170 Gold .2128 oz. AGW **Obverse:** Toughra **Note:** Struck at Bursa.

Date	F	VF	XF	Unc
AH1327//1 (1909)	215	325	400	700

KM# 794 100 KURUS Weight: 7.2160 g. **Composition:** 0.9170 Gold .2128 oz. AGW **Obverse:** Toughra **Note:** Struck at Edirne.

Date	F	VF	XF	Unc
AH1327//2 (1910)	250	350	475	700

KM# 800 100 KURUS Weight: 7.2160 g. **Composition:** 0.9170 Gold .2128 oz. AGW **Obverse:** Toughra **Note:** Struck at Kosova.

Date	Mintage	F	VF	XF	Unc
AH1327//3 (1911)	750	250	300	450	750

KM# 806 100 KURUS Weight: 7.2160 g. **Composition:** 0.9170 Gold .2128 oz. AGW **Obverse:** Toughra **Note:** Struck at Manastir.

Date	Mintage	F	VF	XF	Unc
AH1327//3 (1911)	750	225	350	450	750

KM# 812 100 KURUS Weight: 7.2160 g. **Composition:** 0.9170 Gold .2128 oz. AGW **Obverse:** Toughra **Note:** Struck at Salonika.

Date	Mintage	F	VF	XF	Unc
AH1327//3 (1911)	750	225	350	450	750

KM# 795 500 KURUS Weight: 36.0800 g. **Composition:** 0.9170 Gold 1.0638 oz. AGW **Obverse:** Toughra **Note:** Struck at Edirne.

Date	F	VF	XF	Unc
AH1327//2 (1910)	1,500	2,500	3,500	4,000

KM# 801 500 KURUS Weight: 36.0800 g. **Composition:** 0.9170 Gold 1.0638 oz. AGW **Obverse:** Toughra **Note:** Struck at Kosova.

Date	Mintage	F	VF	XF	Unc
AH1327//3 (1911)	20	3,000	4,000	5,000	6,000

KM# 807 500 KURUS Weight: 36.0800 g. **Composition:** 0.9170 Gold 1.0638 oz. AGW **Obverse:** Toughra **Note:** Struck at Manastir.

Date	Mintage	F	VF	XF	Unc
AH1327//3 (1911)	20	2,500	4,000	5,000	6,250

KM# 813 500 KURUS Weight: 36.0800 g. **Composition:** 0.9170 Gold 1.0638 oz. AGW **Obverse:** Toughra **Note:** Struck at Salonika.

Date	Mintage	F	VF	XF	Unc
AH1327//3 (1911)	20	2,500	4,000	5,250	6,750

Muhammad VI
AH1336-41/1918-23AD

STANDARD COINAGE

KM# 828 40 PARA Composition: Copper-Nickel **Obverse:** Toughra **Note:** Struck at Qustantiniyah.

Date	Mintage	Good	VG	F	VF	XF
AH1336//4 (1920)	6,520,000	—	1.75	2.50	4.00	10.00

KM# 815 2 KURUS Weight: 2.4055 g. **Composition:** 0.8300 Silver .0642 oz. ASW **Obverse:** Toughra **Note:** Struck at Qustantiniyah.

Date	Mintage	Good	VG	F	VF	XF
AH1336//1 (1918)	25,000	—	50.00	100	150	220
AH1336//2 (1918)	3,000	—	75.00	125	200	350

KM# 816 5 KURUS Weight: 6.0130 g. **Composition:** 0.8300 Silver .1605 oz. ASW **Obverse:** Toughra **Note:** Struck at Qustantiniyah.

Date	Mintage	Good	VG	F	VF	XF
AH1336//1 (1917)	10,000	—	50.00	125	175	265
AH1336//2 (1918)	2,000	—	75.00	150	225	385

KM# 817 10 KURUS Weight: 12.0270 g. **Composition:** 0.8300 Silver .3210 oz. ASW **Obverse:** Toughra **Note:** Struck at Qustantiniyah.

Date	Mintage	Good	VG	F	VF	XF
AH1336//1 (1917)	—	—	120	250	400	600
AH1336//2 (1918)	1,000	—	200	400	600	1,000

KM# 818 20 KURUS Weight: 24.0550 g. **Composition** 0.8300 Silver .6419 oz. ASW **Obverse:** Toughra **Note:** Struck at Qustantiniyah.

Date	Mintage	Good	VG	F	VF	X
AH1336//1 (1917)	—	—	30.00	60.00	125	18
AH1336//2 (1918)	1,530	—	350	525	650	92

KM# 819 25 KURUS Weight: 1.8040 g. **Compositio** 0.9170 Gold .0532 oz. AGW **Obverse:** Toughra **Note:** Struc at Qustantiniyah.

Date	Good	VG	F	VF	
AH1336//1 (1917)	—	30.00	40.00	50.00	1
AH1336//2 (1918)	—	30.00	40.00	50.00	1
AH1336//3 (1919)	—	40.00	75.00	150	2
AH1336//4 (1920)	—	50.00	90.00	200	3
AH1336//5 (1921)	—	80.00	140	240	3

KM# 825 25 KURUS Weight: 1.7540 g. **Compositio** 0.9170 Gold .0517 oz. AGW **Series:** Monnaie de Luxe **Obverse:** Toughra **Note:** Struck at Qustantiniyah.

Date	Good	VG	F	VF	XF
AH1336//2	—	60.00	80.00	100	150
AH1336//3	—	60.00	80.00	100	150

KM# 820 50 KURUS Weight: 3.6080 g. **Composition:** 0.9170 Gold .1064 oz. AGW **Obverse:** Toughra **Note:** Struck at Qustantiniyah.

ate	Good	VG	F	VF	XF
AH1336//1 (1917)	—	100	125	150	300
.H1336//2 (1918)	—	100	125	150	300
.H1336//3 (1919)	—	150	200	250	500
.H1336//4 (1920)	—	250	450	750	1,500
H1336//5 (1921)	—	200	300	450	1,000

:M# 821 100 KURUS Weight: 7.2160 g. **Composition:** 0.9170 Gold .2128 oz. AGW **Obverse:** Toughra **Note:** Struck at Qustantiniyah.

ate	Good	VG	F	VF	XF
H1336//1 (1917)	—	BV	110	140	180
11336//2 (1918)	—	BV	110	140	180
11336//3 (1919)	—	150	180	225	450
11336//5 (1921)	—	400	600	800	1,000

M# 826 100 KURUS Weight: 7.0160 g. **Composition:** 0.9170 Gold .2068 oz. AGW **Series:** Monnaie de Luxe **Obverse:** Toughra **Note:** Struck at Qustantiniyah.

e	Good	VG	F	VF	XF
1336//2 (1918)	—	250	300	325	375
1336//3 (1919)	—	250	300	325	375

 # 822 250 KURUS Weight: 18.0400 g. **Composition:** 0.9170 Gold .5319 oz. AGW **Obverse:** Toughra **Note:** Struck at Qustantiniyah.

	Mintage	Good	VG	F	VF	XF
336//1 (1917)	—	—	1,750	3,000	4,500	6,500
336//2 (1918)	26	—	1,750	3,000	4,500	6,500
336//3 (1919)	31	—	1,750	3,000	4,500	6,500

KM# 827 250 KURUS Weight: 17.5400 g. **Composition:** 0.9170 Gold .5169 oz. AGW **Series:** Monnaie de Luxe **Obverse:** Toughra **Note:** Struck at Qustantiniyah.

Date	Mintage	Good	VG	F	VF	XF
AH1336//2 (1918)	19,000	—	300	500	700	900
AH1336//3 (1919)	Inc. above	—	250	425	600	800

KM# 823 500 KURUS Weight: 36.0800 g. **Composition:** 0.9170 Gold 1.0638 oz. AGW **Obverse:** Toughra **Note:** Struck at Qustantiniyah.

Date	Mintage	Good	VG	F	VF	XF
AH1336//1 (1917)	—	—	1,000	1,200	1,450	1,800
AH1336//2 (1918)	—	—	1,000	1,200	1,450	1,800
AH1336//3 (1919)	—	—	1,000	1,200	1,450	1,800
AH1336//4 (1920)	23	—	2,000	4,000	6,000	8,000
AH1336//5 (1921)	22	—	2,000	4,000	6,000	8,000

KM# 824 500 KURUS Weight: 35.0800 g. **Composition:** 0.9170 Gold 1.0338 oz. AGW **Series:** Monnaie de Luxe **Obverse:** Toughra above crossed flage, ornamental base **Note:** Struck at Qustantiniyah.

Date	Mintage	Good	VG	F	VF	XF
AH1336//1 (1917)	—	—	1,000	1,250	1,750	2,400
AH1336//2 (1918)	5,207	—	600	750	950	1,300
AH1336//3 (1919)	Inc. above	—	600	750	950	1,300
AH1336//4 (1920)	88	—	1,500	2,000	2,500	3,200

REPUBLIC

STANDARD COINAGE

Old Monetary System

KM# 830 100 PARA Composition: Aluminum-Bronze

Date	Mintage	F	VF	XF	Unc
AH1340 (1921)	1,798,000	3.00	5.00	10.00	60.00
AH1341 (1922)	5,583,000	1.00	2.50	5.00	30.00

KM# 834 100 PARA Composition: Aluminum-Bronze

Date	Mintage	F	VF	XF	Unc
AH1345 (1926)	4,388,000	1.00	2.50	6.00	32.00
AH1347 (1928)	—	150	225	400	600
AH1347 (1928)	—	150	225	400	600

KM# 831 5 KURUS Composition: Aluminum-Bronze

Date	Mintage	F	VF	XF	Unc
AH1340 (1921)	5,023,000	1.00	2.50	7.00	32.00
AH1341 (1922)	23,545,000	1.00	2.50	7.00	32.00

KM# 835 5 KURUS Composition: Aluminum-Bronze

Date	Mintage	F	VF	XF	Unc
AH1345 (1926)	356,000	1.00	2.50	7.00	32.00
AH1347 (1928)	—	175	250	500	700

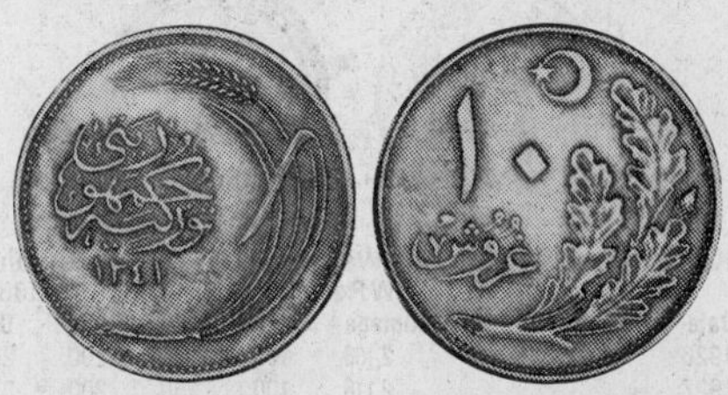

KM# 832 10 KURUS Composition: Aluminum-Bronze **Note:** Varieties exist.

Date	Mintage	F	VF	XF	Unc
AH1340 (1921)	4,836,000	1.50	3.00	8.00	35.00
AH1341 (1922)	14,223,000	1.50	3.00	8.00	35.00

KM# 836 10 KURUS Composition: Aluminum-Bronze

Date	Mintage	F	VF	XF	Unc
1926	856,000	1.50	3.00	8.00	35.00
1928	—	125	200	375	575

KM# 833 25 KURUS **Composition:** Nickel

Date	Mintage	F	VF	XF	Unc
AH1341 (1922)	4,973,000	2.00	4.00	10.00	30.00

KM# 837 25 KURUS **Composition:** Nickel **Note:** Varieties exist.

Date	Mintage	F	VF	XF	Unc
1926	27,000	175	275	475	675
1928	5,794,000	1.50	3.00	8.00	30.00

KM# 840 25 KURUS **Weight:** 1.8040 g. **Composition:** 0.9170 Gold .0532 oz. AGW **Reverse:** AH date: "23 Nisan 1336"

Date	Mintage	F	VF	XF	Unc
1926	4,539	40.00	75.00	140	175
1927	14,000	40.00	75.00	120	150
1928	8,424	40.00	75.00	130	165
1929	—	40.00	75.00	120	150

KM# 844 25 KURUS **Weight:** 1.7540 g. **Composition:** 0.9170 Gold .0517 oz. AGW **Series:** Monnaie de Luxe

Date	Mintage	F	VF	XF	Unc
1927	4,103	50.00	75.00	125	200
1928	4,549	50.00	75.00	125	200

KM# 841 50 KURUS **Weight:** 3.6080 g. **Composition:** 0.9170 Gold .1064 oz. AGW **Reverse:** AH date: "23 Nisan 1336"

Date	Mintage	F	VF	XF	Unc
1926	2,168	100	150	200	275
1927	2,116	100	150	200	275
1928	2,431	100	150	200	275
1929	—	100	150	200	275

KM# 845 50 KURUS **Weight:** 3.5080 g. **Composition:** 0.9170 Gold .1034 oz. AGW **Series:** Monnaie de Luxe

Date	Mintage	F	VF	XF	Unc
1927	3,903	75.00	150	250	375
1928	3,620	75.00	150	250	375

KM# 842 100 KURUS **Weight:** 7.2160 g. **Composition:** 0.9170 Gold .2128 oz. AGW **Reverse:** AH date: "23 Nisan 1336"

Date	Mintage	F	VF	XF	Unc
1926	1,073	120	175	250	350
1927	—	120	175	250	350

Date	Mintage	F	VF	XF	Unc
1928	920	120	175	250	350
1929	—	120	175	250	350

KM# 846 100 KURUS **Weight:** 7.0160 g. **Composition:** 0.9170 Gold .2069 oz. AGW **Series:** Monnaie de Luxe

Date	Mintage	F	VF	XF	Unc
1927	8,676	125	150	250	350
1928	6,092	125	150	250	350

KM# 843 250 KURUS **Weight:** 18.0400 g. **Composition:** 0.9170 Gold .5319 oz. AGW **Reverse:** AH date: "23 Nisan 1336"

Date	Mintage	F	VF	XF	Unc
1926	604	350	450	600	750
1927	886	350	450	600	750
1928	110	350	450	600	750
1929	—	350	450	600	750

KM# 847 250 KURUS **Weight:** 17.5400 g. **Composition:** 0.9170 Gold .5169 oz. AGW **Series:** Monnaie de Luxe

Date	Mintage	F	VF	XF	Unc
1927	7,411	BV	300	450	600
1928	5,045	BV	300	450	600

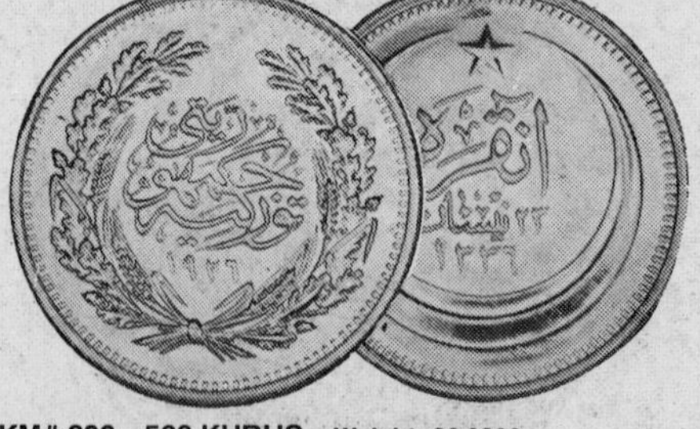

KM# 839 500 KURUS **Weight:** 36.0800 g. **Composition:** 0.9170 Gold 1.0638 oz. AGW **Reverse:** AH date: "23 Nisan 1336"

Date	Mintage	F	VF	XF	Unc
1925	226	BV	700	1,000	1,500
1926	2,268	—	500	600	800
1927	4,011	BV	500	600	800
1928	375	BV	700	1,000	1,500
1929	—	BV	700	1,000	1,500

KM# 848 500 KURUS **Weight:** 35.0800 g. **Composition:** 0.9170 Gold 1.0344 oz. AGW **Series:** Monnaie de Luxe

Date	Mintage	F	VF	XF	U
1927	5,097	BV	500	600	8
1928	2,242	BV	500	600	8

DECIMAL COINAGE

Western numerals and Latin alphabet

40 Para = 1 Kurus; 100 Kurus = 1 Lira

Mintage figures of the 1930's and early 1940's m
not be exact. It is suspected that in some cases, figur
for a particular year may include quantities struck w
the previous year's date.

KM# 868 10 PARA (1/4 Kurus) **Composition:** Aluminum-Bronze

Date	Mintage	VG	F	VF	XF
1940	30,800,000	0.25	0.75	2.50	5.00
1941	22,400,000	0.25	0.75	2.50	5.00
1942	26,800,000	0.25	0.75	2.50	5.00

KM# 884 1/2 KURUS (20 Para) **Composition:** Br

Date	Mintage	F	VF	XF
1948	150	—	—	300

Note: Not released to circulation

KM# 884a 1/2 KURUS (20 Para) **Weight:** 3.9000 **Composition:** 0.9160 Gold .1149 oz. AGW **Series:** Nostalgia **Obverse:** Same as KM#884 **Reverse:** Same KM#884 **Edge:** Plain **Size:** 16 mm.

Date	Mintage	F	VF	XF	
1948	25,000	—	—	—	8

KM# 861 KURUS **Composition:** Copper-Nickel

Date	Mintage	VG	F	VF	XF
1935	784,000	2.00	4.00	6.00	15.00
1936	5,300,000	0.25	1.00	2.50	7.00
1937	4,500,000	0.25	1.00	2.50	7.00

867 KURUS **Composition:** Copper-Nickel

Mintage	VG	F	VF	XF	Unc
16,400,000	0.25	0.50	1.50	4.00	—
21,600,000	0.25	0.50	1.50	4.00	—
8,800,000	0.50	1.00	2.00	8.00	—
6,700,000	0.25	0.75	1.75	5.00	—
10,800,000	0.25	0.50	1.50	4.00	—
4,000,000	0.25	0.75	1.75	5.00	—
6,000,000	0.25	0.75	1.75	5.00	—

881 KURUS **Composition:** Brass

Mintage	F	VF	XF	Unc
890,000	1.00	1.50	2.50	5.00
35,470,000	0.15	0.25	0.50	1.50
29,530,000	0.15	0.25	0.50	1.25
32,800,000	0.15	0.25	0.50	1.25
6,310,000	0.15	0.30	0.75	2.25

881a KURUS **Weight:** 4.9000 g. **Composition:** 9160 Gold .1443 oz. AGW **Series:** Nostalgia **Obverse:** ame as KM#881 **Reverse:** Same as KM#881 **Edge:** Plain ize: 18 mm.

Mintage	F	VF	XF	Unc
25,000	—	—	—	80.00

 # 895 KURUS **Composition:** Brass **Reverse:** Olive ranch

Mintage	F	VF	XF	Unc
1,180,000	—	—	0.10	0.30
3,620,000	—	—	0.10	0.25
1,085,000	—	—	0.10	0.30

 # 895a KURUS **Composition:** Bronze

Mintage	F	VF	XF	Unc
1,180,000	—	—	0.10	0.30
2,520,000	—	—	0.10	0.20
1,860,000	—	—	0.10	0.20
1,820,000	—	—	0.10	0.20
2,410,000	—	—	0.10	0.20
1,040,000	—	—	0.10	0.20
900,000	—	—	0.10	0.20
1,960,000	—	—	0.10	0.20
2,940,000	—	—	0.10	0.20
720,000	—	—	0.10	0.30
540,000	—	—	0.10	0.30
510,000	—	—	0.10	0.30

 # 895b KURUS **Composition:** Aluminum

Mintage	F	VF	XF	Unc
690,000	—	0.10	0.25	1.00
200,000	—	0.10	0.25	1.50
108,000	—	0.10	0.25	1.75

 # 924 KURUS **Composition:** Bronze **Series:** F.A.O.

Mintage	F	VF	XF	Unc
15,000	—	0.25	1.00	3.00

 # 924a KURUS **Composition:** Aluminum **Series:** F.A.O.

Mintage	F	VF	XF	Unc
15,000	—	0.25	1.00	3.00

 # 885 2-1/2 KURUS **Composition:** Brass

Mintage	F	VF	XF	Unc
24,720,000	0.25	0.50	1.00	3.00
23,720,000	0.25	0.50	1.00	3.00

Date	Mintage	F	VF	XF	Unc
1950	11,560,000	0.35	0.65	1.25	4.00
1951	2,000,000	2.00	5.00	12.00	40.00

KM# 885a 2-1/2 KURUS **Weight:** 6.9000 g. **Composition:** 0.9160 Gold .2032 oz. AGW **Series:** Nostalgia **Obverse:** Same as KM#885 **Reverse:** Same as KM#885 **Edge:** Plain **Size:** 21 mm.

Date	Mintage	F	VF	XF	Unc
1950	25,000	—	—	—	85.00

KM# 862 5 KURUS **Composition:** Copper-Nickel

Date	Mintage	VG	F	VF	XF	Unc
1935	100,000	2.00	5.00	8.00	20.00	—
1936	2,900,000	0.50	1.00	2.00	8.00	—
1937	4,060,000	0.30	0.75	1.50	8.00	—
1938	13,380,000	0.25	0.50	1.00	5.00	—
1939	12,520,000	0.25	0.50	1.00	5.00	—
1940	4,340,000	0.30	0.75	1.50	5.00	—
1942	10,160,000	0.20	0.40	1.00	5.00	—
1943	15,360,000	0.20	0.40	1.00	5.00	—

KM# 887 5 KURUS **Composition:** Brass

Date	Mintage	F	VF	XF	Unc
1949	4,500,000	0.25	0.50	1.00	4.00
1950	45,900,000	0.15	0.35	0.75	3.00
1951	29,600,000	0.15	0.35	0.75	3.00
1955	15,300,000	0.15	0.35	0.75	3.00
1956	21,380,000	0.15	0.35	0.75	3.00
1957	3,320,000	0.25	0.50	1.00	4.00

KM# 890.1 5 KURUS **Weight:** 2.5000 g. **Composition:** Bronze

Date	Mintage	F	VF	XF	Unc
1958	25,870,000	0.10	0.25	0.50	1.50
1959	21,580,000	—	—	0.10	0.30
1960	17,150,000	—	—	0.10	0.30
1961	11,110,000	—	—	0.10	0.20
1962	15,280,000	—	—	0.10	0.30
1963	17,680,000	—	—	0.10	0.20
1964	18,190,000	—	—	0.10	0.30
1965	19,170,000	—	—	0.10	0.20
1966	19,840,000	—	—	0.10	0.30
1967	16,170,000	—	—	0.10	0.30
1968	26,050,000	—	—	0.10	0.30

KM# 890.2 5 KURUS **Weight:** 2.0000 g. **Composition:** Bronze **Note:** Reduced weight.

Date	Mintage	F	VF	XF	Unc
1969	33,630,000	—	—	0.10	0.30
1970	29,360,000	—	—	0.10	0.30
1971	17,440,000	—	—	0.10	0.30
1972	22,670,000	—	—	0.10	0.20
1973	17,370,000	—	—	0.10	0.20

KM# 890.3 5 KURUS **Weight:** 1.3500 g. **Composition:** Bronze **Note:** Varieties exist.

Date	Mintage	F	VF	XF	Unc
1974	13,540,000	—	—	0.10	0.20

KM# 890a 5 KURUS **Composition:** Aluminum

Date	Mintage	F	VF	XF	Unc
1975	1,560,000	—	—	0.10	0.30
1976	1,321,000	—	—	0.10	0.30
1977	190,000	—	0.10	0.20	1.00

KM# 906 5 KURUS **Composition:** Aluminum **Series:** F.A.O. **Reverse:** Oak leaf branch with acorn

Date	Mintage	F	VF	XF	Unc
1975	1,019,000	—	—	0.50	1.50

KM# 907 5 KURUS **Composition:** Aluminum **Series:** F.A.O. **Reverse:** Oak leaf branch with acorn

Date	Mintage	F	VF	XF	Unc
1976	17,000	—	0.50	1.50	4.00

KM# 934 5 KURUS **Composition:** Bronze **Series:** F.A.O. **Reverse:** Oak leaf branch with acorn

Date	Mintage	F	VF	XF	Unc
1980	13,000	—	0.25	0.75	2.50

KM# 863 10 KURUS **Composition:** Copper-Nickel

Date	Mintage	VG	F	VF	XF	Unc
1935	60,000	2.00	5.00	8.00	20.00	—
1936	3,580,000	0.75	2.00	5.00	12.50	—
1937	3,020,000	0.50	1.00	4.00	8.00	—
1938	6,610,000	0.50	1.00	4.00	8.00	—
1939	4,610,000	0.50	1.00	2.50	5.00	—
1940	6,960,000	0.50	1.00	2.50	5.00	—

KM# 888 10 KURUS **Composition:** Brass

Date	Mintage	F	VF	XF	Unc
1949	27,000,000	0.10	0.25	0.75	3.00
1951	6,200,000	0.10	0.25	0.75	3.00
1955	10,090,000	0.10	0.25	0.75	3.00
1956	9,910,000	0.10	0.25	0.75	3.00

KM# 891.1 10 KURUS **Weight:** 4.0000 g. **Composition:** Bronze **Reverse:** Sheaf of grain

Date	Mintage	F	VF	XF	Unc
1958	14,770,000	—	0.10	0.25	1.50
1959	11,160,000	—	—	0.10	0.40
1960	9,450,000	—	—	0.10	0.40
1961	5,370,000	—	—	0.10	0.40
1962	9,250,000	—	—	0.10	0.40
1963	10,390,000	—	—	0.10	0.40
1964	9,890,000	—	—	0.10	0.40
1965	10,480,000	—	—	0.10	0.40
1966	12,200,000	—	—	0.10	0.40
1967	11,410,000	—	—	0.10	0.40
1968	1,862,000	—	—	0.10	0.40

KM# 891a 10 KURUS **Composition:** Aluminum

Date	Mintage	F	VF	XF	Unc
1975	2,165,000	—	—	0.10	0.30
1976	559,000	—	0.10	0.20	0.60
1977	106,000	—	0.10	0.50	1.00

KM# 891.2 10 KURUS **Weight:** 3.5000 g. **Composition:** Bronze **Note:** Reduced weight.

Date	Mintage	F	VF	XF	Unc
1969	21,190,000	—	—	0.10	0.20
1970	19,930,000	—	—	0.10	0.20
1971	14,780,000	—	—	0.10	0.20
1972	17,960,000	—	—	0.10	0.20
1973	11,930,000	—	—	0.10	0.20

KM# 891.3 10 KURUS **Weight:** 2.5000 g. **Composition:** Bronze **Note:** Varieties exist.

Date	Mintage	F	VF	XF	Unc
1974	9,280,000	—	—	0.10	0.20

KM# 898.1 10 KURUS **Weight:** 3.5000 g. **Composition:** Bronze **Series:** F.A.O.

Date	Mintage	F	VF	XF	Unc
1971	630,000	—	0.10	0.15	0.75
1972	500,000	—	0.10	0.50	2.00
1973	10,000	—	4.00	10.00	30.00

KM# 898.2 10 KURUS **Weight:** 2.5000 g. **Composition:** Bronze

Date	Mintage	F	VF	XF	Unc
1974	605,000	—	0.10	0.50	1.00

KM# 898a 10 KURUS **Composition:** Aluminum

Date	Mintage	F	VF	XF	Unc
1975	517,000	—	0.10	0.25	0.75

KM# 908 10 KURUS **Composition:** Aluminum **Series:** F.A.O.

Date	Mintage	F	VF	XF	Unc
1976	17,000	—	0.50	2.00	5.00

KM# 935 10 KURUS **Composition:** Bronze **Series:** F.A.O.

Date	Mintage	F	VF	XF	Unc
1980	13,000	—	0.25	1.00	2.50

KM# 864 25 KURUS **Weight:** 3.0000 g. **Composition:** 0.8300 Silver .0801 oz. ASW

Date	Mintage	VG	F	VF	XF	Unc
1935	888,000	1.00	2.00	6.00	15.00	—
1936	10,576,000	1.00	2.00	10.00	20.00	—
1937	8,536,000	1.00	2.00	10.00	20.00	—

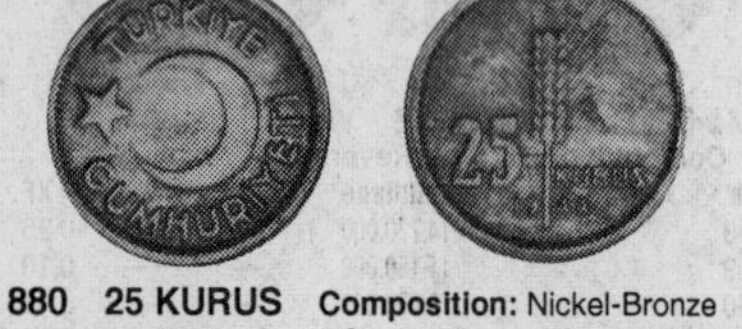

KM# 880 25 KURUS **Composition:** Nickel-Bronze

Date	Mintage	VG	F	VF	XF	Unc
1944	20,000,000	0.25	0.50	1.00	2.50	—
1945	5,328,000	0.50	1.00	1.50	3.00	—
1946	2,672,000	0.50	1.25	2.00	4.00	—

KM# 886 25 KURUS **Composition:** Brass

Date	Mintage	F	VF	XF	Unc
1948	18,000,000	0.10	0.20	0.40	1.25
1949	21,000,000	0.10	0.20	0.40	1.25
1951	2,000,000	0.25	0.50	2.50	10.00
1955	9,624,000	0.10	0.20	0.40	1.25
1956	14,376,000	0.10	0.20	0.40	1.25

KM# 886a 25 KURUS **Weight:** 10.0000 g. **Composition:** 0.9160 Gold .2945 oz. AGW **Series:** Nostalgia **Obverse:** Same as KM#886 **Reverse:** Same as KM#886 **Edge:** Plain **Size:** 22.6 mm.

Date	Mintage	F	VF	XF	Unc
1951	25,000	—	—	—	85.00

KM# 892.1 25 KURUS **Weight:** 5.0000 g. **Composition:** Stainless Steel **Obverse:** Smooth ground under woman's feet

Date	Mintage	F	VF	XF	Unc
1959	21,864,000	0.10	0.15	0.30	0.75

KM# 892.2 25 KURUS **Weight:** 5.0000 g. **Composition:** Stainless Steel **Obverse:** Rough ground under woman's feet

Date	Mintage	F	VF	XF	Unc
1960	14,778,000	—	0.10	0.15	0.70
1961	7,248,000	—	0.10	0.15	1.00
1962	10,722,000	—	0.10	0.15	0.80
1963	11,016,000	—	0.10	0.15	0.80
1964	13,962,000	—	0.10	0.15	0.70
1965	9,816,000	—	0.10	0.15	0.70
1966	2,424,000	—	0.10	0.15	0.80

KM# 892.3 25 KURUS **Weight:** 4.0000 g. **Composition:** Stainless Steel **Note:** Reduced weight

Date	Mintage	F	VF	XF	Unc
1966	7,596,000	—	—	0.10	0.50
1967	17,022,000	—	—	0.10	0.25
1968	31,482,000	—	—	0.10	0.25
1969	34,566,000	—	—	0.10	0.25
1970	32,960,000	—	—	0.10	0.25
1973	20,496,000	—	—	0.10	0.25
1974	16,602,000	—	—	0.10	0.25
1977	10,204,000	—	—	0.10	0.25
1978	185,000	0.35	0.75	1.25	2.00

KM# 865 50 KURUS **Weight:** 6.0000 g. **Composition:** 0.8300 Silver .1601 oz. ASW **Obverse:** Head of Kemal Atatürk left

Date	Mintage	VG	F	VF	XF	Unc
1935	630,000	3.00	6.00	10.00	25.00	—
1936	5,082,000	2.00	5.00	8.00	17.00	—
1937	4,270,000	12.00	30.00	50.00	100	—

KM# 882 50 KURUS **Weight:** 4.0000 g. **Composition:** 0.6000 Silver .0772 oz. ASW **Note:** Edge varieties exist.

Date	Mintage	F	VF	XF	Unc
1947	9,296,000	1.00	2.50	3.50	6.00
1948	12,704,000	1.00	2.50	3.50	6.00

KM# 899 50 KURUS **Composition:** Stainless Steel

Date	Mintage	F	VF	XF	Unc
1971	16,756,000	—	0.10	0.15	0.25
1972	22,152,000	—	0.10	0.15	0.25
1973	18,928,000	—	0.10	0.15	0.25
1974	14,480,000	—	0.10	0.15	0.25
1975	27,714,000	—	0.10	0.15	0.25
1976	27,476,000	—	0.10	0.15	0.25
1977	5,062,000	—	0.10	0.15	0.30
1979	3,714,000	—	0.10	0.15	0.30

KM# 913 50 KURUS **Composition:** Stainless Steel **Series:** F.A.O.

Date	Mintage	F	VF	XF	Unc
1978	10,000	—	0.20	0.50	1.75

KM# 925 50 KURUS **Composition:** Stainless Steel **Series:** F.A.O.

Date	Mintage	F	VF	XF	Un
1979	20,000	—	0.20	0.50	1.7

KM# 936 50 KURUS **Composition:** Stainless Steel **Series:** F.A.O.

Date	Mintage	F	VF	XF	Ur
1980	13,000	—	0.10	0.20	1.0

KM# 860.2 100 KURUS (Lira) **Weight:** 12.0000 g. **Composition:** 0.8300 Silver .3203 oz. ASW **Obverse:** Hea of Kemal Atatürk left **Reverse:** Low star

Date	VG	F	VF	XF	U
1934	10.00	20.00	30.00	50.00	

KM# 860.1 100 KURUS (Lira) **Weight:** 12.0000 g. **Composition:** 0.8300 Silver .3203 oz. ASW **Obverse:** He of Kemal Atatürk left **Reverse:** High star

Date	Mintage	VG	F	VF	XF
1934	718,000	15.00	30.00	40.00	75.00

KM# 860.1a 100 KURUS (Lira) **Weight:** 13.5000 g **Composition:** 0.9250 Silver .4015 oz. ASW **Series:** Nostalgia **Obverse:** Same as KM#860.1 **Reverse:** Same KM#860.1 **Edge:** Plain **Size:** 29.5 mm.

Date	Mintage	F	VF	XF	
1934 Matte	10,000	—	—	—	2(

KM# 941 1/2 LIRA **Weight:** 7.8600 g. **Composition** 0.9250 Silver .2337 oz. ASW **Subject:** 100th Anniversa Ataturk's Birth

Date	Mintage	F	VF	XF	
ND(1981)	25,000	—	—	—	1

KM# 941a 1/2 LIRA **Weight:** 8.0000 g. **Compositio** 0.9170 Gold .2358 oz. AGW **Subject:** 100th Anniversar Ataturk's Birth

Date	Mintage	F	VF	XF	Unc
ND(1981)	25,000	—	—	—	125

KM# 866 LIRA **Weight:** 12.0000 g. **Composition:** 0.8300 Silver .3203 oz. ASW **Subject:** Head of Kemal Atatürk left

Date	Mintage	VG	F	VF	XF	Unc
1937	1,624,000	5.00	10.00	15.00	32.00	—
1938	8,282,000	25.00	50.00	75.00	150	—
1939	376,000	5.00	10.00	15.00	32.00	—

KM# 869 LIRA **Weight:** 12.0000 g. **Composition:** 0.8300 Silver .3203 oz. ASW **Subject:** Head of Ismet Inonu left

Date	Mintage	VG	F	VF	XF	Unc
1940	253,000	7.50	12.50	15.00	25.00	—
1941	6,167,000	4.50	10.00	12.50	22.50	—

KM# 883 LIRA **Weight:** 7.5000 g. **Composition:** 0.6000 Silver .1447 oz. ASW **Note:** Edge varieties exist.

Date	Mintage	F	VF	XF	Unc
1947	11,104,000	1.50	3.50	5.00	8.50
1948	16,896,000	1.50	3.00	4.00	7.50

KM# 889 LIRA **Composition:** Copper-Nickel

Date	Mintage	F	VF	XF	Unc
1957	25,000,000	0.25	0.50	1.00	2.50

KM# 889a.1 LIRA **Weight:** 8.0000 g. **Composition:** Stainless Steel **Obverse:** Head of Kemal Atatürk left

ate	Mintage	F	VF	XF	Unc
959	7,452,000	—	0.10	0.20	0.50
960	11,436,000	—	0.10	0.20	0.50
961	2,100,000	—	0.10	0.20	1.00
962	4,228,000	—	0.10	0.20	0.50
963	4,316,000	—	0.10	0.20	0.50
964	4,976,000	—	0.10	0.20	0.50
965	5,348,000	—	0.10	0.20	0.50
966	8,040,000	—	0.10	0.20	0.50
967	—	—	0.10	0.20	0.50

KM# 889a.2 LIRA **Weight:** 7.0000 g. **Composition:** Stainless Steel **Obverse:** Head of Kemal Atatürk left **Note:** Reduced weight.

ate	Mintage	F	VF	XF	Unc
967	10,444,000	—	0.10	0.20	0.50
968	12,728,000	—	0.10	0.20	0.50

Date	Mintage	F	VF	XF	Unc
1969	6,612,000	—	0.10	0.20	0.50
1970	8,652,000	—	0.10	0.20	0.50
1971	10,504,000	—	0.10	0.20	0.50
1972	26,512,000	—	0.10	0.20	0.50
1973	12,596,000	—	0.10	0.20	0.50
1974	11,596,000	—	0.10	0.20	0.50
1975	20,348,000	—	0.10	0.20	0.50
1976	23,144,000	—	0.10	0.20	0.50
1977	30,244,000	—	0.10	0.20	0.50
1978	22,156,000	—	0.10	0.20	0.50
1979	9,289,000	—	0.10	0.20	0.50
1980	3,585,000	—	0.10	0.20	0.50

KM# 914 LIRA **Weight:** 8.0000 g. **Composition:** Stainless Steel **Series:** F.A.O.

Date	Mintage	F	VF	XF	Unc
1978	20,000	—	0.50	1.00	2.50

KM# 926 LIRA **Weight:** 8.0000 g. **Composition:** Stainless Steel **Series:** F.A.O. **Note:** Similar to 50 Kurus, KM#925.

Date	Mintage	F	VF	XF	Unc
1979	20,000	—	0.50	1.00	2.50

KM# 937 LIRA **Weight:** 8.0000 g. **Composition:** Stainless Steel **Series:** F.A.O.

Date	Mintage	F	VF	XF	Unc
1980	13,000	—	0.40	0.75	2.00

KM# 942 LIRA **Weight:** 16.0000 g. **Composition:** 0.9250 Silver **Subject:** 100th Anniversary of Ataturk's Birth **Reverse:** Head of Kemal Atatürk 3/4 right

Date	F	VF	XF	Unc
ND(1981)	—	—	—	22.50

KM# 942a LIRA **Weight:** 16.0000 g. **Composition:** 0.9170 Gold .4716 oz. AGW **Subject:** 100th Anniversary of Ataturk's Birth **Reverse:** Head of Kemal Atatürk 3/4 right

Date	Mintage	F	VF	XF	Unc
ND(1981)	25,000	—	—	—	250

KM# 943 LIRA **Composition:** Aluminum **Obverse:** Head of Kemal Atatürk left **Reverse:** Crescent opens left

Date	Mintage	F	VF	XF	Unc
1981	14,432,000	—	—	0.10	0.25

KM# 990 LIRA **Composition:** Aluminum **Obverse:** Head of Kemal Atatürk left, Similar to KM#943 **Reverse:** Crescent opens right with thin "1"

Date	Mintage	F	VF	XF	Unc
1982	799,000	—	—	0.10	0.25

KM# 962.1 LIRA **Composition:** Aluminum **Obverse:** Head of Kemal Atatürk left **Reverse:** Large (5mm) "1"

Date	Mintage	F	VF	XF	Unc
1984	498,000	—	—	0.10	0.20

KM# 962.2 LIRA **Composition:** Aluminum **Reverse:** Small (3.5mm) "1" **Note:** Varieties exist.

Date	Mintage	F	VF	XF	Unc
1985	712,000	—	—	0.10	0.20
1986	504,000	—	—	0.10	0.20
1987	500,000	—	—	0.10	0.20
1988	75,000	—	—	0.10	0.20
1989	10,000	—	—	0.10	0.20

KM# 893.1 2-1/2 LIRA **Weight:** 12.0000 g. **Composition:** Stainless Steel

Date	Mintage	F	VF	XF	Unc
1960	4,015,000	—	0.25	1.00	3.00
1961	1,222,000	—	0.25	1.00	6.00
1962	3,636,000	—	0.25	1.00	3.00
1963	3,108,000	—	0.25	1.00	3.00
1964	2,710,000	—	0.25	1.00	3.00
1965	1,246,000	—	0.25	1.00	4.00
1966	1,788,000	—	0.25	1.00	3.00
1967	5,333,000	—	0.25	1.00	3.00
1968	2,707,000	—	0.25	1.00	3.00

KM# 893.1a 2-1/2 LIRA **Weight:** 11.8000 g. **Composition:** 0.9250 Silver .3509 oz. ASW **Series:** Nostalgia **Obverse:** Same as KM#893.1 **Reverse:** Same as KM#893.1 **Edge:** Plain **Size:** 30 mm.

Date	Mintage	F	VF	XF	Unc
1965	10,000	—	—	—	20.00

KM# 893.2 2-1/2 LIRA **Weight:** 9.0000 g. **Composition:** Stainless Steel **Note:** Reduced weight. Varieties exist.

Date	Mintage	F	VF	XF	Unc
1969	1,378,000	—	0.15	0.75	2.00
1970	3,777,000	—	0.15	0.75	2.00
1971	2,170,000	—	0.15	0.75	2.00
1972	9,147,000	—	0.15	0.50	2.00
1973	4,348,000	—	0.15	0.50	3.00
1974	3,816,000	—	0.15	0.50	3.00
1975	9,811,000	—	0.15	0.50	2.50
1976	3,952,000	—	0.15	0.50	2.50
1977	21,473,000	—	0.10	0.25	0.50
1978	15,738,000	—	0.10	0.25	0.50
1979	6,074,000	—	0.10	0.25	0.50
1980	2,621,000	—	0.10	0.25	0.75

KM# 896 2-1/2 LIRA **Composition:** Stainless Steel **Series:** F.A.O.

Date	Mintage	F	VF	XF	Unc
1970	200,000	—	0.10	0.35	1.50

KM# 910 2-1/2 LIRA **Composition:** Stainless Steel **Series:** F.A.O.

Date	Mintage	F	VF	XF	Unc
1977	25,000	—	0.25	0.50	1.75

KM# 915 2-1/2 LIRA **Composition:** Stainless Steel **Series:** F.A.O.

Date	Mintage	F	VF	XF	Unc
1978	10,000	—	1.00	2.00	4.00

KM# 927 2-1/2 LIRA **Composition:** Stainless Steel **Series:** F.A.O.

Date	Mintage	F	VF	XF	Unc
1979	20,000	—	1.00	2.00	4.00

KM# 938 2-1/2 LIRA **Composition:** Stainless Steel **Series:** F.A.O.

Date	Mintage	F	VF	XF	Unc
1980	13,000	—	0.75	2.00	5.00

KM# 905 5 LIRA **Composition:** Stainless Steel

Date	Mintage	F	VF	XF	Unc
1974	2,842,000	—	0.15	0.75	3.00
1975	10,855,000	—	0.15	0.25	2.00
1976	17,532,000	—	0.15	0.25	2.00
1977	6,172,000	—	0.15	0.75	3.00
1978	76,000	1.50	2.50	3.50	6.00
1979	6,054,000	—	0.15	0.30	1.00

KM# 905a 5 LIRA **Weight:** 14.7000 g. **Composition:** 0.9250 Silver .4372 oz. ASW **Series:** Nostalgia **Obverse:** Same as KM#905 **Reverse:** Same as KM#905 **Edge:** Plain **Size:** 32.5 mm.

Date	Mintage	F	VF	XF	Unc
1975	10,000	—	—	—	20.00

KM# 909 5 LIRA **Composition:** Stainless Steel **Series:** International Women's Year; F.A.O.

Date	Mintage	F	VF	XF	Unc
1976	17,000	—	1.50	2.50	6.50

KM# 911 5 LIRA **Composition:** Stainless Steel **Series:** F.A.O.

Date	Mintage	F	VF	XF	Unc
1977	25,000	—	0.75	1.50	3.50

KM# 916 5 LIRA **Composition:** Stainless Steel **Series:** F.A.O.

Date	Mintage	F	VF	XF	Unc
1978	10,000	—	1.25	3.00	7.00

KM# 928 5 LIRA **Composition:** Stainless Steel **Series:** F.A.O.

Date	Mintage	F	VF	XF	Unc
1979	20,000	—	1.25	3.00	7.00

KM# 939 5 LIRA **Composition:** Stainless Steel **Series:** F.A.O.

Date	Mintage	F	VF	XF	Unc
1980	13,000	—	1.25	3.00	7.50

KM# 944 5 LIRA **Composition:** Aluminum **Reverse:** Crescent opens left

Date	Mintage	F	VF	XF	Unc
1981	61,605,000	—	—	0.15	0.35

KM# 949.1 5 LIRA **Composition:** Aluminum **Reverse:** Crescent opens right

Date	Mintage	F	VF	XF	Unc
1982	69,975,000	—	—	0.15	0.35

KM# 949.2 5 LIRA **Composition:** Aluminum **Reverse:** Bolder, larger "5"

Date	Mintage	F	VF	XF	Unc
1983	90,310,000	—	—	0.15	0.35

KM# 963 5 LIRA **Composition:** Aluminum **Obverse:** Head of Kemal Atatürk left **Note:** Varieties exist.

Date	Mintage	F	VF	XF	Unc
1984	17,316,000	—	—	0.15	0.35
1985	9,405,000	—	—	0.15	0.35
1986	9,575,000	—	—	0.20	0.50
1987	500,000	—	—	0.20	0.50
1988	100,000	—	—	0.20	0.50
1989	10,000	—	—	0.20	0.50

KM# 894 10 LIRA **Weight:** 15.0000 g. **Composition:** 0.8300 Silver .4003 oz. ASW **Subject:** 27th May Revolution **Obverse:** Head of Kemal Atatürk left

Date	Mintage	F	VF	XF	Unc
ND(1960)	4,000,000	—	3.00	4.00	8.00
ND(1960) Prooflike	—	—	—	—	12.00

KM# 945 10 LIRA **Composition:** Aluminum **Reverse:** Crescent opens left

Date	Mintage	F	VF	XF	Unc
1981	25,520,000	—	0.10	0.25	0.7

KM# 950.1 10 LIRA **Composition:** Aluminum **Reverse:** Crescent opens right

Date	Mintage	F	VF	XF	Unc
1982	17,092,000	—	0.10	0.25	0.

KM# 950.2 10 LIRA **Composition:** Aluminum

Date	Mintage	F	VF	XF	Unc
1983	2,228,000	—	0.10	0.25	0.

<M# 964 10 LIRA **Composition:** Aluminum **Obverse:** Head of Kemal Atatürk left **Note:** Varieties exist.

ate	Mintage	F	VF	XF	Unc
984	23,360,000	—	0.10	0.25	0.50
985	41,736,000	—	—	0.15	0.30
986	78,224,000	—	—	0.15	0.30
987	62,340,000	—	—	0.15	0.30
988	17,620,000	—	—	0.15	0.30
989	10,000	—	—	0.15	0.30

M# 946 20 LIRA **Composition:** Aluminum **Series:** World Food Day

te	Mintage	F	VF	XF	Unc
81	10,000	—	—	1.25	3.00

M# 965 20 LIRA **Composition:** Copper-Nickel

te	Mintage	F	VF	XF	Unc
34	1,644,000	—	0.10	0.25	1.00
39	—	—	0.10	0.25	1.00

 # 897 25 LIRA **Weight:** 14.6000 g. **Composition:** 0.8300 Silver .3896 oz. ASW **Subject:** 50th Anniversary of National Assembly

	Mintage	F	VF	XF	Unc
1970)	23,000	—	—	6.00	8.00
1970) Proof	Inc. above	Value: 14.00			

 # 975 25 LIRA **Composition:** Aluminum **Note:** Varieties exist.

	Mintage	F	VF	XF	Unc
	37,014,000	—	—	0.15	0.40
	49,611,000	—	—	0.15	0.40
	61,335,000	—	—	0.15	0.40
	39,540,000	—	—	0.15	0.40
	10,000	—	—	0.15	0.40

KM# 900 50 LIRA **Weight:** 19.0000 g. **Composition:** 0.8300 Silver .5070 oz. ASW **Subject:** 900th Anniversary - Battle of Malazgirt

Date	Mintage	F	VF	XF	Unc
ND(1971)	33,000	—	—	7.00	10.00
ND(1971) Proof	Inc. above	Value: 13.50			

KM# 901 50 LIRA **Weight:** 20.1000 g. **Composition:** 0.8300 Silver .5363 oz. ASW

Date	Mintage	F	VF	XF	Unc
ND(1972)	172,000	—	—	6.00	9.00
ND(1972) Proof	—	Value: 11.50			

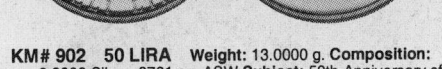

KM# 902 50 LIRA **Weight:** 13.0000 g. **Composition:** 0.9000 Silver .3761 oz. ASW **Subject:** 50th Anniversary of Republic

Date	Mintage	F	VF	XF	Unc
ND(1973)	70,000	—	—	5.00	8.00
ND(1973) Proof	Inc. above	Value: 11.50			

KM# 912 50 LIRA **Weight:** 8.8500 g. **Composition:** 0.8300 Silver .2361 oz. ASW **Series:** F.A.O.

Date	Mintage	F	VF	XF	Unc
1977	25,000	—	—	7.00	10.00

KM# 966 50 LIRA **Composition:** Copper-Nickel-Zinc **Obverse:** Head of Kemal Atatürk left **Note:** Varieties exist.

Date	Mintage	F	VF	XF	Unc
1984	14,731,000	—	0.10	0.25	0.60
1985	52,658,000	—	0.10	0.20	0.50
1986	80,656,000	—	0.10	0.20	0.50
1987	32,078,000	—	0.10	0.20	0.50

KM# 987 50 LIRA **Composition:** Aluminum-Bronze **Obverse:** Head of Kemal Atatürk left **Note:** Varieties exist.

Date	Mintage	F	VF	XF	Unc
1988	3,396,000	—	—	—	0.15
1989	25,463,000	—	—	—	0.15
1990	500,000	—	—	—	0.15
1991	10,000	—	—	—	0.15
1992	10,000	—	—	—	0.15
1993	5,000	—	—	—	0.35
1994	2,500	—	—	—	0.50

KM# 903 100 LIRA **Weight:** 22.0000 g. **Composition:** 0.9000 Silver .6367 oz. ASW **Subject:** 50th Anniversary of Republic

Date	Mintage	F	VF	XF	Unc
1973	65,000	—	—	8.00	15.00
1973 Prooflike	—	—	—	—	20.00

KM# 951 100 LIRA **Composition:** Copper-Nickel **Subject:** World Championship Soccer - Madrid

Date	Mintage	F	VF	XF	Unc
1982	100,000	0.75	1.50	3.00	6.00

KM# 967 100 LIRA **Composition:** Copper-Nickel-Zinc **Obverse:** Head of Kemal Atatürk left **Note:** Varieties exist.

Date	Mintage	F	VF	XF	Unc
1984	758,000	—	0.20	0.40	0.85
1985	866,000	—	0.20	0.40	0.85
1986	12,064,000	—	0.20	0.40	0.85
1987	91,400,000	—	0.15	0.25	0.65
1988	16,184,000	—	0.15	0.25	0.65

KM# 988 100 LIRA **Composition:** Aluminum-Bronze **Obverse:** Head of Kemal Atatürk left **Note:** Varieties exist.

Date	Mintage	F	VF	XF	Unc
1988	10,000,000	—	—	—	0.20
1989	233,750,000	—	—	—	0.20
1990	152,230,000	—	—	—	0.20
1991	49,160,000	—	—	—	0.20
1992	22,930,000	—	—	—	0.20
1993	3,700,000	—	—	—	0.20
1994	2,500	—	—	—	0.50

KM# 988a 100 LIRA **Weight:** 5.1000 g. **Composition:** 0.9250 Silver 0.1517 oz. ASW **Obverse:** Ataturk's portrait **Reverse:** Denomination in wreath **Edge:** Reeded **Size:** 21 mm.

Date	Mintage	F	VF	XF	Unc
1988 Proof	998	Value: 75.00			

KM# 917 150 LIRA **Weight:** 9.0000 g. **Composition:** 0.8000 Silver .2314 oz. ASW **Subject:** World Cup Soccer Championship

Date	Mintage	F	VF	XF	Unc
1978	5,000	—	—	—	22.50

KM# 918.1 150 LIRA **Weight:** 9.0000 g. **Composition:** 0.8000 Silver .2314 oz. ASW **Series:** F.A.O. **Edge:** Reeded

Date	Mintage	F	VF	XF	Unc
1978	10,000	—	—	—	6.50

KM# 918.2 150 LIRA **Weight:** 9.0000 g. **Composition:** 0.8000 Silver .2314 oz. ASW **Series:** F.A.O. **Edge:** Lettered

Date	Mintage	F	VF	XF	Unc
1978 Proof	2,500	Value: 22.50			

KM# 929.1 150 LIRA **Weight:** 9.0000 g. **Composition:** 0.8000 Silver .2314 oz. ASW **Series:** F.A.O. **Edge:** Reeded

Date	Mintage	F	VF	XF	Unc
1979	10,000	—	—	—	6.50

KM# 929.2 150 LIRA **Weight:** 9.0000 g. **Composition:** 0.8000 Silver .2314 oz. ASW **Series:** F.A.O. **Edge:** Lettered

Date	Mintage	F	VF	XF	Unc
1979 Proof	2,500	Value: 22.50			

KM# 919 200 LIRA **Weight:** 9.0000 g. **Composition:** 0.8300 Silver .2402 oz. ASW **Subject:** 705th Anniversary - Death of Jalaladdin Rumi

Date	Mintage	F	VF	XF	Unc
1978	10,000	—	—	—	12.00
1978 Proof	1,000	Value: 25.00			

KM# 904 500 LIRA **Weight:** 6.0000 g. **Composition:** 0.9170 Gold .1769 oz. AGW **Subject:** 50th Anniversary of Republic

Date	Mintage	F	VF	XF	Unc
1973	30,000	—	—	—	100

KM# 920 500 LIRA **Weight:** 8.0000 g. **Composition:** 0.9170 Gold .2358 oz. AGW **Series:** F.A.O.

Date	Mintage	F	VF	XF	Unc
1978 Proof	650	Value: 200			

KM# 921 500 LIRA **Weight:** 8.0000 g. **Composition:** 0.9170 Gold .2358 oz. AGW **Subject:** 705th Anniversary - Death of Jalaladdin Rumi

Date	Mintage	F	VF	XF	Unc
1978 Proof	900	Value: 200			

KM# 930 500 LIRA **Weight:** 8.0000 g. **Composition:** 0.9170 Gold .2358 oz. AGW **Series:** F.A.O.

Date	Mintage	F	VF	XF	Unc
1979 Proof	783	Value: 200			

KM# 931 500 LIRA **Weight:** 23.3300 g. **Composition:** 0.9250 Silver .6938 oz. ASW **Subject:** UNICEF and I.Y.C.

Date	Mintage	F	VF	XF	Unc
1979(1981) Proof	10,000	Value: 20.00			

KM# 940.1 500 LIRA **Weight:** 9.0000 g. **Composition:** 0.9000 Silver .2604 oz. ASW **Series:** F.A.O. **Edge:** Reeded

Date	Mintage	F	VF	XF	Unc
1980	13,000	—	—	—	7.50

KM# 940.2 500 LIRA **Weight:** 9.0000 g. **Composition:** 0.9000 Silver .2604 oz. ASW **Edge:** Lettered

Date	Mintage	F	VF	XF	Unc
1980 Proof	4,000	Value: 20.00			

KM# 952 500 LIRA **Weight:** 23.3300 g. **Composition:** 0.9250 Silver .6938 oz. ASW **Subject:** World Championshi Soccer - Madrid

Date	Mintage	F	VF	XF	U
1982 Proof	12,000	Value: 18.00			

KM# 953 500 LIRA **Weight:** 23.3300 g. **Compositio** 0.9250 Silver .6938 oz. ASW **Subject:** World Championsh Soccer - Madrid

Date	Mintage	F	VF	XF
1982 Proof	12,000	Value: 18.00		

KM# 957 500 LIRA **Composition:** Copper-Nickel **Subject:** Lydia - First Coin in the World

Date	Mintage	F	VF	XF
1983	3,542	—	—	6.50

968 **500 LIRA** **Composition:** Copper-Nickel
ubject: FAO World Fisheries Conference **Obverse:** enomination **Reverse:** Fish

	Mintage	F	VF	XF	Unc
84)	3,000	—	—	6.50	17.50

968a **500 LIRA** **Weight:** 28.2800 g. **Composition:** .9250 Silver .8411 oz. ASW **Series:** World Fisheries Conference

	Mintage	F	VF	XF	Unc
84) Proof	763,000	Value: 75.00			

968b **500 LIRA** **Weight:** 47.5400 g. **Composition:** .9170 Gold 1.4009 oz. AGW **Subject:** World Fisheries Conference

	Mintage	F	VF	XF	Unc
84) Proof	74	Value: 1,250			

979 **500 LIRA** **Composition:** Copper-Nickel
Subject: 40th Anniversary of F.A.O.

	Mintage	F	VF	XF	Unc
86) Proof	3,000	Value: 10.00			

989 **500 LIRA** **Composition:** Aluminum-Bronze
Obverse: Head of Kemal Atatürk left **Note:** Varieties exist.

Mintage	F	VF	XF	Unc
141,813,000	—	—	—	0.60
100,114,000	—	—	—	0.60
30,006,000	—	—	—	0.60
10,000	—	—	—	0.60
5,000	—	—	—	0.75
2,500	—	—	—	0.85
2,500	—	—	—	0.85
10,000	—	—	—	0.60
—	—	—	—	0.60

989a **500 LIRA** **Weight:** 7.6000 g. **Composition:** 0.9250 Silver 0.226 oz. ASW **Obverse:** Ataturk's portrait **Reverse:** Denomination in wreath **Edge:** Reeded **Size:** 24 mm.

	Mintage	F	VF	XF	Unc
Proof	998	Value: 75.00			

KM# 922 1000 LIRA **Weight:** 16.0000 g. **Composition:** 0.9170 Gold .4717 oz. AGW **Series:** F.A.O.

Date	Mintage	F	VF	XF	Unc
1978 Proof	650	Value: 375			

KM# 923 1000 LIRA **Weight:** 16.0000 g. **Composition:** 0.9170 Gold .4717 oz. AGW **Subject:** 705th Anniversary - Death of Rumi

Date	Mintage	F	VF	XF	Unc
1978 Proof	450	Value: 375			

KM# 932 1000 LIRA **Weight:** 16.0000 g. **Composition:** 0.9170 Gold .4717 oz. AGW **Series:** F.A.O.

Date	Mintage	F	VF	XF	Unc
1979 Proof	900	Value: 375			

KM# 985 1000 LIRA **Composition:** Nickel-Bronze
Subject: Peace

Date	F	VF	XF	Unc
1986 Proof	—	Value: 12.00		

KM# 980 1000 LIRA **Composition:** Copper-Nickel
Subject: Shelter for the Homeless

Date	F	VF	XF	Unc
ND(1987) Proof	—	Value: 10.00		

KM# 991 1000 LIRA **Composition:** Copper-Nickel
Subject: 400th Anniversary - Death of Architect Sinan
Reverse: City view

Date	F	VF	XF	Unc
ND(1988) Proof	—	Value: 10.00		

KM# 996 1000 LIRA **Composition:** Copper-Zinc-Nickel
Subject: Environmental Protection

Date	Mintage	F	VF	XF	Unc
1990	500,000	—	—	—	8.50

KM# 997 1000 LIRA **Composition:** Copper-Zinc-Nickel
Obverse: Head of Kemal Atatürk left **Reverse:** Denomination

Date	Mintage	F	VF	XF	Unc
1990	136,480,000	—	0.15	0.25	2.00
1991	110,245,000	—	0.15	0.25	2.00
1992	15,820,000	—	0.15	0.25	2.00

Date	Mintage	F	VF	XF	Unc
1993	11,675,000	—	0.15	0.25	2.00
1994	61,515,000	—	0.15	0.25	2.00

KM# 1028 1000 LIRA **Composition:** Bronze Clad Brass
Obverse: Head of Kemal Atatürk left

Date	Mintage	F	VF	XF	Unc
1995	36,820,000	—	—	—	1.00
1996	3,900,000	—	—	—	1.00
1997	—	—	—	—	1.00

KM# 947 1500 LIRA **Weight:** 16.0000 g. **Composition:** 0.9250 Silver .4758 oz. ASW **Series:** F.A.O.

Date	Mintage	F	VF	XF	Unc
1981	6,000	—	—	—	18.50
1982	500	—	—	—	37.50

KM# 958 1500 LIRA **Weight:** 16.0000 g. **Composition:** 0.9250 Silver .4758 oz. ASW **Series:** FAO World Food Day
Reverse: Goat nursing young ones

Date	Mintage	F	VF	XF	Unc
1983 Proof	1,552	Value: 40.00			

KM# 1015 2500 LIRA **Composition:** Nickel-Bronze
Obverse: Head of Kemal Atatürk left

Date	Mintage	F	VF	XF	Unc
1991	22,938,000	0.10	0.25	0.50	3.00
1992	48,784,000	0.10	0.25	0.50	3.00
1993	2,310,000	0.10	0.25	0.50	3.00
1994	2,500	0.10	0.25	0.50	4.50
1995	2,500	0.10	0.25	0.50	4.50
1996	10,000	0.10	0.25	0.50	3.00
1997	—	0.10	0.25	0.50	3.00

KM# 948 3000 LIRA **Weight:** 28.2800 g. **Composition:** 0.9250 Silver .8411 oz. ASW **Series:** International Year of Disabled Persons

Date	Mintage	F	VF	XF	Unc
1981	14,000	—	—	—	45.00
1981 Proof	16,000	Value: 55.00			

KM# 959 3000 LIRA **Weight:** 28.2800 g. **Composition:** 0.9250 Silver .8411 oz. ASW **Series:** International Year of the Scout **Reverse:** Mountain, trees, river, with a pitched tent

Date	Mintage	F	VF	XF	Unc
ND(1982)	12,000	—	—	—	45.00
ND(1982) Proof	14,000	Value: 55.00			

KM# 970 5000 LIRA **Weight:** 23.3300 g. **Composition:** 0.9250 Silver .6939 oz. ASW **Series:** 1984 Summer Olympics **Reverse:** Olympic athletes around center circle with stylized flame

Date	Mintage	F	VF	XF	Unc
ND(1984) Proof	5,343	Value: 22.50			

KM# 976 5000 LIRA **Weight:** 23.3300 g. **Composition:** 0.9250 Silver .6939 oz. ASW **Subject:** 500th Anniversary of Turkish Navy **Reverse:** Man with Turkish headdress at right, old fleet of masted ships at left

Date	Mintage	F	VF	XF	Un
ND(1985) Proof	1,000	Value: 80.00			

KM# 960 3000 LIRA **Weight:** 16.0000 g. **Composition:** 0.9250 Silver .4758 oz. ASW **Subject:** 60th Anniversary of the Republic **Obverse:** Head of Kemal Atatürk left

Date	Mintage	F	VF	XF	Unc
ND(1983) Proof	4,000	Value: 35.00			

KM# 954 5000 LIRA **Weight:** 7.1300 g. **Composition:** 0.5000 Gold .1146 oz. AGW **Subject:** World Championship Soccer - Madrid **Obverse:** Soccer player kicking the ball **Reverse:** World globe with Spanya '82 across middle

Date	Mintage	F	VF	XF	Unc
ND(1982) Proof	2,400	Value: 135			

KM# 971 5000 LIRA **Weight:** 23.3300 g. **Composition:** 0.9250 Silver .6939 oz. ASW **Series:** 1984 Winter Olympics **Reverse:** Stylized slalom, bobsledder, ski jumper, and figure skater in inner circle, legend around

Date	Mintage	F	VF	XF	Unc
1984 Proof	4,657	Value: 50.00			

KM# 977 5000 LIRA **Weight:** 23.3300 g. **Compositio** 0.9250 Silver .6939 oz. ASW **Subject:** Forestry Conferenc - Mexico **Reverse:** Trees

Date	Mintage	F	VF	XF	U
1985 Proof	2,000	Value: 25.00			

KM# 969 5000 LIRA **Weight:** 23.3300 g. **Composition:** 0.9250 Silver .6939 oz. ASW **Subject:** Decade for Women **Reverse:** Stylized woman holding dove

Date	Mintage	F	VF	XF	Unc
1984 Proof	20,000	Value: 35.00			

KM# 972 5000 LIRA **Weight:** 23.3300 g. **Composition:** 0.9250 Silver .6939 oz. ASW **Subject:** 50th Anniversary of Women's Suffrage **Reverse:** Three women

Date	Mintage	F	VF	XF	Unc
ND(1984) Proof	1,000	Value: 65.00			

KM# 978 5000 LIRA **Weight:** 23.3300 g. **Compositi** 0.9250 Silver .6939 oz. ASW **Subject:** Youth Year

Date	Mintage	F	VF	XF
1985 Proof	2,000	Value: 25.00		

KM# 1011 5000 LIRA **Weight:** 23.3300 g. **Composition:** 0.9250 Silver .6939 oz. ASW **Subject:** Architect - Sinan

Date		F	VF	XF
ND(1988) Proof	—	Value: 35.00		

1005 5000 LIRA **Composition:** Copper-Nickel
Subject: Yunus Emre Sevgi Yili

Date	F	VF	XF	Unc
Proof	—	Value: 7.50		

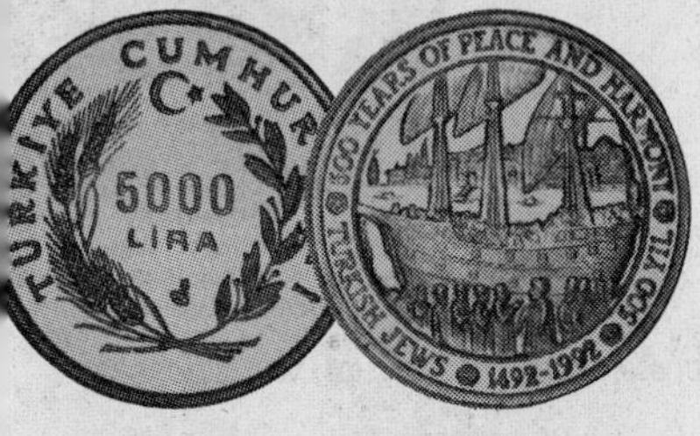

1018 5000 LIRA **Composition:** Copper-Nickel
Subject: Turkish Jews

Date	F	VF	XF	Unc
992) Proof	—	Value: 8.50		

1025 5000 LIRA **Composition:** Nickel-Bronze
Obverse: Head of Kemal Atatürk left

Date	Mintage	F	VF	XF	Unc
	24,904,000	0.10	0.25	0.50	3.00
Proof	—	Value: 6.50			
	15,872,000	0.10	0.25	0.50	3.00
	69,504,000	0.10	0.25	0.50	3.00

1029.1 (KM1029) 5000 LIRA **Composition:**
Brass **Obverse:** Head of Kemal Atatürk left

Date	Mintage	F	VF	XF	Unc
5 Large date	69,550,000	—	—	—	1.50
5 Large date	69,550,000	—	—	—	1.50
5 Small date	Inc. above	—	—	—	0.75
5 Small date	Inc. above	—	—	—	0.75
6	80,506,000	—	—	—	0.75
6	80,506,000	—	—	—	0.75
7	—	—	—	—	0.75
7	—	—	—	—	0.75
8	—	—	—	—	0.75
8	—	—	—	—	0.75
9	—	—	—	—	0.75
9	—	—	—	—	0.75

1029.2 5000 LIRA **Weight:** 3.5000 g. **Composition:** Brass **Obverse:** Head of Kemal Atatürk left **Reverse:** Flower and denomination **Edge:** Reeded **Size:** 19.5 mm. **Note:** Reduced weight version of KM#1029.1

Date	F	VF	XF	Unc
9	—	—	—	0.75

933 10000 LIRA (10 Bin Lira) **Weight:** 17.1700 g. **Composition:** 0.9000 Gold .4900 oz. AGW **Subject:** UNICEF and I.Y.C. **Note:** Similar to 500 Lira, KM#931

Date	Mintage	F	VF	XF	Unc
9(1981) Proof	4,450	Value: 225			

KM# 986 10000 LIRA (10 Bin Lira) Weight: 23.3300 g. **Composition:** 0.9250 Silver .6939 oz. ASW **Subject:** 1986 World Cup Soccer - Mexico

Date	Mintage	F	VF	XF	Unc
1986 Proof	5,000	Value: 18.50			

KM# 1009 10000 LIRA (10 Bin Lira) Weight: 23.3300 g. **Composition:** 0.9250 Silver .6939 oz. ASW **Subject:** 1986 World Cup Soccer **Reverse:** Cactus

Date	Mintage	F	VF	XF	Unc
1986 Proof	7,000	Value: 16.50			

KM# 1010 10000 LIRA (10 Bin Lira) Weight: 23.3300 g. **Composition:** 0.9250 Silver .6939 oz. ASW **Subject:** A. Ersoy - Poet

Date	F	VF	XF	Unc
1986 Proof	—	Value: 35.00		

KM# 1022 10000 LIRA (10 Bin Lira) Weight: 23.3300 g. **Composition:** 0.9250 Silver .6939 oz. ASW **Subject:** World Peace **Reverse:** Dove of Peace in square

Date	Mintage	F	VF	XF	Unc
1986 Proof	Est. 1,200	Value: 60.00			

KM# 981 10000 LIRA (10 Bin Lira) Weight: 22.9700 g. **Composition:** 0.9250 Silver .6832 oz. ASW **Subject:** Shelter for the Homeless

Date	F	VF	XF	Unc
ND(1987) Proof	—	Value: 35.00		

KM# 982 10000 LIRA (10 Bin Lira) Weight: 22.9700 g. **Composition:** 0.9250 Silver .6832 oz. ASW **Subject:** 130 Years of Turkish Forestry

Date	Mintage	F	VF	XF	Unc
ND(1987) Proof	5,000	Value: 40.00			

KM# 983 10000 LIRA (10 Bin Lira) Weight: 23.3300 g. **Composition:** 0.9250 Silver .6939 oz. ASW **Series:** Winter Olympics **Reverse:** Bear holding torch

Date	Mintage	F	VF	XF	Unc
1988 Proof	Est. 10,000	Value: 32.50			

KM# 984 10000 LIRA (10 Bin Lira) Weight: 23.3300 g. **Composition:** 0.9250 Silver .6939 oz. ASW **Series:** 1988 Summer Olympics **Reverse:** Torch

Date	Mintage	F	VF	XF	Unc
1988	—	—	—	—	35.00
1988 Proof	Est. 10,000	Value: 27.50			

KM# 1027.1 10000 LIRA (10 Bin Lira) **Weight:** 9.7500 g. **Composition:** Copper-Nickel-Zinc **Obverse:** Head of Kemal Atatürk left **Edge:** Reeded with legend **Edge Lettering:** TURKIYE CUMHURIYETI

Date	Mintage	F	VF	XF	Unc
1994	17,319,000	—	0.10	0.25	3.00
1995	56,584,000	—	0.10	0.25	3.00
1996	119,572,000	—	0.10	0.25	3.00
1997	—	—	0.10	0.25	3.00

KM# 1042 10000 LIRA (10 Bin Lira) **Composition:** Copper-Nickel-Zinc **Series:** 1994 Olympics

Date	Mintage	F	VF	XF	Unc
1994	500,000	—	—	—	3.75

KM# 1027.2 10000 LIRA (10 Bin Lira) **Weight:** 6.7500 g. **Composition:** Copper-Nickel-Zinc **Edge:** "TC" six times between reeded sections **Note:** Thin planchet. Edge varieties exist.

Date	F	VF	XF	Unc
1998	—	0.10	0.25	3.00
1999	—	0.10	0.25	3.00

KM# 1027.3 10000 LIRA (10 Bin Lira) **Composition:** Copper-Nickel-Zinc **Note:** Like KM#1027.2 but edge: "T.C." repeated twice in groups of three.

Date	F	VF	XF	Unc
1998	—	—	—	—

KM# 998 20000 LIRA (20 Bin Lira) **Weight:** 23.3200 g. **Composition:** 0.9250 Silver .6938 oz. ASW **Subject:** Environmental Protection

Date	Mintage	F	VF	XF	Unc
1988 Proof	Est. 5,000	Value: 40.00			

KM# 1001 20000 LIRA (20 Bin Lira) **Weight:** 23.3200 g. **Composition:** 0.9250 Silver .6938 oz. ASW **Subject:** 400th Anniversary - Death of Architect Sinan **Note:** Similar to 1000 Lira, KM#991.

Date	Mintage	F	VF	XF	Unc
ND(1988) Proof	Est. 5,000	Value: 37.50			

KM# 1003 20000 LIRA (20 Bin Lira) **Weight:** 23.3200 g. **Composition:** 0.9250 Silver .6938 oz. ASW **Subject:** Teacher's Day **Note:** Similar to 200,000 Lira, KM#1004.

Date	Mintage	F	VF	XF	Unc
1989 Proof	1,013	Value: 37.50			

KM# 1013 20000 LIRA (20 Bin Lira) **Weight:** 23.3200 g. **Composition:** 0.9250 Silver .6938 oz. ASW **Subject:** Istanbul Metro **Reverse:** City view

Date	Mintage	F	VF	XF	Unc
ND(1989) Proof	Est. 5,000	Value: 75.00			

KM# 992 20000 LIRA (20 Bin Lira) **Weight:** 23.3200 g. **Composition:** 0.9250 Silver .6938 oz. ASW **Subject:** 1990 World Cup Soccer

Date	Mintage	F	VF	XF	Unc
1990 Proof	14,000	Value: 25.00			

KM# 993 20000 LIRA (20 Bin Lira) **Weight:** 23.3200 g. **Composition:** 0.9250 Silver .6938 oz. ASW **Subject:** 75th Anniversary - Battle of Gallipoli

Date	Mintage	F	VF	XF	Unc
ND(1990) Proof	Est. 5,000	Value: 30.00			

KM# 995 20000 LIRA (20 Bin Lira) **Weight:** 23.3200 g. **Composition:** 0.9250 Silver .6938 oz. ASW **Subject:** Soccer

Date	Mintage	F	VF	XF	U
1990 Proof	14,000	Value: 25.00			

KM# 1014 20000 LIRA (20 Bin Lira) **Weight:** 23.3200 g. **Composition:** 0.9250 Silver .6938 oz. ASW **Subject:** 70th Anniversary of Parliament

Date	Mintage	F	VF	XF	U
1990 Proof	Est. 5,000	Value: 27.50			

KM# 1057 20000 LIRA (20 Bin Lira) **Weight:** 23.3200 g. **Composition:** 0.9250 Silver .6938 oz. ASW

Series: Summer Olympics **Obverse:** National emblem
Reverse: Bicyclist

	F	VF	XF	Unc
990) Proof	—	Value: 30.00		

 # 1077 20000 LIRA (20 Bin Lira) Weight: 23.4200 g. **Composition:** 0.9250 Silver .6965 oz. ASW **Series:** Olympics **Subject:** Speed Skating **Obverse:** Denomination in wreath **Reverse:** Speed skater

	F	VF	XF	Unc
990) Proof	—	Value: 30.00		

 # 1041 25000 LIRA (25 Bin Lira) Composition: Copper-Nickel-Zinc **Edge:** Lettered TC and flower five times

	Mintage	F	VF	XF	Unc
5	13,740,000	0.20	0.30	0.50	3.00
	59,742,000	0.20	0.30	0.50	3.00
	—	0.20	0.30	0.50	3.00
	—	0.20	0.30	0.50	3.00
	—	0.20	0.30	0.50	3.00
	—	0.20	0.30	0.50	3.00

 # 1043 25000 LIRA (25 Bin Lira) Composition: Copper-Nickel-Zinc **Series:** Environmental Protection **Reverse:** Three human heads

	Mintage	F	VF	XF	Unc
5	500,000	—	—	—	5.00

 # 1104 25000 LIRA (25 Bin Lira) Weight: 2.7000 g. **Composition:** Copper-Zinc **Obverse:** Bust of Kemal Atatürk **Reverse:** Denomination **Edge:** Plain **Size:** 17 mm.

	F	VF	XF	Unc
	—	—	—	2.50

 # 955 30000 LIRA Weight: 15.9800 g. **Composition:** 0.9170 Gold .4712 oz. AGW **Series:** International Year of Disabled Persons

	Mintage	F	VF	XF	Unc
	4,000	—	—	—	400
1 Proof	3,000	Value: 450			

KM# 961 30000 LIRA Weight: 15.9800 g. **Composition:** 0.9170 Gold .4712 oz. AGW **Series:** International Year of the Scout **Obverse:** Denomination within sprays

Date	Mintage	F	VF	XF	Unc
ND(1983)	2,000	—	—	—	450
ND(1983) Proof	2,000	Value: 500			

KM# 973 50000 LIRA Weight: 7.1300 g. **Composition:** 0.9000 Gold .2063 oz. AGW **Series:** Decade for Women

Date	Mintage	F	VF	XF	Unc
1984 Proof	800	Value: 135			

KM# 999 50000 LIRA Weight: 28.2800 g. **Composition:** 0.9250 Silver .8411 oz. ASW **Series:** Winter Olympics **Reverse:** Speed skater

Date	Mintage	F	VF	XF	Unc
ND(1990) Proof	15,000	Value: 30.00			

KM# 1000 50000 LIRA Weight: 28.2800 g. **Composition:** 0.9250 Silver .8411 oz. ASW **Series:** 1990 Summer Olympics **Reverse:** Bicyclist

Date	Mintage	F	VF	XF	Unc
ND(1990) Proof	15,000	Value: 30.00			

KM# 1006 50000 LIRA Weight: 22.8700 g. **Composition:** 0.9250 Silver .6801 oz. ASW **Subject:** Yunus Emre Sevgi Yili

Date	Mintage	F	VF	XF	Unc
1991 Proof	5,000	Value: 28.00			

KM# 1007 50000 LIRA Weight: 22.8700 g. **Composition:** 0.9250 Silver .6801 oz. ASW **Subject:** Mozart Opera

Date	Mintage	F	VF	XF	Unc
ND(1991) Proof	5,000	Value: 30.00			

KM# 1019 50000 LIRA Weight: 22.7700 g. **Composition:** 0.9250 Silver .6772 oz. ASW **Subject:** Hmet Adnan Saygun - Musician

Date		F	VF	XF	Unc
ND(1991) Proof	—	Value: 30.00			

KM# 1016 50000 LIRA Weight: 23.3300 g. **Composition:** 0.9250 Silver .6858 oz. ASW **Subject:** Turkish Jews

Date	Mintage	F	VF	XF	Unc
ND(1992) Proof	Est. 5,000	Value: 25.00			

KM# 1023 50000 LIRA Weight: 23.0800 g. **Composition:** 0.9250 Silver .6184 oz. ASW **Subject:** 200th Birthday of Rossini

Date		F	VF	XF	Unc
ND(1992) Proof	—	Value: 25.00			

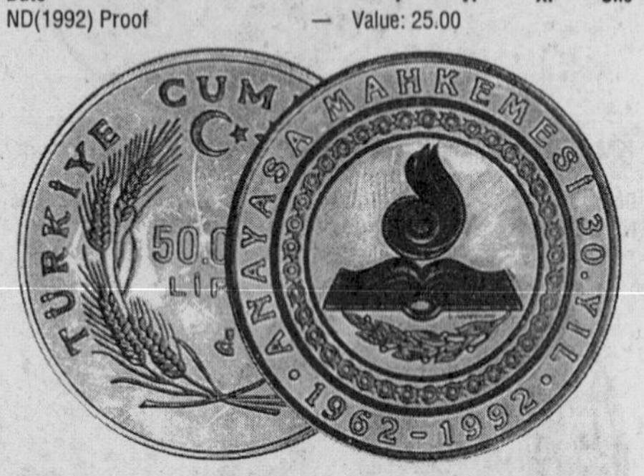

KM# 1136 50000 LIRA Weight: 23.1600 g. **Composition:** 0.9250 Silver 0.6888 oz. ASW **Subject:** 30th Anniversary - Constitution **Obverse:** Denomination **Reverse:** Flame above open book **Edge:** Reeded **Size:** 38.6 mm.

Date	F	VF	XF	Unc
ND(1992) Proof	—	—	—	—

KM# 1020 50000 LIRA Weight: 23.0800 g. **Composition:** 0.9250 Silver .6184 oz. ASW **Subject:** 1994 World Cup Soccer **Reverse:** Torch with ball

Date	Mintage	F	VF	XF	Unc
ND(1993) Proof	Est. 20,000	Value: 28.00			

KM# 1021.1 50000 LIRA Weight: 23.0800 g. **Composition:** 0.9250 Silver .6184 oz. ASW **Subject:** 1994 World Cup Soccer **Reverse:** Bridge behind player, fuzzy looking rock under bridge

Date		F	VF	XF	Unc
ND(1993)		—	—	—	75.00
ND(1993) Proof	Est. 20,000	Value: 25.00			

KM# 1021.2 50000 LIRA Weight: 23.0800 g. **Composition:** 0.9250 Silver .6184 oz. ASW **Subject:** 1994 World Cup Soccer **Reverse:** Bridge behind player, sharp looking rock under bridge

Date	Mintage	F	VF	XF	Unc
ND(1993) Proof	1,000	Value: 40.00			

KM# 1044 50000 LIRA Weight: 23.0800 g. **Composition:** 0.9250 Silver .6184 oz. ASW **Subject:** 125 Years - Turkish Supreme Court

Date		F	VF	XF	Unc
ND(1993) Proof	—	Value: 30.00			

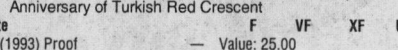

KM# 1024 50000 LIRA Weight: 23.0800 g. **Composition:** 0.9250 Silver .6184 oz. ASW **Subject:** 25th Anniversary of Turkish Red Crescent

Date		F	VF	XF	Unc
ND(1993) Proof	—	Value: 25.00			

KM# 1026 50000 LIRA Weight: 22.8400 g. **Composition:** 0.9250 Silver .6793 oz. ASW **Series:** Olympics **Reverse:** Flag and rings

Date	Mintage	F	VF	XF
ND(1994) Proof	5,000	Value: 25.00		

KM# 1030 50000 LIRA Weight: 31.4700 g. **Composition:** 0.9250 Silver .9359 oz. ASW **Series:** Endangered Wildlife **Reverse:** Ibis

Date	Mintage	F	VF	XF
ND(1994) Proof	10,000	Value: 20.00		

KM# 1031 50000 LIRA Weight: 23.3300 g. **Composition:** 0.9250 Silver .6938 oz. ASW **Subject:** Tschaikovsky

Date	Mintage	F	VF	XF
ND(1994) Proof	5,000	Value: 27.50		

KM# 1033 50000 LIRA **Weight:** 23.3300 g. **Composition:** 0.9250 Silver .6938 oz. ASW **Subject:** 75th Anniversary - Turkish National Assembly

Date	Mintage	F	VF	XF	Unc
1995 Proof	10,000	Value: 25.00			

KM# 1035 50000 LIRA **Weight:** 23.3300 g. **Composition:** 0.9250 Silver .6938 oz. ASW **Subject:** 150th Anniversary - National Police

ate	Mintage	F	VF	XF	Unc
995 Proof	10,000	Value: 22.50			

M# 1037 50000 LIRA **Composition:** Brass **Reverse:** Sea turtle **Note:** Oxidized finish

te	Mintage	F	VF	XF	Unc
95	10,000	—	—	—	17.50

M# 1037a 50000 LIRA **Weight:** 23.3300 g. **Composition:** 0.9250 Silver .6938 oz. ASW **Reverse:** Sea turtle

te	Mintage	F	VF	XF	Unc
95 Proof	15,000	Value: 25.00			

M# 1038 50000 LIRA **Weight:** 23.3300 g. **Composition:** 0.9250 Silver .6938 oz. ASW **Reverse:** Sailing ship - "Piri Reis"

	Mintage	F	VF	XF	Unc
5 Proof	15,000	Value: 27.50			

KM# 1040 50000 LIRA **Weight:** 23.3300 g. **Composition:** 0.9250 Silver .6938 oz. ASW **Series:** 50th Anniversary - F.A.O.

Date	Mintage	F	VF	XF	Unc
1995 Proof	15,000	Value: 25.00			

KM# 1045 50000 LIRA **Weight:** 31.4700 g. **Composition:** 0.9250 Silver .9359 oz. ASW **Series:** Summer Olympics **Reverse:** Wrestlers

Date	Mintage	F	VF	XF	Unc
1995 Proof	15,000	Value: 30.00			

KM# 1050 50000 LIRA **Composition:** Copper-Nickel-Zinc **Series:** F.A.O. **Edge:** "T.C." and four fleur-de-lis repeated four times

Date	Mintage	F	VF	XF	Unc
ND(1996)	500,000	—	—	—	4.50

KM# 1056 50000 LIRA **Composition:** Copper-Nickel-Zinc **Obverse:** Bust **Reverse:** Denomination

Date	Mintage	F	VF	XF	Unc
1996	11,916,000	—	—	—	3.50
1997	—	—	—	—	3.50
1998	—	—	—	—	3.50
1999	—	—	—	—	3.50
2000	—	—	—	—	3.50

KM# 1103 50000 LIRA **Composition:** Aluminum **Series:** F.A.O **Obverse:** Denomination **Reverse:** Ancient vintner **Edge:** Plain **Size:** 20 mm.

Date	F	VF	XF	Unc
1999	—	—	—	0.75

KM# 1105 50000 LIRA **Weight:** 3.2000 g. **Composition:** Copper-Nickel-Zinc **Obverse:** Ataturk's portrait **Reverse:** Denomination **Edge:** Plain **Size:** 17.75 mm.

Date	F	VF	XF	Unc
2001	—	—	—	3.00
2002	—	—	—	3.00

KM# 956 100000 LIRA **Weight:** 33.8200 g. **Composition:** 0.9170 Gold .9972 oz. AGW **Subject:** Islamic World 15th Century

Date	Mintage	F	VF	XF	Unc
1982 Proof	12,000	Value: 650			

KM# 1078 100000 LIRA **Composition:** Copper-Nickel-Zinc **Subject:** 75th Anniversary of Republic **Obverse:** Denomination **Reverse:** Bust of Kemal Atatürk right

Date	F	VF	XF	Unc
1999	—	—	—	3.00
2000	—	—	—	3.00

KM# 1079 100000 LIRA **Composition:** Copper-Nickel-Zinc **Subject:** 75th Anniversary of Republic **Obverse:** Denomination **Reverse:** Anniversary logo and dates

Date	F	VF	XF	Unc
1999	—	—	—	4.00
2000	—	—	—	4.00

KM# 1106 100000 LIRA **Weight:** 4.6000 g. **Composition:** Copper-Nickel-Zinc **Obverse:** Ataturk wearing hat **Reverse:** Denomination **Edge:** Plain **Size:** 21 mm.

Date	F	VF	XF	Unc
2001	—	—	—	3.50
2002	—	—	—	3.50

KM# 974 200000 LIRA **Weight:** 33.8200 g. **Composition:** 0.9170 Gold .9972 oz. AGW **Subject:** 50th Anniversary of Women's Suffrage

Date	Mintage	F	VF	XF	Unc
ND(1984) Proof	58	Value: 1,850			

KM# 1002 200000 LIRA **Weight:** 7.2160 g. **Composition:** 0.9170 Gold .2126 oz. AGW **Subject:** 400th Anniversary - Death of Architect Sinan **Note:** Similar to 1000 Lira, KM#991

Date	Mintage	F	VF	XF	Unc
ND(1988) Proof	500	Value: 325			

KM# 1004 200000 LIRA **Weight:** 7.2160 g. **Composition:** 0.9170 Gold .2126 oz. AGW **Subject:** Teacher's Day

Date	Mintage	F	VF	XF	Unc
1989 Proof	197	Value: 350			

KM# 994 200000 LIRA **Weight:** 7.2160 g. **Composition:** 0.9170 Gold .2126 oz. AGW **Subject:** 75th Anniversary - Battle of Gallipoli

Date	F	VF	XF	Unc
ND(1990) Proof	Est. 500	Value: 325		

KM# 1137 250000 LIRA **Weight:** 6.4200 g. **Composition:** Copper-Nickel-Zinc **Subject:** UNESCO **Obverse:** Portrait **Reverse:** Denomination **Edge Lettering:** "T.C." six times dividing reeded sections **Size:** 23.4 mm.

Date	F	VF	XF	Unc
2002	—	—	—	1.75

KM# 1051 400000 LIRA **Composition:** Bronze **Subject:** Habitat II **Obverse:** City view **Reverse:** Conference logo

Date	Mintage	F	VF	XF	Unc
1996	5,000	—	—	—	12.50

KM# 1008 500000 LIRA **Weight:** 7.1300 g. **Composition:** 0.9000 Gold .2063 oz. AGW **Subject:** Yunus Emre

Date	Mintage	F	VF	XF	Unc
1991 Proof	500	Value: 320			

KM# 1017 500000 LIRA **Weight:** 7.1400 g. **Composition:** 0.9000 Gold .2066 oz. AGW **Subject:** 100 Years of Peace and Harmony - Turkish Jews

Date	Mintage	F	VF	XF	Unc
ND(1992) Proof	—	Value: 320			

KM# 1032 500000 LIRA **Weight:** 7.2160 g. **Composition:** 0.9166 Gold .2126 oz. AGW **Subject:** Southeast Anatolian Project

Date	Mintage	F	VF	XF	Unc
ND(1994) Proof	1,500	Value: 300			

KM# 1034 500000 LIRA **Weight:** 7.2160 g. **Composition:** 0.9166 Gold .2126 oz. AGW **Subject:** 75th Anniversary - Turkish National Assembly

Date	Mintage	F	VF	XF	Unc
1995 Proof	1,000	Value: 300			

KM# 1036 500000 LIRA **Weight:** 7.2160 g. **Composition:** 0.9166 Gold .2126 oz. AGW **Subject:** Istanbul Gold Exchange

Date	Mintage	F	VF	XF	Unc
1995 Proof	1,000	Value: 300			

KM# 1039 500000 LIRA **Weight:** 7.2160 g. **Composition:** 0.9166 Gold .2126 oz. AGW **Subject:** Sailing Ship - "Piri Reis"

Date	Mintage	F	VF	XF	Unc
1995 Proof	1,000	Value: 300			

KM# 1138 500000 LIRA **Weight:** 12.1000 g. **Composition:** Copper Nickel **Subject:** Lira to Euro Transition **Obverse:** Denomination and date in wreath **Reverse:** Ataturk's portrait **Edge:** Reeded **Size:** 32 mm. **Note:** Dual denomination: 500,000 lira-2 euro

Date	F	VF	XF	Unc
1998	—	—	—	18.00

KM# 1081 EURO (500000 Lira) **Weight:** 11.9100 g. **Composition:** Copper-Nickel **Subject:** Trojan Horse **Obverse:** Denomination **Reverse:** Ancient Greek soldier and wooden horse **Edge:** Reeded **Note:** Struck at Istanbul.

Date	F	VF	XF	Unc
1999	—	—	—	15.00

KM# 1046 750000 LIRA **Weight:** 31.4700 g. **Composition:** 0.9250 Silver .9359 oz. ASW **Subject:** Europa - Various Landmarks

Date	Mintage	F	VF	XF	Unc
1996 Proof	Est. 35,000	Value: 22.50			

KM# 1048.1 750000 LIRA **Weight:** 23.2000 g. **Composition:** 0.9250 Silver .6899 oz. ASW **Series:** F.A.O.

Date	F	VF	XF	Unc
1996 Proof	—	Value: 18.50		

KM# 1048.2 750000 LIRA **Weight:** 23.2000 g. **Composition:** 0.9250 Silver .6899 oz. ASW **Reverse:** World globe with corn stalks at right

Date	F	VF	XF	Unc
1996 Proof	—	Value: 22.50		

KM# 1049 750000 LIRA **Weight:** 23.4100 g. **Composition:** 0.9250 Silver .6962 oz. ASW **Subject:** Turkish European Customs Union **Reverse:** Clasped hand

Date	F	VF	XF	Un
1996 Proof	—	Value: 22.50		

KM# 1052 750000 LIRA **Weight:** 23.3700 g. **Composition:** 0.9250 Silver .6950 oz. ASW **Subject:** Nasreddin Hoca

Date	Mintage	F	VF	XF
1996 Proof	5,000	Value: 20.00		

KM# 1063 750000 LIRA **Weight:** 31.4700 g. **Composition:** 0.9250 Silver .9359 oz. ASW **Subject:** World Cup Soccer **Obverse:** Denomination **Reverse:** Goalie catching ball

Date	Mintage	F	VF	XF	Unc
1996 Proof	15,000	Value: 30.00			

KM# 1058 750000 LIRA **Composition:** Bronze **Subject:** First World Air Games - Manned Flight

Date	F	VF	XF	Unc
1997	—	—	—	10.00

M# 1059 750000 LIRA **Composition:** Bronze **Subject:** XI World Forestry Congress **Reverse:** Stylized bird and tree

ate	F	VF	XF	Unc
997	—	—	—	12.50

M# 1068 750000 LIRA **Composition:** Bronze **Subject:** Forestry - "TEMA"

te	F	VF	XF	Unc
98	—	—	—	12.50

KM# 1047 1000000 LIRA **Weight:** 31.7200 g. **Composition:** 0.9250 Silver .9433 oz. ASW **Series:** Endangered Wildlife **Reverse:** Mediterranean seal

Date		F	VF	XF	Unc
1996 Proof	—	Value: 30.00			

KM# 1053 1000000 LIRA **Weight:** 31.4600 g. **Composition:** 0.9250 Silver .9356 oz. ASW **Series:** Endangered Wildlife **Reverse:** Galathus Elwesii flowers

Date	Mintage	F	VF	XF	Unc
1996 Proof	5,000	Value: 22.50			

KM# 1054 1000000 LIRA **Weight:** 31.4600 g. **Composition:** 0.9250 Silver .9356 oz. ASW **Subject:** Habitat II

Date	Mintage	F	VF	XF	Unc
1996 Proof	5,000	Value: 25.00			

KM# 1055 1000000 LIRA **Weight:** 31.7700 g. **Composition:** 0.9250 Silver .9448 oz. ASW **Subject:** Bust of Hulusi Behcet facing

Date	Mintage	F	VF	XF	Unc
1996 Proof	5,000	Value: 22.50			

KM# 1098 1000000 LIRA **Weight:** 1.2200 g. **Composition:** 0.9990 Gold 0.0392 oz. AGW **Obverse:** Denomination in wreath **Reverse:** Sailing ship, Piri Reis **Edge:** Reeded **Size:** 13.9 mm.

Date		F	VF	XF	Unc
1997 Proof	—	Value: 50.00			

KM# 1060 1000000 LIRA **Weight:** 31.5700 g. **Composition:** 0.9250 Silver .9389 oz. ASW **Subject:** Chinese History - Excavation of the Terra Cotta Army **Obverse:** Great Wall of China

Date	Mintage	F	VF	XF	Unc
1997	5,000	—	—	—	22.50

Note: This coin does not have any national identification other than the mintmark and denomination

KM# 1066 1000000 LIRA **Weight:** 1.2441 g. **Composition:** 0.9990 Gold .0400 oz. AGW **Obverse:** Denomination in wreath **Reverse:** Head of King Croesus of Lydia right **Edge:** Reeded **Note:** Struck at Istanbul.

Date		F	VF	XF	Unc
1997 Proof	—	Value: 50.00			

KM# 1067 1000000 LIRA **Weight:** 1.2441 g. **Composition:** 0.9990 Gold **Reverse:** Ancient Lydian coin portraying lion

Date		F	VF	XF	Unc
1997 Proof	—	Value: 50.00			

KM# 1069 1000000 LIRA **Weight:** 31.4400 g. **Composition:** 0.9250 Silver .9350 oz. ASW **Subject:** Mehmed Akif Ersoy **Obverse:** Spiral inscription

Date	Mintage	F	VF	XF	Unc
1997 Proof	Est. 5,000	Value: 22.50			

KM# 1158 1000000 LIRA **Weight:** 11.8700 g. **Composition:** Bi-Metallic **Subject:** Turkish Mint **Obverse:**

Building **Reverse:** "28 KASIM 2002" **Edge:** Plain **Size:** 32.1 mm.

Date	F	VF	XF	Unc
ND(2002)	—	—	—	5.50

KM# 1139 1000000 LIRA **Weight:** 11.8700 g. **Composition:** Bi-Metallic **Subject:** Foundation of the Mint **Obverse:** National arms above building and denomination **Reverse:** Legend and inscription "19 KASIM 2002" **Edge:** Plain **Size:** 32.1 mm.

Date	F	VF	XF	Unc
ND(2002)	—	—	—	15.00

KM# 1141 1000000 LIRA **Weight:** 11.7400 g. **Composition:** Bi-Metallic **Subject:** Turkish Mint **Obverse:** Mint building **Reverse:** Legend around inscription "OCAK 28 JANUARY 2003" **Edge:** Plain **Size:** 32 mm.

Date	F	VF	XF	Unc
ND(2003)	—	—	—	15.00

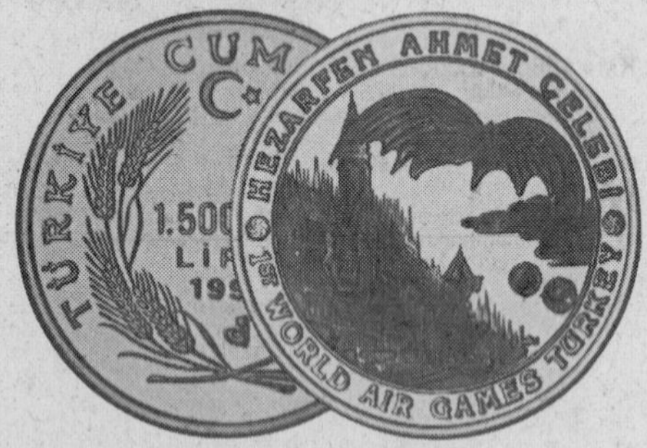

KM# 1061 1500000 LIRA **Weight:** 31.4400 g. **Composition:** 0.9250 Silver .9350 oz. ASW **Subject:** First World Air Games - Manned Flight

Date	Mintage	F	VF	XF	Unc
1997 Proof	5,000	Value: 25.00			

KM# 1062 1500000 LIRA **Weight:** 31.4400 g. **Composition:** 0.9250 Silver .9350 oz. ASW **Subject:** XI World Forestry Conference **Reverse:** Stylized bird and tree

Date	Mintage	F	VF	XF	Unc
1997 Proof	5,000	Value: 22.50			

KM# 1082 1500000 LIRA **Weight:** 31.3300 g. **Composition:** 0.9250 Silver .9317 oz. ASW **Subject:** Barbaros Mayreddin **Obverse:** Denomination in wreath **Reverse:** Two war ships c.1533 **Edge:** Reeded **Note:** Struck at Istanbul.

Date	Mintage	F	VF	XF	Unc
1997 Proof	3,000	Value: 30.00			

KM# 1100 1500000 LIRA **Weight:** 31.3700 g. **Composition:** 0.9250 Silver .9329 oz. ASW **Subject:** Myra'li Aziz Noel Baba and Euro **Obverse:** Denomination **Reverse:** Statue and tower **Edge:** Reeded **Size:** 38.6 mm.

Date	F	VF	XF	Unc
1997 Proof	—	Value: 25.00		

KM# 1064 2500000 LIRA **Weight:** 31.1500 g. **Composition:** 0.9250 Silver .9264 oz. ASW **Reverse:** Hasan-Sali Yucel

Date	Mintage	F	VF	XF	Unc
1998 Proof	Est. 5,000	Value: 22.50			

KM# 1065 2500000 LIRA **Weight:** 31.5800 g. **Composition:** 0.9250 Silver .9392 oz. ASW **Subject:** Forestry - "TEMA" **Reverse:** Wheel of trees design

Date	Mintage	F	VF	XF	Unc
1998 Proof	Est. 5,000	Value: 22.50			

KM# 1070 2500000 LIRA **Weight:** 31.4400 g. **Composition:** 0.9250 Silver .9350 oz. ASW **Subject:** 75 Years of Peace **Reverse:** Doves, treaty, and radiant sun

Date	Mintage	F	VF	XF	Unc
1998 Proof	Est. 5,000	Value: 25.00			

KM# 1083 2500000 LIRA **Weight:** 31.3500 g. **Composition:** 0.9250 Silver .9323 oz. ASW **Series:** 2000 Olympics **Obverse:** Denomination in wreath **Reverse:** Weight lifter and mosque **Edge:** Reeded **Note:** Struck at Istanbul.

Date	Mintage	F	VF	XF	Unc
1998 Proof	3,000	Value: 27.50			

KM# 1084 10 EURO (2500000 Lira) **Weight:** 23.3000 g. **Composition:** 0.9250 Silver .6929 oz. ASW **Subject:** Ataturk **Obverse:** Denomination in wreath **Reverse:** Head of Kemal Atatürk left **Edge:** Reeded **Note:** Struck at Istanbul.

Date	Mintage	F	VF	XF	Unc
1998 Proof	3,000	Value: 35.00			

 # 1071 3000000 LIRA **Weight:** 31.3233 g.
Composition: 0.9250 Silver .9315 oz. ASW **Subject:** 75 Years of Peace **Obverse:** 75th Anniversary logo **Reverse:** Doves, treaty, and radiant sun

	Mintage	F	VF	XF	Unc
998) Proof	Est. 5,000	Value: 30.00			

 # 1072 3000000 LIRA **Weight:** 31.3233 g.
Composition: 0.9250 Silver .9315 oz. ASW **Subject:** 75th Anniversary Republic **Obverse:** 75th Anniversary logo **Reverse:** Two revolutionaries, head of Kemal Atatürk behind

	Mintage	F	VF	XF	Unc
998) Proof	Est. 5,000	Value: 30.00			

 # 1073 3000000 LIRA **Weight:** 31.3233 g.
Composition: 0.9250 Silver .9315 oz. ASW **Subject:** 75th Anniversary of Republic **Obverse:** 75th Anniversary logo **Reverse:** Couple dancing, people in background

		F	VF	XF	Unc
998) Proof	Est. 5,000	Value: 30.00			

KM# 1074 3000000 LIRA **Weight:** 31.3233 g.
Composition: 0.9250 Silver .9315 oz. ASW **Obverse:** 75th Anniversary logo **Reverse:** Ataturk with children

Date	Mintage	F	VF	XF	Unc
ND(1998) Proof	Est. 5,000	Value: 30.00			

KM# 1075 3000000 LIRA **Weight:** 31.3233 g.
Composition: 0.9250 Silver .9315 oz. ASW **Obverse:** 75th Anniversary logo **Reverse:** Ataturk with cane before crowd

Date	Mintage	F	VF	XF	Unc
ND(1998) Proof	Est. 5,000	Value: 30.00			

KM# 1076 3000000 LIRA **Weight:** 31.3233 g.
Composition: 0.9250 Silver .9315 oz. ASW **Obverse:** 75th Anniversary logo **Reverse:** Depictions of arts and sciences in Turkey

Date	Mintage	F	VF	XF	Unc
ND(1998) Proof	Est. 5,000	Value: 30.00			

KM# 1107 3000000 LIRA **Weight:** 31.4700 g.
Composition: 0.9250 Silver .9359 oz. ASW **Series:** Olympics **Obverse:** Denomination **Reverse:** Long jumper and logo **Edge:** Reeded **Size:** 38.6 mm.

Date	Mintage	F	VF	XF	Unc
1999 Proof	31,000	Value: 35.00			
2002	—	—	—	—	—

KM# 1080 EURO (3000000 Lira) **Weight:** 31.4700 g.
Composition: 0.9250 Silver .9359 oz. ASW **Obverse:** Denomination in wreath **Reverse:** Dolmababce Palace

Date		F	VF	XF	Unc
1998 Proof	—	Value: 30.00			

KM# 1086 EURO (3000000 Lira) **Weight:** 31.3600 g.
Composition: 0.9250 Silver .9326 oz. ASW **Subject:** Galata Kulesi **Reverse:** Tower and city view above "EURO"

Date	Mintage	F	VF	XF	Unc
1998 Proof	3,000	Value: 32.50			

KM# 1085 EURO (3000000 Lira) **Weight:** 31.3600 g.
Composition: 0.9250 Silver .9326 oz. ASW **Subject:** Dolmabance Sarayi Palace **Obverse:** Denomination in wreath **Reverse:** Building above "EURO" **Edge:** Reeded **Note:** Struck at Istanbul.

Date	Mintage	F	VF	XF	Unc
1998 Proof	3,000	Value: 32.50			

KM# 1108 4000000 LIRA **Weight:** 31.4700 g.
Composition: 0.9250 Silver .9359 oz. ASW **Subject:** Ataturk **Obverse:** Denomination **Reverse:** Atatruk's portrait below "EURO" **Edge:** Reeded **Size:** 38.6 mm.

Date		F	VF	XF	Unc
1999 Proof	—	Value: 35.00			

KM# 1087 4000000 LIRA **Weight:** 31.4000 g. **Composition:** 0.9250 Silver .9338 oz. ASW **Subject:** Fethiye **Obverse:** Denomination in wreath **Reverse:** Two sailing ships **Edge:** Reeded **Note:** Struck at Istanbul.

Date	Mintage	F	VF	XF	Unc
1999 Proof	13,000	Value: 30.00			

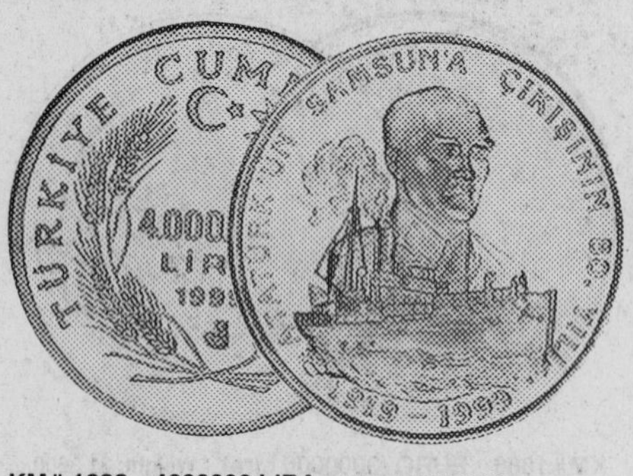

KM# 1088 4000000 LIRA **Weight:** 31.4000 g. **Composition:** 0.9250 Silver .9338 oz. ASW **Subject:** 80th Anniversary - Atatürk's Landing at Samsun **Reverse:** Atatürk's bust above steam ship

Date	Mintage	F	VF	XF	Unc
1999 Proof	27	Value: 27.50			

KM# 1089 4000000 LIRA **Weight:** 31.4000 g. **Composition:** 0.9250 Silver .9338 oz. ASW **Subject:** Istanbul Culture Capital **Reverse:** Topkane Cesmesi

Date	Mintage	F	VF	XF	Unc
1999 Proof	5,000	Value: 32.50			

KM# 1090 4000000 LIRA **Weight:** 31.4000 g. **Composition:** 0.9250 Silver .9338 oz. ASW **Subject:** Solar Eclipse **Reverse:** Eclipse stages above map

Date	Mintage	F	VF	XF	Unc
1999 Proof	35	Value: 35.00			

KM# 1091 4000000 LIRA **Weight:** 31.4000 g. **Composition:** 0.9250 Silver .9338 oz. ASW **Subject:** Solar Eclipse **Reverse:** People watching eclipse

Date	Mintage	F	VF	XF	Unc
1999 Proof	5,000	Value: 35.00			

KM# 1092 4000000 LIRA **Weight:** 31.4000 g. **Composition:** 0.9250 Silver .9338 oz. ASW **Subject:** Silk Road **Obverse:** Scroll design with landmarks **Reverse:** Mounted archer hunting lion **Note:** Antiqued finish.

Date	Mintage	F	VF	XF	Unc
1999 Proof	5,000	Value: 35.00			

KM# 1093 4000000 LIRA **Weight:** 31.4000 g. **Composition:** 0.9250 Silver .9338 oz. ASW **Subject:** Osman Gazi **Reverse:** Turbaned 1/2-length bust of Osman Gazi facing half left

Date	Mintage	F	VF	XF	Unc
1999 Proof	5,000	Value: 32.50			

KM# 1094 4000000 LIRA **Weight:** 31.4000 g. **Composition:** 0.9250 Silver .9338 oz. ASW **Reverse:** Gazi leading mounted troops

Date	Mintage	F	VF	XF	Unc
1999 Proof	5,000	Value: 32.50			

KM# 1095 4000000 LIRA **Weight:** 31.4000 g. **Composition:** 0.9250 Silver .9338 oz. ASW **Reverse:** Mounted archers and prey

Date	Mintage	F	VF	XF	U
1999 Proof	5,000	Value: 32.50			

KM# 1099 4000000 LIRA **Weight:** 31.4100 g. **Composition:** 0.9250 Silver .9341 oz. ASW **Subject:** Lacerta Clarkorum **Obverse:** Denomination **Reverse:** Tv lizards **Edge:** Reeded **Size:** 38.6 mm.

Date		F	VF	XF
1999 Proof	—	Value: 35.00		

KM# 1096 4000000 LIRA **Weight:** 31.4000 g. **Composition:** 0.9250 Silver .9338 oz. ASW **Reverse:** 700-year-old Islamic coin design

Date		F	VF	XF	Unc
1999 Proof		32	Value: 32.50		

KM# 1109 4000000 LIRA **Weight:** 31.4700 g. **Composition:** 0.9250 Silver .9359 oz. ASW **Subject:** "Bogazici" (Bosphorus) **Obverse:** Denomination **Reverse:** Water front mosque above "EURO" **Edge:** Reeded **Size:** 38.6 mm.

Date	Mintage	F	VF	XF	Unc
1999 Proof	23,000	Value: 35.00			

KM# 1110 5000000 LIRA **Weight:** 67.0000 g. **Composition:** Bronze **Subject:** Children's Day **Obverse:** Legend and inscription **Reverse:** Dancing children **Edge:** Plain **Size:** 50 mm.

Date	Mintage	F	VF	XF	Unc
2001 Matte	15,000	—	—	—	10.00

KM# 1097 60000000 LIRA **Weight:** 15.0000 g. **Composition:** 0.9167 Gold .4921 oz. AGW **Subject:** 700th Anniversary - The Ottoman Empire **Obverse:** Denomination in wreath **Reverse:** Ottoman coat of arms **Edge:** Reeded **Note:** Struck at Istanbul.

ate	Mintage	F	VF	XF	Unc
999 Proof	5,000	Value: 300			

M# 1101 7500000 LIRA **Weight:** 31.4000 g. **Composition:** 0.9250 Silver .9338 oz. ASW **Subject:** 34th World Chess Olympiad **Obverse:** World globe with chess pieces **Reverse:** Logo and horse head **Edge:** Reeded **Size:** 38.6 mm.

	Mintage	F	VF	XF	Unc
0 Proof	Est. 1,000	Value: 40.00			

KM# 1102 7500000 LIRA **Weight:** 23.3300 g. **Composition:** 0.9250 Silver .6938 oz. ASW **Subject:** UNICEF **Obverse:** Denomination **Reverse:** Two children candle dancing **Edge:** Reeded **Size:** 38.6 mm.

Date		F	VF	XF	Unc
2000 Proof		—	Value: 50.00		

KM# 1111 7500000 LIRA **Weight:** 31.4700 g. **Composition:** 0.9250 Silver .9359 oz. ASW **Subject:** Ephesus' Celcius Library **Obverse:** Mint logo and denomination **Reverse:** Building **Edge:** Reeded **Size:** 38.6 mm.

Date	Mintage	F	VF	XF	Unc
2000 Matte	15,000	—	—	—	35.00
2000 Proof	15,000	Value: 35.00			

KM# 1112 7500000 LIRA **Weight:** 31.4700 g. **Composition:** 0.9250 Silver .9359 oz. ASW **Subject:** Traditional Turkish Theater **Obverse:** Mint logo and denomination **Reverse:** Marionette theater scene

Date	Mintage	F	VF	XF	Unc
2000 Proof	15,000	Value: 35.00			

KM# 1113 7500000 LIRA **Weight:** 31.4700 g. **Composition:** 0.9250 Silver .9359 oz. ASW **Subject:** United Nations Summit **Obverse:** Coiled rope design **Reverse:** UN logo and stylized 2000

Date	Mintage	F	VF	XF	Unc
2000 Proof	15,000	Value: 35.00			

KM# 1114 7500000 LIRA **Weight:** 31.4700 g. **Composition:** 0.9250 Silver .9359 oz. ASW **Subject:** Turkish European Union Candidacy **Obverse:** Circular design **Reverse:** Cluster of flags behind star and crescent

Date	Mintage	F	VF	XF	Unc
2000 Proof	15,000	Value: 35.00			

KM# 1115 7500000 LIRA **Weight:** 31.4700 g. **Composition:** 0.9250 Silver .9359 oz. ASW **Subject:** First Female Pilots **Obverse:** Turkish pilot's badge **Reverse:** Early female pilot saluting

Date	Mintage	F	VF	XF	Unc
2000 Proof	15,000	Value: 40.00			

KM# 1116 7500000 LIRA **Weight:** 31.4700 g. **Composition:** 0.9990 Silver 1.0108 oz. ASW **Subject:** President Clinton's Turkish Visit **Obverse:** Mint logo **Reverse:** Clinton holding baby

Date	Mintage	F	VF	XF	Unc
2000 Proof	100,000	Value: 40.00			

KM# 1117 7500000 LIRA **Weight:** 31.4700 g. **Composition:** 0.9250 Silver .9359 oz. ASW **Subject:** Iznik Tabak **Obverse:** Two peacocks **Reverse:** Circle of flowers

Date	Mintage	F	VF	XF	Unc
2001 Proof	15,000	Value: 35.00			

KM# 1142 7500000 LIRA **Weight:** 31.2500 g. **Composition:** 0.9250 Silver 0.9294 oz. ASW **Subject:** Cahit Arf, Mathematician **Obverse:** Mathematical formula **Reverse:** Portrait **Edge:** Reeded **Size:** 38.5 mm.

Date		F	VF	XF	Unc
2001 Proof	—	Value: 40.00			

KM# 1143 7500000 LIRA **Weight:** 31.2500 g. **Composition:** 0.9250 Silver 0.9294 oz. ASW **Subject:** Mimar Koca Sinan, Architect **Obverse:** Ornamented circle design **Reverse:** Portrait **Edge:** Reeded **Size:** 38.5 mm.

Date		F	VF	XF	Unc
2001 Proof	—	Value: 40.00			

KM# 1144 7500000 LIRA **Weight:** 31.2500 g. **Composition:** 0.9250 Silver 0.9294 oz. ASW **Subject:** Koca Yusuf Baspehlivan **Obverse:** Two figures wrestling **Reverse:** Portrait on circular background **Edge:** Reeded **Size:** 38.5 mm.

Date		F	VF	XF	Unc
2001 Proof	—	Value: 40.00			

KM# 1120 7500000 LIRA **Weight:** 15.4000 g. **Composition:** 0.9250 Silver 0.458 oz. ASW **Subject:** Bird Series - Saz Horozu **Obverse:** Denomination **Reverse:** Reed cock on ground **Edge:** Plain **Shape:** 28.1 x 28.1mm square

Date		F	VF	XF	Unc
2001 Proof	—	Value: 20.00			

KM# 1121 7500000 LIRA **Weight:** 15.4000 g. **Composition:** 0.9250 Silver 0.458 oz. ASW **Subject:** Bird Series - Toy **Obverse:** Denomination **Reverse:** Greater Bustard on ground **Edge:** Plain **Shape:** 28.1 x 28.1mm square

Date		F	VF	XF	Unc
2001 Proof	—	Value: 20.00			

KM# 1122 7500000 LIRA **Weight:** 15.4000 g. **Composition:** 0.9250 Silver 0.458 oz. ASW **Subject:** Bird Series - Yaz Ordegi **Obverse:** Denomination **Reverse:** Duck on ground **Edge:** Plain **Shape:** 28.1 x 28.1mm square

Date		F	VF	XF	Unc
2001 Proof	—	Value: 20.00			

KM# 1123 7500000 LIRA **Weight:** 15.4000 g. **Composition:** 0.9250 Silver 0.458 oz. ASW **Subject:** Bird Series - Dikkuyruk **Obverse:** Denomination **Reverse:** Duck on water **Edge:** Plain **Shape:** 28.1 x 28.1mm square

Date		F	VF	XF	Unc
2001 Proof	—	Value: 20.00			

KM# 1124 7500000 LIRA **Weight:** 15.4000 g. **Composition:** 0.9250 Silver 0.458 oz. ASW **Subject:** Bird Series - Yesil Arikusu **Obverse:** Denomination **Reverse:** Green Bee-eater on branch **Edge:** Plain **Shape:** 28.1 x 28.1mm square

Date		F	VF	XF	Unc
2001 Proof	—	Value: 20.00			

KM# 1125 7500000 LIRA **Weight:** 15.4000 g. **Composition:** 0.9250 Silver 0.458 oz. ASW **Subject:** Bird Series - Kucuk Karabatak **Obverse:** Denomination **Reverse:** Three Black Cormorants **Edge:** Plain **Shape:** 28.1 x 28.1mm square

Date		F	VF	XF	Unc
2001 Proof	—	Value: 20.00			

KM# 1126 7500000 LIRA **Weight:** 15.4000 g. **Composition:** 0.9250 Silver 0.458 oz. ASW **Subject:** Bird Series - Kizil Akbaba **Obverse:** Denomination **Reverse:** Vulture **Edge:** Plain **Shape:** 28.1 x 28.1mm square

Date		F	VF	XF	Unc
2001 Proof	—	Value: 20.00			

KM# 1127 7500000 LIRA **Weight:** 15.4000 g. **Composition:** 0.9250 Silver 0.458 oz. ASW **Subject:** Bird Series - Sah Kartal **Obverse:** Denomination **Reverse:** Two eagles **Edge:** Plain **Shape:** 28.1 x 28.1mm square

Date		F	VF	XF	Unc
2001 Proof	—	Value: 20.00			

KM# 1128 7500000 LIRA **Weight:** 15.4000 g. **Composition:** 0.9250 Silver 0.458 oz. ASW **Subject:** Bird Series - Ala Sigireik **Obverse:** Denomination **Reverse:** Starling on ground **Edge:** Plain **Shape:** 28.1 x 28.1mm square

Date		F	VF	XF	Unc
2001 Proof	—	Value: 20.00			

KM# 1129 7500000 LIRA **Weight:** 15.4000 g. **Composition:** 0.9250 Silver 0.458 oz. ASW **Subject:** Bird Series - Izmir Yalicapkini **Obverse:** Denomination **Reverse:** Kingfisher on stump **Edge:** Plain **Shape:** 28.1 x 28.1mm square

Date		F	VF	XF	Unc
2001 Proof	—	Value: 20.00			

KM# 1130 7500000 LIRA **Weight:** 15.4000 g. **Composition:** 0.9250 Silver 0.458 oz. ASW **Subject:** Bird Series - Turac **Obverse:** Denomination **Reverse:** Francolin birds on the ground **Edge:** Plain **Shape:** 28.1 x 28.1mm square

Date		F	VF	XF	Unc
2001 Proof	—	Value: 20.00			

KM# 1131 7500000 LIRA **Weight:** 15.4000 g. **Composition:** 0.9250 Silver 0.458 oz. ASW **Subject:** Bird Series - Kelaynak **Obverse:** Denomination **Reverse:** Two long-billed birds on ground **Edge:** Plain **Shape:** 28.1 x 28.1mm square

Date		F	VF	XF	Ur
2001 Proof	—	Value: 20.00			

KM# 1132 7500000 LIRA **Weight:** 15.4000 g. **Composition:** 0.9250 Silver 0.458 oz. ASW **Subject:** Bir Series - Sakalli Akbaba **Obverse:** Denomination **Reverse** Bearded vulture **Edge:** Plain **Shape:** 28.1 x 28.1mm squa

Date		F	VF	XF	U
2001 Proof	—	Value: 20.00			

KM# 1133 7500000 LIRA **Weight:** 15.4000 g. **Composition:** 0.9250 Silver 0.458 oz. ASW **Subject:** Bi Series - Tepeli Pelikan **Obverse:** Denomination **Reverse** Pelican on rock **Edge:** Plain **Shape:** 28.1 x 28.1mm squa

Date		F	VF	XF
2001 Proof	—	Value: 20.00		

1134 7500000 LIRA Weight: 15.4000 g. Composition: 0.9250 Silver 0.458 oz. ASW Subject: Bird Series - Ishakkusu Obverse: Denomination Reverse: Owl on branch Edge: Plain Shape: 28.1 x 28.1mm square

Date	F	VF	XF	Unc
Proof	—	Value: 20.00		

1135 7500000 LIRA Weight: 31.0300 g. Composition: 0.9250 Silver 0.9228 oz. ASW Subject: Mevlana Celaleddin-i Rumi Obverse: Dancer Reverse: Portrait Edge: Reeded Size: 38.5 mm.

Date	F	VF	XF	Unc
1 Proof	—	Value: 30.00		

1145 7500000 LIRA Weight: 15.6100 g. Composition: 0.9250 Silver 0.4642 oz. ASW Subject: Flower Series Obverse: Denomination Reverse: Paeonia Edge: Reeded Shape: Oval Size: 27.9 x 38.6 mm.

Date	F	VF	XF	Unc
2 Proof	—	Value: 17.50		

1146 7500000 LIRA Weight: 15.6100 g. Composition: 0.9250 Silver 0.4642 oz. ASW Subject: Flower Series Obverse: Denomination Reverse: Orchis Edge: Reeded Shape: Oval Size: 27.9 x 38.6 mm.

Date	F	VF	XF	Unc
2 Proof	—	Value: 17.50		

1147 7500000 LIRA Weight: 15.6100 g. Composition: 0.9250 Silver 0.4642 oz. ASW Subject: Flower Series Obverse: Denomination Reverse: Iris Edge: Reeded Shape: Oval Size: 27.9 x 38.6 mm.

Date	F	VF	XF	Unc
2 Proof	—	Value: 17.50		

1148 7500000 LIRA Weight: 15.6100 g. Composition: 0.9250 Silver 0.4642 oz. ASW Subject: Flower Series Obverse: Denomination Reverse: Gladiolus Edge: Reeded Shape: Oval Size: 27.9 x 38.6 mm.

Date	F	VF	XF	Unc
2 Proof	—	Value: 17.50		

M# 1149 7500000 LIRA Weight: 15.6100 g. Composition: 0.9250 Silver 0.4642 oz. ASW Subject: Flower Series Obverse: Denomination Reverse: Crocus Edge: Reeded Shape: Oval Size: 27.9 x 38.6 mm.

Date	F	VF	XF	Unc
02 Proof	—	Value: 17.50		

M# 1150 7500000 LIRA Weight: 15.6100 g. Composition: 0.9250 Silver 0.4642 oz. ASW Subject: Flower Series Obverse: Denomination Reverse: Campanula Edge: Reeded Shape: Oval Size: 27.9 x 38.6 mm.

Date	F	VF	XF	Unc
02 Proof	—	Value: 17.50		

M# 1151 7500000 LIRA Weight: 15.6100 g. Composition: 0.9250 Silver 0.4642 oz. ASW Subject: Flower Series Reverse: Centaurea Edge: Reeded Shape: Oval Size: 27.9 x 38.6 mm.

Date	F	VF	XF	Unc
02 Proof	—	Value: 17.50		

M# 1152 7500000 LIRA Weight: 15.6100 g. Composition: 0.9250 Silver 0.4642 oz. ASW Subject: Flower Series Obverse: Denomination Reverse: Tchihatchewia Edge: Reeded Shape: Oval Size: 27.9 x 38.6 mm.

Date	F	VF	XF	Unc
02 Proof	—	Value: 17.50		

M# 1153 7500000 LIRA Weight: 15.6100 g. Composition: 0.9250 Silver 0.4642 oz. ASW Subject: Flower Series Obverse: Denomination Reverse: Linum Edge: Reeded Shape: Oval Size: 27.9 x 38.6 mm.

Date	F	VF	XF	Unc
02 Proof	—	Value: 17.50		

M# 1154 7500000 LIRA Weight: 15.6100 g. Composition: 0.9250 Silver 0.4642 oz. ASW Subject: Flower Series Obverse: Denomination Reverse: Cyclamen Edge: Reeded Shape: Oval Size: 27.9 x 38.6 mm.

Date	F	VF	XF	Unc
2002 Proof	—	Value: 17.50		

KM# 1155 7500000 LIRA Weight: 15.6100 g. Composition: 0.9250 Silver 0.4642 oz. ASW Subject: Flower Series Obverse: Denomination Reverse: Tulipa Edge: Reeded Shape: Oval Size: 27.9 x 38.6 mm.

Date	F	VF	XF	Unc
2002 Proof	—	Value: 17.50		

KM# 1156 7500000 LIRA Weight: 15.6100 g. Composition: 0.9250 Silver 0.4642 oz. ASW Subject: Flower Series Obverse: Denomination Reverse: Stenbergia Edge: Reeded Shape: Oval Size: 27.9 x 38.6 mm.

Date	F	VF	XF	Unc
2002 Proof	—	Value: 17.50		

KM# 1157 7500000 LIRA Weight: 15.6100 g. Composition: 0.9250 Silver 0.4642 oz. ASW Subject: Flower Series Obverse: Denomination Reverse: Arum Edge: Reeded Shape: Oval Size: 27.9 x 38.6 mm.

Date	F	VF	XF	Unc
2002 Proof	—	Value: 17.50		

KM# 1118 10000000 LIRA Weight: 31.4700 g. Composition: 0.9250 Silver .9359 oz. ASW Subject: Divrigi Ulu Camii Obverse: Art work in center Reverse: Ornate door Edge: Reeded Size: 38.6 mm.

Date	Mintage	F	VF	XF	Unc
2001 Matte	15,000	—	—	—	40.00

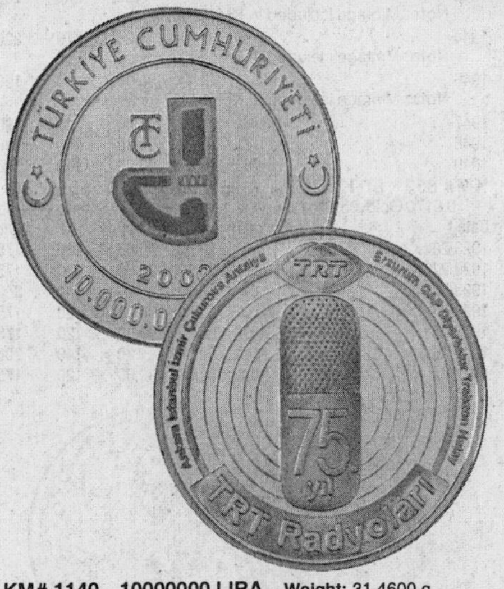

KM# 1140 10000000 LIRA Weight: 31.4600 g. Composition: 0.9250 Silver 0.9356 oz. ASW Subject: Turkish Radio: 75th Anniversary Obverse: Large mint mark Reverse: Radio microphone Edge: Reeded Size: 38.6 mm.

Date	F	VF	XF	Unc
2002 Proof	—	Value: 40.00		

KM# 1119 150000000 LIRA Ring Weight: 17.0000 g. Ring Composition: 0.9250 Silver .5056 oz. ASWCenter Weight: 24.0000 g. Center Composition: 0.9160 Gold .7068 oz. AGW Subject: President Clinton's Turkish Visit Obverse: Mint logo Reverse: Clinton holding baby Edge: Reeded Size: 38.6 mm.

Date	Mintage	F	VF	XF	Unc
2000 Proof	10,000	Value: 300			

GOLD BULLION COINAGE

Since 1943, the Turkish government has issued regular and deluxe gold coins in five denominations corresponding to the old traditional 25, 50, 100, 250, and 500 Kurus of the Ottoman period. The regular coins are all dated 1923, plus the year of the republic (e.g. 1923/40 = 1963), de Luxe coins bear actual AD dates. For a few years, 1944-1950, the bust of Ismet Inonu replaced that of Kemal Ataturk.

KM# 850 25 KURUS Weight: 1.8041 g. Composition: 0.9170 Gold .0532 oz. AGW Obverse: Head of Ismet Inonu left

Date	Mintage	F	VF	XF	Unc
1923/20	—	BV	50.00	65.00	90.00
1923/22	3,228	BV	50.00	75.00	120
1923/23	2,757	BV	50.00	75.00	120
1923/24	46,000	BV	50.00	65.00	90.00
1923/25	20,000	BV	50.00	70.00	110
1923/26	11,000	BV	50.00	70.00	110

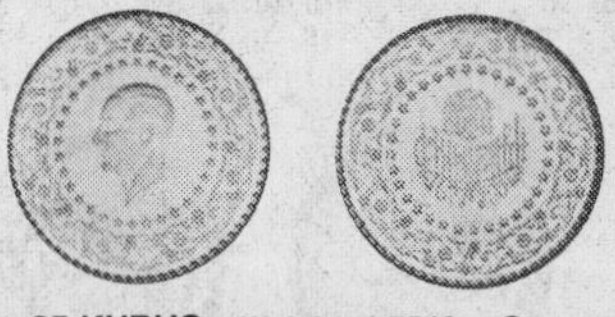

KM# 870 25 KURUS Weight: 1.7540 g. Composition: 0.9170 Gold .0517 oz. AGW Series: Monnaie de Luxe Obverse: Head of Kemal Ataturk left

Date	Mintage	F	VF	XF	Unc
1942	138	—	50.00	75.00	150
1943	386	—	50.00	75.00	125
1944	811	—	50.00	75.00	125
1946	235	—	50.00	75.00	150
1950	2,053	—	22.50	32.50	55.00
1951	2,035	—	22.50	32.50	55.00
1952	3,374	—	22.50	32.50	55.00
1953	1,944	—	22.50	32.50	55.00
1954	2,244	—	22.50	32.50	55.00
1955	2,573	—	22.50	32.50	55.00
1956	4,004	—	22.50	32.50	55.00
1957	8,842	—	22.50	32.50	55.00
1958	9,546	—	22.50	32.50	55.00
1959	17,000	—	20.00	28.00	45.00
1960	19,000	—	20.00	28.00	45.00
1961	35,000	—	20.00	28.00	45.00
1962	31,000	—	20.00	28.00	45.00
1963	47,000	—	20.00	28.00	45.00
1964	57,000	—	20.00	28.00	45.00
1965	78,000	—	20.00	28.00	45.00
1966	106,000	—	20.00	28.00	45.00
1967	114,000	—	20.00	28.00	45.00
1968	152,000	—	20.00	28.00	45.00
1969	163,000	—	20.00	28.00	45.00
1970	224,000	—	20.00	28.00	45.00
1971	306,000	—	20.00	28.00	45.00
1972	271,000	—	20.00	28.00	45.00
1973	162,000	—	20.00	28.00	45.00
1974	141,000	—	20.00	28.00	45.00
1975	202,000	—	20.00	28.00	45.00
1976	583,000	—	20.00	28.00	45.00
1977	1,089,000	—	20.00	28.00	45.00
1978	238,000	—	20.00	28.00	45.00
1980	—	—	20.00	28.00	45.00

KM# 875 25 KURUS **Weight:** 1.7540 g. **Composition:** 0.9170 Gold .0517 oz. AGW **Series:** Monnaie de Luxe **Obverse:** Head of Ismet Inonu left

Date	Mintage	F	VF	XF	Unc
1943	—	70.00	90.00	140	200
Note: Mintage included in KM#870					
1944	—	70.00	90.00	140	200
Note: Mintage included in KM#870					
1945	592	70.00	90.00	140	200
1946	—	70.00	90.00	140	200
Note: Mintage included in KM#870					
1947	3,443	70.00	90.00	125	185
1948	714	70.00	90.00	140	200
1949	552	70.00	90.00	140	200

KM# 851 25 KURUS **Weight:** 1.8041 g. **Composition:** 0.9170 Gold .0532 oz. AGW **Obverse:** Head of Kemal Ataturk left

Date	Mintage	F	VF	XF	Unc
1923/20	14,000	BV	20.00	25.00	40.00
1923/27	18,000	BV	20.00	25.00	40.00
1923/28	15,000	BV	20.00	25.00	40.00
1923/29	15,000	BV	20.00	25.00	40.00
1923/30	17,000	BV	20.00	25.00	40.00
1923/31	19,000	BV	20.00	25.00	40.00
1923/32	5,455	BV	20.00	25.00	40.00
1923/33	11,000	BV	20.00	25.00	40.00
1923/34	20,000	BV	20.00	25.00	40.00
1923/35	25,000	BV	20.00	25.00	40.00
1923/36	34,000	BV	20.00	25.00	40.00
1923/37	31,000	BV	20.00	25.00	40.00
1923/38	35,000	BV	20.00	25.00	40.00
1923/39	46,000	BV	20.00	25.00	40.00
1923/40	49,000	BV	20.00	25.00	40.00
1923/41	59,000	BV	20.00	25.00	40.00
1923/42	74,000	BV	20.00	25.00	40.00
1923/43	90,000	BV	20.00	25.00	40.00
1923/44	85,000	BV	20.00	25.00	40.00
1923/45	73,000	BV	20.00	25.00	40.00
1923/46	89,000	BV	20.00	25.00	40.00
1923/47	119,000	BV	20.00	25.00	40.00
1923/48	112,000	BV	20.00	25.00	40.00
1923/49	112,000	BV	20.00	25.00	40.00
1923/50	67,000	BV	20.00	25.00	40.00
1923/51	40,000	BV	20.00	25.00	40.00
1923/52	71,000	BV	20.00	25.00	40.00
1923/53	124,000	BV	20.00	25.00	40.00
1923/54	196	BV	20.00	25.00	40.00
1923/55	112,000	BV	20.00	25.00	40.00
1923/56	—	BV	20.00	25.00	40.00
1923/57	—	BV	20.00	25.00	40.00

KM# 853 50 KURUS **Weight:** 3.6083 g. **Composition:** 0.9170 Gold .0517 oz. AGW **Obverse:** Head of Kemal Ataturk left

Date	Mintage	F	VF	XF	Unc
1923/20	12,000	BV	40.00	50.00	65.00
1923/27	Inc. above	BV	40.00	50.00	65.00
1923/28	3,300	BV	40.00	50.00	65.00
1923/29	6,384	BV	40.00	50.00	65.00
1923/30	4,590	BV	40.00	50.00	65.00
1923/31	9,068	BV	40.00	50.00	65.00
1923/32	4,344	BV	40.00	50.00	65.00
1923/33	3,958	BV	40.00	50.00	65.00
1923/34	9,499	BV	40.00	50.00	65.00
1923/35	9,307	BV	40.00	50.00	65.00
1923/36	12,000	BV	40.00	50.00	65.00
1923/37	9,049	BV	40.00	50.00	65.00
1923/38	9,854	BV	40.00	50.00	65.00
1923/39	11,000	BV	40.00	50.00	65.00
1923/40	13,000	BV	40.00	50.00	65.00
1923/41	13,000	BV	40.00	50.00	65.00
1923/42	18,000	BV	40.00	50.00	65.00
1923/43	26,000	BV	40.00	50.00	65.00
1923/44	26,000	BV	40.00	50.00	65.00
1923/45	25,000	BV	40.00	50.00	65.00
1923/46	28,000	BV	40.00	50.00	65.00
1923/47	38,000	BV	40.00	50.00	65.00
1923/48	35,000	BV	40.00	50.00	65.00
1923/49	28,000	BV	40.00	50.00	65.00
1923/50	16,000	BV	40.00	50.00	65.00
1923/51	8,000	BV	40.00	50.00	65.00
1923/52	14,000	BV	40.00	50.00	65.00
1923/53	28,000	BV	40.00	50.00	65.00
1923/54	54,000	BV	40.00	50.00	65.00
1923/55	16,000	BV	40.00	50.00	65.00
1923/57	—	BV	40.00	50.00	65.00

KM# 871 50 KURUS **Weight:** 3.5080 g. **Composition:** 0.9170 Gold .1034 oz. AGW **Series:** Monnaie de Luxe **Obverse:** Head of Kemal Ataturk left

Date	Mintage	F	VF	XF	Unc
1942	115	100	150	200	250
1943	91	100	150	200	250
1944	950	70.00	120	140	175
1946	565	70.00	120	140	175
1950	1,971	—	40.00	70.00	140
1951	1,780	—	40.00	70.00	140
1952	2,557	—	40.00	70.00	140
1953	2,392	—	40.00	70.00	140
1954	1,714	—	40.00	70.00	140
1955	4,143	—	40.00	60.00	110
1956	2,956	—	40.00	60.00	110
1957	6,855	—	40.00	60.00	110
1958	6,381	—	40.00	60.00	110
1959	12,000	—	40.00	50.00	65.00
1960	12,000	—	40.00	50.00	65.00
1961	15,000	—	40.00	50.00	65.00
1962	22,000	—	40.00	50.00	65.00
1963	29,000	—	40.00	50.00	65.00
1964	34,000	—	40.00	50.00	65.00
1965	44,000	—	40.00	50.00	65.00
1966	58,000	—	40.00	50.00	65.00
1967	64,000	—	40.00	50.00	65.00
1968	82,000	—	40.00	50.00	65.00
1969	79,000	—	40.00	50.00	65.00
1970	109,000	—	40.00	50.00	65.00
1971	154,000	—	40.00	50.00	65.00
1972	110,000	—	40.00	50.00	65.00
1973	73,000	—	40.00	50.00	65.00
1974	45,000	—	40.00	50.00	65.00
1975	72,000	—	40.00	50.00	65.00
1976	196,000	—	40.00	50.00	65.00
1977	361,000	—	40.00	50.00	65.00
1978	161,000	—	40.00	50.00	65.00
1980	—	—	40.00	50.00	65.00

KM# 876 50 KURUS **Weight:** 3.5080 g. **Composition:** 0.9170 Gold .1034 oz. AGW **Series:** Monnaie de Luxe **Obverse:** Head of Ismet Inonu left

Date	Mintage	F	VF	XF	Unc
1943	—	—	150	200	250
Note: Mintage included in KM#871					
1944	—	—	120	170	220
Note: Mintage included in KM#871					
1946	—	—	90.00	140	190
Note: Mintage included in KM#871					
1947	3,481	—	90.00	140	190
1948	773	—	90.00	140	190
1949	582	—	90.00	140	190

KM# 852 50 KURUS **Weight:** 3.6083 g. **Composition:** 0.9170 Gold .0517 oz. AGW **Obverse:** Head of Ismet Inonu left

Date	Mintage	F	VF	XF	Unc
1923/20	—	50.00	90.00	120	175
1923/22	1,093	50.00	90.00	120	175
1923/23	897	50.00	120	140	200
1923/24	11,000	50.00	90.00	120	175
1923/25	3,004	50.00	90.00	120	175
1923/26	817	50.00	120	140	200
1923/27	5,228	50.00	90.00	120	175

KM# 872 100 KURUS **Weight:** 7.0160 g. **Composition:** 0.9170 Gold .2069 oz. AGW **Series:** Monnaie de Luxe **Obverse:** Head of Kemal Ataturk left

Date	Mintage	F	VF	XF	Unc
1942	8,659	—	110	140	225
1943	6,594	—	110	140	225
1944	7,160	—	110	140	225
1948	14,000	—	110	140	200
1950	25,000	—	110	140	200
1951	35,000	—	110	140	175
1952	41,000	—	110	140	175
1953	32,000	—	110	140	175
1954	24,000	—	110	140	175
1955	4,881	—	110	140	200
1956	11,000	—	80.00	100	130
1957	49,000	—	80.00	100	130
1958	67,000	—	80.00	100	130
1959	89,000	—	80.00	100	130
1960	57,000	—	80.00	100	130
1961	77,000	—	80.00	100	130
1962	108,000	—	80.00	100	130
1963	146,000	—	80.00	100	130
1964	128,000	—	80.00	100	130
1965	157,000	—	80.00	100	130
1966	190,000	—	80.00	100	130
1967	177,000	—	80.00	100	130
1968	143,000	—	80.00	100	130
1969	206,000	—	80.00	100	130
1970	253,000	—	80.00	100	130
1971	293,000	—	80.00	100	130
1972	222,000	—	80.00	100	130
1973	140,000	—	80.00	100	130
1974	82,000	—	80.00	100	130
1975	142,000	—	80.00	100	130
1976	265,000	—	80.00	100	130
1977	277,000	—	80.00	100	130
1978	86,000	—	80.00	100	130
1980	—	—	80.00	100	130

KM# 877 100 KURUS **Weight:** 7.0160 g. **Composition:** 0.9170 Gold .2069 oz. AGW **Series:** Monnaie de Luxe **Obverse:** Head of Ismet Inonu left

Date	Mintage	F	VF	XF	Unc
1943	—	140	190	265	325
Note: Mintage included in KM#872					
1944	—	140	190	265	375
Note: Mintage included in KM#872					
1945	2,202	140	190	265	400
1946	8,863	140	190	265	325
1947	28,000	140	190	265	325
1948	—	140	190	265	325
Note: Mintage included in KM#872					
1949	6,578	140	190	265	325
1950	—	140	190	265	325
Note: Mintage included in KM#872					

KM# 854 100 KURUS **Weight:** 7.2160 g. **Composition:** 0.9170 Gold .2126 oz. AGW **Obverse:** Head of Ismet Inonu left

Date	Mintage	F	VF	XF	Unc
1923/20	—	—	BV	80.00	140
1923/22 Rare	3	—	—	—	—
1923/23	381,000	—	BV	80.00	140
1923/24	2,274	—	BV	80.00	[illegible]
1923/25	28,000	—	BV	80.00	[illegible]
1923/26	2,097	—	BV	80.00	[illegible]
1923/27	17,000	—	BV	80.00	[illegible]

KM# 855 100 KURUS **Weight:** 7.2160 g. **Composition:** 0.9170 Gold .2126 oz. AGW **Obverse:** Head of Kemal Ataturk left

Date	Mintage	F	VF	XF	Unc
1923/20	29,000	—	BV	80.00	[illegible]
1923/27	Inc. above	—	BV	80.00	[illegible]
1923/28 Rare	3	—	—	—	—
1923/29	2,111	—	BV	80.00	[illegible]
1923/30	13,000	—	BV	80.00	[illegible]
1923/31	109,000	—	BV	80.00	[illegible]
1923/32	134,000	—	BV	80.00	[illegible]
1923/33	216,000	—	BV	80.00	[illegible]
1923/34	463,000	—	BV	80.00	[illegible]
1923/35	405,000	—	BV	80.00	[illegible]
1923/36	25,000	—	BV	80.00	[illegible]
1923/37	131,000	—	BV	80.00	[illegible]
1923/38	159,000	—	BV	80.00	[illegible]
1923/39	85,000	—	BV	80.00	[illegible]
1923/40	10,000	—	BV	80.00	[illegible]
1923/41	164,000	—	BV	80.00	[illegible]
1923/42	63,000	—	BV	80.00	[illegible]
1923/43	56,000	—	BV	80.00	[illegible]
1923/44	198,000	—	BV	80.00	[illegible]
1923/45	176,000	—	BV	80.00	[illegible]
1923/46	1,290,000	—	BV	80.00	[illegible]
1923/47	513,000	—	BV	80.00	[illegible]
1923/48	600	90.00	120	145	[illegible]
1923/49	1,300	—	90.00	115	[illegible]
1923/50	47,000	—	BV	80.00	[illegible]
1923/51	240,000	—	BV	80.00	[illegible]
1923/52	1,046,999	—	BV	80.00	[illegible]
1923/53	550,000	—	BV	80.00	[illegible]
1923/54	18,000	—	BV	80.00	[illegible]
1923/55	309,000	—	BV	80.00	[illegible]

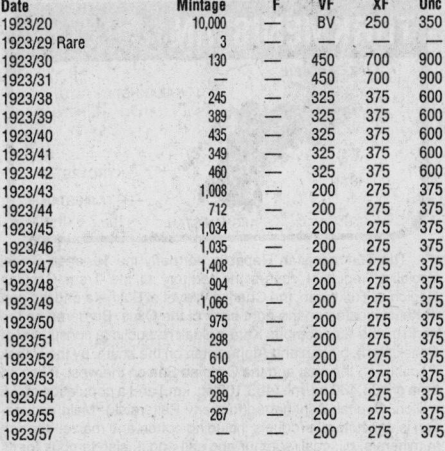

te	Mintage	F	VF	XF	Unc
3/57	—	—	BV	80.00	100
3/58	—	—	BV	80.00	100

M# 873 250 KURUS Weight: 17.5400 g. **Composition:** 0.9170 Gold .5169 oz. AGW **Series:** Monnaie de Luxe **Obverse:** Head of Kemal Ataturk left

te	Mintage	F	VF	XF	Unc
42	10,000	—	250	425	600
43	11,000	—	250	425	600
44	15,000	—	300	650	900
46	16,000	—	300	650	900
47	42,000	—	250	425	600
48	13,000	—	250	425	600
50	45,000	—	250	425	600
51	41,000	—	185	200	275
52	59,000	—	185	200	275
53	45,000	—	185	200	275
54	40,000	—	185	200	275
55	7,067	—	185	200	275
56	14,000	—	185	200	275
57	47,000	—	185	200	275
58	75,000	—	185	200	275
59	93,000	—	185	200	275
60	50,000	—	185	200	275
61	65,000	—	185	200	275
62	99,000	—	185	200	275
63	137,000	—	185	200	275
64	152,000	—	185	200	275
65	194,000	—	185	200	275
66	218,000	—	185	200	275
67	201,000	—	185	200	275
68	150,000	—	185	200	275
69	262,000	—	185	200	275
70	301,000	—	185	200	275
71	356,000	—	185	200	275
72	305,000	—	185	200	275
73	198,000	—	185	200	275
74	142,000	—	185	200	275
75	223,000	—	185	200	275
76	345,000	—	185	200	275
77	227,000	—	185	200	275
78	311,000	—	185	200	275
80	—	—	185	200	275

M# 878 250 KURUS Weight: 17.5400 g. **Composition:** 0.9170 Gold .5169 oz. AGW **Series:** Monnaie de Luxe **Obverse:** Head of Ismet Inonu left

te	Mintage	F	VF	XF	Unc
43	—	—	185	200	250

Note: Mintage included in KM#873

44	—	—	185	200	250

Note: Mintage included in KM#873

45	4,135	—	250	375	550
46	—	—	185	200	250

Note: Mintage included in KM#873

47	—	—	185	200	250

Note: Mintage included in KM#873

48	—	—	185	200	250

Note: Mintage included in KM#873

49	11,000	—	185	200	250
50	—	—	185	200	250

Note: Mintage included in KM#873

M# 856 250 KURUS Weight: 18.0400 g. **Composition:** 0.9170 Gold .5319 oz. AGW **Obverse:** Head of Ismet Inonu left

te	Mintage	F	VF	XF	Unc
23/20	—	—	220	270	375
23/23	14,000	—	220	270	375
23/24	60	—	300	400	500

M# 857 250 KURUS Weight: 18.0400 g. **Composition:** 0.9170 Gold .5319 oz. AGW **Obverse:** Head of Kemal Ataturk left

Date	Mintage	F	VF	XF	Unc
1923/20	10,000	—	BV	250	350
1923/29 Rare	3	—	—	—	—
1923/30	130	—	450	700	900
1923/31	—	—	450	700	900
1923/38	245	—	325	375	600
1923/39	389	—	325	375	600
1923/40	435	—	325	375	600
1923/41	349	—	325	375	600
1923/42	460	—	325	375	600
1923/43	1,008	—	200	275	375
1923/44	712	—	200	275	375
1923/45	1,034	—	200	275	375
1923/46	1,035	—	200	275	375
1923/47	1,408	—	200	275	375
1923/48	904	—	200	275	375
1923/49	1,066	—	200	275	375
1923/50	975	—	200	275	375
1923/51	298	—	200	275	375
1923/52	610	—	200	275	375
1923/53	586	—	200	275	375
1923/54	289	—	200	275	375
1923/55	267	—	200	275	375
1923/57	—	—	200	275	375

KM# 874 500 KURUS Weight: 35.0800 g. **Composition:** 0.9170 Gold 1.0338 oz. AGW **Series:** Monnaie de Luxe **Obverse:** Head of Kemal Ataturk left

Date	Mintage	F	VF	XF	Unc
1942	2,949	—	385	435	520
1943	1,210	—	385	435	520
1944	1,254	—	385	435	520
1947	3,699	—	385	435	520
1950	59	—	500	550	650
1951	21	—	500	550	650
1952	26	—	500	550	650
1953	35	—	500	550	650
1954	182	—	500	550	650
1955	14	—	500	550	650
1956	13	—	500	550	650
1957	68	—	500	550	650
1958	121	—	500	550	650
1959	294	—	500	550	650
1960	208	—	500	550	650
1961	619	—	385	435	520
1962	1,228	—	385	435	520
1963	1,985	—	385	435	520
1964	2,787	—	370	400	485
1965	4,631	—	370	400	485
1966	5,572	—	370	400	485
1967	6,637	—	370	400	485
1968	5,983	—	370	400	485
1969	7,152	—	370	400	485
1970	11,000	—	370	400	485
1971	15,000	—	370	400	485
1972	15,000	—	370	400	485
1973	7,939	—	370	400	485
1974	5,412	—	370	400	485
1975	6,205	—	370	400	485
1976	11,000	—	370	400	485
1977	6,931	—	370	400	485
1978	5,740	—	370	400	485
1980	—	—	370	400	485

KM# 879 500 KURUS Weight: 35.0800 g. **Composition:** 0.9170 Gold 1.0338 oz. AGW **Series:** Monnaie de Luxe **Obverse:** Head of Ismet Inonu left

Date	Mintage	F	VF	XF	Unc
1943	—	—	385	435	520

Note: Mintage included in KM#874

1944	—	—	385	435	520

Note: Mintage included in KM#874

1945	115	—	500	530	575
1946	298	—	500	530	575
1947	—	—	385	435	520

Note: Mintage included in KM#874

1948	40	—	500	530	575

KM# 858 500 KURUS Weight: 36.0800 g. **Composition:** 0.9170 Gold 1.0638 oz. AGW **Obverse:** Head of Ismet Inonu left

Date	Mintage	F	VF	XF	Unc
1923/20	—	—	BV	550	700
1923/23	9,006	—	BV	550	700
1923/24	7,923	—	650	800	900
1923/25	272	—	750	900	1,000

KM# 859 500 KURUS Weight: 36.0800 g. **Composition:** 0.9170 Gold 1.0638 oz. AGW **Obverse:** Head of Kemal Ataturk left

Date	Mintage	F	VF	XF	Unc
1923/20	12,000	—	BV	550	700
1923/27	615	—	650	800	1,000
1923/28	34	—	650	800	1,000
1923/29	137	—	575	700	900
1923/30	45	—	575	700	900
1923/31	100	—	575	700	900
1923/32	74	—	575	700	900
1923/33	268	—	550	650	800
1923/34	758	—	550	650	800
1923/35	1,586	—	BV	385	465
1923/36	765	—	BV	385	465
1923/37	983	—	BV	385	465
1923/38	1,738	—	BV	385	465
1923/39	2,629	—	BV	385	465
1923/40	2,763	—	BV	385	465
1923/41	3,440	—	BV	385	465

Date	Mintage	F	VF	XF	Unc
1923/42	3,335	—	BV	385	465
1923/43	4,914	—	BV	385	465
1923/44	4,308	—	BV	385	465
1923/45	3,488	—	BV	385	465
1923/46	5,636	—	BV	385	465
1923/47	7,588	—	BV	385	465
1923/48	6,060	—	BV	385	465
1923/49	4,235	—	BV	385	465
1923/50	4,733	—	BV	385	465
1923/51	2,757	—	BV	385	465
1923/52	2,041	—	BV	385	465
1923/53	4,819	—	BV	385	465
1923/54	1,401	—	BV	385	465
1923/55	1,484	—	BV	385	465
1923/57	—	—	BV	385	465

PATTERNS

Including off metal strikes

KM#	Date	Mintage	Identification	Mkt Val
Pn2	1948	—	5 Kurus. Brass. KM#887	500
Pn3	1948	—	10 Kurus. Brass. KM#888	500

PIEFORTS

KM#	Date	Mintage	Identification	Mkt Val
P1	1981	2,500	500 Lira. 0.9250 Silver. KM#931	165
P2	1981	1,200	3000 Lira. 0.9250 Silver. KM#948	180
P3	1981	—	30000 Lira. Gold. KM#955	1,350
P4	1982	600	3000 Lira. 0.9250 Silver. KM#959	125

MINT SETS

KM#	Date	Mintage	Identification	Issue Price	Mkt Val
MSA1	1949 (8)	—	KM#881-888	—	—
MS1	1962 (7)	—	KM#889a.1, 890.1, 891.1, 892.2, 893.1, 894 (1960), 895	—	—
MSA2	1963 (6)	—	KM#889a.1, 890.1, 891.1, 892.2, 893.1, 895a	—	—
MS2	1964 (6)	—	KM#889a.1, 890.1, 891.1, 892.2, 893.1, 895a	—	4.50
MS3	1965 (6)	—	KM#889a.1, 890.1, 891.1, 892.2, 893.1, 895a	—	4.50
MS4	1966 (6)	—	KM#889a.1, 890.1, 891.1, 892.2, 893.1, 895a	—	4.50
MSA5	1967 (6)	—	KM#889a.2, 890.1, 891.1, 892.3, 893.1, 895a	—	—
MS5	1968 (6)	—	KM#889a.2, 890.1, 891.1, 892.3, 893.1, 895a	—	4.50
MS6	1969 (6)	—	KM#889a.2, 890.2, 891.2, 892.3, 893.2, 895a	—	3.50
MS7	1970 (6)	—	KM#889a.2, 890.2, 891.2, 892.3, 893.2, 895a	—	3.50
MS8	1971 (6)	—	KM#889a.2, 890.2, 891.2, 893.2, 895a, 899	—	3.50
MS9	1972 (6)	—	KM#889a.2, 890.2, 891.2, 893.2, 895a, 899	—	3.50
MS10	1973 (7)	—	KM#889a.2, 890.2, 891.2, 892.3, 893.2, 895a, 899	—	3.00
MS11	1974 (7)	—	KM#889a.2, 890.3-892.3, 893.2, 895a, 899	—	3.00
MS12	1975 (7)	—	KM#889a.2, 890a, 891a, 893.2, 895c, 899, 905	—	3.00
MS13	1976 (7)	—	KM#889a.2, 890a, 891a, 893.2, 895c, 899, 905	—	3.00
MS14	1977 (8)	—	KM#889a.2, 890a, 891a, 892.3, 893.2, 895c, 899, 905	—	3.50
MS15	1978 (4)	—	KM#889a.2, 892.3, 893.2, 905	—	3.00
MS16	1979 (4)	—	KM#889a.2, 893.2, 899, 905	—	3.00
MS17	1980 (2)	—	KM#889a.2, 893.2	—	2.00
MS18	1981 (3)	—	KM#943-945	—	3.00
MS19	1982 (3)	—	KM#943, 949.1, 950.1	—	3.00
MS20	1983 (2)	—	KM#949.2, 950.2	—	3.00
MS21	1984 (6)	—	KM#962-967	—	5.50
MS22	1985 (6)	—	KM#962-964, 966, 967, 975	—	5.00
MS23	1986 (5)	—	KM#963-967	—	4.00
MS24	1989 (7)	9,350	KM#962-964, 975, 987, 988, and medal	2.00	2.00
MS25	1990 (5)	5,300	KM#987-989, 996, 997, and medal	4.00	8.50
MS26	1991 (5)	2,250	KM#987-989, 997, 1015, and mint medal	—	20.00
MS27	1992 (6)	2,240	KM#987-989, 997, 1015, 1025, and mint medal	—	20.00
MS28	1993 (6)	1,750	KM#987-989, 997, 1015, 1025, and mint medal	—	20.00
MS29	1994 (8)	2,500	KM#987-989, 997, 1015, 1025, 1027, 1042, plus mint medal	—	20.00
MS30	1995 (7)	2,500	KM#989, 1015, 1027-1029, 1041, 1043, plus mint medal	—	15.00
MS31	1996 (8)	10,000	KM#989, 1015, 1027-1029, 1041, 1050, 1056, plus mint medal	—	8.00
MS32	1997 (7)	—	KM#989, 1015, 1027.2, 1028, 1029, 1041, 1056, plus silver mint medal	—	20.00
MS33	2000 (3)	10,000	KM#860.1a, 893.1a, 905a Mixed dates	60.00	—
MS34	2000 (4)	25,000	KM#881a, 884a, 885a, 886a Mixed dates	325	—
MS35	2000 (7)	10,000	KM#860.1a, 881a, 884a, 885a, 886a, 893.1a, 905a Mixed dates	350	—

TURKMENISTAN

The Turkmenistan Republic (formerly the Turkmen Soviet Socialist Republic) covers the territory of the Trans-Caspian Region of Turkestan, the Charjiui Vilayet of Bukhara and the part of Khiva located on the right bank of the Oxus. Bordered on the north by the Autonomous Kara-Kalpak Republic (a constituent of Uzbekistan), by Iran and Afghanistan on the south, by the Usbek Republic on the east and the Caspian Sea on the west. It has an area of 186,400 sq. mi. (488,100 sq. km.) and a population of 3.5 million. Capital: Ashkhabad(formerly Poltoratsk). Main occupation is agricultural products including cotton and maize. It is rich in minerals, oil, coal, sulphur and salt and is also famous for its carpets, Turkoman horses and Karakui sheep.

The Turkomans arrived in Trancaspia as nomadic Seluk Turks in the 11th century. It often became subjected to one of the neighboring states. Late in the 19th century the Czarist Russians invaded with their first victory at Kyzyl Arvat in 1877, arriving in Ashkhabad in 1882 resulting in submission of the Turkmen tribes. By March 18,1884 the Transcaspian province of Russian Turkestan was formed. During WW I the Czarist government tried to conscript the Turkmen; this led to a revolt in Oct. 1916 under the leadership of Aziz Chapykov. In 1918 the Turks captured Baku from the Red army and the British sent a contingent to Merv to prevent a German-Turkish offensive toward Afghanistan and India. In mid-1919 a Bureau of Turkestan Moslem Communist Organization was formed in Moscow hoping to develop one large republic including all surrounding Turkic areas within a Soviet federation. A Turkestan Autonomous Soviet Socialist Republic was formed and plans to partition Turkestan into five republics according to the principle of nationalities was quickly implemented by Joseph Stalin. On Oct. 27, 1924 Turkmenistan became a Soviet Socialist Republic and was accepted as a member of the U.S.S.R. on Jan. 29, 1925. The Bureau of T.M.C.O. was disbanded in 1934. In Aug. 1990 the Turkmen Supreme Soviet adopted a declaration of sovereignty followed by a declaration of independence in Oct. 1991 joining the Commonwealth of Independent States in Dec. A new constitution was adopted in 1992 providing for an executive presidency.

MONETARY SYSTEM

100 Teññesi (Tengngesi) = 1 Manat

REPUBLIC

STANDARD COINAGE

100 Tennesi = 1 Manat

KM# 1 TEññESI Composition: Copper Plated Steel **Reverse:** President Saparmyrat Nyyazow bust left

Date	F	VF	XF	Unc	BU
1993	—	—	—	0.25	—

KM# 2 5 TEññESI Composition: Copper Plated Steel **Reverse:** President Saparmyrat Nyyazow bust left

Date	F	VF	XF	Unc	BU
1993	—	—	—	0.35	—

KM# 3 10 TEññESI Composition: Copper Plated Steel **Reverse:** President Saparmyrat Nyyazow bust left

Date	F	VF	XF	Unc	BU
1993	—	—	—	0.60	—

KM# 4 20 TEññESI Composition: Nickel Plated Ste **Reverse:** President Saparmyrat Nyyazow bust left

Date	F	VF	XF	Unc
1993	—	—	—	1.25

KM# 5 50 TEññESI Composition: Nickel Plated Ste **Reverse:** President Saparmyrat Nyyazow bust left

Date	F	VF	XF	Unc
1993	—	—	—	2.75

KM# 6 500 MANAT Weight: 28.2800 g. **Compositic** 0.9250 Silver .8410 oz. ASW **Series:** Endangered Wildli **Obverse:** Portrait of President Nyyakow **Reverse:** Goiter gazelle

Date	Mintage	F	VF	XF	Unc
1996 Proof	Est. 5,000	Value: 35.00			

KM# 7 500 MANAT Weight: 28.2800 g. **Compositio** 0.9250 Silver .8410 oz. ASW **Series:** Endangered Wildli **Obverse:** Portrait of President Nyyakow **Reverse:** Purpl Swamphen walking right

Date	Mintage	F	VF	XF	Unc
1996 Proof	Est. 5,000	Value: 35.00			

KM# 8 500 MANAT Weight: 28.2800 g. **Compositio** 0.9250 Silver .8410 oz. ASW **Series:** Endangered Wildli

Subject: Kaspi Ular **Obverse:** Portrait of President Nyyakow **Reverse:** Pair of Caspian Ular snowcock

Date	Mintage	F	VF	XF	Unc	BU
1996 Proof	Est. 5,000	Value: 35.00				

KM# 9 500 MANAT **Weight:** 28.2800 g. **Composition:** 0.9250 Silver .8410 oz. ASW **Series:** Endangered Wildlife **Subject:** Manui **Obverse:** Portrait of President Nyyakow **Reverse:** Pallas' cat

Date	Mintage	F	VF	XF	Unc	BU
1996 Proof	Est. 5,000	Value: 35.00				

KM# 10 500 MANAT **Weight:** 28.2800 g. **Composition:** 0.9250 Silver .8410 oz. ASW **Series:** Endangered Wildlife **Subject:** Gulan **Obverse:** Portrait of President Nyyakow **Reverse:** Asian wild ass

Date	Mintage	F	VF	XF	Unc	BU
1996 Proof	Est. 5,000	Value: 35.00				

KM# 11 500 MANAT **Weight:** 28.2800 g. **Composition:** 0.9250 Silver .8410 oz. ASW **Series:** Endangered Wildlife **Subject:** Turkmen Eublefary **Obverse:** Portrait of President Nyyakow **Reverse:** Turkmenic gecko

Date	Mintage	F	VF	XF	Unc	BU
1996 Proof	Est. 5,000	Value: 35.00				

KM# 12 500 MANAT **Composition:** Nickel Clad Steel **Obverse:** Denomination **Reverse:** President Nyyazow head left **Edge:** Reeded

Date	F	VF	XF	Unc	BU
1999	—	—	—	1.25	—

KM# 14 500 MANAT **Weight:** 28.2800 g. **Composition:** 0.9250 Silver .8410 oz. ASW **Series:** Wildlife Series **Subject:** Jaculus Turkmenicus **Obverse:** President Nyyazow head left **Reverse:** 2 Turkmenic Jerboa **Edge:** Reeded

Date	Mintage	F	VF	XF	Unc	BU
1999 Proof	Est. 5,000	Value: 35.00				

KM# 15 500 MANAT **Weight:** 28.2800 g. **Composition:** 0.9250 Silver .8410 oz. ASW **Series:** Wildlife Series **Subject:** Chlamydotis Undulata **Reverse:** 2 Houbara Bustards

Date	Mintage	F	VF	XF	Unc	BU
1999 Proof	Est. 5,000	Value: 35.00				

KM# 16 500 MANAT **Weight:** 28.2800 g. **Composition:** 0.9250 Silver .8410 oz. ASW **Series:** Wildlife Series **Subject:** Falco cherrug **Reverse:** Saker falcon on branch, falconer in back

Date	Mintage	F	VF	XF	Unc	BU
1999 Proof	Est. 5,000	Value: 35.00				

KM# 17 500 MANAT **Weight:** 28.2800 g. **Composition:** 0.9250 Silver .8410 oz. ASW **Series:** Wildlife Series **Subject:** Naja Oxiana **Reverse:** Cobra with hood open

Date	Mintage	F	VF	XF	Unc	BU
1999 Proof	Est. 5,000	Value: 37.50				

KM# 18 500 MANAT **Weight:** 28.2800 g. **Composition:** 0.9250 Silver .8410 oz. ASW **Series:** Wildlife Series **Subject:** Felis Caracal **Reverse:** Caracal seated

Date	Mintage	F	VF	XF	Unc	BU
1999 Proof	Est. 5,000	Value: 35.00				

KM# 19 500 MANAT **Weight:** 28.2800 g. **Composition:** 0.9250 Silver .8410 oz. ASW **Series:** Wildlife Series **Subject:** Panthera tigris

Date	Mintage	F	VF	XF	Unc	BU
1999 Proof	Est. 5,000	Value: 37.50				

KM# 20 500 MANAT **Weight:** 28.2800 g. **Composition:** 0.9250 Silver 0.841 oz. ASW **Subject:** 5th Anniversary of Neutrality **Obverse:** Male bust left. **Reverse:** Map and monument. **Edge:** Reeded. **Size:** 38.5 mm.

Date	Mintage	F	VF	XF	Unc	BU
ND Proof	5,000	Value: 35.00				

KM# 21 500 MANAT **Weight:** 28.2800 g. **Composition:** 0.9250 Silver 0.841 oz. ASW **Subject:** 5th Anniversary of Neutrality **Obverse:** Male bust left. **Reverse:** Astanbaba Mausoleum. **Edge:** Reeded. **Size:** 38.5 mm.

Date	Mintage	F	VF	XF	Unc	BU
2000 Proof	5,000	Value: 35.00				

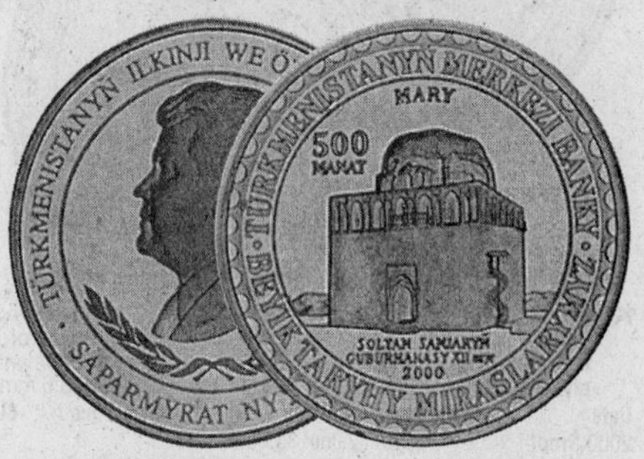

KM# 22 500 MANAT **Weight:** 28.2800 g. **Composition:** 0.9250 Silver 0.841 oz. ASW **Obverse:** Male bust left. **Reverse:** Square based Soltan Sanjar Mausoleum. **Edge:** Reeded. **Size:** 38.5 mm.

Date	Mintage	F	VF	XF	Unc	BU
2000 Proof	5,000	Value: 35.00				

KM# 23 500 MANAT Weight: 28.2800 g. **Composition:** 0.9250 Silver 0.841 oz. ASW **Obverse:** Male bust left. **Reverse:** Shirkebir Mausoleum - Mosque. **Edge:** Reeded. **Size:** 38.5 mm.

Date	Mintage	F	VF	XF	Unc	BU
2000 Proof	5,000	Value: 35.00				

KM# 24 500 MANAT Weight: 28.2800 g. **Composition:** 0.9250 Silver 0.841 oz. ASW **Obverse:** Male bust left. **Reverse:** Nisa Fortress, statue with mountaintop in background. **Edge:** Reeded. **Size:** 38.5 mm.

Date	Mintage	F	VF	XF	Unc	BU
2000 Proof	5,000	Value: 35.00				

KM# 25 500 MANAT Weight: 28.2800 g. **Composition:** 0.9250 Silver 0.841 oz. ASW **Subject:** 10th Anniversary of Independence **Obverse:** Male bust left. **Reverse:** Monument dividing 1991 and 2001 dates. **Edge:** Reeded. **Size:** 38.5 mm.

Date	Mintage	F	VF	XF	Unc	BU
2000 Proof	5,000	Value: 35.00				

KM# 13 1000 MANAT Composition: Nickel Clad Steel **Obverse:** Denomination **Reverse:** President Nyyazow head left **Edge:** Reeded

Date	F	VF	XF	Unc	BU
1999 Proof	—	—	—	2.50	—

PROOF SETS

KM#	Date	Mintage	Identification	Issue Price	Mkt Val
PS1	1996 (6)	5,000	KM#6-11	—	210

TURKS & CAICOS IS.

The Colony of the Turks and Caicos Islands, a British colony situated in the West Indies at the eastern end of the Bahama Islands, has an area of 166 sq. mi. (430 sq.km.) and a population of *10,000. Capital: Cockburn Town, on Grand Turk. The principal industry of the colony is the production of salt, which is gathered by raking. Salt, crayfish, and conch shells are exported.

The Turks and Caicos Islands were discovered by Juan Ponce de Leon in 1512, but were not settled until 1678when Bermudians arrived to rake salt from the salt ponds. The Spanish drove the British settlers from the island in 1710, during the long War of the Spanish Succession. They returned and throughout the remaining years of the war repulsed repeated attacks by France and Spain. In 1799 the islands were granted representation in the Bahamian assembly, but in 1848, on petition of the inhabitants, they were made a separate colony under Jamaica. They were annexed by Jamaica in 1873 and remained a dependency until 1959 when they became a unit territory of the Federation of the West Indies. When the Federation was dissolved in 1962, the Turks and Caicos Islands became a separate Crown Colony.

RULERS
British

MONETARY SYSTEM
100 Cents = 1 East Caribbean Dollar
1 Crown = 1 Dollar U.S.A.

CROWN COLONY

STANDARD COINAGE

1 Crown = 1 Dollar U.S.A.

KM# 51 1/4 CROWN Composition: Copper-Nickel

Date	F	VF	XF	Unc	BU
1981	—	—	—	1.50	—

KM# 52 1/2 CROWN Composition: Copper-Nickel

Date	F	VF	XF	Unc	BU
1981	—	—	—	2.00	—

KM# 1 CROWN Composition: Copper-Nickel

Date	Mintage	F	VF	XF	Unc	BU
1969	50,000	—	—	2.00	4.50	—
1969 Proof	6,000	Value: 6.00				

KM# 5 CROWN Composition: Copper-Nickel

Date	Mintage	F	VF	XF	Unc	BU
1975 Matte	590	—	—	—	10.00	—
1975 Proof	1,370	Value: 6.50				
1976	1,960	—	—	—	6.00	—
1976 Proof	2,270	Value: 6.50				
1977 Proof	1,420	Value: 6.50				

KM# 60 CROWN Composition: Copper-Nickel **Subject:** Prince Andrew's marriage

Date	Mintage	F	VF	XF	Unc	BU
1986	20,000	—	—	—	4.50	—

KM# 60a CROWN Weight: 28.2800 g. **Composition:** 0.9250 Silver .8411 oz. ASW **Subject:** Prince Andrew's marriage

Date	Mintage	F	VF	XF	Unc	BU
1986 Proof	5,000	Value: 13.50				

KM# 122 CROWN Composition: Copper-Nickel

Date	F	VF	XF	Unc	BU
1986	—	—	—	4.00	—

KM# 64 CROWN Composition: Copper-Nickel **Series:** World Wildlife Fund **Reverse:** Iguana

Date	F	VF	XF	Unc
1988	—	—	—	7.50

KM# 64a CROWN **Weight:** 28.2800 g. **Composition:** 0.9250 Silver .8411 oz. ASW **Series:** World Wildlife Fund **Reverse:** Iguana

Date	Mintage	F	VF	XF	Unc	BU
1988 Proof	Est. 25,000	Value: 20.00				

KM# 66 CROWN **Composition:** Copper-Nickel **Subject:** Queen Mother's 90th birthday

Date	F	VF	XF	Unc	BU
ND(1990)	—	—	—	5.50	—

KM# 66a CROWN **Weight:** 28.2800 g. **Composition:** 0.9250 Silver .8411 oz. ASW **Subject:** Queen Mother's 90th birthday

Date	Mintage	F	VF	XF	Unc	BU
ND(1990) Proof	Est. 10,000	Value: 22.50				

KM# 74 CROWN **Composition:** Copper-Nickel **Subject:** Royal birthdays

Date	F	VF	XF	Unc	BU
1991	—	—	—	4.50	—

KM# 74a CROWN **Weight:** 31.1200 g. **Composition:** 0.9990 Silver 0.9995 oz. ASW **Subject:** Royal Birthdays **Obverse:** Bust of Queen Elizabeth II right. **Reverse:** Queen Elizabeth II and Philip. **Edge:** Reeded with plain section containing fineness. **Size:** 39.1 mm.

Date	F	VF	XF	Unc	BU
1991 Proof	—	Value: 27.50			

KM# 76 CROWN **Composition:** Copper-Nickel **Subject:** 10th wedding anniversary - prince and princess of Wales

Date	F	VF	XF	Unc	BU
1991	—	—	—	4.00	—

KM# 76a CROWN **Weight:** 31.1200 g. **Composition:** 0.9990 Silver 0.9995 oz. ASW **Subject:** Tenth Royal Wedding Anniversary **Obverse:** Bust of Queen Elizabeth II right. **Reverse:** Princess Diana. **Edge:** Reeded with plain section containing fineness. **Size:** 39.1 mm.

Date	F	VF	XF	Unc	BU
1991 Proof	—	Value: 40.00			

KM# 121 CROWN **Composition:** Copper-Nickel **Subject:** 10th wedding anniversary - prince and princess of Wales **Reverse:** Prince Charles

Date	F	VF	XF	Unc	BU
1991	—	—	—	4.00	—

KM# 121a CROWN **Weight:** 31.2100 g. **Composition:** 0.9250 Silver .9282 oz. ASW

Date	F	VF	XF	Unc	BU
1991 Proof	—	Value: 35.00			

KM# 143 DOLLAR **Composition:** Copper-Nickel **Series:** Steam Locomotive **Subject:** City of Truro **Note:** Similar to 20 Dollars, KM#145.

Date	F	VF	XF	Unc	BU
1996	—	—	—	5.00	—

KM# 146 DOLLAR **Composition:** Copper-Nickel **Series:** Steam Locomotive **Subject:** Flying Scotsman **Note:** Similar to 20 Dollars, KM#148.

Date	F	VF	XF	Unc	BU
1996	—	—	—	5.00	—

KM# 149 DOLLAR **Composition:** Copper-Nickel **Series:** Steam Locomotive **Subject:** Rocket **Note:** Similar to 20 Dollars, KM#151.

Date	F	VF	XF	Unc	BU
1996	—	—	—	5.00	—

KM# 152 DOLLAR **Composition:** Copper-Nickel **Series:** Steam Locomotive **Subject:** Evening Star **Note:** Similar to 20 Dollars, KM#154.

Date	F	VF	XF	Unc	BU
1996	—	—	—	5.00	—

KM# 155 DOLLAR **Composition:** Copper-Nickel **Series:** Steam Locomotive **Subject:** Mallard **Note:** Similar to 20 Dollars, KM#157.

Date	F	VF	XF	Unc	BU
1996	—	—	—	5.00	—

KM# 158 DOLLAR **Composition:** Copper-Nickel **Series:** Steam Locomotive **Subject:** Princess Elizabeth **Note:** Similar to 20 Dollars, KM#160.

Date	F	VF	XF	Unc	BU
1996	—	—	—	5.00	—

KM# 161 DOLLAR **Composition:** Copper-Nickel **Series:** Steam Locomotive **Subject:** Southern Pacific Lines - Class GS4 **Note:** Similar to 20 Dollars, KM#163.

Date	F	VF	XF	Unc	BU
1996	—	—	—	5.00	—

KM# 164 DOLLAR **Composition:** Copper-Nickel **Series:** Steam Locomotive **Subject:** German States Railway Class 05 **Note:** Similar to 20 Dollars, KM#166.

Date	F	VF	XF	Unc	BU
1996	—	—	—	5.00	—

KM# 167 DOLLAR **Composition:** Copper-Nickel **Series:** Steam Locomotive **Subject:** Japanese National Railways Class 62 **Note:** Similar to 20 Dollars, KM#169.

Date	F	VF	XF	Unc	BU
1996	—	—	—	5.00	—

KM# 170 DOLLAR **Composition:** Copper-Nickel **Series:** Steam Locomotive **Subject:** Chinese State Railways Class RM **Note:** Similar to 20 Dollars, KM#171.

Date	F	VF	XF	Unc	BU
1996	—	—	—	5.00	—

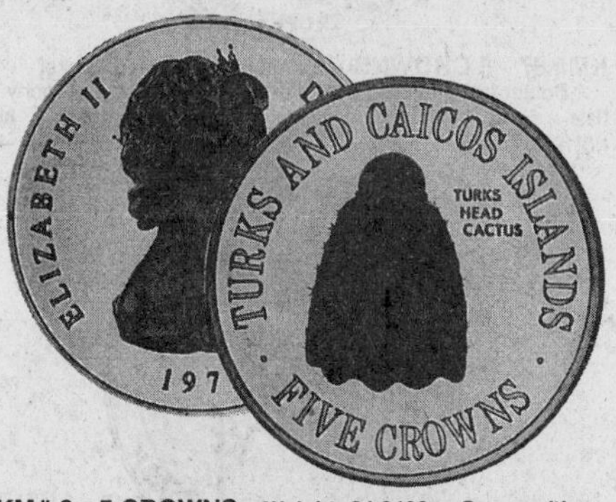

KM# 6 5 CROWNS **Weight:** 24.2400 g. **Composition:** 0.5000 Silver .3897 oz. ASW

Date	Mintage	F	VF	XF	Unc	BU
1975 Matte	440	—	—	—	18.00	—
1975 Proof	1,320	Value: 13.50				
1976	1,760	—	—	—	11.50	—
1976 Proof	2,220	Value: 11.50				
1977 Proof	1,370	Value: 13.50				

KM# 47 5 CROWNS **Weight:** 14.5800 g. **Composition:** 0.5000 Silver .2344 oz. ASW **Subject:** Lord Mountbatten **Obverse:** Similar to 10 Crowns, KM#45

Date	Mintage	F	VF	XF	Unc	BU
1980 Proof	—	Value: 9.50				

KM# 75 5 CROWNS **Composition:** Copper-Nickel **Subject:** Discovery of America **Reverse:** Columbus before Ferdinand and Isabella

Date	F	VF	XF	Unc	BU
1991	—	—	—	7.50	—

KM# 68 5 CROWNS **Composition:** Copper-Nickel **Series:** Olympics **Reverse:** Equestrian and 3 events

Date	F	VF	XF	Unc	BU
1992	—	—	—	4.50	—

KM# 69 5 CROWNS **Composition:** Copper-Nickel **Series:** Olympics **Reverse:** Gymnast on rings and 5 events

Date	F	VF	XF	Unc	BU
1992	—	—	—	4.50	—

KM# 70 5 CROWNS **Composition:** Copper-Nickel **Series:** Olympics **Reverse:** Weighlifting and 3 events

Date	F	VF	XF	Unc	BU
1992	—	—	—	4.50	—

KM# 71 5 CROWNS **Composition:** Copper-Nickel **Series:** Olympics **Reverse:** Rifle shooting and 3 events

Date	F	VF	XF	Unc	BU
1992	—	—	—	4.50	—

KM# 72 5 CROWNS **Composition:** Copper-Nickel **Series:** Olympics **Reverse:** Sail boarding and 3 events

Date	F	VF	XF	Unc	BU
1992	—	—	—	4.50	—

KM# 73 5 CROWNS **Composition:** Copper-Nickel **Series:** Olympics **Reverse:** Ski jumper and 4 events

Date	F	VF	XF	Unc	BU
1992	—	—	—	4.50	—

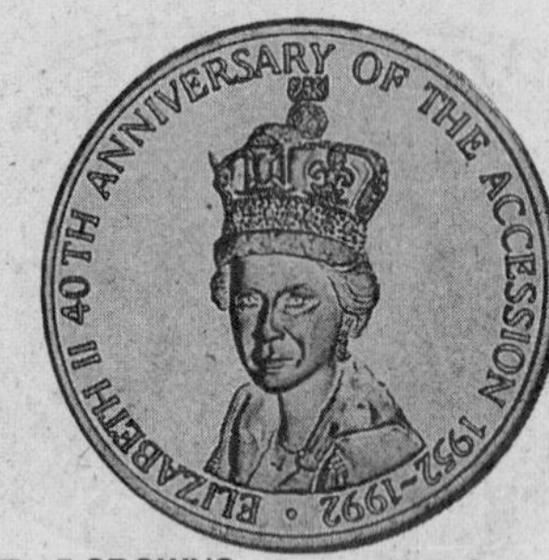

KM# 77 5 CROWNS **Composition:** Copper-Nickel **Subject:** 40th anniversary - reign of Elizabeth II

Date	F	VF	XF	Unc	BU
1992	—	—	—	6.75	—

KM# 77a 5 CROWNS **Weight:** 28.0400 g. **Composition:** 0.9250 Silver .8339 oz. ASW **Subject:** 40th anniversary - reign of Elizabeth II

Date	F	VF	XF	Unc	BU
1992 Proof	—	Value: 40.00			

KM# 84 5 CROWNS **Composition:** Copper-Nickel **Subject:** 40th anniversary - reign of Elizabeth II

Date	F	VF	XF	Unc	BU
1992	—	—	—	6.75	—

KM# 84a 5 CROWNS **Weight:** 28.0400 g. **Composition:** 0.9250 Silver .8339 oz. ASW **Subject:** 40th anniversary - reign of Elizabeth II

Date	F	VF	XF	Unc	BU
1992 Proof	—	Value: 40.00			

KM# 85 5 CROWNS **Composition:** Copper-Nickel **Subject:** 40th anniversary - reign of Elizabeth II **Reverse:** King George VI

Date	F	VF	XF	Unc	BU
1992	—	—	—	6.75	—

KM# 85a 5 CROWNS **Weight:** 28.0400 g. **Composition:** 0.9250 Silver .8339 oz. ASW **Subject:** 40th anniversary - reign of Elizabeth II **Reverse:** King George VI

Date	F	VF	XF	Unc	BU
1992 Proof	—	Value: 40.00			

KM# 86 5 CROWNS **Composition:** Copper-Nickel **Subject:** 40th anniversary - reign of Elizabeth II **Reverse:** Windsor Castle

Date	F	VF	XF	Unc	BU
1992	—	—	—	6.75	—

KM# 86a 5 CROWNS **Weight:** 28.2800 g. **Composition:** 0.9250 Silver .8339 oz. ASW **Subject:** 40th anniversary - reign of Elizabeth II **Reverse:** Windsor Castle

Date	F	VF	XF	Unc	BU
1992 Proof	—	Value: 40.00			

KM# 87 5 CROWNS **Composition:** Copper-Nickel **Subject:** World Cup '94 **Reverse:** Jules Rimet and trophy

Date	F	VF	XF	Unc	BU
ND(1993)	—	—	—	7.50	—

KM# 88 5 CROWNS **Composition:** Copper-Nickel **Subject:** World Cup '94 **Reverse:** Uruguay winners and 2 players

Date	F	VF	XF	Unc	BU
ND(1993)	—	—	—	7.50	—

KM# 89 5 CROWNS **Composition:** Copper-Nickel **Subject:** World Cup '94 **Reverse:** Italy winners - Dino Zoff

Date	F	VF	XF	Unc	BU
ND(1993)	—	—	—	7.50	—

KM# 90 5 CROWNS **Composition:** Copper-Nickel **Subject:** World Cup '94 **Reverse:** West Germany winners - Franz Beckenbauer

Date	F	VF	XF	Unc	BU
ND(1993)	—	—	—	7.50	—

KM# 91 5 CROWNS **Composition:** Copper-Nickel **Subject:** World Cup '94 **Reverse:** Brazil winners - Pele

Date	F	VF	XF	Unc	BU
ND(1993)	—	—	—	7.50	—

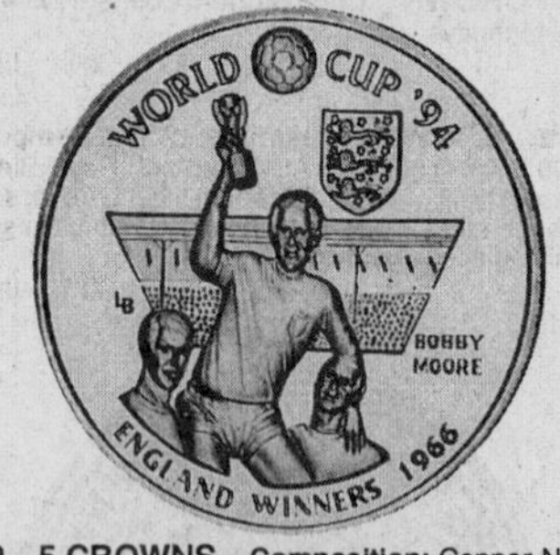

KM# 92 5 CROWNS **Composition:** Copper-Nickel **Subject:** World Cup '94 **Reverse:** England winners - Bobby Moore

Date	F	VF	XF	Unc	BU
ND(1993)	—	—	—	7.50	—

KM# 93 5 CROWNS **Composition:** Copper-Nickel
Subject: World Cup '94 **Reverse:** Argentina winners - Mario Kempes

Date	F	VF	XF	Unc	BU
ND(1993)	—	—	—	7.50	—

KM# 94 5 CROWNS **Composition:** Copper-Nickel
Subject: World Cup '94 **Reverse:** USA host - trophy and flag

Date	F	VF	XF	Unc	BU
ND(1993)	—	—	—	7.50	—

KM# 103 5 CROWNS **Composition:** Copper-Nickel
Subject: 40th anniversary of coronation **Reverse:** Westminster Abbey

Date	F	VF	XF	Unc	BU
ND(1993)	—	—	—	6.00	—

M# 104 5 CROWNS **Composition:** Copper-Nickel
Subject: 40th anniversary of coronation **Reverse:** Crown jewels

ate	F	VF	XF	Unc	BU
D(1993)	—	—	—	6.00	—

M# 105 5 CROWNS **Composition:** Copper-Nickel
Subject: 40th anniversary of coronation **Reverse:** Queen, clergy and Maids of Honor

e	F	VF	XF	Unc	BU
(1993)	—	—	—	6.00	—

KM# 106 5 CROWNS **Composition:** Copper-Nickel
Subject: 40th anniversary of coronation **Reverse:** Consort's homage

Date	F	VF	XF	Unc	BU
ND(1993)	—	—	—	6.00	—

KM# 107 5 CROWNS **Composition:** Copper-Nickel
Subject: 40th anniversary of coronation **Reverse:** Enthroned queen

Date	F	VF	XF	Unc	BU
ND(1993)	—	—	—	6.00	—

KM# 108 5 CROWNS **Composition:** Copper-Nickel
Subject: 40th anniversary of coronation **Reverse:** Queen in coach

Date	F	VF	XF	Unc	BU
ND(1993)	—	—	—	6.00	—

KM# 123 5 CROWNS **Composition:** Copper-Nickel
Series: 1994 Winter Olympics **Subject:** Speed skating

Date	F	VF	XF	Unc	BU
1993 Prooflike	—	—	—	4.75	—

KM# 124 5 CROWNS **Composition:** Copper-Nickel
Series: 1994 Winter Olympics **Subject:** Figure skating

Date	F	VF	XF	Unc	BU
1993 Prooflike	—	—	—	4.75	—

KM# 125 5 CROWNS **Composition:** Copper-Nickel
Series: 1994 Winter Olympics **Subject:** Ice hockey

Date	F	VF	XF	Unc	BU
1993 Prooflike	—	—	—	4.75	—

KM# 126 5 CROWNS **Composition:** Copper-Nickel
Series: 1994 Winter Olympics **Subject:** Slalom skiing

Date	F	VF	XF	Unc	BU
1993 Prooflike	—	—	—	4.75	—

KM# 127 5 CROWNS **Composition:** Copper-Nickel
Series: 1994 Winter Olympics **Subject:** Ski jumping

Date	F	VF	XF	Unc	BU
1993 Prooflike	—	—	—	4.75	—

KM# 128 5 CROWNS **Composition:** Copper-Nickel
Series: 1994 Winter Olympics **Reverse:** Bob sled and team

Date	F	VF	XF	Unc	BU
1993 Prooflike	—	—	—	4.75	—

KM# 177 5 CROWNS Composition: Copper-Nickel
Subject: 25th anniversary 1969-1994 - Apollo 11

Date	F	VF	XF	Unc	BU
1993	—	—	—	6.75	—

KM# 178 5 CROWNS Composition: Copper-Nickel
Subject: 25th anniversary 1969-1994 - Apollo 11 **Reverse:** Lunar landing

Date	F	VF	XF	Unc	BU
1993	—	—	—	6.75	—

KM# 179 5 CROWNS Composition: Copper-Nickel
Subject: 25th anniversary 1969-1994 - Apollo 11 **Reverse:** Astronaut descending ladder

Date	F	VF	XF	Unc	BU
1993	—	—	—	6.75	—

KM# 181 5 CROWNS Composition: Copper-Nickel
Subject: 25th anniversary 1969-1994 - Apollo 11 **Reverse:** Astronaut walking on the moon

Date	F	VF	XF	Unc	BU
1993	—	—	—	6.75	—

KM# 182 5 CROWNS Composition: Copper-Nickel
Subject: 25th anniversary 1969-1994 - Apollo 11 **Reverse:** Ocean recovery

Date	F	VF	XF	Unc	BU
1993	—	—	—	6.75	—

KM# 180 5 CROWNS Composition: Copper-Nickel
Subject: 25th anniversary 1969-1994 - Apollo 11 **Reverse:** Astronauts raising flag on moon

Date	F	VF	XF	Unc	BU
1994	—	—	—	6.75	—

KM# 234 5 CROWNS Weight: 3.1104 g. **Composition:** 0.9995 Platinum 0.1 oz. APW **Subject:** ANA Salute to Coin Collecting **Obverse:** Bust of Queen Elizabeth II right. **Reverse:** Astronaut on the moon, same design as KM#132. **Edge:** Reeded. **Size:** 16.5 mm.

Date	Mintage	F	VF	XF	Unc	BU
1994 Proof	200	Value: 100				

KM# 132 5 CROWNS Composition: Copper-Nickel
Subject: 25th anniversary 1969-1994 - Apollo 11 **Reverse:** First lunar landing, salute to American Numismatic Association and coin collecting

Date	Mintage	F	VF	XF	Unc	BU
1994 Prooflike	10,000	—	—	—	10.00	—

KM# 173 5 CROWNS Composition: Copper-Nickel
Subject: 50th anniversary - Normandy landing **Reverse:** Sir Bertram II Ramsay

Date	F	VF	XF	Unc	BU
1994	—	—	—	9.50	—

KM# 174 5 CROWNS Composition: Copper-Nickel
Subject: 50th anniversary - Normandy landing **Reverse:** Bernard L. Montgomery

Date	F	VF	XF	Unc	BU
1994	—	—	—	9.50	—

KM# 175 5 CROWNS Composition: Copper-Nickel
Subject: 50th anniversary - Normandy landing **Reverse:** Omar N. Bradley

Date	F	VF	XF	Unc	BU
1994	—	—	—	9.50	—

KM# 176 5 CROWNS Composition: Copper-Nickel
Subject: 50th anniversary - Normandy landing **Reverse:** Dwight D. Eisenhower

Date	F	VF	XF	Unc	BU
1994	—	—	—	9.50	—

KM# 133 5 CROWNS Composition: Copper-Nickel
Subject: 50th anniversary - VE Day **Reverse:** Roosevelt, Churchill, and Stalin

Date	F	VF	XF	Unc	B
1995	—	—	—	9.50	-

KM# 134 5 CROWNS Composition: Copper-Nickel
Subject: 50th anniversary - VE Day **Obverse:** Similar to KM#133 **Reverse:** Planes

Date	F	VF	XF	Unc
1995	—	—	—	7.50

 # 135 5 CROWNS **Composition:** Copper-Nickel **Subject:** 50th anniversary - VE Day **Obverse:** Similar to KM#133 **Reverse:** U.S. and Soviet troops meet

	F	VF	XF	Unc	BU
5	—	—	—	7.50	—

 # 136 5 CROWNS **Composition:** Copper-Nickel **Subject:** 50th anniversary - VE Day **Obverse:** Similar to KM#133 **Reverse:** London, Washington and Paris

	F	VF	XF	Unc	BU
5	—	—	—	7.50	—

 # 188 5 CROWNS **Weight:** 10.0000 g. **Composition:** 0.9990 Silver .3212 oz. ASW **Series:** XXVI Summer Olympics **Reverse:** Hurdlers **Note:** Similar to 20 Crowns, KM#189.

	F	VF	XF	Unc	BU
5 Proof	—	Value: 15.00			

 # 190 5 CROWNS **Weight:** 10.0000 g. **Composition:** 0.9990 Silver .3212 oz. ASW **Series:** XXVI Summer Olympics **Reverse:** Cyclist **Note:** Similar to 20 Crowns, KM#191.

	F	VF	XF	Unc	BU
5 Proof	—	Value: 15.00			

 # 192 5 CROWNS **Weight:** 10.0000 g. **Composition:** 0.9990 Silver .3212 oz. ASW **Series:** XXVI Summer Olympics **Reverse:** Fencers **Note:** Similar to 20 Crowns, KM#193.

	F	VF	XF	Unc	BU
5 Proof	—	Value: 15.00			

 # 194 5 CROWNS **Weight:** 10.0000 g. **Composition:** 0.9990 Silver .3212 oz. ASW **Series:** XXVI Summer Olympics **Reverse:** Equestrian **Note:** Similar to 20 Crowns, KM#195.

	F	VF	XF	Unc	BU
5 Proof	—	Value: 15.00			

 # 196 5 CROWNS **Weight:** 10.0000 g. **Composition:** 0.9990 Silver .3212 oz. ASW **Series:** XXVI Summer Olympics **Reverse:** Pole vaulter **Note:** Similar to 20 Crowns, KM#197.

	F	VF	XF	Unc	BU
5 Proof	—	Value: 15.00			

 # 198 5 CROWNS **Weight:** 10.0000 g. **Composition:** 0.9990 Silver .3212 oz. ASW **Series:** XXVI Summer Olympics **Reverse:** Runners **Note:** Similar to 20 Crowns, KM#199.

	F	VF	XF	Unc	BU
5 Proof	—	Value: 15.00			

 # 200 5 CROWNS **Weight:** 10.0000 g. **Composition:** 0.9990 Silver .3212 oz. ASW **Series:** XXVI Summer Olympics **Reverse:** Gymnast **Note:** Similar to 20 Crowns, KM#201.

	F	VF	XF	Unc	BU
5 Proof	—	Value: 15.00			

 # 202 5 CROWNS **Weight:** 10.0000 g. **Composition:** 0.9990 Silver .3212 oz. ASW **Series:** XXVI Summer Olympics **Reverse:** Swimmer **Note:** Similar to 20 Crowns, KM#203.

	F	VF	XF	Unc	BU
5 Proof	—	Value: 15.00			

 # 204 5 CROWNS **Weight:** 10.0000 g. **Composition:** 0.9990 Silver .3212 oz. ASW **Series:** XXVI Summer Olympics **Reverse:** Diver **Note:** Similar to 20 Crowns, KM#205.

	F	VF	XF	Unc	BU
5 Proof	—	Value: 15.00			

KM# 206 5 CROWNS **Weight:** 10.0000 g. **Composition:** 0.9990 Silver .3212 oz. ASW **Series:** XXVI Summer Olympics **Reverse:** Sprinter

Date	F	VF	XF	Unc	BU
1995 Proof	—	Value: 15.00			

KM# 225 5 CROWNS **Weight:** 26.2000 g. **Composition:** Brass **Subject:** Mother Theresa **Obverse:** National arms **Reverse:** Portrait **Edge:** Reeded **Size:** 39.1 mm.

Date	F	VF	XF	Unc	BU
1997	—	—	—	10.00	—

KM# 238 5 CROWNS **Weight:** 1.5600 g. **Composition:** 0.9999 Gold 0.0502 oz. AGW **Obverse:** Queen's portrait **Reverse:** Two Bottle-nosed Dolphins **Edge:** Reeded **Size:** 13.7 mm.

Date	F	VF	XF	Unc	BU
1998	—	Value: 45.00			

Note: Proof

KM# 232 5 CROWNS **Weight:** 26.4300 g. **Composition:** Copper-Nickel **Subject:** Year of the Tiger **Obverse:** Bust of Queen Elizabeth II right. **Reverse:** Stylized tiger. **Edge:** Reeded. **Size:** 39.2 mm.

Date	F	VF	XF	Unc	BU
1998	—	—	—	7.50	—

KM# 233 5 CROWNS **Weight:** 26.4300 g. **Composition:** Copper-Nickel **Subject:** Royal Navy Submarines **Obverse:** Bust of Queen Elizabeth II right. **Reverse:** Old and modern submarines. **Edge:** Reeded. **Size:** 39.2 mm.

Date	F	VF	XF	Unc	BU
2001	—	—	—	7.50	—

KM# 144 5 DOLLARS **Weight:** 10.0000 g. **Composition:** 0.9990 Silver .3212 oz. ASW **Series:** Steam Locomotive **Subject:** City of Truro **Note:** Similar to 20 Dollars, KM#145.

Date	Mintage	F	VF	XF	Unc	BU
1996 Proof	Est. 25,000	Value: 22.00				

KM# 147 5 DOLLARS **Weight:** 10.0000 g. **Composition:** 0.9990 Silver .3212 oz. ASW **Series:** Steam Locomotive **Subject:** Flying Scotsman **Note:** Similar to 20 Dollars, KM#148.

Date	Mintage	F	VF	XF	Unc	BU
1996 Proof	Est. 25,000	Value: 22.00				

KM# 150 5 DOLLARS **Weight:** 10.0000 g. **Composition:** 0.9990 Silver .3212 oz. ASW **Series:** Steam Locomotive **Subject:** Rocket **Note:** Similar to 20 Dollars, KM#151.

Date	Mintage	F	VF	XF	Unc	BU
1996 Proof	Est. 25,000	Value: 22.00				

KM# 153 5 DOLLARS **Weight:** 10.0000 g. **Composition:** 0.9990 Silver .3212 oz. ASW **Series:** Steam Locomotive **Subject:** Evening Star **Note:** Similar to 20 Dollars, KM#154.

Date	Mintage	F	VF	XF	Unc	BU
1996 Proof	Est. 25,000	Value: 22.00				

KM# 156 5 DOLLARS **Weight:** 10.0000 g. **Composition:** 0.9990 Silver .3212 oz. ASW **Series:** Steam Locomotive **Subject:** Mallard **Note:** Similar to 20 Dollars, KM#157.

Date	Mintage	F	VF	XF	Unc	BU
1996 Proof	Est. 25,000	Value: 22.00				

KM# 159 5 DOLLARS **Weight:** 10.0000 g. **Composition:** 0.9990 Silver .3212 oz. ASW **Series:** Steam Locomotive **Subject:** Princess Elizabeth **Note:** Similar to 20 Dollars, KM#160.

Date	Mintage	F	VF	XF	Unc	BU
1996 Proof	Est. 25,000	Value: 22.00				

KM# 162 5 DOLLARS **Weight:** 10.0000 g. **Composition:** 0.9990 Silver .3212 oz. ASW **Series:** Steam Locomotive **Subject:** Southern Pacific Lines - Class GS4 **Note:** Similar to 20 Dollars, KM#163.

Date	Mintage	F	VF	XF	Unc	BU
1996 Proof	Est. 25,000	Value: 22.00				

KM# 165 5 DOLLARS **Weight:** 10.0000 g. **Composition:** 0.9990 Silver .3212 oz. ASW **Series:** Steam Locomotive **Subject:** German States Railway - Class 05 **Note:** Similar to 20 Dollars, KM#166.

Date	Mintage	F	VF	XF	Unc	BU
1996 Proof	Est. 25,000	Value: 22.00				

KM# 168 5 DOLLARS **Weight:** 10.0000 g. **Composition:** 0.9990 Silver .3212 oz. ASW **Series:** Steam Locomotive **Subject:** Japanese National Railways - Class 62 **Note:** Similar to 20 Dollars, KM#169.

Date	Mintage	F	VF	XF	Unc	BU
1996 Proof	Est. 25,000	Value: 22.00				

KM# 171 5 DOLLARS **Weight:** 10.0000 g. **Composition:** 0.9990 Silver .3212 oz. ASW **Series:** Steam Locomotive **Subject:** Chinese State Railways - Class RM **Note:** Similar to 20 Dollars, KM#172.

Date	Mintage	F	VF	XF	Unc	BU
1996 Proof	Est. 25,000	Value: 22.00				

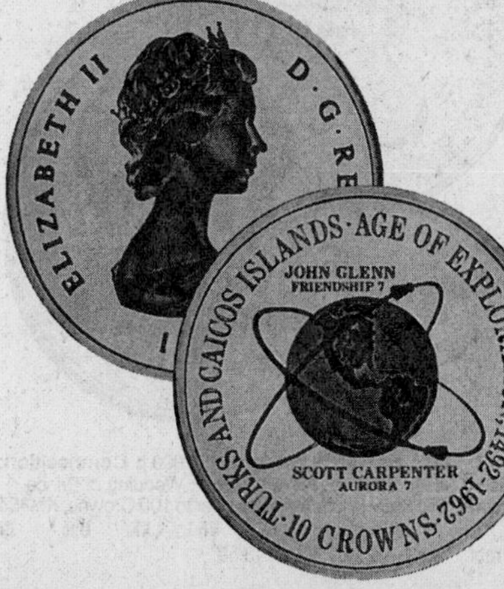

KM# 7 10 CROWNS **Weight:** 29.9800 g. **Composition:** 0.9250 Silver .8916 oz. ASW **Subject:** Age of exploration **Reverse:** Spacecraft

Date	Mintage	F	VF	XF	Unc	BU
1975 Matte	1,250	—	—	—	16.50	—
1975 Proof	2,935	Value: 14.50				

KM# 12 10 CROWNS **Weight:** 29.9800 g. **Composition:** 0.9250 Silver .8916 oz. ASW **Obverse:** Similar to KM#7

Date	Mintage	F	VF	XF	Unc	BU
1976	4,185	—	—	—	12.50	—
1976 Proof	2,220	Value: 15.00				
1977 Proof	1,370	Value: 16.50				

KM# 45 10 CROWNS **Weight:** 29.7000 g. **Composition:** 0.9250 Silver .8832 oz. ASW **Subject:** 10th anniversary - Prince Charles' investiture

Date	Mintage	F	VF	XF	Unc	BU
1979 Proof	25,000	Value: 10.00				

KM# 48 10 CROWNS **Weight:** 23.3300 g. **Composition:** 0.5000 Silver .3750 oz. ASW **Subject:** Lord Mountbatten **Obverse:** Similar to KM#45

Date		F	VF	XF	Unc	BU
1980 Proof	—	Value: 12.50				

KM# 53 10 CROWNS **Weight:** 29.7000 g. **Composition:** 0.9250 Silver .8832 oz. ASW **Subject:** Wedding of Prince Charles and Lady Diana **Note:** Similar to 100 Crowns, KM#54.

Date	Mintage	F	VF	XF	Unc	BU
1981 Proof	40,000	Value: 18.50				

KM# 55 10 CROWNS **Weight:** 23.2800 g. **Composition:** 0.9250 Silver .6923 oz. ASW **Series:** International Year of the Child

Date	Mintage	F	VF	XF	Unc	BU
1982 Proof	7,928	Value: 20.00				

KM# 56 10 CROWNS **Weight:** 23.2800 g. **Composition:** 0.9250 Silver .6923 oz. ASW **Subject:** World Football Chmpionship **Reverse:** 1 player

Date	Mintage	F	VF	XF	Unc	BU
1982 Proof	7,865	Value: 18.50				

KM# 57 10 CROWNS **Weight:** 23.2800 g. **Composition:** 0.9250 Silver .6923 oz. ASW **Subject:** World Football Championship **Reverse:** 2 players

Date	Mintage	F	VF	XF	Unc	BU
1982 Proof	7,165	Value: 18.50				

KM# 58 10 CROWNS **Weight:** 23.2800 g. **Composition:** 0.9250 Silver .6923 oz. ASW **Series:** Summer Olympics **Reverse:** Javelin thrower

Date	Mintage	F	VF	XF	Unc	BU
1984 Proof	2,160	Value: 20.00				

KM# 63 10 CROWNS **Weight:** 23.2800 g. **Composition:** 0.9250 Silver .6923 oz. ASW **Series:** Decade for Women

Date	Mintage	F	VF	XF	Unc	BU
1985 Proof	1,001	Value: 35.00				

KM# 2 20 CROWNS **Weight:** 38.7000 g. **Composition:** 0.9250 Silver 1.1509 oz. ASW **Subject:** Centenary - birth of Churchill

Date	Mintage	F	VF	XF	Unc	BU
1974 Matte	268,000	—	—	—	17.50	—
1974 Proof	8,400	Value: 25.00				

Note: 4,100 issued individually; 4,300 issued in binational sets with Cayman Islands 25 Dollars, KM#10.

KM# 8 20 CROWNS **Weight:** 38.7000 g. **Compositio** 0.9250 Silver 1.1509 oz. ASW **Subject:** Age of Exploratio **Obverse:** Similar to 10 Crowns, KM#7 **Reverse:** Christoph Columbus

Date	Mintage	F	VF	XF	Unc
1975 Matte	1,037	—	—	—	22.50
1975 Proof	2,769	Value: 23.50			

1# 13 20 CROWNS **Weight:** 38.7000 g. **Composition:** 0.9250 Silver 1.1509 oz. ASW **Subject:** U.S. Bicentennial **Obverse:** Similar to 10 Crowns, KM#7

e	Mintage	F	VF	XF	Unc	BU
6 Matte	5,022	—	—	—	20.00	—
6 Proof	4,474	Value: 22.50				

1# 14 20 CROWNS **Weight:** 38.7000 g. **Composition:** 0.9250 Silver 1.1509 oz. ASW **Obverse:** Similar to 10 Crowns, KM#7 **Reverse:** 4 Victoria cameos

e	Mintage	F	VF	XF	Unc	BU
6	25,000	—	—	—	17.50	—
6 Proof	22,000	Value: 22.50				
7 Proof	1,934	Value: 27.50				

1# 18 20 CROWNS **Weight:** 38.7000 g. **Composition:** 0.9250 Silver 1.1509 oz. ASW **Obverse:** Similar to 1/2 Crown, KM#52 **Reverse:** 4 George III cameos

e	Mintage	F	VF	XF	Unc	BU
7	—	—	—	—	27.50	—
7 Proof	1,973	Value: 32.50				

KM# 23 20 CROWNS **Weight:** 38.7000 g. **Composition:** 0.9250 Silver 1.1509 oz. ASW **Subject:** XI Commonwealth Games **Obverse:** Similar to 10 Crowns, KM#55

Date	Mintage	F	VF	XF	Unc	BU
1978 Proof	10,000	Value: 20.00				

KM# 49 20 CROWNS **Weight:** 29.8100 g. **Composition:** 0.5000 Silver .4792 oz. ASW **Subject:** Lord Mountbatten **Obverse:** Similar to 10 Crowns, KM#45

Date	F	VF	XF	Unc	BU
1980 Proof	—	Value: 22.50			

KM# 131.1 20 CROWNS **Weight:** 28.0400 g. **Composition:** 0.9250 Silver .8339 oz. ASW **Subject:** Discovery of America **Obverse:** Crude portrait **Reverse:** Columbus and Indians exchange gifts

Date	F	VF	XF	Unc	BU
1981 Proof	—	Value: 27.50			

KM# 67.1 20 CROWNS **Weight:** 28.0400 g. **Composition:** 0.9250 Silver .8339 oz. ASW **Subject:** Discovery of America **Obverse:** Crude portrait **Reverse:** Santa Maria

Date	F	VF	XF	Unc	BU
1989 Proof	—	Value: 27.50			

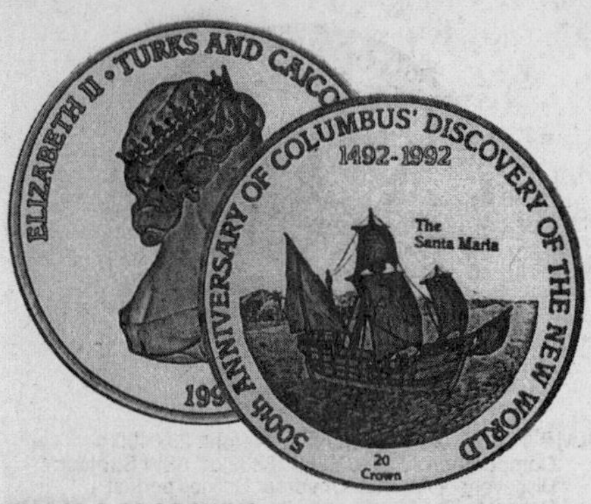

KM# 67.2 20 CROWNS **Weight:** 28.0400 g. **Composition:** 0.9250 Silver .8339 oz. ASW **Subject:** Discovery of America **Obverse:** Refined portrait **Reverse:** Santa Maria

Date	F	VF	XF	Unc	BU
1991 Proof	—	Value: 30.00			

KM# 67.3 20 CROWNS **Weight:** 28.0400 g. **Composition:** 0.9250 Silver .8339 oz. ASW **Subject:** Discovery of America **Obverse:** Refined portrait #2 **Reverse:** Santa Maria

Date	F	VF	XF	Unc	BU
1992 Proof	—	Value: 30.00			

KM# 115.1 20 CROWNS **Weight:** 28.0400 g. **Composition:** 0.9250 Silver .8339 oz. ASW **Subject:** Discovery of America **Obverse:** Crude portrait **Reverse:** The Nina

Date	F	VF	XF	Unc	BU
1989 Proof	—	Value: 27.50			

KM# 115.2 20 CROWNS **Weight:** 28.0400 g. **Composition:** 0.9250 Silver .8339 oz. ASW **Subject:** Discovery of America **Obverse:** Refined portrait **Reverse:** The Nina

Date	F	VF	XF	Unc	BU
1991 Proof	—	Value: 30.00			

KM# 115.3 20 CROWNS **Weight:** 28.0400 g. **Composition:** 0.9250 Silver .8339 oz. ASW **Subject:** Discovery of America **Obverse:** Refined portrait #2, similar to KM#67.3 **Reverse:** The Nina

Date	F	VF	XF	Unc	BU
1992 Proof	—	Value: 30.00			

KM# 116.1 20 CROWNS **Weight:** 28.0400 g. **Composition:** 0.9250 Silver .8339 oz. ASW **Subject:** Discovery of America **Obverse:** Crude portrait **Reverse:** The Pinta

Date	F	VF	XF	Unc	BU
1989 Proof	—	Value: 27.50			

KM# 116.2 20 CROWNS **Weight:** 28.0400 g. **Composition:** 0.9250 Silver .8339 oz. ASW **Subject:** Discovery of America **Obverse:** Refined portrait **Reverse:** The Pinta

Date	F	VF	XF	Unc	BU
1991 Proof	—	Value: 30.00			

KM# 116.3 20 CROWNS **Weight:** 28.0400 g. **Composition:** 0.9250 Silver .8339 oz. ASW **Subject:** Discovery of America **Obverse:** Refined portrait #2, similar to KM#67.3 **Reverse:** The Pinta

Date	F	VF	XF	Unc	BU
1992 Proof	—	Value: 30.00			

KM# 117.1 20 CROWNS **Weight:** 28.0400 g. **Composition:** 0.9250 Silver .8339 oz. ASW **Subject:** Discovery of America **Obverse:** Crude portrait **Reverse:** Ships set sail

Date	F	VF	XF	Unc	BU
1989 Proof	—	Value: 27.50			

KM# 117.2 20 CROWNS **Weight:** 28.0400 g. **Composition:** 0.9250 Silver .8339 oz. ASW **Subject:** Discovery of America **Obverse:** Refined portrait **Reverse:** Ships set sail

Date	F	VF	XF	Unc	BU
1991 Proof	—	Value: 30.00			

KM# 117.3 20 CROWNS **Weight:** 28.0400 g. **Composition:** 0.9250 Silver .8339 oz. ASW **Subject:** Discovery of America **Obverse:** Refined portrait #2, similar to KM#67.3 **Reverse:** Ships set sail

Date	F	VF	XF	Unc	BU
1992 Proof	—	Value: 30.00			

KM# 118.1 20 CROWNS **Weight:** 28.0400 g. **Composition:** 0.9250 Silver .8339 oz. ASW **Subject:** Discovery of America **Obverse:** Crude portrait **Reverse:** Ships crossing the Atlantic

Date	F	VF	XF	Unc	BU
1989 Proof	—	Value: 27.50			

KM# 118.2 20 CROWNS **Weight:** 28.0400 g. **Composition:** 0.9250 Silver .8339 oz. ASW **Subject:** Discovery of America **Obverse:** Refined portrait **Reverse:** Ships crossing the Atlantic

Date	F	VF	XF	Unc	BU
1991 Proof	—	Value: 30.00			

KM# 118.3 20 CROWNS **Weight:** 28.0400 g. **Composition:** 0.9250 Silver .8339 oz. ASW **Subject:** Discovery of America **Obverse:** Refined portrait #2, similar to KM#67.3 **Reverse:** Ships crossing the Atlantic

Date	F	VF	XF	Unc	BU
1992 Proof	—	Value: 30.00			

KM# 119.1 20 CROWNS **Weight:** 28.0400 g. **Composition:** 0.9250 Silver .8339 oz. ASW **Subject:** Discovery of America **Obverse:** Crude portrait **Reverse:** Siting land

Date	F	VF	XF	Unc	BU
1989 Proof	—	Value: 27.50			

KM# 119.2 20 CROWNS **Weight:** 28.0400 g. **Composition:** 0.9250 Silver .8339 oz. ASW **Subject:** Discovery of America **Obverse:** Refined portrait **Reverse:** Siting land

Date	F	VF	XF	Unc	BU
1991 Proof	—	Value: 30.00			

KM# 119.3 20 CROWNS **Weight:** 28.0400 g. **Composition:** 0.9250 Silver .8339 oz. ASW **Subject:** Discovery of America **Obverse:** Refined portrait #2, similar to KM#67.3 **Reverse:** Siting land

Date	F	VF	XF	Unc	BU
1992 Proof	—	Value: 30.00			

KM# 120.1 20 CROWNS **Weight:** 28.0400 g. **Composition:** 0.9250 Silver .8339 oz. ASW **Subject:** Discovery of America **Obverse:** Crude portrait **Reverse:** Columbus explores the Caribbean

Date	F	VF	XF	Unc	BU
1989 Proof	—	Value: 27.50			

KM# 120.2 20 CROWNS **Weight:** 28.0400 g. **Composition:** 0.9250 Silver .8339 oz. ASW **Subject:** Discovery of America **Obverse:** Refined portrait **Reverse:** Columbus explores the Caribbean

Date	F	VF	XF	Unc	BU
1991 Proof	—	Value: 30.00			

KM# 120.3 20 CROWNS **Weight:** 28.0400 g. **Composition:** 0.9250 Silver .8339 oz. ASW **Subject:** Discovery of America **Obverse:** Refined portrait #2, similar to KM#67.3 **Reverse:** Columbus explores the Caribbean

Date	F	VF	XF	Unc	BU
1992 Proof	—	Value: 30.00			

KM# 129.1 20 CROWNS **Weight:** 28.0400 g. **Composition:** 0.9250 Silver .8339 oz. ASW **Subject:** Discovery of America **Obverse:** Crude portrait **Reverse:** Columbus sights new world

Date	F	VF	XF	Unc	BU
1989 Proof	—	Value: 27.50			

KM# 129.2 20 CROWNS **Weight:** 28.0400 g. **Composition:** 0.9250 Silver .8339 oz. ASW **Subject:** Discovery of America **Obverse:** Refined portrait **Reverse:** Columbus sights new world

Date	F	VF	XF	Unc	B
1991 Proof	—	Value: 30.00			

KM# 129.3 20 CROWNS **Weight:** 28.0400 g. **Composition:** 0.9250 Silver .8339 oz. ASW **Subject:** Discovery of America **Obverse:** Refined portrait #2, simila to KM#67.3 **Reverse:** Columbus sights new world

Date	F	VF	XF	Unc	B
1992 Proof	—	Value: 30.00			

KM# 130.1 20 CROWNS **Weight:** 28.0400 g. **Composition:** 0.9250 Silver .8339 oz. ASW **Subject:** Discovery of America **Obverse:** Crude portrait **Reverse:** Columbus claims land for Spain

Date	F	VF	XF	Unc
1989 Proof	—	Value: 27.50		

 # 130.2 20 CROWNS **Weight:** 28.0400 g. **Composition:** 0.9250 Silver .8339 oz. ASW **Subject:** Discovery of America **Obverse:** Refined portrait **Reverse:** Columbus claims land for Spain

		F	VF	XF	Unc	BU
1 Proof	—	Value: 30.00				

 # 130.3 20 CROWNS **Weight:** 28.0400 g. **Composition:** 0.9250 Silver .8339 oz. ASW **Subject:** Discovery of America **Obverse:** Refined portrait #2, similar to KM#67.3 **Reverse:** Columbus claims land for Spain

		F	VF	XF	Unc	BU
2 Proof	—	Value: 30.00				

 # 131.2 20 CROWNS **Weight:** 28.0400 g. **Composition:** 0.9250 Silver .8339 oz. ASW **Subject:** Discovery of America **Obverse:** Refined portrait **Reverse:** Columbus and Indians exchange gifts

		F	VF	XF	Unc	BU
1 Proof	—	Value: 30.00				

 # 131.3 20 CROWNS **Weight:** 28.0400 g. **Composition:** 0.9250 Silver .8339 oz. ASW **Subject:** Discovery of America **Obverse:** Refined portrait #2, similar to KM#67.3 **Reverse:** Columbus and Indians exchange gifts

		F	VF	XF	Unc	BU
2 Proof	—	Value: 30.00				

 # 226 20 CROWNS **Weight:** 31.1700 g. **Composition:** 0.9990 Silver 1.0011 oz. ASW **Subject:** 40th Anniversary of Accession **Obverse:** National arms. **Reverse:** Queen Elizabeth II wearing crown half facing. **Edge:** Reeded. **Size:** 38.9 mm.

		F	VF	XF	Unc	BU
1992) Proof	—	Value: 30.00				
3 Proof	—	Value: 30.00				

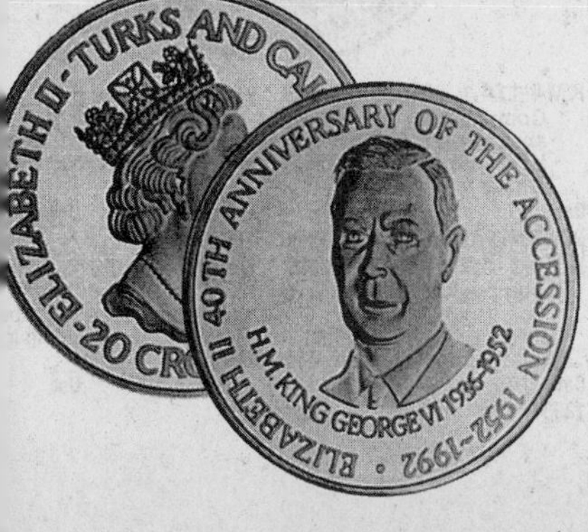

KM# 227.1 20 CROWNS **Weight:** 31.1700 g. **Composition:** 0.9990 Silver 1.0011 oz. ASW **Subject:** 40th Anniversary of the Accession **Obverse:** Bust of Queen Elizabeth II right with wavy truncation. **Reverse:** Bust of George VI facing. **Edge:** Reeded. **Size:** 38.9 mm.

Date		F	VF	XF	Unc	BU
ND(1992) Proof	—	Value: 30.00				

KM# 228.1 20 CROWNS **Weight:** 31.1700 g. **Composition:** 0.9990 Silver 1.0011 oz. ASW **Subject:** 40th Anniversary of the Accession **Obverse:** Bust of Queen Elizabeth II right with wavy truncation. **Reverse:** Windsor castle. **Edge:** Reeded. **Size:** 38.9 mm.

Date		F	VF	XF	Unc	BU
ND(1992) Proof	—	Value: 30.00				

KM# 229.1 20 CROWNS **Weight:** 31.1700 g. **Composition:** 0.9990 Silver 1.0011 oz. ASW **Subject:** 40th Anniversary of the Accession **Obverse:** Bust of Queen Elizabeth II right with wavy truncation. **Reverse:** Facing busts of Prince Philip at left and Queen Elizabeth II at right. **Edge:** Reeded. **Size:** 38.9 mm.

Date		F	VF	XF	Unc	BU
ND(1992) Proof	—	Value: 30.00				

KM# 229.2 20 CROWNS **Weight:** 31.1700 g. **Composition:** 0.9990 Silver 1.0011 oz. ASW **Subject:** 40th Anniversary of the Accession **Obverse:** Bust of Queen Elizabeth II right with smooth truncation. **Reverse:** Busts of Prince Philip at left and Queen Elizabeth II at right facing. **Edge:** Reeded. **Size:** 38.9 mm.

Date		F	VF	XF	Unc	BU
ND(1992) Proof	—	Value: 30.00				

KM# 78 20 CROWNS **Weight:** 31.1000 g. **Composition:** 0.9990 Silver 1 oz. ASW **Series:** Olympics **Obverse:** Similar to KM#2 reverse **Reverse:** Equestrian and 3 events

Date	Mintage	F	VF	XF	Unc	BU
1992 Proof	20,000	Value: 21.50				

KM# 79 20 CROWNS **Weight:** 31.1000 g. **Composition:** 0.9990 Silver 1 oz. ASW **Series:** Olympics **Reverse:** Gymnast on rings and 5 events

Date	Mintage	F	VF	XF	Unc	BU
1992 Proof	Est. 20,000	Value: 21.50				

KM# 80 20 CROWNS **Weight:** 31.1000 g. **Composition:** 0.9990 Silver 1 oz. ASW **Series:** Olympics **Reverse:** Weightlifting and 3 events

Date	Mintage	F	VF	XF	Unc	BU
1992 Proof	Est. 20,000	Value: 21.50				

KM# 81 20 CROWNS **Weight:** 31.1000 g. **Composition:** 0.9990 Silver 1 oz. ASW **Series:** Olympics **Reverse:** Rifle shooting and 3 events

Date	Mintage	F	VF	XF	Unc	BU
1992 Proof	Est. 20,000	Value: 21.50				

KM# 82 20 CROWNS **Weight:** 31.1000 g. **Composition:** 0.9990 Silver 1 oz. ASW **Series:** Olympics **Reverse:** Sail boarding and 3 events

Date	Mintage	F	VF	XF	Unc	BU
1992 Proof	Est. 20,000	Value: 21.50				

KM# 83 20 CROWNS **Weight:** 31.1000 g. **Composition:** 0.9990 Silver 1 oz. ASW **Series:** Olympics **Reverse:** Ski jumper and 4 events

Date	Mintage	F	VF	XF	Unc	BU
1992 Proof	Est. 20,000	Value: 21.50				

KM# 239 20 CROWNS **Composition:** Silver

Date		F	VF	XF	Unc	BU
1993 Proof	—	Value: 27.50				

KM# 95 20 CROWNS **Weight:** 31.1000 g. **Composition:** 0.9990 Silver 1 oz. ASW **Subject:** World Cup '94 - Jules Rimet **Note:** Similar to 5 Crowns, KM#87.

Date	Mintage	F	VF	XF	Unc	BU
ND(1993) Proof	Est. 10,000	Value: 27.50				

KM# 96 20 CROWNS **Weight:** 31.1000 g. **Composition:** 0.9990 Silver 1 oz. ASW **Subject:** World Cup '94 - Uruguay winners **Reverse:** 2 players **Note:** Similar to 5 Crowns, KM#88.

Date	Mintage	F	VF	XF	Unc	BU
ND(1993) Proof	Est. 10,000	Value: 30.00				

KM# 97 20 CROWNS **Weight:** 31.1000 g. **Composition:** 0.9990 Silver 1 oz. ASW **Subject:** World Cup '94 - Italy winners **Reverse:** Dino Zoff **Note:** Similar to 5 Crowns, KM#89.

Date	Mintage	F	VF	XF	Unc	BU
ND(1993) Proof	Est. 10,000	Value: 30.00				

KM# 98 20 CROWNS **Weight:** 31.1000 g. **Composition:** 0.9990 Silver 1 oz. ASW **Subject:** World Cup '94 - West German winners **Reverse:** Franz Breckenbauer **Note:** Similar to 5 Crowns, KM#90.

Date	Mintage	F	VF	XF	Unc	BU
ND(1993) Proof	Est. 10,000	Value: 30.00				

KM# 99 20 CROWNS **Weight:** 31.1000 g. **Composition:** 0.9990 Silver 1 oz. ASW **Subject:** World Cup '94 - Brazil winners **Reverse:** Pele **Note:** Similar to 5 Crowns, KM#91.

Date	Mintage	F	VF	XF	Unc	BU
ND(1993) Proof	Est. 10,000	Value: 27.50				

KM# 100 20 CROWNS **Weight:** 31.1000 g. **Composition:** 0.9990 Silver 1 oz. ASW **Subject:** World Cup '94 - England winners **Reverse:** Bobby Moore **Note:** Similar to 5 Crowns, KM#92.

Date	Mintage	F	VF	XF	Unc	BU
ND(1993) Proof	Est. 10,000	Value: 30.00				

KM# 110.1 20 CROWNS **Weight:** 31.1000 g. **Composition:** 0.9990 Silver 1 oz. ASW **Subject:** 40th anniversary of coronation **Obverse:** Bust of Queen Elizabeth II right with wavy truncation **Reverse:** Crown jewels **Note:** Similar to 5 Crowns, KM#104.

Date	Mintage	F	VF	XF	Unc	BU
ND(1993) Proof	Est. 10,000	Value: 30.00				

KM# 101 20 CROWNS **Weight:** 31.1000 g. **Composition:** 0.9990 Silver 1 oz. ASW **Subject:** World Cup '94 - Argentina winners **Reverse:** Mario Kempes **Note:** Similar to 5 Crowns, KM#93.

Date	Mintage	F	VF	XF	Unc	BU
ND(1993) Proof	Est. 10,000	Value: 30.00				

KM# 110.2 20 CROWNS **Weight:** 31.1700 g. **Composition:** 0.9990 Silver 1.0011 oz. ASW **Subject:** 40th Anniversary of Reign **Obverse:** Bust of Queen Elizabeth II right with smooth truncation. **Reverse:** Jeweled crown on pillow with crossed sceptres. **Edge:** Reeded. **Size:** 38.9 mm.

Date		F	VF	XF	Unc	BU
1993 Proof	—	Value: 30.00				

KM# 102 20 CROWNS **Weight:** 31.1000 g. **Composition:** 0.9990 Silver 1 oz. ASW **Subject:** World Cup '94 - USA host **Reverse:** Trophy and flag

Date	Mintage	F	VF	XF	Unc	BU
ND(1993) Proof	Est. 10,000	Value: 27.50				

KM# 111.1 20 CROWNS **Weight:** 31.1000 g. **Composition:** 0.9990 Silver 1 oz. ASW **Subject:** 40th anniversary of coronation **Obverse:** Bust of Queen Elizabeth II right with wavy truncation **Reverse:** Queen, clergy and maids of honor **Note:** Similar to 5 Crowns, KM#105.

Date	Mintage	F	VF	XF	Unc	BU
ND(1993) Proof	Est. 10,000	Value: 30.00				

KM# 109 20 CROWNS **Weight:** 31.1000 g. **Composition:** 0.9990 Silver 1 oz. ASW **Subject:** 40th anniversary of coronation **Reverse:** Westminster Abbey **Note:** Similar to 5 Crowns, KM#103.

Date	Mintage	F	VF	XF	Unc	BU
ND(1993) Proof	Est. 10,000	Value: 30.00				

KM# 111.2 20 CROWNS **Weight:** 31.1700 g. **Composition:** 0.9990 Silver 1.0011 oz. ASW **Subject:** 40th Anniveresary of Reign **Obverse:** Bust of Queen Elizabeth II right with smooth truncation. **Reverse:** Queen, Clergy and Maids of Honor. **Edge:** Reeded. **Size:** 38.9 mm.

Date		F	VF	XF	Unc	BU
1993 Proof	—	Value: 30.00				

KM# 112.1 20 CROWNS **Weight:** 31.1000 g. **Composition:** 0.9990 Silver 1 oz. ASW **Subject:** 40th anniversary of coronation **Obverse:** Bust of Queen Elizabeth II right with wavy truncation **Reverse:** Consort's homage **Note:** Similar to 5 Crowns, KM#106.

Date	Mintage	F	VF	XF	Unc	BU
ND(1993) Proof	Est. 10,000	Value: 30.00				

KM# 112.2 20 CROWNS **Weight:** 31.1700 g. **Composition:** 0.9990 Silver 1.0011 oz. ASW **Subject:** Coronation Anniversary **Obverse:** Bust of Queen Elizabeth II right with smooth truncation. **Reverse:** Consort's homage. **Edge:** Reeded. **Size:** 38.9 mm.

Date		F	VF	XF	Unc	BU
1993 Proof	—	Value: 30.00				

KM# 113.1 20 CROWNS **Weight:** 31.1000 g. **Composition:** 0.9990 Silver 1 oz. ASW **Subject:** 40th anniversary of coronation **Obverse:** Bust of Queen Elizabeth II right with wavy truncation **Reverse:** Queen on throne **Note** Similar to 5 Crowns, KM#107.

Date	Mintage	F	VF	XF	Unc	B
ND(1993) Proof	Est. 10,000	Value: 30.00				

KM# 113.2 20 CROWNS **Weight:** 31.1700 g. **Composition:** 0.9990 Silver 1.0011 oz. ASW **Subject:** Coronation Anniversary **Obverse:** Bust of Queen Elizabeth II right with smooth truncation. **Reverse:** Queen seated on throne. **Edge:** Reeded. **Size:** 38.9 mm.

Date		F	VF	XF	Unc	B
1993 Proof	—	Value: 30.00				

KM# 114.1 20 CROWNS **Weight:** 31.1000 g. **Composition:** 0.9990 Silver 1 oz. ASW **Subject:** 40th anniversary of coronation **Obverse:** Bust of Queen Elizabe II right with wavy truncation **Reverse:** Queen in coach **No** Similar to 5 Crowns, KM#108.

Date	Mintage	F	VF	XF	Unc
ND(1993) Proof	Est. 10,000	Value: 30.00			

KM# 114.2 20 CROWNS **Weight:** 31.1700 g. **Composition:** 0.9990 Silver 1.0011 oz. ASW **Subject:** Coronation Anniversary **Obverse:** Bust of Queen Elizabe II right with smooth truncation. **Reverse:** Queen riding in coach. **Edge:** Reeded. **Size:** 38.9 mm.

Date		F	VF	XF	Unc
1993 Proof	—	Value: 30.00			

1# 141 20 CROWNS Weight: 31.1000 g. **Composition:** 0.9990 Silver 1 oz. ASW **Series:** 1994 Olympics **Reverse:** Bobsled

e	F	VF	XF	Unc	BU
3 Proof	—	Value: 27.50			

/# 142 20 CROWNS Weight: 31.1000 g. **Composition:** 0.9990 Silver 1 oz. ASW **Subject:** 25th anniversary - Apollo 11 moon landing

e	F	VF	XF	Unc	BU
3 Proof	—	Value: 30.00			

/# 183 20 CROWNS Weight: 28.0400 g. **Composition:** 0.9250 Silver .8339 oz. ASW **Subject:** Apollo 11 series - rocket launch **Obverse:** Queen's portrait **Reverse:** Rocket launch scene **Note:** Similar to 5 Crowns, KM#177.

e	F	VF	XF	Unc	BU
3 Proof	—	Value: 35.00			

/# 184 20 CROWNS Weight: 28.0400 g. **Composition:** 0.9250 Silver .8339 oz. ASW **Subject:** Apollo 11 series - lunar landing **Obverse:** Queen's portrait **Reverse:** Lunar landing scene **Note:** Similar to 5 Crowns, KM#178.

e	F	VF	XF	Unc	BU
3 Proof	—	Value: 30.00			

/# 185 20 CROWNS Weight: 28.0400 g. **Composition:** 0.9250 Silver .8339 oz. ASW **Subject:** Apollo 11 series - leaving lunar lander **Obverse:** Queen's portrait **Reverse:** Astronaut descending ladder **Note:** Similar to 5 Crowns, KM#179.

e	F	VF	XF	Unc	BU
3 Proof	—	Value: 35.00			

/# 186 20 CROWNS Weight: 28.0400 g. **Composition:** 0.9250 Silver .8339 oz. ASW **Subject:** Apollo 11 series - planting American flag **Obverse:** Queen's portrait **Reverse:** Astronauts planting flag on moon **Note:** Similar to 5 Crowns, KM#180.

e	F	VF	XF	Unc	BU
3 Proof	—	Value: 30.00			

/# 187 20 CROWNS Weight: 28.0400 g. **Composition:** 0.9250 Silver .8339 oz. ASW **Subject:** Apollo 11 series - moon walk **Obverse:** Queen's portrait **Reverse:** Astronaut walking on the moon **Note:** Similar to 5 Crowns, KM#181.

e	F	VF	XF	Unc	BU
3 Proof	—	Value: 32.50			

/# 228.2 20 CROWNS Weight: 31.1700 g. **Composition:** 0.9990 Silver 1.0011 oz. ASW **Subject:** 40th Anniversary of the Accession **Obverse:** Bust of Queen Elizabeth II right with smooth truncation. **Reverse:** Windsor castle. **Edge:** Reeded. **Size:** 38.9 mm.

Date	F	VF	XF	Unc	BU
1993 Proof	—	Value: 30.00			

KM# 227.2 20 CROWNS Weight: 31.1700 g. **Composition:** 0.9990 Silver 1.0011 oz. ASW **Subject:** 40th Anniversary of the Accession **Obverse:** Bust of Queen Elizabeth II right with smooth truncation. **Reverse:** Bust of George VI facing. **Edge:** Reeded. **Size:** 38.9 mm.

Date	F	VF	XF	Unc	BU
1993 Proof	—	Value: 30.00			

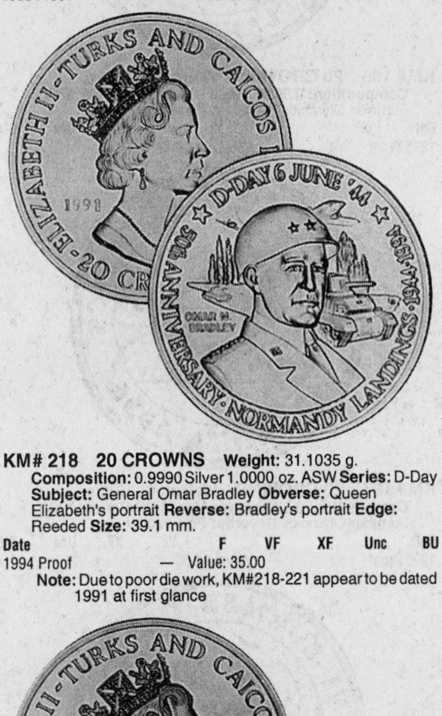

KM# 218 20 CROWNS Weight: 31.1035 g. **Composition:** 0.9990 Silver 1.0000 oz. ASW **Series:** D-Day **Subject:** General Omar Bradley **Obverse:** Queen Elizabeth's portrait **Reverse:** Bradley's portrait **Edge:** Reeded **Size:** 39.1 mm.

Date	F	VF	XF	Unc	BU
1994 Proof	—	Value: 35.00			

Note: Due to poor die work, KM#218-221 appear to be dated 1991 at first glance

KM# 219 20 CROWNS Weight: 31.1035 g. **Composition:** 0.9990 Silver 1.0000 oz. ASW **Series:** D-Day **Subject:** General Montgomery **Obverse:** Queen Elizabeth's portrait **Reverse:** General Montgomery's portrait **Edge:** Reeded **Size:** 39.1 mm.

Date	F	VF	XF	Unc	BU
1994 Proof	—	Value: 35.00			

KM# 220 20 CROWNS Weight: 31.1035 g. **Composition:** 0.9990 Silver 1.0000 oz. ASW **Series:** D-Day **Subject:** Sir Bertram Ramsay **Obverse:** Queen Elizabeth's portrait **Reverse:** Sir Bertram Ramsay's portrait **Edge:** Reeded **Size:** 39.1 mm.

Date	F	VF	XF	Unc	BU
1994 Proof	—	Value: 35.00			

KM# 221 20 CROWNS Weight: 31.1035 g. **Composition:** 0.9990 Silver 1.0000 oz. ASW **Series:** D-Day **Subject:** General Dwight Eisenhower **Obverse:** Queen Elizabeth's portrait **Reverse:** Genreal Dwight Eisenhower's portrait **Edge:** Reeded **Size:** 39.1 mm.

Date	F	VF	XF	Unc	BU
1994 Proof	—	Value: 35.00			

KM# 208 20 CROWNS Weight: 21.1300 g. **Composition:** 0.9990 Silver .9999 oz. ASW **Series:** XVII Winter Olympics **Obverse:** Queen's portrait and date **Reverse:** Figure skater **Note:** Reportedly a mule or pattern.

Date	F	VF	XF	Unc	BU
1994 Proof	—	Value: 125			

KM# 230 20 CROWNS Weight: 31.1700 g. **Composition:** 0.9990 Silver 1.0011 oz. ASW **Subject:** The Lady of the Century - The Queen Mother **Obverse:** Bust of Queen Elizabeth II right with smooth truncation. **Reverse:** Bust of the Queen Mother half right. **Edge:** Reeded. **Size:** 38.9 mm.

Date	F	VF	XF	Unc	BU
1995 Proof	—	Value: 30.00			

KM# 137 20 CROWNS Weight: 31.1035 g. **Composition:** 0.9990 Silver 1 oz. ASW **Subject:** 50th anniversary - VE Day **Reverse:** Churchill, Roosevelt and Stalin

Date	Mintage	F	VF	XF	Unc	BU
1995 Proof	15,000	Value: 32.50				

KM# 138 20 CROWNS Weight: 31.1035 g. **Composition:** 0.9990 Silver 1 oz. ASW **Subject:** 50th anniversary - VE Day **Reverse:** 3 planes

Date	Mintage	F	VF	XF	Unc	BU
1995 Proof	15,000	Value: 32.50				

KM# 139 20 CROWNS Weight: 31.1035 g. **Composition:** 0.9990 Silver 1 oz. ASW **Subject:** 50th anniversary - VE Day **Reverse:** U.S. and Soviet troops meet

Date	Mintage	F	VF	XF	Unc	BU
1995 Proof	15,000	Value: 32.50				

KM# 140 20 CROWNS Weight: 31.1035 g. **Composition:** 0.9990 Silver 1 oz. ASW **Subject:** 50th anniversary - VE Day **Reverse:** London, Washington, Moscow and Paris

Date	Mintage	F	VF	XF	Unc	BU
1995 Proof	15,000	Value: 40.00				

KM# 189 20 CROWNS Weight: 31.1035 g. **Composition:** 0.9990 Silver 1 oz. ASW **Series:** XXVI Summer Olympics **Reverse:** Hurdlers

Date	F	VF	XF	Unc	BU
1995 Proof	—	Value: 28.50			

KM# 191 20 CROWNS Weight: 31.1035 g. **Composition:** 0.9990 Silver 1 oz. ASW **Series:** XXVI Summer Olympics **Reverse:** Cyclist

Date	F	VF	XF	Unc	BU
1995 Proof	—	Value: 28.50			

KM# 193 20 CROWNS Weight: 31.1035 g. **Composition:** 0.9990 Silver 1 oz. ASW **Series:** XXVI Summer Olympics **Reverse:** Fencers

Date	F	VF	XF	Unc	BU
1995 Proof	—	Value: 27.50			

KM# 195 20 CROWNS Weight: 31.1035 g. **Composition:** 0.9990 Silver 1 oz. ASW **Series:** XXVI Summer Olympics **Reverse:** Equestrian

Date	F	VF	XF	Unc	BU
1995 Proof	—	Value: 28.50			

KM# 197 20 CROWNS Weight: 31.1035 g. **Composition:** 0.9990 Silver 1 oz. ASW **Series:** XXVI Summer Olympics **Reverse:** Pole vaulter

Date	F	VF	XF	Unc	BU
1995 Proof	—	Value: 28.50			

KM# 199 20 CROWNS Weight: 31.1035 g. **Composition:** 0.9990 Silver 1 oz. ASW **Series:** XXVI Summer Olympics **Reverse:** Runners

Date	F	VF	XF	Unc	BU
1995 Proof	—	Value: 27.50			

KM# 201 20 CROWNS Weight: 31.1035 g. **Composition:** 0.9990 Silver 1 oz. ASW **Series:** XXVI Summer Olympics **Reverse:** Gymnast

Date	F	VF	XF	Unc	BU
1995 Proof	—	Value: 28.50			

KM# 203 20 CROWNS Weight: 31.1035 g. **Composition:** 0.9990 Silver 1 oz. ASW **Series:** XXVI Summer Olympics **Reverse:** Swimmer

Date	F	VF	XF	Unc	BU
1995 Proof	—	Value: 27.50			

KM# 205 20 CROWNS Weight: 31.1035 g. **Composition:** 0.9990 Silver 1 oz. ASW **Series:** XXVI Summer Olympics **Reverse:** Diver

Date	F	VF	XF	Unc	BU
1995 Proof	—	Value: 28.50			

KM# 207 20 CROWNS Weight: 31.1035 g. **Composition:** 0.9990 Silver 1 oz. ASW **Series:** XXVI Summer Olympics **Reverse:** Sprinter

Date	F	VF	XF	Unc	BI
1995 Proof	—	Value: 28.50			

KM# 231 20 CROWNS Weight: 31.1100 g. **Composition:** 0.9990 Silver 0.9992 oz. ASW **Subject:** T 70th Birthday of H. M. Queen Elizabeth II **Obverse:** Natior arms. **Reverse:** Seated Queen Elizabeth II with her pet corgi's on either side. **Edge:** Reeded. **Size:** 38.9 mm.

Date	F	VF	XF	Unc
1996 Proof	—	Value: 30.00		

KM# 222 20 CROWNS **Weight:** 31.1035 g. **Composition:** 0.9990 Silver 1.0000 oz. ASW **Subject:** Hong Kong's Return to China **Obverse:** Queen's portrait. **Reverse:** City view. **Edge:** Reeded. **Size:** 38.9 mm. **Note:** Struck at North American Mint, Inc.

Date		F	VF	XF	Unc	BU
1997 Proof	—	Value: 28.50				

KM# 217 20 CROWNS **Weight:** 31.2400 g. **Composition:** 0.9990 Silver 1.0034 oz. ASW **Obverse:** Portrait of Queen Elizabeth **Reverse:** Two bottle-nosed dolphins **Edge:** Reeded **Size:** 39 mm.

Date		F	VF	XF	Unc	BU
1998 Proof	—	Value: 30.00				

M# 235 20 CROWNS **Weight:** 31.2000 g. **Composition:** 0.9990 Silver 1.0021 oz. ASW **Subject:** Prince Edward's Wedding **Obverse:** Bust of Queen Elizabeth II right. **Reverse:** Portraits of Edward and Sophie. **Edge:** Reeded. **Size:** 38.9 mm.

te		F	VF	XF	Unc	BU
99 Proof	—	Value: 40.00				

KM# 223 20 CROWNS **Weight:** 31.1035 g. **Composition:** 0.9990 Silver 1.0000 oz. ASW **Subject:** Apollo 11 **Obverse:** Queen's portrait. **Reverse:** Spacecraft in flight. **Edge:** Reeded. **Size:** 38.9 mm.

Date		F	VF	XF	Unc	BU
1999 Proof	—	Value: 30.00				

KM# 224 20 CROWNS **Weight:** 31.1035 g. **Composition:** 0.9990 Silver 1.0000 oz. ASW **Subject:** Apollo 11 **Obverse:** Queen's portrait. **Reverse:** Portraits of three astronauts. **Edge:** Reeded. **Size:** 38.9 mm.

Date		F	VF	XF	Unc	BU
1999 Proof	—	Value: 30.00				

KM# 236 20 CROWNS **Weight:** 31.2000 g. **Composition:** 0.9990 Silver 1.0021 oz. ASW **Subject:** Queen Victoria **Obverse:** Bust of Queen Elizabeth II right. **Reverse:** Queen Victoria. **Edge:** Reeded. **Size:** 38.9 mm.

Date		F	VF	XF	Unc	BU
2001 Proof	—	Value: 40.00				

KM# 145 20 DOLLARS **Weight:** 31.1035 g. **Composition:** 0.9990 Silver 1 oz. ASW **Series:** Steam Locomotive **Subject:** City of Truro

Date	Mintage	F	VF	XF	Unc	BU
1996 Proof	Est. 20,000	Value: 32.50				

KM# 148 20 DOLLARS **Weight:** 31.1035 g. **Composition:** 0.9990 Silver 1 oz. ASW **Series:** Steam Locomotive **Subject:** Flying Scotsman **Obverse:** Similar to KM#145

Date	Mintage	F	VF	XF	Unc	BU
1996 Proof	Est. 20,000	Value: 32.50				

KM# 151 20 DOLLARS **Weight:** 31.1035 g. **Composition:** 0.9990 Silver 1 oz. ASW **Series:** Steam Locomotive **Subject:** Rocket **Obverse:** Similar to KM#145

Date	Mintage	F	VF	XF	Unc	BU
1996 Proof	Est. 20,000	Value: 35.00				

KM# 154 20 DOLLARS **Weight:** 31.1035 g. **Composition:** 0.9990 Silver 1 oz. ASW **Series:** Steam Locomotive **Subject:** Evening Star **Obverse:** Similar to KM#145

Date		F	VF	XF	Unc	BU
1996 Proof	Est. 20,000	Value: 35.00				

KM# 157 20 DOLLARS **Weight:** 31.1035 g. **Composition:** 0.9990 Silver 1 oz. ASW **Series:** Steam Locomotive **Subject:** Mallard **Obverse:** Similar to KM#145

Date	Mintage	F	VF	XF	Unc	BU
1996 Proof	Est. 20,000	Value: 35.00				

KM# 160 20 DOLLARS **Weight:** 31.1035 g. **Composition:** 0.9990 Silver 1 oz. ASW **Series:** Steam Locomotive **Subject:** Princess Elizabeth **Obverse:** Similar to KM#145

Date	Mintage	F	VF	XF	Unc	BU
1996 Proof	Est. 20,000	Value: 32.50				

KM# 163 20 DOLLARS **Weight:** 31.1035 g. **Composition:** 0.9990 Silver 1 oz. ASW **Series:** Steam Locomotive **Subject:** South Pacific Line - Class GS4 **Obverse:** Similar to KM#145

Date	Mintage	F	VF	XF	Unc	BU
1996 Proof	Est. 20,000	Value: 35.00				

KM# 166 20 DOLLARS **Weight:** 31.1035 g. **Composition:** 0.9990 Silver 1 oz. ASW **Series:** Steam Locomotive **Subject:** German State Railway - Class 05 **Obverse:** Similar to KM#145

Date	Mintage	F	VF	XF	Unc	BU
1996 Proof	Est. 20,000	Value: 32.50				

KM# 169 20 DOLLARS **Weight:** 31.1035 g. **Composition:** 0.9990 Silver 1 oz. ASW **Series:** Steam Locomotive **Subject:** Japanese Railway - Class 62 **Obverse:** Similar to KM#145

Date	Mintage	F	VF	XF	Unc	BU
1996 Proof	Est. 20,000	Value: 35.00				

KM# 172 20 DOLLARS **Weight:** 31.1035 g. **Composition:** 0.9990 Silver 1 oz. ASW **Series:** Steam Locomotive **Subject:** Chinese State Railway Class RM **Obverse:** Similar to KM#145

Date	Mintage	F	VF	XF	Unc	BU
1996 Proof	Est. 20,000	Value: 35.00				

KM# 9.1 25 CROWNS **Weight:** 4.5000 g. **Composition:** 0.5000 Gold .0723 oz. AGW

Date	Mintage	F	VF	XF	Unc	BU
1975	1,272	—	—	—	35.00	—
1975 Proof	2,096	Value: 40.00				

KM# 9.2 25 CROWNS **Weight:** 4.5000 g. **Composition:** 0.5000 Gold .0723 oz. AGW **Size:** 19 mm.

Date	Mintage	F	VF	XF	Unc	BU
1976	-	—	—	—	35.00	—
1976 Proof	2,185	Value: 40.00				
1977 Proof	2,125	Value: 40.00				

KM# 19 25 CROWNS **Weight:** 43.7500 g. **Composition:** 0.9250 Silver 1.3012 oz. ASW **Subject:** Queen's silver jubilee **Obverse:** Similar to 10 Crowns, KM#7

Date	Mintage	F	VF	XF	Unc	BU
1977 Matte	—	—	—	—	22.50	—
1977 Proof	13,000	Value: 25.00				

KM# 24 25 CROWNS **Weight:** 43.7500 g. **Composition:** 0.9250 Silver 1.3012 oz. ASW **Subject:** 25th anniversary of coronation **Obverse:** Similar to 50 Crowns, KM#39 **Reverse:** Lion of England

Date	F	VF	XF	Unc	BU
1978 Proof	—	Value: 30.00			

KM# 25 25 CROWNS **Weight:** 43.7500 g. **Composition:** 0.9250 Silver 1.3012 oz. ASW **Subject:** Griffin of Edward III **Obverse:** Similar to 50 Crowns, KM#39

Date	F	VF	XF	Unc	BU
1978 Proof	—	Value: 30.00			

KM# 26 25 CROWNS **Weight:** 43.7500 g. **Composition:** 0.9250 Silver 1.3012 oz. ASW **Subject:** Red dragon of Wales **Obverse:** Similar to 50 Crowns, KM#39

Date	F	VF	XF	Unc	BU
1978 Proof	—	Value: 30.00			

KM# 27 25 CROWNS **Weight:** 43.7500 g. **Composition:** 0.9250 Silver 1.3012 oz. ASW **Subject:** White greyhound o Richmond **Obverse:** Similar to 50 Crowns, KM#39

Date	F	VF	XF	Unc	B
1978 Proof	—	Value: 30.00			

KM# 28 25 CROWNS **Weight:** 43.7500 g. **Composition:** 0.9250 Silver 1.3012 oz. ASW **Subject:** Unicorn of Scotland **Obverse:** Similar to 50 Crowns, KM#

Date	F	VF	XF	Unc
1978 Proof	—	Value: 37.50		

KM# 29 25 CROWNS **Weight:** 43.7500 g. **Compositio** 0.9250 Silver 1.3012 oz. ASW **Subject:** White horse of Hannover **Obverse:** Similar to 50 Crowns, KM#39

Date	F	VF	XF	Unc
1978 Proof	—	Value: 30.00		

 # 30 25 CROWNS **Weight:** 43.7500 g. **Composition:** 0.9250 Silver 1.3012 oz. ASW **Subject:** Black bull of Clarence **Obverse:** Similar to 50 Crowns, KM#39

	F	VF	XF	Unc	BU
Proof	—	Value: 30.00			

 # 31 25 CROWNS **Weight:** 43.7500 g. **Composition:** 0.9250 Silver 1.3012 oz. ASW **Subject:** Yale of Beaufort **Obverse:** Similar to 50 Crowns, KM#41

	F	VF	XF	Unc	BU
Proof	—	Value: 30.00			

 # 32 25 CROWNS **Weight:** 43.7500 g. **Composition:** 0.9250 Silver 1.3012 oz. ASW **Subject:** Falcon of Plantagenets **Obverse:** Similar to 50 Crowns, KM#42

	F	VF	XF	Unc	BU
Proof	—	Value: 30.00			

KM# 33 25 CROWNS **Weight:** 43.7500 g. **Composition:** 0.9250 Silver 1.3012 oz. ASW **Subject:** White lion of Mortimer **Obverse:** Similar to 50 Crowns, KM#43

Date	F	VF	XF	Unc	BU
1978 Proof	—	Value: 30.00			

KM# 209 25 CROWNS **Weight:** 155.4400 g. **Composition:** 0.9990 Silver 4.9925 oz. ASW **Subject:** Purple-throated carib **Obverse:** Queen's portrait **Reverse:** Multicolored purple-throated carib bird **Size:** 63 mm. **Note:** Illustration reduced.

Date	F	VF	XF	Unc	BU
1995 Matte	—	—	—	100	—
1995 Proof	—	Value: 75.00			

KM# 210 25 CROWNS **Weight:** 155.4400 g. **Composition:** 0.9990 Silver 4.9925 oz. ASW **Subject:** Streamertail **Obverse:** Queen's portrait **Reverse:** Multicolored streamertail bird **Size:** 63 mm. **Note:** Illustration reduced.

Date	F	VF	XF	Unc	BU
1995 Matte	—	—	—	100	—
1995 Proof	—	Value: 75.00			

KM# 211 25 CROWNS **Weight:** 155.4400 g. **Composition:** 0.9990 Silver 4.9925 oz. ASW **Subject:** Woodstar **Obverse:** Queen's portrait **Reverse:** Multicolored woodstar bird **Size:** 63 mm. **Note:** Illustration reduced.

Date	F	VF	XF	Unc	BU
1995	—	—	—	100	—
1995 Proof	—	Value: 75.00			

KM# 3 50 CROWNS **Weight:** 9.0000 g. **Composition:** 0.5000 Gold .1447 oz. AGW **Subject:** Centenary - birth of Churchill

Date	Mintage	F	VF	XF	Unc	BU
1974 Matte	30,000	—	—	—	60.00	—
1974 Proof	4,000	Value: 80.00				

KM# 10 50 CROWNS **Weight:** 6.2200 g. **Composition:** 0.5000 Gold .1 oz. AGW **Subject:** Age of Exploration **Reverse:** Christopher Columbus

Date	Mintage	F	VF	XF	Unc	BU
1975	2,863	—	—	—	75.00	—
1975 Proof	1,577	Value: 90.00				

KM# 15 50 CROWNS **Weight:** 6.2200 g. **Composition:** 0.5000 Gold .1 oz. AGW **Subject:** U.S. Bicentennial

Date	Mintage	F	VF	XF	Unc	BU
1976	905	—	—	—	100	—
1976 Proof	2,421	Value: 85.00				

KM# 16 50 CROWNS **Weight:** 55.1800 g. **Composition:** 0.9250 Silver 1.6412 oz. ASW **Reverse:** 4 Victoria cameos **Note:** Similar to 100 Crowns, KM#17.

Date	Mintage	F	VF	XF	Unc	BU
1976 Matte	3,500	—	—	—	40.00	—
1976 Proof	2,908	Value: 45.00				
1977 Proof	940	Value: 50.00				

KM# 20 50 CROWNS **Weight:** 9.0000 g. **Composition:** 0.5000 Gold .1447 oz. AGW **Subject:** Queen's silver jubilee

Date	Mintage	F	VF	XF	Unc	BU
1977	—	—	—	—	65.00	—
1977 Proof	2,903	Value: 85.00				

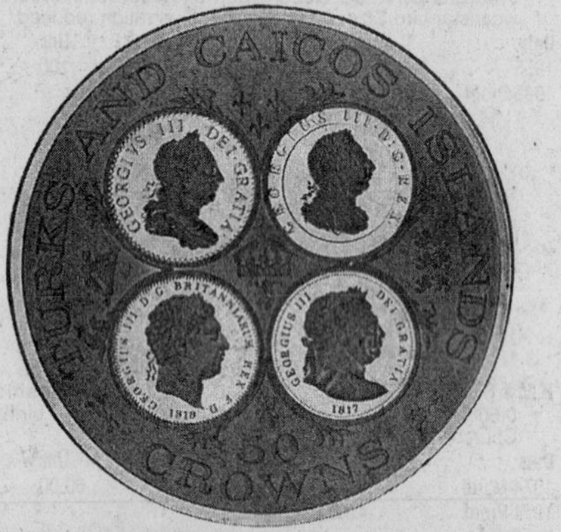

KM# 21 50 CROWNS **Weight:** 55.1800 g. **Composition:** 0.9250 Silver 1.6412 oz. ASW **Reverse:** 4 George III cameos **Note:** Similar to 100 Crowns, KM#22.

Date	Mintage	F	VF	XF	Unc	BU
1977	—	—	—	—	50.00	—
1977 Proof	958	Value: 55.00				

KM# 34 50 CROWNS **Weight:** 9.0000 g. **Composition:** 0.5000 Gold .1447 oz. AGW **Subject:** 25th anniversary of coronation **Reverse:** Lion of England

Date	Mintage	F	VF	XF	Unc	BU
1978 Proof	261	Value: 165				

KM# 35 50 CROWNS **Weight:** 9.0000 g. **Composition:** 0.5000 Gold .1447 oz. AGW **Subject:** Griffin of Edward III

Date	Mintage	F	VF	XF	Unc	BU
1978 Proof	266	Value: 165				

KM# 36 50 CROWNS **Weight:** 9.0000 g. **Composition:** 0.5000 Gold .1447 oz. AGW **Subject:** Red dragon of Wales

Date	Mintage	F	VF	XF	Unc	BU
1978 Proof	266	Value: 165				

KM# 37 50 CROWNS **Weight:** 9.0000 g. **Composition:** 0.5000 Gold .1447 oz. AGW **Subject:** White greyhound of Richmond

Date	Mintage	F	VF	XF	Unc	BU
1978 Proof	270	Value: 165				

KM# 38 50 CROWNS **Weight:** 9.0000 g. **Composition:** 0.5000 Gold .1447 oz. AGW **Subject:** Unicorn of Scotland

Date	Mintage	F	VF	XF	Unc	BU
1978 Proof	268	Value: 165				

KM# 39 50 CROWNS **Weight:** 9.0000 g. **Composition:** 0.5000 Gold .1447 oz. AGW **Subject:** White horse of Hannover

Date	Mintage	F	VF	XF	Unc	BU
1978 Proof	266	Value: 165				

KM# 40 50 CROWNS **Weight:** 9.0000 g. **Composition:** 0.5000 Gold .1447 oz. AGW **Subject:** Black bull of Clarence

Date	Mintage	F	VF	XF	Unc	BU
1978 Proof	269	Value: 165				

KM# 41 50 CROWNS **Weight:** 9.0000 g. **Composition:** 0.5000 Gold .1447 oz. AGW **Subject:** Yale of Beaufort

Date	Mintage	F	VF	XF	Unc	BU
1978 Proof	254	Value: 165				

KM# 42 50 CROWNS **Weight:** 9.0000 g. **Composition:** 0.5000 Gold .1447 oz. AGW **Subject:** Falcon of the Plantagenets

Date	Mintage	F	VF	XF	Unc	BU
1978 Proof	265	Value: 165				

KM# 43 50 CROWNS **Weight:** 9.0000 g. **Composition:** 0.5000 Gold .1447 oz. AGW **Subject:** White lion of Mortimer

Date	Mintage	F	VF	XF	Unc	BU
1978 Proof	265	Value: 165				

KM# 61 50 CROWNS **Weight:** 136.0800 g. **Composition:** 0.9250 Silver 4.0699 oz. ASW **Subject:** Columbus proposes Atlantic voyage to Ferdinand and Isabella **Obverse:** Similar to 5 Crowns, KM#123 **Size:** 63 mm. **Note:** Illustration reduced.

Date	Mintage	F	VF	XF	Unc	BU
1986 Proof	20,000	Value: 85.00				

KM# 4 100 CROWNS **Weight:** 18.0150 g. **Composition:** 0.5000 Gold .2896 oz. AGW **Subject:** Birth of Churchill centenary

Date	Mintage	F	VF	XF	Unc	BU
1974	4,500	—	—	—	165	-
1974 Proof	5,100	Value: 165				

KM# 11 100 CROWNS **Weight:** 12.4400 g. **Composition:** 0.5000 Gold .2000 oz. AGW **Subject:** Age Exploration **Reverse:** Spacecraft

Date	Mintage	F	VF	XF	Unc
1975	756	—	—	—	135
1975 Proof	1,508	Value: 120			

KM# 17 100 CROWNS **Weight:** 18.0150 g. **Compositi**- 0.5000 Gold .2896 oz. AGW **Reverse:** 4 Victoria camec

Date	Mintage	F	VF	XF	Unc
1976	250	—	—	—	160
1976 Proof	350	Value: 175			
1977	1,655	—	—	—	150
1977 Proof	2,648	Value: 165			

 # 22 100 CROWNS **Weight:** 18.0150 g. **Composition:**).5000 Gold .2896 oz. AGW **Reverse:** 4 George III cameos

	Mintage	F	VF	XF	Unc	BU
	—	—	—	—	165	—
Proof	844	Value: 185				

 # 44 100 CROWNS **Weight:** 18.0150 g. **Composition:**).5000 Gold .2896 oz. AGW **Subject:** XI Commonwealth Games

	Mintage	F	VF	XF	Unc	BU
Proof	540	Value: 250				

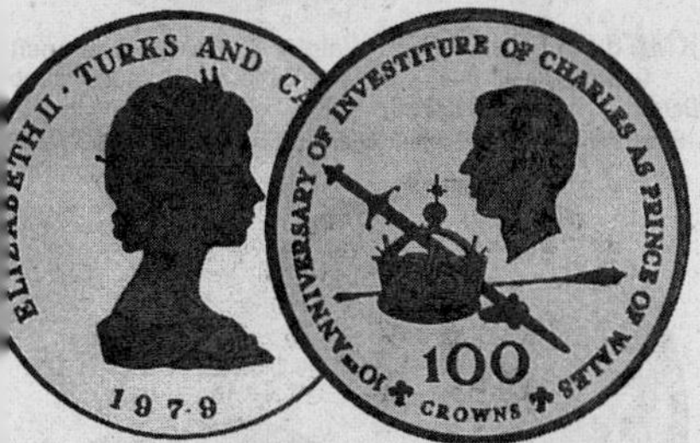

 # 46 100 CROWNS **Weight:** 18.0150 g. **Composition:** 0.5000 Gold .2896 oz. AGW **Subject:** 10th anniversary - Prince Charles' investiture

	Mintage	F	VF	XF	Unc	BU
	10,000	—	—	—	140	—

 # 50 100 CROWNS **Weight:** 12.9600 g. **Composition:** 0.5000 Gold .2083 oz. AGW **Subject:** Lord Mountbatten **Obverse:** Similar to 10 Crowns, KM#45

	F	VF	XF	Unc	BU
Proof	—	Value: 140			

 # 54 100 CROWNS **Weight:** 6.4800 g. **Composition:** 0.9000 Gold .1875 oz. AGW **Subject:** Wedding of Princes Charles and Lady Diana

	Mintage	F	VF	XF	Unc	BU
Proof	1,205	Value: 115				

 # 59 100 CROWNS **Weight:** 6.4800 g. **Composition:** 0.9000 Gold .1875 oz. AGW **Subject:** World Football Championship **Reverse:** 2 players

	Mintage	F	VF	XF	Unc	BU
2 Proof	565	Value: 225				

 # 62 100 CROWNS **Weight:** 7.1300 g. **Composition:** 0.9000 Gold .2063 oz. AGW **Series:** Decade for Women

	Mintage	F	VF	XF	Unc	BU
5 Proof	313	Value: 275				

KM# 65 100 CROWNS **Weight:** 10.0000 g. **Composition:** 0.9170 Gold .2949 oz. AGW **Series:** World Wildlife Fund **Subject:** Jumbo shrimp

Date	Mintage	F	VF	XF	Unc	BU
1988 Proof	Est. 5,000	Value: 200				

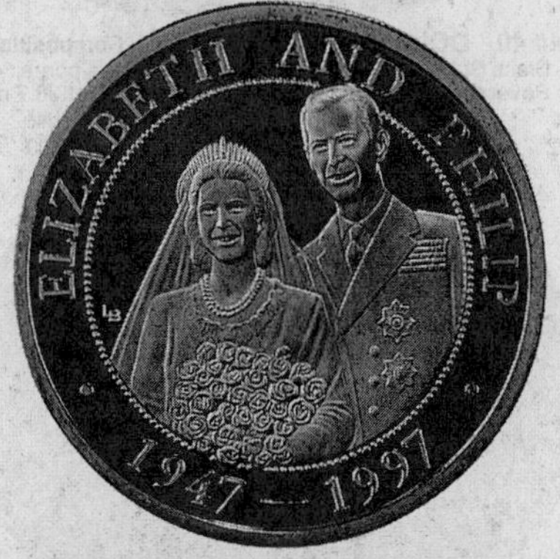

KM# 237 100 CROWNS **Weight:** 155.5175 g. **Composition:** 0.9990 Gold Plated Silver 4.995 oz. ASW AGW **Subject:** Queen's Golden Wedding Anniversary **Obverse:** National arms. **Reverse:** Royal couple's wedding portrait. **Edge:** Reeded and numbered. **Size:** 63.7 mm. **Note:** Illustration reduced.

Date	Mintage	F	VF	XF	Unc	BU
1997 Proof	3,000	Value: 175				

PATTERNS

Standard metals unless noted otherwise

KM#	Date	Mintage	Identification	Issue Price	Mkt Val
Pn1	ND(1993)	50	20 Crowns. Silver. Bobsledders.	—	75.00
Pn2	ND(1993)	50	20 Crowns. Silver. Skier.	—	75.00
Pn3	ND(1993)	50	20 Crowns. Silver. Ski jumper.	—	75.00
Pn4	ND(1993)	50	20 Crowns. Silver. Figure skater.	—	75.00
Pn5	ND(1993)	50	20 Crowns. Silver. Hockey player.	—	75.00
Pn6	ND(1993)	50	20 Crowns. Silver. Speed skater.	—	75.00

PIEFORTS

KM#	Date	Mintage	Identification	Issue Price	Mkt Val
P2	1980	400	10 Crowns. KM48.	95.00	38.00
P3	1980	300	20 Crowns. KM49.	115	40.00
P4	1980	250	100 Crowns. KM50.	825	275
P1	1980	500	5 Crowns. KM47.	79.50	32.00
P5	1982	80	10 Crowns. KM55.	—	135
P6	1991	—	Crown. Silver. KM76.	—	40.00
P7	1991	400	Crown. Silver. KM121.	—	30.00

MINT SETS

KM#	Date	Mintage	Identification	Issue Price	Mkt Val
MS1	1975 (7)	440	KM5-11	214	350
MS2	ND(1993) (8)	—	KM87-94	67.20	45.00
MS3	ND(1993) (6)	—	KM103-108	49.95	35.00
MS4	1995 (4)	—	KM133-136	33.50	33.50
MS5	1996 (10)	—	KM143, 146, 149, 152, 155, 158, 161, 164, 167, 170	33.50	33.50

PROOF SETS

KM#	Date	Mintage	Identification	Issue Price	Mkt Val
PS1	1974 (2)	1,600	KM2, 4	—	170
PS2	1975 (7)	1,270	KM5-8, 9.1, 10-11	313	385
PS3	1976 (4)	2,185	KM5, 6, 9.2, 12	78.00	85.00
PS4	1976 (3)	—	KM14, 16, 17	280	270
PS5	1976 (2)	1,951	KM13, 15	108	115
PS6	1977 (4)	1,370	KM5, 6, 9.2, 12	87.50	100
PS8	1977 (2)	—	KM14, 18	62.00	115
PS7	1977 (3)	—	KM18, 21, 22	280	380
PS10	1978 (10)	—	KM34-43	1,120	1,650
PS9	1978 (10)	—	KM24-33	560	320
PS11	1979 (2)	—	KM45, 46	228	160
PS12	1980 (4)	—	KM47-50	458	195
PS13	1980 (3)	—	KM47-49	108	45.00
PS15	ND(1993) (8)	—	KM95-102	320	325
PS17	ND(1993) (6)	—	KM109-114	234	255
PS18	1995 (4)	15,000	KM137-140	160	160
PS19	1996 (10)	20,000	KM144, 147, 150, 153, 156, 159, 162, 165, 168, 171	220	220
PS20	1996 (10)	20,000	KM145, 148, 151, 154, 157, 160, 163, 166, 169, 172	350	350

TUVALU

Tuvalu (formerly the Ellice or Lagoon Islands of the Gilbert and Ellice Islands), located in the South Pacific north of the Fiji Islands, has an area of 10 sq. mi. (26 sq.km.) and a population of *9,000. Capital: Funafuti. The independent state includes the islands of Nanumanga, Nanumea, Nui, Niutao, Viatupa, Funafuti, Nukufetau, Nukulailai and Nurakita. The latter four islands were claimed by the United States until relinquished by the Feb.7, 1979, Treaty of Friendship signed by the United States and Tuvalu. The principal industries are copra production and phosphate mining.

The islands were discovered in 1764 by John Byron, a British navigator, and annexed by Britain in 1892. In 1915 they became part of the crown colony of the Gilbert and Ellice Islands. In 1974 the islanders voted to separate from the Gilberts, becoming on Jan. 1, 1976, the separate constitutional dependency of Tuvalu. Full independence was attained on Oct. 1, 1978. Tuvalu is a member of the Commonwealth of Nations. Elizabeth II is Head of State as Queen of Tuvalu.

RULERS

British, until 1978

MONETARY SYSTEM

100 Cents = 1 Dollar

BRITISH ADMINISTRATION

STANDARD COINAGE

100 Cents = 1 Dollar

KM# 1 CENT **Composition:** Bronze **Reverse:** Sea shell

Date	Mintage	F	VF	XF	Unc	BU
1976	93,000	—	—	0.10	0.35	0.50
1976 Proof	20,000	Value: 1.00				
1981	—	—	—	0.10	0.35	0.50
1981 Proof	—	Value: 1.00				
1985	—	—	—	0.10	0.35	0.50

KM# 26 CENT **Composition:** Bronze **Obverse:** Queen's portrait by Maklouf

Date	F	VF	XF	Unc	BU
1994	—	—	—	0.35	0.50

KM# 2 2 CENTS **Composition:** Bronze **Reverse:** Stingray

Date	Mintage	F	VF	XF	Unc	BU
1976		—	0.10	0.15	0.50	0.75
1976 Proof	20,000	Value: 1.00				
1981		—	0.10	0.15	0.50	0.75
1981 Proof	—	Value: 1.00				
1985		—	0.10	0.15	0.50	0.75

KM# 30 2 CENTS **Composition:** Bronze **Obverse:** Queen's portrait by Maklouf

Date	F	VF	XF	Unc	BU
1994	—	—	—	0.50	—

KM# 3 5 CENTS **Composition:** Copper-Nickel **Reverse:** Tiger shark

Date	Mintage	F	VF	XF	Unc	BU
1976		—	0.10	0.25	1.50	—
1976 Proof	20,000	Value: 1.50				
1981		—	0.10	0.25	1.50	—
1981 Proof	—	Value: 1.50				
1985		—	0.10	0.25	1.50	—

KM# 31 5 CENTS **Composition:** Copper-Nickel **Obverse:** Queen's portrait by Maklouf

Date	F	VF	XF	Unc	BU
1994	—	—	—	1.50	—

KM# 4 10 CENTS **Composition:** Copper-Nickel **Reverse:** Red-eyed crab

Date	Mintage	F	VF	XF	Unc	BU
1976	26,000	0.15	0.20	0.30	1.00	—
1976 Proof	20,000	Value: 2.00				
1981	—	0.15	0.20	0.30	1.00	—
1981 Proof	—	Value: 2.00				
1985	—	0.15	0.20	0.30	1.00	—

KM# 32 10 CENTS **Composition:** Copper-Nickel **Obverse:** Queen's portrait by Maklouf

Date	F	VF	XF	Unc	BU
1994	—	—	—	1.00	—

KM# 5 20 CENTS **Composition:** Copper-Nickel **Reverse:** Flying fish

Date	Mintage	F	VF	XF	Unc	BU
1976	36,000	0.30	0.40	0.50	1.00	—
1976 Proof	20,000	Value: 2.50				
1981	—	0.30	0.40	0.50	1.00	—
1981 Proof	—	Value: 2.50				
1985	—	0.30	0.40	0.50	1.00	—

KM# 33 20 CENTS **Composition:** Copper-Nickel **Obverse:** Queen's portrait by Maklouf

Date	F	VF	XF	Unc	BU
1994	—	—	—	1.00	—

KM# 6 50 CENTS **Composition:** Copper-Nickel **Reverse:** Octopus

Date	Mintage	F	VF	XF	Unc	BU
1976	19,000	0.50	0.75	1.50	5.00	—
1976 Proof	20,000	Value: 6.00				
1981	—	0.50	0.75	1.50	5.00	—
1981 Proof	—	Value: 6.00				
1985	—	0.50	0.75	1.50	5.00	—

KM# 34 50 CENTS **Composition:** Copper-Nickel **Obverse:** Queen's portrait by Maklouf

Date	F	VF	XF	Unc	BU
1994	—	—	—	4.50	—

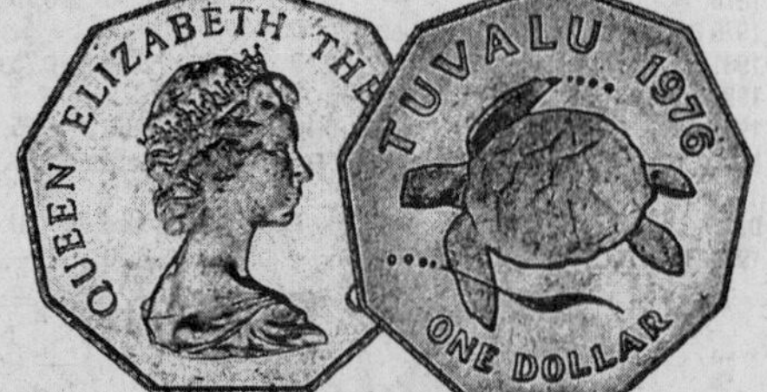

KM#7 DOLLAR **Composition:** Copper-Nickel **Reverse:** Sea turtle

Date	Mintage	F	VF	XF	Unc	BU
1976	21,000	1.00	1.50	2.00	6.00	—
1976 Proof	20,000	Value: 7.00				
1981	—	1.00	1.50	2.00	6.00	—
1981 Proof	—	Value: 7.00				
1985	—	1.00	1.50	2.00	6.00	—

KM# 35 DOLLAR **Composition:** Copper-Nickel **Obverse:** Queen's portrait by Maklouf

Date	F	VF	XF	Unc	BU
1994	—	—	—	5.00	—

KM# 40 DOLLAR **Weight:** 20.0000 g. **Composition:** Brass **Subject:** Dinosaurs **Obverse:** Queen's portrait **Reverse:** Giganotosaurus **Edge:** Reeded **Size:** 38.7 mm.

Date	Mintage	F	VF	XF	Unc	BU
2002	50,000	—	—	—	12.00	—

KM# 41 DOLLAR **Weight:** 20.0000 g. **Composition:** Brass **Subject:** Dinosaurs **Obverse:** Queen's portrait **Reverse:** Dromaeosaurus **Edge:** Reeded **Size:** 38.7 mm.

Date	Mintage	F	VF	XF	Unc	BU
2002	50,000	—	—	—	12.00	—

KM# 42 DOLLAR **Subject:** Dinosaurs **Obverse:** Queen's portrait **Reverse:** Seismosaurus **Edge:** Reeded **Size:** 38.7 mm.

Date	Mintage	F	VF	XF	Unc	BU
2002	50,000	—	—	—	12.00	—

KM# 43 DOLLAR **Weight:** 20.0000 g. **Composition:** Brass **Subject:** Dinosaurs **Obverse:** Queen's portrait **Reverse:** Stegosaurus **Edge:** Reeded **Size:** 38.7 mm.

Date	Mintage	F	VF	XF	Unc	BU
2002	50,000	—	—	—	12.00	—

KM#37 2 DOLLARS **Weight:** 10.0000 g. **Composition:** 0.5000 Silver .1608 oz. ASW **Series:** Olympics **Obverse:** Queen Elizabeth's portrait **Reverse:** Swimmer **Edge:** Reeded **Size:** 30 mm.

Date	F	VF	XF	Unc
1996 Proof	— Value: 15.00			

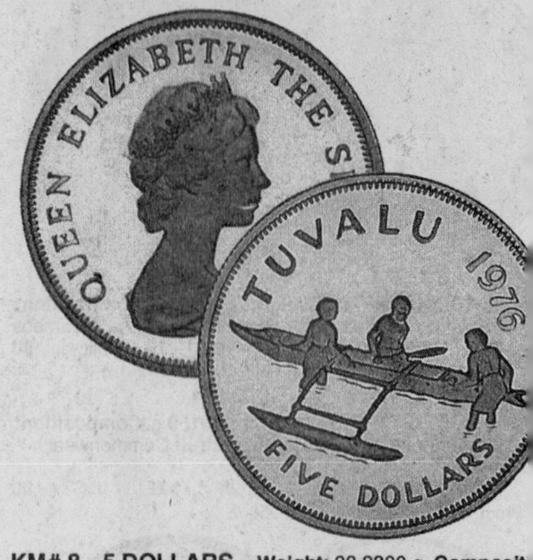

KM# 8 5 DOLLARS **Weight:** 28.2800 g. **Composit** 0.9250 Silver .8411 oz. ASW **Reverse:** Outrigger cano

Date	Mintage	F	VF	XF	Unc
1976 Proof	20,000	Value: 20.00			

KM# 12 5 DOLLARS **Composition:** Copper-Nickel **Subject:** Wedding of Prince Charles and Lady Diana

Date	F	VF	XF	Unc
1981	—	—	—	9.00

KM# 12a 5 DOLLARS **Weight:** 28.2800 g. **Composition:** 0.9250 Silver .8411 oz. ASW

Date	Mintage	F	VF	XF	Unc
1981 Proof	35,000	Value: 17.50			

KM#38 5 DOLLARS **Weight:** 31.6400 g. **Composit** 0.9250 Silver 0.941 oz. ASW **Subject:** Victorian Age **Obverse:** Bust of Queen Elizabeth II right. **Reverse:** 3/ standing figure at left, SS Great Britain in back at right. **Ed** Reeded. **Size:** 38.6 mm.

Date	F	VF	XF	Unc
1997 Proof	— Value: 40.00			

KM#36 5 DOLLARS **Weight:** 31.2200 g. **Compositi** 0.9250 Silver .9285 oz. ASW **Subject:** Millennium 2000 **Obverse:** Queen's portrait. **Reverse:** Seashell, stars, wa above denomination. **Edge:** Reeded, square. **Size:** 30.2 mm.

Date	F	VF	XF	Unc
1998 Proof	— Value: 45.00			

KM#44 5 DOLLARS **Weight:** 31.2000 g. **Compositi** 0.9250 Silver 0.9279 oz. ASW **Subject:** Millennium **Obverse:** Queen's portrait **Reverse:** Sea shell and denomination **Edge:** Reeded **Size:** 30.2 mm.

Date	F	VF	XF	Unc
2000 Proof	— Value: 45.00			

 # 10 10 DOLLARS **Weight:** 35.0000 g. **Composition:** 0.5000 Silver .5627 oz. ASW **Subject:** 1st Anniversary of Independence **Obverse:** Similar to 5 Dollars, KM#8 **Reverse:** Brigantine "Rebecca"

	Mintage	F	VF	XF	Unc	BU
9	5,000	—	—	—	25.00	—

 # 10a 10 DOLLARS **Weight:** 35.0000 g. **Composition:** 0.9250 Silver 1.0409 oz. ASW

	Mintage	F	VF	XF	Unc	BU
9 Proof	2,500	Value: 35.00				

#11 10 DOLLARS **Weight:** 35.0000 g. **Composition:** 0.5000 Silver .5627 oz. ASW **Subject:** 80th Birthday of Queen Mother **Obverse:** Similar to 5 Dollars, KM#8

	F	VF	XF	Unc	BU
0	—	—	—	15.00	—

 # 11a 10 DOLLARS **Weight:** 35.0000 g. **Composition:** 0.9250 Silver 1.0409 oz. ASW

	F	VF	XF	Unc	BU
0 Proof	—	Value: 23.50			

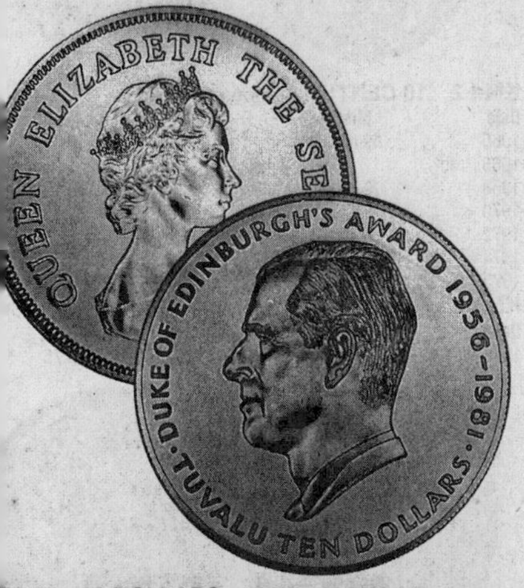

 # 13 10 DOLLARS **Weight:** 35.0000 g. **Composition:** 0.5000 Silver .5627 oz. ASW **Subject:** Duke of Edinburgh Award **Obverse:** Similar to 5 Dollars, KM#8

	Mintage	F	VF	XF	Unc	BU
1	5,000	—	—	—	14.50	—

KM# 13a 10 DOLLARS **Weight:** 35.0000 g. **Composition:** 0.9250 Silver 1.0409 oz. ASW

Date	Mintage	F	VF	XF	Unc	BU
1981 Proof	3,000	Value: 22.50				

KM# 15 10 DOLLARS **Weight:** 35.0000 g. **Composition:** 0.5000 Silver .5627 oz. ASW **Subject:** Royal Visit **Obverse:** Similar to 5 Dollars, KM#8

Date	Mintage	F	VF	XF	Unc	BU
1982	2,500	—	—	—	20.00	—

KM# 15a 10 DOLLARS **Weight:** 35.0000 g. **Composition:** 0.9250 Silver 1.0409 oz. ASW

Date	Mintage	F	VF	XF	Unc	BU
1982 Proof	2,500	Value: 27.50				

KM# 16 20 DOLLARS **Weight:** 31.4700 g. **Composition:** 0.9250 Silver .9359 oz. ASW **Subject:** 40th Anniversary of Coronation

Date	Mintage	F	VF	XF	Unc	BU
1993 Proof	Est. 10,000	Value: 27.50				

KM# 17 20 DOLLARS **Weight:** 31.4700 g. **Composition:** 0.9250 Silver .9359 oz. ASW **Subject:** Sir Isaac Newton

Date	Mintage	F	VF	XF	Unc	BU
1993 Proof	Est. 10,000	Value: 27.50				

KM# 18 20 DOLLARS **Weight:** 31.4700 g. **Composition:** 0.9250 Silver .9359 oz. ASW **Subject:** HMS Royalist

Date	Mintage	F	VF	XF	Unc	BU
1993 Proof	Est. 15,000	Value: 27.50				

KM# 19 20 DOLLARS **Weight:** 31.4700 g. **Composition:** 0.9250 Silver .9359 oz. ASW **Reverse:** Leatherback turtle

Date	Mintage	F	VF	XF	Unc	BU
1993 Proof	Est. 10,000	Value: 32.00				

KM# 20 20 DOLLARS **Weight:** 31.4700 g. **Composition:** 0.9250 Silver .9359 oz. ASW **Reverse:** Dugong - Manatee-like animal

Date	Mintage	F	VF	XF	Unc	BU
1994 Proof	Est. 10,000	Value: 32.00				

KM# 22 20 DOLLARS **Weight:** 31.4700 g. **Composition:** 0.9250 Silver .9359 oz. ASW **Subject:** 1994 World Cup Soccer

Date	Mintage	F	VF	XF	Unc	BU
1994 Proof	Est. 30,000	Value: 32.50				

KM# 24 20 DOLLARS **Weight:** 31.4700 g. **Composition:** 0.9250 Silver .9359 oz. ASW **Series:** Olympics **Subject:** Swimming

Date	Mintage	F	VF	XF	Unc	BU
1994 Proof	Est. 50,000	Value: 21.50				

KM# 25 20 DOLLARS **Weight:** 31.4700 g. **Composition:** 0.9250 Silver .9359 oz. ASW **Series:** Olympics **Subject:** Javelin throwing

Date	Mintage	F	VF	XF	Unc	BU
1994 Proof	Est. 50,000	Value: 22.50				

KM# 27 20 DOLLARS **Weight:** 31.7000 g. **Composition:** 0.9250 Silver .9427 oz. ASW **Series:** Protect Our World **Reverse:** Blue coral seascape

Date	F	VF	XF	Unc	BU
1994 Proof	—	Value: 35.00			

KM# 39 20 DOLLARS **Weight:** 155.5000 g. **Composition:** 0.9990 Silver 4.9944 oz. ASW **Subject:** Birthday of Queen Elizabeth - The Queen Mother **Obverse:** Bust of Queen Elizabeth II right. **Reverse:** Queen Mother and grandchildren. **Edge:** Reeded. **Size:** 65 mm. **Note:** Illustration reduced. Actual size: 65mm.

Date	Mintage	F	VF	XF	Unc	BU
1996 Proof	3,000	Value: 125				

KM# 9 50 DOLLARS **Weight:** 15.9800 g. **Composition:** 0.9170 Gold .4710 oz. AGW **Reverse:** Native meeting hut

Date	Mintage	F	VF	XF	Unc	BU
1976 Proof	2,074	Value: 245				

KM# 14 50 DOLLARS **Weight:** 15.9800 g. **Composition:** 0.9170 Gold .4710 oz. AGW **Subject:** Wedding of Prince Charles and Lady Diana

Date	Mintage	F	VF	XF	Unc	BU
1981 Proof	5,000	Value: 235				

KM# 29 100 DOLLARS **Weight:** 7.7760 g. **Composition:** 0.5833 Gold .1458 oz. AGW **Subject:** 40th Anniversary of Coronation **Obverse:** Similar to 20 Dollars, KM#16

Date	F	VF	XF	Unc	BU
1993 Proof	—	Value: 125			

KM# 21 100 DOLLARS **Weight:** 7.7760 g. **Composition:** 0.5833 Gold .1458 oz. AGW **Subject:** Todos Los Santos

Date	Mintage	F	VF	XF	Unc	BU
1994 Proof	3,000	Value: 135				

KM# 23 100 DOLLARS **Weight:** 7.7760 g. **Composition:** 0.5833 Gold .1458 oz. AGW **Subject:** 1994 World Cup Soccer

Date	Mintage	F	VF	XF	Unc	BU
1994 Proof	3,000	Value: 145				

MINT SETS

KM#	Date	Mintage	Identification	Issue Price	Mkt Val
MS1	1985 (7)	—	KM#1-7	10.00	10.00

PROOF SETS

KM#	Date	Mintage	Identification	Issue Price	Mkt Val
PS1	1976 (7)	20,000	KM#1-7	13.00	16.00
PS2	1981 (7)	—	KM#1-7	—	16.00

UGANDA

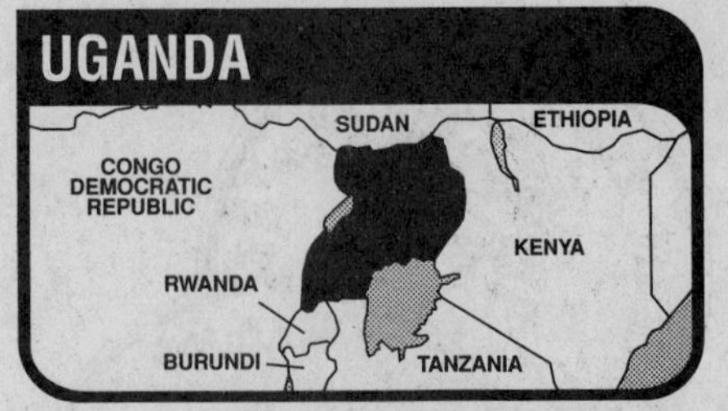

The Republic of Uganda, a former British protectorate located astride the equator in east-central Africa, has an area of 91,134 sq. mi. (236,040 sq. km.) and a population of *17 million. Capital: Kampala. Agriculture, including livestock, is the basis of the economy; there is some mining of copper, tin, gold and lead. Coffee, cotton, copper and tea are exported.

Uganda was first visited by Arab slavers in the 1830s. They were followed in the 1860s by British explorers searching for the headwaters of the Nile. The explorers, and the missionaries who followed them into the Lake Victoria region of south central Africa in 1877-79, found well-developed African kingdoms dating back several centuries. In 1894 the local native Kingdom of Buganda was established as a British protectorate that was extended in 1896 to encompass an area substantially the same as the present Republic of Uganda. The protectorate was given a ministerial form of government in 1955, full internal self-government on March 1, 1962, and complete independence on Oct. 9, 1962. Uganda is a member of the Commonwealth of Nations. The president is Chief of State and Head of Government.

For earlier coinage refer to East Africa.

RULERS
British, until 1962

MONETARY SYSTEM
100 Cents = 1 Shilling

REPUBLIC

STANDARD COINAGE

100 Cents = 1 Shilling

KM# 1 5 CENTS **Composition:** Bronze

Date	Mintage	F	VF	XF	Unc	BU
1966	41,000,000	—	0.10	0.15	0.30	–
1966 Proof	—	Value: 1.00				
1974	10,000,000	—	0.20	0.30	0.75	–
1975	14,784,000	—	0.20	0.30	0.75	–

KM# 1a 5 CENTS **Composition:** Copper Plated Steel

Date	Mintage	F	VF	XF	Unc	B
1976	10,000,000	—	0.20	0.30	0.75	–

KM# 2 10 CENTS **Composition:** Bronze

Date	Mintage	F	VF	XF	Unc
1966	19,100,000	—	0.10	0.15	0.35
1966 Proof	—	Value: 1.00			
1968	20,000,000	—	0.10	0.15	0.35
1970	6,000,000	—	0.20	0.30	0.75
1972	5,000,000	—	0.20	0.30	0.75
1974	5,000,000	—	0.20	0.30	0.75
1975	14,110,000	—	0.20	0.30	0.75

KM# 2a 10 CENTS **Composition:** Copper-Plated-Ste

Date	Mintage	F	VF	XF	Unc
1976	10,000,000	—	0.20	0.30	0.75

KM# 3 20 CENTS **Composition:** Bronze

Date	Mintage	F	VF	XF	Unc	BU
1966	7,000,000	—	0.30	0.70	1.65	—
1966 Proof	—	Value: 2.00				
1974	2,000,000	—	0.50	1.00	2.25	—

KM# 4 50 CENTS **Composition:** Copper-Nickel
Reverse: East African crowned crane

Date	Mintage	F	VF	XF	Unc	BU
1966	16,000,000	—	0.20	0.40	2.00	—
1966 Proof	—	Value: 2.00				
1970	3,000,000	—	0.25	0.65	2.25	—
1974	10,000,000	—	0.25	0.65	2.00	—

KM# 4a 50 CENTS **Composition:** Copper-Nickel Plated Steel

Date	Mintage	F	VF	XF	Unc	BU
1976	10,000,000	—	0.25	0.65	2.00	—

KM# 5 SHILLING **Composition:** Copper-Nickel
Reverse: East African crowned crane

Date	Mintage	F	VF	XF	Unc	BU
1966	24,500,000	—	0.25	0.50	2.50	—
1966 Proof	—	Value: 3.00				
1968	10,000,000	—	0.35	0.85	2.75	—
1972	—	—	0.35	0.85	2.50	—
1975	15,540,000	—	0.35	0.85	2.50	—

KM# 5a SHILLING **Composition:** Copper-Nickel Plated Steel

Date	Mintage	F	VF	XF	Unc	BU
1976	10,000,000	—	0.35	0.85	2.50	—
1978	—	—	0.35	0.85	2.50	—

KM# 27 SHILLING **Composition:** Copper Plated Steel

Date	F	VF	XF	Unc	BU
1987	—	—	—	0.25	—
1987 Proof	—	Value: 2.50			

KM# 6 2 SHILLINGS **Composition:** Copper-Nickel
Reverse: East African crowned crane

Date	Mintage	F	VF	XF	Unc	BU
1966	4,000,000	—	1.00	2.00	5.00	—
1966 Proof	—	Value: 6.00				

KM# 8 2 SHILLINGS **Weight:** 4.0000 g. **Composition:** 0.9990 Silver .1284 oz. ASW **Subject:** Visit of Pope Paul VI

Date	Mintage	F	VF	XF	Unc	BU
1969 Proof	8,170	Value: 10.00				
1970 Proof	Inc. above	Value: 10.00				

KM# 28 2 SHILLINGS **Composition:** Copper Plated Steel

Date	F	VF	XF	Unc	BU
1987	—	—	—	1.00	—
1987 Proof	—	Value: 4.00			

KM# 7 5 SHILLINGS **Composition:** Copper-Nickel
Series: F.A.O.

Date	Mintage	F	VF	XF	Unc	BU
ND(1968)	100,000	—	1.50	2.50	6.00	—
ND(1968) Proof	5,000	Value: 7.50				

KM# 9 5 SHILLINGS **Weight:** 10.0000 g. **Composition:** 0.9990 Silver .3212 oz. ASW **Subject:** Visit of Pope Paul VI **Reverse:** East African crowned crane

Date	Mintage	F	VF	XF	Unc	BU
1969 Proof	7,670	Value: 16.50				
1970 Proof	Inc. above	Value: 16.50				

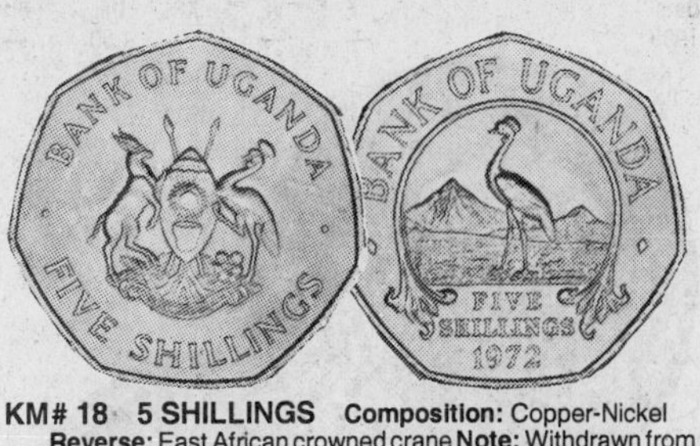

KM# 18 5 SHILLINGS **Composition:** Copper-Nickel
Reverse: East African crowned crane **Note:** Withdrawn from circulation. Almost entire mintage was melted.

Date	F	VF	XF	Unc	BU
1972	—	35.00	55.00	90.00	—

KM# 29 5 SHILLINGS **Composition:** Stainless Steel

Date	F	VF	XF	Unc	BU
1987	—	—	—	2.50	—
1987 Proof	—	Value: 6.50			

KM# 10 10 SHILLINGS **Weight:** 20.0000 g. **Composition:** 0.9990 Silver .6424 oz. ASW **Subject:** Visit of Pope Paul VI **Reverse:** Martyrs' Shrine

Date	Mintage	F	VF	XF	Unc	BU
1969 Proof	6,720	Value: 22.50				
1970 Proof	Inc. above	Value: 22.50				

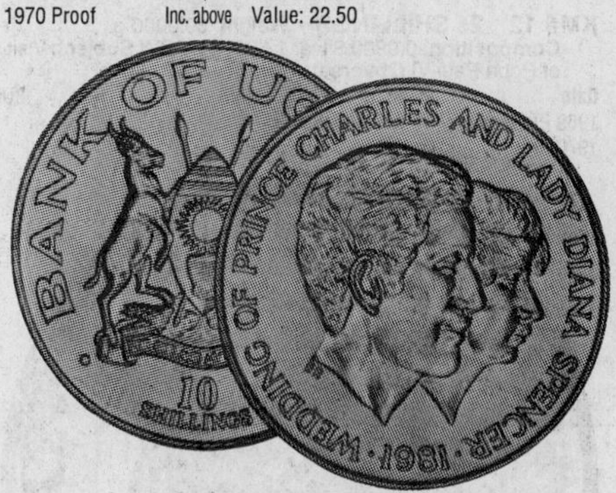

KM# 21 10 SHILLINGS **Composition:** Copper-Nickel
Subject: Wedding of Prince Charles and Lady Diana

Date	Mintage	F	VF	XF	Unc	BU
1981	10,000	—	—	—	7.00	—

KM# 30 10 SHILLINGS **Composition:** Stainless Steel

Date	F	VF	XF	Unc	BU
1987	—	—	—	3.50	—
1987 Proof	—	Value: 12.50			

KM# 11 20 SHILLINGS **Weight:** 40.0000 g. **Composition:** 0.9990 Silver 1.2848 oz. ASW **Subject:** Visit of Pope Paul VI **Obverse:** Arms **Reverse:** Map

Date	Mintage	F	VF	XF	Unc	BU
1969 Proof	6,670	Value: 30.00				
1970 Proof	Inc. above	Value: 32.50				

KM# 12 25 SHILLINGS **Weight:** 50.0000 g. **Composition:** 0.9990 Silver 1.6061 oz. ASW **Subject:** Visit of Pope Paul VI **Obverse:** Arms **Reverse:** Globe

Date	Mintage	F	VF	XF	Unc	BU
1969 Proof	6,070	Value: 35.00				
1970 Proof	Inc. above	Value: 37.50				

KM# 13 30 SHILLINGS **Weight:** 60.0000 g. **Composition:** 0.9990 Silver 1.9273 oz. ASW **Subject:** Visit of Pope Paul VI **Obverse:** Arms **Size:** 60 mm. **Note:** Illustration reduced.

Date	Mintage	F	VF	XF	Unc	BU
1969 Proof	6,720	Value: 40.00				
1970 Proof	Inc. above	Value: 42.50				

KM# 14 50 SHILLINGS **Weight:** 6.9100 g. **Composition:** 0.9000 Gold .1999 oz. AGW **Subject:** Visit of Pope Paul VI **Reverse:** Martyrs' Shrine

Date	Mintage	F	VF	XF	Unc	BU
1969 Proof	4,390	Value: 100				
1970 Proof	Inc. above	Value: 100				

KM# 66 50 SHILLINGS **Composition:** Nickel Plated Steel **Reverse:** Antelope

Date	F	VF	XF	Unc	BU
1998	—	—	—	1.00	—

KM# 15 100 SHILLINGS **Weight:** 13.8200 g. **Composition:** 0.9000 Gold .3999 oz. AGW **Subject:** Visit of Pope Paul VI **Reverse:** Map

Date	Mintage	F	VF	XF	Unc	BU
1969 Proof	4,190	Value: 200				
1970 Proof	Inc. above	Value: 200				

KM# 22 100 SHILLINGS **Weight:** 31.4700 g. **Composition:** 0.9250 Silver .9360 oz. ASW **Subject:** Wedding of Prince Charles and Lady Diana

Date	Mintage	F	VF	XF	Unc	BU
1981 Proof	5,000	Value: 40.00				

KM# 67 100 SHILLINGS **Composition:** Copper-Nickel **Reverse:** African bull

Date	F	VF	XF	Unc	BU
1998	—	—	—	1.50	—

KM# 26 200 SHILLINGS **Weight:** 28.2800 g. **Composition:** 0.9250 Silver .8411 oz. ASW **Series:** International Year of Disabled Persons

Date	Mintage	F	VF	XF	Unc	BU
1981	10,000	—	—	—	25.00	—
1981 Proof	10,000	Value: 37.50				

KM# 68 200 SHILLINGS **Composition:** Copper-Nickel **Reverse:** Cichlid fish

Date	F	VF	XF	Unc	BU
1998	—	—	—	2.00	—

KM# 16 500 SHILLINGS **Weight:** 69.1200 g. **Composition:** 0.9000 Gold 2.0002 oz. AGW **Subject:** Visit of Pope Paul VI **Obverse:** Arms **Reverse:** Globe

Date	Mintage	F	VF	XF	Unc	BU
1969 Proof	1,680	Value: 1,000				
1970 Proof	Inc. above	Value: 1,000				

KM# 23 500 SHILLINGS **Weight:** 136.0000 g. **Composition:** 0.5000 Silver 2.1864 oz. ASW **Series:** Wildlife **Reverse:** Elephants

Date	Mintage	F	VF	XF	Unc
1981	700	—	—	—	110

KM# 23a 500 SHILLINGS **Weight:** 136.0000 g. **Composition:** 9.2500 Silver 4.045 oz. ASW **Series:** Wild **Reverse:** Elephants

Date	Mintage	F	VF	XF	Unc
1981 Proof	700	Value: 185			

KM# 69 500 SHILLINGS **Composition:** Nickel-Brass **Reverse:** East African crowned crane

Date	F	VF	XF	Unc	BU
1998	—	—	—	2.50	—

KM# 17 1000 SHILLINGS **Weight:** 138.2400 g. **Composition:** 0.9000 Gold 4.0005 oz. AGW **Subject:** Visit of Pope John Paul VI

Date	Mintage	F	VF	XF	Unc	BU
1969 Proof	1,390	Value: 2,000				
1970 Proof	Inc. above	Value: 2,000				

M# 24 1000 SHILLINGS **Weight:** 10.0000 g. **Composition:** 0.5000 Gold .1607 oz. AGW **Subject:** Wedding of Prince Charles and Lady Diana **Reverse:** Busts of Charles and Diana right

ate	Mintage	F	VF	XF	Unc	BU
981 Proof	1,500	Value: 125				

M# 35 1000 SHILLINGS **Composition:** Copper-Nickel **Series:** Famous Places **Subject:** Matterhorn Mountain **Reverse:** Multicolored plastic applique

e	Mintage	F	VF	XF	Unc	BU
93 Proof	15,000	Value: 17.50				

M# 49 1000 SHILLINGS **Composition:** Copper-Nickel **Series:** Famous Places **Subject:** Munich

e		F	VF	XF	Unc	BU
4 Proof	—	Value: 17.50				

KM# 40 1000 SHILLINGS **Composition:** Copper-Nickel **Series:** 50th Anniversary - United Nations

Date		F	VF	XF	Unc	BU
1995 Proof	—	Value: 20.00				

KM# 50 1000 SHILLINGS **Composition:** Copper-Nickel **Subject:** Year of the Pig **Reverse:** Stylized pig

Date		F	VF	XF	Unc	BU
1995 Proof	—	Value: 17.50				

KM# 41 1000 SHILLINGS **Composition:** Copper-Nickel **Series:** Endangered Wildlife **Reverse:** Multicolored zebra applique

Date		F	VF	XF	Unc	BU
1996 Proof	—	Value: 17.50				

KM# 44 1000 SHILLINGS **Composition:** Copper-Nickel **Series:** Endangered Wildlife **Reverse:** Rhinoceros

Date	Mintage	F	VF	XF	Unc	BU
1996 Proof	15,000	Value: 22.50				

KM# 45 1000 SHILLINGS **Composition:** Copper-Nickel **Series:** Endangered Wildlife **Reverse:** Lion

Date	Mintage	F	VF	XF	Unc	BU
1996 Proof	15,000	Value: 20.00				

KM# 52 1000 SHILLINGS **Composition:** Copper-Nickel **Subject:** Hong Kong's return to China **Obverse:** National arms **Reverse:** City view

Date	F	VF	XF	Unc	BU
1996	—	—	—	18.00	—

KM# 54 1000 SHILLINGS **Composition:** Copper-Nickel **Subject:** Year of the rat **Obverse:** Pair of rats flanking Chinese symbol **Reverse:** Multicolored rat applique

Date	F	VF	XF	Unc	BU
1996	—	—	—	20.00	—

KM# 55 1000 SHILLINGS **Composition:** Copper-Nickel **Subject:** Africa - protection of endangered wildlife **Obverse:** National arms **Reverse:** Multicolored elephant applique

Date		F	VF	XF	Unc	BU
1996 Proof	—	Value: 22.50				

KM# 56 1000 SHILLINGS Composition: Copper-Nickel **Subject:** Michael Schumacher **Obverse:** National arms **Reverse:** Multicolored applique of Michael Schumacher, car and flag

Date	F	VF	XF	Unc	BU
1996 Proof	—	Value: 28.00			

KM# 74 1000 SHILLINGS Weight: 28.5200 g. **Composition:** Copper-Nickel **Subject:** Birth of Jesus and the Modern Dating System **Obverse:** Jesus' portrait **Reverse:** National arms **Edge:** Reeded **Size:** 38.15 mm.

Date	F	VF	XF	Unc	BU
1996 Proof	—	Value: 20.00			

KM# 57 1000 SHILLINGS Composition: Copper-Nickel **Subject:** Princess Diana - Queen of Hearts **Obverse:** National arms **Reverse:** Multicolored applique of Princess Diana

Date	F	VF	XF	Unc	BU
1997 Proof	—	Value: 28.00			

KM# 70 1000 SHILLINGS Weight: 14.9700 g. **Composition:** 0.9990 Silver .4808 oz. ASW **Series:** XXVII Olympic Games **Obverse:** National arms **Reverse:** Javelin thrower

Date	F	VF	XF	Unc	BU
1999 Proof	—	Value: 25.00			

KM# 77 1000 SHILLINGS Weight: 19.8400 g. **Composition:** Copper-Nickel **Subject:** Colourful Big Five of Africa **Obverse:** National arms. **Reverse:** Multicolor rhinocerous stamp design. **Edge:** Reeded. **Size:** 38.6 mm.

Date	F	VF	XF	Unc	BU
2001 Proof	—	Value: 40.00			

KM# 78 1000 SHILLINGS Weight: 19.8400 g. **Composition:** Copper-Nickel **Subject:** Colourful Big Five of Africa **Obverse:** National arms. **Reverse:** Multicolor lion stamp design. **Edge:** Reeded. **Size:** 38.6 mm.

Date	F	VF	XF	Unc	BU
2001 Proof	—	Value: 40.00			

KM# 79 1000 SHILLINGS Weight: 19.8400 g. **Composition:** Copper-Nickel **Subject:** Coulourful Big Five of Africa **Obverse:** National arms. **Reverse:** Multicolor water buffalo stamp design. **Edge:** Reeded. **Size:** 38.6 mm.

Date	F	VF	XF	Unc	BU
2001 Proof	—	Value: 40.00			

KM# 80 1000 SHILLINGS Weight: 19.8400 g. **Composition:** Copper-Nickel **Subject:** Colourful Big Five of Africa **Obverse:** National arms. **Reverse:** Multicolor leopard stamp design. **Edge:** Reeded. **Size:** 38.6 mm.

Date	F	VF	XF	Unc	BU
2001 Proof	—	Value: 40.00			

KM# 81 1000 SHILLINGS Weight: 19.8400 g. **Composition:** Copper-Nickel **Subject:** Colourful Big Five c Africa **Obverse:** National arms. **Reverse:** Multicolor elephant stamp design. **Edge:** Reeded. **Size:** 38.6 mm.

Date	F	VF	XF	Unc	B
2001 Proof	—	Value: 40.00			

KM# 82 1000 SHILLINGS Weight: 24.8300 g. **Composition:** 0.9990 Silver 0.7975 oz. ASW **Subject:** World of Football **Obverse:** National arms. **Reverse:** Socc ball globe. **Edge:** Reeded. **Size:** 38.6 mm.

Date	F	VF	XF	Unc
2002 Proof	—	Value: 30.00		

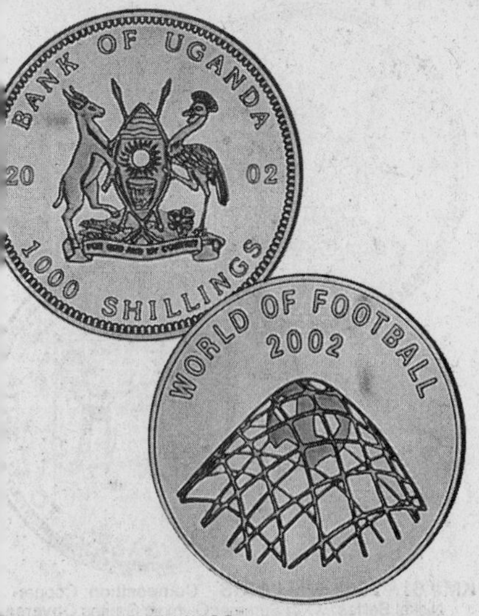

 # 83 1000 SHILLINGS **Weight:** 24.8300 g. **Composition:** 0.9990 Silver 0.7975 oz. ASW **Subject:** World of Football **Obverse:** National arms. **Reverse:** Soccer ball in net. **Edge:** Reeded. **Size:** 38.6 mm.

e	F	VF	XF	Unc	BU
2 Proof	—	Value: 30.00			

 # 84 1000 SHILLINGS **Weight:** 24.8300 g. **Composition:** 0.9990 Silver 0.7975 oz. ASW **Subject:** World of Football **Obverse:** National arms. **Reverse:** Goalie catching ball, red kicker insert at right. **Edge:** Reeded. **Size:** 38.6 mm.

e	F	VF	XF	Unc	BU
2 Proof	—	Value: 30.00			

 # 85 1000 SHILLINGS **Weight:** 24.8300 g. **Composition:** 0.9990 Silver 0.7975 oz. ASW **Subject:** World of Football **Obverse:** National arms. **Reverse:** Two players going after the ball, red runner insert at left. **Edge:** Reeded. **Size:** 38.6 mm.

Date	F	VF	XF	Unc	BU
2002 Proof	—	Value: 30.00			

KM# 86 1000 SHILLINGS **Weight:** 24.8300 g. **Composition:** 0.9990 Silver 0.7975 oz. ASW **Subject:** World of Football **Obverse:** National arms. **Reverse:** Player kicking ball, blue kicker insert at right. **Edge:** Reeded. **Size:** 38.6 mm.

Date	F	VF	XF	Unc	BU
2002 Proof	—	Value: 30.00			

KM# 31 2000 SHILLINGS **Weight:** 15.9800 g. **Composition:** 0.9170 Gold .4710 oz. AGW **Series:** International Year of Disabled Persons

Date	Mintage	F	VF	XF	Unc	BU
1981	2,005	—	—	—	550	—
1981 Proof	2,005	Value: 700				

KM# 38 2000 SHILLINGS **Weight:** 19.8000 g. **Composition:** 0.9990 Silver .6359 oz. ASW **Subject:** World Cup soccer **Reverse:** Player kicking ball

Date	F	VF	XF	Unc	BU
1993 Proof	—	Value: 50.00			

KM# 39 2000 SHILLINGS **Weight:** 19.8000 g. **Composition:** 0.9990 Silver .6359 oz. ASW **Subject:** World Cup soccer **Reverse:** Player kicking ball down field

Date	F	VF	XF	Unc	BU
1993 Proof	—	Value: 50.00			

KM# 42 2000 SHILLINGS **Weight:** 19.9200 g. **Composition:** 0.9990 Silver .6398 oz. ASW **Series:** Famous Places **Subject:** Matterhorn Mountain **Note:** With multicolored applique.

Date	Mintage	F	VF	XF	Unc	BU
1993 Proof	10,000	Value: 30.00				

KM# 64 2000 SHILLINGS **Weight:** 30.4600 g. **Composition:** 0.9990 Silver .9783 oz. ASW **Subject:** Protection of the African elephant **Obverse:** National arms

Date	F	VF	XF	Unc	BU
1993 Proof	—	Value: 50.00			

KM# 43 2000 SHILLINGS **Weight:** 19.9200 g. **Composition:** 0.9990 Silver .6398 oz. ASW **Series:** Famous Places **Subject:** Munich's Frauen Kirche

Date	Mintage	F	VF	XF	Unc	BU
1994 Proof	10,000	Value: 27.50				

KM# 53 2000 SHILLINGS **Composition:** Copper-Nickel **Subject:** Nations United for Peace **Obverse:** National arms **Reverse:** United Nations building

Date	F	VF	XF	Unc	BU
ND(1995)	—	—	—	8.50	—

KM# 58 2000 SHILLINGS **Weight:** 30.8400 g. **Composition:** 0.9990 Silver .9904 oz. ASW **Obverse:** Sow and piglets **Reverse:** Multicolored pig applique

Date	Mintage	F	VF	XF	Unc	BU
1995 Proof	—	Value: 30.00				

KM# 93 2000 SHILLINGS **Weight:** 19.9200 g. **Composition:** 0.9990 Silver .6398 oz. ASW **Reverse:** Multicolored leaning Tower of Pisa

Date	Mintage	F	VF	XF	Unc	BU
1996 Proof	10,000	Value: 35.00				

KM# 94 2000 SHILLINGS **Weight:** 19.9000 g. **Composition:** 0.9990 Silver 0.6392 oz. ASW **Subject:** Christian Dating System **Obverse:** National arms **Reverse:** Jesus portrait **Edge:** Reeded **Size:** 37.9 mm.

Date	Mintage	F	VF	XF	Unc	BU
1996 Proof	—	Value: 35.00				

KM# 46 2000 SHILLINGS **Weight:** 19.9200 g. **Composition:** 0.9990 Silver .6398 oz. ASW **Series:** Endangered Wildlife **Reverse:** Zebra

Date	Mintage	F	VF	XF	Unc	BU
1996 Proof	10,000	Value: 32.50				

KM# 47 2000 SHILLINGS **Weight:** 19.9200 g. **Composition:** 0.9990 Silver .6398 oz. ASW **Series:** Endangered Wildlife **Reverse:** Rhinocerous

Date	Mintage	F	VF	XF	Unc	BU
1996 Proof	10,000	Value: 45.00				

KM# 48 2000 SHILLINGS **Weight:** 19.9200 g. **Composition:** 0.9990 Silver .6398 oz. ASW **Series:** Endangered Wildlife **Reverse:** Lion

Date	Mintage	F	VF	XF	Unc	BU
1996 Proof	10,000	Value: 50.00				

KM# 59 2000 SHILLINGS **Weight:** 30.8400 g. **Composition:** 0.9990 Silver .9904 oz. ASW **Obverse:** Pair of rats flanking Chinese symbols **Reverse:** Multicolored rat applique

Date	Mintage	F	VF	XF	Unc	BU
1996 Proof	—	Value: 40.00				

KM# 60 2000 SHILLINGS **Weight:** 7.1000 g. **Composition:** 0.9990 Silver .228 oz. ASW **Subject:** 1998 World Championship Football **Obverse:** National arms **Reverse:** Soccer player and Eiffel Tower

Date	Mintage	F	VF	XF	Unc	BU
1996 Proof	—	Value: 22.50				

KM# 61 2000 SHILLINGS **Composition:** Copper-Nickel **Series:** XXVI Summer Olympic Games **Obverse:** National arms **Reverse:** 1936 German Olympic stamp

Date	Mintage	F	VF	XF	Unc	BU
1996 Proof	—	Value: 20.00				

KM# 62 2000 SHILLINGS **Composition:** Copper-Nickel **Series:** Olympics **Obverse:** National arms **Reverse:** Spanish postal stamp design

Date	Mintage	F	VF	XF	Unc	BU
1996 Proof	—	Value: 20.00				

KM# 65 2000 SHILLINGS **Weight:** 20.2600 g. **Composition:** 0.9990 Silver .6507 oz. ASW **Series:** Endangered Wildlife **Obverse:** National arms **Reverse:** Multicolored elephant

Date	Mintage	F	VF	XF	Unc	BU
1996 Proof	—	Value: 45.00				

 # 63 2000 SHILLINGS **Composition:** Copper-
lickel **Subject:** Queen's golden wedding anniversary
)bverse: National arms **Reverse:** Queen Elizabeth and
'rince Philip on horseback

	F	VF	XF	Unc	BU
997)	—	—	—	9.00	—

 # 51 2000 SHILLINGS **Weight:** 19.7400 g.
Composition: 0.9990 Silver .6346 oz. ASW **Subject:** Hong
Kong's return to China **Obverse:** National arms
Reverse: City view

	F	VF	XF	Unc	BU
Proof	—	Value: 35.00			

 # 71 2000 SHILLINGS **Weight:** 26.0000 g.
Composition: 0.9990 Silver .8351 oz. ASW **Series:**
Olympics 2000 **Obverse:** Queen Elizabeth II above arms
Reverse: Hurdler **Edge:** Reeded **Size:** 40.1 mm.

		F	VF	XF	Unc	BU
) Proof	5,000	Value: 32.50				

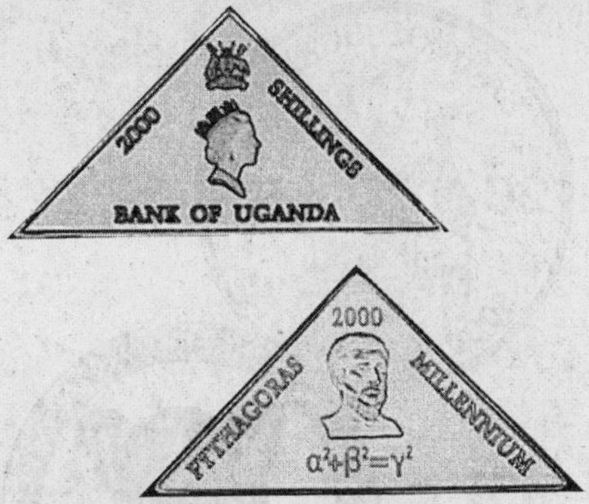

KM# 72 2000 SHILLINGS **Weight:** 15.7500 g.
Composition: 0.9250 Silver .4684 oz. ASW **Series:**
Millennium **Obverse:** National arms above Queen Elizabeth
II **Reverse:** Pythagoras **Edge:** Plain, 3 sided **Size:**
45.2x23.2 mm.

Date	Mintage	F	VF	XF	Unc	BU
2000 Proof	10,000	Value: 30.00				

KM# 73 2000 SHILLINGS **Weight:** 25.0000 g.
Composition: 0.9250 Silver .7435 oz. ASW **Subject:**
Wildlife protection **Obverse:** Queen Elizabeth's portrait
above Ugandan arms **Reverse:** Three zebras drinking in
reflective water **Edge:** Reeded **Size:** 37.9 mm.

Date		F	VF	XF	Unc	BU
2000 Proof	5,000	Value: 32.50				

KM# 75 2000 SHILLINGS **Weight:** 49.9000 g.
Composition: 0.9990 Silver 1.4840 oz. ASW **Subject:**
Illusion: "Spirit of the Mountain" **Obverse:** Ugandan arms
above Queen Elizabeth's portrait **Reverse:** Landscape that
looks like a male portrait **Edge:** Reeded **Size:** 50 mm.

Date		F	VF	XF	Unc	BU
2001 Proof	—	Value: 42.50				

KM# 25 5000 SHILLINGS **Weight:** 33.9300 g.
Composition: 0.9170 Gold 1 oz. AGW **Subject:** Wildlife
Obverse: Facing bust of Dr. Milton Obote **Reverse:** East
African crowned crane

Date	Mintage	F	VF	XF	Unc	BU
1981	100	—	—	—	550	—
1981 Proof	100	Value: 650				

KM# 32 5000 SHILLINGS **Weight:** 12.0000 g.
Composition: 0.9990 Silver .3858 oz. ASW **Subject:**
Soccer **Reverse:** Ball and net

Date	F	VF	XF	Unc	BU
1992	—	—	—	25.00	—

KM# 36 5000 SHILLINGS **Weight:** 500.0000 g.
Composition: 0.9990 Silver 16.0753 oz. ASW **Series:**
Endangered Wildlife **Reverse:** 2 leopards

Date	Mintage	F	VF	XF	Unc	BU
1993 Proof	2,500	Value: 275				

KM# 87 5000 SHILLINGS **Weight:** 33.7300 g. **Composition:** 0.8500 Silver 0.9218 oz. ASW **Subject:** "The Big Five" **Obverse:** National arms. **Reverse:** Rhinoceros. **Edge:** Reeded. **Size:** 38.65 mm.

Date		F	VF	XF	Unc	BU
2002 Proof	—	Value: 45.00				

KM# 88 5000 SHILLINGS **Weight:** 33.7300 g. **Composition:** 0.8500 Silver 0.9218 oz. ASW **Subject:** "The Big Five" **Obverse:** National arms. **Reverse:** Lion. **Edge:** Reeded. **Size:** 38.65 mm.

Date		F	VF	XF	Unc	BU
2002 Proof	—	Value: 45.00				

KM# 89 5000 SHILLINGS **Weight:** 33.7300 g. **Composition:** 0.8500 Silver 0.9218 oz. ASW **Subject:** "The Big Five" **Obverse:** National arms. **Reverse:** Cape Buffalo. **Edge:** Reeded. **Size:** 38.65 mm.

Date		F	VF	XF	Unc	BU
2002 Proof	—	Value: 45.00				

KM# 90 5000 SHILLINGS **Weight:** 33.7300 g. **Composition:** 0.8500 Silver 0.9218 oz. ASW **Subject:** "The Big Five" **Obverse:** National arms. **Reverse:** Leopard. **Edge:** Reeded. **Size:** 38.65 mm.

Date		F	VF	XF	Unc	BU
2002 Proof	—	Value: 45.00				

KM# 91 5000 SHILLINGS **Weight:** 33.7300 g. **Composition:** 0.8500 Silver 0.9218 oz. ASW **Subject:** "The Big Five" **Obverse:** National arms. **Reverse:** Elephant. **Edge:** Reeded. **Size:** 38.65 mm.

Date		F	VF	XF	Unc	BU
2002 Proof	—	Value: 45.00				

KM# 33 10000 SHILLINGS **Weight:** 20.0000 g. **Composition:** 0.9990 Silver .6430 oz. ASW **Subject:** Soccer **Reverse:** Mount Rushmore behind 2 players

Date	Mintage	F	VF	XF	Unc	BU
ND(1992) Proof	Est. 10,000	Value: 45.00				

KM# 34 10000 SHILLINGS **Weight:** 20.0000 g. **Composition:** 0.9990 Silver .6430 oz. ASW **Subject:** Papa visit

Date		F	VF	XF	Unc	B
1993 Proof	—	Value: 37.50				

KM# 37 10000 SHILLINGS **Weight:** 1000.0000 g. **Composition:** 0.9990 Silver 32.1507 oz. ASW **Series:** Endangered Wildlife **Reverse:** 2 rhinoceros

Date	Mintage	F	VF	XF	Unc
1993 Proof	2,000	Value: 350			

KM# 92 10000 SHILLINGS **Weight:** 155.5000 g. **Composition:** 0.9990 Silver 4.9944 oz. ASW **Obverse:** National arms. **Reverse:** Bust of Princess Diana 1/2 facing. **Edge:** Reeded. **Size:** 65 mm. **Note:** Illustration reduced. Actual size: 65mm.

ate	Mintage	F	VF	XF	Unc	BU
998 Proof	2,500	Value: 150				

KM# 76 12000 SHILLINGS **Weight:** 6.2207 g. **Composition:** 0.9999 Gold .2000 oz. AGW **Subject:** Illusion: "Spirit of the Mountain" **Obverse:** Ugandan arms above Queen Elizabeth's portrait **Reverse:** Landscape that looks like a male portrait **Edge:** Reeded **Size:** 22 mm.

ate	F	VF	XF	Unc	BU
001 Proof	—	—	—	—	—

PATTERNS

Including off metal strikes

M#	Date	Mintage	Identification	Mkt Val
1	1994	—	1000 Shillings. Copper-Nickel. Soccer player, 999.	—
2	1994	—	1000 Shillings. Copper-Nickel. 3 soccer players, 999 CuNi.	—
3	1994	—	1000 Shillings. Copper-Nickel. 4 soccer players, 999.	—
4	1996	—	1000 Shillings. Gilt Bronze. Surinam. 100 Guilders.	—

PIEFORTS

#	Date	Mintage	Identification	Mkt Val
	1981	—	200 Shillings. 0.9250 Silver. KM26.	75.00
	1981	505	2000 Shillings. 0.9170 Gold. KM31.	750

TRIAL STRIKES

#	Date	Mintage	Identification	Mkt Val
1	1969	—	500 Shillings. Goldine. KM16.	100

	1970	—	1000 Shillings. Goldine. KM17.	125

MINT SETS

Date	Mintage	Identification	Issue Price	Mkt Val
1987 (4)	—	KM27-30	10.50	11.50

PROOF SETS

Date	Mintage	Identification	Issue Price	Mkt Val
1966 (6)	8,250	KM1-6	7.75	14.50
1969 (10)	1,390	KM8-17	790	3,450
1969 (6)	6,070	KM8-13	78.50	160
1970 (10)	—	KM8-17, including KM-PS2	790	3,300
1970 (6)	—	KM8-13, including KM-PS3	78.50	170
1987 (4)	2,500	KM27-30	25.00	27.50

UKRAINE

Ukraine (formerly the Ukrainian Soviet Socialist Republic) is bordered by Russia to the east, Russia and Belarus to the north, Poland, Slovakia and Hungary to the west, Romania and Moldova to the southwest and in the south by the Black Sea and the Sea of Azov. It has an area of 233,088 sq. mi. (603,700 sq. km.) and a population of 51.9 million. Capital: Kyiv (Kiev). Coal, grain, vegetables and heavy industrial machinery are major exports.

The territory of Ukraine has been inhabited for over 30,000 years. As the result of its location, Ukraine has served as the gateway to Europe for millennia and its early history has been recorded by Arabic, Greek, Roman, as well as Ukrainian historians.

Ukraine, which was known as *Rus'* until the sixteenth century (and from which the name Russia was derived in the 17th century) became the major political and cultural center of Eastern Europe in the 9th century. The Rus' Kingdom, under a dynasty of Varangian origin, due to its position on the intersection of the north-south Scandinavia to Byzantium and the east-west Orient to Europe trade routes, became a focal point of world trade. At its apex Rus' stretched from the Baltic to the Black Sea and from the upper Volga River in the east, almost to the Vistula River in the west. It has family ties to many European dynasties. In 988 knyaz (king) Volodymyr adopted Christianity from Byzantium. With it came church books written in the Cyrillic alphabet, which originated in Bulgaria. The Mongol invasion in 1240 brought an end to the might of the Rus' Kingdom.

In the seventeenth century, after almost four hundred years of Mongol, Lithuanian, Polish, and Turkish domination, the Cosack State under Hetman Bohdan Khmelnytsky regained Ukrainian independence. The Hetman State lasted until the mid-eighteenth century and was followed by a period of foreign rule. Eastern Ukraine was controlled by Russia, which enforced russification through introduction of the Russian language and prohibiting the use of the Ukrainian language in schools, books and public life. Western Ukraine came under relatively benign Austro-Hungarian rule.

With the disintegration of the Russian and Austro-Hungarian Empires in 1917 and 1918. Eastern Ukraine declared its full independence on January 22,1918 and Western Ukraine followed suit on November 1 of that year. On January 22, 1919 both parts united into one state that had to defend itself on three fronts: from the "Red Bolsheviks"and their puppet Ukrainian Soviet Republic formed in Kharkiv, from the "White" czarist Russian forces, and from Poland. Ukraine lost the war. In 1920 Eastern Ukraine was occupied by the Bolsheviks and in 1922 was incorporated into the Soviet Union. There followed a brief resurgence of Ukrainian language and culture which Stalin suppressed in 1928. The artificial famine-genocide of 1932-33 killed 7-10 million Ukrainians, and Stalinist purges in the mid-1930s took a heavy toll. Western Ukraine was partitioned between Poland, Romania, Hungary and Czechoslovakia.

On August 24, 1991 Ukraine once again declared its independence. On December 1, 1991 over 90% of Ukraine's electorate approved full independence from the Soviet Union. On December 5, 1991 the Ukrainian Parliament abrogated the 1922 treaty which incorporated Ukraine into the Soviet Union. Later, Leonid Kravchuk was elected president by a 65% majority.

Ukraine is a charter member of the United Nations and has inherited the third largest nuclear arsenal in the world.

Rulers

Russian (Eastern, Northern, Southern, Central Ukraine), 1654-1917

Austrian (Western Ukraine), 1774-1918

MINT

w/o mm - Lugansk; Kiev (1997-1998)

MONETARY SYSTEM

(1) Kopiyka

(2) Kopiyky КОПіИКН

(5 and up) Kopiyok КОПИОК

100 Kopiyok = 1 Hrynia ГРИВЕНЬ

100,000 Karbovanetsiv = 1 Hryni or Hryven)

REPUBLIC

STANDARD COINAGE

KM# 9 200000 KARBOVANTSIV **Composition:** Copper-Nickel **Subject:** Bohdan Khmelnytsky Monument

Date	Mintage	F	VF	XF	Unc	BU
1995 Prooflike	250,000	—	—	—	5.50	—

KM# 10.1 200000 KARBOVANTSIV **Composition:** Copper-Nickel **Subject:** 50th anniversary - end of World War II **Obverse:** Ukrainian letter "Y" looks similar to "X" **Reverse:** Ukrainian letter "Y" looks similar to "X"

Date	Mintage	F	VF	XF	Unc	BU
1995 Prooflike	10,000	—	—	—	22.50	—

KM# 10.2 200000 KARBOVANTSIV **Composition:** Copper-Nickel **Subject:** 50th Anniversary - End of World War II **Obverse:** Ukrainian letter "Y" like Y/2 in legends **Reverse:** Ukrainian letter "Y" like Y/2 in legends

Date	Mintage	F	VF	XF	Unc	BU
1995 Prooflike	240,000	—	—	—	5.50	—

KM# 11 200000 KARBOVANTSIV **Composition:** Copper-Nickel **Subject:** World War II - Monument at Kerch

Date	Mintage	F	VF	XF	Unc	BU
1995 Prooflike	50,000	—	—	—	10.00	—

KM# 12 200000 KARBOVANTSIV **Composition:** Copper-Nickel **Subject:** World War II - Monument at Odessa

Date	Mintage	F	VF	XF	Unc	BU
1995 Prooflike	75,000	—	—	—	5.50	—

KM# 13 200000 KARBOVANTSIV Composition: Copper-Nickel **Subject:** World War II - Monument at Kiev

Date	Mintage	F	VF	XF	Unc	BU
1995 Prooflike	100,000	—	—	—	5.50	—

KM# 14 200000 KARBOVANTSIV Composition: Copper-Nickel **Subject:** World War II - Monument at Sevastopol

Date	Mintage	F	VF	XF	Unc	BU
1995 Prooflike	75,000	—	—	—	8.00	—

KM# 15 200000 KARBOVANTSIV Composition: Copper-Nickel **Series:** 50th Anniversary - United Nations

Date	Mintage	F	VF	XF	Unc	BU
1995	100,000	—	—	—	5.50	—

KM# 17 200000 KARBOVANTSIV Composition: Copper-Nickel **Reverse:** Half bust of Lesya Ukrainka, poetess, facing

Date	Mintage	F	VF	XF	Unc	BU
1996 Prooflike	100,000	—	—	—	7.50	—

KM# 21 200000 KARBOVANTSIV Composition: Copper-Nickel **Subject:** 10th Anniversary - Chernobyl Disaster

Date	Mintage	F	VF	XF	Unc	BU
1996 Prooflike	250,000	—	—	—	5.50	—

KM# 23 200000 KARBOVANTSIV Composition: Copper-Nickel **Series:** 1st Participation in Summer Olympics **Reverse:** Athletes around octagon

Date	Mintage	F	VF	XF	Unc	BU
1996 Prooflike	100,000	—	—	—	5.50	—

KM# 24 200000 KARBOVANTSIV Composition: Copper-Nickel **Series:** Centennial of Modern Olympics **Reverse:** Flame and logo

Date	Mintage	F	VF	XF	Unc	BU
1996 Prooflike	100,000	—	—	—	5.50	—

KM# 27 200000 KARBOVANTSIV Composition: Copper-Nickel **Subject:** Mikhailo Hrushevsky - 1866-1934

Date	Mintage	F	VF	XF	Unc	BU
1996 Prooflike	75,000	—	—	—	7.50	—

KM# 16 1000000 KARBOVANETS Weight: 16.8110 g. **Composition:** 0.9250 Silver .5 oz. ASW **Subject:** Bohdan Khmelnytsky Monument

Date	Mintage	F	VF	XF	Unc	BU
1996 Proof	10,000	Value: 30.00				

KM# 18 1000000 KARBOVANETS Weight: 16.8110 g. **Composition:** 0.9250 Silver .5 oz. ASW **Reverse:** Half bust of Lesya Ukrainka, poetess, facing

Date	Mintage	F	VF	XF	Unc	BU
1996 Proof	10,000	Value: 30.00				

KM# 20 1000000 KARBOVANETS Weight: 16.8110 g. **Composition:** 0.9250 Silver .5 oz. ASW **Obverse:** Similar to KM#16 **Reverse:** Bust of Grygory Skovoroda facing

Date	Mintage	F	VF	XF	Unc	BU
1996 Proof	10,000	Value: 27.50				

KM# 32 1000000 KARBOVANETS Weight: 16.8110 g. **Composition:** 0.9250 Silver .5 oz. ASW **Obverse:** National arms **Reverse:** Half bust of Mikhailo Hrushevsky - 1866-1934

Date	Mintage	F	VF	XF	Unc	BU
1996 Proof	10,000	Value: 27.50				

KM# 19 2000000 KARBOVANETS Weight: 33.6220 **Composition:** 0.9250 Silver 1 oz. ASW **Series:** 50 Years United Nations

Date	Mintage	F	VF	XF	Unc	B
1995 Proof	10,000	Value: 37.50				

KM# 22 2000000 KARBOVANETS Weight: 33.6220 **Composition:** 0.9250 Silver 1 oz. ASW **Subject:** 10th Anniversary - Chernobyl Disaster

Date	Mintage	F	VF	XF	Unc
1996 Proof	10,000	Value: 40.00			

KM# 25 2000000 KARBOVANETS Weight: 33.622 **Composition:** 0.9250 Silver 1 oz. ASW **Series:** 1st Participation in Summer Olympics **Reverse:** Athletes aro octagon

Date	Mintage	F	VF	XF	Unc
1996 Proof	10,000	Value: 35.00			

KM# 26 2000000 KARBOVANETS **Weight:** 33.6220 g. **Composition:** 0.9250 Silver 1 oz. ASW **Series:** Centennial of Modern Olympics **Reverse:** Flame and logo

ate	Mintage	F	VF	XF	Unc	BU
996 Proof	10,000	Value: 35.00				

M# 33 2000000 KARBOVANETS **Weight:** 33.6220 g. **Composition:** 0.9250 Silver 1 oz. ASW **Subject:** Independence **Obverse:** National arms

ate	Mintage	F	VF	XF	Unc	BU
96 Proof	10,000	Value: 45.00				

REFORM COINAGE

September 2, 1996

100,000 Karbovanets = 1 Hryvnia; 100 Kopiyok = 1 ryvnia; The Kopiyok has replaced the Karbovanet

M# 6 KOPIYKA **Weight:** 1.5000 g. **Composition:** Stainless Steel

te	F	VF	XF	Unc	BU
92	—	—	0.15	0.35	—
94	—	—	5.00	10.00	—
96	—	—	1.00	1.35	—
)0	—	—	0.35	0.75	—
)1	—	—	0.35	0.75	—
2	—	—	0.35	0.75	—

 # 4 2 KOPIYKY **Weight:** 0.6400 g. **Composition:** Aluminum

	F	VF	XF	Unc	BU
3	—	0.20	0.50	1.00	—
4	—	0.20	0.50	1.00	—
5	—	0.20	1.00	2.00	—
	—	0.20	0.50	1.00	—

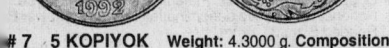

 # 7 5 KOPIYOK **Weight:** 4.3000 g. **Composition:** Stainless Steel

	F	VF	XF	Unc	BU
	—	—	0.35	0.65	—
	—	0.50	1.50	3.00	—
	—	0.50	1.50	3.00	—

KM# 1.1 10 KOPIYOK **Weight:** 1.7000 g. **Composition:** Brass **Reverse:** Five dots right of final "K" in denomination **Note:** Edge varieties - fine or coarse reeding - exist.

Date	F	VF	XF	Unc	BU
1992	—	0.50	1.00	2.25	—
1994	—	0.50	1.00	2.25	—
1996	—	0.60	1.25	2.50	—
2001	—	2.00	3.00	5.00	—
2002	—	0.60	1.25	2.50	—

KM# 1.2 10 KOPIYOK **Composition:** Brass **Reverse:** Six dots right of "K"

Date	F	VF	XF	Unc	BU
1992	—	0.50	1.00	2.25	—

KM# 2.1 25 KOPIYOK **Weight:** 2.9000 g. **Composition:** Brass

Date	F	VF	XF	Unc	BU
1992	—	0.60	1.25	2.50	—
1994	—	0.60	1.25	2.50	—
1995	—	1.50	3.00	6.00	—
1996	—	0.80	2.25	3.50	—
2001	—	0.80	2.25	3.50	—

KM# 2.2 25 KOPIYOK **Composition:** Brass **Reverse:** Berries with dots inside

Date	F	VF	XF	Unc	BU
1992	—	0.60	1.25	2.50	—

KM# 3.1 50 KOPIYOK **Weight:** 4.2000 g. **Composition:** Brass **Reverse:** Five dots grouped in wreath to right of final letter "K" in denomination **Edge:** Reeded sections of 16 grooves each

Date	F	VF	XF	Unc	BU
1992	—	0.85	1.75	3.50	—
1994	—	0.85	1.75	3.50	—

KM# 3.3 50 KOPIYOK **Composition:** Brass **Reverse:** Five dots grouped in wreath to right of final letter "K" in denomination

Date	F	VF	XF	Unc	BU
1992	—	0.85	1.75	3.50	—
1994	—	0.85	1.75	3.50	—
1995	—	2.00	4.00	8.00	—
1996	—	0.85	2.25	4.00	—
2001	—	1.00	2.50	4.00	—

KM# 3.2 50 KOPIYOK **Composition:** Brass **Reverse:** Four dots grouped in wreath to right of final letter "K" in denomination **Edge:** Reeded sections of seven grooves each

Date	F	VF	XF	Unc	BU
1992	—	0.85	1.75	3.50	—

KM# 8 HRYVNIA **Composition:** Brass

Date	F	VF	XF	Unc	BU
1992	—	—	12.50	25.00	—
1995	—	—	3.50	6.50	—
1996	—	—	2.50	4.50	—
2001	—	—	5.00	8.00	—

KM# 28 2 HRYVNI **Composition:** Copper-Nickel **Subject:** 200th Anniversary - Sophiyivka Dendrological Park **Reverse:** Partially overgrown stone face

Date	Mintage	F	VF	XF	Unc	BU
1996 Prooflike	30,000	—	—	—	12.50	—

KM# 29 2 HRYVNI **Composition:** Copper-Nickel **Subject:** Desiatynna Church **Obverse:** National arms above Madonna and child

Date	Mintage	F	VF	XF	Unc	BU
1996 Prooflike	30,000	—	—	—	12.50	—

KM# 30 2 HRYVNI **Composition:** Copper-Nickel-Zinc **Subject:** Modern Ukrainian coinage **Obverse:** National arms

Date	Mintage	F	VF	XF	Unc	BU
1996	200,000	—	—	—	8.00	—

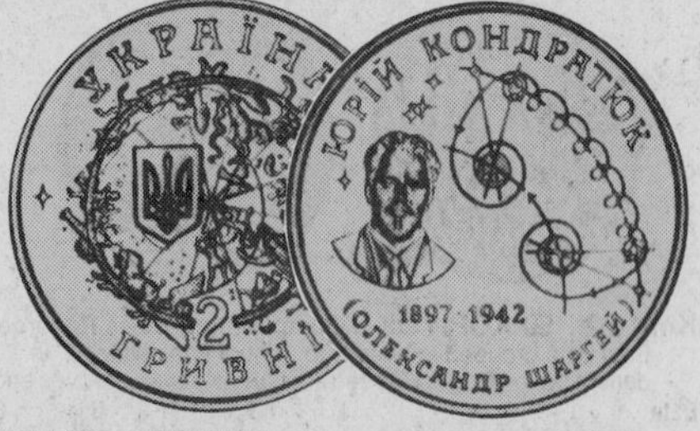

KM# 39 2 HRYVNI **Composition:** Copper-Nickel **Subject:** Yuri Kondratiuk **Obverse:** National arms on astrological design **Reverse:** Scientific drawing

Date	Mintage	F	VF	XF	Unc	BU
1997 Prooflike	20,000	—	—	—	12.50	—

KM# 40 2 HRYVNI **Composition:** Copper-Nickel **Subject:** 1st Anniversary - Constitution **Obverse:** National arms **Reverse:** Scroll

Date	Mintage	F	VF	XF	Unc	BU
1997 Prooflike	20,000	—	—	—	12.50	—

KM# 41 2 HRYVNI **Composition:** Copper-Nickel **Subject:** Solomiya Krushelnytska - 1872-1952 **Obverse:** National arms

Date	Mintage	F	VF	XF	Unc	BU
1997 Prooflike	20,000	—	—	—	12.50	—

KM# 42 2 HRYVNI **Composition:** Copper-Nickel **Subject:** 80 Years of Nationhood **Obverse:** National arms and people above denomination **Reverse:** Cossacks, soldiers

Date	Mintage	F	VF	XF	Unc	BU
ND(1998)	150,000	—	—	—	7.50	—
ND(1998) Prooflike	50,000	—	—	—	10.00	—

Note: Encapsulated

KM# 43 2 HRYVNI **Composition:** Copper-Nickel-Zinc **Subject:** Bolodimir Sosura - 1898-1965 **Obverse:** National arms

Date	Mintage	F	VF	XF	Unc	BU
1998	180,000	—	—	—	7.50	—
1998 Prooflike	20,000	—	—	—	12.00	—

Note: Encapsulated

KM# 47 2 HRYVNI **Composition:** Copper-Nickel-Zinc **Subject:** 80 Years of Nationhood **Obverse:** Family group and national arms **Reverse:** Soldiers on guard

Date	Mintage	F	VF	XF	Unc	BU
1998	150,000	—	—	—	7.50	—
1998 Prooflike	50,000	—	—	—	10.00	—

Note: Encapsulated

KM# 49 2 HRYVNI **Composition:** Copper-Nickel-Zinc **Subject:** 100th Anniversary - Askania-Nova Wildlife Preserve **Obverse:** National arms, denomination, wild animals and plants

Date	Mintage	F	VF	XF	Unc	BU
1998	150,000	—	—	—	7.50	—
1998 Prooflike	50,000	—	—	—	10.00	—

Note: Encapsulated

KM# 51 2 HRYVNI **Composition:** Copper-Nickel-Zinc **Subject:** 100th Anniversary - Polytechnical Institute **Obverse:** National arms in circular design

Date	Mintage	F	VF	XF	Unc	BU
1998	40,000	—	—	—	9.00	—
1998 Prooflike	10,000	—	—	—	13.50	—

Note: Encapsulated

KM# 48 2 HRYVNI **Composition:** Copper-Nickel-Zinc **Subject:** European Bank of Reconstruction and Development **Obverse:** National arms and denomination **Reverse:** Legendary founders at Kiev statue

Date	Mintage	F	VF	XF	Unc	BU
1998	10,000	—	—	—	13.50	—

KM# 72 2 HRYVNI **Composition:** Copper-Nickel-Zinc **Subject:** 50 Years - United Nations Human Rights Declaration **Obverse:** National arms **Reverse:** Logo on globe

Date	Mintage	F	VF	XF	Unc	BU
1998	100,000	—	—	—	7.50	—

KM# 73 2 HRYVNI **Composition:** Copper-Nickel **Subject:** Steppe Eagle **Obverse:** National arms **Reverse:** Eagle in flight

Date	F	VF	XF	Unc	B
1999	—	—	—	7.50	-

KM# 75 2 HRYVNI **Composition:** Copper-Nickel **Subject:** 80th Anniversary - Ukranian State **Obverse:** National arms **Reverse:** Seated woman

Date	F	VF	XF	Unc
1999	—	—	—	7.50

KM# 76 2 HRYVNI **Composition:** Copper-Nickel **Obverse:** National arms **Reverse:** Bust of P.Y. Rudcher (1849-1920) with book and quill

Date	Mintage	F	VF	XF	Unc
1999 Prooflike	50,000	—	—	—	8.00

KM# 78 2 HRYVNI **Composition:** Copper-Nickel **Obve** National arms **Reverse:** Head of Anatolyi Solovianenkc

Date	F	VF	XF	Unc
1999 Prooflike	—	—	—	9.00

KM# 81 2 HRYVNI **Weight:** 12.5500 g. **Composit** Copper-Nickel **Subject:** Platanthera Bifolia **Obverse:** National arms above denomination **Reverse:** Flower **E** Reeded **Size:** 31.1 mm.

Date	Mintage	F	VF	XF	Unc
1999	50,000	—	—	—	7.50

82 2 HRYVNI Composition: Copper-Nickel
ubject: 100 Years - Ukraine's National Mining Academy

Mintage	F	VF	XF	Unc	BU
20,000	—	—	—	8.50	—

83 2 HRYVNI Composition: Copper-Nickel
everse: Dormouse

Mintage	F	VF	XF	Unc	BU
50,000	—	—	—	6.50	—

79 2 HRYVNI Composition: Copper-Nickel
ubject: 55th Annivesary - Freedom From Nazi Occupation
bverse: National arms **Reverse:** Stylized sword design

Mintage	F	VF	XF	Unc	BU
50,000	—	—	—	7.50	—

 # 91 2 HRYVNI Weight: 13.4000 g. **Composition:** Copper-Nickel **Subject:** 55th Annivesary - Victory in World War II **Obverse:** Arms and denomination **Reverse:** Symboblic "Peace" figure **Edge:** Reeded

Mintage	F	VF	XF	Unc	BU
50,000	—	—	—	7.50	—

 # 110 2 HRYVNI Weight: 12.9200 g. **Composition:** Copper-Nickel **Obverse:** Flower cluster **Reverse:** Kateryna Bilokur (1900-1961) - artist **Edge:** Reeded **Size:** 31 mm.

Mintage	F	VF	XF	Unc	BU
50,000	—	—	—	7.00	—

KM# 92 2 HRYVNI Weight: 13.4000 g. **Composition:** Copper-Nickel **Subject:** Archaeologist V. Hvoika **Obverse:** Arms within circles and artifacts **Reverse:** V. Hvoika head facing

Date	Mintage	F	VF	XF	Unc	BU
2000	20,000	—	—	—	7.50	—

KM# 93 2 HRYVNI Weight: 13.4000 g. **Composition:** Copper-Nickel **Series:** Sydney 2000 Olympics **Obverse:** Arms and denomination **Reverse:** Broad jumper

Date	Mintage	F	VF	XF	Unc	BU
2000	50,000	—	—	—	6.50	—

KM# 94 2 HRYVNI Weight: 13.4000 g. **Composition:** Copper-Nickel **Series:** Sydney 2000 Olympics **Obverse:** Arms and denomination **Reverse:** Gymnast on parallel bars

Date	Mintage	F	VF	XF	Unc	BU
2000	50,000	—	—	—	6.50	—

KM# 96 2 HRYVNI Composition: Copper-Nickel **Subject:** Musician Ivan Kozlovsky **Obverse:** Flowery lyre **Reverse:** I. Kozlovsky head left **Edge:** Reeded **Size:** 31 mm.

Date	Mintage	F	VF	XF	Unc	BU
2000	20,000	—	—	—	6.50	—

KM# 97 2 HRYVNI Composition: Copper-Nickel **Series:** Sydney 2000 Olympics **Obverse:** National arms, sports figures, and denomination **Reverse:** Stylized sailing scene

Date	Mintage	F	VF	XF	Unc	BU
2000	50,000	—	—	—	6.50	—

KM# 98 2 HRYVNI Composition: Copper-Nickel **Obverse:** National arms, flowers, and denomination **Reverse:** Bust of Walter O. Gonchar at right with life dates 1918-1995

Date	Mintage	F	VF	XF	Unc	BU
2000	20,000	—	—	—	6.50	—

KM# 99 2 HRYVNI Composition: Copper-Nickel **Obverse:** National arms and denomination **Reverse:** Potamon Tauricum crab

Date	Mintage	F	VF	XF	Unc	BU
2000	50,000	—	—	—	7.50	—

KM# 100 2 HRYVNI Composition: Copper-Nickel **Subject:** 125th Anniversary - Chernivtsy National University **Obverse:** National arms above denomination **Reverse:** University viewed through arch **Edge:** Reeded **Size:** 31 mm.

Date	Mintage	F	VF	XF	Unc	BU
2000	50,000	—	—	—	7.50	—

KM# 101 2 HRYVNI Composition: Copper-Nickel **Series:** Sydney 2000 Olympics **Obverse:** National arms, athletes, and denomination **Reverse:** Gymnast doing floor exercises

Date	Mintage	F	VF	XF	Unc	BU
2000	50,000	—	—	—	7.50	—

KM# 133 2 HRYVNI Weight: 12.8000 g. **Composition:** Copper-Nickel **Subject:** Kindness to Children **Obverse:** National arms above denomination **Reverse:** Two children frlocking under fountain of knowledge **Edge:** Reeded **Size:** 31 mm. **Note:** Struck at Malyn Mint.

Date	Mintage	F	VF	XF	Unc	BU
2001	100,000	—	—	—	7.50	—

KM# 134 2 HRYVNI Weight: 12.8000 g. **Composition:** Copper-Nickel **Subject:** 5th Anniversary of Constitution **Obverse:** National arms above denomination **Reverse:** Building above book **Edge:** Reeded **Size:** 31 mm. **Note:** Struck at Malyn Mint.

Date	Mintage	F	VF	XF	Unc	BU
2001	30,000	—	—	—	7.50	—

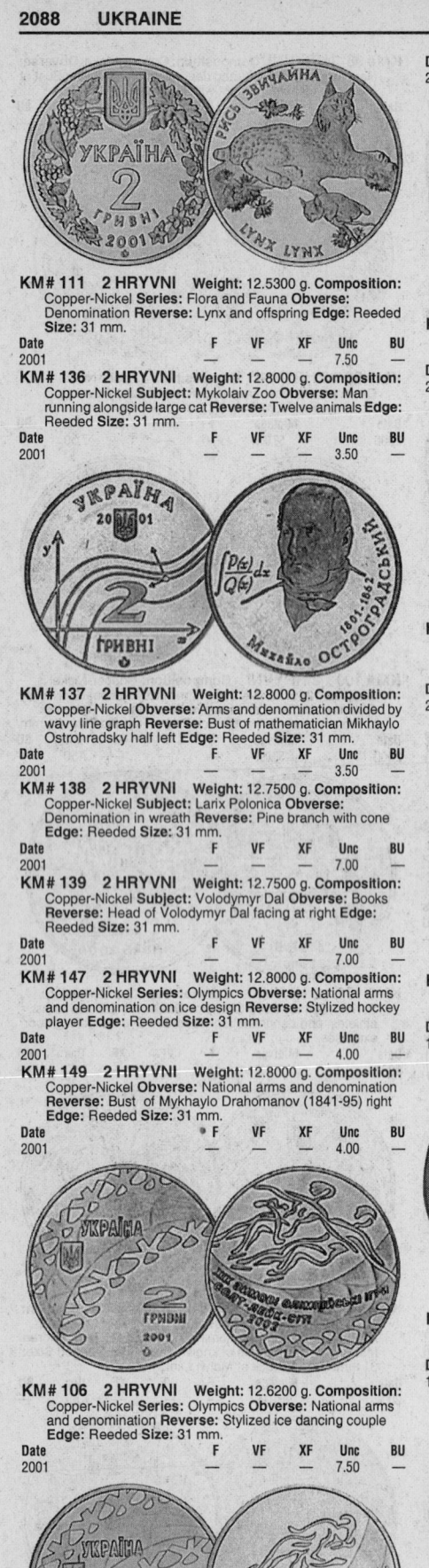

KM# 111 2 HRYVNI **Weight:** 12.5300 g. **Composition:** Copper-Nickel **Series:** Flora and Fauna **Obverse:** Denomination **Reverse:** Lynx and offspring **Edge:** Reeded **Size:** 31 mm.

Date	F	VF	XF	Unc	BU
2001	—	—	—	7.50	—

KM# 136 2 HRYVNI **Weight:** 12.8000 g. **Composition:** Copper-Nickel **Subject:** Mykolaiv Zoo **Obverse:** Man running alongside large cat **Reverse:** Twelve animals **Edge:** Reeded **Size:** 31 mm.

Date	F	VF	XF	Unc	BU
2001	—	—	—	3.50	—

KM# 137 2 HRYVNI **Weight:** 12.8000 g. **Composition:** Copper-Nickel **Obverse:** Arms and denomination divided by wavy line graph **Reverse:** Bust of mathematician Mikhaylo Ostrohradsky half left **Edge:** Reeded **Size:** 31 mm.

Date	F	VF	XF	Unc	BU
2001	—	—	—	3.50	—

KM# 138 2 HRYVNI **Weight:** 12.7500 g. **Composition:** Copper-Nickel **Subject:** Larix Polonica **Obverse:** Denomination in wreath **Reverse:** Pine branch with cone **Edge:** Reeded **Size:** 31 mm.

Date	F	VF	XF	Unc	BU
2001	—	—	—	7.00	—

KM# 139 2 HRYVNI **Weight:** 12.7500 g. **Composition:** Copper-Nickel **Subject:** Volodymyr Dal **Obverse:** Books **Reverse:** Head of Volodymyr Dal facing at right **Edge:** Reeded **Size:** 31 mm.

Date	F	VF	XF	Unc	BU
2001	—	—	—	7.00	—

KM# 147 2 HRYVNI **Weight:** 12.8000 g. **Composition:** Copper-Nickel **Series:** Olympics **Obverse:** National arms and denomination on ice design **Reverse:** Stylized hockey player **Edge:** Reeded **Size:** 31 mm.

Date	F	VF	XF	Unc	BU
2001	—	—	—	4.00	—

KM# 149 2 HRYVNI **Weight:** 12.8000 g. **Composition:** Copper-Nickel **Obverse:** National arms and denomination **Reverse:** Bust of Mykhaylo Drahomanov (1841-95) right **Edge:** Reeded **Size:** 31 mm.

Date	F	VF	XF	Unc	BU
2001	—	—	—	4.00	—

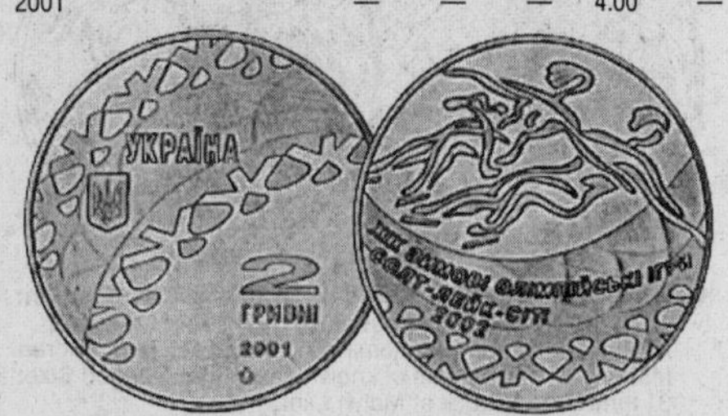

KM# 106 2 HRYVNI **Weight:** 12.6200 g. **Composition:** Copper-Nickel **Series:** Olympics **Obverse:** National arms and denomination **Reverse:** Stylized ice dancing couple **Edge:** Reeded **Size:** 31 mm.

Date	F	VF	XF	Unc	BU
2001	—	—	—	7.50	—

KM# 150 2 HRYVNI **Weight:** 12.8000 g. **Composition:** Copper-Nickel **Series:** Olympics **Obverse:** National arms and denomination on ice design **Reverse:** Speed skater **Edge:** Reeded **Size:** 31 mm.

Date	F	VF	XF	Unc	BU
2002	—	—	—	5.00	—

KM# 155 2 HRYVNI **Weight:** 12.2400 g. **Composition:** Copper-Nickel **Subject:** Owl **Obverse:** Denomination **Reverse:** Owl **Edge:** Reeded **Size:** 31 mm.

Date	F	VF	XF	Unc	BU
2002 Prooflike	—	—	—	—	—

KM# 156 2 HRYVNI **Weight:** 12.2400 g. **Composition:** Copper-Nickel **Subject:** Olympics **Obverse:** Two ancient figures above denomination **Reverse:** Swimmer **Edge:** Reeded **Size:** 31 mm.

Date	F	VF	XF	Unc	BU
2002 Prooflike	—	—	—	—	—

KM# 66 5 HRYVEN **Composition:** Copper-Nickel-Zinc **Subject:** St. Michaels Cathedral **Obverse:** Denomination **Reverse:** Cathedral behind human silhouettes

Date	Mintage	F	VF	XF	Unc	BU
1998	200,000	—	—	—	10.00	—

KM# 69 5 HRYVEN **Composition:** Copper-Nickel-Zinc **Subject:** Kiev-Pechersk Assumption Cathedral **Obverse:** Denomination **Reverse:** Cathedral behind carved ruins

Date	Mintage	F	VF	XF	Unc	BU
1998	200,000	—	—	—	10.00	—

KM# 74 5 HRYVEN **Composition:** Copper-Nickel **Subject:** 900th Anniversary - Novgorad City Charter's **Obverse:** Denomination **Reverse:** Armed horsemen

Date	Mintage	F	VF	XF	Unc	BU
1999	50,000	—	—	—	10.00	—

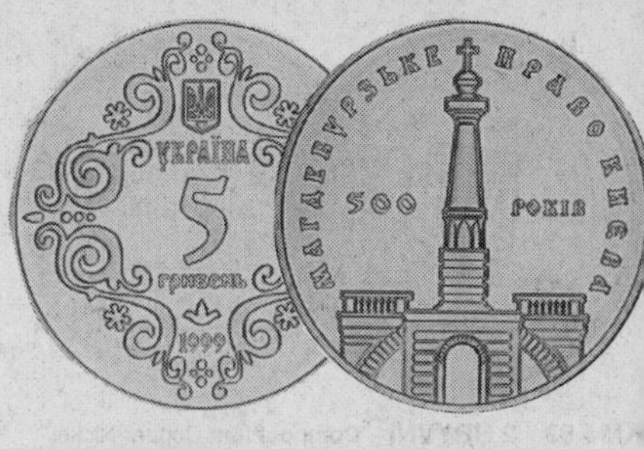

KM# 80 5 HRYVEN **Composition:** Copper-Nickel **Subject:** Kiev Monument to the "Magdeburg Law" of the 13th Century **Obverse:** National arms above denomination **Reverse:** Monument

Date	Mintage	F	VF	XF	Unc	B
1999	50,000	—	—	—	10.00	—

KM# 84 5 HRYVEN **Weight:** 16.3600 g. **Compositior** Copper-Nickel **Subject:** Birth of Jesus **Obverse:** Nationa arms, denomination, and angels **Reverse:** Nativity scene **Edge:** Reeded **Size:** 35.1 mm. **Note:** Struck at Lugansk.

Date	Mintage	F	VF	XF	Unc
1999	100,000	—	—	—	9.00

KM# 95 5 HRYVEN **Weight:** 17.0000 g. **Compositio** Copper-Nickel **Subject:** 2,500 Years - Bilgorod-Dnestrov **Obverse:** Arms above denomination **Reverse:** Castle abc city arms and ancient coins **Edge:** Reeded

Date	Mintage	F	VF	XF	Unc
2000	50,000	—	—	—	8.00

KM# 104 5 HRYVEN **Ring Weight:** 9.5000 g. **Ring Composition:** Copper-Nickel **Center Composition:** Br **Subject:** Third Millennium **Obverse:** National arms **Reverse:** Figure sowing seeds **Edge:** Reeded and plai sections **Size:** 27.9 mm.

Date	Mintage	F	VF	XF	Unc
2000	50,000	—	—	—	7.50

KM# 102 5 HRYVEN **Composition:** Copper-Nicke **Subject:** Russian Conversion to Christianity **Obverse:** National arms and angels **Reverse:** Bearded figure an crowd **Edge:** Reeded **Size:** 35 mm.

Date	Mintage	F	VF	XF	Unc
2000	100,000	—	—	—	9.00

 # 103 5 HRYVEN **Composition:** Copper-Nickel **Subject:** Centennial - Lviv's Opera House **Obverse:** National arms and angels **Reverse:** Opera house

Mintage	F	VF	XF	Unc	BU
50,000	—	—	—	8.50	—

 # 105 5 HRYVEN **Weight:** 16.4500 g. **Composition:** Copper-Nickel-Zinc **Subject:** 2600th Anniversary - City of Kerch's **Obverse:** National arms above bracelet and denomination **Reverse:** Ancient coins above pillar **Edge:** Reeded **Size:** 35 mm.

Mintage	F	VF	XF	Unc	BU
50,000	—	—	—	10.00	—

 # 107 5 HRYVEN **Ring Weight:** 9.4300 g. **Ring Composition:** Copper-Nickel **Center Composition:** Brass **Subject:** New Millennium **Obverse:** Spiral design **Reverse:** Mother and child **Edge:** Segmented reeding **Size:** 28 mm.

Mintage	F	VF	XF	Unc	BU
50,000	—	—	—	9.00	—

 # 112 5 HRYVEN **Weight:** 16.2400 g. **Composition:** Copper-Nickel **Subject:** Ostrozbka Academy **Obverse:** Denomination, old writing and printing artifacts **Reverse:** Teaching scene **Edge:** Reeded **Size:** 35 mm.

Mintage	F	VF	XF	Unc	BU
30,000	—	—	—	9.50	—

 # 140 5 HRYVEN **Ring Composition:** Copper-Nickel **Center Weight:** 9.4400 g. **Center Composition:** Brass **Subject:** 10th Anniversary of Army **Obverse:** Crossed maces **Reverse:** Military decoration in wreath **Edge:** Reeded and plain sections **Size:** 28 mm.

F	VF	XF	Unc	BU
—	—	—	10.00	—

KM# 148 5 HRYVEN **Weight:** 16.2400 g. **Composition:** Copper-Nickel **Obverse:** National arms above gateway **Reverse:** Krolivets city arms **Edge:** Reeded **Size:** 35 mm.

Date	Mintage	F	VF	XF	Unc	BU
2001	30,000	—	—	—	8.00	—

KM# 129 5 HRYVEN **Weight:** 16.2400 g. **Composition:** Copper-Nickel **Subject:** 10th Anniversary - National Bank **Obverse:** National arms between two arches **Reverse:** Large building central entrance **Edge:** Reeded **Size:** 35 mm. **Note:** Struck at Malyn Mint.

Date	Mintage	F	VF	XF	Unc	BU
2001	50,000	—	—	—	9.50	—

KM# 132 5 HRYVEN **Weight:** 16.2400 g. **Composition:** Copper-Nickel **Subject:** 10th Anniversary - National Independence **Obverse:** National arms **Reverse:** Building on map **Edge:** Reeded **Size:** 35 mm. **Note:** Struck at Malyn Mint.

Date	Mintage	F	VF	XF	Unc	BU
2001	100,000	—	—	—	10.00	—

KM# 135 5 HRYVEN **Weight:** 16.5400 g. **Composition:** Copper-Nickel **Subject:** 1100th Anniversary - Poltava **Obverse:** National arms above denomination **Reverse:** Buildings above arms **Edge:** Reeded **Size:** 35 mm. **Note:** Struck at Malyn Mint.

Date	Mintage	F	VF	XF	Unc	BU
2001	50,000	—	—	—	9.00	—

KM# 151 5 HRYVEN **Weight:** 16.2400 g. **Composition:** Copper-Nickel-Zinc **Subject:** City of Khotin **Obverse:** Denomination **Reverse:** Castle **Edge:** Reeded **Size:** 35 mm.

Date	Mintage	F	VF	XF	Unc	BU
2002	30,000	—	—	—	9.50	—

KM# 152 5 HRYVEN **Weight:** 16.2400 g. **Composition:** Copper-Nickel-Zinc **Obverse:** Sun and flying geese **Reverse:** "AN-225 Mrija" cargo jet **Edge:** Reeded **Size:** 35 mm.

Date	Mintage	F	VF	XF	Unc	BU
2002	30,000	—	—	—	9.50	—

KM# 163 5 HRYVEN **Weight:** 16.3200 g. **Composition:** Copper-Nickel **Subject:** Christmas **Obverse:** National arms in star above denomination **Reverse:** Christmas pageant scene **Edge:** Reeded **Size:** 35 mm.

Date	F	VF	XF	Unc	BU
ND(2002)	—	—	—	8.00	—

KM# 157 5 HRYVEN **Weight:** 16.3400 g. **Composition:** Copper-Nickel **Subject:** City of Romny 1100th Anniversary **Obverse:** National arms above denomination **Reverse:** City view **Edge:** Reeded **Size:** 35 mm.

Date	F	VF	XF	Unc	BU
2002	—	—	—	—	6.00

KM# 34 10 HRYVEN **Weight:** 16.8110 g. **Composition:** 0.9250 Silver .5 oz. ASW **Obverse:** National arms, people and building **Reverse:** Bust of Petro Mohyla - 1596-1647 - at left holding scepter

Date	Mintage	F	VF	XF	Unc	BU
1996 Proof	5,000	Value: 45.00				

KM# 44 10 HRYVEN **Weight:** 33.6220 g. **Composition:** 0.9250 Silver 1 oz. ASW **Series:** Nagano Olympics **Obverse:** National arms **Reverse:** Cross-country skier

Date	Mintage	F	VF	XF	Unc	BU
1998 Proof	7,500	Value: 35.00				

KM# 45 10 HRYVEN **Weight:** 33.6220 g. **Composition:** 0.9250 Silver 1 oz. ASW **Series:** Nagano Olympics **Obverse:** National arms **Reverse:** Biathlon shooter

Date	Mintage	F	VF	XF	Unc	BU
1998 Proof	7,500	Value: 35.00				

KM# 50 10 HRYVEN **Weight:** 33.6220 g. **Composition:** 0.9250 Silver 1 oz. ASW **Subject:** 100th Anniversary - Ascania National Park **Obverse:** Plants and animals around national arms, denomination below **Reverse:** Assortment of flora and fauna

Date	Mintage	F	VF	XF	Unc	BU
1998 Proof	10,000	Value: 42.50				

KM# 52 10 HRYVEN **Weight:** 33.6220 g. **Composition:** 0.9250 Silver 1 oz. ASW **Series:** Nagano Olympics **Obverse:** National emblem and denomination **Reverse:** Figure skater

Date	Mintage	F	VF	XF	Unc	BU
1998 Proof	7,500	Value: 40.00				

KM# 53 10 HRYVEN **Weight:** 33.6220 g. **Composition:** 0.9250 Silver 1 oz. ASW **Subject:** Prince Kiy - founder of Kiev **Obverse:** Denomination in ornamental frame **Reverse:** Portrait, riders

Date	Mintage	F	VF	XF	Unc	BU
1998 Proof	10,000	Value: 42.50				

KM# 64 10 HRYVEN **Weight:** 33.6220 g. **Composition:** 0.9250 Silver 1 oz. ASW **Obverse:** Denomination **Reverse:** Half bust of crowned Prince Danylo of Halych, castle behind at left, army behind at right

Date	Mintage	F	VF	XF	Unc	BU
1998 Proof	10,000	Value: 42.50				

KM# 67 10 HRYVEN **Weight:** 33.6220 g. **Composition:** 0.9250 Silver 1 oz. ASW **Obverse:** National arms in ornamental frame **Reverse:** St. Michael's golden-domed cathedral

Date	Mintage	F	VF	XF	Unc	BU
1998 Proof	10,000	Value: 42.50				

KM# 70 10 HRYVEN **Weight:** 33.6220 g. **Composition:** 0.9250 Silver 1 oz. ASW **Reverse:** Kiev-Pechersk Assumption Cathedral behind carved ruins

Date	Mintage	F	VF	XF	Unc	BU
1998 Proof	10,000	Value: 40.00				

KM# 77 10 HRYVEN **Weight:** 33.6220 g. **Composition:** 0.9250 Silver 1 oz. ASW **Obverse:** National arms **Reverse:** 3/4-length figure of Dmitro Vishnevetsky facing with bow and arrow

Date	Mintage	F	VF	XF	Unc	BU
1999 Proof	10,000	Value: 42.50				

KM# 85 10 HRYVEN **Weight:** 33.9000 g. **Composition:** 0.9250 Silver 1.0082 oz. ASW **Subject:** Birth of Jesus **Obverse:** National arms, denomination, and angels **Reverse:** Nativity scene **Edge:** Reeded **Size:** 38.6 mm. **Note:** Struck at Lugansk.

Date	Mintage	F	VF	XF	Unc	BU
1999 Proof	10,000	Value: 40.00				

KM# 86 10 HRYVEN **Weight:** 33.9000 g. **Composition:** 0.9250 Silver 1.0082 oz. ASW **Obverse:** National arms, denomination, and Viking carvings **Reverse:** Prince Askolc and Viking ships

Date	Mintage	F	VF	XF	Unc	B
1999 Proof	10,000	Value: 42.50				

KM# 87 10 HRYVEN **Weight:** 33.9000 g. **Compositio** 0.9250 Silver 1.0082 oz. ASW **Subject:** Magdeburg Righ

Date	Mintage	F	VF	XF	Unc
1999 Proof	5,000	Value: 42.50			

KM# 88 10 HRYVEN **Weight:** 33.9000 g. **Compositic** 0.9250 Silver 1.0082 oz. ASW **Reverse:** Petro Doroshen Cossack, mounted

Date		F	VF	XF	Unc
1999 Proof	—	Value: 40.00			

#89 10 HRYVEN Weight: 33.9000 g. **Composition:** .9250 Silver 1.0082 oz. ASW **Reverse:** Dormouse

Date	Mintage	F	VF	XF	Unc	BU
Proof	5,000	Value: 40.00				

#90 10 HRYVEN Weight: 33.9000 g. **Composition:** .9250 Silver 1.0082 oz. ASW **Reverse:** Steppe Eagle in flight

Date	Mintage	F	VF	XF	Unc	BU
Proof	—	Value: 42.50				

 # 116 10 HRYVEN Weight: 33.6200 g. **Composition:** 0.9250 Silver .9998 oz. ASW **Series:** Olympics **Obverse:** National arms, denomination and Olympic motto **Reverse:** Broad jumper

Date	Mintage	F	VF	XF	Unc	BU
Proof	15,000	Value: 40.00				

 # 117 10 HRYVEN Weight: 33.6200 g. **Composition:** 0.9250 Silver .9998 oz. ASW **Series:** Olympics **Obverse:** National arms, denomination and Olympic motto **Reverse:** Gymnast on parallel bars

Date	Mintage	F	VF	XF	Unc	BU
Proof	15,000	Value: 40.00				

KM# 118 10 HRYVEN Weight: 33.6200 g. **Composition:** 0.9250 Silver .9998 oz. ASW **Subject:** Platanthera Bifolia **Obverse:** National arms, denomination and wreath **Reverse:** Flower

Date	Mintage	F	VF	XF	Unc	BU
1999 Proof	5,000	Value: 40.00				

KM# 119 10 HRYVEN Weight: 33.6200 g. **Composition:** 0.9250 Silver .9998 oz. ASW **Obverse:** National arms, denomination in ornamental frame **Reverse:** Princess Olga and court scene

Date	Mintage	F	VF	XF	Unc	BU
2000 Proof	10,000	Value: 40.00				

KM# 120 10 HRYVEN Weight: 33.6200 g. **Composition:** 0.9250 Silver .9998 oz. ASW **Obverse:** National arms **Reverse:** Ship at left and Petro Sahaydachny cameo at upper right

Date	Mintage	F	VF	XF	Unc	BU
2000 Proof	10,000	Value: 40.00				

KM# 121 10 HRYVEN Weight: 33.6200 g. **Composition:** 0.9250 Silver .9998 oz. ASW **Obverse:** National arms and denomination in wreath **Reverse:** Freshwater crab

Date	Mintage	F	VF	XF	Unc	BU
2000 Proof	5,000	Value: 42.50				

KM# 122 10 HRYVEN Weight: 33.6200 g. **Composition:** 0.9250 Silver .9998 oz. ASW **Obverse:** National arms and denomination in ornamental frame **Reverse:** Crowned Volodymyr the Great with raised hands

Date	Mintage	F	VF	XF	Unc	BU
2000 Proof	5,000	Value: 40.00				

KM# 123 10 HRYVEN Weight: 33.6200 g. **Composition:** 0.9250 Silver .9998 oz. ASW **Obverse:** Two figures on an arch **Reverse:** Lviv Theater and Opera House

Date	Mintage	F	VF	XF	Unc	BU
2000 Proof	3,000	Value: 42.50				

KM# 108 10 HRYVEN Weight: 33.6200 g. **Composition:** 0.9250 Silver .9998 oz. ASW **Subject:** 55th Anniversary - End of WWII **Obverse:** National arms and denomination **Reverse:** Figure holding palm branch **Edge:** Reeded **Size:** 38.6 mm.

Date	Mintage	F	VF	XF	Unc	BU
2000 Proof	3,000	Value: 45.00				

KM# 109 10 HRYVEN **Weight:** 33.6200 g. **Composition:** 0.9250 Silver .9998 oz. ASW **Subject:** Conversion of the Russ to Christianity **Obverse:** National arms, denomination and two angels **Reverse:** Mass baptism scene

Date	Mintage	F	VF	XF	Unc	BU
2000 Proof	3,000	Value: 45.00				

KM# 142 10 HRYVEN **Weight:** 31.1000 g. **Composition:** 0.9250 Silver 0.9249 oz. ASW **Subject:** Khan Palace in Bakhchisarai **Obverse:** Denomination in arch **Reverse:** Courtyard view **Edge:** Reeded **Size:** 38.6 mm.

Date		F	VF	XF	Unc	BU
2001 Proof	3,000	Value: 45.00				

KM# 143 10 HRYVEN **Weight:** 3.8800 g. **Composition:** 0.9000 Gold 0.1123 oz. AGW **Subject:** 10 Years Independence **Obverse:** National arms **Reverse:** Parliament building on map **Edge:** Reeded **Size:** 16 mm.

Date		F	VF	XF	Unc	BU
2001 Proof	3,000	Value: 175				

KM# 141 10 HRYVEN **Weight:** 31.1000 g. **Composition:** 0.9250 Silver 0.9249 oz. ASW **Subject:** Flora and Fauna **Obverse:** National arms and denomination **Reverse:** Pine branch with cone **Edge:** Reeded **Size:** 38.5 mm.

Date	Mintage	F	VF	XF	Unc	BU
2001 Proof	3,000	Value: 40.00				

KM# 113 10 HRYVEN **Weight:** 33.6200 g. **Composition:** 0.9250 Silver .9998 oz. ASW **Obverse:** National arms **Reverse:** Half figure of Ivan Mazepa (1644-1709), palace at lef **Edge:** Reeded **Size:** 38.5 mm.

Date		F	VF	XF	Unc	BU
2001 Proof	—	Value: 45.00				

KM# 114 10 HRYVEN **Weight:** 33.6200 g. **Composition:** 0.9250 Silver .9998 oz. ASW **Reverse:** Mosaic portrait at left and Aroslav Mudriy (1015-1054) with scroll at right

Date		F	VF	XF	Unc	BU
2001 Proof	—	Value: 45.00				

KM# 115 10 HRYVEN **Weight:** 33.6200 g. **Composition:** 0.9250 Silver .998 oz. ASW **Series:** Ukranian Flora and Fauna **Obverse:** Denomination **Reverse:** Lynx with offspring

Date		F	VF	XF	Unc	BU
2001 Proof	—	Value: 47.50				

KM# 130 10 HRYVEN **Weight:** 33.6200 g. **Composition:** 0.9250 Silver .9998 oz. ASW **Subject:** 10th Anniversary - National Bank **Obverse:** National arms between arches **Reverse:** Large building entrance **Edge:** Reeded **Size:** 38.6 mm. **Note:** Struck at Malyn Mint.

Date	Mintage	F	VF	XF	Unc	BU
2001 Proof	3,000	Value: 42.50				

KM# 131 10 HRYVEN **Weight:** 33.6200 g. **Composition:** 0.9250 Silver .9998 oz. ASW **Series:** Olympics **Obverse:** National arms and denomination on ice **Reverse:** Stylized ice dancing couple **Edge:** Reeded **Size:** 38.6 mm. **Note:** Struck at Malyn Mint.

Date	Mintage	F	VF	XF	Unc	B
2001 Proof	3,000	Value: 45.00				

KM# 160 10 HRYVEN **Weight:** 33.9500 g. **Composition:** 0.9250 Silver 1.0097 oz. ASW **Obverse:** Denomination encircled by angels **Reverse:** Church and tower **Edge:** Reeded **Size:** 38.6 mm.

Date		F	VF	XF	Unc
2002 Proof	—	Value: 45.00			

KM# 161 10 HRYVEN **Weight:** 33.9500 g. **Composition:** 0.9250 Silver 1.0097 oz. ASW **Subject:** Holyman **Obverse:** Denomination within jewelry design **Reverse:** Man holding book with buildings and St. Geor in background **Edge:** Reeded **Size:** 38.6 mm.

Date		F	VF	XF	Unc
2002 Proof	—	Value: 45.00			

#162 10 HRYVEN **Weight:** 33.9500 g. **Composition:** 0.9250 Silver 1.0097 oz. ASW **Subject:** Cossack Warrior **Obverse:** Denomination in ornate design **Reverse:** Cossack with sword and shield **Edge:** Reeded **Size:** 38.6 mm.

		F	VF	XF	Unc	BU
2 Proof	—	Value: 45.00				

 # 164 10 HRYVEN **Weight:** 34.0000 g. **Composition:** 0.9250 Silver 1.0111 oz. ASW **Subject:** Christmas **Obverse:** National arms in star above denomination **Reverse:** Christmas pageant scene **Edge:** Reeded **Size:** 38.6 mm.

		F	VF	XF	Unc	BU
2002) Proof	—	Value: 40.00				

 # 145 10 HRYVEN **Weight:** 31.1000 g. **Composition:** 0.9250 Silver 0.9249 oz. ASW **Subject:** Ivan Sirko **Obverse:** National arms **Reverse:** Cossack battle scene **Edge:** Reeded **Size:** 38.5 mm.

		F	VF	XF	Unc	BU
2 Proof	—	Value: 40.00				

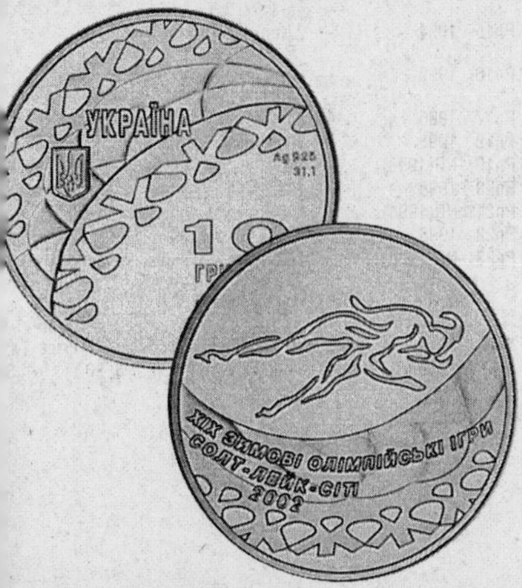

 # 146 10 HRYVEN **Weight:** 31.0000 g. **Composition:** 0.9250 Silver 0.9219 oz. ASW **Obverse:** National arms and denomination on ice **Reverse:** Speed skater **Edge:** Reeded **Size:** 38.5 mm.

		F	VF	XF	Unc	BU
2 Proof	—	Value: 40.00				

KM# 35 20 HRYVEN **Weight:** 33.6220 g. **Composition:** 0.9250 Silver 1 oz. ASW **Obverse:** National arms above Madonna and child **Reverse:** Desyatinna Church

Date	Mintage	F	VF	XF	Unc	BU
1996 Proof	5,000	Value: 45.00				

KM# 36 20 HRYVEN **Weight:** 33.6220 g. **Composition:** 0.9250 Silver 1 oz. ASW **Obverse:** National arms above Madonna and child **Reverse:** St. Spassky Cathedral in Chernigiv

Date	Mintage	F	VF	XF	Unc	BU
1997 Proof	5,000	Value: 45.00				

KM# 46 20 HRYVEN **Weight:** 33.6220 g. **Composition:** 0.9250 Silver 1 oz. ASW **Subject:** Cossacks in Revolt **Obverse:** National arms **Reverse:** Severyn Nalyvayko on horseback leads charge

Date	Mintage	F	VF	XF	Unc	BU
1997 Proof	5,000	Value: 47.50				

KM# 54 20 HRYVEN **Weight:** 33.6220 g. **Composition:** 0.9250 Silver 1 oz. ASW **Subject:** Cossacks Mamay **Obverse:** National arms supported by St. Michael and lion **Reverse:** Cossack playing a bandre

Date	Mintage	F	VF	XF	Unc	BU
1997 Proof	5,000	Value: 55.00				

KM# 57 20 HRYVEN **Weight:** 33.6220 g. **Composition:** 0.9250 Silver 1 oz. ASW **Subject:** 200th Anniversary - Kiev Commodity Futures Market **Obverse:** National arms **Reverse:** Steepled building and sailboat

Date	Mintage	F	VF	XF	Unc	BU
1997 Proof	5,000	Value: 45.00				

KM# 58 20 HRYVEN **Weight:** 33.6220 g. **Composition:** 0.9250 Silver 1 oz. ASW **Subject:** 350th Anniversary - Cossack Revolt **Obverse:** National arms supported by St. Michael and lion **Reverse:** Cossacks attacking Polish cavalrymen

Date	Mintage	F	VF	XF	Unc	BU
1998 Proof	5,000	Value: 50.00				

KM# 126 20 HRYVEN **Ring Weight:** 14.7000 g. **Ring Composition:** 0.9250 Silver .2508 oz. ASW **Center Composition:** 0.9160 Gold .1845 oz. AGW **Subject:** Palcolithic Age **Obverse:** Eagle on wheel **Reverse:** Pottery and petroglyphs **Edge:** Reeded and plain sections **Size:** 31 mm.

Date	Mintage	F	VF	XF	Unc	BU
2000 Proof	3,000	Value: 50.00				

KM# 127 20 HRYVEN **Ring Weight:** 14.7000 g. **Ring Composition:** 0.9250 Silver .2508 oz. ASW **Center Composition:** 0.9160 Gold .1845 oz. AGW **Subject:** Trypolean Culture **Obverse:** Eagle on wheel **Reverse:** Ancient sculptures

Date	Mintage	F	VF	XF	Unc	BU
2000 Proof	3,000	Value: 50.00				

KM# 128 20 HRYVEN **Ring Weight:** 14.7000 g. **Ring Composition:** 0.9250 Silver .2508 oz. ASW **Center Composition:** 0.9160 Gold .1845 oz. AGW **Subject:** The

Olbian City State **Obverse:** Eagle on wheel **Reverse:** Ancient coin and Greek figures

Date	Mintage	F	VF	XF	Unc	BU
2000 Proof	3,000	Value: 50.00				

KM# 144 20 HRYVEN Weight: 62.2000 g. **Composition:** 0.9250 Silver 1.8498 oz. ASW **Subject:** 10 Years Independence **Obverse:** National arms **Reverse:** Parliament building on map **Edge:** Segmented reeding **Size:** 50 mm.

Date	Mintage	F	VF	XF	Unc	BU
2001 Proof	1,000	Value: 75.00				

KM# 153 20 HRYVEN Weight: 62.2070 g. **Composition:** 0.9250 Silver 1.85 oz. ASW **Obverse:** Sun and flying geese **Reverse:** "AN-225 Mrija" cargo jet **Edge:** Reeded **Size:** 50 mm.

Date	Mintage	F	VF	XF	Unc	BU
2002 Proof	2,002	Value: 175				

KM# 59 50 HRYVEN Weight: 3.1104 g. **Composition:** 0.9999 Gold .1 oz. AGW **Subject:** St. Sophia Cathedral in Kiev **Obverse:** Cathedral **Reverse:** Mother of God Mossaic (orante)

Date	Mintage	F	VF	XF	Unc	BU
1996	2,000	—	—	—	175	—

KM# 124 50 HRYVEN Weight: 17.6300 g. **Composition:** 0.9000 Gold .5101 oz. AGW **Subject:** Birth of Jesus **Obverse:** Two angels, arms and denomination **Reverse:** Nativity scene **Edge:** Plain **Size:** 25 mm.

Date	Mintage	F	VF	XF	Unc	BU
1999 Proof	3,000	Value: 450				

KM# 125 50 HRYVEN Weight: 17.6300 g. **Composition:** 0.9000 Gold .5101 oz. AGW **Subject:** Conversion of the Russ to Christianity **Obverse:** Two angels, arms and denomination **Reverse:** Baptism scene

Date	Mintage	F	VF	XF	Unc	BU
2000 Proof	3,000	Value: 450				

KM# 63 100 HRYVEN Weight: 17.2797 g. **Composition:** 0.9000 Gold .5 oz. AGW **Subject:** Kyiv Psalm book **Obverse:** Open book **Reverse:** Monk writing book

Date	Mintage	F	VF	XF	Unc	BU
1997 Proof	2,000	Value: 650				

KM# 65 100 HRYVEN Weight: 17.2797 g. **Composition:** 0.9000 Gold .5 oz. AGW **Subject:** Poem "Aeneld" by Ivan P. Kotlyarevsky **Obverse:** Helmet and musical instruments **Reverse:** Helmeted figure playing stringed instrument

Date	Mintage	F	VF	XF	Unc	BU
1998 Proof	2,000	Value: 550				

KM# 68 100 HRYVEN Weight: 17.2797 g. **Composition:** 0.9000 Gold .5 oz. AGW **Subject:** St. Michael's Cathedral **Obverse:** Denomination **Reverse:** Cathedral behind human silhouettes

Date	Mintage	F	VF	XF	Unc	BU
1998 Proof	3,000	Value: 500				

KM# 71 100 HRYVEN Weight: 17.2797 g. **Composition:** 0.9000 Gold .5 oz. AGW **Subject:** Kyiv-Pechersk Assumption Cathedral **Obverse:** Denomination **Reverse:** Cathedral behind carved ruins

Date	Mintage	F	VF	XF	Unc	BU
1998 Proof	3,000	Value: 500				

KM# 60 125 HRYVEN Weight: 7.7759 g. **Composition:** 0.9999 Gold .25 oz. AGW **Obverse:** St. Sophia Cathedral in Kiev **Reverse:** St. Sophia

Date	Mintage	F	VF	XF	Unc	BU
1996	4,000	—	—	—	350	—

KM# 37 200 HRYVEN Weight: 17.5000 g. **Composition:** 0.9000 Gold .5 oz. AGW **Obverse:** National arms above denomination **Reverse:** Bust of Taras G. Shevchenko

Date	Mintage	F	VF	XF	Unc	BU
1996 Proof	20,000	Value: 400				

KM# 38 200 HRYVEN Weight: 17.5000 g. **Composition:** 0.9000 Gold .5 oz. AGW **Subject:** Pecherska Lavra **Obverse:** Church above date, denomination

Date	Mintage	F	VF	XF	Unc	BU
1996 Proof	20,000	Value: 400				

KM# 61 250 HRYVEN Weight: 15.5518 g. **Composition:** 0.9999 Gold .5 oz. AGW **Obverse:** St. Sophia Cathedral in Kiev **Reverse:** St. Sophia

Date	Mintage	F	VF	XF	Unc	BL
1996	3,000	—	—	—	700	—

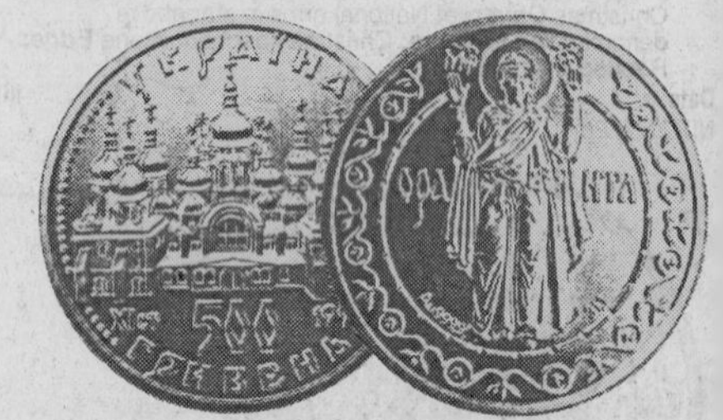

KM# 62 500 HRYVEN Weight: 31.1035 g. **Composition** 0.9999 Gold 1 oz. AGW **Obverse:** St. Sophia Cathedral ir Kiev **Reverse:** St. Sophia

Date	Mintage	F	VF	XF	Unc	B
1996	1,000	—	—	—	1,400	-

PATTERNS

Including off metal strikes

KM#	Date	Mintage	Identification	Mkt V
Pn1	1992	—	Kopiyka. Aluminum.	
Pn2	1922	—	2 Kopiyky. Aluminum.	
Pn3	1992	—	5 Kopiyok. White Brass.	
Pn4	1992	—	10 Kopiyok. Brass. Incuse shield.	20.
Pn5	1992	—	15 Kopiyok. Brass.	35.
Pn6	1992	—	15 Kopiyok. Bronze.	35.
Pn7	1992	—	25 Kopiyok. Brass. Incuse shield.	20.
Pn8	1992	—	50 Kopiyok. Copper-Nickel.	
Pn9	1992	—	50 Kopiyok. Brass. Incuse shield.	20
Pn10	1992	—	50 Kopiyok. Brass Clad Steel.	
Pn11	1993	—	2 Kopiyky. Brass.	
Pn12	1993	—	2 Kopiyky. Aluminum-Zinc.	
Pn13	1993	—	15 Kopiyok. Aluminum.	35.
Pn14	1994	—	Kopiyka. 0.6000 Silver. Specific gravity: 9.8.	
Pn15	1994	—	2 Kopiyky. Bronze. 3.7500 g. Piefort.	
Pn16	1996	—	Kopiyka. 0.3500 Silver. Specific gravity: 9.43.	
Pn17	1996	—	25 Kopiyok. Aluminum.	
Pn18	1998	—	100 Hryvnias. Brass.	
Pn19	ND(1998)	—	100 Hryvnias. Brass.	
Pn20	1998	—	100 Hryvnias. Brass.	
Pn21	ND(1998)	—	100 Hryvnias. Brass.	
Pn22	1998	—	100 Hryvnias. Brass.	
Pn23	ND(1998)	—	100 Hryvnias. Brass.	

MINT SETS

KM#	Date	Mintage	Identification	Issue Price	N V
MS1	1996 (8)	—	KM1, 2, 3.3, 4, 6, 7, 8, 30	—	3

UMM AL QAIWAIN - U.A.E.

This emirate, one of the original members of the United Arab Emirates, is the second smallest, least developed and lowest in population. The area is 300 sq. mi. (800 sq. km.) and the population is 5,000. The first recognition by the West was in 1820. Most of the emirate is uninhabited desert. Native boat building is an important activity.

TITLES

ام القيوين

Umm al Qaiwain

RULERS

Ahmad Bin Abdullah al-Mualla, 1872-1904
Rashid Bin Ahmad al-Mualla, 1904-1929
Ahmad Bin Rashid al-Mualla, 1929-1981
Rashid Bin Ahmad al-Mualla, 1981-

EMIRATE

NON-CIRCULATING LEGAL TENDER COINAGE

KM# 1 RIYAL Weight: 3.0000 g. **Composition:** 1.0000 Silver .0965 oz. ASW **Ruler:** Ahmad bin Rashid al-Mualla **Reverse:** Old cannon

Date	Mintage	F	VF	XF	Unc	BU
AH1389 (1969) Proof	2,050	Value: 17.50				

KM# 2 2 RIYALS Weight: 6.0000 g. **Composition:** 1.0000 Silver .1929 oz. ASW **Ruler:** Ahmad bin Rashid al-Mualla **Reverse:** Fort of the 19th Century

Date	Mintage	F	VF	XF	Unc	BU
AH1389 (1969) Proof	2,050	Value: 27.50				

KM# 3 5 RIYALS Weight: 15.0000 g. **Composition:** 1.0000 Silver .4823 oz. ASW **Ruler:** Ahmad bin Rashid al-Mualla **Reverse:** Gazelles

Date	Mintage	F	VF	XF	Unc	BU
AH1389 (1969) Proof	2,100	Value: 37.50				

KM# 4 10 RIYALS Weight: 30.0000 g. **Composition:** 1.0000 Silver .9646 oz. ASW **Ruler:** Ahmad bin Rashid al-Mualla **Obverse:** Similar to 5 Riyals, KM#3 **Reverse:** Facade of the Great Rock Temple

Date	Mintage	F	VF	XF	Unc	BU
AH1389 (1969) Proof	2,000	Value: 70.00				

KM# 6 25 RIYALS Weight: 5.1800 g. **Composition:** 0.9000 Gold .1499 oz. AGW **Ruler:** Ahmad bin Rashid al-Mualla **Reverse:** Old cannon

Date	Mintage	F	VF	XF	Unc	BU
AH1389 (1969) Proof	500	Value: 150				

KM# 7 50 RIYALS Weight: 10.3600 g. **Composition:** 0.9000 Gold .2998 oz. AGW **Ruler:** Ahmad bin Rashid al-Mualla **Reverse:** Fort of the 19th Century

Date	Mintage	F	VF	XF	Unc	BU
AH1389 (1969) Proof	420	Value: 265				

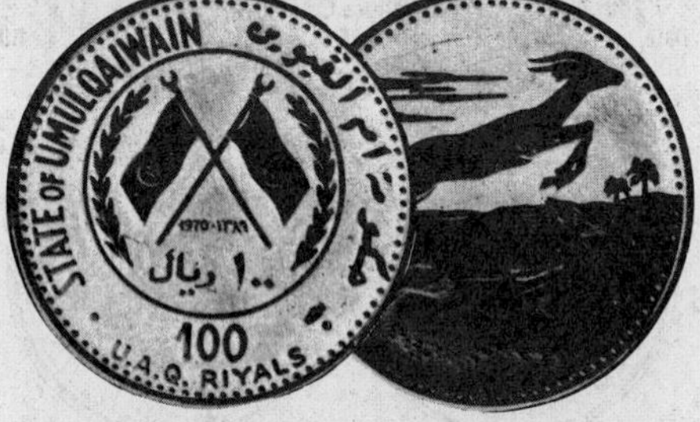

KM# 8 100 RIYALS Weight: 20.7300 g. **Composition:** 0.9000 Gold .5999 oz. AGW **Ruler:** Ahmad bin Rashid al-Mualla **Reverse:** Gazelles

Date	Mintage	F	VF	XF	Unc	BU
AH1389 (1969) Proof	300	Value: 450				

KM# 9 200 RIYALS Weight: 41.4600 g. **Composition:** 0.9000 Gold 1.1998 oz. AGW **Ruler:** Ahmad bin Rashid al-Mualla **Obverse:** Similar to 25 Riyals, KM#6 **Reverse:** Sheik Ahmed Ben Rashid al Moalla Bust Left

Date	Mintage	F	VF	XF	Unc	BU
AH1389 (1969) Proof	230	Value: 775				

PROOF SETS

KM#	Date	Mintage	Identification	Issue Price	Mkt Val
PS1	1970 (4)	2,000	KM#1-4	26.30	150
PS2	1970 (4)	230	KM#6-9	—	1,650
PS3	1970 (8)	—	KM#1-4, 6-9	—	1,800

UNITED ARAB EMIRATES

The seven United Arab Emirates (formerly known as the Trucial Sheikhdoms or States), located along the southern shore of the Persian Gulf, are comprised of the Sheikhdoms of Abu Dhabi, Dubai, al-Sharjah, Ajman, Umm al Qaiwain, Ras al-Khaimah and al-Fujairah. They have a combined area of about 32,000 sq. mi. (83,600 sq. km.) and a population of *2.1 million. Capital: Abu Zaby (Abu Dhabi). Since the oil strikes of 1958-60, the economy has centered about petroleum.

The Trucial States came under direct British influence in 1892 when the Maritime Truce Treaty enacted after the supression of pirate activity along the Trucial Coast was enlarged to enjoin the states from disposing of any territory, or entering into any foreign agreements, without British consent in return for British protection from external aggression. In March of 1971 Britain reaffirmed its decision to terminate its treaty relationships with the Trucial Sheikhdoms, whereupon the seven states joined with Bahrain and Qatar in an effort to form a union of Arab Emirates under British protection. When the prospective members failed to agree on terms of union, Bahrain and Qatar declared their respective independence, Aug. and Sept. of 1971. Six of the sheikhdoms united to form the United Arab Emirates on Dec. 2, 1971. Ras al-Khaimah joined a few weeks later.

TITLES

الامارات العربية المتحدة

al-Imara(t) al-Arabiya(t) al-Muttahida(t)

MONETARY SYSTEM

فلساً فلس فلوس

Falus, Fulus — Fals, Fils — Falsan

100 Fils = 1 Dirham

UNITED EMIRATES

STANDARD COINAGE

KM# 1 FIL Composition: Bronze **Series:** F.A.O. **Reverse:** Date Palms

Date	Mintage	F	VF	XF	Unc	BU
AH1393 (1973)	4,000,000	—	0.10	0.15	0.20	—
AH1395 (1975)	—	—	0.20	0.30	0.50	—
AH1409 (1989)	—	—	0.20	0.30	0.50	—
AH1418 (1997)	—	—	0.20	0.30	0.50	—

KM# 2.1 5 FILS Composition: Bronze **Series:** F.A.O. **Reverse:** Mata Hari Fish

Date	Mintage	F	VF	XF	Unc	BU
AH1393 (1973)	11,400,000	—	0.10	0.15	0.25	—
AH1402 (1982)	—	—	0.10	0.20	0.35	—
AH1407 (1987)	—	—	0.10	0.20	0.35	—
AH1408 (1988)	—	—	0.10	0.20	0.35	—
AH1409 (1989)	—	—	0.10	0.20	0.35	—

KM# 2.2 5 FILS Composition: Bronze **Series:** F.A.O. **Note:** Reduced size.

Date	F	VF	XF	Unc	BU
AH1416 (1996)	—	0.10	0.15	0.25	—

KM# 3.1 10 FILS **Composition:** Bronze **Reverse:** Arab Dhow

Date	Mintage	F	VF	XF	Unc	BU
AH1393 (1973)	6,400,000	—	0.25	0.40	0.90	—
AH1402 (1982)	—	—	0.25	0.45	1.00	—
AH1404 (1984)	—	—	0.25	0.45	1.00	—
AH1407 (1987)	—	—	0.25	0.45	1.00	—
AH1408 (1988)	—	—	0.25	0.45	1.00	—
AH1409 (1989)	—	—	0.25	0.45	1.00	—

KM# 3.2 10 FILS **Composition:** Bronze **Note:** Reduced size.

Date	F	VF	XF	Unc	BU
AH1416 (1996)	—	0.20	0.30	0.70	—

KM# 4 25 FILS **Composition:** Copper-Nickel **Reverse:** Arab Dune Gazelle

Date	Mintage	F	VF	XF	Unc	BU
AH1393 (1973)	10,400,000	—	0.15	0.35	0.65	0.85
AH1402 (1982)	—	—	0.20	0.40	0.75	0.95
AH1403 (1983)	—	—	0.20	0.40	0.75	0.95
AH1404 (1984)	—	—	0.20	0.40	0.75	0.95
AH1406 (1986)	—	—	0.20	0.40	0.75	0.95
AH1407 (1987)	—	—	0.20	0.40	0.75	0.95
AH1408 (1988)	—	—	0.20	0.40	0.75	0.95
AH1409 (1989)	—	—	0.20	0.40	0.75	0.95
AH1410 (1990)	—	—	0.20	0.40	0.75	0.95
AH1415 (1995)	—	—	0.20	0.40	0.75	0.95
AH1416 (1996)	—	—	0.20	0.40	0.75	0.95
AH1419-1998 (1998)	—	—	0.20	0.40	0.75	0.95

KM# 5 50 FILS **Composition:** Copper-Nickel **Reverse:** Oil Derricks

Date	Mintage	F	VF	XF	Unc	BU
AH1393 (1973)	8,400,000	—	0.35	0.50	1.50	—
AH1402 (1982)	—	—	0.35	0.55	1.65	—
AH1404 (1984)	—	—	0.35	0.55	1.65	—
AH1407 (1987)	—	—	0.35	0.55	1.65	—
AH1408 (1988)	—	—	0.35	0.55	1.65	—
AH1409 (1989)	—	—	0.35	0.55	1.65	—

KM# 16 50 FILS **Composition:** Copper-Nickel **Note:** Reduced size, 7-sided coin.

Date	F	VF	XF	Unc	BU
AH1415 (1995)	—	0.25	0.45	1.35	—
AH1419 (1998)	—	0.25	0.45	1.35	—

KM# 6.1 DIRHAM **Composition:** Copper-Nickel **Reverse:** Jug

Date	Mintage	F	VF	XF	Unc	BU
AH1393 (1973)	13,000,000	—	0.50	0.75	2.00	—
AH1402 (1982)	—	—	0.50	0.80	2.25	—
AH1404 (1984)	—	—	0.50	0.80	2.25	—
AH1406 (1986)	—	—	0.50	0.80	2.25	—
AH1407 (1987)	—	—	0.50	0.80	2.25	—
AH1408 (1988)	—	—	0.50	0.80	2.25	—
AH1409 (1989)	—	—	0.50	0.80	2.25	—

KM# 10 DIRHAM **Composition:** Copper-Nickel **Subject:** 27th Chess Olympiad in Dubai

Date	F	VF	XF	Unc	BU
1986	—	2.00	4.50	9.00	—

KM# 11 DIRHAM **Composition:** Copper-Nickel **Subject:** 25th Anniversary - Offshore Oil Drilling

Date	F	VF	XF	Unc	BU
ND(1987)	—	2.00	4.50	9.00	—

KM# 14 DIRHAM **Composition:** Copper-Nickel **Subject:** 10th Anniversary - al-Ain University

Date	F	VF	XF	Unc	BU
ND(1987)	—	1.75	4.00	8.00	—

KM# 15 DIRHAM **Composition:** Copper-Nickel **Subject:** Soccer

Date	F	VF	XF	Unc	BU
ND(1990)	—	1.50	3.00	6.50	—

KM# 6.2a DIRHAM **Composition:** Copper-Nickel **Note:** Reduced size.

Date	F	VF	XF	Unc	BU
AH1415 (1995)	—	0.35	0.65	1.85	—
AH1419 (1999)	—	0.35	0.65	1.85	—

KM# 32 DIRHAM **Composition:** Copper-Nickel **Subject:** Bank of Dubai 35th Anniversary **Obverse:** Denomination **Reverse:** Bank building

Date	F	VF	XF	Unc	BU
ND(1998)	—	—	—	3.50	—

KM# 35 DIRHAM **Composition:** Copper-Nickel **Subject:** College of Technology: 35 Years **Obverse:** Denomination **Reverse:** Bird viewed through window frame

Date	F	VF	XF	Unc	BU
ND(1998)	—	—	—	3.50	—

KM# 38 DIRHAM **Composition:** Copper-Nickel **Subject:** 15th Anniversary - Women's Association **Obverse:** Denomination **Reverse:** Logo

Date	F	VF	XF	Unc	B
ND(1998)	—	—	—	3.50	-

KM# 39 DIRHAM **Composition:** Copper-Nickel **Subjec** Sharjah Cultural City **Obverse:** Denomination **Reverse:** Stylized flame

Date	F	VF	XF	Unc
ND(1998)	—	—	—	3.50

KM# 39 DIRHAM **Composition:** Copper-Nickel **Subje** Sharjah Cultural City **Obverse:** Denomination **Reverse:** Stylized flame

Date	F	VF	XF	Unc
ND(1998)	—	—	—	3.50
ND	—	—	—	3.50

KM# 40 DIRHAM **Weight:** 6.3700 g. **Composition:** Copper-Nickel **Subject:** Abu Al Bukhoosh **Obverse:** Denomination **Reverse:** Ocean oil well **Edge:** Reeded **Size:** 24 mm.

Date	F	VF	XF	Unc
ND(1999)	—	—	—	3.50

KM# 41 DIRHAM **Weight:** 6.3700 g. **Composition:** Copper-Nickel **Subject:** Honor Sheik Zayed **Obverse:** Denomination **Reverse:** Square design

Date	F	VF	XF	Unc
AH1420(1999)	—	—	—	3.50

43 DIRHAM Weight: 6.3700 g. **Composition:** :opper-Nickel **Subject:** Dubai Islamic Bank **Obverse:** enomination **Reverse:** Bank name

	F	VF	XF	Unc	BU
99)	—	—	—	3.50	—

46 DIRHAM Weight: 6.3700 g. **Composition:** :opper-Nickel **Subject:** General Women's Union **Obverse:**)enomination **Reverse:** Stylized gazelle

	F	VF	XF	Unc	BU
)00)	—	—	—	3.50	—

49 DIRHAM Weight: 6.3700 g. **Composition:** :opper-Nickel **Subject:** 25th Anniversary **Obverse:**)enomination. **Reverse:** Heraldic eagle. **Edge:** Reeded. **Size:** 24 mm.

	F	VF	XF	Unc	BU
2001)	—	—	—	4.00	—

9 5 DIRHAMS Composition: Copper-Nickel **Subject:** 1500th Anniversary - al-Hegira

	F	VF	XF	Unc	BU
01 (1981)	—	2.00	4.00	9.00	—

33 25 DIRHAMS Weight: 20.0000 g. **Composition:** 0.9250 Silver .5948 oz. ASW **Subject:** Dubai National Bank: 35 Years **Obverse:** Denomination **Reverse:** Bank building

	F	VF	XF	Unc	BU
998)	—	—	—	35.00	—

44 25 DIRHAMS Weight: 20.1000 g. **Composition:** 0.9250 Silver .5978 oz. ASW **Subject:** Dubai Islamic Bank **Obverse:** Denomination **Reverse:** Bank name **Edge:** Reeded **Size:** 27.9 mm.

	Mintage	F	VF	XF	Unc	BU
000) Proof	1,000	Value: 35.00				

KM# 7 50 DIRHAMS Weight: 27.2200 g. **Composition:** 0.9250 Silver .8095 oz. ASW **Subject:** IYC and UNICEF

Date	Mintage	F	VF	XF	Unc	BU
AH1400 (1980) Proof	8,031	Value: 21.50				

KM# 17 50 DIRHAMS Weight: 40.0000 g. **Composition:** 0.9250 Silver 1.1896 oz. ASW **Subject:** Death of Shaikh Rashid Bin Saeed Al-Maktoum **Obverse:** Portrait **Reverse:** Dubai International Trade Center

Date	F	VF	XF	Unc	BU
AH1410 (1990) Proof	—	Value: 70.00			

KM# 18 50 DIRHAMS Weight: 40.0000 g. **Composition:** 0.9250 Silver 1.1896 oz. ASW **Subject:** 10th Anniversary - UAE Central Bank

Date	F	VF	XF	Unc	BU
AH1410 (1990) Proof	—	Value: 70.00			

KM# 19 50 DIRHAMS Weight: 40.0000 g. **Composition:** 0.9250 Silver 1.1896 oz. ASW **Subject:** 50th Anniversary of the Arab League

Date	F	VF	XF	Unc	BU
AH1415 (1995) Proof	—	Value: 70.00			

KM# 21 50 DIRHAMS Weight: 40.0000 g. **Composition:** 0.9250 Silver 1.1896 oz. ASW **Subject:** 25th Anniversary of the UAE - National Day Issue **Obverse:** Portrait **Reverse:** Heraldic eagle

Date	F	VF	XF	Unc	BU
AH1416 (1996) Proof	—	Value: 65.00			

KM# 22 50 DIRHAMS Weight: 40.0000 g. **Composition:** 0.9250 Silver 1.1896 oz. ASW **Subject:** 30th Anniversary - Reign of Shaikh Zayed **Obverse:** Portrait **Reverse:** Circular design of Arabic lettering

Date	F	VF	XF	Unc	BU
AH1416 (1996) Proof	—	Value: 65.00			

KM# 34 50 DIRHAMS **Weight:** 40.0000 g. **Composition:** 0.9250 Silver 1.1896 oz. ASW **Subject:** Dubai National Bank: 35 Years **Obverse:** Denomination **Reverse:** Bank building

Date	F	VF	XF	Unc	BU
ND(1998) Proof	—	Value: 65.00			

KM# 36 50 DIRHAMS **Weight:** 40.0000 g. **Composition:** 0.9250 Silver 1.1896 oz. ASW **Subject:** Colleges of Technology: 10 Years **Obverse:** Portrait **Reverse:** Bird viewed through window frame

Date	F	VF	XF	Unc	BU
ND(1998) Proof	—	Value: 65.00			

KM# 37 50 DIRHAMS **Weight:** 27.5000 g. **Composition:** 0.9250 Silver .8178 oz. ASW **Series:** UNICEF **Obverse:** Denomination **Reverse:** Two children

Date	F	VF	XF	Unc	BU
1998 Proof	—	Value: 37.50			

KM# 42 50 DIRHAMS **Weight:** 40.2200 g. **Composition:** 0.9250 Silver 1.1961 oz. ASW **Subject:** Honor Sheik Zayed **Obverse:** Portrait **Reverse:** Square design **Edge:** Reeded **Size:** 40 mm.

Date	Mintage	F	VF	XF	Unc	BU
AH1420(1999) Proof	2,000	Value: 90.00				

KM# 45 50 DIRHAMS **Weight:** 40.2200 g. **Composition:** 0.9250 Silver 1.1961 oz. ASW **Subject:** Dubai Islamic Bank **Obverse:** Denomination **Reverse:** Bank name

Date	F	VF	XF	Unc	BU
ND(2000) Proof	—	Value: 55.00			

KM# 47 50 DIRHAMS **Weight:** 40.2200 g. **Composition:** 0.9250 Silver 1.1961 oz. ASW **Subject:** General Women's Union **Obverse:** Portrait **Reverse:** Stylized gazelle

Date	Mintage	F	VF	XF	Unc	BU
ND(2000) Proof	2,000	Value: 55.00				

KM# 48 50 DIRHAMS **Weight:** 40.0000 g. **Composition:** 0.9250 Silver 1.1896 oz. ASW **Subject:** Dubai Airport Terminal **Obverse:** Portrait **Reverse:** Airport scene. **Edge:** Reeded. **Size:** 40 mm.

Date	Mintage	F	VF	XF	Unc	BU
2000 Proof	500	Value: 225				

KM# 12 500 DIRHAMS **Weight:** 19.9700 g. **Composition:** 0.9170 Gold .5886 oz. AGW **Subject:** 5th Anniversary - United Arab Emirates

Date	Mintage	F	VF	XF	Unc	BU
ND(1976) Proof	11,000	Value: 275				

KM# 23 500 DIRHAMS **Weight:** 19.9700 g. **Composition:** 0.9170 Gold .5886 oz. AGW **Subject:** Death of Shaikh Rashid **Obverse:** Bust

Date	F	VF	XF	Unc	BU
1990 Proof	—	Value: 400			

KM# 24 500 DIRHAMS **Weight:** 19.9700 g. **Composition:** 0.9170 Gold .5886 oz. AGW **Subject:** 10th Anniversary - Central Bank **Obverse:** Bust

Date	F	VF	XF	Unc	BU
1990 Proof	—	Value: 400			

KM# 25 500 DIRHAMS **Weight:** 19.9700 g. **Composition:** 0.9170 Gold .5886 oz. AGW **Subject:** 10th Anniversary - Women's Association **Obverse:** Heraldic eagle

Date	Mintage	F	VF	XF	Unc	BU
1995 Proof	1,000	Value: 400				

KM# 8 750 DIRHAMS **Weight:** 17.1700 g. **Composition:** 0.9000 Gold .4969 oz. AGW **Subject:** IYC and UNICEF

Date	Mintage	F	VF	XF	Unc	B
AH1400 (1980) Proof	3,063	Value: 245				

KM# 13 1000 DIRHAMS **Weight:** 39.9400 g. **Composition:** 0.9170 Gold 1.1771 oz. AGW **Subject:** 5th Anniversary - United Arab Emirates

Date	Mintage	F	VF	XF	Unc	
ND(1976) Proof	10,000	Value: 625				

KM# 26 1000 DIRHAMS **Weight:** 39.9400 g. **Compositio** 0.9170 Gold 1.1771 oz. AGW **Subject:** Death of Shaikh Rash Bin Saeed al-Maktoum **Obverse:** Portrait **Reverse:** Dubai International Trade Center **Note:** Similar to 50 Dirhams, KM#

Date	F	VF	XF	Unc	
1990 Proof	—	Value: 700			

KM# 27 1000 DIRHAMS **Weight:** 39.9400 g. **Composition:** 0.9170 Gold 1.1771 oz. AGW **Subject:** 10 Anniversary - UAE Central Bank **Obverse:** Portrait **Revers** Bank building **Note:** Similar to 50 Dirhams, KM#18.

Date	F	VF	XF	Unc
1990 Proof	—	Value: 700		

KM# 28 1000 DIRHAMS **Weight:** 39.9400 g. **Composition:** 0.9170 Gold 1.1771 oz. AGW **Subject:** 1 Anniversary - Women's Association **Obverse:** Heraldic ea **Reverse:** Seal in wreath

Date	F	VF	XF	Unc
1995 Proof	—	Value: 700		

KM# 29 1000 DIRHAMS **Weight:** 39.9400 g. **Compositi** 0.9170 Gold 1.1771 oz. AGW **Subject:** 25th Anniversary the UAE - National Day Issue **Obverse:** Portrait **Reverse** Heraldic eagle **Note:** Similar to 50 Dirhams, KM#21.

Date	F	VF	XF	Unc
1996 Proof	—	Value: 700		

KM# 30 1000 DIRHAMS **Weight:** 39.9400 g. **Composition:** 0.9170 Gold 1.1771 oz. AGW **Subject:** 3 Anniversary - Reign of Shaikh Zayed **Obverse:** Portrait **Reverse:** Circular design of Arabic lettering **Note:** Simila 50 Dirhams, KM#22.

Date	F	VF	XF	Unc
1996 Proof	—	Value: 700		

MEDALLIC COINAGE

KM# M1 5000 DIRHAMS **Weight:** 2000.0000 g. **Composition:** 0.9167 Gold 5.8945 oz. AGW **Subject:** 2 Anniversary of the UAE - National Day Issue **Obverse:** E **Reverse:** Heraldic eagle **Note:** Similar to 50 Dirhams, KM

Date	F	VF	XF	Unc
1996 Proof; Rare	—	—	—	—

KM# M2 5000 DIRHAMS **Weight:** 2000.0000 g. **Composition:** 0.9167 Gold 5.8945 oz. AGW **Subject:** 3 Anniversary - Reign of Shaikh Zayed **Obverse:** Portrait **Reverse:** Circular design of Arabic lettering **Note:** Simila 50 Dirhams, KM#22.

Date	F	VF	XF	Unc
1996 Proof; Rare	—	—	—	—

PIEFORTS

KM#	Date	Mintage	Identification	M
P1	1981	75	50 Dirhams. 0.9250 Silver. KM#7.	
P2	1981	100	750 Dirhams. 0.9000 Gold. KM#8.	

MINT SETS

KM#	Date	Mintage	Identification	Issue Price
MS2	Mixed dates (5)	—	KM#10-11 1987, KM#14 1988, KM#15 1991, KM#9 1981	—
MS1	AH1409/1989 (6)	—	KM#1, 2.1-3.1, 4-5, 6.1	—

UNITED STATES

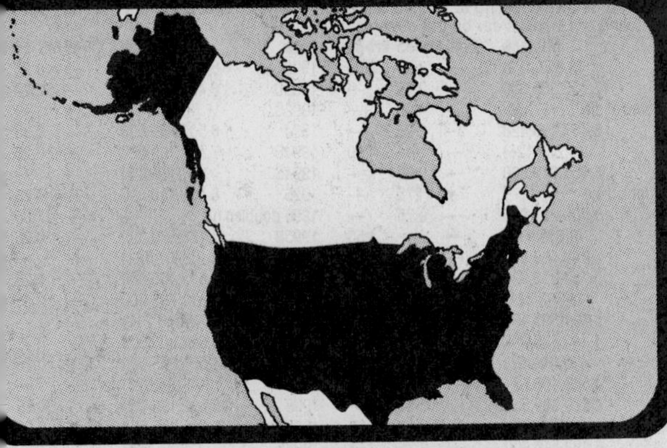

The United States of America as politically organized, under the Articles of ıfederation consisted of the 13 original British-American colonies; New Hamp-'e, Massachusetts, Rhode Island, Connecticut, New York, New Jersey, Penn-vania, Delaware, Virginia, North Carolina, South Carolina, Georgia and ryland. Clustered along the eastern seaboard of North American between the sts of Maine and the marshes of Georgia. Under the Article of Confederation, United States had no national capital: Philadelphia, where the "United States Congress Assembled", was the "seat of government". The population during political phase of America's history (1781-1789) was about 3 million, most of om lived on self-sufficient family farms. Fishing, lumbering and the production grains for export were major economic endeavors. Rapid strides were also ng made in industry and manufacturing by 1775, the (then) colonies were counting for one-seventh of the world's production of raw iron.

On the basis of the voyage of John Cabot to the North American mainland in 7, England claimed the entire continent. The first permanent English settle-nt was established at Jamestown, Virginia, in 1607. France and Spain also med extensive territory in North America. At the end of the French and Indian rs (1763), England acquired all of the territory east of the Mississippi River, uding East and West Florida. From 1776 to 1781, the States were governed the Continental Congress. From 1781 to 1789, they were organized under the icles of Confederation, during which period the individual States had the right ssue money. Independence from Great Britain was attained by the American volution in 1776. The Constitution which organized and governs the present ted States was ratified on Nov. 21, 1788.

CENT

Indian Head.

1864 "L"

90a **Designer:** James B. Longacre. **Diameter:** 19 **Weight:** 3.1100 g. **Composition:** Bronze. **Notes:** The 1864 "L" variety has the designer's initial in Liberty's hair to the right of her neck.

	Mintage	G-4	VG-8	F-12	VF-20	XF-40	AU-50	MS-60	MS-65	Prf-65
)	66,833,764	1.25	1.65	2.00	2.75	11.00	18.00	25.00	175	425
	79,611,143	1.20	1.60	1.80	2.50	7.50	17.00	25.00	140	425
2	87,376,722	1.20	1.60	1.80	2.50	7.25	17.00	25.00	140	425
3	85,094,493	1.20	1.60	1.80	2.50	7.25	17.00	25.00	140	425
4	61,328,015	1.20	1.60	1.80	2.50	8.00	17.00	25.00	140	475
5	80,719,163	1.20	1.60	1.80	2.50	7.25	17.00	25.00	140	475
5	96,022,255	1.20	1.60	1.80	2.50	7.25	17.00	25.00	140	395
7	108,138,618	1.20	1.60	1.80	2.50	7.25	17.00	25.00	145	485
3	32,327,987	1.25	2.00	2.25	2.50	7.50	18.00	26.00	145	395
3S	1,115,000	61.00	62.00	73.00	83.00	125	135	210	650	—
9	14,370,645	2.75	3.00	3.25	4.00	15.00	21.00	30.00	150	400
9S	309,000	285	315	345	400	465	485	565	1,400	—

Lincoln. Wheat.

132 **Designer:** Victor D. Brenner. **Diameter:** 19 **Weight:** 3.1100 g. **Composition:** Bronze. **Notes:** The 1909 "VDB" varieties have the designer's initials inscribed at the 6 o'clock position on the reverse. The initials were removed until 1918, when they were restored on the obverse.

	Mintage	G-4	VG-8	F-12	VF-20	XF-40	AU-50	MS-60	MS-65	Prf-65
	72,702,618	1.35	1.60	1.90	2.10	2.75	9.00	13.50	80.00	520
VDB	27,995,000	3.65	4.00	4.40	4.50	5.25	5.75	9.50	72.50	6,000
S	1,825,000	58.00	67.00	85.00	115	145	175	190	640	—

Date	Mintage	G-4	VG-8	F-12	VF-20	XF-40	AU-50	MS-60	MS-65	Prf-65
1909S VDB	484,000	500	610	670	720	810	870	1,050	5,000	—
1910	146,801,218	0.25	0.30	0.40	0.50	2.00	5.50	14.50	100.00	700
1910S	6,045,000	7.00	8.00	8.50	10.50	23.00	56.00	60.00	375	—
1911	101,177,787	0.25	0.45	1.00	1.35	3.50	7.50	16.00	180	600
1911D	12,672,000	5.00	5.75	8.50	12.50	40.00	62.50	80.00	990	—
1911S	4,026,000	16.00	17.50	19.00	24.00	43.00	85.00	145	1,450	—
1912	68,153,060	1.25	1.50	1.75	4.50	9.00	17.00	30.00	295	950
1912D	10,411,000	6.00	6.50	7.00	18.00	43.00	70.00	135	1,100	—
1912S	4,431,000	10.00	13.50	16.00	24.00	45.00	72.50	115	1,750	—
1913	76,532,352	0.65	0.75	1.40	3.00	12.50	16.00	27.50	265	550
1913D	15,804,000	2.75	3.00	3.50	7.50	25.00	55.00	90.00	1,300	—
1913S	6,101,000	6.25	7.00	7.50	12.00	32.50	70.00	135	2,800	—
1914	75,238,432	0.45	0.70	1.25	3.50	10.00	27.50	38.00	350	600
1914D	1,193,000	110	160	200	275	500	900	1,150	12,000	—
1914S	4,137,000	9.00	12.00	15.00	22.00	50.00	125	240	10,000	—
1915	29,092,120	1.35	1.75	3.50	8.00	40.00	64.00	70.00	575	600
1915D	22,050,000	1.50	1.75	2.00	2.75	11.50	27.00	60.00	700	—
1915S	4,833,000	7.00	8.00	10.00	12.00	37.50	62.50	135	3,300	—
1916	131,833,677	0.20	0.25	0.30	1.25	3.00	7.00	11.00	120	1,650
1916D	35,956,000	0.35	0.40	1.15	2.00	8.50	17.50	52.00	1,800	—
1916S	22,510,000	1.00	1.35	1.50	2.25	9.50	20.00	65.00	4,500	—
1917	196,429,785	0.20	0.25	0.30	1.15	3.00	7.00	11.00	140	—
1917D	55,120,000	0.25	0.35	0.70	1.65	8.50	20.00	54.00	1,450	—
1917S	32,620,000	0.50	0.55	0.75	1.50	7.00	17.00	54.00	4,500	—
1918	288,104,634	0.20	0.25	0.30	0.70	3.50	6.50	11.00	200	—
1918D	47,830,000	0.30	0.50	0.75	1.35	7.00	17.00	54.00	1,800	—
1918S	34,680,000	0.30	0.55	0.70	1.50	7.00	30.00	55.00	5,000	—
1919	392,021,000	0.20	0.25	0.30	0.50	1.35	4.00	8.00	100.00	—
1919D	57,154,000	0.30	0.35	0.45	1.15	4.50	26.50	45.00	1,250	—
1919S	139,760,000	0.20	0.25	1.00	1.20	2.75	12.00	33.50	3,000	—
1920	310,165,000	0.20	0.25	0.30	0.50	1.50	3.50	9.25	110	—
1920D	49,280,000	0.30	0.45	0.95	2.50	8.50	20.00	52.50	950	—
1920S	46,220,000	0.25	0.35	1.10	1.75	6.50	28.00	80.00	4,900	—
1921	39,157,000	0.25	0.30	0.50	1.00	4.50	16.00	35.00	195	—
1921S	15,274,000	1.25	1.35	1.65	3.00	16.50	65.00	85.00	4,500	—
1922D	7,160,000	8.00	9.50	11.00	14.50	23.00	42.00	75.00	930	—
1922 No D-T.2	Inc. above	395	490	550	640	1,525	3,000	5,000	175,000	—
1923	74,723,000	0.20	0.25	0.30	0.60	2.50	7.00	11.00	17,210	—
1923S	8,700,000	1.40	1.65	2.50	4.00	22.50	70.00	185	4,500	—
1924	75,178,000	0.20	0.30	0.40	0.60	3.00	8.00	20.00	150	—
1924D	2,520,000	12.00	13.50	14.50	28.50	83.00	150	235	5,000	—
1924S	11,696,000	0.80	1.00	1.50	2.50	11.00	55.00	95.00	7,800	—
1925	139,949,000	0.20	0.25	0.30	0.50	2.50	6.00	8.50	95.00	—
1925D	22,580,000	0.30	0.60	0.75	1.50	7.50	20.00	45.00	1,800	—
1925S	26,380,000	0.25	0.40	0.70	1.00	6.00	18.00	60.00	6,850	—
1926	157,088,000	0.15	0.20	0.25	0.50	1.35	4.00	7.00	64.00	—
1926D	28,020,000	0.25	0.30	0.50	1.25	6.00	22.50	55.00	1,800	—
1926S	4,550,000	3.00	3.75	6.00	8.00	13.50	55.00	100.00	60,000	—
1927	144,440,000	0.15	0.20	0.25	0.50	1.35	3.25	7.00	95.00	—
1927D	27,170,000	0.20	0.25	0.50	1.25	3.00	13.50	55.00	1,250	—
1927S	14,276,000	0.70	1.00	1.40	3.00	9.00	25.00	60.00	4,100	—
1928	134,116,000	0.15	0.25	0.25	0.50	1.25	3.00	7.50	90.00	—
1928D	31,170,000	0.20	0.25	0.50	0.75	3.00	8.50	26.50	550	—
1928S	17,266,000	0.60	0.75	1.00	1.25	4.00	11.00	60.00	1,800	—
1929	185,262,000	0.15	0.20	0.25	0.40	0.75	4.00	6.00	85.00	—
1929D	41,730,000	0.15	0.20	0.40	0.60	3.00	7.00	16.00	240	—
1929S	50,148,000	0.15	0.20	0.30	0.50	2.75	4.50	11.00	130	—
1930	157,415,000	0.15	0.20	0.30	0.50	1.10	2.25	3.65	35.00	—
1930D	40,100,000	0.20	0.25	0.40	0.60	2.00	5.00	11.00	95.00	—
1930S	24,286,000	0.20	0.25	0.35	0.50	1.10	6.50	10.00	49.00	—
1931	19,396,000	0.50	0.60	1.00	1.20	1.50	6.00	17.50	100.00	—
1931D	4,480,000	3.00	3.25	3.50	4.00	8.00	37.50	52.00	590	—
1931S	866,000	42.50	45.00	55.00	57.50	60.00	76.00	82.50	460	—
1932	9,062,000	1.00	1.25	2.00	2.50	3.00	8.00	18.50	75.00	—
1932D	10,500,000	0.75	1.25	1.35	1.50	2.00	7.00	14.50	80.00	—
1933	14,360,000	0.75	1.00	1.25	1.50	3.00	8.00	16.50	70.00	—
1933D	6,200,000	1.40	1.80	202	3.00	6.00	11.00	16.50	66.00	—
1934	219,080,000	—	0.15	0.20	0.25	0.75	1.50	4.00	27.00	—
1934D	28,446,000	0.15	0.20	0.25	0.45	1.50	5.00	16.50	52.00	—
1935	245,338,000	—	0.10	0.15	0.25	0.75	1.00	2.50	13.00	—
1935D	11,100,000,000	—	0.15	0.20	0.30	0.95	2.50	5.50	9.50	—
1935S	38,702,000	0.10	0.20	0.30	0.40	1.00	3.00	12.00	46.00	—
1936	309,637,569	—	0.10	0.15	0.25	0.75	1.00	2.00	6.00	1,200
1936D	40,620,000	—	0.10	0.15	0.25	0.75	1.50	2.75	8.50	—
1936S	29,130,000	0.10	0.15	0.25	0.35	0.85	1.75	2.75	8.50	—
1937	309,179,320	—	0.10	0.15	0.20	0.70	0.90	1.75	7.00	125
1937D	50,430,000	—	0.10	0.15	0.25	0.70	1.00	2.50	9.50	—
1937S	34,500,000	—	0.10	0.15	0.25	0.60	1.25	3.00	8.50	—
1938	156,696,734	—	0.10	0.15	0.20	0.50	1.00	2.00	5.75	85.00
1938D	20,010,000	0.20	0.25	0.35	0.45	0.75	1.50	3.50	8.50	—
1938S	15,180,000	0.30	0.40	0.50	0.70	0.90	1.90	2.80	8.50	—
1939	316,479,520	—	0.10	0.15	0.20	0.30	0.50	1.00	5.75	78.00
1939D	15,160,000	0.30	0.30	0.35	0.60	0.85	1.90	2.25	8.50	—
1939S	52,070,000	—	0.15	0.20	0.25	0.45	0.90	1.35	9.50	—
1940	586,825,872	—	0.15	0.20	0.25	0.30	0.45	1.00	5.75	70.00
1940D	81,390,000	—	0.15	0.20	0.25	0.35	0.50	1.20	5.75	—
1940S	112,940,000	—	0.15	0.20	0.25	0.30	0.75	1.25	5.85	—
1941	887,039,100	—	—	0.10	0.15	0.25	0.40	0.85	5.75	65.00
1941D	128,700,000	—	—	0.15	0.20	0.25	1.00	2.00	8.50	—
1941S	92,360,000	—	—	0.15	0.20	0.25	1.25	2.25	11.00	—
1942	657,828,600	—	—	0.10	0.15	0.20	0.25	0.50	4.60	78.00
1942D	206,698,000	—	—	0.10	0.15	0.20	0.30	0.50	5.75	—
1942S	85,590,000	—	—	0.10	0.20	0.30	1.50	3.50	16.00	—

Lincoln. Wheat.

KM# 132a **Designer:** Victor D. Brenner. **Diameter:** 19 **Weight:** 2.7000 g. **Composition:** Zinc Coated Steel.

Date	Mintage	G-4	VG-8	F-12	VF-20	XF-40	AU-50	MS-60	MS-65	Prf-65
1943	684,628,670	—	—	0.25	0.30	0.50	0.70	0.85	4.60	—
1943D	217,660,000	—	—	0.25	0.35	0.60	0.65	1.00	6.50	—

Date	Mintage	G-4	VG-8	F-12	VF-20	XF-40	AU-50	MS-60	MS-65	Prf-65
1943S	191,550,000	—	0.30	0.35	0.40	0.70	1.00	1.75	12.50	—

Lincoln. Wheat.

KM# A132 Designer: Victor D. Brenner. **Diameter:** 19 **Weight:** 3.1100 g. **Composition:** Copper-Zinc. **Notes:** KM#132 design and composition resumed.

Date	Mintage	XF-40	MS-65	Prf-65
1944	1,435,400,000	0.20	2.00	—
1944D	430,578,000	0.20	2.00	—
1944D/S	—	175	1,600	—
1944S	282,760,000	0.20	5.50	—
1945	1,040,515,000	0.20	2.00	—
1945D	226,268,000	0.20	2.00	—
1945S	181,770,000	0.20	5.50	—
1946	991,655,000	0.20	2.00	—
1946D	315,690,000	0.20	4.50	—
1946S	198,100,000	0.20	4.60	—
1947	190,555,000	0.20	2.25	—
1947D	194,750,000	0.20	2.00	—
1947S	99,000,000	0.20	5.50	—
1948	317,570,000	0.20	2.00	—
1948D	172,637,000	0.20	2.25	—
1948S	81,735,000	0.20	5.50	—
1949	217,775,000	0.20	3.50	—
1949D	153,132,000	0.20	3.50	—
1949S	64,290,000	0.25	6.00	—
1950	272,686,386	0.20	1.75	40.00
1950D	334,950,000	0.20	1.50	—
1950S	118,505,000	0.20	2.50	—
1951	295,633,500	0.20	2.00	40.00

Date	Mintage	XF-40	MS-65	Prf-65
1951D	625,355,000	0.10	1.65	—
1951S	136,010,000	0.15	3.00	—
1952	186,856,980	0.15	2.75	34.00
1952D	746,130,000	0.10	1.60	—
1952S	137,800,004	0.15	3.00	—
1953	256,883,800	0.10	1.25	28.00
1953D	700,515,000	0.10	1.25	—
1953S	181,835,000	0.15	1.75	—
1954	71,873,350	0.15	1.25	9.00
1954D	251,552,500	0.10	0.50	—
1954S	96,190,000	0.15	0.75	—
1955	330,958,000	0.10	0.75	13.00
1955 doubled die	—	750	33,500	—

Note: The 1955 "doubled die" has distinct doubling of the date and lettering on the obverse.

Date	Mintage	XF-40	MS-65	Prf-65
1955D	563,257,500	0.10	0.75	—
1955S	44,610,000	0.25	1.00	—
1956	421,414,384	—	0.50	3.00
1956D	1,098,201,100	—	0.50	—
1957	283,787,952	—	0.50	2.00
1957D	1,051,342,000	—	0.50	—
1958	253,400,652	—	0.50	3.00
1958D	800,953,300	—	0.50	—

Lincoln. Lincoln Memorial.

KM# 201 Rev. Designer: Frank Gasparro. **Weight:** 3.1100 g. **Composition:** Copper-Zinc. **Notes:** The dates were modified in 1960, 1970 and 1982, resulting in large-date and small-date varieties for those years. The 1972 "doubled die" shows doubling of "In God We Trust." The 1979-S and 1981-S Type II proofs have a clearer mint mark than the Type I proofs of those years. Some 1982 cents have the predominantly copper composition; others have the predominantly zinc composition. They can be distinguished by weight.

Date	Mintage	XF-40	MS-65	Prf-65
1959	610,864,291	—	0.50	1.50
1959D	1,279,760,000	—	0.50	—
1960 small date	588,096,602	2.10	5.00	16.00
1960 large date	Inc. above	—	0.30	1.25
1960D small date	1,580,884,000	—	0.30	—
1960D large date	Inc. above	—	0.30	—
1961	756,373,244	—	0.30	1.00
1961D	1,753,266,700	—	0.30	—
1962	609,263,019	—	0.30	1.00
1962D	1,793,148,400	—	0.30	—
1963	757,185,645	—	0.30	1.00
1963D	1,774,020,400	—	0.30	—
1964	2,652,525,762	—	0.30	1.00
1964D	3,799,071,500	—	0.30	—
1965	1,497,224,900	—	0.30	—
1966	2,188,147,783	—	0.30	—
1967	3,048,667,100	—	0.30	—
1968	1,707,880,970	—	0.30	—
1968D	2,886,269,600	—	0.40	—
1968S	261,311,510	—	0.40	1.00
1969	1,136,910,000	—	0.60	—
1969D	4,002,832,200	—	0.40	—
1969S	547,309,631	—	0.40	1.10
1970	1,898,315,000	—	0.40	—
1970D	2,891,438,900	—	0.40	—
1970S	693,192,814	—	0.40	1.20
1970S small date	—	—	55.00	60.00
1971	1,919,490,000	—	0.35	—
1971D	2,911,045,600	—	0.40	—
1971S	528,354,192	—	0.25	1.20
1972	2,933,255,000	—	0.25	—
1972 doubled die	—	210	500	—
1972D	2,665,071,400	—	0.25	—
1972S	380,200,104	—	0.25	1.15

Date	Mintage	XF-40	MS-65	Prf-65
1973	3,728,245,000	—	0.25	—
1973D	3,549,576,588	—	0.25	—
1973S	319,937,634	—	0.25	0.80
1974	4,232,140,523	—	0.25	—
1974D	4,235,098,000	—	0.25	—
1974S	412,039,228	—	0.25	0.75
1975	5,451,476,142	—	0.25	—
1975D	4,505,245,300	—	0.25	—
1975S	(2,845,450)	—	—	5.50
1976	4,674,292,426	—	0.25	—
1976D	4,221,592,455	—	0.25	—
1976S	(4,149,730)	—	—	5.00
1977	4,469,930,000	—	0.25	—
1977D	4,149,062,300	—	0.25	—
1977S	(3,251,152)	—	—	3.00
1978	5,558,605,000	—	0.25	—
1978D	4,280,233,400	—	0.25	—
1978S	(3,127,781)	—	—	3.50
1979	6,018,515,000	—	0.25	—
1979D	4,139,357,254	—	0.25	—
1979S type I, proof	(3,677,175)	—	—	4.00
1979S type II, proof	Inc. above	—	—	4.25
1980	7,414,705,000	—	0.25	—
1980D	5,140,098,660	—	0.25	—
1980S	(3,554,806)	—	—	2.25
1981	7,491,750,000	—	0.25	—
1981S type II, proof	Inc. above	—	—	60.00
1981D	5,373,235,677	—	0.25	—
1981S type I, proof	(4,063,083)	—	—	3.50
1982 large date	10,712,525,000	—	0.25	—
1982 small date	—	—	0.25	—
1982D large date	6,012,979,368	—	0.25	—

Lincoln. Lincoln Memorial.

KM# 201a Diameter: 19 **Weight:** 2.5000 g. **Composition:** Copper Plated Zinc.

Date	Mintage	XF-40	MS-65	Prf-65
1982 large date	—	—	0.50	—
1982 small date	—	—	2.00	—
1982D large date	—	—	0.30	—
1982D small date	—	—	0.25	—

Lincoln. Lincoln Memorial.

KM# 201b Diameter: 19 **Composition:** Copper Plated Zinc. **Notes:** The 1983 "doubled die reverse" shows doubling of "United States of America." The 1984 "doubled die" shows doubling of Lincoln's ear on the obverse.

Date	Mintage	XF-40	MS-65	Prf-65
1982S	(3,857,479)	—	—	3.00
1983	7,752,355,000	—	0.25	—
1983 doubled die	—	—	400	—
1983D	6,467,199,428	—	0.25	—
1983S	(3,279,126)	—	—	4.00
1984	8,151,079,000	—	0.25	—
1984 doubled die	—	—	275	—
1984D	5,569,238,906	—	0.75	—
1984S	(3,065,110)	—	—	4.50
1985	5,648,489,887	—	0.25	—
1985D	5,287,399,926	—	0.25	—
1985S	(3,362,821)	—	—	6.00
1986	4,491,395,493	—	1.50	—
1986D	4,442,866,698	—	0.75	—
1986S	(3,010,497)	—	—	7.50
1987	4,682,466,931	—	0.25	—
1987D	4,879,389,514	—	0.25	—
1987S	(4,227,728)	—	—	5.00
1988	6,092,810,000	—	0.25	—
1988D	5,253,740,443	—	0.25	—
1988S	(3,262,948)	—	—	12.50
1989	7,261,535,000	—	0.25	—
1989D	5,345,467,111	—	0.25	—
1989S	(3,220,194)	—	—	12.50
1990	6,851,765,000	—	0.25	—
1990D	4,922,894,533	—	0.25	—
1990S	(3,299,559)	—	—	5.75
1990 no S	—	—	—	2,750
1991	5,165,940,000	—	0.25	—
1991D	4,158,442,076	—	0.25	—
1991S	(2,867,787)	—	—	30.00
1992	4,648,905,000	—	0.25	—
1992D	4,448,673,300	—	0.25	—
1992S	(4,176,560)	—	—	5.50

Date	Mintage	XF-40	MS-65	Prf-65
1993	5,684,705,000	—	0.25	—
1993D	6,426,650,571	—	0.25	—
1993S	(3,394,792)	—	—	9.50
1994	6,500,850,000	—	0.25	—
1994D	7,131,765,000	—	0.25	—
1994S	(3,269,923)	—	—	8.50
1995	6,411,440,000	—	0.25	—
1995 doubled die	—	—	27.00	—
1995D	7,128,560,000	—	0.25	—
1995S	(2,707,481)	—	—	9.50
1996	6,612,465,000	—	0.25	—
1996D	6,510,795,000	—	0.25	—
1996S	(2,915,212)	—	—	6.50
1997	4,622,800,000	—	0.25	—
1997D	4,576,555,000	—	0.25	—
1997S	(2,796,678)	—	—	11.50
1998	5,032,155,000	—	0.25	—
1998D	5,255,353,500	—	0.25	—
1998S	(2,957,286)	—	—	9.50
1999	5,237,600,000	—	0.25	—
1999D	6,360,065,000	—	0.25	—
1999S	(3,362,462)	—	—	5.0
2000	5,503,200,000	—	0.25	—
2000D	8,774,220,000	—	0.25	—
2000S	(4,063,361)	—	—	4.0
2001P	4,959,600,000	—	0.25	—
2001D	5,374,990,000	—	0.25	—
2001S	(3,099,096)	—	—	4.0
2002P	3,260,800,000	—	0.25	—
2002D	4,028,055,000	—	0.25	—
2002S	—	—	—	4.0
2003P	—	—	0.25	—
2003S	—	—	—	4.0
2003D	—	—	0.25	—

5 CENTS

Liberty. "Cents" below "V".

KM# 112 Weight: 5.0000 g. **Composition:** Copper Nickel.

Date	Mintage	G-4	VG-8	F-12	VF-20	XF-40	AU-50	MS-60	MS-65	Prf-
1900	27,255,995	1.60	2.00	5.00	9.50	25.00	52.50	75.00	570	5
1901	26,480,213	1.25	2.50	5.50	8.50	25.00	45.00	60.00	570	5
1902	31,480,579	1.25	2.50	4.00	7.00	25.00	45.00	65.00	570	5
1903	28,006,725	1.25	2.50	4.00	8.50	25.00	45.00	60.00	565	5
1904	21,404,984	1.25	1.75	4.25	8.50	26.50	45.00	60.00	565	6
1905	29,827,276	1.25	1.75	3.25	7.50	25.00	45.00	60.00	570	5
1906	38,613,725	1.25	1.75	2.75	7.00	25.00	45.00	60.00	570	5
1907	39,214,800	1.25	1.75	2.75	6.50	25.00	45.00	60.00	1,150	5
1908	22,686,177	1.25	1.75	2.75	6.50	25.00	45.00	60.00	1,100	5
1909	11,590,526	2.25	2.50	3.00	7.50	27.50	45.00	75.00	900	5
1910	30,169,353	1.25	1.75	2.75	6.50	21.50	40.00	60.00	660	4
1911	39,559,372	1.25	1.75	2.75	6.50	21.50	40.00	60.00	565	4
1912	26,236,714	1.25	1.75	2.75	7.50	21.50	40.00	60.00	565	5
1912D	8,474,000	1.75	1.75	5.00	20.00	50.00	120	225	1,200	
1912S	238,000	100.00	125	165	300	625	950	1,125	4,600	
1913 5 known	—	—	—	—	—	—	—	—	—	

Note: 1913, Superior Sale, March 2001, Proof, $1,840,000.

Buffalo. Buffalo standing on a mound.

KM# 133 Designer: James Earle Fraser. **Diameter:** 21.2 **Weight:** 5.0000 g. **Compositi** Copper-Nickel.

Date	Mintage	G-4	VG-8	F-12	VF-20	XF-40	AU-50	MS-60	MS-65	P
1913	30,993,520	7.00	8.00	9.00	9.50	16.00	23.00	32.00	125	2
1913D	5,337,000	9.50	11.50	13.50	15.00	20.00	42.00	50.00	315	
1913S	2,105,000	22.00	25.00	28.00	36.00	54.00	60.00	80.00	670	

Buffalo. Buffalo standing on a line.

1918/17D

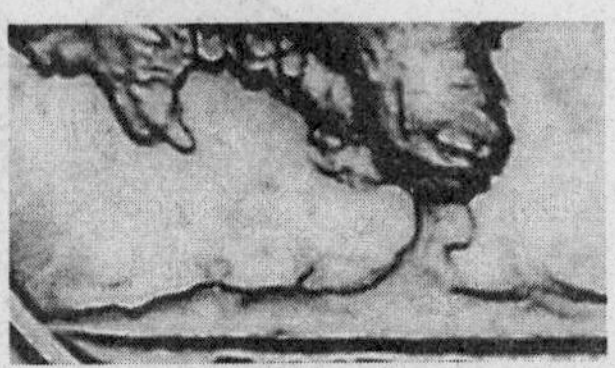

1937D 3-legged

1# 134 Designer: James Earle Fraser. **Diameter:** 21.2 **Weight:** 5.0000 g. **Composition:** Copper Nickel. **Notes:** In 1913 the reverse design was modified so the ground under the buffalo was represented as a line rather than a mound. On the 1937D 3-legged variety, the buffalo's right front leg is missing, the result of a damaged die.

e	Mintage	G-4	VG-8	F-12	VF-20	XF-40	AU-50	MS-60	MS-65	Prf-65
3	29,858,700	7.50	8.50	9.00	10.00	17.00	23.00	30.00	340	1,675
3D	4,156,000	55.00	65.00	85.00	95.00	100.00	125	160	1,400	—
3S	1,209,000	160	230	250	290	300	340	395	3,750	—
4	20,665,738	13.00	15.00	16.00	17.50	20.00	30.00	44.00	440	1,475
4D	3,912,000	55.00	65.00	77.00	90.00	150	160	220	1,650	—
4S	3,470,000	15.00	18.00	24.00	27.50	47.00	82.50	135	2,250	—
5	20,987,270	4.50	5.00	6.00	10.50	17.50	35.00	45.00	290	1,400
5D	7,569,500	12.50	15.00	24.00	40.00	80.00	110	200	2,300	—
5S	1,505,000	24.00	36.50	55.00	95.00	325	320	480	2,950	—
6	63,498,066	3.50	4.25	4.50	5.00	8.00	15.00	40.00	300	2,350
6/16	Inc. above	1,750	3,800	6,600	9,150	12,500	23,500	41,000	330,000	—
6D	13,333,000	8.75	13.50	16.50	25.00	70.00	95.00	140	2,300	—
6S	11,860,000	4.50	6.50	12.50	21.50	50.00	95.00	160	2,250	—
7	51,424,029	3.50	4.00	4.50	6.00	12.00	26.50	50.00	540	—
7D	9,910,800	9.00	13.50	24.00	55.00	110	180	290	4,000	—
7S	4,193,000	15.00	23.00	38.50	66.00	125	250	335	4,750	—
8	32,086,314	3.25	365	4.85	10.00	25.00	40.00	85.00	1,525	—
8/17D	8,362,314	750	1,200	2,200	4,600	7,700	9,400	20,000	280,000	—
8D	Inc. above	7.50	15.00	25.00	92.50	180	290	350	4,750	—
8S	4,882,000	8.00	18.00	30.00	72.00	150	260	400	31,000	—
9	60,868,000	1.25	1.50	1.75	4.00	11.00	25.00	44.00	540	—
9D	8,006,000	9.50	14.50	35.00	80.00	200	320	500	7,500	—
9S	7,521,000	5.25	14.50	29.00	80.00	200	320	460	14,000	—
20	63,093,000	0.75	1.25	1.50	4.00	8.50	23.00	45.00	685	—
20D	9,418,000	5.50	11.00	23.00	85.00	250	300	450	7,250	—
20S	9,689,000	3.00	5.25	16.00	80.00	175	250	435	27,500	—
21	10,663,000	1.80	2.40	2.65	12.50	35.00	50.00	100.00	700	—
21S	1,557,000	40.00	65.00	100.00	475	760	1,100	1,500	7,500	—
23	35,715,000	1.25	1.35	1.50	3.00	8.00	29.00	44.00	580	—
23S	6,142,000	3.90	5.00	9.00	115	240	300	400	9,600	—
24	21,620,000	1.00	1.25	1.50	5.00	11.50	26.50	60.00	875	—
24D	5,258,000	4.00	4.50	14.50	65.00	185	240	330	5,200	—
24S	1,437,000	9.00	17.00	70.00	435	1,100	1,600	2,150	12,000	—
25	35,565,100	2.00	2.10	2.25	4.00	9.00	23.00	38.50	525	—
25D	4,450,000	6.00	13.50	30.00	72.00	145	220	350	6,100	—
25S	6,256,000	3.90	8.50	14.00	66.00	150	230	380	4,400	—
26	44,693,000	0.65	0.75	0.90	1.75	5.50	16.00	29.00	160	—
26D	5,638,000	4.25	8.00	15.00	72.00	140	230	235	5,150	—
26S	970,000	14.00	23.00	50.00	400	750	2,300	3,900	80,000	—
27	37,981,000	0.65	0.75	0.90	1.50	7.50	16.00	26.50	280	—
27D	5,730,000	2.00	4.00	5.00	21.00	70.00	110	145	8,800	—
27S	3,430,000	1.15	2.10	4.00	27.50	75.00	150	480	20,000	—
28	23,411,000	0.85	0.90	1.00	2.00	6.00	18.50	27.50	310	—
28D	6,436,000	1.10	2.00	3.30	11.00	36.00	43.00	45.00	900	—
28S	6,936,000	1.35	1.45	2.10	9.00	21.50	92.50	200	5,200	—
29	36,446,000	0.65	0.75	0.90	1.50	5.75	14.50	29.00	310	—
29D	8,370,000	0.85	1.10	1.75	5.50	30.00	40.00	53.00	1,900	—
29S	7,754,000	0.75	0.85	1.00	1.50	11.50	25.00	45.00	450	—
30	22,849,000	0.65	0.75	0.85	1.10	4.00	14.50	26.50	170	—
30S	5,435,000	0.80	0.80	0.85	1.35	10.00	24.00	40.00	500	—
31S	1,200,000	11.50	12.00	12.50	13.50	19.00	38.00	42.00	265	—
34	20,213,003	0.60	0.75	0.85	1.75	3.75	12.00	46.00	370	—
34D	7,480,000	0.75	0.95	1.35	3.75	13.50	40.00	67.00	810	—
35	58,264,000	0.60	0.75	0.80	1.25	1.75	8.00	19.00	100.00	—
35D	12,092,000	0.80	1.00	1.50	5.00	12.50	36.00	60.00	450	—
35S	10,300,000	0.65	0.75	0.85	1.40	3.00	15.00	49.00	150	—
36	119,001,420	0.60	0.70	0.85	1.00	1.75	6.50	14.50	90.00	1,100
36D	24,814,000	0.60	0.75	0.85	1.00	3.00	11.50	34.00	95.00	—
36S	14,930,000	0.60	0.75	0.85	1.00	1.75	9.50	34.00	105	—
37	79,485,769	0.60	0.75	0.85	0.95	1.50	6.50	14.00	53.00	850
37D	17,826,000	0.60	0.75	0.85	1.10	1.50	8.00	18.00	60.00	—
37D 3-gged	Inc. above	200	335	375	440	500	790	1,450	24,000	—
37S	5,635,000	0.75	0.80	0.90	1.25	2.20	8.00	24.00	65.00	—
38D	7,020,000	1.50	1.60	1.85	2.50	3.00	8.00	17.00	40.00	—
38D/D	—	2.50	4.50	6.00	8.00	10.00	17.00	20.00	60.00	—
38D/S	Inc. above	4.50	6.50	9.00	10.00	12.50	27.50	45.00	180	—

Jefferson.

KM# 192 Designer: Felix Schlag. **Diameter:** 21.2 **Weight:** 5.0000 g. **Composition:** Copper-Nickel. **Notes:** Some 1939 strikes have doubling of the word "Monticello" on the reverse.

Date	Mintage	VG-8	F-12	VF-20	XF-40	MS-60	MS-65	-65FS	Prf-65
1938	19,515,365	0.25	0.40	0.80	1.25	4.00	8.00	125	70.00
1938D	5,376,000	0.90	1.00	1.25	1.75	3.50	8.00	95.00	—
1938S	4,105,000	1.60	1.75	2.00	2.25	4.25	8.50	165	—
1939 T I	—	—	—	—	—	—	—	300	70.00
1939 T II	120,627,535	—	0.20	0.25	0.30	1.75	3.50	40.00	300
1939 doubled Monticello T II	—	20.00	30.00	45.00	75.00	200	550	700	—
1939D T I	—	—	—	—	—	—	—	275	—
1939D T II	3,514,000	3.00	3.50	5.00	10.00	42.00	85.00	250	—
1939S T I	—	—	—	—	—	—	—	250	—
1939S T II	6,630,000	0.45	0.60	1.50	2.75	15.00	40.00	275	—
1940	176,499,158	—	—	—	0.25	1.00	2.50	35.00	65.00
1940D	43,540,000	—	0.20	0.30	0.40	1.50	2.75	25.00	—
1940S	39,690,000	—	0.20	0.25	0.50	2.50	5.00	45.00	—
1941	203,283,720	—	—	—	0.20	0.75	2.00	40.00	60.00
1941D	53,432,000	—	0.20	0.30	0.50	2.50	5.00	25.00	—
1941S	43,445,000	—	0.20	0.30	0.50	3.75	6.75	60.00	—
1942	49,818,600	—	—	—	0.40	5.00	8.50	75.00	55.00
1942D	13,938,000	0.30	0.40	0.60	2.00	27.00	50.00	70.00	—

Note: Fully Struck Full Step nickels command higher prices. Bright, Fully Struck coins command even higher prices. 1938 thru 1989 - 5 Full Steps. 1990 to date - 6 Full Steps. Without bag marks or nicks on steps.

Jefferson. Mint mark above Monticello.

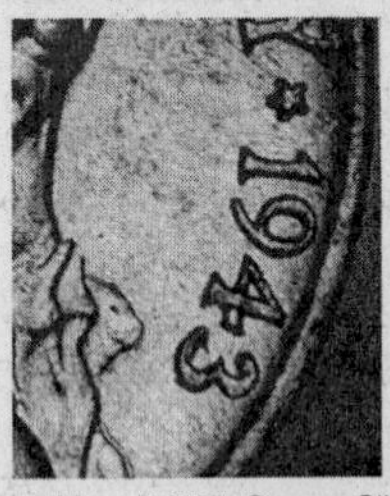

KM# 192a Designer: Felix Schlag. **Diameter:** 21.2 **Composition:** 0.3500 Copper-Silver-Manganese, 0.0563 oz. **Notes:** War-time composition nickels have a large mint mark above Monticello on the reverse.

Date	Mintage	VG-8	F-12	VF-20	XF-40	MS-60	MS-65	-65FS	Prf-65
1942P	57,900,600	0.65	0.85	1.00	1.75	6.00	22.50	70.00	140
1942S	32,900,000	0.70	1.00	1.10	1.75	6.00	20.00	125	—
1943P	271,165,000	0.50	0.85	1.00	1.50	2.75	15.00	35.00	—
1943/2P	Inc. above	15.00	20.00	30.00	40.00	125	450	1,000	—
1943D	15,294,000	0.90	1.20	1.50	1.75	4.00	13.00	30.00	—
1943S	104,060,000	0.55	0.70	1.00	1.50	3.00	13.00	55.00	—
1944P	119,150,000	0.50	0.70	1.00	1.50	4.00	17.00	100.00	—
1944D	32,309,000	0.60	0.80	1.00	1.75	6.50	13.00	30.00	—
1944S	21,640,000	0.70	1.00	1.25	2.00	3.50	13.00	185	—
1945P	119,408,100	0.50	0.70	1.00	1.50	3.50	12.00	125	—
1945D	37,158,000	0.55	0.75	1.00	1.50	3.50	7.00	40.00	—
1945S	58,939,000	0.50	0.70	0.80	0.90	3.00	6.50	250	—

Note: Fully Struck Full Step nickels command higher prices. Bright, Fully Struck coins command even higher prices. 1938 thru 1989 - 5 Full Steps. 1990 to date - 6 Full Steps. Without bag marks or nicks on steps.

Jefferson. Pre-war design resumed.

KM# A192 Designer: Felix Schlag. **Diameter:** 21.2 **Weight:** 5.0000 g. **Composition:** Copper-Nickel. **Notes:** KM#192 design and composition resumed. The 1979-S and 1981-S Type II proofs have clearer mint marks than the Type I proofs of those years.

Date	Mintage	VG-8	F-12	VF-20	XF-40	MS-60	MS-65	-65FS	Prf-65
1946	161,116,000	—	—	0.20	0.25	0.80	1.00	40.00	—
1946D	45,292,200	—	—	0.25	0.35	0.95	1.50	30.00	—
1946S	13,560,000	—	—	0.30	0.40	0.50	1.00	45.00	—
1947	95,000,000	—	—	0.20	0.25	0.75	2.00	30.00	—
1947D	37,822,000	—	—	0.20	0.30	0.90	2.00	30.00	—
1947S	24,720,000	—	—	0.20	0.25	1.00	2.25	55.00	—
1948	89,348,000	—	—	0.20	0.25	0.50	1.50	60.00	—
1948D	44,734,000	—	—	0.25	0.35	1.20	2.75	30.00	—
1948S	11,300,000	—	—	0.25	0.50	1.20	2.25	45.00	—
1949	60,652,000	—	—	0.25	0.30	2.25	4.50	200	—
1949D	36,498,000	—	—	0.30	0.40	1.25	3.00	75.00	—
1949D/S	Inc. above	—	35.00	40.00	65.00	170	325	1,750	—
1949S	9,716,000	0.25	0.35	0.45	0.90	1.50	3.50	145	—
1950	9,847,386	0.20	0.30	0.35	0.75	1.50	3.50	150	45.00
1950D	2,630,030	5.00	5.15	5.25	5.50	6.50	10.00	45.00	—
1951	28,609,500	—	—	0.40	0.50	1.50	2.75	90.00	30.00
1951D	20,460,000	0.25	0.30	0.40	0.50	3.00	6.00	45.00	—

Date	Mintage	VG-8	F-12	VF-20	XF-40	MS-60	MS-65	-65FS	Prf-65
1951S	7,776,000	0.30	0.40	0.50	1.10	1.75	4.00	150	—
1952	64,069,980	—	—	0.20	0.25	0.85	3.00	125	26.00
1952D	30,638,000	—	—	0.30	0.45	2.00	4.50	65.00	—
1952S	20,572,000	—	—	0.20	0.25	0.75	3.50	195	—
1953	46,772,800	—	—	0.20	0.25	0.40	1.50	200	28.00
1953D	59,878,600	—	—	0.20	0.25	0.40	1.50	100.00	—
1953S	19,210,900	—	—	0.20	0.25	0.60	2.50	1,750	—
1954	47,917,350	—	—	—	—	0.60	1.75	95.00	16.00
1954D	117,136,560	—	—	—	—	0.35	2.00	175	—
1954S	29,384,000	—	—	—	0.20	1.00	3.00	1,000	—
1954S/D	Inc. above	—	5.00	8.00	12.00	22.00	65.00	—	—
1955	8,266,200	0.25	0.35	0.40	0.45	0.75	2.00	85.00	16.00
1955D	74,464,100	—	—	—	—	0.40	1.00	150	—
1955D/S	Inc. above	—	5.00	8.50	13.00	33.00	75.00	—	—
1956	35,885,384	—	—	—	—	0.30	0.70	35.00	2.50
1956D	67,222,940	—	—	—	—	0.25	0.60	90.00	—
1957	39,655,952	—	—	—	—	0.25	0.60	40.00	1.50
1957D	136,828,900	—	—	—	—	0.25	0.60	55.00	—
1958	17,963,652	—	—	0.15	0.20	0.30	0.65	80.00	6.00
1958D	168,249,120	—	—	—	—	0.25	0.60	30.00	—

Note: Fully Struck Full Step nickels command higher prices. Bright, Fully Struck coins command even higher prices. 1938 thru 1989 - 5 Full Steps. 1990 to date - 6 Full Steps. Without bag marks or nicks on steps.

Date	Mintage	MS-65-65FS		Prf-65
1959	28,397,291	0.65	30.00	1.25
1959D	160,738,240	0.55	45.00	—
1960	57,107,602	2.00	60.00	1.00
1960D	192,582,180	0.55	650	—
1961	76,668,244	0.55	100.00	1.00
1961D	229,342,760	0.55	800	—
1962	100,602,019	1.50	75.00	1.00
1962D	280,195,720	0.55	600	—
1963	178,851,645	0.55	45.00	1.00
1963D	276,829,460	0.55	650	—
1964	1,028,622,762	0.55	55.00	1.00
1964D	1,787,297,160	0.50	500	—
1965	136,131,380	0.50	225	—
1966	156,208,283	0.50	350	—
1967	107,325,800	0.50	275	—
1968 none minted	—	—	—	—
1968D	91,227,880	0.50	750	—
1968S	103,437,510	0.50	300	0.75
1969 none minted	—	—	—	—
1969D	202,807,500	0.50	—	—
1969S	123,099,631	0.50	450	0.75
1970 none minted	—	—	—	—
1970D	515,485,380	0.50	500	—
1970S	241,464,814	0.50	125	0.75
1971	106,884,000	2.00	35.00	—
1971D	316,144,800	0.50	25.00	—
1971S	(3,220,733)	—	—	2.00
1972	202,036,000	0.50	35.00	—
1972D	351,694,600	0.50	25.00	—
1972S	(3,260,996)	—	—	2.00
1973	384,396,000	0.50	20.00	—
1973D	261,405,000	0.50	20.00	—
1973S	(2,760,339)	—	—	1.75
1974	601,752,000	0.50	75.00	—
1974D	277,373,000	0.50	50.00	—
1974S	(2,612,568)	—	—	2.00
1975	181,772,000	0.75	65.00	—
1975D	401,875,300	0.50	60.00	—
1975S	(2,845,450)	—	—	2.25
1976	367,124,000	0.75	150	—
1976D	563,964,147	0.60	55.00	—
1976S	(4,149,730)	—	—	2.00
1977	585,376,000	0.40	65.00	—
1977D	297,313,460	0.55	35.00	—
1977S	(3,251,152)	—	—	1.75
1978	391,308,000	0.40	40.00	—
1978D	313,092,780	0.40	35.00	—
1978S	(3,127,781)	—	—	1.75
1979	463,188,000	0.40	95.00	—
1979D	325,867,672	0.40	35.00	—
1979S type I, proof	(3,677,175)	—	—	1.50
1979S type II, proof	Inc. above	—	—	1.75
1980P	593,004,000	0.40	30.00	—
1980D	502,323,448	0.40	25.00	—
1980S	(3,554,806)	—	—	1.50
1981P	657,504,000	0.40	70.00	—
1981D	364,801,843	0.40	40.00	—
1981S type I, proof	(4,063,083)	—	—	2.00
1981S type II, proof	Inc. above	—	—	2.50
1982P	292,355,000	4.50	80.00	—
1982D	373,726,544	3.50	45.00	—
1982S	(3,857,479)	—	—	3.50
1983P	561,615,000	4.00	45.00	—
1983D	536,726,276	2.50	35.00	—
1983S	(3,279,126)	—	—	4.00
1984P	746,769,000	3.00	65.00	—
1984D	517,675,146	0.85	30.00	—
1984S	(3,065,110)	—	—	5.00
1985P	647,114,962	0.75	60.00	—
1985D	459,747,446	0.75	35.00	—
1985S	(3,362,821)	—	—	4.00
1986P	536,883,483	1.00	70.00	—
1986D	361,819,140	2.00	60.00	—
1986S	(3,010,497)	—	—	7.00
1987P	371,499,481	0.75	30.00	—
1987D	410,590,604	0.75	25.00	—
1987S	(4,227,728)	—	—	3.50
1988P	771,360,000	0.75	30.00	—
1988D	663,771,652	—	25.00	—
1988S	(3,262,948)	—	—	6.50
1989P	898,812,000	0.75	75.00	—
1989D	570,842,474	0.75	25.00	—
1989S	(3,220,194)	—	—	5.50
1990P	661,636,000	0.75	25.00	—
1990D	663,938,503	0.75	25.00	—
1990S	(3,299,559)	—	—	5.50
1991P	614,104,000	0.75	25.00	—
1991D	436,496,678	0.75	25.00	—
1991S	(2,867,787)	—	—	5.00
1992P	399,552,000	2.00	25.00	—
1992D	450,565,113	0.75	25.00	—
1992S	(4,176,560)	—	—	4.00
1993P	412,076,000	0.75	25.00	—
1993D	406,084,135	0.75	25.00	—
1993S	(3,394,792)	—	—	4.50
1994P	722,160,000	0.75	25.00	—
1994P matte	167,703	75.00	—	—
1994D	715,762,110	0.75	25.00	—
1994S	(3,269,923)	—	—	4.00
1995P	774,156,000	0.75	25.00	—
1995D	888,112,000	0.85	25.00	—
1995S	(2,707,481)	—	—	7.50
1996P	829,332,000	0.75	25.00	—
1996D	817,736,000	0.75	25.00	—
1996S	(2,915,212)	—	—	3.00
1997P	470,972,000	0.75	25.00	—
1997P matte	25,000	250	—	—
1997D	466,640,000	0.80	25.00	—
1997S	(1,975,000)	—	—	5.00
1998P	688,272,000	0.80	25.00	—
1998D	635,360,000	0.80	25.00	—
1998S	(2,957,286)	—	—	4.50
1999P	1,212,000,000	0.80	20.00	—
1999D	1,066,720,000	0.80	20.00	—
1999S	(3,362,462)	—	—	3.50
2000P	846,240,000	0.80	20.00	—
2000D	1,509,520,000	0.80	20.00	—
2000S	(4,063,361)	—	—	2.00
2001P	675,704,000	0.50	20.00	—
2001D	627,680,000	0.50	20.00	—
2001S	(3,099,096)	—	—	2.00
2002P	539,280,000	0.50	—	—
2002D	691,200,000	0.50	—	—
2002S	—	—	—	2.00
2003P	—	0.50	—	—
2003D	—	0.50	—	—
2003S	—	—	—	2.00

DIME

Barber.

KM# 113 **Designer:** Charles E. Barber. **Diameter:** 17.9 **Weight:** 2.5000 g. **Composition:** 0.9000 Silver, 0.0724 oz. ASW. **Notes:** Commonly called "Barber dime."

Date	Mintage	G-4	VG-8	F-12	VF-20	XF-40	AU-50	MS-60	MS-65	Prf-65
1900	17,600,912	2.20	3.90	6.30	10.00	21.00	65.00	95.00	800	1,450
1900O	2,010,000	14.00	34.00	95.00	125	200	340	570	5,800	—
1900S	5,168,270	3.90	4.50	10.00	12.50	23.00	72.00	150	1,750	—
1901	18,860,478	2.10	2.70	5.70	8.00	20.00	60.00	95.00	825	1,450
1901O	5,620,000	2.10	3.90	11.50	20.00	42.00	120	430	3,000	—
1901S	593,022	70.00	115	335	385	415	640	975	5,000	—
1902	21,380,777	2.40	2.70	4.50	6.75	20.00	60.00	95.00	575	1,450
1902O	4,500,000	2.70	4.50	12.00	23.00	42.00	110	370	4,500	—
1902S	2,070,000	5.00	14.00	49.00	65.00	95.00	145	370	3,300	—
1903	19,500,755	2.40	2.70	3.30	7.20	20.00	60.00	95.00	1,150	1,450
1903O	8,180,000	2.40	3.90	10.00	14.50	25.50	85.00	240	4,950	—
1903S	613,300	65.00	115	330	450	800	820	1,100	3,200	—
1904	14,601,027	2.75	3.00	6.00	8.00	20.00	60.00	105	2,250	1,450
1904S	800,000	34.00	58.50	140	190	265	450	720	4,300	—
1905	14,552,350	2.45	2.75	4.50	6.25	18.50	60.00	95.00	575	1,450
1905O	3,400,000	2.65	7.00	29.00	43.00	60.00	115	275	1,800	—
1905S	6,855,199	2.40	2.75	5.75	12.50	31.00	72.00	210	800	—
1906	19,958,406	1.75	2.10	3.25	5.50	20.00	60.00	95.00	575	1,450
1906D	4,060,000	2.40	2.75	5.75	12.50	28.50	72.00	165	1,550	—
1906O	2,610,000	4.25	11.00	43.00	62.50	85.00	130	200	1,250	—
1906S	3,136,640	2.10	4.25	10.00	16.00	38.00	90.00	230	1,250	—
1907	22,220,575	1.75	2.10	2.70	5.50	20.00	60.00	95.00	575	1,450
1907D	4,080,000	2.10	4.00	7.50	14.00	33.50	95.00	270	4,200	—
1907O	5,058,000	2.40	5.50	29.00	44.00	54.00	72.00	200	1,300	—
1907S	3,178,470	2.40	4.00	11.00	17.50	42.00	95.00	380	2,200	—
1908	10,600,545	2.10	2.40	3.30	5.50	20.00	60.00	95.00	575	1,450
1908D	7,490,000	2.10	2.40	4.50	9.00	27.50	60.00	125	950	—
1908O	1,789,000	4.50	11.00	42.00	53.00	72.00	135	290	1,850	—
1908S	3,220,000	2.10	3.70	9.00	15.00	35.00	150	300	2,000	—
1909	10,240,650	2.10	2.40	3.30	5.50	20.00	60.00	100.00	575	1,700
1909D	954,000	5.75	14.50	57.50	85.00	115	200	480	3,000	—
1909O	2,287,000	2.75	5.50	9.50	16.00	27.50	185	180	1,450	—
1909S	1,000,000	6.25	16.00	80.00	120	160	300	515	3,000	—
1910	11,520,551	1.70	2.10	3.30	8.50	20.00	60.00	95.00	575	1,450
1910D	3,490,000	2.00	3.90	7.50	15.00	36.00	90.00	210	1,500	—
1910S	1,240,000	5.00	8.00	47.00	68.50	90.00	155	420	2,200	—
1911	18,870,543	1.70	1.85	2.70	5.00	20.00	60.00	95.00	550	1,700
1911D	11,209,000	1.70	1.85	3.00	5.00	20.00	60.00	95.00	720	—
1911S	3,520,000	2.15	2.75	7.00	14.00	33.00	85.00	200	850	—
1912	19,350,700	1.70	1.85	2.75	5.00	20.00	60.00	95.00	550	1,700
1912D	11,760,000	1.70	1.85	3.20	5.50	20.00	60.00	95.00	550	—
1912S	3,420,000	1.70	2.10	5.00	10.00	28.00	87.50	160	850	—
1913	19,760,622	1.70	2.10	2.75	5.00	20.00	60.00	95.00	550	1,45
1913S	510,000	12.00	20.00	75.00	115	195	265	480	1,400	—
1914	17,360,655	1.70	1.85	2.75	5.50	20.00	60.00	95.00	550	1,70
1914D	11,908,000	1.80	1.85	3.50	5.50	20.00	60.00	95.00	550	—
1914S	2,100,000	2.10	2.70	7.20	14.50	35.00	72.00	145	1,000	—
1915	5,620,450	2.10	2.50	2.75	5.50	20.00	60.00	95.00	550	2,00
1915S	960,000	4.50	8.00	30.00	40.00	54.00	125	240	1,600	—
1916	18,490,000	1.70	2.25	3.00	7.00	20.00	60.00	95.00	540	—
1916S	5,820,000	1.70	2.25	4.00	6.50	20.00	60.00	95.00	850	—

Mercury.

Mint mark

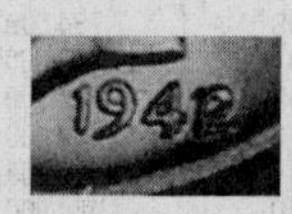

1942/41

KM# 140 **Designer:** Adolph A. Weinman. **Diameter:** 17.9 **Weight:** 2.5000 g. **Composition** 0.9000 Silver, 0.0724 oz. ASW. **Notes:** All specimens listed as -65FSB are for fully struc MS-65 coins with fully split and rounded horizontal bands on the fasces.

Date	Mintage	G-4	VG-8	F-12	VF-20	XF-40	MS-60	MS-65	Prf-65	-65F
1916	22,180,080	3.50	4.50	6.00	6.25	9.00	30.00	90.00	—	1
1916D	264,000	640	975	1,400	1,800	2,800	4,700	19,000	—	38,5
1916S	10,450,000	3.90	4.20	7.75	8.50	18.00	35.00	155	—	6
1917	55,230,000	1.85	2.00	2.50	5.00	7.50	30.00	155	—	4
1917D	9,402,000	3.90	5.00	10.00	21.50	42.00	120	1,100	—	6,0
1917S	27,330,000	1.80	2.00	3.50	5.75	10.00	62.00	470	—	1,1
1918	26,680,000	2.50	2.75	5.50	10.00	25.00	70.00	420	—	1,1
1918D	22,674,800	2.65	3.00	4.50	10.00	21.50	105	600	—	33,5
1918S	19,300,000	2.40	2.75	3.50	8.50	16.00	90.00	660	—	6,6
1919	35,740,000	1.85	2.00	3.00	5.00	10.00	37.00	320	—	7
1919D	9,939,000	3.50	6.00	11.00	21.50	35.00	175	1,400	—	38,5
1919S	8,850,000	2.75	3.00	8.00	15.00	31.00	175	1,000	—	13,0
1920	59,030,000	1.35	1.45	2.00	3.50	6.50	27.50	235	—	5
1920D	19,171,000	2.40	2.75	4.00	7.00	18.00	105	750	—	4,0
1920S	13,820,000	2.40	2.75	4.00	7.50	15.00	110	1,300	—	8,0
1921	1,230,000	33.00	54.00	90.00	200	470	1,000	3,200	—	4,0

Date	Mintage	G-4	VG-8	F-12	VF-20	XF-40	MS-60	MS-65	Prf-65	-65FSB
1921D	1,080,000	42.00	88.00	140	270	525	1,100	2,800	—	5,200
1923	50,130,000	1.20	1.60	2.00	3.50	6.00	27.50	110	—	295
1923S	6,440,000	2.40	2.75	7.00	12.50	65.00	160	1,150	—	6,900
1924	24,010,000	1.35	1.60	2.50	4.25	12.00	42.00	175	—	520
1924D	6,810,000	2.75	4.00	6.00	14.00	44.00	160	950	—	1,400
1924S	7,120,000	2.75	3.50	4.00	8.75	44.00	170	1,100	—	14,000
1925	25,610,000	1.15	1.45	2.00	3.75	7.50	27.00	195	—	1,000
1925D	5,117,000	4.00	4.25	11.50	38.00	110	350	1,750	—	3,500
1925S	5,850,000	2.40	2.75	7.00	12.50	65.00	175	1,400	—	4,400
1926	32,160,000	1.10	1.45	1.70	2.75	4.25	25.00	240	—	525
1926D	6,828,000	2.75	4.00	4.50	8.50	24.00	125	550	—	2,650
1926S	1,520,000	7.00	9.00	22.00	49.00	215	870	3,000	—	6,500
1927	28,080,000	1.10	1.45	1.75	3.50	4.50	26.00	125	—	400
1927D	4,812,000	2.75	5.00	7.25	18.50	65.00	175	1,200	—	8,500
1927S	4,770,000	2.10	3.50	4.75	8.00	23.00	280	1,400	—	7,700
1928	19,480,000	1.10	1.45	1.75	3.50	4.00	27.50	110	—	300
1928D	4,161,000	3.00	3.25	8.00	18.50	44.00	170	875	—	2,500
1928S	7,400,000	1.80	2.10	2.75	5.50	16.00	125	425	—	1,900
1929	25,970,000	1.35	1.60	1.95	2.75	4.00	20.00	60.00	—	265
1929D	5,034,000	1.80	3.00	3.50	6.25	14.50	25.00	70.00	—	225
1929S	4,730,000	1.35	1.60	2.00	4.00	7.00	32.50	120	—	525
1930	6,770,000	1.35	1.50	2.00	3.50	7.00	26.00	115	—	525
1930S	1,843,000	2.50	3.50	4.50	5.50	14.00	70.00	195	—	565
1931	3,150,000	2.10	2.50	2.75	4.25	8.75	35.00	135	—	725
1931D	1,260,000	6.00	7.00	10.00	15.00	28.00	85.00	210	—	350
1931S	1,800,000	2.40	2.75	4.00	6.25	11.50	85.00	210	—	2,100
1934	24,080,000	1.00	1.45	1.75	3.00	5.00	21.50	40.00	—	150
1934D	6,772,000	1.60	2.10	2.75	4.00	8.00	50.00	72.00	—	360
1935	58,830,000	0.80	1.00	1.50	2.15	4.25	8.00	30.00	—	70.00
1935D	10,477,000	1.25	1.75	2.50	3.75	7.50	34.00	72.00	—	600
1935S	15,840,000	1.00	1.50	1.75	3.00	5.50	24.00	31.50	—	500
1936	87,504,130	0.80	1.00	1.50	2.25	3.50	8.00	25.00	2,000	90.00
1936D	16,132,000	1.00	1.25	1.50	3.00	6.50	26.00	42.00	—	295
1936S	9,210,000	1.00	1.25	1.50	2.50	3.00	20.00	31.50	—	85.00
1937	56,865,756	0.80	1.00	1.50	2.00	3.25	8.00	23.00	800	42.00
1937D	14,146,000	1.00	1.25	1.50	3.00	5.50	21.00	43.00	—	100.00
1937S	9,740,000	1.00	1.25	1.50	3.00	5.50	24.00	34.00	—	195
1938	22,198,728	0.80	1.00	1.50	2.25	3.50	13.00	27.50	450	80.00
1938D	5,537,000	1.50	1.75	2.00	3.50	6.00	16.00	26.00	—	65.00
1938S	8,090,000	1.35	1.55	1.75	2.35	3.75	20.00	35.00	—	135
1939	67,749,321	0.80	1.00	1.50	2.00	3.25	8.50	25.00	425	170
1939D	24,394,000	1.00	1.25	1.50	2.00	3.50	7.50	26.00	—	45.00
1939S	10,540,000	1.25	1.50	2.00	2.50	4.25	21.00	35.00	—	750
1940	65,361,827	0.60	0.70	0.90	1.10	2.50	6.00	26.00	385	57.50
1940D	21,198,000	0.60	0.70	0.90	1.10	1.50	8.00	30.00	—	55.00
1940S	21,560,000	0.60	0.70	0.90	1.10	1.50	8.50	30.00	—	95.00
1941	175,106,557	0.60	0.70	0.90	1.10	1.50	5.00	30.00	385	42.00
1941D	45,634,000	0.60	0.70	0.90	1.10	1.50	8.00	23.00	—	40.00
1941S	43,090,000	0.60	0.70	0.90	1.10	1.50	7.00	30.00	—	50.00
1942	205,432,329	0.60	0.70	0.90	1.10	1.50	5.50	24.00	385	52.50
942/41	Inc. above	430	465	520	590	700	1,850	12,500	—	37,000
942D	60,740,000	0.60	0.70	0.90	1.10	1.50	8.00	27.50	—	40.00
942/41D	Inc. above	325	365	450	500	610	1,900	5,400	—	19,000
942S	49,300,000	0.60	0.70	0.90	1.10	1.50	9.50	24.00	—	140
943	191,710,000	0.60	0.70	0.90	1.10	1.50	5.50	30.00	—	50.00
943D	71,949,000	0.60	0.70	0.90	1.10	1.50	7.50	27.50	—	40.00
943S	60,400,000	0.60	0.70	0.90	1.10	1.50	8.25	25.00	—	66.00
944	231,410,000	0.60	0.70	0.90	1.10	1.50	5.50	23.00	—	80.00
944D	62,224,000	0.60	0.70	0.90	1.10	1.50	6.50	23.00	—	40.00
944S	49,490,000	0.60	0.70	0.90	1.10	1.50	6.50	30.00	—	50.00
945	159,130,000	0.60	0.70	0.90	1.10	1.50	5.50	23.00	—	8,000
945D	40,245,000	0.60	0.70	0.90	1.10	1.50	6.00	24.00	—	40.00
945S	41,920,000	0.60	0.70	0.90	1.10	1.50	6.50	24.00	—	135
945S micro	Inc. above	1.00	1.25	1.50	3.00	4.25	26.00	85.00	—	650

Roosevelt.

Mint mark 1946-64

M# 195 **Designer:** John R. Sinnock. **Diameter:** 17.9 **Weight:** 2.5000 g. **Composition:** 0.9000 Silver, 0.0724 oz. ASW.

te	Mintage	G-4	VG-8	F-12	VF-20	XF-40	AU-50	MS-60	MS-65	Prf-65
46	225,250,000	—	—	—	0.50	0.65	0.95	2.30	4.50	—
46D	61,043,500	—	—	—	0.50	0.65	1.10	1.75	8.00	—
46S	27,900,000	—	—	—	0.50	0.65	0.90	2.70	11.00	—
47	121,520,000	—	—	—	0.50	0.65	0.95	3.25	4.75	—
47D	46,835,000	—	—	—	0.50	0.95	1.50	4.50	11.00	—
47S	34,840,000	—	—	—	0.50	0.95	1.25	3.40	13.00	—
48	74,950,000	—	—	—	0.50	0.95	1.50	3.00	14.00	0.50
48D	52,841,000	—	—	—	0.50	1.20	2.00	3.00	10.00	—
48S	35,520,000	—	—	—	0.50	0.95	1.10	3.00	11.00	—
49.	30,940,000	—	—	—	1.00	1.50	4.00	21.50	40.00	—
49D	26,034,000	—	—	0.60	0.80	1.25	2.00	9.30	20.00	—
49S	13,510,000	—	1.00	1.25	1.50	2.75	6.00	33.50	60.00	—
0	50,181,500	—	—	—	0.50	0.95	1.35	6.40	12.00	37.00
0D	46,803,000	—	—	—	0.50	0.65	1.60	3.65	8.00	—
0S	20,440,000	—	0.85	1.00	1.10	1.25	6.00	34.50	50.00	—
1	102,937,602	—	—	—	0.50	0.85	1.00	1.25	3.50	26.00
1D	56,529,000	—	—	—	0.50	0.65	0.95	1.50	5.00	—
1S	31,630,000	—	—	—	0.75	1.05	3.25	8.75	24.00	—
2	99,122,073	—	—	—	0.50	0.90	1.10	1.35	5.00	29.00
2D	122,100,000	—	—	—	0.50	0.65	0.95	1.35	5.00	—
2S	44,419,500	—	—	—	0.75	1.05	1.50	4.25	11.00	—
3	53,618,920	—	—	—	0.50	0.65	1.00	2.15	5.00	24.00
3D	136,433,000	—	—	—	0.50	0.65	0.95	2.15	5.00	—
3S	39,180,000	—	—	—	0.50	0.65	0.75	1.00	4.00	—

Date	Mintage	G-4	VG-8	F-12	VF-20	XF-40	AU-50	MS-60	MS-65	Prf-65
1954	114,243,503	—	—	—	0.50	0.65	0.75	1.00	4.00	11.00
1954D	106,397,000	—	—	—	0.50	0.65	0.75	1.00	3.25	—
1954S	22,860,000	—	—	—	0.50	0.65	0.80	1.00	3.25	—
1955	12,828,381	—	—	—	0.70	0.80	0.85	1.00	5.00	15.00
1955D	13,959,000	—	—	—	0.50	0.55	0.60	0.90	3.50	—
1955S	18,510,000	—	—	—	0.50	0.60	0.65	0.90	4.50	—
1956	109,309,384	—	—	—	0.50	0.50	0.60	0.70	2.50	2.50
1956D	108,015,100	—	—	—	0.50	0.50	0.60	0.70	2.50	—
1957	161,407,952	—	—	—	0.50	0.50	0.60	0.70	2.50	2.00
1957D	113,354,330	—	—	—	0.50	0.50	0.60	0.70	3.50	—
1958	32,785,652	—	—	—	0.50	0.50	0.60	0.70	3.80	2.00
1958D	136,564,600	—	—	—	0.50	0.50	0.60	0.70	3.50	—
1959	86,929,291	—	—	—	0.50	0.50	0.60	0.70	2.50	2.00
1959D	164,919,790	—	—	—	0.50	0.50	0.60	0.70	3.00	—
1960	72,081,602	—	—	—	0.50	0.50	0.60	0.70	2.50	2.00
1960D	200,160,400	—	—	—	0.50	0.50	0.60	0.70	2.50	—
1961	96,758,244	—	—	—	0.50	0.50	0.60	0.70	2.35	2.00
1961D	209,146,550	—	—	—	0.50	0.50	0.60	0.70	2.35	—
1962	75,668,019	—	—	—	0.50	0.50	0.60	0.70	2.35	2.00
1962D	334,948,380	—	—	—	0.50	0.50	0.60	0.70	2.75	—
1963	126,725,645	—	—	—	0.50	0.50	0.60	0.70	2.35	2.00
1963D	421,476,530	—	—	—	0.50	0.50	0.60	0.70	2.35	—
1964	933,310,762	—	—	—	0.50	0.50	0.60	0.70	2.35	2.00
1964D	1,357,517,180	—	—	—	0.50	0.50	0.60	0.70	2.35	—

Roosevelt.

Mint mark 1968 - Present

1982 No mint mark

KM# 195a **Designer:** John R. Sinnock. **Diameter:** 17.9 **Weight:** 2.2700 g. **Composition:** Copper-Nickel Clad Copper. **Notes:** The 1979-S and 1981-S Type II proofs have clearer mint marks than the Type I proofs of those years. On the 1982 no-mint-mark variety, the mint mark was inadvertently left off.

Date	Mintage	MS-65	Prf-65	Date	Mintage	MS-65	Prf-65
1965	1,652,140,570	1.00	—	1985S	(3,362,821)	—	1.10
1966	1,382,734,540	0.80	—	1986P	682,649,693	1.70	—
1967	2,244,007,320	0.80	—	1986D	473,326,970	1.60	—
1968	424,470,000	0.70	—	1986S	(3,010,497)	—	2.50
1968D	480,748,280	0.80	—	1987P	762,709,481	0.75	—
1968S	(3,041,506)	—	0.75	1987D	653,203,402	0.75	—
1969	145,790,000	2.00	—	1987S	(4,227,728)	—	1.50
1969D	563,323,870	1.00	—	1988P	1,030,550,000	0.80	—
1969S	(2,934,631)	—	0.65	1988D	962,385,488	0.80	—
1970	345,570,000	0.70	—	1988S	(3,262,948)	—	3.50
1970D	754,942,100	0.70	—	1989P	1,298,400,000	0.50	—
1970S	(2,632,810)	—	0.65	1989D	896,535,597	0.50	—
1971	162,690,000	1.00	—	1989S	(3,220,194)	—	4.00
1971D	377,914,240	0.80	—	1990P	1,034,340,000	1.00	—
1971S	(3,220,733)	—	0.60	1990D	839,995,824	0.80	—
1972	431,540,000	0.70	—	1990S	(3,299,559)	—	2.75
1972D	330,290,000	0.60	—	1991P	927,220,000	0.80	—
1972S	(3,260,996)	—	1.00	1991D	601,241,114	1.00	—
1973	315,670,000	0.70	—	1991S	(2,867,787)	—	3.25
1973D	455,032,426	0.75	—	1992P	593,500,000	0.75	—
1973S	(2,760,339)	—	1.00	1992D	616,273,932	0.80	—
1974	470,248,000	0.70	—	1992S	(2,858,981)	—	4.00
1974D	571,083,000	0.70	—	1993P	766,180,000	0.80	—
1974S	(2,612,568)	—	1.00	1993D	750,110,166	0.80	—
1975	585,673,900	0.70	—	1993S	(2,633,439)	—	6.00
1975D	313,705,300	0.75	—	1994P	1,189,000,000	0.80	—
1975S	(2,845,450)	—	1.25	1994D	1,303,268,110	0.80	—
1976	568,760,000	0.80	—	1994S	(2,484,594)	—	4.50
1976D	695,222,774	0.80	—	1995P	1,125,500,000	0.80	—
1976S	(4,149,730)	—	1.00	1995D	1,274,890,000	1.20	—
1977	796,930,000	0.70	—	1995S	(2,010,384)	—	20.00
1977D	376,607,228	0.70	—	1996P	1,421,163,000	0.75	—
1977S	(3,251,152)	—	1.00	1996D	1,400,300,000	0.75	—
1978	663,980,000	0.70	—	1996W	1,457,949	15.00	—
1978D	282,847,540	0.70	—	1996S	(2,085,191)	—	2.50
1978S	(3,127,781)	—	1.00	1997P	991,640,000	0.75	—
1979	315,440,000	0.70	—	1997D	979,810,000	0.75	—
1979D	390,921,184	0.70	—	1997S	(1,975,000)	—	6.50
1979 type I	—	—	1.00	1998P	1,163,000,000	0.80	—
1979S type I	(3,677,175)	—	1.00	1998D	1,172,250,000	0.80	—
1979S type II	Inc. above	—	1.25	1998S	(2,078,494)	—	3.50
1980P	735,170,000	0.70	—	1999P	2,164,000,000	0.80	—
1980D	719,354,321	0.70	—	1999D	1,397,750,000	0.80	—
1980S	(3,554,806)	—	1.00	1999S	(2,557,897)	—	3.00
1981P	676,650,000	0.70	—	2000P	1,842,500,000	0.80	—
1981D	712,284,143	0.70	—	2000D	1,818,700,000	0.75	—
1981S type I	—	—	1.00	2000S	(3,097,440)	—	2.00
1981S type II	—	—	4.00	2001P	1,369,590,000	0.80	—
1982P	519,475,000	5.00	—	2001D	1,412,800,000	0.75	—
1982 no mint mark	—	200	—	2001S	(2,249,496)	—	3.00
1982D	542,713,584	3.00	—	2002P	1,187,500,000	0.50	—
1982S	(3,857,479)	—	1.20	2002D	1,379,500,000	0.50	—
1983P	647,025,000	6.00	—	2002S	—	—	2.00
1983D	730,129,224	2.00	—	2003P	—	0.50	—
1983S	(3,279,126)	—	1.10	2003D	—	0.50	—
1984P	856,669,000	0.80	—	2003S	—	—	2.00
1984D	704,803,976	0.90	—				
1984S	(3,065,110)	—	1.60				
1985P	705,200,962	0.80	—				
1985D	587,979,970	0.80	—				

Roosevelt.

KM# A195 **Composition:** Silver.

Date	Mintage	Prf-65	Date	Mintage	Prf-65
1992S	(1,317,579)	4.50	1998S	(878,792)	5.50
1993S	(761,353)	6.00	1999S	(804,565)	5.00
1994S	(785,329)	6.00	2000S	(965,921)	4.50
1995S	(838,953)	18.00	2001S	(849,600)	4.50
1996S	(830,021)	6.00	2002S	—	4.50
1997S	(821,678)	17.50	2003S	—	—

QUARTER

Barber.

KM# 114 **Designer:** Charles E. Barber. **Diameter:** 24.3 **Weight:** 6.2500 g. **Composition:** 0.9000 Silver, 0.1809 oz. ASW. **Notes:** Commonly called "Barber quarter."

Date	Mintage	G-4	VG-8	F-12	VF-20	XF-40	AU-50	MS-60	MS-65	Prf-65
1892	8,237,245	5.00	7.50	21.50	32.50	65.00	115	180	1,100	2,000
1892O	2,640,000	5.75	11.00	30.00	38.00	72.00	135	290	1,600	—
1892S	964,079	16.00	32.00	60.00	80.00	115	265	450	4,700	—
1893	5,484,838	5.00	7.00	22.50	31.50	65.00	115	200	1,700	2,000
1893O	3,396,000	5.00	7.50	25.00	40.00	72.00	145	265	1,850	—
1893S	1,454,535	11.00	20.00	65.00	80.00	110	265	465	8,000	—
1894	3,432,972	5.00	7.50	27.50	40.00	77.00	135	240	1,550	2,000
1894O	2,852,000	5.00	9.00	31.50	50.00	85.00	195	330	2,250	—
1894S	2,648,821	6.25	9.00	31.50	47.00	85.00	175	300	3,300	—
1895	4,440,880	5.00	6.25	24.00	31.50	65.00	135	220	1,850	2,000
1895O	2,816,000	5.00	10.00	35.00	50.00	85.00	200	390	2,650	—
1895S	1,764,681	9.00	15.00	43.00	72.00	95.00	210	360	3,850	—
1896	3,874,762	5.00	6.25	21.50	33.00	65.00	135	230	1,600	2,000
1896O	1,484,000	7.50	21.50	80.00	210	335	625	825	7,500	—
1896S	188,039	390	600	885	1,250	2,500	3,800	5,400	27,000	—
1897	8,140,731	5.00	6.00	20.00	31.50	65.00	115	180	1,100	2,000
1897O	1,414,800	8.00	21.50	75.00	180	335	600	800	3,600	—
1897S	542,229	50.00	70.00	175	235	335	600	950	6,700	—
1898	11,100,735	5.00	5.50	21.50	31.50	65.00	115	180	1,100	2,000
1898O	1,868,000	6.00	14.00	57.50	110	215	370	600	10,000	—
1898S	1,020,592	6.50	15.00	40.00	48.00	65.00	180	400	7,000	—
1899	12,624,846	5.00	5.50	19.00	32.00	65.00	115	180	1,100	2,000
1899O	2,644,000	5.00	11.50	26.50	43.00	85.00	250	380	3,500	—
1899S	708,000	13.00	28.00	60.00	75.00	100.00	225	400	3,650	—
1900	10,016,912	5.50	6.50	19.00	31.50	65.00	135	180	1,100	2,000
1900O	3,416,000	7.50	20.00	55.00	95.00	115	330	550	3,600	—
1900S	1,858,585	6.50	11.50	35.00	49.00	65.00	115	360	5,000	—
1901	8,892,813	6.50	7.00	19.00	31.50	65.00	110	180	2,200	2,200
1901O	1,612,000	27.50	40.00	95.00	185	335	625	800	5,750	—
1901S	72,664	2,600	4,700	6,400	8,200	10,700	14,500	27,500	47,000	—
1902	12,197,744	5.50	6.50	16.00	30.00	65.00	110	180	1,000	2,100
1902O	4,748,000	5.50	12.00	36.00	56.00	100.00	180	385	4,700	—
1902S	1,524,612	8.00	13.50	37.00	60.00	85.00	190	510	3,400	—
1903	9,670,064	5.50	6.50	16.00	30.00	65.00	110	180	2,500	2,000
1903O	3,500,000	5.50	7.00	32.00	48.00	85.00	230	400	5,500	—
1903S	1,036,000	12.00	20.00	40.00	65.00	100.00	260	425	2,800	—
1904	9,588,813	5.50	6.50	16.00	31.50	65.00	110	180	1,400	2,000
1904O	2,456,000	6.25	12.00	45.00	75.00	175	375	775	3,100	—
1905	4,968,250	5.50	6.50	21.50	32.00	65.00	110	180	1,650	2,000
1905O	1,230,000	10.00	20.00	72.00	125	195	340	465	6,500	—
1905S	1,884,000	6.25	11.50	34.00	50.00	90.00	200	325	3,600	—
1906	3,656,435	5.50	6.50	16.00	30.00	65.00	110	170	1,000	2,000
1906D	3,280,000	5.50	6.50	22.00	37.50	65.00	145	210	2,100	—
1906O	2,056,000	5.50	8.50	33.50	47.50	85.00	185	285	1,200	—
1907	7,192,575	5.00	6.00	16.00	30.00	65.00	110	180	1,100	2,000
1907D	2,484,000	5.00	7.50	25.00	44.00	80.00	175	240	2,650	—
1907O	4,560,000	5.00	6.50	16.00	31.50	65.00	135	195	2,400	—
1907S	1,360,000	6.00	9.50	37.00	56.00	100.00	250	440	3,450	—
1908	4,232,545	4.50	5.50	18.00	30.00	65.00	110	195	1,100	2,200
1908D	5,788,000	4.50	5.50	16.00	29.00	65.00	115	215	1,750	—
1908O	6,244,000	4.50	6.50	16.00	29.00	72.00	120	195	1,100	—
1908S	784,000	12.00	28.00	70.00	110	235	415	700	5,200	—
1909	9,268,650	4.50	5.50	16.00	29.00	65.00	110	180	1,100	2,000
1909D	5,114,000	4.50	5.50	17.00	30.00	65.00	145	195	2,300	—
1909O	712,000	12.50	31.50	80.00	175	290	460	800	8,700	—
1909S	1,348,000	5.00	6.25	27.50	42.00	65.00	180	275	2,400	—
1910	2,244,551	5.00	6.50	23.00	33.50	65.00	140	190	1,175	2,000
1910D	1,500,000	5.75	7.00	37.00	56.00	98.00	235	335	2,200	—
1911	3,720,543	5.00	6.00	16.00	31.50	72.00	120	180	1,100	2,000
1911D	933,600	6.00	15.00	75.00	185	300	450	630	6,000	—
1911S	988,000	5.00	7.50	45.00	57.50	135	300	375	1,500	—
1912	4,400,700	5.00	6.00	16.00	32.00	65.00	110	180	1,100	2,000
1912S	708,000	6.00	7.00	40.00	57.50	95.00	220	375	2,700	—
1913	484,613	9.50	18.00	65.00	145	380	480	900	4,200	2,200
1913D	1,450,800	6.00	9.50	30.00	45.00	75.00	160	265	1,150	—
1913S	40,000	580	875	2,100	3,200	4,200	4,700	5,800	14,000	—
1914	6,244,610	4.50	5.50	16.00	26.50	55.00	110	180	1,100	2,200
1914D	3,046,000	4.50	5.50	16.00	26.50	56.00	110	180	1,100	—
1914S	264,000	58.00	80.00	150	190	390	585	850	3,500	—
1915	3,480,450	4.50	5.50	16.00	26.50	65.00	110	180	1,100	2,200
1915D	3,694,000	4.50	5.50	16.00	26.50	65.00	110	180	1,100	—
1915S	704,000	6.00	7.00	23.50	37.50	75.00	185	225	1,100	—
1916	1,788,000	4.50	5.50	16.00	26.50	54.00	110	180	1,100	—
1916D	6,540,800	4.50	5.50	16.00	26.50	54.00	110	180	1,100	—

Standing Liberty. Right breast exposed; Type 1.

KM# 141 **Designer:** Hermon A. MacNeil. **Diameter:** 24.3 **Weight:** 6.2500 g. **Composition:** 0.9000 Silver, 0.1809 oz. ASW.

Date	Mintage	G-4	VG-8	F-12	VF-20	XF-40	AU-50	MS-60	MS-65	-65FH
1916	52,000	1,750	2,400	3,500	4,900	6,100	6,700	8,000	14,500	24,000
1917	8,792,000	20.00	32.00	44.00	56.00	80.00	165	195	750	1,300
1917D	1,509,200	22.50	33.00	45.00	57.50	95.00	165	200	950	1,900
1917S	1,952,000	25.00	33.00	45.00	70.00	135	195	215	1,250	2,600

Standing Liberty. Right breast covered; Type 2. Three stars below eagle.

Mint mark

KM# 145 **Designer:** Hermon A. MacNeil. **Diameter:** 24.3 **Weight:** 6.2500 g. **Composition:** 0.9000 Silver, 0.1809 oz. ASW.

Date	Mintage	G-4	VG-8	F-12	VF-20	XF-40	AU-50	MS-60	MS-65	-65F
1917	13,880,000	17.50	20.00	27.00	29.00	44.00	80.00	125	530	80
1917D	6,224,400	37.50	41.00	65.00	67.50	90.00	125	195	1,200	3,40
1917S	5,522,000	35.00	44.00	61.00	67.00	77.00	105	180	1,150	3,30
1918	14,240,000	15.00	17.50	27.50	30.00	45.00	80.00	125	485	1,70
1918D	7,380,000	22.00	30.00	45.00	62.50	80.00	130	200	1,200	4,50
1918S	11,072,000	16.00	21.00	30.00	35.00	46.50	80.00	175	1,200	9,00
1918/17S	Inc. above	1,100	1,350	2,150	2,800	4,700	8,800	12,500	90,000	300,00
1919	11,324,000	31.00	41.50	52.50	55.00	70.00	100.00	135	500	1,45
1919D	1,944,000	70.00	95.00	145	230	350	480	575	2,400	22,00
1919S	1,836,000	67.00	95.00	160	255	470	520	700	3,100	25,00
1920	27,860,000	12.50	15.00	24.00	27.50	38.00	70.00	120	480	1,9
1920D	3,586,400	42.00	49.00	75.00	90.00	110	165	235	2,000	6,2
1920S	6,380,000	16.00	22.00	28.00	36.00	55.00	100.00	220	2,400	18,5
1921	1,916,000	110	135	180	250	325	380	485	1,525	3,9
1923	9,716,000	13.50	15.00	27.00	30.00	39.00	63.50	125	560	4,0
1923S	1,360,000	230	340	420	520	560	640	750	1,750	4,0
1924	10,920,000	13.50	16.00	21.00	25.00	35.00	73.00	120	450	1,4
1924D	3,112,000	48.00	58.50	77.00	80.00	95.00	125	150	485	4,2
1924S	2,860,000	24.00	28.00	37.50	40.00	90.00	180	250	1,800	5,2
1925	12,280,000	2.50	3.00	4.25	12.50	32.00	68.00	110	450	8
1926	11,316,000	2.50	3.00	4.00	10.00	30.00	63.00	100.00	450	1,8
1926D	1,716,000	5.00	9.00	14.00	26.50	50.00	85.00	135	450	19,0
1926S	2,700,000	3.00	4.00	10.00	20.00	100.00	220	300	2,100	25,0
1927	11,912,000	2.50	3.00	4.00	10.00	30.00	65.00	100.00	450	9
1927D	976,400	6.50	9.00	12.50	35.00	82.50	140	160	2,400	2,5
1927S	396,000	11.00	12.50	50.00	165	1,000	2,750	4,000	9,500	175,0
1928	6,336,000	2.50	3.00	4.25	11.50	29.00	65.00	100.00	450	1,3
1928D	1,627,600	3.50	5.00	8.00	18.00	37.50	75.00	125	450	5,0
1928S	2,644,000	3.00	4.00	6.00	14.00	32.00	72.00	125	450	[illegible]
1929	11,140,000	2.50	3.00	4.00	11.50	30.00	65.00	100.00	450	[illegible]
1929D	1,358,000	3.50	5.00	6.00	14.00	34.00	72.00	125	450	5,2
1929S	1,764,000	3.00	3.50	4.50	14.00	30.00	70.00	125	450	[illegible]
1930	5,632,000	2.50	3.00	4.00	10.00	30.00	65.00	100.00	450	[illegible]
1930S	1,556,000	3.50	4.50	5.00	11.00	30.00	70.00	110	450	[illegible]

Washington.

Mint mark 1932-64

KM# 164 **Designer:** John Flanagan. **Diameter:** 24.3 **Weight:** 6.2500 g. **Composition:** 0.9[illegible] Silver, 0.1809 oz. ASW.

Date	Mintage	G-4	VG-8	F-12	VF-20	XF-40	AU-50	MS-60	MS-65	P[illegible]
1932	5,404,000	3.75	5.25	6.00	7.50	9.50	14.50	22.00	400	
1932D	436,800	85.00	95.00	115	130	185	360	880	15,000	
1932S	408,000	90.00	100.00	105	115	140	160	365	5,500	
1934	31,912,052	2.00	2.25	2.50	3.00	4.00	9.00	25.00	80.00	

	Mintage	G-4	VG-8	F-12	VF-20	XF-40	AU-50	MS-60	MS-65	Prf-65
	3,527,200	3.75	5.50	6.50	10.00	15.00	80.00	210	1,450	—
	32,484,000	1.75	2.00	2.50	2.75	4.00	8.00	21.00	70.00	—
)	5,780,000	2.00	3.00	5.00	10.00	18.50	125	240	800	—
S	5,660,000	2.00	2.50	4.75	5.75	12.00	32.50	80.00	300	—
	41,303,837	1.75	2.00	2.25	2.75	3.50	8.50	21.00	70.00	1,050
	5,374,000	2.50	3.25	4.75	15.00	44.00	220	420	950	—
S	3,828,000	1.75	2.00	3.50	5.00	11.00	45.00	90.00	350	—
	19,701,542	1.75	2.00	3.00	3.50	4.00	16.00	22.00	90.00	380
)	7,189,600	2.00	2.50	3.00	4.50	12.00	28.00	60.00	135	—
S	1,652,000	3.00	4.00	5.00	11.00	18.50	85.00	125	275	—
	9,480,045	4.00	4.50	5.00	6.00	13.50	35.00	70.00	180	225
S	2,832,000	4.50	5.00	5.50	7.00	14.00	38.00	72.00	175	—
	33,548,795	1.75	2.00	2.25	2.50	3.50	7.00	14.00	55.00	150
)	7,092,000	2.00	2.25	3.25	4.00	8.00	16.00	34.00	85.00	—
S	2,628,000	3.00	3.25	3.50	5.00	12.00	45.00	72.00	215	—
	35,715,246	1.75	2.00	2.25	2.50	3.00	6.50	15.00	65.00	150
)	2,797,600	2.00	2.50	6.00	8.50	18.00	55.00	95.00	215	—
S	8,244,000	1.75	2.25	4.75	5.00	6.50	14.00	24.00	55.00	—
	79,047,287	—	—	1.65	1.75	2.50	4.00	9.00	43.00	110
D	16,714,800	—	—	1.75	2.25	3.50	7.50	35.00	110	—
S	16,080,000	—	—	1.75	2.25	3.25	6.50	30.00	85.00	—
	102,117,123	—	—	1.65	1.75	2.50	3.00	6.00	37.50	110
)	17,487,200	—	—	1.75	2.50	3.75	7.00	22.50	65.00	—
S	19,384,000	—	—	2.00	3.00	5.50	16.00	75.00	240	—
	99,700,000	—	—	1.50	1.75	2.10	2.75	5.00	45.00	—
D	16,095,600	—	—	1.75	2.25	4.00	7.00	27.50	75.00	—
S	21,700,000	—	—	1.75	2.25	5.50	11.00	27.50	75.00	—
	104,956,000	—	—	1.50	1.75	2.10	2.85	5.00	44.00	—
D	14,600,800	—	—	1.75	2.50	3.75	8.00	13.00	45.00	—
S	12,560,000	—	—	1.85	2.75	4.00	9.00	14.00	45.00	—
	74,372,000	—	—	1.50	1.75	2.10	2.85	4.50	44.00	—
D	12,341,600	—	—	1.75	3.00	6.00	10.50	16.00	50.00	—
S	17,004,001	—	—	1.65	2.50	3.75	6.00	10.00	45.00	—
	53,436,000	—	—	1.50	1.85	2.25	2.75	5.00	42.00	—
D	9,072,800	—	—	1.50	1.85	2.25	2.75	5.00	42.00	—
S	4,204,000	—	—	1.65	2.00	3.00	4.00	7.00	42.00	—
	22,556,000	—	—	1.65	2.25	2.75	3.50	12.50	55.00	—
D	15,338,400	—	—	1.65	2.25	2.50	2.75	11.00	45.00	—
S	5,532,000	—	—	1.65	2.25	2.75	3.00	10.00	45.00	—
	35,196,000	—	—	1.65	1.85	2.25	2.75	3.50	40.00	—
D	16,766,800	—	—	1.65	1.85	2.25	2.75	10.00	45.00	—
S	15,960,000	—	—	1.75	1.95	2.50	3.00	6.00	50.00	—
	9,312,000	—	—	1.65	2.50	4.50	14.00	36.00	80.00	—
D	10,068,400	—	—	1.60	2.25	4.00	5.00	20.00	70.00	—
	24,971,512	—	—	1.50	1.65	1.75	2.10	4.50	28.00	55.00
0D	21,075,600	—	—	1.65	1.85	2.10	2.40	3.50	30.00	—
0D/S	Inc. above	22.00	25.00	36.00	60.00	150	225	275	650	—
S	10,284,004	—	—	1.65	1.85	2.40	4.50	7.50	30.00	—
S/D	Inc. above	22.00	25.00	36.00	60.00	185	315	400	750	—
	43,505,602	—	—	1.50	1.65	1.75	2.25	7.00	40.00	40.00
D	35,354,800	—	—	1.50	1.75	2.00	2.25	6.50	35.00	—
S	9,048,000	—	—	1.50	1.75	3.75	7.00	22.00	65.00	—
2	38,862,073	—	—	1.50	1.65	1.75	2.25	6.50	35.00	37.00
2D	49,795,200	—	—	1.50	1.65	1.75	2.25	5.00	28.00	—
2S	13,707,800	—	—	1.50	1.75	3.25	7.00	17.50	45.00	—
3	18,664,920	—	—	1.50	1.65	1.75	2.10	7.50	30.00	25.00
3D	56,112,400	—	—	1.50	1.65	1.75	1.95	3.00	25.00	—
3S	14,016,000	—	—	1.50	1.75	2.10	2.75	4.50	28.00	—
4	54,645,503	—	—	—	1.50	1.65	1.75	6.50	30.00	13.00
4D	42,305,500	—	—	—	1.50	1.65	1.75	4.50	28.00	—
4S	11,834,722	—	—	—	1.50	1.75	2.00	4.00	25.00	—
5	18,558,381	—	—	—	1.65	1.75	2.00	3.00	25.00	14.00
5D	3,182,400	—	—	2.00	2.25	2.50	2.75	2.50	25.00	—
6	44,813,384	—	—	—	1.65	1.85	2.00	3.50	22.00	4.00
6D	32,334,500	—	—	—	1.75	1.85	2.10	3.00	24.00	—
7	47,779,952	—	—	—	1.65	1.75	1.95	2.75	26.00	4.00
7D	77,924,160	—	—	—	1.65	1.75	1.95	2.25	20.00	—
8	7,235,652	—	—	—	1.65	1.75	2.00	2.00	20.00	6.00
8D	78,124,900	—	—	—	1.65	1.75	1.95	2.25	20.00	—
9	25,533,291	—	—	—	1.65	1.75	1.95	2.25	20.00	4.25
9D	62,054,232	—	—	—	1.65	1.75	1.95	2.25	20.00	—
0	30,855,602	—	—	—	1.65	1.75	1.95	2.25	17.00	3.75
0D	63,000,324	—	—	—	1.65	1.75	1.95	2.25	17.00	—
1	40,064,244	—	—	—	1.65	1.75	1.95	2.50	18.00	3.50
1D	83,656,928	—	—	—	1.65	1.75	1.95	2.25	16.00	—
2	39,374,019	—	—	—	1.65	1.75	1.95	2.50	18.00	3.50
2D	127,554,756	—	—	—	1.65	1.75	1.95	2.25	16.00	—
3	77,391,645	—	—	—	1.50	1.60	1.75	1.95	15.00	3.50
3D	135,288,184	—	—	—	1.50	1.60	1.75	1.95	15.00	—
4	564,341,347	—	—	—	1.50	1.60	1.75	1.95	15.00	3.50
4D	704,135,528	—	—	—	1.50	1.60	1.75	1.95	15.00	—

Washington.

M# 164a Designer: John Flanagan. **Diameter:** 24.3 **Weight:** 5.6700 g. **Composition:** Copper-Nickel Clad Copper.

e	Mintage	MS-65	Prf-65	Date	Mintage	MS-65	Prf-65
5	1,819,717,540	2.75	—	1971S	(3,220,733)	—	1.05
6	821,101,500	2.75	—	1972	215,048,000	2.00	—
7	1,524,031,848	2.75	—	1972D	311,067,732	2.00	—
8	220,731,500	2.75	—	1972S	(3,260,996)	—	1.10
8D	101,534,000	3.00	—	1973	346,924,000	2.00	—
8S	(3,041,506)	—	1.00	1973D	232,977,400	2.25	—
9	176,212,000	4.50	—	1973S	(2,760,339)	—	1.00
9D	114,372,000	3.00	—	1974	801,456,000	2.00	—
9S	(2,934,631)	—	1.25	1974D	353,160,300	2.25	—
0	136,420,000	2.50	—	1974S	(2,612,568)	—	1.25
0D	417,341,364	2.25	—	1975 none minted	—	—	—
0S	(2,632,810)	—	1.00	1975D none minted	—	—	—
1	109,284,000	2.25	—	1975S none minted	—	—	—
1D	258,634,428	2.25	—				

Washington. Bicentennial design, drummer boy.

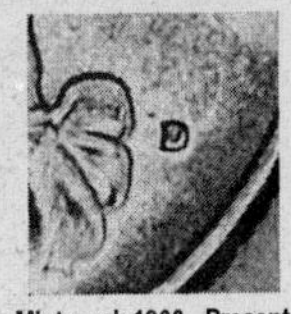

Mint mark 1968 - Present

KM# 204 Rev. Designer: Jack L. Ahr. **Diameter:** 24.3 **Weight:** 5.6700 g. **Composition:** Copper-Nickel Clad Copper.

Date	Mintage	G-4	VG-8	F-12	VF-20	XF-40	MS-60	MS-65	Prf-65
1976	809,784,016	—	—	—	—	—	0.95	1.75	—
1976D	860,118,839	—	—	—	—	—	0.95	1.75	—
1976S	(4,149,730)	—	—	—	—	—	—	—	1.00

Washington. Bicentennial design, drummer boy.

KM# 204a Rev. Designer: Jack L. Ahr. **Diameter:** 24.3 **Weight:** 5.7500 g. **Composition:** Silver Clad, 0.074 oz.

Date	Mintage	G-4	VG-8	F-12	VF-20	XF-40	MS-60	MS-65	Prf-65
1976S	4,908,319(3,998,621)	—	—	—	—	—	1.25	1.75	2.00

Washington. Regular design resumed.

KM# A164a Diameter: 24.3 **Weight:** 5.6700 g. **Composition:** Copper-Nickel Clad Copper. **Notes:** KM#164 design and composition resumed. The 1979-S and 1981 Type II proofs have clearer mint marks than the Type I proofs for those years.

Date	Mintage	MS-65	Prf-65	Date	Mintage	MS-65	Prf-65
1977	468,556,000	1.00	—	1987S	(4,227,728)	—	1.50
1977D	256,524,978	1.00	—	1988P	562,052,000	3.00	—
1977S	(3,251,152)	—	1.10	1988D	596,810,688	1.50	—
1978	521,452,000	1.00	—	1988S	(3,262,948)	—	2.10
1978D	287,373,152	1.00	—	1989P	512,868,000	1.50	—
1978S	(3,127,781)	—	1.20	1989D	896,535,597	1.50	—
1979	515,708,000	1.00	—	1989S	(3,220,194)	—	2.10
1979D	489,789,780	1.00	—	1990P	613,792,000	1.00	—
1979S T-I	—	—	1.00	1990D	927,638,181	1.00	—
1979S T-II	—	—	1.50	1990S	(3,299,559)	—	5.00
1980P	635,832,000	1.00	—	1991P	570,968,000	1.00	—
1980D	518,327,487	1.00	—	1991D	630,966,693	1.00	—
1980S	(3,554,806)	—	1.15	1991S	(2,867,787)	—	2.50
1981P	601,716,000	1.00	—	1992P	384,764,000	1.00	—
1981D	575,722,833	1.00	—	1992D	389,777,107	1.35	—
1981S T-I	—	—	1.10	1992S	(2,858,981)	—	3.00
1981S T-II	—	—	3.00	1993P	639,276,000	1.20	—
1982P	500,931,000	6.50	—	1993D	645,476,128	1.50	—
1982D	480,042,788	3.00	—	1993S	(2,633,439)	—	5.00
1982S	(3,857,479)	—	2.00	1994P	825,600,000	1.25	—
1983P	673,535,000	30.00	—	1994D	880,034,110	1.25	—
1983D	617,806,446	20.00	—	1994S	(2,484,594)	—	4.00
1983S	(3,279,126)	—	2.25	1995P	1,004,336,000	1.20	—
1984P	676,545,000	1.75	—	1995D	1,103,216,000	1.20	—
1984D	546,483,064	2.50	—	1995S	(2,010,384)	—	20.00
1984S	(3,065,110)	—	2.40	1996P	925,040,000	1.20	—
1985P	775,818,962	3.50	—	1996S	—	—	4.00
1985D	519,962,888	5.00	—	1996D	906,868,000	1.20	—
1985S	(3,362,821)	5.00	1.45	1997P	595,740,000	1.25	—
1986P	551,199,333	6.00	—	1997D	599,680,000	1.25	—
1986D	504,298,660	10.00	—	1997S	(1,975,000)	—	10.00
1986S	(3,010,497)	—	2.25	1998P	896,268,000	1.00	—
1987P	582,499,481	1.00	—	1998D	821,000,000	1.00	—
1987D	655,594,696	1.00	—	1998S	—	—	10.00

Washington.

KM# A164b Composition: Silver.

Date	Mintage	Prf-65	Date	Mintage	Prf-65
1992S	(1,317,579)	7.00	1996S	—	18.00
1993S	(761,353)	6.00	1997S	—	7.00
1994S	(785,329)	9.50	1998S	—	9.00
1995S	(838,953)	18.00			

50 State Quarters

Delaware

KM# 290 Diameter: 24.3 **Weight:** 5.6700 g. **Composition:** Copper-Nickel Clad Copper.

Date	Mintage	MS-63	MS-65	Prf-65
1999P	373,400,000	1.25	1.50	—
1999D	401,424,000	1.25	1.50	—
1999S	(3,713,359)	—	—	10.00

KM# 290a Composition: 0.9000 Silver.

Date	Mintage	MS-63	MS-65	Prf-65
1999S	(804,565)	—	—	40.00

Pennsylvania

KM# 291 **Diameter:** 24.3 **Weight:** 5.6700 g. **Composition:** Copper-Nickel Clad Copper.

Date	Mintage	MS-63	MS-65	Prf-65
1999P	349,000,000	1.50	2.00	—
1999D	358,332,000	1.25	1.50	—
1999S	(3,713,359)	—	—	10.00

KM# 291a **Composition:** 0.9000 Silver.

Date	Mintage	MS-63	MS-65	Prf-65
1999S	(804,565)	—	—	40.00

New Jersey

KM# 292 **Composition:** Copper-Nickel Clad Copper.

Date	Mintage	MS-63	MS-65	Prf-65
1999P	363,200,000	1.00	1.50	—
1999D	299,028,000	1.00	1.75	—
1999S	(3,713,359)	—	—	10.00

KM# 292a **Composition:** 0.9000 Silver.

Date	Mintage	MS-63	MS-65	Prf-65
1999S	(804,565)	—	—	40.00

Georgia

KM# 293 **Composition:** Copper-Nickel Clad Copper.

Date	Mintage	MS-63	MS-65	Prf-65
1999P	451,188,000	0.75	1.00	—
1999D	488,744,000	0.75	1.00	—
1999S	(3,713,359)	—	—	10.00

KM# 293a **Composition:** 0.9000 Silver.

Date	Mintage	MS-63	MS-65	Prf-65
1999S	(804,565)	—	—	40.00

Connecticut

KM# 294 **Composition:** Copper-Nickel Clad Copper.

Date	Mintage	MS-63	MS-65	Prf-65
1999P	688,744,000	0.75	1.00	—
1999D	657,480,000	0.75	1.00	—
1999S	(3,713,359)	—	—	10.00

KM# 294a **Composition:** 0.9000 Silver.

Date	Mintage	MS-63	MS-65	Prf-65
1999S	(804,565)	—	—	40.00

Massachusetts

KM# 306 **Composition:** Copper-Nickel Clad Copper.

Date	Mintage	MS-63	MS-65	Prf-65
2000P	629,800,000	0.75	1.00	—
2000D	535,184,000	0.75	1.00	—
2000S	(4,078,747)	—	—	5.00

KM# 306a **Composition:** 0.9000 Silver.

Date	Mintage	MS-63	MS-65	Prf-65
2000S	(965,921)	—	—	7.50

Maryland

KM# 307 **Composition:** Copper-Nickel Clad Copper.

Date	Mintage	MS-63	MS-65	Prf-65
2000P	678,200,000	0.75	1.00	—
2000D	556,526,000	0.75	1.00	—
2000S	(4,078,747)	—	—	5.00

KM# 307a **Composition:** 0.9000 Silver.

Date	Mintage	MS-63	MS-65	Prf-65
2000S	(965,921)	—	—	7.50

South Carolina

KM# 308 **Composition:** Copper-Nickel Clad Copper.

Date	Mintage	MS-63	MS-65	Prf-6
2000P	742,756,000	0.75	1.00	—
2000D	566,208,000	0.75	1.00	—
2000S	(4,078,747)	—	—	5.0

KM# 308a **Composition:** 0.9000 Silver.

Date	Mintage	MS-63	MS-65	Prf-6
2000S	(965,921)	—	—	7.5

New Hampshire

KM# 309 **Composition:** Copper-Nickel Clad Copper.

Date	Mintage	MS-63	MS-65	Prf-6
2000P	673,040,000	0.75	1.00	
2000D	495,976,000	0.75	1.00	
2000S	(4,078,747)	—	—	5.0

KM# 309a **Composition:** 0.9000 Silver.

Date	Mintage	MS-63	MS-65	Prf-6
2000S	(965,921)	—	—	7.

Virginia

KM# 310 **Composition:** Copper-Nickel Clad Copper.

Date	Mintage	MS-63	MS-65	Prf-
2000P	943,000,000	0.75	1.00	
2000D	651,616,000	0.75	1.00	
2000S	(4,078,747)	—	—	5.

KM# 310a **Composition:** 0.9000 Silver.

Date	Mintage	MS-63	MS-65	Prf-
2000S	(965,921)	—	—	7

New York

319 Composition: Copper-Nickel Clad Copper.

	Mintage	MS-63	MS-65	Prf-65
	655,400,000	0.75	1.00	—
	619,640,000	0.75	1.00	—
	(3,009,800)	—	—	6.50

319a Composition: Silver.

	Mintage	MS-63	MS-65	Prf-65
	(849,600)	—	—	20.00

North Carolina

320 Composition: Copper-Nickel Clad Copper.

	Mintage	MS-63	MS-65	Prf-65
	627,600,000	0.75	1.00	—
	427,876,000	0.75	1.00	—
	(3,009,800)	—	—	6.50

320a Composition: Silver.

	Mintage	MS-63	MS-65	Prf-65
	(849,600)	—	—	20.00

Rhode Island

 # 321 Composition: Copper-Nickel Clad Copper.

	Mintage	MS-63	MS-65	Prf-65
P	423,000,000	0.75	1.00	—
D	447,100,000	0.75	1.00	—
S	(3,009,800)	—	—	6.50

 # 321a Composition: Silver..

	Mintage	MS-63	MS-65	Prf-65
S	(849,600)	—	—	20.00

Vermont

 # 322 Composition: Copper-Nickel Clad Copper.

	Mintage	MS-63	MS-65	Prf-65
P	423,400,000	0.75	1.00	—
D	459,404,000	0.75	1.00	—
S	(3,009,800)	—	—	6.50

 # 322a Composition: Silver.

	Mintage	MS-63	MS-65	Prf-65
S	(849,600)	—	—	20.00

Kentucky

 # 323 Composition: Copper-Nickel Clad Copper.

	Mintage	MS-63	MS-65	Prf-65
P	353,000,000	0.75	1.00	—
D	370,564,000	0.75	1.00	—
S	(3,009,800)	—	—	6.50

 # 323a Composition: Silver.

	Mintage	MS-63	MS-65	Prf-65
S	(849,500)	—	—	20.00

Tennessee

KM# 324 Composition: Copper-Nickel Clad Copper.

Date	Mintage	MS-63	MS-65	Prf-65
2002P	361,600,000	0.75	1.00	—
2002D	286,468,000	0.75	1.00	—
2002S	(2,956,721)	—	—	7.50

KM# 324a Composition: Silver.

Date	Mintage	MS-63	MS-65	Prf-65
2002S	(878,542)	—	—	7.50

Ohio

KM# 325 Composition: Copper-Nickel Clad Copper.

Date	Mintage	MS-63	MS-65	Prf-65
2002P	217,200,000	—	—	—
2002D	414,832,000	—	—	—
2002S	(3,009,800)	—	—	6.00

KM# 325a Composition: Silver.

Date	Mintage	MS-63	MS-65	Prf-65
2002S	—	—	—	—

Louisiana

KM# 326 Composition: Copper-Nickel Clad Copper.

Date	Mintage	MS-63	MS-65	Prf-65
2002P	—	—	—	—
2002D	—	—	—	—
2002S	—	—	—	—

KM# 326a Composition: Silver.

Date	Mintage	MS-63	MS-65	Prf-65
2002S	—	—	—	—

Indiana

KM# 327 Composition: Copper-Nickel Clad Copper.

Date	Mintage	MS-63	MS-65	Prf-65
2002P	—	—	—	—
2002D	—	—	—	—
2002S	—	—	—	—

KM# 327a Composition: Silver.

Date	Mintage	MS-63	MS-65	Prf-65
2002S	—	—	—	—

Mississippi

KM# 328 Composition: Copper-Nickel Clad Copper.

Date	Mintage	MS-63	MS-65	Prf-65
2002P	—	—	—	—
2002D	—	—	—	—
2002S	—	—	—	—

KM# 328a **Composition:** Silver.

Date	Mintage	MS-63	MS-65	Prf-65
2002S	—	—	—	—

Alabama

KM# 340 **Composition:** Copper-Nickel Clad Copper, 0 oz.

Date	Mintage	MS-63	MS-65	Prf-65
2003P	—	—	—	—
2003D	—	—	—	—
2003S	—	—	—	—

KM# 340a **Composition:** Silver, 0 oz. ASW.

Date	Mintage	MS-63	MS-65	Prf-65
2003S	—	—	—	—

Arkansas

KM# 343 **Composition:** Copper-Nickel Clad Copper, 0 oz.

Date	Mintage	MS-63	MS-65	Prf-65
2003P	—	—	—	—
2003D	—	—	—	—
2003S	—	—	—	—

KM# 343a **Composition:** Silver, 0 oz. ASW.

Date	Mintage	MS-63	MS-65	Prf-65
2003S	—	—	—	—

Illinois

KM# 339 **Composition:** Copper-Nickel Clad Copper, 0 oz.

Date	Mintage	MS-63	MS-65	Prf-65
2003P	—	—	—	—
2003D	—	—	—	—
2003S	—	—	—	—

KM# 339a **Composition:** Silver, 0 oz. ASW.

Date	Mintage	MS-63	MS-65	Prf-65
2003S	—	—	—	—

Maine

KM# 341 **Composition:** Copper-Nickel Clad Copper, 0 oz.

Date	Mintage	MS-63	MS-65	Prf-65
2003P	—	—	—	—
2003D	—	—	—	—
2003S	—	—	—	—

KM# 341a **Composition:** Silver, 0 oz. ASW.

Date	Mintage	MS-63	MS-65	Prf-65
2003S	—	—	—	—

Missouri

KM# 342 **Composition:** Copper-Nickel Clad Copper, 0 oz.

Date	Mintage	MS-63	MS-65	Prf-65
2003P	—	—	—	—
2003D	—	—	—	—
2003S	—	—	—	—

KM# 342a **Composition:** Silver, 0 oz. ASW.

Date	Mintage	MS-63	MS-65	Prf-65
2003S	—	—	—	—

HALF DOLLAR

Barber.

Mint mark

KM# 116 **Designer:** Charles E. Barber. **Diameter:** 30.6 **Weight:** 12.5000 g. **Composition:** 0.9000 Silver, 0.3618 oz. ASW.

Date	Mintage	G-4	VG-8	F-12	VF-20	XF-40	AU-50	MS-60	MS-65	Prf-6
1892	935,245	25.00	34.00	50.00	90.00	175	280	400	2,750	3,30
1892O	390,000	195	250	335	375	425	450	850	4,200	—
1892 micro o	—	1,500	3,450	4,250	5,750	9,500	16,500	—	55,000	—
1892S	1,029,028	165	250	275	335	375	600	900	5,000	—
1893	1,826,792	14.50	21.50	54.00	85.00	160	310	510	4,000	3,30
1893O	1,389,000	23.00	42.00	75.00	120	275	370	540	8,500	—
1893S	740,000	110	135	200	330	420	540	1,200	26,500	—
1894	1,148,972	19.00	36.00	75.00	100.00	220	350	480	3,000	3,30
1894O	2,138,000	14.50	24.00	65.00	95.00	230	300	510	6,250	—
1894S	4,048,690	15.00	21.50	50.00	72.00	200	330	440	11,000	—
1895	1,835,218	11.50	16.00	52.00	80.00	180	310	570	3,300	3,30
1895O	1,766,000	12.50	23.00	57.50	95.00	230	360	560	7,000	—
1895S	1,108,086	24.00	40.00	80.00	130	275	360	550	7,700	—
1896	950,762	18.00	23.00	60.00	95.00	230	325	540	6,000	3,40
1896O	924,000	25.00	36.00	110	150	365	630	1,200	11,500	—
1896S	1,140,948	70.00	95.00	125	210	375	550	1,200	11,000	—
1897	2,480,731	10.00	12.00	33.50	77.00	135	310	440	3,800	3,30
1897O	632,000	67.00	145	350	680	900	1,200	1,600	6,500	—
1897S	933,900	125	150	270	420	700	1,000	1,350	9,300	—
1898	2,956,735	9.00	11.50	29.00	72.00	135	310	420	3,400	3,30
1898O	874,000	20.00	40.00	110	185	390	500	900	10,000	—
1898S	2,358,550	12.00	20.00	42.00	83.00	200	350	840	8,000	—
1899	5,538,846	10.00	11.50	29.00	72.00	135	300	420	4,250	3,90
1899O	1,724,000	10.00	14.50	50.00	92.50	230	360	630	6,900	—
1899S	1,686,411	14.00	23.00	50.00	85.00	190	340	635	6,000	—
1900	4,762,912	9.00	11.50	27.50	72.00	135	300	400	3,300	3,30
1900O	2,744,000	9.00	14.00	40.00	90.00	250	310	840	15,500	—
1900S	2,560,322	9.00	12.50	42.00	95.00	190	300	625	11,000	—
1901	4,268,813	9.00	11.00	27.50	65.00	135	285	400	4,250	3,5
1901O	1,124,000	10.00	18.00	54.00	115	285	450	1,300	12,000	—
1901S	847,044	19.00	36.00	115	240	550	920	1,500	18,500	—
1902	4,922,777	9.00	11.00	25.00	65.00	135	280	400	4,200	3,7
1902O	2,526,000	9.00	13.00	40.00	80.00	190	350	700	7,200	
1902S	1,460,670	11.00	16.00	50.00	90.00	200	360	635	5,750	
1903	2,278,755	9.00	13.00	40.00	78.00	185	325	450	8,400	3,8
1903O	2,100,000	9.00	12.50	42.00	80.00	200	330	650	9,500	
1903S	1,920,772	9.00	12.50	42.00	78.00	215	365	590	4,800	
1904	2,992,670	9.00	11.00	28.50	65.00	135	300	420	5,500	4,1
1904O	1,117,600	11.50	19.00	55.00	115	310	500	1,100	12,900	
1904S	553,038	20.00	36.00	150	370	690	1,250	3,000	32,000	
1905	662,727	12.50	18.00	57.50	84.00	220	330	550	6,700	3,9
1905O	505,000	16.00	30.00	85.00	150	260	420	730	5,200	
1905S	2,494,000	9.00	11.00	40.00	78.00	190	345	620	9,500	
1906	2,638,675	8.50	9.25	24.00	65.00	135	285	400	3,000	3,3
1906D	4,028,000	8.50	9.50	27.50	72.00	140	300	430	4,250	
1906O	2,446,000	8.50	9.25	36.00	78.00	160	310	600	5,500	
1906S	1,740,154	10.00	14.00	44.00	80.00	190	300	585	5,250	
1907	2,598,575	8.50	9.25	24.00	65.00	135	300	400	3,000	4,0
1907D	3,856,000	8.50	9.50	26.00	65.00	135	300	400	3,000	
1907O	3,946,000	8.50	9.50	27.50	72.00	150	310	570	3,300	
1907S	1,250,000	10.00	14.00	62.50	105	310	625	1,250	13,000	
1908	1,354,545	8.50	9.25	26.00	72.00	135	280	400	3,000	4,0
1908D	3,280,000	8.50	9.25	26.00	72.00	145	310	530	3,000	
1908O	5,360,000	8.50	9.25	26.00	72.00	145	310	530	3,000	
1908S	1,644,828	9.00	13.00	47.00	80.00	210	340	765	5,500	
1909	2,368,650	8.50	9.25	24.00	65.00	135	280	400	3,000	4,
1909O	925,400	10.00	11.50	42.00	84.00	260	480	750	4,500	
1909S	1,764,000	8.50	10.00	30.00	78.00	180	340	570	3,800	
1910	418,551	11.00	20.00	68.00	115	260	400	600	3,300	4,
1910S	1,948,000	9.00	10.00	27.50	72.00	180	330	630	5,000	
1911	1,406,543	9.00	9.25	26.00	65.00	135	300	410	3,000	3,
1911D	695,080	10.00	13.00	35.00	72.00	190	280	545	3,000	
1911S	1,272,000	9.00	10.00	32.50	78.00	160	320	560	5,600	
1912	1,550,700	8.50	9.00	24.00	65.00	135	280	400	3,100	4,
1912D	2,300,800	8.50	9.00	24.00	65.00	135	310	430	3,000	
1912S	1,370,000	8.50	9.00	30.00	72.00	160	320	520	5,750	
1913	188,627	23.00	34.00	115	185	360	670	925	4,100	3
1913D	534,000	10.00	13.00	32.00	72.00	190	295	450	5,200	
1913S	604,000	11.00	15.00	42.00	85.00	190	350	600	4,200	
1914	124,610	37.50	50.00	175	330	500	750	950	7,500	4
1914S	992,000	9.00	10.00	32.50	72.00	180	300	550	3,800	
1915	138,450	25.00	31.00	95.00	200	375	660	1,000	5,350	4
1915D	1,170,400	8.50	9.25	24.00	65.00	135	280	400	3,000	
1915S	1,604,000	8.75	9.25	26.00	65.00	135	280	400	3,000	

Walking Liberty.

Obverse mint mark

Reverse mint mark

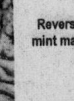

#142 **Designer:** Adolph A. Weinman. **Diameter:** 30.6 **Weight:** 12.5000 g. **Composition:**).9000 Silver, 0.3618 oz. ASW. **Notes:** The mint mark appears on the obverse below the word "Trust" on 1916 and some 1917 issues. Starting with some 1917 issues and continuing hrough the remainder of the series, the mint mark was changed to the reverse, at about he 8 o'clock position near the rim.

	Mintage	G-4	VG-8	F-12	VF-20	XF-40	AU-50	MS-60	MS-65	Prf-65
	608,000	32.50	37.00	57.00	115	145	215	270	1,425	—
D	1,014,400	25.00	29.00	44.00	80.00	135	200	275	1,750	—
S	508,000	110	115	145	330	485	670	950	4,400	—
D obv.	765,400	16.00	23.00	44.00	95.00	130	230	500	5,900	—
S obv.	952,000	19.00	31.00	57.00	265	655	1,125	2,100	16,000	—
	12,292,000	3.75	5.00	8.75	17.00	33.00	60.00	120	775	—
D rev.	1,940,000	10.00	16.00	16.00	90.00	200	485	750	15,000	—
S rev.	5,554,000	4.50	8.00	14.50	29.00	48.00	140	315	10,500	—
	6,634,000	4.50	6.25	16.00	50.00	125	245	525	3,250	—
D	3,853,040	5.75	8.50	20.00	58.00	145	350	900	21,000	—
S	10,282,000	4.50	5.75	14.50	28.00	55.00	150	470	15,500	—
	962,000	18.50	24.00	42.00	160	390	670	1,000	4,700	—
D	1,165,000	14.50	18.50	50.00	160	550	925	3,400	100,000	—
S	1,552,000	15.50	20.00	33.50	160	700	1,500	2,650	13,500	—
	6,372,000	4.50	5.00	11.00	27.50	60.00	95.00	300	5,000	—
D	1,551,000	9.50	11.50	30.00	135	350	750	1,200	10,000	—
S	4,624,000	5.25	8.00	15.00	55.00	210	400	750	11,500	—
	246,000	110	150	200	575	1,350	2,350	3,200	12,000	—
D	208,000	160	200	290	675	2,000	2,750	3,400	15,500	—
S	548,000	29.00	31.50	110	600	4,000	7,500	11,000	60,000	—
3S	2,178,000	8.50	11.00	22.00	65.00	210	625	1,250	12,500	—
'S	2,392,000	4.50	5.75	11.00	31.50	95.00	300	800	8,200	—
3S	1,940,000	4.00	5.75	12.00	38.00	95.00	315	800	8,500	—
9D	1,001,200	6.25	9.00	12.50	21.50	67.00	160	340	2,300	—
9S	1,902,000	4.50	6.25	10.00	21.00	75.00	180	340	2,200	—
3S	1,786,000	6.75	9.00	11.00	15.00	45.00	215	550	3,000	—
4	6,964,000	3.25	3.50	3.75	4.00	8.00	25.00	65.00	390	—
4D	2,361,400	5.00	5.50	6.00	7.50	25.00	85.00	180	850	—
4S	3,652,000	3.75	4.00	4.25	5.00	25.00	105	350	3,400	—
5	9,162,000	3.25	3.50	3.75	4.50	5.50	22.00	44.00	350	—
5D	3,003,800	3.75	4.00	4.25	6.00	22.50	53.00	140	1,525	—
5S	3,854,000	3.25	3.50	3.75	4.50	23.00	100.00	280	1,850	—
6	12,617,901	3.25	3.50	3.75	4.00	5.50	22.00	40.00	145	5,000
6D	4,252,400	3.25	3.50	4.00	4.50	16.00	42.00	80.00	360	—
6S	3,884,000	3.25	3.50	4.00	5.00	19.00	60.00	130	540	—
7	9,527,728	3.25	3.50	3.75	4.50	6.00	22.00	38.00	180	1,250
7D	1,676,000	5.00	5.25	5.50	8.50	26.50	105	205	490	—
7S	2,090,000	3.50	4.00	4.50	6.00	17.00	65.00	155	430	—
8	4,118,152	4.00	4.25	4.50	5.50	9.00	37.00	70.00	340	925
8D	491,600	30.00	32.50	38.50	40.00	95.00	240	400	950	—
9	6,820,808	3.25	3.50	3.75	4.00	5.50	22.00	40.00	135	845
9D	4,267,800	3.25	3.50	3.75	4.00	7.00	23.00	47.00	155	—
9S	2,552,000	4.00	4.25	5.25	6.50	13.00	51.00	110	175	—
0	9,167,279	3.25	3.50	3.75	4.00	4.75	11.00	27.00	145	725
0S	4,550,000	3.30	3.60	3.85	4.00	5.25	16.50	39.00	390	—
1	24,207,412	3.25	3.50	3.75	4.00	4.25	11.00	30.00	115	675
1D	11,248,400	3.25	3.50	3.75	4.00	4.70	14.50	37.00	165	—
1S	8,098,000	3.25	3.50	3.75	4.20	5.75	26.00	72.00	1,100	—
2	47,839,120	3.25	3.50	3.75	4.00	4.25	11.00	32.50	115	675
2D	10,973,800	3.25	3.50	3.75	4.00	4.70	16.00	37.00	265	—
2S	12,708,000	3.25	3.50	3.75	4.00	5.00	16.00	37.00	625	—
3	53,190,000	3.25	3.50	3.75	4.25	4.50	11.00	32.50	110	—
3D	11,346,000	3.25	3.50	3.75	4.00	4.70	20.00	40.00	270	—
3S	13,450,000	3.25	3.50	3.75	4.00	4.70	18.00	40.00	400	—
4	28,206,000	3.25	3.50	3.75	4.00	4.25	11.00	32.50	160	—
4D	9,769,000	3.25	3.50	3.75	4.00	4.70	16.00	34.00	135	—
4S	8,904,000	3.25	3.50	3.75	4.10	4.75	16.00	38.50	600	—
5	31,502,000	3.25	3.50	3.75	4.00	4.25	11.00	31.50	135	—
5D	9,966,800	3.25	3.50	3.75	4.00	4.75	15.00	32.50	135	—
45S	10,156,000	3.25	3.50	3.75	4.00	5.00	15.00	33.00	175	—
46	12,118,000	3.25	3.50	3.75	4.00	4.75	11.00	31.00	220	—
46D	2,151,000	3.75	4.50	5.50	6.50	9.50	19.00	38.00	95.00	—
46S	3,724,000	3.25	3.50	3.75	4.00	5.50	16.00	32.50	135	—
47	4,094,000	3.25	3.50	3.75	4.00	7.25	18.00	38.00	210	—
47D	3,900,600	3.25	3.50	3.75	4.00	7.00	20.00	38.00	135	—

Franklin.

Mint mark

KM# 199 **Designer:** John R. Sinnock. **Diameter:** 30.6 **Weight:** 12.5000 g. **Composition:** 0.9000 Silver, 0.3618 oz. ASW.

Date	Mintage	G-4	VG-8	F-12	VF-20	XF-40	AU-50	MS-60	MS-65	-65FBL	-65CAM
1948	3,006,814	—	3.00	4.00	4.25	4.50	6.00	13.75	90.00	315	—
1948D	4,028,600	—	3.00	3.25	3.50	3.75	5.00	10.00	195	325	—
1949	5,614,000	—	3.00	3.25	3.50	4.00	10.00	28.00	150	290	—
1949D	4,120,600	—	3.00	3.50	3.75	4.00	13.00	29.00	1,050	2,350	—
1949S	3,744,000	—	3.50	4.00	6.25	8.00	21.00	48.00	210	775	—
1950	7,793,509	—	—	3.00	3.50	6.00	7.00	20.00	150	350	3,700
1950D	8,031,600	—	—	3.00	3.50	6.50	7.75	16.00	575	1,150	—
1951	16,859,602	—	—	3.00	3.50	4.00	4.50	9.00	95.00	375	2,200
1951D	9,475,200	—	—	3.00	4.25	5.00	11.50	15.00	300	550	—
1951S	13,696,000	—	—	2.75	3.00	3.50	10.00	18.00	125	775	—
1952	21,274,073	—	—	2.50	2.75	3.00	4.00	7.00	90.00	325	1,100
1952D	25,395,600	—	—	2.50	2.75	3.00	4.00	8.50	250	450	—
1952S	5,526,000	—	—	2.50	3.25	3.75	17.00	38.00	135	1,100	—
1953	2,796,920	3.00	3.00	3.25	3.50	5.00	10.00	14.00	275	1,100	475
1953D	20,900,400	—	—	2.25	3.50	4.00	4.25	7.00	250	400	—
1953S	4,148,000	—	—	2.60	4.25	4.75	8.50	17.00	70.00	9,000	—
1954	13,421,503	—	—	2.25	3.50	3.75	4.00	5.50	85.00	275	250
1954D	25,445,580	—	—	2.25	3.25	3.50	4.00	5.50	165	250	—
1954S	4,993,400	—	—	2.25	3.75	4.00	4.25	8.50	60.00	425	—
1955	2,876,381	5.00	5.00	5.25	5.50	5.75	6.00	8.00	75.00	160	195
1956	4,701,384	—	—	2.50	3.00	3.50	4.25	5.00	50.00	120	75.00
1957	6,361,952	—	—	2.50	2.75	3.00	3.75	6.00	50.00	120	135
1957D	19,966,850	—	—	—	2.10	2.25	2.50	5.00	50.00	105	—
1958	4,917,652	—	—	2.25	2.50	2.75	3.00	5.00	50.00	135	250
1958D	23,962,412	—	—	—	2.25	2.50	2.75	4.25	50.00	105	—
1959	7,349,291	—	—	—	2.25	2.50	2.75	4.50	150	295	475
1959D	13,053,750	—	—	—	2.25	2.50	2.75	5.00	150	275	—
1960	7,715,602	—	—	—	2.25	2.50	2.75	4.25	175	400	75.00
1960D	18,215,812	—	—	—	2.25	2.50	2.75	4.50	750	1,450	—
1961	11,318,244	—	—	—	2.25	2.50	2.75	4.25	275	1,900	75.00
1961D	20,276,442	—	—	—	2.25	2.50	2.75	4.50	450	1,050	—
1962	12,932,019	—	—	—	2.25	2.50	2.75	4.25	290	2,600	50.00
1962D	35,473,281	—	—	—	2.25	2.50	2.75	4.25	400	1,000	—
1963	25,239,645	—	—	—	—	2.50	2.75	4.00	90.00	975	50.00
1963D	67,069,292	—	—	—	—	2.50	2.75	4.00	90.00	250	—

Kennedy.

Mint mark 1964

KM# 202 **Obv. Designer:** Gilroy Roberts. **Rev. Designer:** Frank Gasparro. **Diameter:** 30.6 **Weight:** 12.5000 g. **Composition:** 0.9000 Silver, 0.3618 oz. ASW..

Date	Mintage	G-4	VG-8	F-12	VF-20	XF-40	MS-60	MS-65	Prf-65
1964	277,254,766	—	—	—	—	—	3.00	9.00	10.00
1964D	156,205,446	—	—	—	—	—	3.50	12.00	—

Kennedy.

Mint mark 1968 - Present

KM# 202a **Obv. Designer:** Gilroy Roberts. **Rev. Designer:** Frank Gasparro. **Diameter:** 30.6 **Weight:** 11.5000 g. **Composition:** 0.4000 Silver, 0.1480 oz. ASW.

Date	Mintage	G-4	VG-8	F-12	VF-20	XF-40	MS-60	MS-65	Prf-65
1965	65,879,366	—	—	—	—	—	1.25	9.50	—
1966	108,984,932	—	—	—	—	—	1.40	11.00	—
1967	295,046,978	—	—	—	—	—	1.50	9.50	—
1968D	246,951,930	—	—	—	—	—	1.25	9.00	—
1968S	3,041,506	—	—	—	—	—	—	—	5.00
1969D	129,881,800	—	—	—	—	—	1.25	7.50	—
1969S	2,934,631	—	—	—	—	—	—	—	5.00
1970D	2,150,000	—	—	—	—	—	16.00	32.00	—
1970S	2,632,810	—	—	—	—	—	—	—	10.00

Kennedy.

KM# 202b **Obv. Designer:** Gilroy Roberts. **Rev. Designer:** Frank Gasparro. **Diameter:** 30.6 **Weight:** 11.3400 g. **Composition:** Copper-Nickel Clad Copper.

Date	Mintage	G-4	VG-8	F-12	VF-20	XF-40	MS-60	MS-65	Prf-65
1971	155,640,000	—	—	—	—	—	1.50	12.00	—
1971D	302,097,424	—	—	—	—	—	1.00	5.00	—

Date	Mintage	G-4	VG-8	F-12	VF-20	XF-40	MS-60	MS-65	Prf-65
1971S	3,244,183	—	—	—	—	—	—	—	3.00
1972	153,180,000	—	—	—	—	—	1.00	9.00	—
1972D	141,890,000	—	—	—	—	—	1.00	6.00	—
1972S	3,267,667	—	—	—	—	—	—	—	2.50
1973	64,964,000	—	—	—	—	—	1.00	6.00	—
1973D	83,171,400	—	—	—	—	—	—	5.50	—
1973S	(2,769,624)	—	—	—	—	—	—	—	2.50
1974	201,596,000	—	—	—	—	—	1.00	5.00	—
1974D	79,066,300	—	—	—	—	—	1.00	6.00	—
1974S	(2,617,350)	—	—	—	—	—	—	—	3.00
1975	—	—	—	—	—	—	—	—	—
1975D none minted	—	—	—	—	—	—	—	—	—
1975S none minted	—	—	—	—	—	—	—	—	—

Kennedy. Bicentennial design, Independence Hall.

KM# 205 **Rev. Designer:** Seth Huntington. **Composition:** Copper-Nickel Clad Copper.

Date	Mintage	G-4	VG-8	F-12	VF-20	XF-40	MS-60	MS-65	Prf-65
1976	234,308,000	—	—	—	—	—	1.00	10.00	—
1976D	287,565,248	—	—	—	—	—	1.00	4.50	—
1976S	(7,059,099)	—	—	—	—	—	—	—	2.00

Kennedy. Bicentennial design, Independence Hall.

KM# 205a **Rev. Designer:** Seth Huntington. **Weight:** 11.5000 g. **Composition:** 0.4000 Silver, 0.1480 oz. ASW.

Date	Mintage	G-4	VG-8	F-12	VF-20	XF-40	MS-60	MS-65	Prf-65
1976S	4,908,319(3,998,621)	—	—	—	—	—	—	6.50	5.00

Kennedy. Regular design resumed.

KM# A202b **Diameter:** 30.6 **Weight:** 11.3400 g. **Composition:** Copper-Nickel Clad Copper. **Notes:** KM#202b design and composition resumed. The 1979-S and 1981-S Type II proofs have clearer mint marks than the Type I proofs of those years.

Date	Mintage	MS-65	Prf-65
1977	43,598,000	6.50	—
1977D	31,449,106	6.00	—
1977S	(3,251,152)	—	2.00
1978	14,350,000	6.50	—
1978D	13,765,799	6.50	—
1978S	(3,127,788)	—	2.00
1979	68,312,000	5.50	—
1979D	15,815,422	6.00	—
1979S type I, proof	(3,677,175)	—	2.00
1979S type II, proof	Inc. above	—	18.00
1980P	44,134,000	5.00	—
1980D	33,456,449	4.50	—
1980S	(3,547,030)	—	2.00
1981P	29,544,000	4.50	—
1981D	27,839,533	4.50	—
1981S type I, proof	(4,063,083)	—	2.00
1981S type II, proof	Inc. above	—	14.50
1982P	10,819,000	5.00	—
1982D	13,140,102	5.00	—
1982S	(38,957,479)	—	3.50
1983P	34,139,000	5.00	—
1983D	32,472,244	5.00	—
1983S	(3,279,126)	—	3.00
1984P	26,029,000	5.00	—
1984D	26,262,158	5.00	—
1984S	(3,065,110)	—	4.00
1985P	18,706,962	5.00	—
1985D	19,814,034	5.00	—
1985S	(3,962,138)	—	4.50
1986P	13,107,633	16.00	—
1986D	15,336,145	12.00	—
1986S	(2,411,180)	—	7.50
1987P	2,890,758	9.00	—
1987D	2,890,758	9.00	—
1987S	(4,407,728)	—	3.50
1988P	13,626,000	10.00	—
1988D	12,000,096	6.00	—
1988S	(3,262,948)	—	7.00
1989P	24,542,000	8.00	—
1989D	23,000,216	8.00	—
1989S	(3,220,194)	—	7.00
1990P	22,780,000	15.00	—
1990D	20,096,242	15.00	—
1990S	(3,299,559)	—	5.00
1991P	14,874,000	8.00	—
1991D	15,054,678	12.00	—
1991S	(2,867,787)	—	11.50
1992P	17,628,000	7.00	—
1992D	17,000,106	7.00	—
1992S	(2,858,981)	—	10.00
1993P	15,510,000	1.50	—
1993D	15,000,006	7.00	—
1993S	(2,633,439)	—	14.00
1994P	23,718,000	6.00	—
1994D	23,828,110	6.00	—
1994S	(2,484,594)	—	8.00
1995P	26,496,000	6.00	—
1995D	26,288,000	6.00	—
1995S	(2,010,384)	—	47.50
1996P	24,442,000	6.00	—
1996D	24,744,000	6.00	—
1996S	2,085,191	—	10.00
1997P	20,882,000	7.00	—
1997D	19,876,000	6.00	—
1997S	(1,975,000)	—	25.00
1998P	15,646,000	9.00	—
1998D	15,064,000	8.00	—
1998S	(2,078,494)	—	14.00
1998S matte	62,350	—	400
1999P	8,900,000	6.00	—
1999D	10,682,000	6.00	—
1999S	(2,557,897)	—	10.00
2000P	22,600,000	4.00	—
2000D	19,466,000	4.00	—
2000S	(3,082,944)	—	4.50
2001P	21,200,000	3.00	—
2001D	19,504,000	3.00	—
2001S	(2,235,000)	—	10.00
2002P	3,100,000	15.00	—
2002D	2,500,000	10.00	—
2002S	—	—	7.00
2003P	—	—	—
2003D	—	—	—
2003S	—	—	—

Kennedy.

KM# B202b **Composition:** Silver.

Date	Mintage	Prf-65
1992S	(1,317,579)	15.00
1993S	(761,353)	25.00
1994S	(785,329)	35.00
1995S	(838,953)	100.00
1996S	(830,021)	50.00
1997S	(821,678)	100.00
1998S	(878,792)	30.00
1999S	(804,565)	15.00
2000S	(965,921)	12.50
2001S	(849,600)	12.50
2002S	—	—
2003S	—	—

DOLLAR

Morgan.

KM# 110 **Designer:** George T. Morgan. **Diameter:** 38.1 **Weight:** 26.7300 g. **Composition:** 0.9000 Silver, 0.7736 oz. ASW. **Notes:** "65DMPL" values are for coins grading MS-65 deep-mirror prooflike. The 1878 "8 tail feathers" and "7 tail feathers" varieties are distinguished by the number of feathers in the eagle's tail. On the "reverse of 1878" varieties, the top of the top feather in the arrows held by the eagle is straight across and the eagle's breast is concave. On the "reverse of 1879 varieties," the top feather in the arrows held by the eagle is slanted and the eagle's breast is convex. The 1890-CC "tail-bar variety has a bar extending from the arrow feathers to the wreath on the reverse, the result of a die gouge.

Date	Mintage	VG-8	F-12	VF-20	XF-40	AU-50	MS-60	MS-63	MS-64	MS-65	65DMPL	Prf-65
1900	8,880,938	13.00	15.00	16.00	18.00	19.00	30.00	38.00	55.00	195	11,000	5,500
1900O	12,590,000	13.00	15.00	16.00	20.00	24.00	32.00	42.00	52.00	135	3,000	—
1900O/CC	Inc. above	20.00	25.00	34.00	49.00	120	215	490	725	1,400	19,000	—
1900S	3,540,000	16.00	17.00	19.00	36.00	85.00	245	300	365	1,350	9,450	—
1901	6,962,813	18.50	20.00	30.00	60.00	350	1,675	17,500	55,000	215,000	220,000	8,100
1901O	13,320,000	13.00	14.50	16.00	19.00	20.00	30.00	38.00	52.00	170	3,800	—
1901S	2,284,000	15.00	20.00	29.00	45.00	175	335	575	850	3,500	12,500	—
1902	7,994,777	15.50	16.00	18.00	19.00	23.00	42.00	90.00	130	445	15,750	5,750
1902O	8,636,000	13.50	15.50	16.50	20.00	21.00	29.00	38.00	47.50	140	3,600	—
1902S	1,530,000	27.00	42.00	90.00	105	135	285	365	580	2,700	15,000	—
1903	4,652,755	24.00	28.50	30.00	40.00	46.00	53.00	57.00	72.00	215	9,150	5,500
1903O	4,450,000	175	190	220	255	300	365	400	415	535	4,650	—
1903S	1,241,000	23.00	29.00	90.00	245	1,100	2,900	4,250	5,200	7,000	35,000	—
1904	2,788,650	15.50	16.00	16.50	18.00	30.00	80.00	230	560	4,700	38,000	5,500
1904O	3,720,000	14.50	15.50	16.00	18.00	20.00	30.00	38.00	47.50	105	550	—
1904S	2,304,000	17.00	25.00	46.00	190	540	1,000	2,100	1,750	6,500	19,000	—
1921	44,690,000	10.00	10.25	10.50	11.00	12.00	15.50	25.00	35.00	135	8,800	—
1921D	20,345,000	10.00	10.25	10.50	11.75	13.00	39.50	48.00	100.00	260	15,000	—
1921S	21,695,000	10.00	10.25	11.00	12.00	14.00	26.00	54.00	135	1,700	22,000	—

Peace.

Mint mark

KM# 150 **Designer:** Anthony DeFrancisci. **Diameter:** 38.1 **Weight:** 26.7300 g. **Composition** 0.9000 Silver, 0.7736 oz. ASW. **Notes:** Commonly called Peace dollars.

Date	Mintage	G-4	VG-8	F-12	VF-20	XF-40	AU-50	MS-60	MS-63	MS-64	MS-
1921	1,006,473	29.00	40.00	42.00	46.00	54.00	100.00	170	290	485	2,4
1922	51,737,000	8.00	8.50	8.75	9.00	9.25	9.50	15.50	26.50	36.00	100.
1922D	15,063,000	8.00	8.50	9.00	10.00	11.00	12.00	24.00	44.00	72.00	3
1922S	17,475,000	8.00	8.50	9.00	10.25	12.00	13.00	22.50	65.00	210	2,2
1923	30,800,000	8.00	8.50	8.75	9.00	9.25	9.50	15.50	26.50	36.00	88.
1923D	6,811,000	8.00	8.50	10.00	10.50	11.00	18.00	53.00	120	215	1,0
1923S	19,020,000	8.00	8.50	10.00	10.50	11.00	13.00	26.00	65.00	200	8,4
1924	11,811,000	8.00	8.50	9.50	10.00	10.50	11.00	15.50	27.50	42.00	100.
1924S	1,728,000	8.50	9.00	11.25	14.50	24.00	48.00	195	430	1,000	8,5
1925	10,198,000	8.00	8.50	9.00	9.25	10.00	12.50	15.50	27.50	42.00	95.
1925S	1,610,000	9.00	10.00	12.00	13.00	15.00	30.00	65.00	145	550	20,5
1926	1,939,000	8.00	11.50	12.50	13.50	14.00	16.00	32.00	60.00	95.00	3
1926D	2,348,700	8.00	10.00	11.00	12.50	16.00	25.00	58.50	135	260	6
1926S	6,980,000	8.00	8.50	10.00	10.00	12.00	15.00	35.00	77.00	235	8
1927	848,000	12.00	16.00	20.00	22.00	27.00	45.00	67.00	140	260	2,0
1927D	1,268,900	11.00	14.50	17.00	20.00	24.00	75.00	145	300	625	5,8
1927S	866,000	13.00	15.00	17.00	20.00	25.00	67.00	135	250	725	11,0
1928	360,649	135	165	180	190	200	210	255	360	725	3,7
1928S	1,632,000	11.00	17.50	18.50	18.50	24.00	42.00	140	330	1,000	24,0
1934	954,057	11.00	13.00	14.50	17.50	20.00	36.00	90.00	170	285	8
1934D	1,569,500	11.00	13.00	14.50	17.50	20.00	40.00	95.00	265	500	2,1
1934S	1,011,000	11.00	14.50	15.00	52.50	135	495	1,600	2,700	4,200	6,7
1935	1,576,000	11.00	14.50	15.00	15.50	16.00	30.00	60.00	100.00	160	6
1935S	1,964,000	11.00	13.50	14.00	14.50	24.00	72.00	180	335	485	1,1

Eisenhower.

203 **Designer:** Frank Gasparro. **Diameter:** 38.1 **Weight:** 22.6800 g. **Composition:** Copper-Nickel Clad Copper.

	Mintage	(Proof)	MS-63	Prf-65
	47,799,000	—	3.75	—
D	68,587,424	—	2.00	—
2	75,890,000	—	2.75	—
2D	92,548,511	—	2.25	—
3	2,000,056	—	11.00	—
3D	2,000,000	—	11.00	—
3S	2,769,624	—	—	11.00
4	27,366,000	—	3.00	—
4D	35,466,000	—	2.75	—
4S	—	(2,617,350)	—	6.50

Eisenhower.

203a **Designer:** Frank Gasparro. **Diameter:** 38.1 **Weight:** 24.5900 g. **Composition:** Silver.

	Mintage	(Proof)	MS-63	Prf-65
1S	6,868,530	(4,265,234)	7.00	7.00
2S	2,193,056	(1,811,631)	7.50	7.00
3S	1,833,140	(1,005,617)	8.50	30.00
4S	1,720,000	(1,306,579)	7.50	6.50

Eisenhower.
Bicentennial design, moon behind Liberty Bell.

Type I Type II

M# 206 **Rev. Designer:** Dennis R. Williams. **Diameter:** 38.1 **Weight:** 22.6800 g. **Composition:** Copper-Nickel Clad Copper. **Notes:** In 1976 the lettering on the reverse on the reverse was changed to thinner letters, resulting in Type I and Type II varieties for that year.

te	Mintage	(Proof)	MS-63	Prf-65
76 type I	117,337,000	—	4.00	—
76 type II	Inc. above	—	2.00	—
76D type I	103,228,274	—	3.25	—
76D type II	Inc. above	—	2.00	—
76S type I	—	(2,909,369)	—	5.75
76S type II	—	(4,149,730)	—	5.75

Eisenhower.
Bicentennial design, moon behind Liberty Bell.

M# 206a **Rev. Designer:** Dennis R. Williams. **Weight:** 24.5900 g. **Composition:** 0.4000 Silver, 0.3162 oz. ASW.

te	Mintage	(Proof)	MS-63	Prf-65
76S	4,908,319	(3,998,621)	14.00	12.50

Eisenhower. Regular design resumed.

M# A203 **Diameter:** 38.1 **Composition:** Copper-Nickel Clad Copper.

te	Mintage	(Proof)	MS-63	Prf-65
77	12,596,000	—	4.25	—

Date	Mintage	(Proof)	MS-63	Prf-65
1977D	32,983,006	—	3.25	—
1977S	—	(3,251,152)	—	8.00
1978	25,702,000	—	2.75	—
1978D	33,012,890	—	3.00	—
1978S	—	(3,127,788)	—	10.00

Susan B. Anthony.

KM# 207 **Designer:** Frank Gasparro. **Diameter:** 26.5 **Weight:** 8.1000 g. **Composition:** Copper-Nickel Clad Copper, 0 oz. **Notes:** The 1979-S and 1981-S Type II coins have a clearer mint mark than the Type I varieties for those years.

Date	Mintage	MS-63
1979P	360,222,000	2.00
1979P Near date	Inc. above	12.00
1979D	288,015,744	1.75
1979S	109,576,000	2.00
1979S Proof, Type I	3,677,175	—
1979S Proof, Type II	Inc. above	—
1980P	27,610,000	2.00
1980D	41,628,708	2.00
1980S	20,422,000	2.00
1980S Proof	3,547,030	—
1981P	3,000,000	5.75
1981D	3,250,000	5.75
1981S	3,492,000	6.00
1981S Proof, Type I	4,063,083	—
1981S Proof, Type II	Inc. above	—
1999P	29,592,000	1.50
1999D	11,776,000	1.75
1999P Proof; *maximum mintage	(750,000)	—

Sacagawea.

KM# 311 **Diameter:** 26.4 **Weight:** 8.0700 g. **Composition:** Copper-Zinc-Manganese-Nickel Clad Copper.

Date	Mintage	MS-63	Prf-65
2000P	767,140,000	1.50	—
2000D	518,916,000	1.50	—
2000S	(4,048,865)	—	7.50
2001P	62,468,000	1.50	—
2001D	70,909,500	1.50	—
2001S	(3,084,600)	—	7.50

$2.50 (QUARTER EAGLE)

Coronet Head.

1948 "Cal."

KM# 72 **Designer:** Christian Gobrecht. **Diameter:** 18 **Weight:** 4.1800 g. **Composition:** 0.9000 Gold, 0.121 oz. AGW. **Notes:** Varieties for 1843 are distinguished by the size of the numerals in the date. One 1848 variety has "Cal." inscribed on the reverse, indicating it was made from California gold. The 1873 "closed-3" and "open-3" varieties are distinguished by the amount of space between the upper left and lower left serifs in the 3 in the date.

Date	Mintage	F-12	VF-20	XF-40	AU-50	MS-60	Prf-65
1900	67,205	135	160	250	315	400	13,000
1901	91,322	130	145	170	180	285	13,000
1902	133,733	130	145	170	180	285	13,000
1903	201,257	130	145	170	180	285	13,000
1904	160,960	130	145	170	180	285	13,000
1905	217,944	130	145	170	180	285	13,000
1906	176,490	130	145	170	180	285	13,000
1907	336,448	130	145	170	180	285	13,000

Indian Head.

KM# 128 **Designer:** Bela Lyon Pratt. **Diameter:** 18 **Weight:** 4.1800 g. **Composition:** 0.9000 Gold, 0.121 oz. AGW.

Date	Mintage	VF-20	XF-40	AU-50	MS-60	MS-63	MS-65	Prf-65
1908	565,057	135	175	185	250	800	2,500	15,000
1909	441,899	135	175	185	275	950	2,800	29,000
1910	492,682	135	175	185	265	900	4,900	16,000
1911	704,191	135	175	185	250	900	3,500	15,000
1911D	55,680	700	1,000	1,450	3,100	8,250	44,000	—

Date	Mintage	VF-20	XF-40	AU-50	MS-60	MS-63	MS-65	Prf-65
1912	616,197	135	175	185	285	1,000	5,500	15,500
1913	722,165	135	175	185	270	900	3,500	15,800
1914	240,117	135	175	200	450	2,750	10,000	16,500
1914D	448,000	135	175	185	300	1,300	12,000	—
1915	606,100	135	175	185	240	800	3,500	15,250
1925D	578,000	135	175	185	230	750	2,500	—
1926	446,000	135	175	185	230	725	2,500	—
1927	388,000	135	175	185	230	725	2,500	—
1928	416,000	135	175	185	230	725	2,500	—
1929	532,000	135	175	185	230	725	3,000	—

$5 (HALF EAGLE)

Coronet Head. "In God We Trust" above eagle.

KM# 101 **Designer:** Christian Gobrecht. **Diameter:** 21.6 **Weight:** 8.3590 g. **Composition:** 0.9000 Gold, 0.242 oz. AGW. **Notes:** The 1873 "closed-3" and "open-3" varieties are known and are distinguished by the amount of space between the upper left and lower left serifs of the 3 in the date.

Date	Mintage	VF-20	XF-40	AU-50	MS-60	MS-65	Prf-65
1900	1,405,730	155	165	185	235	2,600	30,000
1900S	329,000	170	180	275	250	11,500	—
1901	616,040	160	175	200	350	3,100	12,500
1901S	3,648,000	155	165	185	230	2,900	—
1902	172,562	165	170	190	240	4,400	22,000
1902S	939,000	160	165	180	230	2,650	—
1903	227,024	160	170	185	240	3,400	22,000
1903S	1,855,000	160	165	180	220	2,700	—
1904	392,136	160	165	180	225	2,700	25,000
1904S	97,000	165	180	265	850	9,000	—
1905	302,308	160	165	180	215	3,300	25,000
1905S	880,700	160	175	195	500	9,200	—
1906	348,820	160	165	185	220	2,950	22,000
1906D	320,000	160	165	185	220	3,500	—
1906S	598,000	160	165	185	250	4,500	—
1907	626,192	160	165	180	215	2,750	23,000
1907D	888,000	160	165	185	215	2,750	—
1908	421,874	160	165	185	215	2,750	—

Indian Head.

KM# 129 **Designer:** Bela Lyon Pratt. **Diameter:** 21.6 **Weight:** 8.3590 g. **Composition:** 0.9000 Gold, .2420 oz. AGW.

Date	Mintage	VF-20	XF-40	AU-50	MS-60	MS-63	MS-65	Prf-65
1908	578,012	180	215	225	325	1,100	11,000	16,000
1908D	148,000	180	215	225	325	1,000	18,000	—
1908S	82,000	195	415	450	1,200	2,500	14,000	—
1909	627,138	180	215	225	325	1,200	11,500	29,000
1909D	3,423,560	175	200	220	310	1,150	11,500	—
1909O	34,200	650	1,350	1,600	6,000	40,000	190,000	—
1909S	297,200	185	240	285	1,300	6,800	39,000	—
1910	604,250	175	215	240	300	1,500	14,000	32,000
1910D	193,600	175	215	240	350	1,750	34,500	—
1910S	770,200	175	230	275	925	5,500	36,000	—
1911	915,139	175	215	240	300	1,200	12,750	26,000
1911D	72,500	350	450	500	2,900	16,500	115,000	—
1911S	1,416,000	180	230	270	550	2,700	31,000	—
1912	790,144	180	210	240	315	1,200	12,900	26,000
1912S	392,000	195	275	310	1,500	7,500	75,000	—
1913	916,099	180	210	230	310	1,150	11,500	26,000
1913S	408,000	200	250	290	1,300	9,800	100,000	—
1914	247,125	180	225	240	335	1,250	12,500	26,000
1914D	247,000	185	235	250	325	2,600	25,000	—
1914S	263,000	260	285	300	1,400	8,000	72,000	—
1915	588,075	190	225	250	335	1,200	14,000	33,000
1915S	164,000	270	350	385	1,900	8,000	85,000	—
1916S	240,000	260	280	295	530	2,800	18,500	—
1929	662,000	2,400	4,800	5,300	6,100	7,800	23,500	—

$10 (EAGLE)

Coronet Head. New-style head. "In God We Trust" above eagle.

KM# 102 **Designer:** Christian Gobrecht. **Diameter:** 27 **Weight:** 16.7180 g. **Composition:** 0.9000 Gold, 0.4839 oz. AGW. **Notes:** The 1873 "closed-3" and "open-3" varieties are distinguished by the amount of space between the upper left and lower left serifs of the 3 in the date.

Date	Mintage	VF-20	XF-40	AU-50	MS-60	MS-65	Prf-65
1900	293,960	200	225	230	300	7,750	30,500
1900S	81,000	210	275	350	850	—	—
1901	1,718,825	200	215	240	285	2,800	30,500
1901O	72,041	225	250	285	400	—	—
1901S	2,812,750	200	215	240	285	2,500	—
1902	82,513	230	260	295	330	—	30,500
1902S	469,500	230	250	260	400	2,700	—
1903	125,926	215	260	290	315	—	30,000
1903O	112,771	225	250	295	375	—	—
1903S	538,000	200	225	250	290	2,650	—
1904	162,038	215	230	260	325	—	31,50
1904O	108,950	220	250	285	360	—	—
1905	201,078	200	220	250	285	4,800	30,000
1905S	369,250	210	230	300	1,100	—	—
1906	165,497	225	230	250	295	7,750	30,00
1906D	981,000	230	245	275	325	3,850	—
1906O	86,895	235	250	330	450	—	—
1906S	457,000	220	250	300	475	12,500	—
1907	1,203,973	195	210	220	275	—	30,00
1907D	1,030,000	230	240	250	310	—	—
1907S	210,500	240	260	280	600	—	—

Indian Head. No motto next to eagle.

KM# 125 **Designer:** Augustus Saint-Gaudens. **Diameter:** 27 **Weight:** 16.7180 g. **Composition:** 0.9000 Gold, 0.4839 oz. AGW. **Notes:** 1907 varieties are distinguished by whether the edge is rolled or wired, and whether the legend "E Pluribus Unum" has periods between each word.

Date	Mintage	VF-20	XF-40	AU-50	MS-60	MS-63	MS-65	Prf-6
1907 wire edge, periods before and after legend	500	—	4,500	6,000	11,500	18,000	45,000	—
1907 same, without stars on edge, unique	—	—	—	—	—	—	—	—
1907 rolled edge, periods	42	13,000	18,000	22,000	28,000	35,000	95,000	—
1907 without periods	239,406	350	375	400	550	2,000	6,100	—
1908 without motto	33,500	350	390	450	625	2,400	9,700	—
1908D without motto	210,000	335	390	425	740	4,800	40,000	—

Indian Head. "In God We Trust" left of eagle.

KM# 130 **Designer:** Augustus Saint-Gaudens. **Diameter:** 27 **Weight:** 16.7180 g. **Composition:** 0.9000 Gold, 0.4839 oz. AGW.

Date	Mintage	VF-20	XF-40	AU-50	MS-60	MS-63	MS-65	Prf
1908	341,486	315	370	385	475	1,400	5,000	29,5
1908D	836,500	320	375	390	650	3,700	18,000	
1908S	59,850	360	390	400	1,675	5,800	20,000	
1909	184,863	330	375	400	485	1,850	8,400	31,5
1909D	121,540	330	380	400	690	2,300	42,000	
1909S	292,350	330	380	395	600	3,200	10,750	
1910	318,704	335	375	400	480	900	5,600	37,
1910D	2,356,640	330	365	390	465	900	5,500	
1910S	811,000	330	370	390	700	3,250	45,000	
1911	505,595	325	345	375	480	1,050	4,875	32,
1911D	30,100	425	690	890	3,900	11,500	100,000	
1911S	51,000	365	550	630	1,100	4,800	10,500	
1912	405,083	330	350	385	450	900	6,800	32,

	Mintage	VF-20	XF-40	AU-50	MS-60	MS-63	MS-65	Prf-65
S	300,000	345	375	390	800	2,750	47,500	—
	442,071	340	360	375	460	925	4,600	32,000
S	66,000	360	640	850	3,650	15,000	100,000	—
	151,050	345	360	350	525	1,525	6,750	32,000
D	343,500	330	360	360	535	1,550	10,000	—
S	208,000	340	365	415	700	4,200	38,000	—
	351,075	340	360	385	525	1,200	5,600	40,000
S	59,000	400	625	775	2,900	8,500	54,000	—
S	138,500	340	375	415	675	2,350	14,250	—
S	126,500	5,000	6,200	8,200	17,000	35,000	195,000	—
	1,014,000	290	325	380	430	615	3,650	—
S	96,000	4,000	5,250	6,500	9,300	11,000	26,750	—
	4,463,000	290	325	380	430	615	2,750	—
	312,500	10,000	30,000	37,500	60,000	100,000	360,000	—

$20 (DOUBLE EAGLE)

Liberty. "Twenty Dollars" below eagle.

 # 74.3 Weight: 33.4360 g. **Composition:** 0.9000 Gold, 0.9677 oz. AGW.

	Mintage	VF-20	XF-40	AU-50	MS-60	MS-65	Prf-65
	1,874,584	390	400	410	425	4,250	49,000
S	2,459,500	390	400	410	425	—	—
	111,526	390	400	410	700	3,200	—
S	1,596,000	390	400	410	465	—	—
2	31,254	400	450	475	875	—	—
2S	1,753,625	400	450	475	425	—	—
3	287,428	400	450	475	450	3,400	51,500
3S	954,000	400	450	475	425	9,750	—
4	6,256,797	400	450	475	425	3,300	50,000
4S	5,134,175	400	450	475	425	4,700	—
5	59,011	400	450	475	875	—	—
5S	1,813,000	400	450	475	550	—	—
6	69,690	400	450	475	525	13,500	52,500
6D	620,250	400	450	475	450	—	—
6S	2,065,750	400	450	475	450	—	—
7	1,451,864	400	450	475	425	6,800	—
7D	842,250	400	450	475	440	4,500	—
7S	2,165,800	400	450	475	440	—	—

Saint-Gaudens.
Roman numerals in date. No motto below eagle.

M# Pn1874 Designer: Augustus Saint-Gaudens. **Diameter:** 34 **Weight:** 33.4360 g. **Composition:** 0.9000 Gold, 0.9677 oz. AGW. **Notes:** The "Roman numerals" varieties for 1907 use Roman numerals for the date instead of Arabic numerals. The lettered-edge varieties have "E Pluribus Unum" on the edge, with stars between the words.

te	Mintage	VF-20	XF-40	AU-50	MS-60	MS-63	MS-65	Prf-65
7 extremely high relief, ique	—	—	—	—	—	—	—	—
)7 extremely high relief, tered edge	—	—	—	—	—	—	—	—

te: 1907 extremely high relief, lettered edge, Prf-68, private sale, 1990, $1,500,000.

Saint-Gaudens.
Roman numerals in date. No motto below eagle.

M# 126 Designer: Augustus Saint-Gaudens. **Diameter:** 34 **Weight:** 33.4360 g. **Composition:** 0.9000 Gold, 0.9677 oz. AGW.

te	Mintage	VF-20	XF-40	AU-50	MS-60	MS-63	MS-65	Prf-65
;MVII (1907) high relief, nique, AU-55, $150,000	—	—	—	—	—	—	—	—
;MVII (1907) high relief, vire rim	11,250	3,500	5,500	5,400	8,500	14,500	29,000	—
;MVII (1907) high relief, at rim	Inc. above	3,600	5,750	5,650	9,000	15,500	30,000	—

Saint-Gaudens.
Arabic numerals in date. No motto below eagle.

KM# 127 Designer: Augustus Saint-Gaudens. **Diameter:** 34 **Weight:** 33.4360 g. **Composition:** 0.9000 Gold, 0.9677 oz. AGW.

Date	Mintage	VF-20	XF-40	AU-50	MS-60	MS-63	MS-65	Prf-65
1907 large letters on edge, unique	—	—	—	—	—	—	—	—
1907 small letters on edge	361,667	430	450	450	565	850	2,500	—
1908	4,271,551	415	435	440	465	550	1,200	—
1908D	663,750	425	440	450	550	900	10,500	—

Saint-Gaudens. "In God We Trust" below eagle.

KM# 131 Designer: Augustus Saint-Gaudens. **Diameter:** 34 **Weight:** 33.4360 g. **Composition:** 0.9000 Gold, 0.9677 oz. AGW.

Date	Mintage	VF-20	XF-40	AU-50	MS-60	MS-63	MS-65	Prf-65
1908	156,359	400	420	430	460	750	1,250	38,000
1908D	349,500	400	400	420	460	800	5,300	—
1908S	22,000	650	1,200	1,250	4,400	11,000	37,000	—
1909/8	161,282	525	580	650	1,150	4,000	26,000	—
1909	Inc. above	450	560	625	700	2,950	48,000	49,000
1909D	52,500	500	690	775	1,200	3,800	36,000	—
1909S	2,774,925	360	415	450	485	675	5,750	—
1910	482,167	365	400	445	485	675	6,750	49,000
1910D	429,000	365	400	425	550	675	3,300	—
1910S	2,128,250	365	425	425	500	750	8,500	—
1911	197,350	365	410	425	515	1,850	11,000	39,500
1911D	846,500	365	410	425	485	650	1,275	—
1911S	775,750	365	400	425	480	750	5,700	—
1912	149,824	385	425	475	520	1,100	16,000	40,000
1913	168,838	365	400	430	500	1,850	26,000	40,000
1913D	393,500	380	415	430	525	900	5,500	—
1913S	34,000	550	800	840	1,250	3,100	43,000	—
1914	95,320	400	515	530	580	1,475	14,750	41,500
1914D	453,000	380	400	430	525	725	3,250	—
1914S	1,498,000	380	450	430	515	625	2,100	—
1915	152,050	390	450	520	625	1,675	14,500	47,500
1915S	567,500	380	400	425	500	725	2,000	—
1916S	796,000	380	400	430	585	750	2,150	—
1920	228,250	380	400	450	590	825	33,500	—
1920S	558,000	4,300	8,000	10,500	25,000	48,500	165,000	—
1921	528,500	8,000	14,000	20,000	35,000	90,000	225,000	—
1922	1,375,500	380	400	420	515	625	3,900	—
1922S	2,658,000	500	750	800	925	2,400	38,000	—
1923	566,000	380	400	440	525	625	1,050	—
1923D	1,702,250	380	410	450	540	740	1,375	—
1924	4,323,500	380	400	430	515	600	1,200	—
1924D	3,049,500	800	1,325	1,500	1,900	5,200	56,000	—
1924S	2,927,500	750	1,200	1,400	2,500	6,100	35,000	—
1925	2,831,750	380	400	425	485	585	1,150	—
1925D	2,938,500	1,000	1,750	2,300	3,400	7,600	52,500	—
1925S	3,776,500	900	1,350	1,550	5,800	16,750	80,000	—
1926	816,750	380	400	425	485	585	1,200	—
1926D	481,000	1,100	2,850	3,200	7,900	18,750	88,000	—
1926S	2,041,500	700	1,250	1,375	1,850	3,350	35,000	—
1927	2,946,750	380	400	425	475	575	1,100	—
1927D	180,000	—	—	225,000	260,000	425,000	750,000	—
1927S	3,107,000	2,500	4,400	4,550	12,500	27,000	100,000	—
1928	8,816,000	380	410	425	500	625	1,050	—
1929	1,779,750	4,750	7,000	8,000	13,000	12,500	35,000	—
1930S	74,000	6,000	8,500	9,300	18,000	35,000	80,000	—
1931	2,938,250	4,250	8,000	9,250	14,000	24,000	50,000	—
1931D	106,500	5,500	8,000	8,500	17,500	20,000	58,000	—
1932	1,101,750	7,000	10,000	11,500	19,000	25,000	36,000	—
1933 Sotheby/Stack Sale, July 2002	445,500	—	—	—	—	—	7,590,000	—

COMMEMORATIVE COINAGE 1892-1954

All commemorative half dollars of 1892-1954 have the following specifications: diameter -- 24.3 millimeters; weight -- 6.2500 grams; composition -- 0.9000 silver, 0.1808 ounces actual silver weight. Values for "PDS sets" contain one example each from the Philadelphia, Denver and San Francisco mints. "Type coin" prices are the most inexpensive single coin available from the date and mint-mark combinations listed.

QUARTER

COLUMBIAN EXPOSITION. **Obverse:** Queen Isabella **Diameter:** 24.3 **Weight:** 6.2500 g. **Composition:** 0.9000 Silver, 0.1808 oz. ASW. **KM#** 115

Date	Mintage	AU-50	MS-60	MS-63	MS-64	MS-65
1893	24,214	425	600	655	1,050	3,000

HALF DOLLAR

COLUMBIAN EXPO. **Obv. Designer:** Charles E. Barber **Rev. Designer:** George T. Morgan **KM#** 117

Date	Mintage	AU-50	MS-60	MS-63	MS-64	MS-65
1892	950,000	16.50	27.00	85.00	200	700
1893	1,550,405	14.00	27.00	85.00	200	715

PANAMA-PACIFIC EXPOSITION. **Designer:** Charles E. Barber. **KM#** 135

Date	Mintage	AU-50	MS-60	MS-63	MS-64	MS-65
1915S	27,134	285	340	625	1,150	2,400

LINCOLN-ILLINOIS. **Obv. Designer:** George T. Morgan **Rev. Designer:** John R. Sinnock **KM#** 143

Date	Mintage	AU-50	MS-60	MS-63	MS-64	MS-65
1918	100,058	80.00	105	115	140	400

MAINE CENTENNIAL. **Designer:** Anthony de Francisci. **KM#** 146

Date	Mintage	AU-50	MS-60	MS-63	MS-64	MS-65
1920	50,028	110	140	145	260	460

PILGRIM TERCENTENARY. **Designer:** Cyrus E. Dallin. **KM#** 147.1

Date	Mintage	AU-50	MS-60	MS-63	MS-64	MS-65
1920	152,112	59.00	70.00	85.00	145	475

2 x 2

ALABAMA CENTENNIAL. **Designer:** Laura G. Fraser. **Obverse:** "2x2" at right above stars **KM#** 148.1

Date	Mintage	AU-50	MS-60	MS-63	MS-64	MS-6
1921	6,006	175	300	525	875	2,38

ALABAMA CENTENNIAL. **Obv. Designer:** Laura G. Fraser **KM#** 148.2

Date	Mintage	AU-50	MS-60	MS-63	MS-64	MS-6
1921	59,038	125	210	450	750	2,27

MISSOURI CENTENNIAL. **Designer:** Robert Aitken. **KM#** 149.1

Date	Mintage	AU-50	MS-60	MS-63	MS-64	MS-
1921	15,428	225	410	775	1,400	5,0

2☆4

MISSOURI CENTENNIAL. **Designer:** Robert Aitken. **Obverse:** 2 star 4 in field at lef **KM#** 149.2

Date	Mintage	AU-50	MS-60	MS-63	MS-64	MS-
1921	5,000	380	470	900	1,650	4,8

PILGRIM TERCENTENARY. **Designer:** Cyrus E. Dallin. **Obverse:** 1921 date next to Pilgrim **KM#** 147.2

Date	Mintage	AU-50	MS-60	MS-63	MS-64	MS-65
1921	20,053	105	120	155	260	575

GRANT MEMORIAL. **Designer:** Laura G. Fraser. **KM#** 151.1

Date	Mintage	AU-50	MS-60	MS-63	MS-64	MS-65
1922	67,405	80.00	85.00	160	295	925

GRANT MEMORIAL. **Designer:** Laura G. Fraser. **Obverse:** Star above the word "Grant" **KM#** 151.2

ate	Mintage	AU-50	MS-60	MS-63	MS-64	MS-65
922	4,256	650	1,200	1,550	2,275	6,900

IONROE DOCTRINE CENTENNIAL. **Designer:** Chester Beach. **KM#** 153

ate	Mintage	AU-50	MS-60	MS-63	MS-64	MS-65
923S	274,077	29.00	41.00	155	400	2,750

UGUENOT-WALLOON TERCENTENARY. **Designer:** George T. Morgan. **KM#** 154

te	Mintage	AU-50	MS-60	MS-63	MS-64	MS-65
24	142,080	95.00	110	170	220	475

ALIFORNIA DIAMOND JUBILEE. **Designer:** Jo Mora. **KM#** 155

te	Mintage	AU-50	MS-60	MS-63	MS-64	MS-65
25S	86,594	105	120	170	300	1,025

RT VANCOUVER CENTENNIAL. **Designer:** Laura G. Fraser. **KM#** 158

Date	Mintage	AU-50	MS-60	MS-63	MS-64	MS-65
1925	14,994	230	295	375	575	1,325

LEXINGTON-CONCORD SESQUICENTENNIAL. **Designer:** Chester Beach. **KM#** 156

Date	Mintage	AU-50	MS-60	MS-63	MS-64	MS-65
1925	162,013	65.00	70.00	105	185	425

STONE MOUNTAIN MEMORIAL. **Designer:** Gutzon Borglum. **KM#** 157.1

Date	Mintage	AU-50	MS-60	MS-63	MS-64	MS-65
1925	1,314,709	42.00	55.00	70.00	90.00	210

OREGON TRAIL MEMORIAL. **Designer:** James E. and Laura G. Fraser. **KM#** 159

Date	Mintage	AU-50	MS-60	MS-63	MS-64	MS-65
1926	47,955	95.00	100.00	110	140	200
1926S	83,055	95.00	100.00	110	140	205
Type coin	—	95.00	100.00	110	140	260
1928	6,028	150	160	170	175	285
1933D	5,008	225	240	260	290	460
1934D	7,006	145	150	160	190	290
1936	10,006	105	115	125	145	200
1936S	5,006	125	135	160	200	285
1937D	12,008	125	140	150	180	225
1938 PDS set	6,005	490	490	600	620	660
1939 PDS set	3,004	1,050	1,200	1,350	1,450	1,750

U.S. SESQUICENTENNIAL. **Designer:** John R. Sinnock. **KM#** 160

Date	Mintage	AU-50	MS-60	MS-63	MS-64	MS-65
1926	141,120	60.00	78.00	155	565	5,100

VERMONT SESQUICENTENNIAL. **Obv. Designer:** Charles Keck **KM#** 162

Date	Mintage	AU-50	MS-60	MS-63	MS-64	MS-65
1927	28,142	150	165	180	290	825

HAWAIIAN SESQUICENTENNIAL. **Designer:** Juliette M. Fraser. KM# 163

Date	Mintage	AU-50	MS-60	MS-63	MS-64	MS-65
1928	10,008	1,050	1,300	1,850	2,600	4,900

DANIEL BOONE BICENTENNIAL. **Designer:** Augustus Lukeman. KM# 165.1

Date	Mintage	AU-50	MS-60	MS-63	MS-64	MS-65
1934	10,007	65.00	72.00	90.00	110	185
1935 PDS set	2,003	210	225	300	325	540

DANIEL BOONE BICENTENNIAL. **Designer:** Augustus Lukeman. **Reverse:** "1934" added above the word "Pioneer." KM# 165.2

Date	Mintage	AU-50	MS-60	MS-63	MS-64	MS-65
1935 PDS set	5,005	550	625	820	1,075	1,850
Type coin	—	65.00	72.00	90.00	110	185
1936 PDS set	5,005	210	225	295	325	550
1937 PDS set	2,506	525	675	660	800	1,050
1938 PDS set	2,100	725	775	975	1,150	1,500

MARYLAND TERCENTENARY. **Designer:** Hans Schuler. KM# 166

Date	Mintage	AU-50	MS-60	MS-63	MS-64	MS-65
1934	25,015	110	125	160	190	330

TEXAS CENTENNIAL. **Designer:** Pompeo Coppini. KM# 167

Date	Mintage	AU-50	MS-60	MS-63	MS-64	MS-65
1934	61,463	90.00	100.00	110	120	170
Type coin	—	90.00	100.00	110	120	180
1935 PDS set	9,994	270	300	320	340	490
1936 PDS set	8,911	270	290	300	320	480
1937 PDS set	6,571	280	300	310	330	510
1938 PDS set	3,775	525	625	740	775	1,150

ARKANSAS CENTENNIAL. **Designer:** Edward E. Burr. KM# 168

Date	Mintage	AU-50	MS-60	MS-63	MS-64	MS-65
Type coin	—	62.00	72.00	78.00	90.00	200
1935 PDS set	5,505	200	215	235	320	750
1936 PDS set	9,600	200	215	235	300	780
1937 PDS set	5,505	210	225	290	325	975
1938 PDS set	3,155	270	360	420	500	1,900
1939 PDS set	—	550	625	900	1,100	3,200

CONNECTICUT TERCENTENARY. **Designer:** Henry Kreiss. KM# 169

Date	Mintage	AU-50	MS-60	MS-63	MS-64
1935	25,018	170	195	215	320

HUDSON, N.Y., SESQUICENTENNIAL. **Designer:** Chester Beach. KM# 170

Date	Mintage	AU-50	MS-60	MS-63	MS-64
1935	10,008	405	465	510	710

OLD SPANISH TRAIL. **Designer:** L.W. Hoffecker. KM# 172

Date	Mintage	AU-50	MS-60	MS-63	MS-64
1935	10,008	725	780	850	950

SAN DIEGO-CALIFORNIA-PACIFIC EXPOSITION. **Designer:** Robert Aitken. KM

Date	Mintage	AU-50	MS-60	MS-63	MS-64
1935S	70,132	58.00	85.00	92.00	100.00
1936D	30,092	59.00	92.00	100.00	110

ALBANY, N.Y., CHARTER ANNIVERSARY. **Designer:** Gertrude K. Lathrop. KM

Date	Mintage	AU-50	MS-60	MS-63	MS-64
1936	17,671	190	205	215	235

ARKANSAS CENTENNIAL. **Obv. Designer:** Henry Kreiss **Rev. Designer:** Edwa Burr **Obverse:** Sen. Joseph T. Robinson KM# 187

Date	Mintage	AU-50	MS-60	MS-63	MS-64
1936	25,265	95.00	100.00	120	130

TLE OF GETTYSBURG 75TH ANNIVERSARY. Designer: Frank Vittor. KM# 81

	Mintage	AU-50	MS-60	MS-63	MS-64	MS-65
	26,928	250	285	320	385	600

DGEPORT, CONN., CENTENNIAL. Designer: Henry Kreiss. KM# 175

	Mintage	AU-50	MS-60	MS-63	MS-64	MS-65
	25,015	105	120	130	150	240

CINNATI MUSIC CENTER. Designer: Constance Ortmayer. KM# 176

	Mintage	AU-50	MS-60	MS-63	MS-64	MS-65
e coin	—	200	215	225	300	600
PDS set	5,005	625	720	765	880	2,475

EVELAND-GREAT LAKES EXPOSITION. Designer: Brenda Putnam. KM# 177

	Mintage	AU-50	MS-60	MS-63	MS-64	MS-65
6	50,030	62.00	68.00	75.00	95.00	220

LUMBIA, S.C., SESQUICENTENNIAL. Designer: A. Wolfe Davidson. KM# 178

	Mintage	AU-50	MS-60	MS-63	MS-64	MS-65
6 PDS set	9,007	490	525	555	600	720
e coin	—	160	170	180	195	240

LAWARE TERCENTENARY. Designer: Carl L. Schmitz. KM# 179

e	Mintage	AU-50	MS-60	MS-63	MS-64	MS-65
6	20,993	200	210	225	265	355

ELGIN, ILL., CENTENNIAL. Designer: Trygve Rovelstad. KM# 180

Date	Mintage	AU-50	MS-60	MS-63	MS-64	MS-65
1936	20,015	160	175	180	195	230

LONG ISLAND TERCENTENARY. Designer: Howard K. Weinman. KM# 182

Date	Mintage	AU-50	MS-60	MS-63	MS-64	MS-65
1936	81,826	58.00	65.00	75.00	120	375

LYNCHBURG, VA., SESQUICENTENNIAL. Designer: Charles Keck. KM# 183

Date	Mintage	AU-50	MS-60	MS-63	MS-64	MS-65
1936	20,013	145	155	170	215	275

NORFOLK, VA., BICENTENNIAL. Designer: William M. and Marjorie E. Simpson. KM# 184

Date	Mintage	AU-50	MS-60	MS-63	MS-64	MS-65
1936	16,936	345	365	385	400	450

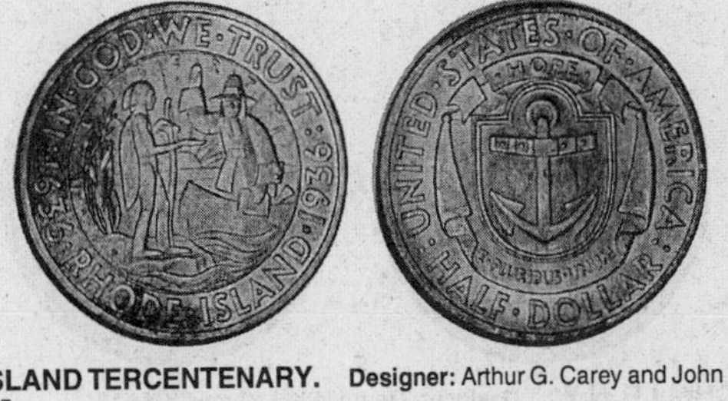

RHODE ISLAND TERCENTENARY. Designer: Arthur G. Carey and John H. Benson. KM# 185

Date	Mintage	AU-50	MS-60	MS-63	MS-64	MS-65
1936 PDS set	15,010	190	210	270	305	700
Type coin	—	65.00	70.00	85.00	115	215

SAN FRANCISCO-OAKLAND BAY BRIDGE. Designer: Jacques Schnier. KM# 174

Date	Mintage	AU-50	MS-60	MS-63	MS-64	MS-65
1936	71,424	100.00	110	120	160	270

WISCONSIN TERRITORIAL CENTENNIAL. **Designer:** David Parsons. **KM#** 188

Date	Mintage	AU-50	MS-60	MS-63	MS-64	MS-65
1936	25,015	140	150	165	210	240

YORK COUNTY, MAINE, TERCENTENARY. **Designer:** Walter H. Rich. **KM#** 189

Date	Mintage	AU-50	MS-60	MS-63	MS-64	MS-65
1936	25,015	135	145	158	168	190

BATTLE OF ANTIETAM 75TH ANNIVERSARY. **Designer:** William M. Simpson. **KM#** 190

Date	Mintage	AU-50	MS-60	MS-63	MS-64	MS-65
1937	18,028	395	430	460	550	650

ROANOKE ISLAND, N.C.. **Designer:** William M. Simpson. **KM#** 186

Date	Mintage	AU-50	MS-60	MS-63	MS-64	MS-65
1937	29,030	160	200	215	220	240

NEW ROCHELLE, N.Y.. **Designer:** Gertrude K. Lathrop. **KM#** 191

Date	Mintage	AU-50	MS-60	MS-63	MS-64	MS-65
1938	15,266	250	270	285	305	355

BOOKER T. WASHINGTON. **Designer:** Isaac S. Hathaway. **KM#** 198

Date	Mintage	AU-50	MS-60	MS-63	MS-64	MS-65
1946 PDS set	200,113	—	43.00	70.00	80.00	130
Type coin	—	13.00	14.50	16.00	20.00	40.00
1947 PDS set	100,017	—	72.00	80.00	110	280

Date	Mintage	AU-50	MS-60	MS-63	MS-64
1948 PDS set	8,005	—	135	140	160
1949 PDS set	6,004	—	215	225	240
1950 PDS set	6,004	—	120	135	140
1951 PDS set	7,004	—	110	140	145

IOWA STATEHOOD CENTENNIAL. **Designer:** Adam Pietz. **KM#** 197

Date	Mintage	AU-50	MS-60	MS-63	MS-64
1946	100,057	60.00	66.00	71.00	80.00

BOOKER T. WASHINGTON AND GEORGE WASHINGTON CARVER. **Designer:** Isaac S. Hathaway. **KM#** 200

Date	Mintage	AU-50	MS-60	MS-63	MS-64
1951 PDS set	10,004	—	80.00	105	120
Type coin	—	13.00	14.00	16.00	17.00
1952 PDS set	8,006	—	80.00	110	125
1953 PDS set	8,003	—	80.00	110	130
1954 PDS set	12,006	—	82.00	90.00	110

DOLLAR

LAFAYETTE. **Designer:** Charles E. Barber. **Diameter:** 38.1 **Weight:** 26.7300 g. **Composition:** 0.9000 Silver, 0.7736 oz. ASW. **KM#** 118

Date	Mintage	AU-50	MS-60	MS-63	MS-64	M
1900	36,026	325	565	1,400	2,850	

LOUISIANA PURCHASE EXPOSITION. **Designer:** Charles E. Barber. **Obvers** Jefferson **Diameter:** 15 **Weight:** 1.6720 g. **Composition:** 0.9000 Gold, 0.0484 oz. AC **KM#** 119

Date	Mintage	AU-50	MS-60	MS-63	MS-64	M
1903	17,500	340	420	670	1,850	3

LOUISIANA PURCHASE EXPOSITION. **Obv. Designer:** Charles E. Barber **Obve** McKinley **Diameter:** 15 **Weight:** 1.6720 g. **Composition:** 0.9000 Gold, 0.0484 oz. AG **KM#** 120

Date	Mintage	AU-50	MS-60	MS-63	MS-64	M
1903	17,500	300	370	650	1,675	3

LEWIS AND CLARK EXPO. **Obv. Designer:** Charles E. Barber **Diameter:** 15 **Weig** 1.6720 g. **Composition:** 0.9000 Gold, 0.7736 oz. AGW. **KM#** 121

Date	Mintage	AU-50	MS-60	MS-63	MS-64	MS
1904	10,025	520	775	1,875	4,275	9
1905	10,041	495	860	2,200	6,100	17

AMA-PACIFIC EXPO. **Obv. Designer:** Charles Keck **Diameter:** 15 **Weight:** 1.6720 **Composition:** 0.9000 Gold, 0.0484 oz. AGW. **KM#** 136

Mintage	AU-50	MS-60	MS-63	MS-64	MS-65
15,000	320	380	500	1,325	2,775

INLEY MEMORIAL. **Obv. Designer:** Charles E. Barber **Rev. Designer:** George T. organ **Diameter:** 15 **Weight:** 1.6720 g. **Composition:** 0.9000 Gold, 0.0484 oz. AGW. M# 144

Mintage	AU-50	MS-60	MS-63	MS-64	MS-65
9,977	270	360	550	1,175	2,700
10,000	365	510	925	2,150	3,725

NT MEMORIAL. **Obv. Designer:** Laura G. Fraser **Obverse:** Without a star above e word "Grant" **Diameter:** 15 **Weight:** 1.6720 g. **Composition:** 0.9000 Gold, 0.0484 oz. GW. **Notes:** The Grant gold-dollar varieties are distinguished by whether a star appears n the obverse above the word 'Grant.' **KM#** 152.1

Mintage	AU-50	MS-60	MS-63	MS-64	MS-65
5,016	1,025	1,150	1,500	2,975	3,650

Star

NT MEMORIAL. **Obv. Designer:** Laura G. Fraser **Obverse:** With a star above the vord "Grant" **Diameter:** 15 **Weight:** 1.6720 g. **Composition:** 0.9000 Gold, 0.0484 oz. AGW. M# 152.3

Mintage	AU-50	MS-60	MS-63	MS-64	MS-65
5,000	1,100	1,300	1,775	2,975	3,650

$2.50 (QUARTER EAGLE)

IAMA PACIFIC EXPO. **Obv. Designer:** Charles E. Barber **Rev. Designer:** George . Morgan **Diameter:** 18 **Weight:** 4.1800 g. **Composition:** 0.9000 Gold, 0.121 oz. AGW. KM# 137

	Mintage	AU-50	MS-60	MS-63	MS-64	MS-65
S	6,749	1,200	1,425	2,750	4,250	5,350

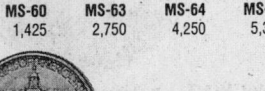

LADELPHIA SESQUICENTENNIAL. **Obv. Designer:** John R. Sinnock **Diameter:** 18 **Weight:** 4.1800 g. **Composition:** 0.9000 Gold, 0.121 oz. AGW. **KM#** 161

Mintage	AU-50	MS-60	MS-63	MS-64	MS-65
46,019	265	295	525	1,075	3,875

$50

NAMA PACIFIC EXPO.. **Obv. Designer:** Robert Aitken **Diameter:** 44 **Weight:** 83.5900 g. **Composition:** 0.9000 Gold, 2.419 oz. AGW. **KM#** 138

Date	Mintage	AU-50	MS-60	MS-63	MS-64	MS-65
1915S	483	22,500	26,500	37,000	47,000	109,000

PANAMA PACIFIC EXPO.. **Obv. Designer:** Robert Aitken **Diameter:** 44 **Weight:** 83.5900 g. **Composition:** 0.9000 Gold, 2.419 oz. AGW. **KM#** 139

Date	Mintage	AU-50	MS-60	MS-63	MS-64	MS-65
1915S	645	20,000	23,500	34,000	46,500	94,500

Note: In 1982, after a hiatus of nearly 20 years, coinage of commemorative half dollars resumed. Those designated with a 'W' were struck at the West Point Mint. Some issues were struck in copper-nickel. Those struck in silver have the same size, weight and composition as the prior commemorative half-dollar series.

COMMEMORATIVE COINAGE 1982-PRESENT

All commemorative silver dollar coins of 1982-present have the following specifications: diameter -- 38.1 millimeters; weight -- 26.7300 grams; composition -- 0.9000 silver, 0.7736 ounces actual silver weight. All commemorative $5 coins of 1982-present have the following specificiations: diameter -- 21.6 millimeters; weight -- 8.3590 grams; composition: 0.9000 gold, 0.242 ounces actual gold weight.

HALF DOLLAR

250TH ANNIVERSARY OF GEORGE WASHINGTON'S BIRTH. **Obv. Designer:** Elizabeth Jones **Diameter:** 30.6 **Weight:** 12.5000 g. **Composition:** 0.9000 Silver, 0.3618 oz. ASW. **KM#** 208

Date	Mintage	Proof	MS-65	Prf-65
1982D	2,210,458	—	6.50	—
1982S	—	(4,894,044)	—	6.00

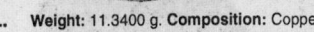

STATUE OF LIBERTY CENTENNIAL. **Weight:** 11.3400 g. **Composition:** Copper-Nickel Clad Copper **KM#** 212

Date	Mintage	Proof	MS-65	Prf-65
1986D	928,008	—	5.75	—
1986S	—	(6,925,627)	—	6.25

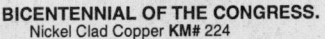

BICENTENNIAL OF THE CONGRESS. **Weight:** 11.3400 g. **Composition:** Copper-Nickel Clad Copper **KM#** 224

Date	Mintage	Proof	MS-65	Prf-65
1989D	163,753	—	7.00	—

Date	Mintage	Proof	MS-65	Prf-65
1989S	—	—	—	6.50

MOUNT RUSHMORE GOLDEN ANNIVERSARY. **Weight:** 11.3400 g. **Composition:** Copper-Nickel Clad Copper **KM#** 228

Date	Mintage	Proof	MS-65	Prf-65
1991D	172,754	—	12.50	—
1991S	—	—	—	12.50

500TH ANNIVERSARY OF COLUMBUS DISCOVERY. **Weight:** 11.3400 g. **Composition:** Copper-Nickel Clad Copper **KM#** 237

Date	Mintage	Proof	MS-65	Prf-65
1992D	135,702	—	10.00	—
1992S	—	(390,154)	—	11.00

OLYMPICS. **Weight:** 11.3400 g. **Composition:** Copper-Nickel Clad Copper **KM#** 233

Date	Mintage	Proof	MS-65	Prf-65
1992P	161,607	—	7.25	—
1992S	—	(519,645)	—	7.50

JAMES MADISON AND BILL OF RIGHTS. **Weight:** 12.5000 g. **Composition:** 0.9000 Silver, 0.3618 oz. ASW. **KM#** 240

Date	Mintage	Proof	MS-65	Prf-65
1993W	173,224	—	14.00	—
1993S	—	(559,758)	—	14.00

WORLD WAR II 50TH ANNIVERSARY. **Weight:** 11.3400 g. **Composition:** Copper-Nickel Clad Copper **KM#** 243

Date	Mintage	Proof	MS-65	Prf-65
1993P	192,968	(290,343)	17.00	17.00

1994 WORLD CUP SOCCER. **Weight:** 11.3400 g. **Composition:** Copper-Nicke Copper **KM#** 246

Date	Mintage	Proof	MS-65
1994D	168,208	—	9.50
1994P	122,412	(609,354)	—

ATLANTA OLYMPICS. **Obverse:** Basketball **Weight:** 11.3400 g. **Composition:** C Nickel Clad Copper **KM#** 257

Date	Mintage	Proof	MS-65
1995S	171,001	(169,655)	21.00

ATLANTA OLYMPICS. **Obverse:** Baseball **Weight:** 11.3400 g. **Composition:** Co Nickel Clad Copper **KM#** 262

Date	Mintage	Proof	MS-65
1995S	164,605	(118,087)	21.00

CIVIL WAR. **Weight:** 11.3400 g. **Composition:** Copper-Nickel Clad Copper **KM#** 2

Date	Mintage	Proof	MS-65
1995S	119,510	(330,099)	29.00

ATLANTA OLYMPICS. **Obverse:** Soccer **Weight:** 11.3400 g. **Composition:** Cop Nickel Clad Copper **KM#** 271

Date	Mintage	Proof	MS-65
1996S	52,836	(122,412)	39.50

ATLANTA OLYMPICS. **Obverse:** Swimming **Weight:** 11.3400 g. **Composition:** Cop Nickel Clad Copper **KM#** 267

Date	Mintage	Proof	MS-65	Prf-65
1996S	49,533	(114,315)	88.00	21.00

CAPITOL VISITOR CENTER. **Weight:** 11.3400 g. **Composition:** Copper-Nickel Clad Copper **KM#** 332

Date	Mintage	Proof	MS-65	Prf-65
2001	99,157	(77,962)	12.00	16.50

DOLLAR

LOS ANGELES XXIII OLYMPIAD. **Obv. Designer:** Elizabeth Jones **KM#** 209

Date	Mintage	Proof	MS-65	Prf-65
1983P	294,543	—	11.00	—
983D	174,014	—	11.00	—
983S	174,014	(1,577,025)	11.00	12.50

OS ANGELES XXIII OLYMPIAD. **Obv. Designer:** Robert Graham **KM#** 210

ate	Mintage	Proof	MS-65	Prf-65
984P	217,954	—	13.50	—
984D	116,675	—	21.00	—
984S	116,675	(1,801,210)	22.00	12.00

TATUE OF LIBERTY CENTENNIAL. **Obv. Designer:** John Mercanti **KM#** 214

te	Mintage	Proof	MS-65	Prf-65
36P	723,635	—	16.00	—
36S	—	(6,414,638)	—	16.00

CONSTITUTION BICENTENNIAL. **Obv. Designer:** Patricia Lewis Verani **KM#** 220

Date	Mintage	Proof	MS-65	Prf-65
1987P	451,629	—	12.50	—
1987S	—	(2,747,116)	—	12.50

OLYMPICS. **Obv. Designer:** Patricia Lewis Verani **Rev. Designer:** Sherl Joseph Winter **KM#** 222

Date	Mintage	Proof	MS-65	Prf-65
1988D	191,368	—	12.50	—
1988S	—	(1,359,366)	—	12.00

BICENTENNIAL OF THE CONGRESS. **Obv. Designer:** William Woodward **KM#** 225

Date	Mintage	Proof	MS-65	Prf-65
1989D	135,203	—	16.00	—
1989S	—	(762,198)	—	17.00

EISENHOWER CENTENNIAL. **Obv. Designer:** John Mercanti **Rev. Designer:** Marcel Jovine **KM#** 227

Date	Mintage	Proof	MS-65	Prf-65
1990W	241,669	—	17.50	—
1990P	—	(638,335)	—	20.00

KOREAN WAR. **Obv. Designer:** John Mercanti **Rev. Designer:** James Ferrell **KM# 231**

Date	Mintage	Proof	MS-65	Prf-65
1991D	213,049	—	14.50	—
1991P	—	(618,488)	—	15.00

OLYMPICS. **Obv. Designer:** John R. Deecken **Rev. Designer:** Marcel Jovine **KM# 234**

Date	Mintage	Proof	MS-65	Prf-65
1992D	187,552	—	24.00	—
1992S	—	(504,505)	—	28.00

MOUNT RUSHMORE GOLDEN ANNIVERSARY. **Obv. Designer:** Marika Somogyi **Rev. Designer:** Frank Gasparro **KM# 229**

Date	Mintage	Proof	MS-65	Prf-65
1991P	133,139	—	29.00	—
1991S	—	(738,419)	—	39.00

WHITE HOUSE BICENTENNIAL. **KM# 236**

Date	Mintage	Proof	MS-65	Prf-6
1992D	123,803	—	38.00	—
1992W	—	(375,851)	—	38.0

USO 50TH ANNIVERSARY. **Obv. Designer:** Robert Lamb **Rev. Designer:** John Mercanti **KM# 232**

Date	Mintage	Proof	MS-65	Prf-65
1991D	124,958	—	16.00	—
1991S	—	(321,275)	—	16.00

JAMES MADISON AND BILL OF RIGHTS. **KM# 241**

Date	Mintage	Proof	MS-65	Prf-6
1993D	98,383	—	19.50	—
1993S	—	(534,001)	—	20.

COLUMBUS QUINCENTENARY. **KM# 238**

Date	Mintage	Proof	MS-65	Prf-65
1992D	106,949	—	29.00	—
1992P	—	(385,241)	—	39.00

THOMAS JEFFERSON 250TH ANNIVERSARY OF BIRTH. **KM# 249**

Date	Mintage	Proof	MS-65	Prf-
1993P	266,927	—	26.50	
1993S	—	(332,891)	—	29

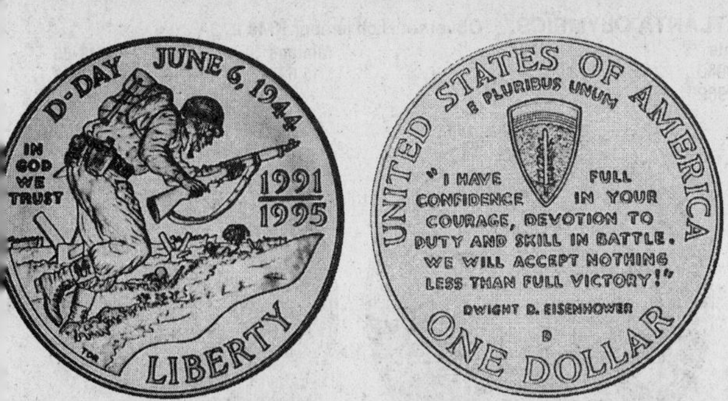

RLD WAR II 50TH ANNIVERSARY. KM# 244

	Mintage	Proof	MS-65	Prf-65
)	94,708	—	26.50	—
V	—	(322,422)	—	33.00

TIONAL PRISONER OF WAR MUSEUM. KM# 251

	Mintage	Proof	MS-65	Prf-65
V	54,790	—	63.00	—
P	—	(220,100)	—	41.00

. CAPITOL BICENTENNIAL. KM# 253

	Mintage	Proof	MS-65	Prf-65
D	68,352	—	22.00	—
S	—	(279,416)	—	24.00

TNAM VETERANS MEMORIAL. KM# 250

	Mintage	Proof	MS-65	Prf-65
4W	57,317	—	56.00	—
4P	—	(226,262)	—	67.00

WOMEN IN MILITARY SERVICE MEMORIAL. KM# 252

Date	Mintage	Proof	MS-65	Prf-65
1994W	53,054	—	28.00	—
1994P	—	(213,201)	—	26.50

WORLD CUP SOCCER. KM# 247

Date	Mintage	Proof	MS-65	Prf-65
1994D	81,698	—	27.00	—
1994S	—	(576,978)	—	29.00

ATLANTA OLYMPICS. **Obverse:** Gymnastics **KM#** 260

Date	Mintage	Proof	MS-65	Prf-65
1995D	42,497	—	60.00	—
1995P	—	(182,676)	—	29.00

ATLANTA OLYMPICS. **Obverse:** Track and field **KM#** 264

Date	Mintage	Proof	MS-65	Prf-65
1995D	24,796	—	60.00	—
1995P	—	(136,935)	—	28.00

ATLANTA OLYMPICS. **Obverse:** Cycling **KM#** 263

Date	Mintage	Proof	MS-65	Prf-65
1995D	19,662	—	88.00	—
1995P	—	(118,795)	—	36.00

ATLANTA OLYMPICS, PARALYMPICS. Obverse: Blind runner KM# 259

Date	Mintage	Proof	MS-65	Prf-65
1995D	28,649	—	85.00	—
1995P	—	(138,337)	—	34.00

CIVIL WAR. KM# 255

Date	Mintage	Proof	MS-65	Prf-65
1995P	45,866	—	40.00	—
1995S	—	(55,246)	—	52.00

SPECIAL OLYMPICS WORLD GAMES. KM# 266

Date	Mintage	Proof	MS-65	Prf-65
1995W	89,301	—	23.00	—
1995P	—	(351,764)	—	20.00

ATLANTA OLYMPICS. Obverse: Tennis KM# 269

Date	Mintage	Proof	MS-65	Prf-65
1996D	15,983	—	155	—
1996P	—	(92,016)	—	56.00

ATLANTA OLYMPICS. Obverse: High jumper KM# 272A

Date	Mintage	Proof	MS-65
1996D	15,697	—	235
1996P	—	(124,502)	—

ATLANTA OLYMPICS. Obverse: Rowing KM# 272

Date	Mintage	Proof	MS-65
1996D	16,258	—	200
1996P	—	(151,890)	—

ATLANTA OLYMPICS, PARALYMPICS. Obverse: Wheelchair racer KM# 26

Date	Mintage	Proof	MS-65
1996D	14,497	—	225
1996P	—	(84,280)	—

NATIONAL COMMUNITY SERVICE. KM# 275

Date	Mintage	Proof	MS-65
1996S	23,500	—	220
1996S	—	(101,543)	—

SMITHSONIAN 150TH ANNIVERSARY. KM# 276

Date	Mintage	Proof	MS-65
1996D	31,230	—	95.00
1996P	—	(129,152)	—

JACKIE ROBINSON 50TH ANNIVERSARY. KM# 279

Date	Mintage	Proof	MS-65	Prf-65
1997S	30,007	(110,495)	57.00	40.00

NATIONAL LAW ENFORCEMENT OFFICERS MEMORIAL. KM# 281

ate	Mintage	Proof	MS-65	Prf-65
997P	28,575	(110,428)	115	110

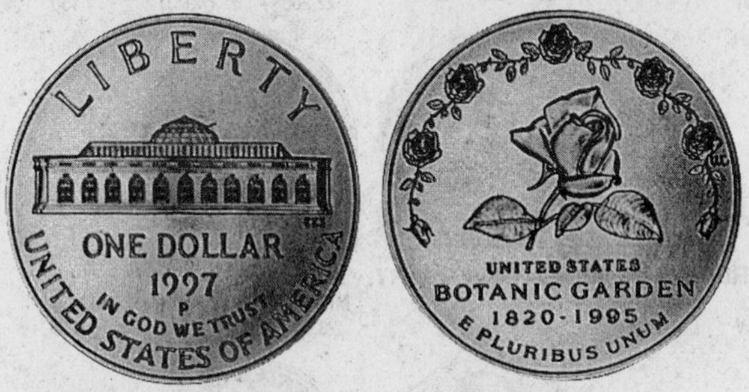

.S. BOTANIC GARDENS 175TH ANNIVERSARY. KM# 278

ate	Mintage	Proof	MS-65	Prf-65
997P	57,272	(264,528)	36.00	40.00

LACK PATRIOTS. **Obverse:** Crispus Attucks KM# 288

te	Mintage	Proof	MS-65	Prf-65
98S	37,210	(75,070)	90.00	73.00

OBERT F. KENNEDY. KM# 287

e	Mintage	Proof	MS-65	Prf-65
8S	106,422	(99,020)	31.00	40.00

DOLLEY MADISON. KM# 299

Date	Mintage	Proof	MS-65	Prf-65
1999P	22,948	(158,247)	40.00	42.50

YELLOWSTONE. KM# 300

Date	Mintage	Proof	MS-65	Prf-65
1999P	23,614	(128,646)	42.50	42.50

LEIF ERICSON. KM# 318

Date	Mintage	Proof	MS-65	Prf-65
2000P	28,150	(58,612)	58.50	47.50
2000 Iceland	—	(15,947)	—	—

LIBRARY OF CONGRESS. KM# 316

Date	Mintage	Proof	MS-65	Prf-65
2000P	52,771	(196,900)	36.00	40.00

AMERICAN BUFFALO. KM# 334

Date	Mintage	Proof	MS-65	Prf-65
2001	197,131	(272,869)	160	160

CAPITOL VISITOR CENTER. KM# 333

Date	Mintage	Proof	MS-65	Prf-65
2001	66,636	(143,793)	44.00	41.00

WEST POINT. KM# 338

Date	Mintage	Proof	MS-65	Prf-65
2002	—	—	40.00	40.00

WINTER OLYMPICS - SALT LAKE CITY. KM# 336

Date	Mintage	Proof	MS-65	Prf-65
2002	—	—	40.00	40.00

$5 (HALF EAGLE)

STATUE OF LIBERTY CENTENNIAL. KM# 215

Date	Mintage	Proof	MS-65	Prf-65
1986W	95,248	(404,013)	100.00	105

CONSTITUTION BICENTENNIAL. **Obv. Designer:** Marcel Jovine KM# 221

Date	Mintage	Proof	MS-65	Prf-65
1987W	214,225	(651,659)	100.00	100.00

OLYMPICS. **Obv. Designer:** Elizabeth Jones **Rev. Designer:** Marcel Jovine KM# 223

Date	Mintage	Proof	MS-65	Prf-65
1988W	62,913	(281,456)	105	100.00

BICENTENNIAL OF THE CONGRESS. **Obv. Designer:** John Mercanti KM# 226

Date	Mintage	Proof	MS-65	Prf-65
1989W	46,899	(164,690)	110	110

MOUNT RUSHMORE GOLDEN ANNIVERSARY. **Obv. Designer:** John Mercanti **Rev. Designer:** Robert Lamb KM# 230

Date	Mintage	Proof	MS-65	Prf-65
1991W	31,959	(111,991)	140	140

COLUMBUS QUINCENTENARY. KM# 239

Date	Mintage	Proof	MS-65	Prf-65
1992W	24,329	(79,730)	160	140

OLYMPICS. **Obv. Designer:** James C. Sharpe **Rev. Designer:** James M. Peed KM# 23

Date	Mintage	Proof	MS-65	Prf-6
1992W	27,732	(77,313)	140	12

JAMES MADISON AND BILL OF RIGHTS. KM# 242

Date	Mintage	Proof	MS-65	Prf-
1993W	22,266	(78,651)	150	13

WORLD WAR II 50TH ANNIVERSARY. KM# 245

Date	Mintage	Proof	MS-65	Prf-
1993W	23,089	—	170	1

WORLD CUP SOCCER. KM# 248

Date	Mintage	Proof	MS-65	Pr
1994W	22,464	(89,619)	150	

CIVIL WAR. KM# 256

Date	Mintage	Proof	MS-65	Pr
1995W	12,735	(55,246)	365	

OLYMPICS. **Obverse:** Torch runner KM# 261

Date	Mintage	Proof	MS-65	Pr
1995W	14,675	(57,442)	225	

PICS. **Obverse:** Stadium **KM# 265**

Mintage	Proof	MS-65	Prf-65
10,579	(43,124)	275	180

PICS. **Obverse:** Flag bearer **KM# 274**

Mintage	Proof	MS-65	Prf-65
9,174	(32,886)	300	240

PICS. **Obverse:** Cauldron **KM# 270**

Mintage	Proof	MS-65	Prf-65
9,210	(38,555)	300	245

HSONIAN 150TH ANNIVERSARY. **KM# 277**

Mintage	Proof	MS-65	Prf-65
9,068	(21,772)	395	260

NKLIN DELANO ROOSEVELT. **KM# 282**

Mintage	Proof	MS-65	Prf-65
11,894	(29,474)	240	230

KIE ROBINSON 50TH ANNIVERSARY. **KM# 280**

Mintage	Proof	MS-65	Prf-65
5,202	(24,546)	1,050	325

RGE WASHINGTON. **KM# 301**

Mintage	Proof	MS-65	Prf-65
—	—	240	260

CAPITOL VISITOR CENTER. **KM# 335**

Date	Mintage	Proof	MS-65	Prf-65
2001	38,017	(27,652)	500	225

WINTER OLYMPICS - SALT LAKE CITY. **KM# 337**

Date	Mintage	Proof	MS-65	Prf-65
2002	—	—	260	230

$10 (EAGLE)

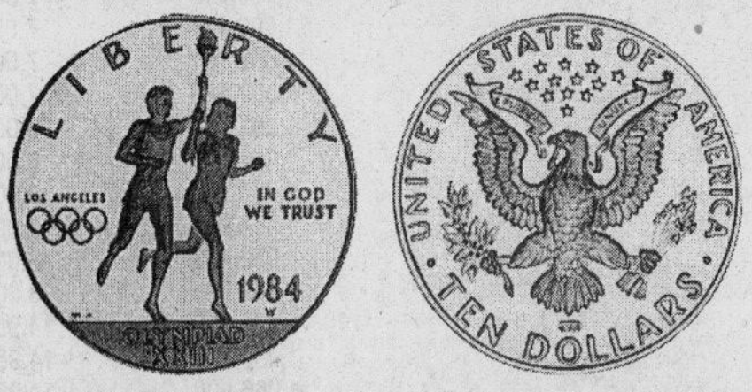

LOS ANGELES XXIII OLYMPIAD. **Diameter:** 27 **Weight:** 16.7180 g. **Composition:** 0.9000 Gold, 0.4839 oz. AGW. **KM# 211**

Date	Mintage	Proof	MS-65	Prf-65
1984W	75,886	(381,085)	180	185
1984P	33,309	—	—	280
1984D	34,533	—	—	280
1984S	48,551	—	—	220

LIBRARY OF CONGRESS. **Weight:** 16.2590 g. **Composition:** Platinum-Gold-Alloy **Notes:** Composition is 48 percent platinum, 48 percent gold, and 4 percent alloy. **KM# 317**

Date	Mintage	Proof	MS-65	Prf-65
2000W	6,683	(27,167)	925	540

MINT SETS

Mint, or uncirculated, sets contain one uncirculated coin of each denomination from each mint produced for circulation that year. Values listed here are only for those sets sold by the U.S. Mint. Sets were not offered in years not listed. In years when the Mint did not offer the sets, some private companies compiled and marketed uncirculated sets. Mint sets from 1947 through 1958 contained two examples of each coin mounted in cardboard holders, which caused the coins to tarnish. Beginning in 1959, the sets have been packaged in sealed Pliofilm packets and include only one specimen of each coin struck for that year. Listings for 1965, 1966 and 1967 are for "special mint sets," which were of higher quality than regular mint sets and were prooflike. They were packaged in plastic cases. The 1970 large-date and small-date varieties are distinguished by the size of the date on the coin. The 1976 three-piece set contains the quarter, half dollar and dollar with the Bicentennial design. The 1971 and 1972 sets do not include a dollar coin; the 1979 set does not include an S-mint-marked dollar.

Date	Sets Sold	Issue Price	Value
1947 Est. 5,000	—	4.87	1,300
1948 Est. 6,000	—	4.92	600
1949 Est. 5,200	—	5.45	900
1950 None issued	—	—	—
1951	8,654	6.75	850
1952	11,499	6.14	750
1953	15,538	6.14	575
1954	25,599	6.19	330
1955	49,656	3.57	180
1956	45,475	3.34	160
1957	32,324	4.40	265
1958	50,314	4.43	170
1959	187,000	2.40	40.00
1960	260,485	2.40	22.00
1961	223,704	2.40	41.00
1962	385,285	2.40	19.00
1963	606,612	2.40	15.00
1964	1,008,108	2.40	10.00
1965 SMS*	2,360,000	4.00	9.50
1966 SMS*	2,261,583	4.00	9.25
1967 SMS*	1,863,344	4.00	10.00
1968	2,105,128	2.50	4.40
1969	1,817,392	2.50	7.00
1970 large date	2,038,134	2.50	20.00
1970 small date	Inc. above	2.50	44.00
1971	2,193,396	3.50	4.00
1972	2,750,000	3.50	4.00
1973	1,767,691	6.00	26.50
1974	1,975,981	6.00	7.50
1975	1,921,488	6.00	12.00
1976 3 coins	4,908,319	9.00	17.50
1976	1,892,513	6.00	12.50
1977	2,006,869	7.00	8.50
1978	2,162,609	7.00	9.00

Date	Sets Sold	Issue Price	Value
1979	2,526,000	8.00	7.00
1980	2,815,066	9.00	7.00
1981	2,908,145	11.00	17.00
1982 & 1983 None issued	—	—	—
1984	1,832,857	7.00	7.50
1985	1,710,571	7.00	7.50
1986	1,153,536	7.00	26.00
1987	2,890,758	7.00	8.50
1988	1,646,204	7.00	9.50
1989	1,987,915	7.00	9.00
1990	1,809,184	7.00	9.00
1991	1,352,101	7.00	13.00
1992	1,500,143	7.00	7.50
1993	1,297,094	8.00	10.00
1994	1,234,813	8.00	12.00
1995	1,038,787	8.00	20.00
1996	1,457,949	8.00	22.50
1997	950,473	8.00	18.00
1998	1,187,325	8.00	20.00
1999	1,421,625	14.95	29.00
2000	1,490,160	14.95	18.00
2001	1,066,900	14.95	22.00
2002	—	14.95	17.00
2003	—	—	—

MODERN COMMEMORATIVE COIN SETS

Olympic, 1983-1984

Date	Price
1983 & 1984 proof dollars	20.00
1983 & 1984S gold and silver proof set: One 1983 and one 1984 proof dollar and one 1984 proof gold $10; KM209, 210, 211.	200
1983 & 1984 6 coin set: One 1983 and one 1984 uncirculated and proof dollar, one uncirculated and one proof gold $10; KM209, 210, 211.	400
1983 collectors set: 1983 PDS uncirculated dollars; KM209.	30.00
1983 & 1984 gold and silver uncirculated set: One 1983 and one 1984 uncirculated dollar and one 1984P uncirculated gold $10; KM209, 210, 211.	210
1984 collectors set: 1984 PDS uncirculated dollars; KM210.	45.00

Statue of Liberty

Date	Price
1986 3 coin set: proof silver dollar, clad half dollar and gold $5; KM212, 214, 215.	120
1986 2 coin set: uncirculated silver dollar and clad half dollar; KM212, 214.	16.00
1986 2 coin set: proof silver dollar and clad half dollar; KM212, 214.	16.50
1986 3 coin set: uncirculated silver dollar, clad half dollar and gold $5; KM212, 214, 215.	120
1986 6 coin set: 1 each of the proof and uncirculated issues; KM212, 214, 215.	230

Constitution

Date	Price
1987 2 coin set: uncirculated silver dollar and gold $5; KM220, 221.	125
1987 2 coin set: proof silver dollar and gold $5; KM220, 221.	105
1987 4 coin set: 1 each of the proof and uncirculated issues; KM220, 221.	195

Olympic, 1988

Date	Price
1988 2 coin set: uncirculated silver dollar and gold $5; KM222, 223.	115
1988 2 coin set: Proof silver dollar and gold $5; KM222, 223.	105
1988 4 coin set: 1 each of proof and uncirculated issues; KM222, 223.	250

Congress

Date	Price
1989 2 coin set: uncirculated silver dollar and clad half dollar; KM224, 225.	20.00
1989 2 coin set: proof silver dollar and clad half dollar; KM224, 225.	19.00
1989 3 coin set: uncirculated silver dollar, clad half and gold $5; KM224, 225, 226.	120
1989 3 coin set: proof silver dollar, clad half and gold $5; KM224, 225, 226.	110
1989 6 coin set: 1 each of the proof and uncirculated issues; KM224, 225, 226.	225

Mt. Rushmore

Date	Price
1991 2 coin set: uncirculated half dollar and silver dollar; KM228, 229.	36.00
1991 2 coin set: proof half dollar and silver dollar; KM228, 229.	35.00
1991 3 coin set: uncirculated half dollar, silver dollar and gold $5; KM228, 229, 230.	160
1991 3 coin set: proof half dollar, silver dollar and gold $5; KM228, 229, 230.	150
1991 6 coin set: 1 each of proof and uncirculated issues; KM228, 229, 230.	325

Columbus Quincentenary

Date	Price
1992 2 coin set: uncirculated half dollar and silver dollar; KM237, 238.	34.00
1992 2 coin set: proof half dollar and silver dollar; KM237, 238.	37.00
1992 3 coin set: uncirculated half dollar, silver dollar and gold $5; KM237, 238, 239.	180
1992 3 coin set: proof half dollar, silver dollar and gold $5; KM237, 238, 239.	160
1992 6 coin set: 1 each of proof and uncirculated issues; KM237, 238, 239.	360

Olympic, 1992

Date	Price
1992 2 coin set: uncirculated half dollar and silver dollar; KM233, 234.	24.00
1992 2 coin set: proof half dollar and silver dollar; KM233, 234.	30.00
1992 3 coin set: uncirculated half dollar, silver dollar and gold $5; KM233, 234, 235.	170
1992 3 coin set: proof half dollar, silver dollar and gold $5; KM233, 234, 235.	145
1992 6 coin set: 1 each of proof and uncirculated issues; KM233, 234, 235.	295

World War II

Date	Price
1993 6 coin set: 1 each of proof and uncirculated issues; KM243, 244, 245.	380
1993 2 coin set: uncirculated half dollar and silver dollar; KM243, 244.	30.00
1993 2 coin set: proof half dollar and silver dollar; KM243, 244.	36.00

Date
1993 3 coin set: uncirculated half dollar, silver dollar and gold $5; KM243, 244, 245.
1993 3 coin set: proof half dollar, silver dollar and gold $5; KM243, 244, 245.

Madison / Bill of Rights

Date
1993 2 coin set: uncirculated half dollar and silver dollar; KM240, 241.
1993 2 coin set: proof half dollar and silver dollar; KM240; 241.
1993 3 coin set: uncirculated half dollar, silver dollar and gold $5; KM240, 241, 242.
1993 3 coin set: proof half dollar, silver dollar and gold $5; KM240, 241, 242.
1993 6 coin set: 1 each of proof and uncirculated issues; KM240, 241, 242.

Jefferson

Date
1993 Jefferson: dollar, nickel and $2 note; KM249, 192.

U.S. Veterans

Date
1994 3 coin set: uncirculated POW, Vietnam, Women dollars; KM250, 251, 252.
1994 3 coin set: proof POW, Vietnam, Women dollars; KM250, 251, 252.

World Cup

Date
1994 2 coin set: uncirculated half dollar and silver dollar; KM246, 247.
1994 2 coin set: proof half dollar and silver dollar; KM246, 247.
1994 3 coin set: uncirculated half dollar, silver dollar and gold $5; KM246, 247, 248.
1994 3 coin set: proof half, silver dollar and gold $5; KM246, 247, 248.
1994 6 coin set: 1 each of proof and uncirculated issues; KM246, 247, 248.

Olympic, 1995-96

Date
1995 4 coin set: uncirculated basketball half, $1 gymnast & blind runner, $5 torch runner; KM257, 259, 260, 261.
1995 4 coin set: proof basketball half, $1 gymnast & blind runner, $5 torch runner; KM257, 259, 260, 261.
1995-96 4 coin set: proof halves, basketball, baseball, swimming, soccer; KM257, 262, 267, 271.
1996P 2 coin set: proof $1 gymnast & blind runner; KM259, 260.
1996P 2 coin set: proof $1 track & field, cycling; KM263, 264.
1996P 2 coin set: proof $1 wheelchair & tennis; KM268, 269.
1996P 2 coin set: proof $1 rowing & high jump; KM272, 272A.

Civil War

Date
1995 2 coin set: uncirculated half and dollar; KM254, 255.
1995 2 coin set: proof half and dollar; KM254, 255.
1995 3 coin set: uncirculated half, dollar and gold $5; KM254, 255, 256.
1995 3 coin set: proof half, dollar and gold $5; KM254, 255, 256.
1995 6 coin set: 1 each of proof and uncirculated issues; KM254, 255, 256.

Smithsonian

Date
1996 2 coin set: proof dollar and $5 gold; KM276, 277.
1996 4 coin set: proof and B.U. ; KM276, 277.

Botanic Garden

Date
1997 2 coin set: dollar, Jefferson nickel and $1 note; KM278, 192.

Jackie Robinson

Date
1997 2 coin set: proof dollar & $5 gold; KM279, 280.
1997 4 coin set: proof & BU; KM279, 280.
1997 legacy set.

Franklin Delano Roosevelt

Date
1997W 2 coin set: uncirculated and proof; KM282.

Kennedy

Date
1998 2 coin set: proof; KM287.
1998 2 coin collectors set: Robert Kennedy dollar and John Kennedy half dollar; KM287, 202b. Matte finished.

Black Patriots

Date
1998S 2 coin set: uncirculated and proof; KM288.

Dolley Madison

Date
1999 2 coin set: proof and uncirculated silver dollars; KM299.

George Washington

Date
1999 2 coin set: proof and uncirculated gold $5; KM301.

Yellowstone National Park

Date
1999 2 coin set: proof and uncirculated silver dollars; KM300.

Leif Ericson

Date
2000 2 coin set: proof and uncirculated silver dollars; KM318.

American Buffalo

Date
2001 2 coin set: 90% Silver unc. & proof $1.; KM334.

	Price
oin & currency set 90% unc. dollar & replicas of 1899 $5 silver cert.; KM334.	135

Capitol Visitor Center

	Price
coin set: proof half, silver dollar, gold $5; KM332, 333, 335.	265

PROOF SETS

oof coins are produced through a special process involving specially selected, highly ed planchets and dies. They usually receive two strikings from the coin press at sed pressure. The result is a coin with mirrorlike surfaces and, in recent years, a ɔ effect on its raised design surfaces. Proof sets have been sold off and on by the U.S. since 1858. Listings here are for sets from what is commonly called the modern era, 1936. Values for earlier proofs are included in regular date listings. Sets were not d in years not listed. Since 1968, proof coins have been produced at the San Francisco before that they were produced at the Philadelphia Mint. In 1942 the five-cent coin truck in two compositions. Some proof sets for that year contain only one type (five-set); others contain both types. Two types of packaging were used in 1955 -- a box flat, plastic holder. The 1960 large-date and small-date sets are distinguished by the of the date on the cent. Some 1968 sets are missing the mint mark on the dime, the of an error in the preparation of an obverse die. The 1970 large-date and small-date re distinguished by the size of the date on the cent. Some 1970 sets are missing the mark on the dime, the result of an error in the preparation of an obverse die. Some sets are missing the mint mark on the five-cent piece, the result of an error in the ration of an obverse die. The 1976 three-piece set contains the quarter, half dollar ollar with the Bicentennial designs. The 1979 and 1981 Type II sets have clearer mint s than the Type I sets for those years. Some 1983 sets are missing the mint mark on me, the result of an error in the preparation of an obverse die. Prestige sets contain ve regular-issue coins plus a commemorative silver dollar from that year.

	Sets Sold	Issue Price	Value
	3,837	1.89	6,400
	5,542	1.89	3,500
	8,045	1.89	1,300
	8,795	1.89	1,400
	11,246	1.89	1,150
	15,287	1.89	1,000
5 coins	21,120	1.89	1,150
5 coins	Inc. above	1.89	1,000
	51,386	2.10	575
	57,500	2.10	600
	81,980	2.10	300
	128,800	2.10	300
	233,300	2.10	165
box	378,200	2.10	110
flat pack	Inc. above	2.10	135
	669,384	2.10	55.00
	1,247,952	2.10	20.00
	875,652	2.10	45.00
	1,149,291	2.10	28.00
large date	1,691,602	2.10	19.00
small date	Inc. above	2.10	39.00
	3,028,244	2.10	10.00
	3,218,019	2.10	10.00
	3,075,645	2.10	13.50
	3,950,762	2.10	11.50
S	3,041,509	5.00	8.00
S no mint mark dime	Inc. above	5.00	9,500
S	2,934,631	5.00	8.50
S large date	2,632,810	5.00	14.00
S small date	Inc. above	5.00	80.00
S no mint mark dime	Inc. above	5.00	1,125
S	3,224,138	5.00	6.50
S no-mint mark nickel Est. 1,655	1,655	5.00	1,100
S	3,267,667	5.50	5.50
S	2,769,624	7.00	14.00
S	2,617,350	7.00	11.00
S	2,909,369	7.00	17.00
S no mint mark dime	Inc. above	7.00	47,000
S 3 coins	3,998,621	12.00	21.50
S	4,149,730	7.00	10.00
S	3,251,152	9.00	8.75
S	3,127,788	9.00	10.00
S Type I	3,677,175	9.00	10.00
S Type II	Inc. above	9.00	120
S	3,547,030	10.00	10.00
S Type I	4,063,083	11.00	8.50
S Type II	Inc. above	11.00	375
S	3,857,479	11.00	5.50
S	3,138,765	11.00	7.00
S Prestige Set	140,361	59.00	83.00
S no mint mark dime	Inc. above	11.00	1,000
S	2,748,430	11.00	12.50
S Prestige Set	316,680	59.00	22.00
S	3,362,821	11.00	7.00
S	2,411,180	11.00	21.50
S Prestige Set	599,317	48.50	38.00
S	3,972,233	11.00	5.50
S Prestige Set	435,495	45.00	25.00
S	3,031,287	11.00	11.00
S Prestige Set	231,661	45.00	32.00
S	3,009,107	11.00	10.00
S Prestige Set	211,087	45.00	39.00
S	2,793,433	11.00	15.00
S no S 1¢	3,555	11.00	3,400
S Prestige Set	506,126	45.00	31.50
S Prestige Set, no S 1¢	Inc. above	45.00	4,200
S	2,610,833	11.00	23.00

Date	Sets Sold	Issue Price	Value
1991S Prestige Set	256,954	59.00	72.00
1992S	2,675,618	12.00	11.25
1992S Prestige Set	183,285	59.00	42.00
1992S Silver	1,009,585	21.00	17.00
1992S Silver premier	308,055	37.00	20.00
1993S	2,337,819	12.50	16.50
1993S Prestige Set	224,045	57.00	52.50
1993S Silver	570,213	21.00	36.00
1993S Silver premier	191,140	37.00	42.50
1994S	2,308,701	13.00	22.00
1994S Prestige Set	175,893	57.00	57.00
1994S Silver	636,009	21.00	40.00
1994S Silver premier	149,320	37.50	50.00
1995S	2,010,384	12.50	63.50
1995S Prestige Set	17,112	57.00	135
1995S Silver	549,878	21.00	100.00
1995S Silver premier	130,107	37.50	110
1996S	2,085,191	16.00	16.00
1996S Prestige Set	55,000	57.00	270
1996S Silver	623,655	21.00	54.00
1996S Silver premier	151,366	37.50	57.50
1997S	1,975,000	12.50	62.50
1997S Prestige Set	80,000	57.00	175
1997S Silver	605,473	21.00	95.00
1997S Silver premier	136,205	37.50	96.00
1998S	2,078,494	12.50	40.00
1998S Silver	638,134	21.00	36.00
1998S Silver premier	240,658	37.50	38.00
1999S	2,543,401	19.95	78.00
1999S 5 quarter set	1,169,958	13.95	52.50
1999S Silver	804,565	—	195
2000S	3,082,944	19.95	40.00
2000S 5 quarter set	995,803	13.95	18.50
2000S Silver	965,921	31.95	38.00
2001S	2,235,000	19.95	57.50
2001S 5 quarter set	774,800	13.95	31.00
2001S Silver	849,600	31.95	105
2002S	—	19.95	23.00
2002S 5 quarter set	—	13.95	17.00
2002S Silver	—	31.95	72.00
2003S	—	—	—
2003S 5 quarter set	—	—	—
2003S Silver	—	—	—

AMERICAN EAGLE BULLION COINS

SILVER DOLLAR

Obv. Designer: Adolph A. Weinman. **Rev. Designer:** John Mercanti. **Diameter:** 40.6 **Weight:** 31.1010 g. **Composition:** 0.9993 SILVER, 1 oz. **Notes:** Prices based on $5.50 spot silver. **KM#273**

Date	Mintage	Unc	Prf.
1986	5,393,005	16.50	—
1986S	1,446,778	—	26.00
1987	11,442,335	8.00	—
1987S	904,732	—	26.00
1988	5,004,646	10.00	—
1988S	557,370	—	90.00
1989	5,203,327	10.00	—
1989S	617,694	—	30.00
1990	5,840,210	12.50	—
1990S	695,510	—	30.00
1991	7,191,066	8.50	—
1991S	511,924	—	60.00
1992	5,540,068	9.50	—
1992S	498,552	—	35.00
1993	6,763,762	9.00	—
1993P	403,625	—	120
1994	4,227,319	14.00	—
1994P	372,168	—	110
1995	4,672,051	12.50	—
1995P	395,400	—	105
1995W 10th Anniversary	30,125	—	2,250
1996	3,603,386	26.00	—
1996P	473,021	—	50.00
1997	4,295,004	12.50	—
1997P	429,682	—	90.00
1998	4,847,549	8.00	—
1998P	452,319	—	40.00
1999	7,408,640	9.50	—

Date	Mintage	Unc	Prf.
1999P	549,769	—	70.00
2000P	—	—	30.00
2000	9,239,132	8.50	—
2001	9,001,711	7.50	—
2001W	—	—	30.00
2002	10,539,026	7.50	—
2002W	—	—	29.00
2003	—	8.00	—
2003W	—	—	—

GOLD $5

Obv. Designer: Augustus Saint-Gaudens. **Rev. Designer:** Miley Busiek. **Diameter:** 16.5 **Weight:** 3.3930 g. **Composition:** 0.9167 GOLD, 0.1 oz. **KM#216**

Date	Mintage	Unc	Prf.
MCMLXXXVI (1986)	912,609	50.00	—
MCMLXXXVII (1987)	580,266	50.00	—
MCMLXXXVIII (1988)	159,500	190	—
MCMLXXXVIIIP (1988)P	143,881	—	56.00
MCMLXXXIX (1989)	264,790	90.00	—
MCMLXXXIXP (1989)P	82,924	—	56.00
MCMXC (1990)	210,210	70.00	—
MCMXCP (1990)P	99,349	—	56.00
MCMXCI (1991)	165,200	115	—
MCMXCIP (1991)P	70,344	—	58.00
1992	209,300	52.00	—
1992P	64,902	—	71.00
1993	210,709	52.00	—
1993P	58,649	—	66.00
1994	206,380	52.00	—
1994W	—	—	60.00
1995	223,025	52.00	—
1995W	—	—	56.00
1996	401,964	47.00	—
1996W	—	—	74.00
1997	528,515	45.00	—
1997W	—	—	91.00
1998	1,344,520	43.00	—
1998W	—	—	58.00
1999	2,750,338	42.00	—
1999W	—	—	58.00
2000	569,153	50.00	—
2000W	—	—	59.00
2001	269,147	50.00	70.00
2001W	—	—	—
2002	230,027	47.00	—
2002W	—	—	70.00
2003	—	50.00	—
2003W	—	—	—

GOLD $10

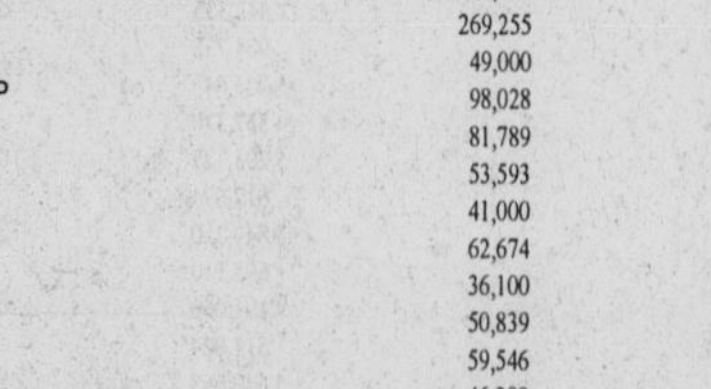

Obv. Designer: Augustus Saint-Gaudens. **Rev. Designer:** Miley Busiek. **Diameter:** 22 **Weight:** 8.4830 g. **Composition:** 0.9167 GOLD, 0.25 oz. **KM#217**

Date	Mintage	Unc	Prf.
MCMLXXXVI (1986)	726,031	125	—
MCMLXXXVII (1987)	269,255	125	—
MCMLXXXVIII (1988)	49,000	140	—
MCMLXXXVIIIP (1988)P	98,028	—	150
MCMLXXXIX (1989)	81,789	130	—
MCMLXXXIX (1989P)	53,593	—	150
MCMXC (1990)	41,000	145	—
MCMXCP (1990)P	62,674	—	150
MCMXCI (1991)	36,100	255	—
MCMXCIP (1991)P	50,839	—	150
1992	59,546	130	—
1992P	46,290	—	150
1993	71,864	130	—
1993P	46,271	—	150
1994	72,650	130	—
1994W	—	—	150
1995	83,752	130	—
1995W	—	—	150
1996	60,318	130	—
1996W	—	—	150
1997	108,805	120	—
1997W	—	—	150
1998	309,829	115	—
1998W	—	—	150
1999	564,232	115	—
1999W	—	—	150

Date	Mintage	Unc
2000	128,964	125
2000W	—	—
2001	71,280	120
2001W	—	—
2002	62,027	115
2002W	—	—
2003	—	125
2003W	—	—

GOLD $25

Obv. Designer: Augustus Saint-Gaudens. **Rev. Designer:** Miley Busiek. **Diameter:** 27 **We**
16.9660 g. **Composition:** 0.9167 GOLD, 0.5 oz. **KM#218**

Date	Mintage	Unc
MCMLXXXVI (1986)	599,566	250
MCMLXXXVII (1987)	131,255	250
MCMLXXXVIIP (1987)P	143,398	—
MCMLXXXVIII (1988)	45,000	290
MCMLXXXVIIIP (1988)P	76,528	—
MCMLXXXIX (1989)	44,829	385
MCMLXXXIXP (1989)P	44,264	—
MCMXC (1990)	31,000	400
MCMXCP (1990)P	51,636	—
MCMXCI (1991)	24,100	540
MCMXCIP (1991)P	53,125	—
1992	54,404	280
1992P	40,982	—
1993	73,324	240
1993P	43,319	—
1994	62,400	240
1994W	—	—
1995	53,474	250
1995W	—	—
1996	39,287	290
1996W	—	—
1997	79,605	225
1997W	—	—
1998	169,029	220
1998W	—	—
1999	263,013	220
1999W	—	—
2000	79,287	230
2000W	—	—
2001	48,047	285
2001W	—	—
2002	70,027	230
2002W	—	—
2003	—	230
2003W	—	—

GOLD $50

Obv. Designer: Augustus Saint-Gaudens. **Rev. Designer:** Miley Busiek. **Diameter:** 32.7 **Weight:** 33.9310 g. **Composition:** 0.9167 GOLD, 1 oz. **KM#219**

Date	Mintage	Unc
MCMLXXXVI (1986)	1,362,650	440
MCMLXXXVIW (1986)W	446,290	—
MCMLXXXVII (1987)	1,045,500	440
MCMLXXXVIIW (1987)W	147,498	—
MCMLXXXVIII (1988)	465,000	440
MCMLXXXVIIIW (1988)W	87,133	—
MCMLXXXIX (1989)	415,790	440
MCMLXXXIXW (1989)W	53,960	—
MCMXC (1990)	373,210	440
MCMXCW (1990)W	62,401	—
MCMXCI (1991)	243,100	450
MCMXCIW (1991)W	50,411	—
1992	275,000	440
1992W	44,835	—
1993	480,192	440
1993W	34,389	—

Date	Mintage	Unc	Prf.
1994	221,633	440	—
1994W	—	—	570
1995	200,636	440	—
1995W	—	—	570
1996	189,148	440	—
1996W	—	—	570
1997	664,508	435	—
1997W	—	—	570
1998	1,468,530	435	—
1998W	—	—	570
1999	1,505,026	430	—
1999W	—	—	570
2000	433,319	440	—
2000W	—	—	570
2001	143,605	440	—
2001W	—	—	—
2002	222,029	430	—
2002W	—	—	570
2003	—	440	—
2003W	—	—	—

PLATINUM $10

Obv. Designer: John Mercanti. **Rev. Designer:** Thomas D. Rogers Sr.. **Composition:** 0.9990 PLATINUM, 0.1 oz. **KM#283**

Date	Mintage	Unc	Prf.
1997	70,250	80.00	—
1997W	—	—	125
1998	39,525	80.00	—
1998W	—	—	125
1999	55,955	85.00	—
1999W	—	—	125
2000	34,027	80.00	—
2000W	—	—	125
2001	52,017	—	—
2001W	—	—	—
2002	23,005	—	—
2002W	—	—	—
2003	—	—	—
2003W	—	—	—

PLATINUM $25

Obv. Designer: John Mercanti. **Rev. Designer:** Thomas D. Rogers Sr. **Composition:** 0.9995 PLATINUM, 0.25 oz. **KM#284**

Date	Mintage	Unc	Prf.
1997	27,100	220	—
1997W	—	—	210
1998	38,887	195	—
1998W	—	—	225
1999	39,734	195	—
1999W	—	—	225
2000	20,054	195	—
2000W	—	—	225
2001	21,815	—	—
2001W	—	—	—
2002	27,405	—	—
2002W	—	—	—
2003	—	—	—
2003W	—	—	—

PLATINUM $50

Obv. Designer: John Mercanti. **Rev. Designer:** Thomas D. Rogers Sr. **Composition:** 0.9995 PLATINUM, 0.5 oz. **KM#285**

Date	Mintage	Unc	Prf.
1997	20,500	430	—
1997W	—	—	370
1998	32,415	350	—
1998W	—	—	410
1999	32,309	300	—
1999W	—	—	410
2000	18,892	340	—
2000W	—	—	415
2001	12,815	550	—
2001W	—	—	430
2002	24,005	—	—
2002W	—	—	405
2003	—	—	—
2003W	—	—	—

PLATINUM $100

Composition: 0.9995 PLATINUM, 1 oz. **Notes:** Prices based on $374.00 spot platinum. **KM#286**

Date	Mintage	Unc	Prf.
1997	56,000	700	—
1997W	—	—	775
1998	133,002	700	—
1998W	—	—	750
1999	56,707	700	—
1999W	—	—	750
2000	18,892	700	—
2000W	—	—	750
2001	14,070	725	—
2001W	—	—	750
2002	11,502	725	—
2002W	—	—	750
2003	—	—	—
2003W	—	—	—

The Oriental Republic of Uruguay (so called because of its location on the east bank of the Uruguay River) is situated on the Atlantic coast of South America between Argentina and Brazil. This South American country has an area of 68,536 sq. mi.(176,220 sq. km.) and a population of *3 million. Capital: Montevideo. Uruguay's chief economic asset is its rich, rolling grassy plains. Meat, wool, hides and skins are exported.

Uruguay was discovered in 1516 by Juan Diaz de Solis, a Spaniard, but settled by the Portuguese who founded Colonia in 1680. Spain contested Portuguese possession and, after a long struggle, gained control of the country in 1778. During the general South American struggle for independence, Uruguay 's first attempt was led by Gaucho soldier Jose Gervasio Artigas leading the Banda Oriental which was quelled by Spanish and Portuguese forces in 1811. The armistice was soon broken and Argentine force from Buenos Aires cast off the Spanish bond in the Plata region in 1814 only to be conquered again by the Portuguese from Brazil in the struggle of 1816-20. Revolt flared anew in 1825 and independence was reasserted in 1828 with the help of Argentina. The Uruguayan Republic was established in1830.

MINT MARKS

A - Paris, Berlin, Vienna
(a) Paris, privy marks only
D - Lyon (France)
H - Birmingham
Mx, Mo - Mexico City
(p) - Poissy, France
So - Santiago (Small O above S)
(u) – Utrecht

MONETARY SYSTEM

100 Centesimo = 1 Peso
1975-1993
1000 Old Pesos = 1 Nuevo (New) Peso
Commencing 1994
1000 Nuevos Pesos = 1 Peso Uruguayo

REPUBLIC

DECIMAL COINAGE

KM#19 CENTESIMO **Weight:** 2.0000 g. **Composition:** Copper Nickel

Date	Mintage	F	VF	XF	Unc	BU
1901A	6,000,000	0.45	1.00	4.00	30.00	—
1901A Proof	—	Value: 225				
1909A	5,000,000	0.45	1.00	3.00	10.00	—
1924(p)	3,000,000	0.45	1.00	3.00	12.00	—
1936A	2,000,000	0.50	1.00	3.00	12.50	—

KM#32 CENTESIMO **Weight:** 1.5000 g. **Composition:** Copper Nickel **Obverse:** Artigas bust right, 'HP' below

Date	Mintage	F	VF	XF	Unc	BU
1953	5,000,000	0.15	0.30	0.50	1.00	—
1953 Proof	—	Value: 100				

KM# 20 2 CENTESIMOS **Weight:** 3.5000 g. **Composition:** Copper Nickel

Date	Mintage	F	VF	XF	Unc	BU
1901A	7,500,000	0.50	2.00	9.00	20.00	—
1909A	10,000,000	0.50	1.00	3.00	10.00	—
1924(p)	11,000,000	0.50	1.00	3.00	10.00	—
1936A	6,500,000	0.50	1.25	7.00	15.00	—
1941So	10,000,000	0.50	1.00	4.00	12.00	—

KM# 20a 2 CENTESIMOS **Weight:** 3.5000 g. **Composition:** Copper

Date	Mintage	F	VF	XF	Unc	BU
1943So	5,000,000	0.25	0.50	2.00	8.00	—
1944So	3,500,000	0.25	0.50	2.00	8.00	—
1945So	2,500,000	0.25	0.50	3.00	9.00	—
1946So	2,500,000	0.25	0.50	3.00	8.00	—
1947So	5,000,000	0.25	0.50	1.50	7.00	—
1948So	7,500,000	0.25	0.50	1.00	6.00	—
1949So	7,400,000	0.25	0.50	1.00	6.00	—
1951So	12,500,000	0.25	0.50	1.00	6.00	—

KM# 33 2 CENTESIMOS **Weight:** 2.5000 g. **Composition:** Copper Nickel **Obverse:** Artigas bust right, 'HP' below

Date	Mintage	F	VF	XF	Unc	BU
1953	50,000,000	0.15	0.30	1.00	3.00	—
1953 Proof	—	Value: 65.00				

KM# 37 2 CENTESIMOS **Weight:** 2.0000 g. **Composition:** Nickel-Brass

Date	Mintage	F	VF	XF	Unc	BU
1960	17,500,000	—	0.15	0.25	1.00	—
1960 Proof	—	Value: 40.00				

KM# 21 5 CENTESIMOS **Weight:** 5.0000 g. **Composition:** Copper Nickel

Date	Mintage	F	VF	XF	Unc	BU
1901A	6,000,000	1.00	2.00	9.00	20.00	—
1901A Proof	—	Value: 325				
1909A	5,000,000	0.25	1.00	8.00	16.00	—
1909A Proof	—	Value: 125				
1924(p)	5,000,000	0.35	1.00	3.50	12.00	—
1936A	3,000,000	0.35	1.00	3.00	12.00	—
1941So	2,400,000	0.25	0.75	2.00	8.00	—
1941So Proof	—	Value: 200				

KM# 21a 5 CENTESIMOS **Weight:** 5.0000 g. **Composition:** Copper

Date	Mintage	F	VF	XF	Unc	BU
1944So	4,000,000	0.20	0.65	2.00	9.00	—
1946So	2,000,000	0.20	0.50	3.00	10.00	—
1947So	2,000,000	0.20	0.50	3.00	10.00	—
1948So	3,000,000	0.20	0.50	2.00	9.00	—
1949So	2,800,000	0.20	0.50	2.00	9.00	—
1951So	15,000,000	0.20	0.50	2.00	6.00	—

KM# 34 5 CENTESIMOS **Weight:** 3.5000 g. **Composition:** Copper Nickel **Obverse:** Artigas bust right, 'HP' below **Reverse:** Value within wreath

Date	Mintage	F	VF	XF	Unc	BU
1953	17,500,000	0.20	0.30	0.50	1.00	—
1953 Proof	—	Value: 75.00				

KM# 38 5 CENTESIMOS **Weight:** 3.5000 g. **Composition:** Nickel-Brass **Obverse:** Bust right **Reverse:** Value within wreath

Date	Mintage	F	VF	XF	Unc	BU
1960	88,000,000	—	0.15	0.25	1.00	—
1960 Proof	—	Value: 40.00				

KM# 25 10 CENTESIMOS **Weight:** 8.0000 g. **Composition:** Aluminum-Bronze **Subject:** Constitutional Centennial **Obverse:** MORLON behind neck **Reverse:** Cornucopia and torch flank denomination

Date	Mintage	F	VF	XF	Unc	BU
1930(a)	5,000,000	1.00	2.50	7.50	25.00	—

KM# 28 10 CENTESIMOS **Weight:** 6.0000 g. **Composition:** Aluminum-Bronze

Date	Mintage	F	VF	XF	Unc	BU
1936A	2,000,000	1.50	3.50	8.50	25.00	—

KM# 35 10 CENTESIMOS **Weight:** 4.5000 g. **Composition:** Copper Nickel **Obverse:** Artigas bust right, 'HP' below

Date	Mintage	F	VF	XF	Unc	BU
1953	28,250,000	0.15	0.20	0.30	1.00	-
1953 Proof	—	Value: 75.00				
1959	10,000,000	0.20	0.30	0.50	2.00	-

KM# 39 10 CENTESIMOS **Weight:** 4.5000 g. **Composition:** Nickel-Brass

Date	Mintage	F	VF	XF	Unc
1960	72,500,000	0.15	0.20	0.30	1.00
1960 Proof	—	Value: 75.00			

KM# 24 20 CENTESIMOS **Weight:** 5.0000 g. **Composition:** 0.8000 Silver .1286 oz. ASW **Obverse:** Radiant sun peeks out over shield of arms within wreath **Reverse:** Bust left

Date	Mintage	F	VF	XF	Unc
1920	2,500,000	2.00	4.00	9.00	25.00

KM# 26 20 CENTESIMOS **Weight:** 5.0000 g. **Composition:** 0.8000 Silver .1286 oz. ASW **Subject:** Constitutional Centennial **Obverse:** Constitution seated left, P. TURIN left of date **Reverse:** Five wheat ears, small cornucopia and torch mintmarks flank stems

Date	Mintage	F	VF	XF	Unc	BU
1930(a)	2,500,000	2.00	3.50	8.00	25.00	—

KM# 29 20 CENTESIMOS **Weight:** 3.0000 g. **Composition:** 0.7200 Silver .0694 oz. ASW

ate	Mintage	F	VF	XF	Unc	BU
942So	18,000,000	1.25	2.50	4.50	7.00	—

M# 36 20 CENTESIMOS **Weight:** 3.0000 g. **Composition:** 0.7200 Silver .0694 oz. ASW

ate	Mintage	F	VF	XF	Unc	BU
954(u)	10,000,000	0.75	1.50	2.50	5.00	—

M# 44 20 CENTESIMOS **Composition:** Aluminum

te	Mintage	F	VF	XF	Unc	BU
65So	40,000,000	0.15	0.20	0.35	1.00	—

M# 40 25 CENTESIMOS **Composition:** Copper Nickel **Obverse:** "HP" below bust

te	Mintage	F	VF	XF	Unc	BU
60	48,000,000	0.20	0.35	0.50	1.00	—
60 Proof	—	Value: 60.00				

22 50 CENTESIMOS **Weight:** 12.5000 g. **Composition:** 0.9000 Silver .3617 oz. ASW

e	Mintage	F	VF	XF	Unc	BU
6	400,000	5.00	10.00	28.00	200	—
7	5,600,000	4.00	7.00	20.00	100	—

31 50 CENTESIMOS **Weight:** 7.0000 g. **Composition:** 0.7000 Silver .1620 oz. ASW

	Mintage	F	VF	XF	Unc	BU
3So	10,800,000	BV	2.00	3.00	8.00	—

KM# 41 50 CENTESIMOS **Composition:** Copper Nickel **Obverse:** Artigas bust right, 'HP' below

Date	Mintage	F	VF	XF	Unc	BU
1960	18,000,000	0.20	0.40	0.60	1.00	—
1960 Proof	—	Value: 60.00				

KM# 45 50 CENTESIMOS **Composition:** Aluminum

Date	Mintage	F	VF	XF	Unc	BU
1965So	50,000,000	0.15	0.25	0.40	1.00	—

KM# 23 PESO **Weight:** 25.0000 g. **Composition:** 0.9000 Silver .7235 oz. ASW

Date	Mintage	F	VF	XF	Unc	BU
1917	2,000,000	10.00	20.00	50.00	250	—

KM# 30 PESO **Weight:** 9.0000 g. **Composition:** 0.7200 Silver .2083 oz. ASW

Date	Mintage	F	VF	XF	Unc	BU
1942So	9,000,000	BV	3.00	8.00	20.00	—

KM# 42 PESO **Composition:** Copper Nickel **Obverse:** Artigas bust right, 'HP' below

Date	Mintage	F	VF	XF	Unc	BU
1960	8,000,000	0.25	0.50	0.75	2.00	—
1960 Proof	—	Value: 75.00				

KM# 46 PESO **Composition:** Aluminum-Bronze

Date	Mintage	F	VF	XF	Unc	BU
1965So	60,000,000	—	0.15	0.35	1.00	—
1965So Proof	25	Value: 65.00				

KM# 49 PESO **Composition:** Nickel-Brass **Reverse:** Ceibo, national flower

Date	Mintage	F	VF	XF	Unc	BU
1968So	103,200,000	—	—	0.15	0.75	—
1968So Proof	50	Value: 50.00				

KM# 52 PESO **Composition:** Aluminum-Brass

Date	Mintage	F	VF	XF	Unc	BU
1969So	51,800,000	—	—	0.15	0.75	—

KM# 27 5 PESOS **Weight:** 8.4850 g. **Composition:** 0.9170 Gold .2501 oz. AGW **Subject:** Constitution Centennial **Obverse:** Artigas head right, L. BAZOR in left field behind neck

Date	F	VF	XF	Unc	BU
1930(a)	100	115	135	175	—

Note: Only 14,415 were released. Remainder withheld

KM# 47 5 PESOS **Composition:** Aluminum-Bronze

Date	Mintage	F	VF	XF	Unc	BU
1965So	18,000,000	0.20	0.30	0.50	1.00	—
1965So Proof	25	Value: 75.00				

KM# 50 5 PESOS **Composition:** Nickel-Brass **Reverse:** Ceibo, national flower

Date	Mintage	F	VF	XF	Unc	BU
1968So	42,680,000	0.10	0.20	0.30	0.40	—
1968So Proof	50	Value: 65.00				

KM# 53 5 PESOS **Composition:** Aluminum-Bronze

Date	Mintage	F	VF	XF	Unc	BU
1969So	42,320,000	—	—	0.10	0.30	—

KM# 43 10 PESOS **Weight:** 12.5000 g. **Composition:** 0.9000 Silver .3617 oz. ASW **Subject:** Sesquicentennial of Revolution Against Spain

Date	Mintage	F	VF	XF	Unc	BU
1961	3,000,000	BV	—	3.50	7.00	—
1961 Proof	—	Value: 600				

KM# 48 10 PESOS **Composition:** Aluminum-Bronze

Date	Mintage	F	VF	XF	Unc	BU
1965So	18,000,000	0.15	0.20	0.35	1.00	—

KM# 51 10 PESOS **Composition:** Nickel-Brass **Reverse:** Ceibo, national flower

Date	Mintage	F	VF	XF	Unc	BU
1968So	90,000,000	0.15	0.20	0.35	0.65	—
1968So Proof	50	Value: 80.00				

KM# 54 10 PESOS **Composition:** Aluminum-Bronze

Date	Mintage	F	VF	XF	Unc	BU
1969So	10,000,000	0.15	0.20	0.35	0.65	—

KM# 56 20 PESOS **Composition:** Copper Nickel **Reverse:** Spears of wheat

Date	Mintage	F	VF	XF	Unc	BU
1970So	50,000,000	0.15	0.25	0.40	0.75	—
1970So Proof	—	Value: 80.00				

KM# 57 50 PESOS **Composition:** Copper Nickel **Reverse:** Spears of wheat

Date	Mintage	F	VF	XF	Unc	BU
1970So	20,000,000	0.20	0.40	0.60	1.50	—
1970So Proof	—	Value: 80.00				

KM# 58 50 PESOS **Composition:** Nickel-Brass **Subject:** Centennial - Birth of Rodo

Date	Mintage	F	VF	XF	Unc	BU
1971So	15,000,000	0.20	0.50	1.00	2.00	—

KM# 58a 50 PESOS **Weight:** 6.0200 g. **Composition:** 0.9000 Silver .1742 oz. ASW **Subject:** Centennial - Birth of Rodo

Date	Mintage	F	VF	XF	Unc	BU
1971So Proof	1,000	Value: 17.50				

KM# 58b 50 PESOS **Composition:** Gold **Subject:** Centennial - Birth of Rodo

Date	Mintage	F	VF	XF	Unc	BU
1971So Proof	100	Value: 350				

KM# 59 100 PESOS **Composition:** Copper Nickel

Date	Mintage	F	VF	XF	Unc	BU
1973Mx	20,000,000	0.25	0.50	1.00	2.50	—

KM# 55 1000 PESOS **Weight:** 25.0000 g. **Composition:** 0.9000 Silver .7234 oz. ASW **Series:** F.A.O

Date	Mintage	F	VF	XF	Unc	BU
1969So	500,000	—	BV	6.50	10.00	—
1969So Proof	350	Value: 150				

KM# 55a 1000 PESOS **Composition:** Bronze **Series:** F.A.O.

Date	Mintage	F	VF	XF	Unc	BU
1969So	11,000	—	—	15.00	28.00	—

KM# 55b 1000 PESOS **Composition:** Gold **Series:** F.A.O

Date	Mintage	F	VF	XF	Unc	BU
1969So	450	—	—	—	725	—

REFORM COINAGE

1000 Old Pesos = 1 Nuevo (New) Peso

KM# 71 CENTESIMO **Composition:** Aluminum **Obverse:** Radiant sun

Date	Mintage	F	VF	XF	Unc	BU
1977So	10,000,000	—	—	0.15	0.25	—

KM# 71a CENTESIMO **Weight:** 3.7000 g. **Composition:** 0.9000 Silver .1071 oz. ASW **Obverse:** Radiant sun

Date	Mintage	F	VF	XF	Unc	BU
1979So Proof	202	Value: 15.00				

KM# 71b CENTESIMO **Weight:** 6.2600 g. **Composition:** 0.9000 Gold .1811 oz. AGW **Obverse:** Radiant sun

Date	Mintage	F	VF	XF	Unc	BU
1979So Proof	50	Value: 175				

KM# 72 2 CENTESIMOS **Composition:** Aluminum **Obverse:** Radiant sun

Date	Mintage	F	VF	XF	Unc	BU
1977So	17,000,000	—	—	0.15	0.25	—
1978So	3,000,000	—	—	0.15	0.25	—

KM# 72a 2 CENTESIMOS **Weight:** 5.2000 g. **Comp.:** 0.9000 Silver .1505 oz. ASW **Obverse:** Radiant sun

Date	Mintage	F	VF	XF	Unc	BU
1979So Proof	202	Value: 20.00				

KM# 72b 2 CENTESIMOS **Weight:** 9.2500 g. **Comp.:** 0.9000 Gold .2676 oz. AGW **Obverse:** Radiant sun

Date	Mintage	F	VF	XF	Unc	BU
1979So Proof	52	Value: 275				

KM# 73 5 CENTESIMOS **Composition:** Aluminum **Obverse:** Steer left

Date	Mintage	F	VF	XF	Unc	BU
1977So	11,000,000	—	—	0.15	0.50	—
1978So	19,000,000	—	—	0.15	0.50	—

KM# 73a 5 CENTESIMOS **Weight:** 7.4000 g. **Composition:** 0.9000 Silver .2141 oz. ASW **Obverse:** Steer left

Date	Mintage	F	VF	XF	Unc	BU
1979So Proof	202	Value: 20.00				

KM# 73b 5 CENTESIMOS **Weight:** 12.5500 g. **Composition:** 0.9000 Gold .3631 oz. AGW **Obverse:** Steer left

Date	Mintage	F	VF	XF	Unc	BU
1979So Proof	52	Value: 350				

KM# 66 10 CENTESIMOS **Composition:** Aluminum-Bronze **Obverse:** Horse left

Date	Mintage	F	VF	XF	Unc	BU
1976So	127,400,000	—	—	0.30	0.80	1.2
1976So Proof	—	—	—	—	—	—
1977So	12,700,000	—	—	0.35	0.85	1.2
1978So	19,900,000	—	—	0.35	0.85	1.2
1981So	—	—	—	0.35	0.85	1.2

KM# 66a 10 CENTESIMOS **Weight:** 3.8000 g. **Composition:** 0.9000 Silver .1100 oz. ASW **Obverse:** Horse left

Date	Mintage	F	VF	XF	Unc	BU
1976So Proof	200	Value: 20.00				
1977So Proof	200	Value: 20.00				

KM# 66b 10 CENTESIMOS **Weight:** 6.0000 g. **Composition:** 0.9000 Gold .1736 oz. AGW **Obverse:** Horse left

Date	Mintage	F	VF	XF	Unc	BU
1976So Proof	50	Value: 175				

KM# 67 20 CENTESIMOS **Comp.:** Aluminum-Bronze

Date	Mintage	F	VF	XF	Unc
1976So	40,000,000	—	—	0.20	0.45
1976So Proof	—	—	—	—	—
1977So	4,700,000	—	—	0.20	0.60
1978So	15,300,000	—	—	0.20	0.45
1981So	—	—	—	0.20	0.45

KM# 67a 20 CENTESIMOS **Weight:** 6.4000 g. **Composition:** 0.9000 Silver .1852 oz. ASW

Date	Mintage	F	VF	XF	Unc
1976So Proof	200	Value: 22.50			
1977So Proof	200	Value: 22.50			

KM# 67b 20 CENTESIMOS **Weight:** 10.5000 g. **Composition:** 0.9000 Gold .3038 oz. AGW

Date	Mintage	F	VF	XF	Unc
1976So Proof	50	Value: 350			

KM# 68 50 CENTESIMOS **Composition:** Aluminum-Bronze **Obverse:** Scale

Date	Mintage	F	VF	XF	Unc
1976So	30,000,000	—	—	0.20	0.50
1976So Proof	—	—	—	—	—
1977So	9,800,000	—	—	0.20	0.50
1978So	200,000	—	—	0.20	0.55
1981So	—	—	—	0.20	0.50

KM# 68a 50 CENTESIMOS **Weight:** 9.0000 g. **Composition:** 0.9000 Silver .2604 oz. ASW **Obverse:** Sc

Date	Mintage	F	VF	XF	Unc
1976So Proof	200	Value: 35.00			
1977So Proof	200	Value: 35.00			

KM# 68b 50 CENTESIMOS **Weight:** 15.0000 g. **Composition:** 0.9000 Gold .4340 oz. AGW **Obverse:** Sc

Date	Mintage	F	VF	XF	Unc	BU
1976So Proof	50	Value: 500				

KM# 69 NUEVO PESO **Composition:** Aluminum-Bronze **Obverse:** Bust of Jose Gervasio Artigas left

ate	Mintage	F	VF	XF	Unc	BU
976So	65,540,000	—	—	0.30	0.60	—
976So Proof	—	—	—	—	—	—
977So	7,360,000	—	—	0.30	0.65	—
978So	27,100,000	—	—	0.30	0.65	—

<M# 69a NUEVO PESO **Weight:** 13.5000 g. **Composition:** 0.9000 Silver .3906 oz. ASW **Obverse:** Bust of Jose Gervasio Artigas left

ate	Mintage	F	VF	XF	Unc	BU
976So Proof	200	Value: 40.00				

<M# 69b NUEVO PESO **Weight:** 23.0000 g. **Composition:** 0.9000 Gold .6655 oz. AGW **Obverse:** Bust of Jose Gervasio Artigas left

ate	Mintage	F	VF	XF	Unc	BU
976So Proof	50	Value: 600				

M# 74 NUEVO PESO **Composition:** Copper Nickel **Obv.:** Radiant sun peeking over shield of arms within wreath

ate	Mintage	F	VF	XF	Unc	BU
980So	50,000,000	—	0.20	0.35	0.65	—

M# 74a NUEVO PESO **Weight:** 7.0000 g. **Composition:** 0.9000 Silver .2026 oz. ASW **Obverse:** Radiant sun peeking over shield of arms within wreath

te	Mintage	F	VF	XF	Unc	BU
80So Proof	300	Value: 25.00				

M# 74b NUEVO PESO **Weight:** 11.6500 g. **Composition:** 0.9000 Gold .3371 oz. AGW **Obverse:** Radiant sun peeking over shield of arms within wreath

te	Mintage	F	VF	XF	Unc	BU
80So Proof	100	Value: 300				

M# 76 NUEVO PESO **Weight:** 6.9400 g. **Composition:** 0.9000 Silver .2008 oz. ASW **Obverse:** National flag

te	Mintage	F	VF	XF	Unc	BU
31 Proof	100	Value: 30.00				

M# 95 NUEVO PESO **Composition:** Stainless Steel

te	F	VF	XF	Unc	BU
39	—	—	0.15	0.35	—

 # 77 2 NUEVO PESOS **Composition:** Copper-Nickel-Zinc **Subject:** World Food Day

	Mintage	F	VF	XF	Unc	BU
	95,000,000	—	0.25	0.50	1.00	—

 # 77a 2 NUEVO PESOS **Weight:** 14.5300 g. **Composition:** 0.9000 Gold .4204 oz. AGW **Subject:** World Food Day

	Mintage	F	VF	XF	Unc	BU
Proof	100	Value: 400				

KM# 65 5 NUEVO PESOS **Comp.:** Copper-Nickel-Aluminum **Subject:** 150th Anniversary - Revolutionary Movement

Date	Mintage	F	VF	XF	Unc	BU
ND(1975)So	3,000,000	0.50	0.75	1.25	3.50	—

KM# 65a 5 NUEVO PESOS **Weight:** 18.4300 g. **Composition:** 0.9000 Silver .5332 oz. ASW **Subject:** 150th Anniversary - Revolutionary Movement

Date	Mintage	F	VF	XF	Unc	BU
ND(1975)So Proof	2,000	Value: 15.00				

KM# 65b 5 NUEVO PESOS **Composition:** Gold **Subject:** 150th Anniversary - Revolutionary Movement

Date	Mintage	F	VF	XF	Unc	BU
ND(1975)So Proof	1,000	Value: 500				

Note: 50 pieces each in aluminum, alpaca and copper are reported to have been struck

KM# 70 5 NUEVO PESOS **Comp.:** Copper-Aluminum **Subject:** 250th Anniversary - Founding of Montevideo

Date	Mintage	F	VF	XF	Unc	BU
1976So	300,000	0.75	1.00	1.50	4.00	—

KM# 70a 5 NUEVO PESOS **Weight:** 30.0000 g. **Composition:** 0.9000 Gold .8681 oz. AGW **Subject:** 250th Anniversary - Founding of Montevideo

Date	Mintage	F	VF	XF	Unc	BU
1976So Proof	100	Value: 650				

KM# 70b 5 NUEVO PESOS **Composition:** Silver **Subject:** 250th Anniversary - Founding of Montevideo

Date	F	VF	XF	Unc	BU
1976So	—	—	—	175	—

KM# 75 5 NUEVO PESOS **Composition:** Copper Nickel **Obverse:** National flag

Date	Mintage	F	VF	XF	Unc	BU
1980So	50,000,000	—	0.20	0.40	1.50	—
1981So	—	—	0.20	0.40	1.50	—

KM# 75a 5 NUEVO PESOS **Weight:** 9.3000 g. **Composition:** 0.9000 Silver .2691 oz. ASW **Obverse:** National flag

Date	Mintage	F	VF	XF	Unc	BU
1980So Proof	300	Value: 30.00				

KM# 75b 5 NUEVO PESOS **Weight:** 15.6000 g. **Composition:** 0.9000 Gold .4514 oz. AGW **Obverse:** National flag

Date	Mintage	F	VF	XF	Unc	BU
1980So Proof	100	Value: 450				

KM# 78 5 NUEVO PESOS **Weight:** 9.3000 g. **Composition:** 0.9000 Silver .2691 oz. ASW **Obverse:** Coat of arms

Date	Mintage	F	VF	XF	Unc	BU
1981 Proof	100	Value: 30.00				

KM# 92 5 NUEVO PESOS **Composition:** Stainless Steel

Date	Mintage	F	VF	XF	Unc	BU
1989	65,000,000	—	—	0.15	0.35	—

KM# 79 10 NUEVO PESOS **Composition:** Copper Nickel **Obverse:** Bust of Jose Gervasio Artigas half left

Date	F	VF	XF	Unc	BU
1981So	—	0.20	0.50	1.75	—

KM# 79a 10 NUEVO PESOS **Weight:** 11.6300 g. **Composition:** 0.9000 Silver .3365 oz. ASW **Obverse:** Bust of Jose Gervasio Artigas half left

Date	Mintage	F	VF	XF	Unc	BU
1981So Proof	100	Value: 35.00				

KM# 79b 10 NUEVO PESOS **Weight:** 19.4800 g. **Composition:** 0.9000 Gold .5637 oz. AGW **Obverse:** Bust of Jose Gervasio Artigas half left

Date	Mintage	F	VF	XF	Unc	BU
1981So Proof	100	Value: 500				

KM# 93 10 NUEVO PESOS **Composition:** Stainless Steel

Date	Mintage	F	VF	XF	Unc	BU
1989	79,000,000	—	—	0.20	0.50	—

KM# 86 20 NUEVO PESOS **Composition:** Copper-Nickel **Subject:** World Fisheries Conference

Date	Mintage	F	VF	XF	Unc	BU
1984	3,771	—	—	—	17.50	—

KM# 86a 20 NUEVO PESOS **Weight:** 11.6600 g. **Composition:** 0.9250 Silver .3468 oz. ASW **Subject:** World Fisheries Conference

Date	Mintage	F	VF	XF	Unc	BU
1984 Proof	25,000	Value: 32.00				

KM# 86b 20 NUEVO PESOS **Weight:** 19.6000 g. **Composition:** 0.9170 Gold .5776 oz. AGW **Subject:** World Fisheries Conference

Date	Mintage	F	VF	XF	Unc	BU
1984 Proof	100	Value: 500				

KM# 94 50 NUEVO PESOS

Date	F	VF	XF	Unc	BU
1989	—	—	0.20	0.50	—

KM# 80 100 NUEVO PESOS **Weight:** 12.0000 g. **Composition:** 0.9000 Silver .3472 oz. ASW **Obverse:** Hydroelectric dam

Date	Mintage	F	VF	XF	Unc	BU
1981So	25,000	—	—	—	6.50	—

KM# 96 100 NUEVO PESOS **Composition:** Stainless Steel **Obverse:** Gaucho bust right

Date	F	VF	XF	Unc	BU
1989	—	—	0.35	0.75	—

KM# 97 200 NUEVO PESOS **Composition:** Copper Nickel **Obverse:** Unchained Liberty

Date	F	VF	XF	Unc	BU
1989	—	—	—	1.50	—

KM# 82 500 NUEVO PESOS **Weight:** 12.0000 g. **Composition:** 0.9000 Silver .3472 oz. ASW **Obverse:** Hydroelectric dam

Date	Mintage	F	VF	XF	Unc	BU
1983So	15,000	—	—	—	6.50	—

KM# 90 500 NUEVO PESOS **Weight:** 12.0000 g. **Composition:** 0.9000 Silver .3473 oz. ASW **Obverse:** Bust of General Leandro Gomez half left

Date	Mintage	F	VF	XF	Unc	BU
1986Mo Proof	6,000	Value: 21.50				

KM# 98 500 NUEVO PESOS **Composition:** Copper Nickel **Obverse:** Bust of Jose Gervasio Artigas half right

Date	F	VF	XF	Unc	BU
1989	—	—	—	3.00	—

KM# 87 2000 NUEVO PESOS **Weight:** 25.0000 g. **Composition:** 0.9000 Silver .7235 oz. ASW **Subject:** 140th Anniversary of Silver Coinage and 25th Meeting of Interamerican Bank Governors **Obverse:** Radiant sun peeking over shield of arms in wreath within inner circle

Date	Mintage	F	VF	XF	Unc	BU
1984 Proof	15,000	Value: 16.50				

KM# 88 2000 NUEVO PESOS **Weight:** 25.0000 g. **Composition:** 0.9000 Silver .7235 oz. ASW **Subject:** 25th Meeting of Interamerican Bank Governors **Obverse:** Radiant sun peeking over shield of arms within wreath

Date	Mintage	F	VF	XF	Unc	BU
1984 Proof	15,000	Value: 16.50				

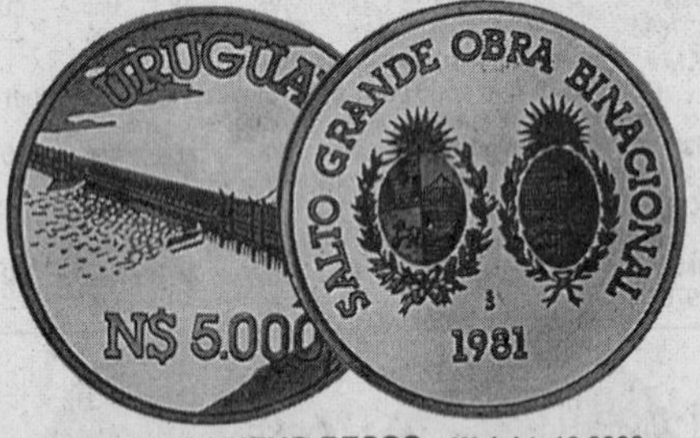

KM# 81 5000 NUEVO PESOS **Weight:** 12.0000 g. **Composition:** 0.9000 Silver .3472 oz. ASW **Obverse:** Hydroelectric dam

Date	Mintage	F	VF	XF	Unc	BU
1981So Proof	15,000	Value: 15.00				

KM# 91 5000 NUEVO PESOS **Weight:** 25.0000 g. **Composition:** 0.9000 Silver .7235 oz. ASW **Subject:** 20th Anniversary of Central Bank

Date	Mintage	F	VF	XF	Unc	BU
1987So Proof	10,000	Value: 13.50				

KM# 91a 5000 NUEVO PESOS **Weight:** 42.7600 g. **Composition:** Gold

Date	F	VF	XF	Unc	BU
1987	—	—	—	—	—

KM# 99 5000 NUEVO PESOS **Weight:** 25.0000 g. **Composition:** 0.9000 Silver .7235 oz. ASW **Subject:** Latin America Presidents' Assembly

Date	F	VF	XF	Unc	BU
1988 Proof	—	Value: 18.50			

KM# 85 20000 NUEVO PESOS **Weight:** 20.0000 g. **Composition:** 0.9000 Gold .5787 oz. AGW **Obverse:** Hydroelectric dam

Date	Mintage	F	VF	XF	Unc	BU
1983So Proof	2,500	Value: 275				

KM# 89 20000 NUEVO PESOS **Subject:** 130th Anniversary of Gold Coinage and 25th Meeting of Interamerican Bank Governors

Date	Mintage	F	VF	XF	Unc	B
1984 Proof	1,500	Value: 275				

KM# 101 25000 PESOS **Weight:** 12.5000 g. **Composition:** 0.9000 Silver .3617 oz. ASW **Subject:** 25t Anniversary of Central Bank

Date	F	VF	XF	Unc	
1992	—	—	—	16.50	

KM# 100 50000 NUEVO PESOS **Weight:** 27.0000 **Composition:** 0.9250 Silver .8029 oz. ASW **Subject:** Ibe - American Series

Date	Mintage	F	VF	XF	Unc
1991 Proof	70,000	Value: 30.00			

GOLD BULLION COINAGE

KM# 108 1/4 GAUCHO **Weight:** 8.6400 g. **Composition:** 0.9000 Gold .2500 oz. AGW **Obverse:** He of Gaucho right **Reverse:** Value 1/4 within wreath

Date	F	VF	XF	Unc
1992 Proof	—	Value: 200		

KM# 109 1/2 GAUCHO **Weight:** 17.2800 g. **Composition:** 0.9000 Gold .5000 oz. AGW **Obverse:** Head of Gaucho right **Reverse:** Value 1/2 within wreath

Date	F	VF	XF	Unc	BU
1992 Proof	—	Value: 300			

KM# 110 GAUCHO **Weight:** 34.5590 g. **Composition:** 0.9000 Gold 1.0000 oz. AGW **Obverse:** Head of Gaucho right **Reverse:** Value of 1 within wreath

Date	F	VF	XF	Unc	BU
1992 Proof	—	Value: 500			

REFORM COINAGE

March 1993

1,000 Nuevos Pesos = 1 Uruguayan Peso; 100 Centesimos = 1 Uruguayan Peso (UYP)

KM# 102 10 CENTESIMOS **Composition:** Stainless Steel

Date	F	VF	XF	Unc	BU
1994	—	—	0.25	0.50	—

KM# 105 20 CENTESIMOS **Composition:** Stainless Steel

Date	F	VF	XF	Unc	BU
1994	—	—	0.30	0.60	—

KM# 106 50 CENTESIMOS **Composition:** Stainless Steel

Date	F	VF	XF	Unc	BU
1994	—	—	0.35	0.75	—

KM# 103.2 URUGUAYAN PESO **Weight:** 3.5200 g. **Composition:** Brass **Obverse:** Mint mark under bust right. **Reverse:** Denomination **Edge:** Plain **Size:** 20 mm.

Date	F	VF	XF	Unc	BU
1998	—	—	—	0.50	—

KM# 104 2 URUGUAYAN PESOS **Composition:** Brass

Date	F	VF	XF	Unc	BU
1994	—	—	0.75	1.50	—
1998	—	—	0.75	1.50	—

Note: Mint mark under bust

KM# 113 50 URUGUAYAN PESOS **Weight:** 12.5000 g. **Composition:** 0.9000 Silver .3617 oz. ASW **Subject:** Bicentennial - City of Melo **Obverse:** National map **Reverse:** City arms

Date	Mintage	F	VF	XF	Unc	BU
1996 Proof	10,000	Value: 20.00				

KM# 111 100 URUGUAYAN PESOS **Weight:** 25.0000 g. **Composition:** 0.9990 Silver .7234 oz. ASW **Subject:** 50th Anniversary - F.A.O **Obverse:** Wheat stalks **Reverse:** F.A.O, logo and dates

Date	F	VF	XF	Unc	BU
ND1995 Proof	—	Value: 20.00			

KM# 112 100 URUGUAYAN PESOS **Weight:** 25.0000 g. **Composition:** 0.9990 Silver .7234 oz. ASW **Subject:** Centennial - Central Bank **Obverse:** Radiant sun face **Reverse:** Central Bank building

Date	Mintage	F	VF	XF	Unc	BU
1996 Proof	50,000	Value: 22.50				

KM# 107 200 URUGUAYAN PESOS **Weight:** 27.0000 g. **Composition:** 0.9250 Silver .8030 oz. ASW **Subject:** Environmental Protection **Reverse:** Pampas deer right

Date	Mintage	F	VF	XF	Unc	BU
1994 Proof	20,000	Value: 35.00				

KM# 116 200 URUGUAYAN PESOS **Weight:** 28.2800 g. **Composition:** 0.9250 Silver .8410 oz. ASW **Subject:** 50th Anniversary - United Nations

Date	F	VF	XF	Unc	BU
1995 Proof	—	Value: 42.50			

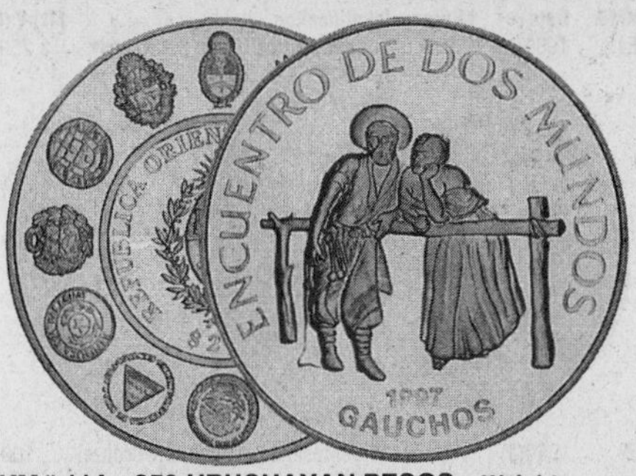

KM# 114 250 URUGUAYAN PESOS **Weight:** 27.0000 g. **Composition:** 0.9000 Silver .8030 oz. ASW **Subject:** Ibero - American Series **Reverse:** Gaucho and lady

Date	Mintage	F	VF	XF	Unc	BU
1997 Proof	11,000	Value: 45.00				

KM# 117 250 URUGUAYAN PESOS **Weight:** 27.0000 g. **Composition:** 0.9000 Silver .8030 oz. ASW **Series:** Ibero-American **Obverse:** National arms coin design within circle of arms **Reverse:** Man and woman on horseback **Edge:** Reeded **Size:** 40 mm.

Date	Mintage	F	VF	XF	Unc	BU
2000 Proof	8,000	Value: 45.00				

ESSAIS

KM#	Date	Mintage	Identification	Mkt Val
E7	1924(p)	12	5 Centesimos. Nickel. KM21.	300
E6	1924(p)	12	2 Centesimos. Nickel. KM20.	275
E5	1924(p)	12	Centesimo. Nickel. KM19.	250
E10	1930(a)	60	10 Centesimos. Gold. 18.3200 g. KM25.	3,000
E11	1930(a)	—	20 Centesimos. Aluminum-Bronze. KM24.	100
E14	1930(a)	60	5 Pesos. Gold. KM27.	1,850
E13	1930(a)	70	5 Pesos. Aluminum-Bronze. KM27.	225
EA12	1930	—	20 Centesimos. Silver. 4.9000 g.	—
	1930	—	20 Centesimos. Silver. 4.9000 g.	—

KM#	Date	Mintage	Identification	Mkt Val
E12	1930(a)	60	20 Centesimos. Gold. 8.9500 g. KM24.	3,250

KM#	Date	Mintage	Identification	Mkt Val
E8	1930(a)	70	10 Centesimos. Aluminum-Bronze. KM25.	100
E17	1983	20	2000 Pesos. Gold. KM83	2,750
E19	1983	1,500	20000 Pesos. Gold. ENSAYO, KM85.	450
E15	1983	100	500 Pesos. Gold. ENSAYO, KM82.	400
E16	1983	200	2000 Pesos. Copper. KM83.	95.00
E18	1983	200	20000 Pesos. Silver. ENSAYO, KM85.	60.00
E21	1984	600	20 Pesos. Gold. ENSAYO, KM86b.	350
E20	1984	20,500	20 Pesos. Silver. ENSAYO, KM86a.	20.00
E22	1984	1,500	20000 Pesos. Gold. ENSAYO, KM89.	400

PATTERNS

Including off metal strikes

KM#	Date	Mintage	Identification	Mkt Val
PnA39	1916	—	50 Centesimos. Silver.	—
Pn39	1916	45	50 Centesimos. Silver.	—
Pn40	1917	20	Peso. Silver.	—
PnA41	1920	—	20 Centesimos. Copper-Nickel. Similar to KM#24.	—
Pn41	1942	10	20 Centesimos. Copper Gilt.	—
PnA42	1942	20	20 Centesimos. Silver Gilt.	—
	1942	20	20 Centesimos. Silver Gilt.	—
Pn42	1942	—	20 Centesimos. Gold. KM29.	450
	1942	—	20 Centesimos. Gold. KM29.	450
Pn43	1942So	—	Peso. Gold. KM30.	1,000
Pn44	1943So	—	2 Centesimos. Gold. KM20a.	935
Pn45	1943So	—	50 Centesimos. Gold. KM31	1,000
PnB51	1953	—	Peso. Brass. Similar to PNA51.	—
PnC51	1953	—	Peso. Copper-Nickel. Similar to PNA51.	—
Pn49	1953	100	5 Centesimos. 0.9160 Gold. KM34.	—
Pn50	1953	100	10 Centesimos. 0.9160 Gold. KM35.	—
PnA51	1953	—	Peso. Aluminum-Bronze.	—
PnD51	1953	—	Peso. Silver. Similar to PNA51.	—
Pn46	1953	100	Centesimo. 0.9160 Gold. KM32.	—
Pn47	1953	—	2 Centesimos. Aluminum. KM33.	—
Pn48	1953	100	2 Centesimos. 0.9160 Gold. KM33.	—
Pn51	1954	100	20 Centesimos. 0.9830 Gold. KM36.	500
Pn52	1959	—	10 Centesimos. 0.9160 Gold. KM35.	—
Pn54	1960	100	5 Centesimos. Gold. KM38.	—
Pn59	1960	—	10 Pesos. Gold.	—
Pn53	1960	100	2 Centesimos. Gold. KM37.	—
Pn55	1960	100	10 Centesimos. Gold. KM39.	—
Pn56	1960	100	25 Centesimos. Gold. KM40.	—
Pn57	1960	100	50 Centesimos. Gold. KM41.	—
Pn58	1960	—	Peso. Gold. KM42.	—
PnB54	ND(1960)	—	5 Centesimos. Aluminum. Similar to KM#34 and KM#38 reverses. With "HA" in the base of the 5 and "MBL" above the 5.	—
PnA60	1961	—	10 Pesos. Gold. KM43.	—
Pn60	1965So	10	20 Centesimos. Copper. KM44.	—
Pn63	1965So	25	50 Centesimos. Aluminum-Bronze. KM45.	—
Pn66	1965So	—	50 Centesimos. Silver. KM45.	—
Pn67	1965So	—	50 Centesimos. Gold. KM45.	—
Pn69	1965So	25	Peso. Copper-Nickel. KM46.	—
Pn71	1965So	—	Peso. Gold. KM46.	—
Pn77	1965So	—	10 Pesos. Silver. KM48.	—
PnA69	1965	—	Peso. Aluminum-Bronze. 24 mm. Similar to KM#46. Planchet is 5 Pesos.	—
Pn61	1965So	—	20 Centesimos. Silver. KM44.	—
Pn62	1965So	—	20 Centesimos. Gold. KM44.	—
Pn70	1965So	—	Peso. Silver. KM46.	—
PnA73	1965	—	5 Pesos. Copper-Nickel. 29 mm. Similar to KM#47. Planchet is 10 Pesos.	—
Pn65	1965So	25	50 Centesimos. Copper-Nickel. KM45.	—
Pn73	1965So	25	5 Pesos. Copper-Nickel. KM47.	—
Pn64	1965So	10	50 Centesimos. Copper. KM45.	—
Pn68	1965So	10	Peso. Copper. KM46.	—
Pn72	1965So	10	5 Pesos. Copper. KM47.	—
Pn74	1965So	—	5 Pesos. Silver. KM47.	—
Pn75	1965So	—	5 Pesos. Gold. KM47.	—
Pn76	1965So	10	10 Pesos. Copper. KM48.	—
PnC84	1968	—	20 Pesos. Silver. Star. Similar to KM#56.	—
PnB85	1968	—	50 Pesos. Copper-Nickel. Similar to KM#57; Proof.	—
PnC85	1968	—	50 Pesos. Silver. Star. Similar to KM#57.	—
Pn78	1968So	100	Peso. Copper-Nickel. KM49.	35.00
PnB84	1968	—	20 Pesos. Copper-Nickel. Similar to KM#56; Proof.	—
Pn79	1968So	1,000	Peso. Silver. KM49.	15.00
Pn80	1968So	100	5 Pesos. Copper-Nickel. KM50.	35.00
Pn81	1968So	1,000	5 Pesos. Silver. KM50.	18.00
Pn82	1968So	100	10 Pesos. Copper-Nickel. KM51.	35.00
Pn83	1968So	1,000	10 Pesos. Silver. KM51.	20.00
PnA84	1968S	—	20 Pesos. Yellow Metal.	—
Pn84	1968So	1,000	20 Pesos. Silver.	25.00
PnA85	1968S	—	50 Pesos. Yellow Metal.	—
Pn85	1968So	1,000	50 Pesos. Silver.	28.00
Pn86	1969So	50	Peso. Copper-Nickel. KM52.	30.00
PnA92	1969	—	10 Pesos. Gold. Similar to KM#54; Proof.	—
Pn87	1969So	1,000	Peso. 0.9000 Silver. KM52.	15.00
PnA88	1969So	—	Peso. Gold. KM52.	125
Pn88	1969So	50	5 Pesos. Copper-Nickel. KM53.	30.00
Pn89	1969So	1,000	5 Pesos. 0.9000 Silver. KM53.	15.00
PnA90	1969So	—	5 Pesos. Gold. KM53.	200
Pn90	1969So	50	10 Pesos. Copper-Nickel. KM54.	30.00
Pn91	1969So	1,000	10 Pesos. 0.9000 Silver. KM54.	15.00
Pn92	1969	20,000	1000 Pesos. Copper.	30.00
Pn93	1969	250	1000 Pesos. Silver.	45.00
Pn96	1970So	—	20 Pesos. Silver. No star on reverse. KM56.	15.00
Pn97	1970So	1,000	20 Pesos. Gold. KM56.	200
Pn99	1970So	1,000	50 Pesos. Gold. KM57.	275
Pn95	1970So	—	20 Pesos. Silver. Star on reverse. KM56.	—
Pn98	1970So	—	50 Pesos. Silver. KM57.	15.00
Pn101	1971So	80	50 Pesos. Copper Nickel. With F. ORRELLANA, P., KM58	55.00
Pn103	1971So	200	50 Pesos. Gold. KM58.	325
Pn100	1971So	—	50 Pesos. Copper Nickel. KM58.	55.00
Pn102	1971So	2,000	50 Pesos. Silver. KM58.	25.00
Pn105	1972So	12	100 Pesos. Alpaca.	—
Pn104	1972So	3	100 Pesos.	—
PnA107	1973	—	100 Pesos. Gold. Similar to KM#59.	—
PnB107	1973	50	100 Pesos. Aluminum.	—
Pn106	1973	—	100 Pesos. Silver. KM59.	40.00
PnC107	1975	50	5 Pesos. Alpaca. Similar to KM#65.	—
Pn110	1976	—	5 Nuevo Pesos. Silver. KM70.	150
PnA108	1976	—	10 Centesimos. Copper. Similar to KM#66.	—
PnB108	1976	—	10 Centesimos. Aluminum. Similar to KM#66.	—
PnC108	1976	—	20 Centesimos. Copper. Similar to KM#67.	—
PnF108	1976	—	50 Centesimos. Aluminum. Similar to KM#68.	—
Pn107	1976	—	5 Nuevo Pesos. Aluminum. KM70.	75.00
PnE108	1976	—	50 Centesimos. Copper. Similar to KM#68.	—
PnH108	1976	—	Nuevo Peso. Aluminum. Similar to KM#69.	—
PnG108	1976	—	Nuevo Peso. Copper. Similar to KM#69.	—
Pn108	1976	—	5 Nuevo Pesos. Copper-Aluminum. KM70.	75.00
Pn109	1976	—	5 Nuevo Pesos. Copper-Nickel. KM70.	100
PnD108	1976	—	20 Centesimos. Aluminum. Similar to KM#67.	—
PnD111	1977	—	Centesimo. Aluminum-Bronze. Similar to KM#71.	—
PnG111	1977	—	2 Centesimos. Copper. Similar to KM#72.	—
PnL111	1977	—	5 Centesimos. Aluminum-Bronze. Similar to KM#73.	—
PnH111	1977	—	2 Centesimos. Aluminum-Bronze. Similar to KM#72.	—
PnK111	1977	—	5 Centesimos. Copper. Similar to KM#73.	—
PnC111	1977	—	Centesimo. Copper. Similar to KM#71.	—
PnF111	1977	—	2 Centesimos. Nickel. Similar to KM#72.	—
PnI111	1977	—	5 Centesimos. Gold. Similar to KM#73.	—
PnJ111	1977	—	5 Centesimos. Nickel. Similar to KM#73.	—
PnA111	1977	—	Centesimo. Gold. Similar to KM#71.	—
PnB111	1977	—	Centesimo. Nickel. Similar to KM#71.	—
PnE111	1977	—	2 Centesimos. Gold. Similar to KM#72.	—
Pn111	1980	—	Peso. Brass. KM74.	—
Pn112	1980	—	5 Pesos. Brass. KM75.	—
PnM111	1980	—	Nuevo Peso. Aluminum. Similar to KM#74.	—
PnN111	1980	—	Nuevo Peso. Copper. Similar to KM#74.	—
PnB112	1980	—	5 Nuevo Pesos. Copper. Similar to KM#75.	—
PnA112	1980	—	5 Nuevo Pesos. Aluminum. Similar to KM#75.	—
Pn113	1981	—	10 Pesos. Brass. KM79.	—
PnB114	1981So	—	5000 Nuevo Pesos. 0.9000 Gold. 20.0000 g. KM81.	275
PnD113	1981	—	10 Nuevo Pesos. Aluminum. Similar to KM#79.	—
PnA114	1981So	—	100 Nuevo Pesos. 0.9000 Gold. 20.0000 g. KM80.	375
PnB113	1981	—	2 Nuevo Pesos. Aluminum-Bronze. Similar to KM#77; Proof.	—
PnC113	1981	—	10 Nuevo Pesos. Copper. Similar to KM#79.	—
PnA113	1981	—	2 Nuevo Pesos. Silver. Similar to KM#77; Proof.	—
PnD114	1983So	—	20000 Nuevo Pesos. Silver. KM85.	—
PnC114	1983So	—	500 Nuevo Pesos. 0.9000 Gold. 20.0000 g. KM82.	500
Pn115	1984	—	2000 Nuevo Pesos. Aluminum. Thick reeded edge. KM87.	—
Pn119	1984	—	20000 Nuevo Pesos. Gold. KM89.	—
PnB119	1984	—	20000 Nuevo Pesos. Copper. Similar to KM#89.	—
PnC119	1984	—	20000 Nuevo Pesos. Brass. Similar to KM#89.	—
Pn116	1984	—	2000 Nuevo Pesos. Aluminum. Thick reeded edge. KM88.	—
Pn117	1984	—	2000 Nuevo Pesos. Aluminum. Thick reeded edge. KM88.	—
Pn114	1984	—	2000 Nuevo Pesos. Copper. Thick reeded edge. KM87.	—
PnA119	1984	—	20000 Nuevo Pesos. Silver. Similar to KM#89.	—
Pn118	1984	—	20000 Nuevo Pesos. Aluminum. KM89.	—
PnA118	1984	40	2000 Nuevo Pesos. Silver. Similar to KM#88. Different obverse and reverse; Proof.	—
Pn121	1987	—	5000 Pesos. Copper. KM91.	—
Pn122	1987	—	5000 Pesos. Bronze. KM91.	—
Pn120	1987	—	5000 Pesos. Alpaca. KM91; Alpaca	—
Pn123	1988	—	5000 Nuevo Pesos. Copper. Similar to KM#99.	—
Pn124	1988	—	5000 Nuevo Pesos. Alpaca. Similar to KM#99.	—

TRIAL STRIKES

KM#	Date	Mintage	Identification	Mkt Val
TS2	1983	—	2000 Nuevo Pesos. Silver. 64.4200 g. PRUEBA. Conjoined busts of the King and Queen of Spain.	15
TS7	1983	—	20000 Nuevo Pesos. Copper. Two shields of arms, one in wreath, one crowned. PRUEBA.	80.0
TS6	1983	—	20000 Nuevo Pesos. Silver. 20.2100 g. Two shields of arms, one in wreath, one crowned. PRUEBA.	12
TS5	1983	—	20000 Nuevo Pesos. Silver. 19.6600 g. PRUEBA. Conjoined busts of the King and Queen of Spain.	12
TS8	1983	—	20000 Nuevo Pesos. Copper. PRUEBA. Conjoined busts of the King and Queen of Spain.	80.0
TS1	1983	—	2000 Nuevo Pesos. Silver. 64.5100 g. Two shields of arms, one in wreath, one crowned.. PRUEBA.	15
TS3	1983	—	2000 Nuevo Pesos. Copper. Two shields of arms, one in wreath, one crowned. PRUEBA.	1
TS4	1983	—	2000 Nuevo Pesos. Copper. PRUEBA. Conjoined busts of the King and Queen of Spain.	1
TS9	1984	—	20000 Nuevo Pesos. Silver. 25.4700 g. Radiant sun peeking over shield of arms in wreath within inner circle. PRUEBA.	1
TS10	1984	—	2000 Nuevo Pesos. Silver. 25.6700 g. PRUEBA. Map of Uruguay at right, map of North and South America above rising sun at lower left.	1
TS11	1984	—	2000 Nuevo Pesos. Copper. Radiant sun peeking over shield of arms in wreath within inner circle. PRUEBA.	85.
TS12	1984	—	2000 Nuevo Pesos. Copper. PRUEBA. Map of Uruguay at right, map of North and South America above rising sun at lower left.	85
TS13	1984	—	2000 Nuevo Pesos. Copper Gilt. Radiant sun peeking over shield of arms in wreath within inner circle. PRUEBA.	[illegible]
TS14	1984	—	2000 Nuevo Pesos. Copper Gilt. PRUEBA. Map of Uruguay at right, map of North and South America above rising sun at lower left.	[illegible]
TS15	1984	—	2000 Nuevo Pesos. Aluminum. Radiant sun peeking over shield of arms in wreath within inner circle. PRUEBA.	85
TS16	1984	—	2000 Nuevo Pesos. Aluminum. PRUEBA. Map of Uruguay at right, map of North and South America above rising sun.	85
TS17	1984	—	2000 Nuevo Pesos. Silver. 25.0000 g. Radiant sun peeking over shield of arms within wreath. PRUEBA.	

KM#	Date	Mintage	Identification	Mkt Val
TS18	1984	—	2000 Nuevo Pesos. Silver. 24.7200 g. PRUEBA. Map of Uruguay at right, map of North and South America above rising sun.	100
TS19	1984	—	2000 Nuevo Pesos. Copper. Radiant sun peeking over shield of arms within wreath. PRUEBA.	85.00
TS20	1984	—	2000 Nuevo Pesos. Copper. PRUEBA. Map of Uruguay at right, map of North and South America above rising sun at lower left.	85.00
TS21	1984	—	2000 Nuevo Pesos. Copper Gilt. Radiant sun peeking over shield of arms within wreath. PRUEBA.	100
TS22	1984	—	2000 Nuevo Pesos. Copper Gilt. PRUEBA. Map of Uruguay at right, map of North and South America above rising sun at lower left.	100
TS23	1984	—	2000 Nuevo Pesos. Aluminum. Radiant sun peeking over shield of arms within wreath. PRUEBA.	85.00
TS24	1984	—	2000 Nuevo Pesos. Aluminum. PRUEBA. Map of Uruguay at right, map of North and South America above rising sun at lower left.	85.00
TS25	1984	—	20000 Nuevo Pesos. Silver. 19.4400 g. Shield of arms flanked by flags in inner circle. PRUEBA.	110
TS26	1984	—	20000 Nuevo Pesos. Silver. 20.2700 g. PRUEBA. Map of Uruguay at right, map of North and South America above rising sun at lower left.	110
TS27	1984	—	20000 Nuevo Pesos. Copper. Shield of arms flanked by flags in inner circle. PRUEBA.	80.00
TS28	1984	—	20000 Nuevo Pesos. Copper. PRUEBA. Map of Uruguay at right, map of North and South America above rising sun at lower left.	80.00
TS29	1984	—	20000 Nuevo Pesos. Copper Gilt. Shield of arms flanked by flags in inner circle. PRUEBA.	90.00
TS30	1984	—	20000 Nuevo Pesos. Copper Gilt. PRUEBA. Map of Uruguay at right, map of North and South America above rising sun at lower left.	90.00

PIEFORTS

Double Thickness

M#	Date	Mintage	Identification	Mkt Val
2	1983	10	2000 Nuevo Pesos. Silver. 64.5700 g. Reeded edge. KM#M1.	300
3	1983	10	2000 Nuevo Pesos. Copper. Plain edge. KM#M1.	100
A4	1983	—	20000 Nuevo Pesos. Gold. KM#M2.	950
4	1983	—	20000 Nuevo Pesos. Silver. 39.7000 g. KM#M3.	165
5	1983	—	20000 Nuevo Pesos. Copper. Plain edge. KM#M2.	65.00
6	1984	600	20 Pesos. Silver. KM86a.	60.00
7	1984	—	2000 Nuevo Pesos. Silver. 50.0000 g. Plain edge. KM87.	185
8	1984	—	2000 Nuevo Pesos. Copper. Thick plain edge. KM87.	65.00
9	1984	—	2000 Nuevo Pesos. Copper Gilt. Thick plain edge. KM87.	75.00
10	1984	—	2000 Nuevo Pesos. Silver. 50.4800 g. Plain edge. KM88.	185
11	1984	—	2000 Nuevo Pesos. Copper. Thick plain edge. KM88.	65.00
2	1984	—	2000 Nuevo Pesos. Copper Gilt. Thick plain edge. KM88.	75.00
3	1984	—	20000 Nuevo Pesos. Silver. 20.7500 g. Reeded edge. KM89.	135
4	1984	—	20000 Nuevo Pesos. Silver. 40.1700 g. Reeded edge. KM89.	200
5	1984	—	20000 Nuevo Pesos. Silver. 40.4400 g. Plain edge. KM89.	200
6	1984	—	20000 Nuevo Pesos. Copper. Thick reeded edge. KM89.	80.00
7	1984	—	20000 Nuevo Pesos. Copper. Reeded edge. KM89.	80.00
8	1984	—	20000 Nuevo Pesos. Copper Gilt. KM89.	100

MINT SETS

#	Date	Mintage	Identification	Issue Price	Mkt Val
S1	1969/70 (5)	—	KM52-54, 56-57 KM#MS1 was issued under the law no. 13,637 of December 21, 1967.	—	3.50
S2	1969/70 (5)	—	KM52-54, 56-57 KM#MS2 was issued for the 11th Assembly of the Interamerica Bank.	—	3.50
3	1976 (4)	—	KM66-69	—	2.50
4	1976 (4)	—	KM#Pn107-110	—	400

PROOF SETS

#	Date	Mintage	Identification	Issue Price	Mkt Val
	1953 (4)	100	KM32-35	—	275
	1968 (3)	50	KM49-51	—	200
	1968 (3)	100	KM#Pn78, 80, 82	—	90.00
	1968 (5)	1,000	KM#Pn79, 81, 83-85	—	78.00
	1969 (3)	50	KM#Pn86, 88, 90	—	75.00
	1969/70 (5)	1,000	KM#Pn87, 89, 91, 96, 98	—	50.00
	1969 (3)	1,000	KM#Pn87, 89, 91	—	30.00

UZBEKISTAN

The Republic of Uzbekistan (formerly the Uzbek S.S.R.), is bordered on the north by Kazakhstan, to the east by Kirghizia and Tajikistan, on the south by Afghanistan and on the west by Turkmenistan. The republic is comprised of the regions of Andizhan, Bukhara, Dzhizak, Ferghana, Kashkadar, Khorezm (Khiva), Namangan, Navoi, Samarkand, Surkhan-.Darya, Syr-Darya, Tashkent and the Karakalpak Autonomous Republic. It has an area of 172,741 sq. mi. (447,400 sq. km.) and a population of 20.3 million. Capital: Tashkent.

Crude oil, natural gas, coal, copper, and gold deposits make up the chief resources, while intensive farming, based on artificial irrigation, provides an abundance of cotton.

On the eve of WW I, Khiva and Bukhara were enclaves within a Russian Turkestan divided into five provinces or oblasti. The czarist government did not attempt to Russify the indigenous Turkic or Tajik populations. The revolution of March 1917 created a confused situation in the area. In Tashkent there was a Turkestan committee of the provisional government; a Communist-controlled council of workers', soldiers' and peasants' deputies; also a Moslem Turkic movement, Shuro-i-Islamiya, and a young Turkestan or Jaddidi (Renovation) party. The last named party claimed full political autonomy for Turkestan and the abolition of the emirate of Bukhara and the khanate of Khiva. After the Communist *coup d'etat in* Petrograd, the council of people's commissars on Nov. 24 (Dec. 7), 1917, published an appeal to "all toiling Moslems in Russia and in the east" proclaiming their right to build their national life "freely and unhindered". In response, the Moslem and Jaddidi organizations in Dec. 1917 convoked a national congress in Khokand, which appointed a provisional government headed by Mustafa Chokayev (or Chokaigolu; 1890-1941) and resolved to elect a constituent assembly to decide whether Turkestan should remain within a Russian federal state or proclaim its independence. In the spring of 1919 a Red army group defeated Kolchak and in September its commander, M.V. Frunze, arrived in Tashkent with V.V.Kuibyshev as political commissar. The Communists were still much too weak in Turkestan to proclaim the country part of Soviet Russia. Faizullah Khojayev organized a young Bukhara movement, which on Sept. 14, 1920, proclaimed the dethronement of Emir Mir Alim. Bukhara was then made a S.S.R. In 1920 the Tashkent Communist government declared war on Junaid, who took to flight, and Khiva became another S.S.R. In Oct. 1921, Enver Pasha, the former leader of the young Turks, appeared in Bukhara and assumed command of the Basmachi movement. In Aug. 1922 he was forced to retreat into Tajikistan and died on Aug. 4, in a battle near Baljuvan. Khiva concluded a treaty of alliance with the Russian S.F.S.R. in Sept. 1920, and Bukhara followed suit in March 1921. Theoretically, a Turkestan Autonomous Soviet Socialist Republic had existed since May 1, 1918; in 1920 this "Turk republic", as it was called, was proclaimed part of the R.S.F.S.R. On Sept. 18, 1924, the Uzbek and Turkmen peoples were authorized to form S.S.R.'s of their own, and the Kazakhs, Kirghiz, and Tajiks to form autonomous S.S.R.'s. On Oct.27, 1924, the Uzbek and Turkmen S.S.R. were officially constituted and the former was formally accepted on Jan.15, 1925, as a member of the U.S.S.R. Tajikistan was an autonomous soviet republic within Uzbekistan until Dec.5, 1929, when it became a S.S.R. On Dec. 5, 1936, incorporating the Kara-Kalpak A.S.S.R., which had belonged to Kazakhstan until 1930 and afterward had come under direct control of the R.S.F.S.R, increased the Uzbekistan territory.

On June 20, 1990 the Uzbek Supreme Soviet adopted a declaration of sovereignty, and in Aug. 1991, following an unsuccessful coup, declared itself independent as the "Republic of Uzbekistan", which was confirmed by referendum in Dec. That same month Uzbekistan became a member of the CIS.

Monetary System

100 Tiyin = 1 Sum or Som

REPUBLIC

STANDARD COINAGE

KM# 1.1 TIYIN Composition: Brass Clad Steel **Reverse:** Small denomination

Date	F	VF	XF	Unc	BU
1994	—	—	—	0.30	—

KM# 1.2 TIYIN Composition: Brass Clad Steel **Reverse:** Large denomination

Date	F	VF	XF	Unc	BU
1994	—	—	—	0.30	—

KM# 2.1 3 TIYIN Composition: Brass Plated Steel **Reverse:** Small denomination

Date	F	VF	XF	Unc	BU
1994	—	—	—	0.40	—

KM# 2.2 3 TIYIN Composition: Brass Plated Steel **Reverse:** Large denomination

Date	F	VF	XF	Unc	BU
1994	—	—	—	0.40	—

KM# 3.1 5 TIYIN Composition: Brass Plated Steel **Reverse:** Small denomination

Date	F	VF	XF	Unc	BU
1994	—	—	—	0.50	—

KM# 3.2 5 TIYIN Composition: Brass Plated Steel **Reverse:** Large denomination

Date	F	VF	XF	Unc	BU
1994	—	—	—	0.50	—

KM# 4.1 10 TIYIN Composition: Nickel Clad Steel **Reverse:** Small denomination

Date	F	VF	XF	Unc	BU
1994	—	—	—	0.60	—

KM# 4.2 10 TIYIN Composition: Nickel Clad Steel **Reverse:** Large denomination

Date	F	VF	XF	Unc	BU
1994	—	—	—	0.60	—

KM# 5.1 20 TIYIN Composition: Nickel Clad Steel **Reverse:** Small denomination

Date	F	VF	XF	Unc	BU
1994	—	—	—	0.75	—

KM# 5.2 20 TIYIN Composition: Nickel Clad Steel **Reverse:** Large denomination

Date	F	VF	XF	Unc	BU
1994	—	—	—	0.75	—

KM# 6 50 TIYIN **Composition:** Nickel Clad Steel

Date	F	VF	XF	Unc	BU
1994	—	—	—	1.00	—

KM# 8 SOM **Composition:** Nickel Clad Steel **Reverse:** Denomination

Date	F	VF	XF	Unc	BU
1997	—	—	—	1.35	—
1999	—	—	—	1.35	—
2000	—	—	—	1.35	—

KM# 12 SOM **Weight:** 2.8300 g. **Composition:** Nickel-Clad Steel **Obverse:** National arms **Reverse:** Denomination and map **Edge:** Reeded **Size:** 18.8 mm.

Date	F	VF	XF	Unc	BU
2000	—	—	—	1.00	—
2001	—	—	—	1.00	—

KM# 9 5 SOM **Composition:** Nickel Clad Steel **Reverse:** Denomination

Date	F	VF	XF	Unc	BU
1997	—	—	—	1.50	—
1999	—	—	—	1.50	—

KM# 13 5 SOM **Weight:** 3.3500 g. **Composition:** Brass Plated Steel **Obverse:** National arms **Reverse:** Denomination and map **Edge:** Plain **Size:** 21.2 mm.

Date	F	VF	XF	Unc	BU
2001	—	—	—	1.35	—

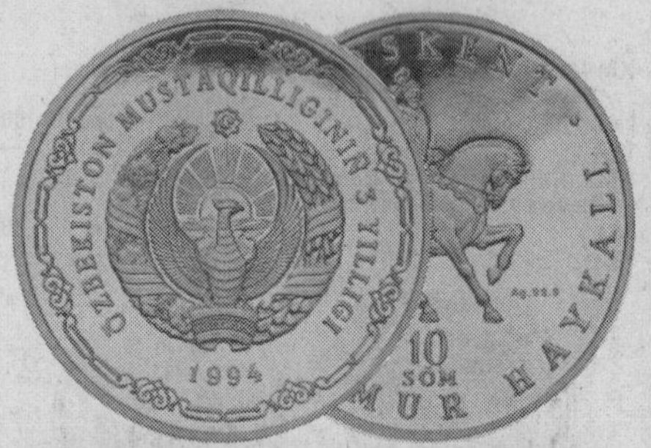

KM# 7 10 SOM **Weight:** 31.1000 g. **Composition:** 0.9990 Silver .9988 oz. ASW **Subject:** 3rd anniversary of independence

Date	Mintage	F	VF	XF	Unc	BU
1994 Proof	Est. 1,000	Value: 60.00				

KM# 10 10 SOM **Composition:** Nickel Clad Steel **Reverse:** Denomination

Date	F	VF	XF	Unc	BU
1997	—	—	—	2.00	—
1999	—	—	—	2.00	—
2000	—	—	—	2.00	—

KM# 14 10 SOM **Weight:** 2.7100 g. **Composition:** Nickel-Clad Steel **Obverse:** National arms **Reverse:** Denomination and map **Edge:** Plain **Size:** 19.75 mm.

Date	F	VF	XF	Unc	BU
2001	—	—	—	2.00	—

KM# 11 25 SOM **Composition:** Nickel Clad Steel **Subject:** Jaloliddin Manguberdi

Date	F	VF	XF	Unc	BU
1999	—	—	—	2.50	—

KM# 15 50 SOM **Weight:** 8.0000 g. **Composition:** Nickel-Clad Steel **Obverse:** National arms **Reverse:** Denomination and map **Edge:** Plain and reeded sections **Size:** 26.2 mm.

Date	F	VF	XF	Unc	BU
2001	—	—	—	3.50	—

KM# 16 50 SOM **Weight:** 7.9000 g. **Composition:** Nickel-Clad Steel **Subject:** Shahrisabz Town: 2700th Anniversary **Obverse:** National arms **Reverse:** Statue and ruins above denomination **Edge:** Reeded and plain sections **Size:** 26.3 mm.

Date	F	VF	XF	Unc	BU
2002	—	—	—	3.50	—

EMIRATE OF BUKHARA

Bukhara, a city and former emirate in southern Russian Turkestan, formed part (Sogdiana) of the Seleucid empire after the conquest of Alexander the Great and remained an important regional center, sometimes city state, until the 19th century. It became virtually a Russian vassal in1868 as a consequence of the Czarist invasion of 1866,following which it gradually became a part of Russian Turkestan and then part of Uzbekistan S.S.R., now Uzbekistan.

RULERS

Russian Vassal, AH1284-1336/1868-1917AD
Independent, AH1336-1338/1917-1920AD

MINTNAME

بخارا

Bukhara

MONETARY SYSTEM

10 Falus = 1 Tenga

KHANATE OF BUKHARA

ANONYMOUS COINAGE

KM# 87 FALUS **Composition:** Copper Or Brass **Note:** In the name of Ma'sum Ibn Danyal. Varieties exist. Previous #Y1.

Date	Good	VG	F	VF	XF
AH1322	12.00	18.00	25.00	35.00	—
AH1324	12.00	18.00	25.00	35.00	—

KM# 63 TENGA **Weight:** 3.2000 g. **Composition:** Silver **Note:** Varieties exist. Previous #Y2 and C#75, 91.

Date	VG	F	VF	XF	Unc
AH1319//1320	10.00	16.50	27.50	40.00	—
AH1319	6.50	12.50	20.00	30.00	—
AH1320	6.50	12.50	20.00	30.00	—
AH1322	6.50	12.50	20.00	30.00	—
AH1323//1322	10.00	16.50	27.50	40.00	—
AH1323	6.50	12.50	20.00	30.00	—

KM# 65 TILLA **Composition:** Gold **Note:** Previous #Y3 and C#85 and 95.

Date	VG	F	VF	XF	Unc
AH1319	75.00	100	135	185	—
AH1324/1324	75.00	100	135	185	—
AH1325	75.00	100	135	185	—
AH1327	75.00	100	135	185	—
AH1328	75.00	100	135	185	—
AH1329	75.00	100	135	185	—

NAMED COINAGE

10 Falus = 1 Tenga

KM# 85 FALUS **Composition:** Copper Or Brass **Ruler:** Alim Ibn Sayyid Mir Amin 1911-1920AD, independent after AH1336 (1917 AD) **Note:** Dates on obverse and reverse. Previous #YA4.

Date	VG	F	VF	XF	Unc
AH132x-1332	—	—	—	—	—

KM# 86 FALUS **Composition:** Copper Or Brass **Ruler:** Alim Ibn Sayyid Mir Amin 1911-1920AD, independent after AH1336 (1917 AD) **Reverse:** "32" or "33" or "302" in a circle **Note:** Many varieties exist. Previous #Y4.1.

Date	VG	F	VF	XF	Unc
AH1321	6.00	10.00	15.00	30.00	–
AH1322	6.00	10.00	15.00	30.00	–
AH1323	6.00	10.00	15.00	30.00	–
AH1324	6.00	10.00	15.00	30.00	–
AH1326	6.00	10.00	15.00	30.00	–
AH1327	6.00	10.00	15.00	30.00	–
AH1329	6.00	10.00	15.00	30.00	–
AH1330	6.00	10.00	15.00	30.00	–
AH1331	6.00	10.00	15.00	30.00	–
AH1332	6.00	10.00	15.00	30.00	–
AH1333	6.00	10.00	15.00	30.00	–
AH1335	6.00	10.00	15.00	30.00	–
AH(13)36	15.00	25.00	40.00	60.00	–

KM# 42 2 FALUS **Composition:** Copper **Ruler:** Alim Ib Sayyid Mir Amin 1911-1920AD, independent after AH133 (1917 AD) **Reverse:** "2" or "4" in a circle **Note:** Date rang 1331-1336 reported but not confirmed. Many varieties exis Previous #Y4.

Date	VG	F	VF	XF	U
AH1332	6.00	10.00	15.00	22.50	
AH1334	8.00	12.00	18.00	25.00	

KM# 44 4 FALUS **Composition:** Copper **Ruler:** Alim Ibn Sayyid Mir Amin 1911-1920AD, independent aft AH1336 (1917 AD) **Note:** Previous #Y5.

Date	VG	F	VF	XF	U
AH1334	6.50	12.50	20.00	35.00	
AH1335	6.50	12.50	20.00	35.00	

45 8 FALUS **Composition:** Copper **Ruler:** lim Ibn Sayyid Mir Amin 1911-1920AD, independent after H1336 (1917 AD) **Note:** Previous #YA5.

	VG	F	VF	XF	Unc
35	6.50	12.50	20.00	35.00	—

A6 1/2 TENGA **Composition:** Bronze **Ruler:** lim Ibn Sayyid Mir Amin 1911-1920AD, independent after H1336 (1917 AD) **Reverse:** Legend in sextagonal frame **ize:** 14-15 mm. **Note:** Previous #Y6.

	VG	F	VF	XF	Unc
36	15.00	30.00	50.00	100	—

46.2 TENGA **Composition:** Bronze **Ruler:** lim Ibn Sayyid Mir Amin 1911-1920AD, independent after H1336 (1917 AD) **Reverse:** Stars **Size:** 17-18 mm. **Note:** arge flan, dotted border. Varieties exist. Previous #Y6a.

	VG	F	VF	XF	Unc
36	7.50	15.00	30.00	60.00	—
37	7.50	15.00	30.00	60.00	—

46.1 TENGA **Composition:** Bronze **Ruler:** lim Ibn Sayyid Mir Amin 1911-1920AD, independent after H1336 (1917 AD) **Reverse:** No stars **Size:** 14-15 mm. **ote:** Small flan, no border.

	VG	F	VF	XF	Unc
36	10.00	15.00	30.00	60.00	—

#47 2 TENGA **Composition:** Bronze Or Brass **Ruler:** Alim Ibn Sayyid Mir Amin 1911-1920AD, independent after AH1336 (1917 AD) **Obverse:** Greek meander pattern border **Reverse:** Star with 5 or 6 rays, Greek meander pattern border **Note:** Varieties exist. Previous #Y7.

	VG	F	VF	XF	Unc
36	9.00	15.00	25.00	55.00	—
37	9.00	15.00	25.00	55.00	—

#48 3 TENGA **Composition:** Bronze Or Brass **Ruler:** Alim Ibn Sayyid Mir Amin 1911-1920AD, independent after AH1336 (1917 AD) **Reverse:** Star with 5 or 6 rays **Note:** Varieties exist. Previous #Y8.

	VG	F	VF	XF	Unc
336	9.00	15.00	25.00	50.00	—
337	9.00	15.00	25.00	50.00	—

#49 4 TENGA **Composition:** Bronze Or Brass **Ruler:** Alim Ibn Sayyid Mir Amin 1911-1920AD, independent after AH1336 (1917 AD) **Note:** Probably a pattern. Previous #Y9.

	VG	F	VF	XF	Unc
336	85.00	140	200	300	—

KM# 50 5 TENGA **Composition:** Bronze Or Brass **Ruler:** Alim Ibn Sayyid Mir Amin 1911-1920AD, independent after AH1336 (1917 AD) **Note:** Previous #Y10.

Date	VG	F	VF	XF	Unc
AH1336	22.50	35.00	50.00	80.00	—
AH1337	22.50	35.00	50.00	80.00	—

KM# 53 10 TENGA **Composition:** Bronze Or Brass **Ruler:** Alim Ibn Sayyid Mir Amin 1911-1920AD, independent after AH1336 (1917 AD) **Note:** Size of squares vary. Previous #Y11.

Date	VG	F	VF	XF	Unc
AH1337	10.00	17.50	35.00	65.00	—
AH1338/1337	10.00	17.50	35.00	65.00	—

KM# 51 20 TENGA **Composition:** Bronze Or Brass **Ruler:** Alim Ibn Sayyid Mir Amin 1911-1920AD, independent after AH1336 (1917 AD) **Note:** Previous #Y12.

Date	VG	F	VF	XF	Unc
AH1336	22.50	35.00	50.00	85.00	—
AH1337	22.50	35.00	50.00	85.00	—

KHANATE OF KHIVA (KHWAREZM)

Khwarezm (Khiva), a present town once a great kingdom under the names of Chorasmia, Khwarezm and Urgenj, is located in Russian Turkestan east of the Caspian Sea and south of the Aral Sea. Russia established relations with Khwarezm (Khiva) in the 17th century, occupied it in 1873, and annexed it in 1875. Revolution concentrated Russia's preoccupation elsewhere during 1917 and Khwarezm (Khiva) seized this opportunity to declare its independence. It was able to sustain this status for a scant two years. By 1919 the Soviet regime had reestablished control over the region and extinguished the independent state. In AH1338/1920AD it became Khwarezm Soviet People's Republic and later became part of the Uzbekistan S.S.R., now Uzbekistan.

RULERS

Sayyid Abdullah Khan and Junaid Khan, AH1337-1338/1918-1920AD

MINTNAME

خوارزم

Khwarezm

INDEPENDANT KHANATE
AH1337-1338 / 1918-1920AD

STANDARD COINAGE

Y# 8 TENGA **Weight:** 2.3000 g. **Composition:** Silver **Note:** Struck in the name of Sayid Muhammad Rahim. Varieties exist.

Date	VG	F	VF	XF	Unc
AH1337	100	175	250	—	—

Y# A9 TENGA **Composition:** Copper, Bronze Or Brass **Reverse:** Date above or below inscription **Note:** Similar to 5 Tenga, Y#10. Varieties exist.

Date	VG	F	VF	XF	Unc
AH1337	20.00	30.00	40.00	75.00	—

Y# 9.3 2-1/2 TENGA **Composition:** Copper, Bronze Or Brass **Obverse:** Full sun in sky, inscription with Falus on left side **Note:** Many die varieties exist. Diameters, ornamentation, die rotation, number of sun rays, and size of circles vary.

Date	VG	F	VF	XF	Unc
AH1337	27.50	37.50	50.00	90.00	—
AH1338	27.50	37.50	50.00	90.00	—

Y# 9.2 2-1/2 TENGA **Comp.:** Copper, Bronze Or Brass **Obverse:** Full sun in sky, inscription with Falus on right side

Date	VG	F	VF	XF	Unc
AH1337	27.50	37.50	50.00	90.00	—
AH1338	27.50	37.50	50.00	90.00	—

Y# 9.1 2-1/2 TENGA **Composition:** Copper, Bronze Or Brass **Obverse:** Sun rising, inscription with Falus on right side

Date	VG	F	VF	XF	Unc
AH1337	27.50	37.50	50.00	90.00	—

Y# 10.1 5 TENGA **Comp.:** Copper, Bronze Or Brass **Obverse:** Full sun in sky, inscription with Falus on right side

Date	VG	F	VF	XF	Unc
AH1337	37.50	52.50	70.00	110	—
AH1338	37.50	52.50	70.00	110	—

Y# 10.2 5 TENGA **Composition:** Copper, Bronze Or Brass **Obverse:** Full sun in sky, inscription with Falus on left side **Note:** Many die varieties exist. Date above or below inscription. Diameters, ornamentation, die rotation, sun rays, and size of circles vary.

Date	VG	F	VF	XF	Unc
AH1337	37.50	52.50	70.00	110	—
AH1338	37.50	52.50	70.00	110	—

Y# 11 15 TENGA **Composition:** Copper, Bronze Or Brass **Note:** Many die varieties exist.

Date	VG	F	VF	XF	Unc
AH1338	100	175	250	—	—

PEOPLES REPUBLIC
AH1338-1343/1920-1924AD

STANDARD COINAGE

Y# 5 20 ROUBLES Composition: Bronze Or Brass

Date	VG	F	VF	XF	Unc
AH1338	20.00	30.00	40.00	75.00	—
AH1339	20.00	30.00	40.00	75.00	—
AH1340	20.00	30.00	40.00	75.00	—

Y# 16 25 ROUBLES Composition: Bronze Or Brass
Reverse: 8-pointed star

Date	VG	F	VF	XF	Unc
AH1339	17.50	30.00	40.00	75.00	—

Y# 16.1 25 ROUBLES Composition: Bronze Or Brass
Reverse: 12-pointed star

Date	VG	F	VF	XF	Unc
AH1339	17.50	30.00	40.00	75.00	—

Y# 17 100 ROUBLES Composition: Bronze Or Brass

Date	VG	F	VF	XF	Unc
AH1339	17.50	25.00	32.50	60.00	—

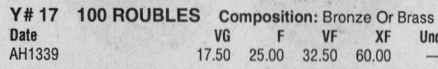

Y# 18 500 ROUBLES Composition: Bronze Or Brass

Date	VG	F	VF	XF	Unc
AH1339	50.00	75.00	200	275	—

Y# 19 500 ROUBLES Composition: Bronze Or Brass
Note: Varieties exist. Similar 200 and 1,000 Rouble strikes with crude inscriptions are considered fantasies.

Date	VG	F	VF	XF	Unc
AH1339	20.00	30.00	40.00	75.00	—
AH1340	20.00	30.00	40.00	75.00	—

VANUATU

The Republic of Vanuatu, formerly New Hebrides Condominium, a group of islands located in the South Pacific 500 miles (800 km.) west of Fiji, were under the joint sovereignty of Great Britain and France. The islands have an area of 5,700 sq. mi. (14,760 sq. km.) and a population of 165,000, mainly Melanesians of mixed blood. Capital: Port-Vila. The volcanic and coral islands, while malaria land subject to frequent earthquakes, are extremely fertile, and produce copra, coffee, tropical fruits and timber for export.

The New Hebrides were discovered by Portuguese navigator Pedro de Quiros in 1606, visited by French explorer Bougainville in 1768, and named by British navigator Capt. James Cook in 1774. Ships of all nations converged on the islands to trade for sandalwood, prompting France and Britain to relinquish their individual claims and declare the islands a neutral zone in 1878. The New Hebrides were placed under the control of a mixed Anglo-French commission of naval officers during the native uprisings of 1887, and established as a condominium under the joint sovereignty of France and Great Britain in 1906.

Vanuatu became an independent republic within the Commonwealth in July 1980. A president is Head of State and the Prime Minister is Head of Government.

MINT MARKS
(a) - Paris, privy marks only

MONETARY SYSTEM
100 Centimes = 1 Franc

REPUBLIC

STANDARD COINAGE

KM# 3 VATU Composition: Nickel-Brass

Date	F	VF	XF	Unc	BU
1983	—	—	0.10	0.35	—
1983 Proof	—	Value: 1.50			
1990	—	—	0.10	0.35	—
1999	—	—	0.10	0.35	—

KM# 4 2 VATU Composition: Nickel-Brass

Date	F	VF	XF	Unc	BU
1983	—	—	0.15	0.50	—
1983 Proof	—	Value: 2.00			
1990	—	—	0.15	0.50	—
1995	—	—	0.15	0.50	—

KM# 5 5 VATU Composition: Nickel-Brass

Date	F	VF	XF	Unc	BU
1983	—	—	0.20	0.75	—
1983 Proof	—	Value: 2.50			
1990	—	—	0.20	0.75	—
1995	—	—	0.20	0.75	—

KM# 6 10 VATU Comp.: Copper-Nickel Series: F

Date	F	VF	XF	Unc
1983	—	—	0.35	1.50
1983 Proof	—	Value: 3.00		
1990	—	—	0.35	1.50
1995	—	—	0.35	1.50

KM#25 10 VATU Composition: Copper-Nickel Sub
End of Victorian Era - Queen Victoria

Date	F	VF	XF	Unc
1995	—	—	—	10.00

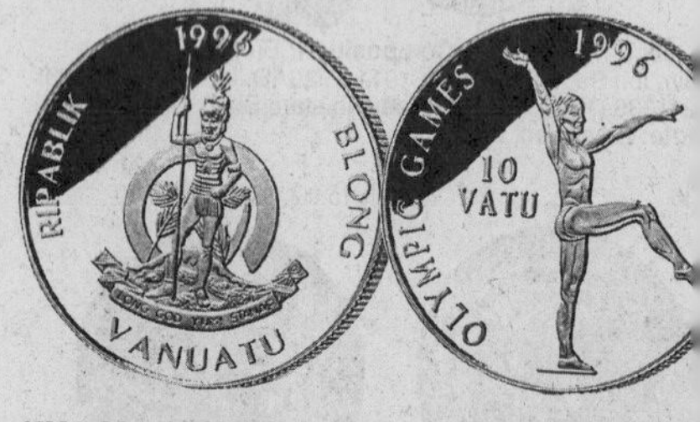

KM# 28 10 VATU Weight: 10.0000 g. Comp.: 0.50
Silver .1607 oz. ASW Series: Olympics Reverse: Gym

Date	F	VF	XF	Unc
1996	—	—	—	14.50

KM# 7 20 VATU Composition: Copper-Nickel Seri
F.A.O Note: Similar 10 10 Vatu, KM#6.

Date	F	VF	XF	Unc
1983	—	—	0.35	1.50
1983 Proof	—	Value: 4.00		
1990	—	—	0.35	1.50
1995	—	—	0.35	1.50

KM# 19 20 VATU Weight: 20.0000 g. Composition
0.5000 Silver .3215 oz. ASW Subject: Captain James C

Date	Mintage	F	VF	XF	Unc
1994 Proof	Est. 25,000	Value: 17.50			

KM# 20 20 VATU **Weight:** 20.0000 g. **Composition:** 0.9250 Silver .5948 oz. ASW **Series:** Endangered Wildlife **Reverse:** Kingfisher

Date	Mintage	F	VF	XF	Unc	BU
1994 Proof	Est. 25,000	Value: 37.50				

KM# 1 50 VATU **Composition:** Nickel **Subject:** 1st Anniversary of Independence

Date	F	VF	XF	Unc	BU
1981	—	—	1.00	2.50	—

KM# 1a 50 VATU **Weight:** 15.0000 g. **Composition:** 0.9250 Silver .4461 oz. ASW

Date	Mintage	F	VF	XF	Unc	BU
1981 Proof	846	Value: 35.00				

KM# 8 50 VATU **Composition:** Copper-Nickel **Series:** F.A.O.

ate	F	VF	XF	Unc	BU
983	—	—	1.00	2.75	—
983 Proof	—	Value: 7.00			
990	—	—	1.00	2.75	—
995	—	—	1.00	2.75	—
999	—	—	1.00	2.75	—

M# 10 50 VATU **Weight:** 34.0000 g. **Composition:** 0.9250 Silver 1.0111 oz. ASW **Series:** Seoul Olympics **Subject:** Boxing

te	Mintage	F	VF	XF	Unc	BU
38 Proof	15,000	Value: 22.50				

KM# 11 50 VATU **Weight:** 31.4700 g. **Composition:** 0.9250 Silver .9359 oz. ASW **Subject:** Voyager I

Date	Mintage	F	VF	XF	Unc	BU
1992 Proof	10,000	Value: 27.50				

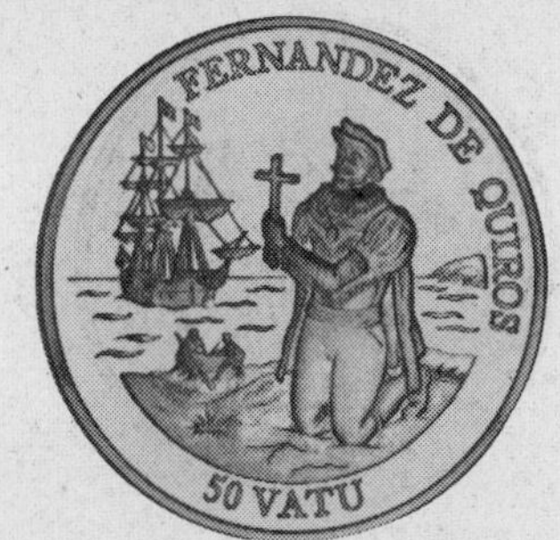

KM# 12 50 VATU **Weight:** 31.4700 g. **Comp.:** 0.9250 Silver .9359 oz. ASW **Subject:** Pedro Fernandez De Quiros

Date	F	VF	XF	Unc	BU
1992 Proof	—	Value: 26.50			

KM# 13 50 VATU **Weight:** 31.4700 g. **Composition:** 0.9250 Silver .9359 oz. ASW **Series:** Endangered Wildlife **Subject:** Earth Pigeons

Date	F	VF	XF	Unc	BU
1992 Proof	—	Value: 30.00			

KM# 14 50 VATU **Weight:** 31.4700 g. **Composition:** 0.9250 Silver .9359 oz. ASW **Series:** Olympics **Subject:** Canoes

Date	Mintage	F	VF	XF	Unc	BU
1992 Proof	Est. 40,000	Value: 15.00				

KM# 15 50 VATU **Weight:** 31.4700 g. **Composition:** 0.9250 Silver .9359 oz. ASW **Subject:** 40th Anniversary of Coronation

Date	Mintage	F	VF	XF	Unc	BU
1993 Proof	Est. 10,000	Value: 45.00				

KM# 16 50 VATU **Weight:** 31.4700 g. **Composition:** 0.9250 Silver .9359 oz. ASW **Subject:** The Boudeuse **Reverse:** Ship

Date	Mintage	F	VF	XF	Unc	BU
1993 Proof	Est. 15,000	Value: 30.00				

KM# 17 50 VATU **Weight:** 31.4700 g. **Composition:** 0.9250 Silver .9359 oz. ASW **Subject:** Protect Our World **Reverse:** Whale

Date	Mintage	F	VF	XF	Unc	BU
1993 Proof	Est. 10,000	Value: 50.00				

KM# 18 50 VATU **Weight:** 31.4700 g. **Composition:** 0.9250 Silver .9359 oz. ASW **Subject:** World Cup Soccer

Date	Mintage	F	VF	XF	Unc	BU
1994 Proof	Est. 15,000	Value: 27.50				

KM# 21 50 VATU **Weight:** 31.4700 g. **Composition:** 0.9250 Silver .9359 oz. ASW **Subject:** De Bougainville

Date	Mintage	F	VF	XF	Unc	BU
1994 Proof	Est. 10,000	Value: 37.50				

KM# 22 50 VATU **Weight:** 31.4700 g. **Composition:** 0.9250 Silver .9359 oz. ASW **Subject:** Queen Victoria

Date	Mintage	F	VF	XF	Unc	BU
1994 Proof	Est. 20,000	Value: 30.00				

KM# 24 50 VATU **Weight:** 31.4700 g. **Composition:** 0.9250 Silver .9359 oz. ASW **Series:** Olympics **Reverse:** Swimmers

Date	Mintage	F	VF	XF	Unc	BU
1994 Proof	Est. 40,000	Value: 25.00				

KM# 30 50 VATU **Weight:** 31.4700 g. **Composition:** 0.9250 Silver .9359 oz. ASW **Series:** Olympic Games 1996 **Obverse:** National emblem **Reverse:** Gymnast

Date		F	VF	XF	Unc	BU
1994 Proof	—	Value: 24.50				

KM# 26 50 VATU **Weight:** 31.4700 g. **Composition:** 0.9250 Silver .9359 oz. ASW **Subject:** Birth of Great Grandson Prince William

Date	Mintage	F	VF	XF	Unc	BU
1995 Proof	Est. 30,000	Value: 35.00				

KM# 29 50 VATU **Weight:** 31.4700 g. **Composition:** 0.9250 Silver .9359 oz. ASW **Subject:** Queen Victoria and Prince Albert

Date	Mintage	F	VF	XF	Unc	BU
1996 Proof	Est. 10,000	Value: 42.50				

KM# 31 50 VATU **Weight:** 1.2441 g. **Composition:** 0.9990 Gold .0400 oz. AGW **Obverse:** National emblem **Reverse:** Spanish 1704 gold coin design

Date		F	VF	XF	Unc	BU
1998 Proof	—	Value: 45.00				

KM# 32 50 VATU **Weight:** 1.2441 g. **Composition:** 0.9990 Gold .0400 oz. AGW **Obverse:** National emblem **Reverse:** Boar tusk necklace

Date		F	VF	XF	Unc	BU
1998 Proof	—	Value: 45.00				

KM# 33 50 VATU **Weight:** 30.9700 g. **Composition:** 0.9250 Silver .9210 oz. ASW **Subject:** Millennium 2000 **Note:** Gold plated shell on reverse.

Date		F	VF	XF	Unc	BU
1998 Proof	—	Value: 45.00				

KM# 9 100 VATU **Composition:** Nickel-Brass

Date	F	VF	XF	Unc	BU
1988	—	—	—	3.75	—
1995	—	—	—	3.75	—

KM# 23 100 VATU **Weight:** 7.7760 g. **Composition:** 0.5830 Gold .1458 oz. AGW **Series:** Endangered Wildlife **Reverse:** Kingfisher

Date	Mintage	F	VF	XF	Unc	BU
1994 Proof	Est. 2,000	Value: 150				

KM# 27 100 VATU **Weight:** 155.5000 g. **Composition:** 0.9250 Silver 4.6245 oz. ASW **Reverse:** Coronation portrait **Size:** 65 mm. **Note:** Illustration reduced.

Date	Mintage	F	VF	XF	Unc	BU
1995 Proof	Est. 2,000	Value: 80.00				

KM# 34 100 VATU **Weight:** 155.5000 g. **Composition:** 0.9250 Silver 4.6245 oz. ASW **Subject:** H.M.S. Resolution **Obverse:** National arms **Reverse:** Sailing ship and carvings **Edge:** Reeded **Size:** 65.7 mm. **Note:** Illustration reduced.

Date	Mintage	F	VF	XF	Unc	BU
1996 Proof	5,000	Value: 150				

KM# 2 10000 VATU **Weight:** 15.9800 g. **Composition:** 0.9170 Gold .4712 oz. AGW **Subject:** 1st Anniversary of Independence

Date		F	VF	XF	Unc	BU
1981		—	—	—	240	—
1981 Proof	1,054	Value: 300				

PROOF SETS

KM#	Date	Mintage	Identification	Issue Price	Mkt Val
PS1	1983 (6)	—	KM#3-8	—	20.00

VATICAN CITY

The State of the Vatican City, a papal state on the right bank of the Tiber River within the boundaries of Rome, has an area of 0.17 sq. mi. (0.44 sq. km.) and a population of *775. Capital: Vatican City.

Vatican City State, comprising the Vatican, St. Peter's and extra territorial right to Castel Gandolfo and 13 buildings in Rome, is all that remains of the extensive papal states over which the Pope exercised temporal power in central Italy. During the struggle for Italian unification, the Papal States, including Rome, were forcibly incorporated into the Kingdom of Italy in 1870. The resultant confrontation of crozier and sword remained unresolved until the signing of the Lateran Treaty, Feb. 11, 1929, between the Vatican and the Kingdom of Italy which recognized the independence and sovereignty of the State of the Vatican City, defined the relationship between the government and the church within Italy, and financially compensated the Holy See for its territorial losses in1870.

Today the Pope exercises supreme legislative, executive and judicial power within the Vatican City, and the State of the Vatican City is recognized by many nations as an independent sovereign state under the temporal jurisdiction of the Pope, even to the extent of ambassadorial exchange.

PONTIFFS

Pius XI, 1922-1939
Sede Vacante, Feb. 10 - Mar. 2, 1939
Pius XII, 1939-1958
Sede Vacante, Oct. 9 - 28, 1958
John XXIII, 1958-1963
Sede Vacante, June 3 - 21,1963
Paul VI, 1963-1978
Sede Vacante, Aug. 6 - 26, 1978
John Paul I, Aug. 26 - Sept. 28, 1978
Sede Vacante, Sept. 28 - Oct. 16, 1978
John Paul II, 1978-

MINT MARKS

Commencing 1981

R – Rome

MONETARY SYSTEM

100 Centesimi = 1 Lira

DATING

Most Vatican coins indicate the regnal year of the pope preceded by the word ***Anno*** (or an abbreviation), even if the anno domini date is omitted.

CITY STATE

STANDARD COINAGE

100 Centesimi = 1 Lira

 # 1 5 CENTESIMI Comp.: Bronze **Ruler:** Pope Pius XI

te	Mintage	F	VF	XF	Unc	BU
29/VIII	10,000	—	5.00	7.50	16.00	—
30/IX	100,000	—	2.50	4.00	6.00	—
31/X	100,000	—	2.50	4.00	6.00	—
32/XI	100,000	—	2.50	4.00	6.00	—
34/XIII	100,000	—	2.50	4.00	6.00	—
35/XIV	44,000	—	5.00	10.00	20.00	—
36/XV	62,000	—	2.50	4.00	6.50	—
37/XVI	62,000	—	2.50	4.00	6.50	—
38/XVII Rare	—	—	—	—	—	—

 # 11 5 CENTESIMI Composition: Bronze **Ruler:** Pope Pius XI **Subject:** Jubilee

e	Mintage	F	VF	XF	Unc	BU
3-34	100,000	—	5.00	10.00	20.00	—

Y# 22 5 CENTESIMI Composition: Aluminum-Bronze **Ruler:** Pope Pius XII

Date	Mintage	F	VF	XF	Unc	BU
1939/I	62,000	—	2.50	4.00	7.50	—
1940/II	62,000	—	2.50	4.00	7.50	—
1941/III	5,000	—	7.50	15.00	27.00	—

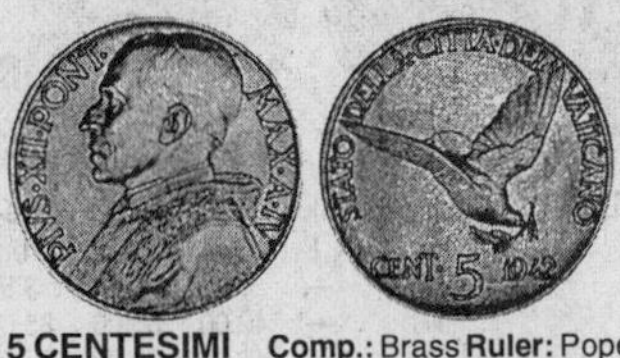

Y# 31 5 CENTESIMI Comp.: Brass **Ruler:** Pope Pius XII

Date	Mintage	F	VF	XF	Unc	BU
1942/IV	5,000	—	15.00	27.50	55.00	—
1943/V	1,000	—	25.00	40.00	85.00	—
1944/VI	1,000	—	25.00	40.00	85.00	—
1945/VII	1,000	—	25.00	40.00	85.00	—
1946/VIII	1,000	—	25.00	40.00	85.00	—

Y# 2 10 CENTESIMI Comp.: Bronze **Ruler:** Pope Pius XII

Date	Mintage	F	VF	XF	Unc	BU
1929/VIII	10,000	—	5.00	7.50	18.00	—
1930/IX	90,000	—	2.00	4.00	6.00	—
1931/X	90,000	—	2.00	4.00	6.00	—
1932/XI	90,000	—	2.00	4.00	6.00	—
1934/XIII	90,000	—	2.00	4.00	6.00	—
1935/XIV	90,000	—	2.00	4.00	6.00	—
1936/XV	81,000	—	2.00	4.00	8.00	—
1937/XVI	81,000	—	2.00	4.00	8.00	—
1938/XVII	—	—	—	—	950	—

Y# 12 10 CENTESIMI Composition: Bronze **Ruler:** Pope Pius XII **Subject:** Jubilee

Date	Mintage	F	VF	XF	Unc	BU
1933-34	90,000	—	5.00	10.00	20.00	—

Y# 23 10 CENTESIMI Composition: Aluminum-Bronze **Ruler:** Pope Pius XII

Date	Mintage	F	VF	XF	Unc	BU
1939/I	81,000	—	2.50	5.00	10.00	—
1940/II	81,000	—	2.50	5.00	10.00	—
1941/III	7,500	—	7.50	15.00	27.00	—

Y# 32 10 CENTESIMI Composition: Brass **Ruler:** Pope Pius XII

Date	Mintage	F	VF	XF	Unc	BU
1942/IV	7,500	—	12.50	25.00	55.00	—
1943/V	1,000	—	40.00	60.00	85.00	—
1944/VI	1,000	—	40.00	60.00	85.00	—
1945/VII	1,000	—	40.00	60.00	85.00	—
1946/VIII	1,000	—	40.00	60.00	85.00	—

Y# 3 20 CENTESIMI Comp.: Nickel **Ruler:** Pope Pius XI

Date	Mintage	F	VF	XF	Unc	BU
1929/VIII	10,000	—	5.00	10.00	18.00	—
1930/IX	80,000	—	2.00	4.00	6.00	—
1931/X	80,000	—	2.00	4.00	6.00	—
1932/XI	80,000	—	2.00	4.00	6.00	—
1934/XIII	80,000	—	2.00	4.00	6.00	—
1935/XIV	11,000	—	25.00	50.00	75.00	—
1936/XV	64,000	—	2.00	4.00	6.00	—
1937/XVI	64,000	—	2.00	4.00	6.00	—

Y# 13 20 CENTESIMI Composition: Nickel **Ruler:** Pope Pius XI **Subject:** Jubilee

Date	Mintage	F	VF	XF	Unc	BU
1933-34	80,000	—	5.00	10.00	20.00	—

Y# 24 20 CENTESIMI Comp.: Nickel **Ruler:** Pope Pius XII

Date	Mintage	F	VF	XF	Unc	BU
1939/I	64,000	—	2.00	4.00	6.00	—

Y# 24a 20 CENTESIMI Composition: Stainless Steel **Ruler:** Pope Pius XII

Date	Mintage	F	VF	XF	Unc	BU
1940/II	64,000	—	2.00	4.00	5.50	—
1941/III	125,000	—	2.00	3.00	4.50	—

Y# 33 20 CENTESIMI Composition: Stainless Steel **Ruler:** Pope Pius XII

Date	Mintage	F	VF	XF	Unc	BU
1942/IV	125,000	—	2.00	2.75	3.50	—
1943/V	1,000	—	40.00	60.00	85.00	—
1944/VI	1,000	—	40.00	60.00	85.00	—
1945/VII	1,000	—	40.00	60.00	85.00	—
1946/VIII	1,000	—	40.00	60.00	85.00	—

Y# 4 50 CENTESIMI Comp.: Nickel **Ruler:** Pope Pius XI

Date	Mintage	F	VF	XF	Unc	BU
1929/VIII	10,000	—	5.00	10.00	18.00	—
1930/IX	80,000	—	2.00	4.00	6.00	—
1931/X	80,000	—	2.00	4.00	6.00	—
1932/XI	80,000	—	2.00	4.00	6.00	—
1934/XIII	80,000	—	2.00	4.00	6.00	—
1935/XIV	14,000	—	6.00	12.00	25.00	—
1936/XV	52,000	—	2.00	4.00	6.00	—
1937/XVI	52,000	—	2.00	4.00	6.00	—

Y# 14 50 CENTESIMI Composition: Nickel **Ruler:** Pope Pius XI **Subject:** Jubilee

Date	Mintage	F	VF	XF	Unc	BU
1933-34	80,000	—	4.00	8.00	16.00	—

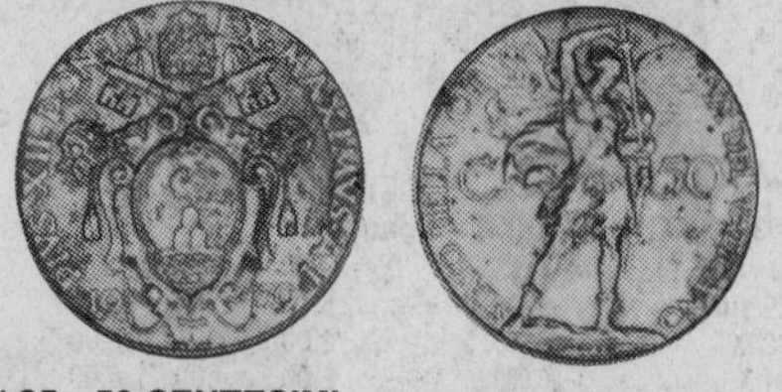

Y# 25 50 CENTESIMI Composition: Nickel **Ruler:** Pope Pius XII

Date	Mintage	F	VF	XF	Unc	BU
1939/I	52,000	—	2.00	4.00	6.00	—

Y# 25a 50 CENTESIMI Composition: Stainless Steel **Ruler:** Pope Pius XII

Date	Mintage	F	VF	XF	Unc	BU
1940/II	52,000	—	2.00	4.00	5.50	—
1941/III	180,000	—	2.00	3.50	5.00	—

Y# 34 50 CENTESIMI Composition: Stainless Steel **Ruler:** Pope Pius XII

Date	Mintage	F	VF	XF	Unc	BU
1942/IV	180,000	—	2.00	3.25	4.50	—
1943/V	1,000	—	40.00	60.00	85.00	—
1944/VI	1,000	—	40.00	60.00	85.00	—
1945/VII	1,000	—	40.00	60.00	85.00	—
1946/VIII	1,000	—	40.00	60.00	85.00	—

Y# 5 LIRA Composition: Nickel **Ruler:** Pope Pius XI

Date	Mintage	F	VF	XF	Unc	BU
1929/VIII	10,000	—	5.00	10.00	18.00	—
1930/IX	80,000	—	2.00	4.00	6.00	—
1931/X	80,000	—	2.00	4.00	6.00	—
1932/XI	80,000	—	2.00	4.00	6.00	—
1934/XIII	80,000	—	2.00	4.00	6.00	—
1935/XIV	40,000	—	2.00	4.00	6.00	—
1936/XV	40,000	—	2.00	4.00	6.00	—
1937/XVI	70,000	—	2.00	4.00	6.00	—

Y# 15 LIRA Composition: Nickel **Ruler:** Pope Pius XI **Subject:** Jubilee **Note:** Enlargement of date area.

Date	Mintage	F	VF	XF	Unc	BU
1933-34	80,000	—	5.00	10.00	20.00	—

Y# 26 LIRA Composition: Nickel **Ruler:** Pope Pius XII

Date	Mintage	F	VF	XF	Unc	BU
1939/I	70,000	—	3.00	5.00	10.00	—

Y# 26a LIRA Composition: Stainless Steel **Ruler:** Pope Pius XII

Date	Mintage	F	VF	XF	Unc	BU
1940/II	70,000	—	3.00	5.00	7.50	—
1941/III	284,000	—	1.00	2.00	4.50	—

Y# 35 LIRA Comp.: Stainless Steel **Ruler:** Pope Pius XII

Date	Mintage	F	VF	XF	Unc	BU
1942/IV	284,000	—	1.00	1.75	3.50	—
1943/V	1,000	—	40.00	60.00	85.00	—
1944/VI	1,000	—	40.00	60.00	85.00	—
1945/VII	1,000	—	40.00	60.00	85.00	—
1946/VIII	1,000	—	40.00	60.00	85.00	—

Y# 40 LIRA Composition: Aluminum **Ruler:** Pope Pius XII

Date	Mintage	F	VF	XF	Unc	BU
1947/IX	120,000	—	1.00	2.00	4.00	—
1948/X	10,000	—	2.00	4.00	7.00	—
1949/XI	10,000	—	2.00	4.00	7.00	—

Y# 44 LIRA Composition: Aluminum **Ruler:** Pope Pius XII **Subject:** Holy Year

Date	Mintage	F	VF	XF	Unc	BU
1950	50,000	—	1.00	2.00	3.50	—

Y# 49.1 LIRA Composition: Aluminum **Ruler:** Pope Pius XII **Obv. Legend:** ANNO

Date	Mintage	F	VF	XF	Unc	BU
1951/XIII	400,000	—	0.25	0.50	1.50	—
1952/XIV	400,000	—	0.25	0.50	1.50	—
1953/XV	400,000	—	0.25	0.50	1.50	—
1955/XVII	10,000	—	1.50	3.00	6.00	—
1957/XIX	30,000	—	0.75	2.00	3.50	—
1958/XX	30,000	—	0.75	2.00	3.50	—

Y# 49.2 LIRA Composition: Aluminum **Ruler:** Pope Pius XII **Obv. Legend:** A

Date	Mintage	F	VF	XF	Unc	BU
1956/XVIII	10,000	—	1.50	3.00	6.00	—

Y# 58.1 LIRA Composition: Aluminum **Ruler:** Pope John XXIII **Obv. Legend:** AN

Date	Mintage	F	VF	XF	Unc	BU
1959/I	25,000	—	1.00	3.50	6.00	—
1960/II	25,000	—	1.00	2.00	4.00	—

Y# 58.2 LIRA Composition: Aluminum **Ruler:** Pope John XXIII **Obv. Legend:** A

Date	Mintage	F	VF	XF	Unc	BU
1961/III	25,000	—	1.00	2.00	4.00	—
1962/IV	25,000	—	1.00	2.00	4.00	—

Y# 67 LIRA Composition: Aluminum **Ruler:** Pope John XXIII **Subject:** 2nd Ecumenical Council

Date	Mintage	F	VF	XF	Unc	BU
1962/IV	50,000	—	1.00	1.50	3.00	—

Y# 76.1 LIRA Composition: Aluminum **Ruler:** Pope Paul VI **Obv. Legend:** AN

Date	Mintage	F	VF	XF	Unc	BU
1963/I	60,000	—	0.75	2.00	4.00	—

Y# 76.2 LIRA Composition: Aluminum **Ruler:** Pope Paul VI **Obv. Legend:** A

Date	Mintage	F	VF	XF	Unc	BU
1964/II	60,000	—	0.50	1.00	2.00	—
1965/III	60,000	—	0.50	1.00	2.00	—

Y# 84 LIRA Composition: Aluminum **Ruler:** Pope Paul VI

Date	Mintage	F	VF	XF	Unc	BU
1966/IV	90,000	—	0.25	0.75	1.25	—

Y# 92 LIRA Composition: Aluminum **Ruler:** Pope Paul VI

Date	Mintage	F	VF	XF	Unc	BU
1967/V	100,000	—	0.25	0.75	1.25	–

Y# 100 LIRA Composition: Aluminum **Ruler:** Pope Paul VI **Series:** F.A.O.

Date	Mintage	F	VF	XF	Unc	BU
ND(1968)/VI	100,000	—	0.25	0.75	1.25	-

Y# 108 LIRA Composition: Aluminum **Ruler:** Pope Paul VI **Series:** F.A.O.

Date	Mintage	F	VF	XF	Unc
1969/VII	100,000	—	0.25	0.75	1.25

Y# 116 LIRA Composition: Aluminum **Ruler:** Pope Paul VI **Series:** F.A.O.

Date	Mintage	F	VF	XF	Unc
1970/VIII	100,000	—	0.25	0.50	1.00
1971/IX	110,000	—	0.25	0.50	1.00
1972/X	110,000	—	0.25	0.50	1.00
1973/XI	132,000	—	0.25	0.50	1.00
1974/XII	132,000	—	0.25	0.50	1.00
1975/XIII	150,000	—	0.25	0.50	1.00
1976/XIV	150,000	—	0.25	0.50	1.00
1977/XV	135,000	—	0.25	0.50	1.00

Y# 124 LIRA **Composition:** Aluminum **Ruler:** Pope Paul VI **Subject:** Holy Year

Date	Mintage	F	VF	XF	Unc	BU
1975	170,000	—	0.25	0.50	1.00	—

Y# 6 2 LIRE **Composition:** Nickel **Ruler:** Pope Pius XI

Date	Mintage	F	VF	XF	Unc	BU
1929/VIII	10,000	—	5.00	10.00	18.00	—
1930/IX	50,000	—	2.00	4.00	5.50	—
1931/X	50,000	—	2.00	4.00	5.50	—
1932/XI	50,000	—	2.00	4.00	5.50	—
1934/XIII	50,000	—	2.00	4.00	5.50	—
1935/XIV	70,000	—	2.00	4.00	5.50	—
1936/XV	40,000	—	2.00	4.00	5.50	—
1937/XVI	70,000	—	2.00	4.00	5.50	—

Y# 16 2 LIRE **Composition:** Nickel **Ruler:** Pope Pius XI **Subject:** Jubilee

ate	Mintage	F	VF	XF	Unc	BU
933-34	50,000	—	4.00	6.00	10.00	—

 # 27 2 LIRE **Composition:** Nickel **Ruler:** Pope Pius XII

te	Mintage	F	VF	XF	Unc	BU
39/I	40,000	—	3.00	5.00	10.00	—

 # 27a 2 LIRE **Composition:** Stainless Steel **Ruler:** Pope Pius XII

te	Mintage	F	VF	XF	Unc	BU
40/II	40,000	—	0.75	1.50	4.00	—
41/III	270,000	—	0.50	1.00	3.00	—

36 2 LIRE **Composition:** Stainless Steel **Ruler:** Pope Pius XII

e	Mintage	F	VF	XF	Unc	BU
2/IV	270,000	—	0.50	1.00	3.50	—
3/V	1,000	—	40.00	60.00	85.00	—
4/VI	1,000	—	40.00	60.00	85.00	—
5/VII	1,000	—	40.00	60.00	85.00	—
6/VIII	1,000	—	40.00	60.00	85.00	—

Y# 41 2 LIRE **Composition:** Aluminum **Ruler:** Pope Pius XII

Date	Mintage	F	VF	XF	Unc	BU
1947/IX	65,000	—	2.00	4.00	8.00	—
1948/X	110,000	—	1.50	3.50	5.00	—
1949/XI	10,000	—	4.00	6.00	10.00	—

Y# 45 2 LIRE **Composition:** Aluminum **Ruler:** Pope Pius XII **Subject:** Holy Year

Date	Mintage	F	VF	XF	Unc	BU
1950	50,000	—	1.25	2.00	4.00	—

Y# 50 2 LIRE **Composition:** Aluminum **Ruler:** Pope Pius XII

Date	Mintage	F	VF	XF	Unc	BU
1951/XIII	400,000	—	0.25	0.50	1.50	—
1952/XIV	400,000	—	0.25	0.50	1.50	—
1953/XV	400,000	—	0.25	0.50	1.50	—
1955/XVII	20,000	—	1.00	2.00	4.00	—
1956/XVIII	20,000	—	1.00	2.00	4.00	—
1957/XIX	30,000	—	0.75	1.25	2.50	—
1958/XX	30,000	—	0.75	1.25	2.50	—

Y# 59.1 2 LIRE **Composition:** Aluminum **Ruler:** Pope John XXIII **Obv. Legend:** AN

Date	Mintage	F	VF	XF	Unc	BU
1959/I	25,000	—	1.50	4.00	6.00	—
1960/II	25,000	—	1.50	3.00	5.00	—

Y# 59.2 2 LIRE **Composition:** Aluminum **Ruler:** Pope John XXIII **Obv. Legend:** A

Date	Mintage	F	VF	XF	Unc	BU
1961/III	25,000	—	1.50	3.00	5.00	—
1962/IV	25,000	—	1.50	3.00	5.00	—

Y# 68 2 LIRE **Composition:** Aluminum **Ruler:** Pope John XXIII **Subject:** Second Ecumenical Council

Date	Mintage	F	VF	XF	Unc	BU
1962/IV	50,000	—	1.00	1.50	3.00	—

Y# 77.1 2 LIRE **Composition:** Aluminum **Ruler:** Pope Paul VI **Obv. Legend:** AN

Date	Mintage	F	VF	XF	Unc	BU
1963/I	60,000	—	0.75	2.00	3.00	—

Y# 77.2 2 LIRE **Composition:** Aluminum **Ruler:** Pope Paul VI **Obv. Legend:** A

Date	Mintage	F	VF	XF	Unc	BU
1964/II	60,000	—	0.75	2.00	3.00	—
1965/III	60,000	—	0.75	1.00	2.00	—

Y# 85 2 LIRE **Composition:** Aluminum **Ruler:** Pope Paul VI

Date	Mintage	F	VF	XF	Unc	BU
1966/IV	90,000	—	0.25	0.75	1.25	—

Y# 93 2 LIRE **Composition:** Aluminum **Ruler:** Pope Paul VI

Date	Mintage	F	VF	XF	Unc	BU
1967/V	100,000	—	0.25	0.75	1.25	—

Y# 101 2 LIRE **Composition:** Aluminum **Ruler:** Pope Paul VI **Series:** F.A.O.

Date	Mintage	F	VF	XF	Unc	BU
ND(1968)/VI	100,000	—	0.25	0.75	1.50	—

Y# 109 2 LIRE **Composition:** Aluminum **Ruler:** Pope Paul VI

Date	Mintage	F	VF	XF	Unc	BU
1969/VII	100,000	—	0.25	0.75	1.50	—

Y# 117 2 LIRE **Comp..:** Aluminum **Ruler:** Pope Paul VI

Date	Mintage	F	VF	XF	Unc	BU
1970/VIII	100,000	—	0.25	0.50	1.00	—
1971/IX	110,000	—	0.25	0.50	1.00	—
1972/X	110,000	—	0.25	0.50	1.00	—
1973/XI	132,000	—	0.25	0.50	1.00	—
1974/XII	132,000	—	0.25	0.50	1.00	—
1975/XIII	150,000	—	0.25	0.50	1.00	—
1976/XIV	150,000	—	0.25	0.50	1.00	—
1977/XV	135,000	—	0.25	0.50	1.00	—

Y# 125 2 LIRE **Composition:** Aluminum **Ruler:** Pope Paul VI **Subject:** Holy Year

Date	Mintage	F	VF	XF	Unc	BU
1975	180,000	—	0.25	0.70	1.00	—

Y# 7 5 LIRE **Weight:** 5.0000 g. **Composition:** 0.8350 Silver .1342 oz. ASW **Ruler:** Pope Pius XI

Date	Mintage	F	VF	XF	Unc	BU
1929/VIII	10,000	—	7.50	15.00	30.00	—
1930/IX	50,000	—	5.00	9.00	20.00	—
1931/X	50,000	—	5.00	9.00	20.00	—
1932/XI	50,000	—	5.00	9.00	20.00	—
1934/XIII	30,000	—	5.00	10.00	20.00	—
1935/XIV	20,000	—	6.00	12.00	22.50	—
1936/XV	40,000	—	5.00	9.00	20.00	—
1937/XVI	40,000	—	5.00	9.00	20.00	—

Y# 17 5 LIRE **Weight:** 5.0000 g. **Composition:** 0.8350 Silver .1342 oz. ASW **Ruler:** Pope Pius XI **Subject:** Jubilee

Date	Mintage	F	VF	XF	Unc	BU
1933-34	50,000	—	5.00	10.00	20.00	—

Y# 20 5 LIRE **Weight:** 5.0000 g. **Composition:** 0.8350 Silver .1342 oz. ASW **Ruler:** Pope Pius XI **Subject:** Sede Vacante

Date	Mintage	F	VF	XF	Unc	BU
1939	40,000	—	7.50	15.00	25.00	—

Y# 28 5 LIRE **Weight:** 5.0000 g. **Composition:** 0.8350 Silver .1342 oz. ASW **Ruler:** Pope Pius XII

Date	Mintage	F	VF	XF	Unc	BU
1939/I	100,000	—	4.00	10.00	18.00	—
1940/II	100,000	—	4.00	10.00	18.00	—
1941/III	4,000	—	25.00	35.00	65.00	—

Y# 37 5 LIRE **Weight:** 5.0000 g. **Composition:** 0.8350 Silver .1342 oz. ASW **Ruler:** Pope Pius XII

Date	Mintage	F	VF	XF	Unc	BU
1942/IV	4,000	—	25.00	40.00	65.00	—
1943/V	1,000	—	50.00	75.00	100	—
1944/VI	1,000	—	50.00	75.00	100	—
1945/VII	1,000	—	50.00	75.00	100	—
1946/VIII	1,000	—	50.00	75.00	100	—

Y# 42 5 LIRE **Composition:** Aluminum **Ruler:** Pope Pius XII

Date	Mintage	F	VF	XF	Unc	BU
1947/IX	50,000	—	2.00	4.00	7.50	—
1948/X	74,000	—	2.00	4.00	7.50	—
1949/XI	74,000	—	2.00	4.00	7.50	—

Y# 46 5 LIRE **Composition:** Aluminum **Ruler:** Pope Pius XII **Subject:** Holy Year

Date	Mintage	F	VF	XF	Unc	BU
1950	50,000	—	3.00	5.00	7.50	—

Y# 51.1 5 LIRE **Composition:** Aluminum **Ruler:** Pope Pius XII **Obv. Legend:** AN

Date	Mintage	F	VF	XF	Unc	BU
1951/XIII	1,500,000	—	0.25	0.50	1.50	—
1952/XIV	1,500,000	—	0.25	0.50	1.50	—
1953/XV	1,500,000	—	0.25	0.50	1.50	—
1955/XVII	30,000	—	0.50	0.75	2.00	—
1956/XVIII	—	—	0.50	0.75	2.00	—
1957/XIX	—	—	0.50	0.75	2.00	—
1958/XX	—	—	0.50	0.75	2.00	—

Y# 51.2 5 LIRE **Composition:** Aluminum **Ruler:** Pope Pius XII **Obv. Legend:** A

Date	Mintage	F	VF	XF	Unc	BU
1956/XVIII	30,000	—	0.50	0.75	2.00	—
1957/XIX	30,000	—	0.50	0.75	2.00	—
1958/XX	30,000	—	0.50	0.75	2.00	—

Y# 60.1 5 LIRE **Composition:** Aluminum **Ruler:** Pope John XXIII **Obv. Legend:** AN

Date	Mintage	F	VF	XF	Unc	BU
1959/I	25,000	—	1.50	4.00	7.00	—

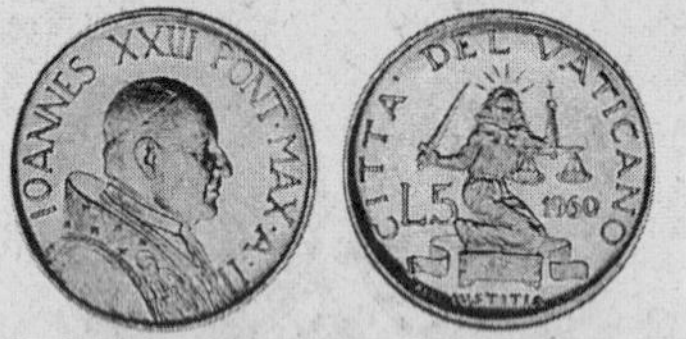

Y# 60.2 5 LIRE **Composition:** Aluminum **Ruler:** Pope John XXIII **Obv. Legend:** A

Date	Mintage	F	VF	XF	Unc	BU
1960/II	25,000	—	1.50	4.00	7.00	—
1961/III	25,000	—	1.50	3.00	4.50	—
1962/IV	25,000	—	1.00	1.50	3.00	—

Y# 69 5 LIRE **Composition:** Aluminum **Ruler:** Pope John XXIII **Subject:** Second Ecumenical Council

Date	Mintage	F	VF	XF	Unc	BU
1962/IV	50,000	—	0.40	0.75	1.50	—

Y# 78.1 5 LIRE **Composition:** Aluminum **Ruler:** Pope Paul VI **Obv. Legend:** AN

Date	Mintage	F	VF	XF	Unc	BU
1963/I	60,000	—	1.00	2.00	3.00	—

Y# 78.2 5 LIRE **Composition:** Aluminum **Ruler:** Pope Paul VI **Obv. Legend:** A

Date	Mintage	F	VF	XF	Unc	BU
1964/II	60,000	—	0.50	1.00	2.00	—
1965/III	60,000	—	0.50	1.00	2.00	—

Y# 86 5 LIRE **Composition:** Aluminum **Ruler:** Pope Paul VI

Date	Mintage	F	VF	XF	Unc	BU
1966/IV	90,000	—	0.25	0.50	1.00	—

Y# 94 5 LIRE **Composition:** Aluminum **Ruler:** Pope Paul VI

Date	Mintage	F	VF	XF	Unc	BU
1967/V	100,000	—	0.25	0.50	1.00	—

Y# 102 5 LIRE **Composition:** Aluminum **Ruler:** Pope Paul VI **Series:** F.A.O.

Date	Mintage	F	VF	XF	Unc	BU
ND(1968)/VI	100,000	—	0.25	0.60	1.00	—

Y# 110 5 LIRE **Composition:** Aluminum **Ruler:** Pope Paul VI

Date	Mintage	F	VF	XF	Unc	BU
1969/VII	100,000	—	0.25	0.60	1.00	—

Y# 118 5 LIRE **Composition:** Aluminum **Ruler:** Pope Paul V

Date	Mintage	F	VF	XF	Unc	BU
1970/VIII	100,000	—	0.25	0.60	1.25	–
1971/IX	110,000	—	0.25	0.60	1.25	–
1972/X	110,000	—	0.25	0.60	1.25	–
1973/XI	132,000	—	0.25	0.60	1.25	–
1974/XII	132,000	—	0.25	0.60	1.25	–
1975/XIII	150,000	—	0.25	0.60	1.25	–
1976/XIV	150,000	—	0.25	0.60	1.25	–
1977/XV	135,000	—	0.25	0.60	1.25	–

Y# 126 5 LIRE **Composition:** Aluminum **Ruler:** Pope Paul VI **Subject:** Holy Year

Date	Mintage	F	VF	XF	Unc	B
1975	380,000	—	0.25	0.35	1.00	–

Y# 133 5 LIRE **Composition:** Aluminum **Ruler:** Pope Paul

Date	Mintage	F	VF	XF	Unc
1978/XVI	120,000	—	0.25	0.40	1.00

Y# 8 10 LIRE **Weight:** 10.0000 g. **Composition:** 0.83 Silver .2684 oz. ASW **Ruler:** Pope Pius XII

Date	Mintage	F	VF	XF	Unc
1929/VIII	10,000	—	7.50	15.00	32.00
1930/IX	50,000	—	8.00	11.50	25.00
1931/X	50,000	—	8.00	11.50	25.00
1932/XI	50,000	—	8.00	11.50	25.00
1934/XIII	60,000	—	8.00	11.50	25.00
1935/XIV	50,000	—	8.00	11.50	25.00
1936/XV	40,000	—	8.00	11.50	25.00
1937/XVI	40,000	—	8.00	11.50	25.00

Y# 18 10 LIRE **Weight:** 10.0000 g. **Composition:** 0.8350 Silver .2684 oz. ASW **Ruler:** Pope Pius XII **Subject:** Jubilee

Date	Mintage	F	VF	XF	Unc	BU
1933-34	50,000	—	8.00	15.00	30.00	—

Y# 21 10 LIRE **Weight:** 10.0000 g. **Composition:** 0.8350 Silver .2684 oz. ASW **Ruler:** Cardinal Eugenio Pacelli **Subject:** Sede Vacante **Obverse:** Arms of Cardinal Pacelli

Date	Mintage	F	VF	XF	Unc	BU
1939	30,000	—	10.00	17.50	35.00	—

Y# 29 10 LIRE **Weight:** 10.0000 g. **Composition:** 0.8350 Silver .2684 oz. ASW **Ruler:** Pope Pius XII

Date	Mintage	F	VF	XF	Unc	BU
939/I	10,000	—	12.00	25.00	45.00	—
940/II	10,000	—	12.00	25.00	45.00	—
941/III	4,000	—	20.00	40.00	80.00	—

Y# 38 10 LIRE **Weight:** 10.0000 g. **Composition:** 0.8350 Silver .2684 oz. ASW **Ruler:** Pope Pius XII

Date	Mintage	F	VF	XF	Unc	BU
942/IV	4,000	—	25.00	50.00	90.00	—
943/V	1,000	—	60.00	85.00	125	—
944/VI	1,000	—	60.00	85.00	125	—
945/VII	1,000	—	60.00	85.00	125	—
946/VIII	1,000	—	60.00	85.00	125	—

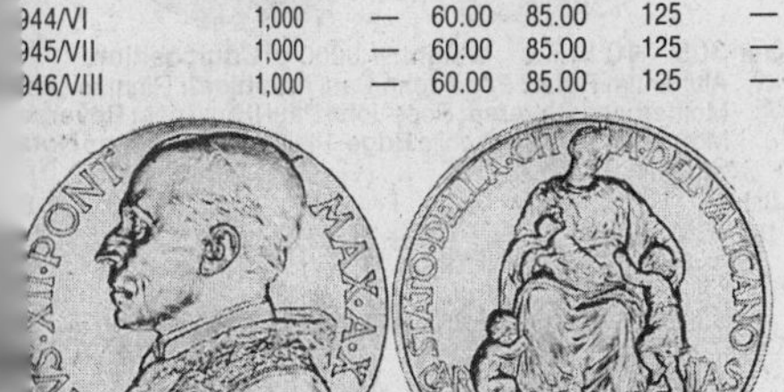

Y# 43 10 LIRE **Composition:** Aluminum **Ruler:** Pope Pius XII

Date	Mintage	F	VF	XF	Unc	BU
47/IX	50,000	—	3.00	5.00	8.00	—
48/X	60,000	—	3.00	5.00	8.00	—
49/XI	60,000	—	3.00	5.00	8.00	—

Y# 47 10 LIRE **Composition:** Aluminum **Ruler:** Pope Pius XII **Subject:** Holy Year

Date	Mintage	F	VF	XF	Unc	BU
0	60,000	—	3.00	5.00	7.50	—

Y# 52.1 10 LIRE **Composition:** Aluminum **Ruler:** Pope Pius XII **Obv. Legend:** AN

Date	Mintage	F	VF	XF	Unc	BU
1951/XIII	1,130,000	—	0.50	0.75	1.50	—
1952/XIV	1,130,000	—	0.50	0.75	1.50	—
1953/XV	1,130,000	—	0.50	0.75	1.50	—
1955/XVII	80,000	—	0.75	1.50	3.00	—

Y# 52.2 10 LIRE **Composition:** Aluminum **Ruler:** Pope Pius XII **Obv. Legend:** A

Date	Mintage	F	VF	XF	Unc	BU
1956/XVIII	80,000	—	0.75	1.50	3.00	—
1957/XIX	36,000	—	0.75	1.50	3.50	—
1958/XX	30,000	—	0.75	1.50	3.50	—

Y# 61.1 10 LIRE **Composition:** Aluminum **Ruler:** Pope John XXIII **Obv. Legend:** AN

Date	Mintage	F	VF	XF	Unc	BU
1959/I	50,000	—	1.00	4.00	6.50	—

Y# 61.2 10 LIRE **Composition:** Aluminum **Ruler:** Pope John XXIII **Obv. Legend:** A

Date	Mintage	F	VF	XF	Unc	BU
1960/II	50,000	—	1.00	3.00	6.00	—
1961/III	50,000	—	1.00	3.00	6.00	—
1962/IV	50,000	—	1.00	2.00	4.00	—

Y# 70 10 LIRE **Composition:** Aluminum **Ruler:** Pope John XXIII **Subject:** Second Ecumenical Council

Date	Mintage	F	VF	XF	Unc	BU
1962/IV	100,000	—	1.00	1.50	3.00	—

Y# 79.1 10 LIRE **Composition:** Aluminum **Ruler:** Pope Paul VI **Obv. Legend:** AN

Date	Mintage	F	VF	XF	Unc	BU
1963/I	90,000	—	1.00	1.50	3.00	—

Y# 79.2 10 LIRE **Composition:** Aluminum **Ruler:** Pope Paul VI **Obv. Legend:** A

Date	Mintage	F	VF	XF	Unc	BU
1964/II	90,000	—	0.75	1.00	2.00	—
1965/III	90,000	—	0.75	1.00	2.00	—

Y# 87 10 LIRE **Composition:** Aluminum **Ruler:** Pope Paul VI

Date	Mintage	F	VF	XF	Unc	BU
1966/IV	100,000	—	0.25	0.75	1.25	—

Y# 95 10 LIRE **Comp.:** Aluminum **Ruler:** Pope Paul VI

Date	Mintage	F	VF	XF	Unc	BU
ND(1967)/V	110,000	—	0.25	0.75	1.25	—

Y# 103 10 LIRE **Composition:** Aluminum **Ruler:** Pope Paul VI **Series:** F.A.O.

Date	Mintage	F	VF	XF	Unc	BU
ND(1968)/VI	110,000	—	0.25	0.80	1.50	—

Y# 111 10 LIRE **Comp.:** Aluminum **Ruler:** Pope Paul VI

Date	Mintage	F	VF	XF	Unc	BU
1969/VII	110,000	—	0.25	0.50	1.25	—

Y# 119 10 LIRE **Comp.:** Aluminum **Ruler:** Pope Paul VI

Date	Mintage	F	VF	XF	Unc	BU
1970/VIII	110,000	—	0.25	0.50	1.00	—
1971/IX	160,000	—	0.25	0.50	1.00	—
1972/X	160,000	—	0.25	0.50	1.00	—
1973/XI	170,000	—	0.25	0.50	1.00	—
1974/XII	170,000	—	0.25	0.50	1.00	—
1975/XIII	200,000	—	0.25	0.50	1.00	—
1976/XIV	200,000	—	0.25	0.50	1.00	—
1977/XV	200,000	—	0.25	0.50	1.00	—

Y# 127 10 LIRE **Composition:** Aluminum **Ruler:** Pope Paul VI **Subject:** Holy Year **Reverse:** Noah's ark

Date	Mintage	F	VF	XF	Unc	BU
1975	400,000	—	0.25	0.75	1.50	—

Y# 134 10 LIRE **Comp.:** Aluminum **Ruler:** Pope Paul VI

Date	Mintage	F	VF	XF	Unc	BU
1978/XVI	250,000	—	0.25	0.50	1.00	—

Y# 143 10 LIRE **Comp.:** Aluminum **Ruler:** Pope John Paul II

Date	Mintage	F	VF	XF	Unc	BU
1979/I	250,000	—	0.25	0.50	1.00	—
1980/II	170,000	—	0.25	0.50	1.00	—

Y# 155 10 LIRE Composition: Aluminum **Ruler:** Pope John Paul II **Reverse:** Jesus given water at the well

Date	Mintage	F	VF	XF	Unc	BU
1981/III	170,000	—	0.25	0.50	1.00	—

Y# 161 10 LIRE Composition: Aluminum **Ruler:** Pope John Paul II **Subject:** Creation of Woman **Obverse:** Similar to 1000 Lire, Y#167

Date	Mintage	F	VF	XF	Unc	BU
1982/IV	220,000	—	0.25	0.50	1.00	—

Y# 170 10 LIRE Composition: Aluminum **Ruler:** Pope John Paul II **Subject:** Work and Teaching

Date	Mintage	F	VF	XF	Unc	BU
1983/V	110,000	—	0.25	0.50	1.00	—

Y# 177 10 LIRE Composition: Aluminum **Ruler:** Pope John Paul II **Subject:** Year of Peace **Obverse:** Similar to 1000 Lire, Y#183

Date	Mintage	F	VF	XF	Unc	BU
1984/VI	110,000	—	0.25	0.50	1.00	—

Y# 185 10 LIRE Composition: Aluminum **Ruler:** Pope John Paul II

Date	Mintage	F	VF	XF	Unc	BU
1985/VII	90,000	—	0.25	0.50	1.00	—

Y# 192 10 LIRE Composition: Aluminum **Ruler:** Pope John Paul II

Date	Mintage	F	VF	XF	Unc	BU
1986/VIII	90,000	—	0.25	0.50	1.00	—

Y# 199 10 LIRE Composition: Aluminum **Ruler:** Pope John Paul II **Obverse:** Similar to 200 Lire, Y#203 **Reverse:** Basilica behind Pieta Statue

Date	F	VF	XF	Unc	BU
1987/IX	—	0.25	0.50	1.00	—

Y# 206 10 LIRE Composition: Aluminum **Ruler:** Pope John Paul II **Subject:** Temptation of Adam and Eve **Obverse:** Similar to 200 Lire, Y#210

Date	F	VF	XF	Unc	BU
1988/X	—	0.25	0.50	1.00	—

Y# 213 10 LIRE Composition: Aluminum **Ruler:** Pope John Paul II **Subject:** Jesus the Teacher

Date	F	VF	XF	Unc	BU
1989/XI	—	0.25	0.50	1.00	—

Y# 220 10 LIRE Composition: Aluminum **Ruler:** Pope John Paul II **Subject:** Saints Peter and Paul

Date	F	VF	XF	Unc	BU
1990/XII	—	0.25	0.50	1.00	—

Y# 228 10 LIRE Composition: Aluminum **Ruler:** Pope John Paul II

Date	F	VF	XF	Unc	BU
1991/XIII	—	0.25	0.50	1.00	—

Y# 236 10 LIRE Composition: Aluminum **Ruler:** Pope John Paul II **Reverse:** Bee on flower

Date	F	VF	XF	Unc	BU
1992/XIV	—	0.25	0.50	1.00	—

Y# 244 10 LIRE Composition: Aluminum **Ruler:** Pope John Paul II **Reverse:** Sailboat

Date	F	VF	XF	Unc	BU
1993/XV	—	0.25	0.50	1.00	—

Y# 252 10 LIRE Composition: Aluminum **Ruler:** Pope John Paul II **Reverse:** Planting trees

Date	F	VF	XF	Unc	BU
1994/XVI	—	0.25	0.50	1.00	—

Y# 262 10 LIRE Composition: Aluminum **Ruler:** Pope John Paul II **Reverse:** Preaching

Date	F	VF	XF	Unc	BU
1995	—	0.25	0.50	1.00	—

Y# 272 10 LIRE Composition: Aluminum **Ruler:** Pope John Paul II **Subject:** Child Carried to Peace

Date	F	VF	XF	Unc	BU
1996	—	0.25	0.50	1.00	—

Y# 280 10 LIRE Composition: Aluminum **Ruler:** Pope John Paul II **Reverse:** Angel and man sowing seeds

Date	F	VF	XF	Unc	BU
1997/XIX	—	0.25	0.50	1.00	—

Y# 293 10 LIRE Composition: Aluminum **Ruler:** Pope John Paul II **Obverse:** Pope with crucifix **Reverse:** Three figures

Date	F	VF	XF	Unc	B
1998	—	0.25	0.50	1.00	—

Y# 305 10 LIRE Weight: 1.6000 g. **Composition:** Aluminum **Ruler:** Pope John Paul II **Subject:** Right to Life Motherhood **Obverse:** Pope John Paul II bust right **Reverse** Mother with baby and child **Edge:** Plain **Size:** 23.3 mm. **Note** Struck at Rome.

Date	F	VF	XF	Unc	E
1999	—	0.25	0.50	1.00	

Y# 323 10 LIRE Weight: 1.6000 g. **Composition:** Aluminum **Ruler:** Pope John Paul II **Obverse:** Papal arm **Reverse:** Pope lifting child **Edge:** Plain **Size:** 23.2 mm.

Date	F	VF	XF	Unc
XXII(2000)	—	—	—	1.00

Y# 331 10 LIRE Weight: 1.6000 g. **Composition:** Aluminum **Ruler:** Pope John Paul II **Obverse:** Bust of Po John Paul I left **Reverse:** Papal arms **Edge:** Plain **Size:** 23.2 mm.

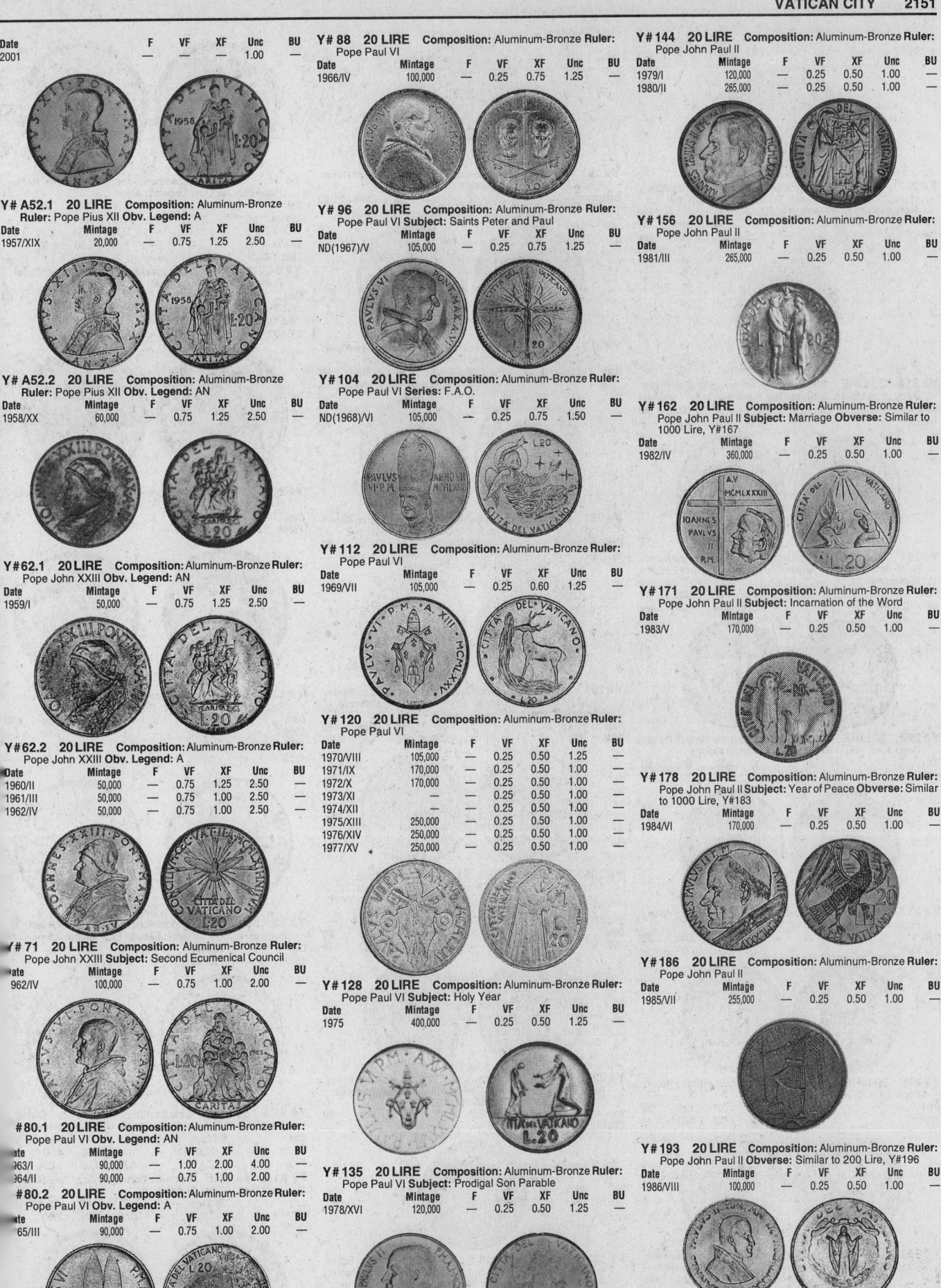

Date	F	VF	XF	Unc	BU
2001	—	—	—	1.00	—

Y# A52.1 20 LIRE Composition: Aluminum-Bronze **Ruler:** Pope Pius XII **Obv. Legend:** A

Date	Mintage	F	VF	XF	Unc	BU
1957/XIX	20,000	—	0.75	1.25	2.50	—

Y# A52.2 20 LIRE Composition: Aluminum-Bronze **Ruler:** Pope Pius XII **Obv. Legend:** AN

Date	Mintage	F	VF	XF	Unc	BU
1958/XX	60,000	—	0.75	1.25	2.50	—

Y#62.1 20 LIRE Composition: Aluminum-Bronze **Ruler:** Pope John XXIII **Obv. Legend:** AN

Date	Mintage	F	VF	XF	Unc	BU
1959/I	50,000	—	0.75	1.25	2.50	—

Y#62.2 20 LIRE Composition: Aluminum-Bronze **Ruler:** Pope John XXIII **Obv. Legend:** A

Date	Mintage	F	VF	XF	Unc	BU
1960/II	50,000	—	0.75	1.25	2.50	—
1961/III	50,000	—	0.75	1.00	2.50	—
1962/IV	50,000	—	0.75	1.00	2.50	—

Y# 71 20 LIRE Composition: Aluminum-Bronze **Ruler:** Pope John XXIII **Subject:** Second Ecumenical Council

Date	Mintage	F	VF	XF	Unc	BU
1962/IV	100,000	—	0.75	1.00	2.00	—

Y#80.1 20 LIRE Composition: Aluminum-Bronze **Ruler:** Pope Paul VI **Obv. Legend:** AN

Date	Mintage	F	VF	XF	Unc	BU
1963/I	90,000	—	1.00	2.00	4.00	—
1964/II	90,000	—	0.75	1.00	2.00	—

Y#80.2 20 LIRE Composition: Aluminum-Bronze **Ruler:** Pope Paul VI **Obv. Legend:** A

Date	Mintage	F	VF	XF	Unc	BU
1965/III	90,000	—	0.75	1.00	2.00	—

Y# 88 20 LIRE Composition: Aluminum-Bronze **Ruler:** Pope Paul VI

Date	Mintage	F	VF	XF	Unc	BU
1966/IV	100,000	—	0.25	0.75	1.25	—

Y# 96 20 LIRE Composition: Aluminum-Bronze **Ruler:** Pope Paul VI **Subject:** Saints Peter and Paul

Date	Mintage	F	VF	XF	Unc	BU
ND(1967)/V	105,000	—	0.25	0.75	1.25	—

Y# 104 20 LIRE Composition: Aluminum-Bronze **Ruler:** Pope Paul VI **Series:** F.A.O.

Date	Mintage	F	VF	XF	Unc	BU
ND(1968)/VI	105,000	—	0.25	0.75	1.50	—

Y# 112 20 LIRE Composition: Aluminum-Bronze **Ruler:** Pope Paul VI

Date	Mintage	F	VF	XF	Unc	BU
1969/VII	105,000	—	0.25	0.60	1.25	—

Y# 120 20 LIRE Composition: Aluminum-Bronze **Ruler:** Pope Paul VI

Date	Mintage	F	VF	XF	Unc	BU
1970/VIII	105,000	—	0.25	0.50	1.25	—
1971/IX	170,000	—	0.25	0.50	1.00	—
1972/X	170,000	—	0.25	0.50	1.00	—
1973/XI	—	—	0.25	0.50	1.00	—
1974/XII	—	—	0.25	0.50	1.00	—
1975/XIII	250,000	—	0.25	0.50	1.00	—
1976/XIV	250,000	—	0.25	0.50	1.00	—
1977/XV	250,000	—	0.25	0.50	1.00	—

Y# 128 20 LIRE Composition: Aluminum-Bronze **Ruler:** Pope Paul VI **Subject:** Holy Year

Date	Mintage	F	VF	XF	Unc	BU
1975	400,000	—	0.25	0.50	1.25	—

Y# 135 20 LIRE Composition: Aluminum-Bronze **Ruler:** Pope Paul VI **Subject:** Prodigal Son Parable

Date	Mintage	F	VF	XF	Unc	BU
1978/XVI	120,000	—	0.25	0.50	1.25	—

Y# 144 20 LIRE Composition: Aluminum-Bronze **Ruler:** Pope John Paul II

Date	Mintage	F	VF	XF	Unc	BU
1979/I	120,000	—	0.25	0.50	1.00	—
1980/II	265,000	—	0.25	0.50	1.00	—

Y# 156 20 LIRE Composition: Aluminum-Bronze **Ruler:** Pope John Paul II

Date	Mintage	F	VF	XF	Unc	BU
1981/III	265,000	—	0.25	0.50	1.00	—

Y# 162 20 LIRE Composition: Aluminum-Bronze **Ruler:** Pope John Paul II **Subject:** Marriage **Obverse:** Similar to 1000 Lire, Y#167

Date	Mintage	F	VF	XF	Unc	BU
1982/IV	360,000	—	0.25	0.50	1.00	—

Y# 171 20 LIRE Composition: Aluminum-Bronze **Ruler:** Pope John Paul II **Subject:** Incarnation of the Word

Date	Mintage	F	VF	XF	Unc	BU
1983/V	170,000	—	0.25	0.50	1.00	—

Y# 178 20 LIRE Composition: Aluminum-Bronze **Ruler:** Pope John Paul II **Subject:** Year of Peace **Obverse:** Similar to 1000 Lire, Y#183

Date	Mintage	F	VF	XF	Unc	BU
1984/VI	170,000	—	0.25	0.50	1.00	—

Y# 186 20 LIRE Composition: Aluminum-Bronze **Ruler:** Pope John Paul II

Date	Mintage	F	VF	XF	Unc	BU
1985/VII	255,000	—	0.25	0.50	1.00	—

Y# 193 20 LIRE Composition: Aluminum-Bronze **Ruler:** Pope John Paul II **Obverse:** Similar to 200 Lire, Y#196

Date	Mintage	F	VF	XF	Unc	BU
1986/VIII	100,000	—	0.25	0.50	1.00	—

Y# 200 20 LIRE Composition: Aluminum-Bronze **Ruler:** Pope John Paul II **Obverse:** Similar to 200 Lire, Y#203 **Reverse:** Assumption of Mother Mary into heaven

Date	F	VF	XF	Unc	BU
1987/IX	—	0.25	0.50	1.00	—

Y# 207 20 LIRE **Composition:** Aluminum-Bronze **Ruler:** Pope John Paul II **Subject:** Temptation of Adam and Eve **Note:** Similar to 200 Lire, Y#210.

Date	F	VF	XF	Unc	BU
1988/X	—	0.25	0.50	1.00	—

Y# 214 20 LIRE **Composition:** Aluminum-Bronze **Ruler:** Pope John Paul II **Subject:** The Harvest

Date	F	VF	XF	Unc	BU
1989/XI	—	0.25	0.50	1.00	—

Y# 221 20 LIRE **Composition:** Aluminum-Bronze **Ruler:** Pope John Paul II **Reverse:** Pope John Paul II and Eastern Rite Bishop

Date	F	VF	XF	Unc	BU
1990/XII	—	0.25	0.50	1.00	—

Y# 229 20 LIRE **Composition:** Aluminum-Bronze **Ruler:** Pope John Paul II **Reverse:** Crane and buildings

Date	F	VF	XF	Unc	BU
1991/XIII	—	0.25	0.50	1.00	—

Y# 237 20 LIRE **Composition:** Aluminum-Bronze **Ruler:** Pope John Paul II **Reverse:** Three children

Date	F	VF	XF	Unc	BU
1992/XIV	—	0.25	0.50	1.00	—

Y# 245 20 LIRE **Composition:** Aluminum-Bronze **Ruler:** Pope John Paul II **Reverse:** Crucifix

Date	F	VF	XF	Unc	BU
1993/XV	—	0.25	0.50	1.00	—

Y# 253 20 LIRE **Composition:** Aluminum-Bronze **Ruler:** Pope John Paul II **Reverse:** Hospital patient with visitors

Date	F	VF	XF	Unc	BU
1994/XVI	—	0.25	0.50	1.00	—

Y# 263 20 LIRE **Composition:** Aluminum-Bronze **Ruler:** Pope John Paul II **Subject:** Euthanasia

Date	F	VF	XF	Unc	BU
1995	—	0.25	0.50	1.00	—

Y# 273 20 LIRE **Composition:** Aluminum-Bronze **Ruler:** Pope John Paul II **Reverse:** Parents praising child

Date	F	VF	XF	Unc	BU
1996	—	0.25	0.50	1.00	—

Y# 281 20 LIRE **Composition:** Aluminum-Bronze **Ruler:** Pope John Paul II **Reverse:** Jesus teaching with book

Date	F	VF	XF	Unc	BU
1997/XIX	—	0.25	0.50	1.00	—

Y# 294 20 LIRE **Composition:** Aluminum-Bronze **Ruler:** Pope John Paul II **Obverse:** Pope with crucifix **Reverse:** Family and sun

Date	F	VF	XF	Unc	BU
1998	—	0.25	0.50	1.00	—

Y# 306 20 LIRE **Weight:** 3.6000 g. **Composition:** Aluminum-Bronze **Ruler:** Pope John Paul II **Subject:** Work - The Right to Fulfill One's Potential **Obverse:** Pope John Paul II bust right **Reverse:** Workers **Edge:** Plain **Size:** 21.3 mm. **Note:** Struck at Rome.

Date	F	VF	XF	Unc	BU
1999	—	0.25	0.50	1.00	—

Y# 324 20 LIRE **Weight:** 3.5700 g. **Composition:** Brass **Ruler:** Pope John Paul II **Obverse:** Papal arms **Reverse:** Pope stargazing **Edge:** Plain **Size:** 21.2 mm.

Date	F	VF	XF	Unc	BU
XXII(2000)	—	—	—	1.00	—

Y# 332 20 LIRE **Weight:** 3.5700 g. **Composition:** Brass **Ruler:** Pope John Paul II **Subject:** Pope Pius XI **Obverse:** Portrait **Reverse:** Papal arms **Edge:** Plain **Size:** 21.2 mm.

Date	F	VF	XF	Unc	BU
2001	—	—	—	1.00	—

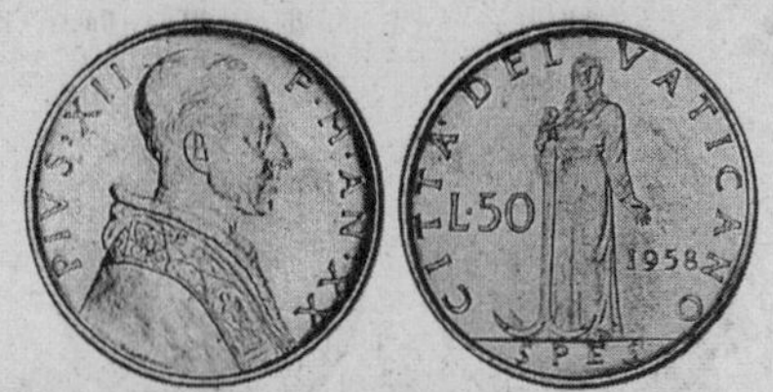

Y# 54.1 50 LIRE **Composition:** Stainless Steel **Ruler:** Pope Pius XII **Obv. Legend:** AN

Date	Mintage	F	VF	XF	Unc	BU
1955/XVII	180,000	—	1.00	1.50	3.00	—
1956/XVIII	—	—	1.00	1.50	3.00	—
1957/XIX	—	—	1.00	1.50	3.00	—
1958/XX	—	—	1.00	1.50	3.00	—

Y# 54.2 50 LIRE **Composition:** Stainless Steel **Ruler:** Pope Pius XII **Obv. Legend:** A

Date	Mintage	F	VF	XF	Unc	BU
1956/XVIII	180,000	—	1.00	1.50	3.00	—
1957/XIX	180,000	—	1.00	1.50	3.00	—
1958/XX	60,000	—	1.00	1.50	3.00	—

Y# 63.1 50 LIRE **Composition:** Stainless Steel **Ruler:** Pope John XXIII **Obverse:** Continuous legend

Date	Mintage	F	VF	XF	Unc	BU
1959/I	100,000	—	1.00	2.50	7.00	—

Y# 63.2 50 LIRE **Composition:** Stainless Steel **Ruler:** Pope John XXIII **Obverse:** Regnal year under bust

Date	Mintage	F	VF	XF	Unc	BU
1960/II	100,000	—	1.00	2.50	6.50	—
1961/III	100,000	—	1.00	2.00	3.50	—
1962/IV	100,000	—	1.00	2.00	3.50	—

Y# 72 50 LIRE **Composition:** Stainless Steel **Ruler:** Pope John XXIII **Subject:** Second Ecumenical Council

Date	Mintage	F	VF	XF	Unc	BU
1962/IV	200,000	—	0.50	1.25	2.50	—

Y# 81.1 50 LIRE **Composition:** Stainless Steel **Ruler:** Pope Paul VI **Subject:** Spes - Hope **Obv. Legend:** AN

Date	Mintage	F	VF	XF	Unc	BU
1963/I	120,000	—	1.00	2.00	4.00	-
1964/II	120,000	—	0.75	1.50	3.00	-

Y# 81.2 50 LIRE **Composition:** Stainless Steel **Ruler:** Pope Paul VI **Obv. Legend:** A

Date	Mintage	F	VF	XF	Unc	BU
1965/III	120,000	—	0.50	1.00	2.00	-

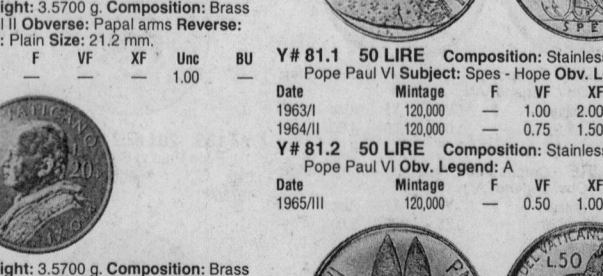

Y# 89 50 LIRE Composition: Stainless Steel **Ruler:** Pope Paul VI

Date	Mintage	F	VF	XF	Unc	BU
1966/IV	150,000	—	0.50	1.00	2.00	—

Y# 97 50 LIRE Composition: Stainless Steel **Ruler:** Pope Paul VI **Subject:** Conversion of Saint Paul

Date	Mintage	F	VF	XF	Unc	BU
1967/V	190,000	—	0.50	1.00	2.00	—

Y# 105 50 LIRE Composition: Stainless Steel **Ruler:** Pope Paul VI **Series:** F.A.O.

Date	Mintage	F	VF	XF	Unc	BU
ND(1968)/VI	190,000	—	0.50	1.00	2.00	—

/# 113 50 LIRE Composition: Stainless Steel **Ruler:** Pope Paul VI **Reverse:** Angel

ate	Mintage	F	VF	XF	Unc	BU
969/VII	190,000	—	0.50	1.00	2.00	—

/# 121 50 LIRE Composition: Stainless Steel **Ruler:** Pope Paul VI

ate	Mintage	F	VF	XF	Unc	BU
970/VIII	190,000	—	0.25	0.75	1.75	—
971/IX	700,000	—	0.25	0.75	1.50	—
972/X	700,000	—	0.25	0.75	1.50	—
973/XI	750,000	—	0.25	0.75	1.50	—
974/XII	750,000	—	0.25	0.75	1.50	—
975/XII	600,000	—	0.25	0.75	1.50	—
976/XIV	600,000	—	0.25	0.75	1.50	—

 # 129 50 LIRE Composition: Stainless Steel **Ruler:** Pope Paul VI **Subject:** Holy Year

te	Mintage	F	VF	XF	Unc	BU
75	500,000	—	0.40	0.75	1.50	—

A121 50 LIRE Composition: Stainless Steel **Ruler:** Pope Paul VI **Reverse:** Wheat and grapes

e	Mintage	F	VF	XF	Unc	BU
7/XV	600,000	—	0.25	0.35	1.25	—

Y# 136 50 LIRE Composition: Stainless Steel **Ruler:** Pope Paul VI **Subject:** 16th Year

Date	Mintage	F	VF	XF	Unc	BU
1978/XVI	223,000	—	0.25	0.50	1.25	—

Y# 145 50 LIRE Composition: Stainless Steel **Ruler:** Pope John Paul II

Date	Mintage	F	VF	XF	Unc	BU
1979/I	223,000	—	0.25	0.50	1.25	—
1980/II	250,000	—	0.25	0.50	1.25	—

Y# 157 50 LIRE Composition: Stainless Steel **Ruler:** Pope John Paul II

Date	Mintage	F	VF	XF	Unc	BU
1981/III	240,000	—	0.25	0.50	1.25	—

Y# 163 50 LIRE Composition: Stainless Steel **Ruler:** Pope John Paul II **Subject:** Maternity **Obverse:** Similar to 1000 Lire, Y#167

Date	Mintage	F	VF	XF	Unc	BU
1982/IV	400,000	—	0.25	0.50	1.25	—

Y# 172 50 LIRE Composition: Stainless Steel **Ruler:** Pope John Paul II **Subject:** Banishment of Adam and Eve

Date	Mintage	F	VF	XF	Unc	BU
1983/V	300,000	—	0.25	0.50	1.25	—

Y# 179 50 LIRE Composition: Stainless Steel **Ruler:** Pope John Paul II **Subject:** Year of Peace **Obverse:** Similar to 1000 Lire, Y#183

Date	Mintage	F	VF	XF	Unc	BU
1984/VI	300,000	—	0.25	0.50	1.25	—

Y# 187 50 LIRE Composition: Stainless Steel **Ruler:** Pope John Paul II

Date	Mintage	F	VF	XF	Unc	BU
1985/VII	360,000	—	0.25	0.50	1.25	—

Y# 194 50 LIRE Composition: Stainless Steel **Ruler:** Pope John Paul II **Obverse:** Similar to 200 Lire, Y#196

Date	Mintage	F	VF	XF	Unc	BU
1986/VIII	100,000	—	0.25	0.50	1.25	—

Y# 201 50 LIRE Composition: Stainless Steel **Ruler:** Pope John Paul II **Obverse:** Similar to 200 LIre, Y#203 **Reverse:** Mother Mary protecting kneeling sinners

Date	F	VF	XF	Unc	BU
1987/IX	—	0.25	0.50	1.25	—

Y# 208 50 LIRE Composition: Stainless Steel **Ruler:** Pope John Paul II **Subject:** Creation of Eve From Adam's Rib

Date	F	VF	XF	Unc	BU
1988	—	0.25	0.50	1.25	—

Y# 215 50 LIRE Composition: Stainless Steel **Ruler:** Pope John Paul II **Subject:** Human Solidarity

Date	F	VF	XF	Unc	BU
1989/XI	—	0.25	0.50	1.25	—

Y# 222 50 LIRE Composition: Stainless Steel **Ruler:** Pope John Paul II **Reverse:** Radiant cross in open door

Date	F	VF	XF	Unc	BU
1990/XII	—	0.25	0.50	1.25	—

Y# 230 50 LIRE Composition: Stainless Steel **Ruler:** Pope John Paul II **Reverse:** Baptism scene

Date	F	VF	XF	Unc	BU
1991/XIII	—	0.25	0.50	1.25	—

Y# 238 50 LIRE **Composition:** Stainless Steel **Ruler:** Pope John Paul II **Reverse:** Cross as balance scale between agriculture and industry

Date	F	VF	XF	Unc	BU
1992/XIV	—	0.25	0.50	1.25	—

Y# 246 50 LIRE **Composition:** Stainless Steel **Ruler:** Pope John Paul II **Reverse:** Chalice

Date	F	VF	XF	Unc	BU
1993/XV	—	0.25	0.50	1.25	—

Y# 254 50 LIRE **Composition:** Stainless Steel **Ruler:** Pope John Paul II **Reverse:** Hands and prison bars

Date	F	VF	XF	Unc	BU
1994/XVI	—	0.25	0.50	1.25	—

Y# 264 50 LIRE **Composition:** Stainless Steel **Ruler:** Pope John Paul II **Reverse:** Dragon on Prone Woman (Abortion)

Date	F	VF	XF	Unc	BU
1995	—	0.25	0.50	1.25	—

Y# 274 50 LIRE **Composition:** Copper-Nickel **Ruler:** Pope John Paul II **Reverse:** Guardian angel protecting child

Date	F	VF	XF	Unc	BU
1996	—	0.25	0.50	1.25	—

Y# 282 50 LIRE **Composition:** Copper-Nickel **Ruler:** Pope John Paul II **Reverse:** One man with lowered sword, the other with dove

Date	F	VF	XF	Unc	BU
1997/XIX	—	0.25	0.50	1.25	—

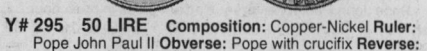

Y# 295 50 LIRE **Composition:** Copper-Nickel **Ruler:** Pope John Paul II **Obverse:** Pope with crucifix **Reverse:** Two figures and hand

Date	F	VF	XF	Unc	BU
1998	—	0.25	0.50	1.25	—

Y# 307 50 LIRE **Weight:** 4.4600 g. **Composition:** Copper-Nickel **Ruler:** Pope John Paul II **Subject:** Ecosystem - Agriculture **Obverse:** Pope John Paul II bust right **Reverse:** Agricultural workers **Edge:** Plain **Size:** 19.2 mm. **Note:** Struck at Rome.

Date	F	VF	XF	Unc	BU
1999	—	0.25	0.50	1.25	—

Y# 325 50 LIRE **Weight:** 4.5000 g. **Comp.:** Copper-Nickel **Ruler:** Pope John Paul II **Obverse:** Papal arms **Reverse:** Pope about to kiss ground **Edge:** Plain **Size:** 19.2 mm.

Date	F	VF	XF	Unc	BU
XXII(2000)	—	—	—	1.25	—

Y# 333 50 LIRE **Weight:** 4.5000 g. **Comp.:** Copper-Nickel **Ruler:** Pope John Paul II **Subject:** Pope Pius XI **Obverse:** Portrait **Reverse:** Papal arms **Edge:** Plain **Size:** 19.2 mm.

Date	F	VF	XF	Unc	BU
2001	—	—	—	1.25	—

Y# 9 100 LIRE **Weight:** 8.8000 g. **Composition:** 0.9000 Gold .2546 oz. AGW **Ruler:** Pope Pius XI

Date	Mintage	F	VF	XF	Unc	BU
1929/VIII	10,000	—	—	175	275	—
1930/IX	2,621	—	—	650	1,000	—
1931/X	3,343	—	—	325	500	—
1932/XI	5,073	—	—	250	375	—
1934/XIII	2,533	—	—	325	500	—
1935/XIV	2,015	—	—	325	500	—

Y# 19 100 LIRE **Weight:** 8.8000 g. **Composition:** 0.9000 Gold .2546 oz. AGW **Ruler:** Pope Pius XI **Subject:** Jubilee

Date	Mintage	F	VF	XF	Unc	BU
1933-34	23,000	—	—	175	245	—

Y# 10 100 LIRE **Weight:** 5.1900 g. **Composition:** 0.9000 Gold .1501 oz. AGW **Ruler:** Pope Pius XI

Date	Mintage	F	VF	XF	Unc	BU
1936/XV	8,239	—	—	220	275	—
1937/XVI	2,000	—	—	2,000	3,000	—
1938 Rare	6	—	—	—	—	—

Y# 30.1 100 LIRE **Weight:** 5.1900 g. **Composition:** 0.9000 Gold .1501 oz. AGW **Ruler:** Pope Pius XII **Obv. Legend:** AN

Date	Mintage	F	VF	XF	Unc	BU
1939/I	2,700	—	—	200	350	—
1940/II	2,000	—	—	250	375	—

Y# 30.2 100 LIRE **Weight:** 5.1900 g. **Composition:** 0.9000 Gold .1501 oz. AGW **Ruler:** Pope Pius XII **Obv. Legend:** A

Date	Mintage	F	VF	XF	Unc	BU
1941/III	2,000	—	—	250	375	—

Y# 39 100 LIRE **Weight:** 5.1900 g. **Composition:** 0.9000 Gold .1501 oz. AGW **Ruler:** Pope Pius XII

Date	Mintage	F	VF	XF	Unc	BU
1942/IV	2,000	—	—	250	375	—
1943/V	1,000	—	—	350	600	—
1944/VI	1,000	—	—	350	600	—
1945/VII	1,000	—	—	350	600	—
1946/VIII	1,000	—	—	350	600	—
1947/IX	1,000	—	—	350	600	—
1948/X	5,000	—	—	200	275	—
1949/XI	1,000	—	—	350	600	—

Y# 48 100 LIRE **Weight:** 5.1900 g. **Composition:** 0.9000 Gold .1501 oz. AGW **Ruler:** Pope Pius XII **Subject:** Holy Year

Date	Mintage	F	VF	XF	Unc	BU
1950	20,000	—	—	200	275	—

Y# 53.1 100 LIRE **Weight:** 5.1900 g. **Composition:** 0.9000 Gold .1501 oz. AGW **Ruler:** Pope Pius XII **Obv. Legend:** AN

Date	Mintage	F	VF	XF	Unc	BU
1951/XIII	1,000	—	—	350	625	—
1952/XIV	1,000	—	—	350	625	—
1953/XV	1,000	—	—	350	625	—
1954/XVI	1,000	—	—	350	625	—
1955/XVII	1,000	—	—	350	625	—

Y# 53.2 100 LIRE **Weight:** 5.1900 g. **Composition:** 0.9000 Gold .1501 oz. AGW **Ruler:** Pope Pius XII **Obv. Legend:** A

Date	Mintage	F	VF	XF	Unc	BU
1956/XVIII	1,000	—	—	350	625	—

Y# 55 100 LIRE **Composition:** Stainless Steel **Ruler:** Pope Pius XII

Date	Mintage	F	VF	XF	Unc
1955/XVII	1,300,000	—	0.50	1.00	2.00
1956/XVII	1,400,000	—	0.50	1.00	2.00
1957/XIX	900,000	—	0.50	1.00	2.00
1958/XX	852,000	—	0.50	1.00	2.00

Y# A53 100 LIRE **Weight:** 5.1900 g. **Composition:** 0.9000 Gold .1501 oz. AGW **Ruler:** Pope Pius XII

Date	Mintage	F	VF	XF	Unc
1957/XIX	2,000	—	—	250	350
1958/XX	3,000	—	—	250	325

Y# 66 100 LIRE **Weight:** 5.1900 g. **Composition:** 0.90 Gold .1501 oz. AGW **Ruler:** Pope John XXIII

Date	Mintage	F	VF	XF	Unc	BU
1959/I	3,000	—	—	750	1,250	—

Y# 64.1 100 LIRE **Composition:** Stainless Steel **Ruler:** Pope John XXIII **Obverse:** Continuous legend

Date	Mintage	F	VF	XF	Unc	BU
1959/I	783,000	—	1.25	2.00	4.00	—

Y# 64.2 100 LIRE **Composition:** Stainless Steel **Ruler:** Pope John XXIII **Obverse:** Regnal year under bust

Date	Mintage	F	VF	XF	Unc	BU
1960/II	783,000	—	1.75	3.00	6.50	—
1961/III	783,000	—	0.75	1.00	2.50	—
1962/IV	783,000	—	0.75	1.00	2.50	—

Y# 73 100 LIRE **Composition:** Stainless Steel **Ruler:** Pope John XXIII **Subject:** Second Ecumenical Council

Date	Mintage	F	VF	XF	Unc	BU
1962/IV	1,566,000	—	0.40	0.75	1.50	—

Y# 82.1 100 LIRE **Composition:** Stainless Steel **Ruler:** Pope Paul VI **Obv. Legend:** AN

ate	Mintage	F	VF	XF	Unc	BU
963/I	558,000	—	1.00	2.00	3.00	—

Y# 82.2 100 LIRE **Composition:** Stainless Steel **Ruler:** Pope Paul VI **Obv. Legend:** A

ate	Mintage	F	VF	XF	Unc	BU
964/II	558,000	—	0.50	1.00	2.00	—
965/III	558,000	—	0.50	1.00	2.00	—

 # 90 100 LIRE **Composition:** Stainless Steel **Ruler:** Pope Paul VI

ate	Mintage	F	VF	XF	Unc	BU
966/IV	388,000	—	0.50	1.00	2.00	—

Y# 98 100 LIRE **Composition:** Stainless Steel **Ruler:** Pope Paul VI

Date	Mintage	F	VF	XF	Unc	BU
1967/V	315,000	—	0.50	1.00	2.00	—

Y# 106 100 LIRE **Composition:** Stainless Steel **Ruler:** Pope Paul VI **Series:** F.A.O.

Date	Mintage	F	VF	XF	Unc	BU
ND(1968)/VI	315,000	—	0.50	1.00	2.00	—

Y# 114 100 LIRE **Composition:** Stainless Steel **Ruler:** Pope Paul VI

Date	Mintage	F	VF	XF	Unc	BU
1969/VII	315,000	—	0.50	1.00	2.00	—

Y# 122 100 LIRE **Composition:** Stainless Steel **Ruler:** Pope Paul VI

Date	Mintage	F	VF	XF	Unc	BU
1970/VIII	315,000	—	0.50	1.00	2.00	—
1971/IX	966,000	—	0.40	0.60	1.50	—
1972/X	966,000	—	0.40	0.60	1.50	—
1973/XI	830,000	—	0.40	0.60	1.50	—
1974/XII	830,000	—	0.40	0.60	1.50	—
1975/XIII	808,000	—	0.40	0.60	1.50	—
1976/XIV	808,000	—	0.40	0.60	1.50	—
1977/XV	819,000	—	0.40	0.60	1.50	—

Y# 130 100 LIRE **Composition:** Stainless Steel **Ruler:** Pope Paul VI **Subject:** Holy Year

Date	Mintage	F	VF	XF	Unc	BU
1975	605,000	—	0.60	1.25	2.00	—

Y# 137 100 LIRE **Composition:** Stainless Steel **Ruler:** Pope Paul VI

Date	Mintage	F	VF	XF	Unc	BU
1978/XVI	399,000	—	0.50	1.00	2.00	—

Y# 146 100 LIRE **Composition:** Stainless Steel **Ruler:** Pope John Paul II

Date	Mintage	F	VF	XF	Unc	BU
1979/I	399,000	—	0.50	1.00	2.00	—
1980/II	485,000	—	0.50	1.00	2.00	—

Y# 158 100 LIRE **Composition:** Stainless Steel **Ruler:** Pope John Paul II

Date	Mintage	F	VF	XF	Unc	BU
1981/III	550,000	—	0.50	1.00	2.00	—

Y# 164 100 LIRE **Composition:** Stainless Steel **Ruler:** Pope John Paul II **Subject:** Family **Obverse:** Similar to 1000 Lire, Y#167

Date	Mintage	F	VF	XF	Unc	BU
1982/IV	656,000	—	0.40	0.60	1.50	—

Y# 173 100 LIRE **Composition:** Stainless Steel **Ruler:** Pope John Paul II **Subject:** God Gives World to Mankind

Date	Mintage	F	VF	XF	Unc	BU
1983/V	455,000	—	0.40	0.60	1.50	—

Y# 180 100 LIRE **Composition:** Stainless Steel **Ruler:** Pope John Paul II **Subject:** Year of Peace **Obverse:** Similar to 1000 Lire, Y#183

Date	Mintage	F	VF	XF	Unc	BU
1984/VI	400,000	—	0.40	0.60	1.50	—

Y# 188 100 LIRE Composition: Stainless Steel **Ruler:** Pope John Paul II

Date	Mintage	F	VF	XF	Unc	BU
1985/VII	800,000	—	0.40	0.60	1.50	—

Y# 195 100 LIRE Composition: Stainless Steel **Ruler:** Pope John Paul II **Obverse:** Similar to 200 Lire, Y#196

Date	Mintage	F	VF	XF	Unc	BU
1986/VIII	100,000	—	0.40	0.60	1.50	—

Y# 202 100 LIRE Composition: Stainless Steel **Ruler:** Pope John Paul II **Subject:** Angel and Mary, The Annunciation

Date	F	VF	XF	Unc	BU
1987/IX	—	0.40	0.60	1.50	—

Y# 209 100 LIRE Composition: Stainless Steel **Ruler:** Pope John Paul II **Subject:** Adam Naming the Animals **Obverse:** Similar to 200 Lire, Y#210

Date	F	VF	XF	Unc	BU
1988/X	—	0.40	0.60	1.50	—

Y# 216 100 LIRE Composition: Stainless Steel **Ruler:** Pope John Paul II **Reverse:** Pelican feeding young

Date	F	VF	XF	Unc	BU
1989/XI	—	0.40	0.60	1.50	—

Y# 223 100 LIRE Composition: Stainless Steel **Ruler:** Pope John Paul II **Subject:** Early Bishop

Date	F	VF	XF	Unc	BU
1990/XII	—	0.40	0.60	1.50	—

Y# 231 100 LIRE Composition: Stainless Steel **Ruler:** Pope John Paul II **Reverse:** Depiction of the risen Christ

Date	F	VF	XF	Unc	BU
1991/XIII	—	0.40	0.60	1.50	—

Y# 239 100 LIRE Composition: Stainless Steel **Ruler:** Pope John Paul II **Reverse:** Open book

Date	F	VF	XF	Unc	BU
1992/XIV	—	0.40	0.60	1.50	—

Y# 247 100 LIRE Composition: Copper-Nickel **Ruler:** Pope John Paul II **Reverse:** Portrait of Jesus

Date	F	VF	XF	Unc	BU
1993/XV	—	0.40	0.60	1.75	—

Y# 255 100 LIRE Composition: Copper-Nickel **Ruler:** Pope John Paul II **Reverse:** Four basketball players - one in wheelchair

Date	F	VF	XF	Unc	BU
1994/XVI	—	0.40	0.60	1.75	—

Y# 265 100 LIRE Composition: Copper-Nickel **Ruler:** Pope John Paul II **Reverse:** Guard and prisoners

Date	F	VF	XF	Unc	BU
1995	—	0.40	0.60	1.75	—

Y# 275 100 LIRE Composition: Copper-Nickel **Ruler:** Pope John Paul II **Reverse:** Women helping children

Date	F	VF	XF	Unc	BU
1996	—	0.40	0.60	1.75	—

Y# 283 100 LIRE Composition: Copper-Nickel **Ruler:** Pope John Paul II **Reverse:** Woman filling birdbath

Date	F	VF	XF	Unc	BU
1997/XIX	—	0.40	0.60	1.75	—

Y# 296 100 LIRE Composition: Copper-Nickel **Ruler:** Pope John Paul II **Obverse:** Pope with crucifix **Reverse:** Female figure in front of globe

Date	F	VF	XF	Unc	BU
1998	—	0.40	0.60	1.75	—

Y# 308 100 LIRE Weight: 4.5000 g. **Composition:** Copper-Nickel **Ruler:** Pope John Paul II **Subject:** The Right to Peace **Obverse:** Pope John Paul II bust right **Reverse:** Children of the world gathered in peace **Edge:** Reeded and plain sections **Size:** 22 mm. **Note:** Struck at Rome.

Date	F	VF	XF	Unc	BU
1999	—	0.40	0.60	1.75	—

Y# 326 100 LIRE Weight: 4.5000 g. **Composition:** Copper-Nickel **Ruler:** Pope John Paul II **Obverse:** Papal arms **Edge:** Plain and reeded sections **Size:** 22 mm.

Date	F	VF	XF	Unc	BU
XXII(2000)	—	—	—	1.75	—

Y# 334 100 LIRE Weight: 4.5000 g. **Composition:** Copper-Nickel **Ruler:** Pope John Paul II **Subject:** Pope Pius XXIII **Obverse:** Portrait **Reverse:** Papal arms **Edge:** Reeded and plain sections **Size:** 22 mm.

Date	F	VF	XF	Unc	BU
2001	—	—	—	1.75	—

Y# 138 200 LIRE Composition: Aluminum-Bronze **Ruler:** Pope Paul VI

Date	Mintage	F	VF	XF	Unc	BU
1978/XVI	355,000	—	0.50	1.00	2.50	—

Y# 147 200 LIRE Composition: Aluminum-Bronze **Ruler:** Pope John Paul II

Date	Mintage	F	VF	XF	Unc	BU
1979/I	355,000	—	0.50	1.00	2.50	—
1980/II	200,000	—	0.50	1.00	2.50	—

Y# 159 200 LIRE Composition: Aluminum-Bronze **Ruler:** Pope John Paul II

Date	Mintage	F	VF	XF	Unc	BU
1981/III	170,000	—	0.50	1.00	2.50	—

Y# 165 200 LIRE Composition: Aluminum-Bronze **Ruler:** Pope John Paul II **Subject:** Labor **Obverse:** Similar to 1000 Lire, Y#167

Date	Mintage	F	VF	XF	Unc	BU
1982/IV	500,000	—	0.50	1.00	2.50	—

Y# 174 200 LIRE Composition: Aluminum-Bronze **Ruler:** Pope John Paul II **Subject:** Creation of Man

Date	Mintage	F	VF	XF	Unc	BU
1983/V	300,000	—	0.40	0.75	2.25	—

Y# 181 200 LIRE Composition: Aluminum-Bronze **Ruler:** Pope John Paul II **Subject:** Year of Peace **Obverse:** Similar to 1000 Lire, Y#183

Date	Mintage	F	VF	XF	Unc	BU
1984/VI	250,000	—	0.40	0.75	2.25	—

Y# 189 200 LIRE Composition: Aluminum-Bronze **Ruler:** Pope John Paul II **Subject:** Winged Ox of St. Luke

Date	Mintage	F	VF	XF	Unc	BU
1985/VII	300,000	—	0.40	0.75	2.25	—

Y# 196 200 LIRE Composition: Aluminum-Bronze **Ruler:** Pope John Paul II **Subject:** Michael the Archangel

Date	Mintage	F	VF	XF	Unc	BU
1986/VIII	100,000	—	0.40	0.75	2.25	—

Y# 203 200 LIRE Composition: Aluminum-Bronze **Ruler:** Pope John Paul II **Subject:** Queen of Peace

Date	F	VF	XF	Unc	BU
1987/IX	—	0.40	0.75	2.25	—

Y# 210 200 LIRE Composition: Aluminum-Bronze **Ruler:** Pope John Paul II **Subject:** Creation of Adam

Date	F	VF	XF	Unc	BU
1988/X	—	0.40	0.75	2.25	—

Y# 217 200 LIRE Composition: Aluminum-Bronze **Ruler:** Pope John Paul II

Date	F	VF	XF	Unc	BU
1989/XI	—	0.40	0.75	2.25	—

Y# 224 200 LIRE Composition: Aluminum-Bronze **Ruler:** Pope John Paul II **Subject:** Blessed Virgin Mary

Date	F	VF	XF	Unc	BU
1990/XII	—	0.40	0.75	2.25	—

Y# 232 200 LIRE Composition: Aluminum-Bronze **Ruler:** Pope John Paul II **Reverse:** Redeemer looking at city views

Date	F	VF	XF	Unc	BU
1991/XIII	—	0.40	0.75	2.25	—

Y# 240 200 LIRE Composition: Aluminum-Bronze **Ruler:** Pope John Paul II **Reverse:** Mother nursing child

Date	F	VF	XF	Unc	BU
1992/XIV	—	0.40	0.75	2.25	—

Y# 248 200 LIRE Composition: Aluminum-Bronze **Ruler:** Pope John Paul II **Subject:** Ten Commandments

Date	F	VF	XF	Unc	BU
1993/XV	—	0.40	0.75	2.25	—

Y# 256 200 LIRE Composition: Aluminum-Bronze **Ruler:** Pope John Paul II **Subject:** Helping Victims of Drug Abuse

Date	F	VF	XF	Unc	BU
1994/XVI	—	0.40	0.75	2.25	—

Y# 266 200 LIRE Composition: Aluminum-Bronze **Ruler:** Pope John Paul II **Reverse:** Family and Farming scene

Date	F	VF	XF	Unc	BU
1995	—	0.40	0.75	2.25	—

Y#276 200 LIRE Composition: Aluminum-Bronze **Ruler:** Pope John Paul II **Reverse:** Display of family togetherness

Date	F	VF	XF	Unc	BU
1996	—	0.40	0.75	2.25	—

Y# 284 200 LIRE Composition: Aluminum-Bronze **Ruler:** Pope John Paul II **Reverse:** Angel guiding two people

Date	F	VF	XF	Unc	BU
1997/XIX	—	0.40	0.75	2.25	—

Y# 297 200 LIRE Composition: Aluminum-Bronze **Ruler:** Pope John Paul II **Obverse:** Pope with crucifix **Reverse:** Two figures, one helping the other

Date	F	VF	XF	Unc	BU
1998	—	0.40	0.75	2.25	—

Y# 309 200 LIRE Weight: 5.0000 g. **Composition:** Aluminum-Bronze **Ruler:** Pope John Paul II **Obverse:** John Paul II bust right **Reverse:** Christ among the poor and outcast **Edge:** Reeded **Size:** 24 mm. **Note:** Struck at Rome.

Date	F	VF	XF	Unc	BU
1999	—	0.40	0.75	2.25	—

Y#327 200 LIRE Weight: 5.0000 g. **Composition:** Brass **Ruler:** Pope John Paul II **Obverse:** Papal arms **Reverse:** Pope praying **Edge:** Reeded **Size:** 22 mm.

Date	F	VF	XF	Unc	BU
XXII(2000)	—	—	—	2.25	—

Y#335 200 LIRE Weight: 5.0000 g. **Composition:** Brass **Ruler:** Pope John Paul II **Subject:** Pope Paul VI **Obverse:** Portrait **Reverse:** Papal arms **Edge:** Reeded **Size:** 22 mm.

Date	F	VF	XF	Unc	BU
2001	—	—	—	2.25	—

Y# 56 500 LIRE **Weight:** 11.0000 g. **Composition:** 0.8350 Silver .2953 oz. ASW **Ruler:** Pope Pius XII

Date	Mintage	F	VF	XF	Unc	BU
1958/XX	20,000	—	6.00	12.50	25.00	—

Y# 57 500 LIRE **Weight:** 11.0000 g. **Composition:** 0.8350 Silver .2953 oz. ASW **Ruler:** Cardinal Benedetto Aloisi-Masella **Subject:** Sede Vacante **Reverse:** Arms of Cardinal Benedetto Aloisi-Masella

Date	Mintage	F	VF	XF	Unc	BU
1958	100,000	—	4.00	6.00	9.00	—

Y# 65 500 LIRE **Weight:** 11.0000 g. **Composition:** 0.8350 Silver .2953 oz. ASW **Ruler:** Pope John XXIII **Obverse:** Continuous legend

Date	Mintage	F	VF	XF	Unc	BU
1959/I	30,000	—	6.00	12.00	22.50	—

Y# 65.1 500 LIRE **Weight:** 11.0000 g. **Composition:** 0.8350 Silver .2953 oz. ASW **Ruler:** Pope John XXIII **Obverse:** Regnal year under bust

Date	Mintage	F	VF	XF	Unc	BU
1960/II	30,000	—	7.00	15.00	30.00	—
1961/III	30,000	—	6.00	12.00	22.50	—
1962/IV	30,000	—	6.00	12.00	22.50	—

Y# 74 500 LIRE **Weight:** 11.0000 g. **Composition:** 0.8350 Silver .2953 oz. ASW **Ruler:** Pope John XXIII **Subject:** Second Ecumenical Council

Date	Mintage	F	VF	XF	Unc	BU
1962/IV	60,000	—	6.00	12.00	22.50	—

Y# 75 500 LIRE **Weight:** 11.0000 g. **Composition:** 0.8350 Silver .2953 oz. ASW **Ruler:** Cardinal Benedetto Aloisi-Masella **Subject:** Sede Vacante **Reverse:** Arms of Cardinal Benedetto Aloisi-Masella

Date	Mintage	F	VF	XF	Unc	BU
1963	200,000	—	4.00	6.00	9.00	—

Y# 83.1 500 LIRE **Weight:** 11.0000 g. **Composition:** 0.8350 Silver .2953 oz. ASW **Ruler:** Pope Paul VI **Obv. Legend:** AN

Date	Mintage	F	VF	XF	Unc	BU
1963/I	70,000	—	8.00	16.00	32.00	—

Y# 83.2 500 LIRE **Weight:** 11.0000 g. **Composition:** 0.8350 Silver .2953 oz. ASW **Ruler:** Pope Paul VI **Obv. Legend:** A

Date	Mintage	F	VF	XF	Unc	BU
1964/II	70,000	—	7.00	15.00	25.00	—
1965/III	70,000	—	6.00	9.00	20.00	—

Y# 91 500 LIRE **Weight:** 11.0000 g. **Composition:** 0.8350 Silver .2953 oz. ASW **Ruler:** Pope Paul VI

Date	Mintage	F	VF	XF	Unc	BU
1966/IV	100,000	—	5.00	8.00	16.00	—

Y# 99 500 LIRE **Weight:** 11.0000 g. **Composition:** 0.8350 Silver .2953 oz. ASW **Ruler:** Pope Paul VI **Subject:** Saint Peter and Paul

Date	Mintage	F	VF	XF	Unc	BU
ND(1967)/V	110,000	—	4.50	7.00	14.00	—

Y# 107 500 LIRE **Weight:** 11.0000 g. **Composition:** 0.8350 Silver .2953 oz. ASW **Ruler:** Pope Paul VI **Series:** F.A.O.

Date	Mintage	F	VF	XF	Unc	BU
ND(1968)/VI	110,000	—	4.50	7.00	14.00	—

Y# 115 500 LIRE **Weight:** 11.0000 g. **Composition:** 0.8350 Silver .2953 oz. ASW **Ruler:** Pope Paul VI **Reverse:** Angel

Date	Mintage	F	VF	XF	Unc	BU
1969/VII	110,000	—	4.50	7.00	14.00	—

Y# 123 500 LIRE **Weight:** 11.0000 g. **Composition:** 0.8350 Silver .2953 oz. ASW **Ruler:** Pope Paul VI **Reverse:** Wheat and grapes

Date	Mintage	F	VF	XF	Unc	BU
1970/VIII	110,000	—	—	5.50	11.00	—
1971/IX	125,000	—	—	5.50	11.00	—
1972/X	125,000	—	—	5.50	11.00	—
1973/XI	145,000	—	—	5.50	11.00	—
1974/XII	145,000	—	—	5.50	11.00	—
1975/XIII	162,000	—	—	5.50	11.00	—
1976/XIV	162,000	—	—	5.50	11.00	—

Y# 131 500 LIRE **Weight:** 11.0000 g. **Composition:** 0.8350 Silver .2953 oz. ASW **Ruler:** Pope Paul VI **Subject:** Holy Year

Date	Mintage	F	VF	XF	Unc	BU
1975	200,000	—	—	7.00	14.00	—

Y# 132 500 LIRE **Weight:** 11.0000 g. **Composition:** 0.8350 Silver .2953 oz. ASW **Ruler:** Pope Paul VI **Subject:** Book of the Evangelists

Date	Mintage	F	VF	XF	Unc	BU
1977/XV	160,000	—	—	7.00	16.50	—

Y# 139 500 LIRE **Weight:** 11.0000 g. **Composition:** 0.8350 Silver .2953 oz. ASW **Ruler:** Pope Paul VI **Reverse:** Jesus walking on water

Date	Mintage	F	VF	XF	Unc	BU
1978/XVI	145,000	—	—	7.00	16.50	—

Y# 140 500 LIRE **Weight:** 11.0000 g. **Composition:** 0.8350 Silver .2953 oz. ASW **Ruler:** Cardinal Jean Villot **Subject:** First Sede Vacante **Reverse:** Arms of Cardinal Jean Villot **Rev. Legend:** SEDE VACANTE MCMLXXVIII

Date	Mintage	F	VF	XF	Unc	BU
1978	500,000	—	—	8.00	17.50	—

41 500 LIRE **Weight:** 11.0000 g. **Composition:** .8350 Silver .2953 oz. ASW **Ruler:** Pope Paul VI **Subject:** Second Sede Vacante **Reverse:** Arms of Cardinal Jean Villot **ev. Legend:** SEDE VACANTE SEPTEMBER MCMLXXVIII

	F	VF	XF	Unc	BU
	—	—	8.00	17.50	—

Note: Mintage included with Y#140.

148 500 LIRE **Weight:** 11.0000 g. **Composition:** .8350 Silver .2953 oz. ASW **Ruler:** Pope John Paul II

	Mintage	F	VF	XF	Unc	BU
I	145,000	—	—	8.00	17.50	—
/II	184,000	—	—	8.00	17.50	—

160 500 LIRE **Weight:** 11.0000 g. **Composition:** 0.8350 Silver .2953 oz. ASW **Ruler:** Pope John Paul II

	Mintage	F	VF	XF	Unc	BU
/III	184,000	—	—	8.00	17.50	—

166 500 LIRE **Ring Composition:** Stainless Steel **Center Composition:** Aluminum-Bronze **Ruler:** Pope John Paul II **Subject:** Education **Obverse:** Similar to 1000 Lire, Y#167

	Mintage	F	VF	XF	Unc	BU
2/IV	1,852,000	—	—	2.75	7.00	—

168 500 LIRE **Weight:** 11.0000 g. **Composition:** 0.8350 Silver .2953 oz. ASW **Ruler:** Pope John Paul II **Subject:** Holy Year

	Mintage	F	VF	XF	Unc	BU
3-84	130,000	—	—	10.00	22.50	—

Y# 175 500 LIRE **Ring Composition:** Stainless Steel **Center Composition:** Aluminum-Bronze **Ruler:** Pope John Paul II **Subject:** Creation of the Universe

Date	F	VF	XF	Unc	BU
1983/V	—	—	2.75	7.00	—

Y# 182 500 LIRE **Ring Composition:** Stainless Steel **Center Composition:** Aluminum-Bronze **Ruler:** Pope John Paul II **Subject:** Year of Peace

Date	Mintage	F	VF	XF	Unc	BU
1984/VI	270,000	—	—	2.75	7.00	—

Y# 184 500 LIRE **Weight:** 11.0000 g. **Composition:** 0.8350 Silver .2953 oz. ASW **Ruler:** Pope John Paul II **Subject:** 2000th Anniversary - Birth of Blessed Virgin Mary

Date	Mintage	F	VF	XF	Unc	BU
1984/VI Proof	105,000	Value: 25.00				

Y# 190 500 LIRE **Ring Composition:** Stainless Steel **Center Composition:** Aluminum-Bronze **Ruler:** Pope John Paul II **Subject:** Saint Peter in boat

Date	Mintage	F	VF	XF	Unc	BU
1985/VII	300,000	—	—	2.50	6.00	—

Y# 197 500 LIRE **Ring Composition:** Stainless Steel **Center Composition:** Aluminum-Bronze **Ruler:** Pope John Paul II **Reverse:** Seated Mary and Jesus

Date	Mintage	F	VF	XF	Unc	BU
1986/VIII	300,000	—	—	2.50	6.00	—

Y# 204 500 LIRE **Ring Composition:** Stainless Steel **Center Composition:** Aluminum-Bronze **Ruler:** Pope John Paul II **Reverse:** Crucified Jesus

Date	F	VF	XF	Unc	BU
1987/IX	—	—	2.50	6.00	—

Y# 211 500 LIRE **Ring Composition:** Stainless Steel **Center Composition:** Aluminum-Bronze **Ruler:** Pope John Paul II **Reverse:** Holy Trinity

Date	F	VF	XF	Unc	BU
1988/X	—	—	2.50	6.00	—

Y# 218 500 LIRE **Ring Composition:** Stainless Steel **Center Composition:** Aluminum-Bronze **Ruler:** Pope John Paul II **Reverse:** Grapevine

Date	F	VF	XF	Unc	BU
1989/XI	—	—	2.50	6.00	—

Y# 225 500 LIRE **Ring Composition:** Stainless Steel **Center Composition:** Aluminum-Bronze **Ruler:** Pope John Paul II **Reverse:** Jesus and two kneeling figures

Date	F	VF	XF	Unc	BU
1990/XII	—	—	2.00	4.00	—

Y# 227 500 LIRE **Weight:** 11.0000 g. **Composition:** 0.8350 Silver .2953 oz. ASW **Ruler:** Pope John Paul II

Date	F	VF	XF	Unc	BU
1991	—	—	—	27.50	—

Y# 233 500 LIRE **Ring Composition:** Stainless Steel **Center Composition:** Aluminum-Bronze **Ruler:** Pope John Paul II **Reverse:** Redeemer sending out missionaries

Date	F	VF	XF	Unc	BU
1991/XIII	—	—	2.00	4.00	—

Y# 235 500 LIRE **Weight:** 11.0000 g. **Composition:** 0.8350 Silver .2953 oz. ASW **Ruler:** Pope John Paul II

Date	F	VF	XF	Unc	BU
1992/XIV	—	—	—	25.00	—

Y# 241 500 LIRE **Ring Composition:** Stainless Steel **Center Composition:** Aluminum-Bronze **Ruler:** Pope John Paul II **Reverse:** Hands holding loaf of bread

Date	F	VF	XF	Unc	BU
1992/XIV	—	—	2.00	4.00	—

Y# 243 500 LIRE **Weight:** 11.0000 g. **Composition:** 0.8350 Silver .2953 oz. ASW **Ruler:** Pope John Paul II **Subject:** World Peace

Date	F	VF	XF	Unc	BU
1993/XV	—	—	—	25.00	—

Y# 249 500 LIRE **Ring Composition:** Stainless Steel **Center Composition:** Aluminum-Bronze **Ruler:** Pope John Paul II **Subject:** Thurible

Date	F	VF	XF	Unc	BU
1993/XV	—	—	2.00	4.00	—

Y# 251 500 LIRE **Weight:** 11.0000 g. **Composition:** 0.8350 Silver .2953 oz. ASW **Ruler:** Pope John Paul II **Subject:** Veritatis Splendor

Date	F	VF	XF	Unc	BU
1994/XVI	—	—	—	25.00	—
1994/XVI Proof	—	Value: 40.00			

Y# 257 500 LIRE **Ring Composition:** Stainless Steel **Center Comp.:** Aluminum-Bronze **Ruler:** Pope John Paul II **Reverse:** People meeting, Golgotha in background

Date	F	VF	XF	Unc	BU
1994/XVI	—	—	2.00	4.00	—

Y# 259 500 LIRE **Weight:** 11.0000 g. **Composition:** 0.8350 Silver .2953 oz. ASW **Ruler:** Pope John Paul II **Series:** International Women's Year **Edge Lettering:** INTERNATIONALIS ANNUS MELIEREI DICATUS

Date	Mintage	F	VF	XF	Unc	BU
1995	20,000	—	—	—	35.00	—
1995 Proof	7,000	Value: 55.00				

Y# 267 500 LIRE **Weight:** 11.0000 g. **Composition:** 0.8350 Silver .2953 oz. ASW **Ruler:** Pope John Paul II **Subject:** Cain Slaying Abel

Date	Mintage	F	VF	XF	Unc	BU
1995	460,000	—	—	2.00	4.00	—

Y# 269 500 LIRE **Weight:** 11.0000 g. **Composition:** 0.8350 Silver .2953 oz. ASW **Ruler:** Pope John Paul II **Subject:** 50th Anniversary - Ordination of Pope John Paul II

Date	Mintage	F	VF	XF	Unc	BU
1996	33,000	—	—	—	30.00	—
1996 Proof	7,000	Value: 55.00				

Y# 277 500 LIRE **Ring Composition:** Stainless Steel **Center Comp.:** Aluminum-Bronze **Ruler:** Pope John Paul II **Reverse:** Male figure protecting child from serpent

Date	Mintage	F	VF	XF	Unc	BU
1996	100,000	—	—	2.00	4.00	—

Y# 279 500 LIRE **Weight:** 11.0000 g. **Composition:** 0.8350 Silver .2953 oz. ASW **Ruler:** Pope John Paul II **Subject:** XII World Youth Conference **Reverse:** Six children with Jesus **Edge Lettering:** IUVENTUTIS XII UNIVERSALIS DIES PARISIIS

Date	Mintage	F	VF	XF	Unc	BU
1997	18,000	—	—	—	35.00	—
1997 Proof	—	Value: 60.00				

Y# 285 500 LIRE **Ring Composition:** Stainless Steel **Center Comp.:** Aluminum-Bronze **Ruler:** Pope John Paul II **Reverse:** One man freeing another from thorns

Date	Mintage	F	VF	XF	Unc	BU
1997/XIX	160,000	—	—	2.00	4.00	—

Y# 292 500 LIRE **Weight:** 11.0000 g. **Composition:** 0.8350 Silver .2953 oz. ASW **Ruler:** Pope John Paul II **Subject:** Shroud of Turin **Edge Lettering:** SACRA SINDON OSTENTATUR AVG. TAVR. MCMXCVIII

Date	Mintage	F	VF	XF	Unc	BU
1998/XX	23,000	—	—	—	35.00	—

Y# 298 500 LIRE **Ring Composition:** Stainless St **Center Comp.:** Aluminum-Bronze **Ruler:** Pope John P **Obverse:** Pope's portrait **Reverse:** Two figures

Date	Mintage	F	VF	XF	Unc
1998	103,500	—	—	2.00	4.00

Y# 322 500 LIRE **Weight:** 11.0000 g. **Composition** 0.8350 Silver .2953 oz. ASW **Ruler:** Pope John Paul II **Subject:** 70th Anniversary - Vatican City Arms of Six P

Date	F	VF	XF	Unc
1999	—	—	—	30.00
1999 Proof	—	Value: 50.00		

Y# 310 500 LIRE **Ring Composition:** Stainless SteelCenter **Weight:** 6.7000 g. **Center Composition:** Aluminum-Bronze **Ruler:** Pope John Paul II **Subject:** T of Choices, Time of Hope **Obverse:** Pope John Paul II right **Reverse:** God's hand above young parent's with b **Edge:** Reeded **Size:** 25.9 mm. **Note:** Struck at Rome.

Date	Mintage	F	VF	XF	Unc
1999	161,000	—	—	2.00	4.00

Y# 328 500 LIRE **Ring Weight:** 6.7700 g. **Ring Com** Stainless Steel **Center Composition:** Brass **Ruler:** Pop John Paul II **Obverse:** Papal arms **Reverse:** Pope turnin page **Edge:** Reeded and plain sections **Size:** 25.7 mm.

Date	F	VF	XF	Unc
XXII(2000)	—	—	—	4.00

Y# 336 500 LIRE **Ring Weight:** 6.7700 g. **Ring Composition:** Stainless Steel **Center Composition:** Br **Ruler:** Pope John Paul II **Subject:** Pope John Paul I **Obverse:** Portrait **Reverse:** Papal arms **Edge:** Reeded a plain sections **Size:** 25.7 mm.

Date	F	VF	XF	Unc
2001	—	—	—	4.00

Y# 142 1000 LIRE **Weight:** 14.6000 g. **Composition** 0.8350 Silver .3920 oz. ASW **Ruler:** Pope John Paul I

Date	F	VF	XF	Unc
1978	—	—	—	25.00

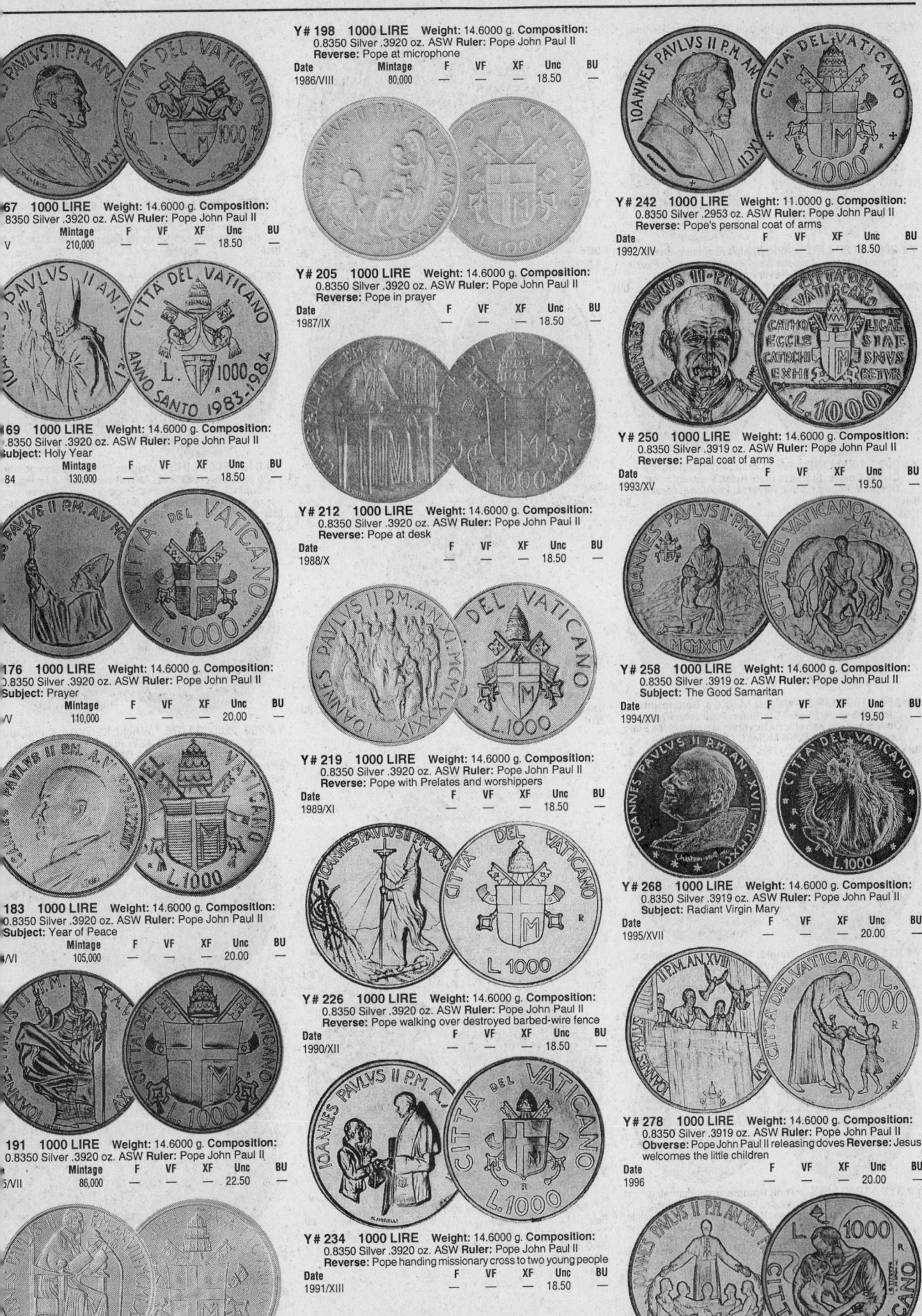

67 **1000 LIRE** **Weight:** 14.6000 g. **Composition:** 8350 Silver .3920 oz. ASW **Ruler:** Pope John Paul II

Date	Mintage	F	VF	XF	Unc	BU
V	210,000	—	—	—	18.50	—

169 **1000 LIRE** **Weight:** 14.6000 g. **Composition:** .8350 Silver .3920 oz. ASW **Ruler:** Pope John Paul II **Subject:** Holy Year

Date	Mintage	F	VF	XF	Unc	BU
84	130,000	—	—	—	18.50	—

176 **1000 LIRE** **Weight:** 14.6000 g. **Composition:** 0.8350 Silver .3920 oz. ASW **Ruler:** Pope John Paul II **Subject:** Prayer

Date	Mintage	F	VF	XF	Unc	BU
/V	110,000	—	—	—	20.00	—

183 **1000 LIRE** **Weight:** 14.6000 g. **Composition:** 0.8350 Silver .3920 oz. ASW **Ruler:** Pope John Paul II **Subject:** Year of Peace

Date	Mintage	F	VF	XF	Unc	BU
/VI	105,000	—	—	—	20.00	—

191 **1000 LIRE** **Weight:** 14.6000 g. **Composition:** 0.8350 Silver .3920 oz. ASW **Ruler:** Pope John Paul II

Date	Mintage	F	VF	XF	Unc	BU
5/VII	86,000	—	—	—	22.50	—

Y# 198 1000 LIRE **Weight:** 14.6000 g. **Composition:** 0.8350 Silver .3920 oz. ASW **Ruler:** Pope John Paul II **Reverse:** Pope at microphone

Date	Mintage	F	VF	XF	Unc	BU
1986/VIII	80,000	—	—	—	18.50	—

Y# 205 1000 LIRE **Weight:** 14.6000 g. **Composition:** 0.8350 Silver .3920 oz. ASW **Ruler:** Pope John Paul II **Reverse:** Pope in prayer

Date	F	VF	XF	Unc	BU
1987/IX	—	—	—	18.50	—

Y# 212 1000 LIRE **Weight:** 14.6000 g. **Composition:** 0.8350 Silver .3920 oz. ASW **Ruler:** Pope John Paul II **Reverse:** Pope at desk

Date	F	VF	XF	Unc	BU
1988/X	—	—	—	18.50	—

Y# 219 1000 LIRE **Weight:** 14.6000 g. **Composition:** 0.8350 Silver .3920 oz. ASW **Ruler:** Pope John Paul II **Reverse:** Pope with Prelates and worshippers

Date	F	VF	XF	Unc	BU
1989/XI	—	—	—	18.50	—

Y# 226 1000 LIRE **Weight:** 14.6000 g. **Composition:** 0.8350 Silver .3920 oz. ASW **Ruler:** Pope John Paul II **Reverse:** Pope walking over destroyed barbed-wire fence

Date	F	VF	XF	Unc	BU
1990/XII	—	—	—	18.50	—

Y# 234 1000 LIRE **Weight:** 14.6000 g. **Composition:** 0.8350 Silver .3920 oz. ASW **Ruler:** Pope John Paul II **Reverse:** Pope handing missionary cross to two young people

Date	F	VF	XF	Unc	BU
1991/XIII	—	—	—	18.50	—

Y# 242 1000 LIRE **Weight:** 11.0000 g. **Composition:** 0.8350 Silver .2953 oz. ASW **Ruler:** Pope John Paul II **Reverse:** Pope's personal coat of arms

Date	F	VF	XF	Unc	BU
1992/XIV	—	—	—	18.50	—

Y# 250 1000 LIRE **Weight:** 14.6000 g. **Composition:** 0.8350 Silver .3919 oz. ASW **Ruler:** Pope John Paul II **Reverse:** Papal coat of arms

Date	F	VF	XF	Unc	BU
1993/XV	—	—	—	19.50	—

Y# 258 1000 LIRE **Weight:** 14.6000 g. **Composition:** 0.8350 Silver .3919 oz. ASW **Ruler:** Pope John Paul II **Subject:** The Good Samaritan

Date	F	VF	XF	Unc	BU
1994/XVI	—	—	—	19.50	—

Y# 268 1000 LIRE **Weight:** 14.6000 g. **Composition:** 0.8350 Silver .3919 oz. ASW **Ruler:** Pope John Paul II **Subject:** Radiant Virgin Mary

Date	F	VF	XF	Unc	BU
1995/XVII	—	—	—	20.00	—

Y# 278 1000 LIRE **Weight:** 14.6000 g. **Composition:** 0.8350 Silver .3919 oz. ASW **Ruler:** Pope John Paul II **Obverse:** Pope John Paul II releasing doves **Reverse:** Jesus welcomes the little children

Date	F	VF	XF	Unc	BU
1996	—	—	—	20.00	—

Y# 287 1000 LIRE **Weight:** 14.0000 g. **Composition:** 0.8350 Silver .3919 oz. ASW **Ruler:** Pope John Paul II **Obverse:** John Paul II teaching people **Reverse:** Saint cradling ill man **Edge Lettering:** TOTVS TVVS MCMXCVII

Date	F	VF	XF	Unc	BU
1997/XIX	—	—	—	20.00	—

Y# 286 1000 LIRE **Ring Comp.:** Aluminum-Bronze **Center Comp.:** Stainless Steel **Ruler:** Pope John Paul II **Obverse:** John Paul II **Reverse:** Papal coat of arms

Date	Mintage	F	VF	XF	Unc	BU
1997/XIX	270,000	—	—	—	7.00	—

Y# 299 1000 LIRE **Ring Comp.:** Aluminum-Bronze **Center Comp.:** Stainless Steel **Ruler:** Pope John Paul II **Obverse:** Pope's portrait **Reverse:** Papal coat of arms

Date	Mintage	F	VF	XF	Unc	BU
1998	306,500	—	—	—	7.00	—

Y# 300 1000 LIRE **Weight:** 14.0000 g. **Composition:** 0.8350 Silver .3919 oz. ASW **Ruler:** Pope John Paul II **Obverse:** Pope with crucifix **Reverse:** Jesus on globe **Edge Lettering:** TOTVS TVVS MCMXCVIII

Date	F	VF	XF	Unc	BU
1998	—	—	—	20.00	—

Y# 312 1000 LIRE **Weight:** 14.0000 g. **Composition:** 0.8350 Silver .3919 oz. ASW **Ruler:** Pope John Paul II **Subject:** The Right to Religous Freedom **Obverse:** Pope John Paul bust right **Reverse:** Family at altar **Edge:** TOTVS TVVS ++ ++ ++ ++ MCMXCIX ++ ++ ++ ++

Date	F	VF	XF	Unc	BU
1999	—	—	—	20.00	—

Y# 311 1000 LIRE **Ring Composition:** Aluminum-Bronze **Center Composition:** Stainless Steel **Ruler:** Pope John Paul II **Obverse:** Pope's arms **Reverse:** Couple at base of Christ on cross **Edge:** Reeded and plain sections **Size:** 26.9 mm. **Note:** 8.85 grams. Struck at Rome.

Date	Mintage	F	VF	XF	Unc	BU
1999	126,100	—	—	—	7.00	—

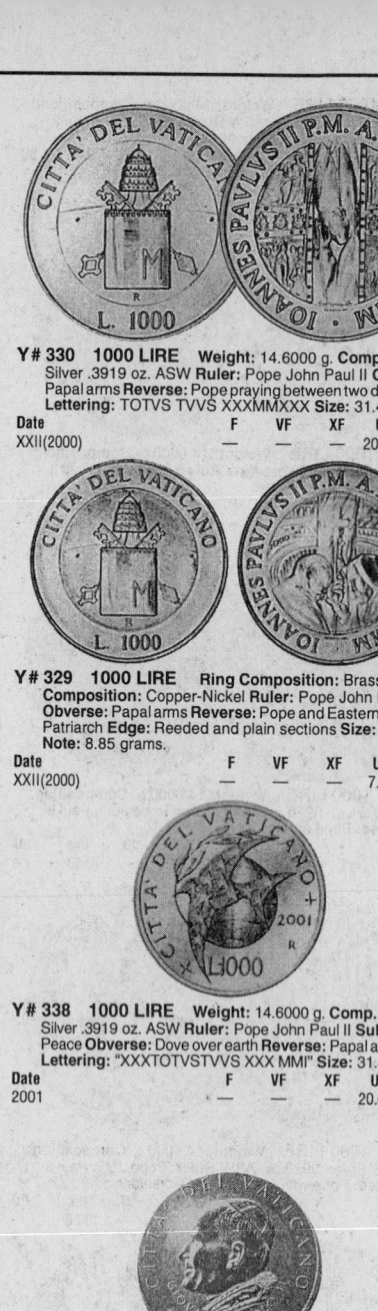

Y# 330 1000 LIRE **Weight:** 14.6000 g. **Comp.:** 0.8350 Silver .3919 oz. ASW **Ruler:** Pope John Paul II **Obverse:** Papal arms **Reverse:** Pope praying between two doors **Edge Lettering:** TOTVS TVVS XXXMMXXX **Size:** 31.4 mm.

Date	F	VF	XF	Unc	BU
XXII(2000)	—	—	—	20.00	—

Y# 329 1000 LIRE **Ring Composition:** Brass **Center Composition:** Copper-Nickel **Ruler:** Pope John Paul II **Obverse:** Papal arms **Reverse:** Pope and Eastern Orthodox Patriarch **Edge:** Reeded and plain sections **Size:** 26.9 mm. **Note:** 8.85 grams.

Date	F	VF	XF	Unc	BU
XXII(2000)	—	—	—	7.00	—

Y# 338 1000 LIRE **Weight:** 14.6000 g. **Comp.:** 0.8350 Silver .3919 oz. ASW **Ruler:** Pope John Paul II **Subject:** Peace **Obverse:** Dove over earth **Reverse:** Papal arms **Edge Lettering:** "XXXTOTVSTVVS XXX MMI" **Size:** 31.4 mm.

Date	F	VF	XF	Unc	BU
2001	—	—	—	20.00	—

Y# 337 1000 LIRE **Weight:** 8.8500 g. **Composition:** Copper-Nickel **Ruler:** Pope John Paul II **Subject:** Pope John Paul I **Obverse:** Portrait **Reverse:** Papal arms **Edge:** Reeded and plain sections **Size:** 26.9 mm.

Date	F	VF	XF	Unc	BU
2001	—	—	—	7.00	—

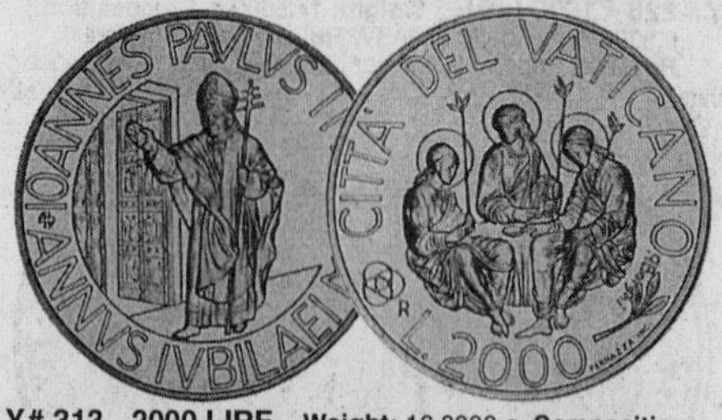

Y# 313 2000 LIRE **Weight:** 16.0000 g. **Composition:** 0.8350 Silver .4295 oz. ASW **Ruler:** Pope John Paul II **Subject:** Holy Year **Obverse:** Pope standing by open door **Reverse:** Three hallowed figures **Edge:** Reeded

Date	Mintage	F	VF	XF	Unc	BU
2000	60,000	—	—	—	25.00	—
2000 Proof	10,000	Value: 35.00				

Y# 339 2000 LIRE **Weight:** 16.0000 g. **Compositi** 0.8350 Silver .4295 oz. ASW **Ruler:** Pope John Paul I **Subject:** Dialog for Peace **Obverse:** Pope holding sta **Reverse:** Dove above crowd **Edge:** Reeded **Size:** 31.4

Date	Mintage	F	VF	XF	Unc
2001	16,000	—	—	—	25.00
2001 Proof	8,000	Value: 35.00			

Y# 340 5000 LIRE **Weight:** 18.0000 g. **Compositi** 0.8350 Silver .4832 oz. ASW **Ruler:** Pope John Paul II **Subject:** Easter **Obverse:** Pope praying **Reverse:** Jes rising **Edge:** Reeded and plain sections **Size:** 32 mm.

Date	Mintage	F	VF	XF	Unc
2001 Proof	16,000	Value: 30.00			

Y# 260 10000 LIRE **Weight:** 22.0000 g. **Compositi** 0.8350 Silver .5906 oz. ASW **Ruler:** Pope John Paul II **Subject:** The Annunciation **Obverse:** Pope John Paul

Date	Mintage	F	VF	XF	Unc
1995 Proof	30,000	Value: 80.00			

Note: Proof sets only

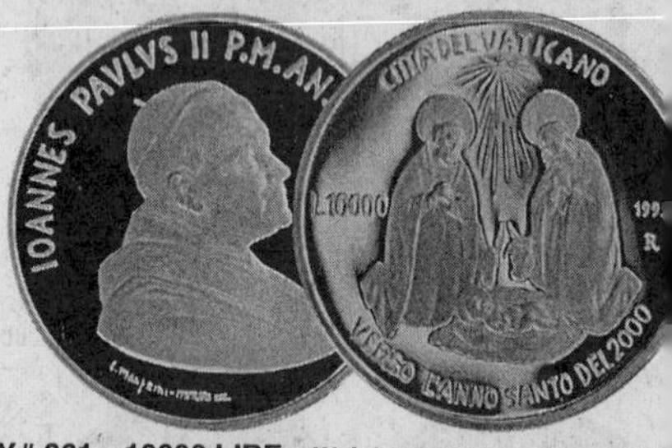

Y# 261 10000 LIRE **Weight:** 22.0000 g. **Compositi** 0.8350 Silver .5906 oz. ASW **Ruler:** Pope John Paul II **Subject:** The Nativity

Date	Mintage	F	VF	XF	Unc
1995 Proof	30,000	Value: 80.00			

Note: Proof sets only

Y# 270 10000 LIRE **Weight:** 22.0000 g. **Compositi** 0.8350 Silver .5906 oz. ASW **Ruler:** Pope John Paul II **Subject:** Holy Year 2000 - Baptism in River Jordan

Date	Mintage	F	VF	XF	Unc
1996 Proof	30,000	Value: 70.00			

Note: Proof sets only

Y# 271 10000 LIRE Weight: 22.0000 g. **Composition:** 0.8350 Silver .5906 oz. ASW **Ruler:** Pope John Paul II **Subject:** Holy Year 2000 - Jesus Teaching

Date	Mintage	F	VF	XF	Unc	BU
1996 Proof	30,000	Value: 70.00				

Note: Proof sets only

Y# 318 10000 LIRE Weight: 22.0000 g. **Composition:** 0.8350 Silver .5906 oz. ASW **Ruler:** Pope John Paul II **Subject:** Cure of the Paralytic

Date		F	VF	XF	Unc	BU
1997 Proof	—	Value: 70.00				

Note: Proof sets only

Y# 319 10000 LIRE Weight: 22.0000 g. **Composition:** 0.8350 Silver .5906 oz. ASW **Ruler:** Pope John Paul II **Subject:** Calming of the Storm

Date		F	VF	XF	Unc	BU
1997 Proof	—	Value: 70.00				

Note: Proof sets only

 # 290 10000 LIRE Weight: 22.0000 g. **Composition:** 0.8350 Silver .5906 oz. ASW **Ruler:** Pope John Paul II **Subject:** Last Supper **Obverse:** Pope John Paul II

ate	Mintage	F	VF	XF	Unc	BU
998 Proof	30,000	Value: 70.00				

 # 291 10000 LIRE Weight: 22.0000 g. **Composition:** 0.8350 Silver .5906 oz. ASW **Ruler:** Pope John Paul II **Subject:** Crucifixion of Jesus **Obverse:** Pope John Paul II

ate	Mintage	F	VF	XF	Unc	BU
998 Proof	30,000	Value: 70.00				

 # 304 10000 LIRE Weight: 22.0000 g. **Composition:** 0.8350 Silver .5906 oz. ASW **Ruler:** Pope John Paul II **Reverse:** Jesus rising from his tomb

e	Mintage	F	VF	XF	Unc	BU
99 Proof	30,000	Value: 70.00				

Y# 303 10000 LIRE Weight: 22.0000 g. **Composition:** 0.8350 Silver .5906 oz. ASW **Ruler:** Pope John Paul II **Obverse:** Pope John Paul II bust right **Reverse:** Group with flames above head **Size:** 34 mm. **Note:** Struck at Rome.

Date	Mintage	F	VF	XF	Unc	BU
1999 Proof	30,000	Value: 70.00				

Y# 314 10000 LIRE Weight: 22.0000 g. **Composition:** 0.8350 Silver .5906 oz. ASW **Ruler:** Pope John Paul II **Obverse:** Pope John Paul II bust right **Reverse:** Angel holding church above "GERUSALEMME"

Date	Mintage	F	VF	XF	Unc	BU
2000 Proof	30,000	Value: 70.00				

Y# 315 10000 LIRE Weight: 22.0000 g. **Composition:** 0.8350 Silver .5906 oz. ASW **Ruler:** Pope John Paul II **Reverse:** Angel holding church above "ROMA"

Date	Mintage	F	VF	XF	Unc	BU
2000 Proof	30,000	Value: 70.00				

Y# 288 50000 LIRE Weight: 7.5000 g. **Composition:** 0.9170 Gold .2211 oz. AGW **Ruler:** Pope John Paul II **Obverse:** Pope John Paul II and Holy Door **Reverse:** St. Paul

Date	Mintage	F	VF	XF	Unc	BU
1997/XIX Proof	6,000	Value: 250				

Y# 301 50000 LIRE Weight: 7.5000 g. **Composition:** 0.9170 Gold .2211 oz. AGW **Ruler:** Pope John Paul II **Obverse:** Pope and Holy Door **Reverse:** Madonna and child **Edge:** Reeded **Size:** 23 mm. **Note:** Struck at Rome.

Date	Mintage	F	VF	XF	Unc	BU
1998 Proof	6,000	Value: 250				

Y# 320 50000 LIRE Weight: 7.5000 g. **Composition:** 0.9170 Gold .2211 oz. AGW **Ruler:** Pope John Paul II **Reverse:** Statue of St. Peter

Date		F	VF	XF	Unc	BU
1999 Proof	—	Value: 250				

Y# 316 50000 LIRE Weight: 7.5000 g. **Composition:** 0.9170 Gold .2211 oz. AGW **Ruler:** Pope John Paul II **Subject:** Prodigal Son **Obverse:** Pope John Paul II bust right **Reverse:** Father embracing son

Date	Mintage	F	VF	XF	Unc	BU
2000 Proof	6,000	Value: 250				

Y# 289 100000 LIRE Weight: 15.0000 g. **Composition:** 0.9170 Gold .4422 oz. AGW **Ruler:** Pope John Paul II **Obverse:** Pope John Paul II and Holy Door **Reverse:** Basilica of St. Paul outside the walls

Date	Mintage	F	VF	XF	Unc	BU
1997/XIX Proof	6,000	Value: 450				

Y# 302 100000 LIRE Weight: 15.0000 g. **Composition:** 0.9170 Gold .4422 oz. AGW **Ruler:** Pope John Paul II **Obverse:** Pope and Holy Door **Reverse:** Basilica of St. Mary Major **Edge:** Reeded **Size:** 28 mm. **Note:** Struck at Rome.

Date	Mintage	F	VF	XF	Unc	BU
1998 Proof	6,000	Value: 450				

Y# 321 100000 LIRE Weight: 15.0000 g. **Composition:** 0.9170 Gold .4422 oz. AGW **Ruler:** Pope John Paul II **Reverse:** St. Peter's Basilica

Date		F	VF	XF	Unc	BU
1999 Proof	—	Value: 450				

Y# 317 100000 LIRE Weight: 15.0000 g. **Composition:** 0.9170 Gold .4422 oz. AGW **Ruler:** Pope John Paul II **Subject:** Crucifixion **Obverse:** John Paul II bust right **Reverse:** Crucifixion scene

Date	Mintage	F	VF	XF	Unc	BU
2000 Proof	6,000	Value: 450				

EURO COINAGE

Y# 341 EURO CENT Weight: 2.2700 g. **Composition:** Copper Plated Steel **Ruler:** Pope John Paul II **Obverse:** Pope's portrait **Reverse:** Denomination and globe **Edge:** Plain **Size:** 16.2 mm.

Date	Mintage	F	VF	XF	Unc	BU
2002R	—	—	—	—	100	—
2002R Proof	9,000	Value: 175				

Y# 342 2 EURO CENTS Weight: 3.0300 g. **Composition:** Copper Plated Steel **Ruler:** Pope John Paul II **Obverse:** Pope's portrait **Reverse:** Denomination and globe **Edge:** Grooved **Size:** 18.7 mm.

Date	Mintage	F	VF	XF	Unc	BU
2002R	—	—	—	—	100	—
2002R Proof	9,000	Value: 175				

Y# 343 5 EURO CENTS Weight: 3.8600 g. **Composition:** Copper Plated Steel **Ruler:** Pope John Paul II **Obverse:** Pope's portrait **Reverse:** Denomination and globe **Edge:** Plain **Size:** 21.2 mm.

Date	Mintage	F	VF	XF	Unc	BU
2002R	—	—	—	—	100	—
2002R Proof	9,000	Value: 175				

Y# 344 10 EURO CENTS Weight: 4.0700 g. **Composition:** Brass **Ruler:** Pope John Paul II **Obverse:** Pope's portrait **Reverse:** Map and denomination **Edge:** Reeded **Size:** 19.7 mm.

Date	Mintage	F	VF	XF	Unc	BU
2002R	—	—	—	—	100	—
2002R Proof	9,000	Value: 175				

Y# 345 20 EURO CENTS **Ruler:** Pope John Paul II **Obverse:** Pope's portrait **Reverse:** Map and denomination **Edge:** Notched **Size:** 22.1 mm.

Date	Mintage	F	VF	XF	Unc	BU
2002R	—	—	—	—	100	—
2002R Proof	9,000	Value: 175				

Y# 346 50 EURO CENTS **Weight:** 7.8100 g. **Composition:** Brass **Ruler:** Pope John Paul II **Obverse:** Pope's portrait **Reverse:** Map and denomination **Edge:** Reeded **Size:** 24.2 mm.

Date	Mintage	F	VF	XF	Unc	BU
2002R	—	—	—	—	100	—
2002R Proof	9,000	Value: 175				

Y# 347 EURO **Weight:** 7.5000 g. **Composition:** Bi-Metallic **Ruler:** Pope John Paul II **Obverse:** Pope's portrait **Reverse:** Denomination and map **Edge:** Reeded and plain sections **Size:** 23.2 mm.

Date	Mintage	F	VF	XF	Unc	BU
2002R	—	—	—	—	95.00	—
2002R Proof	9,000	Value: 185				

Y# 348 2 EUROS **Weight:** 25.7000 g. **Composition:** Bi-Metallic **Ruler:** Pope John Paul II **Obverse:** Pope's portrait **Reverse:** Denomination and map **Edge:** Reeded with"2's" and stars **Size:** 8.52 mm.

Date	Mintage	F	VF	XF	Unc	BU
2002R	—	—	—	—	155	—
2002R Proof	9,000	Value: 215				

PROVAS

KM#	Date	Mintage	Identification	Mkt Val
Pr2	1951	103	2 Lire. Silver. Y#50.	65.00
Pr3	1951	103	5 Lire. Silver. Y#51.	85.00
Pr4	1951	103	10 Lire. Silver. Y#52.	100
Pr1	1951	103	Lira. Silver. Y#49.	50.00
Pr7	1952	103	5 Lire. Silver. Y#51.	85.00
Pr6	1952	103	2 Lire. Silver. Y#50.	65.00
Pr8	1952	103	10 Lire. Silver. Y#52.	100
Pr5	1952	103	Lira. Silver. Y#49.	50.00
Pr9	1953	103	Lira. Silver. Y#49.	50.00
Pr10	1953	103	2 Lire. Silver. Y#50.	65.00
Pr11	1953	103	5 Lire. Silver. Y#51.	85.00
Pr12	1953	103	10 Lire. Silver. Y#52.	100
Pr18	1955	103	100 Lire. Silver. Y#55.	100
Pr13	1955	103	Lira. Silver. Y#49.	40.00
Pr17	1955	103	50 Lire. Silver. Y#54.	90.00
Pr16	1955	103	10 Lire. Silver. Y#52.	75.00
Pr14	1955	103	2 Lire. Silver. Y#50.	55.00
Pr15	1955	103	5 Lire. Silver. Y#51.	65.00
Pr20	1956	103	2 Lire. Silver. Y#50.	55.00
Pr21	1956	103	5 Lire. Silver. Y#51.	65.00
Pr22	1956	103	10 Lire. Silver. Y#52.	75.00
Pr23	1956	103	50 Lire. Silver. Y#54.	90.00
Pr19	1956	103	Lira. Silver. Y#49.	40.00
Pr24	1956	103	100 Lire. Silver. Y#55.	100
Pr26	1957	103	2 Lire. Silver. Y#50.	50.00
Pr27	1957	103	5 Lire. Silver. Y#51.	60.00
Pr30	1957	103	50 Lire. Silver. Y#54.	90.00
Pr31	1957	103	100 Lire. Silver. Y#55.	100
Pr25	1957	103	Lira. Silver. Y#49.	40.00
Pr28	1957	103	10 Lire. Silver. Y#52.	70.00
Pr29	1957	103	20 Lire. Silver. Y-A52.	80.00
Pr32	1958	103	Lira. Silver. Y#49.	40.00
Pr33	1958	103	2 Lire. Silver. Y#50.	50.00
Pr35	1958	103	10 Lire. Silver. Y#52.	70.00
Pr36	1958	103	20 Lire. Silver. Y-A52.	80.00
Pr37	1958	103	50 Lire. Silver. Y#54.	90.00
Pr38	1958	103	100 Lire. Silver. Y#55.	100
Pr39	1958	103	500 Lire. Silver. Y#56.	125
Pr34	1958	103	5 Lire. Silver. Y#51.	60.00
Pr42	1959	103	5 Lire. Silver. Y#60.	60.00
Pr45	1959	103	50 Lire. Silver. Y#63.	90.00
Pr47	1959	103	500 Lire. Silver. Y#65.	125
Pr40	1959	103	Lira. Silver. Y#58.	40.00
Pr46	1959	103	100 Lire. Silver. Y#64.	100
Pr41	1959	103	2 Lire. Silver. Y#59.	50.00
Pr43	1959	103	10 Lire. Silver. Y#61.	70.00
Pr44	1959	103	20 Lire. Silver. Y#62.	80.00
Pr54	1960	103	100 Lire. Silver. Y#64.1.	100
Pr48	1960	103	Lira. Silver. Y#58.	40.00
Pr49	1960	103	2 Lire. Silver. Y#59.	50.00
Pr53	1960	103	50 Lire. Silver. Y#63.1.	90.00
Pr55	1960	103	500 Lire. Silver. Y#65.1.	125
Pr50	1960	103	5 Lire. Silver. Y#60.	60.00
Pr51	1960	103	10 Lire. Silver. Y#61.	70.00
Pr52	1960	103	20 Lire. Silver. Y#62.	80.00
Pr56	1961	103	Lira. Silver. Y#58.	40.00
Pr57	1961	103	2 Lire. Silver. Y#59.	50.00
Pr58	1961	103	5 Lire. Silver. Y#60.	60.00
Pr62	1961	103	100 Lire. Silver. Y#64.1.	100
Pr63	1961	103	500 Lire. Silver. Y#65.1.	125
Pr60	1961	103	20 Lire. Silver. Y#62.	80.00
Pr61	1961	103	50 Lire. Silver. Y#63.1.	90.00
Pr59	1961	103	10 Lire. Silver. Y#61.	70.00
Pr65	1962	103	2 Lire. Silver. Y#59.	50.00
Pr72	1962	103	Lira. Silver. Y#67.	40.00
Pr79	1962	103	500 Lire. Silver. Y#74.	125
Pr70	1962	103	100 Lire. Silver. Y#64.1.	100
Pr71	1962	103	500 Lire. Silver. Y#65.1.	125
Pr73	1962	103	2 Lire. Silver. Y#68.	50.00
Pr68	1962	103	20 Lire. Silver. Y#62.	80.00
Pr69	1962	103	50 Lire. Silver. Y#63.1.	90.00
Pr74	1962	103	5 Lire. Silver. Y#69.	60.00
Pr64	1962	103	Lira. Silver. Y#58.	40.00
Pr66	1962	103	5 Lire. Silver. Y#60.	60.00
Pr67	1962	103	10 Lire. Silver. Y#61.	70.00
Pr75	1962	103	10 Lire. Silver. Y#70.	70.00
Pr76	1962	103	20 Lire. Silver. Y#71.	80.00
Pr77	1962	103	50 Lire. Silver. Y#72.	90.00
Pr78	1962	103	100 Lire. Silver. Y#73.	100
Pr84	1963	103	20 Lire. Silver. Y#80.	80.00
Pr85	1963	103	50 Lire. Silver. Y#81.	90.00
Pr86	1963	103	100 Lire. Silver. Y#82.	100
Pr83	1963	103	10 Lire. Silver. Y#79.	70.00
Pr80	1963	103	Lira. Silver. Y#76.	40.00
Pr81	1963	103	2 Lire. Silver. Y#77.	50.00
Pr82	1963	103	5 Lire. Silver. Y#78.	60.00
Pr87	1963	103	500 Lire. Silver. Y#83.	125
Pr95	1964	103	500 Lire. Silver. Y#83.	125
Pr88	1964	103	Lira. Silver. Y#76.	40.00
Pr89	1964	103	2 Lire. Silver. Y#77.	50.00
Pr90	1964	103	5 Lire. Silver. Y#78.	60.00
Pr91	1964	103	10 Lire. Silver. Y#79.	70.00
Pr94	1964	103	100 Lire. Silver. Y#82.	100
Pr92	1964	103	20 Lire. Silver. Y#80.	80.00
Pr93	1964	103	50 Lire. Silver. Y#81.	90.00
Pr100	1965	103	20 Lire. Silver. Y#80.	80.00
Pr101	1965	103	50 Lire. Silver. Y#81.	90.00
Pr102	1965	103	100 Lire. Silver. Y#82.	100
Pr103	1965	103	500 Lire. Silver. Y#83.	125
Pr96	1965	103	Lira. Silver. Y#76.	40.00
Pr97	1965	103	2 Lire. Silver. Y#77.	50.00
Pr98	1965	103	5 Lire. Silver. Y#78.	60.00
Pr99	1965	103	10 Lire. Silver. Y#79.	70.00
Pr106	1966	103	5 Lire. Silver. Y#86.	60.00
Pr107	1966	103	10 Lire. Silver. Y#87.	70.00
Pr104	1966	103	Lira. Silver. Y#84.	40.00
Pr105	1966	103	2 Lire. Silver. Y#85.	50.00
Pr110	1966	103	100 Lire. Silver. Y#90.	100
Pr111	1966	103	500 Lire. Silver. Y#91.	125
Pr108	1966	103	20 Lire. Silver. Y#88.	80.00
Pr109	1966	103	50 Lire. Silver. Y#89.	90.00
Pr116	ND(1967)	103	20 Lire. Silver. Y#96.	80.00
Pr114	ND(1967)	103	5 Lire. Silver. Y#94.	60.00
Pr117	1967	103	50 Lire. Silver. Y#97.	90.00
Pr118	1967	103	100 Lire. Silver. Y#98.	100
Pr113	ND(1967)	103	2 Lire. Silver. Y#93.	50.00
Pr119	1967	103	500 Lire. Silver. Y#99.	125
Pr112	ND(1967)	103	Lira. Silver. Y#92.	40.00
Pr115	ND(1967)	103	10 Lire. Silver. Y#95.	70.00
Pr122	ND(1968)	103	5 Lire. Silver. Y#102.	60.00
Pr120	ND(1968)	103	Lira. Silver. Y#100.	40.00
Pr121	ND(1968)	103	2 Lire. Silver. Y#101.	50.00
Pr123	ND(1968)	103	10 Lire. Silver. Y#103.	70.00
Pr127	ND(1968)	103	500 Lire. Silver. Y#107.	125
Pr124	ND(1968)	103	20 Lire. Silver. Y#104.	80.00
Pr126	ND(1968)	103	100 Lire. Silver. Y#106.	100
Pr125	ND(1968)	103	50 Lire. Silver. Y#105.	90.00
Pr130	1969	103	5 Lire. Silver. Y#110.	60.00
Pr131	1969	103	10 Lire. Silver. Y#111.	70.00
Pr128	1969	103	Lira. Silver. Y#108.	40.00
Pr134	1969	103	100 Lire. Silver. Y#114.	100
Pr129	1969	103	2 Lire. Silver. Y#109.	50.00
Pr132	1969	103	20 Lire. Silver. Y#112.	80.00
Pr133	1969	103	50 Lire. Silver. Y#113.	90.00
Pr135	1969	103	500 Lire. Silver. Y#115.	125
Pr139	1970	103	10 Lire. Silver. Y#119.	70.00
Pr140	1970	103	20 Lire. Silver. Y#120.	80.00
Pr138	1970	103	5 Lire. Silver. Y#118.	60.00
Pr136	1970	103	Lira. Silver. Y#116.	40.00
Pr142	1970	103	100 Lire. Silver. Y#122.	100
Pr137	1970	103	2 Lire. Silver. Y#117.	50.00
Pr141	1970	103	50 Lire. Silver. Y#121.	90.00
Pr143	1970	103	500 Lire. Silver. Y#123.	125
Pr150	1971	103	100 Lire. Silver. Y#122.	100
Pr151	1971	103	500 Lire. Silver. Y#123.	120
Pr144	1971	103	Lira. Silver. Y#116.	40.00
Pr145	1971	103	2 Lire. Silver. Y#117.	50.00
Pr146	1971	103	5 Lire. Silver. Y#118.	60.00
Pr148	1971	103	20 Lire. Silver. Y#120.	80.00
Pr149	1971	103	50 Lire. Silver. Y#121.	90.00
Pr147	1971	103	10 Lire. Silver. Y#119.	70.00
Pr154	1972	103	5 Lire. Silver. Y#118.	60.00
Pr155	1972	103	10 Lire. Silver. Y#119.	70.00
Pr156	1972	103	20 Lire. Silver. Y#120.	80.00
Pr157	1972	103	50 Lire. Silver. Y#121.	90.00
Pr152	1972	103	Lira. Silver. Y#116.	40.00
Pr153	1972	103	2 Lire. Silver. Y#117.	50.00
Pr158	1972	103	100 Lire. Silver. Y#122.	100
Pr159	1972	103	500 Lire. Silver. Y#123.	125
Pr160	1973	103	Lira. Silver. Y#116.	40.00
Pr166	1973	103	100 Lire. Silver. Y#122.	100
Pr161	1973	103	2 Lire. Silver. Y#117.	50.00
Pr167	1973	103	500 Lire. Silver. Y#123.	125
Pr163	1973	103	10 Lire. Silver. Y#119.	70.00
Pr162	1973	103	5 Lire. Silver. Y#118.	60.00
Pr164	1973	103	20 Lire. Silver. Y#120.	80.00
Pr165	1973	103	50 Lire. Silver. Y#121.	90.00
Pr172	1974	103	20 Lire. Silver. Y#120.	80.00
Pr173	1974	103	50 Lire. Silver. Y#121.	90.00
Pr171	1974	103	10 Lire. Silver. Y#119.	70.00
Pr170	1974	103	5 Lire. Silver. Y#118.	60.00
Pr175	1974	103	500 Lire. Silver. Y#123.	125
Pr168	1974	103	Lira. Silver. Y#116.	40.00
Pr169	1974	103	2 Lire. Silver. Y#117.	50.00
Pr174	1974	103	100 Lire. Silver. q edge. Y#122.	100
Pr176	1975	103	Lira. Silver. Y#116.	40.00
Pr183	1975	103	500 Lire. Silver. Y#123.	125
Pr189	1975	103	50 Lire. Silver. Y#129.	90.00
Pr190	1975	103	100 Lire. Silver. Y#130.	100
Pr181	1975	103	50 Lire. Silver. Y#121.	90.00
Pr182	1975	103	100 Lire. Silver. Y#122.	100
Pr184	1975	103	Lira. Silver. Y#124.	40.00
Pr177	1975	103	2 Lire. Silver. Y#117.	50.00
Pr178	1975	103	5 Lire. Silver. Y#118.	60.00
Pr179	1975	103	10 Lire. Silver. Y#119.	70.00
Pr185	1975	103	2 Lire. Silver. Y#125.	50.00
Pr188	1975	103	20 Lire. Silver. Y#128.	80.00
Pr180	1975	103	20 Lire. Silver. Y#120.	80.00
Pr186	1975	103	5 Lire. Silver. Y#126.	60.00
Pr187	1975	103	10 Lire. Silver. Y#127.	70.00
Pr191	1975	103	500 Lire. Silver. Y#131.	120

MINT SETS

KM#	Date	Mintage	Identification	Issue Price	Mkt Val
MS1	1929 (9)	10,000	Y#1-9	—	470
MS2	1929 (8)	10,000	Y#1-8	—	170
MS3	1930 (9)	2,621	Y#1-9	—	825
MS4	1930 (8)	50,000	Y#1-8	—	75.00
MS5	1931 (9)	3,343	Y#1-9	—	575
MS6	1931 (8)	50,000	Y#1-8	—	75.00
MS7	1932 (9)	5,073	Y#1-9	—	475
MS8	1932 (8)	50,000	Y#1-8	—	75.00
MS10	1933-34 (8)	50,000	Y#11-18	—	125
MS9	1933-34 (9)	23,235	Y#11-19	—	400
MS11	1934 (9)	2,533	Y#1-9	—	575
MS12	1934 (8)	30,000	Y#1-8	—	75.00
MS13	1935 (9)	2,105	Y#1-9	—	685
MS14	1935 (8)	9,000	Y#1-8	—	250
MS15	1936 (9)	8,239	Y#1-8, 10	—	350
MS16	1936 (8)	40,000	Y#1-8	—	75.00
MS17	1937 (9)	2,000	Y#1-8, 10	—	3,075
MS18	1937 (8)	20,000	Y#1-8	—	75.00
MS19	1938 (3)	—	Y#1-2, 10 Rare	—	—
MS20	1939 (9)	2,700	Y#22-30.1	—	435
MS21	1939 (8)	10,000	Y#22-29	—	110
MS22	1939 (2)	30,000	Y#20, 21	—	60.00
MS23	1940 (9)	2,000	Y#22, 23, 24a-27a, 28-30.1	—	470
MS24	1940 (8)	10,000	Y#22, 23, 24a-27a, 28-29	—	100
MS25	1941 (9)	2,000	Y#22, 23, 24a-27a, 28-30.2	—	58
MS26	1941 (8)	4,000	Y#22, 23, 24a-27a, 28-29	—	20
MS27	1942 (9)	2,000	Y#31-39	—	63
MS28	1942 (8)	4,000	Y#31-38	—	23
MSA29	1942 (4)	—	Y#33-36	—	—
MS29	1943 (9)	1,000	Y#31-39	—	82
MS30	1943 (8)	1,000	Y#31-38	—	32
MS31	1944 (9)	1,000	Y#31-39	—	82
MS32	1944 (8)	1,000	Y#31-38	—	32
MS33	1945 (9)	1,000	Y#31-39	—	82
MS34	1945 (8)	1,000	Y#31-38	—	32
MS35	1946 (9)	1,000	Y#31-39	—	82
MS36	1946 (8)	1,000	Y#31-38	—	32
MS37	1947 (5)	1,000	Y#39-43	—	53
MS38	1947 (4)	50,000	Y#40-43	—	28.0
MS39	1947 (2)	—	Y#42-43	—	16.0
MS40	1948 (5)	5,000	Y#39-43	—	28
MS41	1948 (4)	10,000	Y#40-43	—	28.0
MS42	1949 (5)	1,000	Y#39-43	—	53
MS43	1949 (4)	10,000	Y#40-43	—	35.0
MS44	1950 (5)	20,000	Y#44-48	—	26
MS45	1950 (4)	50,000	Y#44-47	—	23.0
MS46	1951 (5)	1,000	Y#49.1-53.1	—	60
MS47	1951 (4)	400,000	Y#49.1, 50, 51.1-52.1	—	5.0
MS54	1956 (7)	1,000	Y#49.2-55	—	60
MS48	1952 (5)	1,000	Y#49.1-52.1, 53.1	—	6
MS49	1952 (4)	400,000	Y#49.1-52.1	—	5.
MS50	1953 (5)	1,000	Y#49.1-52.1, 53.1	—	5
MS51	1953 (4)	400,000	Y#49.1-52.1	—	5.0
MS52	1955 (7)	1,000	Y#49.1-55	—	6
MS53	1955 (6)	10,000	Y#49.1-52.1, 54.1, 55	—	18.
MS55	1956 (6)	10,000	Y#49.2-52.2, 54.2, 55	—	18.
MS56	1957 (8)	2,000	Y#49.1-A52, A53, 54.2, 55	—	3
MS57	1957 (6)	20,000	Y#49.1-52.2, 54.2, 55	—	12.
MS58	1958 (8)	3,000	Y#49.1-52.2, 54.2-57	—	3
MS59	1958 (7)	20,000	Y#49.1-52.2, 54.2-56	—	35.
MS60	1959 (9)	3,000	Y#58.1-64.1, 65-66	—	1,3
MS61	1959 (8)	25,000	Y#58.1-64.1, 65	—	75.
MS62	1960 (8)	25,000	Y#58.1-59.1, 60.2-64.2, 65.1	—	75.
MS63	1961 (8)	25,000	Y#58.2-62.2, 63.2-64.2, 65.1	—	60.
MS64	1962 (8)	25,000	Y#58.2-64.2, 65.1	—	55.
MS65	1962 (8)	50,000	Y#67-74	—	45
MS66	1963 (8)	60,000	Y#76.1-83.1	—	65
MS68	1964 (8)	60,000	Y#76.2-79.2, 80.1-81.1, 82.2-83.2	—	45
MS69	1965 (8)	60,000	Y#76.2-83.2	—	35
MS70	1966 (8)	90,000	Y#84-91	—	28
MS71	1967 (8)	100,000	Y#92-99	3.25	28
MS72	1968 (8)	100,000	Y#100-107	4.20	28
MS73	1969 (8)	100,000	Y#108-115	4.20	25
MS74	1970 (8)	100,000	Y#116-123	5.00	25
MS75	1971 (8)	110,000	Y#116-123	—	25
MS76	1972 (8)	110,000	Y#116-123	6.00	25

KM#	Date	Mintage	Identification	Issue Price	Mkt Val
MS77	1973 (8)	120,000	Y#116-123	6.75	25.00
MS78	1974 (8)	120,000	Y#116-123	7.25	25.00
MS79	1975 (8)	132,000	Y#116-123	9.00	25.00
MS80	1975 (8)	170,000	Y#124-131	—	28.00
MSA80	1975 (5)	—	Y#126-130	—	7.50
MS81	1976 (8)	180,000	Y#116-123	—	22.00
MS82	1977 (7)	180,000	Y#116-120, 122, 132	—	25.00
MS83	1978 (7)	180,000	Y#133-139	—	25.00
MS84	1979 (6)	156,000	Y#143-148	—	25.00
MS85	1980 (6)	—	Y#143-148	18.00	25.00
MS86	1981 (6)	—	Y#155-160	—	25.00
MS87	1982 (7)	120,000	Y#161-167	—	30.00
MS88	1983 (7)	120,000	Y#170-176	—	32.00
MS93	1983/84 (2)	130,000	Y#168-169	—	40.00
MS89	1984 (7)	—	Y#177-183	—	30.00
MS90	1985 (7)	—	Y#185-191	—	35.00
MS91	1986 (7)	—	Y#192-198	23.50	30.00
MS92	1987 (7)	—	Y#199-205	27.00	30.00
MSA93	1987 (5)	—	Y#200-204	—	10.00
MS94	1988 (7)	—	Y#206-212	—	30.00
MS95	1989 (7)	—	Y#213-219	30.00	32.00
MS96	1990 (7)	—	Y#220-226	33.00	35.00
MS97	1991 (7)	—	Y#228-234	25.00	28.00
MS98	1992 (7)	—	Y#236-242	25.00	28.00
MS99	1993 (7)	—	Y#244-250	—	32.00
MS100	1994 (7)	—	Y#252-258	—	32.00
MS101	1995 (7)	—	Y#262-268	32.50	35.00
MS102	1996 (7)	—	Y#272-278	33.00	35.00
MS103	1997 (8)	—	Y#280-287	—	37.50
MS104	1998 (8)	—	Y#293-300	—	37.50
MS105	1999 (8)	—	Y#205-312	—	37.50
MS106	(2000) (8)	—	Y#323-330	37.50	—
MS108	2002 (8)	80,000	Y#341-348	12.00	850

PROOF SETS

M#	Date	Mintage	Identification	Issue Price	Mkt Val
S1	1995 (2)	30,000	Y#260-261	75.00	100
S2	1996 (2)	30,000	Y#270-271	75.00	140
S4	1997 (2)	6,000	Y#288-289	547	625
S3	1998 (2)	30,000	Y#290-291	—	140
S5	2002 (8)	9,000	Y#341-348	75.00	1,450

PROVA SETS

M#	Date	Mintage	Identification	Issue Price	Mkt Val
S1	1951 (4)	103	Pr1-Pr4	—	300
S2	1952 (4)	103	Pr5-Pr8	—	300
S3	1953 (4)	103	Pr9-Pr12	—	300
S4	1955 (6)	103	Pr13-Pr18	—	425
S5	1956 (6)	103	Pr19-Pr24	—	425
S6	1957 (7)	103	Pr25-31	—	425
S7	1958 (8)	103	Pr32-Pr39	—	600
S8	1959 (8)	103	Pr40-Pr47	—	600
S9	1960 (8)	103	Pr48-Pr55	—	600
S10	1961 (8)	103	Pr56-Pr63	—	600
S11	1962 (8)	103	Pr64-Pr71	—	600
S12	1962 (8)	103	Pr72-Pr79	—	600
S13	1963 (8)	103	Pr80-Pr87	—	600
S14	1964 (8)	103	Pr88-Pr95	—	600
S15	1965 (8)	103	Pr96-103	—	600
S16	1966 (8)	103	Pr104-Pr111	—	600
S17	1967 (8)	103	Pr112-Pr119	—	600
S18	1968 (8)	103	Pr120-Pr127	—	600
S19	1969 (8)	103	Pr128-Pr135	—	600
S20	1970 (8)	103	Pr136-Pr143	—	600
S21	1971 (8)	103	Pr144-Pr151	—	600
S22	1972 (8)	103	Pr152-Pr159	—	600
S23	1973 (8)	103	Pr160-Pr167	—	600
S24	1974 (8)	103	Pr168-Pr175	—	600
S25	1975 (8)	103	Pr176-Pr183	—	600
S26	1975 (8)	103	Pr184-Pr191	—	600

VENEZUELA

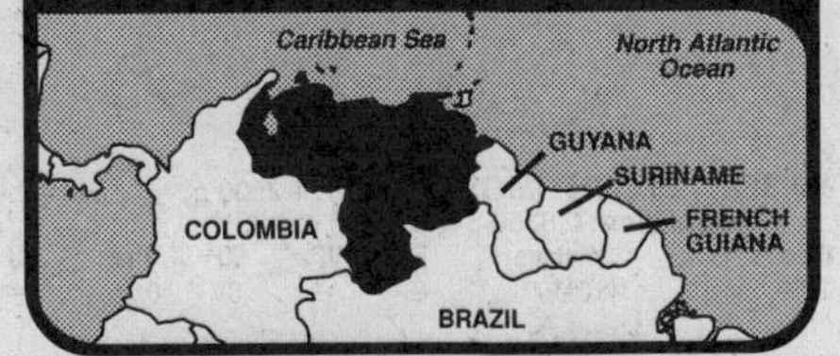

The Republic of Venezuela ("Little Venice"); located on the northern coast of South America between Colombia and Guyana, has an area of 352,145 sq. mi.(912,050 sq. km.) and a population of 20 million. Capital: Caracas. Petroleum and mining provide a significant portion of Venezuela's exports. Coffee, grown on 60,000 plantations, is the chief crop. Metalurgy, refining, oil, iron and steel production are the main employment industries.

Columbus discovered Venezuela on his third voyage in 1498. Initial exploration did not reveal Venezuela to be a land of great wealth. An active pearl trade operated on the offshore islands and slavers raided the interior in search of Indians to be sold into slavery, but no significant mainland settlements were made before 1567 when Caracas was founded. Venezuela, the home of Bolivar, was among the first South American colonies to rebel against Spain in 1810. The declaration of Independence of Venezuela was signed by seven provinces which are represented by the seven stars of the Venezuelan flag. Coinage of Caracas and Margarita use the seven stars in their designs. These original provinces were: Barcelona, Barinas, Caracas, Cumana, Margarita, Merida and Trujillo. The Provinces of Coro, Guyana and Maracaibo were added to Venezuela during the Independence War. Independence was attained in 1821 but not recognized by Spain until 1845. Together with Ecuador, Panama and Colombia, Venezuela was part of "Gran Colombia" until 1830, when it became a sovereign and independent state.

RULERS

Republic, 1823-present

MINT MARKS

A - Paris
(a) - Paris, privy marks only
(aa) - Altena
(b) - Berlin
(bb) - Brussels
(cc) – Canada

(c) - Caracas
(d) - Denver
H, Heaton - Heaton, Birmingham
(l) - London
(m) - Madrid
(mm) - Mexico
(o) - Ontario
(p) - Philadelphia
(s) - San Francisco
(sc) - Schwerte - Vereinigte Deutsche Nickelwerke
(w) - Werdohl - Vereinigte Deutsche Metalwerke

MONETARY SYSTEM

100 Centimos = 1 Bolivar

REPUBLIC OF VENEZUELA

REFORM COINAGE

1896; 100 Centimos = 1 Bolivar

Y# 27 5 CENTIMOS Composition: Copper-Nickel

Date	Mintage	F	VF	XF	Unc	BU
1896(b)	4,000,000	0.50	2.00	17.00	75.00	—
1915(p)	2,000,000	1.00	4.00	40.00	135	—
1921(p)	2,000,000	0.50	2.00	50.00	150	—
1925(p)	2,000,000	0.30	1.00	6.00	15.00	—
1927(p)	2,000,000	0.30	1.00	6.00	15.00	—
1929(p)	2,000,000	0.25	1.00	6.00	15.00	—
1936(p)	5,000,000	0.15	0.50	4.00	10.00	—
1938(p)	6,000,000	0.10	0.20	3.00	8.00	—

Y# 29 5 CENTIMOS Composition: Brass

Date	Mintage	F	VF	XF	Unc	BU
1944(d)	4,000,000	0.50	1.00	4.50	20.00	—

Y# 29a 5 CENTIMOS Composition: Copper-Nickel

Date	Mintage	F	VF	XF	Unc	BU
1945(p)	12,000,000	0.10	0.20	0.50	3.00	—
1946(p)	12,000,000	0.10	0.20	0.50	3.00	—
1948(p)	18,000,000	0.10	0.20	0.50	3.00	—

Y# 38.1 5 CENTIMOS Composition: Copper-Nickel

Date	Mintage	F	VF	XF	Unc	BU
1958(p)	25,000,000	—	—	—	0.75	—

Y# 38.2 5 CENTIMOS Composition: Copper-Nickel

Date	Mintage	F	VF	XF	Unc	BU
1964(m)	40,000,000	—	—	—	0.50	—
1965(m)	60,000,000	—	—	—	0.50	—

Y# 38.3 5 CENTIMOS Composition: Copper-Nickel

Date	Mintage	F	VF	XF	Unc	BU
1971(o)	40,000,000	—	—	—	0.50	—

Y# 49 5 CENTIMOS Composition: Copper Clad Steel

Date	Mintage	F	VF	XF	Unc	BU
1974(w)	200,000,000	—	—	—	0.15	—
1976(w)	200,000,000	—	—	—	0.15	—
1977(l)	600,000,000	—	—	—	0.15	—

Y# 49a 5 CENTIMOS Composition: Nickel Clad Steel

Date	Mintage	F	VF	XF	Unc	BU
1983(w)	600,000,000	—	—	—	0.10	—

Y# 49b 5 CENTIMOS Comp.: Copper-Nickel Clad Steel

Date	Mintage	F	VF	XF	Unc	BU
1986(w)	500,000,000	—	—	—	0.10	—

Y# A40 10 CENTIMOS Composition: Copper-Nickel

Date	Mintage	F	VF	XF	Unc	BU
1971(o)	60,000,000	—	—	0.10	0.25	—

Y# 28 12-1/2 CENTIMOS Composition: Copper-Nickel
Note: Varieties exist.

Date	Mintage	F	VF	XF	Unc	BU
1925(p)	800,000	2.50	6.50	45.00	200	—
1927(p)	800,000	1.00	2.00	12.00	75.00	—
1929(p)	800,000	0.15	0.50	5.00	45.00	—

Date	Mintage	F	VF	XF	Unc	BU
1936(p)	1,200,000	0.15	0.30	2.00	25.00	—
1938(p)	1,600,000	0.15	0.30	1.00	18.00	—

Y# 30 12-1/2 CENTIMOS **Composition:** Brass

Date	Mintage	F	VF	XF	Unc	BU
1944(d)	800,000	2.50	4.50	9.00	60.00	—

Y# 30a 12-1/2 CENTIMOS **Composition:** Copper-Nickel

Date	Mintage	F	VF	XF	Unc	BU
1945(p)	11,200,000	0.10	0.20	0.35	9.00	—
1946(p)	9,200,000	0.10	0.20	0.35	12.00	—
1948(s)	6,000,000	0.10	0.20	0.35	8.00	—

Y# 39 12-1/2 CENTIMOS **Composition:** Copper-Nickel **Reverse:** Value within wreath, knobbed 2

Date	Mintage	F	VF	XF	Unc	BU
1958(p)	10,000,000	—	—	0.20	3.00	—

Y# A39.1 12-1/2 CENTIMOS **Composition:** Copper-Nickel **Obverse:** Flat stars **Reverse:** Plain 2

Date	Mintage	F	VF	XF	Unc	BU
1969(m)	2,000,000	—	—	—	200	—

Y# A39.2 12-1/2 CENTIMOS **Composition:** Copper-Nickel **Obverse:** Raised stars **Reverse:** Outlined stem ends

Date	F	VF	XF	Unc	BU
1969(m)	—	—	—	300	—

Y# A39.3 12-1/2 CENTIMOS **Composition:** Copper-Nickel **Reverse:** Solid stem ends

Date	F	VF	XF	Unc	BU
1969(m)	—	—	—	300	—

Note: 1969 dated strikes were not released into circulation

Y# 20 1/4 BOLIVAR **Weight:** 1.2500 g. **Composition:** 0.8350 Silver .0336 oz. ASW

Date	Mintage	F	VF	XF	Unc	BU
1901(a)	393,000	7.00	25.00	55.00	300	800
1903(p)	400,000	6.00	20.00	50.00	250	750
1911(a)	600,000	2.50	5.00	12.00	75.00	200
1912(a)	800,000	3.00	6.00	15.00	100	300
1919(p)	400,000	2.50	5.00	12.00	75.00	200
1921(p) High 2	800,000	2.00	4.00	10.00	50.00	125
1921(p) Low 2	Inc. above	1.00	3.00	10.00	50.00	125
1924(p)	400,000	1.00	3.00	10.00	35.00	100
1929(p)	1,200,000	—	BV	1.00	6.00	15.00
1935(p)	3,400,000	—	BV	1.00	3.00	8.00
1936(p)	2,800,000	—	BV	1.00	3.00	8.00
1944(p)	1,800,000	—	BV	1.00	2.00	5.00
1945(p)	8,000,000	—	—	BV	1.50	2.50
1946(p)	8,000,000	—	—	BV	1.00	2.00
1948(s)	8,638,000	—	—	BV	1.00	2.00

Y# 35 25 CENTIMOS **Weight:** 1.2500 g. **Composition:** 0.8350 Silver .0336 oz. ASW

Date	Mintage	F	VF	XF	Unc	BU
1954(p)	36,000,000	—	—	BV	1.00	—

Y# 35a 25 CENTIMOS **Weight:** 1.2500 g. **Composition:** 0.8350 Silver .0336 oz. ASW

Date	Mintage	F	VF	XF	Unc	BU
1960(a)	48,000,000	—	—	BV	0.75	—

Y# 40 25 CENTIMOS **Composition:** Nickel

Date	Mintage	F	VF	XF	Unc	BU
1965(l)	240,000,000	—	—	0.10	0.35	—

Y# 50.1 25 CENTIMOS **Weight:** 1.7500 g. **Composition:** Nickel **Note:** 1.18 thick

Date	Mintage	F	VF	XF	Unc	BU
1977(w)	240,000,000	—	—	0.10	0.25	—

Y# 50.2 25 CENTIMOS **Weight:** 1.5000 g. **Composition:** Nickel **Note:** Dies vary for each date; thin.

Date	Mintage	F	VF	XF	Unc	BU
1977(w)	Inc. above	—	—	0.10	0.25	—
1978(w)	200,000,000	—	—	0.10	0.25	—
1987	150,000,000	—	—	0.10	0.25	—

Y# 50a 25 CENTIMOS **Weight:** 1.5000 g. **Composition:** Nickel Clad Steel **Note:** Varieties exist.

Date	Mintage	F	VF	XF	Unc	BU
1989(sc)	510,000,000	—	—	0.10	0.25	—
1990(mm)	400,000,000	—	—	0.10	0.25	—

Y# 21 1/2 BOLIVAR **Weight:** 2.5000 g. **Composition:** 0.8350 Silver .0671 oz. ASW

Date	Mintage	F	VF	XF	Unc	BU
1901(a)	600,000	20.00	50.00	175	1,200	2,500
1903(p)	200,000	75.00	200	600	2,000	5,000
1911(a)	300,000	30.00	60.00	200	600	2,000
1912(a)	1,920,000	5.00	15.00	50.00	300	1,000
1919(p)	400,000	6.00	20.00	80.00	400	1,000
1921(p) Normal date	600,000	2.50	7.00	16.00	100	250
1921(p) Narrow date	Inc. above	3.50	9.00	27.50	125	300
1921(p) Wide date	Inc. above	3.50	9.00	27.50	125	300
1924(p)	800,000	2.50	7.00	16.00	85.00	200
1929(p)	400,000	1.00	2.00	6.00	55.00	135
1935(p)	1,000,000	—	BV	1.00	12.00	28.00
1936(p)	600,000	BV	1.00	5.00	50.00	125

Note: Privy mark placement varies with 1901 and 1911

Y# 21a 1/2 BOLIVAR **Weight:** 2.5000 g. **Composition:** 0.8350 Silver .0671 oz. ASW

Date	Mintage	F	VF	XF	Unc	BU
1944(d) Accent in Bolivar	500,000	1.00	3.00	5.00	15.00	—
1944(d) Without accent in Bolivar	Inc. above	1.50	5.00	10.00	25.00	—
1945(p)	4,000,000	—	BV	1.00	5.00	—
1946(p)	2,500,000	—	BV	1.00	5.00	—

Y# 36 50 CENTIMOS **Weight:** 2.5000 g. **Composition:** 0.8350 Silver .0671 oz. ASW

Date	Mintage	F	VF	XF	Unc	BU
1954(p)	15,000,000	—	—	BV	3.00	—

Y# 36a 50 CENTIMOS **Weight:** 2.5000 g. **Composition:** 0.8350 Silver .0671 oz. ASW

Date	Mintage	F	VF	XF	Unc	BU
1960(a)	20,000,000	—	—	BV	2.00	—

Y# 41 50 CENTIMOS **Composition:** Nickel

Date	Mintage	F	VF	XF	Unc	BU
1965(l)	180,000,000	—	0.10	0.15	0.35	—
1985(o)	50,000,000	—	0.10	0.15	0.35	—

Y# 41a 50 CENTIMOS **Weight:** 3.2000 g. **Composition:** Nickel Clad Steel

Date	Mintage	F	VF	XF	Unc	BU
1988(w)	80,000,000	—	0.10	0.15	0.30	—
1989(w)	260,000,000	—	0.10	0.15	0.30	—
1990(l)	300,000,000	—	0.10	0.15	0.30	—

Note: Die varieties exist for 1990 dated strikes

Y# 22 BOLIVAR **Weight:** 5.0000 g. **Composition:** 0.8350 Silver .1342 oz. ASW

Date	Mintage	F	VF	XF	Unc	BU
1901(a)	323,000	20.00	55.00	150	650	1,25
1903(p)	800,000	5.00	15.00	90.00	350	85
1911(a)	1,500,000	3.00	5.00	40.00	200	65
1912(a) Wide date	820,000	6.00	16.50	75.00	300	80
1912(a) Narrow date	Inc. above	6.00	16.50	75.00	300	80
1919(p)	1,000,000	2.00	3.00	12.00	45.00	1
1921(p)	1,000,000	2.00	3.00	12.00	40.00	1
1924(p)	1,500,000	BV	2.00	6.00	30.00	75.0
1926(p)	1,000,000	BV	2.00	6.00	30.00	75.0
1929(p)	2,500,000	—	BV	1.50	8.00	20.0
1935(p)	5,000,000	—	BV	1.50	5.00	12.
1936(p)	5,000,000	—	BV	1.50	5.00	12.

Y# 22a BOLIVAR **Weight:** 5.0000 g. **Composition:** 0.8350 Silver .1342 oz. ASW

Date	Mintage	F	VF	XF	Unc
1945(p)	8,000,000	—	—	BV	3.50

Y# 37 BOLIVAR **Weight:** 5.0000 g. **Composition:** 0.8350 Silver .1342 oz. ASW

Date	Mintage	F	VF	XF	Unc
1954(p)	13,500,000	—	—	BV	2.50

Y# 37a BOLIVAR **Weight:** 5.0000 g. **Composition:** 0.8350 Silver .1342 oz. ASW

Date	Mintage	F	VF	XF	Unc
1960(a) Thin letters	30,000,000	—	—	BV	1.50

Date	Mintage	F	VF	XF	Unc	BU
1960(a) Thick letters	Inc. above	—	—	BV	1.50	—
1965(l)	20,000,000	—	—	BV	1.50	—

Y# 42 BOLIVAR **Composition:** Nickel

Date	Mintage	F	VF	XF	Unc	BU
1967(l)	180,000,000	—	0.10	0.15	0.75	—

Y# 52 BOLIVAR **Composition:** Nickel **Note:** Dies vary for each date.

Date	Mintage	F	VF	XF	Unc	BU
1977(l)	200,000,000	—	0.10	0.15	0.65	—
1986(w)	200,000,000	—	0.10	0.15	0.50	—
1986(w)	50,000,000	—	—	—	—	—

Y# 52a.2 BOLIVAR **Composition:** Nickel Clad Steel **Obverse:** Large letters and date **Reverse:** Large letters and date **Note:** Dies vary for each date.

Date	Mintage	F	VF	XF	Unc	BU
1989(sc)	600,000,000	—	0.10	0.15	0.45	—
1990(mm)	600,000,000	—	0.10	0.15	0.45	—

Y# 52a.1 BOLIVAR **Comp.:** Nickel Clad Steel **Obverse:** Small letters and date **Reverse:** Small letters and date

Date	Mintage	F	VF	XF	Unc	BU
1989(w)	370,000,000	—	0.10	0.15	0.45	—

 # 23 2 BOLIVARES **Weight:** 10.0000 g. **Composition:** 0.8350 Silver .2685 oz. ASW

ate	Mintage	F	VF	XF	Unc	BU
902(p)	500,000	11.50	45.00	200	700	1,500
903(p)	500,000	11.50	25.00	125	400	1,250
904(a) Large 0, small 4	550,000	11.50	40.00	175	500	1,000
904(a) Large 0, large 4	Inc. above	11.50	40.00	175	650	1,500
904(a) Small 0, large 4	Inc. above	11.50	45.00	200	750	1,500
04(a) Small 0, large lant 4	Inc. above	11.50	45.00	200	750	1,500
04(a) Small 0, small 4	50,000	20.00	55.00	250	900	1,650
05(a) Upright 5	750,000	3.50	16.50	100	400	1,000
05(a) Slant 5	Inc. above	3.50	16.50	120	400	1,000
11(a)	750,000	3.50	16.50	60.00	275	650
12(a)	500,000	3.50	16.50	140	400	1,000
13(a) Normal date	210,000	40.00	250	500	1,000	1,750
13(a) Raised 3	Inc. above	40.00	250	500	1,000	1,750
19(p)	1,000,000	BV	3.50	11.50	125	300
22(p) Narrow date	1,000,000	BV	3.50	11.50	85.00	200
22(p) Wide date	Inc. above	BV	3.50	11.50	85.00	200
22(p) Low first 2	Inc. above	BV	0.50	11.50	85.00	200
24(p)	1,250,000	BV	3.50	11.50	85.00	200
26(p)	1,000,000	BV	3.50	11.50	85.00	200
29(p)	1,500,000	BV	2.75	8.00	20.00	45.00
30(p)	425,000	2.75	7.00	25.00	130	300
35(p)	3,000,000	BV	2.75	4.00	8.00	20.00
36(p)	2,500,000	BV	2.75	4.00	8.00	20.00

 # 23a 2 BOLIVARES **Weight:** 10.0000 g. **Composition:** 0.8350 Silver .2685 oz. ASW

e	Mintage	F	VF	XF	Unc	BU
5(p)	3,000,000	—	—	BV	3.50	—

Y# A37 2 BOLIVARES **Weight:** 10.0000 g. **Composition:** 0.8350 Silver .2685 oz. ASW

Date	Mintage	F	VF	XF	Unc	BU
1960(a)	4,000,000	—	—	BV	3.50	—
1965(l)	7,170,000	—	—	BV	3.50	—

Y# 43 2 BOLIVARES **Composition:** Nickel **Note:** Dies vary for each date.

Date	Mintage	F	VF	XF	Unc	BU
1967(l)	50,000,000	—	—	0.25	1.25	—
1986(w)	50,000,000	—	—	0.25	1.25	—
Note: Die varieites exist for 1986 strikes						
1986(w)	—	—	—	—	—	—
Note: Die varieties exist for 1986 strikes						
1988(c)	80,000,000	—	—	0.25	1.25	—

Y# 43a.1 2 BOLIVARES **Composition:** Nickel Clad Steel **Obverse:** Small letters **Reverse:** Small letters

Date	Mintage	F	VF	XF	Unc	BU
1989(sc)	200,000,000	—	—	0.20	0.75	—
1990(c)	400,000,000	—	—	0.20	0.75	—

Note: Two varieties of 1990 exist

Y# 43a.2 2 BOLIVARES **Composition:** Nickel Clad Steel **Obverse:** Large letters **Reverse:** Large letters

Date	Mintage	F	VF	XF	Unc	BU
1989(w)	100,000,000	—	—	0.20	0.75	—
1989(c)	95,000,000	—	—	0.20	0.75	—

Y# 24.2 (Y24.1) 5 BOLIVARES **Weight:** 25.0000 g. **Composition:** 0.9000 Silver .7234 oz. ASW **Obverse:** Date on ribbon right of arms 13 DE APRIL DE 1864

Date	Mintage	F	VF	XF	Unc	BU
1901(a)	90,000	20.00	100	375	1,500	5,000
1901(a)	90,000	20.00	100	375	1,500	5,000
1902(p) Wide date	500,000	9.00	16.00	120	700	1,500
1902(p) Wide date	500,000	9.00	16.00	120	700	1,500
1902(p) Narrow date	Inc. above	9.00	16.00	120	700	1,500
1902(p) Narrow date	Inc. above	9.00	16.00	120	700	1,500
1903(p)	200,000	9.00	16.00	120	700	1,500
1903(p)	200,000	9.00	16.00	120	700	1,500
1904(a)	200,000	9.00	16.00	150	1,000	3,000
1904(a)	200,000	9.00	16.00	150	1,000	3,000
1905(a)	300,000	9.00	16.00	120	650	1,250
1905(a)	300,000	9.00	16.00	120	650	1,250
1910(a) Oval 0	400,000	9.00	16.00	85.00	450	900
1910(a) Oval 0	400,000	9.00	16.00	85.00	450	900
1910(a) Round 0	Inc. above	12.00	25.00	130	650	1,250
1910(a) Round 0	Inc. above	12.00	25.00	130	650	1,250
1911(a) Normal date	1,104,000	6.50	12.50	45.00	225	500
1911(a) Normal date	1,104,000	6.50	12.50	45.00	225	500
1911(a) Wide date	Inc. above	6.50	12.50	45.00	225	500
1911(a) Wide date	Inc. above	6.50	12.50	45.00	225	500
1911(a) Narrow date	Inc. above	6.50	12.50	45.00	225	500
1911(a) Narrow date	Inc. above	6.50	12.50	45.00	225	500
1912(a) Normal date	696,000	6.50	12.50	45.00	225	500
1912(a) Normal date	696,000	6.50	12.50	45.00	225	500
1912(a) Wide date	Inc. above	6.50	12.50	45.00	225	500
1912(a) Wide date	Inc. above	6.50	12.50	45.00	225	500
1912(a) Narrow date	Inc. above	6.50	12.50	45.00	225	500
1912(a) Narrow date	Inc. above	6.50	12.50	45.00	225	500
1919(p)	400,000	6.50	12.50	30.00	175	350
1919(p)	400,000	6.50	12.50	30.00	175	350
1921(p) Wide date	500,000	6.50	12.50	25.00	100	200
1921(p) Wide date	500,000	6.50	12.50	25.00	100	200
1921(p) Narrow date	Inc. above	6.50	12.50	25.00	100	200
1921(p) Narrow date	Inc. above	6.50	12.50	25.00	100	200
1924(p) Wide date	500,000	6.50	12.50	25.00	100	200
1924(p) Wide date	500,000	6.50	12.50	25.00	100	200
1924(p) Narrow date	Inc. above	6.50	12.50	25.00	100	200
1924(p) Narrow date	Inc. above	6.50	12.50	25.00	100	200
1924(p) Low 9	Inc. above	6.50	12.50	25.00	100	200
1924(p) Low 9	Inc. above	6.50	12.50	25.00	100	200
1926(p)	800,000	BV	8.50	22.50	80.00	150
1926(p)	800,000	BV	8.50	22.50	80.00	150
1929(p) High 9	800,000	BV	8.50	22.00	60.00	120
1929(p) High 9	800,000	BV	8.50	22.00	60.00	120
1929(p) Low 9	Inc. above	BV	8.50	22.00	60.00	120
1929(p) Low 9	Inc. above	BV	8.50	22.00	60.00	120
1935(p)	1,600,000	BV	7.50	16.50	38.00	75.00
1935(p)	1,600,000	BV	7.50	16.50	38.00	75.00

Date	Mintage	F	VF	XF	Unc	BU
1936(p) Normal date	2,000,000	BV	7.50	16.50	38.00	75.00
1936(p) Normal date	2,000,000	BV	7.50	16.50	38.00	75.00
1936(p) High 3	Inc. above	BV	7.50	16.50	38.00	75.00
1936(p) High 3	Inc. above	BV	7.50	16.50	38.00	75.00
1936(p) Low 3	Inc. above	BV	7.50	16.50	38.00	75.00
1936(p) Low 3	Inc. above	BV	7.50	16.50	38.00	75.00

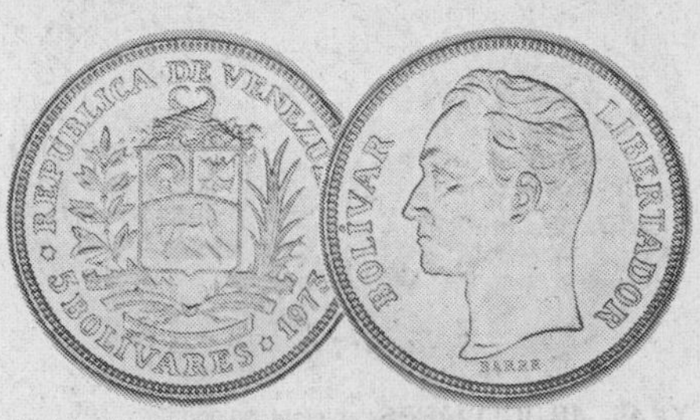

Y# 44 5 BOLIVARES **Composition:** Nickel

Date	Mintage	F	VF	XF	Unc	BU
1973(m)	20,000,000	—	0.45	0.75	1.75	—

Y# 53 5 BOLIVARES **Composition:** Nickel

Date	Mintage	F	VF	XF	Unc	BU
1977(m)	60,000,000	—	—	0.50	1.50	—
1987(c)	25,000,000	—	—	0.50	1.50	—
1987(c)	—	—	—	—	—	—
1988(w)	20,000,000	—	—	0.50	1.50	—

Y# 53a.1 5 BOLIVARES **Weight:** 13.3000 g. **Composition:** Nickel Clad Steel **Obverse:** Small letters **Reverse:** Large letters

Date	Mintage	F	VF	XF	Unc	BU
1989(w)	55,000,000	—	—	0.50	1.50	—
1989(w) Prooflike	26,000,000	—	—	—	—	—

Y# 53a.2 5 BOLIVARES **Weight:** 13.3000 g. **Composition:** Nickel Clad Steel **Obverse:** Large letters **Reverse:** Small letters

Date	Mintage	F	VF	XF	Unc	BU
1989(sc)	100,000,000	—	—	0.50	1.50	—
1990(c)	200,000,000	—	—	0.50	1.50	—

Y# 53a.3 5 BOLIVARES **Weight:** 13.3000 g. **Comp.:** Nickel Clad Steel **Note:** Large letters in legends.

Date	F	VF	XF	Unc	BU
1990	—	—	0.65	1.75	—

Y# 31 10 BOLIVARES **Weight:** 3.2258 g. **Composition:** 0.9000 Gold .0933 oz. AGW

Date	F	VF	XF	Unc	BU
1930(p)	—	BV	40.00	75.00	120

Note: Only 10% of the total mintage was released; the balance remaining as part of the nation's gold reserve

Y# 45 10 BOLIVARES **Weight:** 30.0000 g. **Composition:** 0.9000 Silver .8681 oz. ASW

Date	Mintage	F	VF	XF	Unc	BU
1973(o)	2,000,000	—	—	—	11.50	—
1973(o) Proof	200	Value: 400				

Y# 75 10 BOLIVARES **Composition:** Nickel Clad Steel **Obverse:** National arms above denomination **Reverse:** Bolivar

Date	F	VF	XF	Unc	BU
1998	—	—	0.25	0.50	—

Y# 80 10 BOLIVARES **Weight:** 2.3300 g. **Composition:** Nickel Clad Steel **Obverse:** National arms and denomination. **Reverse:** Bolivar's portrait with new mint mark at left. **Edge:** Reeded. **Size:** 16.85 mm. **Note:** Struck at Maracay Mint.

Date	F	VF	XF	Unc	BU
2000	—	—	—	0.50	—

Y# 32 20 BOLIVARES **Weight:** 6.4516 g. **Composition:** 0.9000 Gold .1867 oz. AGW

Date	Mintage	F	VF	XF	Unc	BU
1904(a)	100,000	BV	70.00	80.00	110	—
1905(a)	100,000	BV	70.00	80.00	110	—
1910(a)	70,000	BV	70.00	80.00	110	—

Note: Die varieties exist in the placement of dot between date and Lei, Type 1 is evenly space, Type 2 had dot closer to L of Lei

Date	Mintage	F	VF	XF	Unc	BU
1911(a)	80,000	BV	70.00	80.00	110	—

Note: Die varieties exist in the placement of dot between date and Lei, Type 1 is evenly space, Type 2 had dot closer to L of Lei

Date	Mintage	F	VF	XF	Unc	BU
1912(a)	150,000	BV	70.00	80.00	110	—

Note: Die varieties exist in the placement of the torch privy mark in relation to bust truncation; Type 1 is well below truncation, Type 2 is slightly below truncation and Type 3 is in line with the truncation

Y# 76 20 BOLIVARES **Composition:** Nickel Clad Steel **Obverse:** National arms above denomination **Reverse:** Bolivar

Date	F	VF	XF	Unc	BU
1998	—	—	0.25	0.50	—

Y# 81 20 BOLIVARES **Weight:** 4.3200 g. **Composition:** Nickel Clad Steel **Obverse:** National arms and denomination. **Reverse:** Bolivar's portrait with new mint mark at left. **Edge:** Plain. **Size:** 20 mm. **Note:** Struck at Maracay Mint.

Date	F	VF	XF	Unc	BU
2000	—	—	—	0.65	—

Y# 46 25 BOLIVARES **Weight:** 28.2800 g. **Composition:** 0.9250 Silver .8411 oz. ASW **Subject:** Conservation **Reverse:** Jaguar

Date	Mintage	F	VF	XF	Unc	BU
1975(l)	38,000	—	—	—	22.50	—
1975(l) Proof	8,000,000	Value: 32.50				

Y# 47 50 BOLIVARES **Weight:** 35.0000 g. **Composition:** 0.9250 Silver 1.0409 oz. ASW **Subject:** Conservation **Obverse:** Similar to 25 Bolivares, Y#46 **Reverse:** Giant Armadillo

Date	Mintage	F	VF	XF	Unc	BU
1975(l)	39,000	—	—	—	25.00	—
1975(l) Proof	8,000,000	Value: 35.00				

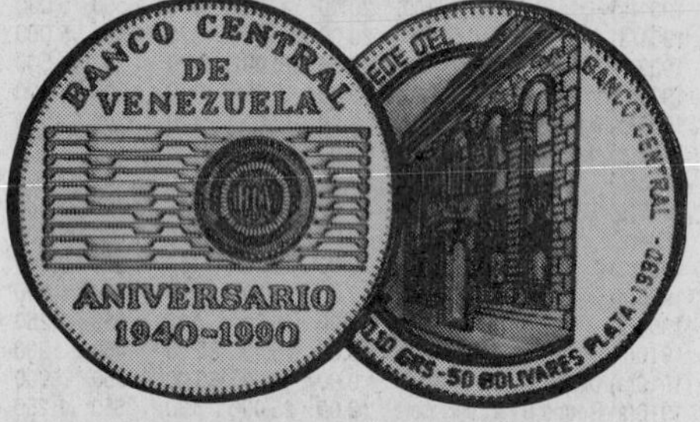

Y# 66 50 BOLIVARES **Weight:** 31.1000 g. **Composition:** 0.9000 Silver .9000 oz. ASW **Subject:** 50th Anniversary of Central Bank

Date	Mintage	F	VF	XF	Unc	BU
1990(c) Proof	10,000	Value: 45.00				

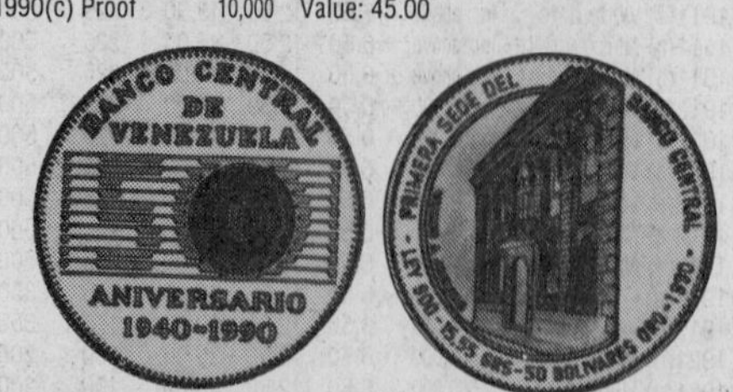

Y# 67 50 BOLIVARES **Weight:** 15.5500 g. **Composition:** 0.9000 Gold .4500 oz. AGW **Subject:** 50th Anniversary of Central Bank

Date	Mintage	F	VF	XF	Unc	BU
1990(c) Proof	5,000	Value: 350				

Y# 77 50 BOLIVARES **Composition:** Nickel Clad Steel **Obverse:** National arms above denomination **Reverse:** Bolivar

Date	F	VF	XF	Unc	BU
1998	—	—	0.35	0.75	—
1999(c)	—	—	0.40	0.80	—

Y# 82 50 BOLIVARES **Weight:** 6.6500 g. **Composition:** Nickel Clad Steel **Obverse:** National arms and denomination. **Reverse:** Bolivar's portrait with new mint mark at left. **Edge:** Reeded. **Size:** 23 mm.

Date	F	VF	XF	Unc	BU
2000	—	—	—	0.80	—

Y# 55 75 BOLIVARES **Weight:** 17.0000 g. **Composition:** 0.9000 Silver .4920 oz. ASW **Subject:** 50th Anniversary - Sucre's Death

Date	Mintage	F	VF	XF	Unc	BU
1980(l)	500,000	—	—	—	10.00	—
1980(l) Proof	200	Value: 450				

Y# 56 100 BOLIVARES **Weight:** 22.0000 g. **Composition:** 0.9000 Silver .6367 oz. ASW **Subject:** 150th Anniversary - Bolivar's Death

Date	Mintage	F	VF	XF	Unc	BU
1980(l)		—	—	—	12.50	—
1980(l) Proof	200	Value: 450				

Y# 57 100 BOLIVARES **Weight:** 27.0000 g. **Composition:** 0.8350 Silver .7249 oz. ASW **Subject:** 200th Anniversary - Birth of Andres Bello

Date	Mintage	F	VF	XF	Unc	BU
ND(1981)(w)		—	—	—	400	
ND(1981)(w) Proof	500,000	Value: 10.00				

Y# 58 100 BOLIVARES Weight: 31.0000 g. **Composition:** 0.9000 Silver .9000 oz. ASW **Subject:** 200th Anniversary - Birth of Simon Bolivar

Date	Mintage	F	VF	XF	Unc	BU
ND(1983)(w) Proof	300,000	Value: 17.50				

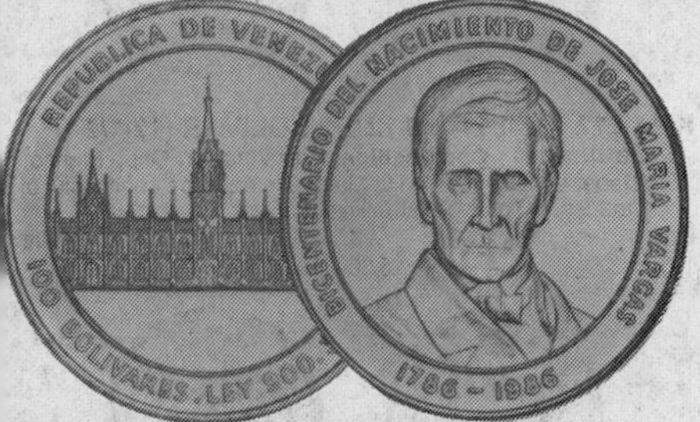

Y# 60 100 BOLIVARES Weight: 31.0000 g. **Composition:** 0.9000 Silver .9000 oz. ASW **Subject:** 200th Anniversary - Birth of Jose M. Vargas

Date	Mintage	F	VF	XF	Unc	BU
ND(1986)(l)	—	—	—	—	8.50	—
ND(1986)(l) Proof	500	Value: 250				

Note: Beware of some altered circulation coins to look like proofs

Y# 78 100 BOLIVARES **Composition:** Nickel Clad Steel **Obverse:** National arms above denomination **Reverse:** Bolivar

Date	F	VF	XF	Unc	BU
1998	—	—	0.50	1.00	—
1999(c)	—	—	0.60	1.20	—

Y# 54 500 BOLIVARES Weight: 18.0000 g. **Composition:** 0.9000 Gold .5209 oz. AGW **Subject:** Nationalization of Oil Industry

Date	Mintage	F	VF	XF	Unc	BU
1975(c) Proof	100	Value: 12,000				

Y# 64 500 BOLIVARES Weight: 31.1000 g. **Composition:** 0.9000 Silver .9000 oz. ASW **Reverse:** Jose Antonio Paez

Date	Mintage	F	VF	XF	Unc	BU
1990(mm) Proof	30,000	Value: 22.50				

Y# 69 500 BOLIVARES Weight: 31.1000 g. **Composition:** 0.9000 Silver .9000 oz. ASW **Subject:** Battle of Matasiete

Date	Mintage	F	VF	XF	Unc	BU
1992(w) Proof	10,000	Value: 25.00				

Y# 71 500 BOLIVARES Weight: 31.1000 g. **Composition:** 0.9000 Silver .9000 oz. ASW **Subject:** 50th Anniversary - United Nations

Date	Mintage	F	VF	XF	Unc	BU
1995(cc) Proof	10,000	Value: 25.00				

Y# 72 500 BOLIVARES Weight: 31.1000 g. **Composition:** 0.9000 Silver .9000 oz. ASW **Subject:** 200th Anniversary - Sucre's Birth

Date	Mintage	F	VF	XF	Unc	BU
1995(cc) Proof	15,000	Value: 25.00				

Y# 74 500 BOLIVARES Weight: 31.1000 g. **Composition:** 0.9000 Silver .9000 oz. ASW **Obverse:** National arms **Reverse:** Two portraits **Note:** Manuel Gual and Jose Maria Espana

Date	Mintage	F	VF	XF	Unc	BU
1997A Proof	10,000	Value: 25.00				

Y# 79 500 BOLIVARES **Composition:** Nickel Clad Steel **Obverse:** National arms above denomination **Reverse:** Bolivar

Date	F	VF	XF	Unc	BU
1998	—	—	0.75	1.50	—

Y# 48.1 1000 BOLIVARES Weight: 33.4370 g. **Comp.:** 0.9000 Gold .9676 oz. AGW **Subject:** Conservation Series - Cock of the Rocks **Reverse:** Feathered wings

Date	Mintage	F	VF	XF	Unc	BU
1975(l)	5,047	—	—	—	475	—
1975(l) Proof	483	Value: 950				

Y# 48.2 1000 BOLIVARES Weight: 33.4370 g. **Composition:** 0.9000 Gold .9676 oz. AGW **Subject:** Conservation Series - Cock of the Rocks **Reverse:** Smooth wings

Date	F	VF	XF	Unc	BU
1975(l)	—	—	—	500	—
1975(l) Proof reported, not confirmed	—	—	—	—	—

Y# 68 1100 BOLIVARES Weight: 27.0000 g. **Composition:** 0.9250 Silver .8029 oz. ASW **Subject:** Ibero - American Series

Date	Mintage	F	VF	XF	Unc	BU
1991(mm) Proof	30,000	Value: 60.00				

Y# 59 3000 BOLIVARES Weight: 31.1000 g. **Composition:** 0.9000 Gold .9000 oz. AGW **Subject:** 200th Anniversary - Birth of Simon Bolivar

Date	Mintage	F	VF	XF	Unc	BU
ND(1983)(w) Proof	10,000	Value: 425				

Y# 62 5000 BOLIVARES Weight: 15.5500 g. **Composition:** 0.9000 Gold .4500 oz. AGW **Reverse:** Rafael Urdaneta

Date	Mintage	F	VF	XF	Unc	BU
1988(cc) Proof	25,000	Value: 200				

Y# 63 5000 BOLIVARES Weight: 15.5500 g. **Composition:** 0.9000 Gold .4500 oz. AGW **Reverse:** Santiago Marino

Date	Mintage	F	VF	XF	Unc	BU
1988(cc) Proof	25,000	Value: 200				

Y# 65 5000 BOLIVARES **Weight:** 15.5500 g. **Composition:** 0.9000 Gold .4500 oz. AGW **Reverse:** Jose Antonio Paez

Date	Mintage	F	VF	XF	Unc	BU
1990(mm) Proof	10,000	Value: 200				

Y# 73 5000 BOLIVARES **Weight:** 15.5500 g. **Composition:** 0.9000 Gold .4500 oz. AGW **Subject:** 200th Anniversary - Sucre's Birth

Date	Mintage	F	VF	XF	Unc	BU
1995(cc) Proof	10,000	Value: 260				

Y# 61 10000 BOLIVARES **Weight:** 31.1000 g. **Composition:** 0.9000 Gold .9000 oz. AGW

Date	Mintage	F	VF	XF	Unc	BU
1987(c) Proof	50,000	Value: 325				

ESSAIS

KM#	Date	Mintage	Identification	Mkt Val
E18	1991(c)	—	1300 Bolivares. 0.9000 Copper. M1, thick planchet.	—

PATTERNS

including off metal strikes

KM#	Date	Mintage	Identification	Mkt Val
Pn46-47	1973(m)	—	5 Bolivares. Nickel.	700
	1973(m)	—	5 Bolivares. Nickel.	700
Pn48	1977(w)	—	25 Centimos. Nickel.	100
Pn49	1977(m)	—	5 Bolivares. Nickel.	200
Pn50	1981(w)	—	100 Bolivares. Silver. Y57, with LEY.	400
Pn53	1990(c)	—	50 Bolivares. Gold. Medal rotation	600
Pn54	1990(c)	—	50 Bolivares. Gold. Coin rotation.	600
Pn52	1990(c)	—	50 Bolivares. Silver.	600
Pn56	1990	—	5000 Bolivares. Copper-Nickel. Y65.	2,000
Pn51	1990(c)	—	50 Bolivares. Lead.	200
Pn55	1990(c)	—	50 Bolivares. Gold.	1,000

TRIAL STRIKES

KM#	Date	Mintage	Identification	Mkt Val
TS10	1973(c)	—	10 Bolivares. Silver. 2 obverses.	400
TS12	1975(c)	—	500 Bolivares. Gold plated; Uniface reverse.	—
TS13	1977(m)	—	5 Bolivares. Nickel. Uniface obverse.	200
TS9	1977	—	10 Bolivares. 0.9000 Silver. Uniface reverse.	1,000
TS19	1990(c)	—	50 Bolivares. Silver. Y#66. Uniface.	600
TS11	1975(c)	—	500 Bolivares. Gold plated; Uniface obverse.	—
TS16	1990(c)	—	50 Bolivares. Bronze. Y66, uniface obverse.	600
TS21	1990(c)	—	50 Bolivares. Copper. Y67, uniface reverse.	600
TS15	1990(c)	—	50 Bolivares. Copper. Y66, uniface reverse.	600
TS14	1990(c)	—	50 Bolivares. Copper. Y66, uniface obverse.	600
TS17	1990(c)	—	50 Bolivares. Bronze. Y66, uniface reverse.	600
TS18	1990(c)	—	50 Bolivares. Silver. Y66, uniface obverse.	1,000
TS20	1990(d)	—	50 Bolivares. Copper. Y67, uniface obverse.	600
TS26	1991(c)	—	1300 Bolivares. Silver. Y79, uniface obverse.	—
TS23	ND (1991)	—	1100 Bolivares. Y68, uniface reverse.	650
TS24	1991(c)	—	1300 Bolivares. Copper. Y79, uniface obverse.	—
TS25	1991(c)	—	1300 Bolivares. Copper. Y79, uniface reverse.	—
TS22	1991	—	1100 Bolivares. Y68, uniface obverse.	650
TS27	1991(c)	—	1300 Bolivares. Silver. Y79, uniface reverse.	—

PRIVATE PATTERNS

KM#	Date	Mintage	Identification	Mkt Val
PPn1	1930	—	5 Bolivares. 0.9000 Silver. Gomez, Bayer Hauptmunzamt, incuse lettered inscription on edge.	7,000

Note: Prepared by Karl Goetz. Later strikes and uniface trial strikes with original dies in various metals exist, as do modern fabrications. Mulings with Goetz German patterns exist but are possible modern restrikes or reproductions, refer to Unusual World Coins for detailed listings

KM#	Date	Mintage	Identification	Mkt Val
PPn2	1973(c)	—	10 Bolivares. Silver. Similar to KM45. (Pn5)	800
PPn3	1973(c)	—	10 Bolivares. Silver. Double obverse similar to KM45.	600

PRIVATE TRIAL STRIKES

KM#	Date	Mintage	Identification	Mkt Val
PTS1	1973	—	10 Bolivares. Uniface obverse similar to KM45. (TS2)	200
PTS2	1973	—	10 Bolivares. Uniface reverse similar to KM45. (TS3)	500

MINT SETS

KM#	Date	Mintage	Identification	Issue Price	Mkt Val
MS1	1975 (3)	—	Y46-48	250	500

PROOF SETS

KM#	Date	Mintage	Identification	Issue Price	Mkt Val
PS1	1975 (3)	—	Y46-48	—	1,000

MARACAIBO

The Venezuelan Government maintained a large leper colony on Providencia Island in Lake Maracaibo, where hundreds of people suffering from Hansen's disease were cared for. To provide a monetary system and prevent regular coinage, handled by lepers, to re-circulate in the general population, the Venezuelan Government created a special currency. They had value only on the island until 30 years ago, when the illness was almost fully extinguished in South America and medical research revealed that little risk was involved in handling these coins.

VENEZUELAN GOVERNMENT CONTROLLED LEPER COLONY

LEPROSARIUM COINAGE

KM# L11 (KML10) 0.05 BOLIVAR (5 Centimos) **Composition:** Brass **Issuer:** Cabo Blanco, A leper hospital located in Maiquetia near the capitol city of Caracas. Coins were struck in 1936 for this colony.

Date	VG	F	VF	XF	Unc
1936	3.00	6.00	10.00	20.00	—

KM# L19 (KML20) 0.05 BOLIVAR (5 Centimos) **Composition:** Brass **Issuer:** Isla De Providencia

Date	VG	F	VF	XF	Unc
1939	2.00	4.00	8.00	16.00	—

KM# L3 (KML1) 1/8 BOLIVAR **Composition:** Brass **Issuer:** Maracaibo Lazareto Nacional

Date	VG	F	VF	XF	Unc
1913	3.50	7.00	12.00	25.00	—
1916	20.00	40.00	80.00	135	—

KM# L3a (KML1a) 1/8 BOLIVAR **Composition:** Copper Nickel **Issuer:** Maracaibo Lazareto Nacional

Date	VG	F	VF	XF	Unc
1913 Rare	—	—	—	—	—

KM# L12 (KML11) 0.12-1/2 BOLIVAR (12-1/2 Centimos) **Composition:** Brass **Issuer:** Cabo Blanco, A leper hospital located in Maiquetia near the capitol city of Caracas. Coins were struck in 1936 for this colony.

Date	VG	F	VF	XF	Unc
1936	25.00	50.00	85.00	135	—

KM# L20 (KML21) 0.12-1/2 BOLIVAR (12-1/2 Centimos) **Comp.:** Brass **Issuer:** Isla De Providencia

Date	VG	F	VF	XF	Unc
1939	2.50	5.00	9.00	18.00	—

KM# L20a (KML21a) 0.12-1/2 BOLIVAR (12-1/2 Centimos) **Composition:** Copper-Nickel **Issuer:** Isla De Providencia

Date	VG	F	VF	XF	Unc
1939 Rare	—	—	—	—	—

KM# L4 (KML2) 1/2 BOLIVAR **Composition:** Brass **Issuer:** Maracaibo Lazareto Nacional **Note:** Similar to 1/8 Bolivar previous KM#L1, now numbered KM#L3.

Date	VG	F	VF	XF	Unc
1913	20.00	35.00	75.00	125	—
1916	35.00	65.00	140	250	—

KM# L13 (KML12) 0.50 BOLIVAR (50 Centimos) **Composition:** Brass **Issuer:** Cabo Blanco, A leper hospital located in Maiquetia near the capitol city of Caracas. Coins were struck in 1936 for this colony.

Date	VG	F	VF	XF	Unc
1936	35.00	65.00	110	185	-

KM# L21 (KML22) 0.50 BOLIVAR (50 Centimos) **Composition:** Brass **Issuer:** Isla De Providencia

Date	VG	F	VF	XF	U
1939	20.00	40.00	75.00	125	

KM# L5 (KML3) BOLIVAR **Composition:** Brass **Issuer:** Maracaibo Lazareto Nacional **Note:** Similar to 1/8 Bolivar, previous KM#L1, now numbered KM#L3.

Date	VG	F	VF	XF	U
1913	20.00	30.00	45.00	75.00	
1916	25.00	40.00	55.00	85.00	

L14 (KML13) **BOLIVAR** **Composition:** Brass
ssuer: Cabo Blanco, A leper hospital located in Maiquetia
ear the capitol city of Caracas. Coins were struck in 1936
r this colony.

VG	F	VF	XF	Unc
50.00	85.00	150	250	—

L22 (KML23) **BOLIVAR** **Composition:** Brass
suer: Isla De Providencia

VG	F	VF	XF	Unc
25.00	50.00	90.00	150	—

L6 (KML4) **2 BOLIVARES** **Composition:** Brass
ssuer: Maracaibo Lazareto Nacional **Obverse:** Similar to
0 Bolivares, previous KM#L7, now numbered KM#L9

VG	F	VF	XF	Unc
25.00	40.00	60.00	100	—
35.00	50.00	70.00	120	—

L15 (KML14) **2 BOLIVARES** **Composition:**
Brass **Issuer:** Cabo Blanco, A leper hospital located in
Maiquetia near the capitol city of Caracas. Coins were struck
n 1936 for this colony.

VG	F	VF	XF	Unc
60.00	100	165	270	—

L23 (KML24) **2 BOLIVARES** **Composition:**
Brass **Issuer:** Isla De Providencia

VG	F	VF	XF	Unc
30.00	60.00	110	185	—

L7 (KML5) **5 BOLIVARES** **Composition:** Brass
Issuer: Maracaibo Lazareto Nacional **Note:** Similar to 1/8
Bolivar, prevous KM#L1, now numbered KM#L3.

	VG	F	VF	XF	Unc
3	55.00	100	175	275	—
6	85.00	120	200	350	—

KM# L16 (KML15) 5 BOLIVARES **Composition:**
Brass **Issuer:** Cabo Blanco, A leper hospital located in
Maiquetia near the capitol city of Caracas. Coins were struck
in 1936 for this colony.

Date	VG	F	VF	XF	Unc
1936	80.00	140	220	375	—

KM# L24 (KML25) 5 BOLIVARES **Composition:**
Brass **Issuer:** Isla De Providencia

Date	VG	F	VF	XF	Unc
1939	40.00	85.00	165	275	—

KM# L8 (KML6) 10 BOLIVARES **Composition:**
Brass **Issuer:** Maracaibo Lazareto Nacional **Note:** Similar to
1/8 Bolivar, previous KM#L1, now numbered KM#L3.

Date	VG	F	VF	XF	Unc
1913	60.00	120	200	350	—
1916	90.00	180	300	500	—

KM# L17 (KML16) 10 BOLIVARES **Composition:**
Brass **Issuer:** Cabo Blanco, A leper hospital located in
Maiquetia near the capitol city of Caracas. Coins were struck
in 1936 for this colony.

Date	VG	F	VF	XF	Unc
1936	120	200	320	500	—

KM# L25 (KML26) 10 BOLIVARES **Composition:**
Brass **Issuer:** Isla De Providencia

Date	VG	F	VF	XF	Unc
1939 Reported, not confirmed	—	—	—	—	—

Note: According to records, coins with the 10 Bolivares denomination were authorized to be struck, but at present none are known to exist in the numismatic community

KM# L9 (KML7) 20 BOLIVARES **Composition:**
Brass **Issuer:** Maracaibo Lazareto Nacional **Reverse:**
Similar to 2 Bolivares, previous KM#L4, now numbered
KM#L6

Date	VG	F	VF	XF	Unc
1913	175	275	400	600	—
1916	250	350	500	700	—

KM# L18 (KML17) 20 BOLIVARES **Composition:**
Brass **Issuer:** Cabo Blanco, A leper hospital located in
Maiquetia near the capitol city of Caracas. Coins were struck
in 1936 for this colony.

Date	VG	F	VF	XF	Unc
1936	175	275	375	650	—

VIET NAM

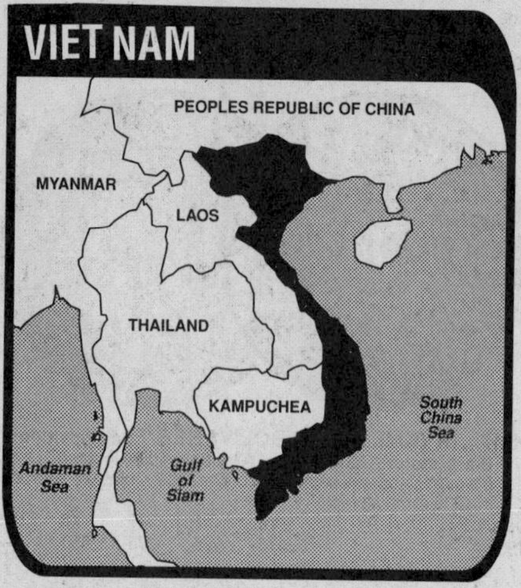

In 207 B.C. a Chinese general set up the Kingdom of Nam-Viet on the Red River. This kingdom was over-thrown by the Chinese under the Han Dynasty in 111 B.C., where upon the country became a Chinese province under the name of Giao-Chi, which was later changed to Annam or peaceful or pacified South. Chinese rule was maintained until 968, when the Vietnamese became independent until 1407 when China again invaded Viet Nam. The Chinese were driven out in 1428 and the country became independent and named Dai-Viet. Gia Long united the North and South as Dai Nam in 1802.

After the French conquered Dai Nam, they split the country into three parts. The South became the Colony of Cochin china; the North became the Protectorate of Tonkin; and the central became the Protectorate of Annam. The emperors were permitted to have their capital in Hue and to produce small quantities of their coins, presentation pieces, and bullion bars. Annam had an area of 57,840 sq. mi. (141,806 sq. km.) and a population of about 6 million. Chief products of the area are silk, cinnamon and rice. There are important mineral deposits in the mountainous inland.

At the start of World War II, Vietnamese Communists fled to China's Kwangsi provinces where Ho Chi Minh organized the Revolution to free Viet Nam of French rule. The Japanese occupied Viet Nam during World War II. As the end of the war drew near, they ousted the Vichy French administration and granted Viet Nam independence under a puppet government headed by Bao Dai, Emperor of Annam. The Bao Dai government collapsed at the end of the war, and on Sept. 2, 1945, Ho Chi Minh proclaimed the existence of an independent Viet Nam consisting of Cochin-China, Annam, and Tonkin, and set up a Communist government. France recognized the new government as a free state, but reneged and in 1949 reinstalled Bao Dai as Ruler of Viet Nam and extended the regime independence within the French Union. Ho Chi Minh led a guerrilla war, in the first Indochina war, against the French which raged on to the disastrous defeat of the French at Dien Bien Phu on May 7,1954.

An agreement signed at Geneva on July 21, 1954, provided for a temporary division of Viet Nam at the 17th parallel of latitude, between a Communist-supported North and a U.S.-supported South. In Oct. 1955, South Viet Nam deposed Bao Dai by referendum and authorized the establishment of a republic with Ngo Dinh Diem as president. The Republic of South Viet Nam was proclaimed on Oct. 26, 1955, and was immediately recognized by some Western Powers.

The activities of Communists in South Viet Nam led to the second Indochina war, which became to a brief halt in 1973 (when a cease-fire was arranged and U.S. forces withdrew), but it didn't end until April 30, 1975 when South Viet Nam surrendered unconditionally. The two Viet Nams were reunited as the Socialist Republic of Viet Nam on July 2, 1976.

NOTE: For earlier coinage refer to French Indo-China or Tonkin.

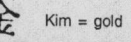

ANNAM

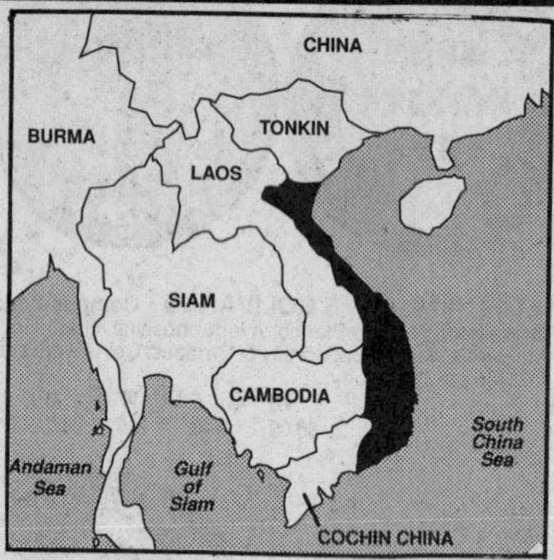

EMPERORS

Thanh Thai, 1888-1907 成泰

Duy Tan, 1907-1916 維新

Khai Dinh, 1916-1925 啓定

Bao Dai, 1926-1945 保大

IDENTIFICATION

Khai 啓

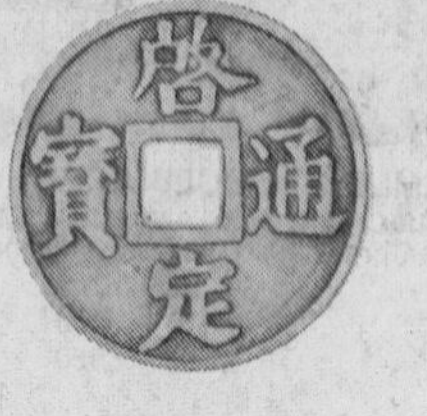

Bao 寶

Thong 通

Dinh 定

CYCLICAL DATES

	庚	辛	壬	癸	甲	乙	丙	丁	戊	己
戌	1850 1910		1862 1922		1874 1934		1886 1946		1838 1898	
亥		1851 1911		1863 1923		1875 1935		1887 1947		1839 1899
子	1840 1900		1852 1912		1864 1924		1876 1936		1888 1948	
丑		1841 1901		1853 1913		1865 1925		1877 1937		1889 1949
寅	1830 1890		1842 1902		1854 1914		1866 1926		1878 1938	
卯		1831 1891		1843 1903		1855 1915		1867 1927		1879 1939
辰	1880 1940		1832 1892		1844 1904		1856 1916		1868 1928	
巳		1881 1941		1833 1893		1845 1905		1857 1917		1869 1929
午	1870 1930		1882 1942		1834 1894		1846 1906		1858 1918	
未		1871 1931		1883 1943		1835 1895		1847 1907		1859 1919
申	1860 1920		1872 1932		1884 1944		1836 1896		1848 1908	
酉		1861 1921		1873 1933		1885 1945		1837 1897		1849 1909

NOTE: This table has been adapted from *Chinese Bank Notes* by Ward Smith and Brian Matravers.

Cyclical dates consist of a pair of characters one of which indicates the animal associated with that year. Every 60 years, this pair of characters is repeated. The first character of a cyclical date corresponds to a character in the first row of the chart above. The second character is taken from the column at left. In this catalog where a cyclical date is used, the abbreviation CD appears before the A.D. date.

Annamese silver and gold coins were sometimes dated according to the year of the emperor's reign. In this case, simply add the year of reign to the year in which the reign would be 1849 (1847 plus 3 = 1850 -1 = 1849 or 1847 = 1; 1848 = 2; 1849 = 3). In this catalog the A.D. date appears in parenthesis followed by the year of reign.

NUMERALS

NUMBER	CONVENTIONAL	FORMAL	COMMER
1	一 元	壹 弌	〡
2	二	弍 貳	〢
3	三	叁 弎	〣
4	四	肆	〤
5	五	伍	〥
6	六	陸	〦
7	七	柒	〧
8	八	捌	〨
9	九	玖	〩
10	十	拾 什	十
20	十 二 or 廿	拾貳	〢十
25	五 十 二 or 五廿	伍拾貳	〢十
30	十 三 or 卅	拾叁	〣十
100	百 一	佰壹	〡百
1,000	千 一	仟壹	〡千
10,000	萬 一	萬壹	〡万
100,000	萬十 億 一	萬拾 億壹	十万
1,000,000	萬百一	萬佰壹	〡百万

NOTE: This table has been adapted from *Chinese Notes* by Ward Smith and Brian Matravers.

MONETARY SYSTEM

10 Dong (zinc) = 1 Dong (copper)
600 Dong (zinc) = 1 Quan (string of cash)
Approx. 2600 Dong (zinc) = 1 Piastre

NOTE: Ratios between metals changed frequently, th fore the above is given as an approximate relationship.

SILVER and GOLD

2-1/2 Quan = 1 Lang
10 Tien (Mace) = 1 Lang (Tael)
14 to 17 Piastres (silver) = 1 Piastre (gold)
14 to 17 Lang (silver) = 1 Lang (gold)

The real currency of Dai Nam and An Nam consisted of per and zinc coins similar to Chinese cash-style coins and called sapeques and dongs by the French.

The smaller gold pieces saw a limited circulation, m among the local merchants and foreign traders. The larger pieces were used mainly for hoarding, while most of these intended as rewards and gifts. Many of these gold pieces ap to have been struck from silver coin dies or vice-versa.

NOTE: Sch# are in reference to Albert Schroeder's *Ann Etudes Numismatiques* or to the same numbering system in *Gold and Silver Coins of Annam"*, by Bernard Permar and Novak.

CHARACTER IDENTIFICATION

The Vietnamese used Chinese-style characters for of documents and coins and bars. Some were modified to thei ing and will sometimes not match the Chinese character fo same word. The above identification and this table will trans most of the Vietnamese characters (Chinese-style) on their c and bars described herein.

Chinese/French
Vietnamese/English

安南 An Nam = name of the French protectorate

大南 Dai Nam = name of the country under Gia Long's Nguye dynasty

越南 Viet Nam = name used briefly during Minh Mang's reign and bec the modern name of the count

河內 Ha Noi = city and province in north Dai NamTonkin

內帑 Noi Thang = court treasury in the capital of Hue

年 Nien = year

造 Tao = made

銀 Ngan = silver

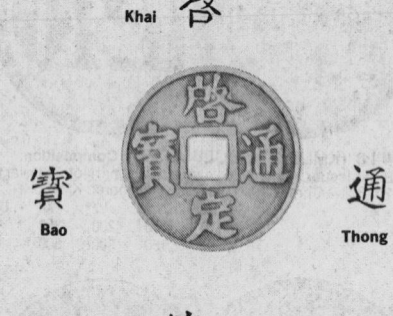

金 Kim = gold

錢 Tien = a weight of about 3.78 grams

兩 Lang = a weight of about 37.78 grams

貫 Quan = a string of cash style coins

分 Phan = a weight of about .38 grams

文 Van = cash-style coins

中平 Trung Binh = a name of weight standard

FRENCH PROTECTORATE

CAST COINAGE

Copper, brass, and zinc cash

M#626 (Y1) PHAN **Composition:** Cast Copper Alloys **Ruler:** Thanh Thai **Obverse:** Inscription: "Thanh Thai Thong Bao" **Reverse:** Plain

te	Good	VG	F	VF	XF
(1888-1907)	2.00	3.50	5.50	9.00	—

M#654 (Y4) PHAN **Composition:** Cast Copper Alloys **Ruler:** Khai Dinh **Obv. Inscription:** "Khai Dinh Thong Bao"

e	Good	VG	F	VF	XF
(1916-25)	5.50	9.00	15.00	25.00	—

 # 661 (Y6a) PHAN **Composition:** Cast Brass **Ruler:** Bao Dai **Obverse:** Inscription: Bao-dai Thong bao

e	Good	VG	F	VF	XF
1926-45)	2.50	5.00	7.50	12.50	—

 # 628 (Y2) 10 VAN **Composition:** Cast Copper Alloys **Ruler:** Thanh Thai **Obv. Inscription:** "Thanh Thai Thong Bao" **Reverse:** "Thap Van" **Rev. Inscription:** "10 Van"

	Good	VG	F	VF	XF
888-1907)	0.50	0.75	1.25	2.50	—

KM# 652 (Y3) 10 VAN **Composition:** Cast Brass **Ruler:** Duy Tan **Obv. Inscription:** "Duy Tan Thong Bao" **Rev. Inscription:** "10 Van"

Date	Good	VG	F	VF	XF
ND(1907-16)	0.50	0.75	1.25	2.50	—

KM# 664 (Y7) 10 VAN **Composition:** Copper Alloys **Ruler:** Bao Dai **Obv. Inscription:** "Bao Dai Thong Bao" **Rev. Inscription:** "10 Van"

Date	Good	VG	F	VF	XF
ND(1926-45)	2.00	3.50	7.50	12.50	—

MILLED COINAGE

Brass

KM# 656 (Y5.2) PHAN **Composition:** Brass **Ruler:** Khai Dinh **Obverse:** Characters slightly different **Obv. Inscription:** "Khai Dinh Thong Bao"

Date	Good	VG	F	VF	XF
ND(1916-25)	2.00	3.50	6.00	10.00	—

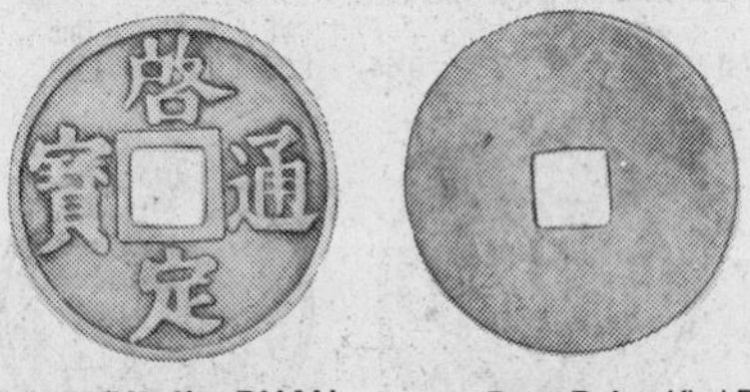

KM# 655 (Y5.1) PHAN **Comp.:** Brass **Ruler:** Khai Dinh **Obv. Inscription:** "Khai Dinh Thong Bao" **Note:** Uniface.

Date	Good	VG	F	VF	XF
ND(1916-25)	1.75	2.75	4.50	7.50	—

KM# 662 (Y6) PHAN **Comp.:** Copper Alloys **Ruler:** Bao Dai **Obv. Inscription:** "Bao Dai Thong Bao" **Size:** 18 mm.

Date	Good	VG	F	VF	XF
ND(1926-45)	2.50	5.00	7.50	12.50	—

HAMMERED COINAGE

KM# 634 TIEN **Weight:** 3.9000 g. **Composition:** Gold **Ruler:** Thanh Thai **Obv. Inscription:** "Thanh Thai Thong Bao" **Rev. Inscription:** "Nhat Nguyen" **Note:** Cross-reference number Schroeder#432.

Date	VG	F	VF	XF	Unc
ND(1888-1907)	325	600	950	1,450	—

KM# 636 1-1/2 TIEN **Weight:** 6.6000 g. **Composition:** Gold **Ruler:** Thanh Thai **Obv. Inscription:** "Thanh Thai Thong Bao" **Reverse:** Legend between moon and sun **Rev. Inscription:** "Nhi Nghi" **Note:** Cross-reference number Schroeder#435.

Date	VG	F	VF	XF	Unc
ND(1888-1907)	240	450	750	1,150	—

KM# 630 3 TIEN **Composition:** Silver **Ruler:** Thanh Thai **Obv. Inscription:** "Thanh Thai Thong Bao" **Reverse:** Dragon **Note:** Cross-reference number Schroeder#428.

Date	VG	F	VF	XF	Unc
ND(1888-1907)	70.00	140	240	400	—

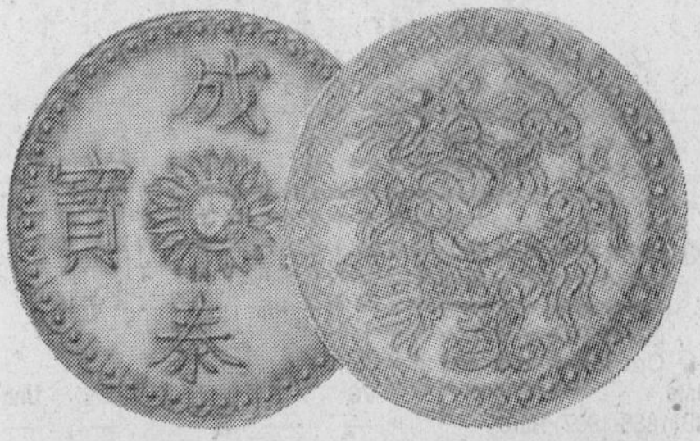

KM# 638 3 TIEN **Composition:** Gold **Ruler:** Thanh Thai **Obv. Inscription:** "Thanh Thai Thong Bao" **Reverse:** Dragon **Note:** Weight varies: 10.50-12.40 grams. Cross-reference number Schroeder#433.

Date	VG	F	VF	XF	Unc
ND(1888-1907)	1,000	2,000	3,250	5,000	—

KM# 639 3 TIEN **Composition:** Gold **Ruler:** Thanh Thai **Obv. Inscription:** "Thanh Thai Thong Bao" **Reverse:** Dragon above three Longevities **Rev. Inscription:** "Tam Tho" **Note:** Weight varies: 10.00-10.50 grams. Cross-reference number Schroeder #436.

Date	VG	F	VF	XF	Unc
ND(1888-1907)	550	1,000	1,700	2,600	—

KM# 641 4 TIEN **Weight:** 14.5000 g. **Composition:** Gold **Ruler:** Thanh Thai **Obv. Inscription:** "Tu My" **Reverse:** Inscription between Four Perfections **Note:** Cross-reference number Schroeder#437.

Date	VG	F	VF	XF	Unc
ND(1888-1907)	650	1,200	2,100	3,200	—

KM# 645 6 TIEN **Weight:** 23.0000 g. **Composition:** Gold **Ruler:** Thanh Thai **Obv. Inscription:** "Thanh Thai Thong Bao" **Reverse:** Large dragon **Note:** Cross-reference number Schroeder#382A.

Date	VG	F	VF	XF	Unc
ND(1888-1907)	1,100	2,200	3,500	5,500	—

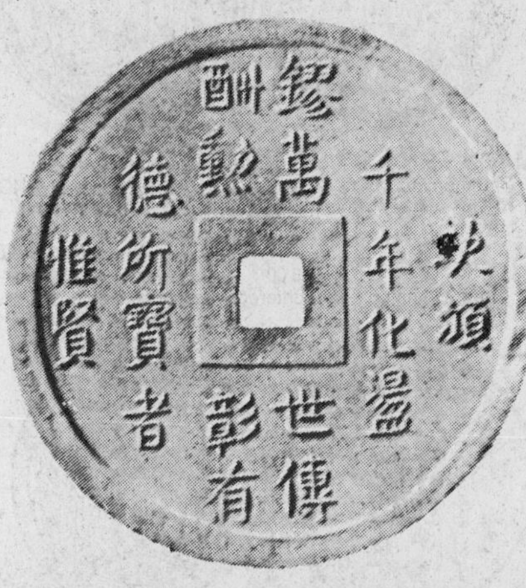

KM# 647 LANG **Composition:** Gold **Ruler:** Thanh Thai **Obverse:** Inscription: "Thanh-thai Thong-bao" at right, "Van The Vinh Lai" at left **Note:** Weight unknown. Cross-reference number Schroeder#431.

Date	VG	F	VF	XF	Unc
ND(1888-1907)	3,000	—	9,500	15,000	—

BULLION GOLD BARS

All of the bars described here are inscribed with their weight, except the 10 Lang "banana bars", and many contain a date or the name of the province in which they were made.

KM# 649 LANG Composition: 0.8500 Gold **Ruler:** Thanh Thai **Obverse:** Inscription: "Thanh-thai Nien-tao" **Reverse:** Inscription: "Noi Thang Kim Nhat Lang" **Note:** Court Treasury. Fineness on edge. 36.10-36.70 grams. Cross-reference number Schroeder#429.

Date	VG	F	VF	XF	Unc
ND(1888-1907) Rare	—	—	—	—	—

KM# 650 LANG Composition: 0.8000 Gold **Ruler:** Thanh Thai **Obverse:** Inscription: "Thanh-thai Nien-tao" **Reverse:** Inscription: "Noi Thang Kim Nhat Lang" **Note:** Court Treasury. Fineness on edge. Cross-reference number Schroeder#429.

Date	VG	F	VF	XF	Unc
ND(1888-1907) Rare	—	—	—	—	—

NORTH VIET NAM

INDEPENDENT COMMUNIST STATE

MILLED COINAGE

KM# 1 20 XU Composition: Aluminum **Obverse:** Star, date below **Obv. Legend:** VIET NAM DAN CHU CHONG HOA **Rev. Inscription:** 20 XU

Date	F	VF	XF	Unc	BU
1945(v)	40.00	125	175	200	—

KM# 2.1 5 HAO Composition: Aluminum **Obverse:** Ceremonial pot **Obv. Legend:** VIET DAM DAN CHU CHONG HAO **Reverse:** Value incused in star **Rev. Inscription:** 5 HAO

Date	F	VF	XF	Unc	BU
1946(v)	3.00	9.00	18.00	40.00	—

Note: Commonly encountered with rotated dies

KM# 2.2 5 HAO Composition: Aluminum **Obverse:** Ceremonial pot **Obv. Legend:** VIET DAM DAN CHU CHONG HAO **Reverse:** Value raised in star **Rev. Inscription:** 5 HAO

Date	F	VF	XF	Unc	BU
1946(v)	20.00	40.00	100	175	—

KM# 3 DONG Composition: Aluminum **Obv. Legend:** VIET DAM DAN CHU CHONG HAO **Reverse:** Value to right of spray **Rev. Inscription:** 1 DONG

Date	F	VF	XF	Unc	BU
1946(v)	30.00	75.00	165	250	—

KM# 4 2 DONG Composition: Bronze **Obverse:** Bust of Ho Chi Minh **Obv. Legend:** CHU TICH HO MIHN **Reverse:** Value above and below in wreath, "Nam II" at bottom **Rev. Legend:** VIET DAM DAN CHU CHONG HAO **Rev. Inscription:** HAI DONG **Note:** Varieties exist.

Date	F	VF	XF	Unc	BU
1946(v)	7.50	15.00	40.00	120	—

REFORM COINAGE

KM# 5 XU Composition: Aluminum **Obverse:** Arms **Obv. Legend:** "NUOC VIET NAM DAN CHU CONG HOA" **Rev. Legend:** "NGAN HANG QUOC GIA VIET NAM" **Rev. Inscription:** Value: "MOT ZU"

Date	F	VF	XF	Unc	BU
1958(s)	0.65	1.25	2.00	3.50	—

KM# 6 2 XU Composition: Aluminum **Obverse:** Arms **Obv. Legend:** "NUOC VIET NAM DAN CHU CONG HOA" **Rev. Legend:** "NGAN HANG QUOC GIA VIET NAM" **Rev. Inscription:** Value: "HAI XU"

Date	F	VF	XF	Unc	BU
1958(s)	0.65	1.25	2.00	3.50	—

KM# 7 5 XU Composition: Aluminum **Obverse:** Arms **Obv. Legend:** "NUOC VIET NAM DAN CHU CONG HOA" **Rev. Legend:** "NGAN HANG QUOC GIA VIET NAM" **Rev. Inscription:** Value: "NAM XU"

Date	F	VF	XF	Unc	BU
1958(s)	0.75	1.50	2.50	4.50	—

PATTERNS

Including off metal strikes

KM#	Date	Mintage	Identification	Mkt Val
Pn1	1946(v)	—	5 Dong. Bronze. VIET NAM DAN CHU CONG HOA.	—

PRESENTATION COINAGE

KM#	Date	Mintage	Identification	Mkt Val
A5	1948(v)	—	10 Viet. Gold. 0.9000 g. Legend, date. "CHU-TICH HO-CHI-MINH".	—
B5	1948(v)	—	20 Viet. Gold. 0.9000 g. Head of Ho Chi Minh right. "CHU-TICH HO-CHI-MINH". Inscription above grain sheaves.	—
C5	1948(v)	—	50 Viet. Gold. 0.9000 g. "CHU-TICH HO-CHI-MINH". "VIET-NAM DAN-CHU CONG-HOA".	—

STATE OF SOUTH VIET NAM

DEMOCRATIC STATE

STANDARD COINAGE

KM# 1 10 SU Composition: Aluminum **Obverse:** Three women's busts left **Obv. Legend:** "QUOC-GIA VIET-NAM" **Reverse:** Rice plant dividing value **Rev. Legend:** "VIET-NAM"

Date	Mintage	F	VF	XF	Unc	B
1953(a)	20,000,000	0.15	0.25	0.50	1.00	–

KM# 2 20 SU Composition: Aluminum **Obverse:** Three women's busts left **Obv. Legend:** "QUOC-GIA VIET-NAM" **Reverse:** Rice plant dividing value **Rev. Legend:** "VIET-NAM"

Date	Mintage	F	VF	XF	Unc
1953(a)	15,000,000	0.30	0.50	0.85	1.75

KM# 3 50 XU Composition: Aluminum **Obverse:** Three women's busts half left, facing, and half right **Obv. Legend:** "QUOC-GIA VIET-NAM" **Rev. Legend:** "VIET-NAM"

Date	Mintage	F	VF	XF	Unc
1953(a)	15,000,000	1.50	3.00	6.00	12.50

REPUBLIC OF VIET NAM

STANDARD COINAGE

KM# 4 50 SU Composition: Aluminum **Obverse:** Bust Ngo Dihn Diem half left **Obv. Legend:** "VIET-NAM CON HOA" **Reverse:** Bamboo **Note:** The 1960 50 Su coin wa minted by the Paris Mint with the French spelling Su for X The coin was restruck with the correct Xu, a new date o 1963, and is cataloged as KM#6.

Date	Mintage	F	VF	XF	Unc
1960(a)	10,000,000	0.25	0.50	1.25	2.50
1960(a) Proof	—	Value: 80.00			

KM# 6 50 XU **Composition:** Aluminum **Obverse:** Bust of Ngo Dihn Diem half left **Obv. Legend:** "VIET-NAM CONG-HOA" **Reverse:** Bamboo

ate	Mintage	F	VF	XF	Unc	BU
963	20,000,000	0.20	0.40	1.00	2.50	—
963 Proof	—	Value: 80.00				

KM# 5 DONG **Composition:** Copper-Nickel **Obverse:** Bust of Ngo Dihn Diem half left **Obv. Legend:** "VIET-NAM CONG-HAO" **Reverse:** Bamboo

ate	Mintage	F	VF	XF	Unc	BU
960(a)	105,000,000	0.15	0.50	1.25	2.50	—
960(a) Proof	—	Value: 80.00				

M# 7 DONG **Composition:** Copper-Nickel **Obv. Legend:** "VIET-NAM CONG-HAO" **Reverse:** Rice stalks

te	Mintage	F	VF	XF	Unc	BU
64	44,000,000	0.15	0.35	0.50	1.00	—
64 Proof	—	—	—	—	—	—

M# 7a DONG **Composition:** Nickel-Clad Steel **Obv. Legend:** "VIET-NAM CONG-HAO" **Reverse:** Rice stalks

te	F	VF	XF	Unc	BU
71	0.10	0.15	0.35	1.00	—

M# 12 DONG **Composition:** Aluminum **Series:** F.A.O. **Obv. Legend:** "VIET-NAM CONG-HAO" **Reverse:** Rice stalks **Rev. Legend:** "TANG-GIA SAN-NUAT LUONG-THUC"

te	Mintage	F	VF	XF	Unc	BU
71	30,000,000	0.10	0.15	0.25	0.50	—

1# 9 5 DONG **Composition:** Copper-Nickel **Obv. Legend:** "VIET-NAM CONG-HAO" **Reverse:** Rice stalks **Rev. Legend:** "NGAN-HANG VIET-NAM CONG-HOA"

	Mintage	F	VF	XF	Unc	BU
6	100,000,000	0.10	0.35	0.50	1.00	—

1# 9a 5 DONG **Composition:** Nickel-Clad Steel **Obv. Legend:** "VIET-NAM CONG-HAO" **Reverse:** Rice stalks **Rev. Legend:** "NGAN-HANG VIET-NAM CONG-HOA"

	Mintage	F	VF	XF	Unc	BU
1	15,000,000	0.10	0.25	0.50	1.00	—

KM# 8 10 DONG **Composition:** Copper-Nickel **Obv. Legend:** "VIET-NAM CONG-HAO" **Reverse:** Rice stalks

Date	Mintage	F	VF	XF	Unc	BU
1964	15,000,000	0.20	0.40	0.60	1.25	—

KM# 8a 10 DONG **Composition:** Nickel-Clad Steel **Obv. Legend:** "VIET-NAM CONG-HAO" **Reverse:** Rice stalks

Date	Mintage	F	VF	XF	Unc	BU
1968	30,000,000	0.10	0.20	0.35	0.75	—
1970	50,000,000	0.10	0.20	0.35	0.75	—

KM# 13 10 DONG **Composition:** Brass-Clad Steel **Series:** F.A.O. **Obv. Legend:** "VIET-NAM CONG-HAO, NGAN-HUAN QUOC-GIA VIET-NAM" **Reverse:** Farmers in rice paddy **Rev. Legend:** "TANG-GIA SAM-XUAT NONG-PHAN"

Date	Mintage	F	VF	XF	Unc	BU
1974	30,000,000	0.10	0.15	0.30	0.60	—

KM# 10 20 DONG **Composition:** Nickel-Clad Steel **Obv. Legend:** "VIET-NAM CONG-HAO" **Reverse:** Farmer in rice paddy **Rev. Legend:** "NGAN-HANG QUOC-GIA VIET-NAM"

Date	F	VF	XF	Unc	BU
1968	0.25	0.50	1.00	2.00	—

KM# 11 20 DONG **Composition:** Nickel-Clad Steel **Series:** F.A.O. **Obv. Legend:** "VIET-NAM CONG-HAO" **Reverse:** Farmer in rice paddy **Rev. Legend:** "CHIEN-TICH THE-GIOI CHONG NAM DOI"

Date	Mintage	F	VF	XF	Unc	BU
1968	500,000	0.30	0.60	1.25	3.00	—

KM# 14 50 DONG **Composition:** Nickel Clad Steel **Series:** F.A.O. **Obv. Legend:** "VIET-NAM CONG-HAO, NGAN-HANG QUOC-GIA VIET-NAM" **Reverse:** Farmers in rice paddy **Rev. Legend:** "TANG-GIA SAM-XUAT NONG-PHAN"

Date	Mintage	F	VF	XF	Unc	BU
1975	1,010,000	160	250	300	500	—

Note: It is reported that all but a few examples were disposed of as scrap metal

PEOPLE'S REVOLUTIONARY GOVERNMENT

STANDARD COINAGE

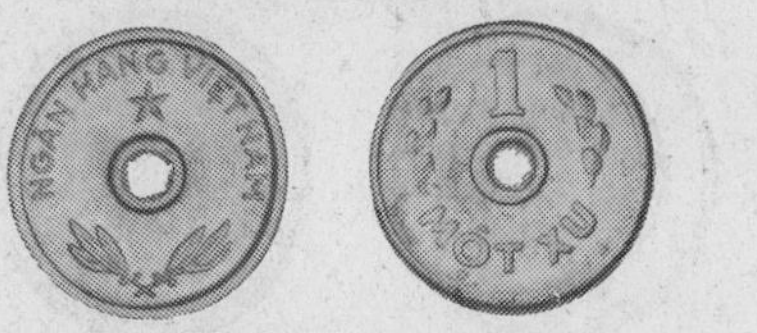

KM# A8 XU **Composition:** Aluminum **Obv. Legend:** "NGAN HANG VIET NAM" **Reverse:** 1 above, MOT XU below grain stalks

Date	F	VF	XF	Unc	BU
ND(1975)	0.50	1.50	2.75	7.50	—

KM# A9 2 XU **Composition:** Aluminum **Obverse:** Legend, HAI XU below **Obv. Legend:** "NGAN HANG VIET NAM" **Reverse:** 2 above, XU below ornamentation

Date	F	VF	XF	Unc	BU
1975	0.50	1.50	2.75	7.50	—

KM# A10 5 XU **Composition:** Aluminum **Obverse:** Value: 5/XU below **Obv. Legend:** "NGAN HANG VIET NAM" **Reverse:** "NAM XU" above, 5 below in stylized sprays

Date	F	VF	XF	Unc	BU
ND(1975)	0.50	1.50	2.75	7.50	—

ESSAIS

Standard metals unless otherwise noted

KM#	Date	Mintage	Identification	Issue Price	Mkt Val
E1	1953	1,200	10 Su. KM#1	—	25.00
E2	1953(a)	1,200	20 Su. KM#2	—	30.00
E3	1953(a)	1,200	50 Su. KM#3	—	35.00

PATTERNS

Including off metal strikes

KM#	Date	Mintage	Identification	Mkt Val
Pn1	1963	—	50 Xu. Aluminum-Bronze.	300
Pn2	1963	—	50 Xu. Copper-Nickel.	300

PIEFORTS WITH ESSAI

Standard metals unless otherwise noted

KM#	Date	Mintage	Identification	Issue Price	Mkt Val
PE1	1953(a)	104	10 Su. KM#1	—	75.00
PE2	1953(a)	104	20 Su. KM#2	—	85.00
PE3	1953(a)	104	50 Xu. KM#3	—	95.00

SOCIALIST REPUBLIC

STANDARD COINAGE

KM# 11 HAO **Composition:** Aluminum **Obverse:** Arms **Rev. Legend:** "NGAN HANG NHA NUOC VIET NAM" **Rev. Inscription:** "1 HAO"

Date	F	VF	XF	Unc	BU
1976(s)	0.25	0.50	1.00	2.50	—

KM# 12 2 HAO Composition: Aluminum **Obverse:** Arms **Rev. Legend:** "NGAN HANG NHA HUOC VIET NAM" **Rev. Inscription:** "5 HOA"

Date	F	VF	XF	Unc	BU
1976(s)	0.35	0.65	1.50	3.50	—

KM# 13 5 HAO Composition: Aluminum

Date	F	VF	XF	Unc	BU
1976	0.35	0.65	1.50	3.50	—

KM# 14 DONG Composition: Aluminum **Obverse:** Arms **Rev. Legend:** "NGAN HANG NHA NUOC VIET NAM" **Rev. Inscription:** "1 DONG"

Date	F	VF	XF	Unc	BU
1976(s)	0.65	1.35	3.50	7.50	—

KM# 36a 5 DONG Weight: 8.7700 g. **Composition:** 0.9000 Silver .2538 oz. ASW **Obverse:** Arms **Obv. Legend:** "CONG HOA XA HOI CHU NGHIA VIET NAM" **Obv. Inscription:** "5 DONG" **Rev. Inscription:** "CHIM PHUONG"

Date	F	VF	XF	Unc	BU
1989(L) Proof	—	Value: 12.50			

KM# 36 5 DONG Composition: Brass **Obverse:** Arms **Obv. Legend:** "CONG HOA XA HOI CHU NGHIA VIET NAM" **Obv. Inscription:** "5 DONG" **Reverse:** Mythological bird - Phoenix **Rev. Legend:** "CHIM PHUONG" **Note:** KM#36 and 36a were minted in the Leningrad (St. Petersburg) Mint (L) as gifts to the Vietnamese government and were not circulated. KM#36a was available in boxed sets of three, with KM#38a and 40a, and KM#36 and 36a were also available as encapsulated individual pieces.

Date	F	VF	XF	Unc	BU
1989(L) Proof	—	Value: 7.50			

KM# 15 10 DONG Composition: Copper-Nickel **Subject:** Nature **Obverse:** Arms, value "10 DONG" below **Obv. Legend:** "CONG HOA XA HOI CHU NGHIA VIET NAM" **Reverse:** Water buffalo, "TRAU" below **Rev. Legend:** "BAO VE THIEN NHIEM"

Date	Mintage	F	VF	XF	Unc	BU
1986(h)	5,000	—	—	—	13.50	16.50

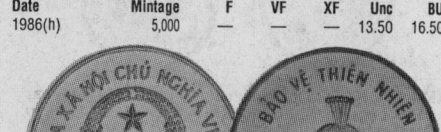

KM# 16 10 DONG Composition: Copper-Nickel **Subject:** Nature **Obverse:** Arms, value below **Obv. Legend:** "CONG HOA XA HOI CHU NGHIA VIET NAM" **Reverse:** Peacock, "CONG" below **Rev. Legend:** "BAO VE THIEN NHIEN"

Date	Mintage	F	VF	XF	Unc	BU
1986(h)	5,000	—	—	—	14.00	17.50

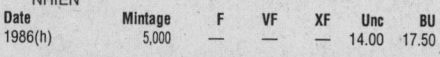

KM# 17 10 DONG Composition: Copper-Nickel **Subject:** Nature **Obverse:** Arms, value "10 DONG" below **Obv. Legend:** "CONG HOA XA HOI CHU NGHIA VIET NAM" **Reverse:** Elephant, "VOI" below **Rev. Legend:** "BAO VE THIEM NHIEN"

Date	Mintage	F	VF	XF	Unc	BU
1986(h)	5,000	—	—	—	17.50	22.50

KM# 28 10 DONG Composition: Copper-Nickel **Subject:** Wildlife Preservation **Obverse:** Arms, value "10 DONG" below **Obv. Legend:** "CONG HOA XA HOI CHU NGHIA VIET NAM" **Reverse:** Orangutan with Wildlife Preservation logo above right **Rev. Legend:** "BAO VE THIEM NHIEN, DUOI UOI"

Date	Mintage	F	VF	XF	Unc	BU
1987(h)	22,000	—	—	—	20.00	25.00

KM# 37 10 DONG Composition: Copper-Nickel **Obverse:** Arms, value "10 DONG" below **Obv. Legend:** "CONG HOA XA HOI CHU NGHIA VIET NAM" **Reverse:** Dragon ship **Rev. Legend:** "THUYEN CO."

Date	F	VF	XF	Unc	BU
1988(h)	—	—	—	8.50	—

KM# 27 10 DONG Composition: Copper-Nickel **Subject:** Soccer - Italy **Obverse:** Arms, value "10 DONG" below **Obv. Legend:** "CONG HOA XA HOI CHU NGHIA VIET NAM" **Reverse:** Legend above, I-TA-LI-A below **Rev. Legend:** "GIAI BONGDA THE GIOI"

Date	F	VF	XF	Unc	BU
1989(h)	—	—	—	10.00	—

KM# 38a 10 DONG Composition: 0.9000 Silver **Obverse:** Arms, value "10 DONG" below **Obv. Legend:** "CONG HOA XA HOI CHU NGHIA VIET NAM" **Rev. Legend:** "CHUA MOT COT-HANOI"

Date	F	VF	XF	Unc	BU
1989(L) Proof	—	Value: 20.00			

KM# 38 10 DONG Composition: Brass **Obverse:** Arms, value "10 DONG" below **Obv. Legend:** "CONG HOA XA HOI CHU NGHIA VIET NAM" **Reverse:** One-pillar Pagoda above water and legend **Rev. Legend:** "CHUA MOT COT-HANOI" **Note:** KM#38 and 38a were minted in the Leningrad (St. Petersburg) Mint (L) as gifts to the Vietnamese government and were not circulated. KM#38a was available in boxed sets of three, with KM#36a and 40a, and KM#38 and 38a were also available as encapsulated individual pieces.

Date	F	VF	XF	Unc	BU
1989(L) Proof	—	Value: 7.00			

KM# 33 10 DONG Composition: Copper-Nickel **Obverse:** Arms, value "10 DONG" below **Obv. Legend:** "CONG HOA XA HOI CHU NGHIA VIET NAM" **Reverse:** Loris **Rev. Legend:** "BAO VE THIEM NHIEN, DUOI UOI"

Date	Mintage	F	VF	XF	Unc	BU
1990(h)	20,000	—	—	—	42.50	55.00

KM# 39 10 DONG Composition: Copper-Nickel **Obverse:** Arms, value "10 DONG" below **Obv. Legend:** "CONG HOA XA HOI CHU NGHIA VIET NAM" **Reverse:** Steam and sail ship - Savannah **Rev. Legend:** "THUYEN CO SAVANNAH"

Date	F	VF	XF	Unc	BU
1991(h)	—	—	—	8.50	—

KM# 46 10 DONG Composition: Copper **Series:** World Cup Soccer **Obverse:** Arms, value "10 DONG" below **Obv. Legend:** "CONG HOA XA HOI CHU NGHIA VIET NAM" **Reverse:** Player and U.S. Capitol **Rev. Legend:** "CUP BONG DA THE GIOI LAN THU XV, HOA KY"

Date	F	VF	XF	Unc	BU
1992(h)	—	—	—	6.50	8.

KM# 44 10 DONG Composition: Copper-Nickel **Series:** Prehistoric Animals **Obverse:** Arms, value "10 DONG" below **Obv. Legend:** "CONG HOA XA HOI CHU NGHIA VIET NA" **Reverse:** Diplodocus **Rev. Legend:** "DONG VAT CO DA

Date	F	VF	XF	Unc	BU
1993(h)	—	—	—	22.00	28

KM# 49 10 DONG Composition: Copper-Nickel **Subject:** World Food Summit **Obverse:** Arms, value "10 DONG" below **Obv. Legend:** "CONG HOA XA HOI CHU NGHIA VIET NAM" **Reverse:** World Food Summit logo above Rice harvesting scene **Rev. Legend:** "MOI NGHI THUONG DINH THE GIOI VE LUOIN THUC"

ate	F	VF	XF	Unc	BU
996(h)	—	—	—	6.00	8.00

KM# 40a 20 DONG Composition: 0.9000 Silver **Obverse:** Arms, value "20 DONG" below **Obv. Legend:** "CONG HOA XA HOI CHU NGHIA VIET NAM" **Rev. Legend:** "HO CHI MINH"

ate	F	VF	XF	Unc	BU
989(L) Proof	—	Value: 37.50			

M# 40 20 DONG Composition: Brass **Subject:** 100th Anniversary - Birth of Ho Chi Minh **Obverse:** Arms, value "20 DONG" below **Obv. Legend:** "CONG HOA XA HOI CHU NGHIA VIET NAM" **Rev. Legend:** "HO CHI MINH" **Note:** KM#40 and 40a were minted in the Leningrad (St. Petersburg) Mint (L) as gifts to the Vietnamese government and were not circulated. KM#40a was available in boxed sets of three, with KM#36a and 38a, and KM#40 and 40a were also available as encapsulated individual pieces.

te	F	VF	XF	Unc	BU
89(L) Proof	—	Value: 14.50			

M# 18 100 DONG Weight: 12.0000 g. **Composition:** 0.9990 Silver .3855 oz. ASW **Obverse:** Arms, value "100 DONG" below **Obv. Legend:** "CONG HOA XA HOI CHU NGHIA VIET NAM" **Reverse:** Junk under sail **Rev. Legend:** "VIETNAM, THUYEN BUOM"

te	Mintage	F	VF	XF	Unc	BU
36(h)	2,000	—	—	—	35.00	—

M# 19 100 DONG Weight: 12.0000 g. **Composition:** 0.9990 Silver .3855 oz. ASW **Subject:** Wildlife **Obverse:** Arms, value "100 DONG" below **Obv. Legend:** "CONG HOA XA HOI CHU NGHIA VIET NAM" **Reverse:** Water buffalo **Rev. Legend:** "BAO VE THIEN KHIEN, TRAU"

e	Mintage	F	VF	XF	Unc	BU
6(h)	5,000	—	—	—	32.50	42.50

KM# 20 100 DONG Weight: 12.0000 g. **Composition:** 0.9990 Silver .3855 oz. ASW **Subject:** Wildlife **Obverse:** Arms, value "100 DONG" below **Obv. Legend:** "CONG HOA XA HOI CHU NGHIA VIET NAM" **Reverse:** Peacock **Rev. Legend:** "BAO VE THIEN NHIEN, CONG"

Date	Mintage	F	VF	XF	Unc	BU
1986(h)	5,000	—	—	—	27.50	35.00

KM# 21 100 DONG Weight: 12.0000 g. **Composition:** 0.9990 Silver .3855 oz. ASW **Subject:** Wildlife **Obverse:** Arms, value "100 DONG" below **Obv. Legend:** "CONG HOA XA HOI CHU NGHIA VIET NAM" **Reverse:** Elephant **Rev. Legend:** "BAO VI THIEN NHIEN, VOI"

Date	Mintage	F	VF	XF	Unc	BU
1986(h)	5,000	—	—	—	45.00	60.00

KM# 22 100 DONG Weight: 12.0000 g. **Composition:** 0.9990 Silver .3855 oz. ASW **Subject:** 100 Years of the Automobile **Obverse:** Arms, value "100 DONG" below **Obv. Legend:** "CONG HOA XA HOI CHU NGHIA VIET NAM" **Rev. Legend:** "100 NAN XE O TO A DOI, 1886-1986"

Date	Mintage	F	VF	XF	Unc	BU
1986(h)	2,000	—	—	—	16.50	—

KM# 23 100 DONG Weight: 6.0000 g. **Composition:** 0.9990 Silver .1927 oz. ASW **Series:** Calgary Olympics **Obverse:** Arms, value "100 DONG" below **Obv. Legend:** "CONG HOA XA HOI CHU NGHIA VIET NAM" **Reverse:** Skier **Rev. Legend:** "THE VAN HOI O-LIM-PIC MUA DONG XV, GAN-GA-RAY 1986"

Date	Mintage	F	VF	XF	Unc	BU
1986(h)	3,700	—	—	—	10.00	—

KM# 24 100 DONG Weight: 12.0000 g. **Composition:** 0.9990 Silver .3855 oz. ASW **Series:** Seoul Olympics **Obverse:** "Arms, value "100 DONG" below **Obv. Legend:** "CONG HOA XA HOI CHU NGHIA VIET NAM" **Reverse:** Fencer **Rev. Legend:** "THE VAN HOI O LIM PIC MUA HE"

Date	Mintage	F	VF	XF	Unc	BU
1986(h)	10,000	—	—	—	10.00	—

KM# 29 100 DONG Weight: 12.0000 g. **Composition:** 0.9990 Silver .3855 oz. ASW **Subject:** Soccer - Mexico **Obverse:** Arms, value "100 DONG" **Obv. Legend:** "CONG HOA XA HOI CHU NGHIA VIET NAM" **Rev. Legend:** "GIAI VO DICH BONG DA THE GIOI LAM THU XIII, ME HI CO"

Date	Mintage	F	VF	XF	Unc	BU
1986(h)	2,000	—	—	—	27.50	—

KM# 25.1 100 DONG Weight: 15.9900 g. **Composition:** 0.9800 Silver .5039 oz. ASW **Obverse:** Arms, value "100 DONG" below **Obv. Legend:** "CONG HOA XA HOI CHU NGHIA VIET NAM" **Rev. Legend:** "THUYEN CO"

Date	Mintage	F	VF	XF	Unc	BU
1988(h)	3,000	—	—	—	20.00	—
1988(h) Proof	—	Value: 27.50				

KM# 25.2 100 DONG Weight: 15.9900 g. **Composition:** 0.9800 Silver .5039 oz. ASW **Obverse:** Small arms with smaller rice grains; "VIET NAM" on ribbon, smaller denomination **Obv. Legend:** "CONG HOA XA HOI CHU NGHIA VIET NAM" **Rev. Legend:** "THUYEN CO"

Date	F	VF	XF	Unc	BU
1988(h)	—	—	—	22.50	—

KM# 26 100 DONG Weight: 12.0000 g. **Composition:** 0.9990 Silver .3855 oz. ASW **Subject:** Soccer - 1988 **Obverse:** ARms, value "100 DONG" below **Obv. Legend:** "CONG HOA XA HOI CHU NGHIA VIET NAM" **Rev. Legend:** "GIAI BONG DA CHAU AU, CONG HOA LIEN BANG DUCTHUYENCO."

Date	Mintage	F	VF	XF	Unc	BU
1988(h)	1,500	—	—	—	20.00	—

KM# 30 100 DONG **Weight:** 16.0000 g. **Composition:** 0.9990 Silver .5145 oz. ASW **Subject:** Soccer - Italy **Obverse:** Arms, value "100 DONG" below **Obv. Legend:** "CONG HOA XA HOI CHU NGHIA VIET NAM" **Rev. Legend:** "GIAI BONG DA THE GIOI, I-TA-LI-A"

Date	Mintage	F	VF	XF	Unc	BU
1989(h) Proof	10,000	Value: 28.50				

KM# 31 100 DONG **Weight:** 16.0000 g. **Composition:** 0.9990 Silver .5145 oz. ASW **Series:** Summer Olympics **Subject:** Rowing **Obverse:** Arms, value "100 DONG" below **Obv. Legend:** "CONG HOA XA HOI CHU NGHIA VIET NAM" **Rev. Legend:** "THE VAN HOI LAN THU XXV, BARCELONA 1992"

Date	Mintage	F	VF	XF	Unc	BU
1989(h) Proof	10,000	Value: 25.00				

KM# 32 100 DONG **Weight:** 16.0000 g. **Composition:** 0.9990 Silver .5145 oz. ASW **Series:** Winter Olympics **Subject:** Hockey **Obverse:** Arms, value "100 DONG" below **Obv. Legend:** "CONG HOA XA HOI CHU NGHIA VIET NAM" **Rev. Legend:** "THE VAN HOI MUA DONG XVI, ALBERTVILLE 1992"

Date	Mintage	F	VF	XF	Unc	BU
1990(h) Proof	10,000	Value: 40.00				

KM# 34 100 DONG **Weight:** 12.0000 g. **Composition:** 0.9990 Silver .3858 oz. ASW **Subject:** Soccer **Obverse:** Arms, Value "100 DONG" below **Obv. Legend:** "CONG HOA XA HOI CHU NGHIA VIET NAM" **Rev. Legend:** "CUP BONG DA THE FIOI LAN THU XV, HOA KY 1994"

Date	F	VF	XF	Unc	BU
1991(h)	—	—	—	22.50	—

KM# 35 100 DONG **Weight:** 16.0000 g. **Composition:** 0.9990 Silver .5145 oz. ASW **Obverse:** Arms, Value "100 DONG" below **Obv. Legend:** "CONG HOA XA HOI CHU NGHIA VIET NAM" **Reverse:** Steamship Savannah **Rev. Legend:** "THUYEN CO SAVANNAH"

Date	F	VF	XF	Unc	BU
1991(h) Proof	—	Value: 35.00			

KM# 42 100 DONG **Weight:** 16.0000 g. **Composition:** 0.9990 Silver .5145 oz. ASW **Series:** Prehistoric Animals **Obverse:** Arms, value "100 DONG" below **Obv. Legend:** "CONG HOA XA HOI CHU NGHIA VIET NAM" **Reverse:** Rhamphorhynchus **Rev. Legend:** "DONG VAT CO DAI"

Date	F	VF	XF	Unc	BU
1993(h) Proof	—	Value: 45.00			

KM# 43 100 DONG **Weight:** 16.0000 g. **Composition:** 0.9990 Silver .5145 oz. ASW **Obverse:** Arms, value "100 DONG" below **Obv. Legend:** "CONG HOA XA HOI CHU NGHIA VIET NAM" **Reverse:** Elephants **Rev. Legend:** "BAO VI THIEN NHIEN - VOI"

Date	F	VF	XF	Unc	BU
1993(h) Proof	—	Value: 40.00			

KM# 45 100 DONG **Weight:** 16.0000 g. **Composition:** 0.9990 Silver .5145 oz. ASW **Series:** Prehistoric Animals **Obverse:** Arms, value "100 DONG" below **Obv. Legend:** "CONG HOA XA HOI CHU NGHIA VIET NAM" **Reverse:** Edaphosaurus **Rev. Legend:** "DONG VAT CO DAI"

Date	F	VF	XF	Unc	BU
1994(h) Proof	—	Value: 45.00			

KM# 47 100 DONG **Weight:** 20.0000 g. **Composition:** 0.9990 Silver .6424 oz. ASW **Series:** Olympics **Obverse:** Arms, value "100 DONG" below **Obv. Legend:** "CONG HO XA HOI CHU NGHIA VIET NAM" **Reverse:** Gymnast on pummel horse **Rev. Legend:** "TU ATEN DEN ATLANTA"

Date	Mintage	F	VF	XF	Unc	B
1995(h) Proof	15,000	Value: 25.00				

KM# 48 100 DONG **Weight:** 20.0000 g. **Composition** 0.9990 Silver And Enamel .6424 oz. **Obverse:** Arms, valu "100 DONG" below **Obv. Legend:** "CONG HOA XA HOI CH NGHIA VIET NAM" **Reverse:** Caracal **Rev. Legend:** "TH AN THIT/CARACAL CARACAL"

Date	F	VF	XF	Unc
1996(h) Proof	—	Value: 60.00		

KM# 50 100 DONG **Weight:** 20.0000 g. **Compositio** 0.9990 Silver And Enamel .6430 oz. **Subject:** World Foo Summit **Obverse:** Arms, value "100 DONG" below **Obv. Legend:** "CONG HOA XA HOI CHU NGHIA VIET NAM" **Reverse:** World Food Summit logo above rice harvestin scene **Rev. Legend:** "HOI NGHI THUONG DINH THE GI VE LUONG THUC"

Date	F	VF	XF	Unc
1996(h) Proof	—	Value: 40.00		

KM# 60 100 DONG **Weight:** 16.0000 g. **Compositic** 0.9990 Silver 0.5139 oz. ASW **Subject:** UNICEF **Obvers** State arms. **Reverse:** Child on water buffalo. **Edge:** Reede **Size:** 38 mm.

Date	Mintage	F	VF	XF	Unc
1997 Proof	25,000	Value: 20.00			

KM# 41 500 DONG **Weight:** 3.1030 g. **Compositior** 0.9990 Gold **Subject:** 100 Anniversary - Birth of Ho Chi M **Obverse:** Arms, value "500 Dong" below **Obv. Legend:** "CONG HOA XA HOI CHU NGHIA VIET NAM" **Note:** KM# was minted in the Leningrad (St. Petersburg) Mint (L) as g to the Vietnamese government and were not circulated. KM#41 was available in a box or as an encapsulated individual piece. This piece is cataloged as A24 and illustra in Gunter Schon's World Coins Catalogue.

ate	F	VF	XF	Unc	BU
989(L)	—	—	—	165	—

KM# 54 5000 DONG Weight: 1.2441 g. **Composition:** 0.9999 Gold .0400 oz. AGW **Subject:** Year of the Dragon **Obverse:** National arms **Obv. Legend:** "CONG HOA XA HOI CHU NGHIA VIET NAM" **Reverse:** Dragon with radiant sun **Rev. Legend:** "RONG VIET NAM" **Edge:** Reeded **Size:** 13.92 mm.

ate		F	VF	XF	Unc	BU
000 (S)	—	Value: 40.00				

KM# 64 5000 DONG Weight: 1.2441 g. **Composition:** 0.9999 Gold 0.04 oz. AGW **Subject:** Year of the Snake **Obverse:** National arms. **Reverse:** Sea snake. **Edge:** Reeded. **Size:** 13.92 mm.

ate	F	VF	XF	Unc	BU
001	—	—	—	50.00	—

KM# 51 10000 DONG Weight: 20.0000 g. **Composition:** 0.9250 Silver .5948 oz. ASW **Subject:** Year of the Dragon **Obverse:** National arms, value "10000 DONG" below **Obv. Legend:** "CONG HOA XA HOI CHU NGHIA VIET NAM" **Reverse:** Dragon with radiant sun **Edge:** Reeded **Size:** 38.7 mm.

ate	Mintage	F	VF	XF	Unc	BU
00 (S) Proof	10,000	Value: 35.00				

M# 52 10000 DONG Weight: 20.0000 g. **Composition:** 0.9250 Silver .5948 oz. ASW **Subject:** Year of the Dragon **Obverse:** National arms, value "10000 DONG" below **Obv. Legend:** "CONG HOA XA HOI CHU NGHIA VIET NAM" **Reverse:** Multi-colored dragon **Rev. Legend:** "RONG VIET NAM" **Edge:** Reeded **Size:** 38.7 mm.

te	Mintage	F	VF	XF	Unc	BU
00 (S) Proof	10,000	Value: 35.00				

M# 53 10000 DONG Weight: 20.0000 g. **Composition:** 0.9250 Silver .5948 oz. ASW **Subject:** Year of the Dragon **Obverse:** National arms **Obv. Legend:** "CONG HOA XA HOI CHU NGHIA VIET NAM" **Reverse:** Two dragons **Edge:** Reeded **Size:** 38.7 mm.

te	Mintage	F	VF	XF	Unc	BU
0 (S) Proof	10,000	Value: 35.00				

KM# 57 10000 DONG Weight: 20.0000 g. **Composition:** 0.9250 Silver .5948 oz. ASW **Subject:** Year of the Snake **Obverse:** Arms, value "10000 DONG" below **Obv. Legend:** "CONG HOA XA HOI CHU NGHIA VIET NAM" **Reverse:** Sea snake **Rev. Legend:** "...VIET NAM" **Edge:** Reeded **Size:** 38.7 mm.

Date	Mintage	F	VF	XF	Unc	BU
2001 (S) Proof	3,500	Value: 40.00				

KM# 58 10000 DONG Weight: 20.0000 g. **Composition:** 0.9250 Silver .5948 oz. ASW **Subject:** Year of the Snake **Obverse:** Arms, value "10000 DONG" below **Obv. Legend:** "CONG HOA XA HOI CHU NGHIA VIET NAM" **Reverse:** Bamboo viper **Rev. Legend:** "...VIET NAM"

Date	Mintage	F	VF	XF	Unc	BU
2001 (S) Proof	3,500	Value: 40.00				

KM# 59 10000 DONG Weight: 20.0000 g. **Composition:** 0.9250 Silver .5948 oz. ASW **Subject:** Year of the Snake **Obverse:** Arms, value "10000 DONG" below **Obv. Legend:** "CONG HOA XA HOI CHU NGHIA VIET NAM" **Reverse:** Multi-colored holographic, cobra in center **Rev. Legend:** "...VIET NAM"

Date	Mintage	F	VF	XF	Unc	BU
2001 (S) Proof	3,500	Value: 40.00				

KM# 61 10000 DONG Weight: 20.0000 g. **Composition:** 0.9990 Silver 0.6424 oz. ASW **Subject:** Year of the Horse **Obverse:** National arms. **Reverse:** Horse with octagonal latent image. **Edge:** Reeded. **Size:** 38.7 mm.

Date	Mintage	F	VF	XF	Unc	BU
2001	3,800	—	—	—	35.00	—

Note: In proof set only

KM# 62 10000 DONG Weight: 20.0000 g. **Composition:** 0.9990 Silver 0.6424 oz. ASW **Subject:** Year of the Horse **Obverse:** National arms. **Reverse:** Horse with multicolor accouterments. **Edge:** Reeded. **Size:** 38.7 mm.

Date	Mintage	F	VF	XF	Unc	BU
2001	3,800	—	—	—	35.00	—

Note: In proof set only

KM# 63 10000 DONG Weight: 20.0000 g. **Composition:** 0.9990 Silver 0.6424 oz. ASW **Subject:** Year of the Horse **Obverse:** National arms. **Reverse:** Multicolor holographic horse in center. **Edge:** Reeded. **Size:** 38.7 mm.

Date	Mintage	F	VF	XF	Unc	BU
2001	3,800	—	—	—	35.00	—

Note: In proof set only

KM# 55 20000 DONG Weight: 7.7749 g. **Composition:** 0.9999 Gold .2500 oz. AGW **Subject:** Year of the Dragon **Obverse:** Arms, value "20000 DONG" below **Obv. Legend:** "CONG HOA XA HOI CHU NGHIA VIET NAM" **Reverse:** Dragon and clouds **Rev. Legend:** "RONG VIET NAM" **Edge:** Reeded **Size:** 22 mm.

Date	Mintage	F	VF	XF	Unc	BU
2000 (S) Proof	1,800	Value: 200				

KM# 65 20000 DONG Weight: 7.7759 g. **Composition:** 0.9999 Gold 0.25 oz. AGW **Subject:** Year of the Snake **Obverse:** National arms. **Reverse:** Sea snake. **Edge:** Reeded. **Size:** 22 mm.

Date		F	VF	XF	Unc	BU
2001 (S) Proof	—	Value: 200				

Note: Issued in a replica Faberge Eggs.

KM# 56 50000 DONG Weight: 15.5518 g. **Composition:** 0.9999 Gold .5000 oz. AGW **Subject:** Year of the Dragon **Obverse:** Arms, value "50000 DONG" below **Obv. Legend:** "CONG HOA XA HOI CHU NGHIA VIET NAM" **Reverse:** Dragon before radiant sun **Rev. Legend:** "RONG VIET NAM" **Edge:** Reeded **Size:** 27 mm.

Date		F	VF	XF	Unc	BU
2000 (S) Proof	3,800	Value: 325				

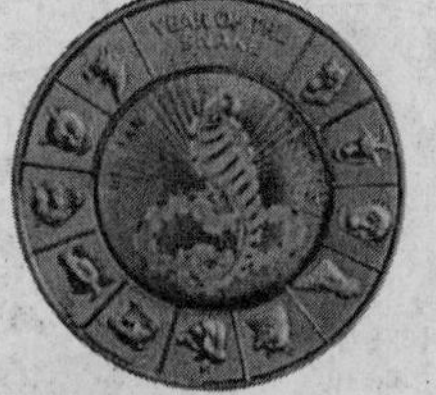

KM# 66 50000 DONG **Weight:** 15.5518 g. **Composition:** 0.9999 Gold 0.5 oz. AGW **Subject:** Year of the Snake **Obverse:** National arms. **Reverse:** Multicolor holographic King Cobra. **Edge:** Reeded. **Size:** 27 mm.

Date		F	VF	XF	Unc	BU
2001 (S) Proof	3,200	Value: 400				

PATTERNS

KM#	Date	Mintage	Identification	Mkt Val
Pn1	1976(s)	—	Hao. Silver. Arms. "NGAN HANG NHA NUOC VIET NAM". KM#11	—
Pn2	1976(s)	—	Dong. Silver. Arms. "NGAN HANG NHA NUOC VIET NAM". KM#14	—

PIEFORTS

KM#	Date	Mintage	Identification	Mkt Val
PE1	1990(h)	110	Dong. KM#32	150

MINT SETS

KM#	Date	Mintage	Identification	Issue Price	Mkt Val
MS1	1958-1976(s) (7)	—	KM#5-7, Democratic Republic; KM#11-14, Socialist Republic	—	85.00
MS2	1975/1976 (s) (7)	—	KM#8-14 NOTE: Created and sold by the Bank for Foreign Trade of Viet Nam to tourists and collectors.	—	15.00

PROOF SETS

KM#	Date	Mintage	Identification	Issue Price	Mkt Val
PS1	1989(L) (3)	—	KM#36a, 38a, 40a	—	—
PS2	2000(S) (3)	2,000	KM#51-53	—	100
PS3	2000(S) (2)	800	KM#55-56	—	525
PS4	2001(S) (3)	3,500	KM#57-59	120	—
PS5	2001(S) (2)	—	KM#59, 66	—	440
PS6	2001(S) (2)	—	KM#65-66	—	600
PS7	2002 (3)	3,800	KM#61-63	—	105

WEST AFRICAN STATES

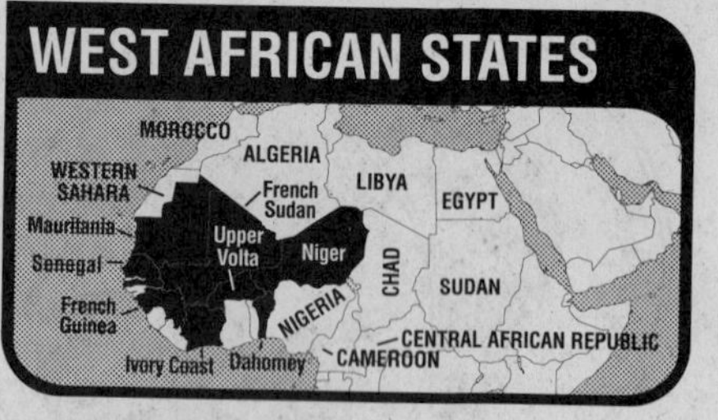

The West African States, a former federation of eight French colonial territories on the northwest coast of Africa, had area of 1,831,079 sq. mi. (4,742,495 sq. km.) and a population of about 17 million. Capital: Dakar. The constituent territories were Mauritania, Senegal, Dahomey, French Sudan, Ivory Coast, Upper Volta, Niger and French Guinea.

The members of the federation were overseas territories within the French Union until Sept. of 1958 when all but French Guinea approved the constitution of the Fifth French Republic, there by electing to become autonomous members of the new French Community. French Guinea voted to become the fully independent Republic of Guinea. The other seven attained independence in 1960. The French West Africa territories were provided with a common currency, a practice which was continued as the monetary union of the West African States which provides a common currency to the autonomous republics of Dahomey (now Benin), Senegal, Upper Volta (now Burkina Faso), Ivory Coast, Mali, Togo and Niger.

For earlier coinage refer to Togo, and French West Africa.

MINT MARKS

(a)- Paris, privy marks only

MONETARY SYSTEM

100 Centimes = 1 Franc

FEDERATION

STANDARD COINAGE

KM# 3.1 FRANC **Composition:** Aluminum

Date	Mintage	F	VF	XF	Unc	BU
1961(a)	3,000,000	—	0.15	0.30	0.60	—
1964(a)	5,000,000	—	0.15	0.30	0.60	—
1965(a)	6,000,000	—	0.15	0.30	0.60	—
1967(a)	2,500,000	—	0.15	0.30	0.60	—
1971(a)	4,000,000	—	0.15	0.30	0.60	—
1972(a)	4,000,000	—	0.15	0.30	0.60	—
1973(a)	4,500,000	—	0.15	0.30	0.60	—
1974(a)	—	—	0.15	0.30	0.60	—
1975(a)	10,080,000	—	0.15	0.30	0.60	—
1976(a)	8,000,000	—	0.15	0.30	0.60	—

KM# 3.2 FRANC **Composition:** Aluminum **Reverse:** Engraver general's name

Date	Mintage	F	VF	XF	Unc	BU
1962(a)	2,000,000	—	2.00	5.00	10.00	—
1963(a)	4,500,000	—	1.50	4.00	7.00	—

KM# 8 FRANC **Composition:** Steel

Date	Mintage	F	VF	XF	Unc	BU
1976(a)	8,000,000	—	—	0.10	0.35	—
1977(a)	14,700,000	—	—	0.10	0.35	—
1978(a)	—	—	—	0.10	0.35	—
1979(a)	—	—	—	0.10	0.35	—
1980(a)	—	—	—	0.10	0.35	—
1981(a)	—	—	—	0.10	0.35	—
1982(a)	—	—	—	0.10	0.35	—
1984(a)	—	—	—	0.10	0.35	—
1985(a)	26,900,000	—	—	—	—	—
1990(a)	—	—	—	0.10	0.35	—
1991(a)	—	—	—	0.10	0.35	—
1992(a)	—	—	—	0.10	0.35	—
1995(a)	—	—	—	0.10	0.35	—
1996(a)	—	—	—	0.10	0.35	—

KM# 2 5 FRANCS **Composition:** Aluminum-Bronze

Date	Mintage	F	VF	XF	Unc	BU
1960(a)	5,000,000	—	0.20	0.40	0.70	—

KM# 2a 5 FRANCS **Composition:** Aluminum-Nickel-Bronze

Date	Mintage	F	VF	XF	Unc	BU
1965(a)	6,510,000	—	0.20	0.40	0.70	—
1967(a)	6,010,000	—	0.20	0.40	0.70	—
1968(a)	6,000,000	—	0.20	0.45	0.75	—
1969(a)	8,000,000	—	0.20	0.40	0.70	—
1970(a)	10,005,000	—	0.20	0.40	0.70	—
1971(a)	10,000,000	—	0.20	0.40	0.70	—
1972(a)	5,000,000	—	0.20	0.40	0.70	—
1973(a)	6,000,000	—	0.20	0.45	0.75	—
1974(a)	13,326,000	—	0.10	0.15	0.30	—
1975(a)	16,840,000	—	0.20	0.40	0.70	—
1976(a)	20,010,000	—	0.20	0.30	0.60	—
1977(a)	16,840,000	—	0.20	0.30	0.60	—
1978(a)	—	—	0.20	0.30	0.60	—
1979(a)	—	—	0.10	0.20	0.40	—
1980(a)	—	—	0.10	0.20	0.40	—
1981(a)	—	—	0.10	0.20	0.40	—
1982(a)	—	—	0.10	0.20	0.40	—
1984(a)	—	—	0.10	0.20	0.40	—
1985(a)	16,000,000	—	0.10	0.20	0.40	—
1986(a)	8,000,000	—	0.10	0.20	0.40	—
1987(a)	—	—	0.10	0.20	0.40	—
1988(a)	—	—	0.10	0.20	0.40	—
1989(a)	—	—	0.10	0.20	0.40	—
1990(a)	—	—	0.10	0.20	0.40	—
1991(a)	—	—	0.10	0.20	0.40	—
1992(a)	—	—	0.10	0.20	0.40	—
1994(a)	—	—	0.10	0.20	0.40	—
1995(a)	—	—	0.10	0.20	0.40	—
1996(a)	—	—	0.10	0.20	0.40	—
1997(a)	—	—	0.10	0.20	0.40	—
1999(a)	—	—	0.10	0.20	0.40	—

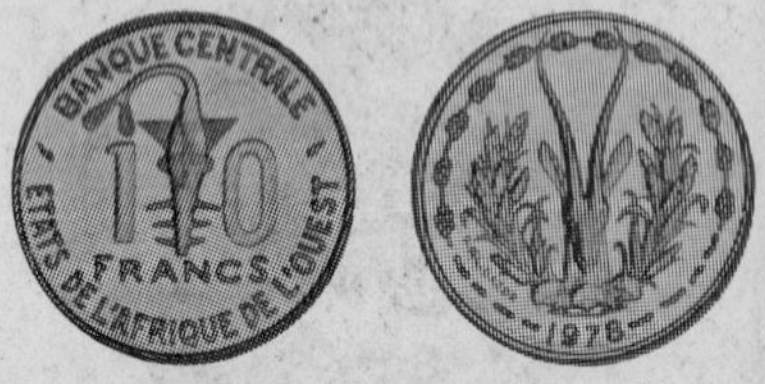

KM# 1 10 FRANCS **Composition:** Aluminum-Bronze

Date	Mintage	F	VF	XF	Unc
1959(a)	10,000,000	—	0.15	0.30	0.60
1964(a)	10,000,000	—	0.20	0.40	0.70

KM# 1a 10 FRANCS **Comp.:** Aluminum-Nickel-Bronze

Date	Mintage	F	VF	XF	Unc
1966(a)	6,000,000	—	0.20	0.40	0.70
1967(a)	3,500,000	—	0.25	0.50	0.90
1968(a)	6,000,000	—	0.20	0.40	0.70
1969(a)	7,000,000	—	0.25	0.50	0.90
1970(a)	7,000,000	—	0.15	0.30	0.60
1971(a)	8,000,000	—	0.15	0.30	0.60
1972(a)	5,500,000	—	0.20	0.40	0.70
1973(a)	3,000,000	—	0.20	0.40	0.70
1974(a)	10,000,000	—	0.15	0.30	0.60
1975(a)	17,000,000	—	0.15	0.30	0.60
1976(a)	18,000,000	—	0.15	0.30	0.60
1977(a)	9,050,000	—	0.15	0.25	0.50
1978(a)	—	—	0.15	0.25	0.50
1979(a)	—	—	0.15	0.25	0.50
1980(a)	—	—	0.15	0.25	0.50
1981(a)	—	—	0.15	0.25	0.50

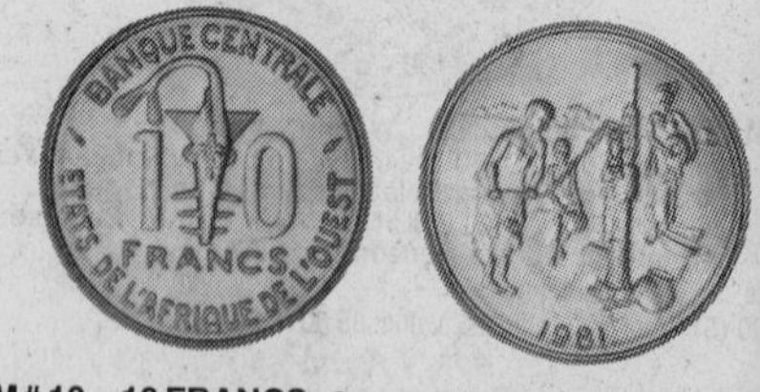

KM# 10 10 FRANCS **Composition:** Brass **Series:** F.A

Date	Mintage	F	VF	XF	Unc
1981(a)	—	—	0.25	0.50	1.25
1982(a)	—	—	0.25	0.50	1.25
1983(a)	—	—	0.25	0.50	1.25
1984(a)	—	—	0.25	0.50	1.25
1985(a)	5,000,000	—	0.25	0.50	1.25
1986(a)	7,500,000	—	0.25	0.50	1.25
1987(a)	—	—	0.25	0.50	1.25
1989(a)	—	—	0.25	0.50	1.25

Date	Mintage	F	VF	XF	Unc	BU
990(a)	—	—	0.25	0.50	1.25	—
991(a)	—	—	0.25	0.50	1.25	—
992(a)	—	—	0.25	0.50	1.25	—
993(a)	—	—	0.25	0.50	1.25	—
994(a)	—	—	0.25	0.50	1.25	—
995(a)	—	—	0.25	0.50	1.25	—
996(a)	—	—	0.25	0.50	1.25	—
997(a)	—	—	0.25	0.50	1.25	—
000(a)	—	—	0.25	0.50	1.25	—

KM# 5 25 FRANCS **Composition:** Aluminum-Bronze

Date	Mintage	F	VF	XF	Unc	BU
970(a)	7,000,000	—	0.25	0.45	0.80	—
971(a)	7,000,000	—	0.50	0.75	1.25	—
972(a)	2,000,000	—	1.50	2.50	4.50	—
975(a)	5,035,000	—	0.25	0.45	0.80	—
976(a)	3,365,000	—	0.25	0.45	0.80	—
977(a)	3,288,000	—	0.25	0.45	0.80	—
978(a)	—	—	0.25	0.45	0.80	—
979(a)	—	—	0.25	0.45	0.80	—

KM# 9 25 FRANCS **Composition:** Aluminum-Bronze **Series:** F.A.O.

Date	Mintage	F	VF	XF	Unc	BU
980(a)	—	—	0.25	0.75	1.75	—
981(a)	—	—	0.25	0.75	1.75	—
982(a)	—	—	0.25	0.75	1.75	—
984(a)	—	—	0.25	0.75	1.75	—
985(a)	8,587,000	—	—	—	—	—
987(a)	—	—	0.25	0.75	1.75	—
989(a)	—	—	0.25	0.75	1.75	—
990(a)	—	—	0.25	0.75	1.75	—
992(a)	—	—	0.25	0.75	1.75	—
994(a)	—	—	0.25	0.75	1.75	—
996(a)	—	—	0.25	0.75	1.75	—
997(a)	—	—	0.25	0.75	1.75	—

KM# 6 50 FRANCS **Composition:** Copper-Nickel **Series:** F.A.O.

Date	Mintage	F	VF	XF	Unc	BU
72(a)	20,000,000	—	0.35	0.50	1.25	—
74(a)	3,000,000	—	0.50	0.75	1.50	—
75(a)	9,000,000	—	0.25	0.40	1.00	—
76(a)	6,002,000	—	0.35	0.50	1.25	—
77(a)	4,832,000	—	0.35	0.50	1.25	—
78(a)	—	—	0.35	0.50	1.25	—
79(a)	—	—	0.35	0.50	1.25	—
80(a)	—	—	0.35	0.50	1.25	—
81(a)	—	—	0.35	0.50	1.25	—
82(a)	—	—	0.35	0.50	1.25	—
84(a)	—	—	0.35	0.50	1.25	—
85(a)	4,120,000	—	—	—	—	—
86(a)	—	—	0.35	0.50	1.25	—
87(a)	—	—	0.35	0.50	1.25	—
89(a)	—	—	0.35	0.50	1.25	—
90(a)	—	—	0.35	0.50	1.25	—
91(a)	—	—	0.35	0.50	1.25	—
92(a)	—	—	0.35	0.50	1.25	—
95(a)	—	—	0.35	0.50	1.25	—
96(a)	—	—	0.35	0.50	1.25	—
97(a)	—	—	0.35	0.50	1.25	—

KM# 4 100 FRANCS **Composition:** Nickel

Date	Mintage	F	VF	XF	Unc	BU
1967(a)	—	—	0.75	1.00	2.50	—
1968(a)	25,000,000	—	0.75	1.00	2.50	—
1969(a)	25,000,000	—	0.75	1.00	2.50	—
1970(a)	4,510,000	—	0.80	1.50	3.50	—
1971(a)	12,000,000	—	0.50	0.75	1.85	—
1972(a)	5,000,000	—	0.60	0.85	2.00	—
1973(a)	5,000,000	—	0.60	0.85	2.00	—
1974(a)	8,500,000	—	0.60	0.75	1.85	—
1975(a)	16,000,000	—	0.60	0.75	1.85	—
1976(a)	11,575,000	—	0.60	0.75	1.85	—
1977(a)	9,355,000	—	0.60	0.75	1.85	—
1978(a)	—	—	0.60	0.75	1.85	—
1979(a)	—	—	0.60	0.85	2.00	—
1980(a)	—	—	0.60	0.75	2.00	—
1981(a)	—	—	0.60	0.75	2.00	—
1982(a)	—	—	0.60	0.75	2.00	—
1984(a)	—	—	0.65	0.85	2.25	—
1985(a)	1,460,000	—	—	—	—	—
1987(a)	—	—	0.65	0.85	2.25	—
1989(a)	—	—	0.65	0.85	2.25	—
1990(a)	—	—	0.65	0.85	2.25	—
1991(a)	—	—	0.65	0.85	2.25	—
1992(a)	—	—	0.65	0.85	2.25	—
1996(a)	—	—	0.65	0.85	2.25	—
1997(a)	—	—	0.65	0.85	2.25	—

KM# 13 250 FRANCS **Ring Composition:** Copper-Nickel **Center Composition:** Brass

Date	F	VF	XF	Unc	BU
1992(a)	—	1.75	2.75	7.00	—
1993(a)	—	1.75	2.75	7.00	—
1996(a)	—	2.00	3.00	8.00	—

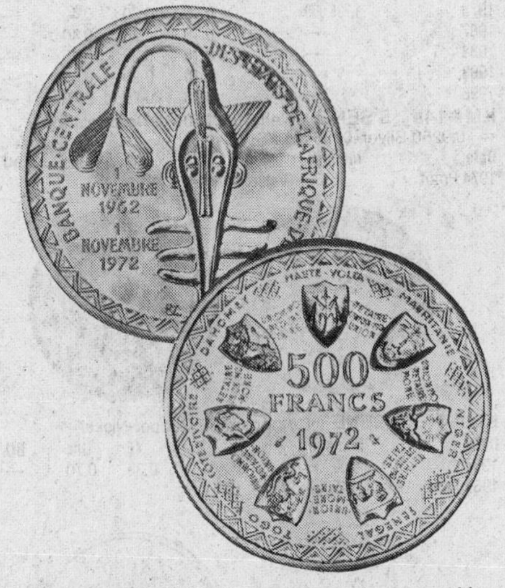

KM# 7 500 FRANCS **Weight:** 25.0000 g. **Composition:** 0.9000 Silver .7234 oz. ASW **Subject:** 10th anniversary of monetary union

Date	Mintage	F	VF	XF	Unc	BU
1972(a)	100,000	—	—	17.50	40.00	—

KM# 11 5000 FRANCS **Weight:** 24.9500 g. **Composition:** 0.9000 Silver .7220 oz. ASW **Subject:** 20th anniversary of monetary union

Date	Mintage	F	VF	XF	Unc	BU
1982(a)	200,000	—	—	15.00	45.00	—

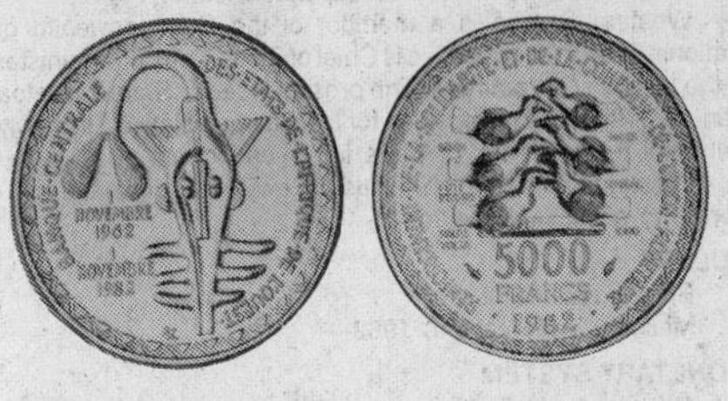

KM# 12 5000 FRANCS **Weight:** 14.4900 g. **Composition:** 0.9000 Gold .4193 oz. AGW **Subject:** 20th anniversary of monetary union

Date	F	VF	XF	Unc	BU
1982(a)	—	—	—	450	—

ESSAIS

KM#	Date	Mintage	Identification	Issue Price	Mkt Val
E1	1959(a)	—	10 Francs. KM1.	—	17.00
E2	1960(a)	—	5 Francs. KM2.	—	15.00
E3	1961(a)	—	Franc. KM3.	—	15.00
E4	1967(a)	1,600	100 Francs. KM4.	—	20.00
E4a	1967(a)	100	100 Francs. Silver. KM4.	—	110
E4b	1967(a)	21	100 Francs. Gold. KM4.	—	750
E5	1970(a)	1,450	25 Francs. KM5.	—	17.00
E6	1972(a)	1,750	50 Francs. KM6.	—	15.00
E7	1972(a)	2,000	500 Francs. KM7.	—	45.00
E6a	1972(a)	120	50 Francs. Silver. KM6.	—	80.00
E6b	1972(a)	17	50 Francs. Gold. KM6.	—	625
E8	1976(a)	—	Franc. KM8.	—	15.00
E10	1980(a)	5	25 Francs. Gold.	—	1,800

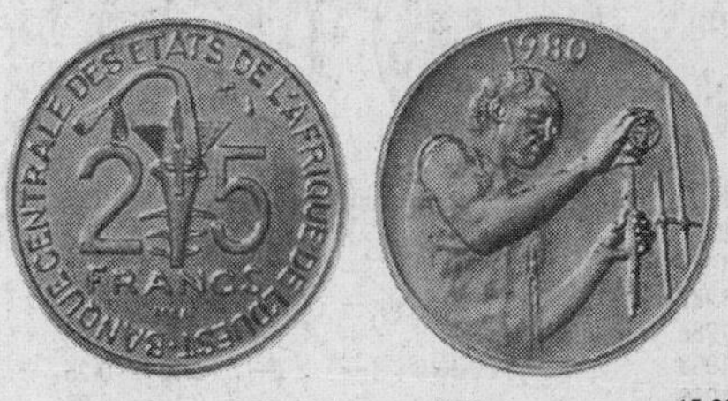

KM#	Date	Mintage	Identification	Issue Price	Mkt Val
E9	1980(a)	3,000	25 Francs. KM9.	—	15.00
E11	1980(a)	—	500 Francs.	—	40.00
E12	1981(a)	1,950	10 Francs. KM10.	—	12.00
E13	1982(a)	1,700	5000 Francs. KM11.	—	85.00
E14	1982(a)	12	5000 Francs. Gold. KM11.	—	1,600

"FDC" SETS

This fleur-de-coin set was issued with New Caledonia and French Polynesia 1967 sets.

KM#	Date	Mintage	Identification	Issue Price	Mkt Val
SS1	1968(a) (3)	—	KM1a, 2a, 4	—	9.50

WESTERN SAMOA

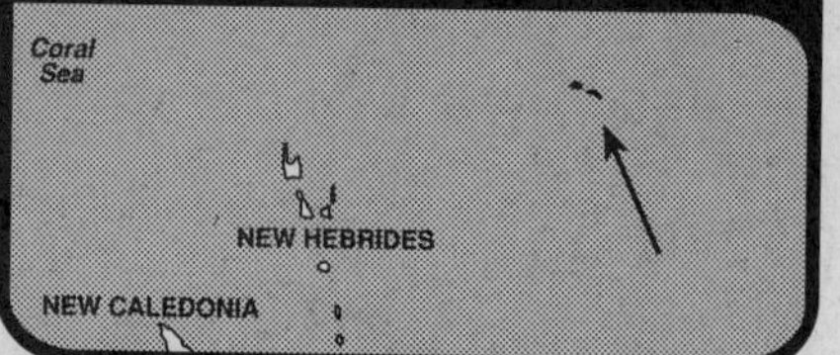

The Independent State of Western Samoa (formerly German Samoa), located in the Pacific Ocean 1,600 miles (2,574 km.) northeast of New Zealand, has an area of 1,097 sq. mi. (2,860 sq. km.) and a population of *182,000. Capital: Apia. The economy is based on agriculture, fishing and tourism. Copra, cocoa and bananas are exported.

The first European to sight the Samoan group of islands was the Dutch navigator Jacob Roggeveen in 1772. Great Britain, the United States and Germany established consular representation at Apia in 1847, 1853 and 1861 respectively. The conflicting interests of the three powers produced the Berlin agreement of 1889, which declared Samoa neutral and had the effect of establishing a tripartite protectorate over the islands. A further agreement, 1899, recognized the rights of the United States in those islands east of 171 deg. west longitude (American Samoa) and of Germany in the other islands (Western Samoa). New Zealand occupied Western Samoa at the start of World War I and administered it as a League of Nations mandate and U. N. trusteeship until Jan. 1, 1962, when it became an independent state.

Western Samoa is a member of the Commonwealth of Nations. The Chief Executive is Chief of State. The prime minister is the Head of Government. The present Head of State, Malietoa Tanumafili II, holds his position for life. The Legislative Assembly will elect future Heads of State for 5-year terms.

Western Samoa, which had used New Zealand coinage, converted to a decimal coinage in 1967.

RULERS

British, until 1962

Malietoa Tanumafili II, 1962—

MONETARY SYSTEM

100 Sene = 1 Tala

BRITISH ADMINISTRATION

STANDARD COINAGE

KM# 1 SENE Composition: Bronze

Date	Mintage	F	VF	XF	Unc	BU
1967	915,000	—	0.10	0.15	0.30	—
1967 Proof	15,000	Value: 0.50				

KM# 12 SENE Composition: Bronze

Date	Mintage	F	VF	XF	Unc	BU
1974	3,380,000	—	—	0.10	0.25	—
1987	—	—	—	0.10	0.25	—
1988	—	—	—	0.10	0.25	—
1993	—	—	—	0.10	0.25	—
1996	—	—	—	0.10	0.25	—

KM# 12a SENE Weight: 1.9500 g. **Composition:** 0.9250 Silver .0579 oz. ASW

Date	Mintage	F	VF	XF	Unc	BU
1974 Proof	5,578	Value: 1.50				

KM# 2 2 SENE Composition: Bronze

Date	Mintage	F	VF	XF	Unc	BU
1967	465,000	—	0.10	0.20	0.40	—
1967 Proof	15,000	Value: 0.50				

KM# 13 2 SENE Composition: Bronze

Date	Mintage	F	VF	XF	Unc	BU
1974	1,640,000	—	0.10	0.15	0.30	—
1988	—	—	0.10	0.15	0.30	—
1996	—	—	0.10	0.15	0.30	—

KM# 13a 2 SENE Weight: 3.8000 g. **Composition:** 0.9250 Silver .1130 oz. ASW

Date	Mintage	F	VF	XF	Unc	BU
1974 Proof	5,578	Value: 2.50				

KM# 122 2 SENE Composition: Bronze **Series:** F.A.O. **Obverse:** King's portrait **Reverse:** Denomination in wreath

Date	F	VF	XF	Unc	BU
2000(1999)	—	—	—	0.35	—

KM# 3 5 SENE Composition: Copper-Nickel

Date	Mintage	F	VF	XF	Unc	BU
1967	495,000	—	0.15	0.25	0.50	—
1967 Proof	15,000	Value: 1.00				

KM# 14 5 SENE Composition: Copper-Nickel

Date	Mintage	F	VF	XF	Unc	BU
1974	1,736,000	—	0.10	0.20	0.40	—
1987	—	—	0.10	0.20	0.40	—
1988	—	—	0.10	0.20	0.40	—
1993	—	—	0.10	0.20	0.40	—
1996	—	—	0.10	0.20	0.40	—

KM# 14a 5 SENE Weight: 3.2500 g. **Composition:** 0.9250 Silver .0966 oz. ASW

Date	Mintage	F	VF	XF	Unc	BU
1974 Proof	5,578	Value: 3.00				

KM# 4 10 SENE Composition: Copper-Nickel

Date	Mintage	F	VF	XF	Unc	BU
1967	400,000	—	0.20	0.35	0.70	—
1967 Proof	15,000	Value: 1.00				

KM# 15 10 SENE Composition: Copper-Nickel

Date	Mintage	F	VF	XF	Unc	BU
1974	1,580,000	—	0.15	0.30	0.60	—
1987	—	—	0.15	0.30	0.60	—
1988	—	—	0.15	0.30	0.60	—
1993	—	—	0.15	0.30	0.60	—
1996	—	—	0.15	0.30	0.60	—

KM# 15a 10 SENE Weight: 6.3700 g. **Composition:** 0.9250 Silver .1894 oz. ASW

Date	Mintage	F	VF	XF	Unc	BU
1974 Proof	5,578	Value: 3.50				

KM# 5 20 SENE Composition: Copper-Nickel

Date	Mintage	F	VF	XF	Unc	BU
1967	400,000	—	0.25	0.50	1.00	—
1967 Proof	15,000	Value: 1.50				

KM# 16 20 SENE Composition: Copper-Nickel

Date	Mintage	F	VF	XF	Unc	BU
1974	1,380,000	—	0.20	0.40	0.80	-
1987	—	—	0.20	0.40	0.80	-
1988	—	—	0.20	0.40	0.80	-
1993	—	—	0.20	0.40	0.80	-
1996	—	—	0.20	0.40	0.80	-

KM# 16a 20 SENE Weight: 12.7000 g. **Composition:** 0.9250 Silver .3776 oz. ASW

Date	Mintage	F	VF	XF	Unc	BU
1974 Proof	5,578	Value: 4.00				

KM# 6 50 SENE Composition: Copper-Nickel

Date	Mintage	F	VF	XF	Unc
1967	80,000	—	0.75	1.25	2.00
1967 Proof	15,000	Value: 2.50			

KM# 17 50 SENE Composition: Copper-Nickel

Date	Mintage	F	VF	XF	Unc
1974	50,000	—	0.75	1.25	2.00
1988	—	—	0.75	1.25	2.00
1996	—	—	0.75	1.25	2.00
2000	—	—	0.75	1.25	2.00

KM# 17a 50 SENE Weight: 15.4000 g. **Composition** 0.9250 Silver .4579 oz. ASW

Date	Mintage	F	VF	XF	Unc
1974 Proof	5,578	Value: 5.00			

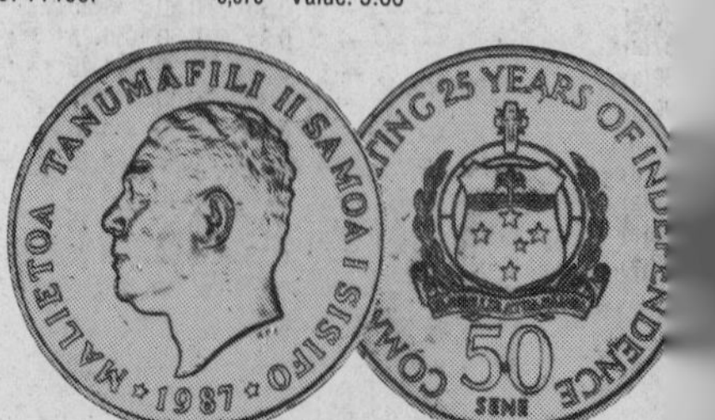

KM# 80 50 SENE Composition: Copper-Nickel **Subje**
25th anniversary of independence

Date		F	VF	XF	Unc	BU
1987		—	—	—	2.50	—

KM# 7 TALA **Composition:** Copper-Nickel **Obverse:** Bust left **Reverse:** Similar to 50 Sene, KM#6

Date	Mintage	F	VF	XF	Unc	BU
1967	20,000	—	—	—	3.00	—
1967 Proof	15,000	Value: 6.00				

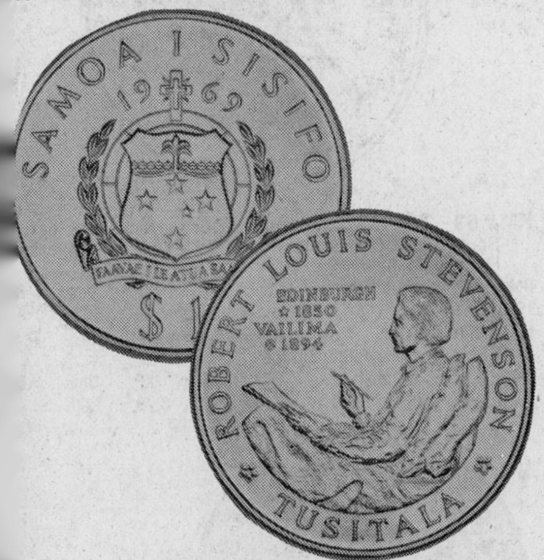

KM# 8 TALA **Composition:** Copper-Nickel **Subject:** 75th anniversary - death of Robert Louis Stevenson

Date	Mintage	F	VF	XF	Unc	BU
1969	25,000	—	—	—	3.00	—
1969 Proof	1,500	Value: 6.00				

KM# 9 TALA **Composition:** Copper-Nickel **Subject:** 200th anniversary - Capt. Cook voyages **Obverse:** Similar to KM#8

Date	Mintage	F	VF	XF	Unc	BU
1970	32,000	—	—	—	3.00	—
1970 Proof	3,000	Value: 6.00				

KM# 10 TALA **Composition:** Copper-Nickel **Subject:** Visit of Pope Paul VI **Obverse:** Similar to KM#8

Date	Mintage	F	VF	XF	Unc	BU
1970	35,000	—	—	—	3.50	—
1970 Proof	3,000	Value: 7.00				

KM# 11 TALA **Composition:** Copper-Nickel **Subject:** Roggeveen's Pacific voyage **Obverse:** Similar to KM#8

Date	Mintage	F	VF	XF	Unc	BU
1972	35,000	—	—	—	3.50	—
1972 Proof	3,000	Value: 8.00				

KM# 18 TALA **Composition:** Copper-Nickel **Subject:** 10th British Commonwealth Games **Obverse:** Similar to KM#8

Date	Mintage	F	VF	XF	Unc	BU
1974	40,000	—	—	—	4.00	—

KM# 18a TALA **Weight:** 27.7000 g. **Composition:** 0.9250 Silver .8239 oz. ASW **Subject:** 10th British Commonwealth Games **Obverse:** Similar to KM#8

Date	Mintage	F	VF	XF	Unc	BU
1974 Proof	1,500	Value: 13.50				

KM# 19 TALA **Composition:** Copper-Nickel **Obverse:** Similar to 50 Sene, KM#17

Date	Mintage	F	VF	XF	Unc	BU
1974	24,000	—	—	—	3.00	—

KM# 19a TALA **Weight:** 31.1500 g. **Composition:** 0.9250 Silver .9263 oz. ASW **Obverse:** Similar to 50 Sene, KM#17

Date	Mintage	F	VF	XF	Unc	BU
1974 Proof	11,000	Value: 10.00				

KM# 20 TALA **Composition:** Copper-Nickel **Subject:** U.S. bicentennial

Date	Mintage	F	VF	XF	Unc	BU
ND(1976)	40,000	—	—	—	3.00	—

KM# 20a TALA **Weight:** 30.4000 g. **Composition:** 0.9250 Silver .9040 oz. ASW **Subject:** U.S. bicentennial

Date	Mintage	F	VF	XF	Unc	BU
ND(1976) Proof	4,127	Value: 10.00				

KM# 22 TALA **Composition:** Copper-Nickel **Series:** Montreal Olympics **Obverse:** Similar to KM#8 **Reverse:** Weight lifter

Date	Mintage	F	VF	XF	Unc	BU
1976	40,000	—	—	—	3.50	—

KM# 22a TALA **Weight:** 30.4000 g. **Composition:** 0.9250 Silver .9040 oz. ASW **Series:** Montreal Olympics **Obverse:** Similar to KM#8 **Reverse:** Weight lifter

Date	Mintage	F	VF	XF	Unc	BU
1976 Proof	6,000	Value: 12.50				

KM# 24 TALA **Composition:** Copper-Nickel **Subject:** Queen's silver jubilee **Obverse:** Similar to KM#8

Date	Mintage	F	VF	XF	Unc	BU
1977	27,000	—	—	—	3.00	—

KM# 24a TALA **Weight:** 30.4000 g. **Composition:** 0.9250 Silver .9040 oz. ASW **Subject:** Queen's silver jubilee **Obverse:** Similar to KM#8

Date	Mintage	F	VF	XF	Unc	BU
1977 Proof	6,171	Value: 10.00				

KM# 26 TALA **Composition:** Copper-Nickel **Subject:** Lindbergh's New York to Paris flight **Obverse:** Similar to KM#8

Date	Mintage	F	VF	XF	Unc	BU
1977	17,000	—	—	—	3.25	—

KM# 26a TALA **Weight:** 30.4000 g. **Composition:** 0.9250 Silver .9040 oz. ASW **Subject:** Lindbergh's New York to Paris flight **Obverse:** Similar to KM#8

Date	Mintage	F	VF	XF	Unc	BU
1977 Proof	4,522	Value: 11.00				

KM# 28 TALA **Comp.:** Copper-Nickel **Subject:** 50th anniversary - first transpacific flight **Obverse:** Similar to KM#8

Date	Mintage	F	VF	XF	Unc	BU
1978	20,000	—	—	—	3.25	—

KM# 28a TALA **Weight:** 30.4000 g. **Composition:** 0.9250 Silver .9040 oz. ASW **Subject:** 50th anniversary - first transpacific flight **Obverse:** Similar to KM#8

Date	Mintage	F	VF	XF	Unc	BU
1978 Proof	5,000	Value: 11.00				

KM# 30 TALA Composition: Copper-Nickel **Subject:** XI Commonwealth Games **Obverse:** Similar to KM#8

Date	Mintage	F	VF	XF	Unc	BU
1978	7,710	—	—	—	4.00	—

KM# 30a TALA Weight: 30.4000 g. **Composition:** 0.9250 Silver .9040 oz. ASW **Subject:** XI Commonwealth Games **Obverse:** Similar to KM#8

Date	Mintage	F	VF	XF	Unc	BU
1978 Proof	5,000	Value: 11.00				

KM# 32 TALA Composition: Copper-Nickel **Subject:** Bicentenary - death of Capt. James Cook **Obverse:** Similar to KM#8

Date	Mintage	F	VF	XF	Unc	BU
1979	5,000	—	—	—	3.00	—

KM# 35 TALA Composition: Copper-Nickel **Series:** 1980 Olympics **Subject:** Hurdles **Obverse:** Similar to KM#8

Date	Mintage	F	VF	XF	Unc	BU
1980	5,000	—	—	—	4.00	—

KM# 38 TALA Composition: Copper-Nickel **Series:** F.A.O. **Obverse:** Similar to KM#8

Date	Mintage	F	VF	XF	Unc	BU
1980	10,000	—	—	—	3.00	—

KM# 40 TALA Composition: Copper-Nickel **Subject:** Gov. Wilhelm Solf **Obverse:** Similar to KM#8

Date	Mintage	F	VF	XF	Unc	BU
1980	5,000	—	—	—	4.00	—

KM# 43 TALA Composition: Copper-Nickel **Subject:** Wedding of Prince Charles and Lady Diana **Obverse:** Similar to KM#8

Date	Mintage	F	VF	XF	Unc	BU
1981	12,000	—	—	—	3.00	—

KM# 47 TALA Composition: Copper-Nickel **Subject:** IYDP - President Franklin Roosevelt **Obverse:** Similar to KM#8

Date	Mintage	F	VF	XF	Unc	BU
1981	8,000	—	—	—	3.00	—

KM# 50 TALA Composition: Copper-Nickel **Subject:** Commonwealth Games **Obverse:** Similar to KM#8 **Reverse:** Javelin thrower

Date	Mintage	F	VF	XF	Unc	BU
1982	6,000	—	—	—	3.50	—

KM# 53 TALA Composition: Copper-Nickel **Subject:** South Pacific Games **Obverse:** Similar to KM#8 **Reverse:** Runner

Date	Mintage	F	VF	XF	Unc	B
1983	8,000	—	—	—	3.25	-

KM# 57 TALA Composition: Aluminum-Bronze **Subject:** Circulation coinage

Date	Mintage	F	VF	XF	Unc	B
1984	1,000,000	—	0.50	0.75	1.00	-

KM# 58 TALA Composition: Copper-Nickel **Series:** Summer Olympics **Reverse:** Boxers

Date	Mintage	F	VF	XF	Unc
1984	5,000	—	—	—	4.50

KM# 63 TALA Composition: Copper-Nickel **Subject:** Prince Andrew's marriage

Date	Mintage	F	VF	XF	Unc
1986	10,000	—	—	—	3.00

74 TALA **Composition:** Copper-Nickel **Subject:** 25th anniversary of World Wildlife Fund **Reverse:** Samoan fantail bird

	F	VF	XF	Unc	BU
	—	—	—	3.00	—

 # 88 TALA **Composition:** Copper-Nickel **Subject:** 40th anniversary - reign of Queen Elizabeth II

	F	VF	XF	Unc	BU
992)	—	—	—	3.50	—

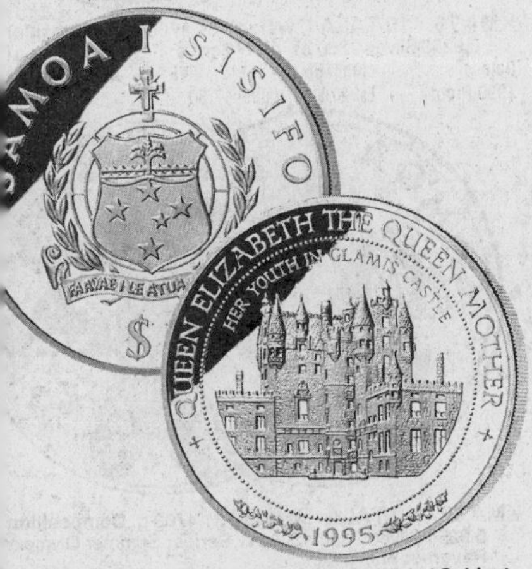

 # 111 TALA **Composition:** Copper-Nickel **Subject:** Queen Mother **Reverse:** Glamis Castle

	F	VF	XF	Unc	BU
5	—	—	—	3.50	—

 # 112 TALA **Weight:** 10.0000 g. **Composition:** 0.5000 Silver .1607 oz. ASW **Series:** Olympics **Reverse:** Gymnast and pummel horse

Date	F	VF	XF	Unc	BU
1996	—	—	—	11.50	—

KM# 120 2 TALA **Weight:** 42.4139 g. **Composition:** 0.9250 Silver 1.3636 oz. ASW **Obverse:** National arms **Reverse:** Denomination and 3 scenes **Note:** Part of a tri-national, three-coin matching set with Cook Islands and Fiji.

Date	Mintage	F	VF	XF	Unc	BU
1998 Proof	Est. 20,000	Value: 50.00				

KM# 125 5 TALA **Weight:** 19.8300 g. **Composition:** Copper Nickel **Subject:** Robert Louis Stevenson **Obverse:** National arms. **Reverse:** Ship, portrait and pirate scene. **Edge:** Reeded. **Size:** 38.7 mm.

Date	Mintage	F	VF	XF	Unc	BU
ND(1994)	100,000	—	—	—	7.50	—

KM# 115 5 TALA **Weight:** 15.5518 g. **Composition:** 0.9250 Silver .4625 oz. ASW **Subject:** War and peace **Obverse:** West Samoan arms **Reverse:** Arrows and sword **Note:** 1/2 of 2-part coin, combined with Kiribati KM#22, issued in sets only; Value is determined by combining the 2 parts.

Date	Mintage	F	VF	XF	Unc	BU
ND(1997) Proof	Est. 10,000	Value: 28.00				

KM# 116 5 TALA **Weight:** 15.5518 g. **Composition:** 0.9250 Silver .4625 oz. ASW **Subject:** Epoch - making events **Reverse:** Helmet and crowns **Note:** 1/2 of 2-part coin, combined with Kiribati KM#23, issued in sets only; Value is determined by combining the 2 parts.

Date	Mintage	F	VF	XF	Unc	BU
ND(1997) Proof	Est. 10,000	Value: 28.00				

KM# 117 5 TALA **Weight:** 15.5518 g. **Composition:** 0.9250 Silver .4625 oz. ASW **Subject:** Tempora mutantur **Reverse:** Man with torch **Note:** 1/2 of 2-part coin, combined with Kiribati KM#24, issued in sets only; Value is determined by combining the 2 parts.

Date	Mintage	F	VF	XF	Unc	BU
ND(1997) Proof	Est. 10,000	Value: 28.00				

KM# 118 5 TALA **Weight:** 15.5518 g. **Composition:** 0.9250 Silver .4625 oz. ASW **Subject:** People and buildings **Reverse:** Working hands **Note:** 1/2 of 2-part coin, combined with Kiribati KM#25, issued in sets only; Value is determined by combining the 2 parts.

Date	Mintage	F	VF	XF	Unc	BU
ND(1997) Proof	Est. 10,000	Value: 28.00				

KM# 33 10 TALA **Weight:** 31.3300 g. **Composition:** 0.5000 Silver .5036 oz. ASW **Subject:** Bicentenary - death of Capt. James Cook

Date	Mintage	F	VF	XF	Unc	BU
1979	3,000	—	—	—	10.00	—

KM# 33a 10 TALA **Weight:** 31.4700 g. **Composition:** 0.9250 Silver .9359 oz. ASW **Subject:** Bicentenary - death of Capt. James Cook

Date	Mintage	F	VF	XF	Unc	BU
1979 Proof	5,000	Value: 12.50				

KM# 36 10 TALA **Weight:** 31.3300 g. **Composition:** 0.5000 Silver .5036 oz. ASW **Series:** 1980 Olympics **Obverse:** Similar to KM#33 **Reverse:** Hurdles

Date	Mintage	F	VF	XF	Unc	BU
1980	3,000	—	—	—	10.00	—

KM# 36a 10 TALA **Weight:** 31.4700 g. **Composition:** 0.9250 Silver .9359 oz. ASW **Series:** 1980 Olympics **Obverse:** Similar to KM#33 **Reverse:** Hurdles

Date	Mintage	F	VF	XF	Unc	BU
1980 Proof	4,000	Value: 12.50				

KM# 39 10 TALA **Weight:** 31.3300 g. **Composition:** 0.5000 Silver .5036 oz. ASW **Series:** F.A.O. **Obverse:** Similar to KM#33

Date	Mintage	F	VF	XF	Unc	BU
1980 Proof	3,000	Value: 12.50				

KM# 41 10 TALA Weight: 31.3300 g. **Composition:** 0.5000 Silver .5036 oz. ASW **Subject:** Gov. Wilhelm Solf **Obverse:** Similar to KM#33

Date	Mintage	F	VF	XF	Unc	BU
1980	3,000	—	—	—	8.50	—

KM# 41a 10 TALA Weight: 31.4700 g. **Composition:** 0.9250 Silver .9359 oz. ASW **Subject:** Gov. Wilhelm Solf **Obverse:** Similar to KM#33

Date	Mintage	F	VF	XF	Unc	BU
1980 Proof	4,000	Value: 13.50				

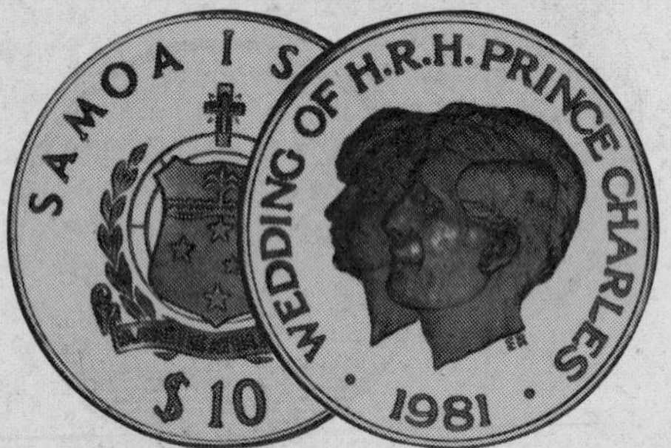

KM# 44 10 TALA Weight: 31.4700 g. **Composition:** 0.9250 Silver .9359 oz. ASW **Subject:** Wedding of Prince Charles and Lady Diana

Date	Mintage	F	VF	XF	Unc	BU
1981 Proof	5,000	Value: 13.50				

KM# 48 10 TALA Weight: 31.4700 g. **Composition:** 0.9250 Silver .9359 oz. ASW **Subject:** IYDP - President Franklin Roosevelt

Date	Mintage	F	VF	XF	Unc	BU
1981 Proof	5,000	Value: 12.50				

KM# 51 10 TALA Weight: 31.4700 g. **Composition:** 0.9250 Silver .9359 oz. ASW **Subject:** Commonwealth Games **Obverse:** Similar to KM#33 **Reverse:** Javelin thrower

Date	Mintage	F	VF	XF	Unc	BU
1982 Proof	4,000	Value: 13.50				

KM# 54 10 TALA Weight: 31.4700 g. **Composition:** 0.9250 Silver .9359 oz. ASW **Subject:** South Pacific Games **Obverse:** Similar to KM#33 **Reverse:** Runner

Date	Mintage	F	VF	XF	Unc	BU
1983 Proof	3,000	Value: 13.50				

KM# 59 10 TALA Weight: 31.4700 g. **Composition:** 0.9250 Silver .9359 oz. ASW **Series:** Summer Olympics **Reverse:** Boxers

Date	Mintage	F	VF	XF	Unc	BU
1984 Proof	2,500	Value: 27.50				

KM# 64 10 TALA Weight: 31.4700 g. **Composition:** 0.9250 Silver .9359 oz. ASW **Subject:** Prince Andrew's marriage **Note:** Similar to Tala, KM#63.

Date	Mintage	F	VF	XF	Unc	BU
1986 Proof	2,500	Value: 12.50				

KM# 72 10 TALA Weight: 31.4700 g. **Composition:** 0.9250 Silver .9360 oz. ASW **Subject:** 25th anniversary of World Wildlife Fund **Reverse:** Samoan Fantail bird

Date	Mintage	F	VF	XF	Unc	BU
1986 Proof	Est. 25,000	Value: 13.50				

KM# 66 10 TALA Weight: 31.1000 g. **Composition:** 0.9990 Silver 1 oz. ASW **Subject:** America's Cup race

Date	Mintage	F	VF	XF	Unc	BU
1987 Proof	Est. 50,000	Value: 11.50				

KM# 70 10 TALA Weight: 31.1000 g. **Compositi**
0.9990 Silver 1 oz. ASW **Series:** 1988 Olympics **Rev**
3 torches and athletes

Date	Mintage	F	VF	XF	Unc
1988	20,000	—	—	—	17.50

KM# 75 10 TALA Weight: 31.1030 g. **Compositic**
0.9990 Silver 1 oz. ASW **Reverse:** Kon-Tiki raft and r

Date	Mintage	F	VF	XF	Unc
1988 Proof	Est. 20,000	Value: 18.50			

KM# 79 10 TALA Weight: 31.4700 g. **Compositio**
0.9250 Silver .9360 oz. ASW **Series:** Save the Children

Date	Mintage	F	VF	XF	Unc
1990 Proof	Est. 20,000	Value: 17.50			

KM# 82 10 TALA Weight: 31.4700 g. **Composition**
0.9250 Silver .9360 oz. ASW **Series:** Summer Olympic
Reverse: Shot putter

Date	Mintage	F	VF	XF	Unc
1991 Proof	Est. 70,000	Value: 12.50			

KM# 83 10 TALA **Weight:** 31.1030 g. **Composition:** 0.9250 Silver .9250 oz. ASW **Subject:** RA expeditions **Obverse:** Similar to KM#82 **Reverse:** RAI

Date	Mintage	F	VF	XF	Unc	BU
1991 Proof	15,000	Value: 20.00				

KM# 85 10 TALA **Weight:** 31.4700 g. **Composition:** 0.9250 Silver .9360 oz. ASW **Series:** Olympics **Reverse:** Javelin thrower

Date	Mintage	F	VF	XF	Unc	BU
1991 Proof	Est. 70,000	Value: 12.50				

KM# 86 10 TALA **Weight:** 31.4700 g. **Composition:** 0.9250 Silver .9360 oz. ASW **Series:** Olympics **Reverse:** Hammer thrower

ate	Mintage	F	VF	XF	Unc	BU
992 Proof	Est. 70,000	Value: 12.50				

M# 89 10 TALA **Weight:** 31.8600 g. **Composition:** 0.9250 Silver .9476 oz. ASW **Subject:** World Cup soccer **Reverse:** Arena

ate	Mintage	F	VF	XF	Unc	BU
992 Proof	Est. 20,000	Value: 16.50				

M# 93 10 TALA **Weight:** 31.4700 g. **Composition:** 0.9250 Silver .9359 oz. ASW **Subject:** Jakob Roggeveen **Obverse:** Coat of arms

ate	Mintage	F	VF	XF	Unc	BU
992 Proof	15,000	Value: 17.50				

KM# 98 10 TALA **Weight:** 31.3500 g. **Composition:** 0.9250 Silver .9323 oz. ASW **Series:** Endangered Wildlife **Reverse:** Bristle-thighed Curlew bird

Date	Mintage	F	VF	XF	Unc	BU
1992 Proof	Est. 20,000	Value: 18.50				

KM# 99 10 TALA **Weight:** 31.7700 g. **Composition:** 0.9250 Silver .9448 oz. ASW **Subject:** Roggeveen's fleet

Date	Mintage	F	VF	XF	Unc	BU
1992 Proof	Est. 15,000	Value: 14.50				

KM# 109 10 TALA **Weight:** 31.4700 g. **Composition:** 0.9250 Silver .9359 oz. ASW **Subject:** 40th anniversary - reign of Queen Elizabeth II **Obverse:** National arms **Reverse:** Royal carriage and guard around Order of the Garter

Date	Mintage	F	VF	XF	Unc	BU
1992 Proof	Est. 5,000	Value: 25.00				

KM# 97 10 TALA **Weight:** 31.8100 g. **Composition:** 0.9250 Silver .9461 oz. ASW **Series:** 1996 Olympics **Reverse:** Gymnast

Date	Mintage	F	VF	XF	Unc	BU
1993 Proof	50,000	Value: 12.50				

KM# 91 10 TALA **Weight:** 31.8100 g. **Composition:** 0.9250 Silver .9461 oz. ASW **Series:** Olympics **Reverse:** Diver

Date	Mintage	F	VF	XF	Unc	BU
1994 Proof	Est. 50,000	Value: 12.50				

KM# 121 10 TALA **Weight:** 31.2300 g. **Composition:** 0.9250 Silver 0.9288 oz. ASW **Subject:** Robert Louis Stephenson **Obverse:** National arms **Reverse:** Seated figure **Edge:** Reeded **Size:** 38.6 mm. **Note:** Struck at Singapore Mint.

Date	Mintage	F	VF	XF	Unc	BU
1994 Proof	10,000	Value: 50.00				

KM# 94 10 TALA **Weight:** 31.1035 g. **Composition:** 0.9990 Silver 1 oz. ASW **Subject:** Tigris expedition **Reverse:** Building Tigris

Date	Mintage	F	VF	XF	Unc	BU
1994 Proof	500	Value: 35.00				

KM# 95 10 TALA **Weight:** 31.1035 g. **Composition:** 0.9990 Silver 1 oz. ASW **Subject:** Tigris expedition **Reverse:** Burning Tigris

Date	Mintage	F	VF	XF	Unc	BU
1994 Proof	500	Value: 35.00				

KM# 100 10 TALA **Weight:** 31.7700 g. **Composition:** 0.9250 Silver .9448 oz. ASW **Reverse:** Jacob Roggeveen sighting land

Date	Mintage	F	VF	XF	Unc	BU
1994 Proof	10,000	Value: 20.00				

KM# 101 10 TALA **Weight:** 31.2300 g. **Composition:** 0.9250 Silver .9288 oz. ASW **Series:** Endangered Wildlife **Reverse:** Samoan Flying fox bat

Date	Mintage	F	VF	XF	Unc	BU
1994 Proof	Est. 20,000	Value: 30.00				

KM# 102 10 TALA **Weight:** 31.4700 g. **Composition:** 0.9250 Silver .9359 oz. ASW **Subject:** Comte de la Perouse

Date	Mintage	F	VF	XF	Unc	BU
1994 Proof	Est. 20,000	Value: 20.00				

KM# 103 10 TALA **Weight:** 31.4700 g. **Composition:** 0.9250 Silver .9359 oz. ASW **Subject:** Protect our world **Reverse:** Flowers

Date	Mintage	F	VF	XF	Unc	BU
1994 Proof	Est. 10,000	Value: 22.50				

KM# 113 10 TALA **Weight:** 1.2442 g. **Composition:** 0.9999 Gold .04 oz. AGW **Series:** Olympics **Reverse:** Discus thrower

Date	F	VF	XF	Unc	BU
1995	—	—	—	60.00	—

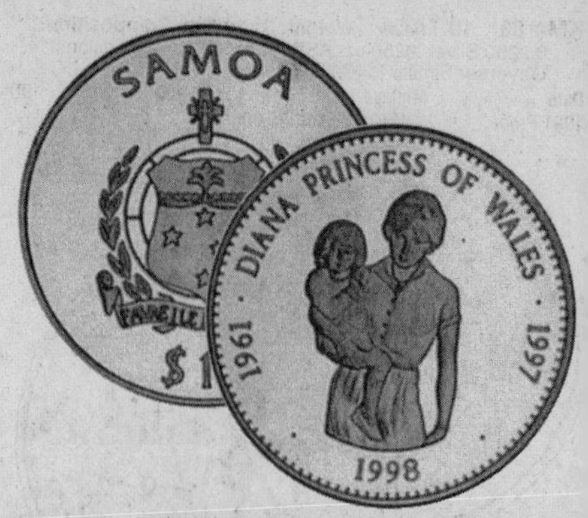

KM# 123 10 TALA **Weight:** 31.5000 g. **Composition:** 0.9250 Silver .9368 oz. ASW **Subject:** Princess Diana **Obverse:** National arms **Reverse:** Diana holding child **Edge:** Reeded **Size:** 38.6 mm.

Date	F	VF	XF	Unc	BU
1998 Proof	—	Value: 22.50			

KM# 104 10 TALA **Weight:** 31.4700 g. **Composition:** 0.9250 Silver .9359 oz. ASW **Subject:** Queen Mother **Reverse:** Glamis Castle

Date	Mintage	F	VF	XF	Unc	BU
1994 Proof	Est. 30,000	Value: 22.50				

KM# 114 10 TALA **Weight:** 31.7000 g. **Composition:** 0.9250 Silver .9427 oz. ASW **Series:** Olympics **Subject:** Jakob le Maire **Obverse:** National arms **Reverse:** Sailing ship

Date	F	VF	XF	Unc	BU
1996 Proof	—	Value: 27.50			

KM# 62 25 TALA **Weight:** 155.5000 g. **Composition:** 0.9990 Silver 5 oz. ASW **Subject:** Kon-Tiki **Size:** 65 mm. **Note:** Illustration reduced.

Date	Mintage	F	VF	XF	Unc	BU
1986 Proof	Est. 25,000	Value: 47.50				

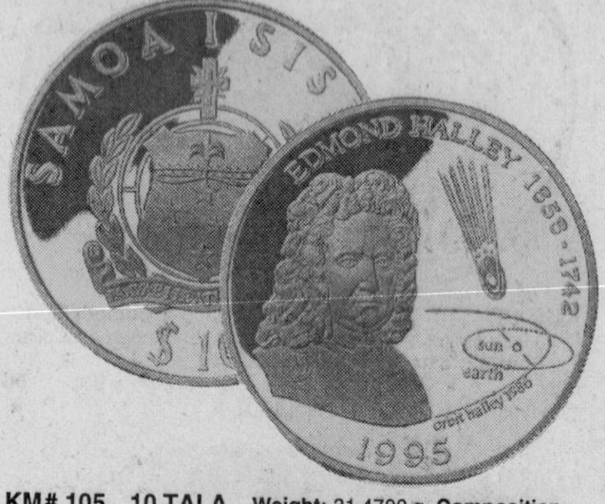

KM# 105 10 TALA **Weight:** 31.4700 g. **Composition:** 0.9250 Silver .9359 oz. ASW **Subject:** Edmond Halley

Date	Mintage	F	VF	XF	Unc	BU
1995 Proof	10,000	Value: 25.00				

KM# 127 10 TALA **Weight:** 31.8000 g. **Composition:** 0.9250 Silver 0.9457 oz. ASW **Subject:** Victorian Age **Obverse:** National arms. **Reverse:** Queen Victoria and family. **Edge:** Reeded. **Size:** 38.6 mm.

Date	F	VF	XF	Unc	BU
1996 Proof	—	Value: 40.00			

KM# 67 25 TALA **Weight:** 155.5000 g. **Composition:** 0.9990 Silver 5 oz. ASW **Subject:** America's Cup race **Size:** 65 mm. **Note:** Illustration reduced.

Date	Mintage	F	VF	XF	Unc	BU
1987 Proof	Est. 35,000	Value: 45.00				

KM# 124 10 TALA **Weight:** 31.6200 g. **Composition:** 0.9250 Silver 0.9404 oz. ASW **Subject:** Queen Elizabeth - Queen Mother **Obverse:** National arms. **Reverse:** Young Lady Elizabeth on Bobs. **Edge:** Reeded. **Size:** 38.5 mm.

Date	F	VF	XF	Unc	BU
1995 Proof	—	Value: 35.00			

KM# 128 10 TALA **Weight:** 31.8000 g. **Composition:** 0.9250 Silver 0.9457 oz. ASW **Subject:** Queen Mother **Obverse:** National arms. **Reverse:** Queen Mother presenting shamrocks to the Irish Guards. **Edge:** Reeded. **Size:** 38.6 mm.

Date	F	VF	XF	Unc	BU
1998 Proof	—	Value: 40.00			

76 50 TALA **Weight:** 31.1030 g. **Composition:** .9990 Palladium 1 oz. **Subject:** Kon-Tiki **Reverse:** Raft and ...mboo poles

	Mintage	F	VF	XF	Unc	BU
...roof	Est. 10,000	Value: 625				

78 50 TALA **Weight:** 7.7700 g. **Composition:** .9990 Gold .25 oz. AGW **Subject:** Trans-Antarctica ...xpedition

	Mintage	F	VF	XF	Unc	BU
Proof	Est. 30,000	Value: 120				

90 50 TALA **Weight:** 7.7760 g. **Composition:** .5833 Gold .1458 oz. AGW **Series:** 1996 Olympics ...everse: Discus thrower

	Mintage	F	VF	XF	Unc	BU
Proof	7,500	Value: 110				

 # 92 50 TALA **Weight:** 7.7760 g. **Composition:** 0.5833 Gold .1458 oz. AGW **Subject:** World Cup soccer

	Mintage	F	VF	XF	Unc	BU
Proof	Est. 3,000	Value: 115				

 # 106 50 TALA **Weight:** 7.7760 g. **Composition:** 0.5833 Gold .1458 oz. AGW **Obverse:** National arms **Reverse:** Portrait

	Mintage	F	VF	XF	Unc	BU
Proof	Est. 3,000	Value: 115				

 # 107 50 TALA **Weight:** 7.7760 g. **Composition:** 0.5833 Gold .1458 oz. AGW **Subject:** The Endeavor

	Mintage	F	VF	XF	Unc	BU
4 Proof	Est. 2,500	Value: 115				

 # 108 50 TALA **Weight:** 7.7760 g. **Composition:** 0.5833 Gold .1458 oz. AGW **Series:** Endangered Wildlife **Reverse:** Dolphins

e	Mintage	F	VF	XF	Unc	BU
95 Proof	Est. 2,500	Value: 115				

 # 119 50 TALA **Weight:** 7.7750 g. **Composition:** 0.9990 Gold .25 oz. AGW **Subject:** Tempora Mutantur **Obverse:** Western Samoan arms **Reverse:** Man with torch **Note:** Similar to 5 Tala, KM#117. 1/2 of 2-part coin, combined with Kiribati KM#26, issued in sets only; Value is determined by combining the 2 parts.

e	Mintage	F	VF	XF	Unc	BU
(1997) Proof	Est. 2,500	Value: 110				

 # 21 100 TALA **Weight:** 15.5500 g. **Composition:** 0.9170 Gold .4583 oz. AGW **Subject:** U.S. bicentennial

te	Mintage	F	VF	XF	Unc	BU
76 Proof	2,000	Value: 210				

KM# 23 100 TALA **Weight:** 15.5500 g. **Composition:** 0.9170 Gold .4583 oz. AGW **Series:** Montreal Olympics **Reverse:** Weight lifter **Note:** Similar to Tala, KM#22.

Date	Mintage	F	VF	XF	Unc	BU
1976 Proof	2,500	Value: 210				

KM# 25 100 TALA **Weight:** 15.5500 g. **Composition:** 0.9170 Gold .4583 oz. AGW **Subject:** Queen's silver jubilee

Date	Mintage	F	VF	XF	Unc	BU
1977 Proof	2,500	Value: 210				

KM# 27 100 TALA **Weight:** 15.5500 g. **Composition:** 0.9170 Gold .4583 oz. AGW **Subject:** Lindbergh's New York to Paris flight

Date	Mintage	F	VF	XF	Unc	BU
1977 Proof	660	Value: 250				

KM# 29 100 TALA **Weight:** 15.5500 g. **Composition:** 0.9170 Gold .4583 oz. AGW **Subject:** 50th anniversary - Transpacific flight **Reverse:** Globe with plane flying across Pacific Ocean, portrait of Lindbergh facing left **Note:** Similar to Tala, KM#28.

Date	Mintage	F	VF	XF	Unc	BU
1978 Proof	1,500	Value: 215				

KM# 31 100 TALA **Weight:** 15.5500 g. **Composition:** 0.9170 Gold .4583 oz. AGW **Subject:** XI Commonwealth Games **Reverse:** Runners **Note:** Similar to Tala, KM#30.

Date	Mintage	F	VF	XF	Unc	BU
1978 Proof	1,000	Value: 215				

KM# 34 100 TALA **Weight:** 12.5000 g. **Composition:** 0.9170 Gold .3686 oz. AGW **Subject:** Bicentenary - death of Capt. James Cook **Reverse:** Portrait of Cook at left of sailing ship **Note:** Similar to 10 Tala, KM#33.

Date	Mintage	F	VF	XF	Unc	BU
1979 Proof	1,000	Value: 200				

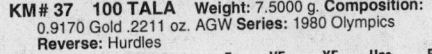

KM# 37 100 TALA **Weight:** 7.5000 g. **Composition:** 0.9170 Gold .2211 oz. AGW **Series:** 1980 Olympics **Reverse:** Hurdles

Date	Mintage	F	VF	XF	Unc	BU
1980	250	—	—	—	165	—
1980 Proof	1,000	Value: 125				

KM# 42 100 TALA **Weight:** 7.5000 g. **Composition:** 0.9170 Gold .2211 oz. AGW **Subject:** Gov. Wilhelm Solf

Date	Mintage	F	VF	XF	Unc	BU
1980	250	—	—	—	150	—
1980 Proof	1,000	Value: 120				

KM# 45 100 TALA **Weight:** 7.5000 g. **Composition:** 0.9170 Gold .2211 oz. AGW **Subject:** Wedding of Prince Charles and Lady Diana

Date	Mintage	F	VF	XF	Unc	BU
1981	250	—	—	—	110	—
1981 Proof	1,500	Value: 120				

KM# 49 100 TALA **Weight:** 7.5000 g. **Composition:** 0.9170 Gold .2211 oz. AGW **Subject:** IYDP - President Franklin Roosevelt **Reverse:** President Roosevelt in wheel chair **Note:** Similar to Tala, KM#47.

Date	Mintage	F	VF	XF	Unc	BU
1981	250	—	—	—	115	—
1981 Proof	1,500	Value: 125				

KM# 52 100 TALA **Weight:** 7.5000 g. **Composition:** 0.9170 Gold .2211 oz. AGW **Subject:** Commonwealth Games **Reverse:** Javelin thrower

Date	Mintage	F	VF	XF	Unc	BU
1982	250	—	—	—	110	—
1982 Proof	1,000	Value: 120				

KM# 55 100 TALA **Weight:** 7.5000 g. **Composition:** 0.9170 Gold .2211 oz. AGW **Subject:** South Pacific Games **Reverse:** Runner

Date	Mintage	F	VF	XF	Unc	BU
1983	—	—	—	—	110	—
1983 Proof	1,000	Value: 120				

KM# 60 100 TALA **Weight:** 7.5000 g. **Composition:** 0.9170 Gold .2211 oz. AGW **Series:** Summer Olympics **Reverse:** Boxers, similar to Tala, KM#58

Date	Mintage	F	VF	XF	Unc	BU
1984	200	—	—	—	200	—
1984 Proof	500	Value: 180				

KM# 68 100 TALA **Weight:** 7.5000 g. **Composition:** 0.9000 Gold .217 oz. AGW **Subject:** America's Cup race

Date	Mintage	F	VF	XF	Unc	BU
1987 Proof	Est. 5,000	Value: 110				

KM# 77 100 TALA **Weight:** 7.5000 g. **Composition:** 0.9000 Gold .217 oz. AGW **Subject:** Kon-Tiki **Reverse:** Raft and inscription

Date	Mintage	F	VF	XF	Unc	BU
1988 Proof	Est. 5,000	Value: 110				

KM# 81 100 TALA **Weight:** 7.5000 g. **Composition:** 0.9170 Gold .2211 oz. AGW **Series:** Save the Children

Date	Mintage	F	VF	XF	Unc	BU
1990 Proof	3,000	Value: 120				

KM# 84 100 TALA **Weight:** 7.5000 g. **Composition:** 0.9170 Gold .2211 oz. AGW **Subject:** RA expeditions **Obverse:** Similar to KM#81 **Reverse:** RA II

Date	Mintage	F	VF	XF	Unc	BU
1991 Proof	5,000	Value: 125				

KM# 87 100 TALA **Weight:** 7.5000 g. **Composition:** 0.9000 Gold .217 oz. AGW **Series:** Olympics **Reverse:** Torch runners

Date	Mintage	F	VF	XF	Unc	BU
1991 Proof	Est. 6,000	Value: 100				

KM# 96 100 TALA **Weight:** 7.5000 g. **Composition:** 0.9170 Gold .2211 oz. AGW **Subject:** Tigris expedition **Reverse:** Tigris sailing

Date	Mintage	F	VF	XF	Unc	BU
1994 Proof	500	Value: 220				

KM# 126 100 TALA **Weight:** 7.5000 g. **Composition:** 0.9160 Gold 0.2209 oz. AGW **Subject:** Robert Louis Stevenson **Obverse:** National arms. **Reverse:** Ship and portrait. **Edge:** Reeded. **Size:** 28.5 mm.

Date	Mintage	F	VF	XF	Unc	BU
ND(1994) Proof	2,000	Value: 135				

KM# 46 1000 TALA **Weight:** 33.9500 g. **Composition:** 0.9170 Gold 1.001 oz. AGW **Subject:** Wedding of Prince Charles and Lady Diana **Note:** Similar to 100 Tala, KM#45.

Date	Mintage	F	VF	XF	Unc	BU
1981 Proof	100	Value: 675				

KM# 56 1000 TALA **Weight:** 31.1000 g. **Composition:** 0.9170 Gold .917 oz. AGW **Subject:** South Pacific Games **Reverse:** Runner **Note:** Similar to 10 Tala, KM#54.

Date	Mintage	F	VF	XF	Unc	BU
1983 Proof	100	Value: 650				

KM# 61 1000 TALA **Weight:** 31.1000 g. **Composition:** 0.9170 Gold .917 oz. AGW **Series:** 1984 Olympics **Reverse:** Boxers

Date	Mintage	F	VF	XF	Unc	BU
1984 Proof	100	Value: 625				

KM# 65 1000 TALA **Weight:** 33.9500 g. **Composition:** 0.9170 Gold 1.001 oz. AGW **Subject:** Prince Andrew's marriage **Obverse:** Similar to Tala, KM#8 **Reverse:** Similar to Tala, KM#63

Date	Mintage	F	VF	XF	Unc	BU
1986 Proof	50	Value: 775				

KM#110 1000TALA **Weight:** 33.9500 g. **Composition:** 0.9170 Gold 1.001 oz. AGW **Subject:** 40th anniversary - reign of Queen Elizabeth II **Obverse:** National arms **Reverse:** Royal carriage and guard around Order of the Garter

Date	Mintage	F	VF	XF	Unc	BU
1992 Proof	Est. 150	Value: 650				

PIEFORTS

KM#	Date	Mintage	Identification	Mkt Val
P1	1984	3,000	Tala. 0.9250 Silver. KM57.	22.00
P2	1992	—	Tala. 0.9250 Silver. KM109.	50.00

COMBINED PROOF SETS (CPS)

KM#	Date	Mintage	Identification	Issue Price	Mkt Val
CPS1	1997 (8)	10,000	West Samoa KM#115-118, Kiribati KM#22-25	—	240

MINT SETS

KM#	Date	Mintage	Identification	Issue Price	Mkt Val
MS1	1967 (6)	—	KM1-6	—	2.50
MS2	1974 (7)	10,740	KM12-17, 19	5.30	5.00

PROOF SETS

KM#	Date	Mintage	Identification	Issue Price	Mkt Val
PS1	1967 (7)	15,000	KM1-7	10.00	7.00
PS2	1974 (7)	5,578	KM12a-17a, 19a	53.00	30.00
PS3	1988 (3)	—	KM75-77	—	910
PS4	1991 (2)	1,000	KM83-84	—	160
PS5	1994 (3)	500	KM94-96	—	345

YEMEN ARAB REPUBLIC

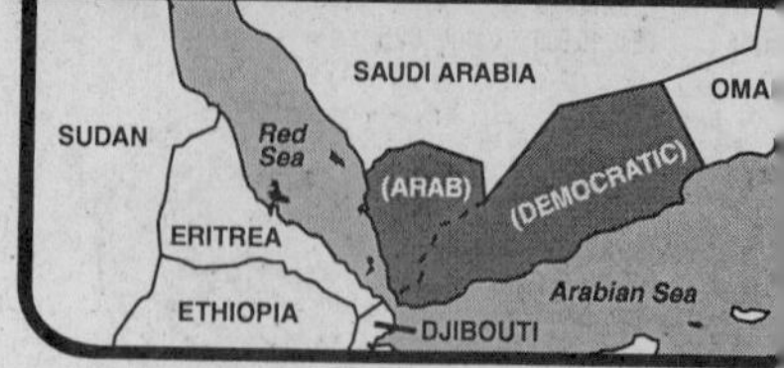

The northwestern region of present day Yemen was inated by Ottoman Turks until 1918. Formal boundarie established in 1934 and a Republic was formed in 1962 l to an eight year civil war between royalist imam and new lican forces.

REPUBLIC

MILLED COINAGE

Y# 20 1/80 RIYAL (1/2 Buqsha) **Composition:** B **Note:** Varieties exist.

Date	F	VF	XF	Unc
AH1382	—	0.50	2.00	5.00

Y# 21.2 1/80 RIYAL (1/2 Buqsha) **Compositio** Bronze **Reverse:** Outlined star **Note:** Varieties exist.

Date	F	VF	XF	Unc
AH13882 (sic)	—	—	—	—
AH1382	—	2.00	6.00	15.00

Y# 21.1 1/80 RIYAL (1/2 Buqsha) **Composition** Bronze **Reverse:** Full star

Date	F	VF	XF	Unc
AH1382	—	2.00	6.00	15.00

Y# 32 1/2 BUQSHA **Composition:** Bronze **Note:** Varieties exist.

Date	F	VF	XF	Unc
AH1382	—	3.00	5.00	9.00

Y# 26 1/2 BUQSHA **Composition:** Copper-Aluminu **Note:** Varieties exist.Struck at Cairo.

Date	Mintage	F	VF	XF	Unc
AH1382 (1962)	10,000,000	—	0.15	0.20	0.30

Y# 22 1/40 RIYAL (1 Buqsha) **Composition:** Brass Bronze **Note:** Dated both sides; AH1382, AH1383 and AH1384/3 are dated AH1382 on obverse, actual date on reverse; AH1384 and AH1384/284 dated AH1384 on bo sides. There are varieties of date size and design.

	F	VF	XF	Unc	BU
2	—	0.75	1.00	2.25	—
3/282	—	—	—	—	—
3	—	1.50	2.25	6.00	—
4/284	—	—	—	—	—
4/3	—	—	—	—	—
4	—	4.00	7.50	20.00	—

7 BUQSHA Composition: Copper-Aluminum **Note:** truck at Cairo.

	Mintage	F	VF	XF	Unc	BU
32 (1962)	10,377,000	—	0.20	0.30	0.50	—

23.1 1/20 RIYAL (2 Buqsha) Composition: 0.7200 Silver **Reverse:** Three stones on top row of wall **Note:** Thick variety, 1.10-1.60 grams

	F	VF	XF	Unc	BU
82	—	6.00	10.00	30.00	—

23.2 1/20 RIYAL (2 Buqsha) Composition: 0.7200 Silver **Reverse:** Two stones on top row of wall **Note:** Thin variety, 0.60-0.90 grams

	F	VF	XF	Unc	BU
82	—	2.00	4.00	10.00	—

A27 2 BUQSHA Composition: Copper-Aluminum

	F	VF	XF	Unc	BU
382 (1962)	—	0.25	0.60	0.85	—

24.1 1/10 RIYAL (4 Buqsha) Composition: 0.7200 Silver **Reverse:** Three or four stones in top row of wall within circle **Note:** Thick variety, 2.40-3.00 grams

	F	VF	XF	Unc	BU
382	—	5.00	10.00	20.00	—

24.2 1/10 RIYAL (4 Buqsha) Composition: 0.7200 Silver **Reverse:** Four stones in top row of wall within circle **Note:** Thin variety, 1.40-1.80 grams. Edge varieties, varying number of stones in wall, exist.

	F	VF	XF	Unc	BU
382	—	2.00	4.00	10.00	—

28 5 BUQSHA Composition: 0.7200 Silver **Note:** Struck at Cairo.

e	Mintage	F	VF	XF	Unc	BU
1382 (1962)	1,600,000	—	1.25	1.50	2.50	—

#25.1 2/10 RIYAL (8 Buqsha) Composition: 0.7200 Silver **Note:** Thick variety, 5.80-6.50 grams.

te	F	VF	XF	Unc	BU
1382	—	8.00	15.00	25.00	—

#25.2 2/10 RIYAL (8 Buqsha) Composition: 0.7200 Silver **Note:** Thin variety, 4.90-5.10 grams.

te	F	VF	XF	Unc	BU
1382	—	60.00	100	150	—

Y# A25.1 1/4 RIYAL (10 Buqsha) Composition: 0.7200 Silver **Note:** Thick variety, 6.00-7.30 grams.

Date	F	VF	XF	Unc	BU
AH1382	—	40.00	65.00	150	—

Y# A25.2 1/4 RIYAL (10 Buqsha) Composition: 0.7200 Silver **Note:** Thin variety, 4.00-4.60 grams. Overstrikes over earlier 1/4 Riyal coins exist.

Date	F	VF	XF	Unc	BU
AH1382	—	40.00	65.00	150	—

Y# 29 10 BUQSHA Weight: 5.0000 g. **Composition:** 0.7200 Silver .1157 oz. ASW

Date	Mintage	F	VF	XF	Unc	BU
AH1382 (1962)	1,024,000	—	2.00	2.25	3.25	—

Y# 30 20 BUQSHA Weight: 9.8500 g. **Composition:** 0.7200 Silver .2280 oz. ASW

Date	Mintage	F	VF	XF	Unc	BU
AH1382 (1962)	1,016,000	—	4.00	5.00	7.00	—

Y# 31 RIYAL Weight: 19.7500 g. **Composition:** 0.7200 Silver .4571 oz. ASW

Date	Mintage	F	VF	XF	Unc	BU
AH1382 (1962)	4,614,000	—	5.00	6.00	9.50	—

DECIMAL COINAGE

100 Fils = 1 Riyal/Rial

Y# 33 FILS Composition: Aluminum

Date	Mintage	F	VF	XF	Unc	BU
AH1394 (1974)		—	3.00	5.00	10.00	—

Note: It is doubtful that the entire mintage was released for circulation

AH1394 (1974) Proof	5,024	Value: 1.50
AH1400 (1980) Proof	10,000	Value: 1.50

Y# 43 FILS Composition: Aluminum **Series:** F.A.O.

Date	Mintage	F	VF	XF	Unc	BU
AH1398 (1978)	7,050	—	—	1.25	3.00	—

Y# 34 5 FILS Composition: Brass

Date	Mintage	F	VF	XF	Unc	BU
AH1394 (1974)	10,000,000	—	0.50	1.00	2.50	—

Y# 38 5 FILS Composition: Brass **Series:** F.A.O.

Date	Mintage	F	VF	XF	Unc	BU
AH1394 (1974)	500,000	—	—	0.10	0.25	—

Y# 35 10 FILS Composition: Brass

Date	Mintage	F	VF	XF	Unc	BU
AH1394 (1974)		—	0.50	1.00	2.50	—
AH1394 (1974) Proof	5,024	Value: 2.50				
AH1400 (1980) Proof	10,000	Value: 2.00				

Y# 39 10 FILS Composition: Brass **Series:** F.A.O.

Date	Mintage	F	VF	XF	Unc	BU
AH1394 (1974)	200,000	—	—	0.10	0.25	—

Y# 36 25 FILS Composition: Copper-Nickel

Date	Mintage	F	VF	XF	Unc	BU
AH1394 (1974)		—	0.25	0.50	1.75	—
AH1394 (1974) Proof	5,024	Value: 3.00				
AH1399 (1979)		—	0.25	0.50	1.75	—
AH1400 (1980) Proof	10,000	Value: 2.25				

Y# 40 25 FILS Composition: Copper-Nickel **Series:** F.A.O.

Date	Mintage	F	VF	XF	Unc	BU
AH1394 (1974)	40,000	—	0.20	0.40	1.00	—

Y# 37 50 FILS **Composition:** Copper-Nickel

Date	Mintage	F	VF	XF	Unc	BU
AH1394 (1974)		—	0.35	0.75	2.50	—
AH1394 (1974) Proof	5,024	Value: 3.50				
AH1399 (1979)		—	0.35	0.75	2.50	—
AH1400 (1980) Proof	10,000	Value: 2.50				
AH1405 (1985)		—	0.35	0.75	2.50	—

Y# 41 50 FILS **Composition:** Copper-Nickel **Series:** F.A.O.

Date	Mintage	F	VF	XF	Unc	BU
AH1394 (1974)	25,000	—	0.25	0.50	1.25	—

KM# 1 RIYAL **Weight:** 12.0000 g. **Composition:** 0.9250 Silver .3569 oz. ASW **Subject:** Qadhi Mohammed Mahmud Azzubairi Memorial

Date	Mintage	F	VF	XF	Unc	BU
1969 Proof	3,200	Value: 15.00				

KM# 1a RIYAL **Weight:** 20.4800 g. **Composition:** 0.9000 Gold .5926 oz. AGW **Subject:** Qadhi Mohammed Mahmud Azzubairi Memorial

Date	Mintage	F	VF	XF	Unc	BU
1969 Proof	100	Value: 375				

Y# 42 RIYAL **Composition:** Copper-Nickel

Date	Mintage	F	VF	XF	Unc	BU
AH1396 (1976)	7,800,000	—	0.50	1.25	4.00	—
AH1400 (1980) Proof	—	Value: 5.00				
AH1405 (1985)	—	—	0.50	1.25	4.00	—

Y# 44 RIYAL **Composition:** Copper-Nickel **Series:** F.A.O.

Date	Mintage	F	VF	XF	Unc	BU
AH1398 (1978)	7,050	—	—	2.00	5.00	—

KM# 2.1 2 RIYALS **Weight:** 25.0000 g. **Composition:** 0.9250 Silver .7435 oz. ASW **Subject:** Apollo II - Cape Kennedy **Note:** Dotter border.

Date	Mintage	F	VF	XF	Unc	BU
1969	7,583	—	—	—	25.00	—
1969 Proof	200	Value: 50.00				

KM# 2.2 2 RIYALS **Weight:** 25.0000 g. **Composition:** 0.9250 Silver .7435 oz. ASW **Note:** Border of dots near rim.

Date	Mintage	F	VF	XF	Unc	BU
1969 Proof; restrike	1,000	Value: 28.50				

KM# 3.1 2 RIYALS **Weight:** 25.0000 g. **Composition:** 0.9250 Silver .7435 oz. ASW **Subject:** Apollo II - Moon Landing **Note:** Dotted border.

Date	Mintage	F	VF	XF	Unc	BU
1969	7,583	—	—	—	25.00	—
1969 Proof	200	Value: 50.00				

KM# 3.2 2 RIYALS **Weight:** 25.0000 g. **Composition:** 0.9250 Silver .7435 oz. ASW **Note:** Border of dots near rim.

Date	Mintage	F	VF	XF	Unc	BU
1969 Proof; restrike	1,000	Value: 28.50				

KM# 4 2 RIYALS **Weight:** 25.0000 g. **Compositi** 0.9250 Silver .7435 oz. ASW **Subject:** Qadhi Moham Mahmud Azzubairi Memorial

Date	Mintage	F	VF	XF	Unc
1969 Proof	4,200	Value: 30.00			

KM# 4a 2 RIYALS **Weight:** 42.2900 g. **Composit** 0.9000 Gold 1.2238 oz. AGW **Subject:** Qadhi Mohar Mahmud Azzubairi Memorial

Date	Mintage	F	VF	XF	Unc
1969 Proof	100	Value: 975			

KM# 14 2-1/2 RIYALS **Weight:** 9.0000 g. **Compos** 0.9250 Silver .2676 oz. ASW **Subject:** Oil Exploration

Date	Mintage	F	VF	XF	Unc
AH1395 (1975)		—	—	—	15.00
AH1395 (1975) Proof	Est. 5,000	Value: 35.00			

KM# 6 5 RIYALS/RIALS **Weight:** 4.9000 g. **Composition:** 0.9000 Gold .1418 oz. AGW **Subject:** C Mohammed Mahmud Azzubairi Memorial

Date	F	VF	XF	Unc
1969 Proof	—	Value: 100		

KM# 15 5 RIYALS/RIALS **Weight:** 18.0000 g. **Composition:** 0.9250 Silver .5353 oz. ASW **Subject:** M Lisa

Date	Mintage	F	VF	XF	Unc
AH1395 (1975)	235,000	—	—	—	20.00
AH1395 (1975) Proof	5,000	Value: 50.00			

KM# 7 10 RIYALS/RIALS **Weight:** 9.8000 g. **Composition:** 0.9000 Gold .2836 oz. AGW **Subject:** Qa Mohammed Mahmud Azzubairi Memorial

Date	F	VF	XF	Unc
1969 Proof	—	Value: 175		

KM# 23 10 RIYALS/RIALS **Weight:** 12.0800 g. **Composition:** 0.9250 Silver .3569 oz. ASW **Obverse:** KM#7 **Reverse:** KM#1 **Note:** Mule.

Date	F	VF	XF	Unc	BU
1969 Proof	—	Value: 40.00			

KM# 16 10 RIYALS/RIALS **Weight:** 36.0000 g. **Composition:** 0.9250 Silver 1.0707 oz. ASW **Series:** Montreal Olympics

ate	Mintage	F	VF	XF	Unc	BU
H1395 (1975)	8,000	—	—	—	90.00	—
H1395 (1975) Proof	4,000	Value: 140				

M# 28 10 RIYALS/RIALS **Weight:** 35.9000 g. **Composition:** 0.9250 Silver 1.0676 oz. ASW **Subject:** Montreal Olympics. **Obverse:** National arms. **Reverse:** Olympic events around coin, Olympic logo in center. **Edge:** Plain. **Size:** 45.6 mm.

ate	Mintage	VG	F	VF	XF	Unc
H1395 (1975) Proof	100	Value: 400				

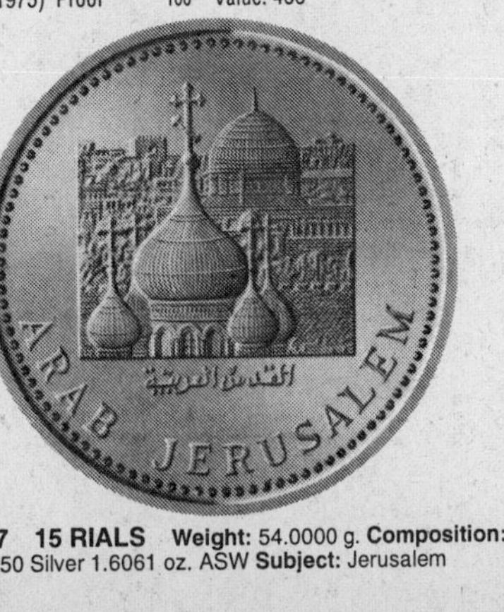

M# 17 15 RIALS **Weight:** 54.0000 g. **Composition:** 0.9250 Silver 1.6061 oz. ASW **Subject:** Jerusalem

Date	Mintage	F	VF	XF	Unc	BU
AH1395 (1975)	70,000	—	—	—	40.00	—
AH1395 (1975) Proof	5,000	Value: 100				

KM# 8 20 RIYALS/RIALS **Weight:** 19.6000 g. **Composition:** 0.9000 Gold .5672 oz. AGW **Subject:** Apollo II - Moon Landing

Date	F	VF	XF	Unc	BU
1969 Proof	—	Value: 350			

KM# 9 20 RIYALS/RIALS **Weight:** 19.6000 g. **Composition:** 0.9000 Gold .5672 oz. AGW **Subject:** Qadhi Mohammed Mahmud Azzubairi Memorial

Date	F	VF	XF	Unc	BU
1969 Proof	—	Value: 365			

KM# 18 20 RIYALS/RIALS **Weight:** 19.6000 g. **Composition:** 0.9000 Gold .5672 oz. AGW **Subject:** Albakiriah Mosque

Date	Mintage	F	VF	XF	Unc	BU
AH1395 (1975)	—	—	—	—	160	—
AH1395 (1975) Proof	3,500	Value: 175				

KM# 19 25 RIYALS/RIALS **Composition:** 0.9000 Gold **Subject:** Oil Exploration

Date	Mintage	F	VF	XF	Unc	BU
AH1395 (1975)	—	—	—	—	135	—
AH1395 (1975) Proof	3,500	Value: 150				

Y# 46 25 RIYALS/RIALS **Weight:** 28.2800 g. **Composition:** 0.9250 Silver .8411 oz. ASW **Series:** International Year of the Disabled Person

Date	Mintage	F	VF	XF	Unc	BU
AH1401 (1981)	—	—	—	—	32.50	—
AH1401 (1981) Proof	Est. 10,000	Value: 50.00				

Y# 47 25 RIYALS/RIALS **Weight:** 28.2800 g. **Composition:** 0.9250 Silver .8411 oz. ASW **Subject:** 20th Anniversary of the Revolution

Date	Mintage	F	VF	XF	Unc	BU
AH1402 (1982) Proof	2,000	Value: 55.00				

Y# 45 25 RIYALS/RIALS **Weight:** 28.2500 g. **Composition:** 0.9250 Silver .8402 oz. ASW **Series:** International Year of the Child

Date	Mintage	F	VF	XF	Unc	BU
AH1403 (1983) Proof	6,604	Value: 18.50				

Y# 49 25 RIYALS/RIALS **Weight:** 28.2500 g. **Composition:** 0.9250 Silver .8402 oz. ASW **Series:** Decade for Women

Date	Mintage	F	VF	XF	Unc	BU
AH1405 (1985) Proof	1,000	Value: 42.50				

KM# 10 30 RIYALS **Weight:** 29.4000 g. **Composition:** 0.9000 Gold .8508 oz. AGW **Subject:** Qadhi Mohammed Mahmud Azzubairi Memorial

Date	F	VF	XF	Unc	BU
1969 Proof	—	Value: 600			

KM# 11 50 RIYALS/RIALS **Weight:** 49.9700 g. **Composition:** Silver **Subject:** Qadhi Mohammed Mahmud Azzubairi Memorial **Reverse:** Lion

Date	F	VF	XF	Unc	BU
1969 Proof; restrike	—	Value: 50.00			

KM# 11a 50 RIYALS/RIALS **Weight:** 49.0000 g. **Composition:** 0.9000 Gold 1.4180 oz. AGW **Subject:** Qadhi Mohammed Mahmud Azzubairi Memorial

Date	F	VF	XF	Unc	BU
1969 Proof	—	Value: 950			

KM# 20 50 RIYALS/RIALS **Weight:** 9.1000 g. **Composition:** 0.9000 Gold .2633 oz. AGW **Subject:** Mona Lisa

Date	Mintage	F	VF	XF	Unc	BU
AH1395 (1975)	—	—	—	—	200	—
AH1395 (1975) Proof	3,500	Value: 350				

KM# 21 75 RIYALS **Weight:** 13.6500 g. **Composition:** 0.9000 Gold .3950 oz. AGW **Series:** Montreal Olympics **Obverse:** Arms **Reverse:** XXI Olympiad

Date	Mintage	F	VF	XF	Unc	BU
AH1395 (1975)	—	—	—	—	250	—
AH1395 (1975) Proof	3,500	Value: 350				

KM# 22 100 RIALS **Weight:** 18.2000 g. **Composition:** 0.9000 Gold .5266 oz. AGW

Date	Mintage	F	VF	XF	Unc	BU
AH1395 (1975)	—	—	—	—	325	—
AH1395 (1975) Proof	3,500	Value: 400				

KM# 24 500 RIYALS/RIALS **Weight:** 15.9800 g. **Composition:** 0.9170 Gold .4711 oz. AGW **Series:** International Year of the Disabled Person

Date	F	VF	XF	Unc	BU
AH1401 (1981)	—	—	—	400	—
AH1401 (1981) Proof	—	Value: 500			

Y# 48 500 RIYALS/RIALS **Weight:** 15.9000 g. **Composition:** 0.9170 Gold .4686 oz. AGW **Subject:** 20th Anniversary of the Revolution

Date	Mintage	F	VF	XF	Unc	BU
AH1402 (1982) Proof	1,000	Value: 350				

ROYALIST GOVERNMENT

MILLED COINAGE

KM# 5 RIAL **Weight:** 24.9200 g. **Composition:** 0.7200 Silver **Subject:** Sir Winston Churchill Memorial

Date	Mintage	F	VF	XF	Unc	BU
AH1385 (1965)	6,000	—	—	8.50	14.50	—

Note: The above coin probably was not intended for circulation, but specimens are known to have been distributed by the exiled monarch to Saudi and other dignitaries

ESSAIS

KM#	Date	Mintage	Identification	Mkt Val
E1	AH1385	500	Rial. 0.7200 Silver.	27.50

PIEFORTS

KM#	Date	Mintage	Identification	Mkt Val
P1	1981	1,150	25 Riyals/Rials. I.Y.D.P.; Y#46	115
P2	1981	—	500 Riyals/Rials. I.Y.P.D.; KM#24	1,000
p3	1983	—	25 Riyals/Rials. 0.9250 Silver. 57.0000 g. Arms, legend, date. Children. I.Y.C.; Y#45	175

TRIAL STRIKES

KM#	Date	Mintage	Identification	Mkt Val

KM#	Date	Mintage	Identification	Mkt Val
TS1	1975	—	100 Rials. Goldine. Uniface.	—

MINT SETS

KM#	Date	Mintage	Identification	Issue Price	Mkt Val
MS1	1975 (4)	—	KM#14-17	50.00	175
MS2	1975 (5)	—	KM#18-22	360	1,130

YEMEN REPUBLIC

The Republic of Yemen, formerly Yemen Arab Republic and Peoples Democratic Republic of Yemen, is located on the southern coast of the Arabian Peninsula. It has an area of 205,020 sq. mi. (531,000 sq. km.) and a population of 12 million. Capital: San'a. The port of Aden is the main commercial center and the area's most valuable natural resource. Recent oil and gas finds and a developing petroleum industry have improved their economic prospects. Agriculture and local handicrafts are the main industries. Cotton, fish, coffee, rock salt and hides are exported.

On May 22, 1990, the Yemen Arab Republic (North Yemen) and Peoples Democratic Republic of Yemen (South Yemen) merged into a unified Republic of Yemen. Disagreements between the two former governments simmered until civil war erupted in 1994, with the northern forces of the old Yemen Arab Republic eventually prevailing.

دار الخلافة

TITLES

Dar al-Khilafa(t)

REPUBLIC

MILLED COINAGE

KM# 25 RIYAL **Composition:** Stainless Steel

Date	F	VF	XF	Unc	B
AH1414 (1993)	—	—	—	1.25	–

KM# 26 5 RIYALS **Composition:** Stainless Steel

Date	F	VF	XF	Unc	B
AH1414 (1993)	—	—	—	1.75	-

KM# 27 10 RIYALS **Composition:** Stainless Steel **Note** Bridge at Shaharah

Date	F	VF	XF	Unc	B
AH1416 (1995)	—	—	—	2.75	-

MEN, DEMOCRATIC REPUBLIC

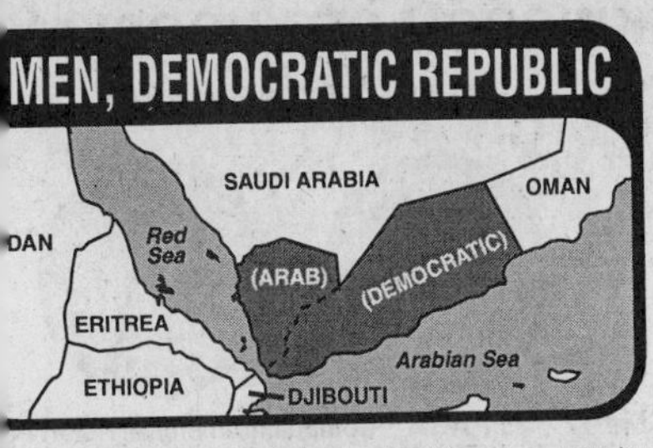

The southeast region of present day Yemen was predom-
ly controlled by the British since their occupation of Aden in
. Independence was declared November 30, 1967 after the
ose of the Federation of South Arabia and the withdrawal of
British.

ES
mhuriya(t) al-Yamaniya(t)
imiqratiya(t) ash-Sha'biya(t)

ETARY SYSTEM

فلوس فلس فلسا

s, Fulus Fals, Fils Falsan, Filsan
) Fils = 1 Dinar

PEOPLES DEMOCRATIC REPUBLIC

DECIMAL COINAGE

3 2-1/2 FILS Composition: Aluminum

	Mintage	F	VF	XF	Unc	BU
393 (1973)	20,000,000	—	0.25	0.65	1.50	—

2 5 FILS Composition: Bronze

e	Mintage	F	VF	XF	Unc	BU
'1	2,000,000	—	0.30	0.60	1.00	—

M# 4 5 FILS Composition: Aluminum

te	Mintage	F	VF	XF	Unc	BU
1393 (1973)	20,000,000	—	0.15	0.30	0.75	—
1404 (1984)	—	—	0.15	0.30	0.75	—

M# 9 10 FILS Composition: Aluminum

te	F	VF	XF	Unc	BU
81	—	0.35	0.75	2.00	—

KM# 5 25 FILS Composition: Copper-Nickel

Date	Mintage	F	VF	XF	Unc	BU
1976	2,000,000	—	0.25	0.50	1.25	—
1977	1,000,000	—	0.25	0.50	1.50	—
1979	—	—	0.25	0.50	1.50	—
1982	—	—	0.25	0.50	1.50	—
1984	—	—	0.25	0.50	1.75	—

KM# 6 50 FILS Composition: Copper-Nickel

Date	Mintage	F	VF	XF	Unc	BU
1976	2,000,000	—	0.35	0.75	2.50	—
1977	2,000,000	—	0.35	0.75	2.50	—
1979	—	—	0.35	0.75	2.50	—
1984	—	—	0.35	0.75	2.50	—

KM# 10 100 FILS Composition: Copper-Nickel

Date	F	VF	XF	Unc	BU
1981	—	0.50	1.00	3.00	—

KM# 7 250 FILS Composition: Copper-Nickel Subject: 10th Anniversary of Independence

Date	Mintage	F	VF	XF	Unc	BU
1977	30,000	2.50	5.00	10.00	25.00	—

KM# 11 250 FILS Composition: Copper-Nickel

Date	F	VF	XF	Unc	BU
1981	—	1.50	3.00	5.50	—

KM# 12 2 DINARS Weight: 28.2800 g. Composition: 0.9250 Silver .8411 oz. ASW Subject: lInternational Year of Disabled Persons - Abdulla Baradoni

Date	Mintage	F	VF	XF	Unc	BU
1981	10,000	—	—	—	47.50	—
1981 Proof	10,000	Value: 52.50				

KM# 8 5 DINARS Weight: 12.5000 g. Composition: 0.9250 Silver .3718 oz. ASW Subject: 10th Anniversary of Independence Note: Similar to 250 Fils, KM#7.

Date	Mintage	F	VF	XF	Unc	BU
1977 Proof	6,000	Value: 60.00				

KM# 13 50 DINARS Weight: 15.9800 g. Composition: 0.9170 Gold .4712 oz. AGW Series: International Year of Disabled Persons

Date	Mintage	F	VF	XF	Unc	BU
1981	2,100	—	—	—	500	—
1981 Proof	1,100	Value: 750				

PIEFORTS

KM#	Date	Mintage	Identification	Mkt Val
P1	1981	1,050	2 Dinars. (No Composition). KM#12.	200
P2	1981	500	50 Dinars. (No Composition). KM#13.	1,500

YUGOSLAVIA

The Federal Republic of Yugoslavia, formerly the Socialist Federal Republic of Yugoslavia, a Balkan country located on the east shore of the Adriatic Sea, has an area of 39,450 sq. mi. (102,173 sq. km.) and a population of 10.5 million. Capital: Belgrade. The chief industries area agriculture, mining, manufacturing and tourism. Machinery, nonferrous metals, meat and fabrics are exported.

Yugoslavia was proclaimed on Dec. 1, 1918, after the union of the Kingdom of Serbia, Montenegro and the South Slav territories of Austria-Hungary; and changed its official name from the Kingdom of the Serbs, Croats and Slovenes to the Kingdom of Yugoslavia on Oct. 3, 1929.The republic was composed of six autonomous republics -Serbia, Croatia, Slovenia, Bosnia-Herzegovina, Macedonia and Montenegro - and two autonomous provinces within Serbia: Kosovo-Melohija and Vojvodina. The government of Yugoslavia attempted to remain neutral in World War II but, yielding to German pressure, aligned itself with the Axis powers in March of 1941; a few days later it was overthrown by revolutionary forces and its neutrality reasserted. The Nazis occupied the country on April 6, and throughout the remaining war years were resisted by a number of guerrilla armies, notably that of Marshal Josip Broz Tito. After the defeat of the Axis powers, a leftist coalition headed by Tito abolished the monarchy and, on Jan. 31, 1946, established a "People's Republic". The collapse of the Federal Republic during 1991-1992 has resulted in the autonomous republics of Croatia, Slovenia, Bosnia-Herzegovina and Macedonia declaring their respective independence. Bosnia-Herzegovina is under military contest with the Serbian, Croat and Muslim populace opposing each other. Besides the remainder of the older Serbian sectors, a Serbian enclave in Knin located in southern Croatia has emerged called REPUBLIKE SRPSKEKRAJINE or Serbian Republic - Krajina whose capital is Knin and has also declared its independence in1992 when the former Republics of Serbia and Montenegro became the Federal Republic of Yugoslavia.

The name Yugoslavia appears on the coinage in letters of the Cyrillic alphabet alone until formation of the Federated Peoples Republic of Yugoslavia in 1953, after which both the Cyrillic and Latin alphabets are employed. From 1965, the coin denomination appears in the 4 different languages of the federated republics in letters of both the Cyrillic and Latin alphabets.

DENOMINATIONS
Para ПАРА
Dinar, ДИНАР, Dinara ДИНАРА
Dinari ДИНАРИ, Dinarjev

RULERS
Petar I, 1918-1921
Alexander I, 1921-1934
Petar II, 1934-1945

MINT MARKS
(a) - Paris, privy marks only
(b) - Brussels
(k) КОВНИЦА,..А.Д. = Kovnica, A.D. (Akcionarno Drustvo) Belgrade
(l) - London
(p) - Poissy (thunderbolt)
(v) – Vienna

MONETARY SYSTEM
100 Para = 1 Dinar

KINGDOM OF THE SERBS, CROATS AND SLOVENES

STANDARD COINAGE

KM# 1 5 PARA **Composition:** Zinc **Ruler:** Petar I **Obv. Designer:** Adolf Hoffmann **Rev. Designer:** Joseph Prinz **Edge:** Plain **Size:** 18.8 mm.

Date	Mintage	F	VF	XF	Unc	BU
1920(v)	3,825,514	3.00	7.50	15.00	42.00	—

KM# 2 10 PARA **Composition:** Zinc **Ruler:** Petar I **Obv. Designer:** Adolf Hoffmann **Rev. Designer:** Joseph Prinz **Edge:** Plain **Size:** 20.85 mm.

Date	Mintage	F	VF	XF	Unc	BU
1920(v)	58,946,122	1.50	3.50	8.00	22.00	—

KM# 3 25 PARA **Composition:** Nickel-Bronze **Ruler:** Petar I **Obv. Designer:** Adolf Hoffmann **Rev. Designer:** Joseph Prinz **Edge:** Plain **Size:** 24 mm.

Date	Mintage	F	VF	XF	Unc	BU
1920(v)	48,173,138	1.50	3.00	7.50	20.00	—

KM# 4 50 PARA **Composition:** Nickel-Bronze **Ruler:** Alexander I **Edge:** Milled **Size:** 18 mm. **Note:** Mint mark: lightning bolt. Struck at Poissy.

Date	Mintage	F	VF	XF	Unc	BU
1925(b)	24,500,000	0.50	1.00	2.00	6.50	—
1925(p)	25,000,000	0.50	1.50	3.00	7.50	—

KM# 5 DINAR **Composition:** Nickel-Bronze **Ruler:** Alexander I **Edge:** Milled **Size:** 23 mm. **Note:** Mint mark: lightning bolt. Struck at Poissy.

Date	Mintage	F	VF	XF	Unc	BU
1925(b)	37,000,000	0.50	1.00	2.00	6.00	—
1925(p)	37,500,410	0.75	1.50	3.00	7.00	—

KM# 6 2 DINARA **Composition:** Nickel-Bronze **Ruler:** Alexander I **Edge:** Milled **Size:** 27 mm. **Note:** Mint mark: lightning bolt.

Date	Mintage	F	VF	XF	Unc	BU
1925(b)	29,500,000	1.00	2.00	5.00	12.00	—
1925(p)	25,004,177	1.00	2.50	5.50	14.00	—

KM# 7 20 DINARA **Weight:** 6.4516 g. **Composition:** 0.9000 Gold .1867 oz. AGW **Ruler:** Alexander I **Edge:** Milled **Size:** 21 mm.

Date	Mintage	F	VF	XF	Unc	BU
1925	1,000	125	145	170	225	—
1925 Proof	—	—	—	—	—	—

KINGDOM OF YUGOSLAV

STANDARD COINAGE

KM# 17 25 PARA **Composition:** Bronze **Ruler:** P **Edge:** Plain **Size:** 20 mm. **Note:** 4 millimeter hole in c of coin.

Date	Mintage	F	VF	XF	Unc
1938	40,000,000	1.25	2.00	5.00	13.00
1938 Proof	—	—	—	—	—

KM# 18 50 PARA **Composition:** Aluminum-Bronz **Ruler:** Petar II **Edge:** Plain **Size:** 18 mm.

Date	Mintage	F	VF	XF	Unc
1938	100,000,000	0.50	1.00	2.50	7.50

KM# 19 DINAR **Composition:** Aluminum-Bronze **R** Petar II **Edge:** Plain **Size:** 21 mm.

Date	Mintage	F	VF	XF	Unc
1938	100,000,000	0.50	0.75	2.00	6.00
1938 Proof	—	—	—	—	—

KM# 20 2 DINARA **Composition:** Aluminum-Bronz **Ruler:** Petar II **Obverse:** 14 millimeter crown **Edge:** Pl **Size:** 24.5 mm.

Date	Mintage	F	VF	XF	Unc
1938	74,250,000	0.50	1.00	3.00	8.00
1938 Proof	—	—	—	—	—

KM# 21 2 DINARA **Composition:** Aluminum-Bronze **Ruler:** Petar II **Obverse:** 12 millimeter crown **Edge:** Pla **Size:** 24.5 mm.

Date	Mintage	F	VF	XF	Unc
1938	750,000	6.00	10.00	18.00	36.00
1938 Proof	—	—	—	—	—

KM# 10 10 DINARA **Weight:** 7.0000 g. **Compositio** 0.5000 Silver .1125 oz. ASW **Ruler:** Alexander I **Edge:** Milled

Date	Mintage	F	VF	XF	Unc
1931(l)	16,000,000	2.00	4.00	8.00	17.50
1931(l) Proof	—	—	—	—	—
1931(a)	4,000,000	3.50	7.00	15.00	32.00
1931(a) Proof	—	—	—	—	—

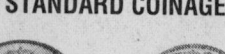

KM# 22 10 DINARA **Composition:** Nickel **Ruler:** Petar II **Edge:** Milled **Size:** 23 mm.

Date	Mintage	F	VF	XF	Unc	BU
1938	25,000,000	0.50	1.00	2.00	4.00	—

KM# 11 20 DINARA **Weight:** 14.0000 g. **Composition:** 0.5000 Silver .2250 oz. ASW **Ruler:** Alexander I **Edge:** Milled **Size:** 31 mm.

Date	Mintage	F	VF	XF	Unc	BU
1931(k)	12,500,000	BV	6.00	12.50	33.00	—
1931(k) Proof	—	—	—	—	—	—

KM# 23 20 DINARA **Weight:** 9.0000 g. **Composition:** 0.7500 Silver .217 oz. ASW **Ruler:** Petar II **Edge Lettering:** BOG CUVA JUGOSLAVIJU ***

ate	Mintage	F	VF	XF	Unc	BU
938	15,000,000	BV	2.50	5.00	12.00	—

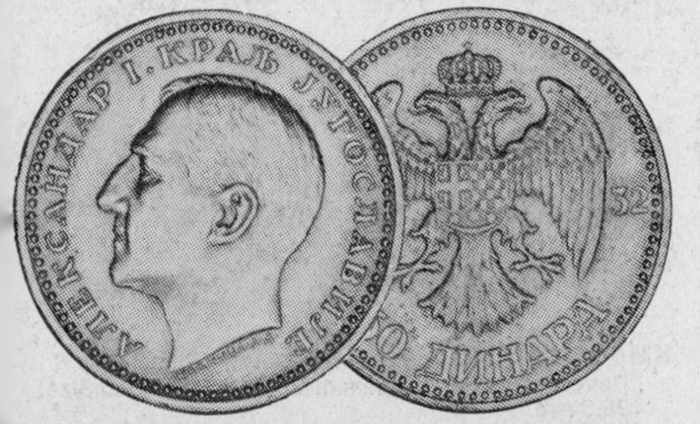

KM# 16 50 DINARA **Weight:** 23.3300 g. **Composition:** 0.7500 Silver .5626 oz. ASW **Ruler:** Alexander I **Edge Lettering:** BOG CUVA JUGOSLAVIJU **Size:** 36 mm.

ate	Mintage	F	VF	XF	Unc	BU
932(k)	5,500,000	10.00	22.00	45.00	180	—
932(l)	5,500,000	10.00	25.00	50.00	200	—
932(l) Proof	—	Value: 2,200				

M# 24 50 DINARA **Weight:** 15.0000 g. **Composition:** 0.7500 Silver .3617 oz. ASW **Ruler:** Petar II **Size:** 31 mm.

te	Mintage	F	VF	XF	Unc	BU
38	10,000,000	3.00	5.00	9.00	18.00	—

TRADE COINAGE

Trade-coinage countermarks were applied by the ugoslav Control Office for Noble Metals to confirm old purity. The initial countermark displayed a sword, ut part way through the first production year, this was retired and the second countermark, showing an ear of corn, was used.

KM# 12.1 DUKAT **Weight:** 3.4900 g. **Composition:** 0.9860 Gold .1106 oz. AGW **Ruler:** Alexander I **Countermark:** Sword **Obverse:** Small legend with ÊÎÂÍÈÖ, À.Ä. below head **Obv. Designer:** Richard Plecht **Reverse:** Small legend with ÊÎÂÍÈÖ, À.Ä. below head **Rev. Designer:** Joseph Prinz **Edge:** Milled

Date	F	VF	XF	Unc	BU
1931(k)	—	80.00	125	185	—
1932(k) Rare	—	—	—	—	—

Note: The 1932(k) examples with sword countermark are believed to be mint sports.

KM# 12.2 DUKAT **Weight:** 3.4900 g. **Composition:** 0.9860 Gold .1106 oz. AGW **Ruler:** Alexander I **Countermark:** Ear of corn **Obverse:** Small legend **Reverse:** Small legend **Note:** Forgeries bearing no countermark exist for 1932 and possibly other dates.

Date	F	VF	XF	Unc	BU
1931(k)	—	70.00	120	165	—
1932(k)	—	80.00	125	175	—
1933(k)	—	125	175	285	—
1934(k)	—	500	800	1,200	—

KM# 12.3 DUKAT **Weight:** 3.4900 g. **Composition:** 0.9860 Gold .1106 oz. AGW **Ruler:** Alexander I **Countermark:** Sword **Obverse:** KM#13.2 **Reverse:** KM#12.1 **Note:** Mule.

Date	F	VF	XF	Unc	BU
1931(k)	—	—	3,000	5,000	—

KM# 13.1 DUKAT **Weight:** 3.4900 g. **Composition:** 0.9860 Gold .1106 oz. AGW **Ruler:** Petar II **Obverse:** Large legend **Reverse:** Large legend

Date	Mintage	F	VF	XF	Unc	BU
1931(k)	2,869	—	—	3,500	5,500	—

KM# 13.2 DUKAT **Weight:** 3.4900 g. **Composition:** 0.9860 Gold .1106 oz. AGW **Ruler:** Alexander I **Countermark:** Sword **Note:** Large-letter varieties bear the Kovnica, A.D. mint mark but were actually struck in Vienna.

Date	F	VF	XF	Unc	BU
1931(k)	—	—	4,000	6,500	—

KM# 14.1 4 DUKATA **Weight:** 13.9600 g. **Composition:** 0.9860 Gold .4425 oz. AGW **Ruler:** Alexander I **Countermark:** Sword **Obverse:** Small legend **Obv. Designer:** Richard Placht **Reverse:** Small legend **Rev. Designer:** Joseph Prinz **Edge:** Milled **Note:** The 1932(k) examples with sword countermark are believed to be mint sports.

Date	F	VF	XF	Unc	BU
1931(k)	—	450	750	950	—
1932(k) Rare	—	—	—	—	—

KM# 14.2 4 DUKATA **Weight:** 13.9600 g. **Composition:** 0.9860 Gold .4425 oz. AGW **Ruler:** Alexander I **Countermark:** Ear of corn

Date	F	VF	XF	Unc	BU
1931(k)	—	450	750	950	—
1932(k)	—	400	725	1,000	—
1933(k)	—	1,000	1,600	2,500	—
1934(k)	—	2,000	3,000	4,500	—

KM# 14.3 4 DUKATA **Weight:** 13.9600 g. **Composition:** 0.9860 Gold .4425 oz. AGW **Ruler:** Alexander I **Obverse:** Without countermark **Reverse:** Without countermark **Note:** Only one genuine piece has been reported.

Date	F	VF	XF	Unc	BU
1931(k) Rare	—	—	—	—	—

KM# A15.1 4 DUKATA **Weight:** 13.9600 g. **Composition:** 0.9860 Gold .4425 oz. AGW **Ruler:** Alexander I **Obverse:** Large legend **Reverse:** Large legend

Date	Mintage	F	VF	XF	Unc	BU
1931(k) Rare	51	—	—	—	—	—

POST WAR COINAGE

KM# 25 50 PARA **Composition:** Zinc **Edge:** Milled **Size:** 18 mm.

Date	Mintage	F	VF	XF	Unc	BU
1945	40,000,000	0.50	1.00	3.00	9.00	—

KM# 26 DINAR **Composition:** Zinc **Edge:** Milled **Size:** 20 mm.

Date	Mintage	F	VF	XF	Unc	BU
1945	90,000,000	0.50	1.00	2.50	7.00	—

KM# 27 2 DINARA **Composition:** Zinc **Edge:** Milled **Size:** 22 mm.

Date	Mintage	F	VF	XF	Unc	BU
1945	70,000,000	0.50	1.25	3.00	9.00	—

KM# 28 5 DINARA Composition: Zinc **Edge:** Milled **Size:** 26.5 mm.

Date	Mintage	F	VF	XF	Unc	BU
1945	50,000,000	1.00	2.00	4.00	12.00	—

FEDERAL PEOPLE'S REPUBLIC

STANDARD COINAGE

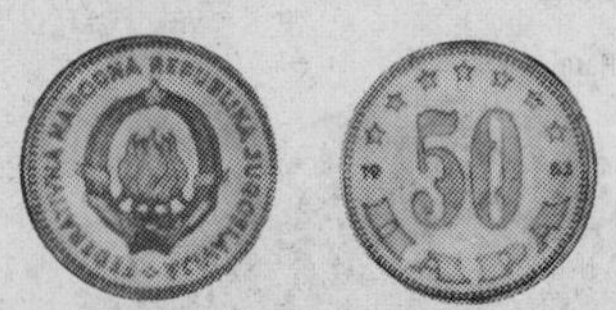

KM# 29 50 PARA Composition: Aluminum **Edge:** Plain **Size:** 17.4 mm.

Date	F	VF	XF	Unc	BU
1953	—	—	0.10	0.25	—

KM# 30 DINAR Composition: Aluminum **Edge:** Plain **Size:** 19.8 mm.

Date	F	VF	XF	Unc	BU
1953	—	0.10	0.15	0.25	—

KM#31 2 DINARA Composition: Aluminum **Edge:** Plain **Size:** 22.2 mm.

Date	F	VF	XF	Unc	BU
1953	—	0.10	0.20	0.30	—

KM#32 5 DINARA Composition: Aluminum **Edge:** Plain **Size:** 24.6 mm.

Date	F	VF	XF	Unc	BU
1953	0.10	0.25	0.50	0.75	—

KM# 33 10 DINARA Composition: Aluminum-Bronze **Edge:** Milled **Size:** 21 mm.

Date	F	VF	XF	Unc	BU
1955	0.15	0.30	0.75	1.50	—

KM# 34 20 DINARA Composition: Aluminum-Bronze **Edge:** Milled **Size:** 25.5 mm.

Date	F	VF	XF	Unc	BU
1955	0.25	0.50	1.00	2.00	—

KM# 35 50 DINARA Composition: Aluminum-Bronze **Edge:** Milled **Size:** 25.5 mm.

Date	F	VF	XF	Unc	BU
1955	0.25	0.50	1.50	3.00	—

SOCIALIST FEDERAL REPUBLIC

STANDARD COINAGE

KM# 42 5 PARA Composition: Copper-Zinc **Edge:** Milled **Size:** 16 mm.

Date	Mintage	F	VF	XF	Unc	BU
1965	23,839,000	—	0.10	0.20	0.40	—

KM# 43 5 PARA Composition: Copper-Zinc **Edge:** Milled **Size:** 16 mm.

Date	Mintage	F	VF	XF	Unc	BU
1965	16,200,000	—	—	0.10	0.20	—
1973	36,384,000	—	—	0.10	0.15	—
1974	3,628,000	—	—	0.10	0.25	—
1975	20,272,000	—	—	0.10	0.15	—
1976	30,490,000	—	—	0.10	0.15	—
1977	10,270,000	—	—	0.10	0.15	—
1978	12,000,000	—	—	0.10	0.15	—
1979	20,414,000	—	—	0.10	0.15	—
1980	22,412,000	—	—	0.10	0.15	—
1981	630,000	—	0.10	0.25	0.50	—

KM# 44 10 PARA Composition: Copper-Zinc **Edge:** Milled **Size:** 21 mm.

Date	Mintage	F	VF	XF	Unc	BU
1965	15,400,000	—	—	0.10	0.20	—
1973	16,647,000	—	—	0.10	0.20	—
1974	60,139,000	—	—	0.10	0.20	—
1975	36,954,000	—	—	0.10	0.15	—
1976	36,111,000	—	—	0.10	0.15	—
1977	40,451,000	—	—	0.10	0.15	—
1978	50,129,000	—	—	0.10	0.15	—
Note: Two varieties of 7 exist						
1979	89,738,000	—	—	0.10	0.15	—
1980	90,111,000	—	—	0.10	0.15	—
1981	14,090,000	—	—	0.10	0.15	—

KM# 139 10 PARA Composition: Copper-Zinc

Date	Mintage	F	VF	XF	Unc	BU
1990	174,028,000	—	—	0.10	0.15	—
1991	60,828,000	—	—	0.15	0.35	—

KM# 45 20 PARA Composition: Copper-Zinc **Edge:** Milled **Size:** 23.2 mm.

Date	Mintage	F	VF	XF	Unc	BU
1965	—	—	—	0.10	0.30	—
1973	30,448,000	—	—	0.10	0.30	—
1974	31,364,000	—	—	0.10	0.30	—
1975	44,683,000	—	—	0.10	0.30	—
1976	33,312,000	—	—	0.10	0.30	—
1977	40,782,000	—	—	0.10	0.30	—
1978	39,999,000	—	—	0.10	0.30	—
1979	49,121,000	—	—	0.10	0.30	—
1980	73,757,000	—	—	0.10	0.30	—
1981	96,144,000	—	—	0.10	0.30	—

KM# 140 20 PARA Composition: Copper-Zinc

Date	Mintage	VG	F	VF	XF	Un
1990	41,353,000	—	—	0.10	0.20	0.5
1991	43,118,000	—	—	0.10	0.20	0.5

KM# 84 25 PARA Composition: Bronze **Edge:** Plain **Size:** 17 mm.

Date	Mintage	F	VF	XF	Unc	B
1982	185,316,000	—	—	0.10	0.25	
1983	65,290,000	—	—	0.15	0.30	

KM# 46.1 50 PARA Composition: Copper-Zinc **Reverse:** Narrow 0 in denomination **Edge:** Milled **Size:** 25.5 mm.

Date	Mintage	F	VF	XF	Unc	B
1965		—	0.10	0.20	0.65	
1973	23,739,000	—	0.10	0.20	0.65	
1974	33,000	1.00	1.50	2.50	5.00	
1975	10,220,000	—	0.10	0.20	0.80	
1976	8,438,000	—	0.10	0.20	1.00	
1977	17,864,000	—	0.10	0.20	0.75	
1978	40,177,000	—	0.10	0.20	0.65	
Note: Two varieties of 7 exist						
1979	3,021,000	0.50	1.00	2.00	5.00	

KM# 46.2 50 PARA Composition: Copper-Zinc **Reverse:** Wide 0 in denomination

Date	Mintage	F	VF	XF	Unc
1979	12,278,000	0.20	0.50	1.00	2.50
1980	24,974,000	—	0.10	0.20	0.65
1981	40,319,000	—	0.10	0.20	0.65

KM# 85 50 PARA **Composition:** Bronze **Edge:** Plain **Size:** 19 mm.

Date	Mintage	F	VF	XF	Unc	BU
1982	79,584,000	—	—	0.10	0.20	—
1983	72,100,000	—	—	0.10	0.20	—
1984	59,642,000	0.25	0.50	1.00	1.50	—

KM# 141 50 PARA **Composition:** Copper-Zinc

Date	Mintage	F	VF	XF	Unc	BU
1990	137,873,000	—	—	0.10	0.20	—
1991	42,152,000	—	0.20	0.40	1.00	—

KM# 36 DINAR **Composition:** Aluminum **Edge:** Plain **Size:** 19.8 mm.

Date	F	VF	XF	Unc	BU
1963	—	—	0.10	0.15	—

KM# 47 DINAR **Composition:** Copper-Nickel **Edge:** Milled **Size:** 21.8 mm.

Date	Mintage	F	VF	XF	Unc	BU
1965	75,822,000	0.10	0.15	0.30	0.60	—

KM# 48 DINAR **Composition:** Copper-Nickel **Edge:** Milled **Size:** 21.8 mm.

Date	Mintage	F	VF	XF	Unc	BU
1968	35,497,000	0.10	0.20	0.40	0.80	—

KM# 59 DINAR **Composition:** Copper-Nickel-Zinc **Edge:** Milled **Size:** 21.8 mm.

Date	Mintage	F	VF	XF	Unc	BU
1973	18,974,000	—	0.10	0.15	0.40	—
1974	42,724,000	—	0.10	0.15	0.35	—
1975	30,260,000	—	0.10	0.15	0.35	—
1976	21,849,000	—	0.10	0.15	0.35	—
1977	30,468,000	—	0.10	0.15	0.35	—
Note: Two varieties of wreath						
1978	35,032,000	—	0.10	0.15	0.35	—
1979	39,848,000	—	0.10	0.15	0.35	—
1980	60,630,000	—	0.10	0.15	0.35	—
1981	56,650,000	—	0.10	0.15	0.35	—

KM# 61 DINAR **Composition:** Copper-Nickel-Zinc **Series:** F.A.O. **Edge:** Milled **Size:** 21.8 mm.

Date	Mintage	F	VF	XF	Unc	BU
1976	500,000	—	0.10	0.30	1.00	—

KM# 86 DINAR **Composition:** Nickel-Brass **Edge:** Milled **Size:** 20 mm.

Date	Mintage	F	VF	XF	Unc	BU
1982	70,105,000	—	—	0.10	0.30	—
1983	114,180,000	—	—	0.10	0.20	—
1984	172,185,000	—	—	0.10	0.20	—
1985	34,436,000	—	—	0.10	0.25	—
1986	122,643,000	—	—	0.10	0.20	—

KM# 142 DINAR **Composition:** Copper-Nickel-Zinc **Edge:** Milled

Date	Mintage	F	VF	XF	Unc	BU
1990	172,105,000	—	—	0.10	0.25	—
1991	79,549,000	—	0.15	0.25	0.75	—

KM# 37 2 DINARA **Composition:** Aluminum **Edge:** Plain **Size:** 22.2 mm.

Date	F	VF	XF	Unc	BU
1963	—	0.10	0.15	0.25	—

KM# 55 2 DINARA **Composition:** Copper-Nickel-Zinc **Series:** F.A.O. **Edge:** Milled **Size:** 24.5 mm.

Date	Mintage	F	VF	XF	Unc	BU
1970	500,000	—	0.20	0.40	1.00	—

KM# 57 2 DINARA **Composition:** Copper-Nickel-Zinc **Edge:** Milled **Size:** 24.5 mm.

Date	Mintage	F	VF	XF	Unc	BU
1971	10,413,000	—	0.10	0.30	0.70	—
1972	18,440,000	—	0.10	0.20	0.50	—
1973	31,848,000	—	0.10	0.20	0.45	—
1974	10,989,000	—	0.10	0.20	0.50	—
1975	92,000	2.00	4.00	7.50	15.00	—
1976	6,092,000	—	0.10	0.20	0.50	—
1977	19,335,000	—	0.10	0.20	0.50	—
1978	13,035,000	—	0.10	0.20	0.50	—
1979	20,069,000	—	0.10	0.20	0.45	—

Date	Mintage	F	VF	XF	Unc	BU
1980	36,088,000	—	0.10	0.20	0.45	—
1981	42,599,000	—	0.10	0.20	0.45	—

KM# 87 2 DINARA **Composition:** Nickel-Brass **Edge:** Milled **Size:** 22 mm.

Date	Mintage	F	VF	XF	Unc	BU
1982	40,632,000	—	0.10	0.15	0.35	—
1983	35,468,000	—	0.10	0.15	0.35	—
1984	51,500,000	—	0.10	0.15	0.35	—
1985	81,100,000	—	0.10	0.15	0.35	—
1986	50,453,000	—	0.10	0.15	0.35	—

KM# 143 2 DINARA **Composition:** Copper-Nickel-Zinc

Date	Mintage	F	VF	XF	Unc	BU
1990	15,936,000	0.15	0.30	0.60	2.00	—
1991	32,836,000	—	0.20	0.40	1.00	—
1992	—	2.50	3.50	7.00	12.50	—

KM# 38 5 DINARA **Composition:** Aluminum **Edge:** Plain **Size:** 24.6 mm.

Date	F	VF	XF	Unc	BU
1963	0.10	0.20	0.35	0.50	—

KM# 56 5 DINARA **Composition:** Copper-Nickel-Zinc **Series:** F.A.O. **Edge:** Milled **Size:** 27.5 mm.

Date	Mintage	F	VF	XF	Unc	BU
1970	500,000	0.20	0.50	1.00	2.50	—

KM# 58 5 DINARA **Composition:** Copper-Nickel-Zinc **Edge:** Milled **Size:** 27.5 mm. **Note:** Regular issue.

Date	Mintage	F	VF	XF	Unc	BU
1971	10,224,000	0.20	0.40	0.60	1.00	—
Note: Two varieties of wreath						
1972	27,974,000	0.10	0.20	0.35	0.60	—
Note: Two varieties of 2 in date						
1973	12,705,000	0.20	0.40	0.60	1.00	—
1974	6,054,000	0.25	0.50	1.00	2.00	—
1975	12,533,000	0.10	0.20	0.35	0.60	—
1976	4,965,000	0.10	0.25	0.40	0.80	—
1977	922,000	0.30	0.60	1.20	2.50	—
1978	1,000,000	0.10	0.25	0.50	1.50	—
1979	3,000,000	0.10	0.25	0.40	0.80	—
1980	9,977,000	0.10	0.20	0.35	0.60	—
1981	15,450,000	0.10	0.20	0.35	0.60	—

KM# 60 5 DINARA **Composition:** Copper-Nickel-Zinc **Subject:** 30th Anniversary of Nazi Defeat **Size:** 27.5 mm.

Date	Mintage	F	VF	XF	Unc	BU
1975	1,020,000	0.25	0.50	1.00	2.50	—

KM# 88 5 DINARA **Composition:** Nickel-Brass **Edge:** Milled **Size:** 24 mm.

Date	Mintage	F	VF	XF	Unc	BU
1982	40,956,000	—	0.10	0.15	0.50	—
1983	40,156,000	—	0.10	0.15	0.50	—
1984	33,023,000	—	0.10	0.15	0.50	—
1985	94,422,000	—	0.10	0.15	0.50	—
1986	37,199,000	—	0.10	0.15	0.50	—

KM# 144 5 DINARA **Composition:** Copper-Nickel-Zinc

Date	Mintage	F	VF	XF	Unc	BU
1990	9,354,000	0.25	0.45	1.00	2.50	—
1991	113,420,000	—	0.25	0.50	1.25	—
1992	—	1.50	2.50	4.00	7.00	—

KM# 145 5 DINARA **Composition:** Copper-Nickel-Zinc **Subject:** 1990 Chess Olympiad **Reverse:** Logo

Date	Mintage	F	VF	XF	Unc	BU
1990 Proof	20,000	Value: 7.00				

KM# 39 10 DINARA **Composition:** Aluminum-Bronze **Edge:** Milled **Size:** 21 mm.

Date	F	VF	XF	Unc	BU
1963	0.15	0.30	0.75	1.25	—

KM# 62 10 DINARA **Composition:** Copper-Nickel **Edge:** Milled **Size:** 30 mm.

Date	Mintage	F	VF	XF	Unc	BU
1976	10,550,000	0.30	0.60	0.75	1.25	—
1977	39,645,000	0.30	0.60	0.75	1.00	—
Note: Two varieties of wreath						
1978	29,834,000	0.30	0.60	0.75	1.00	—
1979	4,969,000	0.30	0.60	0.75	1.00	—
1980	10,139,000	0.30	0.60	0.75	1.00	—
1981	20,116,000	0.30	0.60	0.75	1.00	—

KM# 63 10 DINARA **Composition:** Copper-Nickel-Zinc **Series:** F.A.O. **Size:** 30 mm.

Date	Mintage	F	VF	XF	Unc	BU
1976	500,000	0.50	0.75	1.00	2.50	—

KM# 89 10 DINARA **Composition:** Copper-Nickel **Edge:** Milled **Size:** 23 mm.

Date	Mintage	F	VF	XF	Unc	BU
1982	8,862,000	—	0.10	0.20	0.80	—
1983	42,400,000	—	0.10	0.20	0.75	—
1984	30,900,000	—	0.10	0.20	0.75	—
1985	31,647,000	—	0.10	0.20	0.75	—
1986	40,739,000	—	0.10	0.20	0.75	—
1987	104,988,000	—	0.10	0.20	0.75	—
1988	27,614,000	—	0.10	0.20	0.75	—

KM# 96 10 DINARA **Composition:** Copper-Nickel **Subject:** 40th Anniversary - Battle of Neretva River **Reverse:** Bridge over the River Neretva **Size:** 30 mm.

Date	Mintage	F	VF	XF	Unc	BU
ND(1983)	900,000	—	1.00	2.00	4.00	—
ND(1983) Proof	100,000	Value: 8.00				

KM# 97.1 10 DINARA **Composition:** Copper-Nickel **Subject:** 40th Anniversary - Battle of Sutjeska River **Reverse:** SUTJESKA 1943 **Size:** 30 mm.

Date	Mintage	F	VF	XF	Unc	BU
ND(1983)	900,000	—	1.00	1.50	3.00	—
ND(1983) Proof	100,000	Value: 7.50				

KM# 97.2 10 DINARA **Composition:** Copper-Nickel **Subject:** 40th anniversary - Battle of Sutjeska River **Reverse:** Without pathway in front of monument

Date	F	VF	XF	Unc	BU
ND(1983)	—	3.00	6.00	10.00	—

KM# 131 10 DINARA **Composition:** Brass **Edge:** Plain

Date	Mintage	F	VF	XF	Unc	BU
1988	35,992,000	—	—	0.10	0.25	—
1989	75,000,000	—	—	0.10	0.25	—

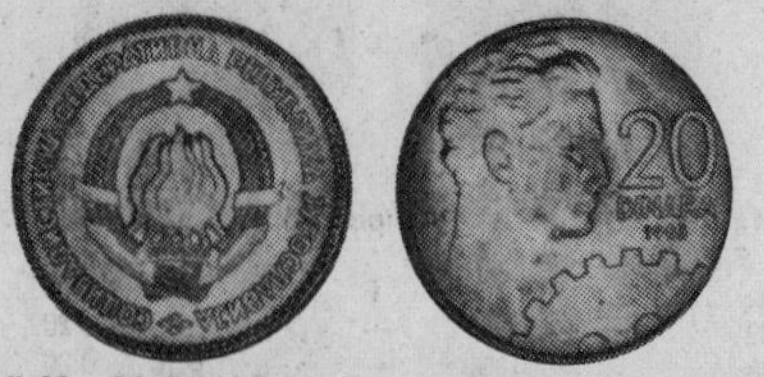

KM# 40 20 DINARA **Composition:** Aluminum-Bronze **Edge:** Milled **Size:** 23.2 mm.

Date	F	VF	XF	Unc	BU
1963	0.50	1.00	1.75	3.50	—

KM# 49 20 DINARA **Weight:** 9.0000 g. **Composition:** 0.9250 Silver .2676 oz. ASW **Subject:** 25th Anniversary of Republic **Edge:** Milled **Size:** 28 mm. **Note:** Similar to 50 Dinara, KM#50. Mint mark: NI (Numismatica Italiana, Milano, Italy).

Date	Mintage	VG	F	VF	XF	Unc
1968 Proof	10,000	Value: 25.00				
1968 NI Proof	Inc. above	Value: 25.00				

KM# 112 20 DINARA **Composition:** Copper-Zinc-Nickel **Edge:** Milled **Size:** 25 mm.

Date	Mintage	F	VF	XF	Unc	BU
1985	5,000,000	—	0.10	0.15	0.50	—
1986	20,932,000	—	0.10	0.15	0.35	—
1987	39,514,000	—	0.10	0.15	0.35	—

KM# 132 20 DINARA **Composition:** Brass **Edge:** Plain

Date	Mintage	F	VF	XF	Unc	BU
1988	29,775,000	—	—	0.10	0.25	—
1989	12,994,000	—	—	0.10	0.25	—

KM# 41 50 DINARA **Composition:** Aluminum-Bronze **Edge:** Milled **Size:** 25.5 mm. **Note:** Exists with filled letter in denomination. Two varieties of the letter P in ANHAPA.

Date	F	VF	XF	Unc	BU
1963	1.00	2.50	6.00	16.00	—

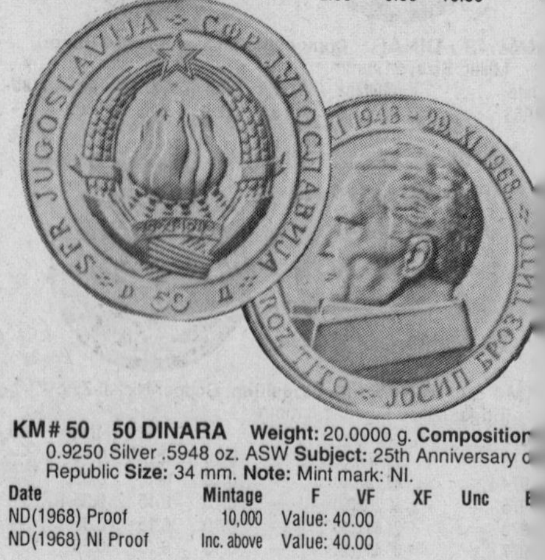

KM# 50 50 DINARA **Weight:** 20.0000 g. **Composition:** 0.9250 Silver .5948 oz. ASW **Subject:** 25th Anniversary of Republic **Size:** 34 mm. **Note:** Mint mark: NI.

Date	Mintage	F	VF	XF	Unc	BU
ND(1968) Proof	10,000	Value: 40.00				
ND(1968) NI Proof	Inc. above	Value: 40.00				

KM# 113 50 DINARA Composition: Copper-Zinc-Nickel **Edge:** Milled **Size:** 27 mm.

Date	Mintage	F	VF	XF	Unc	BU
1985	25,488,000	—	0.10	0.25	0.75	—
1986	20,353,000	—	0.10	0.25	0.75	—
1987	21,792,000	—	0.10	0.25	0.75	—
1988	28,370,000	—	0.10	0.25	0.75	—

KM# 133 50 DINARA Composition: Brass

Date	Mintage	F	VF	XF	Unc	BU
1988	46,973,000	—	—	0.10	0.25	—
1989	2,999,000	—	0.50	1.00	2.00	—

Note: Currently not issued.

KM# 51 100 DINARA Weight: 7.8200 g. **Composition:** 0.9000 Gold .2263 oz. AGW **Subject:** 25th anniversary of republic

Date	Mintage	F	VF	XF	Unc	BU
ND(1968) Proof	10,000	Value: 125				
ND(1968) NI Proof	Inc. above	Value: 125				

KM# 65 100 DINARA Weight: 10.0000 g. **Composition:** 0.9250 Silver .2974 oz. ASW **Subject:** 8th Mediterranean Games at Split **Size:** 28 mm.

Date	Mintage	F	VF	XF	Unc	BU
1978 Proof	71,000	Value: 22.50				

KM# 90 100 DINARA Weight: 13.0000 g. **Composition:** 0.9250 Silver .3867 oz. ASW **Series:** 1984 Winter Olympics **Subject:** Ice hockey **Edge:** Milled **Size:** 30 mm.

Date	Mintage	F	VF	XF	Unc	BU
1982 Proof	110,000	Value: 10.00				

KM# 98 100 DINARA Weight: 13.0000 g. **Composition:** 0.9250 Silver .3867 oz. ASW **Series:** 1984 Winter Olympics **Subject:** Figure skating **Size:** 30 mm.

Date		VG	F	VF	XF	Unc
1983 Proof	—	Value: 10.00				

KM# 99 100 DINARA Weight: 13.0000 g. **Composition:** 0.9250 Silver .3867 oz. ASW **Series:** 1984 Winter Olympics **Subject:** Bobsledding **Size:** 30 mm.

Date	Mintage	F	VF	XF	Unc	BU
1983 Proof	110,000	Value: 10.00				

KM# 105 100 DINARA Weight: 13.0000 g. **Composition:** 0.9250 Silver .3867 oz. ASW **Series:** 1984 Winter Olympics **Subject:** Speed skating **Size:** 30 mm.

Date	Mintage	F	VF	XF	Unc	BU
1984 Proof	110,000	Value: 10.00				

KM# 106 100 DINARA Weight: 13.0000 g. **Composition:** 0.9250 Silver .3867 oz. ASW **Series:** 1984 Winter Olympics **Subject:** Pairs figure skating **Size:** 30 mm.

Date	Mintage	F	VF	XF	Unc	BU
1984 Proof	110,000	Value: 10.00				

KM# 114 100 DINARA Composition: Copper-Zinc-Nickel **Edge:** Milled **Size:** 29 mm.

Date	Mintage	F	VF	XF	Unc	BU
1985	18,684,000	—	0.25	0.65	1.50	—
1986	17,905,000	—	0.20	0.50	1.00	—
1987	94,069,000	—	—	0.40	0.80	—
1988	50,294,000	—	—	0.40	0.80	—

KM# 115 100 DINARA Composition: Copper-Nickel-Zinc **Subject:** 40th anniversary - liberation from fascism

Date	Mintage	F	VF	XF	Unc	BU
ND(1985) Proof	200,000	Value: 4.00				

KM# 127.1 100 DINARA Composition: Copper-Nickel **Subject:** 200th anniversary - birth of Karajich

Date	Mintage	F	VF	XF	Unc	BU
1987 Proof	Est. 200,000	Value: 4.00				

KM# 127.2 100 DINARA Composition: Copper-Nickel **Subject:** 200th anniversary - birth of Karajich

Date	Mintage	F	VF	XF	Unc	BU
1987 Proof	Inc. above	Value: 25.00				

KM# 134 100 DINARA Composition: Brass

Date	Mintage	F	VF	XF	Unc	BU
1988	12,610,000	—	—	0.15	0.30	—
1989	124,260,000	—	—	0.15	0.30	—

KM# 146 100 DINARA Weight: 13.0000 g. **Composition:** 0.9250 Silver .3867 oz. ASW **Subject:** 1990 Chess Olympiad **Reverse:** Petrovaradin clock tower

Date	Mintage	F	VF	XF	Unc	BU
1990 Proof	10,000	Value: 27.50				

KM# 66 150 DINARA **Weight:** 12.5000 g. **Composition:** 0.9250 Silver .3717 oz. ASW **Subject:** 8th Mediterranean Games at Split **Size:** 30 mm.

Date	Mintage	F	VF	XF	Unc	BU
1978 Proof	70,000	Value: 21.50				

KM# 147 150 DINARA **Weight:** 17.0000 g. **Composition:** 0.9250 Silver .5056 oz. ASW **Subject:** 1990 Chess Olympiad **Reverse:** Globe

Date	Mintage	F	VF	XF	Unc	BU
1990 Proof	10,000	Value: 37.50				

KM# 52 200 DINARA **Weight:** 15.6400 g. **Composition:** 0.9000 Gold .4526 oz. AGW **Subject:** 25th Anniversary of Republic **Size:** 30 mm.

Date	Mintage	F	VF	XF	Unc	BU
ND(1968) Proof	10,000	Value: 225				
ND(1968) NI Proof	Inc. above	Value: 225				

KM# 64 200 DINARA **Weight:** 15.0000 g. **Composition:** 0.7500 Silver .3617 oz. ASW **Subject:** Tito's 85th birthday

Date	Mintage	F	VF	XF	Unc	BU
1977 Proof	500,000	Value: 11.50				

KM# 64a 200 DINARA **Weight:** 15.0000 g. **Composition:** 0.7500 Silver .2701 oz. ASW **Subject:** Tito's 85th birthday **Note:** Edge varieties with inscription in cyrillic and western exist.

Date	Mintage	F	VF	XF	Unc	BU
1977	300,000	—	—	—	7.50	—

KM# 67 200 DINARA **Weight:** 15.0000 g. **Composition:** 0.9250 Silver .4461 oz. ASW **Subject:** 8th Mediterranean Games at Split

Date	Mintage	F	VF	XF	Unc	BU
1978 Proof	58,000	Value: 25.00				

KM# 68 250 DINARA **Weight:** 17.5000 g. **Composition:** 0.9250 Silver .5204 oz. ASW **Subject:** 8th Mediterranean Games at Split **Obverse:** Basilica of St. Donat in Zadar **Size:** 34 mm.

Date	Mintage	F	VF	XF	Unc	BU
1979 Proof	48,000	Value: 30.00				

KM# 91 250 DINARA **Weight:** 17.0000 g. **Composition:** 0.9250 Silver .5056 oz. ASW **Series:** 1984 Winter Olympics **Reverse:** Sarajevo view **Size:** 34 mm.

Date	Mintage	F	VF	XF	Unc	BU
1982 Proof	110,000	Value: 11.50				

KM# 100 250 DINARA **Weight:** 17.0000 g. **Composition:** 0.9250 Silver .5056 oz. ASW **Series:** 1984 Winter Olympics **Reverse:** Artifact **Size:** 34 mm.

Date	Mintage	F	VF	XF	Unc	BU
1983 Proof	110,000	Value: 11.50				

KM# 101 250 DINARA **Weight:** 17.0000 g. **Composition:** 0.9250 Silver .5056 oz. ASW **Series:** 1984 Winter Olympics **Reverse:** Radimlja tombs **Size:** 34 mm.

Date	Mintage	F	VF	XF	Unc	BU
1983 Proof	110,000	Value: 11.50				

KM# 107 250 DINARA **Weight:** 17.0000 g. **Composition:** 0.9250 Silver .5056 oz. ASW **Series:** 1984 Winter Olympics **Reverse:** Jajce village **Size:** 34 mm.

Date	Mintage	F	VF	XF	Unc	BU
1984 Proof	110,000	Value: 11.50				

KM# 108 250 DINARA **Weight:** 17.0000 g. **Composition:** 0.9250 Silver .5056 oz. ASW **Series:** 1984 Winter Olympics **Reverse:** Tito **Size:** 34 mm.

Date	Mintage	F	VF	XF	Unc	BU
1984 Proof	110,000	Value: 11.50				

KM# 69 300 DINARA **Weight:** 20.0000 g. **Composition:** 0.9250 Silver .5948 oz. ASW **Subject:** Eighth Mediterranean Games at Split **Obverse:** State emblem, value, church **Size:** 36 mm.

Date	Mintage	F	VF	XF	Unc	BU
1978 Proof	36,000	Value: 35.00				

KM# 70 350 DINARA **Weight:** 22.5000 g. **Composition:** 0.9250 Silver .6692 oz. ASW **Subject:** 8th Mediterranean Games at Split **Obverse:** State emblem, value **Size:** 36 mm.

Date	Mintage	F	VF	XF	Unc	BU
1978 Proof	24,000	Value: 37.50				

KM# 71 400 DINARA **Weight:** 25.0000 g. **Composition:** 0.9250 Silver .7435 oz. ASW **Subject:** 8th Mediterranean Games at Split **Obverse:** State emblem, value, Split... **Size:** 40 mm.

Date	Mintage	F	VF	XF	Unc	BU
1978 Proof	24,000	Value: 37.50				

KM# 53 500 DINARA **Weight:** 39.1000 g. **Composition:** 0.9000 Gold 1.1315 oz. AGW **Subject:** 25th Anniversary of Republic **Size:** 45 mm.

Date	Mintage	F	VF	XF	Unc	BU
ND(1968) Proof	10,000	Value: 550				
ND(1968) NI Proof	Inc. above	Value: 550				

KM# 76 500 DINARA **Weight:** 8.0000 g. **Composition:** 0.9250 Silver .2379 oz. ASW **Subject:** Vukovar Congress **Obverse:** State emblem, value, city hall of Vukovar **Size:** 27 mm.

Date	Mintage	F	VF	XF	Unc	BU
1980 Proof	18,000	Value: 20.00				

KM# 80 500 DINARA **Weight:** 8.0000 g. **Composition:** 0.7500 Silver .1865 oz. ASW **Subject:** World Table Tennis Championship Games **Obverse:** State emblem, value, town Novi Sad **Size:** 27 mm.

Date	Mintage	F	VF	XF	Unc	BU
1981 Proof	18,000	Value: 25.00				

KM# 92 500 DINARA **Weight:** 23.0000 g. **Composition:** 0.9250 Silver .6841 oz. ASW **Series:** 1984 Winter Olympics **Subject:** Downhill skiing

Date	Mintage	F	VF	XF	Unc	BU
1982 Proof	110,000	Value: 13.50				

KM# 102 500 DINARA **Weight:** 23.0000 g. **Composition:** 0.9250 Silver .6841 oz. ASW **Series:** 1984 Winter Olympics **Subject:** Ski jumping **Size:** 38 mm.

Date	Mintage	F	VF	XF	Unc	BU
1983 Proof	110,000	Value: 13.50				

KM# 103 500 DINARA **Weight:** 23.0000 g. **Composition:** 0.9250 Silver .6841 oz. ASW **Series:** 1984 Winter Olympics **Subject:** Biathalon **Size:** 38 mm.

Date	Mintage	F	VF	XF	Unc	BU
1983 Proof	110,000	Value: 13.50				

KM# 109 500 DINARA **Weight:** 23.0000 g. **Composition:** 0.9250 Silver .6841 oz. ASW **Series:** 1984 Winter Olympics **Subject:** Cross country skiing **Size:** 38 mm.

Date	Mintage	F	VF	XF	Unc	BU
1984 Proof	110,000	Value: 13.50				

KM# 110 500 DINARA **Weight:** 23.0000 g. **Composition:** 0.9250 Silver .6841 oz. ASW **Series:** 1984 Winter Olympics **Subject:** Slalom skiing **Size:** 38 mm.

Date	Mintage	F	VF	XF	Unc	BU
1984 Proof	110,000	Value: 13.50				

KM# 116 500 DINARA **Weight:** 13.0000 g. **Composition:** 0.9250 Silver .3867 oz. ASW **Subject:** Ski Jumping Championship **Obverse:** Similar to 10,000 Dinara, KM#123 **Reverse:** Herons

Date	Mintage	F	VF	XF	Unc	BU
1985 Proof	50,000	Value: 15.00				

KM# 54 1000 DINARA **Weight:** 78.2000 g. **Composition:** 0.9000 Gold 2.2630 oz. AGW **Subject:** 25th Anniversary of Republic **Size:** 55 mm.

Date	Mintage	F	VF	XF	Unc	BU
ND(1968) Proof	10,000	Value: 1,150				
ND(1968) NI Proof	Inc. above	Value: 1,150				

KM# 77 1000 DINARA **Weight:** 14.0000 g. **Composition:** 0.9250 Silver .4164 oz. ASW **Subject:** Vukovar Congress **Obverse:** State emblem, value, city hall in Vukovar **Size:** 30 mm.

Date	Mintage	F	VF	XF	Unc	BU
1980 Proof	16,000	Value: 27.50				

KM# 78a 1000 DINARA **Weight:** 26.0000 g. **Composition:** 0.9250 Silver .7733 oz. ASW **Subject:** Tito's death

Date	Mintage	F	VF	XF	Unc	BU
1980 Proof	200,000	Value: 30.00				
1980 ZM Proof	Inc. above	Value: 30.00				

KM# 78 1000 DINARA **Weight:** 25.9000 g. **Composition:** 0.7500 Silver .6245 oz. ASW **Subject:** Tito's death **Obverse:** State emblem, value, map of Yugoslavia **Note:** Eyes with and without pupils.

Date	Mintage	F	VF	XF	Unc	BU
1980	800,000	—	—	—	25.00	—

KM# 81 1000 DINARA **Weight:** 14.0000 g. **Composition:** 0.7500 Silver .4164 oz. ASW **Subject:** World Table Tennis Championship Games **Obverse:** State emblem, value, town Novi Sad **Size:** 30 mm.

Date	Mintage	F	VF	XF	Unc	BU
1981 Proof	16,000	Value: 27.50				

KM# 82 1000 DINARA **Weight:** 14.0000 g. **Composition:** 0.7500 Silver .4164 oz. ASW **Subject:** 40th Anniversary of Uprising and Revolution **Size:** 30 mm.

Date	Mintage	F	VF	XF	Unc	BU
1981 Proof	100,000	Value: 22.00				

KM# 93 1000 DINARA **Weight:** 18.0000 g. **Composition:** 0.9250 Silver .5354 oz. ASW **Subject:** International Canoeing Championships **Reverse:** City view

Date	Mintage	F	VF	XF	Unc	BU
1982 Proof	46,000	Value: 30.00				

KM# 117 1000 DINARA **Weight:** 23.0000 g. **Composition:** 0.9250 Silver .6841 oz. ASW **Subject:** Ski Jumping Championship **Obverse:** Similar to 10,000 Dinara, KM#123 **Reverse:** Bloudek **Size:** 38 mm.

Date	Mintage	F	VF	XF	Unc	BU
1985 Proof	20,000	Value: 30.00				

KM# 118 1000 DINARA **Weight:** 23.0000 g. **Composition:** 0.9250 Silver .6841 oz. ASW **Subject:** Ski Jumping Championship **Obverse:** Similar to 10,000 Dinara, KM#123 **Reverse:** Slovenian cradle **Size:** 38 mm.

Date	Mintage	F	VF	XF	Unc	BU
1985 Proof	20,000	Value: 30.00				

KM# 119 1000 DINARA **Weight:** 6.0000 g. **Composition:** 0.9250 Silver .1784 oz. ASW **Subject:** Sinjska Alka

Date	Mintage	F	VF	XF	Unc	BU
ND(1985) Proof	60,000	Value: 15.00				

KM# 148 1000 DINARA **Weight:** 3.5000 g. **Composition:** 0.9000 Gold .1013 oz. AGW **Subject:** 1990 Chess Olympiad **Reverse:** Logo

Date	Mintage	F	VF	XF	Unc	BU
1990 Proof	2,000	Value: 175				

KM# 72 1500 DINARA **Weight:** 8.8000 g. **Composition:** 0.9000 Gold .2546 oz. AGW **Subject:** 8th Mediterranean Games at Split **Size:** 24 mm.

Date	Mintage	F	VF	XF	Unc	BU
1978 Proof	35,000	Value: 175				

KM# 79 1500 DINARA **Weight:** 22.0000 g. **Composition:** 0.9250 Silver .6542 oz. ASW **Subject:** Vukovar Congress **Obverse:** State emblem, value, city hall in Vukovar **Size:** 34 mm.

Date	Mintage	F	VF	XF	Unc	BU
1980 Proof	16,000	Value: 35.00				

KM# 83 1500 DINARA **Weight:** 22.0000 g. **Composition:** 0.7500 Silver .5329 oz. ASW **Subject:** World Table Tennis Championship Games **Obverse:** State emblem, value, town view **Size:** 34 mm.

Date	Mintage	F	VF	XF	Unc	BU
1981 Proof	16,000	Value: 35.00				

KM# 94 1500 DINARA **Weight:** 22.0000 g. **Composition:** 0.9250 Silver .6542 oz. ASW **Subject:** International Canoeing Championships **Reverse:** Tito **Size:** 36 mm.

Date	Mintage	F	VF	XF	Unc	BU
1982 Proof	36,000	Value: 32.50				

KM# 73 2000 DINARA **Weight:** 11.8000 g. **Composition:** 0.9000 Gold .3414 oz. AGW **Subject:** 8th Mediterranean Games at Split **Size:** 27 mm.

Date	Mintage	F	VF	XF	Unc	BU
1978 Proof	35,000	Value: 225				

KM# 120 2000 DINARA **Weight:** 14.0000 g. **Composition:** 0.9250 Silver .4164 oz. ASW **Subject:** Sinska Alka

Date	Mintage	F	VF	XF	Unc	BU
ND(1985) Proof	20,000	Value: 22.50				

KM# 74 2500 DINARA **Weight:** 14.7000 g. **Composition:** 0.9000 Gold .4254 oz. AGW **Subject:** 8th Mediterranean Games at Split

Date	Mintage	F	VF	XF	Unc	BU
1978 Proof	35,000	Value: 275				

KM# 121 3000 DINARA **Weight:** 26.0000 g. **Composition:** 0.9250 Silver .7733 oz. ASW **Subject:** Sinkska Alka

Date	Mintage	F	VF	XF	Unc	BU
ND(1985) Proof	20,000	Value: 35.00				

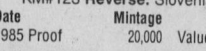

KM# 128 3000 DINARA **Weight:** 13.0000 g. **Composition:** 0.9250 Silver .3867 oz. ASW **Subject:** 200th

Anniversary - Birth of Krajich **Reverse:** Similar to 100 Dinara, KM#127.

Date		F	VF	XF	Unc	BU
1987 Proof	—	Value: 30.00				

KM# 75 5000 DINARA **Weight:** 29.5000 g. **Composition:** 0.9000 Gold .8536 oz. AGW **Subject:** 8th Mediterranean Games at Split **Obverse:** State emblem, value, palace of Diocletian in Split **Size:** 38 mm.

Date	Mintage	F	VF	XF	Unc	BU
1978 Proof	12,000	Value: 450				

KM# 95 5000 DINARA **Weight:** 8.0000 g. **Composition:** 0.9000 Gold .2315 oz. AGW **Series:** 1984 Winter Olympics **Reverse:** Emblem **Size:** 24 mm.

Date	Mintage	F	VF	XF	Unc	BU
1982 Proof	55,000	Value: 120				

KM# 104 5000 DINARA **Weight:** 8.0000 g. **Composition:** 0.9000 Gold .2315 oz. AGW **Series:** 1984 Winter Olympics **Reverse:** Tito **Size:** 24 mm.

Date	Mintage	F	VF	XF	Unc	BU
1983 Proof	55,000	Value: 120				

KM# 111 5000 DINARA **Weight:** 8.0000 g. **Composition:** 0.9000 Gold .2315 oz. AGW **Series:** 1984 Winter Olympics **Reverse:** Flame **Size:** 24 mm.

Date	Mintage	F	VF	XF	Unc	BU
1984 Proof	55,000	Value: 120				

KM# 122 5000 DINARA **Weight:** 23.5000 g. **Composition:** 0.9250 Silver .6989 oz. ASW **Subject:** 400th Anniversary - Liberation from Fascism **Note:** Similar to 100 Dinara, KM#115.

Date	Mintage	F	VF	XF	Unc	BU
1985 Proof	100,000	Value: 40.00				

KM# 129 5000 DINARA **Weight:** 17.0000 g. **Composition:** 0.9250 Silver .5056 oz. ASW **Subject:** 200th Anniversary - Birth of Karajich

Date	Mintage	F	VF	XF	Unc	BU
1987 Proof	Est. 50,000	Value: 35.00				

KM# 135 5000 DINARA **Composition:** Copper-Zinc-Nickel **Subject:** Non-aligned Summit **Reverse:** Symbol

Date	Mintage	F	VF	XF	Unc	BU
ND(1989) Proof	50,000	Value: 4.50				

KM# 123 10000 DINARA **Weight:** 8.0000 g. **Composition:** 0.9000 Gold .2315 oz. AGW **Subject:** World Ski Jumping Championship **Size:** 24 mm.

Date	Mintage	F	VF	XF	Unc	BU
1985 Proof	10,000	Value: 165				

KM# 124 10000 DINARA **Weight:** 5.0000 g. **Composition:** 0.9000 Gold .1447 oz. AGW **Subject:** Sinjska Alka

Date	Mintage	F	VF	XF	Unc	BU
ND(1985) Proof	12,000	Value: 150				

KM#125 20000 DINARA **Weight:** 8.0000 g. **Composition:** 0.9000 Gold .2315 oz. AGW **Subject:** Sinjska Alka

Date	Mintage	F	VF	XF	Unc	BU
ND(1985) Proof	8,000	Value: 250				

KM# 126 40000 DINARA **Weight:** 14.0000 g. **Composition:** 0.9000 Gold .4.083 oz. AGW **Subject:** Sinjska Alka

Date	Mintage	F	VF	XF	Unc	BU
ND(1985) Proof	5,000	Value: 475				

KM# 130 50000 DINARA **Weight:** 8.0000 g. **Composition:** 0.9000 Gold .2315 oz. AGW **Subject:** 200th Anniversary - Birth of Karajich **Note:** Similar to 5,000 Dinar, KM#129.

Date	Mintage	F	VF	XF	Unc	BU
1987 Proof	Est. 10,000	Value: 175				

KM# 136 50000 DINARA **Weight:** 13.0000 g. **Composition:** 0.9250 Silver .3867 oz. ASW **Subject:** Non-aligned Summit **Reverse:** Standing figure

Date	Mintage	F	VF	XF	Unc	BU
ND(1989) Proof	15,000	Value: 25.00				

KM# 137 100000 DINARA **Weight:** 17.0000 g. **Composition:** 0.9250 Silver .5056 oz. ASW **Subject:** Non-aligned Summit **Reverse:** Building

Date	Mintage	F	VF	XF	Unc	BU
ND(1989) Proof	10,000	Value: 35.00				

KM# 138 2000000 DINARA **Weight:** 8.0000 g. **Composition:** 0.9000 Gold .2315 oz. AGW **Subject:** Non-aligned Summit **Reverse:** Symbol

Date	Mintage	F	VF	XF	Unc	BU
ND(1989) Proof	5,000	Value: 240				

FEDERAL REPUBLIC

STANDARD COINAGE

KM# 161 PARA **Composition:** Brass

Date	Mintage	F	VF	XF	Unc	BU
1994	25,350,000	—	—	—	0.35	—

KM# 164.1 5 PARA **Composition:** Brass

Date	Mintage	F	VF	XF	Unc	BU
1994	30,408,000	—	—	—	0.50	—
1995	3,400,000	—	—	—	0.60	—

KM# 164.2 5 PARA **Composition:** Brass **Size:** 17 mm. **Note:** Reduced size.

Date	Mintage	F	VF	XF	Unc	BU
1996	9,951,000	—	—	—	0.50	—

KM# 162.1 10 PARA **Composition:** Copper-Nickel-Zinc

Date	Mintage	F	VF	XF	Unc	BU
1994	52,161,000	—	—	—	0.50	—

KM# 162.2 10 PARA **Composition:** Brass **Note:** Reduced size.

Date	Mintage	F	VF	XF	Unc	BU
1995	31,041,000	—	—	—	0.65	—

KM# 173 10 PARA **Composition:** Brass **Obverse:** Heraldic double eagle shield **Reverse:** Denomination

Date	Mintage	F	VF	XF	Unc	BU
1996	18,129,000	—	—	—	0.50	—
1997	21,384,000	—	—	—	0.50	—
1998	5,153,000	—	—	—	0.50	—

KM# 163 50 PARA **Composition:** Copper-Nickel-Zinc

Date	Mintage	F	VF	XF	Unc	BU
1994	45,013,000	—	—	—	0.75	—

KM# 163a 50 PARA **Composition:** Brass

Date	Mintage	F	VF	XF	Unc	BU
1995	19,193,000	—	—	—	1.00	—

KM# 174 50 PARA **Composition:** Brass **Obverse:** Heraldic double eagle shield

Date	Mintage	F	VF	XF	Unc	BU
1996	3,520,000	—	—	—	1.00	—
1997	14,742,000	—	—	—	1.00	—
1998	20,050,000	—	—	—	1.00	—
1999	18,140,000	—	—	—	1.00	—

KM# 179 50 PARA **Weight:** 3.3000 g. **Composition:** Brass **Obverse:** Female portrait **Reverse:** National arms above denomination **Edge:** Plain **Size:** 18 mm.

Date	Mintage	F	VF	XF	Unc	BU
2000	23,821,000	—	—	—	0.25	—

KM# 149 DINAR **Composition:** Copper-Zinc

Date	Mintage	F	VF	XF	Unc	BU
1992	49,269,000	—	0.10	0.30	0.60	—

KM# 154 DINAR **Composition:** Copper-Zinc-Nickel

Date	Mintage	F	VF	XF	Unc	BU
1993	20,249,000	—	0.10	0.20	0.50	—

KM# 160 DINAR **Composition:** Brass

Date	F	VF	XF	Unc	BU
1994	—	—	—	1.00	—

KM# 180 DINAR **Weight:** 4.4000 g. **Composition:** Copper-Zinc-Nickel **Obverse:** National arms **Reverse:** Large building and denomination **Edge:** Reeded **Size:** 20 mm.

Date	Mintage	F	VF	XF	Unc	BU
2000	20,076,000	—	—	—	0.25	—

KM# 165 NOVI DINAR **Composition:** Copper-Nickel-Zinc

Date	Mintage	F	VF	XF	Unc	BU
1994	47,755,000	—	—	—	1.00	—
1995	10,359,000	—	—	—	1.25	—

KM# 168 NOVI DINAR **Composition:** Copper-Nickel-Zinc **Note:** Reduced size.

Date	Mintage	F	VF	XF	Unc	BU
1996	80,122,000	—	—	—	1.00	—
1999	21,686,000	—	—	—	1.00	—

KM# 150 2 DINARA **Composition:** Copper-Zinc

Date	Mintage	F	VF	XF	Unc	BU
1992	10,571,000	—	0.20	0.40	1.00	—

KM# 155 2 DINARA **Composition:** Copper-Zinc-Nickel

Date	Mintage	F	VF	XF	Unc	BU
1993	10,263,000	—	0.10	0.20	0.50	—

KM# 181 2 DINARA **Weight:** 5.2000 g. **Composition:** Copper-Nickel-Zinc **Obverse:** National arms **Reverse:** Church and denomination **Edge:** Reeded **Size:** 21.9 mm.

Date	Mintage	F	VF	XF	Unc	BU
2000	10,071,000	—	—	—	0.25	—
2002	—	—	—	—	0.25	—

KM# 151 5 DINARA **Composition:** Copper-Zinc

Date	Mintage	F	VF	XF	Unc	BU
1992	26,658,000	—	0.15	0.30	0.75	—

KM# 156 5 DINARA **Composition:** Copper-Zinc-Nickel

Date	Mintage	F	VF	XF	Unc	BU
1993	10,135,000	—	0.10	0.20	0.50	—

KM# 182 5 DINARA **Weight:** 6.3000 g. **Composition:** Copper-Nickel-Zinc **Obverse:** National arms **Reverse:** Domed building and denomination **Edge:** Reeded **Size:** 24 mm.

Date	Mintage	F	VF	XF	Unc	BU
2000	32,762,500	—	—	—	1.25	—

KM# 152 10 DINARA **Composition:** Copper-Zinc-Nickel

Date	Mintage	F	VF	XF	Unc	BU
1992	76,607,000	—	0.10	0.25	0.60	—

KM# 157 10 DINARA **Composition:** Copper-Zinc-Nicke

Date	F	VF	XF	Unc	BU
1993	—	0.15	0.30	0.70	—

KM# 169 20 NOVI DINARA **Composition:** Copper-Zinc-Nickel **Subject:** Nikola Tesla

Date	Mintage	F	VF	XF	Unc	BU
1996 Proof	9,743	Value: 12.50				

KM# 153 50 DINARA **Composition:** Copper-Zinc-Nicke

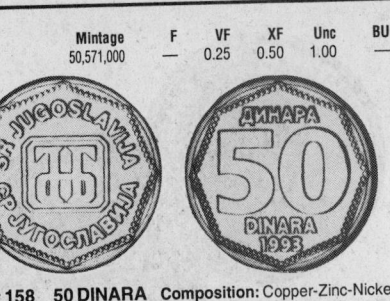

Mintage	F	VF	XF	Unc	BU
50,571,000	—	0.25	0.50	1.00	—

158 50 DINARA **Composition:** Copper-Zinc-Nickel

F	VF	XF	Unc	BU
—	0.20	0.40	0.80	—

 # 159 100 DINARA **Composition:** Brass

F	VF	XF	Unc	BU
—	0.25	0.50	1.00	—

 # 166 150 NOVI DINARA **Weight:** 7.8000 g. **Composition:** 0.9000 Gold .2257 oz. AGW **Subject:** 110th Anniversary - National Bank

	Mintage	F	VF	XF	Unc	BU
1995) Proof	100,000	Value: 175				

 # 170 200 NOVI DINARA **Weight:** 13.0000 g. **Composition:** 0.9250 Silver .3867 oz. ASW **Subject:** Nikola Tesla **Note:** Similar to 20 Novi Dinara, KM#169.

	Mintage	F	VF	XF	Unc	BU
6 Proof	9,847	Value: 32.00				

 # 171 300 NOVI DINARA **Weight:** 26.0000 g. **Composition:** 0.9250 Silver .7734 oz. ASW **Subject:** Nikola Tesla **Note:** Similar to 20 Novi Dinara, KM#169.

e	Mintage	F	VF	XF	Unc	BU
6 Proof	9,034	Value: 45.00				

M# 167 500 DINARA **Composition:** Brass **Note:** All but 1,000 reported melted. Not released for circulation.

te	F	VF	XF	Unc	BU
93	—	—	—	6.50	—

M# 175 600 NOVI DINARA **Weight:** 3.4550 g. **Composition:** 0.9000 Gold .1 oz. AGW **Subject:** Chilander Monastery **Reverse:** Portraits of SS Simon and Sava

ate	Mintage	VG	F	VF	XF	Unc
98(1999)	10,000	—	—	—	—	125

M# 172 1000 NOVI DINARA **Weight:** 8.6400 g. **Composition:** 0.9000 Gold .25 oz. AGW **Subject:** Nikola Tesla **Note:** Similar to 20 Novi Dinara, KM#169.

ate	Mintage	F	VF	XF	Unc	BU
996 Proof	4,617	Value: 250				

M# 176 1500 NOVI DINARA **Weight:** 8.6400 g. **Composition:** 0.9000 Gold .2500 oz. AGW **Subject:** Chilander Monastery **Reverse:** Portraits of SS Simon and Sava

ate	F	VF	XF	Unc	BU
998(1999)	—	—	—	175	—

M# 177 3000 NOVI DINARA **Weight:** 17.2770 g. **Composition:** 0.9000 Gold .4999 oz. AGW **Subject:** Chilander Monastery **Reverse:** Portraits of SS Simon and Sava

Date	Mintage	F	VF	XF	Unc	BU
1998(1999) Proof	300	Value: 400				
1999 Proof	300	Value: 400				

KM# 178 6000 NOVI DINARA **Weight:** 34.5550 g. **Composition:** 0.9000 Gold .9999 oz. AGW **Subject:** Chilander Monastery **Reverse:** Portraits of SS Simon and Sava

Date	Mintage	F	VF	XF	Unc	BU
1998(1999) Proof	300	Value: 650				
1999 Proof	300	Value: 650				

PATTERNS

Including off metal strikes

Patterns Pn1-Pn8 previously listed here are now listed under Serbia.

KM#	Date	Mintage	Identification	Mkt Val
Pn9	1925	—	50 Para. Nickel. KM4. By Pattey.	700
Pn10	1925	—	Dinar. Nickel. KM5. By Pattey.	400
Pn14	1925(a)	—	10 Dinara. Gold.	—
Pn12a	1925	—	2 Dinara. Copper-Nickel. KM6. ESSAI. 3 millimeters thick.	1,000
Pn12	1925	—	2 Dinara. Nickel-Bronze. KM6. ESSAI.	1,000
Pn10a	1925	—	Dinar. Copper. KM5. By Pattey.	400
Pn9a	1925	—	50 Para. Silver. KM4. By Pattey.	500
Pn13	1925	—	2 Dinara. Nickel. KM6.	600
PnA11	1925	—	Dinar. Aluminum. By Pattey.	400
Pn11	1925	—	Dinar. Nickel. KM5.	400
Pn16	1926	—	4 Dukata. Silver. 39.5 mm. River scene.	—
Pn15	1926(k)	—	Dukat. Gold.	—
Pn17	1926(k)	—	4 Dukata. Gold. River scene.	—
Pn19	1931	—	4 Dukata. Gold. 15.0000 g. ESSAI.	—
Pn20	ND	—	4 Dukata. Silver.	—
Pn21	1932	—	50 Dinara. Bronze. Milled edge.	400
Pn21a	1932	—	50 Dinara. Copper.	400
Pn22	1938	—	10 Dinara. Copper.	200
Pn23	1938	—	20 Dinara. Copper.	250
Pn24	1938	—	50 Dinara. Copper.	300
Pn25	1953	—	25 Para. Aluminum. Hole in center.	400
Pn26	1978	20	25 Para. Aluminum.	—
Pn27	1978	19	Dinar. Copper-Nickel.	—
Pn28	1978	15	10 Dinara. Copper-Nickel.	—

PIEFORTS

KM#	Date	Mintage	Identification	Mkt Val
P1	ND(1931-1934)	—	4 Dukata. Gold. 46.4500 g. Conjoined busts.	—

TRIAL STRIKES

KM#	Date	Mintage	Identification	Mkt Val
TS1	1931(a)	—	Dukat. Gold. Uniface. ESSAI Paris/1931.	—
TS2	1931(a)	—	4 Dukata. Gold. Uniface. ESSAI Paris/1931.	—
TS8	1931	2	12 Dukata. 0.9000 Gold. Uniface. ESSAI/PARIS/1931. 45.875-46.45 grams.	—
TS6	1931(k)	—	8 Dukata. Gold. Uniface.	—
TS7	1931	—	8 Dukata. 0.9000 Gold. 30.6180 g. Uniface. ESSAI/PARIS/1931.	—
TS3	1931	—	4 Dukata. Bronze. Uniface.	—
TS4	1931(k)	—	4 Dukata. Gold. Uniface.	—
TS5	1931(k)	—	4 Dukata. Platinum. Uniface.	—

PROOF SETS

KM#	Date	Mintage	Identification	Issue Price	Mkt Val
PS26	1998(1999) (4)	—	KM#175-178	—	1,400
PS27	1998-1999 (4)	—	KM#175-176 dated 1998; KM#177-178 dated 1999	—	1,400

ZAÏRE

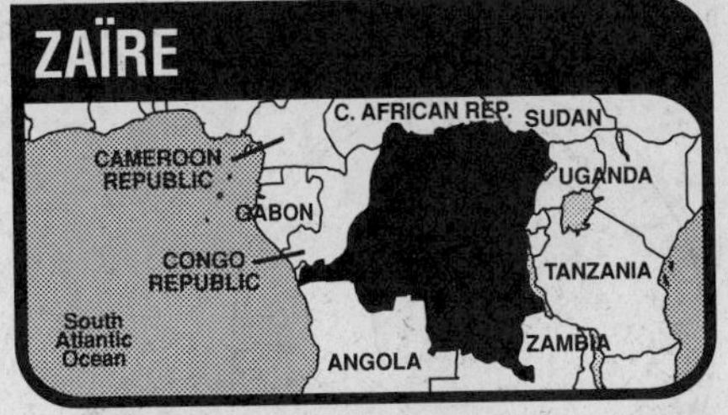

Democratic Republic of the Congo achieved independence on June 30, 1960. It followed the same monetary system as when under the Belgians. Monetary Reform of 1967 introduced new denominations and coins. The name of the country was changed to **Zaire** in 1971.

Under the command of Laurent Kabila, rebel forces overthrew ruler Sese Seko Mobutu in May of 1997. Self appointed President Kabila has officially renamed the country the Democratic Republic of Congo.

MONETARY SYSTEM

100 Makuta = 1 Zaire

1993 -

3,000,000 old Zaires = 1 Nouveau Zaire

REPUBLIC

DECIMAL COINAGE

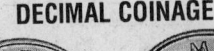

KM# 12 5 MAKUTA **Composition:** Copper-Nickel

Date	Mintage	F	VF	XF	Unc	BU
1977	8,000,000	—	0.50	1.00	3.50	—

KM# 7 10 MAKUTA **Composition:** Copper-Nickel

Date	Mintage	F	VF	XF	Unc	BU
1973	5,000,000	—	2.25	4.00	8.00	—
1975	—	—	2.25	4.00	8.00	—
1976	—	—	2.50	4.50	9.00	—
1978	—	—	2.50	4.50	9.00	—

KM# 8 20 MAKUTA **Composition:** Copper-Nickel

Date	F	VF	XF	Unc	BU
1973	—	3.00	5.50	10.00	—
1976	—	3.50	6.50	12.00	—

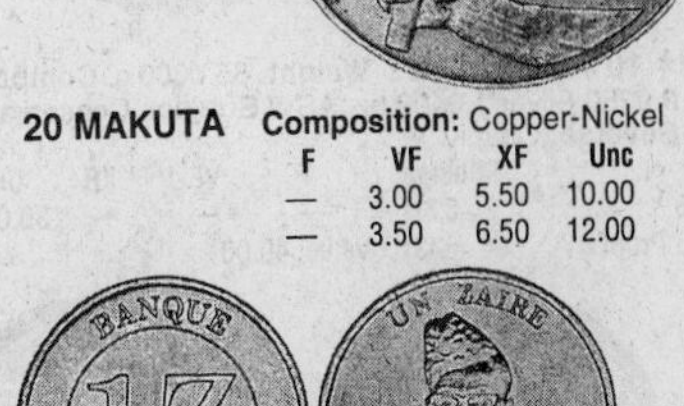

KM# 13 ZAIRE **Composition:** Brass

Date		F	VF	XF	Unc	BU
1987		—	0.50	1.00	2.00	—

KM# 9 2-1/2 ZAIRES **Weight:** 28.2800 g. **Composition:** 0.9250 Silver .8411 oz. ASW **Subject:** Conservation **Reverse:** Mountain gorillas

Date	Mintage	F	VF	XF	Unc	BU
1975	5,735	—	—	—	35.00	—
1975 Proof	6,629	Value: 45.00				

KM# 1 5 ZAIRES **Weight:** 27.8401 g. **Composition:** 0.9250 Silver .8280 oz. ASW **Reverse:** Hotel Intercontinental

Date	F	VF	XF	Unc	BU
1971 Proof	—	Value: 30.00			

KM# 10 5 ZAIRES **Weight:** 35.0000 g. **Composition:** 0.9250 Silver 1.0409 oz. ASW **Subject:** Conservation **Reverse:** Okapi

Date	Mintage	F	VF	XF	Unc	BU
1975	5,734	—	—	—	30.00	—
1975 Proof	6,431	Value: 40.00				

KM# 14 5 ZAIRES **Composition:** Brass

Date	F	VF	XF	Unc	BU
1987	—	0.65	1.25	2.50	—

KM# 2 10 ZAIRES **Weight:** 9.9600 g. **Composition:** 0.9000 Gold .2882 oz. AGW **Reverse:** Hotel Intercontinental

Date	F	VF	XF	Unc	BU
1971 Proof	—	Value: 140			

KM# 3 10 ZAIRES **Weight:** 6.0400 g. **Composition:** 0.9990 Platinum .1940 oz. APW

Date	F	VF	XF	Unc	BU
1971 Proof	—	Value: 210			

KM# 19 10 ZAIRES **Composition:** Brass

Date	F	VF	XF	Unc	BU
1988	—	2.00	4.50	9.00	—

KM# 4 20 ZAIRES **Weight:** 20.9000 g. **Composition:** 0.9000 Gold .6048 oz. AGW **Reverse:** Hotel Intercontinental

Date	F	VF	XF	Unc	BU
1971 Proof	—	Value: 320			

KM# 5 20 ZAIRES **Weight:** 3.8900 g. **Composition:** 0.9990 Platinum .1250 oz. APW

Date	F	VF	XF	Unc	BU
1971 Proof	—	Value: 110			

KM# 6 50 ZAIRES **Weight:** 46.9600 g. **Composit** 0.9000 Gold 1.3590 oz. AGW **Reverse:** Hotel Intercontinental

Date	F	VF	XF	Unc
1971 Proof	—	Value: 675		

KM# 11 100 ZAIRES **Weight:** 33.4370 g. **Composi** 0.9000 Gold .9676 oz. AGW **Subject:** Conservation **Reverse:** Leopard

Date	Mintage	F	VF	XF	Unc
1975	1,415	—	—	—	465
1975 Proof	279	Value: 700			

KM# 20 500 NOUVEAUX ZAIRES **Weight:** 20.0000 g. **Composition:** 0.5000 Silver .3215 oz. ASW **Subject:** Wildlife of Africa **Reverse:** Leopard

Date	Mintage	F	VF	XF	Unc
1996 Proof	10,000	Value: 30.00			

KM# 21 500 NOUVEAUX ZAIRES **Weight:** 20.0000 g. **Composition:** 0.5000 Silver .3215 oz. ASW **Subject:** Wildlife of Africa **Reverse:** Gorilla

Date	Mintage	F	VF	XF	Unc
1996 Proof	Est. 10,000	Value: 30.00			

KM# 22 500 NOUVEAUX ZAIRES Weight: 20.0000 g. **Composition:** 0.5000 Silver .3215 oz. ASW **Subject:** Wildlife of Africa **Reverse:** Two okapi

Date	Mintage	F	VF	XF	Unc	BU
1996 Proof	Est. 10,000	Value: 35.00				

KM# 23 1000 NOUVEAUX ZAIRES Weight: 29.6300 g. **Composition:** 0.9250 Silver .8811 oz. ASW **Subject:** Wildlife of Africa **Obverse:** African map **Reverse:** Hippopotamus

Date	Mintage	F	VF	XF	Unc	BU
1997 Proof	Est. 20,000	Value: 37.50				

KM# 24 1000 NOUVEAUX ZAIRES Weight: 30.0900 g. **Composition:** 0.9250 Silver .8948 oz. ASW **Subject:** Wildlife of Africa **Obverse:** African map **Reverse:** Sailing ship "Portuguese Caravel"

Date	Mintage	F	VF	XF	Unc	BU
1997 Proof	Est. 20,000	Value: 40.00				

KM# 25 5000 NOUVEAUX ZAIRES Weight: 411.4224 g. **Composition:** 0.9990 Silver 13.2143 oz. ASW **Subject:** Wildlife of Africa **Obverse:** Map and national arms **Reverse:** Leopard at rest on branch **Edge:** Reeded

Date	Mintage	F	VF	XF	Unc	BU
1996 Proof	1,000	Value: 225				

KM# 26 10000 NOUVEAUX ZAIRES Weight: 822.8449 g. **Composition:** 0.9990 Silver 26.4286 oz. ASW **Subject:** Wildlife of Africa **Obverse:** Map and national arms **Reverse:** Gorilla **Edge:** Reeded

Date	Mintage	F	VF	XF	Unc	BU
1996 Proof	1,000	Value: 435				

PROOF SETS

KM#	Date	Mintage	Identification	Issue Price	Mkt Val
PS1	1971 (6)	—	KM1-6	—	1,485
PS2	1975 (2)	500	KM9-10	60.00	85.00

ZAMBIA

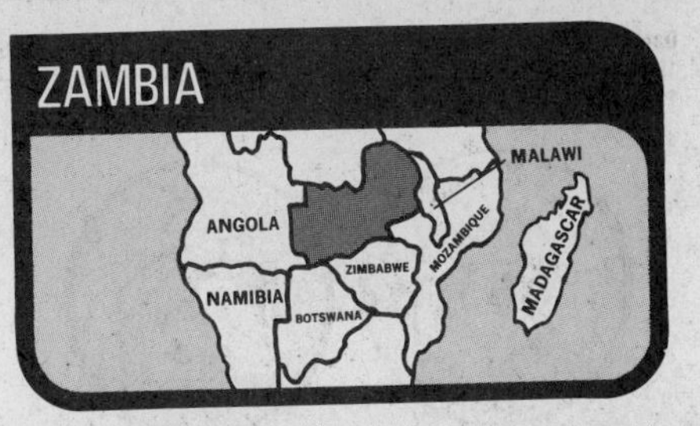

The Republic of Zambia (formerly Northern Rhodesia), a landlocked country in south-central Africa, has an area of 290,586 sq. mi. (752,610 sq. km.) and a population of *7.9 million. Capital: Lusaka. The economy of Zambia is based principally on copper, of which Zambia is the world's third largest producer. Copper, zinc, lead, cobalt and tobacco are exported.

The area that is now Zambia was brought within the British sphere of influence in 1888 by empire builder Cecil Rhodes, who obtained mining concessions in south-central Africa from indigenous chiefs. The territory was ruled by the British South Africa Company, which Rhodes established, until 1924 when its administration was transferred to the British government as a protectorate. In1953, Northern Rhodesia was joined with Nyasaland and the colony of Southern Rhodesia to form the Federation of Rhodesia and Nyasaland. Northern Rhodesia seceded from the Federation on Oct. 24, 1964, and became the independent Republic of Zambia. Zambia is a member of the Commonwealth of Nations. The president is Chief of State.

Zambia converted to a decimal coinage on January 16, 1969. For earlier coinage refer to Rhodesia and Nyasaland.

RULERS
British, until 1964

MONETARY SYSTEM
12 Pence = 1 Shilling
20 Shillings = 1 Pound

REPUBLIC

STANDARD COINAGE

KM# 5 PENNY Composition: Bronze

Date	Mintage	F	VF	XF	Unc	BU
1966	7,200,000	0.15	0.35	0.65	1.75	—
1966 Proof	60	—	—	—	—	—

KM# 1 6 PENCE Composition: Copper-Nickel-Zinc **Reverse:** Morning Glory

Date	Mintage	F	VF	XF	Unc	BU
1964	3,500,000	0.15	0.30	0.60	1.20	—
1964 Proof	5,000	Value: 1.50				

KM# 6 6 PENCE Composition: Copper-Nickel-Zinc

Date	Mintage	F	VF	XF	Unc	BU
1966	7,200,000	0.25	0.50	1.00	2.00	—
1966 Proof	60	—	—	—	—	—

KM# 2 SHILLING Composition: Copper-Nickel **Reverse:** Crowned Hornbill

Date	Mintage	F	VF	XF	Unc	BU
1964	3,510,000	0.25	0.50	1.00	2.00	—
1964 Proof	5,000	Value: 3.50				

KM# 7 SHILLING **Composition:** Copper-Nickel

Date	Mintage	F	VF	XF	Unc	BU
1966	5,000,000	0.35	0.75	1.50	3.25	—
1966 Proof	60	—	—	—	—	—

KM# 3 2 SHILLINGS **Composition:** Copper-Nickel
Note: Bohor Reedbuck

Date	Mintage	F	VF	XF	Unc	BU
1964	3,770,000	0.35	0.75	1.50	3.00	—
1964 Proof	5,000	Value: 4.50				

KM# 8 2 SHILLINGS **Composition:** Copper-Nickel

Date	Mintage	F	VF	XF	Unc	BU
1966	5,000,000	0.45	1.00	2.25	4.50	—
1966 Proof	60	—	—	—	—	—

KM# 4 5 SHILLINGS **Composition:** Copper-Nickel
Subject: 1st Anniversary of Independence

Date	Mintage	F	VF	XF	Unc	BU
1965	10,000	—	2.00	3.50	6.50	—
1965 Proof	20,000	Value: 7.50				

DECIMAL COINAGE

100 Ngwee = 1 Kwacha

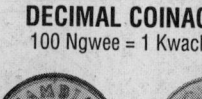

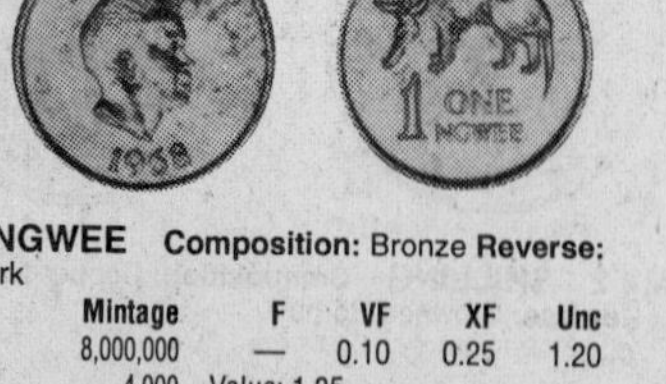

KM# 9 NGWEE **Composition:** Bronze **Reverse:** Aardvark

Date	Mintage	F	VF	XF	Unc	BU
1968	8,000,000	—	0.10	0.25	1.20	—
1968 Proof	4,000	Value: 1.25				
1969	16,000,000	—	0.10	0.20	1.00	—
1972	21,000,000	—	0.10	0.20	1.00	—
1978	23,976,000	—	0.10	0.20	1.00	—
1978 Proof	24,000	Value: 1.50				

KM# 9a NGWEE **Composition:** Copper-Clad Steel

Date	Mintage	F	VF	XF	Unc	BU
1982	10,000,000	—	0.10	0.20	0.85	—
1983	60,000,000	—	0.10	0.15	0.75	—

KM# 10 2 NGWEE **Composition:** Bronze **Reverse:** Martial Eagle

Date	Mintage	F	VF	XF	Unc	BU
1968	19,000,000	—	0.10	0.20	1.00	—
1968 Proof	4,000	Value: 1.50				
1978	—	—	0.15	0.25	1.25	—
1978 Proof	24,000	Value: 1.75				

KM# 10a 2 NGWEE **Composition:** Copper-Clad Steel

Date	Mintage	F	VF	XF	Unc	BU
1982	7,500,000	—	0.10	0.20	1.00	—
1983	60,000,000	—	0.10	0.15	0.50	—

KM# 11 5 NGWEE **Composition:** Copper-Nickel
Reverse: Morning Glory

Date	Mintage	F	VF	XF	Unc	BU
1968	12,000,000	—	0.20	0.30	0.60	—
1968 Proof	4,000	Value: 1.75				
1972	9,000,000	—	0.20	0.30	0.60	—
1978	1,976,000	—	0.20	0.30	0.60	—
1978 Proof	24,000	Value: 2.00				
1982	12,000,000	—	0.20	0.30	0.60	—
1987	10,000,000	—	0.20	0.30	0.60	—

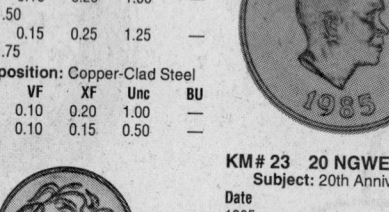

KM# 12 10 NGWEE **Composition:** Copper-Nickel-Zinc
Reverse: Crowned Hornbill

Date	Mintage	F	VF	XF	Unc	BU
1968	1,000,000	—	0.40	0.85	1.75	—
1968 Proof	4,000	Value: 2.00				
1972	1,000,000	—	0.30	0.50	1.00	—
1978	1,976,000	—	0.30	0.50	1.00	—
1978 Proof	24,000	Value: 2.25				
1982	8,000,000	—	0.30	0.50	1.00	—
1983	2,500	—	0.30	0.50	1.00	—
1987	6,000,000	—	0.30	0.50	1.00	—

KM# 13 20 NGWEE **Composition:** Copper-Nickel
Reverse: Bohur Reedbuck, similar to KM#3

Date	Mintage	F	VF	XF	Unc	BU
1968	1,500,000	—	0.75	1.50	2.50	—
1968 Proof	4,000	Value: 2.75				
1972	7,500,000	—	0.50	1.00	2.00	—
1978 Proof	24,000	Value: 3.00				
1983	998,000	—	0.75	1.50	2.50	—
1987	—	—	0.50	1.00	2.00	—
1988	3,000,000	—	0.50	1.00	2.00	—

KM# 22 20 NGWEE **Composition:** Copper-Nickel
Series: F.A.O. - World Food Day

Date	Mintage	F	VF	XF	Unc	BU
1981	970,000	—	0.75	1.50	2.75	—

KM# 23 20 NGWEE **Composition:** Copper-Nickel
Subject: 20th Anniversary - Bank of Zambia

Date	F	VF	XF	Unc	BU
1985	—	0.50	1.00	1.50	—

KM# 23a 20 NGWEE **Weight:** 11.3100 g. **Composition:** 0.9250 Silver .3364 oz. ASW

Date	F	VF	XF	Unc	BU
1985	—	Value: 3.50			

KM# 29 25 NGWEE **Composition:** Nickel Plated Steel
Reverse: Crowned Hornbill

Date	F	VF	XF	Unc	BU
1992	—	—	—	0.75	—

KM# 14 50 NGWEE **Composition:** Copper-Nickel
Series: F.A.O.

Date	Mintage	F	VF	XF	Unc	BU
ND(1969)	70,000	—	2.00	3.50	5.50	—

KM# 15 50 NGWEE **Composition:** Copper-Nickel
Series: F.A.O.

Date	Mintage	F	VF	XF	Unc	BU
1972	510,000	—	1.25	2.50	4.50	—

KM# 16 50 NGWEE Composition: Copper-Nickel
Subject: Second Republic, 13 December 1972

Date	Mintage	F	VF	XF	Unc	BU
1972	6,000,000	—	1.00	2.00	4.00	—
1972 Proof	2,000	Value: 7.00				
1978 Proof	24,000	Value: 5.00				
1983	998,000	—	1.00	2.00	4.00	—

KM# 24 50 NGWEE Composition: Copper-Nickel
Subject: 40th Anniversary of United Nations

Date	F	VF	XF	Unc	BU
1985	—	1.00	1.25	2.50	—

KM# 24a 50 NGWEE Weight: 11.6600 g. Composition: 0.9250 Silver .3468 oz. ASW

Date	F	VF	XF	Unc	BU
1985 Proof	—	—	—	—	—

KM# 30 50 NGWEE Composition: Nickel Plated Steel
Reverse: Kafue Lechwe

Date	F	VF	XF	Unc	BU
1992	—	—	—	1.00	—

KM# 17 KWACHA Composition: Copper-Nickel
Subject: 10th Anniverssary of Independence

Date	Mintage	F	VF	XF	Unc	BU
ND(1974)	4,000	—	—	—	20.00	—
ND(1974) Proof	1,500	Value: 35.00				

KM# 26 KWACHA Composition: Nickel-Brass

Date	Mintage	F	VF	XF	Unc	BU
1989	8,000,000	—	0.75	1.50	3.50	—

KM# 38 KWACHA Composition: Brass

Date	F	VF	XF	Unc	BU
1992	—	—	—	1.00	—

KM# 18 5 KWACHA Weight: 25.3100 g. Composition: 0.9250 Silver .7527 oz. ASW Subject: Conservation
Reverse: Kafue Lechwe

Date	Mintage	F	VF	XF	Unc	BU
1979	3,250	—	—	—	17.50	—

KM# 18a 5 KWACHA Weight: 28.2800 g.
Composition: 0.9250 Silver .8411 oz. ASW

Date	Mintage	F	VF	XF	Unc	BU
1979 Proof	3,407	Value: 22.50				

KM# 31 5 KWACHA Composition: Brass Reverse: Oryx

Date	F	VF	XF	Unc	BU
1992	—	—	—	1.50	—

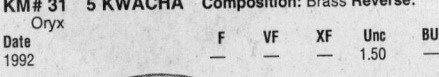

KM# 19 10 KWACHA Weight: 31.6500 g.
Composition: 0.9250 Silver .9398 oz. ASW Subject: Conservation Reverse: Taita Falcon

Date	Mintage	F	VF	XF	Unc	BU
1979	3,250	—	—	—	21.50	—

KM# 19a 10 KWACHA Weight: 35.0000 g.
Composition: 0.9250 Silver 1.0409 oz. ASW

Date	Mintage	F	VF	XF	Unc	BU
1979 Proof	3,256	Value: 27.50				

KM# 21 10 KWACHA Weight: 27.2200 g.
Composition: 0.9250 Silver .8095 oz. ASW Series: International Year of the Child Obverse: Similar to 20 Ngwee, KM#13 Reverse: 3 children on playground equipment

Date	Mintage	F	VF	XF	Unc	BU
1980 Proof	12,000	Value: 15.00				

KM# 25 10 KWACHA Weight: 27.2200 g.
Composition: 0.9250 Silver .8095 oz. ASW Series: World Wildlife Fund Reverse: White-winged Flufftail

Date	Mintage	F	VF	XF	Unc	BU
1986 Proof	25,000	Value: 23.50				

KM# 27 10 KWACHA Weight: 27.2200 g.
Composition: 0.9250 Silver .8095 oz. ASW Subject: 70th Anniversary - Save the Children Fund

Date	Mintage	F	VF	XF	Unc	BU
1989 Proof	Est. 20,000	Value: 22.50				

KM# 32 10 KWACHA **Composition:** Brass **Reverse:** Rhinoceros

Date	F	VF	XF	Unc	BU
1992	—	—	—	2.50	—

KM# 39 10 KWACHA **Weight:** 20.0000 g. **Composition:** 0.9990 Silver .6430 oz. ASW **Subject:** World Cup Soccer **Reverse:** Player kicking ball; .999 in field

Date	F	VF	XF	Unc	BU
1994 Proof	—	Value: 50.00			

KM# 119 10 KWACHA **Weight:** 27.3400 g. **Composition:** Copper-Nickel **Subject:** UNICEF **Obverse:** National arms. **Reverse:** Three boys playing soccer. **Edge:** Reeded. **Size:** 40.1 mm.

Date	F	VF	XF	Unc	BU
2000 Matte	—	—	—	10.00	—

KM# 119a 10 KWACHA **Weight:** 27.2200 g. **Composition:** 0.9250 Silver 0.8095 oz. ASW **Subject:** UNICEF **Obverse:** National arms. **Reverse:** Three boys playing soccer. **Edge:** Reeded. **Size:** 40.1 mm.

Date	Mintage	F	VF	XF	Unc	BU
2000 Proof	25,000	Value: 17.50				

KM# 33 20 KWACHA **Weight:** 10.1700 g. **Composition:** 0.9990 Silver .3266 oz. ASW **Series:** 1994 Olympics **Reverse:** Slalom skier

Date	Mintage	F	VF	XF	Unc	BU
1994 Proof	25,000	Value: 22.50				

KM# 51 75 KWACHA **Weight:** 5.0000 g. **Composition:** 0.9990 Silver .1606 oz. ASW **Subject:** Diana - The People's Princess **Note:** Similar to 200 Kwacha, KM#52

Date	F	VF	XF	Unc	BU
1997 Proof	—	—	—	—	—

KM# 28 100 KWACHA **Weight:** 28.2800 g. **Composition:** 0.9250 Silver .8411 oz. ASW **Series:** Barcelona Summer Olympics **Subject:** Boxing **Obverse:** National arms **Reverse:** 2 Boxers in ring fighting

Date	Mintage	F	VF	XF	Unc	BU
1992 Proof	Est. 50,000	Value: 27.50				

KM# 50 100 KWACHA **Composition:** Copper-Nickel **Reverse:** Charging bull elephant

Date	F	VF	XF	Unc	BU
1997	—	—	—	17.50	—

KM# 56 100 KWACHA **Weight:** 28.2800 g. **Composition:** 0.9990 Silver .9083 oz. ASW **Reverse:** Crocodile

Date	Mintage	F	VF	XF	Unc	BU
1998 Proof	Est. 25,000	Value: 50.00				

KM# 57 100 KWACHA **Weight:** 28.2800 g. **Composition:** 0.9990 Silver .9083 oz. ASW **Reverse:** Leopard

Date	Mintage	F	VF	XF	Unc	BU
1998 Proof	Est. 25,000	Value: 60.00				

KM# 58 100 KWACHA **Weight:** 28.2800 g. **Composition:** 0.9990 Silver .9083 oz. ASW **Reverse:** Black Rhinoceros

Date	Mintage	F	VF	XF	Unc	BU
1998 Proof	Est. 25,000	Value: 60.00				

KM# 59 100 KWACHA **Weight:** 28.2800 g. **Composition:** 0.9990 Silver .9083 oz. ASW **Reverse:** Hippopotamus and calf

Date	Mintage	F	VF	XF	Unc	BU
1998 Proof	Est. 25,000	Value: 60.00				

KM# 60 100 KWACHA **Weight:** 28.2800 g. **Composition:** 0.9990 Silver .9083 oz. ASW **Reverse:** Impala

Date	Mintage	F	VF	XF	Unc	BU
1998 Proof	Est. 25,000	Value: 55.00				

KM# 61 100 KWACHA **Weight:** 28.2800 g. **Composition:** 0.9990 Silver .9083 oz. ASW **Reverse:** Pelican

ate	Mintage	F	VF	XF	Unc	BU
998 Proof	Est. 25,000	Value: 60.00				

KM# 64 100 KWACHA **Weight:** 28.2800 g. **Composition:** 0.9990 Silver .9083 oz. ASW **Reverse:** Flamingos

Date	Mintage	F	VF	XF	Unc	BU
1998 Proof	Est. 25,000	Value: 50.00				

KM# 67 100 KWACHA **Weight:** 28.2800 g. **Composition:** 0.9990 Silver .9083 oz. ASW **Reverse:** Two gazelles

Date	Mintage	F	VF	XF	Unc	BU
1998 Proof	Est. 25,000	Value: 55.00				

KM# 62 100 KWACHA **Weight:** 28.2800 g. **Composition:** 0.9990 Silver .9083 oz. ASW **Reverse:** Stork

ate	Mintage	F	VF	XF	Unc	BU
998 Proof	Est. 25,000	Value: 50.00				

KM# 65 100 KWACHA **Weight:** 28.2800 g. **Composition:** 0.9990 Silver .9083 oz. ASW **Reverse:** Giraffes

Date	Mintage	F	VF	XF	Unc	BU
1998 Proof	Est. 25,000	Value: 60.00				

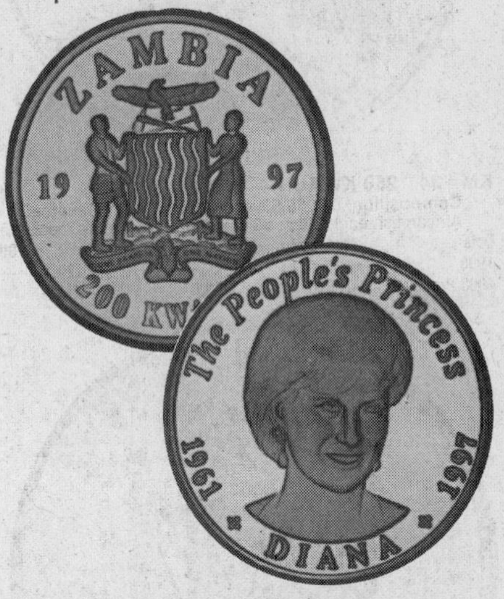

KM# 52 200 KWACHA **Composition:** Copper-Nickel **Subject:** Diana - The People's Princess **Obverse:** National arms **Reverse:** Diana's portrait, dates 1961 at left, 1997 at right

Date	F	VF	XF	Unc	BU
1997 Proof	—	Value: 8.00			

KM# 63 100 KWACHA **Weight:** 28.2800 g. **Composition:** 0.9990 Silver .9083 oz. ASW **Reverse:** Burchell's Zebra

ate	Mintage	F	VF	XF	Unc	BU
998 Proof	Est. 25,000	Value: 55.00				

KM# 66 100 KWACHA **Weight:** 28.2800 g. **Composition:** 0.9990 Silver .9083 oz. ASW **Reverse:** Lion

Date	Mintage	F	VF	XF	Unc	BU
1998 Proof	Est. 25,000	Value: 60.00				

KM# 20 250 KWACHA **Weight:** 33.6300 g. **Composition:** 0.9000 Gold .9371 oz. AGW **Subject:** Conservation **Reverse:** African wild dog

Date	Mintage	F	VF	XF	Unc	BU
1979	455	—	—	—	500	—
1979 Proof	245	Value: 750				

KM# 34 250 KWACHA **Weight:** 136.0800 g. **Composition:** 0.9250 Silver 4.0474 oz. ASW **Reverse:** African fish eagle **Size:** 63 mm. **Note:** Illustration reduced.

Date	Mintage	F	VF	XF	Unc	BU
1993	400	—	—	—	125	—
1993 Proof	5,000	Value: 85.00				

KM# 36 250 KWACHA **Weight:** 136.0800 g. **Composition:** 0.9250 Silver 4.0474 oz. ASW **Reverse:** Paradise Flycatcher **Size:** 63 mm. **Note:** Illustration reduced.

Date	Mintage	F	VF	XF	Unc	BU
1993	400	—	—	—	125	—
1993 Proof	5,000	Value: 85.00				

KM# 40 500 KWACHA **Weight:** 31.7730 g. **Composition:** 0.9990 Silver 1.025 oz. ASW **Subject:** Equality **Reverse:** Black and white face profiles

Date	F	VF	XF	Unc	B
1994 Proof	—	Value: 32.50			

KM# 41 500 KWACHA **Weight:** 31.7730 g. **Composition:** 0.9990 Silver 1.025 oz. ASW **Subject:** Freedom of Speech **Reverse:** Perched African Fish Eagle

Date	F	VF	XF	Unc	B
1994 Proof	—	Value: 30.00			

KM# 35 250 KWACHA **Weight:** 136.0800 g. **Composition:** 0.9250 Silver 4.0474 oz. ASW **Reverse:** Saddle-billed stork **Size:** 63 mm. **Note:** Illustration reduced.

Date	Mintage	F	VF	XF	Unc	BU
1993	400	—	—	—	125	—
1993 Proof	5,000	Value: 85.00				

KM# 37 250 KWACHA **Weight:** 136.0800 g. **Composition:** 0.9250 Silver 4.0474 oz. ASW **Reverse:** Red-breasted Swallow **Size:** 63 mm. **Note:** Illustration reduced.

Date	Mintage	F	VF	XF	Unc	BU
1993	400	—	—	—	135	—
1993 Proof	5,000	Value: 95.00				

KM# 42 500 KWACHA **Weight:** 31.7730 g. **Composition:** 0.9990 Silver 1.025 oz. ASW **Subject:** Rights of Religion and Culture **Reverse:** Books, scroll, and mask

Date	F	VF	XF	Unc	B
1994 Proof	—	Value: 25.00			

 # 43 500 KWACHA **Weight:** 31.7730 g. **Composition:** 0.9990 Silver 1.025 oz. ASW **Subject:** Rights of Association **Reverse:** Lion cub and lamb

	F	VF	XF	Unc	BU
Proof	—	Value: 30.00			

KM# 46 500 KWACHA **Weight:** 31.7730 g. **Composition:** 0.9990 Silver 1.025 oz. ASW **Subject:** Rights of the Disabled **Reverse:** Three elephants

Date	F	VF	XF	Unc	BU
1994 Proof	—	Value: 35.00			

KM# 49 500 KWACHA **Weight:** 31.7730 g. **Composition:** 0.9990 Silver 1.025 oz. ASW **Subject:** Women's Rights **Reverse:** Women with firewood

Date	F	VF	XF	Unc	BU
1994 Proof	—	Value: 22.50			

M# 44 500 KWACHA **Weight:** 31.7730 g. **Composition:** 0.9990 Silver 1.025 oz. ASW **Subject:** Rights to Work **Reverse:** African Masked Weaver Bird building nest

te	F	VF	XF	Unc	BU
94 Proof	—	Value: 30.00			

KM# 47 500 KWACHA **Weight:** 31.7730 g. **Composition:** 0.9990 Silver 1.025 oz. ASW **Subject:** Rights to a Clean Environment **Reverse:** Two South African Shelducks

Date	F	VF	XF	Unc	BU
1994 Proof	—	Value: 30.00			

M# 45 500 KWACHA **Weight:** 31.7730 g. **Composition:** 0.9990 Silver 1.025 oz. ASW **Subject:** Rights to Health **Reverse:** Shaman and Caduceus

ate	F	VF	XF	Unc	BU
994 Proof	—	Value: 25.00			

KM# 48 500 KWACHA **Weight:** 31.7730 g. **Composition:** 0.9990 Silver 1.025 oz. ASW **Subject:** Children's Rights **Reverse:** Fawn

Date	F	VF	XF	Unc	BU
1994 Proof	—	Value: 30.00			

KM# 136 500 KWACHA **Weight:** 223.0000 g. **Composition:** 0.9990 Silver 7.1624 oz. ASW **Subject:** Equality **Obverse:** National arms. **Reverse:** Black and white

facial profiles back to back. **Edge:** Reeded. **Size:** 75.15 mm. **Note:** Illustration reduced. Actual size: 75.15mm.

Date		F	VF	XF	Unc	BU
1995 Proof	—	Value: 175				

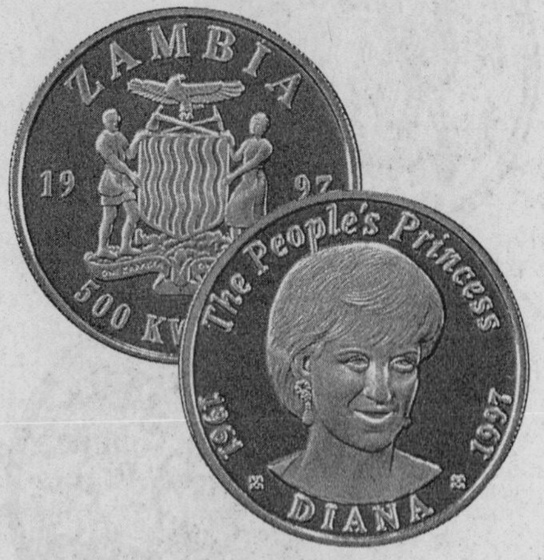

KM# 53 500 KWACHA **Weight:** 31.1035 g. **Composition:** 0.9990 Silver 1.0000 oz. ASW **Subject:** Diana - The People's Princess **Note:** Similar to 200 Kwacha, KM#52

Date	Mintage	F	VF	XF	Unc	BU
1997 Proof	Est. 13,211	Value: 22.50				

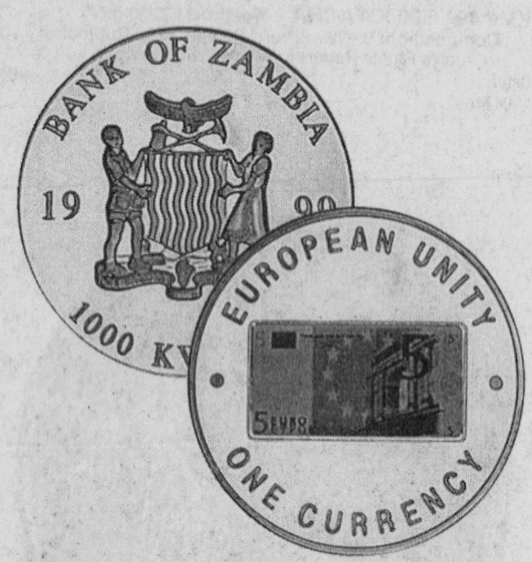

KM# 120 1000 KWACHA **Weight:** 28.5000 g. **Composition:** Silver-Plated Copper-Nickel **Subject:** European Unity - One Currency **Obverse:** National arms. **Reverse:** Multicolor 5 Euro note face design. **Edge:** Reeded. **Size:** 38 mm.

Date		F	VF	XF	Unc	BU
1999 Proof	—	Value: 40.00				

KM# 121 1000 KWACHA **Weight:** 28.5000 g. **Composition:** Silver-Plated Copper-Nickel **Subject:** European Unity - One Currency **Obverse:** National arms. **Reverse:** Multicolor 5 Euro note back design. **Edge:** Reeded. **Size:** 38 mm.

Date		F	VF	XF	Unc	BU
1999 Proof	—	Value: 40.00				

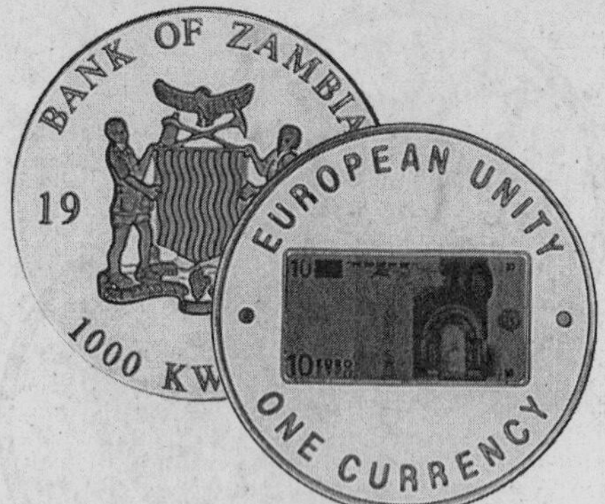

KM# 122 1000 KWACHA **Weight:** 28.5000 g. **Composition:** Silver-Plated Copper-Nickel **Subject:** European Unity - One Currency **Obverse:** National arms. **Reverse:** Multicolor 10 Euro note face design. **Edge:** Reeded. **Size:** 38 mm.

Date		F	VF	XF	Unc	BU
1999 Proof	—	Value: 40.00				

KM# 123 1000 KWACHA **Weight:** 28.5000 g. **Composition:** Silver-Plated Copper-Nickel **Subject:** European Unity - One Currency **Obverse:** National arms. **Reverse:** Multicolor 10 Euro note back design. **Edge:** Reeded. **Size:** 38 mm.

Date		F	VF	XF	Unc	BU
1999 Proof	—	Value: 40.00				

KM# 124 1000 KWACHA **Weight:** 28.5000 g. **Composition:** Silver-Plated Copper-Nickel **Subject:** European Unity - One Currency **Obverse:** National arms. **Reverse:** Multicolor 20 Euro note face design. **Edge:** Reeded. **Size:** 38 mm.

Date		F	VF	XF	Unc	BU
1999 Proof	—	Value: 40.00				

KM# 125 1000 KWACHA **Weight:** 28.5000 g. **Composition:** Silver-Plated Copper-Nickel **Subject:** European Unity - One Currency **Obverse:** National a **Reverse:** Multicolor 20 Euro note back design. **Edge:** Reeded. **Size:** 38 mm.

Date		F	VF	XF	Unc
1999 Proof	—	Value: 40.00			

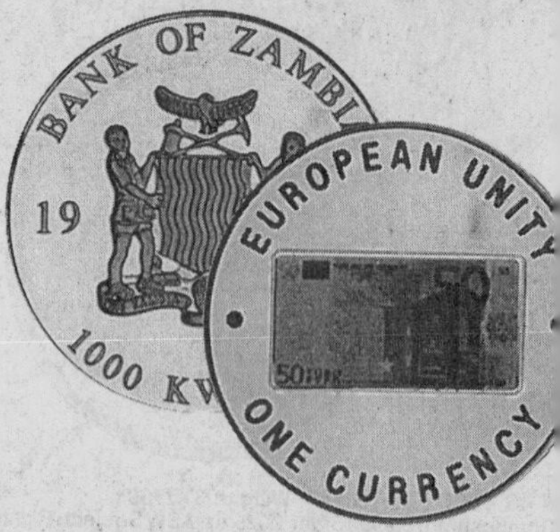

KM# 126 1000 KWACHA **Weight:** 28.5000 g. **Composition:** Silver-Plated Copper-Nickel **Subject:** European Unity - One Currency **Obverse:** National arr **Reverse:** Multicolor 50 Euro note face design. **Edge:** Reeded. **Size:** 38 mm.

Date		F	VF	XF	Unc
1999 Proof	—	Value: 40.00			

KM# 127 1000 KWACHA **Weight:** 28.5000 g. **Composition:** Silver-Plated Copper-Nickel **Subject:** European Unity - One Currency **Obverse:** National arms **Reverse:** Multicolor 50 Euro note back design. **Edge:** Reeded. **Size:** 38 mm.

Date		F	VF	XF	Unc
1999 Proof	—	Value: 40.00			

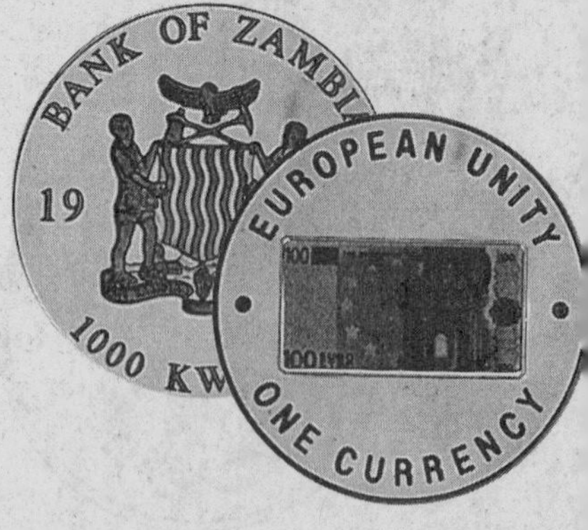

KM# 128 1000 KWACHA **Weight:** 28.5000 g. **Composition:** Silver Plated Copper-Nickel-Zinc **Subject:** Euro Banknotes Series **Obverse:** National arms. **Reverse** Multicolor 100 euro noe face design. **Edge:** Reeded. **Size** 38 mm.

Date		F	VF	XF	Unc	B
1999 Proof	—	Value: 40.00				

 # 129 1000 KWACHA **Weight:** 28.5000 g. **Composition:** Silver Plated Copper-Nickel-Zinc **Subject:** Euro Banknotes Series **Obverse:** National arms. **Reverse:** Multicolor 100 euro note back design. **Edge:** Reeded. **Size:** 38 mm.

	F	VF	XF	Unc	BU
Proof	—	Value: 40.00			

1# 130 1000 KWACHA **Weight:** 28.5000 g. **Composition:** Silver Plated Copper-Nickel-Zinc **Subject:** Euro Banknotes Series **Obverse:** National arms. **Reverse:** Multicolor 200 euro note face design. **Edge:** Reeded. **Size:** 38 mm.

te	F	VF	XF	Unc	BU
99 Proof	—	Value: 40.00			

M# 131 1000 KWACHA **Weight:** 28.5000 g. **Composition:** Silver Plated Copper-Nickel-Zinc **Subject:** Euro Banknotes Series **Obverse:** National arms. **Reverse:** Multicolor 200 euro note back design. **Edge:** Reeded. **Size:** 38 mm.

ate	F	VF	XF	Unc	BU
999 Proof	—	Value: 40.00			

KM# 132 1000 KWACHA **Weight:** 28.5000 g. **Composition:** Silver Plated Copper-Nickel-Zinc **Subject:** Euro Banknotes Series **Obverse:** National arms. **Reverse:** Multicolor 500 euro note face design. **Edge:** Reeded. **Size:** 38 mm.

Date	F	VF	XF	Unc	BU
1999 Proof	—	Value: 40.00			

KM# 133 1000 KWACHA **Weight:** 28.5000 g. **Composition:** Silver Plated Copper-Nickel-Zinc **Subject:** Euro Banknotes Series **Obverse:** National arms. **Reverse:** Multicolor 500 euro note back design. **Edge:** Reeded. **Size:** 38 mm.

Date	F	VF	XF	Unc	BU
1999 Proof	—	Value: 40.00			

KM# 91 1000 KWACHA **Weight:** 28.7200 g. **Composition:** Copper-Nickel **Subject:** European Unity **Obverse:** National arms **Reverse:** Multi-colored 20 euro note **Edge:** Plain **Size:** 38 mm.

Date	F	VF	XF	Unc	BU
1999	—	—	—	15.00	—

KM# 109 1000 KWACHA **Weight:** 20.0000 g. **Composition:** 0.9250 Silver .5948 oz. ASW **Series:** Sydney Olympics **Obverse:** Queen Elizabeth's portrait above Zambian arms **Reverse:** Discus thrower **Edge:** Plain **Size:** 38.6 mm.

Date	F	VF	XF	Unc	BU
1999 Proof	—	Value: 35.00			

KM# 95 1000 KWACHA **Composition:** Copper-Nickel **Series:** 1,000 Years of Exploration **Obverse:** Queen Elizabeth's portrait above Zambian arms **Reverse:** Multicolor portrait of Lief Ericksson and Viking ship **Edge:** Reeded **Size:** 48 x 30.1 mm.

Date	Mintage	F	VF	XF	Unc	BU
2000 Proof	15,000	Value: 10.00				

KM# 96 1000 KWACHA **Composition:** Copper-Nickel **Series:** 1,000 Years of Exploration **Reverse:** Multicolor portrait of Marco Polo and ship

Date	Mintage	F	VF	XF	Unc	BU
2000 Proof	15,000	Value: 10.00				

KM# 97 1000 KWACHA **Composition:** Copper-Nickel **Series:** 1,000 Years of Exploration **Reverse:** Multicolor portrait of Columbus and ship

Date	Mintage	F	VF	XF	Unc	BU
2000 Proof	15,000	Value: 10.00				

KM# 98 1000 KWACHA **Composition:** Copper-Nickel **Series:** 1,000 Years of Exploration **Reverse:** Multicolor portrait of Sir Francis Drake and ship

Date	Mintage	F	VF	XF	Unc	BU
2000 Proof	15,000	Value: 10.00				

KM# 99 1000 KWACHA **Composition:** Copper-Nickel **Series:** 1,000 Years of Exploration **Reverse:** Multicolor portrait of Captain Cook and ship

Date	Mintage	F	VF	XF	Unc	BU
2000 Proof	15,000	Value: 10.00				

KM#100 1000 KWACHA **Composition:** Copper-Nickel **Series:** 1,000 Years of Exploration **Reverse:** Multicolor portrait of Amundsen and ship

Date	Mintage	F	VF	XF	Unc	BU
2000 Proof	15,000	Value: 10.00				

KM# 147 1000 KWACHA **Weight:** 28.9000 g. **Composition:** 0.9250 Silver 0.8595 oz. ASW **Subject:** African Wildlife **Obverse:** Queen's portrait above national arms **Reverse:** Multicolor snarling leopard under protective acrylic. **Edge:** Reeded **Size:** 40.3 mm.

Date		F	VF	XF	Unc	BU
2000 Proof	—	Value: 50.00				

KM# 148 1000 KWACHA **Weight:** 28.9000 g. **Composition:** 0.9250 Silver 0.8595 oz. ASW **Subject:** African Wildlife **Obverse:** Queen's portrait above national arms **Reverse:** Multicolor white storck under protective acrylic **Edge:** Reeded **Size:** 40.3 mm.

Date		F	VF	XF	Unc	BU
2000 Proof	—	Value: 50.00				

KM# 149 1000 KWACHA **Weight:** 28.9000 g. **Composition:** 0.9250 Silver 0.8595 oz. ASW **Subject:** African Wildlife **Obverse:** Queen's portrait above national arms **Reverse:** Multicolor cheetah under protective acrylic **Edge:** Reeded **Size:** 40.3 mm.

Date		F	VF	XF	Unc	BU
2000 Proof	—	Value: 50.00				

KM# 74 1000 KWACHA **Composition:** Copper-Nickel **Reverse:** 2001 calendar

Date		F	VF	XF	Unc	BU
2000 Proof	—	Value: 12.50				

KM# 77 1000 KWACHA **Weight:** 20.0000 g. **Composition:** Copper-Nickel **Subject:** 100th Birthday Queen Mother **Reverse:** Black and white photo of Que Mother as an elderly lady **Note:** Size 48x30mm, similar KM#80.

Date	Mintage	F	VF	XF	Unc
2000 Proof	50,000	Value: 13.50			

KM# 76 1000 KWACHA **Weight:** 20.0000 g. **Composition:** Copper-Nickel **Subject:** 100th Birthday - Queen Mother **Reverse:** Black and white photo of Quee Mother seated on throne at 1937 coronation **Note:** Size 48x30mm.

Date	Mintage	F	VF	XF	Unc
2000 Proof	50,000	Value: 13.50			

KM# 75 1000 KWACHA **Weight:** 20.0000 g. **Composition:** Copper-Nickel **Subject:** 100th Birthday - Queen Mother **Obverse:** Queen's portrait above Zambian arms **Edge:** Reeded **Note:** Size: 48x30mm, similar to KM#78.

Date		F	VF	XF	Unc	B
2000 Proof	—	Value: 13.50				

87 1000 KWACHA **Weight:** 28.9100 g. **Composition:** Copper-Nickel **Series:** Patrons of the Ocean **bverse:** National arms above Queen Elizabeth's portrait **everse:** Sea turtle **Edge:** Reeded **Size:** 38 mm.

		F	VF	XF	Unc	BU
Proof	—	Value: 8.50				

88 1000 KWACHA **Weight:** 28.9100 g. **Composition:** Copper-Nickel **Series:** Patrons of the Ocean **Reverse:** Coclacanth

		F	VF	XF	Unc	BU
Proof	—	Value: 8.50				

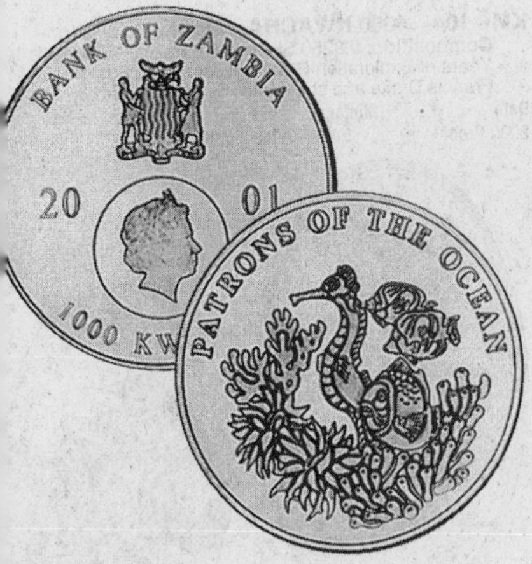

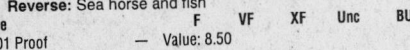

M# 89 1000 KWACHA **Weight:** 28.9100 g. **Composition:** Copper-Nickel **Series:** Patrons of the Ocean **Reverse:** Sea horse and fish

te		F	VF	XF	Unc	BU
01 Proof	—	Value: 8.50				

KM# 90 1000 KWACHA **Weight:** 28.9100 g. **Composition:** Copper-Nickel **Series:** Patrons of the Ocean **Reverse:** Two dolphins

Date		F	VF	XF	Unc	BU
2001 Proof	—	Value: 8.50				

KM# 137 2000 KWACHA **Weight:** 22.5000 g. **Composition:** Copper-Nickel **Subject:** World Cup Soccer **Obverse:** National arms. **Reverse:** Player kicking ball. **Edge:** Reeded. **Size:** 38 mm.

Date		F	VF	XF	Unc	BU
1994 Proof	—	Value: 20.00				

KM# 138 2000 KWACHA **Weight:** 22.5000 g. **Composition:** Copper-Nickel **Subject:** World Cup Soccer **Obverse:** National arms. **Reverse:** Two players in action. **Edge:** Reeded. **Size:** 38 mm.

Date		F	VF	XF	Unc	BU
1994 Proof	—	Value: 20.00				

KM# 139 2000 KWACHA **Weight:** 22.5000 g. **Composition:** Copper-Nickel **Subject:** World Cup Soccer **Obverse:** National arms. **Reverse:** Three players and "Winner Brazil". **Edge:** Reeded. **Size:** 38 mm.

Date		F	VF	XF	Unc	BU
1994 Proof	—	Value: 20.00				

KM# 152 2000 KWACHA **Weight:** 20.2200 g. **Composition:** 0.9999 Silver 0.65 oz. ASW **Subject:** Leonardo Da Vinci **Obverse:** National arms **Reverse:** Humn figure study **Edge:** Reeded **Size:** 38 mm.

Date		F	VF	XF	Unc	BU
1997 Proof	—	Value: 35.00				

KM# 54 2000 KWACHA **Weight:** 3.1103 g. **Composition:** 0.9999 Gold .1000 oz. AGW **Subject:** Diana - The People's Princess **Note:** Similar to 200 Kwacha, KM#52.

Date	F	VF	XF	Unc	BU
1997 Proof	—	—	—	—	—

KM# 68 2000 KWACHA **Weight:** 15.5518 g. **Composition:** 0.9990 Silver .5000 oz. ASW **Subject:** Taipai Subway **Obverse:** National arms **Reverse:** Train with inset diamond headlight **Note:** Struck at Singapore Mint.

Date	Mintage	F	VF	XF	Unc	BU
1998 Proof	9,999	Value: 40.00				

KM# 118 2000 KWACHA **Weight:** 31.1035 g. **Composition:** 0.9990 Silver 1.0000 oz. ASW **Subject:** Centennial of the Anglo-Japanese Alliance **Obverse:** Queen Elizabeth **Reverse:** Fantasy Japanese coin design **Edge:** Reeded **Size:** 38.6 mm.

Date	Mintage	F	VF	XF	Unc	BU
2002	500	—	—	—	55.00	—

KM# 146 2000 KWACHA/100 GUILDERS **Weight:** 25.0000 g. **Composition:** 0.9990 Silver 0.803 oz. ASW **Subject:** World Cup Soccer **Obverse:** Zambian national arms (KM#137-139). **Reverse:** Two soccer players of Suriname KM#43.1. **Edge:** Reeded. **Size:** 38 mm. **Note:** Zambia/Suriname muled dies Error. Obverse is Zambia and the reverse is Suriname.

Date		F	VF	XF	Unc	BU
1994 Proof	—	Value: 100				

KM# 55 2500 KWACHA **Weight:** 155.5175 g. **Composition:** 0.9990 Silver 5.0000 oz. ASW **Subject:** Diana - The People's Princess **Reverse:** With sons, William and Harry **Note:** Similar to 200 Kwacha, KM#52.

Date	Mintage	F	VF	XF	Unc	BU
1997 Proof	Est. 1,997	Value: 115				

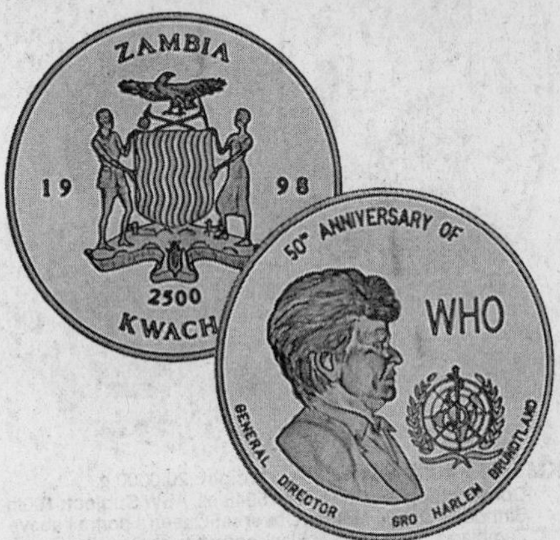

KM# 107 2500 KWACHA **Weight:** 15.5535 g. **Composition:** 0.9250 Silver .4626 oz. ASW **Series:** World Health Organization **Obverse:** Zambian arms **Reverse:** Director Brundtland portrait and logo **Edge:** Reeded **Size:** 36 mm.

Date		F	VF	XF	Unc	BU
1998 Proof	—	Value: 30.00				

KM# 134 4000 KWACHA **Weight:** 31.1035 g. **Composition:** 0.9990 Silver 0.999 oz. ASW **Subject:** Year of the Tiger **Obverse:** National arms. **Reverse:** Gold bat disc mounted above tiger. **Edge:** Reeded. **Size:** 38.5 mm.

Date		F	VF	XF	Unc	BU
1997 Proof	—	Value: 100				

KM# 69 4000 KWACHA **Weight:** 31.1035 g. **Composition:** 0.9990 Silver 1.0000 oz. ASW **Subject:** Taipai Subway **Obverse:** National arms **Reverse:** Train with inset diamond headlight **Note:** Struck at Singapore Mint.

Date	Mintage	F	VF	XF	Unc	BU
1998 Proof	9,999	Value: 60.00				

KM# 85 4000 KWACHA Weight: 25.1000 g. **Composition:** 0.9250 Silver .7465 oz. ASW **Series:** Wildlife Protection **Obverse:** British Queen's portrait below arms **Reverse:** Lion hologram **Edge:** Reeded **Size:** 37.9 mm. **Note:** Lighter weight and smaller diameter than official specifications.

Date	Mintage	F	VF	XF	Unc	BU
2000 Proof	5,000	Value: 47.50				
2001		—	—	—	—	—

KM# 78 4000 KWACHA Weight: 20.0000 g. **Composition:** 0.9250 Silver .5948 oz. ASW **Subject:** 100th Birthday - Queen Mother **Obverse:** Queen's portrait above Zambian arms **Reverse:** Black and white photo of the Queen Mother as a young lady **Edge:** Reeded **Note:** Size: 48x30mm oval.

Date	Mintage	F	VF	XF	Unc	BU
2000 Proof	25,000	Value: 40.00				

KM# 79 4000 KWACHA Weight: 20.0000 g. **Composition:** 0.9250 Silver .5948 oz. ASW **Subject:** 100th Birthday - Queen Mother **Reverse:** Black and white photo of Queen Mother on throne at 1937 coronation **Note:** Size: 48x30mm oval, similar to KM#76.

Date	Mintage	F	VF	XF	Unc	BU
2000 Proof	25,000	Value: 40.00				

KM# 80 4000 KWACHA Weight: 20.0000 g. **Composition:** 0.9250 Silver .5948 oz. ASW **Subject:** 100th Birthday - Queen Mother **Reverse:** Black and white photo of an elderly Queen Mother **Note:** Size: 48x30mm oval.

Date	Mintage	F	VF	XF	Unc	BU
2000 Proof	25,000	Value: 40.00				

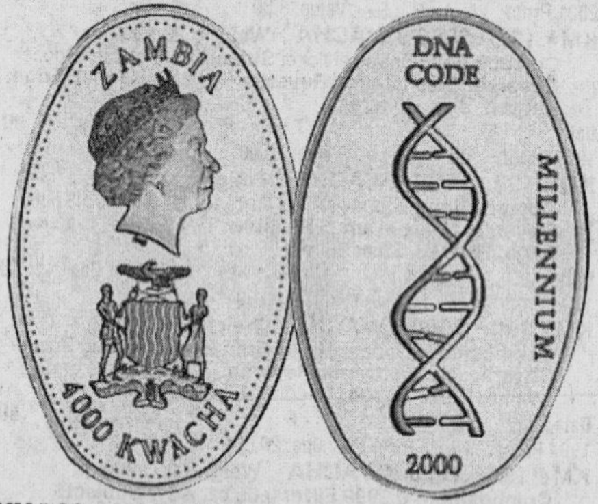

KM# 84 4000 KWACHA Weight: 20.0000 g. **Composition:** 0.9250 Silver .5948 oz. ASW **Subject:** Millennium - DNA Code **Obverse:** British Queen's portrait above arms **Reverse:** DNA chain **Edge:** Reeded **Size:** 30.1x48 mm.

Date		F	VF	XF	Unc	BU
2000 Proof	—	Value: 32.50				

KM# 101 4000 KWACHA Weight: 20.0000 g. **Composition:** 0.9250 Silver .5948 oz. ASW **Series:** 1000 Years of Exploration **Obverse:** Queen Elizabeth's portrait and Zambian arms below **Reverse:** Multi-colored portrait of Lief Erikssson and ship **Edge:** Reeded **Note:** 48x30.1 milimeters

Date	Mintage	F	VF	XF	Unc	BU
2000 Proof	5,000	Value: 40.00				

KM# 102 4000 KWACHA Weight: 20.0000 g. **Composition:** 0.9250 Silver .5948 oz. ASW **Subject** Years of Exploration **Reverse:** Multi-colored portrait of Polo and ship **Note:** Similar to KM#96.

Date	Mintage	F	VF	XF	Unc
2000 Proof	5,000	Value: 40.00			

KM# 103 4000 KWACHA Weight: 20.0000 g. **Composition:** 0.9250 Silver .5948 oz. ASW **Subject:** Years of Exploration **Reverse:** Multi-colored portrait of Columbus and ship **Note:** Similar to KM#97.

Date	Mintage	F	VF	XF	Unc
2000 Proof	5,000	Value: 40.00			

KM# 104 4000 KWACHA Weight: 20.0000 g. **Composition:** 0.9250 Silver .5948 oz. ASW **Subject:** 1(Years of Exploration **Reverse:** Multi-colored portrait of S Francis Drake and ship **Note:** Similar to KM#98.

Date	Mintage	F	VF	XF	Unc
2000 Proof	5,000	Value: 40.00			

KM# 105 4000 KWACHA Weight: 20.0000 g. **Composition:** 0.9250 Silver .5948 oz. ASW **Subject:** 10C Years of Exploration **Reverse:** Multi-colored portrait of Captain Cook and ship **Note:** Similar to KM#99.

Date	Mintage	F	VF	XF	Unc
2000 Proof	5,000	Value: 40.00			

106 4000 KWACHA **Weight:** 20.0000 g. **omposition:** 0.9250 Silver .5948 oz. ASW **Subject:** 1000 ears of Exploration **Reverse:** Multi-colored portrait of mundsen and ship **Note:** Similar to KM#100.

	Mintage	F	VF	XF	Unc	BU
Proof	5,000	Value: 40.00				

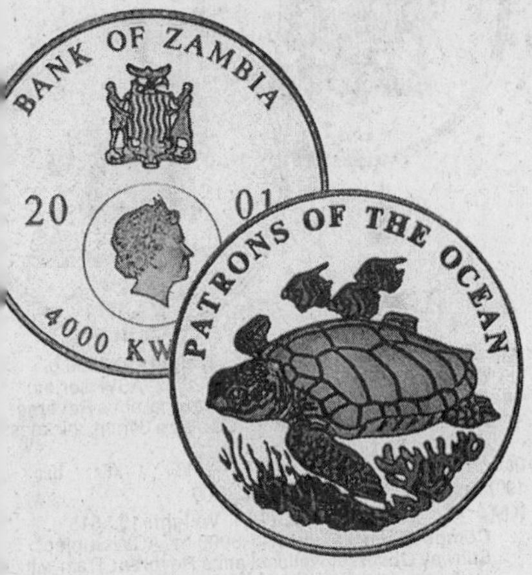

KM# 110 4000 KWACHA **Weight:** 20.0000 g. **Composition:** 0.9990 Silver .6424 oz. ASW **Series:** Patrons of the Ocean **Obverse:** Zambian arms above Queen Elizabeth's portrait **Reverse:** Sea turtle **Edge:** Reeded **Size:** 37.9 mm.

	F	VF	XF	Unc	BU
Proof	—	Value: 40.00			

M# 111 4000 KWACHA **Weight:** 20.0000 g. **Composition:** 0.9990 Silver .6424 oz. ASW **Series:** Patrons of the Ocean **Reverse:** Coclacanth fish

te	F	VF	XF	Unc	BU
01 Proof	—	Value: 50.00			

KM# 112 4000 KWACHA **Weight:** 20.0000 g. **Composition:** 0.9990 Silver .6424 oz. ASW **Series:** Patrons of the Ocean **Reverse:** Sea horse and fish

Date	F	VF	XF	Unc	BU
2001 Proof	—	Value: 40.00			

KM# 113 4000 KWACHA **Weight:** 20.0000 g. **Composition:** 0.9990 Silver .6424 oz. ASW **Series:** Patrons of the Ocean **Reverse:** Two dolphins

Date	F	VF	XF	Unc	BU
2001 Proof	—	Value: 50.00			

KM# 114 4000 KWACHA **Weight:** 50.0000 g. **Composition:** 0.9990 Silver 1.6059 oz. ASW **Subject:** Illusion **Obverse:** Zambian arms below Queen Elizabeth's portrait **Reverse:** "Cat in the Window" **Edge:** Plain **Note:** 50x50 milimeters

Date	F	VF	XF	Unc	BU
2001 Proof	5,000	Value: 40.00			

KM# 144 5000 KWACHA **Composition:** Silver **Reverse:** Lions, map, and arms

Date	F	VF	XF	Unc	BU
1997 Proof	2,000	Value: 210			

KM# 108 5000 KWACHA **Weight:** 31.2100 g. **Composition:** 0.9250 Silver .9282 oz. ASW **Subject:** World Health Organization **Obverse:** Zambian arms **Reverse:** Director Brundtland's portrait **Edge:** Reeded **Size:** 40 mm.

Date	F	VF	XF	Unc	BU
1998 Proof	—	Value: 40.00			

KM# 70 5000 KWACHA **Weight:** 7.7759 g. **Composition:** 0.9990 Gold .2500 oz. AGW **Subject:** Taipai Subway **Obverse:** National arms **Reverse:** Train with inset diamond headlight **Note:** Struck at Singapore Mint.

Date	Mintage	F	VF	XF	Unc	BU
1998 Proof	999	Value: 350				

KM# 92 5000 KWACHA **Weight:** 31.2100 g. **Composition:** 0.9990 Silver 1.0024 oz. ASW **Subject:** African Wildlife **Obverse:** National arms **Reverse:** Elephant mother and calf **Edge:** Reeded **Size:** 38.7 mm.

Date	F	VF	XF	Unc	BU
1999 Proof	—	Value: 35.00			

KM# 73 5000 KWACHA **Weight:** 31.1346 g. **Composition:** 0.9990 Silver 1.0000 oz. ASW **Subject:** African Wildlife **Reverse:** Elephant

Date	F	VF	XF	Unc	BU
1999	—	—	—	20.00	—
1999 Matte	—	—	—	25.00	—

KM# 150 5000 KWACHA **Weight:** 31.1035 g. **Composition:** 0.9999 Silver 0.9999 oz. ASW **Subject:** Chinese Zodiac **Obverse:** Dragon on Chinese map above Zambian arms **Reverse:** Cartoon rabbit **Edge:** Reeded **Size:** 38 mm.

Date	F	VF	XF	Unc	BU
ND Proof	—	Value: 45.00			

KM# 151 5000 KWACHA **Weight:** 31.1035 g. **Composition:** 0.9999 Silver 0.9999 oz. ASW **Subject:** Chinese Zodiac **Obverse:** Dragon on Chinese map above Zambian arms **Reverse:** Cartoon bull **Edge:** Reeded **Size:** 38 mm.

Date	F	VF	XF	Unc	BU
ND Proof	—	Value: 45.00			

KM# 115 5000 KWACHA **Weight:** 31.3600 g. **Composition:** 0.9250 Silver .9326 oz. ASW **Subject:** Olympics **Obverse:** National arms map, Queen Elizabeth's portrait. **Reverse:** Runners and map. **Edge:** Plain. **Size:** 48.7 x 41.75 mm. **Note:** Irregular shape.

Date	F	VF	XF	Unc	BU
2000 Proof	—	Value: 50.00			

KM# 81 5000 KWACHA **Weight:** 27.0000 g. **Composition:** 0.9990 Gold .8672 oz. AGW **Subject:** 100th Birthday - Queen Mother **Obverse:** Queen's portrait above Zambian arms **Reverse:** Black and white photo of the Queen Mother as a young lady **Edge:** Reeded **Note:** Size: 48x30mm oval.

Date	Mintage	F	VF	XF	Unc	BU
2000 Proof	100	Value: 675				

KM# 82 5000 KWACHA **Weight:** 27.0000 g. **Composition:** 0.9990 Gold .8672 oz. AGW **Subject:** 100th Birthday - Queen Mother **Reverse:** Black ad white photo of Queen Mother on throne at 1937 coronation **Note:** Size: 48x30mm oval.

Date	Mintage	F	VF	XF	Unc	BU
2000 Proof	100	Value: 675				

KM# 83 5000 KWACHA **Weight:** 27.0000 g. **Composition:** 0.9990 Gold .8672 oz. AGW **Subject:** 100th Birthday - Queen Mother **Reverse:** Black and white photo of an elderly Queen Mother **Note:** Size: 48x30mm oval.

Date	Mintage	F	VF	XF	Unc	BU
2000 Proof	100	Value: 675				

KM# 117 5000 KWACHA **Weight:** 31.3000 g. **Composition:** 0.9990 Silver 1.0053 oz. ASW **Subject:** African Wildlife **Obverse:** National arms. **Reverse:** Elephant mother and calf grazing on grass. **Edge:** Reeded. **Size:** 38.6 mm.

Date	F	VF	XF	Unc	BU
2001 Proof	—	Value: 45.00			

KM# 143 5000 KWACHA **Weight:** 28.8600 g. **Composition:** 0.9990 Silver 0.9269 oz. ASW **Subject:** African Wildlife **Obverse:** National arms **Reverse:** Elephant **Edge:** Reeded **Size:** 38.5 mm.

Date	F	VF	XF	Unc	BU
2002 Matte	—	—	—	40.00	—

KM# 145 10000 KWACHA **Composition:** Silver **Reverse:** Kudu, map, and arms

Date	Mintage	F	VF	XF	Unc	BU
1997 Proof	2,000	Value: 360				

KM# 116 10000 KWACHA **Weight:** 30.4000 g. **Composition:** 0.9990 Silver .9764 oz. ASW **Subject** Endangered Wildlife **Obverse:** National arms. **Reverse** on branch and one flying. **Edge:** Reeded. **Size:** 34 m

Date	F	VF	XF	Unc
1997 Proof	—	Value: 40.00		

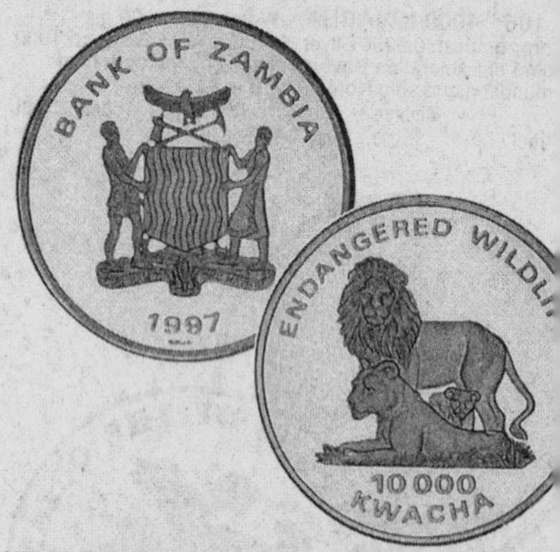

KM# 86 10000 KWACHA **Weight:** 30.2800 g. **Composition:** 0.9990 Silver .9726 oz. ASW **Series:** Endangered Wildlife **Obverse:** National arms **Reverse:** family **Edge:** Reeded **Note:** Coin size 34mm, thicknes 3.8mm.

Date	F	VF	XF	Unc
1997 Proof	—	Value: 35.00		

KM# 71 10000 KWACHA **Weight:** 15.5518 g. **Composition:** 0.9999 Gold .5000 oz. AGW **Subject:** Ta Subway **Obverse:** National arms **Reverse:** Train with i diamond headlight **Note:** Struck at Singapore Mint.

Date	Mintage	F	VF	XF	Unc
1998 Proof	99	Value: 650			

KM# 93 20000 KWACHA **Weight:** 1000.0000 g. **Composition:** 0.9990 Silver 32.1186 oz. ASW **Subject:** K Imari VOC Plate **Obverse:** Queen Elizabeth's portrait **Reverse:** Multi-colored plate design **Edge:** Reeded **Size:**